Familiar Quotations

A collection of passages, phrases and proverbs traced to their sources in ancient and modern literature

FIFTEENTH AND 125TH ANNIVERSARY EDITION
REVISED AND ENLARGED

John Bartlett

Edited by EMILY MORISON BECK
and the editorial staff of Little, Brown and Company

First Edition Published 1855
Fifteenth and 125th Anniversary Edition Published 1980
ISBN 0-333-30917-0

Published by
THE MACMILLAN PRESS LTD
London and Basingstoke
Companies and representatives
throughout the world

PRINTED IN THE UNITED STATES OF AMERICA

Familiar Quotations

Contents

Preface to the Fifteenth Edition vii

Historical Note xi

Guide to the Use of *Familiar Quotations* xiv

Index of Authors xvii

Familiar Quotations, *from ancient Egypt and the Bible to the present* 3

Index 937

Preface to the Fifteenth Edition

"By necessity, by proclivity, and by delight, we all quote," said Emerson, while Montaigne avowed, "I do not speak the minds of others except to speak my own better." Hence the usefulness of a work like Bartlett's *Familiar Quotations,* now in its fifteenth edition and one hundred and twenty-fifth year since John Bartlett, erudite owner of the University Book Store in Cambridge, Massachusetts, published his "small thin volume" in 1855.[1] Intended "to show . . . the obligations our language owes to various authors for numerous phrases and familiar quotations which have become 'household words,' " it has itself become a household word, now even in the comics.

The first mission of a *Bartlett* editor is to assemble appropriate[2] quotations from the years since the previous edition, in this case the fourteenth, published in 1968. The new edition also should reflect recent developments in scholarship regarding earlier authors (from antiquity on down), new editions, and fresh translations. Quotations hitherto not included suddenly take on relevance and significance in the light of emerging interests and changing tastes and attitudes. And every revision discovers old familiar quotations that somehow never before got into *Bartlett.*

Probably the first quotations gathered for this new fifteenth edition were Neil Armstrong's historic statements on the moon landing of July 20, 1969. With that "giant step" we saw for the first time the beautiful blue bubble of planet Earth from outer space. Did we begin then to realize how endangered it was? For the 1970s, finally emerging from domestic upheavals and from Vietnam, found us at last recognizing the fragility of our environment, which Rachel Carson had warned of in 1962. We began in earnest to realize with Thoreau that "in wildness is the preservation of the world." The present edition turns to old and recent works on ecology, and adds quotations from John Muir, Aldo Leopold, and others.

In the interests of enlarging certain sections, we asked experts to look over in particular the quotations from the Koran and from ancient Buddhist and Sanskrit writings, with the result of considerable expansion. Even the great Bible section has been enlarged. Scholarly scrutiny of the sciences has added many quotations; so also with economics. More translations from non-English works heighten the international flavor of *Bart-*

[1] For further information on John Bartlett and the editions, see the Historical Note, page xi. "Small thin volume" is from his preface to the ninth edition.

[2] For the *Bartlett* criteria in selecting quotations, see the Historical Note, page xi.

lett— inspired are the recent translations from ancient Egyptian texts, transforming the archaic English renderings into fresh love lyrics and words of wisdom that bridge thousands of years. Current movements in our society to bring an end to continuing discrimination are represented also by the words of their ancestors, including some of the eloquent statements of North American Indian leaders when, betrayed by the government, they gave up their sacred lands—indeed, gave up their lives as nations and tribes. In the expanded Anonymous sections of this edition African and North American Indian chants, poems, and proverbs appear, as well as sayings from the French, Russian, and Spanish. Cowboy songs, sea shanties, and spirituals are also represented, most of them for the first time.

Time will judge the validity of the fifteenth edition's choices from contemporary life and literature. Altogether we have added more than four hundred new authors—among them the Egyptian queen Hatshepsut, Plotinus, Giordano Bruno, Tecumseh, George Sand, Frederick Douglass, Susan B. Anthony, Chief Joseph, Cavafy, Apollinaire, Knute Rockne, Kenyatta, Cole Porter, Brecht, Borges, Malraux, Margaret Mead, Anaïs Nin, Moss Hart, Neruda, Gwendolyn Brooks, Pope John Paul II, John Berryman, Denise Levertov, John Ashbery, Tom Wolfe, Bob Dylan, Joni Mitchell, Mick Jagger, and Steve Biko.

Famous quotations, both old and new, added to *Bartlett* in this edition include "Inherit the wind" (*Proverbs 11:29*); the riddle of the Sphinx (the "famous riddle" in Sophocles' *Oedipus Rex*); "Speak silver, reply gold" (Swahili proverb); "Living well is the best revenge" (George Herbert); "Amazing grace!" (John Newton); "Remember the ladies" (Abigail Adams); "The sleep of reason produces monsters" (Goya); "Nothing contributes so much to tranquilize the mind as a steady purpose" (Mary Shelley); "Bah! Humbug!" (Dickens); "We hold these truths to be self-evident, that all men and women are created equal" (Elizabeth Cady Stanton); "Good morning—Midnight—I'm coming home" (Dickinson); "The problem of the twentieth century is the problem of the color line" (Du Bois); "Oh bang the drum slowly" (cowboy song); "Never give in, never, never, never, never" (Churchill); "Time the destroyer is time the preserver" (T. S. Eliot); "Wind is in the cane. Come along" (Toomer); "Not waving but drowning" (Stevie Smith); "The medium is the message" (McLuhan); "I could have danced all night" (Lerner); "Catch-22" (Heller); "I'm so lonesome I could cry" (Hank Williams); "Dying / Is an art, like everything else" (Plath); "Float like a butterfly, sting like a bee" (Muhammad Ali).

As before, there is extensive cross-referencing; for example, sending Kaufman and Hart's "You Can't Take It with You" all the way back to the ancient Egyptian *Song of the Harper,* the Bible, and Theognis.

The evolution of an adage is a fascinating aspect of *Bartlett.* Many of the sayings current today derive from earlier, often differently worded versions of unknown authorship. Many of them appear in the collections of proverbs of John Heywood, George Herbert, John Ray, and others. The ancient Egyptians have their proverbs, as of course does the Old Testament, some of them expressing the same observations.

In our time a familiar adage often has evolved from a recognizable though differently worded source. The quotation "A journey of a thousand miles must begin with a single step," made famous by President Kennedy, is a more succinct version than the literal rendering by Lao-tzu. There is also a mystery over the origin of "The only thing necessary for the triumph of evil is for good men to do nothing." It has been ascribed to Edmund Burke, yet has not been found—so far—in his writings. Is it possible that it is a twentieth-century paraphrase of Burke's view that "When bad men combine, the good must associate; else they will fall one by one, an unpitied sacrifice in a contemptible struggle" (from *Thoughts on the Cause of the Present Discontents,* April 23, 1770)? Whatever the credit, it is the shorter version that will continue to be quoted, you may be assured.

A similar case is that of "An idea whose time has come." Everyone agrees that it derives from Victor Hugo's line "On résiste à l'invasion des armées; on ne résiste pas à l'invasion des idées" (One can resist the invasion of armies, but not the invasion of ideas). But today the reference to armies is omitted, while sometimes only part of the quotation, "Whose time has come," is used—frequently in advertising.

Bartlett includes expressions in current use which by the next edition may have vanished from everyday speech, for sayings can be as evanescent as most slang.

The traditional order of Bartlett's *Familiar Quotations* is chronological by author and selection. It is helpful and illuminating to read in sequence a body of quotations from an author, also to compare the work of contemporaries. Next to reading them in the original, the full sections from the Bible, the classics, Shakespeare, Milton, and the rest of the great core of *Bartlett* provide a rich, rewarding experience.

Emerson said, "Language is the archives of history . . . language is fossil poetry." I think of *Bartlett* as literary archaeology in which familiar and noteworthy quotations reveal—as do ancient artifacts, temples and dwellings, frescoes and cave paintings—the nature of the age and the people who created them. Christopher Morley in his preface to the eleventh edition called *Bartlett* "a sort of anthropology; a social history; a diary of the race." It is all these things.

Quotations tell us of the inward thoughts and aspirations of men and women, of their struggle with life and death, with ambition, misfortune, evil, grief, of their experience with love and joy, of their sense of humor. They reveal to us that people from ancient times, from the first written utterances, can speak to us today in ways that inspire, inform, comfort, entertain.

"Books are the treasured wealth of the world and the fit inheritance of generations and nations," said Thoreau. "Their authors are a natural and irresistible aristocracy in every society, and, more than kings and emperors, exert an influence on mankind."

"Words guard the shape of man," wrote George Seferis, "even when man has fled and is no longer there." *Bartlett* goes a long way toward guarding this shape for our posterity.

This fifteenth edition of Bartlett's *Familiar Quotations* has been aided by a staff of experts in various fields, and in addition by the numerous correspondents who steadily over the years write in with information, questions, quotations, and criticisms for which we are continuously grateful. We acknowledge with much thanks the work of our experts: Ruth Adams (Victorian literature), César Albini (French), Bailey Aldrich (law), Lilian Andrews (environment), Edward Applewhite (R. Buckminster Fuller), Emily Marshall Beck (modern poetry), Gordon Morison Beck (environment), William Bentinck-Smith (American history and literature), Paul Brooks (ecology), Lyman Butterfield (American history), Eloise Collingwood (French), the Reverend G. Harris Collingwood (the Bible; the Book of Common Prayer), Hugh B. Cott (zoology), Lois Eliot (general), Robert Epstein (psychology), Doris Eyges (modern poetry), Marc Friedlaender (American history), David Frisch (general), John Kenneth Galbraith (economics), James Nelson Goodsell (Latin American literature), Richard F. Hanser (German), Betty Jane Johnson (general), Ralph Keyes (contemporary life), Elena Levin (Russian), Julie Armstrong Ludwig (songs; general), Dumas Malone (Jefferson), David McCord (American literature), Paul Monette (contemporary literature), Jan Nattier-Barbero (Buddhist and Sanskrit literature), Sari Nuseibah (the Koran), James G. Paradis (literature of science), Lynn H. Parsons (John Quincy Adams), Rachel Phillips (Latin American literature and Spanish), Don K. Price (political science), George Savidis (modern Greek poetry), Richard Sawaya (contemporary literature), Arthur M. Schlesinger, Jr. (history; general), Frank R. Scott (Canada), Edward Spingarn (economics), Zeph Stewart (classics), Joseph Tabler (general), Samuel Taylor (general), Edward A. Weeks (contemporary writers), Mitchell Nelson York (modern poetry).

A very close collaboration has been with Mary Rackliffe, the Little, Brown editor who has overseen and worked on the new *Bartlett* from its earliest stages; her knowledge, insight, taste, and exceptional skill add immeasurably to this edition. She has been ably assisted by Augusta Gelber Devine in many ways, especially in the management of the voluminous index, and also by Melissa Clemence, Natalie Dandekar, Luise Erdmann, Julia Fair, Donna Kaye, Sheila Marian, Lisbeth Murray, Betsy Pitha, and Susan Rous, all of whom we thank for their share in various aspects of putting the book together. We are also grateful to Executive Editor Winthrop M. Hodges for his encouragement and support, and to Moses F. Carr, Jr., General Manager of Manufacturing.

The fifteenth edition appears in a new, larger format, with a newly designed page and typeface, for both clarity and the accommodation of more quotations in less space.

EMILY MORISON BECK, *Editor*

Canton, Massachusetts

Historical Note

"Go, litel bok."[1] Sent forth in 1855, John Bartlett's modest volume of *Familiar Quotations* was destined, like Chaucer's tale, to its own immortality, and it established him as a perpetuator of the immortals.

By the time he brought the book out, Bartlett (1820–1905) was already a figure of eminence in Cambridge, Massachusetts, and its environs. In 1849, at the age of twenty-nine, he had become proprietor of the University Book Store, which in 1836 he had joined straight from the public schools of his native Plymouth. Renowned for his erudition and omnivorous reading, he was constantly called on to answer questions about quotations, and thought of the book as a service. Selecting the most popular quotations from his commonplace book, he published them himself, with their authors and sources, in an edition of a thousand copies. His brief preface told the reader that "the object of this work is to show, to some extent, the obligations our language owes to various authors for numerous phrases and familiar quotations which have become 'household words.' "

Familiar Quotations contained two hundred and fifty-eight pages of quotations from one hundred and sixty-nine authors. The Bible and Shakespeare took up about a third of the text; the balance was chiefly English poetry—Milton, Pope, Wordsworth, and Byron had the greatest number of entries. There was a scattering of prose from Milton, Bacon, Franklin, Tom Paine, Macaulay, and one maxim from La Rochefoucauld: "Hypocrisy is the homage that vice pays to virtue." No Blake, Shelley, or various other authors who could not have been much upon the tongue in the mid-nineteenth century. A mere handful of Americans was included —Irving, Bryant, Longfellow, Lowell—and a line each from "Hail, Columbia," "The Star-Spangled Banner," and "The Old Oaken Bucket." There were no quotations from Washington, Adams, Jefferson, or even Emerson (who made it by the third edition three years later).

The Gettysburg Address had not yet been delivered. Walt Whitman published *Leaves of Grass* that same year, and Thoreau *Walden* the year before. Ahead of their time, neither would be in *Familiar Quotations* until the tenth edition in 1914.

John Bartlett's venture was a success. In 1863 he joined Little, Brown and Company, who published the fourth edition that same year; fifteen years later he was a senior partner. Before his death at the age of eighty-five he had published not only the ninth edition of *Familiar Quotations*

[1] See Chaucer, 145:7.

(1891) but also a *New Method of Chess Notation* (1857), *The Shakespeare Phrase Book* (1882), a *Catalogue of Books on Angling* (1882), and a *Complete Concordance to Shakespeare's Dramatic Works and Plays* (1894). Later editions of *Familiar Quotations* continue the basic patterns and style Bartlett devised for the book. In particular, the chronological order he chose for presenting his authors and their works proves more valuable every year.

In selecting quotations, Bartlett used the criteria of familiarity and worth. In his preface to the fourth edition (1863) he made it plain that though he would try to err if at all "on the side of fullness," quotations would not be admitted "simply on their own merits, without assurance that the general reader would readily recognize them as old friends."

The next editor, Nathan Haskell Dole (1852–1935), poet, editor, and translator, continued to require quotations with "the seal of popular approval" and "distinctly worthy of perpetuation." His tenth edition of *Familiar Quotations* (1914), twice the size and three times the thickness of the first, was to "incorporate . . . quotations from those writers whose place in literature has been achieved since the issue of the ninth edition," and to add selections from other "best writers of their day." "It is not always easy," he wrote, "for Elisha to wear the mantle of Elijah;[1] but it is Elisha's business to carry on his predecessor's work in the same spirit." Among the many new authors now included (besides Thoreau and Whitman) were Lewis Carroll, W. S. Gilbert, Nietzsche, Shaw, novelists George Eliot and George Moore (but not Hawthorne, Melville, or Henry James), poets Swinburne, Hardy, Stevenson, Housman, Kipling, and Yeats (but still not Blake).

For the eleventh edition (1937) Elijah's mantle passed to writer, poet, and editor Christopher Morley, dubbed an "angloliterophile" for his love of the English language for its own sake, and associate editor Louella D. Everett, a noted quotation finder for the *New York Times* who had also published anthologies. Of their joint editorship Morley wrote in his preface: "One of the pleasures of this re-editing has been that one collaborator, by long experience with inquiries for the affable familiar ghosts of print, knows acutely what readers want; and the other believes himself to know what they ought to want. They have striven for a happy compromise."

For the first time the editors grappled with removing quotations no longer relevant or familiar, a delicate task that since then is repeated for every *Bartlett* edition; occasional restorations in later editions are not unknown. The editors added not only to twentieth-century quotations but to every period from ancient times on, reflecting perhaps a broadening cultural outlook on the part of the average American. Between 1914 and 1937 a new age had flowered, and the changes in the text of the eleventh edition are more striking than in any other. Blake, Hawthorne, Melville, Emily Dickinson, the Jameses, Conrad, Wharton, Turgenev, Dostoevski, Du Bois, Bertrand Russell, Cather, Will Rogers, Joyce, Virginia Woolf, Pound, T. S. Eliot, Langston Hughes, and Auden (then just turning thirty) are a small sample of the newcomers. The innovation of a two-column

[1] See *II Kings* 2:13, 14:14.

page allowed a vast increment of new quotations within a single volume.

Morley's preface to the eleventh edition asks at the outset the question every *Bartlett* editor must try to answer: "What makes words memorable?" His theory of selection was broader than John Bartlett's. "Previous editions adhered, almost with pedantry, to the touchstones of familiarity," he wrote. . . . "This edition is not so stringent: we have tried to make literary power the criterion rather than width and vulgarity of fame." "Literary power" is so much more a matter of personal opinion than "familiarity" that this new approach opened up for future *Bartlett* editors the temptation to exploit their literary passions. Restraint has been necessary to keep the volume from becoming idiosyncratic or growing into an anthology.

World War II and the atomic age required an updating of *Bartlett*, and in 1948 the twelfth edition appeared, edited by Morley and Everett and with new quotations from (among many others) Churchill, Hitler, Einstein, the Charter of the United Nations, MacArthur, Truman, and Lippman. "The duty of stoical old *Bartlett,*" Morley wrote, "is to hand on, without fear or favor, what looks to be most memorable of men's joy, suspicion, and dismay," a policy still followed in 1980. Though publisher and editors agreed that "there was no need, at this time, to reconsider *Bartlett* from the beginning," some earlier quotations were added, such as "No man is an island" (Donne) and "I have not yet begun to fight" (John Paul Jones).

The centennial of Bartlett's *Familiar Quotations* was celebrated by the thirteenth edition (1955), edited by the editors of Little, Brown, and continuing the tradition of re-editing throughout the book. New authors included Archimedes, Constantine, James Madison, Bismarck, Baudelaire, Francis Parkman, Alexander Graham Bell, Isak Dinesen, Garbo, and Dylan Thomas.

The fourteenth edition (1968), edited by Emily Morison Beck, expanded the editorial collaboration to include a staff of scholars and experts in a number of fields. Historical and literary figures represented for the first time included Confucius, Columbus, Kierkegaard, Chekhov, and Gandhi, and famous quotations down the ages were added, such as "Man is the measure of all things" (Protagoras); "But it does move" (Galileo); "One man with courage makes a majority" (Andrew Jackson); and "The force that through the green fuse drives the flower / Drives my green age" (Dylan Thomas). Translations were moved from a separate section into the main chronological text; many were greatly improved, and Homer appeared for the first time in direct translation rather than through Pope (see Richard Bentley, 319:3). Like its predecessors since 1937, this *Bartlett* retained its intrinsic character while expanding in the manner Morley initiated—including among the quotations some not necessarily widely familiar but "distinctly worthy of perpetuation," expressing the interests, the ideas, the taste of the period.

Twelve years, embodying the 1970s, have passed since the fourteenth edition. The fifteenth edition is discussed in the preface.

EMILY MORISON BECK, *Editor*

Guide to the Use of FAMILIAR QUOTATIONS

Basic Information

Authors appear chronologically in birth date order. Under each author heading, quotations appear chronologically by date of publication, usually the date of first publication in a book.

To find a particular author, see the Index of Authors, page xvii.

To find a particular quotation, see the Index, page 937. Since we index keywords, not first lines, look up any of the main words in the quotation.

For information on this fifteenth edition of *Bartlett,* see the Preface, page vii. For information on John Bartlett and earlier editions, see the Historical Note, page xi.

Author Headings

The author heading shows the author's name and life dates; the headings run chronologically by birth order. Authors born in the same year are arranged alphabetically. Quotations in the Anonymous section following the last dated author run roughly chronologically (no actual date of origin is known), and the groupings at the end of the book—Anonymous: African; Anonymous: Ballads, and so on—are listed alphabetically. An author heading covering a document appears near the people with whom it is associated; for example, the Constitution of the United States (1787) appears among its creators, such as Franklin (born in 1706), Washington (1732), Madison (1751), and Hamilton (1755).

For an author with a pseudonym, the less familiar name is bracketed after the more familiar one. To find out which name is the pseudonym, see the Index of Authors, page xvii.

The chronological order enhances understanding of the authors and their works by putting them in context. For the reader, simply to meet in one place Ethel Barrymore, James Branch Cabell, Einstein, E. M. Forster, Edmund L. Gruber ("Those caissons go rolling along"), John Haynes Holmes, Vachel Lindsay, Joe Hill, Will Rogers, Jack Norworth ("Take me out to the ball game"), Stalin, Wallace Stevens, and the other authors also born in 1879, is an illumination of their world and ours.

Quotations

Each quotation has a source or identification line intended to give the reader as much information as is needed (or possible) to find the work the quotation comes from, including the date, usually that of publication in book form. *Ib.* (short for *ibidem,* "in the same place") covers everything in the preceding source line that would have to be repeated in the next. For example, in the source line *Ib. 13* following the source line *Light in August* [*1932*], *ch. 4,* the only change is the chapter number.

The chronological arrangement of quotations (usually by publication date) within the author entry helps to put the quotation in context and show the author's development, while the whole entry can often provide a significant sample of style and thought.

Footnotes, Including Cross-References

A footnote can supply information about a quotation—the name of a translator, the original text of a translated quotation, or background such as at Robert Lowell's *Mr. Edwards and the Spider,* page 892. It can also supply quotations related in phrase or content to the footnoted quotation, as well as cross-references to similarly related quotations elsewhere in the book.

Index of Authors (page xvii)

The author index supplies birth and death dates as well as the page number for the entry and for the author's additional quotations in footnotes. Bracketed parts of a name are those not used in the typical "signature"—C[live] S[taples] Lewis.

If you wish to locate a book of the Bible, see the Bible entry, where the books are listed alphabetically. Shakespeare's works are similarly listed at his entry, and the various Anonymous sections at the Anonymous entry.

Index (page 937)

The *Bartlett* index is large because we hope to enable the reader to find even half-remembered or almost forgotten quotations as well as the fully known ones. We also like its aspect as a field for browsing, which can lead to many rewarding new and renewed discoveries among the quotations.

The number at the end of each index entry shows the page on which the quotation starts, and the number of the quotation on the page, either in text (481:6) or in a footnote (481:*n*5).

Spelling follows *Webster's Third New International Dictionary.* Keywords with variant spellings show in the Webster form *(Coming,* not *Comin')* and sometimes in the variant form also. The standard order of plural and possessive keywords is: *Lover's, Lovers, Lovers'.*

The index line is usually a short form of the phrase being indexed, and

the words show in the same order, with the keyword abbreviated unless it starts the entry.

Hope a waking dream, 86 : 16
all we h. in heaven, 525 : 2
Americans h. of world, 368 : 3
animated by faith and h., 352 : 24
beautiful Evelyn H., 542 : 1
thing with feathers, 604 : 17

The first word of a quotation is not necessarily indexed; "I am the captain of the *Pinafore*" is indexed at the two nouns, not at *I.*

If you don't find your quotation under the keyword you're trying, scan the rest of the keyword entry; there are many familiar ways of indexing one phrase (Love, jot of former l.; Love, one jot of former l.). If it isn't there, try another keyword, and if it doesn't emerge from any remembered keyword try related words (*valor* is often remembered as *courage, approbation* as *praise,* and so on).

Under a keyword which is part of a two-word term you're looking for (for example, *old age*), the two-word term can appear in the middle or at the end of the index line as well as at the start, so scanning is needed.

Age, accompany old a., 239 : 31
green old a., 303 : 15
old a. serene and bright, 427 : 20
old a. should burn, 887 : 4
'tis well an old a. is out, 307 : 1

If you are looking for quotations about a topic (*nature* or *bravery* or *wisdom* or *love* or whatever), think also of all the synonyms and related words you can—and then, in addition, browse. You'll find more.

MARY RACKLIFFE
Editor, Little, Brown and Company

Index of Authors

Abbott, Bud [William] (*1895–1974*) 832
Abelard, Peter (*1079–1142*) 136
Abrantès, Andoche Junot, Duc d' (*1771–1813*)
note 86
Abu Muhammad al-Kasim al-Hariri. *See* Hariri
Accius, Lucius (*170–86 B.C.*) 97
Ace, Jane (*1905–1974*) 862
Acton, John Emerich Edward Dalberg-Acton, Lord (*1834–1902*) 615
Adams, Abigail (*1744–1818*) 392
Adams, Charles Francis (*1807–1886*) 509
Adams, Franklin P[ierce] (F.P.A.) (*1881–1960*) 773
note 673
Adams, Henry [Brooks] (*1838–1918*) 634
Adams, John (*1735–1826*) 380
note 367, 450
Adams, John Quincy (*1767–1848*) 417
note 95, 330, 392
Adams, Samuel (*1722–1803*) 365
Adams, Sarah Flower (*1805–1848*) 505
Adamson, Harold (*1906–*) 866
Addams, Jane (*1860–1935*) 694
Addison, Joseph (*1672–1719*) 325
note 159, 325
Ade, George (*1866–1944*) 718
Ady, Thomas (*fl. 1655*) 294
A.E. *See* Russell, George William
Aeschylus (*525–456 B.C.*) 70
note 66
Aesop (*fl. c. 550 B.C.*) 65
African (Anonymous) 925
Agassiz, Jean Louis Rodolphe (*1807–1873*) 509
Agathon (*c. 448–400 B.C.*) 82
Agee, James (*1909–1955*) 875
Agesilaus (*444–400 B.C.*) 82
Agis (*5th century B.C.*) 78
Aïdé, Charles Hamilton (*1826–1906*) 597
Aiken, Conrad (*1889–1973*) 811
Akhmatova, Anna (*pseudonym of* Anna Andreyevna Gorenko) (*1888–1966*) 801
Akins, Zoë (*1886–1958*) 794
Alain. *See* Chartier, Émile Auguste
Alain de Lille (Alanus de Insulis) (*d. 1202*) 137
Alain-Fournier (*pseudonym of* Henri Alban Fournier) (*1886–1914*) 795
Albee, Edward F[rancis] (*1857–1930*) 683
Albee, Edward [Franklin] (*1928–*) 908
Alcaeus (*c. 625 – c. 575 B.C.*) 62
Alcott, [Amos] Bronson (*1799–1888*) 484
Alcott, Louisa May (*1832–1888*) 610
Alcuin (*735–804*) 135
Aldrich, Henry (*1647–1710*) 315
Aldrich, Thomas Bailey (*1836–1907*) 626
Aldus Manutius. *See* Manutius
Alembert, Jean Le Rond d' (*1717–1783*) 363
Alexander II (*1818–1881*) 561
Alexander the Great (*356–323 B.C.*) 90
Alexander, Cecil Frances (*1818–1895*) 561
Alfonso X (Alfonso the Wise) (*1221–1284*) 139
Alford, Henry (*1810–1871*) 536
Algarotti, Francesco (*1712–1764*)
note 486
Ali, Muhammad (*formerly* Cassius Marcellus Clay, Jr.) (*1942–*) 915
Ali ibn-Abi-Talib (*c. 602–661*) 130
Alighieri. *See* Dante
Allainval, Léonor J. C. Soulas, Abbé d' (*1700–1753*)
note 344
Allen, Elizabeth Akers (*1832–1911*) 610
Allen, Ethan (*1738–1789*) 385

Allen, Fred (*1894–1956*) 828
Allen, William (*1803–1879*) 492
Allen, Woody (*1937–*) 913
Allingham, William (*1824–1889*) 594
note 95
Amado, Jorge (*1912–*) 879
Ambrose, Saint (*c. 340–397*) 127
Amenemope (*c. 11th century B.C.*) 6
Ames, Fisher (*1758–1808*) 407
Amiel, Henri Frédéric (*1821–1881*) 580
Ammianus Marcellinus (*c. 330–395*) 127
Ammons, A[rchie] R[andolph] (*1926–*) 905
Anacharsis (*fl. c. 600 B.C.*) 63
Anacreon (*c. 570 – c. 480 B.C.*) 67
Anaxagoras (*c. 500–428 B.C.*) 72
Andersen, Hans Christian (*1805–1875*) 505
Anderson, Maxwell (*1888–1959*) 802
Anderson, Sherwood (*1876–1941*) 757
Angell, Sir Norman (*1872–1967*) 735
Angelus Silesius (*pseudonym of* Johannes Scheffler) (*1624–1677*) 300
Anonymous 916
African 925
Ballads 926
Cowboy Songs 927
Early 132
French 927
Latin 183
North American Indian 928
Nursery Rhymes 929
Russian 934
Shanties 934
Spanish 935
Spirituals 935
Anouilh, Jean (*1910–*) 877
Anselm, Saint (*c. 1033–1109*) 136
Anthony, Susan B[rownell] (*1820–1906*) 577
Antigonus (*c. 382–301 B.C.*) 88
Antiphanes (*c. 388 – c. 311 B.C.*) 86
Apelles (*fl. 325 B.C.*) 90
Apollinaire, Guillaume (Wilhelm Apollinaris de Kostrowitsky) (*1880–1918*) 770
Appleton, Thomas Gold (*1812–1884*)
note 675
Aquinas, Saint Thomas (*c. 1225–1274*) 139
Aratus (*c. 315–240 B.C.*) 92
Arbuthnot, John (*1667–1735*)
note 344
Archilochus (*early 7th century B.C.*) 61
Archimedes (*c. 287–212 B.C.*) 93
Archpoet, The (*12th century*) 137
Arendt, Hannah (*1906–1975*) 866
Ariosto, Ludovico (*1474–1533*) 154
Aristophanes (*c. 450–385 B.C.*) 81
note 113
Aristotle (*384–322 B.C.*) 86
note 60, 73, 75, 87, 115, 137, 307
Armstrong, Louis (Satchmo) (*1900–1971*) 847
Armstrong, Neil [Alden] (*1930–*) 910
Arndt, Ernst Moritz (*1769–1860*) 420
Arno, Peter (*1904–1968*) 858
Arnold, Sir Edwin (*1832–1904*) 610
Arnold, George (*1834–1865*) 616
Arnold, Matthew (*1822–1858*) 584
note 481
Arrianus, Flavius (*c. 100–170*)
note 96
Asaf, George (*pseudonym of* George H. Powell) (*1880–1951*) 770
Asbury, Herbert (*1891–1963*)
note 554
Ashbery, John (*1927–*) 906
Aten, The Great Hymn to the (*c. 1350 B.C.*) 5
Aubigné, Théodore Agrippa d' (*1552–1630*) 171
Aubrey, John (*1626–1697*) 301
note 255, 263
Auden, W[ystan] H[ugh] (*1907–1973*) 868
note 477, 786
Aue, Hartmann von. *See* Hartmann
Augustine, Saint (*354–430*) 128
note 86, 127
Augustus Caesar (*63 B.C.–A.D. 14*) 110
Auslander, Joseph (*1897–1965*) 836
Austen, Jane (*1775–1817*) 440
Austin, Alfred (*1835–1913*)
note 170
Averroës (*1126–1198*) 137
Avonmore, Barry Yelverton, Lord (*1736–1805*)
note 365
Aytoun, William Edmondstoune (*1813–1865*) 551

Babel, Isaac Emmanuelovich (*1894 – c. 1939*) 828

Babeuf, François Noël (*pseudonym* Gracchus) (*1760–1797*) 414
Bacon, Lady Ann (*1528–1610*)
note 148
Bacon, Francis (*1561–1626*) 178
note 86, 99, 100, 110, 111, 119, 206, 285, 372
Bacon, Roger (*c. 1214 – c. 1294*) 139
Baden, Grand Duke Friedrich von (*1826–1907*) 597
Bagehot, Walter (*1826–1877*) 597
Bailey, Philip James (*1816–1902*) 555
note 532
Bairnsfather, Bruce (*1888–1959*) 796
Baker, Sir Henry Williams (*1821–1877*) 580
Baldwin, James (*1924–*) 903
Baldwin, Stanley, Earl Baldwin of Bewdley (*1867–1947*) 720
Balfour, Arthur James, Earl of Balfour (*1848–1930*) 661
Ballads (Anonymous) 926
Balzac, Honoré de (*1790–1850*) 484
note 582
Bancroft, George (*1800–1891*)
note 484
Bangs, John Kendrick (*1862–1922*)
note 270
Bankhead, Tallulah [Brockman] (*1903–1968*) 857
Banville, Théodore de (*1823–1891*) 591
Baraka, Amiri (LeRoi Jones) (*1934–*) 912
Barbauld, Anna Letitia (*1743–1825*) 387
Barbour, John (c. *1316–1395*) 143
Barca the Carthaginian. *See* Maharbal
Barclay, Alexander (*c. 1475–1552*)
note 109, 720
Barère de Vieuzac, Bertrand (*1755–1841*) 401
note 359
Baring, Maurice (*1874–1945*) 741
Baring-Gould, Sabine (*1834–1924*) 616
Barker, George (*1913–*) 881
Barlow, Joel (*1754–1812*) 400
Barnard, Charlotte Alington (*pseudonym* Claribel) (*1830–1869*) 603
Barnfield, Richard (*1574–1627*) 257
Barnum, P[hineas] T[aylor] (*1810–1891*) 536
Barrie, Sir James M[atthew] (*1860–1937*) 694
note 675
Barrington, George (*1755 – c. 1840*)
note 329
Barrymore, Ethel (*1879–1959*) 762
Bartas, Seigneur Du. *See* Du Bartas
Barth, Karl (*1886–1968*) 794
Barthélemy, Auguste Marseille (*1796–1867*)
note 451
Baruch, Bernard M[annes] (*1870–1965*) 729
Barzun, Jacques (*1907–*) 869
Basho (Matsuo, Basho) (*1644–1694*) 313
Basse, William (*died c. 1653*) 265
Bates, Katherine Lee (*1859–1929*) 688
Bath, Sir William Pulteney, Earl of. *See* Pulteney
Baudelaire, Charles (*1821–1867*) 580
Baum, L[yman] Frank (*1856–1919*) 677
Baxter, Richard (*1615–1691*) 294
Bayard, Pierre Terrail, Seigneur de (Chevalier Bayard) (*c. 1473–1524*)
note 163
Bayle, Pierre (*1647–1706*)
note 499
Bayly, T[homas] H[aynes] (*1797–1839*) 481
note 616
Beaconsfield, Benjamin Disraeli, Earl of. *See* Disraeli
Beard, Charles A[ustin] (*1874–1948*) 741
Beard, Mary R[itter] (*1876–1958*) 741
Beaumarchais, Pierre de (*1732–1799*) 378
Beaumont, Francis (*c. 1584–1616*) 263
Beaumont and Fletcher 263
note 101, 111, 155, 168, 176, 191, 205, 509
Beauvoir, Simone de (*1908–*) 870
Beaverbrook, William Maxwell Aiken, Baron (*1879–1964*) 762
Beck, Brooks (*1918–1969*)
note 815
Becker, Carl [Lotus] (*1873–1945*) 738
Beckett, Samuel (*1906–*) 866
Beddoes, Thomas Lovell (*1803–1849*) 492
Bede (Venerable Bede) (*c. 672 – c. 735*) 135
note 116

Bee, Bernard Elliott (1824–1861) 594
Beecher, Henry Ward (1813–1887) 551
Beerbohm, Sir Max (1872–1956) 735
Beers, Ethel Lynn (1827–1879)
note 598
Beethoven, Ludwig van (1770–1827) 421
Beeton, Isabella Mary (1836–1865) 627
Begin, Menachem (1913–) 881
Behn, Aphra (1640–1689) 312
Bell, Alexander Graham (1847–1922) 661
Bellamy, Edward (1850–1898) 665
Bellamy, Francis (1856–1931) 677
Bellay, Joachim du (1522–1560) 162
Belloc, Hilaire (1870–1953) 729
Bellow, Saul (1915–) 887
Benchley, Robert [Charles] (1889–1945) 812
Benda, Julien (1867–1956) 720
Benedict, Saint (480–543) 129
Benedict, Ruth [Fulton] (1887–1948) 796
Benét, Stephen Vincent (1898–1943) 839
Benét, William Rose (1886–1950) 794
Benjamin, Judah P[hilip] (1811–1884)
note 501
Bennard, George (1873–1958) 738
Bennett, [Enoch] Arnold (1867–1931) 720
Bennett, Henry Holcomb (1863–1924)
note 676
Benserade, Isaac de (1612–1691) 290
Benson, A[rthur] C[hristopher] (1862–1925) 698
Benson, Stella (1892–1933) 821
Bentham, Jeremy (1748–1832)
note 342
Bentley, E[dmund] C[lerihew] (1875–1956) 753
Bentley, Richard (1662–1742) 319
Benton, Thomas Hart (1782–1858) 449
Bergerac. *See* Cyrano de Bergerac
Bergson, Henri (1859–1941) 688
Berkeley, Bishop George (1685–1753) 330
Berlin, Irving (1888–) 802
Bernanos, Georges (1888–1948) 802
Bernard, Saint (1091–1153) 136
note 106
Bernard, Claude (1813–1878) 551
Bernard, Tristan (1866–1947) 718
Berra, Yogi [Lawrence Peter] (1925–) 903
Berryman, John (1914–1972) 884
Bertaut, Jean (1552–1611)
note 155
Beston, Henry (1888–1968) 802
Bethell, Richard, Lord Westbury. *See* Westbury
Bethmann-Hollweg, Theobald von (1856–1921) 677
Bethune, Mary McLeod (1875–1955) 753
Betjeman, John (1906–) 866
Beveridge, Albert [Jeremiah] (1862–1927) 698
Beveridge, Sir William Henry (1879–1963) 762
Beyerlinck, Laurens (Laurentius) (1578–1627)
note 126
Beyle, Henri. *See* Stendhal
Bhagavad Gita (250 B.C.–A.D. 250) 94
note 861
Bias (*6th century* B.C.). *See also* Seven Sages
note 73
Bible 6
Old Testament 6
Amos 33
I Chronicles 14
Daniel 32
Deuteronomy 11
Ecclesiastes 26
Esther 14
Exodus 9
Ezekiel 32
Genesis 6
Habakkuk 33
Hosea 33
Isaiah 28
note 48
Jeremiah 31
note 32, 36
Job 14
note 15, 907
Joel 33
Jonah 33
Joshua 11
Judges 12
I Kings 13
II Kings 14
Lamentations 32
Leviticus 10
Malachi 33
Micah 33

Bible (*continued*)
Nahum 33
note 33
Nehemiah 14
Numbers 10
Proverbs 23
note 16, 25
Psalms 17
note 15
Ruth 12
I Samuel 12
II Samuel 13
Song of Solomon 28
Zechariah 33
New Testament 36
Acts 45
Colossians 50
I Corinthians 48
II Corinthians 49
Ephesians 49
Galatians 49
Hebrews 51
James 51
John 44
note 44
I John 52
Jude 52
Luke 42
Mark 41
Matthew 36
note 11, 41, 89, 198
I Peter 52
II Peter 52
Philemon 51
Philippians 50
Revelation 52
Romans 46
note 46
I Thessalonians 50
I Timothy 50
II Timothy 51
Titus 51
Apocrypha 34
Ecclesiasticus (Wisdom of Jesus the Son of Sirach) 34
I Esdras 34
II Esdras 34
History of Susanna 36
Judith 34
II Maccabees 36
Song of the Three Holy Children 36
Tobit 34
Wisdom of Solomon 34
Bichat, Marie François Xavier (*1771–1802*) 429
Bickerstaffe, Isaac (*c. 1735 – c. 1812*) 382
Biel, Gabriel (*c. 1425–1495*) 150
note 137
Bierce, Ambrose (*1842–c. 1914*) 647
Biko, Steve [Stephen Bantu] (*1946–1977*) 916
Billings, Josh (*pseudonym of* Henry Wheeler Shaw) (*1818–1885*) 561
Binyon, Laurence (*1869–1943*) 727
Bion (*c. 325 – c. 255 B.C.*) 92
Birrell, Augustine (*1850–1933*) 666
Bishop, Elizabeth (*1911–1979*) 878
Bishop, Thomas Brigham (*1835–1905*) 619
Bismarck, Otto von (*1815–1898*) 553
note 553
Black, Hugo La Fayette (*1886–1971*) 794
Black Elk (*1863–1950*) 701
Black Hawk (*1767–1838*) 418
Blacker, Valentine (*1778–1823*) 444
Blackstone, Sir William (*1723–1780*) 365
Blair, Eric. *See* Orwell, George
Blair, Robert (*1699–1746*)
note 274, 306, 318
Blake, Charles Dupee (*1846–1903*) 660
Blake, James W. (*1862–1935*) 698
Blake, William (*1757–1827*) 402
note 386, 407
Blanc, Louis (*1811–1882*)
note 563
Bland, James A. (*1854–1911*) 672
Blasco-Ibáñez, Vicente (*1867–1928*) 720
Bliss, Daniel (*1740–1806*) 385
Bliss, Philip Paul (*1838–1876*) 635
Blixen, Karen. *See* Dinesen, Isak
Blok, Alexander (*1880–1921*) 770
Bloomer, Amelia Jenks (*1818–1894*)
note 842
Blount, Sir Thomas Pope (*1649–1697*) 316
Bloy, Léon (*1846–1917*) 661
Blücher, Gebhard Leberecht von (*1742–1819*) 386
Blum, Léon (*1872–1950*) 736
Blunden, Edmund (*1896–1974*) 834
Blunt, Wilfrid Scawen (*1840–1922*) 639
Bly, Robert (*1926–*) 905
Boas, Franz (*1858–1942*) 685
Boccaccio, Giovanni (*1313–1375*)
note 255
Boethius, [Anicius Manlius Severinus] (*480–524*) 129
note 77, 108
Bogan, Louise (*1897–1970*) 836

Bogart, Humphrey [DeForest] (*1899–1957*) 843
note 913
Bogart, John B. (*1845–1921*) 659
Bohn, Henry George (*1796–1884*)
note 186
Bohr, Niels (*1885–1962*) 789
Boileau-Despréaux, Nicolas (*1636–1711*) 311
note 462
Bolingbroke, Henry St. John, Viscount (*1678–1751*) 329
Bolívar, Simón (*1783–1830*) 451
Bond, Carrie Jacobs (*1862–1946*) 698
Bontemps, Arna (*1902–*) 854
Book of Changes, The (*I Ching*) (*c. 12th century B.C.*) 5
Book of Common Prayer 54
note 17, 18, 19, 20, 22, 36, 37, 173, 534
Book of Common Prayer, English 56
Book of the Dead, The (*c. 1700–1000 B.C.*) 4
Booth, Barton (*1681–1733*)
note 291
Booth, John Wilkes (*1838–1865*) 635
Borges, Jorge Luis (*1899–*) 843
Born, Max (*1882–1970*) 775
Borrow, George (*1803–1881*) 492
Bosquet, Pierre [Jean François Joseph] (*1810–1861*) 536
Bossidy, John Collins (*1860–1928*) 694
Bossuet, Jacques Bénigne (*1627–1704*) 301
note 421
Boswell, James (*1740–1795*) 385
note 78, 79, 86, 350, 352, 355
Bottomley, Gordon (*1874–1948*) 741
Boulay de la Meurthe, Antoine [Jacques Claude Joseph] (*1761–1840*) 415
Boulton, Harold Edwin (*1859–1935*) 688
Bourdillon, Francis William (*1852–1921*) 670
Bourget, [Charles Joseph] Paul (*1852–1935*) 670
Bowen, Edward Ernest (*1836–1901*) 627
Bowles, William Lisle (*1762–1850*) 415
Bowring, John (*1792–1872*) 465
Boyle, Robert (*1627–1691*) 301
Bradford, John (*1510–1555*) 162
Bradford, Sarah H. (*b. 1818*)
note 593
Bradford, William (*1590–1657*) 265
Bradley, Omar (*1893–*) 825
Bradstreet, Anne (*c. 1612–1672*) 290
Brady, Nicholas (*1659–1726*) 317
Bragg, Edward Stuyvesant (*1827–1912*) 598
Braley, Berton (*1882–1966*) 775
Brandeis, Louis D[embitz] (*1856–1941*) 677
note 444
Brann, William Cowper (*1855–1898*) 676
note 421
Brant, Sebastian (*1457–1521*) 152
Braque, Georges (*1882–1963*) 776
Brecht, Bertolt (*1898–1956*) 840
Brereton, Jane (*1685–1740*) 330
Breton, André (*1896–1966*) 834
Breton, Nicholas (*c. 1545–1626*)
note 175
Bridges, Robert (*1844–1930*) 654
Bridgman, Percy Williams (*1882–1961*) 776
Briggs, Le Baron Russell (*1855–1934*)
note 890
Bright, John (*1811–1889*) 538
note 683
Brillat-Savarin, Anthelme (*1755–1826*) 401
note 170
Brinnin, John Malcolm (*1916–*) 888
Brogan, D[enis] W[illiam] (*1900–1974*) 847
Bromley, Isaac Hill (*1833–1898*) 614
Bronowski, Jacob (*1908–1974*) 870, 871
Brontë, Charlotte (*1816–1855*) 555
Brontë, Emily (*1818–1848*) 561
Brooke, Fulke Greville, Lord. *See* Greville
Brooke, Henry (*c. 1703–1783*)
note 356
Brooke, Rupert (*1887–1915*) 796
Brooks, Gwendolyn (*1917–*) 889
Brooks, Paul (*1909–*) 875
Brooks, Phillips (*1835–1893*) 619
Brooks, Thomas (*1608–1680*)
note 34
Brougham, Henry Peter, Baron Brougham and Vaux (*1778–1868*) 444
Broun, Heywood (*1888–1939*) 803
note 665
Brown, James (*1934–*) 913

Brown, John (*1800–1859*) 486
Brown, Lew (*1893–1958*) 825
Brown, Rap [Hubert Gerold] (*1943–*) 915
Brown, Thomas (Tom) (*1663–1704*) 319
Brown, Thomas Edward (*1830–1897*) 603
Browne, Charles Farrar (*pseudonym* Artemus Ward) (*1834–1867*) 616
Browne, Matthew. *See* Rands, William Brighty
Browne, Sir Thomas (*1605–1682*) 273
note 108, 116, 121, 153, 169, 181, 262, 270, 308, 657
Browne, William (*1591–1643*) 265
note 181
Browning, Elizabeth Barrett (*1806–1861*) 506
note 120
Browning, Robert (*1812–1889*) 540
note 80, 158, 202, 205, 234, 321, 332, 473
Brownlow, Louis (*1879–1963*) 762
Brownson, Orestes A[ugustus] (*1803–1876*) 492
Bruegel, Pieter (*c. 1525–1569*) 163
Bruner, Jerome S[eymour] (*1915–*) 887
Bruno, Giordano (*1548–1600*) 171
note 179, 387
Bruyère, Jean de La. *See* La Bruyère
Bryan, William Jennings (*1860–1925*) 694
note 694
Bryant, William Cullen (*1794–1878*) 471
Bryce, James (*1838–1922*) 635
Buchan, John, Lord Tweedsmuir (*1875–1940*) 753
Buchanan, Robert (*1841–1901*) 643
Büchner, Georg (*1813–1837*) 552
Buck, Pearl S[ydenstricker] (*1891–1973*) 821
Buckingham, Duke of. *See* Villiers
Buckingham and Normanby, John Sheffield, Duke of. *See* Sheffield
Buffon, Georges Louis Leclerc de (*1707–1788*) 349
Buller, Arthur Henry Reginald (*1874–1944*) 742
Bülow, Bernhard von (*1849–1929*) 663
Bulwer-Lytton, Edward George Earle Lytton, Baron Lytton (*1803–1873*) 493
note 512
Bulwer-Lytton, Edward Robert. *See* Lytton
Bunn, Alfred (*1796–1860*) 480
Bunner, Henry Cuyler (*1855–1896*) 676
Bunyan, John (*1628–1688*) 301
note 145, 193
Burchard, Samuel Dickinson (*1812–1891*) 546
Burdette, Robert Jones (*1844–1914*) 655
Burgess, Gelett (*1866–1951*) 718
note 736
Burgon, John William (*1813–1860*) 552
Burke, Edmund (*1729–1797*) 372
note 350, 799, 894
Burnham, Daniel Hudson (*1846–1912*) 661
Burns, Robert (*1759–1796*) 408
note 159, 218, 259, 333, 382, 919
Burroughs, Edgar Rice (*1875–1950*) 753
Burroughs, Bishop Edward Arthur (*1882–1934*) 776
Burroughs, John (*1837–1921*) 630
Burton, Henry (*1840–1930*) 639
Burton, Sir Richard Francis (*1821–1890*) 581
note 335
Burton, Robert (*1577–1640*) 258
note 96, 106, 116, 117, 120, 148, 156, 158, 159, 160, 161, 177, 186
Busch, Wilhelm (*1832–1908*) 610
Bush, Vannevar (*1890–1974*) 814
Bussy-Rabutin, Roger de (*1618–1693*) 294
note 319
Butler, Nicholas Murray (*1862–1947*) 698
Butler, Samuel (*1612–1680*) 290
note 65, 112, 149, 173, 188, 348
Butler, Samuel (*1835–1902*) 620
Butler, William (*1535–1618*) 166
Butler, William Allen (*1825–1902*) 595
Butterfield, Herbert (*1900–*) 847
Byrd, William (*1543–1623*)
note 167
Byrom, John (*1692–1763*) 341
note 300

Byron, George Noel Gordon, Lord (*1788–1824*) 456
note 91, 108, 145, 258, 261, 295, 306, 364, 432, 743

Cabell, James Branch (*1879–1958*) 762
Caecilius Statius (*220–168 B.C.*) 95
Caedmon (*fl. 670*) 135
Caesar, Augustus. *See* Augustus Caesar
Caesar, Gaius. *See* Caligula
Caesar, [Gaius] Julius (*100–44 B.C.*) 99
note 303
Calderón de la Barca, Pedro (*1600–1681*) 273
Caldwell, Erskine (*1903–*) 857
Calhoun, Arthur Wallace (*1885–*) 789
Calhoun, John C[aldwell] (*1782–1850*) 449
Caligula (Gaius Caesar) (*12–41*) 116
Callimachus (*c. 300–240 B.C.*) 92
Calverley, Charles Stuart (*1831–1884*)
note 546, 602
Cambronne, Pierre Jacques Étienne, Count (*1770–1842*) 421
Camden, William (*1551–1623*) 171
Camões [Camoëns], Luis Vaz de (*c. 1524–1580*) 162
Campanella, Tommaso (*1568–1639*) 250
Campbell, Joseph (*1881–1944*) 773
Campbell, Mrs. Patrick (Beatrice Stella Tanner Campbell) (*1865–1940*) 706
Campbell, Roy (*1901–1957*) 852
Campbell, Thomas (*1777–1844*) 443
note 261, 360
Campbell, Timothy J. (*1840–1904*) 639
Campion, Thomas (*1567–1620*) 250
Camus, Albert (*1913–1960*) 882
Canning, George (*1770–1827*) 421
Cannon, Jimmy (*1910–1973*) 877
Čapek, Karel (*1890–1938*) 814
Capote, Truman (*1924–*) 903
Cardozo, Benjamin Nathan (*1870–1938*) 730
Carew, Richard (*1555–1620*)
note 176
Carew, Thomas (*c. 1595 – c. 1639*) 271
Carey, Henry (*c. 1687–1743*) 331
Carleton, Will[iam McKendree] (*1845–1912*) 660
note 109
Carlyle, Jane [Baillie] Welsh (*1801–1866*) 489
note 473
Carlyle, Thomas (*1795–1881*) 472
note 123, 139, 158, 420, 472, 473, 474, 536
Carman, [William] Bliss (*1861–1929*) 696
Carmichael, Stokely (Kwame Toure) (*1941–*) 914
Carnegie, Andrew (*1835–1919*) 621
Carnegie, Dale (*1888–1955*) 803
Carney, Julia A. Fletcher (*1823–1908*) 591
Carpenter, Joseph Edwards (*1813–1885*)
note 548
Carroll, Lewis (*pseudonym of* Charles Lutwidge Dodgson) (*1832–1898*) 611
Carruth, W[illiam] H[erbert] (*1859–1924*)
note 545
Carryl, Charles Edward (*1842–1920*) 647
Carryl, Guy Wetmore (*1873–1904*) 738
Carson, Rachel [Louise] (*1907–1964*) 869
Carter, Jimmy (James Earl, Jr.) (*1924–*) 903
note 909
Cartier, Jacques (*1491–1557*) 157
Cartwright, William (*1611–1643*) 290
Cary, Phoebe (*1824–1871*) 594
Casement, Sir Roger (*1864–1916*) 704
Cassiodorus, Flavius Magnus Aurelius (*c. 490–583*) 130
Castro, Fidel (*1926–*) 905
Cather, Willa [Sibert] (*1873–1947*) 738
Cato, Marcus Porcius (Cato the Elder, Cato the Censor) (*234–149 B.C.*) 95
note 120
Catt, Carrie Chapman [Lane] (*1859–1947*) 688
Catullus, Gaius Valerius (*87–c. 54 B.C.*) 101
Cavafy, C[onstantine] P[eter] (*1863–1933*) 701
Cavell, Edith [Louisa] (*1865–1915*) 706
Cecil, Robert Arthur Talbot Gascoyne-. *See* Salisbury

Céline, Louis Ferdinand (*pseudonym of* Louis Ferdinand Destouches) (*1894–1961*) 828
Centlivre, Susannah (*c. 1667–1723*) 321
note 564
Cervantes, Miguel de (*1547–1616*) 168
note 96, 103, 110, 111, 119, 120, 123, 146, 148, 149, 158, 225, 261, 321
Cézanne, Paul (*1839–1906*) 638
Chafee, Zechariah, Jr. (*1885–1957*) 789
Chagall, Marc (*1887–*) 797
Chalmers, Patrick Reginald (*1872–1942*) 736
Chamberlain, Joseph (*1836–1914*) 627
Chamberlain, Neville (*1869–1940*) 727
Chamfort, Sébastien Roch Nicolas (*1741–1794*) 386
Chandler, Raymond (*1888–1959*) 803
Chanel, Coco [Gabrielle] (*1883–1970*) 782
Chang Heng (*78–139*) 123
Channing, William Ellery (*1780–1842*) 448
Channing, William Ellery (*1818–1901*) 562
Channing, William Henry (*1810–1884*) 536
Chaplin, Charlie (Sir Charles Spencer) (*1889–1977*) 812
Chapman, Arthur (*1873–1935*) 739
Chapman, George (*c. 1559–1634*) 177
note 152, 155, 158, 159, 183
Chapman, John Jay (*1862–1933*) 699
Charles I (*1600–1649*)
note 370
Charles II (*1630–1685*) 302
Charles V (*1500–1558*) 161
Charles V (Charles the Wise) (*1337–1380*) 143
Charles VIII (*1470–1498*) 154
Charles IX (*1550–1574*) 171
Charles d'Orléans. *See* Orléans
Charles, Prince, of Prussia (*fl. c. 1745*)
note 368
Charles, Hughie (*1907–*) 885
Charron, Pierre (*1541–1603*)
note 337
Charter of the United Nations 788
Chartier, Alain (*c. 1385 – c. 1433*)
note 478
Chartier, Émile Auguste (*pseudonym* Alain) (*1868–1951*) 724
Chase, Salmon P[ortland] (*1808–1873*) 514
Chateaubriand, François René de (*1768–1848*) 419
Chatham, William Pitt, Earl of. *See* Pitt
Chatterton, Thomas (*1752–1770*) 399
Chaucer, Geoffrey (*c. 1343–1400*) 143
note 51, 58, 84, 93, 113, 117, 137, 158, 218
Chavez, Cesar [Estrada] (*1927–*) 906
Chayevsky, Paddy (*1923–*) 901
Cheever, John (*1912–*) 879
Chekhov, Anton Pavlovich (*1860–1904*) 695
note 602
Ch'en Tu-hsiu (*1879–1942*) 763
Cheney, John Vance (*1848–1922*) 661
Cherry, Andrew (*1762–1812*) 415
Chesterfield, Philip Dormer Stanhope, Earl of (*1694–1773*) 341
note 370, 593
Chesterton, G[ilbert] K[eith] (*1874–1936*) 742
Chikamatsu, Monzaemon (*1653–1725*) 317
Child, Lydia Maria (*1802–1880*) 490
Chilon (*6th century B.C.*). *See* Seven Sages
Ching Hao (*fl. 925*) 135
Choate, Rufus (*1799–1859*) 484
Christie, Agatha (*1891–1976*) 817
Christy, David (*1802–c. 1868*) 491
Chrysostom, Saint John (*c. 345–407*) 128
Chuang-tzu (*369–286 B.C.*) 90
Church, Francis Pharcellus (*1839–1906*) 638
Churchill, Charles (*1731–1764*) 375
Churchill, Lord Randolph Spencer (*1849–1895*) 663
Churchill, Sir Winston Spencer (*1874–1965*) 742, 781
note 642, 743
Churchyard, Thomas (*c. 1520–1604*)
note 249
Ciano, Count Galeazzo (*1903–1944*) 857
Ciardi, John (*1916–*) 888
Cibber, Colley (*1671–1757*) 324
note 275, 324
Cicero, Marcus Tullius (*106–43 B.C.*) 98
note 58, 96, 348

Cid, Poem of the (*12th century*) 137
Clapiers, Luc de, Marquis de Vauvenargues. *See* Vauvenargues
Clare, John (*1793–1864*) 470
Clarendon, Edward Hyde, Earl of. *See* Hyde
Clarke, Joseph Ignatius Constantine (*1846–1925*) 661
Claudel, Paul (*1868–1955*) 724
Clausewitz, Karl von (*1780–1831*) 448
Clausius, Rudolf [Julius Emanuel] (*1822–1888*) 589
Clay, Henry (*1777–1852*) 444
note 438
Cleanthes (*c. 330–232 B.C.*) 92
Cleaver, [Leroy] Eldridge (*1935–*) 913
Cleghorn, Sarah N[orcliffe] (*1876–1959*) 757
Clemenceau, Georges (*1841–1929*) 643
Clemens, Samuel Langhorne. *See* Twain, Mark
Cleobulus (*6th century B.C.*). *See* Seven Sages
Cleveland, Grover (*1837–1908*) 631
Cleveland, [James] Harlan (*1918–*) 894
Clifford, William Kingdon (*1845–1879*) 660
Clive, Robert, Lord (*1725–1774*) 367
Clough, Arthur Hugh (*1819–1861*) 564
note 532
Clovis (*466–511*) 129
Cobb, Irvin S[hrewsbury] (*1876–1944*) 757
Cockburn, Alison (*1713–1794*) 359
Cocteau, Jean (*1891–1963*) 818
Cohan, George M[ichael] (*1878–1942*) 759
Coke, Sir Edward (*1552–1634*) 171
Cole, Thomas (*1801–1848*) 490
Coleridge, [David] Hartley (*1796–1849*) 480
note 424
Coleridge, Henry Nelson (*1798–1843*)
note 423
Coleridge, Samuel Taylor (*1772–1834*) 433
note 118, 196, 428, 441, 443
Colette (*pseudonym of* Sidonie Gabrielle Colette) (*1873–1954*) 739
Collins, John Churton (*1848–1908*) 662
Collins, William (*1721–1759*) 364
Collins, [William] Wilkie (*1824–1889*) 594
Colman, George, the Younger (*1762–1836*) 415
note 123
Colton, Charles Caleb (*1780–1832*) 448
Colum, Mary [Maguire] (*c. 1885–1957*)
note 845
Colum, Padraic (*1881–1972*) 774
Columbus, Christopher (*1451–1506*) 150
Comte, Auguste (*1798–1857*) 483
Conan Doyle, Sir Arthur. *See* Doyle
Conant, James Bryant (*1893–1978*) 825
Condillac, Étienne Bonnot de (L'Abbé de Condillac) (*1715–1780*) 360
Confucius (*551–479 B.C.*) 68
Congreve, William (*1670–1729*) 324
note 515, 532
Conkling, Roscoe (*1829–1888*) 602
Connelly, Marc[us Cook] (*1890–*) 814
Connolly, Cyril [Vernon] (*1903–1974*) 857
note 711
Conrad, Joseph (*1857–1924*) 683
Constable, Henry (*1562–1613*)
note 429
Constantine (Flavius Valerius Aurelius Constantinus) (*c. 288–337*) 127
Constitution of the United States (*1787*) 391
Cook, Eliza (*1818–1889*) 562
Cooke, Edmund Vance (*1866–1932*) 718
Coolidge, Calvin (*1872–1933*) 736
Cooper, Anthony Ashley, Earl of Shaftesbury. *See* Shaftesbury
Cooper, George (*1838–1927*) 636
Cooper, James Fenimore (*1789–1851*) 463
Copeland, Charles Townsend (*1860–1952*) 695
Copernicus, Nicholas (*1473–1543*) 154
Corbet, Bishop Richard (*1582–1635*) 262
Corbusier, Le. *See* Le Corbusier
Corneille, Pierre (*1606–1684*) 275
note 117
Cornford, Frances (*1886–1960*) 795
Cornuel, Madame (*1605–1694*)
note 88

Cornwall, Barry (*pseudonym of* Bryan Waller Procter) (*1787–1874*) 456
Corse, John Murray (*1835–1893*)
note 579
Cortés, Hernán (Hernando Cortez) (*1485–1547*) 156
Cory, William Johnson (*1823–1892*) 591
Costello, Lou (Louis Francis Cristillo) (*1906–1959*) 832
Cotton, Nathaniel (*1705–1788*) 346
Coué, Émile (*1857–1926*) 684
Cousin, Victor (*1792–1867*) 465
Coward, Noel (*1899–1973*) 843
Cowboy Songs (Anonymous) 927
Cowley, Abraham (*1618–1667*) 295
note 108, 119
Cowper, William (*1731–1800*) 375
note 118, 304, 320, 336, 375
Crabbe, George (*1754–1832*) 400
note 259, 532
Craig, [Edward] Gordon (*1872–1966*) 736
Craik, Dinah Maria Mulock (*1826–1887*) 597
Crane, Hart (*1899–1932*) 843
Crane, Stephen (*1871–1900*) 732
Cranfield, Lionel, Earl of Middlesex (*1575–1645*)
note 290
Crapsey, Adelaide (*1878–1914*) 759
Crashaw, Richard (*c. 1613–1649*) 292
note 173
Crassus, Marcus Licinius (*fl. 70 B.C.*) 97
Craven, Margaret (*1901–*) 852
Crawford, F[rancis] Marion (*1854–1909*)
note 694
Crawford, Julia (*1800–1885*) 487
Crèvecoeur, Michel Guillaume Jean de (*pseudonym* J. Hector St. John) (*1735–1813*) 382
Crile, George Washington (*1864–1943*)
note 746
Crittenden, John Jordan (*1787–1863*)
note 445
Crockett, David (*1786–1836*) 455
Cromwell, Oliver (*1599–1658*) 272
Cronkite, Walter (*1916–*) 888
Cross, Marian Evans. *See* Eliot, George
Crowfoot (*1821–1890*) 581
Crumb, R[obert] (*1943–*) 915
Cruz, Juana Inés de la (*1648–1695*) 316
Cuauhtémoc (*c. 1495–1525*)
note 721
Culbertson, Ely (*1891–1955*) 818
Cullen, Countee (*1903–1946*) 857
Cumberland, Bishop Richard (*1631–1718*) 303
Cummings, E[dward] E[stlin] (*1894–1962*) 828
Cummings, William Thomas (*1903–1944*) 857
Cunningham, Allan (*1784–1842*) 453
Cunningham, Sir Andrew Browne (*1883–1963*) 782
Cunninghame-Graham, Robert Bontine (*1852–1936*) 670
Curran, John Philpot (*1750–1817*) 397
Curtius, Quintus (*1st century*)
note 172
Custine, Astolphe Louis Léonard, Marquis de (*1790–1857*) 464
Cyprian, Saint (*d. 258*) 126
Cyrano de Bergerac, Savinien (*1619–1655*)
note 298

Dacre, Harry (*d. 1922*) 718
Dana, Richard Henry (*1815–1882*) 553
Daniel, Samuel (*1562–1619*) 182
note 99
Dante Alighieri (*1265–1321*) 140
note 100
Danton, Georges Jacques (*1759–1794*) 412
D'Arcy, Hugh Antoine (*1843–1925*) 652
Darío, Rubén (*pseudonym of* Félix Rubén García Sarmiento) (*1867–1916*) 720
Darion, Joe (*1917–*) 890
Darrow, Clarence [Seward] (*1857–1938*) 684
Darrow, Karl Kelchner (*1891–*) 818
Darwin, Charles Robert (*1809–1882*) 514
Darwin, Erasmus (*1731–1802*) 377
Darwin, Sir Francis (*1848–1925*) 662
Daugherty, Harry M[icajah] (*1860–1941*) 695
Davenant, Sir William (*1606–1668*) 275
David, Hal (*1921–*) 898
Davidson, John (*1857–1909*) 684

Davies, Sir John (*1569–1626*) 251
note 165, 167
Davies, John, of Hereford (*c. 1565–1618*) 250
Davies, W[illiam] H[enry] (*1871–1940*) 732
da Vinci, Leonardo. *See* Vinci
Davis, David (*1815–1886*) 553
Davis, Elmer (*1890–1958*) 814
Davis, James (*pseudonym* Owen Hall) (*1853–1907*) 685
Davis, Thomas Osborne (*1814–1845*) 552
Dawson, Christopher [Henry] (*1889–*) 812
Day, Clarence (*1874–1935*) 746
Day Lewis, Cecil. *See* Lewis
Dazai, Osamu (*pseudonym of* Tsushima Shuji) (*1909–1948*) 875
Debs, Eugene V[ictor] (*1855–1926*) 676
Decatur, Stephen (*1779–1820*) 445
Deffand, Marie de Vichy-Chamrond, Marquise du (*1697–1780*) 344
Defoe, Daniel (*c. 1660–1731*) 318
note 194
de Gaulle, Charles [André Joseph Marie] (*1890–1970*) 815
Dekker, Thomas (*1572–1632*) 251
note 99
Delacroix, Eugène (*1798–1863*) 483
de la Mare, Walter (*1873–1956*) 739
Delille, Jacques (*1738–1813*) 385
Deloria, Vine [Victor], Jr. (*1933–*) 912
Democritus (*c. 460 – c. 400 B.C.*) 79
Demosthenes (*c. 384–322 B.C.*) 88
note 397
Denham, Sir John (*1615–1669*) 294
note 338
Denman, Thomas, Lord (*1779–1854*) 445
Dennis, John (*1657–1734*) 318
De Quincey, Thomas (*1785–1859*) 454
note 351
Derzhavin, Gavriil Romanovich (*1743–1816*) 387
Descartes, René (*1596–1650*) 272
Destouches, Philippe (*pseudonym of* Philippe Néricault) (*1680–1754*) 329
De Sylva, Buddy [George Gard] (*1895–1950*) 825
De Voto, Bernard (*1897–1955*) 837
note 699
Dewar, Sir James (*1842–1923*) 647
Dewey, George (*1837–1917*) 631
Dewey, Thomas E[dmund] (*1902–1971*) 854
Díaz, Porfirio (*1830–1915*) 604
Diaz del Castillo, Bernal (*c. 1492 – c. 1581*) 157
note 481
Dibdin, Charles (*1745–1814*) 393
Dibdin, Thomas (*1771–1841*) 429
Dickens, Charles [John Huffam] (*1812–1870*) 546
note 258, 298, 433, 519
Dickey, James (*1923–*) 901
Dickinson, Emily (*1830–1886*) 604
note 293
Dickinson, Goldsworthy Lowes (*1862–1932*) 699
Dickinson, John (*1732–1808*) 378
Dickman, Franklin J[ackson] (*1827–1908*) 598
Diderot, Denis (*1713–1784*) 359
Didion, Joan (*1934–*) 913
Digby, Sir Kenelm (*1603–1665*) 273
Dillon, Wentworth, Earl of Roscommon. *See* Roscommon
Dinesen, Isak (*pseudonym of* Karen Blixen) (*1885–1962*) 789
Dio Chrysostom (Dio Cocceianus) (*c. 40 – c. 120*) 118
Diogenes the Cynic (*c. 400 – c. 325 B.C.*) 86
Diogenes Laertius (*fl. c. 200*) 125
note 79, 111, 270, 443
Dionysius of Halicarnassus (*c. 54 – c. 7 B.C.*) 112
Disraeli, Benjamin, Earl of Beaconsfield (*1804–1881*) 501
note 349, 922
D'Israeli, Isaac (*1766–1848*) 417
Divine, Father (George Baker) (*c. 1882–1965*) 776
Doane, William Croswell (*1832–1913*) 614
Dobie, J[ames] Frank (*1888–1964*) 803
Dobroliubov, Nikolai Alexandrovich (*1836–1861*)
note 550
Dobson, [Henry] Austin (*1840–1921*) 639
note 107, 179
Dobzhansky, Theodosius (*1900–1975*) 848
Doddridge, Philip (*1702–1751*) 346
Dodgson, Charles Lutwidge. *See* Carroll, Lewis

Donne, John (*1572–1631*) 251
note 743
Dooley, Mr. *See* Dunne
Dos Passos, John [Roderigo] (*1896–1970*) 835
Dostoevski, Fëdor Mikhailovich (*1821–1881*) 581
Douglas, Norman (*1868–1952*) 724
Douglas, Sallie Hume (*fl. c. 1923*)
note 535
Douglas, William O[rville] (*1898–1980*) 841
Douglass, Frederick (*c. 1817–1895*) 556
note 593
Dow, Lorenzo (*1777–1834*) 444
Dowling, Bartholomew (*1823–1863*) 719
Dowson, Ernest (*1867–1900*) 721
Doyle, Sir Arthur Conan (*1859–1930*) 689
note 544
Doyle, Sir Francis Hastings (*1810–1888*) 536
Drake, Joseph Rodman (*1795–1820*) 474
Drayton, Michael (*1563–1631*) 182
Dreiser, Theodore (*1871–1945*) 732
Drennan, William (*1754–1820*) 400
Driver, William (*1803–1886*) 493
Drummond, Thomas (*1797–1840*)
note 501
Drummond, William (*1585–1649*)
note 181
Dryden, John (*1631–1700*) 303
note 76, 78, 113, 115, 167, 175, 185, 192, 259, 260, 394, 567, 926
Du Bartas, Guillaume de Salluste, Seigneur (*1544–1590*) 167
note 111, 116, 117, 147, 158, 169, 284
Du Bois, W[illiam] E[dward] B[urghardt] (*1868–1963*) 724
Dudley, Sir Henry Bate (*1745–1824*) 393
Duffield, George (*1818–1888*) 562
Duhem, Pierre Maurice Marie (*1861–1916*) 696
Dulles, John Foster (*1888–1959*) 803
Dumas, Alexandre, the Elder (*1802–1870*) 491
Dumas, Alexandre, the Younger (*1824–1895*) 594
note 695
du Maurier, George [Louis Palmella Busson] (*1834–1896*) 617
note 362, 498, 546
Dunbar, Paul Laurence (*1872–1906*) 736
Dunbar, William (*c. 1465 – c. 1530*) 153
Dunne, Finley Peter (*creator of* Mr. Dooley) (*1867–1936*) 721
Durant, Will (*1885–*) 789
Durante, Jimmy (James Francis) (*1893–1980*) 825
D'Urfey, Thomas (*1653–1723*)
note 332
Durocher, Leo (*1906–*) 867
Durrell, Lawrence [George] (*1912–*) 880
Dyer, Sir Edward (*c. 1543–1607*) 167
Dyer, John (*c. 1700–1758*) 345
Dykes, Oswald (*fl. c. 1709*)
note 101
Dylan, Bob (Robert Zimmerman) (*1941–*) 915

Earhart [Putnam], Amelia (*1898–1937*) 842
Early Miscellaneous (Anonymous) 132
Eastman, Charles Alexander. *See* Ohiyesa
Ebbinghaus, Hermann (*1850–1909*) 666
Eberhart, Richard (*1904–*) 858
Eckhart, Meister (*c. 1260 – c. 1327*) 140
Eddington, Sir Arthur Stanley (*1882–1944*) 776
Eddy, Mary Baker (*1821–1910*) 583
Eden, Sir Anthony (*1897–1977*) 837
Edison, Thomas A[lva] (*1847–1931*) 661
Edward III (*1312–1377*) 143
Edward VIII. *See* Windsor, Edward, Duke of
Edwards, Jonathan (*1703–1758*) 346
note 892
Edwards, Oliver (*1711–1791*) 357
Edwards, Richard (*c. 1523–1566*)
note 96
Egan, Pierce (*1772–1849*)
note 553
Egan, Raymond B. (*1890–1952*) 795
Ehrlichman, John [Daniel] (*1925–*) 904
Eike von Repkow (*fl. c. 1220*) 138
Einstein, Albert (*1879–1955*) 763
note 763
Eisenhower, Dwight D[avid] (*1890–1969*) 815
Eliot, Charles William (*1834–1926*) 617
Eliot, George (*pseudonym of* Marian Evans Cross) (*1819–1880*) 564

Eliot, T[homas] S[tearns] (*1888–1965*) 803
  note 56, 57, 94, 128, 174, 177, 580, 711
Elizabeth I (*1533–1603*) 163
Elizabeth, Queen Mother of England (*1900–*) 848
Elizabeth, Queen of Belgium (*1876–1965*)
  note 746
Ellerton, John (*1826–1893*) 597
Elliot, Jane (*1727–1805*) 368
Elliott, Ebenezer (*1781–1849*) 449
Ellis, Havelock (*1859–1939*) 689
  note 694
Ellison, Ralph [Waldo] (*1914–*) 885
Éluard, Paul (*1895–1952*) 832
Emerson, Ralph Waldo (*1803–1882*) 493
  note 164, 336, 354, 365, 426, 488, 493, 495, 496, 497, 501, 504, 538, 708
Emmett, Daniel Decatur (*1815–1904*) 554
Empedocles (*c. 490 – c. 430 B.C.*) 75
Engels, Friedrich (*1820–1895*) 563
  note 563
English, Thomas Dunn (*1819–1902*) 566
Ennius, Quintus (*239–169 B.C.*) 94
Epictetus (*c. 50–120*) 121
  note 88, 112
Epicurus (*341–270 B.C.*) 91
Epstein, Julius J. (*1909–*)
  note 913
Epstein, Philip G. (*1909–1952*)
  note 913
Erasmus, Desiderius (*1465–1536*) 153
  note 62, 91, 108, 115, 128
Erickson, Arthur Charles (*1924–*) 903
Erikson, Erik [Homburger] (*1902–*) 854
  note 854
Estienne, Henri (*c. 1531–1598*) 163
Euclid (*fl. 300 B.C.*) 92
Euripides (*c. 485–406 B.C.*) 75
  note 66, 267
Euwer, Anthony [Henderson] (*1877–1955*) 758
Evans, Bergen [Baldwin] (*1904–1978*) 859
Evarts, William Maxwell (*1818–1901*) 562
Everett, Edward (*1794–1865*) 471
Evtushenko, Evgeni. *See* Yevtushenko, Yevgeny
Faber, Frederick William (*1814–1863*) 552
Fabius Maximus (*c. 275–203 B.C.*) 93
Fadiman, Clifton (*1904–*) 859
Fallersleben. *See* Hoffmann, August Heinrich
Farley, James A[loysius] (*1888–1976*)
  note 923
Farquhar, George (*1678–1707*) 329
Farragut, David Glasgow (*1801–1870*) 490
Faulkner, William (*1897–1962*) 837
Fenderson, Mark (*1873–1944*) 740
Fénelon, François de Salignac de la Mothe (*1651–1715*) 316
  note 342
Fern, Fanny (*pseudonym of* Sara Payson Parton) (*1811–1872*) 538
Field, Eugene (*1850–1895*) 666
  note 428, 519, 550
Fielding, Henry (*1707–1754*) 349
  note 79, 192, 345
Fields, James T[homas] (*1817–1881*) 556
Fields, W[illiam] C[laude] (*1880–1946*) 770
  note 683
Filicaja, Vincenzo da (*1642–1707*)
  note 458
Fisher, Dorothy Canfield (*1879–1958*) 764
Fisher, H[erbert] A[lbert] L[aurens] (*1865–1940*) 706
Fiske, John (*1842–1901*)
  note 535
Fitzgeffrey, Charles (*c. 1575–1638*)
  note 329
FitzGerald, Edward (*1809–1883*) 515
Fitzgerald, F[rancis] Scott [Key] (*1896–1940*) 835
  note 855
Fitzsimmons, Robert (Bob) [Prometheus] (*1862–1917*)
  note 78
Flaubert, Gustave (*1821–1880*) 583
  note 504
Flecker, James Elroy (*1884–1915*) 785
Fleming, Sir Alexander (*1881–1955*) 774
Fletcher, Andrew, of Saltoun (*1655–1716*) 317
Fletcher, John (*1579–1625*) 260
  note 118, 229, 261, 262
  See also Beaumont and Fletcher 263
  and Shakespeare *Henry VIII* 248

Fletcher, Phineas (*1582–1650*)
note 338
Florio, John (*c. 1553–1625*) 174
Florus, Lucius Annaeus (*fl. 125*) 123
Flying Hawk (*1852–1931*) 670
Foch, Ferdinand (*1851–1929*) 670
Fontaine, Jean de La. *See* La Fontaine
Fontenelle, Bernard Le Bovier de (*1657–1757*) 318
Foote, Samuel (*1720–1777*) 364
Ford, Ford Madox (*originally* Ford Madox Hueffer) (*1873–1939*) 740
Ford, Gerald R[udolph] (*1913–*) 882
Ford, Henry (*1863–1947*)
note 587
Ford, John (*c. 1586–1639*) 264
Ford, Lena Guilbert (*d. 1918*) 740
Forgy, Howell M[aurice] (*1908–*) 871
Forrest, Nathan Bedford (*1821–1877*) 583
Forster, E[dward] M[organ] (*1879–1970*) 764
Fortescue, John (*c. 1395 – c. 1476*) 149
Fortunatus, Saint Venantius Honorius Clementianus (*c. 530 – c. 610*)
note 139
Fosdick, Harry Emerson (*1878–1969*) 759
Foss, Sam Walter (*1858–1911*) 685
note 671
Foster, Fred 913
Foster, Stephen Collins (*1826–1864*) 598
note 443
Fouché, Joseph (*1763–1820*) 415
note 491
Foullon, Joseph François (*1717–1789*)
note 473
Fournier. *See* Alain-Fournier
Fowler, F[rancis] G[eorge] (*1870–1918*) 685
Fowler, H[enry] W[atson] (*1858–1933*) 685
Fox, Charles James (*1749–1806*) 394
note 450
Fox, George (*1624–1691*) 300
Foxe, John (*1516–1587*)
note 161
F.P.A. *See* Adams, Franklin Pierce
France, Anatole (*pseudonym of* Jacques Anatole François Thibault) (*1844–1924*) 655
note 66
Francis, Saint, of Assisi (*c. 1181–1226*) 138
Francis [François] I (*1494–1547*) 157
note 105
Franck, Johann (*1618–1677*) 295
Franck, Richard (*c. 1624–1708*)
note 117
Frank, Anne (*1929–1945*) 909
Frankfurter, Felix (*1882–1965*) 776
Franklin, Benjamin (*1706–1790*) 346
note 66, 94, 707
Frazer, Sir James George (*1854–1941*) 672
Frederick I (Barbarossa) (*1122–1190*) 137
Frederick the Great (*1712–1786*) 358
Freiligrath, Ferdinand (*1810–1876*) 536
French (Anonymous) 927
Freneau, Philip (*1752–1832*) 399
Freud, Sigmund (*1856–1939*) 678
Freyre, Gilberto (*1900–*) 848
Freytag, Gustav (*1816–1895*) 679
Friedan, Betty [Naomi] (*1921–*) 898
Friedman, Milton (*1912–*) 880
Friedrich Wilhelm IV (*1795–1861*) 480
Frisch, Max (*1911–*) 878
Frith, John (*1503–1533*)
note 161
Frohman, Charles (*1860–1915*)
note 574
Frost, Robert (*1874–1963*) 747
Fry, Christopher (*1907–*) 870
Fujiwara no Teika (*1162–1241*) 138
Fukuzawa, Yukichi (*1834–1901*) 617
Fulbright, J[ames] William (*1905–*) 862
Fuller, Margaret (*1810–1850*) 536
note 170
Fuller, R[ichard] Buckminster (*1895–*) 832
Fuller, Thomas (*1608–1661*) 276
note 126, 158, 166, 172, 180, 269
Fuller, Thomas (*1654–1734*)
note 95, 99
Fyleman, Rose (*1877–1957*) 758

Gage, Thomas (*d. 1656*)
note 412

Gaius Caesar. *See* Caligula
Galbraith, John Kenneth (*1908–*) 871
Galen (*129–199*) 125
Galento, Tony (Two-Ton) (*1910–1979*) 877
Galileo Galilei (*1564–1642*) 182
Galsworthy, John (*1867–1933*) 723
Gander, Joseph (*fl. c. 1703*)
note 181
Gandhi, Mohandas Karamchand (Mahatma) (*1869–1948*) 727
Garbo, Greta (Greta Gustafson) (*1905–*) 863
García Lorca, Federico (*1898–1936*) 841
García Marquez, Gabriel (*1928–*) 908
García Sarmiento, Félix Rubén. *See* Darío, Rubén
Garfield, James A[bram] (*1831–1881*) 609
Garibaldi, Giuseppe (*1807–1882*) 509
Garland, Hamlin (*1860–1940*) 695
Garnett, Richard (*1835–1906*) 621
Garrick, David (*1717–1779*) 363
note 258
Garrison, William Lloyd (*1805–1879*) 505
Garth, Sir Samuel (*1661–1719*) 318
Garvey, Marcus (*1887–1940*) 797
Gascoigne, George (*c. 1525–1577*)
note 97, 215
Gaskell, Elizabeth Cleghorn (*1810–1865*) 536
Gasset. *See* Ortega y Gasset
Gaulle, Charles [André Joseph Marie] de. *See* de Gaulle
Gaultier, Jules de (*b. 1858*)
note 504
Gauss, Carl Friedrich (*1777–1855*) 444
Gautier, Théophile (*1811–1872*) 538
Gavarni [Sulpice Guillaume Chevalier] (*1804–1866*) 502
Gay, John (*1688–1732*) 331
note 326
Gelbart, Larry (*1928–*) 908
Gellert, Christian Fürchtegott (*1715–1769*) 360
Genet, Jean (*1910–*) 877
George V (*1865–1936*) 706
George, Henry (*1839–1897*) 638
Gerhardt, Paul (*1607–1676*) 276
Geronimo (*c. 1829–1909*) 603
Gershwin, George (*1898–1937*) 842
Gershwin, Ira (*1896–*) 835
Gibbon, Edward (*1737–1794*) 383
note 82, 183, 349
Gibbons, James Sloan (*1810–1892*) 537
Gibbons, Stella (*1902–*) 854
Gibbs, Josiah Willard (*1839–1903*)
note 589
Gibbs, Wolcott (*1902–1958*) 854
Gibran, Kahlil (*1883–1931*) 782
Gide, André (*1869–1951*) 727
Gifford, Richard (*1725–1807*)
note 359
Gilbert, Fred (*1850–1903*) 666
Gilbert, Harold N. (*1896–1966*) 836
Gilbert, Sir Humphrey (*c. 1539–1583*) 166
Gilbert, William (*1540–1603*) 166
Gilbert, Sir W[illiam] S[chwenck] (*1836–1911*) 627
Gillilan, Strickland (*1869–1954*) 727
Gillray, James (*1757–1815*) 407
Gilman, Charlotte Perkins (*1860–1935*) 695
Gilman, Samuel (*1791–1858*) 465
Ginsberg, Allen (*1926–*) 906
Giovanni, Nikki (*1943–*) 915
Gipp, George (*1895–1920*)
note 811
Giraudoux, Jean (*1882–1944*) 777
Gladstone, William Ewart (*1809–1898*) 517
note 517
Glasgow, Ellen (*1874–1945*) 750
Gloucester, William Henry, Duke of (*1743–1805*) 387
Goebbels, Paul Joseph (*1897–1945*) 838
note 746
Goering, Hermann (*1893–1946*) 825
Goethe, Johann Wolfgang von (*1749–1832*) 394
note 337, 397
Gogarty, Oliver St. John (*1878–1957*) 759
Gogol, Nikolai Vasilievich (*1809–1852*) 518
Goldberg, Isaac (*1887–1938*) 797
Goldberger, Ludwig Max (*1848–1913*) 662
Golding, William (*1911–*) 878
Goldsmith, Oliver (*1728–1774*) 368
note 91, 123, 144, 180, 310, 315, 318

Goldwater, Barry [Morris] (*1909–*)
note 385
Goldwyn, Samuel (*1882–1974*) 777
Gompers, Samuel (*1850–1924*) 666
Goncharov, Ivan Aleksandrovich (*1812–1891*) 550
Góngora y Argote, Luis de (*1561–1627*)
note 113
Googe, Barnabe (*1540–1594*)
note 148
Gordon, Adam Lindsay (*1833–1870*) 614
Gordon, George Noel. *See* Byron
Gorenko, Anna Andreyevna. *See* Akhmatova, Anna
Gorki, Maxim (*pseudonym of* Aleksei Maksimovich Peshkov) (*1868–1936*) 725
Gosse, Sir Edmund [William] (*1849–1928*) 663
note 171
Goudy, Frederic William (*1865–1947*) 706
Gourmont, Remy de (*1858–1915*) 686
Gower, John (*c. 1325–1408*)
note 159
Goya y Lucientes, Francisco José de (*1746–1828*) 394
note 394
Grafton, Richard (*d. 1572*) 162
Graham, James, Marquess of Montrose. *See* Montrose
Grahame, Kenneth (*1859–1932*) 690
Grant, Sir Robert (*1779–1838*) 445
Grant, Ulysses S[impson] (*1822–1885*) 589
Gratian (Franciscus Gratianus) (*12th century*) 137
Graves, John Woodcock (*1795–1886*) 474
Graves, Robert (*1895–*) 833
Gray, John Chipman (*1839–1915*) 638
Gray, Thomas (*1716–1771*) 361
note 215, 283, 295
Great Hymn to the Aten, The (*c. 1350 B.C.*) 5
Greeley, Horace (*1811–1872*) 538
Green, John Richard (*1837–1883*)
note 345
Green, Matthew (*1696–1737*) 344
Greene, Graham (*1904–*) 859
Greene, Robert (*c. 1560–1592*) 178
note 159, 259
Gregory I, Pope (*540–604*) 130
Gregory XIII, Pope (*1502–1585*) 161
Gregory, Horace (*1898–*) 842
Grellet, Stephen (Étienne de Grellet du Mabillier) (*1773–1855*) 439
Grenville, George (*1712–1770*) 358
Greville, Fulke, Lord Brooke (*1554–1628*) 175
note 148
Grey, Edward, Viscount Grey of Fallodon (*1862–1933*) 699
Gruber, Edmund L. (*1879–1941*) 764
Gualtier, Philippe (*fl. c. 1300*)
note 200
Guedalla, Philip (*1889–1944*) 812
Guest, Edgar A[lbert] (*1881–1959*) 774
Guinan, Texas [Mary Louise Cecilia] (*1884–1933*) 785
note 924
Guiney, Louise Imogen (*1861–1920*) 696
Guiterman, Arthur (*1871–1943*) 732
note 609
Guitry, Sacha (*1885–1957*)
note 692
Guizot, François (*1787–1874*) 456
Guthrie, Woody [Woodrow Wilson] (*1912–1967*) 881
Guyon, Jeanne (*1648–1717*)
note 296
Guzmán, Martin Luis (*1887–*) 797

Haberler, Gottfried (*1900–*) 848
Hadrian (Publius Aelius Hadrianus (*76–138*) 123
Haeckel, Ernst Heinrich (*1834–1919*) 617
Hagedorn, Hermann (*1882–1964*) 777
Hagen, Walter C. (*1892–1969*) 821
Haile Selassie (*1891–1975*) 820
Hakewill, George (*1578–1649*)
note 178
Halberstam, David (*1934–*)
note 452
Haldane, J[ohn] B[urdon] S[anderson] (*1892–1964*) 821
Hale, Edward Everett (*1822–1909*) 590
Hale, Lucretia Peabody (*1820–1900*) 578
Hale, Sir Matthew (*1609–1676*) 289
Hale, Nathan (*1755–1776*) 401
Hale, Sarah Josepha (*1788–1879*) 463

Haliburton, Thomas Chandler. *See* Slick, Sam
Halifax, George Savile, Marquess of. *See* Savile
Hall, Bishop Joseph (*1574–1656*) 257
Hall, Owen. *See* Davis, James
Hall, Robert (*1764–1831*) 416
Halleck, Fitz-Greene (*1790–1867*) 464
Halm, Friedrich (Eligius Franz Josef von Münch-Bellinghausen) (*1806–1871*) 508
Halsey, William Frederick, Jr. (*1882–1959*) 777
Hamann, Johann Georg (*1730–1788*) 374
Hamilton, Alexander (*1755–1804*) 401
note 108
Hamilton, Charles V[ernon] (*1929–*) 914
Hamilton, Edith (*1867–1963*) 723
Hammarskjöld, Dag (*1905–1961*) 863
Hammerstein, Oscar, II (*1895–1960*) 833
Hammett, Dashiell (*1894–1961*) 830
Han Wu-ti (*157–87* *B.C.*) 97
Hand, Learned (*1872–1961*) 737
Handy, W[illiam] C[hristopher] (*1873–1958*) 740
Haraucourt, Edmond (*1856–1941*) 679
Harbach, Otto (*1873–1963*) 740
Harburg, Edgar Y. (*1898–*) 842
Hardenberg, Baron Friedrich von. *See* Novalis
Harding, Warren G[amaliel] (*1865–1923*)
note 890
Hardwick, Elizabeth (*1916–*) 889
Hardy, Godfrey Harold (*1877–1947*) 758
Hardy, Thomas (*1840–1928*) 640
note 281
Harington, Sir John (*1561–1612*) 181
Hariri, Abu Muhammad al-Kasim al- (*1054–1122*) 136
Harlan, John Marshall (*1833–1911*) 615
Harper, Robert Goodloe (*1765–1825*) 416
Harper, The Song of the (*c. 2650 – c. 2600 B.C.*) 3
Harrington, Michael (*1928–*) 908
Harris, Joel Chandler (*1848–1908*) 662
Harris, Thomas Anthony (*1910–*) 877
Harrison, William Henry (*1773–1841*) 439
Hart, Basil Henry Liddell. *See* Liddell Hart
Hart, Lorenz [Milton] (*1895–1943*) 833
Hart, Moss (*1904–1961*) 813, 859
Harte, Bret (Francis Brett Harte) (*1836–1902*) 630
Hartley, L[esley] P[oles] (*1895–*) 833
Hartmann von Aue (*c. 1170 – c. 1215*) 138
Harvey, William (*1578–1657*) 260
Hasegawa, Nyozekan (*1875–1969*) 756
Hatshepsut, Queen (*d. 1468 B.C.*) 5
Hawker, Robert Stephen (*1803–1875*) 500
Hawkins, Anthony Hope. *See* Hope
Hawthorne, Alice. *See* Winner
Hawthorne, Nathaniel (*1804–1864*) 502
Hay, John Milton (*1838–1905*) 636
Hayden, Joseph (*fl. 1896*) 705
Hayden, Robert (*1913–1980*)
note 556
Hayek, Friedrich August von (*1899–*) 844
Hayes, Rutherford B[irchard] (*1822–1893*) 590
Hazlitt, William (*1778–1830*) 445
note 94, 293, 323
Hearst, William Randolph (*1863–1951*) 702
Heath, John (*1758–1810*) 407
Heber, Reginald (*1783–1826*) 452
note 377
Hegel, Georg Wilhelm Friedrich (*1770–1831*) 422
Heine, Heinrich (*1797–1856*) 481
note 83
Heisenberg, Werner Karl (*1901–1976*) 852
Heller, Joseph (*1923–*) 902
Hellman, Lillian (*1905–*) 863
Helmholtz, Hermann Ludwig Ferdinand von (*1821–1894*) 583
Héloïse (*c. 1101 – c. 1164*) 136
Helvétius, Claude Adrien (*1715–1771*) 360
Hemans, Felicia [Dorothea] (*1793–1835*) 470
note 561
Hemingway, Ernest (*1899–1961*) 844
Hendyng (*1272–1307*)
note 148, 160
Henley, William Ernest (*1849–1903*) 663
Henri IV (Henry of Navarre) (*1533–1610*) 174
Henry II (*1133–1189*) 137
Henry VI (*1421–1471*) 150

Henry, Matthew (*1662–1714*) 319
note 250, 261
Henry, O. (*pseudonym of* William Sydney Porter) (*1862–1910*) 699
Henry, Patrick (*1736–1799*) 382
Heraclitus (*c.540 – c.480 B.C.*) 69
Herbart, Johann Friedrich (*1776–1841*) 443
Herbert, Sir Alan Patrick (*1890–1971*) 815
Herbert, George (*1593–1633*) 268
note 66, 91, 93, 115, 119, 120, 136, 156, 160, 161, 172
Herbort von Fritzlar (*fl. c. 1210*) 138
Herder, Johann Gottfried von (*1744–1803*) 393
Herodotus (*c.485 – c.425 B.C.*) 78
note 268
Herrick, Robert (*1591–1674*) 265
note 110, 119, 223
Herschel, John Frederick William (*1792–1871*) 465
Hersey, John (*1914–*) 885
Herwegh, Georg (*1817–1875*) 557
Herzen, Alexander Ivanovich (*1812–1870*) 550
Hesiod (*c. 700 B.C.*) 61
note 58
Heyward, Dorothy (*1890–1961*)
note 836
Heyward, DuBose (*1885–1940*)
note 836
Heywood, John (*c.1497 – c.1580*) 158
note 74, 87, 97, 110, 111, 120, 126, 146, 147, 148, 152, 153, 183, 235
Heywood, Thomas (*c.1574 – c.1641*) 257
note 152, 211
Hidalgo y Costilla, Miguel (*1753–1811*) 400
Higginson, Thomas Wentworth (*1823–1911*) 591
Hill, Aaron (*1685–1750*) 331
note 292
Hill, Benjamin Harvey (*1823–1882*) 591
Hill, Joe (Joseph Hillstrom) (*1879–1915*) 764
Hill, Rowland (*1744–1833*) 393
Hilton, James (*1900–1954*) 848
Hippocrates (*c. 460–400 B.C.*) 79
Hipponax (*c. 570–520 B.C.*) 67
Hitler, Adolf (*1889–1945*) 812
Hobbes, Thomas (*1588–1679*) 264
Hoch, Edward Wallis (*1849–1925*)
note 646
Hodgson, Ralph (*1871–1962*) 732
Hoffenstein, Samuel (*1890–1947*) 816
note 822
Hoffmann, August Heinrich (Hoffmann von Fallersleben) (*1798–1874*) 483
Hogarth, William (*1697–1764*)
note 539
Hogg, James (*1770–1835*) 422
Holland, Josiah Gilbert (*1819–1881*) 566
note 567
Holland, Sir Richard (*fl. 1450*)
note 597
Holmes, John Haynes (*1879–1964*) 764
Holmes, Oliver Wendell (*1809–1894*) 518
note 98, 512, 539
Holmes, Oliver Wendell, Jr. (*1841–1935*) 643
note 739, 890
Homans, Miss A. M.
note 798
Homans, George C[aspar] (*1910–*) 877
Home, John (*1722–1808*) 366
Homer (*c. 700 B.C.*) 57
note 200
Hood, Thomas (*1799–1845*) 485
note 258, 386
Hooke, Robert (*1635–1703*) 311
Hooker, Richard (*c. 1554–1600*) 175
note 160
Hooper, Ellen Sturgis (*1816–1841*) 555
Hoover, Herbert [Clark] (*1874–1964*) 750
Hope, Anthony (*pseudonym of* Anthony Hope Hawkins) (*1863–1933*)
note 627
Hope, Laurence (*pseudonym of* Adela Florence Cory Nicolson) (*1865–1904*) 707
Hopkins, Gerard Manley (*1844–1889*) 655
Hopkins, Jane Ellice (*1836–1904*) 630
Hopkinson, Joseph (*1770–1842*) 422
Hor, Suti and (*15th–14th centuries B.C.*) 5
Horace (Quintus Horatius Flaccus) (*65–8 B.C.*) 106
note 77, 78, 98, 108, 109, 128, 145, 284, 447

Horne, Richard Henry Hengist (*1803–1884*) 500
Horney, Karen (*1885–1952*) 789
Housman, A[lfred] E[dward] (*1859–1936*) 690
Hovey, Richard (*1864–1900*) 705
How, William Walsham (*1823–1897*) 592
Howard, Rowland (*fl. 1876*)
note 347
Howard, Sidney (*1891–1939*)
note 848
Howe, Edgar Watson (*1853–1937*) 671
Howe, Julia Ward (*1819–1910*) 566
Howe, Mark Antony De Wolfe (*1864–1960*) 705
Howell, James (*c. 1594–1666*) 271
note 259
Howells, William Dean (*1837–1920*) 631
note 354, 545
Howitt, Mary (*1799–1888*) 485
Hoyle, Edmond (*1672–1769*) 327
Hoyt, Daniel Webster (*1845–1936*) 660
Hsieh Ho (*fl. 500*) 129
Hu Shih (*1891–1962*) 818
Huai-nan Tzu (*known also as* Liu An) (*2nd century B.C.*) 97
Hubbard, Elbert (*1856–1915*) 679
Hubbard, Frank McKinney "Kin" (*creator of* Abe Martin) (*1868–1930*) 725
Hudson, W[illiam] H[enry] (*1841–1922*) 646
Hughes, Charles Evans (*1862–1948*) 700
Hughes, Langston (*1902–1967*) 854
Hughes, Thomas (*1822–1896*) 590
Hugo, Victor (*1802–1885*) 491
note 491
Humboldt, [Friedrich Heinrich] Alexander von (*1769–1859*) 420
Hume, David (*1711–1776*) 357
note 489
Humphrey, Hubert H[oratio] (*1911–1978*) 879
Hungerford, Margaret Wolfe (*1855–1897*) 676
Hunt, G[eorge] W[illiam] (*c. 1829–1904*) 598
Hunt, Leigh (*1784–1859*) 453
Hupfeld, Herman (*1894–1951*) 830
Hurdis, James (*1763–1801*)
note 175
Huss, John (*c. 1370–1415*) 148
Hutcheson, Francis (*1694–1746*) 342
Hutchins, Robert Maynard (*1899–1977*) 845
Hutton, James (*1726–1797*) 367
Huxley, Aldous [Leonard] (*1894–1963*) 830
note 369
Huxley, T[homas] H[enry] (*1825–1895*) 595
Huysmans, Joris Karl (*1848–1907*) 662
Hyde, Edward, Earl of Clarendon (*1609–1674*) 289
Hymn to the Aten, The Great (*c. 1350 B.C.*) 5

I Ching (The Book of Changes) (*c. 12th century B.C.*) 5
Ibáñez, *See* Blasco-Ibáñez
Ibarruri, Dolores (*pseudonym* La Pasionara) (*1895–*) 833
Ibsen, Henrik (*1828–1906*) 599
Ibycus (*c. 580 B.C.*) 65
Ickes, Harold L[eClair] (*1874–1952*) 751
Ignatius of Loyola, Saint. *See* Loyola
Ignatius Theophorus, Saint (*fl. c. 100*)
note 269
Ihara, Saikaku (*1642–1693*) 312
Ingalls, John James (*1833–1900*) 615
Inge, William Ralph (*1860–1954*) 696
Ingelow, Jean (*1820–1897*) 578
Ingersoll, Robert [Green] (*1833–1899*) 615
Ingram, John Kells (*1823–1907*) 592
Ionesco, Eugène (*1912–*) 881
Iphicrates (*419–348 B.C.*) 86
Iron, Ralph. *See* Schreiner, Olive
Ironquill (*pseudonym of* Eugene Fitch Ware) (*1841–1911*) 647
note 633
Irving, Washington (*1783–1859*) 452
note 271, 290
Isherwood, Christopher [William Bradshaw] (*1904–*) 860
Ishikawa, Takuboku (*1885–1912*) 789
Isocrates (*436–338 B.C.*)
note 261

Jackson, Andrew (*1767–1845*) 418
Jackson, Helen Hunt (*1831–1885*) 609

Jackson, Robert H[oughwout] (*1892–1954*) 821
Jackson, Thomas Jonathan (Stonewall) (*1824–1863*) 594
Jacob, Max (*1876–1944*) 757
Jacobs, Joe (*1896–1940*) 836
Jagger, Mick (Michael Philip) (*1944–*) 916
James, George Payne Rainsford (*1799–1860*)
note 398
James, Henry (*1843–1916*) 652
James, William (*1842–1910*) 647
note 601–602, 650, 652, 688, 893
Jarrell, Randall (*1914–1965*) 885
Jean de Meun (*13th century*)
note 149
Jeanneret, Charles Edouard. *See* Le Corbusier
Jeans, Sir James Hopwood (*1877–1946*) 758
Jefferies, Richard (*1848–1887*) 662
Jeffers, Robinson (*1887–1962*) 797
Jefferson, Thomas (*1743–1826*) 387
note 346, 380, 382, 401, 920
Jeffrey, Francis, Lord Jeffrey (*1773–1850*)
note 428
Jerome, Saint (*c. 342–420*) 127
note 126, 447
Jerome, Jerome K[lapka] (*1859–1927*) 692
Jerrold, Douglas (*1803–1857*) 500
note 185
Jesus, The Sayings of (*3rd century*) 126
Jewett, Sarah Orne (*1849–1909*) 663
John XXIII, Pope (Angelo Giuseppe Roncalli) (*1881–1963*) 774
John Chrysostom, Saint. *See* Chrysostom
John of Damascus, Saint (*c. 700 – c. 760*) 135
John of the Cross, Saint (San Juan de la Cruz) (*1542–1591*) 167
John Paul I, Pope (Albino Luciani) (*1912–1978*) 881
John Paul II, Pope (Karol Wojtyla) (*1920–*) 897
Johnson, George Washington (*1838–1917*) 636
Johnson, Gerald White (*1890–*) 816
note 686
Johnson, James Weldon (*1871–1938*) 733
Johnson, Lyndon B[aines] (*1908–1973*) 872
Johnson, Samuel (*1709–1784*) 351
note 111, 116, 118, 158, 178, 194, 258, 259, 269, 292, 322, 328, 332, 351, 352, 354, 356, 372, 461
Johst, Hanns (*1890–*) 816
Jolson, Al (*1886–1950*) 795
Jones, John Ceredigion (*1883–1947*)
note 427
Jones, John Paul (*1747–1792*) 394
Jones, LeRoi. *See* Baraka, Amiri
Jones, Tom
note 762
Jones, Sir William (*1746–1794*) 394
note 172
Jonson, Ben (*c. 1573–1637*) 255
note 108, 113, 118, 152, 158, 159, 210
Joplin, Janis (*1943–1970*) 916
Jordan, Barbara C. (*1936–*) 913
Jordan, Dorothea (*1762–1816*) 415
Joseph, Chief (*c. 1840–1904*) 642
Joubert, Joseph (*1754–1824*) 400
Joyce, James (*1882–1941*) 777
Joyce, John Alexander (*1842–1915*) 651
Julian (The Apostate) (Flavius Claudius Julianus) (*332–363*) 127
Julius III, Pope (*1487–1555*) 157
Julius Caesar. *See* Caesar, [Gaius] Julius
Jung, Carl Gustav (*1875–1961*) 753
Junius, The Letters of (*1769–1771*) 390
note 122
Junot. *See* Abrantès
Juvenal (Decimus Junius Juvenalis) (*c. 50 – c. 130*) 121
note 96

Kafka, Franz (*1884–1924*) 786
Kahn, Gus (*1886–1941*) 795
Kamo, Mabuchi (*1697–1769*) 344
Kamo no Chomei (*1153–1216*) 137
Kant, Immanuel (*1724–1804*) 366
note 367
Karr, Alphonse (*1808–1890*) 514
Kaufman, George S. (*1889–1961*) 813
Kazantzakis, Nikos (*1883–1957*) 782
Keats, John (*1795–1821*) 474
note 478, 748
Keble, John (*1792–1866*) 465

Keith, George, Earl Marischal (*c. 1553–1623*) 175
Keller, Helen (*1880–1968*) 771
Kelly, Walt[er Crawford] (*1913–1973*)
note 455
Kelvin, William Thomson, Lord (*1824–1907*) 594
Kemble, John Philip (*1757–1823*) 407
Ken, Bishop Thomas (*1637–1711*) 311
Kennan, George (*1845–1924*) 660
Kennan, George F[rost] (*1904–*) 860
Kennedy, John Fitzgerald (*1917–1963*) 890
note 857, 898
Kennedy, Joseph P[atrick] (*1888–1969*) 809
Kenyatta, Jomo (Kamau Wa Ngengi) (*1891–1978*) 818
Kenyon, James Benjamin (*1858–1924*)
note 103
Kepler, Johannes (*1571–1630*) 251
Kerner, Otto, Jr. (*1908–1976*) 872
Kerouac, Jack (*1922–1969*) 901
Kerr, Clark (*1911–*) 879
Kerr, Philip Henry, Marquess of Lothian (*1882–1940*) 778
Kesey, Ken (*1935–*) 913
Kettering, Charles F[ranklin] (*1876–1958*) 757
Key, Francis Scott (*1779–1843*) 446
Keyes, Charlotte (*1914–*)
note 761
Keynes, John Maynard (*1883–1946*) 783
Khrushchev, Nikita Sergeyevich (*1894–1971*) 830
Kieran, James Michael, Jr. (*1901–1952*) 853
Kierkegaard, Sören (*1813–1855*) 552
Kikaku (*1661–1707*) 319
Kilmer, Joyce (*1886–1918*) 795
note 620
King, Benjamin Franklin, Jr. (*1857–1894*) 684
King, Bishop Henry (*1592–1669*) 267
King, Martin Luther, Jr. (*1929–1968*) 909
King, Stoddard (*1889–1933*) 813
King, W[illiam] L[yon] Mackenzie (*1874–1950*) 751
Kinglake, A[lexander] W[illiam] (*1809–1891*)
note 578
Kingsley, Charles (*1819–1875*) 566
note 668
Kipling, Rudyard (*1865–1936*) 707
note 360, 371, 556, 578, 671
Kirchoff, Gustav Robert (*1824–1887*) 594
Kissinger, Henry [Alfred] (*1923–*) 902
Kittredge, Walter (*1834–1905*) 618
Klinger, Friedrich Maximilian von (*1752–1831*) 399
Klopstock, Friedrich Gottlieb (*1724–1803*) 367
Knight, Frank Hyneman (*1885–1974*) 790
Knox, E[dmund George] V[alpy] (*1881–1971*)
note 470
Knox, Henry (*1750–1806*)
note 378
Knox, John (*1505–1572*) 162
Knox, William (*1789–1825*) 463
Koch, Howard (*1902–*)
note 913
Koran, The (*c. 610–632*) 130
note 525
Kotzebue, August Friedrich Ferdinand von (*1761–1819*) 415
Kraus, Karl (*1874–1936*) 751
Kristofferson, Kris (*1936–*) 913
Kronecker, Leopold (*1823–1891*) 592
Kropotkin, Prince Pëtr Alekseevich (*1842–1921*) 651
Krylov, Ivan (*1768–1844*) 420
Kumin, Maxine [Winokur] (*1925–*) 904
Kunitz, Stanley (*1905–*) 863
Kyd, Thomas (*1558–1594*) 176
note 120, 201

Laberius, Decimus (*105–43 B.C.*)
note 111
Labrunie, Gérard. *See* Nerval
La Bruyère, Jean de (*1645–1696*) 315
Lacydes (*fl. c. 241 B.C.*) 93
La Fontaine, Jean de (*1621–1695*) 296
note 66, 168
La Guardia, Fiorello H[enry] (*1882–1947*) 778
Laing, Dilys (*1906–1960*) 867
Laing, R[onald] D[avid] (*1927–*) 906

Lamarck, Jean Baptiste (*1744–1829*) 393
Lamartine, Alphonse de (*1790–1869*) 464
Lamb, Arthur J. (*1870–1928*) 730
Lamb, Lady Caroline (*1785–1828*) 454
Lamb, Charles (*1775–1834*) 441
Lamb, William, Viscount Melbourne (*1779–1848*)
note 487
La Mettrie, Julien Offray de (*1709–1751*) 357
Lampton, William James (*1859–1917*) 693
Land, Edwin [Herbert] (*1909–*) 876
Landon, Letitia Elizabeth (*1802–1838*) 492
Landor, Walter Savage (*1775–1864*) 442
note 753
Lane, George Martin (*1823–1897*) 592
Lang, Andrew (*1844–1912*) 657
note 668
Langland, William (*c. 1330 – c. 1400*) 143
note 148
Lanier, Sidney (*1842–1881*) 651
Lao-tzu (*c. 604 – c. 531 B.C.*) 63
La Pasionara. *See* Ibarruri
Laplace, Pierre Simon de (*1749–1827*) 397
Lardner, Ring (*1885–1933*) 790
Larkin, Philip (*1922–*) 901
La Rochefoucauld, François, Duc de (*1613–1680*) 292
note 166, 587
La Rochefoucauld-Liancourt, François Alexandre Frédéric, Duc de (*1747–1827*) 394
Las Casas, Bartolomé de (*1474–1566*) 154
Laski, Harold [Joseph] (*1893–1950*) 825
Lasswell, Harold [Dwight] (*1902–*) 855
Latham, Peter Mere (*1789–1875*) 463
Latimer, Bishop Hugh (*c. 1485–1555*) 156
note 100
Latin (Anonymous) 133
Lauder, Sir Harry (*1870–1950*) 730
Laurence, William L[eonard] (*1888–*) 809
Laurens, Jacques du (*1583–1650*) 262
Lavater, Johann Kaspar (*1741–1801*) 386
Lavoisier, Antoine Laurent (*1743–1794*) 390
Lawrence, D[avid] H[erbert] (*1885–1930*) 790
note 739
Lawrence, James (*1781–1813*) 449
Lawrence, T[homas] E[dward] (*1888–1935*) 810
Lazarus, Emma (*1849–1887*) 664
Leacock, Stephen [Butler] (*1869–1944*) 728
Lear, Edward (*1812–1888*) 550
Leary, Timothy (*1920–*) 897
Lec, Stanislaw J[erzy] (*1909–1966*) 876
Le Carré, John (*pseudonym of* David John Moore Cornwell) (*1931–*) 911
Lecky, William Edward Hartpole (*1838–1903*) 636
Le Corbusier (*pseudonym of* Charles Édouard Jeanneret) (*1887–1965*) 798
Lee, Charles (*1731–1782*) 378
Lee, Henry (Light-Horse Harry) (*1756–1818*) 402
Lee, Nathaniel (*c. 1653–1692*) 317
Lee, Richard Henry (*1732–1794*) 378
Lee, Robert E[dward] (*1807–1870*) 509
Leeuwenhoek, Anton van (*1632–1723*) 307
Leibnitz, Baron Gottfried Wilhelm von (*1646–1716*) 315
Leighton, Robert (*1611–1684*) 290
note 355
Le May, Curtis [Emerson] (*1906–*) 867
L'Enclos, Ninon de (*1620–1705*) 296
Lenin, Vladimir Ilyich (Ulyanov) (*1870–1924*) 731
note 766
Lennon, John [Ono] (*1940–*) 914
Leo XIII, Pope (Gioacchino Pecci) (*1810–1903*) 537
Leoncavallo, Ruggiero (*1858–1919*) 686
Leonidas of Tarentum (*c. 290 – c. 220 B.C.*) 93
Leopold, Aldo (*1886–1948*) 795
Lermontov, Mikhail Yurievich (*1814–1841*) 553
note 486
Lerner, Alan Jay (*1918–*) 894
Lesage, Alain René (*1668–1747*) 323
note 261
Lespinasse, Julie de (*1732–1776*) 378
Lessing, Doris (*1919–*) 896

Lessing, Gotthold Ephraim (*1729–1781*) 374
note 542
L'Estrange, Sir Roger (*1616–1704*) 294
Letters of Junius, The (*1769–1771*) 390
note 122
Letts, Winifred M[ary] (*1882–c. 1936*) 778
Leveridge, Richard (*c. 1670–1758*)
note 349
Levertov, Denise (*1923–*) 902
Levi, Carlo (*1902–1975*) 855
Lévis, Gaston Pierre Marc, Duc de (*1764–1830*) 416
Lewis, C[ecil] Day (*1904–1972*) 860
Lewis, C[live] S[taples] (*1898–1963*) 842
Lewis, Sam M. (*1885–1959*) 801
Lewis, Sinclair (*1885–1951*) 791
Ley, Robert (*1890–1945*) 816
Leybourne, George (*d. 1884*) 636
Liberace, [Wladziu Valentino] (Lee) (*1919–*) 896
Lichtenberg, Georg Christoph (*1742–1799*) 386
Liddell Hart, Basil Henry (*1895–1970*) 834
Ligne, Charles Joseph, Prince de (*1735–1814*) 382
Liliuokalani, Lydia Kamekeha (*1838–1917*) 636
Lincoln, Abraham (*1809–1865*) 519
note 520, 537
Lindbergh, Anne Morrow (*1906–*) 867
Lindbergh, Charles A[ugustus] (*1902–1974*) 855
Lindsay, Vachel (*1879–1931*) 765
Linnaeus (Carl von Linné) (*1707–1778*) 350
Lippmann, Walter (*1889–1974*) 813
Lisle. *See* Rouget de Lisle
Litvinov, Maxim Maximovich (*1876–1951*) 757
note 757
Liu An. *See* Huai-nan Tzu
Livy (Titus Livius) (*59 B.C.–A.D. 17*) 110
Lloyd, David (*1635–1692*)
note 310
Locke, David Ross. *See* Nasby
Locke, John (*1632–1704*) 307
Locke, John (*1847–1889*) 661
Lodge, Henry Cabot (*1850–1924*) 667
Lodge, Thomas (*c. 1558–1625*) 177
note 120

Logan, Chief (*1725–1780*) 367
Logau, Friedrich von (*1604–1655*) 273
Lombardi, Vince [Vincent Thomas] (*1913–1970*)
note 925
Lombroso, Cesare (*1836–1909*) 630
note 115
Lomonosov, Mikhail Vasilievich (*1711–1765*) 357
Long, John Luther (*1861–1927*) 696
Longfellow, Henry Wadsworth (*1807–1882*) 509
note 78, 166, 171, 173, 188, 307, 395, 496
Longinus (*1st century*) 118
Longus (*3rd century*) 127
Longworth, Alice [Lee] Roosevelt (*1884–1980*) 786
Loos, Anita (*1893–*) 826
Lord, Walter (*1917–*) 892
Lothian, Philip Henry Kerr, Marquess of. *See* Kerr
Louis XIV (*1638–1715*) 312
Louis XVIII (*1755–1824*) 402
Love Songs of the New Kingdom (*c. 1550–1080 B.C.*) 4
Lovecraft, H[oward] P[hillips] (*1890–1937*) 816
Lovelace, Richard (*1618–1658*) 295
Loveman, Robert (*1864–1923*) 705
Lover, Samuel (*1797–1868*) 482
Low, David (*1891–1963*) 818
Lowell, Amy (*1874–1925*) 751
Lowell, James Russell (*1819–1891*) 567
note 66, 223, 332, 495, 500
Lowell, Robert [Traill Spence] (*1917–1977*) 892
note 87
Lowry, Malcolm (*1909–1957*) 876
Loyola, Saint Ignatius of (*1491–1556*) 157
Lucan (Marcus Annaeus Lucanus) (*39–65*) 118
Lucas, E[dward] V[errall] (*1868–1938*) 725
Lucretius (Titus Lucretius Carus) (*99–55 B.C.*) 100
note 59
Luther, Martin (*1483–1546*) 155
Lycurgus (*fl. 820 B.C.*)
note 78
Lydgate, John (*c. 1370 – c. 1451*)
note 137

Lyell, Sir Charles (*1797–1875*) 482
Lyly, John (*c. 1554–1606*) 175
note 86, 94, 96, 100, 158, 159, 160, 172
Lyte, Henry Francis (*1793–1847*) 470
Lyttelton, George, Lord (*1709–1773*) 357
Lytton, Edward George Earle Lytton Bulwer-Lytton, Baron. *See* Bulwer-Lytton
Lytton, Edward Robert Bulwer-Lytton, Earl of (*pseudonym* Owen Meredith) (*1831–1891*) 609
note 331, 494

MacArthur, Douglas (*1880–1964*) 771
Macaulay, Thomas Babington, Lord (*1800–1859*) 487
note 153, 331, 353
Macdonald, George (*1824–1905*) 594
Mach, Ernst (*1838–1916*) 636
Machiavelli, Niccolò (*1469–1527*) 153
note 119
Mackay, Charles (*1814–1889*) 553
Mackintosh, Sir James (*1765–1832*) 416
Macklin, Charles (*c. 1697–1797*) 344
note 301
MacLeish, Archibald (*1892–*) 821
Macleod, Fiona. *See* Sharp, William
MacMahon, Comte Marie Edmé Patrice, Maurice de (*1808–1893*) 514
MacNally, Leonard (*1752–1820*) 399
MacNeice, Louis (*1907–1963*) 870
Madden, Samuel (*1686–1765*) 331
Madison, James (*1751–1836*) 398
Maeterlinck, Maurice (*1862–1949*) 700
Magna Carta (*1215*) 139
Mahan, Alfred Thayer (*1840–1914*) 642
Maharbal (Barca the Carthaginian) (*fl. 210 B.C.*) 94
Maimonides (Moses ben Maimon) (*1135–1204*) 137
Maistre, Joseph de (*1753–1821*) 400
Malcolm X (El-Hajj Malik El-Shabazz) (*1925–1965*) 904
Malherbe, François de (*1555–1628*) 176
Malinowski, Bronislaw (*1884–1942*) 786
Mallarmé, Stéphane (*1842–1898*) 651
note 808
Mallory, George Leigh (*1886–1924*)
note 710
Malone, Dumas (*1892–*)
note 387
Malory, Sir Thomas (*d. 1471*) 149
Malraux, André (*1901–1976*) 853
Malthus, Thomas Robert (*1766–1834*) 417
note 514
Man Who Was Tired of Life, The (*c. 1990 B.C.*) 4
Mandelstam, Osip Emilevich (*1891–1938*) 819
Manilius, Marcus (*1st century A.D.*) 115
Manley, Mary de la Rivière (*1663–1724*) 319
Mann, Horace (*1796–1859*) 480
Mann, Thomas (*1875–1955*) 755
Mansfield, Katherine (*1888–1923*) 810
Mantuanus, Johannes Baptista (*1448–1516*)
note 707
Manutius, Aldus (*1450–1515*) 150
Mao Tse-tung (*1893–1976*) 826
Map (Mapes), Walter (*c. 1140 – c. 1210*) 137
Marcus Aurelius [Antoninus] (*121–180*) 124
Marcy, William Learned (*1786–1857*) 455
Maritain, Jacques (*1882–1973*) 778
Marivaux, Pierre Carlet de Chamblain de (*1688–1763*) 332
Markham, Edwin (*1852–1940*) 670
note 269, 779
Marlowe, Christopher (*1564–1593*) 183
Marquand, John P[hillips] (*1893–1960*) 826
Marquis, Don[ald Robert Perry] (*1878–1937*) 759
Marryat, Frederick (*1792–1848*) 465
Marshall, Alfred (*1842–1924*) 652
Marshall, George C[atlett] (*1880–1959*) 771
Marshall, John (*1755–1835*) 402
Marshall, Thomas Riley (*1854–1925*) 673
Marston, John (*c. 1575 – c. 1634*) 258
note 108, 152, 158, 159
Marston, Philip Bourke (*1850–1887*)
note 614
Martí [y Perez], José [Julian] (*1853–1895*) 671
note 451

Martial (Marcus Valerius Martialis) (*c. 40 – c. 104*) 118
note 145
Martin, Abe. *See* Hubbard, Frank McKinney
Marvell, Andrew (*1621–1678*) 296
Marx, Groucho [Julius Henry] (*1895–1977*) 834
Marx, Karl (*1818–1883*) 562, 563
Mary Stuart (Mary, Queen of Scots) (*1542–1587*) 167
Mary Tudor (Mary II) (*1516–1558*) 162
Masefield, John (*1878–1967*) 760
Maslow, Abraham H[arold] (*1908–1970*) 872
Mason, Daniel Gregory (*1873–1953*) 740
Mason, Donald Francis (*1913–*) 882
Mason, George (*1725–1792*) 367
Massachusetts, Constitution of
note 387
Massinger, Philip (*1583–1640*) 262
note 115, 172, 197, 262
Masson, Thomas Lansing (*1866–1934*) 718
Masters, Edgar Lee (*1869–1950*) 728
Mather, Cotton (*1663–1728*) 319
Matisse, Henri (*1869–1954*) 728
Matsuo, Basho. *See* Basho
Maugham, W[illiam] Somerset (*1874–1965*) 751
Mauldin, Bill [William Henry] (*1921–*) 898
Maupassant, [Henri René Albert] Guy de (*1850–1893*) 667
Mauriac, François (*1885–1970*) 791
Maurois, André (*1885–1967*) 791
note 83
Maxwell, James Clerk (*1831–1979*) 610
Mayakovski, Vladimir Vladimirovich (*1893–1930*) 826
Mazarin, Jules Cardinal (*1602–1661*) 273
Mazlish, Bruce (*1923–*) 871
Mazzini, Giuseppi (*1805–1872*)
note 473
McCarthy, Denis A[loysius] (*1870–1931*)
note 562
McCarthy, Mary [Therese] (*1912–*) 881
McCartney, Paul (*1942–*) 914
McClellan, George B[rinton] (*1826–1885*) 598
McCord, David (*1897–*) 838
McCrae, John (*1872–1918*) 737
McCullers, Carson [Smith] (*1917–1967*) 894
McDougall, William (*1871–1938*) 733
McGahern, John (*1935–*) 913
McGinley, Phyllis (*1905–1977*) 864
McKay, Claude (*1891–1948*) 819
McLeod, Irene Rutherford (*1891–1964*) 819
McLuhan, Marshall [Herbert] (*1911–*) 879
Mead, Margaret (*1901–1978*) 853
Mearns, Hughes (*1875–1965*) 756
Medawar, Sir Peter Brian (*1915–*) 887
Medvedev, Zhores Aleksandrovich (*1925–*) 904
Meir, Golda (*1898–1978*) 842
Melbourne, William Lamb, Viscount. *See* Lamb
Meleager (*1st century B.C.*) 97
note 87
Melville, Herman (*1819–1891*) 569
note 383, 473
Menander (*c. 342–292 B.C.*) 90
note 109
Mencius (*372–289 B.C.*) 89
note 89
Mencken, H[enry] L[ouis] (*1880–1956*) 771
Mercier, Louis Sébastien (*1740–1814*) 386
Meredith, George (*1828–1909*) 600
Meredith, Owen. *See* Lytton, Edward Robert Bulwer
Merikare, The Teaching for (*c. 2135–2040 B.C.*) 3
Merrill, James [Ingram] (*1926–*) 906
Merritt, Dixon Lanier (*1879–1972*) 765
Merwin, W[illiam] S[tanley] (*1927–*) 907
Mesmer, Franz [Friedrich] Anton (*1734–1815*) 380
Mettrie, Julien Offray de La. *See* La Mettrie
Meurier, Gabriel (*1530–1601*) 163
Meynell, Alice (*1847–1922*) 661
Michelangelo [Buonarroti] (*1475–1564*) 154
Michelet, Jules (*1798–1874*) 483
Mickle, William Julius (*1735–1788*) 382
Middlesex, Lionel Cranfield, Earl of. *See* Cranfield

Middleton, Thomas (1580–1627) 261
note 170, 187, 211, 227
Miles, Alfred Hart (1883–1956) 783
Miles, William Porcher (1822–1899) 590
Mill, John Stuart (1806–1873) 508
Millay, Edna St. Vincent (1892–1950) 822
note 507
Miller, Alice Duer (1874–1942) 752
Miller, Arthur (1915–) 888
Miller, Henry (1891–1980) 819
Miller, Joaquin (*pseudonym of* Cincinnatus Hiner *or* Heine Miller) (c. 1841–1913) 646
Miller, William (1810–1872) 537
Milman, Henry Hart (1791–1868) 465
Milne, A[lan] A[lexander] (1882–1956) 778
Milton, John (1608–1674) 277
note 86, 92, 111, 285
Mimnermus (c. 650 – c. 590 B.C.) 62
Miner, Charles (1780–1865) 448
Mirabeau, Honoré Gabriel Riquetti, Comte de (1749–1791) 397
note 346
Mises, Ludwig Edler von (1881–1973) 775
Mishima, Yukio (*pseudonym of* Kimitake Hiraoka) (1925–1970) 905
Missal, The 54
Mitchell, Joni (1943–) 916
Mitchell, Margaret (1900–1949) 848
Mizner, Wilson (1876–1933) 757
Mohr, Joseph (1792–1848) 466
Moir, David Macbeth (1798–1851) 483
Mola, Emilio (1887–1937) 798
Molière (*pseudonym of* Jean Baptiste Poquelin) (1622–1673) 297
note 168, 462
Molina, Tirso de. *See* Tirso de Molina
Moltke, Helmuth von (1800–1891) 489
Monroe, James (1758–1831) 407
Monsell, John Samuel Bewley (1811–1875)
note 292
Montagu, Lady Mary Wortley (1689–1762) 341
Montague, Charles Edward (1867–1928) 723
Montaigne, Michel Eyquem de (1533–1592) 164
note 114, 117, 120, 157, 247
Montalvo, Juan (1832–1889) 614
Montenaeken, Leon (b. 1859)
note 617
Montesquieu, Charles de Secondat, Baron de (1689–1755) 341
Montgomery, Sir Bernard Law, Viscount Montgomery of Alamein (Monty) (1887–1976) 798
Montgomery, James (1771–1854) 429
Montrose, James Graham, Marquess of (1612–1650) 292
Moody, William Vaughn (1869–1910) 728
Moore, Clement Clarke (1779–1863) 446
Moore, Edward (1712–1757) 358
Moore, George (1852–1933) 671
Moore, G[eorge] E[dward] (1873–1958) 740
Moore, John Trotwood (1858–1929) 686
Moore, Julia A. (1847–1920) 661
Moore, Marianne (1887–1972) 798
note 798
Moore, Thomas (Tom) (1779–1852) 446
note 158
Mordaunt, Thomas Osbert (1730–1809) 375
More, Hannah (1745–1833) 393
More, Sir Thomas (1478–1535) 155
note 166
Morehead, John Motley (1796–1866)
note 669
Morell, Thomas (1703–1784) 346
Morelly (*fl.* 1773)
note 563
Morelos y Pavón, José María (1765–1815) 416
Morgan, J[ohn] P[ierpont] (1837–1913)
note 923, 924
Morgan, Junius S. (1813–1890)
note 924
Morgan, Robin (1941–) 915
Morison, Elting E[lmore] (1909–) 876
Morison, Samuel Eliot (1887–1976) 799
note 367
Morley, Christopher (1890–1957) 816
Morley, John, Viscount Morley of Blackburn (1838–1923) 637
Morris, George Pope (1802–1864) 492
note 164, 439

Morris, William (*1834–1896*) 618
Morris, Wright (*1910–*) 877
Morse, Wayne [Lyman] (*1900–1974*) 848
Morton, Charles W. (*1899–1967*) 846
Morton, David (*1886–1957*) 795
Morton, Thomas (*1764–1838*) 416
Motherwell, William (*1797–1835*) 482
Motoori, Norinaga (*1730–1801*) 375
Mott, Lucretia [Coffin] (*1793–1880*) 471
Mowat, R[obert] B[almain] (*1883–1941*)
 note 706
Mozart, Wolfgang Amadè (*1756–1791*) 402
Muggeridge, Malcolm (*1903–*) 858
Muir, Alexander (*1830–1906*) 608
Muir, John (*1838–1914*) 637
Mulligan, James Hilary (*1844–1916*) 657
Mumford, Lewis (*1895–*) 834
Münch-Bellinghausen, Eligius Franz Josef von. *See* Halm
Munro, H[ector] H[ugh]. *See* Saki
Münster, Ernst F[riedrich Herbert von] (*1766–1839*) 417
Münsterberg, Hugo (*1863–1916*) 702
Murasaki, Shikibu (*c. 978–1031*) 135
Murrow, Edward R[oscoe] (*1908–1965*) 872
 note 742–743
Musset, Alfred de (*1810–1857*) 537
Mussolini, Benito (*1883–1945*) 783

Nabokov, Vladimir (*1899–1977*) 846
Nairne, Carolina Oliphant, Baroness (*1766–1845*) 417
Nakae, Toju (*1608–1648*) 289
Napoleon I (Napoleon Bonaparte) (*1769–1821*) 420
 note 110, 294
Nasby, Petroleum V. (*pseudonym of* David Ross Locke) (*1833–1888*) 615
Nash, Ogden (*1902–1971*) 855
 note 686
Nashe, Thomas (*1567–1601*) 250
Naylor, James Ball (*1860–1945*) 696
Neale, John Mason (*1818–1866*) 563
Nehru, Jawaharlal (*1889–1964*) 814
Nekrasov, Nikolai (*1821–1877*) 584
Nelson, Horatio, Viscount Nelson (*1758–1805*) 408
Nemerov, Howard (*1920–*) 897
Nero (*originally* Lucius Domitius Ahenobarbus) (*37–68*) 118
Neruda, Pablo (Neftalí Ricardo Reyes y Basualto) (*1904–1973*) 860
Nerval, Gérard de (*pseudonym of* Gérard Labrunie) (*1808–1855*) 514
Nervo, Amado (*1870–1919*) 731
Nevins, Allan (*1890–1971*) 816
New England Primer, The 320
Newbolt, Sir Henry (*1862–1938*) 700
Newman, John Henry Cardinal (*1801–1890*) 490
Newton, Sir Isaac (*1642–1727*) 313
Newton, John (*1725–1807*) 367
Nicolai, Philip (*1556–1608*) 176
Nicolson, Adela Florence Cory. *See* Hope, Laurence
Niebuhr, Reinhold (*1892–1971*) 823
Niemoeller, Martin (*1892–*) 824
Nietzsche, Friedrich Wilhelm (*1844–1900*) 657
 note 413, 561, 565, 587, 657, 658, 696
Nimitz, Chester William (*1885–1966*) 791
Nin, Anaïs (*1903–1977*) 858
Nivelle, Robert Georges (*1856–1924*)
 note 679
Nixon, Richard M[ilhous] (*1913–*) 882
Nobles, Milton (*1847–1924*) 661
Nock, Albert Jay (*1873–1945*) 740
Noel, Thomas (*1799–1861*) 486
Norris, John (*1657–1711*) 318
North, Christopher. *See* John Wilson
North American Indian (Anonymous) 928
Norton, Caroline Sheridan (*1808–1877*) 514
Norton, Charles Eliot (*1827–1908*) 598
Norworth, Jack (*1879–1959*) 765
Novalis (*pseudonym of* Baron Friedrich von Hardenberg) (*1772–1801*) 438
 note 308
Novello, Ivor (*1893–1951*)
 note 740
Noyes, Alfred (*1880–1958*) 772
Nursery Rhymes (Anonymous) 929
Nyerere, Julius K[ambarage] (*1921–*) 898

O'Casey, Sean (*1884–1964*) 786
Occam (Ockham), William of (*c. 1300 – c. 1348*) 143
Ochs, Adolph S[imon] (*1858–1935*) 686
O'Connor, Edwin (*1918–1968*) 895
O'Connor, Flannery (*1925–1964*) 905
O'Flaherty, Liam (*1896–*) 836
O'Hara, John (*1905–1970*) 865
O'Hara, Theodore (*1820–1867*) 578
Ohiyesa (Charles Alexander Eastman) (*1858–1939*) 686
O'Keeffe, Georgia (*1887–*) 800
O'Keeffe, John (*1747–1833*) 394
O'Kelly, Dennis (*1720–1787*) 364
Oken, Lorenz (*1779–1851*) 447
Oldys, William (*1696–1761*) 344
Oliphant, Carolina, Baroness Nairne. *See* Nairne
Olmsted, Frederick Law (*1822–1903*) 590
Olsen, Tillie (*1913–*) 883
O'Malley, Frank Ward (*1875–1932*) 756
Omar ibn al-Halif
note 109
Omar Khayyám (*died c. 1123*) 516
Onasander (*fl. 49*) 116
O'Neill, Eugene (*1888–1953*) 810
Ono no Komachi (*9th century*) 135
Oppenheimer, J[ulius] Robert (*1904–1967*) 861
O'Reilly, John Boyle (*1844–1890*) 659
Orléans, Charles d' (*1391–1465*) 148
Ortega y Gasset, José (*1883–1955*) 784
Orwell, George (*pseudonym of* Eric Blair) (*1903–1950*) 858
Osborn, Fairfield (*1887–1969*) 801
Osborne, John [James] (*1929–*) 910
O'Shaughnessy, Arthur [William Edgar] (*1844–1881*) 659
Osler, Sir William (*1849–1919*) 664
note 518
O'Sullivan, John Louis (*1813–1895*) 552
Otis, James (*1725–1783*) 367
note 367
Otway, Thomas (*1652–1685*) 316
Overbury, Sir Thomas (*1581–1613*) 262
Ovid (Publius Ovidius Naso) (*43 B.C.–A.D. c. 18*) 113
note 60, 100, 104, 112, 113, 145, 206
Owen, Wilfred (*1893–1918*) 827
Oxenstiern, Axel (*1583–1654*)
note 263

Page, Walter Hines (*1855–1918*) 677
Page, William Tyler (*1868–1942*) 725
Paige, Satchel (Leroy) (*c. 1906–*) 867
Paine, Albert Bigelow (*1861–1937*) 696
Paine, Thomas (*1737–1809*) 384
Palafox [y Melzi], José de (*1775–1847*)
note 457
Paley, William (*1743–1805*) 390
Pali Canon, The (*c. 500 – c. 250 B.C.*) 72
Palladas (*fl. 400*)
note 259
Palmerston, Henry John Temple, Viscount (*1784–1865*) 454
Paracelsus, Philippus Aureolus (*pseudonym of* Theophrastus Bombastus von Hohenheim) (*c. 1493–1541*) 157
note 168
Paramore, Edward E., Jr. (*1895–1956*) 834
Paré, Ambroise (*1517–1590*) 162
Pareto, Vilfredo (*1848–1923*) 662
Parker, Dorothy (*1893–1967*) 827
Parker, John (*1729–1775*) 374
Parker, Martin (*c. 1600 – c. 1656*) 273
Parker, Ross (*1914–*) 885
Parker, Theodore (*1810–1860*) 537
Parkinson, C[yril] Northcote (*1909–*) 876
Parkman, Francis (*1823–1893*) 592
Parnell, Thomas (*1679–1718*) 329
Parra, Nicanor (*1914–*) 885
Parton, James (*1822–1891*)
note 418
Parton, Sara Payson. *See* Fern
Pascal, Blaise (*1623–1662*) 299
note 111, 178, 393
Pasternak, Boris (*1890–1960*) 816
Pasteur, Louis (*1822–1895*) 591
Patchen, Kenneth (*1911–1972*) 879
Pater, Walter (*1839–1894*) 638
note 109
Paterson, Andrew Barton (Banjo) (*1864–1941*) 705
Patmore, Coventry (*1823–1896*) 593
Patten, George Washington (*c. 1808–1882*) 514

Patton, George S[mith] (*1885–1945*) 791
Paul, Elliot (*1891–1958*) 819
Pauling, Linus [Carl] (*1901–*) 854
Pavlov, Ivan Petrovich (*1849–1936*) 665
Payne, John Howard (*1791–1852*) 465
Paz, Octavio (*1914–*) 885
Peacham, Henry (*c. 1576 – c. 1643*) 258
Peacock, Thomas Love (*1785–1866*) 455
Peale, Norman Vincent (*1898–*) 842
Pearce, Donn (*1928–*) 908
Pearson, Karl (*1857–1936*) 684
Peary, Robert E[dwin] (*1856–1920*) 679
Peele, George (*c. 1558 – c. 1597*) 177
note 260, 450
Pegler, Westbrook (*1894–1969*) 830
Péguy, Charles (*1873–1914*) 741
Peirce, Benjamin (*1809–1880*) 525
Peirce, Charles Sanders (*1839–1914*) 639
Penn, William (*1644–1718*) 314
Pepys, Samuel (*1633–1703*) 309
note 99, 926
Percy, Walker (*1916–*) 889
Perelman, S[idney] J[oseph] (*1904–1979*) 861
Periander (*d. 585 B.C.*). *See* Seven Sages
Pericles (*c. 495–429 B.C.*) 73
Perls, Frederick Salomon (*1893–*) 827
Perry, Oliver Hazard (*1785–1819*) 455
Pershing, John Joseph (*1860–1948*)
note 693
Persius (Aulus Persius Flaccus) (*34–62*) 117
Peshkov, Aleksei Maksimovich. *See* Gorki
Pétain, Henri Philippe (*1856–1951*) 679
Peter, Laurence J[ohnston] (*1919–*) 896
Petrarch (Francesco Petrarca) (*1304–1374*) 143
note 113
Petronius, Gaius (Petronius Arbiter) (*died c. 66*) 117
Phaedrus (*fl. c. 8*) 114
note 66
Pheidippides (*d. 490 B.C.*) 71
Philip VI (Philip of Valois) (*1293–1350*) 143
Philips, John (*1676–1709*) 328
Phillips, Wendell (*1811–1884*) 538
note 616
Philostratus (*c. 181–250*)
note 256
Phinehas ben Yair
note 346
Phocion (*c. 402–317 B.C.*) 86
Piave, Francesco Maria (*1810–1879*)
note 105
Picasso, Pablo (*1881–1973*) 774
Pickett, George Edward (*1825–1875*) 596
Pindar (*c. 518 – c. 438 B.C.*) 71
note 71
Pindar, Peter. *See* Wolcot, John
Pinero, Sir Arthur Wing (*1855–1934*) 677
Pinzón, Martín Alonso (*c. 1440–1493*)
note 646
Piozzi, Hester Lynch Thrale (Mrs. Thrale) (*1741–1821*) 386
note 461
Pirandello, Luigi (*1867–1936*) 723
Pitavals, François Goyot de (*1673–1743*) 327
Pitt, William (*1759–1806*) 412
Pitt, William (*d. 1840*) 429
Pitt, William, Earl of Chatham (*1708–1778*) 350
Pittacus (*c. 650 – c. 570 B.C.*). *See* Seven Sages
Pius XII, Pope (Eugenio Pacelli) (*1876–1958*) 757
Planché, James Robinson (*1796–1880*) 480
Planck, Max (*1858–1947*) 686
Plath, Sylvia (*1932–1963*) 911
Plato (*c. 428–348 B.C.*) 83
note 63, 86, 108, 122, 307, 337, 468
Plautus, Titus Maccius (*254–184 B.C.*) 93
Pliny the Elder (Gaius Plinius Secundus) (*23–79*) 116
note 96, 245
Pliny the Younger (Gaius Plinius Caecilius Secundus) (*c. 61 – c. 112*) 123
note 97
Plotinus (*205–270*) 126
Plutarch (*46–120*) 119
note 91, 99, 111, 112, 116, 120, 147, 190, 242, 259, 519
Poe, Edgar Allan (*1809–1849*) 525
note 525, 526, 527, 812
Poem of the Cid (*12th century*) 137

Poincaré, Jules Henri (*1854–1912*) 673
Polanyi, Michael (*1891–1976*) 819
Pollock, Edward (*1823–1858*) 593
Polybius (*c. 208 – c. 126 B.C.*) 95
Pomfret, John (*1667–1702*) 321
note 304, 320
Pompadour, Jeanne Antoinette Poisson, Marquise de (*1721–1764*) 364
Pompey (Gnaeus Pompeius) (*106–48 B.C.*) 99
note 117
Ponting, Herbert George (*1871–1935*) 733
Pope, Alexander (*1688–1744*) 332
note 57, 93, 119, 167, 173, 174, 178, 180, 219, 285, 303, 304, 305, 307, 338
Pope, Walter (*c. 1630–1714*) 302
Popper, Sir Karl Raimund (*1902–*) 856
Poquelin, Jean Baptiste. *See* Molière
Porter, Cole [Albert] (*1891–1964*) 820
Porter, Horace (*1837–1921*) 632
Porter, William Sydney. *See* Henry, O.
Porteus, Beilby (*1731–1808*) 378
note 164
Potter, Beatrix (*1866–1943*) 719
Potter, David Morris (*1910–1971*) 877
Potter, Stephen (*1900–1969*) 848
Pottier, Eugène (*1816–1887*) 555
Pound, Ezra (*1885–1972*) 792
Pound, Roscoe (*1870–1964*) 731
Powell, Adam Clayton, Jr. (*1908–1972*)
note 914–915
Powell, George H. *See* Asaf, George
Powell, Sir John (*1645–1713*)
note 172
Powers, John A. (*1922–1979*)
note 921
Praed, Winthrop Mackworth (*1802–1839*)
note 170, 268
Prescott, William (*1726–1795*) 368
Prescott, William Hickling (*1796–1859*) 480
Previn, Dory (*c. 1929–*) 910
Prévost, Abbé (Antoine François Prévost d'Exiles) (*1697–1763*) 345
Price, Don K[rasher] (*1910–*) 878
Priestley, J[ohn] B[oynton] (*1894–*) 830
Priestley, Joseph (*1733–1804*) 379
note 342
Primary Chronicle, The (*1040–1118*) 136
Prior, Matthew (*1664–1721*) 320
note 256, 270
Proclus (*c. 411–485*)
note 120
Procter, Adelaide Anne (*1825–1864*) 596
Procter, Bryan Waller. *See* Cornwall, Barry
Propertius, Sextus (*54 B.C. – A.D. 2*) 112
Protagoras (*c. 485 – c. 410 B.C.*) 78
Proudhon, Pierre Joseph (*1809–1865*) 527
Proust, Marcel (*1871–1922*) 733
Ptahhotpe (*24th century B.C.*) 3
Ptolemy (Claudius Ptolemaeus) (*c. 100–178*) 124
Publilius Syrus (*fl. 1st century B.C.*) 110
note 78, 96, 103, 107, 110, 111, 128
Pulteney, Sir William, Earl of Bath (*1684–1764*) 330
Punch 660
note 546
Pushkin, Alexander Sergeevich (*1799–1837*) 486
note 357
Putnam, Amelia Earhart. *See* Earhart
Puzo, Mario (*1920–*) 897
Pyle, Ernie (*1900–1945*) 848
Pynchon, Thomas (*1937–*) 914
Pyrrhus (*c. 318–272 B.C.*) 92
Pythagoras (*c. 582–500 B.C.*) 65
Pytheas (*fl. 330 B.C.*) 90

Quarles, Francis (*1592–1644*) 267
note 156
Quesnay, François (*1694–1774*) 342
Quiller-Couch, Sir Arthur [Thomas] (*1863–1944*) 702
Quincy, Josiah (*1744–1775*) 393
Quincy, Josiah, Jr. (*1772–1864*) 438
Quintilian (Marcus Fabius Quintilianus) (*born c. 35*) 117
note 447

Rabelais, François (*c. 1494–1553*) 157
note 60, 62, 63, 86, 91, 95, 110, 261
Racan, Honorat de Bueil, Marquis de (*1589–1670*) 265
Racine, Jean (*1639–1699*) 312
note 96
Radcliffe, Ann (*1764–1823*) 416
Rado, James (*1939–*) 914
Ragni, Gerome (*1942–*) 914
Raimund, Ferdinand (*1790–1836*) 464
Rainsborough, Thomas (*d. 1648*) 264
Ralegh, Sir Walter (*c. 1552–1618*) 172
Raleigh, Sir Walter (*1861–1922*) 697
Ramsay, Allan (*1686–1758*) 331
Rand, Ayn (*1905–*) 865
Randall, James Ryder (*1839–1908*) 639
Randolph, Innes (*1837–1887*) 632
Randolph, John (*1773–1833*) 439
Rands, William Brighty (*pseudonym* Matthew Browne) (*1823–1882*) 593
Ranke, Leopold von (*1795–1886*) 480
Ransetsu (*1653–1708*) 317
Ransom, John Crowe (*1888–1974*) 810
Raspe, Rudolf Erich (*1737–1794*) 385
note 121
Ravenscroft, Thomas (*c. 1592 – c. 1635*) 268
Ray, John (*1627–1705*) 301
note 136, 321
Rayburn, Sam (*1882–1961*) 779
Raymond, Rossiter Worthington (*1840–1918*) 642
Read, Sir Herbert (*1893–1968*) 827
note 655
Read, Thomas Buchanan (*1822–1872*) 591
Rechberg, Johann Bernhard, Graf von (*1806–1899*) 509
Red Cloud (*1822–1909*) 591
Red Jacket (Sagoyewatha) (*c. 1758–1830*) 408
Reddy, Helen (*1941–*) 915
Reed, John (*1887–1920*) 801
Remarque, Erich Maria (*1897–1970*) 839
Remy (Remigius), Saint (*c. 438 – c. 533*) 129
Renan, [Joseph] Ernest (*1823–1892*) 593
Renard, Jules (*1864–1910*) 705
Renoir, [Pierre] Auguste (*1841–1919*) 646
Repkow. *See* Eike von Repkow
Revere, Paul (*1735–1818*) 382
Rexford, Eben Eugene (*1848–1916*) 662
Reynaud, Paul (*1878–1966*) 761
Rhodes, Cecil [John] (*1853–1902*) 672
Rhodes, William Barnes (*1772–1826*) 438
Ricardo, David (*1772–1823*) 438
Rice, Grantland (*1880–1954*) 773
note 704
Rich, Adrienne (*1929–*) 910
Rich, Richard (*fl. 1610*) 261
Richards, Keith (*1944–*) 916
Richards, Laura E[lizabeth] (*1850–1943*) 667
Richardson, Robert (*1850–1901*)
note 625
Richter, Johann Paul Friedrich (Jean Paul) (*1763–1825*) 415
Ridgway, Matthew B[unker] (*1895–*)
note 826
Riley, James Whitcomb (*1849–1916*) 665
Rilke, Rainer Maria (*1875–1926*) 756
Rimbaud, Arthur (*1854–1891*) 673
note 580
Ripley, Robert Leroy (*1893–1949*) 827
Riquetti, Honoré Gabriel de, Comte de Mirabeau. *See* Mirabeau
Rivarol, Antoine de (*1753–1801*) 400
Robbe-Grillet, Alain (*1922–*) 901
Robbins, Lionel [Charles], Lord Robbins (*1898–*) 842
Robin, Leo (*1900–*) 848
Robinson, Edwin Arlington (*1869–1935*) 728
Robinson, James Harvey (*1863–1936*) 703
Rochefoucauld, François, Duc de La. *See* La Rochefoucauld
Rochefoucauld-Liancourt, François Alexandre Frédéric, Duc de La. *See* La Rochefoucauld-Liancourt
Rochester, John Wilmot, Earl of (*1647–1680*) 315
Rockefeller, John D[avison], Jr. (*1874–1960*) 752
Rockne, Knute [Kenneth] (*1888–1931*) 811
Rodó, José Enrique (*1872–1917*) 737
Roethke, Theodore (*1908–1963*) 873

Rogers, Robert Cameron (*1862–1912*) 700
Rogers, Samuel (*1763–1855*) 416
note 114, 180
Rogers, Will[iam Penn Adair] (*1879–1935*) 765
Rojas, Fernando de (*c. 1465 – c. 1538*) 153
Roland, Song of (11th century) 136
Roland de la Platière, Jeanne Manon Phlipon (Madame Roland) (*1754–1793*) 400
Ronsard, Pierre de (*1524–1585*) 162
note 123
Roosevelt, [Anna] Eleanor (*1884–1962*) 786
Roosevelt, Franklin Delano (*1882–1945*) 779, 781
note 741
Roosevelt, Theodore (*1858–1919*) 686
Root, George Frederick (*1820–1895*) 578
Roscommon, Wentworth Dillon, Earl of (*c. 1633–1685*) 309
Ross, A. C. (*fl. c. 1840*)
note 439
Ross, Harold [Wallace] (*1892–1951*) 824
Rossellini, Roberto (*1906–1977*) 867
Rossetti, Christina Georgina (*1830–1894*) 608
Rossetti, Dante Gabriel (*1828–1882*) 601
Rostand, Edmond (*1868–1918*) 726
Rosten, Leo C[alvin] (*1908–*)
note 770
Roszak, Theodore (*1933–*) 912
Rouget de Lisle, [Claude] Joseph (*1760–1836*) 415
Rousseau, Jean Jacques (*1712–1778*) 358
note 890
Rousset, David (*1912–*) 881
Routh, Martin Joseph (*1755–1854*) 402
Rowe, Nicholas (*1674–1718*) 327
Rowley, "Red" (*fl. 1915*) 817
Roydon, Matthew (*c. 1564 – c. 1622*) 184
Rozanov, Vasili (*1856–1919*)
note 746
Rukeyser, Muriel (*1913–*) 883
Rumbold, Richard (*c. 1622–1685*) 298
Runyon, [Alfred] Damon (*1884–1946*) 787
Rusk, Dean (*1909–*)
note 925
Ruskin, John (*1819–1900*) 572
note 280, 619
Russell, Bertrand, Earl Russell (*1872–1970*) 737
Russell, George William (*pseudonym* A.E.) (*1867–1935*) 720
Russell, Lord John (*1792–1878*) 466
note 351, 727, 921
Russell, Sir William Howard (*1820–1907*) 578
Russian (Anonymous) 934
Rutebeuf (*d. 1285*) 139
Rutherford, Ernest (*1871–1937*) 734

Sabatini, Rafael (*1875–1950*) 756
Sacco, Nicola (*1891–1927*) 820
Sadat, Anwar al- (*1918–*) 895
Sagan, Carl (*1934–*) 913
Sainte-Beuve, Charles Augustin (*1804–1869*) 504
Saint-Exupéry, Antoine de (*1900–1944*) 849
St. John, Henry, Viscount Bolingbroke. *See* Bolingbroke
Saint-Simon, Claude Henri de Rouvroy (*1760–1825*)
note 108
Sakharov, Andrei Dmitrievich (*1921–*)
note 448
Saki (*pseudonym of* H[ector] H[ugh] Munro) (*1870–1916*) 731
Salinger, J[erome] D[avid] (*1919–*) 896
Salisbury, Robert Arthur Talbot Gascoyne-Cecil, Marquess of (*1830–1903*) 609
Sallust (Gaius Sallustius Crispus) (*86–34 B.C.*) 102
note 81
Salvandy, Narcisse Achille, Comte de (*1795–1856*) 472
Sand, George (*pseudonym of* Amandine Aurore Lucie Dupin, Baronne Dudevant) (*1804–1876*) 504
Sandburg, Carl (*1878–1967*) 761
note 358, 731–732, 921
Sandys, Sir Edwin (*1561–1629*)
note 164
Sangster, Margaret [Elizabeth] (*1838–1912*) 637
Santayana, George (*1863–1952*) 703
Sappho (*c. 612 B.C.*) 63
Saroyan, William (*1908–*) 875

Sarton, George (*1884–1956*) 787
Sartre, Jean Paul (*1905–1980*) 865
Sassoon, Siegfried (*1886–1967*) 795
Savage, Minot Judson (*1841–1918*) 646
Savile, George, Marquess of Halifax (*1633–1695*) 310
Saxe, John Godfrey (*1816–1887*) 556
Sayers, Dorothy L[eigh] (*1893–1957*) 827
Sayers, Henry J. (*d. 1932*) 719
Sayings of Jesus, The (*3rd century*) 126
Scarborough, William (*fl. c. 1875*)
  note 743
Scheffler, Johannes. *See* Angelus Silesius
Schelling, Friedrich von (*1775–1854*)
  note 396
Schidoni, Bartolommeo (*1560–1616*)
  note 133
Schiller, Johann [Christoph] Friedrich von (*1759–1805*) 412
Schlegel, Friedrich von (*1772–1829*) 438
Schlesinger, Arthur M[eier], Jr. (*1917–*) 894
Schliemann, Heinrich (*1822–1890*) 591
Schneckenburger, Max (*1819–1849*) 573
Schopenhauer, Arthur (*1788–1860*) 463
Schreiner, Olive [Emilie Albertina] (*pseudonym* Ralph Iron) (*1855–1920*) 677
Schultz, Charles M[onroe] (*1922–*) 901
Schumacher, E[rnst] F[riedrich] (*1911–1977*) 879
Schumpeter, Joseph Alois (*1883–1950*) 784
Schurz, Carl (*1829–1906*) 603
Schwartz, Delmore (*1913–1966*) 883
  note 713
Schweitzer, Albert (*1875–1965*) 756
Scott, Charles Prestwick (*1846–1932*) 661
Scott, Clement William (*1841–1904*) 646
Scott, John (*1730–1783*) 375
Scott, Robert Falcon (*1868–1912*) 726
Scott, Sir Walter (*1771–1832*) 429
  note 112, 170, 175, 211, 234, 261, 292, 343, 399, 412, 440, 613
Scott, William, Lord Stowell (*1745–1836*) 393
Scott, Winfield (*1786–1866*) 455
Sears, Edmund Hamilton (*1810–1876*) 537
Seattle (*c. 1786–1866*) 455
Sébastiani, Horace François Bastien (*1772–1851*) 439
Sechenov, Ivan Mikhailovich (*1829–1905*) 603
Secondat, Charles de, Baron de Montesquieu. *See* Montesquieu
Sedgwick, Ellery (*1872–1960*) 738
  note 741
Sedley, Sir Charles (*c. 1639–1701*) 312
Seeger, Alan (*1888–1916*) 811
Seeger, Pete [Peter] (*1919–*) 896
Seferis, George (Giorgios Sefiriades) (*1900–1971*) 849
Sei Shonagon (*b. 966*) 135
Seibert, T. Laurence (*fl. 1900*) 731
Selassie. *See* Haile Selassie
Selden, John (*1584–1654*) 263
  note 179
Seldes, George (*1890–1970*) 817
Seneca, Lucius Annaeus (*c. 4 B.C.–A.D. 65*) 114
  note 80, 157, 497, 602
Service, Robert William (*1874–1958*) 752
Seven Sages, The: Bias, Chilon, Cleobulus, Periander, Pittacus, Solon, Thales (*c. 650 – c. 550 B.C.*) 62
Sévigné, Marie de Rabutin-Chantal, Marquise de (*1626–1696*) 301
Seward, Thomas (*1708–1790*)
  note 257
Seward, William Henry (*1801–1872*)
  note 538
Sexton, Anne (*1928–1974*) 908
Seymour, Charles (*1885–1963*) 793
Shadwell, Thomas (*c. 1642–1692*) 313
Shaftesbury, Anthony Ashley Cooper, Earl of (*1671–1713*) 325
  note 325
Shahn, Ben (*1898–1969*) 843
Shakespeare, William (*1564–1616*) 184
  All's Well That Ends Well 227
    note 184
  Antony and Cleopatra 240
  As You Like It 210
    note 112
  Comedy of Errors, The 187
    note 147
  Coriolanus 242
    note 209
  Cymbeline 243

Shakespeare (continued)
Hamlet 217
note 148, 223
Julius Caesar 214
King Henry IV, Part I 202
note 158, 209
King Henry IV, Part II 205
note 161, 185
King Henry V 207
note 146, 167, 181
King Henry VI, Part I 184
note 160
King Henry VI, Part II 185
note 172
King Henry VI, Part III 186
note 175, 186
King Henry VIII 248
note 147, 249
King John 201
note 168
King Lear 232
note 160, 189, 478
King Richard II 193
note 144
King Richard III 186
note 159, 160, 167, 173
Love's Labour's Lost 190
note 128
Macbeth 235
note 239
Measure for Measure 227
note 205
Merchant of Venice, The 197
note 77, 137, 148, 159
Merry Wives of Windsor, The 225
note 147, 159, 170, 183
Midsummer-Night's Dream, A 195
Much Ado About Nothing 208
Othello 229
note 84, 169
Pericles 243
note 214
Phoenix and the Turtle, The 225
Rape of Lucrece, The 189
Romeo and Juliet 191
note 168, 188
Sonnets 243
Taming of the Shrew, The 188
note 158, 160
Tempest, The 247
note 168
Timon of Athens 242
Titus Andronicus 188
note 148, 160, 161
Troilus and Cressida 225
note 461
Twelfth-Night 213
note 167, 200, 209, 248

Shakespeare (continued)
Two Gentlemen of Verona, The 189
note 160
Venus and Adonis 189
Winter's Tale, The 246
note 158, 159
Shanties (Anonymous) 934
Shapiro, Karl (*1913–*) 883
Sharp, William (*pseudonym* Fiona Macleod) (*1855–1905*) 677
Shaw, George Bernard (*1856–1950*) 680
note 136, 539
Shaw, Henry Wheeler. *See* Billings
Sheed, Wilfrid (*1930–*) 910
Sheehy, Gail (*1937–*) 914
Sheffield, John, Duke of Buckingham and Normanby (*1648–1721*) 316
note 289
Shelley, Mary [Wollstonecraft] (*1797–1851*) 482
Shelley, Percy Bysshe (*1792–1822*) 466
note 234, 436, 467, 488
Shenstone, William (*1714–1763*)
note 355
Sheridan, Philip Henry (*1831–1888*) 610
Sheridan, Richard Brinsley (*1751–1816*) 398
note 117, 193, 213, 236, 349
Sherman, John (*1823–1900*) 593
Sherman, Sidney (*1805–1873*) 506
Sherman, William Tecumseh (*1820–1891*) 578
Sherwood, Robert E[mmet] (*1896–1955*) 836
Shevelove, Burt (*1915–*) 908
Shirley, James (*1596–1666*) 272
Sidney, Algernon (*1622–1683*) 298
note 66, 117, 243
Sidney, Sir Philip (*1554–1586*) 176
note 108
Sieyès, Emmanuel Joseph (*1748–1836*) 394
Sigismund (*1361–1437*)
note 298
Sigourney, Lydia Huntley (*1791–1865*) 465
Silesius, Angelus. *See* Angelus
Silius Italicus (*c. 25–99*)
note 270
Sill, Edward Rowland (*1841–1887*) 646
Silone, Ignazio (Secondo Tranquilli) (*1900–1978*) 851

Silverman, Sime (*1873–1933*) 741
Simon, Paul (*1942–*) 915
Simonides (*c. 556–468 B.C.*) 67
Sims, George Robert (*1847–1922*) 661
Singer, Isaac Bashevis (*1904–*) 861
Sitting Bull (*c. 1831–1890*) 610
Sitwell, Dame Edith (*1887–1964*) 801
Skelton, John (*c. 1460–1529*) 152
Skinner, B[urrhus] F[rederic] (*1904–*) 862
Slick, Sam (*pseudonym of* Thomas Chandler Haliburton) (*1796–1865*) 481
  note 348
Smart, Christopher (*1722–1771*) 365
Smedley, Francis Edward (*1818–1864*) 564
Smiles, Samuel (*1812–1904*) 551
Smith, Adam (*1723–1790*) 366
Smith, Alexander (*1830–1867*) 609
  note 95
Smith, Alfred E[manuel] (*1873–1944*) 741
Smith, Edgar (*1857–1938*) 684
Smith, Edmund (*1672–1710*)
  note 335
Smith, John (*1580–1631*)
  note 412
Smith, Langdon (*1858–1908*) 688
Smith, Logan Pearsall (*1865–1946*) 711
  note 276, 711
Smith, Samuel Francis (*1808–1895*) 514
Smith, Stevie (Margaret Florence) (*1902–1971*) 856
Smith, Sydney (*1771–1845*) 432
  note 298
Smithson, James (*1765–1829*) 417
Smollett, Tobias (*1721–1771*) 365
Snodgrass, William D[eWitt] (*1926–*) 906
Snow, Sir C[harles] P[ercy] (*1905–*) 865
Snowden, Ethel Annakin Snowden, Viscountess (*1881–1951*)
  note 746
Socrates (*469–399 B.C.*) 79
Solomos, Dionysius (*1798–1857*) 484
Solon (*c. 638 – c. 559 B.C.*). *See also* Seven Sages 62
Solzhenitsyn, Alexander Isayevich (*1918–*) 895
Somerville, William (*1675–1742*) 328
Sommer, Robert (*1929–*) 910
Sondheim, Stephen (*1930–*) 910
Song of Roland (*11th century*) 136
Song of the Harper, The (*c. 2650–2600 B.C.*) 3
Sophocles (*c. 495–406 B.C.*) 73
  note 66, 74
Soule, John Babsone Lane (*1815–1891*) 554
South, Robert (*1634–1716*) 310
Southerne, Thomas (*1660–1746*)
  note 176, 260
Southey, Robert (*1774–1843*) 439
  note 145, 295
Southwell, Robert (*c. 1561–1595*) 182
  note 73, 159
Spanish (Anonymous) 935
Spark, Muriel (*1918–*) 896
Speckled Snake (*c. 1729–1829*) 374
Spencer, Herbert (*1820–1903*) 579
Spencer, William Robert (*1770–1834*) 423
  note 227
Spender, Stephen (*1909–*) 876
Spenser, Edmund (*1552–1599*) 173
  note 100
Spinoza, Baruch *or* Benedict (*1632–1677*) 308
Spirituals (Anonymous) 935
Spock, Benjamin (*1903–*) 858
Spofford, Harriet Prescott (*1835–1921*) 621
Spooner, William Archibald (*1844–1930*) 659
Sprague, Charles (*1791–1875*) 465
Staël, Madame de (Germaine, Baronne de Staël-Holstein) (*1766–1817*) 417
  note 417
Stafford, Jean (*1915–*) 888
Stahl, Friedrich Julius (*1802–1861*) 492
Stalin, Joseph (Iosif Vissarionovich Dzhugashvili) (*1879–1953*) 766
Stallings, Laurence (*1894–1968*) 802
Standing Bear, Luther (*1868–1939*) 726
Stanhope, Philip Dormer, Earl of Chesterfield. *See* Chesterfield
Stanislavski, Konstantin Sergeevich Alekseev (*1863–1938*) 704
Stanley, Sir Henry Morton (*1841–1904*) 646
Stanton, Charles E. (*1859–1933*) 693
Stanton, Edwin McMasters (*1814–1869*) 553

Stanton, Elizabeth Cady (*1815–1902*) 554
Stanton, Frank Lebby (*1857–1927*) 684
Stark, John (*1728–1822*) 371
Statius, Caecilius. *See* Caecilius
Steele, Sir Richard (*1672–1729*) 327
note 170, 917
Steffens, Lincoln (*1866–1936*) 719
Stein, Gertrude (*1874–1946*) 752
Steinbeck, John [Ernst] (*1902–1968*) 857
Stendhal (*pseudonym of* Henri Beyle) (*1783–1842*) 453
Stephen, James K[enneth] (*1859–1892*) 693
note 428
Stephen, Leslie (*1832–1904*)
note 349
Stephens, James (*1882–1950*) 781
Sterling, George (*1869–1926*) 729
Stern, G[ladys] B[ronwyn] (*1890–*)
note 548
Sterne, Laurence (*1713–1768*) 359
note 158, 170, 171
Stesichorus (*c. 630 – c. 555 B.C.*) 62
Stevens, Wallace (*1879–1955*) 766
note 437
Stevenson, Adlai E[wing] (*1900–1965*) 851
note 786
Stevenson, Robert Louis (*1850–1894*) 667
note 145, 314, 668
Stevenson, William (*c. 1530–1575*) 163
Stickney, Trumbull (*1874–1904*) 752
Stimson, Henry L[ewis] (*1867–1950*) 723
Stockton, Frank [Richard] (*1834–1902*) 618
Stoppard, Tom (*1937–*) 914
Story, Joseph (*1779–1849*) 447
Story, William Wetmore (*1819–1895*) 573
Stoughton, William (*1631–1701*) 307
Stowe, Harriet Beecher (*1811–1896*) 538
Stowell, William Scott, Lord. *See* Scott
Strafford, Thomas Wentworth, Earl of (*1593–1641*)
note 200
Strand, Mark (*1934–*) 913
Strunk, William, Jr. (*1869–1946*) 729
Strunsky, Simeon (*1879–1948*) 770
Stuart, Mary. *See* Mary Stuart, Queen of Scots
Stubbs, Charles William (*1845–1912*) 660
note 542
Suarès, André (*1868–1948*) 726
Suckling, Sir John (*1609–1642*) 289
note 177
Suetonius (Gaius Suetonius Tranquillus) (*c. 70 – c. 140*) 123
Sullivan, John L[aurence] (*1858–1918*)
note 78
Sullivan, Louis Henri (*1856–1924*) 681
Sully, Maximilien de Béthune, Duc de (*1559–1641*) 178
Sulzberger, Arthur Hays (*1891–1968*) 820
Sumner, Charles (*1811–1874*) 539
Sumner, William Graham (*1840–1910*) 642
Sun Yat-sen (*1866–1925*) 719
Surtees, Robert Smith (*1803–1864*) 500
Suti and Hor (*15th–14th centuries B.C.*) 5
Swenson, May (*1919–*) 896
Swift, Jonathan (*1667–1745*) 321
note 119, 158, 294, 319
Swinburne, Algernon Charles (*1837–1909*) 632
Sydenham, Thomas (*1624–1689*) 301
Symonds, John Addington (*1840–1893*) 643
Symons, Arthur (*1865–1945*) 711
Synge, John Millington (*1871–1909*) 735
Syrus, Publilius. *See* Publilius Syrus
Szent-Györgyi von Nagyrapolt, Albert (*1893–*) 828

Tabb, John Banister (*1845–1909*) 660
Tabrar, Joseph (*fl. 1892*) 677
Tacitus, Cornelius (*c. 55 – c. 117*) 122
note 86, 115, 548
Taggard, Genevieve (*1894–1948*) 830
Tagore, Rabindranath (*1861–1941*) 697
Talleyrand-Périgord, Charles Maurice de (*1754–1838*) 400
note 782
Tanizaki, Junichiro (*1886–1965*) 796

Tarkington, Booth (1869–1946) 729
Tate, Nahum (1652–1715) 317
Tawney, Richard Henry (1880–1962) 773
Taylor, Ann (1782–1866) 449
Taylor, Bayard (1825–1878) 596
Taylor, Bert Leston (1866–1921) 719
Taylor, Edward (c. 1644–1729) 314
Taylor, Jane (1783–1824) 449
Taylor, Bishop Jeremy (1613–1667) 294
Taylor, John (1580–1653)
  note 91, 159
Taylor, Zachary (1784–1850) 454
Teaching for Merikare, The (c. 2135–2040 B.C.) 3
Teasdale, Sara (1884–1933) 787
Tecumseh (1768–1813) 419
Teilhard de Chardin, Pierre (1881–1955) 775
Temple, Sir William (1628–1699) 302
Temple, William (1881–1944) 775
Tennyson, Alfred, Lord (1809–1892) 527
  note 58, 76, 146, 157, 179, 184, 228, 457
Terence (Publius Terentius Afer) (c. 190–159 B.C.) 96
Terkel, Studs [Louis] (1912–) 881
Terman, Lewis M[adison] (1877–1956) 758
Tertullian (Quintus Septimus Tertullianus) (c. 160–240) 126
  note 91, 115
Thackeray, William Makepeace (1811–1863) 539
  note 168, 359
Thales (c. 640 – c. 546 B.C.). *See also* Seven Sages
  note 174
Thaxter, Celia [Laighton] (1835–1894) 621
Thayer, Ernest L[awrence] (1863–1940) 704
Thayer, Louis Edwin (1878–1956) 762
Themistocles (c. 528 – c. 462 B.C.) 70
Theobald, Lewis (1688–1744)
  note 115
Theocritus (c. 310 – c. 250 B.C.) 92
Theognis (fl. c. 545 B.C.) 67
Theophorus, Saint Ignatius. *See* Ignatius Theophorus
Theophrastus (d. 278 B.C.) 91
Thibault, Jacques Anatole François. *See* France, Anatole
Thomas à Kempis (1380–1471) 148
  note 58
Thomas Aquinas, Saint. *See* Aquinas
Thomas, Dylan (1914–1953) 886
Thomas, Lewis (1913–) 883
Thomas, Norman [Mattoon] (1884–1968) 787
Thompson, Sir D'Arcy Wentworth (1860–1948) 696
Thompson, Francis (1859–1907) 693
Thomson, James (1700–1748) 345
  note 268
Thomson, James (1834–1882) 618
Thomson, Sir Joseph John (1856–1940) 681
Thomson, William, Lord Kelvin. *See* Kelvin
Thoreau, Henry David (1817–1862) 557
  note 299, 421, 557, 779
Thorndike, Edward L[ee] (1874–1949) 752
Thorpe, Rose Hartwick (1850–1939) 669
Thorpe, Thomas (c. 1570 – c. 1635)
  note 243
Thrale, Mrs. *See* Piozzi, Hester Lynch Thrale
Thucydides (c. 460–400 B.C.) 80
  note 75
Thurber, James (1894–1961) 831
Tiberius (42 B.C.–A.D. 37)
  note 86
Tibullus, Albius (c. 54 – c. 19 B.C.) 112
Tichborne, Chidiock (c. 1558–1586) 177
Tickell, Thomas (1686–1740)
  note 325
Tillotson, John (1630–1694) 303
Tirso de Molina (*pseudonym of* Gabriel Téllez) (c. 1584–1648) 264
Titchener, Edward B[radford] (1867–1927) 724
Titus Vespasianus (c. 41–81) 119
Tiutchev, Fëdor (1803–1873) 500
Tocqueville, Alexis [Charles Henri Maurice Clérel] de (1805–1859) 506
Toffler, Alvin (1928–) 909
Tolkien, J[ohn] R[onald] R[euel] (1892–1973) 824
Tolstoi, Alexei Konstantinovich (1817–1875) 561
Tolstoi, Leo Nikolaevich (1828–1910) 601
  note 298

Tomlinson, H[enry] M[ajor] (1873–1958) 741
Tommaso di Celano (c. 1185 – c. 1255) 139
Toomer, Jean (1894–1967) 831
Toplady, Augustus Montague (1740–1778) 386
Toure, Kwame. *See* Stokely Carmichael
Tracy, Spencer (1900–1967) 852
Traherne, Thomas (c. 1637–1674) 311
Trench, [Frederic] Herbert (1865–1923) 711
Trenck, Frederick von der (1726–1794)
note 346
Trevelyan, G[eorge] M[acaulay] (1876–1962) 758
Trilling, Lionel (1905–1976) 865
Trollope, Anthony (1815–1882) 554
note 548, 555
Trollope, Frances [Milton] (1780–1863) 449
Tronchin, Theodore (1709–1781) 357
Trotsky, Leon (Leib Davydovich Bronstein) (1870–1940) 770
Truffaut, François (1932–) 911
Truman, Harry S. (1884–1972) 787
note 788
Truth, Sojourner (Isabella Van Wagener) (c. 1797–1883) 482
Tsushima, Shuji. *See* Dazai, Osamu
Tubman, Harriet (c. 1823–1913) 593
Tucker, Josiah (1712–1799) 359
Tucker, Sophie (c. 1884–1966) 788
Tudor, Mary. *See* Mary Tudor
Tung Chung-shu (c. 179 – c. 104 B.C.) 97
Tupper, Martin Farquhar (1810–1889) 537
Turgenev, Ivan Sergeyevich (1818–1883) 564
Turgot, Anne Robert Jacques, Baron de l'Aulne (1727–1781) 368
note 346
Tusser, Thomas (c. 1524–1580) 163
note 111, 159, 160, 161
Twain, Mark (*pseudonym of* Samuel Langhorne Clemens) (1835–1910) 621
note 378, 621
Tweed, William Marcy (Boss Tweed) (1823–1878) 594
Tweedsmuir, John Buchan, Lord. *See* Buchan
Tyler, Royall (1757–1826) 407
note 920
Tyndall, John (1820–1893) 580

Udall, Nicholas (1505–1556)
note 720
Udall, Stewart [Lee] (1920–) 897
Ufford, Edward Smith (1851–1929) 670
Ullman, Liv [Johanne] (1938–) 914
Ulyanov, Vladimir Ilyich. *See* Lenin
Unamuno, Miguel de (1864–1936) 705
United Nations, Charter of the 788
Upanishads, The (800–500 B.C.) 56
Updike, John (1932–) 911
Upham, James B. (1845–1905)
note 677
Urey, Harold [Clayton] (1893–) 828
Ustinov, Peter (1921–) 898

Valéry, Paul (1871–1945) 735
Vallejo, César (1892–1938) 824
Vanbrugh, Sir John (1664–1726) 321
Van Buren, Martin (1782–1862)
note 350
Vanderbilt, William H[enry] (1821–1885) 584
Van der Post, Laurens (1906–) 867
Vandiver, Willard Duncan (1854–1932) 674
Van Doren, Mark (1894–1972) 831
Van Dyke, Henry (1852–1933) 671
Vanzetti, Bartolomeo (1888–1927) 811
Varro, Marcus Terentius (116–27 B.C.) 97
note 91
Vaughan, Henry (1622–1695) 298
Vauvenargues, Luc de Clapiers, Marquis de (1715–1747) 361
note 176
Vaux, Calvert (1824–1895) 590
Vaux, Sir Thomas (1510–1556) 162
Veblen, Thorstein (1857–1929) 685
Vega, Lope de (1562–1635) 182
note 353
Vegetius (Flavius Vegetius Renatus) (*fl. c.* 375) 128
Venable, William Henry (1836–1920)
note 765

Venning, Ralph (*c. 1621–1674*)
note 91, 250
Verlaine, Paul (*1844–1896*) 659
Versailles, Treaty of
note 812–813
Vespucci, Amerigo (*1454–1512*) 152
Vest, George Graham (*1830–1904*) 609
Vichy-Chamrond, Marie de, Marquise du Deffand. *See* Deffand
Vico, Giovanni Battista (Giambattista) (*1668–1774*) 324
Victoria (*1819–1901*) 573
Vidal, Gore (*1925–*)
note 700
Vigny, Alfred de (*1797–1863*) 483
Villars, Claude Louis Hector, Duc de (*1653–1734*)
note 422
Villiers, George, Duke of Buckingham (*1628–1687*) 302
Villiers de L'Isle-Adam, Philippe Auguste (*1838–1889*) 638
Villon, François (*1431–c. 1465*) 150
Vincent of Lerins, Saint (*died c. 450*) 129
Vinci, Leonardo da (*1452–1519*) 152
Vinson, Fred[erick] M[oore] (*1890–1953*) 817
Virchow, Rudolf (*1821–1902*) 584
Virgil (Publius Vergilius Maro) (*70–19 B.C.*) 103
note 117, 200
Volney, Constantin de (*1757–1820*)
note 488
Voltaire (*pseudonym of* François Marie Arouet (*1694–1778*) 342
note 96, 294, 322, 360, 376
Vonnegut, Kurt, Jr. (*1922–*) 901
Voss, Johann Heinrich (*1751–1826*) 399
Voznesensky, Andrei Andreevich (*1933–*) 912
Vulgate, The
note 6, 18, 31, 34, 45

Wagener, Isabella Van. *See* Truth, Sojourner
Wagner, Richard (*1813–1883*) 552
Walaeus, Johannes (Jan van Wale) (*1604–1699*)
note 349
Walcott, Derek (*1930–*) 911
Walker, James J[ohn] (*1881–1946*)
note 651
Walker, Margaret [Abigail] (*1915–*) 888
Walker, William (*1623–1684*) 300
Wallace, Henry A[gard] (*1888–1965*) 811
Wallace, Lew[is] (*1827–1905*) 599
Wallace, William Ross (*1819–1881*) 573
Waller, Edmund (*1606–1687*) 276
note 66
Waller, Thomas (Fats) (*1904–1943*)
note 847
Walpole, Horace (*1717–1797*) 363
Walpole, Sir Robert (*1676–1745*) 328
note 293, 330
Walsh, William (*1663–1708*) 320
Walter, Howard Arnold (*1883–1918*) 785
Walther von der Vogelweide (*c. 1170 – c. 1230*) 138
Walton, Izaak (*1593–1683*) 270
note 251, 253
Warburton, Bishop William (*1698–1779*) 345
Ward, Artemus. *See* Browne, Charles Farrar
Ware, Eugene Fitch. *See* Ironquill
Warhol, Andy (*1927–*) 908
Warner, Anna Bartlett (*1827–1915*) 599
Warner, Charles Dudley (*1829–1900*) 603
Warren, Earl (*1891–1974*) 820
Washburn, Henry Stevenson (*1813–1903*) 552
Washington, Booker T[aliaferro] (*1856–1915*) 681
Washington, George (*1732–1799*) 378
note 170
Waterhouse, Benjamin (*1754–1846*) 401
Watson, John Broadus (*1878–1958*) 762
Watson, Sir William (*1858–1935*) 688
Watts, Isaac (*1674–1748*) 328
note 268
Waugh, Evelyn (*1903–1966*) 858
Wayne, John (*1907–1979*) 870
Weatherly, Frederic Edward (*1848–1929*) 663
Webb, Beatrice (*1858–1943*) 694
Webb, Sidney, Lord Passfield (*1859–1947*) 694
Webster, Daniel (*1782–1852*) 450
note 450

Webster, H[arold] T[ucker] (1885–1952) 793
Webster, John (c. 1580 – c. 1625) 262
note 108, 148, 161, 165
Wedgwood, Josiah (1730–1795) 375
Weems, Mason Locke (1759–1825)
note 378
Weil, Simone (1909–1943) 876
Weisskopf, Victor [Frederick] (1908–) 875
Wellington, Arthur Wellesley, Duke of (1769–1852) 421
Wells, H[erbert] G[eorge] (1866–1946) 719
Welty, Eudora (1909–) 876
Wentworth, Thomas, Earl of Strafford. *See* Strafford
Wesley, Charles (1707–1788) 350
Wesley, John (1703–1791) 346
Wesley, Samuel (1662–1735) 319
West, Mae (1892–) 824
West, Nathanael (1902–1940) 857
West, Dame Rebecca (*pseudonym of* Cicily Isabel Fairfield) (1892–)
note 781
Westbury, Richard Bethell, Lord (1800–1873) 489
Westcott, Edward Noyes (1846–1898) 661
Wharton, Edith [Newbold Jones] (1862–1937) 700
Whewell, William (1794–1866) 471
note 179
Whistler, James McNeill (1834–1903) 619
White, E[lwyn] B[rooks] (1899–) 846
note 558–559
White, James Terry (1845–1920)
note 133
White, T[erence] H[anbury] (1906–1964)
note 419
White, William Allen (1868–1944) 726
White, William Lindsay (1900–1973) 852
Whitefield, George (1714–1770)
note 350
Whitehead, Alfred North (1861–1947) 697
Whitehead, William (1715–1785) 361
Whiting, William (1825–1878) 596
Whitman, Walt (1819–1892) 573
note 751
Whittier, John Greenleaf (1807–1892) 513
note 512, 532, 671
Whittinton, Robert (c. 1480 – c. 1530) 155
Whyte-Melville, George John (1821–1878) 584
Wieland, Christoph Martin (1733–1813) 380
Wiener, Norbert (1894–1964) 831
Wilberforce, Samuel (1805–1873)
note 596
Wilbur, Richard [Purdy] (1921–) 899
Wilcox, Ella Wheeler (1850–1919) 669
note 500
Wilde, Oscar [Fingal O'Flahertie Wills] (1854–1900) 674
note 66, 914
Wilder, Thornton [Niven] (1897–1975) 839
Wiley, Herbert V. (1891–1954) 821
Wilhelm I (1797–1888) 483
Wilkes, John (1727–1797) 368
note 342
Willard, Emma (1787–1870) 456
William I (William the Silent) (1533–1584) 166
William III, Prince of Orange (1650–1702) 316
William of Occam. *See* Occam
William of Wykeham. *See* Wykeham
Williams, Hank (1923–1953) 902
Williams, Harry (1874–1924) 753
Williams, Harry H. (1879–1922)
note 699
Williams, Roger (c. 1603–1683) 273
Williams, Tennessee (Thomas Lanier) (1914–) 887
note 301
Williams, William Carlos (1883–1963) 785
Willich, August (1810–1878)
note 792
Willkie, Wendell L[ewis] (1892–1944) 824
Wilmot, John, Earl of Rochester. *See* Rochester
Wilson, Charles E[rwin] (1890–1961) 817
Wilson, Edmund (1895–1972) 834
Wilson, Harry Leon (1867–1939) 724
Wilson, John (*pseudonym* Christopher North) (1785–1854)
note 412

Wilson, John (*d. 1889*) 643
Wilson, McLandburgh (*fl. 1915*) 758
Wilson, Sloan (*1920–*) 898
Wilson, Woodrow (*1856–1924*) 682
Windsor, Edward, Duke of (Edward VIII) (*1894–1972*) 832
Winner, Septimus (*pseudonym* Alice Hawthorne) (*1827–1902*) 599
Winslow, Edward (*1595–1655*)
note 319
Winthrop, John (*1588–1649*) 264
Winthrop, Robert Charles (*1809–1894*) 535
Wister, Owen (*1860–1938*) 696
Wither, George (*1588–1667*) 264
note 259
Wodehouse, [Sir] P[elham] G[renville] (*1881–1975*) 775
Wolcot, John (*pseudonym* Peter Pindar) (*1738–1819*) 385
note 256, 336
Wolfe, Charles (*1791–1823*) 465
Wolfe, Humbert (*1885–1940*) 793
Wolfe, Thomas (*1900–1938*) 852
Wolfe, Tom [Thomas Kennerly, Jr.] (*1931–*) 911
Wollstonecraft [Godwin], Mary (*1759–1797*) 414
Wonder, Stevie (Steveland Judkins Hardaway) (*1950–*) 916
Woodfall, Henry (*1739–1805*)
note 663
Woodworth, Samuel (*1785–1842*) 455
Woolf, Virginia (*1882–1941*) 781
Woollcott, Alexander (*1887–1943*) 801
Woolman, John (*1720–1772*) 364
Woolsey, John M[unro] (*1877–1945*) 758
Wordsworth, Elizabeth (*1840–1932*) 643
Wordsworth, William (*1770–1850*) 423
note 156, 278, 296
Work, H[enry] C[lay] (*1832–1884*) 614
Wotton, Sir Henry (*1568–1639*) 250
note 166
Wrangel, Count Friedrich Heinrich Ernst von (*1784–1877*)
note 645
Wren, Sir Christopher (*1632–1723*) 309
Wright, Frank Lloyd (*1869–1959*) 729
Wright, Orville (*1871–1948*) 724
Wright, Richard (*1908–1960*) 875
Wright, Wilbur (*1867–1912*) 724
Wundt, Wilhelm Max (*1832–1920*) 614
Wyatt, Sir Thomas (*c. 1503–1542*) 161
note 262
Wycherley, William (*c. 1640–1716*)
note 117
Wycliffe, John (*c. 1320–1384*) 143
Wykeham, William of (*1324–1404*) 143
Wylie, Elinor Hoyt (*1885–1928*) 793

Xenophanes (*c. 570 – c. 475 B.C.*) 67
Xenophon (*c. 430 – c. 355 B.C.*) 83

Yamaga, Soko (*1622–1685*) 299
Ybarra, T[homas] R[ussell] (*1880–*) 773
Yeats, William Butler (*1865–1939*) 711
note 323, 712, 715, 916
Yellen, Jack (*1892–1958*) 824
note 788
Yelverton, Barry. *See* Avonmore
Yevtushenko, Yevgeny Alexandrovich (*1933–*) 912
Yonge, Nicholas (*d. 1619*)
note 111
Yosano, Akiko (*1878–1942*) 759
Yoshida, Kenko (*1283–1350*) 142
Yoshida, Shoin (*1830–1859*) 609
Young, Brigham (*1801–1877*) 490
Young, Edward (*1683–1765*) 329
note 223, 259, 260, 274, 307, 310, 327
Young, George W. (*fl. 1900*) 718
Young, Joe (*1889–1939*) 801
Young, Sir John
note 255
Young, Whitney M[oore], Jr. (*1921–1971*) 900
Youngdahl, Luther W[allace] (*1896–*) 836

Zamoyski, Jan (*1542–1605*) 167
Zangwill, Israel (*1864–1926*) 706
Zapata, Emiliano (*c. 1877–1919*) 759
Zeno (*335–263 B.C.*) 91
Zeuxis (*fl. 400 B.C.*) 83
Zincgref, Julius Wilhelm (*1591–1635*) 267
Zinsser, Hans (*1878–1940*) 762
Zola, Émile (*1840–1902*) 643

Familiar Quotations

The Song of the Harper[1, 2]

c. 2650–2600 B.C.

1 There is no one who can return from there,[3]
To describe their nature, to describe their dissolution,
That he may still our desires,
Until we reach the place where they have gone. *St. 5*

2 Remember: it is not given to man to take his goods with him.[4]
No one goes away and then comes back. *St. 10*

Ptahhotpe[5]

Twenty-fourth century B.C.

3 Teach him what has been said in the past; then he will set a good example to the children of the magistrates, and judgment and all exactitude shall enter into him. Speak to him, for there is none born wise. *The Maxims of Ptahhotpe [c. 2350 B.C.],[6] introduction*

4 Do not be arrogant because of your knowledge, but confer with the ignorant man as with the learned. . . . Good speech is more hidden than malachite, yet it is found in the possession of women slaves at the millstones. *Ib. maxim no. 1*

5 Truth is great and its effectiveness endures.[7] *Ib. 5*

[1]Ancient Egyptian quotations from *The Song of the Harper*, Ptahhotpe, *The Teaching for Merikare, The Man Who Was Tired of Life*, and *Love Songs of the New Kingdom* are from WILLIAM KELLY SIMPSON, ed., *The Literature of Ancient Egypt* [1973]. Those from *The Book of the Dead*, Queen Hatshepsut, Suti and Hor, *The Great Hymn to the Aten*, and Amenemope are from MIRIAM LICHTHEIM, *Ancient Egyptian Literature*, vol. II, *The New Kingdom* [1976].

[2]From the tomb of King Inyotef.
Translated by WILLIAM KELLY SIMPSON.

[3]See Shakespeare, 221:12.

[4]See *Ecclesiastes 5:15*, 27:2; *I Timothy 6:7*, 51:1; Theognis, 67:6; and Kaufman and Hart, 813:4.

[5]Also spelled Ptahhotep. He was city governor and vizier under King Izezi.

[6]Translated from the earliest manuscript of the *Maxims* (the Prisse Papyrus in Paris) by R. O. FAULKNER.

[7]See *I Esdras 4:41*, 34:3.

6 Follow your desire as long as you live and do not perform more than is ordered; do not lessen the time of following desire, for the wasting of time is an abomination to the spirit. . . . When riches are gained, follow desire, for riches will not profit if one is sluggish. *Ib. 11*

7 Beware an act of avarice; it is a bad and incurable disease. *Ib. 19*

8 If you are well-to-do and can maintain your household, love your wife in your home according to good custom. . . . Make her happy while you are alive, for she is land profitable to her lord. *Ib. 21*

9 Do not repeat slander; you should not hear it, for it is the result of hot temper. *Ib. 23*

10 One who is serious all day will never have a good time, while one who is frivolous all day will never establish a household.[8] *Ib. 25*

11 Be cheerful while you are alive. *Ib. 34*

The Teaching for Merikare[9]

c. 2135–2040 B.C.

12 Be skillful in speech, that you may be strong; [. . .][10] it is the strength of [. . .] the tongue, and words are braver than all fighting[11] . . . a wise man is a school for the magnates, and those who are aware of his knowledge do not attack him. *Par. 4*

13 Copy your forefathers,[12] for work is carried out through knowledge; see, their words endure in writing. . . . Do not be evil, for pa-

[8]See Herodotus, 78:9; Cervantes, 169:36; and Howell, 271:17.

[9]A treatise on kingship addressed by a king of Heracleopolis, whose name is lost, to his son and successor Merikare.
Translated by R. O. FAULKNER.

[10]Three bracketed dots represent an unfilled gap in the original; unbracketed dots represent our own omission from the text.

[11]See Cervantes, 169:34; Burton, 259:3; and Bulwer-Lytton, 493:6.

[12]See Tacitus, 123:4.

tience is good; make your lasting monument in the love of you. *Par. 5*

1 Wretched is he who has bound the land to himself [. . .]; a fool is he who is greedy when others possess. Life on earth passes away, it is not long;[1] he is fortunate who has a good remembrance in it. *Par. 6*

2 Do justice, that you may live long upon earth. Calm the weeper, do not oppress the widow, do not oust a man from his father's property, do not degrade magnates from their seats. Beware of punishing wrongfully; do not kill, for it will not profit you. *Par. 8*

3 More acceptable is the character of the straightforward man than the ox of the wrongdoer. Serve God, that He may do the like for you . . . Provide for men, the cattle of God, for He made heaven and earth[2] at their desire. He suppressed the greed of the waters, He gave the breath of life to their noses, for they are likenesses of Him which issued from His flesh.[3] *Par. 22*

4 Instill the love of you into all the world, for a good character is what is remembered. *Par. 24*

The Man Who Was Tired of Life[4]

C. 1990 B.C.

5 To whom can I speak today?
Brothers are evil
And the friends of today unlovable.
Song, st. 9

6 To whom can I speak today?
Gentleness has perished
And the violent man has come down on everyone. *Ib. st. 11*

7 To whom can I speak today?
I am heavy-laden with trouble
Through lack of an intimate friend.

To whom can I speak today?
The wrong which roams the earth,
There is no end to it. *Ib. st. 23, 24*

8 Death is in my sight today
As when a man desires to see home
When he has spent many years in captivity.
Ib. st. 30

[1]See Homer, 58:1; Pindar, 72:2; and Aristophanes, 82:9.
[2]See *Psalm 121:2*, 22:4.
[3]See *Genesis 1:26*, 6:13.
[4]Translated by R. O. FAULKNER.

The Book of the Dead[5]

C. 1700–1000 B.C.

9 Hail to you gods . . .
On that day of the great reckoning.
Behold me, I have come to you,
Without sin, without guilt, without evil,
Without a witness against me,
Without one whom I have wronged. . . .
Rescue me, protect me,
Do not accuse me before the great god!

I am one pure of mouth, pure of hands.
The Address to the Gods

Love Songs of the New Kingdom[6]

C. 1550–1080 B.C.

10 My love for you is mixed throughout my body . . .

So hurry to see your lady,
like a stallion on the track,
or like a falcon swooping down to its papyrus marsh.

Heaven sends down the love of her
as a flame falls in the hay. *Song no. 2*

11 The voice of the wild goose,
caught by the bait, cries out.
Love of you holds me back,
and I can't loosen it at all. . . .

I did not set my traps today;
love of you has thus entrapped me.
Ib. 10

12 Now must I depart from the brother . . .
and as I long for your love,
my heart stands still inside me. . . .

Sweet pomegranate wine in my mouth
is bitter as the gall of birds.

But your embraces
alone give life to my heart;
may Amun give me what I have found
for all eternity. *Ib. 12*

13 The voice of the turtledove speaks out.[7] It says:
Day breaks, which way are you going?
Lay off, little bird,
must you so scold me?

[5]Translated by MIRIAM LICHTHEIM.
"The coming forth by day" . . . the Egyptians called it.
—MIRIAM LICHTHEIM, *Ancient Egyptian Literature, vol. II, The New Kingdom* [1976], *pt. III, introduction*
[6]Translated by WILLIAM KELLY SIMPSON.
[7]See *Song of Solomon 2:12*, 28:7.

I found my lover on his bed,
and my heart was sweet to excess.

Ib. 14

Queen Hatshepsut[1]

d. 1468 B.C.

1 So as regards these two great obelisks,[2]
Wrought with electrum[3] by my majesty for my father Amun,
In order that my name may endure in this temple,
For eternity and everlastingness,
They are each of one block of hard granite,
Without seam, without joining together!

Speech of the Queen

Suti and Hor[4]

Fifteenth–fourteenth centuries B.C.

2 Creator uncreated.
Sole one, unique one, who traverses eternity,
Remote one, with millions under his care;
Your splendor is like heaven's splendor.

First Hymn to the Sun God

3 Beneficent mother[5] of gods and men . . .
Valiant shepherd who drives his flock,
Their refuge, made to sustain them. . . .
He makes the seasons with the months,
Heat as he wishes, cold as he wishes. . . .
Every land rejoices at his rising,
Every day gives praise to him.

Second Hymn to the Sun God

The Great Hymn to the Aten[6]

c. 1350 B.C.

4 Splendid you rise in heaven's lightland,
O living Aten, creator of life! *St. 1*

5 When you set in western lightland,
Earth is in darkness as if in death.[7]

St. 2

6 Every lion comes from its den,
All the serpents bite;
Darkness hovers, earth is silent,
As their maker rests in lightland.[8]

Earth brightens when you dawn in lightland,
When you shine as Aten of daytime;
As you dispel the dark,
As you cast your rays,
The Two Lands are in festivity.
Awake they stand on their feet,
You have roused them.[9] *St. 2, 3*

7 The entire land sets out to work,
All beasts browse on their herbs;
Trees, herbs are sprouting,
Birds fly from their nests . . .
Ships fare north, fare south as well,
Roads lie open when you rise;
The fish in the river dart before you,
Your rays are in the midst of the sea.[9]

St. 3

8 How many are your deeds,
Though hidden from sight,
O Sole God beside whom there is none!
You made the earth as you wished, you alone.[10] *St. 5*

I Ching[11]
[The Book of Changes]

c. Twelfth century B.C.[12]

9 Fire in the lake: the image of revolution.

Book I, ch. 49, Ko/Revolution (Molting)

10 Wind over lake: the image of inner truth.

Ib. 61, Chung Fu/Inner Truth

[1]Translated by MIRIAM LICHTHEIM.

[2]Queen Hatshepsut erected four obelisks in the temple of Amun at Karnak, two of which have disappeared entirely. . . . The obelisks are of pink Assuan granite. — MIRIAM LICHTHEIM, *Ancient Egyptian Literature, vol. II, The New Kingdom* [1976], *pt. I, sec. 2*

[3]"Electrum," or "fine gold," designated the gold with a high silver content which was especially prized. — *Ib. note to Speech of the Queen*

[4]Architects to Amenhotep III (reigned c. 1411–1375 B.C.).

Translated by MIRIAM LICHTHEIM.

[5]See Eddy, 583:1; O'Neill, 810:10; and John Paul I, 881:6.

[6]From the reign [1365–1349 B.C.] of Amenhotep IV Akhenaten.

Translated by MIRIAM LICHTHEIM.

Amenhotep IV . . . converted the supreme god [Aten, the sun disk] into the sole god by denying the reality of all the other gods. — LICHTHEIM, *Ib. pt. II*

[7]See *Psalm 104:20*, 21:11.

The resemblances [between the Great Hymn to the Aten and Psalm 104] are . . . likely to be the result of the generic similarity between Egyptian hymns and Biblical psalms. A specific literary interdependence is not probable. — LICHTHEIM, *Ib. note to The Great Hymn to the Aten*

[8]See *Psalm 104:21*, 21:11.

[9]See *Psalm 104:22, 23*, 21:11.

[10]See *Psalm 104:24*, 21:11.

[11]Translated from Chinese into German by RICHARD WILHELM, and into English by CARY F. BAYNES.

[12]Traditional date of the present collection of sixty-four hexagrams (some of which reach into legendary antiquity) credited to Wen Wang, whose son Wu Wang was the first ruler of the Chou dynasty [c. 1027–256 B.C.].

Amenemope
c. Eleventh century B.C.

1 Beginning of the teaching for life,
The instructions for well-being . . .
Knowing how to answer one who speaks,
To reply to one who sends a message.[1]

The Instruction of Amenemope,[2] *prologue*

2 Give your ears, hear the sayings,
Give your heart to understand them;
It profits to put them in your heart.[3]

Ib. ch. 1

3 Beware of robbing a wretch,
Of attacking a cripple.[4] *Ib. 2*

4 The truly silent, who keep apart,
He is like a tree grown in a meadow.
It greens, it doubles its yield,
It stands in front of its lord.
Its fruit is sweet, its shade delightful,
Its end comes in the garden.[5] *Ib. 4*

5 Do not move the markers on the border of the fields.[6] *Ib. 6*

6 Better is poverty in the hand of the god,
Than wealth in the storehouse;
Better is bread with a happy heart
Than wealth with vexation.[7] *Ib.*

7 Do not set your heart on wealth . . .
Do not strain to seek increases,
What you have, let it suffice you.[8]
If riches come to you by theft,
They will not stay the night with
you. . . .
They made themselves wings like geese,
And flew away to the sky.[9] *Ib. 7*

8 Look to these thirty chapters,
They inform, they educate.[10] *Ib. 30*

9 The scribe who is skilled in his office,
He is found worthy to be a courtier.[11]

Ib.

[1]See *Proverbs 22:20–21,* 25:1.
[2]Translated by MIRIAM LICHTHEIM.
[3]See *Proverbs 22:17–18,* 24:37.
[4]See *Proverbs* 22:22, 25:2, and *Ecclesiasticus 4:1,* 34:29.
[5]See *Psalm 1:1–3,* 17:12, and *Jeremiah 17:8,* 32:11.
[6]See *Proverbs 22:28,* 25:3.
[7]See *Proverbs 15:16–17,* 24:7, and Confucius, 68:21.
[8]See *Proverbs 23:4,* 25:6.
[9]See *Proverbs 23:5,* 25:7.
[10]See *Proverbs 22:20,* 25:1.
[11]See *Proverbs 22:29,* 25:4.

The Holy Bible[12]
The Old Testament[13]

10 In the beginning God created the heaven
and the earth.
And the earth was without form, and void;
and darkness was upon the face of the deep.
And the Spirit of God moved upon the face of
the waters.
And God said, Let there be light:[14] and
there was light.

The First Book of Moses, Called Genesis,[15] *chapter 1, verses 1–3*[16]

11 And the evening and the morning were the
first day. *1:5*

12 And God saw that it was good. *1:10*

13 And God said, Let us make man in our
image, after our likeness.[17] *1:26*

14 Male and female created he them.

1:27

15 Be fruitful, and multiply, and replenish the
earth, and subdue it: and have dominion over
the fish of the sea, and over the fowl of the air,
and over every living thing that moveth upon
the earth. *1:28*

16 And on the seventh day God ended his
work which he had made. *2:2*

17 And the Lord God formed man of the dust
of the ground, and breathed into his nostrils
the breath of life; and man became a living
soul. *2:7*

18 And the Lord God planted a garden eastward in Eden. *2:8*

19 The tree of life also in the midst of the
garden. *2:9*

20 But of the tree of the knowledge of good
and evil, thou shalt not eat of it: for in the day

[12]The oldest part of the Bible, Song of the Sea (*Exodus 15:1–18;* see 9:32–9:35) dates from the tenth century B.C., the era of Solomon, but the material used by the author (called J, or the Yahwist) was much older. Next oldest is the Song of Deborah (*Judges 5:1–12,* 12:3–12:4).

Bible quotations are from the Authorized (King James) Version [1611], which was "translated out of the original tongues: and with the former translations diligently compared and revised."

Among all our joys, there was no one that more filled our hearts, than the blessed continuance of the preaching of God's sacred Word among us; which is that inestimable treasure, which excelleth all the riches of the earth.
— *Epistle Dedicatory from the Translators to James I*

[13]The Hebrew Scriptures. The first five books (the Pentateuch, or the five books of Moses) are the Jewish Torah, embodying the Law revealed to Moses on Mt. Sinai.
[14]Fiat lux. — *The Vulgate*
[15]First of the five books of the Pentateuch.
[16]Numbers in Bible citations represent chapter and verse.
[17]See *The Teaching for Merikare,* 4:3.

that thou eatest thereof thou shalt surely die. *Genesis 2:17*

1 It is not good that the man should be alone; I will make him an help meet for him. *2:18*

2 And the Lord God caused a deep sleep to fall upon Adam, and he slept: and he took one of his ribs, and closed up the flesh instead thereof.

And the rib, which the Lord God had taken from man, made he a woman. *2:21–22*

3 Bone of my bones, and flesh of my flesh. *2:23*

4 Therefore shall a man leave his father and his mother, and shall cleave unto his wife: and they shall be one flesh.

And they were both naked, the man and his wife, and were not ashamed. *2:24–25*

5 Now the serpent was more subtile than any beast of the field. *3:1*

6 Your eyes shall be opened, and ye shall be as gods, knowing good and evil. *3:5*

7 And they sewed fig leaves together, and made themselves aprons.[1]

And they heard the voice of the Lord God walking in the garden in the cool of the day. *3:7–8*

8 The woman whom thou gavest to be with me, she gave me of the tree, and I did eat. *3:12*

9 What is this that thou hast done? And the woman said, The serpent beguiled me, and I did eat.

And the Lord God said unto the serpent, Because thou hast done this, thou art cursed above all cattle, and above every beast of the field; upon thy belly shalt thou go, and dust shalt thou eat all the days of thy life. *3:13–14*

10 And I will put enmity between thee and the woman, and between thy seed and her seed; it shall bruise thy head, and thou shalt bruise his heel. *3:15*

11 In sorrow thou shalt bring forth children. *3:16*

12 In the sweat of thy face shalt thou eat bread, till thou return unto the ground; for out of it wast thou taken: for dust thou art, and unto dust shalt thou return.

[1]The Geneva Bible [1560] was known sometimes as the Breeches Bible because in this passage "aprons" is rendered as "breeches."

And Adam called his wife's name Eve; because she was the mother of all living. *Genesis 3:19–20*

13 So he drove out the man: and he placed at the east of the garden of Eden cherubims, and a flaming sword which turned every way, to keep the way of the tree of life. *3:24*

14 And Abel was a keeper of sheep, but Cain was a tiller of the ground. *4:2*

15 Am I my brother's keeper? *4:9*

16 The voice of thy brother's blood crieth unto me from the ground. *4:10*

17 A fugitive and a vagabond shalt thou be in the earth. *4:12*

18 My punishment is greater than I can bear. *4:13*

19 And the Lord set a mark upon Cain. *4:15*

20 And Cain went out from the presence of the Lord, and dwelt in the land of Nod. *4:16*

21 Jabal: he was the father of such as dwell in tents. *4:20*

22 Jubal: he was the father of all such as handle the harp and organ. *4:21*

23 Tubal-cain, an instructor of every artificer in brass and iron. *4:22*

24 And Enoch walked with God. *5:24*

25 And all the days of Methuselah were nine hundred sixty and nine years. *5:27*

26 And Noah begat Shem, Ham, and Japheth. *5:32*

27 There were giants in the earth in those days . . . mighty men which were of old, men of renown. *6:4*

28 Make thee an ark of gopher wood. *6:14*

29 And of every living thing of all flesh, two of every sort shalt thou bring into the ark. *6:19*

30 And the rain was upon the earth forty days and forty nights. *7:12*

31 But the dove found no rest for the sole of her foot. *8:9*

32 And, lo, in her mouth was an olive leaf pluckt off. *8:11*

33 For the imagination of man's heart is evil from his youth. *8:21*

1 While the earth remaineth, seedtime and harvest, and cold and heat, and summer and winter, and day and night shall not cease. *Genesis 8:22*

2 Whoso sheddeth man's blood, by man shall his blood be shed: for in the image of God made he man. *9:6*

3 I do set my bow in the cloud, and it shall be for a token of a covenant between me and the earth. *9:13*

4 Even as Nimrod the mighty hunter before the Lord. *10:9*

5 Therefore is the name of it called Babel; because the Lord did there confound the language of all the earth. *11:9*

6 Let there be no strife, I pray thee, between me and thee . . . for we be brethren. *13:8*

7 Abram dwelled in the land of Canaan, and Lot dwelled in the cities of the plain, and pitched his tent toward Sodom. *13:12*

8 In a good old age. *15:15*

9 His [Ishmael's] hand will be against every man, and every man's hand against him. *16:12*

10 Thy name shall be Abraham; for a father of many nations have I made thee. *17:5*

11 My Lord, if now I have found favor in thy sight, pass not away, I pray thee, from thy servant. *18:3*

12 But his [Lot's] wife looked back from behind him, and she became a pillar of salt. *19:26*

13 My son, God will provide himself a lamb for a burnt offering. *22:8*

14 Behold behind him a ram caught in a thicket by his horns. *22:13*

15 Esau was a cunning hunter, a man of the field; and Jacob was a plain man, dwelling in tents. *25:27*

16 And he [Esau] sold his birthright unto Jacob.

Then Jacob gave Esau bread and pottage of lentils. *25:33–34*

17 The voice is Jacob's voice, but the hands are the hands of Esau. *27:22*

18 Thy brother came with subtilty, and hath taken away thy blessing. *27:35*

19 He [Jacob] dreamed, and behold a ladder set up on the earth, and the top of it reached to heaven: and behold the angels of God ascending and descending on it. *28:12*

20 Surely the Lord is in this place; and I knew it not. *Genesis 28:16*

21 This is none other but the house of God, and this is the gate of heaven. *28:17*

22 Jacob served seven years for Rachel; and they seemed unto him but a few days, for the love he had to her. *29:20*

23 And Laban said, This heap [of stones] is a witness between me and thee this day. Therefore was the name of it called Galeed;

And Mizpah; for he said, The Lord watch between me and thee, when we are absent one from another. *31:48–49*

24 And Jacob was left alone; and there wrestled a man with him until the breaking of the day. *32:24*

25 I will not let thee go, except thou bless me. *32:26*

26 And Jacob called the name of the place Peniel: for I have seen God face to face, and my life is preserved.[1] *32:30*

27 Behold, this dreamer cometh. *37:19*

28 They stript Joseph out of his coat, his coat of many colors. *37:23*

29 The Lord made all that he did to prosper in his hand. *39:3*

30 And she [Potiphar's wife] caught him by his garment, saying, Lie with me: and he left his garment in her hand, and fled, and got him out. *39:12*

31 The seven good kine are seven years; and the seven good ears are seven years: the dream is one.

And the seven thin and ill-favored kine that came up after them are seven years; and the seven empty ears blasted with the east wind shall be seven years of famine. *41:26–27*

32 Then shall ye bring down my gray hairs with sorrow to the grave. *42:38*

33 But Benjamin's mess was five times so much as any of theirs. *43:34*

34 Wherefore have ye rewarded evil for good? *44:4*

35 God forbid. *44:7*[2]

36 The man in whose hand the cup is found, he shall be my servant. *44:17*

37 And he fell upon his brother Benjamin's neck, and wept; and Benjamin wept upon his neck. *45:14*

[1] See *I Corinthians 13:12*, 48:25.
[2] *Passim* in the Old Testament.

1 And ye shall eat the fat of the land.
Genesis 45:18

2 And they came into the land of Goshen.
46:28

3 But I will lie with my fathers, and thou shalt carry me out of Egypt, and bury me in their buryingplace. And he said, I will do as thou hast said. *47:30*

4 Unstable as water, thou shalt not excel.
49:4

5 I have waited for thy salvation, O Lord.
49:18

6 Unto the utmost bound of the everlasting hills. *49:26*

7 Now there arose up a new king over Egypt, which knew not Joseph.
The Second Book of Moses, Called Exodus[1] *1:8*

8 She took for him an ark of bulrushes, and daubed it with slime and with pitch.
2:3

9 I have been a stranger in a strange land.[2]
2:22

10 Behold, the bush burned with fire, and the bush was not consumed. *3:2*

11 Put off thy shoes from off thy feet, for the place whereon thou standest is holy ground.
3:5

12 And Moses hid his face; for he was afraid to look upon God. *3:6*

13 A land flowing with milk and honey.[3]
3:8

14 And God said unto Moses, I AM THAT I AM. *3:14*

15 I am slow of speech, and of a slow tongue.
4:10

16 Let my people go. *5:1*

17 Ye shall no more give the people straw to make brick. *5:7*

18 Thou shalt say unto Aaron, Take thy rod, and cast it before Pharaoh, and it shall become a serpent. *7:9*

19 They [Pharaoh's wise men] cast down every man his rod, and they became serpents: but Aaron's rod swallowed up their rods.
And he hardened Pharaoh's heart.
7:12–13

20 This is the finger of God. *8:19*

[1]Second of the five books of the Pentateuch.
[2]See Sophocles, 75:9.
[3]Also in *Exodus 33:3* and *Jeremiah 11:5*.

21 Darkness which may be felt.
Exodus 10:21

22 Yet will I bring one plague more upon Pharaoh, and upon Egypt. *11:1*

23 Your lamb shall be without blemish.
12:5

24 And they shall eat the flesh in that night, roast with fire, and unleavened bread; and with bitter herbs they shall eat it.[4]
12:8

25 And thus shall ye eat it; with your loins girded, your shoes on your feet, and your staff in your hand; and ye shall eat it in haste: it is the Lord's passover.
For I will pass through the land of Egypt this night, and will smite all the firstborn in the land of Egypt, both man and beast; and against all the gods of Egypt I will execute judgment: I am the Lord. *12:11–12*

26 This day [Passover] shall be unto you for a memorial; and ye shall keep it a feast to the Lord throughout your generations.[5]
12:14

27 Seven days shall ye eat unleavened bread.
12:15

28 There was a great cry in Egypt; for there was not a house where there was not one dead. *12:30*

29 Remember this day, in which ye came out from Egypt, out of the house of bondage.
13:3

30 And the Lord went before them by day in a pillar of a cloud, to lead them the way; and by night in a pillar of fire, to give them light.
13:21

31 And the children of Israel went into the midst of the sea upon the dry ground: and the waters were a wall unto them on their right hand, and on their left. *14:22*

32 I will sing unto the Lord, for he hath triumphed gloriously: the horse and his rider hath he thrown into the sea.
The Lord is my strength and song, and he is become my salvation. *15:1–2*

33 The Lord is a man of war. *15:3*

34 Thy right hand, O Lord, is become glorious in power: thy right hand, O Lord, hath dashed in pieces the enemy. *15:6*

35 Thou sentest forth thy wrath, which consumed them as stubble.

[4]The feast of the Passover. The origin of the Eucharist.
[5]See *I Corinthians 5:7*, 48:10.

And with the blast of thy nostrils the waters were gathered together, the floods stood upright as an heap, and the depths were congealed in the heart of the sea.
Exodus 15:7–8

1 Would to God we had died by the hand of the Lord in the land of Egypt, when we sat by the fleshpots, and when we did eat bread to the full. *16:3*

2 It is manna. *16:15*

3 I am the Lord thy God. *20:2* [1]

4 Thou shalt have no other gods before me.
Thou shalt not make unto thee any graven image. *20:3–4*

5 For I the Lord thy God am a jealous God, visiting the iniquity of the fathers upon the children unto the third and fourth generation of them that hate me;[2]
And showing mercy unto thousands of them that love me, and keep my commandments.
Thou shalt not take the name of the Lord thy God in vain. *20:5–7*

6 Remember the sabbath day, to keep it holy.
Six days shalt thou labor, and do all thy work:
But the seventh day . . . thou shalt not do any work. *20:8–10*

7 Honor thy father and thy mother: that thy days may be long upon the land which the Lord thy God giveth thee.[3]
Thou shalt not kill.
Thou shalt not commit adultery.
Thou shalt not steal.
Thou shalt not bear false witness against thy neighbor.
Thou shalt not covet thy neighbor's house, thou shalt not covet thy neighbor's wife, nor his manservant, nor his maidservant, nor his ox, nor his ass, nor any thing that is thy neighbor's. *20:12–17*

8 But let not God speak with us, lest we die. *20:19*

9 He that smiteth a man, so that he die, shall be surely put to death. *21:12*

10 Eye for eye, tooth for tooth,[4] hand for hand, foot for foot. *21:24*

11 Behold, I send an Angel before thee, to keep thee in the way. *23:20*

[1] *Exodus 20:2–17* contains the Ten Commandments (the Decalogue), as handed down by God to Moses on Mt. Sinai. Also in *Deuteronomy 5:6–21*.

[2] See Euripides, 77:23.

[3] See Aeschylus, 70:22.

[4] Also in *Matthew 5:38*.

12 A stiffnecked people. *Exodus 32:9*

13 Who is on the Lord's side? let him come unto me. *32:26*

14 Thou canst not see my face: for there shall no man see me, and live. *33:20*

15 And he [Moses] was there with the Lord forty days and forty nights; he did neither eat bread, nor drink water. And he wrote upon the tables the words of the covenant, the ten commandments. *34:28*

16 Whatsoever parteth the hoof, and is clovenfooted, and cheweth the cud, among the beasts, that shall ye eat.
The Third Book of Moses, Called Leviticus[5] *11:3*

17 And the swine . . . is unclean to you.
Of their flesh shall ye not eat. *11:7–8*

18 Let him go for a scapegoat into the wilderness. *16:10*

19 And when ye reap the harvest of your land, thou shalt not wholly reap the corners of thy field, neither shalt thou gather the gleanings of thy harvest.
And thou shalt not glean thy vineyard, neither shalt thou gather every grape of thy vineyard; thou shalt leave them for the poor and stranger. *19:9–10*

20 Thou shalt not go up and down as a talebearer among thy people. *19:16*

21 Thou shalt love thy neighbor as thyself.[6] *19:18*

22 Ye shall hallow the fiftieth year, and proclaim liberty throughout all the land unto all the inhabitants thereof:[7] it shall be a jubilee unto you. *25:10*

23 The Lord bless thee, and keep thee:
The Lord make his face shine upon thee, and be gracious unto thee:
The Lord lift up his countenance upon thee, and give thee peace.
The Fourth Book of Moses, Called Numbers[8] *6:24–26*

24 Sent to spy out the land. *13:16*

25 And your children shall wander in the wilderness forty years. *14:33*

26 Moses lifted up his hand, and with his rod he smote the rock twice: and the water came out abundantly. *20:11*

[5] Third of the five books of the Pentateuch.

[6] Also in *Matthew 19:19* and *22:39* (40:16), *Mark 12:31* and *33*, *Romans 13:9*, *Galatians 5:14*, *James 2:8*.

[7] From "proclaim" through "thereof": inscription on the Liberty Bell, Philadelphia [1751].

[8] Fourth of the five books of the Pentateuch.

1 He whom thou blessest is blessed.
Numbers 22:6

2 The Lord opened the mouth of the ass, and she said unto Balaam, What have I done unto thee? *22:28*

3 Let me die the death of the righteous, and let my last end be like his! *23:10*

4 God is not a man, that he should lie.[1]
23:19

5 What hath God wrought![2] *23:23*

6 How goodly are thy tents, O Jacob, and thy tabernacles, O Israel! *24:5*

7 Be sure your sin will find you out.
32:23

8 I call heaven and earth to witness.
The Fifth Book of Moses, Called Deuteronomy[3] *4:26*

9 Thou shalt love the Lord thy God with all thine heart, and with all thy soul, and with all thy might.[4]
And these words, which I command thee this day, shall be in thine heart:
And thou shalt teach them diligently unto thy children. *6:5–7*

10 Ye shall not tempt the Lord your God.[5]
6:16

11 The Lord thy God hath chosen thee to be a special people unto himself. *7:6*

12 Man doth not live by bread only,[6] but by every word that proceedeth out of the mouth of the Lord doth man live. *8:3*

13 For the Lord thy God bringeth thee into a good land. *8:7*

14 A land of wheat, and barley, and vines, and fig trees, and pomegranates; a land of oil olive, and honey;
A land wherein thou shalt eat bread without scarceness, thou shalt not lack any thing in it; a land whose stones are iron, and out of whose hills thou mayest dig brass.
8:8–9

15 A dreamer of dreams. *13:1*

16 The wife of thy bosom. *13:6*

17 The poor shall never cease out of the land.[7] *15:11*

18 Thou shalt not move a sickle unto thy neighbor's standing corn. *23:25*

[1] See Aeschylus, 71:1.
[2] Quoted by Samuel F. B. Morse in the first telegraph message he sent to his partner, Alfred Vail, from Washington to Baltimore [May 24, 1844].
[3] Last of the five books of the Pentateuch.
[4] See *Matthew 22:37*, 40:16.
[5] Also in *Matthew 4:7*.
[6] Man shall not live by bread alone.—*Matthew 4:4*
[7] See *Matthew 26:11*, 41:4.

19 And thou shalt become an astonishment, a proverb, and a byword, among all nations.
Deuteronomy 28:37

20 In the morning thou shalt say, Would God it were even! and at even thou shalt say, Would God it were morning! *28:67*

21 The secret things belong unto the Lord our God. *29:29*

22 I have set before you life and death, blessing and cursing: therefore choose life, that both thou and thy seed may live.
30:19

23 He is the Rock, his work is perfect: for all his ways are judgment: a God of truth.
32:4

24 Jeshurun waxed fat, and kicked.
32:15

25 As thy days, so shall thy strength be.
33:25

26 The eternal God is thy refuge, and underneath are the everlasting arms. *33:27*

27 No man knoweth of his [Moses'] sepulcher unto this day. *34:6*

28 Be strong and of a good courage;[8] be not afraid, neither be thou dismayed: for the Lord thy God is with thee whithersoever thou goest. *The Book of Joshua 1:9*

29 And the priests that bare the ark of the covenant of the Lord stood firm on dry ground in the midst of Jordan, and all the Israelites passed over on dry ground, until all the people were passed clean over Jordan.
3:17

30 Mighty men of valor. *6:2*

31 And it came to pass, when the people heard the sound of the trumpet, and the people shouted with a great shout, that the wall fell down flat, so that the people went up into the city [Jericho]. *6:20*

32 His fame was noised throughout all the country. *6:27*

33 Hewers of wood and drawers of water.
9:21

34 Sun, stand thou still upon Gibeon; and thou, Moon, in the valley of Ajalon.
10:12

35 Old and stricken in years.[9] *13:1*

36 I am going the way of all the earth.
23:14

[8] Also in *Deuteronomy 31:6, 7, 23*.
[9] Also in *I Kings 1:1*.

1 They shall be as thorns in your sides.[1] *The Book of Judges 2:3*

2 Then Jael, Heber's wife, took a nail of the tent, and took an hammer in her hand, and went softly unto him [Sisera], and smote the nail into his temples, and fastened it into the ground; for he was fast asleep, and weary: so he died. *4:21*

3 I Deborah arose . . . I arose a mother in Israel.[2] *5:7*

4 Awake, awake, Deborah: awake, awake, utter a song: arise, Barak, and lead thy captivity captive. *5:12*

5 The stars in their courses fought against Sisera. *5:20*

6 She [Jael] brought forth butter in a lordly dish. *5:25*

7 At her feet he bowed, he fell, he lay down: at her feet he bowed, he fell: where he bowed, there he fell down dead. *5:27*

8 The mother of Sisera looked out at a window, and cried through the lattice, Why is his chariot so long in coming? why tarry the wheels of his chariots? *5:28*

9 Have they not divided the prey; to every man a damsel or two? *5:30*

10 The sword of the Lord, and of Gideon. *7:18*

11 Is not the gleaning of the grapes of Ephraim better than the vintage of Abiezer? *8:2*

12 Say now Shibboleth: and he said Sibboleth: for he could not frame to pronounce it right. *12:6*

13 There was a swarm of bees and honey in the carcase of the lion. *14:8*

14 Out of the eater came forth meat, and out of the strong came forth sweetness. *14:14*

15 If ye had not plowed with my heifer, ye had not found out my riddle. *14:18*

16 He smote them hip and thigh. *15:8*

17 With the jawbone of an ass . . . have I slain a thousand men. *15:16*

18 The Philistines be upon thee, Samson. *16:9*

19 The Philistines took him [Samson], and put out his eyes, and brought him down to Gaza, and bound him with fetters of brass; and he did grind in the prison house. *16:21*

[1] See *II Corinthians 12:7*, 49:22.
[2] The Song of Deborah; see 6:*n12*.

20 Strengthen me, I pray thee, only this once, O God, that I may be . . . avenged of the Philistines for my two eyes. *Judges 16:28*

21 So the dead which he slew at his death were more than they which he slew in his life. *16:30*

22 From Dan even to Beersheba. *20:1*

23 All the people arose as one man. *20:8*

24 In those days there was no king in Israel: every man did that which was right in his own eyes. *21:25*

25 Whither thou goest, I will go; and where thou lodgest, I will lodge: thy people shall be my people, and thy God my God. *The Book of Ruth 1:16*

26 Let me glean and gather after the reapers among the sheaves. *2:7*

27 Go not empty unto thy mother in law. *3:17*

28 In the flower of their age. *The First Book of Samuel 2:33*

29 The Lord called Samuel: and he answered, Here am I. *3:4*

30 Speak, Lord; for thy servant heareth. *3:9*

31 Be strong, and quit yourselves like men.[3] *4:9*

32 And she named the child Ichabod, saying, The glory is departed from Israel: because the ark of God was taken. *4:21*

33 Is Saul also among the prophets? *10:11*

34 God save the king. *10:24*

35 A man after his own heart. *13:14*

36 Every man's sword was against his fellow. *14:20*

37 But Jonathan heard not when his father charged the people with the oath: wherefore he put forth the end of the rod that was in his hand, and dipped it in an honeycomb, and put his hand to his mouth; and his eyes were enlightened. *14:27*

38 For the Lord seeth not as man seeth; for man looketh on the outward appearance, but the Lord looketh on the heart. *16:7*

39 I know thy pride, and the naughtiness of thine heart. *17:28*

40 Let no man's heart fail because of him [Goliath]. *17:32*

[3] See *I Corinthians 16:13*, 49:9.

1 Go, and the Lord be with thee.
I Samuel 17:37

2 And he [David] . . . chose him five smooth stones out of the brook. *17:40*

3 So David prevailed over the Philistine with a sling and with a stone. *17:50*

4 Saul hath slain his thousands, and David his ten thousands. *18:7*

5 And Jonathan . . . loved him [David] as he loved his own soul. *20:17*

6 Wickedness proceedeth from the wicked. *24:13*

7 I have played the fool. *26:21*

8 Tell it not in Gath, publish it not in the streets of Askelon.
The Second Book of Samuel 1:20

9 Saul and Jonathan were lovely and pleasant in their lives, and in their death they were not divided: they were swifter than eagles, they were stronger than lions. *1:23*

10 How are the mighty fallen in the midst of the battle! *1:25*

11 Thy love to me was wonderful, passing the love of women.
How are the mighty fallen, and the weapons of war perished! *1:26–27*

12 Abner . . . smote him under the fifth rib. *2:23*

13 Know ye not that there is a prince and a great man [Abner] fallen this day in Israel? *3:38*

14 And David and all the house of Israel played before the Lord on all manner of instruments made of fir wood, even on harps, and on psalteries, and on timbrels, and on cornets, and on cymbals.[1] *6:5*

15 Uzzah put forth his hand to the ark of God, and took hold of it . . . and the anger of the Lord was kindled against Uzzah. *6:6*

16 David danced before the Lord. *6:14*

17 Tarry at Jericho until your beards be grown.[2] *10:5*

18 Set ye Uriah in the forefront of the hottest battle. *11:15*

19 The poor man had nothing, save one little ewe lamb. *12:3*

20 Thou art the man. *12:7*

21 Now he is dead, wherefore should I fast? Can I bring him back again? I shall go to him, but he shall not return to me. *12:23*

[1] See *Psalm 150:3–6,* 22:25.
[2] Also in *I Chronicles 19:5.*

22 For we must needs die, and are as water spilt on the ground, which cannot be gathered up again. *II Samuel 14:14*

23 Would God I had died for thee, O Absalom, my son, my son! *18:33*

24 The Lord is my rock, and my fortress, and my deliverer. 22:2

25 David the son of Jesse . . . the sweet psalmist of Israel. *23:1*

26 Went in jeopardy of their lives. *23:17*

27 A wise and an understanding heart.
The First Book of the Kings 3:12

28 Many, as the sand which is by the sea in multitude. *4:20*

29 Judah and Israel dwelt safely, every man under his vine and under his fig tree. *4:25*

30 He [Solomon] spake three thousand proverbs: and his songs were a thousand and five. *4:32*

31 The wisdom of Solomon. *4:34*

32 So that there was neither hammer nor axe nor any tool of iron heard in the house,[3] while it was in building. *6:7*

33 A proverb and a byword among all people. *9:7*

34 When the queen of Sheba heard of the fame of Solomon . . . she came to prove him with hard questions. *10:1*

35 The half was not told me: thy wisdom and prosperity exceedeth the fame which I heard. *10:7*

36 Once in three years came the navy of Tharshish, bringing gold, and silver, ivory, and apes, and peacocks. *10:22*

37 King Solomon loved many strange women. *11:1*

38 My father hath chastised you with whips, but I will chastise you with scorpions. *12:11*

39 To your tents, O Israel. *12:16*

40 He [Elijah] went and dwelt by the brook Cherith, that is before Jordan. *17:5*

41 And the ravens brought him bread and flesh in the morning, and bread and flesh in the evening; and he drank of the brook. *17:6*

42 An handful of meal in a barrel, and a little oil in a cruse. *17:12*

43 And the barrel of meal wasted not, neither did the cruse of oil fail. *17:16*

[3] Solomon's temple (the house of the Lord).

1 How long halt ye between two opinions? *I Kings 18:21*

2 Either he [Baal] is talking, or he is pursuing, or he is in a journey, or peradventure he sleepeth, and must be awaked. *18:27*

3 There ariseth a little cloud out of the sea, like a man's hand. *18:44*

4 And he girded up his loins, and ran before Ahab. *18:46*

5 But the Lord was not in the wind: and after the wind an earthquake; but the Lord was not in the earthquake:

And after the earthquake a fire; but the Lord was not in the fire: and after the fire a still small voice. *19:11–12*

6 Let not him that girdeth on his harness boast himself as he that putteth it off. *20:11*

7 Hast thou found me, O mine enemy? *21:20*

8 The dogs shall eat Jezebel by the wall of Jezreel. *21:23*

9 But there was none like unto Ahab, which did sell himself to work wickedness in the sight of the Lord, whom Jezebel his wife stirred up. *21:25*

10 I saw all Israel scattered upon the hills, as sheep that have not a shepherd. *22:17*

11 Feed him [Micajah] with bread of affliction, and with water of affliction, until I come in peace. *22:27*

12 There appeared a chariot of fire, and horses of fire, and parted them both asunder; and Elijah went up by a whirlwind into heaven. *The Second Book of the Kings 2:11*

13 The chariot of Israel, and the horsemen thereof. And he saw him no more. *2:12*

14 He [Elisha] took up also the mantle of Elijah. *2:13*

15 There is death in the pot. *4:40*

16 Is thy servant a dog, that he should do this great thing? *8:13*

17 What hast thou to do with peace? turn thee behind me. *9:18*

18 The driving is like the driving of Jehu the son of Nimshi; for he driveth furiously. *9:20*

19 Jezebel heard of it; and she painted her face, and tired her head, and looked out at a window. *9:30*

20 The angel of the Lord went out, and smote in the camp of the Assyrians an hundred fourscore and five thousand: and when they arose early in the morning, behold, they were all dead corpses.

So Sennacherib king of Assyria departed. *II Kings 19:35–36*

21 Set thine house in order. *20:1*

22 I will wipe Jerusalem as a man wipeth a dish, wiping it, and turning it upside down. *21:13*

23 His mercy endureth for ever. *The First Book of the Chronicles 16:41*

24 The Lord searcheth all hearts, and understandeth all the imaginations of the thoughts. *28:9*

25 Thine, O Lord, is the greatness, and the power, and the glory, and the victory, and the majesty: for all that is in the heaven and in the earth is thine; thine is the kingdom, O Lord, and thou art exalted as head above all.[1] *29:11*

26 For all things come of thee, and of thine own have we given thee.[2] *29:14*

27 Our days on the earth are as a shadow. *29:15*

28 He [David] died in a good old age, full of days, riches, and honor. *29:28*

29 They which builded on the wall, and they that bare burdens, with those that laded, every one with one of his hands wrought in the work, and with the other hand held a weapon. *The Book of Nehemiah 4:17*

30 And he [Ezra] read therein before the street that was before the water gate from the morning until midday, before the men and the women, and those that could understand; and the ears of all the people were attentive unto the book of the law. *8:3*

31 Thou art a God ready to pardon, gracious and merciful, slow to anger, and of great kindness. *9:17*

32 Mordecai rent his clothes, and put on sackcloth with ashes. *The Book of Esther 4:1*

33 The man whom the king delighteth to honor. *6:6*

34 They hanged Haman on the gallows. *7:10*

35 One that feared God, and eschewed evil. *The Book of Job 1:1*

[1]See *Matthew 6:13*, 37:15.
[2]See Marcus Aurelius, 124:19.

1 Satan came also. *Job 1:6*

2 And the Lord said unto Satan, Whence comest thou? Then Satan answered the Lord, and said, From going to and fro in the earth, and from walking up and down in it. *1:7*

3 Doth Job fear God for nought? *1:9*

4 Naked came I out of my mother's womb, and naked shall I return thither:[1] the Lord gave, and the Lord hath taken away; blessed be the name of the Lord. *1:21*

5 Skin for skin, yea, all that a man hath will he give for his life. *2:4*

6 Curse God, and die. *2:9*

7 Let the day perish wherein I was born, and the night in which it was said, There is a man child conceived.[2] *3:3*

8 For now should I have lain still and been quiet, I should have slept: then had I been at rest,

With kings and counsellors of the earth, which built desolate places for themselves. *3:13–14*

9 There the wicked cease from troubling; and there the weary be at rest. *3:17*

10 Who ever perished, being innocent? or where were the righteous cut off? *4:7*

11 Fear came upon me, and trembling. *4:14*

12 Then a spirit passed before my face; the hair of my flesh stood up. *4:15*

13 Shall mortal man be more just than God? shall a man be more pure than his maker? *4:17*

14 Wrath killeth the foolish man, and envy slayeth the silly one. *5:2*

15 Man is born unto trouble, as the sparks fly upward. *5:7*

16 He taketh the wise in their own craftiness. *5:13*

17 For thou shalt be in league with the stones of the field: and the beasts of the field shall be at peace with thee. *5:23*

18 Thou shalt come to thy grave in a full age, like as a shock of corn cometh in in his season. *5:26*

19 How forcible are right words! *6:25*

20 My days are swifter than a weaver's shuttle, and are spent without hope. *7:6*

[1]See *Ecclesiastes 5:15*, 27:2.
[2]See Euripides, 76:10.

21 He shall return no more to his house, neither shall his place know him any more.[3] *Job 7:10*

22 I would not live alway: let me alone: for my days are vanity. *7:16*

23 But how should man be just with God? *9:2*

24 The land of darkness and the shadow of death. *10:21*

25 Canst thou by searching find out God? *11:7*

26 And thine age shall be clearer than the noonday. *11:17*

27 No doubt but ye are the people, and wisdom shall die with you. *12:2*

28 The just upright man is laughed to scorn. *12:4*

29 But ask now the beasts, and they shall teach thee; and the fowls of the air, and they shall tell thee:

Or speak to the earth, and it shall teach thee; and the fishes of the sea shall declare unto thee. *12:7–8*

30 With the ancient is wisdom; and in length of days understanding. *12:12*

31 He discovereth deep things out of darkness, and bringeth out to light the shadow of death. *12:22*

32 Though he slay me, yet will I trust in him. *13:15*

33 Man that is born of a woman is of few days, and full of trouble.

He cometh forth like a flower, and is cut down: he fleeth also as a shadow, and continueth not. *14:1–2*

34 But man dieth, and wasteth away: yea, man giveth up the ghost, and where is he? *14:10*

35 If a man die, shall he live again? *14:14*

36 Should a wise man utter vain knowledge, and fill his belly with the east wind? *15:2*

37 Miserable comforters are ye all. *16:2*

38 My days are past. *17:11*

39 I have said to corruption, Thou art my father: to the worm, Thou art my mother, and my sister. *17:14*

[3]When a few years are come, then I shall go the way whence I shall not return.—*Job 16:22*

The place thereof shall know it no more.—*Psalm 103:16*

1 The king of terrors. *Job 18:14*

2 I am escaped with the skin of my teeth. *19:20*

3 Oh that my words were now written! oh that they were printed in a book! *19:23*

4 I know that my redeemer liveth, and that he shall stand at the latter day upon the earth:[1]

And though, after my skin, worms destroy this body, yet in my flesh shall I see God. *19:25–26*

5 Seeing the root of the matter is found in me. *19:28*

6 Though wickedness be sweet in his mouth, though he hide it under his tongue. *20:12*

7 Suffer me that I may speak; and after that I have spoken, mock on. *21:3*

8 Shall any teach God knowledge? *21:22*

9 They are of those that rebel against the light. *24:13*

10 The womb shall forget him; the worm shall feed sweetly on him; he shall be no more remembered. *24:20*

11 Yea, the stars are not pure in his sight.

How much less man, that is a worm? and the son of man, which is a worm? *25:5–6*

12 But where shall wisdom be found? and where is the place of understanding? *28:12*

13 The land of the living. *28:13*

14 The price of wisdom is above rubies.[2] *28:18*

15 Behold, the fear of the Lord, that is wisdom; and to depart from evil is understanding. *28:28*

16 I caused the widow's heart to sing for joy. *29:13*

17 I was eyes to the blind, and feet was I to the lame. *29:15*

18 I know that thou wilt bring me to death, and to the house appointed for all living. *30:23*

19 I am a brother to dragons, and a companion to owls. *30:29*

20 My desire is, that the Almighty would answer me, and that mine adversary had written a book. *31:35*

[1] Also in *Book of Common Prayer, Burial of the Dead.*

[2] [Wisdom] is more precious than rubies.—*Proverbs 3:15*

See Sophocles, 75:1.

21 Great men are not always wise. *Job 32:9*

22 For I am full of matter, the spirit within me constraineth me. *32:18*

23 One among a thousand. *33:23*

24 Far be it from God, that he should do wickedness. *34:10*

25 He multiplieth words without knowledge. *35:16*

26 Fair weather cometh out of the north. *37:22*

27 Then the Lord answered Job out of the whirlwind, and said,

Who is this that darkeneth counsel by words without knowledge?

Gird up now thy loins like a man. *38:1–3*

28 Where wast thou when I laid the foundations of the earth? declare, if thou hast understanding. *38:4*

29 The morning stars sang together, and all the sons of God shouted for joy. *38:7*

30 Hitherto shalt thou come, but no further: and here shall thy proud waves be stayed. *38:11*

31 Hast thou entered into the springs of the sea? or hast thou walked in the search of the depth? *38:16*

32 Hath the rain a father? or who hath begotten the drops of dew? *38:28*

33 Canst thou bind the sweet influences of Pleiades, or loose the bands of Orion? *38:31*

34 Canst thou guide Arcturus with his sons? *38:32*

35 Who can number the clouds in wisdom? or who can stay the bottles of heaven. *38:37*

36 Hast thou given the horse strength? hast thou clothed his neck with thunder? *39:19*

37 He paweth in the valley, and rejoiceth in his strength: he goeth on to meet the armed men. *39:21*

38 He swalloweth the ground with fierceness and rage; neither believeth he that it is the sound of the trumpet.

He saith among the trumpets, Ha, ha; and he smelleth the battle afar off, the thunder of the captains, and the shouting. *39:24–25*

1 Doth the eagle mount up at thy command, and make her nest on high?

She dwelleth and abideth on the rock, upon the crag of the rock, and the strong place.

From thence she seeketh the prey, and her eyes behold afar off.

Her young ones also suck up blood: and where the slain are, there is she.

Job 39:27–30

2 Behold, I am vile; what shall I answer thee? *40:4*

3 Behold now behemoth, which I made with thee; he eateth grass as an ox. *40:15*

4 Canst thou draw out leviathan with a hook? *41:1*

5 Who can open the doors of his face? his teeth are terrible round about.

His scales are his pride, shut up together as with a close seal. *41:14,15*

6 His heart is as firm as a stone; yea as hard as a piece of the nether millstone.

41:24

7 He maketh the deep to boil like a pot.

41:31

8 Upon earth there is not his like, who is made without fear. *41:33*

9 He is a king over all the children of pride.

41:34

10 I have heard of thee by the hearing of the ear: but now mine eye seeth thee.

42:5

11 So the Lord blessed the latter end of Job more than his beginning. *42:12*

12 Blessed is the man that walketh not in the counsel of the ungodly, nor standeth in the way of sinners, nor sitteth in the seat of the scornful.

But his delight is in the law of the Lord; and in his law doth he meditate day and night.

And he shall be like a tree planted by the rivers of water, that bringeth forth his fruit in his season; his leaf also shall not wither; and whatsoever he doeth shall prosper.

The ungodly are not so: but are like the chaff which the wind driveth away.

The Book of Psalms 1:1–4 [1]

13 Why do the heathen rage, and the people imagine a vain thing? *2:1*

14 Blessed are all they that put their trust in him. *2:12*

[1]See Amenemope, 6:4, and *Jeremiah 17:5–8*, 32:11.

15 Lord, lift thou up the light of thy countenance upon us. *Psalms 4:6*

16 I will both lay me down in peace, and sleep.[2] *4:8*

17 Out of the mouth of babes and sucklings hast thou ordained strength, because of thine enemies; that thou mightest still the enemy and the avenger.

When I consider thy heavens, the work of thy fingers, the moon and the stars, which thou hast ordained;

What is man, that thou art mindful of him? and the son of man, that thou visitest him?

For thou hast made him a little lower than the angels. *8:2–5*

18 How excellent is thy name in all the earth. *8:9*

19 Flee as a bird to your mountain. *11:1*

20 How long wilt thou forget me, O Lord? *13:1*

21 The fool hath said in his heart, There is no God. *14:1 and 53:1*

22 Lord, who shall abide in thy tabernacle? who shall dwell in thy holy hill? *15:1*

23 He that sweareth to his own hurt, and changeth not. *15:4*

24 The lines are fallen unto me in pleasant places;[3] yea, I have a goodly heritage. *16:6*

25 Keep me as the apple of the eye,[4] hide me under the shadow of thy wings. *17:8*

26 He rode upon a cherub, and did fly: yea, he did fly upon the wings of the wind. *18:10*

27 The heavens declare the glory of God; and the firmament showeth his handiwork.

Day unto day uttereth speech, and night unto night showeth knowledge. *19:1–2*

28 Their line is gone out through all the earth, and their words to the end of the world. In them hath he set a tabernacle for the sun,

Which is as a bridegroom coming out of his chamber, and rejoiceth as a strong man to run a race.

His going forth is from the end of the heaven, and his circuit unto the ends of it: and there is nothing hid from the heat thereof. *19:4–6*

[2]I will lay me down in peace, and take my rest.—*Book of Common Prayer, Psalm 4:9*

[3]The lot is fallen unto me in a fair ground.—*Book of Common Prayer, Psalm 16:7*

[4]Also in *Deuteronomy 32:10* and *Proverbs 7:2*.

1 The judgments of the Lord are true and righteous altogether.
More to be desired are they than gold, yea, than much fine gold: sweeter also than honey and the honeycomb. *Psalms 19:9–10*

2 Cleanse thou me from secret faults. *19:12*

3 Let the words of my mouth, and the meditation of my heart, be acceptable in thy sight, O Lord, my strength, and my redeemer. *19:14*

4 Thou hast given him his heart's desire. *21:2*

5 My God, my God, why hast thou forsaken me?[1] why art thou so far from helping me, and from the words of my roaring? *22:1*

6 They part my garments among them, and cast lots upon my vesture. *22:18*

7 The Lord is my shepherd; I shall not want.
He maketh me to lie down in green pastures: he leadeth me beside the still waters.
He restoreth my soul: he leadeth me in the paths of righteousness for his name's sake.
Yea, though I walk through the valley of the shadow of death, I will fear no evil: for thou art with me; thy rod and thy staff they comfort me.
Thou preparest a table before me in the presence of mine enemies: thou anointest my head with oil; my cup runneth over.
Surely goodness and mercy shall follow me all the days of my life: and I will dwell in the house of the Lord for ever. *23*

8 The earth is the Lord's, and the fullness thereof; the world, and they that dwell therein.[2]
For he hath founded it upon the seas, and established it upon the floods.
Who shall ascend into the hill of the Lord? or who shall stand in his holy place?
He that hath clean hands, and a pure heart; who hath not lifted up his soul unto vanity, nor sworn deceitfully. *24:1–4*

9 Lift up your heads, O ye gates; and be ye lift up, ye everlasting doors; and the King of glory shall come in. *24:7*

10 Who is this King of glory? The Lord of hosts, he is the King of glory. *24:10*

[1]This was the psalm Christ recited on the cross. See *Matthew 27:46*, 41:27.
[2]See *I Corinthians 10:26*, 48:18.

11 The Lord is my light[3] and my salvation; whom shall I fear? the Lord is the strength of my life; of whom shall I be afraid? *Psalms 27:1*

12 Though an host should encamp against me, my heart shall not fear: though war should rise against me, in this will I be confident. *27:3*

13 The Lord is my strength and my shield. *28:7*

14 Worship the Lord in the beauty of holiness. *29:2*

15 Weeping may endure for a night, but joy cometh in the morning. *30:5*

16 I am forgotten as a dead man out of mind: I am like a broken vessel. *31:12*

17 My times are in thy hand. *31:15*

18 From the strife of tongues. *31:20*

19 Sing unto him a new song; play skillfully with a loud noise. *33:3*

20 O taste and see that the Lord is good. *34:8*

21 Keep thy tongue from evil, and thy lips from speaking guile.
Depart from evil, and do good; seek peace, and pursue it. *34:13–14*

22 Rescue my soul from their destructions, my darling from the lions. *35:17*

23 How excellent is thy lovingkindness, O God! *36:7*

24 The meek shall inherit the earth.[4] *37:11*

25 I have been young, and now am old; yet have I not seen the righteous forsaken, nor his seed begging bread. *37:25*

26 I have seen the wicked in great power, and spreading himself[5] like a green bay tree. *37:35*

27 Mark the perfect man, and behold the upright: for the end of that man is peace.[6] *37:37*

28 For thine arrows stick fast in me, and thy hand presseth me sore. *38:2*

29 I said, I will take heed to my ways, that I sin not with my tongue. *39:1*

30 My heart was hot within me, while I was musing the fire burned. *39:3*

[3]Dominus illuminatio mea.—*The Vulgate.* Motto of Oxford University.
[4]See *Matthew 5:5*, 37:4.
[5]Flourishing.—*Book of Common Prayer, Psalm 37:36*
[6]For that shall bring a man peace at the last.—*Book of Common Prayer, Psalm 37:38*

1 Lord, make me to know mine end, and the measure of my days, what it is; that I may know how frail I am. *Psalms 39:4*

2 Every man at his best state is altogether vanity. *39:5*

3 Surely every man walketh in a vain show: surely they are disquieted in vain: he heapeth up riches, and knoweth not who shall gather them. *39:6*

4 For I am a stranger with thee, and a sojourner, as all my fathers were.
O spare me, that I may recover strength, before I go hence, and be no more. *39:12–13*

5 As the hart panteth after the water brooks, so panteth my soul after thee, O God.
My soul thirsteth for God, for the living God. *42:1–2*

6 Why art thou cast down, O my soul? and why art thou disquieted in me? *42:5*[1]

7 Deep calleth unto deep. *42:7*

8 My tongue is the pen of a ready writer. *45:1*

9 The king's daughter is all glorious within. *45:13*

10 God is our refuge and strength, a very present help in trouble.
Therefore will we not fear, though the earth be removed, and though the mountains be carried into the midst of the sea. *46:1–2*

11 There is a river, the streams whereof shall make glad the city of God, the holy place of the tabernacles of the most High.
God is in the midst of her; she shall not be moved: God shall help her, and that right early. *46:4–5*

12 Be still, and know that I am God. *46:10*

13 Every beast of the forest is mine, and the cattle upon a thousand hills. *50:10*

14 I was shapen in iniquity; and in sin did my mother conceive me. *51*[2]*:5*

15 Purge me with hyssop, and I shall be clean: wash me, and I shall be whiter than snow. *51:7*

16 Create in me a clean heart, O God; and renew a right spirit within me. *51:10*

[1] Also in *Psalms 42:11* and *43:5*.
[2] This psalm is known as the Miserere from its opening word in the Vulgate. The first line is: Have mercy upon me, O God.

17 And take not thy holy spirit from me. *Psalms 51:11*

18 Open thou my lips; and my mouth shall show forth thy praise. *51:15*

19 A broken and a contrite heart, O God, thou wilt not despise. *51:17*

20 Oh that I had wings like a dove! for then would I fly away, and be at rest.[3] *55:6*

21 We took sweet counsel together. *55:14*

22 The words of his mouth were smoother than butter, but war was in his heart:[4] his words were softer than oil, yet were they drawn swords. *55:21*

23 They are like the deaf adder that stoppeth her ear;
Which will not hearken to the voice of charmers, charming never so wisely. *58:4–5*

24 Thou hast showed thy people hard things: thou hast made us to drink the wine of astonishment. *60:3*

25 Moab is my washpot; over Edom will I cast out my shoe: Philistia, triumph thou because of me. *60:8*

26 Lead me to the rock that is higher than I. *61:2*

27 He only is my rock and my salvation: he is my defense; I shall not be moved. *62:6*

28 Thou renderest to every man according to his work. *62:12*

29 My soul thirsteth for thee, my flesh longeth for thee in a dry and thirsty land, where no water is. *63:1*

30 Thou crownest the year with thy goodness. *65:11*

31 Make a joyful noise unto God, all ye lands. *66:1*

32 We went through fire and through water. *66:12*

33 God setteth the solitary in families. *68:6*

34 Cast me not off in the time of old age; forsake me not when my strength faileth. *71:9*

35 He shall come down like rain upon the mown grass: as showers that water the earth. *72:6*

[3] See Euripides, 76:24.
[4] The words of his mouth were softer than butter, having war in his heart.—*Book of Common Prayer, Psalm 50:22*

1 His enemies shall lick the dust.
Psalms 72:9

2 His name shall endure for ever.
72:17

3 A stubborn and rebellious generation.
78:8

4 Man did eat angels' food. *78:25*

5 But ye shall die like men, and fall like one of the princes. *82:7*

6 How amiable are thy tabernacles, O Lord of hosts! *84:1*

7 They go from strength to strength.
84:7

8 A day in thy courts is better than a thousand. I had rather be a doorkeeper in the house of my God, than to dwell in the tents of wickedness. *84:10*

9 Mercy and truth are met together; righteousness and peace have kissed each other.
85:10

10 Lord, why castest thou off my soul? why hidest thou thy face from me? *88:14*

11 Lord, thou hast been our dwelling place in all generations.

Before the mountains were brought forth, or ever thou hadst formed the earth and the world, even from everlasting to everlasting, thou art God.

Thou turnest man to destruction; and sayest, Return, ye children of men.

For a thousand years in thy sight are but as yesterday when it is past, and as a watch in the night.

Thou carriest them away as with a flood; they are as a sleep: in the morning they are like grass which groweth up.

In the morning it flourisheth, and groweth up; in the evening it is cut down, and withereth.[1] *90:1–6*

12 We spend our years as a tale that is told.[2]
90:9

13 The days of our years are threescore years and ten; and if by reason of strength they be fourscore years, yet is their strength labor and sorrow; for it is soon cut off, and we fly away.[3] *90:10*

[1]See *Isaiah 40:6* and *40:8*, 30:32 and 30:33, and *I Peter 1:24*, 52:9.

[2]We bring our years to an end, as it were a tale that is told.—*Book of Common Prayer, Psalm 90:9*

[3]The days of our age are threescore and ten; and though men be so strong that they come to fourscore years, yet is their strength then but labor and sorrow; so soon passeth it away, and we are gone.—*Book of Common Prayer, Psalm 90:10*

14 So teach us to number our days, that we may apply our hearts unto wisdom.
Psalms 90:12

15 Establish thou the work of our hands upon us; yea, the work of our hands establish thou it. *90:17*

16 He that dwelleth in the secret place of the most High shall abide under the shadow of the Almighty.

I will say of the Lord, He is my refuge and my fortress: my God; in him will I trust.

Surely he shall deliver thee from the snare of the fowler, and from the noisome pestilence.

He shall cover thee with his feathers, and under his wings shalt thou trust: his truth shall be thy shield and buckler.

Thou shalt not be afraid for the terror by night; nor for the arrow that flieth by day.

Nor for the pestilence that walketh in darkness; nor for the destruction that wasteth at noonday.

A thousand shall fall at thy side, and ten thousand at thy right hand; but it shall not come nigh thee. *91:1–7*

17 He shall give his angels charge over thee, to keep thee in all thy ways.

They shall bear thee up in their hands, lest thou dash thy foot against a stone.[4]

Thou shalt tread upon the lion and adder: the young lion and the dragon shalt thou trample under feet. *91:11–13*

18 The righteous shall flourish like the palm tree: he shall grow like a cedar in Lebanon.
92:12

19 Mightier than the noise of many waters.[5]
93:4

20 O come, let us sing unto the Lord: let us make a joyful noise to the rock of our salvation.

Let us come before his presence with thanksgiving, and make a joyful noise unto him with psalms.

For the Lord is a great God, and a great King above all gods.

In his hand are the deep places of the earth: the strength of the hills is his also.

The sea is his, and he made it: and his hands formed the dry land.

O come, let us worship and bow down: let us kneel before the Lord our maker.

For he is our God; and we are the people of his pasture, and the sheep of his hand.[6]
95:1–7

[4]See *Luke 4:10–11*, 43:1. Also in *Matthew 4:6*.

[5]See *Revelation 14:2*, 53:22.

[6]See *Ephesians 5:19*, 49:37, and *Book of Common Prayer, Morning Prayer (Venite)*, 54:16.

1 O sing unto the Lord a new song.
Psalms 96:1

2 The Lord reigneth; let the earth rejoice.
97:1

3 Make a joyful noise unto the Lord, all ye lands.
Serve the Lord with gladness: come before his presence with singing.
Know ye that the Lord he is God: it is he that hath made us, and not we ourselves; we are his people, and the sheep of his pasture.
Enter into his gates with thanksgiving, and into his courts with praise: be thankful unto him, and bless his name.
For the Lord is good; his mercy is everlasting; and his truth endureth to all generations. *100*

4 My days are consumed like smoke.
102:3

5 I watch, and am as a sparrow alone upon the house top. *102:7*

6 As the heaven is high above the earth, so great is his mercy toward them that fear him.
103:11

7 As for man, his days are as grass: as a flower of the field, so he flourisheth.
For the wind passeth over it, and it is gone; and the place thereof shall know it no more.[1]
103:15–16

8 Who layeth the beams of his chambers in the waters: who maketh the clouds his chariot: who walketh upon the wings of the wind.
104:3

9 Wine that maketh glad the heart of man.
104:15

10 The cedars of Lebanon. *104:16*

11 He appointed the moon for seasons: the sun knoweth his going down.
Thou makest darkness, and it is night: wherein all the beasts of the forest do creep forth.[2]
The young lions roar after their prey, and seek their meat from God.[3]
The sun ariseth, they gather themselves together, and lay them down in their dens.
Man goeth forth unto his work and to his labor until the evening.[4]
O Lord, how manifold are thy works! in wisdom hast thou made them all: the earth is full of thy riches.[5]
So is this great and wide sea, wherein are things creeping innumerable, both small and great beasts.
There go the ships: there is that leviathan, whom thou hast made to play therein.
These wait all upon thee; that thou mayest give them their meat in due season.
Psalms 104:19–27

12 The people asked, and he brought quails, and satisfied them with the bread of heaven.[6]
105:40

13 Such as sit in darkness and in the shadow of death.[7] *107:10*

14 They that go down to the sea in ships, that do business in great waters. *107:23*

15 They mount up to the heaven, they go down again to the depths. *107:26*

16 They reel to and fro, and stagger like a drunken man, and are at their wit's end.
107:27

17 For I am poor and needy, and my heart is wounded within me.
I am gone like the shadow when it declineth: I am tossed up and down as the locust. *109:22–23*

18 Thou hast the dew of thy youth.
110:3

19 The fear of the Lord is the beginning of wisdom. *111:10*

20 From the rising of the sun unto the going down of the same the Lord's name is to be praised. *113:3*

21 The mountains skipped like rams, and the little hills like lambs. *114:4*

22 They have mouths, but they speak not: eyes have they, but they see not.
They have ears, but they hear not.[8]
115:5–6

23 I said in my haste, All men are liars.
116:11

24 Precious in the sight of the Lord is the death of his saints. *116:15*

25 The stone which the builders refused is become the head stone of the corner.[9]
118:22

26 This is the day which the Lord hath made.
118:24

[1] See Homer, 61:1.
[2] See *The Great Hymn to the Aten,* 5:5.
[3] See *The Great Hymn to the Aten,* 5:6.
[4] See *The Great Hymn to the Aten,* 5:6 and 5:7.
[5] See *The Great Hymn to the Aten,* 5:8.

[6] See *John 6:35,* 44:41.
[7] See *Matthew 4:16,* 37:2, and *Luke 1:79,* 42:26.
[8] Also in *Psalm 135:16–17.*
[9] Also in *Matthew 21:42.*

1 Blessed be he that cometh in the name of the Lord.[1] *Psalms 118:26*

2 Thy word is a lamp unto my feet, and a light unto my path. *119:105*

3 I am for peace: but when I speak, they are for war. *120:7*

4 I will lift up mine eyes unto the hills, from whence cometh my help.[2]
My help cometh from the Lord, which made heaven and earth.[3]
He will not suffer thy foot to be moved: he that keepeth thee will not slumber.
Behold, he that keepeth Israel shall neither slumber nor sleep.
The Lord is thy keeper: the Lord is thy shade upon thy right hand.
The sun shall not smite thee by day, nor the moon by night.
The Lord shall preserve thee from all evil: he shall preserve thy soul.
The Lord shall preserve thy going out and thy coming in from this time forth, and even for evermore. *121*

5 I was glad when they said unto me, Let us go into the house of the Lord. *122:1*

6 Peace be within thy walls, and prosperity within thy palaces. *122:7*

7 They that sow in tears shall reap in joy.
He that goeth forth and weepeth, bearing precious seed, shall doubtless come again with rejoicing, bringing his sheaves with him. *126:5–6*

8 Except the Lord build the house, they labor in vain that build it: except the Lord keep the city, the watchman waketh but in vain. *127:1*

9 He giveth his beloved sleep. *127:2*

10 As arrows are in the hand of a mighty man; so are children of the youth.
Happy is the man that hath his quiver full of them. *127:4–5*

11 Out of the depths have I cried unto thee, O Lord. *130:1*

12 My soul waiteth for the Lord more than they that watch for the morning. *130:6*

13 I will not give sleep to mine eyes, or slumber to mine eyelids.[4] *132:4*

[1] Also in *Matthew 21:9, 23:39, Mark 11:9,* and *Luke 13:35.*
[2] I lift up my eyes to the hills. From whence does my help come?—*Revised Standard Version*
[3] See *The Teaching for Merikare,* 4:3.
[4] Also in *Proverbs 6:4.*

14 Behold, how good and how pleasant it is for brethren to dwell together in unity! *Psalms 133:1*

15 By the rivers of Babylon, there we sat down, yea, we wept, when we remembered Zion.[5]
We hanged our harps upon the willows in the midst thereof.
For there they that carried us away captive required of us a song; and they that wasted us required of us mirth, saying, Sing us one of the songs of Zion.
How shall we sing the Lord's song in a strange land?
If I forget thee, O Jerusalem, let my right hand forget her cunning.
If I do not remember thee, let my tongue cleave to the roof of my mouth. *137:1–6*

16 O Lord, thou hast searched me, and known me.
Thou knowest my downsitting and mine uprising; thou understandest my thought afar off. *139:1–2*

17 Whither shall I go from thy Spirit? or whither shall I flee from thy presence?
If I ascend up into heaven, thou art there: if I make my bed in hell, behold, thou art there.
If I take the wings of the morning, and dwell in the uttermost parts of the sea;
Even there shall thy hand lead me, and thy right hand shall hold me. *139:7–10*

18 The darkness and the light are both alike to thee. *139:12*

19 I am fearfully and wonderfully made. *139:14*

20 They have sharpened their tongues like a serpent. *140:3*

21 Thou openest thine hand, and satisfiest the desire of every living thing. *145:16*

22 The Lord is nigh unto all them that call upon him, to all that call upon him in truth. *145:18*

23 Put not your trust in princes. *146:3*

24 He telleth the number of the stars; he calleth them all by their names. *147:4*

25 Praise him with the sound of the trumpet: praise him with the psaltery and harp.
Praise him with the timbrel and dance: praise him with stringed instruments and organs.

[5] By the waters of Babylon we sat down and wept, when we remembered thee, O Sion.—*Book of Common Prayer, Psalm 137:1*

Praise him upon the loud cymbals: praise him upon the high sounding cymbals.[1]
Let every thing that hath breath praise the Lord. *Psalms 150:3–6*

1 To give subtilty to the simple, to the young man knowledge and discretion. *The Proverbs 1:4*

2 My son, if sinners entice thee, consent thou not. *1:10*

3 Wisdom crieth without; she uttereth her voice in the streets. *1:20*

4 Length of days is in her right hand; and in her left hand riches and honor. *3:16*

5 Her ways are ways of pleasantness, and all her paths are peace. *3:17*

6 Be not afraid of sudden fear. *3:25*

7 Wisdom is the principal thing; therefore get wisdom: and with all thy getting get understanding. *4:7*

8 The path of the just is as the shining light, that shineth more and more unto the perfect day. *4:18*

9 Keep thy heart with all diligence; for out of it are the issues of life. *4:23*

10 The lips of a strange woman drop as a honeycomb, and her mouth is smoother than oil:
But her end is bitter as wormwood, sharp as a two-edged sword. *5:3–4*

11 Go to the ant, thou sluggard; consider her ways, and be wise:
Which having no guide, overseer, or ruler,
Provideth her meat in the summer, and gathereth her food in the harvest. *6:6–8*

12 Yet a little sleep, a little slumber, a little folding of the hands to sleep:[2]
So shall thy poverty come as one that traveleth, and thy want as an armed man. *6:10–11*

13 Lust not after her beauty in thine heart; neither let her take thee with her eyelids. *6:25*

14 Can a man take fire in his bosom, and his clothes not be burned?
Can one go upon hot coals, and his feet not be burned? *6:27–28*

15 Jealousy is the rage of a man: therefore he will not spare in the day of vengeance. *6:34*

16 He goeth after her straightway, as an ox goeth to the slaughter. *7:22*

[1]See *II Samuel* 6:5, 13:14.
[2]Also in *Proverbs* 24:33.

17 I love them that love me; and those that seek me early shall find me. *Proverbs 8:17*

18 Wisdom hath builded her house, she hath hewn out her seven pillars. *9:1*

19 Reprove not a scorner, lest he hate thee: rebuke a wise man, and he will love thee. *9:8*

20 Stolen waters are sweet, and bread eaten in secret is pleasant. *9:17*

21 A wise son maketh a glad father: but a foolish son is the heaviness of his mother. *10:1*

22 Blessings are upon the head of the just: but violence covereth the mouth of the wicked.
The memory of the just is blessed: but the name of the wicked shall rot. *10:6–7*

23 Hatred stirreth up strifes: but love covereth all sins. *10:12*

24 In the multitude of counsellors there is safety.[3]
He that is surety for a stranger shall smart for it. *11:14–15*

25 As a jewel of gold in a swine's snout, so is a fair woman which is without discretion. *11:22*

26 He that trusteth in his riches shall fall. *11:28*

27 He that troubleth his own house shall inherit the wind. *11:29*

28 A virtuous woman is a crown to her husband. *12:4*

29 A righteous man regardeth the life of his beast: but the tender mercies of the wicked are cruel. *12:10*

30 The way of a fool is right in his own eyes. *12:15*

31 Hope deferred maketh the heart sick. *13:12*

32 The way of transgressors is hard. *13:15*

33 The desire accomplished is sweet to the soul. *13:19*

34 He that spareth his rod hateth his son: but he that loveth him chasteneth him betimes.[4] *13:24*

35 Fools make a mock at sin. *14:9*

36 The heart knoweth his own bitterness; and a stranger doth not intermeddle with his joy. *14:10*

[3]Also in *Proverbs* 24:6.
[4]See Menander, 91:3, and Butler, 291:19.

1 Even in laughter the heart is sorrowful.
Proverbs 14:13

2 The prudent man looketh well to his going.
14:15

3 In all labor there is profit: but the talk of the lips tendeth only to penury. *14:23*

4 Righteousness exalteth a nation.
14:34

5 A soft answer turneth away wrath.
15:1

6 A merry heart maketh a cheerful countenance: but by sorrow of the heart the spirit is broken. *15:13*

7 He that is of a merry heart hath a continual feast.

Better is little with the fear of the Lord, than great treasure, and trouble therewith.

Better is a dinner of herbs where love is, than a stalled ox and hatred therewith.[1]
15:15–17

8 A wrathful man stirreth up strife: but he that is slow to anger appeaseth strife.
15:18

9 A word spoken in due season, how good is it! *15:23*

10 Before honor is humility.
15:33 and 18:12

11 A man's heart deviseth his way: but the Lord directeth his steps. *16:9*

12 Pride goeth before destruction, and an haughty spirit before a fall.[2] *16:18*

13 The hoary head is a crown of glory, if it be found in the way of righteousness.

He that is slow to anger is better than the mighty; and he that ruleth his spirit than he that taketh a city. *16:31–32*

14 Whoso mocketh the poor reproacheth his Maker. *17:5*

15 He that repeateth a matter separateth very friends. *17:9*

16 Whoso rewardeth evil for good, evil shall not depart from his house. *17:13*

17 A merry heart doeth good like a medicine.
17:22

18 He that hath knowledge spareth his words: and a man of understanding is of an excellent spirit.

Even a fool, when he holdeth his peace, is counted wise. *17:27–28*

[1]See *The Teaching for Merikare,* 4:3, and Amenemope, 6:6.

[2]See Sophocles, 74:3 and 75:4.

19 A fool's mouth is his destruction.
Proverbs 18:7

20 A wounded spirit who can bear?
18:14

21 A brother offended is harder to be won than a strong city: and their contentions are like the bars of a castle. *18:19*

22 Whoso findeth a wife findeth a good thing.
18:22

23 A man that hath friends must show himself friendly: and there is a friend that sticketh closer than a brother. *18:24*

24 Wealth maketh many friends. *19:4*

25 A foolish son is the calamity of his father: and the contentions of a wife are a continual dropping. *19:13*

26 He that hath pity upon the poor lendeth unto the Lord. *19:17*

27 Wine is a mocker, strong drink is raging.
20:1

28 It is an honor for a man to cease from strife: but every fool will be meddling. *20:3*

29 Even a child is known by his doings, whether his work be pure, and whether it be right.

The hearing ear, and the seeing eye, the Lord hath made even both of them.
20:11–12

30 It is naught, it is naught, saith the buyer: but when he is gone his way, then he boasteth. *20:14*

31 Bread of deceit is sweet to a man; but afterwards his mouth shall be filled with gravel.
20:17

32 Meddle not with him that flattereth with his lips. *20:19*

33 It is better to dwell in a corner of the housetop, than with a brawling woman in a wide house. *21:9 and 25:24*

34 A good name is rather to be chosen than great riches. *22:1*

35 Train up a child in the way he should go; and when he is old, he will not depart from it.
22:6

36 The borrower is servant to the lender.
22:7

37 Bow down thine ear, and hear the words of the wise, and apply thine heart unto my knowledge.

For it is a pleasant thing if thou keep them within thee; they shall withal be fitted in thy lips.[3] *22:17–18*

[3]See Amenemope, 6:2.

1 Have I not written to thee excellent things in counsels and knowledge,
That I might make thee know the certainty of the words of truth; that thou mightest answer the words of truth to them that send unto thee?[1] *Proverbs 22:20–21*

2 Rob not the poor, because he is poor: neither oppress the afflicted in the gate.[2] *22:22*

3 Remove not the ancient landmark.[3] *22:28*

4 Seest thou a man diligent in his business? He shall stand before kings.[4] *22:29*

5 Put a knife to thy throat, if thou be a man given to appetite. *23:2*

6 Labor not to be rich: cease from thine own wisdom.[5] *23:4*

7 Riches certainly make themselves wings; they fly away as an eagle toward heaven.[5] *23:5*

8 As he thinketh in his heart, so is he. *23:7*

9 The drunkard and the glutton shall come to poverty: and drowsiness shall clothe a man with rags. *23:21*

10 Despise not thy mother when she is old. *23:22*

11 Look not thou upon the wine when it is red, when it giveth his color in the cup, when it moveth itself aright.
At the last it biteth like a serpent, and stingeth like an adder. *23:31–32*

12 A wise man is strong; yea, a man of knowledge increaseth strength. *24:5*

13 If thou faint in the day of adversity, thy strength is small. *24:10*

14 A word fitly spoken is like apples of gold in pictures of silver. *25:11*

[1] Here I have written out for you thirty sayings, / full of knowledge and wise advice, / to impart to you a knowledge of the truth, / that you may take back a true report to him who sent you.—*The New English Bible with the Apocrypha: Oxford Study Edition* [1976], *Proverbs 22:20–21*

Thirty wise sayings [*Proverbs 22:17–24:22*]. This section is dependent on the Egyptian work by Amenemope, from which ten sayings have been derived and adapted to the Israelite setting. . . . The Masoretic Text reading . . . formerly rendered "excellent things" [22:20] has been corrected to "thirty sayings"—a very minor change in the Hebrew—on the basis of the Amenemope.—*Ib., note to Proverbs 22:17–24:22*

See Amenemope, 6:1 and 6:8.

[2] See Amenemope, 6:3, and *Ecclesiasticus 4:1*, 34:29.

[3] Also in *Proverbs 23:10*.

See Amenemope, 6:5.

[4] See Amenemope, 6:9.

[5] See Amenemope, 6:7.

15 If thine enemy be hungry, give him bread to eat; and if he be thirsty, give him water to drink:
For thou shalt heap coals of fire upon his head.[6] *Proverbs 25:21–22*

16 As cold waters to a thirsty soul, so is good news from a far country. *25:25*

17 For men to search their own glory is not glory. *25:27*

18 Answer a fool according to his folly. *26:5*

19 As a dog returneth to his vomit, so a fool returneth to his folly.
Seest thou a man wise in his own conceit? There is more hope of a fool than of him.
The slothful man saith, There is a lion in the way; a lion is in the streets. *26:11–13*

20 Whoso diggeth a pit shall fall therein: and he that rolleth a stone, it will return upon him. *26:27*

21 Boast not thyself of tomorrow; for thou knowest not what a day may bring forth.[7] *27:1*

22 Let another man praise thee, and not thine own mouth. *27:2*

23 Open rebuke is better than secret love.
Faithful are the wounds of a friend; but the kisses of an enemy are deceitful. *27:5–6*

24 To the hungry soul every bitter thing is sweet. *27:7*

25 Better is a neighbor that is near than a brother far off. *27:10*

26 Iron sharpeneth iron; so a man sharpeneth the countenance of his friend. *27:17*

27 The wicked flee when no man pursueth: but the righteous are bold as a lion. *28:1*

28 He that maketh haste to be rich shall not be innocent. *28:20*

29 He that trusteth in his own heart is a fool. *28:26*

30 He that giveth unto the poor shall not lack. *28:27*

31 A fool uttereth all his mind. *29:11*

32 Where there is no vision, the people perish. *29:18*

33 A man's pride shall bring him low: but honor shall uphold the humble in spirit. *29:23*

[6] Also in *Romans 12:20*.

See Marcus Aurelius, 125:10.

[7] See Sophocles, 75:7.

1 Give me neither poverty nor riches.
Proverbs 30:8

2 Accuse not a servant unto his master.
30:10

3 The horseleach hath two daughters, crying, Give, give. *30:15*

4 There be three things which are too wonderful for me, yea, four which I know not:
The way of an eagle in the air; the way of a serpent upon a rock; the way of a ship in the midst of the sea; and the way of a man with a maid. *30:18–19*

5 Give strong drink unto him that is ready to perish, and wine unto those that be of heavy hearts.
Let him drink, and forget his poverty, and remember his misery no more. *31:6–7*

6 Who can find a virtuous woman? for her price is far above rubies.
The heart of her husband doth safely trust in her. *31:10–11*

7 Her husband is known in the gates, when he sitteth among the elders of the land.
31:23

8 Strength and honor are her clothing.
31:25

9 In her tongue is the law of kindness.
She looketh well to the ways of her household, and eateth not the bread of idleness.
Her children arise up, and call her blessed.
31:26–28

10 Many daughters have done virtuously, but thou excellest them all.
Favor is deceitful, and beauty is vain: but a woman that feareth the Lord, she shall be praised.
Give her of the fruit of her hands; and let her own works praise her in the gates.
31:29–31

11 Vanity of vanities, saith the Preacher, vanity of vanities; all is vanity.
What profit hath a man of all his labor which he taketh under the sun?
One generation passeth away, and another generation cometh: but the earth abideth for ever.
The sun also ariseth.
Ecclesiastes; or, The Preacher 1:2–5

12 All the rivers run into the sea; yet the sea is not full. *1:7*

13 The eye is not satisfied with seeing, nor the ear filled with hearing. *1:8*

14 The thing that hath been, it is that which shall be; and that which is done is that which shall be done: and there is no new thing under the sun. *Ecclesiastes 1:9*

15 There is no remembrance of former things; neither shall there be any remembrance of things that are to come with those that shall come after. *1:11*

16 I have seen all the works that are done under the sun; and, behold, all is vanity and vexation of spirit.
That which is crooked cannot be made straight: and that which is wanting cannot be numbered. *1:14–15*

17 In much wisdom is much grief: and he that increaseth knowledge increaseth sorrow.
1:18

18 Wisdom excelleth folly, as far as light excelleth darkness. *2:13*

19 One event happeneth to them all.
2:14

20 How dieth the wise man? as the fool.
2:16

21 To every thing there is a season, and a time to every purpose under the heaven.
A time to be born, and a time to die; a time to plant, and a time to pluck up that which is planted;
A time to kill, and a time to heal; a time to break down, and a time to build up;
A time to weep, and a time to laugh; a time to mourn, and a time to dance;
A time to cast away stones, and a time to gather stones together; a time to embrace, and a time to refrain from embracing;
A time to get, and a time to lose; a time to keep, and a time to cast away;
A time to rend, and a time to sew; a time to keep silence, and a time to speak;[1]
A time to love, and a time to hate; a time of war, and a time of peace. *3:1–8*

22 Wherefore I praised the dead which are already dead more than the living which are yet alive. *4:2*

23 Better is an handful with quietness, than both the hands full with travail and vexation of spirit. *4:6*

24 A threefold cord is not quickly broken.
4:12

25 Better is a poor and a wise child than an old and foolish king. *4:13*

26 God is in heaven, and thou upon earth: therefore let thy words be few. *5:2*

27 Better is it that thou shouldest not vow, than that thou shouldest vow and not pay.
5:5

[1] See Homer, 60:10.

1 The sleep of a laboring man is sweet . . . but the abundance of the rich will not suffer him to sleep. *Ecclesiastes 5:12*

2 As he came forth of his mother's womb, naked shall he return to go as he came,[1] and shall take nothing of his labor, which he may carry away in his hand.[2] *5:15*

3 A good name is better than precious ointment; and the day of death than the day of one's birth.[3] *7:1*

4 It is better to go to the house of mourning, than to go to the house of feasting. *7:2*

5 As the crackling of thorns under a pot, so is the laughter of the fool. *7:6*

6 Better is the end of a thing than the beginning thereof. *7:8*

7 In the day of prosperity be joyful, but in the day of adversity consider. *7:14*

8 Be not righteous over much. *7:16*

9 There is not a just man upon earth, that doeth good, and sinneth not. *7:20*

10 And I find more bitter than death the woman, whose heart is snares and nets, and her hands as bands. *7:26*

11 One man among a thousand have I found; but a woman among all those have I not found. *7:28*

12 God hath made man upright; but they have sought out many inventions. *7:29*

13 There is no discharge in that war. *8:8*

14 A man hath no better thing under the sun, than to eat, and to drink, and to be merry.[4] *8:15*

15 A living dog is better than a dead lion.
For the living know that they shall die: but the dead know not any thing, neither have they any more a reward; for the memory of them is forgotten. *9:4–5*

16 Whatsoever thy hand findeth to do, do it with thy might; for there is no work, nor device, nor knowledge, nor wisdom, in the grave, whither thou goest. *9:10*

17 I returned, and saw under the sun, that the race is not to the swift, nor the battle to the strong, neither yet bread to the wise, nor yet riches to men of understanding, nor yet favor to men of skill; but time and chance happeneth to them all.

For man also knoweth not his time: as the fishes that are taken in an evil net, and as the birds that are caught in the snare; so are the sons of men snared in an evil time, when it falleth suddenly upon them. *Ecclesiastes 9:11–12*

18 A feast is made for laughter, and wine maketh merry: but money answereth all things. *10:19*

19 A bird of the air shall carry the voice, and that which hath wings shall tell the matter. *10:20*

20 Cast thy bread upon the waters: for thou shalt find it after many days. *11:1*

21 He that observeth the wind shall not sow; and he that regardeth the clouds shall not reap. *11:4*

22 In the morning sow thy seed, and in the evening withhold not thine hand. *11:6*

23 Rejoice, O young man, in thy youth. *11:9*

24 Remember now thy Creator in the days of thy youth, while the evil days come not, nor the years draw nigh, when thou shalt say, I have no pleasure in them;
While the sun, or the light, or the moon, or the stars, be not darkened, nor the clouds return after the rain:
In the day when the keepers of the house shall tremble, and the strong men shall bow themselves, and the grinders cease because they are few, and those that look out of the windows be darkened,
And the doors shall be shut in the streets, when the sound of the grinding is low, and he shall rise up at the voice of the bird, and all the daughters of music shall be brought low. *12:1–4*

25 The almond tree shall flourish, and the grasshopper shall be a burden, and desire shall fail; because man goeth to his long home, and the mourners go about the streets:
Or ever the silver cord be loosed, or the golden bowl be broken, or the pitcher be broken at the fountain, or the wheel broken at the cistern.
Then shall the dust return to the earth as it was: and the spirit shall return unto God who gave it. *12:5–7*

26 The words of the wise are as goads, and as nails fastened by the masters of assemblies. *12:11*

27 Of making many books there is no end; and much study is a weariness of the flesh.
Let us hear the conclusion of the whole

[1] See *Job 1:21*, 15:4.
[2] See *The Song of the Harper*, 3:2, and *I Timothy 6:7*, 51:1.
[3] See Publilius Syrus, 110:19.
[4] See *Luke 12:19*, 43:19.

matter: Fear God, and keep his commandments: for this is the whole duty of man.

For God shall bring every work into judgment, with every secret thing, whether it be good, or whether it be evil.

Ecclesiastes 12:12–14

1 The song of songs, which is Solomon's.

The Song of Solomon 1:1

2 I am black, but comely, O ye daughters of Jerusalem, as the tents of Kedar, as the curtains of Solomon. *1:5*

3 O thou fairest among women. *1:8*

4 I am the rose of Sharon, and the lily of the valleys. *2:1*

5 As the apple tree among the trees of the wood, so is my beloved among the sons. *2:3*

6 His banner over me was love.

Stay me with flagons, comfort me with apples: for I am sick of love. *2:4–5*

7 Rise up, my love, my fair one, and come away.

For, lo, the winter is past, the rain is over and gone;

The flowers appear on the earth; the time of the singing of birds is come, and the voice of the turtle is heard in our land.[1] *2:10–12*

8 The little foxes, that spoil the vines. *2:15*

9 Until the day break, and the shadows flee away. *2:17 and 4:6*

10 By night on my bed I sought him whom my soul loveth: I sought him, but I found him not. *3:1*

11 Thy two breasts are like two young roes that are twins, which feed among the lilies. *4:5*

12 Thou art all fair, my love; there is no spot in thee. *4:7*

13 How much better is thy love than wine! *4:10*

14 Awake, O north wind; and come, thou south; blow upon my garden, that the spices thereof may flow out. Let my beloved come into his garden, and eat his pleasant fruits. *4:16*

15 My beloved put in his hand by the hole of the door, and my bowels were moved for him. *5:4*

16 His mouth is most sweet: yea, he is altogether lovely. This is my beloved, and this is my friend, O daughters of Jerusalem. *5:16*

[1]See *Love Songs of the New Kingdom,* 4:13.

17 Who is she that looketh forth as the morning, fair as the moon, clear as the sun, and terrible as an army with banners?

Song of Solomon 6:10

18 Return, return, O Shulamite. *6:13*

19 Thy belly is like a heap of wheat set about with lilies. *7:2*

20 Thy neck is as a tower of ivory. *7:4*

21 Like the best wine . . . that goeth down sweetly, causing the lips of those that are asleep to speak. *7:9*

22 I am my beloved's, and his desire is toward me. *7:10*

23 Set me as a seal upon thine heart, as a seal upon thine arm: for love is strong as death; jealousy is cruel as the grave. *8:6*

24 Many waters cannot quench love, neither can the floods drown it. *8:7*

25 Make haste, my beloved, and be thou like to a roe or to a young hart upon the mountains of spices. *8:14*

26 The ox knoweth his owner, and the ass his master's crib.

The Book of the Prophet Isaiah 1:3

27 The whole head is sick, and the whole heart faint. *1:5*

28 As a lodge in a garden of cucumbers. *1:8*

29 Bring no more vain oblations. *1:13*

30 Learn to do well; seek judgment, relieve the oppressed, judge the fatherless, plead for the widow.

Come now, and let us reason together . . . though your sins be as scarlet, they shall be as white as snow. *1:17–18*

31 They shall beat their swords into plowshares, and their spears into pruninghooks: nation shall not lift up sword against nation, neither shall they learn war any more.[2] *2:4*

32 In that day a man shall cast his idols . . . to the moles and to the bats. *2:20*

33 Cease ye from man, whose breath is in his nostrils. *2:22*

34 The stay and the staff, the whole stay of bread, and the whole stay of water. *3:1*

35 What mean ye that ye beat my people to pieces and grind the faces of the poor? *3:15*

[2]Also in *Joel 3:10* and *Micah 4:3*.

1 Walk with stretched forth necks and wanton eyes, walking and mincing as they go, and making a tinkling with their feet. *Isaiah 3:16*

2 In that day seven women shall take hold of one man. *4:1*

3 My wellbeloved hath a vineyard in a very fruitful hill. *5:1*

4 And he looked for judgment, but behold oppression; for righteousness, but behold a cry.
Woe unto them that join house to house, that lay field to field, till there be no place, that they may be placed alone in the midst of the earth! *5:7–8*

5 Woe unto them that rise up early in the morning, that they may follow strong drink. *5:11*

6 Woe unto them that draw iniquity with cords of vanity, and sin as it were with a cart rope. *5:18*

7 Woe unto them that call evil good, and good evil. *5:20*

8 I saw also the Lord sitting upon a throne, high and lifted up, and his train filled the temple.
Above it stood the seraphims: each one had six wings; with twain he covered his face, and with twain he covered his feet, and with twain he did fly. *6:1–2*

9 Holy, holy, holy, is the Lord of hosts: the whole earth is full of his glory. *6:3*

10 Woe is me! for I am undone; because I am a man of unclean lips, and I dwell in the midst of a people of unclean lips: for mine eyes have seen the King, the Lord of hosts. *6:5*

11 I heard the voice of the Lord, saying, Whom shall I send, and who will go for us? Then said I, Here am I; send me. *6:8*

12 Then said I, Lord, how long? *6:11*

13 Behold, a virgin shall conceive, and bear a son, and shall call his name Immanuel.[1] *7:14*

14 For a stone of stumbling and for a rock of offense. *8:14*

15 The people that walked in darkness have seen a great light: they that dwell in the land of the shadow of death, upon them hath the light shined. *9:2*

16 For unto us a child is born, unto us a son is given: and the government shall be upon his shoulder: and his name shall be called Wonderful, Counsellor, The mighty God, The everlasting Father, The Prince of Peace.
Of the increase of his government and peace there shall be no end. *Isaiah 9:6–7*

17 The ancient and honorable, he is the head. *9:15*

18 And there shall come forth a rod out of the stem of Jesse, and a Branch shall grow out of his roots:
And the Spirit of the Lord shall rest upon him, the spirit of wisdom and understanding, the spirit of counsel and might, the spirit of knowledge and of the fear of the Lord. *11:1–2*

19 The wolf also shall dwell with the lamb, and the leopard shall lie down with the kid; and the calf and the young lion and the fatling together; and a little child shall lead them.
And the cow and the bear shall feed; their young ones shall lie down together: and the lion shall eat straw like the ox.
And the suckling child shall play on the hole of the asp, and the weaned child shall put his hand on the cockatrice' den.
They shall not hurt nor destroy in all my holy mountain: for the earth shall be full of the knowledge of the Lord, as the waters cover the sea. *11:6–9*

20 For the Lord JEHOVAH is my strength and my song; he also is become my salvation. *12:2*

21 And I will punish the world for their evil, and the wicked for their iniquity; and I will cause the arrogancy of the proud to cease, and will lay low the haughtiness of the terrible. *13:11*

22 How art thou fallen from heaven, O Lucifer, son of the morning! *14:12*

23 Is this the man that made the earth to tremble, that did shake kingdoms. *14:16*

24 The nations shall rush like the rushing of many waters. *17:13*

25 And they shall fight every one against his brother. *19:2*

26 The burden of the desert of the sea. As whirlwinds in the south pass through; so it cometh from the desert, from a terrible land. *21:1*

27 Babylon is fallen, is fallen;[2] and all the graven images of her gods he hath broken unto the ground. *21:9*

[1] See *Matthew 1:23*, 36:19.

[2] See *Revelation 14:8*, 53:23.

1 Watchman, what of the night? *Isaiah 21:11*

2 Let us eat and drink; for tomorrow we shall die. *22:13*

3 I will fasten him as a nail in a sure place. *22:23*

4 Whose merchants are princes. *23:8*

5 As with the maid, so with her mistress. *24:2*

6 For thou hast been a strength to the poor, a strength to the needy in his distress. *25:4*

7 A feast of fat things, a feast of wines on the lees. *25:6*

8 He will swallow up death in victory;[1] and the Lord God will wipe away tears from off all faces.[2] *25:8*

9 Open ye the gates, that the righteous nation which keepeth the truth may enter in.
Thou wilt keep him in perfect peace, whose mind is stayed on thee. *26:2–3*

10 Awake and sing. *26:19*

11 Hide thyself as it were for a little moment, until the indignation be overpast. *26:20*

12 Leviathan that crooked serpent . . . the dragon that is in the sea. *27:1*

13 For precept must be upon precept, precept upon precept; line upon line, line upon line; here a little, and there a little. *28:10*

14 We have made a covenant with death, and with hell are we at agreement. *28:15*

15 It shall be a vexation only to understand the report. *28:19*

16 They are drunken, but not with wine; they stagger, but not with strong drink. *29:9*

17 Their strength is to sit still.
Now go, write it before them in a table, and note it in a book, that it may be for the time to come for ever and ever. *30:7–8*

18 The bread of adversity, and the water of affliction. *30:20*

19 This is the way, walk ye in it. *30:21*

20 Behold, a king shall reign in righteousness. *32:1*

21 And a man shall be as an hiding place from the wind, and a covert from the tempest; as rivers of water in a dry place, as the shadows of a great rock in a weary land. *32:2*

[1] See *Hosea 13:14*, 33:16, and *I Corinthians 15:54*, 49:8.
[2] See *Revelation 21:4*, 53:30.

22 An habitation of dragons, and a court for owls. *Isaiah 34:13*

23 The desert shall rejoice, and blossom as the rose. *35:1*

24 Then the eyes of the blind shall be opened, and the ears of the deaf shall be unstopped.
Then shall the lame man leap as an hart, and the tongue of the dumb sing. *35:5–6*

25 Sorrow and sighing shall flee away. *35:10*

26 Thou trustest in the staff of this broken reed. *36:6*

27 Incline thine ear, O Lord, and hear. *37:17*

28 I shall go softly all my years in the bitterness of my soul. *38:15*

29 Comfort ye, comfort ye my people. *40:1*

30 Speak ye comfortably to Jerusalem, and cry unto her, that her warfare is accomplished, that her iniquity is pardoned: for she hath received of the Lord's hand double for all her sins.
The voice of him that crieth in the wilderness, Prepare ye the way of the Lord, make straight in the desert a highway for our God.[3] *40:2–3*

31 Every valley shall be exalted, and every mountain and hill shall be made low: and the crooked shall be made straight, and the rough places plain. *40:4*

32 The voice said, Cry. And he said, what shall I cry? All flesh is grass, and all the goodliness thereof is as the flower of the field. *40:6*

33 The grass withereth, the flower fadeth;[4] but the word of our God shall stand for ever. *40:8*

34 Get thee up into the high mountain . . . say unto the cities of Judah, Behold your God! *40:9*

35 He shall feed his flock like a shepherd: he shall gather the lambs with his arm, and carry them in his bosom, and shall gently lead those that are with young. *40:11*

36 The nations are as a drop of a bucket, and are counted as the small dust of the balance. *40:15*

[3] See *Matthew 3:3*, 36:26. Also in *Mark 1:3*, *Luke 3:4*, and *John 1:23*.
[4] See *Psalm 90:5–6*, 20:11, and *I Peter 1:24*, 52:9.

1 Have ye not known? have ye not heard? hath it not been told you from the beginning? *Isaiah 40:21*

2 They that wait upon the Lord shall renew their strength; they shall mount up with wings as eagles; they shall run, and not be weary, and they shall walk, and not faint. *40:31*

3 They helped every one his neighbor; and every one said to his brother, Be of good courage. *41:6*

4 A bruised reed shall he not break, and the smoking flax shall he not quench. *42:3*

5 Shall the clay say to him that fashioneth it, What makest thou? *45:9*

6 Behold, I have refined thee, but not with silver; I have chosen thee in the furnace of affliction. *48:10*

7 O that thou hadst hearkened to my commandments! then had thy peace been as a river, and thy righteousness as the waves of the sea. *48:18*

8 There is no peace, saith the Lord, unto the wicked. *48:22*

9 Therefore the redeemed of the Lord shall return, and come with singing unto Zion. *51:11*

10 Thou hast drunken the dregs of the cup of trembling. *51:17*

11 Therefore hear now this. *51:21*

12 How beautiful upon the mountains are the feet of him that bringeth good tidings, that publisheth peace. *52:7*

13 They shall see eye to eye. *52:8*

14 He is despised and rejected of men; a man of sorrows, and acquainted with grief. *53:3*

15 Surely he hath borne our griefs, and carried our sorrows. *53:4*

16 All we like sheep have gone astray.[1] *53:6*

17 He is brought as a lamb to the slaughter.[2] *53:7*

18 Ho, everyone that thirsteth, come ye to the waters. *55:1*

19 Behold, I have given him for a witness to the people, a leader and commander to the people. *55:4*

[1]See *Book of Common Prayer, A General Confession,* 54:12.

[2]Also in *Acts 8:32.*

20 Let the wicked forsake his way, and the unrighteous man his thoughts. *Isaiah 55:7*

21 For my thoughts are not your thoughts, neither are your ways my ways, saith the Lord. *55:8*

22 Peace to him that is far off, and to him that is near. *57:19*

23 Arise, shine; for thy light is come, and the glory of the Lord is risen upon thee. *60:1*

24 A little one shall become a thousand, and a small one a strong nation. *60:22*

25 Give unto them beauty for ashes, the oil of joy for mourning, the garment of praise for the spirit of heaviness. *61:3*

26 I have trodden the winepress alone; and of the people there was none with me: for I will tread them in mine anger, and trample them in my fury; and their blood shall be sprinkled upon my garments, and I will stain all my raiment. *63:3*

27 All our righteousnesses are as filthy rags; and we all do fade as a leaf. *64:6*

28 We all are the work of thy hand. *64:8*

29 I am holier than thou. *65:5*

30 For, behold, I create new heavens and a new earth.[3] *65:17*

31 And they shall build houses, and inhabit them; and they shall plant vineyards, and eat the fruit of them.

They shall not build, and another inhabit; they shall not plant, and another eat. *65:21–22*

32 As one whom his mother comforteth, so will I comfort you. *66:13*

33 They were as fed horses in the morning: every one neighed after his neighbor's wife. *The Book of the Prophet Jeremiah 5:8*

34 Hear now this, O foolish people, and without understanding; which have eyes, and see not; which have ears, and hear not. *5:21*

35 But this people hath a revolting and a rebellious heart. *5:23*

36 Saying, Peace, peace; when there is no peace. *6:14 and 8:11*

37 Stand ye in the ways, and see, and ask for the old paths, where is the good way, and walk therein.[4] *6:16*

[3]See *Revelation 21:1,* 53:29.

[4]Stare super vias antiquas. — *The Vulgate*

1 Amend your ways and your doings. *Jeremiah 7:3 and 26:13*

2 The harvest is past, the summer is ended, and we are not saved. *8:20*

3 Is there no balm in Gilead? *8:22*

4 Oh that I had in the wilderness a lodging place of wayfaring men! *9:2*

5 Thus saith the Lord, Let not the wise man glory in his wisdom, neither let the mighty man glory in his might, let not the rich man glory in his riches:

But let him that glorieth glory in this, that he understandeth and knoweth me. *9:23–24*

6 Can the Ethiopian change his skin, or the leopard his spots? *13:23*

7 Our backslidings are many; we have sinned against thee. *14:7*

8 Her sun is gone down while it was yet day. *15:9*

9 A man of strife and a man of contention. *15:10*

10 The sin of Judah is written with a pen of iron, and with the point of a diamond. *17:1*

11 Cursed be the man that trusteth in man, and maketh flesh his arm, and whose heart departeth from the Lord.

For he shall be like the heath in the desert, and shall not see when good cometh; but shall inhabit the parched places in the wilderness, in a salt land and not inhabited.

Blessed is the man that trusteth in the Lord, and whose hope the Lord is.

For he shall be as a tree planted by the waters, and that spreadeth out her roots by the river, and shall not see when heat cometh, but her leaf shall be green; and shall not be careful in the year of drought, neither shall cease from yielding fruit.[1] *17:5–8*

12 The heart is deceitful above all things, and desperately wicked: who can know it? *17:9*

13 As the partridge sitteth on eggs, and hatcheth them not; so he that getteth riches, and not by right, shall leave them in the midst of his days, and at his end shall be a fool. *17:11*

14 Thou art my hope in the day of evil. *17:17*

[1] See Amenemope, 6:4; see also *Psalm 1:1–4*, 17:12.

15 O earth, earth, earth, hear the word of the Lord. *Jeremiah 22:29*

16 A curse, and an astonishment, and a hissing, and a reproach. *29:18*

17 The fathers have eaten a sour grape, and the children's teeth are set on edge.[2] *31:29*

18 With my whole heart and with my whole soul. *32:41*

19 And seekest thou great things for thyself? seek them not. *45:5*

20 How doth the city sit solitary, that was full of people! how is she become as a widow! *The Lamentations of Jeremiah 1:1*

21 She weepeth sore in the night, and her tears are on her cheeks: among all her lovers she hath none to comfort her. *1:2*

22 Is it nothing to you, all ye that pass by? behold, and see if there be any sorrow like unto my sorrow. *1:12*

23 Remembering mine affliction and my misery, the wormwood and the gall.[3] *3:19*

24 It is good for a man that he bear the yoke in his youth. *3:27*

25 As it were a wheel[4] in the middle of a wheel. *The Book of the Prophet Ezekiel 1:16*

26 As is the mother, so is her daughter. *16:44*

27 The king of Babylon stood at the parting of the way. *21:21*

28 The valley . . . was full of bones . . . and lo, they were very dry. *37:1–2*

29 Can these bones live? *37:3*

30 O ye dry bones, hear the word of the Lord. *37:4*

31 Every man's sword shall be against his brother. *38:21*

32 His legs of iron, his feet part of iron and part of clay. *The Book of Daniel 2:33*

33 Shadrach, Meshach, and Abednego, fell down bound into the midst of the burning fiery furnace. *3:23*

34 Nebuchadnezzar . . . was driven from men, and did eat grass as oxen. *4:33*

35 Belshazzar the king made a great feast to a thousand of his lords. *5:1*

[2] Also in *Ezekiel 18:2*.

[3] I will feed them with wormwood, and make them drink the water of gall.—*Jeremiah 23:15* (also in *Jeremiah 9:15*)

[4] Also in *Ezekiel 10:10*.

1 And this is the writing that was written, MENE, MENE, TEKEL, UPHARSIN.

This is the interpretation of the thing: MENE; God hath numbered thy kingdom, and finished it.

TEKEL; Thou art weighed in the balances, and art found wanting.

PERES; Thy kingdom is divided, and given to the Medes and Persians.

Daniel 5:25–28

2 According to the law of the Medes and Persians, which altereth not. *6:12*

3 They brought Daniel, and cast him into the den of lions. *6:16*

4 So Daniel was taken up out of the den, and no manner of hurt was found upon him, because he believed in his God. *6:23*

5 The Ancient of days. *7:9 and 7:13*

6 Many shall run to and fro, and knowledge shall be increased. *12:4*

7 Ye are the sons of the living God.

Hosea 1:10

8 Like people, like priest. *4:9*

9 After two days will he revive us: in the third day he will raise us up, and we shall live in his sight. *6:2*

10 He shall come unto us as the rain, as the latter and former rain unto the earth.

6:3

11 For I desired mercy, and not sacrifice; and the knowledge of God more than burnt offerings. *6:6*

12 They have sown the wind, and they shall reap the whirlwind. *8:7*

13 Ye have plowed wickedness, ye have reaped iniquity. *10:13*

14 I drew them with . . . bands of love.

11:4

15 I have multiplied visions, and used similitudes, by the ministry of the prophets.

12:10

16 I will ransom them from the power of the grave; I will redeem them from death: O death, I will be thy plagues; O grave, I will be thy destruction.[1] *13:14*

17 Your old men shall dream dreams, your young men shall see visions. *Joel 2:28*

18 Multitudes in the valley of decision.

3:14

[1]See *Isaiah 25:8*, 30:8, and *I Corinthians 15:54*, 49:8.

19 They sold the righteous for silver, and the poor for a pair of shoes. *Amos 2:6*

20 Can two walk together, except they be agreed? *3:3*

21 Woe to them that are at ease in Zion.

6:1

22 And Jonah was in the belly of the fish three days and three nights. *Jonah 1:17*

23 What doth the Lord require of thee, but to do justly, and to love mercy, and to walk humbly with thy God? *Micah 6:8*

24 The faces of them all gather blackness.[2]

Nahum 2:10

25 Write the vision, and make it plain upon tables, that he may run that readeth it.

Habakkuk 2:2

26 The stone shall cry out of the wall,[3] and the beam out of the timber shall answer it.

2:11

27 The Lord is in his holy temple: let all the earth keep silence before him. *2:20*

28 Your fathers, where are they? And the prophets, do they live forever?

Zechariah 1:5

29 I have spread you abroad as the four winds of the heaven. *2:6*

30 Not by might, nor by power, but by my spirit, saith the Lord of hosts. *4:6*

31 For who hath despised the day of small things? *4:10*

32 Behold, thy King cometh unto thee . . . lowly, and riding upon an ass. *9:9*

33 Prisoners of hope. *9:12*

34 So they weighed for my price thirty pieces of silver.[4] *11:12*

35 What are these wounds in thine hands? . . . Those with which I was wounded in the house of my friends. *13:6*

36 Have we not all one father? hath not one God created us? *Malachi 2:10*

37 Behold, I will send my messenger, and he shall prepare the way before me. *3:1*

38 Behold, the day cometh, that shall burn as an oven. *4:1*

39 Unto you that fear my name shall the Sun of righteousness arise with healing in his wings. *4:2*

[2]The faces of them all are as the blackness of a kettle. —*Douay Bible* [1609], *Nahum 2:10*. The English version of the Roman Catholic Bible was first printed in Douay, France.

[3]See *Luke 19:40*, 43:42.

[4]See *Matthew 26:15*, 41:5.

1 Behold, I will send you Elijah the prophet before the coming of the great and dreadful day of the Lord. *Malachi 4:5*

The Apocrypha[1]

2 And when they are in their cups, they forget their love both to friends and brethren, and a little after draw out swords. *I Esdras 3:22*

3 Great is Truth, and mighty above all things.[2] *4:41*

4 What is past I know, but what is for to come I know not. *II Esdras 4:46*

5 Now therefore keep thy sorrow to thyself, and bear with a good courage that which hath befallen thee. *10:15*

6 I shall light a candle of understanding in thine heart, which shall not be put out. *14:25*

7 If thou hast abundance, give alms accordingly: if thou have but a little, be not afraid to give according to that little. *Tobit 4:8*

8 Put on her garments of gladness. *Judith 10:3*

9 The ear of jealousy heareth all things. *The Wisdom of Solomon 1:10*

10 Our time is a very shadow that passeth away. *2:5*

11 Let us crown ourselves with rosebuds, before they be withered. *2:8*

12 For God created man to be immortal, and made him to be an image of his own eternity.
Nevertheless through envy of the devil came death into the world. *2:23–24*

13 The souls of the righteous are in the hand of God, and there shall no torment touch them.
In the sight of the unwise they seemed to die: and their departure is taken for misery,
And their going from us to be utter destruction: but they are in peace.

[1]The Apocrypha (The Hidden Books) is a term used to describe the books found in the Alexandrine Greek Scripture (the Septuagint) but absent from the Orthodox Hebrew Scripture (the Masoretic Text). In the light of recent archaeological discoveries it appears that this difference reflects a conscious exclusion of the debatable books by developing Orthodox Judaism. These books are regarded as canonical only by Roman Catholics.

[2]Magna est veritas et praevalet.—*The Vulgate, Book III* (uncanonical)

See Ptahhotpe, 3:5.

For great is truth, and shall prevail.—THOMAS BROOKS, *The Crown and Glory of Christianity* [1662]

For though they be punished in the sight of men, yet is their hope full of immortality.
And having been a little chastised, they shall be greatly rewarded: for God proved them, and found them worthy for himself. *Wisdom of Solomon 3:1–5*

14 They that put their trust in him shall understand the truth. *3:9*

15 Even so we in like manner, as soon as we were born, began to draw to our end. *5:13*

16 For the hope of the ungodly is like dust that is blown away with the wind . . . and passeth away as the remembrance of a guest that tarrieth but a day. *5:14*

17 For the very true beginning of her [wisdom] is the desire of discipline; and the care of discipline is love. *6:17*

18 And when I was born, I drew in the common air, and fell upon the earth, which is of like nature; and the first voice which I uttered was crying, as all others do. *7:3*

19 All men have one entrance into life, and the like going out. *7:6*

20 The light that cometh from her [wisdom] never goeth out. *7:10*

21 Who can number the sand of the sea, and the drops of rain, and the days of eternity? *The Wisdom of Jesus the Son of Sirach, or Ecclesiasticus, 1:2*

22 To whom hath the root of wisdom been revealed? *1:6*

23 For the Lord is full of compassion and mercy, longsuffering, and very pitiful, and forgiveth sins, and saveth in time of affliction. *2:11*

24 The greater thou art, the more humble thyself. *3:18*

25 Many are in high place, and of renown: but mysteries are revealed unto the meek. *3:19*

26 Seek not out the things that are too hard for thee, neither search the things that are above thy strength. *3:21*

27 Be not curious in unnecessary matters: for more things are showed unto thee than men understand. *3:23*

28 Profess not the knowledge . . . that thou hast not.
A stubborn heart shall fare evil at the last. *3:25–26*

29 Defraud not the poor of his living, and make not the needy eyes to wait long.[3] *4:1*

[3]See Amenemope, 6:3, and *Proverbs* 22:22, 25:2.

1 Wisdom exalteth her children, and layeth hold of them that seek her.
He that loveth her loveth life.
Ecclesiasticus 4:11–12

2 Observe the opportunity. *4:20*

3 Be not as a lion in thy house, nor frantic among thy servants.
Let not thine hand be stretched out to receive, and shut when thou shouldest repay. *4:30–31*

4 Set not thy heart upon thy goods; and say not, I have enough for my life. *5:1*

5 Winnow not with every wind, and go not into every way. *5:9*

6 Let thy life be sincere. *5:11*

7 Be not ignorant of any thing in a great matter or a small. *5:15*

8 If thou wouldest get a friend, prove him first. *6:7*

9 A faithful friend is a strong defense: and he that hath found such an one hath found a treasure. *6:14*

10 A faithful friend is the medicine of life. *6:16*

11 If thou seest a man of understanding, get thee betimes unto him, and let thy foot wear the steps of his door. *6:36*

12 Whatsoever thou takest in hand, remember the end, and thou shalt never do amiss. *7:36*

13 Rejoice not over thy greatest enemy being dead, but remember that we die all. *8:7*

14 Miss not the discourse of the elders. *8:9*

15 Forsake not an old friend; for the new is not comparable to him: a new friend is as new wine; when it is old, thou shalt drink it with pleasure. *9:10*

16 Pride is hateful before God and man. *10:7*

17 He that is today a king tomorrow shall die. *10:10*

18 Pride was not made for men, nor furious anger for them that are born of a woman. *10:18*

19 Be not overwise in doing thy business. *10:26*

20 Many kings have sat down upon the ground; and one that was never thought of hath worn the crown. *11:5*

21 In the day of prosperity there is a forgetfulness of affliction: and in the day of affliction there is no more remembrance of prosperity.
Ecclesiasticus 11:25

22 Judge none blessed before his death.[1] *11:28*

23 A friend cannot be known in prosperity: and an enemy cannot be hidden in adversity. *12:8*

24 He that toucheth pitch shall be defiled therewith. *13:1*

25 How agree the kettle and the earthen pot together? *13:2*

26 All flesh consorteth according to kind, and a man will cleave to his like.[2] *13:16*

27 A rich man beginning to fall is held up of his friends: but a poor man being down is thrust also away by his friends. *13:21*

28 The heart of a man changeth his countenance, whether it be for good or evil. *13:25*

29 So is a word better than a gift. *18:16*

30 Be not made a beggar by banqueting upon borrowing. *18:33*

31 He that contemneth small things shall fall by little and little. *19:1*

32 Whether it be to friend or foe, talk not of other men's lives. *19:8*

33 A man's attire, and excessive laughter, and gait, show what he is. *19:30*

34 A tale out of season [is as] music in mourning. *22:6*

35 I will not be ashamed to defend a friend. *22:25*

36 All wickedness is but little to the wickedness of a woman. *25:19*

37 The discourse of fools is irksome. *27:13*

38 Many have fallen by the edge of the sword: but not so many as have fallen by the tongue. *28:18*

39 Better is the life of a poor man in a mean cottage, than delicate fare in another man's house. *29:22*

40 There is no riches above a sound body. *30:16*

41 Gladness of the heart is the life of a man, and the joyfulness of a man prolongeth his days. *30:22*

[1]See Solon, 62:17; Aeschylus, 71:8; and Sophocles, 74:7.

[2]See Homer, 60:21.

1 Envy and wrath shorten the life, and carefulness bringeth age before the time.
Ecclesiasticus 30:24

2 Watching for riches consumeth the flesh, and the care thereof driveth away sleep.
31:1

3 Let thy speech be short, comprehending much in few words. *32:8*

4 Consider that I labored not for myself only, but for all them that seek learning.
33:17

5 Leave not a stain in thine honor.
33:22

6 Let the counsel of thine own heart stand.
37:13

7 Honor a physician with the honor due unto him for the uses which ye may have of him: for the Lord hath created him. *38:1*

8 When the dead is at rest, let his remembrance rest; and be comforted for him, when his spirit is departed from him. *38:23*

9 How can he get wisdom . . . whose talk is of bullocks? *38:25*

10 Let us now praise famous men, and our fathers that begat us. *44:1*

11 All these were honored in their generations, and were the glory of their times.

There be of them, that have left a name behind them, that their praises might be reported.

And some there be, which have no memorial; who are perished, as though they had never been; and are become as though they had never been born; and their children after them. *44:7–9*

12 Their bodies are buried in peace; but their name liveth for evermore. *44:14*

13 His word burned like a lamp. *48:1*

14 O all ye works of the Lord, bless ye the Lord: praise him and exalt him above all[1] for ever.
The Song of the Three Holy Children 35

15 Daniel had convicted them of false witness by their own mouth.
The History of Susanna 61

16 It is a foolish thing to make a long prologue, and to be short in the story itself.
The Second Book of the Maccabees 2:32

17 When he was at the last gasp. *7:9*

18 Speech finely framed delighteth the ears.
15:39

[1] In the Book of Common Prayer (The Benedicite): magnify him.

The New Testament[2]

19 Behold, a virgin shall be with child, and shall bring forth a son, and they shall call his name Emmanuel, which being interpreted is, God with us.[3]
The Gospel According to St. Matthew 1:23

20 Now when Jesus was born in Bethlehem of Judaea in the days of Herod the king, behold, there came wise men from the east to Jerusalem,

Saying, Where is he that is born King of the Jews? for we have seen his star in the east, and are come to worship him.
2:1–2

21 They saw the young child with Mary his mother, and fell down, and worshipped him: and . . . they presented unto him gifts; gold, and frankincense, and myrrh.

And being warned of God in a dream that they should not return to Herod, they departed into their own country another way.
2:11–12

22 Out of Egypt have I called my son.
2:15

23 Rachel weeping for her children, and would not be comforted, because they are not.[4] *2:18*

24 He shall be called a Nazarene. *2:23*

25 Repent ye: for the kingdom of heaven is at hand. *3:2*

26 The voice of one crying in the wilderness, Prepare ye the way of the Lord, make his paths straight.[5] *3:3*

27 And his meat was locusts and wild honey.
3:4

28 O generation of vipers, who hath warned you to flee from the wrath to come?
3:7

29 Now also the axe is laid unto the root of the trees: therefore every tree which bringeth not forth good fruit is hewn down, and cast into the fire. *3:10*

30 The Spirit of God descending like a dove.
3:16

31 This is my beloved Son, in whom I am well pleased. *3:17*

[2] The earliest Christian writings [A.D. c. 50–c. 64] are the Letters (Epistles) of Paul the Apostle. The Gospels are later, between the years 70 and 100.

[3] See *Isaiah 7:14*, 29:13.

[4] Rachel weeping for her children refused to be comforted . . . because they were not.—*Jeremiah 31:15*

[5] See *Isaiah 40:3*, 30:30.

1 And when he had fasted forty days and forty nights, he was afterward an hungred.
Matthew 4:2

2 The people which sat in darkness saw great light.[1]
4:16

3 Follow me, and I will make you fishers of men.
4:19

4 Blessed are the poor in spirit: for theirs is the kingdom of heaven.

Blessed are they that mourn: for they shall be comforted.

Blessed are the meek: for they shall inherit the earth.[2]

Blessed are they which do hunger and thirst after righteousness: for they shall be filled.

Blessed are the merciful: for they shall obtain mercy.

Blessed are the pure in heart: for they shall see God.

Blessed are the peacemakers: for they shall be called the children of God.

Blessed are they which are persecuted for righteousness' sake: for theirs is the kingdom of heaven.

Blessed are ye, when men shall revile you, and persecute you, and shall say all manner of evil against you falsely, for my sake.
5:3–11[3]

5 Ye are the salt of the earth: but if the salt have lost his savor, wherewith shall it be salted?
5:13

6 Ye are the light of the world. A city that is set on an hill cannot be hid.

Neither do men light a candle, and put it under a bushel, but on a candlestick; and it giveth light unto all that are in the house.

Let your light so shine before men, that they may see your good works, and glorify your Father which is in heaven.

Think not that I am come to destroy the law, or the prophets: I am not come to destroy, but to fulfill.
5:14–17

7 Till heaven and earth pass, one jot or one tittle shall in no wise pass from the law, till all be fulfilled.
5:18

8 Whosoever looketh on a woman to lust after her hath committed adultery with her already in his heart.

And if thy right eye offend thee, pluck it out, and cast it from thee: for it is profitable for thee that one of thy members should perish, and not that thy whole body should be cast into hell.

And if thy right hand offend thee, cut it off.
Matthew 5:28–30

9 Swear not at all; neither by heaven; for it is God's throne:

Nor by the earth; for it is his footstool.
5:34–35

10 Resist not evil: but whosoever shall smite thee on thy right cheek, turn to him the other also.
5:39

11 Love your enemies, bless them that curse you, do good to them that hate you, and pray for them which despitefully use you, and persecute you.
5:44

12 He maketh his sun to rise on the evil and on the good, and sendeth rain on the just and on the unjust.
5:45

13 Be ye therefore perfect, even as your Father which is in heaven is perfect.
5:48

14 When thou doest alms, let not thy left hand know what thy right hand doeth.
6:3

15 After this manner therefore pray ye: Our Father which art in heaven,[4] Hallowed be thy name.

Thy kingdom come. Thy will be done in earth, as it is in heaven.

Give us this day our daily bread.

And forgive us our debts, as we forgive our debtors.[5]

And lead us not into temptation, but deliver us from evil: For thine is the kingdom, and the power, and the glory,[6] for ever. Amen.
6:9–13[7]

16 Lay not up for yourselves treasures upon earth, where moth and rust doth corrupt, and where thieves break through and steal:

But lay up for yourselves treasures in heaven.
6:19–20

17 For where your treasure is, there will your heart be also.
6:21

18 The light of the body is the eye.
6:22

19 If therefore the light that is in thee be darkness, how great is that darkness!
6:23

[1] See *Psalm 107:10*, 21:13, and *Luke 1:79*, 42:26.

[2] See *Psalm 37:11*, 18:24.

[3] The Beatitudes are the opening of the Sermon on the Mount, which continues through *Matthew 7*.
See Lao-tzu, 64:10.

[4] Our Father, who art in heaven.—*Book of Common Prayer, Morning Prayer*

[5] And forgive us our trespasses, As we forgive those who trespass against us.—*Book of Common Prayer, Morning Prayer*

[6] See *Chronicles 29:11*, 14:25.

[7] The Lord's Prayer.

1 No man can serve two masters: for either he will hate the one, and love the other; or else he will hold to the one, and despise the other. Ye cannot serve God and mammon. *Matthew 6:24*

2 Is not the life more than meat, and the body than raiment?
Behold the fowls of the air: for they sow not, neither do they reap, nor gather into barns. *6:25–26*

3 Which of you by taking thought can add one cubit unto his stature? *6:27*

4 Consider the lilies of the field, how they grow; they toil not, neither do they spin. *6:28*

5 Even Solomon in all his glory was not arrayed like one of these. *6:29*

6 Seek ye first the kingdom of God, and his righteousness; and all these things shall be added unto you. *6:33*

7 Take therefore no thought for the morrow: for the morrow shall take thought for the things of itself. Sufficient unto the day is the evil thereof. *6:34*

8 Judge not, that ye be not judged. *7:1*

9 With what measure ye mete, it shall be measured to you again.
And why beholdest thou the mote that is in thy brother's eye, but considerest not the beam that is in thine own eye? *7:2–3*

10 Thou hypocrite, first cast out the beam out of thine own eye. *7:5*

11 Neither cast ye your pearls before swine. *7:6*

12 Ask, and it shall be given you; seek, and ye shall find; knock, and it shall be opened unto you. *7:7*

13 Or what man is there of you, whom if his son ask bread, will he give him a stone? *7:9*

14 Therefore all things whatsoever ye would that men should do to you, do ye even so to them: for this is the law and the prophets.[1] *7:12*

15 Wide is the gate, and broad is the way, that leadeth to destruction, and many there be which go in thereat:
Because strait is the gate, and narrow is the way, which leadeth unto life, and few there be that find it. *7:13–14*[2]

[1]The Golden Rule. Common form: Do as you would be done by.
See Confucius, 69:14, and Aristotle, 87:3.
[2]See Hesiod, 61:17.

16 Beware of false prophets, which come to you in sheep's clothing, but inwardly they are ravening wolves. *Matthew 7:15*

17 Ye shall know them by their fruits. Do men gather grapes of thorns, or figs of thistles? *7:16*

18 By their fruits ye shall know them. *7:20*

19 Not every one that saith unto me, Lord, Lord, shall enter into the kingdom of heaven; but he that doeth the will of my Father which is in heaven. *7:21*

20 [The house] fell not: for it was founded upon a rock. *7:25*

21 A foolish man, which built his house upon the sand. *7:26*

22 But the children of the kingdom shall be cast out into outer darkness: there shall be weeping and gnashing of teeth. *8:12*

23 The foxes have holes, and the birds of the air have nests; but the Son of man hath not where to lay his head. *8:20*

24 Follow me; and let the dead bury their dead. *8:22*

25 Why are ye fearful, O ye of little faith? *8:26*

26 He saw a man, named Matthew, sitting at the receipt of custom. *9:9*

27 They that be whole need not a physician, but they that are sick. *9:12*

28 I am not come to call the righteous, but sinners to repentance. *9:13*

29 Can the children of the bridechamber mourn, as long as the bridegroom is with them? *9:15*

30 Neither do men put new wine into old bottles. *9:17*

31 The maid is not dead, but sleepeth. *9:24*

32 The harvest truly is plenteous, but the laborers are few. *9:37*

33 Go rather to the lost sheep of the house of Israel. *10:6*

34 Freely ye have received, freely give. *10:8*

35 Whosoever shall not receive you, nor hear your words, when ye depart out of that house or city, shake off the dust of your feet. *10:14*

36 Be ye therefore wise as serpents, and harmless as doves.[3] *10:16*

[3]Often quoted as: Wise as the serpent, and harmless as the dove.

1 Ye shall be hated of all men for my name's sake. *Matthew 10:22*

2 The disciple is not above his master, nor the servant above his lord. *10:24*

3 Are not two sparrows sold for a farthing? and one of them shall not fall on the ground without your Father.
But the very hairs of your head are all numbered. *10:29–30*

4 I came not to send peace, but a sword. *10:34*

5 He that taketh not his cross, and followeth after me, is not worthy of me.
He that findeth his life shall lose it: and he that loseth his life for my sake shall find it.[1] *10:38–39*

6 He that hath ears to hear, let him hear. *11:15*

7 The Son of man came eating and drinking, and they say, Behold a man gluttonous, and a winebibber, a friend of publicans and sinners. But wisdom is justified of her children. *11:19*

8 Come unto me, all ye that labor and are heavy laden, and I will give you rest.
Take my yoke upon you, and learn of me; for I am meek and lowly in heart: and ye shall find rest unto your souls.
For my yoke is easy, and my burden is light. *11:28–30*

9 He that is not with me is against me. *12:30*

10 The tree is known by his fruit. *12:33*

11 Out of the abundance of the heart the mouth speaketh. *12:34*

12 Behold, a greater than Solomon is here. *12:42*

13 Some seeds fell by the way side. *13:4*

14 Because they had no root, they withered away. *13:6*

15 But other fell into good ground, and brought forth fruit, some an hundredfold, some sixtyfold, some thirtyfold. *13:8*

16 The care of this world, and the deceitfulness of riches. *13:22*

17 The kingdom of heaven is like to a grain of mustard seed. *13:31*

18 Pearl of great price. *13:46*

[1] See *Matthew 16:25*, 39:38.

19 The kingdom of heaven is like unto a net, that was cast into the sea, and gathered of every kind.[2] *Matthew 13:47*

20 Is not this the carpenter's son? *13:55*

21 A prophet is not without honor, save in his own country. *13:57*

22 [Salome] the daughter of Herodias danced before them, and pleased Herod. *14:6*

23 Give me here John Baptist's head in a charger. *14:8*

24 We have here but five loaves, and two fishes. *14:17*

25 And they did all eat, and were filled: and they took up of the fragments that remained twelve baskets full. *14:20*

26 And in the fourth watch of the night Jesus went unto them, walking on the sea. *14:25*

27 Be of good cheer; it is I; be not afraid. *14:27*

28 O thou of little faith, wherefore didst thou doubt? *14:31*

29 Of a truth thou art the Son of God. *14:33*

30 Not that which goeth into the mouth defileth a man; but that which cometh out of the mouth, this defileth a man. *15:11*

31 They be blind leaders of the blind. And if the blind lead the blind, both shall fall into the ditch. *15:14*

32 The dogs eat of the crumbs which fall from their masters' table. *15:27*

33 When it is evening, ye say, It will be fair weather: for the sky is red. *16:2*

34 The signs of the times. *16:3*

35 Thou art the Christ, the Son of the living God. *16:16*

36 Thou art Peter, and upon this rock I will build my church; and the gates of hell shall not prevail against it.
And I will give unto thee the keys of the kingdom of heaven. *16:18–19*

37 Get thee behind me, Satan. *16:23*

38 Whosoever will save his life shall lose it: and whosoever will lose his life for my sake shall find it.[3]
For what is a man profited, if he shall gain the whole world, and lose his own soul? *16:25–26*

[2] See Lao-tzu, 65:6.
[3] See *Matthew 10:39*, 39:5.

1 Except ye be converted, and become as little children, ye shall not enter into the kingdom of heaven. *Matthew 18:3*

2 He rejoiceth more of that sheep, than of the ninety and nine which went not astray. *18:13*

3 Where two or three are gathered together in my name, there am I in the midst of them.[1] *18:20*

4 Until seventy times seven. *18:22*

5 What therefore God hath joined together, let not man put asunder.[2] *19:6*

6 If thou wilt be perfect, go and sell that thou hast, and give to the poor, and thou shalt have treasure in heaven. *19:21*

7 It is easier for a camel to go through the eye of a needle, than for a rich man to enter into the kingdom of God. *19:24*

8 Many that are first shall be last; and the last shall be first. *19:30*

9 Borne the burden and heat of the day. *20:12*

10 Is it not lawful for me to do what I will with mine own? *20:15*

11 Overthrew the tables of the moneychangers. *21:12*

12 My house shall be called the house of prayer; but ye have made it a den of thieves. *21:13*

13 They made light of it. *22:5*

14 Many are called, but few are chosen. *22:14*

15 Render therefore unto Caesar the things which are Caesar's; and unto God the things that are God's. *22:21*

16 Thou shalt love the Lord thy God with all thy heart, and with all thy soul, and with all thy mind.[3]

This is the first and great commandment.

And the second is like unto it, Thou shalt love thy neighbor as thyself.[4]

On these two commandments hang all the law and the prophets. *22:37–40*

17 Whosoever shall exalt himself shall be abased; and he that shall humble himself shall be exalted. *23:12*

[1]See *Book of Common Prayer, A Prayer of St. Chrysostom,* 55:8.
[2]See *Book of Common Prayer, Solemnization of Matrimony,* 56:11.
[3]See *Deuteronomy 6:5,* 11:9.
[4]See *Leviticus 19:18,* 10:21.

18 Woe unto you, scribes and Pharisees, hypocrites! for ye pay tithe of mint and anise and cumin. *Matthew 23:23*

19 Blind guides, which strain at a gnat, and swallow a camel. *23:24*

20 Whited sepulchers, which indeed appear beautiful outward, but are within full of dead men's bones. *23:27*

21 O Jerusalem, Jerusalem, thou that killest the prophets, and stonest them which are sent unto thee, how often would I have gathered thy children together, even as a hen gathereth her chickens under her wings, and ye would not! *23:37*

22 Ye shall hear of wars and rumors of wars: see that ye be not troubled: for all these things must come to pass, but the end is not yet.

For nation shall rise against nation. *24:6–7*

23 Abomination of desolation. *24:15*

24 Wheresoever the carcase is, there will the eagles be gathered together. *24:28*

25 And he shall send his angels with a great sound of a trumpet. *24:31*

26 Heaven and earth shall pass away, but my words shall not pass away. *24:35*

27 The one shall be taken, and the other left. *24:40*

28 Then shall the kingdom of heaven be likened unto ten virgins, which took their lamps, and went forth to meet the bridegroom.

And five of them were wise, and five were foolish. *25:1–2*

29 Well done, thou good and faithful servant . . . enter thou into the joy of thy lord. *25:21*

30 Unto every one that hath shall be given, and he shall have abundance: but from him that hath not shall be taken away even that which he hath. *25:29*

31 Cast ye the unprofitable servant into outer darkness. *25:30*

32 And before him shall be gathered all nations: and he shall separate them one from another, as a shepherd divideth his sheep from the goats. *25:32*

33 For I was an hungred, and ye gave me meat: I was thirsty, and ye gave me drink: I was a stranger, and ye took me in:

Naked, and ye clothed me: I was sick, and ye visited me: I was in prison, and ye came unto me. *25:35–36*

1 Inasmuch as ye have done it unto one of the least of these my brethren, ye have done it unto me. *Matthew 25:40*

2 There came unto him [Jesus] a woman having an alabaster box of very precious ointment, and poured it on his head, as he sat at meat. *26:7*

3 To what purpose is this waste? *26:8*

4 For ye have the poor always with you; but me ye have not always.[1] *26:11*

5 What will ye give me, and I will deliver him unto you? And they covenanted with him for thirty pieces of silver.[2] *26:15*

6 My time is at hand. *26:18*

7 Verily I say unto you, that one of you shall betray me. *26:21*

8 And they were exceeding sorrowful, and began every one of them to say unto him, Lord, is it I? *26:22*

9 It had been good for that man [Judas] if he had not been born. *26:24*

10 Jesus took bread, and blessed it, and brake it, and gave it to the disciples, and said, Take, eat; this is my body.

And he took the cup, and gave thanks, and gave it to them, saying, Drink ye all of it;

For this is my blood of the new testament, which is shed for many for the remission of sins.

But I say unto you, I will not drink henceforth of this fruit of the vine, until that day when I drink it new with you in my Father's kingdom.[3] *26:26–29*

11 My soul is exceeding sorrowful, even unto death. *26:38*

12 O my Father, if it be possible, let this cup pass from me: nevertheless, not as I will, but as thou wilt. *26:39*

13 Could ye not watch with me one hour? Watch and pray, that ye enter not into temptation: the spirit indeed is willing, but the flesh is weak. *26:40–41*

14 Behold, the hour is at hand, and the Son of man is betrayed into the hands of sinners. *26:45*

15 He came to Jesus, and said, Hail, Master; and kissed him. *26:49*

16 All they that take the sword shall perish with the sword. *26:52*

17 Thy speech bewrayeth thee. *26:73*

[1]See *Deuteronomy 15:11*, 11:17.
[2]See *Zechariah 11:12*, 33:34.
[3]See *I Corinthians 11:24, 25*, 48:20 and 48:21.

18 Then began he to curse and to swear, saying, I know not the man. And immediately the cock crew.

And Peter remembered the word of Jesus . . . Before the cock crow, thou shalt deny me thrice.[4] And he went out, and wept bitterly. *Matthew 26:74–75*

19 The potter's field, to bury strangers in. *27:7*

20 Have thou nothing to do with that just man. *27:19*

21 Let him be crucified. *27:22*

22 [Pilate] took water, and washed his hands before the multitude, saying, I am innocent of the blood of this just person: see ye to it. *27:24*

23 His blood be on us, and on our children. *27:25*

24 A place called Golgotha, that is to say, a place of a skull. *27:33*

25 This is Jesus the King of the Jews. *27:37*

26 He saved others; himself he cannot save. *27:42*

27 Eli, Eli, lama sabachthani? that is to say, My God, my God, why hast thou forsaken me?[5] *27:46*

28 And, behold, the veil of the temple was rent in twain from the top to the bottom; and the earth did quake, and the rocks rent. *27:51*

29 His countenance was like lightning, and his raiment white as snow. *28:3*

30 Go ye therefore, and teach all nations, baptizing them in the name of the Father, and of the Son, and of the Holy Ghost. *28:19*

31 Lo, I am with you alway, even unto the end of the world. *28:20*

32 There cometh one mightier than I[6] after me, the latchet of whose shoes I am not worthy to stoop down and unloose. *The Gospel According to St. Mark 1:7*

33 Arise, and take up thy bed, and walk. *2:9*

34 The sabbath was made for man, and not man for the sabbath. *2:27*

35 If a house be divided against itself, that house cannot stand. *3:25*

[4]This night, before the cock crow, thou shalt deny me thrice.—*Matthew 26:34*
[5]See *Psalm 22:1*, 18:5.
[6]John the Baptist.

1 The earth bringeth forth fruit of herself; first the blade, then the ear, after that the full corn in the ear. *Mark 4:28*

2 What manner of man is this? *4:41*

3 They came . . . into the country of the Gadarenes. *5:1*

4 My name is Legion: for we are many. *5:9*

5 And the unclean spirits went out, and entered the swine: and the herd ran violently down a steep place into the sea . . . and were choked in the sea. *5:13*

6 Clothed, and in his right mind. *5:15*

7 My little daughter lieth at the point of death. *5:23*

8 Knowing in himself that virtue had gone out of him. *5:30*

9 I see men as trees, walking. *8:24*

10 Lord, I believe; help thou mine unbelief. *9:24*

11 Suffer the little children to come unto me, and forbid them not; for of such is the kingdom of God. *10:14*

12 Which devour widows' houses, and for a pretense make long prayers. *12:40*

13 And there came a certain poor widow, and she threw in two mites. *12:42*

14 Watch ye therefore: for ye know not when the master of the house cometh, at even, or at midnight, or at the cockcrowing, or in the morning:
Lest coming suddenly he find you sleeping. *13:35–36*

15 He is risen.[1] *16:6*

16 Go ye into all the world, and preach the gospel to every creature. *16:15*

17 Hail, thou that art highly favored, the Lord is with thee: blessed art thou among women.
The Gospel According to St. Luke 1:28

18 For with God nothing shall be impossible. *1:37*

19 Blessed is the fruit of thy womb. *1:42*

20 My soul doth magnify the Lord. *1:46*

21 For he hath regarded the low estate of his handmaiden: for, behold, from henceforth all generations shall call me blessed. *1:48*

[1]See *Luke 24:34*, 44:16, and *The Book of Common Prayer*, 54:10.

22 He hath scattered the proud in the imagination of their hearts.
He hath put down the mighty from their seats, and exalted them of low degree. *Luke 1:51–52*

23 He hath filled the hungry with good things; and the rich he hath sent empty away. *1:53*

24 Blessed be the Lord God of Israel; for he hath visited and redeemed his people. *1:68*

25 As he spake by the mouth of his holy prophets, which have been since the world began:
That we should be saved from our enemies, and from the hand of all that hate us. *1:70–71*

26 Through the tender mercy of our God; whereby the dayspring from on high hath visited us,
To give light to them that sit in darkness and in the shadow of death.[2] *1:78–79*

27 And she brought forth her firstborn son, and wrapped him in swaddling clothes, and laid him in a manger; because there was no room for them in the inn. *2:7*

28 There were in the same country shepherds abiding in the field, keeping watch over their flock by night.
And, lo, the angel of the Lord came upon them, and the glory of the Lord shone round about them: and they were sore afraid.
And the angel said unto them, Fear not: for, behold, I bring you good tidings of great joy, which shall be to all people.
For unto you is born this day in the city of David a Savior, which is Christ the Lord. *2:8–11*

29 Glory to God in the highest, and on earth peace, good will toward men.[3] *2:14*

30 Lord, now lettest thou thy servant depart in peace. *2:29*

31 A light to lighten the Gentiles, and the glory of thy people Israel. *2:32*

32 Wist ye not that I must be about my Father's business? *2:49*

33 Jesus increased in wisdom and stature, and in favor with God and man. *2:52*

34 [The devil] showed unto him all the kingdoms of the world in a moment of time. *4:5*

[2]See *Psalm 107:10*, 21:13, and *Matthew 4:16*, 37:2.
[3]The Douay Bible has "peace to men of good will."

1 For it is written, He shall give his angels charge over thee, to keep thee:
And in their hands they shall bear thee up, lest at any time thou dash thy foot against a stone. *Luke 4:10–11* [1]

2 Physician, heal thyself. *4:23*

3 Woe unto you, when all men shall speak well of you! *6:26*

4 Her sins, which are many, are forgiven; for she loved much. *7:47*

5 And he said to the woman, Thy faith hath saved thee; go in peace. *7:50*

6 Nothing is secret, that shall not be made manifest. *8:17*

7 No man, having put his hand to the plow, and looking back, is fit for the kingdom of God. *9:62*

8 Nor scrip, nor shoes. *10:4*

9 Peace be to this house. *10:5*

10 The laborer is worthy of his hire. *10:7*

11 I beheld Satan as lightning fall from heaven. *10:18*

12 Many prophets and kings have desired to see those things which ye see, and have not seen them; and to hear those things which ye hear, and have not heard them. *10:24*

13 A certain man went down from Jerusalem to Jericho, and fell among thieves. *10:30*

14 A certain Samaritan . . . had compassion on him. *10:33*

15 Go, and do thou likewise. *10:37*

16 But Martha was cumbered about much serving. *10:40*

17 But one thing is needful: and Mary hath chosen that good part, which shall not be taken away from her. *10:42*

18 This is an evil generation: they seek a sign. *11:29*

19 Soul, thou hast much goods laid up for many years; take thine ease, eat, drink, and be merry.[2] *12:19*

20 Thou fool, this night thy soul shall be required of thee. *12:20*

21 Let your loins be girded about, and your lights burning. *12:35*

22 For unto whomsoever much is given, of him shall be much required: and to whom men have committed much, of him they will ask the more. *Luke 12:48*

[1] See *Psalm 91:11–12*, 20:17. Also in *Matthew 4:6*.
[2] See *Ecclesiastes 8:15*, 27:14.

23 The poor, and the maimed, and the halt, and the blind. *14:21*

24 Which of you, intending to build a tower, sitteth not down first, and counteth the cost, whether he have sufficient to finish it? *14:28*

25 Rejoice with me; for I have found my sheep which was lost. *15:6*

26 [The prodigal son] wasted his substance with riotous living. *15:13*

27 Bring hither the fatted calf, and kill it. *15:23*

28 For this my son was dead, and is alive again; he was lost, and is found. *15:24*

29 Son, thou art ever with me, and all that I have is thine. *15:31*

30 What shall I do? . . . I cannot dig; to beg I am ashamed. *16:3*

31 The children of this world are in their generation wiser than the children of light. *16:8*

32 He that is faithful in that which is least is faithful also in much: and he that is unjust in the least is unjust also in much. *16:10*

33 The beggar died, and was carried by the angels into Abraham's bosom. *16:22*

34 Between us and you there is a great gulf fixed. *16:26*

35 It were better for him that a millstone were hanged about his neck, and he cast into the sea. *17:2*

36 The kingdom of God is within you. *17:21*

37 Remember Lot's wife. *17:32*

38 Two men went up into the temple to pray; the one a Pharisee, and the other a publican. *18:10*

39 God, I thank thee, that I am not as other men are. *18:11*

40 God be merciful to me a sinner. *18:13*

41 Out of thine own mouth will I judge thee. *19:22*

42 If these should hold their peace, the stones would immediately cry out.[3] *19:40*

43 He is not a God of the dead, but of the living. *20:38*

[3] See *Habakkuk 2:11*, 33:26.

1 In your patience possess ye your souls. *Luke 21:19*

2 The Son of man coming in a cloud with power and great glory. *21:27*

3 This do in remembrance of me.[1] *22:19*

4 Not my will, but thine, be done. *22:42*

5 For if they do these things in a green tree, what shall be done in the dry? *23:31*

6 The place, which is called Calvary. *23:33*

7 Father, forgive them; for they know not what they do. *23:34*

8 Lord, remember me when thou comest into thy kingdom. *23:42*

9 To day shalt thou be with me in paradise. *23:43*

10 Father, into thy hands I commend my spirit. *23:46*

11 He gave up the ghost. *Ib.*

12 He was a good man, and a just. *23:50*

13 Why seek ye the living among the dead? *24:5*

14 Their words seemed to them as idle tales. *24:11*

15 Did not our heart burn within us, while he talked with us? *24:32*

16 The Lord is risen indeed.[2] *24:34*

17 In the beginning was the Word, and the Word was with God, and the Word was God. *The Gospel According to St. John 1:1*

18 And the light shineth in darkness; and the darkness comprehended it not. *1:5*

19 There was a man sent from God, whose name was John. *1:6*

20 The true Light, which lighteth every man that cometh into the world. *1:9*

21 The Word was made flesh, and dwelt among us . . . full of grace and truth. *1:14*

22 No man hath seen God at any time. *1:18*

23 Behold the Lamb of God, which taketh away the sin of the world.[3] *1:29*

[1]See *I Corinthians 11:24*, 48:20.
[2]See *Mark 16:6*, 42:15, and *The Book of Common Prayer*, 54:10.
[3]Spoken by John the Baptist.
See *The Missal*, 54:5.

24 Can there any good thing come out of Nazareth? *John 1:46*

25 Hereafter ye shall see heaven open, and the angels of God ascending and descending upon the Son of man. *1:51*

26 Woman, what have I to do with thee? mine hour is not yet come. *2:4*

27 The water that was made wine. *2:9*

28 This beginning of miracles did Jesus in Cana of Galilee,[4] and manifested forth his glory; and his disciples believed on him. *2:11*

29 When he had made a scourge of small cords, he drove them all out of the temple. *2:15*

30 Make not my Father's house an house of merchandise. *2:16*

31 Except a man be born again, he cannot see the kingdom of God. *3:3*

32 The wind bloweth where it listeth, and thou hearest the sound thereof, but canst not tell whence it cometh, and whither it goeth: so is every one that is born of the Spirit. *3:8*

33 How can these things be? *3:9*

34 God so loved the world, that he gave his only begotten Son, that whosoever believeth in him should not perish, but have everlasting life. *3:16*

35 There cometh a woman of Samaria to draw water: Jesus saith unto her, Give me to drink. *4:7*

36 The hour cometh, and now is, when the true worshippers shall worship the Father in spirit and in truth. *4:23*

37 He was a burning and a shining light. *5:35*

38 Search the scriptures. *5:39*

39 What are they among so many? *6:9*

40 Gather up the fragments that remain, that nothing be lost. *6:12*

41 I am the bread of life:[5] he that cometh to me shall never hunger; and he that believeth on me shall never thirst. *6:35*

42 It is the spirit that quickeneth; the flesh profiteth nothing. *6:63*

43 Judge not according to the appearance. *7:24*

[4]There was a marriage in Cana of Galilee.—*John 2:1*
[5]See *Psalm 105:40*, 21:12.

1 Never man spake like this man.
John 7:46

2 He that is without sin among you, let him first cast a stone at her. *8:7*

3 Neither do I condemn thee: go, and sin no more. *8:11*

4 I am the light of the world: he that followeth me shall not walk in darkness, but shall have the light of life. *8:12*

5 The truth shall make you free. *8:32*

6 Ye are of your father the devil . . . there is no truth in him. . . . he is a liar, and the father of it. *8:44*

7 I must work the works of him that sent me, while it is day: the night cometh, when no man can work. *9:4*

8 Whether he be a sinner or no, I know not: one thing I know, that, whereas I was blind, now I see. *9:25*

9 I am the door. *10:9*

10 I am come that they might have life, and that they might have it more abundantly. *10:10*

11 I am the good shepherd: the good shepherd giveth his life for the sheep. *10:11*

12 Other sheep I have, which are not of this fold. *10:16*

13 I am the resurrection, and the life: he that believeth in me, though he were dead, yet shall he live:

And whosoever liveth and believeth in me shall never die.[1] *11:25–26*

14 Jesus wept. *11:35*

15 It is expedient for us, that one man should die for the people. *11:50*

16 Then saith one of his disciples, Judas Iscariot, Simon's son, which should betray him,

Why was not this ointment sold for three hundred pence, and given to the poor.[2] *12:4–5*

17 Yet a little while is the light with you. Walk while ye have the light, lest darkness come upon you. *12:35*

18 That thou doest, do quickly. *13:27*

19 A new commandment I give unto you, That ye love one another. *13:34*

20 Let not your heart be troubled: ye believe in God, believe also in me.

In my Father's house are many mansions: if it were not so, I would have told you. I go to prepare a place for you.
John 14:1–2

21 I will come again, and receive you unto myself; that where I am, there ye may be also. *14:3*

22 I am the way, the truth, and the life. *14:6*

23 I will not leave you comfortless. *14:18*

24 Peace I leave with you, my peace I give unto you: not as the world giveth, give I unto you. Let not your heart be troubled, neither let it be afraid. *14:27*

25 Greater love hath no man than this, that a man lay down his life for his friends. *15:13*

26 Ye have not chosen me, but I have chosen you. *15:16*

27 Whither goest thou?[3] *16:5*

28 Ask, and ye shall receive, that your joy may be full. *16:24*

29 Be of good cheer; I have overcome the world. *16:33*

30 Pilate saith unto him, What is truth? *18:38*

31 Now Barabbas was a robber. *18:40*

32 Behold the man![4] *19:5*

33 Woman, behold thy son! *19:26*

34 It is finished. *19:30*

35 Touch me not.[5] *20:17*

36 Then saith he to Thomas . . . be not faithless, but believing. *20:27*

37 Blessed are they that have not seen, and yet have believed. *20:29*

38 Suddenly there came a sound from heaven as of a rushing mighty wind.
The Acts of the Apostles 2:2

39 There appeared unto them cloven tongues like as of fire, and it sat upon each of them.

And they were all filled with the Holy Ghost, and began to speak with other tongues. *2:3–4*

40 Silver and gold have I none; but such as I have give I thee. *3:6*

41 And distribution was made unto every man according as he had need. *4:35*

[1] Also in *Book of Common Prayer, Burial of the Dead.*
[2] See *Matthew 26:7* and *26:8*, 41:2 and 41:3.

[3] Quo vadis? — *The Vulgate*
[4] Ecce homo. — *The Vulgate*
[5] Noli me tangere. — *The Vulgate*

1 If this counsel or this work be of men, it will come to nought:
But if it be of God, ye cannot overthrow it.
Acts 5:38–39

2 Thy money perish with thee. *8:20*

3 In the gall of bitterness, and in the bond of iniquity. *8:23*

4 Saul, yet breathing out threatenings and slaughter against the disciples of the Lord.
9:1

5 Saul, Saul, why persecutest thou me?
9:4

6 It is hard for thee to kick against the pricks.[1] *9:5*

7 He is a chosen vessel unto me. *9:15*

8 Immediately there fell from his eyes as it had been scales. *9:18*

9 What God hath cleansed, that call not thou common. *10:15*

10 God is no respecter of persons.[2]
10:34

11 The gods are come down to us in the likeness of men. *14:11*

12 We also are men of like passions with you.
14:15

13 Come over into Macedonia, and help us.
16:9

14 Certain lewd fellows of the baser sort.
17:5

15 Ye men of Athens, I perceive that in all things ye are too superstitious.
For as I passed by, and beheld your devotions, I found an altar with this inscription, TO THE UNKNOWN GOD. *17:22–23*

16 God that made the world, and all things therein, seeing that he is Lord of heaven and earth, dwelleth not in temples made with hands;
Neither is worshipped with men's hands, as though he needed any thing, seeing he giveth to all life, and breath, and all things;
And hath made of one blood all nations of men for to dwell on all the face of the earth.
17:24–26

17 For in him we live, and move, and have our being; as certain also of your own poets have said, For we are also his offspring.[3]
17:28

[1] See Aeschylus, 71:12.
[2] For there is no respect of persons with God. — *Romans 2:11*
[3] See Aeschylus, 71:11; Cleanthes, 92:1; and Aratus, 92:11.

18 Your blood be upon your own heads.
Acts 18:6

19 And Gallio cared for none of those things.
18:17

20 Mighty in the Scriptures. *18:24*

21 We have not so much as heard whether there be any Holy Ghost. *19:2*

22 All with one voice about the space of two hours cried out, Great is Diana of the Ephesians. *19:34*

23 It is more blessed to give than to receive.
20:35

24 I [Paul] am . . . a Jew of Tarsus, a city in Cilicia, a citizen of no mean city.
21:39

25 Brought up in this city at the feet of Gamaliel. *22:3*

26 And the chief captain answered, With a great sum obtained I this freedom. And Paul said, But I was free born. *22:28*

27 God shall smite thee, thou whited wall.
23:3

28 Revilest thou God's high priest?
23:4

29 I [Paul] am a Pharisee, the son of a Pharisee. *23:6*

30 A conscience void of offense toward God, and toward men. *24:16*

31 When I have a convenient season, I will call for thee. *24:25*

32 I appeal unto Caesar. *25:11*

33 Paul, thou art beside thyself; much learning doth make thee mad. *26:24*

34 I am not mad . . . but speak forth the words of truth and soberness. *26:25*

35 For this thing was not done in a corner.
26:26

36 Almost thou persuadest me to be a Christian. *26:28*

37 Wherein thou judgest another, thou condemnest thyself.
The Epistle of Paul the Apostle to the Romans 2:1

38 These, having not the law, are a law unto themselves. *2:14*

39 The things that are more excellent.
2:18

40 Where no law is, there is no transgression.
4:15

1 Who against hope believed in hope. *Romans 4:18*

2 Where sin abounded, grace did much more abound. *5:20*

3 Death hath no more dominion over him. *6:9*

4 I speak after the manner of men. *6:19*

5 The wages of sin is death; but the gift of God is eternal life. *6:23*

6 The good that I would I do not: but the evil which I would not, that I do.[1] *7:19*

7 Who shall deliver me from the body of this death? *7:24*

8 Heirs of God, and joint-heirs with Christ. *8:17*

9 For we know that the whole creation groaneth and travaileth in pain together until now. *8:22*

10 All things work together for good to them that love God. *8:28*

11 For whom he did foreknow, he also did predestinate to be conformed to the image of his Son, that he might be the firstborn among many brethren.

Moreover whom he did predestinate, them he also called: and whom he called, them he also justified: and whom he justified, them he also glorified. *8:29–30*

12 If God be for us, who can be against us? *8:31*

13 Who shall lay any thing to the charge of God's elect? It is God that justifieth. *8:33*

14 Who shall separate us from the love of Christ? *8:35*

15 Neither death, nor life, nor angels, nor principalities, nor powers, nor things present, nor things to come,

Nor height, nor depth, nor any other creature, shall be able to separate us from the love of God, which is in Christ Jesus our Lord. *8:38–39*

16 Hath not the potter power over the clay, of the same lump to make one vessel unto honor, and another unto dishonor? *9:21*

17 For who hath known the mind of the Lord? *11:34*

[1] See Euripides, 76:19, and Ovid, 113:21.

18 I beseech you therefore, brethren . . . that ye present your bodies a living sacrifice, holy, acceptable unto God, which is your reasonable service.[2] *Romans 12:1*

19 Let love be without dissimulation. *12:9*

20 Be kindly affectioned one to another with brotherly love. *12:10*

21 Given to hospitality. *12:13*

22 Be not wise in your own conceits.

Recompense to no man evil for evil. *12:16–17*

23 If it be possible, as much as lieth in you, live peaceably with all men. *12:18*

24 Vengeance is mine; I will repay, saith the Lord. *12:19*

25 Be not overcome of evil, but overcome evil with good. *12:21*

26 The powers that be are ordained of God. *13:1*

27 Render therefore to all their dues: tribute to whom tribute is due; custom to whom custom; fear to whom fear; honor to whom honor.

Owe no man anything, but to love one another. *13:7–8*

28 Love is the fulfilling of the law. *13:10*

29 The night is far spent, the day is at hand: let us therefore cast off the works of darkness, and let us put on the armor of light.

Let us walk honestly, as in the day; not in rioting and drunkenness, not in chambering and wantonness, not in strife and envying.

But put ye on the Lord Jesus Christ, and make not provision for the flesh, to fulfil the lusts thereof.[3] *13:12–14*

30 Doubtful disputations. *14:1*

31 Let every man be fully persuaded in his own mind. *14:5*

32 For none of us liveth to himself, and no man dieth to himself.

For whether we live, we live unto the Lord; and whether we die, we die unto the Lord: whether we live therefore, or die, we are the Lord's. *14:7–8*

33 Let us therefore follow after the things which make for peace. *14:19*

34 We then that are strong ought to bear the infirmities of the weak, and not to please ourselves. *15:1*

[2] See *Book of Common Prayer*, 55:19.
[3] See St. Augustine, 129:4, and note.

1 God hath chosen the foolish things of the world to confound the wise; and God hath chosen the weak things of the world to confound the things which are mighty.
The First Epistle of Paul the Apostle to the Corinthians 1:27

2 As it is written,[1] Eye hath not seen, nor ear heard. *2:9*

3 I have planted, Apollos watered; but God gave the increase. *3:6*

4 We are laborers together with God: ye are God's husbandry. *3:9*

5 Every man's work shall be made manifest: for the day shall declare it, because it shall be revealed by fire; and the fire shall try every man's work of what sort it is. *3:13*

6 For the temple of God is holy, which temple ye are. *3:17*

7 We are made a spectacle unto the world, and to angels, and to men. *4:9*

8 Absent in body, but present in spirit. *5:3*

9 A little leaven leaveneth the whole lump. *5:6*

10 For even Christ our Passover is sacrificed for us. *5:7*

11 It is better to marry than to burn. *7:9*

12 The fashion of this world passeth away. *7:31*

13 Knowledge puffeth up, but charity edifieth. *8:1*

14 I am made all things to all men. *9:22*

15 Know ye not that they which run in a race run all, but one receiveth the prize? *9:24*

16 Let him that thinketh he standeth take heed lest he fall. *10:12*

17 All things are lawful for me, but all things are not expedient. *10:23*

18 The earth is the Lord's, and the fullness thereof.[2] *10:26*

19 If a woman have long hair, it is a glory to her. *11:15*

20 Take, eat: this is my body, which is broken for you: this do in remembrance of me.[3] *11:24*

[1] Men have not heard, nor perceived by the ear, neither hath the eye seen.—*Isaiah 64:4*

[2] See *Psalm 24:1*, 18:8.

[3] See *Matthew 26:26*, 41:10, and *Luke 22:19*, 44:3.

21 This cup is the new testament in my blood: this do ye, as oft as ye drink it, in remembrance of me.[4] *I Corinthians 11:25*

22 Though I speak with the tongues of men and of angels, and have not charity,[5] I am become as sounding brass, or a tinkling cymbal. *13:1*

23 Though I have all faith, so that I could remove mountains, and have not charity, I am nothing.

And though I bestow all my goods to feed the poor, and though I give my body to be burned, and have not charity, it profiteth me nothing.

Charity suffereth long, and is kind; charity envieth not; charity vaunteth not itself, is not puffed up. *13:2–4*

24 Beareth all things, believeth all things, hopeth all things, endureth all things.

Charity never faileth. *13:7–8*

25 We know in part, and we prophesy in part.

But when that which is perfect is come, then that which is in part shall be done away.

When I was a child, I spake as a child, I understood as a child, I thought as a child: but when I became a man, I put away childish things.[6]

For now we see through a glass, darkly; but then face to face:[7] now I know in part; but then shall I know even as also I am known.

And now abideth faith, hope, charity, these three; but the greatest of these is charity. *13:9–13*

26 If the trumpet give an uncertain sound, who shall prepare himself to the battle? *14:8*

27 Let all things be done decently and in order. *14:40*

28 And last of all he was seen of me also, as of one born out of due time.

For I am the least of the apostles, that am not meet to be called an apostle, because I persecuted the church of God.

But by the grace of God I am what I am. *15:8–10*

29 But now is Christ risen from the dead, and become the firstfruits of them that slept.

For since by man came death, by man came also the resurrection of the dead.

For as in Adam all die, even so in Christ shall all be made alive. *15:20–22*

[4] See *Matthew 26:27–29*, 41:10.

[5] In the Revised Standard Version *charity* throughout this chapter is translated as *love*—the love of mankind in the sense of the Greek *agapé* and the Latin *caritas*.

[6] See Homer, 59:17.

[7] See *Genesis 32:30*, 8:26.

1 The last enemy that shall be destroyed is death. *I Corinthians 15:26*

2 Evil communications corrupt good manners. *15:33*

3 Thou fool, that which thou sowest is not quickened, except it die. *15:36*

4 One star differeth from another star in glory. *15:41*

5 It is sown in corruption; it is raised in incorruption. *15:42*

6 The first man is of the earth, earthy. *15:47*

7 Behold, I show you a mystery; We shall not all sleep, but we shall all be changed,

In a moment, in the twinkling of an eye, at the last trump: for the trumpet shall sound, and the dead shall be raised incorruptible, and we shall be changed.

For this corruptible must put on incorruption, and this mortal must put on immortality. *15:51–53*

8 Death is swallowed up in victory.[1]

O death, where is thy sting? O grave, where is thy victory? *15:54–55*

9 Watch ye, stand fast in the faith, quit you like men, be strong.[2] *16:13*

10 If any man love not the Lord Jesus Christ, let him be Anathema Maranatha. *16:22*

11 Not of the letter, but of the spirit: for the letter killeth, but the spirit giveth life. *The Second Epistle of Paul the Apostle to the Corinthians 3:6*

12 Seeing then that we have such hope, we use great plainness of speech. *3:12*

13 The things which are seen are temporal; but the things which are not seen are eternal. *4:18*

14 We walk by faith, not by sight. *5:7*

15 Now is the accepted time. *6:2*

16 By honor and dishonor, by evil report and good report. *6:8*

17 As having nothing, and yet possessing all things.[3] *6:10*

18 God loveth a cheerful giver. *9:7*

19 Though I be rude in speech. *11:6*

20 For ye suffer fools gladly, seeing ye yourselves are wise. *11:19*

[1] See *Isaiah 25:8*, 30:8, and *Hosea 13:14*, 33:16.
[2] See *I Samuel 4:9*, 12:31.
[3] See Terence, 96:16, and Wotton, 250:16.

21 Forty stripes save one. *II Corinthians 11:24*

22 A thorn in the flesh.[4] *12:7*

23 My strength is made perfect in weakness. *12:9*

24 The grace of the Lord Jesus Christ, and the love of God, and the communion of the Holy Ghost, be with you all.[5] *13:14*

25 The right hands of fellowship. *The Epistle of Paul the Apostle to the Galatians 2:9*

26 Weak and beggarly elements. *4:9*

27 It is good to be zealously affected always in a good thing. *4:18*

28 Ye are fallen from grace. *5:4*

29 For the flesh lusteth against the Spirit, and the Spirit against the flesh: and these are contrary the one to the other: so that ye cannot do the things that ye would. *5:17*

30 The fruit of the Spirit is love, joy, peace, longsuffering, gentleness, goodness, faith,

Meekness, temperance. *5:22–23*

31 Every man shall bear his own burden. *6:5*

32 Be not deceived; God is not mocked: for whatsoever a man soweth, that shall he also reap. *6:7*

33 Let us not be weary in well doing. *6:9*

34 To be strengthened with might by his Spirit in the inner man. *The Epistle of Paul the Apostle to the Ephesians 3:16*

35 Carried about with every wind of doctrine. *4:14*

36 We are members one of another.

Be ye angry, and sin not: let not the sun go down upon your wrath. *4:25–26*

37 Speaking to yourselves in psalms and hymns and spiritual songs, singing and making melody in your heart to the Lord.[6] *5:19*

38 Put on the whole armor of God. *6:11*

39 For we wrestle not against flesh and blood, but against principalities, against powers, against the rulers of the darkness of this world, against spiritual wickedness in high places.

[4] See *Judges 2:3*, 12:1.
[5] Also in *Book of Common Prayer, Morning Prayer* (end).
[6] See *Psalm 95:1–2*, 20:20, and *Book of Common Prayer, Morning Prayer (Venite)*, 54:16.

Wherefore take unto you the whole armor of God, that ye may be able to withstand in the evil day, and having done all, to stand.
Ephesians 6:12–13

1 To live is Christ, and to die is gain.
The Epistle of Paul the Apostle to the Philippians 1:21

2 Work out your own salvation with fear and trembling. *2:12*

3 For it is God which worketh in you both to will and to do of his good pleasure. *2:13*

4 This one thing I do, forgetting those things which are behind, and reaching forth unto those things which are before,
I press toward the mark. *3:13–14*

5 Whose end is destruction, whose God is their belly, and whose glory is in their shame, who mind earthly things. *3:19*

6 The peace of God, which passeth all understanding, shall keep your hearts and minds through Christ Jesus.[1] *4:7*

7 Whatsoever things are true, whatsoever things are honest, whatsoever things are just, whatsoever things are pure, whatsoever things are lovely, whatsoever things are of good report; if there be any virtue, and if there be any praise, think on these things. *4:8*

8 I have learned, in whatsoever state I am, therewith to be content. *4:11*

9 By him were all things created, that are in heaven, and that are in earth, visible and invisible . . . all things were created by him, and for him:
And he is before all things, and by him all things consist.
The Epistle of Paul the Apostle to the Colossians 1:16–17

10 Touch not; taste not; handle not. *2:21*

11 Set your affection on things above, not on things on the earth. *3:2*

12 Where there is neither Greek nor Jew, circumcision nor uncircumcision, Barbarian, Scythian, bond nor free: but Christ is all, and in all. *3:11*

13 Fathers, provoke not your children to anger, lest they be discouraged. *3:21*

[1]Also in *Book of Common Prayer, Holy Communion (Blessing).*

14 Let your speech be alway with grace, seasoned with salt. *Colossians 4:6*

15 Luke, the beloved physician. *4:14*

16 Labor of love.
The First Epistle of Paul the Apostle to the Thessalonians 1:3

17 Study to be quiet, and to do your own business. *4:11*

18 The day of the Lord so cometh as a thief in the night. *5:2*

19 Ye are all the children of light, and the children of the day: we are not of the night, nor of darkness. *5:5*

20 Putting on the breastplate of faith and love; and for an helmet, the hope of salvation. *5:8*

21 Pray without ceasing. *5:17*

22 Prove all things; hold fast that which is good. *5:21*

23 The law is good, if a man use it lawfully.
The First Epistle of Paul the Apostle to Timothy 1:8

24 Christ Jesus came into the world to save sinners; of whom I am chief. *1:15*

25 For if a man know not how to rule his own house, how shall he take care of the church of God?[2] *3:5*

26 Not greedy of filthy lucre. *3:8*

27 Speaking lies in hypocrisy; having their conscience seared with a hot iron. *4:2*

28 Every creature of God is good, and nothing to be refused, if it be received with thanksgiving. *4:4*

29 Refuse profane and old wives' fables. *4:7*

30 Let them learn first to show piety at home. *5:4*

31 But if any provide not for his own, and specially for those of his own house, he hath denied the faith, and is worse than an infidel. *5:8*

32 They learn to be idle, wandering about from house to house; and not only idle, but tattlers also and busybodies, speaking things which they ought not. *5:13*

33 Drink no longer water, but use a little wine for thy stomach's sake. *5:23*

[2]See Sophocles, 74:19.

1 We brought nothing into this world, and it is certain we can carry nothing out.[1]
I Timothy 6:7

2 The love of money is the root of all evil.[2]
6:10

3 Fight the good fight of faith, lay hold on eternal life. *6:12*

4 Rich in good works. *6:18*

5 O Timothy, keep that which is committed to thy trust, avoiding profane and vain babblings, and oppositions of science falsely so called. *6:20*

6 For God hath not given us the spirit of fear; but of power, and of love, and of a sound mind.
The Second Epistle of Paul the Apostle to Timothy 1:7

7 A workman that needeth not to be ashamed. *2:15*

8 Be instant in season, out of season.
4:2

9 I have fought a good fight, I have finished my course, I have kept the faith. *4:7*

10 The Lord reward him according to his works. *4:14*

11 Unto the pure all things are pure.
The Epistle of Paul to Titus 1:15

12 Making mention of thee always in my prayers.
The Epistle of Paul to Philemon 1:4

13 Who maketh his angels spirits, and his ministers a flame of fire.
The Epistle of Paul the Apostle to the Hebrews 1:7

14 The word of God is quick, and powerful, and sharper than any two-edged sword, piercing even to the dividing asunder of soul and spirit, and of the joints and marrow, and is a discerner of the thoughts and intents of the heart. *4:12*

15 Strong meat belongeth to them that are of full age. *5:14*

16 They crucify to themselves the Son of God afresh, and put him to an open shame.
6:6

17 Without shedding of blood is no remission.
9:22

[1] Also in *Book of Common Prayer, Burial of the Dead.* See also *The Song of the Harper,* 3:2, and *Ecclesiastes* 5:15, 27:2.

[2] See Sophocles, 74:12, and Plato, 84:12.

Radix malorum est cupiditas.—CHAUCER, *The Canterbury Tales* [c. 1387], *The Pardoner's Prologue, l. 6*

18 Faith is the substance of things hoped for, the evidence of things not seen.
Hebrews 11:1

19 Wherefore seeing we also are compassed about with so great a cloud of witnesses . . . let us run with patience the race that is set before us,
Looking unto Jesus the author and finisher of our faith. *12:1–2*

20 Whom the Lord loveth he chasteneth.
12:6

21 The spirits of just men made perfect.
12:23

22 Let brotherly love continue.
Be not forgetful to entertain strangers: for thereby some have entertained angels unawares. *13:1–2*

23 The Lord is my helper, and I will not fear what man shall do unto me. *13:6*

24 Jesus Christ the same yesterday, and to day, and for ever. *13:8*

25 For here have we no continuing city, but we seek one to come. *13:14*

26 To do good and to communicate forget not: for with such sacrifices God is well pleased.
13:16

27 Let patience have her perfect work, that ye may be perfect and entire, wanting nothing.
If any of you lack wisdom, let him ask of God.
The General Epistle of James 1:4–5

28 Blessed is the man that endureth temptation: for when he is tried, he shall receive the crown of life. *1:12*

29 Every good gift and every perfect gift is from above, and cometh down from the Father of lights, with whom is no variableness, neither shadow of turning. *1:17*

30 Be swift to hear, slow to speak, slow to wrath:
For the wrath of man worketh not the righteousness of God. *1:19–20*

31 Be ye doers of the word, and not hearers only.[3] *1:22*

32 Unspotted from the world. *1:27*

33 As the body without the spirit is dead, so faith without works is dead also. *2:26*

34 How great a matter a little fire kindleth!
3:5

35 The tongue can no man tame; it is an unruly evil. *3:8*

[3] See Homer, 58:10.

1 This wisdom descendeth not from above, but is earthly, sensual, devilish.
James 3:15

2 Resist the devil, and he will flee from you.
4:7

3 What is your life? It is even a vapor, that appeareth for a little time, and then vanisheth away. *4:14*

4 Be patient therefore, brethren, unto the coming of the Lord. Behold, the husbandman waiteth for the precious fruit of the earth, and hath long patience for it, until he receive the early and latter rain. *5:7*

5 Ye have heard of the patience of Job.
5:11

6 The effectual fervent prayer of a righteous man availeth much. *5:16*

7 Hope to the end.
The First Epistle General of Peter 1:13

8 The Father, who without respect of persons judgeth according to every man's work.
1:17

9 All flesh is as grass, and all the glory of man as the flower of grass. The grass withereth, and the flower thereof falleth away:
But the word of the Lord endureth for ever.[1] *1:24–25*

10 Abstain from fleshly lusts, which war against the soul. *2:11*

11 Honor all men. Love the brotherhood. Fear God. Honor the king. *2:17*

12 Ornament of a meek and quiet spirit.
3:4

13 Giving honor unto the wife, as unto the weaker vessel. *3:7*

14 Charity shall cover the multitude of sins.
4:8

15 A crown of glory that fadeth not away.
5:4

16 Be sober, be vigilant; because your adversary the devil, as a roaring lion, walketh about, seeking whom he may devour.
5:8

17 And the day star arise in your hearts.
The Second Epistle General of Peter 1:19

18 The dog is turned to his own vomit again.
2:22

[1]See *Psalm 90:5–6,* 20:11, and *Isaiah 40:6* and *40:8,* 30:32 and 30:33.

19 God is light, and in him is no darkness at all.
The First Epistle General of John 1:5

20 If we say that we have no sin, we deceive ourselves, and the truth is not in us.
1:8

21 If any man sin, we have an advocate with the Father, Jesus Christ the righteous:
And he is the propitiation for our sins:[2] and not for ours only, but also for the sins of the whole world. *2:1–2*

22 He is antichrist, that denieth the Father and the Son. *2:22*

23 Whoso hath this world's good, and seeth his brother have need, and shutteth up his bowels of compassion from him, how dwelleth the love of God in him? *3:17*

24 He that loveth not, knoweth not God; for God is love. *4:8*

25 There is no fear in love; but perfect love casteth out fear. *4:18*

26 Raging waves of the sea, foaming out their own shame; wandering stars, to whom is reserved the blackness of darkness for ever.
The General Epistle of Jude 13

27 I John, who also am your brother, and companion in tribulation, and in the kingdom and patience of Jesus Christ, was in the isle that is called Patmos, for the word of God, and for the testimony of Jesus Christ.
The Revelation of St. John the Divine 1:9

28 What thou seest, write in a book, and send it unto the seven churches which are in Asia.
1:11

29 And being turned, I saw seven golden candlesticks. *1:12*

30 His feet like unto fine brass, as if they burned in a furnace; and his voice as the sound of many waters. *1:15*

31 When I saw him, I fell at his feet as dead.
1:17

32 I am he that liveth, and was dead; and, behold, I am alive for evermore, Amen; and have the keys of hell and of death.
1:18

33 I have somewhat against thee, because thou hast left thy first love. *2:4*

34 To him that overcometh will I give to eat of the tree of life. *2:7*

[2]Quoted in *The Book of Common Prayer, Holy Communion, p. 76.*

1 Be thou faithful unto death, and I will give thee a crown of life. *Revelation 2:10*

2 He shall rule them with a rod of iron. *2:27*

3 I will give him the morning star. *2:28*

4 I will not blot out his name out of the book of life. *3:5*

5 I know thy works, that thou art neither cold nor hot: I would thou wert cold or hot.
So then because thou art lukewarm, and neither cold nor hot, I will spew thee out of my mouth. *3:15–16*

6 Behold, I stand at the door, and knock. *3:20*

7 The first beast was like a lion, and the second beast like a calf, and the third beast had a face as a man, and the fourth beast was like a flying eagle.
And the four beasts had each of them six wings about him; and they were full of eyes within: and they rest not day and night, saying, Holy, holy, holy, Lord God Almighty, which was, and is, and is to come. *4:7–8*

8 Thou hast created all things, and for thy pleasure they are and were created. *4:11*

9 A book . . . sealed with seven seals. *5:1*

10 He went forth conquering, and to conquer. *6:2*

11 Behold a pale horse: and his name that sat on him was Death, and Hell followed with him. *6:8*

12 Four angels standing on the four corners of the earth, holding the four winds of the earth. *7:1*

13 Hurt not the earth, neither the sea, nor the trees. *7:3*

14 All nations, and kindreds, and people, and tongues. *7:9*

15 These are they which came out of great tribulation, and have washed their robes, and made them white in the blood of the lamb. *7:14*

16 They shall hunger no more, neither thirst any more; neither shall the sun light on them, nor any heat. *7:16*

17 The name of the star is called Wormwood. *8:11*

18 The kingdoms of this world are become the kingdoms of our Lord and of his Christ. *Revelation 11:15*

19 There was war in heaven: Michael and his angels fought against the dragon; and the dragon fought and his angels,
And prevailed not. *12:7–8*

20 The great dragon was cast out, that old serpent, called the Devil, and Satan, which deceiveth the whole world. *12:9*

21 No man might buy or sell, save he that had the mark, or the name of the beast. *13:17*

22 The voice of many waters.[1] *14:2*

23 Babylon is fallen, is fallen, that great city.[2] *14:8*

24 Blessed are the dead which die in the Lord . . . that they may rest from their labours.[3] *14:13*

25 And he gathered them together into a place called in the Hebrew tongue Armageddon. *16:16*

26 He is Lord of lords, and King of kings. *17:14*

27 He treadeth the winepress of the fierceness and wrath of Almighty God. *19:15*

28 Another book was opened, which is the book of life. *20:12*

29 I saw a new heaven and a new earth:[4] for the first heaven and the first earth were passed away; and there was no more sea.
And I John saw the holy city, new Jerusalem, coming down from God out of heaven, prepared as a bride adorned for her husband. *21:1–2*

30 God shall wipe away all tears[5] from their eyes; and there shall be no more death, neither sorrow, nor crying, neither shall there be any more pain: for the former things are passed away. *21:4*

31 There shall be no night there. *22:5*

32 He that is unjust, let him be unjust still: and he which is filthy, let him be filthy still: and he that is righteous, let him be righteous still: and he that is holy, let him be holy still.
And, behold, I come quickly. *22:11–12*

33 I am Alpha and Omega, the beginning and the end, the first and the last. *22:13*

[1] See *Psalm 93:4*, 20:19.
[2] See *Isaiah 21:9*, 29:27.
[3] Also in *Book of Common Prayer, Burial of the Dead.*
[4] See *Isaiah 65:17*, 31:30.
[5] See *Isaiah 25:8*, 30:8.

The Missal

1 Dominus vobiscum [The Lord be with you]. Et cum spiritu tuo [And with your spirit].
Antiphon

2 Mea culpa, mea culpa, mea maxima culpa [Through my fault, through my fault, through my most grievous fault].
Confession of Sins

3 Kyrie, eleison [Lord, have mercy on us].
Kyrie

4 Gloria in excelsis Deo. Et in terra pax hominibus bonae voluntatis [Glory to God in the highest. And on earth peace to men of good will].[1] *Gloria*

5 Domine Deus, Agnus Dei, Filius Patris: qui tollis peccata mundi, miserere nobis [O Lord God, Lamb of God, Son of the Father: who takest away the sins of the world, have mercy on us].[2] *Ib.*

6 Hoc est enim Corpus meum [For this is My Body].[3] *The Consecration*

7 Hic est enim Calix Sanguinis mei, novi et aeterni testamenti: mysterium fidei: qui pro vobis et pro multis effundetur in remissionem peccatorum [For this is the chalice of My Blood, of the new and eternal covenant; the mystery of faith; which shall be shed for you and for many unto the forgiveness of sins].[4]
Ib.

8 O felix culpa, quae talem ac tantum meruit habere Redemptorem [O happy fault, which has deserved to have such and so mighty a Redeemer].[5]
Exsultet on Holy Saturday

The Book of Common Prayer [1928][6]

9 Movable feasts.
Tables and Rules, p. xxxi

10 He is risen. The Lord is risen indeed.[7]
Morning Prayer, Easter, p. 5

11 The Scripture moveth us, in sundry places, to acknowledge and confess our manifold sins and wickedness.
Ib. Minister's Opening Words, p. 5

12 We have erred, and strayed from thy ways like lost sheep.[8]
Ib. A General Confession, p. 6

13 We have left undone those things which we ought to have done; And we have done those things which we ought not to have done.
Ib.

14 Have mercy upon us, miserable offenders.
Ib.

15 Who desireth not the death of a sinner, but rather that he may turn from his wickedness and live.
Ib. The Declaration of Absolution, p. 7

16 Let us come before his presence with thanksgiving; and show ourselves glad in him with psalms.[9] *Ib. Venite, p. 9*

17 In his hand are all the corners of the earth; and the strength of the hills is his also.
The sea is his, and he made it; and his hands prepared the dry land. *Ib.*

18 Glory be to the Father, and to the Son, and to the Holy Ghost;
As it was in the beginning, is now, and ever shall be, world without end. Amen.
Ib. Gloria Patri, p. 9

19 We praise thee, O God [Te deum laudamus]. *Ib. Te Deum, p. 10*

[1] See *Luke 2:14*, 42:29.

[2] See *John 1:29*, 44:23.

[3] See *Matthew 26:26*, 41:10, and *I Corinthians 11:24*, 48:20.

[4] See *Matthew 26:27–29*, 41:10, and *I Corinthians 11:25*, 48:21.

[5] This dates from the seventh century at the latest, and may be much older. It has been attributed to St. Augustine and St. Ambrose.

[6] THOMAS CRANMER [1489–1556] gathered the western Latin rites as used in England, notably the Sarum rite of Salisbury Cathedral, when he compiled [1549] the English Prayer Book, known as the first Prayer Book of Edward VI. A revised second Prayer Book of Edward VI [1552] was revised again [1559]; finally, the present English Book of Common Prayer was published [1662]. The American Book of Common Prayer [1789], which derives from the English Prayer Book, was revised in 1892, and last revised in 1928. It is this last revision from which the quotations in *Bartlett* are taken. The proposed Book of Common Prayer . . . will be more a new composition than a revision of the Prayer Book of Edward VI. — G. HARRIS COLLINGWOOD, D.D. [1927–1978]

The proposed book was subsequently approved by the General Convention [1979] and is now the official Book of Common Prayer of the Episcopal Church.

It is a most invaluable part of that blessed "liberty wherewith Christ hath made us free," that in his worship different forms and usages may without offense be allowed, provided the substance of the Faith be kept entire; and that, in every Church, what cannot be clearly determined to belong to Doctrine must be referred to Discipline; and therefore, by common consent and authority, may be altered, abridged, enlarged, amended, or otherwise disposed of, as may seem most convenient for the edification of the people, "according to the various exigency of times and occasions." — *Preface to the edition for the Protestant Episcopal Church in the United States of America* [1789]

See Newman, 490:10.

[7] See *Mark 16:6*, 42:15, and *Luke 24:34*, 44:16.

[8] See *Isaiah 53:6*, 31:16.

[9] See *Psalm 95:1–2*, 20:20, and *Ephesians 5:19*, 49:37.

1 The noble army of Martyrs. *Ib.*

2 I believe in God the Father Almighty, Maker of heaven and earth:

And in Jesus Christ his only Son our Lord: Who was conceived by the Holy Ghost, Born of the Virgin Mary: Suffered under Pontius Pilate, Was crucified, dead, and buried: He descended into hell; The third day he rose again from the dead: He ascended into heaven, And sitteth on the right hand of God the Father Almighty: From thence he shall come to judge the quick and the dead.

I believe in the Holy Ghost: The holy Catholic Church; The Communion of Saints: The Forgiveness of sins: The Resurrection of the body: And the Life everlasting.

Ib. Apostles' Creed, p. 15

3 Begotten of his Father before all worlds, God of God, Light of Light, Very God of very God; Begotten, not made; Being of one substance with the Father; By whom all things were made: Who for us men and for our salvation came down from heaven, And was incarnate by the Holy Ghost of the Virgin Mary, And was made man.

Ib. Nicene Creed, p. 16

4 O God, who art the author of peace and lover of concord, in knowledge of whom standeth our eternal life, whose service is perfect freedom; Defend us thy humble servants in all assaults of our enemies.

Ib. A Collect for Peace, p. 17

5 O God, the Creator and Preserver of all mankind, we humbly beseech thee for all sorts and conditions of men; that thou wouldest be pleased to make thy ways known unto them, thy saving health unto all nations.

Ib. A Prayer for All Conditions of Men, p. 18

6 We commend to thy fatherly goodness all those who are any ways afflicted, or distressed, in mind, body, or estate.

Ib. p. 19

7 We, thine unworthy servants, do give thee most humble and hearty thanks for all thy goodness and loving-kindness to us, and to all men; We bless thee for our creation, preservation, and all the blessings of this life; but above all, for thine inestimable love in the redemption of the world by our Lord Jesus Christ; for the means of grace, and for the hope of glory.

Ib. A General Thanksgiving, p. 19

8 Almighty God, who . . . dost promise that when two or three are gathered together in thy Name[1] thou wilt grant their requests; Fulfill now, O Lord, the desires and petitions of thy servants, as may be most expedient for them.

Ib. A Prayer of St. Chrysostom, p. 20

9 Lighten our darkness, we beseech thee, O Lord; and by thy great mercy defend us from all perils and dangers of this night.

Evening Prayer, A Collect for Aid against Perils, p. 31

10 From all blindness of heart, from pride, vainglory, and hypocrisy; from envy, hatred, and malice, and all uncharitableness,

Good Lord, deliver us.

The Litany, p. 54

11 From all the deceits of the world, the flesh, and the devil. *Ib.*

12 From battle and murder, and from sudden death. *Ib.*

13 Give to all nations unity, peace, and concord. *Ib. p. 56*

14 The kindly fruits of the earth.

Ib. p. 57

15 Almighty God, unto whom all hearts are open, all desires known, and from whom no secrets are hid; Cleanse the thoughts of our hearts by the inspiration of thy Holy Spirit, that we may perfectly love thee, and worthily magnify thy holy Name.

Holy Communion, The Collect, p. 67

16 Ye who do truly and earnestly repent you of your sins, and are in love and charity with your neighbors, and intend to lead a new life.

Ib. To those who come to receive the Holy Communion, p. 75

17 We acknowledge and bewail our manifold sins and wickedness, Which we, from time to time, most grievously have committed, By thought, word, and deed, Against thy Divine Majesty, Provoking most justly thy wrath and indignation against us. We do earnestly repent, And are heartily sorry for these our misdoings; The remembrance of them is grievous unto us; The burden of them is intolerable. *Ib. General Confession, p. 75*

18 Therefore with Angels and Archangels, and with all the company of heaven, we laud and magnify thy glorious Name; evermore praising thee. *Ib. Proper Preface, p. 77*

19 And here we offer and present unto thee, O Lord, our selves, our souls and bodies, to be a reasonable, holy, and living sacrifice unto thee.[2] *Ib. The Invocation, p. 81*

[1]See *Matthew 18:20*, 40:3.

[2]See *Romans 12:1*, 47:18.

1 The Peace of God, which passeth all understanding, keep your hearts and minds in the knowledge and love of God, and of his Son Jesus Christ our Lord.

Ib. Blessing, p. 84

2 Miserable sinners.

Ib. The Exhortations, p. 86

3 Read, mark, learn, and inwardly digest [the Scriptures].

The Second Sunday in Advent. The Collect, p. 92

4 Dost thou, therefore, in the name of this Child, renounce the devil and all his works, the vain pomp and glory of the world, with all covetous desires of the same, and the sinful desires of the flesh, so that thou wilt not follow, nor be led by them?

Holy Baptism. To the Godfathers and Godmothers, p. 276

5 An outward and visible sign of an inward and spiritual grace.

Offices of Instruction, Questions on the Sacraments, p. 292

6 Is not by any to be entered into unadvisedly or lightly; but reverently, discreetly, advisedly, soberly, and in the fear of God.

Solemnization of Matrimony, p. 300

7 If any man can show just cause, why they may not lawfully be joined together, let him now speak, or else hereafter for ever hold his peace. *Ib.*

8 Wilt thou . . . forsaking all others, keep thee only unto [him; her], so long as ye both shall live? *Ib. p. 301*

9 To have and to hold from this day forward, for better for worse, for richer for poorer, in sickness and in health, to love and to cherish, till death us do part. *Ib.*

10 With this Ring I thee wed.

Ib. p. 302

11 Those whom God hath joined together let no man put asunder.[1] *Ib. p. 303*

12 In the midst of life we are in death.[2]

Burial of the Dead, p. 332

13 Earth to earth, ashes to ashes, dust to dust; in sure and certain hope of the Resurrection unto eternal life. *Ib. p. 333*

14 The iron entered into his soul.

The Psalter, Psalm 105:18, p. 471

[1]See *Matthew 19:6,* 40:5.

[2]This is derived from a Latin antiphon, said to have been composed by Notker, a monk of St. Gall, in 911, while watching some workmen building a bridge at Martinsbrücke, in peril of their lives. It forms the groundwork of Luther's antiphon *De Morte.*

The Book of Common Prayer [English]

15 Give peace in our time, O Lord.

Morning Prayer, Versicles

16 Grant that the old Adam in this Child may be so buried, that the new man may be raised up in him.

Public Baptism of Infants, Blessing on the Child

17 To love, cherish, and to obey.

Solemnization of Matrimony

18 With all my worldly goods I thee endow.

Ib.

The Upanishads

800–500 B.C.[3]

19 Thou art that.[4]

Chandogya Upanishad, 6.8.7, etc.

20 Lead me from the unreal to the real!
Lead me from darkness to light!
Lead me from death to immortality![5]

Brihadaranyaka Upanishad, 1.3.28

21 Not thus, not thus.[6] *Ib. 2.3.6*

22 This Self is the honey of all beings, and all beings are the honey of this Self.

Ib. 2.5.14

23 The gods love the obscure and hate the obvious.[7] *Ib. 4.2.2*

24 Da da da[8] (that is) Be subdued, Give, Be merciful.[5] *Ib. 5.2.3*

25 If the slayer thinks he slays,
If the slain thinks he is slain,
Both these do not understand:
He slays not, is not slain.[9]

Katha Upanishad, 2.19

[3]Ancient Indian literary chronology is conjectural. The dates given are approximate.

[4]Tat tvam asi (Sanskrit). The context: That which is that subtle essence is the self of this All; it is the true; it is the Self. "Thou art that, O Svetaketu."

[5]Translated by F. MAX MÜLLER.

[6]Neti neti. The only possible description of the world soul self. The context: Not thus, not thus; for there is nothing else higher than this "not thus."

[7]Translated by R. C. ZAEHNER.

[8]The voice of the thunder. The full Sanskrit is: Da da da iti. Damyata datta dayadhvamiti.

"Datta, dayadhvam, damyata" (Give, sympathize, control). — T. S. ELIOT, *The Waste Land* [1922], *note to line 401*

See T. S. Eliot, 805:13.

[9]See Emerson, 495:11.

Bhagavad-Gitā 2.19 is almost identical.

1 Om.[1] *Passim*

2 Shanti.[2] *Passim*

Homer

c. 700 B.C.

3 Sing, goddess, the wrath of Peleus' son Achilles, a destroying wrath which brought upon the Achaeans myriad woes, and sent forth to Hades many valiant souls of heroes. *The Iliad, bk. I, l. 1*

4 And the plan of Zeus was being accomplished. *Ib. l. 5*

5 A dream, too, is from Zeus. *Ib. l. 63*

6 He knew the things that were and the things that would be and the things that had been before. *Ib. l. 70*

7 If you are very valiant, it is a god, I think, who gave you this gift. *Ib. l. 178*

8 Speaking, he addressed her winged words. *Ib. l. 201*

9 Whoever obeys the gods, to him they particularly listen. *Ib. l. 218*

10 From his tongue flowed speech sweeter than honey. *Ib. l. 249*

11 Rosy-fingered dawn appeared, the early-born.[3] *Ib. l. 477 and elsewhere*

12 The son of Kronos [Zeus] spoke, and nodded with his darkish brows, and immortal locks fell forward from the lord's deathless head, and he made great Olympus tremble. *Ib. l. 528*

13 The Olympian is a difficult foe to oppose. *Ib. l. 589*

14 Uncontrollable laughter arose among the blessed gods.[4] *Ib. l. 599*

15 A councilor ought not to sleep the whole night through, a man to whom the populace is entrusted, and who has many responsibilities. *Ib. II, l. 24*

16 Proud is the spirit of Zeus-fostered kings — their honor comes from Zeus, and Zeus, god of council, loves them. *Ib. l. 196*

17 A multitude of rulers is not a good thing. Let there be one ruler, one king. *Ib. l. 204*

[1] Om is a sacred syllable used especially to begin and end a scriptural recitation.

[2] Shanti means "peace." T. S. Eliot, in his note to line 434 of *The Waste Land,* says, " 'The Peace which passeth understanding' is our equivalent to this word."

[3] See Milton, 286:25.

[4] Also in *The Odyssey, bk. VIII, l. 326.*

18 He [Thersites] was the ugliest man who came to Ilium. *Ib. l. 216*

19 I could not tell nor name the multitude, not even if I had ten tongues, ten mouths, not if I had a voice unwearying and a heart of bronze were in me.[5] *Ib. l. 488*

20 Yet with his powers of augury he [Chromis] did not save himself from dark death. *Ib. l. 859*

21 The glorious gifts of the gods are not to be cast aside. *Ib. III, l. 65*

22 Young men's minds are always changeable, but when an old man is concerned in a matter, he looks both before and after. *Ib. l. 108*

23 Like cicadas, which sit upon a tree in the forest and pour out their piping voices, so the leaders of the Trojans were sitting on the tower. *Ib. l. 151*

24 There is no reason to blame the Trojans and the well-greaved Achaeans that for such a woman they long suffer woes. *Ib. l. 156*

25 Words like winter snowflakes. *Ib. l. 222*

26 The sun, which sees all things and hears all things. *Ib. l. 277*

27 Son of Atreus, what manner of speech has escaped the barrier of your teeth? *Ib. IV, l. 350*

28 Far away in the mountains a shepherd hears their thundering. *Ib. l. 455*

29 He lives not long who battles with the immortals, nor do his children prattle about his knees when he has come back from battle and the dread fray.[6] *Ib. V, l. 407*

30 Not at all similar are the race of the immortal gods and the race of men who walk upon the earth.[7] *Ib. l. 441*

31 Great-hearted Stentor with brazen voice, who could shout as loud as fifty other men. *Ib. l. 785*

32 He was a wealthy man, and kindly to his fellow men; for dwelling in a house by the side of the road, he used to entertain all comers.[8] *Ib. VI, l. 14*

[5] See Virgil, 105:20.

[6] See Thomas Gray, 362:1.

[7] See Xenophanes, 67:14.

[8] He held his seat; a friend to human race. / Fast by the road, his ever-open door / Obliged the wealthy and relieved the poor. — ALEXANDER POPE, *translation of The Iliad* [1714]

See Foss, 685:12.

1 A generation of men is like a generation of leaves: the wind scatters some leaves upon the ground, while others the burgeoning wood brings forth—and the season of spring comes on. So of men one generation springs forth and another ceases.[1] *Ib. l. 146*

2 Always to be bravest and to be preeminent above others. *Ib. l. 208*

3 Victory shifts from man to man. *Ib. l. 339*

4 May men say, "He is far greater than his father," when he returns from battle. *Ib. l. 479*

5 Smiling through tears. *Ib. l. 484*

6 Attach a golden chain from heaven, and all of you take hold of it, you gods and goddesses, yet would you not be able to drag Zeus the most high from heaven to earth. *Ib. VIII, l. 19*

7 Hades is relentless and unyielding. *Ib. IX, l. 158*

8 Hateful to me as the gates of Hades is that man who hides one thing in his heart and speaks another. *Ib. l. 312*

9 Even when someone battles hard, there is an equal portion for one who lingers behind, and in the same honor are held both the coward and the brave man; the idle man and he who has done much meet death alike. *Ib. l. 318*

10 To be both a speaker of words and a doer of deeds.[2] *Ib. l. 443*

11 Prayers are the daughters of mighty Zeus, lame and wrinkled and slanting-eyed. *Ib. l. 502*

12 A companion's words of persuasion are effective. *Ib. XI, l. 793*

13 It was built against the will of the immortal gods, and so it did not last for long. *Ib. XII, l. 8*

14 The single best augury is to fight for one's country. *Ib. l. 243*

15 There is a strength in the union even of very sorry men. *Ib. XIII, l. 237*

16 There is a fullness of all things, even of sleep and of love. *Ib. l. 636*

17 You will certainly not be able to take the lead in all things yourself, for to one man a god has given deeds of war, and to another the dance, to another the lyre and song, and in another wide-sounding Zeus puts a good mind. *Ib. l. 729*

18 It is not possible to fight beyond your strength, even if you strive. *Ib. l. 787*

19 She [Aphrodite] spoke and loosened from her bosom the embroidered girdle of many colors into which all her allurements were fashioned. In it was love and in it desire and in it blandishing persuasion which steals the mind even of the wise. *Ib. XIV, l. 214*

20 There she met sleep, the brother of death.[3] *Ib. l. 231 and XVI, l. 672*

21 Ocean, who is the source of all. *Ib. XIV, l. 246*

22 The hearts of the noble may be turned [by entreaty]. *Ib. XV, l. 203*

23 It is not unseemly for a man to die fighting in defense of his country.[4] *Ib. l. 496*

24 Of men who have a sense of honor, more come through alive than are slain, but from those who flee comes neither glory nor any help. *Ib. l. 563*

25 The outcome of the war is in our hands; the outcome of words is in the council. *Ib. XVI, l. 630*

26 But he, mighty man, lay mightily in the whirl of dust, forgetful of his horsemanship. *Ib. l. 775*

27 Once harm has been done, even a fool understands it. *Ib. XVII, l. 32*

28 The most preferable of evils.[5] *Ib. l. 105*

29 Surely there is nothing more wretched than a man, of all the things which breathe and move upon the earth.[6] *Ib. l. 446*

30 Sweeter it [wrath] is by far than the honeycomb dripping with sweetness, and spreads through the hearts of men. *Ib. XVIII, l. 109*

[1] See *The Teaching for Merikare,* 4:1; Pindar, 72:2; and Aristophanes, 82:9.

[2] See *James 1:22,* 51:31.

[3] Sleep, the brother of Death.—HESIOD [c. 700 B.C.], *The Theogony, l. 756*

See Virgil, 105:17; Daniel, 182:4; Shakespeare, 238:6; and Shelley, 466:6.

Sleep, Death's twin brother.—TENNYSON, *In Memoriam* [1850], *pt. LXVIII*

[4] See Horace, 107:27.

[5] See Aristotle, 87:18.

Of two evils, the least should be chosen.—CICERO [106–43 B.C.], *De Officiis, III, 1*

Of harmes two, the lesse is for to chese.—CHAUCER, *Troilus and Criseyde* [1372–1386], *bk. II, l. 470*

Of two evils the less is always to be chosen.—THOMAS À KEMPIS [1380–1471], *Imitation of Christ, bk. III, ch. 12*

[6] See Aristophanes, 82:9.

1 I too shall lie in the dust when I am dead, but now let me win noble renown.
Ib. l. 120

2 Zeus does not bring all men's plans to fulfillment. *Ib. l. 328*

3 The Erinyes, who exact punishment of men underground if one swears a false oath.
Ib. XIX, l. 259

4 Not even Achilles will bring all his words to fulfillment. *Ib. XX, l. 369*

5 Miserable mortals who, like leaves, at one moment flame with life, eating the produce of the land, and at another moment weakly perish. *Ib. XXI, l. 463*

6 It is entirely seemly for a young man killed in battle to lie mangled by the bronze spear. In his death all things appear fair. But when dogs shame the gray head and gray chin and nakedness of an old man killed, it is the most piteous thing that happens among wretched mortals. *Ib. XXII, l. 71*

7 Then the father held out the golden scales, and in them he placed two fates of dread death. *Ib. l. 209*

8 There are no compacts between lions and men, and wolves and lambs have no concord.
Ib. l. 262

9 By the ships there lies a dead man, unwept, unburied: Patroclus.[1] *Ib. l. 386*

10 Remembering this, he wept bitterly, lying now on his side, now on his back, now on his face. *Ib. XXIV, l. 9*

11 The fates have given mankind a patient soul. *Ib. l. 49*

12 Thus have the gods spun the thread for wretched mortals: that they live in grief while they themselves are without cares; for two jars stand on the floor of Zeus of the gifts which he gives, one of evils and another of blessings. *Ib. l. 525*

13 Tell me, muse, of the man of many resources[2] who wandered far and wide after he sacked the holy citadel of Troy, and he saw the cities and learned the thoughts of many men, and on the sea he suffered in his heart many woes. *The Odyssey, bk. I, l. 1*

14 By their own follies they perished, the fools. *Ib. l. 7*

15 Look now how mortals are blaming the gods, for they say that evils come from us, but in fact they themselves have woes beyond their share because of their own follies.
Ib. l. 32

16 Surely these things lie on the knees of the gods.[3] *Ib. l. 267*

17 You ought not to practice childish ways, since you are no longer that age.[4]
Ib. l. 296

18 For rarely are sons similar to their fathers: most are worse, and a few are better than their fathers. *Ib. II, l. 276*

19 Gray-eyed Athena sent them a favorable breeze, a fresh west wind, singing over the wine-dark sea. *Ib. 420*

20 A young man is embarrassed to question an older one. *Ib. III, l. 24*

21 All men have need of the gods.
Ib. l. 48

22 The minds of the everlasting gods are not changed suddenly. *Ib. l. 147*

23 A small rock holds back a great wave.
Ib. l. 296

24 No mortal could vie with Zeus, for his mansions and his possessions are deathless.
Ib. IV, l. 78

25 She [Helen] threw into the wine which they were drinking a drug which takes away grief and passion and brings forgetfulness of all ills. *Ib. l. 220*

26 The immortals will send you to the Elysian plain at the ends of the earth, where fair-haired Rhadamanthys is. There life is supremely easy for men. No snow is there, nor ever heavy winter storm, nor rain, and Ocean is ever sending gusts of the clear-blowing west wind to bring coolness to men.
Ib. l. 563

27 Olympus, where they say there is an abode of the gods, ever unchanging: it is neither shaken by winds nor ever wet with rain, nor does snow come near it, but clear weather spreads cloudless about it, and a white radiance stretches above it.[5] *Ib. VI, l. 42*

28 May the gods grant you all things which your heart desires, and may they give you a husband and a home and gracious concord,

[1] See Horace, 108:13; Chaucer, 144:17; Shakespeare, 219:24; Milton, 284:11; Scott, 430:10; and Byron, 458:26.

[2] See Pope, 334:21.

[3] Also familiar as: In the lap of the gods.

[4] See *I Corinthians 13:11*, 48:25.

[5] The majesty of the gods is revealed, and their peaceful abodes, which neither the winds shake nor clouds soak with showers, nor does the snow congealed with biting frost besmirch them with its white fall, but an ever cloudless sky vaults them over, and smiles with light bounteously spread abroad.—LUCRETIUS [95–55 B.C.], *De Rerum Natura, bk. III, l. 18*

for there is nothing greater and better than this—when a husband and wife keep a household in oneness of mind, a great woe to their enemies and joy to their friends, and win high renown. *Ib. l. 180*

1 All strangers and beggars are from Zeus, and a gift, though small, is precious.[1] *Ib. l. 207*

2 Their ships are swift as a bird or a thought. *Ib. VII, l. 36*

3 We are quick to flare up, we races of men on the earth. *Ib. l. 307*

4 So it is that the gods do not give all men gifts of grace—neither good looks nor intelligence nor eloquence. *Ib. VIII, l. 167*

5 Evil deeds do not prosper; the slow man catches up with the swift. *Ib. l. 329*

6 Even if you gods, and all the goddesses too, should be looking on, yet would I be glad to sleep with golden Aphrodite. *Ib. l. 341*

7 Among all men on the earth bards have a share of honor and reverence, because the muse has taught them songs and loves the race of bards. *Ib. l. 479*

8 Thus she spoke; and I longed to embrace my dead mother's ghost. Thrice I tried to clasp her image, and thrice it slipped through my hands, like a shadow, like a dream.[2] *Ib. XI, l. 204*

9 They strove to pile Ossa on Olympus, and on Ossa Pelion with its leafy forests, that they might scale the heavens.[3] *Ib. l. 315*

10 There is a time for many words, and there is also a time for sleep.[4] *Ib. l. 379*

11 There is nothing more dread and more shameless than a woman who plans such deeds in her heart as the foul deed which she plotted when she contrived her husband's murder. *Ib. l. 427*

12 In the extravagance of her evil she has brought shame both on herself and on all women who will come after her, even on one who is virtuous. *Ib. l. 432*

[1]See Theocritus, 92:16.
[2]See Virgil, 105:5.
[3]See Virgil, 103:29.
Then the omnipotent Father with his thunder made Olympus tremble, and from Ossa hurled Pelion.—OVID [43 B.C.–A.D. 17], *Metamorphoses, I, l. 154*
I would have you call to mind the strength of the ancient giants, that undertook to lay the high mountain Pelion on the top of Ossa, and set among those the shady Olympus.—RABELAIS, *Works, bk. IV* [1548], *ch. 38*
[4]See *Ecclesiastes 3:7*, 26:21.

13 Therefore don't you be gentle to your wife either. Don't tell her everything you know, but tell her one thing and keep another thing hidden.[5] *Ib. l. 441*

14 There is no more trusting in women. *Ib. l. 456*

15 I should rather labor as another's serf, in the home of a man without fortune, one whose livelihood was meager, than rule over all the departed dead. *Ib. l. 489*

16 Friends, we have not till now been unacquainted with misfortunes. *Ib. XII, l. 208*

17 It is tedious to tell again tales already plainly told.[6] *Ib. l. 452*

18 The wine urges me on, the bewitching wine, which sets even a wise man to singing and to laughing gently and rouses him up to dance and brings forth words which were better unspoken. *Ib. XIV, l. 463*

19 It is equally wrong to speed a guest who does not want to go, and to keep one back who is eager. You ought to make welcome the present guest, and send forth the one who wishes to go.[7] *Ib. XV, l. 72*

20 Even his griefs are a joy long after to one that remembers all that he wrought and endured.[8] *Ib. l. 400*

21 God always pairs off like with like.[9] *Ib. XVII, l. 218*

22 Bad herdsmen ruin their flocks. *Ib. l. 246*

23 Wide-sounding Zeus takes away half a man's worth on the day when slavery comes upon him. *Ib. l. 322*

24 Then dark death seized Argus, as soon as he had seen Odysseus in the twentieth year. *Ib. l. 326*

25 The gods, likening themselves to all kinds of strangers, go in various disguises from city to city, observing the wrongdoing and the righteousness of men. *Ib. l. 485*

26 Nothing feebler than a man does the earth raise up, of all the things which breathe and move on the earth, for he believes that he will never suffer evil in the future, as long as the gods give him success and he flourishes in his

[5]See Fuller, 276:16.
[6]See Shakespeare, 202:1.
[7]See Pope, 334:23 and 339:9.
[8]See Virgil, 104:22.
[9]See *Ecclesiasticus 13:16*, 35:26; Heywood, 159:10; and Robert Burton, 259:17.
Like to like.—ARISTOTLE, *Rhetoric, bk. I, ch. 2, sec. 25*

strength; but when the blessed gods bring sorrows too to pass, even these he bears, against his will, with steadfast spirit, for the thoughts of earthly men are like the day which the father of gods and men brings upon them. *Ib. XVIII, l. 130*

1 Men flourish only for a moment.[1] *Ib. XIX, l. 328*

2 Dreams surely are difficult, confusing, and not everything in them is brought to pass for mankind. For fleeting dreams have two gates: one is fashioned of horn and one of ivory. Those which pass through the one of sawn ivory are deceptive, bringing tidings which come to nought, but those which issue from the one of polished horn bring true results when a mortal sees them.[2] *Ib. l. 560*

3 Endure, my heart: you once endured something even more dreadful. *Ib. XX, l. 18*

4 Your heart is always harder than a stone. *Ib. XXIII, l. 103*

5 Therefore the fame of her excellence will never perish, and the immortals will fashion among earthly men a gracious song in honor of faithful Penelope. *Ib. XXIV, l. 196*

Hesiod

c. 700 B.C.

6 With the muses of Helicon let us begin our singing. *The Theogony, l. 1*

7 They once taught Hesiod beauteous song, when he was shepherding his sheep below holy Helicon. *Ib. l. 22*

8 We know how to speak many falsehoods which resemble real things, but we know, when we will, how to speak true things. *Ib. l. 27*

9 On his tongue they pour sweet dew, and from his mouth flow gentle words.[3] *Ib. l. 83*

10 Love, who is most beautiful among the immortal gods, the melter of limbs, overwhelms in their hearts the intelligence and wise counsel of all gods and all men. *Ib. l. 120*

11 From their eyelids as they glanced dripped love. *Ib. l. 910*

12 There was not after all a single kind of strife, but on the earth there are two kinds: one of them a man might praise when he recognized her, but the other is blameworthy. *Works and Days, l. 11*

13 Potter bears a grudge against potter, and craftsman against craftsman, and beggar is envious of beggar, and bard of bard.[4] *Ib. l. 25*

14 Fools, they do not even know how much more is the half than the whole.[5] *Ib. l. 40*

15 Often an entire city has suffered because of an evil man. *Ib. l. 240*

16 He harms himself who does harm to another, and the evil plan is most harmful to the planner. *Ib. l. 265*

17 Badness you can get easily, in quantity: the road is smooth, and it lies close by. But in front of excellence the immortal gods have put sweat, and long and steep is the way to it, and rough at first. But when you come to the top, then it is easy, even though it is hard.[6] *Ib. l. 287*

18 A bad neighbor is a misfortune, as much as a good one is a great blessing. *Ib. l. 346*

19 Do not seek evil gains; evil gains are the equivalent of disaster. *Ib. l. 352*

20 If you should put even a little on a little, and should do this often, soon this too would become big.[7] *Ib. l. 361*

21 At the beginning of a cask and at the end take your fill; in the middle be sparing. *Ib. l. 368*

22 The dawn speeds a man on his journey, and speeds him too in his work. *Ib. l. 579*

23 Observe due measure, for right timing is in all things the most important factor. *Ib. l. 694*

24 Gossip is mischievous, light and easy to raise, but grievous to bear and hard to get rid of. No gossip ever dies away entirely, if many people voice it: it too is a kind of divinity. *Ib. l. 761*

Archilochus

Early seventh century B.C.

25 I have saved myself—what care I for that shield? Away with it! I'll get another one no worse. *Fragment 6*

[1] See *Psalm 103:15*, 21:7.
[2] See Virgil, 105:26.
[3] See Coleridge, 433:27.
[4] See Gay, 331:18, and Meredith, 600:14.
[5] See Browning, 542:24.
[6] See *Matthew 7:13–14*, 38:15.
[7] See Chaucer, 148:9, and Cervantes, 170:9.

1 Old women should not seek to be perfumed.
Fragment 27

2 The fox knows many things, but the hedgehog knows one great thing.[1]
Fragment 103

Mimnermus

c. 650 – c. 590 B.C.

3 What life is there, what delight, without golden Aphrodite? *Fragment 1*

The Seven Sages[2]

c. 650 – c. 550 B.C.

4 Know thyself.
Inscription at the Delphic Oracle. From PLUTARCH, *Morals*

5 Hesiod might as well have kept his breath to cool his pottage.[3]
PERIANDER. *From* PLUTARCH, *The Banquet of the Seven Wise Men, sec. 14*

6 Every one of you hath his particular plague, and my wife is mine; and he is very happy who hath this only.
PITTACUS. *From* PLUTARCH, *Morals, On the Tranquillity of the Mind*

7 Nothing too much.[4]
From DIOGENES LAERTIUS, *Lives of Eminent Philosophers, bk. I, sec. 63*

8 Do not speak ill of the dead.[5] *Ib. 70*

9 Not even the gods fight against necessity.[6] *Ib. 77*

10 Know the right moment.[7] *Ib. 79*

11 Rule will show the man.
BIAS. *From* ARISTOTLE, *Nicomachean Ethics, bk. V, ch. 1*

[1]The fox has many tricks, and the hedgehog has only one, but that is the best of all. — ERASMUS, *Adagia* [1500]

[2]Sayings throughout antiquity were variously attributed to the figures known as the Seven Sages. The list is commonly given as Thales, Solon, Periander, Cleobulus, Chilon, Bias, Pittacus. (See Solon, below.)

[3]Spare your breath to cool your porridge. — RABELAIS, *Works, bk. V* [1552], *ch. 28*

[4]See Terence, 96:1; Horace, 106:12 and 107:20; Lucan, 118:8; Anonymous Latin, 134:12; and Voltaire, 343:23.

[5]The Latin form: De mortuis nil nisi bonum [Of the dead, nothing but good].
See Propertius, 112:23.

[6]See Euripides, 77:11.

[7]Occasionem cognosce.

Solon

c. 638 – c. 559 B.C.

12 Many evil men are rich, and good men poor, but we shall not exchange with them our excellence for riches. *Fragment 4*

13 Poets tell many lies. *Fragment 21*

14 I grow old ever learning many things.[8]
Fragment 22

15 Speech is the image of actions.
From DIOGENES LAERTIUS, *Lives of Eminent Philosophers, bk. I, sec. 58*

16 Let us sacrifice to the Muses.
From PLUTARCH, *The Banquet of the Seven Wise Men*

17 Until he is dead, do not yet call a man happy, but only lucky.[9]
From HERODOTUS,[10] *bk. I, ch. 32*

Stesichorus

c. 630 – c. 555 B.C.

18 This tale is not true: you [Helen] did not even board the well-benched ships, and you did not go to the citadel of Troy.[11]
Fragment 11

Alcaeus

c. 625 – c. 575 B.C.

19 Wine, dear boy, and truth.[12]
Fragment 66

20 Wine is a peep-hole on a man.[12]
Fragment 104

21 Let us run into a safe harbor.[13]
Fragment 120

[8]See Plato, 84:20.

[9]See *Ecclesiasticus 11:28*, 35:22; Aeschylus, 71:8; and Sophocles, 74:7.

[10]Herodotus attributed these words to Solon.

[11]Stesichorus allegedly went blind after writing an account of Helen's perfidy to Menelaus in his *Helen*, but was cured after he composed a palinode, denying that Helen ever went to Troy and blaming Homer for the story.

[12]Earliest references to what became the proverb *In vino veritas* (In wine is truth), which was known to Plato *(Symposium, 217)* and to Pliny the Elder [A.D. 23–79], *Natural History, XIV, 141*.

[13]Part of what is probably the oldest poem using the image of the ship of state.
See Sophocles, 74:9.

Anacharsis

fl. c. 600 B.C.

1 [On learning that the sides of a ship were four fingers thick] The passengers are just that distance from death.[1]

From DIOGENES LAERTIUS, *Lives of Eminent Philosophers, Anacharsis, 5*

2 [Anacharsis] laughed at him [Solon] for imagining the dishonesty and covetousness of his countrymen could be restrained by written laws, which were like spiders' webs, and would catch, it is true, the weak and poor, but easily be broken by the mighty and rich.[2]

From PLUTARCH, *Lives, Life of Solon*

3 In Greece wise men speak and fools decide.[3] *Ib.*

Sappho[4]

c. 612 B.C.

4 Deathless Aphrodite on your rich-wrought throne.[5] *Fragment 1*

5 Equal to the gods seems to me that man who sits facing you and hears you nearby sweetly speaking and softly laughing. This sets my heart to fluttering in my breast, for when I look on you a moment, then can I speak no more, but my tongue falls silent, and at once a delicate flame courses beneath my skin, and with my eyes I see nothing, and my ears hum, and a cold sweat bathes me, and a trembling seizes me all over, and I am paler than grass, and I feel that I am near to death.[6] *Fragment 2*

6 The stars about the lovely moon hide their shining forms when it lights up the earth at its fullest. *Fragment 4*

7 I loved you once long ago, Athis . . . you seemed to me a small, ungainly child. *Fragments 40–41*

8 The moon has set, and the Pleiades; it is midnight, and time passes, and I sleep alone.[7] *Fragment 94*

9 Sweet mother, I cannot ply the loom, vanquished by desire for a youth through the work of soft Aphrodite. *Fragment 114*

10 As an apple reddens on the high bough; high atop the highest bough the apple pickers passed it by—no, not passed it by, but they could not reach it. *Fragment 116*

11 Hesperus, you herd homeward whatever Dawn's light dispersed: you herd sheep—herd goats—herd children home to their mothers.[8] *Fragment 120*

Lao-tzu[9]

c. 604 – c. 531 B.C.

12 The Tao [Way] that can be told of is not the eternal Tao;
The name that can be named is not the eternal name.
The Nameless is the origin of Heaven and Earth;
The Named is the mother of all things.
Therefore let there always be non-being, so we may see their subtlety,
And let there always be being, so we may see their outcome.
The two are the same,
But after they are produced, they have different names.
They both may be called deep and profound.
Deeper and more profound,
The door of all subtleties!

The Way of Lao-tzu, 1

13 When the people of the world all know beauty as beauty,
There arises the recognition of ugliness.
When they all know the good as good,
There arises the recognition of evil.

Ib. 2

14 In the government of the sage,
He keeps their hearts vacuous,
Fills their bellies,
Weakens their ambitions,
And strengthens their bones,
He always causes his people to be without knowledge [cunning] or desire,
And the crafty to be afraid to act.

Ib. 3

[1] "How thick do you judge the planks of our ship to be?" "Some two good inches and upward," returned the pilot. "It seems, then, we are within two fingers' breadth of damnation."—RABELAIS, *Works, bk. IV* [1548], *ch. 23*

[2] See Zincgref, 267:3, and Swift, 321:15.

[3] Literally: Anacharsis said [to Solon] that in Greece wise men spoke and fools decided.

[4] Some say there are nine Muses: but they're wrong. / Look at Sappho of Lesbos; she makes ten.—PLATO, *no. 36;* translated by PETER JAY in his edition of *The Greek Anthology* [1973]

[5] Or "with your intricate charms."

[6] See Catullus, 102:5.

[7] See Housman, 692:8.

[8] Translated by MARY BARNARD [1962]. See Meleager, 97:16, and Housman, 692:2.

[9] From *The Way of Lao-tzu,* translated by WING-TSIT CHAN.

1 Heaven and Earth are not humane.
They regard all things as straw dogs.[1]
Ib. 5

2 The spirit of the valley never dies.
It is called the subtle and profound female.
The gate of the subtle and profound female
Is the root of Heaven and Earth.
It is continuous, and seems to be always existing.
Use it and you will never wear it out.
Ib. 6

3 The best [man] is like water.
Water is good; it benefits all things and does not compete with them.
It dwells in [lowly] places that all disdain.
This is why it is so near to Tao. *Ib. 8*

4 To produce things and to rear them,
To produce, but not to take possession of them,
To act, but not to rely on one's own ability,
To lead them, but not to master them—
This is called profound and secret virtue.
Ib. 10

5 He who loves the world as his body may be entrusted with the empire. *Ib. 13*

6 We look at it [Tao] and do not see it;
Its name is The Invisible.
We listen to it and do not hear it;
Its name is The Inaudible.
We touch it and do not find it;
Its name is The Subtle [formless].
Ib. 14

7 It is The Vague and Elusive.
Meet it and you will not see its head.
Follow it and you will not see its back.
Ib.

8 Manifest plainness,
Embrace simplicity,
Reduce selfishness,
Have few desires. *Ib. 19*

9 Abandon learning and there will be no sorrow. *Ib. 20*

10 To yield is to be preserved whole.
To be bent is to become straight.
To be empty is to be full.
To be worn out is to be renewed.
To have little is to possess.
To have plenty is to be perplexed.[2]
Ib. 22

11 He who knows others is wise;
He who knows himself is enlightened.
Ib. 33

[1] Straw dogs were used in sacrifices and then discarded.
[2] See the Beatitudes, *Matthew 5:3–11*, 37:4.

12 [The sage] never strives himself for the great, and thereby the great is achieved.
Ib. 34

13 Tao invariably takes no action, and yet there is nothing left undone.
Reversion is the action of Tao.
Weakness is the function of Tao.
All things in the world come from being.
And being comes from non-being.
Ib. 40

14 When the highest type of men hear Tao,
They diligently practice it.
When the average type of men hear Tao,
They half believe in it.
When the lowest type of men hear Tao,
They laugh heartily at it. *Ib. 41*

15 The softest things in the world overcome the hardest things in the world.
Non-being penetrates that in which there is no space.
Through this I know the advantage of taking no action. *Ib. 43*

16 There is no calamity greater than lavish desires.
There is no greater guilt than discontentment.
And there is no greater disaster than greed.
Ib. 46

17 One may know the world without going out of doors.
One may see the Way of Heaven without looking through the windows.
The further one goes, the less one knows.[3]
Therefore the sage knows without going about,
Understands without seeing,
And accomplishes without any action.
Ib. 47

18 He who possesses virtue in abundance
May be compared to an infant. *Ib. 55*

19 He who knows does not speak.
He who speaks does not know. *Ib. 56*

20 The more laws and order are made prominent,
The more thieves and robbers there will be.
Ib. 57

21 Ruling a big country is like cooking a small fish.[4] *Ib. 60*

22 Tao is the storehouse of all things.
It is the good man's treasure and the bad man's refuge. *Ib. 62*

[3] I.e., the more one studies, the further one is from the Tao.
[4] I.e., too much handling will spoil it.

1 A journey of a thousand miles must begin with a single step.[1] *Ib. 64*

2 People are difficult to govern because they have too much knowledge. *Ib. 65*

3 I have three treasures. Guard and keep them:
The first is deep love,
The second is frugality,
And the third is not to dare to be ahead of the world.
Because of deep love, one is courageous.
Because of frugality, one is generous.
Because of not daring to be ahead of the world, one becomes the leader of the world. *Ib. 67*

4 When armies are mobilized and issues joined,
The man who is sorry over the fact will win. *Ib. 69*

5 To know that you do not know is the best.
To pretend to know when you do not know is a disease.[2] *Ib. 71*

6 Heaven's net is indeed vast.
Though its meshes are wide, it misses nothing.[3] *Ib. 73*

7 To undertake executions for the master executioner [Heaven] is like hewing wood for the master carpenter.
Whoever undertakes to hew wood for the master carpenter rarely escapes injuring his own hands. *Ib. 74*

8 The Way of Heaven has no favorites.
It is always with the good man. *Ib. 79*

9 Let there be a small country with few people. . . .
Though neighboring communities overlook one another and the crowing of cocks and barking of dogs can be heard,
Yet the people there may grow old and die without ever visiting one another. *Ib. 80*

10 True words are not beautiful;[4]
Beautiful words are not true.
A good man does not argue;
He who argues is not a good man.
A wise man has no extensive knowledge;
He who has extensive knowledge is not a wise man.[5]
The sage does not accumulate for himself.
The more he uses for others, the more he has himself.
The more he gives to others, the more he possesses of his own.
The Way of Heaven is to benefit others and not to injure.
The Way of the sage is to act but not to compete. *Ib. 81*

[1] Traditional translation.
[2] See Confucius, 68:11.
[3] See *Matthew 13:47*, 39:19.
[4] I.e., they are not "fine-sounding."
[5] See Confucius, 68:10; Heraclitus, 69:28; Chaucer, 147:2; Selden, 263:18; Penn, 314:19; and Newman, 490:14.

Pythagoras

c. 582–500 B.C.

11 Friends share all things.[6]
From DIOGENES LAERTIUS, *Lives of Eminent Philosophers,*[7] *bk. VIII, sec. 10*

12 Don't eat your heart. *Ib. 17*

13 Reason is immortal, all else mortal. *Ib. 30*

14 The most momentous thing in human life is the art of winning the soul to good or to evil. *Ib. 32*

Ibycus[8]

c. 580 B.C.

15 There is no medicine to be found for a life which has fled. *Fragment 23*

16 An argument needs no reason, nor a friendship. *Fragment 40*

Aesop[9]

fl. c. 550 B.C.

17 The lamb . . . began to follow the wolf in sheep's clothing.
The Wolf in Sheep's Clothing

18 Appearances often are deceiving. *Ib.*

19 Do not count your chickens before they are hatched.[10]
The Milkmaid and Her Pail

[6] See Plato, 83:8, and Sallust, 102:26.
[7] Translated by R. D. HICKS (Loeb Classical Library).
[8] Associated with Ibycus is the phrase: the cranes of Ibycus. It derives from the legend that Ibycus was murdered at sea and his murderers were discovered through cranes that followed the ship. Hence, "the cranes of Ibycus" became a term for the agency of the gods in revealing crime.
[9] Animal fables from before Aesop's time and after were attributed to him. The first collection was made two hundred years after his death. See also La Fontaine, 296.
[10] To swallow gudgeons ere they're catched / And count their chickens ere they're hatched. — SAMUEL BUTLER, *Hudibras, pt. II* [1664], *canto 3, l. 923*

1 I am sure the grapes are sour.[1]
The Fox and the Grapes

2 No act of kindness, no matter how small, is ever wasted. *The Lion and the Mouse*

3 Slow and steady wins the race.
The Hare and the Tortoise

4 Familiarity breeds contempt.[2]
The Fox and the Lion

5 The boy cried "Wolf, wolf!" and the villagers came out to help him.
The Shepherd Boy and the Wolf

6 A crust eaten in peace is better than a banquet partaken in anxiety.[3]
The Town Mouse and the Country Mouse

7 Borrowed plumes.
The Jay and the Peacock

8 It is not only fine feathers that make fine birds. *Ib.*

9 Self-conceit may lead to self-destruction.
The Frog and the Ox

10 People often grudge others what they cannot enjoy themselves.
The Dog in the Manger

11 It is thrifty to prepare today for the wants of tomorrow.
The Ant[4] and the Grasshopper

12 Be content with your lot; one cannot be first in everything.
Juno and the Peacock[5]

13 A huge gap appeared in the side of the mountain. At last a tiny mouse came forth.[6]
The Mountain in Labor

14 Any excuse will serve a tyrant.
The Wolf and the Lamb

15 Beware lest you lose the substance by grasping at the shadow.
The Dog and the Shadow

[1]The fox, when he cannot reach the grapes, says they are not ripe.—GEORGE HERBERT, *Jacula Prudentum* [1640]

"They are too green," he said, "and only good for fools."—LA FONTAINE, *Fables, bk. III* [1668], *fable 11, The Fox and the Grapes*

[2]See Mark Twain, 626:14.

[3]See *Proverbs 15:17*, 24:7.

[4]See *Proverbs 6:6–8*, 23:11.

[5]See Sean O'Casey, 786:9.

[6]A mountain was in labor, sending forth dreadful groans, and there was in the region the highest expectation. After all, it brought forth a mouse.—PHAEDRUS [fl c. A.D. 8] *IV, 22:1*

See Horace, 109:25.

16 Who shall bell the cat?
The Rats and the Cat

17 I will have nought to do with a man who can blow hot and cold with the same breath.
The Man and the Satyr

18 Thinking to get at once all the gold the goose could give, he killed it and opened it only to find—nothing.
The Goose with the Golden Eggs

19 Put your shoulder to the wheel.
Hercules and the Wagoner

20 The gods help them that help themselves.[7]
Ib.

21 We would often be sorry if our wishes were gratified.[8]
The Old Man and Death

22 Union gives strength.[9]
The Bundle of Sticks

23 While I see many hoof marks going in, I see none coming out. It is easier to get into the enemy's toils than out again.
The Lion, the Fox, and the Beasts

24 The haft of the arrow had been feathered with one of the eagle's own plumes. We often give our enemies the means of our own destruction.[10] *The Eagle and the Arrow*

[7]God loves to help him who strives to help himself.—AESCHYLUS [525–456 B.C.], *Fragment 223*

Heaven helps not the men who will not act.—SOPHOCLES [495–405 B.C.], *Fragment 288*

Try first thyself, and after call in God; / For to the worker God himself lends aid.—EURIPIDES [485–406 B.C.], *Hippolytus, Fragment 435*

See Hippocrates, 80:13.

Help thyself, and God will help thee.—GEORGE HERBERT, *Jacula Prudentum* [1640]

God helps those who help themselves.—ALGERNON SIDNEY, *Discourses on Government* [1698], *sec. 23*, and BENJAMIN FRANKLIN, *Poor Richard's Almanac* [1733–1758]

[8]Granting our wish one of Fate's saddest jokes is!—J. R. LOWELL [1819–1891], *Two Scenes from the Life of Blondel, sc. II, st. 2*

Beware, my lord! Beware lest stern Heaven hate you enough to hear your prayers!—ANATOLE FRANCE, *The Crime of Sylvestre Bonnard* [1881], *pt. II, ch. 4*

When the gods wish to punish us they answer our prayers.—OSCAR WILDE, *An Ideal Husband* [1895], *act II*

[9]See John Dickinson, 378:11.

[10]So in the Libyan fable it is told / That once an eagle, stricken with a dart, / Said, when he saw the fashion of the shaft, / "With our own feathers, not by others' hands, / Are we now smitten."—AESCHYLUS [525–456 B.C.], *Fragment 135;* translated [1868] by EDWARD HAYES PLUMPTRE

That eagle's fate and mine are one, / Which on the shaft that made him die / Espied a feather of his own, / Wherewith he wont to soar so high.—EDMUND WALLER [1605–1687], *To a Lady Singing a Song of His Composing*

See Byron, 456:17.

Theognis
fl. c. 545 B.C.

1 One finds many companions for food and drink, but in a serious business a man's companions are very few. *Elegies, l. 115*

2 Even to a wicked man a divinity gives wealth, Cyrnus, but to few men comes the gift of excellence. *Ib. l. 149*

3 Surfeit begets insolence, when prosperity comes to a bad man. *Ib. l. 153*

4 Adopt the character of the twisting octopus, which takes on the appearance of the nearby rock. Now follow in this direction, now turn a different hue. *Ib. l. 215*

5 The best of all things for earthly men is not to be born and not to see the beams of the bright sun; but if born, then as quickly as possible to pass the gates of Hades, and to lie deep buried.[1] *Ib. l. 425*

6 No man takes with him to Hades all his exceeding wealth.[2] *Ib. l. 725*

7 Bright youth passes swiftly as a thought. *Ib. l. 985*

Anacreon
c. 570 – c. 480 B.C.

8 Bring water, bring wine, boy! Bring flowering garlands to me! Yes, bring them, so that I may try a bout with love.
Fragment 27

9 I both love and do not love, and am mad and am not mad.[3] *Fragment 79*

10 War spares not the brave, but the cowardly.[4]
Fragment 101. From The Palatine Anthology, VII, 160

Hipponax
c. 570–520 B.C.

11 There are two days when a woman is a pleasure: the day one marries her and the day one buries her. *Fragment*

[1]See Sophocles, 75:13; Bacon, 181:19; Yeats, 715:19; and Auden, 868:7.
[2]See *The Song of the Harper*, 3:2; *Ecclesiastes 5:15*, 27:2; *I Timothy 6:7*, 51:1; and Kaufman, 813:4.
[3]See Catullus, 102:17.
[4]See Sophocles, 75:8.

Xenophanes
c. 570 – c. 475 B.C.

12 Homer and Hesiod attributed to the gods everything that is a shame and a reproach among men. *Fragment 11*

13 If cattle and horses, or lions, had hands, or were able to draw with their feet and produce the works which men do, horses would draw the forms of gods like horses, and cattle like cattle, and they would make the gods' bodies the same shape as their own.[5]
Fragment 15

14 One god, greatest among gods and men, similar to mortals neither in shape nor even in thought.[6] *Fragment 23*

15 It takes a wise man to recognize a wise man.
From Diogenes Laertius, Lives of Eminent Philosophers, Xenophanes, IX

Simonides
c. 556–468 B.C.

16 It is hard to be truly excellent, four-square in hand and foot and mind, formed without blemish. *Fragment 4*

17 The city is the teacher of the man.
Fragment 53

18 Fighting in the forefront of the Greeks, the Athenians crushed at Marathon the might of the gold-bearing Medes. *Fragment 88*

19 Go tell the Spartans, thou who passest by,
That here, obedient to their laws, we lie.[7]
Fragment 92

20 If to die honorably is the greatest
Part of virtue, for us fate's done her best.
Because we fought to crown Greece with freedom
We lie here enjoying timeless fame.[8]
For the Athenian Dead at Plataia[9]

21 We did not flinch but gave our lives to save
Greece when her fate hung on a razor's edge.
Cenotaph at the Isthmos[9]

[5]See Montesquieu, 341:7.
[6]See Homer, 57:30.
[7]Translated by W. L. Bowles.
Epitaph for the Lacedaemonian [Spartan] king Leonidas and his small force at Thermopylae, who all died fighting to hold the pass against the invading Persian army [480 B.C.].
Ruskin said of this epitaph that it was the noblest group of words uttered by man.
[8]See Pindar, 72:7; Thucydides, 81:5; and Brandeis, 677:12.
[9]Translated by Peter Jay in his edition of *The Greek Anthology* [1973].

1 Painting is silent poetry, and poetry painting that speaks.
From PLUTARCH, *De Gloria Atheniensium, III, 346*

Confucius

551–479 B.C.

2 Fine words and an insinuating appearance are seldom associated with true virtue.
The Confucian Analects,[1] *bk. 1:3*

3 A youth, when at home, should be filial, and, abroad, respectful to his elders.
Ib. 1:6

4 If a man withdraws his mind from the love of beauty, and applies it as sincerely to the love of the virtuous; if, in serving his parents, he can exert his utmost strength; if, in serving his prince, he can devote his life; if, in his intercourse with his friends, his words are sincere—although men say that he has not learned, I will certainly say that he has.
Ib. 1:7

5 Hold faithfulness and sincerity as first principles. *Ib. 1:8, ii*

6 Have no friends not equal to yourself.
Ib. 1:8, iii

7 When you have faults, do not fear to abandon them. *Ib. 1:8, iv*

8 He who exercises government by means of his virtue may be compared to the north polar star, which keeps its place and all the stars turn towards it. *Ib. 2:1*

9 [The superior man] acts before he speaks, and afterwards speaks according to his actions. *Ib. 2:13*

10 Learning without thought is labor lost; thought without learning is perilous.[2]
Ib. 2:15

11 When you know a thing, to hold that you know it; and when you do not know a thing, to allow that you do not know it—this is knowledge.[3] *Ib. 2:17*

12 Things that are done, it is needless to speak about . . . things that are past, it is needless to blame. *Ib. 3:21, ii*

13 I have not seen a person who loved virtue, or one who hated what was not virtuous. He who loved virtue would esteem nothing above it. *Ib. 4:6, i*

14 If a man in the morning hear the right way, he may die in the evening without regret.
Ib. 4:8

15 The superior man . . . does not set his mind either for anything, or against anything; what is right he will follow.
Ib. 4:10

16 When we see men of worth, we should think of equaling them; when we see men of a contrary character, we should turn inwards and examine ourselves. *Ib. 4:17*

17 The cautious seldom err. *Ib. 4:23*

18 Virtue is not left to stand alone. He who practices it will have neighbors.
Ib. 4:25

19 Man is born for uprightness. If a man lose his uprightness, and yet live, his escape from death is the effect of mere good fortune.
Ib. 6:16

20 The man of virtue makes the difficulty to be overcome his first business, and success only a subsequent consideration.
Ib. 6:20

21 With coarse rice to eat, with water to drink, and my bended arm for a pillow—I have still joy in the midst of these things. Riches and honors acquired by unrighteousness are to me as a floating cloud.[4]
Ib. 7:15

22 I am not one who was born in the possession of knowledge; I am one who is fond of antiquity, and earnest in seeking it there.
Ib. 7:19

23 Is virtue a thing remote? I wish to be virtuous, and lo! virtue is at hand. *Ib. 7:29*

24 The superior man is satisfied and composed; the mean man is always full of distress. *Ib. 7:36*

25 The people may be made to follow a path of action, but they may not be made to understand it. *Ib. 8:9*

26 While you are not able to serve men, how can you serve spirits [of the dead]? . . . While you do not know life, how can you know about death? *Ib. 11:11*

27 To go beyond is as wrong as to fall short.
Ib. 11:15, iii

[1] Sayings attributed to Confucius and his followers from *The Chinese Classics* [1861–1886], vol. I, *The Confucian Analects,* translated by JAMES LEGGE.

[2] See Lao-tzu, 65:10; Heraclitus, 69:28; Chaucer, 147:2; Selden, 263:18; Penn, 314:19; and Newman, 490:14.

[3] See Lao-tzu, 65:5.

[4] See Amenemope, 6:6, and *Proverbs 15:16–17, 24:7.*

1 He with whom neither slander that gradually soaks into the mind, nor statements that startle like a wound in the flesh, are successful may be called intelligent indeed.
Ib. 12:6

2 In carrying on your government, why should you use killing [the unprincipled for the good of the unprincipled] at all? Let your evinced desires be for what is good, and the people will be good. The relation between superiors and inferiors is like that between the wind and the grass. The grass must bend when the wind blows across it.
Ib. 12:19

3 Good government obtains when those who are near are made happy, and those who are far off are attracted. *Ib. 13:16, ii*

4 The firm, the enduring, the simple, and the modest are near to virtue. *Ib. 13:27*

5 The scholar who cherishes the love of comfort is not fit to be deemed a scholar.
Ib. 14:3

6 The man who in the view of gain thinks of righteousness; who in the view of danger is prepared to give up his life; and who does not forget an old agreement however far back it extends—such a man may be reckoned a complete man. *Ib. 14:13, ii*

7 He who speaks without modesty will find it difficult to make his words good.
Ib. 14:21

8 The superior man is modest in his speech, but exceeds in his actions. *Ib. 14:29*

9 Recompense injury with justice, and recompense kindness with kindness.
Ib. 14:36, iii

10 The determined scholar and the man of virtue will not seek to live at the expense of injuring their virtue. They will even sacrifice their lives to preserve their virtue complete.
Ib. 15:8

11 If a man take no thought about what is distant, he will find sorrow near at hand.
Ib. 15:11

12 The superior man is distressed by his want of ability. *Ib. 15:18*

13 What the superior man seeks is in himself. What the mean man seeks is in others.
Ib. 15:20

14 What you do not want done to yourself, do not do to others.[1] *15:23*

15 When a man's knowledge is sufficient to attain, and his virtue is not sufficient to enable him to hold, whatever he may have gained, he will lose again. *Ib. 15:32, i*

16 The superior man cannot be known in little matters, but he may be entrusted with great concerns. The small man may not be entrusted with great concerns, but he may be known in little matters. *Ib. 15:33*

17 Virtue is more to man than either water or fire. I have seen men die from treading on water and fire, but I have never seen a man die from treading the course of virtue.
Ib. 15:34

18 By nature, men are nearly alike; by practice, they get to be wide apart.
Ib. 17:2

19 To be able to practice five things everywhere under heaven constitutes perfect virtue. . . . [They are] gravity, generosity of soul, sincerity, earnestness, and kindness.
Ib. 17:6

20 There are three things which the superior man guards against. In youth . . . lust. When he is strong . . . quarrelsomeness. When he is old . . . covetousness.
Ib. 17:8

21 Without recognizing the ordinances of Heaven, it is impossible to be a superior man.
Ib. 20:3, i

22 Without an acquaintance with the rules of propriety, it is impossible for the character to be established. *Ib. 20:3, ii*

23 Without knowing the force of words, it is impossible to know men. *Ib. 20:3, iii*

Heraclitus

c. 540 – c. 480 B.C.

24 All is flux, nothing stays still.[2]
From DIOGENES LAERTIUS, *Lives of Eminent Philosophers, bk. IX, sec. 8, and* PLATO, *Cratylus, 402A*

25 Nothing endures but change.[3] *Ib.*

26 It is wise to listen, not to me but to the Word, and to confess that all things are one.
On the Universe,[4] *fragment 1*

27 Nature is wont to hide herself.
Ib. 10

28 Much learning does not teach understanding.[5] *Ib. 16*

[1]See *Matthew 7:12*, 38:14, and Aristotle, 87:3.

[2]See Tyndall, 580:3.

[3]See Racan, 265:3; Swift, 321:16; Shelley, 466:11; and Wilde, 676:4.

[4]Translated by W. H. S. JONES (Loeb Classical Library).

[5]See Lao-tzu, 65:10; Confucius, 68:10; Chaucer, 147:2; Selden, 263:18; Penn, 314:19; and Newman, 490:14.

1 This world . . . ever was, and is, and shall be, ever-living Fire, in measures being kindled and in measures going out.

Ib. 20

2 God is day and night, winter and summer, war and peace, surfeit and hunger.

Ib. 36

3 You could not step twice into the same rivers;[1] for other waters are ever flowing on to you. *Ib. 41*

4 The opposite is beneficial; from things that differ comes the fairest attunement; all things are born through strife. *Ib. 46*

5 Couples are wholes and not wholes, what agrees disagrees, the concordant is discordant. From all things one and from one all things. *Ib. 59*

6 The road up and the road down is one and the same. *Ib. 69*

7 Man, like a light in the night, is kindled and put out. *Ib. 77*

8 When is death not within ourselves? . . . Living and dead are the same, and so are awake and asleep, young and old.[2]

Ib. 78

9 The people should fight for their law as for a wall. *Ib. 100*

10 It is better to hide ignorance, but it is hard to do this when we relax over wine.

Ib. 108

11 A man's character is his fate.

Ib. 121

Themistocles

c. 528 – c. 462 B.C.

12 Tuning the lyre and handling the harp are no accomplishments of mine, but rather taking in hand a city that was small and inglorious and making it glorious and great.

From PLUTARCH, *Lives, Themistocles, sec. 2*

13 The wooden wall is your ships.[3]

Ib. 10

14 Strike, but hear me.[4] *Ib. 11*

15 [Of his son] The boy is the most powerful of all the Hellenes; for the Hellenes are commanded by the Athenians, the Athenians by myself, myself by the boy's mother, and the mother by her boy. *Ib. 18*

16 [Of two suitors for his daughter's hand] I choose the likely man in preference to the rich man; I want a man without money rather than money without a man.

From PLUTARCH, *Lives, Themistocles, sec. 18*

17 I have with me two gods, Persuasion and Compulsion.[5] *Ib. 21*

18 The speech of man is like embroidered tapestries, since like them this too has to be extended in order to display its patterns, but when it is rolled up it conceals and distorts them. *Ib. 29*

19 He who commands the sea has command of everything.[6]

From CICERO, *Ad Atticum, X, 8*

20 [Upon being asked whether he would rather be Achilles or Homer] Which would you rather be—a victor in the Olympic games, or the announcer of the victor?

From PLUTARCH, *Apothegms, Themistocles*

Aeschylus

525–456 B.C.

21 I would far rather be ignorant than knowledgeable of evils.

The Suppliants, l. 453

22 "Reverence for parents" stands written among the three laws of most revered righteousness.[7] *Ib. l. 707*

23 Myriad laughter of the ocean waves.

Prometheus Bound, l. 89

24 For somehow this is tyranny's disease, to trust no friends. *Ib. l. 224*

25 Words are the physicians of a mind diseased.[8] *Ib. l. 378*

26 Time as he grows old teaches all things.

Ib. l. 981

[1] Usually quoted as: river.

[2] See Euripides, 77:21; Aristophanes, 82:21; Montaigne, 165:9; and Calderón de la Barca, 273:2.

[3] This was Themistocles' interpretation to the Athenians in 480 B.C. of the second oracle at Delphi: "Safe shall the wooden wall continue for thee and thy children." The account appears in full in HERODOTUS, *Histories, bk. VII, sec. 141–143.*

[4] Said in reply to Eurybiades, commander of the Spartan fleet, when he raised his staff as though to strike.

[5] Said to the Andrians, when demanding money from them, to which they replied that they already had two great gods, Penury and Powerlessness, who hindered them from giving him money.

[6] See Bacon, 181:11; Waller, 276:3; Washington, 379:5; Mahan, 642:8; and Morison, 800:11.

[7] See *Exodus 20:12,* 10:7.

[8] See Milton, 288:24.

1 God's mouth knows not how to speak falsehood, but he brings to pass every word.[1]
Ib. l. 1030

2 On me the tempest falls. It does not make me tremble. O holy Mother Earth, O air and sun, behold me. I am wronged.[2]
Ib. l. 1089

3 I pray the gods some respite from the weary task of this long year's watch that lying on the Atreidae's roof on bended arm, doglike, I have kept, marking the conclave of all the night's stars, those potentates blazing in the heavens that bring winter and summer to mortal men, the constellations, when they wane, when they rise.
Agamemnon, l. 1

4 A great ox stands on my tongue.[3]
Ib. l. 36

5 He who learns must suffer. And even in our sleep pain that cannot forget falls drop by drop upon the heart, and in our own despair, against our will, comes wisdom to us by the awful grace of God. *Ib. l. 177*

6 She [Helen] brought to Ilium her dowry, destruction. *Ib. l. 406*

7 It is in the character of very few men to honor without envy a friend who has prospered. *Ib. l. 832*

8 Only when man's life comes to its end in prosperity can one call that man happy.[4]
Ib. l. 928

9 Alas, I am struck a deep mortal blow!
Ib. l. 1343

10 Death is better, a milder fate than tyranny.[5]
Ib. l. 1364

11 Zeus, first cause, prime mover; for what thing without Zeus is done among mortals?[6]
Ib. l. 1485

12 Do not kick against the pricks.[7]
Ib. l. 1624

13 I know how men in exile feed on dreams of hope. *Ib. l. 1668*

14 Good fortune is a god among men, and more than a god.
The Libation Bearers, l. 59

[1] See *Numbers 23:19*, 11:4.
[2] Translated by EDITH HAMILTON.
[3] A proverbial expression of uncertain origin for enforced silence.
[4] See *Ecclesiasticus 11:28*, 35:22; Solon, 62:17; and Sophocles, 74:7.
[5] See Patrick Henry, 383:5.
[6] See *Acts 17:28*, 46:17; Cleanthes, 92:1; and Aratus, 92:11.
[7] Also in PINDAR, *Pythian Odes, II, l. 174*, and EURIPIDES, *Bacchae, l. 795*. See *Acts 9:5*, 46:6.

15 Destiny waits alike for the free man as well as for him enslaved by another's might.
Ib. l. 103

16 For a deadly blow let him pay with a deadly blow: it is for him who has done a deed to suffer.[8] *Ib. l. 312*

17 What is pleasanter than the tie of host and guest? *Ib. l. 702*

18 His resolve is not to seem, but to be, the best. *The Seven Against Thebes, l. 592*

Pheidippides

d. 490 B.C.

19 Rejoice, we are victorious.
From LUCAN, *Pro Lapsu in Salutado, 3*

Pindar

c. 518 – c. 438 B.C.

20 Water is best. But gold shines like fire blazing in the night, supreme of lordly wealth.
Olympian Odes, I, l. 1

21 The days that are still to come are the wisest witnesses. *Ib. l. 51*

22 If any man hopes to do a deed without God's knowledge, he errs. *Ib. l. 104*

23 Do not peer too far.[9] *Ib. l. 184*

24 I have many swift arrows in my quiver which speak to the wise, but for the crowd they need interpreters. The skilled poet is one who knows much through natural gift, but those who have learned their art chatter turbulently, vainly, against the divine bird of Zeus. *Ib. II, l. 150*

25 I will not steep my speech in lies; the test of any man lies in action.[10]
Ib. IV, l. 27

26 The issue is in God's hands.
Ib. XIII, l. 147

27 Zeus, accomplisher, to all grant grave restraint and attainment of sweet delight.[10]
Ib. last line

28 Seek not, my soul, the life of the immortals; but enjoy to the full the resources that are within thy reach.[11]
Pythian Odes, III, l. 109

[8] See *Exodus 21:12*, 10:9.
[9] Do not set your eyes on things far off. — *Pythian Odes, III, l. 39*
See Euripides, 76:14.
[10] Translated by RICHMOND LATTIMORE.
[11] See Euripides, 76:9.

1 They say that this lot is bitterest: to recognize the good but by necessity to be barred from it.[1] *Ib. IV, l. 510*

2 Creatures of a day, what is a man? What is he not? Mankind is a dream of a shadow. But when a god-given brightness comes, a radiant light rests on men, and a gentle life.[2]
Ib. VIII, l. 135

3 When toilsome contests have been decided, good cheer is the best physician, and songs, the sage daughters of the Muses, soothe with their touch. *Nemean Odes, IV, l. 1*

4 Words have a longer life than deeds.
Ib. l. 10

5 Not every truth is the better for showing its face undisguised; and often silence is the wisest thing for a man to heed.
Ib. V, l. 30

6 One race there is of men, one of gods, but from one mother we both draw our breath.
Ib. VI, l. 1

7 If one but tell a thing well,[3] it moves on with undying voice, and over the fruitful earth and across the sea goes the bright gleam of noble deeds ever unquenchable.[4]
Isthmian Odes, IV, l. 67

8 It is not possible with mortal mind to search out the purposes of the gods.
Fragment 61

9 O bright and violet-crowned and famed in song, bulwark of Greece, famous Athens, divine city! *Fragment 76*

10 Unsung, the noblest deed will die.[5]
Fragment 120

11 What is God? Everything.
Fragment 140d

12 Convention is the ruler of all.
Fragment 169

13 Hope, which most of all guides the changeful mind of mortals. *Fragment 214*

Anaxagoras

c. 500–428 B.C.

14 The descent to Hades is the same from every place.
From DIOGENES LAERTIUS, *Lives of Eminent Philosophers, Anaxagoras, 2*

[1]See Boethius, 129:22; Dante, 141:2; Chaucer, 144:24; and Tennyson, 529:20.
[2]See *The Teaching for Merikare*, 4:1; Homer, 58:1 and 59:5; and Aristophanes, 82:9.
[3]See Chateaubriand, 419:8.
[4]See Simonides, 67:20, and Thucydides, 81:5.
[5]See Horace, 108:13, and Pope, 339:32.

The Pali Canon[6]

c. 500 – c. 250 B.C.[7]

15 All that is comes from the mind; it is based on the mind, it is fashioned by the mind.[8]
Suttapitaka. Dhammapada, ch. 1, verse 1

16 For hatred does not cease by hatred at any time: hatred ceases by love — this is the eternal law.[8] *Ib. 1:5*

17 Avoid what is evil; do what is good; purify the mind — this is the teaching of the Awakened One [Buddha].[8] *Ib. 14:183*

18 Better to live alone; with a fool there is no companionship. With few desires live alone and do no evil, like an elephant in the forest roaming at will. *Ib. 23:330*

19 I have preached the truth without making any distinction between exoteric and esoteric doctrine: for in respect of truths, Ananda, the Tathagata[9] has no such thing as the closed fist of a teacher, who keeps some things back.[10]
Ib. Mahaparinibbana-sutta, 2:32

20 Be lamps [or islands] unto yourselves. Be a refuge unto yourselves. Do not turn to any external refuge. Hold fast to the teaching [dhamma] as a lamp.[8] *Ib. 2:33*

21 Few and far between are the Tathagatas,[9] the Arahat Buddhas, who appear in the world.[10] *Ib. 5:10*

22 Decay is inherent in all component things! Work out your salvation with diligence.[11]
Ib. 6:10

23 This is the noble truth of sorrow. Birth is sorrow, age is sorrow, disease is sorrow, death is sorrow . . . in short, all the five components of individuality [khandas] are sorrow.

And this is the noble truth of the arising of sorrow. It arises from craving, which leads to rebirth, which brings delight and passion . . .

And this is the noble truth of the stopping

[6]The sacred scriptures of Theravada Buddhists.
[7]Ancient Indian literary chronology is conjectural.
[8]Translated by JAN NATTIER-BARBARO.
[9]Tathagata: Thus-come-one, an Indian term designating an enlightened being.
[10]Translated by T. W. RHYS DAVIDS.
[11]Translated by T. W. RHYS DAVIDS. The last words of the Buddha.

of sorrow. It is the complete stopping of that craving . . . being emancipated from it . . .

And this is the noble truth of the way which leads to the stopping of sorrow. It is the noble eightfold path.[1]

Ib. Samyutta-nikaya, 5:421

1 The law that I have preached . . . and the discipline that I have established, will be your master after my disappearance.[2]

Ib. Digha Nikaya, II

2 This noble eightfold path . . . right views, right aspirations, right speech, right conduct, right livelihood, right effort, right mindfulness, and right contemplation.[3]

Ib. Dhammacakkappavattana-sutta, verse 4

3 The wise and moral man
Shines like a fire on a hilltop,
Making money like the bee,
Who does not hurt the flower.[4]

Ib. Singalavada-sutta, Digha-nikaya, 3:180

4 It would be absurd to say of the [enlightened] monk, with his heart set free, that he believes that the perfected being survives after death — or indeed that he does not survive, or that he does and yet does not, or that he neither does nor does not. Because the monk is free his state transcends all expression, predication, communication, and knowledge.[5]

Ib. Digha-nikaya, 2:65

5 If, Ananda, women had not received permission to go out from the household life and enter the homeless state[6] . . . then would the pure religion, Ananda, have lasted long, the good law would have stood fast for a thousand years. But since, Ananda, women have now received that permission, the pure religion, Ananda, will not now last so long, the good law will now stand fast for only five hundred years.[7]

Vinayapitaka. Cullavagga, bk. X, ch. 1, verse 6

[1]Translated by William Theodore de Bary.
See the Pali Canon, 73:2.

[2]Translated by Jan Nattier-Barbaro.

[3]Translated by T. W. Rhys Davids and H. Oldenberg.
See the Pali Canon, 72:23.

[4]Translated by William Theodore de Bary.
A text addressed — exceptionally in the early Buddhist literature — to laity rather than monks.

[5]Translated by William Theodore de Bary.

[6]Enter the Buddhist order.

[7]Translated by T. W. Rhys Davids and H. Oldenberg.

6 I go for refuge to the Buddha.
I go for refuge to the Doctrine.
I go for refuge to the Order [of monks].

Traditional (liturgical), passim

Pericles[8]

c. 495–429 B.C.

7 Wait for that wisest of all counselors, Time.

From Plutarch, Lives, Pericles, sec. 18

8 Trees, though they are cut and lopped, grow up again quickly,[9] but if men are destroyed, it is not easy to get them again.

Ib. 33

Sophocles[10]

c. 495–406 B.C.

9 Silence gives the proper grace to women.

Ajax, l. 293

10 Nobly to live, or else nobly to die,
Befits proud birth.[11] *Ib. l. 480*

11 Of all human ills, greatest is fortune's wayward tyranny. *Ib. l. 486*

12 For kindness begets kindness evermore,
But he from whose mind fades the memory
Of benefits, noble is he no more.

Ib. l. 522

13 Sleep that masters all. *Ib. l. 675*

14 I, whom proof hath taught of late
How so far only should we hate our foes
As though we soon might love them, and so far
Do a friend service as to one most like
Someday to prove our foe, since oftenest men
In friendship but a faithless haven find.[12]

Ib. l. 678

15 Men of ill judgment oft ignore the good
That lies within their hands, till they have lost it. *Ib. l. 964*

16 It is not righteousness to outrage
A brave man dead, not even though you hate him. *Ib. l. 1344*

[8]See Thucydides, *Funeral Oration of Pericles,* 80:17–81:7.

[9]The lopped tree in time may grow again. — Robert Southwell [c. 1561–1595], *Times Go by Turns*

[10]Sophocles said he drew men as they ought to be, and Euripides as they were. — Aristotle, *Poetics, ch. 25*

[11]See Euripides, 77:16, and the Duc de Lévis, 416:7.

[12]They love as though they will someday hate and hate as though they will someday love. — Aristotle quoting Bias [sixth century B.C.], *Rhetoric, II, 13*
See Publilius Syrus, 111:8.

1 Ships are only hulls, high walls are nothing,
When no life moves in the empty passageways.[1] *Oedipus Rex,*[2] *l. 56*

2 How dreadful knowledge of the truth can be
When there's no help in truth!
Ib. l. 316

3 The tyrant is a child of Pride
Who drinks from his great sickening cup
Recklessness and vanity,
Until from his high crest headlong
He plummets to the dust of hope.[3]
Ib. l. 872

4 The greatest griefs are those we cause ourselves. *Ib. l. 1230*

5 Time eases all things.[4] *Ib. l. 1515*

6 Look upon Oedipus
This is the king who solved the famous riddle
[of the Sphinx].[5] *Ib. l. 1524*

7 Let every man in mankind's frailty
Consider his last day; and let none
Presume on his good fortune until he find
Life, at his death, a memory without pain.[6]
Ib. l. 1529

8 For God hates utterly
The bray of bragging tongues.
Antigone[7] *[c. 442 B.C.], l. 123*

9 Our ship of state, which recent storms have threatened to destroy, has come safely to harbor at last.[8] *Ib. l. 163*

10 I have nothing but contempt for the kind of governor who is afraid, for whatever reason, to follow the course that he knows is best for the State; and as for the man who sets private friendship above the public welfare—I have no use for him, either. *Ib. l. 181*

11 Nobody likes the man who brings bad news.[9] *Ib. l. 277*

12 Money: There's nothing in the world so demoralizing as money.[10] *Ib. l. 295*

13 How dreadful it is when the right judge judges wrong! *Ib. l. 323*

14 Numberless are the world's wonders, but
none
More wonderful than man.
Ib. l. 333 (Ode I)

15 It is a good thing
To escape from death, but it is not great
pleasure
To bring death to a friend. *Ib. l. 437*

16 But all your[11] strength is weakness itself
against
The immortal unrecorded laws of God.
They are not merely now: they were and shall
be
Forever, beyond man utterly.
Ib. l. 452

17 Grief teaches the steadiest minds to waver.
Ib. l. 563

18 All that is and shall be,
And all the past, is his [Zeus's].
Ib. l. 611 (Ode II)

19 Show me the man who keeps his house in
hand,
He's fit for public authority.[12]
Ib. l. 660

20 Anarchy, anarchy! Show me a greater evil!
This is why cities tumble and the great
houses rain down,
This is what scatters armies! *Ib. l. 672*

21 Reason is God's crowning gift to man.
Ib. l. 684

22 The ideal condition
Would be, I admit, that men should be right
by instinct;
But since we are all likely to go astray,
The reasonable thing is to learn from those
who can teach. *Ib. l. 720*

23 Love, unconquerable,[13]
Waster of rich men, keeper
Of warm lights and all-night vigil

[1] See Thucydides, 81:8, and Shakespeare, 242:19.
[2] Translated by DUDLEY FITTS and ROBERT FITZGERALD.
[3] See *Proverbs 16:18,* 24:12.
Pride will have a fall.—*English proverb* [c. 1509]
A variant is: Pride goeth before a fall.
Pride goeth before, and shame cometh behind.—*Treatise of a Gallant* [c. 1510]
Pride will have a fall; / For pride goeth before and shame cometh after.—JOHN HEYWOOD, *Proverbs* [1546], *pt. I, ch. 10*
[4] See Terence, 96:9, and La Fontaine, 296:17.
[5] The riddle of the Sphinx: What creature walks in the morning on four feet, at noon upon two, and at evening upon three? Oedipus solved it: Man, as a baby crawling on hands and knees, then erect on his feet, and in old age with a staff. The Sphinx, a monster with a woman's head and bust and a lion's body with wings, waylaid passers on the road to Thebes to propound the riddle, destroying anyone who failed to guess the answer. Oedipus solved the riddle, the Sphinx destroyed herself, and the grateful Thebans made him king. See Seferis, 851:3.
[6] See *Ecclesiasticus 11:28,* 35:22; Solon, 62:17; and Aeschylus, 71:8.
There is a saying among men, put forth of old, that you cannot rightly judge whether a mortal's lot is good or evil, until he dies.—SOPHOCLES, *Trachiniae, l. 1*
[7] Translated by DUDLEY FITTS and ROBERT FITZGERALD.
[8] See Alcaeus, 62:21.

[9] See Shakespeare, 205:20 and 241:4.
[10] See *I Timothy 6:10,* 51:2, and Plato, 84:12.
[11] Creon.
[12] See *I Timothy 3:5,* 50:25.
[13] See Sophocles, 75:5; Virgil, 103:24; and Chaucer, 145:20.

In the soft face of a girl:
Sea-wanderer, forest-visitor!
Even the pure immortals cannot escape you,
And mortal man, in his one day's dusk,
Trembles before your glory.
Ib. l. 781 (Ode III)

1 Wisdom outweighs any wealth.[1]
Ib. l. 1050

2 There is no happiness where there is no wisdom;[2]
No wisdom but in submission to the gods.
Big words are always punished,
And proud men in old age learn to be wise.
Ib. l. 1347, closing lines

3 Death is not the worst; rather, in vain
To wish for death, and not to compass it.
Electra, l. 1008

4 A prudent mind can see room for misgiving, lest he who prospers should one day suffer reverse.[3] *Trachiniae, l. 296*

5 They are not wise, then, who stand forth to buffet against Love; for Love rules the gods as he will, and me.[4] *Ib. l. 441*

6 Knowledge must come through action; you can have no test which is not fanciful, save by trial. *Ib. l. 592*

7 Rash indeed is he who reckons on the morrow, or haply on days beyond it; for tomorrow is not, until today is past.[5] *Ib. l. 943*

8 War never slays a bad man in its course,
But the good always![6]
Philoctetes, l. 436

9 Stranger in a strange country.[7]
Oedipus at Colonus[8] *[406 B.C.], l. 184*

10 The good befriend themselves.
Ib. l. 309

11 The immortal
Gods alone have neither age nor death!
All other things almighty Time disquiets.
Ib. l. 607

12 Athens, nurse of men. *Ib. l. 701*

13 Not to be born surpasses thought and speech.
The second best is to have seen the light
And then to go back quickly whence we came.[9] *Ib. l. 1224*

14 One word
Frees us of all the weight and pain of life:
That word is love. *Ib. l. 1616*

15 It made our hair stand up in panic fear.
Ib. l. 1625

16 A remedy too strong for the disease.
Tereus, fragment 514[10]

17 Truly, to tell lies is not honorable;
But when the truth entails tremendous ruin,
To speak dishonorably is pardonable.
Creusa, fragment 323

18 Sons are the anchors of a mother's life.
Phaedra, fragment 612

19 To him who is in fear everything rustles.
Acrisius, fragment 58

20 No falsehood lingers on into old age.
Ib. 59

21 No man loves life like him that's growing old.[11] *Ib. 64*

22 A woman's vows I write upon the wave.[12]
Unknown Dramas, fragment 694

Empedocles

c. 490 – c. 430 B.C.

23 At one time through love all things come together into one, at another time through strife's hatred they are borne each of them apart. *Fragment 17*

24 The blood around men's heart is their thinking. *Fragment 105*

Euripides[13]

c. 485–406 B.C.

25 Never say that marriage has more of joy than pain. *Alcestis*[14] *[438 B.C.], l. 238*

[1]See *Job 28:18,* 16:14.
[2]See Epicurus, 91:16.
[3]See *Proverbs 16:18,* 24:12.
[4]See Sophocles, 74:23; Virgil, 103:24; and Chaucer, 145:20.
[5]See *Proverbs 27:1,* 25:21.
[6]Translated by SIR GEORGE YOUNG.
See Anacreon, 67:10.
[7]See *Exodus 2:22,* 9:9.
[8]Translated by ROBERT FITZGERALD.
[9]See Theognis, 67:5; Bacon, 181:19; Yeats, 715:19; and Auden, 868:7.
[10]The fragments are from the Everyman edition of *The Dramas of Sophocles.*
[11]See Euripides, 76:5.
[12]See Catullus, 102:12; More, 155:8; Bacon, 181:18; Shakespeare, 249:14; and Keats, 480:7.
[13]All Greece is his monument, though his grave / Lies in Macedon, refuge of his last days. / Hellas of Hellas, Athens his land, who gave / so much joy by his art, whom so many praise. — THUCYDIDES, *Euripides;* translated by PETER JAY in his edition of *The Greek Anthology* [1973]
Sophocles said he drew men as they ought to be, and Euripides as they were. — ARISTOTLE, *Poetics, ch. 25*
[14]Translated by DUDLEY FITTS and ROBERT FITZGERALD.

1 A second wife
is hateful to the children of the first;
a viper is not more hateful. *Ib. l. 309*

2 A sweet thing, for whatever time,
to revisit in dreams the dear dead we have lost. *Ib. l. 355*

3 Oh, if I had Orpheus' voice and poetry
with which to move the Dark Maid and her Lord,
I'd call you back, dear love, from the world below.
I'd go down there for you. Charon or the grim
King's dog could not prevent me then
from carrying you up into the fields of light.
Ib. l. 358

4 Light be the earth upon you, lightly rest.[1]
Ib. l. 462

5 God, these old men!
How they pray for death! How heavy
they find this life in the slow drag of days!
And yet, when Death comes near them,
You will not find one who will rise and walk with him, not one whose years are still a burden to him.[2] *Ib. l. 669*

6 You love the daylight: do you think your
father does not? *Ib. l. 691*

7 Dishonor will not trouble me, once I am dead.
Ib. l. 726

8 Today's today. Tomorrow, we may be
ourselves gone down the drain of Eternity.[3]
Ib. l. 788

9 O mortal man, think mortal thoughts![4]
Ib. l. 799

10 My mother was accursed the night she bore me,
and I am faint with envy of all the dead.[5]
Ib. l. 865

11 You were a stranger to sorrow: therefore Fate
has cursed you. *Ib. l. 927*

12 I have found power in the mysteries of thought,
exaltation in the chanting of the Muses;
I have been versed in the reasonings of men;
but Fate is stronger than anything I have known. *Ib. l. 962*

13 Time cancels young pain. *Ib. l. 1085*

[1]See Anonymous Latin, 134:28; Beaumont and Fletcher, 263:7; and Twain, 625:20.

[2]See Sophocles, 75:21.

[3]See Edward FitzGerald, 516:13.

[4]See Pindar, 71:28.

[5]See *Job 3:3*, 15:7.

14 Slight not what's near through aiming at what's far.[6]
Rhesus [c. 435 B.C.], l. 482

15 There is no benefit in the gifts of a bad man.
Medea [431 B.C.], l. 618

16 When love is in excess it brings a man nor honor
nor any worthiness. *Ib. l. 627*

17 What greater grief than the loss of one's
native land. *Ib. l. 650*

18 I know indeed what evil I intend to do,
but stronger than all my afterthoughts is my fury,
fury that brings upon mortals the greatest evils. *Ib. l. 1078*

19 We know the good, we apprehend it clearly,
but we can't bring it to achievement.[7]
Hippolytus [428 B.C.],[8] l. 380

20 There is one thing alone
that stands the brunt of life throughout its course:
a quiet conscience. *Ib. l. 426*

21 In this world second thoughts, it seems, are best.[9] *Ib. l. 435*

22 Love distills desire upon the eyes,
love brings bewitching grace into the heart
of those he would destroy.
I pray that love may never come to me
with murderous intent,
in rhythms measureless and wild.
Not fire nor stars have stronger bolts
than those of Aphrodite sent
by the hand of Eros, Zeus's child.
Ib. l. 525

23 My tongue swore, but my mind was still unpledged.[10] *Ib. l. 612*

24 Would that I were under the cliffs, in the secret
hiding-places of the rocks,
that Zeus might change me to a winged bird.[11] *Ib. l. 732*

25 I would win my way to the coast,
apple-bearing Hesperian coast
of which the minstrels sing,
where the Lord of the Ocean
denies the voyager further sailing,

[6]See Pindar, 71:23.

[7]See *Romans 7:19*, 47:6, and Ovid, 113:21.

[8]Translated by DAVID GRENE.

[9]Second thoughts, they say, are best.—DRYDEN, *The Spanish Friar* [1681], *act II, sc. ii*
Is it so true that second thoughts are best?—TENNYSON, *Sea Dreams* [1864]

[10]See Sallust, 102:24.

[11]See *Psalm 55:6*, 19:20.

and fixes the solemn limit of Heaven
which giant Atlas upholds.
There the streams flow with ambrosia
by Zeus's bed of love,
and holy Earth, the giver of life,
yields to the gods rich blessedness.[1]

Ib. l. 742

1 In a case of dissension, never dare to judge till you've heard the other side.[2]

Heraclidae[3] *[c. 428 B.C.] (quoted by* ARISTOPHANES, *The Wasps)*

2 Leave no stone unturned. *Ib.*

3 I care for riches, to make gifts
To friends, or lead a sick man back to health
With ease and plenty. Else small aid is wealth
For daily gladness; once a man be done
With hunger, rich and poor are all as one.

Electra [413 B.C.],[1] *l. 427*

4 A coward turns away, but a brave man's choice is danger.

Iphigenia in Tauris [c. 412 B.C.], l. 114

5 The day is for honest men, the night for thieves. *Ib. l. 1026*

6 Mankind . . . possesses two supreme blessings. First of these is the goddess Demeter, or Earth—whichever name you choose to call her by. It was she who gave to man his nourishment of grain. But after her there came the son of Semele, who matched her present by inventing liquid wine as his gift to man. For filled with that good gift, suffering mankind forgets its grief; from it comes sleep; with it oblivion of the troubles of the day. There is no other medicine for misery.[4]

The Bacchae [c. 407 B.C.], l. 274

7 Talk sense to a fool and he calls you foolish. *Ib. l. 480*

8 Slow but sure moves the might of the gods.[5] *Ib. l. 882*

9 What is wisdom? What gift of the gods
is held in glory like this:
to hold your hand victorious
over the heads of those you hate?
Glory is precious forever. *Ib. l. 877*

10 Humility, a sense of reverence before the sons of heaven—
of all the prizes that a mortal man might win,
these, I say, are wisest; these are best.

Ib. l. 1150

[1] Translated by GILBERT MURRAY.
[2] See Protagoras, 78:24, and St. Augustine, 129:7.
[3] Translated by MORRIS HICKEY MORGAN.
[4] Translated by WILLIAM ARROWSMITH.
[5] See George Herbert, 270:14, and von Logau, 273:14.

11 Yet do I hold that mortal foolish who strives against the stress of necessity.[6]

Mad Heracles, l. 281

12 The company of just and righteous men is better than wealth and a rich estate.

Aegeus,[3] *fragment 7*

13 A bad beginning makes a bad ending.

Aeolus,[3] *fragment 32*

14 Time will explain it all. He is a talker, and needs no questioning before he speaks.

Ib. fragment 38

15 Waste not fresh tears over old griefs.

Alexander,[3] *fragment 44*

16 The nobly born must nobly meet his fate.[7] *Alcymene,*[3] *fragment 100*

17 Man's best possession is a sympathetic wife. *Antigone,*[3] *fragment 164*

18 When good men die their goodness does not perish,
But lives though they are gone. As for the bad,
All that was theirs dies and is buried with them.[8] *Temenidae,*[3] *fragment 734*

19 An old man weds a tyrant, not a wife.

Phoenix (quoted by ARISTOPHANES, *Thesmophoriazusae), fragment 413*

20 Every man is like the company he is wont to keep.[9] *Ib. 809*

21 Who knows but life be that which men call death,
And death what men call life?[10]

Phrixus,[3] *fragment 830*

22 Whoso neglects learning in his youth,
Loses the past and is dead for the future.[11]

Ib. 927

23 The gods
Visit the sins of the fathers upon the children.[12] *Ib. 970*

[6] See The Seven Sages, 62:9.
[7] See Sophocles, 73:10, and the Duc de Lévis, 416:7.
If there be any good in nobility, I trow it to be only this, that it imposeth a necessity upon those which are noble, that they should not suffer their nobility to degenerate from the virtues of their ancestors.—BOETHIUS [470–525], *De Consolatione Philosophiae, III, 6:25*
[8] See Shakespeare, 216:17.
[9] Translated by MORRIS HICKEY MORGAN.
Familiar form: A man is known by the company he keeps.
[10] See Heraclitus, 70:8; Aristophanes, 82:21; and Montaigne, 165:9.
[11] See Thucydides, 80:15, and Santayana, 703:11.
[12] See *Exodus 20:5, 10:5*.
For the sins of your fathers you, though guiltless, must suffer.—HORACE, *Odes, III, 6:1*
The sins of the fathers are to be laid upon the children.—SHAKESPEARE, *Merchant of Venice* [1596–1597], *act III, sc. v, l. 1*

1 Those whom God wishes to destroy, he first makes mad.[1] *Fragment*

2 These men won eight victories over the Syracusans when the favor of the gods was equal for both sides.
Epitaph for the Athenians Slain in Sicily

Herodotus

c. 485 – c. 425 B.C.

3 Men trust their ears less than their eyes.
The Histories of Herodotus, bk. I, ch. 8

4 A woman takes off her claim to respect along with her garments.[2] *Ib.*

5 In peace, children inter their parents; war violates the order of nature and causes parents to inter their children. *Ib. 87*

6 [The Persians] are accustomed to deliberate about the most important matters when they are drunk. *Ib. 133*

7 It was a kind of Cadmean victory.[3]
Ib. 166

8 For great wrongdoing there are great punishments from the gods. *Ib. II, 120*

9 If a man insisted always on being serious, and never allowed himself a bit of fun and relaxation, he would go mad or become unstable without knowing it.[4] *Ib. 173*

10 It is better to be envied than pitied.[5]
Ib. III, 52

11 Envy is born in a man from the start.
Ib. 80

12 Force has no place where there is need of skill. *Ib. 127*

13 From the foot, Hercules.[6] *Ib. IV, 82*

14 It is the gods' custom to bring low all things of surpassing greatness.[7] *Ib. VII, 10*

15 Haste in every business brings failures.
Ib.

16 When life is so burdensome, death has become for man a sought-after refuge.
Ib. 46

17 Circumstances rule men; men do not rule circumstances. *Ib. 49*

18 Great deeds are usually wrought at great risks. *Ib. 50*

19 Not snow, no, nor rain, nor heat, nor night keeps them from accomplishing their appointed courses with all speed.[8]
Ib. VIII, 98

20 The king's might is greater than human, and his arm is very long. *Ib. 140*

21 This is the bitterest pain among men, to have much knowledge but no power.
Ib. IX, 16

22 In soft regions are born soft men.
Ib. 122

Protagoras

c. 485 – c. 410 B.C.

23 Man is the measure of all things.
Fragment 1

24 There are two sides to every question.[9]
From DIOGENES LAERTIUS, *Lives of Eminent Philosophers, Protagoras, bk. IX, sec. 51*

Agis

Fifth century B.C.

25 The Lacedemonians are not wont to ask how many the enemy are, but where they are.
From PLUTARCH, *Apothegms, Agis*

[1] See Anonymous Latin, 134:21.
In Boswell's *Life of Johnson* [1791], *vol. 2, pp. 442–443* (Everyman edition), this is quoted as a saying which everybody repeats but nobody knows where to find.
Whom Fortune wishes to destroy she first makes mad. — PUBLILIUS SYRUS [first century B.C.], *Maxim 911*
When falls on man the anger of the gods, / First from his mind they banish understanding. — LYCURGUS [fl. 820 B.C.]
For those whom God to ruin has designed, / He fits for fate, and first destroys their mind. — DRYDEN, *The Hind and the Panther* [1687], *pt. III, l. 1093*
Whom the Gods would destroy they first make mad. — LONGFELLOW, *The Masque of Pandora* [1875], *VI*

[2] See Chaucer, 147:12.

[3] Polyneices and Eteocles, sons of Oedipus and descendants of Cadmus, fought for the possession of Thebes and killed each other. Hence, a Cadmean victory means one where victor and vanquished suffer alike.
See also Pyrrhus, 92:10 ("Pyrrhic victory").

[4] See Ptahhotpe, 3:10; Cervantes, 169:36; and Howell, 271:17.

[5] Also in PINDAR, *Pythian Odes, I, 164*.

[6] Ex pede, Herculem. From AULUS GELLIUS *(Noctes Atticae, I, 1)*, who tells how Pythagoras deduced the stature of Hercules from the length of his foot.
See Anonymous Latin, 133:24.

[7] It is the lofty pine that by the storm / Is oftener tossed; towers fall with heavier crash / Which higher soar. — HORACE [65–8 B.C.], *Odes, II, 10:9*
The bigger they come, the harder they fall. — *Boxing expression attributed to* ROBERT FITZSIMMONS [1862–1917] *and to* JOHN L. SULLIVAN [1858–1918]; *probably much earlier than either*

[8] Neither snow, nor rain, nor heat, nor gloom of night stays these couriers from the swift completion of their appointed rounds. — *Inscription, New York City Post Office, adapted from* HERODOTUS

[9] See Euripides, 77:1, and St. Augustine, 129:7.

Socrates[1]

469–399 B.C.

1 Often when looking at a mass of things for sale, he would say to himself, "How many things I have no need of!"

From DIOGENES LAERTIUS, *Lives of Eminent Philosophers, bk. II, sec. 25*

2 Having the fewest wants, I am nearest to the gods. *Ib. 27*

3 There is only one good, knowledge, and one evil, ignorance. *Ib. 31*

4 My divine sign indicates the future to me. *Ib. 32*

5 I know nothing except the fact of my ignorance.[2] *Ib.*

6 Bad men live that they may eat and drink, whereas good men eat and drink that they may live.[3]

From PLUTARCH, *How a Young Man Ought to Hear Poems, 4*

7 I am not an Athenian or a Greek, but a citizen of the world.[4]

From PLUTARCH, *Of Banishment*

8 Crito, I owe a cock to Asclepius; will you remember to pay the debt?

From PLATO, *Phaedo (Socrates' last words)*

Democritus

c. 460 – c. 400 B.C.

9 Whatever a poet writes with enthusiasm and a divine inspiration is very fine.[5]

Fragment 18

10 In truth we know nothing, for truth lies in the depth. *Fragment 117*

11 By convention there is color, by convention sweetness, by convention bitterness, but in reality there are atoms and space.

Fragment 125

12 Word is a shadow of deed.

Fragment 145

Hippocrates

c. 460–400 B.C.

13 I swear by Apollo Physician, by Asclepius, by Health, by Panacea, and by all the gods and goddesses, making them my witnesses, that I will carry out, according to my ability and judgment, this oath and this indenture. . . . I will use treatment to help the sick according to my ability and judgment, but never with a view to injury and wrongdoing . . . I will keep pure and holy both my life and my art . . . In whatsoever houses I enter, I will enter to help the sick, and I will abstain from all intentional wrongdoing and harm, especially from abusing the bodies of man or woman, bond or free. And whatsoever I shall see or hear in the course of my profession in my intercourse with men, if it be what should not be published abroad, I will never divulge, holding such things to be holy secrets. Now if I carry out this oath, and break it not, may I gain forever reputation among all men for my life and for my art; but if I transgress it and forswear myself, may the opposite befall me.

The Physician's Oath[6]

14 Healing is a matter of time, but it is sometimes also a matter of opportunity.

Precepts,[6] *ch. 1*

15 Time is that wherein there is opportunity, and opportunity is that wherein there is no great time. *Ib.*

16 Sometimes give your services for nothing, calling to mind a previous benefaction or present satisfaction. And if there be an opportunity of serving one who is a stranger in financial straits, give full assistance to all such. For where there is love of man, there is also love of the art. For some patients, though conscious that their condition is perilous, recover their health simply through their contentment with the goodness of the physician. And it is well to superintend the sick to make them well, to care for the healthy to keep them well, also to care for one's own self, so as to observe what is seemly.[7] *Ib. 6*

[1] Much of Plato, especially in the *Apology* and *Phaedo*, is thought to be direct quotation from Socrates. See Plato, 83:16.

[2] See Milton, 288:16.

[3] He used to say that other men lived to eat, but that he ate to live. — DIOGENES LAERTIUS [c. 200], *Lives of Eminent Philosophers, Socrates, sec. 14*

See Molière, 298:4, and Franklin, 347:1.

We must eat to live and live to eat. — FIELDING [1707–1754], *The Miser, act III, sc. iii*

[4] See Bacon, 180:13; Paine, 385:2; Garrison, 505:10; and F. D. Roosevelt, 781:5.

Diogenes, when asked from what country he came, replied, "I am a citizen of the world." — DIOGENES LAERTIUS [c. 200], *Lives of Eminent Philosophers, Diogenes, sec. 6*

Citizen of the world, as I hold myself to be. — BOSWELL, *Life of Johnson* [1791], *vol. I, p. 521* (Everyman edition)

[5] Apparently the earliest reference to the madness or divine inspiration of poets.

See Robert Burton, 258:13; Wordsworth, 425:10; and Robert Lowell, 892:15.

[6] Translated by W. H. S. JONES (Loeb Classical Library).

[7] See Plato, 84:5.

1 In all abundance there is lack. *Ib. 8*

2 If for the sake of a crowded audience you do wish to hold a lecture, your ambition is no laudable one, and at least avoid all citations from the poets, for to quote them argues feeble industry. *Ib. 12*

3 Opposites are cures for opposites. *Breaths, bk. I*

4 Medicine is the most distinguished of all the arts, but through the ignorance of those who practice it, and of those who casually judge such practitioners, it is now of all the arts by far the least esteemed. *Law, bk. I*

5 There are in fact two things, science and opinion; the former begets knowledge, the latter ignorance. *Ib. IV*

6 Things that are holy are revealed only to men who are holy.[1] *Ib. V*

7 Idleness and lack of occupation tend—nay are dragged—towards evil. *Decorum, bk. I*

8 A wise man should consider that health is the greatest of human blessings, and learn how by his own thought to derive benefit from his illnesses. *Regimen in Health, bk. IX*

9 Life is short, the art long, opportunity fleeting, experience treacherous, judgment difficult.[2] *Aphorisms, sec. I, 1*

10 For extreme illnesses extreme treatments are most fitting.[3] *Ib. 6*

11 Many admire, few know. *Regimen, bk. I, sec. 24*

12 Male and female have the power to fuse into one solid, both because both are nourished in both and because soul is the same thing in all living creatures, although the body of each is different. *Ib. 28*

13 Prayer indeed is good, but while calling on the gods a man should himself lend a hand.[4] *Ib. IV, 87*

[1] See Manilius, 115:17.

[2] Vita brevis est, ars longa.—Seneca, *De Brevitate Vitae, I, 1*

See Chaucer, 144:8; Goethe, 395:7; and Longfellow, 509:14.

Art's long, though time is short.—Browning, *The Ring and the Book* [1868–1869], *pt. IX, Juris Doctor Johannes-Baptista Bottinius*

[3] See Shakespeare, 223:14.

[4] See Aesop, 66:20.

Thucydides[5]

c. 460–400 B.C.

14 Thucydides, an Athenian, wrote the history of the war between the Peloponnesians and the Athenians; he began at the moment that it broke out, believing that it would be a great war, and more memorable than any that had preceded it. *The History of the Peloponnesian War [431–413 B.C.], bk. I, sec. 1*

15 With reference to the narrative of events, far from permitting myself to derive it from the first source that came to hand, I did not even trust my own impressions, but it rests partly on what I saw myself, partly on what others saw for me, the accuracy of the report being always tried by the most severe and detailed tests possible. My conclusions have cost me some labor from the want of coincidence between accounts of the same occurrences by different eyewitnesses, arising sometimes from imperfect memory, sometimes from undue partiality for one side or the other. The absence of romance in my history will, I fear, detract somewhat from its interest; but I shall be content if it is judged useful by those inquirers who desire an exact knowledge of the past as an aid to the interpretation of the future,[6] which in the course of human things must resemble if it does not reflect it. My history has been composed to be an everlasting possession, not the showpiece of an hour.[7] *Ib. 22*

16 The great wish of some is to avenge themselves on some particular enemy, the great wish of others to save their own pocket. Slow in assembling, they devote a very small fraction of the time to the consideration of any public object, most of it to the prosecution of their own objects. Meanwhile each fancies that no harm will come of his neglect, that it is the business of somebody else to look after this or that for him; and so, by the same notion being entertained by all separately, the common cause imperceptibly decays.[8] *Ib. 141*

17 Our constitution is named a democracy, because it is in the hands not of the few but of the many. But our laws secure equal justice for all in their private disputes, and our public opinion welcomes and honors talent in every branch of achievement, not for any sec-

[5] Translated by Sir Richard Livingstone.

[6] See Euripides, 77:22, and Santayana, 703:11.

[7] See Ranke, 480:8.

[8] Quoted by President John F. Kennedy in Frankfurt [June 25, 1963].

tional reason but on grounds of excellence alone. And as we give free play to all in our public life, so we carry the same spirit into our daily relations with one another. . . . Open and friendly in our private intercourse, in our public acts we keep strictly within the control of law. We acknowledge the restraint of reverence; we are obedient to whomsoever is set in authority, and to the laws, more especially to those which offer protection to the oppressed and those unwritten ordinances whose transgression brings admitted shame.
Ib. II (Funeral Oration of Pericles), 37

1 We are lovers of beauty without extravagance, and lovers of wisdom without unmanliness. Wealth to us is not mere material for vainglory but an opportunity for achievement; and poverty we think it no disgrace to acknowledge but a real degradation to make no effort to overcome. *Ib. 40*

2 But the bravest are surely those who have the clearest vision of what is before them, glory and danger alike, and yet notwithstanding go out to meet it. *Ib.*

3 We secure our friends not by accepting favors but by doing them.[1] *Ib.*

4 In a word I claim that our city as a whole is an education to Greece. *Ib. 41*

5 Fix your eyes on the greatness of Athens as you have it before you day by day, fall in love with her, and when you feel her great, remember that this greatness was won by men with courage, with knowledge of their duty, and with a sense of honor in action . . . So they gave their bodies to the commonwealth and received, each for his own memory, praise that will never die, and with it the grandest of all sepulchers, not that in which their mortal bones are laid, but a home in the minds of men, where their glory remains fresh to stir to speech or action as the occasion comes by. For the whole earth is the sepulcher of famous men; and their story is not graven only on stone over their native earth, but lives on far away, without visible symbol, woven into the stuff of other men's lives. For you now it remains to rival what they have done and, knowing the secret of happiness to be freedom and the secret of freedom a brave heart, not idly to stand aside from the enemy's onset.[2] *Ib. 43*

[1]Rather by conferring than by accepting favors, they [the Romans] established friendly relations.—SALLUST, *The War with Catiline* [c. 40 B.C.], *6*

[2]See Simonides, 67:20; Pindar, 72:7; and Brandeis, 677:12.

6 Great is the glory of the woman who occasions the least talk among men, whether of praise or of blame. *Ib. 45*

7 For human nature is as surely made arrogant by consideration as it is awed by firmness. *Ib. III, 39*

8 Men make the city, and not walls or ships without men in them.[3]
Ib. VII, 77 (Address of Nicias to the Athenians at Syracuse)

9 This or the like was the cause of the death of a man [Nicias] who, of all the Greeks in my time, least deserved such a fate, for he had lived in the practice of every virtue.
Ib. VIII, 86

10 This was the greatest event in the war, or, in my opinion, in Greek history; at once most glorious to the victors and most calamitous to the conquered. They were beaten at all points and altogether; their sufferings in every way were great. They were totally destroyed—their fleet, their army, everything—and few out of many returned home. So ended the Sicilian expedition. *Ib. 87*

Aristophanes

c. 450–385 B.C.

11 For then, in wrath, the Olympian Pericles
Thundered and lightened, and confounded Hellas
Enacting laws which ran like drinking songs.[4] *Acharnians [425 B.C.], l. 530*

12 When men drink, then they are rich and successful and win lawsuits and are happy and help their friends.
Quickly, bring me a beaker of wine, so that I may wet my mind and say something clever. *Knights [424 B.C.], l. 92*

13 You have all the characteristics of a popular politician: a horrible voice, bad breeding, and a vulgar manner. *Ib. l. 217*

14 To make the worse appear the better reason.[5]
Clouds [423 B.C.], l. 114 and elsewhere

15 Haven't you sometimes seen a cloud that looked like a centaur?
Or a leopard perhaps? Or a wolf? Or a bull?[6] *Ib. l. 346*

[3]See Sophocles, 74:1.

[4]Translated by B. B. ROGERS (Loeb Classical Library).

[5]See Milton, 284:8.

[6]Translated by DUDLEY FITTS.
See Shakespeare, 222:20 and 241:17.

1 Old men are children for a second time.[1]
Ib. l. 1417

2 This is what extremely grieves us, that a man who never fought
Should contrive our fees to pilfer, one who for his native land
Never to this day had oar, or lance, or blister in his hand.
Wasps[2] *[422 B.C.], l. 1117*

3 Let each man exercise the art he knows.
Ib. l. 1431

4 You cannot teach a crab to walk straight.
Peace [421 B.C.], l. 1083

5 [On the nightingale] Lord Zeus, listen to the little bird's voice; he has filled the whole thicket with honeyed song.
Birds [414 B.C.], l. 223

6 Bringing owls to Athens.[3] *Ib. l. 301*

7 The wise learn many things from their enemies. *Ib. l. 375*

8 Full of wiles, full of guile, at all times, in all ways,
Are the children of Men.[2] *Ib. l. 451*

9 Mankind, fleet of life, like tree leaves, weak creatures of clay, unsubstantial as shadows, wingless, ephemeral, wretched, mortal and dreamlike.[4] *Ib. l. 685*

10 Somewhere, what with all these clouds, and all this air,
There must be a rare name, somewhere . . . How do you like "Cloud-Cuckoo-Land"?[5]
Ib. l. 817

11 Halcyon days.[6] *Ib. l. 1594*

12 A woman's time of opportunity is short, and if she doesn't seize it, no one wants to marry her, and she sits watching for omens. *Lysistrata [411 B.C.], l. 596*

13 There is no animal more invincible than a woman, nor fire either, nor any wildcat so ruthless.[7] *Ib. l. 1014*

14 These impossible women! How they do get around us!
The poet was right: can't live with them, or without them![8] *Ib. l. 1038*

[1] See Shakespeare, 220:32.
[2] Translated by B. B. Rogers (Loeb Classical Library).
[3] See Horace, 106:18.
[4] See *The Teaching for Merikare*, 4:1; Homer, 58:1, 58:29, and 59:5; and Pindar, 72:2.
[5] Translated by Dudley Fitts.
[6] See Shakespeare, 184:17.
The appellation of Halcyon days, which was applied to a rare and bloodless week of repose. — Gibbon, *Decline and Fall of the Roman Empire* [1776–1788], *ch. 48*
[7] See Congreve, 324:16, and Nietzsche, 657:21.
[8] Translated by Dudley Fitts.
See Ovid, 113:8, and Martial, 119:17.

15 Under every stone lurks a politician.[9]
Thesmophoriazusae [410 B.C.], l. 530

16 There's nothing worse in the world than shameless woman — save some other woman. *Ib. l. 531*

17 Shall I crack any of those old jokes, master,
At which the audience never fail to laugh?
Frogs[2] *[405 B.C.], l. 1*

18 Brekekekex, ko-ax, ko-ax.[10]
Ib. l. 209 and elsewhere

19 A savage-creating stubborn-pulling fellow,
Uncurbed, unfettered, uncontrolled of speech,
Unperiphrastic, bombastiloquent.[11]
Ib. l. 837

20 High thoughts must have high language.[5]
Ib. l. 1058

21 Who knows whether living is dying, and breathing
Is eating, and sleeping is a wool blanket?[12]
Ib. l. 1477

22 Blest the man who possesses a
Keen intelligent mind. *Ib. l. 1482*

23 I am amazed that anyone who has made a fortune should send for his friends.
Plutus [c. 388 B.C.], l. 340

24 We say that poverty is the sister of beggary.
Ib. l. 549

25 Even if you persuade me, you won't persuade me. *Ib. l. 600*

26 A man's homeland is wherever he prospers.
Ib. l. 1151

Agathon

c. 448–400 B.C.

27 This only is denied to God: the power to undo the past.
From Aristotle, Nicomachean Ethics, bk. VI, ch. 2

Agesilaus

444–400 B.C.

28 If all men were just, there would be no need of valor.
From Plutarch, Lives, Agesilaus, sec. 23

[9] A play on the proverb: Under every stone lurks a scorpion.
[10] Adopted as a Yale College cheer.
[11] Refers to Aeschylus.
[12] See Heraclitus, 70:8; Euripides, 77:21; and Montaigne, 165:9.

1 It is circumstance and proper timing that give an action its character and make it either good or bad. *Ib. 36*

Xenophon

c. 430 – c. 355 B.C.

2 Apollo said that everyone's true worship was that which he found in use in the place where he chanced to be.

Recollections of Socrates, bk. I, ch. 3, sec. 1

3 The sea! The sea![1]

Anabasis, IV, 7, 24

4 I knew my son was mortal.[2]

From DIOGENES LAERTIUS, *Lives of Eminent Philosophers, Xenophon, bk. II, sec. 55*

Zeuxis

fl. 400 B.C.

5 Criticism comes easier than craftsmanship.

From PLINY THE ELDER, *Natural History*

Plato[3]

c. 428–348 B.C.

6 We who of old left the booming surge of the Aegean lie here in the mid-plain of Ecbatana: farewell, renowned Eretria once our country; farewell, Athens nigh to Euboea; farewell, dear sea.[4]

The Greek Anthology [1906],[5] III, 10

7 Beloved Pan, and all ye other gods who haunt this place, give me beauty in the inward soul; and may the outward and inward man be at one. May I reckon the wise to be the wealthy, and may I have such a quantity of gold as none but the temperate can carry.

Dialogues, Phaedrus, sec. 279

8 Friends have all things in common.[6]

Ib.

[1]Thalatta! Thalatta! / Hail to thee, O Sea, ageless and eternal! — HEINRICH HEINE [1797–1856], *Thalatta! Thalatta!, st. 1*

[2]When his son was killed in battle.

[3]Translated by BENJAMIN JOWETT.

Asclepius cured the body: to make men whole / Phoebus sent Plato, healer of the soul. — *On Plato's Grave,* anonymous inscription translated by WILLIAM J. PHILBIN in *The Greek Anthology* [1973], edited by PETER JAY

[4]On the Eretrian exiles settled in Persia by Darius.

[5]Edited by J. W. MACKAIL.

[6]Also in EURIPIDES, *Orestes, l. 735.*

See Pythagoras, 65:11, and Sallust, 102:26.

9 And the true order of going, or being led by another, to the things of love, is to begin from the beauties of earth and mount upwards for the sake of that other beauty, using these steps only, and from one going on to two, and from two to all fair forms to fair practices, and from fair practices to fair notions, until from fair notions he arrives at the notion of absolute beauty, and at last knows what the essence of beauty is.

Ib. Symposium, 211

10 Beholding beauty with the eye of the mind, he will be enabled to bring forth, not images of beauty, but realities (for he has hold not of an image but of a reality), and bringing forth and nourishing true virtue to become the friend of God and be immortal, if mortal man may. *Ib. 212*

11 Socrates is a doer of evil, who corrupts the youth; and who does not believe in the gods of the state, but has other new divinities of his own. Such is the charge.

Ib. Apology, 24

12 The life which is unexamined is not worth living. *Ib. 38*

13 Either death is a state of nothingness and utter unconsciousness, or, as men say, there is a change and migration of the soul from this world to another.[7] . . . Now if death be of such a nature, I say that to die is to gain; for eternity is then only a single night.

Ib. 40

14 No evil can happen to a good man, either in life or after death. *Ib. 41*

15 The hour of departure has arrived, and we go our ways — I to die, and you to live. Which is better God only knows. *Ib. 42*

16 Man is a prisoner who has no right to open the door of his prison and run away. . . . A man should wait, and not take his own life until God summons him.

Ib. Phaedo,[8] 62

17 Must not all things at the last be swallowed up in death? *Ib. 72*

18 Will you not allow that I have as much of the spirit of prophecy in me as the swans? For they, when they perceive that they must die, having sung all their life long, do then sing more lustily than ever, rejoicing in the

[7]Either the soul is immortal and we shall not die, or it perishes with the flesh and we shall not know that we are dead. Live, then, as if you were eternal. — ANDRÉ MAUROIS [1885–1967]. From WILL DURANT, *On the Meaning of Life* [1932], *p. 53.*

[8]See Socrates, 79:*n*1.

thought that they are going to the god they serve.[1] *Ib. 85*

1 The partisan, when he is engaged in a dispute, cares nothing about the rights of the question, but is anxious only to convince his hearers of his own assertions. *Ib. 91*

2 False words are not only evil in themselves, but they infect the soul with evil. *Ib.*

3 The soul takes nothing with her to the other world but her education and culture; and these, it is said, are of the greatest service or of the greatest injury to the dead man, at the very beginning of his journey thither. *Ib. 107*

4 He who is of a calm and happy nature will hardly feel the pressure of age, but to him who is of an opposite disposition youth and age are equally a burden. *The Republic, bk. I, 329–D*

5 No physician, insofar as he is a physician, considers his own good in what he prescribes, but the good of his patient; for the true physician is also a ruler having the human body as a subject, and is not a mere moneymaker.[2] *Ib. 342–D*

6 When there is an income tax, the just man will pay more and the unjust less on the same amount of income. *Ib. 343–D*

7 Mankind censure injustice fearing that they may be the victims of it, and not because they shrink from committing it. *Ib. 344–C*

8 The beginning is the most important part of the work.[3] *Ib. 377–B*

9 The judge should not be young; he should have learned to know evil, not from his own soul, but from late and long observation of the nature of evil in others: knowledge should be his guide, not personal experience. *Ib. III, 409–B*

10 Everything that deceives may be said to enchant. *Ib. 413–C*

11 How, then, might we contrive . . . one noble lie to persuade if possible the rulers themselves, but failing that the rest of the city?[4] *Ib. 414–C*

12 Wealth is the parent of luxury and indolence, and poverty of meanness and viciousness, and both of discontent.[5] *Ib. IV, 422–A*

13 The direction in which education starts a man will determine his future life. *Ib. 425–B*

14 What is the prime of life? May it not be defined as a period of about twenty years in a woman's life, and thirty in a man's? *Ib. V, 460–E*

15 Until philosophers are kings, or the kings and princes of this world have the spirit and power of philosophy, and political greatness and wisdom meet in one, and those commoner natures who pursue either to the exclusion of the other are compelled to stand aside, cities will never have rest from their evils—no, nor the human race, as I believe—and then only will this our State have a possibility of life and behold the light of day. *Ib. 473–C*

16 Let there be one man who has a city obedient to his will, and he might bring into existence the ideal polity about which the world is so incredulous. *Ib. 502–B*

17 Behold! human beings living in an underground den . . . Like ourselves . . . they see only their own shadows, or the shadows of one another, which the fire throws on the opposite wall of the cave. *Ib. VII, 515–B*

18 Astronomy compels the soul to look upwards and leads us from this world to another. *Ib. 529*

19 I have hardly ever known a mathematician who was capable of reasoning. *Ib. 531–E*

20 Solon was under a delusion when he said that a man when he grows old may learn many things[6]—for he can no more learn much than he can run much; youth is the time for any extraordinary toil. *Ib. 536–D*

21 Bodily exercise, when compulsory, does no harm to the body; but knowledge which is acquired under compulsion obtains no hold on the mind. *Ib. 536–E*

[1] The jalous swan, ayens his deth that singeth.—CHAUCER, *The Parliament of Fowls* [1380–1386], *l. 342*
I will play the swan and die in music.—SHAKESPEARE, *Othello* [1604–1605], *act V, sc. ii, l. 245*
See Shakespeare, 199:22 and 202:16; Byron, 461:9; and Anonymous, 918:17.

[2] See Hippocrates, 79:16.

[3] Proverbial. Also in *Laws, VI,* 2.
See Aristotle, 88:11; Horace, 108:20; and Heywood, 159:29.

[4] Translated by PAUL SHOREY (Loeb Classical Library).

[5] See *I Timothy 6:10,* 51:2, and Sophocles, 74:12.

[6] See Solon, 62:14.

1 Let early education be a sort of amusement; you will then be better able to find out the natural bent. *Ib. 537*

2 Oligarchy: A government resting on a valuation of property, in which the rich have power and the poor man is deprived of it. *Ib. VIII, 550–C*

3 Democracy, which is a charming form of government, full of variety and disorder, and dispensing a sort of equality to equals and unequals alike.[1] *Ib. 558–C*

4 Democracy passes into despotism.[2] *Ib. 562–A*

5 The people have always some champion whom they set over them and nurse into greatness. . . . This and no other is the root from which a tyrant springs; when he first appears he is a protector. *Ib. 565–C*

6 In the early days of his power, he is full of smiles, and he salutes everyone whom he meets. *Ib. 566–D*

7 When the tyrant has disposed of foreign enemies by conquest or treaty, and there is nothing to fear from them, then he is always stirring up some war or other, in order that the people may require a leader. *Ib. 566–E*

8 There are three arts which are concerned with all things: one which uses, another which makes, a third which imitates them. *Ib. X, 601–D*

9 No human thing is of serious importance. *Ib. 604–C*

10 The soul of man is immortal and imperishable. *Ib. 608–D*

11 If a person shows that such things as wood, stones, and the like, being many are also one, we admit that he shows the coexistence of the one and many, but he does not show that the many are one or the one many; he is uttering not a paradox but a truism. *Dialogues, Parmenides, 129*

12 The absolute natures or kinds are known severally by the absolute idea of knowledge. *Ib. 134*

13 If a man, fixing his attention on these and the like difficulties, does away with ideas of things and will not admit that every individual thing has its own determinate idea which is always one and the same, he will have nothing on which his mind can rest; and so he will utterly destroy the power of reasoning. *Ib. 135*

[1]See Aristotle, 88:6.

[2]Translated by F. M. Cornford.

14 You cannot conceive the many without the one. *Ib. 166*

15 Let us affirm what seems to be the truth, that, whether one is or is not, one and the others in relation to themselves and one another, all of them, in every way, are and are not, and appear to be and appear not to be. *Ib.*

16 Well, my art of midwifery is in most respects like theirs; but differs, in that I attend men and not women, and I look after their souls when they are in labor, and not after their bodies: and the triumph of my art is in thoroughly examining whether the thought which the mind of the young man brings forth is a false idol or a noble and true birth. *Ib. Theaetetus, 150*

17 He [the philosopher] does not hold aloof in order that he may gain a reputation; but the truth is, that the outer form of him only is in the city: his mind, disdaining the littlenesses and nothingnesses of human beings, is "flying all abroad" as Pindar says, measuring earth and heaven and the things which are under and on the earth and above the heaven, interrogating the whole nature of each and all in their entirety, but not condescending to anything which is within reach. *Ib. 173*

18 I would have you imagine, then, that there exists in the mind of man a block of wax, which is of different sizes in different men; harder, moister, and having more or less of purity in one than another, and in some of an intermediate quality. . . . Let us say that this tablet is a gift of Memory, the mother of the Muses; and that when we wish to remember anything which we have seen, or heard, or thought in our own minds, we hold the wax to the perceptions and thoughts, and in that material receive the impression of them as from the seal of a ring; and that we remember and know what is imprinted as long as the image lasts; but when the image is effaced, or cannot be taken, then we forget and do not know. *Ib. 191*

19 Let us now suppose that in the mind of each man there is an aviary of all sorts of birds—some flocking together apart from the rest, others in small groups, others solitary, flying anywhere and everywhere. . . . We may suppose that the birds are kinds of knowledge, and that when we were children, this receptacle was empty; whenever a man has gotten and detained in the enclosure a kind of knowledge, he may be said to have

learned or discovered the thing which is the subject of the knowledge: and this is to know. *Ib. 197*

1 The greatest penalty of evildoing—namely, to grow into the likeness of bad men. *Laws, 728*

2 Of all the animals, the boy is the most unmanageable. *Ib. 808*

3 You are young, my son, and, as the years go by, time will change and even reverse many of your present opinions. Refrain therefore awhile from setting yourself up as a judge of the highest matters. *Ib. 888*

4 And this which you deem of no moment is the very highest of all: that is whether you have a right idea of the gods, whereby you may live your life well or ill. *Ib.*

5 Not one of them who took up in his youth with this opinion that there are no gods ever continued until old age faithful to his conviction. *Ib.*

Iphicrates

419–348 B.C.

6 My family history begins with me, but yours ends with you.[1]

From Plutarch, Apothegms, Iphicrates

Phocion

c. 402–317 B.C.

7 Have I inadvertently said some evil thing?[2]

From Plutarch, Apothegms, Phocion, sec. 10

8 The good have no need of an advocate. *Ib.*

Diogenes the Cynic

c. 400 – c. 325 B.C.

9 [When asked by Alexander if he wanted anything] Stand a little out of my sun.

From Plutarch, Lives, Alexander, sec. 14

10 Plato having defined man to be a two-legged animal without feathers,[3] Diogenes plucked a cock and brought it into the Academy, and said, "This is Plato's man."[4] On which account this addition was made to the definition: "With broad flat nails."

From Diogenes Laertius, Lives of Eminent Philosophers, Diogenes, sec. 6

11 [When asked what was the proper time for supper] If you are a rich man, whenever you please; and if you are a poor man, whenever you can.[5] *Ib.*

12 I am looking for an honest man.[6] *Ib.*

13 The sun too penetrates into privies, but is not polluted by them.[7] *Ib.*

Antiphanes

c. 388 – c. 311 B.C.

14 We must have richness of soul.

Greek Comic Fragments, no. 570

Aristotle[8]

384–322 B.C.

15 Liars when they speak the truth are not believed.

From Diogenes Laertius, Lives of Eminent Philosophers, bk. V, sec. 17

16 Hope is a waking dream. *Ib. 18*

17 What soon grows old? Gratitude. *Ib.*

18 Beauty is the gift of God. *Ib. 19*

19 Educated men are as much superior to uneducated men as the living are to the dead.[9] *Ib.*

[1]Iphicrates, a shoemaker's son who became a famous general, said this to Harmodius of distinguished ancestry when he reviled him for his mean birth.

Curtius Rufus seems to be descended from himself. — Tiberius. From Tacitus, *Annals, XI, 21*

I am my own ancestor [Moi, je suis mon ancêtre]. — Andoche Junot [1771–1813]

[2]Said when an opinion he delivered pleased the people.

[3]See Dryden, 304:2.

[4]Seeing that the human race falls into the same classification as the feathered creatures, we must divide the biped class into featherless and feathered. — Plato [c. 428–348 B.C.], *The Statesman, 266–E*

[5]The rich when he is hungry, the poor when he has anything to eat. — Rabelais, *Works, bk. IV* [1548], *ch. 64*

[6]Attributed also to Aesop.

[7]The spiritual virtue of a sacrament is like light: although it passes among the impure, it is not polluted. — St. Augustine [354–430], *Tract on St. John, ch. 5:15*

The sun shineth upon the dunghill, and is not corrupted. — Lyly, *Euphues* [1579]

The sun, which passeth through pollutions and itself remains as pure as before. — Bacon, *Advancement of Learning* [1605], *bk. II*

Truth is as impossible to be soiled by any outward touch as the sunbeam. — Milton, *The Doctrine and Discipline of Divorce* [1643]

[8]Chiefly from *The Basic Works of Aristotle,* edited by Richard McKeon.

[9]This used to be quoted "with great warmth" by Dr. Johnson, according to Boswell, *Life of Johnson* [1791].

1 What is a friend? A single soul dwelling in two bodies.[1] *Ib. 20*

2 I have gained this by philosophy: that I do without being commanded what others do only from fear of the law.[2] *Ib. 21*

3 We should behave to our friends as we would wish our friends to behave to us.[3] *Ib.*

4 Education is the best provision for old age. *Ib.*

5 If purpose, then, is inherent in art, so is it in Nature also. The best illustration is the case of a man being his own physician, for Nature is like that—agent and patient at once. *Physics,*[4] *bk. II, ch. 8*

6 Time crumbles things; everything grows old under the power of Time and is forgotten through the lapse of Time. *Ib. IV, 12*

7 The least initial deviation from the truth is multiplied later a thousandfold. *On the Heavens, bk. I, ch. 5*

8 In all things of nature there is something of the marvelous. *Parts of Animals, bk. I, ch. 5*

9 All men by nature desire knowledge. *Metaphysics, bk. I, ch. 1*

10 The final cause, then, produces motion through being loved.[5] *Ib. 7*

11 The actuality of thought is life. *Ib. XII, 7*

12 It is of itself that the divine thought thinks (since it is the most excellent of things), and its thinking is a thinking on thinking. *Ib. 9*

13 Every science and every inquiry, and similarly every activity and pursuit, is thought to aim at some good. *Nicomachean Ethics, bk. I, ch. 1*

14 While both [Plato and truth] are dear, piety requires us to honor truth above our friends.[6] *Ib. 6*

[1] Andrágathos, my soul's half.—MELEAGER [first century B.C.]. From *The Greek Anthology* [1906], edited by J. W. MACKAIL, *XII, 52*

See Zeno, 91:18; Cicero, 99:7; Horace, 106:26; and Donne, 253:4.

[2] Also attributed to Xenocrates [396–314 B.C.] by Cicero.

[3] See *Matthew 7:12*, 38:14; Confucius, 69:14; Chesterfield, 341:19; and Kingsley, 566:16.

[4] Translated by PHILIP H. WICKSTEED and FRANCIS CORNFORD (Loeb Classical Library).

[5] See Dante, 142:20.

[6] Amicus Plato, sed magis amica veritas [Plato is dear to me, but dearer still is truth]. Adapted from a medieval life of Aristotle.

15 One swallow does not make a summer.[7] *Ib. 7*

16 For the things we have to learn before we can do them, we learn by doing them. *Ib. II, 1*

17 It is possible to fail in many ways . . . while to succeed is possible only in one way (for which reason also one is easy and the other difficult—to miss the mark easy, to hit it difficult). *Ib. 6*

18 We must as second best . . . take the least of the evils.[8] *Ib. 9*

19 A man is the origin of his action.[9] *Ib. III, 3*

20 Without friends no one would choose to live, though he had all other goods. *Ib. VIII, 1*

21 To be conscious that we are perceiving or thinking is to be conscious of our own existence.[10] *Ib. IX, 9*

22 To enjoy the things we ought and to hate the things we ought has the greatest bearing on excellence of character. *Ib. X, 1*

23 If happiness is activity in accordance with excellence, it is reasonable that it should be in accordance with the highest excellence. *Ib. 7*

24 We make war that we may live in peace.[11] *Ib.*

25 With regard to excellence, it is not enough to know, but we must try to have and use it. *Ib. 9*

26 Man is by nature a political animal. *Politics, bk. I, ch. 2*

27 Nature does nothing uselessly.[12] *Ib.*

28 He who is unable to live in society, or who has no need because he is sufficient for himself, must be either a beast or a god. *Ib.*

29 The two qualities which chiefly inspire regard and affection [are] that a thing is your own and that it is your only one. *Ib. II, 4*

[7] One swallow maketh not summer.—JOHN HEYWOOD, *Proverbs* [1546], *pt. II, ch. 5*

One swallow makes a summer.—ROBERT LOWELL, *Fall, 1961*

[8] See Homer, 58:28.

[9] See Sallust, 103:5.

[10] See Descartes, 272:10.

[11] See Vegetius, 128:25; Robert Burton, 259:13; Fénelon, 316:12; Washington, 379:9; and Lowell, 568:9.

[12] God and nature do nothing uselessly.—*On the Heavens, bk. I, ch. 4*

1 It is the nature of desire not to be satisfied, and most men live only for the gratification of it. The beginning of reform is not so much to equalize property as to train the noble sort of natures not to desire more, and to prevent the lower from getting more. *Ib. 7*

2 Even when laws have been written down, they ought not always to remain unaltered. *Ib. 8*

3 Again, men in general desire the good, and not merely what their fathers had. *Ib.*

4 They should rule who are able to rule best. *Ib. 11*

5 A state is not a mere society, having a common place, established for the prevention of mutual crime and for the sake of exchange. . . . Political society exists for the sake of noble actions, and not of mere companionship. *Ib. III, 9*

6 If liberty and equality, as is thought by some, are chiefly to be found in democracy, they will be best attained when all persons alike share in the government to the utmost.[1] *Ib. IV, 4*

7 The best political community is formed by citizens of the middle class. *Ib. 11*

8 Democracy arises out of the notion that those who are equal in any respect are equal in all respects; because men are equally free, they claim to be absolutely equal. *Ib. V, 1*

9 Inferiors revolt in order that they may be equal, and equals that they may be superior. Such is the state of mind which creates revolutions. *Ib. 2*

10 In revolutions the occasions may be trifling but great interests are at stake. *Ib. 3*

11 Well begun is half done.[2] *Ib. 4*

12 The basis of a democratic state is liberty. *Ib. VI, 2*

13 Law is order, and good law is good order. *Ib. VII, 4*

14 Evils draw men together.[3] *Rhetoric, bk. I, ch. 6*

15 It is this simplicity that makes the uneducated more effective than the educated when addressing popular audiences. *Ib. II, 22*

16 A tragedy is the imitation of an action that is serious and also, as having magnitude, complete in itself . . . with incidents arousing pity and fear, wherewith to accomplish its catharsis of such emotions. *Poetics, ch. 6*

17 A whole is that which has beginning, middle, and end. *Ib. 7*

18 Poetry is something more philosophic and of graver import than history, since its statements are of the nature of universals, whereas those of history are singulars. *Ib. 9*

19 A likely impossibility is always preferable to an unconvincing possibility. *Ib. 24*

20 Misfortune shows those who are not really friends.[4] *Eudemian Ethics, bk. VII, ch. 2*

Demosthenes

c. 384–322 B.C.

21 Every advantage in the past is judged in the light of the final issue. *First Olynthiac, sec. 11*

22 Nothing is easier than self-deceit. For what each man wishes, that he also believes to be true.[5] *Third Olynthiac, sec. 19*

23 You cannot have a proud and chivalrous spirit if your conduct is mean and paltry; for whatever a man's actions are, such must be his spirit. *Ib. 33*

24 I decline to buy repentance at the cost of ten thousand drachmas.[6] *From* AULUS GELLIUS, *Noctes Atticae, bk. I, ch. 8*

Antigonus

c. 382–301 B.C.

25 But how many ships do you reckon my presence to be worth?[7] *From* PLUTARCH, *Apothegms, Antigonus*

26 [When described by Hermodotus as "Son of the Sun"] My valet is not aware of this.[8] *Ib.*

[1] See Plato, 85:3.
[2] Aristotle is quoting a proverb.
See Plato, 84:8; Horace, 108:20; and Heywood, 159:29.
[3] Aristotle is quoting a proverb.

[4] In prosperity it is very easy to find a friend, but in adversity it is the most difficult of all things. — EPICTETUS, *Fragment 127*
See Cicero, 99:6; Publilius Syrus, 112:10; Ovid, 113:28; and Heywood, 160:19.
[5] See Caesar, 99:15.
[6] In reply to the courtesan Laïs.
[7] His pilot had told him that the enemy outnumbered him in ships.
[8] See Montaigne, 165:17.
The phrase "No man is a hero to his valet" has often been attributed to Madame de Sévigné, but on the authority of Madame Aissé (*Letters*, edited by JULES RAVENAL, 1853) it belongs to Madame Cornuel [1605–1694].

Mencius[1]

372–289 B.C.

1 When one by force subdues men, they do not submit to him in heart. They submit, because their strength is not adequate to resist.
Works, bk. II, 1:3.2

2 There is no attribute of the superior man greater than his helping men to practice virtue.
Ib. 1:8.5

3 The superior man will not manifest either narrow-mindedness or the want of self-respect.
Ib. 1:9.3

4 To give the throne to another man would be easy; to find a man who shall benefit the kingdom is difficult.
Ib. III, 1:4.10

5 Never has a man who has bent himself been able to make others straight.
Ib. 2:1.5

6 If you know that [a] thing is unrighteous, then use all dispatch in putting an end to it —why wait till next year?
Ib. 2:8.3

7 The compass and square produce perfect circles and squares. By the sages, the human relations are perfectly exhibited.
Ib. IV, 1:2.1

8 The root of the kingdom is in the state. The root of the state is in the family. The root of the family is in the person of its head.
Ib. 1:5

9 The people turn to a benevolent rule as water flows downwards, and as wild beasts fly to the wilderness.
Ib. 1:9.2

10 Benevolence is the tranquil habitation of man, and righteousness is his straight path.
Ib. 1:10.2

11 The path of duty lies in what is near, and man seeks for it in what is remote.
Ib. 1:11

12 Sincerity is the way of Heaven.
Ib. 1:12.2

13 There are three things which are unfilial, and to have no posterity is the greatest of them.[2]
Ib. 1:26.1

14 Men must be decided on what they will not do, and then they are able to act with vigor in what they ought to do.
Ib. 2:8

15 The great man does not think beforehand of his words that they may be sincere, nor of his actions that they may be resolute—he simply speaks and does what is right.
Ib. 2:11

16 The great man is he who does not lose his child's-heart.[3]
Ib. 2:12

17 Friendship with a man is friendship with his virtue, and does not admit of assumptions of superiority.
Ib. 2:13.1

18 The tendency of man's nature to good is like the tendency of water to flow downwards.
Ib. VI, 1:2.2

19 From the feelings proper to it, [man's nature] is constituted for the practice of what is good.
Ib. 1:6.5–6

20 Benevolence, righteousness, propriety, and knowledge are not infused into us from without.
Ib. 1:6.7

21 Benevolence is man's mind, and righteousness is man's path.
Ib. 1:11.1

22 The great end of learning is nothing else but to seek for the lost mind.[4]
Ib. 1:11.4

23 All men have in themselves that which is truly honorable. Only they do not think of it.
Ib. 1:17.1

24 If a scholar have not faith [in his principles], how shall he take a firm hold of things?
Ib. 2:12

25 When Heaven is about to confer a great office on any man, it first exercises his mind with suffering, and his sinews and bones with toil.
Ib. 2:15.2

26 Kindly words do not enter so deeply into men as a reputation for kindness.
Ib. VII, 1:14.1

27 Is it only the mouth and belly which are injured by hunger and thirst? Men's minds are also injured by them.
Ib. 1:27.1

28 The people are the most important element in a nation; the spirits of the land and grain are next; the sovereign is the lightest.
Ib. 2:14.1

[1] From *The Chinese Classics* [1861–1886], vol. II, *The Works of Mencius,* translated by JAMES LEGGE.

[2] To be without posterity . . . is an offense against the whole line of ancestors, and terminates the sacrifices to them.—MENCIUS, *Ib.*

[3] "Except ye be converted, and become as little children, ye shall not enter into the kingdom of heaven" [*Matthew 18:3*]. But Christ speaks of the child's-heart as a thing to be regained; Mencius speaks of it as a thing not to be lost. —JAMES LEGGE

See Mencius, 89:22.

[4] The Chinese sages always end with the recovery of "the old heart"; the idea of "a new heart" is unknown to them.—JAMES LEGGE

See Mencius, 89:16.

Chuang-tzu[1]

369–286 B.C.

1 Great wisdom is generous; petty wisdom is contentious. Great speech is impassioned, small speech cantankerous.

On Leveling All Things

2 Take, for instance, a twig and a pillar, or the ugly person and the great beauty, and all the strange and monstrous transformations. These are all leveled together by Tao. Division is the same as creation; creation is the same as destruction. *Ib.*

3 I do not know whether I was then a man dreaming I was a butterfly, or whether I am now a butterfly dreaming I am a man.

Ib.

4 All men know the utility of useful things; but they do not know the utility of futility.

This Human World

5 He who pursues fame at the risk of losing his self is not a scholar.

The Great Supreme

6 Those who seek to satisfy the mind of man by hampering it with ceremonies and music and affecting charity and devotion have lost their original nature. *Joined Toes*

7 In the days of perfect nature, man lived together with birds and beasts, and there was no distinction of their kind . . . they were in a state of natural integrity. . . . When Sages appeared, crawling for charity and limping with duty, doubt and confusion entered men's minds. . . . Destruction of Tao and virtue in order to introduce charity and duty —this is the error of the Sages.

Horses' Hoofs

8 Banish wisdom, discard knowledge, and gangsters will stop!

Opening Trunks; or, A Protest Against Civilization

9 For all men strive to grasp what they do not know, while none strive to grasp what they already know; and all strive to discredit what they do not excel in, while none strive to discredit what they do excel in. This is why there is chaos. *Ib.*

10 Cherish that which is within you, and shut off that which is without; for much knowledge is a curse. *On Tolerance*

[1] From *The Wisdom of China and India* [1942], edited by LIN YUTANG.

11 "The prince keeps [a] tortoise carefully enclosed in a chest in his ancestral temple. Now would this tortoise rather be dead and have its remains venerated, or would it rather be alive and wagging its tail in the mud?"

"It would rather be alive . . . and wagging its tail in the mud."

"Begone!" cried Chuang-tzu. "I too will wag my tail in the mud." *Autumn Floods*

Pytheas[2]

fl. 330 B.C.

12 They smell of the lamp.[3]

From PLUTARCH, *Lives, Demosthenes*

Alexander the Great

356–323 B.C.

13 [At Achilles' tomb] O fortunate youth, to have found Homer as the herald of your glory![4] *From* CICERO, *Pro Archia, 24*

14 If I were not Alexander, I would be Diogenes.

From PLUTARCH, *Lives, Alexander, 14*

Apelles

fl. 325 B.C.

15 Not a day without a line.[5]

Proverbial from PLINY THE ELDER, *Natural History, XXXV, 36*

16 A cobbler should not judge above his last.[6] *Ib. 85*

Menander[7]

c. 342–292 B.C.

17 We live, not as we wish to, but as we can.

Lady of Andros, fragment 50

18 Riches cover a multitude of woes.

The Boeotian Girl, fragment 90

[2] See Virgil, 103:*n*14.

[3] Pytheas refers to the orations of Demosthenes, who worked in an underground cave lighted only by a lamp.

See Cardozo, 730:15.

[4] See Chateaubriand, 419:8.

[5] Nulla dies sine linea.

See Trollope, 555:10.

[6] Ne supra crepidam sutor iudicaret.

The more common rendering is: Cobbler, stick to your last.

[7] Translated by F. C. ALLINSON (Loeb Classical Library).

1 Whom the gods love dies young.[1]
The Double Deceiver, fragment 125

2 At times discretion should be thrown aside, and with the foolish we should play the fool.[2]
Those Offered for Sale, fragment 421

3 The man who has never been flogged has never been taught.[3]
The Girl Who Gets Flogged, fragment 422

4 The truth sometimes not sought for comes forth to the light. *Ib. 433*

5 This is living, not to live unto oneself alone.
The Brothers in Love, fragment 508

6 Deus ex machina [A god from the machine].
The Woman Possessed with a Divinity, fragment 227

7 I call a fig a fig, a spade a spade.[4]
Unidentified fragment 545

8 Even God lends a hand to honest boldness.[5] *Ib. 572*

9 Marriage, if one will face the truth, is an evil, but a necessary evil.[6] *Ib. 651*

10 It is not white hair that engenders wisdom.
Ib. 639

11 Health and intellect are the two blessings of life. *Monostikoi (Single Lines)*

12 The man who runs may fight again.[7]
Ib.

13 Conscience is a God to all mortals.
Ib.

Epicurus

341–270 B.C.

14 Death is nothing to us, since when we are, death has not come, and when death has come, we are not.
From DIOGENES LAERTIUS, *Lives of Eminent Philosophers, bk. X, sec. 125*

15 Pleasure is the beginning and the end of living happily. *Ib. 128*

16 It is impossible to live pleasurably without living wisely, well, and justly, and impossible to live wisely, well, and justly without living pleasurably.[8] *Ib. 140*

Theophrastus

d. 278 B.C.

17 Time is the most valuable thing a man can spend.[9]
From DIOGENES LAERTIUS, *Lives of Eminent Philosophers, bk. V, sec. 40*

Zeno

335–263 B.C.

18 [When asked, "What is a friend?"] Another I.[10]
From DIOGENES LAERTIUS, *Lives of Eminent Philosophers, bk. VII, sec. 23*

19 The goal of life is living in agreement with nature.[11] *Ib. 87*

---

[1] Also in PLAUTUS, *Bacchides, IV, 7:18.*
Those that God loves do not live long. — GEORGE HERBERT, *Jacula Prudentum* [2nd edition, 1651]
See Wordsworth, 428:11.
Heaven gives its favorites — early death. — BYRON, *Childe Harold, canto IV* [1818], *st. 102*

[2] See Horace, 108:15; Montaigne, 166:4; Bacon, 181:3; and Linnaeus, 350:7.

[3] See *Proverbs 13:24*, 23:34, and Samuel Butler, 291:19.
They spare the rod and spoil the child. — RALPH VENNING, *Mysteries and Revelations* [1649]
Also in LUCIAN, *Hermotimus, sec. 86.*

[4] Also attributed to Aristophanes by LUCIAN, *De Conscribend. Hist., 41.*
The Macedonians are a rude and clownish people that call a spade a spade. — PLUTARCH, *Apothegms, Philip of Macedon*
I think it good plain English, without fraud, To call a spade a spade, a bawd a bawd. — JOHN TAYLOR, The Water Poet [1580–1653], *A Kicksey Winsey*

[5] See Terence, 97:1; Virgil, 106:4; and Propertius, 112:22.

[6] Marriage is an evil that most men welcome. — *Monostikoi (Single Lines)*
Motto of *The Spectator* [December 29, 1711].

[7] He who flees will fight again. — TERTULLIAN [c. 155–225], *De Fuga in Persecutione, 10*
That same man that runneth away / May again fight another day. — ERASMUS, *Apothegms* [1542], translated by NICHOLAS UDALL [1505–1556]
Celuy qui fuit de bonne heure / Peut combattre derechef / [Who flies in good time / Can fight anew]. — ANONYMOUS [1594]; *translated from* VARRO [116–27 B.C.], *Saturae Menippeae*
For he who fights and runs away / May live to fight another day; / But he who is in battle slain / Can never rise and fight again. — GOLDSMITH, *The Art of Poetry on a New Plan* [1761]
A version similar to Goldsmith's appears in JAMES RAY, *History of the Rebellion* [1752].

[8] See Sophocles, 75:2.

[9] Nothing is so dear and precious as time. — RABELAIS, *Works, bk. V* [1564], *ch. 5*
See Franklin, 348:1.

[10] In Latin: Alter ego.
See Aristotle, 87:1; Cicero, 99:7; Horace, 106:26; and Donne, 253:4.

[11] See Marcus Aurelius, 124:19.

Cleanthes
c. 330–232 B.C.

1 For we are your offspring.[1]
Hymn to Zeus, l. 4

2 Lead me, Zeus, and you, Fate, wherever you have assigned me. I shall follow without hesitation; but even if I am disobedient and do not wish to, I shall follow no less surely.
From EPICTETUS, *Enchiridion, sec. 53*

Euclid
fl. 300 B.C.

3 Q.E.D. [Quod erat demonstrandum: Which was to be proved.]
Elements, bk. I, proposition 5[2]

4 [To Ptolemy I] There is no royal road to geometry.[3]
From PROCLUS, *Commentary on Euclid, Prologue*

Bion
c. 325 – c. 255 B.C.

5 Old age is the harbor of all ills.
From DIOGENES LAERTIUS, *Lives of Eminent Philosophers, bk. IV, sec. 47*

6 Wealth is the sinews of affairs.[4]
Ib. 48

7 The road to Hades is easy to travel.[5]
Ib. 49

8 He has not acquired a fortune; the fortune has acquired him.[6] *Ib. 50*

9 Though boys throw stones at frogs in sport, the frogs do not die in sport, but in earnest.[7]
From PLUTARCH, *Water and Land Animals, 7*

[1]Possibly the source of *Acts 17:28*, 46:17. See also Aeschylus, 71:11, and Aratus, 92:11.

[2]Proposition 5, too difficult for many students to pass beyond, became known as the asses' bridge [pons asinorum].

[3]Often quoted as: There is no royal road to learning.

[4]See Cicero, 99:11; Rabelais, 157:10; Dryden, 305:22; and Churchill, 746:10.

[5]See *Matthew 7:13, 14*, 38:15; Virgil, 105:15; and Shakespeare, 218:28 and 238:2.
A passage broad, / Smooth, easy, inoffensive, down to Hell. — MILTON, *Paradise Lost, bk. II, l. 432*

[6]See Robert Burton, 258:22, and Ingersoll, 615:9.

[7]See L'Estrange, 294:20.

Pyrrhus
c. 318–272 B.C.

10 Another such victory over the Romans, and we are undone.[8]
From PLUTARCH, *Lives, Pyrrhus, sec. 21*

Aratus
c. 315–240 B.C.

11 From Zeus let us begin, whom we mortals never leave unnamed: full of Zeus are all streets and all gathering places of men, and full are the sea and harbors. Everywhere we all have need of Zeus. For we are also his offspring.[9] *Phaenomena, sec. 1*

Theocritus[10]
c. 310–250 B.C.

12 Sweet is the whispering music of yonder pine
that sings.[11] *Idylls, I*

13 Our concern be peace of mind: some old crone
let us seek,
To spit on us for luck and keep unlovely
things afar. *Ib. VII*

14 Cicala to cicala is dear, and ant to ant,
And kestrels dear to kestrels, but to me the
Muse and song. *Ib. IX*

15 The frog's life is most jolly, my lads; he has no
care
Who shall fill up his cup; for he has drink
enough to spare. *Ib. X*

16 Verily great grace may go
With a little gift; and precious are all things
that come from friends.[12] *Ib. XXVIII*

Callimachus
c. 300–240 B.C.

17 Big book, big bore.[13]
From The Greek Anthology [1973], PETER JAY, *ed., introduction to Callimachus*

18 You're walking by the tomb of Battiades,[14]
Who knew well how to write poetry, and
enjoy
Laughter at the right moment, over the wine.
Ib. no. 150, On Himself[15]

[8]Pyrrhus, king of Epirus, refers to the dearly bought victory at Asculum, 280 B.C. Hence the phrase: Pyrrhic victory. See also Herodotus, 78:7 ("Cadmean victory").

[9]Probably the source of *Acts 17:28*, 46:17.
See also Aeschylus, 71:11, and Cleanthes, 92:1.

[10]Translated by R. C. TREVELYAN.

[11]See Longfellow, 510:26.

[12]See Homer, 60:1.

[13]In reference to the traditional epics.

[14]Callimachus.

[15]Translated by PETER JAY.

1 Someone spoke of your death, Heraclitus.[1] It brought me
Tears, and I remembered how often together
We ran the sun down with talk . . . somewhere
You've long been dust, my Halicarnassian friend.
But your *Nightingales* live on. Though the Death-world
Claws at everything, it will not touch them.[2] *Ib. 152*

Leonidas of Tarentum

C. 290 – C. 220 B.C.

2 Far from Italy, far from my native Tarentum
I lie; and this is the worst of it—worse than death.
An exile's life is no life. But the Muses loved me.
For my suffering they gave me a honeyed gift:
My name survives me. Thanks to the sweet Muses
Leonidas will echo throughout all time.[3]

From The Greek Anthology [1973], PETER JAY, ed., no. 189

3 The season of ships is here,
The west wind and the swallows;
Flowers in the fields appear,
And the ocean of hills and hollows
Has calmed its waves and is clear.

Free that anchor and chain!
Set your full canvas flying,
O men in the harbor lane:
It is I, Priapus, crying.
Sail out on your trades again![4] *Ib. 197*

Archimedes

C. 287–212 B.C.

4 Eureka! [I have found it!][5]

From VITRUVIUS POLLIO [first century B.C.], De Architectura, bk. IX, 215

5 Give me where to stand, and I will move the earth.[6]

From PAPPUS OF ALEXANDRIA, Collectio, bk. VIII, prop. 10, sec. 11

[1] Elegiac poet from Halicarnassus, author of a collection of poems, *Nightingales*, and a friend of Callimachus.

[2] Translated by PETER JAY.

See Cory, 591:9.

[3] Translated by FLEUR ADCOCK.

[4] Translated by CLIVE SANSOM.

[5] On discovery of a method to test the purity of gold.

[6] Said with reference to the lever.

Fabius Maximus

C. 275–203 B.C.

6 To be turned from one's course by men's opinions, by blame, and by misrepresentation shows a man unfit to hold an office.[7]

From PLUTARCH, Lives, Fabius Maximus, sec. 5

Lacydes

fl. C. 241 B.C.

7 [When asked late in life why he was studying geometry] If I should not be learning now, when should I be?

From DIOGENES LAERTIUS, Lives of Eminent Philosophers, Lacydes, sec. 5

Titus Maccius Plautus

254–184 B.C.

8 What is yours is mine, and all mine is yours.[8] *Trinummus, act II, sc. ii, l. 48*

9 Not by age but by capacity is wisdom acquired. *Ib. l. 88*

10 You are seeking a knot in a bulrush.[9] *Menaechmi, act II, sc. i, l. 22*

11 In the one hand he is carrying a stone, while he shows the bread in the other.[10] *Aulularia, act II, sc. ii, l. 18*

12 There are occasions when it is undoubtedly better to incur loss than to make gain. *Captivi, act II, sc. ii, l. 77*

13 Patience is the best remedy for every trouble. *Rudens, act II, sc. v, l. 71*

14 Consider the little mouse, how sagacious an animal it is which never entrusts its life to one hole only.[11] *Truculentus, act IV, sc. iv, l. 15*

[7] See Horace, 107:28.

[8] See Shakespeare, 229:10.

[9] A proverbial expression implying a desire to create doubts and difficulties where there really are none. It occurs in TERENCE, *Andria, V, 4:38;* also in ENNIUS, *Saturae, 46.*

[10] See *Matthew 7:9*, 38:13.

[11] I holde a mouses herte nat worth a leek, / That hath but oon hole for to sterte to, / And if that faille, thanne is al y-do. —CHAUCER, *The Canterbury Tales* [c. 1387], *The Wife of Bath's Prologue, l. 572*

The mouse that hath but one hole is quickly taken. — GEORGE HERBERT, *Jacula Prudentum* [1640]

The mouse that always trusts to one poor hole / Can never be a mouse of any soul. — POPE, *Paraphrase of the Prologue* [1714], *l. 298*

1 No guest is so welcome in a friend's house that he will not become a nuisance after three days.[1]

Miles Gloriosus, act III, sc. i

2 No man is wise enough by himself.

Ib. iii

3 Nothing is there more friendly to a man than a friend in need.[2]

Epidicus, act III, sc. iii, l. 44

4 Things which you do not hope happen more frequently than things which you do hope.[3]

Mostellaria, act I, sc. iii, l. 40

5 To blow and swallow at the same moment is not easy. *Ib. III, ii, l. 104*

6 Practice yourself what you preach.[4]

Asinaria, act III, sc. iii, l. 644

Maharbal [Barca the Carthaginian]

fl. 210 B.C.

7 You know how to win a victory, Hannibal, but not how to use it.[5]

From LIVY, *History, XXII, 51*

Bhagavad Gita[6]

250 B.C.–A.D. 250[7]

8 For certain is death for the born
And certain is birth for the dead;
Therefore over the inevitable
Thou shouldst not grieve.[8]

Chapter 2, verse 27

9 This embodied [soul] is eternally unslayable
In the body of everyone, son of Bharata;
Therefore all beings
Thou shouldst not mourn.

Likewise having regard for thine own [caste] duty
Thou shouldst not tremble;
For another, better thing than a fight required of duty
Exists not for a warrior.

2:30

10 On action alone be thy interest,
Never on its fruits.
Let not the fruits of action be thy motive,
Nor be thy attachment to inaction.[9]

2:47

11 Better one's own duty, [though] imperfect,
Than another's duty well performed.[10]

3:35 and 18:47

12 In whatsoever way any come to Me,
In that same way I grant them favor.[10]

4:11

13 Who sees Me in all,
And sees all in Me,
For him I am not lost,
And he is not lost for Me.[10] *6:30*

14 Whatsoever state [of being] meditating upon
He leaves the body at death,[11]
To just that he goes, son of Kunti,
Always being made to be in the condition of that.[12] *8:6*

15 If the radiance of a thousand suns were to burst forth at once in the sky, that would be like the splendor of the Mighty One [Krishna].[13] *11:12*

Quintus Ennius

239–169 B.C.

16 No sooner said than done—so acts your man of worth.

Annals, bk. 9 (quoted by PRISCIANUS*)*

17 I never indulge in poetics
Unless I am down with rheumatics.

Fragment of a satire (quoted by PRISCIANUS*)*

[1] Fish and guests in three days are stale.—JOHN LYLY, *Euphues* [1579]

Fish and visitors stink in three days.—BENJAMIN FRANKLIN, *Poor Richard's Almanac* [1736], *January*

[2] A friend in need is a friend indeed.—HAZLITT, *English Proverbs*

[3] The unexpected always happens.—*Common saying*

[4] Facias ipse quod faciamus suades.

See St. Jerome, 127:21.

[5] Vincere scis, Hannibal, victoria uti nescis.

Maharbal was commander of cavalry under Hannibal, who had insisted on a day's rest for the army after the victory at Cannae [216 B.C.], thereby enabling the enemy to recoup.

See Polybius, 95:17.

[6] Sanskrit: The Lord's Song.

[7] Ancient Indian literary chronology is conjectural. The dates given are approximate.

[8] Translated by ANNIE BESANT.

[9] Translated by F. EDGERTON.

At the moment which is not of action or inaction / You can receive this: "on whatever sphere of being / The mind of a man may be intent / At the time of death"—that is the one action / (And the time of death is every moment) / Which shall fructify in the lives of others: / And do not think of the fruit of action, / Fare forward.—T. S. ELIOT, *Four Quartets* [1943], *The Dry Salvages, pt. III*

[10] Translated by F. EDGERTON.

[11] See Eliot's lines from *The Dry Salvages* quoted in the note to *Gita 2:47*, 94:10.

[12] Translated by F. EDGERTON.

[13] Translated by SWAMI NIKHILANANDA.

Quoted by J. Robert Oppenheimer when the first atomic bomb exploded [July 16, 1945, near Alamogordo, New Mexico].

1 By delaying he preserved the state.[1]
From Cicero, De Senectute, IV

2 Let no one pay me honor with tears, nor celebrate my funeral rites with weeping.[2]
Ib. XX

3 The ape, vilest of beasts, how like to us.[3]
From Cicero, De Natura Deorum, bk. I, ch. 35

4 No one regards what is before his feet; we all gaze at the stars.
Iphigenia. From Cicero, De Divinatione, bk. II, ch. 13

5 The idle mind knows not what it is it wants. *Ib.*

6 Whom they fear they hate.[4]
Thyestes. From Cicero, De Officiis, II, 7

Marcus Porcius Cato [Cato the Elder][5]

234–149 B.C.

7 A farm is like a man—however great the income, if there is extravagance but little is left. *On Agriculture,[6] bk. I, sec. 6*

8 Even though work stops, expenses run on.
Ib. XXXIX, 2

9 It is a hard matter, my fellow citizens, to argue with the belly, since it has no ears.[7]
From Plutarch, Lives, Cato, sec. 8

10 Wise men profit more from fools than fools from wise men; for the wise men shun the mistakes of fools, but fools do not imitate the successes of the wise. *Ib. 9*

11 I would much rather have men ask why I have no statue, than why I have one.
Ib. 19

12 Carthage must be destroyed.[8] *Ib. 27*

[1]This refers to Quintus Fabius Maximus, "Cunctator." Hence the "Fabian policy" of waiting.

[2]See Tennyson, 535:19.

No funeral gloom, my dears, when I am gone, / Corpse-gazings, tears, black raiment, graveyard grimness.—William Allingham [1828–1889], *Diary*

[3]Simia quam similis, turpissima bestia, nobis!

[4]See Accius, 97:9, and Machiavelli, 153:19.

[5]Also known as Cato the Censor.

[6]Translated by William D. Hooper, revised by Harrison Boyd Ash (Loeb Classical Library).

[7]The belly has no ears nor is it to be filled with fair words.—Rabelais, *Works, IV* [1548], *67*

See La Fontaine, 296:21, and Adlai Stevenson, 851:11.

[8]Delenda est Carthago.

These words were added to every speech Cato made in the senate, preceded by *ceterum censeo* [in my opinion].

13 Grasp the subject, the words will follow.[9]
From Caius Julius Victor, Ars Rhetorica, I [4th century A.D.]

14 An orator is a good man who is skilled in speaking.
From Seneca the Elder [c. 45 B.C.–A.D. 40], Controversiae, I, Preface, and elsewhere

Caecilius Statius

220–168 B.C.

15 He plants trees to benefit another generation.[10]
Synephebi. Quoted by Cicero in De Senectute, VII

Polybius

c. 208 – c. 126 B.C.

16 For peace, with justice and honor, is the fairest and most profitable of possessions, but with disgrace and shameful cowardice it is the most infamous and harmful of all.
History, bk. IV, sec. 31

17 Those who know how to win are much more numerous than those who know how to make proper use of their victories.[11]
Ib. X, 36

18 That historians should give their own country a break, I grant you; but not so as to state things contrary to fact. For there are plenty of mistakes made by writers out of ignorance, and which any man finds it difficult to avoid. But if we knowingly write what is false, whether for the sake of our country or our friends or just to be pleasant, what difference is there between us and hack writers? Readers should be very attentive to and critical of historians, and they in turn should be constantly on their guard.[12]
Ib. XVI

19 There is no witness so dreadful, no accuser so terrible as the conscience that dwells in the heart of every man.[13]
Ib. XVIII, 43

[9]Rem tene; verba sequentur.

[10]Serit arbores quae alteri seculo prosint.

John Quincy Adams used *Alteri seculo* for his seal [c. 1830].

See John Adams, 381:14.

He that plants trees loves others beside himself.—Thomas Fuller, *Gnomologia* [1732]

A man does not plant a tree for himself; he plants it for posterity.—Alexander Smith, *Dreamthorp* [1863], *ch. 11*

[11]See Maharbal, 94:7.

[12]Translated by S. E. Morison.

See Cicero, 98:10.

[13]See Stubbs, 660:9, and R. L. Stevenson, 668:22.

Terence[1] [Publius Terentius Afer]

c. 190–159 B.C.

1 Moderation in all things.[2]
Andria (The Lady of Andros), l. 61

2 Obsequiousness begets friends, truth hatred.[3] *Ib. l. 68*

3 Hence these tears.[4] *Ib. l. 126*

4 I am Davos, not Oedipus.[5] *Ib. l. 194*

5 Lovers' quarrels are the renewal of love.[6] *Ib. l. 555*

6 Charity begins at home.[7] *Ib. l. 635*

7 I am a man: nothing human is alien to me.[8]
Heauton Timoroumenos (The Self-Tormentor), l. 77

8 Draw from others the lesson that may profit yourself.[9] *Ib. l. 221*

9 Time removes distress.[10] *Ib. l. 421*

10 Nothing is so difficult but that it may be found out by seeking.[11] *Ib. l. 675*

[1]Translated by JOHN SARGEAUNT (Loeb Classical Library), with occasional adaptations.

[2]Ne quid nimis.

See The Seven Sages, 62:7; Horace, 106:12 and 107:20; Lucan, 118:8; Anonymous Latin, 134:12; and Voltaire, 343:23.

[3]Obsequium amicos, veritas odium parit.

[4]Hinc illae lacrimae.

The phrase is proverbial for "That's the cause of it," and was often quoted, by Horace in *Epistles, I, xix, 41,* and by others.

Hence rage and tears [Inde irae et lacrimae].—JUVENAL, *Satires, bk. I, l. 168*

[5]Davos sum, non Oedipus.

[6]Amantium irae amoris integratio est.

This was quoted by Winston Churchill in a message to Franklin D. Roosevelt.

The anger of lovers renews the strength of love.—PUBLILIUS SYRUS [first century B.C.], *Maxim 24*

The falling out of faithful friends renewing is of love. —RICHARD EDWARDS, *The Paradise of Dainty Devices* [1576]

Let the falling out of friends be a renewing of affection. —JOHN LYLY, *Euphues* [1579]

The falling out of lovers is the renewing of love.—ROBERT BURTON, *Anatomy of Melancholy* [1621–1651], *pt. III, sec. 2*

[7]Proxumus sum egomet mihi.

See *I Timothy 5:4,* 50:30, and Sir Thomas Browne, 274:19.

[8]Homo sum: humani nil a me alienum puto. Quoted by CICERO in *De Officiis, I, 30.*

[9]Periclum ex aliis facito tibi quod ex usu siet. (A saying.)

Profit by the folly of others.—PLINY THE ELDER [A.D. 23–79], *Natural History, bk. XVIII, 31*

[10]Diem adimere aegritudinem hominibus. (A saying: Time heals all wounds.)

See Sophocles, 74:5, and La Fontaine, 296:17.

[11]Nil tam difficile est quin quaerendo investigari possiet.

11 Some people ask, "What if the sky were to fall?"[12] *Ib. l. 719*

12 Extreme law is often extreme injustice.[13] *Ib. l. 796*

13 There is nothing so easy but that it becomes difficult when you do it reluctantly. *Ib. l. 805*

14 While there's life, there's hope.[14] *Ib. l. 981*

15 In fact, nothing is said that has not been said before.[15]
Eunuchus, l. 41 (Prologue)

16 I have everything, yet have nothing; and although I possess nothing, still of nothing am I in want.[16] *Ib. l. 243*

17 There are vicissitudes in all things.[17] *Ib. l. 276*

18 I don't care one straw.[18] *Ib. l. 411*

19 Take care and say this with presence of mind.[19] *Ib. l. 769*

20 He is wise who tries everything before arms. *Ib. l. 789*

21 I know the disposition of women: when you will, they won't; when you won't, they set their hearts upon you of their own inclination. *Ib. l. 812*

22 I took to my heels as fast as I could. *Ib. l. 844*

23 Many a time . . . from a bad beginning great friendships have sprung up. *Ib. l. 873*

[12]Quid si nunc caelum ruat?

Some ambassadors from the Celtae, being asked by Alexander what in the world they dreaded most, answered, that they feared lest the sky should fall upon them.—ARRIANUS [c. 100–170], *bk. I, 4*

[13]Ius summum saepe summa est malitia.

See Anonymous Latin, 134:29.

Extreme law, extreme injustice, is now become a stale proverb in discourse.—CICERO [106–43 B.C.], *De Officiis, I, 33*

Extreme justice is often injustice.—RACINE, *La Thébaïde* [1664], *act IV, sc. iii*

Mais l'extrême justice est une extrême injure.—VOLTAIRE, *Oedipe* [1718], *act III, sc. iii*

[14]Modo liceat vivere, est spes.

See Cicero, 98:18, and Goldsmith, 368:11.

[15]See *Ecclesiastes 1:9,* 26:14; Robert Burton, 258:6; and La Bruyère, 315:4.

[16]See *II Corinthians 6:10,* 49:17, and Wotton, 250:16.

[17]See Bacon, 181:15, and Sterne, 359:17.

[18]Ego non flocci pendere.

Nor do they care a straw.—CERVANTES, *Don Quixote, pt. I* [1605], *bk. III, ch. 9*

[19]Fac animo haec praesenti dicas. Literally, "with a present mind"—equivalent to Caesar's *praesentia animi (De Bello Gallico, V, 43, 4).*

1 Fortune helps the brave.[1]

Phormio, l. 203

2 So many men, so many opinions; every one his own way.[2] *Ib. l. 454*

3 As they say, I have got a wolf by the ears.[3]

Ib. l. 506

4 I bid him look into the lives of men as though into a mirror, and from others to take an example for himself.

Adelphoe (The Brothers), l. 415

5 According as the man is, so must you humor him. *Ib. l. 431*

6 It is the common vice of all, in old age, to be too intent upon our interests.[4]

Ib. l. 833

Huai-nan Tzu[5]
[Liu An]

Second century B.C.

7 Before heaven and earth had taken form all was vague and amorphous. Therefore it was called the Great Beginning. The Great Beginning produced emptiness and emptiness produced the universe. . . . The combined essences of heaven and earth became the yin and yang, the concentrated essences of the yin and yang became the four seasons, and the scattered essences of the four seasons became the myriad creatures of the world.

Huai-nan Tzu, 3:1a

Tung Chung-shu[5]

c. 179 – c. 104 B.C.

8 He who is the ruler of men takes nonaction as his way and considers impartiality as his treasure. He sits upon the throne of nonaction and rides upon the perfection of his officials. *Ch'un-ch'iu fan-lu*

[1] See Menander, 91:8, and Virgil, 106:4.
Pliny the Younger says *(bk. VI, letter 16)* that Pliny the Elder said this during the eruption of Vesuvius: "Fortune favors the brave."

[2] Quot homines tot sententiae: suo quoque mos.
So many heads so many wits.—JOHN HEYWOOD, *Proverbs* [1546], *pt. I, ch. 2*
So many men so many minds.—GEORGE GASCOIGNE, *The Glass of Government* [1575]

[3] A proverbial expression which, according to Suetonius, was frequently in the mouth of Tiberius Caesar.

[4] Cicero quotes this in *Tusculan Disputations, bk. III.* The maxim was a favorite with the Stoic philosophers.

[5] *Huai-nan Tzu* is from the scholarly court of Liu An (d. 122 B.C.), prince of Huai-nan, known also as Huai-nan Tzu.
From *Sources of Chinese Tradition* [1960], edited by WILLIAM THEODORE DE BARY.

Lucius Accius

170–86 B.C.

9 Let them hate, so long as they fear.[6]

Fragment

Han Wu-ti[7]

157–87 B.C.

10 The sound of her silk skirt has stopped.
On the marble pavement dust grows.
Her empty room is cold and still.
Fallen leaves are piled against the doors.
  Longing for that lovely lady
How can I bring my aching heart to rest?

On the death of his mistress[8]

Marcus Terentius Varro

116–27 B.C.

11 The longest part of the journey is said to be the passing of the gate.

On Agriculture [De Re Rustica],[9] *bk. I, ii, 2*

12 When people come to inspect . . . farmsteads, it is not to see collections of pictures . . . but collections of fruit. *Ib. 10*

13 Not all who own a harp are harpers.

Ib. II, i, 3

14 It was divine nature which gave us the country, and man's skill that built the cities.[10] *Ib. III, i, 4*

Marcus Licinius Crassus

fl. 70 B.C.

15 Those who aim at great deeds must also suffer greatly.

From PLUTARCH, *Lives, Crassus, ch. 26*

Meleager

First century B.C.

16 Farewell, Morning Star, herald of dawn, and quickly come as the Evening Star, bring-

[6] Oderint dum metuant.
From a lost tragedy. Frequently cited by Cicero and others. Suetonius *(Gaius Caligula, 30)* says that the Emperor Caligula was fond of quoting it.
See Ennius, 95:6, and Machiavelli, 153:19.

[7] Sixth emperor of the Han dynasty.

[8] From *Chinese Poems,* ARTHUR WALEY, translator.

[9] Translated by WILLIAM D. HOOPER, revised by HARRISON BOYD ASH (Loeb Classical Library).

[10] Divina natura dedit agros, ars humana aedificavit urbes.

ing again in secret her whom thou takest away.[1]

The Greek Anthology [1906], J. W. Mackail, ed., sec. 1, no. 21

Marcus Tullius Cicero

106–43 B.C.

1 How long, Catiline, will you abuse our patience?[2] *In Catilinam, I, 1*

2 O tempora! O mores! [Oh the times! The customs!] *Ib.*

3 He has departed, withdrawn, gone away, broken out.[3] *Ib. II, 1*

4 I am a Roman citizen.[4] *In Verrem, V, 57*

5 Law stands mute in the midst of arms.[5] *Pro Milone, IV, 11*

6 Cui bono? [To whose advantage?][6] *Ib. XII, 32*

7 These studies are a spur to the young, a delight to the old; an ornament in prosperity, a consoling refuge in adversity; they are pleasure for us at home, and no burden abroad; they stay up with us at night, they accompany us when we travel, they are with us in our country visits.

Pro Archia Poeta, VII, 16

8 Leisure with dignity.[7] *De Oratore, II, 62*

9 History is the witness that testifies to the passing of time; it illumines reality, vitalizes memory, provides guidance in daily life, and brings us tidings of antiquity.

Ib. II, 36

10 The first law for the historian is that he shall never dare utter an untruth. The second is that he shall suppress nothing that is true. Moreover, there shall be no suspicion of partiality in his writing, or of malice.[8]

Ib. 62

11 The freedom of poetic license.[9] *Ib. III, 153*

12 If a man aspires to the highest place, it is no dishonor to him to halt at the second, or even at the third.

Orator ad M. Brutum, 4

13 For just as some women are said to be handsome though without adornment, so this subtle manner of speech, though lacking in artificial graces, delights us.[10] *Ib. 78*

14 Nothing quite new is perfect. *Brutus, 71*

15 There were poets before Homer. *Ib.*

16 The aim of forensic oratory is to teach, to delight, to move.

De Optimo Genere Oratorum, 16

17 The dregs of Romulus.[11] *Ad Atticum, II, 1*

18 While there's life, there's hope.[12] *Ib. IX, 10*

19 What is more agreeable than one's home?[13] *Ad Familiares, IV, 8*

20 I like myself, but I won't say I'm as handsome as the bull that kidnapped Europa.

De Natura Deorum, I, 78

21 It was ordained at the beginning of the world that certain signs should prefigure certain events.[14] *De Divinatione, I, 118*

22 There is nothing so ridiculous but some philosopher has said it.[15] *Ib. II, 119*

23 I would rather be wrong with Plato than right with such men as these [the Pythagoreans].

Tusculanae Disputationes, I, 17

24 O philosophy, you leader of life.[16] *Ib. V, 2*

25 Socrates was the first to call philosophy down from the heavens and to place it in cities, and even to introduce it into homes and compel it to inquire about life and standards and goods and evils. *Ib. V, 4*

26 The highest good.[17] *De Officiis, I, 2*

27 Let arms yield to the toga, the laurel crown to praise.[18] *Ib. I, 22*

[1] See Sappho, 63:11, and Housman, 692:2.

[2] Quo usque, Catilina, abutere patientia nostra?

[3] Abiit, excessit, evasit, erupit.

Depart—be off—excede—evade—erump!—Oliver Wendell Holmes, *The Autocrat of the Breakfast Table* [1858], *Aestivation, ch. II*

[4] Civis Romanus sum.

[5] Silent enim leges inter arma.

[6] In full: Cui bono fuerit? [To whose advantage was it?]

[7] Otium cum dignitate.

[8] See Polybius, 95:18.

[9] Poetarum licentiae liberiora.

[10] See Milton, 286:3, and Thomson, 345:14.

[11] In Romuli faece. That is, the lowest order of society.

[12] Dum anima est, spes est.

See Terence, 96:14, and Goldsmith, 368:11.

[13] Quae est domestica sede iucundior?

[14] See Shakespeare, 226:5; Campbell, 443:14; Shelley, 470:5; and Wells, 720:9.

[15] See Goethe, 396:22, and Descartes, 272:9.

[16] O vitae philosophia dux.

See John Heath, 407:17.

[17] Summum bonum.

See Lucretius, 101:11.

The nature of the good and the highest good.—Horace, *Satires, II, 6, 76*

[18] Cedant arma togae, concedat laurea laudi.

He is quoting from his own poem *De suis temporibus, bk. III.*

1 Never less idle than when wholly idle, nor less alone than when wholly alone.[1]

Ib. III, 1

2 Rome, fortunately natal 'neath my consulship![2] *De Consultatu Suo*

3 The people's good is the highest law.[3]

De Legibus, III, 3

4 He used to raise a storm in a teapot.[4]

Ib. 16

5 Let the punishment match the offense.[5]

Ib. 20

6 The shifts of Fortune test the reliability of friends.[6] *De Amicitia, XVII*

7 A friend is, as it were, a second self.[7]

Ib. XXI

8 Give me a young man in whom there is something of the old, and an old man with something of the young: guided so, a man may grow old in body, but never in mind.

De Senectute, XI

9 Old men are garrulous by nature.

Ib. XVI

10 Old age: the crown of life, our play's last act. *Ib. XXIII*

11 Endless money forms the sinews of war.[8]

Philippics, V, 2:5

Pompey [Gnaeus Pompeius]

106–48 B.C.

12 More worship the rising than the setting sun.[9]

From PLUTARCH, *Lives, Pompey, 14*

13 A dead man cannot bite. *Ib. 77*

[1]See Samuel Rogers, 416:2, and Thoreau, 560:3.

[2]O fortunatam natam me consule Romam!

The verse is quoted disparagingly by Juvenal (*X, 122*), Quintilian (*XI, 1, 24*), and others.

[3]Salus populi suprema est lex.

[4]Excitabat enim fluctus in simpulo.

A tempest in a teapot.—*Proverb*

[5]Noxiae poena par esto.

See W. S. Gilbert, 629:11.

[6]See Aristotle, 88:20; Publilius Syrus, 112:10; Ovid, 113:28; and Heywood, 160:19.

[7]See Aristotle, 87:1; Zeno, 91:18; Horace, 106:26; and Donne, 253:4.

[8]See Bion, 92:6; Rabelais, 157:10; Dryden, 305:22; and Winston Churchill, 746:10.

He who first called money the sinews of affairs seems to have spoken with special reference to the affairs of war.—PLUTARCH, *Lives, Cleomenes 27*

Neither is money the sinews of war (as it is trivially said).—FRANCIS BACON, *Essays* [1625], *Of the True Greatness of Kingdoms*

Money is the sinew of love as well as of war.—THOMAS FULLER, *Gnomonologia* [1732], *no. 3442*

[9]Addressed to Sulla.

See David Garrick, 363:15.

Julius Caesar

100–44 B.C.

14 All Gaul is divided into three parts.[10]

De Bello Gallico, I, 1

15 Men willingly believe what they wish.[11]

Ib. III, 18

16 I love treason but hate a traitor.[12]

From PLUTARCH, *Lives, Romulus, sec. 17*

17 I wished my wife to be not so much as suspected.[13] *Ib. Caesar, sec. 10*

18 I had rather be the first man among these fellows than the second man in Rome.

Ib. 11

19 The die is cast.[14] *Ib. 32*

20 Go on, my friend, and fear nothing; you carry Caesar and his fortune in your boat.

Ib. 38

21 The Ides of March have come.[15]

Ib. 63

22 [In answer to a question as to what sort of death was the best] A sudden death.

Ib.

23 I came, I saw, I conquered.[16]

From SUETONIUS, *Lives of the Caesars, Julius, sec. 37*

24 You also, Brutus my son.[17] *Ib. 82*

25 It is not these well-fed long-haired men that I fear, but the pale and the hungry-looking.[18]

From PLUTARCH, *Lives, Antony, sec. 11*

[10]Gallia est omnis divisa in partes tres.

[11]Fere libenter homines id quod volunt credunt.

See Demosthenes, 88:22.

[12]Princes in this case do hate the traitor, though they love the treason.—SAMUEL DANIEL, *Tragedy of Cleopatra* [1594], *act IV, sc. i*

This principle is old, but true as fate, / Kings may love treason, but the traitor hate.—DEKKER, *The Honest Whore* [1604], *pt. I, act IV, sc. iv*

Though I love the treason, I hate the traitor.—PEPYS, *Diary, March 7, 1667*

See Dryden, 305:26.

[13]Caesar's wife must be above suspicion.—*Traditional saying*

[14]Iacta alea est. Proverb quoted by Caesar as he crossed the Rubicon.

Also in SUETONIUS, *Lives of the Caesars, Julius.*

[15]See Shakespeare, 215:2.

[16]Veni, vidi, vici. Inscription displayed in Caesar's Pontic triumph.

Also in PLUTARCH, *Apothegms, Caesar.*

[17]Et tu, Brute. Suetonius reports that Caesar said this in Greek.

See Shakespeare, 216:5.

[18]The reference is to Brutus and Cassius.

See Shakespeare, 215:8.

Lucretius[1] [Titus Lucretius Carus]

99–55 B.C.

1 Mother of Aeneas and his race, darling of men and gods, nurturing Venus.
De Rerum Natura (On the Nature of Things), bk. I, l. 1 (Invocation)

2 For thee the wonder-working earth puts forth sweet flowers. *Ib. l. 7*

3 The vivid force of his mind prevailed, and he fared forth far beyond the flaming ramparts of the heavens and traversed the boundless universe in thought and mind.
Ib. l. 72

4 Such evil deeds could religion prompt.[2, 6]
Ib. l. 101

5 Nothing can be created from nothing.[3]
Ib. l. 155

6 The first beginnings of things cannot be distinguished by the eye. *Ib. l. 268*

7 The ring on the finger becomes thin beneath by wearing, the fall of dripping water hollows the stone.[4] *Ib. l. 314*

8 Nature works by means of bodies unseen.
Ib. l. 328

9 Material objects are of two kinds, atoms and compounds of atoms. The atoms themselves cannot be swamped by any force, for they are preserved indefinitely by their absolute solidity.[5] *Ib. l. 518*

10 On a dark theme I trace verses full of light, touching all the muses' charm.[6]
Ib. l. 933

[1]Translated by W. H. D. ROUSE (Loeb Classical Library), with adaptations.

[2]Tantum religio potuit suadere malorum.

The reference is to Agamemnon's sacrifice of his daughter Iphigenia.

[3]Nil posse creari de nilo.

See Shakespeare, 232:24.

[4]Anulus in digito subter tenuatur habendo, / Stilicidi casus lapidem cavat.

See also the concluding lines of *Book IV:*

Nonne vides etiam guttas in saxa cadentis / Umoris longo in spatio pertundere saxa? [Do you not see that even drops of water falling upon a stone in the long run beat a way through the stone?]

Drops of water hollow out a stone, a ring is worn thin by use.—OVID, *Ex Ponto, IV, 10:5*

Also in PLUTARCH, *Of the Training of Children.*

The drop of rain maketh a hole in the stone, not by violence, but by oft falling.—HUGH LATIMER, *Seventh Sermon Before Edward VI* [1549]

The soft droppes of rain perce the hard marble.—JOHN LYLY, *Euphues* [1579]

And drizling drops that often doe redound, / The firmest flint doth in continuance wear.—EDMUND SPENSER, *Amoretti* [1595], *sonnet 18*

[5]Translated by R. E. LATHAM.

[6]Translated by CYRIL BAILEY.

11 Truths kindle light for truths.
Ib. l. 1117

12 Pleasant it is, when over a great sea the winds trouble the waters, to gaze from shore upon another's tribulation: not because any man's troubles are a delectable joy, but because to perceive from what ills you are free yourself is pleasant.[7] *Ib. II, l. 1*

13 O miserable minds of men! O blind hearts! In what darkness of life, in what great dangers ye spend this little span of years![6, 8]
Ib. l. 14

14 Life is one long struggle in the dark.
Ib. l. 54

15 Thus the sum of things is ever being renewed, and mortals live dependent one upon another. Some nations increase, others diminish, and in a short space the generations of living creatures are changed and like runners pass on the torch of life.[9]
Ib. l. 75

16 So far as it goes, a small thing may give analogy of great things, and show the tracks of knowledge. *Ib. l. 123*

17 All things must needs be borne on through the calm void, moving at equal rate with unequal weights.[6] *Ib. l. 238*

18 Never trust her at any time, when the calm sea shows her false alluring smile.
Ib. l. 558

19 What once sprung from the earth sinks back into the earth.[6, 10] *Ib. l. 999*

20 That fear of Acheron be sent packing which troubles the life of man from its deepest depths, suffuses all with the blackness of death, and leaves no delight clean and pure.
Ib. III, l. 37

21 So it is more useful to watch a man in times of peril, and in adversity to discern what kind of man he is; for then at last words of truth are drawn from the depths of his heart, and the mask is torn off, reality remains.
Ib. l. 55

22 For as children tremble and fear everything in the blind darkness, so we in the light

[7]It is a pleasure to stand upon the shore, and to see ships tost upon the sea: a pleasure to stand in the window of a castle, and to see a battle and the adventures thereof below: but no pleasure is comparable to the standing upon the vantage ground of truth . . . and to see the errors, and wanderings, and mists, and tempests, in the vale below.—FRANCIS BACON, *Essays* [1625], *Of Truth*

[8]Insensate care of mortals! Oh how false the argument which makes thee downward beat thy wings.—DANTE, *Divine Comedy* [c. 1300], *Paradiso, canto XI, 1*

[9]Et quasi cursores vitae lampada tradunt.

[10]See *The Book of Common Prayer,* 56:13.

sometimes fear what is no more to be feared than the things children in the dark hold in terror and imagine will come true.[1]
Ib. l. 87

1 A tree cannot grow in the sky, nor clouds be in the deep sea, nor fish live in the fields, nor can blood be in sticks nor sap in rocks.
Ib. l. 784

2 Therefore death is nothing to us, it matters not one jot, since the nature of the mind is understood to be mortal.[2] *Ib. l. 831*

3 When immortal Death has taken mortal life.[3] *Ib. l. 869*

4 Why dost thou not retire like a guest sated with the banquet of life, and with calm mind embrace, thou fool, a rest that knows no care?[4] *Ib. l. 938*

5 By protracting life, we do not deduct one jot from the duration of death.[5]
Ib. l. 1087

6 What is food to one, is to others bitter poison.[6] *Ib. IV, l. 637*

7 From the heart of this fountain of delights wells up some bitter taste to choke them even amid the flowers.[7] *Ib. l. 1133*

8 But if one should guide his life by true principles, man's greatest wealth is to live on a little with contented mind; for a little is never lacking. *Ib. V, l. 1117*

9 Men are eager to tread underfoot what they have once too much feared.
Ib. l. 1140

10 Violence and injury enclose in their net all that do such things, and generally return upon him who began.[8] *Ib. l. 1152*

11 [Epicurus] set forth what is the highest good, towards which we all strive, and pointed out the past, whereby along a narrow track we may strain on towards it in a straight course.[9] *Ib. VI, l. 26*

12 [The people] were given over in troops to disease[10] and death. *Ib. l. 1144*

Gaius Valerius Catullus[11]

87 – c. 54 B.C.

13 To whom am I to present my pretty new book, freshly smoothed off with dry pumice stone? To you, Cornelius: for you used to think that my trifles were worth something, long ago. *Carmina, I, l. 1*

14 May it live and last for more than one century. *Ib. l. 10*

15 Mourn, ye Graces and Loves, and all you whom the Graces love. My lady's sparrow is dead, the sparrow, my lady's pet.[12]
Ib. III, l. 1

16 Now he goes along the dark road, thither whence they say no one returns.
Ib. l. 11

17 But these things are past and gone.[13]
Ib. IV, l. 25

18 Let us live and love, my Lesbia, and value at a penny all the talk of crabbed old men. Suns may set and rise again: for us, when our brief light has set, there's the sleep of perpetual night.[14] Give me a thousand kisses.[15]
Ib. V, l. 1

19 Poor Catullus, you should cease your folly.
Ib. VIII, l. 1

20 But you, Catullus, be resolved and firm.
Ib. l. 19

21 And let her not look to find my love, as before; my love, which by her fault has dropped like a flower on the meadow's edge, when it has been touched by the plow passing by. *Ib. XI, l. 21*

22 Over head and heels.[16] *Ib. XX, l. 9*

23 Ah, what is more blessed than to put cares away! *Ib. XXXI, l. 7*

24 Whatever it is, wherever he is, whatever he is doing, he smiles: it is a malady he has,

[1] See Bacon, 180:2.

[2] Nil igitur mors est ad nos neque pertinet hilum, / Quandoquidem natura animi mortalis habetur.

[3] Translated by Cyril Bailey.
Mortalem vitam mors cum immortalis ademit.

[4] Translated by Cyril Bailey.
See Horace 106:13, and Bryant, 471:6.

[5] See Montaigne, 164:10.

[6] Ut quod ali cibus est aliis fuat acre venenum.
What's one man's poison, signor, / Is another's meat or drink.—Beaumont and Fletcher, *Love's Cure* [1647], *act III, sc. ii*
One man's meat is another man's poison.—Oswald Dykes, *English Proverbs* [1709]

[7] Translated by Cyril Bailey.
See Byron, 457:2.

[8] See *Matthew* 26:52, 41:16.

[9] Translated by Cyril Bailey.
The highest good [summum bonum]. See Cicero, 98:26.

[10] The devastating Athenian plague [430 B.C.] described by Thucydides.

[11] Translated by F. W. Cornford (Loeb Classical Library).

[12] Passer, deliciae meae puellae.
This is also the opening line of *Carmina, II.*
See Gogarty, 759:12.

[13] Sed haec prius fuere.

[14] See Shakespeare, 187:10; Campion, 250:3; Jonson, 255:16; Herrick, 266:21; and Fouché, 415:17.

[15] Vivamus, mea Lesbia, atque amemus . . . / Soles occidere et redire possunt: / Nobis cum semel occidit brevis lux / Nox est perpetua una dormienda. / Da mi basia mille.
See Herrick, 266:10.

[16] Per caputque pedesque.

neither an elegant one as I think, nor in good taste. *Ib. XXXIX, l. 6*

1 There is nothing more silly than a silly laugh. *Ib. l. 16*

2 Oh this age! How tasteless and ill-bred it is! *Ib. XLIII, l. 8*

3 Now spring brings back balmy warmth.[1] *Ib. XLVI, l. 1*

4 Catullus, the worst of all poets, gives you [Marcus Tullius] his warmest thanks; he being as much the worst of all poets as you are the best of all patrons. *Ib. XLIX, l. 4*

5 He seems to me to be equal to a god, he, if it may be, seems to surpass the very gods, who sitting opposite you again gazes at you and hears you sweetly laughing.[2] *Ib. LI, l. 1*

6 What an eloquent manikin![3] *Ib. LIII, l. 5*

7 I would see a little Torquatus, stretching his baby hands from his mother's lap, smile a sweet smile at his father with lips half parted. *Ib. LXI, l. 209*

8 The evening is come; rise up, ye youths. Vesper from Olympus now at last is just raising his long-looked-for light. *Ib. LXII, l. 1*

9 What is given by the gods more desirable than the fortunate hour?[4] *Ib. l. 30*

10 Not unknown am I to the goddess [Venus] who mingles with her cares a sweet bitterness. *Ib. LXVIII, l. 17*

11 It is not fit that men should be compared with gods. *Ib. l. 141*

12 What a woman says to her ardent lover should be written in wind and running water.[5] *Ib. LXX*

13 Leave off wishing to deserve any thanks from anyone, or thinking that anyone can ever become grateful. *Ib. LXXIII, l. 1*

14 If a man can take any pleasure in recalling the thought of kindnesses done. *Ib. LXXVI, l. 1*

15 It is difficult suddenly to lay aside a long-cherished love. *Ib. l. 13*

[1] Iam ver egelidos refert tepores.
[2] See Sappho, 63:5.
[3] Salaputtium disertum!
[4] Quid datur a divis felici optatius hora?
[5] See Sophocles, 75:22; More, 155:8; Bacon, 181:18; Shakespeare, 249:14; and Keats, 480:7.

16 O ye gods, grant me this in return for my piety. *Ib. l. 26*

17 I hate and I love. Why I do so, perhaps you ask. I know not, but I feel it and I am in torment.[6] *Ib. LXXXV, l. 1*

18 Wandering through many countries and over many seas, I come, my brother, to these sorrowful obsequies, to present you with the last guerdon of death, and speak, though in vain, to your silent ashes. *Ib. CI, l. 1*

19 And forever, O my brother, hail and farewell![7] *Ib. l. 10*

20 But you shall not escape my iambics.[8] *Fragment*

Sallust[9] [Gaius Sallustius Crispus]

86–34 B.C.

21 All our power lies in both mind and body; we employ the mind to rule, the body rather to serve; the one we have in common with the Gods, the other with the brutes. *The War with Catiline [c. 40 B.C.], sec. 1*

22 The renown which riches or beauty confer is fleeting and frail; mental excellence is a splendid and lasting possession. *Ib.*

23 Covetous of others' possessions, he [Catiline] was prodigal of his own.[10] *Ib. 5*

24 Ambition drove many men to become false; to have one thought locked in the breast, another ready on the tongue.[11] *Ib. 10*

25 In truth, prosperity tries the souls even of the wise.[12] *Ib. 11*

26 To like and dislike the same things, that is indeed true friendship.[13] *Ib. 20*

27 Thus in the highest position there is the least freedom of action.[14] *Ib. 51*

28 On behalf of their country, their children, their altars, and their hearths.[15] *Ib. 59*

[6] Odi et amo. Quare id faciam, fortasse requiris. / Nescio, sed fieri sentio et excrucior.
See Anacreon, 67:9.
[7] Atque in perpetuum, frater, ave atque vale.
[8] At non effugies meos iambos.
[9] Translated by J. C. Rolfe (Loeb Classical Library).
[10] Alieni appetens, sui profusus.
[11] See Euripides, 76:23.
[12] Quippe secundae res sapientium animos fatigant.
[13] Idem velle atque idem nolle, ea demum firma amicitia est.
See Pythagoras, 65:11, and Plato, 83:8.
[14] Ita in maxima fortuna minima licentia est.
[15] Pro patria, pro liberis, pro aris atque focis suis.

1 The soul is the captain and ruler of the life of mortals.[1]

The War with Jugurtha [c. 41 B.C.], sec. 1

2 The splendid achievements of the intellect, like the soul, are everlasting. *Ib. 2*

3 A city for sale and soon to perish if it finds a buyer![2] *Ib. 35*

4 Punic faith.[3] *Ib. 108*

5 Experience has shown that to be true which Appius[4] says in his verses, that every man is the architect of his own fortune.[5]

Speech to Caesar on the State, sec. 1

Virgil [Publius Vergilius Maro]

70–19 B.C.

6 A god has brought us this peace.

Eclogues, I, l. 6

7 To compare great things with small.

Ib. l. 23

8 Happy old man![6] *Ib. l. 46*

9 Ah Corydon, Corydon, what madness has caught you? *Ib. II, l. 69*

10 With Jove I begin.[7] *Ib. III, l. 60*

11 A sad thing is a wolf in the fold, rain on ripe corn, wind in the trees, the anger of Amaryllis. *Ib. l. 80*

12 A snake lurks in the grass.[8]

Ib. l. 93

13 Let us raise a somewhat loftier strain![9]

Ib. IV, l. 1

14 The great cycle of the ages is renewed. Now Justice returns, returns the Golden Age; a new generation now descends from on high.[10] *Ib. l. 5*

15 We have made you [Priapus] of marble for the time being. *Ib. VII, l. 35*

16 We are not all capable of everything.[11]

Ib. VIII, l. 63

17 Draw Daphnis from the town, my songs, draw Daphnis home. *Ib. l. 68*

18 Hylax barks in the doorway.

Ib. l. 107

19 Your descendants shall gather your fruits.[12] *Ib. IX, l. 50*

20 Time bears away all things, even our minds. *Ib. l. 51*

21 Let us go singing as far as we go: the road will be less tedious. *Ib. l. 64*

22 This last labor grant me, O Arethusa.

Ib. X, l. 1

23 What if Amyntas is dark? Violets are dark, too, and hyacinths. *Ib. l. 38*

24 Love conquers all things; let us too surrender to Love.[13] *Ib. l. 69*

25 Utmost [farthest] Thule.[14]

Georgics, I, l. 30

26 Look with favor upon a bold beginning.[15]

Ib. l. 40

27 O farmers, pray that your summers be wet and your winters clear. *Ib. l. 100*

28 Practice and thought might gradually forge many an art. *Ib. l. 133*

29 Thrice they tried to pile Ossa on Pelion, yes, and roll up leafy Olympus upon Ossa; thrice the Father of Heaven split the mountains apart with his thunderbolt.[16]

Ib. l. 281

---

[1] Dux atque imperator vitae mortalium animus est.

See Sallust, 103:5; Bacon, 181:6; Shakespeare, 215:6; Tennyson, 534:7; Henley, 663:11; and Nehru, 814:8.

Be the proud captain still of thine own fate. — J. B. KENYON [1858–1924], *The Black Camel*

[2] Jugurtha's remark as he looked back at Rome upon being ordered by the senate to leave Italy.

[3] Punica fide (treachery).

[4] Appius Claudius Caecus, consul in 307 B.C., the earliest Roman writer known to us.

[5] See Aristotle, 87:19, and Sallust, 103:1.

His own character is the arbiter of everyone's fortune. — PUBLILIUS SYRUS [first century B.C.], *Maxim 283*

The brave man carves out his fortune, and every man is the son of his own works. — CERVANTES, *Don Quixote, pt. I* [1605], *bk. I, ch. 4*

See Bacon, 181:6.

[6] Fortunate senex!

[7] Ab Iove principium.

[8] Latet anguis in herba.

[9] Paulo maiora canamus!

[10] Magnus ab integro saeclorum nascitur ordo. / Iam redit et Virgo, redeunt Saturnia regna; / Iam nova progenies caelo demittitur alto.

Interpreted by the Middle Ages as a prophecy of the birth of Christ. Dante cites the lines in *Purgatorio, canto XXII, l. 70.*

A phrase altered from the first line (Novus ordo seclorum) appears on the reverse of the Great Seal of the United States of America (first used on the silver dollar certificates, series of 1935). Virgil supplied the Latin for other phrases of the Great Seal.

See Virgil, 103:26 and 106:8, and Shelley, 468:17.

[11] Non omnia possumus omnes.

[12] Carpent tua poma nepotes.

[13] Omnia vincit amor: et nos cedamus amori.

See Sophocles, 74:23 and 75:5, and Chaucer, 145:20.

[14] Ultima Thule.

The phrase, designating a far-off land, has been in use since the Greek mariner Pytheas discovered in the fourth century B.C. an island he named Thule six days north of England, thought to be Iceland.

See Seneca, 115:13, and Thomson, 345:15.

[15] Audacibus annue coeptis.

This phrase also (see note 10, above) was adapted for use on the reverse of the Great Seal of the United States of America: Annuit coeptis. See Virgil, 106:*n*5, for the Latin on the face of the Great Seal.

[16] See Homer, 60:9.

1 Frogs in the marsh mud drone their old lament. *Ib. l. 378*

2 Not every soil can bear all things. *Ib. II, l. 109*

3 Ah too fortunate farmers, if they knew their own good fortune! *Ib. l. 458*

4 May the countryside and the gliding valley streams content me. Lost to fame, let me love river and woodland. *Ib. l. 485*

5 Happy the man who could search out the causes of things.[1] *Ib. l. 490*

6 And no less happy he who knows the rural gods.[2] *Ib. l. 493*

7 This life the old Sabines knew long ago; Remus knew it, and his brother. *Ib. l. 532*

8 The best day . . . is the first to flee.[3] *Ib. III, l. 66*

9 Years grow cold to love. *Ib. l. 97*

10 Time is flying never to return.[4] *Ib. l. 284*

11 All aglow is the work.[5] *Ib. IV, l. 169*

12 A sudden madness came down upon the unwary lover [Orpheus]—forgivable, surely, if Death knew how to forgive. *Ib. l. 488*

13 Sweet Parthenope nourished me, flourishing in studies of ignoble ease.[6] *Ib. l. 563*

14 I who once played shepherds' songs and in my brash youth sang of you, O Tityrus, beneath the spreading beech.[7] *Ib. l. 565*

15 Arms and the man I sing.[8] *Aeneid, bk. I, l. 1*

16 Can heavenly minds yield to such rage? *Ib. l. 11*

17 So vast was the struggle to found the Roman state. *Ib. l. 33*

[1]Felix qui potuit rerum cognoscere causas.
The reference is apparently to the scientist-philosopher-poet Lucretius.
[2]Fortunatus et ille deos qui novit agrestis.
[3]Optima . . . dies . . . prima fugit.
[4]Fugit inreparabile tempus.
[5]Fervet opus.
[6]Me . . . dulcis alebat / Parthenope, studiis florentem ignobilis otii.
Parthenope: ancient name of Naples.
See Milton, 284:13, and T. R. Roosevelt, 686:12.
[7]Tityrus is also referred to in *Eclogues I, 1.*
[8]Arma virumque cano.
See Dryden, 306:11.

18 Night, pitch-black, lies upon the deep.[9] *Ib. l. 89*

19 O thrice and four times blessed![10] *Ib. l. 94*

20 Fury provides arms. *Ib. l. 150*

21 You have suffered worse things; God will put an end to these also. *Ib. l. 199*

22 Perhaps someday it will be pleasant to remember even this.[11] *Ib. l. 203*

23 The organizer a woman.[12] *Ib. l. 364*

24 Her walk revealed her as a true goddess. *Ib. l. 405*

25 How happy those whose walls already rise! *Ib. l. 437*

26 Here are the tears of things; mortality touches the heart.[13] *Ib. l. 462*

27 I make no distinction between Trojan and Tyrian. *Ib. l. 574*

28 A mind aware of its own rectitude.[14] *Ib. l. 604*

29 As long as rivers shall run down to the sea, or shadows touch the mountain slopes, or stars graze in the vault of heaven, so long shall your honor, your name, your praises endure. *Ib. l. 607*

30 I have known sorrow and learned to aid the wretched. *Ib. l. 630*

31 Unspeakable, O Queen, is the sorrow you bid me renew. *Ib. II, l. 3*

32 Whatever it is, I fear Greeks even when they bring gifts.[15] *Ib. l. 49*

33 From a single crime know the nation. *Ib. l. 65*

34 I shudder to say it.[16] *Ib. l. 204*

35 O fatherland, O Ilium home of the gods, O Troy walls famed in battle! *Ib. l. 241*

36 Ucalegon's afire next door.[17] *Ib. l. 311*

[9]See *Genesis 1:2*, 6:10.
[10]O terque quaterque beati!
[11]Forsan et haec olim meminisse iuvabit.
See Homer, 60:20.
[12]Dux femina facti.
[13]Sunt lacrimae rerum et mentem mortalia tangunt.
[14]The mind, conscious of rectitude, laughed to scorn the falsehood of report.—OVID [43 B.C.–A.D. 18], *Fasti, bk. IV, l. 311*
[15]Quidquid id est, timeo Danaos et dona ferentis.
[16]Horresco referens.
[17]Iam proximus ardet / Ucalegon.
Ucalegon was one of the ancient counselors who sat with Priam on the wall. His house was next to that of Anchises, father of Aeneas.

1 We have been Trojans; Troy has been.
Ib. l. 325

2 There is but one safety to the vanquished —to hope not safety. *Ib. l. 354*

3 Our foes will provide us with arms.
Ib. l. 391

4 The gods thought otherwise.[1]
Ib. l. 428

5 Thrice would I have thrown my arms about her neck, and thrice the ghost embraced fled from my grasp: like a fluttering breeze, like a fleeting dream.[2] *Ib. l. 793*

6 O accurst craving for gold!
Ib. III, l. 57

7 Rumor flies.[3] *Ib. l. 121*

8 I feel again a spark of that ancient flame.[4] *Ib. IV, l. 23*

9 Deep in her breast lives the silent wound.
Ib. l. 67

10 A woman is always a fickle, unstable thing.[5] *Ib. l. 569*

11 Arise from my bones, avenger of these wrongs! *Ib. l. 625*

12 Thus, thus, it is joy to pass to the world below.[6] *Ib. l. 660*

13 Naked in death upon an unknown shore.
Ib. V, l. 871

14 Yield not to evils, but attack all the more boldly. *Ib. VI, l. 95*

15 It is easy to go down into Hell; night and day, the gates of dark Death stand wide; but to climb back again, to retrace one's steps to the upper air—there's the rub, the task.[7]
Ib. l. 126

16 Faithful Achates.[8]
Ib. l. 158 and elsewhere

[1] Dis aliter visum.

[2] Virgil here translates HOMER, *Odyssey, bk. XI, l. 204.* See 60:8.

[3] Fama volat.

[4] Agnosco veteris vestigia flammae.
See Dante, 142:6.

[5] Varium et mutabile semper femina.
Woman often changes; foolish the man who trusts her. —FRANCIS I OF FRANCE [1494–1547], written by him with his ring on a window of the château of Chambord (BRANTÔME, *Oeuvres, VII, 395)*
La donna è mobile.—FRANCESCO MARIA PIAVE [1810–1879], *libretto of* Verdi's *Rigoletto, Duke's song*
See Scott, 431:2.

[6] Sic, sic, iuvat ire sub umbras.

[7] Facilis descensus Averni: / Noctes atque dies patet atri ianua Ditis; / Sed revocare gradum superasque evadere ad auras, / Hoc opus, hic labor est.
See *Matthew 7:13–14,* 38:15; Bion, 92:7; Shakespeare, 218:28 and 238:2; and Milton, 284:17.

[8] Fidus Achates. Proverbial for a trusty friend; Achates was the faithful comrade of Aeneas.

17 Death's brother, Sleep.[9] *Ib. l. 278*

18 The swamp of Styx, by which the gods take oath. *Ib. l. 323*

19 Unwillingly I left your land, O Queen.[10]
Ib. l. 460

20 Had I a hundred tongues, a hundred mouths, a voice of iron and a chest of brass, I could not tell all the forms of crime, could not name all the types of punishment.[11]
Ib. l. 625

21 That happy place, the green groves of the dwelling of the blest. *Ib. l. 638*

22 The spirit within nourishes, and the mind, diffused through all the members, sways the mass and mingles with the whole frame.
Ib. l. 726

23 Each of us bears his own Hell.[12]
Ib. l. 743

24 Others, I take it, will work better with breathing bronze and draw living faces from marble; others will plead at law with greater eloquence, or measure the pathways of the sky, or forecast the rising stars. Be it your concern, Roman, to rule the nations under law (this is your proper skill) and establish the way of peace; to spare the conquered and put down the mighty from their seat.[13]
Ib. l. 847

25 Give me handfuls of lilies to scatter.[14]
Ib. l. 883

26 There are two gates of Sleep. One is of horn, easy of passage for the shades of truth; the other, of gleaming white ivory, permits false dreams to ascend to the upper air.[15]
Ib. l. 893

27 Prayed to the Genius of the place.
Ib. VII, l. 136

28 We descend from Jove; in ancestral Jove Troy's sons rejoice. *Ib. l. 219*

29 If I cannot bend Heaven, I shall move Hell.
Ib. l. 312

30 An old story, but the glory of it is forever.
Ib. IX, l. 79

[9] See Homer, 58:20; Daniel, 182:4; Shakespeare, 238:6; and Shelley, 466:6.

[10] Aeneas to the ghost of Dido, who had killed herself when he left her.

[11] See Homer, 57:19.

[12] See Marlowe, 183:21 and 184:1; Browne, 274:15; Milton, 283:13 and 285:12; Eliot, 809:1; Sartre, 865:12; and Lowell, 893:7.

[13] See Milton, 281:17.

[14] Quoted by DANTE in *The Divine Comedy, Purgatorio, canto XXX, l. 21.*

[15] See Homer, 61:2.

1 To have died once is enough.
Ib. l. 140

2 I cannot bear a mother's tears.
Ib. l. 289

3 Good speed to your youthful valor, boy! So shall you scale the stars![1] *Ib. l. 641*

4 Fortune favors the brave.[2]
Ib. X, l. 284

5 Dying dreams of his sweet Argos.[3]
Ib. l. 782

6 Believe one who has proved it. Believe an expert.[4] *Ib. XI, l. 283*

7 His limbs were cold in death; his spirit fled with a groan, indignant, to the shades below.
Ib. XII, l. 951

8 One composed of many.[5]
Minor Poems. Moretum, l. 104

9 Death twitches my ear. "Live," he says; "I am coming."[6] *Ib. Copa, l. 38*

Horace
[Quintus Horatius Flaccus]
65–8 B.C.

10 How comes it, Maecenas, that no man living is content with the lot that either his choice has given him, or chance has thrown in his way, but each has praise for those who follow other paths?
Satires, bk. I [35 B.C.], satire i, l. 1

11 The story's about you.[7] *Ib. l. 69*

12 There is measure in all things.[8]
Ib. l. 106

13 We rarely find anyone who can say he has lived a happy life, and who, content with his life, can retire from the world like a satisfied guest.[9] *Ib. l. 117*

14 And all that tribe.[10] *Ib. ii, l. 2*

15 The limbs of a dismembered poet.[11]
Ib. iv, l. 62

16 A man without a flaw.[12] *Ib. v, l. 32*

17 Life grants nothing to us mortals without hard work. *Ib. ix, l. 59*

18 As crazy as hauling timber into the woods.[13] *Ib. x, l. 34*

19 Simplicity and charm.[14] *Ib. l. 44*

20 This used to be among my prayers[15]—a piece of land not so very large, which would contain a garden, and near the house a spring of ever-flowing water, and beyond these a bit of wood.[16] *Ib. II [30 B.C.], vi, l. 1*

21 O nights and feasts of the gods![17]
Ib. l. 65

22 In Rome you long for the country; in the country—oh inconstant!—you praise the distant city to the stars. *Ib. vii, l. 28*

23 Happy the man who far from schemes of business, like the early generations of mankind, works his ancestral acres with oxen of his own breeding, from all usury free.[18]
Epodes [c. 29 B.C.], II, st. 1

24 You ask me why a soft numbness diffuses all my inmost senses with deep oblivion, as though with thirsty throat I'd drained the cup that brings the sleep of Lethe.[19]
Ib. XIV, st. 1

25 But if you name me among the lyric bards, I shall strike the stars with my exalted head.
Odes, bk. I [23 B.C.], ode i, last lines

26 The half of my own soul.[20]
Ib. iii, l. 8

27 No ascent is too steep for mortals. Heaven itself we seek in our folly. *Ib. l. 37*

[1] Macte nova virtute, puer, sic itur ad astra.
See Dante, 142:8.

[2] Audentes fortuna iuvat.
See Menander, 91:8, and Terence, 97:1.

[3] Dulces moriens reminiscitur Argos.

[4] Experto credite.
Believe an expert; believe one who has had experience.
—St. Bernard, *Epistle 106*
Believe the experienced Robert. Believe Robert, who has tried it.—Robert Burton, *Anatomy of Melancholy* [1621–1651], *Introduction*

[5] E pluribus unus.
Adapted (E pluribus unum) for the motto on the face of the Great Seal of the United States, adopted June 20, 1782. For the Latin on the reverse of the Great Seal, see Virgil, 103:*n*9 and 103:*n*15.

[6] Quoted by Justice Oliver Wendell Holmes in a radio address on his ninetieth birthday [March 8, 1931].

[7] De te fabula.

[8] Est modus in rebus.
See The Seven Sages, 62:7; Terence, 96:1; Horace, 107:20; Lucan, 118:8; Anonymous Latin, 134:12; and Voltaire, 343:23.

[9] See Lucretius, 101:4, and Bryant, 471:6.

[10] Hoc genus omne.

[11] Disiecti membra poetae.
The reference is to Orpheus torn apart by the Maenads.

[12] Ad unguem factus homo.

[13] Carrying coals to Newcastle.—*Proverb*
See Aristophanes, 82:6.

[14] Molle atque facetum. This refers to Virgil's poetry.

[15] Hoc erat in votis.

[16] See Pope, 339:10.

[17] O noctes cenaeque deum!

[18] See Pope, 332:10.

[19] See Keats, 476:21.

[20] Animae dimidium meae.
The reference is to Virgil.
See Aristotle, 87:1; Zeno, 91:18; Cicero, 99:7; and Donne, 253:4.

1 Pale Death with impartial tread beats at the poor man's cottage door and at the palaces of kings.[1] *Ib. iv, l. 13*

2 Life's brief span forbids us to enter on far-reaching hopes.[2] *Ib. l. 15*

3 What slender youth, bedewed with liquid odors,
Courts thee on roses in some pleasant cave,
Pyrrha? For whom bind'st thou
In wreaths thy golden hair,
Plain in thy neatness?[3] *Ib. v, l. 1*

4 Never despair.[4] *Ib. vii, l. 27*

5 Tomorrow once again we sail the Ocean Sea.[5] *Ib. last line*

6 Leave all else to the gods.[6] *Ib. ix, l. 9*

7 Cease to ask what the morrow will bring forth, and set down as gain each day that Fortune grants.[7] *Ib. l. 13*

8 Seize the day, put no trust in the morrow![8] *Ib. xi, last line*

9 Happy, thrice happy and more, are they whom an unbroken bond unites and whose love shall know no sundering quarrels so long as they shall live. *Ib. xiii, l. 17*

10 O fairer daughter of a fair mother![9] *Ib. xvi, l. 1*

11 The pure in life and free from sin.[10] *Ib. xxii, l. 1*

12 What restraint or limit should there be to grief for one so dear? *Ib. xxiv, l. 1*

13 Grant me, sound of body and of mind, to pass an old age lacking neither honor nor the lyre.[11] *Ib. xxxi, last lines*

14 A grudging and infrequent worshipper of the gods.[12] *Ib. xxxiv, l. 1*

15 Now is the time for drinking, now the time to beat the earth with unfettered foot.[13] *Ib. xxxvii, l. 1*

[1] See Publilius Syrus, 110:14, and Shirley, 272:15.
[2] Vitae summa brevis spem nos vetat incohare longam. See Dowson, 721:7.
[3] Translated by JOHN MILTON.
[4] Nil desperandum.
[5] Cras ingens iterabimus aequor. Translated by S. E. MORISON.
[6] Permitte divis cetera.
[7] See *Matthew 6:34*, 38:7, and Publilius Syrus, 111:29.
[8] Carpe diem, quam minimum credula postero. See *The Wisdom of Solomon 2:8*, 34:11; Ronsard, 162:13; Spenser, 173:14; and Herrick, 266:11.
[9] O matre pulchra filia pulchrior.
[10] Integer vitae scelerisque purus.
[11] Not to be tuneless in old age!—AUSTIN DOBSON [1840–1921], *Henry Wadsworth Longfellow*
[12] Parcus deorum cultor et infrequens.
[13] Nunc est bibendum, nunc pede libero pulsanda tellus. Ode on the death of Cleopatra.

16 Persian luxury, boy, I hate.[14] *Ib. xxxviii, l. 1*

17 Cease your efforts to find where the last rose lingers.[15] *Ib. l. 3*

18 In adversity remember to keep an even mind.[16] *Ib. II [23 B.C.], iii, l. 1*

19 We are all driven into the same fold.[17] *Ib. l. 25*

20 Whoever cultivates the golden mean[18] avoids both the poverty of a hovel and the envy of a palace. *Ib. x, l. 5*

21 It is the mountaintop that the lightning strikes. *Ib. l. 11*

22 Nor does Apollo always stretch the bow.[19] *Ib. l. 19*

23 Alas, Postumus, Postumus, the fleeting years slip by.[20] *Ib. xiv, l. 1*

24 No lot is altogether happy.[21] *Ib. xvi, l. 27*

25 I hate the common herd of men and keep them afar. Let there be sacred silence: I, the Muses' priest, sing for girls and boys songs not heard before. *Ib. III [23 B.C.], i, l. 1*

26 Dark Care sits enthroned behind the Knight.[22] *Ib. l. 40*

27 It is sweet and honorable to die for one's country.[23] *Ib. ii, l. 13*

28 The man who is tenacious of purpose in a rightful cause is not shaken from his firm resolve by the frenzy of his fellow citizens clamoring for what is wrong, or by the tyrant's threatening countenance.[24] *Ib. iii, l. 1*

29 Force without wisdom falls of its own weight. *Ib. iv, l. 65*

30 Our sires' age was worse than our grandsires'. We their sons are more worthless than

[14] Persicos odi, puer, apparatus.
[15] Mitte sectari, rosa quo locorum / Sera moretur.
[16] Aequam memento rebus in arduis / Servare mentem.
[17] Omnes eodem cogimur.
[18] Auream quisquis mediocritatem / Diliget. Keep the golden mean.—PUBLILIUS SYRUS [first century B.C.], *Maxim 1072*
See The Seven Sages, 62:7; Terence, 96:1; Horace, 106:12; Lucan, 118:8; Anonymous Latin, 134:12; and Voltaire, 343:23.
[19] Neque semper arcum / Tendit Apollo.
[20] Eheu fugaces, Postume, Postume, / Labuntur anni.
[21] Nihil est ab omni / Parte beatum.
[22] Post equitem sedet atra cura.
[23] Dulce et decorum est pro patria mori. See Homer, 58:23.
[24] See Fabius Maximus, 93:6, and Addison, 325:11.

they: so in our turn we shall give the world a progeny yet more corrupt. *Ib. vi, l. 46*

1 Skilled in the works of both languages. *Ib. viii, l. 5*

2 With you I should love to live, with you be ready to die.[1] *Ib. ix, last line*

3 Gloriously perjured,[2] a maiden famous to all time.[3] *Ib. xi, l. 35*

4 O fount Bandusian, more sparkling than glass.[4] *Ib. xiii, l. 1*

5 I would not have borne this in my hot youth when Plancus was consul.[5] *Ib. xiv, l. 27*

6 A pauper in the midst of wealth.[6] *Ib. xvi, l. 28*

7 He will through life be master of himself and a happy man who from day to day can have said, "I have lived: tomorrow the Father may fill the sky with black clouds or with cloudless sunshine."[7] *Ib. xxix, l. 41*

8 I have built a monument more lasting than bronze. *Ib. xxx, l. 1*

9 I shall not wholly die.[8] *Ib. l. 6*

10 I am not what I was in the reign of the good Cinara. Forbear, cruel mother of sweet loves.[9] *Ib. IV [13 B.C.], i, l. 3*

11 The centuries roll back to the ancient age of gold.[10] *Ib. ii, l. 39*

12 We are but dust and shadow. *Ib. vii, l. 16*

13 Many brave men lived before Agamemnon; but all are overwhelmed in eternal night, unwept, unknown, because they lack a sacred poet.[11] *Ib. ix, l. 25*

[1] Tecum vivere amem, tecum obeam libens.

[2] Splendide mendax.

Chosen by Swift as Gulliver's motto.

[3] Hypermnestra.

[4] O fons Bandusiae splendidior vitro.

[5] In my hot youth, when George the Third was king. — BYRON, *Don Juan* [1819–1824], *canto 1, st. 212*

[6] Magnus inter opes inops.

[7] Ille potens sui / Laetusque deget, cui licet in diem / Dixisse "Vixi: cras vel atra / Nube polum pater occupato / Vel sole puro."

Tomorrow let my sun his beams display / Or in clouds hide them; I have lived my day. — COWLEY, *Discourse XI, Of Myself* [1661], *st. 11*

See Dryden, 305:1, and Sydney Smith, 433:12.

[8] Non omnis moriar.

[9] Non sum qualis eram bonae / Sub regno Cinarae. Desine, dulcium / Mater saeva Cupidinum.

Mater saeva Cupidinum. — *Odes, bk. I, xix, l. 1*

See Dowson, 721:4.

[10] See Milton, 277:9, and Macaulay, 489:4.

The golden age, which a blind tradition has hitherto placed in the past, is before us. — C. H. SAINT-SIMON [1760–1825], quoted by CARLYLE in *Sartor Resartus* [1833–1834], *bk. III, ch. 5*

14 It is not the rich man you should properly call happy, but him who knows how to use with wisdom the blessings of the gods, to endure hard poverty, and who fears dishonor worse than death, and is not afraid to die for cherished friends or fatherland. *Ib. l. 45*

15 It is sweet to let the mind unbend on occasion.[12] *Ib. xii, l. 27*

16 I am not bound over to swear allegiance to any master; where the storm drives me I turn in for shelter. *Epistles, bk. I, epistle i, l. 14*

17 To flee vice is the beginning of virtue, and to have got rid of folly is the beginning of wisdom. *Ib. l. 41*

18 Make money, money by fair means if you can, if not, by any means money.[13] *Ib. l. 66*

19 The people are a many-headed beast.[14] *Ib. l. 76*

20 He who has begun has half done. Dare to be wise; begin![15] *Ib. ii, l. 40*

[11] How many, famous while they lived, are utterly forgotten for want of writers! — BOETHIUS [c. 480–524], *De Consolatione Philosophiae, II, 7*

See Pindar, 72:10, and Pope, 339:32.

Brave men were living before Agamemnon / And since, exceeding valorous and sage, / A good deal like him too, but quite the same none; / But then they shone not on the poet's page. — BYRON, *Don Juan* [1819–1824], *canto I, st. 5*

[12] See Menander, 91:2; Montaigne, 166:4; Bacon, 181:3; and Linnaeus, 350:7.

[13] Get money; still get money, boy, no matter by what means. — BEN JONSON, *Every Man in His Humour* [1598], *act II, sc. iii*

See Pope, 339:19.

[14] Belua multorum es capitum.

Plato [c. 429–347 B.C.] describes the multitude as a "great strong beast." — *The Republic, bk. VI, 493-B*

The multitude of the gross people, being a beast of many heads. — ERASMUS [1465–1536], *Adagia, no. 122*

O weak trust of the many-headed multitude. — SIR PHILIP SIDNEY, *Arcadia* [1590], *bk. II*

See Machiavelli, 154:8; Shakespeare, 205:18, 242:14, and 242:21; and Pope, 339:28.

The beast of many heads, the staggering multitude. — MARSTON AND WEBSTER, *The Malcontent* [1604], *act III, sc. iii*

If there be any among those common objects of hatred I do contemn and laugh at, it is that great enemy of reason, virtue, and religion, the multitude . . . one great beast and a monstrosity more prodigious than Hydra. — SIR THOMAS BROWNE, *Religio Medici* [1643], *pt. II, sec. 1*

Sir, your people is a great beast. — *Attributed to* ALEXANDER HAMILTON [1755–1804]

[15] See Plato, 84:8; Aristotle, 88:11; and Heywood, 159:29.

1 The covetous man is ever in want. *Ib. l. 56*

2 Anger is a short madness. *Ib. l. 62*

3 Think to yourself that every day is your last; the hour to which you do not look forward will come as a welcome surprise. As for me, when you want a good laugh, you will find me, in a fine state, fat and sleek, a true hog of Epicurus' herd.[1] *Ib. iv, l. 13*

4 You may drive out Nature with a pitchfork, yet she still will hurry back. *Ib. l. 24*

5 They change their clime, not their disposition, who run across the sea.[2] *Ib. xi, l. 27*

6 He is not poor who has enough of things to use. If it is well with your belly, chest and feet, the wealth of kings can give you nothing more. *Ib. xii, l. 4*

7 Harmony in discord.[3] *Ib. l. 19*

8 For joys fall not to the rich alone, nor has he lived ill, who from birth to death has passed unknown. *Ib. xvii, l. 9*

9 It is not everyone that can get to Corinth.[4] *Ib. l. 36*

10 Once a word has been allowed to escape, it cannot be recalled.[5] *Ib. xviii, l. 71*

11 It is your concern when your neighbor's wall is on fire. *Ib. l. 84*

12 No poems can please for long or live that are written by water-drinkers. *Ib. xix, l. 2*

[1] See Chaucer, 146:2.
[2] See Kipling, 709:7.
[3] Concordia discors.
[4] A rendering of a Greek proverb, "It's not everyone that can make the voyage to Corinth," which referred to the expense of the life there.
There is but one road that leads to Corinth.—WALTER PATER, *Marius the Epicurean* [1885], *ch. 24*
[5] Semel emissum volat irrevocabile verbum.
The written word, unpublished, can be destroyed, but the spoken word can never be recalled.—HORACE, *Ars Poetica* [c. 8 B.C.], *l. 389*
It is as easy to recall a stone thrown violently from the hand as a word which has left your tongue.—MENANDER [c. 342–292 B.C.], *Fragment 1092K*
Four things come not back: the spoken word; the sped arrow; time past; the neglected opportunity.—OMAR IBN AL-HALIF, *Aphorism*
See Chaucer, 148:8.
A word once spoken revoked cannot be.—ALEXANDER BARCLAY, *Shyp of Folys* [1509]
Thoughts unexpressed may sometimes fall back dead; / But God Himself can't kill them when they're said.—WILL CARLETON [1845–1912], *The First Settler's Story, st. 21*

13 O imitators, you slavish herd! *Ib. l. 19*

14 And seek for truth in the groves of Academe.[6] *Ib. II [14 B.C.], ii, l. 45*

15 Barefaced poverty drove me to writing verses. *Ib. l. 51*

16 The years as they pass plunder us of one thing after another. *Ib. l. 55*

17 I have to submit to much in order to pacify the touchy tribe of poets.[7] *Ib. l. 102*

18 "Painters and poets," you say, "have always had an equal license in bold invention." We know; we claim the liberty for ourselves and in turn we give it to others. *Ib. III (Ars Poetica) [c. 8 B.C.], l. 9*

19 It was a wine jar when the molding began: as the wheel runs round why does it turn out a water pitcher? *Ib. l. 21*

20 It is when I struggle to be brief that I become obscure. *Ib. l. 25*

21 Scholars dispute and the case is still before the courts.[8] *Ib. l. 78*

22 Foot-and-a-half-long words.[9] *Ib. l. 97*

23 If you wish me to weep, you yourself
Must first feel grief.[10] *Ib. l. 102*

24 Taught or untaught, we all scribble poetry. *Ib. l. 117*

25 The mountains will be in labor, and a ridiculous mouse will be brought forth.[11] *Ib. l. 139*

26 From the egg.[12] *Ib. l. 147*

27 In the midst of things.[13] *Ib. l. 148*

28 A praiser of past time.[14] *Ib. l. 173*

29 Let a play have five acts, neither more nor less. *Ib. l. 189*

30 Turn the pages of your Greek models night and day.[15] *Ib. l. 268*

[6] Atque inter silvas Academi quaerere verum.
See Milton, 288:14.
[7] Genus irritabile vatum.
[8] Grammatici certant et adhuc sub iudice lis est.
[9] Sesquipedalia verba.
[10] Si vis me flere, dolendum est / Primum ipsi tibi.
[11] Parturient montes, nascetur ridiculus mus.
See Aesop, 66:13.
[12] Ab ovo.
Helen, the cause of the Trojan War, sprang from an egg engendered by Leda and the Swan (Zeus).
[13] In medias res.
[14] Laudator temporis acti.
[15] See Hsieh Ho, 129:20, and Fujiwara no Teika, 138:5.

1 He wins every hand who mingles profit with pleasure, by delighting and instructing the reader at the same time.
Ib. l. 343

2 Sometimes even good old Homer nods.[1]
Ib. l. 359

3 As in painting, so in poetry.[2]
Ib. l. 361

4 He has defiled his father's grave.
Ib. l. 471

Augustus Caesar
63 B.C.–A.D. 14

5 Quintilius Varus, give me back my legions![3]
From SUETONIUS, *Augustus, sec. 23*

6 More haste, less speed.[4] *Ib. 25*

7 Well done is quickly done.[5] *Ib.*

8 I found Rome a city of bricks and left it a city of marble. *Ib. 28*

9 After this time I surpassed all others in authority, but I had no more power than the others who were also my colleagues in office.
Res Gestae, 34

10 Young men, hear an old man to whom old men hearkened when he was young.
From PLUTARCH, *Apothegms, Caesar Augustus*

Livy [Titus Livius]
59 B.C.–A.D. 17

11 We can endure neither our evils nor their cures.[6] *History, Prologue*

12 Better late than never.[7]
Ib. bk. IV, sec. 23

13 Beyond the Alps lies Italy.[8]
Ib. XXI, 30

[1] Quandoque bonus dormitat Homerus.
Homer himself, in a long work, may sleep. — ROBERT HERRICK, *Hesperides* [1648], *no. 95*
See Pope, 332:18.

[2] Ut pictura poesis.

[3] Quintili Vare, legiones redde!

[4] A Greek proverb, a familiar rendering of which is: Festina lente.

[5] A Latin proverb: Sat celeriter fieri quidquid fiat satis bene.
See Publilius Syrus, 110:15, and Anonymous Latin, 133:10.

[6] The two reasons for writing a history.

[7] Potius sero quam numquam.
It is better to learn late than never. — PUBLILIUS SYRUS [first century B.C.], *Maxim 864*

[8] In conspectu Alpes habeant, quarum alterum latus Italiae sit.
Au-delà des Alpes est l'Italie. — NAPOLEON [1797]

Publilius Syrus[9]
fl. First century B.C.

14 As men, we are all equal in the presence of death.[10] *Maxim 1*

15 He doubly benefits the needy who gives quickly.[11] *Maxim 6*

16 To do two things at once is to do neither.
Maxim 7

17 A god could hardly love and be wise.[12]
Maxim 25

18 The loss which is unknown is no loss at all.[13] *Maxim 38*

19 A good reputation is more valuable than money.[14] *Maxim 108*

20 It is well to moor your bark with two anchors. *Maxim 119*

21 Many receive advice, few profit by it.
Maxim 149

22 While we stop to think, we often miss our opportunity. *Maxim 185*

23 Whatever you can lose, you should reckon of no account. *Maxim 191*

24 For a good cause, wrongdoing is virtuous.[15] *Maxim 244*

25 You should hammer your iron when it is glowing hot.[16] *Maxim 262*

26 What is left when honor is lost?
Maxim 265

27 A fair exterior is a silent recommendation.
Maxim 267

28 Fortune is not satisfied with inflicting one calamity. *Maxim 274*

29 When Fortune is on our side, popular favor bears her company. *Maxim 275*

[9] Commonly called Publius, but spelled Publilius by Pliny in his *Natural History, 35, sec. 199*. Translated mainly by DARIUS LYMAN. The numbers are those of the translator.

[10] See Horace, 107:1, and Shirley, 272:15.

[11] See Augustus Caesar, 110:7, and Anonymous Latin, 133:10.

[12] It is impossible to love and be wise. — FRANCIS BACON, *Essays* [1597–1625], *Of Love*

[13] See Shakespeare, 231:10.

[14] See *Ecclesiastes 7:1*, 27:3, and Bacon, 180:11.
A good name is better than riches. — CERVANTES, *Don Quixote, pt. II* [1615], *bk. II, ch. 33*

[15] Honesta turpitudo est pro causa bona.

[16] When the iron is hot, strike. — JOHN HEYWOOD, *Proverbs* [1546], *pt. I, ch. 2*
Strike while the iron is hot. — RABELAIS, *bk. II* [1534], *ch. 31*
Nothing like striking while the iron is hot. — CERVANTES, *Don Quixote, pt. II* [1615], *bk. IV, ch. 71*

1 When Fortune flatters, she does it to betray.[1] *Maxim 277*

2 Fortune is like glass—the brighter the glitter, the more easily broken. *Maxim 280*

3 It is more easy to get a favor from Fortune than to keep it. *Maxim 282*

4 There are some remedies worse than the disease.[2] *Maxim 301*

5 A cock has great influence on his own dunghill.[3] *Maxim 357*

6 Anyone can hold the helm when the sea is calm.[4] *Maxim 358*

7 The bow too tensely strung is easily broken. *Maxim 388*

8 Treat your friend as if he might become an enemy.[5] *Maxim 402*

9 No pleasure endures unseasoned by variety.[6] *Maxim 406*

10 The judge is condemned when the criminal is absolved.[7] *Maxim 407*

11 Practice is the best of all instructors.[8] *Maxim 439*

12 He who is bent on doing evil can never want occasion. *Maxim 459*

13 Never find your delight in another's misfortune. *Maxim 467*

14 It is a bad plan that admits of no modification. *Maxim 469*

15 It is an unhappy lot which finds no enemies. *Maxim 499*

16 The fear of death is more to be dreaded than death itself.[9] *Maxim 511*

[1] See Shakespeare, 202:2.

[2] Marius said, "I see the cure is not worth the pain." —PLUTARCH [A.D. 46–120], *Lives, Caius Marius*

The remedy is worse than the disease.—FRANCIS BACON, *Essays* [1597–1625], *Of Seditions*

I find the medicine worse than the malady.—BEAUMONT AND FLETCHER, *Love's Cure* [1647], *act III, sc. ii*

[3] Every cock is proud on his own dunghill.—JOHN HEYWOOD, *Proverbs* [1546], *pt. I, ch. 2*

[4] See Shakespeare, 225:36.

[5] Treat your friend as if he will one day be your enemy, and your enemy as if he will one day be your friend. —LABERIUS [105–43 B.C.], *Fragment*

See Sophocles, 73:14.

[6] See Johnson, 352:13, and Cowper, 376:22.

[7] Iudex damnatur ubi nocens absolvitur.—*Motto adopted for the Edinburgh Review*

[8] Practice makes perfect.—*Proverb*

The saying "Practice is everything" is Periander's. —DIOGENES LAERTIUS [c. 200], *Lives of Eminent Philosophers, Periander, 6*

[9] See Shakespeare, 228:17.

17 A rolling stone gathers no moss.[10] *Maxim 524*

18 Never promise more than you can perform. *Maxim 528*

19 No one should be judge in his own case.[11] *Maxim 545*

20 Necessity knows no law except to prevail.[12] *Maxim 553*

21 Nothing can be done at once hastily and prudently.[13] *Maxim 557*

22 We desire nothing so much as what we ought not to have. *Maxim 559*

23 It is only the ignorant who despise education. *Maxim 571*

24 Do not turn back when you are just at the goal.[14] *Maxim 580*

25 It is not every question that deserves an answer. *Maxim 581*

26 No man is happy who does not think himself so.[15] *Maxim 584*

27 Never thrust your own sickle into another's corn.[16] *Maxim 593*

28 You cannot put the same shoe on every foot. *Maxim 596*

29 Every day should be passed as if it were to be our last.[17] *Maxim 633*

30 Money alone sets all the world in motion. *Maxim 656*

31 You should go to a pear tree for pears, not to an elm.[18] *Maxim 674*

[10] The rolling stone never gathereth mosse.—JOHN HEYWOOD, *Proverbs* [1546], *pt. I, ch. 2*

The stone that is rolling can gather no moss.—THOMAS TUSSER, *A Hundred Good Points of Husbandry* [1557]

[11] It is not permitted to the most equitable of men to be a judge in his own cause.—PASCAL, *Pensées* [1670], *ch. 4, 1*

[12] Proverbial; attributed to Syrus.

Necessity gives the law and does not itself receive it. —*Maxim 399*

See St. Augustine, 129:9; Cromwell, 272:20; and William Pitt, 412:4.

And with necessity, / The tyrant's plea, excused his devilish deeds.—MILTON, *Paradise Lost* [1667], *bk. IV, l. 393*

[13] See Chaucer, 147:25, and Heywood, 158:18.

[14] When men are arrived at the goal, they should not turn back.—PLUTARCH [A.D. 46–120], *Of the Training of Children*

[15] No man can enjoy happiness without thinking that he enjoys it.—SAMUEL JOHNSON, *The Rambler* [1750–1752]

[16] See *Deuteronomy 23:25*, 11:18.

Did thrust as now in others' corn his sickle.—SEIGNEUR DU BARTAS, *Divine Weeks and Works* [1578], *pt. II, Second Week*

Not presuming to put my sickle in another man's corn. —NICHOLAS YONGE, *Musica Transalpina, Epistle Dedicatory* [1588]

[17] See Horace, 107:7, and Marcus Aurelius, 124:6.

[18] You may as well expect pears from an elm.—CERVANTES, *Don Quixote, pt. II* [1615], *bk. IV, ch. 40*

1 It is a very hard undertaking to seek to please everybody. *Maxim 675*

2 Look for a tough wedge for a tough log. *Maxim 723*

3 Pardon one offense, and you encourage the commission of many. *Maxim 750*

4 In every enterprise consider where you would come out.[1] *Maxim 777*

5 It takes a long time to bring excellence to maturity. *Maxim 780*

6 No one knows what he can do till he tries. *Maxim 786*

7 It is vain to look for a defense against lightning. *Maxim 835*

8 Everything is worth what its purchaser will pay for it.[2] *Maxim 847*

9 Better be ignorant of a matter than half know it.[3] *Maxim 865*

10 Prosperity makes friends, adversity tries them.[4] *Maxim 872*

11 Let a fool hold his tongue and he will pass for a sage. *Maxim 914*

12 You need not hang up the ivy branch over the wine that will sell.[5] *Maxim 968*

13 It is a consolation to the wretched to have companions in misery.[6] *Maxim 995*

14 Unless degree is preserved, the first place is safe for no one.[7] *Maxim 1042*

15 Confession of our faults is the next thing to innocence. *Maxim 1060*

16 I have often regretted my speech, never my silence.[8] *Maxim 1070*

[1] In every affair, consider what precedes and what follows and then undertake it.—EPICTETUS [c. 50–120], *That Everything Is to Be Undertaken with Circumspection, ch. 15*

[2] What is worth in anything / But so much money as 'twill bring?—BUTLER, *Hudibras, pt. I* [1663], *canto I, l. 465*

[3] See Pope, 332:20.

[4] See Aristotle, 88:20; Cicero, 99:6; Ovid, 113:28; and Heywood, 160:19.

[5] Good wine needs no bush.—SHAKESPEARE, *As You Like It* [1598–1600], *Epilogue, l. 4*

Good wine needs neither bush nor preface / To make it welcome.—SIR WALTER SCOTT, *Peveril of the Peak* [1822], *ch. 4*

Bush . . . *archaic:* a bunch or branch of ivy, formerly hung outside a tavern to indicate wine for sale.—*Webster's Third New International Dictionary* [1966]

I.e., good wine needs no advertising.

[6] See John Ray, 301:16.

[7] See Shakespeare, 226:1.

[8] Simonides said that "he never repented that he held his tongue, but often that he had spoken."—PLUTARCH [A.D. 46–120], *Rules for the Preservation of Health*

See Plutarch, 120:10.

17 Speech is a mirror of the soul: as a man speaks, so is he. *Maxim 1073*

Dionysius of Halicarnassus

c. 54 – c. 7 B.C.

18 The contact with manners then is education; and this Thucydides appears to assert when he says history is philosophy learned from examples. *Ars Rhetorica, XI, 2*

Sextus Propertius

54 B.C.–A.D. 2

19 Never change when love has found its home. *Elegies, I, i, 36*

20 The seaman's story is of tempest, the plowman's of his team of bulls; the soldier tells his wounds, the shepherd his tale of sheep. *Ib. II, i, 43*

21 Let each man pass his days in that wherein his skill is greatest. *Ib. 46*

22 What though strength fails? Boldness is certain to win praise. In mighty enterprises, it is enough to have had the determination.[9] *Ib. x, 5*

23 Let no one be willing to speak ill of the absent.[10] *Ib. xix, 32*

24 Let each man have the wit to go his own way.[11] *Ib. xxv, 38*

25 Absence makes the heart grow fonder.[12] *Ib. xxxiii, 43*

26 There is something beyond the grave; death does not end all, and the pale ghost escapes from the vanquished pyre.[13] *Ib. IV, vii, 1*

Albius Tibullus

c. 54 – c. 19 B.C.

27 May I look on you when my last hour comes; may I hold you, as I sink, with my failing hand.[14] *Elegies, I, i, 59*

[9] Quod si deficiant vires, audacia certe / Laus erit: in magnis et voluisse sat est.

See Menander, 91:8.

[10] Absenti nemo non nocuisse velit.

See The Seven Sages 62:8.

[11] Paddle your own canoe.—ANONYMOUS, *Harper's Monthly* [May 1854]

[12] Semper in absentes felicior aestus amantes.

[13] Our souls survive this death.—OVID, *Metamorphoses, XV, l. 158*

[14] Te spectem, suprema mihi cum venerit hora. / Te teneam moriens deficiente manu.

1 Jupiter laughs at the perjuries of lovers.[1] *Ib. III, vi, 49*

2 Jove the Rain-giver. *Ib. vii, 26*

Ovid [Publius Ovidius Naso]
43 B.C.–A.D. c. 18

3 I have faith that yields to none, and ways without reproach, and unadorned simplicity, and blushing modesty. *Amores, I, iii, 13*

4 The rest who does not know?[2] *Ib. v, 25*

5 Every lover is a warrior, and Cupid has his camps.[3] *Ib. ix, 1*

6 Run slowly, horses of the night.[4] *Ib. xiii, 39*

7 Stay far hence, far hence, you prudes![5] *Ib. II, i, 3*

8 So I can't live either without you or with you.[6] *Ib. III, xi, 39*

9 They come to see; they come that they themselves may be seen.[7] *Ars Amatoria, I, 99*

10 It is convenient that there be gods, and, as it is convenient, let us believe there are.[8] *Ib. 637*

11 To be loved, be lovable. *Ib. II, 107*

12 Nothing is stronger than habit. *Ib. 345*

13 Perhaps too my name will be joined to theirs[9] [the names of famous poets]. *Ib. III, 339*

[1] Periuria ridet amantum Iupiter.
Also in Ovid, *Ars Amatoria, I, 633*
See Shakespeare, 192:8.
And Jove but laughs at lovers' perjury.—Dryden, *Palamon and Arcite* [1680], *bk. II, l. 758*, and *Amphitryon* [1690], *act I, sc. ii*

[2] Cetera quis nescit?

[3] Love is a kind of warfare.—Ovid, *Ars Amatoria, II, 233*
A batallas de amor campo de pluma [A field of feathers for the strife of love].—Luis de Góngora y Argote [1561–1627], *Soledad, I*

[4] At si, quem malis, Cephalum complexa teneres, / Clamares "lente currite noctis equi."
See Marlowe, 184:8.

[5] Procul hinc, procul este, severi!

[6] Sic ego nec sine te nec tecum vivere possum.
See Aristophanes, 82:14, and Martial, 119:17.

[7] Spectatum veniunt, veniunt spectentur ut ipsae.
And for to se, and eek for to be seye.—Chaucer, *The Canterbury Tales* [c. 1387], *The Wife of Bath's Prologue, l. 552*
To see and to be seen.—Ben Jonson [1572–1637], *Epithalamion, III, 4*

[8] See Tillotson, 303:1, and Voltaire, 344:2.

[9] Forsitan et nostrum nomen miscebitur istis.

14 Now there are fields of corn where Troy once was. *Heroides, I, i, 2*

15 [Chaos] A rough, unordered mass of things.[10] *Metamorphoses, I, 7*

16 Your lot is mortal: not mortal is what you desire. *Ib. II, 56*

17 You will be safest in the middle.[11] *Ib. 137*

18 I am Actaeon: recognize your master![12] *Ib. III, 230*

19 The cause is hidden, but the result is well known.[13] *Ib. IV, 287*

20 We can learn even from our enemies.[14] *Ib. 428*

21 I see and approve better things, but follow worse.[15] *Ib. VII, 20*

22 The gods have their own rules.[16] *Ib. IX, 500*

23 Time the devourer of all things.[17] *Ib. XV, 234*

24 And now I have finished a work that neither the wrath of love, nor fire, nor the sword, nor devouring age shall be able to destroy. *Ib. 871*

25 Resist beginnings; the prescription comes too late when the disease has gained strength by long delays.[18] *Remedia Amoris, 91*

26 Love yields to business. If you seek a way out of love, be busy; you'll be safe then.[19] *Ib. 143*

27 Poetry comes fine-spun from a mind at peace. *Tristia, I, i, 39*

28 So long as you are secure you will count many friends; if your life becomes clouded you will be alone.[20] *Ib. ix, 5*

29 Whatever I tried to write was verse. *Ib. IV, x, 26*

[10] Rudis indigestaque moles.

[11] Medio tutissimus ibis.

[12] Actaeon ego sum, dominum cognoscite vestrum!

[13] Causa latet, vis est notissima.

[14] Fas est et ab hoste doceri. Imitated from Aristophanes, *The Birds, l. 370:* People before this have learned from their enemies.

[15] Video meliora, proboque, deteriora sequor.
See *Romans 7:19*, 47:6, and Euripides, 76:19.
I know and love the good, yet, ah! the worst pursue.—Petrarch, *Sonnet 225, Canzone 21, To Laura in Life* [c. 1327]

[16] Sunt superis sua iura.

[17] Tempus edax rerum.

[18] See Persius, 117:11.

[19] Qui finem quaeris amoris / Cedit amor rebus; res age, tutus eris.

[20] See Aristotle, 88:20; Cicero, 99:6; Publilius Syrus, 112:10; and Heywood, 160:19.

1 It is annoying to be honest to no purpose. *Ex Ponto, II, iii, 14*

2 Note too that a faithful study of the liberal arts humanizes character and permits it not to be cruel. *Ib. ix, 47*

Phaedrus[1]

fl. c. A.D. 8

3 Submit to the present evil, lest a greater one befall you. *Fables, bk. I, fable 2, l. 31*

4 He was the author, our hand finished it. *Ib. 6, l. 20*

5 That it is unwise to be heedless ourselves while we are giving advice to others, I will show in a few lines. *Ib. 9, l. 1*

6 No one returns with good will to the place which has done him a mischief. *Ib. 18, l. 1*

7 It has been related that dogs drink at the river Nile running along, that they may not be seized by the crocodiles.[2] *Ib. 25, l. 3*

8 Everyone is bound to bear patiently the results of his own example. *Ib. 26, l. 12*

9 Come of it what may, as Sinon said. *Ib. III, prologue, l. 27*

10 Things are not always what they seem.[3] *Ib. IV, 2, l. 5*

11 To add insult to injury. *Ib. V, l. 3*

12 Once lost, Jupiter himself cannot bring back opportunity.[4] *Ib. VII, l. 4*

Lucius Annaeus Seneca[5]

c. 4 B.C.–A.D. 65

13 What fools these mortals be.[6] *Epistles, 1, 3*

14 It is not the man who has too little, but the man who craves more, that is poor. *Ib. 2, 2*

15 Love of bustle is not industry. *Ib. 3, 5*

[1]Translated by Henry Thomas Riley [1816–1878].

[2]Pliny the Elder in his *Natural History (bk. VIII, sec. 148)* and Aelian in his *Various Histories* relate the same fact as to the dogs drinking from the Nile. "To treat a thing as the dogs do the Nile" was a common proverb, signifying superficial treatment.

[3]Non semper ea sunt quae videntur.

See Longfellow, 509:13, and Gilbert, 627:16.

[4]Opportunity knocks only once.—*Proverb*

[5]Translated by R. M. Gummere, J. W. Basore, W. H. D. Rouse, and F. J. Miller (Loeb Classical Library).

[6]Tanta stultitia mortalium est.

See Shakespeare, 197:1.

16 Live among men as if God beheld you; speak to God as if men were listening. *Ib. 10, 5*

17 The best ideas are common property. *Ib. 12, 11*

18 Men do not care how nobly they live, but only how long, although it is within the reach of every man to live nobly, but within no man's power to live long. *Ib. 22, 17*

19 A great pilot can sail even when his canvas is rent. *Ib. 30, 3*

20 Man is a reasoning animal. *Ib. 41, 8*

21 That most knowing of persons—gossip. *Ib. 43, 1*

22 It is quality rather than quantity that matters.[7] *Ib. 45, 1*

23 You can tell the character of every man when you see how he receives praise. *Ib. 52, 12*

24 Nothing is so certain as that the evils of idleness can be shaken off by hard work. *Ib. 56, 9*

25 Not lost, but gone before.[8] *Ib. 63, 16*

26 All art is but imitation of nature. *Ib. 65, 3*

27 It is a rough road that leads to the heights of greatness. *Ib. 84, 13*

28 The pilot . . . who has been able to say, "Neptune, you shall never sink this ship except on an even keel," has fulfilled the requirements of his art.[9] *Ib. 85, 33*

29 I was shipwrecked before I got aboard. *Ib. 87, 1*

30 It is better, of course, to know useless things than to know nothing. *Ib. 88, 45*

31 Do not ask for what you will wish you had not got. *Ib. 95, 1*

32 We are mad, not only individually, but nationally. We check manslaughter and isolated murders; but what of war and the much vaunted crime of slaughtering whole peoples?[10] *Ib. 95, 30*

[7]See Anonymous Latin, 134:13.

[8]Non amittuntur, sed praemittuntur.

Not dead, but gone before.—Samuel Rogers, *Human Life* [1819]

[9]The mariner of old said thus to Neptune in a great tempest, "O God! thou mayest save me if thou wilt, and if thou wilt, thou mayest destroy me; but whether or no, I will steer my rudder true."—Montaigne, *Essays* [1580–1595], *bk. II, ch. 16*

[10]See Edward Young, 330:1; Porteus, 378:3; and J. R. Lowell, 567:20.

1 A great step towards independence is a good-humored stomach, one that is willing to endure rough treatment. *Ib. 123, 3*

2 Fire is the test of gold; adversity, of strong men.[1]
Moral Essays. On Providence, 5, 9

3 Time discovers truth.[2]
Ib. On Anger, 2, 22

4 Whom they have injured they also hate.[3]
Ib. 33

5 I do not distinguish by the eye, but by the mind, which is the proper judge of the man.
Ib. On the Happy Life, 2, 2

6 There is no great genius without some touch of madness.[4]
Ib. On Tranquillity of the Mind, 17, 10

7 A great fortune is a great slavery.
Ib. To Polybius on Consolation, 6, 5

8 Wherever the Roman conquers, there he dwells.
Ib. To Helvia on Consolation, 7, 7

9 He who receives a benefit with gratitude repays the first installment on his debt.
On Benefits, bk. II, 22, 1

10 You roll my log, and I will roll yours.
Apocolocyntosis, sec. 9

11 Do you seek Alcides' equal? None is, except himself.[5] *Hercules Furens, 1, 1, 84*

[1]See Beaumont and Fletcher, 263:10.

[2]Veritatem dies aperit. Omnia tempus revelat [Time reveals all]. — TERTULLIAN [A.D. c. 155–c. 225], *Apologeticus, 7*

Time reveals all things. — ERASMUS [1465–1536], *Adagia*

[3]It is human nature to hate those whom you have injured. — TACITUS [c. 55–c. 117], *Agricola, 42, 15*

Chi fa ingiuria non perdona mai [He never pardons those he injures]. — *Italian proverb*

The offender never pardons. — GEORGE HERBERT, *Jacula Prudentum* [1640]

Forgiveness to the injured does belong; / But they ne'er pardon who have done the wrong. — DRYDEN, *The Conquest of Granada* [1670], *pt. II, act I, sc. ii*

[4]An ancient commonplace, which Seneca says he quotes from ARISTOTLE, *Problemata, 30, 1:* "No excellent soul is exempt from a mixture of madness." It is also in PLATO, *Phaedrus, 245-A.*

Good sense travels on the well-worn paths; genius, never. And that is why the crowd, not altogether without reason, is so ready to treat great men as lunatics. — CESARE LOMBROSO [1836–1909], *The Man of Genius, preface*

See Dryden, 303:20.

[5]And but herself admits no parallel. — MASSINGER [1583–1640], *Duke of Milan, act IV, sc. iii*

None but himself can be his parallel. — LEWIS THEOBALD [1688–1744], *The Double Falsehood*

12 Successful and fortunate crime is called virtue.[6] *Ib. 255*

13 An age will come after many years when the Ocean will loose the chains of things, and a huge land lie revealed; when Tiphys[7] will disclose new worlds and Thule[8] no more be the ultimate.[9] *Medea, l. 374*

14 A good mind possesses a kingdom.[10]
Thyestes, 380

15 Light griefs are loquacious, but the great are dumb.[11] *Hippolytus, II, 3, 607*

Marcus Manilius

First century A.D.

16 [Human reason] freed men's minds from wondering at portents by wresting from Jupiter his bolts and power of thunder, and ascribing to the winds the noise and to the clouds the flame.[12]
Astronomica,[13] bk. I, l. 102

17 Who could know heaven save by heaven's gift and discover God save one who shares himself in the divine?[14] *Ib. II, l. 115*

18 At birth our death is sealed, and our end is consequent upon our beginning.[15]
Ib. IV, l. 16

19 Scorn not your powers as if proportionate to the smallness of the mind: its power has no bounds. *Ib. l. 923*

[6]See Harington, 181:21.

[7]Jason's pilot.

[8]See Virgil, 103:25, and Thomson, 345:15.

[9]Venient annis / Saecula seris, quibus Oceanus / Vincula rerum laxet, et ingens / Pateat tellus, Tiphysque novos / Detegat orbes nec sit terris / Ultima Thule.

Translated by S. E. MORISON.

As one much addicted to prophecies, and who had already voyaged beyond Thule (Iceland), Columbus was much impressed by the passage in Seneca's *Medea.* — S. E. MORISON, *Admiral of the Ocean Sea* [1942], *vol. I, ch. 6*

Next to these lines from *Medea* in an early edition of Seneca's tragedies that belonged to Columbus's son Ferdinand, there is this annotation in the son's hand: Haec profetia impleta est per patrem meum . . . almirantem anno 1492 [The prophecy was fulfilled by my father the Admiral in the year 1492]. — *Ib. 5*

[10]See Dyer, 167:5.

[11]See Ralegh, 172:12.

[12]Cur imbres ruerent, ventosque causa moveret pervidit, solvitque animis miracula rerum eripuitque Jovi fulmen viresque tonandi et sonitum ventis concessit, nubibus ignem.

See Shakespeare, 242:20, and Franklin, 346:*n*5.

[13]Translated by G. P. GOULD (Loeb Classical Library).

[14]See Hippocrates, 80:6.

[15]See *The Wisdom of Solomon 5:13,* 34:15.

Caligula [Gaius Caesar]

A.D. 12–41

1 Would that the Roman people had a single neck [to cut off their head].

From Suetonius, Gaius Caligula, sec. 30

Onasander

fl. A.D. 49

2 Vigor is found in the man who has not yet grown old, and discretion in the man who is not too young.

The General, ch. 1, sec. 10

3 Envy is a pain of mind that successful men cause their neighbors.

Ib. ch. 42, par. 25

Pliny the Elder [Gaius Plinius Secundus][1]

A.D. 23–79

4 In comparing various authors with one another, I have discovered that some of the gravest and latest writers have transcribed, word for word, from former works, without making acknowledgment.

Natural History, bk. I, dedication, sec. 22

5 Everything is soothed by oil, and this is the reason why divers send out small quantities of it from their mouths, because it smooths every part which is rough.[2] *Ib. II, 234*

6 It is far from easy to determine whether she [Nature] has proved to man a kind parent or a merciless stepmother.[3]

Ib. VII, 1

7 Man alone at the very moment of his birth, cast naked upon the naked earth, does she abandon to cries and lamentations.[4]

Ib. 2

8 To laugh, if but for an instant only, has never been granted to man before the fortieth day from his birth, and then it is looked upon as a miracle of precocity.[5] *Ib.*

9 Man is the only one that knows nothing, that can learn nothing without being taught. He can neither speak nor walk nor eat, and in short he can do nothing at the prompting of nature only, but weep.[6] *Ib. VII, 4*

10 With man, most of his misfortunes are occasioned by man.[7] *Ib. 5*

11 Indeed, what is there that does not appear marvelous when it comes to our knowledge for the first time?[8] How many things, too, are looked upon as quite impossible until they have been actually effected? *Ib. 6*

12 The human features and countenance, although composed of but some ten parts or little more, are so fashioned that among so many thousands of men there are no two in existence who cannot be distinguished from one another.[9] *Ib. 8*

13 All men possess in their bodies a poison which acts upon serpents; and the human saliva, it is said, makes them take to flight, as though they had been touched with boiling water. The same substance, it is said, destroys them the moment it enters their throat.[10] *Ib. 15*

14 It has been observed that the height of a man from the crown of the head to the sole of the foot is equal to the distance between the

[1] With some alterations, translated by John Bostock [1773–1846] and Henry Thomas Riley [1816–1878].
See also Pliny the Younger, 123:6.

[2] Why does pouring oil on the sea make it clear and calm? Is it for that the winds, slipping the smooth oil, have no force, nor cause any waves?—Plutarch [A.D. 46–120], *Natural Questions, IX*

Bishop Adain [651] gave to a company about to take a journey by sea "some holy oil, saying, 'I know that when you go abroad you will meet with a storm and contrary wind; but do you remember to cast this oil I give you into the sea, and the wind shall cease immediately.'"—Bede [c. 672–c. 735], *Ecclesiastical History, bk. III, ch. 14*

In Jared Sparks's edition of Benjamin Franklin's *Works, vol. VI, p. 354*, there are letters between Franklin, Brownrigg, and Parish on the stilling of waves by means of oil.

[3] To man the earth seems altogether / No more a mother, but a step-dame rather.—Seigneur Du Bartas, *Divine Weeks and Works* [1578], *First Week, Third Day*

[4] See *The Wisdom of Solomon 7:3, 34:18.*

He is born naked, and falls a-whining at the first.—Robert Burton, *Anatomy of Melancholy* [1621–1651], *pt. I, sec. 2, member 3, subsec. 10*

[5] This term of forty days is mentioned by Aristotle in his *Natural History.*

[6] See Tennyson, 532:10.

[7] See Burns, 408:16, and Wordsworth, 423:4.

[8] See Tacitus, 123:2.

[9] It is the common wonder of all men, how among so many millions of faces there should be none alike.—Sir Thomas Browne, *Religio Medici* [1642], *pt. II, sec. 2*

Of a thousand shavers, two do not shave so much alike as not to be distinguished.—Samuel Johnson [1777]; from Boswell, *Life of Johnson* [1791], *vol. II, p. 120* (Everyman edition)

[10] Madame D'Abrantès relates that when Bonaparte was in Cairo he sent for a serpent-detector (Psylli) to remove two serpents that had been seen in his house. He, having enticed one of them from his hiding place, caught it in one hand, just below the jawbone, in such a manner as to oblige the mouth to open, when, spitting into it, the effect was like magic: the reptile appeared struck with instant death.—*Memoirs, vol. I, ch. 59*

tips of the middle fingers of the two hands when extended in a straight line.
Ib. 77

1 There is always something new out of Africa.[1] *Ib. VIII, 17*

2 When a building is about to fall down, all the mice desert it.[2] *Ib. 103*

3 Bears when first born are shapeless masses of white flesh a little larger than mice, their claws alone being prominent. The mother then licks them gradually into proper shape.[3] *Ib. 126*

4 The agricultural population, says Cato, produces the bravest men, the most valiant soldiers, and a class of citizens the least given of all to evil designs. *Ib. XVIII, 26*

5 The best plan is to profit by the folly of others. *Ib. 31*

6 With a grain of salt.[4] *Ib. XXIII, 8*

7 Why is it that we entertain the belief that for every purpose odd numbers are the most effectual?[5] *Ib. XXVIII, 23*

Persius [Aulus Persius Flaccus]
A.D. 34–62

8 The stomach is the teacher of the arts and the dispenser of invention.[6]
Satires, prologue, l. 10

9 Tell, priests, what is gold doing in a holy place? *Ib. II, l. 69*

[1] Ex Africa semper aliquid novi.
Quoted as a Greek proverb.

[2] This is alluded to by Cicero in his letters to Atticus, and is mentioned by Aelian *(Animated Nature, bk. VI, ch. 41)*. Compare the modern proverb: Rats desert a sinking ship.

[3] Not unlike the bear which bringeth forth / In the end of thirty days a shapeless birth; / But after licking, it in shape she draws, / And by degrees she fashions out the paws, / The head, and neck, and finally doth bring / To a perfect beast that first deformed thing. — SEIGNEUR DU BARTAS, *Divine Weeks and Works* [1578], *First Week, First Day*
I had not time to lick it into form, as a bear doth her young ones. — ROBERT BURTON, *Anatomy of Melancholy* [1621–1651], *Democritus to the Reader*

[4] Cum grano salis.
Pompey's antidote against poison was "to be taken fasting, a grain of salt being added."

[5] The god delights in an odd number. — VIRGIL [70–19 B.C.], *Eclogues, VIII, 75*
See Shakespeare, 225:28, and Samuel Lover, 482:10.

[6] Magister artis ingenique largitor venter.
See Anonymous Latin, 134:9.
Necessity, mother of invention. — WYCHERLEY, *Love in a Wood* [1671], *act III, sc. iii*
Art imitates Nature, and necessity is the mother of invention. — RICHARD FRANCK, *Northern Memoirs* [written 1658, published 1694]
Sheer necessity — the proper parent of an art so nearly allied to invention. — SHERIDAN, *The Critic* [1779], *act I, sc. ii*

10 Let them look upon virtue and pine because they have lost her. *Ib. III, l. 38*

11 Meet the disease at its first stage.[7]
Ib. l. 64

Gaius Petronius [Petronius Arbiter[8]]
died A.D. c. 66

12 He has joined the great majority.[9]
Satyricon, sec. 42

13 A man who is always ready to believe what is told him will never do well. *Ib. 43*

14 One good turn deserves another.
Ib. 45

15 A man must have his faults. *Ib.*

16 Not worth his salt. *Ib. 57*

17 My heart was in my mouth. *Ib. 62*

18 Beauty and wisdom are rarely conjoined.[10]
Ib. 94

19 The studied spontaneity of Horace.[11]
Ib. 118

20 Natural curls.[12] *Ib. 126*

Quintilian
[Marcus Fabius Quintilianus]
born A.D. c. 35

21 We give to necessity the praise of virtue.[13]
De Institutione Oratoria, bk. I, 8, 14

22 A liar should have a good memory.[14]
Ib. IV, 2, 91

[7] Venienti occurrite morbo.
A stitch in time saves nine. — *Proverb*
See Ovid, 113:25.
Also in Publilius Syrus, *Maxim 866.*

[8] Pliny calls Petronius Titus in *Natural History, XXXVII, 8.*
See Tacitus, 122:23.

[9] Abiit ad plures.

[10] See Petrarch, 143:6.

[11] Horatii curiosa felicitas.

[12] Crines ingenio suo flexi.

[13] In the additions of Hadrianus Julius to the *Adages* of Erasmus he remarks under the head of *Necessitatem edere* that a very familiar proverb was current among his countrymen: Necessitatem in virtutem commutare [To make necessity a virtue].
Thus maketh vertue of necessitee. — CHAUCER, *Troilus and Criseyde* [1372–1386], *bk. IV, l. 1586*
See Shakespeare, 194:5.
Make a virtue of necessity. — ROBERT BURTON, *Anatomy of Melancholy* [1621–1651], *pt. III, sec. 3, member 4, subsec. I*

[14] He who has not a good memory should never take upon him the trade of lying. — MONTAIGNE, *Essays* [1580–1595], *bk. I, ch. 9, Of Liars*
Il faut bonne mémoire, après qu'on a menti [You must have a good memory after you have lied]. — CORNEILLE, *Le Menteur* [1642], *act IV, sc. v*
Liars ought to have good memories. — ALGERNON SIDNEY, *Discourses on Government* [1698], *ch. 2, sec. 15*

1 Vain hopes are often like the dreams of those who wake. *Ib. VI, 2, 30*

2 For it is feeling and force of imagination that makes us eloquent.[1] *Ib. X, 7, 15*

3 Those who wish to appear wise among fools, among the wise seem foolish.[2] *Ib. 21*

Nero

A.D. 37–68

4 What an artist dies with me![3] *From* SUETONIUS, *Nero, sec. 49*

Lucan

A.D. 39–65

5 If the victor had the gods on his side, the vanquished had Cato.[4] *The Civil War, bk. I, 128*

6 There stands the shadow of a glorious name.[5] *Ib. 135*

7 Pigmies placed on the shoulders of giants see more than the giants themselves.[6] *Ib. II, 10 (Didacus Stella)*

8 Keep to moderation, keep the end in view, follow nature.[7] *Ib. 381*

9 Thinking nothing done while anything remained to be done.[8] *Ib. 657*

10 More was lost than mere life and existence.[9] *Ib. VII, 639*

11 We all praise fidelity; but the true friend pays the penalty when he supports those whom Fortune crushes.[10] *Ib. VIII, 485*

12 A name illustrious and revered by nations.[11] *Ib. IX, 203*

13 Is the dwelling place of God anywhere but in the earth and sea, the air and sky, and virtue? Why seek we further for deities? Whatever you see, whatever you touch, that is Jupiter. *Ib. 578*

14 The very ruins have been destroyed.[12] *Ib. 969*

Longinus

First century

15 It frequently happens that where the second line is sublime, the third, in which he [Lucan] meant to rise still higher, is perfect bombast. *On the Sublime, sec. 3*

16 Sublimity is the echo of a noble mind. *Ib. 9*

17 In the Odyssey one may liken Homer to the setting sun, of which the grandeur remains without the intensity. *Ib.*

Dio Chrysostom[13] [Dio Cocceianus]

A.D. C. 40 – C. 120

18 *Diogenes:* The man I know not, for I am not acquainted with his mind. *Fourth Discourse, On Kingship, ch. 17*

19 Idleness and lack of occupation are the best things in the world to ruin the foolish. *Tenth Discourse, On Servants, ch. 7*

20 Most men are so completely corrupted by opinion that they would rather be notorious for the greatest calamities than suffer no ill and be unknown. *Eleventh, or Trojan, Discourse, ch. 6*

Martial[14] [Marcus Valerius Martialis]

A.D. C. 40 – C. 104

21 My poems are naughty, but my life is pure.[15] *Epigrams, I, 4*

---

[1] Pectus est enim, quod disertos facit.

[2] See Pope, 340:23.

A fool with judges, amongst fools a judge. — COWPER, *Conversation* [1782], *l. 298*

This man [Chesterfield], I thought, had been a lord among wits; but I find he is only a wit among lords. — SAMUEL JOHNSON; from BOSWELL, *Life of Johnson* [1791], *vol. II, p. 159* (Everyman edition)

[3] Qualis artifex pereo!

[4] Victrix causa deis placuit, sed victa Catoni.

[5] Stat magni nominis umbra.

[6] Pigmei gigantum humeris impositi plusquam ipsi gigantes vident.

See Robert Burton, 258:7, and Sir Isaac Newton, 313:10.

The dwarf sees farther than the giant, when he has the giant's shoulder to mount on. — COLERIDGE, *The Friend* [1828]

[7] Servare modum, finemque tenere, / Naturamque sequi.

See The Seven Sages, 62:7; Terence, 96:1; Horace, 106:12 and 107:20; Anonymous Latin, 134:12; and Voltaire, 343:23.

[8] The reference is to Caesar.

[9] Plus est quam vita salusque / Quod perit.

[10] "Dat poenas laudata fides, dum sustinet," inquit, / "Quos fortuna premit" / [A praised faith / Is her own scourge, when it sustains their states / Whom fortune hath depressed]. — BEN JONSON, *Anglia, 39, 247*

And faith though praised, is punished, that supports / Such as good fate forsakes. — FLETCHER, *The False One* [1647], *act I, sc. i, l. 303*

[11] Clarum et venerabile nomen / Gentibus.

Cato's tribute to the fallen Pompey.

[12] Etiam periere ruinae.

The reference is to Troy.

[13] Translated by J. W. COHOON (Loeb Classical Library).

[14] Translated by DUDLEY FITTS.

[15] Lasciva est nobis pagina, vita proba.

1 Tomorrow's life is too late. Live today. *Ib. 15*

2 Some good, some so-so, and lots plain bad: that's how a book of poems is made, my friend. *Ib. 16*

3 I don't like you, Sabidius, I can't say why; But I can say this: I don't like you, Sabidius.[1] *Ib. 32*

4 Stop abusing my verses, or publish some of your own. *Ib. 91*

5 You complain, friend Swift, of the length of my epigrams, but you yourself write nothing. Yours are shorter. *Ib. 110*

6 Conceal a flaw, and the world will imagine the worst. *Ib. III, 42*

7 The bee is enclosed, and shines preserved in amber, so that it seems enshrined in its own nectar.[2] *Ib. IV, 32*

8 They praise those verses, yes, but read something else. *Ib. 49*

9 You ask what a nice girl will do? She won't give an inch, but she won't say no. *Ib. 71*

10 Our days pass by, and are scored against us.[3] *Ib. V, 20*

11 What's a wretched man? A man whom no man pleases. *Ib. 28*

12 A man who lives everywhere lives nowhere. *Ib. 73*

13 You puff the poets of other days,
The living you deplore.
Spare me the accolade: your praise
Is not worth dying for.[4] *Ib. VIII, 69*

14 Virtue extends our days: he lives two lives who relives his past with pleasure.[5] *Ib. X, 23*

15 Neither fear your death's day nor long for it.[6] *Ib. 47*

16 You'll get no laurel crown for outrunning a burro. *Ib. XII, 36*

[1]See Tom Brown, 319:19.

[2]Whence we see spiders, flies, or ants entombed preserved forever in amber, a more than royal tomb.—FRANCIS BACON, *Historia Vitae et Mortis* [1623], *Sylva Sylvarum, cent. I, exper. 100*

I saw a fly within a bead / Of amber cleanly buried. —HERRICK [1591–1674], *On a Fly Buried in Amber*

See Pope, 338:12.

[3]Nobis pereunt et imputantur.

[4]See Hazlitt, 445:8, and Louis Edwin Thayer, 762:1.

[5]Thus would I double my life's fading space; / For he that runs it well, runs twice his race.—COWLEY [1618–1667], *Discourse XI, Of Myself, st. 11*

For he lives twice who can at once employ / The present well, and ev'n the past enjoy.—POPE [1688–1744], *Imitation of Martial*

[6]See Milton, 287:30.

17 You're obstinate, pliant, merry, morose, all at once. For me there's no living with you, or without you.[7] *Ib. 47*

18 The country in town.[8] *Ib. 57*

19 I know these are nothing.[9] *Ib. XIII, 2*

Titus Vespasianus

A.D. C. 41–81

20 Friends, I have lost a day.[10] *From SUETONIUS, Titus, sec. 8*

Plutarch

A.D. 46–120

21 As geographers, Sosius, crowd into the edges of their maps parts of the world which they do not know about, adding notes in the margin to the effect that beyond this lies nothing but sandy deserts full of wild beasts, and unapproachable bogs.[11] *Lives, Aemilius Paulus, sec. 5*

22 About Theseus began the saying, "He is a second Hercules." *Ib. 29*

23 A Roman divorced from his wife, being highly blamed by his friends, who demanded, "Was she not chaste? Was she not fair? Was she not fruitful?" holding out his shoe, asked them whether it was not new and well made. "Yet," added he, "none of you can tell where it pinches me."[12] *Ib.*

24 Where the lion's skin will not reach, you must patch it out with the fox's.[13] *Ib. Lysander, sec. 7*

25 Moral habits, induced by public practices, are far quicker in making their way into men's private lives, than the failings and faults of individuals are in infecting the city at large. *Ib. 17*

[7]Difficilis facilis fucundus acerbus es idem: / Nec tecum possum vivere nec sine te.

See Aristophanes, 82:14, and Ovid, 113:8.

[8]Rus in urbe.

[9]Nos haec novimus esse nihil.

Said of his own poems. The phrase was used by John Gay as an epigraph for *The Beggar's Opera* [1728].

[10]Amici, diem perdidi.

[11]So geographers, in Afric maps, / With savage pictures fill their gaps, / And o'er unhabitable downs / Place elephants for want of towns.—SWIFT, *On Poetry, A Rhapsody* [1733]

[12]The wearer knows where the shoe wrings.—GEORGE HERBERT, *Jacula Prudentum* [1640]

I can tell where my own shoe pinches me.—CERVANTES, *Don Quixote, pt. I* [1605], *bk. IV, ch. 5*

[13]The prince must be a lion, but he must also know how to play the fox.—NICCOLÒ MACHIAVELLI, *The Prince* [1532]

1 As it is in the proverb, played Cretan against Cretan.[1] *Ib. 20*

2 Perseverance is more prevailing than violence; and many things which cannot be overcome when they are together, yield themselves up when taken little by little.
Ib. Sertorius, sec. 16

3 Good fortune will elevate even petty minds, and give them the appearance of a certain greatness and stateliness, as from their high place they look down upon the world; but the truly noble and resolved spirit raises itself, and becomes more conspicuous in times of disaster and ill fortune.
Ib. Eumenes, sec. 9

4 Authority and place demonstrate and try the tempers of men, by moving every passion and discovering every frailty.
Ib. Demosthenes and Cicero, sec. 3

5 Medicine, to produce health, has to examine disease; and music, to create harmony, must investigate discord.
Ib. Demetrius, sec. 1

6 It is a true proverb, that if you live with a lame man you will learn to limp.
Morals. Of the Training of Children

7 The very spring and root of honesty and virtue lie in good education. *Ib.*

8 It is indeed desirable to be well descended, but the glory belongs to our ancestors.
Ib.

9 Nothing made the horse so fat as the king's eye. *Ib.*

10 It is wise to be silent when occasion requires, and better than to speak, though never so well.[2] *Ib.*

11 An old doting fool, with one foot already in the grave. *Ib.*

12 He is a fool who leaves things close at hand to follow what is out of reach.[3]
Ib. Of Garrulity

13 All men whilst they are awake are in one common world; but each of them, when he is asleep, is in a world of his own.[4]
Ib. Of Superstition

[1]Cheat against cheat. (The Cretans were considered notorious liars.)

[2]Closed lips hurt no one, speaking may.—Cato the Censor [234–149 B.C.], *bk. I, distich 12*
See Publilius Syrus, 112:16.

[3]Better one bird in hand than ten in the wood.—John Heywood, *Proverbs* [1546], *pt. I, ch. 2*
One bird in the hand is worth two in the wood.—Thomas Lodge, *Rosalyne* [1590]
A bird in hand is worth two in the bush.—Cervantes, *Don Quixote, pt. I* [1605], *bk. IV, ch. 4*
A feather in hand is better than a bird in the air.—George Herbert, *Jacula Prudentum* [1640]

[4]A saying attributed to Heraclitus.

14 That proverbial saying, "Bad news travels fast and far."[5] *Ib. Of Inquisitiveness*

15 Spintharus, speaking in commendation of Epaminondas, says he scarce ever met with any man who knew more and spoke less.
Ib. Of Hearing, sec. 6

16 Antiphanes said merrily that in a certain city the cold was so intense that words were congealed as soon as spoken, but that after some time they thawed and became audible; so that the words spoken in winter were articulated next summer.[6]
Ib. Of Man's Progress in Virtue

17 When the candles are out all women are fair.[7] *Ib. Conjugal Precepts*

18 Like watermen, who look astern while they row the boat ahead.[8]
Ib. Whether 'Twas Rightfully Said, Live Concealed

19 The great god Pan is dead.[9]
Ib. Why the Oracles Cease to Give Answers

20 I am whatever was, or is, or will be; and my veil no mortal ever took up.[10]
Ib. Of Isis and Osiris

21 For to err in opinion, though it be not the part of wise men, is at least human.[11]
Ib. Against Colotes

22 Pythagoras, when he was asked what time was, answered that it was the soul of this world. *Ib. Platonic Questions*

[5]Evil news fly faster still than good.—Thomas Kyd, *Spanish Tragedy* [1594], *act I*
See Milton, 289:7.

[6]Rabelais gives a somewhat similar account, referring to Antiphanes, in *Works, bk. IV* [1548], *chs. 55–56.*
See Raspe (Baron Munchausen), 385:8.

[7]When all candles be out, all cats be gray.—John Heywood, *Proverbs* [1546], *pt. I, ch. 5*
See Herrick, 266:9.

[8]Like rowers, who advance backward.—Montaigne, *Essays* [1580–1595], *Of Profit and Honor, bk. III, ch. 1*
Like the watermen that row one way and look another.—Robert Burton, *Anatomy of Melancholy* [1621–1651], *Democritus to the Reader*
See Bunyan, 302:7.

[9]Plutarch says in *Of Isis and Osiris* that a ship well laden with passengers drove with the tide near the Isles of Paxi, when a loud voice was heard by most of the passengers calling one Thanus. The voice then said aloud to him, "When you are arrived at Palodes, take care to make it known that the great god Pan is dead."
Great Pan is dead.—Elizabeth Barrett Browning [1806–1861], *The Dead Pan, st. 26*

[10]I am the things that are, and those that are to be, and those that have been. No one ever lifted my skirts; the fruit which I bore was the sun.—Proclus [c. 411–485], *On Plato's Timaeus* (inscription in the temple of Neith at Sais, in Egypt)

[11]See Anonymous Latin, 133:22; Shirley, 272:12; and Pope, 333:15.

Epictetus[1]

c. 50–120

1 To the rational being only the irrational is unendurable, but the rational is endurable.
Discourses, bk. I, ch. 2

2 When you close your doors, and make darkness within, remember never to say that you are alone, for you are not alone;[2] nay, God is within, and your genius is within. And what need have they of light to see what you are doing?
Ib. 14

3 No thing great is created suddenly, any more than a bunch of grapes or a fig. If you tell me that you desire a fig, I answer you that there must be time. Let it first blossom, then bear fruit, then ripen.
Ib. 15

4 Any one thing in the creation is sufficient to demonstrate a Providence to a humble and grateful mind.
Ib. 16

5 Were I a nightingale, I would sing like a nightingale; were I a swan, like a swan. But as it is, I am a rational being, therefore I must sing hymns of praise to God.
Ib.

6 Practice yourself, for heaven's sake, in little things; and thence proceed to greater.
Ib. 18

7 It is difficulties that show what men are.
Ib. 24

8 The good or ill of man lies within his own will.
Ib. 25

9 In theory there is nothing to hinder our following what we are taught; but in life there are many things to draw us aside.
Ib. 26

10 Appearances to the mind are of four kinds. Things either are what they appear to be; or they neither are, nor appear to be; or they are, and do not appear to be; or they are not, and yet appear to be. Rightly to aim in all these cases is the wise man's task.
Ib. 27

11 Only the educated are free.
Ib. II, 1

12 The materials are indifferent, but the use we make of them is not a matter of indifference.
Ib. 5

13 Shall I show you the sinews of a philosopher? "What sinews are those?"—A will undisappointed; evils avoided; powers daily exercised; careful resolutions; unerring decisions.
Ib. 8

14 What is the first business of one who practices philosophy? To get rid of self-conceit. For it is impossible for anyone to begin to learn that which he thinks he already knows.
Ib. 17

15 Whatever you would make habitual, practice it; and if you would not make a thing habitual, do not practice it, but accustom yourself to something else.
Ib. 18

16 Be not swept off your feet by the vividness of the impression, but say, "Impression, wait for me a little. Let me see what you are and what you represent. Let me try you."
Ib.

17 There are some faults which men readily admit, but others not so readily.
Ib. 21

18 Two principles we should always have ready—that there is nothing good or evil save in the will; and that we are not to lead events, but to follow them.
Ib. III, 10

19 First say to yourself what you would be; and then do what you have to do.
Ib. 23

20 Remember that you ought to behave in life as you would at a banquet. As something is being passed around it comes to you; stretch out your hand, take a portion of it politely. It passes on; do not detain it. Or it has not come to you yet; do not project your desire to meet it, but wait until it comes in front of you. So act toward children, so toward a wife, so toward office, so toward wealth.
The Encheiridion, 15

21 Where do you suppose he got that high brow?
Ib. 22

22 Everything has two handles—by one of which it ought to be carried and by the other not.[3]
Ib. 43

Juvenal
[Decimus Junius Juvenalis]

c. 50 – c. 130

23 Honesty is praised and starves.[4]
Satires, I, l. 74

24 If nature refuses, indignation will produce verses.[5]
Ib. l. 79

[1]Translated by W. A. Oldfather (Loeb Classical Library).

[2]Though in a wilderness, a man is never alone.—Sir Thomas Browne, *Religio Medici* [1642], *p. 82* (Everyman edition)

[3]There is a right and wrong handle to everything. — Raspe, *Travels of Baron Munchausen* [1785], *ch. 30*

[4]Probitas laudatur et alget.
A favorite quotation of Linnaeus.

[5]Si natura negat, facit indignatio versum.

1 All the doings of mankind, their wishes, fears, anger, pleasures, joys, and varied pursuits, form the motley subject of my book.
Ib. l. 85

2 Censure pardons the raven, but is visited upon the dove.[1] *Ib. II, l. 63*

3 No one becomes depraved in a moment.[2]
Ib. l. 83

4 Grammarian, rhetorician, geometrician, painter, trainer, soothsayer, ropedancer, physician, magician—he knows everything. Tell the hungry little Greek to go to heaven; he'll go.[3] *Ib. III, l. 76*

5 Bitter poverty has no harder pang than that it makes men ridiculous.[4]
Ib. l. 152

6 It is not easy for men to rise whose qualities are thwarted by poverty. *Ib. l. 164*

7 We all live in a state of ambitious poverty.
Ib. l. 182

8 A rare bird on earth, comparable to a black swan.[5] *Ib. VI, l. 165*

9 I wish it, I command it. Let my will take the place of reason.[6] *Ib. l. 223*

10 We are now suffering the evils of a long peace. Luxury, more deadly than war, broods over the city, and avenges a conquered world.[7]
Ib. l. 292

11 But who is to guard the guards themselves?[8] *Ib. l. 347*

12 An inveterate and incurable itch for writing besets many, and grows old in their sick hearts. *Ib. VII, l. 51*

13 Nobility is the one and only virtue.[9]
Ib. VIII, l. 20

14 Count it the greatest sin to prefer life to honor, and for the sake of living to lose what makes life worth having.[10] *Ib. l. 83*

15 The people that once bestowed commands, consulships, legions, and all else, now concerns itself no more, and longs eagerly for just two things—bread and circuses![11]
Ib. X, l. 79

16 Put Hannibal in the scales.[12]
Ib. l. 147

17 You should pray for a sound mind in a sound body.[13] *Ib. l. 356*

18 For revenge is always the delight of a mean spirit, of a weak and petty mind! You may immediately draw proof of this—that no one rejoices more in revenge than a woman.
Ib. XIII, l. 189

19 The greatest reverence is due the young.[14]
Ib. XIV, 47

Cornelius Tacitus

c. 55 – c. 117

20 The images of the most illustrious families . . . were carried before it [the bier of Julia]. Those of Brutus and Cassius were not displayed; but for that reason they shone with preeminent luster.[15]
Annals, bk. III, 76

21 He had talents equal to business, and aspired no higher. *Ib. VI, 39*

22 What is today supported by precedents will hereafter become a precedent.[16]
Ib. XI, 24

23 [Of Petronius] Arbiter of taste.[17]
Ib. XVI, 18

24 It is the rare fortune of these days that one may think what one likes and say what one thinks. *Histories, bk. I, 1*

25 [Of Servius Galba] He seemed more important than a private citizen while he was a private citizen, and in the opinion of all he was capable of rule—if he had not ruled.
Ib. 49

26 The desire for glory clings even to the best men longer than any other passion.[18]
Ib. IV, 6

[1] Dat veniam corvis, vexat censura columbas.
[2] Nemo repente fuit turpissimus.
Translated by Gilbert Highet.
See Beaumont and Fletcher, 263:6, and Racine, 312:10.
[3] See Dryden, 304:10.
[4] Nil habet infelix paupertas durius in se, quam quod ridiculos homines facit.
[5] Rara avis in terris nigroque simillima cycno.
[6] Hoc volo, sic iubeo, sit pro ratione voluntas.
[7] Nunc patimur longae pacis mala, saevior armis / Luxuria incubuit victumque ulciscitur orbem.
[8] Sed quis custodiet ipsos Custodes?
What an absurd idea—a guardian to need a guardian!
—Plato [c. 428–348 B.C.], *The Republic, bk. III, 403–E*
[9] Nobilitas sola est atque unica virtus.
[10] Summum crede nefas animam praeferre pudori, / Et propter vitam vivendi perdere causas.
[11] Panem et circenses.
See Bellamy, 666:3.
[12] Expende Hannibalem.
[13] Mens sana in corpore sano.
See John Locke, 307:18.
[14] Maxima debetur puero reverentia.
See Locke, 308:1.
[15] See Lord John Russell, 466:4.
[16] One precedent creates another. They soon accumulate and become law.—Junius, *Letters* [1769–1771], *dedication*
[17] Elegantiae arbiter.
See Petronius, 117.
[18] See Milton, 280:15.

1 The gods are on the side of the stronger.[1]
Ib. 17

2 Whatever is unknown is taken for marvelous;[2] but now the limits of Britain are laid bare. *Agricola, sec. 30*

3 Where they make a desert, they call it peace.[3] *Ib.*

4 Think of your forefathers and posterity.[4]
Ib. 32

5 Fortune favored him . . . in the opportune moment of his death. *Ib. 45*

Pliny the Younger
[Gaius Plinius Caecilius Secundus]

c. 61 – c. 112

6 Modestus said of Regulus that he was "the biggest rascal that walks upon two legs."
Letters,[5] *bk. I, letter 5*

7 There is nothing to write about, you say. Well then, write and let me know just this — that there is nothing to write about; or tell me in the good old style if you are well. That's right. I am quite well.[6] *Ib. 11*

8 An object in possession seldom retains the same charm that it had in pursuit.[7]
Ib. II, 15

9 He [Pliny the Elder] used to say that "no book was so bad but some good might be got out of it."[8] *Ib. III, 5*

10 This expression of ours, "Father of a family."[9] *Ib. V, 19*

11 That indolent but agreeable condition of doing nothing.[10] *Ib. VIII, 9*

[1] Deos fortioribus adesse.
See Bussy-Rabutin, 294:21; Boileau, 311:15; Frederick the Great, 358:4; and Gibbon, 383:13.

[2] Omne ignotum pro magnifico est.
See Pliny the Elder, 116:11.

[3] Calgacus, addressing the Britons at the battle of the Grampians, referring to the Romans.
See Byron, 459:7.

[4] Et maiores vestros et posteros cogitate.
See *The Teaching for Merikare,* 3:13, and Samuel Adams, 365:3.

[5] *Book VI, letter 16,* contains the description of the eruption of Vesuvius [79], as witnessed by Pliny the Elder.

[6] This comes to inform you that I am in a perfect state of health, hoping you are in the same. Ay, that's the old beginning. — GEORGE COLMAN THE YOUNGER, *The Heir at Law* [1797], *act III, sc. ii*

[7] It has been a thousand times observed, and I must observe it once more, that the hours we pass with happy prospects in view are more pleasing than those crowned with fruition. — GOLDSMITH, *The Vicar of Wakefield* [1766], *ch. 10*

[8] "There is no book so bad," said the bachelor, "but something good may be found in it." — CERVANTES, *Don Quixote, pt. II* [1615], *ch. 3*

[9] Paterfamilias.

[10] Dolce far niente [Sweet doing-nothing]. — *Italian proverb*

12 Objects which are usually the motives of our travels by land and by sea are often overlooked and neglected if they lie under our eye. . . . We put off from time to time going and seeing what we know we have an opportunity of seeing when we please.
Ib. 20

13 His only fault is that he has no fault.[11]
Ib. IX, 26

Suetonius
[Gaius Suetonius Tranquillus]

c. 70 – c. 140

14 Hail, Emperor, we who are about to die salute you.[12] *Life of Claudius, 21*

Hadrian
[Publius Aelius Hadrianus]

76–138

15 Little soul, wandering, gentle guest and companion of the body, into what places will you now go, pale, stiff, and naked, no longer sporting as you did![13]
Ad Animam Suam

Chang Heng[14]

78–139

16 Heaven is like an egg, and the earth is like the yolk of the egg. *Saying*

Lucius Annaeus Florus

fl. 125

17 Each year new consuls and proconsuls are made; but not every year is a king or a poet born.[15]
De Qualitate Vitae, fragment 8

[11] The greatest of faults, I should say, is to be conscious of none. — CARLYLE, *Heroes and Hero Worship* [1841], *The Hero as Prophet*

[12] Ave, Caesar, morituri te salutamus.
Also rendered "te salutant": those about to die salute you.

[13] Animula vagula blandula, / Hospes comesque corporis, / Quae nunc abibis in loca / Pallidula rigida nudula, / Nec ut soles dabis iocosi.
Amelette Ronsardelette, / mignonelette doucelette, / très chère hostesse de mon corps, / tu descens là bas foibelette, / pasle, maigrelette, seulette, / dans le froid Royaulme des mors. — RONSARD, *A son âme* [dictated on his deathbed, December 27, 1585]
See Pope, 333:23.

[14] From *Sources of Chinese Tradition* [1960], edited by WILLIAM THEODORE DE BARY.

[15] From this derived the proverb: Poeta nascitur, non fit (The poet is born, not made).
See Ben Jonson, 256:17.

Ptolemy
[Claudius Ptolemaeus]

c. 100–178

1 Everything that is hard to attain is easily assailed by the generality of men.
Tetrabiblos,[1] *bk. I, sec. 1*

2 The length of life takes the leading place among inquiries about events following birth. *Ib. III, 10*

3 As material fortune is associated with the properties of the body, so honor belongs to those of the soul. *Ib. IV, 1*

4 There are three classes of friendship and enmity, since men are so disposed to one another either by preference or by need or through pleasure and pain. *Ib. 7*

Marcus Aurelius Antoninus[2]

121–180

5 This Being of mine, whatever it really is, consists of a little flesh, a little breath, and the part which governs.
Meditations, II, 2

6 You will find rest from vain fancies if you perform every act in life as though it were your last.[3] *Ib. 5*

7 Remember that no man loses other life than that which he lives, nor lives other than that which he loses. *Ib. 14*

8 Each thing is of like form from everlasting and comes round again in its cycle.
Ib.

9 The longest-lived and the shortest-lived man, when they come to die, lose one and the same thing. *Ib.*

10 As for life, it is a battle and a sojourning in a strange land; but the fame that comes after is oblivion. *Ib. 17*

11 A man should *be* upright, not be *kept* upright. *Ib. III, 5*

12 Never esteem anything as of advantage to you that will make you break your word or lose your self-respect. *Ib. 7*

13 By a tranquil mind I mean nothing else than a mind well ordered. *Ib. IV, 3*

14 The universe is change; our life is what our thoughts make it. *Ib.*

[1]Translated by F. E. Robbins (Loeb Classical Library).
[2]Translated by Morris Hickey Morgan, with some adaptations.
[3]See *Matthew 6:34*, 38:7; Horace, 107:7; and Publilius Syrus, 111:29.

15 Death, like birth, is a secret of Nature.
Ib. 5

16 Whatever happens at all happens as it should; you will find this true, if you watch narrowly.[4] *Ib. 10*

17 How much time he gains who does not look to see what his neighbor says or does or thinks, but only at what he does himself, to make it just and holy. *Ib. 18*

18 Whatever is in any way beautiful hath its source of beauty in itself, and is complete in itself; praise forms no part of it. So it is none the worse nor the better for being praised.
Ib. 20

19 All that is harmony for you, my Universe, is in harmony with me as well.[5] Nothing that comes at the right time for you is too early or too late for me. Everything is fruit to me that your seasons bring, Nature. All things come of you, have their being in you, and return to you.[6] *Ib. 23*

20 "Let your occupations be few," says the sage,[7] "if you would lead a tranquil life."
Ib. 24

21 Love the little trade which you have learned, and be content with it. *Ib. 31*

22 There is a proper dignity and proportion to be observed in the performance of every act of life. *Ib. 32*

23 All is ephemeral — fame and the famous as well. *Ib. 35*

24 Search men's governing principles, and consider the wise, what they shun and what they cleave to. *Ib. 38*

25 Time is a sort of river of passing events, and strong is its current; no sooner is a thing brought to sight than it is swept by and another takes its place, and this too will be swept away.[8] *Ib. 43*

26 All that happens is as usual and familiar as the rose in spring and the crop in summer.
Ib. 44

27 Mark how fleeting and paltry is the estate of man — yesterday in embryo, tomorrow a mummy or ashes. So for the hairsbreadth of time assigned to thee, live rationally, and part with life cheerfully, as drops the ripe

[4]See Dryden, 303:14, and Pope, 337:1.
[5]See Zeno, 91:19.
[6]See *I Chronicles 29:14*, 14:26.
[7]Democritus [c. 460 – c. 400 B.C.], *Fragment 3;* also quoted by Seneca [8 B.C.–A.D. 65] in *On Anger, III, 6,* and *On the Happy Life, 13.*
[8]See Isaac Watts, 328:12, and Anonymous, 925:6.

olive, extolling the season that bore it and the tree that matured it. *Ib. 48*

1 In the morning, when you are sluggish about getting up, let this thought be present: "I am rising to a man's work."

Ib. V, 1

2 A man makes no noise over a good deed, but passes on to another as a vine to bear grapes again in season.[1] *Ib. 6*

3 Nothing happens to anybody which he is not fitted by nature to bear. *Ib. 18*

4 Live with the gods. *Ib. 27*

5 Look beneath the surface; let not the several quality of a thing nor its worth escape thee. *Ib. VI, 3*

6 The controlling intelligence understands its own nature, and what it does, and whereon it works. *Ib. 5*

7 Do not think that what is hard for you to master is humanly impossible; but if a thing is humanly possible, consider it to be within your reach. *Ib. 19*

8 What is not good for the swarm is not good for the bee. *Ib. 54*

9 One universe made up of all that is; and one God in it all, and one principle of being, and one law, the reason, shared by all thinking creatures, and one truth.

Ib. VII, 9

10 It is man's peculiar duty to love even those who wrong him.[2] *Ib. 22*

11 Very little is needed to make a happy life. *Ib. 67*

12 To change your mind and to follow him who sets you right is to be nonetheless the free agent that you were before.

Ib. VIII, 16

13 Look to the essence of a thing, whether it be a point of doctrine, of practice, or of interpretation. *Ib. 22*

14 Be not careless in deeds, nor confused in words, nor rambling in thought. *Ib. 51*

15 Think not disdainfully of death, but look on it with favor; for even death is one of the things that Nature wills. *Ib. IX, 3*

16 A wrongdoer is often a man who has left something undone, not always one who has done something.[3] *Ib. 5*

[1]See *Matthew 6:3*, 37:14.
[2]See *Proverbs 25:21*, 25:15.
[3]See *Book of Common Prayer*, 54:13.

17 Blot out vain pomp; check impulse; quench appetite; keep reason under its own control. *Ib. 7*

18 All things are the same—familiar in enterprise, momentary in endurance, coarse in substance. All things now are as they were in the day of those whom we have buried. *Ib. 14*

19 Whatever may befall you, it was preordained for you from everlasting.

Ib. X, 5

Galen

129–199

20 The chief merit of language is clearness, and we know that nothing detracts so much from this as do unfamiliar terms.

On the Natural Faculties,[4] *bk. I, sec.* 2

21 Those who are enslaved to their sects are not merely devoid of all sound knowledge, but they will not even stop to learn!

Ib. 13

22 Nature's artistic skill. *Ib.*

23 It was, of course, a grand and impressive thing to do, to mistrust the obvious, and to pin one's faith in things which could not be seen! *Ib.*

24 Praxiteles and Phidias . . . were unable to . . . reach and handle all portions of the material. It is not so, however, with nature. Every part of a bone she makes bone, every part of the flesh she makes flesh, and so with fat and all the rest; there is no part she has not touched, elaborated, and embellished. *Ib. II, 3*

25 That which *is* grows, while that which *is not* becomes. *Ib.*

Diogenes Laertius

fl. c. 200

26 Ignorance plays the chief part among men, and the multitude of words.

Cleobulus, 4

27 Time is the image of eternity.

Plato, 41

28 There is a written and an unwritten law. The one by which we regulate our constitutions in our cities is the written law; that which arises from custom is the unwritten law. *Ib. 51*

[4]Translated by ARTHUR J. BROCK (Loeb Classical Library).

Tertullian
[Quintus Septimius Tertullianus]
c. 160–240

1 O witness of the soul naturally Christian.
Apologeticus, 17

2 See how these Christians love one another.[1]
Ib. 39

3 We multiply whenever we are mown down by you; the blood of Christians is seed.[2]
Ib. 50

4 Man is one name belonging to every nation upon earth. In them all is one soul though many tongues. Every country has its own language, yet the subjects of which the untutored soul speaks are the same everywhere.
Testimony of the Soul

5 Mother Church.[3] *Ad Martyras, 1*

6 Truth persuades by teaching, but does not teach by persuading.
Adversus Valentinianos, 1

7 Truth does not blush.[4] *Ib. 3*

8 It is to be believed because it is absurd.[5]
De Carne Christi, 5

9 It is certain because it is impossible.[6]
Ib.

10 Out of the frying pan into the fire.[7]
Ib. 6

11 One man's religion neither harms nor helps another man. *Ad Scapulam, 2*

12 It is certainly no part of religion to compel religion. *Ib.*

13 I must dispel vanity with vanity.
Adversus Marcionem, IV, 30

The Sayings of Jesus
Third century

14 Jesus saith, Wherever there are two, they are not without God, and wherever there is one alone, I say, I am with him.[8] Raise the stone, and there thou shalt find Me, cleave the wood and there am I.[9]
The Oxyrhynchus Papyri,[10] Part I [1898], no. 1, ΛΟΓΙΑ ΙΗCΟΥ [Logia Ithcoy], logion 5

15 Jesus saith, Ye ask who are those that draw us to the kingdom, if the kingdom is in Heaven? . . . The fowls of the air, and all beasts that are under the earth or upon the earth, and the fishes of the sea, these are they which draw you, and the kingdom of Heaven is within you.[11]
Ib. IV [1904], no. 654, New Sayings of Jesus, second saying

St. Cyprian
d. 258

16 He cannot have God for his father who has not the Church for his Mother.[12]
De Unitate Ecclesiae [251], ch. 6

17 There is no salvation outside the Church.[13]
Letter 73 [c. 256]

Plotinus
205–270

18 All things are filled full of signs, and it is a wise man who can learn about one thing from another.
Enneads,[14] bk. II, treatise iii, sec. 7

19 One principle must make the universe a single complex living creature, one from all.
Ib. 8

[1] Tertullian is sarcastically repeating what the enemies of Christianity are saying.

[2] Plures efficimur, quoties metimur a vobis; semen est sanguis christianorum.

This is often rendered as: The blood of the martyrs is the seed of the Church.

The Church of Christ has been founded by shedding its own blood, not that of others; by enduring outrage, not by inflicting it. Persecutions have made it grow; martyrdoms have crowned it. — ST. JEROME [c. 342–420], *letter 82*

The blood of martyrs is the seed of Christians. — BEYERLINCK, *Magnum Theatrum Vitae Humanorum* [1665]

The seed of the Church, I mean the blood of primitive martyrs. — THOMAS FULLER, *Church History of Britain* [1665], *pt. IV, bk. I*

See Jefferson, 388:7; Barère, 401:4; and Unamuno, 705:18.

[3] Domina mater ecclesia.

See St. Cyprian, 126:16.

[4] Veritas non erubescit.

[5] Prorsus credibile est, quia ineptum est.

[6] Certum est, quia impossible est.

This is called Tertullian's rule of faith. It is sometimes rendered as: Credo quia impossible [I believe because it is impossible]. St. Augustine expresses the same idea in *Confessions, VI, 5, 7*.

[7] De calcaria in carbonarium.

Leap out of the frying pan into the fire. — JOHN HEYWOOD, *Proverbs* [1546], *pt. II, ch. 5*

[8] See *Matthew 18:20*, 40:3.

[9] See Van Dyke, 671:9.

[10] Translated and edited by BERNARD P. GRENFELL and ARTHUR H. HUNT, who also discovered the papyri. The *Logia* were first published [1897] as ΛΟΓΙΑ ΙΗCΟΥ: *Sayings of Our Lord.*

[11] See *Luke 17:21*, 43:36.

[12] Habere non potest deum patrem qui ecclesiam non habet matrem.

See Tertullian, 126:5.

[13] Salus extra ecclesiam non est.

Quoted by St. Augustine in *De Baptismo*, hence sometimes attributed to him.

[14] Translated by A. H. ARMSTRONG (Loeb Classical Library).

Longus

Third century

1 There was never any yet that wholly could escape love, and never shall there be any, never so long as beauty shall be, never so long as eyes can see.

Daphnis and Chloe, proem, ch. 2

2 He is so poor that he could not keep a dog.

Ib. 15

Constantine[1]

c. 288–337

3 In this sign shalt thou conquer.[2]

From EUSEBIUS, *Life of Constantine, I, 28*

Ammianus Marcellinus

c. 330–395

4 Rose among thorns.

History, bk. XVI, ch. 17

Julian [Flavius Claudius Julianus][3]

332–363

5 You have conquered, Galilean.[4]

From THEODORET, *Church History, III, 20*

St. Ambrose

c. 340–397

6 When you are at Rome live in the Roman style; when you are elsewhere live as they live elsewhere.[5]

Advice to St. Augustine. From JEREMY TAYLOR, *Ductor Dubitantium [1660], I, 1, 5*

[1] Flavius Valerius Aurelius Constantinus.

[2] In hoc signo vinces.

The alleged words of Constantine's vision before his battle with Maxentius at Saxa Rubra, near Rome [312].

[3] Known as Julian the Apostate.

[4] Vicisti, Galilaee.

The Latin translation of the alleged dying words of the emperor.

See Swinburne, 633:6.

[5] Si fueris Romae, Romano vivito more; / Si fueris alibi, vivito sicut ibi.

My mother, having joined me at Milan, found that the church there did not fast on Saturdays as at Rome, and was at a loss what to do. I consulted St. Ambrose, of holy memory, who replied, "When I am at Rome, I fast on a Saturday; when I am at Milan, I do not. Follow the custom of the church where you are." — ST. AUGUSTINE [354–430], *Epistle to Januarius (Epistle 2), sec. 18.* Also *Epistle to Casualanus (Epistle 36), sec. 32*

When in Rome, do as the Romans do. — *Proverb*

St. Jerome[6]

c. 342–420

7 A friend is long sought, hardly found, and with difficulty kept. *Letter 1*

8 Love is not to be purchased, and affection has no price. *Letter 3*

9 The friendship that can cease has never been real. *Ib.*

10 It is easier to mend neglect than to quicken love. *Letter 7*

11 Love knows nothing of order. *Ib.*

12 The fact is that my native land is a prey to barbarism, that in it men's only God is their belly,[7] that they live only for the present, and that the richer a man is the holier he is held to be. *Ib.*

13 An unstable pilot steers a leaking ship, and the blind is leading the blind straight to the pit.[8] The ruler is like the ruled. *Ib.*

14 No athlete is crowned but in the sweat of his brow. *Letter 14*

15 If there is but little water in the stream, it is the fault, not of the channel, but of the source. *Letter 17*

16 You are a Ciceronian, not a Christian.[9] *Letter 22*

17 It is idle to play the lyre for an ass.[10] *Letter 27*

18 Everything must have in it a sharp seasoning of truth. *Letter 31*

19 While truth is always bitter, pleasantness waits upon evildoing. *Letter 40*

20 The line, often adopted by strong men in controversy, of justifying the means by the end.[11] *Letter 48*

21 Do not let your deeds belie your words, lest when you speak in church someone may say to himself, "Why do you not practice what you preach?"[12] *Letter 48*

22 Avoid, as you would the plague, a clergyman who is also a man of business.[13] *Letter 52*

[6] Translated by W. H. FREMANTLE.

[7] See *Philippians 3:19,* 50:5.

[8] See *Matthew 15:14,* 39:31.

[9] This was addressed to Jerome in a dream by Christ the Judge, censuring him for loving the classics more than the Fathers.

[10] A Greek proverb frequently quoted by Jerome.

[11] See Matthew Prior, 320:15.

[12] Cur ergo haec ipse non facis?

See Plautus, 94:6.

[13] Translated by F. A. WRIGHT (Loeb Classical Library).

1 A fat paunch never breeds fine thoughts.[1] *Ib.*

2 No one cares to speak to an unwilling listener. An arrow never lodges in a stone: often it recoils upon the sender of it. *Ib.*

3 That clergyman soon becomes an object of contempt who being often asked out to dinner never refuses to go. *Ib.*

4 The best almoner is he who keeps back nothing for himself. *Ib.*

5 It is worse still to be ignorant of your ignorance. *Letter 53*

6 Even brute beasts and wandering birds do not fall into the same traps or nets twice.[2] *Letter 54*

7 Sometimes the character of the mistress is inferred from the dress of her maids. *Ib.*

8 The face is the mirror of the mind, and eyes without speaking confess the secrets of the heart. *Ib.*

9 The scars of others should teach us caution. *Ib.*

10 When the stomach is full, it is easy to talk of fasting. *Letter 58*

11 Small minds can never handle great themes.[3] *Letter 60*

12 The Roman world is falling, yet we hold our heads erect instead of bowing our necks.[4] *Ib.*

13 Every day we are changing, every day we are dying, and yet we fancy ourselves eternal. *Ib.*

14 Early impressions are hard to eradicate from the mind. When once wool has been dyed purple, who can restore it to its previous whiteness? *Letter 107*

15 The tired ox treads with a firmer step.[5] *Letter 112*

16 Athletes as a rule are stronger than their backers; yet the weaker presses the stronger to put forth all his efforts. *Letter 118*

17 For they wished to fill the winepress of eloquence not with the tendrils of mere words but with the rich grape juice of good sense. *Letter 125*

[1]This is a Greek proverb.
Fat paunches have lean pates, and dainty bits / Make rich the ribs, but bankrupt quite the wits. — SHAKESPEARE, *Love's Labour's Lost, act I, sc. i, l. 26*

[2]Translated by F. A. WRIGHT (Loeb Classical Library).

[3]Translated by W. J. COURTENAY.

[4]Romanus orbis ruit.

[5]An old Roman proverb quoted by St. Jerome to St. Augustine after the latter criticized the elder Jerome.

18 It is no fault of Christianity that a hypocrite falls into sin. *Ib.*

19 The charges we bring against others often come home to ourselves; we inveigh against faults which are as much ours as theirs; and so our eloquence ends by telling against ourselves. *Ib.*

20 Preferring to store her money in the stomachs of the needy rather than hide it in a purse.[6] *Letter 127*

21 The privileges of a few do not make common law.[7] *Exposition on Jona*

22 Never look a gift horse in the mouth.[8] *On the Epistle to the Ephesians*

St. John Chrysostom
c. 345–407

23 Hell is paved with priests' skulls. *De Sacerdotio [c. 390]*

24 No one can harm the man who does himself no wrong.[9] *Letter to Olympia*

Vegetius
[Flavius Vegetius Renatus]
fl. c. 375

25 Let him who desires peace prepare for war.[10] *De Rei Militari, III, prologue*

St. Augustine
354–430

26 Will is to grace as the horse is to the rider.[11] *De Libero Arbitrio [388–395]*

27 The weakness of little children's limbs is innocent, not their souls. *Confessions [397–401], I, 7*

28 To Carthage I came, where all about me resounded a caldron of dissolute loves.[12] *Ib. III, 1*

[6]Translated by F. A. WRIGHT (Loeb Classical Library).

[7]Privilegia paucorum non faciunt legem.
The exception proves the rule.

[8]Noli equi dentes inspicere donati.

[9]No one is injured save by himself. — ERASMUS [1465–1536], *Adagia*

[10]Qui desiderat pacem, praeparet bellum.
See Aristotle, 87:24; Robert Burton, 259:13; Fénelon, 316:12; Washington, 379:9; and Lowell, 568:9.
In peace, like a wise man, he has provided for the needs of war. — HORACE, *Satires, bk. II* [30 B.C.], *ii, 111*
We should provide in peace what we need in war. — PUBLILIUS SYRUS [first century B.C.], *Maxim 709*

[11]This is considered the most important definition of the relation of grace to free will in the Middle Ages.

[12]To Carthage then I came. — T. S. ELIOT, *The Waste Land* [1922], *III, l. 307 and note*

1 I was in love with loving. *Ib.*

2 In the usual course of study I had come to a book of a certain Cicero. *Ib. 4*

3 Give me chastity and continence, but not just now. *Ib. VIII, 7*

4 Take up, read! Take up, read![1]
Ib. 12

5 Too late I loved you, O Beauty ever ancient and ever new! Too late I loved you! And, behold, you were within me, and I out of myself, and there I searched for you.
Ib. X, 27

6 Give what you command, and command what you will. *Ib. 29*

7 Hear the other side.[2]
De Duabus Animabus, XIV, 2

8 I would not have believed the gospel had not the authority of the Church moved me.
Contra Epistulam Fundamenti [c. 410], ch. 5

9 Necessity has no law.[3]
Soliloquiorum. Animae ad Deum [c. 410], 2

10 We make a ladder of our vices, if we trample those same vices underfoot.[4]
Sermons, 3

11 Anger is a weed; hate is the tree.
Ib. 58

12 The dove loves when it quarrels; the wolf hates when it flatters. *Ib. 64*

13 Rome has spoken; the case is closed.[5]
Ib. 131

14 He who created you without you will not justify you without you. *Ib. 169*

15 The most glorious city of God.
City of God [415], I, preface

St. Vincent of Lerins
died c. 450

16 [That faith is catholic] which has been believed always, everywhere, and by all.[6]
Commonitorium, ch. 2

17 Every word [of Tertullian] almost was a sentence; every sentence a victory.
Ib. 18

St. Remy [Remigius]
c. 438 – c. 533

18 Henceforward burn what thou hast worshipped, and worship what thou hast burned.[7]
Said to Clovis at his baptism [496]

Clovis
466–511

19 God of Clotilda,[8] if you grant me victory I shall become a Christian.[9]
Legendary vow before battle

Hsieh Ho[10]
fl. 500

20 By copying, the ancient models should be perpetuated.[11]
Notes Concerning the Classification of Old Paintings, Sixth Principle

St. Benedict[12]
480–543

21 We are therefore about to establish a school of the Lord's service in which we hope to introduce nothing harsh or burdensome.
Rule of St. Benedict, prologue

Boethius
480–524

22 In every adversity of fortune, to have been happy is the most unhappy kind of misfortune.[13]
De Consolatione Philosophiae, bk. II, 4, 4

[1] Tolle lege, tolle lege.
What the bell seemed to say to Augustine at the moment of his conversion. When he opened the Bible, his eyes fell on *Romans 13:12–14*, 47:29.

[2] Audi partem alteram.
See Euripides, 77:1, and Protagoras, 78:24.

[3] See Publilius Syrus, 111:20, and Oliver Cromwell, 272:20.

[4] See Longfellow, 511:22, and Tennyson, 531:19.

[5] Roma locuta est; causa finita est.

[6] Quod semper, quod ubique, quod ab omnibus creditum est.
The definition of the traditional articles of faith.

[7] See Clovis, 129:19.

[8] St. Clotilda, wife of Clovis.

[9] Clovis defeated the Alemanni in 496, and following his vow was baptized with three thousand followers by St. Remy at Rheims.
See St. Remy, 129:18.

[10] From *The Spirit of the Brush*, translated by Shio Sakanishi [Wisdom of the East Series, 1957].

[11] See Horace, 109:30, and Fujiwara no Teika, 138:5.

[12] Founder of Western monasticism.

[13] See Pindar, 72:1; Dante, 141:2; Chaucer, 144:24; and Tennyson, 529:20.

1 Who hath so entire happiness that he is not in some part offended with the condition of his estate? *Ib. 41*

2 Nothing is miserable but what is thought so, and contrariwise, every estate is happy if he that bears it be content. *Ib. 64*

3 From thee, great God, we spring, to thee we
tend—
Path, motive, guide, original and end.[1]
Ib. III, 9, 27

4 Who can give law to lovers? Love is a greater law to itself. *Ib. 12, 47*

Flavius Magnus Aurelius Cassiodorus

c. 490 – c. 583

5 He receives hope in future benefits who recognizes a benefit that has already taken place. *Institutiones*

6 He is invited to great things who receives small things greatly. *Ib.*

Pope Gregory I

540–604

7 [They answered that they were called Angles.] It is well, for they have the faces of angels, and such should be the co-heirs of the angels in heaven.[2]
From BEDE, *Ecclesiastical History of the English People, II, 1*

Ali ibn-Abi-Talib[3]

c. 602–661

8 He who has a thousand friends has not a
friend to spare,
And he who has one enemy will meet him
everywhere.[4]
A Hundred Sayings

[1]Translated by SAMUEL JOHNSON, and used as motto to *The Rambler, no. 7* [1750].

[2]Traditionally quoted "Non Angli sed angeli" (Not Angles but angels), these were the words of Pope Gregory when he beheld two English slaves in a Roman slave market.

[3]Ali ibn-abi-Talib, son-in-law of Muhammad and fourth caliph, who was called the Lion of God, was murdered in 661.

[4]Quoted by RALPH WALDO EMERSON in *The Conduct of Life* [1860], *Considerations by the Way*.
See George Herbert, 270:7.

The Koran[5]

9 In the name of the most merciful God: Praise be to God, the Lord of all Being; the most merciful, the Master of the day of judgment. Thee do we worship, and of Thee do we beg assistance. Direct us in the right path, in the path of those to whom Thou hast been gracious; not of those against whom Thou art incensed, nor of those who go astray.
Chapter 1, verses 1–3

10 Do not veil the truth with falsehood, nor conceal the truth knowingly. *2:42*

11 We believe in God, and in that which has been sent down on us and sent down on Abraham, Ishmael, Isaac and Jacob, and the Tribes, and that which was given to Moses and Jesus and the Prophets, of their Lord; we make no division between any of them, and to Him we surrender.[6] *2:135–136*

12 A believing slave is better than an idolater, even though ye admire him. *2:221*

13 God will not take you to task for vain words in your oaths, but He will take you to task for what your hearts have amassed. *2:225*

14 I [Muhammad] have no power over benefit or hurt to myself except as God willeth . . . I am only a warner, and a bringer of good tidings to a people who believe. *7:188*

15 God sufficeth me: there is no God but He. In Him I put my trust. *9:129*

16 In the alternation of night and day, and what God has created in the heavens and the earth—surely there are signs for a god-fearing people. *10:6*

17 Surely God wrongs not men, but themselves men wrong. *10:44*

18 Not so much as the weight of an ant in earth or heaven escapes from the Lord, neither is aught smaller than that, or greater, but is clearly written in God's book.
10:61

[5]Also spelled Qur'an; Quran. Muslims believe that the Koran is of divine origin, revealed by God to the prophet Muhammad [c. 570–632].

The word Koran, derived from the verb *karaa, to read,* signifies properly in Arabic "the reading," or rather, "that which ought to be read." . . . The Koran is divided into 114 larger portions of very unequal length, which we call chapters, but the Arabians *sowar,* in the singular *sura,* a word rarely used on any other occasion.—GEORGE SALE, *The Koran* [1734], *The Preliminary Discourse, sec. III*

Translations by GEORGE SALE [1734], E. H. PALMER [1900], J. M. RODWELL [1909], RICHARD BELL [1927], M. M. PICKTHALL [1953], and A. J. ARBERRY [1955], edited and adapted by SARI NUSEIBAH.

[6]"Surrender" is the literal translation of the word Islam.

1 God changes not what is in a people, until they change what is in themselves.

13:11

2 We [God] never sent a messenger save with the language of his folk, that he might make (the message)[1] clear for them. *14:4*

3 Seest thou not how God hath coined a parable? A good word is like a good tree whose root is firmly fixed, and whose top is in the sky. And it produces its edible fruit every season, by the permission of its Lord. . . . And a corrupt word is like a corrupt tree which has been torn off the ground, and has no fixity. God makes those who believe stand firm in this life and the next by His firm Word. *14:24–27*

4 Our [God's] word to a thing when We will it, is but to say, "Be," and it is. *16:40*

5 Glory be to Him who carried His servant by night from the sacred temple of Mecca to the temple of Jerusalem that is more remote, whose precinct We have blessed, that We might show him of Our tokens. *17:1*

6 Thy Lord hath decreed that ye worship none save Him, and (that ye show) kindness to parents. . . . Lower unto them the wing of submission through mercy, and say, "My Lord, have mercy on them both as they took care of me when I was little."

17:23–24

7 Walk not on the earth exultantly, for thou canst not cleave the earth, neither shalt thou reach to the mountains in height.

17:37

8 They will question thee concerning the soul. Say: "The soul is the concern of my Lord, and you have been given of knowledge but a little." *17:85*

9 They say: "We will not believe thee till thou makest a spring to gush forth from the earth for us, or . . . bringest God and the angels as a surety" . . . And naught prevented men from believing when the guidance came to them, but that they said, "Has God sent forth a mortal as messenger?" Say: "Had there been in the earth angels walking at peace, We would have sent down upon them out of heaven an angel as messenger."

17:90–95

10 And do not say, regarding anything, "I am going to do that tomorrow," but only, "if God will."[2] *18:23–24*

[1] Throughout the Koran, parentheses indicate additions to the Arabic.

[2] In Arabic: Inshallah.

11 Wealth and children are the adornment of this present life: but good works, which are lasting, are better in the sight of thy Lord as to recompense, and better as to hope.

18:46

12 Man says: "How is it possible, when I am dead, that I shall then be brought forth alive?" Does he not remember that We have created him once, and that he was nothing then? *19:66–67*

13 Do not the unbelievers see that the skies and the earth were both a solid mass, and that We clave them asunder, and that by means of water We give life to everything? Will they not then believe? *21:30*

14 O men, if you are in doubt as to the Resurrection, surely We created you of dust, then of a sperm drop, then of a blood clot, then of a lump of flesh . . . And thou beholdest the earth blackened; then, when We send down water upon it, it quivers, and swells, and puts forth herbs of every joyous kind.

22:5

15 We [God] charge not any soul save to its ability. *23:62*

16 God is the light of the heavens and of the earth. His light is like a niche in which is a lamp—the lamp encased in glass—the glass, as it were, a glistening star. From a blessed tree it is lighted, the olive neither from the East nor of the West, whose oil would well nigh shine out, even though fire touched it not. It is light upon light. God guideth whom He will to His light, and God setteth forth parables to men. *24:35*

17 As for the unbelievers, their works are as a mirage in a spacious plain which the man athirst supposes to be water, till, when he comes to it, he finds it is nothing; there indeed he finds God, and He pays him his account in full; and God is swift at the reckoning.

Or they are as shadows upon a sea obscure, covered by a billow above which is a billow, above which are clouds, shadows piled upon one another; when he puts forth his hand, wellnigh he cannot see it. And to whomsoever God assigns no light, no light has he.

24:39–40

18 Thou seest the mountains and thou deemest them affixed, (verily) they are as fleeting as the clouds. *27:88*

19 Thou truly canst not guide whom thou lovest; but God guideth whom He will; and He best knoweth those who yield to guidance.

28:55

1 The present life is naught but a diversion and a sport; surely the Last Abode is Life, did they but know. *29:64*

2 Whosoever surrenders his face to God and performs good deeds, he verily has grasped the surest handle, and unto God is the sequel of all things. *31:22*

3 If whatever trees are in the earth were pens, and He should after that swell the seas into seven seas of ink, the Words of God would not be exhausted. *31:27*

4 We offered this trust[1] to the heavens and the earth and the mountains, but they were humbled by it, and shrank from bearing it. Yet, man bore it. Truly he is ever in the darkness of injustice, and of ignorance. *33:72*

5 He makes the night seep into the day, and makes the day seep into the night; He has subordinated the sun and the moon, making each of them journey towards a preordained time. *35:13*

6 And on that day no soul shall be wronged at all, nor shall ye be rewarded for aught but that which ye have done. *36:54*

7 They say: "We only have the life of this world. We die and we live, and nothing destroys us but time." Yet, not true knowledge have they of this; only belief. *45:24*

8 O true believers, let not men laugh other men to scorn, who peradventure may be better than themselves. . . . Neither let the one of you speak ill of another in his absence. *49:10–13*

9 The Arabs of the desert say, We believe. Answer, Ye do by no means believe; but say, We have embraced Islam: for the faith hath not yet entered into your hearts. *49:14*

10 We [God] created Man, and We know what his soul whispereth within him; and We are nearer unto him than his jugular vein. *50:16*

11 The heart of Muhammad did not falsely represent that which he saw. Will you therefore dispute with him concerning that which he saw? *53:11–12*

12 O tribe of spirits and of men, if you are able to slip through the parameters of the skies and the earth, then do so. You shall not pass through them save with My [the Lord's] authority. *55:33*

[1]The message conveyed in the Koran.

13 He is the first and the last, the manifest and the hidden: and He knoweth all things. *57:3*

14 Let every soul look upon the morrow for the deed it has performed. *59:18*

15 Is he, therefore, who goeth groveling upon his face, better directed than he who walketh upright in a straight way? *67:22*

16 Man is a witness unto his deeds. *75:14*

17 Recite: In the name of thy Lord who created,
Created Man of a blood clot.
Recite: And thy Lord is the most
Generous, who taught by the Pen,
Taught Man that he knew not. *96:1–5*

18 Whoso has done an atom's weight of good shall see it; and whoso has done an atom's weight of evil shall see it. *99:7–8*

19 Say: "He is God, One God, the Everlasting Refuge, who has not begotten, and has not been begotten, and equal to Him is not anyone." *112*

Anonymous: Miscellaneous [Early]

20 Whatever kind of word thou speakest the like shalt thou hear.
The Greek Anthology,[2] *bk. IX, 382*

21 Envy slays itself by its own arrows.
Ib. X, 111

22 Give a sop to Cerberus.
Greek and Roman saying

23 Give me today, and take tomorrow.
Quoted, and condemned, by St. Chrysostom

24 One picture is worth more than ten thousand words.[3] *Chinese proverb*

25 Keep a green tree in your heart and perhaps the singing bird will come.
Chinese proverb

26 On the day of victory no one is tired.
Arab proverb

27 Death is afraid of him because he has the heart of a lion. *Arab proverb*

28 I came to the place of my birth, and cried, "The friends of my youth, where are they?" And echo answered, "Where are they?"
Arab saying

[2]Translated by W. R. Paton (Loeb Classical Library).
[3]See Turgenev, 564:7.

1 If you have two loaves of bread, sell one and buy a hyacinth. *Persian saying*[1]

2 If only, when one heard
That Old Age was coming
One could bolt the door,
Answer "Not at home"
And refuse to meet him!
Kokinshu (Collection of Ancient and Modern Poems) [905][2]

Anonymous: Latin

3 Ab urbe condita [Since the founding of the city (Rome)]. *Saying*

4 Absit omen [May it not be an omen]. *Saying*

5 Acta est fabula [The play is over]. *Said at ancient dramatic performances and quoted by Augustus on his deathbed*

6 Actus non facit reum, nisi mens sit rea [The act is not criminal unless the intent is criminal]. *Legal maxim*

7 Ad astra per aspera [To the stars through hardships]. *Proverb*

8 Adeste, fideles,
Laeti triumphantes;
Venite, venite in Bethlehem.

[O come, all ye faithful,
Joyful and triumphant,
O come ye, O come ye to Bethlehem.]
Hymn, eighteenth century

9 Anno aetatis suae . . . [In the year of his age . . .]. *Phrase*

10 Bis dat qui cito dat [He gives twice who gives promptly].[3] *Saying*

11 Cave ab homine unius libri [Beware the man of one book].[4] *Quoted by* ISAAC D'ISRAEL *in Curiosities of Literature [1791–1793]*

12 Cave canem [Beware of the dog]. *Proverb*

13 Caveat emptor [Let the buyer beware]. *Proverb*

[1]Quoted also as a Chinese or Greek saying, and in various versions, including: If you have two pieces of silver, take one and buy a lily.

If thou of fortune be bereft, / And in thy store there be but left / Two loaves — sell one, and with the dole / Buy hyacinths to feed thy soul. — JAMES TERRY WHITE [1845–1920], *Not by Bread Alone* [1907]

[2]Translated by ARTHUR WALEY in *Anthology of Japanese Literature* [1955], edited by DONALD KEENE.

[3]See Augustus Caesar, 110:7, and Publilius Syrus, 110:15.

[4]See Sydney Smith, 433:8.

14 Cras amet qui nunquam amavit quique amavit cras amet [Tomorrow let him love who has never loved and tomorrow let him who has loved love].[5] *Pervigilium Veneris [c. 350], refrain*

15 Cucullus non facit monachum [The cowl does not make a monk].[6] *Medieval proverb*

16 Cuius regio eius religio [He who controls the area controls the religion]. *Proverb*

17 De gustibus non disputandum [There is no accounting for tastes]. *Proverb*

18 De minimis non curat lex [The law is not concerned with trifles]. *Legal maxim*

19 Deus vult [God wills it]. *Motto of the Crusades [1095]*

20 Dis manibus sacrum[7] [Sacred to the departed spirit(s)]. *Tombstone inscription*

21 Divide et impera [Divide and rule]. *Ancient political maxim cited by* MACHIAVELLI

22 Errare humanum est [To err is human].[8] *Saying*

23 Et in Arcadia ego [I too am in Arcadia].[9] *Inscription on a tomb in a painting [c. 1623] by* GUERCINO *[1591–1666]*

24 Ex ungue leonem [From his claw one can tell a lion].[10] *Saying*

25 Fiat justitia ruat coelum [Let justice be done though heaven should fall].[11] *Proverb, sometimes attributed to* LUCIUS CALPURNIUS PISO CAESONINUS *[d. 43 B.C.]*

26 Finis coronat opus [The end crowns the work].[12] *Saying*

[5]See Parnell, 329:16.

[6]It takes more than a hood and sad eyes to make a monk. — *Albanian proverb*

[7]Abbreviated DMS.

[8]See Plutarch, 120:21; Shirley, 272:12; and Pope, 333:15.

[9]That is, Even in Arcadia there am I [Death].

Bartolommeo Schidoni [1560–1616] wrote: Et ego in Arcadia vixi [I too have lived in Arcadia]. Poussin, Reynolds, and others used this phrase in their paintings. E. Panofsky discusses the phrase in *Philosophy and History: Essays Presented to E. Cassirer* [1936].

[10]Literally: From the claw a lion.

See Herodotus, 78:13.

[11]Also familiar as: Fiat justitia et ruant coeli [Let justice be done though the heavens fall].

And as: Fiat justitia et pereat mundus [Let justice be done though the world perish].

See J. Q. Adams, 417:17.

[12]See Heywood, 159:28; Shakespeare, 227:5 and 227:18; Herrick, 266:4; and Quarles, 267:18.

1 Flagrante delicto ["Red-handed"].
Saying

2 Fluctuat nec mergitur [It tosses but doesn't sink]. *Saying*

3 Gaudeamus igitur,
Iuvenes dum sumus.

[Let us live then and be glad
While young life is before us.]
Students' song [c. 1267]

4 Habeas corpus [You are to produce the person[1]]. *Legal phrase*

5 Hannibal ad portas! [Hannibal is at the gates!] *Saying*

6 In vino veritas [In wine is truth].[2]
Proverb quoted by PLATO, *Symposium 217*

7 Ipse dixit [He himself said it].[3]
Phrase of "proof"

8 Ius est ars boni et aequi [Legal justice is the art of the good and the fair]. *Saying*

9 Mater artium necessitas [Necessity is the mother of invention].[4] *Saying*

10 Mors ultima ratio [Death is the final accounting]. *Saying*

11 Nemo me impune lacessit [No one provokes me with impunity].
Motto of the Crown of Scotland

12 Nihil nimis [Nothing in excess].[5]
Saying

13 Non multa sed multum [Not many but much].[6] *Proverb*

14 Orare est laborare, laborare est orare [To pray is to work, to work is to pray].
Ancient motto of the Benedictine order

15 Parvis e glandibus quercus [Tall oaks from little acorns grow]. *Saying*

16 Pereant qui nostra ante nos dixerunt [May they perish who have used our words before us]. *Saying*

17 Piscem natare doces [You're teaching a fish to swim]. *Saying*

18 Post hoc, ergo propter hoc [After this, therefore because of this].
Definition of fallacy in logic

[1]The person of the accused.
[2]See Alcaeus, 62:19.
[3]See W. S. Gilbert, 627:17.
[4]See Persius, 117:8.
[5]Also quoted as: Ne quid nimis.
See The Seven Sages, 62:7; Terence, 96:1; Horace, 106:12 and 107:20; Lucan, 118:8; and Voltaire, 343:23.
[6]I.e., Not quantity but quality.
See Seneca, 114:22.

19 Primus inter pares [First among equals].
Saying

20 Pro bono publico [For the public good].
Saying

21 Quos [or Quem] deus vult perdere prius dementat [Those whom God wishes to destroy, he first makes mad.][7] *Saying*

22 Requiescat in pace[8] [May he rest in peace; May she rest in peace]. *Saying*

23 Res iudicata pro veritate habetur [A matter which has been legally decided is considered true]. *Legal maxim*

24 Ruat coelum, fiat voluntas tua [Though heaven should fall, let thy will be done].
Proverb

25 Salus populi suprema lex [The people's safety is the highest law].
Legal and political maxim

26 Semper fidelis [Ever faithful].
Saying

27 Sic semper tyrannis[9] [Thus always to tyrants]. *Saying*

28 Sit tibi terra levis [May the earth rest lightly on you].[10]
Tombstone inscription

29 Summum ius summa iniuria [Extreme justice is extreme injustice].[11]
Legal maxim cited by CICERO *in De Officiis, I, 10, 33*

30 Tempora mutantur, nos et mutamur in illis [Times change, and we change with them too].[12]
From OWEN'S *Epigrammata [1615]*

31 Testis unus testis nullus [A single witness is no witness]. *Legal maxim*

32 Ubi bene ibi patria [Where one is happy, there's one's homeland]. *Saying*

33 Urbi et orbi [To the city[13] and to the world].
Apostolic blessing

34 Vade in pace [Go in peace].
End of confessional absolution

35 Vae victis! [Woe to the conquered!]
From LIVY, *History, bk. V, sec. 48, as said by Brennus to the Romans*

[7]See Euripides, 78:1.
[8]Abbreviated RIP.
[9]See John Wilkes Booth, 635:23.
[10]Abbreviated STTL.
See Euripides, 76:4; Beaumont and Fletcher, 263:7; and Twain, 625:20.
[11]I.e., Extreme legal justice.
See Terence, 96:12.
[12]Translated by JOHN OWEN in *Epigrams* [1615]. Also quoted by RAPHAEL HOLINSHED in *Chronicles of England* [1578].
See Spencer, 174:8.
[13]Rome.

1 Volenti non fit iniuria [To a person who consents no injustice is done].

Legal maxim

Caedmon
fl. 670

2 Light was first
Through the Lord's word
Named day:
Beauteous, bright creation!

Creation.[1] *The First Day*

3 The fiend with all his comrades
Fell then from heaven above,
Through as long as three nights and days,
The angels from heaven into hell;
And them all the Lord transformed to devils,
Because they his deed and word
Would not revere.

Ib. The Fall of the Rebel Angels

Bede [Venerable Bede]
c. 672 – c. 735

4 It is better never to begin a good work than, having begun it, to stop.

Ecclesiastical History of the English People, bk. I, ch. 23

St. John of Damascus
c. 700 – c. 760

5 God is a sea of infinite substance.[2]

De Fide Orthodoxa, bk. I, ch. 9

Alcuin
735–804

6 The voice of the people is the voice of God [Vox populi vox Dei].[3]

Letter to Charlemagne [A.D. 800]

7 Here halt, I pray you, make a little stay,
O wayfarer, to read what I have writ,
And know by my fate what thy fate shall be.
What thou art now, wayfarer, world renowned,
I was: what I am now, so shall thou be.
The world's delight I followed with a heart
Unsatisfied: ashes am I, and dust.

His Own Epitaph[4]

[1]From the text of BENJAMIN THORPE [1782–1870].

[2]This is the most frequently quoted definition of God in the Middle Ages. It is based on ST. GREGORY OF NAZIANZUS [c. 330–390], *Oration 38.*

[3]See Pope, 339:21.

[4]Translated by HELEN WADDELL.

8 Alcuin was my name: learning I loved.

Ib.

Ono no Komachi
Ninth century

9 The flowers withered,
Their color faded away,
While meaninglessly
I spent my days in the world
And the long rains were falling.

Kokinshu [905][5]

10 This night of no moon
There is no way to meet him.
I rise in longing—
My breast pounds, a leaping flame,
My heart is consumed in fire.

Ib.

Ching Hao
fl. 925

11 There are Six Essentials in painting. The first is called *spirit;* the second, *rhythm;* the third, *thought;* the fourth, *scenery;* the fifth, the *brush;* and the last is the *ink.*

Notes on Brushwork[6]

12 Resemblance reproduces the formal aspect of objects, but neglects their spirit; truth shows the spirit and substance in like perfection.

Ib.

Sei Shonagon
b. 966

13 If someone with whom one is having an affair keeps on mentioning some woman whom he knew in the past, however long ago it is since they separated, one is always irritated.

Makura no Soshi [c. 1002][5]

Murasaki Shikibu
c. 978–1031

14 [The art of the novel] happens because the storyteller's own experience of men and things, whether for good or ill—not only what he has passed through himself, but even events which he has only witnessed or been told of—has moved him to an emotion so pas-

[5]Translated by DONALD KEENE in his *Anthology of Japanese Literature* [1955].

[6]From *The Spirit of the Brush,* translated by SHIO SAKANISHI [Wisdom of the East Series, 1957].

sionate that he can no longer keep it shut up in his heart.

The Tale of Genji [c. 1000][1]

1 Anything whatsoever may become the subject of a novel, provided only that it happens in this mundane life and not in some fairyland beyond our human ken. *Ib.*[1]

The Primary Chronicle[2]

1040–1118

2 The Chuds, the Slavs and the Krivchians then said to the peoples of Rus: "Our whole land is great and rich, but there is no order in it. Come to rule and reign over us."

Annal for the years 860–862: Invitation of the Varangians to Novgorod

3 Then we went to Greece, and the Greeks led us to the edifices where they worship their God, and we knew not whether we were in heaven or on earth. For on earth there is no such splendor or such beauty, and we are at a loss how to describe it. We only know that God dwells there among men, and their service is fairer than the ceremonies of other nations.

Annal for the year 987: Vladimir's Christianization of Russia

4 It is the Russians' joy to drink; we cannot do without it. *Ib.*

St. Anselm

c. 1033–1109

5 God is that, the greater than which cannot be conceived.[3] *Proslogion, ch. 3*

Abu Muhammad al-Kasim al-Hariri

1054–1122

6 We praise Thee, O God,
For whatever perspicuity of language Thou
hast taught us
And whatever eloquence Thou hast inspired
us with. *Makamat. Prayer*

[1]Translated by ARTHUR WALEY.
See Motoori, 375:3.

[2]The earliest of the Russian chronicles or annals, begun in 1040 and continued through 1118 by various annalists, gives the record of Russian history since 852. It was copied several times and incorporated into later chronicles as the beginning. These quotations are from the Laurentian version, copied in 1377, translated by SAMUEL CROSS.

[3]This is commonly referred to as the ontological argument for the existence of God, and derives from ST. AUGUSTINE, *De Doctrina Christiana, bk. I, ch. 7.* It is also to be found in DESCARTES, *Third Meditation.*

Peter Abelard

1079–1142

7 O what their joy and their glory must be,
Those endless sabbaths the blessed ones
see![4] *Hymnus Paraclitensis*

8 Against the disease of writing one must take special precautions, since it is a dangerous and contagious disease.

Letter 8, Abelard to Héloise[5]

St. Bernard

1091–1153

9 You will find something more in woods than in books. Trees and stones will teach you that which you can never learn from masters.[6] *Epistle 106*

10 I have liberated my soul.[7] *Ib. 371*

11 Hell is full of good intentions or desires.[8]

Attributed. From ST. FRANCIS DE SALES, Letter 74

Song of Roland

Eleventh century

12 Friend Roland, sound your horn.[9]

La Chanson de Roland, l. 1070

13 Roland is valorous and Oliver is wise.[10]

Ib. l. 1093

Héloise

c. 1101 – c. 1164

14 Riches and power are but gifts of blind fate, whereas goodness is the result of one's own merits. *Letter 2, Héloise to Abelard*

[4]O quanta qualia sunt illa sabbata, / Quae semper celebrat superna curia.
Translated by JOHN MASON NEALE [1884].

[5]See Héloise, 136.

[6]See Shakespeare, 210:24 and 211:17, and Wordsworth, 423:7.

[7]Liberavi animam meam.

[8]Hell is full of good meanings and wishings.—GEORGE HERBERT, *Jacula Prudentum* [1651], *no. 170*
Hell is paved with good intentions.—JOHN RAY, *English Proverbs* [1670]
Quoted by SAMUEL JOHNSON [1775]; from BOSWELL, *Life of Johnson* [1791], *vol. I, p. 555* (Everyman edition)
Hell is paved with good intentions, not with bad ones. —GEORGE BERNARD SHAW [1856–1950], *Maxims for Revolutionists*

[9]Compagnon Roland sonnez de votre oliphant.

[10]Roland est preux et Oliver est sage.
A Roland for an Oliver. I.e., a blow for a blow, tit for tat, referring to the drawn combat between Roland and Oliver.

The Archpoet
Twelfth century

1 Let me die in a tavern so that the wine may be near my dying mouth.[1] *Confessio*

Gratian [Franciscus Gratianus]
Twelfth century

2 Paintings are the Bible of the laity.[2] *Decretum, pt. III*

Poem of the Cid[3]
Twelfth century

3 Were his lord but worthy, God, how fine a vassal. *l. 20*

4 Thus parted the one from the others as the nail from the flesh. *l. 375*

5 Who serves a good lord lives always in luxury. *l. 850*

6 One would grow poor staying in one place always. *l. 948*

Frederick I [Barbarossa]
1122–1190

7 An emperor is subject to no one but God and Justice.
From Julius Wilhelm Zincgref, *Apophthegmata, bk. I [1626]*

Averroës
1126–1198

8 Knowledge is the conformity of the object and the intellect.[4]
Destructio Destructionum

Henry II
1133–1189

9 Who will free me from this turbulent priest?[5] *Attributed*

[1]In taberna mori / ut sint vina proxima / morientis ori. See Walter Map, 137:11, and Johnson, 355:19.
[2]Also attributed to Gregory Sereno, bishop of Massilia (Marseilles), *Letter 9*.
[3]Translated by W. S. Merwin.
[4]The classic definition of epistemology, still commented on today and used by the Neo-Thomists.
[5]Thomas à Becket.

Maimonides [Moses ben Maimon]
1135–1204

10 Anticipate charity by preventing poverty; assist the reduced fellowman, either by a considerable gift, or a sum of money, or by teaching him a trade, or by putting him in the way of business, so that he may earn an honest livelihood, and not be forced to the dreadful alternative of holding out his hand for charity. This is the highest step and the summit of charity's golden ladder.[6]
Charity's Eight Degrees

Walter Map [Mapes]
c. 1140 – c. 1210

11 I intend to die in a tavern; let the wine be placed near my dying mouth,[7] so that when the choirs of angels come, they may say, "God be merciful to this drinker!"
De Nugis Curialium

Alain de Lille [Alanus de Insulis]
d. 1202

12 Do not hold as gold all that shines as gold.[8] *Parabolae*

Kamo no Chomei
1153–1216

13 The flow of the river is ceaseless and its water is never the same. The bubbles that float in the pools, now vanishing, now forming, are not of long duration: so in the world are man and his dwellings. . . . [People] die

[6]See Spinoza, 309:1; Johnson, 354:23; and Andrew Carnegie, 621:10.
[7]Meum est propositum in taberna mori; / Vinum sit appositum morientis ori.
See the Archpoet, 137:1.
[8]Non teneas aurum totum quod splendet ut aurum [All that glitters is not gold].
This was considered a common proverb which had its roots in a Latin translation from Aristotle: Yellow-colored objects appear to be gold. — *Elenchi, bk. I, ch. 1*
Hyt is not al gold that glareth. — Chaucer, *The House of Fame* [1374–1385], *bk. I, l. 272*
But al thyng which that shineth as the gold / Nis nat gold, as that I have herd it told. — *The Canterbury Tales* [c. 1387], *The Canon's Yeoman's Tale, l. 962*
All is not gold that outward showeth bright. — Lydgate [c. 1370–c. 1451], *On the Mutability of Human Affairs*
Non omne quod fulget est aurum. — Gabriel Biel [d. 1495], *Expositio Canonis Messe, lecture 77*, derived from William of Auvergne [d. 1249]. This is the Latin version closest to the proverb as commonly known.
All that glisters is not gold — / Often have you heard that told. — Shakespeare, *Merchant of Venice* [1596–1597], *act II, sc. vii, l. 65*

in the morning, they are born in the evening, like foam on the water.

Hojoki (An Account of My Hut) [1212][1]

1 He who complies with the ways of the world may be impoverished thereby; he who does not, appears deranged. Wherever one may live, whatever work one may do, is it possible even for a moment to find a haven for the body or peace for the mind? *Ib.*

2 Only in a hut built for the moment can one live without fears. *Ib.*

3 My body is like a drifting cloud—I ask for nothing, I want nothing. *Ib.*

Fujiwara no Teika

1162–1241

4 In the expression of the emotions originality merits the first consideration. . . . The words used, however, should be old ones.

Guide to the Composition of Poetry[2]

5 There are no teachers of Japanese poetry. But they who take the old poems as their teachers, steep their minds in the old style, and learn their words from the masters of former time—who of them will fail to write poetry?[3] *Ib.*

Hartmann von Aue

c. 1170 – c. 1215

6 He who helps in the saving of others,
Saves himself as well. *Poor Henry*

Walther von der Vogelweide

c. 1170 – c. 1230

7 Now the summer came to pass
And flowers through the grass
Joyously sprang,
While all the tribes of birds sang.[4]

Dream Song, st. 1[5]

8 This was ever the world's distempered will:
Fools have always mocked and spurned the wise.
These shall be judged according to their lies.[6] *Lament, st. 2*

[1]Translated by Donald Keene in his *Anthology of Japanese Literature* [1955].

[2]From *Sources of Japanese Tradition* [1960], edited by William Theodore de Bary.

[3]See Horace, 109:30, and Hsieh Ho, 129:20.

[4]Dô der sumer komen was, / Und die blumen dur daz gras / Wünneclâchen sprungen, / Aedâ die vogele sungen.

[5]See Anonymous, 916:14, and Pound, 792:8.

[6]Translated by Margaret F. Richey.

9 The sun no longer shows
His face; and treason sows
His secret seeds that no man can detect;
Fathers by their children are undone;
The brother would the brother cheat;
And the cowled monk is a deceit . . .
Might is right, and justice there is none.[7]

Millennium

Herbort von Fritzlar

fl. c. 1210

10 The cart has no place where a fifth wheel could be used. *Saying*

Eike von Repkow

fl. c. 1220

11 He who comes first, eats first.[8]

Sachsenspiegel [1219–1233]

St. Francis of Assisi[9]

c. 1181–1226

12 Praise to thee, my Lord, for all thy creatures,
Above all Brother Sun
Who brings us the day and lends us his light.

The Song of Brother Sun and of All His Creatures [1225]

13 Love is he, radiant with great splendor,
And speaks to us of Thee, O Most High.

Ib.

14 Where there is charity and wisdom, there is neither fear nor ignorance. Where there is patience and humility, there is neither anger nor vexation. Where there is poverty and joy, there is neither greed nor avarice. Where there is peace and meditation, there is neither anxiety nor doubt.

The Counsels of the Holy Father St. Francis. Admonition 27

15 Lord, make me an instrument of Your peace. Where there is hatred let me sow love; where there is injury, pardon; where there is doubt, faith; where there is despair, hope; where there is darkness, light; and where there is sadness, joy.

O divine Master, grant that I may not so much seek to be consoled as to console; to be understood as to understand; to be loved as to love. For it is in giving that we receive; it is in pardoning that we are pardoned; and it is in dying that we are born to eternal life.

Attributed

[7]Translated by Jethro Bithell.

[8]Familiar as: First come first served.

[9]Translated by Leo Sherley-Price.

1 I have sinned against my brother the ass.
Dying words

Magna Carta
1215

2 No freeman shall be taken, or imprisoned, or outlawed, or exiled, or in any way harmed, nor will we go upon him nor will we send upon him, except by the legal judgment of his peers or by the law of the land.
Clause 39

3 To none will we sell, to none deny or delay, right or justice. *Clause 40*

Tommaso di Celano
c. 1185 – c. 1255

4 Day of wrath! O day of mourning!
See fulfilled the prophets' warning,
Heaven and earth in ashes burning![1]
Dies Irae

Roger Bacon
c. 1214 – c. 1294

5 If in other sciences we should arrive at certainty without doubt and truth without error, it behooves us to place the foundations of knowledge in mathematics.[2]
Opus Majus,[3] *bk. I, ch. 4*

Alfonso X [Alfonso the Wise]
1221–1284

6 Had I been present at the creation, I would have given some useful hints for the better ordering of the universe.[4] *Attributed*

Rutebeuf
d. 1285

7 What became of the friends I had
With whom I was always so close
And loved so dearly?
La Complainte Rutebeuf

8 Friendship is dead:
They were friends who go with the wind,[5]
And the wind was blowing at my door.
Ib.

St. Thomas Aquinas
c. 1225–1274

9 Sing, my tongue, the Savior's glory,
Of His Flesh the mystery sing;
Of the Blood, all price exceeding,
Shed by our immortal King.[6]
Pange, Lingua (hymn for Vespers on the Feast of Corpus Christi), st. 1

10 Down in adoration falling,
Lo! the sacred Host we hail;
Lo! o'er ancient forms departing,
Newer rites of grace prevail;
Faith for all defects supplying,
Where the feeble senses fail.
Ib. st. 5 (Tantum Ergo)

11 Thus Angels' Bread is made
The Bread of man today:
The Living Bread from Heaven
With figures doth away:
O wondrous gift indeed!
The poor and lowly may
Upon their Lord and Master feed.[7]
Sacris Solemniis Juncta Sint Gaudia (Matins hymn for Corpus Christi), st. 6 (Panis Angelicus)

12 O saving Victim, opening wide
The gate of of heaven to man below,
Our foes press on from every side,
Thine aid supply, Thy strength bestow.[8]
Verbum Supernum Prodiens (hymn for Lauds on Corpus Christi), st. 5 (O Salutaris Hostia)

13 Lord Jesu, blessed Pelican.
Adoro Te Devote (hymn appointed for the Thanksgiving after Mass), st. 6 (Pie Pellicane Jesu Domine)

14 Three things are necessary for the salvation of man: to know what he ought to be-

[1] Dies irae, dies illa / Solvet saeclum in favilla, / Teste David cum Sibylla.
Translated by W. J. IRONS [1849]. This has been attributed also to ST. GREGORY and ST. BERNARD.
See Roscommon, 309:11, and Scott, 430:12.

[2] See Galileo, 182:20.

[3] Translated by ROBERT BURKE.

[4] Carlyle says, in his *History of Frederick the Great, bk. II, ch. 7,* that this saying of Alfonso about Ptolemy's astronomy, "that it seemed a crank machine; that it was pity the Creator had not taken advice," is still remembered by mankind—this and no other of his many sayings.

[5] See Dowson, 721:5.

[6] Pange, lingua, gloriosi / Corporis mysterium / Sanguinisque pretiosi, / Quem in mundi pretium / Fructus ventris generosi / Rex effudit gentium.
Translated by EDWARD CASWALL.
Now, my tongue, the mystery telling / Of the glorious Body sing.—*Hymnal of the Protestant Episcopal Church*
Pange, lingua, gloriosi proelium certáminis [Sing, my tongue, the glorious battle].—ST. VENANTIUS FORTUNATUS [c. 530–c. 610], bishop of Poitiers

[7] Translated by J. D. CHAMBERS.
See *Psalm 78:25,* 20:4.

[8] Translated by EDWARD CASWALL.

lieve; to know what he ought to desire; and to know what he ought to do.

Two Precepts of Charity [1273]

1 Law: an ordinance of reason for the common good, made by him who has care of the community.

Summa Theologica [1273]

2 Concerning perfect blessedness which consists in a vision of God.[1] *Ib.*

3 Reason in man is rather like God in the world. *Opuscule 11, De Regno*

Meister Eckhart

c. 1260 – c. 1327

4 In silence man can most readily preserve his integrity.

Directions for the Contemplative Life

5 The more wise and powerful a master, the more directly is his work created, and the simpler it is. *Of the Eternal Birth*

6 One must not always think so much about what one should do, but rather what one should be. Our works do not ennoble us; but we must ennoble our works.

Work and Being

Dante Alighieri

1265–1321

7 In that part of the book of my memory before which is little that can be read, there is a rubric, saying, "Incipit Vita Nova [The new life begins]." *La Vita Nuova [1293]*[2]

8 Love hath so long possessed me for his own
And made his lordship so familiar. *Ib.*

9 Love with delight discourses in my mind
Upon my lady's admirable gifts . . .
Beyond the range of human intellect.

Il Convito.[3] *Trattato Terzo, l. 1*

10 In the middle of the journey of our life I came to myself within a dark wood where the straight way was lost.[4]

The Divine Comedy [c. 1310–1320].
Inferno,[5] *canto I, l. 1*

[1]Probably the origin of the phrase: beatific vision.
[2]Translated by Dante Gabriel Rossetti.
[3]Translated by Charles Lyell.
The first line is also in *The Divine Comedy, Purgatorio, canto II, l. 112.*
[4]Nel mezzo del cammin di nostra vita / Mi ritrovai per una selva oscura, / Che la diritta via era smarrita.
[5]Translated by John D. Sinclair unless otherwise noted.

11 And as he, who with laboring breath has escaped from the deep to the shore, turns to the perilous waters and gazes.

Ib. l. 22

12 Thou [Virgil] art my master and my author, thou art he from whom alone I took the style whose beauty has done me honor.

Ib. l. 85

13 All hope abandon, ye who enter here![6]

Ib. III, l. 9

14 Here must all distrust be left behind; all cowardice must be ended. *Ib. l. 14*

15 There sighs, lamentations and loud wailings resounded through the starless air, so that at first it made me weep; strange tongues, horrible language, words of pain, tones of anger, voices loud and hoarse, and with these the sound of hands, made a tumult which is whirling through that air forever dark, as sand eddies in a whirlwind.

Ib. l. 22

16 This miserable state is borne by the wretched souls of those who lived without disgrace and without praise. *Ib. l. 34*

17 Let us not speak of them; but look, and pass on.[7] *Ib. l. 51*

18 These wretches, who never were alive.

Ib. l. 64

19 Into the eternal darkness, into fire and into ice.[7, 8] *Ib. l. 87*

20 Without hope we live in desire.

Ib. IV, l. 42

21 I came into a place void of all light, which bellows like the sea in tempest, when it is combated by warring winds.[7]

Ib. V, l. 28

22 As in the cold season their wings bear the starlings along in a broad, dense flock, so does that blast the wicked spirits. Hither, thither, downward, upward, it drives them.[9]

Ib. l. 40

23 Love, which is quickly kindled in the gentle heart, seized this man for the fair form that was taken from me, and the manner still hurts me. Love, which absolves no beloved one from loving, seized me so strongly with

[6]Lasciate ogni speranza, voi ch'entrate.
Traditional translation.
[7]Translated by John Aitken Carlyle, *The Temple Classics* [1900].
[8]See Housman, 691:6, and Frost, 748:2.
[9]Di qua, di là, di giù, di su li mena.

his charm that, as thou seest, it does not leave me yet.[1] *Ib. l. 100*

1 What sweet thoughts, what longing led them to the woeful pass.[2] *Ib. l. 113*

2 There is no greater sorrow
Than to be mindful of the happy time
In misery.[3] *Ib. l. 121*

3 Galeotto was the book and he that wrote it; that day we read in it no farther.[4] *Ib. l. 137*

4 I fell as a dead body falls. *Ib. Last line*

5 Pride, Envy, and Avarice are the three sparks that have set these hearts on fire. *Ib. VI, l. 74*

6 But when thou shalt be in the sweet world, I pray thee bring me to men's memory.[5] *Ib. l. 88*

7 Ye that are of good understanding, note the doctrine that is hidden under the veil of the strange verses! *Ib. IX, l. 61*

8 Already I had fixed my look on his; and he rose upright with breast and countenance, as if he entertained great scorn of Hell.[6] *Ib. X, l. 34*

9 Necessity brings him [Dante] here, not pleasure. *Ib. XII, l. 87*

10 If thou follow thy star, thou canst not fail of a glorious haven. *Ib. XV, l. 55*

11 So my conscience chide me not, I am ready for Fortune as she wills. *Ib. l. 91*

12 He listens well who takes notes. *Ib. l. 99*

13 A fair request should be followed by the deed in silence. *Ib. XXIV, l. 77*

14 Consider your origin; you were not born to live like brutes, but to follow virtue and knowledge. *Ib. XXVI, l. 118*

15 If I thought my answer were to one who would ever return to the world, this flame should stay without another movement; but since none ever returned alive from this depth, if what I hear is true, I answer thee without fear of infamy.[7] *Ib. XXVII, l. 60*

16 And thence we came forth, to see again the stars.[8] *Ib. XXXIV, l. 139*

17 To run over better waters the little vessel of my genius now hoists her sails, as she leaves behind her a sea so cruel.[9] *Ib. Purgatorio,*[10] *canto I, l. 1*

18 He goes seeking liberty, which is so dear, as he knows who for it renounces life. *Ib. l. 71*

19 O conscience, upright and stainless, how bitter a sting to thee is a little fault! *Ib. III, l. 8*

20 For to lose time is most displeasing to him who knows most. *Ib. l. 78*

21 The Infinite Goodness has such wide arms that it takes whatever turns to it. *Ib. l. 121*

22 Unless, before then, the prayer assist me which rises from a heart that lives in grace: what avails the other, which is not heard in heaven? *Ib. IV, l. 133*

23 "Why is thy mind so entangled," said the Master [Virgil], "that thou slackenest thy pace? What is it to thee what they whisper there? Come after me and let the people talk. Stand like a firm tower that never shakes its top for blast of wind." *Ib. V,*[11] *l. 10*

24 Go right on and listen as thou goest. *Ib. l. 45*

25 [Beatrice] who shall be a light between truth and intellect. *Ib. VI, l. 45*

26 It was now the hour that turns back the longing of seafarers and melts their hearts, the day they have bidden dear friends farewell, and pierces the new traveler with love if he hears in the distance the bell that seems to mourn the dying day.[11] *Ib. VIII, l. 1*

27 Give us this day the daily manna,[12] without which, in this rough desert, he backward goes, who toils most to go on. *Ib. XI, l. 13*

[1] Francesca of Rimini tells of the love she and Paolo, her brother-in-law, bore one another and of its tragic end when her husband surprised and stabbed them.

[2] Translated by JOHN AITKEN CARLYLE, *The Temple Classics* [1900].

[3] Translated by LONGFELLOW.
Nessun maggior dolore / Che ricordarsi del tempo felice / Nella miseria.
See Pindar, 72:1; Boethius, 129:22; Chaucer, 144:24; and Tennyson, 529:20.

[4] Galeotto fu il libro e chi lo scrisse: / Quel giorno più non vi leggemmo avante.
See Hunt, 454:2.

[5] Ciacco (Hog), noted for his gluttony, entreats Dante.

[6] Translated by JOHN AITKEN CARLYLE, *The Temple Classics* [1900].
Dante speaks of Farinata, head of the Uberti family, leaders of the Ghibelline faction in Florence.

[7] Count Guido da Montefeltro, the famous Ghibelline warrior, addresses Dante.
This passage in Italian is the epigraph for T. S. ELIOT, *The Love Song of J. Alfred Prufrock* [1917].

[8] E quindi uscimmo a riveder le stelle.

[9] See Pope, 338:2.

[10] Translated [1902] by CHARLES ELIOT NORTON unless otherwise noted.

[11] Translated by JOHN D. SINCLAIR.

[12] See *Matthew, 6:11*, 37:15.

1 Worldly renown is naught but a breath of wind, which now comes this way and now comes that, and changes name because it changes quarter. *Ib. l. 100*

2 O human race, born to fly upward, wherefore at a little wind dost thou so fall? *Ib. XII, l. 95*

3 To a greater force, and to a better nature, you, free, are subject, and that creates the mind in you, which the heavens have not in their charge. Therefore if the present world go astray, the cause is in you, in you it is to be sought. *Ib. XVI, l. 79*

4 Everyone confusedly conceives of a good in which the mind may be at rest, and desires it; wherefore everyone strives to attain to it. *Ib. XVII, l. 127*

5 Love kindled by virtue always kindles another, provided that its flame appear outwardly. *Ib. XXII, l. 10*

6 Less than a drop of blood remains in me that does not tremble; I recognize the signals of the ancient flame.[1] *Ib. XXX, l. 46*

7 But so much the more malign and wild does the ground become with bad seed and untilled, as it has the more of good earthly vigor. *Ib. l. 118*

8 Pure and disposed to mount unto the stars.[2] *Ib. XXXIII, l. 145*

9 The glory of Him who moves everything penetrates through the universe, and is resplendent in one part more and in another less. *Ib. Paradiso,*[3] *canto I, l. 1*

10 A great flame follows a little spark. *Ib. l. 34*

11 And in His will is our peace.[4] *Ib. III, l. 85*

12 The greatest gift that God in His bounty made in creation, and the most conformable to His goodness, and that which He prizes the most, was the freedom of the will, with which the creatures with intelligence, they all and they alone, were and are endowed. *Ib. V, l. 19*

[1]Men che dramma / Di sangue m'è rimaso, che no tremi; / Conosco i segni dell' antica fiamma.
See Virgil, 105:8.

[2]Puro e disposto a salire alle stelle.
See Virgil, 106:3.

[3]Translated by John D. Sinclair.

[4]E'n la sua volontade e nostra pace.
See T. S. Eliot, 806:7.

13 Thou shalt prove how salt is the taste of another's bread and how hard is the way up and down another man's stairs. *Ib. XVII, l. 58*

14 Overcoming me with the light of a smile, she [Beatrice] said to me: "Turn and listen, for not only in my eyes is Paradise."[5] *Ib. XVIII, l. 19*

15 Therefore the sight that is granted to your world penetrates within the Eternal Justice as the eye into the sea; for though from the shore it sees the bottom, in the open sea it does not, and yet the bottom is there but the depth conceals it. *Ib. XIX, l. 73*

16 The experience of this sweet life.[6] *Ib. XX, l. 47*

17 Like the lark that soars in the air, first singing, then silent, content with the last sweetness that satiates it, such seemed to me that image, the imprint of the Eternal Pleasure. *Ib. l. 73*

18 The night that hides things from us. *Ib. XXIII, l. 3*

19 With the color that paints the morning and evening clouds that face the sun I saw then the whole heaven suffused. *Ib. XXVII, l. 28*

20 The Love that moves the sun and the other stars.[7] *Ib. XXXIII, l. 145*

Yoshida Kenko

1283–1350

21 One should write not unskillfully in the running hand, be able to sing in a pleasing voice and keep good time to music; and, lastly, a man should not refuse a little wine when it is pressed upon him. *Tsurezure-Gusa (Essays in Idleness) [c. 1340]*[8]

22 To sit alone in the lamplight with a book spread out before you, and hold intimate converse with men of unseen generations—such is a pleasure beyond compare. *Ib.*

23 A certain recluse, I know not who, once said that no bonds attached him to this life, and the only thing he would regret leaving was the sky. *Ib.*

[5]See Chaucer, 145:2.

[6]L'esperienza di questa dolce vita.

[7]L'amor che muove il sole e l'altre stelle.
See Aristotle, 87:10.

[8]Translated by Donald Keene in his *Anthology of Japanese Literature* [1955].

Philip VI [Philip of Valois]

1293–1350

1 He who loves me, let him follow me.[1]
Attributed

William of Occam [Ockham]

c. 1300 – c. 1348

2 Entities should not be multiplied unnecessarily.[2] *Quodlibeta Septem [c. 1320]*

Petrarch[3] [Francesco Petrarca]

1304–1374

3 Who overrefines his argument brings himself to grief.
To Laura in Life, canzone 11

4 A good death does honor to a whole life.
To Laura in Death, canzone 16

5 To be able to say how much you love is to love but little. *Ib. 137*

6 Rarely do great beauty and great virtue dwell together.[4] *De Remedies, bk. II*

Edward III

1312–1377

7 Honi soit qui mal y pense. [Evil to him who evil thinks].
Motto of the Order of the Garter [1349]

8 Let the boy win his spurs.
Said of the Black Prince at the battle of Crécy [1345]

John Barbour

c. 1316–1395

9 Freedom all solace to man gives;
He lives at ease that freely lives.
The Bruce [c. 1375], l. 227

John Wycliffe

c. 1320–1384

10 I believe that in the end the truth will conquer.
To the Duke of Lancaster [1381]. From J. R. Green, A Short History of the English People [1874], ch. 5

11 By hook or by crook.[5]
Controversial Tracts [c. 1380]

12 This Bible is for the government of the People, by the People, and for the People.[6]
Attributed [1382]

William of Wykeham

1324–1404

13 Manners maketh man.[7]
Motto of his two foundations, Winchester College and New College, Oxford

William Langland

c. 1330 – c. 1400

14 In a summer season when soft was the sun.[8]
The Vision of Piers Plowman [1362–1390]

15 Who will bell the cat?[9] *Ib.*

Charles V [Charles the Wise]

1337–1380

16 I speak Spanish to God, Italian to women, French to men, and German to my horse.[10]
Attributed

Geoffrey Chaucer[11]

c. 1343–1400

17 To rede, and drive the night away.
The Book of the Duchess [1369], l. 49

18 Soun ys noght but eyr ybroken,
And every speche that ys spoken,

[1] Qui m'aime me suive.

[2] Translated [seventeenth century] by John Ponce of Cork.
The original statement of "Occam's Razor."

[3] Chaucer translated *Sonnet 88 (In Vita), S'amor non è*. See 144:14.

[4] See Petronius, 117:18.

[5] The phrase has been said to derive from the custom of some manors where tenants were authorized to take firebote *by hook or by crook;* that is, so much of the underwood as may be cut with a crook, and so much of the loose timber as may be collected from the boughs by a hook. Quoted by Skelton, Heywood, Spenser, and others.

[6] Supposedly, Wycliffe used this phrase in the general prologue of his translation of the Bible [1382]. However, this editor could not find it in the 1850 edition collated from all the Wycliffe MSS. by Josiah Forshall and Sir Frederick Madden. The closest sentence is: If this book be wel understanden, it is profitable bothe to goostly governours and bodily lordis, and iustisis and comyns also.
See Webster, 450:14; Disraeli, 501:6; Garrison, 505:19; Lincoln, 523:4; and Parker, 537:15.

[7] See Goethe, 397:9.

[8] See Chaucer, 144:12.

[9] Also in Eustache Deschamps [c. 1345–c. 1406].

[10] Je parle espagnol à Dieu, italien aux femmes, français aux hommes, et allemand à mon cheval.

[11] From the text of F. N. Robinson, *The Works of Geoffrey Chaucer, 2nd edition* [1957].

Lowd or pryvee, foul or fair,
In his substaunce ys but air.
The House of Fame [1374–1385], bk. II, l. 765

1 Venus clerk, Ovide,
That hath ysowen wonder wide
The grete god of Loves name.
Ib. III, l. 1487

2 Hard is the herte that loveth nought
In May.
The Romaunt of the Rose [c. 1380],[1] *l. 85*

3 The tyme, that may not sojourne,
But goth, and may never retourne,
As watir that doun renneth ay,
But never drope retourne may.
Ib. l. 381

4 Nakid as a worm was she. *Ib. l. 454*

5 As round as appil was his face.
Ib. l. 819

6 So that the more she yaf awey,
The more, ywis, she hadde alwey.
Ib. l. 1159

7 A ful gret fool is he, ywis,
That bothe riche and nygard is.
Ib. l. 1171

8 The lyf so short, the craft so long to lerne,[2]
Th' assay so hard, so sharp the conqueryinge.
The Parliament of Fowls [1380–1386], l. 1

9 For out of olde feldes, as men seyth,
Cometh al this newe corn fro yer to yere;[3]
And out of olde bokes, in good feyth,
Cometh al this newe science that men lere.
Ib. l. 22

10 Nature, the vicaire of the almyghty lorde.
Ib. l. 379

11 A fol can not be stille.[4] *Ib. l. 574*

12 Now welcome, somer, with thy sonne softe,[5]
That hast this wintres weders overshake.
Ib. l. 680

13 But the Troian gestes, as they felle,
In Omer, or in Dares, or in Dite,
Whoso that kan may rede hem as they write.
Troilus and Criseyde [c. 1385], bk. I, l. 145

[1] Chaucer, and probably others, translated the French *Roman de la Rose* by Guillaume de Lorris [begun 1237] and Jean de Meun [continued c. 1277].

[2] See Hippocrates, 80:9; Goethe, 395:7; and Longfellow, 509:14.

[3] John Bartlett quoted this line at the head of his preface to the ninth edition of *Familiar Quotations* [1891].

[4] See *Proverbs 29:11,* 25:31.

[5] See Langland, 143:14.

14 If no love is, O God, what fele I so?
And if love is, what thing and which is he?
If love be good, from whennes cometh my woo?[6] *Ib. l. 400 (Canticus Troili)*

15 A fool may ek a wys-man ofte gide.
Ib. l. 630

16 Ek som tyme it is craft to seme fle
Fro thyng whych in effect men hunte faste.
Ib. l. 747

17 Unknowe, unkist, and lost, that is unsought.[7] *Ib. l. 809*

18 O wynd, o wynd, the weder gynneth clere.
Ib. II, l. 2

19 Til crowes feet be growen under youre yë.
Ib. l. 403

20 Lord, this is an huge rayn!
This were a weder for to slepen inne!
Ib. III, l. 656

21 It is nought good a slepyng hound to wake.[8]
Ib. l. 764

22 For I have seyn, of a ful misty morwe
Folowen ful often a myrie someris day.
Ib. l. 1060

23 Right as an aspes leef she gan to quake.
Ib. l. 1200

24 For of fortunes sharpe adversitee
The worste kynde of infortune is this,
A man to han ben in prosperitee,
And it remembren, whan it passed is.[9]
Ib. III, l. 1625

25 Oon ere it herde, at tothir out it wente.[10]
Ib. IV, l. 434

26 But manly sette the world on six and sevene;[11]
And if thow deye a martyr, go to hevene!
Ib. l. 622

27 For tyme ylost may nought recovered be.
Ib. l. 1283

28 They take it wisly, faire, and softe.[12]
Ib. V, l. 347

[6] The *Canticus Troili (Song of Troilus)* is a fairly close rendering of Petrarch's *Sonnet 88 (In Vita), S'amor non è.*

[7] See Homer, 59:9; Horace, 108:13; Shakespeare, 219:24; Milton, 284:11; Scott, 430:10; and Byron, 458:26.

[8] See Dickens, 549:5.

[9] See Pindar, 72:1; Boethius, 129:22; Dante, 141:2; and Tennyson, 529:20.

[10] Commonly quoted: In one ear and out the other.

[11] All is uneven, / And everything is left at six and seven.
—Shakespeare, *Richard II* [1595–1596], *act II, sc. ii, l. 120*

Things going on at sixes and sevens.—Goldsmith, *The Good-Natured Man* [1768], *act I*

[12] The proverb is: Fair and softly goes far.
See Shakespeare, 192:22.

1 For he that naught n' assaieth, naught n' acheveth.[1] *Ib. l. 784*

2 Paradis stood formed in her yën.[2] *Ib. l. 817*

3 Trewe as stiel. *Ib. l. 831*

4 This sodeyn Diomede. *Ib. l. 1024*

5 Ye, fare wel al the snow of ferne yere![3] *Ib. l. 1176*

6 Ek gret effect men write in place lite;
Th' entente is al, and nat the lettres space.
Ib. 1629

7 Go, litel bok, go, litel myn tragedye.[4] *Ib. l. 1786*

8 O yonge, fresshe folkes, he or she,
In which that love up groweth with youre age,
Repeyreth hom fro worldly vanyte.
Ib. l. 1835

9 O moral Gower, this book I directe
To the. *Ib. l. 1856*

10 Whan that the month of May
Is comen, and that I here the foules synge,
And that the floures gynnen for to sprynge,
Farewel my bok, and my devocioun!
The Legend of Good Women [c. 1386], l. 36

11 That, of al the floures in the mede,
Thanne love I most thise floures white and rede,
Swiche as men callen daysyes in our toun.
Ib. l. 41

12 Whan that Aprill with his shoures soote
The droghte of March hath perced to the roote.
The Canterbury Tales [c. 1387]. Prologue, l. 1

[1]See Heywood, 160:12, and Gilbert, 629:2.

[2]See Dante, 142:14.

[3]See Villon, 150:7.

[4]Off with you down where you want to go.—HORACE [65–8 B.C.], *Epistles, I, xx, 5*

Little book, you will go without me—I don't mind—to the city.—OVID [43 B.C.–A.D. 18], *Tristia, I, i, 1*

Vade salutatem pro me, liber [Go forth, my book, to bear my greetings].—MARTIAL [A.D. c. 40–c. 104], *Epigrams, I, 70*

Go now, my little book, to every place / Where my first pilgrim has but shown his face.—JOHN BUNYAN, *Pilgrim's Progress* [1678], *Apology*

Go, little Book! From this my solitude / I cast thee on the Waters—go thy ways.—ROBERT SOUTHEY, *Lay of the Laureate* [1815], *L'Envoi*

These lines of Southey's and the next two were quoted by BYRON in *Don Juan* [1818], *canto I, stanza 222,* which ends: The four first rhymes are Southey's, every line: / For God's sake, reader! take them not for mine!

Go, little book, and wish to all / Flowers in the garden, meat in the hall.—R. L. STEVENSON, *Underwoods* [1887], *Envoy*

13 And smale foweles maken melodye,
That slepen al the nyght with open yë,
(So priketh hem nature in hir corages);
Thanne longen folk to goon on pilgrimages.
Ib. l. 9

14 He was a verray, parfit gentil knight.
Ib. l. 72

15 He was as fressh as is the month of May.
Ib. l. 92

16 He koude songes make, and wel endyte.
Ib. l. 95

17 Curteis he was, lowely, and servysable,
And carf beforn his fader at the table.
Ib. l. 99

18 Ful weel she soong the service dyvyne,
Entuned in hir nose ful semely;
And Frenssh she spak ful faire and fetisly,
After the scole of Stratford atte Bowe
For Frenssh of Parys was to hir unknowe.
Ib. l. 122

19 She wolde wepe, if that she saugh a mous
Kaught in a trappe, if it were deed or bledde.
Ib. l. 144

20 And theron heng a brooch of gold ful sheene,
On which ther was first write a crowned *A*,
And after *Amor vincit omnia.*[5]
Ib. l. 160

21 His palfrey was as broun as is a berye.
Ib. l. 207

22 A Frere ther was, a wantowne and a merye.
Ib. l. 208

23 He knew the tavernes wel in every toun.
Ib. l. 240

24 Somwhat he lipsed, for his wantownesse,
To make his Englissh sweete upon his tonge.
Ib. l. 264

25 A Clerk ther was of Oxenford also.
Ib. l. 285

26 As leene was his hors as is a rake.
Ib. l. 287

27 For hym was levere have at his beddes heed
Twenty bookes, clad in blak or reed,
Of Aristotle and his philosophie,
Than robes riche, or fithele, or gay sautrie,
But al be that he was a philosophre,
Yet hadde he but litel gold in cofre.
Ib. l. 293

28 And gladly wolde he lerne, and gladly teche.[6] *Ib. l. 308*

[5]See Sophocles, 74:23 and 75:5, and Virgil, 103:24.

[6]See Pope, 333:21.

1 Nowher so bisy a man as he ther nas,
And yet he semed bisier than he was.
Ib. l. 321

2 For he was Epicurus owene sone.[1]
Ib. l. 336

3 It snewed in his hous of mete and drynke.
Ib. l. 345

4 He was a good felawe.[2] *Ib. l. 395*

5 His studie was but litel on the Bible.
Ib. l. 438

6 For gold in phisik is a cordial,
Therefore he lovede gold in special.
Ib. l. 443

7 She was a worthy womman al hir lyve,
Housbondes at chirche dore she hadde fyve.
Ib. l. 459

8 This noble ensample to his sheep he yaf,
That first he wroghte, and afterward he taughte. *Ib. l. 496*

9 If gold ruste, what shal iren do?
Ib. l. 500

10 But Cristes loore and his apostles twelve
He taughte, but first he folwed it hymselve.
Ib. l. 527

11 And yet he hadde a thombe of gold.[3]
Ib. l. 563

12 That hadde a fyr-reed cherubynnes face.
Ib. l. 624

13 Wel loved he garleek, oynons, and eek lekes,
And for to drynken strong wyn, reed as blood.
Ib. l. 634

14 And whan that he wel dronken hadde the wyn,
Than wolde he speke no word but Latyn.
Ib. l. 637

15 Whoso shal telle a tale after a man,
He moot reherce as ny as evere he kan
Everich a word, if it be in his charge,
Al speke he never so rudeliche and large,
Or ellis he moot telle his tale untrewe,
Or feyne thyng, or fynde wordes new.
Ib. l. 731

16 For May wol have no slogardie anyght.
The sesoun priketh every gentil herte,
And maketh hym out of his slep to sterte.[4]
Ib. The Knight's Tale, l. 1042

[1] See Horace, 109:3.

[2] If he be not fellow with the best king, thou shalt find him the best king of good fellows.—SHAKESPEARE, *King Henry V* [1598–1600], *act V, sc. ii, l. 259*

[3] In allusion to the proverb: An honest miller hath a golden thumb.

[4] See Malory, 149:13.

17 Ech man for hymself. *Ib. l. 1182*

18 The bisy larke, messager of day.
Ib. l. 1491

19 May, with alle thy floures and thy grene,
Welcome be thou, faire, fresshe May.
Ib. l. 1510

20 That "feeld hath eyen, and the wode hath eres."[5] *Ib. l. 1522*

21 Now up, now doun, as boket in a welle.
Ib. l. 1533

22 For pitee renneth soone in gentil herte.
Ib. l. 1761

23 Cupido,
Upon his shuldres wynges hadde he two;
And blynd he was, as it is often seene;
A bowe he bar and arwes brighte and kene.
Ib. l. 1963

24 The smylere with the knyf under the cloke.
Ib. l. 1999

25 Up roos the sonne, and up roose Emelye.
Ib. l. 2273

26 Myn be the travaille, and thyn be the glorie!
Ib. l. 2406

27 And was al his chiere, as in his herte.
Ib. l. 2683

28 What is this world? what asketh men to have?
Now with his love, now in his colde grave
Allone, withouten any compaignye.
Ib. l. 2777

29 This world nys but a thurghfare ful of wo,
And we been pilgrymes, passing to and fro.
Deeth is an ende of every worldly soore.
Ib. l. 2847

30 Jhesu Crist, and seiynte Benedight,
Blesse this hous from every wikked wight.
Ib. The Miller's Tale, l. 3483

31 And broghte of myghty ale a large quart.
Ib. l. 3497

32 "Tehee!" quod she, and clapte the wyndow to.
Ib. l. 3740

[5] The proverb also occurs in the Latin form: Campus habet lumen, et habet nemus auris acumen [The field has sight, and the wood a sharp ear].

Fields have eyes and woods have ears.—JOHN HEYWOOD, *Proverbs* [1546], *pt. II, ch. 5*

Wode has erys, felde has sigt.—*King Edward and the Shepherd, MS* [c. 1300]

Walls have ears.—CERVANTES, *Don Quixote, pt. II* [1615], *ch. 48*

Woods have tongues / As walls have ears.—TENNYSON, *Idylls of the King, Balin and Balan* [1885], *l. 522*

1 Yet in our asshen olde is fyr yreke.[1]
Ib. The Reeve's Prologue, l. 3882

2 The gretteste clerkes been noght the wisest men.[2] *Ib. The Reeve's Tale, l. 4054*

3 Thurgh thikke and thurgh thenne.[3]
Ib. l. 4066

4 So was hir joly whistle wel ywet.
Ib. l. 4155

5 She is mirour of alle curteisye.[4]
Ib. The Man of Law's Tale, l. 166

6 For in the sterres, clerer than is glas,
Is writen, God woot, whoso koude it rede,
The deeth of every man. *Ib. l. 194*

7 Sathan, that evere us waiteth to bigile.
Ib. l. 582

8 In his owene grece I made hym frye.[5]
Ib. The Wife of Bath's Prologue, l. 487

9 What thyng we may nat lightly have,
Thereafter wol we crie alday and crave.
Ib. l. 517

10 Greet prees at market maketh deere ware,
And to greet cheep is holde at litel prys.
Ib. l. 522

11 But yet I hadde alwey a coltes tooth.
Gat-toothed I was, and that bicam me weel.
Ib. l. 601

12 A womman cast hir shame away,
Whan she cast of hir smok.[6] *Ib. l. 782*

13 As thikke as motes in the sonne-beem.
Ib. The Wife of Bath's Tale, l. 868

14 "My lige lady, generally," quod he,
"Wommen desiren have sovereynetee
As well over hir housbond as hir love."
Ib. l. 1037

15 Looke who that is moost vertuous alway,
Pryvee and apert, and most entendeth ay
To do the gentil dedes that he kan;
Taak hym for the grettest gentil man.
Ib. l. 1113

16 That he is gentil that dooth gentil dedis.[7]
Ib. l. 1170

17 For thogh we slepe or wake, or rome, or ryde,
Ay fleeth the tyme, it nyl no man abyde.[8]
Ib. The Clerk's Tale, l. 118

18 Love is noght oold as whan that it is newe.
Ib. l. 857

19 This flour of wyfly pacience. *Ib. l. 919*

20 O stormy peple! unsad and evere untrewe!
Ib. l. 995

21 No wedded man so hardy be t'assaille
His wyves pacience, in trust to fynde
Grisildis, for in certein he shal faille!
Ib. l. 1180

22 It is no childes pley
To take a wyf withoute avysement.
Ib. The Merchant's Tale, l. 1530

23 Love is blynd.[9] *Ib. l. 1598*

24 My wit is thynne. *Ib. l. 1682*

25 Ther nys no werkman, whatsoevere he be,
That may bothe werke wel and hastily;[10]
This wol be doon at leyser parfitly.[11]
Ib. l. 1832

26 Therfore bihoveth hire a ful long spoon
That shal ete with a feend.[12]
Ib. The Squire's Tale, l. 602

27 Men loven of propre kynde newefangelnesse.
Ib. l. 610

28 Fy on possessioun
But if a man be vertuous withal.
Ib. l. 686

29 Pacience is an heigh vertu, certeyn.
Ib. The Franklin's Tale, l. 773

30 Servant in love, and lord in marriage.
Ib. l. 793

31 It is agayns the proces of nature.
Ib. l. 1345

32 Trouthe is the hyeste thyng that men may kepe. *Ib. l. 1479*

[1] See Thomas Gray, 362:15.

[2] See Lao-tzu, 65:10; Confucius, 68:10; Heraclitus, 69:28; Selden, 263:18; Penn, 314:19; and Newman, 490:14.
The greatest clerks be not the wisest men. — JOHN HEYWOOD, *Proverbs* [1546], *pt. II, ch. 5*

[3] Through thick and thin. — SEIGNEUR DU BARTAS, *Divine Weeks and Works* [1578], *Second Week, Fourth Day*

[4] Call him bounteous Buckingham, / The mirror of all courtesy. — SHAKESPEARE, *Henry VIII* [1613], *act II, sc. i, l. 53*

[5] Proverbial.
Fryeth in her own grease. — JOHN HEYWOOD, *Proverbs* [1546], *pt. I, ch. 11*
The best way were to entertain him with hope, till the wicked fire of lust have melted him in his own grease. — SHAKESPEARE, *Merry Wives of Windsor* [1601], *act II, sc. i, l. 60*

[6] See Herodotus, 78:4.

[7] See Goldsmith, 369:9.

[8] See John Heywood, 159:3.

[9] Proverbial.
See Shakespeare, 196:1, and 199:7.

[10] See Publilius Syrus, 111:21, and John Heywood, 158:18.

[11] Ease and speed in doing a thing do not give the work lasting solidity or exactness of beauty. — PLUTARCH [A.D. 46–120], *Life of Pericles*

[12] Proverbial.
He must have a long spoon that must eat with the devil. — SHAKESPEARE, *Comedy of Errors* [1592–1593], *act IV, sc. iii, l. 64*

1 For dronkenesse is verray sepulture
Of mannes wit and his discrecioun.
Ib. The Pardoner's Tale, l. 558

2 Mordre wol out, certeyn, it wol nat faille.[1]
Ib. The Prioress's Tale, l. 1776

3 This may wel be rym dogerel.
Ib. Chaucer's Tale of Sir Thopas, l. 2115

4 Ful wys is he that kan hymselven knowe![2]
Ib. The Monk's Tale, l. 3329

5 He was of knyghthod and of fredom flour.
Ib. l. 3832

6 For whan a man hath over-greet a wit,
Ful oft hym happeth to mysusen it.
Ib. The Canon Yeoman's Prologue, l. 648

7 My sone, keep wel thy tonge, and keep thy freend. *Ib. The Manciple's Tale, l. 319*

8 Thing that is seyd, is seyd; and forth it gooth.[3] *Ib. l. 355*

9 For the proverbe seith that "manye smale maken a greet."[4]
Ib. The Parson's Tale, l. 361

10 Reule wel thyself, that other folk canst rede.
And trouthe thee shal delivere, it is no drede.
Truth [c. 1390], l. 6

11 The wrastling for this world axeth a fal.
Ib. l. 16

John Huss
c. 1370–1415

12 O holy simplicity![5]
Last words, at the stake

[1]Proverbial.
Also in *The Nun's Priest's Tale, ll. 4242 and 4247.*
How easily murder is discovered! — SHAKESPEARE, *Titus Andronicus* [1593–1594], *act II, sc. iii, l. 28*
Truth will come to light; murder cannot be hid long. — SHAKESPEARE, *The Merchant of Venice* [1596–1597], *act II, sc. ii, l. 86*
Murder, though it have no tongue, will speak / With most miraculous organ. — SHAKESPEARE, *Hamlet* [1600–1601], *act II, sc. ii, l. 630*
Murder will out. — CERVANTES, *Don Quixote, pt. I* [1605], *bk. III, ch. 8*
Carcasses bleed at the sight of the murderer. — ROBERT BURTON, *Anatomy of Melancholy* [1621–1651], *pt. I, sec. I member 2, subsec. 5*
Other sins only speak; murder shrieks out. — JOHN WEBSTER, *Duchess of Malfi* [1623], *act IV, sc. ii*
[2]See The Seven Sages, 62:4.
[3]See Horace, 109:10.
[4]The proverb goes back to St. Augustine.
See Hesiod, 61:20, and Cervantes, 170:9.
Many small make a great. — JOHN HEYWOOD, *Proverbs* [1546], *pt. I, ch. II*
[5]O sancta simplicitas!

Thomas à Kempis
1380–1471

13 Sic transit gloria mundi [So passes away the glory of this world].[6]
Imitation of Christ [c. 1420], bk. I, ch. 3

14 Be not angry that you cannot make others as you wish them to be, since you cannot make yourself as you wish to be.
Ib. 16

15 Man proposes, but God disposes.[7]
Ib. 19

16 What canst thou see elsewhere which thou canst not see here? Behold the heaven and the earth and all the elements; for of these are all things created. *Ib. 20*

17 No man ruleth safely but he that is willingly ruled. *Ib.*

18 And when he is out of sight, quickly also is he out of mind.[8] *Ib. 23*

19 First keep the peace within yourself, then you can also bring peace to others.
Ib. II, 3

20 Love is swift, sincere, pious, pleasant, gentle, strong, patient, faithful, prudent, long-suffering, manly and never seeking her own; for wheresoever a man seeketh his own, there he falleth from love.[9] *Ib. III, 5*

Charles d'Orléans
1391–1465

21 I am dying of thirst by the side of the fountain.[10] *Ballades, 2*

22 The season has shed its mantle of wind and chill and rain.[11] *Rondeaux, 63*

[6]These words are used in the crowning of the pope.
[7]Homo proponet et Deus disponit. — WILLIAM LANGLAND [c. 1330–c. 1400], *The Vision of Piers Plowman, l. 13,994* [1550 edition]
Man appoints, and God disappoints. — CERVANTES, *Don Quixote, pt. II* [1615], *bk. IV, ch. 55*
See *Proverbs 16:9*, 24:11.
[8]Out of sight, out of mind. — BARNABE GOOGE, *Eglogs* [1563]
And out of mind as soon as out of sight. — FULKE GREVILLE [1554–1628], *Sonnet 56*
Fer from eze, fer from herte, / Quoth Hendyng. — HENDYNG [1272–1307], *Proverbs, MS*
I do perceive that the old proverbs be not always true, for I do find that the absence of my Nath. doth breed in me the more continual remembrance of him. — LADY ANN BACON [1528–1610], *letter to Lady Jane Cornwallis*
[9]See *I Corinthians 13:4* and *13:7*, 48:23 and 48:24.
[10]Je meurs de soif en cousté la fontaine.
See Wilbur, 900:4.
[11]Le temps a laissé son manteau / De vent, de froidure et de pluie.

1 All by myself, wrapped in my thoughts,
And building castles in Spain and in France.[1] *Ib. 109*

John Fortescue
c. 1395 – c. 1476

2 Much cry and no wool.[2]
De Laudibus Legum Angliae [1471], ch. 10

3 Comparisons are odious.[3] *Ib. 19*

Sir Thomas Malory
d. 1471

4 The noble history of the Sangreal,[4] and of the most renowned Christian king . . . King Arthur.
Le Morte d'Arthur [1485]. Preface by William Caxton *[c. 1422–1491], the first English printer*

5 For herein may be seen noble chivalry, courtesy, humanity, friendliness, hardiness, love, friendship, cowardice, murder, hate, virtue, and sin. Do after the good and leave the evil, and it shall bring you to good fame and renown. *Ib.*

6 Whoso pulleth out this sword of this stone and anvil, is rightwise king born of all England. *Ib. bk. I, ch. 5*

7 And with that the king saw coming toward him the strangest beast that ever he saw or heard of; so the beast went to the well and drank, and the noise was in the beast's belly like unto the questing of thirty couple hounds; but all the while the beast drank there was no noise in the beast's belly: and therewith the beast departed with a great noise . . . Pellinore, that time king, followed the questing beast. *Ib. 19*

8 In the midst of the lake Arthur was ware of an arm clothed in white samite, that held a fair sword in that hand. *Ib. 25*

9 Always Sir Arthur lost so much blood that it was marvel he stood on his feet, but he was so full of knighthood that knightly he endured the pain. *Ib. IV, 9*

10 What, nephew, said the king, is the wind in that door?[5] *Ib. VII, 34*

11 The joy of love is too short, and the sorrow thereof, and what cometh thereof, dureth over long. *Ib. X, 56*

12 It is his day. *Ib. 70*

13 The month of May was come, when every lusty heart beginneth to blossom, and to bring forth fruit; for like as herbs and trees bring forth fruit and flourish in May, in likewise every lusty heart that is in any manner a lover, springeth and flourisheth in lusty deeds. For it giveth unto all lovers courage, that lusty month of May.[6] *Ib. XVIII, 25*

14 All ye that be lovers call unto your remembrance the month of May, like as did Queen Guenever, for whom I make here a little mention, that while she lived she was a true lover, and therefore she had a good end. *Ib.*

15 Such a fellowship of good knights shall never be together in no company. *Ib. XX, 9*

16 I shall curse you with book and bell and candle.[7] *Ib. XXI, 1*

17 Through this man [Launcelot] and me [Guenever] hath all this war been wrought, and the death of the most noblest knights of the world; for through our love that we have loved together is my most noble lord slain. *Ib. 9*

18 For as well as I have loved thee, mine heart will not serve me to see thee, for through thee and me is the flower of kings and knights destroyed. *Ib.*

19 Then Sir Launcelot saw her visage, but he wept not greatly, but sighed. *Ib. 11*

20 Thou Sir Launcelot, there thou liest, that thou were never matched of earthly knight's hand. And thou were the courteoust knight that ever bare shield. And thou were the truest friend to thy lover that ever bestrad horse. And thou were the truest lover of a sinful man that ever loved woman. And thou were the kindest man that ever struck with sword. And thou were the goodliest person

[1] Translated by Norbert Guterman.
Thou shalt make castels thanne in Spayne, / And dreme of joye, all but in vayne. — Jean de Meun, *The Romaunt of the Rose* [c. 1277], *fragment B, l. 2573*, translated by Chaucer

[2] A great cry, but little wool. — Cervantes, *Don Quixote, pt. II* [1615], *bk. III, ch. 13*
All cry and no wool. — Samuel Butler, *Hudibras, pt. I* [1663], *canto 1, l. 852*

[3] This was a well-known phrase in the fourteenth century, and has been repeated by many, including Lydgate, Shakespeare, and Swift.
See Donne, 253:19.

[4] The Holy Grail.

[5] See Shakespeare, 209:17.

[6] See Chaucer, 146:16.

[7] The reference is to the ceremony of excommunication, current since the eighth century, performed with bell, book, and candle.
See Shakespeare, 201:23.

that ever came among press of knights. And thou were the meekest man and the gentlest that ever ate in hall among ladies. And thou were the sternest knight to thy mortal foe that ever put spear in the rest. *Ib. 13*

Henry VI

1421–1471

1 Kingdoms are but cares,
State is devoid of stay;
Riches are ready snares,
And hasten to decay.

From Sir John Harington, *Nugae Antiquae [1769]*

Gabriel Biel

c. 1425–1495

2 To be crushed in the winepress of passion.
Expositio Canonis Missae, lectio 52

3 Always in these matters desiring rather to be taught than to teach. *Ib. 53*

4 No one conquers who doesn't fight.
Ib. 78

5 You get what you pay for.[1] *Ib. 86*

François Villon

1431 – c. 1465

6 Ah God! Had I but studied
In the days of my foolish youth.[2]
Le Grand Testament, 26

7 But where are the snows of yesteryear?[3]
Ib. Ballade des Dames du Temps Jadis

8 In this faith I will to live and die.
Ib. Ballade de l'Homage à Notre Dame

9 There's no good speech save in Paris.[4]
Ib. Ballade des Femmes de Paris

10 But pray God that he absolve us all![5]
Codicile

11 I know all except myself.[6]
Ballade des Menus Propres

[1] Pro tali numismate tales merces.
[2] Hé Dieu! si j'eusse étudié / Au temps de ma jeunesse folle.
[3] Mais où sont les neiges d'antan?
Translated by Dante Gabriel Rossetti.
See Chaucer, 145:5.
[4] Il n'est bon bec que de Paris.
[5] Mais priez Dieu que tous nous veuille absoudre.
[6] Je connais tout, fors moi-même.

Aldus Manutius

1450–1515

12 Talk of nothing but business, and dispatch that business quickly.
Placard on the door of the Aldine Press, Venice, established about 1490[7]

Christopher Columbus

1451–1506

13 "Thanks be to God," says the Admiral; "the air is soft as in April in Seville, and it is a pleasure to be in it, so fragrant it is."
Journal of the First Voyage,[8] *October 8, 1492*

14 Here the people could stand it no longer and complained of the long voyage; but the Admiral cheered them as best he could, holding out good hope of the advantages they would have. He added that it was useless to complain, he had come [to go] to the Indies, and so had to continue it until he found them, with the help of Our Lord.
Ib. October 10, 1492

15 At two hours after midnight appeared the land, at a distance of 2 leagues. They handed all sails and set the *treo,* which is the mainsail without bonnets, and lay-to waiting for daylight Friday, when they arrived at an island of the Bahamas that was called in the Indians' tongue Guanahaní [San Salvador].
Ib. October 12, 1492

16 The Admiral says that he never beheld so fair a thing: trees all along the river, beautiful and green, and different from ours, with flowers and fruits each according to their kind, many birds and little birds which sing very sweetly. *Ib. October 28, 1492*

17 The two Christians met on the way many people who were going to their towns, women and men, with a firebrand in the hand, [and] herbs to drink the smoke thereof, as they are accustomed.[9] *Ib. November 6, 1492*

18 When there are such lands there should be profitable things without number.
Ib. November 27, 1492

[7] Quoted by Thomas Frognall Dibdin in *Introduction to the Knowledge of Rare and Valuable Editions of the Greek and Latin Classics* [1802], *vol. I, p. 436.*
[8] Bartolomé de Las Casas [1474–1566] made an abstract of Columbus's *Journal of the First Voyage (El Libro de la Primera Navegación),* which is the nearest thing to an original journal that we have.
Translated by Samuel Eliot Morison.
[9] The first certain reference in history to smoking tobacco.

1 And I say that Your Highnesses ought not to consent that any foreigner does business or sets foot here, except Christian Catholics, since this was the end and the beginning of the enterprise, that it should be for the enhancement and glory of the Christian religion, nor should anyone who is not a good Christian come to these parts.[1] *Ib.*

2 The Admiral ordered the lord to be given some things, and he and all his folk rested in great contentment, believing truly that they had come from the sky, and to see the Christians they held themselves very fortunate.

Ib. December 22, 1492

3 "Of this voyage, I observe," says the Admiral, "that it has miraculously been shown, as may be understood by this writing, by the many signal miracles that He has shown on the voyage, and for me, who for so great a time was in the court of Your Highnesses with the opposition and against the opinion of so many high personages of your household, who were all against me, alleging this undertaking to be folly, which I hope in Our Lord will be to the greater glory of Christianity, which to some slight extent already has happened." *Ib. March 15, 1493*

4 It is true that after they have been reassured and have lost this fear, they are so artless and so free with all they possess, that no one would believe it without having seen it. Of anything they have, if you ask them for it, they never say no; rather they invite the person to share it, and show as much love as if they were giving their hearts.

Letter to the Sovereigns on the First Voyage, February 15–March 4, 1493[2]

5 And they know neither sect nor idolatry, with the exception that all believe that the source of all power and goodness is in the sky, and they believe very firmly that I, with these ships and people, came from the sky, and in this belief they everywhere received me, after they had overcome their fear.

Ib.

6 I have come to believe that this is a mighty continent which was hitherto unknown. I am greatly supported in this view by reason of this great river [Ozama], and by this sea which is fresh.

Journal of the Third Voyage, May 30–August 31, 1498[3]

7 I have always read that the world, both land and water, was spherical, as the authority and researches of Ptolemy and all the others who have written on this subject demonstrate and prove, as do the eclipses of the moon and other experiments that are made from east to west, and the elevation of the North Star from north to south.

Letter to the Sovereigns on the Third Voyage, October 18, 1498

8 Your Highnesses have an Other World here, by which our holy faith can be so greatly advanced and from which such great wealth can be drawn. *Ib.*

9 I should be judged as a captain who went from Spain to the Indies to conquer a people numerous and warlike, whose manners and religion are very different from ours, who live in sierras and mountains, without fixed settlements, and where by divine will I have placed under the sovereignty of the King and Queen our Lords, an Other World, whereby Spain, which was reckoned poor, is become the richest of countries.

Letter to Doña Juana de Torres, October 1500[4]

10 The tempest was terrible and separated me from my [other] vessels that night, putting every one of them in desperate straits, with nothing to look forward to but death. Each was certain the others had been destroyed. What man ever born, not excepting Job, who would not have died of despair, when in such weather seeking safety for my son, my brother, shipmates, and myself, we were forbidden [access to] the land and the harbors which I, by God's will and sweating blood, had won for Spain?

Lettera Rarissima to the Sovereigns, July 7, 1503 (Fourth Voyage)[5]

11 I came to serve you at the age of 28 and now I have not a hair on me that is not white, and my body is infirm and exhausted. All that was left to me and my brothers has been taken away and sold, even to the cloak that I wore, without hearing or trial, to my great dishonor. *Ib.*

[1] Here may be found the first suggestion of the exclusive colonial policy that Spain and other nations followed. — SAMUEL ELIOT MORISON, *Journals and Other Documents on the Life and Voyages of Christopher Columbus* [1963]

[2] This letter, the first and rarest of all printed Americana, describes the scenery and the natives of Hispaniola.

[3] Translated by SAMUEL ELIOT MORISON and MILTON ANASTOS.

[4] Columbus is coming from the Indies as a prisoner to Cadiz.

[5] Translated by MILTON ANASTOS.

1 Weep for me, whoever has charity, truth and justice! I did not come on this voyage for gain, honor or wealth, that is certain; for then the hope of all such things was dead. I came to Your Highnesses with honest purpose and sincere zeal; and I do not lie. I humbly beseech Your Highnesses that, if it please God to remove me hence, you will help me to go to Rome and on other pilgrimages.
Ib.

Leonardo da Vinci

1452–1519

2 Man and the animals are merely a passage and channel for food, a tomb for other animals, a haven for the dead, giving life by the death of others, a coffer full of corruption.
The Notebooks [1508–1518],[1] *vol. I, ch. 1*

3 Intellectual passion drives out sensuality.
Ib.

4 As a well-spent day brings happy sleep, so life well used brings happy death. *Ib.*

5 Life well spent is long. *Ib.*

6 Shun those studies in which the work that results dies with the worker. *Ib.*

7 Whoever in discussion adduces authority uses not intellect but rather memory.
Ib. 2

8 Iron rusts from disuse; stagnant water loses its purity and in cold weather becomes frozen; even so does inaction sap the vigor of the mind. *Ib.*

9 Savage is he who saves himself. *Ib.*

10 It is easier to resist at the beginning than at the end. *Ib.*

11 Necessity is the mistress and guardian of Nature.[2] *Ib.*

12 Human subtlety . . . will never devise an invention more beautiful, more simple or more direct than does nature, because in her inventions nothing is lacking, and nothing is superfluous. *Ib. 3*

13 Mechanics is the paradise of the mathematical sciences because by means of it one comes to the fruits of mathematics.
Ib. 20

14 O speculators about perpetual motion, how many vain chimeras have you created in the like quest? Go and take your place with the seekers after gold. *Ib. II, 25*

[1]Translated by EDWARD MACCURDY.
[2]See Shakespeare, 217:7.

15 O neglectful Nature, wherefore art thou thus partial, becoming to some of thy children a tender and benignant mother, to others a most cruel and ruthless stepmother? I see thy children given into slavery to others without ever receiving any benefit, and in lieu of any reward for the services they have done for them they are repaid by the severest punishments. *Ib. 45*

16 The Medici created and destroyed me.
Ib. 46

Amerigo Vespucci

1454–1512

17 Those new regions [America] which we found and explored with the fleet . . . we may rightly call a New World . . . a continent more densely peopled and abounding in animals than our Europe or Asia or Africa; and, in addition, a climate milder than in any other region known to us.[3]
Letter called Mundus Novus [1503] to Lorenzo Pier Francesco de'-Medici

Sebastian Brant

1457–1521

18 The world wants to be deceived.
Ship of Fools (Narrenschiff) [1494]

John Skelton

c. 1460–1529

19 I say, thou mad March hare.[4]
Replication Against Certain Young Scholars

20 He ruleth all the roost.[5]
Why Come Ye Not to Court, l. 198

[3]Translated by G. T. NORTHUP, *Vespucci Reprints and Studies* [1916], and S. E. MORISON, *The European Discovery of America: The Southern Voyages* [1974].

This, and a letter of Vespucci to his friend Pier Soderini [1504], led geography professor Martin Waldseemüller to credit Vespucci with discovering "a fourth part of the world" and to issue a map [1507] with a bold AMERICA on the continent now called South America. Vespucci had invented a voyage of 1497, a year before Columbus's Third Voyage to the mainland of South America.

[4]Mad as a March hare.—JOHN HEYWOOD, *Proverbs* [1546], *pt. II, ch. 5*

[5]Rule the rost.—JOHN HEYWOOD, *Proverbs* [1546], *pt. I, ch. 5*

Her that ruled the rost.—THOMAS HEYWOOD, *History of Women* [ed. 1624]

Rules the roast.—JONSON, CHAPMAN, MARSTON, *Eastward Ho* [1605], *act II, sc. ii*

1 The wolf from the door.[1] *Ib. l. 1531*

2 Old proverb says,
That bird is not honest
That filleth his own nest.[2]
Poems Against Garnesche

3 Maid, widow, or wife. *Philip Sparrow*

William Dunbar
c. 1465 – c. 1530

4 London, thou art the flower of Cities all.
London, refrain

5 Gem of all joy, jasper of jocundity.
Ib. st. 3

6 I that in heill wes and gladnes
Am trublit now with gret seiknes
And feblit with infermite:
Timor Mortis conturbat me.[3]
Lament for the Makers (Makaris)[4] *[c. 1508], refrain*

7 Our plesance here is all vain glory,
This false world is but transitory.
Ib. st. 2

Desiderius Erasmus
1465–1536

8 It is folly alone that stays the fugue of Youth and beats off louring Old Age.
The Praise of Folly [1509]

9 They may attack me with an army of six hundred syllogisms; and if I do not recant, they will proclaim me a heretic. *Ib.*

10 A peck of troubles.
Apothegms [1542]

Fernando de Rojas
c. 1465 – c. 1538

11 Goods which are not shared are not goods.
La Celestina, act I

12 The use of riches is better than their possession. *Ib. II*

13 The first step towards madness is to think oneself wise. *Ib.*

14 Riches do not make one rich but busy.
Ib. IV

15 No one is so old that he cannot live yet another year, nor so young that he cannot die today. *Ib.*

16 When God wounds from on high he will follow with the remedy. *Ib. X*

17 When one door closes, fortune will usually open another. *Ib. XV*

Niccolò Machiavelli[5]
1469–1527

18 There is nothing more difficult to take in hand, more perilous to conduct, or more uncertain in its success, than to take the lead in the introduction of a new order of things.
The Prince [1532],[6] *ch. 6*

19 From this arises the question whether it is better to be loved rather than feared, or feared rather than loved. It might perhaps be answered that we should wish to be both: but since love and fear can hardly exist together, if we must choose between them, it is far safer to be feared than loved.[7] *Ib. 8*

20 The chief foundations of all states, new as well as old or composite, are good laws and good arms; and as there cannot be good laws where the state is not well armed, it follows that where they are well armed they have good laws. *Ib. 12*

21 A prince should therefore have no other aim or thought, nor take up any other thing for his study, but war and its organization and discipline, for that is the only art that is necessary to one who commands.
Ib. 14

22 Among other evils which being unarmed brings you, it causes you to be despised.
Ib.

23 Many have imagined republics and principalities which have never been seen or known to exist in reality; for how we live is so far removed from how we ought to live, that he who abandons what is done for what ought to be done, will rather bring about his own ruin than his preservation. *Ib. 15*

24 The prince who relies upon their words, without having otherwise provided for his security, is ruined; for friendships that are won by awards, and not by greatness and nobility

[1] To keep the wolf from the door.—JOHN HEYWOOD, *Proverbs* [1546], *pt. II, ch. 7*

[2] It is a foul bird that filleth his own nest.—JOHN HEYWOOD, *Proverbs* [1546], *pt. II, ch. 5*

[3] Fear of Death troubles me.

[4] Makers: poets.

[5] Every Country hath its Machiavel.—SIR THOMAS BROWNE, *Religio Medici* [1642], *p. 24* (Everyman edition)
Out of his surname they have coined an epithet for a knave, and out of his Christian name a synonym for the Devil.—MACAULAY, *Machiavelli* [1827]
See Butler, 291:28.

[6] Translated by W. K. MARRIOTT.

[7] See Ennius, 95:6, and Accius, 97:9.

of soul, although deserved, yet are not real, and cannot be depended upon in time of adversity. *Ib. 17*

1 A prince being thus obliged to know well how to act as a beast must imitate the fox and the lion, for the lion cannot protect himself from traps, and the fox cannot defend himself from wolves. One must therefore be a fox to recognize traps, and a lion to frighten wolves. *Ib.*

2 When neither their property nor their honor is touched, the majority of men live content. *Ib. 19*

3 There are three classes of intellects: one which comprehends by itself; another which appreciates what others comprehend; and a third which neither comprehends by itself nor by the showing of others; the first is the most excellent, the second is good, the third is useless. *Ib. 22*

4 There is no other way of guarding oneself against flattery than by letting men understand that they will not offend you by speaking the truth; but when everyone can tell you the truth, you lose their respect. *Ib. 23*

5 Where the willingness is great, the difficulties cannot be great. *Ib. 26*

6 God is not willing to do everything, and thus take away our free will and that share of glory which belongs to us. *Ib.*

7 Whoever desires to found a state and give it laws, must start with assuming that all men are bad and ever ready to display their vicious nature, whenever they may find occasion for it.

Discourse upon the First Ten Books of Livy, bk. I, ch. 3

8 The people resemble a wild beast,[1] which, naturally fierce and accustomed to live in the woods, has been brought up, as it were, in a prison and in servitude, and having by accident got its liberty, not being accustomed to search for its food, and not knowing where to conceal itself, easily becomes the prey of the first who seeks to incarcerate it again. *Ib. 16*

Charles VIII

1470–1498

9 This is our gracious will.[2]

Royal Order of March 12, 1497

[1]See Horace, 108:19; Shakespeare, 205:18, 242:14, and 242:21; and Pope, 339:28.

[2]Tel est notre bon plaisir.

Nicholas Copernicus

1473–1543

10 Finally we shall place the Sun himself at the center of the Universe. All this is suggested by the systematic procession of events and the harmony of the whole Universe, if only we face the facts, as they say, "with both eyes open."

De Revolutionibus Orbium Coelestium [1543][3]

Ludovico Ariosto

1474–1533

11 Nature made him, and then broke the mold.[4]

Orlando Furioso [1532], canto X, st. 84

Bartolomé de Las Casas[5]

c. 1474–1566

12 It clearly appears that there are no races in the world, however rude, uncultivated, barbarous, gross, or almost brutal they may be, who cannot be persuaded and brought to a good order and way of life, and made domestic, mild and tractable, provided . . . the method that is proper and natural to men is used; that is, love and gentleness and kindness.[6]

Apologética Historia (Apologetic History) de las Indias [written c. 1530], ch. 48

13 The main goal of divine Providence in [allowing] the discovery of these tribes and lands . . . is . . . the conversion and well-being of souls, and to this goal everything temporal must necessarily be subordinated and directed.[7]

Historia de las Indias [written 1550–1563], prologue

Michelangelo Buonarroti

1475–1564

14 The more the marble wastes, the more the statue grows. *Sonnet*

15 If it be true that any beautiful thing raises the pure and just desire of man from earth to

[3]Translated by John F. Dobson.

[4]Natura il fece, e poi ruppe la stampa. See Byron, 459:20.

[5]Known as the Apostle of the Indies.

[6]Translated by George Sanderlin.

[7]Translated by Rachel Phillips.

God, the eternal fount of all, such I believe my love. *Sonnet*

1 The power of one fair face makes my love sublime, for it has weaned my heart from low desires. *Sonnet*

2 I live and love in God's peculiar light. *Ib.*

Sir Thomas More[1]

1478–1535

3 They wonder much to hear that gold, which in itself is so useless a thing, should be everywhere so much esteemed, that even men for whom it was made, and by whom it has its value, should yet be thought of less value than it is.

Utopia [1516]. Of Jewels and Wealth

4 They have no lawyers among them, for they consider them as a sort of people whose profession it is to disguise matters.

Ib. Of Law and Magistrates

5 Plato by a goodly similitude declareth, why wise men refrain to meddle in the commonwealth. For when they see the people swarm into the streets, and daily wet to the skin with rain, and yet cannot persuade them to go out of the rain, they do keep themselves within their houses, seeing they cannot remedy the folly of the people.[2]

Ib. Concerning the Best State of a Commonwealth

6 A little wanton money, which burned out the bottom of his purse.

Works [c. 1530]

7 This is a fair tale of a tub told of his election.[3]

Confutation of Tyndale's Answers [1532]

8 For men use, if they have an evil turn, to write it in marble: and whoso doth us a good turn we write it in dust.[4]

Richard III and His Miserable End [1543]

9 See me safe up: for my coming down, I can shift for myself.

On ascending the scaffold. From Froude, *History of England [1856–1870]*

10 This hath not offended the king.

As he drew his beard aside upon placing his head on the block. From Bacon, *Apothegms, no. 22*

Robert Whittinton

c. 1480 – c. 1530

11 [Sir Thomas] More is a man of angel's wit and singular learning; I know not his fellow. For where is the man of that gentleness, lowliness and affability? And as time requireth, a man of marvelous mirth and pastimes; and sometimes of as sad a gravity; a man for all seasons.[5]

Passage composed for schoolboys to put into Latin

Martin Luther

1483–1546

12 If it were an art to overcome heresy with fire, the executioners would be the most learned doctors on earth.

To the Christian Nobility of the German States [1520]

13 Here I stand; I can do no other. God help me. Amen.[6]

Speech at the Diet of Worms, [April 18, 1521]

14 The mad mob does not ask how it could be better, only that it be different. And when it then becomes worse, it must change again. Thus they get bees for flies, and at last hornets for bees.

Whether Soldiers Can Also Be in a State of Grace [1526]

15 A mighty fortress is our God,
A bulwark never failing.

---

[1] Canonized [1935] by Pope Pius XI.
See Robert Whittinton, 155:11.

[2] In the modern phrase: Not sense enough to come in out of the rain.

[3] A tale of a tub is a cock-and-bull story. Jonson used it as the title of a comedy [1633], and Swift as the title of a satire [1696].

[4] See Sophocles, 75:22; Catullus, 102:12; Bacon, 181:18; Shakespeare, 249:14; and Keats, 480:7.
Words writ in waters. — George Chapman [c. 1559–1634], *Revenge for Honor, act. V, sc. ii*
L'injure se grave en métal; et le bienfait s'escrit en l'onde [An injury is engraved in metal, but a benefit is written in water]. — Jean Bertaut [1552–1611]
All your better deeds shall be in water writ, but this in marble. — Beaumont and Fletcher, *Philaster* [1620], *act V, sc. iii*

[5] See Ben Jonson, 256:15.

[6] Hier stehe ich, ich kann nicht anders. Gott helfe mir. Amen.
Inscribed on his monument at Worms.
Also translated as: Here I stand, I cannot do otherwise. And: God helping me, I can do no other.
See Wilson, 682:13.

Our helper He amid the flood
Of mortal ills prevailing.[1]

Ein' Feste Burg [1529]

1 What can only be taught by the rod and with blows will not lead to much good; they will not remain pious any longer than the rod is behind them.

The Great Catechism. Second Command [1529]

2 Peace is more important than all justice; and peace was not made for the sake of justice, but justice for the sake of peace.

On Marriage [1530]

3 Justice is a temporary thing that must at last come to an end; but the conscience is eternal and will never die. *Ib.*

4 Superstition, idolatry, and hypocrisy have ample wages, but truth goes a-begging.

Table Talk [1569], 53

5 For where God built a church, there the Devil would also build a chapel[2] . . . Thus is the Devil ever God's ape. *Ib. 67*

6 The Mass is the greatest blasphemy of God, and the highest idolatry upon earth, an abomination the like of which has never been in Christendom since the time of the Apostles. *Ib. 171*

7 There is no more lovely, friendly and charming relationship, communion or company than a good marriage. *Ib. 292*

8 A theologian is born by living, nay dying and being damned, not by thinking, reading, or speculating. *Ib. 352*

9 Reason is the greatest enemy that faith has: it never comes to the aid of spiritual things, but—more frequently than not—struggles against the divine Word, treating with contempt all that emanates from God. *Ib. 353*

10 If I had heard that as many devils would set on me in Worms as there are tiles on the roofs, I should nonetheless have ridden there.

Luthers Sammtliche Schriften [1745], XVI, 14

11 It makes a difference whose ox is gored.[3]

Works [1854 ed.], vol. LXII

Hernán Cortés [Hernando Cortez]

1485–1547

12 It seems most credible that our Lord God has purposefully allowed these lands [Mexico] to be discovered . . . so that Your Majesties may be fruitful and deserving in His sight by causing these barbaric tribes to be enlightened and brought to the faith by Your hand.

First Dispatch [July 10, 1519]. To Queen Juana and her son Charles V from the Vera Cruz town council; probably dictated by Cortés

13 [The Aztecs] said that by no means would they give themselves up, for as long as one of them was left he would die fighting, and that we would get nothing of theirs because they would burn everything or throw it into the water.

Third Dispatch [May 15, 1522]. To Charles V

Hugh Latimer

c. 1485–1555

14 Play the man, Master Ridley; we shall this day light such a candle, by God's grace, in England, as I trust shall never be put out.[4]

To Nicholas Ridley [1500–1555] as they were being burned alive at Oxford for heresy [October 16, 1555].[5] From J. R. Green, A Short History of the English People [1874], ch. 7

[1] Ein' feste burg is unser Gott, / ein gute wehr und waffen. / Er hilft uns frei aus aller not, / die uns itzt hat betroffen.

Translated by FREDERICK HENRY HEDGE.

Great God! there is no safety here below; / Thou art my fortress, thou that seem'st my foe.—FRANCIS QUARLES [1592–1644], *Divine Poems*

See *Psalm 46:1*, 19:10.

[2] Where God hath a temple, the Devil will have a chapel.—ROBERT BURTON, *Anatomy of Melancholy* [1621–1651], *pt. III, sec. 4, member I, subsec. I*

No sooner is a temple built to God but the Devil builds a chapel hard by.—GEORGE HERBERT, *Jacula Prudentum* [1640]

See Defoe, 318:5.

[3] This is the moral of the fable of the lawyer, the farmer, and the farmer's ox, which was included in NOAH WEBSTER, *American Spelling Book* [1802], entitled *The Partial Judge*.

[4] See *II Esdras 14:25*, 34:6.

[5] See Latimer and Ridley in the might / Of Faith stand coupled for a common flight!—WORDSWORTH [1770–1850], *Ecclesiastical Sonnets, pt. II, no. 34, Latimer and Ridley*

Pope Julius III

1487–1555

1 Do you not know, my son, with what little understanding the world is ruled?[1]

To a Portuguese monk who sympathized with the pope's burdens of office

Jacques Cartier

1491–1557

2 I am rather inclined to believe that this is the land God gave to Cain.[2]

La Première Relation

St. Ignatius of Loyola[3]

1491–1556

3 Teach us, good Lord, to serve Thee as Thou
deservest:
To give and not to count the cost;
To fight and not to heed the wounds;
To toil and not to seek for rest;
To labor and not ask for any reward
Save that of knowing that we do Thy will.

Prayer for Generosity [1548]

Bernal Díaz del Castillo

c. 1492 – c. 1581

4 To me it appears that the names of those[4] ought to be written in letters of gold, who died so cruel a death, for the service of God and His Majesty, to give light to those who were in darkness,[5] and to procure wealth which all men desire.[6]

The True History of the Conquest of New Spain (Historia Verdadera de la Conquista de la Nueve Espana) [1800], pt. II, ch. 10

Philippus Aureolus Paracelsus

c. 1493–1541

5 Every experiment is like a weapon which must be used in its particular way—a spear to thrust, a club to strike. Experimenting requires a man who knows when to thrust and when to strike, each according to need and fashion.[7]

Surgeon's Book (Chirurgische Bucher) [1605]

Francis [François] I

1494–1547

6 All is lost save honor.[8]

Letter to his mother after his defeat at Pavia [February 23, 1525]

François Rabelais

c. 1494–1553

7 Break the bone and suck out the substantific marrow.

Gargantua and Pantagruel,[9] bk. I [1532], prologue

8 To laugh is proper to man.[10]

Ib. Rabelais to the Reader

9 Appetite comes with eating[11] . . . but the thirst goes away with drinking.

Ib. ch. 5

10 War begun without good provision of money beforehand for going through with it is but as a breathing of strength and blast that will quickly pass away. Coin is the sinews of war.[12] *Ib. 46*

11 How shall I be able to rule over others, that have not full power and command of myself?[13] *Ib. 52*

12 Do what thou wilt.[14] *Ib. 57*

13 Wisdom entereth not into a malicious mind, and science without conscience is but the ruin of the soul. *Ib. II [1534], 8*

14 Subject to a kind of disease, which at that time they called lack of money.[15]

Ib. 16

[1] An nescis, mi fili, quantilla prudentia mundus regatur?

[2] J'estime mieux que autrement, que c'est la terre que Dieu donna à Caïn.

Upon discovering the bleak shore of the Gulf of St. Lawrence, today's Labrador and Quebec [summer 1534].

[3] Founder of the Society of Jesus.

[4] The five hundred and fifty soldiers who came to Mexico with Cortés [1519], all but five of whom were dead at the time Díaz was writing [1568].

[5] See *Isaiah 9:2*, 29:15.

[6] Translated by MAURICE KEATINGE.

[7] Translated by HENRY M. PACHTER.

[8] Tout est perdu fors l'honneur.

The actual words written were: De toutes choses ne m'est demeuré que l'honneur et la vie qui est sauvé. The letter is in DULAURE, *Histoire Civile, Physique et Morale de Paris* [1821–1825].

[9] Translated by SIR THOMAS URQUHART and PETER ANTHONY MOTTEUX [1653–1694].

[10] Pour ce que rire est le propre de l'homme.

[11] My appetite comes to me while eating. — MONTAIGNE, *Essays* [1580–1595], *III, 9*

[12] See Bion, 92:6; Cicero, 99:11; Dryden, 305:22; and Churchill, 746:10.

[13] He is most powerful who has power over himself. — SENECA [8 B.C.–A.D. 65], *Epistles, 90, 34*

See Massinger, 262:19.

[14] Fais ce que voudras.

[15] See Shakespeare, 206:5.

Or that eternal want of pence, / Which vexes public men. — TENNYSON, *Will Waterproof's Lyrical Monologue [1842], st. 6*

1 So much is a man worth as he esteems himself. *Ib. 29*

2 A good crier of green sauce. *Ib. 31*

3 This flea which I have in mine ear. *Ib. III [1545], 31*

4 Oh thrice and four times happy those who plant cabbages![1] *Ib. IV [1548], 18*

5 Which was performed to a T.[2] *Ib. 41*

6 He that has patience may compass anything. *Ib. 48*

7 We will take the good will for the deed.[3] *Ib. 49*

8 Speak the truth and shame the Devil.[4] *Ib. V [1552], author's prologue*

9 Plain as a nose in a man's face.[5] *Ib.*

10 Like hearts of oak.[6] *Ib.*

11 Go hang yourselves [critics] . . . you shall never want rope enough.[7] *Ib.*

12 Looking as like . . . as one pea does like another.[8] *Ib. ch. 2*

13 It is meat, drink, and cloth to us. *Ib. 7*

14 I am going to seek a grand perhaps; draw the curtain, the farce is played.[9] *Alleged last words. From* MOTTEUX, *Life of Rabelais*

John Heywood[10]

c. 1497 – c. 1580

15 All a green willow, willow, willow,
All a green willow is my garland.[11]
The Green Willow

16 The loss of wealth is loss of dirt,
As sages in all times assert;
The happy man's without a shirt.[12]
Be Merry Friends

17 Let the world slide,[13] let the world go;
A fig for care, and a fig for woe!
If I can't pay, why I can owe,
And death makes equal the high and low.
Ib.

18 Haste maketh waste.[14] *Proverbs [1546], pt. I, ch. 2*

19 Good to be merry and wise. *Ib.*

20 Beaten with his own rod. *Ib.*

21 Look ere ye leap.[15] *Ib.*

22 While between two stools my tail go to the ground.[16] *Ib.*

23 He that will not when he may,
When he would he shall have nay.
Ib. 3

[1] See Montaigne, 164:8, and Voltaire, 343:14.

[2] We could manage this matter to a T. — STERNE, *Tristram Shandy, bk. II* [1760], *ch. 5*
You see they'd have fitted him to a T. — SAMUEL JOHNSON; from BOSWELL, *Life of Johnson* [1791]
You will find it shall echo my speech to a T. — THOMAS MOORE [1779–1852], *Address for the Opening of the New Theatre of St. Stephen*

[3] The will for deed I do accept. — SEIGNEUR DU BARTAS, *Divine Weeks and Works* [1578], *Second Week, Third Day, pt. II*
You must take the will for the deed. — SWIFT, *Polite Conversation* [1738], *Dialogue 2*

[4] While you live, tell truth and shame the devil! — SHAKESPEARE, *Henry IV, pt. I* [1597–1598], *act III, sc. i, l. 58*
I'd tell the truth, and shame the devil. — SAMUEL JOHNSON; from BOSWELL, *Life of Johnson* [1791], *vol. I, p. 460* (Everyman edition)
Truth being truth, / Tell it and shame the devil. — BROWNING, *The Ring and the Book* [1868–1869], *III, The Other Half-Rome*

[5] See Shakespeare, 189:33.
As clear and as manifest as the nose in a man's face. — ROBERT BURTON, *Anatomy of Melancholy* [1621–1651], *pt. III, sec. 3, member 4, subsec. I*

[6] See Garrick, 363:16.

[7] They were suffered to have rope enough till they had haltered themselves. — THOMAS FULLER, *The Historie of the Holy Warre* [1639], *bk. 5, ch. 7*
Give a man enough rope and he'll hang himself. — *Proverb*

[8] As like as one pease is to another. — JOHN LYLY, *Euphues* [1579]
They say we are / Almost as like as eggs. — SHAKESPEARE, *The Winter's Tale* [1608–1611], *act I, sc. ii, l. 130*
As one egg is like another. — CERVANTES, *Don Quixote, pt. II* [1615], *bk. III, ch. 14*

[9] Je m'en vais chercher un grand peut-être; tirez le rideau, la farce est jouée.
His religion, at best, is an anxious wish; like that of Rabelais, "a great Perhaps." — CARLYLE, *Essays, Burns* [1828]
The grand perhaps. — BROWNING, *Bishop Blougram's Apology* [1855]
See Leoncavallo, 686:4.

[10] John Heywood's *Proverbs*, first printed in 1546, is the earliest collection of English colloquial sayings. The selection here given is from the edition of 1874 (a reprint of 1598), edited by JULIAN SHARMAN.
See also *Oxford Dictionary of English Proverbs* [2nd edition, 1948], compiled by WILLIAM G. SMITH and revised by PAUL HARVEY, and *A Dictionary of the Proverbs in English in the 16th and 17th Centuries* [1950], compiled by MORRIS PALMER TILLEY.

[11] The earliest known of the "willow" songs (see Shakespeare, 232:8).

[12] This line is the theme of many poems.

[13] Let the world slide. — *Towneley Mysteries* [1420].
Let the world slide. — SHAKESPEARE, *The Taming of the Shrew* [1593–1594]. *Induction, sc. i, l. 6*

[14] In wikked haste is no profit. — CHAUCER, *The Canterbury Tales* [c. 1387], *Melibee, 2240*
See Publilius Syrus, 111:21, and Chaucer, 147:25.

[15] Thou shouldst have looked before thou hadst leapt. — JONSON, CHAPMAN, MARSTON, *Eastward Ho* [1605], *act V, sc. i*
See Samuel Butler, 291:23.

[16] Between two stools one sits on the ground. — *Les Proverbes del Vilain*, MS Bodleian [c. 1303]

1 The fat is in the fire. *Ib.*

2 When the sun shineth, make hay. *Ib.*

3 The tide tarrieth no man.[1] *Ib.*

4 Fast bind, fast find.[2] *Ib.*

5 And while I at length debate and beat the bush,
There shall step in other men and catch the birds.[3] *Ib.*

6 Wedding is destiny,
And hanging likewise.[4] *Ib.*

7 Happy man, happy dole.[5] *Ib.*

8 God never send'th mouth but he sendeth meat.[6] *Ib. 4*

9 A hard beginning maketh a good ending. *Ib.*

10 Like will to like.[7] *Ib.*

11 When the sky falleth we shall have larks. *Ib.*

12 More afraid than hurt. *Ib.*

13 Nothing is impossible to a willing heart. *Ib.*

14 Let the world wag, and take mine ease in mine inn. *Ib. 5*

15 Hold their noses to grindstone. *Ib.*

[1]See Chaucer, 147:17.
Time nor tide tarrieth no man.—ROBERT GREENE, *Disputations* [1592]
Hoist up sail while gale doth last, / Tide and wind stay no man's pleasure.—ROBERT SOUTHWELL, *St. Peter's Complaint* [1595]
Nae man can tether time or tide.—BURNS, *Tam o' Shanter* [1787]

[2]Dry sun, dry wind; / Safe bind, safe find.—THOMAS TUSSER, *A Hundred Good Points of Husbandry* [1557], *October's Abstract, Washing*
Fast bind, fast find; / A proverb never stale in thrifty mind.—SHAKESPEARE, *The Merchant of Venice* [1596–1597], *act II, sc. v, l. 54*

[3]It is this proverb which Henry V is reported to have uttered at the siege of Orléans: Shall I beat the bush and another take the bird?

[4]Hanging and wiving go by destiny.—*The Schole-hous for Women* [1541]
Marriage and hanging go by destiny; matches are made in heaven.—ROBERT BURTON, *Anatomy of Melancholy* [1621–1651], *pt. III, sec. 2, member 5, subsec. 5*
See Lyly, 176:3.

[5]Happy man be his dole.—SHAKESPEARE, *The Merry Wives of Windsor* [1600–1601], *act III, sc. iv, l. 68*, and *The Winter's Tale* [1609–1611], *act I, sc. ii, l. 163*

[6]God sendeth and giveth both mouth and the meat. —THOMAS TUSSER, *A Hundred Good Points of Husbandry* [1557]
God sends meat, and the Devil sends cooks.—JOHN TAYLOR, *Works* [1630], *vol. II, p. 85*
The holy prophet Zoroaster said, / The Lord who made thy teeth shall give thee bread.—*Persian couplet*

[7]See *Ecclesiasticus 13:16,* 35:26; Homer, 60:21; and Robert Burton, 259:17.

16 A sleeveless errand.[8] *Ib. 7*

17 Reckoners without their host must reckon twice.[9] *Ib. 8*

18 Cut my coat after my cloth. *Ib.*

19 The nearer to the church, the further from God.[10] *Ib. 9*

20 Now for good luck, cast an old shoe after me. *Ib.*

21 Better is to bow than break.[11] *Ib.*

22 It hurteth not the tongue to give fair words.[12] *Ib.*

23 Two heads are better than one. *Ib.*

24 A short horse is soon curried. *Ib. 10*

25 To tell tales out of school. *Ib.*

26 To hold with the hare and run with the hound. *Ib.*

27 Neither fish nor flesh, nor good red herring. *Ib.*

28 All is well that ends well.[13] *Ib.*

29 Of a good beginning cometh a good end.[14] *Ib.*

30 When the steed is stolen, shut the stable door.[15] *Ib.*

31 She looketh as butter would not melt in her mouth. *Ib.*

32 Ill weed groweth fast.[16] *Ib.*

[8]Chaucer and Shakespeare use the phrase.
Sending every one of her children upon some sleeveless errand, as she terms it.—JOSEPH ADDISON, *The Spectator, no. 47* [April 24, 1711] (referring to April Fool errands)

[9]He reckoneth without his hostess. Love knoweth no laws.—JOHN LYLY, *Euphues* [1579]

[10]Qui est près de l'église est souvent loin de Dieu [He who is near the Church is often far from God].—*Les Proverbes Communs* [c. 1500]
See Spenser, 173:6.

[11]Rather to bow than break is profitable: / Humility is a thing commendable.—*The Moral Proverbs of Cristyne* [1390]

[12]Fair words never hurt the tongue.—JONSON, CHAPMAN, MARSTON, *Eastward Ho* [1605], *act IV, sc. i*

[13]Si finis bonus est, totum bonum erit [If the end is good, all will be good].—*Gesta Romanorum* [1472], *tale 67*
See Anonymous Latin, 133:26; Shakespeare, 227:5 and 227:18; Herrick, 266:4; and Quarles, 267:18.

[14]See Plato, 84:8; Aristotle, 88:11; and Horace, 108:20.
Who that well his warke beginneth, / The rather a good end he winneth.—JOHN GOWER, *Confessio Amantis* [c. 1386–1390]

[15]Quant le cheval est emblé dounke ferme fols l'estable [When the horse has been stolen, the fool shuts the stable]. —*Les Proverbes del Vilain* [c. 1303]

[16]Ewyl weed ys sone y-growe.—*MS Harleian* [c. 1490]
Great weeds do grow apace.—SHAKESPEARE, *Richard III* [1592–1593], *act II, sc. iv, l. 13*
An ill weed grows apace.—GEORGE CHAPMAN, *An Humorous Day's Mirth* [1599]

1 It is a dear collop
That is cut out of th' own flesh.[1] *Ib.*

2 Beggars should be no choosers. *Ib.*

3 Merry as a cricket. *Ib. 11*

4 To rob Peter and pay Paul.[2] *Ib.*

5 A man may well bring a horse to the water,
But he cannot make him drink without he will.[3] *Ib.*

6 Kinde will creep where it may not go.[4] *Ib.*

7 The cat would eat fish, and would not wet her feet.[5] *Ib.*

8 Rome was not built in one day. *Ib.*

9 Ye have many strings to your bow.[6] *Ib.*

10 Children learn to creep ere they can learn to go. *Ib.*

11 Better is half a loaf than no bread. *Ib.*

12 Nought venture nought have.[7] *Ib.*

13 Children and fools cannot lie.[8] *Ib.*

14 All is fish that cometh to net.[9] *Ib.*

15 Who is worse shod than the shoemaker's wife?[10] *Ib.*

16 One good turn asketh another. *Ib.*

17 A dog hath a day. *Ib.*

18 A hair of the dog that bit us.[11] *Ib.*

19 But in deed,
A friend is never known till a man have need.[12] *Ib.*

20 Burnt child fire dreadeth.[13] *Ib. 2*

21 There is no fool to the old fool.[14] *Ib.*

22 All is not gospel that thou dost speak. *Ib.*

23 A fool's bolt is soon shot.[15] *Ib. 3*

24 A woman hath nine lives like a cat. *Ib. 4*

25 A penny for your thought. *Ib.*

26 You cannot see the wood for the trees. *Ib.*

27 You stand in your own light. *Ib.*

28 Tit for tat.[16] *Ib.*

29 Three may keep counsel, if two be away.[17] *Ib. 5*

30 Small pitchers have wide ears.[18] *Ib.*

31 Many hands make light work. *Ib.*

32 Out of God's blessing into the warm sun.[19] *Ib.*

33 There is no fire without some smoke.[20] *Ib.*

34 A cat may look on a king. *Ib.*

[1] God knows thou art a collop of my flesh.—SHAKESPEARE, *Henry VI, Part I* [1591], *act V, sc. iv, l. 18*

[2] Give not Saint Peter so much, to leave Saint Paul nothing.—GEORGE HERBERT, *Jacula Prudentum* [1640]

"To rob Peter and pay Paul" is said to have had its origin in the reign of Edward VI when the lands of St. Peter at Westminster were appropriated to raise money for the repair of St. Paul's in London.

The French form of the proverb is: Découvrir saint Pierre pour couvrir saint Paul.

[3] You may bring a horse to the river, but he will drink when and what he pleaseth.—GEORGE HERBERT, *Jacula Prudentum* [1640]

[4] You know that love / Will creep in service when it cannot go.—SHAKESPEARE, *Two Gentlemen of Verona* [1594–1595], *act IV, sc. ii, l. 19*

[5] Cat lufat visch, ac he nele his feth wete.—*MS Trinity College, Cambridge* [c. 1250]

See Shakespeare, 237:2.

[6] Two strings to his bow.—RICHARD HOOKER, *Laws of Ecclesiastical Polity, bk. V* [1597], *ch. 80*

[7] See Chaucer, 145:1, and W. S. Gilbert, 629:2.

[8] 'Tis an old saw, children and fools speak true.—JOHN LYLY, *Endymion* [1591]

[9] All's fish they get that cometh to net.—TUSSER, *A Hundred Good Points of Husbandry* [1557], *February Abstract*

[10] Him that makes shoes go barefoot himself.—ROBERT BURTON, *Anatomy of Melancholy* [1621–1651], *Democritus to the Reader*

[11] Old receipt books advised that an inebriate should drink sparingly in the morning some of the same kind of liquor which he had drunk to excess the night before.

[12] See Aristotle, 88:20; Cicero, 99:6; Publilius Syrus, 112:10; and Ovid, 113:28.

[13] Brend child fur dredth, / Quoth Hendyng.—*Proverbs of Hendyng, MS* [c. 1320]

[14] There is no fool like an old fool.—JOHN LYLY, *Mother Bombie* [1592], *act IV, sc. ii*, and in frequent use thereafter.

[15] Sottes bolt is sone shotte.—*Proverbs of Hendyng, MS* [c. 1320]

[16] This is a corruption of *Tant pour tant.*

See *Song of Roland,* 136:13.

[17] Two may keep counsel when the third's away.—SHAKESPEARE, *Titus Andronicus* [1593–1594], *act IV, sc. ii, l. 145*

Three can hold their peace if two be away.—GEORGE HERBERT, *Jacula Prudentum* [1640]

[18] Pitchers have ears.—SHAKESPEARE, *The Taming of the Shrew* [1593–1594], *act IV, sc. iv, l. 52*, and *Richard III* [1592–1593], *act II, sc. iv, l. 37*

Little pitchers have wide ears.—GEORGE HERBERT, *Jacula Prudentum* [1640]

[19] Thou shalt come out of a warm sun into God's blessing.—JOHN LYLY, *Euphues* [1579]

Thou out of Heaven's benediction comest / To the warm sun.—SHAKESPEARE, *King Lear* [1605–1606], *act II, sc. ii, l. 168*

[20] There can no great smoke arise, but there must be some fire.—LYLY, *Euphues* [1579]

1 Have ye him on the hip.[1] *Ib.*

2 Much water goeth by the mill
That the miller knoweth not of.[2] *Ib.*

3 He must needs go whom the devil doth drive. *Ib. 7*

4 Set the cart before the horse. *Ib.*

5 The more the merrier. *Ib.*

6 It is better to be
An old man's darling than a young man's
warling. *Ib.*

7 Be the day never so long,
Evermore at last they ring to even-song.[3]
Ib.

8 The moon is made of a green cheese.[4]
Ib.

9 I know on which side my bread is buttered.
Ib.

10 The wrong sow by th' ear. *Ib. 9*

11 An ill wind that bloweth no man to good.[5]
Ib.

12 For when I gave you an inch, you took an ell.[6] *Ib.*

13 Would ye both eat your cake and have your cake?[7] *Ib.*

14 Every man for himself and God for us all.[8]
Ib.

15 Though he love not to buy the pig in the poke.[9] *Ib.*

[1] See Shakespeare, 198:20 and 200:18.

[2] More water glideth by the mill / Than wots the miller of. — SHAKESPEARE, *Titus Andronicus* [1593–1594], *act II, sc. i, l. 85*

The miller sees not all the water that goes by his mill. — ROBERT BURTON, *Anatomy of Melancholy* [1621–1651], *pt. III, sec. 3, member 4, subsec. 1*

[3] Be the day short or never so long, / At length it ringeth to evensong. — *Quoted at the stake by George Tankerfield* [1555]. From JOHN FOXE, *Actes and Monuments (The Book of Martyrs)* [1563], *ch. 7*

[4] They would make me believe that the moon was made of green cheese. — JOHN FRITH, *A Pistle to the Christian Reader* [1529]

[5] Except wind stands as never it stood, / It is an ill wind turns none to good. — THOMAS TUSSER [c. 1524–1580], *A Description of the Properties of Winds*

Falstaff. What wind blew you hither, Pistol?
Pistol. Not the ill wind which blows no man to good. — SHAKESPEARE, *Henry IV, Part II* [1597–1598], *act V, sc. iii, l. 87*

[6] Give an inch, he'll take an ell. — JOHN WEBSTER [c. 1580–c. 1625], *Sir Thomas Wyatt*

[7] Wouldst thou both eat thy cake and have it? — GEORGE HERBERT, *The Size* [1633]

[8] Every man for himself, his own ends, the Devil for all. — ROBERT BURTON, *Anatomy of Melancholy* [1621–1651], *pt. III, sec. 1, member 3*

[9] For buying or selling of pig in a poke. — TUSSER, *A Hundred Good Points of Husbandry* [1557], *September Abstract*

16 This hitteth the nail on the head.
Ib. 11

17 Enough is as good as a feast. *Ib.*

Charles V[10]

1500–1558

18 Fortune hath somewhat the nature of a woman; if she be too much wooed, she is the farther off.
From FRANCIS BACON, *The Advancement of Learning [1605], bk. II*

19 Iron hand in a velvet glove.
Attributed. From THOMAS CARLYLE, *Latter-Day Pamphlets, 11*

20 I make war on the living, not on the dead.
Said when advised to hang Luther's corpse on the gallows [1546]

Pope Gregory XIII

1502–1585

21 To the greater glory of God.[11]
From The Canons and Decrees of the Council of Trent [1542–1560]

Sir Thomas Wyatt

c. 1503–1542

22 Forget not yet the tried intent
Of such a truth as I have meant;
My great travail so gladly spent,
Forget not yet! *Forget Not Yet*

23 And wilt thou leave me thus?
Say nay, say nay, for shame!
The Appeal

24 My lute, awake! perform the last
Labor that thou and I shall waste,
And end that I have now begun;
For when this song is sung and past,
My lute, be still, for I have done.
The Lover Complaineth the Unkindness of His Love

25 They flee from me, that sometime did me
seek
With naked foot, stalking in my chamber.
The Lover Showeth How He Is Forsaken of Such as He Sometime Enjoyed

[10] See Lomonosov, 357:19.

[11] Ad maiorem Dei gloriam. Motto of the Society of Jesus.

John Knox
1505–1572

1 The First Blast of the Trumpet Against the Monstrous Regiment [Regimen] of Women.
Title of pamphlet [1558]

2 A man with God is always in the majority.[1]
Inscription on Reformation Monument, Geneva, Switzerland

John Bradford
1510–1555

3 The familiar story, that, on seeing evildoers taken to the place of execution, he was wont to exclaim: "But for the grace of God there goes John Bradford," is a universal tradition, which has overcome the lapse of time.[2]
Biographical notice, Parker Society edition, The Writings of John Bradford [1853]

Sir Thomas Vaux
1510–1556

4 Companion none is like
Unto the mind alone;
For many have been harmed by speech,
Through thinking, few or none.
Of a Contented Mind [1557]

5 I loathe that I did love,
In youth that I thought sweet,
As time requires for my behove,
Methinks they are not meet.
The Aged Lover Renounceth Love, st. 1

6 But age, with his stealing steps,
Hath clawed me in his clutch.[3] *Ib. 3*

Richard Grafton
d. 1572

7 Thirty days hath November,
April, June, and September,
February hath twenty-eight alone,
And all the rest have thirty-one.[4]
Chronicles of England [1562]

Mary Tudor
1516–1558

8 When I am dead and opened, you shall find "Calais" lying in my heart.[5]
From HOLINSHED, *Chronicles [1577], III, 1160*

Ambroise Paré
1517–1590

9 I treated him, God cured him.[6]
His favorite saying

Joachim du Bellay
1522–1560

10 Happy he who like Ulysses has made a glorious voyage.[7]
Les Regrets [1559], XXXI

Luiz Vaz de Camões [Camoëns]
c. 1524–1580

11 The Strait that shall forever bear his name.
The Lusiads [1572], in reference to FERDINAND MAGELLAN'S *discovery of the strait [October 21, 1520]*

Pierre de Ronsard
1524–1585

12 When you are old, at evening candlelit,
Beside the fire bending to your wool,
Read out my verse and murmur, "Ronsard writ
This praise for me when I was beautiful."[8]
Sonnets pour Hélène, I, 43

13 Live now, believe me, wait not till tomorrow;
Gather the roses of life today.[9] *Ib.*

---

[1] Un homme avec Dieu est toujours dans la majorité.
See Phillips, 538:14.

[2] There but for the grace of God goes God.—*Anonymous saying, attributed to* ORSON WELLES, *among others*

[3] Quoted by First Clown in SHAKESPEARE, *Hamlet* [1600–1601], *act V, sc. i, l. 77.*

[4] Thirty days hath September, / April, June, and November; / All the rest have thirty-one, / Excepting February alone, / Which hath but twenty-eight, in fine, / Till leap year gives it twenty-nine.—*Common in the New England states*

Compare the old Latin class mnemonic:

In March, July, October, May, / The Ides are on the fifteenth day, / The Nones the seventh: all other months besides / Have two days less for Nones and Ides.

[5] See Browning, 542:7.

[6] Je le soignay, Dieu le guérit.

[7] Heureux qui, comme Ulysse, a fait un beau voyage.

[8] Quand vous serez bien vieille, au soir à la chandelle, / Assise auprès du feu, devidant et filant, / Direz, chantant mes vers, en vous émerveillant: / "Ronsard me célébrait du temps que j'étais belle."

Translated by HUMBERT WOLFE.

See the adaptation by Yeats: When you are old and gray and full of sleep, 712:8.

[9] Vivez, si m'en croyez, n'attendez à demain: / Cueillez des aujourd'hui les roses de la vie.

See *The Wisdom of Solomon 2:8*, 34:11; Horace, 107:8; Spenser, 173:14; and Herrick, 266:11.

1 Gather, gather your youth:
Just like this flower, old age
Your beauty will wither.[1]
Odes, I, 17. À Cassandre

Thomas Tusser
c. 1524–1580

2 At Christmas play and make good cheer,
For Christmas comes but once a year.
A Hundred Good Points of Husbandry [1557]. The Farmer's Daily Diet

3 Such mistress, such Nan,
Such master, such man.[2]
Ib. April's Abstract

4 Sweet April showers
Do spring May flowers.
Ib. April's Husbandry

5 Who goeth a-borrowing
Goeth a-sorrowing. *Ib. June's Abstract*

6 'Tis merry in hall
Where beards wag all.[3]
Ib. August's Abstract

Pieter Bruegel
c. 1525–1569

7 Because the world is so faithless,
I go my way in mourning.[4]
Inscription in MOLIÈRE, *The Misanthrope [1568]*

Gabriel Meurier
1530–1601

8 He who excuses himself accuses himself.[5]
Trésor des Sentences

William Stevenson
c. 1530–1575

9 I cannot eat but little meat,
My stomach is not good;
But sure I think that I can drink
With him that wears a hood.
Gammer Gurton's Needle [c. 1573], drinking song, act II

10 Back and side go bare, go bare,
Both foot and hand go cold;
But, belly, God send thee good ale enough,
Whether it be new or old. *Ib. refrain*

Henri Estienne
c. 1531–1598

11 Si jeunesse savait, si vieillesse pouvait [If youth but knew, if old age but could].
Les Prémices [1594]

12 God tempers the wind to the shorn lamb.[6]
Ib.

Elizabeth I
1533–1603

13 The use of the sea and air is common to all; neither can a title to the ocean belong to any people or private persons, forasmuch as neither nature nor public use and custom permit any possession thereof.
To the Spanish Ambassador [1580]

14 My care is like my shadow in the sun—
Follows me flying—flies when I pursue it.
On the departure of Alençon [1582]

15 I know I have the body of a weak and feeble woman, but I have the heart and stomach of a king, and of a king of England too; and think foul scorn that Parma or Spain, or any prince of Europe, should dare to invade the borders of my realm.
Speech to the troops at Tilbury on the approach of the Armada [1588]

16 I am your anointed Queen. I will never be by violence constrained to do anything. I thank God I am endued with such qualities that if I were turned out of the Realm in my petticoat I were able to live in any place in Christendom.
From CHAMBERLIN, *Sayings of Queen Elizabeth*

17 I will make you shorter by the head.
Ib.

18 The daughter of debate, that eke discord doth sow.[7] *Ib.*

19 [To the Countess of Nottingham] God may forgive you, but I never can.
From HUME, *History of England Under the House of Tudor, vol. II, ch. 7*

[1] Cueillez, cueillez votre jeunesse: / Comme à cette fleur, la vieillesse / Fera ternir votre beauté.

[2] Tel maître, tel valet.—*Attributed to* PIERRE TERRÀIL, SEIGNEUR DE BAYARD [c. 1473–1524], *known as the* CHEVALIER BAYARD

[3] Merry swithe it is in halle, / When the beards 'waveth alle.—*Life of Alexander* [1312]

[4] Om dat de werelt is soe ongetru / Daer om gha ic in den ru.

[5] Qui s'excuse, s'accuse.
See Shakespeare, 197:21, and 202:6.

[6] Dieu mesure le froid à la brebis tondue.
See Laurence Sterne, 360:25.

[7] Mary, Queen of Scots.

1 Though God hath raised me high, yet this I count the glory of my crown: that I have reigned with your loves.
The Golden Speech [1601]

2 Semper eadem [Ever the same].
Motto

3 I am no lover of pompous title, but only desire that my name may be recorded in a line or two, which shall briefly express my name, my virginity, the years of my reign, the reformation of religion under it, and my preservation of peace.
To her ladies, discussing her epitaph

4 'Twas God the word that spake it,
He took the Bread and brake it;
And what the word did make it,
That I believe, and take it.[1]
From S. Clarke, Marrow of Ecclesiastical History [ed. 1675], pt. II, Life of Queen Elizabeth

Michel Eyquem de Montaigne[2]

1533–1592

5 I want to be seen here in my simple, natural, ordinary fashion, without straining or artifice; for it is myself that I portray. . . . I am myself the matter of my book.[3]
Essays,[4] bk. I [1580], To the Reader

6 Truly man is a marvelously vain, diverse, and undulating object. It is hard to found any constant and uniform judgment on him.[5]
Ib. ch. 1

7 The thing I fear most is fear.[6]
Ib. 18

8 I want death to find me planting my cabbages.[7]
Ib. 20

9 He who would teach men to die would teach them to live.[8] *Ib.*

10 Live as long as you please, you will strike nothing off the time you will have to spend dead.[9] *Ib.*

11 Wherever your life ends, it is all there. The advantage of living is not measured by length, but by use; some men have lived long, and lived little; attend to it while you are in it. It lies in your will, not in the number of years, for you to have lived enough. *Ib.*

12 I do not speak the minds of others except to speak my own mind better. *Ib. 26*

13 Since I would rather make of him [the child] an able man than a learned man, I would also urge that care be taken to choose a guide [tutor] with a well-made rather than a well-filled head.[10] *Ib.*

14 If you press me to say why I loved him, I can say no more than it was because he was he and I was I.[11] *Ib. 28*

15 Nothing is so firmly believed as what is least known. *Ib. 32*

16 A man of understanding has lost nothing, if he has himself.[12] *Ib. 39*

17 We must reserve a back shop all our own,[13] entirely free, in which to establish our real liberty and our principal retreat and solitude. *Ib.*

18 The greatest thing in the world is to know how to belong to oneself.[14] *Ib.*

19 It is a thorny undertaking, and more so than it seems, to follow a movement so wandering as that of our mind, to penetrate the opaque depths of its innermost folds, to pick out and immobilize the innumerable flutterings that agitate it.[15] *Ib. II [1580], 6*

[1] Answer on being asked her opinion of Christ's presence in the Sacrament.

[2] Translated by Donald M. Frame.

[3] Je veux qu'on m'y voit en ma façon simple, naturelle, et ordinaire, sans étude et artifice; car c'est moi que je peins. . . . Je suis moi-même la matière de mon livre.

[4] Books I and II of the *Essays* were published in 1580; republished [1588] with the addition of book III and with many interpolations in books I and II; the whole republished posthumously [1595], incorporating material based on Montaigne's marginal annotations in the 1588 edition.

This book of Montaigne the world has endorsed by translating it into all tongues. — Emerson, *Representative Men* [1850], *Montaigne*

[5] Certes, c'est un subject [sic] merveilleusement vain, divers, et ondoyant, que l'homme. Il est malaisé d'y fonder jugement constant et uniforme.

[6] C'est de quoi j'ai le plus de peur que la peur.

See *Proverbs 3:25*, 23:6; Bacon, 179:13; Wellington, 421:10; Thoreau, 557:9; and Roosevelt, 779:10.

[7] Je veux que la mort me trouve plantant mes choux.

See Rabelais, 158:4, and Voltaire, 343:14.

[8] I have taught you, my dear flock, for above thirty years how to live, and I will show you in a very short time how to die. — Sir Edwin Sandys [1561–1629], *Anglorum Speculum*

Teach him how to live, / And, oh still harder lesson! how to die. — Beilby Porteus [1731–1808], *Death, l. 316*

In teaching me the way to live / It taught me how to die. — George Pope Morris [1802–1864], *My Mother's Bible, st. 4*

[9] See Lucretius, 101:5.

[10] Plutôt la tête bien faite que bien pleine.

[11] Parce que c'était lui; parce que c'était moi.

Translated by Charles Cotton, revised by Hazlitt and Wight.

[12] L'homme d'entendement n'a rien perdu, s'il a soi-même.

[13] Il se faut réserver une arrière boutique toute notre.

[14] La plus grande chose du monde, c'est de savoir être à soi.

See Ibsen, 599:21.

[15] C'est une épineuse entreprise, et plus qu'il ne semble, de suivre une allure si vagabonde que celle de nôtre esprit; de pénétrer les profondeurs opaques de ses replis internes; de choisir et arrêter tant de menus de ses agitations.

1 My trade and my art is living.[1] *Ib.*

2 The easy, gentle, and sloping path . . . is not the path of true virtue. It demands a rough and thorny road. *Ib. 11*

3 When I play with my cat, who knows if I am not a pastime to her more than she is to me? *Ib. 12*

4 The souls of emperors and cobblers are cast in the same mold. . . . The same reason that makes us bicker with a neighbor creates a war between princes. *Ib.*

5 Their [the Skeptics'] way of speaking is: "I settle nothing . . . I do not understand it . . . Nothing seems true that may not seem false." Their sacramental word is Επεχω, which is to say, I suspend my judgment.[2] *Ib.*

6 This notion [skepticism] is more clearly understood by asking "What do I know?"[3] *Ib.*

7 Man is certainly crazy. He could not make a mite, and he makes gods by the dozen.[4] *Ib.*

8 What of a truth that is bounded by these mountains and is falsehood to the world that lives beyond?[5] *Ib.*

9 Those who have compared our life to a dream were right. . . . We sleeping wake, and waking sleep.[6] *Ib.*

[1] Mon métier et mon art, c'est vivre.

[2] Je suspends mon jugement.

Translated by E. J. TRECHMAN.

Greek word (*epecho*) inscribed on a bay in Montaigne's library.—MAURICE RAT, *Oeuvres Complètes de Montaigne, La Pléiade Edition* [1962], *note*

This is one of a dozen maxims from Sextus Empiricus, third-century Greek philosopher, which together with Biblical and Latin quotations comprise the fifty-seven sentences painted on the roof bays of Montaigne's library. About two thirds of the sentences are in *Apologie de Raimond Sebond* (chapter 12 of book II of the *Essays*).

See also the next quotation (Montaigne, 165:6).

[3] Que sais-je?

Translated by E. J. TRECHMAN.

This phrase appeared on a medal Montaigne had struck, which showed also his coat of arms and the collar of the order of St. Michael, and on the reverse side a pair of scales in perfect balance, the date [1576], his age (forty-two), and the Skeptics' motto Επεχω (see Montaigne, 165:5).

[4] L'homme est bien insensé. Il ne saurait forger un ciron, et forge des Dieux à douzaines.

[5] Quelle vérité que ces montagnes bornent, qui est mensonge qui se tient au delà?

[6] Ceux qui ont apparié notre vie à un songe ont eu de la raison. . . . Nous veillons dormants et veillants dormons.

Translated by E. J. TRECHMAN.

See Euripides, 77:21; Aristophanes, 82:21; and Calderón de la Barca, 273:2.

10 How many valiant men we have seen to survive their own reputation![7] *Ib. 16*

11 A man may be humble through vainglory. *Ib. 17*

12 I find that the best goodness I have has some tincture of vice. *Ib. 20*

13 Saying is one thing and doing is another. *Ib. 31*

14 There were never in the world two opinions alike, any more than two hairs or two grains. Their most universal quality is diversity. *Ib. 37*

15 I will follow the good side right to the fire, but not into it if I can help it. *Ib. III [1595], 1*

16 I speak the truth, not my fill of it, but as much as I dare speak; and I dare to do so a little more as I grow old. *Ib.*

17 Few men have been admired by their own households.[8] *Ib.*

18 Every man bears the whole stamp of the human condition.[9] *Ib.*

19 It [marriage] happens as with cages: the birds without despair to get in, and those within despair of getting out.[10] *Ib. 5*

20 Everyone recognizes me in my book, and my book in me. *Ib.*

21 It takes so much to be a king that he exists only as such. That extraneous glare that surrounds him hides him and conceals him from us; our sight breaks and is dissipated by it, being filled and arrested by this strong light.[11] *Ib. 7*

[7] See Bentley, 319:2.

[8] See Antigonus, 88:26.

[9] Chaque homme porte la forme, entière de l'humaîne condition.

Translated by CHARLES COTTON, revised by HAZLITT and WIGHT.

[10] Translated by CHARLES COTTON, revised by HAZLITT and WIGHT.

I myself have loved a lady and pursued her with a great deal of under-age protestation, whom some three or four gallants that have enjoyed would with all their hearts have been glad to have been rid of. 'Tis just like a summer bird-cage in a garden: the birds that are without despair to get in, and the birds that are within despair and are in a consumption for fear they shall never get out.—JOHN WEBSTER, *The White Devil* [1612], *act I, sc. ii*

Wedlock, indeed, hath oft comparèd been / To public feasts, where meet a public rout— / Where they that are without would fain go in, / And they that are within would fain go out.—SIR JOHN DAVIES [1569–1626], *Contention Betwixt a Wife, etc.*

See Emerson, 498:18.

[11] See Shakespeare, 223:27, and Tennyson, 534:1.

1 Our wisdom and deliberation for the most part follow the lead of chance.[1] *Ib. 8*

2 Not because Socrates said so,[2] but because it is in truth my own disposition—and perchance to some excess—I look upon all men as my compatriots, and embrace a Pole as a Frenchman, making less account of the national than of the universal and common bond.[3] *Ib. 9*

3 There is no man so good that if he placed all his actions and thoughts under the scrutiny of the laws, he would not deserve hanging ten times in his life.[4] *Ib.*

4 A man must be a little mad if he does not want to be even more stupid.[5] *Ib.*

5 I have seen no more evident monstrosity and miracle in the world than myself. *Ib. 11*

6 I have here only made a nosegay of culled flowers, and have brought nothing of my own but the thread that ties them together.[6] *Ib. 12*

7 It is more of a job to interpret the interpretations than to interpret the things, and there are more books about books than about any other subject: we do nothing but write glosses about each other. *Ib. 13*

8 For truth itself does not have the privilege to be employed at any time and in every way; its use, noble as it is, has its circumscriptions and limits. *Ib.*

9 No matter that we may mount on stilts, we still must walk on our own legs. And on the highest throne in the world, we still sit only on our own bottom.[7] *Ib.*

[1] Although men flatter themselves with their great actions, they are not so often the result of great design as of chance.—La Rochefoucauld [1613–1680], *Maxim 57*

[2] See Socrates, 79:7.

[3] Translated by Charles Cotton, revised by Hazlitt and Wight.
See Montesquieu, 341:10.

[4] See Shakespeare, 221:5.

[5] See Menander, 91:2; Horace, 108:15; Bacon, 181:3; and Linnaeus, 350:7.

[6] Translated by Charles Cotton, revised by Hazlitt and Wight.
I am but a gatherer and disposer of other men's stuff, at my best value.—Sir Henry Wotton, *The Elements of Architecture* [1624], *preface*
John Bartlett used this passage as an epigraph for the fourth edition of *Familiar Quotations* [1864].

[7] Si, avons nous beau monter sur des échasses, car sur des échasses encore faut-il marcher de nos jambes. Et au plus élevé trône du monde, si ne sommes assis que sur notre cul.
Translated by Walter Kaiser.
See Bunyan, 301:23.

10 Let us give Nature a chance; she knows her business better than we do. *Ib.*

William I [William the Silent]

1533–1584

11 My God, have mercy on my soul and on my poor people.[8]
Last words as he fell under an assassin's bullets

William Butler[9]

1535–1618

12 It is unseasonable and unwholesome in all months that have not an *r* in their name to eat an oyster.
Dyet's Dry Dinner [1599]

Sir Humphrey Gilbert

c. 1539–1583

13 We are as near to heaven by sea as by land![10]
From Hakluyt, Voyages, vol. III [1600], p. 159

William Gilbert

1540–1603

14 Philosophy is for the few.[11]
De Magnete (On the Magnet) [1600]

15 In the discovery of secret things and in the investigation of hidden causes, stronger reasons are obtained from sure experiments and demonstrated arguments than from probable conjectures and the opinions of philosophical speculators of the common sort.[11] *Ib.*

[8] Mon Dieu, ayez pitié de mon âme et de mon pauvre peuple.

[9] Styled by Thomas Fuller in his *Worthies of England* [1662], the "Aesculapius of our age."
See Walton, 271:10.

[10] The way to heaven out of all places is of like length and distance.—Sir Thomas More, *Utopia* [1516]
Gilbert, on the last day of his life, was seen in his tiny pinnace *Squirrel* with a book in hand, probably More's *Utopia*, which inspired his last utterance. He was homeward bound from Newfoundland, which he had just taken possession of in the name of the queen [August 1583].
"Do not fear! Heaven is as near," / He said, "by water as by land!"—Longfellow, *Sir Humphrey Gilbert* [1849], *st. 6*
See Robert Burton, 259:12, and James T. Fields, 556:15.

[11] Translated by P. F. Mottelay.

St. John of the Cross [San Juan de la Cruz]

1542–1591

1 The Dark Night of the Soul.[1]

Title of treatise [c. 1583] based on his poem[2] Songs of the Soul Which Rejoices at Having Reached . . . Union with God by the Road of Spiritual Negation [c. 1578]

Mary Stuart [Mary, Queen of Scots]

1542–1587

2 In my end is my beginning. *Motto*

3 O Lord my God, I have trusted in thee;
O Jesu my dearest one, now set me free.
In prison's oppression, in sorrow's obsession,
I weary for thee.
With sighing and crying bowed down as dying,
I adore thee, I implore thee, set me free![3]

Prayer written in her Book of Devotion before her execution

Jan Zamoyski

1542–1605

4 The king reigns, but does not govern.[4]

Speech in the Polish Parliament [1605], referring to King Sigismund III

Sir Edward Dyer

c. 1543–1607

5 My mind to me a kingdom is;
Such present joys therein I find
That it excels all other bliss
That earth affords or grows by kind:
Though much I want which most would have,
Yet still my mind forbids to crave.

Rawlinson Poetry MS 85,[5] p. 17

6 Some have too much, yet still do crave;
I little have, and seek no more. *Ib.*

7 Fain would I, but I dare not; I dare, and yet I may not;
I may, although I care not, for pleasure when I play not.

Fain Would I (attributed)

Guillaume de Salluste, Seigneur Du Bartas

1544–1590

8 Oft seen in forehead of the frowning skies.[6]

Divine Weeks and Works [1578], First Week, Second Day

9 For where's the state beneath the firmament
That doth excel the bees for government?[7]

Ib. Fifth Day, pt. 1

10 These lovely lamps, these windows of the soul.[8] *Ib. Sixth Day*

11 Or almost like a spider, who, confined
In her web's center, shakt with every wind,
Moves in an instant if the buzzing fly
Stir but a string of her lawn canapie.[9]

Ib.

12 Living from hand to mouth.

Ib. Second Week, First Day, pt. 4

13 In the jaws of death.[10] *Ib.*

14 Only that he may conform
To tyrant custom. *Ib. Third Day, pt. 2*

15 Who breaks his faith, no faith is held with him. *Ib. Fourth Day, bk. 2*

---

[1] La noche oscura del alma.

See Fitzgerald, 835:11.

[2] The poem, often called *Noche oscura* from its first line (En una noche oscura; In a dark night), is one of three poems made up of *canciones del alma* (songs of the soul), on which the author later wrote spiritual treatises. *The Dark Night of the Soul* is sometimes used as a group title for the poems.

[3] Translated by SWINBURNE.

O Domine Deus! speravi in te; / O care mi Jesu! nunc libera me. / In dura catena, in misera poena, / Disidero te. / Languendo, gemendo, et genuflectendo, / Adoro, imploro, ut liberes me!

[4] Thiers adopted the epigram as the motto for his journal *Nationale*, which he established with Mignet and Carrel in 1830.

[5] This poem became popular as a song, altered thus: My mind to me a kingdom is; / Such perfect joy therein I find, / As far exceeds all earthly bliss / That God and Nature hath assigned. / Though much I want that most would have, / Yet still my mind forbids to crave. — WILLIAM BYRD [1543–1623], *Psalms, Sonnets, and Songs of Sadness and Piety* [1588]

See Seneca, 115:14.

[6] See Milton, 281:4.

[7] So work the honeybees, / Creatures that by a rule in Nature teach / The act of order to a peopled kingdom. — SHAKESPEARE, *King Henry V* [1598–1600], *act I, sc. ii, l. 187*

[8] The windows of mine eyes. — SHAKESPEARE, *King Richard III* [1592–1593], *act V, sc. iii, l. 117*

[9] Much like a subtle spider which doth sit / In middle of her web, which spreadeth wide; / If aught do touch the utmost thread of it / She feels it instantly on every side. — SIR JOHN DAVIES, *The Immortality of the Soul* [1599]

Our souls sit close and silently within, / And their own webs from their own entrails spin; / And when eyes meet far off, our sense is such / That, spider-like, we feel the tenderest touch. — DRYDEN, *Marriage à la Mode* [1673], *act II, sc. i*

The spider's touch, how exquisitely fine! / Feels at each thread, and lives along the line. — POPE, *An Essay on Man* [1733–1734], *epistle I, l. 217*

[10] Out of the jaws of death. — SHAKESPEARE, *Twelfth-Night* [1598–1600], *act III, sc. iv, l. 396*

See Tennyson, 533:14.

1 Who well lives, long lives; for this age of ours
Should not be numbered by years, days, and
hours. *Ib.*

2 My lovely living boy,
My hope, my hap, my love, my life, my joy.[1] *Ib.*

3 Out of the book of Nature's learned breast.[2] *Ib.*

4 Flesh of thy flesh, nor yet bone of thy bone. *Ib.*

Miguel de Cervantes

1547–1616

5 You are a king by your own fireside, as much as any monarch in his throne.
Don Quixote de la Mancha [1605–1615][3] *author's preface, p. xix*

6 I was so free with him as not to mince the matter.[4] *p. xx*

7 They can expect nothing but their labor for their pains.[5] *p. xxiii*

8 Time out of mind.[6] *Pt. I [1605], bk. I, ch. 1, p. 4*

9 Which I have earned with the sweat of my brows.[7] *I, 4, p. 22*

10 By a small sample we may judge of the whole piece. *p. 25*

11 Put you in this pickle.[8] *I, 5, p. 30*

12 Can we ever have too much of a good thing? *I, 6, p. 37*

13 The charging of his enemy was but the work of a moment.[9] *I, 8, p. 50*

14 I don't know that ever I saw one in my born days. *II, 2, p. 57*

15 Those two fatal words, Mine and Thine.[10] *II, 3, p. 63*

16 The eyes those silent tongues of Love. *p. 65*

17 And had a face like a benediction.[11] *II, 4, p. 69*

18 There's not the least thing can be said or done, but people will talk and find fault.[12] *p. 70*

19 Without a wink of sleep.[13] *p. 72*

20 Fortune leaves always some door open to come at a remedy. *III, 1, p. 94*

21 Thank you for nothing. *p. 94*

22 No limits but the sky.[14] *III, 3, p. 110*

23 To give the devil his due. *p. 111*

24 You're leaping over the hedge before you come to the stile. *III, 4, p. 117*

25 Paid him in his own coin. *p. 119*

26 The famous Don Quixote de la Mancha, otherwise called the Knight of the Sorrowful Countenance.[15] *III, 5, p. 126*

27 You are come off now with a whole skin. *p. 127*

28 Fear is sharp-sighted, and can see things underground, and much more in the skies. *III, 6, p. 131*

29 A finger in every pie.[16] *p. 133*

30 No better than she should be.[17] *Ib.*

31 That's the nature of women . . . not to love when we love them, and to love when we love them not.[18] *Ib.*

[1] My fair son! / My life, my joy, my food, my all the world. — SHAKESPEARE, *King John* [1596–1597], *act III, sc. iv, l. 103*

[2] The book of Nature is that which the physician must read; and to do so he must walk over the leaves. — PARACELSUS [c. 1493–1541]. From *Encyclopaedia Britannica (11th edition), vol. XX, p. 749*

[3] Translated [1700–1703] by PETER ANTHONY MOTTEUX. Page numbers are those of the Modern Library Giant edition.

[4] See Shakespeare, 230:22.
You mince matters. — MOLIÈRE, *Tartuffe* [1667], *act I, sc. i*

[5] Nothing is to be gotten without pains (labor). — *Old Proverb*
See Shakespeare, 225:33.

[6] Time out o' mind. — SHAKESPEARE, *Romeo and Juliet* [1594–1595], *act I, sc. iv, l. 70*

[7] See *Genesis 3:19*, 7:12.

[8] How cam'st thou in this pickle? — SHAKESPEARE, *The Tempest* [1611], *act V, sc. i, l. 281*

[9] Don Quixote has mistaken windmills for giants, the "enemy," and attacks them. The expression "tilting at windmills" alludes to this incident.

[10] See Boileau, 311:15.

[11] The more familiar translation.

[12] Take wife, or cowl; ride you, or walk: / Doubt not but tongues will have their talk. — LA FONTAINE, *The Miller, His Son, and the Donkey* [1694]
Do you think you could keep people from talking? — MOLIÈRE, *Tartuffe* [1667], *act I, sc. viii*

[13] See Shakespeare, 243:22, and Pope, 339:5.

[14] Modern saying: The sky's the limit.

[15] El Caballero de la Triste Figura.
Translated by TOBIAS SMOLLETT.

[16] No pie was baked at Castlewood but her little finger was in it. — THACKERAY, *The Virginians* [1857–1859], *ch. 5*

[17] An old proverb.
You are no better than you should be. — BEAUMONT AND FLETCHER, *The Coxcomb* [1647], *act IV, sc. iii*

[18] See George Bernard Shaw, 680:3.

1 You may go whistle for the rest. *p. 134*

2 Ill luck, you know, seldom comes alone.[1] *p. 135*

3 Why do you lead me a wild-goose chase? *p. 136*

4 Experience, the universal Mother of Sciences. *III, 7, p. 140*

5 Give me but that, and let the world rub, there I'll stick. *p. 148*

6 Sing away sorrow, cast away care. *III, 8, p. 153*

7 Of good natural parts, and of a liberal education. *p. 154*

8 Let every man mind his own business. *p. 157*

9 Those who'll play with cats must expect to be scratched. *p. 159*

10 Raise a hue and cry. *Ib.*

11 'Tis the part of a wise man to keep himself today for tomorrow, and not venture all his eggs in one basket. *III, 9, p. 162*

12 The ease of my burdens, the staff of my life. *p. 163*

13 Within a stone's throw of it. *p. 170*

14 The very remembrance of my former misfortune proves a new one to me. *III, 10, p. 174*

15 Absence, that common cure of love. *p. 177*

16 From pro's and con's they fell to a warmer way of disputing. *p. 181*

17 Little said is soon amended.[2] *p. 184*

18 Thou hast seen nothing yet. *III, 11, p. 190*

19 Between jest and earnest. *Ib.*

20 My love and hers have always been purely Platonic. *p. 192*

21 'Tis ill talking of halters in the house of a man that was hanged. *p. 195*

22 My memory is so bad that many times I forget my own name! *Ib.*

23 'Twill grieve me so to the heart that I shall cry my eyes out. *p. 197*

24 Ready to split his sides with laughing. *III, 13, p. 208*

[1]See Shakespeare, 223:25.

[2]Often rendered: Least said soonest mended.

25 My honor is dearer to me than my life. *IV, 1, p. 226*

26 On the word of a gentleman, and a Christian. *p. 236*

27 Think before thou speakest. *IV, 3, p. 252*

28 Let us forget and forgive injuries. *p. 254*

29 I must speak the truth, and nothing but the truth. *p. 255*

30 More knave than fool. *IV, 4, p. 261*

31 Here's the devil-and-all to pay. *IV, 10, p. 319*

32 I begin to smell a rat. *Ib.*

33 The proof of the pudding is in the eating. *p. 322*

34 Let none presume to tell me that the pen is preferable to the sword.[3] *p. 325*

35 There's no striving against the stream; and the weakest still goes to the wall. *IV, 20, p. 404*

36 The bow cannot always stand bent, nor can human frailty subsist without some lawful recreation.[4] *IV, 21, p. 412*

37 It is not the hand but the understanding of a man that may be said to write.[5] *Pt. II [1615], bk. III, author's preface, p. 441*

38 When the head aches, all the members partake of the pains.[6] *III, 2, p. 455*

39 Youngsters read it [Don Quixote's story], grown men understand it, and old people applaud it. *III, 3, p. 464*

40 History is in a manner a sacred thing, so far as it contains truth; for where truth is, the supreme Father of it may also be said to be, at least, inasmuch as concerns truth. *p. 465*

[3]See *The Teaching for Merikare,* 3:12; Burton, 259:3; and Bulwer-Lytton, 493:6.

Scholars' pens carry farther, and give a louder report than thunder.—SIR THOMAS BROWNE, *Religio Medici* [1642], *p. 70* (Everyman edition)

[4]See Ptahhotpe, 3:10; Herodotus, 78:9; and Howell, 271:17.

[5]Cervantes's left hand was maimed for life by gunshot wounds in the battle of Lepanto.

[6]When the head is not sound, the rest cannot be well. —DU BARTAS, *Divine Weeks and Works* [1578]

For let our finger ache, and it indues / Our other healthful members even to that sense / Of pain.—SHAKESPEARE, *Othello* [1604–1605], *act III, sc. iv, l. 145*

1 Every man is as Heaven made him, and sometimes a great deal worse. *III, 4, p. 468*

2 There's no sauce in the world like hunger. *III, 5, p. 473*

3 He casts a sheep's eye at the wench. *p. 474*

4 I ever loved to see everything upon the square. *p. 475*

5 Neither will I make myself anybody's laughingstock. *Ib.*

6 Journey over all the universe in a map, without the expense and fatigue of traveling, without suffering the inconveniences of heat, cold, hunger, and thirst. *III, 6, p. 479*

7 Presume to put in her oar. *p. 480*

8 The fair sex.[1] *Ib.*

9 A little in one's own pocket is better than much in another man's purse. 'Tis good to keep a nest egg. Every little makes a mickle.[2] *III, 7, p. 486*

10 Remember the old saying, "Faint heart ne'er won fair lady." *III, 10, p. 501*

11 Forewarned forearmed. *p. 502*

12 As well look for a needle in a bottle of hay.[3] *Ib.*

13 Are we to mark this day with a white or a black stone?[4] *p. 503*

14 The very pink of courtesy. *III, 13, p. 521*

15 I'll turn over a new leaf. *p. 524*

16 He's [Don Quixote's] a muddled fool, full of lucid intervals.[5] *III, 18, p. 556*

17 Marriage is a noose. *III, 19, p. 564*

18 There are only two families in the world, the Haves and the Have-Nots. *III, 20, p. 574*

19 He preaches well that lives well, quoth Sancho; that's all the divinity I understand. *p. 575*

20 Love and War are the same thing, and stratagems and policy are as allowable in the one as in the other. *III, 21, p. 580*

21 A private sin is not so prejudicial in this world as a public indecency. *III, 22, p. 582*

[1]That sex which is therefore called fair.—STEELE, *The Spectator, no. 302* [February 15, 1712]

[2]See Hesiod, 61:20, and Chaucer, 148:9.

[3]A needle in a haystack.

[4]A red-letter day.

[5]See Bacon, 179:12; Dryden, 304:25; and Heine, 482:6.

22 There is no love lost, sir.[6] *Ib.*

23 Come back sound, wind and limb. *p. 587*

24 Patience, and shuffle the cards.[7] *III, 23, p. 592*

25 Tell me thy company, and I'll tell thee what thou art.[8] *p. 594*

26 Tomorrow will be a new day. *III, 26, p. 618*

27 I can see with half an eye. *III, 29, p. 632*

28 Great persons are able to do great kindnesses. *III, 32, p. 662*

29 Honesty's the best policy.[9] *III, 33, p. 666*

30 An honest man's word is as good as his bond. *IV, 34, p. 674*

31 A blot in thy scutcheon to all futurity. *IV, 35, p. 681*

32 They had best not stir the rice, though it sticks to the pot. *IV, 37, p. 691*

33 Good wits jump;[10] a word to the wise is enough. *p. 692*

34 Diligence is the mother of good fortune. *IV, 38, p. 724*

35 What a man has, so much he's sure of. *p. 725*

36 The pot calls the kettle black. *p. 727*

37 Mum's the word.[11] *IV, 44, p. 729*

38 I shall be as secret as the grave. *IV, 62, p. 862*

[6]There is no hate lost between us.—THOMAS MIDDLETON [1580–1627], *The Witch, act IV, sc. iii*

[7]But patience, cousin, and shuffle the cards, till our hand is a stronger one.—SIR WALTER SCOTT, *Quentin Durward* [1823], *ch. 8*

Cut the fiercest quarrels short / With "Patience, gentlemen, and shuffle."—W. M. PRAED [1802–1839], *Quince, st. 5*

Men disappoint me so, I disappoint myself so, yet courage, patience, shuffle the cards.—MARGARET FULLER [1810–1850], *letter to the Reverend W. H. Channing*

[8]Tell me what you eat, and I will tell you what you are. —ANTHELME BRILLAT-SAVARIN [1755–1826], *La Physiologie du Goût, aphorism 4*

Show me your garden and I shall tell you what you are. —ALFRED AUSTIN, *The Garden That I Love* [1905]

[9]I hold the maxim no less applicable to public than to private affairs, that honesty is always the best policy. — GEORGE WASHINGTON, *Farewell Address* [1796]

[10]Great wits jump.—LAURENCE STERNE, *Tristram Shandy, vol. III* [1761–1762], *ch. 9*

[11]Cry "mum."—SHAKESPEARE, *The Merry Wives of Windsor* [1600–1601], *act V, sc. ii, l. 6*

1 Now blessings light on him that first invented this same sleep! It covers a man all over, thoughts and all, like a cloak;[1] 'tis meat for the hungry, drink for the thirsty, heat for the cold, and cold for the hot. 'Tis the current coin that purchases all the pleasures of the world cheap; and the balance that sets the king and the shepherd, the fool and the wise man even. *IV, 68, p. 898*

2 The ass will carry his load, but not a double load; ride not a free horse to death. *IV, 71, p. 917*

3 I thought it working for a dead horse, because I am paid beforehand.[2] *Ib.*

4 He . . . got the better of himself, and that's the best kind of victory one can wish for. *IV, 72, p. 924*

5 Every man was not born with a silver spoon in his mouth. *IV, 73, p. 926*

6 Ne'er look for birds of this year in the nests of the last.[3] *IV, 74, p. 933*

7 There is a strange charm in the thoughts of a good legacy, or the hopes of an estate, which wondrously alleviates the sorrow that men would otherwise feel for the death of friends. *p. 934*

8 For if he like a madman lived,
At least he like a wise one died.
p. 935 (Don Quixote's epitaph)

9 Don't put too fine a point to your wit for fear it should get blunted. *The Little Gypsy (La Gitanilla)*

10 My heart is wax molded as she pleases, but enduring as marble to retain.[4] *Ib.*

Giordano Bruno
1548–1600

11 Time takes all and gives all.[5] *The Candle Bearer [1582],[6] dedication*

12 I who am in the night will move into the day. *Ib.*

13 It is Unity that doth enchant me. By her power I am free though thrall, happy in sorrow, rich in poverty, and quick even in death. *On the Infinite Universe and Worlds [1584],[7] introductory epistle*

14 Our bodily eye findeth never an end, but is vanquished by the immensity of space. *Ib. Fifth Dialogue*

15 There is in the universe neither center nor circumference. *Ib.*

16 Magicians can do more by means of faith than physicians by the truth. *The Heroic Enthusiasts [1585], pt. I, Fifth Dialogue*

Charles IX
1550–1574

17 Horses and poets should be fed, not overfed.[8] *Saying*

William Camden
1551–1623

18 My friend, judge not me,
Thou seest I judge not thee.
Betwixt the stirrup and the ground
Mercy I asked, and mercy found.
Remains Concerning Britain. Epitaph for a man killed by falling from his horse

Théodore Agrippa d'Aubigné
1552–1630

19 Each of us aspires to goodness,
Each of us desires the good
And desires it for himself.[9]
Pièces Épigrammatiques, 49

20 More exquisite than any other is the autumn rose.[10] *Les Tragiques. Les Feux*

Sir Edward Coke
1552–1634

21 Reason is the life of the law; nay, the common law itself is nothing else but reason.

[1] "God's blessing," said Sancho Panza, "be upon the man who first invented this self-same thing called sleep; it covers a man all over like a cloak." — LAURENCE STERNE, *Tristram Shandy*
See Saxe, 556:2.

[2] It is a heartrending delusion and a cruel snare to be paid for your work before you accomplish it. As soon as once your work is finished you ought to be promptly paid; but to receive your lucre one minute before it is due is to tempt Providence to make a Micawber of you. — EDMUND GOSSE, *Gossip in a Library* [1891], *Beau Nash*

[3] For Time will teach thee soon the truth, / There are no birds in last year's nest! — LONGFELLOW [1807–1882], *It Is Not Always May, st. 6*

[4] See Byron, 460:7.

[5] See Eliot, 808:6.

[6] Translated by J. B. HALLE.

[7] Translated by DOROTHEA SINGER.

[8] Equi et poetae alendi, non saginandi.

[9] Chacun au bien aspire, / Chacun le bien désire, / Et le désire sien.

[10] Une rose d'automne est plus qu'une autre exquise.

. . . The law, which is perfection of reason.[1]
First Institute [1628]

1 The gladsome light of jurisprudence.
Ib. epilogue

2 For a man's house is his castle, *et domus sua cuique tutissimum refugium.*[2]
Third Institute [1644]

3 The house of everyone is to him as his castle and fortress, as well for his defense against injury and violence as for his repose.
Semayne's Case. 5 Report 91

4 They [corporations] cannot commit treason, nor be outlawed nor excommunicate, for they have no souls.
Case of Sutton's Hospital. 10 Report 32

5 Magna Carta is such a fellow that he will have no sovereign.
Debate in the Commons [May 17, 1628]

6 Six hours in sleep, in law's grave study six,
Four spend in prayer, the rest on Nature fix.[3]
Translation quoted by Coke. *From The Pandects (Digest of Justinian). De in Ius Vocando*

Sir Walter Ralegh
c. 1552–1618

7 Like to an hermit poor in place obscure,
I mean to spend my days of endless doubt,
To wail such woes as time cannot recure,
Where none but Love shall ever find me out.
The Phoenix Nest [1593]. Sonnet

8 As you came from the holy land
Of Walsinghame,
Met you not with my true Love
By the way as you came?
As You Came from the Holy Land [c. 1599], st. 1

9 But true love is a durable fire,
In the mind ever burning,
Never sick, never old, never dead,
From itself never turning.
Ib. st. 11

[1] Let us consider the reason of the case. For nothing is law that is not reason.—Sir John Powell, *Coggs v. Bernard, 2 Ld. Raym. Rep., p. 911*

[2] One's home is the safest refuge to everyone.—*Pandects* [533], *lib. II, tit. IV, De in Ius Vocando*

I in mine own house am an emperor / And will defend what's mine.—Massinger, *The Roman Actor* [1629], *act I, sc. ii*

[3] Seven hours to law, to soothing slumber seven; / Ten to the world allot, and all to heaven.—Sir William Jones [1746–1794]

10 If all the world and love were young,
And truth in every shepherd's tongue,
These pretty pleasures might me move
To live with thee, and be thy love.[4]
The Nymph's Reply to the Passionate Shepherd[5] *(printed in England's Helicon) [1600], st. 1*

11 Fain would I climb, yet fear I to fall.
Written on a windowpane[6]

12 Our passions are most like to floods and streams,
The shallow murmur, but the deep are dumb.[7]
Sir Walter Ralegh to the Queen [c. 1599], st. 1

13 Silence in love bewrays more woe
Than words, though ne'er so witty;
A beggar that is dumb, you know,
Deserveth double pity.
Ib. st. 5

14 Go, Soul, the body's quest,
Upon a thankless arrant:
Fear not to touch the best,
The truth shall be thy warrant:
Go, since I needs must die,
And give the world the lie.
The Lie (printed in Francis Davison, *Poetical Rhapsody) [1608; manuscript copy traced to 1595], st. 1*

15 Give me my scallop shell of quiet,
My staff of faith to walk upon,
My scrip of joy, immortal diet,
My bottle of salvation,
My gown of glory, hope's true gage
And thus I'll take my pilgrimage.
Diaphantus [1604]. The Passionate Man's Pilgrimage

16 Methought I saw the grave where Laura lay.
Verses to Edmund Spenser

17 Shall I, like a hermit, dwell
On a rock or in a cell?
Poem

[4] See Donne, 253:2.

[5] An answer to Christopher Marlowe, *The Passionate Shepherd to His Love* (see 183:8).

[6] Under this Queen Elizabeth wrote, "If thy heart fails thee, climb not at all."—Thomas Fuller, *Worthies of England* [1662]

[7] See Seneca, 115:15.

Altissima quaeque flumina minimo sono labi [The deepest rivers flow with the least sound].—Quintus Curtius [first century A.D.], *VII, 4, 13*

Where the stream runneth smoothest, the water is deepest.—John Lyly, *Euphues and his England* [1580]

Smooth runs the water where the brook is deep.—Shakespeare, *Henry VI, Part II* [1591], *act III, sc. i, l. 53*

Take heed of still waters, the quick pass away.—George Herbert, *Jacula Prudentum* [1640]

1 What is our life? a play of passion,
Our mirth the music of division,
Our mothers' wombs the tiring houses be
Where we are dressed for this short comedy.
From ORLANDO GIBBONS, *The First Set of Madrigals and Motets [1612]. On the Life of Man*

2 [History] hath triumphed over time, which besides it nothing but eternity hath triumphed over.
History of the World [1614], preface

3 Whosoever, in writing a modern history, shall follow truth too near the heels, it may haply strike out his teeth. *Ib.*

4 O eloquent, just, and mighty Death! whom none could advise, thou hast persuaded; what none hath dared, thou hast done; and whom all the world hath flattered, thou only hast cast out of the world and despised. Thou hast drawn together all the far-stretched greatness, all the pride, cruelty, and ambition of man, and covered it all over with these two narrow words, *Hic jacet!*
Ib. bk. V, pt. I, ch. 6, conclusion

5 Even such is time, that takes in trust
Our youth, our joys, our all we have,
And pays us but with age and dust;
Who in the dark and silent grave,
When we have wandered all our ways,
Shuts up the story of our days.
And from which earth, and grave, and dust,
The Lord shall raise me up, I trust.
A version of one of his earlier poems, found at his death in his Bible in the Gatehouse at Westminster

Edmund Spenser

1552–1599

6 To kirk the nearer, from God more far,
Has been an old-said saw.
And he that strives to touch the stars,
Oft stumbles at a straw.[1]
The Shepherd's Calendar [1579]. July, l. 97

7 Fierce wars and faithful loves shall moralize my song.[2]
The Faerie Queene [1590], introduction, st. 1

8 A gentle knight was pricking on the plain.
Ib. bk. I, canto 1, st. 1

9 A bold bad man. *Ib. st. 37*

[1] See Heywood, 159:19.

[2] And moralized his song. — POPE, *Epistle to Dr. Arbuthnot* [1735], *l. 340*

10 Her angel's face
As the great eye of heaven shined bright,
And made a sunshine in the shady place.
Ib. 3, st. 4

11 Ay me, how many perils do enfold
The righteous man, to make him daily fall.[3]
Ib. 8, st. 1

12 Sleep after toil, port after stormy seas,
Ease after war, death after life does greatly please.[4] *Ib. 9, st. 40*

13 All for love, and nothing for reward.
Ib. II, 8, st. 2

14 Gather therefore the Rose, whilst yet is prime,
For soon comes age, that will her pride deflower:
Gather the Rose of love, whilst yet is time.[5]
Ib. 12, st. 75

15 Her birth was of the womb of morning dew.[6] *Ib. III, 6, st. 3*

16 Roses red and violets blue,
And all the sweetest flowers, that in the forest grew. *Ib. st. 6*

17 All that in this delightful garden grows,
Should happy be, and have immortal bliss.
Ib. st. 41

18 That Squire of Dames. *Ib. 8, st. 44*

19 And painful pleasure turns to pleasing pain.
Ib. 10, st. 60

20 How over that same door was likewise writ,
Be bold, be bold, and everywhere *Be bold.*[7]
Ib. 11, st. 54

21 Another iron door, on which was writ,
Be not too bold.[8] *Ib.*

22 Dan Chaucer, well of English undefiled,
On Fame's eternal beadroll worthy to be filed. *Ib. IV [1596], 2, st. 32*

[3] Ay me! what perils do environ / The man that meddles with cold iron! — SAMUEL BUTLER: *Hudibras, pt. I* [1663], *canto III, l. 1*

[4] These lines are cut on Joseph Conrad's gravestone at Canterbury.

[5] See *The Wisdom of Solomon 2:8,* 34:11; Horace, 107:8; Ronsard, 162:13; and Herrick, 266:11.

[6] The dew of thy birth is of the womb of the morning. — *Book of Common Prayer, Psalter, Psalm 110:3*

[7] See Danton, 412:2; Channing, 448:4; and Patton, 792:3.

[8] Jockey of Norfolk, be not too bold, / For Dickon thy master is bought and sold. — SHAKESPEARE, *Richard III* [1592–1593], *act V, sc. iii, l. 305*

Forbear, said I: be not too bold. / Your fleece is white but 'tis too cold. — RICHARD CRASHAW [c. 1613–1649], *Hymn of the Nativity, l. 50*

Write on your doors the saying wise and old, / "Be bold! be bold!" and everywhere — "Be bold; / Be not too bold!" — LONGFELLOW, *Morituri Salutamus* [1875]

1 For all that nature by her mother wit
Could frame in earth. *Ib. 10, st. 21*

2 Ill can he rule the great, that cannot reach the small. *Ib. V, 2, st. 43*

3 Who will not mercy unto others show,
How can he mercy ever hope to have?[1]
Ib. VI, 1, st. 42

4 The gentle mind by gentle deeds is known.
For a man by nothing is so well bewrayed,
As by his manners. *Ib. 3, st. 1*

5 That here on earth is no sure happiness.
Ib. 11, st. 1

6 The ever-whirling wheel
Of Change; the which all mortal things doth sway. *Ib. VII, 6, st. 1*

7 Wars and alarums unto nations wide.
Ib. st. 3

8 But times do change and move continually.[2]
Ib. st. 47

9 For deeds do die, however nobly done,
And thoughts of men do as themselves decay,
But wise words taught in numbers for to run,
Recorded by the Muses, live for ay.
The Ruines of Time [1591], l. 400

10 Full little knowest thou that hast not tried,
What hell it is, in suing long to bide:
To lose good days, that might be better spent;
To waste long nights in pensive discontent;
To speed today, to be put back tomorrow;
To feed on hope, to pine with fear and sorrow.
Mother Hubberd's Tale [1591], l. 895

11 To fret thy soul with crosses and with cares;
To eat thy heart through comfortless despairs;
To fawn, to crouch, to wait, to ride, to run,
To spend, to give, to want, to be undone.
Unhappy wight, born to disastrous end,
That doth his life in so long tendance spend.
Ib. l. 903

12 What more felicity can fall to creature,
Than to enjoy delight with liberty.
Muiopotmos; or, The Fate of the Butterfly [1591], l. 209

13 I hate the day, because it lendeth light
To see all things, and not my love to see.
Daphnaida [1591], l. 407

14 Death slew not him, but he made death his ladder to the skies.
An Epitaph upon Sir Philip Sidney [1591], l. 20

[1]See *Matthew 5:7*, 37:4, and Pope, 340:4.
[2]See Anonymous Latin, 134:30.

15 Though last not least.[3]
Colin Clouts Come Home Again [1595], l. 144

16 Tell her the joyous time will not be stayed
Unlesse she do him by the forelock take.[4]
Amoretti [1595]. Sonnet 70

17 The woods shall to me answer, and my Echo ring. *Epithalamion [1595], l. 18*

18 Ah! when will this long weary day have end,
And lend me leave to come unto my love?
Ib. l. 278

19 For of the soul the body form doth take:
For soul is form, and doth the body make.
Hymn in Honor of Beauty [1596], l. 132

20 For all that fair is, is by nature good;[5]
That is a sign to know the gentle blood.
Ib. l. 139

21 Sweet Thames! run softly, till I end my Song.[6] *Prothalamion [1596], refrain*

22 I was promised on a time
To have reason for my rhyme;
From that time unto this season,
I received nor rhyme nor reason.
Lines on his promised pension. From THOMAS FULLER, *Worthies of England [1662]*

John Florio
c. 1553–1625

23 England is the paradise of women, the purgatory of men, and the hell of horses.[7]
Second Frutes [1591]

24 Praise the sea; on shore remain. *Ib.*

Henri IV [Henry of Navarre]
1553–1610

25 I want there to be no peasant in my realm so poor that he will not have a chicken in his pot every Sunday. *Attributed*

26 Paris is well worth a Mass.[8]
Attributed[9]

[3]See Shakespeare, 216:10 and 232:23.
The last, not least in honor or applause.—POPE, *The Dunciad* [1728], *bk. IV, l. 577*
[4]Take Time by the forelock.—THALES [c. 640–c. 546 B.C.]
[5]See Shakespeare, 228:22.
[6]Sweet Thames, run softly till I end my song, / Sweet Thames, run softly, for I speak not loud or long.—T. S. ELIOT, *The Waste Land* [1922], *pt. III*
[7]See Robert Burton, 259:22.
[8]Paris vaut bien une messe.
[9]Attributed also to Henri's minister Sully.

1 Let my white panache be your rallying point.[1] *Attributed battle cry*

2 Hang yourself, brave Crillon; we fought at Arques and you were not there.[2]

Letter [1597]. From Lettres missives de Henri IV, Collection des Documents Inédits de l'Histoire de France, vol. IV [1847]

3 The wisest fool in Christendom [James I of England]. *Attributed*[3]

George Keith, Fifth Earl Marischal

c. 1553–1623

4 Thai half said. Quhat say thai? Let thame say.[4]

Family motto, Mitchell Tower, Marischal College, Aberdeen, Scotland [founded 1593]

Fulke Greville, Lord Brooke

1554–1628

5 Oh wearisome condition of humanity!
Born under one law, to another bound.

Mustapha [1609], V, 4

6 Fulke Greville, Servant to Queen Elizabeth, Councillor to King James, and Friend to Sir Philip Sidney.

Epitaph, on his monument in Warwick

Richard Hooker

c. 1554–1600

7 Of Law there can be no less acknowledged than that her seat is the bosom of God, her voice the harmony of the world. All things in heaven and earth do her homage — the very least as feeling her care, and the greatest as not exempted from her power.

Laws of Ecclesiastical Polity [1594], bk. I

8 That to live by one man's will became the cause of all men's misery. *Ib.*

[1] Ralliez-vous à mon panache blanc.

[2] Pends-toi, brave Crillon, nous avons combattu à Arques et tu n'y étais pas.

Louis de Balbes de Berton de Crillon [c. 1541–1615], French soldier of legendary courage, fought as captain under Henri IV in the battle of Ivry and the siege of Paris.

[3] Attributed also to Henri's minister Sully.

[4] They say. What say they? Let them say. — *Motto over the fireplace in George Bernard Shaw's home*

John Lyly

c. 1554–1606

9 Be valiant, but not too venturous. Let thy attire be comely, but not costly.

Euphues: The Anatomy of Wit [1579]. Arber's reprint, p. 39

10 The finest edge is made with the blunt whetstone. *Ib. p. 47*

11 Delays breed dangers.[5] *Ib. p. 65*

12 It seems to me (said she) that you are in some brown study. *Ib. p. 80*

13 Many strokes overthrow the tallest oaks.[6] *Ib. p. 81*

14 Let me stand to the main chance.[7] *Ib. p. 104*

15 It is a world to see. *Ib. p. 116*

16 A clear conscience is a sure card. *Ib. p. 207*

17 Go to bed with the lamb, and rise with the lark.[8]

Euphues and His England, [1580], p. 229

18 A comely old man as busy as a bee. *Ib. p. 252*

19 Maidens, be they never so foolish, yet being fair they are commonly fortunate. *Ib. p. 279*

20 Your eyes are so sharp that you cannot only look through a millstone, but clean through the mind. *Ib. p. 289*

21 I am glad that my Adonis hath a sweet tooth in his head. *Ib. p. 308*

22 A rose is sweeter in the bud than full-blown.[9] *Ib. p. 314*

23 Cupid and my Campaspe played
At cards for kisses: Cupid paid.

Alexander and Campaspe [1584], act III, sc. v

[5] Periculum in mora. — *Latin proverb*

See Shakespeare, 185:4.

All delays are dangerous in war. — DRYDEN, *Tyrannic Love* [1669], *act I, sc. i*

[6] Many strokes, though with a little axe, / Hew down and fell the hardest-timbered oak. — SHAKESPEARE, *Henry VI, Part III* [1591], *act II, sc. i, l. 54*

See Franklin, 347:29.

[7] See Butler, 291:23.

[8] To rise with the lark and go to bed with the lamb. — BRETON, *Court and Country* [1618]

Rise with the lark, and with the lark to bed. — JAMES HURDIS [1763–1801], *The Village Curate*

[9] The rose is fairest when 'tis budding new. — SCOTT, *Lady of the Lake* [1810], *canto III, st. I*

1 How at heaven's gates she claps her wings,
The morn not waking till she sings.[1]
Ib. V, i

2 Night hath a thousand eyes.[2]
Maides Metamorphosis, III, 1

3 Marriages are made in heaven and consummated on earth.[3]
Mother Bombie [1590], act IV, sc. i

Sir Philip Sidney[4]
1554–1586

4 High-erected thoughts seated in the heart of courtesy.[5]
The Arcadia [written 1580], bk. I

5 They are never alone that are accompanied with noble thoughts.[6] *Ib.*

6 My dear, my better half. *Ib. III*

7 My true-love hath my heart, and I have his,
By just exchange one for the other given:
I hold his dear, and mine he cannot miss,
There never was a better bargain driven.
Ib. Sonnet

8 Ring out your bells! Let mourning shows be spread!
For Love is dead. *Ib. Song*

9 Leave me, O Love, which reachest but to dust,
And thou, my mind, aspire to higher things;
Grow rich in that which never taketh rust:
Whatever fades, but fading pleasure brings.
Ib. Sonnet

10 Sweet food of sweetly uttered knowledge.
The Defense of Poesy [written c. 1580]

11 He cometh unto you with a tale which holdeth children from play, and old men from the chimney corner. *Ib.*

[1]See Shakespeare, 243:16.

[2]On the stars thou gazest, my star; would I were heaven to look at thee with many eyes.—*The Greek Anthology* [1906], edited by J. W. MACKAIL, *8, 7*
See Bourdillon, 670:8.

[3]Les mariages se font au ciel, et se consomment sur la terre.—*French proverb*
See Heywood, 159:*n*4.
If marriages / Are made in heaven, they should be happier.—THOMAS SOUTHERNE, *The Fatal Marriage* [1694]

[4]The miracle of our age, Sir Philip Sidney.—RICHARD CAREW [1555–1620]
See Fulke Greville, 175:6; Roydon, 184:12; and Browning, 540:11.

[5]Great thoughts come from the heart.—VAUVENARGUES [1715–1747], *Maxim 127*

[6]He never is alone that is accompanied with noble thoughts.—BEAUMONT AND FLETCHER, *Love's Cure* [1647], *act III, sc. iii*

12 I never heard the old song of Percy and Douglas that I found not my heart moved more than with a trumpet. *Ib.*

13 "Fool!" said my muse to me, "look in thy heart, and write."
Astrophel and Stella [1591]

14 With how sad steps, O Moon, thou climb'st the skies!
How silently, and with how wan a face![7]
Ib.

15 Have I caught my heav'nly jewel.[8]
Ib. Second Song

16 Thy necessity[9] is yet greater than mine.
Said on the battlefield of Zutphen [September 22, 1586] on giving his water bottle to a dying soldier

François de Malherbe[10]
1555–1628

17 And a rose, she lived as roses do, the space of a morn.[11]
Consolation à Monsieur du Périer [1599]

18 And the fruits will outdo what the flowers have promised.[12]
Prière pour le roi Henri le Grand [1605]

19 What Malherbe writes will endure forever.
Sonnet à Louis XIII [1624]

Philip Nicolai
1556–1608

20 Wake, awake, for night is flying:
The watchmen on the heights are crying.[13]
Hymn [1597]

Thomas Kyd
1558–1594

21 What outcries call me from my naked bed?
The Spanish Tragedy [1594],[14] act II, sc. v, l. 1

[7]Wordsworth begins a sonnet [1802] with these two lines.

[8]Quoted by SHAKESPEARE in *The Merry Wives of Windsor* [1600–1601], *act III, sc. iii, l. 45.*

[9]More often quoted as: Thy need.

[10]See Boileau, 311:3.

[11]Et rose, elle a vécu ce que vivent les roses, / L'espace d'un matin.

[12]Et les fruits passeront la promesse des fleurs.

[13]Wachet auf, ruft uns die stimme.
Translated by CATHERINE WINKWORTH.

[14]This play was undoubtedly the most popular drama of its time, outstripping Shakespeare and the other Elizabethans.

1 O eyes, no eyes, but fountains fraught with tears;
O life, no life, but lively form of death;
O world, no world, but mass of public wrongs,
Confused and filled with murder and misdeeds.
Ib. III, ii, 1

2 Hieronymo, beware: go by, go by.
Ib. III, xii, 31

3 Why then I'll fit you,[1] say no more.
When I was young, I gave my mind
And plied myself to fruitless poetry:
Which though it profit the professor naught
Yet it is passing pleasing to the world.
Ib. IV, ii, 70

Thomas Lodge
c. 1558–1625

4 Love in my bosom like a bee
Doth suck his sweet. *Rosalind [1590]*

5 Devils are not so black as they are painted.
A Margarite of America [1596]

George Peele
c. 1558 – c. 1597

6 Fair and fair, and twice so fair,
As fair as any may be.
The Arraignment of Paris [1584]

7 My merry, merry, merry roundelay
Concludes with Cupid's curse:
They that do change old love for new,
Pray gods, they change for worse! *Ib.*

8 His golden locks time hath to silver turned;
O time too swift, O swiftness never ceasing!
His youth 'gainst time and age hath ever spurned,
But spurned in vain; youth waneth by increasing.
Polyhymnia [1590]. The Aged Man-at-Arms, st. 1

9 His helmet now shall make a hive for bees,
And lovers' sonnets turned to holy psalms,
A man-at-arms must now serve on his knees,
And feed on prayers, which are age his alms.
Ib. 2

Chidiock Tichborne[2]
c. 1558–1586

10 My prime of youth is but a frost of cares;
My feast of joy is but a dish of pain;
My crop of corn is but a field of tares;
And all my good is but vain hope of gain:
The day is past, and yet I saw no sun;
And now I live, and now my life is done.
Tichborne's Elegy [1586]

[1]Quoted by T. S. Eliot in *The Waste Land* [1922], *l. 431*, followed by: Hieronymo's mad againe.

[2]He was executed for an attempt on Queen Elizabeth's life.

George Chapman
c. 1559–1634

11 Promise is most given when the least is said.
Hero and Leander [1598]

12 Love calls to war;
Sighs his alarms,
Lips his swords are,
The field his arms.
Ib. Epithalamion Teratos, refrain

13 Young men think old men are fools; but old men know young men are fools.
All Fools [1605], act V, sc. i

14 Keep thy shop, and thy shop will keep thee. Light gains make heavy purses.[3]
Eastward Ho [1605],[4] act I, sc. i

15 Why, do nothing, be like a gentleman, be idle . . . Make ducks and drakes with shillings. *Ib.*

16 Only a few industrious Scots perhaps, who indeed are dispersed over the face of the whole earth. But as for them, there are no greater friends to Englishmen and England, when they are out on't, in the world, than they are. And for my own part, I would a hundred thousand of them were there [Virginia]; for we are all one countrymen now, ye know, and we should find ten times more comfort of them there than we do here.[5]
Ib. III, ii

17 I will neither yield to the song of the siren nor the voice of the hyena, the tears of the crocodile[6] nor the howling of the wolf.
Ib. V, i

18 For one heat, all know, doth drive out another,
One passion doth expel another still.[7]
Monsieur d'Olive [1606], act V, sc. i

[3]Quoted by Benjamin Franklin in *Poor Richard's Almanac* [1735], *June.*

[4]By Chapman, Jonson, and Marston.

[5]This is the famous passage that gave offense to James I and caused the imprisonment of the authors. The leaves containing it were canceled and reprinted, and it only occurs in a few of the original copies.—RICHARD HERNE SHEPHERD

[6]These crocodile tears.—ROBERT BURTON, *Anatomy of Melancholy* [1621–1651], *pt. III, sec. 2, member 2, subsec. 4*

She's false, false as the tears of crocodiles.—SIR JOHN SUCKLING [1609–1642], *The Sad One, act IV, sc. v*

[7]See Shakespeare, 191:19.

1 To put a girdle round about the world.[1]
Bussy d'Ambois [1607], act I, sc. i

2 Speed his plow.[2] *Ib.*

3 So our lives
In acts exemplary, not only win
Ourselves good names, but doth to others give
Matter for virtuous deeds, by which we live.
Ib.

4 Who to himself is law no law doth need,
Offends no law, and is a king indeed.
Ib. II, i

5 Be free, all worthy spirits,
And stretch yourselves, for greatness and for height.
The Conspiracy of Charles, Duke of Byron [1608], act III, sc. i

6 Give me a spirit that on this life's rough sea
Loves t' have his sails filled with a lusty wind,
Even till his sail-yards tremble, his masts crack,
And his rapt ship run on her side so low
That she drinks water, and her keel plows air. *Ib.*

7 Danger, the spur of all great minds.
The Revenge of Bussy d'Ambois [1610], act V, sc. i

8 We have watered our horses in Helicon.
May-Day [1611], act III, sc. iii

Maximilien de Béthune, Duc de Sully[3]

1559–1641

9 Tilling and grazing are the two breasts that feed France.[4] *Economies Royales, III*

Robert Greene

c. 1560–1592

10 Sweet are the thoughts that savor of content;
The quiet mind is richer than a crown.[5]
Farewell to Folly [1591], st. 1

11 A mind content both crown and kingdom is.[5] *Ib. st. 2*

12 For there is an upstart crow, beautified with our feathers, that with his tiger's heart wrapped in a player's hide,[6] supposes he is as well able to bumbast out a blank verse as the best of you; and being an absolute *Johannes fac totum*, is in his own conceit the only Shake-scene in a country.[7]
The Croatsworth of Wit [1592]

13 Hangs in the uncertain balance of proud time.
Friar Bacon and Friar Bungay [acted 1594], act III

14 Hell's broken loose.[8] *Ib. IV*

Francis Bacon[9]

1561–1626

15 I have taken all knowledge to be my province. *Letter to Lord Burleigh [1592]*

16 The monuments of wit survive the monuments of power. *Essex's Device [1595]*

17 Knowledge is power [Nam et ipsa scientia potestas est].[10]
Meditationes Sacrae [1597]. De Haeresibus

18 For all knowledge and wonder (which is the seed of knowledge) is an impression of pleasure in itself.
The Advancement of Learning [1605], bk. I, i, 3

19 Time, which is the author of authors.
Ib. iv, 12

20 If a man will begin with certainties, he shall end in doubts; but if he will be content to begin with doubts he shall end in certainties. *Ib. v, 8*

21 *Antiquitas saeculi juventus mundi.*[11] These times are the ancient times, when the world is ancient, and not those which we account ancient *ordine retrogrado*, by a computation backward from ourselves.[12] *Ib.*

[1] See Shakespeare, 196:16.
[2] Usually quoted: Speed the plow.
[3] See Henri IV of France, 174:26.
[4] Labourage et pâturage sont les deux mamelles dont la France est alimentée.
[5] See stanza 2 (Greene, 178:11) and Shakespeare, 186:8.
[6] See Shakespeare, 186:2.
[7] First known literary reference to Shakespeare.
[8] See Milton, 286:9.
[9] If parts allure thee, think how Bacon shined, / The wisest, brightest, meanest of mankind. — POPE, *Essay on Man* [1733–1734], *epistle IV, l. 281*
See Walton, 271:15.
[10] See *Proverbs 24:5, 25:12*.
Knowledge is more than equivalent to force. — SAMUEL JOHNSON, *Rasselas* [1759], *ch. 13*
[11] The age of antiquity is the youth of the world.
[12] As in the little, so in the great world, reason will tell you that old age or antiquity is to be accounted by the farther distance from the beginning and the nearer approach to the end — the times wherein we now live being in propriety of speech the most ancient since the world's creation. — GEORGE HAKEWILL, *An Apologie or Declaration of the Power and Providence of God in the Government of the World* [1627]
For as old age is that period of life most remote from infancy, who does not see that old age in this universal man ought not to be sought in the times nearest his birth, but in those most remote from it? — PASCAL [1623–1662], *Preface to the Treatise on Vacuum*

1 [Knowledge] is a rich storehouse for the glory of the Creator and the relief of man's estate. *Ib. 11*

2 It [Poesy] was ever thought to have some participation of divineness, because it doth raise and erect the mind by submitting the shows of things to the desires of the mind. *Ib. II, iv, 2*

3 They are ill discoverers that think there is no land, when they can see nothing but sea. *Ib. vii, 5*

4 But men must know that in this theater of man's life it is reserved only for God and angels to be lookers on. *Ib. xx, 8*

5 We are much beholden to Machiavel and others, that write what men do, and not what they ought to do. *Ib. xxi, 9*

6 All good moral philosophy is but the handmaid to religion. *Ib. xxii, 14*

7 There are and can be only two ways of searching into and discovering truth. The one flies from the senses and particulars to the most general axioms . . . this way is now in fashion. The other derives axioms from the senses and particulars, rising by a gradual and unbroken ascent, so that it arrives at the most general axioms last of all. This is the true way, but as yet untried. *Novum Organum [1620]*

8 There are four classes of Idols which beset men's minds. To these for distinction's sake I have assigned names—calling the first class, Idols of the Tribe; the second, Idols of the Cave; the third, Idols of the Market-Place; the fourth, Idols of the Theater. *Ib. Aphorism 39*

9 The human understanding is like a false mirror, which, receiving rays irregularly, distorts and discolors the nature of things by mingling its own nature with it. *Ib. 41*

10 Nature, to be commanded, must be obeyed. *Ib. 129*

11 I do plainly and ingenuously confess that I am guilty of corruption, and do renounce all defense. I beseech your Lordships to be merciful to a broken reed.[1] *On being charged by Parliament with corruption in office [1621]*

12 Lucid intervals and happy pauses.[2] *History of King Henry VII [1622], III*

13 Nothing is terrible except fear itself.[3] *De Augmentis Scientiarum, bk. II, Fortitudo [1623]*

14 Riches are a good handmaid, but the worst mistress. *Ib. Antitheta*

15 Hope is a good breakfast, but it is a bad supper. *Apothegms [1624], no. 36*

16 Like strawberry wives, that laid two or three great strawberries at the mouth of their pot, and all the rest were little ones. *Ib. 54*

17 Sir Amice Pawlet, when he saw too much haste made in any matter, was wont to say, "Stay a while, that we may make an end the sooner." *Ib. 76*

18 Alonso of Aragon was wont to say in commendation of age, that age appears to be best in four things—old wood best to burn, old wine to drink, old friends to trust, and old authors to read.[4] *Ib. 97*

19 Cosmus, Duke of Florence, was wont to say of perfidious friends, that "We read that we ought to forgive our enemies; but we do not read that we ought to forgive our friends." *Ib. 206*

20 Cato said the best way to keep good acts in memory was to refresh them with new. *Ib. 247*

21 My essays . . . come home to men's business and bosoms. *Essays [1625],[5] dedication*

22 What is truth? said jesting Pilate,[6] and would not stay for an answer. *Ib. Of Truth*

It is worthy of remark that a thought which is often quoted from Francis Bacon occurs in [Giordano] Bruno's *Cena di Cenere,* published in 1584: I mean the notion that the later times are more aged than the earlier.—WHEWELL, *Philosophy of the Inductive Sciences* [1847], *vol. II, p. 198*

We are Ancients of the earth, / And in the morning of the times.—TENNYSON, *The Day Dream* [1842], *L'Envoi*

[1] See *Isaiah 36:6,* 30:26.

[2] See Cervantes, 170:16; Dryden, 304:25; and Heine, 482:6.

[3] Nil terribile nisi ipse timor.

See *Proverbs 3:25,* 23:6; Montaigne, 164:7; Wellington, 421:10; Thoreau, 557:9; and F. D. Roosevelt, 779:10.

[4] See Webster, 262:1.

Old friends are best. King James used to call for his old shoes; they were easiest for his feet.—SELDEN, *Table Talk* [1689], *Friends*

See Goldsmith, 371:3.

Old books, old wine, old Nankin blue.—HENRY AUSTIN DOBSON [1840–1921], *Rondeau, To Richard Watson Gilder*

[5] First edition, 1597; first complete edition, 1625.

[6] See *John 18:38,* 45:30.

1 No pleasure is comparable to the standing upon the vantage-ground of truth. *Ib.*

2 Men fear death as children fear to go in the dark; and as that natural fear in children is increased with tales, so is the other.[1] *Ib. Of Death*

3 Revenge is a kind of wild justice, which the more man's nature runs to, the more ought law to weed it out. *Ib. Of Revenge*

4 It was a high speech of Seneca (after the manner of the Stoics), that "The good things which belong to prosperity are to be wished, but the good things that belong to adversity are to be admired." *Ib. Of Adversity*

5 Prosperity is the blessing of the Old Testament; adversity is the blessing of the New. *Ib.*

6 Prosperity is not without many fears and distastes; and adversity is not without comforts and hopes. *Ib.*

7 Prosperity doth best discover vice, but adversity doth best discover virtue. *Ib.*

8 Virtue is like precious odors—most fragrant when they are incensed or crushed.[2] *Ib.*

9 He that hath wife and children hath given hostages to fortune; for they are impediments to great enterprises, either of virtue or mischief. *Ib. Of Marriage and Single Life*

10 Wives are young men's mistresses, companions for middle age, and old men's nurses. *Ib.*

11 A good name is like a precious ointment; it filleth all around about, and will not easily away; for the odors of ointments are more durable than those of flowers.[3] *Ib. Of Praise*

12 In charity there is no excess. *Ib. Of Goodness and Goodness of Nature*

13 If a man be gracious and courteous to strangers, it shows he is a citizen of the world,[4] and that his heart is no island cut off from other lands, but a continent that joins to them.[5] *Ib.*

14 The desire of power in excess caused the angels to fall; the desire of knowledge in excess caused man to fall.[6] *Ib.*

15 Money is like muck, not good except it be spread. *Ib. Of Seditions and Troubles*

16 I had rather believe all the fables in the legends and the Talmud and the Alcoran, than that this universal frame is without a mind. *Ib. Of Atheism*

17 A little philosophy inclineth man's mind to atheism, but depth in philosophy bringeth men's minds about to religion.[7] *Ib.*

18 Travel, in the younger sort, is a part of education; in the elder, a part of experience. He that traveleth into a country before he hath some entrance into the language, goeth to school, and not to travel. *Ib. Of Travel*

19 Princes are like to heavenly bodies, which cause good or evil times, and which have much veneration but no rest.[8] *Ib. Of Empire*

20 Fortune is like the market, where many times, if you can stay a little, the price will fall. *Ib. Of Delays*

21 Nothing doth more hurt in a state than that cunning men pass for wise. *Ib. Of Cunning*

22 Be so true to thyself, as thou be not false to others.[9] *Ib. Of Wisdom for a Man's Self*

23 It is the nature of extreme self-lovers, as they will set an house on fire, and it were but to roast their eggs. *Ib.*

24 He that will not apply new remedies must expect new evils; for time is the greatest innovator. *Ib. Of Innovations*

25 Cure the disease and kill the patient. *Ib. Of Friendship*

[1] See Lucretius, 100:22.

[2] As aromatic plants bestow / No spicy fragrance while they grow; / But crushed or trodden to the ground, / Diffuse their balmy sweets around.—GOLDSMITH, *The Captivity* [1764], *act I*

The good are better made by ill, / As odors crushed are sweeter still.—SAMUEL ROGERS, *Jacqueline* [1814], *st. 3*

[3] See *Ecclesiastes 7:1*, 27:3, and Publilius Syrus, 110:19.

[4] See Socrates, 79:7; Paine, 385:2; Garrison, 505:10; and F. D. Roosevelt, 781:5.

[5] See *Romans 14:7*, 47:32; Donne, 254:22; and Quarles, 267:9.

[6] Pride still is aiming at the blest abodes; / Men would be angels, angels would be gods. / Aspiring to be gods if angels fell, / Aspiring to be angels men rebel.—ALEXANDER POPE, *Essay on Man, epistle I* [1733], *l. 125*

[7] A little skill in antiquity inclines a man to Popery; but depth in that study brings him about again to our religion.—THOMAS FULLER, *The Holy State and the Profane State* [1642], *The True Church Antiquary*

[8] See Shelley, 468:16.

[9] See Shakespeare, 219:2.

1 Riches are for spending.
Ib. Of Expense

2 There is a wisdom in this beyond the rules of physic. A man's own observation, what he finds good of and what he finds hurt of, is the best physic to preserve health.
Ib. Of Regimen of Health

3 Intermingle . . . jest with earnest.[1]
Ib. Of Discourse

4 Nature is often hidden; sometimes overcome; seldom extinguished.
Ib. Of Nature in Men

5 If a man look sharply and attentively, he shall see Fortune; for though she is blind, she is not invisible.[2] *Ib. Of Fortune*

6 Chiefly the mold of a man's fortune is in his own hands.[3] *Ib.*

7 Young men are fitter to invent than to judge, fitter for execution than for counsel, and fitter for new projects than for settled business. *Ib. Of Youth and Age*

8 Virtue is like a rich stone—best plain set.
Ib. Of Beauty

9 There is no excellent beauty that hath not some strangeness in the proportion.
Ib.

10 God Almighty first planted a garden.[4]
Ib. Of Gardens

11 He that commands the sea is at great liberty, and may take as much and as little of the war as he will.[5]
Ib. Of the True Greatness of Kingdoms

12 Some books are to be tasted, others to be swallowed, and some few to be chewed and digested. *Ib. Of Studies*

[1]See Menander, 91:2; Horace, 108:15; Montaigne, 166:4; and Linnaeus, 350:7.

[2]Fortune is painted blind, with a muffler afore her eyes, to signify to you that Fortune is blind.—SHAKESPEARE, *Henry V* [1598–1600], *act III, sc. vi, l. 31*

[3]See Sallust, 103:1 and 103:5; Shakespeare, 215:6; Tennyson, 534:7; Henley, 663:11; and Nehru, 814:8.

[4]See *Genesis 2:8*, 6:18; Varro, 97:14; Shakespeare, 185:26 and 224:5; Tennyson, 528:10; and Kipling, 710:22.

Gardens were before gardeners, and but some hours after the earth.—SIR THOMAS BROWNE, *The Garden of Cyrus* [1658], *ch. 1*

See Cowley, 295:14, and Cowper, 376:17.

[5]See Themistocles, 70:19; Waller, 276:3; Washington, 379:5; Mahan, 642:8; and Morison, 800:11.

He that is master of the sea, may, in some sort, be said to be Master of every country; at least such as are bordering on the sea. For he is at liberty to begin and end War, where, when, and on what terms he pleaseth, and extend his conquests even to the Antipodes.—JOSEPH GANDER, *The Glory of Her Sacred Majesty Queen Anne in the Royal Navy* [1703]

13 Reading maketh a full man, conference a ready man, and writing an exact man.
Ib.

14 Histories make men wise; poets, witty; the mathematics, subtile; natural philosophy, deep; moral, grave; logic and rhetoric, able to contend. *Ib.*

15 The greatest vicissitude of things amongst men is the vicissitude of sects and religions.[6] *Ib. Of Vicissitude of Things*

16 I bequeath my soul to God. . . . My body to be buried obscurely. For my name and memory, I leave it to men's charitable speeches, and to foreign nations, and the next age. *From his will [1626]*

17 The world's a bubble, and the life of man
Less than a span.[7] *The World [1629]*

18 Who then to frail mortality shall trust
But limns on water, or but writes in dust.[8]
Ib.

19 What then remains but that we still should cry
For being born, and, being born, to die?[9]
Ib.

20 Books must follow sciences, and not sciences books.
Proposition touching amendment of laws

Sir John Harington
1561–1612

21 Treason doth never prosper: what's the reason?
For if it prosper, none dare call it treason.[10]
Epigrams. Of Treason

22 The readers and the hearers like my books,
But yet some writers cannot them digest;
But what care I? for when I make a feast
I would my guests should praise it, not the cooks.
Ib. Of Writers Who Carp at Other Men's Books

[6]See Terence, 96:17; and Sterne, 359:17.

[7]Whose life is a bubble, and in length a span.—WILLIAM BROWNE, *Britannia's Pastorals* [1613], *bk. I, song*

See Sir John Davies, 251:7, and *The New England Primer*, 320:11.

[8]See Sophocles, 75:22; Catullus, 102:12; More, 155:8; Shakespeare, 249:14; and Keats, 480:7.

[9]This line frequently occurs in almost exactly the same shape among the minor poems of the time: "Not to be born, or, being born, to die."—WILLIAM DRUMMOND, *Poems* [1656]

See Theognis, 67:5; Sophocles, 75:13; Yeats, 715:19; and Auden, 868:7.

[10]See Seneca, 115:12.

Robert Southwell
c. 1561–1595

1 Times go by turns, and chances change by course,
From foul to fair, from better hap to worse.
Times Go by Turns [c. 1595], st. 1

2 As I in hoary winter night stood shivering in the snow,
Surprised was I with sudden heat which made my heart to glow;
And lifting up a fearful eye to view what fire was near
A pretty Babe all burning bright did in the air appear.
The Burning Babe [written c. 1595]

3 With this he vanished out of sight, and swiftly shrunk away,
And straight I callèd unto mind that it was Christmas Day.
Ib.

Samuel Daniel
1562–1619

4 Care-charmer Sleep, son of the sable Night,
Brother to Death, in silent darkness born.[1]
Sonnets to Delia [1592]

5 Make me to say, when all my griefs are gone,
"Happy the heart that sighed for such a one!"
Ib. Sonnet: I Must Not Grieve

6 Let others sing of knights and paladins
In agèd accents and untimely words.
Ib.

7 These are the arks, the trophies, I erect,
That fortify thy name against old age.
Ib.

8 And for the few that only lend their ear,
That few is all the world.
Musophilus [1599], st. 97

9 This is the thing that I was born to do.
Ib. st. 100

10 Unless above himself he can
Erect himself, how poor a thing is man![2]
To the Countess of Cumberland [c. 1600], st. 12

11 Love is a sickness full of woes,
All remedies refusing.
Hymen's Triumph [1615]

[1]See Homer, 58:20; Virgil, 105:17; Shakespeare, 238:6; and Shelley, 466:6.

[2]Wordsworth, who quotes these lines (*The Excursion*, book iv, line 330), says they are Daniel's translation from Seneca.

Lope de Vega
1562–1635

12 Harmony is pure love, for love is complete agreement.
Fuenteovejuna [c. 1613],[3] act I, l. 381

13 Except for God, the King's our only lord.
Ib. l. 1701

Michael Drayton
1563–1631

14 Fair stood the wind for France.
The Ballad of Agincourt [1606], st. 1

15 O, when shall Englishmen
With such acts fill a pen,
Or England breed again
Such a King Harry?
Ib. st. 15

16 Since there's no help, come let us kiss and part—
Nay, I have done: you get no more of me,
And I am glad, yea glad with all my heart,
That thus so cleanly I myself can free.
Shake hands forever, cancel all our vows,
And when we meet at any time again,
Be it not seen in either of our brows
That we one jot of former love retain.
Poems [1619]. Idea

17 The coast was clear.
Nymphidia [1627]

18 Had in him those brave translunary things
That the first poets had.
Said of MARLOWE. *To Henry Reynolds, Of Poets and Poesy [1627]*

19 For that fine madness still he did retain
Which rightly should possess a poet's brain.
Ib.

Galileo Galilei
1564–1642

20 Philosophy is written in this grand book—I mean the universe—which stands continually open to our gaze, but it cannot be understood unless one first learns to comprehend the language and interpret the characters in which it is written. It is written in the language of mathematics, and its characters are triangles, circles, and other geometrical figures, without which it is humanly impossible to understand a single word of it; without

[3]Translated by ANGEL FLORES and MURIEL KITTEL. From *Spanish Drama* [1962].

these, one is wandering about in a dark labyrinth.[1] *Il Saggiatore [1623]*[2]

1 But it does move![3]
Attributed. From Abbé Irailh, *Querelles littéraires [1761], vol. III, p. 49*

2 Facts which at first seem improbable will, even on scant explanation, drop the cloak which has hidden them and stand forth in naked and simple beauty.
Dialogues Concerning Two New Sciences [1638],[4] *Day 1*

Christopher Marlowe
1564–1593

3 Our swords shall play the orators for us.
Tamburlaine the Great [c. 1587], pt. I, l. 328

4 Accurst be he that first invented war.
Ib. l. 664

5 Is it not passing brave to be a king,
And ride in triumph through Persepolis?
Ib. l. 758

6 Nature that framed us of four elements,
Warring within our breasts for regiment,
Doth teach us all to have aspiring minds:
Our souls, whose faculties can comprehend
The wondrous Architecture of the world:
And measure every wandering planet's course,
Still climbing after knowledge infinite,
And always moving as the restless Spheres,
Will us to wear ourselves and never rest,
Until we reach the ripest fruit of all,
That perfect bliss and sole felicity,
The sweet fruition of an earthly crown.
Ib. l. 869

7 Tamburlaine, the Scourge of God, must die.
Ib. l. 4641

8 Come live with me, and be my love;
And we will all the pleasures prove
That valleys, groves, hills, and fields,[5]
Woods or steepy mountain yields.[6]
The Passionate Shepherd to His Love [c. 1589]

9 By shallow rivers, to whose falls
Melodious birds sing madrigals.[7] *Ib.*

10 And I will make thee beds of roses
And a thousand fragrant posies.[7] *Ib.*

11 I count religion but a childish toy,
And hold there is no sin but ignorance.[8]
The Jew of Malta [c. 1589], prologue

12 Infinite riches in a little room.[9]
Ib. act I, sc. i

13 Excess of wealth is cause of covetousness.
Ib. ii

14 Now will I show myself to have more of the serpent than the dove;[10] that is, more knave than fool. *Ib. II, iii*

15 *Friar Barnadine:* Thou hast committed—
Barabas: Fornication—but that was in another country;
And besides, the wench is dead.
Ib. IV, i

16 My men, like satyrs grazing on the lawns,
Shall with their goat feet dance the antic hay.
Edward II [1593], act I, sc. i

17 Who ever loved that loved not at first sight?[11]
Hero and Leander [1598]

18 Like untuned golden strings all women are,
Which long time lie untouched, will harshly jar.
Vessels of brass oft handled brightly shine.
Ib.

19 Live and die in Aristotle's works.
The Tragical History of Doctor Faustus [1604], sc. i

20 Unhappy spirits that fell with Lucifer,
Conspired against our God with Lucifer,
And are forever damned with Lucifer.
Ib. iii

21 Why this is hell, nor am I out of it:[12]
Think'st thou that I who saw the face of God,
And tasted the eternal joys of Heaven,
Am not tormented with ten thousand hells,
In being deprived of everlasting bliss?
Ib.

[1] See Roger Bacon, 139:5.

[2] The Assayer in *The Controversy on the Comets of 1618* [1960], translated by Stillman Drake and C. D. O'Malley.

[3] E pur si muove!
The remark alleged to have been whispered by Galileo after his abjuration before the Inquisition [1633] of any conception of the earth as a moving body revolving around the sun.

[4] Translated by Henry Crew and Alfonso De Salvio.

[5] Also given as: Hills and valleys, dales, and fields.

[6] See Ralegh, 172:10, and Donne, 253:2.

[7] To shallow rivers, to whose falls / Melodious birds sing madrigals; / There will we make our peds of roses, / And a thousand fragrant posies.—Shakespeare, *Merry Wives of Windsor* [1600–1601], *act III, sc. i, l. 17* (sung by Evans)

[8] See Wilde, 674:21.

[9] Here lyeth muche rychnesse in lytell space.—John Heywood, *The Foure PP* [1521–1525]

[10] See *Matthew 10:16,* 38:36.

[11] Quoted in Shakespeare, *As You Like It, act III, sc. v, l. 82.*
None ever loved but at first sight they loved.—George Chapman, *The Blind Beggar of Alexandria* [1598]
I saw and loved.—Gibbon, *Memoirs* [1796]

[12] See Virgil, 105:23; Marlowe, 184:1; Browne, 274:15; Milton, 283:13 and 285:12; Eliot, 809:1; Sartre, 865:12; and Lowell, 893:7.

1 Hell hath no limits, nor is circumscribed
In one self place; for where we are is hell,
And where hell is there must we ever be.[1]
Ib. v

2 When all the world dissolves,
And every creature shall be purified,
All places shall be hell that is not Heaven.
Ib.

3 Have not I made blind Homer sing to me?
Ib. vi

4 Was this the face that launched a thousand ships,
And burnt the topless towers of Ilium?[2]
Sweet Helen, make me immortal with a kiss.
Her lips suck forth my soul;[3] see, where it flies!
Ib.

5 Oh, thou art fairer than the evening air
Clad in the beauty of a thousand stars.
Ib.

6 Pray for me! and what noise soever ye hear, come not unto me, for nothing can rescue me.
Ib. xvi

7 Now hast thou but one bare hour to live,
And then thou must be damned perpetually!
Stand still, you ever-moving spheres of Heaven,
That time may cease, and midnight never come.
Ib.

8 *O lente, lente currite noctis equi:*[4]
The stars move still, time runs, the clock will strike,
The Devil will come, and Faustus must be damned.
O, I'll leap up to my God! Who pulls me down?
See, see where Christ's blood streams in the firmament!
One drop would save my soul—half a drop: ah, my Christ!
Ib.

9 O soul, be changed into little waterdrops,
And fall into the ocean—ne'er to be found.
My God! my God! look not so fierce on me!
Ib.

10 I'll burn my books!
Ib.

11 Cut is the branch that might have grown full straight,
And burnèd is Apollo's laurel bough,
That sometime grew within this learnèd man.
Ib.

[1] See Virgil, 105:23; Marlowe, 183:21; Browne, 274:15; Milton, 283:13 and 285:12; Eliot, 809:1; Sartre, 865:12; and Lowell, 893:7.

[2] Was this fair face the cause, quoth she, / Why the Grecians sackèd Troy?—SHAKESPEARE, *All's Well That Ends Well* [1601–1603], *act I, sc. iii, l. 75*

[3] Once he drew / With one long kiss my whole soul through / My lips.—TENNYSON, *Fatima* [1833], *st. 3*

[4] Run slowly, slowly, horses of the night.
See Ovid, 113:6.

Matthew Roydon
c. 1564 – c. 1622

12 You knew—who knew not Astrophil?
The Phoenix Nest [1593]; An Elegy, or Friend's Passion for His Astrophil (on the death of Sir Philip Sidney)

13 A sweet attractive kind of grace,
A full assurance given by looks,
Continual comfort in a face,
The lineaments of Gospel books;
I trow that countenance cannot lie.
Whose thoughts are legible in the eye.
Ib.

14 Was never eye, did see that face,
Was never ear, did hear that tongue,
Was never mind, did mind his grace,
That ever thought the travel long,
But eyes, and ears, and ev'ry thought,
Were with his sweet perfections caught.
Ib.

William Shakespeare[5]
1564–1616

15 Hung be the heavens with black, yield day to night!
King Henry the Sixth, Part I [1591], act I, sc. i, l. 1

16 Fight till the last gasp.
I, ii, 127

17 Expect Saint Martin's summer, halcyon days.[6]
I, ii, 131

18 Glory is like a circle in the water,
Which never ceaseth to enlarge itself,
Till by broad spreading it disperse to nought.
I, ii, 133

19 Unbidden guests
Are often welcomest when they are gone.
II, ii, 55

20 Between two hawks, which flies the higher pitch;
Between two dogs, which hath the deeper mouth;
Between two blades, which bears the better temper;
Between two horses, which doth bear him best;

[5] From the text of W. J. Craig, Oxford University Press [1935]. The dates and order, about which there is much conjecture, are those Sir Edmund K. Chambers (*William Shakespeare*, 1930) thinks most probable.

[6] See Aristophanes, 82:11.

Between two girls, which hath the merriest eye;
I have, perhaps, some shallow spirit of judgment;
But in these nice sharp quillets of the law,
Good faith, I am no wiser than a daw.
Henry VI, Part I, II, iv, 12

1 I'll note you in my book of memory.
II, iv, 101

2 Just death, kind umpire of men's miseries.
II, v, 29

3 Choked with ambition of the meaner sort.
II, v, 123

4 Delays have dangerous ends.[1]
III, ii, 33

5 Of all base passions, fear is most accursed.
V, ii, 18

6 She's beautiful and therefore to be wooed,
She is a woman, therefore to be won.[2]
V, iii, 78

7 For what is wedlock forced, but a hell,
An age of discord and continual strife?
Whereas the contrary bringeth bliss,
And is a pattern of celestial peace.
V, v, 62

8 Whose large style
Agrees not with the leanness of his purse.
King Henry the Sixth, Part II [1591], act I, sc. i, l. 112

9 'Tis not my speeches that you do mislike,
But 'tis my presence that doth trouble ye.
Rancor will out. *I, i, 141*

10 Could I come near your beauty with my nails
I'd set my ten commandments in your face.
I, iii, 144

11 Blessèd are the peacemakers on earth.[3]
II, i, 34

12 Now, God be praised, that to believing souls
Gives light in darkness, comfort in despair!
II, i, 66

13 God defend the right! *II, iii, 55*

14 Sometimes hath the brightest day a cloud;
And after summer evermore succeeds
Barren winter, with his wrathful nipping cold:
So cares and joys abound, as seasons fleet.
II, iv, 1

[1]See Lyly, 175:11.
All delays are dangerous in war.—DRYDEN, *Tyrannic Love* [1669], *act I, sc. i*

[2]A similar passage is in *Titus Andronicus, act II, sc. i, l.* 82.

[3]See *Matthew 5:9*, 37:4.

15 Now 'tis the spring, and weeds are shallow-rooted;
Suffer them now and they'll o'ergrow the garden. *Henry VI, Part II, III, i, 31*

16 In thy face I see
The map of honor, truth, and loyalty.
III, i, 202

17 What stronger breastplate than a heart untainted!
Thrice is he armed that hath his quarrel just,
And he but naked, though locked up in steel,
Whose conscience with injustice is corrupted.[4] *III, ii, 232*

18 He dies, and makes no sign.
III, iii, 29

19 Forbear to judge, for we are sinners all.[5]
Close up his eyes and draw the curtain close;
And let us all to meditation.
III, iii, 31

20 The gaudy, blabbing, and remorseful day
Is crept into the bosom of the sea.
IV, i, 1

21 Small things make base men proud.
IV, i, 106

22 True nobility is exempt from fear.
IV, i, 129

23 I will make it felony to drink small beer.[6]
IV, ii, 75

24 The first thing we do, let's kill all the lawyers. *IV, ii, 86*

25 Is not this a lamentable thing, that of the skin of an innocent lamb should be made parchment? that parchment, being scribbled o'er, should undo a man? *IV, ii, 88*

26 Adam was a gardener.[7] *IV, ii, 146*

27 Sir, he made a chimney in my father's house, and the bricks are alive at this day to testify it. *IV, ii, 160*

28 Thou hast most traitorously corrupted the youth of the realm in erecting a grammar-school; and whereas, before, our forefathers had no other books but the score and the tally, thou hast caused printing to be used; and, contrary to the king, his crown, and dignity, thou hast built a paper-mill.
IV, vii, 35

[4]See Milton, 279:24 and 284:21.

[5]See *Matthew 7:1*, 38:8.

[6]Doth it not show vilely in me to desire small beer? —*King Henry IV, Part II* [1597–1598], *I, ii, 7*
See *Othello*, 230:12.
That questionable superfluity—small beer.—DOUGLAS JERROLD [1803–1857], *The Tragedy of the Till*

[7]See *Genesis 2:8*, 6:18; Bacon, 181:10; *Hamlet*, 224:5; Tennyson, 528:10; and Kipling, 710:22.

1 Beggars mounted run their horse to death.[1]
King Henry the Sixth, Part III [1591], act I, sc. iv, l. 127

2 O tiger's heart wrapped in a woman's hide![2]
I, iv, 137

3 To weep is to make less the depth of grief.
II, i, 85

4 The smallest worm will turn being trodden on. *II, ii, 17*

5 Didst thou never hear
That things ill got had ever bad success?
And happy always was it for that son
Whose father for his hoarding went to hell?
II, ii, 45

6 Thou [Death] setter up and plucker down of kings.[3] *II, iii, 37*

7 And what makes robbers bold but too much lenity? *II, vi, 22*

8 My crown is in my heart, not on my head;
Not decked with diamonds and Indian stones,
Nor to be seen: my crown is called content;
A crown it is that seldom kings enjoy.[4]
III, i, 62

9 'Tis a happy thing
To be the father unto many sons.
III, ii, 104

10 Like one that stands upon a promontory,
And spies a far-off shore where he would tread,
Wishing his foot were equal with his eye.
III, ii, 135

11 Yield not thy neck
To fortune's yoke, but let thy dauntless mind
Still ride in triumph over all mischance.
III, iii, 16

12 For how can tyrants safely govern home,
Unless abroad they purchase great alliance?
III, iii, 69

13 Having nothing, nothing can he lose.
III, iii, 152

14 Hasty marriage seldom proveth well.
IV, i, 18

15 Let us be backed with God and with the seas
Which he hath given for fence impregnable,
And with their helps only defend ourselves:
In them and in ourselves our safety lies.
Henry VI, Part III, IV, i, 43

16 What fates impose, that men must needs abide;
It boots not to resist both wind and tide.
IV, iii, 57

17 Now join your hands, and with your hands your hearts. *IV, vi, 39*

18 For many men that stumble at the threshold
Are well foretold that danger lurks within.
IV, vii, 11

19 A little fire is quickly trodden out,
Which, being suffered, rivers cannot quench.
IV, viii, 7

20 When the lion fawns upon the lamb,
The lamb will never cease to follow him.
IV, viii, 49

21 What is pomp, rule, reign, but earth and dust?
And, live we how we can, yet die we must.
V, ii, 27

22 Every cloud engenders not a storm.
V, iii, 13

23 What though the mast be now blown overboard,
The cable broke, the holding anchor lost,
And half our sailors swallowed in the flood?
Yet lives our pilot still. *V, iv, 3*

24 So part we sadly in this troublous world
To meet with joy in sweet Jerusalem.
V, v, 7

25 Men ne'er spend their fury on a child.
V, v, 57

26 He's sudden if a thing comes in his head.
V, v, 86

27 Suspicion always haunts the guilty mind;
The thief doth fear each bush an officer.
V, vi, 11

28 This word "love," which greybeards call divine. *V, vi, 81*

29 Now is the winter of our discontent
Made glorious summer by this sun of York.
King Richard the Third [1592–1593], act I, sc. i, l. 1

30 Grim-visaged war hath smoothed his wrinkled front. *I, i, 9*

31 He capers nimbly in a lady's chamber
To the lascivious pleasing of a lute.
I, i, 12

32 This weak piping time of peace.
I, i, 24

[1] Set a beggar on horseback and he will ride a gallop. — ROBERT BURTON, *Anatomy of Melancholy* [1621–1651], *pt. II, sec. 2, member 2*
Set a beggar on horseback, and he'll outride the Devil. — BOHN, *Foreign Proverbs, German* [1855]

[2] See Robert Greene, 178:12.

[3] Proud setter up and puller down of kings. — *Ib. III, iii, 157*

[4] See Robert Greene, 178:10 and 178:11.

1 No beast so fierce but knows some touch of pity. *Richard III, I, ii, 71*

2 Look, how my ring encompasseth thy finger,
Even so thy breast encloseth my poor heart;
Wear both of them, for both of them are thine. *I, ii, 204*

3 Was ever woman in this humor wooed?
Was ever woman in this humor won?
I, ii, 229

4 Framed in the prodigality of nature.
I, ii, 245

5 The world is grown so bad,
That wrens make prey where eagles dare not perch.[1] *I, iii, 70*

6 And thus I clothe my naked villany
With odd old ends stol'n forth of holy writ,
And seem a saint when most I play the devil.
I, iii, 336

7 Talkers are no good doers. *I, iii, 351*

8 O, I have passed a miserable night,
So full of ugly sights, of ghastly dreams,
That, as I am a Christian faithful man,
I would not spend another such a night,
Though 'twere to buy a world of happy days.
I, iv, 2

9 Lord, Lord! methought, what pain it was to drown:
What dreadful noise of waters in mine ears!
What ugly sights of death within mine eyes!
Methought I saw a thousand fearful wracks;
A thousand men that fishes gnaw upon.
I, iv, 21

10 The kingdom of perpetual night.[2]
I, iv, 47

11 Sorrow breaks seasons and reposing hours,
Makes the night morning, and the noontide night. *I, iv, 76*

12 A parlous boy. *II, iv, 35*

13 So wise so young, they say, do never live long.[3] *III, i, 79*

14 Off with his head![4] *III, iv, 75*

15 Lives like a drunken sailor on a mast,
Ready with every nod to tumble down
Into the fatal bowels of the deep.
III, iv, 98

16 I am not in the giving vein today.
IV, ii, 115

[1] See Pope, 333:20.
[2] See Catullus, 101:18; Campion, 250:3; Jonson, 255:16; Herrick, 266:21; and Fouché, 415:17.
[3] A little too wise, they say, do ne'er live long.—MIDDLETON [1580–1627]. *The Phoenix, act I, sc. i*
[4] See Colley Cibber, 324:27, and Lewis Carroll, 612:1.

17 The sons of Edward sleep in Abraham's bosom.[5] *Richard III, IV, iii, 38*

18 A grievous burden was thy birth to me;
Tetchy and wayward was thy infancy.
IV, iv, 168

19 An honest tale speeds best being plainly told.
IV, iv, 359

20 Harp not on that string. *IV, iv, 365*

21 Relenting fool, and shallow changing woman!
IV, iv, 432

22 Is the chair empty? is the sword unswayed?
Is the king dead? the empire unpossessed?
IV, iv, 470

23 Thus far into the bowels of the land
Have we marched on without impediment.
V, ii, 3

24 True hope is swift, and flies with swallow's wings;
Kings it makes gods, and meaner creatures kings. *V, ii, 23*

25 The king's name is a tower of strength.
V, iii, 12

26 Give me another horse! bind up my wounds!
V, iii, 178

27 O coward conscience, how dost thou afflict me! *V, iii, 180*

28 My conscience hath a thousand several tongues,
And every tongue brings in a several tale,
And every tale condemns me for a villain.
V, iii, 194

29 By the apostle Paul, shadows tonight
Have struck more terror to the soul of Richard
Than can the substance of ten thousand soldiers. *V, iii, 217*

30 Conscience is but a word that cowards use,
Devised at first to keep the strong in awe.
V, iii, 310

31 A horse! a horse! my kingdom for a horse!
V, iv, 7

32 I have set my life upon a cast,
And I will stand the hazard of the die.
I think there be six Richmonds in the field.
V, iv, 9

33 The pleasing punishment that women bear.
The Comedy of Errors [1592–1593], act I, sc. i, l. 46

34 We may pity, though not pardon thee.
I, i, 97

[5] See *Luke 16:22*, 43:33.

1 Why, headstrong liberty is lashed with woe.
There's nothing situate under heaven's eye
But hath his bound, in earth, in sea, in sky.
The Comedy of Errors, II, i, 15

2 Every why hath a wherefore.[1]
II, ii, 45

3 There's no time for a man to recover his hair that grows bald by nature.
II, ii, 74

4 What he hath scanted men in hair, he hath given them in wit. *II, ii, 83*

5 Small cheer and great welcome makes a merry feast. *III, i, 26*

6 There is something in the wind.
III, i, 69

7 We'll pluck a crow together. *III, i, 83*

8 For slander lives upon succession,
Forever housèd where it gets possession.
III, i, 105

9 Be not thy tongue thy own shame's orator.
III, ii, 10

10 Ill deeds are doubled with an evil word.
III, ii, 20

11 A back-friend, a shoulder-clapper.
IV, ii, 37

12 Give me your hand and let me feel your pulse. *IV, iv, 54*

13 The venom clamors of a jealous woman
Poison more deadly than a mad dog's tooth.
V, i, 69

14 Unquiet meals make ill digestions.
V, i, 74

15 One Pinch, a hungry lean-faced villain,
A mere anatomy, a mountebank,
A threadbare juggler, and a fortune-teller,
A needy, hollow-eyed, sharp-looking wretch,
A living-dead man. *V, i, 238*

16 Sweet mercy is nobility's true badge.
Titus Andronicus [1593–1594], act I, sc. i, l. 119

17 These words are razors to my wounded heart.
I, i, 314

18 He lives in fame that died in virtue's cause.
I, i, 390

19 These dreary dumps.[2] *I, i, 391*

20 What you cannot as you would achieve,
You must perforce accomplish as you may.
II, i, 106

[1]See *King Henry V*, 208:13.
For every why he had a wherefore.—Samuel Butler, *Hudibras, pt. I* [1663], *canto 1, l. 132*

[2]And doleful dumps the mind oppress.—*Romeo and Juliet* [1594–1595], *act IV, sc. v, l. 129*

21 The eagle suffers little birds to sing.
And is not careful what they mean thereby.
Titus Andronicus, IV, iv, 82

22 Tut! I have done a thousand dreadful things
As willingly as one would kill a fly.
V, i, 141

23 I'll not budge an inch.
The Taming of the Shrew [1593–1594], Induction, sc. i, l. 13

24 And if the boy have not a woman's gift
To rain a shower of commanded tears,
An onion will do well for such a shift.
i, 124

25 No profit grows where is no pleasure ta'en;
In brief, sir, study what you most affect.
Act I, sc. i, l. 39

26 There's small choice in rotten apples.
I, i, 137

27 To seek their fortunes further than at home,
Where small experience grows.
I, ii, 51

28 Nothing comes amiss, so money comes withal. *I, ii, 82*

29 And do as adversaries do in law,
Strive mightily, but eat and drink as friends.
I, ii, 281

30 I must dance barefoot on her wedding day,
And, for your love to her, lead apes in hell.
II, i, 33

31 Asses are made to bear, and so are you.
II, i, 200

32 Kiss me, Kate, we will be married o' Sunday.
II, i, 318

33 Old fashions please me best. *III, i, 81*

34 Who wooed in haste and means to wed at leisure.[3] *III, ii, 11*

35 Such an injury would vex a saint.
III, ii, 28

36 A little pot and soon hot.[4] *IV, i, 6*

37 It was the friar of orders gray
As he forth walkèd on his way.[5]
IV, i, 148

38 Sits as one new-risen from a dream.
IV, i, 189

39 This is a way to kill a wife with kindness.
IV, i, 211

[3]See Congreve, 324:5.

[4]He is a little chimney, and heated hot in a moment.
—Longfellow, *The Courtship of Miles Standish* [1858]

[5]See Anonymous, 917:19.

1 Kindness in women, not their beauteous looks,
Shall win my love.
The Taming of the Shrew, IV, ii, 41

2 Our purses shall be proud, our garments poor:
For 'tis the mind that makes the body rich;
And as the sun breaks through the darkest clouds,
So honor peereth in the meanest habit.
IV, iii, 173

3 Forward, I pray, since we have come so far,
And be it moon, or sun, or what you please:
An if you please to call it a rush-candle,
Henceforth I vow it shall be so for me.
IV, v, 12

4 He that is giddy thinks the world turns round. *V, ii, 20*

5 A woman moved is like a fountain troubled,
Muddy, ill-seeming, thick, bereft of beauty.
V, ii, 143

6 Such duty as the subject owes the prince,
Even such a woman oweth to her husband.
V, ii, 156

7 Bid me discourse, I will enchant thine ear.
Venus and Adonis [1593], l. 145

8 Love is a spirit all compact of fire,
Not gross to sink, but light, and will aspire.
l. 149

9 O! What a war of looks was then between them. *l. 355*

10 Like a red morn, that ever yet betokened
Wrack to the seaman, tempest to the field.
l. 453

11 The owl, night's herald. *l. 531*

12 Love comforteth like sunshine after rain.
l. 799

13 The text is old, the orator too green.
l. 806

14 For he being dead, with him is beauty slain,
And, beauty dead, black chaos comes again.[1] *l. 1019*

15 The grass stoops not, she treads on it so light.
l. 1028

16 Beauty itself doth of itself persuade
The eyes of men without an orator.
The Rape of Lucrece [1594], l. 29

17 This silent war of lilies and of roses,
Which Tarquin viewed in her fair face's field.
l. 71

[1]See *Othello*, 230:30.

18 Those that much covet are with gain so fond,
For what they have not, that which they possess
They scatter and unloose it from their bond,
And so, by hoping more, they have but less.
The Rape of Lucrece, l. 134

19 One for all, or all for one we gage.[2]
l. 144

20 Who buys a minute's mirth to wail a week?
Or sells eternity to get a toy?
For one sweet grape who will the vine destroy? *l. 213*

21 Extreme fear can neither fight nor fly.
l. 230

22 All orators are dumb when beauty pleadeth.
l. 268

23 Time's glory is to calm contending kings,
To unmask falsehood, and bring truth to light. *l. 939*

24 For greatest scandal waits on greatest state.
l. 1006

25 To see sad sights moves more than hear them told. *l. 1324*

26 Cloud-kissing Ilion. *l. 1370*

27 Lucrece swears he did her wrong.[3]
l. 1462

28 Home-keeping youth have ever homely wits.
The Two Gentlemen of Verona [1594–1595], act I, sc. i, l. 2

29 I have no other but a woman's reason:
I think him so, because I think him so.
I, ii, 23

30 *Julia:* They do not love that do not show their love.
Lucetta: O! they love least that let men know their love. *I, ii, 31*

31 Since maids, in modesty, say "No" to that
Which they would have the profferer construe "Aye." *I, ii, 53*

32 O! how this spring of love resembleth
The uncertain glory of an April day!
I, iii, 84

33 O jest unseen, inscrutable, invisible,
As a nose on a man's face,[4] or a weathercock on a steeple! *II, i, 145*

34 He makes sweet music with th' enamelled stones. *II, vii, 28*

[2]See Dumas, 491:5.
[3]Some villain hath done me wrong.—*King Lear* [1605–1606], *act I, sc. ii, l. 186*
See Anonymous, 923:8.
[4]See Rabelais, 158:9.

1 That man that hath a tongue, I say, is no man,
If with his tongue he cannot win a woman.
The Two Gentlemen of Verona, III, i, 104

2 Except I be by Silvia in the night,
There is no music in the nightingale.
III, i, 178

3 Much is the force of heaven-bred poesy.
III, ii, 72

4 Who is Silvia? what is she,
That all our swains commend her?
Holy, fair, and wise is she;
The heaven such grace did lend her,
That she might admired be. *IV, ii, 40*

5 Alas, how love can trifle with itself!
IV, iv, 190

6 Black men are pearls in beauteous ladies' eyes. *V, ii, 12*

7 How use doth breed a habit in a man![1]
V, iv, 1

8 Spite of cormorant devouring Time.
Love's Labour's Lost [1594–1595], act I, sc. i, l. 4

9 Make us heirs of all eternity. *I, i, 7*

10 Why, all delights are vain; but that most vain
Which, with pain purchased doth inherit pain. *I, i, 72*

11 Light seeking light doth light of light beguile.
I, i, 77

12 Study is like the heaven's glorious sun,
That will not be deep-searched with saucy looks;
Small have continual plodders ever won,
Save base authority from others' books.
These earthly godfathers of heaven's lights
That give a name to every fixèd star,
Have no more profit of their shining nights
Than those that walk and wot not what they are. *I, i, 84*

13 At Christmas I no more desire a rose
Than wish a snow in May's newfangled mirth;
But like of each thing that in season grows.
I, i, 105

14 And men sit down to that nourishment which is called supper. *I, i, 237*

15 That unlettered small-knowing soul.
I, i, 251

[1] Custom is almost second nature. — PLUTARCH [A.D. 46–120], *Rules for the Preservation of Health, 18*

16 A child of our grandmother Eve, a female; or, for thy more sweet understanding, a woman. *Love's Labour's Lost, I, i, 263*

17 Affiction may one day smile again; and till then, sit thee down, sorrow! *I, i, 312*

18 Devise, wit; write, pen; for I am for whole volumes in folio. *I, ii, 194*

19 Beauty is bought by judgment of the eye,
Not uttered by base sale of chapmen's tongues. *II, i, 15*

20 A man of sovereign parts he is esteemed;
Well fitted in arts, glorious in arms:
Nothing becomes him ill that he would well.
II, i, 44

21 A merrier man,
Within the limit of becoming mirth,
I never spent an hour's talk withal.
II, i, 66

22 Your wit's too hot, it speeds too fast, 'twill tire. *II, i, 119*

23 Warble, child; make passionate my sense of hearing. *III, i, 1*

24 Remuneration! O! that's the Latin word for three farthings. *III, i, 143*

25 A very beadle to a humorous sigh.
III, i, 185

26 This wimpled, whining, purblind, wayward boy,
This senior-junior, giant-dwarf, Dan Cupid;
Regent of love-rimes, lord of folded arms,
The anointed sovereign of sighs and groans,
Liege of all loiters and malcontents.
III, i, 189

27 He hath not fed of the dainties that are bred of a book; he hath not eat paper, as it were; he hath not drunk ink.
IV, ii, 25

28 Many can brook the weather that love not the wind. *IV, ii, 34*

29 You two are book-men. *IV, ii, 35*

30 These are begot in the ventricle of memory, nourished in the womb of pia mater, and delivered upon the mellowing of occasion.
IV, ii, 70

31 By heaven, I do love, and it hath taught me to rime, and to be melancholy.
IV, iii, 13

32 The heavenly rhetoric of thine eye.
IV, iii, 60

33 Young blood doth not obey an old decree:
We cannot cross the cause why we were born.
IV, iii, 217

1 For where is any author in the world
Teaches such beauty as a woman's eye?
Learning is but an adjunct to ourself.
Love's Labour's Lost, IV, iii, 312

2 But love, first learnèd in a lady's eyes,
Lives not alone immurèd in the brain.
IV, iii, 327

3 It adds a precious seeing to the eye.
IV, iii, 333

4 As sweet and musical
As bright Apollo's lute,[1] strung with his hair;
And when Love speaks, the voice of all the gods
Makes heaven drowsy with the harmony.
IV, iii, 342

5 From women's eyes this doctrine I derive:
They sparkle still the right Promethean fire;
They are the books, the arts, the academes,
That show, contain, and nourish all the world. *IV, iii, 350*

6 He draweth out the thread of his verbosity finer than the staple of his argument.
V, i, 18

7 *Moth:* They have been at a great feast of languages, and stolen the scraps.

Costard: O! they have lived long on the alms-basket of words. I marvel thy master hath not eaten thee for a word; for thou art not so long by the head as *honorificabilitudinitatibus;* thou art easier swallowed than a flap-dragon. *V, i, 39*

8 In the posteriors of this day, which the rude multitude call the afternoon.
V, i, 96

9 Taffeta phrases, silken terms precise,
Three-piled hyperboles, spruce affectation,
Figures pedantical. *V, ii, 407*

10 Let me take you a button-hole lower.
V, ii, 705

11 The naked truth of it is, I have no shirt.
V, ii, 715

12 A jest's prosperity lies in the ear
Of him that hears it, never in the tongue
Of him that makes it. *V, ii, 869*

13 When daisies pied and violets blue,
And lady-smocks all silver-white,
And cuckoo-buds of yellow hue
Do paint the meadows with delight,
The cuckoo then, on every tree,
Mocks married men; for thus sings he,
Cuckoo;
Cuckoo, cuckoo: O word of fear,
Unpleasing to a married ear.
V, ii, 902

[1]See Milton, 279:25.

14 When icicles hang by the wall,
And Dick, the shepherd, blows his nail,
And Tom bears logs into the hall,
And milk comes frozen home in pail,
When blood is nipped and ways be foul,
Then nightly sings the staring owl,
Tu-who;
Tu-whit, tu-who—a merry note,
While greasy Joan doth keel the pot.
Love's Labour's Lost, V, ii, 920

15 When all aloud the wind doth blow,
And coughing drowns the parson's saw,
And birds sit brooding in the snow,
And Marian's nose looks red and raw,
When roasted crabs hiss in the bowl.
V, ii, 929

16 The words of Mercury are harsh after the songs of Apollo. *V, ii, 938*

17 A pair of star-crossed lovers.
Romeo and Juliet [1594–1595], prologue, l. 6

18 Saint-seducing gold. *Act I, sc. i, l. 220*

19 One fire burns out another's burning,[2]
One pain is lessened by another's anguish.
I, ii, 47

20 I will make thee think thy swan a crow.
I, ii, 92

21 For I am proverbed with a grandsire phrase.
I, iv, 37

22 We burn daylight. *I, iv, 43*

23 O! then, I see Queen Mab hath been with you! . . .
She is the fairies' midwife, and she comes
In shape no bigger than an agate-stone
On the forefinger of an alderman,
Drawn with a team of little atomies
Athwart men's noses as they lie asleep.
I, iv, 53

24 True, I talk of dreams,
Which are the children of an idle brain,
Begot of nothing but vain fantasy.
I, iv, 97

25 For you and I are past our dancing days.[3]
I, v, 35

26 It seems she hangs upon the cheek of night
Like a rich jewel in an Ethiop's ear;
Beauty too rich for use, for earth too dear!
I, v, 49

27 My only love sprung from my only hate!
Too early seen unknown, and known too late!
I, v, 142

[2]See Chapman, 177:18.

[3]My dancing days are done.—BEAUMONT AND FLETCHER, *The Scornful Lady* [1616], *act V, sc. iii*

1 Young Adam Cupid, he that shot so trim
When King Cophetua loved the beggar-maid.[1] *Romeo and Juliet, II, i, 13*

2 He jests at scars, that never felt a wound.
But, soft! what light through yonder window breaks?
It is the east, and Juliet is the sun!
II, ii, 1

3 She speaks, yet she says nothing.
II, ii, 12

4 See! how she leans her cheek upon her hand:
O! that I were a glove upon that hand,
That I might touch that cheek.
II, ii, 23

5 O Romeo, Romeo! wherefore art thou Romeo?[2]
Deny thy father, and refuse thy name;
Or, if thou wilt not, be but sworn my love,
And I'll no longer be a Capulet.
II, ii, 33

6 What's in a name? That which we call a rose
By any other name would smell as sweet.
II, ii, 43

7 For stony limits cannot hold love out.
II, ii, 67

8 At lovers' perjuries,
They say, Jove laughs.[3] *II, ii, 92*

9 In truth, fair Montague, I am too fond.
II, ii, 98

10 I'll prove more true
Than those that have more cunning to be strange. *II, ii, 100*

11 *Romeo:* Lady, by yonder blessèd moon I swear
That tips with silver all these fruit-tree tops—
Juliet: O! swear not by the moon, the inconstant moon,
That monthly changes in her circled orb,
Lest that thy love prove likewise variable.
II, ii, 107

12 Do not swear at all;
Or, if thou wilt, swear by thy gracious self,
Which is the god of my idolatry.
II, ii, 112

[1]See Tennyson, 530:17, and Anonymous, 917:18.

[2]*Huncamunca:* O Tom Thumb! Tom Thumb! wherefore art thou Tom Thumb?—HENRY FIELDING, *Life and Death of Tom Thumb the Great* [1730], *act II, sc. iii*

[3]See Tibullus, 113:1.
And Jove but laughs at lovers' perjury.—DRYDEN, *Palamon and Arcite* [1680], *bk. II, l. 758,* and *Amphitryon* [1690], *act I, sc. ii*

13 It is too rash, too unadvised, too sudden;
Too like the lightning, which doth cease to be
Ere one can say it lightens.
Romeo and Juliet, II, ii, 118

14 This bud of love, by summer's ripening breath,
May prove a beauteous flower when next we meet. *II, ii, 121*

15 Love goes toward love, as schoolboys from their books;
But love from love, toward school with heavy looks. *II, ii, 156*

16 O! for a falconer's voice,
To lure this tassel-gentle back again.
II, ii, 158

17 How silver-sweet sound lovers' tongues by night,
Like softest music to attending ears!
II, ii, 165

18 I would have thee gone;
And yet no further than a wanton's bird,
Who lets it hop a little from her hand,
Like a poor prisoner in his twisted gyves,
And with a silk thread plucks it back again,
So loving-jealous of his liberty.
II, ii, 176

19 Good night, good night! parting is such sweet sorrow,
That I shall say good night till it be morrow.
II, ii, 184

20 Virtue itself turns vice, being misapplied;
And vice sometime's by action dignified.
II, iii, 21

21 Care keeps his watch in every old man's eye,
And where care lodges, sleep will never lie.
II, iii, 35

22 Wisely and slow; they stumble that run fast.[4] *II, iii, 94*

23 One, two, and the third in your bosom.
II, iv, 24

24 O flesh, flesh, how art thou fishified!
II, iv, 41

25 The very pink of courtesy. *II, iv, 63*

26 A gentleman, nurse, that loves to hear himself talk, and will speak more in a minute than he will stand to in a month.
II, iv, 156

27 These violent delights have violent ends.
II, vi, 9

[4]See Chaucer, 144:28.

1 Therefore love moderately; long love doth so;[1]
Too swift arrives as tardy as too slow.
Romeo and Juliet, II, vi, 14

2 Here comes the lady: O! so light a foot
Will ne'er wear out the everlasting flint.
II, vi, 16

3 Thy head is as full of quarrels as an egg is full of meat.[2] *III, i, 23*

4 A word and a blow.[3] *III, i, 44*

5 No, 'tis not so deep as a well, nor so wide as a church door; but 'tis enough, 'twill serve: ask for me tomorrow, and you shall find me a grave man. *III, i, 101*

6 A plague o' both your houses!
They have made worms' meat of me.
III, i, 112

7 O! I am Fortune's fool. *III, i, 142*

8 Gallop apace, you fiery-footed steeds,
Towards Phoebus' lodging. *III, ii, 1*

9 When he shall die,
Take him and cut him out in little stars,
And he will make the face of heaven so fine
That all the world will be in love with night,
And pay no worship to the garish sun.
III, ii, 21

10 He was not born to shame:
Upon his brow shame is ashamed to sit.
III, ii, 91

11 Romeo, come forth; come forth, thou fearful man:
Affliction is enamored of thy parts,
And thou art wedded to calamity.
III, iii, 1

12 Adversity's sweet milk, philosophy.
III, iii, 54

13 Hang up philosophy!
Unless philosophy can make a Juliet.
III, iii, 56

14 The lark, the herald of the morn.
III, v, 6

15 Night's candles are burnt out, and jocund day
Stands tiptoe on the misty mountaintops.
III, v, 9

16 Villain and he be many miles asunder.
III, v, 82

17 Thank me no thankings, nor proud me no prouds. *III, v, 153*

[1]See Herrick, 266:8, and Anonymous, 917:12.

[2]It's as full of good-nature as an egg's full of meat. — RICHARD BRINSLEY SHERIDAN, *A Trip to Scarborough* [1777], *act III, sc. iv*

[3]Word and a blow. — BUNYAN, *Pilgrim's Progress* [1678], *pt. I*

18 Is there no pity sitting in the clouds,
That sees into the bottom of my grief?
Romeo and Juliet, III, v, 198

19 Past hope, past cure, past help!
IV, i, 45

20 'Tis an ill cook that cannot lick his own fingers. *IV, ii, 6*

21 *Apothecary:* My poverty, but not my will, consents.
Romeo: I pay thy poverty, and not thy will.
V, i, 75

22 The strength
Of twenty men. *V, i, 78*

23 The time and my intents are savage-wild,
More fierce and more inexorable far
Than empty tigers or the roaring sea.
V, iii, 39

24 Tempt not a desperate man. *V, iii, 59*

25 One writ with me in sour misfortune's book.
V, iii, 82

26 How oft when men are at the point of death
Have they been merry! *V, iii, 88*

27 Beauty's ensign yet
Is crimson in thy lips and in thy cheeks,
And death's pale flag is not advancèd there.
V, iii, 94

28 O! here
Will I set up my everlasting rest,
And shake the yoke of inauspicious stars
From this world-wearied flesh. Eyes, look your last!
Arms, take your last embrace!
V, iii, 109

29 O true apothecary!
Thy drugs are quick. *V, iii, 119*

30 See what a scourge is laid upon your hate,
That heaven finds means to kill your joys with love. *V, iii, 292*

31 For never was a story of more woe
Than this of Juliet and her Romeo.
V, iii, 309

32 The purest treasure mortal times afford
Is spotless reputation.
King Richard the Second [1595–1596], act I, sc. i, l. 177

33 Mine honor is my life; both grow in one;
Take honor from me, and my life is done.
I, i, 182

34 We were not born to sue, but to command.
I, i, 196

35 The daintiest last, to make the end most sweet. *I, iii, 68*

1 Truth hath a quiet breast.
Richard II, I, iii, 96

2 How long a time lies in one little word!
I, iii, 213

3 Things sweet to taste prove in digestion sour.
I, iii, 236

4 Must I not serve a long apprenticehood
To foreign passages, and in the end,
Having my freedom, boast of nothing else
But that I was a journeyman to grief?
I, iii, 271

5 All places that the eye of heaven visits
Are to a wise man ports and happy havens.
Teach thy necessity to reason thus;
There is no virtue like necessity.[1]
Think not the king did banish thee,
But thou the king. *I, iii, 275*

6 For gnarling sorrow hath less power to bite
The man that mocks at it and sets it light.
I, iii, 292

7 O! who can hold a fire in his hand
By thinking on the frosty Caucasus?
Or cloy the hungry edge of appetite
By bare imagination of a feast?
Or wallow naked in December snow
By thinking on fantastic summer's heat?
O, no! the apprehension of the good
Gives but the greater feeling to the worse.
I, iii, 294

8 Where'er I wander, boast of this I can,
Though banished, yet a true-born Englishman.[2] *I, iii, 308*

9 The tongues of dying men
Enforce attention like deep harmony.
II, i, 5

10 The setting sun, and music at the close,
As the last taste of sweets, is sweetest last,
Writ in remembrance more than things long past. *II, i, 12*

11 Report of fashions in proud Italy,
Whose manners still our tardy apish nation
Limps after in base imitation. *II, i, 21*

12 For violent fires soon burn out themselves;
Small showers last long, but sudden storms are short. *II, i, 34*

13 This royal throne of kings, this sceptered isle,
This earth of majesty, this seat of Mars,
This other Eden, demi-paradise,
This fortress built by Nature for herself
Against infection and the hand of war,
This happy breed of men, this little world,
This precious stone set in the silver sea,
Which serves it in the office of a wall,
Or as a moat defensive to a house,
Against the envy of less happier lands,
This blessed plot, this earth, this realm, this England,
This nurse, this teeming womb of royal kings,
Feared by their breed and famous by their birth. *Richard II, II, i, 40*

14 England, bound in with the triumphant sea,
Whose rocky shore beats back the envious siege
Of watery Neptune. *II, i, 61*

15 That England, that was wont to conquer others,
Hath made a shameful conquest of itself.
II, i, 65

16 A lunatic lean-witted fool,
Presuming on an ague's privilege.
II, i, 115

17 The ripest fruit first falls. *II, i, 154*

18 Each substance of a grief hath twenty shadows. *II, ii, 14*

19 I count myself in nothing else so happy
As in a soul remembering my good friends.
II, iii, 46

20 Evermore thanks, the exchequer of the poor.
II, iii, 65

21 Grace me no grace, nor uncle me no uncle.
II, iii, 87

22 The caterpillars of the commonwealth,
Which I have sworn to weed and pluck away.
II, iii, 166

23 Things past redress are now with me past care. *II, iii, 171*

24 I see thy glory like a shooting star
Fall to the base earth from the firmament.
II, iv, 19

25 Eating the bitter bread of banishment.[3]
III, i, 21

26 Not all the water in the rough rude sea
Can wash the balm from an anointed king.
III, ii, 54

27 O! call back yesterday, bid time return.[4]
III, ii, 69

28 The worst is death, and death will have his day. *III, ii, 103*

[1] See Quintilian, 117:21.
[2] A stern, a true-born Englishman.—SAMUEL JOHNSON; from BOSWELL, *Life of Johnson* [1791]
The True-born Englishman [1701]. Title of satire by DANIEL DEFOE.

[3] See *Isaiah 30:20*, 30:18.
[4] See Thomas Heywood, 257:17.

1 Of comfort no man speak:
Let's talk of graves, of worms, and epitaphs;
Make dust our paper, and with rainy eyes
Write sorrow on the bosom of the earth;
Let's choose executors and talk of wills.
Richard II, III, ii, 144

2 And nothing can we call our own but death,
And that small model of the barren earth
Which serves as paste and cover to our bones.
For God's sake, let us sit upon the ground
And tell sad stories of the death of kings:
How some have been deposed, some slain in war,
Some haunted by the ghosts they have deposed,
Some poisoned by their wives, some sleeping killed;
All murdered: for within the hollow crown
That rounds the mortal temples of a king
Keeps Death his court. *III, ii, 152*

3 Comes at the last, and with a little pin
Bores through his castle wall, and farewell king! *III, ii, 169*

4 He is come to open
The purple testament of bleeding war.
III, iii, 93

5 O! that I were as great
As is my grief, or lesser than my name,
Or that I could forget what I have been,
Or not remember what I must be now.
III, iii, 136

6 I'll give my jewels for a set of beads,
My gorgeous palace for a hermitage,
My gay apparel for an almsman's gown.
III, iii, 147

7 And my large kingdom for a little grave,
A little little grave, an obscure grave.
III, iii, 153

8 And there at Venice gave
His body to that pleasant country's earth,
And his pure soul unto his captain Christ,
Under whose colors he had fought so long.
IV, i, 97

9 Peace shall go sleep with Turks and infidels.
IV, i, 139

10 So Judas did to Christ: but he, in twelve,
Found truth in all but one; I, in twelve thousand, none.
God save the king! Will no man say, amen?
IV, i, 170

11 Now is this golden crown like a deep well
That owes two buckets filling one another;
The emptier ever dancing in the air,
The other down, unseen and full of water:
That bucket down and full of tears am I,
Drinking my griefs, whilst you mount up on high. *Richard II, IV, i, 184*

12 You may my glories and my state depose,
But not my griefs; still am I king of those.
IV, i, 192

13 Some of you with Pilate wash your hands,[1]
Showing an outward pity. *IV, i, 239*

14 A mockery king of snow. *IV, i, 260*

15 As in a theater, the eyes of men,
After a well-graced actor leaves the stage,
Are idly bent on him that enters next,
Thinking his prattle to be tedious.
V, ii, 23

16 How sour sweet music is
When time is broke and no proportion kept!
So is it in the music of men's lives.
V, v, 42

17 I wasted time, and now doth time waste me;
For now hath time made me his numbering clock;
My thoughts are minutes. *V, v, 49*

18 This music mads me: let it sound no more.
V, v, 61

19 Mount, mount, my soul! thy seat is up on high,
Whilst my gross flesh sinks downward, here to die. *V, v, 112*

20 To live a barren sister all your life,
Chanting faint hymns to the cold fruitless moon.
A Midsummer-Night's Dream [1595–1596], act I, sc. i, l. 72

21 But earthlier happy is the rose distilled,
Than that which withering on the virgin thorn
Grows, lives and dies, in single blessedness.
I, i, 76

22 For aught that I could ever read,
Could ever hear by tale or history,
The course of true love never did run smooth.
I, i, 132

23 Swift as a shadow, short as any dream,
Brief as the lightning in the collied night,
That, in a spleen, unfolds both heaven and earth,
And ere a man hath power to say, "Behold!"
The jaws of darkness do devour it up:
So quick bright things come to confusion.
I, i, 144

[1] See *Matthew 27:24*, 41:22.

1 Love looks not with the eyes, but with the mind,
And therefore is winged Cupid painted blind.[1]
A Midsummer-Night's Dream, I, i, 234

2 The most lamentable comedy, and most cruel death of Pyramus and Thisby.
I, ii, 11

3 Masters, spread yourselves. *I, ii, 16*

4 This is Ercles' vein, a tyrant's vein.
I, ii, 43

5 I'll speak in a monstrous little voice.
I, ii, 55

6 I am slow of study. *I, ii, 70*

7 That would hang us, every mother's son.
I, ii, 81

8 I will aggravate my voice so that I will roar you as gently as any sucking dove; I will roar you as 'twere any nightingale.
I, ii, 85

9 A proper man, as one shall see in a summer's day; a most lovely, gentleman-like man. *I, ii, 89*

10 Over hill, over dale,[2]
Thorough bush, thorough brier,
Over park, over pale,
Thorough flood, thorough fire. *II, i, 2*

11 I must go seek some dew drops here,
And hang a pearl in every cowslip's ear.
II, i, 14

12 I am that merry wanderer of the night.
I jest to Oberon, and make him smile
When I a fat and bean-fed horse beguile,
Neighing in likeness of a filly foal:
And sometimes lurk I in a gossip's bowl,
In very likeness of a roasted crab.
II, i, 43

13 Ill met by moonlight, proud Titania.
II, i, 60

14 Since once I sat upon a promontory,
And heard a mermaid on a dolphin's back
Uttering such dulcet and harmonious breath,
That the rude sea grew civil at her song,
And certain stars shot madly from their spheres
To hear the sea-maid's music.
II, i, 149

[1] See Chaucer, 147:23, and *Merchant of Venice*, 199:7.
I have heard of reasons manifold / Why Love must needs be blind, / But this the best of all I hold— / His eyes are in his mind.—COLERIDGE, *Reason for Love's Blindness* [1828]

[2] See Gruber, 764:11.

15 And the imperial votaress passed on,
In maiden meditation, fancy-free.
Yet marked I where the bolt of Cupid fell:
It fell upon a little western flower,
Before milk-white, now purple with love's wound,
And maidens call it, Love-in-idleness.
A Midsummer-Night's Dream, II, i, 163

16 I'll put a girdle round about the earth
In forty minutes.[3] *II, i, 175*

17 For you in my respect are all the world:
Then how can it be said I am alone,
When all the world is here to look on me?
II, i, 224

18 I know a bank whereon the wild thyme blows,
Where oxlips and the nodding violet grows
Quite over-canopied with luscious woodbine,
With sweet musk-roses, and with eglantine:
There sleeps Titania some time of the night,
Lulled in these flowers with dances and delight;
And there the snake throws her enamelled skin,
Weed wide enough to wrap a fairy in.
II, i, 249

19 Some to kill cankers in the musk-rose buds,
Some war with rere-mice for their leathern wings,
To make my small elves coats.
II, ii, 3

20 The clamorous owl, that nightly hoots, and wonders
At our quaint spirits. *II, ii, 6*

21 You spotted snakes with double tongue,
Thorny hedge-hogs, be not seen;
Newts, and blind-worms, do no wrong;
Come not near our fairy queen.
II, ii, 9

22 Night and silence! who is here?
Weeds of Athens he doth wear.
II, ii, 70

23 As a surfeit of the sweetest things
The deepest loathing to the stomach brings.[4] *II, ii, 137*

24 To bring in—God shield us!—a lion among ladies, is a most dreadful thing, for there is not a more fearful wild-fowl than your lion living. *III, i, 32*

25 A calendar, a calendar! look in the almanack; find out moonshine. *III, i, 55*

26 Bless thee, Bottom! bless thee! thou art translated. *III, i, 124*

[3] See Chapman, 178:1.

[4] See *King Henry IV, Part I*, 204:20.

1 Lord, what fools these mortals be![1]
A Midsummer-Night's Dream, III, ii, 115

2 So we grew together,
Like to a double cherry, seeming parted,
But yet an union in partition;
Two lovely berries molded on one stem.
III, ii, 208

3 Though she be but little, she is fierce.
III, ii, 325

4 I have a reasonable good ear in music: let us have the tongs and the bones.
IV, i, 32

5 Truly, a peck of provender: I could munch your good dry oats. Methinks I have a great desire to a bottle of hay: good hay, sweet hay, hath no fellow. *IV, i, 36*

6 I have an exposition of sleep come upon me.
IV, i, 44

7 My Oberon! what visions have I seen!
Methought I was enamored of an ass.
IV, i, 82

8 I never heard
So musical a discord, such sweet thunder.
IV, i, 123

9 I have had a dream, past the wit of man to say what dream it was. *IV, i, 211*

10 The eye of man hath not heard, the ear of man hath not seen,[2] man's hand is not able to taste, his tongue to conceive, nor his heart to report, what my dream was.
IV, i, 218

11 Eat no onions nor garlic, for we are to utter sweet breath. *IV, ii, 44*

12 The lunatic, the lover, and the poet,
Are of imagination all compact:
One sees more devils than vast hell can hold,
That is, the madman; the lover, all as frantic,
Sees Helen's beauty in a brow of Egypt:
The poet's eye, in a fine frenzy rolling,
Doth glance from heaven to earth, from earth to heaven;
And, as imagination bodies forth
The forms of things unknown, the poet's pen
Turns them to shapes, and gives to airy nothing
A local habitation and a name.
Such tricks hath strong imagination,
That, if it would but apprehend some joy,
It comprehends some bringer of that joy;
Or in the night, imagining some fear,
How easy is a bush supposed a bear!
V, i, 7

[1] See Seneca, 114:13.
[2] See *I Corinthians* 2:9, 48:2.

13 Very tragical mirth.
A Midsummer-Night's Dream, V, i, 57

14 The true beginning of our end.[3]
V, i, 111

15 The best in this kind are but shadows.
V, i, 215

16 A very gentle beast, and of a good conscience. *V, i, 232*

17 All that I have to say, is, to tell you that the lanthorn is the moon; I, the man in the moon; this thorn-bush, my thorn-bush; and this dog, my dog. *V, i, 263*

18 Well roared, Lion! *V, i, 272*

19 This passion, and the death of a dear friend, would go near to make a man look sad.
V, i, 295

20 With the help of a surgeon, he might yet recover, and prove an ass. *V, i, 318*

21 No epilogue, I pray you, for your play needs no excuse. Never excuse.[4] *V, i, 363*

22 The iron tongue of midnight hath told twelve;
Lovers, to bed; 'tis almost fairy time.
V, i, 372

23 If we shadows have offended,
Think but this, and all is mended,
That you have but slumbered here
While these visions did appear.
V, ii, 54

24 Your mind is tossing on the ocean.
The Merchant of Venice [1596–1597], act I, sc. i, l. 8

25 My ventures are not in one bottom trusted,
Nor to one place. *I, i, 42*

26 Nature hath framed strange fellows in her time. *I, i, 51*

27 You have too much respect upon the world:
They lose it that do buy it with much care.
I, i, 74

28 I hold the world but as the world, Gratiano;
A stage, where every man must play a part,[5]
And mine a sad one. *I, i, 77*

29 Why should a man, whose blood is warm within,
Sit like his grandsire cut in alabaster?
I, i, 83

[3] I see the beginning of my end. — MASSINGER, *The Virgin Martyr* [1622], *act III, sc. iii*
[4] See Meurier, 163:8, and *King John*, 202:6.
[5] See *As You Like It*, 211:15.

1 There are a sort of men whose visages
Do cream and mantle like a standing pond.
The Merchant of Venice, I, i, 88

2 I am Sir Oracle,
And when I ope my lips let no dog bark!
I, i, 93

3 I do know of these,
That therefore only are reputed wise
For saying nothing. *I, i, 95*

4 Fish not, with this melancholy bait,
For this fool-gudgeon, this opinion.
I, i, 101

5 Gratiano speaks an infinite deal of nothing, more than any man in all Venice. His reasons are as two grains of wheat hid in two bushels of chaff: you shall seek all day ere you find them, and, when you have them, they are not worth the search. *I, i, 114*

6 In my school-days, when I had lost one shaft,
I shot his fellow of the selfsame flight
The selfsame way with more advisèd watch,
To find the other forth, and by adventuring both,
I oft found both. *I, i, 141*

7 They are as sick that surfeit with too much as they that starve with nothing.
I, ii, 5

8 Superfluity comes sooner by white hairs, but competency lives longer. *I, ii, 9*

9 If to do were as easy as to know what were good to do, chapels had been churches, and poor men's cottages princes' palaces.
I, ii, 13

10 The brain may devise laws for the blood, but a hot temper leaps o'er a cold decree.
I, ii, 19

11 He doth nothing but talk of his horse.
I, ii, 43

12 I fear he will prove the weeping philosopher when he grows old, being so full of unmannerly sadness in his youth.
I, ii, 51

13 God made him, and therefore let him pass for a man. *I, ii, 59*

14 When he is best, he is a little worse than a man, and when he is worst, he is little better than a beast. *I, ii, 93*

15 I dote on his very absence. *I, ii, 118*

16 My meaning in saying he is a good man is to have you understand me that he is sufficient. *I, iii, 15*

17 Ships are but boards, sailors but men: there be land-rats and water-rats, land-thieves and water-thieves. *I, iii, 22*

18 Yes, to smell pork; to eat of the habitation which your prophet the Nazarite[1] conjured the devil into. I will buy with you, sell with you, talk with you, walk with you, and so following; but I will not eat with you, drink with you, nor pray with you. What news on the Rialto?
The Merchant of Venice, I, iii, 34

19 How like a fawning publican he looks!
I hate him for he is a Christian.
I, iii, 42

20 If I can catch him once upon the hip,[2]
I will feed fat the ancient grudge I bear him.
I, iii, 47

21 Cursèd be my tribe,
If I forgive him. *I, iii, 52*

22 The devil can cite Scripture for his purpose.
I, iii, 99

23 A goodly apple rotten at the heart.
O, what a goodly outside falsehood hath!
I, iii, 102

24 For sufferance is the badge of all our tribe.
You call me misbeliever, cut-throat dog,
And spit upon my Jewish gaberdine.
I, iii, 111

25 Shall I bend low, and in a bondman's key,
With bated breath and whispering humbleness,
Say this. *I, iii, 124*

26 I'll seal to such a bond,
And say there is much kindness in the Jew.
I, iii, 153

27 O father Abram! what these Christians are,
Whose own hard dealing teaches them suspect
The thoughts of others. *I, iii, 161*

28 I like not fair terms and a villain's mind.
I, iii, 180

29 Mislike me not for my complexion,
The shadowed livery of the burnished sun.
II, i, 1

30 If Hercules and Lichas play at dice
Which is the better man, the greater throw
May turn by fortune from the weaker hand.
II, i, 32

31 O heavens! this is my true-begotten father.
II, ii, 36

[1]That hee shall be called a Nazarite.—*The Geneva Bible* [1557–1560], *Matthew* 2:23
The Geneva version of the Bible is the one Shakespeare was familiar with.

[2]See Heywood, 161:1, and *The Merchant of Venice,* 200:18.

1 An honest, exceeding poor man.
The Merchant of Venice, II, ii, 54

2 The very staff of my age, my very prop.
II, ii, 71

3 It is a wise father that knows his own child.
II, ii, 83

4 And the vile squealing of the wry-necked fife.
II, v, 30

5 Who riseth from a feast
With that keen appetite that he sits down?
II, vi, 8

6 All things that are,
Are with more spirit chasèd than enjoyed.
How like a younker or a prodigal
The scarfèd bark puts from her native bay,
Hugged and embracèd by the strumpet wind!
How like the prodigal doth she return,
With over-weathered ribs and ragged sails,
Lean, rent, and beggared by the strumpet wind!
II, vi, 12

7 But love is blind,[1] and lovers cannot see
The pretty follies that themselves commit.
II, vi, 36

8 Must I hold a candle to my shames?
II, vi, 41

9 Men that hazard all
Do it in hope of fair advantages:
A golden mind stoops not to show of dross.
II, vii, 18

10 Young in limbs, in judgment old.
II, vii, 71

11 My daughter! O my ducats! O my daughter!
Fled with a Christian! O my Christian ducats!
Justice! the law! my ducats, and my daughter!
A sealed bag, two sealed bags of ducats,
Of double ducats, stol'n from me by my daughter!
II, viii, 15

12 The fool multitude, that choose by show.
II, ix, 26

13 I will not jump with common spirits
And rank me with the barbarous multitude.
II, ix, 32

14 Let none presume
To wear an undeservèd dignity.
O! that estates, degrees, and offices
Were not derived corruptly, and that clear honor
Were purchased by the merit of the wearer.
II, ix, 39

[1]See Chaucer, 147:23, and *A Midsummer-Night's Dream*, 196:1.

15 Some there be that shadows kiss;
Such have but a shadow's bliss.
The Merchant of Venice, II, ix, 66

16 Let him look to his bond. *III, i, 49*

17 I am a Jew. Hath not a Jew eyes? hath not a Jew hands, organs, dimensions, senses, affections, passions? *III, i, 62*

18 If you prick us, do we not bleed? if you tickle us, do we not laugh? if you poison us, do we not die? and if you wrong us, shall we not revenge? *III, i, 65*

19 The villainy you teach me I will execute, and it shall go hard but I will better the instruction. *III, i, 76*

20 I would not have given it for a wilderness of monkeys. *III, i, 130*

21 There's something tells me, but it is not love,
I would not lose you; and you know yourself,
Hate counsels not in such a quality.
III, ii, 4

22 Makes a swanlike end,
Fading in music.[2] *III, ii, 44*

23 Tell me where is fancy bred,
Or in the heart or in the head?
How begot, how nourished?
Reply, reply. *III, ii, 63*

24 In law, what plea so tainted and corrupt
But, being seasoned with a gracious voice,
Obscures the show of evil? *III, ii, 75*

25 There is no vice so simple but assumes
Some mark of virtue on his outward parts.
III, ii, 81

26 Thus ornament is but the guilèd shore
To a most dangerous sea. *III, ii, 97*

27 The seeming truth which cunning times put on
To entrap the wisest. *III, ii, 100*

28 How all the other passions fleet to air,
As doubtful thoughts, and rash-embraced despair,
And shuddering fear, and green-eyed jealousy. *III, ii, 108*

29 An unlessoned girl, unschooled, unpracticed;
Happy in this, she is not yet so old
But she may learn. *III, ii, 160*

30 Here are a few of the unpleasant'st words
That ever blotted paper. *III, ii, 252*

31 Thou call'dst me dog before thou hadst a cause,
But, since I am a dog, beware my fangs.
III, iii, 6

[2]See Plato, 83:18; *King John*, 202:16; Byron, 461:9; and Anonymous, 918:17.

1 Thus when I shun Scylla, your father, I fall into Charybdis, your mother.[1]
The Merchant of Venice, III, v, 17

2 Some men there are love not a gaping pig;
Some, that are mad if they behold a cat.
IV, i, 47

3 A harmless necessary cat. *IV, i, 55*

4 *Bassanio:* Do all men kill the things they do not love?[2]
Shylock: Hates any man the thing he would not kill? *IV, i, 66*

5 What! wouldst thou have a serpent sting thee twice? *IV, i, 69*

6 The weakest kind of fruit
Drops earliest to the ground.
IV, i, 115

7 To hold opinion with Pythagoras
That souls of animals infuse themselves
Into the trunks of men.[3] *IV, i, 131*

8 I never knew so young a body with so old a head.[4] *IV, i, 163*

9 The quality of mercy is not strained,
It droppeth as the gentle rain from heaven
Upon the place beneath: it is twice blessed;
It blesseth him that gives and him that takes:
'Tis mightiest in the mightiest; it becomes
The thronèd monarch better than his crown;
His scepter shows the force of temporal power,
The attribute to awe and majesty,
Wherein doth sit the dread and fear of kings,[5]
But mercy is above this sceptered sway,
It is enthronèd in the hearts of kings,
It is an attribute to God himself,
And earthly power doth then show likest God's
When mercy seasons justice.[6] Therefore, Jew,
Though justice be thy plea, consider this,
That in the course of justice, none of us
Should see salvation: we do pray for mercy,
And that same prayer doth teach us all to render
The deeds of mercy.
The Merchant of Venice, IV, i, 184

10 To do a great right, do a little wrong.
IV, i, 216

11 A Daniel come to judgment! yea, a Daniel!
IV, i, 223

12 How much more elder art thou than thy looks! *IV, i, 251*

13 Is it so nominated in the bond?
IV, i, 260

14 'Tis not in the bond. *IV, i, 263*

15 For herein Fortune shows herself more kind
Than is her custom: it is still her use
To let the wretched man outlive his wealth,
To view with hollow eye and wrinkled brow
An age of poverty. *IV, i, 268*

16 I have a daughter;
Would any of the stock of Barabbas
Had been her husband rather than a Christian! *IV, i, 296*

17 An upright judge, a learnèd judge!
IV, i, 324

18 Now, infidel, I have thee on the hip.[7]
IV, i, 334

19 A Daniel, still say I; a second Daniel!
I thank thee, Jew, for teaching me that word.
IV, i, 341

20 You take my house when you do take the prop
That doth sustain my house; you take my life
When you do take the means whereby I live.
IV, i, 376

21 He is well paid that is well satisfied.
IV, i, 416

22 *Lorenzo:* The moon shines bright: in such a night as this . . .
Troilus methinks mounted the Troyan walls,
And sighed his soul toward the Grecian tents,
Where Cressid lay that night.
Jessica: In such a night
Did Thisbe fearfully o'ertrip the dew,
And saw the lion's shadow ere himself,
And ran dismayed away.
Lorenzo: In such a night
Stood Dido with a willow in her hand

[1] Scylla to port, and on our starboard beam Charybdis, dire gorge of the salt sea tide. — HOMER, *Odyssey, bk. XII, l. 232*

Scylla guards the right side; implacable Charybdis the left. — VIRGIL, *Aeneid, bk. III, l. 420*

Incidis in Scyllam cupiens vitare Charybdim [You fall into Scylla in seeking to avoid Charybdis]. — PHILIPPE GUALTIER, *Alexandreis* [c. 1300], *bk. V, l. 301*

[2] See Oscar Wilde, 676:8.

[3] *Clown:* What is the opinion of Pythagoras concerning wild-fowl? / *Malvolio:* That the soul of our grandam might haply inhabit a bird. — *Twelfth-Night* [1598–1600], *act IV, sc. ii, l. 55*

[4] He is young, but take it from me, a very staid head. — THOMAS WENTWORTH, EARL OF STRAFFORD [1593–1641], *letter commending the Earl of Ormond to Charles I for appointment as councilor*

[5] See *Measure for Measure,* 228:6.

[6] See Milton, 287:25.

[7] See Heywood, 161:1, and *The Merchant of Venice,* 198:20.

Upon the wild sea-banks, and waft her love
To come again to Carthage.
Jessica: In such a night
Medea gathered the enchanted herbs
That did renew old Aeson.
The Merchant of Venice, V, i, 1

1 How sweet the moonlight sleeps upon this bank!
Here we will sit, and let the sounds of music
Creep in our ears: soft stillness and the night
Become the touches of sweet harmony.
Sit, Jessica: look, how the floor of heaven
Is thick inlaid with patines of bright gold:
There's not the smallest orb which thou behold'st
But in his motion like an angel sings,
Still quiring to the young-eyed cherubins.
Such harmony is in immortal souls;
But, whilst this muddy vesture of decay
Doth grossly close it in, we cannot hear it.
V, i, 54

2 I am never merry when I hear sweet music.
V, i, 69

3 The man that hath no music in himself,
Nor is not moved with concord of sweet sounds,
Is fit for treasons, stratagems, and spoils;
The motions of his spirit are dull as night,
And his affections dark as Erebus:
Let no such man be trusted. *V, i, 83*

4 How far that little candle throws his beams!
So shines a good deed in a naughty world.[1]
V, i, 90

5 How many things by season seasoned are
To their right praise and true perfection!
V, i, 107

6 This night methinks is but the daylight sick.
V, i, 124

7 A light wife doth make a heavy husband.
V, i, 130

8 These blessed candles of the night.
V, i, 220

9 For new-made honor doth forget men's names.
King John [1596–1597], act I, sc. i, l. 187

10 Sweet, sweet, sweet poison for the age's tooth.
I, i, 213

11 Bearing their birthrights proudly on their backs,
To make a hazard of new fortunes here.
II, i, 70

[1]See *Matthew 5:15,* 37:6, and William Bradford, 265:13.

12 For courage mounteth with occasion.
King John, II, i, 82

13 The hare of whom the proverb goes,
Whose valor plucks dead lions by the beard.[2] *II, i, 137*

14 A woman's will. *II, i, 194*

15 Saint George, that swinged the dragon, and e'er since
Sits on his horse back at mine hostess' door.
II, i, 288

16 He is the half part of a blessèd man,
Left to be finished by such a she;
And she a fair divided excellence,
Whose fullness of perfection lies in him.
II, i, 437

17 'Zounds! I was never so bethumped with words
Since I first called my brother's father dad.
II, i, 466

18 Mad world! mad kings! mad composition!
II, i, 561

19 That smooth-faced gentleman, tickling Commodity,
Commodity, the bias of the world.
II, i, 573

20 I will instruct my sorrows to be proud;
For grief is proud and makes his owner stoop.
III, i, 68

21 Thou wear a lion's hide! doff it for shame,
And hang a calf's-skin on those recreant limbs. *III, i, 128*

22 The sun's o'ercast with blood: fair day, adieu!
Which is the side that I must go withal?
I am with both: each army hath a hand;
And in their rage, I having hold of both,
They whirl asunder and dismember me.
III, i, 326

23 Bell, book and candle shall not drive me back.[3] *III, iii, 12*

24 Look, who comes here! a grave unto a soul.
III, iv, 17

25 Death, death: O, amiable lovely death![4]
III, iv, 25

26 Grief fills the room up of my absent child,
Lies in his bed, walks up and down with me,
Puts on his pretty looks, repeats his words,
Remembers me of all his gracious parts,
Stuffs out his vacant garments with his form.
III, iv, 93

[2]So hares may pull dead lions by the beard. — KYD, *The Spanish Tragedy* [1594], *act I, sc. ii, l. 172*
[3]See Malory, 149:16.
[4]See Whitman, 576:4.

1 Life is as tedious as a twice-told tale,[1]
Vexing the dull ear of a drowsy man.
King John, III, iv, 108

2 When Fortune means to men most good,
She looks upon them with a threatening eye.[2]
III, iv, 119

3 A scepter snatched with an unruly hand
Must be as boisterously maintained as gained;
And he that stands upon a slippery place
Makes nice of no vile hold to stay him up.
III, iv, 135

4 As quiet as a lamb. *IV, i, 80*

5 To gild refinèd gold, to paint the lily,
To throw a perfume on the violet,
To smooth the ice, or add another hue
Unto the rainbow, or with taper-light
To seek the beauteous eye of heaven to garnish,
Is wasteful and ridiculous excess.
IV, ii, 11

6 And oftentimes excusing of a fault
Doth make the fault the worse by the excuse.[3]
IV, ii, 30

7 We cannot hold mortality's strong hand.
IV, ii, 82

8 There is no sure foundation set on blood,
No certain life achieved by others' death.
IV, ii, 104

9 Make haste; the better foot before.[4]
IV, ii, 170

10 Another lean unwashed artificer.
IV, ii, 201

11 How oft the sight of means to do ill deeds
Makes ill deeds done! *IV, ii, 219*

12 Heaven take my soul, and England keep my bones! *IV, iii, 10*

13 I am amazed, methinks, and lose my way
Among the thorns and dangers of this world.
IV, iii, 140

14 Unthread the rude eye of rebellion,
And welcome home again discarded faith.
V, iv, 11

15 The day shall not be up so soon as I,
To try the fair adventure of tomorrow.
V, v, 21

[1]See Homer, 60:17.
[2]See Publilius Syrus, 111:1.
[3]See Meurier, 163:8, and *A Midsummer-Night's Dream*, 197:21.
[4]Put forward your best foot! — BROWNING, *Respectability* [1855], *st. 3*

16 'Tis strange that death should sing.
I am the cygnet to this pale faint swan,
Who chants a doleful hymn to his own death.[5]
King John, V, vii, 20

17 Now my soul hath elbow-room.
V, vii, 28

18 I do not ask you much:
I beg cold comfort.[6] *V, vii, 41*

19 This England never did, nor never shall,
Lie at the proud foot of a conqueror.
V, vii, 112

20 Come the three corners of the world in arms,
And we shall shock them. Nought shall make us rue,
If England to itself do rest but true.
V, vii, 116

21 So shaken as we are, so wan with care.
King Henry the Fourth, Part I [1597–1598], act I, sc. i, l. 1

22 In those holy fields
Over whose acres walked those blessèd feet
Which fourteen hundred years ago were nailed
For our advantage on the bitter cross.
I, i, 24

23 Unless hours were cups of sack, and minutes capons, and clocks the tongues of bawds, and dials the signs of leaping houses, and the blessèd sun himself a fair hot wench in flame-colored taffeta, I see no reason why thou shouldst be so superfluous to demand the time of the day. *I, ii, 7*

24 Diana's foresters, gentlemen of the shade, minions of the moon. *I, ii, 29*

25 A purse of gold most resolutely snatched on Monday night and most dissolutely spent on Tuesday morning. *I, ii, 38*

26 Thy quips and thy quiddities.
I, ii, 51

27 So far as my coin would stretch; and where it would not, I have used my credit.
I, ii, 61

28 Old father antick the law. *I, ii, 69*

29 I am as melancholy as a gib cat, or a luggèd bear. *I, ii, 82*

30 I would to God thou and I knew where a commodity of good names were to be bought.
I, ii, 92

[5]See Plato, 83:18; *The Merchant of Venice*, 199:22; Byron, 461:9; and Anonymous, 918:17.
[6]See *The Tempest*, 247:25, and William Bradford, 265:11.

1 O! thou hast damnable iteration, and art indeed able to corrupt a saint.
Henry IV, Part I, I, ii, 101

2 Now am I, if a man should speak truly, little better than one of the wicked.
I, ii, 105

3 'Tis my vocation, Hal; 'tis no sin for a man to labor in his vocation. *I, ii, 116*

4 There's neither honesty, manhood, nor good fellowship in thee. *I, ii, 154*

5 I know you all, and will a while uphold
The unyoked humor of your idleness:
Yet herein will I imitate the sun,
Who doth permit the base contagious clouds
To smother up his beauty from the world,
That when he please again to be himself,
Being wanted, he may be more wondered at,
By breaking through the foul and ugly mists
Of vapors that did seem to strangle him.
If all the year were playing holidays,
To sport would be as tedious as to work.
I, ii, 217

6 You tread upon my patience. *I, iii, 4*

7 Came there a certain lord, neat, and trimly dressed,
Fresh as a bridegroom; and his chin new-reaped,
Showed like a stubble-land at harvest-home.
He was perfumèd like a milliner,
And 'twixt his finger and his thumb he held
A pouncet-box, which ever and anon
He gave his nose and took 't away again.
I, iii, 33

8 And as the soldiers bore dead bodies by.
He called them untaught knaves, unmannerly,
To bring a slovenly unhandsome corpse
Betwixt the wind and his nobility.
I, iii, 42

9 So pestered with a popinjay. *I, iii, 50*

10 God save the mark! *I, iii, 56*

11 And but for these vile guns,
He would himself have been a soldier.
I, iii, 63

12 To put down Richard, that sweet lovely rose,
And plant this thorn, this canker, Bolingbroke. *I, iii, 176*

13 Or sink or swim. *I, iii, 194*

14 O! the blood more stirs
To rouse a lion than to start a hare!
I, iii, 197

15 By heaven methinks it were an easy leap
To pluck bright honor from the pale-faced moon,
Or dive into the bottom of the deep,
Where fathom-line could never touch the ground,
And pluck up drowned honor by the locks.
Henry IV, Part I, I, iii, 201

16 Why, what a candy deal of courtesy
This fawning greyhound then did proffer me!
I, iii, 251

17 I know a trick worth two of that.
II, i, 40

18 If the rascal have not given me medicines to make me love him, I'll be hanged.
II, ii, 20

19 I'll starve ere I'll rob a foot further.
II, ii, 24

20 It would be argument for a week, laughter for a month, and a good jest forever.
II, ii, 104

21 Falstaff sweats to death
And lards the lean earth as he walks along.
II, ii, 119

22 Out of this nettle, danger, we pluck this flower, safety. *II, iii, 11*

23 I could brain him with his lady's fan.
II, iii, 26

24 Constant you are,
But yet a woman: and for secrecy,
No lady closer; for I well believe
Thou wilt not utter what thou dost not know;
And so far will I trust thee, gentle Kate.
II, iii, 113

25 A Corinthian, a lad of mettle, a good boy.
II, iv, 13

26 I am not yet of Percy's mind, the Hotspur of the North; he that kills me some six or seven dozen of Scots at a breakfast, washes his hands, and says to his wife, "Fie upon this quiet life! I want work." *II, iv, 116*

27 A plague of all cowards, I say.
II, iv, 129

28 There live not three good men unhanged in England, and one of them is fat and grows old. *II, iv, 146*

29 You care not who sees your back: call you that backing of your friends? A plague upon such backing! *II, iv, 168*

30 I have peppered two of them. . . . I tell thee what, Hal, if I tell thee a lie, spit in my face; call me horse. *II, iv, 216*

31 Give you a reason on compulsion! If reasons were as plenty as blackberries, I would give no man a reason upon compulsion, I.
II, iv, 267

1 Mark now, how a plain tale shall put you down. *Henry IV, Part I, II, iv, 285*

2 What doth gravity out of his bed at midnight? *II, iv, 328*

3 A plague of sighing and grief! It blows a man up like a bladder. *II, iv, 370*

4 I must speak in passion, and I will do it in King Cambyses' vein. *II, iv, 429*

5 That reverend vice, that gray iniquity, that father ruffian, that vanity in years. *II, iv, 505*

6 If sack and sugar be a fault, God help the wicked! If to be old and merry be a sin, then many an old host that I know is damned: if to be fat be to be hated, then Pharaoh's lean kine are to be loved. *II, iv, 524*

7 Banish plump Jack, and banish all the world. *II, iv, 534*

8 Play out the play. *II, iv, 539*

9 O, monstrous! but one half-penny-worth of bread to this intolerable deal of sack! *II, iv, 597*

10 Diseased nature oftentimes breaks forth
In strange eruptions. *III, i, 27*

11 I am not in the roll of common men. *III, i, 43*

12 *Glendower:* I can call spirits from the vasty deep.
Hotspur: Why, so can I, or so can any man;
But will they come when you do call for them? *III, i, 53*

13 I had rather be a kitten and cry mew,
Than one of these same meter ballad mongers. *III, i, 128*

14 Mincing poetry:
'Tis like the forced gait of a shuffling nag. *III, i, 133*

15 But in the way of bargain, mark you me,
I'll cavil on the ninth part of a hair. *III, i, 138*

16 A deal of skimble-skamble stuff. *III, i, 153*

17 I understand thy kisses and thou mine,
And that's a feeling disputation. *III, i, 204*

18 *Lady Percy:* . . . Lie still, ye thief, and hear the lady sing in Welsh.
Hotspur: I had rather hear Lady, my brach, howl in Irish. *III, i, 238*

19 A good mouth-filling oath. *III, i, 258*

20 They surfeited with honey and began
To loathe the taste of sweetness, whereof a little
More than a little is by much too much.[1] *Henry IV, Part I, III, ii, 71*

21 He was but as the cuckoo is in June,
Heard, not regarded. *III, ii, 75*

22 My near'st and dearest enemy.[2] *III, ii, 123*

23 The end of life cancels all bands. *III, ii, 157*

24 An I have not forgotten what the inside of a church is made of, I am a peppercorn, a brewer's horse. *III, iii, 8*

25 Company, villanous company, hath been the spoil of me. *III, iii, 10*

26 I make as good use of it [Bardolph's face] as many a man doth of a Death's head, or a *memento mori.* *III, iii, 32*

27 I have more flesh than another man, and therefore more frailty. *III, iii, 187*

28 The very life-blood of our enterprise. *IV, i, 28*

29 Were it good
To set the exact wealth of all our states
All at one cast? to set so rich a main
On the nice hazard of one doubtful hour? *IV, i, 45*

30 Baited like eagles having lately bathed . . .
As full of spirit as the month of May,
And gorgeous as the sun at midsummer. *IV, i, 99*

31 I saw young Harry, with his beaver on. *IV, i, 104*

32 To turn and wind a fiery Pegasus
And witch the world with noble horsemanship. *IV, i, 109*

33 Worse than the sun in March
This praise doth nourish agues. *IV, i, 111*

34 Doomsday is near; die all, die merrily. *IV, i, 134*

35 The cankers of a calm world and a long peace. *IV, ii, 32*

36 To the latter end of a fray and the beginning of a feast
Fits a dull fighter and a keen guest. *IV, ii, 86*

37 Greatness knows itself. *IV, iii, 74*

[1] See *A Midsummer-Night's Dream,* 196:23.
[2] See *Hamlet,* 218:14.

1 I could be well content
To entertain the lag-end of my life
With quiet hours.
Henry IV, Part I, V, i, 23

2 Rebellion lay in his way, and he found it.
V, i, 28

3 Never yet did insurrection want
Such water-colors to impaint his cause.
V, i, 79

4 I would it were bed-time, Hal, and all well.
V, i, 126

5 Honor pricks me on. Yea, but how if honor prick me off when I come on? how then? Can honor set to a leg? No. Or an arm? No. Or take away the grief of a wound? No. Honor hath no skill in surgery, then? No. What is honor? a word. What is that word, honor? Air. A trim reckoning! Who hath it? he that died o' Wednesday. Doth he feel it? No. Doth he hear it? No. It is insensible then? Yea, to the dead. But will it not live with the living? No. Why? Detraction will not suffer it. Therefore I'll none of it: honor is a mere scutcheon; and so ends my catechism. *V, i, 131*

6 Suspicion all our lives shall be stuck full of eyes;
For treason is but trusted like the fox.
V, ii, 8

7 Let me tell the world.[1] *V, ii, 65*

8 The time of life is short;
To spend that shortness basely were too long.
V, ii, 81

9 Two stars keep not their motion in one sphere. *V, iv, 65*

10 But thought's the slave of life, and life time's fool;
And time, that takes survey of all the world,
Must have a stop. O! I could prophesy,
But that the earthy and cold hand of death
Lies on my tongue. *V, iv, 81*

11 This earth, that bears thee dead,
Bears not alive so stout a gentleman.
V, iv, 92

12 Thy ignominy sleep with thee in the grave,
But not remembered in thy epitaph!
V, iv, 100

13 I could have better spared a better man.
V, iv, 104

[1] I'll tell the world.—SHAKESPEARE, *Measure for Measure* [1604–1605], *act II, sc. iv, l. 154*
Ay, tell the world!—BROWNING, *Paracelsus* [1835], *pt. II*

14 The better part of valor is discretion.[2]
Henry IV, Part I, V, iv, 120

15 Full bravely hast thou fleshed
Thy maiden sword. *V, iv, 132*

16 Lord, Lord, how this world is given to lying!
V, iv, 148

17 I'll purge, and leave sack, and live cleanly.
V, iv, 168

18 Rumor is a pipe
Blown by surmises, jealousies, conjectures,
And of so easy and so plain a stop
That the blunt monster with uncounted heads,
The still-discordant wavering multitude,[3]
Can play upon it.
King Henry the Fourth, Part II [1597–1598], Induction, l. 15

19 Even such a man, so faint, so spiritless,
So dull, so dead in look, so woe-begone,
Drew Priam's curtain in the dead of night,
And would have told him half his Troy was burned. *Act I, sc. i, l. 70*

20 Yet the first bringer of unwelcome news
Hath but a losing office, and his tongue
Sounds ever after as a sullen bell,
Remembered knolling a departing friend.[4]
I, i, 100

21 I am not only witty in myself, but the cause that wit is in other men.[5] *I, ii, 10*

22 A rascally yea-forsooth knave.
I, ii, 40

23 You lie in your throat. *I, ii, 97*

24 Your lordship, though not clean past your youth, hath yet some smack of age in you, some relish of the saltness of time.
I, ii, 112

25 It is the disease of not listening, the malady of not marking, that I am troubled withal.
I, ii, 139

26 I am as poor as Job, my lord, but not so patient. *I, ii, 145*

27 We that are in the vaward of our youth.
I, ii, 201

28 Have you not a moist eye, a dry hand, a yellow cheek, a white beard, a decreasing leg, an increasing belly? *I, ii, 206*

[2] It showed discretion the best part of valor.—BEAUMONT AND FLETCHER, *A King and No King* [1619], *act II, sc. iii*

[3] See Horace, 108:19; Machiavelli, 154:8; *Coriolanus*, 242:14 and 242:21; and Pope, 339:28.

[4] See Sophocles, 74:11, and *Antony and Cleopatra*, 241:4.

[5] See Samuel Johnson, 356:28.

1 Every part about you blasted with antiquity. *Henry IV, Part II, I, ii, 210*

2 For my voice, I have lost it with hollaing and singing of anthems. *I, ii, 215*

3 It was always yet the trick of our English nation, if they have a good thing, to make it too common. *I, ii, 244*

4 I were better to be eaten to death with rust than to be scoured to nothing with perpetual motion. *I, ii, 249*

5 I can get no remedy against this consumption of the purse: borrowing only lingers and lingers it out, but the disease is incurable.[1] *I, ii, 267*

6 Who lined himself with hope,
Eating the air on promise of supply.
I, iii, 27

7 A habitation giddy and unsure
Hath he that buildeth on the vulgar heart.
I, iii, 89

8 Past and to come seem best; things present worst. *I, iii, 108*

9 A poor lone woman. *II, i, 37*

10 Away, you scullion! you rampallian! you fustilarian! I'll tickle your catastrophe. *II, i, 67*

11 He hath eaten me out of house and home. *II, i, 82*

12 Let the end try the man. *II, ii, 52*

13 Thus we play the fools with the time, and the spirits of the wise sit in the clouds and mock us. *II, ii, 155*

14 He was indeed the glass
Wherein the noble youth did dress themselves. *II, iii, 21*

15 And let the welkin roar. *II, iv, 181*

16 Is it not strange that desire should so many years outlive performance? *II, iv, 283*

17 O sleep! O gentle sleep![2]
Nature's soft nurse, how have I frighted thee,
That thou no more wilt weigh my eyelids down
And steep my senses in forgetfulness?
III, i, 5

18 With all appliances and means to boot.
III, i, 29

[1] See Rabelais, 157:14.
[2] Sleep, most gentle sleep.—Ovid [43 B.C.–A.D. 18]. *Metamorphoses, bk. II, l. 624*

19 Uneasy lies the head that wears a crown.
Henry IV, Part II, III, i, 31

20 O God! that one might read the book of fate.
III, i, 45

21 There is a history in all men's lives.
III, i, 80

22 Death, as the Psalmist saith, is certain to all; all shall die. *III, ii, 41*

23 Most forcible Feeble. *III, ii, 181*

24 We have heard the chimes at midnight.
III, ii, 231

25 A man can die but once; we owe God a death. *III, ii, 253*

26 We see which way the stream of time doth run
And are enforced from our most quiet sphere
By the rough torrent of occasion.
IV, i, 70

27 We ready are to try our fortunes
To the last man. *IV, ii, 43*

28 I may justly say, with the hook-nosed fellow of Rome, "I came, saw, and overcame."[3] *IV, iii, 44*

29 O polished perturbation! golden care!
That keep'st the ports of slumber open wide
To many a watchful night! *IV, v, 22*

30 See, sons, what things you are!
How quickly nature falls into revolt
When gold becomes her object!
IV, v, 63

31 Thy wish was father, Harry, to that thought.[4]
IV, v, 91

32 Before thy hour be ripe.[5] *IV, v, 95*

33 Commit
The oldest sins the newest kind of ways.
IV, v, 124

34 His cares are now all ended. *V, ii, 3*

35 This is the English, not the Turkish court;
Not Amurath an Amurath succeeds,
But Harry Harry. *V, ii, 47*

36 I know thee not, old man: fall to thy prayers;
How ill white hairs become a fool and jester!
V, v, 52

37 Master Shallow. I owe you a thousand pound. *V, v, 78*

[3] See Julius Caesar, 99:23.
[4] Men's thoughts are much according to their inclination, their discourse and speeches according to their learning and infused opinions.—Francis Bacon, *Essays* [1597–1625], *Of Custom and Education*
[5] See Blake, 404:17.

1 O! for a Muse of fire, that would ascend
The brightest heaven of invention!
King Henry the Fifth [1598–1600], Chorus, l. 1

2 Or may we cram
Within this wooden O the very casques
That did affright the air at Agincourt?
l. 12

3 Consideration like an angel came,
And whipped the offending Adam out of him.[1] *Act I, sc. i, l. 28*

4 Hear him debate of commonwealth affairs,
You would say it hath been all in all his study. *I, i, 41*

5 Turn him to any cause of policy,
The Gordian knot of it he will unloose,
Familiar as his garter; that, when he speaks,
The air, a chartered libertine, is still.
I, i, 45

6 Therefore doth heaven divide
The state of man in divers functions,
Setting endeavor in continual motion;
To which is fixèd, as an aim or butt,
Obedience: for so work the honeybees,
Creatures that by a rule in nature teach
The act of order to a peopled kingdom.
I, ii, 183

7 The singing masons building roofs of gold.
I, ii, 198

8 Many things, having full reference
To one consent, may work contrariously;
As many arrows, loosèd several ways,
Fly to one mark; as many ways meet in one town;
As many fresh streams meet in one salt sea;
As many lines close in the dial's center;
So may a thousand actions, once afoot,
End in one purpose, and be all well borne
Without defeat. *I, ii, 205*

9 'Tis ever common
That men are merriest when they are from home. *I, ii, 271*

10 Now all the youth of England are on fire,
And silken dalliance in the wardrobe lies.
II, Chorus, 1

11 O England! model to thy inward greatness,
Like little body with a mighty heart,
What mightst thou do, that honor would thee do,
Were all thy children kind and natural!
II, Chorus, 16

12 That's the humor of it. *II, i, 63*

[1]See *The Book of Common Prayer, English,* 56:16.

13 He's [Falstaff's] in Arthur's bosom, if ever man went to Arthur's bosom. A' made a finer end and went away an it had been any christom child; a' parted even just between twelve and one, even at the turning o' the tide: for after I saw him fumble with the sheets and play with flowers and smile upon his fingers' ends, I knew there was but one way; for his nose was as sharp as a pen, and a' babbled of green fields. *Henry V, II, iii, 11*

14 As cold as any stone. *II, iii, 26*

15 Trust none;
For oaths are straws, men's faiths are wafer-cakes,
And hold-fast is the only dog, my duck.
II, iii, 53

16 Once more unto the breach, dear friends, once more;
Or close the wall up with our English dead!
In peace there's nothing so becomes a man
As modest stillness and humility:
But when the blast of war blows in our ears,
Then imitate the action of the tiger;
Stiffen the sinews, summon up the blood,
Disguise fair nature with hard-favored rage;
Then lend the eye a terrible aspect.
III, i, 1

17 And sheathed their swords for lack of argument. *III, i, 21*

18 I see you stand like greyhounds in the slips,
Straining upon the start. The game's afoot:[2]
Follow your spirit; and upon this charge
Cry "God for Harry! England and Saint George!" *III, i, 31*

19 I would give all my fame for a pot of ale, and safety. *III, ii, 14*

20 Men of few words are the best men.
III, ii, 40

21 He will maintain his argument as well as any military man in the world.
III, ii, 89

22 I know the disciplines of wars.
III, ii, 156

23 I thought upon one pair of English legs
Did march three Frenchmen.
III, vi, 161

24 We are in God's hand. *III, vi, 181*

25 That island of England breeds very valiant creatures: their mastiffs are of unmatchable courage. *III, vii, 155*

26 Give them great meals of beef and iron and steel, they will eat like wolves and fight like devils. *III, vii, 166*

[2]See Conan Doyle, 689:12.

1 The hum of either army stilly sounds,
That the fixed sentinels almost receive
The secret whispers of each other's watch:
Fire answers fire, and through their paly flames
Each battle sees the other's umbered face:
Steed threatens steed, in high and boastful neighs
Piercing the night's dull ear; and from the tents
The armorers, accomplishing the knights,
With busy hammers closing rivets up,
Give dreadful note of preparation.
Henry V, IV, Chorus, 5

2 A little touch of Harry in the night.
IV, Chorus, 47

3 There is some soul of goodness in things evil,
Would men observingly distill it out.
IV, i, 4

4 When blood is their argument.
IV, i, 151

5 Every subject's duty is the king's; but every subject's soul is his own. *IV, i, 189*

6 What infinite heart's ease
Must kings neglect that private men enjoy!
And what have kings that privates have not too,
Save ceremony, save general ceremony?
And what art thou, thou idol[1] ceremony?
What kind of god art thou, that suffer'st more
Of mortal griefs than do thy worshippers?
What are thy rents? what are thy comings-in?
O ceremony! show me but thy worth.
IV, i, 256

7 'Tis not the balm, the scepter and the ball,
The sword, the mace, the crown imperial,
The intertissued robe of gold and pearl,
The farcèd title running 'fore the king,
The throne he sits on, nor the tide of pomp
That beats upon the high shore of this world,
No, not all these, thrice-gorgeous ceremony,
Not all these, laid in bed majestical,
Can sleep so soundly as the wretched slave,
Who with a body filled and vacant mind
Gets him to rest, crammed with distressful bread. *IV, i, 280*

8 O God of battles! steel my soldiers' hearts;
Possess them not with fear; take from them now
The sense of reckoning, if the opposèd numbers
Pluck their hearts from them.
IV, i, 309

[1]Sometimes rendered: idle.

9 But if it be a sin to covet honor,
I am the most offending soul alive.
Henry V, IV, iii, 28

10 This day is called the feast of Crispian:
He that outlives this day, and comes safe home,
Will stand a-tiptoe when this day is named.
And rouse him at the name of Crispian.
IV, iii, 40

11 We few, we happy few, we band of brothers;
For he today that sheds his blood with me
Shall be my brother. *IV, iii, 60*

12 The saying is true, "The empty vessel makes the greatest sound." *IV, iv, 72*

13 There is occasions and causes why and wherefore[2] in all things. *V, i, 3*

14 By this leek, I will most horribly revenge. I eat and eat, I swear. *V, i, 49*

15 All hell shall stir for this. *V, i, 72*

16 The naked, poor, and mangled Peace,
Dear nurse of arts, plenties, and joyful births.
V, ii, 34

17 Grow like savages—as soldiers will,
That nothing do but meditate on blood.
V, ii, 59

18 For these fellows of infinite tongue, that can rime themselves into ladies' favors, they do always reason themselves out again.
V, ii, 162

19 My comfort is, that old age, that ill layer-up of beauty, can do no more spoil upon my face. *V, ii, 246*

20 O Kate! nice customs curtsy to great kings.
V, ii, 291

21 He hath indeed better bettered expectation than you must expect of me to tell you how.
Much Ado About Nothing [1598–1600], act I, sc. i, l. 15

22 How much better is it to weep at joy than to joy at weeping. *I, i, 28*

23 A very valiant trencher-man.
I, i, 52

24 There's a skirmish of wit between them.
I, i, 64

25 He wears his faith but as the fashion of his hat. *I, i, 76*

26 I see, lady, the gentleman is not in your books. *I, i, 79*

27 What! my dear Lady Disdain, are you yet living? *I, i, 123*

[2]See *The Comedy of Errors*, 188:2.

1 Shall I never see a bachelor of threescore again?
Much Ado About Nothing, I, i, 209

2 In time the savage bull doth bear the yoke.
I, i, 271

3 Benedick the married man. *I, i, 278*

4 I could not endure a husband with a beard on his face: I had rather lie in the woollen.
II, i, 31

5 As merry as the day is long.
II, i, 52

6 Would it not grieve a woman to be overmastered with a piece of valiant dust? to make an account of her life to a clod of wayward marl? *II, i, 64*

7 I have a good eye, uncle: I can see a church by daylight. *II, i, 86*

8 Speak low, if you speak love.
II, i, 104

9 Friendship is constant in all other things
Save in the office and affairs of love:
Therefore all hearts in love use their own tongues;
Let every eye negotiate for itself
And trust no agent.[1] *II, i, 184*

10 She speaks poniards, and every word stabs: if her breath were as terrible as her terminations, there were no living near her; she would infect to the north star.
II, i, 257

11 Silence is the perfectest herald of joy: I were but little happy, if I could say how much. *II, i, 319*

12 It keeps on the windy side of care.[2]
II, i, 328

13 There was a star danced, and under that was I born. *II, i, 351*

14 I will tell you my drift.[3] *II, i, 406*

15 He was wont to speak plain and to the purpose. *II, iii, 19*

16 Sigh no more, ladies, sigh no more.
Men were deceivers ever;
One foot in sea, and one on shore;
To one thing constant never.
II, iii, 65

17 Sits the wind in that corner?[4]
II, iii, 108

[1]See Longfellow, 511:21.

[2]The windy side of the law.—*Twelfth-Night* [1598–1600], *act III, sc. iv, l. 183*

[3]We know your drift.—*Coriolanus* [1607–1608], *act III, sc. iii, l. 114*

[4]See Malory, 149:10.

18 Bait the hook well: this fish will bite.
Much Ado About Nothing, II, iii, 121

19 Shall quips and sentences and these paper bullets of the brain awe a man from the career of his humor? No; the world must be peopled. When I said I would die a bachelor, I did not think I should live till I were married. *II, iii, 260*

20 From the crown of his head to the sole of his foot, he is all mirth. *III, ii, 9*

21 He hath a heart as sound as a bell, and his tongue is the clapper; for what his heart thinks his tongue speaks. *III, ii, 12*

22 Everyone can master a grief but he that has it. *III, ii, 28*

23 Are you good men and true?
III, iii, 1

24 To be a well-favored man is the gift of fortune; but to write and read comes by nature.
III, iii, 14

25 If they make you not then the better answer, you may say they are not the men you took them for. *III, iii, 49*

26 They that touch pitch will be defiled.[5]
III, iii, 61

27 The fashion wears out more apparel than the man. *III, iii, 147*

28 A good old man, sir; he will be talking: as they say, When the age is in, the wit is out.
III, v, 36

29 O! what men dare do! what men may do! what men daily do, not knowing what they do! *IV, i, 19*

30 O! what authority and show of truth
Can cunning sin cover itself withal.
IV, i, 35

31 For it so falls out
That what we have we prize not to the worth
Whiles we enjoy it, but being lacked and lost,
Why, then we rack the value, then we find
The virtue that possession would not show us
Whiles it was ours. *IV, i, 219*

32 Masters, it is proved already that you are little better than false knaves, and it will go near to be thought so shortly.
IV, ii, 23

33 Flat burglary as ever was committed.
IV, ii, 54

[5]See *Ecclesiasticus 13:1*, 35:24.
This pitch, as ancient writers do report, doth defile; so doth the company thou keepest.—*King Henry IV, Part I* [1597–1598], *act II, sc. iv, l. 460*

1 Thou wilt be condemned into everlasting redemption for this.
Much Ado About Nothing, IV, ii, 60

2 O that he were here to write me down an ass! *IV, ii, 80*

3 Patch griefs with proverbs. *V, i, 17*

4 Charm ache with air, and agony with words. *V, i, 26*

5 For there was never yet philosopher
That could endure the toothache patiently. *V, i, 35*

6 Some of us will smart for it. *V, i, 108*

7 What though care killed a cat,[1] thou hast mettle enough in thee to kill care. *V, i, 135*

8 I was not born under a riming planet. *V, ii, 40*

9 The trumpet of his own virtues. *V, ii, 91*

10 Done to death by slanderous tongues. *V, iii, 3*

11 Fleet the time carelessly, as they did in the golden world.
As You Like It [1598–1600], act I, sc. i, l. 126

12 Always the dullness of the fool is the whetstone of the wits. *I, ii, 59*

13 The little foolery that wise men have makes a great show. *I, ii, 97*

14 Well said: that was laid on with a trowel. *I, ii, 113*

15 Your heart's desires be with you! *I, ii, 214*

16 One out of suits with fortune. *I, ii, 263*

17 My pride fell with my fortunes. *I, ii, 269*

18 Hereafter, in a better world than this,
I shall desire more love and knowledge of you. *I, ii, 301*

19 Heavenly Rosalind! *I, ii, 306*

20 O, how full of briers is this working-day world! *I, iii, 12*

21 Beauty provoketh thieves sooner than gold. *I, iii, 113*

[1] Let care kill a cat, / We'll laugh and grow fat.—*Shirburn Ballads* [1585], *91*
Hang sorrow, care'll kill a cat.—JONSON, *Every Man in His Humour* [1598], *act I, sc. i*

22 We'll have a swashing and a martial outside,
As many other mannish cowards have.
As You Like It, I, iii, 123

23 Hath not old custom made this life more sweet
Than that of painted pomp? Are not these woods
More free from peril than the envious court?
II, i, 2

24 Sweet are the uses of adversity,
Which, like the toad, ugly and venomous,
Wears yet a precious jewel in his head;
And this our life, exempt from public haunt,
Finds tongues in trees, books in the running brooks,
Sermons in stones, and good in everything.[2]
II, i, 12

25 The big round tears
Coursed one another down his innocent nose
In piteous chase. *II, i, 38*

26 "Poor deer," quoth he, "thou mak'st a testament
As worldlings do, giving thy sum of more
To that which had too much."
II, i, 47

27 Sweep on, you fat and greasy citizens.
II, i, 55

28 And He that doth the ravens feed,
Yea, providently caters for the sparrow,
Be comfort to my age! *II, iii, 43*

29 Though I look old, yet I am strong and lusty;
For in my youth I never did apply
Hot and rebellious liquors in my blood.
II, iii, 47

30 Therefore my age is as a lusty winter,
Frosty, but kindly. *II, iii, 52*

31 Thou art not for the fashion of these times,
Where none will sweat but for promotion.
II, iii, 59

32 Ay, now am I in Arden; the more fool I: when I was at home, I was in a better place: but travelers must be content.
II, iv, 16

33 If you remember'st not the slightest folly
That ever love did make thee run into,
Thou hast not loved. *II, iv, 34*

34 We that are true lovers run into strange capers. *II, iv, 53*

35 Thou speakest wiser than thou art ware of. *II, iv, 57*

36 I shall ne'er be ware of mine own wit, till I break my shins against it. *II, iv, 59*

[2] See St. Bernard, 136:9; *As You Like It,* 211:17; and Wordsworth, 423:7.

1 Under the greenwood tree
Who loves to lie with me,
And turn his merry note
Unto the sweet bird's throat,
Come hither, come hither, come hither:
Here shall he see
No enemy
But winter and rough weather.
As You Like It, II, v, 1

2 I can suck melancholy out of a song as a weasel sucks eggs. *II, v, 12*

3 Who doth ambition shun,
And loves to live i' the sun,
Seeking the food he eats,
And pleased with what he gets.
II, v, 38

4 I met a fool i' the forest,
A motley fool. *II, vii, 12*

5 And then he drew a dial from his poke,
And looking on it with lack-luster eye,
Says, very wisely, "It is ten o'clock;
Thus may we see," quoth he, "how the world wags."[1] *II, vii, 20*

6 And so, from hour to hour we ripe and ripe,
And then from hour to hour we rot and rot;
And thereby hangs a tale.[2] *II, vii, 26*

7 My lungs began to crow like chanticleer,
That fools should be so deep-contemplative,
And I did laugh sans intermission
An hour by his dial. *II, vii, 30*

8 Motley's the only wear. *II, vii, 34*

9 If ladies be but young and fair,
They have the gift to know it.
II, vii, 37

10 I must have liberty
Withal, as large a charter as the wind,
To blow on whom I please. *II, vii, 47*

11 The "why" is plain as way to parish church.
II, vii, 52

12 But whate'er you are
That in this desert inaccessible,
Under the shade of melancholy boughs,
Lose and neglect the creeping hours of time;
If ever you have looked on better days,
If ever been where bells have knolled to church,
If ever sat at any good man's feast,
If ever from your eyelids wiped a tear,
And know what 'tis to pity, and be pitied,
Let gentleness my strong enforcement be.
II, vii, 109

[1]So wags the world.—SIR WALTER SCOTT, *Ivanhoe* [1819], *ch. 37*

[2]Also elsewhere in Shakespeare.

13 True is it that we have seen better days.
As You Like It, II, vii, 120

14 Oppressed with two weak evils, age and hunger. *II, vii, 132*

15 All the world's a stage,
And all the men and women merely players:[3]
They have their exits and their entrances;
And one man in his time plays many parts,
His acts being seven ages. At first the infant,
Mewling and puking in the nurse's arms.
And then the whining school-boy, with his satchel,
And shining morning face, creeping like snail
Unwillingly to school. And then the lover,
Sighing like furnace, with a woful ballad
Made to his mistress' eyebrow. Then a soldier,
Full of strange oaths, and bearded like the pard,
Jealous in honor, sudden and quick in quarrel,
Seeking the bubble reputation
Even in the cannon's mouth. And then the justice,
In fair round belly with good capon lined,
With eyes severe and beard of formal cut,
Full of wise saws and modern instances;
And so he plays his part. The sixth age shifts
Into the lean and slippered pantaloon,
With spectacles on nose and pouch on side,
His youthful hose well saved, a world too wide
For his shrunk shank; and his big manly voice,
Turning again toward childish treble, pipes
And whistles in his sound. Last scene of all,
That ends this strange eventful history,
Is second childishness, and mere oblivion,
Sans teeth, sans eyes, sans taste, sans everything. *II, vii, 139*

16 Blow, blow, thou winter wind!
Thou art not so unkind
As man's ingratitude. *II, vii, 174*

17 These trees shall be my books.[4]
III, ii, 5

18 The fair, the chaste, and unexpressive she.
III, ii, 10

19 It goes much against my stomach. Hast any philosophy in thee, shepherd?
III, ii, 21

[3]See *The Merchant of Venice,* 197:28.
The world's a theater, the earth a stage, / Which God and Nature do with actors fill.—THOMAS HEYWOOD, *Apology for Actors* [1612]
The world's a stage on which all the parts are played.—MIDDLETON, *A Game of Chess* [1624], *act V, sc. i*

[4]See St. Bernard, 136:9; *As You Like It,* 210:24; and Wordsworth, 423:7.

1 He that wants money, means, and content, is without three good friends.
As You Like It, III, ii, 25

2 I am a true laborer: I earn that I eat, get that I wear, owe no man hate, envy no man's happiness, glad of other men's good, content with my harm. *III, ii, 78*

3 From the east to western Ind,
No jewel is like Rosalind. *III, ii, 94*

4 This is the very false gallop of verses.
III, ii, 120

5 Let us make an honorable retreat; though not with bag and baggage, yet with scrip and scrippage. *III, ii, 170*

6 O, wonderful, wonderful, and most wonderful, wonderful! and yet again wonderful! and after that out of all whooping.
III, ii, 202

7 Answer me in one word. *III, ii, 238*

8 Do you not know I am a woman? when I think, I must speak. *III, ii, 265*

9 I do desire we may be better strangers.
III, ii, 276

10 *Jacques:* What stature is she of?
Orlando: Just as high as my heart.
III, ii, 286

11 Time travels in divers paces with divers persons. I'll tell you who Time ambles withal, who Time trots withal, who Time gallops withal, and who he stands still withal.
III, ii, 328

12 Every one fault seeming monstrous till his fellow fault came to match it.
III, ii, 377

13 Everything about you demonstrating a careless desolation. *III, ii, 405*

14 Truly, I would the gods had made thee poetical. *III, iii, 16*

15 The wounds invisible
That love's keen arrows make.
III, v, 30

16 Down on your knees,
And thank heaven, fasting, for a good man's love. *III, v, 57*

17 I am falser than vows made in wine.
III, v, 73

18 It is a melancholy of mine own, compounded of many simples, extracted from many objects, and indeed the sundry contemplation of my travels, which, by often rumination, wraps me in a most humorous sadness. *As You Like It, IV, i, 16*

19 I had rather have a fool to make me merry than experience to make me sad.
IV, i, 28

20 Farewell, Monsieur Traveler: look you lisp and wear strange suits, disable all the benefits of your own country, be out of love with your nativity, and almost chide God for making you that countenance you are; or I will scarce think you have swam in a gondola.
IV, i, 35

21 I'll warrant him heart-whole.
IV, i, 51

22 Very good orators, when they are out, they will spit; and for lovers lacking—God warn us!—matter, the cleanliest shift is to kiss.
IV, i, 77

23 Men have died from time to time, and worms have eaten them, but not for love.
IV, i, 110

24 Forever and a day. *IV, i, 151*

25 Men are April when they woo, December when they wed: maids are May when they are maids, but the sky changes when they are wives. *IV, i, 153*

26 My affection hath an unknown bottom, like the bay of Portugal. *IV, i, 219*

27 The horn, the horn, the lusty horn
Is not a thing to laugh to scorn.
IV, ii, 17

28 Chewing the food of sweet and bitter fancy.
IV, iii, 103

29 "So so" is good, very good, very excellent good: and yet it is not; it is but so so.
V, i, 30

30 The fool doth think he is wise, but the wise man knows himself to be a fool.
V, i, 35

31 No sooner met, but they looked; no sooner looked but they loved; no sooner loved but they sighed; no sooner sighed but they asked one another the reason; no sooner knew the reason but they sought the remedy.
V, ii, 37

32 But, O! how bitter a thing it is to look into happiness through another man's eyes!
V, ii, 48

33 It was a lover and his lass,
With a hey, and a ho, and a hey nonino,
That o'er the green corn-field did pass,
In the spring time, the only pretty ring time,

When birds do sing, hey ding a ding, ding;
Sweet lovers love the spring.
As You Like It, V, iii, 18

1 Here comes a pair of very strange beasts, which in all tongues are called fools. *V, iv, 36*

2 An ill-favored thing, sir, but mine own.[1] *V, iv, 60*

3 Rich honesty dwells like a miser, sir, in a poor house, as your pearl in your foul oyster. *V, iv, 62*

4 "The retort courteous." . . . "the quip modest." . . . "the reply churlish." . . . "the reproof valiant" . . . "the countercheck quarrelsome." . . . "the lie circumstantial," and "the lie direct." *V, iv, 75*

5 Your "if" is the only peacemaker; much virtue in "if." *V, iv, 108*

6 He uses his folly like a stalking horse, and under the presentation of that he shoots his wit. *V, iv, 112*

7 If music be the food of love,[2] play on;
Give me excess of it, that, surfeiting,
The appetite may sicken, and so die.
That strain again! it had a dying fall:
O! it came o'er my ear like the sweet sound
That breathes upon a bank of violets,
Stealing and giving odor!
Twelfth-Night [1598–1600], act I, sc. i, l. 1

8 O spirit of love! how quick and fresh art thou,
That, notwithstanding thy capacity
Receiveth as the sea, nought enters there,
Of what validity and pitch soe'er,
But falls into abatement and low price,
Even in a minute: so full of shapes is fancy,
That it alone is high fantastical.
I, i, 9

9 When my tongue blabs, then let mine eyes not see. *I, ii, 61*

10 I am sure care's an enemy to life. *I, iii, 2*

11 Let them hang themselves in their own straps. *I, iii, 13*

12 I am a great eater of beef, and I believe that does harm to my wit. *I, iii, 92*

13 Wherefore are these things hid? *I, iii, 135*

[1]"A poor thing but mine own" is the popular version.
[2]See *Antony and Cleopatra*, 241:3.
Is not music the food of love?—RICHARD BRINSLEY SHERIDAN, *The Rivals* [1775], *act II, sc. i*

14 Is it a world to hide virtues in?
Twelfth-Night, I, iii, 142

15 God give them wisdom that have it; and those that are fools, let them use their talents. *I, v, 14*

16 One draught above heat makes him a fool, the second mads him, and a third drowns him. *I, v, 139*

17 'Tis beauty truly blent, whose red and white
Nature's own sweet and cunning hand laid on:
Lady, you are the cruel'st she alive,
If you will lead these graces to the grave
And leave the world no copy. *I, v, 259*

18 Make me a willow cabin at your gate,
And call upon my soul within the house.
I, v, 289

19 Holla your name to the reverberate hills,
And make the babbling gossip of the air
Cry out, "Olivia!" *I, v, 293*

20 Farewell, fair cruelty. *I, v, 309*

21 O mistress mine! where are you roaming?
II, iii, 42

22 Journeys end in lovers meeting,
Every wise man's son doth know.
II, iii, 46

23 What is love? 'tis not hereafter;
Present mirth hath present laughter.
What's to come is still unsure:
In delay there lies no plenty;
Then come kiss me, sweet and twenty,
Youth's a stuff will not endure.
II, iii, 50

24 He does it with a better grace, but I do it more natural. *II, iii, 91*

25 Is there no respect of place, persons, nor time, in you?[3] *II, iii, 100*

26 *Sir Toby:* Dost thou think, because thou art virtuous, there shall be no more cakes and ale?
Clown: Yes, by Saint Anne; and ginger shall be hot i' the mouth too.
II, iii, 124

27 My purpose is, indeed, a horse of that color.[4] *II, iii, 184*

28 These most brisk and giddy-paced times.
II, iv, 6

29 If ever thou shalt love,
In the sweet pangs of it remember me;
For such as I am all true lovers are:
Unstaid and skittish in all motions else

[3]See *Acts 10:34*, 46:10.
[4]A play on "horse of a different color."

Save in the constant image of the creature
That is beloved.
Twelfth-Night, II, iv, 15

1 Let still the woman take
An elder than herself, so wears she to him,
So sways she level in her husband's heart:
For, boy, however we do praise ourselves,
Our fancies are more giddy and unfirm,
More longing, wavering, sooner lost and worn,
Than women's are. *II, iv, 29*

2 Then, let thy love be younger than thyself,
Or thy affection cannot hold the bent;
For women are as roses, whose fair flower
Being once displayed, doth fall that very hour. *II, iv, 36*

3 The spinsters and the knitters in the sun,
And the free maids that weave their thread with bones,
Do use to chant it: it is silly sooth,
And dallies with the innocence of love,
Like the old age. *II, iv, 44*

4 Come away, come away, death,
And in sad cypress let me be laid;
Fly away, fly away, breath;
I am slain by a fair cruel maid.
II, iv, 51

5 *Duke:* And what's her history?
Viola: A blank, my lord. She never told her love,
But let concealment, like a worm i' the bud,
Feed on her damask cheek: she pined in thought,
And with a green and yellow melancholy,
She sat like Patience on a monument,
Smiling at grief. *II, iv, 112*

6 I am all the daughters of my father's house,
And all the brothers too. *II, iv, 122*

7 Here comes the trout that must be caught with tickling. *II, v, 25*

8 I may command where I adore.
II, v, 116

9 Be not afraid of greatness: some are born great, some achieve greatness, and some have greatness thrust upon them. *II, v, 159*

10 Remember who commended thy yellow stockings, and wished to see thee ever cross-gartered. *II, v, 168*

11 Foolery, sir, does walk about the orb like the sun; it shines everywhere.
III, i, 44

12 This fellow's wise enough to play the fool,
And to do that well craves a kind of wit.
III, i, 68

13 Music from the spheres.[1]
Twelfth-Night, III, i, 122

14 How apt the poor are to be proud.
III, i, 141

15 Then westward-ho! *III, i, 148*

16 O! what a deal of scorn looks beautiful
In the contempt and anger of his lip.
III, i, 159

17 Love sought is good, but giv'n unsought is better. *III, i, 170*

18 You will hang like an icicle on a Dutchman's beard. *III, ii, 30*

19 Let there be gall enough in thy ink.
III, ii, 54

20 Laugh yourselves into stitches.
III, ii, 75

21 I think we do know the sweet Roman hand.
III, iv, 31

22 This is very midsummer madness.
III, iv, 62

23 More matter for a May morning.
III, iv, 158

24 He's a very devil. *III, iv, 304*

25 Out of my lean and low ability
I'll lend you something. *III, iv, 380*

26 I hate ingratitude more in a man
Than lying, vainness, babbling drunkenness,
Or any taint of vice whose strong corruption
Inhabits our frail blood. *III, iv, 390*

27 As the old hermit of Prague, that never saw pen and ink, very wittily said to a niece of King Gorboduc, "That that is, is."
IV, ii, 14

28 Thus the whirligig of time brings in his revenges. *V, i, 388*

29 When that I was and a little tiny boy,
With hey, ho, the wind and the rain;
A foolish thing was but a toy,
For the rain it raineth every day.[2]
V, i, 404

30 A surgeon to old shoes.
Julius Caesar [1598–1600], act I, sc. i, l. 26

31 As proper men as ever trod upon neat's leather. *I, i, 27*

[1] The music of the spheres. —*Pericles, act V, sc. i, l. 231*
A phrase that stems from the Pythagorean Theory (sixth century B.C.) of the music or harmony of the spheres.
See Sir Thomas Browne, 274:20.

[2] Parodied by the Fool in *King Lear,* 234:1.

1 Have you not made a universal shout,
That Tiber trembled underneath her banks,
To hear the replication of your sounds
Made in her concave shores?
Julius Caesar, I, i, 48

2 Beware the ides of March.[1] *I, ii, 18*

3 Set honor in one eye and death i' the other,
And I will look on both indifferently.
I, ii, 86

4 Well, honor is the subject of my story.
I cannot tell what you and other men
Think of this life; but, for my single self,
I had as lief not to be as live to be
In awe of such a thing as I myself.
I, ii, 92

5 Stemming it with hearts of controversy.
I, ii, 109

6 Why, man, he doth bestride the narrow world
Like a Colossus; and we petty men
Walk under his huge legs, and peep about
To find ourselves dishonorable graves.
Men at some time are masters of their fates:[2]
The fault, dear Brutus, is not in our stars,
But in ourselves, that we are underlings.
I, ii, 134

7 Upon what meat doth this our Caesar feed,
That he is grown so great? *I, ii, 148*

8 Let me have men about me that are fat;
Sleek-headed men, and such as sleep o' nights.
Yond Cassius has a lean and hungry look;[3]
He thinks too much: such men are dangerous. *I, ii, 191*

9 He reads much;
He is a great observer, and he looks
Quite through the deeds of men.
I, ii, 200

10 Seldom he smiles, and smiles in such a sort
As if he mocked himself, and scorned his spirit
That could be moved to smile at anything.
I, ii, 204

11 But, for my own part, it was Greek to me.[4]
I, ii, 288

12 Yesterday the bird of night did sit,
Even at noonday, upon the marketplace,
Hooting and shrieking. *I, iii, 26*

13 So every bondman in his own hand bears
The power to cancel his captivity.
I, iii, 101

[1]See Julius Caesar, 99:21.

[2]See Sallust, 103:1 and 103:5; Bacon, 181:6; Tennyson, 534:7; Henley, 663:11; and Nehru, 814:8.

[3]See Julius Caesar, 99:25.

[4]This geare is Greeke to me.—GASCOIGNE, *Supposes, I* [1573]

14 O! he sits high in all the people's hearts:
And that which would appear offense in us,
His countenance, like richest alchemy,
Will change to virtue and to worthiness.
Julius Caesar, I, iii, 157

15 The abuse of greatness is when it disjoins
Remorse from power. *II, i, 18*

16 'Tis a common proof,
That lowliness is young ambition's ladder,
Whereto the climber-upward turns his face;
But when he once attains the upmost round,
He then unto the ladder turns his back,
Looks in the clouds, scorning the base degrees
By which he did ascend. *II, i, 21*

17 Therefore think him as a serpent's egg
Which, hatched, would, as his kind, grow mischievous,
And kill him in the shell. *II, i, 32*

18 Between the acting of a dreadful thing
And the first motion, all the interim is
Like a phantasma, or a hideous dream:
The genius and the mortal instruments
Are then in council; and the state of man,
Like to a little kingdom, suffers then
The nature of an insurrection.
II, i, 63

19 O conspiracy!
Sham'st thou to show thy dangerous brow by night,
When evils are most free? *II, i, 77*

20 Let's carve him as a dish fit for the gods,
Not hew him as a carcass fit for hounds.
II, i, 173

21 But when I tell him he hates flatterers,
He says he does, being then most flattered.
II, i, 207

22 Enjoy the honey-heavy dew of slumber.
II, i, 230

23 You are my true and honorable wife,
As dear to me as are the ruddy drops
That visit my sad heart.[5] *II, i, 288*

24 Think you I am no stronger than my sex,
Being so fathered and so husbanded?
II, i, 296

25 When beggars die, there are no comets seen;
The heavens themselves blaze forth the death of princes. *II, ii, 30*

26 Cowards die many times before their deaths;
The valiant never taste of death but once.
Of all the wonders that I yet have heard,
It seems to me most strange that men should fear;

[5]Dear as the ruddy drops that warm my heart.—THOMAS GRAY, *The Bard* [1757], *act I, sc. iii, l. 12*

Seeing that death, a necessary end,
Will come when it will come.
Julius Caesar, II, ii, 32

1 Antony, that revels long o' nights.
II, ii, 116

2 How hard it is for women to keep counsel!
II, iv, 9

3 But I am constant as the northern star,
Of whose true-fixed and resting quality
There is no fellow in the firmament.
III, i, 60

4 Speak, hands, for me! *III, i, 76*

5 Et tu, Brute![1] *III, i, 77*

6 Some to the common pulpits, and cry out,
"Liberty, freedom, and enfranchisement."
III, i, 79

7 How many ages hence
Shall this our lofty scene be acted o'er,
In states unborn and accents yet unknown!
III, i, 111

8 O mighty Caesar! dost thou lie so low?
Are all thy conquests, glories, triumphs, spoils,
Shrunk to this little measure?
III, i, 148

9 The choice and master spirits of this age.
III, i, 163

10 Though last, not least in love.[2]
III, i, 189

11 O! pardon me, thou bleeding piece of earth,
That I am meek and gentle with these butchers;
Thou art the ruins of the noblest man
That ever lived in the tide of times.
III, i, 254

12 Cry "Havoc!" and let slip the dogs of war.
III, i, 273

13 Romans, countrymen, and lovers! hear me for my cause; and be silent, that you may hear. *III, ii, 13*

14 Not that I loved Caesar less, but that I loved Rome more. *III, ii, 22*

15 As he was valiant, I honor him; but, as he was ambitious, I slew him. *III, ii, 27*

16 If any, speak; for him have I offended. I pause for a reply. *III, ii, 36*

17 Friends, Romans, countrymen, lend me your ears;
I come to bury Caesar, not to praise him.
The evil that men do lives after them,
The good is oft interred with their bones.[3]
Julius Caesar, III, ii, 79

18 For Brutus is an honorable man;
So are they all, all honorable men.
III, ii, 88

19 When that the poor have cried, Caesar hath wept;
Ambition should be made of sterner stuff.
III, ii, 97

20 O judgment! thou art fled to brutish beasts,
And men have lost their reason.
III, ii, 110

21 But yesterday the word of Caesar might
Have stood against the world; now lies he there,
And none so poor to do him reverence.
III, ii, 124

22 If you have tears, prepare to shed them now.
III, ii, 174

23 See what a rent the envious Casca made.
III, ii, 180

24 This was the most unkindest cut of all.
III, ii, 188

25 Great Caesar fell.
O! what a fall was there, my countrymen;
Then I, and you, and all of us fell down,
Whilst bloody treason flourished over us.
III, ii, 194

26 What private griefs they have, alas! I know not. *III, ii, 217*

27 I come not, friends, to steal away your hearts:
I am no orator, as Brutus is;
But, as you know me all, a plain blunt man.
III, ii, 220

28 For I have neither wit, nor words, nor worth,
Action, nor utterance, nor the power of speech,
To stir men's blood: I only speak right on.
III, ii, 225

29 Put a tongue
In every wound of Caesar, that should move
The stones of Rome to rise and mutiny.
III, ii, 232

30 When love begins to sicken and decay,
It useth an enforcèd ceremony.
There are no tricks in plain and simple faith.
IV, ii, 20

31 An itching palm. *IV, iii, 10*

32 I had rather be a dog, and bay the moon,
Than such a Roman. *IV, iii, 27*

[1]See Julius Caesar, 99:24.
[2]See Spenser, 174:15, and *King Lear*, 232:23.
[3]See Euripides, 77:18.

1 I'll use you for my mirth, yea, for my laughter,
When you are waspish.
Julius Caesar, IV, iii, 49

2 There is no terror, Cassius, in your threats;
For I am armed so strong in honesty
That they pass by me as the idle wind,
Which I respect not. *IV, iii, 66*

3 A friend should bear his friend's infirmities,
But Brutus makes mine greater than they are. *IV, iii, 85*

4 All his faults observed,
Set in a notebook, learned, and conned by rote. *IV, iii, 96*

5 There is a tide in the affairs of men,
Which, taken at the flood, leads on to fortune;
Omitted, all the voyage of their life
Is bound in shallows and in miseries.
IV, iii, 217

6 We must take the current when it serves,
Or lose our ventures. *IV, iii, 222*

7 The deep of night is crept upon our talk,
And nature must obey necessity.[1]
IV, iii, 225

8 But for your words, they rob the Hybla bees,
And leave them honeyless. *V, i, 34*

9 Forever, and forever, farewell, Cassius!
If we do meet again, why, we shall smile;
If not, why then, this parting was well made.
V, i, 117

10 O! that a man might know
The end of this day's business, ere it come.
V, i, 123

11 O Julius Caesar! thou art mighty yet!
Thy spirit walks abroad, and turns our swords
In our own proper entrails. *V, iii, 94*

12 The last of all the Romans, fare thee well!
V, iii, 99

13 This was the noblest Roman of them all.
V, v, 68

14 His life was gentle, and the elements
So mixed in him that Nature might stand up
And say to all the world, "This was a man!"[2]
V, v, 73

15 For this relief much thanks; 'tis bitter cold,
And I am sick at heart.
Hamlet [1600–1601], act I, sc. i, l. 8

16 Not a mouse stirring.[3] *I, i, 10*

[1] See Leonardo da Vinci, 152:11.
[2] See *Hamlet*, 218:16.
[3] See Clement Clarke Moore, 446:3.

17 Thou art a scholar; speak to it, Horatio.
Hamlet, I, i, 42

18 But in the gross and scope of my opinion,
This bodes some strange eruption to our state. *I, i, 68*

19 Whose sore task
Does not divide the Sunday from the week.
I, i, 75

20 This sweaty haste
Doth make the night joint-laborer with the day. *I, i, 77*

21 In the most high and palmy state of Rome,
A little ere the mightiest Julius fell,
The graves stood tenantless and the sheeted dead
Did squeak and gibber in the Roman streets.
I, i, 113

22 The moist star
Upon whose influence Neptune's empire stands
Was sick almost to doomsday with eclipse.
I, i, 118

23 And then it started like a guilty thing
Upon a fearful summons. *I, i, 148*

24 The cock, that is the trumpet to the morn.
I, i, 150

25 Whether in sea or fire, in earth or air,
The extravagant and erring spirit hies
To his confine. *I, i, 153*

26 It faded on the crowing of the cock.
Some say that ever 'gainst that season comes
Wherein our Savior's birth is celebrated,
The bird of dawning singeth all night long;
And then, they say, no spirit can walk abroad;
The nights are wholesome; then no planets strike,
No fairy takes, nor witch hath power to charm,
So hallowed and so gracious is the time.
I, i, 157

27 But, look, the morn in russet mantle clad,
Walks o'er the dew of yon high eastern hill.
I, i, 166

28 The memory be green.[4] *I, ii, 2*

29 With one auspicious and one dropping eye,
With mirth in funeral and with dirge in marriage,
In equal scale weighing delight and dole.
I, ii, 11

30 So much for him. *I, ii, 25*

31 A little more than kin, and less than kind.
I, ii, 65

[4] See Thomas Moore, 446:8.

1 Thou know'st 'tis common; all that live must die,
Passing through nature to eternity.
Hamlet, I, ii, 72

2 Seems, madam! Nay, it is; I know not "seems."
'Tis not alone my inky cloak, good mother,
Nor customary suits of solemn black.
I, ii, 76

3 But I have that within which passeth show;
These but the trappings and the suits of woe.
I, ii, 85

4 To persever
In obstinate condolement is a course
Of impious stubbornness; 'tis unmanly grief:
It shows a will most incorrect to heaven,
A heart unfortified, a mind impatient.
I, ii, 92

5 O! that this too too solid[1] flesh would melt,
Thaw and resolve itself into a dew;
Or that the Everlasting had not fixed
His canon 'gainst self-slaughter! O God! O God!
How weary, stale, flat, and unprofitable
Seem to me all the uses of this world.
I, ii, 129

6 Things rank and gross in nature
Possess it merely. That it should come to this!
I, ii, 136

7 So excellent a king; that was, to this,
Hyperion to a satyr; so loving to my mother
That he might not beteem the winds of heaven
Visit her face too roughly. *I, ii, 139*

8 Why, she would hang on him,
As if increase of appetite had grown
By what it fed on. *I, ii, 143*

9 Frailty, thy name is woman! *I, ii, 146*

10 Like Niobe, all tears. *I, ii, 149*

11 A beast, that wants discourse of reason.
I, ii, 150

12 It is not nor it cannot come to good.
I, ii, 158

13 A truant disposition. *I, ii, 169*

14 Thrift, thrift, Horatio! the funeral baked meats
Did coldly furnish forth the marriage tables.
Would I had met my dearest foe[2] in heaven
Ere I had ever seen that day.
I, ii, 180

15 In my mind's eye, Horatio. *I, ii, 185*

[1]Alternative readings are "sallied" and "sullied."
[2]See *Henry IV, Part I,* 204:22.

16 He was a man, take him for all in all,[3]
I shall not look upon his like again.
Hamlet, I, ii, 187

17 Season your admiration for a while.
I, ii, 192

18 In the dead vast and middle of the night.
I, ii, 198

19 Armed at points exactly, cap-a-pe.
I, ii, 200

20 Distilled
Almost to jelly with the act of fear.
I, ii, 204

21 A countenance more in sorrow than in anger.
I, ii, 231

22 While one with moderate haste might tell a hundred. *I, ii, 237*

23 *Hamlet:* His beard was grizzled, no?
Horatio: It was, as I have seen it in his life,
A sable silvered. *I, ii, 239*

24 Give it an understanding, but no tongue.
I, ii, 249

25 All is not well;
I doubt some foul play. *I, ii, 254*

26 Foul deeds will rise,
Though all the earth o'erwhelm them, to men's eyes. *I, ii, 256*

27 The chariest maid is prodigal enough
If she unmask her beauty to the moon;
Virtue itself 'scapes not calumnious strokes;
The canker galls the infants of the spring
Too oft before their buttons be disclosed,
And in the morn and liquid dew of youth
Contagious blastments are most imminent.
I, iii, 36

28 Do not, as some ungracious pastors do,
Show me the steep and thorny way to heaven,
Whiles, like a puffed and reckless libertine,
Himself the primrose path of dalliance treads.[4]
And recks not his own rede.[5] *I, iii, 47*

29 Give thy thoughts no tongue. *I, iii, 59*

30 Be thou familiar, but by no means vulgar;
Those friends thou hast, and their adoption tried,
Grapple them to thy soul with hoops of steel.
I, iii, 61

[3]See *Julius Caesar,* 217:14.
[4]See Bion, 92:7, and *Macbeth,* 238:2.
[5]Wel oghte a preest ensample for to yive. / By his clennesse, how that his sheep shold live. — CHAUCER, *Canterbury Tales* [c. 1387], *prologue, l. 504*
And may ye better reck the rede, / Than ever did th' adviser. — BURNS, *Epistle to a Young Friend* [1786]

1 Beware
Of entrance to a quarrel, but, being in,
Bear 't that th' opposed may beware of thee.
Give every man thy ear, but few thy voice;
Take each man's censure, but reserve thy judgment.
Costly thy habit as thy purse can buy,
But not expressed in fancy; rich, not gaudy;[1]
For the apparel oft proclaims the man.
Hamlet, I, iii, 65

2 Neither a borrower, nor a lender be;
For loan oft loses both itself and friend,
And borrowing dulls the edge of husbandry.
This above all: to thine own self be true,
And it must follow, as the night the day,
Thou canst not then be false to any man.[2]
I, iii, 75

3 'Tis in my memory locked,
And you yourself shall keep the key of it.
I, iii, 85

4 You speak like a green girl,
Unsifted in such perilous circumstance.
I, iii, 101

5 Springes to catch woodcocks. *I, iii, 115*

6 When the blood burns, how prodigal the soul
Lends the tongue vows. *I, iii, 116*

7 Be somewhat scanter of your maiden presence. *I, iii, 121*

8 The air bites shrewdly. *I, iv, 1*

9 But to my mind—though I am native here
And to the manner born—it is a custom
More honored in the breach than the observance. *I, iv, 14*

10 Angels and ministers of grace defend us!
I, iv, 39

11 Be thy intents wicked or charitable,
Thou com'st in such a questionable shape
That I will speak to thee. *I, iv, 42*

12 What may this mean,
That thou, dead corse, again in complete steel
Revisit'st thus the glimpses of the moon,
Making night hideous;[3] and we fools of nature
So horridly to shake our disposition
With thoughts beyond the reaches of our souls? *I, iv, 51*

13 I do not set my life at a pin's fee.
I, iv, 65

14 The dreadful summit of the cliff
That beetles o'er his base into the sea.
I, iv, 70

[1]See Samuel Wesley, 319:18.
[2]See Bacon, 180:22.
[3]And makes night hideous.—ALEXANDER POPE, *The Dunciad, bk. III* [1728], *l. 166*

15 My fate cries out,
And makes each petty artery in this body
As hardy as the Nemean lion's nerve.
Hamlet, I, iv, 81

16 Unhand me, gentlemen,
By heaven! I'll make a ghost of him that lets me. *I, iv, 84*

17 Something is rotten in the state of Denmark.
I, iv, 90

18 I could a tale unfold whose lightest word
Would harrow up thy soul, freeze thy young blood,
Make thy two eyes, like stars, start from their spheres,
Thy knotted and combined locks to part,
And each particular hair to stand an end,
Like quills upon the fretful porpentine.
I, v, 15

19 And duller shouldst thou be than the fat weed
That rots itself in ease on Lethe wharf.
I, v, 32

20 O my prophetic soul!
My uncle! *I, v, 40*

21 O Hamlet! what a falling-off was there.
I, v, 47

22 But virtue, as it never will be moved,
Though lewdness court it in a shape of heaven,
So lust, though to a radiant angel linked,
Will sate itself in a celestial bed,
And prey on garbage. *I, v, 53*

23 In the porches of mine ears. *I, v, 63*

24 Cut off even in the blossoms of my sin,
Unhouseled, disappointed, unaneled,
No reckoning made, but sent to my account
With all my imperfections on my head.[4]
I, v, 76

25 Leave her to heaven,
And to those thorns that in her bosom lodge,
To prick and sting her. *I, v, 86*

26 The glowworm shows the matin to be near,
And 'gins to pale his uneffectual fire.
I, v, 89

27 While memory holds a seat
In this distracted globe. Remember thee!
Yea, from the table of my memory
I'll wipe away all trivial fond records.
I, v, 96

28 Within the book and volume of my brain.
I, v, 103

[4]See Homer, 59:9; Horace, 108:13; Chaucer, 144:17; Milton, 284:11; Scott, 430:10; and Byron, 458:26.

1 O villain, villain, smiling, damned villain!
My tables—meet it is I set it down,
That one may smile, and smile, and be a villain;
At least I'm sure it may be so in Denmark.
Hamlet, I, v, 106

2 There's ne'er a villain dwelling in all Denmark,
But he's an arrant knave. *I, v, 123*

3 There are more things in heaven and earth, Horatio,
Than are dreamt of in your philosophy.
I, v, 166

4 To put an antic disposition on.
I, v, 172

5 Rest, rest, perturbed spirit! *I, v, 182*

6 The time is out of joint; O cursed spite,
That ever I was born to set it right!
I, v, 188

7 Your bait of falsehood takes this carp of truth;
And thus do we of wisdom and of reach,
With windlasses and with assays of bias,
By indirections find directions out.
II, i, 63

8 Ungartered, and down-gyved to his ankle.
II, i, 80

9 This is the very ecstasy of love.
II, i, 102

10 Brevity is the soul of wit. *II, ii, 90*

11 More matter, with less art. *II, ii, 95*

12 That he is mad, 'tis true; 'tis true 'tis pity;
And pity 'tis 'tis true. *II, ii, 97*

13 Find out the cause of this effect,
Or rather say, the cause of this defect,
For this effect defective comes by cause.
II, ii, 101

14 Doubt thou the stars are fire;
Doubt that the sun doth move;
Doubt truth to be a liar;
But never doubt I love. *II, ii, 115*

15 *Polonius:* Do you know me, my lord?
Hamlet: Excellent well; you are a fishmonger. *II, ii, 173*

16 To be honest, as this world goes, is to be one man picked out of ten thousand.
II, ii, 179

17 *Hamlet:* For if the sun breed maggots in a dead dog, being a god[1] kissing carrion—Have you a daughter?
Polonius: I have, my lord.
Hamlet: Let her not walk i' the sun.
Hamlet, II, ii, 183

[1] In some editions: good.

18 Still harping on my daughter.
II, ii, 190

19 *Polonius:* What do you read, my lord?
Hamlet: Words, words, words.
II, ii, 195

20 They have a plentiful lack of wit.
II, ii, 204

21 Though this be madness, yet there is method in 't. *II, ii, 211*

22 These tedious old fools! *II, ii, 227*

23 The indifferent children of the earth.
II, ii, 235

24 Happy in that we are not over happy.
II, ii, 236

25 There is nothing either good or bad, but thinking makes it so. *II, ii, 259*

26 O God! I could be bounded in a nutshell, and count myself a king of infinite space, were it not that I have bad dreams.
II, ii, 263

27 Beggar that I am, I am even poor in thanks.
II, ii, 286

28 This goodly frame, the earth, seems to me a sterile promontory; this most excellent canopy, the air, look you, this brave o'erhanging firmament, this majestical roof fretted with golden fire, why, it appears no other thing to me but a foul and pestilent congregation of vapors. What a piece of work is a man! How noble in reason! how infinite in faculty! in form, in moving, how express and admirable! in action how like an angel! in apprehension how like a god! *II, ii, 317*

29 And yet, to me, what is this quintessence of dust? man delights not me; no, nor woman neither. *II, ii, 328*

30 There is something in this more than natural, if philosophy could find it out.
II, ii, 392

31 I am but mad north-northwest: when the wind is southerly I know a hawk from a handsaw.[2] *II, ii, 405*

32 They say an old man is twice a child.[3]
II, ii, 413

[2] The hawk is the basic tool of the plasterer, the handsaw the basic tool of the carpenter. Both tools are easy to distinguish. Handsaw by some thought to be corruption of heronshaw, a young heron.—*Morris Dictionary of Word and Phrase Origins* [1977]

[3] See Aristophanes, 82:1.

1 One fair daughter and no more,
The which he loved passing well.
Hamlet, II, ii, 435

2 Come, give us a taste of your quality.
II, ii, 460

3 The play, I remember, pleased not the million; 'twas caviare to the general.
II, ii, 465

4 They are the abstracts and brief chronicles of the time: after your death you were better have a bad epitaph than their ill report while you live. *II, ii, 555*

5 Use every man after his desert, and who should 'scape whipping?[1] *II, ii, 561*

6 O! what a rogue and peasant slave am I.
II, ii, 584

7 What's Hecuba to him or he to Hecuba,
That he should weep for her?
II, ii, 593

8 Who calls me villain? breaks my pate across?
Plucks off my beard and blows it in my face?
II, ii, 607

9 But I am pigeon-livered, and lack gall
To make oppression bitter. *II, ii, 613*

10 The play's the thing
Wherein I'll catch the conscience of the king.
II, ii, 641

11 With devotion's visage
And pious action we do sugar o'er
The devil himself. *III, i, 47*

12 To be, or not to be: that is the question:
Whether 'tis nobler in the mind to suffer
The slings and arrows of outrageous fortune,
Or to take arms against a sea of troubles,
And by opposing end them? To die: to sleep;
No more; and, by a sleep to say we end
The heartache and the thousand natural shocks
That flesh is heir to, 'tis a consummation
Devoutly to be wished. To die, to sleep;
To sleep: perchance to dream: ay, there's the rub;
For in that sleep of death what dreams may come,
When we have shuffled off this mortal coil,
Must give us pause. There's the respect
That makes calamity of so long life;
For who would bear the whips and scorns of time,
The oppressor's wrong, the proud man's contumely,
The pangs of disprized love, the law's delay.
The insolence of office, and the spurns
That patient merit of the unworthy takes,
When he himself might his quietus make
With a bare bodkin? who would fardels bear,
To grunt and sweat under a weary life,
But that the dread of something after death,
The undiscovered country from whose bourn
No traveler returns,[2] puzzles the will,
And makes us rather bear those ills we have
Than fly to others that we know not of?
Thus conscience does make cowards of us all;[3]
And thus the native hue of resolution
Is sicklied o'er with the pale cast of thought,
And enterprises of great pith and moment
With this regard their currents turn awry,
And lose the name of action.
Hamlet, III, i, 56

13 Nymph, in thy orisons
Be all my sins remembered. *III, i, 89*

14 To the noble mind
Rich gifts wax poor when givers prove unkind. *III, i, 100*

15 Get thee to a nunnery. *III, i, 124*

16 What should such fellows as I do crawling between heaven and earth? We are arrant knaves, all. *III, i, 128*

17 Be thou as chaste as ice, as pure as snow, thou shalt not escape calumny.
III, i, 142

18 I have heard of your paintings too, well enough; God has given you one face, and you make yourselves another. *III, i, 150*

19 O! what a noble mind is here o'erthrown:
The courtier's, soldier's, scholar's, eye, tongue, sword. *III, i, 159*

20 The glass of fashion and the mould of form,
The observed of all observers!
III, i, 162

21 Now see that noble and most sovereign reason,
Like sweet bells jangled, out of tune and harsh. *III, i, 166*

22 O! woe is me,
To have seen what I have seen, see what I see!
III, i, 169

23 Speak the speech, I pray you, as I pronounced it to you, trippingly on the tongue; but if you mouth it, as many of your players do, I had as lief the towncrier spoke my lines.

[1]See Montaigne, 166:3.

[2]See *The Song of the Harper,* 3:1.
[3]See Wilde, 675:4.

Nor do not saw the air too much with your hand, thus; but use all gently: for in the very torrent, tempest, and—as I may say—whirlwind of passion, you must acquire and beget a temperance, that may give it smoothness. O! it offends me to the soul to hear a robustious periwig-pated fellow tear a passion to tatters, to very rags, to split the ears of the groundlings, who for the most part are capable of nothing but inexplicable dumb-shows and noise: I would have such a fellow whipped for o'erdoing Termagant; it out-herods Herod. *Hamlet, III, ii, 1*

1 Suit the action to the word, the word to the action; with this special observance, that you o'erstep not the modesty of nature. *III, ii, 20*

2 To hold, as 'twere, the mirror up to nature; to show virtue her own feature, scorn her own image, and the very age and body of the time his form and pressure. *III, ii, 25*

3 I have thought some of nature's journeymen had made men and not made them well, they imitated humanity so abominably. *III, ii, 38*

4 No; let the candied tongue lick absurd pomp,
And crook the pregnant hinges of the knee
Where thrift may follow fawning. *III, ii, 65*

5 A man that fortune's buffets and rewards
Hast ta'en with equal thanks. *III, ii, 72*

6 They are not a pipe for fortune's finger
To sound what stop she please. Give me that man
That is not passion's slave, and I will wear him
In my heart's core, ay, in my heart of heart,
As I do thee. Something too much of this. *III, ii, 75*

7 My imaginations are as foul
As Vulcan's stithy. *III, ii, 88*

8 The chameleon's dish: I eat the air, promise-crammed; you cannot feed capons so. *III, ii, 98*

9 Nav, then, let the devil wear black, for I'll have a suit of sables. *III, ii, 138*

10 There's hope a great man's memory may outlive his life half a year. *III, ii, 141*

11 Marry, this is miching mallecho; it means mischief. *III, ii, 148*

12 *Ophelia:* 'Tis brief, my lord.
Hamlet: As woman's love. *III, ii, 165*

13 Where love is great, the littlest doubts are fear;
When little fears grow great, great love grows there. *Hamlet, III, ii, 183*

14 Wormwood, wormwood.[1] *III, ii, 193*

15 The lady doth protest too much, methinks. *III, ii, 242*

16 Let the galled jade wince, our withers are unwrung. *III, ii, 256*

17 Why, let the stricken deer go weep,[2]
The hart ungallèd play;
For some must watch, while some must sleep:
So runs the world away. *III, ii, 287*

18 You would pluck out the heart of my mystery. *III, ii, 389*

19 Do you think I am easier to be played on than a pipe? *III, ii, 393*

20 *Hamlet:* Do you see yonder cloud that's almost in shape of a camel?
Polonius: By the mass, and 'tis like a camel, indeed.
Hamlet: Methinks it is like a weasel.
Polonius: It is backed like a weasel.
Hamlet: Or like a whale?
Polonius: Very like a whale.[3] *III, ii, 400*

21 They fool me to the top of my bent. *III, ii, 408*

22 By and by is easily said. *III, ii, 411*

23 'Tis now the very witching time of night,
When churchyards yawn and hell itself breathes out
Contagion to this world. *III, ii, 413*

24 I will speak daggers to her, but use none. *III, ii, 421*

25 O! my offense is rank, it smells to heaven;
It hath the primal eldest curse upon 't,
A brother's murder! *III, iii, 36*

26 Now might I do it pat, now he is praying;
And now I'll do 't: and so he goes to heaven;
And so I am revenged. *III, iii, 73*

27 With all his crimes broad blown, as flush as May. *III, iii, 81*

28 My words fly up, my thoughts remain below:
Words without thoughts never to heaven go. *III, iii, 97*

29 How now! a rat? Dead, for a ducat, dead! *III, iv, 23*

[1] See *Lamentations of Jeremiah 3:19*, 32:23.
[2] See Cowper, 376:25.
[3] See Aristophanes, 81:15, and *Antony and Cleopatra*, 241:17.

1 False as dicers' oaths.
Hamlet, III, iv, 45

2 A rhapsody of words. *III, iv, 48*

3 See, what a grace was seated on this brow;
Hyperion's curls; the front of Jove himself,
An eye like Mars, to threaten and command,
A station like the herald Mercury
New-lighted on a heaven-kissing hill.
A combination and a form indeed,
Where every god did seem to set his seal,
To give the world assurance of a man.
III, iv, 55

4 At your age
The heyday in the blood is tame, it's humble.
III, iv, 68

5 O shame! where is thy blush? Rebellious hell,
If thou canst mutine in a matron's bones,
To flaming youth let virtue be as wax,
And melt in her own fire: proclaim no shame
When the compulsive ardor gives the charge,
Since frost itself as actively doth burn,
And reason panders will. *III, iv, 82*

6 A king of shreds and patches.[1]
III, iv, 102

7 Lay not that flattering unction to your soul.
III, iv, 145

8 Confess yourself to heaven;
Repent what's past; avoid what is to come.
III, iv, 149

9 For in the fatness of these pursy times
Virtue itself of vice must pardon beg.
III, iv, 153

10 Assume a virtue, if you have it not.
III, iv, 160

11 Refrain tonight;
And that shall lend a kind of easiness
To the next abstinence: the next more easy;
For use almost can change the stamp of nature. *III, iv, 165*

12 I must be cruel, only to be kind.
III, iv, 178

13 For 'tis the sport to have the enginer
Hoist with his own petar. *III, iv, 206*

14 Diseases desperate grown
By desperate appliance are relieved,
Or not at all.[2] *IV, iii, 9*

15 A man may fish with the worm that hath eat of a king, and eat of the fish that hath fed of that worm. *IV, iii, 29*

16 We go to gain a little patch of ground,
That hath in it no profit but the name.
IV, iv, 18

[1] See W. S. Gilbert, 629:4.
[2] See Hippocrates, 80:10.

17 How all occasions do inform against me,
And spur my dull revenge! What is a man,
If his chief good and market of his time
Be but to sleep and feed? a beast, no more.[3]
Sure he that made us with such large discourse,
Looking before and after, gave us not
That capability and godlike reason
To fust in us unused.
Hamlet, IV, iv, 32

18 Some craven scruple
Of thinking too precisely on the event.
IV, iv, 40

19 Rightly to be great
Is not to stir without great argument,
But greatly to find quarrel in a straw
When honor's at the stake. *IV, iv, 53*

20 So full of artless jealousy is guilt,
It spills itself in fearing to be spilt.
IV, v, 19

21 How should I your true love know
From another one?
By his cockle hat and staff,
And his sandal shoon.[4] *IV, v, 23*

22 He is dead and gone, lady,
He is dead and gone;
At his head a grass-green turf,
At his heels a stone. *IV, v, 29*

23 We know what we are, but know not what we may be. *IV, v, 43*

24 Come, my coach! Good night, ladies; good night, sweet ladies; good night, good night.
IV, v, 72

25 When sorrows come, they come not single spies,
But in battalions.[5] *IV, v, 78*

26 We have done but greenly,
In hugger-mugger to inter him.
IV, v, 84

27 There's such divinity doth hedge a king,
That treason can but peep to what it would.[6]
IV, v, 123

[3] The unmotivated herd that only sleep and feed.—JAMES RUSSELL LOWELL [1819–1891], *Under the Old Elm, pt. VII, st. 3*

[4] Ophelia is quoting a version of a poem by Sir Walter Ralegh.

[5] See Cervantes, 169:2.

One woe doth tread upon another's heel, / So fast they follow.—*Hamlet, act IV, sc. vii, l. 164*

Thus woe succeeds a woe, as wave a wave.—HERRICK, *Sorrows Succeed* [1648]

Woes cluster; rare are solitary woes; / They love a train, they tread each other's heel.—EDWARD YOUNG, *Night Thoughts* [1742–1745], *Night III, l. 63*

[6] See Montaigne, 165:21, and Tennyson, 534:1.

1 There's rosemary, that's for remembrance . . . and there is pansies, that's for thoughts. *Hamlet, IV, v, 174*

2 O! you must wear your rue with a difference. There's a daisy; I would give you some violets, but they withered all when my father died. *IV, v, 181*

3 A very riband in the cap of youth. *IV, vii, 77*

4 Nature her custom holds,
Let shame say what it will. *IV, vii, 188*

5 There is no ancient gentlemen but gardeners, ditchers, and grave-makers; they hold up Adam's profession.[1] *V, i, 32*

6 Cudgel thy brains no more about it. *V, i, 61*

7 Has this fellow no feeling of his business, that he sings at grave-making? *V, i, 71*

8 Custom hath made it in him a property of easiness. *V, i, 73*

9 A politician . . . one that would circumvent God. *V, i, 84*

10 Why may not that be the skull of a lawyer? Where be his quiddities now, his quillets, his cases, his tenures, and his tricks? *V, i, 104*

11 One that was a woman, sir; but, rest her soul, she's dead. *V, i, 145*

12 How absolute the knave is! we must speak by the card, or equivocation will undo us. *V, i, 147*

13 The age is grown so picked that the toe of the peasant comes so near the heel of the courtier, he galls his kibe. *V, i, 150*

14 Alas! poor Yorick. I knew him, Horatio; a fellow of infinite jest, of most excellent fancy; he hath borne me on his back a thousand times; and now, how abhorred in my imagination it is! my gorge rises at it. Here hung those lips that I have kissed I know not how oft. Where be your gibes now? your gambols? your songs? your flashes of merriment, that were wont to set the table on a roar? Not one now, to mock your own grinning? quite chapfallen? Now get you to my lady's chamber, and tell her, let her paint an inch thick, to this favor she must come; make her laugh at that. *V, i, 201*

[1]See *Genesis 2:8*, 6:18; Bacon, 181:10; *King Henry VI, Part II*, 185:26; and Kipling, 710:22.

15 To what base uses we may return, Horatio! Why may not imagination trace the noble dust of Alexander, till he find it stopping a bung-hole? *Hamlet, V, i, 222*

16 Imperious Caesar, dead and turned to clay,
Might stop a hole to keep the wind away. *V, i, 235*

17 Lay her i' the earth;
And from her fair and unpolluted flesh
May violets spring![2] *V, i, 260*

18 A ministering angel shall my sister be.[3] *V, i, 263*

19 Sweets to the sweet: farewell! *V, i, 265*

20 I thought thy bride-bed to have decked, sweet maid,
And not have strewed thy grave. *V, i, 267*

21 Though I am not splenetive and rash
Yet have I in me something dangerous. *V, i, 283*

22 I loved Ophelia: forty thousand brothers
Could not, with all their quantity of love,
Make up my sum. *V, i, 291*

23 Nay, an thou'lt mouth,
I'll rant as well as thou. *V, i, 305*

24 Let Hercules himself do what he may,
The cat will mew and dog will have his day.[4] *V, i, 313*

25 There's a divinity that shapes our ends,
Rough-hew them how we will. *V, ii, 10*

26 I once did hold it, as our statists do,
A baseness to write fair. *V, ii, 33*

27 It did me yeoman's service. *V, ii, 36*

28 Not a whit, we defy augury; there's a special providence in the fall of a sparrow.[5] If it be now, 'tis not to come; if it be not to come, it will be now; if it be not now, yet it will come: the readiness is all. *V, ii, 232*

29 A hit, a very palpable hit. *V, ii, 295*

30 This fell sergeant, death,
Is strict in his arrest. *V, ii, 350*

31 Report me and my cause aright. *V, ii, 353*

32 I am more an antique Roman than a Dane. *V, ii, 355*

[2]See FitzGerald, 516:12, and Tennyson, 531:22.
[3]See Sir Walter Scott, 431:2.
[4]See Borrow, 492:18, and Kingsley, 566:14.
[5]See *Matthew 10:29*, 39:3, and Alexander Pope, 336:14.

1 O God! Horatio, what a wounded name,
Things standing thus unknown, shall live behind me.
If thou didst ever hold me in thy heart,
Absent thee from felicity awhile,
And in this harsh world draw thy breath in pain,
To tell my story. *Hamlet, V, ii, 358*

2 The rest is silence. *V, ii, 372*

3 Now cracks a noble heart. Good night, sweet prince,
And flights of angels sing thee to thy rest!
V, ii, 373

4 O proud death![1]
What feast is toward in thine eternal cell?
V, ii, 378

5 I will make a Star Chamber matter of it.
The Merry Wives of Windsor [1600–1601], act I, sc. i, l. 2

6 She has brown hair, and speaks small like a woman. *I, i, 48*

7 Seven hundred pounds and possibilities is goot gifts. *I, i, 65*

8 I had rather than forty shillings I had my Book of Songs and Sonnets here.
I, i, 205

9 "Convey," the wise it call. "Steal!" foh! a fico for the phrase! *I, iii, 30*

10 I am almost out at heels. *I, iii, 32*

11 Thou art the Mars of malcontents.
I, iii, 111

12 Here will be an old abusing of God's patience and the king's English. *I, iv, 5*

13 Dispense with trifles. *II, i, 47*

14 Faith, thou hast some crotchets in thy head now. *II, i, 158*

15 Why, then the world's mine oyster,
Which I with sword will open. *II, ii, 2*

16 This is the short and the long of it.
II, ii, 62

17 Like a fair house built upon another man's ground. *II, ii, 229*

18 Better three hours too soon than a minute too late. *II, ii, 332*

19 I cannot tell what the dickens his name is.
III, ii, 20

20 He capers, he dances, he has eyes of youth, he writes verses, he speaks holiday, he smells April and May. *III, ii, 71*

[1]See Donne, 254:11.

21 O, what a world of vile ill-favored faults
Looks handsome in three hundred pounds a year!
The Merry Wives of Windsor, III, iv, 32

22 A woman would run through fire and water for such a kind heart.
III, iv, 106

23 I have a kind of alacrity in sinking.
III, v, 13

24 As good luck would have it.[2]
III, v, 86

25 A man of my kidney. *III, v, 119*

26 [He] curses all Eve's daughters, of what complexion soever. *IV, ii, 24*

27 Wives may be merry, and yet honest too.
IV, ii, 110

28 This is the third time; I hope good luck lies in odd numbers. . . . There is divinity in odd numbers, either in nativity, chance, or death.[3] *V, i, 2*

29 Better a little chiding than a great deal of heartbreak. *V, iii, 10*

30 Property was thus appalled,
That the self was not the same;
Single nature's double name
Neither two nor one was called.
The Phoenix and the Turtle [1601], l. 37

31 Reason, in itself confounded,
Saw division grow together. *l. 41*

32 The chance of war.
Troilus and Cressida [1601–1603], prologue, l. 31

33 I have had my labor for my travail.[4]
Act I, sc. i, l. 73

34 Women are angels, wooing:
Things won are done; joy's soul lies in the doing. *I, ii, 310*

35 Men prize the thing ungained more than it is.
I, ii, 313

36 The sea being smooth,
How many shallow bauble boats dare sail
Upon her patient breast.[5] *I, iii, 34*

37 The heavens themselves, the planets, and this center,
Observe degree, priority, and place,

[2]As ill luck would have it.—CERVANTES, *Don Quixote, pt. I* [1605], *bk. I, ch. 2*

[3]See Pliny the Elder, 117:7, and Samuel Lover, 482:10.

[4]See Cervantes, 168:7.

[5]See Publilius Syrus, 111:6.

Insisture, course, proportion, season, form,
Office, and custom, in all line of order.
Troilus and Cressida, I, iii, 85

1 O! when degree is shaked,
Which is the ladder to all high designs,
The enterprise is sick.[1] *I, iii, 101*

2 Take but degree away, untune that string,
And, hark! what discord follows; each thing meets
In mere oppugnancy: the bounded waters
Should lift their bosoms higher than the shores
And make a sop of all this solid globe.
I, iii, 109

3 Then everything includes itself in power,
Power into will, will into appetite;
And appetite, an universal wolf,
So doubly seconded with will and power,
Must make perforce a universal prey,
And last eat up himself. *I, iii, 119*

4 Like a strutting player, whose conceit
Lies in his hamstring, and doth think it rich
To hear the wooden dialogue and sound
'Twixt his stretched footing and the scaffoldage. *I, iii, 153*

5 And in such indexes, although small pricks
To their subsequent volumes, there is seen
The baby figure of the giant mass
Of things to come.[2] *I, iii, 343*

6 Who wears his wit in his belly, and his guts in his head. *II, i, 78*

7 Modest doubt is called
The beacon of the wise, the tent that searches
To the bottom of the worst. *II, ii, 15*

8 'Tis mad idolatry
To make the service greater than the god.
II, ii, 56

9 He that is proud eats up himself; pride is his own glass, his own trumpet, his own chronicle. *II, iii, 165*

10 I am giddy, expectation whirls me round.
The imaginary relish is so sweet
That it enchants my sense. *III, ii, 17*

11 Words pay no debts. *III, ii, 56*

12 To fear the worst oft cures the worse.
III, ii, 77

13 All lovers swear more performance than they are able, and yet reserve an ability that they never perform; vowing more than the perfection of ten, and discharging less than the tenth part of one. *III, ii, 89*

[1] See Publilius Syrus, 112:14.
[2] See Cicero, 98:21; Thomas Campbell, 443:14; Shelley, 470:5; and H. G. Wells, 720:9.

14 For to be wise, and love,
Exceeds man's might; that dwells with gods above.
Troilus and Cressida, III, ii, 163

15 If I be false, or swerve a hair from truth,
When time is old and hath forgot itself,
When waterdrops have worn the stones of Troy,
And blind oblivion swallowed cities up.
And mighty states characterless are grated
To dusty nothing, yet let memory,
From false to false, among false maids in love
Upbraid my falsehood! when they have said "as false
As air, as water,[3] wind, or sandy earth,
As fox to lamb, as wolf to heifer's calf,
Pard to the hind, or stepdame to her son";
Yea, let them say, to stick the heart of falsehood,
"As false as Cressid." *III, ii, 191*

16 Time hath, my lord, a wallet at his back,
Wherein he puts alms for oblivion.
III, iii, 145

17 Perseverance, dear my lord,
Keeps honor bright: to have done, is to hang
Quite out of fashion, like a rusty mail
In monumental mockery. *III, iii, 150*

18 For honor travels in a strait so narrow
Where one but goes abreast.
III, iii, 154

19 Time is like a fashionable host,
That slightly shakes his parting guest by the hand,
And with his arms outstretched, as he would fly,
Grasps in the comer: welcome ever smiles,
And farewell goes out sighing.
III, iii, 168

20 Beauty, wit,
High birth, vigor of bone, desert in service,
Love, friendship, charity, are subjects all
To envious and calumniating time.
One touch of nature makes the whole world kin. *III, iii, 171*

21 And give to dust that is a little gilt
More laud than gilt o'er-dusted.
III, iii, 178

22 My mind is troubled, like a fountain stirred;
And I myself see not the bottom of it.
III, iii, 314

23 You do as chapmen do,
Dispraise the thing that you desire to buy.
IV, i, 75

24 As many farewells as be stars in heaven.
IV, iv, 44

[3] See *Othello*, 232:16.

1 And sometimes we are devils to ourselves
When we will tempt the frailty of our powers,
Presuming on their changeful potency.
Troilus and Cressida, IV, iv, 95

2 The kiss you take is better than you give.
IV, v, 38

3 Fie, fie upon her!
There's language in her eye, her cheek, her lip,
Nay, her foot speaks; her wanton spirits look out
At every joint and motive of her body.
IV, v, 54

4 What's past and what's to come is strewed with husks
And formless ruin of oblivion.
IV, v, 165

5 The end crowns all,[1]
And that old common arbitrator, Time,
Will one day end it. *IV, v, 223*

6 Words, words, mere words, no matter from the heart. *V, iii, 109*

7 Hector is dead; there is no more to say.
V, x, 22

8 O world! world! world! thus is the poor agent despised. *V, x, 36*

9 Love all, trust a few,
Do wrong to none: be able for thine enemy
Rather in power than use, and keep thy friend
Under thy own life's key: be checked for silence,
But never taxed for speech.
All's Well That Ends Well [1601–1603],[2] act I, sc. i, l. 74

10 It were all one
That I should love a bright particular star
And think to wed it, he is so above me.
I, i, 97

11 The hind that would be mated by the lion
Must die for love. *I, i, 103*

12 My friends were poor, but honest.[3]
I, iii, 203

13 Oft expectation fails, and most oft there
Where most it promises. *II, i, 145*

14 They say miracles are past. *II, iii, 1*

15 A young man married is a man that's marred. *II, iii, 315*

[1]See Anonymous Latin, 133:26; Heywood, 159:28; *All's Well That Ends Well,* 227:18; Herrick, 266:4; and Quarles, 267:18.

[2]See 227:18.

[3]Though I be poor, I'm honest.—THOMAS MIDDLETON, *The Witch* [c. 1627], *III,* 2
See Anonymous, 924:10.

16 The web of our life is of a mingled yarn, good and ill together.
All's Well That Ends Well, IV, iii, 83

17 There's place and means for every man alive.
IV, iii, 379

18 All's well that end's well: still the fine's the crown;
Whate'er the course, the end is the renown.[4]
IV, iv, 35

19 I am a man whom Fortune hath cruelly scratched. *V, ii, 28*

20 Praising what is lost
Makes the remembrance dear.
V, iii, 19

21 The inaudible and noiseless foot of time.[5]
V, iii, 41

22 Love that comes too late,
Like a remorseful pardon slowly carried.
V, iii, 57

23 All impediments in fancy's course
Are motives of more fancy. *V, iii, 216*

24 Spirits are not finely touched
But to fine issues.
Measure for Measure [1604–1605], act I, sc. i, l. 35

25 Good counselors lack no clients.
I, ii, 115

26 And liberty plucks justice by the nose.
I, iii, 29

27 I hold you as a thing enskyed and sainted.
I, iv, 34

28 A man whose blood
Is very snow-broth; one who never feels
The wanton stings and motions of the sense.
I, iv, 57

29 Our doubts are traitors,
And make us lose the good we oft might win,
By fearing to attempt.[6] *I, iv, 78*

30 We must not make a scarecrow of the law,
Setting it up to fear the birds of prey,
And let it keep one shape, till custom make it
Their perch, and not their terror.
II, i, 1

31 The jury, passing on the prisoner's life,
May in the sworn twelve have a thief or two
Guiltier than him they try. *II, i, 19*

[4]See Anonymous Latin, 133:26; Heywood, 159:28; *Hamlet,* 227:5; Herrick, 266:4; and Quarles, 267:18.

[5]How noiseless falls the foot of time!—W. R. SPENCER [1770–1834], *Lines to Lady A. Hamilton*

[6]See *Macbeth,* 237:2.

1 Some rise by sin, and some by virtue fall.
Measure for Measure, II, i, 38

2 Great with child, and longing . . . for stewed prunes. *II, i, 94*

3 This will last out a night in Russia,
When nights are longest there.
II, i, 144

4 His face is the worst thing about him.
II, i, 167

5 Condemn the fault, and not the act of it?
II, ii, 37

6 No ceremony that to great ones 'longs,
Not the king's crown, nor the deputed sword,
The marshal's truncheon, nor the judge's robe,
Become them with one half so good a grace
As mercy does.[1] *II, ii, 59*

7 Why, all the souls that were were forfeit once;
And He that might the vantage best have took,
Found out the remedy. How would you be,
If He, which is the top of judgment, should
But judge you as you are? *II, ii, 73*

8 The law hath not been dead, though it hath slept. *II, ii, 90*

9 O! it is excellent
To have a giant's strength; but it is tyrannous
To use it like a giant. *II, ii, 107*

10 But man, proud man,
Drest in a little brief authority,
Most ignorant of what he's most assured,
His glassy essence, like an angry ape,
Plays such fantastic tricks before high heaven
As make the angels weep. *II, ii, 117*

11 That in the captain's but a choleric word,
Which in the soldier is flat blasphemy.
II, ii, 130

12 It oft falls out,
To have what we would have, we speak not what we mean. *II, iv, 118*

13 The miserable have no other medicine
But only hope. *III, i, 2*

14 Be absolute for death. *III, i, 5*

15 A breath thou art,
Servile to all the skyey influences.
III, i, 8

16 Thou hast nor youth nor age;
But, as it were, an after-dinner's sleep,
Dreaming on both; for all thy blessed youth
Becomes as aged, and doth beg the alms
Of palsied eld; and when thou art old and rich,
Thou hast neither heat, affection, limb, nor beauty,
To make thy riches pleasant.
Measure for Measure, III, i, 32

17 The sense of death is most in apprehension,[2]
And the poor beetle, that we tread upon,
In corporal sufferance finds a pang as great
As when a giant dies. *III, i, 76*

18 If I must die,
I will encounter darkness as a bride,
And hug it in my arms. *III, i, 81*

19 The cunning livery of hell. *III, i, 93*

20 Ay, but to die, and go we know not where;
To lie in cold obstruction and to rot;
This sensible warm motion to become
A kneaded clod; and the delighted spirit
To bathe in fiery floods, or to reside
In thrilling region of thick-ribbèd ice;
To be imprisoned in the viewless winds,
And blown with restless violence round about
The pendant world. *III, i, 116*

21 The weariest and most loathed worldly life
That age, ache, penury, and imprisonment
Can lay on nature, is a paradise
To what we fear of death. *III, i, 127*

22 The hand that hath made you fair hath made you good.[3] *III, i, 182*

23 Virtue is bold, and goodness never fearful.
III, i, 214

24 There, at the moated grange, resides this dejected Mariana.[4] *III, i, 279*

25 This news is old enough, yet it is every day's news. *III, ii, 249*

26 He who the sword of heaven will bear
Should be as holy as severe.
III, ii, 283

27 O, what may man within him hide,
Though angel on the outward side!
III, ii, 293

28 Take, O take those lips away,
That so sweetly were forsworn;
And those eyes, the break of day,
Lights that do mislead the morn:
But my kisses bring again, bring again;

[1] See *The Merchant of Venice*, 200:9.

[2] See Publilius Syrus, 111:16.

[3] See Spenser, 174:20.

[4] "Mariana in the moated grange."—*Motto used by* TENNYSON *for the poem Mariana* [1830]

Seals of love, but sealed in vain, sealed in vain[1] *Measure for Measure, IV, i, 1*

1 Music oft hath such a charm
To make bad good, and good provoke to harm.[2]
IV, i, 16

2 Every true man's apparel fits your thief.
IV, ii, 46

3 I am a kind of burr; I shall stick.
IV, iii, 193

4 We would, and we would not.
IV, iv, 37

5 A forted residence 'gainst the tooth of time
And razure of oblivion. *V, i, 12*

6 Truth is truth
To the end of reckoning. *V, i, 45*

7 Neither maid, widow, nor wife.
V, i, 173

8 Haste still pays haste, and leisure answers leisure,
Like doth quit like, and measure still for measure. *V, i, 411*

9 They say best men are molded out of faults,
And, for the most, become much more the better
For being a little bad. *V, i, 440*

10 What's mine is yours, and what is yours is mine.[3] *V, i, 539*

11 Horribly stuffed with epithets of war.
Othello [1604–1605], act I, sc. i, l. 14

12 A fellow almost damned in a fair wife.
I, i, 21

13 The bookish theoric. *I, i, 24*

14 We cannot all be masters. *I, i, 43*

15 And when he's old, cashiered. *I, i, 48*

16 In following him, I follow but myself.
I, i, 58

17 But I will wear my heart upon my sleeve
For daws to peck at. *I, i, 64*

18 An old black ram
Is tupping your white ewe. *I, i, 88*

19 You are one of those that will not serve God if the devil bid you. *I, i, 108*

20 Your daughter and the Moor are now making the beast with two backs. *I, i, 117*

[1]This song occurs in act V, sc. ii, of FLETCHER'S *Bloody Brother* [c. 1616], with an additional stanza:
Hide, O hide those hills of snow, / Which thy frozen bosom bears, / On whose tops the pinks that grow / Are of those that April wears! / But first set my poor heart free, / Bound in those icy chains by thee.

[2]See Congreve, 324:14.

[3]See Plautus, 93:8.

21 Keep up your bright swords, for the dew will rust them. *Othello, I, ii, 59*

22 The wealthy curled darlings of our nation.
I, ii, 68

23 The bloody book of law
You shall yourself read in the bitter letter
After your own sense. *I, iii, 67*

24 Rude am I in my speech,
And little blessed with the soft phrase of peace. *I, iii, 81*

25 Little shall I grace my cause
In speaking for myself. Yet, by your gracious patience,
I will a round unvarnished tale deliver
Of my whole course of love. *I, iii, 88*

26 A maiden never bold;
Of spirit so still and quiet, that her motion
Blushed at herself. *I, iii, 94*

27 Still questioned me the story of my life
From year to year, the battles, sieges, fortunes
That I have passed. *I, iii, 129*

28 Wherein I spake of most disastrous chances,
Of moving accidents by flood and field,
Of hair-breadth 'scapes i' the imminent deadly breach. *I, iii, 134*

29 Hills whose heads touch heaven.
I, iii, 141

30 And of the Cannibals that each other eat,
The Anthropophagi, and men whose heads
Do grow beneath their shoulders.
I, iii, 143

31 My story being done,
She gave me for my pains a world of sighs:
She swore, in faith, 'twas strange, 'twas passing strange,
'Twas pitiful, 'twas wondrous pitiful:
She wished she had not heard it, yet she wished
That heaven had made her such a man; she thanked me,
And bade me, if I had a friend that loved her,
I should but teach him how to tell my story,
And that would woo her. Upon this hint I spake:
She loved me for the dangers I had passed,
And I loved her that she did pity them.
This only is the witchcraft I have used.
I, iii, 158

32 I do perceive here a divided duty.
I, iii, 181

33 To mourn a mischief that is past and gone
Is the next way to draw new mischief on.
I, iii, 204

1 The robbed that smiles steals something from the thief. *Othello, I, iii, 208*

2 Our bodies are our gardens, to the which our wills are gardeners. *I, iii, 324*

3 Put money in thy purse. *I, iii, 345*

4 The food that to him now is as luscious as locusts, shall be to him shortly as bitter as coloquintida. *I, iii, 354*

5 Framed to make women false. *I, iii, 404*

6 The enchafèd flood. *II, i, 17*

7 One that excels the quirks of blazoning pens. *II, i, 63*

8 You are pictures out of doors,
Bells in your parlors, wildcats in your kitchens,
Saints in your injuries, devils being offended,
Players in your housewifery, and housewives in your beds. *II, i, 109*

9 For I am nothing if not critical. *II, i, 119*

10 I am not merry, but I do beguile
The thing I am, by seeming otherwise. *II, i, 122*

11 She that was ever fair and never proud,
Had tongue at will and yet was never loud. *II, i, 148*

12 *Iago:* To suckle fools and chronicle small beer.[1]
Desdemona: O most lame and impotent conclusion! *II, i, 160*

13 You may relish him more in the soldier than in the scholar. *II, i, 165*

14 If it were now to die,
'Twere now to be most happy. *II, i, 192*

15 Base men being in love have then a nobility in their natures more than is native to them. *II, i, 218*

16 Egregiously an ass. *II, i, 321*

17 I have very poor and unhappy brains for drinking. *II, iii, 34*

18 Potations pottle deep. *II, iii, 57*

19 Well, God's above all; and there be souls must be saved, and there be souls must not be saved. *II, iii, 106*

20 Silence that dreadful bell! it frights the isle
From her propriety. *II, iii, 177*

[1]See *King Henry VI, Part II*, 185:23.

21 But men are men; the best sometimes forget. *Othello, II, iii, 243*

22 Thy honesty and love doth mince this matter.[2] *II, iii, 249*

23 Reputation, reputation, reputation! O! I have lost my reputation. I have lost the immortal part of myself, and what remains is bestial. *II, iii, 264*

24 Reputation is an idle and most false imposition; oft got without merit, and lost without deserving. *II, iii, 270*

25 O thou invisible spirit of wine! if thou hast no name to be known by, let us call thee devil! *II, iii, 285*

26 O God! that men should put an enemy in their mouths to steal away their brains; that we should, with joy, pleasance, revel, and applause, transform ourselves into beasts. *II, iii, 293*

27 Good wine is a good familiar creature if it be well used. *II, iii, 315*

28 Play the villain. *II, iii, 345*

29 How poor are they that have not patience!
What wound did ever heal but by degrees? *II, iii, 379*

30 Excellent wretch! Perdition catch my soul
But I do love thee! and when I love thee not,
Chaos is come again.[3] *III, iii, 99*

31 Men should be what they seem. *III, iii, 126*

32 Speak to me as to thy thinkings,
As thou dost ruminate, and give thy worst of thoughts
The worst of words. *III, iii, 131*

33 Good name in man and woman, dear my lord,
Is the immediate jewel of their souls:
Who steals my purse steals trash; 'tis something, nothing;
'Twas mine, 'tis his, and has been slave to thousands;
But he that filches from me my good name
Robs me of that which not enriches him,
And makes me poor indeed. *III, iii, 155*

34 O! beware, my lord, of jealousy;
It is the green-eyed monster which doth mock
The meat it feeds on; that cuckold lives in bliss
Who, certain of his fate, loves not his wronger;
But, O! what damned minutes tells he o'er

[2]See Cervantes, 168:6.
[3]See *Venus and Adonis*, 189:14.

Who dotes, yet doubts; suspects, yet soundly loves! *Othello, III, iii, 165*

1 Poor and content is rich, and rich enough. *III, iii, 172*

2 Think'st thou I'd make a life of jealousy,
To follow still the changes of the moon
With fresh suspicions? No; to be once in doubt
Is once to be resolved. *III, iii, 177*

3 I humbly do beseech you of your pardon
For too much loving you. *III, iii, 212*

4 If I do prove her haggard,
Though that her jesses were my dear heart-strings,
I'd whistle her off and let her down the wind,
To prey at fortune. *III, iii, 260*

5 I am declined
Into the vale of years. *III, iii, 265*

6 O curse of marriage!
That we can call these delicate creatures ours,
And not their appetites. I had rather be a toad,
And live upon the vapor of a dungeon,
Than keep a corner in the thing I love
For others' uses. *III, iii, 268*

7 Trifles light as air
Are to the jealous confirmations strong
As proofs of holy writ. *III, iii, 323*

8 Not poppy, nor mandragora,[1]
Nor all the drowsy syrups of the world,
Shall ever medicine thee to that sweet sleep
Which thou ow'dst yesterday. *III, iii, 331*

9 I swear 'tis better to be much abused
Than but to know 't a little. *III, iii, 337*

10 He that is robbed, not wanting what is stol'n,
Let him not know 't and he's not robbed at all.[2] *III, iii, 343*

11 O! now, forever
Farewell the tranquil mind; farewell content!
Farewell the plumed troop and the big wars
That make ambition virtue! O, farewell!
Farewell the neighing steed, and the shrill trump,
The spirit-stirring drum, the ear-piercing fife,
The royal banner, and all quality,
Pride, pomp, and circumstance of glorious war!
And, O you mortal engines, whose rude throats
The immortal Jove's dread clamors counterfeit,
Farewell! Othello's occupation's gone! *Othello, III, iii, 348*

12 Be sure of it; give me the ocular proof. *III, iii, 361*

13 No hinge nor loop
To hang a doubt on. *III, iii, 366*

14 On horror's head horrors accumulate. *III, iii, 371*

15 Take note, take note, O world!
To be direct and honest is not safe. *III, iii, 378*

16 But this denoted a foregone conclusion. *III, iii, 429*

17 Swell, bosom, with thy fraught,
For 'tis of aspics' tongues! *III, iii, 450*

18 Like to the Pontick sea,
Whose icy current and compulsive course
Ne'er feels retiring ebb, but keeps due on
To the Propontic and the Hellespont,
Even so my bloody thoughts, with violent pace,
Shall ne'er look back, ne'er ebb to humble love,
Till that a capable and wide revenge
Swallow them up. *III, iii, 454*

19 Our new heraldry is hands not hearts. *III, iv, 48*

20 But jealous souls will not be answered so;
They are not ever jealous for the cause,
But jealous for they are jealous; 'tis a monster
Begot upon itself, born on itself. *III, iv, 158*

21 'Tis the strumpet's plague
To beguile many and be beguiled by one. *IV, i, 97*

22 They laugh that win. *IV, i, 123*

23 My heart is turned to stone; I strike it, and it hurts my hand. O! the world hath not a sweeter creature; she might lie by an emperor's side and command him tasks. *IV, i, 190*

24 O, she will sing the savageness out of a bear. *IV, i, 198*

25 But yet the pity of it, Iago! O! Iago, the pity of it, Iago! *IV, i, 205*

26 Is this the noble nature
Whom passion could not shake? whose solid virtue
The shot of accident nor dart of chance,
Could neither graze nor pierce? *IV, i, 276*

[1] See *Antony and Cleopatra*, 240:20.
[2] See Publilius Syrus, 110:18.

1 I understand a fury in your words,
But not the words. *Othello, IV, ii, 31*

2 Steeped me in poverty to the very lips.
IV, ii, 49

3 But, alas! to make me
A fixed figure for the time of scorn
To point his slow and moving finger at.
IV, ii, 52

4 Patience, thou young and rose-lipped cherubin. *IV, ii, 62*

5 O thou weed!
Who art so lovely fair and smell'st so sweet
That the sense aches at thee, would thou hadst ne'er been born. *IV, ii, 66*

6 O heaven! that such companions thou'dst unfold,
And put in every honest hand a whip
To lash the rascals naked through the world.
IV, ii, 141

7 Unkindness may do much;
And his unkindness may defeat my life,
But never taint my love. *IV, ii, 159*

8 The poor soul sat sighing by a sycamore tree,
Sing all a green willow;[1]
Her hand on her bosom, her head on her knee,
Sing willow, willow, willow. *IV, iii, 41*

9 It makes us, or it mars us. *V, i, 4*

10 Every way makes my gain. *V, i, 14*

11 He hath a daily beauty in his life.
V, i, 19

12 This is the night
That either makes me or fordoes me quite.
V, i, 128

13 And smooth as monumental alabaster.
V, ii, 5

14 Put out the light, and then put out the light:
If I quench thee, thou flaming minister,
I can again thy former light restore,
Should I repent me; but once put out thy light,
Thou cunning'st pattern of excelling nature,
I know not where is that Promethean heat
That can thy light relume. *V, ii, 7*

15 It is the very error of the moon;
She comes more near the earth than she was wont,
And makes men mad. *V, ii, 107*

16 She was as false as water.[2] *V, ii, 132*

[1]See Heywood, 158:15.
[2]See *Troilus and Cressida,* 226:15.

17 Curse his better angel from his side,
And fall to reprobation.
Othello, V, ii, 206

18 Here is my journey's end, here is my butt,
And very sea-mark of my utmost sail.
V, ii, 266

19 An honorable murderer, if you will;
For naught I did in hate, but all in honor.
V, ii, 293

20 I have done the state some service, and they know 't;
No more of that. I pray you, in your letters,
When you shall these unlucky deeds relate,
Speak of me as I am; nothing extenuate,
Nor set down aught in malice: then, must you speak
Of one that loved not wisely but too well;
Of one not easily jealous, but, being wrought,
Perplexed in the extreme; of one whose hand,
Like the base Indian, threw a pearl away
Richer than all his tribe; of one whose subdued eyes
Albeit unused to the melting mood,
Drop tears as fast as the Arabian trees
Their med'cinable gum. *V, ii, 338*

21 In Aleppo once,
Where a malignant and a turbaned Turk
Beat a Venetian and traduced the state,
I took by the throat the circumcised dog,
And smote him thus. *V, ii, 354*

22 My love's
More richer than my tongue.
King Lear [1605–1606], act I, sc. 1, l. 79

23 Now, our joy,
Although our last, not least.[3] *I, i, 84*

24 Nothing will come of nothing.[4] *I, i, 92*

25 Mend your speech a little,
Lest you may mar your fortunes.
I, i, 96

26 *Lear:* So young, and so untender?
Cordelia: So young, my lord, and true.
I, i, 108

27 Come not between the dragon and his wrath.
I, i, 124

28 Kill thy physician, and the fee bestow
Upon the foul disease. *I, i, 166*

29 I want that glib and oily art,
To speak and purpose not. *I, i, 227*

30 A still-soliciting eye. *I, i, 234*

[3]See Spenser, 174:15, and *Julius Caesar,* 216:10.
[4]See Lucretius, 100:5.

1 Time shall unfold what plighted cunning hides;
Who covers faults, at last shame them derides. *King Lear, I, i, 282*

2 The infirmity of his age. *I, i, 296*

3 Who in the lusty stealth of nature take
More composition and fierce quality
Than doth, within a dull, stale, tired bed,
Go to the creating a whole tribe of fops.
I, ii, 11

4 We have seen the best of our time: machinations, hollowness, treachery, and all ruinous disorders, follow us disquietly to our graves. *I, ii, 125*

5 This is the excellent foppery of the world, that, when we are sick in fortune—often the surfeit of our own behavior—we make guilty of our disasters the sun, the moon, and the stars; as if we were villains by necessity, fools by heavenly compulsion, knaves, thieves, and teachers by spherical predominance, drunkards, liars, and adulterers by an enforced obedience of planetary influence.
I, ii, 129

6 Edgar—
[*Enter Edgar*]
and pat he comes, like the catastrophe of the old comedy: my cue is villainous melancholy, with a sigh like Tom o' Bedlam.
I, ii, 149

7 That which ordinary men are fit for, I am qualified in, and the best of me is diligence.
I, iv, 36

8 Truth's a dog must to kennel; he must be whipped out, when Lady the brach may stand by the fire and stink. *I, iv, 125*

9 Have more than thou showest,
Speak less than thou knowest,
Lend less than thou owest. *I, iv, 132*

10 Ingratitude, thou marble-hearted fiend,
More hideous, when thou show'st thee in a child,
Than the sea-monster. *I, iv, 283*

11 How sharper than a serpent's tooth it is
To have a thankless child! *I, iv, 312*

12 Striving to better, oft we mar what's well.
I, iv, 371

13 The son and heir of a mongrel bitch.
II, ii, 23

14 I have seen better faces in my time
Than stands on any shoulder that I see
Before me at this instant. *II, ii, 99*

15 A good man's fortune may grow out at heels.
II, ii, 164

16 Fortune, good night, smile once more; turn thy wheel! *King Lear, II, ii, 180*

17 *Hysterica passio!* down, thou climbing sorrow!
Thy element's below. *II, iv, 57*

18 That sir which serves and seeks for gain,
And follows but for form,
Will pack when it begins to rain,
And leave thee in the storm. *II, iv, 79*

19 Nature in you stands on the very verge
Of her confine. *II, iv, 149*

20 Necessity's sharp pinch! *II, iv, 214*

21 Our basest beggars
Are in the poorest thing superfluous:
Allow not nature more than nature needs,
Man's life is cheap as beast's.
II, iv, 267

22 Let not women's weapons, waterdrops,
Stain my man's cheeks! *II, iv, 280*

23 I have full cause of weeping, but this heart
Shall break into a hundred thousand flaws
Or e'er I'll weep. O fool! I shall go mad.
II, iv, 287

24 Blow, winds, and crack your cheeks! rage! blow!
You cataracts and hurricanoes, spout
Till you have drenched our steeples, drowned the cocks!
You sulphurous and thought-executing fires,
Vaunt-couriers to oak-cleaving thunderbolts,
Singe my white head! And thou, all-shaking thunder,
Strike flat the thick rotundity o' the world!
Crack nature's molds, all germens spill at once
That make ingrateful man! *III, ii, 1*

25 I tax not you, you elements, with unkindness.
III, ii, 16

26 A poor, infirm, weak, and despised old man.
III, ii, 20

27 There was never yet fair woman but she made mouths in a glass. *III, ii, 35*

28 I will be the pattern of all patience.
III, ii, 37

29 I am a man
More sinned against than sinning.
III, ii, 59

30 The art of our necessities is strange,
That can make vile things precious.
III, ii, 70

1 He that has and a little tiny wit,
With hey, ho, the wind and the rain.
Must make content with his fortunes fit,
Though the rain it raineth every day.[1]
King Lear, III, ii, 76

2 O! that way madness lies; let me shun that.
III, iv, 21

3 Poor naked wretches, wheresoe'er you are,
That bide the pelting of this pitiless storm,
How shall your houseless heads and unfed sides,
Your looped and windowed raggedness, defend you
From seasons such as these?
III, iv, 28

4 Take physic, pomp;
Expose thyself to feel what wretches feel.
III, iv, 33

5 Pillicock sat on Pillicock-hill:
Halloo, halloo, loo, loo! *III, iv, 75*

6 Out-paramoured the Turk.
III, iv, 91

7 Is man no more than this? Consider him well. Thou owest the worm no silk, the beast no hide, the sheep no wool, the cat no perfume. Ha! here's three on 's are sophisticated; thou art the thing itself; unaccommodated man is no more but such a poor, bare, forked animal as thou art. Off, off, you lendings! Come; unbutton here. *III, iv, 105*

8 'Tis a naughty night to swim in.
III, iv, 113

9 The green mantle of the standing pool.
III, iv, 137

10 But mice and rats and such small deer
Have been Tom's food for seven long year.
III, iv, 142

11 The prince of darkness is a gentleman.[2]
III, iv, 147

12 Poor Tom's a-cold. *III, iv, 151*

13 Child Rowland to the dark tower came,[3]
His word was still, Fie, foh, and fum,
I smell the blood of a British man.
III, iv, 185

14 He's mad that trusts in the tameness of a wolf, a horse's health, a boy's love, or a whore's oath. *III, vi, 20*

[1]See *Twelfth-Night,* 214:29.

[2]The Devil is a gentleman.—SHELLEY, *Peter Bell the Third* [1819], *pt. II, st.* 2

[3]Child Roland to the dark tower came.—SIR WALTER SCOTT, *The Bridal of Triermain* [1813]

Dauntless the slug-horn to my lips I set, / And blew. *"Childe Roland to the Dark Tower came."*—BROWNING, *Child Roland to the Dark Tower Came* [1855], *st.* 34

15 The little dogs and all,
Tray, Blanch, and Sweetheart, see, they bark at me. *King Lear, III, vi, 65*

16 Is there any cause in nature that makes these hard hearts? *III, vi, 81*

17 I am tied to the stake, and I must stand the course. *III, vii, 54*

18 Out, vile jelly! *III, vii, 83*

19 The lowest and most dejected thing of fortune. *IV, i, 3*

20 The worst is not,
So long as we can say, "This is the worst."
IV, i, 27

21 As flies to wanton boys, are we to the gods;
They kill us for their sport. *IV, i, 36*

22 You are not worth the dust which the rude wind
Blows in your face. *IV, ii, 30*

23 She that herself will sliver and disbranch
From her material sap, perforce must wither
And come to deadly use. *IV, ii, 34*

24 Wisdom and goodness to the vile seem vile;
Filths savor but themselves. *IV, ii, 38*

25 Tigers, not daughters. *IV, ii, 39*

26 It is the stars,
The stars above us, govern our conditions.
IV, iii, 34

27 Our foster-nurse of nature is repose.
IV, iv, 12

28 How fearful
And dizzy 'tis to cast one's eyes so low!
The crows and choughs that wing the midway air
Show scarce so gross as beetles; halfway down
Hangs one that gathers samphire, dreadful trade!
Methinks he seems no bigger than his head.
The fishermen that walk upon the beach
Appear like mice, and yond tall anchoring bark
Diminished to her cock, her cock a buoy
Almost too small for sight. The murmuring surge,
That on the unnumbered idle pebbles chafes,
Cannot be heard so high. *IV, vi, 12*

29 Nature's above art in that respect.
IV, vi, 87

30 Ay, every inch a king. *IV, vi, 110*

31 The wren goes to 't, and the small gilded fly
Does lecher in my sight.
Let copulation thrive. *IV, vi, 115*

1 Give me an ounce of civet, good apothecary, to sweeten my imagination.
King Lear, IV, vi, 133

2 A man may see how this world goes with no eyes. Look with thine ears: see how yond justice rails upon yon simple thief. Hark, in thine ear: change places; and, handy-dandy, which is the justice, which is the thief?
IV, vi, 154

3 Through tattered clothes small vices do appear;
Robes and furred gowns hide all. Plate sin with gold,
And the strong lance of justice hurtless breaks;
Arm it in rags, a pigmy's straw does pierce it.
IV, vi, 169

4 Get thee glass eyes;
And, like a scurvy politician, seem
To see the things thou dost not.
IV, vi, 175

5 When we are born, we cry that we are come
To this great stage of fools. *IV, vi, 187*

6 Then, kill, kill, kill, kill, kill, kill!
IV, vi, 192

7 Mine enemy's dog,
Though he had bit me, should have stood that night
Against my fire. *IV, vii, 36*

8 Thou art a soul in bliss; but I am bound
Upon a wheel of fire, that mine own tears
Do scald like molten lead. *IV, vii, 46*

9 I am a very foolish fond old man,
Fourscore and upward, not an hour more or less;
And, to deal plainly,
I fear I am not in my perfect mind.
IV, vii, 60

10 Pray you now, forget and forgive.[1]
IV, vii, 84

11 Men must endure
Their going hence, even as their coming hither:
Ripeness is all. *V, ii, 9*

12 Come, let's away to prison;
We two alone will sing like birds i' the cage:
When thou dost ask me blessing, I'll kneel down,
And ask of thee forgiveness: so we'll live,
And pray, and sing, and tell old tales, and laugh
At gilded butterflies, and hear poor rogues
Talk of court news; and we'll talk with them too,
Who loses and who wins; who's in, who's out;
And take upon's the mystery of things,
As if we were God's spies: and we'll wear out,
In a walled prison, packs and sets of great ones
That ebb and flow by the moon.
King Lear, V, iii, 8

13 Upon such sacrifices, my Cordelia,
The gods themselves throw incense.
V, iii, 20

14 The gods are just, and of our pleasant vices
Make instruments to plague us.
V, iii, 172

15 The wheel is come full circle.
V, iii, 176

16 Howl, howl, howl, howl! O! you are men of stones:
Had I your tongues and eyes, I'd use them so
That heaven's vaults should crack. She's gone forever. *V, iii, 259*

17 Her voice was ever soft,
Gentle, and low, an excellent thing in woman. *V, iii, 274*

18 And my poor fool is hanged! No, no, no life!
Why should a dog, a horse, a rat, have life,
And thou no breath at all? Thou'lt come no more,
Never, never, never, never, never![2]
Pray you, undo this button. *V, iii, 307*

19 Vex not his ghost: O! let him pass; he hates him
That would upon the rack of this tough world
Stretch him out longer. *V, iii, 315*

20 The weight of this sad time we must obey;
Speak what we feel, not what we ought to say.
The oldest hath borne most: we that are young,
Shall never see so much, nor live so long.
V, iii, 325

21 *First Witch:* When shall we three meet again
In thunder, lightning, or in rain?
Second Witch: When the hurlyburly's done,
When the battle's lost and won.
Macbeth [1605–1606], act I, sc. i, l. 1

22 Fair is foul, and foul is fair:
Hover through the fog and filthy air.
I, i, 12

23 Banners flout the sky. *I, ii, 50*

[1] All our great fray . . . is forgiven and forgotten between us quite.—HEYWOOD, *Proverbs* [1546], *pt. II, ch. 3*

[2] See Pitt, 351:5, and Churchill, 745:6.

1 A sailor's wife had chestnuts in her lap,
And munched, and munched, and munched:
"Give me," quoth I:
"Aroint thee, witch!" the rump-fed ronyon cries. *Macbeth, I, iii, 4*

2 Sleep shall neither night nor day
Hang upon his pent-house lid.
I, iii, 19

3 Dwindle, peak, and pine. *I, iii, 23*

4 So foul and fair a day I have not seen.
I, iii, 38

5 If you can look into the seeds of time,
And say which grain will grow and which will not,
Speak. *I, iii, 58*

6 And to be king
Stands not within the prospect of belief.
I, iii, 73

7 The earth hath bubbles, as the water has,
And these are of them. *I, iii, 79*

8 Or have we eaten on the insane root
That takes the reason prisoner?
I, iii, 84

9 And oftentimes, to win us to our harm,
The instruments of darkness tell us truths,
Win us with honest trifles, to betray 's
In deepest consequence. *I, iii, 123*

10 As happy prologues to the swelling act
Of the imperial theme. *I, iii, 128*

11 I am Thane of Cawdor:
If good, why do I yield to that suggestion
Whose horrid image doth unfix my hair
And make my seated heart knock at my ribs,
Against the use of nature? Present fears
Are less than horrible imaginings.
I, iii, 134

12 If chance will have me king, why, chance may crown me,
Without my stir. *I, iii, 143*

13 Come what come may,
Time and the hour runs through the roughest day. *I, iii, 146*

14 Nothing in his life
Became him like the leaving it; he died
As one that had been studied in his death
To throw away the dearest thing he ow'd,
As 'twere a careless trifle. *I, iv, 7*

15 There's no art
To find the mind's construction in the face:
He was a gentleman on whom I built
An absolute trust. *I, iv, 11*

16 Glamis thou art, and Cawdor; and shalt be
What thou art promised. Yet do I fear thy nature;
It is too full o' the milk of human kindness[1]
To catch the nearest way.
Macbeth, I, v, 16

17 The raven himself is hoarse
That croaks the fatal entrance of Duncan
Under my battlements. Come, you spirits
That tend on mortal thoughts! unsex me here,
And fill me from the crown to the toe top full
Of direst cruelty; make thick my blood,
Stop up the access and passage to remorse,
That no compunctious visitings of nature
Shake my fell purpose, nor keep peace between
The effect and it! Come to my woman's breasts,
And take my milk for gall, you murdering ministers. *I, v, 38*

18 Nor heaven peep through the blanket of the dark,
To cry, "Hold, hold!" *I, v, 54*

19 Your face, my thane, is as a book where men
May read strange matters. *I, v, 63*

20 Look like the innocent flower,
But be the serpent under 't. *I, v, 66*

21 *Duncan:* This castle hath a pleasant seat; the air
Nimbly and sweetly recommends itself
Unto our gentle senses.
Banquo: This guest of summer,
The temple-haunting martlet, does approve
By his loved mansionry that the heaven's breath
Smells wooingly here: no jutty, frieze,
Buttress, nor coign of vantage, but this bird
Hath made his pendent bed and procreant cradle:
Where they most breed and haunt, I have observed
The air is delicate. *I, vi, 1*

22 If it were done when 'tis done, then 'twere well
It were done quickly; if the assassination
Could trammel up the consequence, and catch
With his surcease success; that but this blow
Might be the be-all and the end-all here,
But here, upon this bank and shoal of time,
We'd jump the life to come. *I, vii, 1*

23 This even-handed justice. *I, vii, 10*

24 Besides, this Duncan
Hath borne his faculties so meek, hath been

[1]The thunder of your words has soured the milk of human kindness in my heart.—Richard Brinsley Sheridan, *The Rivals* [1775], *act III, sc. iv*

So clear in his great office, that his virtues
Will plead like angels trumpet-tongued[1] against
The deep damnation of his taking-off;
And pity, like a naked new-born babe,
Striding the blast, or heaven's cherubin, horsed
Upon the sightless couriers of the air,
Shall blow the horrid deed in every eye,
That tears shall drown the wind. I have no spur
To prick the sides of my intent, but only
Vaulting ambition, which o'erleaps itself
And falls on the other.
Macbeth, I, vii, 16

1 I have bought
Golden opinions from all sorts of people.
I, vii, 32

2 Letting "I dare not" wait upon "I would,"
Like the poor cat i' the adage.[2]
I, vii, 44

3 I dare do all that may become a man;
Who dares do more is none. *I, vii, 46*

4 Nor time nor place
Did then adhere. *I, vii, 51*

5 I have given suck, and know
How tender 'tis to love the babe that milks me:
I would, while it was smiling in my face,
Have plucked my nipple from his boneless gums,
And dashed the brains out, had I so sworn as you
Have done to this. *I, vii, 54*

6 *Macbeth:* If we should fail—
Lady Macbeth: We fail!
But screw your courage to the sticking-place,
And we'll not fail. *I, vii, 59*

7 Memory, the warder of the brain.
I, vii, 65

8 Away, and mock the time with fairest show:
False face must hide what the false heart doth know. *I, vii, 81*

9 The moon is down. *II, i, 2*

10 There's husbandry in heaven;
Their candles are all out. *II, i, 4*

11 Merciful powers!
Restrain in me the cursèd thoughts that nature
Gives way to in repose. *II, i, 7*

12 Shut up
In measureless content. *II, i, 16*

[1]See *Matthew 24:31*, 40:25.
[2]See Heywood, 160:7, and *Measure for Measure*, 227:29.

13 Is this a dagger which I see before me,
The handle toward my hand? Come, let me clutch thee:
I have thee not, and yet I see thee still.
Art thou not, fatal vision, sensible
To feeling as to sight? or art thou but
A dagger of the mind, a false creation,
Proceeding from the heat-oppressed brain?
Macbeth, II, i, 33

14 Now o'er the one half-world
Nature seems dead; and wicked dreams abuse
The curtained sleep; witchcraft celebrates
Pale Hecate's offerings. *II, i, 49*

15 Thou sure and firm-set earth,
Hear not my steps, which way they walk, for fear
The very stones prate of my whereabout.[3]
II, i, 56

16 The bell invites me.
Hear it not, Duncan; for it is a knell
That summons thee to heaven or to hell.
II, i, 62

17 It was the owl that shrieked, the fatal bellman,
Which gives the stern'st good-night.
II, ii, 4

18 The attempt and not the deed
Confounds us. *II, ii, 12*

19 Had he not resembled
My father as he slept I had done 't.
II, ii, 14

20 I had most need of blessing, and "Amen"
Stuck in my throat. *II, ii, 33*

21 Methought I heard a voice cry, "Sleep no more!
Macbeth does murder sleep!" the innocent sleep,
Sleep that knits up the raveled sleave of care,
The death of each day's life, sore labor's bath,
Balm of hurt minds, great nature's second course,
Chief nourisher in life's feast.
II, ii, 36

22 Glamis hath murdered sleep, and therefore Cawdor
Shall sleep no more, Macbeth shall sleep no more! *II, ii, 43*

23 Infirm of purpose!
Give me the daggers. The sleeping and the dead
Are but as pictures; 'tis the eye of childhood
That fears a painted devil. *II, ii, 53*

[3]See *Habakkuk 2:11*, 33:26, and *Luke 19:40*, 43:42.

1 Will all great Neptune's ocean wash this blood
Clean from my hand? No, this my hand will rather
The multitudinous seas incarnadine,
Making the green one red.
Macbeth, II, ii, 61

2 The primrose way to the everlasting bonfire.[1] *II, iii, 22*

3 It [drink] provokes the desire, but it takes away the performance. *II, iii, 34*

4 The labor we delight in physics pain.
II, iii, 56

5 Confusion now hath made his masterpiece!
Most sacrilegious murder hath broke ope
The Lord's anointed temple, and stole thence
The life o' the building! *II, iii, 72*

6 Shake off this downy sleep, death's counterfeit.[2] *II, iii, 83*

7 Had I but died an hour before this chance
I had lived a blessed time; for, from this instant,
There's nothing serious in mortality,
All is but toys; renown and grace is dead,
The wine of life is drawn, and the mere lees
Is left this vault to brag of. *II, iii, 98*

8 Who can be wise, amazed, temperate and furious,
Loyal and neutral, in a moment? No man.
II, iii, 115

9 In the great hand of God I stand, and thence
Against the undivulged pretense I fight
Of treasonous malice. *II, iii, 137*

10 To show an unfelt sorrow is an office
Which the false man does easy.
II, iii, 143

11 A falcon, towering in her pride of place,
Was by a mousing owl hawked at and killed.
II, iv, 12

12 I must become a borrower of the night
For a dark hour or twain. *III, i, 27*

13 To be thus is nothing;
But to be safely thus. *III, i, 48*

14 *Murderer:* We are men, my liege.
Macbeth: Ay, in the catalogue ye go for men.
III, i, 91

15 I am one, my liege,
Whom the vile blows and buffets of the world
Have so incensed that I am reckless what
I do to spite the world. *III, i, 108*

[1] See Bion, 92:7, and *Hamlet,* 218:28.
[2] See Homer, 58:20; Virgil, 105:17; Daniel, 182:4; and Shelley, 466:6.

16 So weary with disasters, tugged with fortune,
That I would set my life on any chance,
To mend it or be rid on 't.
Macbeth, III, i, 112

17 Things without all remedy
Should be without regard: what's done is done. *III, ii, 11*

18 We have scotched the snake, not killed it.
III, ii, 13

19 Duncan is in his grave;
After life's fitful fever he sleeps well;
Treason has done his worst: nor steel, nor poison,
Malice domestic, foreign levy, nothing
Can touch him further. *III, ii, 22*

20 Then be thou jocund. Ere the bat hath flown
His cloistered flight, ere, to black Hecate's summons
The shard-borne beetle with his drowsy hums
Hath rung night's yawning peal, there shall be done
A deed of dreadful note. *III, ii, 40*

21 Come, seeling night,
Scarf up the tender eye of pitiful day,
And with thy bloody and invisible hand
Cancel and tear to pieces that great bond
Which keeps me pale! Light thickens, and the crow
Makes wing to the rooky wood.
III, ii, 46

22 Now spurs the lated traveler apace
To gain the timely inn. *III, iii, 6*

23 But now I am cabined, cribbed, confined, bound in
To saucy doubts and fears. *III, iv, 24*

24 Now good digestion wait on appetite,
And health on both! *III, iv, 38*

25 Thou canst not say I did it: never shake
Thy gory locks at me. *III, iv, 50*

26 The air-drawn dagger. *III, iv, 62*

27 I drink to the general joy of the whole table.
III, iv, 89

28 What man dare, I dare:
Approach thou like the rugged Russian bear,
The armed rhinoceros, or the Hyrcan tiger,
Take any shape but that, and my firm nerves
Shall never tremble. *III, iv, 99*

29 Hence, horrible shadow!
Unreal Mockery, hence! *III, iv, 106*

30 Stand not upon the order of your going,
But go at once. *III, iv, 119*

1 It will have blood, they say; blood will have blood:
Stones have been known to move and trees to speak. *Macbeth, III, iv, 122*

2 *Macbeth:* What is the night?
Lady Macbeth: Almost at odds with morning, which is which. *III, iv, 126*

3 I am in blood
Stepped in so far, that, should I wade no more,
Returning were as tedious as go o'er.
III, iv, 136

4 Double, double toil and trouble;
Fire burn and cauldron bubble.
IV, i, 10

5 Eye of newt, and toe of frog,
Wool of bat, and tongue of dog.
IV, i, 14

6 Finger of birth-strangled babe,
Ditch-delivered by a drab. *IV, i, 30*

7 By the pricking of my thumbs,
Something wicked this way comes.
Open, locks,
Whoever knocks! *IV, i, 44*

8 How now, you secret, black, and midnight hags! *IV, i, 48*

9 A deed without a name.[1] *IV, i, 49*

10 Be bloody, bold, and resolute; laugh to scorn
The power of man, for none of woman born
Shall harm Macbeth. *IV, i, 79*

11 But yet I'll make assurance double sure,
And take a bond of fate. *IV, i, 83*

12 Macbeth shall never vanquished be until
Great Birnam wood to high Dunsinane hill
Shall come against him.[2] *IV, i, 92*

13 Show his eyes, and grieve his heart;
Come like shadows, so depart.
IV, i, 110

14 What! will the line stretch out to the crack of doom? *IV, i, 117*

15 The weird sisters. *IV, i, 136*

16 When our actions do not,
Our fears do make us traitors.
IV, ii, 3

17 He wants the natural touch. *IV, ii, 9*

18 Angels are bright still, though the brightest fell. *IV, iii, 22*

19 Pour the sweet milk of concord into hell,
Uproar the universal peace, confound
All unity on earth. *IV, iii, 98*

[1]See Ann Radcliffe, 416:11.

[2]Till Birnam wood remove to Dunsinane / I cannot taint with fear.—*Macbeth, act V, sc. iii, l. 2*

20 Give sorrow words; the grief that does not speak
Whispers the o'er-fraught heart and bids it break. *Macbeth, IV, iii, 209*

21 All my pretty ones?
Did you say all? O hell-kite! All?
What! all my pretty chickens and their dam
At one fell swoop? *IV, iii, 216*

22 *Malcolm:* Dispute it like a man.
Macbeth: I shall do so;
But I must also feel it as a man:
I cannot but remember such things were
That were most precious to me.
IV, iii, 219

23 Out, damned spot! out, I say!
V, i, 38

24 Fie, my lord, fie! a soldier, and afeard?
V, i, 40

25 Who would have thought the old man to have had so much blood in him?
V, i, 42

26 The Thane of Fife had a wife: where is she now? *V, i, 46*

27 All the perfumes of Arabia will not sweeten this little hand. *V, i, 56*

28 Those he commands move only in command,
Nothing in love; now does he feel his title
Hang loose about him, like a giant's robe
Upon a dwarfish thief. *V, ii, 19*

29 The devil damn thee black, thou cream-faced loon
Where gott'st thou that goose look?
V, iii, 11

30 Thou lily-livered boy. *V, iii, 15*

31 I have lived long enough: my way of life
Is fall'n into the sere, the yellow leaf;[3]
And that which should accompany old age,
As honor, love, obedience, troops of friends,
I must not look to have; but, in their stead,
Curses, not loud but deep, mouth-honor, breath,
Which the poor heart would fain deny, and dare not. *V, iii, 22*

32 *Macbeth:* Canst thou not minister to a mind diseased,
Pluck from the memory a rooted sorrow,
Raze out the written troubles of the brain,
And with some sweet oblivious antidote
Cleanse the stuffed bosom of that perilous stuff
Which weighs upon the heart?

[3]See Byron, 462:18.

Doctor: Therein the patient
Must minister to himself.
Macbeth: Throw physic to the dogs; I'll none of it. *Macbeth, V, iii, 40*

1 I would applaud thee to the very echo,
That should applaud again. *V, iii, 53*

2 Hang out our banners on the outward walls;
The cry is still, "They come"; our castle's strength
Will laugh a siege to scorn. *V, v, 1*

3 My fell of hair
Would at a dismal treatise rouse and stir
As life were in 't. I have supped full with horrors. *V, v, 11*

4 She should have died hereafter;
There would have been a time for such a word.
Tomorrow, and tomorrow, and tomorrow,
Creeps in this petty pace from day to day,
To the last syllable of recorded time;
And all our yesterdays have lighted fools
The way to dusty death. Out, out, brief candle!
Life's but a walking shadow, a poor player
That struts and frets his hour upon the stage,
And then is heard no more; it is a tale
Told by an idiot, full of sound and fury,
Signifying nothing. *V, v, 17*

5 I 'gin to be aweary of the sun,
And wish the estate o' the world were now undone. *V, v, 49*

6 Blow, wind! come, wrack!
At least we'll die with harness on our back. *V, v, 51*

7 Why should I play the Roman fool, and die
On mine own sword? *V, vii, 30*

8 I bear a charmèd life. *V, vii, 41*

9 And be these juggling fiends no more believed,
That palter with us in a double sense;
That keep the word of promise to our ear
And break it to our hope. *V, vii, 48*

10 Live to be the show and gaze o' the time. *V, vii, 53*

11 Lay on, Macduff,
And damned be him that first cries, "Hold, enough!" *V, vii, 62*

12 You shall see in him
The triple pillar of the world transformed
Into a strumpet's fool.
Antony and Cleopatra [1606–1607], act I, sc. i, l. 12

13 There's beggary in the love that can be reckoned. *Antony and Cleopatra, I, i, 15*

14 Let Rome in Tiber melt, and the wide arch
Of the ranged empire fall! Here is my space.
Kingdoms are clay. *I, i, 33*

15 In nature's infinite book of secrecy
A little I can read. *I, ii, 11*

16 I love long life better than figs. *I, ii, 34*

17 On the sudden
A Roman thought hath struck him. *I, ii, 90*

18 Eternity was in our lips and eyes,
Bliss in our brows bent. *I, iii, 35*

19 O! my oblivion is a very Antony,
And I am all forgotten. *I, iii, 90*

20 Give me to drink mandragora.[1] . . .
That I might sleep out this great gap of time
My Antony is away. *I, v, 4*

21 O happy horse, to bear the weight of Antony! *I, v, 21*

22 The demi-Atlas of this earth, the arm
And burgonet of men. *I, v, 23*

23 Where's my serpent of old Nile? *I, v, 25*

24 A morsel for a monarch. *I, v, 31*

25 My salad days,
When I was green in judgment. *I, v, 73*

26 We, ignorant of ourselves,
Beg often our own harms, which the wise powers
Deny us for our good; so find we profit
By losing of our prayers. *II, i, 5*

27 Epicurean cooks
Sharpen with cloyless sauce his appetite. *II, i, 24*

28 No worse a husband than the best of men. *II, ii, 135*

29 The barge she sat in, like a burnished throne,
Burned on the water; the poop was beaten gold,
Purple the sails, and so perfumed, that
The winds were love-sick with them; the oars were silver,
Which to the tune of flutes kept stroke, and made
The water which they beat to follow faster,
As amorous of their strokes. For her own person,
It beggared all description. *II, ii, 199*

[1] See *Othello,* 231:8.

1 Age cannot wither her, nor custom stale
Her infinite variety; other women cloy
The appetites they feed, but she makes hungry
Where most she satisfies; for vilest things
Become themselves in her, that the holy priests
Bless her when she is riggish.
Antony and Cleopatra, II, ii, 243

2 I have not kept my square; but that to come
Shall all be done by the rule. *II, iii, 6*

3 Music, moody food
Of us that trade in love.[1] *II, v, 1*

4 Though it be honest, it is never good
To bring bad news.[2] *II, v, 85*

5 Come, thou monarch of the vine,
Plumpy Bacchus, with pink eyne!
II, vii, 120

6 Ambition,
The soldier's virtue. *III, i, 22*

7 Celerity is never more admired
Than by the negligent. *III, vii, 24*

8 We have kissed away
Kingdoms and provinces. *III, viii, 17*

9 He wears the rose
Of youth upon him. *III, xi, 20*

10 Men's judgments are
A parcel of their fortunes, and things outward
Do draw the inward quality after them,
To suffer all alike. *III, xi, 31*

11 I found you as a morsel, cold upon
Dead Caesar's trencher. *III, xi, 116*

12 Let's have one other gaudy night.
III, xi, 182

13 Now he'll outstare the lightning. To be furious
Is to be frightened out of fear.
III, xi, 194

14 To business that we love we rise betime,
And go to 't with delight. *IV, iv, 20*

15 O infinite virtue! com'st thou smiling from
The world's great snare uncaught?
IV, viii, 17

16 The shirt of Nessus is upon me.
IV, x, 56

17 Sometimes we see a cloud that's dragonish;
A vapor sometime like a bear or lion,
A towered citadel, a pendant rock,
A forked mountain, or blue promontory
With trees upon 't.[3]
Antony and Cleopatra, IV, xii, 2

18 Unarm, Eros; the long day's task is done,
And we must sleep. *IV, xii, 35*

19 But I will be
A bridegroom in my death, and run into 't
As to a lover's bed. *IV, xii, 99*

20 O sun!
Burn the great sphere thou mov'st in; darkling stand
The varying shore[4] o' the world.
IV, xiii, 10

21 I am dying, Egypt, dying; only
I here importune death awhile, until
Of many thousand kisses the poor last
I lay upon thy lips. *IV, xiii, 18*

22 O! withered is the garland of the war,
The soldier's pole is fall'n; young boys and girls
Are level now with men; the odds is gone,
And there is nothing left remarkable
Beneath the visiting moon.
IV, xiii, 64

23 Let's do it after the high Roman fashion,
And make death proud to take us.
IV, xiii, 87

24 And it is great
To do that thing that ends all other deeds,
Which shackles accidents, and bolts up change. *V, ii, 4*

25 His legs bestrid the ocean; his reared arm
Crested the world; his voice was propertied
As all the tunèd spheres, and that to friends;
But when he meant to quail and shake the orb,
He was as rattling thunder. For his bounty,
There was no winter in 't, an autumn 'twas
That grew the more by reaping; his delights
Were dolphin-like, they showed his back above
The element they lived in; in his livery
Walked crowns and crownets, realms and islands were
As plates dropped from his pocket.
V, ii, 82

26 The bright day is done,
And we are for the dark. *V, ii, 192*

27 Antony
Shall be brought drunken forth, and I shall see
Some squeaking Cleopatra boy my greatness
I' the posture of a whore. *V, ii, 217*

[1] See *Twelfth-Night,* 213:7.

[2] See Sophocles, 74:11, and *King Henry IV, Part II,* 205:20.

[3] See Aristophanes, 81:15, and *Hamlet,* 222:20.

[4] In some editions: star.

1 A woman is a dish for the gods, if the devil dress her not.
Antony and Cleopatra, V, ii, 274

2 I have
Immortal longings in me. *V, ii, 282*

3 If thou and nature can so gently part,
The stroke of death is as a lover's pinch,
Which hurts, and is desired. *V, ii, 296*

4 Dost thou not see my baby at my breast,
That sucks the nurse asleep?
V, ii, 311

5 Now boast thee, death, in thy possession lies
A lass unparalleled. *V, ii, 317*

6 *First Guard:* . . . Charmian, is this well done?
Charmian: It is well done, and fitting for a princess
Descended of so many royal kings.[1]
V, ii, 327

7 As she would catch another Antony
In her strong toil of grace. *V, ii, 348*

8 The gods sent not
Corn for the rich men only.
Coriolanus [1607–1608], act I, sc. i, l. 213

9 They threw their caps
As they would hang them on the horns o' the moon,
Shouting their emulation. *I, i, 218*

10 All the yarn she spun in Ulysses' absence did but fill Ithaca full of moths.
I, iii, 93

11 Nature teaches beasts to know their friends. *II, i, 6*

12 A cup of hot wine with not a drop of allaying Tiber in 't.[2] *II, i, 52*

13 My gracious silence, hail! *II, i, 194*

14 He himself stuck not to call us the many-headed multitude.[3] *II, iii, 18*

15 Bid them wash their faces,
And keep their teeth clean. *II, iii, 65*

16 I thank you for your voices, thank you,
Your most sweet voices. *II, iii, 179*

17 The mutable, rank-scented many.
III, i, 65

[1]One of the soldiers seeing her, angrily said unto her: Is that well done Charmian? Very well said she again, and meet for a princess descended of so many noble kings. — PLUTARCH, *Lives;* translated [1579] by SIR THOMAS NORTH

[2]See Lovelace, 296:3.

[3]See Horace, 108:19; Machiavelli, 154:8; *King Henry IV, Part II,* 205:18; *Coriolanus,* 242:21; and Pope, 339:28.

18 Hear you this Triton of the minnows? mark you
His absolute "shall"?
Coriolanus, III, i, 88

19 What is the city but the people?[4]
III, i, 198

20 His nature is too noble for the world:
He would not flatter Neptune for his trident,
Or Jove for 's power to thunder.[5] His heart's his mouth:
What his breast forges, that his tongue must vent. *III, i, 254*

21 The beast
With many heads butts me away.[6]
IV, i, 1

22 O! a kiss
Long as my exile, sweet as my revenge![7]
V, iii, 44

23 Chaste as the icicle
That's curdied by the frost from purest snow,
And hangs on Dian's temple.
V, iii, 65

24 He wants nothing of a god but eternity and a heaven to throne in. *V, iv, 25*

25 They'll give him death by inches.
V, iv, 43

26 If you have writ your annals true, 'tis there,
That, like an eagle in a dovecote, I
Fluttered your Volscians in Corioli:
Alone I did it. *V, v, 114*

27 Thou hast done a deed whereat valor will weep. *V, v, 135*

28 He shall have a noble memory.
V, v, 155

29 'Tis not enough to help the feeble up,
But to support him after.
Timon of Athens [1607–1608], act I, sc. i, l. 108

30 I call the gods to witness.[8] *I, i, 138*

31 I wonder men dare trust themselves with men. *I, ii, 45*

32 Here's that which is too weak to be a sinner,
Honest water, which ne'er left man i' the mire.[9] *I, ii, 60*

[4]See Sophocles, 74:1.

[5]See Manilius, 115:16, and Benjamin Franklin, 346:*n*5.

[6]See Horace, 108:19; Machiavelli, 154:8; *King Henry IV, Part II,* 205:18; *Coriolanus,* 242:14; and Pope, 339:28.

[7]See Byron, 460:17.

[8]See *Deuteronomy 4:26,* 11:8.

[9]Inscribed on the drinking fountain in the market square of Stratford-on-Avon.

1 Immortal gods, I crave no pelf;
I pray for no man but myself:
Grant I may never prove so fond,
To trust man on his oath or bond.
Timon of Athens, I, ii, 64

2 Men shut their doors against a setting sun.
I, ii, 152

3 Every man has his fault, and honesty is his.
III, i, 30

4 Nothing emboldens sin so much as mercy.
III, v, 3

5 You fools of fortune, trencher-friends, time's flies. *III, vi, 107*

6 We have seen better days. *IV, ii, 27*

7 O! the fierce wretchedness that glory brings us. *IV, ii, 30*

8 I am Misanthropos, and hate mankind.
IV, iii, 53

9 Life's uncertain voyage. *V, i, 207*

10 See, where she comes appareled like the spring.
Pericles [1608–1609], act I, sc. i, l. 12

11 Few love to hear the sins they love to act.
I, i, 92

12 The sad companion, dull-eyed melancholy.
I, ii, 2

13 *Third Fisherman:* . . . Master, I marvel how the fishes live in the sea.
First Fisherman: Why, as men do a-land; the great ones eat up the little ones.[1]
II, i, 29

14 Lest the bargain should catch cold and starve.
Cymbeline [1609–1610], act I, sc. iv, l. 186

15 Hath his bellyful of fighting.
II, i, 24

16 Hark! hark! the lark at heaven's gate sings,
And Phoebus 'gins arise,[2]
His steeds to water at those springs
On chaliced flowers that lies;
And winking Mary-buds begin
To ope their golden eyes:
With everything that pretty is,
My lady sweet, arise. *II, iii, 22*

17 As chaste as unsunned snow. *II, v, 13*

18 Some griefs are med'cinable. *III, ii, 33*

[1]Men lived like fishes; the great ones devoured the small.—ALGERNON SIDNEY, *Discourses on Government* [1698], *ch. 2, sec. 18*

[2]See Lyly, 176:1.

19 O! for a horse with wings!
Cymbeline, III, ii, 49

20 The game is up. *III, iii, 107*

21 Slander,
Whose edge is sharper than the sword, whose tongue
Outvenoms all the worms of Nile, whose breath
Rides on the posting winds and doth belie
All corners of the world. *III, iv, 35*

22 I have not slept one wink.[3] *III, iv, 103*

23 Weariness
Can snore upon the flint when resty sloth
Finds the down pillow hard.
III, vi, 33

24 An angel! or, if not,
An earthly paragon! *III, vi, 42*

25 Society is no comfort
To one not sociable. *IV, ii, 12*

26 I wear not
My dagger in my mouth. *IV, ii, 78*

27 Fear no more the heat o' the sun,
Nor the furious winter's rages;
Thou thy worldly task hast done,
Home art gone, and ta'en thy wages.
Golden lads and girls all must,
As chimney-sweepers, come to dust.
IV, ii, 258

28 Quiet consummation have;
And renowned be thy grave!
IV, ii, 280

29 Fortune brings in some boats that are not steered. *IV, iii, 46*

30 Hang there like fruit, my soul,
Till the tree die! *V, v, 264*

31 From fairest creatures we desire increase,
That thereby beauty's rose might never die.
Sonnets[4] *[1609], 1, l. 1*

[3]See Cervantes, 168:19, and Pope, 339:5.

[4]The sonnets were written definitely before 1598, according to the *Palladis Tamia* [1598] of Francis Mere [1565–1647], and according to Leslie Hotson in *Mr. W. H.* [1964] they bear strong evidence of all being written in 1588–1589. They were published [1609] by THOMAS THORPE, who wrote the dedication:

TO THE ONLIE BEGETTER OF
THESE INSUING SONNETS
MR. W. H., ALL HAPPINESSE
AND THAT ETERNITIE
PROMISED
BY
OUR EVER-LIVING POET
WISHETH
THE WELL-WISHING
ADVENTURER IN
SETTING
FORTH

T.T.

1 When forty winters shall besiege thy brow,
And dig deep trenches in thy beauty's field.
Sonnet 2, l. 1

2 Thou art thy mother's glass, and she in thee
Calls back the lovely April of her prime.
Sonnet 3, l. 9

3 Music to hear, why hear'st thou music sadly?
Sweets with sweet war not, joy delights in joy.
Sonnet 8, l. 1

4 Everything that grows
Holds in perfection but a little moment.
Sonnet 15, l. 1

5 Shall I compare thee to a summer's day?
Thou art more lovely and more temperate:
Rough winds do shake the darling buds of May,
And summer's lease hath all too short a date.
Sonnet 18, l. 1

6 But thy eternal summer shall not fade.
l. 9

7 The painful warrior famoused for fight,
After a thousand victories, once foiled,
Is from the books of honor razed quite,
And all the rest forgot for which he toiled.
Sonnet 25, l. 9

8 When in disgrace with fortune and men's eyes
I all alone beweep my outcast state,
And trouble deaf heaven with my bootless cries.
Sonnet 29, l. 1

9 Desiring this man's art, and that man's scope,
With what I most enjoy contented least;
Yet in these thoughts myself almost despising,
Haply I think on thee.
Sonnet 29, l. 7

10 For thy sweet love remembered such wealth brings
That then I scorn to change my state with kings.
l. 13

11 When to the sessions of sweet silent thought
I summon up remembrance of things past,
I sigh the lack of many a thing I sought,
And with old woes new wail my dear times' waste.
Sonnet 30, l. 1

12 But if the while I think on thee, dear friend,
All losses are restored and sorrows end.
l. 13

13 Full many a glorious morning have I seen.
Sonnet 33, l. 1

14 Roses have thorns, and silver fountains mud;
Clouds and eclipses stain both moon and sun,
And loathsome canker lives in sweetest bud.
All men make faults.
Sonnet 35, l. 2

15 Be thou the tenth Muse.
Sonnet 38, l. 9

16 For nimble thought can jump both sea and land.
Sonnet 44, l. 7

17 Against that time when thou shalt strangely pass,
And scarcely greet me with that sun, thine eye,
When love, converted from the thing it was,
Shall reasons find of settled gravity.
Sonnet 49, l. 5

18 Not marble, nor the gilded monuments
Of princes, shall outlive this powerful rime.
Sonnet 55, l. i.

19 Like as the waves make towards the pebbled shore,
So do our minutes hasten to their end.
Sonnet 60, l. 1

20 Time doth transfix the flourish set on youth
And delves the parallels in beauty's brow.
l. 9

21 When I have seen by Time's fell hand defaced
The rich-proud cost of outworn buried age.
Sonnet 64, l. 1

22 When I have seen the hungry ocean gain
Advantage on the kingdom of the shore,
And the firm soil win of the watery main,
Increasing store with loss, and loss with store.
l. 5

23 Tired with all these, for restful death I cry.
Sonnet 66, l. 1

24 And art made tongue-tied by authority.
l. 9

25 And simple truth miscalled simplicity,
And captive good attending captain ill.
l. 11

26 No longer mourn for me when I am dead
Than you shall hear the surly sullen bell
Give warning to the world that I am fled
From this vile world, with vilest worms to dwell.
Sonnet 71, l. 1

27 That time of year thou mayst in me behold
When yellow leaves, or none, or few, do hang
Upon those boughs which shake against the cold,[1]
Bare ruined choirs, where late the sweet birds sang.
Sonnet 73, l. 1

28 Clean starved for a look.
Sonnet 75, l. 10

29 Who is it that says most? which can say more
Than this rich praise—that you alone are you?
Sonnet 84, l. 1

[1]See Byron, 462:18.

1 Farewell! thou art too dear for my possessing,
And like enough thou know'st thy estimate.
Sonnet 87, l. 1

2 In sleep a king, but, waking, no such matter.
l. 14

3 Ah! do not, when my heart hath 'scaped this sorrow,
Come in the rearward of a conquered woe;
Give not a windy night a rainy morrow,
To linger out a purposed overthrow.
Sonnet 90, l. 5

4 They that have power to hurt and will do none,
That do not do the thing they most do show,
Who, moving others, are themselves as stone,
Unmoved, cold, and to temptation slow.
Sonnet 94, l. 1

5 They are the lords and owners of their faces,
Others but stewards of their excellence.
The summer's flower is to the summer sweet,
Though to itself it only live and die.
l. 7

6 Lilies that fester smell far worse than weeds.[1]
l. 14

7 The hardest knife ill-used doth lose his edge.
Sonnet 95, l. 14

8 How like a winter hath my absence been.
Sonnet 97, l. 1

9 From you have I been absent in the spring,
When proud-pied April, dressed in all his trim,
Hath put a spirit of youth in everything.
Sonnet 98, l. 1

10 Sweets grown common lose their dear delight. *Sonnet 102, l. 12*

11 To me, fair friend, you never can be old,
For as you were when first your eye I eyed,
Such seems your beauty still.
Sonnet 104, l. 1

12 When in the chronicle of wasted time
I see descriptions of the fairest wights,
And beauty making beautiful old rime,
In praise of ladies dead and lovely knights,
Then, in the blazon of sweet beauty's best,
Of hand, of foot, of lip, of eye, of brow,
I see their antique pen would have expressed
Even such a beauty as you master now.
Sonnet 106, l. 1

[1] As in the nature of things, those which most admirably flourish, most swiftly fester or putrefy, as roses, lilies, violets, while others last: so in the lives of men, those that are most blooming, are soonest turned into the opposite. —PLINY [A.D. 23–79], *Natural History, bk. XVI, ch. 15*

13 Not mine own fears, nor the prophetic soul
Of the wide world dreaming on things to come,
Can yet the lease of my true love control,
Supposed as forfeit to a confined doom.
The mortal moon hath her eclipse endured,
And the sad augurs mock their own presage;
Incertainties now crown themselves assured,
And peace proclaims olives of endless age.
Sonnet 107, l. 1

14 O! never say that I was false of heart,
Though absence seemed my flame to qualify.
Sonnet 109, l. 1

15 That is my home of love: if I have ranged,
Like him that travels, I return again.
l. 5

16 Alas! 'tis true I have gone here and there,
And made myself a motley to the view,
Gored mine own thoughts, sold cheap what is most dear,
Made old offenses of affections new.
Sonnet 110, l. 1

17 My nature is subdued
To what it works in, like the dyer's hand.
Sonnet 111, l. 6

18 Let me not to the marriage of true minds
Admit impediments. Love is not love
Which alters when it alteration finds,
Or bends with the remover to remove:
O, no! it is an ever-fixèd mark,
That looks on tempests and is never shaken;
It is the star to every wandering bark,
Whose worth's unknown, although his height be taken.
Love's not Time's fool, though rosy lips and cheeks
Within his bending sickle's compass come;
Love alters not with his brief hours and weeks,
But bears it out even to the edge of doom.
If this be error, and upon me proved,
I never writ, nor no man ever loved.
Sonnet 116

19 What potions have I drunk of Siren tears,
Distilled from limbecks foul as hell within.
Sonnet 119, l. 1

20 O benefit of ill! *l. 9*

21 And ruined love, when it is built anew,
Grows fairer than at first, more strong, far greater. *l. 11*

22 'Tis better to be vile than vile esteemed,
When not to be receives reproach of being.
Sonnet 121, l. 1

23 The expense of spirit in a waste of shame
Is lust in action; and till action, lust
Is perjured, murderous, bloody, full of blame,

Savage, extreme, rude, cruel, not to trust;
Enjoyed no sooner but despised straight;
Past reason hunted; and no sooner had,
Past reason hated, as a swallowed bait,
On purpose laid to make the taker mad:
Mad in pursuit, and in possession so;
Had, having, and in quest to have, extreme;
A bliss in proof—and proved, a very woe;
Before, a joy proposed; behind, a dream.
All this the world well knows; yet none knows well
To shun the heaven that leads men to this hell. *Sonnet 129*

1 My mistress' eyes are nothing like the sun;
Coral is far more red than her lips' red:
If snow be white, why then her breasts are dun;
If hairs be wires, black wires grow on her head. *Sonnet 130, l. 1*

2 When my love swears that she is made of truth,
I do believe her, though I know she lies. *Sonnet 138, l. 1*

3 Two loves I have of comfort and despair,
Which like two spirits do suggest me still. *Sonnet 144, l. 1*

4 Poor soul, the center of my sinful earth. *Sonnet 146, l. 1*

5 So shalt thou feed on Death, that feeds on men,
And Death once dead, there's no more dying then. *l. 13*

6 Past cure I am, now Reason is past care,
And frantic-mad with evermore unrest. *Sonnet 147, l. 9*

7 For I have sworn thee fair, and thought thee bright,
Who art as black as hell, as dark as night. *l. 13*

8 You pay a great deal too dear for what's given freely. *The Winter's Tale [1610–1611], act I, sc. i, l. 18*

9 Two lads that thought there was no more behind
But such a day tomorrow as today,
And to be boy eternal. *I, ii, 63*

10 We were as twinned lambs that did frisk i' the sun,
And bleat the one at the other: what we changed
Was innocence for innocence. *I, ii, 67*

11 Paddling palms and pinching fingers. *I, ii, 116*

12 Affection! thy intention stabs the center:
Thou dost make possible things not so held,
Communicat'st with dreams. *The Winter's Tale, I, ii, 139*

13 He makes a July's day short as December. *I, ii, 169*

14 A sad tale's best for winter.
I have one of sprites and goblins. *II, i, 24*

15 The silence often of pure innocence
Persuades when speaking fails. *II, ii, 41*

16 It is a heretic that makes the fire,
Not she which burns in 't. *II, iii, 115*

17 I am a feather for each wind that blows. *II, iii, 153*

18 What's gone and what's past help
Should be past grief. *III, ii, 223*

19 Exit, pursued by a bear.[1] *III, iii, 57*

20 This is fairy gold, boy, and 'twill prove so. *III, iii, 127*

21 Then comes in the sweet o' the year. *IV, ii, 3*

22 A snapper-up of unconsidered trifles. *IV, ii, 26*

23 For the life to come, I sleep out the thought of it. *IV, ii, 30*

24 Jog on, jog on, the footpath way,
And merrily hent the stile-a:
A merry heart goes all the day,
Your sad tires in a mile-a. *IV, ii, 133*

25 For you there's rosemary and rue; these keep
Seeming and savor all the winter long. *IV, iii, 74*

26 Daffodils,
That come before the swallow dares, and take
The winds of March with beauty. *IV, iii, 118*

27 What you do
Still betters what is done. *IV, iii, 135*

28 When you do dance, I wish you
A wave o' the sea, that you might ever do
Nothing but that. *IV, iii, 140*

29 Lawn as white as driven snow. *IV, iii, 220*

30 I love a ballad in print, a-life, for then we are sure they are true. *IV, iii, 262*

[1] This is perhaps the most famous stage direction in English.

1 The self-same sun that shines upon his court
Hides not his visage from our cottage, but
Looks on alike.
The Winter's Tale, IV, iii, 457

2 I'll queen it no inch further,
But milk my ewes and weep.
IV, iii, 462

3 Prosperity's the very bond of love,
Whose fresh complexion and whose heart together
Affliction alters. *IV, iii, 586*

4 Let me have no lying; it becomes none but tradesmen. *IV, iii, 747*

5 To purge melancholy. *IV, iii, 792*

6 There's time enough for that.
V, iii, 128

7 He hath no drowning mark upon him; his complexion is perfect gallows.
The Tempest [1611–1612], act I, sc. i, l. 33

8 Now would I give a thousand furlongs of sea for an acre of barren ground.
I, i, 70

9 I would fain die a dry death. *I, i, 73*

10 What seest thou else
In the dark backward and abysm of time?
I, ii, 49

11 By telling of it,
Made such a sinner of his memory,
To credit his own lie. *I, ii, 100*

12 Your tale, sir, would cure deafness.
I, ii, 106

13 My library
Was dukedom large enough. *I, ii, 109*

14 The very rats
Instinctively have quit it. *I, ii, 147*

15 Knowing I loved my books, he furnished me,
From mine own library with volumes that
I prize above my dukedom. *I, ii, 166*

16 From the still-vexed Bermoothes.[1]
I, ii, 229

17 I [Ariel] will be correspondent to command,
And do my spiriting gently. *I, ii, 297*

18 You taught me language; and my profit on 't
Is, I know how to curse: the red plague rid you,
For learning me your language!
I, ii, 363

[1]See Richard Rich, 261:*n*11.

19 Come unto these yellow sands,
And then take hands:
Curtsied when you have, and kissed—
The wild waves whist—
Foot it featly here and there.
The Tempest, I, ii, 375

20 This music crept by me upon the waters,
Allaying both their fury, and my passion,
With its sweet air. *I, ii, 389*

21 Full fathom five thy father lies;
Of his bones are coral made:
Those are pearls that were his eyes:
Nothing of him that doth fade,
But doth suffer a sea-change
Into something rich and strange.[2]
I, ii, 394

22 The fringed curtains of thine eye advance.
I, ii, 405

23 Lest too light winning
Make the prize light. *I, ii, 448*

24 There's nothing ill can dwell in such a temple:
If the ill spirit have so fair a house,
Good things will strive to dwell with 't.
I, ii, 454

25 He receives comfort like cold porridge.[3]
II, i, 10

26 I' the commonwealth I would by contraries
Execute all things; for no kind of traffic
Would I admit; no name of magistrate;
Letters should not be known; riches, poverty,
And use of service, none; contract, succession,
Bourn, bound of land, tilth, vineyard, none;
No use of metal, corn, or wine, or oil;
No occupation; all men idle, all;
And women too, but innocent and pure.[4]
II, i, 154

27 What's past is prologue. *II, i, 261*

28 Open-eyed Conspiracy
His time doth take. *II, i, 309*

29 A very ancient and fish-like smell.
II, ii, 27

30 Misery acquaints a man with strange bedfellows.
II, ii, 42

[2]The last three lines are inscribed on Shelley's gravestone.

[3]See *King John*, 202:18, and William Bradford, 265:11.

[4]It is a nation, would I answer Plato, that hath no kind of traffic, no knowledge of letters, no intelligence of numbers, no name of magistrate, nor of politic superiority; no use of service, of riches or poverty, no contracts, no successions, no partitions, no occupation but idle; no respect of kindred, but common, no apparel but natural, no manuring of lands, no use of wine, corn, or metal.—MONTAIGNE, *Essays, bk. I* [1580], *ch. 30, Of the Cannibals*

1 I shall laugh myself to death.
The Tempest, II, ii, 167

2 'Ban, 'Ban, Ca—Caliban,
Has a new master—Get a new man.
II, ii, 197

3 For several virtues
Have I liked several women. *III, i, 42*

4 *Ferdinand:* . . . Here's my hand.
Miranda: And mine, with my heart in't.
III, i, 89

5 Moon-calf. *III, ii, 25*

6 Thou deboshed fish thou. *III, ii, 30*

7 Keep a good tongue in your head.
III, ii, 41

8 Flout 'em, and scout 'em; and scout 'em, and flout 'em;
Thought is free.[1] *III, ii, 133*

9 He that dies pays all debts.
III, ii, 143

10 The isle is full of noises,
Sounds and sweet airs, that give delight, and hurt not.
Sometimes a thousand twangling instruments
Will hum about mine ears; and sometimes voices,
That, if I then had waked after long sleep,
Will make me sleep again. *III, ii, 146*

11 A kind
Of excellent dumb discourse.
III, iii, 38

12 Do not give dalliance
Too much the rein. *IV, i, 51*

13 Our revels now are ended. These our actors,
As I foretold you, were all spirits and
Are melted into air, into thin air;
And, like the baseless fabric of this vision,
The cloud-capped towers, the gorgeous palaces,
The solemn temples, the great globe itself,
Yea, all which it inherit, shall dissolve;
And, like this insubstantial pageant faded,
Leave not a rack behind. We are such stuff
As dreams are made on, and our little life
Is rounded with a sleep. *IV, i, 148*

14 With foreheads villainous low.
IV, i, 252

15 I'll break my staff,
Bury it certain fathoms in the earth,
And, deeper than did ever plummet sound,
I'll drown my book. *V, i, 54*

[1]Thought is free.—*Twelfth-Night, act I, sc. iii, l. 73*

16 Where the bee sucks, there suck I
In a cowslip's bell I lie;
There I couch when owls do cry.
On the bat's back I do fly
After summer merrily:
Merrily, merrily shall I live now
Under the blossom that hangs on the bough.
The Tempest, V, i, 88

17 O brave new world,
That has such people in't! *V, i, 183*

18 Let us not burden our remembrances
With a heaviness that's gone.
V, i, 199

19 My ending is despair. *Epilogue, l. 15*

20 No man's pie is freed
From his ambitious finger.
King Henry the Eighth [1613],[2] *act I, sc. i, l. 52*

21 The force of his own merit makes his way.
I, i, 64

22 Heat not a furnace for your foe so hot
That it do singe yourself. *I, i, 140*

23 If I chance to talk a little wild, forgive me;
I had it from my father. *I, iv, 26*

24 The mirror of all courtesy. *II, i, 53*

25 Go with me, like good angels, to my end;
And, as the long divorce of steel falls on me,
Make of your prayers one sweet sacrifice,
And lift my soul to heaven. *II, i, 75*

26 This bold bad man. *II, ii, 44*

27 'Tis better to be lowly born,
And range with humble livers in content,
Than to be perked up in a glist'ring grief
And wear a golden sorrow. *II, iii, 19*

28 I would not be a queen
For all the world. *II, iii, 45*

29 Orpheus with his lute made trees,
And the mountain-tops that freeze,
Bow themselves when he did sing.
III, i, 3

30 Heaven is above all yet; there sits a judge
That no king can corrupt. *III, i, 99*

31 'Tis well said again;
And 'tis a kind of good deed to say well:
And yet words are no deeds.
III, ii, 153

32 And then to breakfast with
What appetite you have. *III, ii, 203*

[2]Written by Shakespeare and John Fletcher; see pages 260 and 263.

1 I have touched the highest point of all my greatness;
And from that full meridian of my glory,
I haste now to my setting: I shall fall
Like a bright exhalation in the evening,
And no man see me more.
Henry VIII, III, ii, 224

2 Press not a falling man too far.[1]
III, ii, 334

3 Farewell! a long farewell, to all my[2] greatness!
This is the state of man: today he puts forth
The tender leaves of hopes; tomorrow blossoms,
And bears his blushing honors thick upon him;
The third day comes a frost, a killing frost;
And, when he thinks, good easy man, full surely
His greatness is a-ripening, nips his root,
And then he falls, as I do. I have ventured,
Like little wanton boys that swim on bladders,
This many summers in a sea of glory,
But far beyond my depth: my high-blown pride
At length broke under me, and now has left me,
Weary and old with service, to the mercy
Of a rude stream, that must forever hide me.
Vain pomp and glory of this world,[3] I hate ye:
I feel my heart new opened. O! how wretched
Is that poor man that hangs on princes' favors!
There is, betwixt that smile we would aspire to,
That sweet aspect of princes, and their ruin,
More pangs and fears than wars or women have;
And when he falls, he falls like Lucifer,
Never to hope again. *III, ii, 352*

4 A peace above all earthly dignities,
A still and quiet conscience.
III, ii, 380

5 A load would sink a navy. *III, ii, 384*

6 And sleep in dull cold marble.
III, ii, 434

7 Cromwell, I charge thee, fling away ambition:
By that sin fell the angels. *III, ii, 441*

8 Love thyself last: cherish those hearts that hate thee;
Corruption wins not more than honesty.
Still in thy right hand carry gentle peace,
To silence envious tongues: be just, and fear not.
Let all the ends thou aim'st at be thy country's,
Thy God's, and truth's; then if thou fall'st, O Cromwell!
Thou fall'st a blessed martyr!
Henry VIII, III, ii, 444

9 Had I but served my God with half the zeal[4]
I served my king, he would not in mine age
Have left me naked to mine enemies.
III, ii, 456

10 An old man, broken with the storms of state,
Is come to lay his weary bones among ye;
Give him a little earth for charity.
IV, ii, 21

11 He gave his honors to the world again,
His blessed part to heaven, and slept in peace. *IV, ii, 29*

12 So may he rest; his faults lie gently on him!
IV, ii, 31

13 He was a man
Of an unbounded stomach. *IV, ii, 33*

14 Men's evil manners live in brass; their virtues
We write in water.[5] *IV, ii, 45*

15 He was a scholar, and a ripe and good one;
Exceeding wise, fair-spoken, and persuading:
Lofty and sour to them that loved him not;
But, to those men that sought him sweet as summer. *IV, ii, 51*

16 To dance attendance on their lordships' pleasures. *V, ii, 30*

17 Nor shall this peace sleep with her; but as when
The bird of wonder dies, the maiden phoenix,
Her ashes new-create another heir
As great in admiration as herself.
V, v, 40

18 Whenever the bright sun of heaven shall shine,
His honor and the greatness of his name
Shall be, and make new nations.
V, v, 51

19 Some come to take their ease
And sleep an act or two. *Epilogue, l. 2*

[1] 'Tis a cruelty / To load a falling man.—*Henry VIII, act V, sc. iii, l. 76*

[2] Cardinal Wolsey.

[3] See *The Book of Common Prayer,* 56:4.

[4] Had I served God as well in every part / As I did serve my king and master still, / My scope had not this season been so short, / Nor would have had the power to do me ill.—THOMAS CHURCHYARD, *Death of Morton* [1593]

[5] See Sophocles, 75:22; Catullus, 102:12; Sir Thomas More, 155:8; Bacon, 181:18; and Keats, 480:7.

1 Good friend, for Jesus' sake forbear
To dig the dust enclosèd here;
Blest be the man that spares these stones,
And curst be he that moves my bones.
Shakespeare's epitaph

John Davies of Hereford
c. 1565–1618

2 Beauty's but skin deep.[1]
A Select Second Husband for Sir Thomas Overburie's Wife [1616], VI

Thomas Campion
1567–1620

3 My sweetest Lesbia, let us live and love,
And though the sager sort our deeds reprove,
Let us not weigh them. Heaven's great lamps do dive
Into their west, and straight again revive,
But soon as once set is our little light,
Then must we sleep one ever-during night.[2]
A Book of Airs [1601; with PHILIP ROSSETER*]. My Sweetest Lesbia, st. 1*

4 Never love unless you can
Bear with all the faults of man.
Third Book of Airs [1617]. Never Love, st. 1

5 There is a garden in her face
Where roses and white lilies grow;
A heavenly paradise is that place
Wherein all pleasant fruits do flow.
There cherries grow which none may buy,
Till "cherry-ripe"[3] themselves do cry.
Fourth Book of Airs [1617]. Cherry-Ripe, st. 1

6 Those cherries fairly do enclose
Of orient pearl a double row,[4]
Which when her lovely laughter shows,
They look like rosebuds filled with snow.
Ib. st. 2

7 The summer hath his joys,
And winter his delights;
Though love and all his pleasures are but toys,
They shorten tedious nights.
Ib. Winter Nights, st. 2

[1] All the beauty of the world, 'tis but skin deep.— RALPH VENNING, *Orthodox Paradoxes* [3d edition, 1650], *The Triumph of Assurance, p. 41*

Many a dangerous temptation comes to us in fine gay colors that are but skin-deep.— MATHEW HENRY [1662–1714], *Commentaries, Genesis, III*

[2] See Catullus, 101:18; Jonson, 255:16; Herrick, 266:21; and Fouché, 415:17.

[3] "Cherry-ripe" was a familiar street cry of the time. See Herrick, 266:3.

[4] See Herrick, 266:5.

Thomas Nashe
1567–1601

8 Spring, the sweet spring, is the year's pleasant king;
Then blooms each thing, then maids dance in a ring,
Cold doth not sting, the pretty birds do sing.
Cuckoo, jug-jug, pu-we, to-witta-woo!
Summer's Last Will and Testament [1600]. Spring, st. 1

9 From winter, plague and pestilence, good Lord, deliver us!
Ib. Autumn, refrain

10 Brightness falls from the air;
Queens have died young and fair;
Dust hath closed Helen's eye.
I am sick, I must die.
Lord, have mercy on us!
Ib. Adieu! Farewell Earth's Bliss!

Tommaso Campanella
1568–1639

11 Now that they are called masters, [they] are ashamed again to become disciples.
The Defense of Galileo[5]

12 The new philosophy proceeds from the world, the book of God. *Ib.*

Sir Henry Wotton
1568–1639

13 Love lodged in a woman's breast
Is but a guest.
A Woman's Heart [1651]

14 How happy is he born and taught,
That serveth not another's will;
Whose armor is his honest thought,
And simple truth his utmost skill!
The Character of a Happy Life [1614], st. 1

15 Who God doth late and early pray,
More of his grace than gifts to send,
And entertains the harmless day
With a well-chosen book or friend.
Ib. st. 5

16 Lord of himself, though not of lands;
And having nothing, yet hath all.[6]
Ib. st. 6

[5] Translated by GRANT MCCOLLEY.

[6] See *II Corinthians 6:10*, 49:17, and Terence, 96:16.

1 You meaner beauties of the night,
That poorly satisfy our eyes
More by your number than your light;
You common people of the skies,
What are you when the sun shall rise?
On His Mistress, the Queen of Bohemia,[1] *st. 1*

2 He first deceased; she for a little tried
To live without him, liked it not, and died.
Upon the Death of Sir Albert Morton's Wife [1651]

3 Hanging was the worst use a man could be put to.
The Disparity Between Buckingham and Essex [1651]

4 An ambassador is an honest man sent to lie abroad for the commonwealth.[2]
Reliquiae Wottonianae [1651]

5 The itch of disputing will prove the scab of churches.[3]
A Panegyric to King Charles [1651]

Sir John Davies
1569–1626

6 I know my soul hath power to know all things,
Yet is she blind and ignorant in all:
I know I'm one of Nature's little kings,
Yet to the least and vilest things am thrall.
Nosce Teipsum [1599], st. 44

7 I know my life's a pain, and but a span;[4]
I know my sense is mocked in ev'ry thing:
And to conclude, I know myself a man,
Which is a proud, and yet a wretched thing.
Ib. st. 45

Johannes Kepler
1571–1630

8 So long as the mother, Ignorance, lives, it is not safe for Science, the offspring, to divulge the hidden causes of things.[5]
Somnium [1634][6]

[1] This was printed with music as early as 1624, in East's *Sixth Set of Books,* and is found in many manuscripts.

[2] In a letter to Velserus [1612], Wotton says that this "merry definition of an ambassador . . . I had chanced to set down at my friend's, Mr. Christopher Fleckmore, in his Album."

[3] He directed that the stone over his grave be inscribed: Hic jacet hujus sententiae primus auctor: DISPUTANDI PRURITUS ECCLESIARUM SCABIES. Nomen alias quaere [Here lies the author of this phrase: "The itch for disputing is the sore of churches." Seek his name elsewhere]. — IZAAK WALTON, *Life of Wotton* [1651]

[4] See Bacon, 181:17, and *The New England Primer,* 320:11.

[5] A footnote of Kepler's in the text.

[6] Translated by PATRICIA KIRKWOOD.

Thomas Dekker
1572–1632

9 This age thinks better of a gilded fool
Than of a threadbare saint in wisdom's school.
Old Fortunatus [1600]

10 Honest labor bears a lovely face.
Patient Grissell [1603], act I, sc. i

11 The best of men
That e'er wore earth about him, was a sufferer,
A soft, meek, patient, humble, tranquil spirit,
The first true gentleman that ever breathed.
The Honest Whore, pt. I [1604] (in collaboration with THOMAS MIDDLETON*), act I, sc. ii*

12 We are ne'er like angels till our passion dies.
Ib. pt. II [1630], I, ii

13 Cast away care, he that loves sorrow
Lengthens not a day, nor can buy tomorrow;
Money is trash, and he that will spend it,
Let him drink merrily, fortune will send it.
The Sun's Darling [1656] (in collaboration with JOHN FORD*)*

John Donne[7]
1572–1631

14 I wonder by my troth, what thou, and I
Did, till we loved? were we not weaned till then?
But sucked on country pleasures, childishly?
Or snorted we in the seven sleepers' den?
The Good Morrow, st. 1[8]

15 And now good morrow to our waking souls,
Which watch not one another out of fear;
For love, all love of other sights controls,
And makes one little room, an everywhere.
Let sea-discoverers to new worlds have gone,
Let maps to other, worlds on worlds have shown,
Let us possess one world, each hath one, and is one.
Ib. st. 2

16 My face in thine eye, thine in mine appears,
And true plain hearts do in the faces rest,
Where can we find two better hemispheres
Without sharp North, without declining West?
Ib. st. 3

[7] See Izaak Walton, 270:28, and Carew, 271:18.
John Donne, Anne Donne, Un-done.—*Attributed; letter to his wife* [1602]

[8] The poems we quote from were published, for the first time unless otherwise noted, in Donne's posthumous *Poems* [1633; further editions 1635–1669]. The general composition dates are: Songs and Sonnets (through *Farewell to Love,* 253:15) about 1593–1601, with some considerably later; Elegies about 1593–1598; and Holy Sonnets about 1609–1611, 1615–1617.

1 Go, and catch a falling star,
Get with child a mandrake root,
Tell me, where all past years are,
Or who cleft the Devil's foot.
Teach me to hear mermaids singing.[1]
Song (Go and Catch a Falling Star), st. 1

2 And swear
No where
Lives a woman true, and fair. *Ib. st. 2*

3 Though she were true, when you met her,
And last, till you write your letter,
Yet she
Will be
False, ere I come, to two, or three.
Ib. st. 3

4 I have done one braver thing
Than all the Worthies did;
And yet a braver thence doth spring,
Which is, to keep that hid.
The Undertaking, st. 1

5 But he who loveliness within
Hath found, all outward loathes,
For he who color loves, and skin,
Loves but their oldest clothes. *Ib. st. 4*

6 And dare love that, and say so too,
And forget the He and She. *Ib. st. 5*

7 Busy old fool, unruly Sun,
Why dost thou thus,
Through windows, and through curtains call on us?
Must to thy motions lovers' seasons run?
The Sun Rising, st. 1

8 Love, all alike, no season knows, nor clime,
Nor hours, days, months, which are the rags of time. *Ib.*

9 She is all states, and all princes, I,
Nothing else is. *Ib. st. 3*

10 For God sake hold your tongue, and let me love. *The Canonization, st. 1*

11 The Phoenix riddle hath more wit
By us, we two being one, are it.
So to one neutral thing both sexes fit,
We die and rise the same, and prove
Mysterious by this love. *Ib. st. 3*

12 As well a well-wrought urn becomes
The greatest ashes, as half-acre tombs.
Ib. st. 4

13 I am two fools, I know,
For loving, and for saying so
In whining poetry.
The Triple Fool, st. 1

[1] See T. S. Eliot, 803:19.

14 Who are a little wise, the best fools be.
Ib. st. 2

15 Sweetest love, I do not go,
For weariness of thee,
Nor in hope the world can show
A fitter love for me;
But since that I
Must die at last, 'tis best,
To use my self in jest
Thus by feigned deaths to die.
Song (Sweetest Love, I Do Not Go), st. 1

16 Yesternight the sun went hence,
And yet is here today. *Ib. st. 2*

17 But think that we
Are but turned aside to sleep. *Ib. st. 5*

18 When I died last, and dear, I die
As often as from thee I go.
The Legacy, st. 1

19 Oh do not die, for I shall hate
All women so, when thou art gone.
A Fever, st. 1

20 Twice or thrice had I loved thee,
Before I knew thy face or name.
Air and Angels, st. 1

21 'Tis true, 'tis day; what though it be?
O wilt thou therefore rise from me?
Why should we rise, because 'tis light?
Did we lie down, because 'twas night?
Love which in spite of darkness brought us hither
Should in despite of light keep us together.
Break of Day, st. 1

22 All Kings, and all their favorites,
All glory of honors, beauties, wits,
The sun itself, which makes times, as they pass,
Is elder by a year, now, than it was
When thou and I first one another saw:
All other things, to their destruction draw,
Only our love hath no decay;
This, no tomorrow hath, nor yesterday,
Running, it never runs from us away,
But truly keeps his first, last, everlasting day.
The Anniversary, st. 1

23 Send home my long strayed eyes to me,
Which (Oh) too long have dwelt on thee.
The Message, st. 1

24 'Tis the year's midnight, and it is the day's.
A Nocturnal upon St. Lucy's Day, being the shortest day, st. 1

25 The world's whole sap is sunk:
The general balm th' hydroptic earth hath drunk,

Whither, as to the bed's-feet, life is shrunk,
Dead and interred; yet all these seem to laugh,
Compared with me, who am their epitaph.
Ib.

1 For I am every dead thing,
In whom love wrought new alchemy.
For his art did express
A quintessence even from nothingness,
From dull privations, and lean emptiness
He ruined me, and I am re-begot
Of absence, darkness, death; things which are not.
Ib. st. 2

2 Come live with me, and be my love,
And we will some new pleasures prove
Of golden sands, and crystal brooks,
With silken lines, and silver hooks.
The Bait,[1] *st. 1*

3 Dull sublunary lovers' love
(Whose soul is sense) cannot admit
Absence, because it doth remove
Those things which elemented it.
A Valediction Forbidding Mourning, st. 4

4 Our two souls therefore which are one,[2]
Though I must go, endure not yet
A breach, but an expansion,
Like gold to airy thinness beat.
Ib. st. 6

5 If they be two, they are two so
As stiff twin compasses are two,
Thy soul the fixt foot, makes no show
To move, but doth, if the other do.
Ib. st. 7

6 Our eye-beams twisted, and did thread
Our eyes, upon one double string;
So to entergraft our hands, as yet
Was all the means to make us one,
And pictures in our eyes to get
Was all our propagation.
The Extasy, l. 7

7 That subtle knot which makes us man:
So must pure lovers' souls descend
T' affections, and to faculties,
Which sense may reach and apprehend,
Else a great Prince in prison lies.
Ib. l. 64

8 Love's mysteries in souls do grow,
But yet the body is his book.
Ib. l. 71

[1]Included by Izaak Walton in *The Compleat Angler* [1653], *ch. 9*, as "made by Dr. Donne, and made to shew the world that he could make soft verses, when he thought them fit and worth his labor."

See Ralegh, 172:10, and Marlowe, 183:8.

[2]See Aristotle, 87:1; Zeno, 91:18; Cicero, 99:7; and Horace, 106:26.

9 I long to talk with some old lover's ghost,
Who died before the god of love was born.
Love's Deity, st. 1

10 To rage, to lust, to write to, to commend,
All is the purlieu of the god of love.
Ib. st. 3

11 Who ever comes to shroud me, do not harm
Nor question much
That subtle wreath of hair, which crowns my arm;
The mystery, the sign you must not touch,
For 'tis my outward soul,
Viceroy to that, which then to heaven being gone,
Will leave this to control,
And keep these limbs, her provinces, from dissolution.
The Funeral, st. 1

12 A bracelet of bright hair about the bone.
The Relic, st. 1

13 Take heed of loving me.
The Prohibition, st. 1

14 So, so, break off this last lamenting kiss,
Which sucks two souls, and vapors both away.
The Expiration, st. 1

15 Ah cannot we
As well as cocks and lions jocund be,
After such pleasures?
Farewell to Love, st. 3

16 Love built on beauty, soon as beauty, dies.
Elegies, no. 2, The Anagram, l. 27

17 Nature's lay idiot, I taught thee to love.
Ib. 7, Nature's Lay Idiot, l. 1

18 The Alphabet
Of flowers.
Ib. l. 9

19 She, and comparisons are odious.[3]
Ib. 8, The Comparison, l. 54

20 No spring, nor summer beauty hath such grace,
As I have seen in one autumnal face.
Ib. 9, The Autumnal, l. 1

21 The heavens rejoice in motion, why should I
Abjure my so much loved variety.
Ib. 17, Variety, l. 1

22 Who ever loves, if he do not propose
The right true end of love, he's one that goes
To sea for nothing but to make him sick.
Ib. 18, Love's Progress, l. 1

23 The Sestos and Abydos of her breasts
Not of two lovers, but two loves the nests.
Ib. l. 61

[3]See Fortescue, 149:3.

1 Those set our hairs, but these our flesh upright.

Ib. 19, To His Mistress Going to Bed, l. 24

2 O my America! my new-found land.

Ib. l. 27

3 Full nakedness! All joys are due to thee,
As souls unbodied, bodies unclothed must be,
To taste whole joys. *Ib. l. 33*

4 Sir, more than kisses, letters mingle souls;
For, thus friends absent speak.

Verse Letter to Sir Henry Wotton, written before April 1598, l. 1

5 And new philosophy calls all in doubt,
The element of fire is quite put out;
The sun is lost, and the earth, and no man's wit
Can well direct him where to look for it.
And freely men confess that this world's spent,
When in the planets, and the firmament
They seek so many new; then see that this
Is crumbled out again to his atomies.
'Tis all in pieces, all coherence gone;
All just supply, and all relation:
Prince, subject, Father, Son, are things forgot.

An Anatomy of the World. The First Anniversary [first published 1611],[1] l. 205

6 Her pure, and eloquent blood
Spoke in her cheeks, and so distinctly wrought,
That one might almost say, her body thought.

Of the Progress of the Soul. The Second Anniversary [first published 1612],[1] l. 244

7 I am a little world made cunningly
Of elements, and an angelic sprite.

Holy Sonnets, no. 5, l. 1

8 At the round earth's imagined corners, blow
Your trumpets, angels, and arise, arise
From death, you numberless infinities
Of souls. *Ib. 7, l. 1*

9 All whom war, dearth, age, agues, tyrannies,
Despair, law, chance, hath slain.

Ib. l. 6

10 If poisonous minerals, and if that tree,
Whose fruit threw death on else immortal us,
If lecherous goats, if serpents envious
Cannot be damned; alas; why should I be?

Ib. 9, l. 1

[1] "Anniversary" of the death of Elizabeth Drury [c. 1595–1610].

11 Death be not proud,[2] though some have called thee
Mighty and dreadful, for thou art not so,
For those whom thou think'st thou dost overthrow,
Die not, poor death, nor yet canst thou kill me. *Ib. 10, l. 1*

12 Thou art slave to fate, chance, kings, and desperate men. *Ib. l. 9*

13 One short sleep past, we wake eternally,
And death shall be no more;[3] death, thou shalt die. *Ib. l. 13*

14 What if this present were the world's last night? *Ib. 13, l. 1*

15 Batter my heart, three-personed God; for you
As yet but knock, breathe, shine, and seek to mend. *Ib. 14, l. 1*

16 Show me, dear Christ, Thy spouse, so bright and clear. *Ib. 18,[4] l. 1*

17 Since I am coming to that holy room,
Where, with thy choir of saints forevermore,
I shall be made thy music; as I come
I tune the instrument here at the door,
And what I must do then, think here before.

Hymn to God My God, in My Sickness [written c. 1623 or 1631], st. 1

18 Whilst my physicians by their love are grown
Cosmographers, and I their map, who lie
Flat on this bed. *Ib. st. 2*

19 I observe the physician with the same diligence as he the disease.

Devotions upon Emergent Occasions [1624], no. 6

20 I do nothing upon myself, and yet am mine own executioner.[5] *Ib. 12*

21 The flea, though he kill none, he does all the harm he can. *Ib.*

22 No man is an island, entire of itself; every man is a piece of the continent,[6] a part of the main; if a clod be washed away by the sea, Europe is the less, as well as if a promontory were, as well as if a manor of thy friends or of thine own were; any man's death diminishes me, because I am involved in mankind; and therefore never send to know for whom the bell tolls; it tolls for thee. *Ib. 17*

23 What gnashing is not a comfort, what gnawing of the worm is not a tickling, what

[2] See Shakespeare, 225:4.
[3] See *Revelation 21:4*, 53:30.
[4] First published in 1899.
[5] See Browne, 274:19.
[6] See *Romans 14:7*, 47:32; Bacon, 180:13; and Quarles, 267:9.

torment is not a marriage bed to this damnation, to be secluded eternally, eternally, eternally from the sight of God?

LXXX Sermons [1640], no. 76, preached to the Earl of Carlisle, c. autumn 1622

1 Now God comes to thee, not as in the dawning of the day, not as in the bud of the spring, but as the sun at noon to illustrate all shadows, as the sheaves in harvest, to fill all penuries, all occasions invite his mercies, and all times are his seasons.

Ib. 3, preached on Christmas Day, 1625

2 I throw myself down in my chamber, and I call in and invite God and his angels thither, and when they are there, I neglect God and his angels, for the noise of a fly, for the rattling of a coach, for the whining of a door.

Ib. 80, preached at the funeral of Sir William Cokayne, December 12, 1626

3 And what is so intricate, so entangling as death? Who ever got out of a winding sheet?

Ib. 54, preached to the King at Whitehall, April 5, 1628

4 Poor intricated soul! Riddling, perplexed, labyrinthical soul!

Ib. 48, preached upon the Day of St. Paul's Conversion, January 25, 1629

5 When my mouth shall be filled with dust, and the worm shall feed, and feed sweetly upon me,[1] when the ambitious man shall have no satisfaction if the poorest alive tread upon him, nor the poorest receive any contentment in being made equal to princes, for they shall be equal but in dust.

XXVI Sermons [1661], no. 26, Death's Duel, last sermon, February 15, 1631[2]

Ben Jonson[3]

c. 1573–1637

6 As sure as death.[4]

Every Man in His Humour [1598], act II, sc. i

[1]See *Job 24:20*, 16:10.

[2]Called by His Majesty's household the Doctor's Own Funeral Sermon.—*Preface to the first edition* [1632]

[3]O rare Ben Jonson!—Sir John Young, *Epitaph*
Which was done at the charge of Jack Young, who, walking there when the grave was covering, gave the fellow 18 pence to cut it.—John Aubrey [1626–1697], *Brief Lives*

[4]Come del morire [Sure as death].—Giovanni Boccaccio [1313–1375], *Il Filostrato, canto IV, st. 140*

7 As he brews, so shall he drink. *Ib.*

8 It must be done like lightning.

Ib. IV, 5

9 Art hath an enemy called Ignorance.

Every Man out of His Humour [1599], act I, sc. i

10 There shall be no love lost. *Ib. II, i*

11 True happiness
Consists not in the multitude of friends,
But in the worth and choice.

Cynthia's Revels [1600], act III, sc. ii

12 Queen and huntress, chaste and fair,
Now the sun is laid to sleep,
Seated in thy silver chair,
State in wonted manner keep:
Hesperus entreats thy light,
Goddess, excellently bright.

Ib. V, iii

13 That old bald cheater, Time.

The Poetaster [1601], act I, sc. i

14 Of all wild beasts preserve me from a tyrant; and of all tame, a flatterer.

Sejanus [1603], act I

15 Calumnies are answered best with silence.

Volpone [1606], act II, sc. ii

16 Come my Celia, let us prove,
While we can, the sports of love;
Time will not be ours forever,
He at length our good will sever.
Spend not then his gifts in vain;
Suns that set may rise again,
But if once we lose this light,
'Tis with us perpetual night.[5]

Song, To Celia [1607]

17 Still to be neat, still to be drest,
As you were going to a feast.

Epicene; or, The Silent Woman [1609], act I, sc. i

18 Give me a look, give me a face,
That makes simplicity a grace;
Robes loosely flowing, hair as free,
Such sweet neglect more taketh me
Than all the adulteries of art:
They strike mine eyes, but not my heart.[6]

Ib.

19 The dignity of truth is lost with much protesting.

Catiline's Conspiracy [1611], act III, sc. ii

[5]See Catullus, 101:18; Shakespeare, 187:10; Campion, 250:3; Herrick, 266:21; and Fouché, 415:17.

[6]See Herrick, 266:7.

1 Truth is the trial of itself
And needs no other touch,
And purer than the purest gold,
Refine it ne'er so much.

On Truth [1616], st. 1

2 Preserving the sweetness of proportion and expressing itself beyond expression.

The Masque of Hymen [1616]

3 Farewell, thou child of my right hand, and joy!
My sin was too much hope of thee, loved boy.

Epigrams [1616]. On My First Son [written c. 1603]

4 Rest in soft peace, and, asked, say here doth lie
Ben Jonson his best piece of poetry:
For whose sake, henceforth, all his vows be such,
As what he loves may never like too much.

Ib.

5 Underneath this stone doth lie
As much beauty as could die;
Which in life did harbor give
To more virtue than doth live.

Ib. Epitaph on Elizabeth, Lady H——

6 Follow a shadow, it still flies you;
Seem to fly it, it will pursue:
So court a mistress, she denies you;
Let her alone, she will court you.

The Forest [1616]. Follow a Shadow, st. 1

7 Whilst that for which all virtue now is sold,
And almost every vice—almighty gold.[1]

Ib. Epistle to Elizabeth, Countess of Rutland

8 Drink to me only with thine eyes,
And I will pledge with mine;
Or leave a kiss but in the cup
And I'll not look for wine.[2]
The thirst that from the soul doth rise
Doth ask a drink divine;
But might I of Jove's nectar sup,
I would not change for thine.

Ib. To Celia, st. 1

9 I sent thee late a rosy wreath,
Not so much honoring thee
As giving it a hope that there
It could not withered be.
But thou thereon didst only breathe,
And sent'st it back to me;
Since when it grows and smells, I swear,
Not of itself, but thee.

Ib. st. 2

10 Reader, look,
Not at his picture, but his book.

On the portrait of Shakespeare prefixed to the First Folio [1623]

11 Soul of the age!
The applause, delight, the wonder of our stage!
My Shakespeare, rise; I will not lodge thee by
Chaucer or Spenser, or bid Beaumont lie
A little further, to make thee a room;
Thou art a monument, without a tomb,
And art alive still, while thy book doth live,
And we have wits to read, and praise to give.[3]

To the Memory of My Beloved, the Author, Mr. William Shakespeare [1623]

12 Marlowe's mighty line. *Ib.*

13 And though thou hadst small Latin and less Greek. *Ib.*

14 Call forth thundering Aeschylus. *Ib.*

15 He was not of an age but for all time.[4] *Ib.*

16 Who casts to write a living line, must sweat. *Ib.*

17 For a good poet's made, as well as born.[5] *Ib.*

18 Sweet Swan of Avon! *Ib.*

19 Those that merely talk and never think,
That live in the wild anarchy of drink.[6]

Underwoods [1640]. An Epistle, Answering to One That Asked to Be Sealed of the Tribe of Ben

20 In small proportions we just beauties see,
And in short measures life may perfect be.

Ib. To the Immortal Memory of Sir Lucius Cary and Sir Henry Morison

21 The players have often mentioned it as an honor to Shakespeare that in his writing (whatsoever he penned) he never blotted out a line. My answer hath been, "Would he had blotted a thousand."

Timber; or, Discoveries Made upon Men and Matter [1640]

[1] The flattering, mighty, nay, almighty gold.—JOHN WOLCOT [PETER PINDAR], *To Kien Long* [1792], *ode IV*
See Irving, 453:6.

[2] Drink to me with your eyes alone. . . . And if you will, take the cup to your lips and fill it with kisses, and give it so to me.—PHILOSTRATUS [c. 181–250], *Letter 24*

[3] See William Basse, 265:14.

[4] See Robert Whittinton, 155:11.

[5] See Florus, 123:17.

[6] See Dryden, 304:9.
They never taste who always drink; / They always talk who never think.—MATTHEW PRIOR [1664–1721], *Upon a Passage in the Scaligerana*

1 I loved the man [Shakespeare] and do honor his memory, on this side idolatry, as much as any. *Ib.*

2 Greatness of name in the father oft-times overwhelms the son; they stand too near one another. The shadow kills the growth: so much, that we see the grandchild come more and oftener to be heir of the first. *Ib.*

3 Though the most be players, some must be spectators. *Ib.*

4 Talking and eloquence are not the same: to speak, and to speak well, are two things. A fool may talk, but a wise man speaks. *Ib.*

Richard Barnfield
1574–1627

5 The waters were his winding sheet, the sea
was made for his tomb;
Yet for his fame the ocean sea, was not sufficient room.
Epitaph on Hawkins[1] *[1595]*

6 As it fell upon a day
In the merry month of May,
Sitting in a pleasant shade
Which a grove of myrtles made.
Poems: In Divers Humours [1598]. Ode

7 King Pandion, he is dead,
All thy friends are lapped in lead. *Ib.*

8 Every one that flatters thee
Is no friend in misery.
Words are easy, like the wind;
Faithful friends are hard to find.
Every man will be thy friend
Whilst thou hast wherewith to spend;
But if store of crowns be scant,
No man will supply thy want. *Ib.*

9 If music and sweet poetry agree.
Ib. To His Friend, Mr. R. L.

Joseph Hall
1574–1656

10 So little in his purse, so much upon his back.
Portrait of a Poor Gallant

11 'Mongst all these stirs of discontented strife,
O, let me lead an academic life;

[1]Sir John Hawkins [1532–1595], second in command to Drake on the expedition to the West Indies, died at sea off Puerto Rico.

To know much, and to think for nothing, know
Nothing to have, yet think we have enow.
Discontent of Men with Their Condition

12 Death borders upon our birth, and our cradle stands in the grave.[2]
Epistles [1608–1611]. Decade III, epistle 2

13 There is many a rich stone laid up in the bowels of the earth, many a fair pearl laid up in the bosom of the sea, that never was seen, nor never shall be.[3]
Contemplations [c. 1630], bk. IV, The Veil of Moses

14 Moderation is the silken string running through the pearl chain of all virtues.
Christian Moderation [1640], introduction

Thomas Heywood
c. 1574 – c. 1641

15 Within the red-leaved table of my heart.
A Woman Killed with Kindness [1607], act II, sc. iii

16 I will walk on eggs. *Ib. IV, vi*

17 O God! O God! that it were possible
To undo things done; to call back yesterday![4]
That Time could turn up his swift sandy glass,
To untell the days, and to redeem these hours. *Ib.*

18 Pack clouds away, and welcome day,
With night we banish sorrow.
Pack Clouds Away [1630], st. 1

19 I hold he loves me best that calls me Tom.
Hierarchie of the Blessed Angels [1635]

20 Seven cities warred for Homer being dead,
Who living had no roof to shroud his head.[5] *Ib.*

[2]See *The Wisdom of Solomon 5:13*, 34:15; Nabokov, 846:2; and Beckett, 866:13.

[3]See Thomas Gray, 362:8.

[4]See Shakespeare, 194:27.

[5]Seven cities strive for the learnèd root of Homer: / Smyrna, Chios, Colophon, Ithaca, Pylos, Argos, Athens. — ANONYMOUS; *from The Greek Anthology* [1906], *ed.* J. W. MACKAIL, *bk. VI, epigram 298*

Seven wealthy towns contend for Homer dead, / Through which the living Homer begged his bread. — THOMAS SEWARD [1708–1790], *On Homer*

John Marston

c. 1575 – c. 1634

1 Oblivioni sacrum [Sacred to oblivion]. *Epitaph*

Henry Peacham

c. 1576 – c. 1643

2 Affect not as some do that bookish ambition to be stored with books and have well-furnished libraries, yet keep their heads empty of knowledge; to desire to have many books, and never to use them, is like a child that will have a candle burning by him all the while he is sleeping. *The Compleat Gentleman [1622]*

Robert Burton

1577–1640

3 All my joys to this are folly,
Naught so sweet as melancholy.[1]
The Anatomy of Melancholy [1621–1651].[2] *The Author's Abstract*

4 I would help others, out of a fellow-feeling.[3] *Ib. Democritus to the Reader*

5 They lard their lean books with the fat of others' works.[4] *Ib.*

6 We can say nothing but what hath been said.[5] Our poets steal from Homer. . . . Our story-dressers do as much; he that comes last is commonly best. *Ib.*

7 I say with Didacus Stella, a dwarf standing on the shoulders of a giant may see farther than a giant himself.[6] *Ib.*

8 It is most true, *stilus virum arguit*— our style betrays us.[7] *Ib.*

[1] See Fletcher, 261:4, and Milton, 277:17.
There's not a string attuned to mirth / But has its chord in melancholy.—THOMAS HOOD [1799–1845], *Ode to Melancholy*

[2] Burton's *Anatomy of Melancholy,* he said, was the only book that ever took him out of bed two hours sooner than he wished to rise.—SAMUEL JOHNSON; from BOSWELL, *Life of Johnson* [1791]
If the reader has patience to go through his volumes, he will be more improved for literary conversation than by the perusal of any twenty other works with which I am acquainted.—BYRON [1807]; from Moore's *Life*

[3] A fellow-feeling makes one wondrous kind.—GARRICK, *Prologue on Quitting the Stage* [1776]

[4] See Shakespeare, 203:21.

[5] See *Ecclesiastes 1:9,* 26:14; Terence, 96:15; and La Bruyère, 315:4.

[6] See Lucan, 118:7, and Newton, 313:10.

[7] Latin proverb.
See Buffon, 349:2.

9 Old friends become bitter enemies on a sudden for toys and small offenses.[8] *Ib.*

10 Penny wise, pound foolish. *Ib.*

11 Women wear the breeches . . . in a word, the world turned upside downward. *Ib.*

12 Like Aesop's fox, when he had lost his tail, would have all his fellow foxes cut off theirs. *Ib.*

13 All poets are mad.[9] *Ib.*

14 Every man hath a good and a bad angel attending on him in particular, all his life long. *Ib. pt. I, sec. 2, member 1, subsec. 2*

15 That which Pythagoras said to his scholars of old, may be forever applied to melancholy men, *A fabis abstinete,* eat no beans. *Ib. member 2, subsec. 1*

16 Cookery is become an art, a noble science; cooks are gentlemen. *Ib. subsec. 2*

17 No rule is so general, which admits not some exception.[10] *Ib. subsec. 3*

18 Idleness is an appendix to nobility. *Ib. subsec. 6*

19 Why doth one man's yawning make another yawn? *Ib. member 3, subsec. 2*

20 They do not live but linger. *Ib. subsec. 10*

21 [Desire] is a perpetual rack, or horsemill, according to Austin [St. Augustine], still going round as in a ring. *Ib. subsec. 11*

22 [The rich] are indeed rather possessed by their money than possessors.[11] *Ib. subsec. 12*

23 Were it not that they are loath to lay out money on a rope, they would be hanged forthwith, and sometimes die to save charges. *Ib.*

24 A mere madness, to live like a wretch and die rich.[12] *Ib.*

25 I may not here omit those two main plagues and common dotages of human kind, wine and women, which have infatuated and besotted myriads of people; they go commonly together. *Ib. subsec. 13*

26 All our geese are swans.[13] *Ib. subsec. 14*

[8] See Pope, 333:24.

[9] See Democritus, 79:*n*5; Wordsworth, 425:10; and Robert Lowell, 892:15.

[10] The exception proves the rule.—*Proverb*

[11] See Bion, 92:8, and Ingersoll, 615:9.

[12] See Samuel Johnson, 356:7.

[13] Every man thinks his own geese swans.—DICKENS, *The Cricket on the Hearth* [1845], *Chirp the Second*
See Matthew Arnold, 588:2.

1 They are proud in humility; proud in that they are not proud.[1] *Ib.*

2 We can make majors and officers every year, but not scholars. *Ib. subsec. 15*

3 *Hinc quam sic calamus saevior ense, patet.* The pen worse than the sword.[2]
Ib. member 4, subsec. 4

4 See one promontory (said Socrates of old), one mountain, one sea, one river, and see all.[3] *Ib. subsec. 7*

5 One was never married, and that's his hell; another is, and that's his plague. *Ib.*

6 Aristotle said melancholy men of all others are most witty.
Ib. sec. 3, member 1, subsec. 3

7 Seneca thinks the gods are well pleased when they see great men contending with adversity.
Ib. pt. II, sec. 2, member 1, subsec. 1

8 Machiavel says virtue and riches seldom settle on one man. *Ib. member 2*

9 As he said in Machiavel, *omnes eodem patre nati,* Adam's sons, conceived all and born in sin, etc. "We are by nature all as one, all alike, if you see us naked; let us wear theirs and they our clothes, and what is the difference?" *Ib.*

10 Who cannot give good counsel? 'Tis cheap, it costs them nothing. *Ib. member 3*

11 Many things happen between the cup and the lip.[4] *Ib.*

12 All places are distant from heaven alike.[5]
Ib. member 4

13 The commonwealth of Venice in their armory have this inscription: "Happy is that city which in time of peace thinks of war."[6]
Ib. member 6

14 Every man, as the saying is, can tame a shrew but he that hath her. *Ib.*

15 Tobacco, divine, rare, superexcellent tobacco, which goes far beyond all the panaceas, potable gold, and philosopher's stones, a sovereign remedy to all diseases . . . but as it is commonly abused by most men, which take it as tinkers do ale, 'tis a plague, a mischief, a violent purger of goods, lands, health, hellish, devilish and damned tobacco, the ruin and overthrow of body and soul.
Ib. sec. 4, member 2, subsec. 2

16 "Let me not live," said Aretine's Antonia, "if I had not rather hear thy discourse than see a play."
Ib. pt. III, sec. 1, member 1, subsec. 1

17 Birds of a feather will gather together.[7]
Ib. subsec. 2

18 No cord nor cable can so forcibly draw, or hold so fast, as love can do with a twined thread.[8] *Ib. sec. 2, member 1, subsec. 2*

19 To enlarge or illustrate this power and effect of love is to set a candle in the sun.[9]
Ib.

20 [Quoting Seneca] Cornelia kept her in talk till her children came from school, "and these," said she, "are my jewels." *Ib.*

21 Diogenes struck the father when the son swore. *Ib. subsec. 5*

22 England is a paradise for women and hell for horses; Italy a paradise for horses, hell for women, as the diverb goes.[10]
Ib. sec. 3, member 1, subsec. 2

23 For "ignorance is the mother of devotion," as all the world knows.
Ib. sec. 4, member 1, subsec. 2

24 The fear of some divine and supreme powers keeps men in obedience.[11] *Ib.*

[1] See Coleridge, 435:17, and Southey, 440:15.

[2] See *The Teaching for Merikare,* 3:12; Cervantes, 169:34; and Bulwer-Lytton, 493:6.

Pyrrhus was used to say that Cineas had taken more towns with his words than he with his arms.—PLUTARCH [A.D. 46–120], *Pyrrhus*

[3] A blade of grass is always a blade of grass, whether in one country or another.—SAMUEL JOHNSON, in Mrs. Piozzi's *Anecdotes of Johnson* [1786]

[4] A very ancient proverb, sometimes attributed to Homer.

There is many a slip 'twixt the cup and the lip.—PALLADAS [fl. 400], in *The Greek Anthology* [1906], ed. J. W. MACKAIL, *bk. X, epigram 32*

Though men determine, the gods do dispose; and ofttimes many things fall out between the cup and the lip. —ROBERT GREENE, *Perimedes the Blacksmith* [1588]

[5] See Gilbert, 166:13, and Fields, 556:15.

[6] See Aristotle, 87:24; Vegetius, 128:25; Fénelon, 316:12; Washington, 379:9; and Lowell, 568:9.

[7] See *Ecclesiasticus 13:16,* 35:26; Homer, 60:21; and Heywood, 159:10.

Birds of a feather flock together.—GEORGE WITHER, *Abuses* [1613], 72

[8] One hair of a woman can draw more than a hundred pair of oxen.—JAMES HOWELL, *Letters* [1621], *bk. II, 4*

She knows her man, and when you rant and swear, / Can draw you to her with a single hair.—DRYDEN, *Persius* [1693], *satire V, l. 246*

See Pope, 334:3.

[9] See Algernon Sidney, 298:20.

And hold their farthing candle to the sun.—EDWARD YOUNG, *Satire VII* [1725–1728], *l. 56*

And hold their glimmering tapers to the sun.—GEORGE CRABBE, *The Parish Register* [1807], *pt. I, Introduction*

[10] See Florio, 174:23.

[11] The fear o' hell's a hangman's whip / To haud the wretch in order.—ROBERT BURNS [1759–1796], *Epistle to a Young Friend*

1 One religion is as true as another.
Ib. member 2, subsec. 1

2 Melancholy and despair, though often, do not always concur; there is much difference: melancholy fears without a cause, this upon great occasion; melancholy is caused by fear and grief, but this torment procures them and all extremity of bitterness.
Ib. subsec. 3

3 A good conscience is a continual feast.
Ib.

4 Our conscience, which is a great ledger book, wherein are written all our offenses . . . grinds our souls with the remembrance of some precedent sins, makes us reflect upon, accuse and condemn ourselves.
Ib.

5 What physic, what chirurgery, what wealth, favor, authority can relieve, bear out, assuage, or expel a troubled conscience? A quiet mind cureth all. *Ib. subsec. 5*

6 Be not solitary, be not idle.[1]
Ib. subsec. 6

William Harvey
1578–1657

7 The heart of animals is the foundation of their life, the sovereign of everything within them, the sun of their microcosm.
De Motu Cordis et Sanguinis [1628],[2] dedication to King Charles

8 All we know is still infinitely less than all that still remains unknown.
Ib. dedication to Dr. Argent and Other Learned Physicians

9 I profess both to learn and to teach anatomy, not from books but from dissections; not from positions of philosophers but from the fabric of nature. *Ib.*

10 I avow myself the partisan of truth alone.
Ib.

11 As art is a habit with reference to things to be done, so is science a habit in respect to things to be known.
De Generatione Animalium (On the Generation of Animals) [1651],[3] introduction

12 I appeal to your own eyes as my witness and judge. *Ib.*

[1] See Johnson, 356:13.
[2] *An Anatomical Disquisition on the Motion of the Heart and Blood in Animals.*
Translated by Robert Willis.
[3] Translated by Robert Willis.

John Fletcher[4]
1579–1625

13 Drink today, and drown all sorrow;
You shall perhaps not do 't tomorrow.
Rollo, Duke of Normandy [1639] (in collaboration with Jonson *and others), act II, sc. ii*

14 And he that will to bed go sober
Falls with the leaf in October.[5] *Ib.*

15 Three merry boys, and three merry boys,
And three merry boys are we.[6]
As ever did sing in a hempen string
Under the gallows tree. *Ib. III, iii*

16 O woman, perfect woman! what distraction
Was meant to mankind when thou wast made a devil!
Monsieur Thomas [1639], act III, sc. i

17 Man is his own star, and the soul that can
Render an honest and a perfect man
Commands all light, all influence, all fate.
Nothing to him falls early, or too late.
Our acts our angels are, or good or ill,
Our fatal shadows that walk by us still.
The Honest Man's Fortune [1647] (in collaboration with three other authors), epilogue

18 That soul that can
Be honest is the only perfect man.[7] *Ib.*

19 Weep no more, nor sigh, nor groan,
Sorrow calls no time that's gone;
Violets plucked, the sweetest rain
Makes not fresh nor grow again.
The Queen of Corinth [1647] (in collaboration with Massinger *and a third author), act III, sc. ii*

20 Of all the paths lead to a woman's love
Pity's the straightest.[8]
The Knight of Malta [1647] (in collaboration with Massinger*), act I, sc. i*

[4] See also Shakespeare, 248:*n2*, and Beaumont and Fletcher, 263.
[5] The following well-known catch, or glee, is formed on this song:
He who goes to bed, and goes to bed sober, / Falls as the leaves do, and dies in October; / But he who goes to bed, and goes to bed mellow, / Lives as he ought to do, and dies an honest fellow.
[6] Three merry men be we. — Peele, *Old Wives' Tale* [1595]
[7] See Pope, 337:13, and Burns, 408:18.
[8] Pity's akin to love. — Thomas Southerne, *Oroonoko* [1696], *act II, sc. i*
For pity melts the mind to love. — Dryden, *Alexander's Feast* [1697], *l. 96*
Pity swells the tide of love. — Edward Young, *Night Thoughts* [1742–1745], *Night III, l. 107*

1 Go to grass.
The Little French Lawyer [1647] (in collaboration with MASSINGER*), act IV, sc. vii*

2 There is no jesting with edge tools.
Ib.

3 Let's meet, and either do or die.[1]
The Island Princess [1647], act II, sc. iv

4 Hence, all you vain delights,
As short as are the nights
Wherein you spend your folly!
There's naught in this life sweet
But only melancholy;
O sweetest melancholy!
The Nice Valor [1647]. Melancholy[2]

Thomas Middleton
1580–1627

5 Better the day, better the deed.[3]
Michaelmas Term [1607], act III, sc. i

6 Since the worst comes to the worst.[4]
Ib. III, iv

7 What is got over the Devil's back (that's by knavery), is spent under the belly (that's by lechery).[5] *Ib. IV, i*

8 As true as I live.
The Family of Love [1608], act V, sc. iii

9 Have you summoned your wits from wool-gathering?[6] *Ib. V, v*

[1] See Burns, 411:16.
This expression is a kind of common property, being the motto, we believe, of a Scottish family.—SIR WALTER SCOTT [1771–1832], review of Thomas Campbell's *Gertrude of Wyoming* [1809], where it appears (*pt. III, l. 37*): Tomorrow let us do or die!

[2] This poem is frequently and with some likelihood attributed to WILLIAM STRODE [1602–1645].
See Robert Burton, 258:3, and Milton, 277:17.

[3] The better the day, the worse deed.—MATHEW HENRY [1662–1714], *Commentaries, Genesis, III*

[4] If the worst comes to the worst.—*Discovery of the Knights of the Poste* [1597]

[5] What is got over the Devil's back is spent under the belly.—RABELAIS, *Works, bk. V* [1552], *ch. 11*
Isocrates was in the right to insinuate that what is got over the Devil's back is spent under his belly.—ALAIN RENÉ LESAGE, *Gil Blas* [1715–1735], *bk. VIII, ch. 9*

[6] My understanding has forsook me, and is gone a-woolgathering.—CERVANTES, *Don Quixote, pt. II* [1605–1615], *bk. IV, ch. 38*

10 By my faith the fool has feathered his nest well.[7]
The Roaring Girl [1611], act I, sc. i

11 That disease of which all old men sicken — avarice.[8] *Ib.*

12 Beat all your feathers as flat down as pancakes. *Ib.*

13 As the case stands.
The Old Law [1656], act II, sc. i

14 On his last legs. *Ib. V, i*

15 As old Chaucer was wont to say, that broad famous English poet.
More Dissemblers Besides Women [1657], act I, sc. iv

16 'Tis a stinger.[9] *Ib. III, ii*

17 How many honest words have suffered corruption since Chaucer's days!
No Wit, No Help, Like a Woman's [1657], act II, sc. i

18 By many a happy accident. *Ib. IV, i*

19 Anything for a Quiet Life.
Title of play [1662]

20 This was a good week's labor.
Anything for a Quiet Life, act V, sc. iii

21 There's no hate lost between us.
The Witch [written c. 1627], act IV, sc. iii

22 Black spirits and white, red spirits and gray,
Mingle, mingle, mingle, you that mingle may.[10] *Ib. V, ii*

Richard Rich
fl. 1610

23 God will not let us fall . . .
For . . . our work is good,
We hope to plant a nation,
Where none before hath stood.
Newes from Virginia: The Flock Triumphant [1610][11]

[7] We will feather our nests ere time may us espy.—*A Merry Interlude Entitled Respublica* [1553], *act III, sc. vi*

[8] So for a good old-gentlemanly vice / I think I must take up with avarice.—BYRON, *Don Juan* [1819–1824], *canto I, st. 216*

[9] He 'as had a stinger.—FLETCHER, *Wit Without Money* [1639], *act IV, sc. i*

[10] These lines are introduced into *Macbeth, act IV, sc. i.* According to George Steevens, "the song was, in all probability, a traditional one."

[11] Narrative poem about Rich's voyage to Virginia [1609] with Captain Christopher Newport. Its account of a shipwreck on the Bermudas may have been a source for scenes in Shakespeare's *The Tempest.*

John Webster
c. 1580 – c. 1625

1 Is not old wine wholesomest, old pippins toothsomest, old wood burn brightest, old linen wash whitest? Old soldiers, sweethearts, are surest, and old lovers are soundest.[1]

Westward Hoe [1607], (in collaboration with Dekker*), act II, sc. ii*

2 I saw him now going the way of all flesh.

Ib.

3 Call for the robin redbreast and the wren,
Since o'er shady groves they hover,
And with leaves and flowers do cover
The friendless bodies of unburied men.

The White Devil [1612], act V, sc. iv

4 But keep the wolf far thence, that's foe to men,
For with his nails he'll dig them up again.

Ib.

5 Prosperity doth bewitch men, seeming clear;
But seas do laugh, show white, when rocks are near. *Ib. V, vi*

6 Glories, like glowworms, afar off shine bright,
But looked to near have neither heat nor light.

Duchess of Malfi [1623], act IV, sc. ii

7 Of what is't fools make such vain keeping?
Sin their conception, their birth, weeping:
Their life, a general mist of error,
Their death, a hideous storm of terror.

Ib.

8 I know death hath ten thousand several doors
For men to take their exits.[2] *Ib.*

9 Heaven-gates are not so highly arched
As princes' palaces; they that enter there
Must go upon their knees. *Ib.*

10 *Ferdinand:* Cover her face; mine eyes dazzle;[3] she died young.
Bosola: I think not so; her infelicity
Seemed to have years too many. *Ib.*

11 Vain the ambition of kings
Who seek by trophies and dead things
To leave a living name behind,
And weave but nets to catch the wind.[4]

The Devil's Law Case [1623], song

[1] See Bacon, 179:18, and Goldsmith, 371:3.

[2] Death hath a thousand doors to let out life.—Massinger, *A Very Woman* [1665], *act V, sc. iv*

Death hath so many doors to let out life.—Fletcher and Massinger, *The Custom of the Country* [1647], *act II, sc. ii*

The thousand doors that lead to death.—Sir Thomas Browne, *Religio Medici* [1642], *pt. I, sec. 44*

See Swift, 321:10.

[3] See O. W. Holmes, 643:18.

Sir Thomas Overbury
1581–1613

12 Give me, next good, an understanding wife,
By nature wise, not learnèd much by art.

A Wife [1614]

13 He disdains all things above his reach, and preferreth all countries before his own.[5]

An Affectate Traveller [1614]

Richard Corbet
1582–1635

14 Farewell, rewards and fairies,[6]
Good housewives now may say.

Farewell to the Fairies, st. 1

15 Who of late for cleanliness,
Finds sixpence in her shoe? *Ib.*

16 Nor too much wealth nor wit come to thee,
So much of either may undo thee.

To His Son, Vincent Corbet

Jacques du Laurens
1583–1650

17 I do not attack fools, but foolishness.

Satires [1624]

Philip Massinger
1583–1640

18 Be wise;
Soar not too high to fall; but stoop to rise.[7]

Duke of Milan [1623], act I, sc. ii

19 He that would govern others, first should be
Master of himself.[8]

The Bondman [1624], act I, sc. iii

20 To be nobly born
Is now a crime.

The Roman Actor [1629], act I, sc. i

21 Whose wealth
Arithmetic cannot number. *Ib. iii*

22 Grim death.[9] *Ib. IV, ii*

[4] Since in a net I seek to hold the wind.—Wyatt, *Sonnet, Whoso List to Hunt* [c. 1557]

[5] See Shakespeare, 212:20; Canning, 422:3; and Gilbert, 629:7.

[6] See Kipling, 710:15.

[7] See Mather, 320:1.

[8] See Rabelais, 157:11.

[9] See Milton, 284:26.

1 A New Way to Pay Old Debts.
Title of play [1632]

Francis Beaumont[1]
c. 1584–1616

2 What things have we seen
Done at the Mermaid! heard words that have been
So nimble, and so full of subtle flame,
As if that everyone from whence they came,
Had meant to put his whole wit in a jest,
And resolved to live a fool, the rest
Of his dull life.
Letter to Ben Jonson [1640]

Beaumont and Fletcher[2]
[Francis Beaumont c. 1584–1616]
[John Fletcher 1579–1625][3]

3 It is always good
When a man has two irons in the fire.
The Faithful Friends [c. 1608], act I, sc. ii

4 As cold as cucumbers.
Cupid's Revenge [1615], act I, sc. i

5 Kiss till the cow comes home.[4]
Scornful Lady [1616], act III, sc. i

6 There is a method in man's wickedness—
It grows up by degrees.[5]
A King and No King [1619], act V, sc. iv

7 Upon my buried body lie lightly, gentle earth.[6]
The Maid's Tragedy [1619], act I, sc. ii

8 The devil take the hindmost!
Philaster [1620], act V

9 Whistle, and she'll come to you.[7]
Wit Without Money [1639], act IV, sc. iv

10 Calamity is man's true touchstone.[8]
Four Plays in One. The Triumph of Honour [1647], sc. i

[1] See also Beaumont and Fletcher below.

[2] Of whose partnership John Aubrey [1626–1697] said: "There was a wonderful consimility of fancy. They lived together not far from the playhouse, had one wench in the house between them, the same clothes and cloak, &c."

[3] Also on 260.

[4] Also familiar as: Till the cows come home.

[5] See Juvenal, 122:3, and Racine, 312:10.

[6] See Euripides, 76:4; Anonymous Latin, 134:28; and Twain, 625:20.

[7] See Burns, 410:10.

[8] See Seneca, 115:2.

11 Though I say it that should not say it.
Wit at Several Weapons (probably in collaboration with WILLIAM ROWLEY *[c. 1585–c. 1642]), act II, sc. ii*

John Selden
1584–1654

12 *Scrutamini scripturas* [Let us look at the scriptures]. These two words have undone the world.
Table Talk [1689]. Bible, Scripture

13 Equity is a roguish thing. For Law we have a measure, know what to trust to; Equity is according to the conscience of him that is Chancellor, and as that is larger or narrower, so is Equity. 'Tis all one as if they should make the standard for the measure we call a "foot" a Chancellor's foot; what an uncertain measure would this be! One Chancellor has a long foot, another a short foot, a third an indifferent foot. 'Tis the same thing in the Chancellor's conscience. *Ib. Equity*

14 Humility is a virtue all preach, none practice; and yet everybody is content to hear.
Ib. Humility

15 Tis not the drinking that is to be blamed, but the excess. *Ib.*

16 Commonly we say a judgment falls upon a man for something in him we cannot abide.
Ib. Judgments

17 Ignorance of the law excuses no man; not that all men know the law, but because 'tis an excuse every man will plead, and no man can tell how to refute him. *Ib. Law*

18 No man is the wiser for his learning.[9]
Ib. Learning

19 Wit and wisdom are born with a man.
Ib.

20 Few men make themselves masters of the things they write or speak. *Ib.*

21 Take a straw and throw it up into the air —you may see by that which way the wind is.
Ib. Libels

22 Philosophy is nothing but discretion.
Ib. Philosophy

23 Marriage is a desperate thing.
Ib. Marriage

24 Thou little thinkest what a little foolery governs the world.[10] *Ib. Pope*

[9] See Lao-tzu, 65:10; Confucius, 68:10; Heraclitus, 69:28; Chaucer, 147:2; Penn, 314:19; and Newman, 490:14.

[10] Behold, my son, with how little wisdom the world is governed.—AXEL OXENSTIERN [1583–1654]

1 They that govern the most make the least noise. *Ib. Power*

2 Syllables govern the world. *Ib.*

3 Never tell your resolution beforehand. *Ib. Wisdom*

4 Wise men say nothing in dangerous times. *Ib.*

5 Pleasure is nothing else but the intermission of pain. *Ib. Pleasure*

6 Preachers say, Do as I say, not as I do. *Ib. Preaching*

7 A king is a thing men have made for their own sakes, for quietness' sake. Just as in a family one man is appointed to buy the meat. *Ib. Of a King*

Tirso de Molina [Gabriel Téllez]

c. 1584–1648

8 Through his honor I conquered him. For these peasants carry their honor in their hands so that they may constantly consult it; this same honor that once felt so much at home in the city but now has taken refuge in a more rural setting.

El Burlador de Sevilla (The Rogue of Seville) [1630],[1] *act III, sc. iii*

John Ford

c. 1586–1639

9 Diamond cut diamond.

The Lover's Melancholy [1629], act I, sc. i

10 'Tis Pity She's a Whore.

Title of play [1633]

Thomas Rainsborough

d. 1648

11 The poorest he that is in England hath a life to live as the greatest he.

In the army debates at Putney [October 29, 1647]

Thomas Hobbes

1588–1679

12 The condition of man . . . is a condition of war of everyone against everyone.[2]

Leviathan [1651], pt. I, ch. 4

[1]Translated by Robert O'Brien.
This is the original Don Juan play.
[2]See Swift, 322:20.

13 Words are wise men's counters, they do but reckon with them, but they are the money of fools. *Ib.*

14 The privilege of absurdity; to which no living creature is subject but man only. *Ib. 5*

15 Sudden glory is the passion which maketh those grimaces called laughter. *Ib. 6*

16 The secret thoughts of a man run over all things, holy, profane, clean, obscene, grave, and light, without shame or blame. *Ib. 8*

17 [In a state of nature] No arts; no letters; no society; and which is worst of all, continual fear and danger of violent death; and the life of man, solitary, poor, nasty, brutish, and short. *Ib. 13*

18 The Papacy is not other than the Ghost of the deceased Roman Empire, sitting crowned upon the grave thereof.

Ib. pt. IV, ch. 47

19 The praise of ancient authors proceeds not from the reverence of the dead, but from the competition and mutual envy of the living. *Ib. Review and Conclusion*

20 Such truth as opposeth no man's profit nor pleasure is to all men welcome. *Ib.*

21 I am about to take my last voyage, a great leap in the dark. *Last words*

John Winthrop

1588–1649

22 For we must consider that we shall be a city upon a hill.[3] The eyes of all people are upon us, so that if we shall deal falsely with our God in this work we have undertaken, and so cause Him to withdraw His present help from us, we shall be made a story and a byword through the world.

A Model of Christian Charity [1630], a sermon delivered on board the Arbella

George Wither

1588–1667

23 Shall I wasting in despair
Die because a woman's fair?
Or make pale my cheeks with care
'Cause another's rosy are?
Be she fairer than the day,
Or the flow'ry meads in May,

[3]See *Matthew 5:14,* 37:6.

If she be not so to me,
What care I how fair she be?
Fair Virtue [1622]. Sonnet 4, st. 1

1 'Twas I that beat the bush,
The bird to others flew.
A Love Sonnet [1622], st. 11

2 Though I am young, I scorn to flit
On the wings of borrowed wit.
The Shepherd's Hunting [1622]

Honorat de Bueil, Marquis de Racan
1589–1670

3 Nothing in the world lasts
Save eternal change.[1]
Odes. The Coming of Spring

4 The good effect of Fortune may be short-lived. To build on it is to build on sand.[2]
Poésies Diverses

William Bradford
1590–1657

5 They knew they were pilgrims.[3]
Of Plymouth Plantation [1620–1647], ch. 7

6 So they committed themselves to the will of God and resolved to proceed. *Ib. 9*

7 Being thus arrived in a good harbor, and brought safe to land, they fell upon their knees[4] and blessed the God of Heaven who had brought them over the vast and furious ocean, and delivered them from all the perils and miseries thereof, again to set their feet on the firm and stable earth, their proper element. *Ib.*

8 Our fathers were Englishmen which came over this great ocean, and were ready to perish in this wilderness. *Ib.*

9 The loss of . . . honest and industrious men's lives cannot be valued at any price. *Ib. 12*

10 But it pleased God to visit us then with death daily, and with so general a disease that the living were scarce able to bury the dead. *Ib.*

11 Cold comfort to fill their hungry bellies.[5] *Ib. 13*

12 Behold, now, another providence of God. A ship comes into the harbor. *Ib.*

13 Thus out of small beginnings greater things have been produced by His hand that made all things of nothing,[6] and gives being to all things that are; and, as one small candle may light a thousand, so the light here kindled hath shone unto many, yea in some sort to our whole nation.[7] *Ib. 21*

William Basse
died c. 1653

14 Renownèd Spenser, lie a thought more nigh
To learnèd Chaucer; and rare Beaumont, lie
A little nearer Spenser; to make room
For Shakespeare in your threefold fourfold tomb.
To lodge all four in one bed make a shift
Until Doomsday; for hardly will a fift,
Betwixt this day and that, by fate be slain,
For whom your curtains may be drawn again.[8]
On Mr. Wm. Shakespeare [c. 1616]

William Browne
1591–1643

15 Underneath this sable hearse
Lies the subject of all verse:
Sidney's sister, Pembroke's mother.
Death, ere thou hast slain another
Fair and learned and good as she,
Time shall throw a dart at thee.
Epitaph on the Countess of Pembroke [1621]

16 There is no season such delight can bring,
As summer, autumn, winter, and the spring.
Variety

Robert Herrick
1591–1674

17 I sing of brooks, of blossoms, birds, and bowers:
Of April, May, of June, and July flowers.
I sing of Maypoles, Hock-carts, wassails, wakes,
Of bridegrooms, brides, and of their bridal cakes.
Hesperides [1648]. Argument of His Book

[1] Rien au monde ne dure / Qu'un éternel changement.
See Heraclitus, 69:25; Swift, 321:16; Shelley, 466:11; and Wilde, 676:4.

[2] Le bien de la fortune est un bien périssable; quand on bâtit sur elle, on bâtit sur le sable.
See *Matthew 7:26,* 38:21.

[3] It was owing to this passage, first printed in 1669, that the *Mayflower's* company came eventually to be called the Pilgrim Fathers.

[4] See Evarts, 562:14.

[5] See Shakespeare, 202:18 and 247:25.

[6] See Dryden, 303:4.

[7] See *Matthew 5:15,* 37:6, and Shakespeare, 201:4.

[8] See Jonson, 256:11.

1 What is a kiss? Why this, as some approve:
The sure, sweet cement, glue, and lime of love.
Ib. A Kiss

2 Bid me to live, and I will live
Thy Protestant to be,
Or bid me love, and I will give
A loving heart to thee.
Ib. To Anthea

3 Cherry ripe,[1] ripe, ripe, I cry,
Full and fair ones; come and buy!
If so be you ask me where
They do grow, I answer, there,
Where my Julia's lips do smile;
There's the land, or cherry-isle.
Ib. Cherry Ripe

4 It is the end that crowns us, not the fight.[2]
Ib. The End

5 Some asked how pearls did grow, and where?
Then spoke I to my girl
To part her lips, and showed them there
The quarelets of pearl.[3]
Ib. The Rock of Rubies, and the Quarrie of Pearls

6 A sweet disorder in the dress
Kindles in clothes a wantonness.
Ib. Delight in Disorder

7 A winning wave, deserving note,
In the tempestuous petticoat,
A careless shoestring, in whose tie
I see a wild civility,
Do more bewitch me than when art
Is too precise in every part.[4]
Ib.

8 You say to me-wards your affection's strong;
Pray love me little, so you love me long.[5]
Ib. Love Me Little, Love Me Long

9 Night makes no difference 'twixt the Priest and Clerk;
Joan as my Lady is as good i' the dark.[6]
Ib. No Difference i' th' Dark

10 Give me a kiss, and to that kiss a score;
Then to that twenty, add a hundred more:
A thousand to that hundred: so kiss on,[7]
To make that thousand up a million.
Treble that million, and when that is done,
Let's kiss afresh, as when we first begun.
Ib. To Anthea: Ah, My Anthea!

[1] See Campion, 250:5.
[2] See Anonymous Latin, 133:26; Heywood, 159:28; Shakespeare, 227:5 and 227:18; and Quarles, 267:18.
[3] See Campion, 250:6.
[4] See Jonson, 255:18.
[5] See Shakespeare, 193:1, and Anonymous, 917:12.
[6] See Plutarch, 120:17.
[7] See Catullus, 101:18.

11 Gather ye rosebuds while ye may,
Old Time is still a-flying,
And this same flower that smiles today
Tomorrow will be dying.[8]
Ib. To the Virgins to Make Much of Time

12 Fair daffodils, we weep to see
You haste away so soon.
Ib. To Daffodils

13 Her pretty feet, like snails, did creep
A little out, and then,[9]
As if they playèd at bo-peep,
Did soon draw in again.
Ib. To Mistress Susanna Southwell

14 Her eyes the glowworm lend thee,
The shooting stars attend thee;
And the elves also,
Whose little eyes glow
Like the sparks of fire, befriend thee.
Ib. The Night Piece to Julia

15 Thus times do shift, each thing his turn does hold;
New things succeed, as former things grow old.[10]
Ib. Ceremonies for Candlemas Eve

16 Made us nobly wild, not mad.
Ib. Ode for Ben Jonson

17 Outdid the meat, outdid the frolic wine.
Ib.

18 Attempt the end, and never stand to doubt;
Nothing's so hard but search will find it out.
Ib. Seek and Find

19 Get up, sweet Slug-a-bed, and see
The dew bespangling herb and tree.
Ib. Corinna's Going A-Maying

20 'Tis sin,
Nay, profanation to keep in.
Ib.

21 So when or you or I are made
A fable, song, or fleeting shade,
All love, all liking, all delight
Lies drowned with us in endless night.[11]
Ib.

22 Whenas in silks my Julia goes,
Then, then (methinks) how sweetly flows
That liquefaction of her clothes.

[8] See *Wisdom of Solomon 2:8*, 34:11; Horace, 107:8; Ronsard, 162:13; and Spenser, 173:14.
[9] See Suckling, 289:21.
[10] See Tennyson, 534:31.
[11] See Catullus, 101:18; Campion, 250:3; Jonson, 255:16; and Fouché, 415:17.

Next, when I cast mine eyes and see
That brave vibration each way free;
Oh how that glittering taketh me!
Ib. Upon Julia's Clothes

1 Here a little child I stand
Heaving up my either hand.
Cold as paddocks though they be,
Here I lift them up to Thee,
For a benison to fall
On our meat, and on us all.
Noble Numbers [1648]. A Child's Grace

Julius Wilhelm Zincgref

1591–1635

2 One who longs for death is miserable, but more miserable is he who fears it.
Apophthegmata, bk. II [1628]

3 Laws and police regulations can be compared to a spider's web that lets the big mosquitoes through and catches the small ones.[1] *Ib.*

Henry King

1592–1669

4 Thou art the book,
The library whereon I look.
The Exequy [1657]

5 Then we shall rise
And view ourselves with clearer eyes
In that calm region where no night
Can hide us from each other's sight.
Ib.

6 Sleep on, my Love, in thy cold bed,
Never to be disquieted!
My last good-night! Thou wilt not wake,
Till I thy fate shall overtake;
Till age, or grief, or sickness, must
Marry my body to that dust
It so much loves, and fill the room
My heart keeps empty in thy tomb.
Stay for me there; I will not fail
To meet thee in that hollow vale. *Ib.*

7 I am content to live
Divided, with but half a heart. *Ib.*

8 We that did nothing study but the way
To love each other, with which thoughts the day
Rose with delight to us, and with them set,
Must learn the hateful art, how to forget.
The Surrender

[1]See Anacharsis, 63:2, and Swift, 321:15.

Francis Quarles

1592–1644

9 No man is born unto himself alone;[2]
Who lives unto himself, he lives to none.
Esther [1621], Sec. 1, Meditation 1

10 The way to bliss lies not on beds of down,
And he that has no cross deserves no crown.[3] *Ib. Sec. 9, Meditation 9*

11 Death aims with fouler spite
At fairer marks.[4]
Divine Fancies [1632]

12 We spend our midday sweat, our midnight oil;
We tire the night in thought, the day in toil.
Emblems [1635], bk. II, no. 2

13 Be wisely worldly, be not worldly wise.
Ib.

14 This house is to be let for life or years;
Her rent is sorrow, and her income tears.
Cupid, 't has long stood void; her bills make known,
She must be dearly let, or let alone.
Ib. 10, Epigram

15 The slender debt to Nature's quickly paid,[5]
Discharged, perchance, with greater ease than made. *Ib. 13*

16 The road to resolution lies by doubt:
The next way home's the farthest way about.[6] *Ib. IV, 2, Epigram*

17 It is the lot of man but once to die.
Ib. V, 7

18 My soul, sit thou a patient looker-on;
Judge not the play before the play is done:
Her plot hath many changes; every day
Speaks a new scene; the last act crowns the play.[7] *Epigram. Respice Finem*

19 And what's a life?—a weary pilgrimage,
Whose glory in one day doth fill the stage
With childhood, manhood, and decrepit age.
What Is Life?

20 Let all thy joys be as the month of May,
And all thy days be as a marriage day:
Let sorrow, sickness, and a troubled mind
Be stranger to thee. *To a Bride*

[2]See *Romans 14:7,* 47:32; Bacon, 180:13; and Donne, 254:22.
[3]See *Matthew 10:38,* 39:5; Penn, 314:9; and Bennard, 738:11.
[4]See Edward Young, 330:16.
[5]To die is a debt we must all of us discharge.—EURIPIDES, *Alcestis, l. 418*
[6]The longest way round is the shortest way home. —*Proverb*
[7]See Anonymous Latin, 133:26; Heywood, 159:28; Shakespeare, 227:5 and 227:18; and Herrick, 266:4.

Thomas Ravenscroft

c. 1592 – c. 1635

1 Nose, nose, nose, nose!
And who gave thee this jolly red nose?
Nutmegs and ginger, cinnamon and cloves,
And they gave me this jolly red nose.
Deuteromelia [1609]. Song no. 7 [1]

George Herbert

1593–1633

2 A verse may find him who a sermon flies.[2]
The Temple [1633]. The Church Porch, st. 1

3 Drink not the third glass,[3] which thou canst not tame
When once it is within thee. *Ib. st. 5*

4 Dare to be true: nothing can need a lie:
A fault, which needs it most, grows two thereby.[4] *Ib. st. 13*

5 By all means use sometimes to be alone.
Ib. st. 25

6 By no means run in debt: take thine own measure.
Who cannot live on twenty pound a year,
Cannot on forty. *Ib. st. 30*

7 Wit's an unruly engine, wildly striking
Sometimes a friend, sometimes the engineer.
Ib. st. 41

8 Be useful where thou livest. *Ib. st. 55*

9 Man is God's image; but a poor man is
Christ's stamp to boot: both images regard.
Ib. st. 64

10 Was ever grief like mine?
Ib. The Church. The Sacrifice, refrain

11 For thirty pence he did my death devise,[5]
Who at three hundred did the ointment prize.[6] *Ib. st. 5*

12 Man stole the fruit, but I must climb the tree.
Ib. st. 51

13 I got me flowers to strew Thy way,
I got me boughs off many a tree:
But Thou wast up by break of day,
And brought'st Thy sweets along with Thee.
Ib. Easter, st. 4

14 Who says that fictions only and false hair
Become a verse? Is there in truth no beauty?[7] *Ib. Jordan, st. 1*

15 Sweet day, so cool, so calm, so bright,
The bridal of the earth and sky.
Ib. Virtue, st. 1

16 Sweet spring, full of sweet days and roses,
A box where sweets compacted lie.
Ib. st. 3

17 Only a sweet and virtuous soul,
Like seasoned timber, never gives.
Ib. st. 4

18 Who goes to bed and does not pray,
Maketh two nights to every day.
Ib. Charms and Knots, st. 4

19 Nothing wears clothes, but Man; nothing doth need
But he to wear them.
Ib. Providence, st. 28

20 Most things move th' under-jaw, the crocodile not.[8]
Most things sleep lying, th' elephant leans or stands.[9] *Ib. st. 35*

21 I struck the board, and cried, No more:
I will abroad.
What? shall I ever sigh and pine?
My lines and life are free; free as the road,
Loose as the wind, as large as store.
Shall I be still in suit?
Have I no harvest but a thorn
To let me blood, and not restore
What I have lost with cordial fruit?
Sure there was wine
Before my sighs did dry it; there was corn
Before my tears did drown it;
Is the year only lost to me?
Have I no bays to crown it?
Ib. The Collar

22 Call in thy death's head there: tie up thy fears. *Ib.*

23 But as I raved and grew more fierce and wild
At every word,
Methought I heard one calling, *Child!*
And I replied, *My Lord.* *Ib.*

[1] Quoted by Beaumont and Fletcher, *The Knight of the Burning Pestle* [1613], *act I, sc. iii.* Ravenscroft's *Deuteromelia* was a supplement to his *Pammelia,* which was the earliest collection of rounds, catches, and canons printed in England.

[2] That many people read a song / Who will not read a sermon. — Winthrop Mackworth Praed [1802–1839], *The Chant of the Brazenhead, st. 1*

[3] See Addison, 326:18; Hugo, 491:22; and Sill, 646:12.

[4] And he that does one fault at first, / And lies to hide it, makes it two. — Isaac Watts [1674–1748], *Song 15*

[5] See *Zechariah 11:12,* 33:34, and *Matthew 26:15,* 41:5.

[6] See *John 12:4–5,* 45:16.

[7] See Keats, 477:11.

[8] The crocodile does not move the lower jaw, but is the only animal that brings down its upper jaw to the under one. — Herodotus [c. 485–c. 425 B.C.], *Customs of the Egyptians*

[9] Leans the huge elephant. — James Thomson, *The Seasons, Summer* [1727], *l.* 725

1 He would adore my gifts instead of me,
And rest in Nature, not the God of Nature:
So both should losers be.
Ib. The Pulley, st. 3

2 Let him be rich and weary, that at least,
If goodness lead him not, yet weariness
May toss him to my breast. *Ib. st. 4*

3 Grief melts away
Like snow in May,
As if there were no such cold thing.
Ib. The Flower, st. 1

4 Who would have thought my shriveled heart
Could have recovered greenness?
Ib. st. 2

5 And now in age I bud again,
After so many deaths I live and write;
I once more smell the dew and rain,
And relish versing: O my only light,
It cannot be
That I am he
On whom thy tempests fell all night.
Ib. st. 6

6 The harbingers are come. See, see their mark;
White is their color, and behold my head.
Ib. The Forerunners, st. 1

7 Teach me, my God and King,
In all things thee to see
And what I do in any thing,
To do it as for thee.
Ib. The Elixir, st. 1

8 A servant with this clause
Makes drudgery divine:
Who sweeps a room, as for thy laws,
Makes that and th' action fine.
Ib. st. 5

9 Love bade me welcome: yet my soul drew back,
Guilty of dust and sin.
But quick-eyed Love, observing me grow slack
From my first entrance in,
Drew nearer to me, sweetly questioning,
If I lacked anything. *Ib. Love, st. 1*

10 You must sit down, says Love, and taste my meat:
So I did sit and eat. *Ib. st. 3*

11 Religion stands on tiptoe in our land,
Ready to pass to the American strand.
The Church Militant [1633], l. 235

12 Love, and a cough, cannot be hid.[1]
Jacula Prudentum [1651], no. 49

13 Ill ware is never cheap. Pleasing ware is half sold. *Ib. 61*

[1] See Anonymous: Spanish, 935:17.

14 When a dog is drowning, everyone offers him drink. *Ib. 77*

15 Deceive not thy physician, confessor, nor lawyer. *Ib. 105*

16 Who would do ill ne'er wants occasion.
Ib. 116

17 A snow year, a rich year. *Ib. 125*

18 Well may he smell fire, whose gown burns.
Ib. 138

19 Love your neighbor, yet pull not down your hedge.[2] *Ib. 141*

20 Marry your son when you will; your daughter when you can. *Ib. 149*

21 The mill cannot grind with the water that's past. *Ib. 153*

22 Good words are worth much, and cost little.
Ib. 155

23 Hell is full of good meanings and wishings.[3]
Ib. 170

24 Where the drink goes in, there the wit goes out. *Ib. 187*

25 Whose house is of glass, must not throw stones at another.[4] *Ib. 196*

26 By suppers more have been killed than Galen ever cured. *Ib. 272*

27 The lion is not so fierce as they paint him.[5]
Ib. 289

28 Go not for every grief to the physician, nor for every quarrel to the lawyer, nor for every thirst to the pot. *Ib. 290*

29 The best mirror is an old friend.
Ib. 296

30 When you are an anvil, hold you still; when you are a hammer, strike your fill.[6]
Ib. 338

31 He that lies with the dogs, riseth with fleas.
Ib. 343

32 He that is not handsome at twenty, nor strong at thirty, nor rich at forty, nor wise at fifty, will never be handsome, strong, rich, or wise. *Ib. 349*

[2] See Robert Frost, 747:5.

[3] Sir, Hell is paved with good intentions.—SAMUEL JOHNSON [1775]; from BOSWELL, *Life of Johnson* [1791], *vol. I, p. 555* (Everyman edition)

[4] People in glass houses shouldn't throw stones.—*Proverb*

See Franklin, 347:16.

[5] The lion is not so fierce as painted.—THOMAS FULLER [1608–1661], *Expecting Preferment*

[6] Stand like an anvil when it is beaten upon.—ST. IGNATIUS THEOPHORUS, bishop of Antioch [fl. c. 100]

When you are the anvil, bear— / When you are the hammer, strike.—EDWIN MARKHAM [1852–1940], *Preparedness*

1 The buyer needs a hundred eyes, the seller not one.[1] *Ib. 390*

2 My house, my house, though thou art small, thou art to me the Escurial. *Ib. 413*

3 Trust not one night's ice. *Ib. 453*

4 For want of a nail the shoe is lost, for want of a shoe the horse is lost, for want of a horse the rider is lost.[2] *Ib. 499*

5 Pension never enriched young man. *Ib. 515*

6 Living well is the best revenge. *Ib. 520*

7 One enemy is too much.[3] *Ib. 523*

8 Thursday come, and the week is gone. *Ib. 587*

9 Time is the rider that breaks youth. *Ib. 615*

10 Show me a liar, and I'll show thee a thief. *Ib. 652*

11 One father is more than a hundred schoolmasters. *Ib. 686*

12 Reason lies between the spur and the bridle. *Ib. 711*

13 One sword keeps another in the sheath. *Ib. 725*

14 God's mill grinds slow, but sure.[4] *Ib. 747*

15 He that lends, gives. *Ib. 787*

16 Words are women, deeds are men.[5] *Ib. 842*

17 Poverty is no sin. *Ib. 844*

18 None knows the weight of another's burthen. *Ib. 880*

19 One hour's sleep before midnight is worth three after. *Ib. 882*

20 He hath no leisure who useth it not. *Ib. 897*

21 Half the world knows not how the other half lives. *Ib. 907*

22 Life is half spent before we know what it is. *Ib. 917*

23 Every mile is two in winter. *Ib. 949*

24 The eye is bigger than the belly. *Ib. 1018*

[1] Caveat emptor [Buyer, beware]. —*Proverb*
[2] See Benjamin Franklin, 347:35.
[3] See Ali ibn-Abi-Talib, 130:8.
[4] See Euripides, 77:8, and von Logau, 273:14.
[5] See Johnson, 352:6.
Fatti maschii parole femine [Manly deeds, womanly words]. —*State motto of Maryland*

25 His bark is worse than his bite. *Ib. 1090*

26 There is an hour wherein a man might be happy all his life, could he find it. *Ib. 1143*

27 Woe be to him that reads but one book. *Ib. 1146*

Izaak Walton

1593–1683

28 But God, who is able to prevail, wrestled with him, as the Angel did with Jacob, and marked him; marked him for his own.[6] *Life of Donne [1640]*

29 I have laid aside business, and gone a-fishing. *The Compleat Angler [1653–1655]. Epistle to the Reader*

30 Angling may be said to be so like the mathematics that it can never be fully learnt. *Ib.*

31 As no man is born an artist, so no man is born an angler. *Ib.*

32 I shall stay him no longer than to wish him a rainy evening to read this following discourse; and that if he be an honest angler, the east wind may never blow when he goes a-fishing. *Ib.*

33 I am, Sir, a brother of the Angle. *Ib. pt. I, ch. 1*

34 Doubt not but angling will prove to be so pleasant that it will prove to be, like virtue, a reward to itself.[7]

Sir Henry Wotton . . . was a most dear lover, and a frequent practicer of the art of angling; of which he would say, "it was an employment for his idle time, which was then not idly spent . . . a rest to his mind, a cheerer of his spirits, a diverter of sadness, a calmer of unquiet thoughts, a moderator of passions, a procurer of contentedness; and

[6] See *Genesis 32:24*, 8:24, and Gray, 362:17.
[7] Ipsa quidem virtus sibimet pulcherrima merces [Virtue herself is her own fairest reward]. —SILIUS ITALICUS [A.D. c. 25–99], *Punica, bk. XIII, l. 663*
Virtue was sufficient of herself for happiness. —DIOGENES LAERTIUS [c. 200], *Lives of Eminent Philosophers, XLII, Plato*
That virtue is her own reward, is but a cold principle. —SIR THOMAS BROWNE, *Religio Medici* [1642], *pt. I, sec. 47*
Virtue is its own reward. —PRIOR [1664–1721], *Imitations of Horace, bk. III, ode 2*
I think mankind by thee would be less bored / If only thou wert not thine own reward. —JOHN KENDRICK BANGS [1862–1922], *A Hint to Virtue*

that it begat habits of peace and patience in those that professed and practiced it." *Ib.*

1 You will find angling to be like the virtue of humility, which has a calmness of spirit and a world of other blessings attending upon it.[1] *Ib.*

2 I remember that a wise friend of mine did usually say, "That which is everybody's business is nobody's business." *Ib. 2*

3 An honest ale-house where we shall find a cleanly room, lavender in the windows, and twenty ballads stuck about the wall. *Ib.*

4 Good company and good discourse are the very sinews of virtue. *Ib.*

5 The Chavender or Chub. *Ib. 3*

6 An excellent angler, and now with God. *Ib. 4*

7 Old-fashioned poetry, but choicely good. *Ib.*

8 I love such mirth as does not make friends ashamed to look upon one another next morning. *Ib. 5*

9 No man can lose what he never had. *Ib.*

10 We may say of angling as Dr. Boteler[2] said of strawberries: "Doubtless God could have made a better berry, but doubtless God never did"; and so, if I might be judge, God never did make a more calm, quiet, innocent recreation than angling. *Ib.*

11 Thus use your frog. . . . Put your hook through his mouth, and out at his gills; . . . and then with a fine needle and silk sew the upper part of his leg, with only one stitch, to the arming-wire of your hook; or tie the frog's leg, above the upper joint, to the armed-wire; and in so doing use him as though you loved him. *Ib. 8*

12 This dish of meat is too good for any but anglers, or very honest men. *Ib.*

13 Look to your health; and if you have it, praise God, and value it next to a good conscience; for health is the second blessing that we mortals are capable of; a blessing that money cannot buy. *Ib. 21*

[1]There is certainly something in angling . . . that tends to produce a gentleness of spirit, and a pure serenity of mind.—WASHINGTON IRVING, *The Sketch-Book* [1819–1820], *The Angler*

[2]See William Butler, 166.

This praise of the strawberry first appeared in the second edition of *The Angler* [1655].

14 Let the blessing of St. Peter's Master be . . . upon all that are lovers of virtue, and dare trust in his Providence, and be quiet and go a-angling. *Ib.*

15 The great secretary of Nature and all learning, Sir Francis Bacon.[3]
Life of Herbert [1670]

James Howell
c. 1594–1666

16 Plato, Aristotle, and Socrates are secretaries of Nature.[4] *Letters, bk. II, letter 2*

17 All work and no play makes Jack a dull boy.[5] *Proverbs [1659]*

Thomas Carew
c. 1595 – c. 1639

18 Here lies a King that ruled, as he thought fit
The universal monarchy of wit;
Here lies two flamens, and both those the best:
Apollo's first, at last the true God's priest.
Elegy on the Death of Donne [1633]

19 Ask me no more where Jove bestows,
When June is past, the fading rose;
For in your beauty's orient deep
These flowers, as in their causes, sleep.
Poems [1640]. To Celia, st. 1

20 Ask me no more whither doth haste
The nightingale when May is past;
For in your sweet dividing throat
She winters and keeps warm her note.
Ib. st. 3

21 Ask me no more if east or west
The Phoenix builds her spicy nest;
For unto you at last she flies,
And in your fragrant bosom dies.
Ib. st. 5

22 Give me more love or more disdain;
The torrid or the frozen zone:
Bring equal ease unto my pain;
The temperate affords me none.
Ib. Mediocrity in Love Rejected, st. 1

23 Thou shalt confess the vain pursuit
Of human glory yields no fruit
But an untimely grave.[6]
Ib. On the Duke of Buckingham

[3]See Howell, 271:16.

[4]See Walton, 271:15.

[5]See Ptahhotpe, 3:10; Herodotus, 78:9; and Cervantes, 169:36.

[6]See Gray, 362:3.

1 He that loves a rosy cheek,
Or a coral lip admires,
Or, from starlike eyes, doth seek
Fuel to maintain his fires;
As old Time makes these decay,
So his flames must waste away.

Ib. Disdain Returned, st. 1

2 The firstling of the infant year.

Ib. The Primrose

3 Then fly betimes, for only they
Conquer Love that run away.

Ib. Conquest by Flight

4 The magic of a face.

Ib. Epitaph on the Lady S——

René Descartes

1596–1650

5 Good sense is of all things in the world the most equally distributed, for everybody thinks he is so well supplied with it, that even those most difficult to please in all other matters never desire more of it than they already possess.

Le Discours de la Méthode [1637], I

6 It is not enough to have a good mind. The main thing is to use it well. *Ib.*

7 The greatest minds are capable of the greatest vices as well as of the greatest virtues. *Ib.*

8 The first precept was never to accept a thing as true until I knew it as such without a single doubt. *Ib.*

9 One cannot conceive anything so strange and so implausible that it has not already been said by one philosopher or another.[1]

Ib. II

10 I think, therefore I am [Cogito, ergo sum; Je pense, donc je suis].[2] *Ib. IV*

James Shirley

1596–1666

11 How little room
Do we take up in death that, living, know
No bounds! *The Wedding [1626]*

12 I presume you're mortal, and may err.[3]

The Lady of Pleasure [1635]

13 Only the actions of the just
Smell sweet and blossom in their dust.

Ib.

14 Death calls ye to the crowd of common men.

Cupid and Death [1653]

15 The glories of our blood and state
Are shadows, not substantial things;
There is no armor against fate;
Death lays his icy hand on kings.[4]

Contention of Ajax and Ulysses [1659], sc. iii

Oliver Cromwell

1599–1658

16 A few honest men are better than numbers.

Letter to Sir W. Spring [September 1643]

17 The State, in choosing men to serve it, takes no notice of their opinions. If they be willing faithfully to serve it, that satisfies.

Before the battle of Marston Moor [July 2, 1644]

18 I beseech you, in the bowels of Christ, think it possible you may be mistaken.[5]

Letter to the General Assembly of the Church of Scotland [August 3, 1650]

19 It is not fit that you sit here any longer! . . . you shall now give place to better men.

To the Rump Parliament [January 22, 1654]

20 Necessity hath no law.[6] Feigned necessities, imaginary necessities . . . are the greatest cozenage that men can put upon the Providence of God, and make pretenses to break known rules by.

To Parliament [September 12, 1654]

21 I would have been glad to have lived under my woodside, and to have kept a flock of sheep, rather than to have undertaken this government. *To Parliament [1658]*

22 Mr. Lely, I desire you would use all your skill to paint my picture truly like me, and not flatter me at all; but remark all these roughnesses, pimples, warts, and everything as you see me, otherwise I will never pay a farthing for it.[7]

From HORACE WALPOLE, *Anecdotes of Painting in England [1762–1771]*

[1] See Cicero, 98:22, and Goethe, 396:22.
[2] See Aristotle, 87:21.
[3] See Plutarch, 120:21; Anonymous Latin, 133:22; and Pope, 333:15.

[4] See Horace, 107:1, and Publilius Syrus, 110:14.
[5] Said before his defeat of the Royalist Scots at the battle of Dunbar [September 3, 1650].
See Hand, 737:5.
[6] See Publilius Syrus, 111:20, and St. Augustine, 129:9.
[7] Warts and all. — *Saying*

1 It is not my design to drink or to sleep, but my design is to make what haste I can to be gone. *Dying words*

Pedro Calderón de la Barca
1600–1681

2 What is life? A madness. What is life? An illusion, a shadow, a story. And the greatest good is little enough: for all life is a dream, and dreams themselves are only dreams.[1]
Life Is a Dream, act II, l. 1195

3 But whether it be dream or truth, to do well is what matters. If it be truth, for truth's sake. If not, then to gain friends for the time when we awaken. *Ib. III, 236*

4 The treason past, the traitor is no longer needed. *Ib. III, 1109*

5 What surprises you, if a dream taught me this wisdom, and if I still fear I may wake up and find myself once more confined in prison? And even if this should not happen, merely to dream it is enough. For this I have come to know, that all human happiness finally ceases, like a dream. *Ib. III, 1114*

Martin Parker
c. 1600 – c. 1656

6 Ye gentlemen of England
That live at home at ease,
Ah! little do you think upon
The dangers of the seas. *Song*

7 When the stormy winds do blow.[2] *Ib.*

Jules Cardinal Mazarin
1602–1661

8 I must leave all that! Farewell, dear paintings that I have loved so much and which have cost me so much.[3]
Remark shortly before his death

Sir Kenelm Digby
1603–1665

9 The hot water is to remain upon it [the tea] no longer than whiles you can say the Miserere Psalm[4] very leisurely.
The Closet Opened. Tea with Eggs

[1] Que es la pequeño: / Que toda la vida es sueño, / y los sueños sueños son.
Translated by Edward and Elizabeth Huberman.
See Heraclitus, 70:8, and Montaigne, 165:9.
[2] See Campbell, 443:11.
[3] Il faut quitter tout cela! Adieu, chers tableaux que j'ai tant aimés et qui m'ont tant coûté.
[4] Psalm 51.

10 All matter is indifferent to form.
Of the Vegetation of Plants [1660]

Roger Williams
c. 1603–1683

11 There goes many a ship to sea, with many hundred souls in one ship, whose weal and woe is common, and is a true picture of a commonwealth or a human combination or society. It hath fallen out sometimes that both Papists and Protestants, Jews and Turks may be embarked in one ship; upon which supposal I affirm that all the liberty of conscience that ever I pleaded for turns upon these two hinges—that none of the papists, Protestants, Jews or Turks be forced to come to the ship's prayers or worship, nor compelled from their own particular prayers or worship, if they practice any. I further add that I never denied that, notwithstanding this liberty, the commander of this ship ought to command the ship's course, yea, and also command that justice, peace, and sobriety be kept and practiced, both among the seamen and all the passengers.
Letter to the Town of Providence [January 1655]

Friedrich von Logau
1604–1655

12 Armed peace.
Poetic Aphorisms[5] *[1654]*

13 This month is a kiss
Which heaven gives the earth
That she now become a bride
And then a future mother.
Ib. Characteristics of May

14 Though the mills of God grind slowly, yet
they grind exceeding small.[6]
Ib. Retribution

Sir Thomas Browne
1605–1682

15 I dare, without usurpation, assume the honorable style of a Christian.
Religio Medici [1642], pt. I, sec. 1

16 I could never divide myself from any man upon the difference of an opinion, or be angry with his judgment for not agreeing with me in that from which perhaps within a few days I should dissent myself. *Ib. 6*

[5] Sinngedichten.
[6] Translated by Longfellow.
See Euripides, 77:8, and Herbert, 270:14.

1 Many . . . have too rashly charged the troops of error, and remain as trophies unto the enemies of truth. *Ib.*

2 A man may be in as just possession of truth as of a city, and yet be forced to surrender. *Ib.*

3 As for those wingy mysteries in divinity, and airy subtleties in religion, which have unhinged the brains of better heads, they never stretched the pia mater of mine. *Ib. 9*

4 I love to lose myself in a mystery, to pursue my Reason to an *O altitudo!*[1] *Ib.*

5 Rich with the spoils of Nature.[2] *Ib. 13*

6 We carry with us the wonders we seek without us: There is all Africa and her prodigies in us. *Ib. 15*

7 All things are artificial, for nature is the art of God.[3] *Ib. 16*

8 Obstinacy in a bad cause is but constancy in a good.[4] *Ib. 25*

9 Persecution is a bad and indirect way to plant religion. *Ib.*

10 Not picked from the leaves of any author, but bred amongst the weeds and tares of mine own brain. *Ib. 35*

11 This reasonable moderator, and equal piece of justice, Death. *Ib. 38*

12 I am not so much afraid of death, as ashamed thereof. 'Tis the very disgrace and ignominy of our natures, that in a moment can so disfigure us, that our nearest friends, wife, and children, stand afraid and start at us. *Ib. 40*

13 Whosoever enjoys not this life, I count him but an apparition, though he wear about him the sensible affections of flesh. In these moral acceptions, the way to be immortal is to die daily. *Ib. 45*

14 How shall the dead arise, is no question of my faith; to believe only possibilities, is not faith, but mere philosophy. *Ib. 48*

15 The heart of man is the place the devils dwell in: I feel sometimes a hell within myself.[5] *Ib. 51*

[1] See Aiken, 812:1.
[2] See Thomas Gray, 362:7.
[3] The course of Nature is the art of God.—EDWARD YOUNG, *Night Thoughts* [1742–1745], *Night IX, l. 1267*
[4] See Sterne, 359:24.
[5] See Virgil, 105:23; Marlowe, 183:21 and 184:1; Milton, 283:13 and 285:12; Eliot, 809:1; Sartre, 865:12; and Lowell, 893:7.

16 There is no road or ready way to virtue. *Ib. 54*

17 All places, all airs make unto me one country; I am in England, everywhere, and under any meridian. *Ib. II, 1*

18 They that endeavor to abolish vice, destroy also virtue; for contraries, though they destroy one another, are yet the life of one another. *Ib. 4*

19 But how shall we expect charity towards others, when we are uncharitable to ourselves? *Charity begins at home,*[6] is the voice of the world; yet is every man his greatest enemy, and, as it were, his own executioner.[7] *Ib.*

20 Sure there is music even in the beauty, and the silent note which Cupid strikes, far sweeter than the sound of an instrument. For there is a music wherever there is a harmony, order, or proportion; and thus far we may maintain the music of the spheres.[8] *Ib. 9*

21 For the world, I count it not an inn, but a hospital; and a place not to live, but to die in. *Ib. 11*

22 There is surely a piece of divinity in us, something that was before the elements, and owes no homage unto the sun.[9] *Ib.*

23 Sleep is a death; O, make me try,
By sleeping what it is to die,
And as gently lay my head
On my grave, as now my bed. *Ib. 12*

24 When we desire to confine our words, we commonly say they are spoken under the rose.[10] *Vulgar Errors [1645]*

25 An old and gray-headed error. *Ib.*

26 Times before you, when even living men were antiquities; when the living might exceed the dead, and to depart this world could not be properly said to go unto the greater number.[11]

Urn-Burial; or, Hydriotaphia [1658]. Dedication

[6] See *I Timothy 5:4*, 50:30, and Terence, 96:6.
[7] See Donne, 254:20.
[8] See Shakespeare, 214:13.
[9] See Addison, 326:3, and Emerson, 496:20.
[10] Sub rosa.
This phrase, meaning secretly, is of unknown origin. With the ancients the rose was emblematic of secrecy, and when a host hung a rose above his tables, his guests understood that all words spoken under it were to remain secret. Later, roses were carved as decorations on the ceilings of council chambers and confessionals, with the same significance.
[11] 'Tis long since Death had the majority.—ROBERT BLAIR, *The Grave* [1743], *pt. II, l. 449*

1 With rich flames, and hired tears, they solemnized their obsequies. *Ib. ch. 3*

2 Were the happiness of the next world as closely apprehended as the felicities of this, it were a martyrdom to live. *Ib. 4*

3 These dead bones have . . . quietly rested under the drums and tramplings of three conquests. *Ib. 5*

4 Time which antiquates antiquities, and hath an art to make dust of all things. *Ib.*

5 What song the Sirens sang, or what name Achilles assumed when he hid himself among women, though puzzling questions, are not beyond all conjecture. *Ib.*

6 The long habit of living indisposeth us for dying. *Ib.*

7 The iniquity of oblivion blindly scattereth her poppy, and deals with the memory of men without distinction to merit of perpetuity. *Ib.*

8 Herostratus lives that burnt the Temple of Diana—he is almost lost that built it.[1] *Ib.*

9 Oblivion is not to be hired: the greater part must be content to be as though they had not been, to be found in the register of God, not in the record of man. *Ib.*

10 The night of time far surpasseth the day, and who knows when was the equinox? *Ib.*

11 Man is a noble animal, splendid in ashes, and pompous in the grave. *Ib.*

12 That unextinguishable laugh in heaven. *The Garden of Cyrus [1658], ch. 2*

13 Life itself is but the shadow of death, and souls departed but the shadows of the living. All things fall under this name. The sun itself is but the dark simulacrum, and light but the shadow of God. *Ib. 4*

14 To keep our eyes open longer were but to act our Antipodes. The huntsmen are up in America, and they are already past their first sleep in Persia. But who can be drowsy at that hour which freed us from everlasting sleep? or have slumbering thoughts at that time, when sleep itself must end, and, as some conjecture, all shall awake again? *Ib. 5*

[1]The aspiring youth that fired the Ephesian dome / Outlives in fame the pious fool that raised it.—COLLEY CIBBER [1671–1757], *Richard III, act III, sc. i*

15 The created world is but a small parenthesis in eternity. *Christian Morals [1716], III, 29*

Pierre Corneille
1606–1684

16 To conquer without risk is to triumph without glory. *Le Cid [1636], act II, sc. ii*

17 Brave men are brave from the very first. *Ib. II, iii*

18 And the combat ceased for want of combatants. *Ib. IV, iii*

19 Do your duty, and leave the rest to heaven. *Horace [1639], act II, sc. viii*

20 All evils are equal when they are extreme. *Ib. III, iv*

21 The worst of all states is the people's state. *Cinna [1640], act II, sc. i*

22 Who is all-powerful should fear everything. *Ib. IV, ii*

23 By speaking of our misfortunes we often relieve them. *Polyeucte [1640], act I, sc. iii*

24 The manner of giving is worth more than the gift. *Le Menteur [1642], act I, sc. i*

25 A liar is always lavish of oaths. *Ib. III, v*

26 The fire which seems extinguished often slumbers beneath the ashes. *Rodogune [1644], act III, sc. iv*

27 Guess if you can, choose if you dare. *Héraclius [1646], act IV, sc. iv*

28 A service beyond all recompense
Weighs so heavy that it almost gives offense.
Suréna [1674], act III, sc. i

29 I owe my fame only to myself. *Poésies Diverses, 23*

Sir William Davenant
1606–1668

30 The lark now leaves his wat'ry nest
And, climbing, shakes his dewy wings.
Song [1638], st. 1

31 Who dares doubt the poet wise?
The Philosopher and the Lover: To a Mistress Dying [1638]

32 I shall ask leave to desist, when I am interrupted by so great an experiment as dying. *His apology, in illness, for not having finished Gondibert*

1 How much pleasure they lose (and even the pleasures of heroic poesy are not unprofitable) who take away the liberty of a poet, and fetter his feet in the shackles of a historian.

Prefatory letter to Thomas Hobbes. From S. T. Coleridge, Biographia Literaria [1817], ch. 22

Edmund Waller
1606–1687

2 Illustrious acts high raptures do infuse,
And every conqueror creates a muse.

Panegyric to My Lord Protector

3 Guarded with ships, and all our sea our own.[1] *To My Lord of Falkland*

4 To man, that was in th' evening made,
Stars gave the first delight;
Admiring, in the gloomy shade,
Those little drops of light.

An Apology for Having Loved Before [1664]

5 That which her slender waist confined
Shall now my joyful temples bind;
No monarch but would give his crown
His arms might do what this has done.

On a Girdle [1664], st. 1

6 My joy, my grief, my hope, my love,
Did all within this circle move!

Ib. st. 2

7 Go, lovely rose![2]
Tell her that wastes her time and me
That now she knows,
When I resemble her to thee,
How sweet and fair she seems to be.

Go, Lovely Rose [1664], st. 1

8 So all we know
Of what they do above
Is that they happy are, and that they love.

Upon the Death of My Lady Rich [1664]

9 Poets that lasting marble seek
Must come in Latin or in Greek.

Of English Verse [1668]

10 And keeps the palace of the soul.[3]

Of Tea

11 Poets lose half the praise they should have got,
Could it be known what they discreetly blot.

Upon Roscommon's Translation of Horace, De Arte Poetica

12 The soul's dark cottage, battered and decayed,
Lets in new light through chinks that Time has made;
Stronger by weakness, wiser, men become
As they draw near to their eternal home.
Leaving the old, both worlds at once they view,
That stand upon the threshold of the new.

On the Divine Poems [1686]

[1]See Themistocles, 70:19; Bacon, 181:11; Washington, 379:5; Mahan, 642:8; and Morison, 800:11.

[2]Most of all I envy the octogenarian poet who joined three words—"Go, lovely Rose"—so happily together, that he left his name to float down through Time on the wings of a phrase and a flower.—Logan Pearsall Smith, *Afterthoughts* [1931]

[3]See Byron, 457:6.

Paul Gerhardt
1607–1676

13 O sacred head, now wounded,
With grief and shame bowed down;
Now scornfully surrounded
With thorns, thy only crown.[4]

Passion Chorale [1656], based on twelfth-century Latin hymn, st. 1

Thomas Fuller
1608–1661

14 Drawing near her death, she sent most pious thoughts as harbingers to heaven; and her soul saw a glimpse of happiness through the chinks of her sickness-broken body.

Life of Monica [1642]

15 He was one of a lean body and visage, as if his eager soul, biting for anger at the clog of his body, desired to fret a passage through it.[5] *Life of the Duke of Alva [1642]*

16 He knows little who will tell his wife all he knows.[6]

The Holy State and the Profane State [1642]. The Good Husband

17 One that will not plead that cause wherein his tongue must be confuted by his conscience. *Ib. The Good Advocate*

18 Light, God's eldest daughter,[7] is a principal beauty in a building. *Ib. Of Building*

19 Learning hath gained most by those books by which the printers have lost.

Ib. Of Books

[4]O Haupt vol Blut and Wunden / Vol Schmerz und voller Hohn! / O Haupt zum Spott gebunden / Mit einer Dornen Krohn!
Translated by James Waddell Alexander.

[5]See Dryden, 303:20.

[6]See Homer, 60:13.

[7]See *Genesis 1:3*, 6:10, and Milton, 285:4.

1 Deceive not thyself by overexpecting happiness in the married estate. Remember the nightingales which sing only some months in the spring, but commonly are silent when they have hatched their eggs.

Ib. Of Marriage

2 They that marry ancient people, merely in expectation to bury them, hang themselves in hope that one will come and cut the halter.

Ib.

3 Fame sometimes hath created something of nothing. *Ib. Fame*

4 Anger is one of the sinews of the soul; he that wants it hath a maimed mind.

Ib. Of Anger

5 It is always darkest just before the day dawneth.

Pisgah Sight [1650], bk. II, ch. 2

John Milton[1]

1608–1674

6 This is the month, and this the happy morn,
Wherein the Son of Heav'n's eternal King,
Of wedded maid and virgin mother born,
Our great redemption from above did bring;
For so the holy sages once did sing,
That He our deadly forfeit should release,
And with His Father work us a perpetual peace.

On the Morning of Christ's Nativity [1629], st. 1, l. 1

7 It was the winter wild
While the Heav'n-born child
All meanly wrapt in the rude manger lies.

Ib. Hymn, st. 1, l. 29

8 No war, or battle's sound
Was heard the world around.
The idle spear and shield were high up hung.

Ib. st. 4, l. 53

9 Time will run back and fetch the Age of Gold.[2] *Ib. st. 14, l. 135*

10 The Oracles are dumb.

Ib. st. 19, l. 173

11 From haunted spring and dale
Edged with poplar pale
The parting genius is with sighing sent.

Ib. st. 20, l. 184

12 Peor and Baalim
Forsake their temples dim.

Ib. st. 22, l. 197

[1] See Wordsworth, 425:22.
[2] See Horace, 108:11, and Macaulay, 489:4.

13 What needs my Shakespeare for his honored bones,
The labor of an age in pilèd stones,
Or that his hallowed relics should be hid
Under a star-y-pointing pyramid?
Dear son of memory, great heir of fame,
What need'st thou such weak witness of thy name? *On Shakespeare [1630]*

14 How soon hath Time, the subtle thief of youth,
Stol'n on his wing my three-and-twentieth year.

On His Having Arrived at the Age of Twenty-three [1631]

15 As ever in my great Taskmaster's eye.

Ib.

16 Such sweet compulsion doth in music lie.

Arcades [1630–1634], l. 68

17 Hence, loathèd Melancholy,
Of Cerberus and blackest Midnight born,
In Stygian cave forlorn,
'Mongst horrid shapes, and shrieks, and sights unholy.[3] *L'Allegro [1631], l. 1*

18 So buxom, blithe, and debonair.

Ib. l. 24

19 Haste thee, Nymph, and bring with thee
Jest, and youthful jollity,
Quips and cranks and wanton wiles,
Nods and becks and wreathèd smiles.

Ib. l. 25

20 Sport, that wrinkled Care derides,
And Laughter, holding both his sides.
Come, and trip it, as you go,
On the light fantastic toe. *Ib. l. 31*

21 The mountain nymph, sweet liberty.

Ib. l. 36

22 Mirth, admit me of thy crew,
To live with her, and live with thee,
In unreprovèd pleasures free. *Ib. l. 38*

23 While the cock with lively din
Scatters the rear of darkness thin,
And to the stack, or the barn door,
Stoutly struts his dames before,
Oft list'ning how the hounds and horn
Cheerly rouse the slumb'ring morn.

Ib. l. 49

24 And every shepherd tells his tale
Under the hawthorn in the dale.

Ib. l. 67

25 Meadows trim, with daisies pied,
Shallow brooks, and rivers wide;
Towers and battlements it sees

[3] See Burton, 258:3, and Fletcher, 261:4.

Bosomed high in tufted trees,
Where perhaps some beauty lies,
The cynosure of neighboring eyes.
Ib. l. 75

1 And the jocund rebecks sound
To many a youth, and many a maid,
Dancing in the checkered shade.
And young and old come forth to play
On a sunshine holiday. *Ib. l. 94*

2 Then to the spicy nut-brown ale.
Ib. l. 100

3 Then lies him down the lubber fiend,
And stretched out all the chimney's length,
Basks at the fire his hairy strength.
Ib. l. 110

4 Towered cities please us then,
And the busy hum of men. *Ib. l. 117*

5 Ladies, whose bright eyes
Rain influence, and judge the prize.
Ib. l. 121

6 And pomp, and feast, and revelry,
With mask, and antique pageantry,
Such sights as youthful poets dream
On summer eves by haunted stream.
Then to the well-trod stage anon,
If Jonson's learned sock be on,
Or sweetest Shakespeare, Fancy's child,
Warble his native wood-notes wild,
And ever, against eating cares,
Lap me in soft Lydian airs,
Married to immortal verse[1]
Such as the meeting soul may pierce,
In notes with many a winding bout
Of linked sweetness long drawn out.
Ib. l. 127

7 Untwisting all the chains that tie
The hidden soul of harmony.
Ib. l. 143

8 Such strains as would have won the ear
Of Pluto, to have quite set free
His half-regained Eurydice.
These delights, if thou canst give,
Mirth, with thee, I mean to live.
Ib. l. 148

9 Hence vain deluding Joys,
The brood of Folly without father bred!
Il Penseroso [1631], l. 1

10 The gay motes that people the sunbeams.
Ib. l. 8

11 Hail divinest Melancholy. *Ib. l. 12*

12 Sober, steadfast, and demure. *Ib. l. 32*

[1] Wisdom married to immortal verse.—WORDSWORTH, *The Excursion* [1814], *bk. VII*

13 And looks commercing with the skies,
Thy rapt soul sitting in thine eyes.
Ib. l. 39

14 Forget thyself to marble. *Ib. l. 42*

15 And join with thee, calm Peace and Quiet,
Spare Fast, that oft with gods doth diet.
Ib. l. 45

16 And add to these retired Leisure,
That in trim gardens takes his pleasure.
Ib. l. 49

17 Sweet bird, that shunn'st the noise of folly,
Most musical, most melancholy!
Ib. l. 61

18 I walk unseen
On the dry smooth-shaven green,
To behold the wandering moon,
Riding near her highest noon,
Like one that had been led astray
Through the heav'n's wide pathless way,
And oft, as if her head she bowed,
Stooping through a fleecy cloud.
Ib. l. 65

19 Oft, on a plat of rising ground,
I hear the far-off curfew sound
Over some wide-watered shore,
Swinging low with sullen roar.
Ib. l. 73

20 Where glowing embers through the room
Teach light to counterfeit a gloom,
Far from all resort of mirth,
Save the cricket on the hearth.
Ib. l. 79

21 Sometime let gorgeous Tragedy
In sceptered pall come sweeping by,
Presenting Thebes, or Pelops' line,
Or the tale of Troy divine. *Ib. l. 97*

22 Or bid the soul of Orpheus sing
Such notes as, warbled to the string,
Drew iron tears down Pluto's cheek.
Ib. l. 105

23 Or call up him that left half told
The story of Cambuscan bold.
Ib. l. 109

24 Where more is meant than meets the ear.
Ib. l. 120

25 Hide me from day's garish eye,
While the bee with honied thigh,
That at her flowery work doth sing,
And the waters murmuring
With such consort as they keep,
Entice the dewy-feathered sleep.
Ib. l. 141

26 And storied windows richly dight,
Casting a dim religious light.
There let the pealing organ blow,

To the full-voiced choir below,
In service high, and anthems clear
As may, with sweetness, through mine ear
Dissolve me into ecstasies,
And bring all Heaven before mine eyes.
Ib. l. 159

1 Till old experience do attain
To something like prophetic strain.
Ib. l. 173

2 Before the starry threshold of Jove's Court[1]
My mansion is. *Comus [1634], l. 1*

3 Above the smoke and stir of this dim spot
Which men call earth. *Ib. l. 5*

4 Yet some there be that by due steps aspire
To lay their just hands on that golden key
That opes the palace of Eternity.
Ib. l. 12

5 An old, and haughty nation proud in arms.
Ib. l. 33

6 What never yet was heard in tale or song,
From old or modern bard, in hall or bower.
Ib. l. 44

7 Bacchus, that first from out the purple grape
Crushed the sweet poison of misused wine.
Ib. l. 46

8 These my sky-robes, spun out of Iris' woof.
Ib. l. 83

9 The star that bids the shepherd fold.
Ib. l. 93

10 And the gilded car of day,
His glowing axle doth allay
In the steep Atlantic stream. *Ib. l. 95*

11 Midnight shout and revelry,
Tipsy dance and jollity. *Ib. l. 103*

12 What hath night to do with sleep?
Ib. l. 122

13 Ere the blabbing eastern scout,
The nice morn on th' Indian steep,
From her cabined loophole peep.
Ib. l. 138

14 Come, knit hands, and beat the ground,
In a light fantastic round. *Ib. l. 143*

15 When the gray-hooded Even,
Like a sad votarist in palmer's weed,
Rose from the hindmost wheels of Phoebus' wain. *Ib. l. 188*

16 A thousand fantasies
Begin to throng into my memory,
Of calling shapes, and beck'ning shadows dire,
And airy tongues that syllable men's names
On sands and shores and desert wildernesses.
Ib. l. 205

[1]See Blake, 405:2.

17 Was I deceived or did a sable cloud
Turn forth her silver lining on the night?
Ib. l. 221

18 Sweet Echo, sweetest nymph, that liv'st unseen
Within thy airy shell
By slow Meander's margent green,
And in the violet-embroidered vale.
Ib. l. 230

19 How sweetly did they float upon the wings
Of silence, through the empty-vaulted night,
At every fall smoothing the raven down
Of darkness till it smiled! *Ib. l. 249*

20 Such sober certainty of waking bliss.
Ib. l. 263

21 With thy long leveled rule of streaming light.
Ib. l. 340

22 Virtue could see to do what Virtue would
By her own radiant light, though sun and moon
Were in the flat sea sunk. And Wisdom's self
Oft seeks to sweet retired solitude,
Where, with her best nurse Contemplation,
She plumes her feathers, and lets grow her wings. *Ib. l. 373*

23 The unsunned heaps
Of miser's treasure. *Ib. l. 398*

24 Tis Chastity, my brother, Chastity:
She that has that, is clad in complete steel.[2]
Ib. l. 420

25 How charming is divine philosophy!
Not harsh and crabbèd, as dull fools suppose,
But musical as is Apollo's lute,[3]
And a perpetual feast of nectared sweets
Where no crude surfeit reigns.
Ib. l. 476

26 Filled the air with barbarous dissonance.
Ib. l. 550

27 I was all ear,
And took in strains that might create a soul
Under the ribs of Death. *Ib. l. 560*

28 That power
Which erring men call Chance.
Ib. l. 587

29 Thou canst not touch the freedom of my mind. *Ib. l. 663*

30 Praising the lean and sallow abstinence.
Ib. l. 709

31 Beauty is Nature's coin, must not be hoarded,
But must be current, and the good thereof
Consists in mutual and partaken bliss.
Ib. l. 739

[2]See Shakespeare, 185:17.
[3]See Shakespeare, 191:4.

1 Beauty is Nature's brag, and must be shown
In courts, at feasts, and high solemnities,
Where most may wonder at the workmanship;
It is for homely features to keep home—
They had their name thence; coarse complexions
And cheeks of sorry grain will serve to ply
The sampler, and to tease the huswife's wool.
What need a vermeil-tinctured lip for that,
Love-darting eyes, or tresses like the morn?
Ib. l. 745

2 Enjoy your dear wit, and gay rhetoric,
That hath so well been taught her dazzling fence. *Ib. l. 790*

3 Sabrina fair,
Listen where thou art sitting
Under the glassy, cool, translucent wave,
In twisted braids of lilies knitting
The loose train of thy amber-dropping hair;
Listen for dear honor's sake,
Goddess of the silver lake,
Listen and save. *Ib. l. 859*

4 But now my task is smoothly done:
I can fly, or I can run. *Ib. l. 1012*

5 Love Virtue, she alone is free,
She can teach ye how to climb
Higher than the sphery chime;
Or, if Virtue feeble were,
Heav'n itself would stoop to her.
Ib. l. 1019

6 Yet once more, O ye laurels, and once more
Ye myrtles brown, with ivy never sere,
I come to pluck your berries harsh and crude,
And with forced fingers rude
Shatter your leaves before the mellowing year. *Lycidas [1637], l. 1*

7 He knew
Himself to sing, and build the lofty rhyme.
Ib. l. 10

8 Without the meed of some melodious tear.
Ib. l. 14

9 Hence with denial vain, and coy excuse.
Ib. l. 18

10 Under the opening eyelids of the morn,
We drove afield; and both together heard
What time the gray-fly winds her sultry horn,
Batt'ning our flocks with the fresh dews of night. *Ib. l. 26*

11 But O the heavy change, now thou art gone,
Now thou art gone and never must return!
Ib. l. 37

12 The gadding vine. *Ib. l. 40*

13 As killing as the canker to the rose.
Ib. l. 45

14 Whom universal Nature did lament.
Ib. l. 60

15 Alas! what boots it with incessant care
To tend the homely slighted shepherd's trade,
And strictly meditate the thankless Muse?
Were it not better done as others use,
To sport with Amaryllis in the shade,
Or with the tangles of Neaera's hair?
Fame is the spur that the clear spirit doth raise[1]
(That last infirmity of noble mind)[2]
To scorn delights, and live laborious days;
But the fair guerdon when we hope to find,
And think to burst out into sudden blaze,
Comes the blind Fury with th' abhorrèd shears,
And slits the thin-spun life. *Ib. l. 64*

16 Fame is no plant that grows on mortal soil.
Ib. l. 78

17 That strain I heard was of a higher mood.
Ib. l. 87

18 It was that fatal and perfidious bark,
Built in th' eclipse, and rigged with curses dark,
That sunk so low that sacred head of thine.
Ib. l. 100

19 Last came, and last did go,
The Pilot of the Galilean lake;
Two massy keys he bore of metals twain,
(The golden opes, the iron shuts amain).
Ib. l. 108

20 Such as for their bellies' sake,
Creep and intrude, and climb into the fold.
Ib. l. 114

21 Blind mouths! That scarce themselves know how to hold
A sheep-hook. *Ib. l. 119*

22 The hungry sheep look up, and are not fed,
But swoln with wind and the rank mist they draw,
Rot inwardly, and foul contagion spread:
Besides what the grim wolf with privy paw
Daily devours apace, and nothing said;
But that two-handed engine at the door
Stands ready to smite once, and smite no more. *Ib. l. 123*

[1]See Tacitus, 122:26.

[2]That thirst [for applause], if the last infirmity of noble minds, is also the first infirmity of weak ones; and on the whole, the strongest impulsive influence of average humanity.—RUSKIN, *Sesame and Lilies* [1865], *Of Kings' Treasuries, sec. 3*

1 Throw hither all your quaint enameled eyes,
That on the green turf suck the honied showers,
And purple all the ground with vernal flowers.
Bring the rathe primrose that forsaken dies.
Ib. l. 139

2 Whether beyond the stormy Hebrides,[1]
Where thou perhaps under the whelming tide
Visit'st the bottom of the monstrous world.
Ib. l. 156

3 Look homeward, Angel, now, and melt with ruth.[2] *Ib. l. 163*

4 For Lycidas your sorrow is not dead,
Sunk though he be beneath the watery floor;
So sinks the day-star in the ocean bed;
And yet anon repairs his drooping head,
And tricks his beams, and with new-spangled ore
Flames in the forehead of the morning sky.[3]
So Lycidas sunk low, but mounted high,
Through the dear might of him that walked the waves. *Ib. l. 166*

5 He touched the tender stops of various quills,
With eager thought warbling his Doric lay.
Ib. l. 188

6 At last he rose, and twitched his mantle blue:
Tomorrow to fresh woods and pastures new.
Ib. l. 192

7 The lazy leaden-stepping Hours,
Whose speed is but the heavy plummet's pace. *On Time [c. 1637]*

8 O nightingale, that on yon bloomy spray
Warbl'st at eve, when all the woods are still.
Sonnet, To the Nightingale [c. 1637]

9 Thy liquid notes that close the eye of day.
Ib.

10 Where the bright seraphim in burning row
Their loud uplifted angel trumpets blow.
At a Solemn Music [c. 1637]

11 A poet soaring in the high reason of his fancies, with his garland and singing robes about him.
The Reason of Church Government [1641], bk. II, introduction

12 By labor and intent study (which I take to be my portion in this life), joined with the strong propensity of nature, I might perhaps leave something so written to after-times, as they should not willingly let it die. *Ib.*

[1]See Thomson, 345:15.
[2]See Wolfe, 852:6.
[3]See Du Bartas, 167:8.

13 Beholding the bright countenance of truth in the quiet and still air of delightful studies.
Ib.

14 He who would not be frustrate of his hope to write well hereafter in laudable things ought himself to be a true poem.
Apology for Smectymnuus [1642]

15 His words . . . like so many nimble and airy servitors trip about him at command.
Ib.

16 Truth . . . never comes into the world but like a bastard, to the ignominy of him that brought her forth.[4]
The Doctrine and Discipline of Divorce [1643], introduction

17 Let not England forget her precedence of teaching nations how to live.[5] *Ib.*

18 Litigious terms, fat contentions, and flowing fees.
Tractate of Education [1644]

19 Inflamed with the study of learning and the admiration of virtue; stirred up with high hopes of living to be brave men and worthy patriots, dear to God, and famous to all ages.
Ib.

20 Ornate rhetoric taught out of the rule of Plato. . . . To which poetry would be made subsequent, or indeed rather precedent, as being less subtle and fine, but more simple, sensuous, and passionate. *Ib.*

21 In those vernal seasons of the year, when the air is calm and pleasant, it were an injury and sullenness against Nature not to go out, and see her riches, and partake in her rejoicing with heaven and earth. *Ib.*

22 Books are not absolutely dead things, but do contain a potency of life in them to be as active as that soul was whose progeny they are; nay they do preserve as in a vial the purest efficacy and extraction of that living intellect that bred them.
Areopagitica [1644]

23 As good almost kill a man as kill a good book: who kills a man kills a reasonable creature, God's image; but he who destroys a good book kills reason itself. *Ib.*

24 A good book is the precious lifeblood of a master spirit, embalmed and treasured up on purpose to a life beyond life. *Ib.*

[4]Still rule those minds on earth / At whom sage Milton's wormwood words were hurled: / "Truth like a bastard comes into the world / Never without ill-fame to him who gives her birth"? — THOMAS HARDY, *Lausanne* [1897]
[5]See Virgil, 105:24.

1 I cannot praise a fugitive and cloistered virtue, unexercised and unbreathed, that never sallies out and sees her adversary, but slinks out of the race, where that immortal garland is to be run for, not without dust and heat. *Ib.*

2 Where there is much desire to learn, there of necessity will be much arguing, much writing, many opinions; for opinion in good men is but knowledge in the making. *Ib.*

3 Methinks I see in my mind a noble and puissant nation rousing herself like a strong man after sleep, and shaking her invincible locks. Methinks I see her as an eagle mewing her mighty youth, and kindling her undazzled eyes at the full midday beam. *Ib.*

4 Give me the liberty to know, to utter, and to argue freely according to conscience, above all liberties. *Ib.*

5 Though all the winds of doctrine[1] were let loose to play upon the earth, so Truth be in the field, we do injuriously, by licensing and prohibiting, to misdoubt her strength. Let her and Falsehood grapple; who ever knew Truth put to the worse, in a free and open encounter?[2] *Ib.*

6 As that dishonest victory
At Chaeronea, fatal to liberty,
Killed with report that old man eloquent.[3]
To the Lady Margaret Ley [c. 1644]

7 Men of most renowned virtue have sometimes by transgressing most truly kept the law. *Tetrachordon [1644–1645]*

8 That would have made Quintilian stare and gasp.
On the Detraction Which Followed upon My Writing Certain Treatises [1645]

9 In mirth, that after no repenting draws.
To Cyriack Skinner [1646–1647?]

10 For other things mild Heav'n a time ordains,
And disapproves that care, though wise in show,
That with superfluous burden loads the day,
And, when God sends a cheerful hour, refrains. *Ib.*

11 For such kind of borrowing as this, if it be not bettered by the borrower, among good authors is accounted Plagiarè.
Eikonoklastes [1649], 23

[1] See *Ephesians 4:14*, 49:35.
[2] See Jefferson, 388:16, and Holmes, 645:1.
[3] Athenian teacher and orator Isocrates [436–338 B.C.]. See John Quincy Adams, 417.

12 None can love freedom heartily, but good men; the rest love not freedom, but license.
Tenure of Kings and Magistrates [1649]

13 No man who knows aught, can be so stupid to deny that all men naturally were born free.[4] *Ib.*

14 Peace hath her victories
No less renowned than war.
To the Lord General Cromwell [1652]

15 When I consider how my light is spent,
Ere half my days, in this dark world and wide,
And that one talent which is death to hide
Lodged with me useless.
On His Blindness [1652]

16 Doth God exact day-labor, light denied? *Ib.*

17 Who best
Bear his mild yoke, they serve him best: his state
Is kingly; thousands at his bidding speed,
And post o'er land and ocean without rest;
They also serve who only stand and wait. *Ib.*

18 Avenge, O Lord, thy slaughtered saints, whose bones
Lie scattered on the Alpine mountains cold;
Ev'n them who kept thy truth so pure of old
When all our fathers worshipped stocks and stones
Forget not.
On the Late Massacre in Piedmont [1655]

19 Yet I argue not
Against Heav'n's hand or will, nor bate one jot
Of heart or hope; but still bear up, and steer
Right onward.
To Cyriack Skinner, upon His Blindness [c. 1655]

20 Methought I saw my late espousèd saint
Brought to me like Alcestis from the grave.
On His Deceased Wife [c. 1658]

21 But oh! as to embrace me she inclined,
I waked, she fled, and day brought back my night. *Ib.*

22 Of Man's first disobedience, and the fruit
Of that forbidden tree whose mortal taste
Brought death into the world, and all our woe,
With loss of Eden.
Paradise Lost [1667], bk. I, l. 1

[4] See *Acts 22:28*, 46:26; Rousseau, 358:12; and Davis, 814:20.

1 Things unattempted yet in prose or rhyme.
Ib. l. 16

2 What in me is dark
Illumine, what is low raise and support;
That to the height of this great argument
I may assert eternal Providence,
And justify the ways of God to men.[1]
Ib. l. 22

3 The infernal serpent; he it was, whose guile,
Stirred up with envy and revenge, deceived
The mother of mankind. *Ib. l. 34*

4 Him the Almighty Power
Hurled headlong flaming from th' ethereal sky[2]
With hideous ruin and combustion down
To bottomless perdition, there to dwell
In adamantine chains and penal fire,
Who durst defy th' Omnipotent to arms.
Ib. l. 44

5 As far as angels' ken. *Ib. l. 59*

6 No light, but rather darkness visible.
Ib. l. 63

7 Regions of sorrow, doleful shades, where peace
And rest can never dwell, hope never comes
That comes to all. *Ib. l. 65*

8 What though the field be lost?
All is not lost; th' unconquerable will,
And study of revenge, immortal hate,
And courage never to submit or yield.
Ib. l. 105

9 Vaunting aloud, but racked with deep despair. *Ib. l. 126*

10 To be weak is miserable,
Doing or suffering. *Ib. l. 157*

11 And out of good still to find means of evil.
Ib. l. 165

12 The seat of desolation, void of light.
Ib. l. 181

13 A mind not to be changed by place or time.
The mind is its own place, and in itself
Can make a heav'n of hell, a hell of heav'n.[3] *Ib. l. 253*

14 To reign is worth ambition though in hell:
Better to reign in hell than serve in heav'n.
Ib. l. 262

15 His spear, to equal which the tallest pine
Hewn on Norwegian hills, to be the mast
Of some great ammiral, were but a wand,
He walked with, to support uneasy steps
Over the burning marle. *Ib. l. 292*

16 Thick as autumnal leaves that strow the brooks
In Vallombrosa. *Ib. l. 302*

17 Awake, arise, or be forever fallen!
Ib. l. 330

18 Spirits, when they please,
Can either sex assume, or both.
Ib. l. 423

19 When night
Darkens the streets, then wander forth the sons
Of Belial, flown with insolence and wine.
Ib. l. 500

20 Th' imperial ensign, which, full high advanced,
Shone like a meteor, streaming to the wind.[4] *Ib. l. 536*

21 Sonorous metal blowing martial sounds:
At which the universal host up sent
A shout that tore hell's concave, and beyond
Frighted the reign of Chaos and old Night.
Ib. l. 540

22 Anon they move
In perfect phalanx, to the Dorian mood
Of flutes and soft recorders. *Ib. l. 549*

23 His form had yet not lost
All her original brightness, nor appeared
Less than archangel ruined, and th' excess
Of glory obscured. *Ib. l. 591*

24 The sun . . .
In dim eclipse, disastrous twilight sheds
On half the nations, and with fear of change
Perplexes monarchs. *Ib. l. 594*

25 Care
Sat on his faded cheek, but under brows
Of dauntless courage. *Ib. l. 601*

26 Thrice he assayed, and thrice, in spite of scorn,
Tears, such as angels weep, burst forth.
Ib. l. 619

27 Who overcomes
By force hath overcome but half his foe.
Ib. l. 648

28 Mammon, the least erected spirit that fell
From heaven; for ev'n in heaven his looks and thoughts
Were always downward bent, admiring more

[1] See *Samson Agonistes,* 288:26; Pope, 336:11; and Housman, 691:17.

[2] See *Luke 10:18,* 43:11.

[3] See Virgil, 105:23; Marlowe, 183:21 and 184:1; Browne, 274:15; Milton, 285:12; Eliot, 809:1; Sartre, 865:12; and Lowell, 893:7.

[4] Streamed like a meteor to the troubled air.—THOMAS GRAY, *The Bard* [1757], *sec. I, st. 2, l. 6*

The riches of heaven's pavement, trodden gold,
Than aught divine or holy else enjoyed
In vision beatific. *Ib. l. 679*

1 Let none admire
That riches grow in hell; that soil may best
Deserve the precious bane. *Ib. l. 690*

2 From morn
To noon he fell, from noon to dewy eve,
A summer's day; and with the setting sun
Dropped from the zenith like a falling star.
Ib. l. 742

3 High on a throne of royal state, which far
Outshone the wealth of Ormus and of Ind,
Or where the gorgeous East with richest hand
Showers on her kings barbaric pearl and gold,
Satan exalted sat, by merit raised
To that bad eminence; and from despair
Thus high uplifted beyond hope, aspires
Beyond thus high, insatiate to pursue
Vain war with heav'n. *Ib. II, l. 1*

4 Moloch, sceptered king,
Stood up, the strongest and the fiercest spirit
That fought in heav'n; now fiercer by despair.
Ib. l. 44

5 Rather than be less
Cared not to be at all. *Ib. l. 47*

6 My sentence is for open war. *Ib. l. 51*

7 Which if not victory is yet revenge.
Ib. l. 105

8 But all was false and hollow; through his tongue
Dropped manna, and could make the worse appear
The better reason.[1] *Ib. l. 112*

9 For who would lose,
Though full of pain, this intellectual being,
Those thoughts that wander through eternity,
To perish rather, swallowed up and lost
In the wide womb of uncreated night,
Devoid of sense and motion? *Ib. l. 146*

10 His red right hand.[2] *Ib. l. 174*

11 Unrespited, unpitied, unreprieved.[3]
Ib. l. 185

12 The never-ending flight
Of future days. *Ib. l. 221*

13 Thus Belial with words clothed in reason's garb
Counseled ignoble ease,[4] and peaceful sloth,
Not peace. *Ib. l. 226*

14 With grave
Aspect he rose, and in his rising seemed
A pillar of state; deep on his front engraven
Deliberation sat and public care;
And princely counsel in his face yet shone,
Majestic though in ruin. *Ib. l. 300*

15 To sit in darkness here
Hatching vain empires. *Ib. l. 377*

16 The palpable obscure. *Ib. l. 406*

17 Long is the way
And hard, that out of hell leads up to light.[5] *Ib. l. 432*

18 Their rising all at once was as the sound
Of thunder heard remote. *Ib. l. 476*

19 Others apart sat on a hill retired,
In thoughts more elevate, and reasoned high
Of Providence, foreknowledge, will, and fate,
Fixed fate, free will, foreknowledge absolute,
And found no end, in wand'ring mazes lost.
Ib. l. 557

20 Vain wisdom all, and false philosophy.
Ib. l. 565

21 Arm th' obdured breast
With stubborn patience as with triple steel.[6] *Ib. l. 568*

22 Far off from these a slow and silent stream,
Lethe the river of oblivion rolls.
Ib. l. 582

23 At certain revolutions all the damned
Are brought: and feel by turns the bitter change
Of fierce extremes, extremes by change more fierce. *Ib. l. 597*

24 The other shape,
If shape it might be called. *Ib. l. 666*

25 Whence and what art thou, execrable shape?
Ib. l. 681

26 Before mine eyes in opposition sits
Grim Death[7] my son and foe.
Ib. l. 803

27 Hot, cold, moist, and dry, four champions fierce,[8]
Strive here for mast'ry. *Ib. l. 898*

[1] See Aristophanes, 81:14.
[2] Rubente dextera.—HORACE [65–8 B.C.], *Odes, I, ii, 2, To Caesar Augustus*
[3] See Homer, 59:9; Horace, 108:13; Chaucer, 144:17; Shakespeare, 219:24; Scott, 430:10; and Byron, 458:26.
[4] See Virgil, 104:13, and T. R. Roosevelt, 686:12.
[5] See Virgil, 105:15.
[6] See Shakespeare, 185:17.
[7] See Massinger, 262:22.
[8] Hot and cold, and moist and dry.—SEIGNEUR DU BARTAS, *Divine Weeks and Works* [1578], *Second Day*
See Dryden, 305:9.

1 To compare
Great things with small. *Ib. l. 921*

2 With ruin upon ruin, rout on rout,
Confusion worse confounded.
Ib. l. 995

3 And fast by hanging in a golden chain,
This pendent world, in bigness as a star
Of smallest magnitude close by the moon.
Ib. l. 1051

4 Hail, holy light! offspring of heav'n first born.[1] *Ib. III, l. 1*

5 Thus with the year
Seasons return; but not to me returns
Day, or the sweet approach of ev'n or morn,
Or sight of vernal bloom, or summer's rose,
Or flocks, or herds, or human face divine;[2]
But cloud instead, and ever-during dark
Surrounds me, from the cheerful ways of men
Cut off, and for the book of knowledge fair
Presented with a universal blank
Of Nature's works to me expunged and razed,
And wisdom at one entrance quite shut out.
Ib. l. 40

6 See golden days, fruitful of golden deeds,
With Joy and Love triumphing.
Ib. l. 337

7 Dark with excessive bright. *Ib. l. 380*

8 Into a limbo large and broad, since called
The Paradise of Fools, to few unknown.
Ib. l. 495

9 The hell within him. *Ib. IV, l. 20*

10 At whose sight all the stars
Hide their diminished heads.[3]
Ib. l. 34

11 A grateful mind
By owing owes not, but still pays, at once
Indebted and discharged. *Ib. l. 55*

12 Me miserable! which way shall I fly
Infinite wrath, and infinite despair?
Which way I fly is hell; myself am hell;[4]
And in the lowest deep a lower deep,
Still threat'ning to devour me, opens wide,
To which the hell I suffer seems a heaven.
Ib. l. 73

13 So farewell hope, and with hope farewell fear,
Farewell remorse: all good to me is lost;
Evil, be thou my good. *Ib. l. 108*

14 And on the Tree of Life,
The middle tree and highest there that grew,
Sat like a cormorant. *Ib. l. 194*

15 A heaven on earth. *Ib. l. 208*

16 Flowers of all hue, and without thorn the rose. *Ib. l. 256*

17 Two of far nobler shape erect and tall,
Godlike erect, with native honor clad
In naked majesty seemed lords of all.
Ib. l. 288

18 For contemplation he and valor formed,
For softness she and sweet attractive grace;
He for God only, she for God in him.
Ib. l. 297

19 Implied
Subjection, but required with gentle sway,
And by her yielded, by him best received,
Yielded with coy submission, modest pride,
And sweet reluctant amorous delay.
Ib. l. 307

20 Adam the goodliest man of men since born
His sons, the fairest of her daughters Eve.
Ib. l. 323

21 So spake the Fiend, and with necessity,
The tyrant's plea,[5] excused his devilish deeds. *Ib. l. 393*

22 Imparadised in one another's arms.
Ib. l. 506

23 Live while ye may,
Yet happy pair. *Ib. l. 533*

24 Now came still evening on, and twilight gray
Had in her sober livery all things clad.
Ib. l. 598

25 The wakeful nightingale,
She all night long her amorous descant sung;
Silence was pleased: now glowed the firmament
With living sapphires: Hesperus, that led
The starry host, rode brightest, till the moon,
Rising in clouded majesty, at length
Apparent queen unveiled her peerless light,
And o'er the dark her silver mantle threw.
Ib. l. 602

26 The timely dew of sleep. *Ib. l. 614*

27 With thee conversing I forget all time,
All seasons, and their change; all please alike.
Sweet is the breath of morn, her rising sweet,
With charm of earliest birds.
Ib. l. 639

[1] See *Genesis 1:3*, 6:10, and Fuller, 276:18.
God's first creature, which was light.—BACON, *The New Atlantis* [1626]
Light, the prime work of God.—MILTON, *Samson Agonistes* [1671], *l. 70*

[2] See Blake, 403:11 and 405:14.

[3] Ye little stars! hide your diminished rays.—POPE, *Moral Essays* [1731–1735], *Epistle III, l. 282*

[4] See Virgil, 105:23; Marlowe, 183:21 and 184:1; Browne, 274:15; Milton, 283:13; Eliot, 809:1; Sartre, 865:12; and Lowell, 893:7.

[5] See Publilius Syrus, 111:20, and William Pitt, 412:4.

1 Sweet the coming on
Of grateful ev'ning mild, then silent night
With this her solemn bird, and this fair moon,
And these the gems of heaven, her starry train. *Ib. l. 646*

2 Millions of spiritual creatures walk the earth
Unseen, both when we wake, and when we sleep. *Ib. l. 677*

3 In naked beauty more adorned,
More lovely, than Pandora.[1] *Ib. l. 713*

4 Eased the putting off
These troublesome disguises which we wear.
Ib. l. 739

5 Hail wedded love, mysterious law, true source
Of human offspring. *Ib. l. 750*

6 Squat like a toad, close at the ear of Eve.
Ib. l. 800

7 Not to know me argues yourselves unknown.
Ib. l. 830

8 Abashed the Devil stood,
And felt how awful goodness is, and saw
Virtue in her shape how lovely.
Ib. l. 846

9 All hell broke loose.[2] *Ib. l. 918*

10 Like Teneriff or Atlas unremoved.
Ib. l. 987

11 The starry cope
Of heaven. *Ib. l. 992*

12 His sleep
Was airy light from pure digestion bred.
Ib. V, l. 3

13 My latest found,
Heaven's last, best gift, my ever new delight!
Ib. l. 18

14 Good, the more
Communicated, more abundant grows.
Ib. l. 71

15 These are thy glorious works, Parent of good.
Ib. l. 153

16 Him first, him last, him midst, and without end. *Ib. l. 165*

17 A wilderness of sweets. *Ib. l. 294*

18 So saying, with dispatchful looks in haste
She turns, on hospitable thoughts intent.
Ib. l. 331

[1] See Cicero, 98:13, and Thomson, 345:14.
[2] See Robert Greene, 178:14.

19 Nor jealousy
Was understood, the injured lover's hell.
Ib. l. 449

20 Freely we serve,
Because we freely love, as in our will
To love or not; in this we stand or fall.
Ib. l. 538

21 What if earth
Be but the shadow of heaven, and things therein
Each to other like, more than on earth is thought? *Ib. l. 574*

22 Hear all ye Angels, progeny of light,
Thrones, Dominations, Princedoms, Virtues, Powers. *Ib. l. 600*

23 All seemed well pleased, all seemed but were not all. *Ib. l. 617*

24 Among the faithless, faithful only he.
Ib. l. 897

25 Morn,
Waked by the circling hours, with rosy hand[3]
Unbarred the gates of light.
Ib. VI, l. 2

26 Servant of God, well done,[4] well hast thou fought
The better fight, who single hast maintained
Against revolted multitudes the cause
Of truth, in word mightier than they in arms.
Ib. l. 29

27 He onward came; far off his coming shone.
Ib. l. 768

28 More safe I sing with mortal voice, unchanged
To hoarse or mute, though fall'n on evil days,
On evil days though fall'n, and evil tongues;
In darkness, and with dangers compassed round,
And solitude. *Ib. VII, l. 24*

29 Out of one man a race
Of men innumerable. *Ib. l. 155*

30 There Leviathan
Hugest of living creatures, on the deep
Stretched like a promontory sleeps or swims,
And seems a moving land, and at his gills
Draws in, and at his trunk spouts out a sea.
Ib. l. 412

31 Endued
With sanctity of reason. *Ib. l. 507*

[3] See Homer, 57:11.
[4] See *Matthew* 25:21, 40:29.

1 The planets in their stations list'ning stood,
While the bright pomp ascended jubilant.
Open, ye everlasting gates, they sung,
Open, ye heavens, your living doors;[1] let in
The great Creator from his work returned
Magnificent, his six days' work, a world.
Ib. l. 563

2 The angel ended, and in Adam's ear
So charming left his voice that he awhile
Thought him still speaking, still stood fixed to hear.
Ib. VIII, l. 1

3 To know
That which before us lies in daily life
Is the prime wisdom. *Ib. l. 192*

4 Liquid lapse of murmuring streams.
Ib. l. 263

5 And feel that I am happier than I know.
Ib. l. 282

6 Her virtue and the conscience of her worth,
That would be wooed, and not unsought be won. *Ib. l. 502*

7 The sum of earthly bliss. *Ib. l. 522*

8 So absolute she seems
And in herself complete, so well to know
Her own, that what she wills to do or say,
Seems wisest, virtuousest, discreetest, best.
Ib. l. 547

9 Accuse not Nature, she hath done her part;
Do thou but thine. *Ib. l. 561*

10 Ofttimes nothing profits more
Than self-esteem, grounded on just and right
Well managed. *Ib. l. 571*

11 My unpremeditated verse.
Ib. IX, l. 24

12 Pleased me long choosing, and beginning late. *Ib. l. 26*

13 Unless an age too late, or cold
Climate, or years damp my intended wing.
Ib. l. 44

14 The serpent subtlest beast of all the field.[2]
Ib. l. 86

15 For solitude sometimes is best society,
And short retirement urges sweet return.
Ib. l. 249

16 At shut of evening flowers. *Ib. l. 278*

17 As one who long in populous city pent.[3]
Ib. l. 445

18 God so commanded, and left that command
Sole daughter of his voice;[4] the rest, we live
Law to ourselves, our reason is our law.
Ib. l. 652

19 Her rash hand in evil hour
Forth reaching to the fruit, she plucked, she eat:
Earth felt the wound, and Nature from her seat,
Sighing through all her works, gave signs of woe
That all was lost. *Ib. l. 780*

20 So dear I love him, that with him all deaths
I could endure, without him live no life.
Ib. l. 832

21 In her face excuse
Came prologue, and apology too prompt.
Ib. l. 853

22 O fairest of creation! last and best
Of all God's works! creature in whom excelled
Whatever can to sight or thought be formed,
Holy, divine, good, amiable, or sweet!
How art thou lost, how on a sudden lost,
Defaced, deflowered, and now to Death devote? *Ib. l. 896*

23 I feel
The link of nature draw me: flesh of flesh,
Bone of my bone thou art,[5] and from thy state
Mine never shall be parted, bliss or woe.
Ib. l. 913

24 Our state cannot be severed; we are one,
One flesh; to lose thee were to lose myself.
Ib. l. 958

25 I shall temper so
Justice with mercy.[6] *Ib. X, l. 77*

26 Pandemonium, city and proud seat
Of Lucifer. *Ib. l. 424*

27 A dismal universal hiss, the sound
Of public scorn. *Ib. l. 508*

28 Death . . . on his pale horse.[7]
Ib. l. 588

29 Demoniac frenzy, moping melancholy,
And moon-struck madness.
Ib. XI, l. 485

30 Nor love thy life, nor hate; but what thou liv'st
Live well; how long or short permit to Heaven.[8] *Ib. l. 553*

31 A bevy of fair women. *Ib. l. 582*

32 The evening star,
Love's harbinger. *Ib. l. 588*

33 The brazen throat of war. *Ib. l. 713*

[1] See *Psalm 24:7*, 18:9.
[2] See *Genesis 3:1*, 7:5.
[3] See Keats, 475:4.
[4] See Wordsworth, 427:12.
[5] See *Genesis 2:23*, 7:3.
[6] See Shakespeare, 200:9.
[7] See *Revelation 6:8*, 53:11.
[8] See Martial, 119:15.

1 For now I see
Peace to corrupt no less than war to waste.
Ib. l. 783

2 An olive leaf he brings, pacific sign.
Ib. l. 860

3 In me is no delay; with thee to go,
Is to stay here; without thee here to stay,
Is to go hence unwilling; thou to me
Art all things under heaven, all places thou,
Who for my willful crime art banished hence.
Ib. XII, l. 615

4 The world was all before them, where to choose
Their place of rest, and Providence their guide:
They hand in hand with wand'ring steps and slow
Through Eden took their solitary way.
Ib. l. 646

5 Most men admire
Virtue who follow not her lore.
Paradise Regained [1671], bk. I, l. 482

6 Skilled to retire, and in retiring draw
Hearts after them tangled in amorous nets.
Ib. II, l. 161

7 Beauty stands
In the admiration only of weak minds
Led captive. *Ib. l. 220*

8 Rocks whereon greatest men have oftest wrecked. *Ib. l. 228*

9 Of whom to be dispraised were no small praise. *Ib. III, l. 56*

10 Elephants endorsed with towers.
Ib. l. 329

11 Dusk faces with white silken turbans wreathed. *Ib. IV, l. 76*

12 The childhood shows the man,
As morning shows the day.[1] *Ib. l. 220*

13 Athens, the eye of Greece, mother of arts
And eloquence. *Ib. l. 240*

14 The olive grove of Academe,[2]
Plato's retirement, where the Attic bird
Trills her thick-warbled notes the summer long. *Ib. l. 244*

15 Socrates . . .
Whom well inspired the oracle pronounced
Wisest of men. *Ib. l. 274*

16 The first and wisest of them all professed
To know this only, that he nothing knew.[3]
Ib. l. 293

[1]See Wordsworth, 425:7.
[2]See Horace, 109:14.
[3]See Socrates, 79:5.

17 Deep versed in books and shallow in himself.
Ib. l. 327

18 Till morning fair
Came forth with pilgrim steps, in amice gray.
Ib. l. 426

19 Eyeless in Gaza, at the mill with slaves.[4]
Samson Agonistes [1671], l. 41

20 O dark, dark, dark, amid the blaze of noon,
Irrecoverably dark, total eclipse
Without all hope of day! *Ib. l. 80*

21 The sun to me is dark
And silent as the moon,
When she deserts the night,
Hid in her vacant interlunar cave.
Ib. l. 86

22 To live a life half dead, a living death.
Ib. l. 100

23 Ran on embattled armies clad in iron,
And, weaponless himself,
Made arms ridiculous. *Ib. l. 129*

24 Apt words have power to suage
The tumors of a troubled mind.[5]
Ib. l. 184

25 Wisest men
Have erred, and by bad women been deceived. *Ib. l. 210*

26 Just are the ways of God,
And justifiable to men;[6]
Unless there be who think not God at all.
Ib. l. 293

27 A grain of manhood. *Ib. l. 408*

28 What boots it at one gate to make defense,
And at another to let in the foe?
Ib. l. 560

29 My race of glory run, and race of shame,
And I shall shortly be with them at rest.
Ib. l. 597

30 But who is this, what thing of sea or land?
Female of sex it seems,
That so bedecked, ornate, and gay,
Comes this way sailing
Like a stately ship
Of Tarsus, bound for th' isles
Of Javan or Gadire,
With all her bravery on, and tackle trim,
Sails filled, and streamers waving,
Courted by all the winds that hold them play;
An amber scent of odorous perfume
Her harbinger? *Ib. l. 710*

[4]See *Judges 16:21*, 12:19.
[5]See Aeschylus, 70:25.
[6]See *Paradise Lost*, 283:2; Pope, 336:11; and Housman, 691:17.

1 *Dalila:* In argument with men a woman ever
Goes by the worse, whatever be her cause.
Samson: For want of words, no doubt, or lack of breath! *Ib. l. 903*

2 Fame, if not double-faced, is double-mouthed,
And with contrary blast proclaims most deeds;
On both his wings, one black, the other white,
Bears greatest names in his wild airy flight. *Ib. l. 971*

3 Yet beauty, though injurious, hath strange power,
After offense returning, to regain
Love once possessed. *Ib. l. 1003*

4 Love-quarrels oft in pleasing concord end;
Not wedlock-treachery. *Ib. l. 1008*

5 Boast not of what thou would'st have done, but do
What then thou would'st. *Ib. l. 1104*

6 He's gone; and who knows how he may report
Thy words by adding fuel to the flame? *Ib. l. 1350*

7 For evil news rides post, while good news baits.[1] *Ib. l. 1538*

8 Suspense in news is torture. *Ib. l. 1569*

9 Nothing is here for tears, nothing to wail
Or knock the breast, no weakness, no contempt,
Dispraise, or blame, nothing but well and fair,
And what may quiet us in a death so noble. *Ib. l. 1721*

10 All is best, though we oft doubt,
What the unsearchable dispose
Of highest Wisdom brings about. *Ib. l. 1745*

11 Calm of mind, all passion spent. *Ib. l. 1758*

12 Such bickerings to recount, met often in these our writers, what more worth is it than to chronicle the wars of kites or crows flocking and fighting in the air?
The History of England [1670], bk. IV

Nakae Toju
1608–1648

13 Filial piety is the root of man. When it is lost from one's heart, then one's life becomes like a rootless plant, and if one does not expire instantly, it is nothing but sheer luck.[2]
Toju Sensei Zenshu (Collected Works), vol. I

[1] See Plutarch, 120:14.

Sir Matthew Hale[3]
1609–1676

14 Be not biased with compassion to the poor, or favor to the rich, in point of justice.
Things Necessary to Be Continually Had in Remembrance

15 Not to be solicitous what men will say or think. *Ib.*

Edward Hyde, Earl of Clarendon
1609–1674

16 He [Hampden] had a head to contrive, a tongue to persuade, and a hand to execute any mischief.[4]
History of the Rebellion [1702–1704], vol. III, bk. VII, sec. 84

Sir John Suckling
1609–1642

17 Why so pale and wan, fond lover?
Prithee, why so pale?
Will, when looking well can't move her,
Looking ill prevail?
Aglaura [1638]. Song, st. 1

18 Quit, quit, for shame, this will not move,
This cannot take her.
If of herself she will not love,
Nothing can make her.
The devil take her! *Ib. st. 3*

19 But as when an authentic watch is shown,
Each man winds up and rectifies his own,
So in our very judgments.[5]
Ib. epilogue

20 High characters (cries one), and he would see
Things that ne'er were, nor are, nor ne'er will be.[6] *The Goblins [1639], epilogue*

21 Her feet beneath her petticoat
Like little mice, stole in and out,[7]
As if they feared the light;

[2] From *Sources of Japanese Tradition* [1960], edited by William Theodore de Bary.

[3] Lord Chief Justice of England.

[4] See *The Letters of Junius*, 391:4.

[5] See Pope, 332:15.

[6] See Pope, 333:2.

There's no such thing in Nature, and you'll draw / A faultless monster which the world ne'er saw. —John Sheffield, Duke of Buckingham and Normanby [1648–1721], *Essay on Poetry*

[7] See Herrick, 266:13.

But oh, she dances such a way!
No sun upon an Easter-day
Is half so fine a sight.
A Ballad upon a Wedding [1641], st. 8

1 Her lips were red, and one was thin,
Compared with that was next her chin,
Some bee had stung it newly.
Ib. st. 11

2 I prithee send me back my heart,
Since I cannot have thine;
For if from yours you will not part,
Why then shouldst thou have mine?
Fragmenta Aurea [1646]. Song, st. 1

3 'Tis not the meat, but 'tis the appetite
Makes eating a delight.
Ib. Of Thee, Kind Boy, st. 3

4 Out upon it, I have loved
Three whole days together;
And am like to love three more,
If it prove fair weather.
Ib. A Poem with the Answer, st. 1

5 'Tis expectation makes a blessing dear,
Heaven were not heaven, if we knew what it
were. *Ib. Against Fruition, st. 4*

William Cartwright
1611–1643

6 Love makes those young whom age doth chill,
And whom he finds young, keeps young still.
To Chloe [1651]

Robert Leighton
1611–1684

7 Deliver me, O Lord, from the errors of wise men, yea, and of good men. *Saying*

Isaac de Benserade
1612–1691

8 In bed we laugh, in bed we cry;
And, born in bed, in bed we die.
The near approach a bed may show
Of human bliss to human woe.
À Son Lit[1]

Anne Bradstreet
c. 1612–1672

9 Youth is the time of getting, middle age of improving, and old age of spending.
Meditations Divine and Moral [1664], 3

[1]Translated by Samuel Johnson.

10 Authority without wisdom is like a heavy axe without an edge, fitter to bruise than polish. *Ib. 12*

11 If we had no winter, the spring would not be so pleasant: if we did not sometimes taste of adversity, prosperity would not be so welcome. *Ib. 14*

12 If ever two were one, then surely we.
If ever man were loved by wife, then thee;
If ever wife was happy in a man,
Compare with me ye women if you can.
To My Dear and Loving Husband [1678]

Samuel Butler
1612–1680

13 When civil fury first grew high,
And men fell out they knew not why.
Hudibras, pt. I [1663], canto I, l. 1

14 And pulpit, drum ecclesiastic,[2]
Was beat with fist, instead of a stick.
Ib. l. 11

15 Beside, 'tis known he could speak Greek
As naturally as pigs squeak:[3]
That Latin was no more difficile
Than to a blackbird 'tis to whistle.
Ib. l. 51

16 He could distinguish and divide
A hair 'twixt south and southwest side,
On either which he would dispute,
Confute, change hands, and still confute.
Ib. l. 67

17 He'd run in debt by disputation,
And pay with ratiocination. *Ib. l. 77*

18 For rhetoric, he could not ope
His mouth, but out there flew a trope.
Ib. l. 81

19 For all a rhetorician's rules
Teach nothing but to name his tools.
Ib. l. 89

20 A Babylonish dialect
Which learned pedants much affect.
Ib. l. 93

21 For he by geometric scale,
Could take the size of pots of ale.
Ib. l. 121

[2]This is the first we hear of the "drum ecclesiastic" beating up for recruits in worldly warfare in our country. — Washington Irving, *Knickerbocker's History of New York* [1809], *bk. V, ch. 7*

[3]He Greek and Latin speaks with greater ease / Than hogs eat acorns, and tame pigeons peas. — Lionel Cranfield, Earl of Middlesex [1575–1645], *Panegyric on Tom Coriate*

1 And wisely tell what hour o' th' day
The clock doth strike, by algebra.
Ib. l. 125

2 Where entity and quiddity,
The ghosts of defunct bodies, fly.
Ib. l. 145

3 'Twas Presbyterian true blue.
Ib. l. 189

4 Such as do build their faith upon
The holy text of pike and gun.
Ib. l. 193

5 And prove their doctrine orthodox,
By apostolic blows and knocks.
Ib. l. 197

6 Compound for sins they are inclined to,
By damning those they have no mind to.
Ib. l. 213

7 The trenchant blade, Toledo trusty,
For want of fighting was grown rusty,
And ate into itself, for lack
Of somebody to hew and hack.
Ib. l. 357

8 For rhyme the rudder is of verses,
With which like ships they steer their courses.
Ib. l. 457

9 And force them, though it was in spite
Of Nature and their stars, to write.
Ib. l. 647

10 Great actions are not always true sons
Of great and mighty resolutions.
Ib. l. 885

11 I'll make the fur
Fly 'bout the ears of the old cur.
Ib. canto III, l. 277

12 These reasons made his mouth to water.
Ib. l. 379

13 I am not now in fortune's power:
He that is down can fall no lower.[1]
Ib. l. 871

14 Cheered up himself with ends of verse,
And sayings of philosophers.
Ib. l. 1011

15 Cleric before, and Lay behind;
A lawless linsey-woolsey brother,
Half of one order, half another.
Ib. l. 1226

16 Some have been beaten till they know
What wood a cudgel's of by th' blow;
Some kicked, until they can feel whether
A shoe be Spanish or neat's leather.
Ib. pt. II [1664], canto I, l. 221

[1]See Bunyan, 302:13.

17 For what is worth in anything
But so much money as 'twill bring?
Ib. l. 465

18 She that with poetry is won
Is but a desk to write upon. *Ib. l. 591*

19 Love is a boy by poets styled;
Then spare the rod, and spoil the child.[2]
Ib. l. 843

20 Oaths are but words, and words but wind.
Ib. canto II, l. 107

21 For truth is precious and divine—
Too rich a pearl for carnal swine.
Ib. l. 257

22 He that imposes an oath makes it,
Not he that for convenience takes it;
Then how can any man be said
To break an oath he never made?
Ib. l. 377

23 As the ancients
Say wisely, have a care o' th' main chance,[3]
And look before you ere you leap;[4]
For as you sow, ye are like to reap.[5]
Ib. l. 501

24 Doubtless the pleasure is as great
Of being cheated as to cheat.
Ib. canto III, l. 1

25 He made an instrument to know
If the moon shine at full or no.
Ib. l. 261

26 As men of inward light are wont
To turn their optics in upon 't.
Ib. pt. III [1678], canto I, l. 481

27 What makes all doctrines plain and clear?
About two hundred pounds a year.
And that which was proved true before,
Prove false again? Two hundred more.
Ib. l. 1277

28 Nick Machiavel had ne'er a trick,
Though he gave his name to our Old Nick.
Ib. l. 1313

29 True as the dial to the sun,[6]
Although it be not shined upon.
Ib. canto II, l. 175

30 He that complies against his will
Is of his own opinion still.
Ib. canto III, l. 547

[2]See *Proverbs, 13:24*, 23:34, and Menander, 91:3.
[3]See Lyly, 175:14.
[4]See Heywood, 158:21.
[5]See *Galatians 6:7*, 49:32.
[6]True as the needle to the pole, / Or as the dial to the sun.—BARTON BOOTH [1681–1733], *Song*

1 Neither have the hearts to stay,
Nor wit enough to run away.
Ib. l. 569

2 And poets by their sufferings grow,[1]
As if there were no more to do,
To make a poet excellent,
But only want and discontent.
Fragments

James Graham, Marquess of Montrose
1612–1650

3 He either fears his fate too much,
Or his deserts are small,
That puts it not unto the touch
To win or lose it all.
My Dear and Only Love, st. 2

4 I'll make thee glorious by my pen,
And famous by my sword.[2] *Ib. st. 5*

Richard Crashaw
c. 1613–1649

5 The conscious water saw its God, and blushed.[3]
Epigrammata Sacra [1634]. Aquae in Vinum Versae

6 Two went to pray? Oh, rather say
One went to brag, the other to pray.
Steps to the Temple [1648]. Two Went Up into the Temple to Pray[4]

7 Whoe'er she be,
That not impossible she
That shall command my heart and me.
Ib. Wishes to His Supposed Mistress, l. 1

8 Where'er she lie,
Locked up from mortal eye,
In shady leaves of destiny. *Ib. l. 4*

9 Life that dares send
A challenge to his end,
And when it comes, say, Welcome, friend!
Ib. l. 85

10 Sidnaeian showers
Of sweet discourse, whose powers
Can crown old Winter's head with flowers.
Ib. l. 88

11 I would be married, but I'd have no wife,
I would be married to a single life.
Ib. On Marriage

12 All is Caesar's, and what odds
So long as Caesar's self is God's?
Ib. Mark XII

13 All those fair and flagrant things.
The Flaming Heart upon the Book of Saint Teresa [1652], l. 34

14 Love's passives are his activ'st part.
The wounded is the wounding heart.
Ib. l. 73

15 O thou undaunted daughter of desires!
Ib. l. 93

16 By all the eagle in thee, all the dove.
Ib. l. 95

17 Poor world (said I) what wilt thou do
To entertain this starry stranger?
Is this the best thou canst bestow?
A cold, and not too cleanly, manger?
Contend, ye powers of heav'n and earth,
To fit a bed for this huge birth.
Hymn of the Nativity [1652], st. 6

18 Proud world, said I, cease your contest,
And let the mighty babe alone.
The phoenix builds the phoenix' nest.
Love's architecture is his own.
The babe whose birth embraves this morn,
Made his own bed ere he was born.
Ib. st. 7

19 Welcome, all wonders in one sight!
Eternity shut in a span.
Ib. Full Chorus

20 The modest front of this small floor,
Believe me, reader, can say more
Than many a braver marble can—
"Here lies a truly honest man!"
Epitaph upon Mr. Ashton

François, Duc de La Rochefoucauld
1613–1680

21 Our virtues are most frequently but vices in disguise.[5]
Reflections; or, Sentences and Moral Maxims.[6] *Epigraph*

[1] See Shelley, 467:15.

[2] I'll make thee famous by my pen, / And glorious by my sword.—SCOTT, *Legend of Montrose* [1819], *ch. 15*

[3] Nympha pudica Deum vidit, et erubuit.—Quoted by SAMUEL JOHNSON [1778]; from BOSWELL, *Life of Johnson* [1791], *vol. II, p. 218* (Everyman edition). A footnote states that this line has frequently been attributed to Dryden, but appeared in Crashaw's *Epigrammata Sacra* [1634].

The bashful stream hath seen its God and blushed.—AARON HILL [1685–1750]

The water hears thy faintest word, / And blushes into wine.—JOHN SAMUEL BEWLEY MONSELL [1811–1875], *Mysterious Is Thy Presence, Lord, st. 1*

[4] See *Luke 18:10*, 43:38.

[5] This epigraph, which is the key to the system of La Rochefoucauld, is found in another form as no. 179 of the *Maxims* of the first edition, 1665; it is omitted from the second and third, and reappears for the first time in the fourth edition at the head of the Reflections.—LOUIS AIMÉ MARTIN [1786–1847]

[6] The fifth edition [1678] is the standard one.

1 Self-love is the greatest of all flatterers.
Maxims, 2

2 We all have strength enough to endure the misfortunes of others.[1] *Ib. 19*

3 Philosophy triumphs easily over past evils and future evils; but present evils triumph over it.[2] *Ib. 22*

4 We need greater virtues to sustain good fortune than bad. *Ib. 25*

5 If we had no faults of our own, we would not take so much pleasure in noticing those of others. *Ib. 31*

6 Jealousy feeds upon suspicion, and it turns into fury or it ends as soon as we pass from suspicion to certainty. *Ib. 32*

7 Self-interest speaks all sorts of tongues, and plays all sorts of roles, even that of disinterestedness. *Ib. 39*

8 We are never so happy nor so unhappy as we imagine. *Ib. 49*

9 To succeed in the world, we do everything we can to appear successful. *Ib. 56*

10 There is no disguise which can for long conceal love where it exists or simulate it where it does not. *Ib. 70*

11 There are very few people who are not ashamed of having been in love when they no longer love each other. *Ib. 71*

12 True love is like ghosts, which everybody talks about and few have seen. *Ib. 76*

13 The love of justice in most men is simply the fear of suffering injustice. *Ib. 78*

14 Silence is the best tactic for him who distrusts himself. *Ib. 79*

15 It is more ignominious to mistrust our friends than to be deceived by them.
Ib. 84

16 Everyone complains of his memory, and no one complains of his judgment. *Ib. 89*

17 Old people like to give good advice, as solace for no longer being able to provide bad examples.[3] *Ib. 93*

18 A man who is ungrateful is sometimes less to blame for it than his benefactor.
Ib. 96

19 The mind is always the dupe of the heart.[4]
Ib. 102

[1] See Pope, 340:9.
[2] See Goldsmith, 369:22.
[3] See Pope, 340:12.
[4] The mind lives on the heart / Like any parasite.—EMILY DICKINSON, *The Mind Lives on the Heart* [c. 1876]

20 Nothing is given so profusely as advice.
Ib. 110

21 The true way to be deceived is to think oneself more clever than others.
Ib. 127

22 We would rather speak ill of ourselves than not talk about ourselves at all. *Ib. 138*

23 Usually we praise only to be praised.
Ib. 146

24 Our repentance is not so much regret for the ill we have done as fear of the ill that may happen to us in consequence. *Ib. 180*

25 Who lives without folly is not so wise as he thinks. *Ib. 209*

26 Most people judge men only by their success or their good fortune. *Ib. 212*

27 Hypocrisy is the homage that vice pays to virtue. *Ib. 218*

28 Too great haste in paying off an obligation is a kind of ingratitude. *Ib. 226*

29 There is great skill in knowing how to conceal one's skill. *Ib. 245*

30 The pleasure of love is in loving. We are happier in the passion we feel than in that we arouse.[5] *Ib. 259*

31 Absence diminishes mediocre passions and increases great ones, as the wind blows out candles and fans fire. *Ib. 276*

32 We always like those who admire us; we do not always like those whom we admire.
Ib. 294

33 The gratitude of most men is merely a secret desire to receive greater benefits.[6]
Ib. 298

34 We frequently forgive those who bore us, but cannot forgive those whom we bore.
Ib. 304

35 Lovers never get tired of each other, because they are always talking about themselves. *Ib. 312*

36 In jealousy there is more self-love than love. *Ib. 324*

37 We confess to little faults only to persuade ourselves that we have no great ones.
Ib. 327

38 We pardon to the extent that we love.
Ib. 330

[5] See Shelley, 467:5.
[6] A lively sense of future favors.—SIR ROBERT WALPOLE, *definition of the gratitude of place-expectants;* from WILLIAM HAZLITT, *English Comic Writers* [1819], *Wit and Humor*

1 We rarely find that people have good sense unless they agree with us.[1] *Ib. 347*

2 Jealousy is always born together with love, but it does not always die when love dies. *Ib. 361*

3 Mediocre minds usually dismiss anything which reaches beyond their own understanding.[2] *Ib. 375*

4 The greatest fault of a penetrating wit is to go beyond the mark. *Ib. 377*

5 We may give advice, but we do not inspire conduct. *Ib. 378*

6 The veracity which increases with old age is not far from folly. *Ib. 416*

7 Few people know how to be old. *Ib. 423*

8 Nothing prevents our being natural so much as the desire to appear so. *Ib. 431*

9 In their first passion women love their lovers, in the others they love love.[3] *Ib. 471*

10 Quarrels would not last long if the fault were only on one side. *Ib. 496*

11 In the misfortune of our best friends we often find something that is not displeasing.[4] *Ib. 583*

Jeremy Taylor
1613–1667

12 Too quick a sense of constant infelicity.
Holy Dying [1650–1651]

13 Every schoolboy knows it.
On the Real Presence, V

14 The union of hands and hearts.
Sermons [1653], The Marriage Ring, pt. I

15 No man ever repented that he arose from the table sober, healthful, and with his wits about him. *Ib.*

Thomas Ady
fl. 1655

16 Matthew, Mark, Luke, and John,
The bed be blest that I lie on.
Four angels to my bed,
Four angels round my head,[5]
One to watch, and one to pray,
And two to bear my soul away.
A Candle in the Dark [1655]

Richard Baxter
1615–1691

17 I preached as never sure to preach again,
And as a dying man to dying men.
Poetical Fragments [1681]. Love Breathing Thanks and Praise

18 In necessary things, unity; in doubtful things, liberty; in all things, charity.[6]
Motto

Sir John Denham
1615–1669

19 Oh, could I flow like thee,[7] and make thy stream
My great example, as it is my theme!
Though deep yet clear, though gentle yet not dull;
Strong without rage, without o'erflowing full.
Cooper's Hill [1642], l. 189

Sir Roger L'Estrange
1616–1704

20 Though this may be play to you, 'tis death to us.[8]
Fables [1692]. Fable 398, Boys and Frogs

Roger de Bussy-Rabutin
1618–1693

21 God is usually on the side of the big squadrons and against the small ones.[9]
Letter to the Comte de Limoges [October 18, 1677]

[1] "That was excellently observed," say I when I read a passage in another where his opinion agrees with mine. When we differ, then I pronounce him to be mistaken.
— SWIFT [1667–1745], *Thoughts on Various Subjects*

[2] See Schopenhauer, 463:10.

[3] See Byron, 460:24.

[4] In all distresses of our friends / We first consult our private ends; / While Nature, kindly bent to ease us, / Points out some circumstance to please us. — SWIFT [1667–1745], *A Paraphrase of Rochefoucauld's Maxim*

Maxim 583 is one of the "maximes supprimées" discarded before the 1678 edition.

[5] Usual version: Bless the bed that I lie on. / Four corners to my bed, / Four angels round my head.

[6] In necessariis, unitas; in dubiis libertas; in omniis caritas.

[7] The river Thames.

[8] See Bion, 92:9.

[9] It is said that God is always for the big battalions.
— VOLTAIRE, *letter to M. le Riche, February 6, 1770*

Providence is always on the side of the last reserve.
— *Attributed to* NAPOLEON

See Tacitus, 123:1; Boileau, 311:15; Frederick the Great, 358:4; and Gibbon, 383:13.

Abraham Cowley
1618–1667

1 What shall I do to be forever known,
And make the age to come my own?
The Motto

2 This only grant me, that my means may lie
Too low for envy, for contempt too high.
The Vote [1636]

3 Well then; I now do plainly see
This busy world and I shall ne'er agree;
The very honey of all earthly joy
Does of all meats the soonest cloy,
And they (methinks) deserve my pity,
Who for it can endure the stings,
The crowd, and buzz and murmurings,
Of this great hive, the city.
The Wish [1647]

4 Ah yet, ere I descend to the grave
May I a small house and large garden have;
And a few friends, and many books, both true,
Both wise, and both delightful too! *Ib.*

5 A mistress moderately fair. *Ib.*

6 The world's a scene of changes, and to be
Constant, in Nature were inconstancy.
Inconstancy [1647]

7 The thirsty earth soaks up the rain,
And drinks, and gapes for drink again.
The plants suck in the earth, and are
With constant drinking fresh and fair.
Anacreon [1656], II, Drinking

8 Fill all the glasses there, for why
Should every creature drink but I,
Why, man of morals, tell me why? *Ib.*

9 A mighty pain to love it is,
And 'tis a pain that pain to miss;
But of all pains, the greatest pain
It is to love, but love in vain.
Ib. VII, Gold

10 His time is forever, everywhere his place.
Friendship in Absence

11 Nothing is there to come, and nothing past,
But an eternal now does always last.[1]
Davideis [1656], bk. I, l. 25

12 Life is an incurable disease.[2]
To Dr. Scarborough [1656]

13 Ye fields of Cambridge, our dear Cambridge, say,
Have ye not seen us walking every day?
Was there a tree about which did not know
The love betwixt us two?
On the Death of Mr. William Harvey [1657][3]

14 God the first garden made, and the first city.[4]
The Garden [1664], essay 5

15 Hence ye profane! I hate ye all,
Both the great vulgar and the small.[5]
Horace, bk. III, ode 1

16 Charmed with the foolish whistling of a name.[6] *Virgil, Georgics, bk. II, l. 72*

17 Words that weep and tears that speak.[7]
The Prophet

18 Poet and Saint! to thee alone are given
The two most sacred names of earth and Heaven.
On the Death of Mr. Crashaw[8] *[1668]*

19 His faith, perhaps, in some nice tenets might
Be wrong; his life, I'm sure, was in the right.[9]
Ib.

Johann Franck
1618–1677

20 Deck thyself, my soul, with gladness.[10]
Hymn [1649]

Richard Lovelace
1618–1658

21 Oh, could you view the melody
Of every grace
And music of her face,[11]
You'd drop a tear;
Seeing more harmony
In her bright eye
Than now you hear.
Lucasta [1649]. Orpheus to Beasts

22 Tell me not, sweet, I am unkind,
That from the nunnery
Of thy chaste breast and quiet mind,
To war and arms I fly.
Ib. To Lucasta: Going to the Wars, st. 1

[1] One of our poets (which is it?) speaks of an everlasting now.—SOUTHEY, *The Doctor* [1834–1847], *ch.* 25

[2] See Pope, 338:11, and Arnold, 586:1.

[3] See William Harvey, 260.

[4] See *Genesis* 2:8, 6:18; Bacon, 181:10; Shakespeare, 185:26 and 224:5; and Cowper, 376:17.

[5] Odi profanum vulgus.

[6] See Pope, 337:15.

[7] Thoughts that breathe, and words that burn.—THOMAS GRAY, *Progress of Poesy* [1754], *III, 3, 4*

[8] See Crashaw, 292.

[9] See Pope, 337:9.

[10] Translated by CATHERINE WINKWORTH [1863].

[11] The mind, the music breathing from her face.—BYRON, *Bride of Abydos* [1813], *canto I, st. 6*

1 I could not love thee, dear, so much,
Loved I not honor more. *Ib. st. 3*

2 When I lie tangled in her hair,
And fettered to her eye,
The gods that wanton in the air
Know no such liberty.
Ib. To Althea: From Prison, st. 1

3 When flowing cups pass swiftly round
With no allaying Thames.[1] *Ib. st. 2*

4 Stone walls do not a prison make,[2]
Nor iron bars a cage;
Minds innocent and quiet take
That for an hermitage;
If I have freedom in my love,
And in my soul am free,
Angels alone that soar above
Enjoy such liberty.[3] *Ib. st. 4*

5 If to be absent were to be
Away from thee;
Or that when I am gone,
You and I were alone;
Then, my Lucasta, might I crave
Pity from blust'ring wind, or swallowing
wave.
Ib. To Lucasta: Going Beyond the Seas, st. 1

Ninon de L'Enclos
1620–1705

6 Old age is woman's hell.[4]
Attributed

Jean de La Fontaine
1621–1695

7 We believe no evil till the evil's done.
Fables, bk. I [1668], fable 8

8 We heed no instincts but our own.
Ib.

9 The opinion of the strongest is always the best.[5] *Ib. 10*

10 Better to suffer than to die: that is mankind's motto. *Ib. 16*

11 By the work one knows the workman.
Ib. 21

12 I bend but do not break. *Ib. 22*

[1] See Shakespeare, 242:12.
[2] Stone walls a prisoner make, but not a slave. — WORDSWORTH [1770–1850], *Humanity*
[3] But though my wing is closely bound, / My heart's at liberty; / My prison walls cannot control / The flight, the freedom of the soul. — JEANNE GUYON [1648–1717], *A Prisoner's Song, Castle of Vincennes, France, st. 4*
[4] La vieillesse est l'enfer des femmes.
[5] See Krylov, 420:4.

13 It is a double pleasure to deceive the deceiver. *Ib. II [1668], fable 15*

14 It is impossible to please all the world and one's father. *Ib. III [1668], fable 1*

15 In everything one must consider the end.[6]
Ib. 5

16 Beware, as long as you live, of judging people by appearances.
Ib. VI [1668], fable 5

17 On the wings of Time grief flies away.[7]
Ib. 21

18 The sign brings customers.
Ib. VII [1678–1679], fable 15

19 People who make no noise are dangerous.
Ib. VIII [1678–1679], fable 23

20 He knows the universe, and himself he does not know. *Ib. 26*

21 A hungry stomach cannot hear.[8]
Ib. IX [1678–1679], fable 17

Andrew Marvell
1621–1678

22 The inglorious arts of peace.
Upon Cromwell's Return from Ireland [1650]

23 He[9] nothing common did or mean
Upon that memorable scene,
But with his keener eye
The axe's edge did try. *Ib.*

24 But bowed his comely head
Down as upon a bed. *Ib.*

25 So much one man can do,
That does both act and know. *Ib.*

26 Had we but world enough, and time,
This coyness, lady, were no crime.
To His Coy Mistress [1650–1652]

27 I would
Love you ten years before the Flood,
And you should, if you please, refuse
Till the conversion of the Jews.
My vegetable love should grow
Vaster than empires, and more slow.
Ib.

28 But at my back I always hear
Time's wingèd chariot hurrying near;
And yonder all before us lie
Deserts of vast eternity. *Ib.*

[6] See *Ecclesiasticus* 7:36, 35:12.
[7] See Sophocles, 74:5, and Terence, 96:9.
[8] Ventre affamé n'a point d'oreilles.
See Cato the Elder, 95:9, and Stevenson, 851:11.
[9] King Charles I.

1 Then worms shall try
That long preserved virginity,
And your quaint honor turn to dust,
And into ashes all my lust.
The grave's a fine and private place,
But none, I think, do there embrace.
Ib.

2 Though we cannot make our sun Stand still, yet we will make him run. *Ib.*

3 Annihilating all that's made
To a green thought in a green shade.[1]
The Garden [1650–1652]

4 Casting the body's vest aside,
My soul into the boughs does glide.
Ib.

5 The world in all doth but two nations bear —
The good, the bad; and these mixed everywhere. *The Loyal Scot [1650–1652]*

6 My love is of a birth as rare
As 'tis for object strange and high;
It was begotten by despair
Upon impossibility.
The Definition of Love [1650–1652], st. 1

7 As lines, so loves oblique, may well
Themselves in every angle greet;
But ours, so truly parallel,
Though infinite, can never meet.
Ib. st. 7

8 Where the remote Bermudas ride,
In th' ocean's bosom unespied.
Bermudas [1657]

9 Orange bright,
Like golden lamps in a green light.
Ib.

10 And all the way, to guide their chime,
With falling oars they kept the time.[2]
Ib.

Molière
[Jean Baptiste Poquelin]
1622–1673

11 To pull the chestnuts out of the fire with the cat's paw.[3]
L'Étourdi [1655], act III, sc. vi

12 We die only once, and for such a long time!
Le Dépit Amoureux [1656], act V, sc. iii

[1] The same phrase is in VIRGIL, *Eclogues, IX, 20.*
[2] See Thomas Moore, 446:5.
[3] Tirer les marrons du feu avec la patte du chat. — *Proverb in many languages*

13 I always make the first verse well, but I have trouble making the others.
Les Précieuses Ridicules [1659], act I, sc. xi

14 The world, dear Agnes, is a strange affair.
L'École des Femmes [1662], act II, sc. vi

15 There is no rampart that will hold out against malice.
Tartuffe [1664], act I, sc. i

16 Those whose conduct gives room for talk are always the first to attack their neighbors.
Ib.

17 You are a fool in four letters, my son.[4]
Ib.

18 She is laughing up her sleeve at you.
Ib. vi

19 A woman always has her revenge ready.
Ib. II, ii

20 Cover that bosom that I must not see: souls are wounded by such things.[5]
Ib. III, ii

21 Although I am a pious man, I am not the less a man. *Ib. III, iii*

22 To create a public scandal is what's wicked; to sin in private is not a sin. *Ib. IV, v*

23 I saw him, I say, saw him with my own eyes. *Ib. V, iii*

24 We have changed all that.[6]
Le Médecin Malgré Lui [1666], act II, sc. vi

25 On some preference esteem is based; to esteem everything is to esteem nothing.
Le Misanthrope [1666], act I, sc. i

26 He's a wonderful talker, who has the art of telling you nothing in a great harangue.
Ib. II, v

27 He makes his cook his merit, and the world visits his dinners and not him. *Ib.*

28 You see him laboring to produce *bons mots.*
Ib.

29 The more we love our friends, the less we flatter them; it is by excusing nothing that pure love shows itself. *Ib.*

30 Doubts are more cruel than the worst of truths. *Ib. III, vii*

31 Anyone may be an honorable man, and yet write verse badly. *Ib. IV, i*

[4] Vous êtes un sot en trois lettres, mon fils.
[5] Couvrez ce sein que je ne saurais voir: / Par de pareils objets les âmes sont blessées.
[6] Nous avons changé tout cela.

1 If everyone were clothed with integrity, if every heart were just, frank, kindly, the other virtues would be well-nigh useless, since their chief purpose is to make us bear with patience the injustice of our fellows.
Ib. V, i

2 It is a wonderful seasoning of all enjoyments to think of those we love. *Ib. iv*

3 I prefer an accommodating vice to an obstinate virtue.
Amphitryon [1666], act I, sc. iv

4 One must eat to live, and not live to eat.[1]
Ib. III, i

5 The true Amphitryon is the Amphitryon who gives dinners.[2] *Ib. v*

6 My Lord Jupiter knows how to sugarcoat the pill. *Ib. x*

7 You've asked for it, Georges Dandin, you've asked for it.[3]
Georges Dandin [1668], act I, sc. ix

8 Good Heavens! For more than forty years I have been speaking prose without knowing it.
Le Bourgeois Gentilhomme [1670], act II, sc. iv

9 All that is not prose is verse; and all that is not verse is prose. *Ib.*

10 My fair one, let us swear an eternal friendship.[4] *Ib. IV, i*

11 I will maintain it before the whole world.
Ib. IV, v

12 What the devil was he doing in that galley?[5]
Les Fourberies de Scapin [1671], act II, sc. xi

[1]See Socrates, 79:6, and Franklin, 347:1.

[2]Le véritable Amphitryon est l'Amphitryon où l'on dine.

See Dryden, 306:5.

[3]Vous l'avez voulu, Georges Dandin, vous l'avez voulu.

[4]Madam, I have been looking for a person who disliked gravy all my life; let us swear eternal friendship.—SYDNEY SMITH, *Lady Holland's Memoir,* [1855], *vol. I, ch. 9*

[5]Que diable allait-il faire dans cette galère?

Que diable aller faire aussi dans la galère d'un Turc? d'un Turc! [What the deuce did he want on board a Turk's galley? A Turk!] —CYRANO DE BERGERAC, *Le Pédant Joué* [1654], *act II, sc. iv*

The saying of Molière came into his head: "But what the devil was he doing in that galley?" and he laughed at himself.—TOLSTOI, *War and Peace* [1865–1872], *pt. IV, ch. 6*

Often misquoted "in that gallery," as in DICKENS, *A Tale of Two Cities* [1859], *bk. I, ch. 5:* What the devil do you do in that gallery there!

13 Grammar, which knows how to control even kings.[6]
Les Femmes Savantes [1672], act II, sc. vi

14 It is seasoned throughout with Attic salt.
Ib. III, ii

15 A learned fool is more foolish than an ignorant one. *Ib. IV, iii*

16 Ah, there are no longer any children!
Le Malade Imaginaire [1673], act II, sc. xi

17 Nearly all men die of their remedies, and not of their illnesses. *Ib. III, iii*

Richard Rumbold
c. 1622–1685

18 I never could believe that Providence had sent a few men into the world, ready booted and spurred to ride, and millions ready saddled and bridled to be ridden.
On the scaffold [1685]. From MACAULAY, History of England, ch. 1

Algernon Sidney
1622–1683

19 This hand, unfriendly to tyrants,
Seeks with the sword placid repose under liberty.[7]
Life and Memoirs of Algernon Sidney

20 It is not necessary to light a candle to the sun.[8]
Discourses on Government [1698], sec. 23

Henry Vaughan
1622–1695

21 Dear Night! this world's defeat;
The stop to busy fools; care's check and curb;
The day of spirits; my soul's calm retreat
Which none disturb!
Christ's progress, and His prayer-time;
The hours to which high Heaven doth chime.
Silex Scintillans [1655]. The Night, l. 25

[6]Sigismund [1361–1437], Holy Roman emperor, at the Council of Constance [1414], said to a prelate who had objected to His Majesty's grammar: Ego sum rex Romanus, et supra grammaticam [I am the Roman king, and am above grammar].

[7]Manus haec, inimica tyrannis, / Ense petit placidam sub libertate quietem.

The second line is the motto of the Commonwealth of Massachusetts: By the sword we seek peace, but peace only under liberty.

[8]See Robert Burton, 259:19.

1 There is in God, some say,
A deep but dazzling darkness.
Ib. l. 49

2 Happy those early days, when I
Shined in my angel-infancy![1]
Before I understood this place
Appointed for my second race.
Ib. The Retreat, l. 1

3 But felt through all this fleshly dress
Bright shoots of everlastingness.
Ib. l. 19

4 Some men a forward motion love,
But I by backward steps would move.
Ib. l. 29

5 I cannot reach it, and my striving eye
Dazzles at it, as at eternity.
Ib. Childhood

6 I saw Eternity the other night
Like a great ring of pure and endless light.
All calm, as it was bright;
And round beneath it, Time in hours, days, years,
Driv'n by the spheres
Like a vast shadow moved; in which the world
And all her train were hurled.
Ib. The World

7 They are all gone into the world of light!
And I alone sit lingering here;
Their very memory is fair and bright,
And my sad thoughts doth clear.
Ib. They Are All Gone, st. 1

8 I see them walking in an air of glory
Whose light doth trample on my days,
My days, which are at best but dull and hoary,
Mere glimmering and decays. *Ib. st. 3*

9 Dear, beauteous death, the jewel of the just!
Shining nowhere but in the dark;
What mysteries do lie beyond thy dust,
Could man outlook that mark!
Ib. st. 5

10 My soul, there is a country
Far beyond the stars
Where stands a wingèd sentry
All skillful in the wars:
There, above noise and danger,
Sweet Peace is crowned with smiles,
And One born in a manger
Commands the beauteous files.
Ib. Peace, st. 1

[1] See Traherne, 311:22; Wordsworth, 426:14; and Lowell, 567:11.

Yamaga Soko
1622–1685

11 The business of the samurai consists in reflecting on his own station in life, in discharging loyal service to his master if he has one, in deepening his fidelity in associations with friends, and, with due consideration of his own position, in devoting himself to duty above all.[2] *The Way of the Samurai*

Blaise Pascal
1623–1662

12 Things are always at their best in their beginning.
Lettres Provinciales [1656–1657], no. 4

13 I have made this letter longer than usual, because I lack the time to make it short.[3]
Ib. 16

14 True eloquence takes no heed of eloquence, true morality takes no heed of morality.
Pensées [1670], no. 4

15 Do you wish people to think well of you? Don't speak well of yourself. *Ib. 44*

16 Physical science will not console me for the ignorance of morality in the time of affliction.
Ib. 67

17 What is man in nature? Nothing in relation to the infinite, everything in relation to nothing, a mean between nothing and everything.[4] *Ib. 72*

18 I lay it down as a fact that if all men knew what others say of them, there would not be four friends in the world. *Ib. 101*

19 The state of man: inconstancy, boredom, anxiety.[5] *Ib. 127*

20 I have discovered that all human evil comes from this, man's being unable to sit still in a room.[6] *Ib. 139*

[2] From *Sources of Japanese Tradition* [1960], edited by William Theodore de Bary.

[3] Je n'ai fait celle-ci plus longue parceque je n'ai pas eu le loisir de la faire plus courte.

Not that the story need be long, but it will take a long while to make it short. — Thoreau, *Letter to Mr. B* [November 16, 1857]

[4] Qu'est-ce que l'homme dans la nature? Un néant a l'égard de l'infini, un tout a l'égard du néant, un milieu entre rien et tout.

See Disraeli, 502:4, and Darwin, 515:7.

[5] Condition de l'homme: inconstance, ennui, inquiétude.

See Bossuet, 301:10.

[6] See Bagehot, 597:4.

1 Cleopatra's nose, had it been shorter, the whole face of the world would have been changed. *Ib. 162*

2 The eternal silence of these infinite spaces terrifies me.[1] *Ib. 206*

3 We shall die alone.[2] *Ib. 211*

4 The heart has its reasons which reason knows nothing of.[3] *Ib. 277*

5 We know the truth, not only by the reason, but by the heart. *Ib. 282*

6 Justice without strength is helpless, strength without justice is tyrannical. . . . Unable to make what is just strong, we have made what is strong just. *Ib. 298*

7 Man is but a reed, the weakest in nature, but he is a thinking reed.[4] *Ib. 347*

8 Man is neither angel nor beast; and the misfortune is that he who would act the angel acts the beast.[5] *Ib. 358*

9 Evil is easy, and has infinite forms. *Ib. 408*

10 To ridicule philosophy is really to philosophize.[6] *Ib. 430*

11 What a chimera then is man! What a novelty! What a monster, what a chaos, what a contradiction, what a prodigy! Judge of all things, feeble earthworm, depository of truth, a sink of uncertainty and error, the glory and the shame of the universe.[7] *Ib. 434*

12 Self is hateful.[8] *Ib. 455*

13 Men blaspheme what they do not know. *Ib. 556*

14 Men never do evil so completely and cheerfully as when they do it from religious conviction. *Ib. 894*

15 "The God of Abraham, the God of Isaac, the God of Jacob," not of philosophers and scholars.

Writing found in Pascal's effects after his death

[1] Le silence eternel de ces espaces infinis m'effraie.
[2] On mourra seul.
[3] Le coeur a ses raisons que la raison ne connaît point.
[4] L'homme n'est qu'un roseau, le plus faible de la nature, mais c'est un roseau pensant.
[5] L'homme n'est ni ange ni bête; et le malheur veut que qui veut faire l'ange fait la bête.
[6] Se moquer de la philosophie, c'est vraiment philosopher.
[7] See Pope, 337:2.
[8] Le moi est haïssable.

William Walker
1623–1684

16 Learn to read slow: all other graces
Will follow in their proper places.[9]

The Art of Reading

Angelus Silesius [Johannes Scheffler]
1624–1677

17 God lives not without me.
I know that without me God cannot live at all;
Were I to go, he also to his death must fall.

The Cherubic Wanderer [1657–1675]

18 I am like God, and God like me.
I am as large as God, he is as small as I:
He cannot above me, nor I beneath him be. *Ib.*

19 Everyone to his own.
The bird is in the sky, the stone rests on the land,
In water lives the fish, my spirit in God's hand. *Ib.*

George Fox[10]
1624–1691

20 The Lord showed me, so that I did see clearly, that he did not dwell in these temples which men had commanded and set up, but in people's hearts . . . his people were his temple, and he dwelt in them.[11]

Journal [1694]

21 When the Lord sent me forth into the world, He forbade me to put off my hat to any, high or low. *Ib.*

22 Justice Bennet of Derby, was the first that called us Quakers, because I bid them tremble at the word of the Lord. This was in the year 1650. *Ib.*

23 He [Oliver Cromwell] said: "I see there is a people risen, that I cannot win either with gifts, honors, offices or places; but all other sects and people I can." *Ib.*

[9] Take time enough; all other graces / Will soon fill up their proper places.—JOHN BYROM [1692–1763], *Advice to Preach Slow*
[10] Founder of the Society of Friends (Quakers).
[11] See *I Corinthians 3:17*, 48:6.

Thomas Sydenham
1624–1689

1 Fever itself is Nature's instrument.
Quoted in Bulletin of the New York Academy of Medicine, vol. IV [1928], p. 922

2 Gout, unlike any other disease, kills more rich men than poor, more wise men than simple. Great kings, emperors, generals, admirals and philosophers have all died of gout.
Ib. 993

3 A man is as old as his arteries. *Ib.*

John Aubrey
1626–1697

4 He [Hobbes] had read much, but his contemplation was much more than his reading. He was wont to say that if he had read as much as other men, he should have known no more than other men.
Brief Lives [ed. 1898], I, 349

5 He [Milton] was so fair that they called him *the lady of* Christ's College. *Ib.*

6 Mr. William Shakespeare was born at Stratford upon Avon in the county of Warwick. His father was a butcher, and I have been told heretofore by some of the neighbors, that when he was a boy he exercised his father's trade, but when he killed a calf he would do it in a high style and make a speech.

Ben Jonson and he did gather humors of men daily wherever they came.
Ib. II, 225

Marie de Rabutin-Chantal, Marquise de Sévigné
1626–1696

7 True friendship is never serene.
Lettres. À Madame de Grignan [September 10, 1671]

8 Racine will go out of style like coffee.
Attributed

Jacques Bénigne Bossuet
1627–1704

9 The greatest weakness of all weaknesses is to fear too much to appear weak.
Politique Tirée de l'Écriture Sainte

10 The inexorable boredom that is at the core of life.[1]
From M. A. Couturier, Se Garder Libre

[1] See Pascal, 299:19.

Robert Boyle
1627–1691

11 I am not ambitious to appear a man of letters: I could be content the world should think I had scarce looked upon any other book than that of nature.
The Philosophical Works of Robert Boyle [1738], vol. I, preliminary discourse

John Ray
1627–1705

12 In a calm sea every man is a pilot.
English Proverbs [1670]

13 If wishes were horses, beggars might ride.
Ib.

14 Money begets money. *Ib.*

15 Blood is thicker than water. *Ib.*

16 Misery loves company.[2] *Ib.*

17 To go like a cat upon a hot bakestone.[3]
Ib.

John Bunyan
1628–1688

18 Some said, "John, print it"; others said, "Not so."
Some said, "It might do good"; others said, "No."
The Pilgrim's Progress [1678]. Apology for His Book

19 As I walked through the wilderness of this world. *Ib. pt. I*

20 I saw a man clothed with rags . . . a book in his hand, and a great burden upon his back. *Ib.*

21 The name of the one was Obstinate and the name of the other was Pliable. *Ib.*

22 The name of the slough was Despond.
Ib.

23 Every fat [vat] must stand upon his bottom.[4] *Ib.*

24 The gentleman's name was Mr. Worldly-Wise-Man. *Ib.*

[2] See Publilius Syrus, 112:13.
[3] *Cat on a Hot Tin Roof*—TENNESSEE WILLIAMS, *title of play* [1955]
[4] See Montaigne, 166:9.
Every tub must stand upon its bottom.—CHARLES MACKLIN, *The Man of the World* [1781], *act I, sc. ii*

1 A very stately palace before him, the name of which was Beautiful. *Ib.*

2 The valley of Humiliation. *Ib.*

3 A foul Fiend coming over the field to meet him; his name is Apollyon. *Ib.*

4 I will talk of things heavenly, or things earthly; things moral, or things evangelical; things sacred, or things profane; things past, or things to come; things foreign, or things at home; things more essential, or things circumstantial. *Ib.*

5 It beareth the name of Vanity Fair, because the town where 'tis kept is lighter than vanity. *Ib.*

6 Hanging is too good for him, said Mr. Cruelty. *Ib.*

7 My great-grandfather was but a waterman, looking one way, and rowing another.[1] *Ib.*

8 A castle called Doubting Castle, the owner whereof was Giant Despair. *Ib.*

9 They came to the Delectable Mountains. *Ib.*

10 A great horror and darkness fell upon Christian. *Ib.*

11 So I awoke, and behold it was a dream. *Ib.*

12 A man that could look no way but downwards with a muckrake in his hand.[2] *Ib. pt. II*

13 He that is down, needs fear no fall,
He that is low, no pride.[3]
Ib. Shepherd Boy's Song

14 Who would true valor see,
Let him come hither;
One here will constant be,
Come wind, come weather.[4]
There's no discouragement
Shall make him once relent
His first avowed intent
To be a pilgrim. *Ib.*

15 My sword I give to him that shall succeed me in my pilgrimage, and my courage and skill to him that can get it. My marks and scars I carry with me, to be a witness for me, that I have fought His battles who now will be my rewarder. *Ib.*

[1] See Plutarch, 120:18.
[2] See Roosevelt, 687:11.
[3] See Butler, 291:13.
[4] He who would valiant be / 'Gainst all disaster, / Let him in constancy / Follow the Master. —*Alternate version, as a hymn* [1906]

16 So he passed over, and all the trumpets sounded for him on the other side. *Ib.*

17 The captain of all these men of death that came against him to take him away, was the Consumption, for it was that that brought him down to the grave.
The Life and Death of Mr. Badman [1680]

Sir William Temple
1628–1699

18 Books, like proverbs, receive their chief value from the stamp and esteem of ages through which they have passed.
Miscellanea, pt. II [1690]. Ancient and Modern Learning

19 When all is done, human life is, at the greatest and the best, but like a froward child, that must be played with and humored a little to keep it quiet till it falls asleep, and then the care is over. *Ib. Of Poetry*

George Villiers, Duke of Buckingham
1628–1687

20 Ay, now the plot thickens very much upon us.
The Rehearsal [written 1663, performed 1671], act III, sc. ii

Charles II
1630–1685

21 This is very true: for my words are my own, and my actions are my ministers'.
Reply to Lord Rochester[5]

22 Let not poor Nelly starve.
On his deathbed. From Gilbert Burnet, *The History of My Own Times [1724–1734], vol. I, bk. 2, ch. 17*

23 He had been, he said, an unconscionable time dying; he hoped that they would excuse it.
From Macaulay, *History of England [1849], vol. I, ch. 4*

Walter Pope
c. 1630–1714

24 May I govern my passions with absolute sway,
And grow wiser and better, as strength wears away,

[5] See Rochester, 315:14.

Without gout or stone, by a gentle decay.
The Old Man's Wish [1685]

John Tillotson
1630–1694

1 If God were not a necessary Being of Himself, He might almost seem to be made for the use and benefit of men.[1] *Sermon*

2 They who are in highest places, and have the most power, have the least liberty, because they are most observed.
Reflections

Richard Cumberland
1631–1718

3 It is better to wear out than to rust out.
From BISHOP GEORGE HORNE *[1730–1792], Sermon on the Duty of Contending for the Truth*

John Dryden
1631–1700

4 By viewing Nature, Nature's handmaid Art,
Makes mighty things from small beginnings grow.[2]
Annus Mirabilis [1667], st. 155

5 He [Shakespeare] was the man who of all modern, and perhaps ancient poets, had the largest and most comprehensive soul.
Essay of Dramatic Poesy [1668]

6 He was naturally learnèd; he needed not the spectacles of books to read Nature; he looked inwards, and found her there.
Ib.

7 Pains of love be sweeter far
Than all other pleasures are.
Tyrannic Love [1669], act IV, sc. i

8 I am as free as Nature first made man,
Ere the base laws of servitude began,
When wild in woods the noble savage ran.
The Conquest of Granada [1669–1670], pt. I, act I, sc. i

9 Death in itself is nothing; but we fear
To be we know not what, we know not where.
Aureng-Zebe [1676], act IV, sc. i

10 When I consider life, 'tis all a cheat;
Yet, fooled with hope, men favor the deceit;
Trust on, and think tomorrow will repay.
Tomorrow's falser than the former day.
Ib.

[1]See Ovid, 113:10, and Voltaire, 344:2.
[2]See William Bradford, 265:13.

11 None would live past years again,
Yet all hope pleasure in what yet remain;
And from the dregs of life think to receive
What the first sprightly running could not give. *Ib.*

12 The wretched have no friends.
All for Love [1678], act III, sc. i

13 Your Cleopatra; Dolabella's Cleopatra; every man's Cleopatra. *Ib. IV, i*

14 With how much ease believe we what we wish![3]
Whatever is, is in its causes just.[4]
Oedipus [1679] (with NATHANIEL LEE*), act III, sc. i*

15 His hair just grizzled,
As in a green old age.[5] *Ib.*

16 Of no distemper, of no blast he died,
But fell like autumn fruit that mellowed long—
Even wondered at, because he dropped no sooner.
Fate seemed to wind him up for fourscore years,
Yet freshly ran he on ten winters more;
Till like a clock worn out with eating time,
The wheels of weary life at last stood still.
Ib. IV, i

17 In pious times, ere priestcraft did begin,
Before polygamy was made a sin.
Absalom and Achitophel, pt. I [1680], l. 1

18 Whate'er he did was done with so much ease,
In him alone, 'twas natural to please.
Ib. l. 27

19 Plots, true or false, are necessary things,
To raise up commonwealths and ruin kings.
Ib. l. 83

20 Of these the false Achitophel was first,
A name to all succeeding ages cursed.
For close designs and crooked counsels fit,
Sagacious, bold, and turbulent of wit,
Restless, unfixed in principles and place,
In power unpleased, impatient of disgrace;
A fiery soul, which working out its way,
Fretted the pygmy-body to decay:[6]
And o'er-informed the tenement of clay.
A daring pilot in extremity;
Pleased with the danger, when the waves went high

[3]Men freely believe that which they desire.—CAESAR [c. 102–44 B.C.], *De Bello Gallico, bk. III, sec. 18*
[4]See Marcus Aurelius, 124:16, and Pope, 337:1.
[5]A green old age, unconscious of decays.—POPE, *Translation of the Iliad* [1715], *bk. XXIII, l. 929*
[6]See Thomas Fuller, 276:15.

He sought the storms; but for a calm unfit,
Would steer too nigh the sands to boast his wit.
Great wits are sure to madness near allied,
And thin partitions do their bounds divide.[1]
Ib. l. 150

1 Bankrupt of life, yet prodigal of ease.
Ib. l. 168

2 And all to leave what with his toil he won
To that unfeathered two-legged thing,[2] a son.
Ib. l. 169

3 In friendship false, implacable in hate,
Resolved to ruin or to rule the state.
Ib. l. 173

4 And Heaven had wanted one immortal song.
Ib. l. 197

5 The people's prayer, the glad diviner's theme,
The young men's vision, and the old men's dream![3] *Ib. l. 238*

6 His courage foes, his friends his truth proclaim. *Ib. l. 357*

7 All empire is no more than power in trust.
Ib. l. 411

8 Better one suffer, than a nation grieve.
Ib. l. 416

9 Who think too little, and who talk too much.[4] *Ib. l. 534*

10 A man so various that he seemed to be
Not one, but all mankind's epitome:
Stiff in opinions, always in the wrong;
Was everything by starts, and nothing long:
But, in the course of one revolving moon,
Was chemist, fiddler, statesman, and buffoon.[5] *Ib. l. 545*

11 So over violent, or over civil,
That every man with him was God or Devil.
Ib. l. 557

12 His tribe were God Almighty's gentlemen.
Ib. l. 645

13 Nor is the people's judgment always true:
The most may err as grossly as the few.
Ib. l. 781

14 Large was his wealth, but larger was his heart. *Ib. l. 826*

[1]Remembrance and reflection how allied! / What thin partitions sense from thought divide! — POPE, *Essay on Man* [1733–1734], *epistle I, l. 225*
See Seneca, 115:6.
[2]See Diogenes the Cynic, 86:10.
[3]See *Joel 2:28,* 33:17.
[4]See Jonson, 256:*n*6.
[5]See Juvenal, 122:4.

15 Of ancient race by birth, but nobler yet
In his own worth. *Ib. l. 900*

16 Beware the fury of a patient man.
Ib. l. 1005

17 Made still a blund'ring kind of melody;
Spurred boldly on, and dashed through thick and thin,
Through sense and nonsense, never out nor in.
Free from all meaning, whether good or bad,
And in one word, heroically mad.
Ib. pt. II [1682],[6] *l. 413*

18 For every inch that is not fool is rogue.
Ib. l. 463

19 There is a pleasure sure
In being mad which none but madmen know.[7]
The Spanish Friar [1681], act II, sc. i

20 And, dying, bless the hand that gave the blow.[8] *Ib.*

21 He's a sure card. *Ib.*

22 They say everything in the world is good for something. *Ib. III, ii*

23 Or break the eternal Sabbath of his rest.
Ib. V, ii

24 All human things are subject to decay,
And, when fate summons, monarchs must obey. *Mac Flecknoe [1682], l. 1*

25 The rest to some faint meaning make pretense,
But Shadwell[9] never deviates into sense.
Some beams of wit on other souls may fall,
Strike through and make a lucid interval;[10]
But Shadwell's genuine night admits no ray,
His rising fogs prevail upon the day.
Ib. l. 19

26 And torture one poor word ten thousand ways. *Ib. l. 208*

27 Wit will shine
Through the harsh cadence of a rugged line.
To the Memory of Mr. Oldham [1684], l. 15

[6]In collaboration with NAHUM TATE. See 317.
[7]There is a pleasure in poetic pains / Which only poets know. — COWPER, *The Task* [1785], *II, The Timepiece, l. 285*
[8]Adore the hand that gives the blow. — JOHN POMFRET [1667–1702], *Verses to His Friend*
[9]See Shadwell, 313.
[10]See Cervantes, 170:16; Bacon, 179:12; and Heine, 482:6.

1 Happy the man, and happy he alone,
He who can call today his own;
He who, secure within, can say,
Tomorrow, do thy worst, for I have lived today.[1]
Imitation of Horace, bk. III, ode 29 [1685], l. 65

2 Not heaven itself upon the past has power;
But what has been, has been, and I have had my hour. *Ib. l. 71*

3 I can enjoy her [Fortune] while she's kind;
But when she dances in the wind,
And shakes the wings and will not stay,
I puff the prostitute away. *Ib. l. 81*

4 And virtue, though in rags, will keep me warm. *Ib. l. 87*

5 Men met each other with erected look,
The steps were higher that they took;
Friends to congratulate their friends made haste,
And long inveterate foes saluted as they passed.
Threnodia Augustalis [1685], l. 124

6 Since heaven's eternal year is thine.
To the Pious Memory of Mrs. Anne Killegrew [1686], l. 15

7 O gracious God! how far have we
Profaned thy heavenly gift of poesy!
Ib. l. 56

8 Her wit was more than man, her innocence a child.[2] *Ib. l. 70*

9 Then cold, and hot, and moist, and dry,[3]
In order to their stations leap,
And Music's power obey.
From harmony, from heavenly harmony,
This universal frame began:
From harmony to harmony
Through all the compass of the notes it ran,
The diapason closing full in Man.
A Song for St. Cecilia's Day [1687], st. 1

10 What passion cannot Music raise and quell?
Ib. st. 2

11 The trumpet's loud clangor
Excites us to arms. *Ib. st. 3*

12 The soft complaining flute,
In dying notes, discovers
The woes of hopeless lovers.
Ib. st. 4

13 The trumpet shall be heard on high
The dead shall live, the living die,
And Music shall untune the sky!
Ib. Grand Chorus

14 She feared no danger, for she knew no sin.
The Hind and the Panther [1687], pt. I, l. 4

15 And doomed to death, though fated not to die.
Ib. l. 8

16 For truth has such a face and such a mien
As to be loved needs only to be seen.[4]
Ib. l. 33

17 Of all the tyrannies on human kind
The worst is that which persecutes the mind.
Ib. l. 239

18 Reason to rule, mercy to forgive:
The first is law, the last prerogative.
Ib. l. 261

19 And kind as kings upon their coronation day.
Ib. l. 271

20 And leaves the private conscience for the guide. *Ib. l. 478*

21 All have not the gift of martyrdom.
Ib. II, l. 59

22 War seldom enters but where wealth allures.[5] *Ib. l. 706*

23 Much malice mingled with a little wit.
Ib. III, l. 1

24 Jealousy, the jaundice of the soul.
Ib. l. 73

25 For present joys are more to flesh and blood
Than a dull prospect of a distant good.
Ib. l. 364

26 T' abhor the makers, and their laws approve,
Is to hate traitors and the treason love.[6]
Ib. l. 706

27 Secret guilt by silence is betrayed.
Ib. l. 763

28 Possess your soul with patience.[7]
Ib. l. 839

29 Our vows are heard betimes! and Heaven takes care
To grant, before we can conclude the prayer:
Preventing angels met it half the way,
And sent us back to praise, who came to pray.[8]
Britannia Rediviva [1688], l. 1

[1] See Horace, 108:7, and Sydney Smith, 433:12.

[2] Of manners gentle, of affections mild, / In wit a man; simplicity a child.—Pope, *Epitaph on Gay* [1730]

[3] See Milton, 284:27.

[4] See Pope, 337:5.

[5] See Bion, 92:6; Cicero, 99:11; and Rabelais, 157:10.

[6] See Caesar, 99:16.

[7] See *Luke 21:19*, 44:1.

[8] See Goldsmith, 370:8.

1 Three poets, in three distant ages born,
Greece, Italy, and England did adorn.
The first in loftiness of thought surpassed;
The next, in majesty; in both the last.
The force of Nature could no further go.
To make a third, she joined the former two.
Under Mr. Milton's Picture [1688]

2 This is the porcelain clay of humankind.[1]
Don Sebastian [1690], act I, sc. i

3 A knockdown argument: 'tis but a word and a blow.
Amphitryon [1690], act I, sc. i

4 Whistling to keep myself from being afraid.[2] *Ib. III, iii, i*

5 I am the true Amphitryon.[3] *Ib. V, i*

6 Fairest Isle, all isles excelling,
Seat of pleasures, and of loves;
Venus here will choose her dwelling,
And forsake her Cyprian groves.
King Arthur [1691], act II, sc. v, Song of Venus

7 Theirs was the giant race, before the flood.[4]
Epistle to Congreve [1693], l. 5

8 Genius must be born, and never can be taught. *Ib. l. 60*

9 Be kind to my remains; and oh defend,
Against your judgment, your departed friend! *Ib. l. 72*

10 Look round the habitable world: how few
Know their own good, or knowing it, pursue.
Juvenal, Satire X [1693]

11 Arms, and the man I sing,[5] who, forced by fate,
And haughty Juno's unrelenting hate.
Virgil, Aeneid [1697], bk. I, l. 1

12 None but the brave deserves the fair.
Alexander's Feast [1697], l. 15

13 With ravished ears
The monarch hears;
Assumes the god,
Affects to nod,
And seems to shake the spheres.
Ib. l. 37

14 Sound the trumpets; beat the drums . . .
Now give the hautboys breath; he comes, he comes.[6] *Ib. l. 50*

15 Bacchus, ever fair and ever young.
Ib. l. 54

16 Rich the treasure,
Sweet the pleasure—
Sweet is pleasure after pain. *Ib. l. 58*

17 The king grew vain;
Fought all his battles o'er again;
And thrice he routed all his foes, and thrice he slew the slain. *Ib. l. 68*

18 Fallen, fallen, fallen, fallen,
Fallen from his high estate,
And welt'ring in his blood;
Deserted, at his utmost need,
By those his former bounty fed,
On the bare earth exposed he lies,
With not a friend to close his eyes.
Ib. l. 77

19 Softly sweet, in Lydian measures,
Soon he soothed his soul to pleasures.
War, he sung, is toil and trouble;
Honor but an empty bubble;
Never ending, still beginning,
Fighting still, and still destroying.
If all the world be worth thy winning.
Think, oh think it worth enjoying:
Lovely Thaïs sits beside thee,
Take the good the gods provide thee.
Ib. l. 97

20 Sighed and looked, and sighed again.
Ib. l. 120

21 And, like another Helen, fired another Troy.
Ib. l. 154

22 Could swell the soul to rage, or kindle soft desire. *Ib. l. 160*

23 He raised a mortal to the skies,
She drew an angel down. *Ib. l. 169*

24 Words, once my stock, are wanting to commend
So great a poet and so good a friend.
Epistle to Peter Antony Motteux [1698], l. 54

25 Lord of yourself, uncumbered with a wife.
Epistle to John Driden of Chesterton [1700], l. 18

26 Better to hunt in fields, for health unbought,
Than fee the doctor for a nauseous draught.
The wise, for cure, on exercise depend;
God never made his work for man to mend.
Ib. l. 92

27 A very merry, dancing, drinking,
Laughing, quaffing, and unthinking time.
The Secular Masque [1700], l. 38

28 The sword within the scabbard keep,
And let mankind agree. *Ib. l. 61*

[1] The precious porcelain of human clay.—BYRON, *Don Juan* [1819–1824], *canto iv, st. 11*

[2] Whistling aloud to bear his courage up.—BLAIR, *The Grave* [1743], *l. 58*

[3] See Molière, 298:5.

[4] See *Genesis 6:4*, 7:27.

[5] See Virgil, 104:15.

[6] See Morell, 346:7.

1 All, all of a piece throughout:
Thy chase had a beast in view;
Thy wars brought nothing about;
Thy lovers were all untrue.
'Tis well an old age is out,
And time to begin a new.[1] *Ib. l. 86*

2 Ill habits gather by unseen degrees—
As brooks make rivers, rivers run to seas.
Ovid, Metamorphoses [1700], bk. XV, The Worship of Aesculapius, l. 155

3 [Of Chaucer's *Canterbury Tales*] Here is God's plenty.
Fables Ancient and Modern [1700], preface

4 For Art may err, but Nature cannot miss.
Ib. The Cock and the Fox, l. 452

5 Old as I am, for ladies' love unfit,
The power of beauty I remember yet.
Ib. Cymon and Iphigenia, l. 1

6 He trudged along unknowing what he sought,
And whistled as he went, for want of thought.
Ib. l. 84

7 She hugged the offender, and forgave the offense:
Sex to the last.[2] *Ib. l. 367*

8 Of seeming arms to make a short essay,
Then hasten to be drunk—the business of the day. *Ib. l. 407*

9 He was exhaled; his great Creator drew
His spirit, as the sun the morning dew.[3]
On the Death of a Very Young Gentleman [1700]

10 Here lies my wife: here let her lie!
Now she's at rest, and so am I.
Epitaph intended for his wife

William Stoughton
1631–1701

11 God hath sifted a nation that he might send choice grain into this wilderness.[4]
Election sermon at Boston [April 29, 1669]

[1] See Tennyson, 532:22.
[2] And love the offender, yet detest the offense.—POPE, *Eloisa to Abelard* [1717], *l. 192*
[3] Early, bright, transient, chaste as morning dew, / She sparkled, was exhaled, and went to heaven.—EDWARD YOUNG, *Night Thoughts* [1742–1745], *Night V, l. 600*
[4] God had sifted three kingdoms to find the wheat for this planting.—LONGFELLOW, *Courtship of Miles Standish* [1858], *IV*

Anton van Leeuwenhoek
1632–1723

12 We cannot in any better manner glorify the Lord and Creator of the universe than that in all things, how small soever they appear to our naked eyes, but which have yet received the gift of life and power of increase, we contemplate the display of his omnificence and perfections with the utmost admiration.
The Select Works of Anthony van Leeuwenhoek [1798][5]

John Locke
1632–1704

13 New opinions are always suspected, and usually opposed, without any other reason but because they are not already common.
Essay Concerning Human Understanding [1690], dedicatory epistle

14 No man's knowledge here can go beyond his experience. *Ib. bk. II, ch. 1, sec. 19*

15 It is one thing to show a man that he is in error, and another to put him in possession of truth. *Ib. IV, 7, 11*

16 All men are liable to error; and most men are, in many points, by passion or interest, under temptation to it. *Ib. 20, 17*

17 Wherever Law ends, Tyranny begins.[6]
Second Treatise of Government [1690], sec. 202

18 A sound mind in a sound body,[7] is a short but full description of a happy state in this world.
Some Thoughts Concerning Education [1693], sec. 1

19 Good and evil, reward and punishment, are the only motives to a rational creature: these are the spur and reins whereby all mankind are set on work, and guided.[8] *Ib. 54*

20 Virtue is harder to be got than knowledge of the world; and, if lost in a young man, is seldom recovered. *Ib. 64*

[5] Translated by SAMUEL HOOLE.
[6] See William Pitt, 351:1.
[7] See Juvenal, 122:17.
[8] By education, then, I mean goodness in the form in which it is first acquired by a child . . . the rightly disciplined state of pleasures and pains whereby a man from his first beginnings on will abhor what he should abhor and relish what he should relish.—PLATO, *Laws, bk. II*
In educating the young we use pleasure and pain as rudders to steer their course.—ARISTOTLE, *Nichomachean Ethics, bk. X*

1 He that will have his son have a respect for him and his orders, must himself have a great reverence for his son.[1] *Ib. 65*

2 The only fence against the world is a thorough knowledge of it. *Ib. 88*

Benedict [Baruch] Spinoza[2]

1632–1677

3 Peace is not an absence of war, it is a virtue, a state of mind, a disposition for benevolence, confidence, justice.
Theological-Political Treatise [1670]

4 Nature abhors a vacuum.
Ethics [1677],[3] *pt. I, proposition 15: note*

5 God and all the attributes of God are eternal. *Ib. 19*

6 Nothing exists from whose nature some effect does not follow. *Ib. 36*

7 He who would distinguish the true from the false must have an adequate idea of what is true and false. *Ib. II, 42: proof*

8 Will and Intellect are one and the same thing. *Ib. 49: corollary*

9 He that can carp in the most eloquent or acute manner at the weakness of the human mind is held by his fellows as almost divine.
Ib. III: preface

10 Surely human affairs would be far happier if the power in men to be silent were the same as that to speak. But experience more than sufficiently teaches that men govern nothing with more difficulty than their tongues.
Ib. 2: note

11 Pride is therefore pleasure arising from a man's thinking too highly of himself.
Ib. 26: note

12 It may easily come to pass that a vain man may become proud and imagine himself pleasing to all when he is in reality a universal nuisance. *Ib. 30: note*

13 Self-complacency is pleasure accompanied by the idea of oneself as cause.
Ib. 51: note

[1] See Juvenal, 122:19.

[2] Ein Gottbetrunkener Mensch [A God-intoxicated man]. —NOVALIS (FRIEDRICH VON HARDENBERG) [1772–1801]
The Lord blot out his name under heaven. The Lord set him apart for destruction from all the tribes of Israel, with all the curses of the firmament which are written in the Book of the Law. . . . There shall no man speak to him, no man write to him, no man show him any kindness, no man stay under the same roof with him, no man come nigh him.—*Amsterdam synagogue's curse on Spinoza* [1656]

[3] Everyman edition, translated by ANDREW BOYLE.

14 It therefore comes to pass that everyone is fond of relating his own exploits and displaying the strength both of his body and his mind, and that men are on this account a nuisance one to the other. *Ib. 54: note*

15 I refer those actions which work out the good of the agent to courage, and those which work out the good of others to nobility. Therefore temperance, sobriety, and presence of mind in danger, etc., are species of courage; but modesty, clemency, etc., are species of nobility. *Ib. 59: note*

16 Fear cannot be without hope nor hope without fear.
Ib. definition 13: explanation

17 So long as a man imagines that he cannot do this or that, so long is he determined not to do it: and consequently, so long it is impossible to him that he should do it.
Ib. 28: explanation

18 Those who are believed to be most abject and humble are usually most ambitious and envious.
Ib. proposition 29: explanation

19 One and the same thing can at the same time be good, bad, and indifferent, e.g., music is good to the melancholy, bad to those who mourn, and neither good nor bad to the deaf.
Ib. IV: preface

20 Man is a social animal.[4]
Ib. proposition 35: note

21 Men will find that they can prepare with mutual aid far more easily what they need, and avoid far more easily the perils which beset them on all sides, by united forces.
Ib.

22 Avarice, ambition, lust, etc., are nothing but species of madness.[5] *Ib. 44: note*

23 He whose honor depends on the opinion of the mob must day by day strive with the greatest anxiety, act and scheme in order to retain his reputation. For the mob is varied and inconstant, and therefore if a reputation is not carefully preserved it dies quickly.
Ib. 58: note

24 In refusing benefits caution must be used lest we seem to despise or to refuse them for fear of having to repay them in kind.
Ib. 70: note

[4] See Blackstone, 365:15.

[5] To me, avarice seems not so much a vice, as a deplorable piece of madness.—SIR THOMAS BROWNE, *Religio Medici* [1642]

1 To give aid to every poor man is far beyond the reach and power of every man. . . . Care of the poor is incumbent on society as a whole.[1] *Ib. appendix, 17*

2 None are more taken in by flattery than the proud, who wish to be the first and are not. *Ib. 21*

3 Those are most desirous of honor and glory who cry out the loudest of its abuse and the vanity of the world.
Ib. V, proposition 10: note

4 We feel and know that we are eternal.
Ib. 23: note

5 All excellent things are as difficult as they are rare. *Ib. 42: note*

6 The things which . . . are esteemed as the greatest good of all . . . can be reduced to these three headings: to wit, Riches, Fame, and Pleasure. With these three the mind is so engrossed that it cannot scarcely think of any other good.
Tractatus de Intellectus Emendatione [1677], I, 3

Sir Christopher Wren
1632–1723

7 Si monumentum requiris circumspice [If you would see the man's monument, look around].
Inscription in St. Paul's Cathedral, London. Written by Wren's son

Wentworth Dillon, Earl of Roscommon
c. 1633–1685

8 Choose an author as you choose a friend.
Essay on Translated Verse [1684], l. 96

9 Immodest words admit of no defense,
For want of decency is want of sense.
Ib. l. 113

10 The multitude is always in the wrong.
Ib. l. 183

11 My God, my Father, and my Friend,
Do not forsake me in my end.[2]
Translation of Dies Irae

Samuel Pepys
1633–1703

12 I pray God to keep me from being proud.
Diary, March 22, 1660

[1]See Maimonides, 137:10; Johnson, 354:23; and Carnegie, 621:10.
[2]See Tommaso di Celano, 139:4.

13 This morning came home my fine camlet cloak, with gold buttons, and a silk suit, which cost me much money, and I pray God to make me able to pay for it.
Ib. July 1, 1660

14 And so to bed.
Ib. July 22, 1660, passim

15 I am unwilling to mix my fortune with him that is going down the wind.
Ib. September 6, 1660

16 A good honest and painful sermon.
Ib. March 17, 1661

17 One, by his own confession to me, that can put on two several faces, and look his enemies in the face with as much love as his friends. But, good God! what an age is this, and what a world is this! that a man cannot live without playing the knave and dissimulation.
Ib. September 1, 1661

18 Though he be a fool, yet he keeps much company, and will tell all he sees or hears, so a man may understand what the common talk of the town is.
Ib. September 2, 1661

19 My wife, poor wretch.
Ib. September 18, 1661, passim

20 Thanks be to God, since my leaving drinking of wine, I do find myself much better, and do mind my business better, and do spend less money, and less time lost in idle company.
Ib. January 26, 1662

21 As happy a man as any in the world, for the whole world seems to smile upon me.
Ib. October 31, 1662

22 Bought *Hudibras* again, it being certainly some ill humor to be so against that which all the world cries up to be the example of wit; for which I am resolved once more to read him, and see whether I can find it or no.[3]
Ib. February 6, 1663

23 To the Trinity House, where a very good dinner among the old soakers.
Ib. February 15, 1665

24 But Lord! how everybody's looks, and discourse in the street, is of death, and nothing else; and few people going up and down, that the town is like a place distressed and forsaken.[4] *Ib. August 30, 1665*

25 Strange to see how a good dinner and feasting reconciles everybody.
Ib. November 9, 1665

[3]Pepys had bought *Hudibras* on December 26, 1662, but thought it "so silly an abuse of the Presbyter Knight going to the wars" that he sold it the same day.
[4]The time of the Great Plague.

1 Saw a wedding in the church; and strange to see what delight we married people have to see these poor fools decoyed into our condition. *Ib. December 25, 1665*

2 Musick and women I cannot but give way to, whatever my business is.
Ib. March 9, 1666

3 The truth is, I do indulge myself a little the more in pleasure, knowing that this is the proper age of my life to do it; and, out of my observation that most men that do thrive in the world do forget to take pleasure during the time that they are getting their estate, but reserve that till they have got one, and then it is too late for them to enjoy it.
Ib. March 10, 1666

4 Home, and, being washing-day, dined upon cold meat. *Ib. April 4, 1666*

5 Musick is the thing of the world that I love most. *Ib. July 30, 1666*

6 Busy till night, pleasing myself mightily to see what a deal of business goes off a man's hands when he stays by it.
Ib. January 14, 1667

7 Did satisfy myself mighty fair in the truth of the saying that the world do not grow old at all, but is in as good condition in all respects as ever it was.
Ib. February 3, 1667

8 This day I am, by the blessing of God, 34 years old, in very good health and mind's content, and in condition of estate much beyond whatever my friends could expect of a child of theirs, this day 34 years. The Lord's name be praised! and may I be thankful for it.
Ib. February 23, 1667

9 But it is pretty to see what money will do.
Ib. March 21, 1667

10 To church; and with my mourning, very handsome, and new periwig, make a great show. *Ib. March 31, 1667*

11 But to think of the clatter they make with his coach, and their own fine clothes, and yet how meanly they live within doors, and nastily, and borrowing everything of neighbors.
Ib. April 1, 1667

12 Whose red nose makes me ashamed to be seen with him. *Ib. May 3, 1667*

13 Gives me some kind of content to remember how painful it is sometimes to keep money, as well as to get it.
Ib. October 11, 1667

14 I find my wife hath something in her gizzard, that only waits an opportunity of being provoked to bring up; but I will not, for my content-sake, give it. *Ib. June 17, 1668*

15 In appearance, at least, he being on all occasions glad to be at friendship with me, though we hate one another, and know it on both sides. *Ib. September 22, 1668*

16 I do hate to be unquiet at home.
Ib. January 22, 1669

17 And so I betake myself to that course, which is almost as much as to see myself go into my grave; for which, and all the discomforts that will accompany my being blind, the good God prepare me!
Ib. May 31, 1669 (final entry)

George Savile, Marquess of Halifax

1633–1695

18 Children and fools want everything, because they want wit to distinguish; there is no stronger evidence of a crazy understanding than the making too large a catalogue of things necessary.
Advice to a Daughter [1688]

19 Popularity is a crime from the moment it is sought; it is only a virtue where men have it whether they will or no.
Political, Moral, and Miscellaneous Reflections [1750]

20 Misspending a man's time is a kind of self-homicide. *Ib.*

21 Men are not hanged for stealing horses, but that horses may not be stolen. *Ib.*

Robert South

1634–1716

22 Speech was given to the ordinary sort of men whereby to communicate their mind; but to wise men, whereby to conceal it.[1]
Sermon [1676]

[1]Speech was made to open man to man, and not to hide him; to promote commerce, and not betray it.—DAVID LLOYD [1635–1692], *The Statesmen and Favorites of England Since the Reformation* [1665, edited by WHITWORTH], *vol. I, p. 503*

Men talk only to conceal the mind.—EDWARD YOUNG, *Love of Fame* [1725–1728], *satire II, l. 208*

The true use of speech is not so much to express our wants as to conceal them.—GOLDSMITH, *The Bee, no. 3* [October 20, 1759]

See Voltaire, 343:24.

Robert Hooke

1635–1703

1 The truth is, the science of Nature has been already too long made only a work of the brain and the fancy: It is now high time that it should return to the plainness and soundness of observations on material and obvious things. *Micrographia [1665]*

Nicolas Boileau-Despréaux

1636–1711

2 Happy who in his verse can gently steer
From grave to light, from pleasant to severe.[1]
The Art of Poetry [1674], canto I, l. 75

3 At last comes Malherbe[2] and, the first to do so in France, brings to his verse a smooth cadence. *Ib. l. 131*

4 Whate'er is well conceived is clearly said,
And the words to say it flow with ease.
Ib. l. 153

5 Every age has its pleasures, its style of wit, and its own ways. *Ib. III, l. 374*

6 The wisest man is he who does not fancy that he is so at all. *Satire 1, l. 46*

7 A Cat's a cat, and Rolet is a knave.
Ib. l. 52

8 He [Molière] pleases all the world, but cannot please himself. *Ib. l. 94*

9 In spite of every sage whom Greece can show,
Unerring wisdom never dwelt below;
Folly in all of every age we see,
The only difference lies in the degree.
Satire 4, l. 37

10 Greatest fools are oft most satisfied.
Ib. l. 128

11 If your descent is from heroic sires,
Show in your life a remnant of their fires.
Satire 5, l. 43

12 Of all the creatures that creep, swim, or fly,
Peopling the earth, the waters, and the sky,
From Rome to Iceland, Paris to Japan,
I really think the greatest fool is man.
Satire 8, l. 1

13 But satire, ever moral, ever new,
Delights the reader and instructs him, too.
She, if good sense refine her sterling page,
Oft shakes some rooted folly of the age.
Satire 8, l. 257

14 Honor is like an island, rugged and without a beach; once we have left it, we can never return. *Satire 10, l. 167*

15 Now two punctilious envoys, Thine and Mine,
Embroil the earth about a fancied line;
And, dwelling much on right and much on wrong,
Prove how the right is chiefly with the strong.[3]
Satire 11, l. 141

16 Nothing but truth is lovely, nothing fair.
Epistle 9

17 The terrible burden of having nothing to do.
Epistle 11

[1] See Pope, 338:1.
Translated by DRYDEN.
[2] Enfin Malherbe vint.

Thomas Ken

1637–1711

18 Awake, my soul, and with the sun
Thy daily stage of duty run.
Morning Hymn [1695]

19 Praise God, from whom all blessings flow!
Praise Him, all creatures here below!
Praise Him above, ye heavenly host!
Praise Father, Son, and Holy Ghost!
Doxology [1709]

Thomas Traherne

c. 1637–1674

20 You never enjoy the world aright, till the sea itself floweth in your veins, till you are clothed with the heavens, and crowned with the stars: and perceive yourself to be the sole heir of the whole world.
Centuries of Meditations [1908], Century I, sec. 29

21 The corn was orient and immortal wheat, which never should be reaped, nor was ever sown. I thought it had stood from everlasting to everlasting.[4] *Ib. III, 3*

22 How like an angel came I down![5]
Wonder [1910], st. 1

23 I within did flow
With seas of life like wine. *Ib. st. 3*

[3] See Tacitus, 123:1; Bussy-Rabutin, 294:21; Frederick the Great, 358:4; and Gibbon, 383:13.
[4] See *Psalm 90:2, 20:11.*
[5] See Vaughan, 299:2; Wordsworth, 426:14; and Lowell, 567:11.

Louis XIV
1638–1715

1 I am the state.[1]
Attributed remark before the parliament in 1651

2 Has God forgotten all I have done for him?[2]
Attributed remark upon hearing the news of the French defeat at Malplaquet [1709]

3 I almost had to wait.[3]
Attributed remark when a coach he had ordered arrived just in time

Jean Racine
1639–1699

4 I loved him too much not to hate him at all!
Andromaque [1667], act II

5 You are Emperor, my lord, and yet you weep? *Bérénice [1670], act IV, sc. v*

6 My only hope lies in my despair.
Bajazet [1672], act I, sc. iv

7 You have named him, not I.[4]
Phèdre [1677], act I, sc. iii

8 It is no longer a passion hidden in my heart: it is Venus herself fastened to her prey.[5] *Ib.*

9 Innocence has nothing to dread.
Ib. III, vi

10 Crime like virtue has its degrees; and timid innocence was never known to blossom suddenly into extreme license.[6]
Ib. IV, ii

11 To repair the irreparable ravages of time.
Athalie [1691], act II, sc. v

Sir Charles Sedley
c. 1639–1701

12 Phyllis is my only joy,
Faithless as the winds or seas;
Sometimes coming, sometimes coy,
Yet she never fails to please.
Song [1702], st. 1

[1] L'état c'est moi.
See Napoleon, 420:11.
[2] Dieu a donc oublié tout ce que j'ai fait pour lui?
[3] J'ai failli attendre.
[4] C'est toi qui l'a nommé.
[5] Ce n'est plus une ardeur dans mes veines cachée: / C'est Vénus toute entière à sa proie attachée.
[6] See Juvenal, 122:3, and Beaumont and Fletcher, 263:6.

Aphra Behn
1640–1689

13 A brave world, sir, full of religion, knavery, and change: we shall shortly see better days.
The Roundheads [1677]

14 Variety is the soul of pleasure.
The Rover, Part II [1680], act I

15 Come away; poverty's catching. *Ib.*

16 Money speaks sense in a language all nations understand. *Ib. III, sc. i*

17 Beauty unadorned. *Ib. IV, ii*

18 Faith, sir, we are here today, and gone tomorrow.
The Lucky Chance [1686–1687], act IV

19 Oh, what a dear ravishing thing is the beginning of an Amour!
The Emperor of the Moon [1687], act I, sc. i

Ihara Saikaku
1642–1693

20 Heaven says nothing, and the whole earth grows rich beneath its silent rule. Men, too, are touched by heaven's virtue; yet, in their greater part, they are creatures of deceit. They are born, it seems, with an emptiness of soul, and must take their qualities wholly from things without. To be born thus empty into this modern age, this mixture of good and ill, and yet to steer through life on an honest course to the splendors of success — this is a feat reserved for paragons of our kind, a task beyond the nature of the normal man.
The Japanese Family Storehouse; or, The Millionaires' Gospel,[7] bk. I, 1

21 The first consideration for all, throughout life, is the earning of a living. *Ib.*

22 Though mothers and fathers give us life, it is money alone which preserves it. *Ib.*

23 In life it is training rather than birth which counts. *Ib. 3*

24 Ancient simplicity is gone . . . the people of today are satisfied with nothing but finery.
Ib. 4

25 Take care! Kingdoms are destroyed by bandits, houses by rats, and widows by suitors.
Ib. 5

[7] Edited and translated by G. W. Sargent.

1 There is always something to upset the most careful of human calculations.[1]
Ib. II, 2

2 When you send a clerk on business to a distant province, a man of rigid morals is not your best choice. *Ib. 5*

3 To think twice in every matter and follow the lead of others is no way to make money. *Ib.*

4 For each of the four hundred and four bodily ailments celebrated physicians have produced infallible remedies, but the malady which brings the greatest distress to mankind — to even the wisest and cleverest of us — is the plague of poverty. *Ib. III, 1*

5 To make a fortune some assistance from fate is essential. Ability alone is insufficient. *Ib. 4*

6 If we live by subhuman means we might as well never have had the good fortune to be born human. *Ib.*

7 Like ice beneath the sun's rays — to such poverty did he fall . . . his fortune melted to water. *Ib. 5*

8 If making money is a slow process, losing it is quickly done. *Ib.*

9 Harshness is for the good of a boy, softheartedness will ruin him.[2] *Ib. V, 5*

Sir Isaac Newton
1642–1727

10 If I have seen further (than you and Descartes) it is by standing upon the shoulders of Giants.[3]
Letter to Robert Hooke, February 5, 1675/1676

11 I frame no hypotheses; for whatever is not deduced from the phenomena is to be called an hypothesis; and hypotheses, whether metaphysical or physical, whether of occult qualities or mechanical, have no place in experimental philosophy. *Ib.*

12 Errors are not in the art but in the artificers.
Philosophiae Naturalis Principia Mathematica [1687],[4] preface

13 Every body continues in its state of rest, or of uniform motion in a right line, unless it is compelled to change that state by forces impressed upon it. *Ib. Laws of Motion, I*

14 The change of motion is proportional to the motive force impressed; and is made in the direction of the right line in which that force is impressed.[5] *Ib. II*

15 To every action there is always opposed an equal reaction: or, the mutual actions of two bodies upon each other are always equal, and directed to contrary parts. *Ib. III*

16 God in the beginning formed matter in solid, massy, hard, impenetrable, movable particles, of such sizes and figures, and with such other properties, and in such proportion to space, as most conduced to the end for which he formed them. *Optics [1704]*

17 I do not know what I may appear to the world; but to myself I seem to have been only like a boy playing on the seashore, and diverting myself in now and then finding a smoother pebble or a prettier shell than ordinary, whilst the great ocean of truth lay all undiscovered before me.
From BREWSTER, *Memoirs of Newton [1855], vol. II, ch. 27*

18 O Diamond! Diamond! thou little knowest the mischief done!
Said to a pet dog who knocked over a candle and set fire to his papers

Thomas Shadwell[6]
c. 1642–1692

19 And wit's the noblest frailty of the mind.
A True Widow [1679], act II, sc. i

20 The haste of a fool is the slowest thing in the world. *Ib. III, i*

21 I am, out of the ladies' company, like a fish out of the water. *Ib.*

22 Every man loves what he is good at. *Ib. V, i*

Matsuo Basho
1644–1694

23 The months and days are the travelers of eternity. The years that come and go are also voyagers. . . . I too for years past have been stirred by the sight of a solitary cloud drifting

[1] See Robert Burns, 408:14.
[2] See *Proverbs 13:24*, 23:34.
[3] See Lucan, 118:7, and Burton, 258:7.
[4] *Mathematical Principles of Natural Philosophy* [1729], translated by ANDREW MOTTE.
[5] In modern terms, acceleration is directly proportional to applied force.
[6] Shadwell was at open feud with Dryden from 1682, and the two poets repeatedly attacked one another in satires, the most famous of which is Dryden's *Mac Flecknoe*. See Dryden, 304:25.

with the wind to ceaseless thoughts of roaming.

The Narrow Road of Oku (Oku no Hosomichi)[1]

1 Such stillness—
The cries of the cicadas
Sink into the rocks. *Ib.*

2 My body, now close to fifty years of age, has become an old tree that bears bitter peaches, a snail which has lost its shell, a bagworm separated from its bag; it drifts with the winds and clouds that know no destination. Morning and night I have eaten traveler's fare, and have held out for alms a pilgrim's wallet.

Prose Poem on The Unreal Dwelling (Genjuan no Fu)[1]

3 My poetry is like a stove in the summer or a fan in the winter. It runs against the popular tastes and has no practical use.[2]

The Rustic Gate. From the collection Basho Bunshu

4 Do not seek to follow in the footsteps of the men of old; seek what they sought. *Ib.*

5 The white chrysanthemum
Even when lifted to the eye
Remains immaculate.[2]

Conversations with Basho. From the collection Kyoraisho Hyokai

6 Clear cascades!
Into the waves scatter
Blue pine needles. *Ib.*

7 An old pond—
A frog leaping in—
The sound of water.[3] *Poem*

8 A rough sea!
Stretched out over Sado
The Milky Way.[3] *Poem*

William Penn

1644–1718

9 No Cross, No Crown.[4]

Title of pamphlet [1669]

10 Any government is free to the people under it where the laws rule and the people are a party to the laws.

Frame of Government [1682]

11 Truth often suffers more by the heat of its defenders than from the arguments of its opposers.

Some Fruits of Solitude [1693][5]

12 It is a reproach to religion and government to suffer so much poverty and excess. *Ib.*

13 They that love beyond the world cannot be separated by it. Death is but crossing the world, as friends do the seas; they live in one another still. *Ib.*

14 Men are generally more careful of the breed of their horses and dogs than of their children. *Ib.*

15 It were endless to dispute upon everything that is disputable. *Ib.*

16 Have a care where there is more sail than ballast. *Ib.*

17 Passion is a sort of fever in the mind, which ever leaves us weaker than it found us. *Ib.*

18 The public must and will be served. *Ib.*

19 Much reading is an oppression of the mind, and extinguishes the natural candle, which is the reason of so many senseless scholars in the world.[6]

Advice to His Children [1699]

Edward Taylor

c. 1644–1729

20 Who spread its canopy? Or curtains spun?
Who in this bowling alley bowled the sun?

Poetical Works [1939]. God's Determinations Touching His Elect, preface

21 For in Christ's coach saints sweetly sing
As they to glory ride therein.

Ib. The Joy of Church Fellowship Rightly Attended

22 Make me, O Lord, thy spinning-wheel complete. *Ib. Housewifery*

23 It's food too fine for angels; yet come, take
And eat thy fill! It's Heaven's sugar cake.[7]

Ib. Sacramental Meditations, 8

[1] From *Anthology of Japanese Literature* [1955], edited by DONALD KEENE.

[2] From *Sources of Japanese Tradition* [1960], edited by WILLIAM THEODORE DE BARY.

[3] Translated by DANA B. YOUNG.

[4] See *Matthew 10:38*, 39:5; Quarles, 267:10; and Bennard, 738:11.

[5] A copy of this little book, wrote Robert Louis Stevenson, "I carried in my pocket all about the San Francisco streets, read in streetcars and ferryboats when I was sick unto death, and found in all times and places a peaceful and sweet companion."

[6] See Lao-tzu, 65:10; Confucius, 68:10; Heraclitus, 69:28; Chaucer, 147:2; Selden, 263:18; and Newman, 490:14.

[7] Based on *John 6:51*.

1 This bread of life dropped in thy mouth doth cry:
Eat, eat me, soul, and thou shalt never die.
Ib.

2 Is Christ thy advocate to plead thy cause?[1]
Art thou his client? Such shall never slide.
He never lost his case. *Ib. 38*

3 My case is bad. Lord, be my advocate.
My sin is red: I'm under God's arrest.
Ib.

Jean de La Bruyère
1645–1696

4 We come too late to say anything which has not been said already.[2]
Les Caractères [1688]. Des Ouvrages de l'Esprit

5 Liberality consists less in giving a great deal than in gifts well timed.
Ib. Du Coeur

6 Time, which strengthens friendship, weakens love. *Ib.*

7 We must laugh before we are happy, for fear we die before we laugh at all.[3]
Ib.

8 To laugh at men of sense is the privilege of fools. *Ib. De la Société*

9 There are but three events in a man's life: birth, life and death. He is not conscious of being born, he dies in pain, and he forgets to live. *Ib. De l'Homme*

10 Most men make use of the first part of their life to render the last part miserable.
Ib.

11 Women run to extremes; they are either better or worse than men.
Ib. Des Femmes

Baron Gottfried Wilhelm von Leibnitz
1646–1716

12 I often say a great doctor kills more people than a great general.[4]
Quoted in Bulletin of the New York Academy of Medicine, vol. V [1929], p. 152

[1] See *I John 2:1–2*, 52:21.
[2] See *Ecclesiastes 1:9*, 26:14; Terence, 96:15, and Burton, 258:6.
[3] See Beaumarchais, 378:6, and Byron, 461:10.
[4] See Prior, 320:20.

Henry Aldrich
1647–1710

13 If all be true that I do think,
There are five reasons we should drink:
Good wine—a friend—or being dry—
Or lest we should be by and by—
Or any other reason why.
Five Reasons for Drinking

John Wilmot, Earl of Rochester
1647–1680

14 Here lies our sovereign lord the King,
Whose promise none relies on;
He never said a foolish thing,
Nor ever did a wise one.
Written on the bedchamber door of Charles II[5]

15 For pointed satire I would Buckhurst choose,
The best good man with the worst-natured muse.[6]
An Allusion to Horace, bk. I, satire X

16 A merry monarch, scandalous and poor.
A Satire on King Charles II

17 The world appears like a great family,
Whose lord, oppressed with pride and poverty,
(That to the few great bounty he may show)
Is fain to starve the numerous train below.
Like a Great Family

18 There's not a thing on earth that I can name,
So foolish, and so false, as common fame.
Did E'er This Saucy World

19 Reason, which fifty times to one does err,
Reason, an ignis fatuus of the mind.
A Satire Against Mankind [1675], l. 11

20 Books bear him up a while, and make him try
To swim with bladders of philosophy.
Ib. l. 20

21 Then Old Age and Experience, hand in hand,
Lead him to death, and make him understand,
After a search so painful and so long,
That all his life he has been in the wrong.
Ib. l. 25

22 Dead, we become the lumber of the world.
Seneca's Troas, act 2, chorus

[5] See Charles II, 302.
[6] Thou best-humored man with the worst-humored muse!—Goldsmith, *Retaliation* [1774], *Postscript*

Juana Inés de la Cruz
1648–1695

1 Foolish men who accuse
a woman mindlessly—
you cannot even see
you cause what you abuse.
Hombres Necios (Foolish Men),[1] *st. 1*

2 Has anyone ever seen
a stranger moral fervor?
You who dirty the mirror
cry that it isn't clean. *Ib. st. 6*

3 I became a nun, because although I recognized it as having many ramifications . . . foreign to my temperament, still, given my completely negative feelings about marriage, it was the least disproportionate and most fitting thing I could do.
Reply to Sor Filotea de la Cruz[2] *[1691]*

4 Since I first gained the use of reason my inclination towards learning has been so violent and strong that neither the scoldings of other people . . . nor my own reflections . . . have been able to stop me from following this natural impulse that God gave me. He alone must know why; and He knows too that I have begged Him to take away the light of my understanding, leaving only enough for me to keep His law, for anything else is excessive in a woman, according to some people, and others say it is even harmful.
Ib.

John Sheffield, Duke of Buckingham and Normanby
1648–1721

5 Of all those arts in which the wise excel,
Nature's chief masterpiece is writing well.
Essay on Poetry [1682]

6 Read Homer once, and you can read no more;
For all books else appear so mean, so poor,
Verse will seem prose; but still persist to read,
And Homer will be all the books you need.
Ib.

7 And when I feigned an angry look,
Alas! I loved you best.
The Reconcilement [1701]

[1]Translated by Willis and Alicki Barnstone.

[2]Name used by Manuel Fernández de la Cruz, bishop of Puebla, in signing an angry letter attacking Sor Juana's scholarly work as inappropriate.

Translated by Rachel Phillips.

Sir Thomas Pope Blount
1649–1697

8 Every flower of the field, every fiber of a plant, every particle of an insect, carries with it the impress of its Maker, and can—if duly considered—read us lectures of ethics or divinity.[3] *A Natural History [1693]*

William III[4]
1650–1702

9 There is one certain means by which I can be sure never to see my country's ruin: I will die in the last ditch.
From Hume, History of England [1754–1757], ch. 65

10 Every bullet has its billet.
From John Wesley, Journal [June 6, 1765]

François de Salignac de la Mothe Fénelon
1651–1715

11 Do not men die fast enough without being destroyed by each other? Can any man be insensible of the brevity of life? and can he who knows it, think life too long!
Télémaque [1699], bk. VII

12 To be always ready for war, said Mentor, is the surest way to avoid it.[5] *Ib. X*

13 Some of the most dreadful mischiefs that afflict mankind proceed from wine; it is the cause of disease, quarrels, sedition, idleness, aversion to labor, and every species of domestic disorder. *Ib.*

14 The blood of a nation ought never to be shed except for its own preservation in the utmost extremity. *Ib. XIII*

15 Mankind, by the perverse depravity of their nature, esteem that which they have most desired as of no value the moment it is possessed, and torment themselves with fruitless wishes for that which is beyond their reach. *Ib. XVIII*

Thomas Otway
1652–1685

16 What mighty ills have not been done by woman!

[3]See Tennyson, 535:10.

[4]Prince of Orange; joint sovereign of England with his wife Mary II.

[5]See Aristotle, 87:24; Vegetius, 128:25; Robert Burton, 259:13; Washington, 379:9; and Lowell, 568:9.

Who was 't betrayed the Capitol?—A woman!
Who lost Mark Antony the world?—A woman!
Who was the cause of a long ten years' war,
And laid at last old Troy in ashes?—Woman!
Destructive, damnable, deceitful woman!
The Orphan [1680], act III, sc. i

1 Let us embrace, and from this very moment vow an eternal misery together.
Ib. IV, ii

2 O woman! lovely woman! Nature made thee
To temper man: we had been brutes without you;
Angels are painted fair, to look like you.
Venice Preserved [1682], act I, sc. i

Nahum Tate

1652–1715

3 When I am laid in earth.
Dido and Aeneas [c. 1690][1]

4 While shepherds watched their flocks by night,
All seated on the ground,
The angel of the Lord came down,
And glory shone around.[2]
Christmas Hymn [1700], st. 1

5 Glad tidings of great joy I bring
To you and all mankind.[3] *Ib.*

Nahum Tate

1652–1715

and

Nicholas Brady

1659–1726

6 Through all the changing scenes of life,
In trouble and in joy.
New Version of the Psalms of David [1696], Psalm 34

7 As pants the hart for cooling streams
When heated in the chase.
Ib. Psalm 42

8 Jesus Christ is risen today,
Alleluia!
Easter Hymn [1698], translated from the Latin [fourteenth century]

[1]Libretto for the famous opera by Henry Purcell.
[2]See *Luke 2:8–9*, 42:28.
[3]See *Luke 2:10*, 42:28.

Chikamatsu Monzaemon

1653–1725

9 In writing *joruri*,[4] one attempts first to describe facts as they really are, but in so doing one writes things which are not true, in the interest of art.
Preface to Hozumi Ikan, *Naniwa Miyage*[5]

10 It is essential that one not say of a thing that "it is sad," but that it be sad of itself.
Ib.

11 [Literary composition] should have stylization; this makes it art, and is what delights men's minds. *Ib.*

Nathaniel Lee[6]

c. 1653–1692

12 Then he will talk—good gods! how he will talk!
The Rival Queens; or, The Death of Alexander the Great [1677], act I, sc. iii

13 When Greeks joined Greeks, then was the tug of war. *Ib. IV, ii*

14 'Tis beauty calls, and glory shows the way.
Ib.

15 Man, false man, smiling, destructive man!
Theodosius [1680], act III, sc. ii

Ransetsu

1653–1708

16 Against the blue stands
A pine tree etched
By tonight's moon.[7] *Harvest Moon*

Andrew Fletcher of Saltoun

1655–1716

17 If a man were permitted to make all the ballads, he need not care who should make the laws of a nation.
Conversation Concerning a Right Regulation of Governments for the Common Good of Mankind [1704]

[4]Plays for life-size puppets.
[5]From *Sources of Japanese Tradition* [1960], edited by William Theodore de Bary.
[6]Lee collaborated with Dryden on *Oedipus* (see 303:14).
[7]Translated by Prescott B. Wintersteen, Jr.

John Dennis
1657–1734

1 A man who could make so vile a pun would not scruple to pick a pocket.
The Gentleman's Magazine, vol. LI [1781], p. 324

2 They will not let my play run; and yet they steal my thunder.[1] *Remark*

Bernard Le Bovier de Fontenelle
1657–1757

3 The geometrical mind is not so closely bound to geometry that it cannot be drawn aside and transferred to other departments of knowledge. A work of morality, politics, criticism, perhaps even eloquence will be more elegant, other things being equal, if it is shaped by the hand of geometry.[2]
Préface sur l'Utilité des Mathématiques et la Physique [1729]

John Norris
1657–1711

4 How fading are the joys we dote upon!
Like apparitions seen and gone.
But those which soonest take their flight
Are the most exquisite and strong—
Like angels' visits, short and bright;[3]
Mortality's too weak to bear them long.
The Parting [1678]

Daniel Defoe
c. 1660–1731

5 Wherever God erects a house of prayer,
The Devil always builds a chapel there;[4]
And 'twill be found, upon examination,
The latter has the largest congregation.
The True-Born Englishman [1701], pt. I, l. 1

[1] For his play *Appius and Virginia* [1709], Dennis had invented a new species of thunder. "The tragedy however was coldly received, notwithstanding such assistance, and was acted but a short time. Some nights after, Mr. Dennis, being in the pit at the representation of *Macbeth*, heard his own thunder made use of; upon which he rose in a violent passion, and exclaimed, with an oath, that it was his thunder. 'See,' said he, 'how the rascals use me! They will not let my play run, and yet they steal my thunder!' " —*Biographia Britannica, vol. V, p. 103*

[2] Translated by F. CAJORI.

[3] Like those of angels, short and far between.—ROBERT BLAIR, *The Grave* [1743], *l. 588*
See Campbell, 443:8.

[4] See Luther, 156:5.

6 From this amphibious ill-born mob began
That vain, ill-natured thing, an Englishman.
Ib. l. 132

7 Great families of yesterday we show,
And lords whose parents were the Lord knows who.
Ib. l. 374

8 In their religion they are so uneven,
That each man goes his own byway to heaven.
Ib. II, l. 104

9 And of all plagues with which mankind are cursed,
Ecclesiastic tyranny's the worst.
Ib. l. 299

10 When kings the sword of justice first lay down,
They are no kings, though they possess the crown.
Titles are shadows, crowns are empty things,
The good of subjects is the end of kings.
Ib. l. 313

11 All men would be tyrants if they could.
The Kentish Petition [1712–1713]

12 The best of men cannot suspend their fate:
The good die early, and the bad die late.
Character of the Late Dr. S. Annesley [1715]

13 He bade me [Robinson Crusoe] observe it, and I should always find that the calamities of life were shared among the upper and lower part of mankind; but that the middle station had the fewest disasters.
Robinson Crusoe[5] [1719]

14 One day, about noon, going towards my boat, I was exceedingly surprised with the print of a man's naked foot on the shore, which was very plain to be seen on the sand.
Ib.

15 My man Friday. *Ib.*

Sir Samuel Garth
1661–1719

16 A barren superfluity of words.
The Dispensary [1699], canto II, l. 95

17 Hard was their lodging, homely was their food;
For all their luxury was doing good.[6]
Claremont, l. 148

[5] See Rousseau, 358:23.

[6] And learn the luxury of doing good.—GOLDSMITH, *The Traveller* [1764], *l. 22*

Kikaku
1661–1707

1 A harvest moon!
And on the mats—
Shadows of pine boughs.[1]

Harvest Moon

Richard Bentley
1662–1742

2 No man was ever written out of reputation but by himself.[2]

From J. H. MONK, *Life of Bentley [1831]*

3 It is a pretty poem, Mr. Pope, but you must not call it Homer.[3]

From JOHNSON, *Life of Pope*

Matthew Henry
1662–1714

4 He rolls it under his tongue as a sweet morsel.

Commentaries [1708–1710], Psalm 36

5 Our creature comforts. *Ib. Psalm 37*

6 They that die by famine die by inches. *Ib. Psalm 59*

7 To fish in troubled waters. *Ib. Psalm 60*

8 Here is bread, which strengthens man's heart, and therefore called the staff of life.[4] *Ib. Psalm 104*

9 Hearkeners, we say, seldom hear good of themselves. *Ib. Ecclesiastes 7*

10 It was a common saying among the Puritans, "Brown bread and the Gospel is good fare." *Ib. Isaiah 30*

11 None so blind as those that will not see.[5] *Ib. Jeremiah 20*

12 Judas had given them the slip. *Ib. Matthew 22*

13 After a storm comes a calm. *Ib. Acts 9*

14 Men of polite learning and a liberal education. *Ib. 10*

15 It is good news, worthy of all acceptation! and yet not too good to be true. *Ib. Timothy 1*

16 It is not fit the public trusts should be lodged in the hands of any, till they are first proved and found fit for the business they are to be entrusted with.[6] *Ib. 3*

17 All this and heaven too. *Life of Philip Henry*

Samuel Wesley
1662–1735

18 Style is the dress of thought;[7] a modest dress,
Neat, but not gaudy,[8] will true critics please.

An Epistle to a Friend Concerning Poetry [1700]

Thomas [Tom] Brown
1663–1704

19 I do not love thee, Doctor Fell.
The reason why I cannot tell;
But this alone I know full well,
I do not love thee, Doctor Fell.[9]

Written while a student at Christ Church, Oxford

20 To treat a poor wretch with a bottle of Burgundy, and fill his snuffbox, is like giving a pair of laced ruffles to a man that has never a shirt on his back.[10]

Laconics [1707]

Mary de la Rivière Manley
1663–1724

21 No time like the present.

The Lost Lover [1696], act IV, sc. i

Cotton Mather
1663–1728

22 I write the wonders of the Christian religion, flying from the depravations of Europe, to the American strand: and, assisted by the Holy Author of that religion, I do, with all conscience of truth, required therein by Him, who is the Truth itself, report the wonderful displays of His infinite power, wisdom, goodness, and faithfulness, wherewith his Divine

[1] Translated by PRESCOTT B. WINTERSTEEN, JR.
[2] See Montaigne, 165:10.
[3] The reference is to Pope's translation of *The Iliad.* See Pope, 334:18.
[4] See *Isaiah 3:1,* 28:34.
Bread is the staff of life.—SWIFT, *Tale of a Tub* [1704]
Corn, which is the staff of life.—EDWARD WINSLOW, *Good News from New England* [1624]
[5] See *Jeremiah 5:21,* 31:34.
[6] See Clay, 444:3; Calhoun, 449:8; Sumner, 539:4; and Cleveland, 631:7.
[7] See Chesterfield, 342:7.
[8] See Shakespeare, 219:1.
[9] See Martial, 119:3.
Je ne vous aime pas, Hylas; / Je n'en saurois dire la cause, / Je sais seulement une chose; / C'est que je ne vous aime pas.—ROGER DE BUSSY-RABUTIN [1618–1693]
[10] See Goldsmith, 371:22.

Providence hath irradiated an Indian wilderness.

Magnalia Christi Americana [1702], introduction

1 You are young and have the world before you; stoop as you go through it, and you will miss many hard bumps.

Advice to Benjamin Franklin upon approaching a low-hanging beam in his parsonage[1]

William Walsh

1663–1708

2 Of all the plagues a lover bears,
Sure rivals are the worst. *Song, st. 1*

3 I can endure my own despair,
But not another's hope. *Ib. st. 2*

The New England Primer[2]

4 In Adam's fall
We sinned all.

5 My book and heart
Must never part.

6 Young Obadias,
David, Josias—
All were pious.

7 Peter denied
His Lord, and cried.

8 Young Timothy
Learnt sin to fly.

9 Xerxes did die,
And so must I.

10 Zaccheus he
Did climb the tree
Our Lord to see.

11 Our days begin with trouble here,
Our life is but a span,[3]
And cruel death is always near,
So frail a thing is man.

12 Now I lay me down to sleep,[4]
I pray the Lord my soul to keep;
If I should die before I wake,
I pray the Lord my soul to take.

[1] From *Sailor Historian: The Best of Samuel Eliot Morison* [1977], edited by Emily Morison Beck.
See Massinger, 262:18.

[2] As early as 1691, Benjamin Harris of Boston advertised the forthcoming second impression of the *New England Primer.* The oldest known copy extant is dated 1737.

[3] See Bacon, 181:17, and Davies, 251:7.

[4] The first record of this prayer is found in the *Enchiridion Leonis* [1160]. The early editions of the *Primer* give the first line of the prayer as: Now I lay me down to take my sleep. The familiar version of the line appeared in the edition of 1784. In the edition of 1814 the second line reads: I pray thee, Lord, my soul to keep.

Matthew Prior

1664–1721

13 All jargon of the schools.[5]

I Am That I Am, An Ode [1688]

14 Our hopes, like towering falcons, aim
At objects in an airy height;
The little pleasure of the game
Is from afar to view the flight.

To the Honorable Charles Montague [1692]

15 The end must justify the means.[6]

Hans Carvel [1700]

16 Lays the rough paths of peevish Nature even,
And opens in each heart a little heaven.

Charity [1703]

17 Be to her virtues very kind;
Be to her faults a little blind;
Let all her ways be unconfined;
And clap your padlock—on her mind!

An English Padlock [1707]

18 And thought the nation ne'er would thrive
Till all the whores were burnt alive.

Paulo Purganti and His Wife [1708]

19 He ranged his tropes, and preached up patience;
Backed his opinion with quotations. *Ib.*

20 Cured yesterday of my disease,
I died last night of my physician.[7]

The Remedy Worse than the Disease [1714]

21 And often took leave, but was loth to depart.

The Thief and the Cordelier [1718]

22 Odds life! must one swear to the truth of a song? *A Better Answer [1718]*

23 His noble negligences teach
What others' toils despair to reach.

Alma [1718], canto II, l. 7

24 Till their own dreams at length deceive 'em,
And oft repeating, they believe 'em.

Ib. III, l. 13

25 Abra was ready ere I called her name;
And though I called another, Abra came.

Solomon on the Vanity of the World [1718], bk. II, l. 364

26 To John I owed great obligation;
But John, unhappily, thought fit

[5] Noisy jargon of the schools.—John Pomfret [1667–1702], *Reason*
The sounding jargon of the schools.—Cowper, *Truth* [1782], *l. 367*

[6] See St. Jerome, 127:20.

[7] See Leibnitz, 315:12.

To publish it to all the nation:
Sure John and I are more than quit.
Epigram [1718]

1 Venus, take my votive glass;
Since I am not what I was,
What from this day I shall be,
Venus, let me never see.
The Lady Who Offers Her Looking-Glass to Venus [1718]. From an epigram attributed to Plato in The Greek Anthology[1]

2 Nobles and heralds, by your leave,
Here lies what once was Matthew Prior;
The son of Adam and of Eve:
Can Bourbon or Nassau claim higher?[2]
Epitaph [1721]

Sir John Vanbrugh
1664–1726

3 Once a woman has given you her heart you can never get rid of the rest of her.
The Relapse [1697], act II, sc. i

4 No man worth having is true to his wife, or can be true to his wife, or ever was, or ever will be so. *Ib. III, ii*

5 *Belinda:* Ay, but you know we must return good for evil.
Lady Brute: That may be a mistake in the translation.
The Provoked Wife [1698], act I, sc. i

6 He laughs best who laughs last.[3]
The Country House [1706], act II, sc. v

7 Much of a muchness.
The Provoked Husband [1728] (completed by COLLEY CIBBER*) act I, sc. i*

Susannah Centlivre
c. 1667–1723

8 The real Simon Pure.
A Bold Stroke for a Wife [1718], act V, sc. i

[1] Edited by J. W. MACKAIL.

[2] The following epitaph was written long before the time of Prior:
Johnnie Carnegie lais heer. / Descendit of Adam and Eve. / Gif ony con gang hieher, / Ise willing give him leve.

[3] Better the last smile than the first laughter. — JOHN RAY, *Proverbs* [1670]

John Pomfret
1667–1702

9 We live and learn, but not the wiser grow.[4]
Reason, l. 112

Jonathan Swift
1667–1745

10 Books, like men their authors, have no more than one way of coming into the world, but there are ten thousand to go out of it, and return no more.[5]
A Tale of a Tub [1704], dedication

11 Books, the children of the brain.
Ib. sec. 1

12 As boys do sparrows, with flinging salt upon their tails. *Ib. 7*

13 Satire is a sort of glass, wherein beholders do generally discover everybody's face but their own.
The Battle of the Books [1704], preface

14 Instead of dirt and poison we have rather chosen to fill our hives with honey and wax; thus furnishing mankind with the two noblest of things, which are sweetness and light.[6] *Ib.*

15 Laws are like cobwebs, which may catch small flies, but let wasps and hornets break through.[7]
A Critical Essay upon the Faculties of the Mind [1707]

16 There is nothing in this world constant, but inconstancy.[8] *Ib.*

17 'Tis very warm weather when one's in bed.
Journal to Stella [November 8, 1710]

18 With my own fair hands.
Ib. [January 4, 1711]

19 We are so fond of one another, because our ailments are the same.
Ib. [February 1, 1711]

20 I love good creditable acquaintance; I love to be the worst of the company.
Ib. [May 17, 1711]

[4] It is good to live and learn. — CERVANTES, *Don Quixote, pt. II* [1615], *ch. 32*
Live and learn, / Not first learn and then live. — BROWNING, *Parleyings with Certain People, With Christopher Smart* [1887], *IX*

[5] See Webster, 262:8.

[6] See Matthew Arnold, 588:18.

[7] See Anacharsis, 63:2, and Zincgref, 267:3.

[8] See Heraclitus, 69:25; Racan, 265:3; Shelley, 466:11; and Wilde, 676:4.

1 We were to do more business after dinner; but after dinner is after dinner—an old saying and a true, "much drinking, little thinking." *Ib. [February 26, 1712]*

2 We have just enough religion to make us hate, but not enough to make us love one another.
Thoughts on Various Subjects; from Miscellanies [1711]

3 Censure is the tax a man pays to the public for being eminent. *Ib.*

4 Every man desires to live long, but no man would be old. *Ib.*

5 A nice man is a man of nasty ideas. *Ib.*

6 Vision is the art of seeing things invisible. *Ib. [1726]*

7 'Tis an old maxim in the schools,
That flattery's the food of fools;
Yet now and then your men of wit
Will condescend to take a bit.
Cadenus and Vanessa [1713][1]

8 Proper words in proper places, make the true definition of a style.
Letter to a Young Clergyman [January 9, 1720]

9 If Heaven had looked upon riches to be a valuable thing, it would not have given them to such a scoundrel.
Letter to Miss Vanhomrigh [August 12, 1720]

10 He [the Emperor] is taller by almost the breadth of my nail, than any of his court, which alone is enough to strike an awe into the beholders.
Gulliver's Travels [1726]. Voyage to Lilliput, ch. 2

11 I cannot but conclude the bulk of your natives to be the most pernicious race of little odious vermin that nature ever suffered to crawl upon the surface of the earth.
Ib. Voyage to Brobdingnag, ch. 6

12 And he gave it for his opinion, that whoever could make two ears of corn or two blades of grass to grow upon a spot of ground where only one grew before, would deserve better of mankind, and do more essential service to his country, than the whole race of politicians put together.[2] *Ib.*

13 He had been eight years upon a project for extracting sunbeams out of cucumbers, which were to be put in vials hermetically sealed, and let out to warm the air in raw inclement summers.
Ib. Voyage to Laputa, ch. 5

14 I said the thing which was not. (For they have no word in their language to express lying or falsehood.)[3]
Ib. Voyage to the Houyhnhnms

15 I told him . . . that we ate when we were not hungry, and drank without the provocation of thirst. *Ib. 6*

16 A set of phrases learnt by rote;
A passion for a scarlet coat;
When at a play to laugh, or cry,
Yet cannot tell the reason why:
Never to hold her tongue a minute;
While all she prates has nothing in it.
The Furniture of a Woman's Mind [1727]

17 For conversation well endued;
She calls it witty to be rude;
And, placing raillery in railing,
Will tell aloud your greatest failing. *Ib.*

18 Not die here in a rage, like a poisoned rat in a hole.
Letter to Bolingbroke [March 21, 1729]

19 Yet malice never was his aim;
He lashed the vice but spared the name.
No individual could resent,
Where thousands equally were meant.
His satire points at no defect
But what all mortals may correct;
For he abhorred that senseless tribe
Who call it humor when they gibe.
Verses on the Death of Dr. Swift [1731], l. 459

20 Hobbes clearly proves that every creature
Lives in a state of war by nature.[4]
On Poetry. A Rhapsody [1733]

21 So, naturalists observe, a flea
Hath smaller fleas that on him prey;
And these have smaller still to bite 'em;
And so proceed *ad infinitum.*

[1] When the poem of "Cadenus and Vanessa" was the general topic of conversation, someone said, "Surely that Vanessa must be an extraordinary woman that could inspire the Dean to write so finely upon her." Mrs. Johnson smiled, and answered that "she thought that point not quite so clear; for it was well known the Dean could write finely upon a broomstick."—SAMUEL JOHNSON, *Lives of the Poets* [1779–1781], *Life of Swift*

[2] He who makes two blades of grass grow in place of one renders a service to the state.—VOLTAIRE, *Letter to M. Moreau* [1765]

[3] Gulliver has been trying to describe his voyage in a ship to his Houyhnhnm "Master," who doesn't believe him, and accuses him of being mistaken or of saying "the thing which was not."

[4] See Hobbes, 264:12.

Thus every poet, in his kind,
Is bit by him that comes behind. *Ib.*

1 Conversation is but carving!
Give no more to every guest
Than he's able to digest.
Give him always of the prime,
And but little at a time.
Carve to all but just enough,
Let them neither starve nor stuff,
And that you may have your due,
Let your neighbor carve for you.
Conversation

2 Under an oak, in stormy weather,
I joined this rogue and whore together;
And none but he who rules the thunder
Can put this rogue and whore asunder.
Marriage certificate. From The Oxford Book of Literary Anecdotes, JAMES SUTHERLAND, ed. [1975], no. 77

3 The sight of you is good for sore eyes.[1]
Polite Conversation [1738?], dialogue 1

4 'Tis as cheap sitting as standing. *Ib.*

5 I hate nobody: I am in charity with the world.[2] *Ib.*

6 You were half seas over. *Ib.*

7 I won't quarrel with my bread and butter. *Ib.*

8 She's no chicken; she's on the wrong side of thirty, if she be a day. *Ib.*

9 She wears her clothes, as if they were thrown on her with a pitchfork. *Ib.*

10 He was a bold man that first eat an oyster. *Ib. 2*

11 That's as well said, as if I had said it myself. *Ib.*

12 Fingers were made before forks, and hands before knives. *Ib.*

13 She has more goodness in her little finger, than he has in his whole body. *Ib.*

14 Lord, I wonder what fool it was that first invented kissing! *Ib.*

15 The best doctors in the world are Doctor Diet, Doctor Quiet, and Doctor Merryman.[3] *Ib.*

[1]What a sight for sore eyes that would be! — WILLIAM HAZLITT [1778–1830], *Of Persons One Would Have Seen*

[2]See *The Book of Common Prayer, Holy Communion,* 55:16.

[3]Use three physicians — / First, Dr. Quiet; / Next, Dr. Merryman, / And Dr. Dyet. — *Regimen Sanitatis Salernitanum* [1607]

16 May you live all the days of your life. *Ib.*

17 I always love to begin a journey on Sundays, because I shall have the prayers of the church to preserve all that travel by land, or by water. *Ib.*

18 I thought you and he were hand-in-glove. *Ib.*

19 She watches him, as a cat would watch a mouse. *Ib. 3*

20 She pays him in his own coin. *Ib.*

21 There was all the world and his wife. *Ib.*

22 Hail, fellow, well met,
All dirty and wet:
Find out if you can,
Who's master, who's man.
My Lady's Lamentation [1765], l. 171

23 I shall be like that tree, I shall die at the top.
From SIR WALTER SCOTT, Life of Swift [1814]

24 Good God! What a genius I had when I wrote that book [*A Tale of a Tub*]. *Ib.*

25 Ubi saeva indignatio ulterius cor lacerare nequit [Where savage indignation can lacerate his heart no more].[4]
Epitaph. Inscribed on Swift's grave, St. Patrick's, Dublin

Alain René Lesage
1668–1747

26 It may be said that his wit shines at the expense of his memory.[5]
Gil Blas [1715–1735], bk. III, ch. 11

27 A flatterer can risk everything with great personages. *Ib. IV, 7*

28 Pride and conceit were the original sin of man. *Ib. VII, 3*

29 I wish you all sorts of prosperity with a little more taste. *Ib. 4*

30 The pleasure of talking is the inextinguishable passion of a woman, coeval with the act of breathing. *Ib. 7*

31 Facts are stubborn things. *Ib. X, 1*

[4]Swift sleeps under the greatest epitaph in history. — YEATS
See Yeats, 716:6.

[5]See Sheridan, 399:13.

Giovanni Battista [Giambattista] Vico

1668–1774

1 The nature of things is nothing other than that they come into being at certain times and in certain ways. Wherever the same circumstances are present, the same phenomena arise and no others.

Scienza Nuova [1725][1]

2 In that dark night which shrouds from our eyes the most remote antiquity, a light appears which cannot lead us astray; I speak of this incontestable truth: the social world is certainly the work of man. *Ib.*

3 Governments must be conformable to the nature of the governed; governments are even a result of that nature.[2] *Ib.*

William Congreve

1670–1729

4 Eternity was in that moment.

The Old Bachelor [1693], act IV, sc. vii

5 Married in haste, we may repent at leisure.[3]

Ib. V, viii

6 It is the business of a comic poet to paint the vices and follies of human kind.

The Double Dealer [1694], epistle dedicatory

7 Retired to their tea and scandal, according to their ancient custom.[4]

Ib. act I, sc. i

8 Though marriage makes man and wife one flesh, it leaves 'em still two fools.

Ib. II, iii

9 No mask like open truth to cover lies,
As to go naked is the best disguise.

Ib. V, iv

10 Thou liar of the first magnitude.

Love for Love [1695], act II, sc. ii

11 I warrant you, if he danced till doomsday, he thought I was to pay the piper.[5]

Ib.

12 O fie, miss, you must not kiss and tell.

Ib. x

13 Women are like tricks by sleight of hand,
Which, to admire, we should not understand.

Ib. IV, iii

[1]Translated by JULES MICHELET.
[2]See Jefferson, 387:9.
[3]See Shakespeare, 188:34.
[4]See Fielding, 349:16.
[5]Pay the piper: phrase for settling the score. He who pays the piper calls the tune. — *Proverb*

14 Music has charms to soothe a savage breast,[6]
To soften rocks, or bend a knotted oak.

The Mourning Bride [1697], act I, sc. i

15 By magic numbers and persuasive sound.

Ib.

16 Heaven has no rage like love to hatred turned,
Nor hell a fury like a woman scorned.[7]

Ib. III, viii

17 Love's but a frailty of the mind,
When 'tis not with ambition joined.

The Way of the World [1700], act III, sc. xii

18 I nauseate walking; 'tis a country diversion, I loathe the country. *Ib. IV, v*

19 Let us be very strange and well-bred: Let us be as strange as if we had been married a great while; and as well-bred as if we were not married at all. *Ib.*

20 Thou art a retailer of phrases, and dost deal in remnants of remnants. *Ib. ix*

21 O, she is the antidote to desire.

Ib. xiv

22 Careless she is with artful care,
Affecting to seem unaffected. *Amoret*

23 Defer not till tomorrow to be wise,
Tomorrow's sun to thee may never rise.[8]

Letter to Cobham

Colley Cibber

1671–1757

24 As good be out of the world as out of the fashion.

Love's Last Shift [1696], act II

25 Possession is eleven points in the law.

Woman's Wit [1697], act I

26 Words are but empty thanks. *Ib. V*

27 Off with his head[9] — so much for Buckingham.

Richard III (altered) [1700], act IV, sc. iii

28 Perish the thought! *Ib. V, v*

29 This business will never hold water.

She Wou'd and She Wou'd Not [1703], act IV

[6]See Shakespeare, 229:1.
[7]See Aristophanes, 82:13, and Nietzche, 657:21.
We shall find no fiend in hell can match the fury of a disappointed woman. — COLLEY CIBBER, *Love's Last Shift* [1696], *act IV*
[8]See Euripides, 76:8, and Edward Young, 330:8.
[9]See Shakespeare, 187:14, and Carroll, 612:1.

1 Old houses mended,
Cost little less than new before they're ended.
The Double Gallant [1707], prologue

2 Oh, how many torments lie in the small circle of a wedding ring!
Ib. act I, sc. ii

3 Stolen sweets are best.
The Rival Fools [1709], act I

Anthony Ashley Cooper, Earl of Shaftesbury

1671–1713

4 How comes it to pass, then, that we appear such cowards in reasoning, and are so afraid to stand the test of ridicule?[1]
A Letter Concerning Enthusiasm [1708],[2] *sec. 2*

5 Truth, 'tis supposed, may bear all lights; and one of those principal lights or natural mediums by which things are to be viewed in order to a thorough recognition is ridicule itself.[3]
Essay on the Freedom of Wit and Humor [1709],[4] *pt. I, sec. 1*

Joseph Addison[5]

1672–1719

6 For wheresoe'er I turn my ravished eyes,
Gay gilded scenes and shining prospects rise,
Poetic fields encompass me around,
And still I seem to tread on classic ground.
A Letter from Italy [1703]

7 And, pleased the Almighty's orders to perform,
Rides in the whirlwind and directs the storm.[6]
The Campaign [1704], l. 91

[1] See Chesterfield, 342:12.

[2] Later included in *Characteristics of Men, Manners, Opinions, Times* [1711].

[3] See Chesterfield, 342:12.

'Twas the saying of an ancient sage (Gorgias Leontinus, *apud* Aristotle's *Rhetoric*) that humor was the only test of gravity, and gravity of humor. For a subject which would not bear raillery was suspicious; and a jest which would not bear serious examination was certainly false wit. — SHAFTESBURY, *Essay on the Freedom of Wit and Humor* [1709], *pt. I, sec. 5*

[4] Later included in *Characteristics of Men, Manners, Opinions, Times* [1711].

[5] There taught us how to live; and (oh! too high / The price for knowledge) taught us how to die. — THOMAS TICKELL [1686–1740], *On the Death of Mr. Addison* [1719], *l. 81*

See Montaigne, 164:9.

[6] This line is repeated by Pope in his *Dunciad, bk. III* [1728], *l. 264*. See 340:22.

8 The spacious firmament on high,
With all the blue ethereal sky,
And spangled heavens, a shining frame,
Their great Original proclaim.[7]
Ode [in The Spectator, no. 465, August 23, 1712]

9 Soon as the evening shades prevail,
The moon takes up the wondrous tale,
And nightly to the listening earth
Repeats the story of her birth;
While all the stars that round her burn,
And all the planets in their turn,
Confirm the tidings as they roll,
And spread the truth from pole to pole.
Ib.

10 Forever singing as they shine,
"The Hand that made us is divine."
Ib.

11 Should the whole frame of Nature round him break,
In ruin and confusion hurled,
He, unconcerned, would hear the mighty crack,
And stand secure amidst a falling world.
Horace, Odes, bk. III, ode iii[8]

12 'Tis not in mortals to command success,
But we'll do more, Sempronius; we'll deserve it.
Cato[9] *[1713], act I, sc. ii*

13 Blesses his stars and thinks it luxury.
Ib. iv

14 'Tis pride, rank pride, and haughtiness of soul;
I think the Romans call it stoicism.
Ib.

15 Were you with these, my prince, you'd soon forget
The pale, unripened beauties of the north.
Ib.

16 Beauty soon grows familiar to the lover,
Fades in his eye, and palls upon the sense.
Ib.

17 My voice is still for war.
Gods! can a Roman senate long debate
Which of the two to choose, slavery or death?
Ib. II, i

18 The woman that deliberates is lost.
Ib. IV, i

19 Curse on his virtues! they've undone his country.
Ib. iv

[7] See *Psalm 19:1*, 17:27.

[8] See Horace, 107:28.

[9] The *Massachusetts Spy* used the following lines from *Cato* as its motto from November 22, 1771, to April 6, 1775: Do thou Great Liberty inspire our Souls— / And make our Lives in thy Possession happy— / Or, our Deaths glorious in thy just Defense.

1 What pity is it
That we can die but once to serve our country![1] *Ib.*

2 When vice prevails, and impious men bear sway,
The post of honor is a private station.[2]
Ib.

3 It must be so—Plato, thou reasonest well!
Else whence this pleasing hope, this fond desire,
This longing after immortality?
Or whence this secret dread, and inward horror,
Of falling into naught? Why shrinks the soul
Back on herself, and startles at destruction?
'Tis the divinity that stirs within us;[3]
'Tis heaven itself, that points out an hereafter,
And intimates eternity to man.
Eternity! thou pleasing, dreadful thought!
Ib. V, i

4 Sweet are the slumbers of the virtuous man.
Ib. iv

5 From hence, let fierce contending nations know
What dire effects from civil discord flow.
Ib.

6 Round-heads and Wooden-shoes are standing jokes.
The Drummer [1716], prologue, l. 8

7 If I can any way contribute to the diversion or improvement of the country in which I live, I shall leave it, when I am summoned out of it, with the secret satisfaction of thinking that I have not lived in vain.[4]
The Spectator, no. 1 [March 1, 1711]

8 Thus I live in the world rather as a spectator of mankind than as one of the species.
Ib.

9 I shall endeavor to enliven morality with wit, and to temper wit with morality.
Ib. 10 [March 11, 1711]

10 True happiness is of a retired nature, and an enemy to pomp and noise; it arises, in the first place, from the enjoyment of one's self; and, in the next, from the friendship and conversation of a few select companions.
Ib. 15 [March 17, 1711]

[1] See Nathan Hale, 401:9.
[2] Give me, kind Heaven, a private station, / A mind serene for contemplation! / Title and profit I resign; / The post of honor shall be mine.—GAY, *Fables, pt. II* [1738], *The Vulture, the Sparrow, and Other Birds*
[3] See Browne, 274:22, and Emerson, 496:20.
[4] See Grellet, 439:2.

11 There is not a more unhappy being than a superannuated idol.
Ib. 73 [May 24, 1711]

12 A man that has a taste of music, painting, or architecture, is like one that has another sense, when compared with such as have no relish of those arts.
Ib. 93 [June 16, 1711]

13 There is no defense against reproach but obscurity. *Ib. 101 [June 26, 1711]*

14 Much might be said on both sides.
Ib. 122 [July 20, 1711]

15 Authors have established it as a kind of rule, that a man ought to be dull sometimes; as the most severe reader makes allowances for many rests and nodding places in a voluminous writer. *Ib. 124 [July 23, 1711]*

16 Books are the legacies that a great genius leaves to mankind, which are delivered down from generation to generation, as presents to the posterity of those who are yet unborn.
Ib. 166 [September 10, 1711]

17 Good nature is more agreeable in conversation than wit, and gives a certain air to the countenance which is more amiable than beauty. *Ib. 169 [September 13, 1711]*

18 Were I to prescribe a rule for drinking, it should be formed upon a saying quoted by Sir William Temple: the first glass for myself, the second for my friends, the third for good humor, and the fourth for mine enemies.[5]
Ib. 195 [October 13, 1711]

19 A true critic ought to dwell rather upon excellencies than imperfections, to discover the concealed beauties of a writer, and communicate to the world such things as are worth their observation.
Ib. 291 [February 2, 1712]

20 These widows, sir, are the most perverse creatures in the world.
Ib. 335 [March 25, 1712]

21 Mirth is like a flash of lightning, that breaks through a gloom of clouds, and glitters for a moment; cheerfulness keeps up a kind of daylight in the mind, and fills it with a steady and perpetual serenity.
Ib. 381 [May 17, 1712]

22 Sir Roger made several reflections on the greatness of the British Nation; as, that one Englishman could beat three Frenchmen; that we could never be in danger of Popery so long as we took care of our fleet; that the

[5] See Herbert, 268:3; Hugo, 491:22; and Sill, 646:12.

Thames was the noblest river in Europe . . . with many other honest prejudices which naturally cleave to the heart of a true Englishman. *Ib. 383 [May 20, 1712]*

1 Our disputants put me in mind of the skuttle fish, that when he is unable to extricate himself, blackens all the water about him, till he becomes invisible.
Ib. 476 [September 5, 1712]

2 The fraternity of the henpecked.[1]
Ib. 482 [September 12, 1712]

3 A man should always consider how much he has more than he wants, and how much more unhappy he might be than he really is.
Ib. 574 [July 30, 1714]

4 We are always doing something for Posterity, but I would fain see Posterity do something for us. *Ib. 587 [August 20, 1714]*

5 See in what peace a Christian can die.
Dying words [1719]. From EDWARD YOUNG, *Conjectures on Original Composition [1759]*

Edmond Hoyle[2]

1672–1769

6 When in doubt, win the trick.
Twenty-four Rules for Learners, rule 12

Sir Richard Steele

1672–1729

7 I am come to a tavern alone to eat a steak, after which I shall return to the office.
Letters to His Wife [October 28, 1707]

8 I was going home two hours ago, but was met by Mr. Griffith, who has kept me ever since. I will come within a pint of wine.
Ib. [Eleven at night, January 5, 1708]

9 A little in drink, but at all times yr faithful husband. *Ib. [September 27, 1708]*

10 The finest woman in nature should not detain me an hour from you; but you must sometimes suffer the rivalship of the wisest men. *Ib. [September 17, 1712]*

[1]See Byron, 460:11.
[2]Hoyle published a *Short Treatise on Whist* [1742], which in subsequent editions added rules for playing piquet, backgammon, chess, and other games. His *Laws* [1760] ruled whist playing until 1864, hence the saying, "according to Hoyle."

11 Though her mien carries much more invitation than command, to behold her is an immediate check to loose behavior; to love her is a liberal education.[3]
Tatler [1709–1711], no. 49

12 Reading is to the mind what exercise is to the body. *Ib. no. 147*

13 When you fall into a man's conversation, the first thing you should consider is, whether he has a greater inclination to hear you, or that you should hear him.
The Spectator, no. 49 [April 26, 1711]

14 Of all the affections which attend human life, the love of glory is the most ardent.
Ib. 139 [August 9, 1711]

15 Age in a virtuous person, of either sex, carries in it an authority which makes it preferable to all the pleasures of youth.
Ib. 153 [August 25, 1711]

16 Among all the diseases of the mind there is not one more epidemical or more pernicious than the love of flattery.
Ib. 238 [December 3, 1711]

17 Will Honeycomb calls these over-offended ladies the outrageously virtuous.
Ib. 266 [January 4, 1712]

18 A favor well bestowed is almost as great an honor to him who confers it as to him who receives it.
Ib. 497 [September 30, 1712]

François Goyot de Pitavals

1673–1743

19 Causes Célèbres.
Title of book recounting famous trials and judgments

Nicholas Rowe

1674–1718

20 As if Misfortune made the throne her seat,
And none could be unhappy but the great.[4]
The Fair Penitent [1703], prologue

21 At length the morn and cold indifference
came. *Ib. act I, sc. i*

22 Is this that haughty gallant, gay Lothario?
Ib. V, i

[3]Lady Elizabeth Hastings [1682–1739].
[4]None think the great unhappy, but the great.— EDWARD YOUNG, *The Love of Fame* [1725–1728], *satire I, l. 238*

Isaac Watts
1674–1748

1 Were I so tall to reach the pole,
Or grasp the ocean with my span,
I must be measured by my soul;
The mind's the standard of the man.
Horae Lyricae [1706], bk. II, False Greatness

2 Let dogs delight to bark and bite,
For God hath made them so;
Divine Songs [1715], 16, Against Quarreling and Fighting

3 But, children, you should never let
Such angry passions rise;
Your little hands were never made
To tear each other's eyes. *Ib.*

4 Birds in their little nests agree;
And 'tis a shameful sight,
When children of one family
Fall out, and chide, and fight.
Ib. 17, Love Between Brothers and Sisters

5 How doth the little busy bee
Improve each shining hour,[1]
And gather honey all the day
From every opening flower!
Ib. 20, Against Idleness and Mischief

6 For Satan finds some mischief still
For idle hands to do. *Ib.*

7 Let me be dressed fine as I will,
Flies, worms, and flowers, exceed me still.
Ib. 22, Against Pride in Clothes

8 Hush! my dear, lie still and slumber,
Holy angels guard thy bed!
Heavenly blessings without number
Gently falling on thy head.
Ib. 35, A Cradle Hymn

9 'Tis the voice of the sluggard; I heard him complain,
"You have waked me too soon, I must slumber again."[2] *Ib. The Sluggard*

10 O God, our help in ages past,
Our hope for years to come,
Our shelter from the stormy blast,
And our eternal home.
Psalm 90 [1719], st. 1

11 A thousand ages in Thy sight
Are like an evening gone;
Short as the watch that ends the night
Before the rising sun. *Ib. st. 4*

12 Time, like an ever-rolling stream,
Bears all its sons away;
They fly forgotten, as a dream
Dies at the opening day.[3] *Ib. st. 5*

13 Joy to the world! the Lord is come;
Let earth receive her King.
Let ev'ry heart prepare Him room,
And heav'n and nature sing.
Psalm 98 [1719], st. 1

14 When I can read my title clear
To mansions in the skies,
I'll bid farewell to every fear,
And wipe my weeping eyes.
Hymns and Spiritual Songs, bk. II, hymn 65

15 There is a land of pure delight,
Where saints immortal reign;
Infinite day excludes the night,
And pleasures banish pain. *Ib. 66*

William Somerville[4]
1675–1742

16 Let all the learned say what they can,
'Tis ready money makes the man.
Ready Money [1727]

17 There is something in a face,
An air, and a peculiar grace,
Which boldest painters cannot trace.
The Lucky Hit [1727]

18 The chase, the sport of kings;
Image of war, without its guilt.
The Chase [1735], I, 13

John Philips
1676–1709

19 Happy the man who, void of care and strife,
In silken or in leathern purse retains
A Splendid Shilling.
The Splendid Shilling [1701], l. 1

Sir Robert Walpole
1676–1745

20 The balance of power.
Speech in the House of Commons [February 13, 1741]

21 All those men have their price.
From WILLIAM COXE, *Memoirs of Walpole [1798], vol. IV, p. 369*

[1]See Lewis Carroll, 611:5.
[2]See Lewis Carroll, 612:10.

[3]See Marcus Aurelius, 124:25, and Anonymous, 925:6.
[4]Of whom Johnson, in his *Lives of the Poets,* made the famous remark, "He writes very well for a gentleman." See Johnson, 356:22.

1 Anything but history, for history must be false. *Walpoliana, no. 141*

Henry St. John, Viscount Bolingbroke
1678–1751

2 Truth lies within a little and certain compass, but error is immense.
Reflections upon Exile [1716]

3 Nations, like men, have their infancy.
On the Study and Use of History [1752], letter 4

4 They [Thucydides and Xenophon] maintained the dignity of history. *Ib. 5*

5 It is the modest, not the presumptuous, inquirer who makes a real and safe progress in the discovery of divine truths. One follows Nature and Nature's God; that is, he follows God in his works and in his word.[1]
Letter to Alexander Pope

George Farquhar
1678–1707

6 Reason still keeps its throne, but it nods a little, that's all.
The Recruiting Officer [1706], act III, sc. ii

7 I have fed purely upon ale; I have eat my ale, and I always sleep upon ale.
The Beaux' Stratagem [1707], act I, sc. i

8 My Lady Bountiful. *Ib.*

9 I believe they talked of me, for they laughed consumedly. *Ib. III, i*

10 'Twas for the good of my country that I should be abroad.[2]—Anything for the good of one's country—I'm a Roman for that.
Ib. III, ii

11 How a little love and good company improves a woman! *Ib. IV, i*

12 Spare all I have, and take my life.
Ib. V, ii

[1] See Pope, 337:16, and Jefferson, 387:9.
[2] Leaving his country for his country's sake.—CHARLES FITZGEFFREY, *The Life and Death of Sir Francis Drake* [1596], *st. 213*
True patriots all; for, be it understood, / We left our country for our country's good.—*Prologue for opening of playhouse at New South Wales* [January 16, 1796]; attributed to the famous pickpocket known as GEORGE BARRINGTON [1755–c. 1840]

Thomas Parnell
1679–1718

13 My days have been so wondrous free,
The little birds that fly
With careless ease from tree to tree,
Were but as blessed as I.
Song [1714],[3] st. 1

14 Still an angel appear to each lover beside,
But still be a woman to you.
When Thy Beauty Appears [1722], st. 3

15 We call it only pretty Fanny's way.
An Elegy to an Old Beauty [1722], st. 4

16 Let those love now who never loved before;
Let those who always loved, now love the more.
Translation of the Pervigilium Veneris[4]

Destouches [Philippe Néricault]
1680–1754

17 Those not present are always wrong.[5]
L'Obstacle Imprévu [1717], act I, sc. vi

18 Criticism is easy, art is difficult.
Le Glorieux [1732], act II, sc. v

Edward Young
1683–1765

19 The love of praise, howe'er concealed by art,
Reigns more or less, and glows in ev'ry heart.
Love of Fame [1725–1728], satire I, l. 51

20 Some for renown, on scraps of learning dote,
And think they grow immortal as they quote.
Ib. l. 89

21 Be wise with speed;
A fool at forty is a fool indeed.
Ib. II, l. 282

22 Forever most divinely in the wrong.
Ib. VI, l. 105

23 For her own breakfast she'll project a scheme,
Nor take her tea without a stratagem.
Ib. l. 187

[3] Set to music by Francis Hopkinson; one of the earliest American songs.
[4] See Anonymous Latin, 133:14, and Freiligrath, 536:8.
[5] Les absents ont toujours tort.

1 One to destroy, is murder by the law;
And gibbets keep the lifted hand in awe;
To murder thousands takes a specious name,
War's glorious art, and gives immortal fame.[1]
Ib. VII, l. 55

2 The man that makes a character makes foes.
To Mr. Pope, epistle I, l. 28

3 In records that defy the tooth of time.
The Statesman's Creed

4 Tired nature's sweet restorer, balmy sleep!
Night Thoughts [1742–1745]. Night I, l. 1

5 Night, sable goddess! from her ebon throne,
In rayless majesty, now stretches forth
Her leaden scepter o'er a slumbering world.
Ib. l. 18

6 Creation sleeps! 'Tis as the general pulse
Of life stood still, and Nature made a pause;
An awful pause! prophetic of her end.
Ib. l. 23

7 The bell strikes one. We take no note of time
But from its loss.
Ib. l. 55

8 Be wise today; 'tis madness to defer.[2]
Ib. l. 390

9 Procrastination is the thief of time.
Ib. l. 393

10 At thirty, man suspects himself a fool;
Knows it at forty, and reforms his plan;
At fifty chides his infamous delay,
Pushes his prudent purpose to resolve;
In all the magnanimity of thought
Resolves, and re-resolves; then dies the same.
Ib. l. 417

11 All men think all men mortal but themselves.
Ib. l. 424

12 Man wants but little, nor that little long.[3]
Ib. Night IV, l. 118

13 A God all mercy is a God unjust.
Ib. l. 233

14 By night an atheist half believes a God.[4]
Ib. Night V, l. 177

15 Like our shadows,
Our wishes lengthen as our sun declines.
Ib. l. 661

16 Death loves a shining mark, a signal blow.[5]
Ib. l. 1011

[1] See Seneca, 114:32; Porteus, 378:3; and J. R. Lowell, 567:20.
[2] See Euripides, 76:8, and Congreve, 324:23.
[3] See Goldsmith, 369:12, and John Quincy Adams, 418:7.
[4] See W. T. Cummings, 857:17.
[5] See Quarles, 267:11.

17 Too low they build, who build beneath the stars.
Ib. Night VIII, l. 215

18 Final Ruin fiercely drives
Her plowshare o'er creation.[6]
Ib. Night IX, l. 167

19 An undevout astronomer is mad.
Ib. l. 771

Sir William Pulteney,[7] Earl of Bath
1684–1764

20 Since twelve honest men have decided the cause,
And were judges of facts, though not judges of laws.
The Honest Jury [1731], III

George Berkeley
1685–1753

21 And what are these fluxions? The velocities of evanescent increments. And what are these same evanescent increments? They are neither finite quantities, nor quantities infinitely small, nor yet nothing. May we not call them ghosts of departed quantities?
The Analyst [1734], sec. 4

22 [Tar water] is of a nature so mild and benign and proportioned to the human constitution, as to warm without heating, to cheer but not inebriate.[8]
Siris [1744], par. 217

23 Truth is the cry of all, but the game of the few.
Ib. par. 368

24 He who says there is no such thing as an honest man, you may be sure is himself a knave.
Maxims Concerning Patriotism

25 Westward the course of empire takes its way;[9]
The four first acts already past,
A fifth shall close the drama with the day:
Time's noblest offspring is the last.
On the Prospect of Planting Arts and Learning in America [1752], st. 6

Jane Brereton
1685–1740

26 The picture placed the busts between,
Adds to the thought much strength,

[6] See Burns, 409:10.
[7] One of "the three grand allies," the others being Stanhope and Walpole. Walpole said that he feared Pulteney's tongue more than another man's sword.
[8] See Cowper, 377:3.
[9] Westward the star of empire takes its way.—JOHN QUINCY ADAMS, *Oration at Plymouth* [1802]

Wisdom, and Wit are little seen,
But Folly's at full length.
On Beau Nash's Picture at Full Length Between the Busts of Sir Isaac Newton and Mr. Pope[1]

Aaron Hill
1685–1750

1 Tender-handed stroke a nettle,
And it stings you for your pains;
Grasp it like a man of mettle,
And it soft as silk remains.[2]
Verses Written on a Window in Scotland

Samuel Madden
1686–1765

2 In an orchard there should be enough to eat, enough to lay up, enough to be stolen, and enough to rot upon the ground.
Quoted by SAMUEL JOHNSON *[1783]. From* BOSWELL, *Life of Johnson [1791], vol. II, p. 457 (Everyman edition)*

Allan Ramsay
1686–1758

3 Farewell to Lochaber, farewell to my Jean.
Lochaber No More [1724], st. 1

Henry Carey
c. 1687–1743

4 Namby Pamby's little rhymes,
Little jingle, little chimes.
Namby Pamby[3]

5 Of all the girls that are so smart,
There's none like pretty Sally.
She is the darling of my heart,
And she lives in our alley.
Sally in Our Alley [1729], st. 1

6 God save our gracious king!
Long live our noble king!
God save the king!
God Save the King [c. 1740]

[1] In ALEXANDER DYCE [1798–1869], *Specimens of British Poetesses.* This epigram is generally ascribed to CHESTERFIELD.

[2] The world's a nettle; disturb it, it stings: / Grasp it firmly, it stings not.—OWEN MEREDITH [E. R. BULWER-LYTTON], *Lucile* [1860], *pt. I, canto 3, st. 2*

[3] Ambrose Phillips . . . who had the honor of bringing into fashion a species of composition which has been called, after his name, Namby Pamby.—MACAULAY, *Review of Aikin's Life of Addison* [1843]

John Gay[4]
1688–1732

7 'Twas when the seas were roaring
With hollow blasts of wind,
A damsel lay deploring,
All on a rock reclined.
The What D'ye Call It [1715], act II, sc. viii

8 Now Cynthia, named fair regent of the night.
Trivia [1716], bk. III

9 All in the Downs the fleet was moored.
Sweet William's Farewell to Black-eyed Susan [1720]

10 Adieu! she cries; and waved her lily hand.
Ib.

11 My lodging is on the cold ground,
And hard, very hard, is my fare,
But that which grieves me more
Is the coldness of my dear.
My Lodging Is on the Cold Ground [1720], st. 1

12 Whence is thy learning? Hath thy toil
O'er books consumed the midnight oil?
Fables, pt. I [1727]. The Shepherd and the Philosopher

13 Where yet was ever found a mother
Who'd give her booby for another?
Ib. The Mother, the Nurse, and the Fairy

14 When we risk no contradiction,
It prompts the tongue to deal in fiction.
Ib. The Elephant and the Bookseller

15 Those who in quarrels interpose
Must often wipe a bloody nose.
Ib. The Mastiffs

16 I hate the man who builds his name
On ruins of another's fame.
Ib. The Poet and the Rose

17 And when a lady's in the case,
You know all other things give place.
Ib. The Hare and Many Friends

18 In every age and clime we see
Two of a trade can never agree.[5]
Ib. The Rat-catcher and Cat

19 From wine what sudden friendship springs!
Ib. II [1738]. The Squire and His Cur

20 O Polly, you might have toyed and kissed,
By keeping men off, you keep them on.
The Beggar's Opera [1728],[6] *act I, sc. iv, air 9*

[4] See Pope's *Epitaph on Gay,* 336:9.

[5] See Hesiod, 61:13, and Meredith, 600:14.

[6] See Brecht, 840:*n*1.

1 If with me you'd fondly stray.
Over the hills and far away.[1]
Ib. xiii, air 16

2 Fill ev'ry glass, for wine inspires us,
And fires us
With courage, love and joy.
Women and wine should life employ.
Is there ought else on earth desirous?
Ib. II, i, air 19

3 If the heart of a man is depressed with cares,
The mist is dispelled when a woman appears.
Ib. iii, air 21

4 Youth's the season made for joys,
Love is then our duty. *Ib. iv, air 22*

5 Man may escape from rope and gun;
Nay, some have outlived the doctor's pill:
Who takes a woman must be undone,
That basilisk is sure to kill.
The fly that sips treacle is lost in the sweets,
So he that tastes woman, woman, woman,
He that tastes woman, ruin meets.
Ib. viii, air 26

6 How happy could I be with either,
Were t'other dear charmer away!
Ib. xiii, air 35

7 The charge is prepared; the lawyers are met;
The Judges all ranged (a terrible show!)
Ib. III, xi, air 57

8 Life is a jest; and all things show it.
I thought so once; but now I know it.[2]
My Own Epitaph

Pierre Carlet de Chamblain de Marivaux
1688–1763

9 In this world, you must be a bit too kind in order to be kind enough.
Le Jeu de l'Amour et du Hasard [1730], act I, sc. ii

Alexander Pope[3]
1688–1744

10 Happy the man whose wish and care
A few paternal acres bound,
Content to breathe his native air
In his own ground.[4]
Ode on Solitude [c. 1700], st. 1

11 Thus let me live, unseen, unknown,
Thus unlamented let me die,
Steal from the world, and not a stone
Tell where I lie. *Ib. st. 5*

12 Where'er you walk, cool gales shall fan the glade,
Trees, where you sit, shall crowd into a shade:
Where'er you tread, the blushing flow'rs shall rise,
And all things flourish where you turn your eyes.
Pastorals [written 1704]. Summer, l. 73

13 Nor Fame I slight, nor for her favors call;
She comes unlooked for, if she comes at all.
The Temple of Fame [1711], l. 513

14 How vast a memory has Love!
Sappho to Phaon [1712], l. 52

15 'Tis with our judgments as our watches, none
Go just alike, yet each believes his own.[5]
An Essay on Criticism [1711], pt. I, l. 9

16 Let such teach others who themselves excel,
And censure freely who have written well.
Ib. l. 15

17 Some are bewildered in the maze of schools,
And some made coxcombs nature meant but fools. *Ib. l. 26*

18 Those oft are stratagems which errors seem,
Nor is it Homer nods, but we that dream.[6]
Ib. l. 177

19 Of all the causes which conspire to blind
Man's erring judgment, and misguide the mind,
What the weak head with strongest bias rules,
Is pride, the never-failing vice of fools.
Ib. II, l. 1

20 A little learning is a dangerous thing;[7]
Drink deep, or taste not the Pierian spring:
There shallow draughts intoxicate the brain,
And drinking largely sobers us again.
Ib. l. 15

21 Hills peep o'er hills, and Alps on Alps arise!
Ib. l. 32

[1] See Tennyson, 530:13, and Anonymous, 931:12.
O'er the hills and far away.—THOMAS D'URFEY [1653–1723], *Pills to Purge Melancholy* [1719]

[2] Life is an empty dream.—BROWNING, *Paracelsus II* [1835]
Life seems a jest of Fate's contriving.—J. R. LOWELL, *Harvard Commemoration Ode* [1865], *IV*

[3] A thousand years may elapse before there shall appear another man with a power of versification equal to that of Pope.—JOHNSON [1781]; *from* BOSWELL, *Life of Johnson* [1791]

[4] See Horace, 106:23.

[5] See Suckling, 289:19.

[6] See Horace, 110:2.

[7] See Publilius Syrus, 112:9.

1 'Tis not a lip, or eye, we beauty call,
But the joint force and full result of all.
Ib. l. 45

2 Whoever thinks a faultless piece to see,
Thinks what ne'er was, nor is, nor e'er shall be.[1]
Ib. l. 53

3 True wit is nature to advantage dressed,
What oft was thought, but ne'er so well expressed.
Ib. l. 97

4 Words are like leaves; and where they most abound,
Much fruit of sense beneath is rarely found.
Ib. l. 109

5 Such labored nothings, in so strange a style,
Amaze th' unlearned, and make the learned smile.
Ib. l. 126

6 Be not the first by whom the new are tried,
Nor yet the last to lay the old aside.
Ib. l. 135

7 As some to church repair,
Not for the doctrine, but the music there.
These equal syllables alone require,
Though oft the ear the open vowels tire;
While expletives their feeble aid do join,
And ten low words oft creep in one dull line.
Ib. l. 142

8 Then, at the last and only couplet fraught
With some unmeaning thing they call a thought,
A needless Alexandrine ends the song,
That, like a wounded snake, drags its slow length along.
Ib. l. 156

9 True ease in writing comes from art, not chance,
As those move easiest who have learned to dance.[2]
'Tis not enough no harshness gives offense;
The sound must seem an echo to the sense.
Ib. l. 162

10 At ev'ry trifle scorn to take offense.
Ib. l. 186

11 Yet let not each gay turn thy rapture move;
For fools admire, but men of sense approve.
Ib. l. 190

12 Some judge of authors' names, not works, and then
Nor praise nor blame the writings, but the men.
Ib. l. 212

13 What woeful stuff this madrigal would be,
In some starved hackney sonneteer, or me!
But let a lord once own the happy lines,
How the wit brightens! how the style refines!
Ib. l. 218

14 Some praise at morning what they blame at night,
But always think the last opinion right.
Ib. l. 230

15 To err is human, to forgive divine.[3]
Ib. l. 325

16 All seems infected that th' infected spy,
As all looks yellow to the jaundiced eye.
Ib. l. 358

17 Be silent always when you doubt your sense.
Ib. III, l. 6

18 Men must be taught as if you taught them not,
And things unknown proposed as things forgot.
Ib. l. 15

19 The bookful blockhead ignorantly read,
With loads of learned lumber in his head,
With his own tongue still edifies his ears,
And always list'ning to himself appears.
All books he reads, and all he reads assails.
Ib. l. 53

20 For fools rush in where angels fear to tread.[4]
Ib. l. 66

21 But where's the man who counsel can bestow,
Still pleased to teach, and yet not proud to know?[5]
Ib. l. 72

22 Careless of censure, nor too fond of fame,
Still pleased to praise, yet not afraid to blame,
Averse alike to flatter or offend,
Not free from faults, nor yet too vain to mend.
Ib. l. 182

23 Vital spark of heav'nly flame!
Quit, oh quit, this mortal frame:
Trembling, hoping, ling'ring, flying,
Oh the pain, the bliss of dying![6]
The Dying Christian to His Soul [1712], st. 1

24 What dire offense from amorous causes springs,
What mighty contests rise from trivial things![7]
The Rape of the Lock [1712], canto I, l. 1

[1] See Suckling, 289:20.
[2] Also in *Imitations of Horace* [1737], *epistle II, bk. II, l. 178.*

[3] See Plutarch, 120:21; Anonymous Latin, 133:22; and Shirley, 272:12.
Then gently scan your brother man, / Still gentler sister woman; / Though they may gang a kennin' wrang. / To step aside is human.—ROBERT BURNS, *Address to the Unco Guid* [1787]
[4] See Shakespeare, 187:5.
[5] See Chaucer, 145:28.
[6] See Hadrian, 123:15.
[7] See Robert Burton, 258:9.

1 On her white breast a sparkling cross she wore,
Which Jews might kiss, and infidels adore.
Ib. II, l. 7

2 If to her share some female errors fall,
Look on her face, and you'll forget 'em all.
Ib. l. 17

3 Fair tresses man's imperial race ensnare,
And beauty draws us with a single hair.[1]
Ib. l. 27

4 Here thou, great Anna![2] whom three realms obey,
Dost sometimes counsel take—and sometimes tea. *Ib. III, l. 7*

5 At every word a reputation dies.
Ib. l. 16

6 The hungry judges soon the sentence sign,
And wretches hang that jurymen may dine.
Ib. l. 21

7 Let spades be trumps! she said, and trumps they were. *Ib. l. 46*

8 Coffee, which makes the politician wise.
Ib. l. 117

9 But when to mischief mortals bend their will,
How soon they find fit instruments of ill!
Ib. l. 125

10 The meeting points the sacred hair dissever
From the fair head, forever, and forever!
Then flashed the living lightning from her eyes,
And screams of horror rend th' affrighted skies. *Ib. l. 153*

11 Charms strike the sight, but merit wins the soul. *Ib. V, l. 34*

12 To wake the soul by tender strokes of art,
To raise the genius, and to mend the heart;
To make mankind, in conscious virtue bold,
Live o'er each scene, and be what they behold:
For this the Tragic Muse first trod the stage.
Prologue to Mr. Addison's Cato [1713], l. 1

13 A brave man struggling in the storms of fate,
And greatly falling with a falling state.
Ib. l. 21

14 Ignobly vain, and impotently great.
Ib. l. 29

15 Here hills and vales, the woodland and the plain,
Here earth and water seem to strive again,
Not chaos-like together crushed and bruised,
But, as the world, harmoniously confused:
Where order in variety we see,
And where, though all things differ, all agree.
Windsor Forest [1713], l. 11

[1]See Robert Burton, 259:18.
[2]Queen Anne [1665–1714].

16 Oft, as in airy rings they skim the heath,
The clam'rous lapwings feel the leaden death;
Oft, as the mounting larks their notes prepare,
They fall, and leave their little lives in air.
Ib. l. 131

17 Party-spirit, which at best is but the madness of many for the gain of a few.[3]
Letter to E. Blount [August 27, 1714]

18 The wrath of Peleus' son, the direful spring
Of all the Grecian woes, O goddess sing![4]
Translation of the Iliad [1715],[5] bk I, l. 1

19 She moves a goddess, and she looks a queen.
Ib. III, 1

20 Absent or dead, still let a friend be dear.
Epistle to Robert, Earl of Oxford and Mortimer [1721]

21 Tell me, Muse, of the man of many wiles.[6]
Translation of the Odyssey [1725–1756], bk. I, l. 1

22 So perish all who do the like again.
Ib. l. 37

23 True friendship's laws are by this rule expressed,
Welcome the coming, speed the parting guest.[7] *Ib. XV, l. 83*

24 Dear, damned, distracting town, farewell!
Thy fools no more I'll tease:
This year in peace, ye critics, dwell,
Ye harlots, sleep at ease!
A Farewell to London [1715], st. 1

25 Luxurious lobster-nights, farewell,
For sober, studious days! *Ib. st. 12*

26 Oh name forever sad! forever dear!
Still breathed in sighs, still ushered with a tear. *Eloisa to Abelard [1717], l. 31*

27 Now warm in love, now with'ring in my bloom,
Lost in a convent's solitary gloom!
Ib. l. 37

[3]See Pope, 340:13.
[4]Another version is:
Achilles' wrath, to Greece the direful spring / Of woes unnumbered, heavenly goddess, sing!
[5]See Bentley, 319:3.
[6]See Homer, 59:13.
[7]See Homer, 60:19, and Pope, 339:9.

1 Speed the soft intercourse from soul to soul,
And waft a sigh from Indus to the Pole.
Ib. l. 57

2 No, make me mistress to the man I love;
If there be yet another name more free,
More fond than mistress, make me that to thee!
Ib. l. 88

3 And if I lose thy love, I lose my all.
Ib. l. 118

4 How happy is the blameless vestal's lot!
The world forgetting, by the world forgot.
Ib. l. 207

5 One thought of thee puts all the pomp to flight,
Priests, tapers, temples, swim before my sight.[1]
Ib. l. 273

6 He best can paint them who shall feel them most.
Ib. l. 366

7 What beck'ning ghost, along the moonlight shade
Invites my steps, and points to yonder glade?
Elegy to the Memory of an Unfortunate Lady [1717], l. 1

8 Is it, in Heav'n, a crime to love too well?
To bear too tender, or too firm a heart,
To act a lover's or a Roman's part?
Is there no bright reversion in the sky,
For those who greatly think, or bravely die?
Ib. l. 6

9 Ambition first sprung from your blest abodes;
The glorious fault of Angels and of Gods.
Ib. l. 13

10 By foreign hands thy dying eyes were closed,
By foreign hands thy decent limbs composed,
By foreign hands thy humble grave adorned,
By strangers honored, and by strangers mourned!
Ib. l. 51

11 How loved, how honored once, avails thee not,
To whom related, or by whom begot;
A heap of dust alone remains of thee;
'Tis all thou art, and all the proud shall be!
Ib. l. 71

12 The fate of all extremes is such,
Men may be read, as well as books, too much.
To observations which ourselves we make,
We grow more partial for th' observer's sake.
Moral Essays [1720–1735]. Epistle I, To Lord Cobham [1734], l. 9

[1] Priests, altars, victims, swam before my sight.—EDMUND SMITH, *Phaedra and Hippolytus, adapted from Racine* [1707], *act I, sc. i*

13 Like following life through creatures you dissect,
You lose it in the moment you detect.
Ib. l. 29

14 Not always actions show the man: we find
Who does a kindness is not therefore kind.
Ib. l. 109

15 'Tis education forms the common mind:
Just as the twig is bent, the tree's inclined.
Ib. l. 149

16 Most women have no characters at all.
Ib. II, To Mrs. M. Blount [1735], l. 2

17 Choose a firm cloud before it fall, and in it
Catch, ere she change, the Cynthia of this minute.
Ib. l. 19

18 Chaste to her husband, frank to all beside,
A teeming mistress, but a barren bride.
Ib. l. 71

19 Wise wretch! with pleasures too refined to please;
With too much spirit to be e'er at ease;
With too much quickness ever to be taught;
With too much thinking to have common thought.
You purchase pain with all that joy can give,
And die of nothing but a rage to live.
Ib. l. 95

20 "With ev'ry pleasing, ev'ry prudent part,
Say, what can Chloe want?"—She wants a heart.
Ib. l. 159

21 In men, we various ruling passions find;
In women, two almost divide the kind;
Those, only fixed, they first or last obey,
The love of pleasure, and the love of sway.
Ib. l. 207

22 Men, some to business, some to pleasure take;
But every woman is at heart a rake.
Ib. l. 215

23 She who ne'er answers till a husband cools,
Or, if she rules him, never shows she rules;
Charms by accepting, by submitting, sways,
Yet has her humor most, when she obeys.
Ib. l. 261

24 And mistress of herself, though china fall.
Ib. l. 268

25 Woman's at best a contradiction still.
Ib. l. 270

26 Who shall decide when doctors disagree?[2]
Ib. III, To Lord Bathurst [1732], l. 1

[2] When doctors differ who decides amid the milliard-headed throng?—SIR RICHARD FRANCIS BURTON [1821–1890], *The Kasidah of Haji Abdu El-Yazdi, VIII, 29*

1 But thousands die, without or this or that,
Die, and endow a college, or a cat.
Ib. l. 95

2 The ruling passion, be it what it will,
The ruling passion conquers reason still.
Ib. l. 153

3 Satan now is wiser than of yore,
And tempts by making rich, not making poor.
Ib. l. 351

4 Good sense, which only is the gift of Heaven,
And though no science, fairly worth the seven.
Ib. IV, To Lord Burlington [1731], l. 43

5 Statesman, yet friend to truth! of soul sincere,
In action faithful, and in honor clear;
Who broke no promise, served no private end,
Who gained no title, and who lost no friend.
Ib. VII, To Mr. Addison [1720], l. 67

6 "Blessed is the man who expects nothing, for he shall never be disappointed" was the ninth beatitude.[1]
Letter to Fortescue [September 23, 1725]

7 You beat your pate, and fancy wit will come:
Knock as you please, there's nobody at home.[2]
Epigram: An Empty House [1727]

8 Ye Gods! annihilate but space and time,
And make two lovers happy.
Martinus Scriblerus on the Art of Sinking in Poetry [1728], ch. 11

9 In wit a man, simplicity a child.
Epitaph on Gay [1732][3]

10 Awake, my St. John![4] leave all meaner things
To low ambition, and the pride of kings.
Let us, since life can little more supply
Than just to look about us, and to die,
Expatiate free o'er all this scene of man;
A mighty maze! but not without a plan.
An Essay on Man [1733–1734]. Epistle I, l. 1

11 Eye Nature's walks, shoot folly as it flies,
And catch the manners living as they rise:
Laugh where we must, be candid where we can;
But vindicate the ways of God to man.[5]
Ib. l. 13

12 Say first, of God above or man below,
What can we reason but from what we know?
Ib. l. 17

13 Pleased to the last, he crops the flowery food,
And licks the hand just raised to shed his blood.
Ib. l. 83

14 Who sees with equal eye, as God of all,
A hero perish or a sparrow fall,[6]
Atoms or systems into ruin hurled,
And now a bubble burst, and now a world.
Ib. l. 87

15 Hope springs eternal in the human breast:
Man never is, but always to be blest.
Ib. l. 95

16 Lo, the poor Indian! whose untutored mind
Sees God in clouds, or hears him in the wind;
His soul proud Science never taught to stray
Far as the solar walk or milky way;
Yet simple nature to his hope has giv'n,
Behind the cloud-topped hill, an humbler heav'n.
Ib. l. 99

17 But thinks, admitted to that equal sky,
His faithful dog shall bear him company.
Ib. l. 111

18 In pride, in reas'ning pride, our error lies;
All quit their sphere, and rush into the skies!
Pride still is aiming at the blessed abodes,
Men would be Angels, Angels would be Gods.
Aspiring to be Gods if Angels fell,
Aspiring to be Angels men rebel.
Ib. l. 123

19 Seas roll to waft me, suns to light me rise;
My footstool earth, my canopy the skies.[7]
Ib. l. 139

20 Die of a rose in aromatic pain?
Ib. l. 200

21 All are but parts of one stupendous whole,
Whose body Nature is, and God the soul.
Ib. l. 267

22 As full, as perfect, in vile man that mourns
As the rapt seraph that adores and burns.
To Him no high, no low, no great, no small;[8]
He fills, he bounds, connects, and equals all!
Ib. l. 277

[1] Blessed are those that nought expect, / For they shall not be disappointed.—JOHN WOLCOT [PETER PINDAR] [1738–1819], *Ode to Pitt*

[2] His wit invites you by his looks to come, / But when you knock, it never is at home.—COWPER, *Conversation* [1782], *l. 303*

[3] See Gay, 331.

[4] Bolingbroke.

[5] See Milton, 283:2 and 288:26, and Housman, 691:17.

[6] See *Matthew 10:29*, 39:3, and Shakespeare, 224:28.

[7] See *Matthew 5:35*, 37:9; Wells, 720:6; and Day, 746:20.

[8] There is no great and no small / To the Soul that maketh all.—EMERSON [1803–1882], *Epigraph to History*

1 All nature is but art unknown to thee,
All chance, direction which thou canst not see;
All discord, harmony not understood;
All partial evil, universal good;
And, spite of pride, in erring reason's spite,
One truth is clear, Whatever is, is right.[1]
Ib. l. 289

2 Know then thyself, presume not God to scan;
The proper study of mankind is man.[2]
Placed on this isthmus of a middle state,
A being darkly wise and rudely great:
With too much knowledge for the skeptic side,
With too much weakness for the stoic's pride,
He hangs between; in doubt to act or rest;
In doubt to deem himself a god, or beast;
In doubt his mind or body to prefer;
Born but to die, and reas'ning but to err;
Alike in ignorance, his reason such,
Whether he thinks too little or too much;
Chaos of thought and passion, all confused;
Still by himself abused, or disabused;
Created half to rise, and half to fall;
Great lord of all things, yet a prey to all;
Sole judge of truth, in endless error hurled;
The glory, jest, and riddle of the world![3]
Ib. II, l. 1

3 Fixed like a plant on his peculiar spot,
To draw nutrition, propagate, and rot.
Ib. l. 63

4 And hence one master passion in the breast,
Like Aaron's serpent, swallows up the rest.[4]
Ib. l. 131

5 Vice is a monster of so frightful mien,
As to be hated needs but to be seen;[5]
Yet seen too oft, familiar with her face,
We first endure, then pity, then embrace.
Ib. l. 217

6 The learned is happy Nature to explore,
The fool is happy that he knows no more;
The rich is happy in the plenty giv'n,
The poor contents him with the care of Heav'n. *Ib. l. 263*

[1] See Marcus Aurelius, 124:16, and Dryden, 303:14.
[2] See The Seven Sages, 62:4.
Trees and fields tell me nothing: men are my teachers. —PLATO [c. 428–348 B.C.], *Phaedrus*
La vraie science et la vraie étude de l'homme, c'est l'homme [The true science and the true study of man is man]. —PIERRE CHARRON, *Traité de la Sagesse* [1601], *bk. I, preface*
Das eigentliche Studium der Menschheit ist der Mensch [The proper study of mankind is man]. —GOETHE, *Elective Affinities* [1808], *bk. II, ch. 7*
[3] See Pascal, 300:11.
[4] See *Exodus 7:12*, 9:19.
[5] See Dryden, 305:16.

7 Behold the child, by Nature's kindly law,
Pleased with a rattle, tickled with a straw:
Some livelier plaything gives his youth delight,
A little louder, but as empty quite:
Scarfs, garters, gold, amuse his riper stage,
And beads and prayer books are the toys of age!
Pleased with this bauble still, as that before;
Till tired he sleeps, and life's poor play is o'er.
Ib. l. 274

8 Learn of the little nautilus to sail,
Spread the thin oar, and catch the driving gale. *Ib. III, l. 177*

9 For forms of government let fools contest;
Whate'er is best administered is best:
For modes of faith let graceless zealots fight;
His can't be wrong whose life is in the right.[6]
In faith and hope the world will disagree,
But all mankind's concern is charity.
Ib. l. 303

10 O happiness! our being's end and aim!
Good, pleasure, ease, content! whate'er thy name:
That something still which prompts the eternal sigh,
For which we bear to live, or dare to die.
Ib. IV, l. 1

11 Worth makes the man, and want of it the fellow;
The rest is all but leather or prunella.
Ib. l. 203

12 What's Fame? a fancied life in others' breath,
A thing beyond us, ev'n before our death.
Ib. l. 237

13 A wit's a feather, and a chief a rod;
An honest man's the noblest work of God.[7]
Ib. l. 247

14 One self-approving hour whole years outweighs
Of stupid starers and of loud huzzas:
And more true joy Marcellus exiled feels
Than Caesar with a senate at his heels.
Ib. l. 255

15 If parts allure thee, think how Bacon shined,
The wisest, brightest, meanest of mankind!
Or ravished with the whistling of a name,[8]
See Cromwell, damned to everlasting fame!
Ib. l. 281

16 Slave to no sect, who takes no private road,
But looks through Nature up to Nature's God.[9] *Ib. l. 331*

[6] See Cowley, 295:19.
[7] See Fletcher, 260:18, and Burns, 408:18.
[8] See Cowley, 295:16.
[9] See Bolingbroke, 329:5, and Jefferson, 387:9.

1 Formed by thy converse, happily to steer
From grave to gay, from lively to severe.[1]
Ib. l. 379

2 Say, shall my little bark attendant sail,
Pursue the triumph and partake the gale?[2]
Ib. l. 385

3 Thou wert my guide, philosopher, and friend.[3] *Ib. l. 390*

4 That true self-love and social are the same.[4]
Ib. l. 396

5 Shut, shut the door, good John! fatigued, I said;
Tie up the knocker! say I'm sick, I'm dead.
The Dog-star rages!
Epistle to Dr. Arbuthnot [1734]. Prologue to Imitations of Horace, l. 1

6 Fire in each eye, and papers in each hand,
They rave, recite, and madden round the land. *Ib. l. 5*

7 Fired that the house[5] reject him,
"'S death, I'll print it,
And shame the fools." *Ib. l. 61*

8 No creature smarts so little as a fool.
Ib. l. 84

9 Destroy his fib, or sophistry—in vain!
The creature's at his dirty work again.
Ib. l. 91

10 As yet a child, nor yet a fool to fame,
I lisped in numbers, for the numbers came.
Ib. l. 127

11 This long disease, my life.[6] *Ib. l. 132*

12 Pretty! in amber to observe the forms
Of hairs, or straws, or dirt, or grubs, or worms![7]
The things, we know, are neither rich nor rare,
But wonder how the devil they got there.
Ib. l. 169

13 Means not, but blunders round about a meaning;
And he whose fustian's so sublimely bad,
It is not poetry, but prose run mad.
Ib. l. 186

14 Were there one whose fires
True Genius kindles, and fair Fame inspires,
Blessed with each talent, and each art to please,
And born to write, converse, and live with ease;
Should such a man, too fond to rule alone,
Bear, like the Turk, no brother near the throne;[8]
View him with scornful, yet with jealous eyes,
And hate for arts that caused himself to rise;
Damn with faint praise, assent with civil leer,
And, without sneering, teach the rest to sneer;[9]
Willing to wound, and yet afraid to strike,
Just hint a fault, and hesitate dislike;
Alike reserved to blame or to commend,
A tim'rous foe, and a suspicious friend;
Dreading e'en fools, by flatterers besieged,
And so obliging that he ne'er obliged;
Like Cato, give his little Senate laws,[10]
And sit attentive to his own applause.
Ib. l. 193

15 Who but must laugh, if such a man there be?
Who would not weep, if Atticus were he!
Ib. l. 213

16 Oh let me live my own, and die so too
(To live and die is all I have to do)!
Maintain a poet's dignity and ease,
And see what friends, and read what books I please. *Ib. l. 261*

17 Cursed be the verse, how well soe'er it flow,
That tends to make one worthy man my foe.
Ib. l. 283

18 Let Sporus tremble—"What? that thing of silk,
Sporus, that mere white curd of ass's milk?
Satire or sense, alas! can Sporus feel?
Who breaks a butterfly upon a wheel?"
Ib. l. 305

19 Yet let me flap this bug with gilded wings,
This painted child of dirt, that stinks and stings;
Whose buzz the witty and the fair annoys,
Yet wit ne'er tastes, and beauty ne'er enjoys.
Ib. l. 309

[1] See Boileau, 311:2.

[2] See Dante, 141:17.

[3] Is this my guide, philosopher, and friend?—POPE, *Imitations of Horace* [1733–1738], *Epistle I, bk. I, l. 177*

[4] See John Quincy Adams, 418:9.

[5] The theater.

[6] See Cowley, 295:12, and Arnold, 586:1.

[7] See Martial, 119:7.

[8] Nor is thy fame on lesser ruins built; / Nor needs thy juster title the foul guilt / Of Eastern kings, who, to secure their reign, / Must have their brothers, sons, and kindred slain.—SIR JOHN DENHAM, *On Mr. John Fletcher's Works* [1668]

[9] When needs he must, yet faintly then he praises; / Somewhat the deed, much more the means he raises: / So marreth what he makes, and praising most, dispraises. —PHINEAS FLETCHER, *The Purple Island* [1633], *canto 7*

[10] While Cato gives his little senate laws.—*Prologue to Mr. Addison's Cato* [1713], *l. 23*

1 Eternal smiles his emptiness betray,
As shallow streams run dimpling all the way.
Ib. l. 315

2 And he himself one vile antithesis.
Ib. l. 325

3 Wit that can creep, and pride that licks the dust.
Ib. l. 333

4 Unlearned, he knew no schoolman's subtle art,
No language, but the language of the heart.
Ib. l. 398

5 I cannot sleep a wink.[1]
Imitations of Horace [1733–1738], satire I, bk. II, l. 12

6 Satire's my weapon, but I'm too discreet
To run amuck, and tilt at all I meet.
Ib. l. 69

7 But touch me, and no minister so sore.
Ib. l. 76

8 There St. John mingles with my friendly bowl
The feast of reason and the flow of soul.
Ib. l. 127

9 For I, who hold sage Homer's rule the best,
Welcome the coming, speed the going guest.[2]
Ib. II, II, l. 159

10 I've often wished that I had clear,
For life, six hundred pounds a year;
A handsome house to lodge a friend,
A river at my garden's end,
A terrace walk, and half a rood
Of land set out to plant a wood.[3]
Ib. VI, II, l. 1

11 Give me again my hollow tree,
A crust of bread, and liberty.
Ib. l. 220

12 A patriot is a fool in ev'ry age.
Ib. Epilogue to the Satires, Dialogue I, l. 41

13 Laugh then at any but at fools or foes;
These you but anger, and you mend not those.
Laugh at your friends, and if your friends are sore,
So much the better, you may laugh the more.
Ib. l. 53

14 Let humble Allen, with an awkward shame,
Do good by stealth, and blush to find it fame.
Ib. l. 135

15 Never gallop Pegasus to death.
Ib. Epistle I, bk. I, l. 14

[1]See Cervantes, 168:19, and Shakespeare, 243:22.
[2]See Homer, 60:19, and Pope, 334:23.
[3]See Horace, 106:20.

16 When the brisk minor pants for twenty-one.
Ib. l. 38

17 Not to go back is somewhat to advance,
And men must walk, at least, before they dance.
Ib. l. 53

18 He's armed without that's innocent within.
Ib. l. 94

19 Get place and wealth, if possible with grace;
If not, by any means get wealth and place.[4]
Ib. l. 103

20 Above all Greek, above all Roman fame.
Ib. II, l. 26

21 The people's voice is odd,
It is, and it is not, the voice of God.[5]
Ib. l. 89

22 In quibbles angel and archangel join,
And God the Father turns a school-divine.
Ib. l. 101 (on Paradise Lost)

23 The mob of gentlemen who wrote with ease.
Ib. l. 108

24 One simile that solitary shines
In the dry desert of a thousand lines.
Ib. l. 111

25 Who says in verse what others say in prose.
Ib. l. 202

26 What will a child learn sooner than a song?
Ib. l. 205

27 Ev'n copious Dryden wanted, or forgot,
The last and greatest art—the art to blot.
Ib. l. 280

28 There still remains, to mortify a wit,
The many-headed monster of the pit.[6]
Ib. l. 304

29 We poets are (upon a poet's word)
Of all mankind the creatures most absurd:
The season when to come, and when to go,
To sing, or cease to sing, we never know.[7]
Ib. l. 358

30 Call, if you will, bad rhyming a disease,
It gives men happiness, or leaves them ease.
Ib. II, II, l. 182

31 The worst of madmen is a saint run mad.
Ib. VI, I, l. 27

32 Vain was the chief's, the sage's pride!
They had no poet, and they died.[8]
Ib. Odes, bk. IV, ode 9, st. 4

[4]See Horace, 108:18.
[5]See Alcuin, 135:6.
[6]See Horace, 108:19; Machiavelli, 154:8; and Shakespeare, 205:18, 242:14, and 242:21.
[7]See Robert Frost, 747:2.
[8]See Pindar, 72:10, and Horace, 108:13.

1 Father of all! in every age,
In every clime adored,
By saint, by savage, and by sage,
Jehovah, Jove, or Lord!
The Universal Prayer [1738], st. 1

2 And binding Nature fast in fate,
Left free the human will. *Ib. st. 3*

3 And deal damnation round the land.
Ib. st. 7

4 Teach me to feel another's woe,
To hide the fault I see;
That mercy I to others show,
That mercy show to me.[1] *Ib. st. 10*

5 I am his Highness'[2] dog at Kew;
Pray tell me, sir, whose dog are you?
On the collar of a dog

6 Nature and Nature's laws lay hid in night:
God said, Let Newton be! and all was light.
Epitaph intended for Sir Isaac Newton

7 Who dare to love their country, and be poor.
On his grotto at Twickenham [1740]

8 This is the Jew
That Shakespeare drew.
Of Macklin's performance in 1741 of Shylock in The Merchant of Venice (attributed to Pope)

9 I never knew any man in my life who could not bear another's misfortunes perfectly like a Christian.[3]
Thoughts on Various Subjects; published in Swift's Miscellanies [1727]

10 A man should never be ashamed to own he has been in the wrong, which is but saying, in other words, that he is wiser today than he was yesterday. *Ib.*

11 It is with narrow-souled people as with narrow-necked bottles; the less they have in them the more noise they make in pouring out. *Ib.*

12 When men grow virtuous in their old age, they only make a sacrifice to God of the devil's leavings.[4] *Ib.*

13 Party is the madness of many, for the gain of a few.[5] *Ib.*

14 Whether thou choose Cervantes' serious air,
Or laugh and shake in Rabelais' easy chair.
The Dunciad [1728–1743], bk. I, l. 21

[1]See Spenser, 174:3.
[2]Frederick, Prince of Wales.
[3]See La Rochefoucauld, 293:2.
[4]See La Rochefoucauld, 293:17.
[5]See Pope, 334:17.

15 Poetic Justice, with her lifted scale,
Where, in nice balance, truth with gold she weighs,
And solid pudding against empty praise.
Ib. l. 52

16 While pensive poets painful vigils keep,
Sleepless themselves to give their readers sleep. *Ib. l. 93*

17 Next o'er his books his eyes begin to roll,
In pleasing memory of all he stole.
Ib. l. 127

18 Or where the pictures for the page atone,
And Quarles is saved by beauties not his own.
Ib. l. 139

19 And gentle Dullness ever loves a joke.
Ib. II, l. 34

20 A brain of feathers, and a heart of lead.
Ib. l. 44

21 Peeled, patched, and piebald, linsey-woolsey brothers,
Grave mummers! sleeveless some, and shirtless others.
That once was Britain. *Ib. III, l. 115*

22 And proud his mistress' order to perform,
Rides in the whirlwind and directs the storm.[6] *Ib. l. 263*

23 A wit with dunces, and a dunce with wits.[7]
Ib. IV, l. 90

24 The Right Divine of Kings to govern wrong.
Ib. l. 188

25 Stuff the head
With all such reading as was never read:
For thee explain a thing till all men doubt it,
And write about it, Goddess, and about it.
Ib. l. 249

26 To happy convents, bosomed deep in vines,
Where slumber abbots, purple as their wines.
Ib. l. 301

27 Led by my hand, he sauntered Europe round,
And gathered every vice on Christian ground. *Ib. l. 311*

28 Religion blushing veils her sacred fires,
And unawares Morality expires.
Nor public flame, nor private, dares to shine;
Nor human spark is left, nor glimpse divine!
Lo! thy dread empire Chaos! is restored:
Light dies before thy uncreating word;
Thy hand, great Anarch! lets the curtain fall,
And universal darkness buries all.
Ib. l. 649

[6]See Addison, 325:7.
[7]See Quintilian, 118:3.

Lady Mary Wortley Montagu

1689–1762

1 And we meet, with champagne and a
chicken, at last. *The Lover [1748]*

2 Be plain in dress, and sober in your diet;
In short, my deary, kiss me, and be quiet.
A Summary of Lord Lyttelton's Advice

3 Satire should, like a polished razor keen,
Wound with a touch that's scarcely felt or seen.
To the Imitator of the First Satire of Horace, bk. II

4 But the fruit that can fall without shaking
Indeed is too mellow for me.
Letters and Works [1837]. The Answer

Charles de Secondat, Baron de Montesquieu[1]

1689–1755

5 How can anyone be Persian? *Lettres Persanes [1721], no. 30*

6 A man should be mourned at his birth, not at his death. *Ib. 40*

7 If triangles had a god, he would have three sides.[2] *Ib. 59*

8 Liberty is the right of doing whatever the laws permit. *De l'Esprit des Lois [1748], XI, 3*

9 Useless laws weaken the necessary laws. *Ib. XXIX, 16*

10 If I knew of something that could serve my nation but would ruin another, I would not propose it to my prince, for I am first a man and only then a Frenchman . . . because I am necessarily a man, and only accidentally am I French.[3] *Pensées et Fragments Inédits de Montesquieu [1899], I*

11 You have to study a great deal to know a little. *Ib.*

John Byrom

1692–1763

12 God bless the King, I mean the Faith's Defender;
God bless—no harm in blessing—the Pretender;
But who Pretender is, or who is King,
God bless us all—that's quite another thing.[4]
Miscellaneous Poems [1773]. To an Officer in the Army, Extempore; Intended to Allay the Violence of Party Spirit

13 Some say, that Signor Bononcini,
Compared to Handel's a mere ninny;
Others aver, to him, that Handel
Is scarcely fit to hold a candle.[5]
Strange! that such high dispute should be
'Twixt Tweedledum and Tweedledee.
Ib. On the Feuds Between Handel and Bononcini

14 As clear as a whistle. *Epistle to Lloyd*

Philip Dormer Stanhope, Earl of Chesterfield

1694–1773

15 Measures not men.[6] *Letters to His Son [1774]. March 6, 1742*

16 Whatever is worth doing at all, is worth doing well. *Ib. March 10, 1746*

17 The knowledge of the world is only to be acquired in the world, and not in a closet. *Ib. October 4, 1746*

18 An injury is much sooner forgotten than an insult. *Ib. October 9, 1746*

19 Do as you would be done by, is the surest method of pleasing.[7] *Ib. October 9, 1747*

20 Take the tone of the company that you are in. *Ib.*

21 I knew once a very covetous, sordid fellow,[8] who used to say, "Take care of the pence, for the pounds will take care of themselves." *Ib. November 6, 1747*

22 Advice is seldom welcome; and those who want it the most always like it the least. *Ib. January 29, 1748*

23 Speak of the moderns without contempt, and of the ancients without idolatry. *Ib. February 22, 1748*

[1] See Carlyle, 474:15.
[2] See Xenophanes, 67:13.
[3] See Montaigne, 166:2.

[4] Quoted by Sir Walter Scott in *Redgauntlet, vol. II, ch. 1* [Edinburgh edition, 1832].
[5] See Lamb, 442:4.
[6] See Goldsmith, 369:27; Burke, 372:5; and Adams, 381:1.
[7] See *Matthew 7:12*, 38:14; Confucius, 69:14; Aristotle, 87:3; and Kingsley, 566:16.
[8] William Lowndes [1652–1724], Secretary of the Treasury in the reigns of William III, Queen Anne, and George I.

1 Wear your learning, like your watch, in a private pocket: and do not pull it out and strike it, merely to show that you have one. *Ib.*

2 Manners must adorn knowledge, and smooth its way through the world. Like a great rough diamond, it may do very well in a closet by way of curiosity, and also for its intrinsic value. *Ib. July 1, 1748*

3 Women, then, are only children of a larger growth. *Ib. September 5, 1748*

4 Women who are either indisputably beautiful, or indisputably ugly, are best flattered upon the score of their understandings; but those who are in a state of mediocrity are best flattered upon their beauty, or at least their graces; for every woman who is not absolutely ugly thinks herself handsome. *Ib.*

5 Without some dissimulation no business can be carried on at all. *Ib. May 22, 1749*

6 Idleness is only the refuge of weak minds. *Ib. July 20, 1749*

7 Style is the dress of thoughts.[1] *Ib. November 24, 1749*

8 Whatever subject he [Bolingbroke] either speaks or writes upon, he adorns with the most splendid eloquence.[2] *Ib. December 12, 1749*

9 Dispatch is the soul of business. *Ib. February 5, 1750*

10 Knowledge may give weight, but accomplishments give luster, and many more people see than weigh. *Ib. May 8, 1750*

11 Let blockheads read what blockheads write. *Ib. November 1, 1750*

12 It is commonly said, and more particularly by Lord Shaftesbury,[3] that ridicule is the best test of truth. *Ib. February 6, 1752*

13 Every woman is infallibly to be gained by every sort of flattery, and every man by one sort or other. *Ib. March 16, 1752*

14 The chapter of knowledge is a very short, but the chapter of accidents is a very long one.[4]
To Solomon Dayrolles, February 16, 1753

[1]See Samuel Wesley, 319:18.
[2]Il embellit tout ce qu'il touche [He adorns whatever he touches].—FÉNELON [1651–1715], *Lettre sur les Occupations de l'Académie Française, sec. 4*
See Johnson, 354:2.
[3]See Shaftesbury, 325:4 and 325:5.
[4]The Chapter of Accidents is the longest chapter in the book.—*Attributed to* JOHN WILKES *by* SOUTHEY, *The Doctor* [1837], *ch. 118*

15 I assisted at the birth of that most significant word "flirtation," which dropped from the most beautiful mouth in the world.
The World [December 5, 1754], no. 101

16 Unlike my subject will I frame my song,
It shall be witty, and it shan't be long.
Epigram on ("Long") Sir Thomas Robinson

17 The dews of the evening most carefully shun—
Those tears of the sky for the loss of the sun.
Advice to a Lady in Autumn

18 Give Dayrolles a chair. *Last words*

Francis Hutcheson
1694–1746

19 That action is best which procures the greatest happiness for the greatest numbers.[5]
Inquiry Concerning Moral Good and Evil [1720], sec. 3

François Quesnay
1694–1774

20 Laissez faire, laissez passer.[6] *Attributed*

Voltaire
[François Marie Arouet]
1694–1778

21 Virtue debases itself in justifying itself. *Oedipe [1718], act I, sc. iv*

22 O what fine times, this age of iron! *Le Mondain [1736]*

23 Paradise is where I am. *Ib.*

24 The superfluous, a very necessary thing.[7] *Ib.*

[5]Priestley was the first (unless it was Beccaria) who taught my lips to pronounce this sacred truth—that the greatest happiness of the greatest number is the foundation of morals and legislation.—JEREMY BENTHAM [1748–1832], *Works, vol. X, p. 142*
[6]Let it be, let it pass.
The phrase is not readily translatable, and also appears as: Laissez faire, laissez aller. It has also been attributed to PIERRE LE PESANT BOISGUILBERT [1676–1714] and JEAN CLAUDE GOURNAY [1712–1759]. It was widely used by the Physiocrats in urging freedom from government interference, and was adopted by Adam Smith [1723–1790].
[7]See Holmes, 645:8.

1 The secret of being a bore is to tell everything.

Sept Discours en Vers sur l'Homme [1738]

2 Love truth, but pardon error. *Ib.*

3 He who is merely just is severe.

Letter to Frederick the Great [1740]

4 The first who was king was a fortunate soldier:
Who serves his country well has no need of ancestors.[1]

Mérope [1743], act I, sc. iii

5 It is better to risk saving a guilty person than to condemn an innocent one.[2]

Zadig [1747], ch. 6

6 They squeeze the orange and throw away the skin.

Letter to Madame Denis [September 2, 1751] referring to his quarrel with Frederick the Great

7 This agglomeration which was called and which still calls itself the Holy Roman Empire is neither holy, nor Roman, nor an Empire. *Essai sur les Moeurs [1756]*

8 In this best of possible worlds . . . all is for the best[3] [Dr. Pangloss].

Candide [1759], ch. 1

9 If this is the best of possible worlds, what then are the others? *Ib. 6*

10 Optimism, said Candide, is a mania for maintaining that all is well when things are going badly. *Ib. 19*

11 In this country [England] it is good to kill an admiral from time to time, to encourage the others.[4] *Ib. 23*

12 This is the happiest of mortals, for he is above everything he possesses. *Ib. 26*

13 Work keeps us from three great evils, boredom, vice, and need.[5] *Ib. 30*

14 We must cultivate our garden.[6] *Ib.*

15 There are truths which are not for all men, nor for all times.

Letter to Cardinal de Bernis [April 23, 1761]

16 One feels like crawling on all fours after reading your work.

Letter to Rousseau [August 31, 1761]

17 Whatever you do, crush the infamous thing [superstition], and love those who love you.[7]

Letter to d'Alembert [November 28, 1762]

18 Common sense is not so common.

Dictionnaire Philosophique [1764]. Self-Love

19 In general, the art of government consists in taking as much money as possible from one class of citizens to give to the other.

Ib. Money

20 We have a natural right to make use of our pens as of our tongue, at our peril, risk and hazard. *Ib. Liberty of the Press*

21 The best is the enemy of the good.[8]

Ib. Dramatic Art

22 Very learned women are to be found, in the same manner as female warriors; but they are seldom or never inventors.

Ib. Women

23 The proper mean.[9]

Letter to Count d'Argental [November 28, 1765]

24 Men use thought only to justify their wrongdoings, and speech only to conceal their thoughts.[10]

Dialogue 14. Le Chapon et la Poularde [1766]

25 I have never made but one prayer to God, a very short one: "O Lord, make my enemies ridiculous." And God granted it.

Letter to M. Damilaville [May 16, 1767]

26 History is no more than the portrayal of crimes and misfortunes.[11]

L'Ingénu [1767], ch. 10

[1] What can they see in the longest kingly line in Europe, save that it runs back to a successful soldier? — SIR WALTER SCOTT, *Woodstock* [1826], *ch. 37*

[2] See Blackstone, 365:19.

[3] Dans ce meilleur des mondes possibles . . . tout est au mieux.

Often quoted: All is for the best in the best of all possible worlds.

[4] Pour encourager les autres.

The reference is to Admiral John Byng, who was executed in 1757 for failing to relieve Minorca.

[5] Le travail éloigne de nous trois grands maux, l'ennui, le vice, et le besoin.

[6] Il faut cultiver notre jardin.

See Rabelais, 158:4, and Montaigne, 164:8.

[7] Quoi que vous fassiez, écrasez l'infâme, et aimez qui vous aime.

[8] Le mieux est l'ennemi du bien.

[9] Le juste milieu.

See The Seven Sages, 62:7; Terence, 96:1; Horace, 106:12 and 107:20; Lucan, 118:8; and Anonymous Latin, 134:12.

[10] See Robert South, 310:22.

[11] L'histoire n'est que le tableau des crimes et des malheurs.

See Gibbon, 383:10.

1 Thought depends absolutely on the stomach, but in spite of that, those who have the best stomachs are not the best thinkers.
Letter to d'Alembert [August 20, 1770]

2 If God did not exist, it would be necessary to invent him.[1]
Épître à l'Auteur du Livre des Trois Imposteurs [November 10, 1770]

3 Change everything, except your loves.
Sur l'Usage de la Vie

4 I am very fond of truth, but not at all of martyrdom.
Letter to d'Alembert [February 1776]

5 The embarrassment of riches.[2]
Le Droit du Seigneur, act II, sc. vi

6 He who thinks himself wise, O heavens! is a great fool. *Ib. IV, i*

7 Who has not the spirit of his age,
Of his age has all the unhappiness.[3]
Letter to Madame du Châtelet

8 I advise you to go on living solely to enrage those who are paying your annuities. It is the only pleasure I have left.
Letter to Madame du Deffand

9 Liberty of thought is the life of the soul.
Essay on Epic Poetry (written in English)

10 Whoever you are, behold your master,
He is, or was, or has to be.[4]
On a statuette of Cupid in the Cirey Gardens

11 I disapprove of what you say, but I will defend to the death your right to say it.
Attributed[5]

12 I die adoring God, loving my friends, not hating my enemies, and detesting superstition. *Written February 28, 1778*

[1]See Ovid, 113:10, and Tillotson, 303:1.

[2]L'embarras des richesses. — ABBÉ D'ALLAINVAL [1700–1753], *title of play* [1726]

[3]Qui n'a pas l'esprit de son âge, / De son âge a tout le malheur.
See Carlyle, 472:16.

[4]Qui que tu sois, voici ton maître; / Il l'est — le fut — ou le doit être.

[5]This sentence is not Voltaire's, but was first used in quoting a letter from Voltaire to Helvétius in *The Friends of Voltaire* [1906] by S. G. Tallentyre (E. Beatrice Hall). She claims it was a paraphrase of Voltaire's words in the *Essay on Tolerance:* Think for yourselves and let others enjoy the privilege to do so too.

Norbert Guterman, in *A Book of French Quotations* [1963], suggests that the probable source for the quotation is from a line in a letter to M. le Riche [February 6, 1770]: "Monsieur l'abbé, I detest what you write, but I would give my life to make it possible for you to continue to write."

Matthew Green
1696–1737

13 They politics like ours profess,
The greater prey upon the less.
The Grotto, l. 69

14 Fling but a stone, the giant dies.
Laugh and be well.
The Spleen [1737], l. 92

15 By happy alchemy of mind
They turn to pleasure all they find.
Ib. l. 610

William Oldys
1696–1761

16 Busy, curious, thirsty fly,
Drink with me, and drink as I.
On a Fly Drinking out of a Cup of Ale, st. 1

Marie de Vichy-Chamrond, Marquise du Deffand
1697–1780

17 [Of Voltaire] He has invented history.
From FOURNIER, *L'Esprit dans l'Histoire [1857]*

18 The first step is the hardest.[6]
Letter to d'Alembert [July 7, 1763]

Kamo Mabuchi
1697–1769

19 Japanese poetry has as its subject the human heart. It may seem to be of no practical use and just as well left uncomposed, but when one knows poetry well, one understands also without explanation the reasons governing order and disorder in the world.[7]
Writings

Charles Macklin
c. 1697–1797

20 The law is a sort of hocus-pocus science.[8]
Love à la Mode [1759], act II, sc. i

[6]This remark refers to the legend that Saint Denis, carrying his head in his hands, walked from Montmartre to St. Denis, a few miles north of Paris. Voltaire wrote to Madame du Deffand [January 1764] that one of her bon mots was quoted in the notes of *La Pucelle, canto 1:* Il n'y a que le premier pas qui coûte.

[7]From *Sources of Japanese Tradition* [1960], edited by WILLIAM THEODORE DE BARY.

[8]Hocus was an old cunning attorney. — DR. JOHN ARBUTHNOT, *Law Is a Bottomless Pit; or, History of John Bull* [1712], *ch. 5*

The words of consecration, "Hoc est corpus," were trav-

Abbé Prévost
[Antoine François Prévost d'Exiles]
1697–1763

1 And that is the story of Manon Lescaut.
Histoire du Chevalier des Grieux et de Manon Lescaut [1731; translated 1831]

William Warburton
1698–1779

2 Orthodoxy is my doxy; heterodoxy is another man's doxy.[1]
From Joseph Priestley *[1733–1804], Memoirs, vol. I, p. 572*

John Dyer
c. 1700–1758

3 A little rule, a little sway,
A sunbeam in a winter's day,
Is all the proud and mighty have
Between the cradle and the grave.[2]
Grongar Hill [1726], l. 89

James Thomson
1700–1748

4 See, Winter comes to rule the varied year,[3]
Sullen and sad.
The Seasons. Winter [1726], l. 1

5 Welcome, kindred glooms!
Congenial horrors, hail! *Ib. l. 5*

6 Cruel as death, and hungry as the grave.
Ib. l. 393

7 There studious let me sit,
And hold high converse with the mighty dead. *Ib. l. 431*

8 Ships dim-discovered dropping from the clouds. *Ib. Summer [1727], l. 946*

9 Sighed and looked unutterable things.
Ib. l. 1188

10 Come, gentle Spring! ethereal mildness, come. *Ib. Spring [1728], l. 1*

11 Delightful task! to rear the tender thought,
To teach the young idea how to shoot.
Ib. l. 1149

12 An elegant sufficiency, content,
Retirement, rural quiet, friendship, books.
Ib. l. 1158

13 Crowned with the sickle, and the wheaten sheaf,
While Autumn, nodding o'er the yellow plain,
Comes jovial on.
Ib. Autumn [1730], l. 1

14 For loveliness
Needs not the foreign aid of ornament,
But is when unadorned adorned the most.[4]
Ib. l. 208

15 Or where the Northern ocean, in vast whirls,
Boils round the naked melancholy isles
Of farthest Thulè,[5] and th' Atlantic surge
Pours in among the stormy Hebrides.[6]
Ib. l. 871

16 Come then, expressive silence, muse His praise. *Hymn [1730], l. 118*

17 O Sophonisba! Sophonisba, O![7]
Sophonisba [1730], act III, sc. ii

18 Forever, Fortune, wilt thou prove
An unrelenting foe to love,
And, when we meet a mutual heart,
Come in between and bid us part?
To Fortune

19 When Britain first, at Heaven's command,
Arose from out the azure main,
This was the charter of the land,
And guardian angels sung this strain:
Rule, Britannia, rule the waves;
Britons never will be slaves.
Alfred [1740], act II, sc. v

20 A pleasing land of drowsyhead it was.
The Castle of Indolence [1748], canto I, st. 6

21 A bard here dwelt, more fat than bard beseems,
Who, void of envy, guile, and lust of gain,
On virtue still, and nature's pleasing themes,
Poured forth his unpremeditated strain.
Ib. st. 68

22 A little round, fat, oily man of God.
Ib. st. 69

---

estied into a nickname for jugglery, as "Hocus-pocus." — John Richard Green, *A Short History of the English People* [1874], *ch. 7*

[1] Priestley relates that in a debate on the Test Laws, Lord Sandwich said, "I have heard frequent use of the words 'orthodoxy' and 'heterodoxy' but I confess myself at a loss to know precisely what they mean." Bishop Warburton whispered his definition to him.
See Carlyle, 473:19.

[2] See Shelley, 467:9; Bellamy, 665:17; and Hoffenstein, 816:2.

[3] See Cowper, 377:5.

[4] See Cicero, 98:13, and Milton, 286:3.

[5] See Virgil, 103:25, and Seneca, 115:13.

[6] See Milton, 281:2.

[7] This line was parodied by Fielding in his *Tom Thumb* [acted 1730]: O Huncamunca, Huncamunca, O.

Philip Doddridge
1702–1751

1 Awake my soul! stretch every nerve,
And press with vigor on;
A heavenly race demands thy zeal,
And an immortal crown.
Hymns [1755]. Zeal and Vigor in the Christian Race, st. 1

Jonathan Edwards
1703–1758

2 Resolved, never to do anything which I should be afraid to do if it were the last hour of my life.[1] *Seventy Resolutions*

3 Intend to live in continual mortification, and never to expect or desire any worldly ease or pleasure. *Diary [1723]*

4 A little, wretched, despicable creature; a worm, a mere nothing, and less than nothing; a vile insect that has risen up in contempt against the majesty of Heaven and earth.
The Justice of God in the Damnation of Sinners [1734]

5 I assert that nothing ever comes to pass without a cause.
The Freedom of the Will [1754]

6 This dictate of common sense. *Ib.*

Thomas Morell
1703–1784

7 See, the conquering hero comes!
Sound the trumpet, beat the drums![2]
Joshua [1748], pt. III

John Wesley
1703–1791

8 I look upon the world as my parish.
Journal [1909–1916]. June 11, 1739

9 That execrable sum of all villainies, commonly called the Slave Trade.
Ib. February 12, 1772

10 Though I am always in haste, I am never in a hurry.
Letters [1831]. December 10, 1777

11 Let it be observed, that slovenliness is no part of religion; that neither this nor any text of Scripture, condemns neatness of apparel. Certainly this is a duty, not a sin. "Cleanliness is, indeed, next to godliness."[3]
Sermon 93, On Dress

[1]See Gellert, 360:28.

[2]Handel used this in his oratorios *Judas Maccabaeus* [April 1, 1747] and *Joshua* [March 9, 1748], the libretti of which were written by Morell.
See Dryden, 306:14.

12 Do all the good you can,
By all the means you can,
In all the ways you can,
In all the places you can,
At all the times you can,
To all the people you can,
As long as ever you can.
John Wesley's Rule

Nathaniel Cotton
1705–1788

13 Yet still we hug the dear deceit.
Content. Vision IV

14 Hold the fleet angel fast until he bless thee.[4]
Tomorrow

Benjamin Franklin[5]
1706–1790

15 The body of Benjamin Franklin, Printer (like the cover of an old book, its contents torn out and stripped of its lettering and gilding), lies here, food for worms; but the work shall not be lost, for it will (as he believed) appear once more in a new and more elegant edition, revised and corrected by the Author.[6]
Epitaph on Himself [composed in 1728]

[3]According to Rabbi A. S. Bettelheim, this is found in the Hebrew fathers. He cites Phinehas ben Yair as follows: "The doctrines of religion are resolved into carefulness; carefulness into vigorousness; vigorousness into guiltlessness; guiltlessness into abstemiousness; abstemiousness into cleanliness; cleanliness into godliness"—literally, next to godliness.

[4]See *Genesis 32:26*, 8:25, and Whittier, 513:5.

[5]Eripuit coelo fulmen mox sceptra tyrannis [He snatched the thunderbolt from heaven, then the scepter from tyrants].—*Attributed to* TURGOT
This line was inscribed on Houdon's bust of Franklin in 1778. FREDERICK VON DER TRENCK [1726–1794] asserted in 1794 that he was the author of the line.
See Manilius, 115:16, and Shakespeare, 242:20.
Antiquity would have rasied altars to this mighty genius, who, to the advantage of mankind, compassing in his mind the heavens and the earth, was able to restrain alike thunderbolts and tyrants.—MIRABEAU, *Address upon the Death of Franklin*
I succeed him; no one could replace him.—THOMAS JEFFERSON (to the Comte de Vergennes, who had remarked, "You replace Mr. Franklin" as envoy to France)
See Byron, 462:15.

[6]See Clare, 470:12.

1 Eat to live, and not live to eat.[1]
Poor Richard's Almanac [1733]. May

2 After three days men grow weary, of a wench, a guest, and weather rainy.
Ib. June

3 There is no little enemy.
Ib. September

4 Without justice, courage is weak.
Ib. [1734]. January

5 Blame-all and Praise-all are two blockheads.
Ib. February

6 Where there's marriage without love, there will be love without marriage.
Ib. May

7 Avarice and happiness never saw each other, how then should they become acquainted.
Ib. November

8 A little house well filled, a little field well tilled, and a little wife well willed, are great riches.
Ib. [1735]. February

9 Necessity never made a good bargain.
Ib. April

10 Three may keep a secret, if two of them are dead.
Ib. July

11 Opportunity is the great bawd.
Ib. September

12 Early to bed and early to rise, makes a man healthy, wealthy, and wise.
Ib. October

13 Here comes the orator! with his flood of words, and his drop of reason.
Ib.

14 Some are weatherwise, some are otherwise.
Ib. December

15 God helps them that help themselves.[2]
Ib. [1736]. June

16 Don't throw stones at your neighbors', if your own windows are glass.[3]
Ib. August

17 There are three faithful friends—an old wife, an old dog, and ready money.
Ib. [1738]. January

18 If you would not be forgotten,
As soon as you are dead and rotten,
Either write things worthy reading,
Or do things worth the writing.
Ib. May

[1]See Socrates, 79:6, and Molière, 298:4.
[2]See Aesop, 66:20.
[3]See Herbert, 269:25.

19 Keep your eyes wide open before marriage, half shut afterwards.
Ib. June

20 None but the well-bred man knows how to confess a fault, or acknowledge himself in an error.
Ib. November

21 An empty bag cannot stand upright.
Ib. [1740]. January

22 He that riseth late, must trot all day, and shall scarce overtake his business at night.
Ib. [1742]. August

23 Experience keeps a dear school, but fools will learn in no other.[4]
Ib. [1743]. December

24 The used key is always bright.
Ib. [1744]. July

25 When the well's dry, we know the worth of water.[5]
Ib. [1746]. January

26 Dost thou love life? Then do not squander time; for that's the stuff life is made of.
Ib. June

27 Lost time is never found again.
Ib. [1748]. January

28 He that's secure is not safe.
Ib. August

29 Little strokes,
Fell great oaks.[6]
Ib. [1750]. August

30 The cat in gloves catches no mice.
Ib. [1754]. February

31 Work as if you were to live a hundred years,
Pray as if you were to die tomorrow.
Ib. [1757]. May

32 A word to the wise is enough, and many words won't fill a bushel.
Ib. [1758]. Preface: Courteous Reader

33 He that lives upon hope will die fasting.
Ib.

34 Three removes is as bad as a fire.
Ib.

35 A little neglect may breed great mischief . . . for want of a nail the shoe was lost; for want of a shoe the horse was lost; and for want of a horse the rider was lost.[7]
Ib.

36 Eighth and lastly. They are so grateful!!
Reasons for Preferring an Elderly Mistress [1745]

[4]See Burke, 374:8.
[5]Do not let your chances like sunbeams pass you by, / For you never miss the water till the well runs dry. — Rowland Howard, *You Never Miss the Water* [1876]
[6]See Lyly, 175:13.
[7]See Herbert, 270:4.

1 Remember that time is money.[1]
Advice to a Young Tradesman [1748]

2 They that can give up essential liberty to obtain a little temporary safety deserve neither liberty nor safety.
Historical Review of Pennsylvania [1759]

3 Idleness and pride tax with a heavier hand than kings and parliaments. If we can get rid of the former, we may easily bear the latter.
Letter on the Stamp Act [July 11, 1765]

4 The grand leap of the whale up the Fall of Niagara is esteemed, by all who have seen it, as one of the finest spectacles in nature.
To the editor of a London newspaper [1765], intended to chaff the English for their ignorance of America

5 Here Skugg lies snug
As a bug in a rug.
Letter to Miss Georgiana Shipley [September 1772]

6 There never was a good war or a bad peace.[2]
Letter to Josiah Quincy [September 11, 1773]

7 You and I were long friends: you are now my enemy, and I am
Yours,
B. Franklin
Letter to William Strahan [July 5, 1775]

8 We must all hang together, or assuredly we shall all hang separately.
At the signing of the Declaration of Independence [July 4, 1776]

9 Poor man, said I, you pay too much for your whistle. *The Whistle [1779]*

10 Here you would know and enjoy what posterity will say of Washington. For a thousand leagues have nearly the same effect with a thousand years.
Letter to Washington [March 5, 1780]

11 George Washington, Commander of the American armies, who, like Joshua of old, commanded the sun and the moon to stand still, and they obeyed him.
A toast at a dinner in Versailles[3]

12 No nation was ever ruined by trade.
Thoughts on Commercial Subjects

13 I wish the bald eagle had not been chosen as the representative of our country; he is a bird of bad moral character; like those among men who live by sharping and robbing, he is generally poor, and often very lousy.

The turkey is a much more respectable bird, and withal a true original native of America.
Letter to Sarah Bache [January 26, 1784]

14 He [the sun] gives light as soon as he rises.
An Economical Project [1784][4]

15 A republic if you can keep it.[5]
Response [September 18, 1787]

16 Our Constitution is in actual operation; everything appears to promise that it will last; but in this world nothing is certain but death and taxes. *Letter to M. Leroy [1789]*

17 The next thing most like living one's life over again seems to be a recollection of that life, and to make that recollection as durable as possible by putting it down in writing.
Autobiography [1731–1759],[6] *ch. 1*

18 Eat not to dullness; drink not to elevation.
Ib. 6

19 I shall never ask, never refuse, nor ever resign an office. *Ib. 8*

20 Human felicity is produced not so much by great pieces of good fortune that seldom happen, as by little advantages that occur every day. *Ib. 9*

21 When men are employed, they are best contented; for on the days they worked they were good-natured and cheerful, and, with the consciousness of having done a good day's

[1] We reckon hours and minutes to be dollars and cents.
—T. C. Haliburton [1796–1865], *The Clockmaker*
See Theophrastus, 91:17.

[2] I cease not to advocate peace; even though unjust it is better than the most just war.—Cicero [106–43 B.C.], *Epistolae ad Atticum, bk. VII, epistle 14*
It hath been said that an unjust peace is to be preferred before a just war.—Samuel Butler, *Butler's Remains* [1759], *Speeches in the Rump Parliament*

[3] The British minister had proposed a toast to George III, in which he likened him to the sun, and the French minister had toasted Louis XVI, comparing him with the moon.

[4] Letter to the *Journal de Paris* advocating Daylight Saving Time.

[5] In Philadelphia, a Mrs. Powel "asked Dr. Franklin Well Doctor what have we got a republic or a monarchy? A republic replied the Doctor if you can keep it." Recorded by James McHenry, one of Washington's aides, in his diary; published in the *American Historical Review, XI* [1906], *618.*

[6] The *Autobiography,* begun in 1771, was first published (unauthorized, mangled, and in French) in 1791, and in complete and accurate form in 1868.

work, they spent the evening jollily; but on our idle days they were mutinous and quarrelsome. *Ib. 10*

George Louis Leclerc de Buffon

1707–1788

1 [Of the horse] The noblest conquest man has ever made.
L'Histoire des Mammifères. Le Cheval

2 The style is the man himself.[1]
Discourse (on his admission to the French Academy [1753])

3 Genius is nothing but a greater aptitude for patience. *Attributed*[2]

Henry Fielding

1707–1754

4 All Nature wears one universal grin.
Tom Thumb the Great [1730], act I, sc. i

5 Today it is our pleasure to be drunk;
And this our queen shall be as drunk as we.
Ib. ii

6 When I'm not thanked at all, I'm thanked enough;
I've done my duty, and I've done no more.
Ib. iii

7 Oh, the roast beef of England,
And old England's roast beef![3]
The Grub Street Opera [1731], act III, sc. ii

8 I am as sober as a judge.
Don Quixote in England [1734], act III, sc. xiv

9 This story will never go down.
Tumble-Down Dick

[1]Le style c'est l'homme même.
See Burton, 258:8.

[2]Le génie n'est qu'une plus grande aptitude à la patience.
Hérault de Séchelles, in *Voyage à Montbard,* first attributed this to Buffon. It is quoted by Matthew Arnold in "A French Coleridge" [*Essays in Criticism,* 1865]. There is also a popular proverb: Genius is patience. Lord Sydenham [1799–1841] defined genius as a consummate sense of proportion.
See Carlyle, 474:14; Butler, 620:21; and Hopkins, 630:17.
Patience is a necessary ingredient of genius. — DISRAELI, *The Young Duke* [1831]
Genius is capacity for taking trouble. — LESLIE STEPHEN [1832–1904]
Genius is an intuitive talent for labor. — JOHANNES WALAEUS [JAN VAN WALE] [1604–1699]

[3]The Roast Beef of Old England. — RICHARD LEVERIDGE [c. 1670–1758], *title of poem*

10 The dusky night rides down the sky,
And ushers in the morn;
The hounds all join in glorious cry,
The huntsman winds his horn,
And a-hunting we will go.[4]
A-Hunting We Will Go [1734], st. 1

11 To whom nothing is given, of him can nothing be required.[5]
Joseph Andrews [1742], bk. II, ch. 8

12 I describe not men, but manners; not an individual, but a species. *Ib. III, 1*

13 They are the affectation of affectation.
Ib. 3

14 Public schools are the nurseries of all vice and immorality. *Ib. 5*

15 Some folks rail against other folks, because other folks have what some folks would be glad of. *Ib. IV, 6*

16 Love and scandal are the best sweeteners of tea.[6]
Love in Several Masques [1743]

17 Every physician almost hath his favorite disease.
Tom Jones [1749],[7] bk. II, ch. 9

18 Thwackum was for doing justice, and leaving mercy to heaven. *Ib. III, 10*

19 Can any man have a higher notion of the rule of right and the eternal fitness of things?
Ib. IV, 4

20 Distinction without a difference.
Ib. VI, 13

21 O! more than Gothic ignorance.
Ib. VII, 3

22 An amiable weakness.[8] *Ib. X, 8*

23 His designs were strictly honorable, as the phrase is; that is, to rob a lady of her fortune by way of marriage. *Ib. XI, 4*

24 Hairbreadth missings of happiness look like the insults of Fortune. *Ib. XIII, 2*

25 The republic of letters. *Ib. XIV, 1*

26 It hath been often said, that it is not death, but dying which is terrible.
Amelia [1751], bk. III, ch. 4

[4]It's of three jovial huntsmen, and a-hunting they did go; / And they hunted, and they holloed, and they blew their horns also; / Look ye there! — *The Three Jovial Huntsmen* (old English ballad), *st. 1*

[5]See *Luke 12:48,* 43:22.

[6]See Congreve, 324:7.

[7]See Gibbon, 383:16.

[8]Amiable weaknesses of human nature. — GIBBON, *Decline and Fall of the Roman Empire* [1776–1788], *ch. 14*
It was an amiable weakness. — SHERIDAN, *The School for Scandal* [1777]

1 These are called the pious frauds of friendship. *Ib. VI, 6*

2 When widows exclaim loudly against second marriages, I would always lay a wager that the man, if not the wedding day, is absolutely fixed on. *Ib. 8*

3 There is not in the universe a more ridiculous, nor a more contemptible animal, than a proud clergyman. *Ib. VI, 10*

4 One of my illustrious predecessors.[1]
Covent Garden Journal [January 11, 1752]

Linnaeus
[Carl von Linné]
1707–1778

5 To live by medicine is to live horribly.
Diaeta Naturalis, introduction

6 Nature does not proceed by leaps.[2]
Philosophia Botanica [1750], sec. 77

7 Mingle your joys sometimes with your earnest occupation.[3]
From biography of Linnaeus by BENJAMIN DAYDON JONES, *ch. 9*

8 A professor can never better distinguish himself in his work than by encouraging a clever pupil, for the true discoverers are among them, as comets amongst the stars. *Ib.*

9 Live innocently; God is here.
Ib. 15 (inscribed over the door of Linnaeus's bedchamber)

10 If a tree dies, plant another in its place. *Ib.*

Charles Wesley
1707–1788

11 "Christ, the Lord, is risen today,"
Sons of men and angels say,
Raise your joys and triumphs high,
Sing, ye heavens, and earth reply.
Hymns and Sacred Poems [1739]. Christ, the Lord, Is Risen Today

12 Jesus, lover of my soul,
Let me to Thy bosom fly,
While the waters nearer roll,
While the tempest still is high;
Hide me, O my Savior, hide,
Till the storm of life is past;
Safe into the haven glide,
O receive my soul at last.
Ib. [1740]. Jesus, Lover of My Soul

13 Gentle Jesus, meek and mild,
Look upon a little child;
Pity my simplicity,
Suffer me to come to thee.
Ib. [1742]. Gentle Jesus, Meek and Mild

14 Soldiers of Christ, arise,
And put your armor on.
Ib. [1749]. Soldiers of Christ, Arise

15 Hark! the herald angels sing
Glory to the newborn King;
Peace on earth, and mercy mild,
God and sinners reconciled!
Joyful all ye nations rise,
Join the triumph of the skies;
With th' angelic host proclaim
Christ is born in Bethlehem.[4]
Ib. [1753]. Christmas Hymn: Hark! the Herald Angels Sing

William Pitt, Earl of Chatham
1708–1778

16 The atrocious crime of being a young man, which the honorable gentleman [Walpole] has with such spirit and decency charged upon me, I shall neither attempt to palliate nor deny; but content myself with wishing that I may be one of those whose follies may cease with their youth, and not of that number who are ignorant in spite of experience.
Speech in the House of Commons [March 6, 1741][5]

17 I rejoice that America has resisted. Three millions of people, so dead to all the feelings of liberty, as voluntarily to submit to be slaves, would have been fit instruments to make slaves of the rest.
Ib. [January 14, 1766]

18 Confidence is a plant of slow growth in an aged bosom; youth is the season of credulity.
Speech in the House of Commons [January 14, 1766]

[1] Illustrious predecessor. — BURKE, *The Present Discontents* [1770]
I tread in the footsteps of illustrious men. . . . In receiving from the people the sacred trust twice confined to my illustrious predecessor [Andrew Jackson]. — MARTIN VAN BUREN, *Inaugural Address* [March 4, 1837]

[2] Natura non facit saltus.

[3] See Menander, 91:2; Horace, 108:15; Montaigne, 166:4; and Bacon, 181:3.

[4] GEORGE WHITEFIELD [1714–1770] altered lines 1 and 2, 7 and 8, from Wesley's original:
Hark, how all the welkin rings, / "Glory to the King of kings." . . . / Universal nature say, / "Christ the Lord is born today."

[5] This is the composition of Johnson, founded on some note or statement of the actual speech. Johnson said, "That speech I wrote in a garret, in Exeter Street." — BOSWELL, *Life of Johnson* [1791]

1 Unlimited power is apt to corrupt the minds of those who possess it;[1] and this I know, my lords, that where laws end, tyranny begins.[2]

Case of Wilkes. Speech [January 9, 1770]

2 There is something behind the throne greater than the King himself.

Speech in the House of Lords [March 2, 1770]

3 I love the Americans because they love liberty, and I love them for the noble efforts they made in the last war. *Ib.*

4 Reparation for our rights at home, and security against the like future violations.[3]

Letter to the Earl of Shelburne [September 29, 1770]

5 If I were an American, as I am an Englishman, while a foreign troop was landed in my country, I never would lay down my arms — never — never — never![4] You cannot conquer America.

Speech [November 18, 1777]

6 I invoke the genius of the Constitution.

Ib.

7 The poorest man may in his cottage bid defiance to all the forces of the Crown. It may be frail — its roof may shake — the wind may blow through it — the storm may enter — the rain may enter — but the King of England cannot enter — all his force dares not cross the threshold of the ruined tenement!

Speech on the Excise Bill

Samuel Johnson

1709–1784

8 Of all the griefs that harass the distrest,
Sure the most bitter is a scornful jest.

London [1738] (an imitation of the Third Satire of Juvenal), l. 166

9 This mournful truth is ev'rywhere confessed —
Slow rises worth, by poverty depressed.[5]

Ib. l. 176

[1] See Shelley, 466:7, and Lord Acton, 615:15.

[2] See John Locke, 307:17.

[3] Indemnity for the past and security for the future. — LORD JOHN RUSSELL, *Life and Times of Charles James Fox* [1859–1860], *vol. III, p. 345, letter to the Honorable T. Maitland*

[4] See Shakespeare, 235:18, and Churchill, 745:6.

[5] Three years later Johnson wrote, "Mere unassisted merit advances slowly, if — what is not very common — it advances at all."

10 When learning's triumph o'er her barb'rous foes
First reared the stage, immortal Shakespeare rose;
Each change of many-colored life he drew,
Exhausted worlds, and then imagined new:
Existence saw him spurn her bounded reign,
And panting Time toiled after him in vain.

Prologue at the Opening of Drury Lane Theatre [1747]

11 Cold approbation gave the ling'ring bays,
For those who durst not censure, scarce could praise. *Ib.*

12 Declamation roared, while Passion slept.

Ib.

13 The wild vicissitudes of taste. *Ib.*

14 For we that live to please must please to live.

Ib.

15 Studious to please, yet not ashamed to fail.

Prologue to the Tragedy of Irene [1749]

16 Let observation with extensive view
Survey mankind, from China to Peru.[6]

Vanity of Human Wishes [1749], l. 1

17 Deign on the passing world to turn thine eyes,
And pause a while from learning to be wise.
There mark what ills the scholar's life assail —
Toil, envy, want, the patron, and the jail.

Ib. l. 157

18 A frame of adamant, a soul of fire,
No dangers fright him, and no labors tire.

Ib. l. 191

19 He left the name at which the world grew pale,
To point a moral, or adorn a tale.

Ib. l. 221

20 "Enlarge my life with multitude of days!"
In health, in sickness, thus the suppliant prays:
Hides from himself his state, and shuns to know
That life protracted is protracted woe.

Ib. l. 255

21 Superfluous lags the vet'ran on the stage.

Ib. l. 308

[6] De Quincey quotes with approval, but without naming him, the criticism of a writer who contends that this couplet amounts in effect to this: "Let observation with extensive observation observe mankind extensively." — *Rhetoric* [1828]

1 Must helpless man, in ignorance sedate,
Roll darkling down the torrent of his fate?
Ib. l. 345

2 Secure, whate'er he gives, he gives the best.
Ib. l. 356

3 With these celestial Wisdom calms the mind,
And makes the happiness she does not find.
Ib. l. 367

4 Curiosity is one of the permanent and certain characteristics of a vigorous mind.
The Rambler[1] *[March 12, 1751]*

5 No place affords a more striking conviction of the vanity of human hopes than a public library. *Ib. [March 23, 1751]*

6 I am not so lost in lexicography as to forget that words are the daughters of earth, and that things are the sons of heaven.[2]
Dictionary [1755], preface

7 CLUB—An assembly of good fellows, meeting under certain conditions. *Ib.*

8 ESSAY—A loose sally of the mind; an irregular indigested piece; not a regular and orderly composition. *Ib.*

9 EXCISE—A hateful tax levied upon commodities, and adjudged not by the common judges of property, but wretches hired by those to whom excise is paid. *Ib.*

10 GRUBSTREET—The name of a street near Moorsfield, London, much inhabited by writers of small histories, dictionaries, and temporary poems. *Ib.*

11 LEXICOGRAPHER—A writer of dictionaries, a harmless drudge. *Ib.*

12 OATS—A grain which in England is generally given to horses, but in Scotland supports the people.[3] *Ib.*

13 The joy of life is variety;[4] the tenderest love requires to be renewed by intervals of absence. *The Idler [1758–1760], no. 39*

14 He is no wise man that will quit a certainty for an uncertainty. *Ib. 57*

15 Ye who listen with credulity to the whispers of fancy, and pursue with eagerness the phantoms of hope; who expect that age will perform the promises of youth, and that the deficiencies of the present day will be supplied by the morrow; attend to the history of Rasselas, Prince of Abyssinia.
Rasselas [1759], ch. 1

16 To a poet nothing can be useless.
Ib. 10

17 Human life is everywhere a state in which much is to be endured and little to be enjoyed.
Ib. 11

18 Marriage has many pains, but celibacy has no pleasures. *Ib. 26*

19 Example is always more efficacious than precept. *Ib. 29*

20 The endearing elegance of female friendship. *Ib. 45*

21 How small, of all that human hearts endure,
That part which laws or kings can cause or cure!
Still to ourselves in every place consigned,
Our own felicity we make or find.
Lines added to GOLDSMITH, *The Traveller [1763–1764]*

22 That man is little to be envied whose patriotism would not gain force upon the plain of Marathon, or whose piety would not grow warmer among the ruins of Iona.
Journey to the Western Islands [1775]. Inch Kenneth

23 Whoever wishes to attain an English style, familiar but not coarse, and elegant but not ostentatious, must give his days and nights to the volumes of Addison.
Lives of the Poets [1779–1781]. Addison

24 To be of no church is dangerous. Religion, of which the rewards are distant, and which is animated only by faith and hope, will glide by degrees out of the mind unless it be invigorated and reimpressed by external ordinances, by stated calls to worship, and the salutary influence of example.
Ib. Milton

25 The father of English criticism.
Ib. Dryden

26 He delighted to tread upon the brink of meaning. *Ib.*

27 The *Churchyard* abounds with images which find a mirror in every mind, and with sentiments to which every bosom returns an echo. *Ib. Gray*[5]

[1] For the *Rambler* motto, see Johnson's translation of BOETHIUS, *De Consolatione Philosophiae, III, 9*, 27, 130:3.

[2] See Herbert, 270:16.

[3] It was pleasant to me to find, that "oats," the "food of horses," were so much used as the food of the people in Dr. Johnson's own town.—BOSWELL, *Life of Johnson* [1791], *vol. I, p. 628* (Everyman edition)

I own that by my definition of *oats* I meant to vex them [the Scotch].—JOHNSON, *from Ib. II, 434*

[4] See Publilius Syrus, 111:9, and Cowper, 376:22.

[5] See Gray, 361:20.

1 His [Garrick's] death has eclipsed the gaiety of nations, and impoverished the public stock of harmless pleasure.

Ib. Edmund Smith

2 New things are made familiar, and familiar things are made new. *Ib. Pope*

3 Tomorrow I purpose to regulate my room.

Prayers and Meditations [1785]. 1764

4 Preserve me from unseasonable and immoderate sleep. *Ib. 1767*

5 Every man naturally persuades himself that he can keep his resolutions, nor is he convinced of his imbecility but by length of time and frequency of experiment.

Ib. 1770

6 This world, where much is to be done and little to be known.

Ib. Against Inquisitive and Perplexing Thoughts

7 I have, all my life long, been lying till noon; yet I tell all young men, and tell them with great sincerity, that nobody who does not rise early will ever do any good.

From BOSWELL, *Journal of a Tour to the Hebrides [1785]. September 14, 1773*

8 Wickedness is always easier than virtue; for it takes the short cut to everything.

Ib. September 17, 1773

9 Gratitude is a fruit of great cultivation; you do not find it among gross people.

Ib. September 20, 1773

10 Here closed in death th' attentive eyes
That saw the manners in the face.

Epitaph on Hogarth [1786]

11 When the hoary Sage replied,
"Come, my lad, and drink some beer."

From MRS. PIOZZI, *Anecdotes of Samuel Johnson [1786]*

12 If the man who turnips cries,
Cry not when his father dies,
'Tis a proof that he had rather
Have a turnip than his father.[1] *Ib.*

13 He was a very good hater. *Ib.*

14 The law is the last result of human wisdom acting upon human experience for the benefit of the public. *Ib.*

15 The use of traveling is to regulate imagination by reality, and instead of thinking how things may be, to see them as they are.

Ib.

[1]Burlesque of Lope de Vega's lines: "Se acquien los leones vence," etc.

16 Dictionaries are like watches; the worst is better than none, and the best cannot be expected to go quite true. *Ib.*

17 Books that you may carry to the fire, and hold readily in your hand, are the most useful after all.

From SIR JOHN HAWKINS, *Life of Johnson [1787]. Apothegms*

18 As with my hat[2] upon my head
I walked along the Strand,
I there did meet another man
With his hat in his hand.[3]

Anecdotes of Johnson by GEORGE STEEVENS

19 Abstinence is as easy to me as temperance would be difficult.

Anecdotes of Johnson by HANNAH MORE

20 *Boswell:* That, sir, was great fortitude of mind.

Johnson: No, sir; stark insensibility.

From JAMES BOSWELL, *Life of Johnson*[4] *[1791], November 5, 1728*

21 [Of Pembroke College] Sir, we are a nest of singing birds. *Ib. 1730*

22 Tom Birch is as brisk as a bee in conversation; but no sooner does he take a pen in his hand than it becomes a torpedo to him, and benumbs all his faculties. *Ib. 1743*

23 I'll come no more behind your scenes, David [Garrick]; for the silk stockings and white bosoms of your actresses excite my amorous propensities. *Ib. 1750*

24 A man may write at any time, if he will set himself doggedly to it. *Ib. March 1750*

25 Wretched un-ideaed girls. *Ib. 1753*

26 Is not a patron, my lord, one who looks with unconcern on a man struggling for life in the water, and when he has reached ground encumbers him with help? The notice which you have been pleased to take of my labors, had it been early, had been kind; but it has been delayed till I am indifferent, and cannot enjoy it; till I am solitary, and cannot impart it; till I am known, and do not want it.

Ib. February 7, 1754 (Letter to Lord Chesterfield)

[2]Elsewhere found: I put my hat.

[3]A parody on the ballad *The Hermit of Warkworth.*

[4]Edited by G. B. HILL and revised by L. F. POWELL [1934].

The *Life of Johnson* is assuredly a great, a very great work. Homer is not more decidedly the first of heroic poets, Shakespeare is not more decidedly the first of dramatists, Demosthenes is not more decidedly the first of orators, than Boswell is the first of biographers. He has no second. — MACAULAY, *Samuel Johnson* [1831]

1 [Of Lord Chesterfield] This man, I thought, had been a Lord among wits; but, I find, he is only a wit among Lords! *Ib. 1754*

2 Sir, he [Bolingbroke] was a scoundrel, and a coward: a scoundrel, for charging a blunderbuss against religion and morality; a coward, because he had not resolution to fire it off himself, but left half a crown to a beggarly Scotchman to draw the trigger at his death.[1] *Ib. March 6, 1754*

3 Ignorance, madame, pure ignorance.[2] *Ib. 1755*

4 If a man does not make new acquaintances as he advances through life, he will soon find himself left alone. A man, sir, should keep his friendship in a constant repair.[3] *Ib. 1755*

5 Towering in the confidence of twenty-one. *Ib. January 9, 1758*

6 Being in a ship is being in a jail, with the chance of being drowned. *Ib. March 1759*

7 Nothing is little to him that feels it with great sensibility. *Ib. July 20, 1762*

8 A man of genius has been seldom ruined but by himself. *Ib. December 21, 1762*

9 Sir, I think all Christians, whether Papists or Protestants, agree in the essential articles, and that their differences are trivial, and rather political than religious.[4] *Ib. 1763*

10 The noblest prospect which a Scotchman ever sees is the high-road that leads him to England! *Ib. July 6, 1763*

11 A man ought to read just as inclination leads him; for what he reads as a task will do him little good.[5] *Ib. July 14, 1763*

12 If he does really think that there is no distinction between virtue and vice, why, sir, when he leaves our houses let us count our spoons. *Ib.*

13 Sir, your levelers wish to level *down* as far as themselves; but they cannot bear leveling *up* to themselves. *Ib. July 21, 1763*

14 Sherry[6] is dull, naturally dull; but it must have taken him a great deal of pains to become what we now see him. Such an excess of stupidity, sir, is not in Nature. *Ib. July 28, 1763*

15 Sir, a woman preaching is like a dog's walking on his hind legs. It is not done well; but you are surprised to find it done at all. *Ib. July 31, 1763*

16 I look upon it, that he who does not mind his belly will hardly mind anything else. *Ib. August 5, 1763*

17 This was a good dinner enough, to be sure, but it was not a dinner to *ask* a man to. *Ib.*

18 The gloomy calm of idle vacancy.[7] *Ib. December 8, 1763*

19 [Of Sir John Hawkins] A very unclubable man. *Ib. 1764*

20 It matters not how a man dies, but how he lives. *Ib. October 26, 1769*

21 That fellow seems to me to possess but one idea, and that is a wrong one. *Ib. 1770*

22 A gentleman who had been very unhappy in marriage, married immediately after his wife died: Johnson said, it was the triumph of hope over experience.[8] *Ib.*

23 A decent provision for the poor is the true test of civilization.[9] *Ib.*

24 All denominations of Christians have really little difference in point of doctrine, though they may differ widely in external forms.[10] *Ib. 1772*

25 Nobody can write the life of a man, but those who have eat and drunk and lived in social intercourse with him.[11] *Ib. March 31, 1772*

[1] See Chesterfield, 342:8.

[2] When asked by a lady why he defined "pastern" as the "knee" of a horse in his Dictionary.

[3] Keep your friendships in repair. — EMERSON, *Table Talk* [1864]

[4] See Johnson, 354:24.

I do not find that the age or country makes the least difference; no, nor the language the actor spoke, nor the religion which they professed — whether Arab in the desert, or Frenchman in the Academy. I see that sensible men and conscientious men all over the world were of one religion of well-doing and daring. — EMERSON, *Lectures and Biographical Sketches* [1884], *The Preacher*

See Disraeli, 502:23.

[5] The book which you read from a sense of duty, or because for any reason you must, does not commonly make friends with you. — WILLIAM DEAN HOWELLS, *My Literary Passions* [1895], *ch. 7*

[6] Thomas Sheridan [1719–1788], actor, lecturer, and author.

[7] See Cowper, 377:7.

[8] See Wilde; 675:5.

[9] See Maimonides, 137:10; Spinoza, 309:1; and Carnegie, 621:10.

[10] See first entry for 1763.

[11] They only who live with a man can write his life with any genuine exactness and discrimination; and few people who have lived with a man know what to remark about him. — *vol. I, p. 617* (Everyman edition)

1 I am a great friend to public amusements; for they keep people from vice. *Ib.*

2 There is more knowledge of the heart in one letter of Richardson's than in all *Tom Jones.* *Ib. April 6, 1772*

3 Why, sir, if you were to read Richardson for the story, your impatience would be so much fretted that you would hang yourself. But you must read him for the sentiment, and consider the story as only giving occasion to the sentiment. *Ib.*

4 A cow is a very good animal in the field; but we turn her out of a garden. *Ib. April 15, 1772*

5 Much may be made of a Scotchman if he be caught young.[1] *Ib. Spring 1772*

6 It is a foolish thing well done.[2] *Ib. April 3, 1773*

7 No, sir, do *you* read books *through?*[3] *Ib. April 19, 1773*

8 An old tutor of a college said to one of his pupils: Read over your compositions, and wherever you meet with a passage which you think is particularly fine, strike it out.[4] *Ib. April 30, 1773*

9 You are the most unscottified of your countrymen. *Ib. May 1, 1773*

10 The woman's a whore, and there's an end on 't.[5] *Ib. May 7, 1773*

11 Was ever poet so trusted before?[6] *Ib. July 4, 1774*

12 Attack is the reaction; I never think I have hit hard unless it rebounds. *Ib. April 2, 1775*

13 Most vices may be committed very genteelly: a man may debauch his friend's wife genteelly: he may cheat at cards genteelly. *Ib. April 6, 1775*

14 A man will turn over half a library to make one book. *Ib.*

15 Patriotism is the last refuge of a scoundrel.[7] *Ib. April 7, 1775*

16 That is the happiest conversation where there is no competition, no vanity, but a calm quiet interchange of sentiments. *Ib. April 14, 1775*

17 Knowledge is of two kinds. We know a subject ourselves, or we know where we can find information upon it. *Ib. April 18, 1775*

18 In lapidary inscriptions a man is not upon oath. *Ib. 1775*

19 There is nothing which has yet been contrived by man by which so much happiness is produced as by a good tavern or inn.[8] *Ib. March 21, 1776*

20 No man but a blockhead ever wrote except for money. *Ib. April 5, 1776*

21 Life is a progress from want to want, not from enjoyment to enjoyment. *Ib. May 1776*

22 Sir, you have but two topics, yourself and me. I am sick of both. *Ib.*

23 Olivarii Goldsmith, Poetae, Physici, Historici, qui nullum fere scribendi genus non tetigit, Nullum quod tetigit non ornavit [To Oliver Goldsmith, Poet, Naturalist, Historian, who left scarcely any style of writing untouched, and touched nothing that he did not adorn]. *Ib. June 22, 1776*

24 Life admits not of delays; when pleasure can be had, it is fit to catch it. Every hour takes away part of the things that please us, and perhaps part of our disposition to be pleased. *Ib. September 1, 1777*

25 Depend upon it, sir, when a man knows he is to be hanged in a fortnight, it concentrates his mind wonderfully. *Ib. September 19, 1777*

26 When a man is tired of London, he is tired of life; for there is in London all that life can afford. *Ib. September 20, 1777*

27 It is a man's own fault, it is from want of use, if his mind grows torpid in old age. *Ib. April 9, 1778*

[1] Of Lord Mansfield, educated in England.

[2] Of Goldsmith's apology in the *London Chronicle* for beating Evans the bookseller.

[3] Upon being asked by Elphinstone if he had read a new book through.

[4] See Sydney Smith, 433:14.

[5] Of Lady Diana Beauclerk, divorced.

[6] Of Oliver Goldsmith.

[7] Patriotism having become one of our topics, Johnson suddenly uttered, in a strong, determined tone, an apothegm, at which many will start: "Patriotism is the last refuge of a scoundrel." But let it be considered, that he did not mean a real and generous love of our country, but that pretended patriotism which so many, in all ages and countries, have made a cloak for self-interest. I maintained that certainly all patriots were not scoundrels. — BOSWELL, *Life of Johnson* [1791], *April 7, 1775*

[8] Following this remark, Johnson quoted (not quite correctly):

Whoe'er has traveled life's dull round, / Whate'er his various tour has been, / May sigh to think how oft he found / His warmest welcome at an inn. — WILLIAM SHENSTONE [1714–1763]; *written on a window of an inn at Henley*

Robert Leighton [1611–1684], archbishop of Glasgow, often said that if he were to choose a place to die in, it should be an inn. — *Works, vol. I, p. 76*

See the Archpoet, 137:1.

1 Johnson had said that he could repeat a complete chapter of *The Natural History of Iceland,* from the Danish of Horrebow, the whole of which was exactly thus: "Ch. LXXII. *Concerning snakes.* There are no snakes to be met with throughout the whole island."[1]
Ib. April 13, 1778

2 Every state of society is as luxurious as it can be. Men always take the best they can get. *Ib. April 14, 1778*

3 A country governed by a despot is an inverted cone. *Ib.*

4 I am willing to love all mankind, except an American. *Ib. April 15, 1778*

5 Pleasure of itself is not a vice. *Ib.*

6 As the Spanish proverb says, "He, who would bring home the wealth of the Indies, must carry the wealth of the Indies with him," so it is in traveling, a man must carry knowledge with him if he would bring home knowledge. *Ib. April 17, 1778*

7 It is better to live rich, than to die rich.[2]
Ib.

8 Were it not for imagination, sir, a man would be as happy in the arms of a chambermaid as a duchess. *Ib. May 9, 1778*

9 I would rather be attacked than unnoticed. For the worst thing you can do to an author is to be silent as to his works.
Ib. March 26, 1779

10 I remember a passage in Goldsmith's *Vicar of Wakefield,* which he was afterwards a fool enough to expunge: "I do not love a man who is zealous for nothing." *Ib.*

11 Claret is the liquor for boys; port for men; but he who aspires to be a hero must drink brandy. *Ib. April 7, 1779*

12 Worth seeing? yes; but not worth going to see. *Ib. October 12, 1779*

13 If you are idle, be not solitary; if you are solitary, be not idle.[3]
Ib. October 27, 1779

14 A Frenchman must be always talking, whether he knows anything of the matter or not; an Englishman is content to say nothing, when he has nothing to say. *Ib. 1780*

[1] Chapter XLII is still shorter: "There are no owls of any kind in the whole island."

[2] See Robert Burton, 258:24.

[3] The great direction which Burton has left to men disordered like you, is this: Be not solitary, be not idle. — JOHNSON, *Ib.*
See Burton, 260:6.

15 Greek, sir, is like lace; every man gets as much of it as he can. *Ib.*

16 [Of Oliver Goldsmith] No man was more foolish when he had not a pen in his hand, or more wise when he had. *Ib.*

17 The applause of a single human being is of great consequence. *Ib.*

18 Come to me, my dear Bozzy, and let us be as happy as we can.
Ib. March 14, 1781

19 There are people whom one should like very well to drop, but would not wish to be dropped by. *Ib. March 1781*

20 We are not here to sell a parcel of boilers and vats, but the potentiality of growing rich beyond the dreams of avarice.[4]
Ib. April 4, 1781

21 Classical quotation is the *parole* of literary men all over the world.
Ib. May 8, 1781

22 My friend was of opinion that when a man of rank appeared in that character [as an author], he deserved to have his merit handsomely allowed.[5] *Ib. May 1781*

23 A jest breaks no bones.
Ib. June 4, 1781

24 Officious, innocent, sincere,
Of every friendless name the friend.
Ib. January 20, 1782 (on the death of Robert Levett)

25 To let friendship die away by negligence and silence, is certainly not wise. It is voluntarily to throw away one of the greatest comforts of this weary pilgrimage.
Ib. March 20, 1782

26 Whatever you have, spend less.
Ib. December 7, 1782

27 I never have sought the world; the world was not to seek me.[6]
Ib. March 23, 1783

28 He is not only dull himself, but the cause of dullness in others.[7] *Ib. 1783*

29 Clear your mind of cant.[8]
Ib. May 15, 1783

30 Who drives fat oxen should himself be fat.[9] *Ib. June 1784*

[4] See Edward Moore, 358:8.

[5] Usually quoted as: When a nobleman writes a book, he ought to be encouraged.
See Somerville, 328.

[6] See Byron, 458:3, and Emerson, 493:12.

[7] See Shakespeare, 205:21.

[8] See Carlyle, 473:10.

[9] Parody on: Who rules o'er freemen should himself be free. — HENRY BROOKE, *Gustavus Vasa* [1739]

1 I have found you an argument; I am not obliged to find you an understanding.

Ib.

2 Blown about by every wind of criticism.[1]

Ib.

3 Don't attitudenize. *Ib.*

4 I look upon every day to be lost, in which I do not make a new acquaintance.

Ib. November 1784

5 God bless you, my dear!

Ib. December 13, 1784 (last words)

Julien Offray de La Mettrie

1709–1751

6 Man is a machine and . . . in the whole universe there is but a single substance variously modified.

L'Homme Machine [1748],[2] *conclusion*

George, Lord Lyttelton

1709–1773

7 Women, like princes, find few real friends.

Advice to a Lady

8 What is your sex's earliest, latest care,
Your heart's supreme ambition? To be fair.

Ib.

9 The lover in the husband may be lost.

Ib.

10 Where none admire, 'tis useless to excel;
Where none are beaux, 'tis vain to be a belle.

Soliloquy on a Beauty in the Country

Theodore Tronchin

1709–1781

11 In medicine, sins of commission are mortal, sins of omission venial.

Quoted in Bulletin of New York Academy of Medicine, V [1929], 151

Oliver Edwards

1711–1791

12 I have tried too in my time to be a philosopher; but I don't know how, cheerfulness was always breaking in.

From JAMES BOSWELL, *Life of Johnson [1791]. April 17, 1778*

[1]See *Ephesians 4:14*, 49:35.
[2]Translated by M. W. CALKINS.

David Hume

1711–1776

13 Avarice, the spur of industry.

Essays [1741–1742]. Of Civil Liberty

14 Beauty in things exists in the mind which contemplates them.[3] *Ib. Of Tragedy*

15 Custom, then, is the great guide of human life.

An Enquiry Concerning Human Understanding [1748], pt. 1

16 No testimony is sufficient to establish a miracle, unless the testimony be of such a kind that its falsehood would be more miraculous than the fact which it endeavors to establish. *Ib. Of Miracles*

17 Opposing one species of superstition to another, set them a-quarreling; while we ourselves, during their fury and contention, happily make our escape into the calm, though obscure, regions of philosophy.

The Natural History of Religion [1757]

18 Never literary attempt was more unfortunate than my Treatise of Human Nature. It fell dead-born from the press.

My Own Life [1777], ch. 1

Mikhail Lomonosov[4]

1711–1765

19 Carolus V,[5] Emperor of Rome, was wont to say that the Hispanic tongue was seemly for converse with God, the French with friends, the German with enemies, the Italian with the feminine sex. Had he been versed in the Russian tongue, however, he would of a certainty have added to this that it is appropriate to converse with all of the above, inasmuch as he would have found in it the magnificence of the Hispanic tongue, the sprightliness of the French, the sturdiness of the German, the tenderness of the Italian and, over and above all that, the richness and conciseness of powerful imagery, of the Greek and Latin tongues.

Russian Grammar [1755][6]

[3]See Hungerford, 676:20.
[4]Lomonosov created our first university. To put it better, he himself was our first university.—ALEXANDER PUSHKIN, *The Trip from Moscow to Petersburg* [1834]
[5]See Charles V, 161.
[6]Translated by B. G. GUERNEY.

Frederick the Great

1712–1786

1 By push of bayonets, no firing till you see the whites of their eyes.[1]

At Prague [May 6, 1757]

2 Rascals, would you live forever?[2]

When the Guards hesitated at Kolin [June 18, 1757]

3 The prince is the first servant of his state.

Memoirs of the House of Brandenburg [1758]

4 God is always with the strongest battalions.[3]

Letter to the Duchess Luise Dorothea von Gotha [May 8, 1760]

5 I am tired of ruling over slaves.

Last words [April 1, 1786]

George Grenville

1712–1770

6 A wise government knows how to enforce with temper or to conciliate with dignity.

Speech against expulsion of John Wilkes, in Parliament [1769]

Edward Moore

1712–1757

7 This is adding insult to injury.[4]

The Foundling [1748], act V, sc. ii

8 I am rich beyond the dreams of avarice.[5]

The Gamester [1753], act II, sc. ii

Jean Jacques Rousseau[6]

1712–1778

9 The first man who, having fenced in a piece of land, said, "This is mine," and found people naïve enough to believe him, that man was the true founder of civil society.

Discours sur l'Origine et le Fondement de l'Inégalité Parmi les Hommes [1754]

10 Never exceed your rights, and they will soon become unlimited. *Ib.*

[1]See William Prescott, 368:1.

[2]Ihr Racker, wollt ihr ewig leben?

That sergeant at Belleau Woods . . . / "Come on, you . . . Do you want to live forever?"—SANDBURG, *Losers* [1921]

[3]See Tacitus, 123:1; Bussy-Rabutin, 294:21; Boileau, 311:15; and Gibbon, 383:13.

[4]See Phaedrus, 114:11.

[5]See Johnson, 356:20.

[6]See Voltaire, 343:16.

11 Money is the seed of money, and the first guinea is sometimes more difficult to acquire than the second million. *Ib.*

12 Man is born free, and everywhere he is in chains.[7]

Du Contrat Social [1762], I, ch. 1

13 The strongest is never strong enough to be always the master, unless he transforms his strength into right, and obedience into duty. *Ib. 3*

14 The right of conquest has no foundation other than the right of the strongest. *Ib. 4*

15 In the strict sense of the term, a true democracy has never existed, and never will exist. *Ib. III, 4*

16 The body politic, like the human body, begins to die from its birth, and bears in itself the causes of its destruction. *Ib. 11*

17 Good laws lead to the making of better ones; bad ones bring about worse. *Ib. 15*

18 Everything is good when it leaves the hands of the Creator; everything degenerates in the hands of man.

Émile; ou, De l'Éducation [1762], I

19 I shall always maintain that whoso says in his heart, "There is no God," while he takes the name of God upon his lips, is either a liar or a madman. *Ib.*

20 People who know little are usually great talkers, while men who know much say little. *Ib.*

21 What wisdom can you find that is greater than kindness?[8] *Ib. II*

22 Nature never deceives us; it is always we who deceive ourselves. *Ib. III*

23 There exists one book, which, to my taste, furnishes the happiest treatise of natural education. What then is this marvelous book? Is it Aristotle? Is it Pliny, is it Buffon? No— it is *Robinson Crusoe*. *Ib.*

24 Self-love makes more libertines than love. *Ib. IV*

25 Provided a man is not mad, he can be cured of every folly but vanity. *Ib.*

26 A man says what he knows, a woman says what will please. *Ib. V*

[7]L'homme est né libre, et partout il est dans les fers.

See *Acts* 22:28, 46:26; Milton, 282:13; Bliss, 385:14; Schiller, 413:2; and Davis, 814:20.

[8]See *I Corinthians, 13:1*, 48:22.

1 Where is the man who owes nothing to the land in which he lives? Whatever that land may be, he owes to it the most precious thing possessed by man, the morality of his actions and the love of virtue.[1] *Ib.*

2 I have entered on an enterprise which is without precedent, and will have no imitator. I propose to show my fellows a man as nature made him, and this man shall be myself.
Les Confessions [1781–1788], I

3 Remorse sleeps during a prosperous period but wakes up in adversity. *Ib. II*

4 It is too difficult to think nobly when one only thinks to get a living. *Ib. II*

5 Hatred, as well as love, renders its votaries credulous. *Ib. V*

6 At length I recollected the thoughtless saying of a great princess, who, on being informed that the country people had no bread, replied, "Let them eat cake."[2] *Ib. VI*

7 The thirst after happiness is never extinguished in the heart of man. *Ib. IX*

8 He[3] thinks like a philosopher, but governs like a king. *Ib. XII*

Josiah Tucker

1712–1799

9 What is true of a shopkeeper is true of a shopkeeping nation.[4]
Tract Against Going to War for the Sake of Trade [1763]

Alison Cockburn

1713–1794

10 I've seen the smiling of Fortune beguiling,
I've felt all its favors and found its decay.
The Flowers of the Forest [1764]

11 The flowers of the forest are withered away.[5] *Ib.*

[1]See John F. Kennedy, 890:12.

[2]Qu'ils mangent de la brioche.

This remark is usually attributed to Marie Antoinette, after her arrival in France in 1770, but the sixth book of the *Confessions* was written two or three years before that date.

[3]Frederick the Great, king of Prussia [1740–1786].

[4]See Adam Smith, 366:6.

Let Pitt then boast of his victory to his nation of shopkeepers.—BERTRAND BARÈRE, *Speech* [June 11, 1794]

But it may be said as a rule, that every Englishman in the Duke of Wellington's army paid his way. The remembrance of such a fact surely becomes a nation of shopkeepers.—THACKERAY, *Vanity Fair* [1847–1848], *vol. I, ch. 28*

[5]See Jane Elliott, 368:2.

Denis Diderot

1713–1784

12 My thoughts are my trollops.[6]
Le Neveu de Rameau, ch. 1

13 I can be expected to look for truth but not to find it.
Pensées Philosophiques [1746], no. 29

14 L'esprit de l'escalier [staircase wit].[7]
Paradoxe sur le Comédien

15 From fanaticism to barbarism is only one step. *Essai sur le Mérite de la Vertu*

Laurence Sterne

1713–1768

16 Only the brave know how to forgive. . . . A coward never forgave; it is not in his nature. *Sermons, vol. I [1760], no. 12*

17 This sad vicissitude of things.[8]
Ib. 15

18 I wish either my father or my mother, or indeed both of them, as they were in duty both equally bound to it, had minded what they were about when they begot me.
Tristram Shandy, bk. I [1760], ch. 1

19 "Pray, my dear," quoth my mother, "have you not forgot to wind up the clock?"—"Good G—!" cried my father, making an exclamation, but taking care to moderate his voice at the same time—"Did ever woman, since the creation of the world, interrupt a man with such a silly question?" *Ib.*

20 So long as a man rides his hobbyhorse peaceably and quietly along the king's highway, and neither compels you or me to get up behind him—pray, sir, what have either you or I to do with it? *Ib. 7*

21 For every ten jokes, thou hast got an hundred enemies. *Ib. 12*

22 He was within a few hours of giving his enemies the slip forever. *Ib.*

23 Whistled up to London, upon a Tom Fool's errand. *Ib. 16*

24 'Tis known by the name of perseverance in a good cause—and of obstinacy in a bad one.[9] *Ib. 17*

[6]Mes pensées sont mes catins.

[7]The witty retort thought up after the conversation is finished and one is on one's way downstairs.

[8]See Terence, 96:17, and Bacon, 181:15.

Revolves the sad vicissitude of things.—RICHARD GIFFORD [1725–1807], *Contemplation*

[9]See Browne, 274:8.

1 Persuasion hung upon his lips. *Ib. 19*

2 Digressions, incontestably, are the sunshine—they are the life, the soul of reading; take them out of this book for instance—you might as well take the book along with them. *Ib. 22*

3 The history of a soldier's wound beguiles the pain of it. *Ib. 25*

4 The desire of knowledge, like the thirst of riches, increases ever with the acquisition of it. *Ib. II [1760], ch. 3*

5 Writing, when properly managed (as you may be sure I think mine is), is but a different name for conversation. *Ib. 11*

6 Go, poor devil, get thee gone! Why should I hurt thee? This world surely is wide enough to hold both thee and me. *Ib. 12 (Uncle Toby to the fly)*

7 That's another story,[1] replied my father. *Ib. 17*

8 Trust that man in nothing who has not a conscience in everything. *Ib.*

9 Good—bad—indifferent. *Ib. III [1761–1762], ch. 2*

10 "Our armies swore terribly in Flanders," cried my uncle Toby—"but nothing to this." *Ib. 11*

11 Of all the cants which are canted in this canting world, though the cant of hypocrites may be the worst, the cant of criticism is the most tormenting! *Ib. 12*

12 'Twould be as much as my life was worth. *Ib. 20*

13 One of the two horns of my dilemma. *Ib. IV [1761–1762], ch. 26*

14 The feather put into his cap of having been abroad. *Ib. 31*

15 Now or never was the time. *Ib.*

16 There is a Northwest Passage to the intellectual world. *Ib. V [1761–1762], ch. 42*

17 The Accusing Spirit, which flew up to heaven's chancery with the oath, blushed as he gave it in; and the Recording Angel, as he wrote it down, dropped a tear upon the word and blotted it out forever.[2] *Ib. VI [1761–1762], ch. 8*

18 A man should know something of his own country, too, before he goes abroad. *Ib. VII [1765], ch. 2*

19 Ho! 'tis the time of salads. *Ib. 17*

20 L—d! said my mother, what is all this story about?—A Cock and a Bull, said Yorick. *Ib. IX [1767], ch. 33*

21 They order, said I, this matter better in France. *A Sentimental Journey [1768], l. 1*

22 I pity the man who can travel from Dan to Beersheba and cry, 'Tis all barren! *Ib. In the Street, Calais*

23 *Tant pis* and *tant mieux,* being two of the great hinges in French conversation, a stranger would do well to set himself right in the use of them before he gets to Paris. *Ib. Montreuil*

24 Hail, ye small, sweet courtesies of life! for smooth do ye make the road of it. *Ib. The Pulse, Paris*

25 God tempers the wind, said Maria, to the shorn lamb.[3] *Ib. Maria*

Étienne Bonnot de Condillac [L'Abbé de Condillac]

1715–1780

26 We cannot recollect the ignorance in which we were born. *Traité des Sensations [1754], dedication*

27 The statue is therefore nothing but the sum of all it has acquired. May not this be the same with man? *Ib. conclusion*

Christian Fürchtegott Gellert

1715–1769

28 Live as you will have wished to have lived when you are dying.[4] *Of Death, st. 2*

Claude Adrien Helvétius

1715–1771

29 Truth is a torch that gleams through the fog without dispelling it. *De l'Esprit [1758],[5] preface*

[1] But that is another story.—KIPLING, *Plain Tales from the Hills* [1888], *Three and—An Extra*

[2] But sad as angels for the good man's sin, / Weep to record, and blush to give it in.—THOMAS CAMPBELL, *Pleasures of Hope* [1799], *pt. II, l. 357*

[3] See Estienne, 163:12.

[4] See Jonathan Edwards, 346:2.

[5] Voltaire, when he read *De l'Esprit,* wrote the author: "Your book is dictated by the soundest reason. You had better get out of France as quickly as you can." The book was condemned by the *parlement* and burned.

1 What makes men happy is liking what they have to do. This is a principle on which society is not founded. *Ib.*

2 We don't call a man mad who believes that he eats God, but we do the one who says he is Jesus Christ. *Ib.*

Luc de Clapiers, Marquis de Vauvenargues

1715–1747

3 Great thoughts come from the heart.
Réflexions et Maximes, [c. 1747] no. 127

4 Lazy people are always looking for something to do. *Ib. 458*

5 The things we know best are those we have not learned. *Ib. 479*

William Whitehead

1715–1785

6 Yes, I'm in love, I feel it now
And Caelia has undone me;
And yet I swear I can't tell how
The pleasing plague stole on me.
The Je ne sçay quoi song

7 An old tale which every schoolboy knows.
The Roman Father, prologue

Thomas Gray

1716–1771

8 Ye distant spires, ye antique towers,
That crown the wat'ry glade.
On a Distant Prospect of Eton College [1742], st. 1

9 Still as they run they look behind,
They hear a voice in every wind,
And snatch a fearful joy. *Ib. st. 4*

10 Alas, regardless of their doom,
The little victims play!
No sense have they of ills to come,
Nor care beyond today. *Ib. st. 6*

11 Grim-visaged comfortless Despair.
Ib. st. 7

12 To each his suff'rings: all are men,
Condemned alike to groan,
The tender for another's pain,
Th' unfeeling for his own.
Yet ah! why should they know their fate,
Since sorrow never comes too late,
And happiness too swiftly flies?
Thought would destroy their paradise.
No more; where ignorance is bliss,
'Tis folly to be wise.[1] *Ib. st. 10*

13 Daughter of Jove, relentless power,
Thou tamer of the human breast,
Whose iron scourge and tort'ring hour
The bad affright, afflict the best!
Hymn to Adversity [1742], st. 1

14 What sorrow was, thou bad'st her know,
And from her own she learned to melt at others' woe. *Ib. st. 2*

15 What female heart can gold despise?
What cat's averse to fish?
On the Death of a Favorite Cat [1747], st. 4

16 A fav'rite has no friend! *Ib. st. 6*

17 As sickly plants betray a niggard earth,
Whose barren bosom starves her gen'rous birth.
The Alliance of Education and Government [c. 1748], l. 1

18 The social smile, the sympathetic tear.
Ib. l. 37

19 When love could teach a monarch to be wise,
And gospel-light first dawned from Bullen's eyes.[2] *Ib. l. 108*

20 The curfew tolls the knell of parting day,
The lowing herd wind slowly o'er the lea,
The plowman homeward plods his weary way,
And leaves the world to darkness and to me.
Elegy Written in a Country Churchyard [1750],[3] st. 1

21 Now fades the glimmering landscape on the sight,
And all the air a solemn stillness holds,
Save where the beetle wheels his droning flight,
And drowsy tinklings lull the distant folds.
Ib. st. 2

22 Save that from yonder ivy-mantled tow'r
The moping owl does to the moon complain.
Ib. st. 3

23 Each in his narrow cell forever laid,
The rude forefathers of the hamlet sleep.
Ib. st. 4

24 The breezy call of incense-breathing Morn.
Ib. st. 5

[1] See *Ecclesiastes 1:18*, 26:17.
[2] The monarch is Henry VIII; Anne Boleyn's name is here spelled (as it is in Shakespeare's *Henry VIII*) as it is pronounced.
[3] See Samuel Johnson, 352:27.

1 For them no more the blazing hearth shall burn,
Or busy housewife ply her evening care.[1]
Ib. st. 6

2 Let not ambition mock their useful toil,
Their homely joys, and destiny obscure;
Nor grandeur hear with a disdainful smile,
The short and simple annals of the poor.
Ib. st. 8

3 The boast of heraldry, the pomp of pow'r,
And all that beauty, all that wealth e'er gave,
Awaits alike the inevitable hour:
The paths of glory lead but to the grave.[2]
Ib. st. 9

4 Where thro' the long-drawn aisle and fretted vault
The pealing anthem swells the note of praise.
Ib. st. 10

5 Can storied urn, or animated bust
Back to its mansion call the fleeting breath?
Can honor's voice provoke the silent dust,
Or flatt'ry soothe the dull cold ear of death?
Ib. st. 11

6 Hands, that the rod of empire might have swayed,
Or waked to ecstasy the living lyre.
Ib. st. 12

7 But knowledge to their eyes her ample page
Rich with the spoils of time did ne'er unroll;[3]
Chill penury repressed their noble rage,
And froze the genial current of the soul.
Ib. st. 13

8 Full many a gem of purest ray serene,[4]
The dark unfathomed caves of ocean bear:
Full many a flower is born to blush unseen,
And waste its sweetness on the desert air.
Ib. st. 14

9 Some village Hampden, that with dauntless breast
The little tyrant of his fields withstood;
Some mute inglorious Milton here may rest,
Some Cromwell guiltless of his country's blood.[5]
Ib. st. 15

10 To scatter plenty o'er a smiling land,
And read their hist'ry in a nation's eyes.
Ib. st. 16

[1]See Homer, 57:29.
[2]See Carew, 271:23.
[3]See Sir Thomas Browne, 274:5.
[4]Every single phrase is a string of perfect gems, of purest ray serene, strung together on a loose golden thread.
—GEORGE DU MAURIER, *Trilby, pt. VI* [1894]
See Joseph Hall, 257:13.
[5]See Mencken, 772:7.

11 Forbade to wade through slaughter to a throne,
And shut the gates of mercy on mankind.
Ib. st. 17

12 Far from the madding crowd's ignoble strife,
Their sober wishes never learned to stray;
Along the cool sequestered vale of life
They kept the noiseless tenor of their way.
Ib. st. 19

13 Implores the passing tribute of a sigh.
Ib. st. 20

14 For who to dumb forgetfulness a prey,
This pleasing anxious being e'er resigned,
Left the warm precincts of the cheerful day,
Nor cast one longing ling'ring look behind?
Ib. st. 22

15 E'en from the tomb the voice of nature cries,
E'en in our ashes live their wonted fires.[6]
Ib. st. 23

16 Mindful of th' unhonored dead.
Ib. st. 24

17 Here rests his head upon the lap of Earth
A youth to fortune and to fame unknown.
Fair Science frowned not on his humble birth.
And Melancholy marked him for her own.[7]
Ib. The Epitaph, st. 1

18 Large was his bounty, and his soul sincere,
Heav'n did a recompense as largely send:
He gave to mis'ry all he had, a tear,
He gained from Heav'n ('twas all he wished) a friend.
Ib. st. 2

19 No farther seek his merits to disclose,
Or draw his frailties from their dread abode,
(There they alike in trembling hope repose,)
The bosom of his Father and his God.
Ib. st. 3

20 The meanest floweret of the vale,
The simplest note that swells the gale,
The common sun, the air, the skies,
To him are opening paradise.
Ode on the Pleasure Arising from Vicissitude [1754], l. 49

21 O'er her warm cheek and rising bosom move
The bloom of young Desire and purple light of Love.
The Progress of Poesy [1754], I. 3, l. 16

22 Far from the sun and summer-gale,
In thy green lap was Nature's Darling[8] laid.
Ib. III. 1, l. 1

[6]See Chaucer, 147:1.
[7]See Walton, 270:28.
[8]Shakespeare.

1 Or ope the sacred source of sympathetic tears. *Ib. l. 12*

2 He[1] passed the flaming bounds of place and time:
The living throne, the sapphire-blaze,
Where angels tremble, while they gaze,
He saw; but blasted with excess of light,
Closed his eyes in endless night.
Ib. 2, l. 4

3 Thoughts that breathe, and words that burn.
Ib. 3, l. 4

4 Ruin seize thee, ruthless King!
Confusion on thy banners wait,
Though fanned by Conquest's crimson wing
They mock the air with idle state.
The Bard [1757], I. 1, l. 1

5 Weave the warp, and weave the woof,
The winding sheet of Edward's race.
Give ample room and verge enough,
The characters of hell to trace.
Ib. II. 1, l. 1

6 Fair laughs the morn, and soft the zephyr blows,
While proudly riding o'er the azure realm
In gallant trim the gilded vessel goes;
Youth on the prow, and Pleasure at the helm;
Regardless of the sweeping whirlwind's sway,
That, hushed in grim repose, expects his evening prey. *Ib. 2, l. 9*

7 Visions of glory, spare my aching sight,
Ye unborn ages, crowd not on my soul!
Ib. III, 1, l. 11

8 And truth severe, by fairy fiction drest.
Ib. 3, l. 3

9 Now my weary lips I close;
Leave me, leave me to repose!
Descent of Odin [1761], l. 71

10 Iron sleet of arrowy shower
Hurtles in the darkened air.
The Fatal Sisters [1761]

11 Too poor for a bribe, and too proud to importune,
He had not the method of making a fortune.
On His Own Character [1761]

12 I shall be but a shrimp of an author.
Letter to Horace Walpole [February 25, 1768]

13 Sweet is the breath of vernal shower,
The bee's collected treasures sweet,
Sweet music's melting fall, but sweeter yet
The still small voice[2] of gratitude.
Ode for Music [1769]

[1] Milton.
[2] See *I Kings 19:12*, 14:5.

Jean Le Rond d'Alembert

1717–1783

14 Nothing is more indisputable than the existence of our senses.
The Encyclopedia (L'Encyclopédie), vol. I [1751], preliminary discourse[3]

David Garrick

1717–1779

15 Let others hail the rising sun:
I bow to that whose course is run.[4]
On the Death of Mr. Pelham

16 Heart of oak[5] are our ships,
Heart of oak are our men:
We always are ready;
Steady, boys, steady;
We'll fight, and we'll conquer again and again. *Heart of Oak [c. 1770]*

17 Here lies Nolly Goldsmith, for shortness called Noll,
Who wrote like an angel, but talked like poor Poll.
Impromptu epitaph on Goldsmith

Horace Walpole

1717–1797

18 Our supreme governors, the mob.
Letters. To Horace Mann [September 7, 1743]

19 Every drop of ink in my pen ran cold.
Ib. To George Montagu [July 3, 1752]

20 It is charming to totter into vogue.
Ib. To G. A. Selwyn [December 2, 1765]

21 The next Augustan age will dawn on the other side of the Atlantic. There will, perhaps, be a Thucydides at Boston, a Xenophon at New York, and, in time, a Virgil at Mexico, and a Newton at Peru. At last, some curious traveler from Lima will visit England and give a description of the ruins of St. Paul's, like the editions of Balbec and Palmyra.[6]
Ib. To Mann [November 24, 1774]

22 This world is a comedy to those that think, a tragedy to those that feel.
Ib. To the Countess of Upper Ossory [August 16, 1776]

[3] Translated by R. N. Schwab.
[4] See Pompey, 99:12.
[5] See Rabelais, 158:10.
[6] See Macaulay, 488:7.

1 Prognostics do not always prove prophecies—at least the wisest prophets make sure of the event first.

Ib. To Thomas Walpole [February 19, 1785]

2 All his [Sir Joshua Reynolds's] own geese are swans, as the swans of others are geese.

Ib. [December 1, 1786]

Samuel Foote
1720–1777

3 Born in a cellar . . . and living in a garret.[1]

The Author [1757], act II

4 Matt Minikin won't set fire to the Thames though he lives near the Bridge.

Trip to Calais [1776]

5 So she went into the garden to cut a cabbage leaf to make an apple pie; and at the same time a great she-bear, coming up the street, pops its head into the shop. "What! no soap?" So he died, and she very imprudently married the barber; and there were present the Picninnies, and the Joblillies, and the Garyalies, and the grand Panjandrum himself, with the little round button at top, and they all fell to playing the game of catch as catch can, till the gunpowder ran out at the heels of their boots.

Nonsense written to test the boasted memory of Charles Macklin, The Quarterly Review [1854]. Credited to Foote by MARIA EDGEWORTH, *Harry and Lucy Concluded [1825], vol. II*

Dennis O'Kelly
1720–1787

6 It will be Eclipse first, the rest nowhere.

Declaration at Epsom [May 3, 1769], when the great racehorse Eclipse was to run his first race. Annals of Sporting, vol. II, p. 271

John Woolman
1720–1772

7 Though I felt uneasy at the thought of writing an instrument of slavery . . . through weakness I gave way and wrote it; but . . . said before my master and the Friend that I believed slavekeeping to be a practice inconsistent with the Christian religion. This, in some degree, abated my uneasiness; yet . . . I should have been clearer if I had desired to be excused from it, as a thing against my conscience.

Journal [1774]

[1] Born in the garret, in the kitchen bred.—BYRON, *A Sketch* [1816]

William Collins
1721–1759

8 How sleep the brave, who sink to rest,
By all their country's wishes blessed!

Ode Written in the Year 1746, st. 1

9 By fairy hands their knell is rung,
By forms unseen their dirge is sung;
There Honor comes, a pilgrim gray,
To bless the turf that wraps their clay,
And Freedom shall awhile repair,
To dwell a weeping hermit there!

Ib. st. 2

10 In numbers warmly pure and sweetly strong.

Ode to Simplicity [1747], st. 1

11 If aught of oaten stop or pastoral song
May hope, O pensive Eve, to soothe thine ear.

Ode to Evening [1747], l. 1

12 Now air is hushed, save where the weak-eyed bat,
With short shrill shriek flits by on leathern wing,
Or where the beetle winds
His small but sullen horn.

Ib. l. 9

13 'Twas sad by fits, by starts 'twas wild.

The Passions [1747], l. 28

14 With eyes upraised, as one inspired,
Pale Melancholy sate retired,
And from her wild sequestered seat,
In notes by distance made more sweet,
Poured through the mellow horn her pensive soul.

Ib. l. 57

15 In hollow murmurs died away.

Ib. l. 68

16 O Music, sphere-descended maid,
Friend of Pleasure, Wisdom's aid!

Ib. l. 95

Jeanne Antoinette Poisson, Marquise de Pompadour
1721–1764

17 Après nous le déluge [After us the deluge].[2]

Reputed reply to Louis XV [November 5, 1757] after the defeat of the French and Austrian armies by Frederick the Great in the battle of Rossbach

[2] The attribution to Madame de Pompadour is made by Després *(Mémoires de Madame de Hausset);* also by Sainte-Beuve and La Tour. Larousse *(Fleurs Historiques)* attributes the saying to the king. It was original with neither, for it is an old French proverb.

Tobias Smollett

1721–1771

1 He was formed for the ruin of our sex.

The Adventures of Roderick Random [1748], ch. 22

2 8 June. At London. I am pent up in frowsy lodgings, where there is not room enough to swing a cat.

The Expedition of Humphry Clinker [1771], vol. II

Samuel Adams

1722–1803

3 Let us contemplate our forefathers, and posterity,[1] and resolve to maintain the rights bequeathed to us from the former, for the sake of the latter. The necessity of the times, more than ever, calls for our utmost circumspection, deliberation, fortitude and perseverance. Let us remember that "if we suffer tamely a lawless attack upon our liberty, we encourage it, and involve others in our doom." It is a very serious consideration . . . that millions yet unborn may be the miserable sharers of the event.

Speech [1771]

4 What a glorious morning for America![2]

Upon hearing the gunfire at Lexington [April 19, 1775]

5 Driven from every other corner of the earth, freedom of thought and the right of private judgment in matters of conscience direct their course to this happy country as their last asylum.[3]

Speech, Philadelphia [August 1, 1776]

Christopher Smart

1722–1771

6 Tell them I Am, Jehovah said
To Moses; while earth heard in dread,
And smitten to the heart,
At once above, beneath, around,
All nature, without voice or sound,
Replied, O Lord, Thou art.

A Song to David [1763], st. 40

7 For adoration all the ranks
Of angels yield eternal thanks,
And David in the midst. *Ib. st. 51*

8 Where ask is have, where seek is find,
Where knock is open wide.[4] *Ib. st. 77*

9 And now the matchless deed's achieved,
Determined, dared, and done.

Ib. st. 86

10 For I bless God in the libraries of the learned and for all the booksellers in the world.

Jubilate Agno, frag. B1, l. 79

11 Let James rejoice with the Skuttle-Fish who foils his foe by the effusion of his ink.

Ib. l. 125

12 For the Mouse (mus) prevails in Latin.
For Edi-mus, bibi-mus, vivi-mus, oremus.

Ib. frag. B2, l. 638

13 For I will consider my Cat Jeoffrey,
For he is the servant of the Living God, duly and daily serving him. *Ib. l. 697*

14 For he counteracts the Devil, who is Death, by brisking about the life. *Ib. l. 722*

Sir William Blackstone[5]

1723–1780

15 Man was formed for society.[6]

Commentaries [1765–1769], introduction

16 The royal navy of England hath ever been its greatest defense and ornament; it is its ancient and natural strength; the floating bulwark of our island. *Ib. bk. I, ch. 13*

17 Time whereof the memory of man runneth not to the contrary.[7] *Ib. 18*

18 That the king can do no wrong is a necessary and fundamental principle of the English constitution. *Ib. III, 17*

19 It is better that ten guilty persons escape than one innocent suffer.[8] *Ib. IV, 27*

[1] See *The Teaching for Merikare,* 3:13, and Tacitus, 123:4.

[2] The phrase was adopted by the town of Lexington as a legend for the town seal.

[3] See Thomas Paine, 384:12.

[4] See *Matthew* 7:7, 38:12.

[5] He it was that first gave the law the air of a science. He found it a skeleton, and clothed it with life, color, and complexion; he embraced the cold statue, and by his touch it grew into youth, health, and beauty. — Barry Yelverton, Lord Avonmore [1736–1805], *On Blackstone*

[6] See Spinoza, 308:20.

[7] The favorite phrase of their law is "a custom whereof the memory of man runneth not back to the contrary." — Emerson, *English Traits* [1856]

[8] See Voltaire, 343:5.

Adam Smith

1723–1790

1 A monopoly granted either to an individual or to a trading company has the same effect as a secret in trade or manufactures. The monopolists, by keeping the market constantly understocked, by never fully supplying the effectual demand, sell their commodities much above the natural price, and raise their emoluments, whether they consist in wages or profit, greatly above their natural rate.

Wealth of Nations [1776], vol. I, bk. I, ch. 7

2 People of the same trade seldom meet together, even for merriment and diversion, but the conversation ends in a conspiracy against the public, or in some contrivance to raise prices. It is impossible indeed to prevent such meetings by any law which either could be executed, or would be consistent with liberty and justice. *Ib. 10, pt. 2*

3 It is the highest impertinence and presumption, therefore, in kings and ministers to pretend to watch over the economy of private people, and to restrain their expense. . . . They are themselves always, and without any exception, the greatest spendthrifts in the society. Let them look well after their own expense, and they may safely trust private people with theirs. *Ib. bk. II, ch. 3*

4 Every individual necessarily labors to render the annual revenue of the society as great as he can. He generally indeed neither intends to promote the public interest, nor knows how much he is promoting it. . . . He intends only his own gain, and he is in this, as in many other cases, led by an invisible hand to promote an end which was no part of his intention. . . . By pursuing his own interest he frequently promotes that of the society more effectually than when he really intends to promote it. I have never known much good done by those who affected to trade for the public good.

Ib. bk. IV, ch. 2

5 Defense, however, is of much more importance than opulence. *Ib.*

6 To found a great empire for the sole purpose of raising up a people of customers, may at first sight appear a project fit only for a nation of shopkeepers. It is, however, a project altogether unfit for a nation of shopkeepers; but extremely fit for a nation whose government is influenced by shopkeepers.[1]

Ib. II, bk. IV, ch. 7, pt. 3

[1] See Josiah Tucker, 359:9.

7 Consumption is the sole end and purpose of production; and the interest of the producer ought to be attended to only so far as it may be necessary for promoting that of the consumer. *Ib. ch. 8*

8 All systems either of preference or of restraint, therefore, being thus completely taken away, the obvious and simple system of natural liberty establishes itself of its own accord. Every man, as long as he does not violate the laws of justice, is left perfectly free to pursue his own interest his own way, and to bring both his industry and capital into competition with those of any other man or order of men. The sovereign is completely discharged from a duty, in the attempting to perform which he must always be exposed to innumerable delusions, and for the proper performance of which no human wisdom or knowledge could ever be sufficient: the duty of superintending the industry of private people. *Ib. 9*

John Home

1722–1808

9 I'll woo her as the lion woos his brides.

Douglas [1756], act I, sc. i

10 My name is Norval; on the Grampian hills
My father feeds his flocks; a frugal swain,
Whose constant cares were to increase his store,
And keep his only son, myself, at home.

Ib. III, i

11 Like Douglas conquer, or like Douglas, die.

Ib. V, i

Immanuel Kant

1724–1804

12 Two things fill the mind with ever-increasing wonder and awe, the more often and the more intensely the mind of thought is drawn to them: the starry heavens above me and the moral law within me.

Critique of Pure Reason [1781], conclusion

13 Morality is not properly the doctrine of how we may make ourselves happy, but how we may make ourselves worthy of happiness.

Critique of Practical Reason [1788]

14 There is . . . only a single categorical imperative and it is this: Act only on that maxim through which you can at the same

time will that it should become a universal law.[1]

The Metaphysic of Morals [1797], ch. 11

Friedrich Gottlieb Klopstock

1724–1803

1 The immortality of poetry is worth the sweat of noblemen.

Lake Zurich [1750]

Robert, Lord Clive

1725–1774

2 By God, Mr. Chairman, at this moment I stand astonished at my own moderation!

Reply During Parliamentary Inquiry [1773]

Logan[2]

1725–1780

3 I appeal to any white man to say if he ever entered Logan's cabin hungry and he gave him not meat; if ever he came cold and naked and he clothed him not?[3]

Message to Lord Dunmore, governor of Virginia [November 11, 1774]. From THOMAS JEFFERSON, *Notes on Virginia [1784–1785]*

George Mason

1725–1792

4 That all men are by nature equally free and independent, and have certain inherent rights, of which, when they enter into a state of society, they cannot by any compact deprive or divest their posterity; namely, the enjoyment of life and liberty, with the means of acquiring and possessing property, and pursuing and obtaining happiness and safety.

Virginia Bill of Rights[4] [June 12, 1776], article 1

5 Government is, or ought to be instituted for the common benefit, protection, and security of the people, nation, or community; of all the various modes and forms of government, that is best which is capable of producing the greatest degree of happiness and safety, and is most effectually secured against the danger of maladministration.[5] *Ib. 3*

6 The freedom of the press is one of the great bulwarks of liberty, and can never be restrained but by despotic governments.

Ib. 12

John Newton[6]

1725–1807

7 Amazing grace! How sweet the sound
That saved a wretch like me!
I once was lost, but now am found,
Was blind, but now I see.

Olney Hymns [1779].[7] Amazing Grace

8 Glorious things of thee are spoken,
Zion, city of our God.

Ib. Glorious Things

James Otis[8]

1725–1783

9 An act against the Constitution is void; an act against natural equity is void.

Argument Against the Writs of Assistance [1761]

10 Taxation without representation is tyranny.[9] *Attributed [1763]*

11 Ubi libertas ibi patria [Where liberty is, there is my country]. *His motto*

James Hutton

1726–1797

12 The result, therefore, of this physical inquiry [into the age of the earth] is, that we find no vestige of a beginning — no prospect of an end.

The Theory of the Earth [1795]

[1] Translated by A. D. LINDSAY.
Categorical imperative. — KANT, *Fundamental Principles of Ethics* [1785], *Part 2*

[2] Mingo chief.

[3] See *Matthew 25:35–36*, 40:33.

[4] The parent of all American bills of rights. — SAMUEL ELIOT MORISON, *The Oxford History of the American People* [1965]
See Patrick Henry, 383:6. Henry drafted Article 16, on religious freedom.

[5] See Jefferson, 389:4.

[6] Newton wrote his own epitaph: John Newton, clerk, once an infidel and libertine, a servant of slaves in Africa, was by the rich mercy of our Lord and Savior Jesus Christ preserved, restored, pardoned, and appointed to preach the Faith he had long labored to destroy.

[7] See Cowper, 375:14.

[8] [Otis arguing] was a flame of fire . . . the seeds of patriots and heroes were then and there sown. — JOHN ADAMS, *Works* [1850–1856], *vol. II, p. 522*

[9] This maxim was the guide and watchword of all the friends of liberty. Otis actually said: No parts of His Majesty's dominions can be taxed without their consent. — *Rights of the Colonies* [1764], *p. 64*

William Prescott

1726–1795

1 Don't one of you fire until you see the whites of their eyes.[1]

At Bunker Hill [June 17, 1775]

Jane Elliot

1727–1805

2 I've heard them lilting, at the ewe milking,
Lasses a' lilting, before dawn of day;
But now they are moaning, on ilka green loaning;
The flowers of the forest are a' wede away.

The Flowers of the Forest[2]

Anne Robert Jacques Turgot, Baron de l'Aulne

1727–1781

3 They [the Americans] are the hope of this world. They may become its model.[3]

Letter to Dr. Richard Price [March 22, 1778]

John Wilkes

1727–1797

4 *Earl of Sandwich:* 'Pon my honor, Wilkes, I don't know whether you'll die on the gallows or of the pox.

Wilkes: That must depend, my Lord, upon whether I first embrace your Lordship's principles, or your Lordship's mistresses.

From SIR CHARLES PETRIE, *The Four Georges [1935]*

Oliver Goldsmith

1728–1774

5 One writer, for instance, excels at a plan or a title page, another works away the body of the book, and a third is a dab at an index.

The Bee [1759], no. 1

6 As writers become more numerous, it is natural for readers to become more indolent.

Ib. 175. Upon Unfortunate Merit

[1]Also attributed to ISRAEL PUTNAM [1718–1790].
See Frederick the Great, 358:1.
Silent till you see the whites of their eyes. — PRINCE CHARLES OF PRUSSIA, *at Jagerndorf* [May 23, 1745]

[2]Sir Walter Scott in *Minstrelsy of the Scottish Border* says that *The Flowers of the Forest* was written to an ancient tune and that the last line, the refrain, is indisputably ancient. The air was also used for verses by Alison Cockburn. See 359:11.

[3]This is the origin of: America the hope of the world.

7 Good people all, with one accord,
Lament for Madame Blaize,
Who never wanted a good word —
From those who spoke her praise.

Ib. Elegy on Mrs. Mary Blaize [1759], st. 1

8 A nightcap decked his brows instead of bay,
A cap by night — a stocking all the day!

Description of an Author's Bedchamber [1760]

9 That strain once more; it bids remembrance rise.

The Captivity, An Oratorio [1764], act I

10 O Memory! thou fond deceiver. *Ib.*

11 To the last moment of his breath
On hope the wretch relies;
And e'en the pang preceding death
Bids expectation rise.[4] *Ib. II*

12 Hope, like the gleaming taper's light,
Adorns and cheers our way;
And still, as darker grows the night,
Emits a brighter ray. *Ib.*

13 Remote, unfriended, melancholy, slow,
Or by the lazy Scheldt, or wandering Po.

The Traveller [1764], l. 1

14 Where'er I roam, whatever realms to see,
My heart untraveled fondly turns to thee;
Still to my brother turns with ceaseless pain,
And drags at each remove a lengthening chain. *Ib. l. 7*

15 Such is the patriot's boast, where'er we roam,
His first, best country ever is, at home.

Ib. l. 73

16 Where wealth and freedom reign contentment fails,
And honor sinks where commerce long prevails. *Ib. l. 91*

17 Man seems the only growth that dwindles here.[5] *Ib. l. 126*

18 But winter lingering chills the lap of May.

Ib. l. 172

19 They please, are pleased, they give to get esteem,
Till, seeming blest, they grow to what they seem.[6] *Ib. l. 265*

20 To men of other minds my fancy flies,
Embosomed in the deep where Holland lies.

[4]See Terence, 96:14, and Cicero, 98:18.

[5]Italy.

[6]The character of the French.

Methinks her patient sons before me stand,
Where the broad ocean leans against the land. *Ib. l. 281*

1 Pride in their port, defiance in their eye,
I see the lords of humankind[1] pass by. *Ib. l. 327*

2 The land of scholars, and the nurse of arms.[2] *Ib. l. 356*

3 For just experience tells; in every soil,
That those that think must govern those that toil. *Ib. l. 371*

4 Laws grind the poor,[3] and rich men rule the law. *Ib. l. 386*

5 Vain, very vain, my weary search to find
That bliss which only centers in the mind. *Ib. l. 423*

6 A book may be very amusing with numerous errors, or it may be very dull without a single absurdity. *The Vicar of Wakefield [1766], preface*

7 I . . . chose my wife, as she did her wedding gown, not for a fine glossy surface, but such qualities as would wear well. *Ib. ch. 1*

8 We sometimes had those little rubs which Providence sends to enhance the value of its favors. *Ib.*

9 Handsome is that handsome does.[4] *Ib.*

10 That virtue which requires to be ever guarded is scarce worth the sentinel. *Ib. 5*

11 I find you want me to furnish you with argument and intellects too. *Ib. 7*

12 Man wants but little here below,
Nor wants that little long.[5] *Ib. 8 [The Hermit (Edwin and Angelina), st. 8]*

13 She was all of a muck of sweat. *Ib. 9*

14 They would talk of nothing but high life, and high-lived company, with other fashionable topics, such as pictures, taste, Shakespeare, and the musical glasses.[6] *Ib.*

[1] The British.
[2] England.
[3] See *Isaiah 3:15*, 28:35.
[4] See Chaucer, 147:16.
[5] See Edward Young, 330:12, and John Quincy Adams, 418:7.
[6] "Shall we talk about Shakespeare?" he asked sarcastically. "Or the musical glasses?"—ALDOUS HUXLEY, *Point Counter Point* [1928], *ch. 21*

15 Conscience is a coward, and those faults it has not strength enough to prevent it seldom has justice enough to accuse. *Ib. ch. 13*

16 The naked every day he clad
When he put on his clothes. *Ib. 17. An Elegy on the Death of a Mad Dog, st. 3*

17 And in that town a dog was found,
As many dogs there be,
Both mongrel, puppy, whelp, and hound,
And curs of low degree. *Ib. st. 4*

18 The dog, to gain some private ends,
Went mad, and bit the man. *Ib. st. 5*

19 The man recovered of the bite,
The dog it was that died. *Ib. st. 8*

20 When lovely woman stoops to folly,
And finds too late that men betray,
What charm can soothe her melancholy?
What art can wash her guilt away?[7] *Ib. 29. Song, st. 1*

21 The only art her guilt to cover,
To hide her shame from every eye,
To give repentance to her lover,
And wring his bosom, is—to die. *Ib. st. 2*

22 This same philosophy is a good horse in the stable, but an arrant jade on a journey.[8] *The Good-Natured Man [1768], act I*

23 He calls his extravagance, generosity; and his trusting everybody, universal benevolence. *Ib.*

24 All his faults are such that one loves him still the better for them. *Ib.*

25 Friendship is a disinterested commerce between equals; love, an abject intercourse between tyrants and slaves. *Ib.*

26 Silence gives consent. *Ib. II*

27 Measures, not men, have always been my mark.[9] *Ib.*

28 Sweet Auburn! loveliest village of the plain. *The Deserted Village [1770], l. 1*

29 The bashful virgin's sidelong looks of love,
The matron's glance that would those looks reprove. *Ib. l. 29*

30 Ill fares the land, to hastening ills a prey,
Where wealth accumulates, and men decay;
Princes and lords may flourish, or may fade;[10]

[7] See T. S. Eliot, 805:8.
[8] See La Rochefoucauld, 293:3.
[9] See Chesterfield, 341:15; Burke, 372:5; and John Adams, 381:1.
[10] See Burns, 408:18.

A breath can make them, as a breath has made;
But a bold peasantry, their country's pride,
When once destroyed, can never be supplied.
Ib. l. 51

1 His best companions, innocence and health;
And his best riches, ignorance of wealth.
Ib. l. 61

2 How happy he who crowns in shades like these,
A youth of labor with an age of ease.
Ib. l. 99

3 Bends to the grave with unperceived decay,
While resignation gently slopes the way;
And, all his prospects brightening to the last,
His heaven commences ere the world be past.
Ib. l. 109

4 The watchdog's voice that bayed the whispering wind,
And the loud laugh that spoke the vacant mind.[1] *Ib. l. 121*

5 A man he was to all the country dear,
And passing rich with forty pounds a year.
Ib. l. 141

6 Careless their merits or their faults to scan,
His pity gave ere charity began.
Thus to relieve the wretched was his pride,
And e'en his failings leaned to Virtue's side.
Ib. l. 161

7 And, as a bird each fond endearment tries
To tempt its new-fledged offspring to the skies,
He tried each art, reproved each dull delay,
Allured to brighter worlds, and led the way.
Ib. l. 167

8 Truth from his lips prevailed with double sway,
And fools, who came to scoff, remained to pray.[2] *Ib. l. 179*

9 Even children followed with endearing wile,
And plucked his gown, to share the good man's smile. *Ib. l. 183*

10 A man severe he was, and stern to view;
I knew him well, and every truant knew:
Well had the boding tremblers learned to trace
The day's disasters in his morning face;
Full well they laughed with counterfeited glee,
At all his jokes, for many a joke had he;
Full well the busy whisper, circling round,
Conveyed the dismal tidings when he frowned;
Yet he was kind; or if severe in aught,
The love he bore to learning was in fault;
The village all declared how much he knew;
'Twas certain he could write, and cipher too.
Ib. l. 197

11 In arguing too, the parson owned his skill,
For e'en though vanquished, he could argue still;
While words of learned length, and thundering sound
Amazed the gazing rustics ranged around;
And still they gazed, and still the wonder grew,
That one small head could carry all he knew.
Ib. l. 211

12 Where village statesmen talked with looks profound,
And news much older than their ale went round. *Ib. l. 223*

13 The whitewashed wall, the nicely sanded floor,
The varnished clock that clicked behind the door;
The chest contrived a double debt to pay,
A bed by night, a chest of drawers by day.
Ib. l. 227

14 The twelve good rules, the royal game of goose.[3] *Ib. l. 232*

15 To me more dear, congenial to my heart,
One native charm, than all the gloss of art.
Ib. l. 253

16 And, ev'n while fashion's brightest arts decoy,
The heart distrusting asks, if this be joy.
Ib. l. 263

17 Her modest looks the cottage might adorn,
Sweet as the primrose peeps beneath the thorn. *Ib. l. 329*

18 In all the silent manliness of grief.
Ib. l. 384

[1] Frequent and loud laughter is the characteristic of folly and ill manners: it is the manner in which the mob express their silly joy at silly things, and they call it being merry. In my mind there is nothing so illiberal and so ill-bred as audible laughter. — Lord Chesterfield, *Letters* [March 9, 1748]

See *Ecclesiastes 7:6*, 27:5.

[2] See Dryden, 305:29.

[3] The twelve good rules were ascribed to Charles I: (1) Urge no healths; (2) profane no divine ordinances; (3) touch no state matters; (4) reveal no secrets; (5) pick no quarrels; (6) make no comparisons; (7) maintain no ill opinions; (8) keep no bad company; (9) encourage no vice; (10) make no long meals; (11) repeat no grievances; (12) lay no wagers.

Goose. A game played with counters on a board divided into compartments, in some of which a goose was depicted. — *Oxford English Dictionary*

1 Thou source of all my bliss, and all my woe,
That found'st me poor at first, and keep'st me so. *Ib. l. 413*

2 In my time, the follies of the town crept slowly among us, but now they travel faster than a stagecoach.
She Stoops to Conquer [1775], act I

3 I love everything that's old: old friends, old times, old manners, old books, old wines.[1]
Ib.

4 The very pink of perfection. *Ib.*

5 Let schoolmasters puzzle their brain,
With grammar, and nonsense, and learning;
Good liquor, I stoutly maintain,
Gives genius a better discerning. *Ib.*

6 I'll be with you in the squeezing of a lemon.
Ib.

7 A modest woman, dressed out in all her finery, is the most tremendous object of the whole creation. *Ib. II*

8 This is Liberty Hall, gentlemen. *Ib.*

9 The first blow is half the battle. *Ib.*

10 We are the boys
That fear no noise
Where the thundering cannons roar.
Ib.

11 They liked the book the better the more it made them cry. *Ib.*

12 Ask me no questions, and I'll tell you no fibs.[2] *Ib. III*

13 Our Garrick's a salad; for in him we see
Oil, vinegar, sugar, and saltness agree!
Retaliation [1774], l. 11

14 Here lies our good Edmund,[3] whose genius was such,
We scarcely can praise it, or blame it too much;
Who, born for the universe, narrowed his mind,
And to party gave up what was meant for mankind . . .
Who, too deep for his hearers, still went on refining,
And thought of convincing, while they thought of dining;
Though equal to all things, for all things unfit;
Too nice for a statesman, too proud for a wit.
Ib. l. 29

[1] See Bacon, 179:18, and Webster, 262:1.
[2] Them that asks no questions isn't told a lie. — KIPLING [1865–1936], *A Smuggler's Song, st. 6*
[3] Edmund Burke.

15 His conduct still right, with his argument wrong. *Ib. l. 46*

16 Here lies David Garrick, describe me, who can,
An abridgment of all that was pleasant in man. *Ib. l. 93*

17 As a wit, if not first, in the very first line.
Ib. l. 96

18 On the stage he was natural, simple, affecting;
'Twas only that when he was off he was acting. *Ib. l. 101*

19 He cast off his friends as a huntsman his pack,
For he knew when he pleased he could whistle them back. *Ib. l. 107*

20 Who peppered the highest was surest to please. *Ib. l. 112*

21 When they talked of their Raphaels, Correggios, and stuff,
He shifted his trumpet and only took snuff.[4]
Ib. l. 145

22 Such dainties to them, their health it might hurt;
It's like sending them ruffles, when wanting a shirt.[5]
The Haunch of Venison [1776]

23 There is no arguing with Johnson: for if his pistol misses fire, he knocks you down with the butt end of it.
From JAMES BOSWELL, Life of Johnson [1791]. October 26, 1769

24 [To Dr. Johnson] If you were to make little fishes talk, they would talk like whales.
Ib. April 27, 1773

25 You may all go to pot.
Verses in reply to an invitation to dine at Dr. Baker's

John Stark
1728–1822

26 My men, yonder are the Hessians. They were bought for seven pounds and ten pence a man. Are you worth more? Prove it. Tonight, the American flag floats from yonder hill or Molly Stark sleeps a widow!
Before the battle of Bennington [August 16, 1777]

[4] Sir Joshua Reynolds, who was exceedingly deaf.
[5] See Tom Brown, 319:20.

Edmund Burke[1]

1729–1797

1 Custom reconciles us to everything.[2]

On the Sublime and Beautiful [1756], sec. 18

2 There is, however, a limit at which forbearance ceases to be a virtue.

Observations on a Late Publication on the Present State of the Nation [1769]

3 The wisdom of our ancestors.[3] *Ib.*

4 When bad men combine, the good must associate; else they will fall one by one, an unpitied sacrifice in a contemptible struggle.

Thoughts on the Cause of the Present Discontents [April 23, 1770]

5 Of this stamp is the cant of, Not men, but measures;[4] a sort of charm by which many people get loose from every honorable engagement. *Ib.*

6 So to be patriots as not to forget we are gentlemen. *Ib.*

7 Public life is a situation of power and energy; he trespasses against his duty who sleeps upon his watch, as well as he that goes over to the enemy. *Ib.*

8 Reflect how you are to govern a people who think they ought to be free, and think they are not. Your scheme yields no revenue; it yields nothing but discontent, disorder, disobedience; and such is the state of America, that after wading up to your eyes in blood, you could only end just where you begun; that is, to tax where no revenue is to be found, to—my voice fails me; my inclination indeed carries me no farther—all is confusion beyond it.

First Speech on the Conciliation with America. American Taxation [April 19, 1774]

9 Your representative owes you, not his industry only, but his judgment; and he betrays instead of serving you if he sacrifices it to your opinion.

Speech to the Electors of Bristol [November 3, 1774]

[1]You could not stand five minutes with that man [Burke] beneath a shed while it rained, but you must be convinced you had been standing with the greatest man you had ever seen.—SAMUEL JOHNSON, *Johnsonian Miscellanies* [1897], *edited by* G. B. HILL, *vol. I, p. 290*

[2]See Pushkin, 486:7.

[3]*De Sapienta Veterum* [*The Wisdom of the Ancients*].—FRANCIS BACON [1609], *title of work*

The phrase is also in BURKE, *Discussion on the Traitorous Correspondence Bill* [1793].

[4]See Chesterfield, 341:15; Goldsmith, 369:27; and John Adams, 381:1.

10 I have in general no very exalted opinion of the virtue of paper government.

Second Speech on Conciliation with America. The Thirteen Resolutions [March 22, 1775]

11 The concessions of the weak are the concessions of fear. *Ib.*

12 Young man, there is America—which at this day serves for little more than to amuse you with stories of savage men and uncouth manners; yet shall, before you taste of death, show itself equal to the whole of that commerce which now attracts the envy of the world. *Ib.*

13 When we speak of the commerce with our colonies, fiction lags after truth; invention is unfruitful, and imagination cold and barren. *Ib.*

14 A people who are still, as it were, but in the gristle, and not yet hardened into the bone of manhood. *Ib.*

15 Through a wise and salutary neglect [of the colonies], a generous nature has been suffered to take her own way to perfection; when I reflect upon these effects, when I see how profitable they have been to us, I feel all the pride of power sink and all presumption in the wisdom of human contrivances melt and die away within me. My rigor relents. I pardon something to the spirit of liberty. *Ib.*

16 The use of force alone is but *temporary.* It may subdue for a moment; but it does not remove the necessity of subduing again: and a nation is not governed, which is perpetually to be conquered. *Ib.*

17 Nothing less will content me, than *whole America.* *Ib.*

18 Abstract liberty, like other mere abstractions, is not to be found. *Ib.*

19 The religion most prevalent in our northern colonies is a refinement on the principles of resistance: it is the dissidence of dissent, and the protestantism of the Protestant religion. *Ib.*

20 In no country perhaps in the world is law so general a study [as in America]. . . . This study renders men acute, inquisitive, dexterous, prompt in attack, ready in defense, full of resources. . . . They augur misgovernment at a distance, and snuff the approach of tyranny in every tainted breeze. *Ib.*

21 I do not know the method of drawing up an indictment against an whole people. *Ib.*

1 It is not, what a lawyer tells me I *may* do; but what humanity, reason, and justice, tell me I ought to do. *Ib.*

2 The march of the human mind is slow. *Ib.*

3 Freedom and not servitude is the cure of anarchy; as religion, and not atheism, is the true remedy for superstition. *Ib.*

4 All government—indeed, every human benefit and enjoyment, every virtue and every prudent act—is founded on compromise and barter. *Ib.*

5 Slavery they can have anywhere. It is a weed that grows in every soil. *Ib.*

6 Deny them [the colonies] this participation of freedom, and you break that sole bond, which originally made, and must still preserve the unity of the empire. *Ib.*

7 It is the love of the [British] people; it is their attachment to their government, from the sense of the deep stake they have in such a glorious institution, which gives you both your army and your navy, and infuses into both that liberal obedience, without which your army would be a base rabble, and your navy nothing but rotten timber. *Ib.*

8 Magnanimity in politics is not seldom the truest wisdom; and a great empire and little minds go ill together. *Ib.*

9 By adverting to the dignity of this high calling our ancestors have turned a savage wilderness into a glorious empire: and have made the most extensive, and the only honorable conquests, not by destroying, but by promoting the wealth, the number, the happiness of the human race. *Ib.*

10 Corrupt influence, which is itself the perennial spring of all prodigality, and of all disorder; which loads us, more than millions of debt; which takes away vigor from our arms, wisdom from our councils, and every shadow of authority and credit from the most venerable parts of our constitution.
Speech on the Economical Reform [1780]

11 He was not merely a chip of the old block, but the old block itself.
On Pitt's first speech [February 26, 1781]

12 A rapacious and licentious soldiery.
Speech on Fox's East India Bill [1783]

13 The people never give up their liberties but under some delusion.
Speech at County Meeting of Buckinghamshire [1784]

14 There never was a bad man that had ability for good service.
Impeachment of Warren Hastings [February 15, 1788]

15 Religious persecution may shield itself under the guise of a mistaken and over-zealous piety. *Ib. [February 17, 1788]*

16 An event has happened, upon which it is difficult to speak, and impossible to be silent. *Ib. [May 5, 1789]*

17 Resolved to die in the last dike of prevarication. *Ib. [May 7, 1789]*

18 There is but one law for all, namely, that law which governs all law, the law of our Creator, the law of humanity, justice, equity —the law of nature, and of nations.
Ib. [May 28, 1794]

19 They made and recorded a sort of institute and digest of anarchy, called the Rights of Man. *On the Army Estimates [1790]*

20 People will not look forward to posterity who never look backward to their ancestors.
Reflections on the Revolution in France [1790]

21 Government is a contrivance of human wisdom to provide for human wants. Men have a right that these wants should be provided for by this wisdom. *Ib.*

22 The age of chivalry has gone. That of sophisters, economists, and calculators has succeeded, and the glory of Europe is extinguished forever. *Ib.*

23 The unbought grace of life, the cheap defense of nations, the nurse of manly sentiment and heroic enterprise is gone! *Ib.*

24 That chastity of honor, which felt a stain like a wound. *Ib.*

25 Vice itself lost half its evil, by losing all its grossness. *Ib.*

26 Kings will be tyrants from policy, when subjects are rebels from principle. *Ib.*

27 Learning will be cast into the mire, and trodden down under the hoofs of a swinish multitude. *Ib.*

28 Because half a dozen grasshoppers under a fern make the field ring with their importunate chink, whilst thousands of great cattle,

reposed beneath the shadow of the British oak, chew the cud and are silent, pray do not imagine that those who make the noise are the only inhabitants of the field; that, of course, they are many in number; or that, after all, they are other than the little shriveled, meager, hopping, though loud and troublesome *insects* of the hour. *Ib.*

1 Superstition is the religion of feeble minds. *Ib.*

2 He that wrestles with us strengthens our nerves, and sharpens our skill. Our antagonist is our helper. *Ib.*

3 To execute laws is a royal office; to execute orders is not to be a king. However, a political executive magistracy, though merely such, is a great trust.[1] *Ib.*

4 You can never plan the future by the past.[2]
Letter to a member of the National Assembly [1791]

5 Old religious factions are volcanoes burnt out.
Speech on the Petition of the Unitarians [1792]

6 The cold neutrality of an impartial judge.
Preface to Brissot's Address [1794]

7 All men that are ruined, are ruined on the side of their natural propensities.
Letters on a Regicide Peace [1796], no. 1

8 Example is the school of mankind, and they will learn at no other.[3] *Ib.*

9 Mere parsimony is not economy. . . . Expense, and great expense, may be an essential part of true economy.
Letter to a Noble Lord [1796]

10 Economy is a distributive virtue, and consists not in saving but selection. Parsimony requires no providence, no sagacity, no powers of combination, no comparison, no judgment. *Ib.*

11 And having looked to Government for bread, on the very first scarcity they will turn and bite the hand that fed them.
Thoughts and Details on Scarcity [1800]

12 The only thing necessary for the triumph of evil is for good men to do nothing.
Attributed[4]

[1]See Clay, 444:3; Calhoun, 449:8; Sumner, 539:4; and Cleveland, 631:7.
[2]See Patrick Henry, 383:2.
[3]See Franklin, 347:23.
[4]See Burke, 372:4, and the preface, page ix.

Gotthold Ephraim Lessing
1729–1781

13 He who doesn't lose his wits over certain things has no wits to lose.
Emilia Galotti [1772], act IV, sc. vii

14 No person must have to.
Nathan der Weise [1779], act I, sc. iii

15 People are not always what they seem.
Ib. vi

16 The true beggar is the true king.
Ib. II, end

17 Not all are free who scorn their chains.
Ib. IV, iv

18 One can drink too much, but one never drinks enough. *Lieder*

John Parker
1729–1775

19 Stand your ground. Don't fire unless fired upon, but if they mean to have a war let it begin here!
To his Minute Men at Lexington [April 19, 1775]

Speckled Snake[5]
c. 1729–1829

20 When the white man had warmed himself before the Indians' fire and filled himself with their hominy, he became very large. With a step he bestrode the mountains, and his feet covered the plains and the valleys. His hand grasped the eastern and the western sea, and his head rested on the moon.
Statement when President Andrew Jackson recommended that the Cherokees, Chickasaws, Choctaws, Creeks, and Seminoles move west beyond the Mississippi [1829]

21 Brothers, I have listened to a great many talks from our great father.[6] But they always began and ended in this: "Get a little further; you are too near me." *Ib.*

Johann Georg Hamann
1730–1788

22 Poetry is the mother tongue of mankind.
Aesthetica in Nuce [1762]

[5]A Creek.
[6]President Jackson.

Thomas Osbert Mordaunt

1730–1809

1 One crowded hour of glorious life
Is worth an age without a name.[1]

Verses Written During the War [1756–1763]. From the Bee [October 12, 1791]

Motoori Norinaga[2]

1730–1801

2 Sages are superior to other people only in their cleverness. The fact is that they were all impostors. Among them the least blameworthy was Confucius. *Arrowroot*

3 *The Tale of Genji*[3] is simply a tale of human life which leaves aside and does not profess to take up at all the question of good and bad, and which dwells only upon the goodness of those who are aware of the sorrow of human existence.

Tama no Ogushi

John Scott

1730–1783

4 I Hate That Drum's Discordant Sound.

Title of poem

Josiah Wedgwood

1730–1795

5 Am I not a man and a brother?

On a medallion[4] *[1787]*

Charles Churchill

1731–1764

6 Genius is of no country.

The Rosciad [1761], l. 207

7 Learned without sense, and venerably dull.

Ib. l. 591

8 Those who would make us feel—must feel themselves.[5] *Ib. l. 962*

9 Apt alliteration's artful aid.

The Prophecy of Famine [1763], l. 86

10 Fame
Is nothing but an empty name.

The Ghost [1763], bk. I, l. 229

11 Just to the windward of the law.

Ib. III, l. 56

12 Though by whim, envy, or resentment led,
They damn those authors whom they never read. *The Candidate [1764], l. 57*

13 Be England what she will,
With all her faults she is my country still.[6]

The Farewell, l. 27

William Cowper

1731–1800

14 Oh! for a closer walk with God.

Olney Hymns [1779],[7] *no. 1*

15 What peaceful hours I once enjoyed!
How sweet their memory still!
But they have left an aching void
The world can never fill. *Ib.*

16 God moves in a mysterious way
His wonders to perform;
He plants his footsteps in the sea
And rides upon the storm. *Ib. 35*

17 Behind a frowning providence
He hides a smiling face. *Ib.*

18 Happiness depends, as Nature shows,
Less on exterior things than most suppose.

Table Talk [1782], l. 246

19 Freedom has a thousand charms to show,
That slaves, howe'er contented, never know.

Ib. l. 260

20 Manner is all in all, whate'er is writ,
The substitute for genius, sense, and wit.

Ib. l. 542

21 Low ambition and the thirst of praise.

Ib. l. 591

22 [Pope] Made poetry a mere mechanic art.

Ib. l. 656

23 Lights of the world, and stars of human race.

The Progress of Error [1782], l. 97

24 How much a dunce that has been sent to roam
Excels a dunce that has been kept at home!

Ib. l. 415

25 A fool must now and then be right, by chance.

Conversation [1782], l. 96

[1] Quoted by Sir Walter Scott in *Old Mortality* [1816], *ch. 34.*
See Scott, 432:16.

[2] From *Sources of Japanese Tradition* [1960], edited by William Theodore de Bary.

[3] See Murasaki Shikibu, 135:14.

[4] Representing a Negro in chains, with one knee on the ground and both hands lifted up to heaven. This was adopted as a seal by the Anti-Slavery Society of London.

[5] See Frost, 750:3.

[6] England, with all thy faults I love thee still, / My country!—Cowper, *The Task* [1784], *bk. II, The Timepiece, l. 206*
See John Quincy Adams, 417:17; Decatur, 445:19; and Carl Schurz, 603:4.

[7] See John Newton, 367:7.

1 He would not, with a peremptory tone,
Assert the nose upon his face his own.
Ib. l. 121

2 A moral, sensible, and well-bred man
Will not affront me, and no other can.
Ib. l. 193

3 Pernicious weed![1] whose scent the fair annoys,
Unfriendly to society's chief joys,
Thy worst effect is banishing for hours
The sex whose presence civilizes ours.
Ib. l. 251

4 I cannot talk with civet in the room,
A fine puss-gentleman that's all perfume.
Ib. l. 283

5 His wit invites you by his looks to come,
But when you knock it never is at home.
Ib. l. 303

6 Our wasted oil unprofitably burns,
Like hidden lamps in old sepulchral urns.
Ib. l. 357

7 A business with an income at its heels
Furnishes always oil for its own wheels.
Retirement [1782], l. 615

8 Absence of occupation is not rest,
A mind quite vacant is a mind distressed.
Ib. l. 623

9 Built God a church, and laughed His word to scorn.[2] *Ib. l. 688*

10 Philologists, who chase
A panting syllable through time and space,
Start it at home, and hunt it in the dark
To Gaul, to Greece, and into Noah's ark.
Ib. l. 691

11 I praise the Frenchman,[3] his remark was shrewd—
How sweet, how passing sweet, is solitude!
But grant me still a friend in my retreat
Whom I may whisper—solitude is sweet.
Ib. l. 739

12 I am monarch of all I survey,
My right there is none to dispute.
Verses Supposed to Be Written by Alexander Selkirk [1782], st. 1

13 O Solitude! where are the charms
That sages have seen in thy face? *Ib.*

14 Though on pleasure she was bent,
She had a frugal mind.
History of John Gilpin [1785], st. 8

[1]Tobacco.

[2]Voltaire, who built a church at Ferney [1760–1761], with the inscription *Deo erexit Voltaire.*

[3]La Bruyère.

15 A hat not much the worse for wear.
Ib. st. 46

16 Now let us sing—Long live the king,
And Gilpin, long live he;
And, when he next doth ride abroad,
May I be there to see! *Ib. st. 63*

17 God made the country, and man made the town.[4]
The Task [1785], bk. I, The Sofa, l. 749

18 Oh for a lodge in some vast wilderness,[5]
Some boundless contiguity of shade,
Where rumor of oppression and deceit,
Of unsuccessful or successful war,
Might never reach me more.
Ib. II, The Timepiece, l. 1

19 Mountains interposed
Make enemies of nations, who had else
Like kindred drops, been mingled into one.[6]
Ib. l. 17

20 Slaves cannot breathe in England; if their lungs
Receive our air, that moment they are free!
They touch our country, and their shackles fall. *Ib. l. 40*

21 Presume to lay their hand upon the ark[7]
Of her magnificent and awful cause.
Ib. l. 231

22 Variety's the very spice of life.[8]
Ib. l. 606

23 His head,
Not yet by time completely silvered o'er,
Bespoke him past the bounds of freakish youth,
But strong for service still, and unimpaired.
Ib. l. 702

24 Guilty splendor.
Ib. III, The Garden, l. 70

25 I was a stricken deer[9] that left the herd
Long since. *Ib. l. 108*

26 Great contest follows, and much learned dust
Involves the combatants. *Ib. l. 161*

27 From reveries so airy, from the toil
Of dropping buckets into empty wells,
And growing old in drawing nothing up.[10]
Ib. l. 188

[4]See *Genesis 2:8,* 6:18; Varro, 97:14; Bacon, 181:10; Shakespeare, 224:5; and Cowley, 295:14.

[5]See *Jeremiah 9:2,* 32:4, and Byron, 458:23.

[6]See Tecumseh, 419:9.

[7]See *II Samuel 6:6,* 13:15.

[8]See Publilius Syrus, 111:9, and Johnson, 352:13.

[9]See Shakespeare, 222:17.

[10]See Sydney Smith, 432:25.

1 Riches have wings,[1] and grandeur is a dream.
Ib. l. 265

2 Who loves a garden loves a greenhouse too.
Ib. l. 566

3 Now stir the fire, and close the shutters fast,
Let fall the curtains, wheel the sofa round,
And, while the bubbling and loud-hissing urn
Throws up a steamy column, and the cups,
That cheer but not inebriate,[2] wait on each,
So let us welcome peaceful evening in.
Ib. IV, The Winter Evening, l. 36

4 'Tis pleasant, through the loopholes of retreat,
To peep at such a world; to see the stir
Of the great Babel, and not feel the crowd.
Ib. l. 88

5 O Winter, ruler of the inverted year![3]
Ib. l. 120

6 With spots quadrangular of diamond form,
Ensanguined hearts, clubs typical of strife,
And spades, the emblems of untimely graves.
Ib. l. 217

7 In indolent vacuity of thought.[4]
Ib. l. 297

8 It seems the part of wisdom. *Ib. l. 336*

9 All learned, and all drunk! *Ib. l. 478*

10 Gloriously drunk, obey th' important call.
Ib. l. 510

11 Silently as a dream the fabric rose—
No sound of hammer or of saw was there.[5]
Ib. V, The Winter Morning Walk, l. 144

12 But war's a game, which, were their subjects wise,
Kings would not play at. *Ib. l. 187*

13 There is in souls a sympathy with sounds;
And as the mind is pitched the ear is pleased
With melting airs or martial, brisk, or grave:
Some chord in unison with what we hear
Is touched within us, and the heart replies.
Ib. VI, Winter Walk at Noon, l. 1

14 Here the heart
May give a useful lesson to the head,
And Learning wiser grow without his books.
Ib. l. 85

[1]See Amenemope, 6:7, and *Proverbs* 23:5, 25:7.
[2]See Berkeley, 330:22.
[3]See Thomson, 345:4.
[4]See Samuel Johnson, 354:18.
[5]See *I Kings* 6:7, 13:32.
No hammers fell, no ponderous axes rung, / Like some tall palm the mystic fabric sprung. / Majestic silence!
— Reginald Heber [1783–1826], *Palestine*

15 Knowledge is proud that he has learned so much;
Wisdom is humble that he knows no more.
Ib. l. 96

16 Nature is but a name for an effect,
Whose cause is God. *Ib. l. 223*

17 An honest man, close-buttoned to the chin,
Broadcloth without, and a warm heart within.
Epistle to Joseph Hill [1785], l. 62

18 Shine by the side of every path we tread
With such a luster, he that runs may read.[6]
Tirocinium [1785], l. 79

19 Toll for the brave—
The brave! that are no more;
All sunk beneath the wave,
Fast by their native shore!
On the Loss of the Royal George[7] *[1791], st. 1*

20 And still to love, though prest with ill,
In wintry age to feel no chill,
With me is to be lovely still,
My Mary! *To Mary [1791], st. 11*

21 Beware of desp'rate steps! The darkest day
(Live till tomorrow) will have passed away.
The Needless Alarm [1794]. Moral

22 The British warrior queen,
Bleeding from the Roman rods.
Boadicea [1782]

23 I shall not ask Jean Jacques Rousseau
If birds confabulate or no.
Pairing Time Anticipated [c. 1794]

24 Misses! the tale that I relate
This lesson seems to carry—
Choose not alone a proper mate,
But proper time to marry. *Ib. Moral*

25 Misery still delights to trace
Its semblance in another's case.
The Castaway [1799]

Erasmus Darwin

1731–1802

26 Soon shall thy arm, unconquered steam! afar
Drag the slow barge, or drive the rapid car;
Or on wide-waving wings expanded bear
The flying-chariot through the fields of air.
The Botanic Garden, pt. I [1789], l. 289

[6]See *Habakkuk* 2:2, 33:25.
[7]The *Royal George* was an English man-of-war of 108 guns, which suddenly heeled over, under the strain caused by the shifting of her guns, while being refitted at Spithead, August 29, 1782. The commander, Admiral Kempenfeldt, and eight hundred of the sailors, marines, and visitors on board were drowned.

1 Would it be too bold to imagine, that in the great length of time, since the earth began to exist, perhaps millions of ages before the commencement of the history of mankind, would it be too bold to imagine, that all warm-blooded animals have arisen from one living filament which the Great First Cause endued with animality . . . and thus possessing the faculty of continuing to improve by its own inherent activity, and of delivering down those improvements by generation to its posterity, world without end![1]

Zoonomia [1794]

Charles Lee

1731–1782

2 Beware that your Northern laurels do not change to Southern willows.[2]

To General Horatio Gates after the surrender of Burgoyne at Saratoga [October 17, 1777]

Beilby Porteus

1731–1808

3 One murder made a villain,[3]
Millions, a hero. *Death [1759], l. 154*

4 War its thousands slays, Peace, its ten thousands.[4] *Ib. l. 178*

Pierre de Beaumarchais

1732–1799

5 Judging by the virtues expected of a servant, does your Excellency know many masters who would be worthy valets?

Le Barbier de Séville [1775], act I, sc. ii

6 I quickly laugh at everything, for fear of having to cry.[5] *Ib.*

7 If you assure me that your intentions are honorable. *Ib. IV, vi*

8 If you are mediocre and you grovel, you shall succeed.

Le Mariage de Figaro [1784], act III, sc. iii

9 You went to some trouble to be born, and that's all.[6] *Ib. V, iii*

10 If censorship reigns there cannot be sincere flattery, and only small men are afraid of small writings. *Ib.*

John Dickinson

1732–1808

11 Then join hand in hand, brave Americans all!
By uniting we stand, by dividing we fall.[7]

The Liberty Song [1768]

Richard Henry Lee

1732–1794

12 That these united colonies are, and of right ought to be, free and independent states; that they are absolved from all allegiance to the British crown; and that all political connection between them and the State of Great Britain is, and ought to be, totally dissolved.

Resolution moved at the Continental Congress [June 7, 1776; adopted July 2][8]

Julie de Lespinasse

1732–1776

13 The logic of the heart is absurd.

Letter to M. Guibert [August 27, 1774]

George Washington[9]

1732–1799

14 Discipline is the soul of an army. It makes small numbers formidable; procures success to the weak, and esteem to all.

Letter of Instructions to the Captains of the Virginia Regiments [July 29, 1759]

[1]Here the grandfather of Charles Darwin announces his own early theory of organic evolution.

[2]Gates was later defeated by Cornwallis at Camden, South Carolina [August 16, 1780], and was relieved of his command.

[3]See Seneca, 114:32; Young, 330:1; and J. R. Lowell, 567:20.

[4]See *I Samuel 18:7*, 13:4.

[5]Je me presse de rire de tout, de peur d'être obligé d'en pleurer.

See La Bruyère, 315:7, and Byron, 461:10.

[6]Vous vous êtes donné la peine de naître, et rien de plus.

[7]United we stand, divided we fall.—*A watchword of the American Revolution*

See Aesop, 66:22.

[8]See John Adams, 381:6.

[9]The Father of your Country.—HENRY KNOX, *Letter to Washington* [March 19, 1787]

See Henry (Light-Horse Harry) Lee, 402:10, and Franklin, 348:11.

I can't tell a lie. I did it [cut the cherry tree] with my hatchet.—*Attributed to Washington as a child;* MASON LOCKE WEEMS [1759–1825], *The Life of George Washington* [1800]

Father, I cannot tell a lie. I did it with my little hatchet. —MARK TWAIN [1835–1910], *Mark Twain as Washington*

1 Let us therefore animate and encourage each other, and show the whole world that a Freeman, contending for liberty on his own ground, is superior to any slavish mercenary on earth.

General Orders, Headquarters, New York [July 2, 1776]

2 The time is now near at hand which must probably determine whether Americans are to be freemen or slaves; whether they are to have any property they can call their own; whether their houses and farms are to be pillaged and destroyed, and themselves consigned to a state of wretchedness from which no human efforts will deliver them. The fate of unborn millions will now depend, under God, on the courage and conduct of this army. Our cruel and unrelenting enemy leaves us only the choice of brave resistance, or the most abject submission. We have, therefore, to resolve to conquer or die.

Address to the Continental Army before the battle of Long Island [August 27, 1776]

3 There is nothing that gives a man consequence, and renders him fit for command, like a support that renders him independent of everybody but the State he serves.

Letter to the president of Congress, Heights of Harlem [September 24, 1776]

4 To place any dependence upon militia, is, assuredly, resting upon a broken staff.

Ib.

5 Without a decisive naval force we can do nothing definitive. And with it, everything honorable and glorious.[1]

To Lafayette [November 15, 1781]

6 If men are to be precluded from offering their sentiments on a matter which may involve the most serious and alarming consequences that can invite the consideration of mankind, reason is of no use to us; the freedom of speech may be taken away, and dumb and silent we may be led, like sheep to the slaughter.

Address to officers of the Army [March 15, 1783]

7 The preservation of the sacred fire of liberty, and the destiny of the republican model of government, are justly considered as deeply, perhaps as finally staked, on the experiment entrusted to the hands of the American people.

First Inaugural Address [April 30, 1789]

8 Happily the Government of the United States, which gives to bigotry no sanction, to persecution no assistance, requires only that they who live under its protection should demean themselves as good citizens in giving it on all occasions their effectual support.

Letter to the Jewish congregation of Newport, Rhode Island [1790]

9 To be prepared for war is one of the most effectual means of preserving peace.[2]

First Annual Address [to both houses of Congress, January 8, 1790]

10 The basis of our political system is the right of the people to make and to alter their constitutions of government.

Farewell Address [September 17, 1796]

11 Let me now . . . warn you in the most solemn manner against the baneful effects of the spirit of party. *Ib.*

12 Observe good faith and justice toward all nations. Cultivate peace and harmony with all. . . . The Nation which indulges toward another an habitual hatred or an habitual fondness is in some degree a slave. It is a slave to its animosity or to its affection, either of which is sufficient to lead it astray from its duty and its interest. *Ib.*

13 'Tis our true policy to steer clear of permanent alliances, with any portion of the foreign world. *Ib.*

14 There can be no greater error than to expect or calculate upon real favors from nation to nation. *Ib.*

15 It is well, I die hard, but I am not afraid to go. *Last words [December 14, 1799]*

Joseph Priestley[3]

1733–1804

16 It was ill policy in Leo the Tenth to patronize polite literature. He was cherishing an enemy in disguise. And the English hierar-

[1]See Themistocles, 70:19; Bacon, 181:11; Waller, 276:3; Mahan, 642:8; and Morison, 800:11.

[2]See Aristotle, 87:24; Vegetius, 128:25; Robert Burton, 259:13; Fénelon, 316:12; and Lowell, 568:9.

[3]See the Bentham footnote to Francis Hutcheson, 342:19. Bentham credits Priestley's *Essay on Government* [1768] —or the work of Cesare Bonesana, Marchese di Beccaria [1738–1794]—with inspiring his concept of "the greatest happiness of the greatest number."

chy (if there be anything unsound in its constitution) has equal reason to tremble even at an air pump or an electrical machine.

Experiments and Observations on Different Kinds of Air [1775–1786]

1 In completing one discovery we never fail to get an imperfect knowledge of others of which we could have no idea before, so that we cannot solve one doubt without creating several new ones. *Ib.*

Christoph Martin Wieland
1733–1813

2 To be not as eloquent would be more eloquent.

The Journal Merkur [January 1774]

3 An illusion which makes me happy is worth a verity which drags me to the ground. *Idris und Zenide [1768], canto III*

4 Too much light often blinds gentlemen of this sort. They cannot see the forest for the trees. *Musarion [1768], canto II*

Franz [Friedrich] Anton Mesmer
1734–1815

5 There is only one illness and one cure.

Aphorismes de M. Mesmer [1785],[1] *ch. 16*

John Adams[2]
1735–1826

6 Now to what higher object, to what greater character, can any mortal aspire than to be possessed of all this knowledge, well digested and ready at command, to assist the feeble and friendless, to discountenance the haughty and lawless, to procure redress of wrongs, the advancement of right, to assert and maintain liberty and virtue, to discourage and abolish tyranny and vice?

Letter to Jonathan Sewall [October 1759]

7 A pen is certainly an excellent instrument to fix a man's attention and to inflame his ambition. *Diary [November 14, 1760]*

8 I always consider the settlement of America with reverence and wonder, as the opening of a grand scene and design in providence, for the illumination of the ignorant and the emancipation of the slavish part of mankind all over the earth.

Notes for "A Dissertation on the Canon and Feudal Law" [1765]

9 Liberty cannot be preserved without a general knowledge among the people, who have a right . . . and a desire to know; but besides this, they have a right, an indisputable, unalienable, indefeasible, divine right to that most dreaded and envied kind of knowledge, I mean of the characters and conduct of their rulers.

A Dissertation on the Canon and Feudal Law [1765]

10 Let us . . . cherish, therefore, the means of knowledge. Let us dare to read, think, speak, and write. . . . Let every sluice of knowledge be opened and set a-flowing.

Ib.

11 Facts are stubborn things; and whatever may be our wishes, our inclinations, or the dictates of our passions, they cannot alter the state of facts and evidence.

Argument in Defense of the [British] Soldiers in the Boston Massacre Trials [December 1770]

12 The law . . . will not bend to the uncertain wishes, imaginations and wanton tempers of men. . . . On the one hand it is inexorable to the cries and lamentations of the prisoners; on the other it is deaf, deaf as an adder,[3] to the clamors of the populace.

Ib.

13 There is danger from all men. The only maxim of a free government ought to be to trust no man living with power to endanger the public liberty.

Notes for an Oration at Braintree [Spring 1772]

14 This is the most magnificent movement of all! There is a dignity, a majesty, a sublimity, in this last effort of the patriots that I greatly admire. The people should never rise without doing something to be remembered — something notable and striking. This destruction of the tea is so bold, so daring, so firm, intrepid and inflexible, and it must have so important consequences, and so lasting, that I can't but consider it as an epocha in history!

Diary [on the Boston Tea Party, December 17, 1773]

[1] Recorded by Dr. Caullet de Veaumorel; translated by Jerome Eden.

[2] He is as disinterested as the being who made him: he is profound in his view; and accurate in his judgment, except where knowledge of the world is necessary to form a judgment. — Jefferson [January 30, 1787]
See Webster, 450:n2.

[3] See *Psalm 58:4–5*, 19:23.

1 A government of laws, and not of men.[1]

"Novanglus"[2] papers, Boston Gazette [1774], no. 7. Incorporated [1780] in the Massachusetts Constitution[3]

2 Metaphysicians and politicians may dispute forever, but they will never find any other moral principle or foundation of rule or obedience, than the consent of governors and governed.[4] *Ib.*

3 I agree with you that in politics the middle way is none at all.

Letter to Horatio Gates [March 23, 1776]

4 You bid me burn your letters. But I must forget you first.

Letter to Abigail Adams [April 28, 1776]

5 There is something very unnatural and odious in a government a thousand leagues off. A whole government of our own choice, managed by persons whom we love, revere, and can confide in, has charms in it for which men will fight. *Ib. [May 17, 1776]*

6 Yesterday, the greatest question was decided which ever was debated in America, and a greater perhaps never was nor will be decided among men. A resolution was passed without one dissenting colony, "that these United Colonies are, and of right ought to be, free and independent States."[5]

Ib. [July 3, 1776]

7 The second day of July, 1776,[6] will be the most memorable epoch in the history of America. I am apt to believe that it will be celebrated by succeeding generations as the great anniversary festival. It ought to be commemorated as the day of deliverance, by solemn acts of devotion to God Almighty. It ought to be solemnized with pomp and parade, with shows, games, sports, guns, bells, bonfires, and illuminations, from one end of this continent to the other, from this time forward forevermore.

Second Letter to Abigail Adams [July 3, 1776]

8 The happiness of society[7] is the end of government.

Thoughts on Government [1776]

9 Fear is the foundation of most governments. *Ib.*

10 When annual elections end, there slavery begins. *Ib.*

11 The judicial power ought to be distinct from both the legislative and executive, and independent upon both, that so it may be a check upon both, as both should be checks upon that. *Ib.*

12 Virtue is not always amiable.

Diary [February 9, 1779]

13 By my physical constitution I am but an ordinary man. . . . Yet some great events, some cutting expressions, some mean hypocrisies, have at times thrown this assemblage of sloth, sleep, and littleness into rage like a lion.[8] *Ib. [April 26, 1779]*

14 I must study politics and war that my sons may have liberty to study mathematics and philosophy. My sons ought to study mathematics and philosophy, geography, natural history, naval architecture, navigation, commerce, and agriculture, in order to give their children a right to study painting, poetry, music, architecture, statuary, tapestry, and porcelain.[9]

Letter to Abigail Adams [May 12, 1780]

15 You will never be alone with a poet in your pocket.[10]

Letter to John Quincy Adams [May 14, 1781]

16 My country has in its wisdom contrived for me the most insignificant office [the vice-presidency] that ever the invention of man contrived or his imagination conceived; and as I can do neither good nor evil, I must be borne away by others and meet the common fate.[11]

Letter to Abigail Adams [December 19, 1793]

[1] Adams credits this formulation to James Harrington [1611–1677], with whose work *The Commonwealth of Oceana* [1656] he was familiar. Adams's use of the phrase gave it wide circulation in America.

See Chesterfield, 341:15; Goldsmith, 369:27; and Burke, 372:5.

[2] Pseudonym of John Adams.

[3] Article 30 of the Declaration of Rights.

[4] See Jefferson, 387:9.

[5] See Richard Henry Lee, 378:12.

[6] On July 2, 1776, the resolution for independence, drafted by Richard Henry Lee of Virginia, was adopted by a committee including John Adams. On July 4 the Declaration of Independence was agreed to, engrossed, signed by John Hancock, and sent to the legislatures of the States.

[7] See Gibbon, 383:9, and Jefferson, 387:9.

[8] These lines are as expressive as any that John Adams ever wrote about his own character. They were set down while he waited at the French port of St. Nazaire to sail home after his first and, as he believed, fruitless, mission to Europe. His lion-like rages were already well known and were to become more so in his later public life.—LYMAN H. BUTTERFIELD [1976]

[9] See Caecilius Statius, 95:15.

[10] See Martí, 671:19.

[11] See Jefferson, 388:13.

1 I pray Heaven to bestow the best of blessings on this house and all that shall hereafter inhabit it. May none but honest and wise men ever rule under this roof.[1]

Letter to Abigail Adams [November 2, 1800]

2 I had heard my father say that he never knew a piece of land [to] run away or break.[2]

Autobiography [1802–1807]

3 You and I ought not to die before we have explained ourselves to each other.

Letter to Thomas Jefferson [July 15, 1813]

4 The fundamental article of my political creed is that despotism, or unlimited sovereignty, or absolute power, is the same in a majority of a popular assembly, an aristocratical council, an oligarchical junto, and a single emperor.

Letter to Thomas Jefferson [November 13, 1815]

5 Thomas—Jefferson—still surv—[3]

Last words [July 4, 1826]

Isaac Bickerstaffe
c. 1735–c. 1812

6 There was a jolly miller once
Lived on the River Dee;
He worked and sang from morn till night
No lark more blithe than he.

Love in a Village [1762], act I, sc. ii

7 And this the burthen of his song
Forever used to be,
"I care for nobody, not I,
If no one cares for me."[4]

Ib.

Michel Guillaume Jean de Crèvecoeur [J. Hector St. John]
1735–1813

8 Here [in America] individuals of all nations are melted into a new race of men, whose labors and posterity will one day cause great changes in the world.[5]

Letters from an American Farmer [1782], III

[1]Written the day after Adams moved into the new White House. President Franklin D. Roosevelt had it inscribed on the mantelpiece of the State Dining Room.

[2]See Trollope, 555:4.

[3]Jefferson at Monticello died the same day—the fiftieth anniversary of the adoption of the Declaration of Independence—murmuring, "This is the Fourth?"—SAMUEL ELIOT MORISON, *The Oxford History of the American People* [1965]

[4]Naebody cares for me, / I care for naebody.—ROBERT BURNS [1759–1796], *I Hae a Wife o' My Ain, st. 4*

[5]See Zangwill, 706:15.

Charles Joseph, Prince de Ligne
1735–1814

9 The Congress doesn't run—it waltzes.[6]

Comment to La Garde-Chambonacs [1814]

William Julius Mickle
1735–1788

10 For there's nae luck about the house,
There's nae luck at a';
There's little pleasure in the house
When our gudeman's awa.

The Mariner's Wife, st. 1

Paul Revere
1735–1818

11 To the memory of the glorious Ninety-two: members of the Honorable House of Representatives of the Massachusetts Bay who, undaunted by the insolent menaces of villains in power, from a strict regard to conscience and the liberties of their constituents on the 30th of June 1768 voted NOT TO RESCIND.

Inscription on Revere's silver "Liberty" bowl [1768]

12 If the British went out by water, to show two lanterns in the North Church steeple; and if by land, one as a signal, for we were apprehensive it would be difficult to cross the Charles River or get over Boston Neck.[7]

Signal code arranged with Colonel Conant of the Charlestown Committee of Safety [April 16, 1775]. Letter to Dr. Jeremy Belknap

Patrick Henry
1736–1799

13 Caesar had his Brutus; Charles the First his Cromwell; and George the Third ["Treason!" cried the Speaker]—*may profit by their example.* If *this* be treason, make the most of it.

Speech on the Stamp Act, House of Burgesses, Williamsburg, Virginia [May 29, 1765]

14 I am not a Virginian, but an American.

Speech in the First Continental Congress, Philadelphia [October 14, 1774]

[6]Le Congrès ne marche pas, il danse [said of the Congress of Vienna].

[7]See Longfellow, 512:7.

1 It is natural for man to indulge in the illusions of hope. We are apt to shut our eyes against a painful truth, and listen to the song of that siren till she transforms us into beasts. Is this the part of wise men, engaged in a great and arduous struggle for liberty? Are we disposed to be the number of those who, having eyes, see not, and having ears, hear not,[1] the things which so nearly concern their temporal salvation? For my part, whatever anguish of spirit it may cost, I am willing to know the whole truth; to know the worst, and to provide for it.

Speech in Virginia Convention, Richmond [March 23, 1775]

2 I have but one lamp by which my feet are guided, and that is the lamp of experience. I know no way of judging of the future but by the past.[2] *Ib.*

3 We are not weak if we make a proper use of those means which the God of Nature has placed in our power. . . . The battle, sir, is not to the strong alone;[3] it is to the vigilant, the active, the brave. *Ib.*

4 If we wish to be free; if we mean to preserve inviolate those inestimable privileges for which we have been so long contending; if we mean not basely to abandon the noble struggle in which we have been so long engaged, and which we have pledged ourselves never to abandon until the glorious object of our contest shall be obtained—we must fight! I repeat it, sir, we must fight! An appeal to arms, and to the God of hosts, is all that is left us. *Ib.*

5 It is vain, sir, to extenuate the matter. The gentlemen may cry, Peace, peace! but there is no peace.[4] The war has actually begun! The next gale that sweeps from the north will bring to our ears the clash of resounding arms! Our brethren are already in the field! Why stand we here idle? What is it that the gentlemen wish? What would they have? Is life so dear or peace so sweet as to be purchased at the price of chains and slavery? Forbid it, Almighty God. I know not what course others may take, but as for me, give me liberty or give me death![5] *Ib.*

6 That religion, or the duty which we owe to our Creator, and the manner of discharging it, can be directed only by reason and conviction, not by force or violence; and therefore all men are equally entitled to the free exercise of religion, according to the dictates of conscience; and that it is the mutual duty of all to practice Christian forbearance, love, and charity towards each other.

Virginia Bill of Rights [June 12, 1776],[6] article 16

[1] See *Jeremiah 5:21*, 31:34.
[2] See Burke, 374:4.
[3] See *Ecclesiastes 9:11*, 27:17.
[4] See *Jeremiah 6:14*, 31:36.
[5] See Aeschylus, 71:10.

Edward Gibbon

1737–1794

7 The various modes of worship, which prevailed in the Roman world, were all considered by the people, as equally true; by the philosopher, as equally false; and by the magistrate, as equally useful.

Decline and Fall of the Roman Empire [1776–1788], ch. 2

8 The principles of a free constitution are irrevocably lost, when the legislative power is nominated by the executive. *Ib. 3*

9 Their united reigns [the Antonines'] are possibly the only period of history in which the happiness of a great people was the sole object of government.[7] *Ib.*

10 History . . . is indeed little more than the register of the crimes, follies, and misfortunes of mankind.[8] *Ib.*

11 Corruption, the most infallible symptom of constitutional liberty. *Ib. 21*

12 Our sympathy is cold to the relation of distant misery. *Ib. 49*

13 The winds and waves are always on the side of the ablest navigators.[9] *Ib. 68*

14 Vicissitudes of fortune, which spares neither man nor the proudest of his works, which buries empires and cities in a common grave. *Ib. 71*

15 All that is human must retrograde if it does not advance. *Ib.*

16 The successors of Charles the Fifth may disdain their brethren of England; but the romance of *Tom Jones,* that exquisite picture of human manners, will outlive the palace of the Escurial and the imperial eagle of the house of Austria.

Memoirs (Autobiography) [1796]

[6] See George Mason, 367:*n*4. Mason drafted Articles 1, 3, and 12.
[7] See John Adams, 381:8, and Jefferson, 387:9.
Ah, might we read in America's signs / The Age restored of the Antonines.—HERMAN MELVILLE, *Timoleon* [1891], *The Age of the Antonines, st. 3*
[8] See Voltaire, 343:26.
[9] See Tacitus, 123:1; Bussy-Rabutin, 294:21; Boileau, 311:15; and Frederick the Great, 358:4.

1 Decent easy men, who supinely enjoyed the gifts of the founder. *Ib.*

2 It was here [at the age of seventeen] that I suspended my religious inquiries. *Ib.*

3 I saw and loved. *Ib.*

4 I sighed as a lover, I obeyed as a son. *Ib.*

5 [Of London] Crowds without company, and dissipation without pleasure. *Ib.*

6 The captain of the Hampshire grenadiers[1] . . . has not been useless to the historian of the Roman Empire. *Ib.*

7 It was at Rome, on the fifteenth of October 1764, as I sat musing amidst the ruins of the Capitol, while the barefoot friars were singing vespers in the Temple of Jupiter, that the idea of writing the decline and fall of the city first started to my mind. *Ib.*

Thomas Paine

1737–1809

8 From the east to the west blow the trumpet to arms!
Through the land let the sound of it flee;
Let the far and the near all unite, with a cheer,
In defense of our Liberty Tree.
The Liberty Tree [July 1775], st. 4

9 Society in every state is a blessing, but Government, even in its best state, is but a necessary evil; in its worst state, an intolerable one. *Common Sense [1776]*

10 Suspicion is the companion of mean souls, and the bane of all good society. *Ib.*

11 When we are planning for posterity, we ought to remember that virtue is not hereditary. *Ib.*

12 O! ye that love mankind! Ye that dare oppose not only the tyranny but the tyrant, stand forth! Every spot of the Old World is overrun with oppression. Freedom hath been hunted round the globe. Asia and Africa have long expelled her. Europe regards her as a stranger and England hath given her warning to depart. O! receive the fugitive and prepare in time an asylum for mankind.[2] *Ib.*

13 These are the times that try men's souls. The summer soldier and the sunshine patriot will, in this crisis, shrink from the service of their country; but he that stands it *now,* deserves the love and thanks of man and woman. Tyranny, like hell, is not easily conquered; yet we have this consolation with us, that the harder the conflict, the more glorious the triumph. What we obtain too cheap, we esteem too lightly; 'tis dearness only that gives everything its value. Heaven knows how to put a proper price upon its goods; and it would be strange indeed, if so celestial an article as *Freedom* should not be highly rated.
The American Crisis, no. 1 [December 23, 1776]

14 Panics, in some cases, have their uses; they produce as much good as hurt. Their duration is always short; the mind soon grows through them and acquires a firmer habit than before. But their peculiar advantage is, that they are the touchstone of sincerity and hypocrisy, and bring things and men to light, which might otherwise have lain forever undiscovered. *Ib.*

15 Not a place upon earth might be so happy as America. Her situation is remote from all the wrangling world, and she has nothing to do but to trade with them. *Ib.*

16 A bad cause will ever be supported by bad means and bad men.
Ib. 2 [January 13, 1777]

17 Those who expect to reap the blessings of freedom must, like men, undergo the fatigue of supporting it.
Ib. 4 [September 12, 1777]

18 It is not a field of a few acres of ground, but a cause, that we are defending, and whether we defeat the enemy in one battle, or by degrees, the consequences will be the same. *Ib.*

19 We fight not to enslave, but to set a country free, and to make room upon the earth for honest men to live in. *Ib.*

20 It is the object only of war that makes it honorable. And if there was ever a *just* war since the world began, it is this in which America is now engaged.
Ib. 5 [March 21, 1778]

21 Character is much easier kept than recovered. *Ib. 13 [April 19, 1783]*

22 War involves in its progress such a train of unforeseen and unsupposed circumstances that no human wisdom can calculate the end. It has but one thing certain, and that is to increase taxes.
Prospects on the Rubicon [1787]

[1] Gibbon was a captain in the Hampshire militia from June 12, 1759, to December 23, 1762.

[2] See Samuel Adams, 365:5.

1 [Burke] is not affected by the reality of distress touching his heart, but by the showy resemblance of it striking his imagination. He pities the plumage, but forgets the dying bird. *The Rights of Man, pt. I [1791]*

2 My country is the world and my religion is to do good.[1] *Ib. II [1792], ch. 5*

3 Every religion is good that teaches man to be good. *Ib.*

4 A thing moderately good is not so good as it ought to be. Moderation in temper is always a virtue; but moderation in principle is always a vice.[2] *Ib.*

5 I believe in one God and no more, and I hope for happiness beyond this life. I believe in the equality of man; and I believe that religious duties consist in doing justice, loving mercy, and endeavoring to make our fellow creatures happy.
The Age of Reason [1793], pt. I

6 It is with a pious fraud as with a bad action; it begets a calamitous necessity of going on. *Ib.*

7 When authors and critics talk of the sublime, they see not how nearly it borders on the ridiculous.[3] *Ib. II, note*

Rudolf Erich Raspe

1737–1794

8 His tunes were frozen up in the horn, and came out now by thawing.[4]
Travels of Baron Munchausen [1785], ch. 6

9 If any of the company entertain a doubt of my veracity, I shall only say to such, I pity their want of faith. *Ib.*

10 A traveler has a right to relate and embellish his adventures as he pleases, and it is very impolite to refuse that deference and applause they deserve. *Ib. 21*

Ethan Allen

1738–1789

11 [Captain Delaplace[5]] gazed at Allen in bewildered astonishment. "By whose authority do you act?" exclaimed he. "In the name of the great Jehovah, and the Continental Congress!" replied Allen.
From Washington Irving, *Life of Washington [1855–1859], vol. I, ch. 38*

[1]See Socrates, 79:7; Bacon, 180:13; Garrison, 505:10; and F. D. Roosevelt, 781:5.

[2]See Garrison, 505:12.

Extremism in the defense of liberty is no vice. And . . . moderation in the pursuit of justice is no virtue. — Barry Goldwater, *Acceptance speech, Republican presidential nomination* [July 16, 1964]

[3]See Napoleon, 420:9.

[4]See Plutarch, 120:16.

[5]Commandant at Fort Ticonderoga, New York [May 10, 1775].

Jacques Delille

1738–1813

12 Fate chooses our relatives, we choose our friends.[6]
Malheur et Pitié [1803], canto I

John Wolcot
[Peter Pindar]

1738–1819

13 What rage for fame attends both great and small!
Better be damned than mentioned not at all!
To the Royal Academicians [1782–1785]

Daniel Bliss

1740–1806

14 God wills us free, man wills us slaves,
I will as God wills, God's will be done.
Epitaph on gravestone of John Jack, "A Native of Africa, who died March 1773, aged about 60 years. Tho' born in a land of slavery he was born free."[7]

James Boswell[8]

1740–1795

15 That favorite subject, Myself.
Letter to Temple [July 26, 1763]

16 He who praises everybody, praises nobody.
Life of Johnson [1791], footnote [March 30, 1778]

17 We cannot tell the precise moment when friendship is formed. As in filling a vessel drop by drop, there is at last a drop which makes it run over; so in a series of kindnesses there is at last one which makes the heart run over. *Ib. [September 1777]*

[6]Le sort fait les parents, le choix fait les amis.

[7]See Rousseau, 358:12, and Schiller, 413:2.

[8]See also excerpts from Boswell, *Life of Johnson* [1791], 353:20–357:5.

1 I think no innocent species of wit or pleasantry should be suppressed; and that a good pun may be admitted among the smaller excellencies of lively conversation.

Ib. [June 1784]

Louis Sébastien Mercier

1740–1814

2 Extremes Meet.[1]

Tableaux de Paris [1782], vol. IV, ch. 348, title

Augustus Montague Toplady

1740–1778

3 Rock of Ages, cleft for me,
Let me hide myself in thee.

Rock of Ages [1775], st. 1

Sébastien Roch Nicolas Chamfort

1741–1794

4 The most wasted day of all is that on which we have not laughed.

Maxims and Thoughts, 1

5 Chance is a nickname for Providence.

Ib. 62

6 Be my brother, or I will kill you.[2]

From Carlyle, *French Revolution [1837], vol. II, pt. 1, ch. 12*

Johann Kaspar Lavater

1741–1801

7 Say not you know another entirely, till you have divided an inheritance with him.

Aphorisms on Man [c. 1788], no. 157

8 He who, when called upon to speak a disagreeable truth, tells it boldly and has done is both bolder and milder than he who nibbles in a low voice and never ceases nibbling.[3]

Ib. 302

9 Trust not him with your secrets, who, when left alone in your room, turns over your papers.

Ib. 449

10 The public seldom forgive twice.

Ib. 606

[1] "Extremes meet," as the whiting said with its tail in its mouth. — Thomas Hood [1799–1845], *The Doves and the Crows*

[2] Sois mon frère ou je te tue.
A paraphrase of the revolutionary watchword: Fraternity or death.

[3] Blake's marginal comment on this aphorism was "Damn such!"

11 Venerate four characters: the sanguine who has checked volatility and the rage for pleasure; the choleric who has subdued passion and pride; the phlegmatic emerged from indolence; and the melancholy who has dismissed avarice, suspicion and asperity.

Ib. 609

12 If you mean to know yourself, interline such of these aphorisms as affect you agreeably in reading, and set a mark to such as left a sense of uneasiness with you; and then show your copy to whom you please.

Ib. 643

Hester Lynch Thrale Piozzi [Mrs. Thrale]

1741–1821

13 Johnson's conversation was by much too strong for a person accustomed to obsequiousness and flattery; it was *mustard in a young child's mouth!*

From James Boswell, *Life of Johnson [1791]. May 1781*

Gebhard Leberecht von Blücher

1742–1819

14 Ever forward, but slowly.

While leading the Russians at Leipzig [October 19, 1813]

15 May the pens of the diplomats not ruin again what the people have attained with such exertions.

After the battle of Waterloo [1813]

Georg Christoph Lichtenberg

1742–1799

16 A knife without a blade, for which the handle is missing.

Göttingen Pocket Calendar [1798], describing an impossible existence

17 Nothing contributes more to peace of soul than having no opinion at all.

Aphorismen [1902–1908][4]

18 To do just the opposite is also a form of imitation. *Ib.*

19 I am always grieved when a man of real talent dies. The world needs such men more than Heaven does. *Ib.*

20 Soothsayers make a better living in the world than truthsayers. *Ib.*

[4] Edited by Albert Leitzmann.

1 It may not be natural for man to walk on two legs, but it was a noble invention.[1]

Ib.

2 The thing that astonished him was that cats should have two holes cut in their coat exactly at the place where their eyes are.

Ib.

Anna Letitia Barbauld
1743–1825

3 Say not "Good night"; but in some brighter
clime
Bid me "Good morning."

Ode to Life, st. 3

4 This dead of midnight is the noon of thought.

A Summer's Evening Meditation

Gavriil Romanovich Derzhavin
1743–1816

5 I am a czar—a slave, I am a worm—a god.

God [1784]

William Henry, Duke of Gloucester
1743–1805

6 Another damned, thick, square book! Always scribble, scribble, scribble! Eh! Mr. Gibbon?

Upon receiving from EDWARD GIBBON *volume II of the Decline and Fall of the Roman Empire [1781]. From Best's Literary Memorials*

Thomas Jefferson[2]
1743–1826

7 A lively and lasting sense of filial duty is more effectually impressed on the mind of a son or daughter by reading *King Lear,* than by all the dry volumes of ethics, and divinity, that ever were written.

Letter to Robert Skipwith [August 3, 1771]

8 The God who gave us life, gave us liberty at the same time.

Summary View of the Rights of British America [1774]

9 When, in the course of human events, it becomes necessary for one people to dissolve the political bands which have connected them with another, and to assume among the powers of the earth the separate and equal station to which the laws of nature and of nature's God[3] entitle them, a decent respect to the opinions of mankind requires that they should declare the causes which impel them to the separation. We hold these truths to be self-evident; that all men are created equal; that they are endowed by their creator with certain unalienable rights;[4] that among these are life, liberty, and the pursuit of happiness;[5] that to secure these rights, governments are instituted among men, deriving their just powers from the consent of the governed;[6] that whenever any form of government becomes destructive to these ends, it is the right of the people to alter or to abolish it, and to institute new government, laying its foundation on such principles, and organizing its powers in such form, as to them shall seem most likely to effect their safety and happiness.

Declaration of Independence [July 4, 1776]

10 We must therefore . . . hold them [the British] as we hold the rest of mankind, enemies in war, in peace friends. *Ib.*

11 And for the support of this declaration, with a firm reliance on the protection of divine providence, we mutually pledge to each other our lives, our fortunes, and our sacred honor. *Ib.*

12 Ignorance is preferable to error; and he is less remote from the truth who believes nothing, than he who believes what is wrong.

Notes on the State of Virginia [1781–1785]. Query 6

13 The Newtonian principle of gravitation is now more firmly established, on the basis of reason, than it would be were the government to step in, and to make it an article of necessary faith. Reason and experiment have been indulged, and error has fled before them. *Ib. 17*

14 Subject opinion to coercion: whom will you make your inquisitors? Fallible men; men governed by bad passions, by private as well as public reasons. *Ib. 17*

15 Is uniformity [of opinion] attainable? Millions of innocent men, women, and children,

[1] Se non è vero è ben trovato [If it is not true it is a happy invention].—*Attributed to* GIORDANO BRUNO

[2] His eye, like his mind, sought an extended view. — DUMAS MALONE, *Jefferson the Virginian* [1940]
See Morison, 382:*n*3.

[3] See Bolingbroke, 329:5, and Pope, 337:16.

[4] The phrase is frequently misquoted "inalienable."
All men are born free and equal, and have certain natural, essential and unalienable rights.—*Constitution of Massachusetts* [1778]

[5] See John Adams, 381:8, and Gibbon, 383:9.

[6] See Vico, 324:3, and John Adams, 381:2.

since the introduction of Christianity, have been burnt, tortured, fined, imprisoned; yet we have not advanced one inch towards uniformity. What has been the effect of coercion? To make one half the world fools, and the other half hypocrites. *Ib.*

1 Indeed, I tremble for my country when I reflect that God is just. *Ib. 18*

2 Those who labor in the earth are the chosen people of God, if ever he had a chosen people, whose breasts He has made His peculiar deposit for substantial and genuine virtue. *Ib. 19*

3 He who permits himself to tell a lie once, finds it much easier to do it a second and third time, till at length it becomes habitual; he tells lies without attending to it, and truths without the world's believing him. This falsehood of the tongue leads to that of the heart, and in time depraves all its good dispositions.

Letter to Peter Carr [August 19, 1785]

4 The basis of our government being the opinion of the people, the very first object should be to keep that right; and were it left to me to decide whether we should have a government without newspapers, or newspapers without a government, I should not hesitate a moment to prefer the latter.

Letter to Colonel Edward Carrington [January 16, 1787]

5 Experience declares that man is the only animal which devours his own kind; for I can apply no milder term to the governments of Europe, and to the general prey of the rich on the poor. *Ib.*

6 I hold it, that a little rebellion, now and then, is a good thing, and as necessary in the political world as storms in the physical.

Letter to James Madison [January 30, 1787]

7 What country before ever existed a century and a half without a rebellion? . . . The tree of liberty must be refreshed from time to time with the blood of patriots and tyrants.[1] It is its natural manure.

Letter to William Stevens Smith [November 13, 1787]

8 The republican is the only form of government which is not eternally at open or secret war with the rights of mankind.

Letter to William Hunter [March 11, 1790]

[1]See Tertullian, 126:3, and Barère, 401:4.

9 We are not to expect to be translated from despotism to liberty in a featherbed.

Letter to Lafayette [April 2, 1790]

10 Let what will be said or done, preserve your *sang-froid* immovably, and to every obstacle, oppose patience, perseverance, and soothing language.

Letter to William Short [March 18, 1792]

11 Delay is preferable to error.

Letter to George Washington [May 16, 1792]

12 We confide in our strength, without boasting of it; we respect that of others, without fearing it.

Letter to William Carmichael and William Short [1793]

13 The second office of the government is honorable and easy, the first is but a splendid misery.[2]

Letter to Elbridge Gerry [May 13, 1797]

14 Offices are as acceptable here as elsewhere, and whenever a man has cast a longing eye on them, a rottenness begins in his conduct.

Letter to Tench Coxe [May 21, 1799]

15 I have sworn upon the altar of God, eternal hostility against every form of tyranny over the mind of man.

Letter to Dr. Benjamin Rush [September 23, 1800]

16 We are all Republicans—we are all Federalists. If there be any among us who would wish to dissolve this Union or to change its republican form, let them stand undisturbed as monuments of the safety with which error of opinion may be tolerated where reason is left free to combat it.[3]

First Inaugural Address [March 4, 1801]

17 But would the honest patriot, in the full tide of successful experiment, abandon a government which has so far kept us free and firm, on the theoretic and visionary fear that this government, the world's best hope, may by possibility want energy to preserve itself? *Ib.*

18 Sometimes it is said that man cannot be trusted with the government of himself. Can he, then, be trusted with the government of others? Or have we found angels in the forms of kings to govern him? Let history answer this question. *Ib.*

[2]See John Adams, 381:16.

[3]See Milton, 282:5, and Holmes, 645:1.

1 Still one thing more, fellow citizens—a wise and frugal government, which shall restrain men from injuring one another, which shall leave them otherwise free to regulate their own pursuits of industry and improvement, and shall not take from the mouth of labor the bread it has earned. This is the sum of good government, and this is necessary to close the circle of our felicities. *Ib.*

2 Equal and exact justice to all men, of whatever state or persuasion, religious or political; peace, commerce, and honest friendship with all nations, entangling alliances with none. . . . Freedom of religion; freedom of the press, and freedom of person under the protection of the *habeas corpus,* and trial by juries impartially selected. These principles form the bright constellation which has gone before us, and guided our steps through an age of revolution and reformation. The wisdom of our sages and the blood of our heroes have been devoted to their attainment. They should be the creed of our political faith, the text of civil instruction, the touchstone by which we try the services of those we trust; and should we wander from them in moments of error or alarm, let us hasten to retrace our steps and to regain the road which alone leads to peace, liberty, and safety.

Ib.

3 Whensoever hostile aggressions . . . require a resort to war, we must meet our duty and convince the world that we are just friends and brave enemies.

Letter to Andrew Jackson [December 3, 1806]

4 The care of human life and happiness, and not their destruction, is the first and only legitimate object of good government.[1]

To the Republican Citizens of Washington County, Maryland [March 31, 1809]

5 Politics, like religion, hold up the torches of martyrdom to the reformers of error.

Letter to James Ogilvie [August 4, 1811]

6 But though an old man, I am but a young gardener.

Letter to Charles Wilson Peale [August 20, 1811]

7 The earth belongs to the living, not to the dead.

Letter to John W. Eppes [June 24, 1813]

[1]See George Mason, 367:5.

8 I agree with you that there is a natural aristocracy among men. The grounds of this are virtue and talents.

Letter to John Adams [October 28, 1813]

9 Merchants have no country. The mere spot they stand on does not constitute so strong an attachment as that from which they draw their gains.

Letter to Horatio G. Spafford [March 17, 1814]

10 I cannot live without books.

Letter to John Adams [June 10, 1815]

11 If a nation expects to be ignorant and free, in a state of civilization, it expects what never was and never will be.

Letter to Colonel Charles Yancey [January 6, 1816]

12 Enlighten the people generally, and tyranny and oppressions of body and mind will vanish like evil spirits at the dawn of day.

Letter to Du Pont de Nemours [April 24, 1816]

13 I have the consolation to reflect that during the period of my administration not a drop of the blood of a single fellow citizen was shed by the sword of war or of the law.

Letter to papal nuncio Count Dugnani [February 14, 1818]

14 But this momentous question [the Missouri Compromise], like a firebell in the night awakened and filled me with terror. I considered it the knell of the Union.

Letter to John Holmes [April 22, 1820]

15 I know no safe depository of the ultimate powers of the society but the people themselves; and if we think them not enlightened enough to exercise their control with a wholesome discretion, the remedy is not to take it from them, but to inform their discretion.

Letter to William Charles Jarvis [September 28, 1820]

16 We are not afraid to follow truth wherever it may lead, nor to tolerate any error so long as reason is left free to combat it.

Letter to William Roscoe [December 27, 1820]

17 That one hundred and fifty lawyers should do business together ought not to be expected.

Autobiography [January 6, 1821], on the United States Congress

1 And even should the cloud of barbarism and despotism again obscure the science and libraries of Europe, this country remains to preserve and restore light and liberty to them. In short, the flames kindled on the fourth of July, 1776, have spread over too much of the globe to be extinguished by the feeble engines of despotism; on the contrary, they will consume these engines and all who work them.

Letter to John Adams [September 12, 1821]

2 Men by their constitutions are naturally divided into two parties: (1) Those who fear and distrust the people, and wish to draw all powers from them into the hands of the higher classes. (2) Those who identify themselves with the people, have confidence in them, cherish and consider them as the most honest and safe, although not the most wise depository of the public interests. In every country these two parties exist; and in every one where they are free to think, speak, and write, they will declare themselves.

Letter to Henry Lee [August 10, 1824]

3 Never buy what you do not want, because it is cheap; it will be dear to you.

A Decalogue of Canons for Observation in Practical Life [February 21, 1825]

4 When angry, count ten before you speak; if very angry, an hundred.[1] *Ib.*

5 The good old Dominion, the blessed mother of us all. *Thoughts on Lotteries [1826]*

6 This is the Fourth?

Last words [July 4, 1826][2]

Antoine Laurent Lavoisier

1743–1794

7 It is impossible to dissociate language from science or science from language, because every natural science always involves three things: the sequence of phenomena on which the science is based; the abstract concepts which call these phenomena to mind; and the words in which the concepts are expressed. To call forth a concept a word is needed; to portray a phenomenon, a concept is needed. All three mirror one and the same reality.[3]

Traité Elémentaire de Chimie [1789]

8 If, by the term *elements,* we mean to express the simple and indivisible molecules that compose bodies, it is probable that we know nothing about them; but if, on the contrary, we express by the term *elements* or *principles of bodies* the idea of the last point reached by analysis, all substances that we have not yet been able to decompose by any means are elements to us.[4] *Ib.*

William Paley

1743–1805

9 Who can refute a sneer?

Moral Philosophy [1785], vol. II, bk. V, ch. 9

The Letters of Junius[5]

1769–1771

10 One precedent creates another. They soon accumulate and constitute law. What yesterday was fact, today is doctrine.

Dedication to the English Nation

11 The liberty of the press is the palladium of all the civil, political, and religious rights of an Englishman. *Ib.*

12 I believe there is yet a spirit of resistance in this country, which will not submit to be oppressed; but I am sure there is a fund of good sense in this country, which cannot be deceived.

No. 16, to the Printer of the Public Advertiser (H. S. Woodfall) [July 19, 1769]

13 We owe it to our ancestors to preserve entire those rights, which they have delivered to our care: we owe it to our posterity, not to suffer their dearest inheritance to be destroyed.

No. 20, to the Printer of the Public Advertiser [August 8, 1769]

14 When the constitution is openly invaded, when the first original right of the people, from which all laws derive their authority, is directly attacked, inferior grievances naturally lose their force, and are suffered to pass by without punishment or observation.

No. 30, to the Printer of the Public Advertiser [October 17, 1769]

[1] See Mark Twain, 624:20.

[2] John Adams died the same day. See his last words, 382:5.

[3] Translated by J. Lipetz, D. E. Gershenson, and D. A. Greenberg.

[4] Translated by D. McKie.

[5] Pseudonym of the author of a series of letters [1769–1771] in the London *Public Advertiser* (published in book form, 1772). They have been attributed to, among others, Sir Philip Francis, Lord Shelburne, Lord George Sackville, and Lord Temple.

1 There is a moment of difficulty and danger at which flattery and falsehood can no longer deceive, and simplicity itself can no longer be misled.

No. 35, [1] *to the Printer of the Public Advertiser [December 19, 1769]*

2 They [the Americans] equally detest the pageantry of a king, and the supercilious hypocrisy of a bishop.[2] *Ib.*

3 There is a holy mistaken zeal in politics as well as in religion. By persuading others, we convince ourselves. *Ib.*

4 The least considerable man among us has an interest equal to the proudest nobleman, in the laws and constitution of his country, and is equally called upon to make a generous contribution in support of them— whether it be the heart to conceive, the understanding to direct, or the hand to execute.[3]

No. 37, to the Printer of the Public Advertiser [March 19, 1770]

5 We lament the mistakes of a good man, and do not begin to detest him until he affects to renounce his principles.

No. 41, to Lord Mansfield [November 14, 1770]

6 The injustice done to an individual is sometimes of service to the public. Facts are apt to alarm us more than the most dangerous principles. *Ib.*

7 An honest man, like the true religion, appeals to the understanding, or modestly confides in the internal evidence of his conscience. The impostor employs force instead of argument, imposes silence where he cannot convince, and propagates his character by the sword. *Ib.*

8 If individuals have no virtues, their vices may be of use to us.

No. 59, to the Printer of the Public Advertiser [October 5, 1771]

9 The temple of fame is the shortest passage to riches and preferment. *Ib.*

[1]This letter is of great significance in the history of freedom of the press. The publisher was prosecuted for seditious libel, and the jury brought in a verdict of "guilty of printing and publishing only." After a second trial, Woodfall was freed on payment of costs.

[2]See Rufus Choate, 484:20.

[3]See Hyde, 289:16.

Constitution of the United States

1787

10 We the people of the United States, in order to form a more perfect Union, establish justice, insure domestic tranquillity, provide for the common defense, promote the general welfare, and secure the blessings of liberty to ourselves and our posterity, do ordain and establish this Constitution for the United States of America. *Preamble*

11 The President, Vice-President, and all civil officers of the United States, shall be removed from office on impeachment for, and conviction of, treason, bribery, or other high crimes and misdemeanors. *Article II, sec. 4*

12 Treason against the United States, shall consist only in levying war against them, or in adhering to their enemies, giving them aid and comfort. No person shall be convicted of treason unless on the testimony of two witnesses to the same overt act, or on confession in open court. *Article III, sec. 3*

13 This Constitution, and the laws of the United States, which shall be made in pursuance thereof; and all treaties made, or which shall be made, under the authority of the United States, shall be the Supreme Law of the land; and the judges in every State shall be bound thereby, any thing in the Constitution or laws of any State to the contrary notwithstanding. *Article VI, sec. 2*

14 Congress shall make no law respecting an establishment of religion, or prohibiting the free exercise thereof; or abridging the freedom of speech, or of the press; or the right of the people peaceably to assemble, and to petition the government for a redress of grievances. *First Amendment [1791]*[4]

15 A well-regulated militia, being necessary to the security of a free State, the right of the people to keep and bear arms, shall not be infringed. *Second Amendment [1791]*

16 The right of the people to be secure . . . against unreasonable searches and seizures, shall not be violated, and no warrants shall issue, but upon probable cause.

Fourth Amendment [1791]

17 Nor shall any person be subject for the same offense to be twice put in jeopardy of life or limb; nor shall be compelled in any criminal case to be a witness against himself, nor be deprived of life, liberty, or property, without due process of law.

Fifth Amendment [1791]

[4]The first ten amendments are known as the Bill of Rights.

1 In all criminal prosecutions, the accused shall enjoy the right to a speedy and public trial, by an impartial jury of the State and district wherein the crime shall have been committed. *Sixth Amendment [1791]*

2 The right to trial by jury shall be preserved. *Seventh Amendment [1791]*

3 Excessive bail shall not be required, nor excessive fines imposed, nor cruel and unusual punishment inflicted.
Eighth Amendment [1791]

4 All persons born or naturalized in the United States, and subject to the jurisdiction thereof, are citizens of the United States and of the State wherein they reside. No State shall . . . abridge the privileges or immunities of citizens of the United States; nor shall any State deprive any person of life, liberty, or property, without due process of law; nor deny to any person within its jurisdiction the equal protection of the laws.
Fourteenth Amendment [1868], sec. 1

5 The right of citizens of the United States to vote shall not be denied or abridged . . . on account of race, color, or previous condition of servitude.
Fifteenth Amendment [1870], sec. 1

6 The right of citizens of the United States to vote shall not be abridged . . . on account of sex.
Nineteenth Amendment [1920], sec. 1

Abigail Adams[1]
1744–1818

7 In the new code of laws which I suppose it will be necessary for you to make I desire you would remember the ladies, and be more generous and favorable to them than your ancestors. Do not put such unlimited power into the hands of the husbands. Remember all men would be tyrants if they could. If particular care and attention is not paid to the ladies we are determined to foment a rebellion, and will not hold ourselves bound by any laws in which we have no voice, or representation.
Letter to John Adams [March 31, 1776]

8 Shall we not be despised by foreign powers for hesitating so long at a word?
Ib. [May 7, 1776]

[1] Had she lived to the age of the Patriarchs . . . every day of her life would have been filled with clouds of goodness and love.—JOHN QUINCY ADAMS, *Memoirs, vol. IV, 157–158, 202*

9 Whilst you are proclaiming peace and good will to men, emancipating all nations, you insist upon retaining an absolute power over wives. But you must remember that arbitrary power is like most other things which are very hard, very liable to be broken—and notwithstanding all your wise laws and maxims we have it in our power not only to free ourselves but to subdue our masters, and without violence throw both your natural and legal authority at our feet. *Ib.*

10 Deliver me from your cold phlegmatic preachers, politicians, friends, lovers and husbands. *Ib. [August 5, 1776]*

11 If we mean to have heroes, statesmen and philosophers, we should have learned women. . . . If much depends as is allowed upon the early education of youth and the first principles which are instilled take the deepest root, great benefit must arise from literary accomplishments in women.
Ib. [August 14, 1776]

12 It is really mortifying, sir, when a woman possessed of a common share of understanding considers the difference of education between the male and female sex, even in those families where education is attended to . . . Nay why should your sex wish for such a disparity in those whom they one day intend for companions and associates. Pardon me, sir, if I cannot help sometimes suspecting that this neglect arises in some measure from an ungenerous jealousy of rivals near the throne.[2]
Letter to John Thaxter [February 15, 1778]

13 I regret the trifling narrow contracted education of the females of my own country.
Letter to John Adams [June 30, 1778]

14 If we do not lay out ourselves in the service of mankind whom should we serve?
Letter to John Thaxter [September 29, 1778]

15 Luxury, that baneful poison, has unstrung and enfeebled her sons.
Letter to John Adams [February 13, 1779]

16 These are times in which a genius would wish to live. It is not in the still calm of life, or in the repose of a pacific station, that great challenges are formed. . . . Great necessities call out great virtues.
Letter to John Quincy Adams [January 19, 1780]

[2] See Sand, 504:9.

1 A little of what you call frippery is very necessary towards looking like the rest of the world.

Letter to John Adams [May 1, 1780]

2 Learning is not attained by chance, it must be sought for with ardor and attended to with diligence.

Letter to John Quincy Adams [May 8, 1780]

3 Patriotism in the female sex is the most disinterested of all virtues. Excluded from honors and from offices, we cannot attach ourselves to the State or Government from having held a place of eminence. Even in the freest countries our property is subject to the control and disposal of our partners, to whom the laws have given a sovereign authority. Deprived of a voice in legislation, obliged to submit to those laws which are imposed upon us, is it not sufficient to make us indifferent to the public welfare? Yet all history and every age exhibit instances of patriotic virtue in the female sex; which considering our situation equals the most heroic of yours.

Letter to John Adams [June 17, 1782]

Johann Gottfried von Herder

1744–1803

4 A gain it is to find a beautiful human soul.

Der Gerettete Jungling [1797]

5 Light, love, life.

Herder's Epitaph [1803]

Rowland Hill

1744–1833

6 He did not see any reason why the devil should have all the good tunes.

Sermons. From E. W. BROOME, The Reverend Rowland Hill, p. 93

Jean Baptiste Lamarck

1744–1829

7 FIRST LAW. In every animal . . . a more frequent and continuous use of any organ gradually strengthens, develops and enlarges that organ . . . while the permanent disuse of any organ imperceptibly weakens and deteriorates it, and progressively diminishes its functional capacity, until it finally disappears.

SECOND LAW. All the acquisitions or losses wrought by nature in individuals . . . are preserved by reproduction to the new individuals which arise.

Philosophie Zoologique [1809],[1] *pt. II, ch. 7*

8 Habits form a second nature.[2] *Ib.*

Josiah Quincy

1744–1775

9 Blandishments will not fascinate us, nor will threats of a "halter" intimidate. For, under God, we are determined that wheresoever, whensoever, or howsoever we shall be called to make our exit, we will die free men.

Observations on the Boston Port Bill [1774]

Charles Dibdin

1745–1814

10 Did you ever hear of Captain Wattle?
He was all for love, and a little for the bottle.

Captain Wattle and Miss Roe

11 Here, a sheer hulk, lies poor Tom Bowling,
The darling of our crew;
No more he'll hear the tempest howling,
For death has broached him to.

Tom Bowling

Sir Henry Bate Dudley

1745–1824

12 Wonders will never cease.

Letter to Garrick [September 13, 1776]

Hannah More

1745–1833

13 Since trifles make the sum of human things,
And half our misery from our foibles springs.

Sensibility

14 Small habits well pursued betimes
May reach the dignity of crimes.

Florio and His Friend

William Scott, Lord Stowell

1745–1836

15 A dinner lubricates business.

From BOSWELL, Life of Johnson [1791]

[1] Translated by HUGH ELLIOT.

[2] Habit is a second nature and it destroys the first. — PASCAL, *Pensées* [1670], *no. 376*

1 The elegant simplicity of the three per cents.

From CAMPBELL, *Lives of the Lord Chancellors [1857], vol. X, ch. 212*

Francisco José de Goya y Lucientes

1746–1828

2 The sleep of reason produces monsters [El sueño de la razón produce monstruos].

Los Caprichos [1799]. Plate 43 [1]

Sir William Jones

1746–1794

3 On parent knees, a naked newborn child,
Weeping thou sat'st while all around thee smiled;
So live, that sinking in thy last long sleep,
Calm thou mayst smile, while all around thee weep.

From the Persian [1786]

John Paul Jones

1747–1792

4 I have not yet begun to fight.

Aboard the Bonhomme Richard [2] *[September 23, 1779]*

François Alexandre Frédéric, Duc de La Rochefoucauld-Liancourt

1747–1827

5 *Louis XVI:* Is it a revolt?
La Rochefoucauld-Liancourt: No, Sire, it is a revolution.

Upon learning at Versailles of the fall of the Bastille [1789]

John O'Keeffe

1747–1833

6 Amo, amas,
I love a lass,
As a cedar tall and slender;
Sweet cowslip's grace
Is her nominative case,
And she's of the feminine gender!

The Agreeable Surprise [1783], act II, sc. ii, Song

7 You should always except the present company.

The London Hermit; or, Rambles in Dorsetshire [1793]

8 Fat, fair and forty [3] were all the toasts of the young men.

The Irish Mimic; or, Blunders at Brighton [1795]

Emmanuel Joseph Sieyès

1748–1836

9 I survived [J'ai vécu].

Upon being asked what he had done during the Terror

Charles James Fox

1749–1806

10 [On the fall of the Bastille] How much the greatest event it is that ever happened in the world! and how much the best!

Letter to Richard Fitzpatrick [July 30, 1789]. From LORD JOHN RUSSELL, *Life and Times of C. J. Fox [1859–1866], vol. II, p. 361*

Johann Wolfgang von Goethe

1749–1832

11 There is strong shadow where there is much light.

Götz von Berlichingen [1773], act I

12 One lives but once in the world.

Clavigo [1774], act I, sc. i.

13 If you inquire what the people are like here,
I must answer, "The same as everywhere!"

Die Leiden des Jungen Werthers [1774–1787]. May 17

14 Radiant misery. *Ib. December 24*

15 Getting along with women,
Knocking around with men,
Having more credit than money,
Thus one goes through the world.

Claudine von Villa Bella [1776]

16 Noble be man,
Helpful and good!
For that alone

[1] Translated by HILDA HARRIS.
In plate 43 the artist rests, his head in his arms, on a desk inscribed with the Spanish line. Behind him hover monstrous owls, bats, and a great cat. Goya's text for the plate:
Imagination abandoned by Reason produces impossible monsters: united with her, she is the mother of the arts and the source of their wonders.

[2] Engaged with the British frigate *Serapis* off Flamborough Head, England.

[3] I am resolved to grow fat, and look young till forty! — DRYDEN, *Secret Love; or, The Maiden Queen* [1667], *act III, sc. i*

Sets him apart
From every other creature
On earth.

Das Göttliche (The Divine) [1783]

1 I sing as the bird sings
That lives in the boughs.[1]

Wilhelm Meisters Lehrjahre (Apprenticeship) [1786–1830], bk. II, ch. 11

2 Who ne'er his bread in sorrow ate,
Who ne'er the mournful midnight hours
Weeping upon his bed has sate,
He knows you not, ye Heavenly Powers.[2]

Ib. 13

3 Knowst thou the land where the lemon trees bloom,[3]
Where the gold orange glows in the deep thicket's gloom,
Where a wind ever soft from the blue heaven blows,
And the groves are of laurel and myrtle and rose?[4] *Ib. III, 1*

4 If I love you, what business is it of yours? *Ib. IV, 9*

5 One ought, every day at least, to hear a little song, read a good poem, see a fine picture, and, if it were possible, to speak a few reasonable words.[5] *Ib. V, 1*

6 To know of someone here and there whom we accord with, who is living on with us, even in silence—this makes our earthly ball a peopled garden. *Ib. VII, 5*

7 Art is long, life short;[6] judgment difficult, opportunity transient. *Ib. 9*

8 Seeking with the soul the land of the Greeks.

Iphigenie auf Tauris [1787], act I, sc. i

9 A useless life is an early death. *Ib. ii*

10 One says a lot in vain, refusing;
The other mainly hears the "No."

Ib. iii

11 Pleasure and love are the pinions of great deeds. *Ib. II, i*

[1] Ich singe, wie der Vogel singt / Der in den Zweigen wohnet.

See Tennyson, 532:1.

[2] Wer nie sein Brod mit Tränen ass, / Wer nie die kummervollen Nächte / Auf seinem Bette weinend sass, / Der kennt euch nicht, ihr himmlischen Mächte.

Translated by LONGFELLOW as motto for book I of *Hyperion* [1839].

[3] Kennst du das Land, wo die Zitronen blühn?

[4] See Byron, 459:5.

[5] See Charles Eliot Norton, 598:14.

[6] See Hippocrates, 80:9; Chaucer, 144:8; and Longfellow, 509:14.

12 Life teaches us to be less harsh with ourselves and with others. *Ib. IV, iv*

13 In art the best is good enough.[7]

Italian Journey. March 3, 1787

14 A noble person attracts noble people, and knows how to hold on to them.

Torquato Tasso [1790], act I, sc. i

15 A talent is formed in stillness, a character in the world's torrent. *Ib. ii*

16 We can't form our children on our own concepts; we must take them and love them as God gives them to us.[8]

Hermann und Dorothea [1797]

17 The spirits that I summoned up
I now can't rid myself of.

Der Zauberlehrling (The Sorcerer's Apprentice) [1797]

18 Three things are to be looked to in a building: that it stand on the right spot; that it be securely founded; that it be successfully executed.

Elective Affinities[9] *[1808], bk. I, ch. 9*

19 The sum which two married people owe to one another defies calculation. It is an infinite debt, which can only be discharged through all eternity. *Ib.*

20 One is never satisfied with a portrait of a person that one knows. *Ib. II, 2*

21 Time does not relinquish its rights, either over human beings or over monuments. *Ib.*

22 The fate of the architect is the strangest of all. How often he expends his whole soul, his whole heart and passion, to produce buildings into which he himself may never enter. *Ib. 3*

23 Let us live in as small a circle as we will, we are either debtors or creditors before we have had time to look round. *Ib. 4*

24 No one would talk much in society, if he knew how often he misunderstands others. *Ib.*

25 A teacher who can arouse a feeling for one single good action, for one single good poem, accomplishes more than he who fills our memory with rows on rows of natural objects, classified with name and form. *Ib. 7*

[7] In der Kunst ist das Beste gut genug.

[8] See Gibran, 782:15.

[9] Translated by JAMES ANTHONY FROUDE.

1 One never goes so far as when one doesn't know where one is going.

Letter to Karl Friedrich Zelter [December 3, 1812]

2 Who wants to understand the poem
Must go to the land of poetry;
Who wishes to understand the poet
Must go to the poet's land.

West-östlicher Diwan [1819], motto

3 For I have been a man, and that means to have been a fighter.

Ib. Buch des Paradies

4 One must *be* something to be able to *do* something.

Conversation with Eckermann [October 20, 1828]

5 If I work incessantly to the last, nature owes me another form of existence when the present one collapses.

Letter to Eckermann [February 4, 1829]

6 I call architecture frozen music.[1]

Ib. [March 23, 1829]

7 The artist may be well advised to keep his work to himself till it is completed, because no one can readily help him or advise him with it . . . but the scientist is wiser not to withhold a single finding or a single conjecture from publicity.

Essay on Experimentation

8 Age does not make us childish, as they say.
It only finds us true children still.

Faust [1808–1832]. The First Part. Prelude on the Stage

9 Man errs as long as he strives.[2]

Ib. Prologue in Heaven

10 And here, poor fool! with all my lore
I stand! no wiser than before.[3]

Ib. Night, Faust in His Study

11 Am I a god? I see so clearly! *Ib.*

12 Two souls alas! dwell in my breast.

Ib. Outside the Gate of the Town

13 I am the Spirit that always denies![4]

Ib. Faust's Study

[1] Ich die Baukunst eine erstarrte Musik nenne.
Since it [architecture] is music in space, as it were a frozen music.—FRIEDRICH VON SCHELLING [1775–1854], *Philosophie der Kunst, p. 576*
See Madame de Staël, 417:14.

[2] Es irrt der Mensch, so lang er strebt.

[3] Da stehe ich nun, ich armer Thor! / Und bin so klug als wie zuvor.
Translated by BAYARD TAYLOR.

[4] Ich bin der Geist der stets verneint.

14 Dear friend, all theory is gray,
And green the golden tree of life.

Ib. Mephistopheles and the Student

15 Just trust yourself, then you will know how to live. *Ib.*

16 A true German can't stand the French,
Yet willingly he drinks their wines.

Ib. Auerbach's Cellar

17 He who maintains he's right—if his the gift of tongues—
Will have the last word certainly.[5]

Ib. Faust and Gretchen. A Street

18 My peace is gone,
My heart is heavy.[6]

Ib. Gretchen's Room

19 Fair I was also, and that was my ruin.[7]

Ib. A Prison

20 Law is mighty, mightier necessity.

Ib. The Second Part, act I, A Spacious Hall

21 Once a man's thirty, he's already old,
He is indeed as good as dead.
It's best to kill him right away.

Ib. II, The Gothic Chamber

22 What wise or stupid thing can man conceive
That was not thought of in ages long ago?[8]

Ib.

23 I love those who yearn for the impossible.

Ib. Classical Walpurgis Night

24 The deed is everything, the glory nothing.

Ib. IV, A High Mountain Range

25 Of freedom and of life he only is deserving
Who every day must conquer them anew.[9]

Ib. V, Court of the Palace

26 Who strives always to the utmost,
For him there is salvation.[10]

Ib. Mountain Gorges

27 The Eternal Feminine draws us on.[11]

Ib. Heaven, last line

28 Do you wish to roam farther and farther?
See! The Good lies so near.
Only learn to seize good fortune,
For good fortune's always here.

Erinnerung

[5] Translated by GEORGE MADISON PRIEST.

[6] Meine Ruh' ist hin, / Mein Herz ist schwer.

[7] Schön war ich auch, und das war mein Verderben.

[8] See Cicero, 98:22, and Descartes, 272:9.

[9] Nur der verdient sich Freiheit wie das Leben der täglich sie erobern muss.

[10] Wer immer strebend sich bemüht, / Den können wir erlösen.

[11] Das Ewig-Weibliche zieht uns hinan.

1 In limitations he first shows himself the master,
And the law can only bring us freedom.
Was Wir Bringen [1802]

2 Create, artist! Do not talk! *Saying*

3 O'er all the hilltops
Is quiet now,
In all the treetops
Hearest thou
Hardly a breath;
The birds are asleep in the trees:
Wait; soon like these
Thou too shalt rest.[1]
Wandrers Nachtlied (Wanderer's Nightsong)

4 Individuality of expression is the beginning and end of all art.
Sprüche in Prosa (Proverbs in Prose)

5 Nothing is more damaging to a new truth than an old error. *Ib.*

6 Doubt grows with knowledge. *Ib.*

7 The greatest happiness for the thinking man is to have fathomed the fathomable, and to quietly revere the unfathomable.
Ib.

8 First and last, what is demanded of genius is love of truth. *Ib.*

9 A man's manners are a mirror in which he shows his portrait.[2] *Ib.*

10 All intelligent thoughts have already been thought; what is necessary is only to try to think them again.[3] *Ib.*

11 Nothing is more terrible than ignorance in action.[3] *Ib.*

12 Of all peoples the Greeks have dreamt the dream of life best.[4] *Ib.*

13 Everything that emancipates the spirit without giving us control over ourselves is harmful. *Ib.*

14 America, you have it better than our continent, the old one.[5]
Wendts Musen-Almanach [1831]

15 Without haste, but without rest. *Motto*

16 More light![6] *Last words*

[1] Translated by LONGFELLOW.
[2] See William of Wykeham, 143:13.
[3] Translated by NORBERT GUTERMAN.
[4] Translated by BAILEY SAUNDERS.
[5] Amerika, du hast es besser — als unser Kontinent, das alte.
[6] Someday perhaps the inner light will shine forth from us, and then we shall need no other light. — GOETHE, *Elective Affinities* [1808], *pt. II, ch. 3*

Pierre Simon de Laplace

1749–1827

17 Given for one instant an intelligence which could comprehend all the forces by which nature is animated and the respective positions of the beings which compose it, if moreover this intelligence were vast enough to submit these data to analysis, it would embrace in the same formula both the movements of the largest bodies in the universe and those of the lightest atom; to it nothing would be uncertain, and the future as the past would be present to its eyes.
Oeuvres, vol. VII, Théorie Analytique des Probabilités [1812–1820], introduction

18 The theory of probabilities is at bottom nothing but common sense reduced to calculus. *Ib.*

19 Sire, I have no need of that hypothesis.[7]
From ERIC TEMPLE BELL, *Men of Mathematics [1937]*

Honoré Gabriel Riquetti, Comte de Mirabeau

1749–1791

20 Go and tell those who have sent you that we are here by the will of the nation and that we shall not leave save at the point of bayonets.
Speech in the States-General [June 23, 1789]

John Philpot Curran

1750–1817

21 The condition upon which God hath given liberty to man is eternal vigilance;[8] which condition if he break, servitude is at once the consequence of his crime and the punishment of his guilt.
Speech upon the Right of Election of the Lord Mayor of Dublin [July 10, 1790]

[7] Reply to Napoleon Bonaparte's remark upon receiving a copy of Laplace's *Mécanique Céleste:* You have written this huge book on the system of the world without once mentioning the author of the universe.
[8] Attributed also to JEFFERSON.
Commonly quoted: Eternal vigilance is the price of liberty.
There is one safeguard known generally to the wise, which is an advantage and security to all, but especially to democracies as against despots. What is it? Distrust. — DEMOSTHENES [c. 384–322 B.C.], *Philippic 2, sec. 24*

James Madison
1751–1836

1 By a faction, understand a number of citizens, whether amounting to a majority or minority of the whole, who are united and actuated by some common impulse of passion, or of interest, adverse to the rights of other citizens, or to the permanent and aggregate interests of the community.
The Federalist [1787], no. 10

2 A zeal for different opinions concerning religion, concerning government, and many other points, as well of speculation as of practice; an attachment of different leaders ambitiously contending for pre-eminence and power; or to persons of other descriptions whose fortunes have been interesting to the human passions, have, in turn, divided mankind into parties, inflamed them with mutual animosity, and rendered them much more disposed to vex and oppress each other than to cooperate for their common good. . . . But the most common and durable source of factions has been the various and unequal distribution of property. *Ib.*

3 To secure the public good, and private rights, against the danger of . . . faction, and at the same time to preserve the spirit and form of popular government, is then the great object to which our inquiries are directed. *Ib.*

4 I believe there are more instances of the abridgment of the freedom of the people by gradual and silent encroachments of those in power than by violent and sudden usurpations.
Speech in the Virginia Convention [June 16, 1788]

Richard Brinsley Sheridan
1751–1816

5 *Mrs. Malaprop:* Illiterate him, I say, quite from your memory.
The Rivals [1775], act I, sc. ii

6 'Tis safest in matrimony to begin with a little aversion. *Ib.*

7 A progeny of learning. *Ib.*

8 Never say more than is necessary.
Ib. II, i

9 I know you are laughing in your sleeve.
Ib.

10 He is the very pineapple of politeness!
Ib. III, iii

11 If I reprehend anything in this world, it is the use of my oracular tongue, and a nice derangement of epitaphs! *Ib.*

12 As headstrong as an allegory on the banks of the Nile. *Ib.*

13 Too civil by half. *Ib. iv*

14 Our ancestors are very good kind of folks; but they are the last people I should choose to have a visiting acquaintance with.
Ib. IV, i

15 No caparisons, miss, if you please. Caparisons don't become a young woman.
Ib. ii

16 You are not like Cerberus, three gentlemen at once, are you? *Ib.*

17 The quarrel is a very pretty quarrel as it stands; we should only spoil it by trying to explain it. *Ib. iii*

18 My valor is certainly going!—it is sneaking off! I feel it oozing out, as it were, at the palm of my hands! *Ib. V, iii*

19 I own the soft impeachment. *Ib.*

20 Through all the drama—whether damned or not—
Love gilds the scene, and women guide the plot. *Ib. Epilogue*

21 An apothecary should never be out of spirits. *St. Patrick's Day [1775], act I, sc. i*

22 Death's a debt; his mandamus binds all alike—no bail, no demurrer. *Ib. II, iv*

23 I ne'er could any luster see
In eyes that would not look on me.
The Duenna [1775], act I, sc. ii

24 I loved him for himself alone. *Ib. iii*

25 I was struck all of a heap. *Ib. II, ii*

26 A bumper of good liquor
Will end a contest quicker
Than justice, judge, or vicar.[1] *Ib. iii*

27 Conscience has no more to do with gallantry than it has with politics. *Ib. iv*

28 Tale-bearers are as bad as the tale-makers.
The School for Scandal [1777], act I, sc. i

29 You shall see them on a beautiful quarto page, where a neat rivulet of text shall meander through a meadow of margin. *Ib.*

30 You had no taste when you married me.
Ib. ii

[1] The government of a nation is often decided over a cup of coffee, or the fate of empires changed by an extra bottle of Johannisberg.—G.P.R. JAMES, *Richelieu* [1829], *ch. 16*

1 Here's to the maiden of bashful fifteen;
Here's to the widow of fifty;
Here's to the flaunting, extravagant quean,
And here's to the housewife that's thrifty.
Let the toast pass—
Drink to the lass;
I'll warrant she'll prove an excuse for the glass.
Ib. III, iii

2 An unforgiving eye, and a damned disinheriting countenance. *Ib. IV, i*

3 Be just before you're generous. *Ib.*

4 There is not a passion so strongly rooted in the human heart as envy.
The Critic [1779], act I, sc. i

5 The newspapers! Sir, they are the most villainous — licentious — abominable — infernal—Not that I ever read them—no—I make it a rule never to look into a newspaper. *Ib.*

6 Egad, I think the interpreter is the hardest to be understood of the two! *Ib. ii*

7 A practitioner in panegyric, or, to speak more plainly, a professor of the art of puffing. *Ib.*

8 The number of those who undergo the fatigue of judging for themselves is very small indeed.[1] *Ib.*

9 Certainly nothing is unnatural that is not physically impossible. *Ib. II, i*

10 I wish, sir, you would practice this without me. I can't stay dying here all night.
Ib. III, i

11 You write with ease to show your breeding,
But easy writing's curst hard reading.
Clio's Protest [1819]

12 An oyster may be crossed in love.[2]
Ib.

13 The right honorable gentleman is indebted to his memory for his jests, and to his imagination for his facts.[3]
Sheridaniana. Speech in Reply to Mr. Dundas

Johann Heinrich Voss

1751–1826

14 Who does not love wine, women, and song
Remains a fool his whole life long.[4]
Attributed

[1] See J. R. Lowell, 569:7, and Bryce, 635:25.

[2] From the interpolated tragedy, *The Spanish Armada.*

[3] See Lesage, 323:26.

[4] Wer nicht liebt Wein, Weib und Gesang, / Der bleibt ein Narr sein Leben lang.

The couplet has also been attributed to Luther, apparently on no better authority than an eighteenth-century jingle in which "Luther" is needed to rhyme with "Futter." Redlich ascribes it to Voss in *Die Poetischen Beiträge zum Waudsbecker Bothen* [1871]

Thomas Chatterton[5]

1752–1770

15 Mie love ys dedde,
Gon to hys death-bedde,
Al under the wyllowe-tree.
Mynstrelles Songe[6]

Philip Freneau

1752–1832

16 An age employed in edging steel
Can no poetic raptures feel . . .
No shaded stream, no quiet grove
Can this fantastic century move.
Poems [1795]. To an Author, st. 6

17 Then rushed to meet the insulting foe;
They took the spear—but left the shield.[7]
To the Memory of the Brave Americans Who Fell at Eutaw Springs, S.C., September 8, 1781 [1786], st. 5

18 O come the time, and haste the day,
When man shall man no longer crush,
When Reason shall enforce her sway,
Nor these fair regions raise our blush,
Where still the African complains,
And mourns his yet unbroken chains.
On the Emigration to America and Peopling the Western Country [1786]

Friedrich Maximilian von Klinger

1752–1831

19 Sturm und Drang [Storm and Stress].
Title of play [1776]

Leonard MacNally

1752–1820

20 On Richmond Hill there lives a lass
More bright than Mayday morn;
Whose charms all other maids' surpass—
A rose without a thorn.
The Lass of Richmond Hill,[8] *st. 1*

[5] See Wordsworth, 425:10.

[6] This is from the poems of "Thomas Rowley," an imaginary fifteenth-century Bristol poet invented by Chatterton. Editions of the poems appeared in 1778 and 1782, and were exposed [1777–1778] by Thomas Tyrwhitt.

[7] When Prussia hurried to the field, / And snatched the spear, but left the shield.—SCOTT, *Marmion* [1808], *canto III, introduction*

[8] Also attributed to JAMES UPTON [1670–1749] and W. HUDSON.

Miguel Hidalgo y Costilla
1753–1811

1 Hail Our Lady of Guadalupe! Long live Independence! (Viva Nuestra Señora de Guadalupe! Viva la Independencia!)
The Cry of Dolores (El Grito de Dolores) [September 16, 1810], launching the Mexican War of Independence from Spain

Joseph de Maistre
1753–1821

2 Every nation has the government it deserves. *Letter to X [1811]*

3 The sword of justice has no scabbard.
Les Soirées de Saint-Petersbourg [1821]. Premier Entretien

Antoine de Rivarol
1753–1801

4 What is not clear is not French.
Discours sur l'Universalité de la Langue Française [1784]

Joel Barlow
1754–1812

5 My morning incense, and my evening meal—
The sweets of Hasty Pudding.
The Hasty Pudding [1792], canto I

George Crabbe[1]
1754–1832

6 Habit with him was all the test of truth,
"It must be right: I've done it from my youth."
The Borough [1810]. Letter 3, The Vicar

7 In idle wishes fools supinely stay;
Be there a will, and wisdom finds a way.
The Birth of Flattery [1807]

8 Cut and come again.
Tales [1812]. VII, The Widow's Tale

9 The ring, so worn as you behold,
So thin, so pale, is yet of gold.
His Mother's Wedding Ring

[1]See Byron, 456:18.

William Drennan
1754–1820

10 Nor one feeling of vengeance presume to defile
The cause, or the men, of the Emerald Isle.[2]
Erin [1795], st. 3

Joseph Joubert
1754–1824

11 I had to grow old to learn what I wanted to know, and I should need to be young to say well what I know. *Pensées [1842]*

12 Ask the young: they know everything! *Ib.*

13 To teach is to learn twice. *Ib.*

Jeanne Manon Roland
1754–1793

14 O liberty! O liberty! What crimes are committed in thy name!
Last words, before her death on the guillotine. From LAMARTINE, *Histoire des Girondins [1847]*

Charles Maurice de Talleyrand-Périgord
1754–1838

15 Black as the devil,
Hot as hell,
Pure as an angel,
Sweet as love.[3] *Recipe for coffee*

16 [Of the Bourbons] They have learned nothing, and forgotten nothing.[4]
From CHEVALIER DE PANAT, *letter to Mallet du Pan [January 1796]*

17 [Of the battle of Borodino, 1812] It is the beginning of the end.[5]
From EDOUARD FOURNIER, *L'Esprit dans l'Histoire [1857]*

18 The United States has thirty-two religions but only one dish. *Attributed*

19 Women sometimes forgive a man who forces the opportunity, but never a man who misses one. *Attributed*

[2]The first known use of this appellation for Ireland.
[3]Noir comme le diable, / Chaud comme l'enfer, / Pur comme un ange, / Doux comme l'amour.
This appears as an inscription on many old coffeepots.
[4]Ils n'ont rien appris, ni rien oublié.
[5]Voilà le commencement de la fin.
See Churchill, 746:1.

1 [To a young diplomat] Don't be eager![1]
From CHARLES AUGUSTIN SAINT-BEUVE, *Portraits de Femmes [1858]. Madame de Staël*

2 War is much too serious a matter to be entrusted to the military.[2]
Attributed. Quoted by Briand to Lloyd George during World War I. Also attributed to Clemenceau

Benjamin Waterhouse

1754–1846

3 Tobacco is a filthy weed,
That from the devil does proceed;
It drains your purse, it burns your clothes,
And makes a chimney of your nose.
From OLIVER WENDELL HOLMES *[1809–1894], who was vaccinated by Dr. Waterhouse*

Bertrand Barère de Vieuzac

1755–1841

4 The tree of liberty only grows when watered by the blood of tyrants.[3]
Speech in the National Convention [January 16, 1793]

5 It is only the dead who do not return.
Speech [1794]

Anthelme Brillat-Savarin

1755–1826

6 Tell me what you eat, and I will tell you what you are.[4]
Physiologie du Goût [1825], ch. 4

7 A dessert without cheese is like a beautiful woman with only one eye. *Ib. 14*

8 A meal without wine is like a day without sunshine. *Ib.*

Nathan Hale

1755–1776

9 I only regret that I have but one life to lose for my country.[5]
Last words, before being hanged by the British as a spy [September 22, 1776]

[1] Pas de zèle!

[2] La guerre! C'est une chose trop grave pour la confier à des militaires.
Sometimes quoted as: War is much too serious to leave to the generals.

[3] See Tertullian, 126:3, and Jefferson, 388:7.

[4] See Ruskin, 573:5.

[5] See Addison, 326:1.

Alexander Hamilton

1755–1804

10 A national debt, if it is not excessive, will be to us a national blessing.[6]
Letter to Robert Morris [April 30, 1781]

11 I believe the British government forms the best model the world ever produced. . . . This government has for its object public strength and individual security.
Debates of the Federal Convention [May 14–September 17, 1787].[7] June 18, 1787

12 All communities divide themselves into the few and the many. The first are the rich and wellborn, the other the mass of the people. . . . The people are turbulent and changing; they seldom judge or determine right. Give therefore to the first class a distinct, permanent share in the government. They will check the unsteadiness of the second, and as they cannot receive any advantage by a change, they therefore will ever maintain good government. *Ib.*

13 We are now forming a republican government. Real liberty is neither found in despotism or the extremes of democracy, but in moderate governments.
Ib. June 26, 1787

14 Let Americans disdain to be the instruments of European greatness. Let the thirteen States, bound together in a strict and indissoluble Union, concur in erecting one great American system, superior to the control of all transatlantic force or influence, and able to dictate the terms of the connection between the old and the new world!
The Federalist [1787–1788], no. 11

15 Government implies the power of making laws. It is essential to the idea of a law, that it be attended with a sanction; or, in other words, a penalty or punishment for disobedience. *Ib. 15*

16 Why has government been instituted at all? Because the passions of men will not conform to the dictates of reason and justice, without constraint. *Ib.*

17 Every power vested in a government is in its nature sovereign, and includes by force of

[6] At the time we were funding our national debt, we heard much about "a public debt being a public blessing." —THOMAS JEFFERSON, *Letter to John W. Epps* [November 6, 1813]
See Webster, 450:12.

[7] At which the Constitution was written.

the term a right to employ all the means requisite . . . to the attainment of the ends of such power.

Opinion on the Constitutionality of the Bank [February 23, 1791]

1 If the end be clearly comprehended within any of the specified powers, and if the measure have an obvious relation to that end, and is not forbidden by any particular provision of the Constitution, it may safely be deemed to come within the compass of the national authority. *Ib.*

Louis XVIII

1755–1824

2 Punctuality is the politeness of kings.[1]

A favorite saying

John Marshall

1755–1835

3 It is emphatically the province and duty of the judicial department to say what the law is. . . . If two laws conflict with each other, the courts must decide on the operation of each. . . . This is of the very essence of judicial duty.

Marbury v. Madison, 1 Cranch, 1317 [1803]

4 We must never forget that it is a *constitution* we are expounding.

McCulloch v. Maryland, 4 Wheaton 316, 407 [1819]

5 This provision is made in a constitution, intended to endure for ages to come, and consequently, to be adapted to the various *crises* of human affairs. *Ib. 415*

6 Let the end be legitimate, let it be within the scope of the constitution, and all means which are appropriate, which are plainly adapted to that end, which are not prohibited, but consist with the letter and spirit of the constitution, are constitutional.

Ib. 421

7 The power to tax involves the power to destroy.[2] *Ib. 431*

8 The people made the Constitution, and the people can unmake it. It is the creature of their own will, and lives only by their will.

Cohens v. Virginia, 6 Wheaton (19 U.S.) 264, 389 [1821]

[1] L'exactitude est la politesse des rois.

[2] See Oliver Wendell Holmes, Jr., 645:9.

Martin Joseph Routh

1755–1854

9 You will find it a very good practice always to verify your references, sir.

From J. W. BURGON, Memoir of Dr. Routh, Quarterly Review [July 1878]

Henry [Light-Horse Harry] Lee

1756–1818

10 To the memory of the Man, first in war, first in peace, and first in the hearts of his countrymen.

Resolutions presented to the House of Representatives on the death of Washington [December 1799]

Wolfgang Amadè Mozart

1756–1791

11 Neither a lofty degree of intelligence nor imagination nor both together go to the making of genius. Love, love, love, that is the soul of genius. *Attributed*

William Blake

1757–1827

12 How sweet I roamed from field to field,
And tasted all the summer's pride,
Till I the prince of love beheld,
Who in the sunny beams did glide!

Poetical Sketches [1783]. Song (How Sweet I Roamed), st. 1

13 He loves to sit and hear me sing,
Then, laughing, sports and plays with me;
Then stretches out my golden wing,
And mocks my loss of liberty. *Ib. st. 4*

14 My silks and fine array,
My smiles and languished air,
By love are driv'n away;
And mournful lean Despair
Brings me yew to deck my grave:
Such end true lovers have.

Ib. Song (My Silks and Fine Array), st. 1

15 Like a fiend in a cloud,
With howling woe,
After night I do crowd,
And with night will go;
I turn my back to the east,
From whence comforts have increased;
For light doth seize my brain
With frantic pain. *Ib. Mad Song, st. 3*

1 How have you left the ancient love
That bards of old enjoyed in you!
The languid strings do scarcely move!
The sound is forced, the notes are few!
Ib. To the Muses, st. 4

2 Piping down the valleys wild,
Piping songs of pleasant glee,
On a cloud I saw a child,
And he laughing said to me:

"Pipe a song about a Lamb."
So I piped with merry cheer;
"Piper, pipe that song again."
So I piped; he wept to hear.
Songs of Innocence [1789–1790]. Introduction, st. 1, 2

3 And I made a rural pen,
And I stained the water clear,
And I wrote my happy songs
Every child may joy to hear. *Ib. st. 5*

4 Sing louder around
To the bells' cheerful sound,
While our sports shall be seen
On the echoing green.
Ib. The Echoing Green, st. 1

5 Little Lamb, who made thee?
Dost thou know who made thee?
Gave thee life and bid thee feed
By the stream and o'er the mead;
Gave thee clothing of delight,
Softest clothing, woolly bright.
Ib. The Lamb, st. 1

6 My mother bore me in the southern wild,
And I am black, but O! my soul is white;
White as an angel is the English child,
But I am black as if bereaved of light.
Ib. The Little Black Boy, st. 1

7 And we are put on earth a little space,
That we may learn to bear the beams of love,
And these black bodies and this sunburnt face
Is but a cloud, and like a shady grove.
Ib. st. 4

8 I'll shade him from the heat till he can bear
To lean in joy upon our Father's knee;
And then I'll stand and stroke his silver hair,
And be like him and he will then love me.
Ib. st. 7

9 When my mother died I was very young,
And my father sold me while yet my tongue
Could scarcely cry 'weep! 'weep! 'weep! 'weep!
So your chimneys I sweep, and in soot I sleep.
Ib. The Chimney Sweeper, st. 1

10 To Mercy, Pity, Peace, and Love
All pray in their distress;
And to these virtues of delight
Return their thankfulness.
Ib. The Divine Image, st. 1

11 For Mercy has a human heart,
Pity, a human face,
And Love, the human form divine,[1]
And Peace, the human dress.[2]
Ib. st. 3

12 The moon like a flower
In heaven's high bower,
With silent delight,
Sits and smiles on the night.
Ib. Night, st. 1

13 And there the lion's ruddy eyes
Shall flow with tears of gold,
And pitying the tender cries,
And walking round the fold,
Saying: "Wrath by his meekness,
And by his health, sickness,
Is driven away
From our immortal day." *Ib. st. 5*

14 "For washed in life's river,
My bright mane forever
Shall shine like the gold
As I guard o'er the fold." *Ib. st. 6*

15 When the voices of children are heard on the green
And laughing is heard on the hill,
My heart is at rest within my breast
And everything else is still.
Ib. Nurse's Song, st. 1

16 Can I see another's woe,
And not be in sorrow too?
Can I see another's grief,
And not seek for kind relief?
Ib. On Another's Sorrow, st. 1

17 Does the Eagle know what is in the pit?
Or wilt thou go ask the Mole?
Can Wisdom be put in a silver rod?
Or Love in a golden bowl?
The Book of Thel [1789–1792]. Thel's Motto

18 Rintrah roars and shakes his fires in the burdened air;
Hungry clouds swag on the deep.
The Marriage of Heaven and Hell [1790–1793]. The Argument

19 The reason Milton wrote in fetters when he wrote of Angels and God, and at liberty when of Devils and Hell, is because he was a true poet and of the Devil's party without knowing it.
Ib. note to The Voice of the Devil

[1]See Milton, 285:5, and *A Divine Image,* 405:14.
[2]See *A Divine Image,* 405:14.

1 The busy bee has no time for sorrow.
Ib. Proverbs of Hell, l. 11

2 No bird soars too high, if he soars with his own wings. *Ib. l. 15*

3 The pride of the peacock is the glory of God.
The lust of the goat is the bounty of God.
The wrath of the lion is the wisdom of God.
The nakedness of woman is the work of God.
Ib. l. 22

4 The cistern contains: the fountain overflows.
Ib. l. 35

5 Think in the morning. Act in the noon. Eat in the evening. Sleep in the night.
Ib. l. 41

6 You never know what is enough unless you know what is more than enough.
Ib. l. 46

7 Improvement makes straight roads; but the crooked roads without improvement are roads of genius. *Ib. l. 66*

8 Truth can never be told so as to be understood, and not be believed. *Ib. l. 69*

9 Enough! or too much. *Ib. l. 70*

10 Never seek[1] to tell thy love
Love that never told can be;
For the gentle wind does move
Silently, invisibly.

I told my love, I told my love,
I told her all my heart;
Trembling, cold, in ghastly fears—
Ah, she doth depart.

Soon as she was gone from me
A traveler came by
Silently, invisibly—
Oh, was no deny.[2]
Poems [written c. 1791–1792] from Blake's Notebook. Never Seek to Tell

11 I asked a thief to steal me a peach:
He turned up his eyes.
I asked a lithe lady to lie her down:
Holy and meek, she cries.

As soon as I went
An angel came.
He winked at the thief
And smiled at the dame—

And without one word said[3]
Had a peach from the tree,
And still as a maid[4]
Enjoyed the lady. *Ib. I Asked a Thief*

[1] Alternate: Never pain to tell thy love.
[2] Alternate: He took her with a sigh.
[3] Alternate: And without one word spoke.
[4] Alternate: And 'twixt earnest and joke.

12 Sleep, sleep, beauty bright,
Dreaming o'er the joys of night.
Sleep, sleep: in thy sleep
Little sorrows sit and weep.
Ib. A Cradle Song, st. 1

13 Why art thou silent and invisible,
Father of Jealousy?
Ib. To Nobodaddy, st. 1

14 Love to faults is always blind,
Always is to joy inclined,
Lawless, winged, and unconfined,
And breaks all chains from every mind.
Ib. Love to Faults

15 The sword sung on the barren heath,
The sickle in the fruitful field;
The sword he sung a song of death,
But could not make the sickle yield.
Ib. The Sword Sung

16 Abstinence sows sand all over
The ruddy limbs and flaming hair,
But desire gratified
Plants fruits of life and beauty there.
Ib. Abstinence Sows Sand

17 If you trap the moment before it's ripe,[5]
The tears of repentance you'll certainly wipe;
But if once you let the ripe moment go
You can never wipe off the tears of woe.
Ib. If You Trap the Moment

18 He who binds to himself a joy
Does the wingèd life destroy;
But he who kisses the joy as it flies
Lives in eternity's sunrise.
Ib. Several Questions Answered, no. 1, He Who Binds

19 The look of love alarms
Because 'tis filled with fire;
But the look of soft deceit
Shall win the lover's hire.
Ib. 2, The Look of Love

20 What is it men in women do require?
The lineaments of gratified desire.
What is it women do in men require?
The lineaments of gratified desire.
Ib. 4, What Is It

21 You'll quite remove the ancient curse.
Ib. 5, An Ancient Proverb

22 Then old Nobodaddy aloft
Farted and belched and coughed,
And said, "I love hanging and drawing and quartering
Every bit as well as war and slaughtering."
Ib. Let the Brothels of Paris, st. 2

[5] See Shakespeare, 206:32.

1 Hear the voice of the Bard!
Who Present, Past, and Future sees,
Whose ears have heard
The Holy Word
That walked among the ancient trees.
Songs of Experience [1794]. Introduction, st. 1

2 Turn away no more.
Why wilt thou turn away?
The starry floor,
The wat'ry shore
Is giv'n thee till the break of day.[1]
Ib. st. 4

3 Love seeketh not itself to please,
Nor for itself hath any care,
But for another gives its ease,
And builds a Heaven in Hell's despair.
Ib. The Clod and the Pebble, st. 1

4 Love seeketh only self to please,
To bind another to its delight,
Joys in another's loss of ease,
And builds a Hell in Heaven's despite.
Ib. st. 3

5 O Rose, thou art sick.
The invisible worm
That flies in the night,
In the howling storm,

Has found out thy bed
Of crimson joy,
And his dark secret love
Does thy life destroy.
Ib. The Sick Rose

6 Little Fly,
Thy summer's play
My thoughtless hand
Has brushed away.

Am not I
A fly like thee?
Or art not thou
A man like me?

For I dance
And drink and sing,
Till some blind hand
Shall brush my wing.
Ib. The Fly, st. 1–3

7 Tiger, Tiger, burning bright
In the forests of the night,
What immortal hand or eye
Could frame thy fearful symmetry?

In what distant deeps or skies
Burnt the fire of thine eyes?
On what wings dare he aspire?
What the hand dare seize the fire?
Ib. The Tiger, st. 1, 2

[1]See Milton, 279:2.

8 What the hammer? what the chain?
In what furnace was thy brain?
What the anvil? what dread grasp
Dare its deadly terrors clasp?

When the stars threw down their spears
And watered heaven with their tears,
Did he smile his work to see?
Did he who made the Lamb make thee?
Ib. st. 4, 5

9 In every cry of every man,
In every infant's cry of fear,
In every voice, in every ban,
The mind-forged manacles I hear.
Ib. London, st. 2

10 But most through midnight streets I hear
How the youthful harlot's curse
Blasts the newborn infant's tear
And blights with plagues the marriage hearse.
Ib. st. 4

11 Pity would be no more,
If we did not make somebody poor;
And Mercy no more could be,
If all were as happy as we.
Ib. The Human Abstract, st. 1

12 My mother groaned! my father wept.
Into the dangerous world I leapt:
Helpless, naked, piping loud,
Like a fiend hid in a cloud.
Ib. Infant Sorrow, st. 1

13 I was angry with my friend;
I told my wrath, my wrath did end.
I was angry with my foe;
I told it not, my wrath did grow.
Ib. A Poison Tree, st. 1

14 Cruelty has a human heart,
And Jealousy a human face;
Terror, the human form divine,[2]
And Secrecy, the human dress.
A Divine Image,[3] st. 1

15 Degrade first the arts if you'd mankind degrade,
Hire idiots to paint with cold light and hot shade.
Annotations [c. 1798–1809] to Sir Joshua Reynolds's Discourses,[4] title page

16 To generalize is to be an idiot. To particularize is the alone distinction of merit—general

[2]See Milton, 285:5, and *The Divine Image*, 403:11.

[3]This poem was written and etched by Blake [1790–1791] as a "Song of Experience" linked with *The Divine Image* in *Songs of Innocence* (see 403:10 and 403:11), but in the published *Songs of Experience* it was replaced by *The Human Abstract* (405:11).

[4]Volume I of Reynolds's *Works*, edited by Edmond Malone [second edition, 1798].

knowledges are those knowledges that idiots possess. *Ib. pp. xcvii–xcviii*

1 My specter around me night and day
Like a wild beast guards my way.
My emanation far within
Weeps incessantly for my sin.
Poems [written c. 1804] from Blake's Notebook. My Specter, st. 1

2 And throughout all eternity
I forgive you, you forgive me.
Ib. st. 14

3 Mock on, mock on,[1] Voltaire, Rousseau.
Mock on, mock on—'tis all in vain!
You throw the sand against the wind,
And the wind blows it back again.
Ib. Mock On, st. 1

4 Terror in the house does roar,
But Pity stands before the door.
Ib. Terror in the House

5 There is a smile of love,
And there is a smile of deceit,
And there is a smile of smiles
In which these two smiles meet.
Poems from the Pickering Manuscript [c. 1805].[2] *The Smile, st. 1*

6 This cabinet is formed of gold
And pearl and crystal shining bright,
And within it opens into a world
And a little lovely moony night.
Ib. The Crystal Cabinet, st. 2

7 For a tear is an intellectual thing,
And a sigh is the sword of an Angel King,
And the bitter groan of the martyr's woe
Is an arrow from the Almighty's bow.[3]
Ib. The Gray Monk, st. 8

8 To see a world in a grain of sand
And a heaven in a wild flower,
Hold infinity in the palm of your hand
And eternity in an hour.
Ib. Auguries of Innocence, l. 1

9 A robin redbreast in a cage
Puts all Heaven in a rage. *Ib. l. 5*

10 A dog starved at his master's gate
Predicts the ruin of the state. *Ib. l. 9*

11 He who shall hurt the little wren
Shall never be beloved by men.
Ib. l. 29

[1]See *Job 21:3*, 16:7.
[2]The manuscript, a fair copy, is named after a nineteenth-century owner.
[3]This stanza is also in *Jerusalem* [1804–1820], preface (*To the Deists*) to chapter 3.

12 A truth that's told with bad intent
Beats all the lies you can invent.
Ib. l. 53

13 Man was made for joy and woe,
And when this we rightly know
Through the world we safely go.
Ib. l. 56

14 Every tear from every eye
Becomes a babe in eternity. *Ib. l. 67*

15 He who shall teach the child to doubt
The rotting grave shall ne'er get out.
Ib. l. 87

16 The strongest poison ever known
Came from Caesar's laurel crown.
Ib. l. 97

17 He who doubts from what he sees
Will ne'er believe, do what you please.
If the sun and moon should doubt
They'd immediately go out. *Ib. l. 107*

18 The harlot's cry from street to street
Shall weave old England's winding sheet.
Ib. l. 115

19 Some are born to sweet delight.
Some are born to endless night.
Ib. l. 123

20 Rouse up, O young men of the new age! Set your foreheads against the ignorant hirelings! For we have hirelings in the camp, the court, and the university who would, if they could, forever repress mental and prolong corporeal war.
Milton [c. 1809], preface

21 And did those feet in ancient time
Walk upon England's mountains green?
And was the holy Lamb of God
On England's pleasant pastures seen?

And did the Countenance Divine
Shine forth upon our clouded hills?
And was Jerusalem builded here
Among those dark Satanic mills?

Bring me my bow of burning gold,
Bring me my arrows of desire,
Bring me my spear—O clouds, unfold!
Bring me my chariot of fire!

I will not cease from mental fight,
Nor shall my sword sleep in my hand,
Till we have built Jerusalem
In England's green and pleasant land.
Ib. prefatory poem

1 Great things are done when men and mountains meet;
This is not done by jostling in the street.
Poems [written c. 1807–1809] from Blake's Notebook. Great Things Are Done

2 If you have formed a circle to go into,
Go into it yourself and see how you would do.
Ib. To God

3 The Angel that presided o'er my birth
Said, "Little creature, formed of joy and mirth,
Go love without the help of any thing on earth."
Ib. The Angel That Presided

4 Grown old in love from seven till seven times seven,
I oft have wished for Hell for ease from Heaven.
Ib. Grown Old in Love

5 Poetry fettered fetters the human race. Nations are destroyed, or flourish, in proportion as their poetry, painting, and music are destroyed or flourish!
Jerusalem [c. 1818–1820]. To the Public, plate 1

6 He who would do good to another must do it in minute particulars;
General good is the plea of the scoundrel, hypocrite, and flatterer:
For art and science cannot exist but in minutely organized particulars.
Ib. ch. 3, plate 55, l. 60

7 England! awake! awake! awake!
Jerusalem thy sister calls!
Why wilt thou sleep the sleep of death
And close her from thy ancient walls?
Ib. 4, prefatory poem, plate 77, st. 1

8 The vision of Christ that thou dost see
Is my vision's greatest enemy.
The Everlasting Gospel [written c. 1818], sec. 4, l. 1

9 Both read the Bible day and night,
But thou read'st black where I read white.
Ib. l. 13

10 This life's dim windows of the soul
Distorts the heavens from pole to pole
And leads you to believe a lie
When you see with, not through, the eye.[1]
Ib. 5, l. 101

11 I am sure this Jesus will not do
Either for Englishman or Jew.
Ib. 8

[1] We are led to believe a lie / When we see not through the eye.— BLAKE, *Auguries of Innocence, l. 125*

James Gillray
1757–1815

12 The Old Lady of Threadneedle Street.[2]
Title of cartoon [1797]

John Philip Kemble
1757–1823

13 Perhaps it was right to dissemble your love,
But—why did you kick me down stairs?
The Panel,[3] act I, sc. i

Royall Tyler
1757–1826

14 Since General Shays[4] has sneaked off and given us the bag to hold.
The Contrast [1787], act II, sc. ii

15 I am at the end of my tether.
Ib. III, i

Fisher Ames
1758–1808

16 A monarchy is a merchantman which sails well, but will sometimes strike on a rock, and go to the bottom; a republic is a raft which will never sink, but then your feet are always in the water.
Speech in the House of Representatives [1795]

John Heath
1758–1810

17 Love of wisdom [philosophy] the guide of life.[5]
Greek phrase for Phi Beta Kappa, society founded at the College of William and Mary [December 5, 1776]

James Monroe
1758–1831

18 National honor is national property of the highest value.
First Inaugural Address [March 4, 1817]

[2] The Bank of England.
[3] An adaptation of Isaac Bickerstaffe's *'Tis Well It's No Worse* [1770].
[4] Tyler was involved in suppressing Shays's Rebellion.
[5] Philosophia Biou Kybernetes. The name Phi Beta Kappa is from the Greek initial letters in the phrase. See Cicero, 98:24.

1 The American continents . . . are henceforth not to be considered as subjects for future colonization by any European powers.

Annual Message to Congress [December 2, 1823]. The Monroe Doctrine

2 In the wars of the European powers in matters relating to themselves we have never taken any part, nor does it comport with our policy so to do. *Ib.*

3 We owe it, therefore, to candor, and to the amicable relations existing between the United States and those powers to declare that we should consider any attempt on their part to extend their system to any portion of this hemisphere as dangerous to our peace and safety. With the existing colonies or dependencies of any European power we . . . shall not interfere. But with the governments . . . whose independence we have . . . acknowledged, we could not view any interposition for the purpose of oppressing them, or controlling, in any other manner, their destiny, by any European power, in any other light than as a manifestation of an unfriendly disposition towards the United States. *Ib.*

Horatio Nelson

1758–1805

4 Westminster Abbey, or victory!

At the battle of Cape St. Vincent [February 14, 1797]. From Robert Southey, *Life of Nelson [1813], ch. 4*

5 I have only one eye, I have a right to be blind sometimes . . . I really do not see the signal.

At the battle of Copenhagen [1801]. Ib. 9

6 Something must be left to chance; nothing is sure in a sea fight beyond all others.

Memorandum to the fleet, off Cadiz [October 9, 1805]

7 But, in case signals can neither be seen or perfectly understood, no captain can do very wrong if he places his ship alongside that of the enemy. *Ib.*

8 England expects every man will do his duty.[1]

At the battle of Trafalgar [October 21, 1805]. From Robert Southey, *Life of Nelson [1813], ch. 9*

9 Thank God, I have done my duty. *Ib.*

10 Kiss me, Hardy. *Ib.*

Red Jacket[2]
[Sagoyewatha]

c. 1758–1830

11 We first knew you a feeble plant which wanted a little earth whereon to grow. We gave it to you; and afterward, when we could have trod you under our feet, we watered and protected you; and now you have grown to be a mighty tree, whose top reaches the clouds, and whose branches overspread the whole land, whilst we, who were the tall pine of the forest, have become a feeble plant and need your protection. *Statement [c. 1792]*

Robert Burns

1759–1796

12 Wee, sleekit, cow'rin, tim'rous beastie,
O, what a panic's in thy breastie!
Thou need na start awa sae hasty,
Wi' bickering brattle!

To a Mouse [1785], st. 1

13 I'm truly sorry man's dominion
Has broken Nature's social union.

Ib. st. 2

14 The best laid schemes o' mice and men
Gang aft a-gley.[3] *Ib. st. 7*

15 Nature's law,
That man was made to mourn.

Man Was Made to Mourn [1786], st. 4

16 Man's inhumanity to man.[4]
Makes countless thousands mourn!

Ib. st. 7

17 He wales a portion with judicious care;
And "Let us worship God" he says, with solemn air.

The Cotter's Saturday Night [1786], st. 12

18 From scenes like these, old Scotia's grandeur springs,
That makes her loved at home, revered abroad:

[1]This famous sentence is thus first reported: Say to the fleet, England confides that every man will do his duty. Captain Pasco, Nelson's flag lieutenant, suggested substituting "expects" for "confides," which was adopted. Captain Blackwood, who commanded the *Euryalus*, says that the correction suggested was from "Nelson expects" to "England expects."

[2]Seneca chief.

[3]See Ihara Saikaku, 313:1.

[4]See Pliny, 116:10, and Wordsworth, 423:4.

Princes and lords are but the breath of kings,[1]
"An honest man's the noblest work of God."[2] *Ib. st. 19*

1 Gie me ae spark o' Nature's fire,
That's a' the learning I desire.
First Epistle to J. Lapraik [1786], st. 13

2 The social, friendly, honest man,
Whate'er he be,
'Tis he fulfills great Nature's plan,
And none but he!
Second Epistle to J. Lapraik [1786], st. 15

3 On ev'ry hand it will allowed be,
He's just—nae better than he should be.
A Dedication to Gavin Hamilton [1786]

4 It's hardly in a body's pow'r,
To keep, at times, frae being sour.
Epistle to Davie [1786], st. 2

5 Misled by fancy's meteor ray,
By passion driven;
But yet the light that led astray
Was light from heaven.
The Vision [1786], II, st. 18

6 His lockèd, lettered, braw brass collar
Showed him the gentleman an' scholar.
The Twa Dogs [1786], st. 3

7 An' there began a lang digression
About the lords o' the creation.
Ib. st. 6

8 Oh wad some power the giftie gie us
To see oursels as others see us!
It wad frae monie a blunder free us,
An' foolish notion.
To a Louse [1786], st. 8

9 Wee, modest, crimson-tippèd flow'r,
Thou's met me in an evil hour;
For I maun crush amang the stoure
Thy slender stem:
To spare thee now is past my pow'r,
Thou bonie gem.
To a Mountain Daisy [1786], st. 1

10 Stern Ruin's plowshare drives elate,
Full on thy bloom.[3] *Ib. st. 9*

11 Perhaps it may turn out a sang,
Perhaps turn out a sermon.
Epistle to a Young Friend [1786], st. 1

12 I waive the quantum o' the sin,
The hazard of concealing:
But, och! it hardens a' within,
And petrifies the feeling! *Ib. st. 6*

13 An atheist-laugh's a poor exchange
For Deity offended. *Ib. st. 9*

14 There's nought but care on ev'ry han',
In every hour that passes, O:
What signifies the life o' man,
An' 't were nae for the lasses, O.
Green Grow the Rashes, O [1787], st. 1

15 Auld Nature swears, the lovely dears
Her noblest work she classes, O:
Her prentice han' she tried on man,
An' then she made the lasses, O.
Ib. st. 5

16 Green grow the rashes, O;
Green grow the rashes, O;
The sweetest hours that e'er I spend
Are spent among the lasses, O.
Ib. chorus

17 I wasna fou, but just had plenty.
Death and Dr. Hornbook [1787], st. 3

18 John Barleycorn got up again,
And sore surprised them all.
John Barleycorn [1787], st. 3

19 The heart benevolent and kind
The most resembles God.
A Winter Night [1787]

20 Ye're aiblins nae temptation.
Address to the Unco Guid [1787], st. 6

21 Then gently scan your brother man,
Still gentler sister woman;
Tho' they may gang a kennin wrang,
To step aside is human. *Ib. st. 7*

22 O, my Luve is like a red, red rose,
That's newly sprung in June.
O, my Luve is like the melodie,
That's sweetly played in tune.
Johnson's Musical Museum [1787–1796]. A Red, Red Rose, st. 1

23 Contented wi' little and cantie wi' mair.
Ib. Contented wi' Little, st. 1

24 Ye banks and braes o' bonny Doon,
How can ye bloom sae fresh and fair?
How can ye chant, ye little birds,
And I sae weary fu' o' care!
Thou'll break my heart, thou warbling bird,
That wantons thro' the flowering thorn!
Thou minds me o' departed joys,
Departed never to return.
Ib. The Banks o' Doon, st. 1

[1] See Goldsmith, 369:30.
[2] See Fletcher, 260:18, and Pope, 337:13.
[3] See Edward Young, 330:18.

1 Chords that vibrate sweetest pleasure
Thrill the deepest notes of woe.
Ib. Sensibility How Charming, st. 4

2 Ae fond kiss, and then we sever;
Ae farewell and then forever![1]
Ib. Ae Fond Kiss, st. 1

3 But to see her was to love her,
Love but her, and love forever.[2]
Had we never loved sae kindly,
Had we never loved sae blindly,
Never met — or never parted —
We had ne'er been brokenhearted.
Ib. st. 2

4 It was a' for our rightfu' King
We left fair Scotland's strand.
Ib. It Was A' for Our Rightfu' King, st. 1

5 Now a' is done that men can do,
And a' is done in vain. *Ib. st. 2*

6 He turn'd him right and round about
Upon the Irish shore;
And gae his bridle reins a shake,
With adieu forevermore,
My dear —
And adieu forevermore! *Ib. st. 3*

7 John Anderson my jo, John,
When we were first acquent,
Your locks were like the raven,
Your bonie brow was brent;
But now your brow is beld, John,
Your locks are like the snaw,
But blessings on your frosty pow,
John Anderson my jo!
Ib. John Anderson My Jo, st. 1

8 Farewell to the Highlands, farewell to the North,
The birthplace of valor, the country of worth!
Wherever I wander, wherever I rove,
The hills of the Highlands for ever I love.
Ib. My Heart's in the Highlands, st. 1

9 My heart's in the Highlands, my heart is not here,
My heart's in the Highlands a-chasing the deer;
A-chasing the wild deer, and following the roe,
My heart's in the Highlands wherever I go.
Ib. chorus

10 O whistle, and I'll come to you,[3] my lad:
Tho' father and mither and a' should gae mad.
Whistle, and I'll Come to You, My Lad

11 Should auld acquaintance be forgot,
And never brought to mind?
Should auld acquaintance be forgot,
And auld lang syne!
Auld Lang Syne [1788], st. 1

12 For auld lang syne, my dear,
For auld lang syne,
We'll tak a cup o' kindness yet
For auld lang syne! *Ib. chorus*

13 Flow gently, sweet Afton, among thy green braes,
Flow gently, I'll sing thee a song in thy praise.
My Mary's asleep by thy murmuring stream,
Flow gently, sweet Afton, disturb not her dream. *Afton Water [1789], st. 1*

14 This day Time winds th' exhausted chain,
To run the twelvemonth's length again.
New Year's Day [1791], st. 1

15 The voice of Nature loudly cries,
And many a message from the skies,
That something in us never dies.
Ib. st. 3

16 When Nature her great masterpiece designed,
And framed her last, best work, the human mind,
Her eye intent on all the wondrous plan,
She formed of various stuff the various Man.
To Robert Graham [1791], st. 1

17 She is a winsome wee thing,
She is a handsome wee thing,
She is a lo'esome wee thing,
This sweet wee wife o' mine.
My Wife's a Winsome Wee Thing [1792], chorus

18 The golden hours on angel wings
Flew o'er me and my dearie;
For dear to me as light and life
Was my sweet Highland Mary.
Highland Mary [1792], st. 2

19 But, oh! fell death's untimely frost,
That nipt my flower sae early. *Ib. st. 3*

20 If there's a hole in a' your coats,
I rede you tent it;
A chield's amang you takin' notes,
And faith he'll prent it.
On the Late Captain Grose's Peregrinations Thro' Scotland [1793], st. 1

[1] See Byron, 459:19.
[2] See Halleck, 464:11, and Tennyson, 529:19.
[3] See Beaumont and Fletcher, 263:9.

1 Some hae meat and canna eat,
And some wad eat that want it;
But we hae meat, and we can eat,
And sae the Lord be thankit.
The Selkirk Grace [1793] (attributed)

2 O Mary, at thy window be!
It is the wished, the trysted hour.
Mary Morison [1793], st. 1

3 The lovely Mary Morison! *Ib.*

4 Whare sits our sulky, sullen dame,
Gathering her brows like gathering storm,
Nursing her wrath to keep it warm.
Tam o' Shanter [1793], l. 10

5 Ah, gentle dames! it gars me greet
To think how monie counsels sweet,
How monie lengthened, sage advices,
The husband frae the wife despises.
Ib. l. 33

6 His ancient, trusty, drouthy crony;
Tam lo'ed him like a vera brither—
They had been fou for weeks thegither.
Ib. l. 43

7 Kings may be blest, but Tam was glorious,
O'er a' the ills o' life victorious.
Ib. l. 57

8 But pleasures are like poppies spread—
You seize the flow'r, its bloom is shed;
Or like the snow falls in the river—
A moment white—then melts forever.
Ib. l. 59

9 That hour, o' night's black arch the keystane.
Ib. l. 69

10 Inspiring bold John Barleycorn!
What dangers thou canst make us scorn!
Wi' tippenny, we fear nae evil;
Wi' usquebae, we'll face the devil!
Ib. l. 105

11 As Tammie glow'red, amazed, and curious,
The mirth and fun grew fast and furious.
Ib. l. 143

12 Her cutty sark, o' Paisley harn,
That while a lassie she had worn,
In longitude tho' sorely scanty,
It was her best, and she was vauntie.
Ib. l. 171

13 "Weel done, Cutty Sark!"[1] *Ib. l. 189*

[1]The famous tea clipper *Cutty Sark,* designed by Hercules Linton and built in 1869, had the story of Tam o' Shanter carved upon her bow and counter. Nannie, with flying locks and scanty shift, was the figurehead.

14 Ah, Tam! Ah! Tam! Thou'll get thy fairin!
In hell they'll roast you like a herrin!
Ib. l. 201

15 Scots wha hae wi' Wallace bled,
Scots wham Bruce has aften led,
Welcome to your gory bed
Or to victorie.

Now's the day, and now's the hour;
See the front o' battle lour!
See approach proud Edward's power—
Chains and slaverie!
Scots Wha Hae [1794], st. 1, 2

16 Lay the proud usurpers low!
Tyrants fall in every foe!
Liberty's in every blow!
Let us do or die![2] *Ib. st. 6*

17 The rank is but the guinea's stamp,
The man's the gowd for a' that.
For A' That and A' That [1795], st. 1

18 A prince can mak a belted knight,
A marquis, duke, and a' that;
But an honest man's aboon his might,
Guid faith, he mauna fa' that.
Ib. st. 4

19 For a' that and a' that,
It's coming yet, for a' that,
That man to man the world o'er
Shall brothers be for a' that. *Ib. st. 5*

20 For a' that, and a' that,
An' twice as muckle 's a' that,
I've lost but ane, I've twa behin',
I've wife eneugh for a' that.
Posthumous Pieces [1799]. The Jolly Beggars, chorus

21 God knows, I'm no the thing I should be,
Nor am I even the thing I could be.
Ib. To the Reverend John M'Math, st. 8

22 If there's another world, he lives in bliss;
If there is none, he made the best of this.
Ib. Epitaph on William Muir

23 In durance vile here must I wake and weep,
And all my frowsy couch in sorrow steep.
Ib. Epistle from Esopus to Maria

24 It's guid to be merry and wise,
It's guid to be honest and true,
It's guid to support Caledonia's cause
And bide by the buff and the blue.
Ib. Here's a Health to Them That's Awa', st. 1

[2]See Fletcher, 261:3.

Georges Jacques Danton

1759–1794

1 Everything belongs to the fatherland when the fatherland is in danger.

Speech to the Legislative Assembly [August 28, 1792]

2 Audacity, more audacity, always audacity.[1] *Ib. [September 2, 1792]*

3 Show my head to the people, it is worth seeing.

Last words, addressed to the executioner

William Pitt

1759–1806

4 Necessity is the plea for every infringement of human freedom. It is the argument of tyrants; it is the creed of slaves.[2]

Speech in the House of Commons [November 18, 1783]

Johann Christoph Friedrich von Schiller

1759–1805

5 I feel an army in my fist.

Die Räuber (The Robbers) [1781], act II, end

6 The lemonade is weak, like your soul.

Kabala und Liebe [1784], act V, sc. vii

7 The joke loses everything when the joker laughs himself.

The Conspiracy of Fiesco (Die Verschwörung des Fiesco, 1783), act I, sc. vii

8 Did you think the lion was sleeping because he didn't roar? *Ib. xviii*

9 Joy, thou spark from Heav'n immortal,
Daughter of Elysium!
Drunk with fire, toward Heaven advancing
Goddess, to thy shrine we come.
Thy sweet magic brings together
What stern Custom spreads afar;
All men become brothers
Where thy happy wing-beats are.[3]

An die Freude (Ode to Joy)[4] [1785], st. 1

10 Be embraced, ye millions!
This kiss is for the whole world!
Brothers, above the arch of stars
A loving Father surely dwells.

Ib. st. 5

11 There are three lessons I would write,
Three words as with a burning pen,
In tracings of eternal light
Upon the hearts of men.

Hope, Faith, and Love [c. 1786], st. 1

12 World history is the world's court.[5]

Resignation [1786]

13 What one refuses in a minute
No eternity will return. *Ib.*

14 O who knows what slumbers in the background of the times?

Don Carlos [1787], act I, sc. i

15 O the idea was childish, but divinely beautiful. *Ib. ii*

16 Great souls suffer in silence. *Ib. iv*

17 A moment lived in paradise
Is not atoned for too dearly by death.

Ib. v

18 The richest monarch in the Christian world;
The sun in my own dominions never sets.[6]

Ib. vi

19 What the inner voice says
Will not disappoint the hoping soul.

Hope [1797], last stanza

---

[1] Il nous faut de l'audace, encore de l'audace, toujours de l'audace.

Translated by S. E. Morison.

See Spenser, 173:20; Channing, 448:4; and Patton, 792:3.

[2] See Publilius Syrus, 111:20, and Milton, 285:21.

[3] Alle Menschen werden Brüder, / Wo dein sanfter Flügel weilt.

[4] Adapted from the translation by Theodore Spencer for the Boston Symphony Orchestra, for the performance of Beethoven's Ninth Symphony.

It was during his student days in Bonn that Beethoven fastened upon Schiller's poem. . . . The heady sense of liberation in the verses must have appealed to him as they appealed to every German. They were in the spirit of the times, the spirit that had swept Europe and America, and Beethoven belonged to his time. — John N. Burk, *program notes for the Boston Symphony Orchestra* [October 1, 1965]

[5] Die Weltgeschichte ist das Weltgericht.

[6] Why should the brave Spanish soldier brag the sun never sets in the Spanish dominions, but ever shineth on one part or other we have conquered for our king? — Captain John Smith, *Advertisements for the Unexperienced, etc.* [1631]

It may be said of them [the Hollanders] as of the Spaniards, that the sun never sets on their dominions. — Thomas Gage, *New Survey of the West Indies* [1648], *Epistle Dedicatory*

The sun never sets on the immense empire of Charles V. — Scott, *Life of Napoleon* [1827]

His Majesty's dominions, on which the sun never sets. — John Wilson [Christopher North], *Noctes Ambrosianae, no.* 20 [April 1829]

See Daniel Webster, 451:2.

1 If you want to know yourself,
Just look how others do it;
If you want to understand others,
Look into your own heart.
Tabulae Votivae [1797]

2 Man is created free, and is free,
Though he be born in chains.[1]
Die Worte des Glaubens (The Word of the Faithful) [1797], st. 2

3 Virtue is no empty echo. *Ib. st. 3*

4 Posterity weaves no garlands for imitators.
Wallensteins Lager (Wallenstein's Camp) [1798], prologue

5 He who has done his best for his own time has lived for all times. *Ib.*

6 Life is earnest, art is gay. *Ib.*

7 Whatever is not forbidden is permitted.
Ib. sc. vi

8 Man is made of ordinary things, and habit is his nurse.
Wallensteins Tod (The Death of Wallenstein) [1798], act I, sc. iv

9 I have only an office here, and no opinion.
Ib. v

10 Virtue has her heroes too
As well as Fame and Fortune.[2] *Ib. vii*

11 Many a crown shines spotless now
That yet was deeply sullied in the winning.[2]
Ib. II, ii

12 There's no such thing as chance;
And what to us seems merest accident
Springs from the deepest source of destiny.[2]
Ib. II, iii

13 What is life without the radiance of love?
Ib. IV, xii

14 Time is man's angel. *Ib. V, xi*

15 What is the short meaning of the long speech?
Die Piccolomini [1799], act I, sc. ii

16 War nourishes war.[3] *Ib.*

17 In thy breast are the stars of thy fate.
Ib. II, vi

18 You say it as you understand it. *Ib.*

[1] See Rousseau, 358:12, and Bliss, 385:14.
[2] Translated by Coleridge.
[3] Der Krieg ernährt den Krieg.

19 When the wine goes in, strange things come out. *Ib. xii*

20 The dictates of the heart are the voice of fate. *Ib. III, viii*

21 O tender yearning, sweet hoping!
The golden time of first love!
The eye sees the open heaven,
The heart is intoxicated with bliss;
O that the beautiful time of young love
Could remain green forever.
The Song of the Bell [1799]

22 Appearance should never attain reality,
And if nature conquers, then must art retire.
To Goethe, when he put Voltaire's Mahomet on the stage [1800]

23 Life is only error,
And death is knowledge.
Cassandra [1802]

24 I am better than my reputation.
Maria Stuart [1801], act III, sc. iv

25 For this should the singer accompany the king:
Both dwell on the heights of mankind.
Die Jungfrau von Orleans (Joan of Arc) [1801], act I, sc. ii

26 Against stupidity the very gods
Themselves contend in vain.[4]
Ib. III, vi

27 Pain is short, and joy is eternal.
Ib. last lines

28 What are hopes, what are plans?
Die Braut von Messina (The Bride of Messina) [1803], act III, sc. v

29 Don't let your heart depend on things
That ornament life in a fleeting way!
He who possesses, let him learn to lose,
He who is fortunate, let him learn pain.
Ib. IV, iv

30 On the mountains there is freedom!
The world is perfect everywhere,
Save where man comes with his torment.
Ib. IV, vii

31 The mountain cannot frighten one who was born on it.
Wilhelm Tell [1804], act III, sc. i

32 Who reflects too much will accomplish little.
Ib.

33 You saw his weakness, and he will never forgive you. *Ib.*

[4] Against boredom even the gods themselves struggle in vain. — Nietzsche, *The Antichrist* [1888], 48

1 This feat of Tell, the archer, will be told
While yonder mountains stand upon their base.
By heaven! The apple's cleft right through the core. *Ib. iii*

2 What's old collapses, times change,
And new life blossoms in the ruins.
Ib. IV, ii

3 The most pious man can't stay in peace
If it doesn't please his evil neighbor.
Ib. IV, iii

Mary Wollstonecraft
[Mary Wollstonecraft Godwin]

1759–1797

4 Nothing, I am sure, calls forth the faculties so much as the being obliged to struggle with the world.

Thoughts on the Education of Daughters [1787]. Matrimony

5 No man chooses evil because it is evil; he only mistakes it for happiness, the good he seeks.

A Vindication of the Rights of Men [1790]

6 Virtue can only flourish amongst equals. *Ib.*

7 Till women are more rationally educated, the progress in human virtue and improvement in knowledge must receive continual checks.

A Vindication of the Rights of Women [1792], ch. 3

8 If women be educated for dependence; that is, to act according to the will of another fallible being, and submit, right or wrong, to power, where are we to stop? *Ib.*

9 How can a rational being be ennobled by anything that is not obtained by its own exertions? *Ib.*

10 Women are systematically degraded by receiving the trivial attentions which men think it manly to pay to the sex, when, in fact, men are insultingly supporting their own superiority. *Ib. 4*

11 It would be an endless task to trace the variety of meannesses, cares, and sorrows into which women are plunged by the prevailing opinion that they were created rather to feel than reason, and that all the power they obtain must be obtained by their charms and weakness. *Ib.*

12 It is justice, not charity, that is wanting in the world. *Ib.*

13 Women ought to have representatives, instead of being arbitrarily governed without any direct share allowed them in the deliberations of government. *Ib. 9*

14 Till society is very differently constituted, parents, I fear, will still insist on being obeyed because they will be obeyed, and constantly endeavor to settle that power on a divine right which will not bear the investigation of reason. *Ib. 11*

15 Every political good carried to the extreme must be productive of evil.[1]

The French Revolution [1794], bk. V, ch. 4

16 The endeavor to keep alive any hoary establishment beyond its natural date is often pernicious and always useless. *Ib.*

17 Executions, far from being useful examples to the survivors, have, I am persuaded, a quite contrary effect, by hardening the heart they ought to terrify. Besides, the fear of an ignominious death, I believe, never deterred anyone from the commission of a crime, because in committing it the mind is roused to activity about present circumstances.

Letters Written During a Short Residence in Sweden, Norway, and Denmark [1796]. Letter 19

18 The same energy of character which renders a man a daring villain would have rendered him useful to society, had that society been well organized. *Ib.*

19 We reason deeply, when we forcibly feel. *Ib.*

20 It is the preservation of the species, not of individuals, which appears to be the design of Deity throughout the whole of nature.[2]

Ib. 22

François Noël Babeuf
[Gracchus]

1760–1797

21 Let the revolting distinction of rich and poor disappear once and for all, the distinction of great and small, of masters and valets, of governors and governed. Let there be no other difference between human beings than those of age and sex. Since all have the same needs and the same faculties, let there be one education for all, one food for all.

Manifesto of the Equals [c. 1795]

22 We aim at something more sublime and more equitable—the common good, or the

[1] See Coleridge, 437:2.
[2] See Tennyson, 532:11.

community of goods. . . . We demand, we would have, the communal enjoyment of the fruits of the earth, fruits which are for everyone. *Ib.*

Joseph Rouget de Lisle
1760–1836

1 Allons, enfants de la patrie,
Le jour de gloire est arrivé! . . .
Aux armes, citoyens!
Formez vos bataillons!
Marchons! Marchons! Qu'un sang impur
Abreuve nos sillons!
The Marseillaise [1792][1]

Antoine Boulay de la Meurthe
1761–1840

2 It is worse than a crime, it is a blunder [C'est pire qu'un crime, c'est une faute].[2]
On the execution of the Duc d'Enghien [1804]

August Friedrich Ferdinand von Kotzebue
1761–1819

3 There is another and a better world.
The Stranger [1798], act I, sc. i

William Lisle Bowles[3]
1762–1850

4 The cause of Freedom is the cause of God!
The Right Honorable Edmund Burke [1791], l. 78

Andrew Cherry
1762–1812

5 Loud roared the dreadful thunder,
The rain a deluge show'rd.
The Bay of Biscay

6 Till next day,
There she lay,
In the Bay of Biscay, O! *Ib.*

[1]Forward, sons of France, the day of glory has come! . . . To arms, citizens! Line up in battalions! Let us march on! And let the impure blood [of our enemies] drench our fields.

Composed in the garrison at Strasbourg and originally called *Chant de guerre de l'armée du Rhin*, the *Marseillaise* took its name from the patriots of Marseilles, who first made it known in Paris.

[2]Attributed also to TALLEYRAND and FOUCHÉ. Sainte-Beuve attributed it to BOULAY DE LA MEURTHE.

[3]See Simonides, 67:19.

George Colman the Younger
1762–1836

7 Tell 'em Queen Anne's dead.[4]
The Heir-at-Law [1797], act I, sc. i

8 Not to be sneezed at. *Ib. II, i*

9 Like two single gentlemen rolled into one.
Broad Grins [1802]. Lodgings for Single Gentlemen

10 When taken,
To be well shaken.
Ib. The Newcastle Apothecary

11 John Bull;[5] or, The Englishman's Fireside.
Title of play [1803]

12 His heart runs away with his head.
Who Wants a Guinea? [1805], act I, sc. i

13 O Miss Bailey!
Unfortunate Miss Bailey!
Love Laughs at Locksmiths [1806], act II, song

14 Says he, "I am a handsome man, but I'm a gay deceiver." *Ib.*

15 I had a soul above buttons.
Sylvester Daggerwood; or, New Hay at the Old Market [1808], sc. i

Dorothea Jordan
1762–1816

16 "Oh where, and Oh! where is your Highland laddie gone?"
"He's gone to fight the French, for King George upon the throne,
And it's Oh! in my heart, how I wish him safe at home!" *The Blue Bells of Scotland*

Joseph Fouché
1763–1820

17 Death is an eternal sleep.[6]
Inscription placed by his orders on cemetery gates [1794]

Johann Paul Friedrich Richter [Jean Paul]
1763–1825

18 Weltschmerz.[7]
Selina; oder, Über die Unsterblichkeit (or, Above Immortality) [1827], 2

[4]The phrase became proverbial for telling what everybody knows.

[5]The origin of the supposed type of the British character.

[6]See Catullus, 101:18; Campion, 250:3; Jonson, 255:16; and Herrick, 266:21.

[7]Literally, world pain.

Samuel Rogers
1763–1855

1 Think nothing done while aught remains to do. *Human Life, l. 49*

2 Never less alone than when alone.[1] *Ib. l. 756*

3 By many a temple half as old as Time.[2] *Italy. A Farewell*

4 Go! you may call it madness, folly;
You shall not chase my gloom away!
There's such a charm in melancholy
I would not if I could be gay.
To——— [1814], st. 1

5 It doesn't much signify whom one marries, for one is sure to find next morning that it was someone else. *Table Talk*

Robert Hall
1764–1831

6 Call things by their right names. . . . Glass of brandy and water! That is the current but not the appropriate name: ask for a glass of liquid fire and distilled damnation.
From OLINTHUS GREGORY, *Brief Memoir of the Life of Hall*

Gaston Pierre Marc, Duc de Lévis
1764–1830

7 Noblesse oblige [Rank has its obligations].[3] *Maxims and Reflections [1808]*

Thomas Morton
1764–1838

8 Push on—keep moving. *A Cure for the Heartache [1797], act II, sc. i*

9 Approbation from Sir Hubert Stanley is praise indeed. *Ib. V, ii*

10 What will Mrs. Grundy say? What will Mrs. Grundy think?[4] *Speed the Plow [1798], act I, sc. i*

[1] See Cicero, 99:1, and Thoreau, 560:3.
[2] See John William Burgon, 552:9.
[3] See Sophocles, 73:10, and Euripides, 77:16.
[4] See Spencer, 579:13.

Ann Radcliffe
1764–1823

11 Fate sits on these dark battlements and frowns,
And as the portal opens to receive me,
A voice in hollow murmurs through the courts
Tells of a nameless deed.[5]
The Mysteries of Udolpho [1794], motto

Robert Goodloe Harper
1765–1825

12 Millions for defense, but not one cent for tribute.[6]
Toast at banquet for John Marshall [June 18, 1798]

Sir James Mackintosh
1765–1832

13 Diffused knowledge immortalizes itself. *Vindiciae Gallicae [1791]*

14 The Commons, faithful to their system, remained in a wise and masterly inactivity. *Ib.*

15 The frivolous work of polished idleness. *Dissertation on Ethical Philosophy [1830]. Remarks on Thomas Brown*

16 Disciplined inaction. *History of the Revolution in England in 1688 [1834], ch. 7*

José María Morelos y Pavón
1765–1815

17 The government has properly devolved upon the American nation, which has created a *junta* of individuals, natives of the country, in which resides the exercise of sovereignty. Let no European remain in governance of the nation. *Order [March 23, 1813]*

18 Long live Spain—but Sister Spain, and not the ruler of America. *After capturing Acapulco [August 20, 1813]*

[5] See Shakespeare, 239:9.
[6] In 1797 a secret agent from Talleyrand told Charles Cotesworth Pinckney, minister to the French republic, that the American commissioners in Paris to protest French attacks on U.S. shipping would be received only if they paid a $50,000 bribe and made a large loan to the French government. Pinckney's reply was: "Not a sixpence, sir." Later, Harper's remark was attributed to him.

James Smithson
1765–1829

1 To found at Washington, under the name of the Smithsonian Institution, an establishment for the increase and diffusion of knowledge among men.[1]

Bequest [1829] with which the Smithsonian Institution was established [1846]

Isaac D'Israeli
1766–1848

2 Whatever is felicitously expressed risks being worse expressed: it is a wretched taste to be gratified with mediocrity when the excellent lies before us.

Curiosities of Literature [1834]. On Quotation

Thomas Robert Malthus
1766–1834

3 Population, when unchecked, increases in a geometrical ratio. Subsistence increases only in an arithmetical ratio. A slight acquaintance with numbers will show the immensity of the first power in comparison of the second.

An Essay on the Principle of Population [1798]

Ernst Friedrich Herbert von Münster
1766–1839

4 Absolutism tempered by assassination.

Description of the Russian Constitution

Carolina Oliphant, Baroness Nairne
1766–1845

5 Better lo'ed ye canna be,
Will ye no come back again?

Life and Songs [1869]. Bonnie Charlie's Now Awa'[2]

6 Charlie is my darling, the young Chevalier.

Ib. Charlie Is My Darling[2]

7 We'll up an' gie them a blaw, a blaw,
Wi' a hundred pipers an' a', an' a'.

Ib. The Hundred Pipers

[1]Quoted by John Quincy Adams in the *Committee Report on the Smithson Bequest* [March 5, 1840].
See John Quincy Adams, 418:10.
[2]Also attributed to JAMES HOGG [1770–1835].

8 Gude nicht, and joy be wi' you a'.

Ib. Gude Nicht

9 A penniless lass wi' a lang pedigree.

Ib. The Laird o' Cockpen

10 I'm wearin' awa'
To the land o' the leal.

Ib. The Land o' the Leal

11 There's nae sorrow there, John,
There's neither cauld nor care, John,
The day is aye fair,
In the land o' the leal.

Ib.

Madame de Staël
[Germaine, Baronne de Staël-Holstein]
1766–1817

12 Love is the whole history of a woman's life, it is but an episode in a man's.[3]

De l'Influence des Passions [1796]

13 A man must know how to defy opinion; a woman how to submit to it.

Delphine [1802]

14 The sight of such a monument is like a continuous and stationary music.[4]

Corinne [1807], bk. IV, ch. 3

15 To understand everything makes one tolerant.[5] *Ib. XVIII, 5*

16 I would gladly give half of the wit with which I am credited for half of the beauty you possess. *Letter to Madame Récamier*

John Quincy Adams[6]
1767–1848

17 I can never join with my voice in the toast which I see in the papers attributed to one of our gallant naval heroes. I cannot ask of heaven success, even for my country, in a cause where she should be in the wrong.[7] *Fiat justitia, pereat coelum.*[8] My toast would be, may our country be always successful, but whether successful or otherwise, always right.

Letter to John Adams [August 1, 1816]

[3]L'amour est l'histoire de la vie des femmes, c'est un episode dans celle des hommes.
[4]See Goethe, 396:6.
[5]Tout comprendre rend très indulgent.
Attributed to Madame de Staël are similar phrases: Comprendre c'est pardonner [To understand is to forgive]. Tout comprendre c'est tout pardonner [To know everything is to forgive everything].
[6]Known as "Old Man Eloquent."
See Milton, 282:6.
[7]See Charles Churchill, 375:13; Decatur, 445:19; and Schurtz, 603:4.
[8]See Anonymous Latin, 133:25.

1 America, with the same voice which spoke herself into existence as a nation, proclaimed to mankind the inextinguishable rights of human nature, and the only lawful foundations of government.

Address [July 4, 1821]

2 America . . . well knows that by once enlisting under other banners than her own, were they even the banners of foreign independence, she would involve herself beyond the power of extraction, in all the wars of interest and intrigue, of individual avarice, envy, and ambition, which assume the colors and usurp the standard of freedom. The fundamental maxims of her policy would insensibly change from liberty to force. . . . She might become dictatress of the world. She would be no longer the ruler of her own spirit. *Ib.*

3 Individual liberty is individual power, and as the power of a community is a mass compounded of individual powers, the nation which enjoys the most freedom must necessarily be in proportion to its numbers the most powerful nation.

Letter to James Lloyd [October 1, 1822]

4 Who but shall learn that freedom is the prize
Man still is bound to rescue or maintain;
That nature's God commands the slave to rise,
And on the oppressor's head to break the chain.
Roll, years of promise, rapidly roll round,
Till not a slave shall on this earth be found.

Poem

5 This house will bear witness to his piety; this town, his birthplace, to his munificence; history to his patriotism; posterity to the depth and compass of his mind.

From his epitaph for John Adams [1829][1]

6 In charity to all mankind, bearing no malice or ill will to any human being, and even compassionating those who hold in bondage their fellow men, not knowing what they do.[2]

Letter to A. Bronson [July 30, 1838]

7 My wants are many,[3] and, if told,
Would muster many a score.

The Wants of Man [1841], st. 1

[1] Inscribed on one of the portals of the United First Parish Church Unitarian (Church of the Presidents), Quincy, Massachusetts.
[2] See Lincoln, 524:7.
[3] See Young, 330:12, and Goldsmith, 369:12.

8 I want the seals of power and place,
The ensigns of command,
Charged by the people's unbought grace,
To rule my native land.
Nor crown, nor scepter would I ask
But from my country's will,
By day, by night, to ply the task
Her cup of bliss to fill. *Ib. st. 22*

9 The great problem of legislation is, so to organize the civil government of a community . . . that in the operation of human institutions upon social action, self-love and social may be made the same.[4]

Society and Civilization; in the American Review [July 1845]

10 To furnish the means of acquiring knowledge is . . . the greatest benefit that can be conferred upon mankind. It prolongs life itself and enlarges the sphere of existence.[5]

Report on the establishment of the Smithsonian Institution [c. 1846]

11 This is the last of earth! I am content.

Last words [February 21, 1848]

Black Hawk[6]

1767–1838

12 I saw my evil day at hand. The sun rose dim on us in the morning, and at night it sank in a dark cloud, and looked like a ball of fire. That was the last sun that shone on Black Hawk. His heart is dead . . . He is now a prisoner to the white man.

Speech upon surrender, Prairie du Chien, Wisconsin [August 27, 1832]

13 [Black Hawk] has done nothing for which an Indian ought to be ashamed. He has fought for his countrymen, the squaws and papooses, against white men, who came year after year, to cheat them and take away their lands. You know the cause of our making war.[7] It is known to all white men. They ought to be ashamed of it. *Ib.*

Andrew Jackson[8]

1767–1845

14 The individual who refuses to defend his rights when called by his Government, de-

[4] See Pope, 338:4.
[5] See Smithson, 417:1.
[6] Ma-ke-tai-me-she-kia-kiak.
Chief of the Sauk and Fox Indians.
[7] The Black Hawk War [1832].
[8] He was the most American of Americans — an embodied Declaration of Independence — the Fourth of July incarnate. — JAMES PARTON, *Life of Andrew Jackson* [1859]

serves to be a slave, and must be punished as an enemy of his country and friend to her foe.

Proclamation to the people of Louisiana from Mobile [September 21, 1814]

1 The brave man inattentive to his duty, is worth little more to his country, than the coward who deserts her in the hour of danger.

To troops who had abandoned their lines during the battle of New Orleans [January 8, 1815]

2 Our Federal Union! it must be preserved!

Toast at Jefferson Birthday Celebration [1830]

3 Every man is equally entitled to protection by law; but when the laws undertake to add . . . artificial distinctions, to grant titles, gratuities, and exclusive privileges, to make the rich richer and the potent more powerful, the humble members of society—the farmers, mechanics, and laborers—who have neither the time nor the means of securing like favors to themselves, have a right to complain of the injustice of their government.

Veto of the Bank Bill [July 10, 1832]

4 There are no necessary evils in government. Its evils exist only in its abuses. If it would confine itself to equal protection, and, as Heaven does its rains, shower its favors alike on the high and the low, the rich and the poor, it would be an unqualified blessing.

Ib.

5 One man with courage makes a majority.

Saying

François René de Chateaubriand

1768–1848

6 [On his conversion to Christianity] I wept and I believed.[1]

Le Génie du Christianisme [1802]

7 The original writer is not one who imitates nobody, but one whom nobody can imitate.[2]

Ib.

8 Achilles exists only through Homer. Take away the art of writing from this world, and you will probably take away its glory.[3]

Les Natchez [1826], preface

[1] J'ai pleuré et j'ai cru.

[2] L'écrivain original n'est pas celui qui n'imite personne, mais celui que personne ne peut imiter.

[3] See Pindar, 72:7; Alexander the Great, 90:13; and Horace, 108:13.

Tecumseh[4]

1768–1813

9 These lands are ours. No one has a right to remove us, because we were the first owners. The Great Spirit above has appointed this place for us, on which to light our fires, and here we will remain. As to boundaries, the Great Spirit knows no boundaries, nor will his red children acknowledge any.[5]

To Joseph Barron, messenger of President James Madison [1810]

10 My father! The Great Spirit is my father! The earth is my mother—and on her bosom I will recline.

Council at Vincennes, Indiana Territory [August 14, 1810]. Answer to request to sit at "his father's" (Governor William Henry Harrison's) side

11 I am a Shawnee. My forefathers were warriors. Their son is a warrior. From them I take only my existence. From my tribe I take nothing. I am the maker of my own fortune. And oh, that I might make the fortunes of my red people, and of my country, as great as the conceptions of my mind, when I think of the Great Spirit that rules this universe.

Ib. Speech to Harrison

12 Once they were a happy race. Now they are made miserable by the white people, who are never contented but are always encroaching.

Ib.

13 Sell a country! Why not sell the air, the clouds and the great sea, as well as the earth? Did not the Great Spirit make them all for the use of his children? *Ib.*

14 Our lives are in the hands of the Great Spirit. He gave to our ancestors the lands which we possess. We are determined to defend them, and if it is His will, our bones shall whiten on them, but we will never give them up.[6]

Speech to Major General Henry Procter, British commander, Fort Malden [September 1813]

[4] Chief of the Shawnees.

[5] See Cowper, 376:19.

He remembered the belligerent ants, who claimed their boundaries, and the pacific geese, who did not. . . . All those puffins, razorbills, guillemots and kittiwakes had lived together peacefully, preserving their own kinds of civilization without war—because they claimed no boundaries.—T. H. WHITE, *The Once and Future King* [1939], *bk. IV, ch. 14*

[6] Tecumseh was killed in the battle of the Thames River [October 5, 1813].

Ernst Moritz Arndt
1769–1860

1 What is the German Fatherland?
Wherever the German tongue is heard.
Was Ist des Deutschen Vaterland [1813]

2 The Rhine: Germany's River, but Not Germany's Border. *Title of work [1813]*

Alexander von Humboldt
1769–1859

3 Insight into universal nature provides an intellectual delight and sense of freedom that no blows of fate and no evil can destroy.
Statement [1805]

Ivan Krylov
1768–1844

4 Your guilt consists in this: I want to eat you up![1] *Fables [1809].[2] Wolf and Lamb*

5 Heaven save you from a foolish friend;
The too officious fool is worse than any foe.
Ib. Hermit and Bear

Napoleon I
[Napoleon Bonaparte]
1769–1821

6 Soldiers, from the summit of yonder pyramids forty centuries look down upon you.
In Egypt [July 21, 1798]

7 Go, sir, gallop, and don't forget that the world was made in six days. You can ask me for anything you like, except time.
To an aide [1803]. From R. M. Johnston, The Corsican

8 A form of government that is not the result of a long sequence of shared experiences, efforts, and endeavors can never take root.
[1803]. From J. Christopher Herold, The Mind of Napoleon [1955]

9 From the sublime to the ridiculous is but a step.[3]
To the Abbé du Pradt, on the return from Russia [1812], referring to the retreat from Moscow

[1] See La Fontaine, 296:9.
[2] Translated by Sir Bernard Pares.
[3] Du sublime au ridicule il n'y a qu'un pas.
The saying has been attributed also to Talleyrand. See Paine, 385:7.

10 You write to me that it's impossible; the word is not French.
Letter to General Lemarois [July 9, 1813]

11 What is the throne?—a bit of wood gilded and covered with velvet. I am the state[4]—I alone am here the representative of the people. Even if I had done wrong you should not have reproached me in public—people wash their dirty linen at home.[5] France has more need of me than I of France.
To the Senate [1814]

12 France is invaded; I am leaving to take command of my troops, and, with God's help and their valor, I hope soon to drive the enemy beyond the frontier.
At Paris [January 23, 1814]

13 The bullet that will kill me is not yet cast.
At Montereau [February 17, 1814]

14 The Allied Powers having proclaimed that the Emperor Napoleon is the sole obstacle to the re-establishment of peace in Europe, he, faithful to his oath, declares that he is ready to descend from the throne, to quit France, and even to relinquish life, for the good of his country.
Act of Abdication [April 4, 1814]

15 Unite for the public safety, if you would remain an independent nation.
Proclamation to the French People [June 22, 1815]

16 Wherever wood can swim, there I am sure to find this flag of England.
At Rochefort [July 1815]

17 Whatever shall we do in that remote spot? Well, we will write our memoirs. Work is the scythe of time.
On board H.M.S. Bellerophon [August 1815]

18 [Of his relations with the Empress Josephine] I generally had to give in.
On St. Helena [May 19, 1816]

19 My maxim was, *la carrière est ouverte aux talents,* without distinction of birth or fortune.[6] *Ib. [March 3, 1817]*

20 Our hour is marked, and no one can claim a moment of life beyond what fate has predestined. *To Dr. Arnott [April 1821]*

[4] See Louis XIV, 312:1.
[5] Il faut laver son linge sale en famille [One should wash one's dirty linen at home].—*Saying current since about 1720*
[6] To the very last, he [Napoleon] had a kind of idea; that, namely, of *La carrière ouverte aux talents,* The tools to him that can handle them.—Thomas Carlyle, *Critical and Miscellaneous Essays, Sir Walter Scott* [1838]

1 Two o'clock in the morning courage: I mean unprepared courage.[1]

[December 4, 5, 1815]. From LAS CASES, *Mémorial de Ste-Hélène [1823]*

2 Madame Montholon having inquired what troops he considered the best, "Those which are victorious, Madame," replied the Emperor.

From BOURRIENNE, *Memoirs [1829]*

3 A silk stocking filled with mud.

Description of Talleyrand[2]

4 An army marches on its stomach.[3]

Attributed

5 Every French soldier carries a marshal's baton in his knapsack.[4] *Attributed*

6 Perfidious Albion.[5] *Attributed*

7 Chief of the Army.[6] *Last words*

Arthur Wellesley, Duke of Wellington

1769–1852

8 Nothing except a battle lost can be half so melancholy as a battle won.

Dispatch from the field of Waterloo [June 1815]

9 I used to say of him [Napoleon] that his presence on the field made the difference of forty thousand men.

[November 2, 1831]. From PHILIP HENRY, EARL OF STANHOPE, *Notes of Conversations with the Duke of Wellington [1888]*

10 The only thing I am afraid of is fear.[7]

Ib. [November 3, 1831]

11 Ours [our army] is composed of the scum of the earth—the mere scum of the earth.

Ib. [November 4, 1831]

12 My rule always was to do the business of the day in the day.

Ib. [November 2, 1835]

13 They wanted this iron fist to command them.

Ib. [November 8, 1840]; of troops sent by Wellington to the Canadian frontier in the war with America

14 There is no mistake; there has been no mistake; and there shall be no mistake.

Wellingtoniana [1832], p. 78

15 I don't care a twopenny damn what becomes of the ashes of Napoleon Buonaparte. *Attributed*

16 The battle of Waterloo was won on the playing fields of Eton.

From SIR WILLIAM FRASER, *Words on Wellington [1889]*

17 Publish and be damned.

Attributed; when the courtesan Harriette Wilson threatened to publish her memoirs and his letters

Ludwig van Beethoven

1770–1827

18 I want to seize fate by the throat.

Letter to Dr. Franz Wegeler [November 16, 1801]

19 Art! Who comprehends her? With whom can one consult concerning this great goddess?

Letter to Bettina von Arnim [August 11, 1810]

20 The world is a king, and, like a king, desires flattery in return for favor; but true art is selfish and perverse—it will not submit to the mold of flattery.

Conversations [March 1820]

Pierre Jacques Étienne, Count Cambronne

1770–1842

21 The Guards die, but never surrender.[8]

Attributed

George Canning

1770–1827

22 When our perils are past, shall our gratitude sleep?

[1] Le courage de l'improviste.
The three o'clock in the morning courage, which Bonaparte thought was the rarest.—THOREAU, *Walden* [1854], *ch. 4, Sounds*
See F. Scott Fitzgerald, 835:11.

[2] Attributed by SAINTE-BEUVE.

[3] No man can be a patriot on an empty stomach.—WILLIAM COWPER BRANN, *The Iconoclast, Old Glory* [July 4, 1893]

[4] Tout soldat français porte dans sa giberne le bâton de maréchal de France.

[5] L'Angleterre, ah! la perfide Angleterre.—JACQUES BÉNIGNE BOSSUET [1627–1704], *Sermon sur la Circoncision*
Napoleon used the phrase in 1803, and it became widespread during the French Revolution.

[6] Tête d'armée.

[7] See *Proverbs 3:25*, 23:6; Montaigne, 164:7; Bacon, 179:13; Thoreau, 557:9; and Roosevelt, 779:10.

[8] La Garde meurt, mais ne se rend pas.
Cambronne denied having said this phrase, which was invented by Rougemont after the battle of Waterloo, in the *Indépendent*.—FOURNIER, *L'Esprit dans l'Histoire* [1857]

No—here's to the pilot that weathered the storm.

Song for the Inauguration of the Pitt Club [May 25, 1802]

1 I give thee sixpence! I will see thee damned first.

The Anti-Jacobin, no. 11 [1797]. The Friend of Humanity and the Knife-Grinder, st. 9

2 I think of those companions true
Who studied with me at the U-
niversity of Göttingen.

Ib. no. 30 [1798]. The Rovers, song, st. 1

3 A steady patriot of the world alone,
The friend of every country but his own.[1]

Ib. no 36 [1798]. New Morality, l. 113

4 And finds, with keen, discriminating sight,
Black's not so black—nor white so *very* white. *Ib. l. 199*

5 Give me the avowed, erect, and manly foe,
Firm I can meet, perhaps return the blow;
But of all plagues, good Heaven, thy wrath can send,
Save, save, oh save me from the candid friend![2] *Ib. l. 207*

6 In matters of commerce the fault of the Dutch
Is offering too little and asking too much.

Dispatch to Sir Charles Bagot, British minister at The Hague [January 31, 1826]

7 I called the New World into existence to redress the balance of the Old.

The King's Message [December 12, 1826]

Georg Wilhelm Friedrich Hegel

1770–1831

8 What is reasonable is real; that which is real is reasonable.

Philosophy of Right [1821]

9 What experience and history teach is this—that people and governments never have learned anything from history, or acted on principles deduced from it.

Philosophy of History [1832],[3] introduction

10 Amid the pressure of great events, a general principle gives no help. *Ib.*

11 To him who looks upon the world rationally, the world in its turn presents a rational aspect. The relation is mutual. *Ib.*

12 The history of the world is none other than the progress of the consciousness of freedom. *Ib.*

13 We may affirm absolutely that nothing great in the world has been accomplished without passion. *Ib.*

14 It is easier to discover a deficiency in individuals, in states, and in Providence, than to see their real import and value. *Ib.*

15 Life has a value only when it has something valuable as its object. *Ib.*

16 Serious occupation is labor that has reference to some want.

Ib. pt. I, sec. 2, ch. 1

17 It is a matter of perfect indifference where a thing originated; the only question is: "Is it true in and for itself?" *Ib. III, 3, 2*

18 The Few assume to be the *deputies,* but they are often only the *despoilers* of the Many. *Ib. IV, 3, 3*

James Hogg[4]

1770–1835

19 We'll o'er the water, we'll o'er the sea,
We'll o'er the water to Charlie;
Come weal, come woe, we'll gather and go,
And live and die wi' Charlie.

O'er the Water to Charlie

20 For Kilmeny had been she knew not where,
And Kilmeny had seen what she could not declare. *Kilmeny, l. 38*

Joseph Hopkinson

1770–1842

21 Hail, Columbia! happy land!
Hail, ye heroes! heaven-born band!
Who fought and bled in Freedom's cause.

Hail, Columbia [1798],[5] st. 1

[1] This refers to the Jacobin.
See Shakespeare, 212:20; Overbury, 262:13; and Gilbert, 629:7.

[2] Defend me from my friends; I can defend myself from my enemies.—*Attributed to* MARÉCHAL VILLARS, *when taking leave of Louis XIV*

[3] Translated by J. SIBREE.
Quoted by G. B. Shaw in *The Revolutionist's Handbook.*

[4] The Ettrick Shepherd.

[5] The music, generally attributed to Philip Phile, was Washington's inaugural march. Hopkinson supplied verses at a singer's request, and the song won instant acclaim.

William Robert Spencer

1770–1834

1 Oh! where does faithful Gêlert roam,
The flow'r of all his race?
So true, so brave; a lamb at home,
A lion in the chase!
Beth-Gêlert, st. 4

William Wordsworth[1]

1770–1850

2 And homeless near a thousand homes I stood,
And near a thousand tables pined and wanted food.
Guilt and Sorrow [written 1791–1794],[2] st. 41

3 ——A simple child,[3]
That lightly draws its breath,
And feels its life in every limb,
What should it know of death?
We Are Seven [1798], st. 1

4 Have I not reason to lament
What man has made of man?[4]
Lines Written in Early Spring [1798], st. 6

5 Nor less I deem that there are Powers
Which of themselves our minds impress;
That we can feed this mind of ours
In a wise passiveness.
Expostulation and Reply [1798], st. 6

6 Come forth into the light of things,
Let Nature be your teacher.
The Tables Turned [1798], st. 4

7 One impulse from a vernal wood
May teach you more of man,
Of moral evil and of good,
Than all the sages can.[5]
Ib. st. 6

8 Sensations sweet,
Felt in the blood, and felt along the heart.
Lines Composed a Few Miles Above Tintern Abbey [1798], l. 27

9 That best portion of a good man's life,
His little, nameless, unremembered acts
Of kindness and of love.
Ib. l. 33

10 Blessed mood,
In which the burthen of the mystery,
In which the heavy and the weary weight
Of all this unintelligible world,
Is lightened.
Ib. l. 37

11 While with an eye made quiet by the power
Of harmony, and the deep power of joy,
We see into the life of things.
Ib. l. 47

12 The sounding cataract
Haunted me like a passion: the tall rock,
The mountain, and the deep and gloomy wood,
Their colors and their forms, were then to me
An appetite; a feeling and a love,
That had no need of a remoter charm,
By thought supplied, nor any interest
Unborrowed from the eye.
Ib. l. 76

13 I have learned
To look on nature, not as in the hour
Of thoughtless youth; but hearing oftentimes
The still, sad music of humanity,
Nor harsh nor grating, though of ample power
To chasten and subdue. And I have felt
A presence that disturbs me with the joy
Of elevated thoughts; a sense sublime
Of something far more deeply interfused,
Whose dwelling is the light of setting suns,
And the round ocean and the living air,
And the blue sky, and in the mind of man:
A motion and a spirit, that impels
All thinking things, all objects of all thought,
And rolls through all things.[6]
Ib. l. 88

14 All the mighty world
Of eye and ear, both what they half create,
And what perceive.
Ib. l. 105

15 Knowing that Nature never did betray
The heart that loved her.
Ib. l. 122

16 A primrose by a river's brim
A yellow primrose was to him,
And it was nothing more.
Peter Bell [written 1798],[7] pt. I, st. 12

17 Fair seedtime had my soul, and I grew up
Fostered alike by beauty and by fear.
The Prelude [written 1799–1805],[8] bk. I, l. 301

18 Dust as we are, the immortal spirit grows
Like harmony in music; there is a dark
Inscrutable workmanship that reconciles
Discordant elements, makes them cling together
In one society.
Ib. l. 340

[1] Coleridge said to Wordsworth, "Since Milton, I know of no poet with so many *felicities* and unforgettable lines and stanzas as you."—Henry Nelson Coleridge, *Memoir* [1847]

[2] Published 1842.

[3] In the first edition the line is: A simple child, dear brother Jim. It was reduced to the current text in the 1815 edition of his poems.

[4] See Pliny, 116:10, and Burns, 408:16.

[5] See St. Bernard, 136:9, and Shakespeare, 210:24 and 211:17.

[6] See Shelley, 466:8.

[7] Published 1819.

[8] Published 1850.

1 The grim shape
Towered up between me and the stars, and still,
For so it seemed, with purpose of its own
And measured motion like a living thing,
Strode after me. *Ib. l. 381*

2 Where the statue stood
Of Newton with his prism and silent face,
The marble index of a mind forever
Voyaging through strange seas of thought, alone. *Ib. III, l. 60*

3 When from our better selves we have too long
Been parted by the hurrying world, and droop,
Sick of its business, of its pleasures tired,
How gracious, how benign, is Solitude.
Ib. IV, l. 354

4 Brothers all
In honor, as in one community,
Scholars and gentlemen. *Ib. IX, l. 227*

5 Bliss was it in that dawn to be alive,
But to be young was very heaven![1]
Ib. XI, l. 108

6 There is
One great society alone on earth:
The noble Living and the noble Dead.
Ib. l. 393

7 Poetry is the breath and finer spirit of all knowledge; it is the impassioned expression which is in the countenance of all Science.
Lyrical Ballads [2nd ed., 1800]. Preface

8 In spite of difference of soil and climate, of language and manners, of laws and customs—in spite of things silently gone out of mind, and things violently destroyed, the Poet binds together by passion and knowledge the vast empire of human society, as it is spread over the whole earth, and over all time.
Ib.

9 I have said that poetry is the spontaneous overflow of powerful feelings: it takes its origin from emotion recollected in tranquillity.
Ib.

10 One of those heavenly days that cannot die.
Nutting [1800], l. 3

11 What fond and wayward thoughts will slide
Into a lover's head!
"O mercy!" to myself I cried,
"If Lucy should be dead!"
Strange Fits of Passion Have I Known [1800], st. 7

[1]Also in *French Revolution as It Appears to Enthusiasts* [1804].

12 She dwelt among the untrodden ways
Beside the springs of Dove,
A maid whom there were none to praise
And very few to love:[2]

A violet by a mossy stone
Half hidden from the eye!
—Fair as a star, when only one
Is shining in the sky.

She lived unknown, and few could know
When Lucy ceased to be;
But she is in her grave, and, oh,
The difference to me!
She Dwelt Among the Untrodden Ways [1800]

13 Three years she grew in sun and shower,
Then Nature said, "A lovelier flower
On earth was never sown;
This Child I to myself will take;
She shall be mine, and I will make
A Lady of my own."
Three Years She Grew in Sun and Shower [1800], st. 1

14 A slumber did my spirit seal;
I had no human fears:
She seemed a thing that could not feel
The touch of earthly years.

No motion has she now, no force;
She neither hears nor sees;
Rolled round in earth's diurnal course,
With rocks, and stones, and trees.
A Slumber Did My Spirit Seal [1800]

15 A fingering slave,
One that would peep and botanize
Upon his mother's grave.
A Poet's Epitaph [1800], st. 5

16 A reasoning, self-sufficing thing,
An intellectual All-in-all! *Ib. st. 8*

17 And you must love him, ere to you
He will seem worthy of your love.
Ib. st. 11

18 The harvest of a quiet eye. *Ib. st. 13*

19 The sweetest thing that ever grew
Beside a human door.
Lucy Gray [1800], st. 2

20 And sings a solitary song
That whistles in the wind. *Ib. st. 16*

[2]He lived amidst th' untrodden ways / To Rydal Lake that lead; / A bard whom there were none to praise, / And very few to read. / Unread his works—his "Milk White Doe" / With dust is dark and dim; / It's still in Longmans' shop, and oh! / The difference to him!—*Parody by* HARTLEY COLERIDGE [1796–1849]

1 A youth to whom was given
So much of earth—so much of heaven,
And such impetuous blood.
Ruth [1800], st. 21

2 Something between a hindrance and a help.
Michael [1800], l. 189

3 Drink, pretty creature, drink!
The Pet Lamb [1800], st. 1

4 May no rude hand deface it,
And its forlorn *Hic jacet!*
Ellen Irwin [1800], st. 7

5 She gave me eyes, she gave me ears;
And humble cares, and delicate fears;
A heart, the fountain of sweet tears;
And love, and thought, and joy.
The Sparrows' Nest [1807], st. 2

6 I traveled among unknown men,
In lands beyond the sea;
Nor, England! did I know till then
What love I bore to thee.
I Traveled Among Unknown Men [1807], st. 1

7 My heart leaps up when I behold
A rainbow in the sky:
So was it when my life began;
So is it now I am a man;
So be it when I shall grow old,
Or let me die!
The child is father of the man;[1]
And I could wish my days to be
Bound each to each by natural piety.
My Heart Leaps Up [1807][2]

8 Sweet childish days, that were as long
As twenty days are now.
To a Butterfly (I've Watched You Now a Full Half-Hour) [1807], st. 2

9 Pleasures newly found are sweet
When they lie about our feet.
To the Same Flower (the Small Celandine) [1807], st. 1

10 I thought of Chatterton, the marvelous boy,
The sleepless soul that perished in his pride;
Of him[3] who walked in glory and in joy
Following his plow, along the mountainside:
By our own spirits are we deified:
We Poets in our youth begin in gladness;
But thereof come in the end despondency and madness.[4]
Resolution and Independence [1807], st. 7

[1] See Milton, 288:12.
[2] The last three lines are the epigraph for *Intimations of Immortality*, 426:10.
[3] Robert Burns.
[4] See Democritus, 79:*n*5; Robert Burton, 258:13; and Robert Lowell, 892:15.

11 Choice word and measured phrase, above the reach
Of ordinary men.
Ib. st. 14

12 And mighty poets in their misery dead.
Ib. st. 17

13 Earth has not anything to show more fair:
Dull would he be of soul who could pass by
A sight so touching in its majesty.
Composed upon Westminster Bridge, September 3, 1802 [1807], l. 1

14 Ne'er saw I, never felt, a calm so deep!
The river glideth at his own sweet will!
Dear God! the very houses seem asleep;
And all that mighty heart is lying still!
Ib. l. 11

15 Plain living and high thinking are no more:
The homely beauty of the good old cause
Is gone; our peace, our fearful innocence,
And pure religion breathing household laws.
Written in London, September 1802 [1807]

16 It is a beauteous evening, calm and free,
The holy time is quiet as a nun
Breathless with adoration.
It Is a Beauteous Evening [1807], l. 1

17 Thou liest in Abraham's bosom all the year;
And worship'st at the Temple's inner shrine,
God being with thee when we know it not.
Ib. l. 12

18 Once did she hold the gorgeous east in fee:
And was the safeguard of the west.
On the Extinction of the Venetian Republic [1807], l. 1

19 And, when she took unto herself a mate,
She must espouse the everlasting sea.
Ib. l. 7

20 Men are we, and must grieve when even the shade
Of that which once was great is passed away.
Ib. l. 13

21 Thou hast great allies;
Thy friends are exultations, agonies,
And love, and man's unconquerable mind.
To Toussaint L'Ouverture [1807], l. 12

22 Milton! thou shouldst be living at this hour:
England hath need of thee: she is a fen
Of stagnant waters.
London, 1802 [1807], l. 1

23 Thy soul was like a star, and dwelt apart;
Thou hadst a voice whose sound was like the sea:
Pure as the naked heavens, majestic, free,
So didst thou travel on life's common way,
In cheerful godliness.
Ib. l. 9

1 We must be free or die, who speak the tongue
That Shakespeare spake; the faith and morals hold
Which Milton held.
It Is Not to Be Thought Of [1807], l. 11

2 Thou unassuming commonplace
Of nature.
To the Same Flower (the Daisy) [1807], st. 1

3 Oft on the dappled turf at ease
I sit, and play with similes,
Loose types of things through all degrees.
Ib. st. 2

4 And stepping westward seemed to be
A kind of heavenly destiny.
Stepping Westward [1807], st. 2

5 Old, unhappy, far-off things,
And battles long ago.
The Solitary Reaper [1807], st. 3

6 The music in my heart I bore
Long after it was heard no more.
Ib. st. 4

7 The good old rule
Sufficeth them, the simple plan,
That they should take, who have the power,
And they should keep who can.
Rob Roy's Grave [1807], st. 9

8 A brotherhood of venerable trees.
Sonnet. Composed at —— Castle [1807], l. 6

9 O for a single hour of that Dundee,
Who on that day the word of onset gave!
Sonnet. In the Pass of Killicranky [1803], l. 11

10 There was a time when meadow, grove, and stream,
The earth, and every common sight,
To me did seem
Appareled in celestial light,
The glory and the freshness of a dream.
It is not now as it hath been of yore—
Turn wheresoe'er I may,
By night or day,
The things which I have seen I now can see no more.
Ode. Intimations of Immortality from Recollections of Early Childhood [1807],[1] st. 1

11 The Rainbow comes and goes,
And lovely is the Rose.
Ib. st. 2

[1]The *Ode on Immortality* is the high water mark which the intellect has reached in this age. — EMERSON, *English Traits* [1856]

12 The sunshine is a glorious birth;
But yet I know, where'er I go,
That there hath passed away a glory from the earth.
Ib.

13 Whither is fled the visionary gleam?
Where is it now, the glory and the dream?
Ib. st. 4

14 Our birth is but a sleep and a forgetting:
The soul that rises with us, our life's star,
Hath had elsewhere its setting,
And cometh from afar:
Not in entire forgetfulness,
And not in utter nakedness,
But trailing clouds of glory do we come
From God, who is our home:
Heaven lies about us in our infancy![2]
Shades of the prison-house begin to close
Upon the growing boy.
Ib. st. 5

15 The youth, who daily farther from the east
Must travel, still is Nature's priest,
And by the vision splendid
Is on his way attended;
At length the man perceives it die away,
And fade into the light of common day.
Ib.

16 As if his whole vocation
Were endless imitation.
Ib. st. 7

17 O joy! that in our embers
Is something that doth live,
That nature yet remembers
What was so fugitive!
Ib. st. 9

18 High instincts before which our mortal nature
Did tremble like a guilty thing surprised.
Ib.

19 Truths that wake,
To perish never.
Ib.

20 Though inland far we be,
Our souls have sight of that immortal sea
Which brought us hither.
Ib.

21 Though nothing can bring back the hour
Of splendor in the grass, of glory in the flower.
Ib. st. 10

22 In years that bring the philosophic mind.
Ib.

23 The clouds that gather round the setting sun
Do take a sober coloring from an eye
That hath kept watch o'er man's mortality;
Another race hath been, and other palms are won.
Thanks to the human heart by which we live,
Thanks to its tenderness, its joys, and fears,

[2]See Vaughan, 299:2; Traherne, 311:22; and Lowell, 567:11.

To me the meanest flower that blows can give
Thoughts that do often lie too deep for tears.
Ib. st. 11

1 O blithe newcomer! I have heard,
I hear thee and rejoice.
O Cuckoo! shall I call thee bird,
Or but a wandering voice?
To the Cuckoo [1807], st. 1

2 No bird, but an invisible thing,
A voice, a mystery. *Ib. st. 4*

3 She was a phantom of delight
When first she gleamed upon my sight;
A lovely apparition, sent
To be a moment's ornament.
She Was a Phantom of Delight [1807], st. 1

4 A spirit, yet a woman too! *Ib. st. 2*

5 And now I see with eye serene
The very pulse of the machine.
Ib. st. 3

6 A perfect woman, nobly planned,
To warn, to comfort, and command.
Ib.

7 I wandered lonely as a cloud
That floats on high o'er vales and hills,
When all at once I saw a crowd,
A host, of golden daffodils.
I Wandered Lonely as a Cloud [1807], st. 1

8 Continuous as the stars that shine
And twinkle on the milky way.
Ib. st. 2

9 Ten thousand saw I at a glance,
Tossing their heads in sprightly dance.
Ib.

10 A poet could not but be gay,
In such a jocund company. *Ib. st. 3*

11 That inward eye
Which is the bliss of solitude. *Ib. st. 4*

12 Stern daughter of the voice of God![1]
O Duty! *Ode to Duty [1807], st. 1*

13 A light to guide, a rod
To check the erring, and reprove. *Ib.*

14 Me this unchartered freedom tires;
I feel the weight of chance desires;
My hopes no more must change their name,
I long for a repose that ever is the same.
Ib. st. 5

15 Stern Lawgiver! *Ib. st. 7*

16 Thou dost preserve the stars from wrong;
And the most ancient heavens, through
Thee, are fresh and strong. *Ib.*

[1]See Milton, 287:18.

17 The light that never was, on sea or land,
The consecration, and the poet's dream.
Elegiac Stanzas. Suggested by a Picture of Peele Castle in a Storm [1807], st. 4

18 Dear child of Nature, let them rail!
To a Young Lady [1807], st. 1

19 Thou, while thy babes around thee cling,
Shalt show us how divine a thing
A woman may be made. *Ib. st. 2*

20 But an old age serene and bright,
And lovely as a Lapland night,
Shall lead thee to thy grave. *Ib. st. 3*

21 Who is the happy Warrior?[2] Who is he
That every man in arms would wish to be?
Character of the Happy Warrior [1807], l. 1

22 Who, doomed to go in company with pain,
And fear, and bloodshed, miserable train!
Turns his necessity to glorious gain.
Ib. l. 12

23 More skillful in self-knowledge, even more pure,
As tempted more; more able to endure,
As more exposed to suffering and distress.
Ib. l. 23

24 But who, if he be called upon to face
Some awful moment to which Heaven has joined
Great issues, good or bad for humankind,
Is happy as a lover. *Ib. l. 48*

25 And, through the heat of conflict, keeps the law
In calmness made, and sees what he foresaw.
Ib. l. 53

26 Whom neither shape of danger can dismay,
Nor thought of tender happiness betray.
Ib. l. 72

27 Like—but oh how different!
Yes, It Was the Mountain Echo [1807], st. 2

28 Nuns fret not at their convent's narrow room. *Nuns Fret Not [1807], l. 1*

29 The world is too much with us; late and soon,
Getting and spending, we lay waste our powers:
Little we see in Nature that is ours;
We have given our hearts away, a sordid boon!
The World Is Too Much with Us [1807], l. 1

[2]All's well, for over there among his peers / A happy warrior sleeps.—John Ceredigion Jones [1883–1947], *The Returning Man, st. 4*
See Alfred E. Smith, 741:*n*3.

1 Great God! I'd rather be
A pagan suckled in a creed outworn;
So might I, standing on this pleasant lea,
Have glimpses that would make me less forlorn;
Have sight of Proteus rising from the sea;
Or hear old Triton blow his wreathèd horn.
Ib. l. 9

2 Where lies the land to which yon ship must go?[1]
Fresh as a lark mounting at break of day,
Festively she puts forth in trim array.
Where Lies the Land [1807], l. 1

3 Blessed barrier between day and day.
To Sleep (A Flock of Sheep) [1807], l. 13

4 Dreams, books, are each a world; and books, we know,
Are a substantial world, both pure and good:
Round these, with tendrils strong as flesh and blood,
Our pastime and our happiness will grow.
Personal Talk [1807], sonnet 3

5 A power is passing from the earth.
Lines on the Expected Dissolution of Mr. Fox [1807], st. 5

6 Two voices are there: one is of the sea,[2]
One of the mountains; each a mighty voice.
Thought of a Briton on the Subjugation of Switzerland [1807], l. 1

7 The silence that is in the starry sky,
The sleep that is among the lonely hills.
Song at the Feast of Brougham Castle [1807], l. 163

8 Every great and original writer, in proportion as he is great or original, must himself create the taste by which he is to be relished.
Letter to Lady Beaumont [May 21, 1807]

9 Strongest minds
Are often those of whom the noisy world
Hears least.
The Excursion [1814],[3] bk. I, l. 91

10 The imperfect offices of prayer and praise.
Ib. l. 216

[1] See Clough, 564:13.

[2] Two voices are there: one is of the deep; / And one is of an old half-witted sheep / Which bleats articulate monotony, / And indicates that two and one are three. / And, Wordsworth, both art thine.—JAMES KENNETH STEPHEN, *Sonnet, Wordsworth* [1891]

[3] This will never do.—FRANCIS JEFFREY, *opening sentence, review of* WORDSWORTH, *Excursion, Edinburgh Review* [1814]

11 The good die first,[4]
And they whose hearts are dry as summer dust
Burn to the socket.
Ib. l. 500

12 Wrongs unredressed, or insults unavenged.
Ib. III, l. 374

13 Society became my glittering bride.
Ib. l. 735

14 There is a luxury in self-dispraise;
And inward self-disparagement affords
To meditative spleen a grateful feast.
Ib. IV, l. 475

15 I have seen
A curious child, who dwelt upon a tract
Of inland ground, applying to his ear
The convolutions of a smooth-lipped shell,
To which, in silence hushed, his very soul
Listened intensely; and his countenance soon
Brightened with joy, for from within were heard
Murmurings, whereby the monitor expressed
Mysterious union with its native sea.[5]
Ib. l. 1132

16 One in whom persuasion and belief
Had ripened into faith, and faith become
A passionate intuition.
Ib. l. 1293

17 Spires whose "silent finger points to heaven."[6]
Ib. VI, l. 19

18 A man he seems of cheerful yesterdays
And confident tomorrows.
Ib. VII, l. 557

19 A few strong instincts, and a few plain rules.
Alas! What Boots the Long Laborious Quest? [1815], l. 11

20 Surprised by joy—impatient as the wind.
Surprised by Joy [1815], l. 1

21 The gods approve
The depth, and not the tumult, of the soul.
Laodamia [1815], st. 13

22 An ampler ether, a diviner air.
Ib. st. 18

23 And beauty, for confiding youth,
Those shocks of passion can prepare
That kill the bloom before its time;

[4] See Menander, 91:1.

[5] See Landor, 442:16.
Upon a mountain height, far from the sea, / I found a shell, / And to my listening ear the lonely thing / Ever a song of ocean seemed to sing, / Ever a tale of ocean seemed to tell.—EUGENE FIELD [1850–1895], *The Wanderer, st. 1*

[6] An instinctive taste teaches men to build their churches in flat countries with spire steeples, which, as they cannot be referred to any other object, point as with silent finger to the sky and stars.—COLERIDGE, *The Friend* [1809], *no. 14*

And blanch, without the owner's crime,
The most resplendent hair.
Lament of Mary Queen of Scots [1820], st. 6

1 Enough, if something from our hands have power
To live, and act, and serve the future hour.
The River Duddon [1820], sonnet 34, Afterthought, l. 10

2 We feel that we are greater than we know.
Ib. l. 14

3 Habit rules the unreflecting herd.
Ecclesiastical Sonnets [1822], pt. II, sonnet 28, Reflections, l. 10

4 The feather, whence the pen
Was shaped that traced the lives of these good men,
Dropped from an angel's wing.[1]
Ib. III, 5. Walton's Book of Lives, l. 2

5 The unimaginable touch of Time.
Ib. 34. Mutability

6 Give all thou canst; high Heaven rejects the lore
Of nicely calculated less or more.
Ib. 43. Inside of King's College Chapel, Cambridge, l. 6

7 But hushed be every thought that springs
From out the bitterness of things.
Elegiac Stanzas. Addressed to Sir G. H. B. [1827], st. 7

8 Ethereal minstrel! pilgrim of the sky!
To a Skylark [1827], l. 1

9 Type of the wise who soar, but never roam,
True to the kindred points of heaven and home! *Ib.*

10 Scorn not the sonnet; Critic, you have frowned,
Mindless of its just honors; with this key
Shakespeare unlocked his heart.
Scorn Not the Sonnet [1827], l. 1

11 Small service is true service while it lasts:
Of humblest friends, bright creature! scorn not one:
The daisy, by the shadow that it casts,
Protects the lingering dewdrop from the sun.
To a Child. Written in Her Album [1835]

12 How does the meadow flower its bloom unfold?
Because the lovely little flower is free
Down to its root, and, in that freedom, bold.
A Poet!—He Hath Put His Heart to School [1842], l. 9

13 Minds that have nothing to confer
Find little to perceive.
Yes, Thou Art Fair [1845], st. 2

[1] The pen wherewith thou dost so heavenly sing / Made of a quill from an angel's wing.—Henry Constable [1562–1613], *Sonnet*

Marie François Xavier Bichat

1771–1802

14 Life is the totality of those functions which resist death.
Physiological Researches upon Life and Death [1800]

Thomas Dibdin

1771–1841

15 Oh, it's a snug little island!
A right little, tight little island.
The Snug Little Island

James Montgomery

1771–1854

16 Give me the hand that is honest and hearty,
Free as the breeze and unshackled by party.
Give Me Thy Hand, st. 2

17 Here in the body pent,
Absent from Him I roam,
Yet nightly pitch my moving tent
A day's march nearer home.
At Home in Heaven

18 Prayer is the soul's sincere desire,
Uttered or unexpressed;
The motion of a hidden fire
That trembles in the breast.
What Is Prayer? st. 1

William Pitt

d. 1840

19 A strong nor'wester's blowing, Bill,
Hark! Don't ye hear it roar, now?
Lord help 'em, how I pities all
Unhappy folks on shore now!
The Sailor's Consolation, st. 1

Sir Walter Scott

1771–1832

20 The way was long, the wind was cold,
The Minstrel was infirm and old;
His withered cheek, and tresses gray,
Seemed to have known a better day.
The Lay of the Last Minstrel [1805], introduction

1 The unpremeditated lay. *Ib.*

2 Such is the custom of Branksome Hall.
Ib. canto I, st. 7

3 Steady of heart, and stout of hand.
Ib. st. 21

4 If thou would'st view fair Melrose aright,
Go visit it by the pale moonlight.
Ib. II, st. 1

5 I cannot tell how the truth may be;
I say the tale as 'twas said to me.
Ib. II, st. 22

6 In peace, Love tunes the shepherd's reed;
In war, he mounts the warrior's steed;
In halls, in gay attire is seen;
In hamlets, dances on the green.
Love rules the court, the camp, the grove,
And men below, and saints above;
For love is heaven, and heaven is love.
Ib. III, st. 2

7 For ne'er
Was flattery lost on poet's ear:
A simple race! they waste their toil
For the vain tribute of a smile.
Ib. IV, conclusion

8 Call it not vain; they do not err
Who say, that when the Poet dies,
Mute Nature mourns her worshipper,
And celebrates his obsequies.
Ib. V, st. 1

9 True love's the gift which God has given
To man alone beneath the heaven:
It is not fantasy's hot fire,
Whose wishes, soon as granted, fly;
It liveth not in fierce desire,
With dead desire it doth not die;
It is the secret sympathy,
The silver link, the silken tie,
Which heart to heart and mind to mind
In body and in soul can bind.
Ib. st. 13

10 Breathes there the man, with soul so dead,
Who never to himself hath said,
This is my own, my native land!
Whose heart hath ne'er within him burned[1]
As home his footsteps he hath turned
From wandering on a foreign strand!
If such there breathe, go, mark him well;
For him no Minstrel raptures swell;
High though his titles, proud his name,
Boundless his wealth as wish can claim;
Despite those titles, power, and pelf,
The wretch, concentered all in self,
Living, shall forfeit fair renown,
And, doubly dying, shall go down
To the vile dust, from whence he sprung,
Unwept, unhonored, and unsung.[2]
Ib. VI, st. 1

11 O Caledonia! stern and wild,
Meet nurse for a poetic child!
Land of brown heath and shaggy wood;
Land of the mountain and the flood!
Ib. st. 2

12 That day of wrath, that dreadful day,
When heaven and earth shall pass away.[3]
Ib. st. 31

13 November's sky is chill and drear,
November's leaf is red and sear.
Marmion [1808], canto I, introduction, st. 1

14 Stood for his country's glory fast,
And nailed her colors to the mast!
Ib. st. 10

15 But search the land of living men,
Where wilt thou find their like again?
Ib. st. 11

16 And come he slow, or come he fast,
It is but Death who comes at last.
Ib. II, introduction, st. 30

17 Oh, young Lochinvar is come out of the West,
Through all the wide Border his steed was the best.
Ib. V, st. 12 [Lochinvar, st. 1]

18 So faithful in love, and so dauntless in war,
There never was knight like the young Lochinvar. *Ib.*

19 For a laggard in love, and a dastard in war,
Was to wed the fair Ellen of brave Lochinvar.
Ib. [Lochinvar, st. 2]

20 With a smile on her lips, and a tear in her eye. *Ib. [Lochinvar, st. 5]*

21 Heap on more wood!—the wind is chill;
But let it whistle as it will,
We'll keep our Christmas merry still.
Ib. VI, introduction, st. 1

22 England was merry England, when
Old Christmas brought his sports again.
'Twas Christmas broached the mightiest ale;
'Twas Christmas told the merriest tale;
A Christmas gambol oft could cheer
The poor man's heart through half the year.
Ib. st. 4

23 And dar'st thou, then,
To beard the lion in his den,
The Douglas in his hall? *Ib. st. 14*

[1]See *Luke* 24:32, 44:15.

[2]See Homer, 59:9; Horace, 108:13; Chaucer, 144:17; Shakespeare, 219:24; Milton, 284:11; and Byron, 458:26.

[3]See Tommaso di Celano, 139:4.

1 Oh, what a tangled web we weave,
When first we practice to deceive!
Ib. st. 17

2 O Woman! in our hours of ease,
Uncertain, coy, and hard to please,
And variable as the shade[1]
By the light quivering aspen made;
When pain and anguish wring the brow,
A ministering angel thou![2] *Ib. st. 30*

3 "Charge, Chester, charge! On, Stanley, on!"
Were the last words of Marmion.
Ib. st. 32

4 To all, to each, a fair goodnight,
And pleasing dreams, and slumbers light!
Ib. L'Envoy

5 The stag at eve had drunk his fill,
Where danced the moon on Monan's rill,
And deep his midnight lair had made
In lone Glenartney's hazel shade.
The Lady of the Lake [1810], canto I, st. 1

6 In listening mood she seemed to stand,
The guardian Naiad of the strand.
Ib. st. 17

7 The will to do, the soul to dare.
Ib. st. 21

8 Soldier, rest! thy warfare o'er,
Sleep the sleep that knows not breaking,
Dream of battled fields no more,
Days of danger, nights of waking.
Ib. st. 31

9 Hail to the Chief who in triumph advances![3]
Ib. II, st. 19

10 Some feelings are to mortals given,
With less of earth in them than heaven.
Ib. st. 22

11 Like the dew on the mountain,
Like the foam on the river,
Like the bubble on the fountain,
Thou art gone, and forever!
Ib. III, st. 16 [Coronach, st. 3]

12 And, Saxon—I am Roderick Dhu!
Ib. V, st. 9

13 Come one, come all! this rock shall fly
From its firm base as soon as I.
Ib. st. 10

14 Respect was mingled with surprise,
And the stern joy which warriors feel
In foemen worthy of their steel. *Ib.*

[1]See Virgil, 105:10.
[2]See Shakespeare, 224:18.
[3]The verses beginning with this line were set to music by James Sanderson [1769–c. 1841]. The march has become traditionally attached to the President of the United States.

15 Where, where was Roderick then!
One blast upon his bugle horn
Were worth a thousand men!
Ib. VI, st. 18

16 Still are the thoughts to memory dear.
Rokeby [1813], canto I, st. 33

17 A mother's pride, a father's joy.
Ib. III, st. 15

18 Oh, Brignal banks are wild and fair,
And Greta woods are green,
And you may gather garlands there
Would grace a summer's queen.
Ib. st. 16

19 O! many a shaft at random sent
Finds mark the archer little meant!
And many a word, at random spoken,
May soothe or wound a heart that's broken!
The Lord of the Isles [1815], canto V, st. 18

20 Randolph, thy wreath has lost a rose.[4]
Ib. VI, st. 18

21 A lawyer without history or literature is a mechanic, a mere working mason; if he possesses some knowledge of these, he may venture to call himself an architect.
Guy Mannering [1815], ch. 37

22 It's no fish ye're buying, it's men's lives.[5]
The Antiquary [1816], ch. 11

23 Come as the winds come, when
Forests are rended,
Come as the waves come, when
Navies are stranded.
Pibroch of Donald Dhu [1816], st. 4

24 Time will rust the sharpest sword,
Time will consume the strongest cord;
That which molders hemp and steel,
Mortal arm and nerve must feel.
Harold the Dauntless [1817], canto I, st. 4

25 Sea of upturned faces.
Rob Roy [1817], ch. 20

26 There's a gude time coming. *Ib. 32*

27 My foot is on my native heath, and my name is MacGregor. *Ib. 34*

28 Jock, when ye hae naething else to do, ye may be ay sticking in a tree; it will be growing, Jock, when ye're sleeping.[6]
The Heart of Midlothian [1818], ch. 8

[4]Robert Bruce's censure of Randolph for permitting a body of English cavalry to pass his flank on the day before the battle of Bannockburn [June 24, 1314].
[5]See Thomas Hood, 485:19.
[6]The dying words of a Highland laird to his son.

1 Vacant heart, and hand, and eye,
Easy live and quiet die.
The Bride of Lammermoor [1819], ch. 3. Lucy Ashton's Song

2 There is a southern proverb—fine words butter no parsnips.
The Legend of Montrose [1819], ch. 3

3 The happy combination of fortuitous circumstances.[1]
The Monastery [1820]. Answer of the Author of Waverley to the Letter of Captain Clutterbuck

4 As old as the hills. *Ib. ch. 9*

5 Within that awful volume[2] lies
The mystery, of mysteries! *Ib. ch. 12*

6 And better had they ne'er been born,
Who read to doubt, or read to scorn.
Ib.

7 Spur not an unbroken horse; put not your plowshare too deep into new land.
Ib. 25

8 Oh, poverty parts good company.
The Abbot [1820], ch. 7

9 Ah! County Guy, the hour is nigh,
The sun has left the lea.
Quentin Durward [1823], ch. 4

10 Tell that to the marines—the sailors won't believe it.[3]
Redgauntlet [1824], vol. II, ch. 7

11 Rouse the lion from his lair.
The Talisman [1825], heading, ch. 6

12 Recollect that the Almighty, who gave the dog to be companion of our pleasures and our toils, hath invested him with a nature noble and incapable of deceit. *Ib. 24*

13 A miss is as good as a mile.
Journal [December 3, 1825]

14 If you keep a thing seven years, you are sure to find a use for it.
Woodstock [1826], ch. 28

15 Come fill up my cup, come fill up my can,
Come saddle your horses, and call up your men;
Come open the West Port, and let me gang free,
And it's room for the bonnets of Bonny Dundee!
The Doom of Devorgoil [1830]. Bonny Dundee, chorus

16 One hour of life, crowded to the full with glorious action, and filled with noble risks, is worth whole years of those mean observances of paltry decorum.[4]
Count Robert of Paris [1832], ch. 25

[1]See Daniel Webster, 450:19.
[2]The Bible.
[3]"Right," quoth Ben, "that will do for the marines." — BYRON, *The Island* [1823], *canto II, last line*
"That will do for the marines, but the sailors won't believe it" is an old saying.

Sydney Smith

1771–1845

17 If you choose to represent the various parts in life by holes upon a table, of different shapes—some circular, some triangular, some square, some oblong—and the persons acting these parts by bits of wood of similar shapes, we shall generally find that the triangular person has got into the square hole, the oblong into the triangular, and a square person has squeezed himself into the round hole. The officer and the office, the doer and the thing done, seldom fit so exactly that we can say they were almost made for each other.[5]
Sketches of Moral Philosophy [1850]

18 That knuckle-end of England—that land of Calvin, oatcakes, and sulphur.
Lady Holland's Memoir [1855], vol. I, ch. 2

19 Preaching has become a byword for long and dull conversation of any kind; and whoever wishes to imply, in any piece of writing, the absence of everything agreeable and inviting, calls it a sermon. *Ib. 3*

20 Avoid shame, but do not seek glory,—nothing so expensive as glory. *Ib. 4*

21 Take short views, hope for the best, and trust in God. *Ib. 6*

22 Looked as if she had walked straight out of the ark. *Ib. 7*

23 No furniture so charming as books.
Ib. 9

24 Not body enough to cover his mind decently with; his intellect is improperly exposed. *Ib.*

25 He has spent all his life in letting down empty buckets into empty wells; and he is frittering away his age in trying to draw them up again.[6] *Ib.*

[4]See Mordaunt, 375:1.
[5]Generally accepted as the origin of the phrase: A square peg in a round hole.
See Twain, 625:22.
[6]See Cowper, 376:27.

1 Ah, you flavor everything; you are the vanilla of society. *Ib.*

2 As the French say, there are three sexes — men, women, and clergymen. *Ib.*

3 My living in Yorkshire was so far out of the way, that it was actually twelve miles from a lemon. *Ib.*

4 Praise is the best diet for us, after all. *Ib.*

5 Daniel Webster struck me much like a steam engine in trousers. *Ib.*

6 Live always in the best company when you read. *Ib. 10*

7 Never give way to melancholy; resist it steadily, for the habit will encroach. *Ib.*

8 He was a one-book man. Some men have only one book in them; others, a library.[1] *Ib. 11*

9 Marriage resembles a pair of shears, so joined that they can not be separated; often moving in opposite directions, yet always punishing anyone who comes between them.[2] *Ib.*

10 Macaulay is like a book in breeches . . . He has occasional flashes of silence, that make his conversation perfectly delightful. *Ib.*

11 Let onion atoms lurk within the bowl
And, scarce suspected, animate the whole.[3]
Ib. Recipe for Salad

12 Serenely full, the epicure would say,
Fate cannot harm me, I have dined today.[4]
Ib.

13 What you don't know would make a great book. *Ib.*

14 In composing, as a general rule, run your pen through every other word you have written; you have no idea what vigor it will give your style.[5] *Ib.*

15 Thank God for tea! What would the world do without tea?—how did it exist? I am glad I was not born before tea. *Ib.*

16 That sign of old age, extolling the past at the expense of the present. *Ib.*

17 We know nothing of tomorrow; our business is to be good and happy today. *Ib. 12*

[1]See Anonymous Latin, 133:11.
[2]We are the two halves of a pair of scissors, when apart, Pecksniff, but together we are something.—DICKENS, *Martin Chuzzlewit* [1843–1844], *ch. 11*
[3]See R. L. Stevenson, 668:18.
[4]See Horace, 108:7, and Dryden, 305:1.
[5]See Samuel Johnson, 355:8.

Samuel Taylor Coleridge

1772–1834

18 Poor little foal of an oppressèd race!
I love the languid patience of thy face.
To a Young Ass [1794], l. 1

19 Blest hour! it was a luxury—to be!
Reflections on Having Left a Place of Retirement [1795], l. 43

20 This Lime Tree Bower My Prison.
Title of poem [1797]

21 In Xanadu did Kubla Khan
A stately pleasure dome decree:
Where Alph, the sacred river, ran
Through caverns measureless to man
Down to a sunless sea.
So twice five miles of fertile ground
With walls and towers were girdled round.
Kubla Khan [1798]

22 A savage place! as holy and enchanted
As e'er beneath a waning moon was haunted
By woman wailing for her demon-lover!
Ib.

23 Five miles meandering with a mazy motion.
Ib.

24 Ancestral voices prophesying war! *Ib.*

25 It was a miracle of rare device,
A sunny pleasure dome with caves of ice!
Ib.

26 A damsel with a dulcimer
In a vision once I saw:
It was an Abyssinian maid,
And on her dulcimer she played,
Singing of Mount Abora. *Ib.*

27 That sunny dome! those caves of ice!
And all who heard should see them there,
And all should cry, Beware! Beware!
His flashing eyes, his floating hair!
Weave a circle round him thrice,
And close your eyes with holy dread,
For he on honeydew hath fed,[6]
And drunk the milk of Paradise. *Ib.*

28 Sir Leoline, the Baron rich,
Hath a toothless mastiff bitch.
Christabel [1797–1800], pt. I, l. 6

29 And the spring comes slowly up this way.
Ib. l. 22

30 The one red leaf, the last of its clan,
That dances as often as dance it can.
Ib. l. 49

31 Her gentle limbs did she undress,
And lay down in her loveliness.
Ib. l. 237

[6]See Hesiod, 61:9.

1 A sight to dream of, not to tell!
Ib. l. 252

2 Saints will aid if men will call:
For the blue sky bends over all!
Ib. l. 330

3 And constancy lives in realms above;
And life is thorny; and youth is vain;
And to be wroth with one we love
Doth work like madness in the brain.
Ib. II, l. 410

4 It is an ancient Mariner,
And he stoppeth one of three.
"By thy long gray beard and glittering eye,
Now wherefore stopp'st thou me?"
The Ancient Mariner [1798], pt. I, st. 1

5 The guests are met, the feast is set:
May'st hear the merry din. *Ib. st. 2*

6 He holds him with his glittering eye—
The Wedding Guest stood still,
And listens like a three years' child:
The Mariner hath his will. *Ib. st. 4*

7 The ship was cheered, the harbor cleared,
Merrily did we drop
Below the kirk, below the hill,
Below the lighthouse top. *Ib. st. 6*

8 The Wedding Guest here beat his breast,
For he heard the loud bassoon.
Ib. st. 8

9 The bride hath paced into the hall,
Red as a rose is she. *Ib. st. 9*

10 And now there came both mist and snow,
And it grew wondrous cold:
And ice, mast-high, came floating by,
As green as emerald. *Ib. st. 13*

11 The ice was here, the ice was there,
The ice was all around:
It cracked and growled, and roared and howled,
Like noises in a swound! *Ib. st. 15*

12 "God save thee, ancient Mariner!
From the fiends, that plague thee thus!—
Why look'st thou so?"—"With my crossbow
I shot the Albatross." *Ib. st. 20*

13 The fair breeze blew, the white foam flew,
The furrows followed free;
We were the first that ever burst
Into that silent sea. *Ib. II, st. 5*

14 As idle as a painted ship
Upon a painted ocean. *Ib. st. 8*

15 Water, water, everywhere,
Nor any drop to drink. *Ib. st. 9*

16 The very deep did rot: O Christ!
That ever this should be!
Yea, slimy things did crawl with legs
Upon the slimy sea. *Ib. st. 10*

17 About, about, in reel and rout
The death fires danced at night.
Ib. st. 11

18 I bit my arm, I sucked the blood,
And cried, A sail! a sail! *Ib. III, st. 4*

19 Her lips were red, her looks were free,
Her locks were yellow as gold:
Her skin was white as leprosy,
The nightmare Life-in-Death was she,
Who thicks man's blood with cold.
Ib. st. 11

20 "The game is done! I've won, I've won!"
Quoth she, and whistles thrice.
Ib. st. 12

21 The sun's rim dips, the stars rush out:
At one stride comes the dark;
With far-heard whisper o'er the sea
Off shot the specter bark. *Ib. st. 13*

22 We listened and looked sideways up!
Fear at my heart, as at a cup,
My lifeblood seemed to sip. *Ib. st. 14*

23 The hornèd Moon, with one bright star
Within the nether tip. *Ib.*

24 Each turned his face with a ghastly pang,
And cursed me with his eye. *Ib. st. 15*

25 I fear thee, ancient Mariner!
I fear thy skinny hand!
And thou art long, and lank, and brown,
As is the ribbed sea-sand.[1] *Ib. IV, st. 1*

26 Alone, alone, all, all alone;
Alone on a wide, wide sea. *Ib. st. 3*

27 The moving moon went up the sky,
And nowhere did abide;
Softly she was going up,
And a star or two beside. *Ib. st. 10*

28 Her beams bemocked the sultry main,
Like April hoarfrost spread;
But where the ship's huge shadow lay,
The charmed water burnt alway
A still and awful red. *Ib. st. 11*

29 A spring of love gushed from my heart,
And I blessed them unaware.
Ib. st. 14

30 Oh sleep! it is a gentle thing,
Beloved from pole to pole. *Ib. V, st. 1*

31 We were a ghastly crew. *Ib. st. 11*

[1] A note by Coleridge in *Sibylline Leaves* [1817] says: "For [these] lines I am indebted to Mr. Wordsworth."

1 A noise like of a hidden brook
In the leafy month of June,
That to the sleeping woods all night
Singeth a quiet tune. *Ib. st. 17*

2 The man hath penance done,
And penance more will do. *Ib. st. 25*

3 Like one that on a lonesome road
Doth walk in fear and dread,
And having once turned round walks on,
And turns no more his head;
Because he knows a frightful fiend
Doth close behind him tread.
Ib. VI, st. 10

4 Is this the hill? is this the kirk?
Is this mine own countree? *Ib. st. 14*

5 No voice; but oh! the silence sank
Like music on my heart. *Ib. st. 22*

6 And the owlet whoops to the wolf below,
That eats the she-wolf's young.
Ib. VII, st. 5

7 "Ha! ha!" quoth he, "full plain I see,
The Devil knows how to row."
Ib. st. 12

8 "O shrieve me, shrieve me, holy man!"
Ib. st. 14

9 O Wedding Guest! This soul hath been
Alone on a wide wide sea:
So lonely 'twas, that God himself
Scarce seemèd there to be. *Ib. st. 19*

10 He prayeth well who loveth well
Both man and bird and beast.
Ib. st. 22

11 He prayeth best who loveth best
All things both great and small;
For the dear God who loveth us,
He made and loveth all.[1] *Ib. st. 23*

12 A sadder and a wiser man
He rose the morrow morn. *Ib. st. 25*

13 With what deep worship I have still adored
The spirit of divinest Liberty.
France: An Ode [1798], st. 1

14 The frost performs its secret ministry,
Unhelped by any wind.
Frost at Midnight [1798], l. 1

15 Or if the secret ministry of frost
Shall hang them up in silent icicles,
Quietly shining to the quiet moon.
Ib. l. 72

16 Forth from his dark and lonely hiding place
(Portentous-sight!) the owlet Atheism,
Sailing on obscene wings athwart the noon,
Drops his blue-fringèd lids, and holds them close,
And hooting at the glorious sun in Heaven,
Cries out, "Where is it?"
Fears in Solitude [1798], l. 81

17 And the Devil did grin, for his darling sin
Is pride that apes humility.[2]
The Devil's Thoughts[3] *[1799], st. 6*

18 Strongly it bears us along in swelling and limitless billows,
Nothing before and nothing behind but the sky and the ocean.
The Homeric Hexameter (translated from SCHILLER*) [1799?]*

19 In the hexameter rises the fountain's silvery column;
In the pentameter aye falling in melody back.
The Ovidian Elegiac Metre (translated from SCHILLER*) [1799]*

20 All thoughts, all passions, all delights,
Whatever stirs this mortal frame,
All are but ministers of Love,
And feed his sacred flame.
Love [1799], st. 1

21 Aloof with hermit-eye I scan
The present works of present man—
A wild and dreamlike trade of blood and guile,
Too foolish for a tear, too wicked for a smile!
Ode to Tranquillity [1801], st. 4

22 Hast thou a charm to stay the morning star
In his steep course?[4]
Hymn in the Vale of Chamouni [1802], l. 1

23 Earth, with her thousand voices, praises God.
Ib. last line

24 What is an epigram? A dwarfish whole,
Its body brevity, and wit its soul.[5]
An Epigram [1802]

25 I see, not feel, how beautiful they are!
Dejection: An Ode [1802], st. 2

26 O lady! we receive but what we give
And in our life alone does Nature live.
Ib. st. 4

27 A light, a glory, a fair luminous cloud
Enveloping the earth. *Ib.*

[1] See Alexander, 561:8.

[2] See Robert Burton, 259:1.

[3] This poem was written in collaboration with Southey, who also imitated it in *The Devil's Walk,* 440:15.

[4] See *Job 38:31,* 16:33.

[5] See Shakespeare, 220:10.

1 Joy is the sweet voice, joy the luminous cloud—
We in ourselves rejoice!
And thence flows all that charms or ear or sight,
All melodies the echoes of that voice,
All colors a suffusion from that light.
Ib. st. 5

2 How seldom, friend! a good great man inherits
Honor or wealth, with all his worth and pains!
It sounds like stories from the land of spirits
If any man obtain that which he merits,
Or any merit that which he obtains.
The Good Great Man [1802]

3 Trochee trips from long to short;
From long to long in solemn sort
Slow Spondee stalks.
Metrical Feet [1806]

4 The knight's bones are dust,
And his good sword rust;
His soul is with the saints, I trust.
The Knight's Tomb [c. 1817]

5 With Donne, whose muse on dromedary trots,
Wreathe iron pokers into true-love knots.
On Donne's Poetry [c. 1818]

6 The Eighth Commandment was not made for bards. *The Reproof and Reply [1823]*

7 Nought cared this body for wind or weather,
When youth and I lived in 't together.
Youth and Age [1823–1832], st. 1

8 Flowers are lovely; love is flower-like;
Friendship is a sheltering tree.
Ib. st. 2

9 All Nature seems at work. Slugs leave their lair—
The bees are stirring—birds are on the wing—
And Winter slumbering in the open air,
Wears on his smiling face a dream of Spring!
And I the while, the sole unbusy thing,
Nor honey make, nor pair, nor build, nor sing.
Work Without Hope [February 21, 1825], l. 1

10 Work without Hope draws nectar in a sieve,
And Hope without an object cannot live.
Ib. l. 13

11 In many ways doth the full heart reveal
The presence of the love it would conceal.
Poems Written in Later Life [1826], motto

12 I counted two and seventy stenches,
All well defined, and several stinks.
Cologne [1828]

13 The river Rhine, it is well known,
Doth wash your city of Cologne;
But tell me, nymphs! what power divine
Shall henceforth wash the river Rhine?
Ib.

14 Poetry is not the proper antithesis to prose, but to science. Poetry is opposed to science, and prose to metre. The proper and immediate object of science is the acquirement, or communication, of truth; the proper and immediate object of poetry is the communication of immediate pleasure.
Definitions of Poetry [1811]

15 Reviewers are usually people who would have been poets, historians, biographers, etc., if they could; they have tried their talents at one or at the other, and have failed; therefore they turn critics.[1]
Lectures on Shakespeare and Milton [1811–1812]

16 The last speech [Iago's soliloquy], the motive-hunting of a motiveless malignity—how awful! *Notes on Shakespeare [c. 1812]*

17 Taste is the intermediate faculty which connects the active with the passive powers of our nature, the intellect with the senses; and its appointed function is to elevate the *images* of the latter, while it realizes the *ideas* of the former.
On the Principles of Genial Criticism [1814]

18 The most general definition of beauty . . . Multeity in Unity. *Ib.*

19 The Good consists in the congruity of a thing with the laws of the reason and the nature of the will, and in its fitness to determine the latter to actualize the former: and it is always discursive. The Beautiful arises from the perceived harmony of an object, whether sight or sound, with the inborn and constitutive rules of the judgment and imagination: and it is always intuitive. *Ib.*

20 The imagination . . . that reconciling and mediatory power, which incorporating the reason in images of the sense and organizing (as it were) the flux of the senses by the permanence and self-circling energies of the reason, gives birth to a system of symbols, har-

[1] Reviewers, with some rare exceptions, are a most stupid and malignant race. As a bankrupt thief turns thief-taker in despair, so an unsuccessful author turns critic. —SHELLEY, *Fragments of Adonais* [1821]

See Disraeli, 502:12; Lowell, 567:19; and Flaubert, 583:8.

monious in themselves, and consubstantial with the truths of which they are the conductors. *The Statesman's Manual [1816]*

1 Not the poem which we have *read,* but that to which we *return,* with the greatest pleasure, possesses the genuine power, and claims the name of *essential poetry.* [1]
Biographia Literaria [1817], ch. 1

2 Every reform, however necessary, will by weak minds be carried to an excess, that itself will need reforming. [2] *Ib.*

3 Experience informs us that the first defense of weak minds is to recriminate.
Ib. 2

4 Indignation at literary wrongs I leave to men born under happier stars. I cannot afford it. *Ib.*

5 Milton had a highly imaginative, Cowley a very fanciful mind. *Ib. 4*

6 An idea, in the highest sense of that word, cannot be conveyed but by a symbol.
Ib. 9

7 Veracity does not consist in saying, but in the intention of communicating truth.
Ib.

8 Never pursue literature as a trade.
Ib. 11

9 Until you understand a writer's ignorance, presume yourself ignorant of his understanding. *Ib. 12*

10 During the act of knowledge itself, the objective and subjective are so instantly united, that we cannot determine to which of the two the priority belongs. *Ib.*

11 The primary imagination I hold to be the living power and prime agent of all human perception, and as a repetition in the finite mind of the eternal act of creation in the infinite I Am. *Ib. 13*

12 The secondary imagination . . . dissolves, diffuses, dissipates, in order to re-create; or where this process is rendered impossible, yet still at all events it struggles to idealize and to unify. It is essentially vital, even as all objects (*as* objects) are essentially fixed and dead. *Ib.*

13 The fancy is indeed no other than a mode of memory emancipated from the order of time and space. *Ib.*

14 The two cardinal points of poetry, the power of exciting the sympathy of the reader by a faithful adherence to the truth of nature, and the power of giving the interest of novelty by the modifying colors of imagination. *Ib. 14*

15 That willing suspension of disbelief for the moment, which constitutes poetic faith.
Ib.

16 The poet, described in *ideal* perfection, brings the whole soul of man into activity, with the subordination of its faculties to each other, according to their relative worth and dignity. He diffuses a tone and spirit of unity, that blends, and (as it were) *fuses,* each into each, by that synthetic and magical power . . . imagination. *Ib.*

17 [Imagination] reveals itself in the balance or reconciliation of opposite or discordant qualities: of sameness, with difference; of the general, with the concrete; the idea, with the image; the individual, with the representative; the sense of novelty and freshness, with old and familiar objects; a more than usual state of emotion, with more than usual order; judgment ever awake and steady self-possession, with enthusiasm and feeling profound or vehement; and while it blends and harmonizes the natural and the artificial, still subordinates art to nature; the manner to the matter; and our admiration of the poet to our sympathy with the poetry. *Ib.*

18 No man was ever yet a great poet, without being at the same time a profound philosopher. *Ib. 15*

19 While [Shakespeare] darts himself forth and passes into all the forms of human character and passion, the one Proteus of the fire and the flood, [Milton] attracts all forms and things to himself, into the unity of his own *Ideal.* All things and modes of action shape themselves anew in the being of Milton; while Shakespeare becomes all things, yet ever remaining himself. *Ib.*

20 Our myriad-minded Shakespeare. [3]
Ib.

21 The best part of human language, properly so called, is derived from reflection on the acts of the mind itself. [4] *Ib. 17*

22 Now Art, used collectively for painting, sculpture, architecture and music, is the mediatress between, and reconciler of, nature and man. It is, therefore, the power of

[1] See Robert Frost, 749:20 and 750:4.
[2] See Wollstonecraft, 414:15.

[3] A phrase which I have borrowed from a Greek monk, who applies it to a patriarch of Constantinople.—COLERIDGE'S *footnote*

[4] The poem of the act of the mind.—WALLACE STEVENS [1879–1955], *Collected Poems, Of Modern Poetry*

humanizing nature, of infusing the thoughts and passions of man into everything which is the object of his contemplation.

On Poesy or Art [1818]

1 The artist must imitate that which is within the thing, that which is active through form and figure, and discourses to us by symbols. *Ib.*

2 The heart should have fed upon the truth, as insects on a leaf, till it be tinged with the color, and show its food in every . . . minutest fiber. *Ib.*

3 Schiller has the material sublime.

Table Talk [December 29, 1822]

4 I wish our clever young poets would remember my homely definitions of prose and poetry; that is, prose = words in their best order; poetry = the best words in their best order. *Ib. [July 12, 1827]*

5 The man's desire is for the woman; but the woman's desire is rarely other than for the desire of the man. *Ib. [July 23, 1827]*

6 Poetry is certainly something more than good sense, but it must be good sense at all events; just as a palace is more than a house, but it must be a house, at least.

Ib. [May 9, 1830]

7 That passage is what I call the sublime dashed to pieces by cutting too close with the fiery four-in-hand round the corner of nonsense. *Ib.*

8 The happiness of life is made up of minute fractions—the little soon forgotten charities of a kiss or smile, a kind look, a heartfelt compliment, and the countless infinitesimals of pleasurable and genial feeling.

The Friend. The Improvisatore [1828]

9 Beneath this sod
A poet lies, or that which once seemed he—
Oh, lift a thought in prayer for S.T.C.!
That he, who many a year, with toil of breath,
Found death in life, may here find life in death.

Epitaph written for himself [1833]

Novalis [Baron Friedrich von Hardenberg]

1772–1801

10 We are near awakening when we dream that we dream.

Blütenstaub (Pollen) [1798]

Josiah Quincy, Jr.

1772–1864

11 If this bill [for the admission of Orleans Territory as a State] passes, I am compelled to declare it as my deliberate opinion that the bonds of this Union are virtually dissolved; that the States which compose it are free from their moral obligations; and that, as it will be the right of all, so it will be the duty of some, to prepare definitely for a separation—amicably if they can; violently if they must.[1]

Speech in the House of Representatives [January 14, 1811]

William Barnes Rhodes

1772–1826

12 *Bombastes:* So have I heard on Afric's burning shore
A hungry lion give a grievous roar;
The grievous roar echoed along the shore.
Artaxaminous: So have I heard on Afric's burning shore
Another lion give a grievous roar;
And the first lion thought the last a bore.

Bombastes Furioso [1810], act I, sc. iv

David Ricardo

1772–1823

13 Labor, like all other things which are purchased and sold, and which may be increased or diminished in quantity, has its natural and its market price. The natural price of labor is that price which is necessary to enable the laborers, one with another, to subsist and perpetuate their race, without either increase or diminution.

On the Principles of Political Economy and Taxation [1817]

14 There is no way of keeping profits up but by keeping wages down.

On Protection to Agriculture [1820]

Friedrich von Schlegel

1772–1829

15 The historian is a prophet in reverse.

Athenaeum [1798–1800]

[1]The gentleman [Quincy] cannot have forgotten his own sentiment, uttered even on the floor of this House, "Peaceably if we can, forcibly if we must."—Henry Clay, *Speech* [January 8, 1813]

Horace François Bastien Sébastiani
1772–1851

1 Peace reigns in Warsaw [La tranquillité règne à Varsovie].[1]

Announcement of the fall of Warsaw [1831]

Stephen Grellet [Étienne de Grellet du Mabillier]
1773–1855

2 I expect to pass through this world but once; any good thing therefore that I can do, or any kindness that I can show to any fellow creature, let me do it now; let me not defer or neglect it, for I shall not pass this way again.[2] *Attributed*

William Henry Harrison[3]
1773–1841

3 We admit of no government by divine right . . . the only legitimate right to govern is an express grant of power from the governed.

Inaugural Address [March 4, 1841]

4 Never with my consent shall an officer of the people, compensated for his services out of their pockets, become the pliant instrument of the Executive will. *Ib.*

5 A decent and manly examination of the acts of government should be not only tolerated, but encouraged. *Ib.*

John Randolph
1773–1833

6 The surest way to prevent war is not to fear it.

Speech in the House of Representatives [March 5, 1806]

7 [Of Edward Livingston] He is a man of splendid abilities, but utterly corrupt. He shines and stinks like rotten mackerel by moonlight.

From W. CABELL BRUCE, *John Randolph of Roanoke [1923], vol. II, p. 197*

8 [Of Martin Van Buren] He rowed to his object with muffled oars. *Ib. p. 203*

Robert Southey
1774–1843

9 As frozen as charity.[4]

The Soldier's Wife [1795], st. 4

10 It was a summer evening;
Old Kaspar's work was done,
And he before his cottage door
Was sitting in the sun;
And by him sported on the green
His little grandchild Wilhelmine.

The Battle of Blenheim [1798], st. 1

11 He came to ask what he had found,
That was so large, and smooth, and round.

Ib. st. 2

12 " 'Tis some poor fellow's skull," said he,
"Who fell in the great victory."

Ib. st. 3

13 But what they fought each other for,
I could not well make out. *Ib. st. 6*

14 "And everybody praised the duke,
Who this great fight did win."
"But what good came of it at last?"
Quoth little Peterkin.
"Why, that I cannot tell," said he;
"But 'twas a famous victory."

Ib. st. 11

15 "You are old, Father William," the young man cried,
"The few locks which are left you are gray;
You are hale, Father William — a hearty old man:
Now tell me the reason, I pray."

The Old Man's Comforts and How He Gained Them [1779],[5] st. 1

16 "In the days of my youth, I remembered my God,
And he hath not forgotten my age."

Ib. st. 6

17 And then they knew the perilous rock,
And blessed the Abbot of Aberbrothok.

The Inchcape Rock [1802],[6] st. 4

[1] More familiar as: Order reigns in Warsaw [L'ordre règne à Varsovie].

[2] This is not found in any of Grellet's writings, and has been attributed to many others.
See Addison, 326:7.

[3] Tippecanoe and Tyler, Too. — A. C. Ross, *Presidential campaign song* [1840]
The iron-armed soldier, the true-hearted soldier, / The gallant old soldier of Tippecanoe. — GEORGE POPE MORRIS, *campaign song for Harrison* [1840], *sung to the tune of The Old Oaken Bucket*

[4] See Hood, 485:22, and O'Reilly, 659:8.

[5] Of several parodies of this poem, the one by Lewis Carroll is probably better known than the original. See 611:9–611:11.

[6] A rock in the North Sea, off the Firth of Tay, Scotland, dangerous to navigators because it is covered with every tide. There is a tradition that a warning bell was fixed on the rock by the Abbot of Aberbrothok, which was stolen by a sea pirate, who perished on the rock a year later.

1 Till the vessel strikes with a shivering shock—
"O Christ! It is the Inchcape Rock."
Ib. st. 15

2 Blue, darkly, deeply, beautifully blue.[1]
Madoc in Wales [1805], pt. I, 5

3 Curses are like young chickens, they always come home to roost.
The Curse of Kehama [1810], motto

4 They sin who tell us love can die;
With life all other passions fly,
All others are but vanity.
Ib. canto X, st. 10

5 Thou hast been called, O sleep! the friend of woe;
But 'tis the happy that have called thee so.
Ib. XV, st. 12

6 My days among the dead are past;
Around me I behold,
Where'er these casual eyes are cast,
The mighty minds of old.
My Days Among the Dead Are Past [1818], st. 1

7 Yet leaving here a name, I trust,
That will not perish in the dust.
Ib. st. 4

8 So I told them in rhyme,
For of rhymes I had store.
The Cataract of Lodore [1820]

9 Agreed to differ.
Life of Wesley [1820]

10 The Satanic school.
Vision of Judgment [1821], original preface

11 The arts babblative and scribblative.
Colloquies on the Progress and Prospects of Society [1829], no. 1, pt. 2

12 The march of intellect. *Ib. 14*

13 From his brimstone bed, at break of day,
A-walking the Devil is gone,
To look at his little snug farm of the world,
And see how his stock went on.
The Devil's Walk [1830],[2] *st. 1*

14 His coat was red, and his breeches were blue,
And there was a hole where his tail came through.
Ib. st. 3

15 And he owned with a grin,
That his favorite sin
Is pride that apes humility.[3] *Ib. st. 8*

[1] See Byron, 461:13.
[2] See Shelley, 466:5.
[3] See Robert Burton, 259:1, and Coleridge, 435:17.

Jane Austen[4]

1775–1817

16 It is a truth universally acknowledged, that a single man in possession of a good fortune, must be in want of a wife.
Pride and Prejudice [1813], ch. 1

17 She [Mrs. Bennet] was a woman of mean understanding, little information, and uncertain temper. *Ib.*

18 A lady's imagination is very rapid; it jumps from admiration to love, from love to matrimony in a moment. *Ib. 6*

19 Mr. Collins had only to change from Jane to Elizabeth—and it was soon done—done while Mrs. Bennet was stirring the fire.
Ib. 15

20 You have delighted us long enough.
Ib. 18

21 Mrs. Bennet was restored to her usual querulous serenity. *Ib. 42*

22 You ought certainly to forgive them, as a Christian, but never to admit them in your sight, or allow their names to be mentioned in your hearing. *Ib. 57*

23 For what do we live, but to make sport for our neighbors, and laugh at them in our turn? *Ib.*

24 I have been a selfish being all my life, in practice, though not in principle.
Ib. 58

25 One half of the world cannot understand the pleasures of the other.
Emma [1815], ch. 9

26 It was a delightful visit—perfect, in being much too short. *Ib. 13*

27 Nobody who has not been in the interior of a family can say what the difficulties of any individual of that family may be.
Ib. 18

28 Business, you know, may bring money, but friendship hardly ever does. *Ib. 34*

29 "Only a novel" . . . in short, only some work in which the greatest powers of the mind are displayed, in which the most thorough knowledge of human nature, the happiest delineation of its varieties, the liveliest

[4] [Miss Austen] had a talent for describing the involvements and feelings and characters of ordinary life which is to me the most wonderful I ever met with. The Big Bow-Wow strain I can do myself like any now going; but the exquisite touch, which renders ordinary commonplace things and characters interesting, from the truth of the description and the sentiment, is denied to me.—SCOTT, *Journal* [March 14, 1826]

effusions of wit and humor are conveyed to the world in the best chosen language.

Northanger Abbey [1818], ch. 5

1 She had been forced into prudence in her youth, she learned romance as she grew older — the natural sequence of an unnatural beginning. *Persuasion [1818], ch. 4*

2 I do not want people to be very agreeable, as it saves me the trouble of liking them a great deal.

Letters. To her sister Cassandra [December 24, 1798]

3 The little bit (two inches wide) of ivory on which I work with so fine a brush as produces little effect after much labor.

Ib. To J. Edward Austen [December 16, 1816]

Charles Lamb

1775–1834

4 I have something more to do than feel.

Letter to Coleridge after the death of Lamb's mother [1796]

5 I have had playmates, I have had companions,
In my days of childhood, in my joyful school days —
All, all are gone, the old familiar faces.

Old Familiar Faces [1798]

6 For God's sake (I never was more serious) don't make me ridiculous any more by terming me gentlehearted in print[1] . . . substitute drunken dog, ragged head, seld-shaven, odd-eyed, stuttering, or any other epithet which truly and properly belongs to the gentleman in question.

Letter to Coleridge [August 1800]

7 Separate from the pleasure of your company, I don't much care if I never see a mountain in my life.

Letter to Wordsworth [1801]

8 The man must have a rare recipe for melancholy, who can be dull in Fleet Street.

Letter to Thomas Manning [February 15, 1802]

9 Nursed amid her [London's] noise, her crowds, her beloved smoke — what have I been doing all my life, if I have not lent out my heart with usury to such scenes?

Ib.

[1] For thee, my gentlehearted Charles, to whom / No sound is dissonant which tells of life. — COLERIDGE, *This Lime Tree Bower My Prison* [1797]

10 Gone before
To that unknown and silent shore.

Hester [1803], st. 7

11 A good-natured woman, which is as much as you can expect from a friend's wife, whom you got acquainted with a bachelor.

Letter to Hazlitt [1805]

12 This very night I am going to leave off tobacco! Surely there must be some other world in which this unconquerable purpose shall be realized.

Letter to Thomas Manning [1815]

13 Anything awful makes me laugh. I misbehaved once at a funeral.

Letter to Southey [1815]

14 [Of Coleridge] An archangel a little damaged. *Letter to Wordsworth [1816]*

15 Fanny Kelly's divine plain face.

Letter to Mrs. Wordsworth [1818]

16 The red-letter days, now become, to all intents and purposes, dead-letter days.

Essays of Elia [1823]. Oxford in the Vacation[2]

17 The human species, according to the best theory I can form of it, is composed of two distinct races, the men who borrow, and the men who lend.

Ib. The Two Races of Men

18 Your borrowers of books — those mutilators of collections, spoilers of the symmetry of shelves, and creators of odd volumes.

Ib.

19 A clear fire, a clean hearth, and the rigor of the game.

Ib. Mrs. Battle's Opinions on Whist

20 I have no ear.

Ib. A Chapter on Ears

21 Sentimentally I am disposed to harmony; but organically I am incapable of a tune.

Ib.

22 Credulity is the man's weakness, but the child's strength.

Ib. Witches, and Other Night Fears

23 Not many sounds in life, and I include all urban and all rural sounds, exceed in interest a knock at the door.

Ib. Valentine's Day

24 It is good to love the unknown. *Ib.*

25 Presents, I often say, endear absents.

Ib. A Dissertation upon Roast Pig

[2] Which, it has been pointed out, was actually written at Cambridge. See E. V. LUCAS, *Lamb and the Universities.*

1 I came home forever!

Letter to Bernard Barton [1825], on leaving his "33 years' desk" at the East India House

2 Who first invented work, and bound the free
And holiday-rejoicing spirit down?

Work

3 Riddle of destiny, who can show
What thy short visit meant, or know
What thy errand here below?

On an Infant Dying as Soon as Born [1827]

4 Some cry up Haydn, some Mozart,
Just as the whim bites. For my part,
I do not care a farthing candle
For either of them, nor for Handel.[1]

Letter to Mrs. William Hazlitt [1830]

5 For thy sake, Tobacco, I
Would do anything but die.

A Farewell to Tobacco

6 A poor relation—is the most irrelevant thing in nature.

Last Essays of Elia [1833]. Poor Relations

7 I love to lose myself in other men's minds.

Ib. Detached Thoughts on Books and Reading

8 Books think for me. *Ib.*

9 Things in books' clothing. *Ib.*

10 How sickness enlarges the dimensions of a man's self to himself.

Ib. The Convalescent

11 Your absence of mind we have borne, till your presence of body came to be called in question by it. *Ib. Amicus Redivivus*

12 A pun is a pistol let off at the ear; not a feather to tickle the intellect.

Ib. Popular Fallacies: IX, That the Worst Puns Are the Best

13 A presentation copy . . . is a copy of a book which does not sell, sent you by the author, with his foolish autograph at the beginning of it; for which, if a stranger, he only demands your friendship; if a brother author, he expects from you a book of yours, which does not sell, in return.

Ib. XI, That We Must Not Look a Gift Horse in the Mouth

14 The good things of life are not to be had singly, but come to us with a mixture.

Ib. XIII, That You Must Love Me and Love My Dog

[1]See John Byrom, 341:13.

15 The greatest pleasure I know is to do a good action by stealth, and to have it found out by accident.

Table Talk. In the Athenaeum [1834]

Walter Savage Landor

1775–1864

16 But I have sinuous shells of pearly hue . . .
Shake one, and it awakens; then apply
Its polished lips to your attentive ear,
And it remembers its august abodes,
And murmurs as the ocean murmurs there.[2]

Gebir, bk. I [1798]

17 Ah what avails the sceptered race,
Ah what the form divine!

Rose Aylmer [1806]

18 Rose Aylmer, whom these wakeful eyes
May weep, but never see,
A night of memories and of sighs
I consecrate to thee. *Ib.*

19 There are no fields of amaranth on this side of the grave: there are no voices, O Rhodopè! that are not soon mute, however tuneful: there is no name, with whatever emphasis of passionate love repeated, of which the echo is not faint at last.

Imaginary Conversations [1824–1829]. Aesop and Rhodopè, I

20 Of all failures, to fail in a witticism is the worst, and the mishap is the more calamitous in a drawn-out and detailed one.

Ib. Chesterfield and Chatham

21 'Tis verse that gives
Immortal youth to mortal maids.

Verse

22 When we play the fool, how wide
The theatre expands! beside,
How long the audience sits before us!
How many prompters! what a chorus!

Plays [1846], st. 2

23 There is delight in singing, though none hear
Beside the singer.

To Robert Browning [1846]

24 Shakespeare is not our poet, but the world's,
Therefore on him no speech! and brief for thee,
Browning! Since Chaucer was alive and hale,
No man hath walked along our roads with step
So active, so inquiring eye, or tongue
So varied in discourse. *Ib.*

[2]See Wordsworth, 428:15.

1 I strove with none, for none was worth my strife;
Nature I loved; and next to Nature, Art.
I warmed both hands before the fire of life;
It sinks, and I am ready to depart.
I Strove with None [1853]

2 Around the child bend all the three
Sweet Graces: Faith, Hope, Charity.
Around the man bend other faces;
Pride, Envy, Malice, are his Graces.
Dry Sticks [1858]. Different Graces

Johann Friedrich Herbart
1776–1841

3 Psychology cannot experiment with men, and there is no apparatus for this purpose. So much the more carefully must we make use of mathematics.
Lehrbuch zur Psychologie [1816; A Textbook in Psychology, 1891][1]

Thomas Campbell
1777–1844

4 'Tis distance lends enchantment to the view,
And robes the mountain in its azure hue.[2]
Pleasures of Hope [1799], pt. I, l. 7

5 Hope, for a season, bade the world farewell,
And Freedom shrieked—as Kosciusko fell!
Ib. l. 381

6 Who hath not owned, with rapture-smitten frame,
The power of grace, the magic of a name?
Ib. II, l. 5

7 And muse on Nature with a poet's eye.
Ib. l. 98

8 Cease, every joy, to glimmer on my mind,
But leave, oh! leave the light of Hope behind!
What though my wingèd hours of bliss have been
Like angel visits, few and far between?[3]
Ib. l. 375

9 On the green banks of Shannon, when Sheelah was nigh,
No blithe Irish lad was so happy as I;
No harp like my own could so cheerily play,
And wherever I went was my poor dog Tray.[4]
The Harper [1799], st. 1

10 Ye mariners of England,
That guard our native seas;
Whose flag has braved, a thousand years,
The battle and the breeze!
Ye Mariners of England [1800], st. 1

11 While the battle rages loud and long,
And the stormy winds do blow.[5] *Ib.*

12 Britannia needs no bulwarks,
No towers along the steep;
Her march is o'er the mountain waves,
Her home is on the deep. *Ib. st. 3*

13 The meteor flag of England
Shall yet terrific burn,
Till danger's troubled night depart,
And the star of peace return. *Ib. st. 4*

14 'Tis the sunset of life gives me mystical lore,
And coming events cast their shadows before.[6] *Lochiel's Warning [1802]*

15 The combat deepens. On, ye brave,
Who rush to glory or the grave!
Wave, Munich! all thy banners wave,
And charge with all thy chivalry!
Hohenlinden [1802], st. 7

16 There was silence deep as death,
And the boldest held his breath,
For a time.
Battle of the Baltic [1805], st. 2

17 Ye are brothers! ye are men!
And we conquer but to save. *Ib. st. 5*

18 Oh, how hard it is to find
The one just suited to our mind!
Song, st. 1

19 Oh leave this barren spot to me!
Spare, woodman, spare the beechen tree![7]
The Beech Tree's Petition, st. 1

20 A stoic of the woods—a man without a tear.
Gertrude of Wyoming [1809], pt. I, st. 23

21 Oh! once the harp of Innisfail
Was strung full high to notes of gladness;
But yet it often told a tale
Of more prevailing sadness.
O'Connor's Child [1810], st. 1

[1] Translated by MARGARET K. SMITH.

[2] The mountains too, at a distance, appear airy masses and smooth, but seen near at hand they are rough.—DIOGENES LAERTIUS [c. 200], *Pyrrho, sec. 9*

[3] See John Norris, 318:4.

[4] My Old Dog Tray.—STEPHEN C. FOSTER [1826–1864], *title of song*

[5] See Parker, 273:7.

[6] See Cicero, 98:21; Shakespeare, 226:5; Shelley, 470:5; and Wells, 720:9.
Often do the spirits / Of great events stride on before the events, / And in today already walks tomorrow.—COLERIDGE, *Wallenstein* [1799–1800], *pt. II, act V, sc. i*

[7] See George Pope Morris, 492:10.

Henry Clay

1777–1852

1 How often are we forced to charge fortune with partiality towards the unjust!

Letter [December 4, 1801]

2 If you wish to avoid foreign collision, you had better abandon the ocean.

Speech in the House of Representatives [January 22, 1812]

3 Government is a trust, and the officers of the government are trustees; and both the trust and the trustees are created for the benefit of the people.[1]

Speech at Ashland, Kentucky [March 1829]

4 The arts of power and its minions are the same in all countries and in all ages. It marks its victim; denounces it; and excites the public odium and the public hatred, to conceal its own abuses and encroachments.

Speech in the Senate [March 14, 1834]

5 Precedents deliberately established by wise men are entitled to great weight. They are evidence of truth, but *only* evidence. . . . But a solitary precedent . . . which has never been reexamined, cannot be conclusive.

Speech in the Senate [February 18, 1835]

6 I have heard something said about allegiance to the South. I know no South, no North, no East, no West, to which I owe any allegiance. . . . The Union, sir, is my country. *Speech in the Senate [1848]*

7 The Constitution of the United States was made not merely for the generation that then existed, but for posterity—unlimited, undefined, endless, perpetual posterity.

Speech in the Senate [January 29, 1850]

8 I would rather be right than be President.[2]

Speech in the Senate [1850]

Lorenzo Dow

1777–1834

9 You will be damned if you do.—And you will be damned if you don't [definition of Calvinism]. *Reflections on the Love of God*

[1]See Mathew Henry, 319:16; Burke, 374:3; Calhoun, 449:8; Sumner, 539:4; and Cleveland, 631:7.

Our government is the potent, the omnipresent teacher.—LOUIS D. BRANDEIS, *Olmstead v. U.S.* [1928]

[2]Said when told that his defense of the Compromise would endanger his chances for the presidency.

Carl Friedrich Gauss

1777–1855

10 It may be true that people who are *merely* mathematicians have certain specific shortcomings; however, that is not the fault of mathematics, but is true of every exclusive occupation.

Letter to H. C. Schumacher [1845]

11 Mathematics is the queen of the sciences.

From SARTORIUS VON WALTERSHAUSEN, Gauss zum Gedächtniss [1856]

Valentine Blacker

1778–1823

12 Put your trust in God, my boys, and keep your powder dry!

From EDWARD HAYES, Ballads of Ireland [1856]. Oliver's Advice, An Orange Ballad

Henry Peter Brougham, Baron Brougham and Vaux

1778–1868

13 What is valuable is not new, and what is new is not valuable.[3]

From The Edinburgh Review [c. 1802], The Work of Thomas Young

14 The schoolmaster is abroad,[4] and I trust to him, armed with his primer, against the soldier in full military array.

Speech, Opening of Parliament [January 29, 1828]

15 In my mind, he was guilty of no error he—was chargeable with no exaggeration—he was betrayed by his fancy into no metaphor, who once said that all we see about us, Kings, Lords, and Commons, the whole machinery of the State, all the apparatus of the system, and its varied workings, end in simply bringing twelve good men into a box.

Present State of the Law [February 7, 1828]

16 Pursuit of Knowledge Under Difficulties.

Title of book [1830]

[3]See Daniel Webster, 451:13.

[4]At the first meeting of the London Mechanics' Institution [1825], John Reynolds, head of a school in Clerkenwell, acted as secretary of the meeting. Lord Brougham, who spoke at this meeting, said in the course of his remarks, "Look out, gentlemen, the schoolmaster is abroad." The phrase attracted little attention at that time, but when used in a speech three years later, it at once became popular.

1 Education makes a people easy to lead, but difficult to drive; easy to govern but impossible to enslave. *Attributed*

2 The great unwashed. *Attributed*

William Hazlitt

1778–1830

3 One has no notion of him [William Cobbett] as making use of a fine pen, but a great mutton-fist; his style stuns readers. . . . He is too much for any single newspaper antagonist; "lays waste" a city orator or Member of Parliament, and bears hard upon the government itself. He is a kind of *fourth estate* in the politics of the country.[1]

Table Talk [1821–1822]. Character of Cobbett

4 It is better to be able neither to read nor write than to be able to do nothing else.

Ib. On the Ignorance of the Learned

5 What I mean by living to one's self is living in the world, as in it, not of it. . . . It is to be a silent spectator of the mighty scene of things; . . . to take a thoughtful, anxious interest or curiosity in what is passing in the world, but not to feel the slightest inclination to make or meddle with it.

Ib. On Living to One's Self

6 Even in the common affairs of life, in love, friendship, and marriage, how little security have we when we trust our happiness in the hands of others! *Ib.*

7 There is not a more mean, stupid, dastardly, pitiful, selfish, spiteful, envious, ungrateful animal than the Public. It is the greatest of cowards, for it is afraid of itself. *Ib.*

8 When a man is dead, they put money in his coffin, erect monuments to his memory, and celebrate the anniversary of his birthday in set speeches. Would they take any notice of him if he were living? No![2] *Ib.*

9 One of the pleasantest things in the world is going a journey; but I like to go by myself.

Ib. On Going a Journey

10 When I am in the country I wish to vegetate like the country. *Ib.*

11 The soul of a journey is liberty, perfect liberty, to think, feel, do just as one pleases. *Ib.*

12 Give me a clear blue sky over my head, and the green turf beneath my feet, a winding road before me, and a three hours' march to dinner—and then to thinking! It is hard if I cannot start some game on these lone heaths. *Ib.*

13 No young man ever thinks he shall die.

Ib. On the Fear of Death

14 *Horus non numero nisi serenas*[3] is the motto of a sundial near Venice. There is a softness and a harmony in the words and in the thought unparalleled.

Ib. Of a Sundial in Venice

15 The love of liberty is the love of others; the love of power is the love of ourselves.

Political Essays. The Times Newspaper

16 We never do anything well till we cease to think about the manner of doing it.

Sketches and Essay. On Prejudice

17 Men of genius do not excel in any profession because they labor in it, but they labor in it because they excel.

Characteristics, no. 416 [c. 1821]

18 We are not hypocrites in our sleep.

On Dreams

Stephen Decatur

1779–1820

19 Our country! In her intercourse with foreign nations may she always be in the right; but our country, right or wrong.[4]

Toast given at Norfolk [April 1816]

Thomas, Lord Denman

1779–1854

20 Trial by jury, instead of being a security to persons who are accused, will be a delusion, a mockery, and a snare.

O'Connell v. The Queen [September 4, 1844]

Sir Robert Grant

1779–1838

21 Our shield and defender, the Ancient of
Days,[5]
Pavilioned in splendor, and girded with
praise.

Hymn. O Worship the King [1833]

[1]See Carlyle, 472:17; Macaulay, 487:13; and Thackeray, 539:15.

[2]See Martial, 119:13, and Thayer, 762:1.

[3]I count only the hours that are serene.—*Proverb*
Also quoted as: I count only the sunny hours.

[4]I hope to find my country in the right: however, I will stand by her, right or wrong.—JOHN JORDAN CRITTENDEN [1787–1863], *On the Mexican War*
See Charles Churchill, 375:13; John Quincy Adams, 417:17; and Schurz, 603:4.

[5]See *Daniel 7:9*, 33:5.

Francis Scott Key
1779–1843

1 Oh, say, can you see by the dawn's early light,
What so proudly we hailed at the twilight's last gleaming?
Whose broad stripes and bright stars, through the perilous fight,
O'er the ramparts we watched were so gallantly streaming?
And the rockets' red glare, the bombs bursting in air,
Gave proof through the night that our flag was still there.
Oh, say, does that star-spangled banner yet wave
O'er the land of the free and the home of the brave?
The Star-Spangled Banner [September 14, 1814], st. 1

2 Blessed with victory and peace, may the Heaven-rescued land
Praise the Power that hath made and preserved us a nation.
Then conquer we must, when our cause it is just,
And this be our motto, "In God is our trust."
Ib. st. 4

Clement Clarke Moore
1779–1863

3 'Twas the night before Christmas, when all through the house
Not a creature was stirring—not even a mouse;[1]
The stockings were hung by the chimney with care,
In hopes that St. Nicholas soon would be there.
A Visit from St. Nicholas [December 1823]

4 "Happy Christmas to all, and to all a good-night!" *Ib.*

Thomas Moore
1779–1852

5 Faintly as tolls the evening chime,
Our voices keep tune and our oars keep time.[2]
Poems Relating to America. A Canadian Boat Song, st. 1

[1] See Shakespeare, 217:16.
[2] See Marvell, 297:10.

6 Go where glory waits thee![3]
But while fame elates thee,
Oh, still remember me!
Irish Melodies [1807–1834]. Go Where Glory Waits Thee, st. 1

7 Oh, breathe not his name! let it sleep in the shade,
Where cold and unhonored his relics are laid.
Ib. Oh Breathe Not His Name, st. 1

8 And the tear that we shed, though in secret it rolls,
Shall long keep his memory green in our souls.[4] *Ib. st. 2*

9 The harp that once through Tara's halls
The soul of music shed,
Now hangs as mute on Tara's walls
As if that soul were fled.
Ib. The Harp That Once Through Tara's Halls, st. 1

10 Rich and rare were the gems she wore,
And a bright gold ring on her wand she bore.
Ib. Rich and Rare Were the Gems She Wore, st. 1

11 Believe me, if all those endearing young charms
Which I gaze on so fondly today,
Were to change by tomorrow and fleet in my arms,
Like fairy gifts fading away,
Thou would'st still be adored as this moment thou art,
Let thy loveliness fade as it will,
And around the dear ruin each wish of my heart
Would entwine itself verdantly still.
Ib. Believe Me, If All Those Endearing Young Charms, st. 1

12 But there's nothing half so sweet in life
As love's young dream.
Ib. Love's Young Dream, st. 1

13 Eyes of unholy blue.
Ib. By That Lake Whose Gloomy Shore, st. 2

14 'Tis the last rose of summer,
Left blooming alone;
All her lovely companions
Are faded and gone.
Ib. The Last Rose of Summer, st. 1

15 The Minstrel Boy to the war is gone,
In the ranks of death you'll find him.
His father's sword he has girded on,
And his wild harp slung behind him.
Ib. The Minstrel Boy, st. 1

[3] See Lowell, 567:22.
[4] See Shakespeare, 217:28.

1 And the best of all ways
To lengthen our days
Is to steal a few hours from the night, my dear.

Ib. The Young May Moon, st. 1

2 You may break, you may shatter the vase, if you will,
But the scent of the roses will hang round it still.[1]

Ib. Farewell! But Whenever, st. 3

3 No eye to watch, and no tongue to wound us,
All earth forgot, and all heaven around us.

Ib. Come O'er the Sea, st. 2

4 The light that lies
In woman's eyes,
Has been my heart's undoing.

Ib. The Time I've Lost in Wooing, st. 1

5 My only books
Were woman's looks,
And folly's all they've taught me. *Ib.*

6 A Persian's heaven is easily made:
'Tis but black eyes and lemonade.

Intercepted Letters; or, The Two-Penny Post Bag [1813], VI

7 Oft in the stilly night,
Ere Slumber's chain has bound me,
Fond Memory brings the light
Of other days around me;
The smiles, the tears,
Of boyhood's years,
The words of love then spoken;
The eyes that shone
Now dimmed and gone,
The cheerful hearts now broken.

National Airs [1815]. Oft in the Stilly Night, st. 1

8 I feel like one,
Who treads alone
Some banquet hall deserted,
Whose lights are fled,
Whose garlands dead,
And all but he departed. *Ib. st. 2*

9 What though youth gave love and roses,
Age still leaves us friends and wine.

Ib. Spring and Autumn, st. 1

10 Sound the loud timbrel o'er Egypt's dark sea!
Jehovah has triumphed—his people are free.

Sacred Songs. Sound the Loud Timbrel, st. 1

11 Oh, call it by some better name,
For friendship sounds too cold.

Ballads and Songs. Oh, Call It by Some Better Name, st. 1

12 There's a bower of roses by Bendemeer's stream,
And the nightingale sings round it all the day long. *Lalla Rookh [1817], pt. II*

13 Some flow'rets of Eden ye still inherit,
But the trail of the serpent is over them all.

Ib.

14 Oh! ever thus, from childhood's hour,
I've seen my fondest hope decay;
I never loved a tree or flower,
But 'twas the first to fade away.
I never nursed a dear gazelle
To glad me with its soft black eye,
But when it came to know me well,
And love me, it was sure to die. *Ib. V*

15 Like Dead Sea fruits, that tempt the eye,
But turn to ashes on the lips.[2] *Ib.*

16 Paradise itself were dim
And joyless, if not shared with him!

Ib. VI

Lorenz Oken

1779–1851

17 The universe is the language of God.

Elements of Physiophilosophy [1847],[3] pt. I, par. 64

Joseph Story

1779–1849

18 I will not say with Lord Hale, that "The Law will admit of no rival" . . . but I will say that it is a jealous mistress, and requires a long and constant courtship. It is not to be won by trifling favors, but by lavish homage.[4]

The Value and Importance of Legal Studies [August 5, 1829][5]

[1] The jar will long keep the fragrance of what it was once steeped in when new.—HORACE [65–8 B.C.], *Epistles, I, 2, 69*

That flavor, absorbed when new, remains.—QUINTILIAN [born c. 35]

But, somehow or other, though you fill it with water, the jar retains the odor which it acquired when first used. —ST. JEROME [c. 342–420]

The image was frequently used in the classical period; unglazed ware is more absorbent than glazed.

[2] See Byron, 457:20.

[3] Translated by ALFRED TURK.

[4] See Emerson, 498:25.

[5] Inaugural address as Dane Professor of Law at Harvard University.

William Ellery Channing

1780–1842

1 We do, then, with all earnestness, though without reproaching our brethren, protest against the irrational and unscriptural doctrine of the Trinity. "To us," as to the Apostle and the primitive Christians, "there is one God, even the Father." With Jesus, we worship the Father, as the only living and true God. We are astonished, that any man can read the New Testament, and avoid the conviction, that the Father alone is God.

Unitarian Christianity [Baltimore, 1819]

2 The office of government is not to confer happiness, but to give men opportunity to work out happiness for themselves.

Review of Sir Walter Scott, The Life of Napoleon Bonaparte [1827]. From the Christian Examiner [September and October 1827]

3 I see the marks of God in the heavens and the earth, but how much more in a liberal intellect, in magnanimity, in unconquerable rectitude, in a philanthropy which forgives every wrong, and which never despairs of the cause of Christ and human virtue! I do and I must reverence human nature.[1] . . . I thank God that my own lot is bound up with that of the human race.[2]

Likeness to God [Providence, Rhode Island, 1828]

4 There are seasons, in human affairs, of inward and outward revolution, when new depths seem to be broken up in the soul, when new wants are unfolded in multitudes, and a new and undefined good is thirsted for. There are periods when . . . *to dare,* is the highest wisdom.[3]

Complete Works [1879]. The Union [1829]

5 It is chiefly through books that we enjoy intercourse with superior minds. . . . God be thanked for books. They are the voices of the distant and the dead, and make us heirs of the spiritual life of past ages. Books are true levelers. They give to all, who will faithfully use them, the society, the spiritual presence, of the best and greatest of our race.

Self-Culture [Boston, September 1838]

[1]See Albert Schweitzer, 756:16.

[2]Inscription on Channing Memorial, Public Garden, Boston.

[3]See Spenser, 173:20; Danton, 412:2; and Patton, 792:3.

6 The mind, in proportion as it is cut off from free communication with nature, with revelation, with God, with itself, loses its life, just as the body droops when debarred from the air and the cheering light from heaven.

Remarks on the Character and Writings of Fénelon [1843]

7 I call that mind free which jealously guards its intellectual rights and powers, which calls no man master, which does not content itself with a passive or hereditary faith, which opens itself to light whencesoever it may come, which receives new truth as an angel from Heaven. *Spiritual Freedom*

Karl von Clausewitz

1780–1831

8 War is not merely a political act, but also a political instrument, a continuation of political relations, a carrying out of the same by other means.[4]

Vom Kriege (On War) [1833]

Charles Caleb Colton

1780–1832

9 When you have nothing to say, say nothing.

Lacon [1820–1822], vol. I, no. 183

10 Imitation is the sincerest of flattery.

Ib. 217

11 The debt which cancels all others.

Ib. II, 66

Charles Miner

1780–1865

12 When I see a merchant overpolite to his customers, begging them to taste a little brandy and throwing half his goods on the counter—thinks I, that man has an ax to grind.

Essays from the Desk of Poor Robert the Scribe [1815]. Who'll Turn Grindstones[5]

[4]Der Krieg ist nichts anderes als die Fortsetzung der Politik mit anderen Mitteln.

See Mao Tse-tung, 826:10.

A thermonuclear war cannot be considered a continuation of politics by other means. It would be a means to universal suicide.—Andrei D. Sakharov, *Progress, Coexistence, and Intellectual Freedom* [1966]

[5]First published in *Luzerne Federalist* [September 7, 1810]. Because of the similarity of the title to *Poor Richard,* the phrase "an ax to grind" has often been attributed to Franklin.

Frances Trollope
1780–1863

1 Let no one who wishes to receive agreeable impressions of American manners, commence their travels in a Mississippi steamboat.

Domestic Manners of the Americans [1832]

Ebenezer Elliott
1781–1849

2 Not kings and lords, but nations!
Not thrones and crowns, but men!

Corn Law Rhymes [1828]. When Wilt Thou Save the People? st. 1

3 God save the people! *Ib.*

4 What is a communist? One who hath yearnings
For equal division of unequal earnings.

Poetical Works [1846]. Epigram

James Lawrence
1781–1813

5 Tell the men to fire faster and not to give up the ship; fight her till she sinks.[1]

On board the U.S. frigate Chesapeake [June 1, 1813]

Thomas Hart Benton
1782–1858

6 This new page opened in the book of our public expenditures, and this new departure taken, which leads into the bottomless gulf of civil pensions and family gratuities.

Speech in the Senate against a grant to President Harrison's widow [April 1841]

John Caldwell Calhoun
1782–1850

7 Protection and patriotism are reciprocal.

Speech in the House of Representatives [December 12, 1811]

[1] Usually quoted as "Don't give up the ship." Captain Lawrence's final order as he was carried below, fatally wounded, before the capture of his ship by the British frigate *Shannon.*

8 The very essence of a free government consists in considering offices as public trusts,[2] bestowed for the good of the country, and not for the benefit of an individual or a party.

Speech [February 13, 1835]

9 A power has risen up in the government greater than the people themselves, consisting of many and various and powerful interests, combined into one mass, and held together by the cohesive power of the vast surplus in the banks.[3]

Speech [May 27, 1836]

10 The surrender of life is nothing to sinking down into acknowledgment of inferiority.

Speech in the Senate [February 19, 1847]

11 It is harder to preserve than to obtain liberty.[4]

Speech in the Senate [January 1848]

Ann Taylor
1782–1866
Jane Taylor
1783–1824

12 Who ran to help me when I fell,
And would some pretty story tell,
Or kiss the place to make it well?
My mother.

Original Poems for Infant Minds [1804]. My Mother [by ANN TAYLOR], st. 6

13 Twinkle, twinkle, little star,
How I wonder what you are,
Up above the world so high,
Like a diamond in the sky![5]

Rhymes for the Nursery [1806]. The Star, st. 1

14 I like little pussy, her coat is so warm;
And if I don't hurt her she'll do me no harm.

Ib. I Like Little Pussy [by JANE TAYLOR], st. 1

15 Oh, that it were my chief delight
To do the things I ought!
Then let me try with all my might
To mind what I am taught.

Hymns for Infant Minds [1810]. For a Very Little Child

[2] See Henry, 319:16; Burke, 374:3; Clay, 444:3; Sumner, 539:4; and Cleveland, 631:7.

[3] From this speech comes the phrase: Cohesive power of public plunder.

[4] See S. E. Morison, 800:7.

[5] See Lewis Carroll, 611:20.

1 And willful waste, depend upon 't,
Brings, almost always, woeful want!
Ib. The Pin [by ANN TAYLOR*], st. 6*

Daniel Webster[1]

1782–1852

2 It is, sir, as I have said, a small college, and yet there are those who love it.
Dartmouth College Case [1818]

3 Whatever makes men good Christians, makes them good citizens.
Speech at Plymouth, Massachusetts [December 22, 1820][2]

4 Labor in this country is independent and proud. It has not to ask the patronage of capital, but capital solicits the aid of labor.[3]
Speech [April 2, 1824]

5 We wish that this column, rising towards heaven among the pointed spires of so many temples dedicated to God, may contribute also to produce in all minds a pious feeling of dependence and gratitude. We wish, finally, that the last object to the sight of him who leaves his native shore, and the first to gladden his who revisits it, may be something which shall remind him of the liberty and the glory of his country.
Address on Laying the Cornerstone of the Bunker Hill Monument [June 17, 1825]

6 Mind is the great lever of all things; human thought is the process by which human ends are ultimately answered. *Ib.*

7 Knowledge, in truth, is the great sun in the firmament. Life and power are scattered with all its beams. *Ib.*

8 Let our object be our country, our whole country, and nothing but our country. *Ib.*

9 Sink or swim, live or die, survive or perish, I give my hand and my heart to this vote.[4]
Discourse in Commemoration of Adams and Jefferson, Faneuil Hall, Boston [August 2, 1826]

10 It is my living sentiment, and by the blessing of God it shall be my dying sentiment —Independence now and Independence forever.[5] *Ib.*

11 Washington is in the clear upper sky. *Ib.*

12 The gentleman has not seen how to reply to this, otherwise than by supposing me to have advanced the doctrine that a national debt is a national blessing.[6]
Second Speech on Foote's Resolution [January 26, 1830]

13 I shall enter on no encomium upon Massachusetts; she needs none. There she is.[7] Behold her, and judge for yourselves. There is her history; the world knows it by heart. The past, at least, is secure. There is Boston and Concord and Lexington and Bunker Hill; and there they will remain forever. *Ib.*

14 The people's government, made for the people, made by the people, and answerable to the people.[8] *Ib.*

15 When my eyes shall be turned to behold for the last time the sun in heaven, may I not see him shining on the broken and dishonored fragments of a once glorious Union; on States disevered, discordant, belligerent; on a land rent with civil feuds, or drenched, it may be, in fraternal blood. *Ib.*

16 Liberty and Union, now and forever, one and inseparable. *Ib.*

17 There is no refuge from confession but suicide; and suicide is confession.
Argument on the murder of Captain White [April 6, 1830]

18 There is nothing so powerful as truth— and often nothing so strange.[9] *Ib.*

19 Fearful concatenation of circumstances.[10] *Ib.*

20 A sense of duty pursues us ever. It is omnipresent, like the Deity. If we take to ourselves the wings of the morning, and dwell in the uttermost parts of the sea, duty performed or duty violated is still with us, for our happi-

[1] See Sydney Smith, 433:5.

[2] This oration will be read five hundred years hence with as much rapture as it was heard. It ought to be read at the end of every century, and indeed at the end of every year, forever and ever.—JOHN ADAMS, *Letter to Webster* [December 23, 1821]

[3] See Lincoln, 522:3.

[4] Live or die, sink or swim.—GEORGE PEELE, *Edward I* [c. 1584]

[5] On the day of his [John Adams's] death, hearing the noise of bells and cannon, he asked the occasion. On being reminded that it was "Independent Day," he replied, "Independence forever."—DANIEL WEBSTER, *Works* [1903], *vol. I, p. 150*

[6] See Hamilton, 401:10.

[7] Generally misquoted as "Massachusetts, there she stands."

[8] Our sovereign, the people.—CHARLES JAMES FOX, *toast* [1798], *for which his name was erased from the Privy Council*

See Wycliffe, 143:12; Disraeli, 501:6; Garrison, 505:19; Lincoln, 523:4; and Parker, 537:15.

[9] See Byron, 462:2.

[10] See Scott, 432:3.

ness or our misery. If we say the darkness shall cover us, in the darkness as in the light our obligations are yet with us.[1] *Ib.*

1 He smote the rock of the national resources, and abundant streams of revenue gushed forth.[2] He touched the dead corpse of Public Credit, and it sprung upon its feet.
Speech on Hamilton [March 10, 1831]

2 On this question of principle, while actual suffering was yet afar off, they [the Colonies] raised their flag against a power to which, for purposes of foreign conquest and subjugation, Rome in the height of her glory is not to be compared — a power which has dotted over the surface of the whole globe with her possessions and military posts, whose morning drumbeat, following the sun,[3] and keeping company with the hours, circles the earth with one continuous and unbroken strain of the martial airs of England.
Speech [May 7, 1834]

3 God grants liberty only to those who love it, and are always ready to guard and defend it.
Speech [June 3, 1834]

4 One country, one constitution, one destiny.
Speech [March 15, 1837]

5 There are persons who constantly clamor. They complain of oppression, speculation, and pernicious influence of wealth. They cry out loudly against all banks and corporations, and a means by which small capitalists become united in order to produce important and beneficial results. They carry on mad hostility against all established institutions. They would choke the fountain of industry and dry all streams.
Speech in the Senate [March 12, 1838]

6 When tillage begins, other arts follow. The farmers therefore are the founders of human civilization.
On Agriculture [January 13, 1840]

7 America has furnished to the world the character of Washington. And if our American institutions had done nothing else, that alone would have entitled them to the respect of mankind.
On the Completion of the Bunker Hill Monument [June 17, 1843]

8 Thank God! I — I also — am an American! *Ib.*

9 Justice, sir, is the great interest of man on earth.
On Mr. Justice Story [September 12, 1845]

10 Inconsistencies of opinion, arising from changes of circumstances, are often justifiable.[4] *Speech [July 25 and 27, 1846]*

11 Liberty exists in proportion to wholesome restraint.
Speech at the Charleston Bar Dinner [May 10, 1847]

12 The law: It has honored us; may we honor it. *Ib.*

13 I have read their platform, and though I think there are some unsound places in it, I can stand upon it pretty well. But I see nothing in it both new and valuable. "What is valuable is not new, and what is new is not valuable."[5]
Speech at Marshfield, Massachusetts [September 1, 1848]

14 I was born an American; I will live an American; I shall die an American.
Speech [July 17, 1850]

15 Faneuil Hall, the cradle of American liberty. *Letter [April 1851]*

16 Men hang out their signs indicative of their respective trades: shoemakers hang out a gigantic shoe; jewelers, a monster watch; and the dentist hangs out a gold tooth; but up in the mountains of New Hampshire, God Almighty has hung out a sign to show that there He makes men.
On the Old Man of the Mountain[6]*; attributed*

17 I still live.
Last words [October 24, 1852]

Simón Bolívar[7]
1783–1830

18 A state too extensive in itself, or by virtue of its dependencies, ultimately falls into decay; its free government is transformed into a tyranny; it disregards the principles

[1] See *Psalm 139:9*, 22:17.
[2] See *Numbers 20:11*, 10:26.
[3] See Schiller, 412:18.

[4] L'homme absurde est celui qui ne change jamais [The absurd man is he who never changes]. — AUGUSTE MARSEILLE BARTHÉLEMY, *Ma Justification* [1832]
[5] See Lord Brougham, 444:13.
[6] Natural rock formation in the shape of a human profile, in the Presidential Range of the White Mountains. It gave Hawthorne the theme of his story *The Great Stone Face.*
[7] One must speak of Bolívar from the tribune of a mountain, or amidst thunder and lightning . . . He lived as if among flames, and he was flame. He loved, and spoke flowers of fire. — JOSÉ MARTÍ, *Bolívar* [1893]

which it should preserve, and finally degenerates into despotism. The distinguishing characteristic of small republics is stability: the character of large republics is mutability.
Letter from Jamaica [Summer, 1815]

1 Among the popular and representative systems of government I do not approve of the federal system: it is too perfect; and it requires virtues and political talents much superior to our own. *Ib.*

2 Let us give to our republic a fourth power with authority over the youth, the hearts of men, public spirit, habits, and republican morality. Let us establish this Areopagus to watch over the education of the children, to supervise national education, to purify whatever may be corrupt in the republic, to denounce ingratitude, coldness in the country's service, egotism, sloth, idleness, and to pass judgment upon the first signs of corruption and pernicious example.
Address to the Congress of Angostura [February 15, 1819]

3 Those who have served the cause of the revolution have plowed the sea.
Attributed

4 The three greatest dolts in the world: Jesus Christ, Don Quixote, and I. *Attributed*

Reginald Heber
1783–1826

5 Brightest and best[1] of the sons of the morning,
Dawn on our darkness, and lend us thine aid.
Hymns. Epiphany [1811], st. 1

6 By cool Siloam's shady rill
How sweet the lily grows!
Ib. First Sunday After Epiphany [1812], no. 2

7 The Son of God goes forth to war,
A kingly crown to gain;
His blood-red banner streams afar;
Who follows in His train?
Ib. The Son of God Goes Forth to War [1812], st. 1

8 From Greenland's icy mountains,
From India's coral strand,
Where Afric's sunny fountains
Roll down their golden sand.
Ib. Missionary Hymn [1819], st. 1

[1]The Best and the Brightest. — David Halberstam, *title of book* [1972]
See Shelley, 470:2.

9 Though every prospect pleases,
And only man is vile.[2] *Ib. st. 2*

10 The heathen in his blindness
Bows down to wood and stone. *Ib.*

11 Holy, Holy, Holy! Lord God Almighty!
Early in the morning our song shall rise to Thee:
Holy, Holy, Holy! Merciful and Mighty!
God in Three Persons, Blessed Trinity.
Ib. Holy, Holy, Holy! [1827]

Washington Irving
1783–1859

12 How convenient it would be to many of our great men and great families of doubtful origin, could they have the privilege of the heroes of yore, who, whenever their origin was involved in obscurity, modestly announced themselves descended from a god.
Knickerbocker's History of New York [1809], bk. II, ch. 3

13 His wife "ruled the roast," and in governing the governor, governed the province, which might thus be said to be under petticoat government. *Ib. IV, 4*

14 They claim to be the first inventors of those recondite beverages, cocktail, stonefence, and sherry cobbler. *Ib. 241*

15 There is in every true woman's heart a spark of heavenly fire, which lies dormant in the broad daylight of prosperity; but which kindles up, and beams and blazes in the dark hour of adversity.
The Sketch-Book [1819–1820]. The Wife

16 Those men are most apt to be obsequious and conciliating abroad, who are under the discipline of shrews at home.
Ib. Rip Van Winkle[3]

17 A sharp tongue is the only edge tool that grows keener with constant use. *Ib.*

18 That happy age when a man can be idle with impunity. *Ib.*

19 A woman's whole life is a history of the affections. *Ib. The Broken Heart*

20 Language gradually varies, and with it fade away the writings of authors who have flourished their allotted time.
Ib. The Mutabilities of Literature

[2]Stanza 2 was dropped from the *Hymnal* in 1940.

[3]The theme of Irving's story derives from Diogenes Laertius, *Epimenides* [c. 200]. Epimenides was sent by his father into the field to look for a sheep; he turned out of the road at midday and lay down in a certain cave and fell asleep, and slept there fifty-seven years; and after that, when awake, he went on looking for the sheep, thinking that he had been taking a short nap.

1 There rise authors now and then, who seem proof against the mutability of language, because they have rooted themselves in the unchanging principles of human nature. *Ib.*

2 His [the author's] renown has been purchased, not by deeds of violence and blood, but by the diligent dispensation of pleasure.
Ib. Westminster Abbey [The Poets' Corner]

3 The sorrow for the dead is the only sorrow from which we refuse to be divorced.
Ib. Rural Funerals

4 Whenever a man's friends begin to compliment him about looking young, he may be sure that they think he is growing old.
Bracebridge Hall [1822]. Bachelors

5 I am always at a loss to know how much to believe of my own stories.
Tales of a Traveler [1824]. To the Reader

6 The almighty dollar,[1] that great object of universal devotion throughout our land, seems to have no genuine devotees in these peculiar villages.
Wolfert's Roost [1855]. The Creole Village

Stendhal
[Henri Beyle]
1783–1842

7 Almost all our misfortunes in life come from the wrong notions we have about the things that happen to us. To know men thoroughly, to judge events sanely is, therefore, a great step towards happiness.
Journal [December 10, 1801]

8 I call "crystallization" that action of the mind that discovers fresh perfections in its beloved at every turn of events.
De l'Amour [1822], ch. 1

9 A wise woman never yields by appointment. It should always be an unforeseen happiness. *Ib. 60*

10 One can acquire everything in solitude — except character. *Ib. Fragments*

11 Prudery is a kind of avarice, the worst of all. *Ib.*

12 In matters of sentiment, the public has very crude ideas; and the most shocking fault of women is that they make the public the supreme judge of their lives. *Ib.*

[1]See Jonson, 256:7.

13 A novel is a mirror that strolls along a highway. Now it reflects the blue of the skies, now the mud puddles underfoot.
Le Rouge et le Noir (The Red and the Black)[2] *[1830]*

14 There is no such thing as "natural law": this expression is nothing but old nonsense. Prior to laws, what is natural is only the strength of the lion, or the need of the creature suffering from hunger or cold, in short, need. *Ib.*

15 I see but one rule: to be clear. If I am not clear, all my world crumbles to nothing.
Reply to Balzac [October 30, 1840][3]

16 Wit lasts no more than two centuries.
Ib.

17 It is the nobility of their style which will make our writers of 1840 unreadable forty years from now.
Manuscript note [1840]

18 Love has always been the most important business in my life, I should say the only one.
La Vie d'Henri Brulard [1890]

Allan Cunningham
1784–1842

19 A wet sheet and a flowing sea,
A wind that follows fast,
And fills the white and rustling sail,
And bends the gallant mast.
The Songs of Scotland [1825]. A Wet Sheet and a Flowing Sea, st. 1

20 The hollow oak our palace is,
Our heritage the sea. *Ib. st. 3*

21 It's hame and it's hame, hame fain wad I be—
O, hame, hame, hame to my ain countree!
Ib. It's Hame and It's Hame, refrain

Leigh Hunt
1784–1859

22 This Adonis in loveliness was a corpulent man of fifty.[4]
The Examiner [March 22, 1812]

23 Where the light woods go seaward from the town.
The Story of Rimini [1816], canto I, l. 18

[2]Translated by Norbert Guterman.
[3]In reference to *La Chartreuse de Parme* [1839].
[4]For this reference to the Prince Regent, Hunt was imprisoned. But he was allowed to redecorate the walls of his prison with a trellis of roses, had his family with him, and visitors were freely admitted; Byron, indeed, gave a dinner party in his honor at the jail.

1 But most he loved a happy human face.
Ib. III, l. 110

2 The world was all forgot, the struggle o'er,
Desperate the joy.—That day they read no more.[1]
Ib. l. 607

3 Green little vaulter in the sunny grass.
To the Grasshopper and the Cricket [1817]

4 Abou Ben Adhem (may his tribe increase!)
Awoke one night from a deep dream of peace.
Abou Ben Adhem [1838]

5 An angel writing in a book of gold.
Ib.

6 Write me as one that loves his fellow men.
Ib.

7 And showed the names whom love of God had blessed,
And lo! Ben Adhem's name led all the rest.
Ib.

8 Jenny kissed me when we met,
Jumping from the chair she sat in;
Time, you thief, who love to get
Sweets into your list, put that in:
Say I'm weary, say I'm sad,
Say that health and wealth have missed me,
Say I'm growing old, but add,
Jenny kissed me.[2]
Rondeau [1838]

9 A Venus grown fat!
Blue-Stocking Revels

10 "No love," quoth he, "but vanity, sets love a task like that."
The Glove and the Lions,[3] st. 4

11 A pleasure so exquisite as almost to amount to pain.
Letter to Alexander Ireland [June 2, 1848]

Henry John Temple, Viscount Palmerston
1784–1865

12 We have no eternal allies and we have no perpetual enemies. Our interests are eternal and perpetual, and these interests it is our duty to follow.
Speech on the Polish Question in the House of Commons [1848]

[1] See Dante, 141:3.
[2] Jenny was Jane Welsh Carlyle, who kissed Hunt when he brought Carlyle good news.
[3] Schiller wrote a poem on the same theme, and Browning's *The Glove* [1845] is a later version of the familiar legend.

Zachary Taylor
1784–1850

13 Hurrah for Old Kentuck! That's the way to do it. Give 'em hell, damn 'em.
Shouted to the 2nd Kentucky Regiment on seeing them rally in battle [Buena Vista, Mexico, February 23, 1847]

14 A little more grape, Captain Bragg.
Attributed [Ib.]

15 Tell him to go to hell.
Reply to Santa Anna's demand for surrender [Ib.]

Thomas De Quincey
1785–1859

16 The burden of the incommunicable.
Confessions of an English Opium-Eater [1822–1856], pt. I

17 Call for the grandest of all earthly spectacles, what is that? It is the sun going to his rest. Call for the grandest of all human sentiments, what is that? It is that man should forget his anger before he lies down to sleep.[4]
Ib.

18 So, then, Oxford Street, stonyhearted stepmother, thou that listenest to the sighs of orphans, and drinkest the tears of children, at length I was dismissed from thee.
Ib.

19 Everlasting farewells! and again, and yet again reverberated—everlasting farewells!
Ib. III

20 Dyspepsy is the ruin of most things: empires, expeditions, and everything else.
Letter to Hessey [1823]

21 If once a man indulges himself in murder, very soon he comes to think little of robbing; and from robbing he comes next to drinking and Sabbath-breaking, and from that to incivility and procrastination.
Murder Considered as One of the Fine Arts [1827]

Lady Caroline Lamb
1785–1828

22 [Of Byron] Mad, bad, and dangerous to know.
Journal [March 1812]

[4] See *Ephesians 4:26*, 49:36.

Thomas Love Peacock
1785–1866

1 Not drunk is he who from the floor
Can rise alone and still drink more;
But drunk is he who prostrate lies,
Without the power to drink or rise.
The Misfortunes of Elphin [1829], ch. 3, heading (translated from the Welsh)

2 The mountain sheep are sweeter,
But the valley sheep are fatter;
We therefore deemed it meeter
To carry off the latter. *Ib. 11*

3 Ancient sculpture is the true school of modesty. But where the Greeks had modesty, we have cant; where they had poetry, we have cant; where they had patriotism, we have cant; where they had anything that exalts, delights, or adorns humanity, we have nothing but cant, cant, cant.
Crotchet Castle [1831], ch. 7

4 A book that furnishes no quotations is, *me judice,* no book—it is a plaything.
Ib. 9

Oliver Hazard Perry
1785–1819

5 We have met the enemy, and they are ours.[1]
Dispatch from U.S. brig Niagara to General William Henry Harrison, announcing his victory at the battle of Lake Erie [September 10, 1813]

Samuel Woodworth
1785–1842

6 How dear to this heart are the scenes of my childhood,
When fond recollection presents them to view! *The Old Oaken Bucket*

7 The old oaken bucket, the iron-bound bucket,
The moss-covered bucket which hung in the well. *Ib.*

8 Pickaxe, shovel, spade, crowbar, hoe, and barrow,
Better not invade, Yankees have the marrow.
The Patriotic Diggers [1814], st. 1

[1] We has met the enemy, and it is us.—WALT KELLY [1913–1973], *Pogo*

David Crockett
1786–1836

9 I leave this rule for others when I'm dead,
Be always sure you're right—then go ahead.[2]
Autobiography [1834]

10 Don't shoot, Colonel, I'll come down: I know I'm a gone coon.[3]
Story told by Crockett of a treed raccoon

William Learned Marcy
1786–1857

11 They see nothing wrong in the rule that to the victor belong the spoils of the enemy.
Speech in the Senate [January 1832]

Winfield Scott[4]
1786–1866

12 The enemy say that Americans are good at a long shot, but cannot stand the cold iron. I call upon you instantly to give a lie to the slander. Charge!
Address to the 11th Infantry Regiment [Chippewa, Canada, June 5, 1814]

13 Say to the seceded States, "Wayward sisters, depart in peace."
Letter to W. H. Seward [March 3, 1861]

Seattle[5]
c. 1786–1866

14 My people are few. They resemble the scattering trees of a storm-swept plain. . . . There was a time when our people covered the land as the waves of a wind-ruffled sea cover its shell-paved floor, but that time long since passed away with the greatness of tribes that are now but a mournful memory.
Statement on surrendering tribal lands on site of Seattle to Isaac Stevens, governor of Washington Territory [1855]

[2] Crockett's motto in the War of 1812.

[3] The expression "gone coon" was current during the Revolutionary War, originating in the plea of a spy, dressed in raccoon skins, to his discoverer, an English rifleman.—*Century Cyclopedia of Names*

[4] Known as "Old Fuss 'n Feathers" by his troops during the Black Hawk War [1832].

[5] Chief of the Dwamish and allied tribes of Puget Sound. The city of Seattle was named for him.

1 What is man without the beasts? If all the beasts were gone, men would die from great loneliness of spirit, for whatever happens to the beasts also happens to the man.

Ib.

2 At night when the streets of your cities and villages are silent and you think them deserted, they will throng with the returning hosts that once filled them and still love this beautiful land. The white man will never be alone. *Ib.*

Barry Cornwall [Bryan Waller Procter]

1787–1874

3 The sea! the sea! the open sea!
The blue, the fresh, the ever free.

The Sea, st. 1

François Guizot

1787–1874

4 Enrich yourselves![1]

Speech [March 1, 1843]

Emma Willard

1787–1870

5 Rocked in the cradle of the deep.

The Cradle of the Deep [1831]

George Noel Gordon, Lord Byron

1788–1824

6 "Friendship is Love without his wings!"

L'Amitié Est l'Amour sans Ailes[2] *[written 1806]*

7 I only know we loved in vain;
I only feel—farewell! farewell!

Farewell! If Ever Fondest Prayer [1808], st. 2

8 When we two parted
In silence and tears,
Half brokenhearted,
To sever for years.

When We Two Parted [1808], st. 1

9 Near this spot are deposited the remains of one who possessed beauty without vanity, strength without insolence, courage without ferocity, and all the virtues of Man, without his vices. This praise, which would be unmeaning flattery if inscribed over human ashes, is but a just tribute to the memory of Boatswain, a dog.

Inscription on the monument of a Newfoundland dog [1808]

10 The poor dog, in life the firmest friend,
The first to welcome, foremost to defend.[3]

Ib.

11 I'll publish right or wrong:
Fools are my theme, let satire be my song.

English Bards and Scotch Reviewers [1809], l. 5

12 'Tis pleasant, sure, to see one's name in print;
A book's a book, although there's nothing in 't.

Ib. l. 51

13 A man must serve his time to every trade
Save censure—critics all are ready-made.

Ib. l. 63

14 With just enough of learning to misquote.

Ib. l. 66

15 As soon
Seek roses in December, ice in June;
Hope constancy in wind, or corn in chaff;
Believe a woman or an epitaph,
Or any other thing that's false, before
You trust in critics. *Ib. l. 75*

16 Better to err with Pope, than shine with Pye.

Ib. l. 102

17 'Twas thine own genius gave the final blow,
And helped to plant the wound that laid thee low:
So the struck eagle, stretched upon the plain,
No more through rolling clouds to soar again,
Viewed his own feather on the fatal dart,
And winged the shaft that quivered in his heart.[4] *Ib. l. 826*

18 Though Nature's sternest painter, yet the best.[5] *Ib. l. 839*

19 Maid of Athens, ere we part,
Give, oh give me back my heart!

Maid of Athens [1810], st. 1

20 Vexed with mirth the drowsy ear of night.

Childe Harold's Pilgrimage, canto I [1812], st. 2

21 Had sighed to many, though he loved but one.

Ib. st. 5

22 Maidens, like moths, are ever caught by glare,
And Mammon wins his way where seraphs might despair. *Ib. st. 9*

23 Might shake the saintship of an anchorite.

Ib. st. 11

[1] Enrichissez-vous!
[2] A French proverb.

[3] See Vest, 609:4.
[4] See Aesop, 66:24.
[5] Crabbe.

1 My native land, good night!
Ib. st. 13 (song)

2 Still from the fount of joy's delicious springs
Some bitter o'er the flowers its bubbling venom flings.[1] *Ib. st. 82*

3 War, war is still the cry, "War even to the knife!"[2] *Ib. st. 86*

4 Gone—glimmering through the dream of things that were.
Ib. canto II [1812], st. 2

5 A schoolboy's tale, the wonder of an an hour!
Ib.

6 The dome of thought, the palace of the soul.[3]
Ib. st. 6

7 Fair Greece! sad relic of departed worth!
Immortal, though no more; though fallen, great! *Ib. st. 73*

8 Who would be free themselves must strike the blow. *Ib. st. 76*

9 Where'er we tread 'tis haunted, holy ground.
Ib. st. 88

10 What is the worst of woes that wait on age?
What stamps the wrinkle deeper on the brow?
To view each loved one blotted from life's page,
And be alone on earth, as I am now.
Ib. st. 98

11 Once more upon the waters, yet once more!
And the waves bound beneath me as a steed
That knows his rider!
Ib. canto III [1816], st. 2

12 Years steal
Fire from the mind as vigor from the limb;
And life's enchanted cup but sparkles near the brim. *Ib. st. 8*

13 And Harold stands upon this place of skulls.
Ib. st. 18

14 There was a sound of revelry by night,
And Belgium's capital had gathered then
Her beauty and her chivalry, and bright
The lamps shone o'er fair women and brave men.
A thousand hearts beat happily; and when
Music arose with its voluptuous swell,
Soft eyes looked love to eyes which spake again,
And all went merry as a marriage bell.
But hush! hark! a deep sound strikes like a rising knell! *Ib. st. 21*

[1] See Lucretius, 101:7.
[2] War even to the knife!—JOSÉ DE PALAFOX Y MELZI [1775–1847]
Palafox, governor of Saragossa, had been summoned by the besieging French to surrender the city [1808].
[3] See Waller, 276:10.

15 Did ye not hear it?—No! 'twas but the wind,
Or the car rattling o'er the stony street.
On with the dance! let joy be unconfined;
No sleep till morn, when Youth and Pleasure meet
To chase the glowing hours with flying feet.
Ib. st. 22

16 Arm! Arm! it is—it is—the cannon's opening roar! *Ib.*

17 And there was mounting in hot haste.
Ib. st. 25

18 Or whispering, with white lips, "The foe. They come! they come!" *Ib.*

19 Battle's magnificently stern array!
Ib. st. 28

20 Like to the apples on the Dead Sea's shore,
All ashes to the taste.[4] *Ib. st. 34*

21 Thou fatal Waterloo.
Millions of tongues record thee, and anew
Their children's lips shall echo them, and say—
"Here, where the sword united nations drew,
Our countrymen were warring on that day!"
And this is much, and all which will not pass away.[5] *Ib. st. 35*

22 He who ascends to mountaintops, shall find
The loftiest peaks most wrapt in clouds and snow;
He who surpasses or subdues mankind
Must look down on the hate of those below.
Ib. st. 45

23 All tenantless, save to the crannying wind.
Ib. st. 47

24 History's purchased page to call them great.
Ib. st. 48

25 The castled crag of Drachenfels
Frowns o'er the wide and winding Rhine.
Ib. st. 55

26 To fly from, need not be to hate, mankind.
Ib. st. 69

27 By the blue rushing of the arrowy Rhone.
Ib. st. 71

28 I live not in myself, but I become
Portion of that around me:[6] and to me
High mountains are a feeling, but the hum
Of human cities torture. *Ib. st. 72*

[4] See Thomas Moore, 447:15.
[5] This was the passage Sir Winston Churchill quoted to President Franklin D. Roosevelt when both agreed to substitute the term United Nations for Associated Powers in the pact that the two leaders wished all the free nations to sign. [In a conference at the White House, December 1941.]
[6] I am a part of all that I have met.—TENNYSON, *Ulysses* [1842]

1 Sapping a solemn creed with solemn sneer.
Ib. st. 107

2 Fame is the thirst of youth. *Ib. st. 112*

3 I have not loved the world, nor the world me;[1]
I have not flattered its rank breath, nor bowed
To its idolatries a patient knee.
Ib. st. 113

4 I stood
Among them, but not of them; in a shroud
Of thoughts which were not their thoughts.
Ib.

5 I stood in Venice on the Bridge of Sighs,
A palace and a prison on each hand.
Ib. canto IV [1818], st. 1

6 Where Venice sate in state, throned on her hundred isles. *Ib.*

7 She looks a sea Cybele, fresh from ocean,
Rising with her tiara of proud towers
At airy distance, with majestic motion,
A ruler of the waters and their powers.
Ib. st. 2

8 'Tis solitude should teach us how to die;
It hath no flatterers; vanity can give
No hollow aid; alone—man with his God must strive. *Ib. st. 33*

9 The Ariosto of the North.[2] *Ib. st. 40*

10 Italia! O Italia! thou who hast
The fatal gift of beauty.[3] *Ib. st. 42*

11 Let these describe the undescribable.
Ib. st. 53

12 The starry Galileo, with his woes.
Ib. st. 54

13 The poetry of speech. *Ib. st. 58*

14 Then farewell, Horace; whom I hated so,
Not for thy faults, but mine. *Ib. st. 77*

15 O Rome! my country! city of the soul!
Ib. st. 78

16 The Niobe of nations! there she stands,
Childless and crownless, in her voiceless woe.
Ib. st. 79

17 Yet, Freedom! yet thy banner, torn, but flying,
Streams like the thunderstorm against the wind. *Ib. st. 98*

18 Alas! our young affections run to waste,
Or water but the desert. *Ib. st. 120*

[1]See Johnson, 356:27, and Emerson, 493:12.
[2]Sir Walter Scott.
[3]Based on the famous sonnet of VINCENZO DA FILICAJA [1642–1707]: Italia, Italia! O tu cui feo la sorte.

19 Of its own beauty is the mind diseased.
Ib. st. 122

20 Time, the avenger! unto thee I lift
My hands, and eyes, and heart, and crave of thee a gift. *Ib. st. 130*

21 Butcher'd to make a Roman holiday!
Ib. st. 141

22 "While stands the Coliseum, Rome shall stand;
When falls the Coliseum, Rome shall fall;
And when Rome falls—the world."[4]
Ib. st. 145

23 Oh! that the desert were my dwelling place.[5]
Ib. st. 177

24 There is a pleasure in the pathless woods,
There is a rapture on the lonely shore,
There is society, where none intrudes,
By the deep sea, and music in its roar:
I love not man the less, but Nature more.
Ib. st. 178

25 Roll on, thou deep and dark blue ocean—roll!
Ten thousand fleets sweep over thee in vain;
Man marks the earth with ruin—his control
Stops with the shore. *Ib. st. 179*

26 He sinks into thy depths with bubbling groan,
Without a grave, unknelled, uncoffined, and unknown.[6] *Ib.*

27 Time writes no wrinkle on thine azure brow—
Such as creation's dawn beheld, thou rollest now. *Ib. st. 182*

28 Thou glorious mirror, where the Almighty's form
Glasses itself in tempests. *Ib. st. 183*

29 Dark-heaving—boundless, endless, and sublime—
The image of Eternity. *Ib.*

30 And I have loved thee, Ocean! and my joy
Of youthful sports was on thy breast to be
Borne, like thy bubbles, onward: from a boy
I wantoned with thy breakers.
Ib. st. 184

31 And trusted to thy billows far and near,
And laid my hand upon thy mane—as I do here. *Ib.*

[4]The saying of the ancient pilgrims, quoted from Bede by Gibbon in *The Decline and Fall of the Roman Empire* [1781], *ch. 71.*
[5]See *Jeremiah 9:2, 32:4*, and Cowper, 376:18.
[6]See Homer, 59:9; Horace, 108:13; Chaucer, 144:17; Shakespeare, 219:24; Milton, 284:11; and Scott, 430:10.

1 I awoke one morning and found myself famous.

Entry in Memoranda after publication of first two cantos of Childe Harold's Pilgrimage. From THOMAS MOORE, *Life of Byron [1830], ch. 14*

2 Climë of the unforgotten brave!

The Giaour [1813], l. 103

3 And lovelier things have mercy shown
To every failing but their own;
And every woe a tear can claim,
Except an erring sister's shame.

Ib. l. 418

4 I die—but first I have possessed,
And come what may, I have been blessed.

Ib. l. 1114

5 Know ye the land where the cypress and myrtle
Are emblems of deeds that are done in their clime?[1]
Where the rage of the vulture, the love of the turtle,
Now melt into sorrow, now madden to crime.

The Bride of Abydos [1813], canto I, st. 1

6 Where the virgins are soft as the roses they twine,
And all, save the spirit of man, is divine?

Ib.

7 Mark! where his carnage and his conquests cease!
He makes a solitude, and calls it—peace![2]

Ib. canto II, st. 20

8 The fatal facility of the octosyllabic verse.

The Corsair [1814]. Dedication

9 Such hath it been—shall be—beneath the sun
The many still must labor for the one.

Ib. canto I, st. 8

10 He left a corsair's name to other times,
Linked with one virtue, and a thousand crimes.

Ib. canto III, st. 24

11 The Cincinnatus of the West,
Whom envy dared not hate,
Bequeathed the name of Washington
To make man blush there was but one![3]

Ode to Napoleon Bonaparte [1814], II

12 Lord of himself—that heritage of woe.

Lara [1814], canto I, st. 2

[1] See Goethe, 395:3.
[2] See Tacitus, 123:3.
[3] See *The Age of Bronze,* 462:15.

13 She walks in beauty, like the night
Of cloudless climes and starry skies;
And all that's best of dark and bright
Meet in her aspect and her eyes:
Thus mellowed to that tender light
Which heaven to gaudy day denies.

Hebrew Melodies [1815]. She Walks in Beauty, st. 1

14 The Assyrian came down like the wolf on the fold,
And his cohorts were gleaming in purple and gold;
And the sheen of their spears was like stars on the sea,
When the blue wave rolls nightly on deep Galilee.

Ib. The Destruction of Sennacherib,[4] *st. 1*

15 For the Angel of Death spread his wings on the blast.

Ib. st. 3

16 And the might of the Gentile, unsmote by the sword,
Hath melted like snow in the glance of the Lord!

Ib. st. 6

17 The glory and the nothing of a name.

Churchill's Grave, l. 43

18 For years fleet away with the wings of the dove.

The First Kiss of Love, st. 7

19 Fare thee well! and if forever,
Still forever, fare thee well.[5]

Fare Thee Well [1816], st. 1

20 Sighing that Nature formed but one such man,
And broke the die, in molding Sheridan.[6]

Monody on the Death of Sheridan [1816], l. 117

21 My hair is gray, but not with years,
Nor grew it white
In a single night,
As men's have grown from sudden fears.

The Prisoner of Chillon [1816], st. 1

22 O God! it is a fearful thing
To see the human soul take wing
In any shape, in any mood.

Ib. st. 8

23 A light broke in upon my brain—
It was the carol of a bird;
It ceased, and then it came again,
The sweetest song ear ever heard.

Ib. st. 10

[4] See *II Kings, 19:35,* 14:20.
[5] See Burns, 410:2.
[6] See Ariosto, 154:11.

1 There be none of Beauty's daughters
With a magic like thee;
And like music on the waters
Is thy sweet voice to me.
Stanzas for music [1816], st. 1

2 I had a dream which was not all a dream.
Darkness [1816]

3 Though the day of my destiny's over,
And the star of my fate hath declined.
Stanzas to Augusta [1816], st. 1

4 My boat is on the shore,
And my bark is on the sea;
But, before I go, Tom Moore,
Here's a double health to thee!

Here's a sigh to those who love me,
And a smile to those who hate;
And, whatever sky's above me,
Here's a heart for every fate.[1]
To Thomas Moore [1817], st. 1, 2

5 So we'll go no more a-roving
So late into the night,
Though the heart be still as loving,
And the moon be still as bright.

For the sword outwears its sheath,
And the soul wears out the breast,
And the heart must pause to breathe,
And love itself have rest.

Though the night was made for loving,
And the day returns too soon,
Yet we'll go no more a-roving
By the light of the moon.
So, We'll Go No More A-Roving [1817]

6 Mont Blanc is the monarch of mountains;
They crowned him long ago
On a throne of rocks, in a robe of clouds,
With a diadem of snow.
Manfred [1817], act I, sc. i

7 His heart was one of those which most enamor us,
Wax to receive, and marble to retain.[2]
Beppo [1818], st. 34

8 I love the language, that soft bastard Latin,
Which melts like kisses from a female mouth.
Ib. st. 44

9 I wish he[3] would explain his explanation.
Don Juan. Dedication [written 1818], st. 2

10 In virtues nothing earthly could surpass her,
Save thine "incomparable oil," Macassar!
Ib. canto I, st. 17

[1]See Longfellow, 509:16.
[2]See Cervantes, 171:10.
[3]Coleridge.

11 But—Oh! ye lords of ladies intellectual,
Inform us truly, have they not henpecked you all?[4]
Ib. st. 22

12 Her stature tall—I hate a dumpy woman.
Ib. st. 61

13 What men call gallantry, and gods adultery,
Is much more common where the climate's sultry.
Ib. st. 63

14 Christians have burnt each other, quite persuaded
That all the Apostles would have done as they did.
Ib. st. 83

15 A little still she strove, and much repented,
And whispering "I will ne'er consent"—consented.
Ib. st. 117

16 'Tis sweet to hear the watchdog's honest bark
Bay deep-mouthed welcome as we draw near home;
'Tis sweet to know there is an eye will mark
Our coming, and look brighter when we come.
Ib. st. 123

17 Sweet is revenge—especially to women.[5]
Ib. st. 124

18 Pleasure's a sin, and sometimes sin's a pleasure.
Ib. st. 133

19 Man's love is of man's life a thing apart,
'Tis woman's whole existence.[6]
Ib. st. 194

20 There's nought, no doubt, so much the spirit calms
As rum and true religion.
Ib. canto II [1819], st. 34

21 A solitary shriek, the bubbling cry
Of some strong swimmer in his agony.
Ib. st. 53

22 If this be true, indeed,
Some Christians have a comfortable creed.
Ib. st. 86

23 Let us have wine and women, mirth and laughter,
Sermons and soda water the day after.[7]
Ib. st. 178

24 In her first passion woman loves her lover,
In all the others, all she loves is love.[8]
Ib. canto III [1821], st. 3

25 Think you, if Laura had been Petrarch's wife,
He would have written sonnets all his life?
Ib. st. 7

26 He was the mildest-mannered man
That ever scuttled ship or cut a throat.
Ib. st. 41

[4]See Addison, 327:2.
[5]See Shakespeare, 242:22.
[6]See Wilcox, 670:2.
[7]See Dickens, 547:23, and Ade, 718:12.
[8]See La Rochefoucauld, 294:9.

1 Even good men like to make the public stare.
Ib. st. 81

2 The isles of Greece, the isles of Greece![1]
Where burning Sappho loved and sung.
Ib. st. 86 [song, st. 1]

3 Eternal summer gilds them yet,
But all, except their sun, is set. *Ib.*

4 The mountains look on Marathon,
And Marathon looks on the sea;
And musing there an hour alone,
I dreamed that Greece might still be free.
Ib. [st. 3]

5 And where are they? and where art thou,
My country? On thy voiceless shore
The heroic lay is tuneless now—
The heroic bosom beats no more!
And must thy lyre, so long divine,
Degenerate into hands like mine?
Ib. [st. 5]

6 Earth! render back from out thy breast
A remnant of our Spartan dead!
Of the three hundred grant but three,
To make a new Thermopylae.
Ib. [st. 7]

7 You have the Pyrrhic dance as yet,
Where is the Pyrrhic phalanx gone?
Of two such lessons, why forget
The nobler and the manlier one?
You have the letters Cadmus gave—
Think ye he meant them for a slave?
Ib. [st. 10]

8 Fill high the bowl with Samian wine!
Ib. [st. 11]

9 Place me on Sunium's marble steep,
Where nothing save the waves and I
May hear our mutual murmurs sweep;
There, swanlike, let me sing and die.[2]
A land of slaves shall ne'er be mine—
Dash down yon cup of Samian wine!
Ib. [st. 16]

10 And if I laugh at any mortal thing,
'Tis that I may not weep.[3]
Ib. canto IV [1821], st. 4

11 These two hated with a hate
Found only on the stage. *Ib. st. 93*

12 I've stood upon Achilles' tomb,
And heard Troy doubted; time will doubt of
Rome. *Ib. st. 101*

[1] From isles of Greece / The princes orgulous, their high blood chafed, / Have to the port of Athens sent their ships. —SHAKESPEARE, *Troilus and Cressida* [1601–1603], *prologue*

[2] See Plato, 83:18; Shakespeare, 199:22 and 202:16; and Anonymous, 918:17.

[3] See La Bruyère, 315:7, and Beaumarchais, 378:6.

13 Oh! "darkly, deeply, beautifully blue,"[4]
As someone somewhere sings about the sky.
Ib. st. 110

14 There's not a sea the passenger e'er pukes in,
Turns up more dangerous breakers than the
Euxine. *Ib. canto V [1821], st. 5*

15 And put himself upon his good behavior.
Ib. st. 47

16 That all-softening, overpowering knell,
The tocsin of the soul—the dinner bell.
Ib. st. 49

17 The women pardoned all except her face.
Ib. st. 113

18 Polygamy may well be held in dread,
Not only as a sin, but as a bore.
Ib. canto VI [1823], st. 12

19 A lady of "a certain age," which means
Certainly aged. *Ib. st. 69*

20 Not so Leonidas and Washington,
Whose every battlefield is holy ground,
Which breathes of nations saved, not worlds
undone. *Ib. canto VIII [1823], st. 5*

21 "Gentlemen farmers"—a race worn out
quite. *Ib. canto IX [1823], st. 32*

22 When Bishop Berkeley said "there was no
matter,"
And proved it—twas no matter what he said.
Ib. canto XI [1823], st. 1

23 And, after all, what is a lie? 'Tis but
The truth in masquerade. *Ib. st. 37*

24 'Tis strange the mind, that very fiery parti-
cle,
Should let itself be snuffed out by an article.
Ib. st. 60 (of John Keats)[5]

25 Ready money is Aladdin's lamp.
Ib. canto XII [1823], st. 12

26 Cervantes smiled Spain's chivalry away.
Ib. canto XIII [1823], st. 11

27 The English winter—ending in July,
To recommence in August. *Ib. st. 42*

28 Society is now one polished horde,
Formed of two mighty tribes, the Bores and
Bored. *Ib. st. 95*

29 All human history attests
That happiness for man—the hungry sinner!—
Since Eve ate apples, much depends on dinner.[6] *Ib. st. 99*

[4] See Southey, 440:2.

[5] See Byron, 462:11, and Shelley, 468:22.

[6] For a man seldom thinks with more earnestness of anything than he does of his dinner. —JOHNSON; from MRS. PIOZZI, *Anecdotes of Samuel Johnson* [1786]
See Fanny Fern, 538:6.

1 Of all the horrid, hideous notes of woe,
Sadder than owl songs or the midnight blast,
Is that portentous phrase, "I told you so."
Ib. canto XIV [1823], st. 50

2 'Tis strange—but true; for truth is always strange;
Stranger than fiction.[1] *Ib. st. 101*

3 The Devil hath not, in all his quiver's choice,
An arrow for the heart like a sweet voice.
Ib. canto XV [1824], st. 13

4 The antique Persians taught three useful things—
To draw the bow, to ride, and speak the truth.
Ib. canto XVI [1824], st. 1

5 In truth he was a noble steed.
Mazeppa [1819], st. 9

6 Oh, talk not to me of a name great in story;
The days of our youth are the days of our glory;
And the myrtle and ivy of sweet two and twenty
Are worth all your laurels, though ever so plenty.
Stanzas Written on the Road Between Florence and Pisa [1821], st. 1

7 All farewells should be sudden.
Sardanapalus [1821], act V

8 The best of prophets of the future is the past. *Journal [January 28, 1821]*

9 The world is a bundle of hay,
Mankind are the asses that pull,
Each tugs in a different way—
And the greatest of all is John Bull!
Letter to Thomas Moore [June 22, 1821]

10 Because
He is all-powerful, must all-good, too, follow?
I judge but by the fruits—and they are bitter—
Which I must feed on for a fault not mine.
Cain [1821], act I, sc. i

11 Who killed John Keats?
"I," says the Quarterly,
So savage and Tartarly;
" 'Twas one of my feats."[2]
John Keats [c. 1821]

12 He seems
To have seen better days, as who has not
Who has seen yesterday?
Werner [1822], act I, sc. i

13 The "good old times"—all times when old are good—
Are gone.
The Age of Bronze [1823], st. 1

14 Whose[3] game was empires and whose stakes were thrones,
Whose table earth—whose dice were human bones. *Ib. st. 3*

15 While Franklin's quiet memory climbs to heaven,
Calming the lightning which he thence had riven,
Or drawing from the no less kindled earth
Freedom and peace to that which boasts his birth;[4]
While Washington's a watchword, such as ne'er
Shall sink while there's an echo left to air.[5]
Ib. st. 5

16 Sublime tobacco! which from east to west
Cheers the tar's labor or the Turkman's rest.[6]
The Island [1823], canto II, st. 19

17 What's drinking?
A mere pause from thinking!
The Deformed Transformed [1824], act III, sc. i

18 My days are in the yellow leaf;[7]
The flowers and fruits of love are gone;
The worm, the canker, and the grief
Are mine alone!
On My Thirty-sixth Year [1824], st. 2

19 Seek out—less often sought than found—
A soldier's grave, for thee the best;
Then look around, and choose thy ground,
And take thy rest. *Ib. st. 10*

20 Now Barabbas was a publisher.
Alleged alteration in the Bible, John 18:40[8]

[1]Le vrai peut quelquefois n'etre pas vraisemblable [Truth may sometimes be improbable].—BOILEAU [1636–1711], *L'Art Poétique, III, l. 48*

See Daniel Webster, 450:18.

Truth is stranger than fiction, but not so popular.—*Anonymous*

[2]See *Don Juan,* 461:24; Shelley, 468:22; and Anonymous, 930:9.

[3]Napoleon.

[4]See Franklin, 346:*n*5.

[5]See *Ode to Napoleon,* 459:11.

[6]Let Aristotle and all your philosophers say what they like, there is nothing to be compared with tobacco.—MOLIÈRE [1622–1673], *Don Juan; or, Le Festin de Pierre* [1665], *act I, sc. i*

Translated by CURTIS HIDDEN PAGE.

[7]See Shakespeare, 239:31 and 244:27.

[8]The publisher John Murray sent Byron a lavish copy of the Bible in acknowledgment of a favor, and the poet returned it with the word "robber" changed to "publisher."

Sarah Josepha Hale
1788–1879

1 Mary had a little lamb,
Its fleece was white as snow,
And everywhere that Mary went,
The lamb was sure to go.

Mary's Lamb,[1] *st. 1, 2. From The Juvenile Miscellany [September 1830]*

Arthur Schopenhauer
1788–1860

2 To marry is to halve your rights and double your duties.

The World as Will and Idea [1819], vol. II

3 Hatred comes from the heart; contempt from the head; and neither feeling is quite within our control.

Studies in Pessimism [1851].[2] *Psychological Observations*

4 Every man takes the limits of his own field of vision for the limits of the world.

Ib.

5 Every parting gives a foretaste of death;[3] every coming together again a foretaste of the resurrection. *Ib.*

6 Dissimulation is innate in woman, and almost as much a quality of the stupid as of the clever. *Ib. On Women*

7 Noise is the most impertinent of all forms of interruption. It is not only an interruption, but also a disruption of thought.

Ib. On Noise

8 The two foes of human happiness are pain and boredom.

Essays. Personality; or, What a Man Is

9 A man who has no mental needs, because his intellect is of the narrow and normal amount, is, in the strict sense of the word, what is called a philistine.[4] *Ib.*

10 Intellect is invisible to the man who has none.[5]

Ib. Our Relation to Others, sec. 23

[1] According to *The Story of Mary's Little Lamb* [1928], published by Mr. and Mrs. Henry Ford, the first three stanzas of the poem are by John Roulstone [1805–1822]; Sarah Josepha Hale's "genius completed the poem in its present form" (six stanzas); "Mary" was Mary Elizabeth Sawyer [1806–1889] of Sterling, Massachusetts; and the events of the poem are true.

[2] Translated by T. Bailey Saunders.

[3] Partir c'est mourir un peu [To part is to die a little]. — *French proverb*
See Haraucourt, 679:9.

[4] See Matthew Arnold, 587:3.

[5] See La Rochefoucauld, 294:3.

11 There is no more mistaken path to happiness than worldliness, revelry, high life.

Ib. Our Relation to Ourselves, sec. 24

12 Do not shorten the morning by getting up late; look upon it as the quintessence of life, as to a certain extent sacred.

Counsels and Maxims, ch. 2

James Fenimore Cooper
1789–1851

13 Few men exhibit greater diversity, or, if we may so express it, greater antithesis of character than the native warrior of North America. In war, he is daring, boastful, cunning, ruthless, self-denying, and self-devoted; in peace, just, generous, hospitable, revengeful, superstitious, modest, and commonly chaste.

The Last of the Mohicans [1826]

14 'Tis grand! 'tis solemn! 'tis an education of itself to look upon!

The Deerslayer [1841], ch. 2

15 Those families, you know, are our upper crust — not upper ten thousand.[6]

The Ways of the Hour [1850], ch. 6

William Knox
1789–1825

16 Oh why should the spirit of mortal be proud?

Songs of Israel [1824]. Mortality, st. 1

Peter Mere Latham
1789–1875

17 The practice of physic is jostled by quacks on the one side, and by science on the other.

Collected Works, bk. I, ch. 25

18 There is nothing so captivating as *new* knowledge. *Ib. 51*

19 Truth in all its kinds is most difficult to win; and truth in medicine is the most difficult of all. *Ib. 60*

20 Beware of language, for it is often a great cheat. *Ib. 138*

21 The diagnosis of disease is often easy, often difficult, and often impossible. *Ib. 173*

22 We should always presume the disease to be curable, until its own nature prove it otherwise. *Ib. 174*

[6] See Sam Slick, 481:3.

1 Fortunate, indeed, is the man who takes exactly the right measure of himself, and holds a just balance between what he can acquire and what he can use, be it great or be it small! *Ib. II, 11*

2 Common sense is in medicine the master workman. *Ib. 389*

3 It takes as much time and trouble to pull down a falsehood as to build up a truth. *Ib. 398*

4 Faith and knowledge lean largely upon each other in the practice of medicine. *Ib. 408*

5 It is no easy task to pick one's way from truth to truth through besetting errors. *Ib. 415*

6 It would be a great thing to understand pain in all its meanings. *Ib. 474*

7 It is the great mystery of life itself which is at the bottom of all the mysterious language we are obliged to employ concerning it. *Ib. 494*

8 People in general have no notion of the sort and amount of evidence often needed to prove the simplest matter of fact. *Ib. 525*

Astolphe Louis Léonard, Marquis de Custine

1790–1857

9 This empire [Russia], vast as it is, is only a prison to which the emperor holds the key.[1] *La Russie en 1839.*[2] *Peterhof, July 23, 1839*

10 Whoever has really seen Russia will find himself content to live anywhere else. It is always good to know that a society exists where no happiness is possible because, by a law of nature, man cannot be happy unless he is free. *Ib. Conclusion*

Fitz-Greene Halleck

1790–1867

11 Green be the turf above thee,
Friend of my better days!
None knew thee but to love thee,[3]
Nor named thee but to praise.
On the Death of Joseph Rodman Drake [1820], st. 1

[1] See Stalin, 766:9.
[2] Translated by Phyllis Penn Kohler.
[3] See Burns, 410:3, and Tennyson, 529:19.

12 Strike—till the last armed foe expires,
Strike—for your altars and your fires;
Strike—for the green graves of your sires;
God—and your native land!
Marco Bozzaris[4] *[1855], st. 3*

13 One of the few, the immortal names
That were not born to die. *Ib. st. 7*

Alphonse de Lamartine

1790–1869

14 O time, arrest your flight! and you, propitious hours, arrest your course! Let us savor the fleeting delights of our most beautiful days![5] *The Lake [1820], st. 6*

15 I say to this night: "Pass more slowly"; and the dawn will come to dispel the night.[6] *Ib. st. 8*

16 Limited in his nature, infinite in his desires, man is a fallen god[7] who remembers the heavens. *Méditations Poétiques [1820]. Sermon 2*

17 What is our life but a succession of preludes to that unknown song whose first solemn note is sounded by death?[8] *Ib. 2nd series. Sermon 15*

18 Experience is the only prophecy of wise men. *Speech at Mâcon [1847]*

19 To love for the sake of being loved is human, but to love for the sake of loving is angelic. *Graziella [1849], pt. IV, ch. 5*

20 The more I see of the representatives of the people, the more I admire my dogs. *From Count d'Orsay, Letter to John Forster [1850]*

Ferdinand Raimund

1790–1836

21 No matter how fair the sun shines,
Still it must set.
Das Mädchen aus der Feenwelt (The Maiden from Fairyland) [1826]

[4] A Greek patriot, born about 1788, killed in a night attack against the Turks, near Missolonghi, Greece [August 20, 1823].
[5] O temps, suspends ton vol! et vous, heures propices, / Suspendez votre cours! / Laissez-nous savourer les rapides délices / Des plus beaux de nos jours!
[6] Je dis à cette nuit: "Sois plus lente"; et l'aurore / Va dissiper la nuit.
[7] See Emerson, 496:8.
[8] This passage was used by Liszt as a heading for his tone poem *Les Préludes.*

Samuel Gilman
1791–1858

1 Fair Harvard! Thy sons to thy Jubilee throng.
Ode, Bicentennial, Harvard University [September 8, 1836], st. 1

2 First flower of their wilderness, star of their night,
Calm rising through change and through storm. *Ib.*

Henry Hart Milman
1791–1868

3 Ride on! ride on in majesty!
In lowly pomp ride on to die.
Hymns. Ride On!

John Howard Payne
1791–1852

4 'Mid pleasures and palaces though we may roam,
Be it ever so humble, there's no place like home.[1]
Home, Sweet Home. From the opera Clari, the Maid of Milan [1823]

Lydia Huntley Sigourney
1791–1865

5 Their name[2] is on your waters—
Ye may not wash it out.
Select Poems [1841]. Indian Names, st. 1

Charles Sprague
1791–1875

6 Here lived and loved another race of beings. Beneath the same sun that rolls over your heads the Indian hunter pursued the panting deer. . . . The Indian of falcon glance and lion bearing, the theme of the touching ballad, the hero of the pathetic tale, is gone.
American Independence [1849; delivered July 4, 1825]

Charles Wolfe
1791–1823

7 Not a drum was heard, not a funeral note,
As his corse to the rampart we hurried.
The Burial of Sir John Moore at Corunna [1817], st. 1

[1] Home is home, be it never so homely.—*English proverb* [c. 1300]

[2] American Indian names.

8 But he lay like a warrior taking his rest,
With his martial cloak around him.
Ib. st. 3

9 We carved not a line, and we raised not a stone—
But we left him alone with his glory.
Ib. st. 8

John Bowring
1792–1872

10 Watchman, tell us of the night,[3]
What its signs of promise are.
Hymn [1825]

Victor Cousin
1792–1867

11 We need religion for religion's sake, morality for morality's sake, art for art's sake.
Cours de Philosophie [1818]

John Frederick William Herschel
1792–1871

12 Science is the knowledge of many, orderly and methodically digested and arranged, so as to become attainable by one. The knowledge of reasons and their conclusions constitutes *abstract,* that of causes and their effects, and of the laws of nature, *natural science.*
A Preliminary Discourse on the Study of Natural Philosophy [1830]

John Keble
1792–1866

13 The voice that breathed o'er Eden
That earliest wedding day.
Poems [1869]. Holy Matrimony, st. 1

Frederick Marryat
1792–1848

14 All zeal, Mr. Easy.
Midshipman Easy [1836], ch. 9

15 I haven't the gift of the gab, my sons—because I'm bred to the sea.
The Old Navy, st. 1

16 It's just six of one and half a dozen of the other. *The Pirate, ch. 4*

[3] See *Isaiah 21:11, 30:1.*

1 Every man paddle his own canoe.
Settlers in Canada [1844], ch. 8

Joseph Mohr
1792–1848

2 Silent night, holy night,[1]
All is calm, all is bright.
Holy Night [1818]

Lord John Russell
1792–1878

3 If peace cannot be maintained with honor, it is no longer peace.[2]
Speech at Greenock [September 19, 1853]

4 Among the defects of the bill, which were numerous, one provision was conspicuous by its presence and another by its absence.[3]
Speech to the electors of the City of London [April 1859]

Percy Bysshe Shelley
1792–1822

5 Once, early in the morning,
Beelzebub arose,
With care his sweet person adorning,
He put on his Sunday clothes.[4]
The Devil's Walk [1812], st. 1

6 How wonderful is Death,
Death and his brother Sleep![5]
Queen Mab [1813], I

7 Power, like a desolating pestilence,
Pollutes whate'er it touches;[6] and obedience,
Bane of all genius, virtue, freedom, truth,
Makes slaves of men, and, of the human frame,
A mechanized automation. *Ib. III*

8 The awful shadow of some unseen Power
Floats though unseen among us[7]—visiting
This various world with as inconstant wing
As summer winds that creep from flower to flower.
Hymn to Intellectual Beauty [1816], st. 1

[1]Stille Nacht! Heilige Nacht!
[2]See Disraeli, 502:18, and Chamberlain, 727:2.
[3]See Tacitus, 122:20.
[4]See Southey, 440:13 and 440:14.
[5]See Homer, 58:20; Virgil, 105:17; Daniel, 182:4; and Shakespeare, 238:6.
[6]See Pitt, 351:1, and Lord Acton, 615:15.
[7]See Wordsworth, 423:13.

9 Spirit of Beauty, that dost consecrate
With thine own hues all thou dost shine upon
Of human thought or form. *Ib. st. 2*

10 Some say that gleams of a remoter world
Visit the soul in sleep—that death is slumber,
And that its shapes the busy thoughts outnumber
Of those who wake and live.
Mont Blanc [1816], st. 3

11 Man's yesterday may ne'er be like his morrow;
Nought may endure but Mutability.[8]
Mutability [1816], I, st. 4

12 I met a traveler from an antique land
Who said: "Two vast and trunkless legs of stone
Stand in the desert. Near them, on the sand,
Half sunk, a shattered visage lies, whose frown,
And wrinkled lip, and sneer of cold command,
Tell that its sculptor well those passions read." *Ozymandias [1817]*

13 "My name is Ozymandias, king of kings:
Look on my works, ye Mighty, and despair!"
Nothing beside remains. Round the decay
Of that colossal wreck, boundless and bare,
The lone and level sands stretch far away.
Ib.

14 With hue like that when some great painter dips
His pencil in the gloom of earthquake and eclipse.
The Revolt of Islam [1817], canto V, st. 23

15 I could lie down like a tired child,
And weep away the life of care
Which I have borne and yet must bear,
Till death like sleep might steal on me.
Stanzas Written in Dejection near Naples [1818], st. 4

16 Ere Babylon was dust,
The Magus Zoroaster, my dead child,
Met his own image walking in the garden,
That apparition, sole of men, he saw.
Prometheus Unbound [1818–1819], act I, l. 191

17 The good want power, but to weep barren tears.
The powerful goodness want: worse need for them.
The wise want love; and those who love want wisdom;

[8]See Heraclitus, 69:25; Racan, 265:3; Swift, 321:16; and Wilde, 676:4.

And all best things are thus confused with ill. *Ib. l. 625*

1 Peace is in the grave.
The grave hides all things beautiful and good:
I am a God and cannot find it there.
Ib. l. 638

2 From the dust of creeds outworn.
Ib. l. 697

3 Forms more real than living man,
Nurslings of immortality! *Ib. l. 748*

4 To know nor faith, nor love nor law; to be
Omnipotent but friendless is to reign.
Ib. act II, sc. iv, l. 47

5 All love is sweet,
Given or returned. Common as light is love,
And its familiar voice wearies not ever. . . .
They who inspire it most are fortunate,
As I am now; but those who feel it most
Are happier still.[1] *Ib. II, v, 39*

6 Death is the veil which those who live call life:
They sleep, and it is lifted.[2]
Ib. III, iii, 113

7 Nor yet exempt, though ruling them like slaves,
From chance, and death, and mutability,
The clogs of that which else might overscar
The loftiest star of unascended heaven,
Pinnacled dim in the intense inane.
Ib. III, iv, 200

8 Familiar acts are beautiful through love.
Ib. IV, l. 403

9 Man, who wert once a despot and a slave;
A dupe and a deceiver; a decay;
A traveler from the cradle to the grave[3]
Through the dim light of this immortal day.
Ib. l. 549

10 Good, great and joyous, beautiful and free;
This is alone Life, Joy, Empire, and Victory.
Ib. closing lines

11 I love all waste
And solitary places; where we taste
The pleasure of believing what we see
Is boundless, as we wish our souls to be.
Julian and Maddalo [1819], l. 14

12 Thou paradise of exiles, Italy! *Ib. l. 57*

13 It is our will
That thus enchains us to permitted ill—
We might be otherwise—we might be all
We dream of happy, high majestical.
Where is the love, beauty and truth we seek,
But in our mind? *Ib. l. 170*

14 *Me*—who am as a nerve o'er which do creep
The else unfelt oppressions of this earth.
Ib. l. 449

15 Most wretched men
Are cradled into poetry by wrong;
They learn in suffering what they teach in song.[4] *Ib. l. 543*

16 Chameleons feed on light and air:
Poets' food is love and fame.
An Exhortation [1819], st. 1

17 O wild West Wind, thou breath of Autumn's being,
Thou, from whose unseen presence the leaves dead
Are driven, like ghosts from an enchanter fleeing,
Yellow, and black, and pale, and hectic red,
Pestilence-stricken multitudes.
Ode to the West Wind [1819], l. 1

18 Wild Spirit, which art moving everywhere;
Destroyer and preserver; hear, oh, hear!
Ib. l. 13

19 Thou dirge
Of the dying year, to which this closing night
Will be the dome of a vast sepulcher.
Ib. l. 23

20 Oh, lift me as a wave, a leaf, a cloud!
I fall upon the thorns of life! I bleed!
Ib. l. 44

21 Make me thy lyre, even as the forest is:
What if my leaves are falling like its own!
The tumult of thy mighty harmonies
Will take from both a deep, autumnal tone,
Sweet though in sadness. Be thou, Spirit fierce,
My spirit! Be thou me, impetuous one!
Ib. l. 57

22 The trumpet of a prophecy! O Wind,
If winter comes, can spring be far behind?
Ib. l. 69

23 Men of England, wherefore plow
For the lords who lay ye low?
Song to the Men of England [1819], st. 1

24 Nothing in the world is single,
All things by a law divine
In one spirit meet and mingle.
Love's Philosophy [1819], st. 1

[1] See La Rochefoucauld, 293:30.

[2] Lift not the painted veil which those who live / Call Life.—SHELLEY, *Sonnet* [1818]

[3] See Dyer, 345:3; Bellamy, 665:17; and Hoffenstein, 816:2.

[4] See Butler, 292:2.

1 I arise from dreams of thee
In the first sweet sleep of night,
When the winds are breathing low,
And the stars are shining bright.
The Indian Serenade [1819], st. 1

2 Hell is a city much like London—
A populous and smoky city.
Peter Bell the Third [1819], pt. III, st. 1

3 Teas,
Where small talk dies in agonies.
Ib. st. 12

4 An old, mad, blind, despised and dying king.[1]
England in 1819 [written 1819], l. 1

5 I met Murder on the way—
He had a mask like Castlereagh.
The Mask of Anarchy [written 1819], st. 2

6 One by one, and two by two,
He tossed them human hearts to chew.
Ib. st. 3

7 A lovely lady, garmented in light
From her own beauty.
The Witch of Atlas [1820], st. 5

8 A Sensitive Plant in a garden grew.
The Sensitive Plant [1820], pt. I, st. 1

9 I bring fresh showers for the thirsting flowers,
From the seas and the streams.
The Cloud [1820], st. 1

10 I am the daughter of earth and water,
And the nursling of the sky;
I pass through the pores of the ocean and shores,
I change, but I cannot die. *Ib. st. 6*

11 Hail to thee, blithe spirit!
Bird thou never wert,
That from Heaven, or near it,
Pourest thy full heart
In profuse strains of unpremeditated art.
To a Skylark [1821], st. 1

12 And singing still dost soar, and soaring ever singest. *Ib. st. 2*

13 Thou art unseen—but yet I hear thy shrill delight. *Ib. st. 4*

14 We look before and after,
And pine for what is not;
Our sincerest laughter
With some pain is fraught;
Our sweetest songs are those that tell of saddest thought. *Ib. st. 18*

[1]George III.

15 Teach me half the gladness
That thy brain must know,
Such harmonious madness,
From my lips would flow,
The world should listen then, as I am listening now. *Ib. st. 21*

16 Kings are like stars—they rise and set, they have
The worship of the world, but no repose.[2]
Hellas [1821], l. 195

17 The world's great age begins anew,
The golden years return,[3]
The earth doth like a snake renew
Her winter weeds outworn. *Ib. l. 1060*

18 The world is weary of the past,
Oh, might it die or rest at last!
Ib. final chorus

19 What! alive, and so bold, O earth?
Written on Hearing the News of the Death of Napoleon [1821], st. 1

20 The fields of immortality.
Epipsychidion [1821], l. 133

21 I never was attached to that great sect,
Whose doctrine is, that each one should select
Out of the crowd a mistress or a friend,
And all the rest, though fair and wise, commend
To cold oblivion, though 'tis in the code
Of modern morals, and the beaten road
Which those poor slaves with weary footsteps tread
Who travel to their home among the dead
By the broad highway of the world, and so
With one chained friend, perhaps a jealous foe,
The dreariest and the longest journey go.[4]
Ib. l. 149

22 I weep for Adonais[5]—he is dead!
Oh, weep for Adonais! though our tears
Thaw not the frost which binds so dear a head! *Adonais [1821], st. 1*

23 Till the Future dares
Forget the Past, his fate and fame shall be
An echo and a light unto eternity! *Ib.*

24 Most musical of mourners, weep again!
Ib. st. 4

[2]See Bacon, 180:19.
[3]See Virgil, 103:14.
[4]See Hammarskjöld, 863:4.
[5]John Keats.
Morning star, you shone among the living; and now in death you shine, evening star, on the dead.—PLATO, *Aster (Star), epigraph (in Greek) for Shelley's Adonais*
See Byron, 461:24 and 462:11.

1 To that high capital, where kingly Death
Keeps his pale court in beauty and decay,
He came. *Ib. st. 7*

2 Lost Angel of a ruined Paradise!
Ib. st. 10

3 Desires and Adorations,
Winged Persuasions and veiled Destinies,
Splendors, and Glooms, and glimmering Incarnations
Of hopes and fears, and twilight Fantasies;
And Sorrow, with her family of Sighs,
And Pleasure, blind with tears, led by the gleam
Of her own dying smile instead of eyes,
Came in slow pomp. *Ib. st. 13*

4 Ah woe is me! Winter is come and gone,
But grief returns with the revolving year.
Ib. st. 18

5 The intense atom glows
A moment, then is quenched in a most cold repose. *Ib. st. 20*

6 Alas! that all we loved of him should be,
But for our grief, as if it had not been,
And grief itself be mortal! *Ib. st. 21*

7 As long as skies are blue, and fields are green,
Evening must usher night, night urge the morrow,
Month follow month with woe, and year wake year to sorrow. *Ib.*

8 The Pilgrim of Eternity,[1] whose fame
Over his living head like heaven is bent,
An early but enduring monument,
Came, veiling all the lightnings of his song
In sorrow. *Ib. st. 30*

9 A pardlike spirit, beautiful and swift.
Ib. st. 32

10 In mockery of monumental stone.
Ib. st. 35

11 He hath awakened from the dream of life.
Ib. st. 39

12 He has outsoared the shadow of our night;
Envy and calumny and hate and pain,
And that unrest which men miscall delight
Can touch him not and torture not again;
From the contagion of the world's slow stain
He is secure, and now can never mourn
A heart grown cold, a head grown gray in vain. *Ib. st. 40*

13 He lives, he wakes—tis Death is dead, not he.
Ib. st. 41

14 He is made one with Nature: there is heard
His voice in all her music, from the moan
Of thunder to the song of night's sweet bird.
Ib. st. 42

[1] Byron.

15 He is a portion of the loveliness
Which once he made more lovely.
Ib. st. 43

16 The One remains, the many change and pass;
Heaven's light forever shines, earth's shadows fly;
Life, like a dome of many-colored glass,
Stains the white radiance of eternity,
Until Death tramples it to fragments.
Ib. st. 52

17 The soul of Adonais, like a star,
Beacons from the abode where the Eternal are. *Ib. st. 55*

18 Music, when soft voices die,
Vibrates in the memory;
Odors, when sweet violets sicken,
Live within the sense they quicken.

Rose leaves, when the rose is dead,
Are heaped for the beloved's bed;
And so thy thoughts, when thou art gone,
Love itself shall slumber on.
To ——: Music, When Soft Voices Die [1821]

19 One word is too often profaned
For me to profane it,
One feeling too falsely disdained
For thee to disdain it.
To ——: One Word Is Too Often Profaned [1821], st. 1

20 The desire of the moth for the star,
Of the night for the morrow,
The devotion to something afar
From the sphere of our sorrow.
Ib. st. 2

21 Swiftly walk o'er the western wave, Spirit of Night! *To Night [1821], st. 1*

22 I ask of thee, beloved Night—
Swift be thine approaching flight,
Come soon, soon! *Ib. st. 5*

23 Rarely, rarely, comest thou,
Spirit of Delight!
Song: Rarely, Rarely, Comest Thou [1821], st. 1

24 Let me set my mournful ditty
To a merry measure;
Thou wilt never come for pity,
Thou wilt come for pleasure. *Ib. st. 4*

25 I love tranquil solitude
And such society
As is quiet, wise, and good. *Ib. st. 7*

26 There is no sport in hate when all the rage
Is on one side.
Lines to a Reviewer [1821]

1 When the lamp is shattered
The light in the dust lies dead—
When the cloud is scattered
The rainbow's glory is shed.

When the Lamp Is Shattered [1822], st. 1

2 Best and brightest,[1] come away!

To Jane: The Invitation [1822], l. 1

3 Away, away, from men and towns,
To the wild wood and the downs.

Ib. l. 21

4 I am gone into the fields
To take what this sweet hour yields—
Reflection, you may come tomorrow,
Sit by the fireside with Sorrow.—
You with the unpaid bill, Despair—
You, tiresome verse-reciter, Care—
I will pay you in the grave. *Ib. l. 31*

5 Poets are the hierophants of an unapprehended inspiration; the mirrors of the gigantic shadows which futurity casts upon the present.[2] *A Defense of Poetry [1821]*

6 Poetry is the record of the best and happiest moments of the happiest and best minds. *Ib.*

7 Poets are the unacknowledged legislators of the world. *Ib.*

John Clare
1793–1864

8 I am! yet what I am who cares, or knows?
My friends forsake me like a memory lost.

I Am

9 Untroubling and untroubled where I lie—
The grass below—above the vaulted sky.

Ib.

10 The wind and clouds, now here, now there,
Hold no such strange dominion
As woman's cold, perverted will,
And soon estranged opinion.

When Lovers Part

11 Till kicked and torn and beaten out he lies
And leaves his hold and cackles, groans, and
dies. *Badger*

12 If life had a second edition, how I would correct the proofs.[3]

Letter to a friend. From J. W. AND ANNE TIBBLE, John Clare: A Life [1932]

[1] See Heber, 452:5.
[2] See Cicero, 98:21; Shakespeare, 226:5; Campbell, 443:14; and Wells, 720:9.
[3] See Benjamin Franklin, 346:15.

Felicia Dorothea Hemans
1793–1835

13 The stately homes of England!
How beautiful they stand,
Amidst their tall ancestral trees,
O'er all the pleasant land![4]

The Homes of England, st. 1

14 The breaking waves dashed high
On a stern and rock-bound coast,
And the woods, against a stormy sky,
Their giant branches tossed.

The Landing of the Pilgrim Fathers, st. 1

15 A band of exiles moored their bark
On a wild New England shore.

Ib. st. 2

16 Ay, call it holy ground,
The soil where first they trod!
They have left unstained what there they
found—
Freedom to worship God. *Ib. st. 10*

17 The boy[5] stood on the burning deck,
Whence all but he had fled.

Casabianca, st. 1

18 The flames rolled on; he would not go
Without his father's word. *Ib. st. 3*

19 Come to the sunset tree!
The day is past and gone.

Tyrolese Evening Song, st. 1

20 Thou hast *all* seasons for thine own, O death!

The Hour of Death, st. 1

21 In the busy haunts of men.

Tale of the Secret Tribunal, pt. I

22 He Never Smiled Again.

Title and refrain of poem

Henry Francis Lyte
1793–1847

23 Abide with me: fast falls the eventide;
The darkness deepens; Lord, with me abide:
When other helpers fail, and comforts flee,
Help of the helpless, O abide with me.

Eventide [1847], st. 1

[4] See Woolf, 781:16.
The stately homes of England, / How beautiful they stood / Before their recent owners / Relinquished them for good.—E. V. KNOX [1881–1971], *The Stately Homes*

[5] Giacomo Casabianca, whose father, Louis, at the battle of the Nile [1798], commanded the flagship *Orient*. It took fire and blew up, the commander was mortally wounded, and when most of the crew fled, Giacomo remained aboard, in an effort to help his gallant father.

Lucretia Mott
1793–1880

1 Let woman then go on—not asking favors, but claiming as a right the removal of all hindrances to her elevation in the scale of being—let her receive encouragement for the proper cultivation of all her powers, so that she may enter profitably into the active business of life . . . Then in the marriage union, the independence of the husband and wife will be equal, their dependence mutual, and their obligations reciprocal.

Discourse on Woman [delivered December 17, 1849], last paragraph

William Cullen Bryant
1794–1878

2 To him who in the love of Nature holds
Communion with her visible forms, she speaks
A various language.

Thanatopsis [1817–1821], l. 1

3 Go forth, under the open sky, and list
To Nature's teachings. *Ib. l. 14*

4 The hills,
Rock-ribbed, and ancient as the sun.

Ib. l. 37

5 Old ocean's gray and melancholy waste.

Ib. l. 43

6 So live, that when thy summons comes to join
The innumerable caravan which moves
To that mysterious realm, where each shall take
His chamber in the silent halls of death,
Thou go not, like the quarry-slave at night,
Scourged to his dungeon, but, sustained and soothed
By an unfaltering trust, approach thy grave,
Like one that wraps the drapery of his couch
About him, and lies down to pleasant dreams.[1] *Ib. l. 73*

7 He who, from zone to zone,
Guides through the boundless sky thy certain flight,
In the long way that I must tread alone,
Will lead my steps aright.

To a Waterfowl [1818], st. 8

8 The groves were God's first temples.

A Forest Hymn [1824]

9 Loveliest of lovely things are they,
On earth, that soonest pass away.
The rose that lives its little hour
Is prized beyond the sculptured flower.

A Scene on the Banks of the Hudson [1828], st. 3

10 The melancholy days are come, the saddest of the year,
Of wailing winds, and naked woods, and meadows brown and sere.[2]

The Death of the Flowers [1832], st. 1

11 These are the gardens of the desert, these
The unshorn fields, boundless and beautiful,
For which the speech of England has no name—
The prairies. *The Prairies [1833]*

12 Truth, crushed to earth, shall rise again.

The Battlefield [1839], st. 9

Edward Everett[3]
1794–1865

13 The days of palmy prosperity are not those most favorable to the display of public virtue or the influence of wise and good men. In hard, doubtful, unprosperous, and dangerous times, the disinterested and patriotic find their way, by a species of public instinct, unopposed, joyfully welcomed, to the control of affairs.

Mount Vernon Papers [1860], no. 14

William Whewell
1794–1866

14 And so no force however great can stretch a cord however fine into an horizontal line which is accurately straight.[4]

Elementary Treatise on Mechanics [1819]. The Equilibrium of Forces on a Point

15 Man is the interpreter of nature, science the right interpretation.

Philosophy of the Inductive Sciences [1840], aphorism 17

16 In art, truth is a means to an end; in science, it is the only end. *Ib. 25*

17 The catastrophist constructs theories, the uniformitarian demolishes them.

Ib. 36

[1] See Lucretius, 101:4, and Horace, 106:13.

[2] See William Carlos Williams, 785:14.

[3] His best-known wartime oration was delivered at the dedication of the national cemetery at Gettysburg [November 19, 1863], the same occasion on which Lincoln made his famous address.

[4] In a slightly altered form ("line that shall be absolutely straight"), this was reputed to be an example of unconscious but perfect rhyme.

1 It is a test of true theories not only to account for but to predict phenomena.
Ib. 39

Narcisse Achille, Comte de Salvandy
1795–1856

2 We are dancing on a volcano.
At a fête given by the Duc d'Orléans for the King of Naples [1830]

Thomas Carlyle
1795–1881

3 A well-written Life is almost as rare as a well-spent one.
Critical and Miscellaneous Essays. Richter [1827]

4 The great law of culture is: Let each become all that he was created capable of being.
Ib.

5 The three great elements of modern civilization, gunpowder, printing, and the Protestant religion.
Ib. The State of German Literature [1827]

6 Literary men are . . . a perpetual priesthood. *Ib.*

7 In every man's writings, the character of the writer must lie recorded.
Ib. Goethe [1828]

8 A poet without love were a physical and metaphysical impossibility.
Ib. Burns [1828]

9 There is no heroic poem in the world but is at bottom a biography, the life of a man; also, it may be said, there is no life of a man, faithfully recorded, but is a heroic poem of its sort, rhymed or unrhymed.
Ib. Sir Walter Scott [1838]

10 No man lives without jostling and being jostled; in all ways he has to elbow himself through the world, giving and receiving offense. *Ib.*

11 All greatness is unconscious, or it is little and naught. *Ib.*

12 The uttered part of a man's life, let us always repeat, bears to the unuttered, unconscious part a small unknown proportion. He himself never knows it, much less do others.
Ib.

13 It can be said of him [Scott], when he departed he took a man's life along with him. No sounder piece of British manhood was put together in that eighteenth century of time.
Ib.

14 Nothing that was worthy in the past departs; no truth or goodness realized by man ever dies, or can die. *Ib.*

15 Aesop's Fly, sitting on the axle of the chariot, has been much laughed at for exclaiming: What a dust I do raise!
On Boswell's Life of Johnson [1832]

16 Whoso belongs only to his own age, and reverences only its gilt Popinjays or soot-smeared Mumbojumbos, must needs die with it.[1] *Ib.*

17 The stupendous Fourth Estate, whose wide world-embracing influences what eye can take in?[2] *Ib.*

18 All work is as seed sown; it grows and spreads, and sows itself anew. *Ib.*

19 The courage we desire and prize is not the courage to die decently, but to live manfully.
Ib.

20 No man who has once heartily and wholly laughed can be altogether irreclaimably bad.[3]
Sartor Resartus [1833–1834], bk. I, ch. 4

21 He who first shortened the labor of copyists by device of movable types was disbanding hired armies, and cashiering most kings and senates, and creating a whole new democratic world: he had invented the art of printing. *Ib. 5*

22 Man is a tool-using animal. . . . Without tools he is nothing, with tools he is all.
Ib.

23 The Everlasting No.
Ib. 7 (chapter title)

24 Be not the slave of Words. *Ib. 8*

25 The Everlasting Yea.
Ib. 9 (chapter title)

26 Man's unhappiness, as I construe, comes of his greatness; it is because there is an Infinite in him, which with all his cunning he cannot quite bury under the Finite. *Ib.*

27 Close thy Byron; open thy Goethe.
Ib.

[1] See Voltaire, 344:7.

[2] See Hazlitt, 445:3; Macaulay, 487:13; and Thackeray, 539:15.
Burke said there were Three Estates in Parliament; but, in the Reporters' Gallery yonder, there sat a Fourth Estate more important far than they all.—CARLYLE, *On Heroes and Hero Worship* [1841], *The Hero as Man of Letters*

[3] See W. C. Fields, 770:18.

1 Wonder is the basis of worship. *Ib. 10*

2 What you see, yet can not see over, is as good as infinite. *Ib. II, 1*

3 Sarcasm I now see to be, in general, the language of the Devil; for which reason I have, long since, as good as renounced it. *Ib. II, 4*

4 With stupidity and sound digestion man may front much. *Ib.*

5 Alas! the fearful Unbelief is unbelief in yourself. *Ib. 7*

6 Great men are the inspired (speaking and acting) texts of that divine Book of Revelations, whereof a chapter is completed from epoch to epoch, and by some named History. *Ib. 8*

7 Love not Pleasure; love God. *Ib. 9*

8 "Do the Duty which lies nearest thee," which thou knowest to be a Duty! Thy second Duty will already have become clearer. *Ib.*

9 As the Swiss inscription says: *Sprechen ist silbern, Schweigen ist golden*—"Speech is silvern, Silence is golden"; or, as I might rather express it, speech is of time, silence is of eternity.[1] *Ib. III, 3*

10 It is now almost my sole rule of life to clear myself of cants[2] and formulas, as of poisonous Nessus shirts.
Letter to His Wife [1835]

11 France was long a despotism tempered by epigrams.
History of the French Revolution [1837], pt. I, bk. I, ch. 1

12 No lie you can speak or act but it will come, after longer or shorter circulation, like a bill drawn on Nature's Reality, and be presented there for payment—with the answer, No effects. *Ib. III, 1*

13 To a shower of gold most things are penetrable. *Ib. 7*

14 "The people may eat grass":[3] hasty words, which fly abroad irrevocable—and will send back tidings. *Ib. 9*

15 A whiff of grapeshot. *Ib. V, 3*

16 O poor mortals, how ye make this earth bitter for each other. *Ib. 5*

17 Battles, in these ages, are transacted by mechanism; with the slightest possible development of human individuality or spontaneity; men now even die, and kill one another, in an artificial manner. *Ib. VII, 4*

18 History a distillation of rumor. *Ib. 5*

19 The difference between Orthodoxy or My-doxy and Heterodoxy or Thy-doxy.[4]
Ib. pt. II, bk. IV, ch. 2

20 The sea-green Incorruptible [Robespierre]. *Ib. VI, 7*

21 Aristocracy of the Moneybag. *Ib. VII, 7*

22 Democracy is, by the nature of it, a self-canceling business; and gives in the long run a net result of zero.
Chartism [1839], ch. 6, Laissez-Faire

23 No sadder proof can be given by a man of his own littleness than disbelief in great men.
Heroes and Hero Worship [1840]. The Hero as Divinity

24 The history of the world is but the biography of great men.[5] *Ib.*

25 We must get rid of fear. *Ib.*

26 A vein of poetry exists in the hearts of all men. *Ib. The Hero as Poet*

27 The Age of Miracles is forever here!
Ib. The Hero as Priest

28 In books lies the soul of the whole Past Time; the articulate audible voice of the Past, when the body and material substance of it has altogether vanished like a dream.
Ib. The Hero as Man of Letters

29 All that mankind has done, thought, gained or been: it is lying as in magic preservation in the pages of books. *Ib.*

30 The true university of these days is a collection of books. *Ib.*

31 The suffering man ought really to consume his own smoke; there is no good in emitting smoke till you have made it into fire.[6] *Ib.*

[1] Silence is deep as Eternity; speech is shallow as Time.
—CARLYLE, *Sir Walter Scott* [1838]
[Carlyle] loves silence somewhat platonically.—GIUSEPPI MAZZINI [1805–1872]; *from* JANE WELSH CARLYLE, *Letter to Mrs. Stirling* [October 1843]

[2] See Johnson, 356:29.

[3] Response of JOSEPH FRANÇOIS FOULLON, Comptroller General of Finance, when his finance scheme raised the question: What will the people do?

[4] See William Warburton, 345:2.

[5] History is the essence of innumerable biographies.
—CARLYLE, *On History* [1830]
See Emerson, 496:16.

[6] Consume your own smoke.—BROWNING, *Pacchiarotto* [1876], 25
Would that he consumed his own smoke.—MELVILLE, *Moby-Dick* [1858], *ch. 96*

1 Adversity is sometimes hard upon a man; but for one man who can stand prosperity, there are a hundred that will stand adversity.[1] *Ib.*

2 "A fair day's wages for a fair day's work": it is as just a demand as governed men ever made of governing. It is the everlasting right of man.

Past and Present [1843], bk. I, ch. 3

3 Fire is the best of servants; but what a master![2] *Ib. II, 9*

4 All work, even cotton spinning, is noble; work is alone noble. . . . A life of ease is not for any man, nor for any god.

Ib. III, 4

5 Every noble crown is, and on earth will forever be, a crown of thorns. *Ib. 7*

6 Blessed is he who has found his work; let him ask no other blessedness. *Ib. 4*

7 He who takes not counsel of the Unseen and Silent, from him will never come real visibility and speech. *Ib. 11*

8 Captains of Industry.

Ib. IV, 4 (chapter title)

9 There is endless merit in a man's knowing when to have done. *Francia [1845]*

10 He that works and *does* some Poem, not he that merely *says* one, is worthy of the name of Poet.

Introduction to Cromwell's Letters and Speeches [1845]

11 Respectable Professors of the Dismal Science.[3]

Latter Day Pamphlets, no. 1 [1850]

12 A Parliament speaking through reporters to Buncombe and the twenty-seven millions, mostly fools. *Ib. 6*

13 A healthy hatred of scoundrels.

Ib. 12

14 "Genius" (which means transcendent capacity of taking trouble, first of all).[4]

Life of Frederick the Great [1858–1865], bk. IV, ch. 3

[1]See Samuel Butler, 620:6.

[2]Mammon is like fire: the usefulest of all servants, if the frightfulest of all masters!—CARLYLE, *Ib. IV, 7*

[3]Referring to political economy and social science, Carlyle also in his *Occasional Discourse on the Negro Question* [1849] speaks of: What we might call, by way of eminence, the Dismal Science.

See Galbraith, 872:5.

[4]See Buffon, 349:3; Butler, 620:21; and Hopkins, 630:17.

15 Happy the people whose annals are blank in history books![5] *Ib. XVI, 1*

16 So here hath been dawning
Another blue day:
Think, wilt thou let it
Slip useless away? *Today*

17 Lord Bacon could as easily have created the planets as he could have written Hamlet.

Remark in discussion

Joseph Rodman Drake

1795–1820

18 When Freedom from her mountain height,
Unfurled her standard to the air,
She tore the azure robe of night,
And set the stars of glory there;
She mingled with its gorgeous dyes
The milky baldric of the skies,
And striped its pure, celestial white
With streakings of the morning light.
Then from his mansion in the sun
She called her eagle bearer down,
And gave into his mighty hand
The symbol of her chosen land.

The American Flag [1819], st. 1

John Woodcock Graves

1795–1886

19 D' ye ken John Peel with his coat so gay?
D' ye ken John Peel at the break of day?
D' ye ken John Peel when he's far far away
With his hounds and his horn in the morning?

'Twas the sound of his horn brought me from my bed,
And the cry of his hounds, has me ofttimes led;
For Peel's view-hollo would waken the dead,
Or the fox from his lair in the morning.

John Peel [1832]

John Keats

1795–1821

20 I stood tiptoe upon a little hill.

Poems [1817]. I Stood Tiptoe, l. 1

21 And then there crept
A little noiseless noise among the leaves,
Born of the very sigh that silence heaves.

Ib. l. 10

22 Open afresh your round of starry folds,
Ye ardent marigolds! *Ib. l. 47*

[5]Carlyle identifies this as "Montesquieu's aphorism." See George Eliot, 565:18.

1 Where swarms of minnows show their little heads,
Staying their wavy bodies 'gainst the streams.
Ib. l. 72

2 Sometimes goldfinches one by one will drop
From low-hung branches; little space they stop;
But sip, and twitter, and their feathers sleek;
Then off at once, as in a wanton freak:
Or perhaps, to show their black, and golden wings,
Pausing upon their yellow flutterings.
Ib. l. 87

3 Woman! when I behold thee flippant, vain,
Inconstant, childish, proud, and full of fancies.
Ib. Woman! When I Behold Thee Flippant, Vain

4 To one who has been long in city pent,[1]
'Tis very sweet to look into the fair
And open face of heaven.
Ib. Sonnet. To One Who Has Been Long in City Pent

5 E'en like the passage of an angel's tear
That falls through the clear ether silently.
Ib.

6 Much have I traveled in the realms of gold,
And many goodly states and kingdoms seen;
Round many western islands have I been
Which bards in fealty to Apollo hold.
Ib. On First Looking into Chapman's Homer

7 Then felt I like some watcher of the skies
When a new planet swims into his ken;
Or like stout Cortez when with eagle eyes
He stared at the Pacific—and all his men
Looked at each other with a wild surmise—
Silent, upon a peak in Darien. *Ib.*

8 And other spirits there are standing apart
Upon the forehead of the age to come;
These, these will give the world another heart,
And other pulses. Hear ye not the hum
Of mighty workings in a distant mart?
Listen awhile, ye nations, and be dumb.
Ib. Sonnet. Addressed to the Same (Benjamin Robert Haydon)

9 The poetry of earth is never dead.
Ib. Sonnet. On the Grasshopper and the Cricket

10 Life is but a day;
A fragile dewdrop on its perilous way
From a tree's summit.
Ib. Sleep and Poetry, l. 85

[1]See Milton, 287:17.

11 O for ten years, that I may overwhelm
Myself in poesy; so I may do the deed
That my own soul has to itself decreed.
Ib. l. 96

12 A drainless shower
Of light is poesy; 'tis the supreme of power;
'Tis might half slumb'ring on its own right arm.
Ib. l. 235

13 But strength alone though of the Muses born
Is like a fallen angel: trees uptorn,
Darkness, and worms, and shrouds, and sepulchers
Delight it; for it feeds upon the burrs
And thorns of life; forgetting the great end
Of poesy, that it should be a friend
To soothe the cares, and lift the thoughts of man.
Ib. l. 241

14 There is not a fiercer hell than the failure in a great object.
Endymion [1818], preface

15 The imagination of a boy is healthy, and the mature imagination of a man is healthy; but there is a space of life between, in which the soul is in a ferment, the character undecided, the way of life uncertain, the ambition thicksighted: thence proceeds mawkishness, and the thousand bitters which those men I speak of must necessarily taste in going over the following pages. *Ib.*

16 A thing of beauty is a joy forever:
Its loveliness increases; it will never
Pass into nothingness; but still will keep
A bower quiet for us, and a sleep
Full of sweet dreams, and health, and quiet breathing.
Ib. bk. I, l. 1

17 The grandeur of the dooms
We have imagined for the mighty dead.
Ib. l. 20

18 O magic sleep! O comfortable bird,
That broodest o'er the troubled sea of the mind
Till it is hushed and smooth!
Ib. l. 453

19 Time, that aged nurse,
Rocked me to patience. *Ib. l. 705*

20 Wherein lies happiness? In that which becks
Our ready minds to fellowship divine,
A fellowship with essence; till we shine,
Full alchemized, and free of space. Behold
The clear religion of heaven!
Ib. l. 777

21 The crown of these
Is made of love and friendship, and sits high
Upon the forehead of humanity.
Ib. l. 800

1 A hope beyond the shadow of a dream.
Ib. l. 857

2 Pleasure is oft a visitant; but pain
Clings cruelly to us. *Ib. l. 906*

3 'Tis the pest
Of love, that fairest joys give most unrest.
Ib. II, l. 365

4 To sorrow,
I bade good-morrow,
And thought to leave her far away behind;
But cheerly, cheerly,
She loves me dearly;
She is so constant to me, and so kind.
Ib. IV, l. 173

5 Love in a hut, with water and a crust,
Is—Love, forgive us!—cinders, ashes, dust.
Poems [1820]. Lamia, pt. II, l. 1

6 Philosophy will clip an angel's wings.
Ib. l. 234

7 "For cruel 'tis," said she,
"To steal my Basil-pot away from me."
Ib. Isabella; or, The Pot of Basil, st. 62

8 St. Agnes' Eve—Ah, bitter chill it was!
The owl, for all his feathers, was a-cold.
The hare limped trembling through the frozen grass,
And silent was the flock in wooly fold
Ib. The Eve of St. Agnes, st. 1

9 The silver, snarling trumpets 'gan to chide.
Ib. st. 4

10 The music, yearning like a God in pain.
Ib. st. 7

11 She sighed for Agnes' dreams, the sweetest of the year. *Ib.*

12 Asleep in lap of legends old. *Ib. st. 15*

13 Sudden a thought came like a full-blown rose,
Flushing his brow, and in his pained heart
Made purple riot. *Ib. st. 16*

14 A poor, weak, palsy-stricken, churchyard thing. *Ib. st. 18*

15 As though a tongueless nightingale should swell
Her throat in vain, and die, heart-stifled in her dell. *Ib. st. 23*

16 Full on this casement shone the wintry moon,
And threw warm gules on Madeline's fair breast. *Ib. st. 25*

17 Unclasps her warmed jewels one by one;
Loosens her fragrant bodice; by degrees
Her rich attire creeps rustling to her knees.
Ib. st. 26

18 And still she slept an azure-lidded sleep.
Ib. st. 30

19 And the long carpets rose along the gusty floor. *Ib. st. 40*

20 And they are gone: aye, ages long ago
These lovers fled away into the storm.
Ib. st. 42

21 My heart aches, and a drowsy numbness pains
My sense, as though of hemlock I had drunk,
Or emptied some dull opiate to the drains
One minute past, and Lethe-wards had sunk.[1]
Ib. Ode to a Nightingale, st. 1

22 That thou, light-winged Dryad of the trees,
In some melodious plot
Of beechen green, and shadows numberless,
Singest of summer in full-throated ease.
Ib.

23 O, for a draught of vintage! that hath been
Cooled a long age in the deep-delved earth,
Tasting of Flora and the country green,
Dance, and Provençal song, and sunburnt mirth!
O, for a beaker full of the warm South,
Full of the true, the blushful Hippocrene,
With beaded bubbles winking at the brim,
And purple-stained mouth. *Ib. st. 2*

24 Fade far away, dissolve, and quite forget
What thou among the leaves hast never known,
The weariness, the fever, and the fret
Here, where men sit and hear each other groan;
Where palsy shakes a few, sad, last gray hairs,
Where youth grows pale, and specter-thin, and dies;
Where but to think is to be full of sorrow
And leaden-eyed despairs. *Ib. st. 3*

25 Already with thee! tender is the night.
Ib. st. 4

26 I cannot see what flowers are at my feet,
Nor what soft incense hangs upon the boughs,
But, in embalmed darkness, guess each sweet. *Ib. st. 5*

27 The murmurous haunt of flies on summer eves. *Ib.*

28 Darkling I listen; and, for many a time
I have been half in love with easeful Death,
Called him soft names in many a mused rhyme,
To take into the air my quiet breath;
Now more than ever seems it rich to die,

[1] See Horace, 106:24.

To cease upon the midnight with no pain,
While thou art pouring forth thy soul abroad
In such an ecstasy!
Still wouldst thou sing, and I have ears in vain—
To thy high requiem become a sod.
Ib. st. 6

1 Thou wast not born for death, immortal Bird!
No hungry generations tread thee down;
The voice I hear this passing night was heard
In ancient days by emperor and clown:
Perhaps the self-same song that found a path
Through the sad heart of Ruth, when, sick for home,
She stood in tears amid the alien corn;
The same that oft-times hath
Charmed magic casements, opening on the foam
Of perilous seas, in faery lands forlorn.
Ib. st. 7

2 Forlorn! the very word is like a bell
To toll me back from thee to my sole self!
Ib. st. 8

3 Was it a vision, or a waking dream?
Fled is that music:—Do I wake or sleep?
Ib.

4 Thou still unravished bride of quietness,
Thou foster-child of silence and slow time,
Sylvan historian, who canst thus express
A flowery tale more sweetly than our rhyme:
What leaf-fringed legend haunts about thy shape?
Ib. Ode on a Grecian Urn, st. 1

5 What men or gods are these? What maidens loth?
What mad pursuit? What struggle to escape?
What pipes and timbrels? What wild ecstasy?
Ib.

6 Heard melodies are sweet, but those unheard
Are sweeter. *Ib. st. 2*

7 Forever wilt thou love, and she be fair!
Ib.

8 Forever piping songs forever new.
Ib. st. 3

9 Who are these coming to the sacrifice?
To what green altar, O mysterious priest,
Lead'st thou that heifer lowing at the skies,
And all her silken flanks with garlands drest?
Ib. st. 4

10 O Attic shape! Fair attitude! *Ib.*

11 "Beauty is truth, truth beauty,"[1]—that is all
Ye know on earth, and all ye need to know.
Ib.

12 To make delicious moan
Upon the midnight hours.
Ib. Ode to Psyche, st. 3

13 A bright torch, and a casement ope at night,
To let the warm Love in! *Ib. st. 5*

14 Ever let the fancy roam,
Pleasure never is at home.
Ib. Fancy, l. 1

15 Bards of Passion and of Mirth,
Ye have left your souls on earth!
Have ye souls in heaven too?
Ib. Ode written on the blank page before Beaumont and Fletcher, *The Fair Maid of the Inn*

16 Souls of Poets dead and gone,
What Elysium have ye known,
Happy field or mossy cavern,
Choicer than the Mermaid Tavern?
Have ye tippled drink more fine
Than mine host's Canary wine?
Ib. Lines on the Mermaid Tavern

17 Season of mists and mellow fruitfulness,
Close bosom-friend of the maturing sun.
Ib. To Autumn, st. 1

18 Who hath not seen thee oft amid thy store?
Sometimes whoever seeks abroad may find
Thee sitting careless on a granary floor,
Thy hair soft-lifted by the winnowing wind;
Or on a half-reaped furrow sound asleep,
Drows'd with the fume of poppies while thy hook
Spares the next swath and all its twined flowers. *Ib. st. 2*

19 Then in a wailful choir the small gnats mourn
Among the river sallows. *Ib. st. 3*

20 No, no, go not to Lethe, neither twist
Wolf's-bane, tight-rooted, for its poisonous wine. *Ib. Ode on Melancholy, st. 1*

21 Nor let the beetle, nor the death-moth be
Your mournful Psyche. *Ib.*

22 Then glut thy sorrow on a morning rose.
Ib. st. 2

23 She dwells with Beauty—Beauty that must die. *Ib. st. 3*

[1] See Herbert, 268:14.
If asked who said "Beauty is truth, truth beauty!" a great many readers would answer "Keats." But Keats said nothing of the sort. It is what he said the Grecian Urn said, his description and criticism of a certain kind of work of art, the kind from which the evils and problems of this life, the "heart high sorrowful and cloyed," are deliberately excluded. The Urn, for example, depicts, among other beautiful sights, the citadel of a hill town; it does not depict warfare, the evil which makes the citadel necessary.—W. H. Auden, *The Dyer's Hand* [1962], *Robert Frost*

1 Ay, in the very temple of Delight
Veiled Melancholy has her sovran shrine,
Though seen of none save him whose strenuous tongue
Can burst Joy's grape against his palate fine;
His soul shall taste the sadness of her might,
And be among her cloudy trophies hung.
Ib.

2 Deep in the shady sadness of a vale
Far sunken from the healthy breath of morn,
Far from the fiery noon, and eve's one star,
Sat gray-haired Saturn, quiet as a stone.
Ib. Hyperion: A Fragment, bk. I, l. 1

3 That large utterance of the early Gods!
Ib. l. 51

4 As when, upon a tranced summer-night,
Those green-robed senators of mighty woods,
Tall oaks, branch-charmed by the earnest stars,
Dream, and so dream all night without a stir.
Ib. l. 72

5 For to bear all naked truths,
And to envisage circumstance, all calm,
That is the top of sovereignty.
Ib. II, l. 203

6 Knowledge enormous makes a God of me.
Ib. III, l. 113

7 My spirit is too weak—mortality
Weighs heavily on me like unwilling sleep,
And each imagined pinnacle and steep
Of godlike hardship, tells me I must die
Like a sick Eagle looking at the sky.[1]
Life, Letters and Literary Remains of John Keats, edited by RICHARD MONCKTON MILNES *[1848]. On Seeing the Elgin Marbles*

8 This living hand, now warm and capable
Of earnest grasping, would, if it were cold
And in the icy silence of the tomb,
So haunt thy days and chill thy dreaming nights
That thou would wish thine own heart dry of blood
So in my veins red life might stream again,
And thou be conscience-calmed—see here it is—
I hold it towards you.
Ib. Fragment: This Living Hand

9 Shed no tear! O shed no tear!
The flower will bloom another year.
Weep no more! O weep no more!
Young buds sleep in the root's white core.
Ib. Faery Songs, I [written 1818]

10 O, what can ail thee, knight-at-arms,
Alone and palely loitering?
The sedge has withered from the lake,
And no birds sing!
Ib. La Belle Dame Sans Merci,[2] *st. 1*

11 I met a lady in the meads
Full beautiful, a faery's child;
Her hair was long, her foot was light,
And her eyes were wild. *Ib. st. 4*

12 She looked at me as she did love,
And made sweet moan. *Ib. st. 5*

13 "La Belle Dame sans Merci
Hath thee in thrall!" *Ib. st. 10*

14 In a drear-nighted December
Too happy, happy tree,
Thy branches ne'er remember
Their green felicity. *Ib. Stanzas*

15 But were there ever any
Writhed not at passing joy? *Ib.*

16 It keeps eternal whisperings around
Desolate shores, and with its mighty swell
Gluts twice ten thousand caverns.
Ib. On the Sea[3]

17 When I have fears that I may cease to be
Before my pen has gleaned my teeming brain. *Ib. Sonnet. When I Have Fears*

18 When I behold, upon the night's starred face,
Huge cloudy symbols of a high romance.
Ib.

19 Then on the shore
Of the wide world I stand alone, and think
Till love and fame to nothingness do sink.
Ib.

20 Bright star, would I were steadfast as thou art—
Not in lone splendor hung aloft the night
And watching, with eternal lids apart,
Like nature's patient, sleepless Eremite,
The moving waters at their priestlike task
Of pure ablution round earth's human shores. *Ib. Sonnet. Bright Star*[4]

21 None can usurp this height . . .
But those to whom the miseries of the world
Are misery, and will not let them rest.
The Fall of Hyperion: A Dream, canto I, l. 147[5]

[1]Printed in the *Examiner* [February 23, 1817].

[2]Title of a French poem by ALAIN CHARTIER [c. 1385–c. 1433].
First printed by Leigh Hunt in the *Indicator* [May 10, 1820].

[3]From want of regular rests, I have been rather *narvus*, and the passage in *Lear*—"Do you not hear the sea?"—has haunted me intensely.—KEATS, *Letter to John Hamilton Reynolds* [April 17, 1817]
Edgar: . . . Hark! do you hear the sea?—SHAKESPEARE, *King Lear, act IV, sc. vi, l. 4*

[4]Written on a blank page in Shakespeare's *Poems*.

[5]From *The Letters of John Keats* [1867], edited by RICHARD MONCKTON MILNES.

1 I am certain of nothing but the holiness of the heart's affections and the truth of imagination—what the imagination seizes as beauty must be truth—whether it existed before or not.

Letter to Benjamin Bailey [November 22, 1817]

2 The imagination may be compared to Adam's dream—he awoke and found it truth. *Ib.*

3 O for a life of Sensations rather than of Thoughts! *Ib.*

4 I scarcely remember counting upon happiness—I look not for it if it be not in the present hour—nothing startles me beyond the moment. The setting sun will always set me to rights—or if a sparrow come before my window I take part in its existence and pick about the gravel. *Ib.*

5 At once it struck me what quality went to form a man of achievement, especially in literature, and which Shakespeare possessed so enormously—I mean *negative capability,* that is, when a man is capable of being in uncertainties, mysteries, doubts, without any irritable reaching after fact and reason.

Letter to George and Thomas Keats [December 22, 1817]

6 We hate poetry that has a palpable design upon us—and if we do not agree, seems to put its hand in its breeches pocket. Poetry should be great and unobtrusive, a thing which enters into one's soul, and does not startle or amaze with itself, but with its subject.

Letter to John Hamilton Reynolds [February 3, 1818]

7 Poetry should surprise by a fine excess, and not by singularity. It should strike the reader as a wording of his own highest thoughts, and appear almost as a remembrance.

Letter to John Taylor [February 27, 1818]

8 If poetry comes not as naturally as leaves to a tree it had better not come at all.

Ib.

9 Scenery is fine—but human nature is finer.

Letter to Benjamin Bailey [March 13, 1818]

10 Axioms in philosophy are not axioms until they are proved upon our pulses: we read fine things but never feel them to the full until we have gone the same steps as the author.

Letter to John Hamilton Reynolds [May 3, 1818]

11 I compare human life to a large mansion of many apartments, two of which I can only describe, the doors of the rest being as yet shut upon me. *Ib.*

12 There is an awful warmth about my heart like a load of immortality.

Ib. [September 22, 1818]

13 I begin to get a little acquainted with my own strength and weakness. Praise or blame has but a momentary effect on the man whose love of beauty in the abstract makes him a severe critic on his own works.

Letter to James Hessey [October 9, 1818]

14 The genius of poetry must work out its own salvation in a man; it cannot be matured by law and precept, but by sensation and watchfulness in itself. That which is creative must create itself—

In *Endymion,* I leaped headlong into the sea, and thereby have become better acquainted with the soundings, the quicksands, and the rocks, than if I had stayed upon the green shore, and piped a silly pipe, and took tea and comfortable advice. *Ib.*

15 I would sooner fail than not be among the greatest. *Ib.*

16 I think I shall be among the English Poets after my death.

Letter to George and Georgiana Keats [October 14, 1818]

17 The poetical character . . . is not itself—it has no self—it is everything and nothing. . . . It has as much delight in conceiving an Iago as an Imogen.

Letter to Richard Woodhouse [October 27, 1818]

18 A poet is the most unpoetical of anything in existence; because he has no identity—he is continually infor[ming]—and filling some other body. *Ib.*

19 A man's life of any worth is a continual allegory—and very few eyes can see the mystery of his life—a life like the Scriptures, figurative. . . . Lord Byron cuts a figure, but he is not figurative. Shakespeare led a life of allegory: his works are the comments on it.

Letter to George and Georgiana Keats [February 14–May 3, 1819]

20 Nothing ever becomes real till it is experienced—Even a proverb is no proverb to you till your Life has illustrated it.

Ib.

1 I myself am pursuing the same instinctive course as the veriest human animal you can think of—I am, however young, writing at random—straining at particles of light in the midst of a great darkness—without knowing the bearing of any one assertion, of any one opinion. Yet may I not in this be free from sin? *Ib. [March 19, 1819]*

2 Call the world if you please "The vale of soul-making." *Ib. [April 21, 1819]*

3 I have two luxuries to brood over in my walks, your loveliness and the hour of my death. O that I could have possession of them both in the same minute.
To Fanny Brawne [July 25, 1819]

4 "If I should die," said I to myself, "I have left no immortal work behind me—nothing to make my friends proud of my memory—but I have loved the principle of beauty in all things, and if I had had time I would have made myself remembered."
Ib. [c. February 1820]

5 You might curb your magnanimity, and be more of an artist, and load every rift of your subject with ore.
Letter to Shelley [August 1820]

6 I can scarcely bid you good-bye, even in a letter. I always made an awkward bow. God bless you!
Letter to Charles Armitage Brown; Keats's last letter [November 30, 1820]

7 Here lies one whose name was writ in water.[1] *Epitaph for himself [1821]*

Leopold von Ranke
1795–1886

8 You have reckoned that history ought to judge the past and to instruct the contemporary world as to the future. The present attempt does not yield to that high office. It will merely tell how it really was.[2]
Geschichten der Romanischen und Germanischen Volker (History of the Romanic and Germanic Peoples) von 1492 bis 1535 [1824], preface

[1] Among the many things he has requested of me tonight, this is the principal—that on his gravestone shall be this inscription.—*Letter from Severn, in* RICHARD MONCKTON MILNES, *Life, Letters, and Literary Remains of John Keats* [1848]

See Sophocles, 75:22; Catullus, 102:12; More, 155:8; Bacon, 181:18; and Shakespeare, 249:14.

[2] Wie es eigentlich gewesen.

See Thucydides, 80:15.

Friedrich Wilhelm IV
1795–1861

9 I love an opposition that has convictions.
Speech [April 11, 1847]

10 Henceforth Prussia goes forward as part of Germany.
Proclamation: To My People, to the German Nation [March 21, 1848]

Alfred Bunn
1796–1860

11 I dreamt that I dwelt in marble halls,
With vassals and serfs at my side.
The Bohemian Girl [1843], act II, song

David Hartley Coleridge
1796–1849

12 The soul of man is larger than the sky,
Deeper than ocean, or the abysmal dark
Of the unfathomed center.[3]
To Shakespeare

Horace Mann
1796–1859

13 Lost, yesterday, somewhere between sunrise and sunset, two golden hours, each set with sixty diamond minutes. No reward is offered, for they are gone forever.
Aphorism

14 Be ashamed to die until you have won some victory for humanity.
Commencement Address, Antioch College [1859]

James Robinson Planché
1796–1880

15 It would have made a cat laugh.
The Queen of the Frogs [1879], act I, sc. iv

William Hickling Prescott
1796–1859

16 What, then, must have been the emotions of the Spaniards, when, after working their toilsome way into the upper air, the cloudy tabernacle parted before their eyes, and they beheld these fair scenes in all their pristine

[3] See Millay, 822:12.

magnificence and beauty![1] It was like the spectacle which greeted the eyes of Moses from the summit of Pisgah, and, in the warm glow of their feelings, they cried out, "It is the promised land!"

The Conquest of Mexico [1843], bk. III, ch. 8

1 The surest test of the civilization of a people—at least, as sure as any—afforded by mechanical art is to be found in their architecture, which presents so noble a field for the display of the grand and the beautiful, and which, at the same time, is so intimately connected with the essential comforts of life.

The Conquest of Peru [1847], bk. I, ch. 5

2 Drawing his sword he [Pizarro] traced a line with it on the sand from East to West. Then, turning towards the South, "Friends and comrades!" he said, "on that side are toil, hunger, nakedness, the drenching storm, desertion, and death; on this side ease and pleasure.[2] There lies Peru with its riches; here, Panama and its poverty. Choose, each man, what best becomes a brave Castilian. For my part, I go to the South." So saying, he stepped across the line. *Ib. II, 4*

Sam Slick
[Thomas Chandler Haliburton]
1796–1865

3 I want you to see Peel, Stanley, Graham, Shiel, Russell, Macaulay, Old Joe, and so on. These men are all upper crust here.[3]

Sam Slick in England [1843–1844],[4] ch. 24

4 Circumstances alter cases.

The Old Judge [1849], ch. 15

Thomas Haynes Bayly
1797–1839

5 Tell me the tales that to me were so dear,
Long, long ago, long, long ago.

Long, Long Ago

[1] From this summit [Popocatépetl, 17,887 feet] could be seen the great city of Mexico, and the whole of the lake, and all the towns which were built in it.—BERNAL DÍAZ DEL CASTILLO [c. 1492–1581], *Historia Verdadera de la Conquista de la Nueva España, pt. IV, ch. 53*

[2] See Garibaldi, 509:7, and Churchill, 743:19.

[3] See James Fenimore Cooper, 463:15.

[4] The "Sam Slick" papers first appeared in a weekly paper in Nova Scotia [1836].

Heinrich Heine[5]
1797–1856

6 Out of my own great woe
I make my little songs.[6]

Aus Meinen Grossen Schmerzen (Out of My Great Woe), st. 1

7 I cannot explain the sadness
That's fallen on my breast.
An old, old fable haunts me,
And will not let me rest.[7]

Die Lorelei, st. 1

8 You're lovely as a flower,
So pure and fair to see;
I look at you, and sadness
Comes stealing over me.[8]

Du Bist Wie eine Blume, st. 1

9 At first I was almost about to despair, I thought I never could bear it—but I *did* bear it. The question remains: how?

An Karl von U.

10 A knight of the holy spirit.

Harzreise

11 Wherever they burn books they will also, in the end, burn human beings.

Almansor: A Tragedy [1823]

12 Every woman is the gift of a world to me.

Ideas: The Book Le Grand [1826]

13 On the wings of song.[9]

Lyrisches Intermezzo [1823], no. 9, On the Wings of Song

14 Don't send a poet to London.

English Fragments [1828], ch. 2, London

15 Christianity is an idea, and as such is indestructible and immortal, like every idea.

History of Religion and Philosophy in Germany [1834], vol. I

16 Mark this well, you proud men of action: You are nothing but the unwitting agents of the men of thought who often, in quiet self-effacement, mark out most exactly all your doings in advance. *Ib. III*

[5] Therefore a secret unrest / Tortured thee, brilliant and bold.—MATTHEW ARNOLD, *Heine's Grave* [1867]

[6] Translated by ELIZABETH BARRETT BROWNING.

[7] Ich weiss nicht, was soll es bedeuten, / Dass ich so traurig bin; / Ein Märchen aus alten Zeiten, / Das kommt mir nicht aus dem Sinn.

Translated by AARON KRAMER.

[8] Du bist wie eine Blume, / So hold und schön und rein; / Ich schau dich an, und Wehmut / Schleicht mir ins Herz hinein.

Translated by AARON KRAMER.

[9] Auf Flügeln des Gesanges.

1 People in those old times had convictions; we moderns only have opinions. And it needs more than a mere opinion to erect a Gothic cathedral.

The French Stage (Französische Bühne) [1837], ch. 9

2 If one has no heart, one cannot write for the masses.

Letter to Julius Campe [March 18, 1840]

3 Wild, dark times are rumbling toward us, and the prophet who wishes to write a new apocalypse will have to invent entirely new beasts, and beasts so terrible that the ancient animal symbols of St. John[1] will seem like cooing doves and cupids in comparison.[2]

Lutetia; or, Paris [1842]. From the Augsberg Gazette, 12, VII

4 The future smells of Russian leather, of blood, of godlessness and of much whipping. I advise our grandchildren to come into the world with very thick skin on their backs.

Ib.

5 No talent, but a character.

Atta Troll [1843], ch. 24

6 Ordinarily he is insane, but he has lucid moments when he is only stupid.[3]

Of Savoye, appointed ambassador to Frankfurt by Lamartine [1848]

7 So we keep asking, over and over,
Until a handful of earth
Stops our mouths—
But is that an answer?

Lazarus, I [1854]

8 Of course he [God] will forgive me; that's his business [Bien sûr, il me pardonnera; c'est son métier]. *Last words [1856]*

Samuel Lover
1797–1868

9 Reproof on her lip, but a smile in her eye.

Rory O'More [1836], st. 1

10 "For there's luck in odd numbers," says Rory O'More.[4] *Ib. st. 3*

Sir Charles Lyell[5]
1797–1875

11 Although we are mere sojourners on the surface of the planet, chained to a mere point in space, enduring but for a moment of time, the human mind is not only enabled to number worlds beyond the unassisted ken of mortal eye, but to trace the events of indefinite ages before the creation of our race, and is not even withheld from penetrating into the dark secrets of the ocean, or the interior of the solid globe; free, like the spirit which the poet described as animating the universe.

Principles of Geology, vol. I [1830], ch. 13

12 It may be said that, so far from having a materialistic tendency, the supposed introduction into the earth at successive geological periods of life—sensation, instinct, the intelligence of the higher mammalia bordering on reason, and lastly, the improvable reason of Man himself—presents us with a picture of the ever-increasing dominion of mind over matter.

The Geological Evidences of the Antiquity of Man [1863]

William Motherwell
1797–1835

13 I've wandered east, I've wandered west,
Through many a weary way;
But never, never can forget
The love o' life's young day!

Jeannie Morrison [1832], st. 1

Mary Wollstonecraft Shelley
1797–1851

14 I beheld the wretch—the miserable monster whom I had created.

Frankenstein [1818], ch. 5

15 Nothing contributes so much to tranquilize the mind as a steady purpose—a point on which the soul may fix its intellectual eye.

Ib.

Sojourner Truth
[Isabella Van Wagener]
c. 1797–1883

16 Frederick, is God dead?

Question to speaker FREDERICK DOUGLASS[6] *[c. 1850]*

17 That man . . . says that women need to be helped into carriages, and lifted over ditches, and to have the best place everywhere. No-

[1] In *The Revelation of St. John the Divine.*
[2] See Yeats, 714:13.
[3] See Cervantes, 170:16; Bacon, 179:12; and Dryden, 304:25.
[4] See Pliny, 117:7, and Shakespeare, 225:28.
[5] See Gosse, 663:5.

[6] According to Garrison [December 9, 1878], Douglass, "under the tremendous pressure of the hour, spoke in a somewhat desponding tone."

body ever helps me into carriages, or over mud puddles, or gives me any best place, and aren't I a woman? . . . I have plowed, and planted, and gathered into barns, and no man could head me—and aren't I a woman? I could work as much and eat as much as a man (when I could get it), and bear the lash as well—and aren't I a woman? I have borne thirteen children and seen them most all sold off into slavery, and when I cried out with a mother's grief, none but Jesus heard—and aren't I a woman?

Speech at Woman's Rights Convention, Akron, Ohio [1851]

1 That . . . man . . . says women can't have as much rights as man, cause Christ wasn't a woman. Where did your Christ come from? . . . From God and a woman. Man had nothing to do with him. *Ib.*

2 The rich rob the poor and the poor rob one another. *Saying*

Alfred de Vigny

1797–1863

3 I love the sound of the horn, at night, in the depth of the woods.[1] *Le Cor [1826]*

4 God! how sad is the sound of the horn deep in the woods![2] *Ib.*

5 I [Nature] am called a mother, but I am a grave. *La Maison du Berger [1864]*

6 Love that which will never be seen twice. *Ib.*

7 Silence alone is great; all else is weakness. *La Mort du Loup [1864]*

Wilhelm I

1797–1888

8 In Germany, Prussia must make moral conquests through legislation.

Speech to the Cabinet [November 8, 1858]

9 The Prussian army is the people in arms. *As Prince Regent [1860]*

10 I now have no time to be tired. *On his deathbed [March 8, 1888]*

Auguste Comte

1798–1857

11 Love our principle, order our foundation, progress our goal.

Système de Politique Positive [1851–1854]

[1] J'aime le son du cor, le soir, au fond des bois.

[2] Dieu! que le son du cor est triste au fond des bois!

12 Nothing at bottom is real except humanity.[3] *Ib.*

13 The dead govern the living. *Catéchisme Positiviste [1852]*

Eugène Delacroix

1798–1863

14 O young artist, you search for a subject—everything is a subject. Your subject is yourself, your impressions, your emotions in the presence of nature. *Oeuvres Littéraires*

15 The first virtue of a painting is to be a feast for the eyes. *Journal [1893–1895]*

16 Painting is only a bridge linking the painter's mind with that of the viewer. *Ib.*

August Heinrich Hoffmann [Hoffmann von Fallersleben]

1798–1874

17 Deutschland, Deutschland über Alles.[4] *Title of poem [September 1, 1841]*

Jules Michelet

1798–1874

18 England is an empire, Germany is a nation, a race, France is a person. *Histoire de France [1833–1867]*

19 What is the first part of politics? Education. The second? Education. And the third? Education. *Le Peuple [1846]*

David Macbeth Moir

1798–1851

20 From the lone sheiling of the misty island
Mountains divide us, and the waste of seas—
Yet still the blood is strong, the heart is Highland,
And we in dreams behold the Hebrides.[5]

The Lone Sheiling [Canadian Boat Song, 1829]

[3] Il n'y a, au fond, de réel que l'humanité.

[4] Germany before everything.

[5] This poem, entitled *Canadian Boat Song,* appeared [September 1829] anonymously in the *Noctes Ambrosianae* series in *Blackwood's Edinburgh Magazine.* It has been attributed to (among others) John Wilson ("Christopher North"), John Galt, John Lockhart, Scott, and to David Macbeth Moir, who is now generally accepted as the author.

Dionysios Solomos
1798–1857

1 We knew thee of old,
O divinely restored,
By the light of thine eyes
And the light of thy sword.

From the graves of our slain
Shall thy valor prevail
As we greet thee again—
Hail, Liberty! Hail!

Hymn to Liberty [1823],[1] *st. 1, 2*

2 On the blackened spine of Psara,
Glory, pacing alone,
Broods on her shining heroes;
She crowns her hair with a band
Born from the spare, few grasses
That are left in the ruined land.

The Destruction of Psara [1825][2]

3 Enclose in your soul Greece (or something equal) and you shall feel every kind of grandeur.

Note to "Free Besieged" [c. 1833][3]

4 The nation must learn to consider as national whatever is true.

Table Talk [c. 1850][3]

Amos Bronson Alcott
1799–1888

5 The true teacher defends his pupils against his own personal influence. He inspires self-trust. He guides their eyes from himself to the spirit that quickens him. He will have no disciple.

Orphic Sayings. From The Dial [July 1840]. The Teacher

6 Who loves a garden still his Eden keeps,
Perennial pleasures plants, and wholesome
harvests reaps. *Tablets [1868]*

7 One must be a wise reader to quote wisely and well.

Table Talk [1877]. Quotation

8 To be ignorant of one's ignorance is the malady of the ignorant. *Ib. Discourse*

9 I press thee to my heart as Duty's faithful
child.

Sonnet to Louisa May Alcott [1882]

[1]Translated by Rudyard Kipling.
Out of a total of 158 stanzas in the hymn, the first four have been adopted as the Greek national anthem.
[2]Translated by Cedric Whitman.
[3]Translated by George Savidis.

Honoré de Balzac
1799–1850

10 It is easier to be a lover than a husband for the simple reason that it is more difficult to be witty every day than to say pretty things from time to time.

Physiologie du Mariage [1829]

11 I am a galley slave to pen and ink.

Lettres [1832]

12 Fame is the sun of the dead.

La Recherche de l'Absolu [1834]

13 Our heart is a treasury; if you spend all its wealth at once you are ruined. We find it as difficult to forgive a person for displaying his feeling in all its nakedness as we do to forgive a man for being penniless.

Le Père Goriot [1835][4]

14 Man is no angel. He is sometimes more of a hypocrite and sometimes less, and then fools say that he has or has not principles.

Ib.

15 "Temptations can be got rid of." "How?" "By yielding to them."[5] *Ib.*

16 I believe in the incomprehensibility of God.

Letter to Madame de Hanska [1837]

17 Those sweetly smiling angels with pensive looks, innocent faces, and cash-boxes for hearts. *Cousin Bette [1846], ch. 15*

Rufus Choate
1799–1859

18 The courage of New England was the "courage of conscience." It did not rise to that insane and awful passion, the love of war for itself.

Address at Ipswich Centennial [1834]

19 The final end of government is not to exert restraint but to do good.

Speech in the Senate [July 2, 1841]

20 There was a state without king or nobles; there was a church without a bishop;[6] there was a people governed by grave magistrates which it had selected, and by equal laws which it had framed.

Speech before the New England Society [December 22, 1843]

[4]Translated by Marion Ayton Crawford.
[5]See Wilde, 674:27.
[6]See Junius, 391:2.
It [Calvinism] established a religion without a prelate, a government without a king.—George Bancroft, *History of the United States* [1834–1876], *vol. III, ch. 6*

1 We join ourselves to no party that does not carry the flag and keep step to the music of the Union.

Letter to the Whig Convention, Worcester [October 1, 1855]

2 The glittering and sounding generalities[1] of natural right which make up the Declaration of Independence.

Letter to the Maine Whig Committee [1856]

Thomas Hood

1799–1845

3 They went and told the sexton, and
The sexton tolled the bell.

Faithless Sally Brown [1826], st. 17

4 I remember, I remember
The house where I was born,
The little window where the sun
Came peeping in at morn.

I Remember, I Remember [1827], st. 1

5 Now 'tis little joy
To know I'm farther off from heaven
Than when I was a boy. *Ib. st. 4*

6 And there is even a happiness
That makes the heart afraid.

Ode to Melancholy [1827]

7 There's not a string attuned to mirth
But has its chord in melancholy. *Ib.*

8 But evil is wrought by want of thought,
As well as want of heart.

The Lady's Dream [1827], st. 16

9 I saw old Autumn in the misty morn
Stand shadowless like silence, listening
To silence. *Autumn [1827], st. 1*

10 Straight down the Crooked Lane,
And all round the Square.

A Plain Direction, st. 1

11 Never go to France
Unless you know the lingo,
If you do, like me,
You will repent, by jingo.

French and English [1839], st. 1

12 No warmth, no cheerfulness, no healthful ease,
No comfortable feel in any member—
No shade, no shine, no butterflies, no bees,
No fruits, no flowers, no leaves, no birds,
November! *No!*

13 Seemed washing his hands with invisible soap
In imperceptible water.

Miss Kilmansegg and Her Precious Leg [1841–1843]. Her Christening, st. 10

14 O bed! O bed! delicious bed!
That heaven upon earth to the weary head.

Ib. Her Dream, st. 7

15 Another tumble!—that's his precious nose!

Parental Ode to My Infant Son, st. 3

16 With fingers weary and worn,
With eyelids heavy and red,
A woman sat in unwomanly rags
Plying her needle and thread—
Stitch! stitch! stitch!
In poverty, hunger, and dirt.

The Song of the Shirt [1843], st. 1

17 She sang the Song of the Shirt. *Ib.*

18 Work! work! work! *Ib. st. 2*

19 O men, with sisters dear!
O men, with mothers and wives!
It is not linen you're wearing out,
But human creatures' lives![2] *Ib. st. 4*

20 O God! that bread should be so dear,
And flesh and blood so cheap! *Ib. st. 5*

21 One more unfortunate,
Weary of breath,
Rashly importunate,
Gone to her death!

Take her up tenderly,
Lift her with care;
Fashioned so slenderly,
Young, and so fair!

The Bridge of Sighs [1844], st. 1, 2

22 Alas for the rarity
Of Christian charity
Under the sun![3] *Ib. st. 9*

Mary Howitt

1799–1888

23 "Will you walk into my parlor?" said the spider to the fly;

The Spider and the Fly [1844]

24 Oh! poverty is a weary thing, 'tis full of grief and pain;
It keepeth down the soul of man, as with an iron chain.

The Sale of the Pet Lamb [1844], last stanza

[1] See Dickman, 598:12.

[2] See Scott, 431:22.

[3] See Southey, 439:9, and O'Reilly, 659:8.

Thomas Noel

1799–1861

1 Rattle his bones over the stones!
He's only a pauper, whom nobody owns!

The Pauper's Drive, st. 1

Alexander Pushkin[1]

1799–1837

2 Reason's icy intimations,
and records of a heart in pain.

Eugene Onegin [1823],[2] *dedication*

3 Unforced, as conversation passed,
he had the talent of saluting
felicitously every theme,
of listening like a judge supreme
while serious topics were disputing,
or, with an epigram-surprise,
of kindling smiles in ladies' eyes.

Ib. ch. 1, st. 5

4 Always contented with his life,
and with his dinner, and his wife.

Ib. st. 12

5 Why fight what's known to be decisive?
Custom is despot of mankind.

Ib. st. 25

6 The illness with which he'd been smitten
should have been analyzed when caught,
something like *spleen,* that scourge of Britain,
or Russia's *chondria,* for short.

Ib. st. 38

7 Habit is Heaven's own redress:
it takes the place of happiness.[3]

Ib. 2, st. 31

8 Love passed, the muse appeared, the weather
of mind got clarity newfound;
now free, I once more weave together
emotion, thought, and magic sound.

Ib. st. 59

9 Moscow . . . how many strains are fusing
in that one sound, for Russian hearts!
What store of riches it imparts!

Ib. 7, st. 36

10 *Pimen* [*writing by lamplight*]: One more, the final record, and my annals
Are ended, and fulfilled the duty laid
By God on me, a sinner. Not in vain
Hath God appointed me for many years
A witness, teaching me the art of letters;
A day will come when some laborious monk
Will bring to light my zealous, nameless toil,
Kindle, as I, his lamp, and from the parchment
Shaking the dust of ages, will transcribe
My chronicles.

Boris Godunov [written 1825][4]

11 Like to some magistrate grown gray in office
Calmly he contemplates alike the just
And unjust, with indifference he notes
Evil and good, and knows not wrath nor pity.

Ib.

12 Ah! heavy art thou, crown of Monomakh!

Ib.

13 *Mosalsky:* Good folk! Maria Godunov and her son Feodor have poisoned themselves. We have seen their dead bodies. [*The people are silent with horror.*] Why are you silent? Cry, Long live Czar Dimitri Ivanovich! [*The people are speechless.*] *Ib.*

14 And thus he[5] mused: "From here, indeed
Shall we strike terror in the Swede;
And here a city, by our labor
Founded, shall gall our haughty neighbor;
"Here cut"—so Nature gives command—
"Your window through on Europe:[6] stand
Firm-footed by the sea, unchanging!"

The Bronze Horseman [written 1833][7]

John Brown

1800–1859

15 Had I so interfered in behalf of the rich, the powerful, the intelligent, the so-called great, or in behalf of any of their friends . . . every man in this court would have deemed it an act worthy of reward rather than punishment.

Last speech to the court [November 2, 1859]

16 I am yet too young to understand that God is any respecter of persons.[8] I believe that to have interfered as I have done . . . in behalf of His despised poor, was not wrong, but right. Now, if it is deemed necessary that I should forfeit my life for the furtherance of

[1] The great music's unforgotten strain / Ceased . . . and shall not resound on earth again.—MIKHAIL LERMONTOV, *The Poet's Death* [written January 1837]

[2] Translated by CHARLES JOHNSTON.

[3] See Burke, 372:1.

[4] Translated by ALFRED HAYES.

[5] Peter I (the Great) [1672–1725].

[6] Algarotti has somewhere said: Pétersbourg est la fenêtre, par laquelle la Russie regarde en Europe.—*Author's Note, The Bronze Horseman*

I am at length going to give you some account of this new city, of the great window lately opened in the North, through which Russia looks into Europe.—FRANCESCO ALGAROTTI, *Letters About Russia* [June 30, 1739]

[7] Translated by OLIVER ELTON.

[8] See *Acts 10:34,* 46:10, and *I Peter 1:17,* 52:8.

the ends of justice, and mingle my blood further with the blood of my children, and with the blood of millions in this slave country whose rights are disregarded by wicked, cruel, and unjust enactments, I submit: so let it be done! *Ib.*

1 This *is* a beautiful country.
Remark as he rode to the gallows, seated on his coffin [December 2, 1859]

Julia Crawford
1800–1885

2 Kathleen Mavourneen! the gray dawn is breaking,
The horn of the hunter is heard on the hill.
Kathleen Mavourneen [1835], st. 1

3 Oh! hast thou forgotten this day we must part?
It may be for years, and it may be forever;
Then why art thou silent, thou voice of my heart? *Ib.*

Thomas Babington, Lord Macaulay[1]
1800–1859

4 That is the best government which desires to make the people happy, and knows how to make them happy.
Essay on Mitford's History of Greece [1824]

5 Free trade, one of the greatest blessings which a government can confer on a people, is in almost every country unpopular. *Ib.*

6 Press where ye see my white plume shine, amidst the ranks of war,
And be your oriflamme today the helmet of Navarre.
Ivry: A Song of the Huguenots [1824], l. 29

7 Nobles by the right of an earlier creation, and priests by the imposition of a mightier hand. *On Milton [1825]*

8 The dust and silence of the upper shelf. *Ib.*

[1] I wish I was as cocksure of anything as Tom Macaulay is of everything.—William Lamb, Viscount Melbourne [1779–1848]; *from Melbourne's Papers,* edited by L. C. Sanders [1889], preface by the Earl Cowper

9 As civilization advances, poetry almost necessarily declines. *Ib.*

10 Perhaps no person can be a poet, or even can enjoy poetry, without a certain unsoundness of mind. *Ib.*

11 There is only one cure for the evils which newly acquired freedom produces, and that cure is freedom. *Ib.*

12 Nothing is so useless as a general maxim.
On Machiavelli [1827]

13 The gallery in which the reporters sit has become a fourth estate of the realm.[2]
On Hallam's Constitutional History [1828]

14 The English Bible—a book which if everything else in our language should perish, would alone suffice to show the whole extent of its beauty and power.
On John Dryden [1828]

15 His imagination resembled the wings of an ostrich. It enabled him to run, though not to soar. *Ib.*

16 Men are never so likely to settle a question rightly as when they discuss it freely.
Southey's Colloquies on Society [1830]

17 A single breaker may recede; but the tide is evidently coming in.[3] *Ib.*

18 That wonderful book, while it obtains admiration from the most fastidious critics, is loved by those who are too simple to admire it.
On Southey's edition of Bunyan's Pilgrim's Progress [1830]

19 We know no spectacle so ridiculous as the British public in one of its periodical fits of morality.
On Moore's Life of Lord Byron [1831]

20 From the poetry of Lord Byron they drew a system of ethics compounded of misanthropy and voluptuousness—a system in which the two great commandments were to hate your neighbor and to love your neighbor's wife. *Ib.*

21 Reform, that you may preserve.
Debate on the First Reform Bill [March 2, 1831]

[2] See Hazlitt, 445:3; Carlyle, 472:17; and Thackeray, 539:15.
[3] See Arthur Hugh Clough, 564:17.

1 Ye diners-out from whom we guard our spoons.[1] *Political Georgics*[2]

2 The conformation of his mind was such that whatever was little seemed to him great, and whatever was great seemed to him little.
On Horace Walpole [1833]

3 Such night in England ne'er had been, nor
ne'er again shall be.
The Armada [1833], l. 34

4 To sum up the whole, we should say that the aim of the Platonic philosophy was to exalt man into a god.
On Lord Bacon [1837]

5 An acre in Middlesex is better than a principality in Utopia. *Ib.*

6 Every schoolboy knows who imprisoned Montezuma, and who strangled Atahualpa.
On Lord Clive [1840]

7 She [the Roman Catholic Church] may still exist in undiminished vigor when some traveler from New Zealand shall, in the midst of a vast solitude, take his stand on a broken arch of London Bridge to sketch the ruins of St. Paul's.[3]
On Leopold von Ranke's History of the Popes [1840]

8 She [the Catholic Church] thoroughly understands what no other Church has ever understood, how to deal with enthusiasts.
Ib.

9 The Chief Justice was rich, quiet, and infamous. *On Warren Hastings [1841]*

[1]The louder he talked of his honor, the faster we counted our spoons.—EMERSON, *Conduct of Life* [1860], *Worship*

[2]Poem in a letter to his sister Hannah More Macaulay [June 29, 1831]; published earlier [c. 1828] anonymously in *The Times.*

[3]Macaulay used a similar image in his review [1824] of MITFORD, *Greece,* and in his review [1829] of MILL, *Essay on Government.*

Who knows but that hereafter some traveler like myself will sit down upon the banks of the Seine, the Thames, or the Zuyder Zee, where now, in the tumult of enjoyment, the heart and the eyes are too slow to take in the multitude of sensations? Who knows but he will sit down solitary amid silent ruins, and weep a people inurned and their greatness changed into an empty name?—CONSTANTIN DE VOLNEY [1757–1820], *Ruins, ch. II*

See Horace Walpole, 363:21.

In the firm expectation that when London shall be a habitation of bitterns, when St. Paul and Westminster Abbey shall stand shapeless and nameless ruins in the midst of an unpeopled marsh, when the piers of Waterloo Bridge shall become the nuclei of islets of reeds and osiers, and cast the jagged shadows of their broken arches on the solitary stream, some transatlantic commentator will be weighing in the scales of some new and now unimagined system of criticism the respective merits of the Bells and the Fudges and their historians.—SHELLEY, *Peter Bell the Third* [1819], *dedication*

10 I shall not be satisfied unless I produce something which shall for a few days supersede the last fashionable novel on the tables of young ladies.
Letter to Macvey Napier [November 5, 1841]

11 In order that he might rob a neighbor whom he had promised to defend, black men fought on the coast of Coromandel and red men scalped each other by the great lakes of North America.
On Frederick the Great [1842]

12 We hardly know an instance of the strength and weakness of human nature so striking and so grotesque as the character of this haughty, vigilant, resolute, sagacious blue-stocking, half Mithridates and half Trissotin, bearing up against a world in arms, with an ounce of poison in one pocket and a quire of bad verses in the other. *Ib.*

13 Lars Porsena of Clusium
By the Nine Gods he swore
That the great house of Tarquin
Should suffer wrong no more.
By the Nine Gods he swore it,
And named a trysting day,
And bade his messengers ride forth
East and west and south and north,
To summon his array.
Lays of Ancient Rome [1842]. Horatius, st. 1

14 To every man upon this earth
Death cometh soon or late;
And how can man die better
Than facing fearful odds
For the ashes of his fathers,
And the temples of his gods? *Ib. st. 27*

15 But those behind cried "Forward!"
And those before cried "Back!"
Ib. st. 50

16 Oh, Tiber! father Tiber!
To whom the Romans pray,
A Roman's life, a Roman's arms,
Take thou in charge this day.
Ib. st. 59

17 And even the ranks of Tuscany
Could scarce forbear to cheer.
Ib. st. 60

18 The highest proof of virtue is to possess boundless power without abusing it.
Review of Lucy Aikin's Life and Writings of Addison [1843]

19 He [Richard Steele] was a rake among scholars, and a scholar among rakes.
Ib.

1 A man who has never looked on Niagara has but a faint idea of a cataract; and he who has not read Barère's *Memoirs* may be said not to know what it is to lie.
On Mémoires de Bertrand Barère [1844]

2 There you [Sir Robert Peel] sit, doing penance for the disingenuousness of years.
Speech in the House of Commons [April 14, 1845]

3 Forget all feuds, and shed one English tear
O'er English dust. A broken heart lies here.
Epitaph on a Jacobite [1845]

4 Those who compare the age in which their lot has fallen with a golden age[1] which exists only in imagination, may talk of degeneracy and decay; but no man who is correctly informed as to the past will be disposed to take a morose or desponding view of the present.
History of England [1849–1861], vol. I, ch. 1

5 I shall cheerfully bear the reproach of having descended below the dignity of history if I can succeed in placing before the English of the nineteenth century a true picture of the life of their ancestors. *Ib.*

6 The Puritan hated bear-baiting, not because it gave pain to the bear, but because it gave pleasure to the spectators.[2] *Ib. 2*

7 There were gentlemen and there were seamen in the navy of Charles II. But the seamen were not gentlemen, and the gentlemen were not seamen. *Ib. 3*

8 The ambassador [of Russia] and the grandees who accompanied him were so gorgeous that all London crowded to stare at them, and so filthy that nobody dared to touch them. They came to the court balls dropping pearls and vermin. *Ib. V, 23*

9 Your Constitution is all sail and no anchor.
Letter to H. S. Randall, author of a Life of Thomas Jefferson [May 23, 1857]

10 Soon fades the spell, soon comes the night;
Say will it not be then the same,
Whether we played the black or white,
Whether we lost or won the game?
Sermon in a Churchyard, st. 8

[1] See Horace, 108:11, and Milton, 277:9.

[2] Even bear-baiting was esteemed heathenish and unchristian: the sport of it, not the inhumanity, gave offense. —HUME, *History of England* [1754–1757], *vol. I, ch. 62*

Helmuth von Moltke
1800–1891

11 First ponder, then dare.[3] *Attributed*

12 The fate of every nation rests in its own power.
To the German Reichstag [March 1, 1880]

13 A war, even the most victorious, is a national misfortune. *Letter [1880]*

Richard Bethell, Lord Westbury
1800–1873

14 Take a note of that; his Lordship says he will turn it over in what he is pleased to call his mind. *Attributed*[4]

Jane Welsh Carlyle
1801–1866

15 A positive engagement to marry a certain person at a certain time, at all haps and hazards, I have always considered the most ridiculous thing on earth.
To Thomas Carlyle [January 1825]

16 In spite of the honestest efforts to annihilate my *I-ity,* or merge it in what the world doubtless considers my better half, I still find myself a self-subsisting and alas! self-seeking *me.* *To John Sterling [June 15, 1835]*

17 Oh Lord! If you but knew what a brimstone of a creature I am behind all this beautiful amiability!
To Eliza Stodart [February 29, 1836]

18 Instead of boiling up individuals into the species, I would draw a chalk circle round every individuality, and preach to it to keep within that, and preserve and cultivate its identity.
To John Sterling [August 5, 1845]

19 I can see that the Lady has a genius for ruling, whilst I have a genius for *not being ruled.*
To Thomas Carlyle [September 28, 1845]

20 The surest way to get a thing in this life is to be prepared for doing without it, to the exclusion even of hope.
Journal, August 1849

[3] Erst wägen, dann wagen.

[4] Reportedly an audible aside from the barristers' table in reference to a presiding judge. According to T. A. NASH, *Life of Lord Westbury* [1888], *vol. I, p. 158,* Westbury disclaimed invention of the mot.

1 Not a hundredth part of the thoughts in my head have ever been or ever will be spoken or written—as long as I keep my senses, at least. *Ib. July 16, 1858*

2 The triumphal procession air which, in our manners and customs, is given to marriage at the outset—that singing of *Te Deum* before the battle has begun.
To Miss Barnes [August 24, 1859]

Thomas Cole
1801–1848

3 Over all, rocks, wood, and water, brooded the spirit of repose, and the silent energy of nature stirred the soul to its inmost depths.
Essay on American Scenery [1835]

David Glasgow Farragut
1801–1870

4 Damn the torpedoes—full speed ahead!
At the battle of Mobile Bay [August 5, 1864]

John Henry Cardinal Newman
1801–1890

5 Time hath a taming hand.
Persecution [1832], st. 3

6 Lead, kindly Light, amid the encircling gloom;
Lead thou me on!
The night is dark, and I am far from home;
Lead thou me on!
Keep thou my feet: I do not ask to see
The distant scene; one step enough for me.
The Pillar of Cloud [1833]. Lead Kindly Light, st. 1

7 Growth is the only evidence of life.
Apologia pro Vita Sua [1864]

8 It is thy very energy of thought
Which keeps thee from thy God.
Dream of Gerontius [1866], pt. III

9 Living Nature, not dull Art
Shall plan my ways and rule my heart.
Nature and Art [1868], st. 12

10 O Lord, support us all the day long, until the shadows lengthen and the evening comes, and the busy world is hushed, and the fever of life is over, and our work is done. Then in thy mercy grant us a safe lodging, and a holy rest, and peace at the last.
Sermon [1834]. Included in the Book of Common Prayer

11 There is a knowledge which is desirable, though nothing come of it, as being of itself a treasure, and a sufficient remuneration of years of labor.
The Idea of a University [1873]. Discourse V, pt. 6

12 Knowledge is one thing, virtue is another.
Ib. 9

13 The world is content with setting right the surface of things. *Ib. VIII, 8*

14 A great memory does not make a philosopher, any more than a dictionary can be called a grammar.[1] *Ib. 10*

15 Ex umbris et imaginibus in veritatem [From shadows and symbols into the truth]!
His own epitaph at Edgbaston

Brigham Young
1801–1877

16 This is the place!
On first seeing the valley of the Great Salt Lake [July 24, 1847][2]

Lydia Maria Child
1802–1880

17 We first crush people to the earth, and then claim the right of trampling on them forever, because they are prostrate.
An Appeal on Behalf of That Class of Americans Called Africans [1833]

18 They [the slaves] have stabbed themselves for freedom—jumped into the waves for freedom—starved for freedom—fought like very tigers for freedom! But they have been hung, and burned, and shot—and their tyrants have been their historians! *Ib.*

19 I will work in my own way, according to the light that is in me.
Letter to Ellis Gray Loring [1843]

20 Over the river and through the wood,
To grandfather's house we go;
The horse knows the way
To carry the sleigh,
Through the white and drifted snow.
Flowers for Children [1844–1846]. Thanksgiving Day, st. 1

[1] See Lao-tzu, 65:10; Confucius, 68:10; Heraclitus, 69:28; Chaucer, 147:2; Selden, 263:18; and Penn, 314:19.

[2] Brigham Young and 142 men, three women, and two children were the vanguard of Mormon pioneers who explored westward from Nebraska. Mahonri M. Young, noted sculptor and grandson of Brigham Young, designed the "This Is the Place Monument" [dedicated 1947].

1 Woman stock is rising in the market. I shall not live to see women vote, but I'll come and rap on the ballot box.

Letter to Sarah Shaw [1856]

2 The United States is . . . a warning rather than an example to the world.

To the twenty-fifth-anniversary meeting of the Massachusetts Anti-Slavery Society [1857]

3 Yours for the unshackled exercise of every faculty by every human being.

Message to woman suffrage supporters [c. 1875]

David Christy

1802 – c. 1868

4 Cotton Is King; or, The Economical Relations of Slavery. *Title of book [1855]*[1]

Alexandre Dumas the Elder

1802–1870

5 All for one, one for all, that is our device.[2]

The Three Musketeers [1844], ch. 9

6 Nothing succeeds like success.[3]

Ange Pitou [1854], vol. I

7 Let us look for the woman.[4]

The Mohicans of Paris [1854–1855], vol. III, ch. 10, 11

Victor Hugo

1802–1885

8 These two halves of God, the Pope and the emperor. *Hernani [1830], act IV, sc. ii*

9 God became a man, granted. The devil became a woman.[5]

Ruy Blas [1838], act II, sc. v

10 Popularity? It is glory's small change.

Ib. III, v

11 An invasion of armies can be resisted, but not an idea whose time has come.[6]

Histoire d'un Crime [written 1852], conclusion

[1] Take away *time is money,* and what is left of England? take away *cotton is king,* and what is left of America? — VICTOR HUGO, *Les Misérables* [1862]. *Marius, bk. IV, ch. 4*

[2] See Shakespeare, 189:19.

[3] Rien ne réussit comme le succès. —*French proverb*

[4] The phrase "Cherchez la femme" is attributed to JOSEPH FOUCHÉ [1763–1820].

[5] Dieu s'est fait homme; soit. Le diable s'est fait femme.

[6] On résiste à l'invasion des armées; on ne résiste pas à l'invasion des idées. (Literally, one can resist the invasion of armies, but not the invasion of ideas.)

See Bellamy, 666:5, and Catt, 689:1.

12 Waterloo! Waterloo! Waterloo! Dismal plain[7]

Les Châtiments [1853]. L'Expiation

13 The eye was in the tomb and stared at Cain. *La Conscience [1859]*

14 You have created a new thrill.[8]

Letter to Baudelaire [October 6, 1859]

15 The supreme happiness of life is the conviction that we are loved.

Les Misérables [1862].[9] *Fantine, bk. V, ch. 4*

16 Great grief is a divine and terrible radiance which transfigures the wretched.

Ib. 13

17 Napoleon . . . mighty somnambulist of a vanished dream.

Ib. Cosette, bk. I, ch. 13

18 Waterloo is a battle of the first rank won by a captain of the second. *Ib. 16*

19 Would you realize what Revolution is, call it Progress; and would you realize what Progress is, call it Tomorrow. *Ib. 17*

20 What is that to the Infinite? *Ib. 18*

21 Great blunders are often made, like large ropes, of a multitude of fibers.

Ib. V, 10

22 Upon the first goblet he read this inscription, *monkey wine;* upon the second, *lion wine;* upon the third, *sheep wine;* upon the fourth, *swine wine.* These four inscriptions expressed the four descending degrees of drunkenness: the first, that which enlivens; the second, that which irritates; the third, that which stupefies; finally the last, that which brutalizes.[10] *Ib. VI, 9*

23 A man is not idle because he is absorbed in thought. There is a visible labor and there is an invisible labor. *Ib. VII, 8*

24 No one ever keeps a secret so well as a child. *Ib. VIII, 8*

25 Social prosperity means man happy, the citizen free, the nation great.

Ib. Saint Denis, bk. I, ch. 4

26 Nothing is more dangerous than discontinued labor; it is habit lost. A habit easy to abandon, difficult to resume. *Ib. II, 1*

[7] Waterloo! Waterloo! Waterloo! Morne plaine!

[8] Vous créez un frisson nouveau.

[9] Translated by CHARLES E. WILBOUR.

[10] See George Herbert, 268:3; Addison, 326:18; and Sill, 646:12.

1 Thought is the labor of the intellect, reverie is its pleasure. *Ib.*

2 Where the telescope ends, the microscope begins. Which of the two has the grander view? *Ib. III, 3*

3 A compliment is something like a kiss through a veil. *Ib. VIII, 1*

4 Great perils have this beauty, that they bring to light the fraternity of strangers. *Ib. XII, 4*

5 Philosophy is the microscope of thought. *Ib. Jean Valjean, bk. II, ch. 2*

6 To rise at six, to dine at ten,
To sup at six, to sleep at ten,
Makes a man live for ten times ten.
Inscription over the door of Hugo's study

7 I represent a party which does not yet exist: the party of revolution, civilization.
This party will make the twentieth century.
There will issue from it first the United States of Europe, then the United States of the World.
On the wall of the room in which Hugo died, Place des Vosges, Paris

Letitia Elizabeth Landon
1802–1838

8 Few, save the poor, feel for the poor.
The Poor

9 Were it not better to forget
Than but remember and regret?[1]
Despondency

George Pope Morris
1802–1864

10 Woodman, spare that tree!
Touch not a single bough![2]
In youth it sheltered me,
And I'll protect it now.
Woodman, Spare That Tree [1830], st. 1

11 The union of hearts—the union of hands—
And the flag of our Union forever!
The Flag of Our Union [1851]

[1] See Christina Rossetti, 608:15.
[2] See Campbell, 443:19.

Friedrich Julius Stahl
1802–1861

12 Authority, not majority.
Speech before the Erfurt Parliament [April 11, 1850]

William Allen
1803–1879

13 Fifty-four forty, or fight![3]
Speech in the Senate [1844]

Thomas Lovell Beddoes
1803–1849

14 The anchor heaves, the ship swings free,
The sails swell full. To sea, to sea!
Sailor's Song, st. 2

15 If there were dreams to sell,
What would you buy?
Some cost a passing-bell;
Some a light sigh. *Dream Pedlary*

George Borrow
1803–1881

16 There's night and day, brother, both sweet things; sun, moon, and stars, brother, all sweet things; there's likewise a wind on the heath. Life is very sweet, brother; who would wish to die? *Lavengro [1851], ch. 25*

17 I learned . . . to fear God, and to take my own part. *Ib. 86*

18 Youth will be served, every dog has his day, and mine has been a fine one.[4] *Ib. 92*

19 Youth is the only season for enjoyment, and the first twenty-five years of one's life are worth all the rest of the longest life of man, even though those five-and-twenty be spent in penury and contempt, and the rest in the possession of wealth, honors, respectability.
The Romany Rye [1857], ch. 30

Orestes Augustus Brownson
1803–1876

20 The English laborer does not find his worst enemy in the nobility, but in the middling class. *Boston Quarterly Review [1840]*

[3] Slogan of expansionist Democrats in the 1844 presidential campaign, in which the Oregon boundary definition was a pressing issue. The new Democratic President, James K. Polk, compromised [1846] with Great Britain on the 49th parallel.
[4] See Shakespeare, 224:24, and Kingsley, 566:14.

Edward Bulwer-Lytton, Baron Lytton

1803–1873

1 A good heart is better than all the heads in the world.

The Disowned [1828], ch. 33

2 The easiest person to deceive is one's own self. *Ib. 42*

3 In other countries poverty is a misfortune —with us it is a crime.

England and the English [1833]

4 Rank is a great beautifier.

The Lady of Lyons [1838], act II, sc. i

5 Love, like Death,
Levels all ranks, and lays the shepherd's crook
Beside the scepter. *Ib. III, ii*

6 Beneath the rule of men entirely great,
The pen is mightier than the sword.[1]

Richelieu [1839], act II, sc. ii

7 In the lexicon of youth, which fate reserves
For a bright manhood, there is no such word
As—*fail.* *Ib.*

8 Out-babying Wordsworth and outglittering Keats.[2]

The New Timon [1846], pt. I

9 In science, read, by preference, the newest works; in literature, the oldest. The classic literature is always modern.

Caxtonia. Hints on Mental Culture

10 In science, address the few, in literature the many. In science, the few must dictate opinion to the many; in literature, the many, sooner or later, force their judgment on the few. *Ib. Readers and Writers*

William Driver

1803–1886

11 I name thee Old Glory.

As the flag was hoisted to the masthead of his brig[3]

[1]See *The Teaching for Merikare*, 3:12; Cervantes, 169:34; and Burton, 259:3.

Eloquence a hundred times has turned the scale of war and peace at will.—EMERSON, *Progress of Culture* [1867]

[2]Tennyson.

[3]On August 10, 1831, a large American flag was presented to Driver, captain of the *Charles Doggett*, by a band of women in recognition of his bringing the British mutineers of the ship *Bounty* from Tahiti back to their former home, Pitcairn Island. The flag is now in the Smithsonian Institution, Washington, D.C.

Ralph Waldo Emerson

1803–1882

12 Good-bye, proud world! I'm going home;
Thou art not my friend and I'm not thine.[4]

Poems [1847]. Good-bye, st. 1

13 For what are they all in their high conceit,
When man in the bush with God may meet?

Ib. st. 4

14 Nor knowest thou what argument
Thy life to thy neighbor's creed has lent.
All are needed by each one;
Nothing is fair or good alone.

Ib. Each and All, st. 1

15 I wiped away the weeds and foam,
I fetched my sea-born treasures home;
But the poor, unsightly, noisome things
Had left their beauty on the shore,
With the sun and the sand and the wild uproar. *Ib. st. 3*

16 I like a church; I like a cowl;
I love a prophet of the soul;
And on my heart monastic aisles
Fall like sweet strains or pensive smiles;
Yet not for all his faith can see
Would I that cowlèd churchman be.

Ib. The Problem, st. 1

17 Not from a vain or shallow thought
His awful Jove young Phidias brought.

Ib. st. 2

18 The hand that rounded Peter's dome,
And groined the aisles of Christian Rome,
Wrought in a sad sincerity;
Himself from God he could not free;
He builded better than he knew—
The conscious stone to beauty grew.

Ib.

19 Earth proudly wears the Parthenon
As the best gem upon her zone.

Ib. st. 3

20 The passive Master lent his hand
To the vast soul that o'er him planned.[5]

Ib.

21 Announced by all the trumpets of the sky,
Arrives the snow. *Ib. The Snowstorm*

22 Enclosed
In a tumultuous privacy of storm. *Ib.*

23 The frolic architecture of the snow.

Ib.

[4]See Johnson, 356:27, and Byron, 458:3.

[5]This couplet is inscribed on the boulder marking Emerson's grave in Sleepy Hollow Cemetery, Concord, Massachusetts.

1 Life is too short to waste
In critic peep or cynic bark,
Quarrel or reprimand:
'Twill soon be dark;
Up! mind thine own aim, and
God speed the mark! *Ib. To J.W.*

2 There's no rood has not a star above it.
Ib. Musketaquid

3 All sorts of things and weather
Must be taken in together,
To make up a year
And a Sphere.
Ib. Fable, The Mountain and the Squirrel

4 In May, when sea winds pierced our solitudes,
I found the fresh Rhodora in the woods.
Ib. The Rhodora

5 Rhodora! if the sages ask thee why
This charm is wasted on the earth and sky,
Tell them, dear, that if eyes were made for seeing,
Then Beauty is its own excuse for being.
Ib.

6 For Nature beats in perfect tune,
And rounds with rhyme her every rune,
Whether she work in land or sea,
Or hide underground her alchemy.
Thou canst not wave thy staff in air,
Or dip thy paddle in the lake,
But it carves the bow of beauty there,
And the ripples in rhymes the oar forsake.[1]
Ib. Woodnotes II

7 Things are in the saddle,
And ride mankind.
Ib. Ode Inscribed to W. H. Channing

8 There are two laws discrete,
Not reconciled—
Law for man, and law for thing. *Ib.*

9 Olympian bards who sung
Divine ideas below,
Which always find us young,
And always keep us so.
Ib. Ode to Beauty

10 Give all to love;
Obey thy heart;
Friends, kindred, days,
Estate, good fame,
Plans, credit and the Muse,
Nothing refuse.
Ib. Give All to Love, st. 1

11 Heartily know,
When half-gods go,
The gods arrive. *Ib. st. 4*

[1]See Muir, 637:15.

12 Love not the flower they pluck, and know it not,
And all their botany is Latin names.
Ib. Blight

13 By the rude bridge that arched the flood,
Their flag to April's breeze unfurled,
Here once the embattled farmers stood,
And fired the shot heard round the world.
Ib. Hymn Sung at the Completion of the Battle Monument, Concord [July 4, 1837], st. 1

14 Hast thou named all the birds without a gun?[2]
Loved the wood-rose, and left it on its stalk?[3] *Ib. Forbearance*

15 "Pass in, pass in," the angels say,
"In to the upper doors,
Nor count compartments of the floors,
But mount to paradise
By the stairway of surprise."
Ib. Merlin I

16 God said, I am tired of kings,
I suffer them no more;
Up to my ear the morning brings
The outrage of the poor.
May-Day and Other Pieces [1867]. Boston Hymn,[4] *st. 2*

17 Today unbind the captive,
So only are ye unbound;
Lift up a people from the dust,
Trump of their rescue, sound!
Ib. st. 17

18 Oh, tenderly the haughty day
Fills his blue urn with fire.
Ib. Ode, st. 1

19 Go put your creed into your deed,
Nor speak with double tongue.
Ib. st. 5

20 I think no virtue goes with size.
Ib. The Titmouse

21 So nigh is grandeur to our dust,
So near is God to man,
When Duty whispers low, *Thou must,*
The youth replies, *I can.*
Ib. Voluntaries, III

22 Nor sequent centuries could hit
Orbit and sum of Shakespeare's wit.
Ib. Solution

23 Nor mourn the unalterable Days
That Genius goes and Folly stays.
Ib. In Memoriam E.B.E.

[2]See Foss, 685:10.
[3]Love thou the rose, yet leave it on its stem.—LYTTON, *The Wanderer* [1857], *prologue, pt. I, l. 19*
[4]Read at a celebration in Boston of Emancipation Day [January 1, 1863].

1 Fear not, then, thou child infirm,
There's no god dare wrong a worm.
Ib. Compensation, I

2 He thought it happier to be dead,
To die for Beauty, than live for bread.
Ib. Beauty

3 Wilt thou seal up the avenues of ill?
Pay every debt, as if God wrote the bill.
Ib. "Suum Cuique"

4 Too busied with the crowded hour to fear to live or die. *Ib. Nature*

5 Daughters of Time, the hypocritic Days,
Muffled and dumb like barefoot dervishes,
And marching single in an endless file,
Bring diadems and fagots in their hands.
Ib. Days

6 I, too late,
Under her solemn fillet saw the scorn.
Ib.

7 It is time to be old,
To take in sail. *Ib. Terminus*

8 Obey the voice at eve obeyed at prime.
Ib.

9 Though love repine, and reason chafe,
There came a voice without reply—
" 'Tis man's perdition to be safe,
When for the truth he ought to die."
Ib. Sacrifice

10 For what avail the plow or sail,
Or land or life, if freedom fail?
Ib. Boston, st. 5

11 If the red slayer think he slays,
Or if the slain think he is slain,
They know not well the subtle ways
I keep, and pass, and turn again.[1]
Ib. Brahma

12 They reckon ill who leave me out;
When me they fly, I am the wings;
I am the doubter and the doubt,
And I the hymn the Brahmin sings.
Ib.

13 That book is good
Which puts me in a working mood.
Unless to Thought is added Will,
Apollo is an imbecile.
Ib. Fragments on the Poetic Gift

14 In the vaunted works of Art
The master stroke is Nature's part.[2]
Ib. Art

15 I am the owner of the sphere,
Of the seven stars and the solar year,
Of Caesar's hand, and Plato's brain,
Of Lord Christ's heart, and Shakespeare's strain. *Ib. History*

16 Ever from one who comes tomorrow
Men wait their good and truth to borrow.
Ib. Merlin's Song

17 The music that can deepest reach,
And cure all ill, is cordial speech. *Ib.*

18 Some of your hurts you have cured,
And the sharpest you still have survived,
But what torments of grief you endured
From evils which never arrived![3]
Ib. Borrowing [from the French]

19 A ruddy drop of manly blood
The surging sea outweighs,
The world uncertain comes and goes,
The lover rooted stays. *Ib. Friendship*

20 To different minds, the same world is a hell, and a heaven.
Journal. December 20, 1822

21 Four snakes gliding up and down a hollow for no purpose that I could see—not to eat, not for love, but only gliding.
Ib. April 11, 1834

22 I wish to write such rhymes as shall not suggest a restraint, but contrariwise the wildest freedom. *Ib. June 27, 1839*

23 You shall have joy, or you shall have power, said God; you shall not have both.
Ib. October 1842

24 The sky is the daily bread of the eyes.
Ib. May 25, 1843

25 Poetry must be as new as foam, and as old as the rock. *Ib. March 1845*

26 I hate quotations. Tell me what you know.
Ib. May 1849

27 Blessed are those who have no talent!
Ib. February 1850

28 The word *liberty* in the mouth of Mr. Webster sounds like the word *love* in the mouth of a courtesan.
Ib. February 12 (?), 1851

29 I trust a good deal to common fame, as we all must. If a man has good corn, or wood, or boards, or pigs, to sell, or can make better chairs or knives, crucibles or church organs,

[1]See *The Upanishads*, 56:25.

[2]Nature paints the best part of a picture, carves the best part of the statue, builds the best part of the house, and speaks the best part of the oration.—EMERSON, *Society and Solitude* [1870], *Art*

[3]Let us be of good cheer, however, remembering that the misfortunes hardest to bear are those which never come.—JAMES RUSSELL LOWELL, *Democracy and Addresses* [1884]

than anybody else, you will find a broad hard-beaten road to his house, though it be in the woods.[1] *Ib. February 1855*

1 The blazing evidence of immortality is our dissatisfaction with any other solution.
Ib. July 1855

2 Undoubtedly we have no questions to ask which are unanswerable. We must trust the perfection of the creation so far as to believe that whatever curiosity the order of things has awakened in our minds, the order of things can satisfy.
Nature [1836], introduction

3 Nature never wears a mean appearance. Neither does the wisest man extort her secret and lose his curiosity by finding out all her perfection. *Ib. sec. 1*

4 Standing on the bare ground . . . all mean egotism vanishes. I become a transparent eyeball; I am nothing; I see all; the currents of the Universal Being circulate through me; I am part and parcel of God.
Ib.

5 Give me health and a day and I will make the pomp of emperors ridiculous. *Ib. 3*

6 Every natural fact is a symbol of some spiritual fact. *Ib. 4*

7 We are like Nebuchadnezzar, dethroned, bereft of reason, and eating grass like an ox.
Ib. 8

8 A man is a god in ruins.[2] *Ib.*

9 He who has mastered any law in his private thoughts, is master to that extent of all men whose language he speaks, and of all into whose language his own can be translated.
The American Scholar [1837], sec. 3

10 Wherever Macdonald[3] sits, there is the head of the table. *Ib.*

11 What would we really know the meaning of? The meal in the firkin; the milk in the pan; the ballad in the street; the news of the boat. *Ib.*

[1] If a man can write a better book, preach a better sermon, or make a better mousetrap than his neighbor, though he builds his house in the woods the world will make a beaten path to his door.—*Attributed to* EMERSON *(in a lecture) by* SARAH S. B. YULE and MARY S. KEENE, *Borrowings* [1889]

[2] See Lamartine, 464:16.

[3] Often quoted as: Macgregor.

12 If the single man plant himself indomitably on his instincts, and there abide, the huge world will come round to him.[4] *Ib.*

13 Men grind and grind in the mill of a truism, and nothing comes out but what was put in. But the moment they desert the tradition for a spontaneous thought, then poetry, wit, hope, virtue, learning, anecdote, all flock to their aid. *Literary Ethics [1838]*

14 I have no expectation that any man will read history aright who thinks that what was done in a remote age, by men whose names have resounded far, has any deeper sense than what he is doing today.
Essays: First Series [1841]. History

15 Time dissipates to shining ether the solid angularity of facts. *Ib.*

16 There is properly no history; only biography.[5] *Ib.*

17 Nature is a mutable cloud, which is always and never the same. *Ib.*

18 It is the fault of our rhetoric that we cannot strongly state one fact without seeming to belie some other. *Ib.*

19 To believe your own thought, to believe that what is true for you in your private heart is true for all men—that is genius.
Ib. Self-Reliance

20 We but half express ourselves, and are ashamed of that divine idea which each of us represents.[6] *Ib.*

21 Accept the place the divine providence has found for you, the society of your contemporaries, the connection of events. *Ib.*

22 Society everywhere is in conspiracy against the manhood of every one of its members. . . . The virtue in most request is conformity. Self-reliance is its aversion. It loves not realities and creators, but names and customs. *Ib.*

23 Whoso would be a man must be a nonconformist. *Ib.*

24 The doctrine of hatred must be preached, as the counteraction of the doctrine of love, when that pules and whines. I shun father and mother and wife and brother when my genius calls me. *Ib.*

[4] See Disraeli, 501:26, and Burroughs, 630:21.
All things come round to him who will but wait.—LONGFELLOW, *Tales of a Wayside Inn, The Student's Tale* [1863]

[5] See Carlyle, 473:24.

[6] See Browne, 274:22, and Addison, 326:3.

1 It is easy in the world to live after the world's opinion; it is easy in solitude to live after our own; but the great man is he who in the midst of the crowd keeps with perfect sweetness the independence of solitude. *Ib.*

2 A foolish consistency is the hobgoblin of little minds, adored by little statesmen and philosophers and divines. With consistency a great soul has simply nothing to do. . . . Speak what you think today in hard words and tomorrow speak what tomorrow thinks in hard words again, though it contradict everything you said today. *Ib.*

3 To be great is to be misunderstood. *Ib.*

4 An institution is the lengthened shadow of one man. *Ib.*

5 I like the silent church before the service begins, better than any preaching. *Ib.*

6 Discontent is the want of self-reliance: it is infirmity of will. *Ib.*

7 Traveling is a fool's paradise. . . . My giant goes with me wherever I go. *Ib.*

8 For every Stoic was a Stoic; but in Christendom where is the Christian?[1] *Ib.*

9 Nothing can bring you peace but yourself. *Ib.*

10 Every sweet has its sour; every evil its good. *Ib. Compensation*

11 For everything you have missed, you have gained something else; and for everything you gain, you lose something else. *Ib.*

12 Everything in Nature contains all the powers of Nature. Everything is made of one hidden stuff. *Ib.*

13 It is as impossible for a man to be cheated by anyone but himself, as for a thing to be, and not to be, at the same time. *Ib.*

14 All mankind love a lover. *Ib. Love*

15 Thou art to me a delicious torment. *Ib. Friendship*

16 Almost all people descend to meet.[2] *Ib.*

17 Happy is the house that shelters a friend. *Ib.*

18 A friend is a person with whom I may be sincere. Before him, I may think aloud. *Ib.*

[1] See Melville, 570:2.

[2] Men descend to meet. — EMERSON, *Essays. First Series, The Over-Soul*

19 A friend may well be reckoned the masterpiece of Nature. *Ib.*

20 Two may talk and one may hear, but three cannot take part in a conversation of the most sincere and searching sort. *Ib.*

21 The only reward of virtue is virtue; the only way to have a friend is to be one. *Ib.*

22 I do then with my friends as I do with my books. I would have them where I can find them, but I seldom use them. *Ib.*

23 In skating over thin ice our safety is in our speed. *Ib. Prudence*

24 Heroism feels and never reasons and therefore is always right. *Ib. Heroism*

25 Beware when the great God lets loose a thinker on this planet. *Ib. Circles*

26 One man's justice is another's injustice; one man's beauty another's ugliness; one man's wisdom another's folly. *Ib.*

27 Nature abhors the old, and old age seems the only disease;[3] all others run into this one. *Ib.*

28 Nothing great was ever achieved without enthusiasm. *Ib.*

29 Nothing astonishes men so much as common sense and plain dealing. *Ib. Art*

30 Beauty will not come at the call of a legislature, nor will it repeat in England or America its history in Greece. It will come, as always, unannounced, and spring up between the feet of brave and earnest men. *Ib.*

31 I fancy I need more than another to speak (rather than write), with such a formidable tendency to the lapidary style. I build my house of boulders. *Letter to Carlyle [October 30, 1841]*

32 A man may love a paradox without either losing his wit or his honesty. *Walter Savage Landor. From The Dial [1841], XII*

33 Literature is the effort of man to indemnify himself for the wrongs of his condition. *Ib.*

34 There is always a certain meanness in the argument of conservatism, joined with a certain superiority in its fact. *The Conservative [1842]*

[3] Old age is an incurable disease. — SENECA, *Epistulae ad Lucilium, no. 108*

1 For it is not meters, but a metermaking argument that makes a poem—a thought so passionate and alive that like the spirit of a plant or an animal it has an architecture of its own, and adorns nature with a new thing.

Essays: Second Series [1844]. The Poet

2 We are symbols, and inhabit symbols. *Ib.*

3 Language is the archives of history. . . . Language is fossil poetry. *Ib.*

4 Nature and books belong to the eyes that see them. *Ib. Experience*

5 Of what use is genius, if the organ is too convex or too concave and cannot find a focal distance within the actual horizon of human life? *Ib.*

6 The only gift is a portion of thyself.[1] *Ib. Gifts*

7 The less government we have, the better—the fewer laws, and the less confided power. *Ib. Politics*

8 We think our civilization near its meridian, but we are yet only at the cock-crowing and the morning star. In our barbarous society the influence of character is in its infancy. *Ib.*

9 Money, which represents the prose of life, and which is hardly spoken of in parlors without an apology, is, in its effects and laws, as beautiful as roses.

Ib. Nominalist and Realist

10 Every man is wanted, and no man is wanted much. *Ib.*

11 The reward of a thing well done, is to have done it. *Ib.*

12 He is great who is what he is from Nature, and who never reminds us of others.

Representative Men [1850]. Uses of Great Men

13 When nature removes a great man, people explore the horizon for a successor; but none comes, and none will. His class is extinguished with him. In some other and quite different field, the next man will appear. *Ib.*

14 Every hero becomes a bore at last. *Ib.*

15 Great geniuses have the shortest biographies. *Ib. Plato; or, The Philosopher*

[1]See Lowell, 567:14; Whitman, 574:26; and Gibran, 782:16.

16 Things added to things, as statistics, civil history, are inventories. Things used as language are inexhaustibly attractive. *Ib.*

17 Keep cool: it will be all one a hundred years hence.[2] *Ib. Montaigne; or, The Skeptic*

18 Is not marriage an open question, when it is alleged, from the beginning of the world, that such as are in the institution wish to get out, and such as are out wish to get in?[3] *Ib.*

19 Self-reliance, the height and perfection of man, is reliance on God.

The Fugitive Slave Law [1854]

20 Classics which at home are drowsily read have a strange charm in a country inn, or in the transom of a merchant brig.

English Traits [1856]

21 Great men, great nations, have not been boasters and buffoons, but perceivers of the terror of life, and have manned themselves to face it.

The Conduct of Life [1860]. Fate

22 Men are what their mothers made them.[4] *Ib.*

23 Coal is a portable climate. *Ib. Wealth*

24 The world is his, who has money to go over it. *Ib.*

25 Art is a jealous mistress.[5] *Ib.*

26 All educated Americans, first or last, go to Europe. *Ib. Culture*

27 Solitude, the safeguard of mediocrity, is to genius the stern friend. *Ib.*

28 There is always a best way of doing everything, if it be to boil an egg. Manners are the happy ways of doing things. *Ib. Behavior*

29 Fine manners need the support of fine manners in others. *Ib.*

30 The highest compact we can make with our fellow is—"Let there be truth between us two forevermore." *Ib.*

31 Shallow men believe in luck.[6] *Ib. Worship*

[2]What matters what anybody thinks? "It will be all the same a hundred years hence." That is the most sensible proverb ever invented.—GEORGE DU MAURIER, *Peter Ibbetson* [1891]

[3]See Montaigne, 165:19.

[4]See Freud, 679:6.

[5]See Story, 447:18.

[6]Luck is infatuated with the efficient.—*Persian proverb*

1 I wish that life should not be cheap, but sacred. I wish the days to be as centuries, loaded, fragrant.

Ib. Considerations by the Way

2 Our chief want in life is somebody who shall make us do what we can. *Ib.*

3 Make yourself necessary to somebody. *Ib.*

4 Beauty without grace is the hook without the bait. *Ib. Beauty*

5 Never read any book that is not a year old. *Ib. In Praise of Books*

6 The key to the period appeared to be that the mind had become aware of itself. . . . The young men were born with knives in their brain, a tendency to introversion, self-dissection, anatomizing of motives.

Life and Letters in New England [1867]

7 God may forgive sins, he said, but awkwardness has no forgiveness in heaven or earth.

Society and Solitude [1870]. Society and Solitude

8 The most advanced nations are always those who navigate the most.

Ib. Civilization

9 Hitch your wagon to a star.[1] *Ib.*

10 The true test of civilization is, not the census, nor the size of cities, nor the crops—no, but the kind of man the country turns out. *Ib.*

11 Every genuine work of art has as much reason for being as the earth and the sun. *Ib. Art*

12 A masterpiece of art has in the mind a fixed place in the chain of being, as much as a plant or a crystal. *Ib.*

13 We boil at different degrees. *Ib. Eloquence*

14 The best university that can be recommended to a man of ideas is the gauntlet of the mobs. *Ib.*

15 The ornament of a house is the friends who frequent it. *Ib. Domestic Life*

16 Can anybody remember when the times were not hard and money not scarce? *Ib. Works and Days*

17 'Tis the good reader that makes the good book; in every book he finds passages which seem confidences or asides hidden from all else and unmistakably meant for his ear; the profit of books is according to the sensibility of the reader; the profoundest thought or passion sleeps as in a mine, until it is discovered by an equal mind and heart.

Ib. Success

[1]See Carl Schurz, 603:2.

18 We do not count a man's years until he has nothing else to count. *Ib. Old Age*

19 A mollusk is a cheap edition [of man] with a suppression of the costlier illustrations, designed for dingy circulation, for shelving in an oyster-bank or among the seaweed.

Power and Laws of Thought [c. 1870]

20 Poetry teaches the enormous force of a few words, and, in proportion to the inspiration, checks loquacity.

Parnassus [1874]. Preface

21 There are two classes of poets—the poets by education and practice, these we respect; and poets by nature, these we love. *Ib.*

22 Life is not so short but that there is always time enough for courtesy.

Letters and Social Aims [1875]. Social Aims

23 I have heard with admiring submission the experience of the lady who declared that the sense of being perfectly well-dressed gives a feeling of inward tranquillity which religion is powerless to bestow. *Ib.*

24 Do not say things. What you are stands over you the while, and thunders so that I cannot hear what you say to the contrary. *Ib.*

25 Every really able man, in whatever direction he work . . . if you talk sincerely with him, considers his work, however much admired, as far short of what it should be.

Ib. Immortality

26 Great men are they who see that spiritual is stronger than any material force, that thoughts rule the world.

Ib. Progress and Culture, Phi Beta Kappa Address [July 18, 1876]

27 Next to the originator of a good sentence is the first quoter of it.[2]

Ib. Quotation and Originality

[2]There is not less wit nor less invention in applying rightly a thought one finds in a book, than in being the first author of that thought.—PIERRE BAYLE, *Dictionnaire Historique et Critique* [1697–1702]
See James Russell Lowell, 568:21.

1 When Shakespeare is charged with debts to his authors, Landor replies, "Yet he was more original than his originals. He breathed upon dead bodies and brought them into life." *Ib.*

2 By necessity, by proclivity, and by delight, we all quote. *Ib.*

3 A good symbol is the best argument, and is a missionary to persuade thousands.
Ib. Poetry and Imagination

4 Wit makes its own welcome, and levels all distinctions. *Ib. The Comic*

5 The perception of the comic is a tie of sympathy with other men. *Ib.*

6 What is a weed? A plant whose virtues have not yet been discovered.[1]
Fortune of the Republic [1878]

7 To live without duties is obscene.
Lectures and Biographical Sketches [1883]. Aristocracy

8 Speak the affirmative; emphasize your choice by utter ignoring of all that you reject.
Ib. The Preacher

9 Genius has no taste for weaving sand.
Ib. The Scholar

10 A poet in verse or prose must have a sensuous eye, but an intellectual co-perception.
Ib. Plutarch

11 All the thoughts of a turtle are turtles, and of a rabbit, rabbits.
The Natural History of Intellect [1893]

12 When you strike at a king, you must kill him.
Recollected by OLIVER WENDELL HOLMES, JR. *From* MAX LERNER, *The Mind and Faith of Justice Holmes [1943]*

Robert Stephen Hawker
1803–1875

13 And shall Trelawny die?
Here's twenty thousand Cornish men
Will know the reason why.
The Song of the Western Men [1825],[2] st. 1

[1] A weed is no more than a flower in disguise.—JAMES RUSSELL LOWELL, *A Fable for Critics* [1848]
A weed is but an unloved flower!—ELLA WHEELER WILCOX [1850–1919], *The Weed, st. 1*

[2] "And shall Trelawny die?" has been a popular phrase throughout Cornwall since the imprisonment in the Tower of London [1688] of Sir Jonathan Trelawny [1650–1721] with six other prelates for refusing to recognize the Declaration of Indulgence issued by James II.

Richard Henry Hengist Horne
1803–1884

14 'Tis always morning somewhere in the world.[3]
Orion [1843], bk. III, canto 2

Douglas Jerrold
1803–1857

15 Dogmatism is puppyism come to its full growth.
Wit and Opinions of Douglas Jerrold [1859]

16 That fellow would vulgarize the day of judgment. *Ib. A Comic Author*

17 Some people are so fond of ill luck that they run halfway to meet it.
Ib. Meeting Troubles Halfway

18 Talk to him of Jacob's ladder, and he would ask the number of the steps.
Ib. A Matter-of-fact Man

Robert Smith Surtees
1803–1864

19 Jorrocks' Jaunts and Jollities.
Title of novel [1838]

20 Full o' beans and benevolence.
Handley Cross [1843], ch. 27

21 Three things I never lends—my 'oss, my wife, and my name.
Hillingdon Hall [1845], ch. 33

22 More people are flattered into virtue than bullied out of vice.
The Analysis of the Hunting Field [1846], ch. 1

23 Better be killed than frightened to death.
Mr. Facey Romford's Hounds [1864], ch. 32

Fëdor Tiutchev
1803–1873

24 A thought, once uttered, is a lie.
Silentium [1830]

25 Like first love, the heart of Russia will not forget you.
Tribute to Pushkin [January 29, 1837]

26 Homeland of patience, land of the Russian people. *These Poor Villages [1855]*

[3] See Longfellow, 513:2.

Benjamin Disraeli, Earl of Beaconsfield
1804–1881

1 The microcosm of a public school.
Vivian Grey [1826], bk. I, ch. 2

2 I hate definitions. *Ib. II, 6*

3 Experience is the child of Thought, and Thought is the child of Action. We cannot learn men from books. *Ib. V, 1*

4 Variety is the mother of Enjoyment.
Ib. 4

5 There is moderation even in excess.
Ib. VI, 1

6 I repeat . . . that all power is a trust; that we are accountable for its exercise; that, from the people, and for the people, all springs, and all must exist.[1] *Ib. 7*

7 Man is not the creature of circumstances. Circumstances are the creatures of men.
Ib.

8 A *dark* horse, which had never been thought of, and which the careless St. James had never even observed in the list, rushed past the grandstand in sweeping triumph.
The Young Duke [1831], bk. I, ch. 5

9 Yes, I am a Jew, and when the ancestors of the right honorable gentleman were brutal savages in an unknown island, mine were priests in the temple of Solomon.[2]
Reply to a taunt by Daniel O'Connell

10 What we anticipate seldom occurs; what we least expected generally happens.
Henrietta Temple [1837], bk. II, ch. 4

11 Though I sit down now, the time will come when you will hear me.[3]
Maiden speech in the House of Commons [1837]

12 Free trade is not a principle, it is an expedient.[4]
Speech on import duties [April 25, 1843]

[1]See Wycliffe, 143:12; Webster, 450:14; Garrison, 505:19; Lincoln, 523:4; and Parker, 537:15.

[2]The gentleman will please remember that when his half-civilized ancestors were hunting the wild boar in the forests of Silesia, mine were the princes of the earth. — Judah P. Benjamin [1811–1884], *reply to a senator; from* Ben Perley Poore, *Reminiscences of Sixty Years in the National Metropolis* [1886]

[3]See Garrison, 505:13.

[4]See Grover Cleveland, 631:10.

13 The noble lord [Lord Stanley] is the Rupert[5] of Parliamentary discussion.
Speech [April 1844]

14 A government of statesmen or of clerks? Of Humbug or Humdrum?
Coningsby [1844], bk. II, ch. 4

15 Youth is a blunder; manhood a struggle; old age a regret. *Ib. III, 1*

16 Man is only truly great when he acts from the passions. *Ib. IV, 13*

17 I rather like bad wine . . . one gets so bored with good wine.
Sybil [1845], bk. I, ch. 1

18 Two nations, between whom there is no intercourse and no sympathy; who are as ignorant of each other's habits, thoughts, and feelings as if they were dwellers in different zones, or inhabitants of different planets; who are formed by a different breeding, are fed by a different food, are ordered by different manners, and are not governed by the same laws . . . *the rich and the poor.*
Ib. II, 5

19 Property has its duties as well as its rights.[6] *Ib. 11*

20 Little things affect little minds.
Ib. III, 2

21 We all of us live too much in a circle.[7]
Ib. 7

22 The right honorable gentleman[8] caught the Whigs bathing and walked away with their clothes.
Speech in the House of Commons [February 28, 1845]

23 A conservative government is an organized hypocrisy.
Speech on Agricultural Interests [March 17, 1845]

24 Duty cannot exist without faith.
Tancred [1847], bk. II, ch. 1

25 He was fresh and full of faith that "something would turn up."[9] *Ib. III, 6*

26 Everything comes if a man will only wait.[10] *Ib. IV, 8*

[5]Prince Rupert [1619–1682], nephew of Charles I.

[6]Property has its duties as well as its rights. — Captain Thomas Drummond (inventor of the Drummond light), *Letter to the Landlords of Tipperary* [May 22, 1838]

[7]The life of man is a self-evolving circle. — Emerson, *Essays [1st series, 1841], Circles*

[8]Sir Robert Peel.

[9]See Dickens, 548:25.

[10]See Emerson, 496:12, and Burroughs, 630:21.

1 A precedent embalms a principle.
Speech on the expenditures of the country [February 22, 1848]

2 Justice is truth in action.
Speech [February 11, 1851]

3 How much easier it is to be critical than to be correct. *Speech [January 24, 1860]*

4 Is man an ape or an angel?[1] I, my lord, I am on the side of the angels. I repudiate with indignation and abhorrence those newfangled theories.
Speech at Oxford Diocesan Conference [November 25, 1864]

5 In the character of the victim [Lincoln], and even in the accessories of his last moments, there is something so homely and innocent that it takes the question, as it were, out of all the pomp of history and the ceremonial of diplomacy—it touches the heart of nations and appeals to the domestic sentiment of mankind.
Speech in the House of Commons [May 1, 1865]

6 Ignorance never settles a question.
Ib. [May 14, 1866]

7 Individualities may form communities, but it is institutions alone that can create a nation. *Speech at Manchester [1866]*

8 However gradual may be the growth of confidence, that of credit requires still more time to arrive at maturity.
Speech [November 9, 1867]

9 I have climbed to the top of the greasy pole.
To friends, on being made prime minister [1868]

10 When a man fell into his anecdotage, it was a sign for him to retire.
Lothair [1870], ch. 28

11 Every woman should marry—and no man.
Ib. 30

12 You know who the critics are? The men who have failed in literature and art.[2]
Ib. 35

13 "My idea of an agreeable person," said Hugo Bohun, "is a person who agrees with me." *Ib.*

14 Increased means and increased leisure are the two civilizers of man.
Speech to the Conservatives of Manchester [April 3, 1872]

[1]See Pascal, 299:17, and Darwin, 515:7.
[2]See Coleridge, 436:15; Lowell, 567:19; and Flaubert, 583:8.

15 The secret of success is constancy to purpose. *Speech [June 24, 1872]*

16 A university should be a place of light, of liberty, and of learning.
Speech in the House of Commons [March 11, 1873]

17 The health of the people is really the foundation upon which all their happiness and all their powers as a state depend.
Speech [July 24, 1877]

18 Lord Salisbury and myself have brought you back peace—but a peace I hope with honor.[3]
Speech in the House of Commons [July 16, 1878]

19 A series of congratulatory regrets.[4]
Speech at Knightsbridge [July 27, 1878]

20 A sophistical rhetorician [Gladstone], inebriated with the exuberance of his own verbosity, and gifted with an egotistical imagination that can at all times command an interminable and inconsistent series of arguments to malign an opponent and to glorify himself. *Ib.*

21 The harebrained chatter of irresponsible frivolity.
Speech at the Guildhall, London [November 9, 1878]

22 The Athanasian Creed is the most splendid ecclesiastical lyric ever poured forth by the genius of man. *Ib. 52*

23 "As for that," said Waldershare, "sensible men are all of the same religion." "And pray, what is that?" inquired the prince. "Sensible men never tell."[5] *Ib. 81*

Gavarni
[Sulpice Guillaume Chevalier]
1804–1866

24 Les Enfants Terribles [The Terrible Children]. *Title of series of prints [1865]*

Nathaniel Hawthorne
1804–1864

25 Amid the seeming confusion of our mysterious world, individuals are so nicely adjusted to a system, and systems to one another and to a whole, that, by stepping aside

[3]See Russell, 466:3, and Chamberlain, 727:2.
[4]Lord Hartington's Resolution on the Berlin Treaty.
[5]See Samuel Johnson, 354:*n*4.

for a moment, a man exposes himself to a fearful risk of losing his place forever.

Wakefield [1835]

1 His hour is one of darkness, and adversity, and peril. But should domestic tyranny oppress us, or the invader's step pollute our soil, still may the Gray Champion come, for he is the type of New England's hereditary spirit; and his shadowy march, on the eve of danger, must ever be the pledge, that New England's sons will vindicate their ancestry.

The Gray Champion [1835]

2 By the sympathy of your human hearts for sin ye shall scent out all the places—whether in church, bedchamber, street, field, or forest—where crime has been committed, and shall exult to behold the whole earth one stain of guilt, one mighty blood spot.

Young Goodman Brown [1835]

3 As the moral gloom of the world overpowers all systematic gaiety, even so was their home of wild mirth made desolate amid the sad forest.

The Maypole of Merrymount [1836]

4 "What is the Unpardonable Sin?" asked the lime-burner. . . .

"It is a sin that grew within my own breast," replied Ethan Brand. . . . "The sin of an intellect that triumphed over the sense of brotherhood with man and reverence for God." *Ethan Brand [1850]*

5 On the breast of her gown, in red cloth, surrounded with an elaborate embroidery and fantastic flourishes of gold thread, appeared the letter A.

The Scarlet Letter [1850], ch. 2

6 My heart was a habitation large enough for many guests, but lonely and chill, and without a household fire. I longed to kindle one! It seemed not so wild a dream. *Ib. 4*

7 There is a fatality, a feeling so irresistible and inevitable that it has the force of doom, which almost invariably compels human beings to linger around and haunt, ghostlike, the spot where some great and marked event has given the color to their lifetime; and still the more irresistibly, the darker the tinge that saddens it. *Ib. 5*

8 Wherever there is a heart and an intellect, the diseases of the physical frame are tinged with the peculiarities of these. *Ib. 9*

9 Let the black flower blossom as it may!

Ib. 14

10 Let men tremble to win the hand of woman, unless they win along with it the utmost passion of her heart. *Ib. 15*

11 "Never, never!" whispered she. "What we did had a consecration of its own."

Ib. 17

12 The scarlet letter was her passport into regions where other women dared not tread. Shame, Despair, Solitude! These had been her teachers—stern and wild ones—and they had made her strong, but taught her much amiss. *Ib. 18*

13 No man, for any considerable period, can wear one face to himself, and another to the multitude, without finally getting bewildered as to which may be the true. *Ib. 20*

14 Among many morals which press upon us from the poor minister's miserable experience, we put only this into a sentence: "Be true! Be true! Show freely to the world, if not your worst, yet some trait whereby the worst may be inferred." *Ib. 24*

15 The book, if you would see anything in it, requires to be read in the clear, brown, twilight atmosphere in which it was written; if opened in the sunshine, it is apt to look exceedingly like a volume of blank pages.

Twice-Told Tales [1851], preface

16 Not to be deficient in this particular, the author has provided himself with a moral—the truth, namely, that the wrongdoing of one generation lives into the successive ones.

The House of the Seven Gables [1851], preface

17 God will give him blood to drink!

Ib. ch. 1

18 Life is made up of marble and mud.

Ib. 2

19 What other dungeon is so dark as one's own heart! What jailer so inexorable as one's self!

Ib. 11

20 Of all the events which constitute a person's biography, there is scarcely one . . . to which the world so easily reconciles itself as to his death. *Ib. 21*

21 The greatest obstacle to being heroic is the doubt whether one may not be going to prove one's self a fool; the truest heroism is, to resist the doubt; and the profoundest wisdom, to know when it ought to be resisted, and when to be obeyed.

The Blithedale Romance [1852], ch. 2

22 It is because the spirit is inestimable that the lifeless body is so little valued.

Ib. 28

1 In youth men are apt to write more wisely than they really know or feel; and the remainder of life may be not idly spent in realizing and convincing themselves of the wisdom they uttered long ago.
The Snow Image [1852], preface

2 No author, without a trial, can conceive of the difficulty of writing a romance about a country where there is no shadow, no antiquity, no mystery, no picturesque and gloomy wrong, nor anything but a commonplace prosperity, in broad and simple daylight, as is happily the case with my dear native land. . . . Romance and poetry, ivy, lichens and wallflowers need ruin to make them grow.
The Marble Faun [1860], preface

3 Nobody, I think, ought to read poetry, or look at pictures or statues, who cannot find a great deal more in them than the poet or artist has actually expressed.[1] *Ib. 41*

4 Mountains are earth's undecaying monuments.
Sketches from Memory [1868]. The Notch of the White Mountains

Charles Augustin Sainte-Beuve
1804–1869

5 Vigny, more secret,
As if in his tower of ivory, retired before noon.[2]
Pensées d'Août, à M. Villemain [1837], st. 3

6 Silence is the sovereign contempt.[3]
Mes Poisons

George Sand[4] [Amandine Aurore Lucie Dupin, Baronne Dudevant]
1804–1876

7 Love, bumping his head blindly against all the obstacles of civilization.
Indiana [1832], preface

[1] Every book is written with a constant secret reference to the few intelligent persons whom the writer believes to exist in the million. . . . The artist has always the masters in his eye. — EMERSON, *Progress of Culture* [1867]

[2] Vigny, plus secret, / Comme en sa tour d'ivoire, avant midi, rentrait.

The poet, retired in his Tower of Ivory, isolated, according to his desire, from the world of man, resembles, whether he so wishes or not, another solitary figure, the watcher enclosed for months at a time in a lighthouse at the head of a cliff. — JULES DE GAULTIER [b. 1858], *La Guerre et les Destinées de l'Art*

[3] Le silence seul est le souverain mépris.

[4] See Elizabeth Barrett Browning, 506:13.

She will remain one of the radiant splendors of France, unequaled in her glory. — GUSTAVE FLAUBERT [1821–1880], *Letter to Mademoiselle de Chantepie*

8 No human creature can give orders to love.
Jacques [1834]

9 Deliberately, women are given a deplorable education . . . While man frees himself from constraining civil and religious bonds, he is only too glad to have woman hold tightly to the Christian principle of suffering and keeping her silence.[5]
Letters to Marcie [1837]

10 We cannot tear out a single page of our life, but we can throw the whole book in the fire.
Mauprat [1837]

11 Charity degrades those who receive it and hardens those who dispense it. All that is not a true change will disappear in the future society. *Consuelo [1842]*

12 They [the peasants] were born kings of the earth far more truly than those who possess it only from having bought it.
The Haunted Pool [1851]

13 Life in common among people who love each other is the ideal of happiness.
Histoire de Ma Vie [1856]

14 In our wholly factitious society, to have no cash at all means frightful want or absolute powerlessness. *Ib.*

15 There is only one happiness in life, to love and be loved.
Letter to Lina Calamatta [March 31, 1862]

16 Faith is an excitement and an enthusiasm: it is a condition of intellectual magnificence to which we must cling as to a treasure, and not squander . . . in the small coin of empty words, or in exact and priggish argument.
Letter to Des Planches [May 25, 1866]

17 The whole secret of the study of nature lies in learning how to use one's eyes.
Nouvelles Lettres d'un Voyageur [1869]

18 Art for art's sake is an empty phrase. Art for the sake of the true, art for the sake of the good and the beautiful, that is the faith I am searching for.
Letter to Alexandre Saint-Jean [1872]

19 I would rather believe that God did not exist than believe that He was indifferent.
Impressions et Souvenirs [1896]

[5] See Abigail Adams, 392:12.

Sarah Flower Adams
1805–1848

1 Yet in my dreams I'd be
Nearer, my God, to Thee,
Nearer to Thee.

Nearer, My God, to Thee, st. 2

Hans Christian Andersen
1805–1875

2 They could see she was a real princess and no question about it, now that she had felt one pea all the way through twenty mattresses and twenty more feather beds. Nobody but a princess could be so delicate.

Fairy Tales [1835].[1] *The Princess and the Pea*

3 Far out in the ocean the water is as blue as the petals of the loveliest cornflower, and as clear as the purest glass. But it is very deep too. . . . Many, many steeples would have to be stacked one on top of another to reach from the bottom to the surface of the sea. It is down there that the sea folk live.

Ib. The Little Mermaid

4 We [sea folk] can live to be three hundred years old, but when we perish we turn into mere foam on the sea. *Ib.*

5 The Emperor's New Clothes.

Ib. Title of story

6 "But he hasn't got anything on," a little child said.

Ib. The Emperor's New Clothes

7 The little live nightingale . . . had come to sing of comfort and hope. As he sang, the phantoms grew pale, and still more pale, and the blood flowed quicker and quicker through the Emperor's feeble body. Even Death listened, and said, "Go on, little nightingale, go on!" *Ib. The Nightingale*

8 His own image . . . was no longer the reflection of a clumsy, dirty, gray bird, ugly and offensive. He himself was a swan! Being born in a duck yard does not matter, if only you are hatched from a swan's egg.

Ib. The Ugly Duckling

9 The Little Match Girl.

Ib. Title of story

[1]Translated by JEAN HERSHOLT.

William Lloyd Garrison
1805–1879

10 Our country is the world—our countrymen are all mankind.[2]

Motto of The Liberator [1831]

11 Let Southern oppressors tremble—let their secret abettors tremble—let their Northern apologists tremble—let all the enemies of the persecuted blacks tremble.

The Liberator, no. 1 [January 1, 1831]

12 I will be as harsh as truth and as uncompromising as justice. On this subject I do not wish to think, or speak, or write, with moderation. No! No! Tell a man whose house is on fire to give a moderate alarm; tell him to moderately rescue his wife from the hands of the ravisher; tell the mother to gradually extricate her babe from the fire into which it has fallen; but urge me not to use moderation.[3]

Ib.

13 I am in earnest—I will not equivocate—I will not excuse—I will not retreat a single inch; and I will be heard![4] *Ib.*

14 The compact which exists between the North and the South is a covenant with death and an agreement with hell.[5]

Resolution adopted by the Anti-Slavery Society [January 27, 1843]

15 With reasonable men, I will reason; with humane men I will plead; but to tyrants I will give no quarter, nor waste arguments where they will certainly be lost.

W. P. and F. J. T. GARRISON, William Lloyd Garrison [1885–1889], vol. I, p. 188

16 Since the creation of the world there has been no tyrant like Intemperance, and no slaves so cruelly treated as his.

Ib. p. 268

17 We may be personally defeated, but our principles never. *Ib. p. 402*

18 Wherever there is a human being, I see God-given rights inherent in that being, whatever may be the sex or complexion.

Ib. III, p. 390

19 You cannot possibly have a broader basis for any government than that which includes all the people, with all their rights in their

[2]See Socrates, 79:7; Bacon, 180:13; Paine, 385:2; and F. D. Roosevelt, 781:5.
[3]See Paine, 385:4.
[4]See Disraeli, 501:11.
[5]See *Isaiah 28:15, 30:14*.

hands, and with an equal power to maintain their rights.[1] *Ib. IV, p. 224*

Sidney Sherman
1805–1873

1 Remember the Alamo![2]
Battle cry, San Jacinto [April 21, 1836]; attributed

Alexis de Tocqueville
1805–1859

2 I know of no country, indeed, where the love of money has taken stronger hold on the affections of men and where a profounder contempt is expressed for the theory of the permanent equality of property.
Democracy in America,[3] pt. I [1835], ch. 3

3 Within these limits the power vested in the American courts of justice of pronouncing a statute to be unconstitutional forms one of the most powerful barriers that have ever been devised against the tyranny of political assemblies. *Ib. 6*

4 I have never been more struck by the good sense and the practical judgment of the Americans than in the manner in which they elude the numberless difficulties resulting from their Federal Constitution. *Ib. 8*

5 In order to enjoy the inestimable benefits that the liberty of the press ensures, it is necessary to submit to the inevitable evils that it creates. *Ib. 9*

6 They [the Americans] have all a lively faith in the perfectibility of man, they judge that the diffusion of knowledge must necessarily be advantageous, and the consequences of ignorance fatal; they all consider society as a body in a state of improvement, humanity as a changing scene, in which nothing is, or ought to be, permanent; and they admit that what appears to them today to be good, may be superseded by something better tomorrow. *Ib. 18*

7 America is a land of wonders, in which everything is in constant motion and every change seems an improvement. The idea of novelty is there indissolubly connected with the idea of amelioration. No natural boundary seems to be set to the efforts of man; and in his eyes what is not yet done is only what he has not yet attempted to do. *Ib.*

8 Democratic nations care but little for what has been, but they are haunted by visions of what will be; in this direction their unbounded imagination grows and dilates beyond all measure. . . . Democracy, which shuts the past against the poet, opens the future before him.
Ib. pt. II [1840], bk. I, ch. 17

9 Thus not only does democracy make every man forget his ancestors, but it hides his descendants and separates his contemporaries from him; it throws him back forever upon himself alone and threatens in the end to confine him entirely within the solitude of his own heart. *Ib. II, 2*

10 If I were asked . . . to what the singular prosperity and growing strength of that people [the Americans] ought mainly to be attributed, I should reply: To the superiority of their women. *Ib. III, 12*

11 The love of wealth is therefore to be traced, as either a principal or accessory motive, at the bottom of all that the Americans do; this gives to all their passions a sort of family likeness. . . . It may be said that it is the vehemence of their desires that makes the Americans so methodical; it perturbs their minds, but it disciplines their lives.
Ib. 17

12 Democracy and socialism have nothing in common but one word: equality. But notice the difference: while democracy seeks equality in liberty, socialism seeks equality in restraint and servitude.
Speech in the Constituent Assembly [September 12, 1848]

Elizabeth Barrett Browning
1806–1861

13 Thou large-brained woman and large-
hearted man.
To George Sand, A Desire [1844]

14 Or from Browning some "Pomegranate,"
which, if cut deep down the middle,
Shows a heart within blood-tinctured of a
veined humanity.
Lady Geraldine's Courtship [1844], st. 41

[1]See Wycliffe, 143:12; Webster, 450:14; Disraeli, 501:6; Lincoln, 523:4; and Parker, 537:15.

[2]On March 6, 1836, five days after Texas declared her independence from Mexico, President Antonio López de Santa Anna attacked the Alamo, the fortified mission at San Antonio; captured it after every Texan had been killed or wounded; and put the wounded to death. He was defeated and captured at San Jacinto [April 21, 1836] by the Texas army under Commander in Chief Samuel Houston. Sidney Sherman was a colonel in the army.

[3]The Henry Reeve text, as revised by Francis Bowen, corrected and edited by Phillips Bradley [1945].

1 Knowledge by suffering entereth,
And life is perfected by death.
A Vision of Poets [1844], last lines

2 Do ye hear the children weeping, O my brothers,
Ere the sorrow comes with years?
The Cry of the Children [1844], st. 1

3 I tell you hopeless grief is passionless.
Grief [1844], l. 1

4 Therefore to this dog will I,
Tenderly not scornfully,
Render praise and favor.
To Flush, My Dog [1844], st. 14

5 "Yes," I answered you last night;
"No," this morning, sir, I say:
Colors seen by candlelight
Will not look the same by day.[1]
The Lady's "Yes" [1844], st. 1

6 By thunders of white silence overthrown.
Hiram Power's Greek Slave [1850], last line

7 Unless you can dream that his faith is fast,
Through behoving and unbehoving;
Unless you can die when the dream is past—
Oh, never call it loving!
A Woman's Shortcomings [1850], st. 5

8 "Guess now who holds thee?"—"Death," I said. But there
The silver answer rang—"Not Death, but Love."
Sonnets from the Portuguese [1850], no. 1

9 Go from me. Yet I feel that I shall stand
Henceforward in thy shadow. *Ib. 6*

10 If thou must love me, let it be for naught
Except for love's sake only. *Ib. 14*

11 When our two souls stand up erect and strong,
Face to face, silent, drawing nigh and nigher. *Ib. 22*

12 God only, who made us rich, can make us poor. *Ib. 24*

13 Because God's gifts put man's best dreams to shame. *Ib. 26*

[1] And if I loved you Wednesday, / Well, what is that to you? / I do not love you Thursday— / So much is true.
— EDNA ST. VINCENT MILLAY [1892–1950], *Thursday*

14 How do I love thee? Let me count the ways.
I love thee to the depth and breadth and height
My soul can reach, when feeling out of sight
For the ends of Being and ideal Grace.
Ib. 43

15 I love thee with the breath,
Smiles, tears, of all my life!—and, if God choose,
I shall but love thee better after death.
Ib.

16 Life, struck sharp on death,
Makes awful lightning.
Aurora Leigh[2] [1857], bk. I, l. 210

17 I should not dare to call my soul my own.
Ib. II, l. 786

18 God answers sharp and sudden on some prayers,
And thrusts the thing we have prayed for in our face,
A gauntlet with a gift in 't. *Ib. l. 952*

19 A little sunburnt by the glare of life.
Ib. IV, l. 1140

20 Nay, if there's room for poets in this world
A little overgrown (I think there is),
Their sole work is to represent the age,
Their age, not Charlemagne's.
Ib. V, l. 200

21 Since when was genius found respectable?
Ib. VI, l. 275

22 Earth's crammed with heaven,
And every common bush afire with God.
Ib. VII, l. 820

23 What was he doing, the great god Pan,
Down in the reeds by the river?
Spreading ruin and scattering ban,
Splashing and paddling with hoofs of a goat,
And breaking the golden lilies afloat
With the dragonfly on the river.
A Musical Instrument [1860]

24 Grief may be joy misunderstood;
Only the Good discerns the good.
De Profundis [1862], st. 21

25 The fireflies and the nightingales,
Throbbed each to either, flame and song.
The nightingales, the nightingales!
Bianca Among the Nightingales [1862], st. 1

[2] See Edward FitzGerald, 517:16.

Friedrich Halm [Eligius Franz Josef von Münch-Bellinghausen]

1806–1871

1 Two souls with but a single thought,
Two hearts that beat as one.[1]

Der Sohn der Wildness [1842], act II

John Stuart Mill

1806–1873

2 Jeremy Bentham and Samuel Taylor Coleridge—the two great seminal minds of England in their age. *Bentham [1838]*

3 The sole end for which mankind are warranted, individually or collectively, in interfering with the liberty of action of any of their number is self-protection.

On Liberty [1859], introduction

4 If all mankind minus one were of one opinion, and only one person were of the contrary opinion, mankind would be no more justified in silencing that one person than he, if he had the power, would be justified in silencing mankind. *Ib. ch. 2*

5 There is no such thing as absolute certainty, but there is assurance sufficient for the purposes of human life. *Ib.*

6 He who knows only his own side of the case, knows little of that. *Ib.*

7 The fatal tendency of mankind to leave off thinking about a thing when it is no longer doubtful is the cause of half their errors.

Ib.

8 We can never be sure that the opinion we are endeavoring to stifle is a false opinion; and if we were sure, stifling it would be an evil still. *Ib.*

9 The liberty of the individual must be thus far limited; he must not make himself a nuisance to other people. *Ib. 3*

10 All good things which exist are the fruits of originality. *Ib.*

11 Whatever crushes individuality is despotism, by whatever name it may be called.

Ib.

12 Everyone who receives the protection of society owes a return for the benefit.

Ib. 4

[1] Zwei Sellen und en Gedanke, / Zwei Herzen und ein Schlag!
Translated by MARIA LOVELL.

13 The individual is not accountable to society for his actions, insofar as these concern the interests of no person but himself.

Ib. 5

14 The worth of a state, in the long run, is the worth of the individuals composing it.

Ib.

15 Liberty consists in doing what one desires.

Ib.

16 Unearned increment.

Dissertations and Discussions [1859]

17 Instead of the function of governing, for which it is radically unfit, the proper office of a representative assembly is to watch and control the government. *Ib.*

18 The creed which accepts as the foundation of morals Utility, or the Greatest Happiness Principle, holds that actions are right in proportion as they tend to promote happiness, wrong as they tend to produce the reverse of happiness.

Utilitarianism [1863], ch. 2

19 It is better to be Socrates dissatisfied than a pig satisfied. *Ib.*

20 The social state is at once so natural, so necessary, and so habitual to man, that . . . he never conceives himself otherwise than as a member of a body. *Ib. 3*

21 It is only a man here and there who has any tolerable knowledge of the character even of the women of his own family.

The Subjection of Women [1869], ch. 1

22 The generality of the male sex cannot yet tolerate the idea of living with an equal.

Ib. 2

23 Ask yourself whether you are happy, and you cease to be so.

Autobiography [1873], ch. 5

24 Human existence is girt round with mystery; the narrow region of our experiences is a small island in the midst of a boundless sea.

Utility of Religion [1874]

25 The prose of human life. *Ib.*

26 The essence of religion is the strong and earnest direction of the emotions and desires toward an ideal object, recognized as of the highest excellence and as rightfully paramount over all selfish objects of desire. This condition is fulfilled by the Religion of Humanity in as eminent a degree and in as high a sense as by the supernatural religions even in their best manifestations, and far more so than in any of their others. *Ib.*

Johann Bernhard, Graf von Rechberg
1806–1899

1 Guarantees which are not worth the paper they are written on.

In a dispatch concerning the recognition of Italy [1861]

Charles Francis Adams
1807–1886

2 It would be superfluous in me to point out to your Lordship that this is war.

Dispatch to Earl Russell [September 5, 1863]

Jean Louis Rodolphe Agassiz
1807–1873

3 The time has come when scientific truth must cease to be the property of the few, when it must be woven into the common life of the world.

Methods of Study in Natural History [1863], ch. 4

4 The eye of the trilobite tells us that the sun shone on the old beach where he lived; for there is nothing in nature without a purpose, and when so complicated an organ was made to receive the light, there must have been light to enter it.

Geological Sketches [1870], ch. 2

5 The facts will eventually test all our theories, and they form, after all, the only impartial jury to which we can appeal. *Ib. 9*

6 The world has arisen in some way or another. How it originated is the great question, and Darwin's theory, like all other attempts to explain the origin of life, is thus far merely conjectural. I believe he has not even made the best conjecture possible in the present state of our knowledge.

Evolution and Permanence of Type [1874]

Giuseppe Garibaldi
1807–1882

7 I offer neither pay, nor quarters, nor provisions; I offer hunger, thirst, forced marches, battles and death. Let him who loves his country in his heart, and not with his lips only, follow me.[1]

From G. M. Trevelyan, Garibaldi's Defense of the Roman Republic [1907–1911]

[1]See Prescott, 481:2, and Churchill, 743:19.

Robert Edward Lee
1807–1870

8 It is well that war is so terrible, or we should grow too fond of it.[2]

On seeing a Federal charge repulsed at Fredericksburg [December 1862]

9 Duty is the sublimest word in our language. Do your duty in all things. You cannot do more. You should never wish to do less.

Inscribed beneath his bust in the Hall of Fame

10 Strike the tent.

Last words [October 12, 1870]

Henry Wadsworth Longfellow
1807–1882

11 Music is the universal language of mankind—poetry their universal pastime and delight. *Outre-Mer [1833–1834]*

12 I heard the trailing garments of the Night
Sweep through her marble halls.

Hymn to Night [1839], st. 1

13 Tell me not, in mournful numbers,
Life is but an empty dream!
For the soul is dead that slumbers,
And things are not what they seem.[3]

Life is real! Life is earnest!
And the grave is not its goal;
Dust thou art, to dust returnest,
Was not spoken of the soul.

A Psalm of Life [1839], st. 1, 2

14 Art is long, and Time is fleeting,[4]
And our hearts, though stout and brave,
Still, like muffled drums, are beating
Funeral marches to the grave.[5]

Ib. st. 4

15 Lives of great men all remind us
We can make our lives sublime.
And, departing, leave behind us
Footprints on the sands of time.

Ib. st. 7

16 Let us, then, be up and doing,
With a heart for any fate;[6]
Still achieving, still pursuing,
Learn to labor and to wait. *Ib. st. 9*

[2]See William T. Sherman, 579:3.
[3]See Phaedrus, 114:10, and Gilbert, 627:16.
[4]See Hippocrates, 80:9; Chaucer, 144:8; and Goethe, 395:7.
[5]Our lives are but our marches to the grave.—Beaumont and Fletcher, *The Humorous Lieutenant* [1619], *act III, sc. v*
[6]See Byron, 460:4.

1 There is a Reaper whose name is Death,
And, with his sickle keen,
He reaps the bearded grain at a breath,
And the flowers that grow between.
The Reaper and the Flowers [1839], st. 1

2 Look not mournfully into the Past. It comes not back again. Wisely improve the Present. It is thine.[1] Go forth to meet the shadowy Future, without fear, and with a manly heart.[2]
Hyperion [1839], bk. IV, ch. 8

3 Skoal! to the Northland! skoal!
Thus the tale ended.
The Skeleton in Armor [1841], st. 20

4 It was the schooner Hesperus,
That sailed the wintry sea;
And the skipper had taken his little daughter,
To bear him company.
The Wreck of the Hesperus [1842], st. 1

5 But the father answered never a word,
A frozen corpse was he. *Ib. st. 12*

6 Christ save us all from a death like this,
On the reef of Norman's Woe!
Ib. st. 22

7 Under the spreading chestnut tree
The village smithy stands;
The smith a mighty man is he
With large and sinewy hands.
And the muscles of his brawny arms
Are strong as iron bands.
The Village Blacksmith [1842], st. 1

8 His brow is wet with honest sweat,
He earns whate'er he can,
And looks the whole world in the face,
For he owes not any man. *Ib. st. 2*

9 Something attempted, something done,
Has earned a night's repose. *Ib. st. 7*

10 No one is so accursed by fate,
No one so utterly desolate,
But some heart, though unknown,
Responds unto his own.
Endymion [1842], st. 8

11 Into each life some rain must fall,
Some days must be dark and dreary.
The Rainy Day [1842], st. 3

[1]See Whittier, 513:5.
[2]Blicke nicht trauernd in die Vergangenheit, / Sie kommt nicht wieder, nutze weise die Gegenwart, / Sie ist dein, der düsteren Zukunft geh ohne / Furcht mit männliche Sinne entgegen. —*Inscription, Chapel of St. Gilgen, near Salzburg*

12 I like that ancient Saxon phrase, which calls
The burial ground God's Acre!
God's Acre [1842], st. 1

13 Standing with reluctant feet,
Where the brook and river meet,
Womanhood and childhood fleet!
Maidenhood [1842], st. 3

14 A banner with the strange device,
Excelsior! *Excelsior [1842], st. 1*

15 Stars of the summer night!
Far in yon azure deeps.
The Spanish Student [1843], act I, sc. iii (serenade)

16 I stood on the bridge at midnight,
As the clocks were striking the hour.
The Bridge [1845]

17 The day is done, and the darkness
Falls from the wings of Night,
As a feather is wafted downward
From an eagle in his flight.
The Day Is Done [1845], st. 1

18 A feeling of sadness and longing,
That is not akin to pain. *Ib. st. 3*

19 Some simple and heartfelt lay.
Ib. st. 4

20 The bards sublime,
Whose distant footsteps echo
Through the corridors of Time.
Ib. st. 5

21 Read from some humbler poet.
Ib. st. 7

22 And the night shall be filled with music,
And the cares, that infest the day,
Shall fold their tents, like the Arabs,
And as silently steal away. *Ib. st. 11*

23 The horologe of Eternity
Sayeth this incessantly—
"Forever—never!
Never—forever!"
The Old Clock on the Stairs [1845], st. 9

24 I shot an arrow into the air,
It fell to earth, I knew not where.
The Arrow and the Song [1845], st. 1

25 And the song, from beginning to end,
I found in the heart of a friend.
Ib. st. 3

26 This is the forest primeval. The murmuring pines and the hemlocks[3] . . .
Stand like Druids of old.
Evangeline [1847], l. 1

[3]See Theocritus, 92:12.

1 Alike were they free from
Fear, that reigns with the tyrant, and envy, the vice of republics.
Ib. pt. I, sec. 1

2 When she had passed, it seemed like the ceasing of exquisite music. *Ib.*

3 Silently one by one, in the infinite meadows of heaven
Blossomed the lovely stars, the forget-me-nots of the angels. *Ib. 3*

4 Talk not of wasted affection! affection never was wasted;
If it enrich not the heart of another, its waters, returning
Back to their springs, like the rain, shall fill them full of refreshment:
That which the fountain sends forth returns again to the fountain. *Ib. II, 1*

5 Give what you have. To someone, it may be better than you dare to think.
Kavanagh [1849]

6 Build me straight, O worthy Master!
Staunch and strong, a goodly vessel.
The Building of the Ship [1849], l. 1

7 And see! she stirs!
She starts—she moves—she seems to feel
The thrill of life along her keel.
Ib. l. 349

8 Sail on, O Ship of State!
Sail on, O Union, strong and great!
Humanity with all its fears,
With all the hopes of future years,
Is hanging breathless on thy fate!
Ib. l. 378

9 Our hearts, our hopes, our prayers, our tears,
Our faith triumphant o'er our fears,
Are all with thee—are all with thee!
Ib. l. 397

10 There is no fireside, howsoe'er defended,
But has one vacant chair!
Resignation [1849], st. 1

11 There is no Death! What seems so is transition;
This life of mortal breath
Is but a suburb of the life elysian,
Whose portal we call Death. *Ib. st. 5*

12 Nothing useless is, or low.
The Builders [1849], st. 2

13 God sent his Singers upon earth
With songs of sadness and of mirth.
The Singers [1849], st. 1

14 But the great Master said, "I see
No best in kind, but in degree;
I gave a various gift to each,
To charm, to strengthen, and to teach."
Ib. st. 6

15 All your strength is in your union.
All your danger is in discord;
Therefore be at peace henceforward,
And as brothers live together.
The Song of Hiawatha [1855], pt. I

16 By the shores of Gitche Gumee,
By the shining Big-Sea-Water,
Stood the wigwam of Nokomis,
Daughter of the Moon, Nokomis.
Ib. III

17 From the waterfall he named her,
Minnehaha, Laughing Water. *Ib. IV*

18 As unto the bow the cord is,
So unto the man is woman,
Though she bends him, she obeys him,
Though she draws him, yet she follows,
Useless each without the other! *Ib. X*

19 If we could read the secret history of our enemies, we should find in each man's life sorrow and suffering enough to disarm all hostility. *Driftwood [1857]*

20 If I am not worth the wooing, I surely am not worth the winning.
The Courtship of Miles Standish [1858], pt. III

21 "Why don't you speak for yourself, John?"[1]
Ib.

22 Saint Augustine! well hast thou said,
That of our vices we can frame
A ladder, if we will but tread
Beneath our feet each deed of shame.[2]
The Ladder of St. Augustine [1858], st. 1

23 The heights by great men reached and kept
Were not attained by sudden flight,
But they, while their companions slept,
Were toiling upward in the night.
Ib. st. 10

24 The long mysterious Exodus of death.
The Jewish Cemetery at Newport [1858], st. 1

25 A boy's will is the wind's will,
And the thoughts of youth are long, long thoughts.
My Lost Youth [1858], refrain

[1] See Shakespeare, 209:9.
[2] See St. Augustine, 129:10, and Tennyson, 531:19.

1 A Lady with a Lamp[1] shall stand
In the great history of the land,
A noble type of good,
Heroic womanhood.
Santa Filomena [1858], st. 10

2 Ye are better than all the ballads
That ever were sung or said;
For ye are living poems,
And all the rest are dead.
Children [1858], st. 9

3 Between the dark and the daylight,
When the night is beginning to lower,
Comes a pause in the day's occupations,
That is known as the Children's Hour.
The Children's Hour [1860], st. 1

4 I hear in the chamber above me
The patter of little feet. *Ib. st. 2*

5 Grave Alice, and laughing Allegra,
And Edith with golden hair. *Ib. st. 3*

6 Listen, my children, and you shall hear,
Of the midnight ride of Paul Revere,
On the eighteenth of April, in Seventy-five;
Hardly a man is now alive
Who remembers that famous day and year.
Tales of a Wayside Inn [1863–1874], pt. I, The Landlord's Tale: Paul Revere's Ride, st. 1

7 One if by land, and two if by sea;[2]
And I on the opposite shore will be,
Ready to ride and spread the alarm
Through every Middlesex village and farm.
Ib. st. 2

8 The fate of a nation was riding that night.
Ib. st. 8

9 He seemed the incarnate "Well, I told you so!"
Ib. The Poet's Tale: The Birds of Killingworth, st. 9

10 Ships that pass in the night, and speak each other in passing,
Only a signal shown and a distant voice in the darkness;
So on the ocean of life we pass and speak one another,[3]
Only a look and a voice; then darkness again and a silence.
Ib. III, The Theologian's Tale: Elizabeth, IV

[1] Florence Nightingale [1820–1910].
[2] See Paul Revere, 382:12.
[3] Two lives that once part are as ships that divide. — EDWARD BULWER-LYTTON [1803–1873], *A Lament*
As vessels starting from ports thousands of miles apart pass close to each other in the naked breadths of the ocean, nay, sometimes even touch in the dark. — OLIVER WENDELL HOLMES, *Professor at the Breakfast Table* [1860]

11 Time has laid his hand
Upon my heart, gently, not smiting it,
But as a harper lays his open palm
Upon his harp to deaden its vibrations.
The Golden Legend [1872], pt. IV, The Cloisters

12 The grave itself is but a covered bridge
Leading from light to light, through a brief darkness.[4]
Ib. V, A Covered Bridge at Lucerne

13 Let him not boast who puts his armor on
As he who puts it off, the battle done.
Morituri Salutamus [1875], st. 9

14 Ye, against whose familiar names not yet
The fatal asterisk of death is set.
Ib. st. 11

15 The love of learning, the sequestered nooks,
And all the sweet serenity of books.
Ib. st. 21

16 Ah, nothing is too late,
Till the tired heart shall cease to palpitate.
Ib. st. 22

17 For age is opportunity no less
Than youth itself. *Ib. st. 24*

18 Not in the clamor of the crowded street,
Not in the shouts and plaudits of the throng,
But in ourselves, are triumph and defeat.
The Poets

19 Nothing that is can pause or stay;
The moon will wax, the moon will wane,
The mist and cloud will turn to rain,
The rain to mist and cloud again,
Tomorrow be today. *Kéramos [1878]*

20 Three silences there are: the first of speech,
The second of desire, the third of thought;
This is the lore a Spanish monk, distraught
With dreams and visions, was the first to teach.
The Three Silences of Molinos[5]

21 In the long, sleepless watches of the night.
The Cross of Snow [1879]

22 The holiest of all holidays are those
Kept by ourselves in silence and apart;
The secret anniversaries of the heart.
Holidays

23 Great is the art of beginning, but greater the art is of ending;
Many a poem is marred by a superfluous verse. *Elegiac Verse, st. 14*

[4] Death seems but a covered way / Which opens into light. — WHITTIER [1807–1892], *My Psalm, st. 14*
[5] Miguel Molinos [1640–1696], Spanish mystic, one of the early Quietists.

1 There was a little girl
Who had a little curl
Right in the middle of her forehead;
And when she was good
She was very, very good,
But when she was bad she was horrid.
There Was a Little Girl[1]

2 Out of the shadows of night
The world rolls into light;
It is daybreak everywhere.[2]
The Bells of San Blas [March 15, 1882],[3] *st. 11*

John Greenleaf Whittier
1807–1892

3 No fetters in the Bay State—no slave upon our land!
Massachusetts to Virginia [1843], st. 24

4 What calls back the past, like the rich pumpkin pie?
The Pumpkin [1844], st. 3

5 The Present, the Present is all thou hast
For thy sure possessing;[4]
Like the patriarch's angel hold it fast
Till it gives its blessing.[5]
My Soul and I [1847], st. 34

6 The Night is mother of the Day,
The Winter of the Spring,
And ever upon old Decay
The greenest mosses cling.
A Dream of Summer [1847], st. 4

7 So fallen! so lost! the light withdrawn
Which once he wore!
The glory from his gray hairs gone
Forevermore! *Ichabod [1850],*[6] *st. 1*

8 From those great eyes
The soul has fled:
When faith is lost, when honor dies,
The man is dead! *Ib. st. 8*

[1] Blanche Roosevelt Tucker, in *The Home Life of Henry W. Longfellow* [1882], states that these lines were written by the poet for his children on a day when Edith did not want to have her hair curled.

[2] See Horne, 500:14.

[3] The last poem written by Longfellow. He died on March 24, 1882.

[4] See Longfellow, 510:2.

[5] See *Genesis 32:26,* 8:25, and Cotton, 346:14.

[6] This poem was the outcome of the surprise and grief and forecast of evil consequences which I felt on reading the seventh of March speech of Daniel Webster in support of the "compromise," and the Fugitive Slave Law. No partisan or personal enmity dictated it.—WHITTIER'S *Note*

See *I Samuel 4:21,* 12:32.

9 Search thine own heart. What paineth thee
In others in thyself may be.
The Chapel of the Hermits [1853], st. 85

10 Blessings on thee, little man,
Barefoot boy, with cheek of tan!
The Barefoot Boy [1856], st. 1

11 Health that mocks the doctor's rules,
Knowledge never learned of schools.
Ib. st. 2

12 The age is dull and mean. Men creep,
Not walk.
Lines Inscribed to Friends under Arrest for Treason Against the Slave Power [1856], st. 1

13 Nature speaks in symbols and in signs.
To Charles Sumner

14 For of all sad words of tongue or pen,
The saddest are these: "It might have been!"[7] *Maud Muller [1856], st. 53*

15 The windows of my soul I throw
Wide open to the sun. *My Psalm, st. 2*

16 Up from the meadows rich with corn,
Clear in the cool September morn.
Barbara Frietchie [1864], st. 1

17 The clustered spires of Frederick stand
Green-walled by the hills of Maryland.
Ib. st. 2

18 "Shoot, if you must, this old gray head,
But spare your country's flag," she said.
Ib. st. 18

19 "Who touches a hair of yon gray head
Dies like a dog! March on!" he said.
Ib. st. 21

20 The sun that brief December day
Rose cheerless over hills of gray,
And, darkly circled, gave at noon
A sadder light than waning moon.
Snowbound [1866], l. 1

21 Shut in from all the world without,
We sat the clean-winged hearth about.
Ib. l. 155

22 The low green tent
Whose curtain never outward swings!
Ib. l. 389

23 Angel of the backward look. *Ib. l. 714*

24 I know not where His islands lift
Their fronded palms in air;
I only know I cannot drift
Beyond His love and care.
The Eternal Goodness [1867], st. 20

[7] See Guiterman, 732:15.

1 Dear Lord and Father of mankind,
Forgive our foolish ways!
Reclothe us in our rightful mind,
In purer lives Thy service find,
In deeper reverence, praise.

The Brewing of Soma [1872]

2 God is and all is well.[1]

My Birthday, st. 2

3 He brings cool dew in his little bill,
And lets it fall on the souls of sin:
You can see the mark on his red breast still
Of fires that scorch as he drops it in.[2]

The Robin, st. 4

Salmon Portland Chase
1808–1873

4 The Constitution, in all its provisions, looks to an indestructible Union composed of indestructible States.

Decision in Texas v. White, 7 Wallace 725 [1868]

Alphonse Karr
1808–1890

5 The more things change, the more they remain the same.[3]

Les Guêpes [Janvier 1849]

Maurice de MacMahon
1808–1893

6 Here I am, and here I stay.[4]

At Sevastopol [September 1855]

Gérard de Nerval [Gérard Labrunie]
1808–1855

7 Despair and suicide are the result of certain fatal situations for those who have no faith in immortality, its joys and sorrows.

Le Rêve et la Vie, II

8 The jailer is another kind of captive—is the jailer envious of his prisoner's dreams?

Fragments de Faust

[1] See Browning, 540:15.

[2] Far, far away, is a land of woe and darkness, spirits of evil and fire. Day after day a little bird flies there, bearing in his bill a drop of water to quench the flame. So near the burning stream does he fly that his feathers are scorched by it, and hence he is named "Bron-rhuddyn"—breast-burned. —*Carmarthenshire legend of the robin*

[3] Plus ça change, plus c'est la même chose.

[4] J'y suis, j'y reste.

Reply to the commander in chief, from the trenches before Malakoff, in the siege of Sevastopol, when warned to beware of an explosion which might follow the retreat of the Russians.

9 I am the somber one, the unconsoled widower,
The Prince of Aquitaine whose tower was destroyed.[5]
My only star is dead, and my star-studded lute
Wears the black sun of Melancholy.

Les Chimères [1854]. El Desdichado

Caroline Sheridan Norton
1808–1877

10 A soldier of the Legion lay dying in Algiers.

Bingen on the Rhine, st. 1

George Washington Patten
c. 1808–1882

11 If we must perish in the fight,
Oh! let us die like men.

Oh! Let Us Die Like Men, st. 4

Samuel Francis Smith
1808–1895

12 My country, 'tis of thee,
Sweet land of liberty,
Of thee I sing:
Land where my fathers died,
Land of the pilgrims' pride,
From every mountainside
Let freedom ring.

America [1831], st. 1

13 Long may our land be bright
With freedom's holy light;
Protect us by thy might,
Great God, our King! *Ib. st. 4*

Charles Robert Darwin
1809–1882

14 I have called this principle, by which each slight variation, if useful, is preserved, by the term Natural Selection.

The Origin of Species [1859], ch. 3

15 The expression often used by Mr. Herbert Spencer, of the Survival of the Fittest, is more accurate, and is sometimes equally convenient.[6] *Ib.*

16 We will now discuss in a little more detail the Struggle for Existence.[7] *Ib.*

[5] Je suis le ténébreux, le veuf, l'inconsolé, / Le Prince d'Aquitaine à la tour abolie.

T. S. Eliot quotes the second line in *The Waste Land* [1922], line 429.

[6] See Spencer, 579:20.

[7] The perpetual struggle for room and food. —Malthus, *On Population* [1798], *ch. 3*

1 It is interesting to contemplate an entangled bank, clothed with many plants of many kinds, with birds singing on the bushes, with various insects flitting about, and with worms crawling through the damp earth, and to reflect that these elaborately constructed forms, so different from each other, and dependent on each other in so complex a manner, have all been produced by laws acting around us. *Ib.*

2 Each organic being is striving to increase in a geometrical ratio . . . each at some period of its life, during some season of the year, during each generation or at intervals, has to struggle for life and to suffer great destruction . . . The vigorous, the healthy, and the happy survive and multiply. *Ib.*

3 From the war of nature, from famine and death, the most exalted object which we are capable of conceiving, namely, the production of the higher animals, directly follows. There is grandeur in this view of life, with its several powers, having been originally breathed by the Creator into a few forms or into one, and that . . . from so simple a beginning endless forms most beautiful and most wonderful have been and are being evolved. *Ib. 15*

4 The highest possible stage in moral culture is when we recognize that we ought to control our thoughts.
The Descent of Man [1871], ch. 4

5 The presence of a body of well-instructed men, who have not to labor for their daily bread, is important to a degree which cannot be overestimated; as all high intellectual work is carried on by them, and on such work material progress of all kinds mainly depends, not to mention other and higher advantages. *Ib. 5*

6 Progress has been much more general than retrogression. *Ib.*

7 The Simiadae then branched off into two great stems, the New World and Old World monkeys; and from the latter at a remote period, Man, the wonder and the glory of the universe, proceeded.[1] *Ib. 6*

8 A hairy quadruped, furnished with a tail and pointed ears, probably arboreal in its habits. *The Descent of Man, ch. 21*

9 For my own part I would as soon be descended from that heroic little monkey, who braved his dreaded enemy in order to save the life of his keeper; or from that old baboon, who, descending from the mountains, carried away in triumph his young comrade from a crowd of astonished dogs — as from a savage who delights to torture his enemies, offers up bloody sacrifices, practices infanticide without remorse, treats his wives like slaves, knows no decency, and is haunted by the grossest superstitions. *Ib.*

10 Man with all his noble qualities . . . with his godlike intellect which has penetrated into the movements and constitution of the solar system . . . still bears in his bodily frame the indelible stamp of his lowly origin.
Ib. Conclusion

11 The plow is one of the most ancient and most valuable of man's inventions; but long before he existed the land was in fact regularly plowed, and still continues to be thus plowed by earthworms. It may be doubted whether there are many other animals which have played so important a part in the history of the world, as have these lowly organized creatures.
The Formation of Vegetable Mold Through the Action of Worms [1881], ch. 7

12 Physiological experiment on animals is justifiable for real investigation, but not for mere damnable and detestable curiosity.
Letter to E. Ray Lankester

13 As for a future life, every man must judge for himself between conflicting vague probabilities.
From Life and Letters of Charles Darwin [1887], edited by FRANCIS DARWIN

14 I love fools' experiments. I am always making them. *Ib.*

15 Believing as I do that man in the distant future will be a far more perfect creature than he now is, it is an intolerable thought that he and all other sentient beings are doomed to complete annihilation after such long-continued slow progress. To those who fully admit the immortality of the human soul, the destruction of our world will not appear so dreadful. *Ib.*

Edward FitzGerald

1809–1883

16 Wake! For the Sun who scattered into flight
The Stars before him from the Field of night,

[1] I confess freely to you, I could never look long upon a monkey, without very mortifying reflections. — CONGREVE, *Letter to Dennis* [1695]
See Pascal, 299:17, and Disraeli, 502:4.

Drives Night along with them from Heaven and strikes
The Sultan's Turret with a Shaft of Light.
The Rubáiyát of Omar Khayyám,[1] *st. 1*

1 Awake! for Morning in the Bowl of Night
Has flung the Stone that puts the Stars to flight:
And Lo! the Hunter of the East has caught
The Sultan's Turret in a Noose of Light.
Ib. [first edition]

2 Now the New Year reviving old Desires,
The thoughtful Soul to Solitude retires.
Ib. st. 4

3 Iram indeed is gone with all his Rose.
Ib. st. 5

4 Come, fill the Cup, and in the fire of Spring
The Winter garment of Repentance fling:
The Bird of Time has but a little way
To fly—and Lo! the Bird is on the Wing.
Ib. st. 7 [first edition]

5 The Leaves of Life keep falling one by one.
Ib. st. 8

6 Each Morn a thousand Roses brings, you say:
Yes, but where leaves the Rose of Yesterday?
Ib. st. 9

7 A Book of Verses underneath the Bough,
A Jug of Wine, a Loaf of Bread—and Thou
Beside me singing in the Wilderness—
Oh, Wilderness were Paradise enow!
Ib. st. 12

8 Ah, take the Cash, and let the Credit go,
Nor heed the rumble of a distant Drum!
Ib. st. 13

9 The Worldly Hope men set their Hearts upon
Turns Ashes—or it prospers; and anon,
Like Snow upon the Desert's dusty Face,
Lighting a little hour or two—is gone.
Ib. st. 16

10 Think, in this battered Caravanserai
Whose Portals are alternate Night and Day,
How Sultan after Sultan with his Pomp
Abode his destined Hour, and went his way.
Ib. st. 17

11 They say the Lion and the Lizard keep
The Courts where Jamshyd gloried and drank deep:
And Bahram, that great Hunter—the Wild Ass
Stamps o'er his Head, but cannot break his sleep.
Ib. st. 18

[1]Translated from the Persian of OMAR KHAYYÁM [died c. 1123] in four editions, 1859, 1868, 1872, and 1879. The fourth edition is used here, unless otherwise stated.

12 I sometimes think that never blows so red
The Rose as where some buried Caesar bled;
That every Hyacinth the Garden wears
Dropt in her Lap from some once lovely Head.[2]
Ib. st. 19

13 Ah, my Belovèd, fill the Cup that clears
Today of past Regrets and future Fears:
Tomorrow!—Why, Tomorrow I may be
Myself with Yesterday's Seven thousand Years.[3]
Ib. st. 21

14 For some we loved, the loveliest and the best
That from his Vintage rolling Time hath prest.
Ib. st. 22

15 Ah, make the most of what we yet may spend,
Before we too into the Dust descend;
Dust into Dust, and under Dust, to lie,
Sans Wine, sans Song, sans Singer, and—sans End!
Ib. st. 24

16 Myself when young did eagerly frequent
Doctor and Saint, and heard great argument
About it and about: but evermore
Came out by the same door wherein I went.
Ib. st. 27

17 And this was all the Harvest that I reaped—
"I came like Water, and like Wind I go."
Ib. st. 28

18 There was the Door to which I found no Key;
There was the Veil through which I might not see.
Some little talk awhile of Me and Thee
There was—and then no more of Thee and Me.
Ib. st. 32

19 "While you live,
Drink!—for, once dead, you never shall return."
Ib. st. 35

20 For I remember stopping by the way
To watch a Potter thumping his wet Clay:
And with its all-obliterated Tongue
It murmured—"Gently, Brother, gently, pray!"
Ib. st. 37

21 And fear not lest Existence closing your
Account, and mine, should know the like no more;
The Eternal Saki from that Bowl has poured
Millions of Bubbles like us, and will pour.[4]
Ib. st. 46

22 'Tis all a Checkerboard of Nights and Days
Where Destiny with Men for Pieces plays:
Hither and thither moves, and mates, and slays,
And one by one back in the Closet lays.
Ib. st. 49 [first edition]

[2]See Shakespeare, 224:17, and Tennyson, 531:22.
[3]See Euripides, 76:8.
[4]See Tennyson, 527:21.

1 Striking from the Calendar
Unborn Tomorrow and dead Yesterday.
Ib. st. 57

2 The Moving Finger writes; and, having writ,
Moves on: nor all your Piety nor Wit
Shall lure it back to cancel half a Line,
Nor all your Tears wash out a Word of it.
Ib. st. 71

3 That inverted Bowl we call The Sky,
Whereunder crawling cooped we live and die.
Ib. st. 72 [first edition]

4 Ah, Moon of my Delight who know'st no wane. *Ib. st. 74 [first edition]*

5 One Flash of it within the Tavern caught
Better than in the Temple lost outright.
Ib. st. 77

6 What! out of senseless Nothing to provoke
A conscious Something to resent the yoke.[1]
Ib. st. 78

7 And He that with his hand the Vessel made
Will surely not in after Wrath destroy.
Ib. st. 85

8 After a momentary silence spake
Some Vessel of a more ungainly Make;
"They sneer at me for leaning all awry:
What! did the Hand then of the Potter shake?" *Ib. st. 86*

9 Who *is* the Potter, pray, and who the Pot?
Ib. st. 87

10 Indeed the Idols I have loved so long
Have done my credit in this World much wrong:
Have drowned my Glory in a shallow Cup,
And sold my Reputation for a Song.
Ib. st. 93

11 I wonder often what the Vintners buy
One half so precious as the stuff they sell.
Ib. st. 95

12 Yet Ah, that Spring should vanish with the Rose!
That Youth's sweet-scented manuscript should close! *Ib. st. 96*

13 Ah Love! could you and I with Him conspire
To grasp this Sorry Scheme of Things entire,
Would not we shatter it to bits—and then
Remold it nearer to the Heart's Desire!
Ib. st. 99

14 And when like her, O Saki, you shall pass
Among the Guests Star-scattered on the Grass,
And in your joyous errand reach the spot
Where I made One—turn down an empty Glass! *Ib. st. 101*

[1]See Poe, 527:3.

15 The King in a carriage may ride,
And the Beggar may crawl at his side;
But in the general race,
They are traveling all the same pace.
Chronomoros

16 Mrs. Browning's death was rather a relief to me, I must say; no more Aurora Leighs, thank God! *Letter [July 15, 1861]*[2]

William Ewart Gladstone
1809–1898

17 Decision by majorities is as much an expedient as lighting by gas.
Speech in the House of Commons [1858]

18 You cannot fight against the future. Time is on our side.
Speech on the Reform Bill [1866]

19 The disease of an evil conscience is beyond the practice of all the physicians of all the countries in the world.
Speech at Plumstead [1878]

20 National injustice is the surest road to national downfall. *Ib.*

21 Out of the range of practical politics.
Speech at Dalkeith [November 26, 1879]

22 The resources of civilization are not yet exhausted.
Speech at Leeds [October 7, 1881]

23 All the world over, I will back the masses against the classes.
Speech at Liverpool [June 28, 1886]

24 I have always regarded that Constitution as the most remarkable work known to me in modern times to have been produced by the human intellect, at a single stroke (so to speak), in its application to political affairs.[3]
Letter to the committee in charge of the celebration of the centennial of the American Constitution [July 20, 1887]

25 Selfishness is the greatest curse of the human race.
Speech at Hawarden [May 28, 1890]

[2]See E. B. Browning, 507:16.

[3]As the British Constitution is the most subtle organism which has proceeded from progressive history, so the American Constitution is the most wonderful work ever struck off at a given time by the brain and purpose of man.—GLADSTONE, *Kin Beyond the Sea; from the North American Review* [September 1878]

Nikolai Gogol
1809–1852

1 It is no use to blame the looking glass if your face is awry.

The Inspector-General [1836], epigraph

2 Of course, Alexander the Great was a hero, but why smash the chairs? *Ib.*

3 The more destruction there is everywhere, the more it shows the activity of town authorities. *Ib. act I, sc. i*

4 I tell everyone very plainly that I take bribes, but what kind of bribes? Why, greyhound puppies. That's a totally different matter. *Ib.*

5 The sergeant's widow told you a lie when she said I flogged her. I never flogged her. She flogged herself. *Ib. IV, xv*

6 What are you laughing at? You are laughing at yourselves! *Ib. V, viii*

7 And for a long time yet, led by some wondrous power, I am fated to journey hand in hand with my strange heroes and to survey the surging immensity of life, to survey it through the laughter that all can see and through the tears unseen and unknown by anyone.

Dead Souls [1842], vol. I, ch. 7

8 Rus! Rus! I see you, from my lovely enchanted remoteness I see you: a country of dinginess, and bleakness and dispersal; no arrogant wonders of nature crowned by the arrogant wonders of art appear within you to delight or terrify the eyes. . . . So what is the incomprehensible secret force driving me towards you? Why do I constantly hear the echo of your mournful song as it is carried from sea to sea through your entire expanse? . . . And since you are without end yourself, is it not within you that a boundless thought will be born?[1] *Ib. II, 11*

9 Oh troika, winged troika, tell me who invented you? Surely, nowhere but among a nimble nation could you have been born: in a country which has taken itself in earnest and has evenly spread far and wide over half of the globe, so that once you start counting the milestones you may count on till a speckled haze dances before your eyes. . . .

Rus, are you not similar in your headlong motion to one of those nimble troikas that none can overtake? The flying road turns into smoke under you, bridges thunder and pass, all falls back and is left behind! . . . And what does this awesome motion mean? What is the passing strange force contained in these passing strange steeds? Steeds, steeds, what steeds! Has the whirlwind a home in your manes? . . . Rus, whither are you speeding so? Answer me. No answer. The middle bell trills out in a dream its liquid soliloquy; the roaring air is torn to pieces and becomes wind; all things on earth fly by and other nations and states gaze askance as they step aside and give her the right of way.[1]

Ib. II, concluding paragraphs

10 In the course of the reading he [Pushkin] became more and more melancholy and finally became completely gloomy. When the reading was over he uttered in a voice full of sorrow: "Goodness, how sad is our Russia!"

Four Letters Concerning Dead Souls [1843]

11 I shall laugh my bitter laugh.

Epitaph on Gogol's tombstone

[1]Translated by Vladimir Nabokov.

Oliver Wendell Holmes[2]
1809–1894

12 Ay, tear her tattered ensign down!
Long has it waved on high,
And many an eye has danced to see
That banner in the sky;
Beneath it rung the battle shout,
And burst the cannon's roar—
The meteor of the ocean air
Shall sweep the clouds no more.

Old Ironsides [1830],[3] st. 1

13 And silence, like a poultice, comes
To heal the blows of sound.

The Music Grinders, st. 10

14 When the last reader reads no more.

The Last Reader

15 One flag, one land, one heart, one hand,
One Nation, evermore!

Voyage of the Good Ship Union, st. 12

16 Where we love is home,
Home that our feet may leave, but not our hearts. *Homesick in Heaven, st. 5*

[2]The most successful combination the world has ever seen, of physician and man of letters.—Sir William Osler; *from* Harvey Cushing, *Life of Sir William Osler* [1925], *vol. I, ch. 15*

[3]This poem roused such popular feeling that it is generally credited with saving the frigate *Constitution* from being destroyed as unfit for service.

1 There is no time like the old time, when you
and I were young.[1]
No Time Like the Old Time, st. 1

2 A thought is often original, though you have uttered it a hundred times.
The Autocrat of the Breakfast Table [1858], ch. 1

3 Insanity is often the logic of an accurate mind overtaxed. *Ib. 2*

4 Man has his will—but woman has her way! *Ib.*

5 Put not your trust in money, but put your money in trust. *Ib.*

6 I find the great thing in this world is not so much where we stand, as in what direction we are moving: To reach the port of heaven, we must sail sometimes with the wind and sometimes against it—but we must sail, and not drift, nor lie at anchor. *Ib. 4*

7 Build thee more stately mansions, O my soul,
As the swift seasons roll!
Leave thy low-vaulted past!
Ib. [The Chambered Nautilus, st. 5]

8 Leaving thine outgrown shell by life's unresting sea! *Ib.*

9 Sin has many tools, but a lie is the handle which fits them all. *Ib. ch. 6*

10 There is that glorious Epicurean paradox uttered by my friend the Historian,[2] in one of his flashing moments: "Give us the luxuries of life, and we will dispense with its necessaries."[3] *Ib.*

11 Boston State-House is the hub of the solar system. You couldn't pry that out of a Boston man, if you had the tire of all creation straightened out for a crowbar. *Ib.*

12 The axis of the earth sticks out visibly through the center of each and every town or city. *Ib.*

13 The world's great men have not commonly been great scholars, nor its great scholars great men. *Ib.*

14 Knowledge and timber shouldn't be much used till they are seasoned. *Ib.*

[1]The good old times, the grand old times, the great old times!—DICKENS, *The Chimes* [1844], *First Quarter*
There are no days like the good old days, / The days when we were youthful!—EUGENE FIELD [1850–1895], *Old Times, Old Friends, Old Love*

[2]John Lothrop Motley [1814–1877].

[3]Said Scopas of Thessaly, "We rich men count our felicity and happiness to lie in these superfluities, and not in those necessary things."—PLUTARCH [A.D. 46–120], *On the Love of Wealth*

15 Have you heard of the wonderful one-hoss
shay,
That was built in such a logical way
It ran a hundred years to a day?
Ib. 11 [The Deacon's Masterpiece, st. 1]

16 End of the wonderful one-hoss shay.
Logic is logic. That's all I say.
Ib. [st. 12]

17 He comes of the Brahmin caste of New England. This is the harmless, inoffensive, untitled aristocracy.
The Brahmin Caste of New England [1860]

18 Science is a first-rate piece of furniture for a man's upper chamber, if he has common sense on the ground floor.
The Poet at the Breakfast Table [1872], ch. 5

19 And if I should live to be
The last leaf upon the tree
In the spring,
Let them smile, as I do now,
At the old forsaken bough
Where I cling.
The Last Leaf [1831], st. 8

Abraham Lincoln[4]

1809–1865

20 If the good people, in their wisdom, shall see fit to keep me in the background, I have been too familiar with disappointments to be very much chagrined.
Address at New Salem, Illinois [March 9, 1832]

21 I go for all sharing the privileges of the government who assist in bearing its burdens.
Letter to the Editor, Sangamon Journal, New Salem, Illinois [June 13, 1836]

22 If destruction be our lot we must ourselves be its author and finisher. As a nation of freemen we must live through all time, or die by suicide.
Address at the Young Men's Lyceum, Springfield, Illinois [January 27, 1838]

23 There is no grievance that is a fit object of redress by mob law. *Ib.*

24 Towering genius disdains a beaten path. It seeks regions hitherto unexplored. *Ib.*

[4]Old Abe Lincoln came out of the wilderness / Down in Illinois.—ANONYMOUS [c. 1860]

1 No man is good enough to govern another man without that other's consent.

Speech at Peoria, Illinois [October 16, 1854]

2 I am not a Know-Nothing . . . How could I be? How can anyone who abhors the oppression of Negroes be in favor of degrading classes of white people? Our progress in degeneracy appears to me to be pretty rapid. As a nation we began by declaring that "all men are created equal." We now practically read it "all men are created equal, except Negroes." When the Know-Nothings get control, it will read "all men are created equal, except Negroes and foreigners and Catholics." When it comes to this, I shall prefer emigrating to some country where they make no pretense of loving liberty—to Russia, for instance, where despotism can be taken pure, and without the base alloy of hypocrisy.[1]

Letter to Joshua F. Speed [August 24, 1855]

3 The ballot is stronger than the bullet.

Speech at Bloomington, Illinois [May 19, 1856]

4 "A house divided against itself cannot stand."[2] I believe this government cannot endure permanently half slave and half free. I do not expect the Union to be dissolved—I do not expect the house to fall—but I do expect it will cease to be divided. It will become all one thing, or all the other. Either the opponents of slavery will arrest the further spread of it, and place it where the public mind shall rest in the belief that it is in the course of ultimate extinction; or its advocates will push it forward till it shall become alike lawful in all the states, old as well as new, North as well as South.

Speech at the Republican State Convention, Springfield, Illinois [June 16, 1858]

5 Nobody has ever expected me to be President. In my poor, lean, lank face nobody has ever seen that any cabbages were sprouting out.[3]

Second campaign speech against Douglas, Springfield, Illinois [July 17, 1858]

6 As I would not be a *slave,* so I would not be a *master.* This expresses my idea of democracy. Whatever differs from this, to the extent of the difference, is no democracy.[4]

Fragment [August 1, 1858?]. From Roy P. Basler, *The Collected Works of Abraham Lincoln [1953], vol. II, p. 532*

7 When . . . you have succeeded in dehumanizing the Negro; when you have put him down and made it impossible for him to be but as the beasts of the field; when you have extinguished his soul in this world and placed him where the ray of hope is blown out as in the darkness of the damned, are you quite sure that the demon you have roused will not turn and rend you? What constitutes the bulwark of our own liberty and independence? It is not our frowning battlements, our bristling sea coasts, our army and our navy. These are not our reliance against tyranny. All of those may be turned against us without making us weaker for the struggle. Our reliance is in the love of liberty which God has planted in us. Our defense is in the spirit which prized liberty as the heritage of all men, in all lands everywhere. Destroy this spirit and you have planted the seeds of despotism at your own doors. Familiarize yourselves with the chains of bondage and you prepare your own limbs to wear them. Accustomed to trample on the rights of others, you have lost the genius of your own independence and become the fit subjects of the first cunning tyrant who rises among you.[5]

Speech at Edwardsville, Illinois [September 11, 1858]

8 That is the issue that will continue in this country when these poor tongues of Judge Douglas and myself shall be silent. It is the eternal struggle between these two principles—right and wrong—throughout the world. They are the two principles that have stood face to face from the beginning of time; and will ever continue to struggle. The one is the common right of humanity, and the other the divine right of kings. It is the same principle in whatever shape it develops itself. It is the same spirit that says, "You toil and work and earn bread, and I'll eat it." No matter in what shape it comes, whether from the mouth of a king who seeks to bestride the people of his own nation and live by the fruit of their labor, or from one race of men as an apology for enslaving another race, it is the same tyrannical principle.

Reply, seventh and last joint debate, Alton, Illinois [October 15, 1858]

[1] See Niemoeller, 824:1.

[2] See *Mark 3:25,* 41:35.

[3] They have seen in his [Douglas's] round, jolly, fruitful face, post offices, land offices, marshalships and cabinet appointments, chargeships and foreign missions, bursting and sprouting out in wonderful exuberance, ready to be laid hold of by their greedy hands.—Lincoln, *ib.*

[4] See *Address to Indiana Regiment,* 524:8.

[5] See Einstein, 764:4.

1 This is a world of compensation; and he who would be no slave must consent to have no slave. Those who deny freedom to others deserve it not for themselves, and, under a just God, cannot long retain it.

Letter to H. L. Pierce and others [April 6, 1859]

2 Public opinion in this country is everything.

Speech at Columbus, Ohio [September 16, 1859]

3 It is said an Eastern monarch once charged his wise men to invent him a sentence to be ever in view, and which should be true and appropriate in all times and situations. They presented him the words: "And this, too, shall pass away." How much it expresses! How chastening in the hour of pride! How consoling in the depths of affliction!

Address to the Wisconsin State Agricultural Society, Milwaukee [September 30, 1859]

4 What is conservatism? Is it not adherence to the old and tried, against the new and untried?

Address at Cooper Union, New York [February 27, 1860]

5 Let us have faith that right makes might, and in that faith let us to the end dare to do our duty as we understand it. *Ib.*

6 No one, not in my situation, can appreciate my feeling of sadness at this parting. To this place, and the kindness of these people, I owe everything. Here I have lived a quarter of a century, and have passed from a young to an old man. Here my children have been born, and one is buried. I now leave, not knowing when or whether ever I may return, with a task before me greater than that which rested upon Washington. Without the assistance of that Divine Being who ever attended him, I cannot succeed. With that assistance I cannot fail. Trusting in Him who can go with me, and remain with you, and be everywhere for good, let us confidently hope that all will yet be well.

Farewell Address, Springfield, Illinois [February 11, 1861]

7 If we do not make common cause to save the good old ship of the Union on this voyage, nobody will have a chance to pilot her on another voyage.

Address at Cleveland, Ohio [February 15, 1861]

8 I have never had a feeling, politically, that did not spring from the sentiments embodied in the Declaration of Independence. . . . I have often inquired of myself what great principle or idea it was that kept this Confederacy so long together. It was not the mere matter of separation of the colonies from the motherland, but that sentiment in the Declaration of Independence which gave liberty not alone to the people of this country, but hope to all the world, for all future time. It was that which gave promise that in due time the weights would be lifted from the shoulders of all men, and that all should have an equal chance. This is the sentiment embodied in the Declaration of Independence. . . . I would rather be assassinated on this spot than surrender it.

Speech at Independence Hall, Philadelphia [February 22, 1861]

9 It is safe to assert that no government proper ever had a provision in its organic law for its own termination.

First Inaugural Address [March 4, 1861]

10 If by the mere force of numbers a majority should deprive a minority of any clearly written constitutional right, it might, in a moral point of view, justify revolution—certainly would if such a right were a vital one.

Ib.

11 This country, with its institutions, belongs to the people who inhabit it. Whenever they shall grow weary of the existing government, they can exercise their constitutional right of amending it, or their revolutionary right to dismember or overthrow it. *Ib.*

12 Why should there not be a patient confidence in the ultimate justice of the people? Is there any better or equal hope in the world?

Ib.

13 While the people retain their virtue and vigilance, no administration, by any extreme of wickedness or folly, can very seriously injure the government in the short space of four years. *Ib.*

14 We are not enemies, but friends. We must not be enemies. Though passion may have strained, it must not break, our bonds of affection. The mystic chords of memory, stretching from every battlefield and patriot grave to every living heart and hearthstone all over this broad land, will yet swell the chorus of the Union when again touched, as surely they will be, by the better angels of our nature. *Ib.*

1 I think the necessity of being *ready* increases. Look to it.

Letter (this is the whole message) to Governor Andrew G. Curtin of Pennsylvania [*April 8, 1861*]

2 This is essentially a people's contest . . . It is a struggle for maintaining in the world that form and substance of government whose leading object is to elevate the condition of men — to lift artificial weights from all shoulders — to clear the paths of laudable pursuit for all — to afford all an unfettered start, and a fair chance, in the race of life.

Message to Congress in Special Session [July 4, 1861]

3 Labor is prior to, and independent of, capital. Capital is only the fruit of labor, and could never have existed if labor had not first existed. Labor is the superior of capital, and deserves much the higher consideration. Capital has its rights, which are as worthy of protection as any other rights.[1]

First Annual Message to Congress [December 3, 1861]

4 It is called the Army of the Potomac but it is only McClellan's bodyguard . . . If McClellan is not using the army, I should like to borrow it for a while.

Washington, D.C. [April 9, 1862]

5 It is difficult to make a man miserable while he feels he is worthy of himself and claims kindred to the great God who made him.

Address on colonization to a Negro deputation at Washington [August 14, 1862]

6 My paramount object in this struggle is to save the Union, and is not either to save or to destroy slavery. If I could save the Union without freeing any slave, I would do it; and if I could save it by freeing all the slaves, I would do it; and if I could do it by freeing some and leaving others alone, I would also do that.

Letter to Horace Greeley [August 22, 1862]

7 I shall try to correct errors when shown to be errors; and I shall adopt new views so fast as they shall appear to be true views. . . . I intend no modification of my oft-expressed personal wish that all men, everywhere, could be free. *Ib.*

8 On the first day of January in the year of our Lord, one thousand eight hundred and sixty-three, all persons held as slaves within any state, or designated part of a state, the people whereof shall then be in rebellion against the United States shall be then, thenceforward, and forever free.

Preliminary Emancipation Proclamation [September 22, 1862][2]

9 [I feel] somewhat like the boy in Kentucky who stubbed his toe while running to see his sweetheart. The boy said he was too big to cry, and far too badly hurt to laugh.

Reply as to how he felt about the New York elections.[3] *From Frank Leslie's Illustrated Weekly [November 22, 1862]*

10 A nation may be said to consist of its territory, its people, and its laws. The territory is the only part which is of certain durability.

Second Annual Message to Congress [December 1, 1862]

11 If there ever could be a proper time for mere catch arguments, that time surely is not now. In times like the present, men should utter nothing for which they would not willingly be responsible through time and in eternity. *Ib.*

12 The dogmas of the quiet past are inadequate to the stormy present. The occasion is piled high with difficulty, and we must rise with the occasion. As our case is new, so we must think anew and act anew. We must disenthrall ourselves, and then we shall save our country.

Fellow citizens, we cannot escape history. We of this Congress and this administration will be remembered in spite of ourselves. No personal significance or insignificance can spare one or another of us. The fiery trial through which we pass will light us down in honor or dishonor to the last generation. We say we are for the Union. The world will not forget that we say this. We know how to save the Union. The world knows we do know how to save it. We, even we here, hold the power and bear the responsibility. In giving freedom to the slave, we assure freedom to the free — honorable alike in what we give and what we preserve. We shall nobly save or meanly lose the last, best hope of earth. Other means may succeed; this could not fail. The way is plain, peaceful, generous, just

[1]See Webster, 450:4.

[2]The Emancipation Proclamation was issued one hundred days later [January 1, 1863].

[3]The election was a victory for Horatio Seymour, Democratic candidate for governor of New York. Moreover, throughout the North the Democrats picked up a number of congressional seats and won a number of state elections.

—a way which if followed the world will forever applaud and God must forever bless.

Ib.

1 Beware of rashness, but with energy and sleepless vigilance go forward and give us victories.

Letter to Major General Joseph Hooker [January 26, 1863]

2 The Father of Waters again goes unvexed to the sea.

Letter to James C. Conkling [August 26, 1863]

3 I have endured a great deal of ridicule without much malice; and have received a great deal of kindness, not quite free from ridicule. I am used to it.

Letter to James H. Hackett [November 2, 1863]

4 Fourscore and seven years ago our fathers brought forth on this continent, a new nation, conceived in Liberty, and dedicated to the proposition that all men are created equal.

Now we are engaged in a great civil war, testing whether that nation or any nation so conceived and so dedicated can long endure. We are met on a great battlefield of that war. We have come to dedicate a portion of that field, as a final resting place for those who here gave their lives that that nation might live. It is altogether fitting and proper that we should do this.

But, in a larger sense, we cannot dedicate—we cannot consecrate—we cannot hallow—this ground. The brave men, living and dead, who struggled here, have consecrated it far above our poor power to add or detract. The world will little note nor long remember what we say here, but it can never forget what they did here. It is for us, the living, rather to be dedicated here to the unfinished work which they who fought here have thus far so nobly advanced. It is rather for us to be here dedicated to the great task remaining before us—that from these honored dead we take increased devotion to that cause for which they gave the last full measure of devotion; that we here highly resolve that these dead shall not have died in vain; that this nation, under God, shall have a new birth of freedom; and that government of the people, by the people, for the people, shall not perish from the earth.[1]

Address at Gettysburg [November 19, 1863]

[1]See Wycliffe, 143:12; Webster, 450:14; Disraeli, 501:6; Garrison, 505:19; and Parker, 537:15.

5 The President last night had a dream. He was in a party of plain people and as it became known who he was they began to comment on his appearance. One of them said, "He is a common-looking man." The President replied, "Common-looking people are the best in the world: that is the reason the Lord makes so many of them."

From Letters of John Hay and Extracts from His Diary, edited by C. L. HAY [December 23, 1863]

6 I claim not to have controlled events, but confess plainly that events have controlled me.

Letter to A. G. Hodges [April 4, 1864]

7 The world has never had a good definition of the word liberty. And the American people just now are much in want of one. We all declare for liberty; but in using the same word we do not mean the same thing. With some, the word liberty may mean for each man to do as he pleases with himself and the product of his labor; while with others the same word may mean for some men to do as they please with other men and the product of other men's labor. Here are two, not only different, but incompatible things, called by the same name, liberty. And it follows that each of the things is by the respective parties called by two different and incompatible names, liberty and tyranny.

The shepherd drives the wolf from the sheep's throat, for which the sheep thanks the shepherd as his liberator, while the wolf denounces him for the same act. . . . Plainly the sheep and the wolf are not agreed upon a definition of liberty.

Address at the Sanitary Fair, Baltimore [April 18, 1864]

8 I do not allow myself to suppose that either the convention or the League have concluded to decide that I am either the greatest or best man in America, but rather they have concluded that it is not best to swap horses while crossing the river, and have further concluded that I am not so poor a horse that they might not make a botch of it in trying to swap.

Reply to the National Union League [June 9, 1864]

9 Truth is generally the best vindication against slander.

Letter to Secretary Stanton, refusing to dismiss Postmaster-General Montgomery Blair [July 18, 1864]

1 It has long been a grave question whether any government, not too strong for the liberties of its people, can be strong enough to maintain its existence in great emergencies.

Response to a serenade [November 10, 1864]

2 Human nature will not change. In any future great national trial, compared with the men of this, we shall have as weak and as strong, as silly and as wise, as bad and as good. *Ib.*

3 I desire so to conduct the affairs of this administration that if at the end, when I come to lay down the reins of power, I have lost every other friend on earth, I shall at least have one friend left, and that friend shall be down inside me.

Reply to the Missouri Committee of Seventy [1864]

4 Dear Madam, I have been shown in the files of the War Department a statement of the Adjutant-General of Massachusetts that you are the mother of five[1] sons who have died gloriously on the field of battle. I feel how weak and fruitless must be any words of mine which should attempt to beguile you from the grief of a loss so overwhelming. But I cannot refrain from tendering to you the consolation that may be found in the thanks of the Republic they died to save. I pray that our heavenly Father may assuage the anguish of your bereavement, and leave you only the cherished memory of the loved and lost, and the solemn pride that must be yours to have laid so costly a sacrifice upon the altar of freedom.

Letter to Mrs. Bixby [November 21, 1864]

5 It may seem strange that any men should dare to ask a just God's assistance in wringing their bread from the sweat of other men's faces,[2] but let us judge not, that we be not judged.[3]

Second Inaugural Address [March 4, 1865]

6 The Almighty has His own purposes.

Ib.

7 Fondly do we hope, fervently do we pray, that this mighty scourge of war may speedily pass away. Yet, if God wills that it continue until all the wealth piled by the bondsman's two hundred and fifty years of unrequited toil shall be sunk, and until every drop of blood drawn with the lash shall be paid by another drawn with the sword, as was said three thousand years ago, so still it must be said, "The judgments of the Lord are true and righteous altogether."[4]

With malice toward none, with charity for all, with firmness in the right as God gives us to see the right,[5] let us strive on to finish the work we are in, to bind up the nation's wounds, to care for him who shall have borne the battle and for his widow and his orphan, to do all which may achieve and cherish a just and lasting peace among ourselves and with all nations. *Ib.*

8 I have always thought that all men should be free; but if any should be slaves, it should be first those who desire it for themselves, and secondly those who desire it for others. Whenever I hear anyone arguing for slavery, I feel a strong impulse to see it tried on him personally.[6]

Address to an Indiana Regiment [March 17, 1865]

9 Important principles may and must be inflexible.

Last public address, Washington, D.C. [April 11, 1865]

10 If you once forfeit the confidence of your fellow citizens, you can never regain their respect and esteem. It is true that you may fool all the people some of the time; you can even fool some of the people all the time; but you can't fool all of the people all the time.

To a caller at the White House. From ALEXANDER K. MCCLURE, *Lincoln's Yarns and Stories [1904]*

11 If I were to try to read, much less answer, all the attacks made on me, this shop might as well be closed for any other business. I do the very best I know how—the very best I can; and I mean to keep doing so until the end. If the end brings me out all right, what is said against me won't amount to anything. If the end brings me out wrong, ten angels swearing I was right would make no difference.

Conversation at the White House. From FRANCIS B. CARPENTER, *Six Months at the White House with Abraham Lincoln [1866]*

12 Love is the chain whereby to bind a child to his parents.

Ib. Washington, D.C. [c. 1860]

[1] Later, the records were revised; the correct number was two.

[2] See *Genesis 3:19,* 7:12.

[3] See *Matthew 7:1,* 38:8.

[4] See *Psalms 19:9,* 18:1.

[5] See John Quincy Adams, 418:6.

[6] See *Fragment,* 520:6.

Benjamin Peirce
1809–1880

1 Mathematics is the science which draws necessary conclusions.

Linear Associative Algebra [1870], first sentence

Edgar Allan Poe[1]
1809–1849

2 O, human love! thou spirit given,
On Earth, of all we hope in Heaven!

Tamerlane [1827], l. 177

3 All that we see or seem
Is but a dream within a dream.

A Dream Within a Dream [1827],[2] *l. 10*

4 The happiest day—the happiest hour
My seared and blighted heart hath known,
The highest hope of pride and power,
I feel hath flown.

The Happiest Day [1827], st. 1

5 From childhood's hour I have not been
As others were—I have not seen
As others saw.

Alone [written 1829, published 1875], l. 1

6 And the cloud that took the form
When the rest of Heaven was blue
Of a demon in my view. *Ib. l. 20*

7 Hast thou not torn the Naiad from her flood,
The Elfin from the green grass, and from me
The summer dream beneath the tamarind tree?

Sonnet. To Science [1829], l. 12

8 It is with literature as with law or empire—an established name is an estate in tenure, or a throne in possession.

Poems [1831]. Preface, Letter to Mr. B——

9 Helen, thy beauty is to me
Like those Nicean barks of yore,
That gently, o'er a perfumed sea,
The weary, wayworn wanderer bore
To his own native shore.

On desperate seas long wont to roam,
Thy hyacinth hair, thy classic face,
Thy Naiad airs have brought me home
To the glory that was Greece,
And the grandeur that was Rome.

To Helen [1831], st. 1, 2

[1] See James Russell Lowell, 567:18.

[2] Actually a late poem (written 1849), *A Dream Within a Dream* is a completely revised descendant of the 1827 poem *Imitation.*

10 If I could dwell
Where Israfel[3]
Hath dwelt, and he where I,
He might not sing so wildly well
A mortal melody,
While a bolder note than this might swell
From my lyre within the sky.

Israfel [1831], st. 8

11 Lo! Death has reared himself a throne
In a strange city, lying alone
Far down among the dim West,
Where the good and the bad and the worst and the best
Have gone to their eternal rest.

The City in the Sea [1831], st. 1

12 The viol, the violet, and the vine.

Ib. st. 2

13 While from a proud tower in the town
Death looks gigantically down.[4] *Ib.*

14 And when, amid no earthly moans,
Down, down that town shall settle hence,
Hell, rising from a thousand thrones,
Shall do it reverence. *Ib. st. 5*

15 A dirge for the most lovely dead
That ever died so young!

Lenore [1831],[5] *st. 1*

16 Vastness! and Age! and Memories of Eld!
Silence! and Desolation! and dim Night!

The Coliseum [1833], st. 1

17 Thou wast that all to me, love,
For which my soul did pine—
A green isle in the sea, love,
A fountain and a shrine,
All wreathed with fairy fruits and flowers,
And all the flowers were mine.

To One in Paradise [1834], st. 1

18 And all my days are trances,
And all my nightly dreams
Are where thy gray eye glances,
And where thy footstep gleams—
In what ethereal dances,
By what eternal streams. *Ib. st. 4*

19 During the whole of a dull, dark, and soundless day in the autumn of the year, when the clouds hung oppressively low in the heavens, I had been passing alone, on horseback, through a singularly dreary tract

[3] Poe's epigraph for the poem:
And the angel Israfel, whose heartstrings are a lute, and who has the sweetest voice of all God's creatures.—*Koran*

[4] See Hart Crane, 844:2.

[5] First published in 1843, *Lenore* descends from *A Paean* [1831].
A dirge for her the doubly dead in that she died so young.—Poe, *Lenore* [1849 version], *st. 1*

of country, and at length found myself, as the shades of the evening drew on, within view of the melancholy House of Usher.
The Fall of the House of Usher [1839]

1 In the greenest of our valleys
By good angels tenanted,
Once a fair and stately palace—
Radiant palace—reared its head.
The Haunted Palace [1839], st. 1

2 While, like a ghastly rapid river,
Through the pale door,
A hideous throng rush out forever
And laugh—but smile no more.
Ib. st. 6

3 They who dream by day are cognizant of many things which escape those who dream only by night. *Eleonora [1841]*

4 And much of Madness, and more of Sin,
And Horror the soul of the plot.
The Conqueror Worm [1843], st. 3

5 While the angels, all pallid and wan,
Uprising, unveiling, affirm
That the play is the tragedy, "Man,"
And its hero the Conqueror Worm.
Ib. st. 5

6 There is something in the unselfish and self-sacrificing love of a brute, which goes directly to the heart of him who has had frequent occasion to test the paltry friendship and gossamer fidelity of mere Man.
The Black Cat [1843]

7 The boundaries which divide Life from Death are at best shadowy and vague. Who shall say where the one ends, and where the other begins?
The Premature Burial [1844]

8 From a wild weird clime that lieth, sublime,
Out of Space—out of Time.
Dreamland [1845], st. 1

9 With me poetry has been not a purpose, but a passion; and the passions should be held in reverence: they must not—they cannot at will be excited, with an eye to the paltry compensations, or the more paltry commendations, of mankind.
The Raven and Other Poems [1845], preface

10 Once upon a midnight dreary, while I pondered, weak and weary,
Over many a quaint and curious volume of forgotten lore—
While I nodded, nearly napping, suddenly there came a tapping,
As of someone gently rapping, rapping at my chamber door.
The Raven [1845], st. 1

11 Ah, distinctly I remember it was in the bleak December;
And each separate dying ember wrought its ghost upon the floor. *Ib. st. 2*

12 Sorrow for the lost Lenore—
For the rare and radiant maiden whom the angels name Lenore—
Nameless *here* for evermore. *Ib.*

13 The silken, sad, uncertain rustling of each purple curtain. *Ib. st. 3*

14 Deep into that darkness peering, long I stood there wondering, fearing,
Doubting, dreaming dreams no mortal ever dared to dream before. *Ib. st. 5*

15 "Ghastly grim and ancient Raven wandering from the Nightly shore—
Tell me what thy lordly name is on the Night's Plutonian shore!"
Quoth the Raven, "Nevermore."
Ib. st. 8

16 Whom unmerciful Disaster
Followed fast and followed faster.
Ib. st. 11

17 "Prophet!" said I, "thing of evil!—prophet still, if bird or devil!" *Ib. st. 15*

18 "Take thy beak from out my heart, and take thy form from off my door!"
Quoth the Raven, "Nevermore."
Ib. st. 17

19 And the Raven, never flitting, still is sitting, *still* is sitting
On the pallid bust of Pallas just above my chamber door. *Ib. st. 18*

20 And my soul from out that shadow that lies floating on the floor
Shall be lifted—nevermore! *Ib.*

21 The Imp of the Perverse.[1]
Title of story [1845]

22 The skies they were ashen and sober;
The leaves they were crispèd and sere—
The leaves they were withering and sere:
It was night in the lonesome October
Of my most immemorial year.
Ulalume [1847], st. 1

23 It was down by the dank tarn of Auber,
In the ghoul-haunted woodland of Weir.
Ib.

[1] Perverseness is one of the primitive impulses of the human heart.—POE, *The Black Cat* [1843]

1 Here once, through an alley Titanic,
Of cypress, I roamed with my Soul—
Of cypress, with Psyche, my Soul.

Ib. st. 2

2 Thus I pacified Psyche and kissed her,
And tempted her out of her gloom.

Ib. st. 8

3 Can it be fancied that Deity ever vindictively
Made in his image a mannikin merely to madden it?[1]

The Rationale of Verse [1848], III

4 A Quixotic sense of the honorable—of the chivalrous.

Letter to Mrs. Whitman [October 18, 1848]

5 "Over the Mountains
Of the Moon,
Down the Valley of the Shadow,
Ride, boldly ride,"
The shade replied—
"If you seek for Eldorado!"

Eldorado [1849], st. 4

6 And the fever called "Living"
Is conquered at last.

For Annie [1849], st. 1

7 And this maiden she lived with no other thought
Than to love and be loved by me.

Annabel Lee [1849], st. 1

8 *I* was a child and *she* was a child,[2]
In this kingdom by the sea,
But we loved with a love that was more than love—
I and my Annabel Lee—
With a love that the wingèd seraphs of Heaven
Coveted her and me. *Ib. st. 2*

9 And neither the angels in Heaven above
Nor the demons down under the sea,
Can ever dissever my soul from the soul
Of the beautiful Annabel Lee. *Ib. st. 5*

10 In her sepulcher there by the sea—
In her tomb by the sounding sea.[3]

Ib. st. 6

11 Keeping time, time, time,
In a sort of Runic rhyme,
To the tintinnabulation that so musically wells
From the bells, bells, bells, bells,
Bells, bells, bells.

The Bells [1849], st. 1

[1] See FitzGerald, 517:6.

[2] Poe's latest manuscript version [September 1849] reads: *She* was a child and *I* was a child.

[3] Poe's latest manuscript version [September 1849] reads: In her tomb by the side of the sea.

12 I hold that a long poem does not exist. I maintain that the phrase "a long poem" is simply a flat contradiction in terms.

The Poetic Principle [1850]

13 There neither exists nor can exist any work more thoroughly dignified—more supremely noble than this very poem—this poem *per se*—this poem which is a poem and nothing more—this poem written solely for the poem's sake. *Ib.*

14 I would define, in brief, the poetry of words as the rhythmical creation of Beauty. Its sole arbiter is taste. With the intellect or with the conscience, it has only collateral relations. Unless incidentally, it has no concern whatever either with duty or with truth.

Ib.

Pierre Joseph Proudhon

1809–1865

15 Property is theft [La propriété c'est le vol]!

Qu'est-ce que la Propriété? [1840], ch. 1

Alfred, Lord Tennyson

1809–1892

16 O damned vacillating state!

Supposed Confessions [1830], last line

17 Weeded and worn the ancient thatch
Upon the lonely moated grange.

Mariana[4] [1830], st. 1

18 She said, "I am aweary, aweary,
I would that I were dead!" *Ib. refrain*

19 A still small voice[5] spake unto me,
"Thou art so full of misery,
Were it not better not to be?"

The Two Voices [1832], st. 1

20 This truth within thy mind rehearse,
That in a boundless universe
Is boundless better, boundless worse.

Ib. st. 9

21 Though thou wert scattered to the wind,
Yet is there plenty of the kind.[6]

Ib. st. 11

22 I know that age to age succeeds,
Blowing a noise of tongues and deeds,
A dust of systems and of creeds.

Ib. st. 69

[4] See Shakespeare, 228:24.

[5] See *I Kings 19:12*, 14:5.

[6] See FitzGerald, 516:21.

1 Like glimpses of forgotten dreams.
Ib. st. 127

2 No life that breathes with human breath
Has ever truly longed for death.
Ib. st. 132

3 In after-dinner talk,
Across the walnuts and the wine.
The Miller's Daughter [1832], st. 4

4 O mother Ida, many-fountained Ida,
Dear mother Ida, hearken ere I die.
Oenone [1832], l. 22

5 Self-reverence, self-knowledge, self-control,
These three alone lead life to sovereign power.
Ib. l. 142

6 I built my soul a lordly pleasure-house,
Wherein at ease for aye to dwell.
The Palace of Art [1832], st. 1

7 The daughter of a hundred Earls,
You are not one to be desired.
Lady Clara Vere de Vere [1832], st. 1

8 A simple maiden in her flower
Is worth a hundred coats-of-arms.
Ib. st. 2

9 The lion on your old stone gates
Is not more cold to you than I.
Ib. st. 3

10 The gardener Adam[1] and his wife
Smile at the claims of long descent.
Ib. st. 7

11 'Tis only noble to be good.
Kind hearts are more than coronets,
And simple faith than Norman blood.
Ib.

12 You must wake and call me early, call me early, mother dear;
Tomorrow 'ill be the happiest time of all the glad New Year;
Of all the glad New Year, mother, the maddest, merriest day;
For I'm to be Queen o' the May, mother, I'm to be Queen o' the May.
The May Queen [1832], st. 1

13 In the afternoon they came unto a land
In which it seemed always afternoon.
The Lotos-Eaters [1832], st. 1

14 Music that gentlier on the spirit lies,
Than tired eyelids upon tired eyes.
Ib. Choric Song, st. 1

15 There is no joy but calm!
Ib. st. 2

[1]See *Genesis* 2:8, 6:18; Bacon, 181:10; Shakespeare, 185:26 and 224:5; and Kipling, 710:22.

16 Ah, why
Should life all labor be?
Ib. st. 4

17 Let us alone. Time driveth onward fast,
And in a little while our lips are dumb.
Let us alone. What is it that will last?
All things are taken from us, and become
Portions and parcels of the dreadful Past.
Ib.

18 Give us long rest or death, dark death or dreamful ease.
Ib.

19 Live and lie reclined
On the hills like Gods together, careless of mankind.
Ib. st. 8

20 Surely, surely, slumber is more sweet than toil, the shore
Than labor in the deep mid-ocean, wind and wave and oar;
Oh rest ye, brother mariners, we will not wander more.
Ib. last lines

21 Dan Chaucer, the first warbler, whose sweet breath
Preluded those melodious bursts that fill
The spacious times of great Elizabeth
With sounds that echo still.
A Dream of Fair Women [1832]

22 A daughter of the gods, divinely tall,
And most divinely fair.
Ib. st. 22

23 Many-towered Camelot.
The Lady of Shalott [1832], pt. I, st. 1

24 Willows whiten, aspens quiver,
Little breezes dusk and shiver.
Ib. st. 2

25 All in the blue unclouded weather.
Ib. III, st. 3

26 "Tirra lirra," by the river
Sang Sir Lancelot.
Ib. st. 4

27 She left the web, she left the loom,
She made three paces thro' the room,
She saw the water lily bloom,
She saw the helmet and the plume,
She looked down to Camelot.
Out flew the web and floated wide;
The mirror cracked from side to side.
"The curse has come upon me," cried
The Lady of Shalott.
Ib. st. 5

28 But Lancelot mused a little space;
He said, "She has a lovely face;
God in his mercy lend her grace,
The Lady of Shalott."
Ib. IV, st. 6

29 The great brand
Made lightnings in the splendor of the moon,

And flashing round and round, and whirled in an arch,
Shot like a streamer of the northern morn,
Seen where the moving isles of winter shock
By night, with noises of the northern sea,
So flashed and fell the brand Excalibur.
Morte d'Arthur [1842], l. 133

1 Lo! the level lake
And the long glories of the winter moon.
Ib. l. 184

2 Half light, half shade,
She stood, a sight to make an old man young.
The Gardener's Daughter [1842], l. 139

3 The long mechanic pacings to and fro,
The set gray life, and apathetic end.
Love and Duty [1842], l. 17

4 Meet is it changes should control
Our being, lest we rest in ease.
Love Thou Thy Land [1842], st. 11

5 Ah! when shall all men's good
Be each man's rule, and universal peace
Lie like a shaft of light across the land,
And like a lane of beams athwart the sea,
Through all the circle of the golden year?
The Golden Year [1842], l. 47

6 It little profits that an idle king,
By this still hearth, among these barren crags,
Matched with an aged wife, I mete and dole
Unequal laws unto a savage race.
Ulysses [1842], l. 1

7 I will drink
Life to the lees. *Ib. l. 6*

8 Much have I seen and known; cities of men
And manners, climates, councils, governments,
Myself not least, but honored of them all;
And drunk delight of battle with my peers,
Far on the ringing plains of windy Troy.
I am a part of all that I have met;
Yet all experience is an arch wherethrough
Gleams that untraveled world.[1]
Ib. l. 13

9 How dull it is to pause, to make an end,
To rust unburnished, not to shine in use,
As though to breathe were life!
Ib. l. 22

10 And this gray spirit yearning in desire
To follow knowledge like a sinking star,
Beyond the utmost bound of human thought.
Ib. l. 30

11 This is my son, mine own Telemachus.
Ib. l. 33

[1] See Henry Adams, 634:18.

12 Death closes all: but something ere the end,
Some work of noble note, may yet be done,
Not unbecoming men that strove with gods.
Ib. l. 51

13 The deep
Moans round with many voices.[2] Come, my friends,
'Tis not too late to seek a newer world.
Push off, and sitting well in order smite
The sounding furrows, for my purpose holds
To sail beyond the sunset, and the baths
Of all the western stars, until I die.
It may be that the gulfs will wash us down;
It may be we shall touch the Happy Isles,
And see the great Achilles, whom we knew.
Ib. l. 55

14 To strive, to seek, to find, and not to yield.[3]
Ib. l. 70

15 Comrades, leave me here a little, while as yet 'tis early morn:
Leave me here, and when you want me, sound upon the bugle horn.
Locksley Hall [1842], l. 1

16 In the spring a young man's fancy lightly turns to thoughts of love. *Ib. l. 19*

17 He will hold thee, when his passion shall have spent its novel force,
Something better than his dog, a little dearer than his horse. *Ib. l. 49*

18 The many-wintered crow that leads the clanging rookery home. *Ib. l. 68*

19 Such a one do I remember, whom to look at was to love.[4] *Ib. l. 72*

20 This is the truth the poet sings,
That a sorrow's crown of sorrow is remembering happier things.[5] *Ib. l. 75*

21 Like a dog, he hunts in dreams.
Ib. l. 79

22 With a little hoard of maxims preaching down a daughter's heart. *Ib. l. 94*

23 But the jingling of the guinea helps the hurt that Honor feels. *Ib. l. 105*

24 For I dipped into the future, far as human eye could see,
Saw the Vision of the world, and all the wonder that would be;
Saw the heavens fill with commerce, argosies of magic sails,

[2] See *Revelation 14*:2, 53:22, and Eliot, 808:2.

[3] Inscribed on the cross erected to the memory of Captain Robert Falcon Scott [1868–1912] and his men at Hut Point in the Antarctic.

[4] See Burns, 410:3, and Halleck, 464:11.

[5] See Pindar, 72:1; Boethius, 129:22; Dante, 141:2; and Chaucer, 144:24.

Pilots of the purple twilight, dropping down with costly bales;
Heard the heavens fill with shouting, and there rained a ghastly dew
From the nations' airy navies grappling in the central blue. *Ib. l. 119*

1 Till the war drum throbbed no longer and the battle flags were furled
In the Parliament of man, the Federation of the world. *Ib. l. 127*

2 And the kindly earth shall slumber, lapped in universal law. *Ib. l. 130*

3 Yet I doubt not through the ages one increasing purpose runs,
And the thoughts of men are widened with the process of the suns. *Ib. l. 137*

4 Knowledge comes, but wisdom lingers. *Ib. l. 141*

5 Woman is the lesser man, and all thy passions, matched with mine,
Are as moonlight unto sunlight, and as water unto wine. *Ib. l. 151*

6 I will take some savage woman, she shall rear my dusky race. *Ib. l. 168*

7 I the heir of all the ages, in the foremost files of time. *Ib. l. 178*

8 Let the great world spin forever down the ringing grooves of change. *Ib. l. 182*

9 Better fifty years of Europe than a cycle of Cathay. *Ib. l. 184*

10 This proverb flashes through his head,
"The many fail, the one succeeds."
The Day Dream [1842]. The Arrival, st. 2

11 And on her lover's arm she leant,
And round her waist she felt it fold,
And far across the hills they went
In that new world which is the old.
Ib. The Departure, st. 1

12 O love, thy kiss would wake the dead!
Ib. st. 3

13 And o'er the hills and far away[1]
Beyond their utmost purple rim,
Beyond the night, across the day,
Through all the world she followed him.
Ib. st. 4

14 And is there any moral shut
Within the bosom of the rose?
Ib. Moral, st. 1

[1]See Gay, 332:1, and Nursery Rhymes, 931:12.

15 My strength is as the strength of ten,
Because my heart is pure.
Sir Galahad [1842], st. 1

16 Or that eternal lack of pence,
Which vexes public men.
Will Waterproof's Lyrical Monologue [1842], st. 6

17 Cophetua sware a royal oath;
"This beggar maid shall be my queen!"[2]
The Beggar Maid [1842], st. 2

18 A little grain of conscience made him sour.
The Vision of Sin [1842], sec. 5

19 Break, break, break,
On thy cold gray stones, O Sea!
And I would that my tongue could utter
The thoughts that arise in me.

Oh well for the fisherman's boy,
That he shouts with his sister at play!
Oh well for the sailor lad,
That he sings in his boat on the bay!

And the stately ships go on
To their haven under the hill;
But Oh for the touch of a vanished hand,
And the sound of a voice that is still!
Break, Break, Break [1842], st. 1–3

20 But the tender grace of a day that is dead
Will never come back to me. *Ib. st. 4*

21 Sweet girl graduates[3] in their golden hair.
The Princess [1847]. Prologue, l. 141

22 A rosebud set with little willful thorns,
And sweet as English air could make her, she. *Ib. l. 153*

23 We fell out, my wife and I,
Oh we fell out I know not why
And kissed again with tears.
Ib. pt. II [song, As Through the Land, l. 4]

24 And quoted odes, and jewels five-words-long
That on the stretched forefinger of all Time
Sparkle forever. *Ib. l. 355*

25 Sweet and low, sweet and low,
Wind of the western sea,
Low, low, breathe and blow,
Wind of the western sea!
Over the rolling waters go,
Come from the dying moon, and blow,
Blow him again to me;
While my little one, while my pretty one, sleeps.
Ib. III [song, Sweet and Low, st. 1]

26 The splendor falls on castle walls
And snowy summits old in story:

[2]See Shakespeare, 192:1, and Anonymous, 917:18.
[3]See Huxley, 595:9.

The long light shakes across the lakes,
And the wild cataract leaps in glory.
Blow, bugle, blow, set the wild echoes flying,
Blow, bugle; answer, echoes, dying, dying, dying.

Ib. IV [song, The Splendor Falls, st. 1]

1 The horns of Elfland faintly blowing.

Ib. [st. 2]

2 Our echoes roll from soul to soul,
And grow forever and forever.

Ib. [st. 3]

3 Tears, idle tears, I know not what they mean,
Tears from the depth of some divine despair
Rise in the heart, and gather to the eyes,
In looking on the happy autumn fields,
And thinking of the days that are no more.

Ib. [song, Tears, Idle Tears, st. 1]

4 Dear as remembered kisses after death,
And sweet as those by hopeless fancy feigned
On lips that are for others; deep as love,
Deep as first love, and wild with all regret;
O Death in Life, the days that are no more.

Ib. [st. 4]

5 O Swallow, Swallow, flying, flying South,
Fly to her, and fall upon her gilded eaves,
And tell her, tell her, what I tell to thee.

Ib. [song, O Swallow, st. 1]

6 Man is the hunter; woman is his game.

Ib. V, l. 147

7 Man for the field and woman for the hearth:
Man for the sword and for the needle she:
Man with the head and woman with the heart:
Man to command and woman to obey;
All else confusion. *Ib. l. 427*

8 Home they brought her warrior dead.
She nor swooned nor uttered cry:
All her maidens, watching, said,
"She must weep or she will die."

Ib. VI [song, Home They Brought Her Warrior, st. 1]

9 The woman is so hard
Upon the woman. *Ib. l. 205*

10 Ask me no more: thy fate and mine are sealed:
I strove against the stream and all in vain:
Let the great river take me to the main:
No more, dear love, for at a touch I yield;
Ask me no more.

Ib. VII [song, Ask Me No More, st. 3]

11 Now sleeps the crimson petal, now the white;
Nor waves the cypress in the palace walk;
Nor winks the gold fin in the porphyry font:
The firefly wakens: waken thou with me.

Ib. [song, Now Sleeps the Crimson Petal, st. 1]

12 Now lies the Earth all Danaë to the stars,
And all thy heart lies open unto me.

Ib. [st. 3]

13 Sweet is every sound,
Sweeter thy voice, but every sound is sweet;
Myriads of rivulets hurrying through the lawn,
The moan of doves in immemorial elms,
And murmuring of innumerable bees.

Ib. l. 203

14 Happy he
With such a mother! faith in womankind
Beats with his blood. *Ib. l. 308*

15 Some sense of duty, something of a faith,
Some reverence for the laws ourselves have made,
Some patient force to change them when we will,
Some civic manhood firm against the crowd.

Ib. Conclusion, l. 54

16 Believing where we cannot prove.

In Memoriam[1] *[1850]. Prologue, st. 1*

17 Our little systems have their day.

Ib. st. 5

18 Let knowledge grow from more to more,
But more of reverence in us dwell;
That mind and soul, according well,
May make one music as before.

Ib. st. 7

19 I held it truth, with him who sings[2]
To one clear harp in divers tones
That men may rise on stepping-stones
Of their dead selves to higher things.[3]

Ib. 1, st. 1

20 I sometimes hold it half a sin
To put in words the grief I feel;
For words, like Nature, half reveal
And half conceal the Soul within.

Ib. 5, st. 2

21 But, for the unquiet heart and brain
A use in measured language lies;
The sad mechanic exercise,
Like dull narcotics numbing pain. *Ib.*

22 And from his ashes may be made
The violet of his native land.[4]

Ib. 18, st. 1

[1] In memory of Arthur Henry Hallam [1811–1833].
[2] Goethe.
[3] See St. Augustine, 129:10, and Longfellow, 511:22.
[4] See Shakespeare, 224:17, and FitzGerald, 516:12.

1 I do but sing because I must,
And pipe but as the linnets sing.[1]
Ib. 21, st. 6

2 And Thought leaped out to wed with Thought
Ere Thought could wed itself with Speech.
Ib. 23, st. 4

3 'Tis better to have loved and lost
Than never to have loved at all.[2]
Ib. 27, st. 4

4 How fares it with the happy dead?
Ib. 44, st. 1

5 Be near me when my light is low.
Ib. 50, st. 1

6 And Time, a maniac scattering dust,
And Life, a Fury slinging flame.
Ib. st. 2

7 Do we indeed desire the dead
Should still be near us at our side?
Ib. 51, st. 1

8 Hold thou the good; define it well;
For fear divine Philosophy
Should push beyond her mark, and be
Procuress to the Lords of Hell.
Ib. 53, st. 4

9 Oh yet we trust that somehow good
Will be the final goal of ill.
Ib. 54, st. 1

10 But what am I?
An infant crying in the night:
An infant crying for the light:
And with no language but a cry.[3]
Ib. st. 5

11 So careful of the type she seems,
So careless of the single life.[4]
Ib. 55, st. 2

12 The great world's altar stairs,
That slope through darkness up to God.
Ib. st. 4

13 Nature, red in tooth and claw.
Ib. 56, st. 4

14 O Sorrow, wilt Thou live with me
No casual mistress, but a wife.
Ib. 59, st. 1

[1]See Goethe, 395:1.
[2]Say what you will, 'tis better to be left than never to have been loved.—CONGREVE, *The Way of the World* [1700], *act II, sc. vi*
Better to love amiss than nothing to have loved.—CRABBE, *Tales* [1812], *XIV, The Struggles of Conscience*
'Tis better to have fought and lost / Than never to have fought at all.—ARTHUR HUGH CLOUGH [1819–1861], *Peschiera*
[3]See Pliny, 116:9.
[4]See Wollstonecraft, 414:20.

15 So many worlds, so much to do,
So little done, such things to be.[5]
Ib. 73, st. 1

16 O last regret, regret can die!
Ib. 78, st. 5

17 God's finger touched him, and he slept.
Ib. 85, st. 5

18 Fresh from brawling courts
And dusty purlieus of the law.
Ib. 89, st. 3

19 There lives more faith in honest doubt,[6]
Believe me, than in half the creeds.
Ib. 96, st. 3

20 He seems so near, and yet so far.
Ib. 97, st. 6

21 Ring out, wild bells, to the wild sky!
Ib. 106, st. 1

22 Ring out the old, ring in the new,
Ring, happy bells, across the snow:
The year is going, let him go;
Ring out the false, ring in the true.[7]
Ib. st. 2

23 Ring out old shapes of foul disease,
Ring out the narrowing lust of gold;
Ring out the thousand wars of old,
Ring in the thousand years of peace.
Ib. st. 7

24 There rolls the deep where grew the tree.
Ib. 123, st. 1

25 Love is and was my lord and king.
Ib. 126, st. 1

26 Wearing all that weight
Of learning lightly like a flower.
Ib. Conclusion, st. 10

27 One God, one law, one element,
And one far-off divine event,
To which the whole creation moves.
Ib. st. 36

28 He clasps the crag with crooked hands;
Close to the sun in lonely lands,
Ringed with the azure world he stands.

The wrinkled sea beneath him crawls;
He watches from his mountain walls,
And like a thunderbolt he falls.
The Eagle [1851]

[5]How little I have gained, / How vast the unattained.—WHITTIER [1807–1892], *My Triumph, st. 7*
[6]Who never doubted never half believed. / Where doubt there truth is—'tis her shadow.—P. J. BAILEY [1816–1902], *Festus: A Country Town*
[7]See Dryden, 307:1.

1 Bury the Great Duke
With an empire's lamentation.
Ode on the Death of the Duke of Wellington [1852], st. 1

2 The last great Englishman is low.
Ib. st. 3

3 Rich in saving common sense,
And, as the greatest only are,
In his simplicity sublime.
O good gray head which all men knew!
Ib. st. 4

4 O iron nerve to true occasion true,
O fallen at length, that tower of strength
Which stood four-square to all the winds that blew.
Ib.

5 Not once or twice in our rough island story
The path of duty was the way to glory.
Ib. st. 8

6 Speak no more of his renown.
Lay your earthly fancies down,
And in the vast cathedral leave him.
God accept him, Christ receive him.
Ib. st. 9

7 And yet, my Lords, not well: there is a higher law.
The Third of February, 1852, st. 2

8 We are not cotton-spinners all.
Ib. st. 8

9 Half a league, half a league,
Half a league onward,
All in the valley of death
Rode the six hundred.
The Charge of the Light Brigade [1854],[1] st. 1

10 "Forward, the Light Brigade!"
Was there a man dismayed?
Ib. st. 2

11 Someone had blundered.
Ib.

12 Theirs not to make reply,
Theirs not to reason why,
Theirs but to do and die.
Ib.

13 Cannon to right of them,
Cannon to left of them,
Cannon in front of them
Volleyed and thundered.
Ib. st. 3

14 Into the jaws of death,
Into the mouth of hell
Rode the six hundred.
Ib.

15 I come from haunts of coot and hern,
I make a sudden sally
And sparkle out among the fern,
To bicker down a valley.
The Brook [1855], song, st. 1

16 For men may come and men may go,
But I go on forever.
Ib. st. 6

17 Faultily faultless,[2] icily regular, splendidly null,
Dead perfection, no more.
Maud [1855], pt. I, sec. ii

18 And ah for a man to arise in me,
That the man I am may cease to be!
Ib. st. 6

19 Gorgonized me from head to foot,
With a stony British stare.
Ib. xiii, st. 2

20 Come into the garden, Maud,
For the black bat, night, has flown,
Come into the garden, Maud,
I am here at the gate alone.
Ib. xxii, st. 1

21 For a breeze of morning moves,
And the planet of Love is on high,
Beginning to faint in the light that she loves
On a bed of daffodil sky.
Ib. st. 2

22 All night have the roses heard
The flute, violin, bassoon;
All night has the casement jessamine stirred
To the dancers dancing in tune;
Till a silence fell with the waking bird,
And a hush with the setting moon.
Ib. st. 3

23 Queen rose of the rosebud garden of girls.
Ib. st. 9

24 There has fallen a splendid tear
From the passion flower at the gate.
Ib. st. 10

25 She is coming, my own, my sweet;
Were it ever so airy a tread,
My heart would hear her and beat,
Were it earth in an earthy bed;
My dust would hear her and beat,
Had I lain for a century dead;
Would start and tremble under her feet,
And blossom in purple and red.
Ib. st. 11

26 Ah Christ, that it were possible
For one short hour to see
The souls we loved, that they might tell us
What and where they be.
Ib. II, iv, st. 3

27 The woods decay, the woods decay and fall,
The vapors weep their burthen to the ground,
Man comes and tills the field and lies beneath,
And after many a summer dies the swan.
Tithonus [1860], l. 1

28 Here at the quiet limit of the world.
Ib. l. 7

[1] See Bosquet, 536:5.

[2] See Tennyson, 534:12, and Browning, 545:8.

1 Wearing the white flower of a blameless life,
Before a thousand peering littlenesses,
In that fierce light which beats upon a throne,[1]
And blackens every blot.
Idylls of the King [1859–1885], dedication, l. 24

2 Man's word is God in man.
Ib. The Coming of Arthur, l. 132

3 Large, divine, and comfortable words.[2]
Ib. l. 267

4 Clothed in white samite, mystic, wonderful.[3]
Ib. l. 284

5 Live pure, speak true, right wrong, follow the King—
Else, wherefore born?
Ib. Gareth and Lynette, l. 117

6 Our hoard is little, but our hearts are great.
Ib. The Marriage of Geraint, l. 352

7 For man is man and master of his fate.[4]
Ib. l. 355

8 The useful trouble of the rain.
Ib. Geraint and Enid, l. 770

9 It is the little rift within the lute,
That by and by will make the music mute,
And ever widening slowly silence all.
Ib. Merlin and Vivien, l. 386

10 Blind and naked Ignorance
Delivers brawling judgments, unashamed,
On all things all day long. *Ib. l. 662*

11 Elaine the fair, Elaine the lovable,
Elaine, the lily maid of Astolat.
Ib. Lancelot and Elaine, l. 1

12 But, friend, to me
He is all fault who hath no fault at all:
For who loves me must have a touch of earth.[5] *Ib. l. 131*

13 In me there dwells
No greatness, save it be some far-off touch
Of greatness to know well I am not great.
Ib. l. 447

14 The shackles of an old love straitened him,
His honor rooted in dishonor stood,
And faith unfaithful kept him falsely true.
Ib. l. 870

15 Sweet is true love though given in vain, in vain;
And sweet is death who puts an end to pain.
Ib. l. 1000

[1] See Montaigne, 165:21, and Shakespeare, 223:27.
[2] Hear what comfortable words our Saviour Christ saith unto all who truly turn to him.—*Book of Common Prayer, Holy Communion*
[3] Also *The Passing of Arthur, l. 199.*
[4] See Sallust, 103:1 and 103:5; Bacon, 181:6; Shakespeare, 215:6; Henley, 663:11; and Nehru, 814:8.
[5] See Tennyson, 533:17, and Browning, 545:8.

16 He makes no friend who never made a foe.
Ib. l. 1082

17 Figs out of thistles.[6]
Ib. The Last Tournament, l. 356

18 The greater man the greater courtesy.
Ib. l. 628

19 The vow that binds too strictly snaps itself.
Ib. l. 652

20 For courtesy wins woman all as well
As valor may. *Ib. l. 702*

21 For manners are not idle, but the fruit
Of loyal nature and of noble mind.
Ib. Guinevere, l. 333

22 To love one maiden only, cleave to her,
And worship her by years of golden deeds.
Ib. l. 472

23 No more subtle master under Heaven
Than is the maiden passion for a maid,
Not only to keep down the base in man,
But teach high thought, and amiable words
And courtliness, and the desire of fame,
And love of truth, and all that makes a man.
Ib. l. 475

24 Let no man dream but that I love thee still.
Ib. l. 557

25 The days will grow to weeks, the weeks to months,
The months will add themselves and make the years,
The years will roll into the centuries,
And mine will ever be a name of scorn.
Ib. l. 619

26 To where beyond these voices there is peace.
Ib. l. 692

27 I found Him in the shining of the stars,
I marked Him in the flowering of His fields,
But in His ways with men I find Him not.
Ib. The Passing of Arthur, l. 9

28 For why is all around us here
As if some lesser god had made the world,
But had not force to shape it as he would?
Ib. l. 13

29 So all day long the noise of battle rolled
Among the mountains by the winter sea.
Ib. l. 170

30 Authority forgets a dying king.
Ib. l. 289

31 And slowly answered Arthur from the barge:
The old order changeth, yielding place to new;
And God fulfills himself in many ways,

[6] See *Matthew 7:16*, 38:17.

Lest one good custom should corrupt the world.[1] *Ib. l. 407*

1 More things are wrought by prayer
Than this world dreams of. Wherefore, let thy voice
Rise like a fountain for me night and day.[2]
Ib. l. 414

2 From the great deep to the great deep he goes. *Ib. l. 445*

3 Cast all your cares on God; that anchor holds.
Enoch Arden [1864], l. 222

4 Insipid as the queen upon a card.
Aylmer's Field [1864], l. 28

5 The worst is yet to come.
Sea Dreams [1864], l. 301

6 He said likewise
That a lie which is half a truth is ever the blackest of lies,
That a lie which is all a lie may be met and fought with outright,
But a lie which is part a truth is a harder matter to fight.
The Grandmother [1864], st. 8

7 Dosn't thou 'ear my 'erse's legs, as they canters awaäy?
Proputty, proputty, proputty—that's what I 'ears 'em saäy.
Northern Farmer: New Style [1869], st. 1

8 Doänt thou marry for munny, but goä wheer munny is! *Ib. st. 5*

9 Speak to Him thou for He hears, and Spirit with Spirit can meet—
Closer is He than breathing, and nearer than hands and feet.
The Higher Pantheism [1869], st. 6

10 Flower in the crannied wall,
I pluck you out of the crannies,
I hold you here, root and all, in my hand,
Little flower—but *if* I could understand
What you are, root and all, and all in all,
I should know what God and man is.[3]
Flower in the Crannied Wall [1869]

11 At Flores in the Azores Sir Richard Grenville lay,
And a pinnace, like a fluttered bird, came flying from far away;
"Spanish ships of war at sea! we have sighted fifty-three!"
The Revenge [1878], st. 1

[1] Also in *Morte d'Arthur* [1842].
See Herrick, 266:15.
[2] Also in *Morte d'Arthur* [1842].
[3] See Blount, 316:8.

12 I should count myself the coward if I left them, my Lord Howard,
To these Inquisition dogs and the devildoms of Spain. *Ib. st. 2*

13 Let us bang these dogs of Seville, the children of the devil,
For I never turned my back upon Don or devil yet. *Ib. st. 4*

14 The little *Revenge* ran on sheer into the heart of the foe. *Ib. st. 5*

15 All the charm of all the Muses often flowering in a lonely word.
To Virgil [1882], st. 3

16 Cleave ever to the sunnier side of doubt.
The Ancient Sage [1885], l. 68

17 That man's the best Cosmopolite
Who loves his native country best.
Hands All Round [1885], l. 3

18 I am Merlin
Who follow the Gleam.[4]
Merlin and the Gleam [1889], st. 1

19 Sunset and evening star,
And one clear call for me!
And may there be no moaning of the bar,
When I put out to sea,[5]

But such a tide as moving seems asleep,
Too full for sound and foam,
When that which drew from out the boundless deep
Turns again home.
Crossing the Bar [1889], st. 1, 2

20 Twilight and evening bell,
And after that the dark. *Ib. st. 3*

21 I hope to see my Pilot face to face
When I have crossed the bar. *Ib. st. 4*

Robert Charles Winthrop
1809–1894

22 Our Country—whether bounded by the St. John's and the Sabine, or however otherwise bounded[6] or described, and be the measurements more or less—still our Country, to be

[4] The Gleam . . . signifies . . . the higher poetic imagination.—TENNYSON; *from* HALLAM TENNYSON, *Alfred, Lord Tennyson, A Memoir* [1897], *vol. II, p. 366*

Follow, follow, follow the gleam, / Banners unfurled o'er all the world. / Follow, follow, follow the gleam / Of the chalice that is the Grail.—SALLIE HUME DOUGLAS, *Follow the Gleam* [1923], *refrain*

[5] See Ennius, 95:2.

[6] The United States—bounded on the north by the Aurora Borealis, on the south by the precession of the equinoxes, on the east by the primeval chaos, and on the west by the Day of Judgment.—JOHN FISKE [1842–1901], *Bounding the United States*

cherished in all our hearts, to be defended by all our hands.

Toast at Faneuil Hall [Fourth of July, 1845]

1 A star for every State, and a State for every star.

Address on Boston Common [1862]

Henry Alford

1810–1871

2 Come, ye thankful people, come,
Raise the song of Harvest-home;
All is safely gathered in,
Ere the winter storms begin.

Come, Ye Thankful People, Come [1844]

3 Ten thousand times ten thousand
In sparkling raiment bright,
The armies of the ransomed saints
Throng up the steeps of light:
'Tis finished! all is finished,
Their fight with death and sin:
Fling open wide the golden gates,
And let the victors in.

Hymn [1867], st. 1

Phineas Taylor Barnum

1810–1891

4 There's a sucker born every minute.

Attributed

Pierre Jean François Joseph Bosquet

1810–1861

5 It is magnificent, but it is not war.[1]

On the charge of the Light Brigade at Balaklava [October 25, 1854]

William Henry Channing

1810–1884

6 To live content with small means; to seek elegance rather than luxury, and refinement rather than fashion; to be worthy, not respectable, and wealthy, not rich; to study hard, think quietly, talk gently, act frankly; to listen to stars and birds, to babes and sages, with open heart; to bear all cheerfully, do all bravely, await occasions, hurry never. In a word, to let the spiritual, unbidden and unconscious, grow up through the common. This is to be my symphony.

My Symphony

[1] C'est magnifique, mais ce n'est pas la guerre. See Tennyson, 533:9.

Sir Francis Hastings Doyle

1810–1888

7 Last night, among his fellow roughs,
He jested, quaffed, and swore;
A drunken private of the Buffs,
Who never looked before.
Today, beneath the foeman's frown,
He stands in Elgin's place,
Ambassador from Britain's crown,
And type of all her race.

The Private of the Buffs, st. 1

Ferdinand Freiligrath

1810–1876

8 Oh love, as long as you can love.[2]

Der Liebe Dauer [1830]

Margaret Fuller

1810–1850

9 I myself am more divine than any I see.

Letter to Emerson [March 1, 1838]

10 It does not follow because many books are written by persons born in America that there exists an American literature. Books which imitate or represent the thoughts and life of Europe do not constitute an American literature. Before such can exist, an original idea must animate this nation and fresh currents of life must call into life fresh thoughts along its shores.

In the New York Tribune [1846]

11 For precocity some great price is always demanded sooner or later in life.

Diary. From THOMAS WENTWORTH HIGGINSON, *Life of Margaret Fuller Ossoli [1884], ch. 18*

12 Genius will live and thrive without training, but it does not the less reward the watering pot and pruning knife. *Ib.*

13 I accept the universe.[3] *Attributed*

Elizabeth Cleghorn Gaskell

1810–1865

14 A man is *so* in the way in the house.

Cranford [1851–1853], ch. 1

15 A little credulity helps one on through life very smoothly. *Ib. ch. 11*

[2] See Anonymous Latin, 133:14, and Parnell, 329:16.
[3] By God! she'd better. —*Carlyle's reported comment*

1 I'll not listen to reason. . . . Reason always means what someone else has got to say. *Ib. ch. 14*

James Sloan Gibbons
1810–1892

2 We are coming, Father Abraham, three hundred thousand more.
Three Hundred Thousand More [1862],[1] *st. 1*

Pope Leo XIII [Gioacchino Pecci]
1810–1903

3 Every man has by nature the right to possess property as his own.
Rerum Novarum [encyclical on the condition of labor, May 15, 1891]

4 It is impossible to reduce human society to one level. *Ib.*

5 It is one thing to have a right to the possession of money, and another to have a right to use money as one pleases. *Ib.*

William Miller
1810–1872

6 Wee Willie Winkie rins through the town,
Upstairs and downstairs, in his nichtgown,
Tirlin' at the window, cryin' at the lock,
"Are the weans in their bed? for it's now ten o'clock."
Willie Winkie

Alfred de Musset
1810–1857

7 I have come too late into a world too old.[2]
Rolla [1833]

8 Do Not Trifle with Love.[3]
Title of a comedy [1834]

9 The most despairing songs are the loveliest of all,
I know immortal ones composed only of tears.
Poésies Nouvelles. La Nuit de Mai [1835]

10 How glorious it is, but how painful it is also, to be exceptional in this world!
La Merle Blanc [1842]

[1]Song to help raise volunteers for the Union Army.
[2]Je suis venu trop tard dans un monde trop vieux.
[3]On Ne Badine Pas avec l'Amour.

Theodore Parker
1810–1860

11 Truth never yet fell dead in the streets; it has such affinity with the soul of man, the seed however broadcast will catch somewhere and produce its hundredfold.
A Discourse of Matters Pertaining to Religion [1842]

12 Truth stood on one side and Ease on the other; it has often been so. *Ib.*

13 Man never falls so low that he can see nothing higher than himself.
Essay, A Lesson for the Day

14 All men desire to be immortal.
A Sermon on the Immortal Life [September 20, 1846]

15 A democracy—that is a government of all the people, by all the people, for all the people;[4] of course, a government of the principles of eternal justice, the unchanging law of God; for shortness' sake I will call it the idea of Freedom.
The American Idea [May 29, 1850][5]

Edmund Hamilton Sears
1810–1876

16 It came upon the midnight clear,
That glorious song of old,
From Angels bending near the earth
To touch their harps of gold:
"Peace on the earth, good will to men
From heav'n's all-gracious King."
The world in solemn stillness lay
To hear the angels sing.
The Angel's Song [1850], st. 1

Martin Farquhar Tupper
1810–1889

17 Error is a hardy plant: it flourisheth in every soil.
Proverbial Philosophy [1838–1842]. Of Truth in Things False

[4]See Wycliffe, 143:12; Webster, 450:14; Disraeli, 501:6; Garrison, 505:19; and Lincoln, 523:4.
Parker used the same phrase in a speech delivered in Boston [May 31, 1854] and in a sermon in the Music Hall, Boston [July 4, 1858]. William H. Herndon visited Boston and on his return to Springfield, Illinois, took with him some of Parker's sermons and addresses. In his *Abraham Lincoln, vol. II, p. 65,* Herndon says that Lincoln marked with pencil the portion of the Music Hall address, "Democracy is direct self-government, over all the people, by all the people, for all the people."
[5]Speech at the New England Anti-Slavery Convention, Boston.

1 Well-timed silence hath more eloquence than speech. *Ib. Of Discretion*

2 A good book is the best of friends, the same today and forever. *Ib. Of Reading*

3 Nature's own Nobleman, friendly and frank,
Is a man with his heart in his hand!
Nature's Nobleman [1844], st. 1

John Bright
1811–1889

4 Force is not a remedy.
Speech at Birmingham [November 16, 1880]

5 My opinion is that the Northern States will manage somehow to muddle through.
Said during the American Civil War. From JUSTIN MCCARTHY, *Reminiscences [1899]*

Fanny Fern [Sara Payson Parton]
1811–1872

6 The way to a man's heart is through his stomach.[1] *Willis Parton*

Théophile Gautier
1811–1872

7 Everything passes — Robust art
Alone is eternal.
The bust
Survives the city.[2] *L'Art [1832]*

Horace Greeley
1811–1872

8 The best business you can go into you will find on your father's farm or in his workshop. If you have no family or friends to aid you, and no prospect opened to you there, turn your face to the great West,[3] and there build up a home and fortune.
From JAMES PARTON, *Life of Horace Greeley [1855]. To Aspiring Young Men*

9 The illusion that times that were are better than those that are, has probably pervaded all ages.
The American Conflict [1864–1866]

[1]See Byron, 461:29.
[2]Tout passe — L'art robuste / Seul a l'éternité; / Le buste / Survit à la cité.
See Dobson, 640:1, and Anonymous: French, 928:3.
[3]See J. B. L. Soule, 554:3.

10 Wisdom is never dear, provided the article be genuine.
Address on Agriculture, Houston, Texas [May 23, 1871]

Wendell Phillips
1811–1884

11 Revolutions are not made; they come. A revolution is as natural a growth as an oak. It comes out of the past. Its foundations are laid far back.
Speech [January 8, 1852]

12 The best use of laws is to teach men to trample bad laws under their feet.
Speech [April 12, 1852]

13 What the Puritans gave the world was not thought, but action.
Speech [December 21, 1855]

14 One on God's side is a majority.[4]
Speech [November 1, 1859]

15 Every man meets his Waterloo at last.
Ib.

16 Whether in chains or in laurels, Liberty knows nothing but victories. *Ib.*

17 Truth is one forever absolute, but opinion is truth filtered through the moods, the blood, the disposition of the spectator.
Idols [October 4, 1859]

18 Difference of religion breeds more quarrels than difference of politics.
Speech [November 7, 1860]

19 Revolutions never go backward.[5]
Speech [February 17, 1861]

20 Aristocracy is always cruel.
Address on Toussaint L'Ouverture [1861]

Harriet Beecher Stowe[6]
1811–1896

21 Eliza made her desperate retreat across the river just in the dusk of twilight. The gray mist of evening, rising slowly from the river, enveloped her as she disappeared up the

[4]See Knox, 162:2.
[5]I know, and all the world knows, that revolutions never go backward. — WILLIAM HENRY SEWARD, *Speech at Rochester on the Irrepressible Conflict* [October 1858]
[6]We have seen an American woman write a novel of which a million copies were sold in all languages, and which had one merit, of speaking to the universal heart, and was read with equal interest to three audiences, namely, in the parlor, in the kitchen, and in the nursery of every house. — EMERSON, *Society and Solitude* [1870], *Success*

bank, and the swollen current and floundering masses of ice presented a hopeless barrier between her and her pursuer.

Uncle Tom's Cabin [1852], ch. 8

1 I [Topsy] 'spect I growed. Don't think nobody never made me. *Ib. 20*

Charles Sumner
1811–1874

2 Where Slavery is, there Liberty cannot be; and where Liberty is, there Slavery cannot be.

Slavery and the Rebellion; speech at Cooper Institute [November 5, 1864]

3 There is the National flag. He must be cold, indeed, who can look upon its folds rippling in the breeze without pride of country. If in a foreign land, the flag is companionship, and country itself, with all its endearments.

Are We a Nation? [November 19, 1867]

4 The phrase, "public office is a public trust," has of late become common property.[1]

Speech in the Senate [May 31, 1872]

William Makepeace Thackeray
1811–1863

5 This I set down as a positive truth. A woman with fair opportunities, and without a positive hump, may marry whom she likes.[2]

Vanity Fair [1847–1848], vol. I, ch. 4

6 Them's my sentiments. *Ib. 21*

7 Everybody in Vanity Fair must have remarked how well those live who are comfortably and thoroughly in debt; how they deny themselves nothing; how jolly and easy they are in their minds. *Ib. 22*

8 How to Live Well on Nothing a Year.

Ib. 36 (title)

9 I think I could be a good woman if I had five thousand a year.[3] *Ib. II, 1*

[1]See Matthew Henry, 319:16; Burke, 374:3; Clay, 444:3; Calhoun, 449:8; and Cleveland, 631:7.

[2]I should like to see any kind of a man, distinguishable from a gorilla, that some good and even pretty woman could not shape a husband out of. — OLIVER WENDELL HOLMES, *The Professor at the Breakfast-Table* [1860]

The whole world is strewn with snares, traps, gins and pitfalls for the capture of men by women. — GEORGE BERNARD SHAW, *Man and Superman* [1903], *Epistle Dedicatory*

[3]See Huxley, 596:2.

10 Ah! *Vanitas vanitatum!*[4] Which of us is happy in this world? Which of us has his desire? or, having it, is satisfied? — Come, children, let us shut up the box and the puppets, for our play is played out. *Ib. 27*

11 He who meanly admires mean things is a Snob. *The Book of Snobs [1848], ch. 2*

12 Rake's Progress.[5]

Pendennis [1848–1850], ch. 19 (title)

13 Yes, I am a fatal man, Madame Fribsbi. To inspire hopeless passion is my destiny.

Ib. 23

14 Remember, it's as easy to marry a rich woman as a poor woman. *Ib. 28*

15 Of the Corporation of the Goosequill — of the Press . . . of the fourth estate.[6] . . . There she is — the great engine — she never sleeps. She has her ambassadors in every quarter of the world — her courtiers upon every road. Her officers march along with armies, and her envoys walk into statesmen's cabinets. They are ubiquitous. *Ib. 30*

16 'Tis not the dying for a faith that's so hard, Master Harry — every man of every nation has done that — 'tis the living up to it that's difficult.

Henry Esmond [1852], bk. I, ch. 6

17 'Tis strange what a man may do, and a woman yet think him an angel. *Ib. 7*

18 The wicked are wicked, no doubt, and they go astray and they fall, and they come by their deserts; but who can tell the mischief which the very virtuous do?

The Newcomes [1853–1855], ch. 20

19 This Bouillabaisse a noble dish is —
A sort of soup, or broth, or brew.

Ballads [1855]. The Ballad of Bouillabaisse, st. 2

20 A pedigree reaching as far back as the Deluge.

The Rose and the Ring [1855], ch. 2

21 The book of female logic is blotted all over with tears, and Justice in their courts is forever in a passion.

The Virginians [1857–1859], ch. 4

22 Women like not only to conquer, but to be conquered. *Ib.*

23 Next to the very young, I suppose the very old are the most selfish. *Ib. 61*

[4]See *Ecclesiastes 1:2, 26:11.*

[5]The Rake's Progress. — WILLIAM HOGARTH, *title of series of paintings and engravings* [1735]

[6]See Hazlitt, 445:3; Carlyle, 472:17; and Macaulay, 487:13.

1 To endure is greater than to dare; to tire out hostile fortune; to be daunted by no difficulty; to keep heart when all have lost it; to go through intrigue spotless; to forgo even ambition when the end is gained — who can say this is not greatness? *Ib. 92*

2 Bravery never goes out of fashion.
The Four Georges [1860]. George II

3 It is to the middle class we must look for the safety of England. *Ib. George III*

4 George, be a King!
Ib. Princess Augusta to her son George III

Robert Browning
1812–1889

5 Sun-treader,[1] life and light be thine forever!
Pauline [1833]

6 I go to prove my soul!
I see my way as birds their trackless way.
Paracelsus [1835], pt. I

7 He guides me and the bird. In His good time!
Ib.

8 Measure your mind's height by the shade it casts! *Ib. III*

9 Every joy is gain
And gain is gain, however small.
Ib. IV

10 I give the fight up: let there be an end,
A privacy, an obscure nook for me.
I want to be forgotten even by God.
Ib. V

11 Sidney's self, the starry paladin.
Sordello[2] [1840], pt. I

12 Would you have your songs endure?
Build on the human heart. *Ib. II*

13 Any nose
May ravage with impunity a rose.
Ib. VI

14 Day!
Faster and more fast,
O'er night's brim, day boils at last.
Pippa Passes [1841], introduction

15 The year's at the spring
And day's at the morn;
Morning's at seven;
The hillside's dew-pearled;
The lark's on the wing;
The snail's on the thorn:
God's in his heaven —
All's right with the world.[3] *Ib. pt. I*

[1] Shelley.
[2] See Lombroso, 630:*n*2.
[3] See Whittier, 514:2.

16 Speak to me — not of me! *Ib.*

17 Some unsuspected isle in far-off seas.
Ib. II

18 In the morning of the world,
When earth was nigher heaven than now.
Ib. III

19 All service ranks the same with God:
With God, whose puppets, best and worst,
Are we; there is no last nor first.
Ib. IV

20 You know, we French stormed Ratisbon.
Incident of the French Camp [1842], st. 1

21 "You're wounded!" "Nay," the soldier's pride
Touched to the quick, he said:
"I'm killed, Sire!" And his chief beside,
Smiling the boy fell dead. *Ib. st. 5*

22 That's my last Duchess painted on the wall,
Looking as if she were alive.
My Last Duchess [1842], l. 1

23 She had
A heart — how shall I say? — too soon made glad. *Ib. l. 21*

24 I gave commands;
Then all smiles stopped together.
Ib. l. 45

25 Marching along, fifty-score strong,
Great-hearted gentlemen, singing this song.
Cavalier Tunes [1842]. Marching Along, st. 1

26 Boot, saddle, to horse, and away!
Ib. Boot and Saddle, refrain

27 She never should have looked at me
If she meant I should not love her!
Cristina [1842], l. 1

28 The moth's kiss, first!
In a Gondola [1842], l. 49

29 The bee's kiss, now! *Ib. l. 56*

30 O world, as God has made it! All is beauty.
The Guardian Angel [1842], l. 33

31 Just my vengeance complete,
The man sprang to his feet,
Stood erect, caught at God's skirts, and prayed!
— So, *I* was afraid!
Instans Tyrannus [1845], st. 7

32 Hamelin Town's in Brunswick,
By famous Hanover city.
The Pied Piper of Hamelin [1845], st. 1

1 Rats!
They fought the dogs and killed the cats,
And bit the babies in the cradles,
And ate the cheeses out of the vats,
And licked the soup from the cooks' own ladles.
Ib. st. 2

2 And out of the houses the rats came tumbling.
Great rats, small rats, lean rats, brawny rats,
Brown rats, black rats, gray rats, tawny rats.
Grave old plodders, gay young friskers,
Fathers, mothers, uncles, cousins,
Cocking tails and pricking whiskers,
Families by tens and dozens,
Brothers, sisters, husbands, wives—
Followed the Piper for their lives.
Ib. st. 7

3 When the liquor's out, why clink the cannikin?
The Flight of the Duchess [1845], st. 16

4 It's a long lane that knows no turnings.
Ib. st. 17

5 Just for a handful of silver he left us,
Just for a riband to stick in his coat.
The Lost Leader[1] *[1845], st. 1*

6 We that had loved him so, followed him, honored him,
Lived in his mild and magnificent eye,
Learned his great language, caught his clear accents,
Made him our pattern to live and to die!
Ib.

7 Shakespeare was of us, Milton was for us,
Burns, Shelley, were with us—they watch from their graves!
Ib.

8 One more devils'-triumph and sorrow for angels,
One more wrong to man, one more insult to God!
Ib. st. 2

9 Let him never come back to us!
There would be doubt, hesitation and pain,
Forced praise on our part—the glimmer of twilight,
Never glad confident morning again!
Ib.

10 It was roses, roses all the way.
The Patriot [1845], st. 1

11 I sprang to the stirrup, and Joris, and he;
I galloped, Dirck galloped, we galloped all three.
How They Brought the Good News from Ghent to Aix [1845], st. 1

[1]Often assumed to refer to Wordsworth.

12 And into the midnight we galloped abreast.
Ib.

13 The gray sea and the long black land;
And the yellow half-moon large and low.
Meeting at Night [1845], st. 1

14 Then a mile of warm, sea-scented beach.
Ib. st. 2

15 Round the cape of a sudden came the sea,
And the sun looked over the mountain's rim:
And straight was a path of gold for him,
And the need of a world of men for me.
Parting at Morning [1845]

16 Oh, to be in England now that April's there,
And whoever wakes in England sees, some morning, unaware,
That the lowest boughs and the brushwood sheaf
Round the elm tree bole are in tiny leaf,
While the chaffinch sings on the orchard bough
In England—now!
Home Thoughts, from Abroad [1845], l. 1

17 That's the wise thrush; he sings each song twice over,
Lest you should think he never could recapture
The first fine careless rapture!
Ib. l. 12

18 Nobly, nobly Cape St. Vincent to the northwest died away;
Sunset ran, one glorious blood-red, reeking into Cadiz Bay.
Home Thoughts, from the Sea [1845], l. 1

19 The Savior at his sermon on the mount,
St. Praxed in a glory, and one Pan
Ready to twitch the Nymph's last garment off.
The Bishop Orders His Tomb at St. Praxed's Church [1845], l. 59

20 How I shall lie through centuries,
And hear the blessed mutter of the mass,
And see God made and eaten all day long,
And feel the steady candle flame, and taste
Good strong thick stupefying incense smoke!
Ib. l. 80

21 Let's contend no more, Love,
Strive nor weep:
All be as before, Love,
—Only sleep!
A Woman's Last Word [1855], st. 1

22 Where the apple reddens
Never pry—
Lest we lose our Edens,
Eve and I.
Ib. st. 5

1 Beautiful Evelyn Hope is dead!
Evelyn Hope [1855], st. 1

2 You will wake, and remember, and understand.
Ib. st. 7

3 Where the quiet-colored end of evening smiles.
Love Among the Ruins [1855], st. 1

4 Oh heart! oh blood that freezes, blood that burns!
Earth's returns
For whole centuries of folly, noise and sin!
Shut them in,
With their triumphs and their glories and the rest!
Love is best!
Ib. st. 7

5 'Tis a lifelong toil till our lump be leaven—[1]
The better! What's come to perfection perishes.
Things learned on earth, we shall practice in heaven:
Works done least rapidly, Art most cherishes.
Old Pictures in Florence [1855], st. 17

6 Your ghost will walk, you lover of trees,
(If our loves remain)
In an English lane.
De Gustibus [1855], st. 1

7 Open my heart, and you will see
Graved inside of it, "Italy."[2]
Ib. st. 2

8 Oh, the little more, and how much it is!
And the little less, and what worlds away!
By the Fireside [1855], st. 39

9 If two lives join, there is oft a scar.
They are one and one, with a shadowy third;
One near one is too far.
Ib. st. 46

10 Only I discern
Infinite passion, and the pain
Of finite hearts that yearn.
Two in the Campagna [1855], st. 12

11 Escape me?
Never—
Beloved!
While I am I, and you are you.
Life in a Love [1855], st. 1

12 To dry one's eyes and laugh at a fall,
And baffled, get up and begin again.
Ib. st. 2

13 Ah, did you once see Shelley plain,
And did he stop and speak to you,
And did you speak to him again?
How strange it seems, and new![3]
Memorabilia [1855], st. 1

14 Who knows but the world may end tonight?
The Last Ride Together [1855], st. 2

15 Sing, riding's a joy! For me I ride.
Ib. st. 7

16 The instant made eternity—
And heaven just prove that I and she
Ride, ride together, forever ride?
Ib. st. 10

17 He said, "What's time? Leave Now for dogs and apes!
Man has Forever."
A Grammarian's Funeral [1855], l. 81

18 He ventured neck or nothing—heaven's success
Found, or earth's failure.
Ib. l. 109

19 That low man seeks a little thing to do,
Sees it and does it;
This high man, with a great thing to pursue,
Dies ere he knows it.
That low man goes on adding one to one,
His hundred's soon hit;
This high man, aiming at a million,
Misses an unit.
That, has the world here—should he need the next,
Let the world mind him!
This, throws himself on God, and unperplexed
Seeking shall find Him.
Ib. l. 113

20 Feeling, the East's gift,
Is quick and transient—comes, and lo, is gone—
While Northern thought is slow and durable.
Luria [1855], act V

21 A common grayness silvers everything.
Andrea del Sarto [1855], l. 35

22 Days decrease,
And autumn grows, autumn in everything.
Ib. l. 44

23 So free we seem, so fettered fast we are.
Ib. l. 51

24 Less is more.[4]
Ib. l. 78

[1] See *I Corinthians 5:6*, 48:9.
[2] See Mary Tudor, 162:8.

[3] And did you once find Browning plain? / And did he really seem quite clear? / And did you read the book again? / How strange it seems, and queer.—CHARLES WILLIAM STUBBS [1845–1912], *Parody*

[4] See Hesiod, 61:14.
Not so honest would be more honest.—G. E. LESSING, *Emilia Galotti* [1722], *act I, sc. iv*
A popular aphorism with the architect Ludwig Mies van der Rohe.

1 Ah, but a man's reach should exceed his grasp,
Or what's a heaven for? *Ib. l. 97*

2 I am grown peaceful as old age tonight.
Ib. l. 244

3 Truth that peeps
Over the glass's edge when dinner's done.
Bishop Blougram's Apology [1855], l. 17

4 The common problem, yours, mine, everyone's,
Is—not to fancy what were fair in life
Provided it could be—but, finding first
What may be, then find how to make it fair
Up to our means. *Ib. l. 87*

5 Just when we are safest, there's a sunset touch,
A fancy from a flower bell, someone's death,
A chorus ending from Euripides.
Ib. l. 183

6 One wise man's verdict outweighs all the fools'. *Ib. l. 373*

7 Our interest's on the dangerous edge of things.
The honest thief, the tender murderer,
The superstitious atheist, demirep
That loves and saves her soul in new French books. *Ib. l. 396*

8 You call for faith:
I show you doubt, to prove that faith exists.
The more of doubt, the stronger faith, I say,
If faith o'ercomes doubt. *Ib. l. 601*

9 When the fight begins within himself,
A man's worth something. *Ib. l. 793*

10 While you sat and played toccatas, stately at the clavichord.
A Toccata of Galuppi's [1855], st. 6

11 What of soul was left, I wonder, when the kissing had to stop? *Ib. st. 14*

12 Dear dead women, with such hair, too—what's become of all the gold
Used to hang and brush their bosoms? I feel chilly and grown old. *Ib. st. 15*

13 'Tis an awkward thing to play with souls.
A Light Woman [1855], st. 12

14 Stake your counter as boldly every whit,
Venture as warily, use the same skill,
Do your best, whether winning or losing it,
If you choose to play!
The Statue and the Bust [1855], l. 238

15 The sin I impute to each frustrate ghost
Is—the unlit lamp and the ungirt loin.
Ib. l. 246

16 How good is man's life, the mere living! how fit to employ
All the heart and the soul and the senses forever in joy! *Saul [1855], st. 9*

17 Death was past, life not come: so he waited.
Ib. st. 10

18 All's love, yet all's law. *Ib. st. 17*

19 God is seen God
In the star, in the stone, in the flesh, in the soul and the clod. *Ib.*

20 Do I find love so full in my nature, God's ultimate gift,
That I doubt his own love can compete with it? Here, the parts shift? *Ib.*

21 In the first is the last, in thy will is my power to believe. *Ib. st. 18*

22 'Tis not what man does which exalts him, but what man would do! *Ib.*

23 Thou shalt love and be loved by, forever: a Hand like this hand
Shall throw open the gates of new life to thee! See the Christ stand! *Ib.*

24 The sprinkled isles,
Lily on lily, that o'erlace the sea.
Cleon [1855], l. 1

25 And I have written three books on the soul,
Proving absurd all written hitherto,
And putting us to ignorance again.
Ib. l. 57

26 Why stay we on the earth except to grow?
Ib. l. 114

27 Most progress is most failure.
Ib. l. 271

28 So, the All-Great, were the All-loving too.
An Epistle of Karshish [1855], l. 305

29 We're made so that we love
First when we see them painted, things we have passed
Perhaps a hundred times nor cared to see;
And so they are better, painted—better to us,
Which is the same thing. Art was given for that. *Fra Lippo Lippi [1855], l. 300*

30 Rafael made a century of sonnets.
One Word More [1855], 2

31 Does he paint? he fain would write a poem—
Does he write? he fain would paint a picture.
Ib. 8

1 Where my heart lies, let my brain lie also.
Ib. 14

2 Oh, their Rafael of the dear Madonnas,
Oh, their Dante of the dread Inferno,
Wrote one song—and in my brain I sing it,
Drew one angel—borne, see, on my bosom!
Ib. 19

3 That out of three sounds he frame, not a fourth sound, but a star.
Abt Vogler[1] *[1864], st. 7*

4 On the earth the broken arcs; in the heaven, a perfect round.
Ib. st. 9

5 The high that proved too high, the heroic for earth too hard,
The passion that left the ground to lose itself in the sky,
Are music sent up to God by the lover and the bard.
Ib. st. 10

6 Each sufferer says his say, his scheme of the weal and woe.
Ib. st. 11

7 The C Major of this life.
Ib. st. 12

8 Grow old along with me!
The best is yet to be,
The last of life, for which the first was made.
Our times are in his hand.
Rabbi Ben Ezra [1864], st. 1

9 Irks care the crop-full bird? Frets doubt the maw-crammed beast?
Ib. st. 4

10 Then welcome each rebuff
That turns earth's smoothness rough,
Each sting that bids nor sit nor stand, but go!
Be our joys three parts pain!
Strive, and hold cheap the strain;
Learn, nor account the pang; dare, never grudge the throe!
Ib. st. 6

11 What I aspired to be,
And was not, comforts me.
Ib. st. 7

12 Therefore I summon age
To grant youth's heritage.
Ib. st. 13

13 Look not thou down but up!
Ib. st. 30

14 Such ever was love's way: to rise, it stoops.
A Death in the Desert [1864], l. 134

15 To test man, the proofs shift.
Ib. l. 420

16 Progress, man's distinctive mark alone,
Not God's, and not the beasts': God is, they are;
Man partly is, and wholly hopes to be.
Ib. l. 586

[1]The Abt or Abbé George Joseph Vogler [1749–1824] was a composer, professor, Kapellmeister, and writer on music.

17 Setebos, Setebos, and Setebos!
'Thinketh, He dwelleth i' the cold o' the moon.
Caliban upon Setebos [1864], l. 24

18 Believeth with the life, the pain shall stop.
Ib. l. 250

19 The best way to escape His ire
Is, not to seem too happy.
Ib. l. 256

20 How sad and bad and mad it was[2]—
But then, how it was sweet!
Confessions [1864], st. 9

21 Fear death?—to feel the fog in my throat,
The mist in my face.
Prospice [1864], l. 1

22 No! let me taste the whole of it, fare like my peers,
The heroes of old,
Bear the brunt, in a minute pay glad life's arrears
Of pain, darkness, and cold.
Ib. l. 17

23 Hold me but safe again within the bond
Of one immortal look.
Eurydice to Orpheus [1864], l. 5

24 This could but have happened once—
And we missed it, lost it forever.
Youth and Art [1864], st. 17

25 All that I own is a print,
An etching, a mezzotint.
A Likeness [1864], st. 4

26 A face to lose youth for, to occupy age
With the dream of, meet death with.[3]
Ib. st. 6

27 We find great things are made of little things,
And little things go lessening till at last
Comes God behind them.
Mr. Sludge, "The Medium" [1864], l. 1112

28 'Tis because stiffish cock-tail, taken in time,
Is better for a bruise than arnica.
Ib. l. 1478

29 It's wiser being good than bad;
It's safer being meek than fierce;
It's fitter being sane than mad.
My own hope is, a sun will pierce
The thickest cloud earth ever stretched;
That, after Last, returns the First,
Though a wide compass round be fetched;
That what began best can't end worst,
Nor what God blessed once, prove accursed.
Apparent Failure [1864], st. 7

[2]See Swinburne, 634:11.
[3]A face that a man might die for.—Sir Arthur Conan Doyle, *The Adventures of Sherlock Holmes: A Scandal in Bohemia* [1892]

1 O Lyric Love, half angel and half bird,
And all a wonder and a wild desire.
The Ring and the Book [1868–1869], bk. I, l. 1391

2 That's all we may expect of man, this side
The grave: his good is—knowing he is bad.
Ib. VI, Giuseppe Caponsacchi, l. 142

3 'Twas a thief said the last kind word to Christ:
Christ took the kindness and forgave the theft. *Ib. l. 869*

4 All poetry is difficult to read,
—The sense of it is, anyhow.
Ib. VII, Pompilia, l. 1144

5 No work begun shall ever pause for death!
Ib. l. 1770

6 Let him wait God's instant men call years.
Ib. l. 1824

7 Through such souls alone
God stooping shows sufficient of His light
For us i' the dark to rise by. And I rise.
Ib. l. 1827

8 Faultless to a fault.[1]
Ib. IX, Juris Doctor Johannes-Baptista Bottinius, l. 1170

9 The curious crime, the fine
Felicity and flower of wickedness.
Ib. X, The Pope, l. 590

10 What I call God,
And fools call Nature.[2] *Ib. l. 1073*

11 Why comes temptation, but for man to meet
And master and make crouch beneath his foot,
And so be pedestaled in triumph?
Ib. l. 1185

12 White shall not neutralize the black, nor good
Compensate bad in man, absolve him so:
Life's business being just the terrible choice.
Ib. l. 1236

13 Waived all reward, loved but for loving's sake,
And what my heart taught me, I taught the world. *Ib. l. 1706*

14 You never know what life means till you die:
Even throughout life, 'tis death that makes life live,
Gives it whatever the significance.
Ib. XI, Guido, l. 2375

[1]See Tennyson, 533:17 and 534:12.

[2]Some call it Evolution, / And others call it God. . . . / Some of us call it Autumn, / And others call it God.—W. H. CARRUTH [1859–1924], *Each in His Own Tongue*

15 Save the squadron, honor France, love thy wife the Belle Aurore!
Hervé Riel [1871], st. 11

16 A man in armor is his armor's slave.
Herakles [1871]

17 In God's good time,
Which does not always fall on Saturday
When the world looks for wages.[3] *Ib.*

18 So absolutely good is truth, truth never hurts
The teller.
Fifine at the Fair [1872], st. 32

19 That far land we dream about,
Where every man is his own architect.
Red Cotton Nightcap Country [1873], II

20 A secret's safe
'Twixt you, me, and the gatepost!
The Inn Album [1875], II

21 Ignorance is not innocence but sin.
Ib. V

22 Have you found your life distasteful?
My life did and does smack sweet.
Was your youth of pleasure wasteful?
Mine I saved and hold complete.
Do your joys with age diminish?
When mine fail me, I'll complain.
Must in death your daylight finish?
My sun sets to rise again.
At the "Mermaid" [1876], st. 10

23 I find earth not gray but rosy,
Heaven not grim but fair of hue.
Do I stoop? I pluck a posy.
Do I stand and stare?[4] All's blue.
Ib. st. 12

24 Good, to forgive;
Best, to forget!
Living, we fret;
Dying, we live.
La Saisiaz [1877]. Introduction, st. 1

25 Sky—what a scowl of cloud
Till, near and far,
Ray on ray split the shroud:
Splendid, a star!
The Two Poets of Croisic [1878]. Introduction, st. 2

26 As if true pride
Were not also humble!
Lines written in an album [1882]

[3]The old Tuscan proverb: Iddio non paga sabato [God does not pay Saturdays].—*Life in Letters of William Dean Howells* [1928], *vol. II, p. 169, letter to Mrs. James T. Fields* [February 23, 1903]

[4]See Davies, 732:9.

1 Wanting is — what?
Summer redundant,
Blueness abundant,
— Where is the blot?
Wanting Is — What?[1] *[1883]*

2 Out of the wreck I rise. *Ixion [1883]*

3 Never the time and the place
And the loved one all together!
Never the Time and the Place [1883]

4 Help me with knowledge — for Life's Old
— Death's New!
Epitaph on Levi Lincoln Thaxter, 1824–1884

5 But little do or can the best of us:
That little is achieved through Liberty.
Why I Am a Liberal [1885], l. 9

6 A minute's success pays the failure of years.
Apollo and the Fates [1886], st. 42

7 One who never turned his back but marched
breast forward,
Never doubted clouds would break,
Never dreamed though right were worsted,
wrong would triumph,
Held we fall to rise, are baffled to fight better,
Sleep to wake.
Asolando [1889]. Epilogue, st. 3

Samuel Dickinson Burchard
1812–1891

8 We are Republicans, and don't propose to leave our party and identify ourselves with the party whose antecedents have been Rum, Romanism, and Rebellion.
Speaking for a deputation of clergymen calling upon James G. Blaine, the Republican presidential candidate, in New York [October 29, 1884]

Charles Dickens
1812–1870

9 A smattering of everything, and a knowledge of nothing.
Sketches by Boz [1836–1837]. Tales, ch. 3

10 He had used the word [humbug] in its Pickwickian sense.
Pickwick Papers [1836–1837], ch. 1

[1] Browning is — what? / Riddle redundant, / Baldness abundant, / Sense, who can spot? — ANONYMOUS, in *Punch* [April 21, 1883]

11 "An observer of human nature, sir," said Mr. Pickwick. *Ib. 2*

12 "It wasn't the wine," murmured Mr. Snodgrass, in a broken voice. "It was the salmon." *Ib. 8*

13 I wants to make your flesh creep. *Ib.*

14 Can I unmoved see thee dying
On a log
Expiring frog! *Ib. 15*

15 Tongue; well that's a wery good thing when it an't a woman's. *Ib. 19*

16 Mr. Weller's knowledge of London was extensive and peculiar. *Ib. 20*

17 I took a good deal o' pains with his eddication, sir; let him run in the streets when he was very young, and shift for hisself. It's the only way to make a boy sharp, sir. *Ib.*

18 Be wery careful o' vidders all your life. *Ib.*

19 The wictim o' connubiality, as Blue Beard's domestic chaplain said, with a tear of pity, ven he buried him. *Ib.*

20 Dumb as a drum vith a hole in it, sir. *Ib. 25*

21 Eccentricities of genius. *Ib. 30*

22 Keep yourself *to* yourself. *Ib. 32*

23 Poetry's unnat'ral; no man ever talked poetry 'cept a beadle on Boxin' Day. *Ib. 33*

24 She'll wish there was more, and that's the great art o' letter-writin'. *Ib.*

25 Never mind the character, stick to the aleybi. *Ib.*

26 She knows wot's wot, she does. *Ib. 37*

27 *They* don't mind it; it's a regular holiday to them — all porter and skittles.[2] *Ib. 41*

28 Anythin' for a quiet life, as the man said wen he took the sitivation at the lighthouse. *Ib. 43*

29 Right as a trivet. *Ib. 50*

30 Oliver Twist has asked for more!
Oliver Twist [1837–1838], ch. 2

31 "The artful Dodger." *Ib. 8*

[2] Life is with such all beer and skittles; / They are not difficult to please / About their victuals. — CHARLES STUART CALVERLEY [1831–1884], *Contentment*
Life ain't all beer and skittles, and more's the pity. — GEORGE DU MAURIER, *Trilby* [1894], *pt. I*
See Hughes, 590:10.

1 "Hard," replied the Dodger. "As nails," added Charley Bates. *Ib. 9*

2 There is a passion for hunting something deeply implanted in the human breast. *Ib. 10*

3 I'll eat my head. *Ib.*

4 I only know two sorts of boys. Mealy boys, and beef-faced boys. *Ib.*

5 There's light enough for wot I've got to do. *Ib. 47*

6 "If the law supposes that," said Mr. Bumble . . . "the law is a ass, a idiot." *Ib. 51*

7 He had but one eye, and the popular prejudice runs in favor of two.
Nicholas Nickleby [1838–1839], ch. 4

8 Subdue your appetites, my dears, and you've conquered human natur. *Ib. 5*

9 There are only two styles of portrait painting; the serious and the smirk. *Ib. 10*

10 Oh! they're too beautiful to live, much too beautiful! *Ib. 14*

11 I pity his ignorance and despise him. *Ib. 15*

12 The infant phenomenon. *Ib. 23*

13 The unities, sir . . . are a completeness — a kind of universal dove-tailedness with regard to place and time. *Ib. 24*

14 The two countesses had no outlines at all, and the dowager's was a demd outline. *Ib. 34*

15 A demd, damp, moist, unpleasant body! *Ib.*

16 Bring in the bottled lightning, a clean tumbler, and a corkscrew. *Ib. 49*

17 All is gas and gaiters. *Ib.*

18 My life is one demd horrid grind. *Ib. 64*

19 He has gone to the demnition bowwows. *Ib.*

20 What is the odds so long as the fire of soul is kindled at the taper of conwiviality, and the wing of friendship never moults a feather!
The Old Curiosity Shop [1841], ch. 2

21 She's the ornament of her sex. *Ib. 5*

22 In love of home, the love of country has its rise. *Ib. 38*

23 That vague kind of penitence which holidays awaken next morning.[1] *Ib. 40*

[1] See Byron, 460:23, and Ade, 718:12.

24 "Did you ever taste beer?" "I had a sip of it once," said the small servant. "Here's a state of things!" cried Mr. Swiveller. . . . "She *never* tasted it — it can't be tasted in a sip!" *Ib. 57*

25 It was a maxim with Foxey — our revered father, gentlemen — "Always suspect everybody." *Ib. 66*

26 Rather a tough customer in argyment.
Barnaby Rudge [1841], ch. 1

27 "There are strings," said Mr. Tappertit, " . . . in the human heart that had better not be wibrated." *Ib. 22*

28 Oh gracious, why wasn't I born old and ugly? *Ib. 70*

29 Any man may be in good spirits and good temper when he's well dressed. There ain't much credit in that.
Martin Chuzzlewit [1843–1844], ch. 5

30 With affection beaming in one eye, and calculation shining out of the other. *Ib. 8*

31 "Do not repine, my friends," said Mr. Pecksniff, tenderly. "Do not weep for me. It is chronic." *Ib. 9*

32 Keep up appearances whatever you do. *Ib. 11*

33 "Do other men for they would do you." That's the true business precept. *Ib.*

34 Buy an annuity cheap, and make your life interesting to yourself and everybody else that watches the speculation. *Ib. 18*

35 Leave the bottle on the chimleypiece, and don't ask me to take none, but let me put my lips to it when I am so dispoged. *Ib. 19*

36 Rich folks may ride on camels, but it ain't so easy for 'em to see out of a needle's eye [Sairey Gamp]. *Ib. 25*

37 "She's the sort of woman now," said Mould . . . "one would almost feel disposed to bury for nothing: and do it neatly, too!" *Ib.*

38 He'd make a lovely corpse. *Ib.*

39 Gamp is my name, and Gamp my nater. *Ib. 26*

40 Our fellow-countryman is a model of a man, quite fresh from Natur's mold! *Ib. 34*

1 Oh Sairey, Sairey, little do we know wot lays afore us! *Ib. 40*

2 I don't believe there's no sich a person! *Ib. 49*

3 The words she spoke of Mrs. Harris, lambs could not forgive . . . nor worms forget. *Ib.*

4 Oh, but he was a tightfisted hand at the grindstone. Scrooge! a squeezing, wrenching, grasping, scraping, clutching, covetous old sinner! Hard and sharp as flint, from which no steel had ever struck out generous fire; secret, and self-contained, and solitary as an oyster.
A Christmas Carol [1843], stave 1

5 "Bah," said Scrooge. "Humbug!" *Ib.*

6 I wear the chain I forged in life [Marley's Ghost]. *Ib.*

7 "I am the Ghost of Christmas Past." "Long past?" inquired Scrooge . . . "No. Your past." *Ib. 2*

8 In came a fiddler — and tuned like fifty stomachaches. In came Mrs. Fezziwig, one vast substantial smile. *Ib.*

9 I am the Ghost of Christmas Present. *Ib. 3*

10 As good as gold [Tiny Tim]. *Ib.*

11 "God bless us every one!" said Tiny Tim, the last of all. *Ib.*

12 "I am in the presence of the Ghost of Christmas Yet to Come?" said Scrooge. *Ib. 4*

13 I will honor Christmas in my heart, and try to keep it all the year. *Ib.*

14 It *was* a turkey! He could never have stood upon his legs, that bird! He would have snapped 'em off short in a minute, like sticks of sealing wax. *Ib. 5*

15 Oh let us love our occupations,
Bless the squire and his relations,
Live upon our daily rations,
And always know our proper stations.
The Chimes [1844], second quarter

16 He's tough, ma'am, tough, is J.B. Tough and devilish sly!
Dombey and Son [1848], ch. 7

17 I want to know what it says. . . . The sea, Floy, what it is that it keeps on saying.[1] *Ib. 8*

[1]What are the wild waves saying, / Sister, the whole day long? — JOSEPH EDWARDS CARPENTER [1813–1885], *What Are the Wild Waves Saying? st. 1*

18 "Wal'r, my boy," replied the Captain, "in the Proverbs of Solomon you will find the following words, 'May we never want a friend in need, nor a bottle to give him!' When found, make a note of." *Ib. 15*

19 Cows are my passion. *Ib. 21*

20 The bearings of this observation lays in the application on it. *Ib. 23*

21 You'll find us rough, sir, but you'll find us ready.
David Copperfield [1849–1850], ch. 3

22 I am a lone lorn creetur . . . and everythink goes contrairy with me. *Ib.*

23 Barkis is willin'. *Ib. 5*

24 Experientia does it[2] — as Papa used to say. *Ib. 11*

25 "In case anything turned up," which was his [Mr. Micawber's] favorite expression.[3] *Ib.*

26 I never will desert Mr. Micawber. *Ib. 12*

27 Annual income twenty pounds, annual expenditure nineteen nineteen six, result happiness. Annual income twenty pounds, annual expenditure twenty pounds ought and six, result misery. *Ib.*

28 It's a mad world. Mad as Bedlam. *Ib. 14*

29 Never . . . be mean in anything; never be false; never be cruel. *Ib. 15*

30 I'm a very umble person.[4] *Ib. 16*

31 The mistake was made of putting some of the trouble out of King Charles's head into my head.[5] *Ib. 17*

32 It was as true . . . as turnips is. It was as true . . . as taxes is. And nothing's truer than them. *Ib. 21*

33 What a world of gammon and spinach it is, though, ain't it! *Ib. 22*

34 Nobody's enemy but his own. *Ib. 25*

35 Accidents will occur in the best-regulated families. *Ib. 28*

[2]Experientia docet [Experience teaches]. — TACITUS [c. 55 – c. 117], *History, bk. V, ch. 6*

[3]See Disraeli, 501:25.

[4]Not only humble but umble, which I look upon to be the comparative, or, indeed, superlative degree. — ANTHONY TROLLOPE, *Doctor Thorne* [1858], *ch. 4*

[5]"King Charles's head" has passed into common use in the English language as a phrase meaning some whimsical obsession. — G. B. STERN, *Monogram* [1936]

1 Ride on! Rough-shod if need be, smooth-shod if that will do, but ride on! Ride on over all obstacles, and win the race! *Ib.*

2 A long pull, and a strong pull, and a pull all together. *Ib. 30*

3 He's a-going out with the tide.[1] *Ib.*

4 I ate umble pie with an appetite. *Ib. 39*

5 Let sleeping dogs lie—who wants to rouse 'em?[2] *Ib.*

6 Skewered through and through with office pens, and bound hand and foot with red tape. *Ib. 43*

7 It's only my child-wife. *Ib. 44*

8 There can be no disparity in marriage like unsuitability of mind and purpose. *Ib. 45*

9 A man must take the fat with the lean. *Ib. 51*

10 Trifles make the sum of life. *Ib. 53*

11 The seamen said it blew great guns. *Ib. 55*

12 He is an honorable, obstinate, truthful, high-spirited, intensely prejudiced, perfectly reasonable man.
Bleak House [1852–1858], ch. 2

13 This is a London particular. . . . A fog, miss. *Ib. 3*

14 Not to put too fine a point upon it. *Ib. 11*

15 [Old Mr. Turveydrop] was not like anything in the world but a model of Deportment. *Ib. 14*

16 What I want is Facts. Teach these boys and girls nothing but Facts. Facts alone are wanted in life. Plant nothing else, and root out everything else.
Hard Times [1854], bk. I, ch. 1

17 There is a wisdom of the head, and . . . a wisdom of the heart. *Ib. III, 1*

18 I am the only child of parents who weighed, measured, and priced everything; for whom what could not be weighed, measured, and priced had no existence.
Little Dorrit [1857–1858], bk. I, ch. 2

19 Whatever was required to be done, the Circumlocution Office was beforehand with all the public departments in the art of perceiving—HOW NOT TO DO IT. *Ib. 10*

[1] See Shakespeare, 207:13, and Frazer, 672:20.
[2] See Chaucer, 144:21.

20 Papa, potatoes, poultry, prunes, and prism, are all very good words for the lips: especially prunes and prism. *Ib. II, 5*

21 Once a gentleman, and always a gentleman. *Ib. 28*

22 It was the best of times, it was the worst of times.
A Tale of Two Cities [1859], bk. I, ch. 1

23 A wonderful fact to reflect upon, that every human creature is constituted to be that profound secret and mystery to every other. *Ib. 3*

24 It is a far, far better thing that I do, than I have ever done; it is a far, far better rest that I go to, than I have ever known. *Ib. III, 15*

25 In the little world in which children have their existence, whosoever brings them up, there is nothing so finely perceived and so finely felt, as injustice.
Great Expectations [1860–1861], ch. 9

26 Ever the best of friends! *Ib. 18*

27 My guiding star always is, Get hold of portable property. *Ib. 24*

28 Take nothing on its looks; take everything on evidence. There's no better rule. *Ib. 40*

29 Money and goods are certainly the best of references.
Our Mutual Friend [1864–1865], bk. I, ch. 4

30 Professionally he declines and falls, and as a friend he drops into poetry [Mr. Boffin on Silas Wegg]. *Ib. 5*

31 People now call him the Golden Dustman [Mr. Boffin]. *Ib. 11*

32 The gay, the gay and festive scene. *Ib. 15*

33 I want to be something so much worthier than the doll in the doll's house.[3] *Ib. 55*

34 I don't care whether I am a Minx or a Sphinx [Lavvy]. *Ib. II, 8*

35 That's the state to live and die in! . . . R-r-rich! *Ib. III, 5*

36 We must scrunch or be scrunched. *Ib.*

[3] See Ibsen, 599:9.

Ivan Goncharov
1812–1891

1 "And he was as intelligent as other people, his soul was pure and clear as crystal; he was noble and affectionate—and yet he did nothing!"

"But why? What was the reason?"

"The reason . . . what reason was there? Oblomovism!"[1]

Oblomov [1859], pt. IV, ch. 12

Alexander Ivanovich Herzen
1812–1870

2 Communism is a Russian autocracy turned upside down.

The Development of Revolutionary Ideas in Russia [1851]

3 Russia's future will be a great danger for Europe and a great misfortune for Russia if there is no emancipation of the individual. One more century of present despotism will destroy all the good qualities of the Russian people. *Ib.*

Edward Lear
1812–1888

4 There was an Old Man with a beard,
Who said: "It is just as I feared!
  Two owls and a hen,
  Four larks and a wren
Have all built their nests in my beard."

Book of Nonsense [1846]. Limerick

5 How pleasant to know Mr. Lear![2]
Who has written such volumes of stuff!
Some think him ill-tempered and queer,
But a few think him pleasant enough.

Nonsense Songs [1871]. Preface, st. 1

6 His body is perfectly spherical,
He weareth a runcible hat. *Ib. st. 5*

7 The Owl and the Pussycat went to sea
In a beautiful pea-green boat,
They took some honey, and plenty of money,
Wrapped up in a five-pound note.
The Owl looked up to the stars above,
And sang to a small guitar,
"O lovely Pussy! O Pussy, my love,
What a beautiful Pussy you are."

The Owl and the Pussycat [1871], st. 1

8 Pussy said to the Owl, "You elegant fowl!
How charmingly sweet you sing!
O let us be married! too long we have tarried:
But what shall we do for a ring?"
They sailed away, for a year and a day,
To the land where the Bong-tree grows
And there in a wood a Piggy-wig stood
With a ring at the end of his nose.

Ib. st. 2

9 "Dear Pig, are you willing to sell for one shilling
Your ring?" Said the Piggy, "I will."

Ib. st. 3

10 They dined on mince, and slices of quince,
Which they ate with a runcible spoon;
And hand in hand, on the edge of the sand,
They danced by the light of the moon.

Ib.

11 Far and few, far and few,
Are the lands where the Jumblies live;
Their heads are green, and their hands are blue,
And they went to sea in a sieve.

The Jumblies [1871], st. 1

12 Calico Pie,
  The little Birds fly
Down to the calico tree,
  Their wings were blue,
  And they sang "Tilly-loo!"
  Till away they flew—
And they never came back to me!

Calico Pie [1871], st. 1

13 Calico Jam,
  The little Fish swam,
Over the syllabub sea. *Ib. st. 2*

14 Who, or why, or which, or what,
Is the Akond of Swat?

The Akond of Swat[3] [1877], l. 1

15 On the top of the Crumpetty Tree
The Quangle Wangle sat,
But his face you could not see,
On account of his Beaver Hat.

The Quangle Wangle's Hat [1877], st. 1

16 On the coast of Coromandel
  Where the early pumpkins blow,
    In the middle of the woods
  Lived the Yonghy-Bonghy-Bò.

[1] That word is Oblomovism.
Now, when I hear a country squire talking about the rights of man and urging the necessity of developing personality, I know from the first word he utters that he is an Oblomov.
When I hear a government official complaining that the system of administration is too complicated and cumbersome, I know that he is an Oblomov. — NIKOLAI DOBROLIUBOV, *What Is Oblomovism?* [1859]

[2] See T. S. Eliot, 806:14.

[3] Pray tell me, good reader, if tell me you can, / What's the Ahkoond of Swat to you folks or to me? — EUGENE FIELD, *The Ahkoond of Swat* [1884]

Two old chairs, and half a candle,
One old jug without a handle—
These were all his worldly goods.
The Courtship of the Yonghy-Bongy-Bò [1877], st. 1

1 There he heard a Lady talking,
To some milk-white Hens of Dorking—
'Tis the Lady Jingly Jones! *Ib. st. 2*

2 "I would be your wife most gladly!"
(Here she twirled her fingers madly),
"But in England I've a mate!"
Ib. st. 5

3 When awful darkness and silence reign
Over the great Gromboolian plain,
Through the long, long wintry nights.
The Dong with the Luminous Nose [1877], st. 1

4 When storm-clouds brood on the towering heights
Of the hills of the Chankly Bore.
Ib.

5 The Pobble who has no toes
Had once as many as we;
When they said, "Some day you may lose them all"—
He replied, "Fish fiddle de-dee!"
The Pobble Who Has No Toes [1877], st. 1

6 It's a fact the whole world knows,
That Pobbles are happier without their toes.
Ib. 6

7 Ploffskin, Pluffskin, Pelican jee!
We think no Birds so happy as we!
Plumpskin, Ploshkin, Pelican jill!
We think so then, and we thought so still.
The Pelican Chorus [1877], chorus

Samuel Smiles
1812–1904

8 The spirit of self-help is the root of all genuine growth in the individual; and, exhibited in the lives of many, it constitutes the true source of national vigor and strength. Help from without is often enfeebling in its effects, but help from within invariably invigorates.
Self-Help [1859]

William Edmondstoune Aytoun
1813–1865

9 Nowhere beats the heart so kindly
As beneath the tartan plaid!
Charles Edward at Versailles [1849], l. 219

10 The deep, unutterable woe
Which none save exiles feel.
The Island of the Scots [1849], st. 12

Henry Ward Beecher
1813–1887

11 A thoughtful mind, when it sees a nation's flag, sees not the flag only, but the nation itself; and whatever may be its symbols, its insignia, he reads chiefly in the flag the government, the principles, the truths, the history which belongs to the nation that sets it forth. *The American Flag*

12 Where is human nature so weak as in the bookstore!
Star Papers [1855]. Subtleties of Book Buyers

13 Now comes the mystery.
Last words [March 8, 1887]

Claude Bernard
1813–1878

14 Observation is a passive science, experimentation an active science.
Introduction à l'Étude de la Médecine Expérimentale [1865][1]

15 The science of life is a superb and dazzlingly lighted hall which may be reached only by passing through a long and ghastly kitchen. *Ib.*

16 Science repulses the indefinite. *Ib.*

17 Science admits no exceptions; otherwise there would be no determinism in science, or rather, there would be no science.
Leçons de Pathologie Expérimentale [1872]

18 The stability of the *internal medium* is a primary condition for the freedom and independence of certain living bodies in relation to the environment surrounding them.
Leçons sur les Phénomènes de la Vie Communs aux Animaux et aux Végétaux [1878–1879][2]

19 All the vital mechanisms, varied as they are, have only one object, that of preserving constant the conditions of life in the internal environment. *Ib.*

[1] *An Introduction to the Study of Experimental Medicine,* translated by Henry Copley Greene.
[2] *Lessons on Reactions Common to Animals and Plants,* translated by J. M. D. Olmstead.

1 True science teaches us to doubt and to abstain from ignorance.

From Bulletin of New York Academy of Medicine, vol. IV [1928], p. 997

2 Science increases our power in proportion as it lowers our pride. *Ib.*

3 If I had to define life in a word, it would be: Life is creation. *Ib.*

4 A modern poet has characterized the personality of art and the impersonality of science as follows: Art is I: Science is We. *Ib.*

5 Man can learn nothing unless he proceeds from the known to the unknown. *Ib.*

6 We must never make experiments to confirm our ideas, but simply to control them. *Ib.*

7 The mental never influences the physical. It is always the physical that modifies the mental, and when we think that the mind is diseased, it is always an illusion.

Pensées [1937]

Georg Büchner
1813–1837

8 The Revolution is like Saturn—it eats its own children. *Danton's Death [1835]*

John William Burgon
1813–1860

9 A rose-red city half as old as time.[1]

Petra [1845]

Sören Kierkegaard
1813–1855

10 Life can only be understood backwards; but it must be lived forwards. *Life*

11 All essential knowledge relates to existence, or only such knowledge as has an essential relationship to existence is essential knowledge.

Concluding Unscientific Postscript

12 The absurd . . . the fact that with God all things are possible. The absurd is not one of the factors which can be discriminated within the proper compass of the understanding: it is not identical with the improbable, the unexpected, the unforeseen.

Fear and Trembling [1843]. Problemata: Preliminary Expectoration

[1] See Samuel Rogers, 416:3.

John Louis O'Sullivan
1813–1895

13 Our manifest destiny is to overspread the continent allotted by Providence for the free development of our yearly multiplying millions.

United States Magazine and Democratic Review [July–August 1845]

Richard Wagner
1813–1883

14 O thou, my gracious evening star.

Tannhäuser [1845]

15 To be German means to carry on a matter for its own sake.

Deutsche Kunst und Deutsche Politik[2] *[1867]*

16 Ride of the Valkyries.

Die Walküre [1876]

17 The pure fool. *Parsifal [1882]*

Henry Stevenson Washburn
1813–1903

18 We shall meet, but we shall miss him,
There will be one vacant chair.

The Vacant Chair, st. 1

Thomas Osborne Davis
1814–1845

19 Come in the evening, or come in the morning,
Come when you're looked for, or come without warning. *The Welcome, st. 1*

20 Sheep without a Shepherd,
When the snow shuts out the sky—
Oh, why did you leave us, Owen?
Why did you die?

Lament for the Death of Eoghan Ruadh O'Neill, st. 7

Frederick William Faber
1814–1863

21 Faith of our fathers! holy faith!
We will be true to thee till death.

A Pledge of Faithfulness [1849]

22 Hark! Hark! my soul, angelic songs are swelling
O'er earth's green fields, and ocean's wave-beat shore;

[2] *German Art and German Politics.*

How sweet the truth those blessed strains are
telling
Of that new life when sin shall be no more!
Pilgrims of the Night [1854]

Mikhail Lermontov
1814–1841

1 *A Hero of Our Time,* gentlemen, is indeed a portrait, but not of a single individual; it is a portrait composed of all the vices of our generation in the fullness of their development.
A Hero of Our Time [1840]. Author's Introduction

2 A solitary sail that rises
White in the blue mist on the foam—
What is it in far lands it prizes?
What does it leave behind at home?
A Sail [1841],[1] *st. 1*

3 Beneath, the azure current floweth,
Above, the golden sunlight glows.
Rebellious, the storms it wooeth,
As if the storms could give repose.
Ib. st. 3

Charles Mackay
1814–1889

4 There's a good time coming, boys!
A good time coming.
The Good Time Coming, st. 1

Edwin McMasters Stanton
1814–1869

5 Now he [Lincoln] belongs to the ages.
On the death of Lincoln [April 15, 1865]

Otto von Bismarck
1815–1898

6 The great questions of the time are not decided by speeches and majority decisions—that was the error of 1848 and 1849—but by iron and blood.[2]
Speech to the Prussian Diet [September 30, 1862]

7 Politics is not an exact science.[3]
Speech to the Herrenhaus [December 13, 1863]

[1] Translated by C. M. Bowra.
[2] Eisen und Blut.
[3] Politics is not a science . . . but an art.—Bismarck, *speech* [March 15, 1884]
Politics is the art of the possible.—*Attributed to* Bismarck

8 The glass house of German statecraft.
Concerning Austro-German power, to a commission of the Prussian Landtag [1864]

9 Only a completely ready state can permit the luxury of a liberal government.
Speech [1866]

10 Let us put Germany in the saddle, so to speak—it already knows how to ride.
Speech to the North German Reichstag [March 11, 1867]

11 A conquering army on the border will not be halted by the power of eloquence.
Ib. [September 24, 1867]

12 He who has his thumb on the purse has the power. *Ib. [May 21, 1869]*

13 The luxury of one's own opinion.
Speech to the Prussian Diet [December 17, 1873]

14 The right people in the right jobs.
Speech to the North German Reichstag [1875]

15 Politics ruins the character.
Reported by Bernhard Brigl in the Berlin Tägliche Rundschau [1881]

16 We Germans fear God, but nothing else in the world.
Speech to the Reichstag [February 6, 1888]

Richard Henry Dana
1815–1882

17 Six days shalt thou labor and do all thou art
able,
And on the seventh—holystone the decks
and scrape the cable.
Two Years Before the Mast [1840], ch. 3

18 He seldom went up to town without coming down "three sheets in the wind."[4]
Ib. 20

19 Everything was "shipshape and Bristol fashion." *Ib. 22*

David Davis
1815–1886

20 The Constitution of the United States is a law for rulers and people, equally in war and in peace, and covers with the shield of its protection all classes of men, at all times, and

[4] Old Wax and Bristles is about three sheets in the wind.—Pierce Egan, *Life in London* [1821]

under all circumstances. No doctrine, involving more pernicious consequences, was ever invented by the wit of man than that any of its provisions can be suspended during any of the great exigencies of government.

Ex Parte Milligan, 4 Wallace 2, 120–121 [1866]

Daniel Decatur Emmett

1815–1904

1 I wish I was in de land ob cotton,
Old times dar am not forgotten.
Look away, look away,
Look away, Dixie[1] Land.

Dixie [1859], st. 1

2 In Dixie's land, we'll took our stand,
To lib an' die in Dixie! *Ib. st. 3*

John Babsone Lane Soule

1815–1891

3 Go west, young man.[2]

Article in the Terre Haute (Indiana) Express [1851]

Elizabeth Cady Stanton

1815–1902

4 We hold these truths to be self-evident, that all men and women are created equal.

First Woman's Rights Convention, Seneca Falls, New York [July 19–20, 1848]. Declaration of Sentiments

5 Resolved, That it is the duty of the women of this country to secure to themselves their sacred right to the elective franchise.

Ib. Resolution IX

[1]Originally this word [Dixie] applied only to New Orleans; not until the Civil War, when D. D. Emmett's famous song . . . became the favorite battle song of the Confederacy, was it in general use to designate the entire South. It came about in this fashion:

A few years after Louisiana became a part of the United States . . . one of the New Orleans banks began issuing ten-dollar notes, one side of which was printed in English and the other in French. On the latter, in large letters, was the French word for ten, *dix*. . . . One of these notes was known simply as a dix; collectively they were dixies, a name which was soon applied to the city of issue as well.—Herbert Asbury, *The French Quarter* [1936], *ch. 3*

[2]Horace Greeley [1811–1872] used the expression in an editorial in the *New York Tribune.* As the saying "Go west, young man, and grow up with the country" gained popularity, Greeley printed Soule's article, to show the source of his inspiration.

Many men have stated that the advice was given to them by Greeley, among them William S. Verity [1837–1930], who said Greeley had given it to him in 1859.

See Greeley, 538:8.

6 The prejudice against color, of which we hear so much, is no stronger than that against sex. It is produced by the same cause, and manifested very much in the same way. The Negro's skin and the woman's sex are both prima facie evidence that they were intended to be in subjection to the white Saxon man.

Speech before the New York Legislature [February 18, 1860]

7 Woman's degradation is in man's idea of his sexual rights. Our religion, laws, customs, are all founded on the belief that woman was made for man. Come what will, my whole soul rejoices in the truth that I have uttered.[3]

Letter to Susan B. Anthony [June 14, 1860]

8 Our "pathway" is straight to the ballot box, with no variableness nor shadow of turning. . . . We demand in the Reconstruction suffrage for all the citizens of the Republic. I would not talk of Negroes or women, but of citizens.

Letter to Thomas Wentworth Higginson [January 13, 1868]

9 Women have crucified the Mary Wollstonecrafts, the Fanny Wrights, and the George Sands of all ages. Men mock us with the fact and say we are ever cruel to each other. . . . If this present woman[4] must be crucified, let men drive the spikes.

Letter to Lucretia Mott [April 1, 1872]

Anthony Trollope

1815–1882

10 The tenth Muse who now governs the periodical press.

The Warden [1855], ch. 14

11 One of her instructors in fashion had given her to understand that curls were not the thing. "They'll always pass muster," Miss Dunstable had replied, "when they are done up with bank notes."

Doctor Thorne [1858], ch. 16

12 There is no road to wealth so easy and respectable as that of matrimony. *Ib. 18*

[3]Referring to resolutions she had introduced at the tenth National Woman's Rights Convention [May 10, 1860], declaring that under certain circumstances divorce was justifiable.

[4]Victoria Woodhull.

1 I cannot hold with those who wish to put down the insignificant chatter of the world.
Framley Parsonage [1861]

2 She understood how much louder a cock can crow in its own farmyard than elsewhere.
The Last Chronicle of Barset [1867], vol. I, ch. 17

3 Always remember that when you go into an attorney's office door, you will have to pay for it, first or last. *Ib. 20*

4 It is a comfortable feeling to know that you stand on your own ground. Land is about the only thing that can't fly away.[1]
Ib. II, 58

5 It's dogged as does it. It ain't thinking about it. *Ib. 61*

6 Nothing reopens the springs of love so fully as absence, and no absence so thoroughly as that which must needs be endless.
Ib. 67

7 She knew how to allure by denying, and to make the gift rich by delaying it.
Phineas Finn [1869], ch. 57

8 There are worse things than a lie . . . I have found . . . that it may be well to choose one sin in order that another may be shunned.
Doctor Wortle's School [1879], ch. 6

9 *Barchester Towers* has become one of those novels which do not die quite at once, which live and are read for perhaps a quarter of a century.
An Autobiography [1883], ch. 6

10 A small daily task, if it be really daily,[2] will beat the labors of a spasmodic Hercules.
Ib. 7

11 Of all the needs a book has, the chief need is that it be readable.[3] *Ib. 19*

Philip James Bailey
1816–1902

12 Let each man think himself an act of God,
His mind a thought, his life a breath of God.
Festus [1839]. Proem

[1] See John Adams, 382:2.

[2] Nulla dies sine linea [No day without a line]. Let that be their motto. . . . No gigantic efforts will then be necessary.—TROLLOPE, *An Autobiography* [1883], *ch. 20, advice to young writers*

See Apelles, 90:15.

[3] See Henry James, 652:12.

13 We live in deeds, not years; in thoughts, not breaths;
In feelings, not in figures on a dial.
Ib. A Country Town

14 Envy's a coal comes hissing hot from hell.
Ib.

15 America, thou half-brother of the world;
With something good and bad of every land.
Ib. The Surface

Charlotte Brontë
1816–1855

16 We wove a web in childhood,
A web of sunny air.
Retrospection [1846], st. 1

17 The human heart has hidden treasures,
In secret kept, in silence sealed.
Evening Solace [1846], st. 1

18 Conventionality is not morality. Self-righteousness is not religion. To attack the first is not to assail the last.
Jane Eyre [1847], preface

19 Reader, I married him. *Ib. ch. 38*

20 An abundant shower of curates has fallen upon the north of England.
Shirley [1849], ch. 1

21 Unromantic as Monday morning.
Ib.

Gustav Freytag
1816–1895

22 Madness of the Caesars.[4]
Die Verlorene Handschrift [1864]

Ellen Sturgis Hooper
1816–1841

23 I slept and dreamed that life was beauty.
I woke—and found that life was duty.
Beauty and Duty

Eugène Pottier
1816–1887

24 Arise, ye prisoners of starvation,
Arise, ye wretched of the earth,
For justice thunders condemnation—
A better world's in birth.
L'Internationale [1871][5]

[4] Concerning the proposition that power is intrinsically evil.

[5] ADOLPHE DEGEYTER wrote the music for "The International," which was adopted as the rallying song of Communism.

John Godfrey Saxe
1816–1887

1 In battle or business, whatever the game,
In law or in love, it is ever the same;
In the struggle for power, or the scramble for pelf,
Let this be your motto—Rely on yourself!
For, whether the prize be a ribbon or throne,
The victor is he who can go it alone![1]

The Game of Life, st. 7

2 "God bless the man who first invented sleep!"[2]
So Sancho Panza said, and so say I.[3]

Early Rising, st. 1

Frederick Douglass[4]
c. 1817–1895

3 Every tone [of the songs of the slaves] was a testimony against slavery, and a prayer to God for deliverance from chains.

Narrative of the Life of Frederick Douglass [1845], ch. 2

4 The whole history of the progress of human liberty shows that all concessions yet made to her august claims have been born of earnest struggle. . . . If there is no struggle, there is no progress. Those who profess to favor freedom, and yet deprecate agitation, are men who want crops without plowing up the ground, they want rain without thunder and lightning. They want the ocean without the awful roar of its many waters.[5]

From JOHN W. BLASSINGAME, *Frederick Douglass: The Clarion Voice [1976]*

5 What, to the American slave, is your Fourth of July? I answer: A day that reveals to him, more than all other days of the year, the gross injustices and cruelty to which he is the constant victim. To him your celebration is a sham.

What to the Slave Is the Fourth of July? Speech at Rochester, New York [July 4, 1852]

6 You profess to believe that "of one blood God made all nations of men to dwell on the face of all the earth"—and hath commanded all men, everywhere, to love one another—yet you notoriously hate (and glory in your hatred!) all men whose skins are not colored like your own! *Ib.*

7 The ground which a colored man occupies in this country is, every inch of it, sternly disputed.

Speech at the American and Foreign Anti-Slavery Society annual meeting, New York City [May 1853]

8 The destiny of the colored American . . . is the destiny of America.[6]

Speech at the Emancipation League, Boston [February 12, 1862]

9 The relation between the white and colored people of this country is the great, paramount, imperative, and all-commanding question for this age and nation to solve.[6]

Speech at the Church of the Puritans, New York City [May 1863]

10 Despite of it all, the Negro remains . . . cool, strong, imperturbable, and cheerful.

Speech on the twenty-first anniversary of Emancipation in the District of Columbia, Washington, D.C. [April 1883]

11 In all the relations of life and death, we are met by the color line.

Speech at the Convention of Colored Men, Louisville, Kentucky [September 24, 1883]

12 No man can put a chain about the ankle of his fellow man without at last finding the other end fastened about his own neck.

Speech at Civil Rights Mass Meeting, Washington, D.C. [October 22, 1883]

13 The life of the nation is secure only while the nation is honest, truthful, and virtuous.

Speech on the twenty-third anniversary of Emancipation in the District of Columbia, Washington, D.C. [April 1885]

14 Where justice is denied, where poverty is enforced, where ignorance prevails, and where any one class is made to feel that society is in an organized conspiracy to oppress, rob, and degrade them, neither persons nor property will be safe.

Speech on the twenty-fourth anniversary of Emancipation in the District of Columbia, Washington, D.C. [April 1886]

James Thomas Fields
1817–1881

15 But his little daughter whispered,
As she took his icy hand,

[1] He travels the fastest who travels alone.—KIPLING [1865–1936], *The Winners*

[2] See Cervantes, 171:1.

[3] See F. P. Adams, 773:14.

[4] This man, this Douglass . . . superb in love and logic.—ROBERT HAYDEN [1913–1980], *A Ballad of Remembrance* [1962], *Frederick Douglass*

[5] See *Psalm 93:4*, 20:19.

[6] See Du Bois, 724:15.

"Isn't God upon the ocean,
Just the same as on the land?"[1]

The Captain's Daughter; or, The Ballad of the Tempest [1858], st. 5

Georg Herwegh
1817–1875

1 The poor human heart must break piecemeal.

Strophen aus der Fremde [1840]. From Rückert's Musenalmanach

Henry David Thoreau
1817–1862

2 I am a parcel of vain strivings tied
By a chance bond together.

Sic Vita [1841], st. 1

3 We are as much as we see. Faith is sight and knowledge. The hands only serve the eyes. *Journal [1906]. April 9, 1841*

4 The Indian . . . stands free and unconstrained in Nature, is her inhabitant and not her guest, and wears her easily and gracefully. But the civilized man has the habits of the house. His house is a prison.

Ib. April 26, 1841

5 It is a great art to saunter.[2] *Ib.*

6 A slight sound at evening lifts me up by the ears, and makes life seem inexpressibly serene and grand. It may be in Uranus, or it may be in the shutter.

Ib. July 10–12, 1841

7 For many years I was self-appointed inspector of snowstorms and rainstorms, and did my duty faithfully, though I never received one cent for it.

Ib. February 22, 1845–1847[3]

8 And now, at half-past ten o'clock, I hear the cockerels crow in Hubbard's barns, and morning is already anticipated. It is the feathered, wakeful thought in us that anticipates the following day.

Ib. July 11, 1851

[1]See Sir Humphrey Gilbert, 166:13, and Robert Burton, 259:12.

[2]*Sauntering,* which word is beautifully derived "from idle people who roved about the country, in the Middle Ages, and asked charity, under pretense of going *à la Sainte Terre,*" to the Holy Land, till the children exclaimed, "There goes a Sainte-Terrer."—THOREAU, *Walking* [1862]

[3]No year in Thoreau's dateline.

9 Nothing is so much to be feared as fear.[4]

Ib. September 7, 1851

10 The bluebird carries the sky on his back.

Ib. April 3, 1852

11 The perception of beauty is a moral test.

Ib. June 21, 1852

12 The youth gets together his materials to build a bridge to the moon, or, perchance, a palace or temple on the earth, and, at length, the middle-aged man concludes to build a woodshed with them. *Ib. July 14, 1852*

13 Fire is the most tolerable third party.

Ib. January 2, 1853

14 Some circumstantial evidence is very strong, as when you find a trout in the milk.

Ib. November 11, 1854

15 Nature is full of genius, full of the divinity; so that not a snowflake escapes its fashioning hand. *Ib. January 5, 1856*

16 The same law that shapes the earth-star shapes the snow-star. As surely as the petals of a flower are fixed, each of these countless snow-stars comes whirling to earth . . . these glorious spangles, the sweeping of heaven's floor. *Ib.*

17 That man is the richest whose pleasures are the cheapest. *Ib. March 11, 1856*

18 This bird [the crow] sees the white man come and the Indian withdraw, but it withdraws not. Its untamed voice is still heard above the tinkling of the forge. . . . It remains to remind us of aboriginal nature.

Ib. March 23, 1856

19 The savage in man is never quite eradicated. *Ib. September 26, 1859*

20 Great God, I ask thee for no meaner pelf
Than that I may not disappoint myself,
That in my action I may soar as high
As I can now discern with this clear eye.

A Prayer [1842], st. 1

21 Talk of mysteries! Think of our life in nature—daily to be shown matter, to come in contact with it—rocks, trees, wind on our cheeks! the *solid* earth! the *actual* world! the *common sense! Contact! Contact! Who* are we? *where* are we?

The Maine Woods, Ktaadn [1848]

22 I think that we should be men first, and subjects afterward. It is not desirable to cultivate a respect for the law, so much as for the right. *Civil Disobedience [1849]*

[4]See *Proverbs 3:25,* 23:6; Montaigne, 164:7; Bacon, 179:13; Wellington, 421:10; and Roosevelt, 779:10.

1 How does it become a man to behave toward this American government today? I answered that he cannot without disgrace be associated with it. *Ib.*

2 When a sixth of the population of a nation which has undertaken to be the refuge of liberty are slaves, and a whole country [Mexico] is unjustly overrun and conquered by a foreign army, and subjected to military law, I think that it is not too soon for honest men to rebel and revolutionize. What makes this duty the more urgent is the fact that the country so overrun is not our own, but ours is the invading army. *Ib.*

3 A wise man will not leave the right to the mercy of chance, nor wish it to prevail through the power of the majority. There is but little virtue in the action of masses of men. *Ib.*

4 I came into this world, not chiefly to make this a good place to live in, but to live in it, be it good or bad. *Ib.*

5 Any man more right than his neighbors constitutes a majority of one. *Ib.*

6 Under a government which imprisons any unjustly, the true place for a just man is also a prison . . . the only house in a slave State in which a free man can abide with honor. *Ib.*

7 I saw that the State was half-witted, that it was timid as a lone woman with her silver spoons, and that it did not know its friends from its foes, and I lost all my remaining respect for it, and pitied it. *Ib.*

8 My life is like a stroll upon the beach,
As near the ocean's edge as I can go.
My Life Is Like a Stroll upon the Beach [1849], st. 1

9 The vessel, though her masts be firm,
Beneath her copper bears a worm.
A Week on the Concord and Merrimack Rivers [1849]. Monday [Though All the Fates Should Prove Unkind, st. 2]

10 Far from New England's blustering shore,
New England's worm her hulk shall bore,
And sink her in the Indian seas,
Twine, wine, and hides, and China teas.
Ib.

11 Methinks my own soul must be a bright invisible green. *Ib. Wednesday*

12 It takes two to speak the truth—one to speak, and another to hear. *Ib.*

13 Even the death of friends will inspire us as much as their lives. . . . Their memories will be encrusted over with sublime and pleasing thoughts, as monuments of other men are overgrown with moss; for our friends have no place in the graveyard. *Ib.*

14 This world is but canvas to our imaginations. *Ib.*

15 Dreams are the touchstones of our characters. *Ib.*

16 Go where we will on the *surface* of things, men have been there before us. *Ib. Thursday*

17 The frontiers are not east or west, north or south, but wherever a man *fronts* a fact. *Ib.*

18 A true account of the actual is the rarest poetry, for common sense always takes a hasty and superficial view. *Ib.*

19 Here while I lie beneath this walnut bough,
What care I for the Greeks or for Troy town,
If juster battles are enacted now
Beneath the ants upon this hummock's crown?
Ib. My Books I'd Fain Cast Off, st. 3

20 As if our birth had at first sundered things, and we had been thrust up through into nature like a wedge, and not till the wound heals and the scar disappears, do we begin to discover where we are, and that nature is one and continuous everywhere. *Ib. Friday*

21 What are the earth and all its interests beside the deep surmise which pierces and scatters them? *Ib.*

22 It is so rare to meet with a man outdoors who cherishes a worthy thought in his mind, which is independent of the labor of his hands. *Ib.*

23 The eye may see for the hand, but not for the mind. *Ib.*

24 My life has been the poem I would have writ,
But I could not both live and utter it.
Ib. My Life Has Been the Poem I Would Have Writ

25 The fate of the country . . . does not depend on what kind of paper you drop into the ballot box once a year, but on what kind of man you drop from your chamber into the street every morning. *Slavery in Massachusetts [1854]*

26 I should not talk so much about myself if there were anybody else whom I knew as well. *Walden [1854],*[1] *1, Economy*

[1] *Walden* is the only book I own, although there are some others unclaimed on my shelves. Every man, I

1 I have traveled a good deal in Concord. *Ib.*

2 Public opinion is a weak tyrant compared with our own private opinion. What a man thinks of himself, that is which determines, or rather, indicates, his fate. *Ib.*

3 As if you could kill time without injuring eternity. *Ib.*

4 The mass of men lead lives of quiet desperation. *Ib.*

5 It is characteristic of wisdom not to do desperate things. *Ib.*

6 It is never too late to give up our prejudices. *Ib.*

7 Age is no better, hardly so well, qualified for an instructor as youth, for it has not profited so much as it has lost. *Ib.*

8 Most of the luxuries, and many of the so-called comforts, of life are not only not indispensable, but positive hindrances to the elevation of mankind. *Ib.*

9 To be a philosopher is not merely to have subtle thoughts, nor even to found a school, but so to love wisdom as to live accordingly to its dictates, a life of simplicity, independence, magnanimity, and trust. *Ib.*

10 Beware of all enterprises that require new clothes. *Ib.*

11 Our moulting season, like that of the fowls, must be a crisis in our lives. *Ib.*

12 In the long run men hit only what they aim at. *Ib.*

13 The swiftest traveler is he that goes afoot. *Ib.*

14 It is not necessary that a man should earn his living by the sweat of his brow[1] unless he sweats easier than I do. *Ib.*

15 The man who goes alone can start today; but he who travels with another must wait till that other is ready. *Ib.*

16 When a man dies he kicks the dust. *Ib.*

17 As for doing good, that is one of the professions which are full. *Ib.*

think, reads one book in his life, and this one is mine. It is not the best book I ever encountered, perhaps, but it is for me the handiest, and I keep it about me in much the same way one carries a handkerchief—for relief in moments of defluxion or despair.—E. B. WHITE, *The New Yorker* [May 23, 1953]

See E. B. White, 846.

[1]See *Genesis 3:19*, 7:12.

18 There is no odor so bad as that which arises from goodness tainted.[2] *Ib.*

19 There are a thousand hacking at the branches of evil to one who is striking at the root. *Ib.*

20 Philanthropy is almost the only virtue which is sufficiently appreciated by mankind. *Ib.*

21 A man is rich in proportion to the number of things which he can afford to let alone. *Ib. 2, Where I Lived, and What I Lived For*

22 To him whose elastic and vigorous thought keeps pace with the sun, the day is a perpetual morning. *Ib.*

23 To be awake is to be alive. *Ib.*

24 I know of no more encouraging fact than the unquestionable ability of man to elevate his life by a conscious endeavor. *Ib.*

25 I went to the woods because I wished to live deliberately, to front only the essential facts of life, and see if I could not learn what it had to teach, and not, when I came to die, discover that I had not lived. *Ib.*

26 Our life is frittered away by detail . . . Simplify, simplify. *Ib.*

27 We do not ride on the railroad; it rides upon us. *Ib.*

28 Time is but the stream I go a-fishing in. *Ib.*

29 Books must be read as deliberately and reservedly as they are written. *Ib. 3, Reading*

30 What is called eloquence in the forum is commonly found to be rhetoric in the study. *Ib.*

31 Books are the treasured wealth of the world and the fit inheritance of generations and nations. . . . Their authors are a natural and irresistible aristocracy in every society, and, more than kings or emperors, exert an influence on mankind. *Ib.*

32 The works of the great poets have never yet been read by mankind, for only great poets can read them. *Ib.*

33 It is not all books that are as dull as their readers. *Ib.*

34 How many a man has dated a new era in his life from the reading of a book. *Ib.*

[2]See Shakespeare, 245:6.

1 I love a broad margin to my life.
Ib. 4, Sounds

2 Our horizon is never quite at our elbows.
Ib. 5, Solitude

3 I never found the companion that was so companionable as solitude. We are for the most part more lonely when we go abroad among men than when we stay in our chambers. A man thinking or working is always alone, let him be where he will.[1] *Ib.*

4 I had three chairs in my house: one for solitude, two for friendship, three for society.
Ib. 6, Visitors

5 Ministers who spoke of God as if they enjoyed a monopoly of the subject. *Ib.*

6 I was determined to know beans.
Ib. 7, The Beanfield

7 Through want of enterprise and faith men are where they are, buying and selling, and spending their lives like serfs.
Ib. 10, Baker Farm

8 There is never an instant's truce between virtue and vice. Goodness is the only investment that never fails.
Ib. 11, Higher Laws

9 They [wood stumps] warmed me twice — once while I was splitting them, and again when they were on the fire.[2]
Ib. 13, Housewarming

10 Heaven is under our feet as well as over our heads. *Ib. 16, The Pond in Winter*

11 While men believe in the infinite, some ponds will be thought to be bottomless.
Ib.

12 What is man but a mass of thawing clay?
Ib. 17, Spring

13 Through our own recovered innocence we discern the innocence of our neighbors.
Ib.

14 We need the tonic of wildness . . . We can never have enough of nature. *Ib.*

15 As if there were safety in stupidity alone.
Ib. 18, Conclusion

16 If one advances confidently in the direction of his dreams, and endeavors to live the life which he has imagined, he will meet with a success unexpected in common hours.
Ib.

17 If a man does not keep pace with his companions, perhaps it is because he hears a different drummer. Let him step to the music which he hears, however measured or far away. *Ib.*

18 Love your life, poor as it is. You may perhaps have some pleasant, thrilling, glorious hours, even in a poorhouse. The setting sun is reflected from the windows of the almshouse as brightly as from the rich man's abode.
Ib.

19 It is life near the bone where it is sweetest.
Ib.

20 Rather than love, than money, than fame, give me truth. *Ib.*

21 He would have left a Greek accent slanting the wrong way, and righted up a falling man.
A Plea for Captain John Brown [1859]

22 I hear many condemn these men because they were so few. When were the good and the brave ever in a majority? *Ib.*

23 It was his peculiar doctrine that a man has a perfect right to interfere by force with the slaveholder, in order to rescue the slave. I agree with him. They who are continually shocked by slavery have some right to be shocked by the violent death of the slaveholder, but no others. *Ib.*

24 I speak for the slave when I say that I prefer the philanthropy of Captain Brown to that philanthropy which neither shoots me nor liberates me. *Ib.*

25 So we defend ourselves and our henroosts, and maintain slavery. *Ib.*

26 He is not Old Brown any longer; he is an angel of light. *Ib.*

27 In wildness is the preservation of the world.[3] *Walking [1862]*

28 Life consists with wildness. The most alive is the wildest. Not yet subdued to man, its presence refreshes him. *Ib.*

29 Men will lie on their backs, talking about the fall of man, and never make an effort to get up. *Life Without Principle [1863]*

30 I'm contented you should stay
For ever and aye
If you can take yourself away
Any day.
I'm Contented You Should Stay [1943]

[1] See Cicero, 99:1, and Samuel Rogers, 416:2.

[2] Who splits his own wood warms himself twice. — *Saying*

[3] Motto of the Wilderness Society. See Muir, 637:16.

1 What sought they thus afar
They sought a faith's pure shrine.[1]

Seek! shall I seek! The Gods above should give,
They have enough and we do poorly live.
What Sought They Thus Afar [1943], st. 1, 2

Alexei Konstantinovich Tolstoi
1817–1875

2 His pen is breathing revenge.
Vaska Shibanov [1855–1865]

3 No one can encompass the unencompassable.
Collected Works of Kosma Prutkov [1884][2]

4 If thou hast a fountain, shut it up: let even a fountain have a rest. *Ib.*

5 Many men are like unto sausages: whatever you stuff them with, that they will bear in them. *Ib.*

6 If you want to be happy, be. *Ib.*

Alexander II
1818–1881

7 Better to abolish serfdom from above than to wait till it begins to abolish itself from below.
Speech in Moscow [March 30, 1856]

Cecil Frances Alexander
1818–1895

8 All things bright and beautiful,
All creatures great and small,
All things wise and wonderful,
The Lord God made them all.[3]
All Things Bright and Beautiful [1848], st. 1

9 There is a green hill far away,
Without a city wall,
Where the dear Lord was crucified,
Who died to save us all.
There Is a Green Hill [1848], st. 1

10 Once in royal David's city
Stood a lowly cattle shed,
Where a Mother laid her Baby
In a manger for his bed:
Mary was that Mother mild,
Jesus Christ her little Child.
Once in Royal David's City [1848], st. 1

Josh Billings [Henry Wheeler Shaw]
1818–1885

11 A sekret ceases tew be a sekret if it iz once confided — it iz like a dollar bill, once broken, it iz never a dollar agin.
Affurisms [1865]. From Josh Billings: His Sayings

12 Love iz like the meazles; we kant have it bad but onst, and the later in life we have it the tuffer it goes with us. *Ib.*

13 Put an Englishman into the garden of Eden, and he would find fault with the whole blarsted consarn; put a Yankee in, and he would see where he could alter it to advantage; put an Irishman in, and he would want tew boss the thing; put a Dutchman in, and he would proceed tew plant it. *Ib.*

14 Better make a weak man your enemy than your friend. *Ib.*

15 Nature never makes any blunders; when she makes a fool she means it. *Ib.*

16 I don't care how much a man talks, if he only says it in a few words. *Ib.*

17 As scarce as truth is, the supply has always been in excess of the demand. *Ib.*

18 Poverty iz the stepmother ov genius. *Ib.*

19 The wheel that squeaks the loudest
Is the one that gets the grease.
The Kicker

20 It is better to know nothing than to know what ain't so.[4] *Proverb [1874]*

Emily Brontë
1818–1848

21 Sleep not, dream not; this bright day
Will not, cannot last for aye;
Bliss like thine is bought by years
Dark with torment and with tears.
Sleep Not [1846], st. 1

[1] What sought they thus afar? Bright jewels of the mine? / The wealth of seas, the spoils of war? — / They sought a faith's pure shrine! — FELICIA DOROTHEA HEMANS, *The Landing of the Pilgrim Fathers, st. 9*

[2] Kosma Prutkov, a pompous and platitudinous clerk who dabbled in the muses, was invented by Tolstoi and the brothers Zhemchuzhnikov, who supplied him with a biography, a portrait, and *Collected Works*, published in 1884. Individual satirical pieces had been appearing under his name since 1851. He became a classic of Russian satirical humor.
Translated by B. G. GURNEY.

[3] See Coleridge, 435:11.

[4] Better know nothing than half-know many things. — NIETZSCHE, *Thus Spake Zarathustra* [1883–1891], *pt. IV, 64*

1 Cold in the earth — and fifteen wild Decembers
From those brown hills have melted into spring. *Remembrance [1846], st. 3*

2 Once drinking deep of that divinest anguish,
How could I seek the empty world again?
Ib. st. 8

3 Yes, as my swift days near their goal,
'Tis all that I implore:
In life and death a chainless soul,
With courage to endure.
The Old Stoic [1846], st. 3

4 No coward soul is mine,
No trembler in the world's storm-troubled sphere:
I see Heaven's glories shine,
And faith shines equal, arming me from fear.
Last Lines [1846], st. 1

5 There is not room for Death. *Ib. st. 7*

6 I *am* Heathcliff.
Wuthering Heights [1847], ch. 9

7 I lingered round them, under that benign sky: watched the moths fluttering among the heath and harebells; listened to the soft wind breathing through the grass; and wondered how anyone could ever imagine unquiet slumbers for the sleepers in that quiet earth.
Ib. last words

William Ellery Channing

1818–1901

8 Habitant of castle gray,
Creeping thing in sober way,
Visible sage mechanician,
Skillfulest arithmetician. *The Spider*

9 I laugh, for hope hath happy place with me—
If my bark sinks, 'tis to another sea.
A Poet's Hope

10 The hills are reared, the seas are scooped in vain
If learning's altar vanish from the plain.
Inscription for the Alcott house[1]

Eliza Cook

1818–1889

11 I love it, I love it; and who shall dare
To chide me for loving that old armchair?
The Old Armchair

[1]This couplet is painted over the mantel of the Alcott house, Concord, Massachusetts.

12 Better build schoolrooms for "the boy"
Than cells and gibbets for "the man."[2]
A Song for the Ragged Schools, st. 12

George Duffield

1818–1888

13 Stand up! — stand up for Jesus! *Hymn*

William Maxwell Evarts

1818–1901

14 The pious ones of Plymouth, who, reaching the Rock, first fell upon their own knees and then upon the aborigines.[3]
From HENRY WATTERSON *in the Louisville Courier-Journal [July 4, 1913]*

Karl Marx

1818–1883

15 Religion . . . is the opium of the people.[4]
Critique of the Hegelian Philosophy of Right [1844], introduction

16 It is not the consciousness of men that determines their existence, but on the contrary it is their social existence that determines their consciousness.
Critique of Political Economy [1859], preface

17 Nothing can have value without being an object of utility. If it be useless, the labor contained in it is useless, cannot be reckoned as labor, and cannot therefore create value.
Capital[5] *[1867–1883], pt. II, ch. 3*

18 The intellectual desolation, artificially produced by converting immature human beings into mere machines. *Ib. 10*

19 Capitalist production begets, with the inexorability of a law of nature, its own negation.
Ib. 15

20 When commercial capital occupies a position of unquestioned ascendancy, it everywhere constitutes a system of plunder.
Ib. 21

[2]Give them a chance — if you stint them now, tomorrow you'll have to pay / A larger bill for a darker ill. — DENIS A. MCCARTHY [1870–1931], *Give Them a Place to Play, st. 4*

[3]This pun has also been attributed to Oliver Wendell Holmes, Bill Nye, and George Frisbie Hoar.
See William Bradford, 265:7.

[4]See Unamuno, 706:6.

[5]Abridged edition prepared by JULIAN BORCHARDT, translated by STEPHEN L. TRASK.

1 From each according to his abilities, to each according to his needs.

Critique of the Gotha Program[1] *[1875]*

Karl Marx
1818–1883
and
Friedrich Engels
1820–1895

2 A specter is haunting Europe—the specter of Communism. All the powers of old Europe have entered into a holy alliance to exorcise this specter: Pope and Czar, Meternich and Guizot, French Radicals and German police spies.

The Communist Manifesto [1848],[2] *opening lines*

3 The history of all hitherto existing society is the history of class struggles. Freeman and slave, patrician and plebian, lord and serf, guild master and journeyman, in a word, oppressor and oppressed, stood in constant opposition to each other, carried on an uninterrupted, now hidden, now open fight, a fight that each time ended, either in a revolutionary reconstitution of society at large, or in the common ruin of the contending classes.

Ib. sec. 1

4 The executive of the modern state is but a committee for managing the common affairs of the whole bourgeoisie.[3] The bourgeoisie has, historically, played a most revolutionary role. *Ib.*

5 The bourgeoisie, by the rapid improvement of all instruments of production, by the immensely facilitated means of communication, draws all, even the most barbarian, nations into civilization. *Ib.*

[1]This phrase is in quotation marks, and it is believed that Marx is quoting or paraphrasing either Louis Blanc or Morelly:

Let each produce according to his aptitudes and his force; let each consume according to his need.—LOUIS BLANC, *Organisation du Travail* [1840]

Nothing in society will belong to anyone, either as a personal possession or as capital goods, except the things for which the person has immediate use, for either his needs, his pleasures, or his daily work. Every citizen will make his particular contribution to the activities of the community according to his capacity, his talent and his age; it is on this basis that his duties will be determined, in conformity with the distributive laws.—MORELLY, *Le Code de la Nature* [1755]

See *Acts 4:35, 45:41*.

[2]Translated by SAMUEL MOORE.

[3]By bourgeoisie is meant the class of modern capitalists, owners of the means of social production and employers of wage labor.—ENGELS, *notes to The Communist Manifesto* [1888 edition]

6 Of all the classes that stand face to face with the bourgeoisie today, the proletariat alone is a really revolutionary class. The other classes decay and finally disappear in the race of modern industry; the proletariat is its special and essential product.[4] *Ib.*

7 In this sense, the theory of the Communists may be summed up in the single sentence: Abolition of private property. *Ib. 2*

8 In proportion as the antagonism between classes within the nation vanishes, the hostility of one nation to another will come to an end. *Ib.*

9 The ruling ideas of each age have ever been the ideas of its ruling class. *Ib.*

10 The communists disdain to conceal their views and aims. They openly declare that their ends can be obtained only by forcible overthrow of all existing social conditions. Let the ruling classes tremble at a communist revolution. The proletarians have nothing to lose but their chains. They have a world to win. Working men of all countries, unite![5] *Ib. 4*

John Mason Neale
1818–1866

11 Good King Wenceslas looked out
On the feast of Stephen,
When the snow lay round about,
Deep and crisp and even.

Good King Wenceslas, st. 1

12 Brief life is here our portion.

Hymn from the Latin of ST. BERNARD OF CLUNY *[c. 1145], pt. II, Hic Breve Vivitur [translated 1851], st. 1*

13 Jerusalem the golden, with milk and honey blest,
Beneath thy contemplation sink heart and voice oppressed.

Ib. III, Urbs Syon Aurea [translated 1858], st. 1

14 O come, O come, Emmanuel,
And ransom captive Israel.

Hymn from the Latin, Veni, Veni, Emmanuel [twelfth century], st. 1 [translated 1861]

[4]By proletariat [is meant] the class of modern wage laborers who, having no means of production of their own, are reduced to selling their labor power in order to live.—ENGELS, *notes to The Communist Manifesto* [1888 edition]

[5]More familiar as: Workers of the world, unite!

Francis Edward Smedley
1818–1864

1 You are looking as fresh as paint.
Frank Fairlegh [1850], ch. 41

2 All's fair in love and war.[1] *Ib. 50*

Ivan Sergeyevich Turgenev
1818–1883

3 A nihilist is a man who does not bow to any authorities, who does not take any principle on trust, no matter with what respect that principle is surrounded.
Fathers and Sons [1862],[2] ch. 5

4 That vague, crepuscular time, the time of regrets that resemble hopes, of hopes that resemble regrets, when youth has passed, but old age has not yet arrived. *Ib. 7*

5 I share no man's opinions; I have my own.
Ib. 13

6 The courage not to believe in anything.
Ib. 14

7 A picture shows me at a glance what it takes dozens of pages of a book to expound.[3]
Ib. 16

8 Whatever a man prays for, he prays for a miracle. Every prayer reduces itself to this: "Great God, grant that twice two be not four." *Prayer*

9 In days of doubt, in days of sad brooding on my country's fate, thou alone art my rod and my staff—mighty, true, free Russian speech! But for thee, how not to fall into despair, seeing all that happens at home? Yet who can think that such a tongue is not given to a great people? *Senilia [1882]*

Arthur Hugh Clough
1819–1861

10 Grace is given of God, but knowledge is bought in the market.
The Bothie of Tober-na-Vuolich [1848], pt. IV

11 A world where nothing is had for nothing.
Ib. VIII

12 Hope conquers cowardice, joy grief;
Or at least, faith unbelief.
Easter Day II [1849], l. 34

[1] All policy's allowed in war and love.—SUSANNAH CENTLIVRE, *Love at a Venture* [1706], *act I*
[2] Translated by HARRY STEVENS.
[3] See Anonymous (Early), 132:23.

13 Where lies the land to which the ships would go?
Far, far ahead, is all her seamen know.
And where the land she travels from? Away,
Far, far behind, is all that they can say.[4]
Where Lies the Land to Which the Ship Would Go? [1852], st. 1

14 And almost everyone when age,
Disease, or sorrows strike him,
Inclines to think there is a God,
Or something very like Him.
Dipsychus [1862], pt. I, sc. v

15 How pleasant it is to have money! *Ib.*

16 Say not the struggle naught availeth,
The labor and the wounds are vain,
The enemy faints not, nor faileth,
And as things have been they remain.
Say Not the Struggle Naught Availeth [1862], st. 1

17 For while the tired waves, vainly breaking,
Seem here no painful inch to gain,
Far back, through creeks and inlets making,
Comes silent flooding in, the main.[5]

In front, the sun climbs slow, how slowly,
But westward, look, the land is bright.[6]
Ib. st. 3, 4

18 No graven images may be
Worshipped, except the currency.
The Latest Decalogue [1862]

19 Honor thy parents; that is, all
From whom advancement may befall.
Thou shalt not kill; but needst not strive
Officiously to keep alive. *Ib.*

20 Thou shalt not covet, but tradition
Approves all forms of competition. *Ib.*

George Eliot
[Marian Evans Cross]
1819–1880

21 'Tis God gives skill,
But not without men's hands: He could not make
Antonio Stradivari's violins
Without Antonio. *Stradivarius*

22 O may I join the choir invisible
Of those immortal dead who live again
In minds made better by their presence.
O May I Join the Choir Invisible

[4] See Wordsworth, 428:2.
[5] See Macaulay, 487:17.
[6] Both Sir Winston Churchill and John F. Kennedy liked to quote this line.

1 Any coward can fight a battle when he's sure of winning; but give me the man who has pluck to fight when he's sure of losing. That's my way, sir; and there are many victories worse than a defeat.
Janet's Repentance [1857], ch. 6

2 Opposition may become sweet to a man when he has christened it persecution.
Ib. 8

3 These fellow mortals, every one, must be accepted as they are.
Adam Bede [1859], ch. 17

4 There's no real making amends in this world, any more nor you can mend a wrong subtraction by doing your addition right.
Ib. 18

5 It's but little good you'll do a-watering the last year's crops. *Ib.*

6 It was a pity he couldna be hatched o'er again, an' hatched different. *Ib.*

7 A patronizing disposition always has its meaner side. *Ib. 27*

8 It's them that take advantage that get advantage i' this world. *Ib. 32*

9 He was like a cock who thought the sun had risen to hear him crow. *Ib. 33*

10 Deep, unspeakable suffering may well be called a baptism, a regeneration, the initiation into a new state. *Ib. 42*

11 We hand folks over to God's mercy, and show none ourselves. *Ib.*

12 I'm not denyin' the women are foolish; God Almighty made 'em to match the men.
Ib. 53

13 The law's made to take care o' raskills.
The Mill on the Floss [1860], bk. III, ch. 4

14 There is no hopelessness so sad as that of early youth, when the soul is made up of wants, and has no long memories, no superadded life in the life of others. *Ib. 5*

15 In natural science, I have understood, there is nothing petty to the mind that has a large vision of relations, and to which every single object suggests a vast sum of conditions. It is surely the same with the observation of human life. *Ib. IV, 1*

16 Not let them want bread, but only require them to eat it with bitter herbs.[1] *Ib.*

[1]See *Exodus 12:8*, 9:24.

17 I've never any pity for conceited people, because I think they carry their comfort about with them.[2] *Ib. V, 4*

18 The happiest women, like the happiest nations, have no history.[3] *Ib. VI, 3*

19 Nothing is so good as it seems beforehand.
Silas Marner [1861], ch. 18

20 In our springtime every day has its hidden growth in the mind, as it has in the earth when the little folded blades are getting ready to pierce the ground.
Felix Holt, the Radical [1866], ch. 18

21 One way of getting an idea of our fellow-countrymen's miseries is to go and look at their pleasures. *Ib. 28*

22 Prophecy is the most gratuitous form of error.
Middlemarch [1871–1872], ch. 10

23 If we had a keen vision of all that is ordinary in human life, it would be like hearing the grass grow or the squirrel's heart beat, and we should die of that roar which is the other side of silence. *Ib. 22*

24 If youth is the season of hope, it is often so only in the sense that our elders are hopeful about us. *Ib. 55*

25 There is no creature whose inward being is so strong that it is not greatly determined by what lies outside it. *Ib. Finale*

26 Hostesses who entertain much must make up their parties as ministers make up their cabinets, on grounds other than personal liking.
Daniel Deronda [1876], bk. I, ch. 5

27 A difference of taste in jokes is a great strain on the affections. *Ib. II, 15*

28 Men's men: gentle or simple, they're much of a muchness. *Ib. IV, 31*

29 A new Judea, poised between East and West—a covenant of reconciliation.
Ib. VI, 42

30 Blessed is the man who, having nothing to say, abstains from giving in words evidence of the fact.
Impressions of Theophrastus Such [1879]

[2]There is not enough of love and goodness in the world to throw any of it away on conceited people.—NIETZSCHE [1844–1900], *Human, All Too Human, 129*

[3]See Carlyle, 474:15.

Thomas Dunn English

1819–1902

1 Oh! don't you remember sweet Alice, Ben
Bolt?
Sweet Alice, whose hair was so brown.
Ben Bolt [1843]

Josiah Gilbert Holland

1819–1881

2 Heaven is not reached at a single bound.
Gradatim [1872], st. 1

3 God give us men! A time like this demands
Strong minds, great hearts, true faith, and ready hands;
Men whom the lust of office does not kill;
Men whom the spoils of office cannot buy;
Men who possess opinions and a will;
Men who have honor; men who will not lie.
Wanted [1872], l. 1

Julia Ward Howe

1819–1910

4 Mine eyes have seen the glory of the coming of the Lord;
He is trampling out the vintage where the grapes of wrath are stored;[1]
He hath loosed the fateful lightning of His terrible, swift sword;
His truth is marching on.
Battle Hymn of the Republic [1862], st. 1

5 In the beauty of the lilies Christ was born across the sea,
With a glory in His bosom that transfigures you and me;
As He died to make men holy, let us die to make men free.
Ib. st. 5

Charles Kingsley[2]

1819–1875

6 Give me the political economist, the sanitary reformer, the engineer; and take your saints and virgins, relics and miracles. The spinning-jenny and the railroad, Cunard's liners and the electric telegraph, are to me . . . signs that we are, on some points at least, in harmony with the universe.
Yeast [1848], ch. 5

7 Oh Mary, go and call the cattle home . . .
Across the sands of Dee.
The Sands of Dee [1849], st. 1

[1] See *Isaiah 63:3*, 31:26, and *Revelation 19:15*, 53:27.
[2] See Anonymous, 922:*n*3.

8 The cruel crawling foam.[3] *Ib. st. 4*

9 For men must work, and women must weep,
And there's little to earn and many to keep,
Though the harbor bar be moaning.
The Three Fishers [1851], st. 1

10 And the sooner it's over, the sooner to sleep;
And good-bye to the bar and it's moaning.
Ib. st. 3

11 In the light of fuller day,
Of purer science, holier laws.
On the Death of a Certain Journal[4] [1852], st. 5

12 Be good, sweet maid, and let who will be clever;
Do noble things, not dream them, all day long;
And so make Life, and Death, and that For Ever
One grand sweet song.
A Farewell [1856], st. 3

13 Clear and cool, clear and cool,
By laughing shallow, and dreaming pool.
Water Babies [1863]. Song I, st. 1

14 When all the world is young, lad,
And all the trees are green;
And every goose a swan, lad,
And every lass a queen;
Then hey for boot and horse, lad,
And round the world away:
Young blood must have its course, lad,
And every dog his day.[5]
Ib. Song II, st. 1

15 God grant you find one face there
You loved when all was young! *Ib.*

16 The loveliest fairy in the world; and her name is Mrs. Doasyouwouldbedoneby.[6]
Ib. ch. 5

17 Science frees us in many ways . . . from the bodily terror which the savage feels. But she replaces that, in the minds of many, by a moral terror which is far more overwhelming.
Sermon, The Meteor Shower [November 26, 1866]

18 Tell us not that the world is governed by universal law; the news is not comfortable, but simply horrible, unless you can tell us . . . that there is a loving giver, and a just administrator of that law. *Ib.*

[3] See Ruskin, 572:10.
[4] *The Christian Socialist.*
[5] See Shakespeare, 224:24, and Borrow, 492:18.
[6] See *Matthew 7:12*, 38:14; Confucius, 69:14; Aristotle, 87:3; and Chesterfield, 341:19.

1 To be discontented with the divine discontent, and to be ashamed with the noble shame, is the very germ and first upgrowth of all virtue.

Health and Education [1874]. The Science of Health

James Russell Lowell
1819–1891

2 Blessèd are the horny hands of toil!
A Glance Behind the Curtain [1843]

3 They are slaves who fear to speak
For the fallen and the weak.
Stanzas on Freedom [1843], st. 4

4 They are slaves who dare not be
In the right with two or three. *Ib.*

5 The nurse of full-grown souls is solitude.
Columbus [1844]

6 Once to every man and nation comes the moment to decide,
In the strife of Truth with Falsehood, for the good or evil side.
The Present Crisis [1844], st. 5

7 Truth forever on the scaffold, Wrong forever on the throne[1]—
Yet that scaffold sways the future, and, behind the dim unknown,
Standeth God within the shadow, keeping watch above his own. *Ib. st. 8*

8 New occasions teach new duties; time makes ancient good uncouth;
They must upward still, and onward, who would keep abreast of Truth.
Ib. st. 18

9 I first drew in New England's air, and from her hardy breast
Sucked in the tyrant-hating milk that will not let me rest;
On the Capture of Fugitive Slaves Near Washington [1845], st. 2

10 The birch, most shy and ladylike of trees.
An Indian Summer Reverie [1846], st. 8

11 Not only around our infancy
Doth heaven with all its splendors lie;
Daily, with souls that cringe and plot,
We Sinais climb and know it not.[2]
The Vision of Sir Launfal [1848], prelude to pt. I, st. 2

[1] Worth on foot, and rascals in the coach.—DRYDEN, *Art of Poetry* [1685], *l. 376*
Wrong rules the land, and waiting Justice sleeps!—J. G. HOLLAND [1819–1881], *Wanted*

[2] See Vaughn, 299:2; Traherne, 311:22; and Wordsworth, 426:14.

12 For a cap and bells our lives we pay,
Bubbles we buy with a whole soul's tasking:
'Tis heaven alone that is given away,
'Tis only God may be had for the asking.
Ib. st. 4

13 And what is so rare as a day in June?
Then, if ever, come perfect days.
Ib. st. 5

14 Not what we give, but what we share—
For the gift without the giver is bare;[3]
Who gives himself with his alms feeds three—
Himself, his hungering neighbor, and me.
Ib. pt. II, st. 8

15 In creating, the only hard thing's to begin;
A grass-blade's no easier to make than an oak. *A Fable for Critics [1848]*

16 For though he[4] builds glorious temples, 'tis odd
He leaves never a doorway to get in a god.
Ib.

17 And I honor the man who is willing to sink
Half his present repute for the freedom to think,
And, when he has thought, be his cause strong or weak,
Will risk t' other half for the freedom to speak. *Ib.*

18 There comes Poe, with his raven, like Barnaby Rudge,
Three fifths of him genius and two fifths sheer fudge.[5] *Ib.*

19 Nature fits all her children with something to do,
He who would write and can't write, can surely review.[6] *Ib.*

20 Ez fer war, I call it murder[7]—
There you hev it plain an' flat;
I don't want to go no furder
Than my Testyment fer that.
The Biglow Papers. Series I [1848], no. 1, st. 5

21 You've gut to git up airly
Ef you want to take in God. *Ib.*

22 This goin' ware glory waits ye haint one agreeable feetur.[8] *Ib. 2, st. 6*

23 A marciful Providunce fashioned us holler
O' purpose thet we might our principles swaller. *Ib. 4, st. 2*

[3] See Emerson, 498:6; Whitman, 574:26; and Gibran, 782:16.

[4] Emerson.

[5] See Poe, 525.

[6] See Coleridge, 436:15; Disraeli, 502:12; and Flaubert, 583:8.

[7] See Seneca, 114:32; Young, 330:1; and Porteus, 378:3.

[8] See Thomas Moore, 446:6.

1 I du believe with all my soul
In the gret Press's freedom,
To pint the people to the goal
An' in the traces lead 'em. *Ib. 6, st. 7*

2 I *don't* believe in princerple,
But oh I *du* in interest. *Ib. st. 9*

3 It ain't by princerples nor men
My preudunt course is steadied—
I scent wich pays the best, an' then
Go into it baldheaded. *Ib. st. 10*

4 God makes sech nights, all white an' still,
Fur'z you can look or listen,
Moonshine an' snow on field an' hill,
All silence an' all glisten.
Ib. Series II [1866]. The Courtin', st. 1

5 His heart kep' goin' pity-pat,
But hern went pity-Zekle. *Ib. st. 15*

6 My gran'ther's rule was safer 'n 'tis to crow:
Don't never prophesy—onless ye know.
Ib. No. 2

7 It's 'most enough to make a deacon swear.
Ib.

8 Folks never understand the folks they hate.
Ib.

9 Ef you want peace, the thing you've gut tu du
Is jes' to show you're up to fightin', tu.[1]
Ib.

10 Bad work follers ye ez long's ye live.
Ib.

11 The surest plan to make a Man
Is, think him so. *Ib.*

12 Our papers don't purtend to print on'y wut Guv'ment choose,
An' thet insures us all to git the very best o' noose. *Ib. 3*

13 No, never say nothin' without you're compelled tu,
An' then don't say nothin' thet you can be held tu. *Ib. 5*

14 They came three thousand miles, and died,
To keep the Past upon its throne;
Unheard, beyond the ocean tide,
Their English mother made her moan.[2]
Graves of Two English Soldiers on Concord Battleground [1849], st. 3

15 The snow had begun in the gloaming,
And busily all the night
Had been heaping field and highway
With a silence deep and white.
The First Snowfall [1849], st. 1

16 There is nothing so desperately monotonous as the sea, and I no longer wonder at the cruelty of pirates.
Fireside Travels [1864]. At Sea

17 It is by presence of mind in untried emergencies that the native metal of a man is tested. *Abraham Lincoln [1864]*

18 What men call treasure and the gods call dross.
Ode Recited at the Harvard Commemoration [1865], 4

19 They come transfigured back,
Secure from change in their high-hearted ways,
Beautiful evermore, and with the rays
Of morn on their white Shields of Expectation![3] *Ib. 8*

20 When I was a beggarly boy,
And lived in a cellar damp,
I had not a friend nor a toy,
But I had Aladdin's lamp.
Aladdin [1868], st. 1

21 Though old the thought and oft expressed,
'Tis his at last who says it best.[4]
For an Autograph [1868]

22 Safe in the hallowed quiets of the past.
The Cathedral[5] [1869], st. 9

23 The wisest man could ask no more of Fate
Than to be simple, modest, manly, true,
Safe from the many, honored by the few;
To count as naught in world, or church, or state;
But inwardly in secret to be great.
Sonnet, Jeffries Wyman [1874]

24 For me Fate gave, whate'er she else denied,
A nature sloping to the southern side.
Epistle to George William Curtis [1874]. Postscript

25 The maple puts her corals on in May.
The Maple [1875]

26 The soil out of which such men as he are made is good to be born on, good to live on, good to die for and to be buried in.
Garfield [September 24, 1881]

27 There is no good in arguing with the inevitable. The only argument available with an east wind is to put on your overcoat.
Democracy [October 6, 1884]

[1] See Aristotle, 87:24; Vegetius, 128:25; Robert Burton, 259:13; Fénelon, 316:12; and Washington, 379:9.
[2] Inscribed on the memorial to the two British soldiers, Concord, Massachusetts.
[3] See Masefield 761:1.
[4] See Emerson, 499:27.
[5] Chartres.

1 In vain we call old notions fudge,
And bend our conscience to our dealing;
The Ten Commandments will not budge,
And stealing *will* continue stealing.[1]
International Copyright [November 20, 1885]

2 These pearls of thought in Persian gulfs were bred,
Each softly lucent as a rounded moon;
The diver Omar plucked them from their bed,
Fitzgerald strung them on an English thread.
In a Copy of Omar Khayyám [1888], st. 1

3 As life runs on, the road grows strange
With faces new, and near the end
The milestones into headstones change,
'Neath every one a friend.
Sixty-eighth Birthday [1889]

4 Things always seem fairer when we look back at them, and it is out of that inaccessible tower of the past that Longing leans and beckons.
Literary Essays, vol. I [1864–1890]. A Few Bits of Roman Mosaic

5 Mishaps are like knives, that either serve us or cut us, as we grasp them by the blade or the handle.
Ib. Cambridge Thirty Years Ago

6 What a sense of security in an old book which Time has criticized for us!
Ib. A Library of Old Authors

7 It is curious how tyrannical the habit of reading is, and what shifts we make to escape thinking.[2] There is no bore we dread being left alone with so much as our own minds.
Ib. A Moosehead Journal

8 There is no better ballast for keeping the mind steady on its keel, and saving it from all risk of crankiness, than business.
Ib. II [1870–1890], New England Two Centuries Ago

9 Puritanism, believing itself quick with the seed of religious liberty, laid, without knowing it, the egg of democracy. *Ib.*

10 It was in making education not only common to all, but in some sense compulsory on all, that the destiny of the free republics of America was practically settled. *Ib.*

11 Talent is that which is in a man's power; genius is that in whose power a man is.
Ib. Rousseau and the Sentimentalists

[1]Motto of the American Copyright League.
[2]See Sheridan, 399:8, and Bryce, 635:25.

12 Every man feels instinctively that all the beautiful sentiments in the world weigh less than a single lovely action. *Ib.*

13 An umbrella is of no avail against a Scotch mist.
Ib. III [1870–1890], On a Certain Condescension in Foreigners

14 Solitude is as needful to the imagination as society is wholesome for the character.
Ib. Dryden

15 A wise skepticism is the first attribute of a good critic. *Ib. Shakespeare Once More*

Herman Melville
1819–1891

16 This great power of blackness in him [Hawthorne] derives its force from its appeals to that Calvinistic sense of innate depravity and original sin from whose visitations, in some shape or other, no deeply thinking mind is always and wholly free.
Hawthorne and His Mosses [1850]

17 You must have plenty of sea-room to tell the truth in. *Ib.*

18 Genius all over the world stands hand in hand, and one shock of recognition runs the whole circle round. *Ib.*

19 Many sensible things banished from high life find an asylum among the mob.
White Jacket [1850], ch. 7

20 Oh, give me again the rover's life — the joy, the thrill, the whirl! Let me feel thee again, old sea! let me leap into thy saddle once more. I am sick of these terra-firma toils and cares; sick of the dust and reek of towns. Let me hear the clatter of hailstones on icebergs, and not the dull tramp of these plodders, plodding their dull way from their cradles to their graves. Let me snuff thee up, sea breeze! and whinny in thy spray. Forbid it, sea gods! intercede for me with Neptune, O sweet Amphitrite,[3] that no dull clod may fall on my coffin! Be mine the tomb that swallowed up Pharaoh and all his hosts; let me lie down with Drake where he sleeps in the sea.
Ib. 19

21 Familiarity with danger makes a brave man braver, but less daring. Thus with seamen: he who goes the oftenest round Cape Horn goes the most circumspectly.
Ib. 23

[3]Wife of Neptune.

1 In time of peril, like the needle to the lodestone, obedience, irrespective of rank, generally flies to him who is best fitted to command. *Ib. 27*

2 Are there no Moravians in the Moon, that not a missionary has yet visited this poor pagan planet of ours, to civilize civilization and christianize Christendom?[1] *Ib. 64*

3 Call me Ishmael.

Moby-Dick [1851], ch. 1

4 Yes, as everyone knows, meditation and water are wedded forever . . . Why did the old Persians hold the sea holy? Why did the Greeks give it a separate deity, and own brother of Jove? Surely all this is not without meaning. And still deeper the meaning of that story of Narcissus, who because he could not grasp the tormenting, mild image he saw in the fountain, plunged into it and was drowned. But that same image, we ourselves see in all rivers and oceans. It is the image of the ungraspable phantom of life; and this is the key to it all. *Ib.*

5 But oh! shipmates! on the starboard hand of every woe, there is a sure delight; and higher the top of that delight, than the bottom of the woe is deep. Is not the main-truck higher than the kelson is low? Delight is to him—a far, far upward, and inward delight—who against the proud gods and commodores of this earth, ever stands forth his own inexorable self. *Ib. 9*

6 And eternal delight and deliciousness will be his, who coming to lay him down, can say with his final breath—O Father!—chiefly known to me by Thy rod—mortal or immortal, here I die. I have striven to be Thine, more than to be this world's, or mine own. Yet this is nothing; I leave eternity to Thee; for what is man that he should live out the lifetime of his God? *Ib.*

7 With the landless gull, that at sunset folds her wings and is rocked to sleep between billows; so at nightfall, the Nantucketer, out of sight of land, furls his sails, and lays him to his rest, while under his very pillow rush herds of walruses and whales. *Ib. 14*

8 But when a man's religion becomes really frantic; when it is a positive torment to him; and, in fine, makes this earth of ours an uncomfortable inn to lodge in; then I think it high time to take that individual aside and argue the point with him. *Ib. 17*

9 In one word, Queequeg, said I, rather digressively; hell is an idea first born on an undigested apple dumpling; and since then perpetuated through the hereditary dyspepsias nurtured by Ramadans. *Ib.*

10 If, at my death, my executors, or more properly my creditors, find any precious MSS. in my desk, then here I prospectively ascribe all the honor and the glory to whaling; for a whaleship was my Yale College and my Harvard. *Ib. 24*

11 Thou great democratic God! who didst not refuse to the swart convict, Bunyan, the pale poetic pearl; Thou who didst clothe with doubly hammered leaves of finest gold, the stumped and paupered arm of old Cervantes; Thou who didst pick up Andrew Jackson from the pebbles; who didst hurl him upon a warhorse; who didst thunder him higher than a throne! Thou who, in all Thy mighty, earthly marchings, ever cullest thy selectest champions from the kingly commons! *Ib. 26*

12 This it is, that forever keeps God's true princes of the Empire from the world's hustings; and leaves the highest honors that this air can give, to those men who become famous more through their infinite inferiority to the choice hidden handful of the Divine Inert, than through their undoubted superiority over the dead level of the mass. *Ib. 33*

13 All that most maddens and torments; all that stirs up the lees of things; all truth with malice in it; all that cracks the sinews and cakes the brain; all the subtle demonisms of life and thought; all evil, to crazy Ahab, were visibly personified, and made practically assailable in Moby Dick. He piled upon the whale's white hump the sum of all the general rage and hate felt by his whole race from Adam down; and then, as if his chest had been a mortar, he burst his hot heart's shell upon it. *Ib. 41*

14 For as this appalling ocean surrounds the verdant land, so in the soul of man there lies one insular Tahiti, full of peace and joy, but encompassed by all the horrors of the half known life. *Ib. 58*

15 O Nature, and O soul of man! how far beyond all utterance are your linked analogies! not the smallest atom stirs or lives on matter, but has its cunning duplicate in mind. *Ib. 70*

16 So, therefore, that mortal man who hath more of joy than sorrow in him, that mortal man cannot be true—not true, or undeveloped. With books the same. The truest

[1] See Emerson, 497:8.

of all men was the Man of Sorrows, and the truest of all books is Solomon's and Ecclesiastes is the fine hammered steel of woe. *Ib. 96*

1 Give me a condor's quill! Give me Vesuvius' crater for an inkstand! . . . To produce a mighty book, you must choose a mighty theme. *Ib. 104*

2 Seat thyself sultanically among the moons of Saturn, and take high abstracted man alone; and he seems a wonder, a grandeur, and a woe. But from the same point, take mankind in mass, and for the most part, they seem a mob of unnecessary duplicates, both contemporary and hereditary. *Ib. 107*

3 There is, one knows not what sweet mystery about this sea, whose gently awful stirrings seem to speak of some hidden soul beneath; like those fabled undulations of the Ephesian sod over the buried Evangelist St. John. And meet it is, that over these sea pastures, wide-rolling watery prairies and Potters' Fields of all four continents, the waves should rise and fall, and ebb and flow unceasingly; for here, millions of mixed shades and shadows, drowned dreams, somnambulisms, reveries; all that we call lives and souls, lie dreaming, dreaming, still; tossing like slumberers in their beds; the ever-rolling waves but made so by their restlessness. *Ib. 111*

4 There is no steady unretracing progress in this life; we do not advance through fixed gradations, and at the last one pause: through infancy's unconscious spell, boyhood's thoughtless faith, adolescence' doubt (the common doom), then skepticism, then disbelief, resting at last in manhood's pondering repose of If. But once gone through, we trace the round again; and are infants, boys, and men, and Ifs eternally. Where lies the final harbor, whence we unmoor no more? *Ib. 114*

5 But if the great sun move not of himself; but is as an errand boy in heaven; nor one single star can revolve, but by some invisible power; how then can this one small heart beat; this one small brain think thoughts; unless God does that beating, does that thinking, does that living, and not I. By heaven, man, we are turned round and round in this world, like yonder windlass, and Fate is the handspike. *Ib. 132*

6 Who's to doom, when the judge himself is dragged to the bar? *Ib.*

7 It is a mild, mild wind, and a mild-looking sky; and the air smells now as if it blew from a faraway meadow; they have been making hay somewhere under the slopes of the Andes, Starbuck, and the mowers are sleeping among the new-mown hay. *Ib.*

8 An old, old sight, and yet somehow so young; aye, and not changed a wink since I first saw it, a boy, from the sandhills of Nantucket! The same!—the same!—the same to Noah as to me. There's a soft shower to leeward. Such lovely leewardings! They must lead somewhere—to something else than common land, more palmy than the palms. *Ib. 135*

9 A sky-hawk that tauntingly had followed the main-truck downwards from its natural home among the stars, pecking at the flag, and incommoding Tashtego there; this bird now chanced to intercept its broad fluttering wings between the hammer and the wood; and simultaneously feeling that ethereal thrill, the submerged savage beneath, in his death grasp, kept his hammer frozen there; and so the bird of heaven, with archangelic shrieks, and his imperial beak thrust upwards, and his whole captive form folded in the flag of Ahab, went down with his ship, which, like Satan, would not sink to hell till she had dragged a living part of heaven along with her, and helmeted herself with it.

Now small fowls flew screaming over the yet yawning gulf; a sullen white surf beat against its steep sides; then all collapsed, and the great shroud of the sea rolled on as it rolled five thousand years ago. *Ib.*

10 What we take to be our strongest tower of delight, only stands at the caprice of the minutest event—the falling of a leaf, the hearing of a voice, or the receipt of one little bit of paper scratched over with a few small characters by a sharpened feather. *Pierre [1852], bk. IV*

11 One trembles to think of that mysterious thing in the soul, which seems to acknowledge no human jurisdiction, but in spite of the individual's own innocent self, will still dream horrid dreams, and mutter unmentionable thoughts. *Ib.*

12 A smile is the chosen vehicle for all ambiguities. *Ib.*

13 Say what some poets will, Nature is not so much her own ever-sweet interpreter, as the mere supplier of that cunning alphabet, whereby selecting and combining as he pleases, each man reads his own peculiar lesson according to his own peculiar mind and mood. *Ib. XXV*

1 With shouts the torrents down the gorges go,
And storms are formed behind the storm we feel:
The hemlock shakes in the rafter, the oak in the driving keel.

Battle-Pieces [1860], Misgivings, st. 2

2 The poor old Past,
The Future's slave.

Ib. The Conflict of Convictions, st. 6

3 At the height of their madness
The night winds pause,
Recollecting themselves;
But no lull in these wars.

Ib. The Armies of the Wilderness, pt. II, st. 5

4 What troops
Of generous boys in happiness thus bred—
Saturnians through life's Tempe led,
Went from the North and came from the South,
With golden mottoes in the mouth,
To lie down midway on a bloody bed.

Ib. On the Slain Collegians, st. 2

5 Instinct and study; love and hate;
Audacity—reverence. These must mate,
And fuse with Jacob's mystic heart,
To wrestle with the angel—Art.

Timoleon [1891]. Art

6 Indolence is heaven's ally here,
And energy the child of hell:
The Good Man pouring from his pitcher clear,
But brims the poisoned well.

Ib. Fragments of a Lost Gnostic Poem of the Twelfth Century, fragment 2

7 But me they'll lash in hammock, drop me deep.
Fathoms down, fathoms down, how I'll dream fast asleep.
I feel it stealing now. Sentry, are you there?
Just ease these darbies[1] at the wrist,
And roll me over fair.
I am sleepy, and the oozy weeds about me twist.

Billy Budd, Foretopman [1924]. Billy in the Darbies

John Ruskin

1819–1900

8 He is the greatest artist who has embodied, in the sum of his works, the greatest number of the greatest ideas.

Modern Painters, vol. I [1843], pt. I, ch. 2

[1] Manacles.

9 To know anything well involves a profound sensation of ignorance. *Ib. 3*

10 The foam is not cruel.[2] The state of mind which attributes to it these characteristics of a living creature is one in which the reason is unhinged by grief. All violent feelings . . . produce in us a falseness in all our impressions of external things, which I would generally characterize as the "Pathetic Fallacy."

Ib. III [1856], pt. IV, ch. 12

11 To see clearly is poetry, prophecy, and religion—all in one. *Ib. 16*

12 The essence of lying is in deception, not in words. *Ib. V, pt. IX, ch. 7*

13 In order that people may be happy in their work, these three things are needed: They must be fit for it. They must not do too much of it. And they must have a sense of success in it. *Pre-Raphaelitism [1851]*

14 Remember that the most beautiful things in the world are the most useless; peacocks and lilies for instance.

The Stones of Venice [1851–1853], vol. I, ch. 2

15 All great art is the work of the whole living creature, body and soul, and chiefly of the soul. *Ib. 4*

16 Blue color is everlastingly appointed by the Deity to be a source of delight.

Lectures on Architecture and Painting [1853], I

17 There is no wealth but life.

Unto This Last [1862], sec. 77

18 Let us reform our schools, and we shall find little reform needed in our prisons.

Ib. essay 2

19 That country is the richest which nourishes the greatest number of noble and happy human beings. *Ib. essay 4*

20 Value is the life-giving power of anything; cost, the quantity of labor required to produce it; price, the quantity of labor which its possessor will take in exchange for it.

Munera Pulveris [1862], ch. 1

21 There is no law of history any more than of a kaleidoscope.

Letter to James Anthony Froude [February 1864]

[2] See Kingsley, 566:8.

1 Life being very short, and the quiet hours of it few, we ought to waste none of them in reading valueless books.

Sesame and Lilies [1865], preface

2 All books are divisible into two classes: the books of the hour, and the books of all time.

Ib. Of Kings' Treasuries, sec. 8

3 Borrowers are nearly always ill-spenders, and it is with lent money that all evil is mainly done and all unjust war protracted.

The Crown of Wild Olive [1866], lecture 1

4 Give a little love to a child, and you get a great deal back. *Ib.*

5 Taste is the *only* morality. . . . Tell me what you like, and I'll tell you what you are.[1] *Ib. 2*

6 There's no music in a "rest," Katie, that I know of: but there's the making of music in it. And people are always missing that part of the life-melody.

Ethics of the Dust [1866]. Lecture 4, The Crystal Orders

7 Life without industry is guilt, industry without art is brutality.

Lectures on Art [1870]. III, The Relation of Art to Morals

8 Every increased possession loads us with a new weariness.

The Eagle's Nest [1872], ch. 5

9 Architecture . . . the adaptation of form to resist force.

Val d'Arno [1874], ch. 6

10 The first duty of government is to see that people have food, fuel, and clothes. The second, that they have means of moral and intellectual education.

Fors Clavigera [1876], letter 67

11 Great nations write their autobiographies in three manuscripts—the book of their deeds, the book of their words, and the book of their art.

St. Mark's Rest [1877], preface

Max Schneckenburger

1819–1849

12 Dear Fatherland, no danger thine:
Firm stands thy watch along the Rhine.[2]

The Watch on the Rhine (Die Wacht am Rhein) [1840], chorus

[1]See Brillat-Savarin, 401:6.

[2]Lieb Vaterland, magst ruhig sein, / Fest steht und treu die Wacht am Rhein.

William Wetmore Story

1819–1895

13 Of every noble work the silent part is best,
Of all expression that which cannot be expressed. *The Unexpressed*

Victoria

1819–1901

14 I will be good.

On first seeing a chart of the line of succession to the throne [March 11, 1830]

15 *Great* events make me quiet and calm; it is only trifles that irritate my nerves.

Letter to King Leopold of Belgium [April 4, 1848]

16 We are not interested in the possibilities of defeat.

To A. J. Balfour [December 1899]

17 We are not amused.

Upon seeing an imitation of herself by the Honorable Alexander Grantham Yorke, groom-in-waiting to the Queen. From Notebooks of a Spinster Lady [January 2, 1900]

William Ross Wallace

1819–1881

18 The hand that rocks the cradle is the hand
that rules the world.

The Hand That Rules the World, st. 1

Walt Whitman

1819–1892

19 The United States themselves are essentially the greatest poem. . . . Here at last is something in the doings of man that corresponds with the broadcast doings of the day and night.

Preface to the first edition of Leaves of Grass [1855]

20 The proof of a poet is that his country absorbs him as affectionately as he has absorbed it. *Ib.*

21 Me imperturbe, standing at ease in nature.

Leaves of Grass [1855–1892]. Me Imperturbe[3]

[3]The first edition of *Leaves of Grass* consisted of 94 quarto pages and included the preface which set forth Whitman's faith and his poetic theory. Enlarged and revised editions followed. The tenth edition (from which the text used here is taken) was the last edition supervised by

1 O to be self-balanced for contingencies,
To confront night, storms, hunger, ridicule, accidents, rebuffs, as the trees and animals do. *Ib.*

2 I hear America singing, the varied carols I hear. *Ib. I Hear America Singing*

3 Starting from fish-shape Paumanok where I was born,
Well-begotten, and raised by a perfect mother,
After roaming many lands, lover of populous pavements,
Dweller in Mannahatta my city, or on southern savannas.
Ib. Starting from Paumanok, 1

4 Solitary, singing in the West, I strike up for a New World. *Ib.*

5 Americanos! conquerors! marches humanitarian! *Ib. 3*

6 I will put in my poems that with you is heroism upon land and sea,
And I will report all heroism from an American point of view. *Ib. 6*

7 I say the whole earth and all the stars in the sky are for religion's sake. *Ib. 7*

8 I say that the real and permanent grandeur of these States must be their religion. *Ib.*

9 And I will show of male and female that either is but the equal of the other. *Ib. 12*

10 Nothing can happen more beautiful than death.[1] *Ib.*

11 I celebrate myself, and sing myself,
And what I assume you shall assume.
Ib. Song of Myself, 1

12 I loafe and invite my soul. *Ib.*

13 Urge and urge and urge,
Always the procreant urge of the world. *Ib. 3*

14 A kelson of the creation is love. *Ib. 5*

15 A child said *What is the grass?* fetching it to me with full hands. *Ib. 6*

16 Or I guess it is the handkerchief of the Lord. *Ib.*

17 And now it seems to me the beautiful uncut hair of graves. *Ib.*

18 Has anyone supposed it lucky to be born?
I hasten to inform him or her, it is just as lucky to die, and I know it. *Ib. 7*

19 I am he that walks with the tender and growing night,
I call to the earth and sea half-held by the night.
Press close bare-bosomed night—press close magnetic nourishing night!
Night of south winds—night of the large few stars![2]
Still nodding night—mad naked summer night. *Ib. 21*

20 Walt Whitman, a kosmos, of Manhattan the son,
Turbulent, fleshy, sensual, eating, drinking and breeding,
No sentimentalist, no stander above men and women or apart from them,
No more modest than immodest. *Ib. 24*

21 I dote on myself, there is that lot of me and all so luscious. *Ib.*

22 I hear the violoncello ('tis the young man's heart's complaint). *Ib. 26*

23 I believe a leaf of grass is no less than the journey-work of the stars. *Ib. 31*

24 I think I could turn and live with animals, they are so placid and self-contained,
I stand and look at them long and long.
They do not sweat and whine about their condition,
They do not lie awake in the dark and weep for their sins,
They do not make me sick discussing their duty to God,
Not one is dissatisfied, not one is demented with the mania of owning things,
Not one kneels to another, nor to his kind that lived thousands of years ago,
Not one is respectable or unhappy over the whole earth. *Ib. 32*

25 I am the man, I suffered, I was there. *Ib. 33*

26 Behold, I do not give lectures or a little charity,
When I give I give myself.[3] *Ib. 40*

27 I have said that the soul is not more than the body,
And I have said that the body is not more than the soul,

Whitman himself, literally from his deathbed, and hence it is sometimes called the "Deathbed Edition." Whitman wrote of it: "As there are now several editions of *Leaves of Grass,* different texts and dates, I wish to say that I prefer and recommend this present one."

[1] Why fear death? Death is only a beautiful adventure. —CHARLES FROHMAN [1860–1915], last words to a group of friends as the *Lusitania* was sinking [May 7, 1915]

[2] See Flecker, 785:17.

[3] See Emerson, 498:6; Lowell, 567:14; and Gibran, 782:16.

And nothing, not God, is greater to one than one's self is. *Ib. 48*

1 In the faces of men and women I see God. *Ib.*

2 Do I contradict myself?
Very well then I contradict myself,
(I am large, I contain multitudes.) *Ib. 51*

3 I sound my barbaric yawp over the roofs of the world. *Ib. 52*

4 I bequeath myself to the dirt to grow from the grass I love,
If you want me again look for me under your boot-soles. *Ib.*

5 If any thing is sacred the human body is sacred. *Ib. I Sing the Body Electric, 8*

6 A woman waits for me, she contains all, nothing is lacking. *Ib. A Woman Waits for Me*

7 I hear it was charged against me that I sought to destroy institutions,
But really I am neither for nor against institutions. *Ib. I Hear It Was Charged Against Me*

8 When I peruse the conquered fame of heroes and the victories of mighty generals, I do not envy the generals. *Ib. When I Peruse the Conquered Fame*

9 Afoot and light-hearted I take to the open road,
Healthy, free, the world before me,
The long brown path before me leading wherever I choose. *Ib. Song of the Open Road, 1*

10 Henceforth I ask not good fortune, I myself am good fortune. *Ib.*

11 The earth, that is sufficient,
I do not want the constellations any nearer,
I know they are very well where they are,
I know they suffice for those who belong to them. *Ib.*

12 A great city is that which has the greatest men and women. *Ib. Song of the Broad-Axe, 4*

13 Youth, large, lusty, loving—youth full of grace, force, fascination,
Do you know that Old Age may come after you with equal grace, force, fascination? *Ib. Youth, Day, Old Age and Night*

14 Come my tan-faced children,
Follow well in order, get your weapons ready,
Have you your pistols? have you your sharp-edged axes?
Pioneers! O Pioneers! *Ib. Pioneers! O Pioneers! 1*

15 For we cannot tarry here,
We must march my darlings, we must bear the brunt of danger,
We the youthful sinewy races, all the rest on us depend. *Ib. 2*

16 Through the battle, through defeat, moving yet and never stopping. *Ib. 13*

17 Out of the cradle endlessly rocking,
Out of the mockingbird's throat, the musical shuttle,
Out of the Ninth-month midnight. *Ib. Out of the Cradle Endlessly Rocking*

18 Whereto answering, the sea,
Delaying not, hurrying not,
Whispered me through the night, and very plainly before daybreak,
Lisped to me the low and delicious word death. *Ib.*

19 Aboard at a ship's helm,
A young steersman steering with care. *Ib. Aboard at a Ship's Helm*

20 But O the ship, the immortal ship! O ship aboard the ship!
Ship of the body, ship of the soul, voyaging, voyaging, voyaging. *Ib.*

21 Today a rude brief recitative,
Of ships sailing the seas, each with its special flag or ship-signal. *Ib. Song for All Seas, All Ships, 1*

22 Of sea captains young or old, and the mates, and of all intrepid sailors . . .
Picked sparingly without noise by thee old ocean, chosen by thee,
Thou sea that pickest and cullest the race in time, and unitest nations,
Suckled by thee, old husky nurse, embodying thee,
Indomitable, untamed as thee. *Ib.*

23 Silent and amazed even when a little boy,
I remember I heard the preacher every Sunday put God in his statements,
As contending against some being or influence. *Ib. A Child's Amaze*

24 Give me the splendid silent sun with all his beams full-dazzling. *Ib. Give Me the Splendid Silent Sun, 1*

1 Word over all, beautiful as the sky,
Beautiful that war and all its deeds of carnage must in time be utterly lost,
That the hands of the sisters Death and Night incessantly softly wash again, and ever again, this soiled world;
For my enemy is dead, a man divine as myself is dead. *Ib. Reconciliation*

2 When lilacs last in the dooryard bloomed,
And the great star early drooped in the western sky in the night,
I mourned, and yet shall mourn with ever-returning spring.
Ib. When Lilacs Last in the Dooryard Bloomed, 1

3 O sane and sacred death. *Ib. 7*

4 Come lovely and soothing death,[1]
Undulate round the world, serenely arriving, arriving,
In the day, in the night, to all, to each,
Sooner or later delicate death. *Ib. 14*

5 Praised be the fathomless universe,
For life and joy, and for objects and knowledge curious,
And for love, sweet love—but praise! praise! praise!
For the sure-enwinding arms of cool-enfolding death. *Ib.*

6 O Captain! my Captain! our fearful trip is done,
The ship has weathered every rack, the prize we sought is won,
The port is near, the bells I hear, the people all exulting.
Ib. O Captain! My Captain! 1

7 Exult O shores, and ring O bells!
But I with mournful tread,
Walk the deck my Captain lies,
Fallen cold and dead. *Ib. 3*

8 This dust was once the man,
Gentle, plain, just and resolute, under whose cautious hand,
Against the foulest crime in history known in any land or age,
Was saved the Union of these States.
Ib. This Dust Was Once the Man

9 Underneath all, individuals,
I swear nothing is good to me now that ignores individuals.
Ib. By Blue Ontario's Shore, 15

10 The whole theory of the universe is directed unerringly to one single individual—namely to You. *Ib.*

[1] See Shakespeare, 201:25.

11 Liberty is to be subserved whatever occurs.
Ib. To a Foiled European Revolutionaire

12 What do you suppose will satisfy the soul, except to walk free and own no superior?
Ib. Laws for Creations

13 Not till the sun excludes you do I exclude you.
Ib. To a Common Prostitute

14 To me every hour of the light and dark is a miracle,
Every cubic inch of space is a miracle.
Ib. Miracles

15 O we can wait no longer,
We too take ship O soul,
Joyous we too launch out on trackless seas,
Fearless for unknown shores.
Ib. Passage to India, 8

16 Passage, immediate passage! the blood burns in my veins!
Away O soul! hoist instantly the anchor!
Cut the hawsers—haul out—shake out every sail!
Have we not stood here like trees in the ground long enough?
Have we not groveled here long enough, eating and drinking like mere brutes?
Ib. 9

17 Darest thou now O soul,
Walk out with me toward the unknown region,
Where neither ground is for the feet nor any path to follow?
Ib. Darest Thou Now O Soul

18 At the last, tenderly,
From the walls of the powerful fortressed house,
From the clasp of the knitted locks, from the keep of the well-closed doors,
Let me be wafted.
Ib. The Last Invocation

19 Tenderly—be not impatient,
(Strong is your hold O mortal flesh,
Strong is your hold O love.) *Ib.*

20 Our life is closed, our life begins,
The long, long anchorage we leave,
The ship is clear at last, she leaps!
She swiftly courses from the shore,
Joy, shipmate, joy.
Ib. Joy, Shipmate, Joy!

21 Camerado, this is no book,
Who touches this touches a man.
Ib. So Long!

22 The world, the race, the soul—in space and time the universes,

All bound as is befitting each—all surely going somewhere.

Ib. "Going Somewhere"

1 Political democracy, as it exists and practically works in America, with all its threatening evils, supplies a training school for making first-class men. It is life's gymnasium, not of good only, but of all.

Democratic Vistas [1871]

2 It is native personality, and that alone, that endows a man to stand before presidents or generals, or in any distinguished collection, with *aplomb*—and *not* culture, or any knowledge or intellect whatever. *Ib.*

3 I never see that man [Lincoln] without feeling that he is one to become personally attached to, for his combination of purest, heartiest tenderness, and native western form of manliness.

Specimen Days [1882]. The Inauguration [March 4, 1865]

4 He leaves for America's history and biography, so far, not only its most dramatic reminiscence—he leaves, in my opinion, the greatest, best, most characteristic, artistic, moral personality.

Ib. Death of President Lincoln [April 16, 1865]

5 The real war will never get in the books.

Ib. The Real War

6 After you have exhausted what there is in business, politics, conviviality, and so on—have found that none of these finally satisfy, or permanently wear—what remains? Nature remains.

Ib. New Themes Entered Upon

7 Hast Thou, pellucid, in Thy azure depths, medicine for case like mine?

Ib. The Sky [October 20, 1876]

8 You must not know too much, or be too precise or scientific about birds and trees and flowers and watercraft; a certain free margin, and even vagueness—perhaps ignorance, credulity—helps your enjoyment of these things. *Ib. Birds [May 14, 1881]*

9 To have great poets, there must be great audiences, too.

Notes Left Over. Ventures on an Old Theme

10 A Backward Glance o'er Traveled Roads.[1]

November Boughs [1888], title of preface

[1]See Wharton, 701:4.

11 *Leaves of Grass* . . . has mainly been . . . an attempt, from first to last, to put *a Person*, a human being (myself, in the latter half of the nineteenth century, in America) freely, fully and truly on record. *Ib.*

12 No one will get at my verses who insists upon viewing them as a literary performance, or attempt at such performance, or as aiming mainly toward art or aestheticism.

Ib.

13 Concluding with two items for the imaginative genius of the West, when it worthily rises—First, what Herder taught to the young Goethe, that really great poetry is always (like the Homeric or Biblical canticles) the result of a national spirit, and not the privilege of a polished and select few; Second, that the strongest and sweetest songs yet remain to be sung. *Ib.*

14 No really great song can ever attain full purport till long after the death of its singer—till it has accrued and incorporated the many passions, many joys and sorrows, it has itself aroused. *Ib. The Bible as Poetry*

15 There is no week nor day nor hour, when tyranny may not enter upon this country, if the people lose their supreme confidence in themselves—and lose their roughness and spirit of defiance—Tyranny may always enter—there is no charm, no bar against it—the only bar against it is a large resolute breed of men.

From C. J. Furness, Walt Whitman's Workshop [1928]

Susan Brownell Anthony

1820–1906

16 The men and women of the North are slaveholders, those of the South slaveowners. The guilt rests on the North equally with the South.

Speech on No Union with Slaveholders [1857]

17 Cautious, careful people, always casting about to preserve their reputation and social standing, never can bring about a reform. Those who are really in earnest must be willing to be anything or nothing in the world's estimation.

On the campaign for divorce law reform [1860]

18 Many Abolitionists have yet to learn the ABC of woman's rights.

Journal, June 1860

1 Make [your employers] understand that you are in their service as workers, not as women.[1]

The Revolution (woman suffrage newspaper), October 8, 1868

2 Join the union, girls, and together say *Equal Pay for Equal Work.*[1]

Ib. March 18, 1869

3 Woman must not depend upon the protection of man, but must be taught to protect herself.

Speech in San Francisco [July 1871]

4 I shall work for the Republican party and call on all women to join me, precisely . . . for what that party has done and promises to do for women, nothing more, nothing less.

Letter to Elizabeth Cady Stanton [autumn 1872]

5 Here, in the first paragraph of the Declaration [of Independence], is the assertion of the natural right of all to the ballot; for how can "the consent of the governed" be given, if the right to vote be denied?

Is It a Crime for a Citizen of the United States to Vote? Speech [1873] before her trial for voting

6 Marriage, to women as to men, must be a luxury, not a necessity; an incident of life, not all of it. And the only possible way to accomplish this great change is to accord to women equal power in the making, shaping and controlling of the circumstances of life.

Speech on Social Purity [spring 1875]

7 Failure is impossible.

At her eighty-sixth birthday celebration [February 15, 1906]

Lucretia Peabody Hale

1820–1900

8 At last Elizabeth Eliza said, "They say that the lady from Philadelphia, who is staying in town, is very wise. Suppose I go and ask her what is best to be done."

The Peterkin Papers [1880]

Jean Ingelow

1820–1897

9 There's no dew left on the daisies and clover,
There's no rain left in heaven:
I've said my "seven times" over and over,
Seven times one are seven.

Songs of Seven. Seven Times One, st. 1

[1]See Friedan, 898:6.

Theodore O'Hara

1820–1867

10 On Fame's eternal camping ground
Their silent tents are spread,
And Glory guards, with solemn round,
The bivouac of the dead.

The Bivouac of the Dead[2] *[1847], st. 1*

11 Sons of the dark and bloody ground.[3]

Ib. st. 9

George Frederick Root

1820–1895

12 Tramp! Tramp! Tramp! the boys are marching,
Cheer up, comrades, they will come,
And beneath the starry flag
We shall breathe the air again
Of the free land in our own beloved home.

Tramp! Tramp! Tramp! [1862]

13 Yes, we'll rally round the flag, boys, we'll rally once again,
Shouting the battle cry of Freedom.

The Battle Cry of Freedom [1863]

Sir William Howard Russell

1820–1907

14 The Russians dashed on towards that thin red-line streak tipped with a line of steel.[4]

To The Times of London from the Crimea, describing the British infantry at Balaklava [October 25, 1854]

William Tecumseh Sherman

1820–1891

15 You cannot qualify war in harsher terms than I will. War is cruelty, and you cannot refine it.

Letter to James M. Calhoun, mayor of Atlanta, and others [September 12, 1864]

[2]Written to commemorate Americans slain in the battle of Buena Vista [February 22–23, 1847].

[3]Translation of the Indian name Kentucky.

[4]Soon the men of the column began to see that though the scarlet line was slender, it was very rigid and exact. — A. W. KINGLAKE [1809–1891], *Invasion of the Crimea, vol. III, p. 455*

It's "Thin red line of 'eroes" when the drums begin to roll. — KIPLING [1865–1936], *Tommy, st. 3*

See Kipling, 708:3.

1 Hold the fort! I am coming![1]

Signal from Kenesaw Mountain to General John Murray Corse at Allatoona Pass [October 5, 1864]

2 The legitimate object of war is a more perfect peace.

Speech at St. Louis [July 20, 1865]

3 War is at best barbarism. . . . Its glory is all moonshine. It is only those who have neither fired a shot nor heard the shrieks and groans of the wounded who cry aloud for blood, more vengeance, more desolation. War is hell.[2]

Attributed to a graduation address at Michigan Military Academy [June 19, 1879]. From the National Tribune, Washington, D.C. [November 26, 1914]

4 I will not accept if nominated and will not serve if elected.[3]

Message to Republican National Convention [June 5, 1884]

Herbert Spencer

1820–1903

5 Progress, therefore, is not an accident, but a necessity. . . . It is a part of nature.

Social Statics [1851], pt. I, ch. 2

6 Education has for its object the formation of character. *Ib. II, 17*

7 The poverty of the incapable, the distresses that come upon the imprudent, the starvation of the idle, and those shoulderings aside of the weak by the strong, which leave so many "in shallows and in miseries,"[4] are the decrees of a large, farseeing benevolence.

Ib. III, 25

8 Opinion is ultimately determined by the feelings, and not by the intellect.

Ib. IV, 30

9 Morality knows nothing of geographical boundaries or distinctions of race. *Ib.*

10 No one can be perfectly free till all are free; no one can be perfectly moral till all are moral; no one can be perfectly happy till all are happy. *Ib.*

[1] He actually said: "Hold out. Relief is coming." General Corse replied: "I am short a cheekbone and an ear, but am able to whip all hell yet."
See Philip Bliss, 635:22.

[2] See Robert E. Lee, 509:8.

[3] The familiar version is: If nominated I will not run; if elected I will not serve.

[4] See Shakespeare, 217:5.

11 Architecture, sculpture, painting, music, and poetry, may truly be called the efflorescence of civilized life.

Essays on Education [1861]. Education: What Knowledge Is of Most Worth?

12 Every cause produces more than one effect.

Ib. On Progress: Its Law and Cause

13 The tyranny of Mrs. Grundy[5] is worse than any other tyranny we suffer under.

Ib. On Manners and Fashion

14 Old forms of government finally grow so oppressive that they must be thrown off even at the risk of reigns of terror. *Ib.*

15 Music must take rank as the highest of the fine arts — as the one which, more than any other, ministers to human welfare.

Ib. On the Origin and Function of Music

16 We too often forget that not only is there "a soul of goodness in things evil,"[6] but very generally a soul of truth in things erroneous.

First Principles [1861]

17 The fact disclosed by a survey of the past that majorities have been wrong must not blind us to the complementary fact that majorities have usually not been entirely wrong. *Ib.*

18 Volumes might be written upon the impiety of the pious. *Ib.*

19 We have unmistakable proof that throughout all past time, there has been a ceaseless devouring of the weak by the strong.

Ib.

20 This survival of the fittest which I have here sought to express in mechanical terms, is that which Mr. Darwin has called "natural selection, or the preservation of favored races in the struggle for life."[7]

Principles of Biology [1864–1867], pt. III, ch. 12

21 The Republican form of government is the highest form of government: but because of this it requires the highest type of human nature — a type nowhere at present existing.

Essays [1891]. The Americans

22 The ultimate result of shielding men from the effects of folly is to fill the world with fools.

Ib. State Tamperings with Money Banks

[5] See Thomas Morton, 416:10.

[6] See Shakespeare, 208:3.

[7] See Darwin, 514:15.

1 Time: That which man is always trying to kill, but which ends in killing him.
Definitions

John Tyndall
1820–1893

2 Heat Considered as a Mode of Motion.
Title of treatise [1863]

3 Life is a wave, which in no two consecutive moments of its existence is composed of the same particles.[1]
Fragments of Science, vol. II, Vitality

4 The mind of man may be compared to a musical instrument with a certain range of notes, beyond which in both directions we have an infinitude of silence.
Ib. Matter and Force

5 The brightest flashes in the world of thought are incomplete until they have been proved to have their counterparts in the world of fact.
Ib. Scientific Materialism

6 It is as fatal as it is cowardly to blink facts because they are not to our taste.
Ib. Science and Man

7 Charles Darwin, the Abraham of scientific men—a searcher as obedient to the command of truth as was the patriarch to the command of God. *Ib.*

8 Superstition may be defined as constructive religion which has grown incongruous with intelligence. *Ib.*

9 Religious feeling is as much a verity as any other part of human consciousness; and against it, on the subjective side, the waves of science beat in vain.
Ib. Professor Virchow and Evolution

Henri-Frédéric Amiel
1821–1881

10 To know how to grow old is the masterwork of wisdom, and one of the most difficult chapters in the great art of living.
Journal Intime [1883]

11 An error is the more dangerous the more truth it contains. *Ib.*

12 Truth is the secret of eloquence and of virtue, the basis of moral authority; it is the highest summit of art and of life. *Ib.*

[1]See Heraclitus, 69:24.

13 Charm: the quality in others that makes us more satisfied with ourselves. *Ib.*

14 If ignorance and passion are the foes of popular morality, it must be confessed that moral indifference is the malady of the cultivated classes. *Ib.*

Sir Henry Williams Baker
1821–1877

15 The King of love my shepherd is,
Whose goodness faileth never;
I nothing lack if I am his,
And he is mine forever.
Hymn [1868][2]

Charles Baudelaire[3]
1821–1867

16 Hypocrite lecteur—mon semblable—mon frère[4] [Hypocrite reader—my double—my brother]!
Les Fleurs du Mal [1861]. Au Lecteur

17 The poet is like the prince of the clouds
Who haunts the tempest and laughs at the archer;
Exiled on the ground in the midst of jeers,
His giant wings prevent him from walking.[5]
Ib. L'Albatros, st. 4

18 Perfumes, colors and sounds echo one another.[6] *Ib. Correspondances*

19 Mother of memories, mistress of mistresses.[7] *Ib. Le Balcon, st. 1*

20 There, there is nothing else but grace and measure,
Richness, quietness and pleasure.[8]
Ib. L'Invitation au Voyage, refrain

21 I have more memories than if I were a thousand years old.[9] *Ib. Spleen, l. 1*

[2]Based on the first verse of Psalm 23, 18:7.

[3]Baudelaire is the foremost seer, king of poets, a *true God.* Even so, he lived in too artistic a milieu; his so highly praised form is meager. Ventures into the unknown demand new forms.—ARTHUR RIMBAUD, *Lettre à Paul Demeny* [May 15, 1871]

[4]You! hypocrite lecteur!—mon semblable—mon frère! —T. S. ELIOT, *The Waste Land* [1922], *l. 76*

[5]Le Poète est semblable au prince des nuées / Qui hante la tempête et se rit de l'archer; / Exilé sur le sol au milieu des huées, / Ses ailes de géant l'empêchent de marcher.

[6]Les parfums, les couleurs, les sons se répondent.

[7]Mère des souvenirs, maîtresse des maîtresses.

[8]Là, tout n'est qu'ordre et beauté, / Luxe, calme et volupté.
Translated by RICHARD WILBUR.

[9]J'ai plus de souvenirs que si j'avais mille ans.

1 I am the wound and the knife!
I am the blow and the cheek!
I am the limbs and the wheel—
The victim and the executioner![1]
Ib. L'Héautontimoroumenos

2 Here is the charming evening, the criminal's friend;
It comes like an accomplice, with stealthy tread.[2] *Ib. Le Crépuscule du Soir*

3 What is that sad, dark island?—It is Cythera,
They tell us, a country famous in song,
Banal Eldorado of all the old bachelors.
Look! after all, it is a poor land![3]
Ib. Un Voyage à Cythère

4 O Death, old captain, it is time! raise the anchor! *Ib. Le Voyage, VIII*

5 What do I care that you are good?
Be beautiful! and be sad![4]
Nouvelles Fleurs du Mal [1866–1868]. Madrigal Triste, st. 1

6 There can be no progress (real, that is, moral) except in the individual and by the individual himself.
Mon Coeur Mis à Nu [1887], XV

7 There are in every man, at every hour, two simultaneous postulations, one towards God, the other towards Satan. *Ib. XIX*

8 There exist only three beings worthy of respect: the priest, the soldier, the poet. To know, to kill, to create.[5] *Ib. XXII*

9 To be a great man and a saint for oneself, that is the one important thing.
Ib. LII

10 Theory of the true civilization. It is not to be found in gas or steam or table turning. It consists in the diminution of the traces of original sin. *Ib. LIX*

11 You must shock the bourgeois.[6]
Attributed

[1] Je suis la plaie et le couteau! / Je suis le soufflet et la joue! / Je suis les membres et la roue, / Et la victime et le bourreau!

[2] Voici le soir charmant, ami du criminel; / Il vient comme un complice, à pas de loup.

[3] Quelle est cette île triste et noire?—C'est Cythère, / Nous dit-on, un pays fameux dans les chansons, / Eldorado banal de tous les vieux garçons. / Regardez! après tout c'est un pauvre terre.

[4] Que m'importe que tu sois sage? / Sois belle! et sois triste!

[5] Il n'existe que trois êtres respectables: le prêtre, le guerrier, le poète. Savoir, tuer, et creer.

[6] Il faut épater le bourgeois.

Sir Richard Francis Burton

1821–1890

12 Why meet we on the bridge of Time to 'change one greeting and to part?
The Kasidah of Haji Abdu El-Yazdi, I, 11

13 Indeed he knows not how to know who knows not also how to un-know.
Ib. VI, 18

14 Do what thy manhood bids thee do, from none but self expect applause;
He noblest lives and noblest dies who makes and keeps his self-made laws.
Ib. VIII, 37

Crowfoot[7]

1821–1890

15 What is life? It is the flash of a firefly in the night. It is the breath of a buffalo in the wintertime. It is the little shadow which runs across the grass and loses itself in the sunset.
Last words [1890]

Fëdor Mikhailovich Dostoevski

1821–1881

16 Petersburg, the most theoretical and intentional town on the whole terrestrial globe.
Notes from the Underground [1864],[8] ch. 2

17 Man is sometimes extraordinarily, passionately, in love with suffering. *Ib. 9*

18 Man grows used to everything, the scoundrel!
Crime and Punishment [1866],[8] book I, ch. 2

19 If you were to destroy in mankind the belief in immortality, not only love but every living force maintaining the life of the world would at once be dried up.
The Brothers Karamazov [1879–1880],[8] bk. II, ch. 6

20 I want to tell you now about the insects to whom God gave "sensual lust." . . . I am that insect, brother, and it is said of me especially. All we Karamazovs are such insects, and, angel as you are, that insect lives in you too, and will stir a tempest in your blood. Tempests, because sensual lust is a tempest — worse than a tempest! Beauty is a terrible

[7] Blackfoot warrior and orator.

[8] Translated by CONSTANCE GARNETT.

and awful thing! It is terrible because it has not been fathomed, for God sets us nothing but riddles.[1] Here the boundaries meet and all contradictions exist side by side. *Ib. III, 3*

1 What to the mind is shameful is beauty and nothing else to the heart. Is there beauty in Sodom? Believe me, that for the immense mass of mankind beauty is found in Sodom. Did you know that secret? The awful thing is that beauty is mysterious as well as terrible. God and devil are fighting there, and the battlefield is the heart of man. *Ib.*

2 I want to travel in Europe . . . I know that I am only going to a graveyard, but it's a most precious graveyard. *Ib. V, 3*

3 If the devil doesn't exist, but man has created him, he has created him in his own image and likeness. *Ib. V, 4*

4 Is there in the whole world a being who would have the right to forgive and could forgive? I don't want harmony. From love of humanity I don't want it. . . . I would rather remain with my unavenged suffering and unsatisfied indignation, *even if I were wrong.* Besides, too high a price is asked for harmony; it's beyond our means to pay so much to enter on it. And so I hasten to give back my entrance ticket . . . It's not God that I don't accept, Alyosha, only I most respectfully return Him the ticket. *Ib.*

5 Imagine that you are creating a fabric of human destiny with the object of making men happy in the end, giving them peace and rest at last, but that it was essential and inevitable to torture to death only one tiny creature . . . and to found that edifice on its unavenged tears, would you consent to be the architect on those conditions? Tell me, and tell the truth.[2] *Ib.*

6 So long as man remains free he strives for nothing so incessantly and so painfully as to find someone to worship. *Ib. 5*

7 We have corrected Thy work and have founded it upon *miracle, mystery* and *authority.* And men rejoiced that they were again led like sheep, and that the terrible gift that brought them such suffering, was, at last, lifted from their hearts. *Ib. 5*

[1] See Einstein, 764:1.

[2] "Do you remember the passage where he [Rousseau] asks the reader what he would do if he could make a fortune by killing an old mandarin in China by simply exerting his will, without stirring from Paris?" "Yes." "Well?" "Bah! I'm at my thirty-third mandarin." "Don't play the fool. Look here, if it were proved to you that the thing was possible and you only needed to nod your head, would you do it?" "Is your mandarin well stricken in years? But, bless you, young or old, paralytic or healthy, upon my word—The devil take it! Well, no."—BALZAC, *Le Père Goriot* [1835]

8 "How will you escape it? By what will you escape it? That's impossible with your ideas."
"In the Karamazov way, again."
" 'Everything is lawful,' you mean?" *Ib.*

9 Men reject their prophets and slay them, but they love their martyrs and honor those whom they have slain. *Ib. VI, 3*

10 The jealous are the readiest of all to forgive, and all women know it. *Ib. VIII, 3*

11 Who doesn't desire his father's death? *Ib. XII, 5*

12 Our fatal troika dashes on in her headlong flight perhaps to destruction, and in all Russia for long past men have stretched out imploring hands and called a halt to its furious reckless course. And if other nations stand aside from that troika that may be not from respect, as the poet would fain believe, but simply from horror. And well it is that they stand aside, but maybe they will cease one day to do so and will form a firm wall confronting the hurrying apparition and will check the frenzied rush of our lawlessness, for the sake of their own safety, enlightenment and civilization. *Ib. 9*

13 They have their Hamlets, but we still have our Karamazovs! *Ib.*

14 But profound as psychology is, it's a knife that cuts both ways. *Ib. 10*

15 For a moment the lie becomes truth. *Ib. Epilogue, ch. 2*

16 We have all come out of Gogol's *Overcoat.*[3] *Attributed*

[3] This statement, traditionally attributed to Dostoevski and quoted by most writers on Dostoevski and on Russian realism, appears in EUGÈNE MELCHIOR, vicomte de Vogüé [1848–1910], *Le Roman Russe* [1886], ch. 3: The more I read the Russians, the more I understand the observation one of them made to me . . . "We have all come out of Gogol's *Overcoat.*" We see further how evident the connection is with Dostoevski: the formidable novelist is all in his first book, *Poor People,* and *Poor People* has its origin in the *Overcoat.*

De Vogüé reiterated this statement in the speech he made on the occasion of unveiling a centennial monument to Gogol in Moscow in 1909.

Mary Baker Eddy

1821–1910

1 Our Father-Mother God, all-harmonious.[1]

Science and Health with Key to the Scriptures [1875], p. 16

2 Jesus of Nazareth was the most scientific man that ever trod the globe. He plunged beneath the material surface of things, and found the spiritual cause. *Ib. p. 313*

3 Spirit is the real and eternal; matter is the unreal and temporal. *Ib. p. 468*

4 Sickness, sin and death, being inharmonious, do not originate in God nor belong to His government. *Ib. p. 472*

5 How would you define Christian Science?
As the law of God, the law of good, interpreting and demonstrating the divine Principle and rule of universal harmony.

Rudimental Divine Science [1891], p. 1

Gustave Flaubert

1821–1880

6 One must not always think that feeling is everything. Art is nothing without form.

Letter to Madame Louise Colet [August 12, 1846]

7 What a horrible invention, the bourgeois, don't you think?[2]

Ib. [September 22, 1846]

8 One becomes a critic when one cannot be an artist, just as a man becomes a stool pigeon when he cannot be a soldier.[3]

Ib. [October 22, 1846]

9 There was an air of indifference about them [the male guests], a calm produced by the gratification of every passion . . . that special brutality which comes from the habit of breaking down half-hearted resistances that keep one fit and tickle one's vanity—the handling of blooded horses, the pursuit of loose women.

Madame Bovary [1857],[4] *pt. I, ch. 8*

10 It never occurred to her that if the drainpipes of a house are clogged, the rain may collect in pools on the roof; and she suspected no danger until suddenly she discovered a crack in the wall. *Ib. II, 5*

11 Human speech is like a cracked kettle on which we tap crude rhythms for bears to dance to, while we long to make music that will melt the stars.[5] *Ib. 12*

12 She [Madame Bovary] had that indefinable beauty that comes from happiness, enthusiasm, success—a beauty that is nothing more or less than a harmony of temperament and circumstances. *Ib.*

13 We shouldn't maltreat our idols: the gilt comes off on our hands.[6] *Ib. III, 6*

14 There isn't a bourgeois alive who in the ferment of his youth, if only for a day or for a minute, hasn't thought himself capable of boundless passions and noble exploits. The sorriest little woman-chaser has dreamed of Oriental queens; in a corner of every notary's heart lie the moldy remains of a poet.

Ib.

15 Of all the icy blasts that blow on love, a request for money is the most chilling and havoc-wreaking. *Ib. 8*

16 Anyone's death always releases something like an aura of stupefaction, so difficult is it to grasp this irruption of nothingness and to believe that it has actually taken place.

Ib. 9

17 Axiom: hatred of the bourgeois is the beginning of wisdom.

Letter to George Sand [May 10, 1867]

18 I call a bourgeois anyone whose thinking is vulgar. *Quoted by Maupassant*

19 What is beautiful is moral, that is all there is to it.

Letter to Maupassant [October 26, 1880]

Nathan Bedford Forrest

1821–1877

20 Get there first with the most men.[7]

Reported by General Basil Duke and General Richard Taylor

Hermann Ludwig Ferdinand von Helmholtz

1821–1894

21 Nature as a whole possesses a store of force which cannot in any way be either increased

[1] See Suti and Hor, 5:3; O'Neill, 810:10; and John Paul I, 881:6.

[2] Quelle atroce invention que celle du bourgeois, n'est-ce pas?

[3] See Coleridge, 436:15; Disraeli, 502:12; and Lowell, 567:19.

[4] Translated by FRANCIS STEEGMULLER.

[5] La parole humaine est comme un chaudron fêlé où nous battons des melodies à faire danser les ours, quand on voudrait attendrir les étoiles.

[6] Il ne faut pas toucher aux idoles: la dorure en reste aux mains.

[7] Erroneous version usually rendered: Git thar fustest with the mostest.

or diminished . . . therefore, the quantity of force in Nature is just as eternal and unalterable as the quantity of matter. . . . I have named [this] general law "The Principle of the Conservation of Force."[1]

Über die Erhaltung der Kraft [1847]

1 Whoever, in the pursuit of science, seeks after immediate practical utility, may generally rest assured that he will seek in vain. All that science can achieve is a perfect knowledge and a perfect understanding of the action of natural and moral forces.

Academic discourse, Heidelberg [1862]

Nikolai Nekrasov

1821–1877

2 You do not have to be a poet, but you are obliged to be a citizen.

Poet and Citizen

3 Wretched and abundant,
Oppressed and powerful,
Weak and mighty,
Mother Russia!

Who Is Happy in Russia? [1873–1876]

William Henry Vanderbilt

1821–1885

4 The public be damned.

Reply to a newspaper reporter [October 2, 1882]

Rudolf Virchow

1821–1902

5 I formulate the doctrine of pathological generation . . . in simple terms: *omnis cellula a cellula.*[2]

Cellular Pathology [1858].[3] *Disease, Life and Man*

George John Whyte-Melville

1821–1878

6 In the choice of a horse and a wife, a man must please himself, ignoring the opinion and advice of friends.

Riding Recollections [1878]

[1] Translated by E. Atkinson.
Helmholtz's "force" is equivalent to the modern physicist's "energy."
[2] All cells come from [pre-existing] cells.
[3] Essays translated by Lelland J. Rather.

Matthew Arnold

1822–1888

7 Who prop, thou askst, in these bad days, my mind?

To a Friend [1849], l. 1

8 Be his[4]
My special thanks, whose even-balanced soul,
From first youth tested up to extreme old age,
Business could not make dull, nor passion wild:
Who saw life steadily and saw it whole.

Ib. l. 8

9 Others abide our question. Thou art free.
We ask and ask: Thou smilest and art still,
Out-topping knowledge.

Shakespeare [1849], l. 1

10 Strong is the soul, and wise, and beautiful:
The seeds of godlike power are in us still:
Gods are we, bards, saints, heroes, if we will.

Written in Emerson's Essays [1849]

11 Come, dear children, let us away;
Down and away below!
Now my brothers call from the bay,
Now the great winds shorewards blow,
Now the salt tides seawards flow;
Now the wild white horses play,
Champ and chafe and toss in the spray.

The Forsaken Merman [1849], st. 1

12 Sand-strewn caverns, cool and deep,
Where the winds are all asleep.

Ib. st. 4

13 Where great whales come sailing by,
Sail and sail, with unshut eye,
Round the world forever and aye. *Ib.*

14 Singing, "Here came a mortal,
But faithless was she.
And alone dwell forever
The kings of the sea." *Ib. st. 8*

15 Fate gave, what Chance shall not control,
His sad lucidity of soul.

Resignation [1849], l. 197

16 The world in which we live and move
Outlasts aversion, outlasts love:
Outlasts each effort, interest, hope,
Remorse, grief, joy. *Ib. l. 215*

17 Yet they, believe me, who await
No gifts from Chance, have conquered Fate.

Ib. l. 248

18 We cannot kindle when we will
The fire that in the heart resides,
The spirit bloweth and is still,
In mystery our soul abides.

Morality [1852], st. 1

[4] Sophocles.

1 Calm Soul of all things! make it mine
To feel, amid the city's jar,
That there abides a peace of thine,
Man did not make, and can not mar.
Lines Written in Kensington Gardens [1852], st. 10

2 Goethe in Weimar sleeps, and Greece,
Long since, saw Byron's struggle cease.
Memorial Verses, April 1850 [1852], st. 1

3 Physician of the Iron Age,
Goethe has done his pilgrimage.
He took the suffering human race,
He read each wound, each weakness clear;
And struck his finger on the place,
And said: Thou ailest here, and here!
Ib. st. 3

4 This iron time
Of doubt, disputes, distractions, fears.
Ib. st. 4

5 Hither and thither spins
The windborne, mirroring soul;
A thousand glimpses wins,
And never sees a whole.
Empedocles on Etna [1852], act I, sc. ii, l. 82

6 Be neither saint- nor sophist-led, but be a man! *Ib. l. 136*

7 Thou hast no *right* to bliss. *Ib. l. 160*

8 We do not what we ought;
What we ought not, we do;[1]
And lean upon the thought
That chance will bring us through.
Ib. l. 237

9 Nature, with equal mind,
Sees all her sons at play;
Sees man control the wind,
The wind sweep man away. *Ib. l. 257*

10 So, loath to suffer mute,
We, peopling the void air,
Make Gods to whom to impute
The ills we ought to bear. *Ib. l. 277*

11 Is it so small a thing
To have enjoyed the sun,
To have lived light in the spring,
To have loved, to have thought, to have done;
To have advanced true friends, and beat down baffling foes? *Ib. II, l. 397*

12 The day in its hotness,
The strife with the palm;
The night in her silence,
The stars in their calm. *Ib. l. 465*

[1]See *Book of Common Prayer*, 54:13.

13 Yes, in the sea of life enisled,
With echoing straits between us thrown,
Dotting the shoreless watery wild,
We mortal millions live *alone*.
To Marguerite. Continued [1852], l. 1

14 The unplumbed, salt, estranging sea.
Ib. l. 24

15 But often in the world's most crowded streets,
But often, in the din of strife,
There rises an unspeakable desire
After the knowledge of our buried life.
The Buried Life [1852], l. 45

16 And long we try in vain to speak and act
Our hidden self, and what we say and do
Is eloquent, is well—but 'tis not true!
Ib. l. 64

17 What shelter to grow ripe is ours?
What leisure to grow wise?
Stanzas in Memory of the Author of "Obermann"[2] [1852], st. 18

18 Ah! two desires toss about
The poet's feverish blood;
One drives him to the world without,
And one to solitude. *Ib. st. 24*

19 What actions are the most excellent? Those, certainly, which most powerfully appeal to the great primary human affections: to those elementary feelings which subsist permanently in the race, and which are independent of time. These feelings are permanent and the same; that which interests them is permanent and the same also.
Preface to Poems [1853]

20 Go, for they call you, Shepherd, from the hill.
The Scholar Gypsy [1853], st. 1

21 Crossing the stripling Thames at Bablockhithe,
Trailing in the cool stream thy fingers wet,
As the slow punt swings round.
Ib. st. 8

22 Thou waitest for the spark from heaven: and we,
Light half-believers of our casual creeds,
Who never deeply felt, nor clearly willed . . .
Who hesitate and falter life away,
And lose tomorrow the ground won today—
Ah! do not we, wanderer! await it too?
Ib. st. 18

23 And amongst us one,
Who most has suffered, takes dejectedly
His seat upon the intellectual throne.
Ib. st. 19

[2]Étienne Pivert de Sénancour [1770–1846]. His most notable work was *Obermann* [1804].

1 Oh, born in days when wits were fresh and clear,
And life ran gaily as the sparkling Thames;
Before this strange disease of modern life,[1]
With its sick hurry, its divided aims,
Its heads o'ertaxed, its palsied hearts, was rife. *Ib. st. 21*

2 Still nursing the unconquerable hope,
Still clutching the inviolable shade.
Ib. st. 22

3 Strew on her roses, roses,
And never a spray of yew!
In quiet she reposes;
Ah, would that I did too!
Requiescat [1853], st. 1

4 The vasty hall of death. *Ib. st. 4*

5 Hark! ah, the nightingale—
The tawny-throated!
Philomela [1853], st. 1

6 Eternal passion!
Eternal pain! *Ib. st. 3*

7 Truth sits upon the lips of dying men.
Sohrab and Rustum, l. 656

8 Sanity—that is the great virtue of the ancient literature; the want of that is the great defect of the modern, in spite of its variety and power. *Preface to Poems [1854]*

9 For rigorous teachers seized my youth,
And purged its faith, and trimmed its fire,
Showed me the high, white star of Truth,
There bade me gaze, and there aspire.
Stanzas from the Grande Chartreuse [1855], st. 12

10 Wandering between two worlds, one dead,
The other powerless to be born.[2]
Ib. st. 15

11 And we forget because we must
And not because we will.
Absence [1857], st. 3

12 Peace, peace is what I seek, and public calm;
Endless extinction of unhappy hates.
Merope [1858], l. 100

13 With women the heart argues, not the mind.
Ib. l. 341

14 The translator of Homer should above all be penetrated by a sense of four qualities of his author: that he is eminently rapid; that he is eminently plain and direct, both in the evolution of his thought and in the expression of it, that is, both in his syntax and in his words; that he is eminently plain and direct in the substance of his thought, that is, in his matter and ideas; and, finally, that he is eminently noble.
On Translating Homer [1861]

15 Of these two literatures [French and German], as of the intellect of Europe in general, the main effort, for now many years, has been a *critical* effort; the endeavor, in all branches of knowledge—theology, philosophy, history, art, science—to see the object as in itself it really is. *Ib.*

16 The grand style arises in poetry, when a noble nature, poetically gifted, treats with simplicity or with severity a serious subject. *Ib.*

17 Nations are not truly great solely because the individuals composing them are numerous, free, and active; but they are great when these numbers, this freedom, and this activity are employed in the service of an ideal higher than that of an ordinary man, taken by himself. *Democracy [1861]*

18 It is a very great thing to be able to think as you like; but, after all, an important question remains: *what* you think. *Ib.*

19 For the creation of a masterwork of literature two powers must concur, the power of the man and the power of the moment, and the man is not enough without the moment.
The Function of Criticism at the Present Time [1864]

20 The critical power . . . tends to make an intellectual situation of which the creative power can profitably avail itself . . . to make the best ideas prevail. *Ib.*

21 There is the world of ideas and the world of practice; the French are often for suppressing the one and the English the other; but neither is to be suppressed. *Ib.*

22 Burke is so great because, almost alone in England, he brings thought to bear upon politics, he saturates politics with thought.
Ib.

23 The notion of the free play of the mind upon all subjects being a pleasure in itself, being an object of desire, being an essential provider of elements without which a nation's spirit, whatever compensations it may have for them, must, in the long run, die of inanition, hardly enters into an Englishman's thoughts. *Ib.*

24 I am bound by my own definition of criticism: a disinterested endeavor to learn and propagate the best that is known and thought in the world. *Ib.*

[1] See Cowley, 295:12, and Pope, 338:11.
[2] See T. S. Eliot, 805:7.

1 Whispering from her towers [Oxford] the last enchantments of the Middle Age . . . Home of lost causes, and forsaken beliefs, and unpopular names, and impossible loyalties!
Essays in Criticism, first series [1865], preface

2 Poetry is simply the most beautiful, impressive and wisely effective mode of saying things, and hence its importance.
Ib. Heinrich Heine

3 *Philistine* must have originally meant, in the mind of those who invented the nickname, a strong, dogged, unenlightened opponent of the children of the light.[1] *Ib.*

4 On the breast of that huge Mississippi of falsehood called *History,* a foam-bell more or less is no consequence.[2]
Ib. Literary Influence of Academies [1864]

5 The great apostle of the Philistines, Lord Macaulay. *Ib. Joubert*

6 Are ye too changed, ye hills?
See, 'tis no foot of unfamiliar men
Tonight from Oxford up your pathway strays!
Here came I often, often, in old days—
Thyrsis[3] and I; we still had Thyrsis then.
Thyrsis [1866], st. 1

7 That sweet city[4] with her dreaming spires.
Ib. st. 2

8 He went; his piping took a troubled sound
Of storms that rage outside our happy ground;
He could not wait their passing; he is dead.
Ib. st. 5

9 The bloom is gone, and with the bloom go I.
Ib. st. 6

10 Yes, thou art gone! and round me too the night
In ever-nearing circle weaves her shade.
Ib. st. 14

11 Hear it, O Thyrsis, still our tree is there!—
Ah, vain! These English fields, this upland dim,
These brambles pale with mist engarlanded,
That lone, sky-pointing tree, are not for him;
To a boon southern country he is fled,
And now in happier air,
Wandering with the great Mother's train divine . . .
Within a folding of the Apennine.
Ib. st. 18

12 Why faintest thou? I wandered till I died.
Roam on! The light we sought is shining still,
Dost thou ask proof? Our tree yet crowns the hill,
Our Scholar travels yet the loved hillside.
Ib. st. 24

13 The sea is calm tonight.
The tide is full, the moon lies fair
Upon the straits; on the French coast, the light
Gleams, and is gone; the cliffs of England stand,
Glimmering and vast, out in the tranquil bay.
Dover Beach [1867], st. 1

14 Listen! you hear the grating roar
Of pebbles which the waves draw back, and fling,
At their return, up the high strand,
Begin, and cease, and then again begin,
With tremulous cadence slow, and bring
The eternal note of sadness in. *Ib.*

15 Sophocles long ago
Heard it on the Aegean. *Ib. st. 2*

16 The sea of faith
Was once, too, at the full, and round earth's shore
Lay like the folds of a bright girdle furled;
But now I only hear
Its melancholy, long, withdrawing roar,
Retreating, to the breath
Of the night wind down the vast edges drear
And naked shingles of the world.

Ah, love, let us be true
To one another! for the world, which seems
To lie before us like a land of dreams,
So various, so beautiful, so new,
Hath really neither joy, nor love, nor light,
Nor certitude, nor peace, nor help for pain;
And we are here as on a darkling plain
Swept with confused alarms of struggle and flight,
Where ignorant armies clash by night.
Ib. st. 3, 4

17 It is—last stage of all—
When we are frozen up within, and quite
The phantom of ourselves,
To hear the world applaud the hollow ghost
Which blamed the living man.
Growing Old [1867], st. 7

[1] See Schopenhauer, 463:9.

[2] This passage appeared only in the first appearance of the essay in *Cornhill Magazine* [August 1864].

History never embraces more than a small part of reality.—LA ROCHEFOUCAULD [1613–1680], *Paul Sabatier*

History is nothing more than the belief in the senses, the belief in falsehood.—NIETZSCHE [1844–1900], *The Twilight of the Idols, "Reason" in Philosophy, I*

History is more or less bunk.—HENRY FORD [1863–1947], interview with Charles N. Wheeler, *Chicago Tribune* [May 25, 1916]

[3] Arthur Hugh Clough [1819–1861].

[4] Oxford.

1 Creep into thy narrow bed,
Creep, and let no more be said!
The Last Word [1867], st. 1

2 Let the long contention cease!
Geese are swans, and swans are geese.[1]
Ib. st. 2

3 Charge once more, then, and be dumb!
Let the victors, when they come,
When the forts of folly fall,
Find thy body by the wall.
Ib. st. 4

4 Cruel, but composed and bland,
Dumb, inscrutable and grand,
So Tiberius might have sat,
Had Tiberius been a cat.
Poor Matthias [1867]

5 Coldly, sadly descends
The autumn evening. The field
Strewn with its dank yellow drifts
Of withered leaves, and the elms,
Fade into dimness apace,
Silent; hardly a shout
From a few boys late at their play!
Rugby Chapel[2] [1867], st. 1

6 O strong soul, by what shore
Tarriest thou now? For that force,
Surely, has not been left vain!
Ib. st. 4

7 Most men eddy about
Here and there, eat and drink,
Chatter and love and hate,
Gather and squander.
Ib. st. 6

8 Therefore to thee it was given
Many to save with thyself;
And, at the end of thy day,
O faithful shepherd, to come,
Bringing thy sheep in thy hand.[3]
Ib. st. 9

9 Style . . . is a peculiar recasting and heightening, under a certain condition of spiritual excitement, of what a man has to say, in such a manner as to add dignity and distinction to it.
On the Study of Celtic Literature [1867], sec. 6

10 The Celts certainly have it [style] in a wonderful measure.
Ib.

11 The power of the Latin classic is in *character*, that of the Greek is in *beauty*. Now character is capable of being taught, learnt, and assimilated: beauty hardly.
Schools and Universities on the Continent [1868]

[1]See Burton, 258:26.
[2]Arnold's father. Thomas Arnold [1795–1842], the great headmaster of Rugby, is buried in Rugby Chapel.
[3]See *Psalm* 95:7, 20:20.

12 The whole scope of the essay is to recommend culture as the great help out of our present difficulties; culture being a pursuit of our total perfection by means of getting to know, on all the matters which most concern us, the best which has been thought and said in the world.
Culture and Anarchy [1869], preface

13 Our society distributes itself into Barbarians, Philistines, and Populace; and America is just ourselves, with the Barbarians quite left out, and the Populace nearly.
Ib.

14 I am a Liberal, yet I am a Liberal tempered by experience, reflection, and renouncement, and I am, above all, a believer in culture.
Ib. Introduction

15 Culture is then properly described not as having its origin in curiosity, but as having its origin in the love of perfection; it is *a study of perfection.*
Ib. Sweetness and Light

16 Greatness is a spiritual condition worthy to excite love, interest, and admiration.
Ib.

17 Not a having and a resting, but a growing and a becoming is the character of perfection as culture conceives it.
Ib.

18 He who works for sweetness and light[4] united, works to make reason and the will of God prevail.
Ib.

19 The men of culture are the true apostles of equality.
Ib.

20 Everything in our political life tends to hide from us that there is anything wiser than our ordinary selves.
Ib. Barbarians, Philistines, Populace

21 The governing idea of Hellenism is spirit of consciousness, that of Hebraism, strictness of conscience.
Ib. Hebraism and Hellenism

22 Below the surface stream, shallow and light,
Of what we say and feel—below the stream,
As light, of what we think we feel, there flows
With noiseless current, strong, obscure and
deep,
The central stream of what we feel indeed.
St. Paul and Protestantism [1870]

23 Conduct is three-fourths of our life and its largest concern.
Literature and Dogma [1873], ch. 1

[4]See Swift, 321:14.

1 The freethinking of one age is the common sense of the next.
God and the Bible [1875]

2 Choose equality.
Mixed Essays [1879]. Equality

3 We have the religion of inequality.
Ib.

4 Inequality has the natural and necessary effect, under the present circumstances, of materializing our upper class, vulgarizing our middle class, and brutalizing our lower class. *Ib.*

5 For poetry the idea is everything; the rest is a world of illusion, of divine illusion. Poetry attaches its emotion to the idea; the idea *is* the fact. The strongest part of our religion today is its unconscious poetry.
Introduction to WARD, *English Poets [1880]*

6 *Eutrapelia.* "A happy and gracious flexibility," Pericles calls this quality of the Athenians . . . lucidity of thought, clearness and propriety of language, freedom from prejudice and freedom from stiffness, openness of mind, amiability of manners.
Irish Essays [1882]. A Speech at Eton

7 English civilization — the humanizing, the bringing into one harmonious and truly humane life, of the whole body of English society — that is what interests me.
Ib. Ecce, Convertimur ad Gentes

8 That which in England we call the middle class is in America virtually the nation.
A Word About America [1882]

9 The American Philistine was a livelier sort of Philistine than ours.
A Word More About America [1885]

10 What really dissatisfies in American civilization is the want of the *interesting,* a want due chiefly to the want of those two great elements of the interesting, which are elevation and beauty.
Civilization in the United States [1888]

11 The best poetry will be found to have a power of forming, sustaining, and delighting us, as nothing else can.
Essays in Criticism, second series [1888]. The Study of Poetry

12 Coleridge, poet and philosopher wrecked in a mist of opium. *Ib. Byron*

13 A beautiful and ineffectual angel [Shelley], beating in the void his luminous wings in vain. *Ib.*

Rudolf Julius Emanuel Clausius
1822–1888

14 Heat cannot of itself pass from a colder to a hotter body.
The Second Law of Thermodynamics [1850]. From Die Mechanische Wärmetheorie [1865–1867; On the Mechanical Theory of Heat, 1879][1]

Ulysses Simpson Grant
1822–1885

15 The art of war is simple enough. Find out where your enemy is. Get at him as soon as you can. Strike at him as hard as you can and as often as you can, and keep moving on.[2]
On the art of war

16 No terms except an unconditional and immediate surrender can be accepted. I propose to move immediately upon your works.
To General S. B. Buckner, Fort Donelson [February 16, 1862]

17 I propose to fight it out on this line, if it takes all summer.
Dispatch to Washington, before Spottsylvania Court House [May 11, 1864]

18 Wherever the enemy goes let our troops go also.
Dispatch to General Henry W. Halleck from City Point, Virginia [August 1, 1864]

19 The war is over — the rebels are our countrymen again.
Upon stopping his men from cheering after Lee's surrender at Appomattox Court House [April 9, 1865]

20 Let us have peace.
Accepting nomination for the presidency [May 29, 1868]

21 I know no method to secure the repeal of bad or obnoxious laws so effective as their stringent execution.
Inaugural Address [March 4, 1869]

[1]Translated by WALTER D. BROWN.
Heat will of its own accord flow only from a hot object to a cold object. — JOSIAH WILLARD GIBBS, *Scientific Papers* [1906], *The Second Law of Thermodynamics*
[2]See Halsey, 777:12.

1 Let no guilty man escape, if it can be avoided. No personal considerations should stand in the way of performing a public duty.

Indorsement of a letter relating to the Whiskey Ring [July 29, 1875]

2 Leave the matter of religion to the family altar, the church, and the private school, supported entirely by private contributions. Keep the church and the State forever separate.

Speech at Des Moines, Iowa [1875]

3 Labor disgraces no man; unfortunately you occasionally find men disgrace labor.

Speech at Midland International Arbitration Union, Birmingham, England [1877]

4 They [the Pilgrim Fathers] fell upon an ungenial climate, where there were nine months of winter and three months of cold weather, and that called out the best energies of the men, and of the women too, to get a mere subsistence out of the soil, with such a climate. In their efforts to do that they cultivated industry and frugality at the same time—which is the real foundation of the greatness of the Pilgrims.

Speech at New England Society Dinner [December 22, 1880]

Edward Everett Hale
1822–1909

5 I am only one,
But still I am one.
I cannot do everything,
But still I can do something;
And because I cannot do everything
I will not refuse to do the something that I can do.

For the Lend-a-Hand Society

6 Behind all these men you have to do with, behind officers, and government, and people even, there is the country herself, your country, and . . . you belong to her as you belong to your own mother. Stand by her, boy, as you would stand by your mother.

The Man Without a Country [1863]

7 He loved his country as no other man has loved her, but no man deserved less at her hands. *Ib. Epitaph of Philip Nolan*

8 To look up and not down,
To look forward and not back,
To look out and not in, and
To lend a hand.[1]

Ten Times One Is Ten [1870]

[1]Rule of the Harry Wadsworth Club.

Rutherford Birchard Hayes
1822–1893

9 He serves his party best who serves the country best.

Inaugural Address [March 5, 1877]

Thomas Hughes
1822–1896

10 Life isn't all beer and skittles;[2] but beer and skittles, or something better of the same sort, must form a good part of every Englishman's education.

Tom Brown's Schooldays [1857], pt. I, ch. 2

11 He never wants anything but what's right and fair; only when you come to settle what's right and fair, it's everything that he wants and nothing that you want. *Ib. II, 2*

William Porcher Miles
1822–1899

12 "Vote early and vote often," the advice openly displayed on the election banners in one of our northern cities.

Speech in the House of Representatives [March 31, 1858]

Frederick Law Olmsted
1822–1903
and
Calvert Vaux
1824–1895

13 The Park [Central Park, New York City] throughout is a single work of art, and as such subject to the primary law of every work of art, namely, that it shall be framed upon a single, noble motive, to which the design of all its parts, in some more or less subtle way, shall be confluent and helpful.

Report submitted with "Greensward"[3] Plan, awarded first prize by the Board of Commissioners of the Central Park [April 28, 1858]

14 It is one great purpose of the Park to supply to the hundreds of thousands of tired workers, who have no opportunity to spend their summers in the country, a specimen of God's handiwork that shall be to them, inexpensively, what a month or two in the White

[2]See Dickens, 546:27.
[3]Pseudonym of Olmsted and Vaux in submitting their plan.

Mountains or the Adirondacks is, at great cost, to those in easier circumstances.

Ib.

Louis Pasteur

1822–1895

1 No, a thousand times no; there does not exist a category of science to which one can give the name applied science. There are science and the applications of science, bound together as the fruit to the tree which bears it.[1]

Pourquoi la France n'a pas trouvé des hommes supérieurs au moment du péril. From Revue Scientifique [1871]

2 In the fields of observation, chance favors only the mind that is prepared.

Quoted by René Vallery-Radot *in The Life of Pasteur [1927]*

Thomas Buchanan Read

1822–1872

3 The terrible grumble, and rumble, and roar,
Telling the battle was on once more,
And Sheridan twenty miles away.

Sheridan's Ride [1865], st. 1

Red Cloud[2]

1822–1909

4 We were told that they [federal troops] wished merely to pass through our country . . . to seek for gold in the far west . . . Yet before the ashes of the council fire are cold, the Great Father is building his forts among us. You have heard the sound of the white soldier's axe upon the Little Piney. His presence here is . . . an insult to the spirits of our ancestors. Are we then to give up their sacred graves to be plowed for corn? Dakotas, I am for war.

Speech at council at Fort Laramie, Wyoming [1866]

Heinrich Schliemann

1822–1890

5 I have gazed on the face of Agamemnon.

Telegram to the king of Greece, upon excavating the fifth and last grave at Mycenae [August 1876]

[1]Translated by I. Bernard Cohen.

[2]Mahpiua Luta, Oglala Sioux chief.

Théodore de Banville

1823–1891

6 We'll to the woods no more,
The laurels all are cut.[3]

Nous n'Irons Plus aux Bois

Julia A. Fletcher Carney

1823–1908

7 Little drops of water
Little grains of sand,
Make the mighty ocean
And the pleasant land.

Little Things [1845], st. 1

8 Little deeds of kindness,
Little words of love,
Help to make earth happy
Like the heaven above.

Ib. st. 4

William Johnson Cory

1823–1892

9 They told me, Heraclitus, they told me you were dead;
They brought me bitter news to hear and bitter tears to shed.
I wept as I remembered how often you and I
Had tired the sun with talking and sent him down the sky.
And now that thou art lying, my dear old Carian guest,
A handful of gray ashes, long, long ago at rest,
Still are thy pleasant voices, thy *Nightingales,* awake,
For Death, he taketh all away, but them he cannot take.

Heraclitus. Translated from Callimachus[4]

Thomas Wentworth Higginson

1823–1911

10 When a thought takes one's breath away, a lesson on grammar seems an impertinence.

Preface to Emily Dickinson's *Poems, first series [1890]*

Benjamin Harvey Hill

1823–1882

11 He [Lee] was a foe without hate, a friend without treachery, a soldier without cruelty,

[3]Nous n'irons plus aux bois,/Les lauriers sont coupés. From an old nursery rhyme.
Translated by A. E. Housman.

[4]See Callimachus, 93:1.

and a victim without murmuring. He was a public officer without vices, a private citizen without wrong, a neighbor without reproach, a Christian without hypocrisy, and a man without guile. He was a Caesar without his ambition, a Frederick without his tyranny, a Napoleon without his selfishness, and a Washington without his reward.

Tribute to Robert E. Lee; from THOMAS NELSON PAGE, *Robert E. Lee [1911]*

William Walsham How
1823–1897

1 For all the saints, who from their labors rest.

Hymn [1864], st. 1

John Kells Ingram
1823–1907

2 Who fears to speak of Ninety-eight?[1]
Who blushes at the name?
When cowards mock the patriot's fate,
Who hangs his head for shame?

The Memory of the Dead,[2] st. 1

Leopold Kronecker
1823–1891

3 God made integers, all else is the work of man.

Jahresberichte der Deutschen Mathematiker Vereinigung, bk. 2

George Martin Lane
1823–1897

4 The waiter roars it through the hall:
"We don't give bread with one fish ball!"

Lay of the Lone Fish Ball[3] [1855], st. 10

Francis Parkman
1823–1893

5 The growth of New England was a result of the aggregate efforts of a busy multitude, each in his narrow circle toiling for himself, to gather competence or wealth. The expansion of New France was the achievement of a gigantic ambition striving to grasp a continent. It was a vain attempt.

Pioneers of France in the New World [1865], introduction

6 A boundless vision grows upon us; an untamed continent; vast wastes of forest verdure; mountains silent in primeval sleep; river, lake, and glimmering pool; wilderness oceans mingling with the sky. Such was the domain which France conquered for civilization. Plumed helmets gleamed in the shade of its forests, priestly vestments in its dens and fastnesses of ancient barbarism. Men steeped in antique learning, pale with the close breath of the cloister, here spent the noon and evening of their lives, ruled savage hordes with a mild, parental sway, and stood serene before the direst shapes of death. Men of courtly nurture, heirs to the polish of a far-reaching ancestry, here, with their dauntless hardihood, put to shame the boldest sons of toil. *Ib.*

7 Faithfulness to the truth of history involves far more than a research, however patient and scrupulous, into special facts. Such facts may be detailed with the most minute exactness, and yet the narrative, taken as a whole, may be unmeaning or untrue. The narrator must seek to imbue himself with the life and spirit of the time. He must study events in their bearings near and remote; in the character, habits, and manners of those who took part in them.[4] He must himself be, as it were, a sharer or a spectator of the action he describes. *Ib.*

8 If any pale student, glued to his desk, here seek an apology for a way of life whose natural fruit is that pallid and emasculate scholarship of which New England has had too many examples, it will be far better that this sketch had not been written. For the student there is, in its season, no better place than the saddle, and no better companion than the rifle or the oar.

Autobiography [1868][5]

9 The most momentous and far-reaching question ever brought to issue on this continent was: Shall France remain here or shall she not?

Montcalm and Wolfe [1884], introduction

10 Versailles was a gulf into which the labor of France poured its earnings, and it was never full. *Ib. ch. 1*

[1] Struggle for Irish independence led by Wolfe Tone, Napper Tandy, and others.

[2] First published anonymously in the *Dublin Nation* [April 1, 1843].

[3] Lane was professor of Latin at Harvard; the embarrassment of the "lone fish ball" was an actual experience.

[4] See Tolstoi, 602:8.

[5] Published in *Proceedings of the Massachusetts Historical Society, vol. VIII, p. 353.*

1 The [French] Revolution began at the top—in the world of fashion, birth, and intellect—and propagated itself downwards.

Ib.

2 France built its best colony on a principle of exclusion, and failed: England reversed the system, and succeeded. *Ib.*

Coventry Patmore

1823–1896

3 A Woman is a foreign land,
Of which, though there he settle young,
A man will ne'er quite understand
The customs, politics, and tongue.

The Angel in the House [1854–1856], bk. I, canto 9. Prelude 2, Woman

4 It was not like your great and gracious ways!
Do you, that have naught other to lament,
Never, my Love, repent
Of how, that July afternoon,
You went,
With sudden, unintelligible phrase,
And frightened eye,
Upon your journey of so many days
Without a single kiss, or a good-bye?

The Unknown Eros [1877], bk. I, 8, The Departure, l. 1

Edward Pollock

1823–1858

5 The one who goes is happier
Than those he leaves behind.

The Parting Hour

William Brighty Rands [Matthew Browne]

1823–1882

6 Never do today what you can
Put off till tomorrow.[1] *Lilliput Levee*

7 Great wide, beautiful, wonderful world,
With the wonderful waters round you curled,
And the wonderful grass upon your breast,
World, you are beautifully dressed.

The Child's World, st. 1

[1] No idleness, no laziness, no procrastination; never put off till tomorrow what you can do today.—LORD CHESTERFIELD, *Letters* [December 26, 1749]

Ernest Renan

1823–1892

8 The whole of history is incomprehensible without him [Jesus].

La Vie de Jésus [1863], introduction

9 O Lord, if there is a Lord, save my soul, if I have a soul. *Prière d'un Sceptique*

10 Religion is not a popular error; it is a great instinctive truth, sensed by the people, expressed by the people.

Les Apôtres [1866]

11 An immense river of oblivion is sweeping us away into a nameless abyss.

Souvenirs d'Enfance et de Jeunesse [1883]

12 Immortality is to labor at an eternal task.

L'Avenir de la Science [1890], preface

13 Nothing great is achieved without chimeras. *Ib. ch. 19*

John Sherman

1823–1900

14 I have come home to look after my fences.[2]

Speech to his neighbors, Mansfield, Ohio

Harriet Tubman[3]

c. 1823–1913

15 When I found I had crossed that line,[4] I looked at my hands to see if I was the same person. There was such a glory over everything.

To her biographer Sarah H. Bradford [c. 1868]

16 I started with this idea in my head, "There's two things I've got a right to . . . death or liberty." *Ib.*

17 'Twant me, 'twas the Lord. I always told him, "I trust to you. I don't know where to go or what to do, but I expect you to lead me," and he always did. *Ib.*

[2] Senator Sherman referred to the fences around his farm. Said to be the origin of the political phrase often rendered: to mend fences.

[3] Well has she been called "Moses," for she has been a leader and deliverer unto hundreds of her people.—SARAH H. BRADFORD [b. 1818], *Scenes in the Life of Harriet Tubman* [1869]

Excepting John Brown—of sacred memory—I know of no one who has willingly encountered more perils and hardships to serve our enslaved people than you have.—FREDERICK DOUGLASS, *Letter to Harriet Tubman* [August 29, 1868]

[4] On her first escape from slavery [1845].

William Marcy Tweed
1823–1878

1 As long as I count the votes, what are you going to do about it?

Statement by the "Boss" of Tammany Hall on the ballot in New York City [November 1871]

William Allingham
1824–1889

2 Up the airy mountain,
Down the rushy glen,
We daren't go a-hunting
For fear of little men.

The Fairies, st. 1

3 Four ducks on a pond,
A grass bank beyond,
A blue sky of spring,
White clouds on the wing;
What a little thing
To remember for years—
To remember with tears!

Four Ducks on a Pond

Bernard Elliott Bee
1824–1861

4 There is Jackson, standing like a stone wall!

Of General T. J. Jackson at the battle of Bull Run[1] *[July 21, 1861]*

Phoebe Cary
1824–1871

5 And though hard be the task,
"Keep a stiff upper lip."

Keep a Stiff Upper Lip

6 One sweetly solemn thought
Comes to me o'er and o'er;
I am nearer home today
Than I ever have been before.

Nearer Home, st. 1

Wilkie Collins
1824–1889

7 "I haven't much time to be fond of anything," says Sergeant Cuff. "But when I *have* a moment's fondness to bestow, most times . . . the roses get it."

The Moonstone [1868]. First Period, ch. 12

[1] Bee was killed in this battle.

Alexandre Dumas the Younger
1824–1895

8 Business? It's quite simple. It's other people's money.[2]

La Question d'Argent [1857], act II, sc. vii

Thomas Jonathan [Stonewall] Jackson[3]
1824–1863

9 My duty is to obey orders.

A favorite aphorism

10 Let us cross over the river, and rest under the trees. *Last words [May 10, 1863]*

William Thomson, Lord Kelvin
1824–1907

11 When you can measure what you are speaking about, and express it in numbers, you know something about it; but when you cannot measure it, when you cannot express it in numbers, your knowledge is of a meager and unsatisfactory kind: it may be the beginning of knowledge, but you have scarcely, in your thoughts, advanced to the stage of *science.*

Popular Lectures and Addresses [1891–1894]

Gustav Robert Kirchoff
1824–1887

12 The highest object at which the natural sciences are constrained to aim, but which they will never reach, is the determination of the forces which are present in nature, and of the state of matter at any given moment — in one word, the reduction of all the phenomena of nature to mechanics.[4]

Über das Ziel der Naturwissenschaften [1865]

George Macdonald
1824–1905

13 Said the Wind to the Moon, "I will blow you out!" *The Wind and the Moon, st. 1*

14 Here lie I, Martin Elginbrodde:
Hae mercy o' my soul, Lord God;

[2] Les affaires, c'est bien simple, c'est l'argent des autres.
[3] See Bee, 594:4.
[4] Translated by J. B. STALLO.

As I wad do, were I Lord God,
And ye were Martin Elginbrodde.
David Elginbrod [1863], bk. I, ch. 13

1 There is no feeling in a human heart which exists in that heart alone—which is not, in some form or degree, in every heart.
Unspoken Sermons, second series [1885]

2 You will be dead so long as you refuse to die. *What's Mine's Mine [1886], ch. 31*

3 The world and my being, its life and mine, were one. The microcosm and macrocosm were at length atoned, at length in harmony. I lived in everything; everything entered and lived in me. *Lilith [1895], ch. 45*

William Allen Butler

1825–1902

4 This same Miss McFlimsey of Madison Square,
The last time we met was in utter despair,
Because she had nothing whatever to wear!
Nothing to Wear [1857], st. 3

Thomas Henry Huxley

1825–1895

5 I cannot but think that he who finds a certain proportion of pain and evil inseparably woven up in the life of the very worms, will bear his own share with more courage and submission.
On the Educational Value of the Natural History Sciences [1854]

6 To a person uninstructed in natural history, his country or seaside stroll is a walk through a gallery filled with wonderful works of art, nine-tenths of which have their faces turned to the wall. *Ib.*

7 Extinguished theologians lie about the cradle of every science as the strangled snakes beside that of Hercules.
Darwiniana. The Origin of Species [1860]

8 The method of scientific investigation is nothing but the expression of the necessary mode of working of the human mind.
Our Knowledge of the Causes of the Phenomena of Organic Nature [1863]

9 Let us have "sweet girl graduates"[1] by all means. They will be none the less sweet for a little wisdom; and the "golden hair" will not curl less gracefully outside the head by reason of there being brains within.
Emancipation—Black and White [1865]

10 The improver of natural knowledge absolutely refuses to acknowledge authority, as such. For him, skepticism is the highest of duties, blind faith the one unpardonable sin.
On the Advisableness of Improving Natural Knowledge [1866]

11 For every man the world is as fresh as it was at the first day, and as full of untold novelties for him who has the eyes to see them. *A Liberal Education [1868]*

12 The chess board is the world, the pieces are the phenomena of the universe, the rules of the game are what we call the laws of Nature. The player on the other side is hidden from us. We know that his play is always fair, just, and patient. But also we know, to our cost, that he never overlooks a mistake, or makes the smallest allowance for ignorance.
Ib.

13 M. Comte's philosophy in practice might be compendiously described as Catholicism *minus* Christianity.
On the Physical Basis of Life [1868]

14 Education is the instruction of the intellect in the laws of Nature, under which name I include not merely things and their forces but men and their ways, and the fashioning of the affections and of the will into an earnest and loving desire to move in harmony with these laws.
Science and Education [1868], ch. 4

15 The only medicine for suffering, crime, and all the other woes of mankind, is wisdom.
Ib.

16 If some great Power would agree to make me always think what is true and do what is right, on condition of being turned into a sort of clock and wound up every morning before I got out of bed, I should instantly close with the offer.
On Descartes' Discourse on Method [1870]. Method and Results

17 There is the greatest practical benefit in making a few failures early in life.
On Medical Education [1870]

18 That mysterious independent variable of political calculation, Public Opinion.
Universities, Actual and Ideal [1874]

[1] See Tennyson, 530:21.

1 Veracity is the heart of morality.

Ib.

2 Becky Sharp's acute remark that it is not difficult to be virtuous on ten thousand a year[1] has its application to nations; and it is futile to expect a hungry and squalid population to be anything but violent and gross.

Joseph Priestley [1874]

3 Logical consequences are the scarecrows of fools and the beacons of wise men.

Animal Automatism [1874]

4 Size is not grandeur, and territory does not make a nation.

On University Education [1876]

5 Perhaps the most valuable result of all education is the ability to make yourself do the thing you have to do, when it ought to be done, whether you like it or not;[2] it is the first lesson that ought to be learned; and however early a man's training begins, it is probably the last lesson that he learns thoroughly.

Technical Education [1877]

6 The great end of life is not knowledge but action. *Ib.*

7 If a little knowledge is dangerous, where is the man who has so much as to be out of danger?

On Elemental Instruction in Physiology [1877]

8 Irrationally held truths may be more harmful than reasoned errors.

The Coming of Age of The Origin of Species [1880]

9 It is the customary fate of new truths to begin as heresies and to end as superstitions.

Ib.

10 Social progress means a checking of the cosmic process at every step and the substitution for it of another, which may be called the ethical process.

Evolution and Ethics [1893]

11 I asserted—and I repeat—that a man has no reason to be ashamed of having an ape for his grandfather. If there were an ancestor whom I should feel shame in recalling it would rather be a man—a man of restless and versatile intellect—who, not content with an equivocal success in his own sphere of activity, plunges into scientific questions with which he has no real acquaintance, only to obscure them by an aimless rhetoric, and distract the attention of his hearers from the real point at issue by eloquent digressions and skilled appeals to religious prejudice.

Reply to Wilberforce's question.[3] *From* LEONARD HUXLEY, *Life and Letters of Thomas Henry Huxley [1900], vol. I*

[1] See Thackeray, 539:9.
[2] See William James, 648:9, and Maugham, 751:12.

George Edward Pickett
1825–1875

12 Up, men, and to your posts! Don't forget today that you are from Old Virginia.

Command at the beginning of his division's charge at Gettysburg [July 3, 1863]

Adelaide Anne Procter
1825–1864

13 Seated one day at the organ,
I was weary and ill at ease,
And my fingers wandered idly
Over the noisy keys.

A Lost Chord, st. 1

14 But I struck one chord of music
Like the sound of a great Amen.

Ib. st. 2

Bayard Taylor
1825–1878

15 From the desert I come to thee
On a stallion shod with fire,
And the winds are left behind
In the speed of my desire.

Bedouin Song, st. 1

16 Till the sun grows cold,
And the stars are old,
And the leaves of the Judgment Book unfold. *Ib. refrain*

17 They sang of love, and not of fame;
Forgot was Britain's glory;
Each heart recalled a different name,
But all sang "Annie Laurie."

The Song of the Camp, st. 5

William Whiting
1825–1878

18 Eternal Father, strong to save,
Whose arm doth bind the restless wave,
Who bidd'st the mighty ocean deep

[3] If anyone were to be willing to trace his descent through an ape as his *grandfather*, would he be willing to trace his descent similarly on the side of his *grandmother?*—BISHOP SAMUEL WILBERFORCE, *at the British Association for the Advancement of Science* [1860]

Its own appointed limits keep,
O, hear us when we cry to Thee
For those in peril on the sea!

The Hymn of the U.S. Navy [1860]. Eternal Father, Strong to Save, st. 1

Charles Hamilton Aïdé
1826–1906

1 I sit beside my lonely fire
And pray for wisdom yet:
For calmness to remember
Or courage to forget.

Remember or Forget

Grand Duke Friedrich von Baden
1826–1907

2 Unity makes strength, and, since we must be strong, we must also be one.

On German unity under Prussian hegemony, Versailles [January 18, 1871]

Walter Bagehot
1826–1877

3 One of the greatest pains to human nature is the pain of a new idea.

Physics and Politics [1869], ch. 5

4 An inability to stay quiet . . . is one of the most conspicuous failings of mankind.[1]

Ib.

5 The most melancholy of human reflections, perhaps, is that on the whole it is a question whether the benevolence of mankind does most good or harm. *Ib.*

6 To a great experience one thing is essential —an experiencing nature.

Literary Studies [1879]. Shakespeare

7 The reason why so few good books are written is, that so few people that can write know anything. In general an author has always lived in a room, has read books, has cultivated science, is acquainted with the style and sentiments of the best authors, but he is out of the way of employing his own eyes and ears. He has nothing to hear and nothing to see. His life is a vacuum. *Ib.*

8 A highly developed moral nature joined to an undeveloped intellectual nature, an undeveloped artistic nature, and a very limited religious nature, is of necessity repulsive. It represents a bit of human nature—a good bit, of course, but a bit only—in disproportionate, unnatural and revolting prominence.

Ib. Wordsworth, Tennyson and Browning

9 A constitutional statesman is in general a man of common opinions and uncommon abilities.

Biographical Studies [1907]. Sir Robert Peel

10 You may talk of the tyranny of Nero and Tiberius; but the real tyranny is the tyranny of your next-door neighbor. . . . Public opinion is a permeating influence, and it exacts obedience to itself; it requires us to think other men's thoughts, to speak other men's words, to follow other men's habits.

Ib.

11 It is good to be without vices, but it is not good to be without temptations.

Ib. Sir George Cornewall Lewis

12 [Of Guizot] A Puritan born in France by mistake. *Ib. Guizot*

Dinah Maria Mulock Craik
1826–1887

13 Douglas, Douglas, tender and true!

Douglas, Tender and True,[2] *refrain*

14 Oh, my son's my son till he gets him a wife,
But my daughter's my daughter all her life.

Young and Old

John Ellerton
1826–1893

15 Now the laborer's task is o'er;
Now the battle day is past;
Now upon the farther shore
Lands the voyager at last.

Hymn [1870], st. 1

16 Father, in thy gracious keeping
Leave we now thy servant sleeping.

Ib. refrain

17 The day thou gavest, Lord, is ended,
The darkness falls at thy behest;
To thee our morning hymns ascended,
Thy praise shall sanctify our rest.

Hymn [1870], st. 1

18 So be it, Lord; thy throne shall never,
Like earth's proud empires, pass away:
Thy kingdom stands, and grows forever,
Till all thy creatures own thy sway.

Ib. st. 5

[1] See Pascal, 299:20; quoted by Bagehot in the same chapter.

[2] O Douglas, O Douglas! / Tendir and trewe.—Sir Richard Holland, *The Buke of the Howlat* [c.1450], *st. 31*

Stephen Collins Foster
1826–1864

1 O, Susanna! O, don't you cry for me,
I've come from Alabama, with my banjo on my knee.
O, Susanna[1] *[1848], chorus*

2 Gwine to run all night!
Gwine to run all day!
I'll bet my money on de bobtail nag—
Somebody bet on de bay.
Camptown Races [1850], chorus

3 Way down upon the Swanee River,
Far, far away,
There's where my heart is turning ever;
There's where the old folks stay.
The Old Folks at Home [1851], st. 1

4 All the world is sad and dreary
Everywhere I roam,
Oh! darkies, how my heart grows weary,
Far from the old folks at home.
Ib. chorus

5 Weep no more, my lady,
Oh! weep no more today!
We will sing one song for the old Kentucky home,
For the old Kentucky home far away.
My Old Kentucky Home [1853], chorus

6 I dream of Jeanie with the light brown hair,
Floating, like a vapor, on the soft summer air.
Jeanie with the Light Brown Hair [1854], st. 1

7 I'm coming, I'm coming, for my head is bending low;
I hear those gentle voices calling, "Old Black Joe."
Old Black Joe [1860], st. 3

8 Beautiful dreamer, wake unto me,
Starlight and dewdrop are waiting for thee.
Beautiful Dreamer [1864], st. 1

G. W. Hunt
c. 1829–1904

9 We don't want to fight, but, by jingo, if we do,
We've got the ships, we've got the men, we've got the money, too.
Song [1878][2]

[1]Sung for the first time by Nelson Kneass in Andrews' Eagle Ice Cream Saloon, Pittsburgh, Pennsylvania [September 11, 1847]. It shortly became a worldwide hit.

[2]Sung by Gilbert Hastings Macdermott (Farrell) [1845–1901], "the Great Macdermott." The song gave the terms "jingo" and "jingoism" to the political vocabulary, though the phrase "by jingo" had been used earlier by Goldsmith and Thomas Hood.

George Brinton McClellan
1826–1885

10 All quiet along the Potomac.[3]
Frequent report from his Union headquarters [1861]

Edward Stuyvesant Bragg
1827–1912

11 They love him most for the enemies he has made.[4]
Speech seconding the presidential nomination of Grover Cleveland [July 9, 1884]

Franklin Jackson Dickman
1827–1908

12 Glittering generalities.
Letter reviewing a speech by RUFUS CHOATE, *Providence Journal [December 14, 1849]*[5]

Charles Eliot Norton
1827–1908

13 A knowledge of Greek thought and life, and of the arts in which the Greeks expressed their thought and sentiment, is essential to high culture. A man may know everything else, but without this knowledge he remains ignorant of the best intellectual and moral achievements of his own race.
Letter to F. A. Tupper [1885]

14 Whatever your occupation may be and however crowded your hours with affairs, do not fail to secure at least a few minutes every day for refreshment of your inner life with a bit of poetry.[6]
Used by a Boston newspaper as a heading for a column of reprinted poems

15 The voice of protest, of warning, of appeal is never more needed than when the clamor of fife and drum, echoed by the press and too often by the pulpit, is bidding all men fall in and keep step and obey in silence the tyran-

[3]All quiet along the Potomac tonight, / No sound save the rush of the river, / While soft falls the dew on the face of the dead— / The picket's off duty forever.—ETHEL LYNN BEERS [1827–1879], *The Picket Guard* [1861], *st. 6*

[4]An adaptation of Governor Bragg's expression became a Cleveland campaign slogan: We love him for the enemies he has made.

[5]See Choate, 485:2.

[6]See Goethe, 395:5.

nous word of command. Then, more than ever, it is the duty of the good citizen not to be silent. *True Patriotism [1898]*

1 The old America, the America of our hopes and our dreams, has come to an end, and a new America is entering on the false course which has been tried so often and which has often led to calamity. This war will in the long run result in far more evil to the United States than to Spain. We shall nominally win, but at the cost of what infinite loss!

Letter to Edward Lee-Childe [1898]

Lew [Lewis] Wallace
1827–1905

2 A man is never so on trial as in the moment of excessive good fortune.

Ben Hur: A Tale of the Christ [1880], bk. V, ch. 7

3 Would you hurt a man keenest, strike at his self-love. *Ib. VI, 2*

Anna Bartlett Warner
1827–1915

4 Jesus loves me—this I know,
For the Bible tells me so.

The Love of Jesus [1858]

Septimus Winner [Alice Hawthorne]
1827–1902

5 Listen to the mockingbird, listen to the mockingbird,
Still singing where the weeping willows wave.

Listen to the Mockingbird [1855]

Henrik Ibsen
1828–1906

6 All or nothing. *Brand [1866]*

7 Look into any man's heart you please, and you will always find, in every one, at least one black spot which he has to keep concealed.

Pillars of Society [1877], act III

8 The spirit of truth and the spirit of freedom—they are the pillars of society.

Ib. IV

9 There can be no freedom or beauty about a home life that depends on borrowing and debt. *A Doll's House [1879],*[1] *act I*

[1]See Dickens, 549:33.

10 Our house has never been anything but a playroom. I have been your doll wife, just as at home I was Daddy's doll child. And the children in turn have been my dolls. I thought it was fun when you came and played with me, just as they thought it was fun when I went and played with them. That's been our marriage, Torvald.

Ib. act III

11 If I'm ever to reach any understanding of myself and the things around me, I must learn to stand alone. That's why I can't stay here with you any longer. *Ib.*

12 I have another duty equally sacred . . . My duty to myself. *Ib.*

13 *Helmer:* First and foremost, you are a wife and mother.

Nora: That I don't believe any more. I believe that first and foremost I am an individual, just as much as you are. *Ib.*

14 To crave for happiness in this world is simply to be possessed by a spirit of revolt. What right have we to happiness?

Ghosts [1881], act I

15 I am half inclined to think we are all ghosts, Mr. Manders. It is not only what we have inherited from our fathers that exists again in us, but all sorts of old dead ideas and all kinds of old dead beliefs and things of that kind. They are not actually alive in us; but there they are dormant, all the same, and we can never be rid of them. Whenever I take up a newspaper and read it, I fancy I see ghosts creeping between the lines. There must be ghosts all over the world. They must be as countless as grains of the sands, it seems to me. And we are so miserably afraid of the light, all of us. *Ib. II*

16 Mother, give me the sun. *Ib. III*

17 I hold that man is in the right who is most closely in league with the future.

Letter to Georg Brandes [January 3, 1882]

18 A community is like a ship; everyone ought to be prepared to take the helm.

An Enemy of the People [1882], act I

19 The minority is always right. *Ib. IV*

20 You should never wear your best trousers when you go out to fight for freedom and truth. *Ib. V*

21 The strongest man in the world is he who stands most alone.[2] *Ib.*

[2]See Montaigne, 164:18.

1 Always do that, wild ducks do. Go plunging right to the bottom . . . as deep as they can get . . . hold on with their beaks to the weeds and stuff—and all the other mess you find down there. Then they never come up again. *The Wild Duck [1884], act II*

2 Take the life-lie away from the average man and straightaway you take away his happiness. *Ib. V*

3 Our common lust for life.
Hedda Gabler [1890], act II

4 Oh courage . . . oh yes! If only one had that . . . Then life might be livable, in spite of everything. *Ib.*

5 Back he'll come . . . With vine leaves in his hair. Flushed and confident. *Ib.*

6 Everything I touch seems destined to turn into something mean and farcical.
Ib. IV

7 The younger generation will come knocking at my door.
The Master Builder [1892], act I

George Meredith
1828–1909

8 I expect that Woman will be the last thing civilized by Man.
The Ordeal of Richard Feverel [1859], ch. 1

9 Who rises from prayer a better man, his prayer is answered. *Ib. 12*

10 The sun is coming down to earth, and the fields and the waters shout to him golden shouts. *Ib. 19*

11 Kissing don't last; cookery do!
Ib. 28

12 Speech is the small change of Silence.
Ib. 34

13 See ye not, courtesy
Is the true alchemy,
Turning to gold all it touches and tries?
The Song of Courtesy [1859], IV

14 Two of a trade, lass, never agree.[1]
Juggling Jerry [1859], IX

15 Not till the fire is dying in the grate,
Look we for any kinship with the stars.
Oh, wisdom never comes when it is gold,
And the great price we pay for it full worth;
We have it only when we are half earth.
Modern Love [1862], 4

[1]See Hesiod, 61:13, and Gay, 331:18.

16 And if I drink oblivion of a day,
So shorten I the stature of my soul.
Ib. 12

17 What are we first? First, animals; and next
Intelligences at a leap; on whom
Pale lies the distant shadow of the tomb.
Ib. 30

18 In tragic life, God wot,
No villain need be! Passions spin the plot:
We are betrayed by what is false within.
Ib. 43

19 More brain, O Lord, more brain! Or we shall mar
Utterly this fair garden we might win.
Ib. 48

20 Ah, what a dusty answer gets the soul
When hot for certainties in this our life!
Ib. 50

21 Into the breast that gives the rose
Shall I with shuddering fall!
The Spirit of Earth in Autumn [1862] st. 1

22 [Comedy] it is who proposes the correcting of pretentiousness, of inflation, of dullness, and of the vestiges of rawness and grossness yet to be found among us. She is the ultimate civilizer, the polisher.
The Egoist [1879]. Prelude

23 Cynicism is intellectual dandyism.
Ib. ch. 7

24 In . . . the book of Egoism, it is written, possession without obligation to the object possessed approaches felicity. *Ib. 14*

25 For singing till his heaven fills,
'Tis love of earth that he instills,
And ever winging up and up,
Our valley is his golden cup,
And he the wine which over flows
To lift us with him as he goes.
The Lark Ascending [1881], l. 65

26 The song seraphically free
Of taint of personality. *Ib. l. 95*

27 On a starred night Prince Lucifer uprose.
Tired of his dark dominion swung the fiend.
Lucifer in Starlight [1883]

28 Around the ancient track marched, rank on rank,
The army of unalterable law.[2] *Ib.*

29 Enter these enchanted woods,
You who dare.
The Woods of Westermain [1883], st. 1

[2]See T. S. Eliot, 804:7.

1 She whom I love is hard to catch and conquer,
Hard, but O the glory of the winning were she won!
Love in the Valley [1883], st. 2

2 Darker grows the valley, more and more forgetting:
So were it with me if forgetting could be willed.
Tell the grassy hollow that holds the bubbling well-spring,
Tell it to forget the source that keeps it filled.
Ib. st. 5

3 Civil limitation daunts
His utterance never; the nymphs blush, not he.
An Orson of the Muse (Walt Whitman) [1883]

4 A witty woman is a treasure; a witty beauty is a power.
Diana of the Crossways [1885], ch. 1

5 What a woman thinks of women is the test of her nature. *Ib.*

6 The well of true wit is truth itself. *Ib.*

7 Ireland gives England her soldiers, her generals too. *Ib. 2*

8 How divine is utterance! . . . As we to the brutes, poets are to us. *Ib. 16*

9 With patient inattention hear him prate.
Bellerophon [1887], st. 4

10 Full lasting is the song, though he,
The singer, passes.
The Thrush in February [1888], st. 17

11 Behold the life at ease; it drifts,
The sharpened life commands its course.
Hard Weather [1888], l. 71

12 Cannon his name,
Cannon his voice, he came.
Napoléon [1898], I

Dante Gabriel Rossetti

1828–1882

13 The blessed damozel leaned out
From the gold bar of Heaven;
Her eyes were deeper than the depth
Of waters stilled at even;
She had three lilies in her hand,
And the stars in her hair were seven.
The Blessed Damozel [1850], st. 1

14 And the souls mounting up to God
Went by her like thin flames. *Ib. st. 7*

15 One thing then learned remains to me—
The woodspurge has a cup of three.
The Woodspurge [1870], st. 4

16 Tell me now in what hidden way is
Lady Flora the lovely Roman?
Where's Hipparchia, and where is Thaïs,
Neither of them the fairer woman.
Where is Echo, beheld of no man
Only heard on river and mere—
She whose beauty was more than human? . . .
But where are the snows of yesteryear?
The Ballad of Dead Ladies (After François Villon) [1870], st. 1

17 A sonnet is a moment's monument—
Memorial from the soul's eternity
To one dead deathless hour.
Sonnets from the House of Life [1870–1881].[1] *Proem*

18 Beauty like hers is genius.
Ib. 18, Genius in Beauty

19 And though thy soul sail leagues and leagues beyond—
Still, leagues beyond those leagues, there is more sea. *Ib. 73, The Choice—III*

20 My name is Might-have-been;
I am also called No-more, Too-late, Farewell.
Ib. no. 97, A Superscription

21 When vain desire at last, and vain regret
Go hand in hand to death, and all is vain,
What shall assuage the unforgotten pain
And teach the unforgetful to forget?
Ib. 101, The One Hope

22 The Stealthy School of Criticism.[2]
Letter to the Athenaeum [1871]

23 I have been here before,
But when or how I cannot tell;
I know the grass beyond the door,
The sweet keen smell,
The sighing sound, the lights around the shore. *Sudden Light [1881], st. 1*

Leo Nikolaevich Tolstoi[3]

1828–1910

24 The hero of my tale, whom I love with all the power of my soul, whom I have tried to

[1] See Buchanan, 643:10.

[2] Reply to Buchanan's attack.

[3] Of course you have read Tolstoi's *War and Peace* and *Anna Karenina*. I never had that exquisite felicity before the summer, and now I feel as if I knew the *perfection* in the representation of human life. Life indeed seems less real than his tale of it. Such infallible veracity! The impression haunts me as nothing literary ever haunted me

portray in all his beauty, who has been, is, and will be beautiful, is Truth.
Sevastopol in May 1855 [1855]

1 "What's this? am I falling? my legs are giving way under me," he thought, and fell on his back. He opened his eyes, hoping to see how the struggle of the French soldiers with the artilleryman was ending, and eager to know whether the red-haired artilleryman was killed or not, whether the cannons had been taken or saved. But he saw nothing of all that. Above him there was nothing but the sky—the lofty sky, not clear, but still immeasurably lofty, with gray clouds creeping quietly over it.
War and Peace [1865–1869],[1] *bk. III, ch. 16*

2 Three days afterwards the little princess was buried, and Prince Andrey went to the steps of the tomb to take his last farewell of her. Even in the coffin the face was the same, though the eyes were closed. "Ah, what have you done to me?" it still seemed to say.
Ib. IV, 9

3 In historical events great men—so called—are but the labels that serve to give a name to an event, and like labels, they have the least possible connection with the event itself. Every action of theirs, that seems to them an act of their own free will, is in an historical sense not free at all, but in bondage to the whole course of previous history, and predestined from all eternity.
Ib. IX, 1

4 The strongest of all warriors are these two—Time and Patience. *Ib. X, 16*

5 He [Platon Karataev] did not understand, and could not grasp the significance of words taken apart from the sentence. Every word and every action of his was the expression of a force uncomprehended by him, which was his life. *Ib. XII, 13*

6 For us, with the rule of right and wrong given us by Christ, there is nothing for which we have no standard. And there is no greatness where there is not simplicity, goodness, and truth. *Ib. XIV, 18*

before.—William James, *letter to Henry James* [1872], in *Letters of William James, vol. II* [1896], *p. 48*

Tolstoi stands unshaken; his authority is tremendous, and while he lives, bad taste in literature, all sorts of vulgarity, insolence and sentimentality, all kinds of shoddy irascible vanities will remain deep in the shadow.
—Chekhov, *Letter to M. O. Menshikov* [January 28, 1900]

[1]Translated by Constance Garnett.

7 Pure and complete sorrow is as impossible as pure and complete joy. *Ib. XV, 1*

8 The subject of history is the life of peoples and of humanity. To catch and pin down in words—that is, to describe directly the life, not only of humanity, but even of a single people, appears to be impossible.[2]
Ib. epilogue, pt. II, ch. 1

9 Happy families are all alike; every unhappy family is unhappy in its own way.
Anna Karenina [1875–1877], pt. I, ch. 1

10 Ivan Ilych's life had been most simple and most ordinary and therefore most terrible.
The Death of Ivan Ilych [1886][3]

11 Ivan Ilych saw that he was dying, and he was in continuous despair.

In the depth of his heart he knew he was dying, but not only was he not accustomed to the thought, he simply did not and could not grasp it.

The syllogism he had learned from Kiezewetter's Logic: "Caius is a man, men are mortal, therefore Caius is mortal," had always seemed to him correct as applied to Caius, but certainly not as applied to himself. That Caius—man in the abstract—was mortal, was perfectly correct, but he was not Caius, not an abstract man, but a creature quite, quite separate from all others. *Ib.*

12 Six feet of land was all that he needed.
How Much Land Does a Man Need? [1886]

13 The more is given the less the people will work for themselves, and the less they work the more their poverty will increase.[4]
Help for the Starving, pt. III [January 1892]

14 Art is a human activity having for its purpose the transmission to others of the highest and best feelings to which men have risen.
What Is Art? [1898], ch. 8

Roscoe Conkling
1829–1888

15 He [President Grant] will hew to the line of right, let the chips fall where they may.[5]
Speech [June 5, 1880]

[2]See Francis Parkman, 592:7.

[3]Translated by Aylmer Maude.

[4]If you stop supporting that crowd, it will support itself.
—Seneca [4 b.c.–a.d. 65], *Epistle 20, 7*

[5]See Anonymous, 917:2.

Geronimo[1]

c. 1829–1909

1 It [Arizona] is my land, my home, my father's land, to which I now ask to be allowed to return. I want to spend my last days there, and be buried among those mountains. If this could be I might die in peace, feeling that my people, placed in their native homes, would increase in numbers, rather than diminish as at present, and that our name would not become extinct.

To President Grant from the reservation at Fort Sill, Oklahoma, after surrender [1877]

Carl Schurz

1829–1906

2 Ideals are like stars; you will not succeed in touching them with your hands. But like the seafaring man on the desert of waters, you choose them as your guides, and following them you will reach your destiny.[2]

Address, Faneuil Hall, Boston [April 18, 1859]

3 I will make a prophecy that may now sound peculiar. In fifty years Lincoln's name will be inscribed close to Washington's on this Republic's roll of honor.

Letter to Theodore Petrasch [October 12, 1864]

4 Our country, right or wrong.[3] When right, to be kept right; when wrong, to be put right.

Address, Anti-Imperialistic Conference, Chicago [October 17, 1899]

Ivan Mikhailovich Sechenov

1829–1905

5 All psychical acts without exception, if they are not complicated by elements of emotion . . . develop by way of reflex. Hence, all conscious movements resulting from these acts and usually described as voluntary, are reflex movements in the strict sense of the term.

Reflexes of the Brain [1863],[4] ch. 2

6 The initial cause of any action always lies in external sensory stimulation, because without this thought is inconceivable.

Ib.

[1]Goyathlay, Apache chief.

[2]See Emerson, 499:9.

[3]See Charles Churchill, 375:13; John Quincy Adams, 417:17; and Decatur, 445:19.

[4]Translated by S. Belsky.

Charles Dudley Warner[5]

1829–1900

7 To own a bit of ground, to scratch it with a hoe, to plant seeds, and watch the renewal of life—this is the commonest delight of the race, the most satisfactory thing a man can do.

My Summer in a Garden [1870]. Preliminary

8 No man but feels more of a man in the world if he have a bit of ground that he can call his own. However small it is on the surface, it is four thousand miles deep; and that is a very handsome property. *Ib.*

9 What a man needs in gardening is a cast-iron back, with a hinge in it.

Ib. Third Week

10 The toad, without which no garden would be complete. *Ib. Thirteenth Week*

11 Politics makes strange bedfellows.

Ib. Fifteenth Week

12 What small potatoes we all are, compared with what we might be! *Ib.*

13 Public opinion is stronger than the legislature, and nearly as strong as the Ten Commandments. *Ib. Sixteenth Week*

14 The thing generally raised on city land is taxes. *Ib.*

15 Everybody talks about the weather, but nobody does anything about it.[6]

Editorial, Hartford Courant [August 24, 1897]

Charlotte Alington Barnard [Claribel]

1830–1869

16 I cannot sing the old songs I sang long years ago. *I Cannot Sing the Old Songs*[7]

Thomas Edward Brown

1830–1897

17 A Garden is a lovesome thing, God wot!

My Garden

[5]Warner collaborated with Mark Twain on *The Gilded Age*. See 622:8.

[6]The phrase is commonly attributed to Mark Twain, but the *Hartford Courant* has the exact statement in the aforementioned editorial, which is of course unsigned. Warner was associate editor of the paper [1867–1900]. See Mark Twain, 622:18.

[7]I cannot sing the old songs now! / It is not that I deem them low: / 'Tis that I can't remember how / They go. — C. S. Calverley [1831–1884], *Changed*

1 Not God! in Gardens! when the eve is cool?
Nay, but I have a sign:
'Tis very sure God walks in mine. *Ib.*

Porfirio Díaz
1830–1915

2 Poor Mexico, so far from God and so close to the United States. *Attributed*

Emily Dickinson[1]
1830–1886

3 I never lost as much but twice,
And that was in the sod.
Twice have I stood a beggar
Before the door of God!

Angels—twice descending
Reimbursed my store—
Burglar! Banker!—Father!
I am poor once more! *No. 49 [c. 1858]*

4 Surgeons must be very careful
When they take the knife!
Underneath their fine incisions
Stirs the Culprit—*Life!*
No. 108 [c. 1859]

5 Our share of night to bear—
Our share of morning—
Our blank in bliss to fill
Our blank in scorning—

Here a star, and there a star,
Some lose their way!
Here a mist, and there a mist,
Afterwards—Day! *No. 113 [c. 1859]*

6 For each ecstatic instant
We must an anguish pay
In keen and quivering ratio
To the ecstasy. *No. 125 [c. 1859], st. 1*

7 To fight aloud, is very brave—
But *gallanter*, I know
Who charge within the bosom
The Cavalry of Woe—
No. 126 [c. 1859], st. 1

8 Who counts the wampum of the night
To see that none is due?
No. 128 [c. 1859], st. 3

9 These are the days when Birds come back—
A very few—a Bird or two—
To take a backward look.

These are the days when skies resume
The old—old sophistries of June—
A blue and gold mistake.
No. 130 [c. 1859], st. 1, 2

10 Oh Sacrament of summer days,
Oh Last Communion in the Haze—
Permit a child to join.

Thy sacred emblems to partake—
Thy consecrated bread to take
And thine immortal wine! *Ib. st. 5, 6*

11 Just lost when I was saved!
Just felt the world go by!
Just girt me for the onset with Eternity,
When breath blew back,
And on the other side
I heard recede the disappointed tide!
No. 160 [c. 1860], st. 1

12 The thought beneath so slight a film—
Is more distinctly seen—
As laces just reveal the surge—
Or Mists—the Apennine—
No. 210 [c. 1860]

13 I taste a liquor never brewed,
From Tankards scooped in Pearl—
No. 214 [c. 1860], st. 1

14 Inebriate of Air—am I—
And Debauchee of Dew—
Reeling—through endless summer days—
From inns of Molten Blue— *Ib. st. 2*

15 Till Seraphs swing their snowy Hats—
And Saints—to windows run—
To see the little Tippler
Leaning against the—Sun— *Ib. st. 4*

16 Blazing in Gold and quenching in Purple
Leaping like Leopards to the Sky . . .
And the Juggler of Day is gone.
No. 228 [c. 1861]

17 "Hope" is the thing with feathers—
That perches in the soul—
And sings the tune without the words—
And never stops—at all—
No. 254 [c. 1861], st. 1

18 There's a certain Slant of light,
Winter Afternoons—
That oppresses, like the Heft
Of Cathedral Tunes—
No. 258 [c. 1861], st. 1

19 I'm Nobody! Who are you?
Are you—Nobody—too?
Then there's a pair of us!
Don't tell! they'd advertise—you know!

How dreary—to be—Somebody!
How public—like a Frog—
To tell one's name—the livelong June—
To an admiring Bog! *No. 288 [c. 1861]*

[1] *The Complete Poems of Emily Dickinson* [1960], edited by Thomas H. Johnson. Dates are of composition, not publication.

1 I tasted—careless—then—
I did not know the Wine
Came once a World—Did you?
Oh, had you told me so—
This Thirst would blister—easier—now—
No. 296 [c. 1861], st. 3

2 The Soul selects her own Society—
Then—shuts the Door—
To her divine Majority—
Present no more—
No. 303 [c. 1862], st. 1

3 I'll tell you how the Sun rose—
A Ribbon at a time— *No. 318 [1862]*

4 Some keep the Sabbath going to Church—
I keep it, staying at Home—
With a bobolink for a Chorister—
And an Orchard, for a Dome—
No. 324 [1862], st. 1

5 So instead of getting to Heaven, at last—
I'm going, all along. *Ib. st. 3*

6 After great pain, a formal feeling comes.
No. 341 [c. 1862], st. 1

7 Of Course—I prayed—
And did God Care?
He cared as much as on the Air
A Bird—had stamped her foot—
And cried "Give Me"—
No. 376 [c. 1862]

8 No Rack can torture me—
My Soul—at Liberty—
Behind this mortal Bone
There knits a bolder One—
No. 384 [c. 1862], st. 1

9 Except Thyself may be
Thine Enemy—
Captivity is Consciousness—
So's Liberty. *Ib. st. 4*

10 Good Morning—Midnight—
I'm coming Home—
Day—got tired of Me—
How could I—of Him?
No. 425 [c. 1862], st. 1

11 Much Madness is divinest Sense—
To a discerning Eye—
Much Sense—the starkest Madness—
'Tis the Majority
In this, as All, prevail—
Assent—and you are sane—
Demur—you're straightway dangerous—
And handled with a Chain.
No. 435 [c. 1862]

12 This is my letter to the World
That never wrote to Me—
The simple News that Nature told—
With tender Majesty.
No. 441 [c. 1862], st. 1

13 I died for Beauty—but was scarce
Adjusted in the Tomb
When One who died for Truth, was lain
In an adjoining Room—
No. 449 [c. 1862], st. 1

14 And so, as Kinsmen, met a Night—
We talked between the Rooms—
Until the Moss had reached our lips—
And covered up—our names—
Ib. st. 3

15 It was not Death, for I stood up,
And all the Dead, lie down—
No. 510 [c. 1862], st. 1

16 It was not Frost, for on my Flesh
I felt Siroccos—crawl— *Ib. st. 2*

17 I reckon—when I count at all—
First—Poets—Then the Sun—
Then Summer—Then the Heaven of God—
And then—the List is done—

But, looking back—the First so seems
To Comprehend the Whole—
The Others look a needless Show—
So I write—Poets—All—
No. 569 [c. 1862], st. 1, 2

18 I like to see it lap the Miles—
And lick the Valleys up—
No. 585 [c. 1862], st. 1

19 And neigh like Boanerges—
Then punctual as a Star
Stop—docile and omnipotent
At its own stable door— *Ib. st. 4*

20 I asked no other thing—
No other—was denied—
I offered Being—for it—
The Mighty Merchant sneered—

Brazil? He twirled a Button—
Without a glance my way—
"But—Madam—is there nothing else—
That We can show—Today?"
No. 621 [c. 1862]

21 The Brain—is wider than the Sky—
For—put them side by side—
The one the other will contain
With ease—and You—beside.
No. 632 [1862], st. 1

22 I cannot live with You—
It would be Life—
And Life is over there—
Behind the Shelf.
No. 640 [c. 1862], st. 1

1 And that White Sustenance—
Despair— *Ib. st. 12*

2 Pain—has an Element of Blank—
It cannot recollect
When it begun—or if there were
A time when it was not—
No. 650 [c. 1862], st. 1

3 The Soul unto itself
Is an imperial friend—
Or the most agonizing Spy—
An Enemy—could send—
No. 683 [c. 1862], st. 1

4 Because I could not stop for Death,
He kindly stopped for me—
The Carriage held but just Ourselves
And Immortality.
No. 712 [c. 1863], st. 1

5 Alter! When the Hills do—
Falter! When the Sun
Question if His Glory
Be the Perfect One—

Surfeit! When the Daffodil
Doth of the Dew—
Even as Herself—Sir—
I will—of You— *No. 729 [c. 1863]*

6 God gave a Loaf to every Bird—
But just a Crumb—to Me—
No. 791 [c. 1863], st. 1

7 This quiet Dust was Gentlemen and Ladies
And Lads and Girls—[1]
Was laughter and ability and Sighing,
And Frocks and Curls.
No. 813 [c. 1864], st. 1

8 Adventure most unto itself
The Soul condemned to be—
Attended by a single Hound
Its own identity.
No. 822 [c. 1864], st. 4

9 Dying! To be afraid of thee
One must to thine Artillery
Have left exposed a Friend—
Than thine old Arrow is a Shot
Delivered straighter to the Heart
The leaving Love behind.
No. 831 [c. 1864], st. 1

10 The Poets light but Lamps—
Themselves—go out—
The Wicks they stimulate—
If vital Light

Inhere as do the Suns—
Each Age a Lens
Disseminating their
Circumference— *No. 883 [c. 1864]*

[1] See Shakespeare, 243:27.

11 Love—is anterior to Life—
Posterior—to Death—
Initial of Creation, and
The Exponent of Earth.
No. 917 [c. 1864]

12 If I can stop one Heart from breaking
I shall not live in vain
If I can ease one Life the Aching
Or cool one Pain

Or help one fainting Robin
Unto his Nest again
I shall not live in Vain.
No. 919 [c. 1864]

13 A narrow Fellow in the Grass
Occasionally rides—
No. 986 [c. 1865], st. 1

14 But never met this Fellow
Attended or alone
Without a tighter breathing
And Zero at the Bone—
Ib. last stanza

15 The Dying, is a trifle, past
But living, this include
The dying multifold—without
The Respite to be dead.
No. 1013 [c. 1865]

16 'Twas my one Glory—
Let it be
Remembered
I was owned of Thee—
No. 1028 [c. 1865]

17 I never saw a Moor—
I never saw the Sea—
Yet know I how the Heather looks
And what a Billow be.

I never spoke with God
Nor visited in Heaven—
Yet certain am I of the spot
As if the Checks were given—
No. 1052 [c. 1865]

18 Experiment to me
Is every one I meet
If it contain a Kernel?
The Figure of a Nut

Presents upon a Tree
Equally plausibly,
But Meat within, is requisite
To Squirrels, and to Me.
No. 1073 [c. 1865]

19 Nature, like Us is sometimes caught
Without her Diadem.
No. 1075 [c. 1866], st. 2

1 The Sweeping up the Heart,
And putting Love away
We shall not want to use again
Until Eternity.
No. 1078 [c. 1866], st. 2

2 We never know how high we are
Till we are called to rise
And then, if we are true to plan
Our statures touch the skies.[1]
No. 1176 [c. 1870], st. 1

3 A word is dead
When it is said,
Some say.
I say it just
Begins to live
That day.
No. 1212 [c. 1872]

4 There is no Frigate like a Book
To take us Lands away
Nor any Coursers like a Page
Of prancing Poetry—
This Traverse may the poorest take
Without oppress of Toll—
How frugal is the Chariot
That bears the Human Soul!
No. 1263 [c. 1873]

5 I thought that nature was enough
Till Human nature came
But that the other did absorb
As Parallax a Flame—
No. 1286 [c. 1873], st. 1

6 Until the Desert knows
That Water grows
His Sands suffice
But let him once suspect
That Caspian Fact
Sahara dies.
No. 1291 [c. 1873], st. 1

7 Not with a Club, the Heart is broken
Nor with a Stone—
A Whip so small you could not see it
I've known
To lash the Magic Creature
Till it fell.
No. 1304 [c. 1874], st. 1

8 That short—potential stir
That each can make but once—
That Bustle so illustrious
'Tis almost Consequence—

Is the éclat of Death.
Oh, thou unknown Renown
That not a Beggar would accept
Had he the power to spurn—
No. 1307 [c. 1874]

9 A little Madness in the Spring
Is wholesome even for the King.
No. 1333 [c. 1875]

[1] See William James, 648:3.

10 Love's stricken "why"
Is all that love can speak—
Built of but just a syllable
The hugest hearts that break.
No. 1368 [c. 1876]

11 Bees are Black, with Gilt Surcingles—
Buccaneers of Buzz.
No. 1405 [c. 1877], st. 1

12 A Route of Evanescence
With a revolving Wheel—
A Resonance of Emerald—
A Rush of Cochineal—
And every Blossom on the Bush
Adjusts its tumbled Head—
The mail from Tunis, probably,
An easy Morning's ride.
No. 1463 [c. 1879]

13 The Pedigree of Honey
Does not concern the Bee—
A Clover, any time, to him,
Is Aristocracy.
No. 1627 [c. 1884], version II

14 A Drunkard cannot meet a Cork
Without a Revery—
And so encountering a Fly
This January Day
Jamaicas of Remembrance stir
That send me reeling in.
No. 1628 [c. 1884]

15 Beauty crowds me till I die
Beauty mercy have on me
But if I expire today
Let it be in sight of thee—
No. 1654 [n.d.]

16 Eden is that old-fashioned House
We dwell in every day
Without suspecting our abode
Until we drive away.
No. 1657 [n.d.], st. 1

17 I took one Draught of Life—
I'll tell you what I paid—
Precisely an existence—
The market price, they said.

They weighed me, Dust by Dust—
They balanced Film with Film,
Then handed me my Being's worth—
A single Dram of Heaven!
No. 1725 [n.d.]

18 My life closed twice before its close—
It yet remains to see
If Immortality unveil
A third event to me

So huge, so hopeless to conceive
As these that twice befell.

Parting is all we know of heaven,
And all we need of hell.
No. 1732 [n.d.]

1 That it will never come again
Is what makes life so sweet.
No. 1741 [n.d.], st. 1

2 The only secret people keep
Is Immortality. *No. 1748 [n.d.]*

3 To make a prairie it takes a clover and one bee,
One clover, and a bee,
And revery.
The revery alone will do,
If bees are few. *No. 1755 [n.d.]*

4 Elysium is as far as to
The very nearest Room
If in that Room a Friend await
Felicity or Doom—

What Fortitude the Soul contains,
That it can so endure
The accent of a coming Foot—
The opening of a Door—
No. 1760 [n.d.]

5 That Love is all there is,
Is all we know of Love;
It is enough, the freight should be
Proportioned to the groove.
No. 1765 [n.d.]

6 If I read a book and it makes my whole body so cold no fire can ever warm me, I know that is poetry. If I feel physically as if the top of my head were taken off, I know that is poetry. These are the only ways I know it. Is there any other way?[1]
From MARTHA GILBERT DICKINSON BIANCHI, *Life and Letters of Emily Dickinson [1924]*

7 Little Cousins—Called back. Emily.
Last message to cousins. From WILLIAM LUCE, *The Belle of Amherst [1976], preface*

8 *Phosphorescence.* Now, there's a word to lift your hat to. . . . To find that phosphorescence, that light within, that's the genius behind poetry. *Ib. act I*

Alexander Muir
1830–1906

9 And joined in love together,
The Thistle, Shamrock, Rose entwine
The Maple Leaf forever!
The Maple Leaf Forever [1867]

[1]See Housman, 692:14, and Graves, 833:6.

Christina Georgina Rossetti
1830–1894

10 Does the road wind uphill all the way?
Yes, to the very end.
Will the day's journey take the whole long day?
From morn to night, my friend.
Up-Hill [1861], st. 1

11 My heart is like a singing bird.
A Birthday [1861], st. 1

12 The birthday of my life
Is come, my love is come to me. *Ib. st. 2*

13 When I am dead, my dearest,
Sing no sad songs for me;
Plant thou no roses at my head,
Nor shady cypress tree.
Be the green grass above me
With showers and dewdrops wet;
And if thou wilt, remember
And if thou wilt, forget.
Song [1862], st. 1

14 Remember me when I am gone away,
Gone far away into the silent land.
Remember [1862], l. 1

15 Better by far you should forget and smile
Than that you should remember and be sad.[2] *Remember [1862], l. 13*

16 For there is no friend like a sister
In calm or stormy weather.
Goblin Market [1862], last lines

17 In the bleak midwinter
Frosty wind made moan,
Earth stood hard as iron,
Water like a stone;
Snow had fallen, snow on snow,
Snow on snow,
In the bleak midwinter,
Long ago. *Mid-Winter*

18 Oh roses for the flush of youth,
And laurel for the perfect prime;
But pluck an ivy branch for me
Grown old before my time. *Song [1862]*

19 Who has seen the wind?
Neither you nor I:
But when the trees bow down their heads,
The wind is passing by.
Who Has Seen the Wind? [1872], st. 2

20 Sleeping at last, the trouble and turmoil over,
Sleeping at last, the struggle and horror past,
Cold and white, out of sight of friend and of lover,
Sleeping at last.
Sleeping at Last [1893], st. 1

[2]See Landon, 492:9.

Robert Arthur Talbot Gascoyne-Cecil, Marquess of Salisbury
1830–1903

1 If you believe the doctors, nothing is wholesome; if you believe the theologians, nothing is innocent; if you believe the soldiers, nothing is safe.

Letter to Lord Lytton, Viceroy of India [June 15, 1877]

Alexander Smith
1830–1867

2 It is not of so much consequence what you say, as how you say it. Memorable sentences are memorable on account of some single irradiating word.

Dreamthorp [1863]. On the Writing of Essays

3 Death is the ugly fact which Nature has to hide, and she hides it well.

Ib. Of Death and the Fear of Dying

George Graham Vest
1830–1904

4 The one absolutely unselfish friend that man can have in this selfish world, the one that never deserts him, the one that never proves ungrateful or treacherous, is his dog. . . . When all other friends desert, he remains.[1] *Speech in the Senate [1884]*

Yoshida Shoin[2]
1830–1859

5 To consider oneself different from ordinary men is wrong, but it is right to hope that one will not remain like ordinary men.

Yoshida Shoin Zenshu, vol. II

6 The mind of the superior man is like Heaven. When it is resentful or angry, it thunders forth its indignation. But once having loosed its feelings, it is like a sunny day with a clear sky: within the heart there remains not the trace of a cloud. Such is the beauty of true manliness. *Ib. III*

7 Neither the lords nor the shogun can be depended upon [to save the country], and so our only hope lies in grass-roots heroes.

Ib. V

[1] A man's best friend is his dog. — *Saying*
See Byron, 456:10.

[2] From *Sources of Japanese Tradition* [1960], edited by WILLIAM THEODORE DE BARY.

James Abram Garfield
1831–1881

8 Fellow citizens! God reigns, and the Government at Washington still lives!

Speech on the assassination of Lincoln, New York [April 15, 1865]

9 For mere vengeance I would do nothing. This nation is too great to look for mere revenge. But for the security of the future I would do everything. *Ib.*

10 I am not willing that this discussion should close without mention of the value of a true teacher. Give me a log hut, with only a simple bench, Mark Hopkins[3] on one end and I on the other, and you may have all the buildings, apparatus and libraries without him.

Address to Williams College Alumni, New York [December 28, 1871][4]

Helen Hunt Jackson
1831–1885

11 O suns and skies and clouds of June,
And flowers of June together,
Ye cannot rival for one hour
October's bright blue weather.

October's Bright Blue Weather, st. 1

12 Oh, write of me, not "Died in bitter pains,"
But "Emigrated to another star!"

Emigravit

Edward Robert Bulwer-Lytton, Earl of Lytton [Owen Meredith]
1831–1891

13 We may live without poetry, music and art;
We may live without conscience, and live without heart;
We may live without friends; we may live without books;
But civilized man cannot live without cooks.

Lucile [1860], pt. I, canto 2, st. 19

14 Genius does what it must, and talent does what it can.

Last Words of a Sensitive Second-Rate Poet

[3] Mark Hopkins [1802–1887], president of Williams College [1836–1872] and president of the American Board of Commissioners for Foreign Missions [1857–1881].
For Education is Making Men; / So is it now, so was it when / Mark Hopkins sat on one end of a log / And James Garfield sat on the other. — ARTHUR GUITERMAN [1871–1943], *Education*

[4] In BURKE A. HINSDALE, *President Garfield and Education* [1882], p. 43.

James Clerk Maxwell
1831–1879

1 All the mathematical sciences are founded on relations between physical laws and laws of numbers, so that the aim of exact science is to reduce the problems of nature to the determination of quantities by operations with numbers.
On Faraday's Lines of Force [1856]

2 For the sake of persons of . . . different types, scientific truth should be presented in different forms, and should be regarded as equally scientific, whether it appears in the robust form and the vivid coloring of a physical illustration, or in the tenuity and paleness of a symbolic expression.
Address to the Mathematics and Physics Section, British Association for the Advancement of Science [1870]

3 When at last this little instrument appeared, consisting, as it does, of parts every one of which is familiar to us, and capable of being put together by an amateur, the disappointment arising from its humble appearance was only partially relieved on finding that it was really able to talk.
The Telephone [1878]

Philip Henry Sheridan
1831–1888

4 The only good Indians I ever saw were dead.[1]
Remark at Fort Cobb, Indian Territory [January 1869]

Sitting Bull[2]
c. 1831–1890

5 What treaty that the white man ever made with us have they kept? Not one. When I was a boy the Sioux owned the world; the sun rose and set on their land; they sent ten thousand men to battle. Where are the warriors today? Who slew them? Where are our lands? Who owns them? . . . . What law have I broken? Is it wrong for me to love my own? Is it wicked for me because my skin is red? Because I am a Sioux; because I was born where my father lived; because I would die for my people and my country?
Statement

[1] Edward Sylvester Ellis [1840–1916] reported that after Custer's fight with Black Kettle's band of Cheyenne Indians, the Comanche Chief Toch-a-way (Turtle Dove) was presented to General Sheridan. The Indian said: "Me Toch-a-way, me good Indian." The general's reply, as reported by Ellis, is given in the text; the phrase is more often heard in the version: The only good Indian is a dead Indian.

[2] Tatanka Yotanka, Sioux warrior.

Louisa May Alcott
1832–1888

6 Christmas won't be Christmas without any presents.
Little Women [1868], ch. 1

7 Resolved to take Fate by the throat and shake a living out of her.
From Ednah D. Cheney, *Louisa May Alcott, Her Life, Letters, and Journals [1889], ch. 5*

8 Above man's aims his nature rose.
The wisdom of a just content
Made one small spot a continent,
And tuned to poetry Life's prose.[3]
Ib. 7 [Thoreau's Flute,[4] st. 2]

9 My definition [of a philosopher] is of a man up in a balloon, with his family and friends holding the ropes which confine him to earth and trying to haul him down.
Ib. 10

Elizabeth Akers Allen
1832–1911

10 Backward, turn backward, O Time, in your flight,
Make me a child again just for tonight!
Rock Me to Sleep [1860], st. 1

Sir Edwin Arnold
1832–1904

11 Nor ever once ashamed
So we be named
Pressmen; Slaves of the Lamp; Servants of Light.
The Tenth Muse, st. 18

Wilhelm Busch
1832–1908

12 Becoming a father is easy enough,
But being one can be rough.[5]
Julchen [1877]

[3] The word "tuned" is frequently misprinted as "turned."

[4] In the *Atlantic Monthly* [September 1863].

[5] Vater werden ist nicht schwer, / Vater sein dagegen sehr.
Translated by Richard Hanser.

Lewis Carroll
[Charles Lutwidge Dodgson]
1832–1898

1 All in the golden afternoon
Full leisurely we glide,
For both our oars with little skill
By little arms are plied
While little hands make vain pretense
Our wanderings to guide.
Alice's Adventures in Wonderland [1865], introduction, st. 1

2 "What is the use of a book," thought Alice, "without pictures or conversations?" *Ib. ch. 1*

3 Do cats eat bats? . . . Do bats eat cats? *Ib.*

4 Curiouser and curiouser! *Ib. 2*

5 How doth the little crocodile
Improve his shining tail,
And pour the waters of the Nile
On every golden scale![1]

How cheerfully he seems to grin,
How neatly spreads his claws,
And welcomes little fishes in
With gently smiling jaws! *Ib.*

6 "I'll be judge, I'll be jury," said cunning old Fury; "I'll try the whole cause, and condemn you to death." *Ib. 3*

7 Oh my fur and whiskers! *Ib. 4*

8 "I can't explain *myself,* I'm afraid, sir," said Alice, "because I'm not myself, you see."
"I don't see," said the Caterpillar. *Ib. 5*

9 "You are old, Father William," the young man said,
"And your hair has become very white;
And yet you incessantly stand on your head—
Do you think, at your age, it is right?"[2]
Ib. [You are old, Father William, st. 1]

10 "In my youth," said his father, "I took to the law,
And argued each case with my wife;
And the muscular strength, which it gave to my jaw,
Has lasted the rest of my life."
Ib. [st. 6]

11 "I have answered three questions, and that is enough,"
Said his father. "Don't give yourself airs!
Do you think I can listen all day to such stuff?
Be off, or I'll kick you downstairs!"
Ib. [st. 8]

12 Those serpents! There's no pleasing them! *Ib.*

13 "If everybody minded their own business," said the Duchess in a hoarse growl, "the world would go round a deal faster than it does." *Ib.*

14 "Talking of axes," said the Duchess, "chop off her head!" *Ib.*

15 Speak roughly to your little boy,
And beat him when he sneezes:
He only does it to annoy,
Because he knows it teases. *Ib.*

16 "If it had grown up," she said to herself, "it would have made a dreadfully ugly child; but it makes rather a handsome pig, I think." *Ib.*

17 "All right," said the [Cheshire] Cat; and this time it vanished quite slowly, beginning with the end of the tail, and ending with the grin, which remained some time after the rest of it had gone. *Ib.*

18 "Then you should say what you mean," the March Hare went on.
"I do," Alice hastily replied; "at least—at least I mean what I say—that's the same thing, you know."
"Not the same thing a bit!" said the Hatter. "Why, you might just as well say that 'I see what I eat' is the same thing as 'I eat what I see'!" *Ib. 7*

19 "It was the *best* butter," the March Hare meekly replied. *Ib.*

20 Twinkle, twinkle, little bat!
How I wonder what you're at!
Up above the world you fly,
Like a teatray in the sky.[3] *Ib.*

21 "Take some more tea," the March Hare said to Alice, very earnestly.
"I've had nothing yet," Alice replied in an offended tone: "so I can't take more."
"You mean you can't take *less,*" said the Hatter: "it's very easy to take *more* than nothing." *Ib.*

22 They drew all manner of things—everything that begins with an M . . . such as mousetraps, and the moon, and memory, and muchness—you know you say things are "much of a muchness." *Ib.*

[1] See Isaac Watts, 328:5.
[2] See Southey, 439:15.
[3] See Ann and Jane Taylor, 449:13.

1 The Queen turned crimson with fury, and after glaring at her for a moment like a wild beast, began screaming, "Off with her head![1] Off with—" *Ib. 8*

2 "Tut, tut, child," said the Duchess. "Everything's got a moral if only you can find it." *Ib. 9*

3 Take care of the sense and the sounds will take care of themselves. *Ib.*

4 "We called him Tortoise because he taught us," said the Mock Turtle angrily. "Really you are very dull!" *Ib.*

5 "Reeling and Writhing, of course, to begin with," the Mock Turtle replied, "and the different branches of Arithmetic—Ambition, Distraction, Uglification, and Derision." *Ib.*

6 Advance twice, set to partners . . . change lobsters, and retire in same order.[2] *Ib. 10*

7 "Will you walk a little faster?" said a whiting to a snail,
"There's a porpoise close behind us, and he's treading on my tail."
Ib. [The Lobster-Quadrille, st. 1]

8 Will you, won't you, will you, won't you, will you join the dance? *Ib.*

9 The further off from England the nearer is to France—
Then turn not pale, beloved snail, but come and join the dance. *Ib. [st. 3]*

10 'Tis the voice of the Lobster: I heard him declare
"You have baked me too brown, I must sugar my hair."[3]
Ib. ['Tis the Voice of the Lobster]

11 Soup of the evening, beautiful soup!
Ib. [Turtle Soup]

12 Sentence first—verdict afterwards. *Ib. 12*

13 Begin at the beginning . . . and go on till you come to the end: then stop. *Ib.*

14 You're nothing but a pack of cards! *Ib.*

15 Child of the pure, unclouded brow
And dreaming eyes of wonder!
Though time be fleet and I and thou
Are half a life asunder,
Thy loving smile will surely hail
The love-gift of a fairy tale.
Through the Looking-Glass [1872], introduction, st. 1

16 "The horror of that moment," the King went on, "I shall never, *never* forget!"
"You will, though," the Queen said, "if you don't make a memorandum of it." *Ib. ch. 1*

17 'Twas brillig, and the slithy toves
Did gyre and gimble in the wabe;
All mimsy were the borogoves,
And the mome raths outgrabe.

Beware the Jabberwock, my son!
The jaws that bite, the claws that catch!
Beware the Jubjub bird, and shun
The frumious Bandersnatch!
Ib. [Jabberwocky, st. 1, 2]

18 And, as in uffish thought he stood,
The Jabberwock, with eyes of flame,
Came whiffling through the tulgey wood,
And burbled as it came!

One, two! One, two! And through and through
The vorpal blade went snicker-snack!
He left it dead, and with its head
He went galumphing back.

"And hast thou slain the Jabberwock?
Come to my arms, my beamish boy!
O frabjous day! Callooh! Callay!"
He chortled in his joy. *Ib. [st. 4–6]*

19 Curtsy while you're thinking what to say. It saves time. *Ib. 2*

20 "Now! Now!" cried the Queen. "Faster! Faster!" *Ib.*

21 "A slow sort of country!" said the Queen. "Now, *here*, you see, it takes all the running you can do, to keep in the same place. If you want to get somewhere else, you must run at least twice as fast as that!" *Ib.*

22 Speak in French when you can't think of the English for a thing—turn out your toes when you walk—and remember who you are! *Ib.*

23 "If you think we're waxworks," he said, "you ought to pay, you know. Waxworks weren't made to be looked at for nothing. Nohow!" *Ib. 4*

24 "Contrariwise," continued Tweedledee, "if it was so, it might be; and if it were so, it would be; but as it isn't, it ain't. That's logic." *Ib.*

[1] See Shakespeare, 187:14, and Cibber, 324:27.
[2] Familiar version: Change lobsters and dance.
[3] See Isaac Watts, 328:9.

1 The sun was shining on the sea,
Shining with all his might:
He did his very best to make
The billows smooth and bright—
And this was odd, because it was
The middle of the night.
Ib. [The Walrus and the Carpenter, st. 1]

2 The Walrus and the Carpenter
Were walking close at hand:
They wept like anything to see
Such quantities of sand:
"If this were only cleared away,"
They said, "it would be grand!"

"If seven maids with seven mops
Swept it for half a year,
Do you suppose," the Walrus said,
"That they could get it clear?"
"I doubt it," said the Carpenter,
And shed a bitter tear. *Ib. [st. 4, 5]*

3 "O Oysters, come and walk with us!"
The Walrus did beseech.
"A pleasant walk, a pleasant talk,
Along the briny beach." *Ib. [st. 6]*

4 And thick and fast they came at last,
And more, and more, and more—
All hopping through the frothy waves,
And scrambling to the shore.
Ib. [st. 9]

5 "The time has come," the Walrus said,
"To talk of many things:
Of shoes—and ships—and sealing wax—
Of cabbages—and kings—
And why the sea is boiling hot—
And whether pigs have wings."
Ib. [st. 11]

6 "But wait a bit," the Oysters cried,
"Before we have our chat;
For some of us are out of breath,
And all of us are fat!" *Ib. [st. 12]*

7 The Carpenter said nothing but
"The butter's spread too thick!"
Ib. [st. 16]

8 "I weep for you," the Walrus said:
"I deeply sympathize."
With sobs and tears he sorted out
Those of the largest size,
Holding his pocket-handkerchief
Before his streaming eyes. *Ib. [st. 17]*

9 But answer came there none[1]—
And this was scarcely odd, because
They'd eaten every one. *Ib. [st. 18]*

[1] But answer came there none.—Scott, *The Bridal of Triermain* [1813], *canto III, st. 10*

10 Twopence a week, and jam every other day. *Ib. 5*

11 "The rule is, jam tomorrow, and jam yesterday—but never jam today."
"It must come sometimes to 'jam today,'" Alice objected.
"No, it can't," said the Queen. "It's jam every other day: today isn't any other day, you know." *Ib.*

12 "It's a poor sort of memory that only works backwards," the Queen remarked. *Ib.*

13 Consider anything, only don't cry! *Ib.*

14 "There's no use trying," she said: "one *can't* believe impossible things."
"I daresay you haven't had much practice," said the Queen. "When I was your age, I always did it for half-an-hour a day. Why, sometimes I've believed as many as six impossible things before breakfast." *Ib.*

15 They gave it me—for an unbirthday present. *Ib. 6*

16 "But 'glory' doesn't mean 'a nice knock-down argument,'" Alice objected.
"When *I* use a word," Humpty Dumpty said, in rather a scornful tone, "it means just what I choose it to mean—neither more nor less."
"The question is," said Alice, "whether you *can* make words mean so many different things."
"The question is," said Humpty Dumpty, "which is to be master—that's all." *Ib.*

17 It's as large as life and twice as natural. *Ib. 7*

18 His answer trickled through my head,
Like water through a sieve. *Ib. 8*

19 What's the French for fiddle-de-dee? *Ib. 9*

20 It isn't etiquette to cut anyone you've been introduced to. Remove the joint! *Ib.*

21 He would answer to "Hi!" or to any loud cry
Such as "Fry me!" or "Fritter my wig!"
To "What-you-may-call-um!" or "What-was-his-name!"
But especially "Thing-um-a-jig!"
The Hunting of the Snark [1876]. Fit I, st. 9

22 "What's the good of Mercator's North Poles and Equators,
Tropics, Zones and Meridian Lines?"
So the Bellman would cry: and the crew would reply,
"They are merely conventional signs!"
Ib. Fit II, st. 3

1 It frequently breakfasts at five-o'clock tea,
And dines on the following day.
Ib. st. 17

2 There was silence supreme! Not a shriek, not a scream,
Scarcely even a howl or a groan,
As the man they called "Ho!" told his story of woe
In an antediluvian tone.
Ib. Fit III, st. 3

3 It is this, it is this that oppresses my soul.
Ib. st. 11

4 They sought it with thimbles, they sought it with care;
They pursued it with forks and hope;
They threatened its life with a railway share;
They charmed it with smiles and soap.
Ib. Fit V, st. 1

5 For the Snark *was* a Boojum, you see.
Ib. Fit VIII, st. 9

6 He thought he saw an Elephant,
That practiced on a fife:
He looked again, and found it was
A letter from his wife.
"At length I realize," he said,
"The bitterness of Life!"
Sylvie and Bruno [1889], ch. 5

7 He thought he saw a Buffalo
Upon the chimneypiece:
He looked again, and found it was
His sister's husband's niece. *Ib. 6*

8 He thought he saw an Albatross
That fluttered round the lamp:
He looked again, and found it was
A penny postage stamp.
"You'd best be getting home," he said,
"The nights are very damp." *Ib. 12*

William Croswell Doane
1832–1913

9 Ancient of Days, who sittest throned in glory,
To thee all knees are bent, all voices pray.
Hymn [1886], st. 1

Juan Montalvo
1832–1889

10 Old age is an island surrounded by death.
On Beauty

11 There is nothing harder than the softness of indifference.
Chapters Forgotten by Cervantes [1895]. Epilogue

Henry Clay Work
1832–1884

12 Father, dear father, come home with me now,
The clock in the belfry strikes one;
You said you were coming right home from the shop
As soon as your day's work was done.
Come Home, Father [1864], st. 1

13 Bring the good old bugle, boys, we'll sing another song.
Marching Through Georgia [1865], st. 1

14 "Hurrah! hurrah! we bring the Jubilee!
Hurrah! Hurrah! the flag that makes you free!"
So we sang the chorus from Atlanta to the sea,
While we were marching through Georgia.
Ib. chorus

Wilhelm Max Wundt
1832–1920

15 We take issue . . . with every treatment of psychology that is based on simple self-observation or on philosophical presuppositions.[1]
Grundsuge der Physiologischen Psychologie (Principles of Physiological Psychology) [1874]

Isaac Hill Bromley
1833–1898

16 Conductor, when you receive a fare,
Punch in the presence of the passenjare! . . .
Punch, brothers! Punch with care!
Punch in the presence of the passenjare!
Punch, Brother, Punch [1875][2]

Adam Lindsay Gordon
1833–1870

17 A little season of love and laughter,
Of light and life, and pleasure and pain,
And a horror of outer darkness after,
And dust returneth to dust again.[3]
The Swimmer

[1]Translated by EDWARD TITCHENER.

[2]Based on a New York streetcar sign. Erroneously attributed to Mark Twain, who wrote about the verse in *A Literary Nightmare* [1876].

[3]See Du Maurier, 617:3.
A little time for laughter, / A little time to sing, / A little time to kiss and cling, / And no more kissing after.— PHILIP BOURKE MARSTON [1850–1887], *After, st. 1*

John Marshall Harlan
1833–1911

1 In view of the Constitution, in the eye of the law, there is in this country no superior, dominant, ruling class of citizens. There is no caste here. Our Constitution is color-blind, and neither knows nor tolerates classes among citizens. In respect of civil rights, all citizens are equal before the law. The humblest is the peer of the most powerful.
Dissenting opinion, Plessy v. Ferguson 163 U.S. 537, 559 [1896]

John James Ingalls
1833–1900

2 Every man is the center of a circle, whose fatal circumference he cannot pass.
Eulogy on Benjamin Hill given in the Senate [January 23, 1882]

3 The purification of politics is an iridescent dream. Government is force.
Article in the New York World [1890]

Robert Green Ingersoll
1833–1899

4 Like an armed warrior, like a plumed knight, James G. Blaine marched down the halls of the American Congress and threw his shining lance full and fair against the brazen forehead of every traitor to his country and every maligner of his fair reputation.
Speech nominating Blaine for President, National Republican Convention [June 15, 1876]

5 I am the inferior of any man whose rights I trample under foot. Men are not superior by reason of the accidents of race or color. They are superior who have the best heart—the best brain. *Liberty*

6 The superior man is the providence of the inferior. He is eyes for the blind, strength for the weak, and a shield for the defenseless. He stands erect by bending above the fallen. He rises by lifting others. *Ib.*

7 Every cradle asks us, "Whence?" and every coffin, "Whither?" The poor barbarian, weeping above his dead, can answer these questions as intelligently as the robed priest of the most authentic creed.
Address at a child's grave

8 We, too, have our religion, and it is this: Help for the living, hope for the dead.
Ib.

9 Few rich men own their own property. The property owns them.[1]
Address to the McKinley League, New York [October 29, 1896]

10 An honest God is the noblest work of man.
The Gods [1876]

11 In nature there are neither rewards nor punishments—there are consequences.
Some Reasons Why [1896]

12 Justice is the only worship.
Love is the only priest.
Ignorance is the only slavery.
Happiness is the only good.
The time to be happy is now,
The place to be happy is here,
The way to be happy is to make others so.
Creed

Petroleum V. Nasby [David Ross Locke]
1833–1888

13 The contract 'twixt Hannah, God and me,
Was not for one or twenty years, but for eternity. *Hannah Jane [1871], st. 29*

John Emerich Edward Dalberg-Acton, Lord Acton
1834–1902

14 There is no error so monstrous that it fails to find defenders among the ablest men. Imagine a congress of eminent celebrities such as More, Bacon, Grotius, Pascal, Cromwell, Bossuet, Montesquieu, Jefferson, Napoleon, Pitt, etc. The result would be an Encyclopedia of Error.
Letter to Mary Gladstone [April 24, 1881]

15 Power tends to corrupt and absolute power corrupts absolutely.[2]
Letter to Bishop Mandell Creighton [April 5, 1887]

16 Advice to Persons About to Write History —Don't.[3] *Ib. postscript*

17 Liberty is not a means to a higher political end. It is itself the highest political end.
The History of Freedom and Other Essays [1907], ch. 1

[1] See Bion, 92:8, and Robert Burton, 258:22.
[2] See Pitt, 351:1, and Shelley, 466:7.
[3] See *Punch*, 660:11.

1 It was from America that the plain ideas that men ought to mind their business, and that the nation is responsible to Heaven for the acts of the State—ideas long locked in the breast of solitary thinkers, and hidden among Latin folios—burst forth like a conqueror upon the world they were destined to transform, under the title of the Rights of Man . . . and the principle gained ground, that a nation can never abandon its fate to an authority it cannot control. *Ib.* 2

2 The one pervading evil of democracy is the tyranny of the majority, or rather of that party, not always the majority, that succeeds, by force or fraud, in carrying elections. *Ib. 3*

3 Truth is the only merit that gives dignity and worth to history. *Ib. 4*

4 Writers the most learned, the most accurate in details, and the soundest in tendency, frequently fall into a habit which can neither be cured nor pardoned—the habit of making history into the proof of their theories. *Ib. 8*

George Arnold
1834–1865

5 Life for the living, and rest for the dead!
The Jolly Old Pedagogue, st. 2

Sabine Baring-Gould
1834–1924

6 Onward, Christian soldiers,
Marching as to war,
With the Cross of Jesus
Going on before!
Onward, Christian Soldiers [1864], st. 1

7 Now the day is over,
Night is drawing nigh;
Shadows of the evening
Steal across the sky.
Now the Day Is Over [1865], st. 1

8 Through the night of doubt and sorrow
Onward goes the pilgrim band,
Singing songs of expectation,
Marching to the promised land.
Through the Night of Doubt and Sorrow [1867], st. 1[1]

[1]Translated from the Danish of B. S. INGEMANN [1825].

Charles Farrar Browne [Artemus Ward]
1834–1867

9 I now bid you a welcome adoo.
Artemus Ward, His Book [1862]

10 My pollertics, like my religion, being of an exceedin' accommodatin' character.
Ib. The Crisis

11 N.B. This is rote sarcastikul.
Ib. A Visit to Brigham Young

12 The female woman is one of the greatest institooshuns of which this land can boste.
Ib. Woman's Rights

13 I am not a politician, and my other habits are good, also.[2]
Fourth of July Oration

14 The prevailin' weakness of most public men is to Slop over. G. Washington never slopt over. *Ib.*

15 I can't sing. As a singist I am not a success. I am saddest when I sing.[3] So are those who hear me. They are sadder even than I am.
Artemus Ward, His Travels [1865]. Lecture

16 Did you ever have the measels, and if so, how many? *Ib. The Census*

17 The Puritans nobly fled from a land of despotism to a land of freedim, where they could not only enjoy their own religion, but could prevent everybody else from enjoyin *his.*[4]
London Punch Letters, no. 5 [1866]

18 Why is this thus? What is the reason of this thusness? *Moses, the Sassy*

19 He [Brigham Young] is dreadfully married. He's the most married man I ever saw in my life. *Ib.*

20 Let us all be happy and live within our means, even if we have to borrow the money to do it with. *Natural History*

21 The sun has a right to "set" where it wants to, and so, I may add, has a hen.
A Mormon Romance, ch. 4

22 They cherish his mem'ry, and them as sell picturs of his birthplace, etc., make it prof'tible cherishin' it.
At the Tomb of Shakespeare

[2]A favorite quotation of John F. Kennedy.
[3]I'm Saddest When I Sing.—T. H. BAYLY [1797–1839], *title of poem*
[4]The Puritan's idea of Hell is a place where everybody has to mind his own business.—*Attributed to* WENDELL PHILLIPS [1811–1884]

George Louis Palmella Busson du Maurier
1834–1896

1 The wretcheder one is, the more one smokes; and the more one smokes, the wretcheder one gets—a vicious circle!
Peter Ibbetson [1891]

2 Songs without words are best. *Ib.*

3 A little work, a little play,
To keep us going—and so, good day!

A little warmth, a little light,
Of love's bestowing—and so, good night![1]

A little fun, to match the sorrow
Of each day's growing—and so, good morrow!

A little trust that when we die
We reap our sowing! and so—good-bye!
Trilby [1894], pt. VIII

Charles William Eliot
1834–1926

4 In the modern world the intelligence of public opinion is the one indispensable condition of social progress.
Inaugural address as president of Harvard [1869]

5 Enter to grow in wisdom.
Depart to serve better thy country and mankind.
Inscriptions on the 1890 Gate to Harvard Yard

6 To the Fifty-fourth Regiment of Massachusetts Infantry:

The white officers, taking life and honor in their hands, cast in their lot with men of a despised race unproved in war, and risked death as inciters of servile insurrection if taken prisoners, besides encountering all the common perils of camp march and battle.

The black rank and file volunteered when disaster clouded the Union cause, served without pay for eighteen months till given that of white troops, faced threatened enslavement if captured, were brave in action, patient under heavy and dangerous labors, and cheerful amid hardships and privations.

Together they gave to the nation and the world undying proof that Americans of African descent possess the pride, courage, and devotion of the patriot soldier. One hundred and eighty thousand such Americans enlisted under the Union flag in 1863–1865.
Inscription on the Robert Gould Shaw Monument, Boston Common [1897][2]

7 Carrier of news and knowledge, instrument of trade and commerce, promoter of mutual acquaintance among men and nations and hence of peace and goodwill.

Carrier of love and sympathy, messenger of friendship, consoler of the lonely, servant of the scattered family, enlarger of the public life.
Inscriptions for the East and West Pavilions, Post Office, Washington, D.C.[3]

Fukuzawa Yukichi[4]
1834–1901

8 The final purpose of all my work was to create in Japan a civilized nation as well equipped in both the arts of war and peace as those of the Western world.
Autobiography [1898]

9 As long as I remain in private life, I can watch and laugh. But joining the government would draw me into the practice of those ridiculous pretensions which I cannot allow myself to do. *Ib.*

Ernst Heinrich Haeckel
1834–1919

10 Ontogenesis, or the development of the individual, is a short and quick recapitulation of phylogenesis,[5] or the development of the tribe to which it belongs, determined by the laws of inheritance and adaptation.
The History of Creation [1868][6]

11 The general theory of evolution . . . assumes that in nature there is a great, unital, continuous and everlasting process of devel-

[1] La vie est vaine: / Un peu d'amour, / Un peu de haine . . . / Et puis—bonjour! // La vie est brève: / Un peu d'espoir, / Un peu de rêve / Et puis—bonsoir!—LEON MONTENAEKEN [b. 1859], *Peu de Chose*
See A. L. Gordon, 614:17.

[2] See William James, 650:13; Paul Laurence Dunbar, 737:1; and Robert Lowell, 893:12.

[3] These inscriptions were edited by Woodrow Wilson to read:
Carrier of news and knowledge, instrument of trade and promoter of mutual acquaintance, of peace and good will among men and nations.
Messenger of sympathy and love, servant of parted friends, consoler of the lonely, bond of the scattered family, enlarger of the common life.

[4] From *Sources of Japanese Tradition* [1960], edited by WILLIAM THEODORE DE BARY.

[5] Frequently quoted: Ontogeny recapitulates phylogeny.
See Freud, 678:9.

[6] Translated by E. R. LANKESTER.

opment, and that all natural phenomena without exception, from the motion of the celestial bodies and the fall of the rolling stone up to the growth of the plant and the consciousness of man, are subject to the same great law of causation—that they are ultimately to be reduced to atomic mechanics.

Freie Wissenschaft und Freie Lehre [1878][1]

Walter Kittredge
1834–1905

1 We're tenting tonight on the old campground,
Give us a song to cheer
Our weary hearts, a song of home
And friends we love so dear.

Tenting on the Old Campground [1864], st. 1

William Morris
1834–1896

2 Well, if this is poetry, it is very easy to write.

Remark [1854]. From J. W. Mackail, *Life of William Morris [1899]*

3 I went half mad with beauty on that day.

The Defense of Guinevere [1858], l. 109

4 Had she come all the way for this,
To part at last without a kiss?
Yea, had she borne the dirt and rain
That her own eyes might see him slain
Beside the haystack in the floods?

The Haystack in the Floods [1858], l. 1

5 I know a little garden close,
Set thick with lily and red rose,
Where I would wander if I might
From dewy morn to dewy night.

The Life and Death of Jason [1867]. A Garden by the Sea, st. 1

6 The idle singer of an empty day.

The Earthly Paradise [1868–1870]. An Apology, st. 1

7 Dreamer of dreams,[2] born out of my due time,
Why should I strive to set the crooked straight?[3] *Ib. st. 4*

[1]Translated by J. B. Stallo.
[2]See O'Shaughnessy, 659:9.
[3]See *Ecclesiastes 1:15*, 26:16, and *Isaiah 40:4*, 30:31.

8 Love is enough, though the world be awaning. *Love Is Enough [1872]*

9 If you want a golden rule that will fit everybody, this is it: Have nothing in your houses that you do not know to be useful, or believe to be beautiful.

The Beauty of Life [1880]

10 What I mean by Socialism is a condition of society in which there should be neither rich nor poor, neither master nor master's man, neither idle nor overworked, neither brain-sick brain workers nor heart-sick hand workers, in a word, in which all men would be living in equality of condition, and would manage their affairs unwastefully, and with the full consciousness that harm to one would mean harm to all—the realization at last of the meaning of the word *commonwealth.*

Written for "Justice" [1884]

11 Wonderful days a-coming, when all shall be better than well.

The Day Is Coming [1884], l. 2

12 Then more than one in a thousand in the days that are yet to come,
Shall have some hope of the morrow, some joy of the ancient home. *Ib. l. 5*

13 Come, shoulder to shoulder ere earth grows older!
The Cause spreads over land and sea!
Now the world shaketh, and fear awaketh,
And joy at last for thee and me.

The Voice of Toil [1884], l. 37

14 The reward of labor is life.

News from Nowhere [1891], ch. 15

Frank Richard Stockton
1834–1902

15 Which came out of the opened door—the lady or the tiger?

The Lady or the Tiger? [1884]

16 The board money is in the ginger jar and our conscience is clear.

The Casting Away of Mrs. Lecks and Mrs. Aleshine [1886]

James Thomson
1834–1882

17 Statues and pictures and verse may be grand,
But they are not the Life for which they stand. *Art [1865], st. 3, l. 19*

18 The City is of Night; perchance of Death,
But certainly of Night.

The City of Dreadful Night [1874]. st. 1, l. 1

1 That positive eternity of pain,
Instead of this insufferable inane.
Ib. st. 6, l. 23

2 What never has been, yet may have its when;
The thing which has been, never is again.
Ib. st. 18, l. 77

James McNeill Whistler
1834–1903

3 Two and two continue to make four, in spite of the whine of the amateur for three, or the cry of the critic for five.
Whistler v. Ruskin [1878][1]

4 The rare few, who, early in life, have rid themselves of the friendship of the many.
The Gentle Art of Making Enemies [1890], dedication

5 To say of a picture, as is often said in its praise, that it shows great and earnest labor, is to say that it is incomplete and unfit for view. *Ib. Propositions, 2*

6 Industry in art is a necessity—not a virtue—and any evidence of the same, in the production, is a blemish, not a quality; a proof, not of achievement, but of absolutely insufficient work, for work alone will efface the footsteps of work.[2] *Ib.*

7 The masterpiece should appear as the flower to the painter—perfect in its bud as in its bloom—with no reason to explain its presence—no mission to fulfill—a joy to the artist, a delusion to the philanthropist—a puzzle to the botanist—an accident of sentiment and alliteration to the literary man.
Ib.

8 Art should be independent of all claptrap—should stand alone, and appeal to the artistic sense of eye and ear, without confounding this with emotions entirely foreign to it, as devotion, pity, love, patriotism, and the like. All these have no kind of concern with it.
Ib.

9 It is for the artist . . . in portrait painting to put on canvas something more than the face the model wears for that one day; to paint the man, in short, as well as his features. *Ib.*

[1]Whistler's lawsuit for libel. Ruskin had written of Whistler's *Nocturne in Black and Gold,* "I have seen, and heard, much of Cockney impudence before now; but never expected to hear a coxcomb ask two hundred guineas for flinging a pot of paint in the public's face."—JOHN RUSKIN, *Fors Clavigera, Letter 79* [1877]

[2]Ars est celare artem [Art lies in concealing art].—*Latin proverb*

10 One cannot continually disappoint a Continent.[3] *Ib.*

11 I am not arguing with you—I am telling you. *Ib.*

12 *Wilde:* I wish I'd said that.
Whistler: You will, Oscar, you will.
From L. C. INGLEBY, Oscar Wilde [1907]

13 "I only know of two painters in the world," said a newly introduced feminine enthusiast to Whistler, "yourself and Velasquez." "Why," answered Whistler in dulcet tones, "why drag in Velasquez?"
From D. C. SEITZ, Whistler Stories [1913]

Thomas Brigham Bishop
1835–1905

14 John Brown's body lies a-moldering in the grave,
His soul is marching on.
John Brown's Body, st. 1

15 Shoo, fly! don't bodder me! I belong to Company G,
I feel like a morning star.
Shoo, Fly. Refrain

Phillips Brooks
1835–1893

16 O little town of Bethlehem!
How still we see thee lie;
Above thy deep and dreamless sleep
The silent stars go by;
Yet in thy dark streets shineth
The everlasting Light;
The hopes and fears of all the years
Are met in thee tonight.
O Little Town of Bethlehem [1867], st. 1

17 Life comes before literature, as the material always comes before the work. The hills are full of marble before the world blooms with statues. *Literature and Life*

18 Do not pray for easy lives. Pray to be stronger men! Do not pray for tasks equal to your powers. Pray for powers equal to your tasks.
Sermons. Going Up to Jerusalem

19 Greatness after all, in spite of its name, appears to be not so much a certain size as a certain quality in human lives. It may be present in lives whose range is very small.
Ib. Purpose and Use of Comfort

[3]Referring to a contemplated visit to the United States.

Samuel Butler

1835–1902

1 The man who lets himself be bored is even more contemptible than the bore.

The Fair Haven [1873]. Memoir, ch. 3

2 A hen is only an egg's way of making another egg.

Life and Habit [1877], ch. 8

3 Stowed away in a Montreal lumber room
The Discobolus standeth and turneth his face to the wall;
Dusty, cobweb-covered, maimed and set at naught,
Beauty crieth in an attic and no man regardeth.
O God! O Montreal!

A Psalm of Montreal [1884], st. 1

4 The Discobolus is put here because he is vulgar—
He has neither vest nor pants with which to cover his limbs. *Ib. st. 5*

5 It is far safer to know too little than too much. People will condemn the one, though they will resent being called upon to exert themselves to follow the other.

The Way of All Flesh [1903], ch. 5

6 Adversity, if a man is set down to it by degrees, is more supportable with equanimity by most people than any great prosperity arrived at in a single lifetime.[1]

Ib.

7 It is our less conscious thoughts and our less conscious actions which mainly mold our lives and the lives of those who spring from us. *Ib.*

8 Youth is like spring, an overpraised season.

Ib. 6

9 Taking numbers into account, I should think more mental suffering had been undergone in the streets leading from St. George's, Hanover Square, than in the condemned cells of Newgate. *Ib. 13*

10 Every man's work, whether it be literature or music or pictures or architecture or anything else, is always a portrait of himself.

Ib. 14

11 One great reason why clergymen's households are generally unhappy is because the clergyman is so much at home and close about the house. *Ib. 24*

[1]See Carlyle, 474:1.

12 The advantage of doing one's praising for oneself is that one can lay it on so thick and exactly in the right places. *Ib. 34*

13 The best liar is he who makes the smallest amount of lying go the longest way.

Ib. 39

14 An empty house is like a stray dog or a body from which life has departed.[2]

Ib. 72

15 A man's friendships are, like his will, invalidated by marriage—but they are also no less invalidated by the marriage of his friends. *Ib. 75*

16 Life is the art of drawing sufficient conclusions from insufficient premises.

Notebooks [1912]. Life

17 All progress is based upon a universal innate desire on the part of every organism to live beyond its income. *Ib.*

18 Though analogy is often misleading, it is the least misleading thing we have.

Ib. Music, Pictures, and Books

19 The phrase "unconscious humor" is the one contribution I have made to the current literature of the day.

Ib. Homo Unius Libri

20 Ideas and opinions, like living organisms, have a normal rate of growth which cannot be either checked or forced beyond a certain point. The more unpopular an opinion is, the more necessary is it that the holder should be somewhat punctilious in his observance of conventionalities generally.

Ib. The Art of Propagating Opinion

21 Genius . . . has been defined as a supreme capacity for taking trouble.[3] . . . It might be more fitly described as a supreme capacity for getting its possessors into trouble of all kinds and keeping them therein so long as the genius remains. *Ib. Genius*

22 I am the *enfant terrible* of literature and science. *Ib. Enfant Terrible: Myself*

23 An apology for the Devil: It must be remembered that we have only heard one side of the case. God has written all the books.

Ib. Higgledy-Piggledy: An Apology for the Devil

24 God is Love—I dare say. But what a mischievous devil Love is!

Ib. God Is Love

[2]The tragic house, the house with nobody in it.—JOYCE KILMER [1886–1918], *The House with Nobody in It*

[3]See Buffon, 349:3; Carlyle, 474:14; and Hopkins, 630:17.

1 To live is like to love—all reason is against it, and all healthy instinct for it.
Ib. Life and Love

2 *The Ancient Mariner* would not have taken so well if it had been called *The Old Sailor.*
Ib. Titles and Subjects

3 The public buys its opinions as it buys its meat, or takes in its milk, on the principle that it is cheaper to do this than to keep a cow. So it is, but the milk is more likely to be watered.
Ib. Sequel to "Alps and Sanctuaries"

4 I do not mind lying, but I hate inaccuracy.
Ib. Truth and Convenience: Falsehood

Andrew Carnegie
1835–1919

5 The problem of our age is the proper administration of wealth, so that the ties of brotherhood may still bind together the rich and poor in harmonious relationship.
Wealth. From the North American Review [June 1889]

6 While the law [of competition] may be sometimes hard for the individual, it is best for the race, because it insures the survival of the fittest in every department. We accept and welcome, therefore, as conditions to which we must accommodate ourselves, great inequality of environment, the concentration of business, industrial and commercial, in the hands of a few, and the law of competition between these, as being not only beneficial, but essential for the future progress of the race. *Ib.*

7 Upon the sacredness of property civilization itself depends—the right of the laborer to his hundred dollars in the savings bank, and equally the legal right of the millionaire to his millions. *Ib.*

8 Surplus wealth is a sacred trust which its possessor is bound to administer in his lifetime for the good of the community.
Ib.

9 Those who would administer wisely must, indeed, be wise, for one of the serious obstacles to the improvement of our race is indiscriminate charity. *Ib.*

10 Thus is the problem of Rich and Poor to be solved. The law of accumulation will be left free; the laws of distribution free. Individualism will continue, but the millionaire will be but a trustee of the poor; entrusted for a season with a great part of the increased wealth of the community, but administering it for the community far better than it could or would have done for itself.[1] *Ib.*

11 The man who dies . . . rich dies disgraced.
Ib.

12 Such, in my opinion, is the true Gospel concerning Wealth, obedience to which is destined some day to solve the problem of the Rich and the Poor, and to bring "Peace on earth, among men Good Will." *Ib.*

13 Three generations from shirtsleeves to shirtsleeves.[2] *Attributed*

Richard Garnett
1835–1906

14 When Silence speaks for Love she has much to say.
De Flagello Myrteo [1905], 99

15 Ascend above the restrictions and conventions of the world, but not so high as to lose sight of them. *Ib. 333*

Harriet Prescott Spofford
1835–1921

16 The awful phantom of the hungry poor.
A Winter's Night

Celia Laighton Thaxter
1835–1894

17 Across the narrow beach we flit,
One little sandpiper and I;
And fast I gather, bit by bit,
The scattered driftwood, bleached and dry.
The Sandpiper, st. 1

Mark Twain[3]
[Samuel Langhorne Clemens]
1835–1910

18 I'll resk forty dollars that he can outjump any frog in Calaveras county.
The Celebrated Jumping Frog [1865]

[1]See Maimonides, 137:10; Spinoza, 309:1; and Johnson, 354:23.

[2]There's nobbut three generations atween clog and clog.—*Lancashire proverb, which Carnegie liked to quote*

[3]I was a fresh, new journalist, and needed a *nom de guerre;* so I confiscated the ancient mariner's discarded one ["Mark Twain"], and have done my best to make it remain what it was in his hands—a sign and symbol and warrant that whatever is found in its company may be gambled on as being the petrified truth.—TWAIN, *Life on the Mississippi* [1883], *ch. 50*

1 I don't see no p'ints about that frog that's any better'n any other frog. *Ib.*

2 Soap and education are not as sudden as a massacre, but they are more deadly in the long run.

The Facts Concerning the Recent Resignation [1867]

3 Tomorrow night I appear for the first time before a Boston audience—4000 critics.

Letter to Pamela Clemens Moffet [November 9, 1869]

4 They spell it Vinci and pronounce it Vinchy; foreigners always spell better than they pronounce.

The Innocents Abroad [1869], ch. 19

5 I do not want Michael Angelo for breakfast —for luncheon—for dinner—for tea—for supper—for between meals. *Ib. 27*

6 Lump the whole thing! say that the Creator made Italy from designs by Michael Angelo! *Ib.*

7 Guides cannot master the subtleties of the American joke. *Ib.*

8 There's millions in it!

The Gilded Age [1873][1]

9 Barring that natural expression of villainy which we all have, the man looked honest enough. *A Mysterious Visit [1875]*

10 This poor little one-horse town.

The Undertaker's Chat [1875]

11 Tom appeared on the sidewalk with a bucket of whitewash and a long-handled brush. He surveyed the fence, and all gladness left him and a deep melancholy settled down upon his spirit. Thirty yards of board fence nine feet high. Life to him seemed hollow, and existence but a burden.

The Adventures of Tom Sawyer [1876], ch. 2

12 Work consists of whatever a body is *obliged* to do . . . Play consists of whatever a body is not obliged to do. *Ib.*

13 The minister gave out his text and droned along monotonously through an argument that was so prosy that many a head by and by began to nod—and yet it was an argument that dealt in limitless fire and brimstone and thinned the predestined elect[2] down to a company so small as to be hardly worth the saving. *Ib. 5*

14 There was no getting around the stubborn fact that taking sweetmeats was only "hooking," while taking bacon and hams and such valuables was plain simple *stealing*—and there was a command against that in the Bible. So they inwardly resolved that so long as they remained in the business, their piracies should not again be sullied with the crime of stealing. *Ib. 13*

15 To promise not to do a thing is the surest way in the world to make a body want to go and do that very thing. *Ib. 22*

16 She makes me wash, they comb me all to thunder . . . The widder eats by a bell; she goes to bed by a bell; she gits up by a bell —everything's so awful reg'lar a body can't stand it. *Ib. 35*

17 A baby is an inestimable blessing and bother.

Letter to Annie Webster [September 1, 1876]

18 There is a sumptuous variety about the New England weather that compels the stranger's admiration—and regret. The weather is always doing something there; always attending strictly to business; always getting up new designs and trying them on people to see how they will go. But it gets through more business in spring than in any other season. In the spring I have counted one hundred and thirty-six different kinds of weather inside of twenty-four hours.[3]

New England Weather. Speech to the New England Society [December 22, 1876]

19 Probable nor'east to sou'west winds, varying to the southard and westard and eastard and points between; high and low barometer, sweeping round from place to place; probable areas of rain, snow, hail, and drought, succeeded or preceded by earthquakes with thunder and lightning. *Ib.*

20 One of the brightest gems in the New England weather is the dazzling uncertainty of it. *Ib.*

21 We haven't all had the good fortune to be ladies; we haven't all been generals, or poets,

---

The earlier use of the pen name was by Captain Isaiah Sellers, in the *New Orleans Picayune*.

The phrase "mark twain," meaning "two fathoms deep," was employed in making soundings on the Mississippi riverboats.

[1]Written in collaboration with CHARLES DUDLEY WARNER.

See Warner, 603.

[2]See *Romans 8:29–30*, 47:11, and *Romans 8:33*, 47:13.

[3]See Warner, 603:15.

or statesmen; but when the toast works down to the babies, we stand on common ground.

Answering a toast, "To the babies," at a banquet in honor of General U. S. Grant [November 14, 1879]

1 Among the three or four million cradles now rocking in the land are some which this nation would preserve for ages as sacred things, if we could know which ones they are. *Ib.*

2 It is the longest river[1] in the world — four thousand three hundred miles. . . . It is also the crookedest river in the world, since in one part of its journey it uses up one thousand three hundred miles to cover the same ground that the crow would fly over in six hundred and seventy-five.

Life on the Mississippi [1883], ch. 1

3 The world and the books are so accustomed to use, and over-use, the word "new" in connection with our country, that we early get and permanently retain the impression that there is nothing old about it. *Ib.*

4 Sired by a hurricane, dam'd by an earthquake. *Ib. 3*

5 When I'm playful I use the meridians of longitude and parallels of latitude for a seine, and drag the Atlantic Ocean for whales. I scratch my head with the lightning and purr myself to sleep with the thunder. *Ib.*

6 The Child of Calamity. *Ib.*

7 I was gratified to be able to answer promptly, and I did. I said I didn't know. *Ib. 6*

8 Your true pilot cares nothing about anything on earth but the river, and his pride in his occupation surpasses the pride of kings. *Ib. 7*

9 By the Shadow of Death, but he's a lightning pilot! *Ib.*

10 A limb of Satan.[2] *Ib. 8*

11 I'll learn him or kill him. *Ib.*

12 Give an Irishman lager for a month, and he's a dead man. An Irishman is lined with copper, and the beer corrodes it. But whiskey polishes the copper and is the saving of him. *Ib. 23*

13 All the modern inconveniences. *Ib. 43*

14 The educated Southerner has no use for an *r*, except at the beginning of a word. *Ib. 44*

[1] Mississippi: big river (in Ojibwa, misi sibi).
[2] Also in *The Prince and the Pauper,* ch. 13.

15 In the South the war is what A.D. is elsewhere; they date from it. *Ib. 45*

16 War talk by men who have been in a war is always interesting; whereas moon talk by a poet who has not been in the moon is likely to be dull. *Ib.*

17 Sir Walter [Scott] had so large a hand in making Southern character as it existed before the war that he is in great measure responsible for the war. *Ib. 46*

18 It was without a compeer among swindles. It was perfect, it was rounded, symmetrical, complete, colossal. *Ib. 52*

19 Persons attempting to find a motive in this narrative will be prosecuted; persons attempting to find a moral in it will be banished; persons attempting to find a plot in it will be shot.

BY ORDER OF THE AUTHOR.

Adventures of Huckleberry Finn [1884]. Notice

20 You don't know about me without you have read a book by the name of *The Adventures of Tom Sawyer;* but that ain't no matter. That book was made by Mr. Mark Twain, and he told the truth, mainly. There was things which he stretched, but mainly he told the truth. *Ib. ch. 1*

21 Jim was most ruined for a servant, because he got stuck up on account of having seen the devil and been rode by witches. *Ib. 2*

22 We catched fish and talked, and we took a swim now and then to keep off sleepiness. It was kind of solemn, drifting down the big, still river, laying on our backs looking up at the stars, and we didn't ever feel like talking loud, and it warn't often that we laughed — only a little kind of a low chuckle. We had mighty good weather as a general thing, and nothing ever happened to us at all. *Ib. 12*

23 It most froze me to hear such talk. . . . Thinks I, this is what comes of my not thinking. Here was this nigger, which I had as good as helped to run away, coming right out flat-footed and saying he would steal his children — children that belonged to a man I didn't even know, a man that hadn't ever done me no harm. *Ib. 16*

24 *Pilgrim's Progress,* about a man that left his family, it didn't say why. I read considerable in it now and then. The statements was interesting but tough. *Ib. 17*

25 There warn't anybody at the church, except maybe a hog or two, for there warn't any

lock on the door, and hogs likes a puncheon floor in summertime because it's cool. If you notice, most folks don't go to church only when they've got to; but a hog is different.
Ib. 18

1 We said there warn't no home like a raft, after all. Other places do seem so cramped up and smothery, but a raft don't. You feel mighty free and easy and comfortable on a raft. *Ib.*

2 A monstrous big river. *Ib. 19*

3 Hain't we got all the fools in town on our side? And ain't that a big enough majority in any town?[1] *Ib. 26*

4 I was trying to make my mouth *say* I would do the right thing and the clean thing, and go and write to that nigger's owner and tell where he was; but deep down in me I knowed it was a lie, and He knowed it. You can't pray a lie—I found that out. *Ib. 31*

5 I was a-trembling because I'd got to decide forever betwixt two things, and I knowed it. I studied for a minute, sort of holding my breath, and then says to myself, "All right, then, I'll *go* to hell." *Ib.*

6 An experienced, industrious, ambitious, and often quite picturesque liar.
The Private History of a Campaign That Failed [1885]

7 He is now fast rising from affluence to poverty.
Henry Ward Beecher's Farm [1885]

8 He [George Washington Cable] has taught me to abhor and detest the Sabbath day and hunt up new and troublesome ways to dishonor it.
Letter to William Dean Howells [February 27, 1885]

9 Whenever the literary German dives into a sentence, that is the last you are going to see of him till he emerges on the other side of his Atlantic with his verb in his mouth.
A Connecticut Yankee at King Arthur's Court [1889], ch. 22

10 Weather is a literary speciality, and no untrained hand can turn out a good article on it.
The American Claimant [1892], foreword

11 Tell the truth or trump—but get the trick.
Pudd'nhead Wilson [1894]. Pudd'nhead Wilson's Calendar, ch. 1

12 Adam was but human—this explains it all. He did not want the apple for the apple's sake, he wanted it only because it was forbidden. *Ib. 2*

13 Whoever has lived long enough to find out what life is, knows how deep a debt of gratitude we owe to Adam, the first great benefactor of our race. He brought death into the world. *Ib. 3*

14 Training is everything. The peach was once a bitter almond; cauliflower is nothing but cabbage with a college education.
Ib. 5

15 Habit is habit, and not to be flung out of the window by any man, but coaxed downstairs a step at a time. *Ib. 6*

16 One of the most striking differences between a cat and a lie is that a cat has only nine lives. *Ib. 7*

17 The holy passion of Friendship is of so sweet and steady and loyal and enduring a nature that it will last through a whole lifetime, if not asked to lend money. *Ib. 8*

18 Why is it that we rejoice at a birth and grieve at a funeral? It is because we are not the person involved. *Ib. 9*

19 All say, "How hard it is that we have to die"—a strange complaint to come from the mouths of people who have had to live.
Ib. 10

20 When angry, count four; when very angry, swear.[2] *Ib.*

21 Courage is resistance to fear, mastery of fear—not absence of fear. *Ib. 12*

22 Nothing so needs reforming as other people's habits. *Ib. 15*

23 Put all your eggs in the one basket and —WATCH THAT BASKET. *Ib.*

24 If you pick up a starving dog and make him prosperous, he will not bite you. This is the principal difference between a dog and a man. *Ib. 16*

25 Few things are harder to put up with than the annoyance of a good example.
Ib. 19

26 It were not best that we should all think alike; it is difference of opinion that makes horse races. *Ib.*

27 Be good and you will be lonesome.
Following the Equator [1897]. Caption for author's photograph on shipboard, frontispiece of first edition

[1]See *Pudd'nhead Wilson's New Calendar*, 625:12.

[2]See Jefferson, 390:4.

1 When in doubt tell the truth.
Ib. vol. I, Pudd'nhead Wilson's New Calendar, ch. 2

2 Truth is the most valuable thing we have. Let us economize it. *Ib. 7*

3 It could probably be shown by facts and figures that there is no distinctly native American criminal class except Congress.
Ib. 8

4 Everything human is pathetic. The secret source of Humor itself is not joy but sorrow. There is no humor in heaven. *Ib. 10*

5 We should be careful to get out of an experience only the wisdom that is in it—and stop there; lest we be like the cat that sits down on a hot stove lid. She will never sit down on a hot stove lid again—and that is well; but also she will never sit down on a cold one any more. *Ib. 11*

6 We can secure other people's approval, if we do right and try hard; but our own is worth a hundred of it, and no way has been found out of securing that. *Ib. 14*

7 It is easier to stay out than get out.
Ib. 18

8 Pity is for the living, envy is for the dead.
Ib. 19

9 It is by the goodness of God that in our country we have those three unspeakably precious things: freedom of speech, freedom of conscience, and the prudence never to practice either of them. *Ib. 20*

10 *"Classic."* A book which people praise and don't read. *Ib. 25*

11 Man is the only animal that blushes. Or needs to. *Ib. 27*

12 Let us be thankful for the fools. But for them the rest of us could not succeed.[1]
Ib. 28

13 There are several good protections against temptations, but the surest is cowardice.[2]
Ib. 36

14 There is an old-time toast which is golden for its beauty. "When you ascend the hill of prosperity may you not meet a friend."
Ib. II, 5

15 Each person is born to one possession which outvalues all his others—his last breath. *Ib. 6*

[1]See *Huckleberry Finn*, 624:3.
[2]See Wilde, 674:25.

16 It takes your enemy and your friend, working together, to hurt you to the heart; the one to slander you and the other to get the news to you. *Ib. 9*

17 Grief can take care of itself, but to get the full value of a joy you must have somebody to divide it with. *Ib. 12*

18 In statesmanship get the formalities right, never mind about the moralities.
Ib. 29

19 Everyone is a moon, and has a dark side which he never shows to anybody.
Ib. 30

20 Warm summer sun, shine kindly here;
Warm southern wind, blow softly here;
Green sod above, lie light, lie light—
Good-night, dear heart, good-night, good-night.[3]
Epitaph for his daughter[4] [1896]

21 The reports of my death are greatly exaggerated.
Cable from London to the Associated Press [1897]

22 A round man cannot be expected to fit in a square hole right away. He must have time to modify his shape.[5]
More Tramps Abroad [1897]

23 In Boston they ask, How much does he know? In New York, How much is he worth? In Philadelphia, Who were his parents?
What Paul Bourget Thinks of Us [1899]

24 The silent colossal National Lie that is the support and confederate of all the tyrannies and shams and inequalities and unfairnesses that afflict the peoples—that is the one to throw bricks and sermons at.
My First Lie, and How I Got Out of It [1900]

25 The blessings-of-civilization trust, wisely and cautiously administered, is a daisy. There is more money in it, more territory, more sovereignty, and other kinds of emolument, than there is in any other game that is played. But Christendom . . . has been so eager to get every stake that appeared on the

[3]Adapted from:
Warm summer sun, shine friendly here; / Warm western wind, blow kindly here; / Green sod above, rest light, rest light— / Good-night, Annette! Sweetheart, good-night.—Robert Richardson [1850–1901], *To Annette*
See Euripides, 76:4; Anonymous Latin, 134:28; and Beaumont and Fletcher, 263:7.
[4]Olivia Susan Clemens, who died August 18, 1896, aged twenty-four.
[5]See Sydney Smith, 432:17.

green cloth, that the people who sit in darkness[1] have noticed it . . . and have become suspicious of the blessings of civilization.

To the Person Sitting in Darkness [1901]

1 Always do right. This will gratify some people, and astonish the rest.[2]

To the Young People's Society, Greenpoint Presbyterian Church, Brooklyn [February 16, 1901]

2 A powerful agent is the right word. Whenever we come upon one of those intensely right words in a book or a newspaper the resulting effect is physical as well as spiritual, and electrically prompt.

Essay on William Dean Howells [1906]

3 It may be called the Master Passion, the hunger for self-approval.

What Is Man? [1906], ch. 6

4 The fact that man knows right from wrong proves his *intellectual* superiority to the other creatures; but the fact that he can *do* wrong proves his *moral* inferiority to any creature that *cannot.* *Ib.*

5 Customs do not concern themselves with right or wrong or reason. But they have to be obeyed; one reasons all around them until he is tired, but he must not transgress them, it is sternly forbidden.

The Gorky Incident [1906]

6 Laws are sand, customs are rock. Laws can be evaded and punishment escaped, but an openly transgressed custom brings sure punishment. *Ib.*

7 Thunder is good, thunder is impressive; but it is lightning that does the work.

Letter to an Unidentified Person [1908]

8 As out of place as a Presbyterian in Hell.

From ALBERT BIGELOW PAINE, *Mark Twain [1912]*

9 Biographies are but the clothes and buttons of the man — the biography of the man himself cannot be written.

Autobiography [1924], vol. I, p. 2

10 Of all the creatures that were made he [man] is the most detestable. Of the entire brood he is the only one — the solitary one — that possesses malice. That is the basest of all instincts, passions, vices — the most hateful. . . . He is the only creature that inflicts pain for sport, knowing it to *be* pain. . . . Also — in all the list he is the only creature that has a nasty mind. *Ib. II, p. 7*

11 The trade of critic, in literature, music, and the drama, is the most degraded of all trades. *Ib. p. 69*

12 You tell me whar a man gits his corn pone, en I'll tell you what his 'pinions is.

Europe and Elsewhere [1925]. Corn Pone Opinions

13 Its name is Public Opinion. It is held in reverence. It settles everything. Some think it is the voice of God. *Ib.*

14 Familiarity breeds contempt — and children.[3] *Notebooks [1935]*

15 Good breeding consists in concealing how much we think of ourselves and how little we think of the other person. *Ib.*

16 Death, the only immortal who treats us all alike, whose pity and whose peace and whose refuge are for all — the soiled and the pure, the rich and the poor, the loved and the unloved.

Ib. Memorandum written on his deathbed

17 I believe that our Heavenly Father invented man because he was disappointed in the monkey.

From BERNARD DE VOTO, *Mark Twain in Eruption [1940]*

18 Man seems to be a rickety poor sort of a thing, any way you take him; a kind of British Museum of infirmities and inferiorities. He is always undergoing repairs. A machine that was as unreliable as he is would have no market.

Letters from the Earth [1962].[4] *The Damned Human Race*

19 Loyalty to petrified opinion never yet broke a chain or freed a human soul.

Inscription beneath his bust in the Hall of Fame.

20 The calm confidence of a Christian with four aces. *Attributed*

Thomas Bailey Aldrich
1836–1907

21 Somewhere — in desolate windswept space —
In Twilight land — in No-man's land —
Two hurrying Shapes met face to face,
And bade each other stand.

[1] See *Psalm 107:10,* 21:13, and *Matthew 4:16,* 37:2.
[2] President Truman kept this saying on his desk in the White House.
[3] See Aesop, 66:4.
[4] Edited by BERNARD DE VOTO from unpublished manuscripts.

"And who are you?" cried one agape,
Shuddering in the gloaming light.
"I know not," said the second Shape,
"I only died last night!"

Identity [1877]

1 We knew it would rain, for the poplars showed
The white of their leaves.

Before the Rain, st. 3

2 My mind lets go a thousand things,
Like dates of wars and deaths of kings.

Memory

Isabella Mary Beeton
1836–1865

3 A place for everything and everything in its place.

The Book of Household Management [1861]

4 Clear as you go. *Ib.*

Edward Ernest Bowen
1836–1901

5 Forty years on, when afar and asunder
Parted are those who are singing today.

Forty Years On [1872][1]

Joseph Chamberlain
1836–1914

6 The day of small nations has long passed away. The day of Empires has come.

Speech, Birmingham [May 12, 1904]

Sir William Schwenck Gilbert[2]
1836–1911

7 Oh, I am a cook and a captain bold
And the mate of the *Nancy* brig,
And a bo'sun tight, and a midshipmite,
And the crew of the captain's gig.

The "Bab" Ballads [1866–1871]. The Yarn of the "Nancy Bell," st. 3

8 As innocent as a new-laid egg.

Engaged [1877], act I

[1] Harrow school song.

[2] Collaborator with composer Sir Arthur Sullivan [1842–1900] in the "Savoy" operas produced in London by Richard D'Oyly Carte [1844–1901].

His foe was folly and his weapon wit.—Sir Anthony Hope Hawkins [Anthony Hope, 1863–1933], *inscription on Gilbert Memorial, Victoria Embankment, London*

9 I'm called Little Buttercup—dear little Buttercup,
Though I could never tell why.

H.M.S. Pinafore [1878], act I

10 I am the Captain of the *Pinafore;*
And a right good captain too! *Ib.*

11 And I'm never, never sick at sea!
What, never?
No, never!
What, *never?*
Hardly ever!
He's hardly ever sick at sea!
Then give three cheers, and one cheer more
For the hardy Captain of the *Pinafore!*

Ib.

12 I never use a big, big D. *Ib.*

13 And so do his sisters, and his cousins, and his aunts!
His sisters and his cousins,
Whom he reckons up by dozens,
And his aunts! *Ib.*

14 When I was a lad I served a term
As office boy to an Attorney's firm.
I cleaned the windows and I swept the floor
And I polished up the handle of the big front door.
I polished up that handle so carefullee
That now I am the Ruler of the Queen's Navee! *Ib.*

15 Stick close to your desks and *never go to sea,*
And you all may be Rulers of the Queen's Navee! *Ib.*

16 Things are seldom what they seem,
Skim milk masquerades as cream.[3]

Ib. II

17 He is an Englishman!
For he himself has said it,[4]
And it's greatly to his credit,
That he is an Englishman! *Ib.*

18 For he might have been a Roosian,
A French or Turk or Proosian,
Or perhaps Itali-an.
But in spite of all temptations
To belong to other nations,
He remains an Englishman. *Ib.*

19 It is, it is a glorious thing
To be a Pirate King.

Pirates of Penzance [1879], act I

20 I am the very model of a modern Major-General. *Ib.*

[3] See Phaedrus, 114:10, and Longfellow, 509:13.

[4] See Anonymous Latin, 134:7.

1 I know the Kings of England, and I quote the fights historical,
From Marathon to Waterloo, in order categorical. *Ib.*

2 When the foeman bares his steel,
Tarantara, tarantara!
We uncomfortable feel,
Tarantara. *Ib. II*

3 When constabulary duty's to be done,
The policeman's lot is not a happy one. *Ib.*

4 Come, friends, who plow the sea,
Truce to navigation,
Take another station;
Let's vary piracee
With a little burglaree.[1] *Ib.*

5 Twenty love-sick maidens we,
Love-sick all against our will.
Patience [1881], act I

6 You must lie upon the daisies and discourse in novel phrases of your complicated state of mind,
The meaning doesn't matter if it's only idle chatter of a transcendental kind.
And everyone will say,
As you walk your mystic way,
"If this young man expresses himself in terms too deep for *me,*
Why, what a very singularly deep young man this deep young man must be!" *Ib.*

7 If you walk down Piccadilly with a poppy or a lily in your medieval hand.
And everyone will say,
As you walk your flowery way,
"If he's content with a vegetable love, which would certainly not suit *me,*
Why, what a most particularly pure young man this pure young man must be!" *Ib.*

8 Prithee, pretty maiden, will you marry me?
(Hey, but I'm hopeful, willow, willow, waly!) *Ib.*

9 While this magnetic,
Peripatetic
Lover, he lived to learn,
By no endeavor,
Can magnet ever
Attract a silver churn! *Ib. II*

10 Sing "Hey to you—good day to you"—
Sing "Bah to you—ha! ha! to you"—
Sing "Booh to you—pooh, pooh to you." *Ib.*

11 Francesca di Rimini, miminy, piminy,
Je-ne-sais-quoi young man! *Ib.*

[1] The roistering chorus "Hail, hail, the gang's all here" is sung to Sir Arthur Sullivan's music for these lines.

12 A greenery-yallery, Grosvenor Gallery,
Foot-in-the-grave young man! *Ib.*

13 I see no objection to stoutness, in moderation.
Iolanthe [1882], act I

14 None shall part us from each other,
One in life and death are we:
All in all to one another—
I to thee and thou to me!
Thou the tree and I the flower—
Thou the idol; I the throng—
Thou the day and I the hour—
Thou the singer; I the song! *Ib.*

15 Bow, bow, ye lower middle classes!
Bow, bow, ye tradesmen, bow, ye masses. *Ib.*

16 The Law is the true embodiment
Of everything that's excellent.
It has no kind of fault or flaw,
And I, my Lords, embody the Law. *Ib.*

17 Pretty young wards in Chancery. *Ib.*

18 A pleasant occupation for
A rather susceptible Chancellor! *Ib.*

19 For I'm not so old, and not so plain,
And I'm quite prepared to marry again. *Ib.*

20 Hearts just as pure and fair
May beat in Belgrave Square
As in the lowly air
Of Seven Dials. *Ib.*

21 Here's a pretty kettle of fish! *Ib. II*

22 When I went to the Bar as a very young man
(Said I to myself, said I). *Ib.*

23 I am an intellectual chap,
And think of things that would astonish you.
I often think it's comical
How nature always does contrive
That every boy and every gal,
That's born into the world alive,
Is either a little Liberal,
Or else a little Conservative! *Ib.*

24 The House of Peers, throughout the war,
Did nothing in particular,
And did it very well. *Ib.*

25 Oh, Captain Shaw!
Type of true love kept under!
Could thy Brigade
With cold cascade
Quench my great love, I wonder! *Ib.*

26 When you're lying awake with a dismal headache, and repose is tabooed by anxiety,
I conceive you may use any language you choose to indulge in, without impropriety. *Ib.*

1 For you dream you are crossing the Channel, and tossing about in a steamer from Harwich—
Which is something between a large bathing machine and a very small second class carriage. *Ib.*

2 Faint heart never won fair lady!
Nothing venture, nothing win[1]—
Blood is thick, but water's thin—
In for a penny, in for a pound—
It's Love that makes the world go round![2] *Ib.*

3 I love my fellow creatures—I do all the good I can—
Yet everybody says I'm such a disagreeable man!
And I can't think why!
Princess Ida [1884], act I

4 A wandering minstrel I—
A thing of shreds and patches,[3]
Of ballads, songs and snatches,
And dreamy lullaby!
The Mikado [1885], act I

5 I can't help it. I was born sneering. *Ib.*

6 As some day it may happen that a victim must be found,
I've got a little list—I've got a little list.
Of society offenders who might well be underground,
And who never would be missed—who never would be missed. *Ib.*

7 The idiot who praises, with enthusiastic tone,
All centuries but this, and every country but his own.[4] *Ib.*

8 Three little maids from school are we,
Pert as a schoolgirl well can be,
Filled to the brim with girlish glee. *Ib.*

9 Ah, pray make no mistake,
We are not shy;
We're very wide awake,
The moon and I! *Ib.*

10 Here's a pretty state of things!
Here's a pretty how-de-do. *Ib.*

11 My object all sublime
I shall achieve in time—
To make the punishment fit the crime.[5] *Ib. II*

[1]See Chaucer, 145:1, and Heywood, 160:12.
[2]See Anonymous: French, 928:5.
[3]See Shakespeare, 223:6.
[4]See Shakespeare, 212:20; Overbury, 262:13; and Canning, 422:3.
[5]See Cicero, 99:5.

12 A source of innocent merriment! *Ib.*

13 On a cloth untrue
With a twisted cue
And elliptical billiard balls. *Ib.*

14 I drew my snickersnee! *Ib.*

15 The flowers that bloom in the spring, tra la,
Have nothing to do with the case. *Ib.*

16 On a tree by a river a little tomtit
Sang "Willow, titwillow, titwillow!"
And I said to him, "Dicky-bird, why do you sit
Singing 'Willow, titwillow, titwillow!'
"Is it weakness of intellect, birdie?" I cried,
"Or a rather tough worm in your little inside?"
With a shake of his poor little head he replied,
"Oh, willow, titwillow, titwillow!" *Ib.*

17 There's a fascination frantic
In a ruin that's romantic;
Do you think you are sufficiently decayed? *Ib.*

18 He uses language that would make your hair curl. *Ruddigore [1887], act I*

19 For you are such a smart little craft—
Such a neat little, sweet little craft,
Such a bright little, tight little,
Slight little, light little
Trim little, prim little craft! *Ib. II*

20 When the footpads quail at the night bird's wail, and black dogs bay the moon,
Then is the specters' holiday—then is the ghosts' high noon! *Ib.*

21 I have a song to sing O!
Sing me your song. O!
The Yeomen of the Guard [1888], act I

22 It's a song of a merryman, moping mum,
Whose soul was sad, and whose glance was glum,
Who sipped no sup, and who craved no crumb,
As he sighed for the love of a lady. *Ib.*

23 Is life a boon?
If so, it must befall
That Death, whene'er he call,
Must call too soon. *Ib.*

24 Is life a thorn?
Then count it not a whit!
Man is well done with it. *Ib.*

25 He led his regiment from behind—
He found it less exciting.
The Gondoliers [1889], act I

1 That celebrated,
Cultivated,
Underrated nobleman,
The Duke of Plaza Toro! *Ib.*

2 No soldier in that gallant band
Hid half as well as he did.
He lay concealed throughout the war,
And this preserved his gore, O! *Ib.*

3 Of that there is no manner of doubt—
No probable, possible shadow of doubt—
No possible doubt whatever. *Ib.*

4 Life's a pudding full of plums;
Care's a canker that benumbs,
Wherefore waste our elocution
On impossible solution?
Life's a pleasant institution,
Let us take it as it comes! *Ib.*

5 Life's perhaps the only riddle
That we shrink from giving up. *Ib.*

6 The gratifying feeling that our duty has been done. *Ib.*

7 Take a pair of sparkling eyes. *Ib.*

8 When everyone is somebodee,
Then no one's anybody. *Ib.*

9 The world has joked incessantly for over fifty centuries.
And every joke that's possible has long ago been made.
His Excellency: The Played-Out Humorist [1894]

10 Humor is a drug which it's the fashion to abuse. *Ib.*

Bret Harte
[Francis Brett Harte]
1836–1902

11 Tell the boys I've got the Luck with me now.
The Luck of Roaring Camp [1868]

12 Beneath this tree lies the body of JOHN OAKHURST, who struck a streak of bad luck on the 23rd of November, 1850, and handed in his checks on the 7th of December, 1850.
The Outcasts of Poker Flat [1869]

13 I reside at Table Mountain, and my name is Truthful James;
I am not up to small deceit, or any sinful games.
The Society upon the Stanislaus, st. 1

14 And he smiled a kind of sickly smile, and curled up on the floor,
And the subsequent proceedings interested him no more. *Ib. st. 7*

15 Oh, yer's yer good old whiskey,
Drink it down.
Two Men of Sandy Bar [1876], act IV

16 Give me a man that is capable of a devotion to anything, rather than a cold, calculating average of all the virtues! *Ib.*

Jane Ellice Hopkins
1836–1904

17 Genius is an infinite capacity for taking pains.[1]
Work Amongst Working Men [1870]

Cesare Lombroso
1836–1909

18 Klopstock was questioned regarding the meaning of a passage in his poem. He replied, "God and I both knew what it meant once; now God alone knows."[2]
The Man of Genius [1891], pt. I, ch. 2

19 The appearance of a single great genius is more than equivalent to the birth of a hundred mediocrities. *Ib. II, 2*

20 "Lawsuit mania" . . . a continual craving to go to law against others, while considering themselves the injured party.
Ib. III, 3

John Burroughs
1837–1921

21 Serene, I fold my hands and wait,
Nor care for wind, nor tide, nor sea;
I rave no more 'gainst time or fate,
For lo! my own shall come to me.[3]
Waiting [1876] st. 1

22 I was born with a chronic anxiety about the weather. *Is It Going to Rain? [1877]*

23 Literature is an investment of genius which pays dividends to all subsequent times.
Literary Fame

24 One goes to Nature only for hints and half-truths. Her facts are crude until you have absorbed them or translated them. . . . It is not so much what we see as what the thing seen suggests.
Signs and Seasons [1886]

[1] See Buffon, 349:3; Carlyle, 474:14; and Butler, 620:21.
[2] Also attributed to Browning, apropos of his *Sordello*.
[3] See Emerson, 496:12, and Disraeli, 501:26.

1 It is always easier to believe than to deny. Our minds are naturally affirmative.

The Light of Day [1900]. The Modern Skeptic

2 Time does not become sacred to us until we have lived it.

The Spell of the Past [1904]

3 Nature teaches more than she preaches. There are no sermons in stones. It is easier to get a spark out of a stone than a moral.

Time and Change [1912]. The Gospel of Nature

4 Life is a struggle, but not a warfare.

The Summit of the Years [1913]

5 I see on an immense scale, and as clearly as in a demonstration in a laboratory, that good comes out of evil; that the impartiality of the Nature Providence is best; that we are made strong by what we overcome; that man is man because he is as free to do evil as to do good; that life is as free to develop hostile forms as to develop friendly; that power waits upon him who earns it; that disease, wars, the unloosened, devastating elemental forces have each and all played their part in developing and hardening man and giving him the heroic fiber.

Accepting the Universe [1922]

Grover Cleveland

1837–1908

6 Public officers are the servants and agents of the people, to execute the laws which the people have made.

Letter accepting the nomination for governor of New York [October 1882]

7 Your every voter, as surely as your chief magistrate, exercises a public trust.[1]

Inaugural Address [March 4, 1885]

8 After an existence of nearly twenty years of almost innocuous desuetude these laws are brought forth.

Message [March 1, 1886]

9 When more of the people's sustenance is exacted through the form of taxation than is necessary to meet the just obligations of government and expenses of its economical administration, such exaction becomes ruthless extortion and a violation of the fundamental principles of a free government.

Second Annual Message [December 1886]

10 It is a condition which confronts us—not a theory.[2]

Third Annual Message [December 6, 1887]

11 The lessons of paternalism ought to be unlearned and the better lesson taught that while the people should patriotically and cheerfully support their government, its functions do not include the support of the people.

Inaugural Address [March 4, 1893]

12 I have tried so hard to do the right.

Last words

George Dewey[3]

1837–1917

13 You may fire when you are ready, Gridley.

To the captain of Admiral Dewey's flagship at the battle of Manila Bay [May 1, 1898]

William Dean Howells

1837–1920

14 We live, but a world has passed away
With the years that perished to make us men.

The Mulberries [1871]

15 Lord, for the erring thought
Not into evil wrought:
Lord, for the wicked will
Betrayed and baffled still:
For the heart from itself kept,
Our thanksgiving accept.

A Thanksgiving

16 And before you know me gone
Eternity and I are one. *Time*

17 He who sleeps in continual noise is wakened
by silence. *Pordenone, IV*

18 See how today's achievement is only tomorrow's confusion;
See how possession always cheapens the thing that was precious. *Ib.*

19 The wrecks of slavery are fast growing a fungus crop of sentiment.

Their Wedding Journey [1872]

20 The mortality of all inanimate things is terrible to me, but that of books most of all.

Letter to Charles Eliot Norton [April 6, 1903]

[1] "Public office is a public trust" was used by the Cleveland administration as its motto.
See Matthew Henry, 319:16; Burke, 374:3; Clay, 444:3; Calhoun, 449:8; and Sumner, 539:4.

[2] See Disraeli, 501:12.

[3] See Ironquill, 647:2.

1 I am not sorry for having wrought in common, crude material so much; that is the right American stuff; and perhaps hereafter, when my din is done, if anyone is curious to know what that noise was, it will be found to have proceeded from a small insect which was scraping about on the surface of our life and trying to get into its meaning for the sake of the other insects larger or smaller. That is, such has been my unconscious work; consciously, I was always, as I still am, trying to fashion a piece of literature out of the life next at hand. *Ib. [April 26, 1903]*

2 Clemens was sole, incomparable, the Lincoln of our literature.
My Mark Twain [1910]

3 Some people can stay longer in an hour than others can in a week. *Attributed*

Horace Porter
1837–1921

4 A mugwump is a person educated beyond his intellect.
A slogan of the Cleveland-Blaine campaign [1884]

Innes Randolph
1837–1887

5 Oh, I'm a good old rebel, that's what I am.
A Good Old Rebel [c. 1870], st. 1

6 I won't be reconstructed, and I don't give a damn. *Ib. st. 4*

Algernon Charles Swinburne
1837–1909

7 When the hounds of spring are on winter's traces,
The mother of months in meadow or plain
Fills the shadows and windy places
With lisp of leaves and ripple of rain;
And the brown bright nightingale amorous
Is half assuaged for Itylus,
For the Thracian ships and the foreign faces,
The tongueless vigil, and all the pain.
Atalanta in Calydon [1865], chorus, st. 1

8 For winter's rains and ruins are over,
And all the season of snows and sins;
The days dividing lover and lover,
The light that loses, the night that wins;
And time remembered is grief forgotten,
And frosts are slain and flowers begotten,
And in green underwood and cover
Blossom by blossom the spring begins.
Ib. st. 4

9 Before the beginning of years
There came to the making of man
Time, with a gift of tears;
Grief, with a glass that ran;
Pleasure, with pain for leaven;
Summer, with flowers that fell;
Remembrance fallen from heaven,
And madness risen from hell;
Strength without hands to smite;
Love that endures for a breath;
Night, the shadow of light,
And life, the shadow of death.
Ib. chorus, st. 1

10 For words divide and rend;
But silence is most noble till the end.
Ib.

11 Change in a trice
The lilies and languors of virtue
For the raptures and roses of vice.
Dolores [1866], st. 9

12 O splendid and sterile Dolores,
Our Lady of Pain. *Ib.*

13 Ah beautiful passionate body
That never has ached with a heart!
Ib. st. 11

14 The delight that consumes the desire,
The desire that outruns the delight.
Ib. st. 14

15 For the crown of our life as it closes
Is darkness, the fruit there of dust.
Ib. st. 20

16 What ailed us, O gods, to desert you
For creeds that refuse and restrain?
Come down and redeem us from virtue,
Our Lady of Pain. *Ib. st. 35*

17 Lo, this is she that was the world's delight.
Laus Veneris [1866], st. 3

18 Ah, yet would God this flesh of mine might be
Where air might wash and long leaves cover me;
Where tides of grass break into foam of flowers,
Or where the wind's feet shine along the sea.
Ib. st. 14

19 O sad kissed mouth, how sorrowful it is!
Ib. st. 79

20 To have known love, how bitter a thing it is.
Ib. st. 103

21 There will no man do for your sake, I think,
What I would have done for the least word said.

I had wrung life dry for your lips to drink,
Broken it up for your daily bread.
The Triumph of Time [1866], st. 12

1 At the door of life, by the gate of breath,
There are worse things waiting for men than death. *Ib. st. 20*

2 I will go back to the great sweet mother,
Mother and lover of men, the sea.
Ib. st. 33

3 I shall never be friends again with roses;
I shall loathe sweet tunes. *Ib. st. 45*

4 Marvelous mercies and infinite love.
Les Noyades [1866], st. 1

5 I have lived long enough, having seen one thing, that love hath an end.
Hymn to Proserpine [1866]

6 Thou hast conquered, O pale Galilean;[1] the world has grown gray from thy breath;
We have drunken of things Lethean, and fed on the fullness of death.
Laurel is green for a season, and love is sweet for a day;
But love grows bitter with treason, and laurel outlives not May.
Sleep, shall we sleep after all? for the world is not sweet in the end;
For the old faiths loosen and fall, the new years ruin and rend. *Ib.*

7 I shall die as my fathers died, and sleep as they sleep; even so.
For the glass of the years is brittle wherein we gaze for a span. *Ib.*

8 For there is no God found stronger than death; and death is a sleep. *Ib.*

9 If you loved me ever so little,
I could bear the bonds that gall,
I could dream the bonds were brittle;
You do not love me at all.
Satia Te Sanguine [1866], st. 1

10 While he lives let a man be glad,
For none hath joy of his death.
A Lamentation [1866]. I, st. 4

11 If love were what the rose is,
And I were like the leaf,
Our lives would grow together
In sad or singing weather.
A Match [1866], st. 1

12 If you were April's lady,
And I were lord in May. *Ib. st. 5*

13 If you were queen of pleasure,
And I were king of pain,
We'd hunt down love together,
Pluck out his flying feather,
And teach his feet a measure,
And find his mouth a rein. *Ib. st. 6*

[1] See Julian, 127:5.

14 For in the time we know not of
Did fate begin
Weaving the web of days that wove
Your doom, Faustine.
Faustine [1866], st. 24

15 Take hand and part with laughter;
Touch lips and part with tears;
Once more and no more after,
Whatever comes with years.
Rococo [1866], st. 1

16 Forget that I remember,
And dream that I forget. *Ib. st. 2*

17 The burden of long living. Thou shalt fear
Waking, and sleeping mourn upon thy bed;
And say at night "Would God the day were here,"
And say at dawn "Would God the day were dead."[2]
A Ballad of Burdens [1866], st. 4

18 For life is sweet, but after life is death.
This is the end of every man's desire.
Ib. L'Envoy

19 Here, where the world is quiet;
Here, where all trouble seems
Dead winds' and spent waves' riot
In doubtful dreams of dreams.
The Garden of Proserpine [1866], st. 1

20 I am tired of tears and laughter,
And men that laugh and weep;
Of what may come hereafter
For men that sow and reap:
I am weary of days and hours,
Blown buds of barren flowers,
Desires and dreams and powers
And everything but sleep. *Ib. st. 2*

21 We are not sure of sorrow,
And joy was never sure. *Ib. st. 10*

22 From too much love of living,
From hope and fear set free,
We thank with brief thanksgiving
Whatever gods may be
That no life lives forever;
That dead men rise up never;
That even the weariest river
Winds somewhere safe to sea.[3]
Ib. st. 11

[2] See *Deuteronomy 28:67*, 11:20.

[3] No matter how long the river, the river will reach the sea. — IRONQUILL (EUGENE FITCH WARE) [1841–1911], *The Blizzard*

1 Ah that such sweet things should be fleet,
Such fleet things sweet!
Félise [1866], st. 22

2 I remember the way we parted,
The day and the way we met;
You hoped we were both broken-hearted
And knew we should both forget.
An Interlude [1866], st. 11

3 And the best and the worst of this is
That neither is most to blame,
If you have forgotten my kisses
And I have forgotten your name.
Ib. st. 14

4 I am that which began;
Out of me the years roll;
Out of me God and man;
I am equal and whole;
God changes, and man, and the form of them bodily; I am the soul.
Hertha [1871], st. 1

5 Before ever land was,
Before ever the sea,
Or soft hair of the grass,
Or fair limbs of the tree,
Or the flesh-colored fruit of my branches, I was, and thy soul was in me.
Ib. st. 2

6 A creed is a rod,
And a crown is of night;
But this thing is God,
To be man with thy might,
To grow straight in the strength of thy spirit, and to live out thy life as the light.
Ib. st. 15

7 In the gray beginning of years, in the twilight of things that began,
The word of the earth in the ears of the world, was it God? was it man?
Hymn of Man [1871]

8 Glory to Man in the highest! for Man is the master of things. *Ib.*

9 A blatant Bassarid of Boston, a rampant Maenad of Massachusetts.[1]
Under the Microscope [1872]

10 Poor splendid wings so frayed and soiled and torn!
A Ballad of François Villon [1878], st. 3

11 Villon, our sad bad glad mad brother's name.[2] *Ib. refrain*

[1]Harriet Beecher Stowe, whose accusations against Byron in "The True Story of Lady Byron's Life" [*Atlantic Monthly*, September 1869] and in *Lady Byron Vindicated* [1870] aroused strong protests in England.

[2]See Browning, 544:20.

12 In a coign of the cliff between lowland and highland,
At the sea-down's edge between windward and lee,
Walled round with rocks as an inland island,
The ghost of a garden fronts the sea.
A Forsaken Garden [1878], st. 1

13 Sleep; and if life was bitter to thee, pardon,
If sweet, give thanks; thou hast no more to live;
And to give thanks is good, and to forgive.
Ave Atque Vale: In Memory of Charles Baudelaire [1878], st. 17

14 Body and spirit are twins: God only knows which is which.
The Higher Pantheism in a Nutshell [1880], st. 7

15 God, whom we see not, is: and God, who is not, we see:
Fiddle, we know, is diddle: and diddle, we take it, is dee. *Ib. st. 12*

Henry Brooks Adams
1838–1918

16 Accident counts for much in companionship as in marriage.
The Education of Henry Adams [1907], ch. 4

17 Women have, commonly, a very positive moral sense; that which they will, is right; that which they reject, is wrong; and their will, in most cases, ends by settling the moral. *Ib. 6*

18 All experience is an arch, to build upon.[3] *Ib.*

19 Only on the edge of the grave can man conclude anything. *Ib.*

20 Although the Senate is much given to admiring in its members a superiority less obvious or quite invisible to outsiders, one Senator seldom proclaims his own inferiority to another, and still more seldom likes to be told of it. *Ib. 7*

21 Friends are born, not made. *Ib.*

22 A friend in power is a friend lost.[4] *Ib.*

23 The effect of power and publicity on all men is the aggravation of self, a sort of tumor that ends by killing the victim's sympathies. *Ib. 10*

24 Young men have a passion for regarding their elders as senile. *Ib. 11*

[3]See Tennyson, 529:8.

[4]See below, 635:16.

1 Knowledge of human nature is the beginning and end of political education. *Ib. 12*

2 These questions of taste, of feeling, of inheritance, need no settlement. Everyone carries his own inch-rule of taste, and amuses himself by applying it, triumphantly, wherever he travels. *Ib.*

3 Intimates are predestined. *Ib. 13*

4 Chaos often breeds life, when order breeds habit. *Ib.*

5 At best, the renewal of broken relations is a nervous matter. *Ib.*

6 Sumner's[1] mind had reached the calm of water which receives and reflects images without absorbing them; it contained nothing but itself. *Ib.*

7 The difference is slight, to the influence of an author, whether he is read by five hundred readers, or by five hundred thousand; if he can select the five hundred, he reaches the five hundred thousand. *Ib. 17*

8 A teacher affects eternity; he can never tell where his influence stops. *Ib. 20*

9 One friend in a lifetime is much; two are many; three are hardly possible. Friendship needs a certain parallelism of life, a community of thought, a rivalry of aim. *Ib.*

10 What one knows is, in youth, of little moment; they know enough who know how to learn. *Ib. 21*

11 He had often noticed that six months' oblivion amounts to newspaper death, and that resurrection is rare. Nothing is easier, if a man wants it, than rest, profound as the grave. *Ib. 22*

12 Morality is a private and costly luxury. *Ib.*

13 Practical politics consists in ignoring facts. *Ib.*

14 Nothing in education is so astonishing as the amount of ignorance it accumulates in the form of inert facts. *Ib. 25*

15 Power when wielded by abnormal energy is the most serious of facts. *Ib. 28*

16 Those who seek education in the paths of duty are always deceived by the illusion that power in the hands of friends is an advantage to them.[2] *Ib.*

[1]Charles Sumner [1811–1874].
[2]See above, 634:22.

17 Modern politics is, at bottom, a struggle not of men but of forces. *Ib.*

18 We combat obstacles in order to get repose, and, when got, the repose is insupportable. *Ib. 29*

19 Simplicity is the most deceitful mistress that ever betrayed man. *Ib. 30*

20 No one means all he says, and yet very few say all they mean, for words are slippery and thought is viscous. *Ib. 31*

21 Even in America, the Indian summer of life should be a little sunny and a little sad, like the season, and infinite in wealth and depth of tone—but never hustled. *Ib. 35*

Philip Paul Bliss
1838–1876

22 Hold the fort, for I am coming![3]
Gospel Songs [1874]. Hold the Fort, refrain

John Wilkes Booth
1838–1865

23 Sic semper tyrannis![4] The South is avenged!
After shooting President Lincoln [April 14, 1865]

James Bryce
1838–1922

24 Law will never be strong or respected unless it has the sentiment of the people behind it. If the people of a state make bad laws, they will suffer for it. They will be the first to suffer. Suffering, and nothing else, will implant that sentiment of responsibility which is the first step to reform.
The American Commonwealth [1888], vol. I, p. 352

25 To most people nothing is more troublesome than the effort of thinking.[5]
Studies in History and Jurisprudence [1901]. Obedience

[3]Popular version of what General William Tecumseh Sherman signaled to General John Murray Corse from Kenesaw Mountain when Corse was attacked at Allatoona Pass [October 5, 1864]: "Hold out; relief is coming."
See Sherman, 579:1.
[4]Thus always to tyrants.—*Motto of Virginia*
[5]See R. B. Sheridan, 399:8, and J. R. Lowell, 569:7.

1 The greatest liberty that man has taken with Nature.[1] *South America [1912]*

George Cooper
1838–1927

2 Sweet Genevieve,
The days may come, the days may go,
But still the hands of memory weave
The blissful dreams of long ago.
Sweet Genevieve [c. 1877]

John Milton Hay
1838–1905

3 I'll hold her nozzle agin the bank
Till the last galoot's ashore.
Pike County Ballads [1871]. Jim Bludso, st. 5

4 And Christ ain't a-going to be too hard
On a man that died for men. *Ib. st. 7*

5 And I think that saving a little child,
And fotching him to his own,
Is a derned sight better business
Than loafing around The Throne.
Ib. Little Breeches, last stanza

6 Who would succeed in the world should be wise in the use of his pronouns.
Utter the You twenty times, where you once utter the I. *Distichs, no. 13*

7 True luck consists not in holding the best of the cards at the table:
Luckiest he who knows just when to rise and go home. *Ib. 15*

8 The open door.
To the Cabinet regarding completion of negotiations for the "open door" in China [January 2, 1900]

George Washington Johnson
1838–1917

9 Let us sing of the days that are gone, Maggie,
When you and I were young.
When You and I Were Young, Maggie [1866], refrain

William Edward Hartpole Lecky
1838–1903

10 Offspring of an idle hour,
Whence has come thy lasting power?
On an old song

[1]The Panama Canal.

11 And while the great and wise decay,
And all their trophies pass away,
Some sudden thought, some careless rhyme,
Still floats above the wrecks of Time.
Ib.

George Leybourne
d. 1884

12 He flies through the air with the greatest of ease,
This daring young man on the flying trapeze;
His figure is handsome, all girls he can please,
And my love he purloined her away!
The Man on the Flying Trapeze [1860]

Lydia Kamekeha Liliuokalani
1838–1917

13 Farewell to thee,[2] farewell to thee . . .
Until we meet again.
Aloha Oe (Farewell to Thee) [1878]

Ernst Mach
1838–1916

14 Physics is experience, arranged in economical order.
The Economical Nature of Physical Inquiry [1882]

15 Science throws her treasures, not like a capricious fairy into the lap of a favored few, but into the laps of all humanity, with a lavish extravagance that no legend ever dreamed of. *Ib.*

16 Intelligible as it is . . . that the efforts of thinkers have always been bent upon the "reduction of all physical processes to the motions of atoms," it must yet be affirmed that this is a chimerical ideal. This ideal has often played an effective part in popular lectures, but in the workshop of the serious inquirer it has discharged scarcely the least function.
On the Principle of the Conservation of Energy [1894]

17 [If we suppose that physical events can be reduced to spatial motions of material particles] we impose on the creations of thought the limitations of the visible and tangible.
Ib.

[2]Aloha oe.

John, Viscount Morley of Blackburn
1838–1923

1 Evolution is not a force but a process; not a cause but a law.
On Compromise [1874]

2 Those who would treat politics and morality apart will never understand the one or the other. *Rousseau [1876]*

3 You cannot demonstrate an emotion or prove an aspiration. *Ib.*

4 It is not enough to do good; one must do it the right way. *Ib.*

5 You have not converted a man because you have silenced him. *Ib.*

6 A great interpreter of life ought not himself to need interpretation.
Emerson [1884]

7 The great business of life is to be, to do, to do without, and to depart.
Address on Aphorisms [1887]

8 Simplicity of character is no hindrance to subtlety of intellect.
Life of Gladstone [1903]

9 No man can climb out beyond the limitations of his own character.
Critical Miscellanies [1908]. Robespierre

10 There are some books which cannot be adequately reviewed for twenty or thirty years after they come out.
Recollections [1917], vol. I, bk. 2, ch. 8

11 The proper memory for a politician is one that knows what to remember and what to forget. *Ib. II, 4, 2*

12 In my creed, waste of public money is like the sin against the Holy Ghost.
Ib. 5, 3

13 Success depends on three things: who says it, what he says, how he says it; and of these three things, what he says is the least important. *Ib. 4*

14 Excess of severity is not the path to order. On the contrary, it is the path to the bomb.
Ib.

John Muir
1838–1914

15 "The water in music the oar forsakes."[1] The air in music the wing forsakes. All things move in music and write it. The mouse, lizard, and grasshopper sing together on the Turlock sands, sing with the morning stars.
Letter to Jeanne C. Carr, Yosemite [1874]

16 In God's wildness lies the hope of the world —the great fresh unblighted, unredeemed wilderness.[2] *Alaska Fragment [1890]*

17 On no subject are our ideas more warped and pitiable than on death. . . . Let children walk with nature, let them see the beautiful blendings and communions of death and life, their joyous inseparable unity, as taught in woods and meadows, plains and mountains and streams of our blessed star, and they will learn that death is stingless indeed, and as beautiful as life, and that the grave has no victory,[3] for it never fights. All is divine harmony.
A Thousand-Mile Walk to the Gulf [1916]

18 The clearest way into the Universe is through a forest wilderness.
John of the Mountains [1938]

19 The mountains are fountains of men as well as of rivers, of glaciers, of fertile soil. The great poets, philosophers, prophets, able men whose thought and deeds have moved the world, have come down from the mountains — mountain-dwellers who have grown strong there with the forest trees in Nature's workshops. *Ib.*

20 Most people are *on* the world, not in it — have no conscious sympathy or relationship to anything about them — undiffused, separate, and rigidly alone like marbles of polished stone, touching but separate.
Ib.

21 How hard to realize that every camp of men or beast has this glorious starry firmament for a roof! In such places standing alone on the mountaintop it is easy to realize that whatever special nests we make — leaves and moss like the marmots and birds, or tents or piled stone — we all dwell in a house of one room — the world with the firmament for its roof — and are sailing the celestial spaces without leaving any track.[4] *Ib.*

Margaret Elizabeth Sangster
1838–1912

22 Never yet was a springtime
When the buds forgot to blow.
Awakening

[1] See Emerson, 494:6, last line.

[2] See Thoreau, 560:27.

[3] See *I Corinthians 15:55*, 49:8.

[4] Written while camping in Alaska [July 18, 1890].

Philippe Auguste Villiers de L'Isle-Adam
1838–1889

1 Living? We'll leave that to the servants.[1]
Axel [1890]

2 I have thought too much to stoop to action![2] *Ib.*

Paul Cézanne
1839–1906

3 Treat nature in terms of the cylinder, the sphere, the cone, all in perspective.
From EMILE BERNARD, *Paul Cézanne [1925]*

4 Right now a moment of time is fleeting by! Capture its reality in paint! To do that we must put all else out of our minds. We must become that moment, make ourselves a sensitive recording plate . . . give the image of what we actually see, forgetting everything that has been seen before our time.
From JOACHIM GASQUET, *Paul Cézanne [1926]*[3]

5 The day is coming when a single carrot, freshly observed [in a painting], will set off a revolution. *Ib.*

Francis Pharcellus Church
1839–1906

6 No Santa Claus! Thank God, he lives, and he lives forever. A thousand years from now, Virginia, nay, ten times ten thousand years from now, he will continue to make glad the heart of childhood.
Is There a Santa Claus? [1897][4]

Henry George
1839–1897

7 So long as all the increased wealth which modern progress brings goes but to build up great fortunes, to increase luxury and make sharper the contrast between the House of Have and the House of Want, progress is not real and cannot be permanent.
Progress and Poverty [1879]. Introductory: The Problem

[1] Vivre? Les serviteurs feront cela pour nous.
[2] J'ai trop pensé pour daigner agir!
[3] Translated by NORBERT GUTERMAN.
[4] Usually quoted: Yes, Virginia, there is a Santa Claus. Editorial first published in the *New York Sun* [September 21, 1897] in reply to an inquiry from Virginia O'Hanlon.

John Chipman Gray
1839–1915

8 Dirt is only matter out of place; and what is a blot on the escutcheon of the Common Law may be a jewel in the crown of the Social Republic.[5]
Restraints on the Alienation of Property, second edition [1895], preface

Walter Pater
1839–1894

9 Every intellectual product must be judged from the point of view of the age and the people in which it was produced.
The Renaissance [1873]. Mirandola

10 Hers is the head upon which all "the ends of the world are come," and the eyelids are a little weary. It is a beauty wrought out from within upon the flesh, the deposit, little cell by cell, of strange thoughts and fantastic reveries and exquisite passions. Set it for a moment beside one of those white Greek goddesses or beautiful women of antiquity, and how would they be troubled by this beauty, into which the soul with all its maladies has passed?
Ib. Leonardo da Vinci [Mona Lisa]

11 She is older than the rocks among which she sits; like the vampire, she has been dead many times, and learned the secrets of the grave; and has been a diver in deep seas, and keeps their fallen day about her; and trafficked for strange webs with Eastern merchants: and as Leda, was the mother of Helen of Troy, and, as Saint Anne, the mother of Mary; and all this has been to her but as the sound of lyres and flutes, and lives only in the delicacy with which it has molded the changing lineaments, and tinged the eyelids and the hands. *Ib.*

12 Not the fruit of experience, but experience itself, is the end. *Ib. Conclusion*

13 To burn always with this hard, gemlike flame, to maintain this ecstasy, is success in life. *Ib.*

14 What we have to do is to be forever curiously testing new opinions and courting new impressions. *Ib.*

15 Art comes to you proposing frankly to give nothing but the highest quality to your moments as they pass. *Ib.*

[5] The reference is to "spendthrift trusts," which Gray believed had "no place in the system of the Common Law."

1 A book, like a person, has its fortunes with one; is lucky or unlucky in the precise moment of its falling in our way, and often by some happy accident counts with us for something more than its independent value.
Marius the Epicurean [1885], ch. 6

2 To know when one's self is interested, is the first condition of interesting other people.
Ib.

3 We need some imaginative stimulus, some not impossible ideal such as may shape vague hope, and transform it into effective desire, to carry us year after year, without disgust, through the routine work which is so large a part of life. *Ib. 25*

4 It is the addition of strangeness to beauty that constitutes the romantic character in art. *Appreciation [1889]. Postscript*

Charles Sanders Peirce[1]
1839–1914

5 Do not block the way of inquiry.
Collected Papers [1931–1958], vol. I, par. 135

6 The idea does not belong to the soul; it is the soul that belongs to the idea.
Ib. 216

7 Effort supposes resistance. *Ib. 320*

8 Every man is fully satisfied that there is such a thing as truth, or he would not ask any question. *Ib. V, 211*

9 Let us not pretend to doubt in philosophy what we do not doubt in our hearts.
Ib. 265

10 All the evolution we know of proceeds from the vague to the definite. *Ib. VI, 191*

11 Mere imagination would indeed be mere trifling; only no imagination is *mere*.
Ib. 286

12 Our whole past experience is continually in our consciousness, though most of it sunk to a great depth of dimness. I think of consciousness as a bottomless lake, whose waters seem transparent, yet into which we can clearly see but a little way.[2]
Ib. VII, 547

13 Unless man have a natural bent in accordance with nature's, he has no chance of understanding nature at all.
A Neglected Argument for the Reality of God [Hibbert Journal VII:90]

[1] See William James, 650:*n*1.
[2] See Freud, 678:11, and Bergson, 688:8.

14 It is the man of science, eager to have his every opinion regenerated, his every idea rationalized, by drinking at the fountain of fact, and devoting all the energies of his life to the cult of truth, not as he understands it, but as he does not yet understand it, that ought properly to be called a philosopher.
Review of the Nineteenth Century [1900]

James Ryder Randall
1839–1908

15 Hark to an exiled son's appeal,
Maryland, my Maryland!
My Mother State to thee I kneel.
Maryland, My Maryland [1861], st. 2

Wilfrid Scawen Blunt
1840–1922

16 Ay, this is the famed rock, which Hercules
And Goth and Moor bequeathed us. At this door
England stands sentry. *Gibraltar*

Henry Burton
1840–1930

17 Have you had a kindness shown?
Pass it on. *Pass It On, st. 1*

Timothy J. Campbell
1840–1904

18 What's the Constitution between friends?[3]
Attributed [c. 1885]

Henry Austin Dobson
1840–1921

19 Time goes, you say? Ah no!
Alas, Time stays, *we* go.
The Paradox of Time [1875], st. 1

20 I intended an ode,
And it turned to a sonnet.
It began à la mode,
I intended an ode;
But Rose crossed the road
In her latest new bonnet;
I intended an ode;
And it turned to a sonnet.
Rose Leaves [1874]. Urceus Exit

[3] Reported comment to President Cleveland, who refused to support a bill on the grounds that it was unconstitutional.

1 All passes. Art alone
Enduring stays to us;
The bust outlasts the throne—
The coin, Tiberius.[1]

Ars Victrix [1876], st. 8

2 The ladies of St. James's!
They're painted to the eyes;
Their white it stays forever,
Their red it never dies:
But Phyllida, my Phyllida!
Her color comes and goes;
It trembles to a lily—
It wavers to a rose.

The Ladies of St. James's [1883], st. 4

Thomas Hardy
1840–1928

3 These purblind Doomsters had as readily strown
Blisses about my pilgrimage as pain.

Hap [1866]

4 When I set out for Lyonnesse,
A hundred miles away,
The rime was on the spray,
And starlight lit my lonesomeness.

When I Set Out for Lyonnesse [1870], st. 1

5 Good, but not religious-good.

Under the Greenwood Tree [1872], ch. 2

6 The kingly brilliance of Sirius pierced the eye with a steely glitter, the star called Capella was yellow, Aldebaran and Betelgueux shone with a fiery red. To persons standing alone on a hill during a clear midnight such as this, the roll of the world eastward is almost a palpable movement.

Far from the Madding Crowd [1874], ch. 2

7 Like the British Constitution, she owes her success in practice to her inconsistencies in principle.

The Hand of Ethelberta [1876]

8 A lover without indiscretion is no lover at all. *Ib.*

9 In fact, precisely at this transitional point of its nightly roll into darkness the great and particular glory of the Egdon waste began, and nobody could be said to understand the heath who had not been there at such a time. It could best be felt when it could not clearly be seen.

The Return of the Native [1878], ch. 1

[1] See Théophile Gautier, 538:7.

10 The place became full of a watchful intentness now; for when other things sank brooding to sleep the heath appeared slowly to awake and listen. *Ib.*

11 The great inviolate place had an ancient permanence which the sea cannot claim. Who can say of a particular sea that it is old? Distilled by the sun, kneaded by the moon, it is renewed in a year, in a day, or in an hour. The sea changed, the fields changed, the rivers, the villages, and the people changed, yet Egdon remained. *Ib.*

12 The hard, half-apathetic expression of one who deems anything possible at the hands of Time and Chance, except, perhaps, fair play.

The Mayor of Casterbridge [1886], ch. 1

13 And all her shining keys will be took from her, and her cupboards opened, and little things 'a didn't wish seen, anybody will see; and her wishes and ways will be as nothing! *Ib. 18*

14 Who is such a reprobate as I [Michael Henchard]! And yet it seems that even I be in Somebody's hand! *Ib. 41*

15 The ingenious machinery contrived by the gods for reducing human possibilities of amelioration to a minimum. *Ib. 44*

16 That Elizabeth-Jane Farfrae be not told of my death, or be made to grieve on account of me. And that I be not buried in consecrated ground. And that no sexton be asked to toll the bell. And that nobody is wished to see my dead body. And that no murners walk behind me at my funeral. And that no flours be planted on my grave. And that no man remember me. *Ib. 45 [Henchard's will]*

17 She [Elizabeth-Jane Farfrae] did not cease to wonder at the persistence of the unforeseen, when the one to whom such unbroken tranquility had been accorded in the adult stage was she whose youth had seemed to teach that happiness was but the occasional episode in a general drama of pain.

Ib. Last sentence

18 That cold accretion called the world, which, so terrible in the mass, is so unformidable, even pitiable, in its units.

Tess of the D'Urbervilles [1891], ch. 13

19 That shabby corner of God's allotment where He lets the nettles grow, and where all unbaptized infants, notorious drunkards,

suicides, and others of the conjecturally damned are laid. *Ib. 14*

1 The chronic melancholy which is taking hold of the civilized races with the decline of belief in a beneficent power. *Ib. 18*

2 The debatable land between predilection and love. *Ib. 20*

3 Patience, that blending of moral courage with physical timidity. *Ib. 43*

4 "Justice" was done, and the President of the Immortals (in Aeschylean phrase) had ended his sport with Tess. *Ib. 59*

5 But nobody did come, because nobody does. *Jude the Obscure [1895], pt. I, ch. 4*

6 The fundamental error of their matrimonial union; that of having based a permanent contract on a temporary feeling. *Ib. 11*

7 But sometimes a woman's love of being loved gets the better of her conscience. *Ib. IV, 5*

8 Done because we are too menny. *Ib. VI, 2*

9 Do not do an immoral thing for moral reasons. *Ib. 3*

10 William Dewy, Tranter Reuben, Farmer Ledlow late at plow,
Robert's kin, and John's and Ned's,
And the Squire, and Lady Susan, lie in Mellstock churchyard now!
Friends Beyond [1898], st. 1

11 I leant upon a coppice gate
When Frost was specter-gray,
And Winter's dregs made desolate
The weakening eye of day.
The Darkling Thrush [1900], st. 1

12 An aged thrush, frail, gaunt, and small,
In blast-beruffled plume. *Ib. st. 3*

13 So little cause for carolings
Of such ecstatic sound
Was written on terrestrial things
Afar or nigh around,
That I could think there trembled through
His happy good-night air
Some blessed hope, whereof he knew
And I was unaware. *Ib. st. 4*

14 Here by the baring bough
Raking up leaves,
Often I ponder how
Springtime deceives—
I, an old woman now,
Raking up leaves.
Autumn in King's Hintock Park [1901], st. 1

15 Yes; quaint and curious war is!
You shoot a fellow down
You'd treat if met where any bar is,
Or help to half-a-crown.
The Man He Killed [1902], st. 5

16 The Earth, sayest thou? The Human race?
By Me created? Sad its lot?
Nay; I have no remembrance of such place—
Such world I fashioned not.
God-Forgotten [1902], st. 2

17 What of the Immanent Will and its designs?
It works unconsciously as heretofore,
External artistries in circumstance.
The Dynasts [1904–1908], pt. I, forescene

18 A local cult called Christianity.
Ib. Spirit of the Years, sc. vi

19 Ere systemed suns were globed and lit
The slaughters of the race were writ.
Ib. II, v, semichorus

20 My argument is that War makes rattling good history; but Peace is poor reading. *Ib. Spirit Sinister*

21 A star looks down at me,
And says: "Here I and you
Stand, each in our degree:
What do you mean to do?"
Waiting Both, st. 1

22 We two kept house, the Past and I,
The Past and I;
I tended while it hovered nigh,
Leaving me never alone.
The Ghost of the Past, st. 1

23 I seem but a dead man held on end
To sink down soon. . . . O you could not know
That such swift fleeing
No soul foreseeing—
Not even I—would undo me so!
The Going [1912], st. 6

24 Woman much missed, how you call to me, call to me,
Saying that now you are not as you were
When you had changed from the one who was all to me,
But as at first, when our day was fair.
The Voice [1912], st 1

25 What of the faith and fire within us
Men who march away
Ere the barn cocks say
Night is growing gray,
Leaving all that here can win us?
Men Who March Away [1914], st. 1

1 That night your great guns, unawares,
Shook all our coffins as we lay,
And broke the chancel window-squares,
We thought it was the Judgment Day.
Channel Firing [1914], st. 1

2 Only a man harrowing clods
In a slow silent walk
With an old horse that stumbles and nods
Half asleep as they stalk.

Only thin smoke without flame
From the heaps of couch grass:
Yet this will go onward the same
Though dynasties pass.

Yonder a maid and her wight
Come whispering by;
War's annals will cloud into night
Ere their story die.
In Time of "The Breaking of Nations" [1915]

3 When the Present has latched its postern behind my tremulous stay,
And the May month flaps its glad green leaves like wings,
Delicate-filmed as new-spun silk, will the neighbors say,
"He was a man who used to notice such things"? *Afterwards, st. 1*

4 Ah, no; the years O!
Down their chiseled names the raindrop plows.
During Wind and Rain, st. 4

5 This is the weather the shepherd shuns,
And so do I. *Weathers [1922], st. 2*

6 And meadow rivulets overflow,
And drops on gate bars hang in a row,
And rooks in families homeward go,
And so do I. *Ib.*

Chief Joseph[1]

c. 1840–1904

7 Our chiefs are killed. . . . The old men are all dead. . . . The little children are freezing to death. My people, some of them have run away to the hills and have no blankets, no food. No one knows where they are, perhaps freezing to death. I want to have time to look for my children and see how many of them I can find. Maybe I can find them among the dead. Hear me, my chiefs. My heart is sick and sad. From where the sun now stands I will fight no more forever.

To the Nez Percé tribe after surrender to General Nelson A. Miles [battle of Bear Paw Mountains, Montana, September 30–October 5, 1877]

[1]Hinmaton-Yalaktit: Thunder Rolling in the Mountains.

Alfred Thayer Mahan

1840–1914

8 The world has never seen a more impressive demonstration of the influence of sea power upon its history. Those far distant, storm-beaten ships, upon which the Grand Army never looked, stood between it and the dominion of the world.[2]

The Influence of Sea Power upon the French Revolution and Empire, 1793–1812 [1892], vol. II, p. 118

9 Whether they will or no, Americans must begin to look outward.

The Interest of America in Sea Power [1897]

Rossiter Worthington Raymond

1840–1918

10 Life is eternal; and love is immortal; and death is only a horizon; and a horizon is nothing save the limit of our sight.

A Commendatory Prayer

William Graham Sumner

1840–1910

11 The Forgotten Man[3] . . . delving away in patient industry, supporting his family, paying his taxes, casting his vote, supporting the church and the school . . . but he is the only one for whom there is no provision in the great scramble and the big divide. Such is the Forgotten Man. He works, he votes, generally he prays—but his chief business in life is to pay. . . . Who and where is the Forgotten Man in this case, who will have to pay for it all?

Speech, The Forgotten Man [1883]

[2]Apart from the accidents of weather and the tides and currents, about which he admits he could not obtain trustworthy information, Julius Caesar saw no difficulty in invading the Island. There was not then that far-off line of storm-beaten ships which about two thousand years later stood between the great Corsican conqueror and the dominion of the world.—WINSTON CHURCHILL, *A History of the English-Speaking Peoples. The Birth of Britain* [1956], *p. 5*

Also quoted by Churchill in the same work under *The Age of Revolution*, p. 300.

See Themistocles, 70:19; Bacon, 181:11; Waller, 276:3; Washington, 379:5; and Morison, 800:11.

[3]See Franklin D. Roosevelt, 779:6.

John Addington Symonds

1840–1893

1 These things shall be — a loftier race
Than e'er the world hath known shall rise
With flame of freedom in their souls,
And light of knowledge in their eyes.
The Days That Are to Be

2 They shall be gentle, brave and strong
To spill no drop of blood, but dare
All that may plant man's lordship firm
On earth and fire and sea and air. *Ib.*

John Wilson[1]

d. 1889

3 Oh for a book and a shady nook, either in door or out.
Poem for a catalogue of secondhand books

Elizabeth Wordsworth

1840–1932

4 If all the good people were clever,
And all clever people were good,
The world would be nicer than ever
We thought that it possibly could.
The Clever and the Good [1890]

Émile Zola

1840–1902

5 I am little concerned with beauty or perfection. I don't care for the great centuries. All I care about is life, struggle, intensity. I am at ease in my generation.
Mes Haines (My Hates) [1866]

6 A work of art is a corner of creation seen through a temperament. *Ib.*

7 My own art is a negation of society, an affirmation of the individual, outside all rules and demands of society. *Ib.*

8 Truth is on the march and nothing can stop it.
Article in Le Figaro [November 25, 1897]

9 J'accuse.
Title of letter to the president of the République, L'Aurore [January 13, 1898]

[1]A London bookseller, friend of Austin Dobson.

Robert Buchanan

1841–1901

10 The Fleshly School of Poetry.
Title of article [1871][2]

Georges Clemenceau

1841–1929

11 The good Lord had only ten.
In reference to Wilson's Fourteen Points

12 America is the only nation in history which miraculously has gone directly from barbarism to degeneration without the usual interval of civilization. *Attributed*

13 There is nothing harder for the human spirit to bear than being cold-shouldered.
Quoted by CHARLES DE GAULLE, *Le Fil de l'Épée [1932], ch.* 2

Oliver Wendell Holmes, Jr.

1841–1935

14 The life of the law has not been logic: it has been experience.
The Common Law [1881]

15 The law embodies the story of a nation's development through many centuries, and it cannot be dealt with as if it contained only the axioms and corollaries of a book of mathematics. *Ib.*

16 I think that, as life is action and passion, it is required of a man that he should share the passion and action of his time at peril of being judged not to have lived.
Memorial Day Address [1884]

17 Through our great good fortune, in our youth our hearts were touched with fire. *Ib.*

18 The Law, wherein, as in a magic mirror, we see reflected not only our own lives, but the lives of all men that have been! When I think on this majestic theme, my eyes dazzle.[3]
To the Suffolk Bar Association [1885]

19 I say to you in all sadness of conviction, that to think great thoughts you must be heroes as well as idealists.
The Profession of the Law [1886]

[2]Attack on the Pre-Raphaelites occasioned by some sonnets in Rossetti's *The House of Life*.
See D. G. Rossetti, 601:17 and 601:22.
[3]See John Webster, 262:10.

1 Thus only can you gain the secret isolated joy of the thinker, who knows that, a hundred years after he is dead and forgotten, men who never heard of him will be moving to the measure of his thought—the subtle rapture of a postponed power, which the world knows not because it has no external trappings, but which to his prophetic vision is more real than that which commands an army.
Ib.

2 The prophecies of what the courts will do in fact, and nothing more pretentious, are what I mean by the law.
The Path of the Law [1897]

3 Certainty generally is illusion, and repose is not the destiny of man. *Ib.*

4 The remoter and more general aspects of the law are those which give it universal interest. It is through them that you not only become a great master in your calling, but connect your subject with the universe and catch an echo of the infinite, a glimpse of its unfathomable process, a hint of the universal law. *Ib.*

5 The rule of joy and the law of duty seem to me all one.
Speech at Bar Association Dinner, Boston [1900]

6 Life is an end in itself, and the only question as to whether it is worth living is whether you have enough of it.[1] *Ib.*

7 A great man represents a great ganglion in the nerves of society, or, to vary the figure, a strategic point in the campaign of history, and part of his greatness consists in his being *there.* *John Marshall [1901]*

8 Taxes are what we pay for civilized society.
Compañía de Tabacos v. Collector, 275 U.S. 87, 100 [1904]

9 Great cases like hard cases make bad law.
Northern Securities Co. v. United States, 193 U.S. 197, 400 [1904]

10 The Fourteenth Amendment does not enact Mr. Herbert Spencer's *Social Statics.*
Lochner v. New York, 198 U.S. 45, 75 [1905]

11 General propositions do not decide concrete cases. The decision will depend on a judgment or intuition more subtle than any articulate major premise. *Ib. 78*

12 The great act of faith is when man decides that he is not God.
Letter to William James [1907]

[1]See William James, 649:13, and Santayana, 703:9.

13 Life is painting a picture, not doing a sum.
The Class of '61. From Speeches [1913]

14 I learned in the regiment and in the class the conclusion, at least, of what I think the best service that we can do for our country and for ourselves: To see so far as one may, and to feel the great forces that are behind every detail . . . to hammer out as compact and solid a piece of work as one can, to try to make it first rate, and to leave it unadvertised. *Ib.*

15 The only prize much cared for by the powerful is power. The prize of the general is not a bigger tent, but command.
Law and the Court [1913]

16 Judges are apt to be naïf, simple-minded men, and they need something of Mephistopheles. We too need education in the obvious—to learn to transcend our own convictions and to leave room for much that we hold dear to be done away with short of revolution by the orderly change of law. *Ib.*

17 I do not think the United States would come to an end if we lost our power to declare an Act of Congress void. I do think the Union would be imperiled if we could not make that declaration as to the laws of the several states. *Ib.*

18 The attacks upon the Court are merely an expression of the unrest that seems to wonder vaguely whether law and order pay. When the ignorant are taught to doubt, they do not know what they safely may believe.
Ib.

19 I do not think we need trouble ourselves with the thought that my view depends upon differences of degree. The whole law does so as soon as it is civilized.
LeRoy Fibre Co. v. C., M. & St. P. Ry., 232 U.S. 340, 354 [1914]

20 I recognize without hesitation that judges do and must legislate, but they can do so only interstitially; they are confined from molar to molecular motions.
Southern Pacific Co. v. Jensen, 244 U.S. 205, 221 [1917]

21 The common law is not a brooding omnipresence in the sky but the articulate voice of some sovereign or quasi sovereign that can be identified. *Ib. 222*

22 Certitude is not the test of certainty.
Natural Law [1918]

23 The most stringent protection of free speech would not protect a man in falsely

shouting fire in a theater and causing a panic. . . . The question in every case is whether the words used are used in such circumstances and are of such a nature as to create a clear and present danger that they will bring about the substantive evils that Congress has a right to prevent.

Schenck v. United States, 249 U.S. 47 [1919]

1 When men have realized that time has upset many fighting faiths, they may come to believe even more than they believe the very foundations of their own conduct that the ultimate good desired is better reached by free trade in ideas—that the best test of truth is the power of the thought to get itself accepted in the competition of the market, and that truth is the only ground upon which their wishes safely can be carried out.[1] That at any rate is the theory of our Constitution. It is an experiment, as all life is an experiment.

Abrams v. United States, 250 U.S. 616, 630 [1919]

2 I dare say that I have worked off my fundamental formula on you that the chief end of man is to frame general propositions and that no general proposition is worth a damn.

Letter to Sir Frederick Pollock [1920]

3 Have faith and pursue the unknown end.

Letter to John C. H. Wu [1924]

4 Upon this point a page of history is worth a volume of logic.

New York Trust Co. v. Eisner, 256 U.S. 345, 349 [1921]

5 It is said that this manifesto is more than a theory, that it was an incitement. Every idea is an incitement.

Gitlow v. New York, 268 U.S. 652, 673 [1925]

6 We learn how to behave as lawyers, soldiers, merchants, or whatnot by being them. Life, not the parson, teaches conduct.

Letter to Sir Frederick Pollock [1926]

7 Three generations of imbeciles are enough.

Buck v. Bell, 274 U.S. 200, 207 [1927]

8 But if we are to yield to fashionable conventions, it seems to me that theaters are as much devoted to public use as anything well can be. We have not that respect for art that is one of the glories of France. But to many the superfluous is the necessary,[2] and it seems to me that Government does not go beyond its sphere in attempting to make life livable for them.

Tyson & Bro. v. Banton, 273 U.S. 418, 447 [1927]

[1] See Milton, 282:5.
[2] See Voltaire, 342:24.

9 The power to tax is not the power to destroy while this Court sits.[3]

Panhandle Oil Co. v. Knox, 277 U.S. 223 [1928]

10 For my part I think it a less evil that some criminals should escape than that the government should play an ignoble part. . . . If the existing code does not permit district attorneys to have a hand in such dirty business [wiretapping], it does not permit the judge to allow such iniquities to succeed.

Olmstead v. United States, 277 U.S. 438, 470 [1928]

11 If there is any principle of the Constitution that more imperatively calls for attachment than any other it is the principle of free thought—not free thought for those who agree with us but freedom for the thought that we hate.

United States v. Schwimmer, 279 U.S. 644, 653 [1928]

12 The riders in a race do not stop short when they reach the goal. There is a little finishing canter before coming to a standstill. There is time to hear the kind voice of friends and to say to one's self: "The work is done." But just as one says that, the answer comes: "The race is over, but the work never is done while the power to work remains." The canter that brings you to a standstill need not be only coming to rest. It cannot be, while you still live. For to live is to function. That is all there is in living.

Radio address on his ninetieth birthday [March 8, 1931]

13 Young man, the secret of my success is that at an early age I discovered I was not God.

Reply to a reporter's question on his ninetieth birthday [March 8, 1931]

14 Oh, to be seventy again![4]

At ninety, upon seeing a beautiful young woman. Attributed

15 Life seems to me like a Japanese picture which our imagination does not allow to end with the margin. We aim at the infinite and when our arrow falls to earth it is in flames.

Message to the Federal Bar Association [February 29, 1932]

[3] See John Marshall, 402:7.
[4] If only one were eighty!—FIELD MARSHAL COUNT FRIEDRICH VON WRANGEL [1784–1877]; *attributed*

William Henry Hudson
1841–1922

1 I . . . thanked the Author of my being for the gift of that wild forest, those green mansions where I had found so great a happiness!
Green Mansions [1904], ch. 5

2 In this wild solitary girl [Rima] I had at length discovered the mysterious warbler that so often followed me in the wood.
Ib.

3 You cannot fly like an eagle with the wings of a wren.
Afoot in England [1909], ch. 6

Joaquin [Cincinnatus Hiner or Heine] Miller
c. 1841–1913

4 I only know that creeds to me
Are but new names for mystery,
That good is good from east to east,
And more I do not know nor need
To know, to love my neighbor well.
The Tale of the Tall Alcalde

5 In men whom men condemn as ill
I find so much of goodness still,[1]
In men whom men pronounce divine
I find so much of sin and blot,
I do not dare to draw a line
Between the two, where God has not.[2]
Byron

6 Behind him lay the gray Azores,
Behind the Gates of Hercules;
Before him not the ghost of shores,
Before him only shoreless seas.
Columbus, st. 1

7 He gained a world; he gave that world
Its grandest lesson: "On! sail on!"[3]
Ib. st. 5

Pierre Auguste Renoir
1841–1919

8 I have a predilection for painting that lends joyousness to a wall.
From AMBROISE VOLLARD, *Renoir [1919]*

9 In a few generations you can breed a racehorse. The recipe for making a man like Delacroix is less well known.
From JEAN RENOIR, *Renoir My Father [1958]*

Minot Judson Savage
1841–1918

10 A man's truest monument must be a man.
The Song of a Man,[4] *st. 8*

Clement William Scott
1841–1904

11 Oh, promise me that some day you and I
Will take our love together to some sky
Where we can be alone and faith renew,
And find the hollows where those flowers
grew.
Oh, Promise Me [1888][5]

Edward Rowland Sill
1841–1887

12 At the punch bowl's brink
Let the thirsty think
What they say in Japan:
"First the man takes a drink,
Then the drink takes a drink,
Then the drink takes the man!"[6]
An Adage from the Orient

13 But Lord,
Be merciful to me, a fool!
The Fool's Prayer

14 The ill-timed truth we might have kept—
Who knows how sharp it pierced and stung?
The word we had not sense to say—
Who knows how grandly it had rung?
Ib.

Sir Henry Morton Stanley
1841–1904

15 Doctor Livingstone, I presume?
On meeting David Livingstone in Ujiji, Central Africa [November 10, 1871]

[1] See Shakespeare, 208:3.

[2] There is so much good in the worst of us, / And so much bad in the best of us, / That it hardly behooves any of us / To talk about the rest of us.—First printed in the *Marion* (Kansas) *Record*, owned by Governor Edward Wallis Hoch [1849–1925]; assumed to have been written by him

[3] Actually, it was MARTÍN ALONSO PINZÓN who said, "Adelante, adelante, I can't hold with turning back without sighting land."

[4] Phillips Brooks.

[5] Reginald De Koven wrote the music for Scott's ballad, which was first sung in Chicago at the second performance of his opera *Robin Hood* [June 10, 1890] by the famous contralto Jessie Bartlett Davis.

[6] See Herbert, 268:3; Addison, 326:18; and Hugo, 491:22.

Ironquill
[Eugene Fitch Ware]
1841–1911

1 Human hopes and human creeds
Have their root in human needs.
The Rhymes of Ironquill, preface

2 O Dewey[1] was the morning
Upon the first of May,
And Dewey was the Admiral
Down in Manila Bay;
And Dewey were the Regent's eyes,
"Them" orbs of royal blue!
And Dewey feel discouraged?
I Dew not think we Dew.
In the Topeka (Kansas) Daily Capital [May 3, 1898]

3 No evil deed live oN. *The Palindrome*

Ambrose Bierce[2]
1842 – c. 1914

4 Mark how my fame rings out from zone to zone:
A thousand critics shouting: "He's unknown!" *Couplet*

5 Peyton Farquhar was dead; his body, with a broken neck, swung gently from side to side beneath the timbers of the Owl Creek bridge.
In the Midst of Life [1891].[3] An Occurrence at Owl Creek Bridge

6 To men a man is but a mind. Who cares
What face he carries or what form he wears?
But woman's body is the woman. O
Stay thou, my sweetheart, and do never go.
The Devil's Dictionary [1906][4]

7 *Achievement, n.* the death of endeavor and the birth of disgust. *Ib.*

8 *Advice, n.* the smallest current coin. *Ib.*

9 *Bore, n.* a person who talks when you wish him to listen. *Ib.*

10 *Cynic, n.* a blackguard whose faulty vision sees things as they are, not as they ought to be. *Ib.*

11 *Edible, adj.* good to eat, and wholesome to digest, as a worm to a toad, a toad to a snake, a snake to a pig, a pig to a man, and a man to a worm.[5] *Ib.*

[1] See Dewey, 631:13.
[2] In 1913 Bierce wearied of American civilization and disappeared into Mexico, to seek "the good, kind darkness."
[3] First published as *Tales of Soldiers and Civilians,* retitled in 1892.
[4] First published as *The Cynic's Word Book,* retitled in 1911.
[5] See Wallace Stevens, 767:8.

12 *Habit, n.* a shackle for the free. *Ib.*

13 *Labor, n.* one of the processes by which A acquires property for B. *Ib.*

14 *Lawsuit, n.* a machine which you go into as a pig and come out as a sausage. *Ib.*

15 *Marriage, n.* a community consisting of a master, a mistress, and two slaves, making in all, two. *Ib.*

16 *Prejudice, n.* a vagrant opinion without visible means of support. *Ib.*

17 *Saint, n.* a dead sinner revised and edited. *Ib.*

18 Woman would be more charming if one could fall into her arms without falling into her hands. *Epigrams*

19 You are not permitted to kill a woman who has wronged you, but nothing forbids you to reflect that she is growing older every minute. You are avenged 1440 times a day. *Ib.*

20 Self-denial is indulgence of a propensity to forego. *Ib.*

Charles Edward Carryl
1842–1920

21 A capital ship for an ocean trip
Was the *Walloping Window Blind*—
No gale that blew dismayed her crew
Or troubled the captain's mind.
The man at the wheel was taught to feel
Contempt for the wildest blow.
And it often appeared, when the weather had cleared,
That he'd been in his bunk below.
Davy and the Goblin: A Nautical Ballad [1886], st. 1

Sir James Dewar
1842–1923

22 Minds are like parachutes. They only function when they are open. *Attributed*

William James
1842–1910

23 I have often thought that the best way to define a man's character would be to seek out the particular mental or moral attitude in which, when it came upon him, he felt himself most deeply and intensely active and

alive. At such moments there is a voice inside which speaks and says: "This is the real me!"

The Letters of William James [1920]. To his wife, Alice Gibbons James, 1878

1 Nothing so fatiguing as the eternal hanging on of an uncompleted task.

Ib. To Carl Stumpf, January 1, 1886

2 The difference between the first- and second-best things in art absolutely seems to escape verbal definition—it is a matter of a hair, a shade, an inward quiver of some kind—yet what miles away in the point of preciousness!

Ib. To Henry Rutgers Marshall, February 7, 1899

3 Most people live, whether physically, intellectually or morally, in a very restricted circle of their potential being. They *make use* of a very small portion of their possible consciousness, and of their soul's resources in general, much like a man who, out of his whole bodily organism, should get into a habit of using and moving only his little finger. Great emergencies and crises show us how much greater our vital resources are than we had supposed.[1]

Ib. To W. Lutoslawski, May 6, 1906

4 The moral flabbiness born of the exclusive worship of the bitch-goddess SUCCESS. That—with the squalid cash interpretation put on the word success—is our national disease.

Ib. To H. G. Wells, September 11, 1906

5 The concrete man has but one interest—to be right. That to him is the art of all arts, and all means are fair which help him to it.

The Sentiment of Rationality [1882]

6 All our scientific and philosophic ideals are altars to unknown gods.

The Dilemma of Determinism [1884]

7 Habit is . . . the enormous flywheel of society, its most precious conservative agent. It alone is what keeps us all within the bounds of ordinance.

The Principles of Psychology [1890], ch. 4

8 There is no more miserable human being than one in whom nothing is habitual but indecision. *Ib.*

9 Keep the faculty of effort alive in you by a little gratuitous exercise every day. That is, be systematically ascetic or heroic in little unnecessary points, do every day or two something for no other reason than that you would rather not do it,[2] so that when the hour of dire need draws nigh, it may find you not unnerved and untrained to stand the test. *Ib.*

10 The hell to be endured hereafter, of which theology tells, is no worse than the hell we make for ourselves in this world by habitually fashioning our characters in the wrong way. *Ib.*

11 We are spinning our own fates, good or evil, and never to be undone. Every smallest stroke of virtue or of vice leaves its never so little scar . . . Nothing we ever do is, in strict scientific literalness, wiped out. *Ib.*

12 Consciousness . . . does not appear to itself chopped up in bits. . . . A "river" or a "stream" are the metaphors by which it is most naturally described. In talking of it hereafter, let us call it the stream of thought, of consciousness, or of subjective life.

Ib. 9

13 As we take, in fact, a general view of the wonderful stream of our consciousness, what strikes us first is this different pace of its parts. Like a bird's life, it seems to be made of an alternation of flights and perchings. *Ib.*

14 As the brain changes are continuous, so do all these consciousnesses melt into each other like dissolving views. Properly they are but one protracted consciousness, one unbroken stream. *Ib.*

15 The last peculiarity of consciousness to which attention is to be drawn in this first rough description of its stream is that . . . it is always interested more in one part of its object [thought] than in another, and welcomes and rejects, or chooses, all the while it thinks. *Ib.*

16 An act has no ethical quality whatever unless it be chosen out of several all equally possible. *Ib.*

17 In its widest possible sense, however, a man's Self is the sum total of all that he *can* call his, not only his body and his psychic powers, but his clothes and his house, his wife and children, his ancestors and friends, his reputation and works, his lands and horses, and yacht and bank account. All these things give him the same emotions. If they wax and

[1]See Emily Dickinson, 607:2.

[2]See Huxley, 596:5, and Maugham, 751:12.

prosper, he feels triumphant; if they dwindle and die away, he feels cast down.
Ib. 10

1 So our self-feeling in this world depends entirely on what we *back* ourselves to be and do. *Ib.*

2 Creatures extremely low in the intellectual scale may have conception. All that is required is that they should recognize the same experience again. A polyp would be a conceptual thinker if a feeling of "Hello! thingumbob again!" ever flitted through its mind.
Ib. 12

3 Let anyone try, I will not say to arrest, but to notice or attend to, the *present* moment of time. One of the most baffling experiences occurs. Where is it, this present? It has melted in our grasp, fled ere we could touch it, gone in the instant of becoming.
Ib. 15

4 Genius . . . means little more than the faculty of perceiving in an unhabitual way.
Ib. 19

5 The impulse to take life strivingly is indestructible in the race. *Ib. 21*

6 The art of being wise is the art of knowing what to overlook. *Ib. 22*

7 The more rational statement is that we feel sorry because we cry, angry because we strike, afraid because we tremble, and not that we cry, strike, or tremble because we are sorry, angry, or fearful, as the case may be. Without the bodily states following on the perception, the latter would be purely cognitive in form, pale, colorless, destitute of emotional warmth. *Ib. 25*

8 A purely disembodied human emotion is a nonentity. *Ib.*

9 A thing is important if anyone *think* it important. *Ib. 28, note*

10 In the deepest heart of all of us there is a corner in which the ultimate mystery of things works sadly.
The Will to Believe [1897]. Is Life Worth Living?

11 Need and struggle are what excite and inspire us; our hour of triumph is what brings the void. Not the Jews of the captivity, but those of the days of Solomon's glory are those from whom the pessimistic utterances in our Bible come. *Ib.*

12 It is only by risking our persons from one hour to another that we live at all. And often enough our faith beforehand in an uncertified result is the only thing that makes the result come true. *Ib.*

13 This life is worth living, we can say, since it is what we make it, from the moral point of view.[1] *Ib.*

14 If this life be not a real fight, in which something is eternally gained for the universe by success, it is no better than a game of private theatricals from which one may withdraw at will. But it *feels* like a real fight.
Ib.

15 Be not afraid of life. Believe that life *is* worth living, and your belief will help create the fact. *Ib.*

16 Man's chief difference from the brutes lies in the exuberant excess of his subjective propensities—his preeminence over them simply and solely in the number and in the fantastic and unnecessary character of his wants, physical, moral, aesthetic, and intellectual. Had his whole life not been a quest for the superfluous, he would never have established himself as inexpugnably as he has done in the necessary.
Ib. Reflex Action and Theism

17 All the higher, more penetrating ideals are revolutionary. They present themselves far less in the guise of effects of past experience than in that of probable causes of future experience.
Ib. The Moral Philosopher and the Moral Life

18 There is but one unconditional commandment, which is that we should seek incessantly, with fear and trembling, so to vote and to act as to bring about the very largest total universe of good which we can see.
Ib.

19 An unlearned carpenter of my acquaintance once said in my hearing: "There is very little difference between one man and another; but what little there is, is very important." This distinction seems to me to go to the root of the matter.
Ib. The Importance of Individuals

20 Wherever you are it is your own friends who make your world.
From RALPH BARTON PERRY, *The Thought and Character of William James [1935], vol. II [1899], ch. 91, conclusion*

[1] See Oliver Wendell Holmes, Jr., 644:6, and Santayana, 703:9.

1 Tell him to live by yes and no—yes to everything good, no to everything bad.

Ib.

2 Religion . . . shall mean for us the feelings, acts, and experiences of individual men in their solitude.

The Varieties of Religious Experience [1902]. Lecture 2

3 Religion . . . is a man's total reaction upon life. *Ib.*

4 We can act *as if* there were a God; feel *as if* we were free; consider Nature *as if* she were full of special designs; lay plans *as if* we were to be immortal; and we find then that these words do make a genuine difference in our moral life. *Ib. 3*

5 There is no worse lie than a truth misunderstood by those who hear it.

Ib. 14 and 15

6 The God whom science recognizes must be a God of universal laws exclusively, a God who does a wholesale, not a retail business. He cannot accommodate his processes to the convenience of individuals. *Ib. 20*

7 The philosophy which is so important in each of us is not a technical matter; it is our more or less dumb sense of what life honestly and deeply means. It is only partly got from books; it is our individual way of just seeing and feeling the total push and pressure of the cosmos.

Pragmatism [1907].[1] *Lecture 1*

8 No particular results then, so far, but only an attitude of orientation, is what the pragmatic method means. The attitude of looking away from first things, principles, "categories," supposed necessities; and of looking toward last things, fruits, consequences, facts.

Ib. 2

9 I myself believe that the evidence for God lies primarily in inner personal experiences.

Ib. 3

10 Our minds thus grow in spots; and like grease spots, the spots spread. But we let them spread as little as possible: we keep unaltered as much of our old knowledge, as many of our old prejudices and beliefs, as we can. We patch and tinker more than we renew. The novelty soaks in; it stains the ancient mass; but it is also tinged by what absorbs it. *Ib. 5*

11 Truth *happens* to an idea. It *becomes* true, is *made* true by events. Its verity *is* in fact an event, a process: the process namely of its verifying itself, its veri-*fication.* Its validity is the process of its valid-*ation.* *Ib. 6*

12 Pluralism lets things really exist in the each-form or distributively. Monism thinks that the all-form or collective-unit form is the only form that is rational.

A Pluralistic Universe [1909]. Lecture 8

13 What we really need the poet's and orator's help to keep alive in us is not . . . the common and gregarious courage which Robert Shaw showed when he marched with you, men of the Seventh Regiment. It is that more lonely courage which he showed when he dropped his warm commission in the glorious Second to head your dubious fortunes, Negroes of the Fifty-fourth. That lonely kind of courage (civic courage, as we call it in times of peace) is the kind of valor to which the monuments of nations should most of all be reared.[2]

Memories and Studies [1911]. Robert Gould Shaw: Oration upon the Unveiling of the Shaw Monument [May 31, 1897]

14 The deadliest enemies of nations are not their foreign foes; they always dwell within their borders. And from these internal enemies civilization is always in need of being saved. The nation blessed above all nations is she in whom the civic genius of the people does the saving day by day, by acts without external picturesqueness; by speaking, writing, voting reasonably; by smiting corruption swiftly; by good temper between parties; by the people knowing true men when they see them, and preferring them as leaders to rabid partisans or empty quacks. *Ib.*

15 Democracy is still upon its trial. The civic genius of our people is its only bulwark.

Ib.

16 So long as antimilitarists propose no substitute for war's disciplinary function, no *moral equivalent* of war, analogous, as one might say, to the mechanical equivalent of heat, so long they fail to realize the full inwardness of the situation.

Ib. The Moral Equivalent of War

[1]The term [pragmatism] . . . was first introduced into philosophy by Mr. Charles Peirce in 1878 [in] an article entitled "How to Make Our Ideas Clear" in the *Popular Science Monthly* for January of that year.—WILLIAM JAMES, *Pragmatism* [1907], *Lecture 1*

See Charles Sanders Peirce, page 639.

[2]See C. W. Eliot, 617:6; Paul Laurence Dunbar, 737:1; and Robert Lowell, 893:12.

1 Our colleges ought to have lit up in us a lasting relish for the better kind of man, a loss of appetite for mediocrities.

Ib. The Social Value of the College-Bred

2 Real culture lives by sympathies and admirations, not by dislikes and disdains; under all misleading wrappings it pounces unerringly upon the human core. *Ib.*

3 The "through-and-through" universe seems to suffocate me with its infallible impeccable all-pervasiveness. . . . It seems too buttoned-up and white-chokered and clean-shaven a thing to speak for the vast slow-breathing unconscious Kosmos with its dread abysses and its unknown tides.

Essays in Radical Empiricism [1912], ch. 12, Absolutism and Empiricism

4 The union of the mathematician with the poet, fervor with measure, passion with correctness, this surely is the ideal.

Collected Essays and Reviews [1920], ch. 11, Clifford's "Lectures and Essays" [1879]

5 I wished, by treating Psychology *like* a natural science, to help her to become one.

Ib. A Plea for Psychology as a Natural Science [1892]

John Alexander Joyce

1842–1915

6 I shall love you in December
With the love I gave in May![1]

Question and Answer, st. 8

Prince Pëtr Alekseevich Kropotkin

1842–1921

7 Sociability is as much a law of nature as mutual struggle . . . mutual aid is as much a law of animal life as mutual struggle.

Mutual Aid [1902]

Sidney Lanier

1842–1881

8 Ye marshes, how candid and simple and nothing-withholding and free
Ye publish yourselves to the sky and offer yourselves to the sea!

The Marshes of Glynn [1877], l. 65

[1] Will you love me in December as you do in May? — JAMES J. WALKER; *set to music by* ERNEST R. BALL [1905]

9 As the marsh hen secretly builds on the watery sod,
Behold I will build me a nest on the greatness of God:
I will fly in the greatness of God as the marsh hen flies
In the freedom that fills all the space 'twixt the marsh and the skies:
By so many roots as the marsh grass sends in the sod
I will heartily lay me a-hold on the greatness of God:
Oh, like to the greatness of God is the greatness within
The range of the marshes, the liberal marshes of Glynn. *Ib. l. 71*

10 Out of the hills of Habersham,
Down the valleys of Hall.

Song of the Chattahoochee [1877], st. 1

11 Into the woods my Master went,
Clean forspent, forspent.
Into the woods my Master came,
Forspent with love and shame.

A Ballad of Trees and the Master [1877], st. 1

12 'Twas on a tree they slew Him — last
When out of the woods He came.

Ib. st. 2

Stéphane Mallarmé

1842–1898

13 The flesh is sad, alas, and I have read all the books.[2] *Poésies. Brise Marine*

14 Such as into himself at last Eternity has changed him.[3]

Ib. Le Tombeau d'Edgar Poe

15 A Throw of the Dice Will Never Abolish Chance.[4] *Ib. Title of poem*

16 To *name* an object is to take away three-fourths of the pleasure given by a poem. This pleasure consists in guessing little by little: to *suggest* it, that is the ideal.[5]

Réponse à une Enquête sur l'Évolution Littéraire [1891]

17 You don't make a poem with ideas, but with words.[6]

From PAUL VALÉRY, Degas, Danse, Dessin

[2] La chair est triste, hélas! et j'ai lu tous les livres.

[3] Tel qu'en Lui-Même enfin l'éternité le change.

[4] Un coup de dés n'abolira jamais le hasard.

[5] *Nommer* un objet, c'est supprimer les trois-quarts de la jouissance du poème qui est fait peu à peu: le *suggérer*.

[6] Ce n'est point avec des idées que l'on fait des vers, c'est avec des mots.

Alfred Marshall
1842–1924

1 Thus progress itself increases the urgency of the warning that in the economic world, *Natura non facit saltum.*[1] Progress must be slow. *Principles of Economics [1890]*

2 We might as reasonably dispute whether it is the upper or the under blade of a pair of scissors that cuts a piece of paper, as whether value is governed by utility or cost of production. *Ib.*

Hugh Antoine D'Arcy
1843–1925

3 "Say, boys! if you give me just another whiskey I'll be glad,
And I'll draw right here a picture of the face that drove me mad.
Give me that piece of chalk with which you mark the baseball score,
You shall see the lovely Madeleine upon the bar-room floor."
The Face upon the Floor [1887][2]

Henry James[3]
1843–1916

4 The face of nature and civilization in this our country is to a certain point a very sufficient literary field. But it will yield its secrets only to a really *grasping* imagination. . . . To write well and worthily of American things one need even more than elsewhere to be a *master.*
Letter to Charles Eliot Norton [January 16, 1871]

5 It's a complex fate, being an American, and one of the responsibilities it entails is fighting against a superstitious valuation of Europe.
Letter [1872] quoted in PERCY LUBBOCK, *Letters of Henry James [1920], vol. I, Biographical note*

[1] Nature does not make a leap.

[2] Often called "The Face on the Barroom Floor."

[3] You know how opposed your whole "third manner" of execution is to the literary ideals which animate my crude and Orson-like breast, mine being to say a thing in one sentence as straight and explicit as it can be made, and then to drop it forever; yours being to avoid naming it straight, but by dint of breathing and sighing all round and round it, to arouse in the reader who may have had a similar perception already . . . the illusion of a solid object, made . . . wholly out of impalpable materials, air, and the prismatic interference of light, ingeniously focused by mirrors upon empty space. But you *do* it, that's the queerness! — WILLIAM JAMES, *letter to his brother Henry James* [1907]

See Vidal, 700:*n*3; Wharton, 701:7; and Guedalla, 812:12.

6 It takes a great deal of history to produce a little literature.
Hawthorne [1879], ch. 1

7 Whatever question there may be of his [Thoreau's] talent, there can be none, I think, of his genius. It was a slim and crooked one, but it was eminently personal. He was unperfect, unfinished, inartistic; he was worse than provincial — he was parochial. *Ib. 4*

8 Cats and monkeys, monkeys and cats — all human life is there.
The Madonna of the Future [1879]

9 The real offense, as she ultimately perceived, was her having a mind of her own at all. Her mind was to be his — attached to his own like a small garden plot to a deer park.
The Portrait of a Lady [1881]

10 You were ground in the very mill of the conventional! *Ib.*

11 The only reason for the existence of a novel is that it does attempt to represent life.
The Art of Fiction [1888]

12 The only obligation to which in advance we may hold a novel, without incurring the accusation of being arbitrary, is that it be interesting.[4] *Ib.*

13 The advantage, the luxury, as well as the torment and responsibility of the novelist, is that there is no limit to what he may attempt as an executant — no limit to his possible experiments, efforts, discoveries, successes. *Ib.*

14 The power to guess the unseen from the seen, to trace the implications of things, to judge the whole piece by the pattern, the condition of feeling life in general so completely that you are well on your way to knowing any particular corner of it — this cluster of gifts may almost be said to constitute experience. . . . If experience consists of impressions, it may be said that impressions *are* experience. . . . Therefore, if I should certainly say to a novice, "Write from experience and experience only," I should feel that this was rather a tantalizing monition if I were not careful immediately to add, "Try to be one of the people on whom nothing is lost." *Ib.*

15 We must grant the artist his subject, his idea, his *donnée:* our criticism is applied only to what he makes of it. . . . If we pretend to respect the artist at all, we must allow him his freedom of choice, in the face, in particular cases, of innumerable presumptions that the choice will not fructify. Art derives a con-

[4] See Trollope, 555:11.

siderable part of its beneficial exercise from flying in the face of presumptions. *Ib.*

1 There are few things more exciting to me . . . than a psychological reason. *Ib.*

2 The practice of "reviewing" . . . in general has nothing in common with the art of criticism. *Criticism [1893]*

3 The critical sense is so far from frequent that it is absolutely rare, and the possession of the cluster of qualities that minister to it is one of the highest distinctions. . . . In this light one sees the critic as the real helper of the artist, a torchbearing outrider, the interpreter, the brother. . . . Just in proportion as he is sentient and restless, just in proportion as he reacts and reciprocates and penetrates, is the critic a valuable instrument. *Ib.*

4 However incumbent it may be on most of us to do our duty, there is, in spite of a thousand narrow dogmatisms, nothing in the world that anyone is under the least obligation to *like*—not even (one braces one's self to risk the declaration) a particular kind of writing. *Flaubert [1893]*

5 We work in the dark—we do what we can—we give what we have. Our doubt is our passion, and our passion is our task. The rest is the madness of art. *The Middle Years [1893]*

6 The time-honored bread sauce of the happy ending. *Theatricals: Second Series [1895]*

7 Vereker's secret . . . the general intention of his books: the string the pearls were strung on, the buried treasure, the figure in the carpet. *The Figure in the Carpet [1896]*

8 I caught him, yes, I held him—it may be imagined with what passion; but at the end of a minute I began to feel what it truly was that I held. We were alone with the quiet day, and his little heart, dispossessed, had stopped. *The Turn of the Screw [1898], ending*

9 Live all you can; it's a mistake not to. It doesn't so much matter what you do in particular, so long as you have had your life. If you haven't had that what *have* you had? . . . What one loses one loses; make no mistake about that. . . . The right time is *any* time that one is still so lucky as to have. . . . Live! *The Ambassadors [1903], bk. V, ch. 2*

10 Really, universally, relations stop nowhere, and the exquisite problem of the artist is eternally but to draw, by a geometry of his own, the circle within which they shall happily *appear* to do so. *Prefaces [1907–1909]. Roderick Hudson*

11 There is, I think, no more nutritive or suggestive truth . . . than that of the perfect dependence of the "moral" sense of a work of art on the amount of felt life concerned in producing it. The question comes back thus, obviously, to the kind and the degree of the artist's prime sensibility, which is the soil out of which his subject springs. *Ib. The Portrait of a Lady*

12 To see deep difficulty braved is at any time, for the really addicted artist, to feel almost even as a pang the beautiful incentive, and to feel it verily in such sort as to wish the danger intensified. The difficulty most worth tackling can only be for him, in these conditions, the greatest the case permits of. *Ib.*

13 Life being all inclusion and confusion, and art being all discrimination and selection, the latter, in search of the hard latent *value* with which it alone is concerned, sniffs round the mass as instinctively and unerringly as a dog suspicious of some buried bone. *Ib. The Spoils of Poynton*

14 The fatal futility of Fact. *Ib.*

15 No themes are so human as those that reflect for us, out of the confusion of life, the close connection of bliss and bale, of the things that help with the things that hurt, so dangling before us forever that bright hard medal, of so strange an alloy, one face of which is somebody's right and ease and the other somebody's pain and wrong. *Ib. What Maisie Knew*

16 The effort really to see and really to represent is no idle business in face of the *constant* force that makes for muddlement. The great thing is indeed that the muddled state too is one of the very sharpest of the realities, that it also has color and form and character, has often in fact a broad and rich comicality. *Ib.*

17 To criticize is to appreciate, to appropriate, to take intellectual possession, to establish in fine a relation with the criticized thing and to make it one's own. *Ib.*

1 The historian, essentially, wants more documents than he can really use; the dramatist only wants more liberties than he can really take. *Ib. The Aspern Papers*

2 The ever importunate murmur, "Dramatize it, dramatize it!"
Ib. The Altar of the Dead

3 In art economy is always beauty.
Ib.

4 The terrible *fluidity* of self-revelation.
Ib. The Ambassadors

5 The anomalous fact is that the theater, so called, can flourish in barbarism, but that any *drama* worth speaking of can develop but in the air of civilization.
Letter to C. E. Wheeler [April 9, 1911]

6 I'm glad you like adverbs—I adore them; they are the only qualifications I really much respect.
Letter to Miss M. Betham Edwards [January 5, 1912]

7 We must know, as much as possible, in our beautiful art . . . what we are talking about —and the only way to know is to have lived and loved and cursed and floundered and enjoyed and suffered. I think I don't regret a single "excess" of my responsive youth—I only regret, in my chilled age, certain occasions and possibilities I didn't embrace.
Letter to Hugh Walpole [August 21, 1913]

8 I still, in presence of life . . . have reactions—as many as possible. . . . It's, I suppose, because I am that queer monster, the artist, an obstinate finality, an inexhaustible sensibility. Hence the reactions—appearances, memories, many things, go on playing upon it with consequences that I note and "enjoy" (grim word!) noting. It all takes doing —and I *do*. I believe I shall do yet again — it is still an act of life.
Letter to Henry Adams [March 21, 1914]

9 The effect, if not the prime office, of criticism is to make our absorption and our enjoyment of the things that feed the mind as aware of itself as possible, since that awareness quickens the mental demand, which thus in turn wanders further and further for pasture. This action on the part of the mind practically amounts to a reaching out for the reasons of its interest, as only by its ascertaining them can the interest grow more various. This is the very education of our imaginative life. *The New Novel [1914]*

10 It is art that *makes* life, makes interest, makes importance, for our consideration and application of these things, and I know of no substitute whatever for the force and beauty of its process.
Letter to H. G. Wells [July 10, 1915]

11 The full, the monstrous demonstration that Tennyson was not Tennysonian.
The Middle Years (autobiography) [1917], ch. 6

12 Summer afternoon—summer afternoon; to me those have always been the two most beautiful words in the English language.
Quoted by EDITH WHARTON, *A Backward Glance [1934], ch. 10*

13 To take what there *is*, and use it, without waiting forever in vain for the preconceived —to dig deep into the actual and get something out of *that*—this doubtless is the right way to live. *Notebooks [1948]*

Robert Bridges
1844–1930

14 For beauty being the best of all we know
Sums up the unsearchable and secret aims
Of nature.
The Growth of Love [1876]. Sonnet 8

15 Whither, O splendid ship, thy white sails crowding,
Leaning across the bosom of the urgent West,
That fearest nor sea rising, nor sky clouding,
Whither away, fair rover, and what thy quest?
Shorter Poems, bk. II [1879], no. 2 (A Passer-By), st. 1

16 I have loved flowers that fade,
Within whose magic tents
Rich hues have marriage made
With sweet unmemoried scents.
Ib. no. 13, st. 1

17 So sweet love seemed that April morn,
When first we kissed beside the thorn,
So strangely sweet, it was not strange
We thought that love could never change.
Ib. V [1893], no. 5, st. 1

18 My delight and thy delight
Walking, like two angels white,
In the gardens of the night.
New Poems [1899], no. 9

19 Man, in the unsearchable darkness, knoweth one thing
That as he is, so was he made.
The Testament of Beauty [1929]

Robert Jones Burdette
1844–1914

1 There are two days in the week about which and upon which I never worry. Two carefree days, kept sacredly free from fear and apprehension. One of these days is Yesterday. . . . And the other day I do not worry about is Tomorrow.
The Golden Day

Anatole France
[Jacques Anatole François Thibault]
1844–1924

2 I do not know any reading more easy, more fascinating, more delightful than a catalogue.
The Crime of Sylvestre Bonnard [1881].[1] *The Log, December 24, 1849*

3 All the historical books which contain no lies are extremely tedious. *Ib.*

4 Lovers who love truly do not write down their happiness.
Ib. November 30, 1859

5 To know is nothing at all; to imagine is everything. *Ib. pt. II, ch. 2*

6 He flattered himself on being a man without any prejudices; and this pretension itself is a very great prejudice. *Ib. 4*

7 Those who have given themselves the most concern about the happiness of peoples have made their neighbors very miserable.
Ib.

8 Man is so made that he can only find relaxation from one kind of labor by taking up another. *Ib.*

9 People who have no weaknesses are terrible; there is no way of taking advantage of them. *Ib.*

10 The whole art of teaching is only the art of awakening the natural curiosity of young minds for the purpose of satisfying it afterwards. *Ib.*

11 The good critic is one who tells of his mind's adventures among masterpieces.
La Vie Littéraire [1888], preface

12 We reproach people for talking about themselves; but it is the subject they treat best. *Ib. Journal des Goncourt*

[1]Translated by LAFCADIO HEARN.

13 Chance is perhaps the pseudonym of God when He did not want to sign.[2]
Le Jardin d'Épicure [1894]

14 The law, in its majestic equality, forbids the rich as well as the poor to sleep under bridges, to beg in the streets, and to steal bread. *Le Lys Rouge [1894], ch. 7*

15 We have medicines to make women speak; we have none to make them keep silence.
The Man Who Married a Dumb Wife [1912],[3] *act II, sc. iv*

16 A tale without love is like beef without mustard: insipid.
La Révolte des Anges [1914], ch. 8

Gerard Manley Hopkins[4]
1844–1889

17 And I have asked to be
Where no storms come,
Where the green swell is in the havens dumb,
And out of the swing of the sea.
Poems [1918].[5] *No. 20, Heaven-Haven, st. 2*

18 Elected Silence, sing to me
And beat upon my whorlèd ear,
Pipe me to pastures still and be
The music that I care to hear.
No. 24, The Habit of Perfection, st. 1

19 Thou mastering me
God! giver of breath and bread;
World's strand, sway of the sea;
Lord of living and dead;
Thou hast bound bones and veins in me, fastened me flesh,
And after it almost unmade, what with dread,
Thy doing: and dost thou touch me afresh?
Over again I feel thy finger and find thee.
No. 28, The Wreck of the Deutschland, st. 1

20 The world is charged with the grandeur of God. *No. 31, God's Grandeur, l. 1*

21 Look at the stars! look, look up at the skies!
O look at all the fire-folk sitting in the air!
No. 32, The Starlight Night, l. 1

[2]See Einstein, 763:16.

[3]Translated by CURTIS HIDDEN PAGE.

[4]He has left us only ninety poems—but so essential that they will color and convert the development of English poetry for many decades to come.—HERBERT READ, in *The Criterion* [April 1931]

[5]First published in 1918, edited by ROBERT BRIDGES. Poem numbers are from the third edition [1948], edited by W. H. GARDNER.

1 I caught this morning morning's minion, king-
dom of daylight's dauphin, dapple-dawn-drawn Falcon, in his riding
Of the rolling level underneath him steady air, and striding
High there, how he rung upon the rein of a wimpling wing
In his ecstasy!
No. 36, The Windhover, l. 1

2 The achieve of, the mastery of the thing!
Ib. l. 8

3 Brute beauty and valor and act, oh, air, pride, plume, here
Buckle! *Ib. l. 9*

4 Glory be to God for dappled things.
No. 37, Pied Beauty, l. 1

5 All things counter, original, spare, strange;
Whatever is fickle, freckled (who knows how?)
With swift, slow; sweet, sour; adazzle, dim;
He fathers-forth whose beauty is past change:
Praise him. *Ib. l. 7*

6 Summer ends now; now, barbarous in beauty, the stooks arise
Around; up above, what wind-walks! what lovely behavior
Of silk-sack clouds! Has wilder, willful-wavier
Meal-drift molded ever and melted across skies?
No. 38, Hurrahing in Harvest, st. 1

7 Felix Randal the farrier, O is he dead then? My duty all ended,
Who have watched his mold of man, big-boned and hardy-handsome,
Pining, pining.
No. 53, Felix Randal, st. 1

8 When thou at the random grim forge, powerful amidst peers,
Didst fettle for the great gray drayhorse his bright and battering sandal! *Ib. st. 4*

9 Margaret, are you grieving
Over Goldengrove unleaving?
No. 55, Spring and Fall, l. 1

10 Nor mouth had, no nor mind, expressed
What heart heard of, ghost guessed:
It is the blight man was born for,
It is Margaret you mourn for. *Ib. l. 12*

11 As kingfishers catch fire, dragonflies draw flame. *No. 57, l. 1*

12 How to keep—is there any any, is there none such, nowhere known some, bow or brooch or braid or brace, lace, latch or catch or key to keep
Back beauty, keep it, beauty, beauty, beauty . . . from vanishing away?
No. 59, The Leaden Echo and the Golden Echo, l. 1

13 I say that we are wound
With mercy round and round
As if with air.
No. 60, The Blessed Virgin Compared to the Air We Breathe, l. 34

14 World-mothering air, air wild,
Wound with thee, in thee isled,
Fold home, fast fold thy child.
Ib. l. 124

15 Not, I'll not, carrion comfort, Despair, not feast on thee;
Not untwist—slack they may be—these last strands of man
In me or, most weary, cry *I can no more.* I can;
Can something, hope, wish day come, not choose not to be.
No. 64, Carrion Comfort, l. 1

16 That night, that year
Of now done darkness I wretch lay wrestling with (my God!) my God. *Ib. l. 13*

17 No worst, there is none. Pitched past pitch of grief,
More pangs will, schooled at forepangs, wilder wring. *No. 65, l. 1*

18 O the mind, mind has mountains; cliffs of fall
Frightful, sheer, no-man-fathomed.
Ib. l. 9

19 I wake and feel the fell of dark, not day.
What hours, O what black hours we have spent
This night. *No. 69, l. 1*

20 I am gall, I am heartburn. *Ib. l. 9*

21 I am all at once what Christ is, since he was what I am, and
This Jack, joke, poor potsherd, patch, matchwood, immortal diamond,
Is immortal diamond.
No. 72, That Nature Is a Heraclitean Fire and of the Comfort of the Resurrection, last lines

22 No doubt my poetry errs on the side of oddness. I hope in time to have a more balanced and Miltonic style. But as air, melody, is what strikes me most of all in music, and design in painting, so design, pattern, or what I am in the habit of calling *inscape* is what I above all aim at in poetry. Now it is the virtue of design, pattern, or inscape to be distinctive, and

it is the vice of distinctiveness to become queer. This vice I cannot have escaped.

Letter to Robert Bridges [February 15, 1879]

1 The poetical language of an age should be the current language heightened, to any degree heightened and unlike itself, but not . . . an obsolete one.

Ib. [August 14, 1879]

Andrew Lang
1844–1912

2 You can cover a great deal of country in
books. *To the Gentle Reader, st. 5*

3 Why, why are rhymes so rare to *love?*

Ballade of Difficult Rhymes

4 The surge and thunder of the Odyssey.

Sonnet, The Odyssey

5 Behind all creeds the Spirit that is One.

Herodotus in Egypt[1] *[1888]*

James Hilary Mulligan
1844–1916

6 The moonlight is the softest, in Kentucky,
Summer days come oftest, in Kentucky,
Friendship is the strongest,
Love's fires glow the longest,
Yet a wrong is always wrongest,
In Kentucky. *In Kentucky, st. 1*

Friedrich Wilhelm Nietzsche
1844–1900

7 Our destiny exercises its influence over us even when, as yet, we have not learned its nature: it is our future that lays down the law of our today.

Human, All Too Human [1878],[2] *7*

8 One must have a good memory to be able to keep the promises one makes. *Ib. 59*

9 One will rarely err if extreme actions be ascribed to vanity, ordinary actions to habit, and mean actions to fear. *Ib. 74*

10 Every tradition grows ever more venerable —the more remote is its origin, the more confused that origin is. The reverence due to it increases from generation to generation. The tradition finally becomes holy and inspires awe. *Ib. 96*

11 When Zarathustra was alone . . . he said to his heart: "Could it be possible! This old saint in the forest hath not yet heard of it, that *God is dead!*"[3]

Thus Spake Zarathustra [1883–1891],[4] *prologue, ch. 2*

12 Man is a rope stretched between the animal and the Superman—a rope over an abyss. *Ib. 3*

13 I want to teach men the sense of their existence, which is the Superman, the lightning out of the dark cloud man. *Ib. 7*

14 This is the hardest of all: to close the open hand out of love, and keep modest as a giver.

Ib. pt. II, ch. 23

15 Distrust all in whom the impulse to punish is powerful. *Ib. 29*

16 We ought to learn from the kine one thing: ruminating. *Ib. IV, 68*

17 If ye would go up high, then use your own legs! Do not get yourselves *carried* aloft; do not seat yourselves on other people's backs and heads! *Ib. 73*

18 It is certainly not the least charm of a theory that it is refutable.

Beyond Good and Evil [1885–1886],[5] *I, 18*

19 No one is such a liar as the indignant man.

Ib. II, 26

20 It is not the strength but the duration of great sentiments that makes great men.

Ib. IV, 72

21 In revenge and in love woman is more barbarous than man.[6] *Ib. 139*

22 Whoever fights monsters should see to it that in the process he does not become a monster. And when you look long into an abyss, the abyss also looks into you. *Ib. 146*

23 The thought of suicide is a great consolation:[7] by means of it one gets successfully through many a bad night. *Ib. 157*

24 Blessed are the forgetful: for they get the better even of their blunders. *Ib. 217*

25 Is not life a hundred times too short for us to bore ourselves? *Ib. 227*

[1] Dedicatory poem in *Euterpe: Being the Second Book of the Famous History of Herodotus* [1888], edited by ANDREW LANG.

[2] Translated by ALEXANDER HARVEY.

[3] God is dead. God remains dead. And we have killed him.—NIETZSCHE, *The Gay Science (Die Fröhliche Wissenschaft)* [1882], *ch. 125*

[4] Translated by THOMAS COMMON.

[5] Translated by HELEN ZIMMERN.

[6] See Aristophanes, 82:13, and Congreve, 324:16.

[7] We are in the power of no calamity while death is in our own.—SIR THOMAS BROWNE, *Religio Medici* [1642], *p. 50* (Everyman ed.)

1 Mozart, the last chord of a centuries-old great European taste. *Ib. 245*

2 One does not know—cannot know—the best that is in one. *Ib. 240*

3 The melancholia of everything completed! *Ib. IX, 277*

4 The masters have been done away with; the morality of the common man has triumphed.
Genealogy of Morals [1887], essay 1, aphorism 9

5 At the core of all these aristocratic races the beast of prey is not to be mistaken, the magnificent *blond beast,* avidly rampant for spoil and victory. *Ib. 11*

6 The broad effects which can be obtained by punishment in man and beast are the increase of fear, the sharpening of the sense of cunning, the mastery of the desires; so it is that punishment tames man, but does not make him "better." *Ib. 2, 15*

7 The sick are the greatest danger for the healthy; it is not from the strongest that harm comes to the strong, but from the weakest. *Ib. 3, 14*

8 A strong and well-constituted man digests his experiences (deeds and misdeeds all included) just as he digests his meats, even when he has some tough morsels to swallow. *Ib. 16*

9 Two great European narcotics, alcohol and Christianity.
The Twilight of the Idols [1888]. Things the Germans Lack, 2

10 What is it: is man only a blunder of God, or God only a blunder of man? *Ib.*

11 If a man have a strong faith he can indulge in the luxury of skepticism. *Ib. 12*

12 Liberal institutions straightway cease from being liberal the moment they are soundly established: once this is attained no more grievous and more thorough enemies of freedom exist than liberal institutions. *Ib. 38*

13 It is my ambition to say in ten sentences what everyone else says in a whole book—what everyone else does *not* say in a whole book. *Ib. 51*

14 Love is the state in which man sees things most widely different from what they are. The force of illusion reaches its zenith here, as likewise the sweetening and transfiguring power. When a man is in love he endures more than at other times; he submits to everything.
The Antichrist [1888],[1] *aphorism 23*

15 God created woman. And boredom did indeed cease from that moment—but many other things ceased as well! Woman was God's *second* mistake. *Ib. 48*

16 Life always gets harder toward the summit—the cold increases, responsibility increases. *Ib. 57*

17 I call Christianity the one great curse, the one enormous and innermost perversion, the one great instinct of revenge, for which no means are too venomous, too underhand, too underground and too petty—I call it the one immortal blemish of mankind. *Ib. 62*

18 My doctrine is: Live that thou mayest desire to live again—that is thy duty—for in any case thou wilt live again!
Eternal Recurrence,[1] *27*

19 Even a thought, even a possibility, can shatter us and transform us. *Ib. 30*

20 Nothing on earth consumes a man more quickly than the passion of resentment.
Ecce Homo [1888][1]

21 I believe only in French culture, and regard everything else in Europe which calls itself "culture" as a misunderstanding. I do not even take the German kind into consideration. *Ib.*

22 Wherever Germany extends her sway, she ruins culture. *Ib.*

23 As an artist, a man has no home in Europe save in Paris. *Ib.*

24 Simply by being compelled to keep constantly on his guard, a man may grow so weak as to be unable any longer to defend himself. *Ib.*

25 My time has not yet come either; some are born posthumously. *Ib.*

26 No one can draw more out of things, books included, than he already knows. A man has no ears for that to which experience has given him no access. *Ib.*

27 The Germans are like women, you can scarcely ever fathom their depths—they haven't any.[2] *Ib.*

[1]Translated by ANTHONY M. LUDOVICI.

[2]Man thinks woman profound—why? Because he can never fathom her depths. Woman is not even shallow. —NIETZSCHE, *The Twilight of the Idols, Maxims and Missiles, 27*

1 All prejudices may be traced back to the intestines. A sedentary life is the real sin against the Holy Ghost.[1] *Ib.*

2 One must separate from anything that forces one to repeat No again and again. *Ib.*

3 The Will to Power.[2] *Title of book [1888]*

John Boyle O'Reilly
1844–1890

4 They who see the Flying Dutchman never,
never reach the shore.
The Flying Dutchman

5 Doubt is brother-devil to Despair.
Prometheus

6 The red rose whispers of passion
And the white rose breathes of love;
O, the red rose is a falcon,
And the white rose is a dove.
A White Rose, st. 1

7 This truth keep in sight—every man on the planet
Has just as much right as yourself to the road. *Ib.*

8 The organized charity, scrimped and iced,
In the name of a cautious, statistical Christ.[3] *In Bohemia, st. 5*

Arthur William Edgar O'Shaughnessy
1844–1881

9 We are the music-makers,
And we are the dreamers of dreams,[4]
Wandering by lone sea breakers,
And sitting by desolate streams;
World-losers and world-forsakers,
On whom the pale moon gleams:
Yet we are the movers and shakers
Of the world forever, it seems.
Ode, st. 1

William Archibald Spooner[5]
1844–1930

10 Kinquering Congs their titles take.
Announcing the hymn in college chapel

11 You have deliberately tasted two worms and you can leave Oxford by the next town drain.
Dismissing a student. Attributed

Paul Verlaine
1844–1896

12 The long sobs
Of the violins
Of autumn
Pierce my heart
With monotonous languor.[6]
Poèmes Saturniens [1866]. Chanson d'Automne

13 There is weeping in my heart
Like the rain falling on the city.[7]
Romances sans Paroles [1874], III

14 Here are fruits, flowers, leaves and branches,
And here is my heart which beats only for you.[8] *Ib. Green*

15 What have you done, you there
Weeping without cease,
Tell me, yes you, what have you done
With all your youth?[9]
Sagesse [1881], III, st. 6

16 Music above all, and for this
Choose the irregular.[10]
Jadis et Naguère [1884]. L'Art Poetique

17 Take eloquence and wring its neck![11]
Ib.

18 And all else is literature.[12] *Ib.*

John B. Bogart[13]
1845–1921

19 When a dog bites a man, that is not news, because it happens so often. But if a man bites a dog, that is news.
From Frank M. O'Brien, *The Story of The (New York) Sun [1918]*

[1] Translated by Clifton P. Fadiman.
[2] Der Wille zur Macht.
[3] See Southey, 439:9, and Hood, 485:22.
[4] See William Morris, 618:7.
[5] Canon Spooner, for many years warden of New College, Oxford, was famous for unintentional transposition of (usually initial) word sounds, giving rise to the term "spoonerism."

[6] Les sanglots longs / Des violons / De l'automne / Blessent mon coeur / D'une langueur / Monotone.
[7] Il pleure dans mon coeur / Comme il pleut sur la ville. See Rimbaud, 674:11.
[8] Voici des fruits, des fleurs, des feuilles et des branches, / Et puis voici mon coeur qui ne bat que pour vous.
[9] Qu'as-tu fait, O toi que voilà / Pleurant sans cesse, / Dis, qu'as-tu fait, toi que voilà / De ta jeunesse?
[10] De la musique avant toute chose, / Et pour cela préfère l'Impair.
[11] Prends l'éloquence et tords-lui son cou!
[12] Et tout le reste est littérature.
[13] City editor [1873–1890] of *The Sun,* New York.

William McKendree [Will] Carleton

1845–1912

1 Worm or beetle—drought or tempest—on a farmer's land may fall,
Each is loaded full o' ruin, but a mortgage beats 'em all. *The Tramp's Story*

2 Draw up the papers, lawyer, and make 'em good and stout,
For things at home are crossways, and Betsey and I are out.
Betsey and I Are Out, st. 1

3 And so we've agreed together that we can't never agree. *Ib. st. 3*

4 To appreciate heaven well
'Tis good for a man to have some fifteen minutes of hell.
Gone with a Handsomer Man, st. 20

5 Over the hill to the poorhouse I'm trudgin' my weary way.
Over the Hill to the Poorhouse, st. 1

William Kingdon Clifford

1845–1879

6 Remember, then, that it [science] is the guide of action; that the truth which it arrives at is not that which we can ideally contemplate without error, but that which we may act upon without fear; and you cannot fail to see that scientific thought is not an accompaniment or condition of human progress, but human progress itself.
Aims and Instruments of Scientific Thought [1872]

Daniel Webster Hoyt

1845–1936

7 Why should good words ne'er be said
Of a friend till he is dead?
A Sermon in Rhyme [1878], st. 1

George Kennan

1845–1924

8 Heroism, the Caucasian mountaineers say, is endurance for one moment more.
Letter to Henry Munroe Rogers [July 25, 1921]

Charles William Stubbs

1845–1912

9 To sit alone with my conscience
Will be judgment enough for me.[1]
Conscience and Future Judgment [1876]

John Banister Tabb

1845–1909

10 Out of the dusk a shadow,
Then a spark;
Out of the clouds a silence,
Then a lark;
Out of the heart a rapture,
Then a pain;
Out of the dead, cold ashes,
Life again. *Evolution*

Punch

11 Advice to persons about to marry.—"Don't."[2] *Vol. VIII, p. 1 [1845]*

12 You pays your money and you takes your choice. *X, 16 [1846]*

13 What is Matter?—Never mind.
What is Mind?—No matter.
XXIX, 19 [1855]

14 It ain't the 'unting as 'urts 'un, it's the 'ammer, 'ammer, 'ammer along the 'ard 'igh road. *XXX, 218 [1856]*

15 There was an old owl lived in an oak,
The more he heard, the less he spoke;
The less he spoke, the more he heard,
O, if men were all like that wise bird!
LXVIII, 155 [1875]

16 It's worse than wicked, my dear, it's vulgar.
Almanac [1876]

17 Don't look at me, sir, with—ah—in that tone of voice. *XCVII, 38 [1884]*

18 I'm afraid you've got a bad egg, Mr. Jones.
Oh no, my Lord, I assure you! Parts of it are excellent! *CIX, 222 [1895]*

Charles Dupee Blake

1846–1903

19 Rock-a-bye-baby on the tree top,
When the wind blows the cradle will rock,
When the bough breaks the cradle will fall,
And down will come baby, cradle and all.
Attributed

[1] See Polybius, 95:19, and Stevenson, 668:22.
[2] See Acton, 615:16.

Léon Bloy
1846–1917

1 Suffering is an auxiliary of creation.
Pages de Léon Bloy, Choisies par Raïssa Maritain [1951]

2 When you ask God to send you trials, you may be sure your prayer will be granted.
Ib. Pensées Détachées

Daniel Hudson Burnham
1846–1912

3 Make no little plans; they have no magic to stir men's blood. *Attributed*[1]

Joseph Ignatius Constantine Clarke
1846–1925

4 "Well, here's to good honest fighting blood!"
Said Kelly and Burke and Shea.
The Fighting Race, st. 4

Charles Prestwick Scott
1846–1932

5 The primary office of a newspaper is the gathering of news . . . comment is free, but facts are sacred.
In the Manchester Guardian [May 6, 1926][2]

Edward Noyes Westcott
1846–1898

6 The' ain't nothin' truer in the Bible 'n that sayin' thet them that has gits.
David Harum [1898], ch. 35

Alexander Graham Bell
1847–1922

7 Mr. Watson, come here, I want you.[3]
To his assistant [March 10, 1876]

Thomas Alva Edison
1847–1931

8 There is no substitute for hard work.
Life [1932], ch. 24

9 Genius is one percent inspiration and ninety-nine percent perspiration. *Ib.*

John Locke
1847–1889

10 O Ireland, isn't it grand you look—
Like a bride in her rich adornin'?
And with all the pent-up love of my heart
I bid you the top o' the mornin'!
The Exile's Return (Th' an'am an Dhia: My Soul to God), st. 1

Alice Meynell
1847–1922

11 She walks—the lady of my delight—
A shepherdess of sheep.
The Shepherdess, st. 1

Julia A. Moore[4]
1847–1920

12 Leave off the agony, leave off style,
Unless you've got money by you all the while.
Leave Off the Agony in Style

Milton Nobles
1847–1924

13 The villain still pursued her.
The Phoenix [1875], act I, sc. iii

George Robert Sims
1847–1922

14 It was Christmas Day in the workhouse.
Christmas Day in the Workhouse, st. 1

Arthur James Balfour
1848–1930

15 Biography should be written by an acute enemy.
Quoted by S. K. Ratcliffe *in the London Observer [January 30, 1927]*

John Vance Cheney
1848–1922

16 Who drives the horses of the sun
Shall lord it but a day.
The Happiest Heart, st. 1

[1] This quotation is now doubted. See Henry M. Saylor, " 'Make No Little Plans': Daniel Burnham Thought It but Did He Say It?," *Journal of the American Institute of Architects*, 27 [1957]: 3.
[2] Its one hundredth anniversary.
[3] The first intelligible words transmitted by telephone.
[4] "The Sweet Singer of Michigan."

John Churton Collins

1848–1908

1 Truth is the object of philosophy, but not always of philosophers.

From LOGAN PEARSALL SMITH, *A Treasury of English Aphorisms [1928]*

2 Mistrust a subordinate who never finds fault with his superior. *Ib.*

Sir Francis Darwin

1848–1925

3 But in science the credit goes to the man who convinces the world, not to the man to whom the idea first occurs.[1]

First Galton Lecture before the Eugenics Society [1914]

Ludwig Max Goldberger

1848–1913

4 America, the land of unlimited possibilities.

Land of Unlimited Possibilities: Observations on Economic Life in the United States of America [1903]

Joel Chandler Harris

1848–1908

5 Hit look lak sparrer-grass, hit feel lak sparrer-grass, hit tas'e lak sparrer-grass, en I bless ef 'taint sparrer-grass.

Nights with Uncle Remus [1883], ch. 27

6 Tar-baby ain't sayin' nuthin', en Brer Fox, he lay low.

Uncle Remus and His Friends [1892]

7 Ez soshubble ez a baskit er kittens. *Ib.*

8 Bred en bawn in a brier-patch, Brer Fox. *Ib.*

9 You do de pullin', Sis Cow, en I'll do de gruntin'. *Ib.*

10 W'en ole man Rabbit say "scoot," dey scooted, en w'en old Miss Rabbit say "scat," dey scatted. *Ib.*

11 Lazy fokes' stummucks don't git tired.

Uncle Remus: Plantation Proverbs

12 Jaybird don't rob his own nes'. *Ib.*

[1] See Zinsser, 762:5, and Fleming, 774:2.

13 Licker talks mighty loud w'en it gits loose fum de jug. *Ib.*

14 Hongry rooster don't cackle w'en he fine a wum. *Ib.*

15 Youk'n hide de fier, but w'at you gwine do wid de smoke? *Ib.*

16 Watch out w'en youer gittin' all you want. Fattenin' hogs ain't in luck. *Ib.*

17 Hop light, ladies,
Oh, Miss Loo!
Oh, swing dat yaller gal!
Do, boys, do! *Plantation Play Song*

Joris Karl Huysmans

1848–1907

18 The loveliest tune imaginable becomes vulgar and insupportable as soon as the public begins to hum it and the hurdygurdies make it their own.

À Rebours (Against the Grain) [1884],[2] *ch. 9*

19 Art is the only clean thing on earth, except holiness.

Les Foules de Lourdes [1906]

Richard Jefferies

1848–1887

20 It is eternity now. I am in the midst of it. It is about me in the sunshine; I am in it, as the butterfly in the light-laden air. Nothing has to come; it is now. Now is eternity; now is the immortal life.

The Story of My Heart [1883]

Vilfredo Pareto

1848–1923

21 Give me a fruitful error any time, full of seeds, bursting with its own corrections. You can keep your sterile truth for yourself.

Comment on Kepler

Eben Eugene Rexford

1848–1916

22 Darling, I am growing old,
Silver threads among the gold
Shine upon my brow today;
Life is fading fast away.

Silver Threads Among the Gold [1873], st. 1

[2] Translated by JOHN HOWARD.

Frederic Edward Weatherly
1848–1929

1 Always the same, Darby, my own,
Always the same to your old wife Joan.
Darby and Joan,[1] *refrain*

Bernhard von Bülow
1849–1929

2 A place in the sun.
A Promise for Germany. Speech before the Reichstag [December 6, 1897]

3 The king in Prussia—forward; Prussia in Germany—forward; Germany in the world—forward! *Ib.*

Lord Randolph Spencer Churchill
1849–1895

4 The old gang [members of the Conservative government].
Speech in the House of Commons [March 7, 1878]

Sir Edmund Gosse
1849–1928

5 My father's theory[2] . . . was defined by a hasty press as being this—that God hid the fossils in the rocks in order to tempt geologists into infidelity.
Father and Son [1907], ch. 5

6 The Victorians . . . carried admiration to the highest pitch. . . . They turned it from a virtue into a religion, and called it Hero Worship.
The Agony of the Victorian Age [1918]

William Ernest Henley
1849–1903

7 Bland as a Jesuit, sober as a hymn.
In Hospital [1888]. No. 16, House Surgeon

8 Valiant in velvet, light in ragged luck,
Most vain, most generous, sternly critical,
Buffoon and poet, lover and sensualist:
A deal of Ariel, just a streak of Puck,
Much Antony, of Hamlet most of all,
And something of the Shorter-Catechist.
Ib. 25, Apparition (Robert Louis Stevenson)[3]

9 As dust that drives, as straws that blow,
Into the night go one and all.
Ballade of Dead Actors [1888]

10 Out of the night that covers me,
Black as the Pit from pole to pole,
I thank whatever gods may be
For my unconquerable soul.

In the fell clutch of circumstance,
I have not winced nor cried aloud;
Under the bludgeonings of chance
My head is bloody, but unbowed.
Echoes [1888]. No. 4, In Memoriam R. T. Hamilton Bruce ("Invictus"), st. 1, 2

11 I am the master of my fate;
I am the captain of my soul.[4] *Ib. st. 4*

12 Night with her train of stars
And her great gift of sleep.
Ib. 35, In Memoriam Margaritae Sororis, st. 2

13 Or ever the knightly years were gone
With the old world to the grave,
I was a King in Babylon
And you were a Christian Slave.
Ib. 37, To W. A., st. 1

14 What have I done for you,
England, my England?
What is there I would not do,
England, my own?
For England's Sake. Pro Rege Nostro [1892], st. 1

Sarah Orne Jewett
1849–1909

15 A harbor, even if it is a little harbor, is a good thing, since adventures come into it as well as go out, and the life in it grows strong, because it takes something from the world and has something to give in return.
Country Byways. River Driftwood

16 Captain Littlepage had overset his mind with too much reading.
The Country of the Pointed Firs [1896], ch. 5

17 The old poets little knew what comfort they could be to man. *Ib.*

[1] Old Darby with Joan by his side, / You've often regarded with wonder; / He's dropsical, she is sore-eyed, / Yet they're ever uneasy asunder.—HENRY WOODFALL, *The Gentleman's Magazine* [March 1735]

[2] British naturalist Philip Henry Gosse [1810–1888], who opposed the uniformitarian geological theory of Sir Charles Lyell [1797–1875].
See Lyell, 482:11.

[3] See R. L. Stevenson, 667.

[4] See Sallust, 103:1 and 103:5; Bacon, 181:6; Shakespeare, 215:6; Tennyson, 534:7; and Nehru, 814:8.

1 Wrecked on the lee shore of age.
Ib. 7

2 We were standing where there was a fine view of the harbor and its long stretches of shore all covered by the great army of the pointed firs, darkly cloaked and standing as if they waited to embark. As we looked far seaward among the outer islands, the trees seemed to march seaward still, going steadily over the heights and down to the water's edge. *Ib.*

3 Tact is after all a kind of mind-reading.
Ib. 10

4 Yes'm, old friends is always best, 'less you can catch a new one that's fit to make an old one out of. *Ib. 12*

5 In the life of each of us, I said to myself, there is a place remote and islanded, and given to endless regret or secret happiness.
Ib. 15

6 'Tain't worthwhile to wear a day all out before it comes. *Ib. 16*

7 The road was new to me, as roads always are, going back. *Ib. 19*

8 So we die before our own eyes; so we see some chapters of our lives come to their natural end. *Ib.*

9 The thing that teases the mind over and over for years, and at last gets itself put down rightly on paper—whether little or great, it belongs to Literature.
Letter to Willa Cather. Quoted in preface to The Country of the Pointed Firs and Other Stories [*1925*]

Emma Lazarus
1849–1887

10 Give me your tired, your poor,
Your huddled masses yearning to breathe free,
The wretched refuse of your teeming shore,
Send these, the homeless, tempest-tossed, to me:
I lift my lamp beside the golden door.
The New Colossus: Inscription for the Statue of Liberty, New York Harbor

Sir William Osler
1849–1919

11 The greater the ignorance the greater the dogmatism.
Montreal Medical Journal [1902]

12 The philosophies of one age have become the absurdities of the next, and the foolishness of yesterday has become the wisdom of tomorrow. *Ib.*

13 The natural man has only two primal passions, to get and to beget.
Science and Immortality [1904], ch. 2

14 The desire to take medicine is perhaps the greatest feature which distinguishes man from animals. *Ib. 14*

15 We are here to add what we can *to,* not to get what we can *from,* Life.[1]
From HARVEY CUSHING, *The Life of Sir William Osler [1925], vol. I, ch. 14*

16 Humanity has but three great enemies: fever, famine and war; of these by far the greatest, by far the most terrible, is fever.
Ib.

17 The master word [work] . . . is the open sesame to every portal, the great equalizer in the world, the true philosopher's stone which transmutes all the base metal of humanity into gold.[2] *Ib. 22*

18 Things cannot always go your way. Learn to accept in silence the minor aggravations, cultivate the gift of taciturnity and consume your own smoke with an extra draught of hard work, so that those about you may not be annoyed with the dust and soot of your complaints. *Ib.*

19 Take the sum of human achievement in action, in science, in art, in literature—subtract the work of the men above forty, and while we should miss great treasures, even priceless treasures, we would practically be where we are today. . . . The effective, moving, vitalizing work of the world is done between the ages of twenty-five and forty.[3]
Ib. 24 [The Fixed Period]

20 My second fixed idea is the uselessness of men above sixty years of age, and the incalculable benefit it would be in commercial, political, and in professional life, if as a matter of course, men stopped work at this age.[4]
Ib.

[1] Also in *Doctor and Nurse,* in *Aequanimitas and Other Addresses* [1904].

[2] Lecture, *The Master Word in Medicine,* Toronto [October 1, 1903]; also in *Aequanimitas.*

[3] Address at Johns Hopkins University, Baltimore [February 22, 1905].

[4] This valedictory address caused much discussion and misquotation. It was headlined in the press: OSLER RECOMMENDS CHLOROFORM AT SIXTY, and occasioned many columns of letters, caustic cartoons, and the like, until to "Oslerize" became a byword.

1 I have three personal ideals. One, to do the day's work well and not to bother about tomorrow. . . . The second ideal has been to act the Golden Rule, as far as in me lay, toward my professional brethren and toward the patients committed to my care. And the third has been to cultivate such a measure of equanimity as would enable me to bear success with humility, the affection of my friends without pride, and to be ready when the day of sorrow and grief came to meet it with the courage befitting a man.

Ib. [Farewell Dinner, May 2, 1905]

2 Nothing in life is more wonderful than faith — the one great moving force which we can neither weigh in the balance nor test in the crucible. *Ib. II, 30*

Ivan Petrovich Pavlov

1849–1936

3 The naturalist must consider only one thing: what is the relation of this or that external reaction of the animal to the phenomena of the external world?

Scientific Study of So-Called Psychical Processes in the Higher Animals [1906]

4 Mankind will possess incalculable advantages and extraordinary control over human behavior when the scientific investigator will be able to subject his fellow men to the same external analysis he would employ for any natural object, and when the human mind will contemplate itself not from within but from without. *Ib.*

5 Learn the ABC of science before you try to ascend to its summit.

Bequest to the Academic Youth of Soviet Russia [1936]

6 Learn, compare, collect the facts!

Ib.

James Whitcomb Riley

1849–1916

7 O'er folded blooms
On swirls of musk,
The beetle booms adown the glooms
And bumps along the dusk.

The Beetle, st. 7

8 The ripest peach is highest on the tree.

The Ripest Peach, st. 1

9 There! little girl; don't cry!

A Life Lesson, st. 3

10 That old sweetheart of mine.

An Old Sweetheart of Mine, st. 12

11 An' all us other children, when the supper things is done,
We set around the kitchen fire an' has the mostest fun
A-list'nin' to the witch-tales 'at Annie tells about,
An' the Gobble-uns 'at gits you Ef you don't watch out!

Little Orphant Annie [1883], st. 1

12 'Long about knee-deep in June,
'Bout the time strawberries melts
On the vine.

Knee-Deep in June [1883], st. 1

13 Oh! the old swimmin' hole! When I last saw the place,
The scenes was all changed, like the change in my face.

The Old Swimmin' Hole [1883], st. 5

14 O, it sets my heart a-clickin' like the tickin' of a clock,
When the frost is on the punkin and the fodder's in the shock.

When the Frost Is on the Punkin [1883], st. 3

Edward Bellamy[1]

1850–1898

15 We hold the period of youth sacred to education, and the period of maturity, when the physical forces begin to flag, equally sacred to ease and agreeable relaxation.

Looking Backward, 2000–1887[2] *[1888], ch. 6*

16 Buying and selling is essentially antisocial.

Ib. 9

17 The nation guarantees the nurture, education, and comfortable maintenance of every citizen from the cradle to the grave.[3]

Ib.

18 Love of money[4] . . . was the general impulse to effort in your day. *Ib.*

19 Badly off as the men . . . were in your day, they were more fortunate than their mothers and wives. *Ib. 11*

[1] There is at least a fair chance that another fifty years will confirm Edward Bellamy's position as one of the most authentic prophets of our age. — HEYWOOD BROUN [1931]

[2] Looking back at 1887 from the year 2000.

[3] See Dyer, 345:3; Shelley, 467:9; and Hoffenstein, 816:2.

[4] See *I Timothy 6:10*, 51:2, and Keynes, 783:10.

1 An American credit card . . . is just as good in Europe as American gold used to be.
Ib. 13

2 Equal wealth and equal opportunities of culture . . . have simply made us all members of one class.
Ib. 14

3 If bread is the first necessity of life, recreation is a close second.[1]
Ib. 18

4 Your system was liable to periodical convulsions . . . business crises at intervals of five to ten years, which wrecked the industries of the nation.
Ib. 22

5 On no other stage are the scenes shifted with a swiftness so like magic as on the great stage of history when once the hour strikes.[2]
Ib. Author's postscript

6 *Looking Backward* was written in the belief that the Golden Age lies before us and not behind us.
Ib.

Augustine Birrell
1850–1933

7 Libraries are not made; they grow.
Obiter Dicta. Book Buying

8 That great dust heap called "history."
Ib. Carlyle

Hermann Ebbinghaus
1850–1909

9 From the most ancient subject we shall produce the newest science.[3]
Inscription on the title page of Über das Gedachtnis (Memory) [1885]

10 Psychology has a long past, but only a short history.
Abriss der Psychologie (Summary of Psychology) [1908], opening sentence

Eugene Field
1850–1895

11 I feel a sort of yearnin' 'nd a chokin' in my throat
When I think of Red Hoss Mountain 'nd of Casey's tabble dote!
Casey's Table d'Hôte, st. 1

12 He could whip his weight in wildcats.
Modjesky as Cameel, st. 10

[1]See Juvenal, 122:15.
[2]See Hugo, 491:11.
[3]De subjecto vetustissimo novissimam promovemus scientiam.

13 The best of all physicians
Is apple pie and cheese!
Apple Pie and Cheese, st. 5

14 It always was the biggest fish I caught that got away.
Our Biggest Fish, st. 2

15 When I demanded of my friend what viands he preferred,
He quoth: "A large cold bottle, and a small hot bird!"
The Bottle and the Bird, st. 1

16 Wynken, Blynken, and Nod[4] one night
Sailed off in a wooden shoe—
Sailed on a river of crystal light
Into a sea of dew.
Wynken, Blynken, and Nod, st. 1

17 The little toy dog is covered with dust,
But sturdy and staunch he stands;
And the little toy soldier is red with rust,
And his musket molds in his hands;
Time was when the little toy dog was new,
And the soldier was passing fair;
And that was the time when our Little Boy Blue
Kissed them and put them there.
Little Boy Blue, st. 1

18 The gingham dog went "Bow-wow-wow!"
And the calico cat replied "Mee-ow!"
The air was littered, an hour or so,
With bits of gingham and calico.
The Duel, st. 2

19 Father calls me William, sister calls me Will,
Mother calls me Willie, but the fellers call me Bill!
Jest 'Fore Christmas, st. 1

20 'Most all the time, the whole year round, there ain't no flies on me,
But jest 'fore Christmas I'm as good as I kin be!
Ib.

Fred Gilbert
1850–1903

21 The Man Who Broke the Bank at Monte Carlo.
Title of song [1892]

Samuel Gompers
1850–1924

22 To protect the workers in their inalienable rights to a higher and better life; to protect them, not only as equals before the law, but also in their health, their homes, their firesides, their liberties as men, as workers, and as citizens; to overcome and conquer prejudices and antagonism; to secure to them the right to life, and the opportunity to maintain

[4]See Braley, 775:14.

that life; the right to be full sharers in the abundance which is the result of their brain and brawn, and the civilization of which they are the founders and the mainstay. . . . The attainment of these is the glorious mission of the trade unions. *Speech [1898]*

Henry Cabot Lodge

1850–1924

1 Let every man honor and love the land of his birth and the race from which he springs and keep their memory green. It is a pious and honorable duty. But let us have done with British-Americans and Irish-Americans and German-Americans, and so on, and all be Americans. . . . If a man is going to be an American at all let him be so without any qualifying adjectives; and if he is going to be something else, let him drop the word American from his personal description.

The Day We Celebrate (Forefathers' Day). Address, New England Society of Brooklyn [December 21, 1888]

2 It is the flag just as much of the man who was naturalized yesterday as of the man whose people have been here many generations. *Address [1915]*

3 He was a great patriot, a great man; above all, a great American. His country was the ruling, mastering passion of his life from the beginning even unto the end.

Theodore Roosevelt. Address Before Congress [February 9, 1919]

Guy de Maupassant

1850–1893

4 A man who looks a part has the soul of that part.[1] *Mont-Oriol [1887]*

5 Conversation . . . is the art of never appearing a bore, of knowing how to say everything interestingly, to entertain with no matter what, to be charming with nothing at all.

Sur l'Eau (On the Water) [1888]

6 History, that excitable and lying old lady.[2] *Ib.*

Laura Elizabeth Richards

1850–1943

7 Be you clown or be you king,
Still your singing is the thing.

Tirra Lirra [1930], dedication, l. 7

[1]Quand on a le physique d'un emploi, on en a l'âme.
[2]L'histoire, cette vieille dame exaltée et menteuse.

8 Every little wave had its nightcap on.

Song for Hal, refrain

9 Once there was an elephant
Who tried to use the telephant—
No! No! I mean an elephone
Who tried to use the telephone.

Eletelephony, l. 1

Robert Louis Stevenson[3]

1850–1894

10 Mankind was never so happily inspired as when it made a cathedral.

An Inland Voyage [1878]. Noyon

11 Every man is his own doctor of divinity, in the last resort. *Ib.*

12 For my part, I travel not to go anywhere, but to go. I travel for travel's sake. The great affair is to move.

Travels with a Donkey [1878]

13 Marriage is like life in this—that it is a field of battle, and not a bed of roses.

Virginibus Puerisque [1881], I, ch. 1

14 Times are changed with him who marries; there are no more bypath meadows, where you may innocently linger, but the road lies long and straight and dusty to the grave. *Ib.*

15 Man is a creature who lives not upon bread alone but principally by catchwords. *Ib.*

16 The cruelest lies are often told in silence.

Ib. 4, Truth of Intercourse

17 Old and young, we are all on our last cruise. *Ib. II, Crabbed Age and Youth*

18 It is better to be a fool than to be dead. *Ib.*

19 Give me the young man who has brains enough to make a fool of himself! *Ib.*

20 Every heart that has beat strong and cheerfully has left a hopeful impulse behind it in the world, and bettered the tradition of mankind. *Ib. Aes Triplex*

21 Books are good enough in their own way, but they are a mighty bloodless substitute for life. *Ib. III, An Apology for Idlers*

22 Perpetual devotion to what a man calls his business, is only to be sustained by perpetual neglect of many other things. *Ib.*

23 There is no duty we so much underrate as the duty of being happy. *Ib.*

[3]See Henley, 663:8.

1 To travel hopefully is a better thing than to arrive. *Ib. VI, El Dorado*

2 To be what we are, and to become what we are capable of becoming, is the only end of life.
Familiar Studies of Men and Books [1882]

3 I am in the habit of looking not so much to the nature of a gift as to the spirit in which it is offered.
New Arabian Nights [1882]. The Suicide Club

4 Fifteen men on the Dead Man's Chest—[1]
Yo-ho-ho, and a bottle of rum!
Drink and the devil had done for the rest—
Yo-ho-ho, and a bottle of rum!
Treasure Island [1883], ch. 1

5 Doctors is all swabs. *Ib. 3*

6 "What is the Black Spot, Captain?" "That's a summons, mate." *Ib.*

7 Pieces of eight, pieces of eight, pieces of eight! *Ib. 10*

8 Many's the long night I've dreamed of cheese—toasted, mostly. *Ib. 15*

9 In winter I get up at night
And dress by yellow candlelight.
In summer, quite the other way,
I have to go to bed by day.
A Child's Garden of Verses [1885]. Bed in Summer, st. 1

10 A child should always say what's true
And speak when he is spoken to,
And behave mannerly at table;
At least as far as he is able.
Ib. Whole Duty of Children

11 Whenever the moon and stars are set,
Whenever the wind is high,
All night long in the dark and wet,
A man goes riding by.
Late in the night when the fires are out,
Why does he gallop and gallop about?
Ib. Windy Nights, st. 1

[1] Treasure Island came out of Kingsley's *At Last,* where I got the Dead Man's Chest—and that was the seed. — R. L. STEVENSON, *Letter to Sidney Colvin*

We were crawling slowly along, looking out for Virgin Gorda; the first of those numberless isles which Columbus, so goes the tale, discovered on St. Ursula's day, and named them after the saint and her eleven thousand mythical virgins. Unfortunately, English buccaneers have since given to most of them less poetic names. The Dutchman's Cap, Broken Jerusalem, The Dead Man's Chest, Rum Island, and so forth, mark a time and race more prosaic.—CHARLES KINGSLEY, *At Last* [1870], *ch. 1*

12 I have a little shadow that goes in and out with me,
And what can be the use of him is more than I can see.
He is very, very like me from the heels up to the head;
And I see him jump before me, when I jump into my bed. *Ib. My Shadow, st. 1*

13 The friendly cow all red and white,
I love with all my heart:
She gives me cream with all her might,
To eat with apple tart.
Ib. The Cow, st. 1

14 The world is so full of a number of things,
I'm sure we should all be as happy as kings.
Ib. Happy Thought

15 Dr. Jekyll and Mr. Hyde.
Title of novel [1886]

16 Am I no a bonny fighter?
Kidnapped [1886], ch. 10 (Alan Breck)

17 Of all my verse, like not a single line;
But like my title, for it is not mine.
That title from a better man[2] I stole:
Ah, how much better, had I stol'n the whole!
Underwoods [1887], title page poem

18 Let first the onion flourish there,
Rose among roots, the maiden-fair,
Wine-scented and poetic soul
Of the capacious salad bowl.[3]
Ib. bk. I, In English. To a Gardener

19 Dear Andrew, with the brindled hair.[4]
Ib. To Andrew Lang

20 Under the wide and starry sky,
Dig the grave and let me lie.
Glad did I live and gladly die,
And I laid me down with a will.

This be the verse you grave for me:
Here he lies where he longed to be;
Home is the sailor, home from sea,
And the hunter home from the hill.
Ib. Requiem

21 My body which my dungeon is,
And yet my parks and palaces.
Ib. My Body Which My Dungeon Is

22 There's just ae thing I cannae bear,
An' that's my conscience.[5]
Ib. II, In Scots. My Conscience

23 I have thus played the sedulous ape to Hazlitt, to Lamb, to Wordsworth, to Sir Thomas

[2] Ben Jonson.

[3] See Sydney Smith, 433:11.

[4] Dear Louis of the awful cheek! / Who told you it was right to speak, / Where all the world might hear and stare, / Of other fellows' "brindled hair"?—ANDREW LANG [1844–1912], *To R.L.S.*

[5] See Polybius, 95:19, and Stubbs, 660:9.

Browne, to Defoe, to Hawthorne, to Montaigne, to Baudelaire and to Obermann.
Memories and Portraits [1887]. A College Magazine

1 A Penny Plain and Twopence Colored.
Ib. Essay About Skelt's Juvenile Drama

2 Wealth I ask not, hope nor love,
Nor a friend to know me;
All I ask, the heaven above
And the road below me.
Songs of Travel. The Vagabond, st. 4

3 The untented Kosmos my abode,
I pass, a willful stranger;
My mistress still the open road
And the bright eyes of danger.
Ib. Youth and Love

4 I will make you brooches and toys for your delight
Of birdsong at morning and starshine at night.
Ib. Romance, st. 1

5 God, if this were enough,
That I see things bare to the buff.
Ib. If This Were Faith

6 Bright is the ring of words
When the right man rings them.
Ib. no. 14

7 In the highlands, in the country places,
Where the old plain men have rosy faces,
And the young fair maidens
Quiet eyes.
Ib. 15

8 Trusty, dusky, vivid, true,
With eyes of gold and bramble dew,
Steel-true and blade-straight
The great artificer
Made my mate.
Ib. 25, To My Wife, st. 1

9 Be it granted me to behold you again in dying,
Hills of home!
Ib. 45, To S. R. Crockett

10 Not every man is so great a coward as he thinks he is—nor yet so good a Christian.
The Master of Ballantrae [1889]. Mr. Mackellar's Journey

11 Nothing like a little judicious levity.
The Wrong Box [1889], ch. 7

12 Do you know what the Governor of South Carolina said to the Governor of North Carolina? It's a long time between drinks, observed that powerful thinker.[1]
Ib. 8

13 So long as we love we serve; so long as we are loved by others, I would almost say that we are indispensable; and no man is useless while he has a friend.
Across the Plains [1892]. Lay Morals

14 If your morals make you dreary, depend upon it, they are wrong. I do not say give them up, for they may be all you have, but conceal them like a vice lest they should spoil the lives of better and simpler people.
Ib.

15 Here lies one who meant well, tried a little, failed much:—surely that may be his epitaph of which he need not be ashamed.
Ib.

16 Ice and iron cannot be welded.
Weir of Hermiston [1896]

17 Give us grace and strength to forbear and to persevere. Give us courage and gaiety and the quiet mind, spare to us our friends, soften to us our enemies.
Prayer[2]

18 Youth is wholly experimental.
Letter to a Young Gentleman

Rose Hartwick Thorpe

1850–1939

19 She breathed the husky whisper—
"Curfew must not ring tonight."
Curfew Must Not Ring Tonight [1882], st. 2

20 Out she swung—far out; the city seemed a speck of light below,
There 'twixt heaven and earth suspended as the bell swung to and fro.
Ib. st. 7

Ella Wheeler Wilcox

1850–1919

21 One ship drives east and another drives west
With the selfsame winds that blow.
'Tis the set of sails and not the gales
Which tells us the way to go.
Winds of Fate

---

[1] Of the several traditions relating to the origin of this remark, the most reasonable one traces it to John Motley Morehead [1796–1866], who was Governor of North Carolina 1841–1845. He was visited by James H. Hammond [1807–1864], who was Governor of South Carolina 1842–1844. They engaged in discussion and argument, and when the latter waxed hot, Governor Morehead was reported by a servant to have exclaimed: "It's a long time between drinks."—John Motley Morehead, *letter* [November 21, 1934]

[2] On the bronze memorial to Stevenson in St. Giles Cathedral, Edinburgh, Scotland.

1 No! the two kinds of people on earth that I mean
Are the people who lift and the people who lean.
To Lift or to Lean

2 Love is a mood — no more — to man,
And love to woman is life or death.[1]
Blind, st. 1

3 Laugh, and the world laughs with you;
Weep, and you weep alone.
Solitude, st. 1

4 So many gods, so many creeds,
So many paths that wind and wind,
When just the art of being kind
Is all this sad world needs.
The World's Need

5 No question is ever settled
Until it is settled right.
Settle the Question Right

Ferdinand Foch

1851–1929

6 My center is giving way, my right is pushed back, situation excellent, I am attacking.[2]
At the second battle of the Marne [1918]. From B. H. LIDDELL HART, *Reputations Ten Years After [1928]*

Edward Smith Ufford

1851–1929

7 Throw out the lifeline, throw out the lifeline,
Someone is sinking today.
Throw Out the Lifeline [1884], refrain

Francis William Bourdillon

1852–1921

8 The night has a thousand eyes,[3]
And the day but one;
Yet the light of the bright world dies
With the dying sun.
The mind has a thousand eyes,
And the heart but one;
Yet the light of a whole life dies
When love is done.
Among the Flowers [1878]. The Night Has a Thousand Eyes

[1] See Byron, 460:19.
[2] Mon centre cède, ma droite recule, situation excellente, j'attaque.
[3] On the stars thou gazest, my star; would I were heaven to look at thee with many eyes. — *Greek Anthology, pt. VIII, no. 7; translated by* J. W. MACKAIL
See Lyly, 176:2.

Paul Bourget

1852–1935

9 Ideas are to literature what light is to painting.[4]
La Physiologie de l'Amour Moderne [1890]

10 We must live as we think, otherwise we shall end up by thinking as we have lived.[5]
Le Démon de Midi [1914], conclusion

Robert Bontine Cunninghame-Graham

1852–1936

11 Success, which touches nothing that it does not vulgarize, should be its own reward . . . the odium of success is hard enough to bear, without the added ignominy of popular applause.[6]
Success [1902]

12 God forbid that I should go to any heaven in which there are no horses.
Letter to Theodore Roosevelt [1917]

Flying Hawk[7]

1852–1931

13 The tepee is much better to live in: always clean, warm in winter, cool in summer; easy to move . . . Indians and animals know better how to live than white man; nobody can be in good health if he does not have all the time fresh air, sunshine, and good water.
Statement in old age

Edwin Markham

1852–1940

14 Bowed by the weight of centuries he leans
Upon his hoe and gazes on the ground,
The emptiness of ages in his face,
And on his back the burden of the world.
The Man with the Hoe [1899],[8] st. 1

15 O masters, lords and rulers in all lands,
Is this the handiwork you give to God?
Ib. st. 3

[4] La pensée est à la littérature ce que la lumière est à la peinture.
[5] Il faut vivre comme on pense, sans quoi l'on finira par penser comme on a vécu.
[6] See Lowry, 876:9.
[7] Oglala Sioux chief.
[8] Inspired by Millet's painting.

1 A man to match the mountains[1] and the sea.
Lincoln, The Man of the People [1901], st. 1

2 The color of the ground was in him, the red earth,
The smack and tang of elemental things.[2]
Ib. st. 2

3 He went down
As when a lordly cedar, green with boughs,
Goes down with a great shout upon the hills,
And leaves a lonesome place against the sky.
Ib. st. 4

4 He drew a circle that shut me out—
Heretic, rebel, a thing to flout.
But Love and I had the wit to win:
We drew a circle that took him in.
Outwitted

George Moore
1852–1933

5 After all there is but one race—humanity.
The Bending of the Bough [1900], act III

6 The difficulty in life is the choice.
Ib. IV

7 The wrong way always seems the more reasonable. *Ib.*

8 A man travels the world over in search of what he needs and returns home to find it.
The Brook Kerith [1916], ch. 11

Henry Van Dyke
1852–1933

9 Raise the stone, and thou shalt find me; cleave the wood and there am I.[3]
The Toiling of Felix [1900], pt. I, prelude

10 So it's home again, and home again, America for me.
My heart is turning home again, and there I long to be. *America for Me, st. 2*

11 Not to the swift, the race:
Not to the strong, the fight:[4]
Not to the righteous, perfect grace:
Not to the wise, the light.
Reliance, st. 1

12 The lintel low enough to keep out pomp and pride:
The threshold high enough to turn deceit aside.
For the Friends at Hurstmont. The Door

13 Self is the only prison that can ever bind the soul. *The Prison and the Angel*

14 The first day of spring is one thing, and the first spring day is another. The difference between them is sometimes as great as a month.
Fisherman's Luck [1899], ch. 5

Edgar Watson Howe
1853–1937

15 What people say behind your back is your standing in the community.
Country Town Sayings [1911]

16 There is nothing so well known as that we should not expect something for nothing—but we all do and call it Hope. *Ib.*

José Martí
1853–1895

17 Life on earth is a hand-to-hand mortal combat . . . between the law of love and the law of hate.[5] *Letter [1881]*

18 Love is . . . born with the pleasure of looking at each other, it is fed with the necessity of seeing each other, it is concluded with the impossibility of separation!
Amor [1881]

19 Oh, what company good poets are![6]
Longfellow [1882]

20 A knowledge of different literatures is the best way to free one's self from the tyranny of any of them.
On Oscar Wilde [1882]

21 To beautify life is to give it an object.
Ib.

22 Man needs to suffer. When he does not have real griefs he creates them. Griefs purify and prepare him.
Adúltera (Adulterous Thoughts) [1883]

[1] A man to match his mountains, not to creep / Dwarfed and abased below them.—WHITTIER, *Among the Hills* [1869], *prelude*

Bring me men to match my mountains.—SAM WALTER FOSS [1858–1911], *The Coming American*

[2] See Beston, 802:17.

[3] See *The Sayings of Jesus*, 126:14.

Raise ye the stone or cleave the wood to make a path more fair or flat; / Lo, it is black already with blood some Son of Martha spilled for that.—RUDYARD KIPLING, *The Sons of Martha* [1907]

[4] See *Ecclesiastes 9:11*, 27:17, and John Davidson, 684:13.

[5] Translated by JAMES NELSON GOODSELL.

[6] See John Adams, 381:15.

1 Terrible times in which priests no longer merit the praise of poets and in which poets have not yet begun to be priests.

On "El Poema de Niágara" of Pérez Bonalde [1883]

2 A nation is not a complex of wheels, nor a wild horse race, but a stride upward concerted by real men.

A Glance at the North American's Soul Today [1886]

3 Men are products, expressions, reflections; they live to the extent that they coincide with their epoch, or to the extent that they differ markedly from it.

Henry Ward Beecher [1887]

4 A grain of poetry suffices to season a century.

Dedication of the Statue of Liberty [1887]

5 Hatred, slavery's inevitable aftermath.

Woman Suffrage [1887]

6 Others go to bed with their mistresses; I with my ideas. *Letter [1890]*

7 Man needs to go outside himself in order to find repose and reveal himself.

Vivir en Sí (To Live in Oneself) [1891]

8 Poetry is the work of the bard and of the people who inspire him. *Poesia [1891]*

9 Mankind is composed of two sorts of men — those who love and create, and those who hate and destroy.

Letter to a Cuban farmer [1893]

10 Men have no special right because they belong to one race or another: the word man defines all rights.

Mi Raza (My Race) [1893]

11 I wish to leave the world
By its natural door;
In my tomb of green leaves
They are to carry me to die.
Do not put me in the dark
To die like a traitor;
I am good, and like a good thing
I will die with my face to the sun.

A Morir (To Die) [1894]

12 This is the age in which hills can look down upon the mountains. *Ib.*

13 Only those who hate the Negro see hatred in the Negro.

Manifesto of Montecristi [1895]

14 The spirit of a government must be that of the country. The form of a government must come from the makeup of the country. Government is nothing but the balance of the natural elements of a country.

Our America [1891]

15 I have lived in the monster [the United States] and I know its insides; and my sling is the sling of David.

Letter to Manuel Mercado [1895]

Cecil John Rhodes

1853–1902

16 I desire to encourage and foster an appreciation of the advantages which will result from the union of the English-speaking peoples throughout the world, and to encourage in the students from the United States of America an attachment to the country from which they have sprung without I hope withdrawing them or their sympathies from the land of their adoption or birth.

His will, establishing the Rhodes Scholarships

17 Educational relations make the strongest tie. *Ib.*

18 So little done — so much to do.

Last words

James A. Bland

1854–1911

19 Carry me back to old Virginny,
There's where the cotton and the corn and taters grow;
There's where the birds warble sweet in the springtime,
There's where this old darky's heart am longed to go.

Carry Me Back to Old Virginny [1875], st. 1

Sir James George Frazer

1854–1941

20 Dwellers by the sea cannot fail to be impressed by the sight of its ceaseless ebb and flow, and are apt, on the principles of that rude philosophy of sympathy and resemblance . . . to trace a subtle relation, a secret harmony, between its tides and the life of man. . . . The belief that most deaths happen at ebb tide is said to be held along the east coast of England from Northumberland to Kent.[1]

The Golden Bough [1922],[2] ch. 3

[1] See Shakespeare, 207:13, and Dickens, 549:3.

[2] Abridged one-volume edition. The original appeared in twelve volumes [1890–1915].

1 The heaviest calamity in English history, the breach with America, might never have occurred if George the Third had not been an honest dullard.[1] *Ib.*

2 By religion, then, I understand a propitiation or conciliation of powers superior to man which are believed to direct and control the course of nature and of human life. *Ib. 4*

3 It is a common rule with primitive people not to waken a sleeper, because his soul is away and might not have time to get back. *Ib. 18*

4 The awe and dread with which the untutored savage contemplates his mother-in-law are amongst the most familiar facts of anthropology. *Ib.*

5 The world cannot live at the level of its great men. *Ib. 37*

Thomas Riley Marshall

1854–1925

6 What this country needs is a good five-cent cigar.[2]

Remark to John Crockett, chief clerk of the Senate

Jules Henri Poincaré

1854–1912

7 To doubt everything or to believe everything are two equally convenient solutions; both dispense with the necessity of reflection.

Quoted by BERTRAND RUSSELL *in preface to Science and Method [1913] (La Science et l'Hypothèse, 1903)*[3]

8 Science is built up with facts, as a house is with stones. But a collection of facts is no more a science than a heap of stones is a house. *Ib.*

9 Sociology is the science with the greatest number of methods and the least results. *Ib. ch. 1*

10 The advance of science is not comparable to the changes of a city, where old edifices are pitilessly torn down to give place to new, but to the continuous evolution of zoologic types which develop ceaselessly and end by becoming unrecognizable to the common sight, but where an expert eye finds always traces of the prior work of the past centuries.

Valeur de la Science [1904][3]

[1]See Bentley, 753:5.
[2]What this country needs is a good five-cent nickel. — FRANKLIN P. ADAMS [1932]
[3]Translated by G. B. HALSTED.

Arthur Rimbaud

1854–1891

11 I went out under the sky, Muse! and I was your vassal.[4]

Ma Bohème. Fantaisie

12 My tavern was the Big Bear.
My stars in the sky rustled softly.[5]

Ib.

13 My sad heart foams at the stern.[6]

Le Coeur Volé

14 Lighter than a cork I danced on the waves.[7]

Le Bateau Ivre [1871]

15 Sweeter than apples to children
The green water spurted through my wooden hull.[8] *Ib.*

16 I have bathed in the Poem
Of the Sea . . .
Devouring the green azures.[9] *Ib.*

17 I have seen the sunset, stained with mystic horrors,
Illumine the rolling waves with long purple forms,
Like actors in ancient plays.[10] *Ib.*

18 I long for Europe of the ancient parapets.[11] *Ib.*

19 I have seen starry archipelagoes! and islands
Whose raving skies are opened to the voyager:
Is it in these bottomless nights that you sleep, in exile,
A million golden birds, O future Vigor?[12]

Ib.

20 Black A, white E, red I, green U, blue O: vowels,
Someday I shall recount your latent births.[13]

Voyelles [1871]

[4]J'allais sous le ciel, Muse! et j'étais ton féal.
[5]Mon auberge était à la Grande Ourse. / Mes étoiles au ciel avaient un doux frou-frou.
[6]Mon triste coeur bave à la poupe.
[7]Plus léger qu'un bouchon j'ai dansé sur les flots.
[8]Plus douce qu'aux enfants la chair des pommes sures, / L'eau verte pénétra ma coque de sapin.
[9]Je me suis baigné dans le Poème / De la Mer . . . / Dévorant les azurs verts.
[10]J'ai vu le soleil bas, taché d'horreurs mystiques, / Illuminant de longs figements violets, / Pareils à des acteurs des drames très antiques.
[11]Je regrette l'Europe aux anciens parapets!
[12]J'ai vu des archipels sidéraux! et des îles / Dont les cieux délirants sont ouverts au voyageur: / Est-ce en ces nuits sans fonds que tu dors et t'exiles, / Million d'oiseaux d'or, ô future Vigueur?
[13]A noir, E blanc, I rouge, U vert, O bleu: voyelles, / Je dirai quelque jour vos naissances latantes!

1 It is found again.
What? Eternity.
It is the sea
Gone with the sun.[1] *L'Éternité [1872]*

2 O seasons, O châteaux,
What soul is without flaws?[2]
Bonheur, refrain

3 One evening, I sat Beauty in my lap.—And I found her bitter.—And I cursed her.
Une Saison en Enfer [1873]

4 I found I could extinguish all human hope from my soul. *Ib.*

5 Baptism enslaved me.
Ib. Nuit de l'Enfer

6 I am the master of fantasy. *Ib.*

7 Old poetics played a large part in my alchemy of the word. *Ib. Délires*

8 I! I who fashioned myself a sorcerer or an angel, who dispensed with all morality, I have come back to the earth.
Ib. Adieu

9 One must be absolutely modern. *Ib.*

10 I have embraced the summer dawn.
Illuminations [1874]. Aube

11 It rains softly on the town.[3]
From a lost poem

12 I say one must be a *seer,* make oneself a *seer.* The poet makes himself a *seer* by an immense, long, deliberate *derangement* of all the senses.[4]
Lettre à Paul Demeny [May 15, 1871]

Willard Duncan Vandiver
1854–1932

13 I come from a state that raises corn and cotton and cockleburs and Democrats, and frothy eloquence neither convinces nor satisfies me. I am from Missouri. You have got to show me.
Speech at a naval banquet in Philadelphia [1899]

[1] Elle est retrouvée, / Quoi? — L'Éternité. / C'est la mer allée / Avec le soleil.
[2] O saisons, O châteaux / Quelle âme est sans défauts?
[3] Il pleut doucement sur la ville.
Verlaine used this as an epigraph for his *Ariettes Oubliées,* III.
See Verlaine, 659:13.
[4] Je dis qu'il faut être *voyant,* se faire *voyant.* Le poète se fait *voyant* par un long, immense et raisonné *dérèglement* de tous les sens.
See Baudelaire, 580:*n*3.

Oscar Fingal O'Flahertie Wills Wilde
1854–1900

14 Tread lightly, she is near
Under the snow,
Speak gently, she can hear
The daisies grow. *Requiescat, st. 1*

15 And down the long and silent street,
The dawn, with silver-sandaled feet,
Crept like a frightened girl.
The Harlot's House

16 Lo! with a little rod
I did but touch the honey[5] of romance—
And must I lose a soul's inheritance?
Hélas [1881], l. 12

17 A poet can survive everything but a misprint. *The Children of the Poets*

18 Meredith is a prose Browning, and so is Browning. He used poetry as a medium for writing in prose.
The Critic as Artist [1891], pt. I

19 It is through art, and through art only, that we can realize our perfection; through art and art only that we can shield ourselves from the sordid perils of actual existence.
Ib. II

20 As long as war is regarded as wicked, it will always have its fascination. When it is looked upon as vulgar, it will cease to be popular.
Ib.

21 There is no sin except stupidity.[6]
Ib.

22 There is no such thing as a moral or an immoral book. Books are well written, or badly written. That is all.
The Picture of Dorian Gray [1891], preface

23 All art is quite useless. *Ib.*

24 There is only one thing in the world worse than being talked about, and that is not being talked about. *Ib. ch. 1*

25 Conscience and cowardice are really the same things.[7] *Ib.*

26 A man cannot be too careful in the choice of his enemies.[8] *Ib.*

27 The only way to get rid of a temptation is to yield to it.[9] *Ib. 2*

[5] See *I Samuel 14:27,* 12:37.
[6] See Marlowe, 183:11.
[7] See Mark Twain, 625:13.
[8] See Conrad, 683:9.
[9] See Balzac, 484:15.

1 He knew the precise psychological moment[1] when to say nothing. *Ib.*

2 The only difference between a caprice and a lifelong passion is that the caprice lasts a little longer. *Ib.*

3 Children begin by loving their parents; as they grow older they judge them; sometimes they forgive them. *Ib. 5*

4 Conscience makes egotists of us all.[2] *Ib. 8*

5 When a woman marries again it is because she detested her first husband. When a man marries again, it is because he adored his first wife.[3] Women try their luck; men risk theirs. *Ib. 15*

6 Over the piano was printed a notice: Please do not shoot the pianist. He is doing his best.
Impressions of America. Leadville

7 Nowadays we are all of us so hard up that the only pleasant things to pay are compliments. They're the only things we can pay.
Lady Windermere's Fan [1892], act I

8 I can resist everything except temptation. *Ib.*

9 We are all in the gutter, but some of us are looking at the stars. *Ib. III*

10 In this world there are only two tragedies. One is not getting what one wants, and the other is getting it.[4] *Ib.*

11 What is a cynic? A man who knows the price of everything, and the value of nothing. *Ib.*

12 Experience is the name everyone gives to their mistakes. *Ib.*

13 I have never admitted that I am more than twenty-nine, or thirty at the most. Twenty-nine when there are pink shades, thirty when there are not.[5] *Ib. IV*

[1] In all considerations the psychological momentum or factor must be allowed to play a prominent part, for without its cooperation there is little to be hoped from the work of the artillery.—*Neue Preussische Kreuzzeitung* [December 16, 1870], *commenting upon the siege of Paris*
An error in translation gave us "psychological moment" (i.e., the critical moment). The Parisians ridiculed the phrase as an example of German pedantry, but it speedily became universal.

[2] See Shakespeare, 221:12.

[3] See Samuel Johnson, 354:22.

[4] See Shaw, 680:21.

[5] When you come to write my epitaph, Charles, let it be in these delicious words, "She had a long twenty-nine."—JAMES M. BARRIE [1860–1937], *Rosalind*

14 *Mrs. Allonby:* They say, Lady Hunstanton, that when good Americans die they go to Paris.[6]
Lady Hunstanton: Indeed? And when bad Americans die, where do they go to?
Lord Illingworth: Oh, they go to America.
A Woman of No Importance [1893], act I

15 The youth of America is their oldest tradition. It has been going on now for three hundred years. *Ib.*

16 *Lord Illingworth:* The Book of Life begins with a man and a woman in a garden.
Mrs. Allonby: It ends with Revelations. *Ib.*

17 I suppose society is wonderfully delightful. To be in it is merely a bore. But to be out of it simply a tragedy. *Ib. III*

18 Really, if the lower orders don't set us a good example, what on earth is the use of them?
The Importance of Being Earnest [1895], act I

19 I have invented an invaluable permanent invalid called Bunbury, in order that I may be able to go down into the country whenever I choose. *Ib.*

20 Of course the music is a great difficulty. You see, if one plays good music, people don't listen, and if one plays bad music people don't talk. *Ib.*

21 To lose one parent . . . may be regarded as a misfortune; to lose both looks like carelessness. *Ib.*

22 Relations are simply a tedious pack of people, who haven't got the remotest knowledge of how to live, nor the smallest instinct about when to die. *Ib.*

23 I never travel without my diary. One should always have something sensational to read in the train. *Ib. II*

24 Democracy means simply the bludgeoning of the people by the people for the people.[7]
The Soul of Man Under Socialism [1895]

25 The fact is, that civilization requires slaves. The Greeks were quite right there. Unless there are slaves to do the ugly, horrible, uninteresting work, culture and contemplation become almost impossible. Human

[6] Good Americans, when they die, go to Paris.—THOMAS GOLD APPLETON [1812–1884]; *from* OLIVER WENDELL HOLMES, *The Autocrat of the Breakfast Table* [1858]

[7] See Lincoln, 523:4.

slavery is wrong, insecure, and demoralizing. On mechanical slavery, on the slavery of the machine, the future of the world depends.[1]
Ib.

1 Charity creates a multitude of sins.
Ib.

2 Art is the most intense mode of individualism that the world has known. *Ib.*

3 Now art should never try to be popular. The public should try to make itself artistic.
Ib.

4 The only thing that one really knows about human nature is that it changes. Change is the one quality we can predicate on it.[2]
Ib.

5 Anybody can make history. Only a great man can write it. *Aphorisms*

6 I never saw a man who looked
With such a wistful eye
Upon that little tent of blue
Which prisoners call the sky.
The Ballad of Reading Gaol [1898], pt. I, st. 3

7 When a voice behind me whispered low,
"That fellow's got to swing." *Ib. st. 4*

8 Yet each man kills the thing he loves,[3]
By each let this be heard,
Some do it with a bitter look,
Some with a flattering word.
The coward does it with a kiss,
The brave man with a sword! *Ib. st. 7*

9 It is sweet to dance to violins
When Love and Life are fair:
To dance to flutes, to dance to lutes
Is delicate and rare:
But it is not sweet with nimble feet
To dance upon the air! *Ib. II, st. 9*

10 Something was dead in each of us,
And what was dead was Hope.
Ib. st. 31

11 And the wild regrets, and the bloody sweats,
None knew so well as I:
For he who lives more lives than one
More deaths than one must die.
Ib. st. 37

12 I know not whether laws be right,
Or whether laws be wrong;
All that we know who lie in gaol
Is that the wall is strong;
And that each day is like a year,
A year whose days are long.
Ib. V, st. 1

[1] See Havelock Ellis, 689:27.
[2] See Heraclitus, 69:25; Racan, 265:3; Swift, 321:16; and Shelley, 466:11.
[3] See Shakespeare, 200:4.

13 The vilest deeds like poison weeds
Bloom well in prison air:
It is only what is good in man
That wastes and withers there:
Pale Anguish keeps the heavy gate
And the Warder is Despair. *Ib. st. 5*

14 How else but through a broken heart
May Lord Christ enter in? *Ib. st. 14*

15 Where there is sorrow there is holy ground.
De Profundis [1905]

William Cowper Brann[4]

1855–1898

16 Boston runs to brains as well as to beans and brown bread. But she is cursed with an army of cranks whom nothing short of a straitjacket or a swamp elm club will ever control.
From The Iconoclast. Beans and Blood

Henry Cuyler Bunner

1855–1896

17 Off with your hat as the flag goes by![5]
Airs from Arcady [1888]. The Old Flag,[6] st. 1

Eugene Victor Debs

1855–1926

18 While there is a lower class I am in it, while there is a criminal element I am of it; while there is a soul in prison, I am not free.
On labor and freedom

19 The savings of many in the hands of one.
On wealth

Margaret Wolfe Hungerford

1855–1897

20 Beauty is in the eye of the beholder.[7]
Molly Bawn [1878]

[4] Known as "The Iconoclast" from the name of his paper, first published in Austin, Texas, and later in Waco.
[5] Hats off! / Along the street there comes / A blare of bugles, a ruffle of drums, / A flash of color beneath the sky: / Hats off! / The flag is passing by. — HENRY HOLCOMB BENNETT [1863–1924], *The Flag Goes By, st. 1*
[6] Written on Evacuation Day [March 17], 1883.
[7] See Hume, 357:14.

Walter Hines Page
1855–1918

1 There is one thing better than good government, and that is government in which all the people have a part.

Life and Letters [1922–1925], vol. III, p. 31

Sir Arthur Wing Pinero
1855–1934

2 From forty till fifty a man is at heart either a stoic or a satyr.

The Second Mrs. Tanqueray [1893], act I

Olive Schreiner
[Ralph Iron]
1855–1920

3 The barb in the arrow of childhood suffering is this: its intense loneliness, its intense ignorance.

The Story of an African Farm [1884], ch. 1

4 There never was a man who said one word for woman but he said two for man and three for the whole human race. *Ib. 4*

William Sharp
[Fiona Macleod]
1855–1905

5 My heart is a lonely hunter that hunts on a
lonely hill.

The Lonely Hunter, st. 6

Joseph Tabrar
fl. 1892

6 I've got a little cat,
And I'm very fond of that,
But I'd rather have a bowwow, wow.

Daddy Wouldn't Buy Me a Bowwow [1892]

Lyman Frank Baum
1856–1919

7 The Wonderful Wizard of Oz.[1]

Title of book [1900]

8 The Yellow Brick Road [the road to Oz].

The Wonderful Wizard of Oz [1900]

9 The Wicked Witch of the West. *Ib.*

[1]See Harburg, 842:6.

Francis Bellamy
1856–1931

10 I pledge allegiance to the flag of the United States of America and to the republic for which it stands, one nation, under God, indivisible, with liberty and justice for all.

The Pledge of Allegiance to the Flag [1892][2]

Theobald von Bethmann-Hollweg
1856–1921

11 Just for a word—"neutrality," a word which in wartime has so often been disregarded, just for a scrap of paper—Great Britain is going to make war.

To Sir Edward Goschen [August 4, 1914]

Louis Dembitz Brandeis
1856–1941

12 Those who won our independence believed that the final end of the State was to make men free to develop their faculties; and that in its government the deliberative forces should prevail over the arbitrary. They valued liberty both as an end and as a means. They believed liberty to be the secret of happiness and courage to be the secret of liberty.[3]

Whitney v. California, 274 U.S. 357, 375 [1927]

13 Fear of serious injury cannot alone justify suppression of free speech and assembly. Men feared witches and burned women. It is the function of speech to free men from the bondage of irrational fears. *Ib. 376*

14 They [the makers of the Constitution] conferred, as against the Government, the right to be let alone—the most comprehensive of rights and the right most valued by civilized men.

Olmstead v. United States, 277 U.S. 438, 478 [1928]

15 The greatest dangers to liberty lurk in insidious encroachment by men of zeal, well-meaning but without understanding.

Ib. 479

[2]In 1888 James B. Upham [1845–1905] wrote a draft which Bellamy, chairman of a national celebration of the 400th anniversary of America's discovery, helped put in final form (later amendments were voted by Congress): I pledge allegiance to my flag and to the republic for which it stands: one nation indivisible, with liberty and justice for all.

[3]See Simonides, 67:20, and Thucydides, 81:5.

1 Our Government is the potent, the omnipresent teacher. For good or for ill, it teaches the whole people by its example.

Ib. 485

2 If we would guide by the light of reason, we must let our minds be bold.

New State Ice Co. v. Liebmann, 285 U.S. 262, 311 [1932]

3 *Stare decisis* is usually the wise policy, because in most matters it is more important that the applicable rule of law be settled than that it be settled right. . . . But in cases involving the Federal Constitution, where correction through legislative action is practically impossible, this Court has often overruled its earlier decisions. The Court bows to the lessons of experience and the force of better reasoning, recognizing that the process of trial and error, so fruitful in the physical sciences, is appropriate also in the judicial function.

Burnet v. Coronado Oil and Gas Co., 285 U.S. 393, 406 [1932]

4 There is in most Americans some spark of idealism, which can be fanned into a flame. It takes sometimes a divining rod to find what it is; but when found, and that means often, when disclosed to the owners, the results are often extraordinary.

The Words of Justice Brandeis [1953]

Sigmund Freud[1]

1856–1939

5 Being entirely honest with oneself is a good exercise.

Origins of Psychoanalysis. Letter to Fliess [October 15, 1897]

6 No one who, like me, conjures up the most evil of those half-tamed demons that inhabit the human breast, and seeks to wrestle with them, can expect to come through the struggle unscathed.

Complete Psychological Works. Dora [1905]

7 Conscience is the internal perception of the rejection of a particular wish operating within us.

Ib. Totem and Taboo [1912–1913]

8 At bottom God is nothing more than an exalted father. *Ib.*

[1]See Whitehead, 698:4, and Auden, 868:14.

9 The psychic development of the individual is a short repetition of the course of development of the race.[2]

Leonardo da Vinci [1916]

10 When the wayfarer whistles in the dark, he may be disavowing his timidity, but he does not see any the more clearly for doing so.

The Problem of Anxiety [1925]

11 The poets and philosophers before me discovered the unconscious; what I discovered was the scientific method by which the unconscious can be studied.[3]

On his seventieth birthday [1926]; from LIONEL TRILLING, *The Liberal Imagination*

12 The voice of the intellect is a soft one, but it does not rest until it has gained a hearing. Ultimately, after endlessly repeated rebuffs, it succeeds. This is one of the few points in which one may be optimistic about the future of mankind, but in itself it signifies not a little.

Future of an Illusion [1928]

13 Analogies prove nothing, that is quite true, but they can make one feel more at home.

New Introductory Lectures on Psychoanalysis [1932]

14 One might compare the relation of the ego to the id with that between a rider and his horse. The horse provides the locomotor energy, and the rider has the prerogative of determining the goal and of guiding the movements of his powerful mount towards it. But all too often in the relations between the ego and the id we find a picture of the less ideal situation in which the rider is obliged to guide his horse in the direction in which it itself wants to go.

Ib. The Anatomy of the Mental Personality (Lecture 31)

15 The poor ego has a still harder time of it; it has to serve three harsh masters, and has to do its best to reconcile the claims and demands of all three. . . . The three tyrants are the external world, the superego and the id. *Ib.*

16 Where id was, there shall ego be.

Ib.

17 Thinking is an experimental dealing with small quantities of energy, just as a general moves miniature figures over a map before setting his troops in action.

Ib. Anxiety and Instinctual Life (Lecture 32)

[2]See Haeckel, 617:10.
[3]See Peirce, 639:12, and Bergson, 688:8.

1 If one wishes to form a true estimate of the full grandeur of religion, one must keep in mind what it undertakes to do for men. It gives them information about the source and origin of the universe, it assures them of protection and final happiness amid the changing vicissitudes of life, and it guides their thoughts and motions by means of precepts which are backed by the whole force of its authority.

Ib. A Philosophy of Life (Lecture 35)

2 Religion is an attempt to get control over the sensory world, in which we are placed, by means of the wish-world, which we have developed inside us as a result of biological and psychological necessities. *Ib.*

3 Religion is an illusion and it derives its strength from the fact that it falls in with our instinctual desires. *Ib.*

4 The Mosaic religion had been a Father religion; Christianity became a Son religion. The old God, the Father, took second place; Christ, the Son, stood in His stead, just as in those dark times every son had longed to do.

Moses and Monotheism [1938]

5 Man found that he was faced with the acceptance of "spiritual" forces, that is to say such forces as cannot be apprehended by the senses, particularly not by sight, and yet having undoubted, even extremely strong, effects. If we may trust to language, it was the movement of the air that provided the image of spirituality, since the spirit borrows its name from the breath of wind (animus, spiritus, Hebrew: ruach = smoke). The idea of the soul was thus born as the spiritual principle in the individual. . . . Now the realm of spirits had opened for man, and he was ready to endow everything in nature with the soul he had discovered in himself. *Ib.*

6 A man who has been the indisputable favorite of his mother keeps for life the feeling of a conqueror, that confidence of success that often induces real success.[1]

From Ernest Jones, *Life and Works of Sigmund Freud, vol. I [1953], ch. 1*

7 The great question . . . which I have not been able to answer, despite my thirty years of research into the feminine soul, is "What does a woman want?"

Quoted in Charles Rolo, *Psychiatry in American Life [1963]*

8 Sometimes a cigar is just a cigar.

Attributed

[1] See Emerson, 498:22.

Edmond Haraucourt

1856–1941

9 To leave is to die a little;
To die to what we love.
We leave behind a bit of ourselves
Wherever we have been.[2]

Choix de Poésies [1891]. Rondel de l'Adieu

Elbert Hubbard

1856–1915

10 It is not book learning young men need, nor instruction about this and that, but a stiffening of the vertebrae which will cause them to be loyal to a trust, to act promptly, concentrate their energies, do a thing—"carry a message to Garcia."[3]

A Message to Garcia [March 1899]

11 So long as governments set the example of killing their enemies, private individuals will occasionally kill theirs.

Contemplations [1902]

Robert Edwin Peary

1856–1920

12 The Eskimo, Ootah, had his own explanation. Said he: "The devil is asleep or having trouble with his wife, or we should never have come back so easily."

The North Pole [1910]

Henri Philippe Pétain

1856–1951

13 They shall not pass.[4]

Attributed. Verdun [February 26, 1916]

[2] Partir, c'est mourir un peu; / C'est mourir à ce qu'on aime. / On laisse un peu de soi-même / En toute heure et dans tout lieu.

Translated by Norbert Guterman.

See Schopenhauer, 463:5.

[3] After the declaration of the Spanish-American War, Andrew Summers Rowan, then lieutenant, United States Bureau of Military Intelligence, was sent to communicate with General Calixto Garcia. He landed in an open boat near Turquino Peak [April 24, 1898], executed the mission, and brought back information regarding the insurgent army.

[4] Ils ne passeront pas.

The first official record of the expression appears in General Nivelle's Order of the Day [June 23, 1916] to his troops at the height of battle: Vous ne les laisserez pas passer [You will not let them pass]!—Alan Horne, *New York Times Magazine* [February 20, 1966]

The inscription on the Verdun medal is: On ne passe pas.

See Ibarruri, 833:21.

George Bernard Shaw
1856–1950

1 My method is to take the utmost trouble to find the right thing to say, and then to say it with the utmost levity.
Answers to Nine Questions

2 It's well to be off with the Old Woman before you're on with the New.[1]
The Philanderer [1893], act II

3 The fickleness of the women I love is only equaled by the infernal constancy of the women who love me.[2] *Ib.*

4 The test of a man or woman's breeding is how they behave in a quarrel. *Ib. IV*

5 People are always blaming their circumstances for what they are. I don't believe in circumstances. The people who get on in this world are the people who get up and look for the circumstances they want, and, if they can't find them, make them.
Mrs. Warren's Profession [1893], act II

6 There are no secrets better kept than the secrets that everybody guesses. *Ib. III*

7 A great devotee of the Gospel of Getting On. *Ib. IV*

8 We have no more right to consume happiness without producing it than to consume wealth without producing it.
Candida [1898], act I

9 I'm only a beer teetotaler, not a champagne teetotaler. *Ib. III*

10 We don't bother much about dress and manners in England, because as a nation we don't dress well and we've no manners.
You Never Can Tell [1898], act I

11 The great advantage of a hotel is that it's a refuge from home life. *Ib. II*

12 There is only one religion, though there are a hundred versions of it.
Plays Pleasant and Unpleasant [1898], vol. II, preface

13 You're not a man, you're a machine.
Arms and the Man [1898], act III

14 The worst sin towards our fellow creatures is not to hate them, but to be indifferent to them: that's the essence of inhumanity.
The Devil's Disciple [1901], act II

[1] See Anonymous, 921:9.
[2] See Cervantes, 168:31.

15 This is the true joy in life, the being used for a purpose recognized by yourself as a mighty one; the being thoroughly worn out before you are thrown on the scrap heap; the being a force of nature instead of a feverish selfish little clod of ailments and grievances complaining that the world will not devote itself to making you happy.
Man and Superman [1903], epistle dedicatory

16 A lifetime of happiness! No man alive could bear it: it would be hell on earth.
Ib. act I

17 The more things a man is ashamed of, the more respectable he is. *Ib.*

18 Marry Ann; and at the end of a week you'll find no more inspiration in her than in a plate of muffins. *Ib. II*

19 Hell is full of musical amateurs: music is the brandy of the damned. *Ib. III*

20 An Englishman thinks he is moral when he is only uncomfortable. *Ib.*

21 There are two tragedies in life. One is to lose your heart's desire. The other is to gain it.[3] *Ib. IV*

22 The golden rule is that there is no golden rule. *Ib. Maxims for Revolutionists*

23 He who can, does. He who cannot, teaches. *Ib.*

24 Marriage is popular because it combines the maximum of temptation with the maximum of opportunity. *Ib.*

25 If you strike a child, take care that you strike it in anger, even at the risk of maiming it for life. A blow in cold blood neither can nor should be forgiven. *Ib.*

26 Virtue consists, not in abstaining from vice, but in not desiring it. *Ib.*

27 Lack of money is the root of all evil.[4] *Ib.*

28 The greatest of evils and the worst of crimes is poverty.
Major Barbara [1907], preface

29 I can't talk religion to a man with bodily hunger in his eyes.[5] *Ib. act II*

30 Blood and fire! *Ib.*

31 Home life as we understand it is no more natural to us than a cage is natural to a cockatoo. *Getting Married [1908], preface*

[3] See Wilde, 675:10.
[4] See *I Timothy 6:10*, 51:2.
[5] See Conrad, 683:18.

1 When two people are under the influence of the most violent, most insane, most delusive, and most transient of passions, they are required to swear that they will remain in that excited, abnormal, and exhausting condition continuously until death do them part.
Ib.

2 The whole strength of England lies in the fact that the enormous majority of the English people are snobs. *Ib.*

3 You don't learn to hold your own in the world by standing on guard, but by attacking, and getting well hammered yourself.
Ib.

4 Religion is a great force—the only real motive force in the world; but what you fellows don't understand is that you must get at a man through his own religion and not through yours. *Ib.*

5 I like a bit of a mongrel myself, whether it's a man or a dog; they're the best for every day.
Misalliance [1910], episode I

6 If parents would only realize how they bore their children! *Ib.*

7 Women upset everything. When you let them into your life, you find that the woman is driving at one thing and you're driving at another. *Pygmalion [1912], act II*

8 I have to live for others and not for myself; that's middle-class morality. *Ib. V*

9 Independence? That's middle-class blasphemy. We are all dependent on one another, every soul of us on earth. *Ib.*

10 All great truths begin as blasphemies.
Annajanska [1919]

11 You see things; and you say, "Why?" But I dream things that never were; and I say, "Why not?"
Back to Methuselah [1921], pt. I, act I

12 The nauseous sham goodfellowship our democratic public men get up for shop use.
Ib. pt. II

13 Everything happens to everybody sooner or later if there is time enough.
Ib. pt. V

14 Silence is the most perfect expression of scorn. *Ib.*

15 The worst cliques are those which consist of one man. *Ib.*

16 Assassination is the extreme form of censorship. *The Rejected Statement, pt. I*

17 The Jews generally give value. They make you pay; but they deliver the goods. In my experience the men who want something for nothing are invariably Christians.
Saint Joan [1923], sc. iv

18 One man that has a mind and knows it can always beat ten men who haven't and don't.
The Apple Cart [1929], act I

19 I have defined the hundred per cent American as ninety-nine per cent an idiot.
Remarks on Sinclair Lewis receiving the Nobel Prize [1930]

20 An American has no sense of privacy. He does not know what it means. There is no such thing in the country.
Speech at New York [April 11, 1933]

21 You in America should trust to that volcanic political instinct which I have divined in you. *Ib.*

Louis Henri Sullivan
1856–1924

22 Form ever follows function.
The Tall Office Building Artistically Considered. From Lippincott's Magazine [March 1896]

Sir Joseph John Thomson
1856–1940

23 From the point of view of the physicist, a theory of matter is a policy rather than a creed; its object is to connect or coordinate apparently diverse phenomena, and above all to suggest, stimulate and direct experiment.
The Corpuscular Theory of Matter [1907]

Booker Taliaferro Washington
1856–1915

24 In all things that are purely social we [black and white] can be as separate as the fingers, yet one as the hand in all things essential to mutual progress.
Speech at the Cotton States and International Exposition, Atlanta [September 18, 1895]

25 No race can prosper till it learns that there is as much dignity in tilling a field as in writing a poem. *Up from Slavery [1901]*

26 You can't hold a man down without staying down with him. *Attributed*

Woodrow Wilson

1856–1924

1 The United States must be neutral in fact as well as in name. . . . We must be impartial in thought as well as in action.

Message to the Senate [August 19, 1914]

2 You deal in the raw material of opinion, and, if my convictions have any validity, opinion ultimately governs the world.

Address to the Associated Press [April 20, 1915]

3 There is such a thing as a man being too proud to fight.

Address to Foreign-Born Citizens [May 10, 1915]

4 [The Civil War] created in this country what had never existed before—a national consciousness. It was not the salvation of the Union; it was the rebirth of the Union.

Memorial Day Address [1915]

5 The flag is the embodiment, not of sentiment, but of history. It represents the experiences made by men and women, the experiences of those who do and live under that flag.

Address [June 14, 1915]

6 We have stood apart, studiously neutral.

Message to Congress [December 7, 1915]

7 America cannot be an ostrich with its head in the sand.

Speech at Des Moines [February 1, 1916]

8 There must be, not a balance of power, but a community of power; not organized rivalries, but an organized common peace.

Address to the Senate [January 22, 1917]

9 It must be a peace without victory. . . . Victory would mean peace forced upon the loser, a victor's terms imposed upon the vanquished. It would be accepted in humiliation, under duress, at an intolerable sacrifice, and would leave a sting, a resentment, a bitter memory upon which terms of peace would rest, not permanently, but only as upon quicksand. Only a peace between equals can last. *Ib.*

10 A little group of willful men, representing no opinion but their own, have rendered the great Government of the United States helpless and contemptible.

Statement made in reference to certain members of the Senate [March 4, 1917][1]

11 Armed neutrality is ineffectual enough at best.

Address to Congress, asking for a declaration of war [April 2, 1917]

12 The world must be made safe for democracy.[2] *Ib.*

13 It is a fearful thing to lead this great peaceful people into war, into the most terrible and disastrous of all wars, civilization itself seeming to be in the balance. But the right is more precious than peace, and we shall fight for the things which we have always carried nearest our hearts—for democracy, for the right of those who submit to authority to have a voice in their own governments, for the rights and liberties of small nations, for a universal dominion of right by such a concert of free peoples as shall bring peace and safety to all nations and make the world itself at last free. To such a task we can dedicate our lives and our fortunes, everything that we are and everything that we have, with the pride of those who know that the day has come when America is privileged to spend her blood and her might for the principles that gave her birth and happiness and the peace which she has treasured. God helping her, she can do no other.[3] *Ib.*

14 1. Open covenants of peace, openly arrived at.

2. Absolute freedom of navigation upon the seas. . . .

5. A free, open-minded, and absolutely impartial adjustment of all colonial claims.

Address to Congress (The Fourteen Points) [January 8, 1918][4]

15 14. A general association of nations must be formed . . . for the purpose of affording mutual guarantees of political independence and territorial integrity to great and small states alike. *Ib.*

16 Sometimes people call me an idealist. Well, that is the way I know I am an American. America is the only idealistic nation in the world.

Address at Sioux Falls [September 8, 1919]

17 The highest and best form of efficiency is the spontaneous cooperation of a free people.

From BERNARD BARUCH, *American Industry at War: A Report of the War Industries Board [March 1921]*

---

[1] Eleven senators had conducted a filibuster against a bill authorizing the arming of American merchant vessels.

[2] See James Harvey Robinson, 703:2.

[3] See Luther, 155:13.

[4] See Clemenceau, 643:11.

Edward Francis Albee
1857–1930

1 Never give a sucker an even break.[1]
Remark

Joseph Conrad
1857–1924

2 A work that aspires, however humbly, to the condition of art should carry its justification in every line.
The Nigger of the Narcissus [1898], preface

3 But the artist appeals to that part of our being which is not dependent on wisdom; to that in us which is a gift and not an acquisition—and, therefore, more permanently enduring. He speaks to our capacity for delight and wonder, to the sense of mystery surrounding our lives: to our sense of pity, and beauty, and pain. *Ib.*

4 The ship, a fragment detached from the earth, went on lonely and swift like a small planet. *Ib. ch. 2*

5 Goodbye, brothers! You were a good crowd. As good a crowd as ever fisted with wild cries the beating canvas of a heavy foresail; or tossing aloft, invisible in the night, gave back yell for yell to a westerly gale. *Ib. 5*

6 I am a great foe of favoritism in public life, in private life, and even in the delicate relationship of an author to his works.
Lord Jim [1900], author's note

7 There is a weird power in a spoken word. . . . And a word carries far—very far—deals destruction through time as the bullets go flying through space. *Ib. ch. 15*

8 That faculty of beholding at a hint the face of his desire and the shape of his dream, without which the earth would know no lover and no adventurer. *Ib. 16*

9 You shall judge of a man by his foes as well as by his friends.[2] *Ib. 34*

10 Vanity plays lurid tricks with our memory. *Ib. 41*

11 Only a moment; a moment of strength, of romance, of glamour—of youth! . . . A flick of sunshine upon a strange shore, the time to remember, the time for a sigh, and—goodbye!—Night—Goodbye . . . !
Youth [1902]

12 She strode like a grenadier, was strong and upright like an obelisk, had a beautiful face, a candid brow, pure eyes, and not a thought of her own in her head.
Tales of Unrest [1902]. The Return

13 Running all over the sea trying to get behind the weather.
Typhoon [1902], ch. 2

14 The sea never changes and its works, for all the talk of men, are wrapped in mystery.
Ib.

15 We live, as we dream—alone.
Heart of Darkness [1902],[3] I

16 I don't like work—no man does—but I like what is in work—the chance to find yourself. Your own reality—for yourself, not for others—what no other man can ever know.
Ib.

17 The mind of man is capable of anything—because everything is in it, all the past as well as all the future. *Ib. II*

18 No fear can stand up to hunger, no patience can wear it out, disgust simply does not exist where hunger is; and as to superstition, beliefs, and what you may call principles, they are less than chaff in a breeze.[4]
Ib.

19 Exterminate all the brutes![5] *Ib.*

20 The horror! The horror! *Ib.*

21 Mistah Kurtz—he dead.[6] *Ib.*

22 The air of the New World seems favorable to the art of declamation.
Nostromo [1904], ch. 6

[1]Often attributed to W. C. Fields, who uttered it in *Poppy* [1923]. He made the quote famous.—*Morris Dictionary of Word and Phrase Origins* [1977]
See F. P. Adams, 773:13.

[2]See Wilde, 674:26.

[3]"Heart of Darkness" is experience . . . but it is experience pushed a little (and only very little) beyond the actual facts of the case for the perfectly legitimate, I believe, purpose of bringing it home to the minds and bosoms of the readers. . . . That somber theme had to be given a sinister resonance, a tonality of its own, a continued vibration that, I hoped, would hang in the air and dwell on the ear after the last note had been struck. —CONRAD, *Youth: A Narrative, and Two Other Stories, author's preface*

[4]See G. B. Shaw, 680:29.

[5]For two hundred years, the Judges of England sat on the Bench, condemning to the penalty of death every man, woman, and child who stole property to the value of five shillings; and, during all that time, not one Judge ever remonstrated against the law. We English are a nation of brutes, and ought to be exterminated to the last man.—JOHN BRIGHT [1888]; in HENRY ADAMS, *The Education of Henry Adams* [1907], *ch. 12*

[6]Used by T. S. Eliot as an epigraph for *The Hollow Men* [1925].

1 Efficiency of a practically flawless kind may be reached naturally in the struggle for bread. But there is something beyond—a higher point, a subtle and unmistakable touch of love and pride beyond mere skill; almost an inspiration which gives to all work that finish which is almost art—which *is* art.

The Mirror of the Sea [1906]. The Fine Art

2 A man's real life is that accorded to him in the thoughts of other men by reason of respect or natural love.

Under Western Eyes [1911], pt. I

3 Let a fool be made serviceable according to his folly. *Ib. ch. 3*

4 The belief in a supernatural source of evil is not necessary; men alone are quite capable of every wickedness. *Ib. II, 4*

5 All ambitions are lawful except those which climb upward on the miseries or credulities of mankind.

A Personal Record [1912], preface

6 Only in men's imagination does every truth find an effective and undeniable existence. Imagination, not invention, is the supreme master of art as of life.

Ib. ch. 1

7 In plucking the fruit of memory one runs the risk of spoiling its bloom.

The Arrow of Gold [1919], author's note

8 Historian of fine consciences.

Notes on Life and Letters [1921]. Henry James, An Appreciation

Émile Coué
1857–1926

9 Every day, in every way, I'm getting better and better.[1]

Formula of his faith cures, inscribed in his sanitarium, Nancy, France

Clarence Seward Darrow
1857–1938

10 I do not consider it an insult, but rather a compliment to be called an agnostic. I do not pretend to know where many ignorant men are sure—that is all that agnosticism means.

Scopes trial, Dayton, Tennessee [July 13, 1925]

11 I don't believe in God because I don't believe in Mother Goose.

Speech at Toronto [1930]

12 There is no such thing as justice—in or out of court.

Interview at Chicago [April 1936]

John Davidson
1857–1909

13 In anguish we uplift
A new unhallowed song:
The race is to the swift;
The battle to the strong.[2]

War Song, st. 1

14 And blood in torrents pour
In vain—always in vain,
For war breeds war again. *Ib. st. 7*

Benjamin Franklin King, Jr.
1857–1894

15 Nowhere to go but out,
Nowhere to come but back.

The Pessimist, st. 4

Karl Pearson
1857–1936

16 Modern science, as training the mind to an exact and impartial analysis of facts, is an education specially fitted to promote sound citizenship.

The Grammar of Science [1892]

Edgar Smith
1857–1938

17 You may tempt the upper classes
With your villainous demitasses,
But Heaven will protect the working girl.

Heaven Will Protect the Working Girl[3]

Frank Lebby Stanton
1857–1927

18 Jest a-wearyin' fer you—
All the time a-feelin' blue.

Wearyin' for You, st. 1

[1] Tous les jours, à tous les points de vue, je vais de mieux en mieux.

[2] See *Ecclesiastes 9:11*, 27:17, and Van Dyke, 671:11.

[3] Sung by Marie Dressler [1873–1934] in *Tillie's Nightmare.*

1 Sweetes' li'l' feller—
Everybody knows;
Dunno what ter call 'im,
But he's mighty lak' a rose!
Mighty Lak' a Rose, st. 1

Thorstein Veblen

1857–1929

2 Conspicuous consumption of valuable goods is a means of reputability to the gentleman of leisure.
The Theory of the Leisure Class [1899], ch. 4

3 With the exception of the instinct of self-preservation, the propensity for emulation is probably the strongest and most alert and persistent of the economic motives proper.
Ib. 5

4 The requirement of conspicuous wastefulness is not commonly present, consciously, in our canons of taste, but it is none the less present as a constraining norm selectively shaping and sustaining our sense of what is beautiful, and guiding our discrimination with respect to what may legitimately be approved as beautiful and what may not.
Ib. 6

Franz Boas

1858–1942

5 The passion for seeking the truth for truth's sake . . . can be kept alive only if we continue to seek the truth for truth's sake.
Race and Democratic Society [1945], introduction

6 The behavior of an individual is determined not by his racial affiliation, but by the character of his ancestry and his cultural environment.[1] *Ib. ch. 2*

7 No one has ever proved that a human being, through his descent from a certain group of people, must of necessity have certain mental characteristics. *Ib. 7*

James Davis [Owen Hall]

1853–1907

8 O tell me, pretty maiden, are there any more at home like you?
Floradora [1900], act II

[1]See Benedict, 796:4.

Sam Walter Foss

1858–1911

9 And men two centuries and a half
Trod in the footsteps of that calf.
The Calf-Path,[2] st. 6

10 A rodless Walton of the brooks,
A bloodless sportsman, I.[3]
The Bloodless Sportsman

11 The woods are made for the hunters of dreams,
The brooks for the fishers of song;
To the hunters who hunt for the gunless game
The streams and the woods belong.
Ib.

12 Let me live in my house by the side of the road
And be a friend of man.
The House by the Side of the Road,[4] st. 5

Henry Watson Fowler

1858–1933

and

Francis George Fowler

1870–1918

13 Prefer geniality to grammar.
The King's English [1906], ch. 2

14 HACKNEYED PHRASES. . . . The purpose with which these phrases are introduced is for the most part that of giving a fillip to a passage that might be humdrum without them . . . but their true use when they come into the writer's mind is as danger signals; he should take warning that when they suggest themselves it is because what he is writing is bad stuff, or it would not need such help; let him see to the substance of his cake instead of decorating with sugarplums.
A Dictionary of Modern English Usage [1926][5]

15 QUOTATION. . . . A writer expresses himself in words that have been used before because they give his meaning better than he can give it himself, or because they are beautiful or witty, or because he expects them to touch a chord of association in his reader, or because he wishes to show that he is learned

[2]The reference is to the streets of Boston.
[3]See Emerson, 494:14.
[4]See Homer, 57:32.
[5]To the memory of my brother Francis George Fowler . . . who shared with me the planning of this book, but did not live to share the writing.—H. W. FOWLER, *preface to the first edition*

and well read. Quotations due to the last motive are invariably ill-advised; the discerning reader detects it and is contemptuous; the undiscerning is perhaps impressed, but even then is at the same time repelled, pretentious quotations being the surest road to tedium.
Ib.

1 THAT, *relative pronoun* . . . The two kinds of relative clause, to one of which *that* and to the other of which *which* is appropriate, are the defining and the nondefining;[1] and if writers would agree to regard *that* as the defining relative pronoun, and *which* as the nondefining, there would be much gain both in lucidity and in ease. Some there are who follow this principle now, but it would be idle to pretend that it is the practice either of the most or of the best writers. *Ib.*

Remy de Gourmont
1858–1915

2 Aesthetic emotion puts man in a state favorable to the reception of erotic emotion. Art is the accomplice of love. Take love away and there is no longer art.
Décadence[2]

3 Man is a successful animal, that's all.
Promenades Philosophiques

Ruggiero Leoncavallo
1858–1919

4 The comedy is finished.[3]
I Pagliacci (The Clowns) [1892], last words

John Trotwood Moore
1858–1929

5 Only the gamefish swims upstream.[4]
The Unafraid

Adolph Simon Ochs
1858–1935

6 All the news that's fit to print.
Motto of the New York Times[5]

[1] In American English, restrictive and nonrestrictive.
[2] Translated by W. A. BRADLEY.
[3] La commedia è finita.
See Rabelais, 158:14.
[4] Quoted by GRANTLAND RICE [1880–1954] in *The Ballade of the Gamefish* and *Expanding the Theme.*
Only the gamefish swims upstream, / But the sensible fish swims down. — OGDEN NASH [1902–1971], *When You Say That, Smile*
[5] When Adolph Ochs bought the *New York Times* in 1896 he adopted this motto, which has been printed in every issue since.

Ohiyesa [Charles Alexander Eastman][6]
1858–1939

7 [The Indian] sees no need for setting apart one day in seven as a holy day, since to him all days are God's.
The Soul of the Indian [1911]

8 Nearness to nature . . . keeps the spirit sensitive to impressions not commonly felt, and in touch with the unseen powers.
Ib.

Max Planck
1858–1947

9 We have no right to assume that any physical laws exist, or if they have existed up to now, that they will continue to exist in a similar manner in the future.
The Universe in the Light of Modern Physics [1931]

10 Anybody who has been seriously engaged in scientific work of any kind realizes that over the entrance to the gates of the temple of science are written the words: *Ye must have faith.* It is a quality which the scientist cannot dispense with.
Where Is Science Going? [1932]

11 An important scientific innovation rarely makes its way by gradually winning over and converting its opponents: it rarely happens that Saul becomes Paul. What does happen is that its opponents gradually die out and that the growing generation is familiarized with the idea from the beginning.
The Philosophy of Physics [1936]

Theodore Roosevelt
1858–1919

12 I wish to preach, not the doctrine of ignoble ease,[7] but the doctrine of the strenuous life.
Speech before the Hamilton Club, Chicago [April 10, 1899]

13 Far better it is to dare mighty things, to win glorious triumphs, even though checkered by failure, than to take rank with those poor spirits who neither enjoy much nor suffer much, because they live in the gray twilight that knows not victory nor defeat.
Ib.

It is hard to think of any group of seven words that have aroused more newspaper controversy. — GERALD W. JOHNSON, *An Honorable Titan* [1946]
[6] Santee Dakota.
[7] See Virgil, 104:13, and Milton, 284:13.

1 Death is always and under all circumstances a tragedy, for if it is not, then it means that life itself has become one.

Letter to Cecil Spring-Rice [March 12, 1900]

2 I am as strong as a bull moose and you can use me to the limit.

Letter to Mark Hanna [June 27, 1900]

3 No man is justified in doing evil on the ground of expediency.

The Strenuous Life: Essays and Addresses [1900]. The Strenuous Life

4 If we seek merely swollen, slothful ease and ignoble peace, if we shrink from the hard contests where men must win at the hazard of their lives and at the risk of all they hold dear, then bolder and stronger peoples will pass us by, and will win for themselves the domination of the world. *Ib.*

5 In life, as in a football game, the principle to follow is: Hit the line hard.

Ib. The American Boy

6 There is a homely adage which runs, "Speak softly and carry a big stick; you will go far." If the American nation will speak softly and yet build and keep at a pitch of the highest training a thoroughly efficient navy, the Monroe Doctrine will go far.

Speech at Minnesota State Fair [September 2, 1901]

7 The first requisite of a good citizen in this Republic of ours is that he shall be able and willing to pull his weight.

Speech at New York [November 11, 1902]

8 A man who is good enough to shed his blood for his country is good enough to be given a square deal afterwards. More than that no man is entitled to, and less than that no man shall have.

Speech at Springfield, Illinois [July 4, 1903]

9 No man is above the law and no man is below it; nor do we ask any man's permission when we require him to obey it. Obedience to the law is demanded as a right; not asked as a favor.

Third Annual Message [December 7, 1903]

10 In the Western Hemisphere the adherence of the United States to the Monroe Doctrine may force the United States, however reluctantly, in flagrant cases of such wrongdoing or impotence, to the exercise of an international police power.

Annual Message to Congress: Corollary to the Monroe Doctrine [December 6, 1904]

11 Men with the muckrake are often indispensable to the well-being of society, but only if they know when to stop raking the muck.[1]

Address on the laying of the cornerstone of the House Office Building, Washington [April 14, 1906]

12 Malefactors of great wealth.

Speech at Provincetown, Massachusetts [August 20, 1907]

13 Nature-faker.

Everybody's Magazine [September 1907]

14 To waste, to destroy, our natural resources, to skin and exhaust the land instead of using it so as to increase its usefulness, will result in undermining in the days of our children the very prosperity which we ought by right to hand down to them amplified and developed.

Message to Congress [December 3, 1907]

15 The object of government is the welfare of the people. The material progress and prosperity of a nation are desirable chiefly so far as they lead to the moral and material welfare of all good citizens.

The New Nationalism [1910]

16 Every man holds his property subject to the general right of the community to regulate its use to whatever degree the public welfare may require it.

Speech at Osawatomie [August 31, 1910]

17 We stand at Armageddon and we battle for the Lord.

Speech at Progressive Party Convention, Chicago [June 17, 1912]

18 The lunatic fringe in all reform movements. *Autobiography [1913]*

19 We demand that big business give the people a square deal; in return we must insist that when anyone engaged in big business honestly endeavors to do right he shall himself be given a square deal. *Ib.*

20 We stand equally against government by a plutocracy and government by a mob. There

[1] See John Bunyan, 302:12.

is something to be said for government by a great aristocracy which has furnished leaders to the nation in peace and war for generations; even a democrat like myself must admit this. But there is absolutely nothing to be said for government by a plutocracy, for government by men very powerful in certain lines and gifted with "the money touch," but with ideals which in their essence are merely those of so many glorified pawnbrokers.

Letter to Sir Edward Grey [November 15, 1913]

1 There is no room in this country for hyphenated Americanism. . . . The one absolutely certain way of bringing this nation to ruin, of preventing all possibility of its continuing to be a nation at all, would be to permit it to become a tangle of squabbling nationalities.

Speech before the Knights of Columbus, New York [October 12, 1915]

2 Put out the light.

Last words [January 6, 1919]

Langdon Smith
1858–1908

3 When you were a tadpole and I was a fish,
In the Paleozoic time.

Evolution [1895], st. 1

Sir William Watson
1858–1935

4 April, April,
Laugh thy girlish laughter;
Then, the moment after,
Weep thy girlish tears.

Song

Katharine Lee Bates
1859–1929

5 O beautiful for spacious skies,
For amber waves of grain,
For purple mountain majesties
Above the fruited plain!
America! America!
God shed his grace on thee
And crown thy good with brotherhood
From sea to shining sea!

America the Beautiful [1893], st. 1

Henri Bergson
1859–1941

6 Only those ideas that are least truly ours can be adequately expressed in words.

Essai sur les Données Immédiates de la Conscience [1899; Time and Free Will, 1910]

7 We are free when our actions emanate from our total personality, when they express it, when they resemble it in the indefinable way a work of art sometimes does the artist. *Ib.*

8 The major task of the twentieth century will be to explore the unconscious, to investigate the subsoil of the mind.[1]

Le Rêve (The Dream) [1901]

9 The present contains nothing more than the past, and what is found in the effect was already in the cause.

L'Evolution Créatrice (Creative Evolution) [1907],[2] ch. 1

10 Intelligence . . . is the faculty of making artificial objects, especially tools to make tools. *Ib. 2*

11 L'élan vital [the vital spirit]. *Ib.*

Harold Edwin Boulton
1859–1935

12 Speed, bonnie boat, like a bird on the wing;
Onward, the sailors cry:
Carry the lad that's born to be king
Over the sea to Skye.

Skye Boat Song, st. 1

Carrie Chapman Catt
1859–1947

13 No written law has ever been more binding than unwritten custom supported by popular opinion.

Speech, Why We Ask for the Submission of an Amendment, at Senate hearing on woman's suffrage [February 13, 1900]

[1] See Peirce, 639:12, and Freud, 678:11.

[2] O my Bergson, you are a magician, and your book is a marvel, a real wonder in the history of philosophy. . . . In finishing it I found . . . such a flavor of persistent *euphony*, as of a rich river that never foamed or ran thin, but steadily and firmly proceeded with its banks full to the brim.—WILLIAM JAMES, *The Letters of William James, vol. II* [1907], *p. 290*

1 When a just cause reaches its flood tide . . . whatever stands in the way must fall before its overwhelming power.[1]

Speech at Stockholm, Is Woman Suffrage Progressing? [1911]

Sir Arthur Conan Doyle

1859–1930

2 London, that great cesspool into which all the loungers of the Empire are irresistibly drained. *A Study in Scarlet [1887]*

3 When you have eliminated the impossible, whatever remains, *however improbable*, must be the truth.

The Sign of Four [1890], ch. 6

4 The Baker Street irregulars. *Ib.*

5 The Speckled Band.

The Adventures of Sherlock Holmes [1891]. Title of story

6 It is my belief, Watson, founded upon my experience, that the lowest and vilest alleys of London do not present a more dreadful record of sin than does the smiling and beautiful countryside. *Ib.*

7 To Sherlock Holmes she is always *the* woman. *Ib. A Scandal in Bohemia*

8 ". . . the curious incident of the dog in the nighttime."

"The dog did nothing in the nighttime."

"That was the curious incident," remarked Sherlock Holmes.

The Memoirs of Sherlock Holmes [1894]. Silver Blaze

9 You know my methods, Watson.

Ib. The Crooked Man

10 "Excellent!" I [Watson] cried.

"Elementary," said he [Holmes]. *Ib.*

11 They were the footprints of a gigantic hound!

The Hound of the Baskervilles [1902], ch. 2

12 Come, Watson, come! The game is afoot.[2]

The Return of Sherlock Holmes [1904]. The Adventure of the Abbey Grange

13 The fair sex is your department.

Ib. The Second Stain

14 It is a great thing to start life with a small number of really good books which are your very own.

Through the Magic Door [1908]

15 Mediocrity knows nothing higher than itself, but talent instantly recognizes genius.

The Valley of Fear [1914]

16 The bow was made in England:
Of true wood, of yew wood,
The wood of English bows.

The Song of the Bow, st. 1

Havelock Ellis

1859–1939

17 To be a leader of men one must turn one's back on men.

Introduction to HUYSMANS, *A Rebours (Against the Grain) [1884]*

18 The text of the Bible is but a feeble symbol of the Revelation held in the text of Men and Women. *Impressions and Comments*

19 The omnipresent process of sex, as it is woven into the whole texture of our man's or woman's body, is the pattern of all the process of our life. *The New Spirit*

20 Every artist writes his own autobiography. *Ib.*

21 If men and women are to understand each other, to enter into each other's nature with mutual sympathy, and to become capable of genuine comradeship, the foundation must be laid in youth.

The Task of Social Hygiene, ch. 1

22 There has never been any country at every moment so virtuous and so wise that it has not sometimes needed to be saved from itself. *Ib. 10*

23 The family only represents one aspect, however important an aspect, of a human being's functions and activities. . . . A life is beautiful and ideal or the reverse, only when we have taken into our consideration the social as well as the family relationship.

Little Essays of Love and Virtue [1922], ch. 1

24 One can know nothing of giving aught that is worthy to give unless one also knows how to take. *Ib.*

25 The byproduct is sometimes more valuable than the product. *Ib. 3*

26 All civilization has from time to time become a thin crust over a volcano of revolution. *Ib. 7*

27 The greatest task before civilization at present is to make machines what they ought to be, the slaves, instead of the masters of men.[3] *Ib.*

[1]See Hugo, 491:11.

[2]See Shakespeare, 207:18.

[3]See Oscar Wilde, 675:25.

1 The art of dancing stands at the source of all the arts that express themselves first in the human person. The art of building, or architecture, is the beginning of all the arts that lie outside the person; and in the end they unite.

The Dance of Life [1923], ch. 2

2 Dancing is the loftiest, the most moving, the most beautiful of the arts, because it is no mere translation or abstraction from life; it is life itself. *Ib.*

3 The place where optimism most flourishes is the lunatic asylum. *Ib. 3*

4 Thinking in its lower grades is comparable to paper money, and in its higher forms it is a kind of poetry. *Ib.*

5 In philosophy, it is not the attainment of the goal that matters, it is the things that are met with by the way. *Ib.*

6 The mathematician has reached the highest rung on the ladder of human thought. *Ib.*

7 A man must not swallow more beliefs than he can digest. *Ib. 5*

8 The Promised Land always lies on the other side of a wilderness. *Ib.*

9 What we call "morals" is simply blind obedience to words of command. *Ib. 6*

10 The sun and the moon and the stars would have disappeared long ago . . . had they happened to be within the reach of predatory human hands. *Ib. 7*

11 Had there been a lunatic asylum in the suburbs of Jerusalem, Jesus Christ would infallibly have been shut up in it at the outset of his public career. That interview with Satan on a pinnacle of the Temple would alone have damned him, and everything that happened after could but have confirmed the diagnosis.

Impressions and Comments, series 3

Kenneth Grahame

1859–1932

12 As a rule, indeed, grown-up people are fairly correct on matters of fact; it is in the higher gift of imagination that they are so sadly to seek.

The Golden Age [1895]. The Finding of the Princess

13 Monkeys, who very sensibly refrain from speech, lest they should be set to earn their livings. *Ib. "Lusisti Satis"*

14 There is nothing—absolutely nothing—half so much worth doing as simply messing about in boats . . . or with boats. . . . In or out of 'em, it doesn't matter.

The Wind in the Willows [1908], ch. 1

15 "Glorious, stirring sight!" murmured Toad . . . "The poetry of motion! The *real* way to travel! The *only* way to travel! Here today — in next week tomorrow! Villages skipped, towns and cities jumped—always somebody else's horizons! O bliss! O poop-poop! O my! O my!" *Ib. 2*

Alfred Edward Housman[1]

1859–1936

16 Loveliest of trees, the cherry now
Is hung with bloom along the bough.

A Shropshire Lad [1896], no. 2, st. 1

17 Now, of my threescore years and ten,
Twenty will not come again,
And take from seventy springs a score,
It only leaves me fifty more.

And since to look at things in bloom
Fifty springs are little room,
About the woodlands I will go
To see the cherry hung with snow.

Ib. st. 2, 3

18 Clay lies still, but blood's a rover;
Breath's a ware that will not keep.
Up, lad: when the journey's over
There'll be time enough to sleep.

Ib. 4 (Reveille), st. 6

19 Lovers lying two and two
Ask not whom they sleep beside,
And the bridegroom all night through
Never turns him to the bride.

Ib. 12, st. 4

20 When I was one-and-twenty
I heard a wise man say,
"Give crowns and pounds and guineas
But not your heart away. *Ib. 13, st. 1*

21 When I was one-and-twenty
I heard him say again,
"The heart out of the bosom
Was never given in vain;

[1] I am not a pessimist but a pejorist (as George Eliot said she was not an optimist but a meliorist); and that philosophy is founded on my observation of the world, not on anything so trivial and irrelevant as personal history. —*Autobiographical note written for a French translation of his poems*

’Tis paid with sighs aplenty
And sold for endless rue.”
And I am two-and-twenty,
And Oh, ’tis true, ’tis true. *Ib. st. 2*

1 His folly has not fellow
Beneath the blue of day
That gives to man or woman
His heart and soul away. *Ib. 14*

2 Oh, when I was in love with you,
Then I was clean and brave,
And miles around the wonder grew
How well I did behave.

And now the fancy passes by,
And nothing will remain,
And miles around they’ll say that I
Am quite myself again. *Ib. 18, st. 1, 2*

3 And silence sounds no worse than cheers
After earth has stopped the ears.
Ib. 19 (To an Athlete Dying Young), st. 4

4 The bells they sound on Bredon,
And still the steeples hum.
"Come all to church, good people"—
Oh, noisy bells, be dumb;
I hear you, I will come. *Ib. 21, st. 7*

5 The lads that will die in their glory and never be old. *Ib. 23, st. 4*

6 And fire and ice within me fight
Beneath the suffocating night.[1]
Ib. 30, st. 4

7 There, like the wind through woods in riot,
Through him the gale of life blew high;
The tree of man was never quiet:
Then ’twas the Roman, now ’tis I.
Ib. 31, st. 4

8 Oh tarnish late on Wenlock Edge,
Gold that I never see. *Ib. 39, st. 3*

9 Into my heart an air that kills
From yon far country blows:
What are those blue remembered hills,
What spires, what farms are those?

That is the land of lost content,
I see it shining plain,
The happy highways where I went
And cannot come again. *Ib. 40, st. 1, 2*

10 Earth and high heaven are fixed of old and founded strong. *Ib. 48, st. 1*

11 Far in a western brookland
That bred me long ago
The poplars stand and tremble
By pools I used to know. *Ib. 52, st. 1*

[1]See Dante, 140:19, and Frost, 748:2.

12 There, by the starlit fences,
The wanderer halts and hears
My soul that lingers sighing
About the glimmering weirs. *Ib. st. 4*

13 With rue my heart is laden
For golden friends I had,
For many a rose-lipped maiden
And many a lightfoot lad. *Ib. 54, st. 1*

14 By brooks too broad for leaping
The lightfoot boys are laid. *Ib. st. 2*

15 Now hollow fires burn out to black,
And lights are guttering low:
Square your shoulders, lift your pack,
And leave your friends and go. *Ib. 60*

16 In all the endless road you tread
There’s nothing but the night. *Ib.*

17 Oh many a peer of England brews
Livelier liquor than the Muse,
And malt does more than Milton can
To justify God’s ways to man.[2]
Ale, man, ale’s the stuff to drink
For fellows whom it hurts to think.
Ib. 62, st. 2

18 Mithridates, he died old.[3] *Ib. st. 4*

19 Pass me the can, lad; there’s an end of May.
Last Poems, 9, st. 1

20 The troubles of our proud and angry dust
Are from eternity, and shall not fail.
Bear them we can, and if we can we must.
Shoulder the sky, my lad, and drink your ale.
Ib. st. 7

21 But men at whiles are sober
And think by fits and starts.
And if they think, they fasten
Their hands upon their hearts.
Ib. 10, st. 2

22 The laws of God, the laws of man,
He may keep that will and can;
Not I: let God and man decree
Laws for themselves and not for me.
Ib. 12

23 And how am I to face the odds
Of man’s bedevilment and God’s?
I, a stranger and afraid
In a world I never made. *Ib.*

24 He stood, and heard the steeple
Sprinkle the quarters on the morning town.
Ib. 15 (Eight O’Clock), st. 1

[2]See Milton, 283:2 and 288:26, and Pope, 336:11.

[3]Housman’s passage is based on the belief of the ancients that Mithridates the Great [c. 135–63 B.C.] had so saturated his body with poisons that none could injure him. When captured by the Romans he tried in vain to poison himself, then ordered a Gallic mercenary to kill him.

1 Strapped, noosed, nighing his hour,
He stood and counted them and cursed his luck;
And then the clock collected in the tower
Its strength, and struck. *Ib. st. 2*

2 Happy bridegroom, Hesper brings
All desired and timely things.
All whom morning sends to roam,
Hesper loves to lead them home.
Home return who him behold,
Child to mother, sheep to fold,
Bird to nest from wandering wide:[1]
Happy bridegroom, seek your bride.
Ib. 24 (Epithalamium), st. 3

3 These, in the day when heaven was falling,
The hour when earth's foundations fled,
Followed their mercenary calling
And took their wages and are dead.
Ib. 37 (Epitaph on an Army of Mercenaries),[2] st. 1

4 What God abandoned, these defended.
Ib. 37, st. 2

5 Tell me not here, it needs not saying,
What tune the enchantress plays
In aftermaths of soft September
Or under blanching mays,
For she and I were long acquainted
And I knew all her ways. *Ib. 40, st. 1*

6 They say my verse is sad: no wonder;
Its narrow measure spans
Tears of eternity, and sorrow,
Not mine, but man's.
More Poems [1936], foreword

7 Hope lies to mortals
And most believe her,
But man's deceiver
Was never mine. *Ib. 6, st. 1*

8 The rainy Pleiads wester,
Orion plunges prone,
And midnight strikes and hastens,
And I lie down alone.[3] *Ib. 11, st. 1*

9 Life, to be sure, is nothing much to lose,
But young men think it is, and we were young. *Ib. 36*

10 We now to peace and darkness
And earth and thee restore
Thy creature that thou madest
And wilt cast forth no more.
Ib. 47 (For My Funeral), st. 3

[1]See Sappho, 63:11, and Meleager, 97:16.
[2]The British regulars who made the retreat from Mons, beginning August 24, 1914.
[3]See Sappho, 63:8.

11 Good night; ensured release,
Imperishable peace,
Have these for yours.[4]
While sky and sea and land
And earth's foundations stand
And heaven endures.
More Poems, 48 (Alta Quies), st. 1

12 Oh they're taking him to prison for the color of his hair.
Additional Poems [1937], 18, st. 1

13 Good literature continually read for pleasure must, let us hope, do some good to the reader: must quicken his perception though dull, and sharpen his discrimination though blunt, and mellow the rawness of his personal opinions.
The Name and Nature of Poetry[5]

14 Experience has taught me, when I am shaving of a morning, to keep watch over my thoughts, because, if a line of poetry strays into my memory, my skin bristles so that the razor ceases to act. . . . The seat of this sensation is the pit of the stomach.[6] *Ib.*

Jerome Klapka Jerome
1859–1927

15 Let your boat of life be light, packed with only what you need—a homely home and simple pleasures, one or two friends, worth the name, someone to love and someone to love you,[7] a cat, a dog, and a pipe or two, enough to eat and enough to wear, and a little more than enough to drink; for thirst is a dangerous thing.
Three Men in a Boat [1889], ch. 3

16 It is impossible to enjoy idling thoroughly unless one has plenty of work to do.
Idle Thoughts of an Idle Fellow [1889]. On Being Idle

17 "Nothing, so it seems to me," said the stranger, "is more beautiful than the love that has weathered the storms of life. . . . The love of the young for the young, that is the beginning of life. But the love of the old for the old, that is the beginning of—of things longer."
The Passing of the Third Floor Back [1908]

[4]These three lines are on the tablet over Housman's grave in the parish church at Ludlow, Shropshire.
[5]The Leslie Stephen Lecture, Cambridge University [May 9, 1933].
[6]See Dickinson, 608:6, and Graves, 833:6.
[7]Find someone to love . . . and, oh, someone to love you.—SACHA GUITRY, *Deburau* [1918]

William James Lampton
1859–1917

1 Same old slippers,
Same old rice,
Same old glimpse of
Paradise. *June Weddings, st. 10*

2 Where the corn is full of kernels
And the colonels full of corn.
Kentucky

Charles E. Stanton[1]
1859–1933

3 Lafayette, we are here.[2]
Address at the tomb of Lafayette, Picpus Cemetery, Paris [July 4, 1917]

James Kenneth Stephen
1859–1892

4 When the Rudyards cease from Kipling
And the Haggards ride no more.
Lapsus Calami. To R. K.

5 Of sentences that stir my bile,
Of phrases I detest,
There's one beyond all others vile:
"He did it for the best."
Ib. The Malefactor's Plea, st. 1

Francis Thompson
1859–1907

6 The fairest things have fleetest end,
Their scent survives their close:
But the rose's scent is bitterness
To him that loved the rose.
Daisy [1893], st. 10

7 Nothing begins, and nothing ends,
That is not paid with moan;
For we are born in other's pain,
And perish in our own. *Ib. st. 15*

[1]Chief disbursing officer of the American Expeditionary Forces in France [1917], deputed by General Pershing to speak on behalf of the A.E.F. on this occasion. He used the phrase again on July 14.

[2]The remark has also been attributed to General Pershing, who in *My Experiences in the World War* [1931] says he cannot remember having said "anything so splendid." However Naboth Hedin, one of the uniformed American correspondents present upon the July 4, 1917, occasion, states that he heard Pershing pronounce the phrase three weeks earlier, on June 14, his second day in Paris:

"Pershing stepped up to it [Lafayette's grave] and saluted in his best manner and then said in a loud voice, 'Lafayette, we are here.' I was about twenty feet away." —*Letter from Naboth Hedin to Samuel Eliot Morison* [June 21, 1954]

8 Look for me in the nurseries of Heaven.[3]
To My Godchild

9 The innocent moon, which nothing does but shine,
Moves all the laboring surges of the world.
Sister Songs, pt. II

10 I fled Him, down the nights and down the days;
I fled Him, down the arches of the years;
I fled Him, down the labyrinthine ways
Of my own mind; and in the mist of tears
I hid from Him, and under running laughter.
The Hound of Heaven [1893], l. 1

11 But with unhurrying chase,
And unperturbèd pace,
Deliberate speed, majestic instancy,
They beat—and a Voice beat
More instant than the Feet—
"All things betray thee, who betrayest Me."
Ib. l. 10

12 Across the margent of the world I fled,
And troubled the gold gateways of the stars.
Ib. l. 25

13 I said to dawn, Be sudden; to eve, Be soon.
Ib. l. 30

14 My days have crackled and gone up in smoke.
Ib. l. 122

15 All which I took from thee I did but take,
Not for thy harms,
But just that thou might'st seek it in My arms. *Ib. l. 171*

16 O world invisible, we view thee,
O world intangible, we touch thee,
O world unknowable, we know thee.
The Kingdom of God ("In No Strange Land") [1913], st. 1

17 The drift of pinions, would we hearken,
Beats at our own clay-shuttered doors.
Ib. st. 3

18 The angels keep their ancient places;
Turn but a stone, and start a wing!
'Tis ye, 'tis your estrangèd faces,
That miss the many-splendored thing.
Ib. st. 4

19 Upon thy so sore loss
Shall shine the traffic of Jacob's ladder
Pitched betwixt Heaven and Charing Cross.
Ib. st. 5

20 Short arm needs man to reach to Heaven
So ready is Heaven to stoop to him.
Grace of the Way, st. 6

[3]This line is inscribed on Thompson's tombstone in Kensal Green.

1 Know you what it is to be a child? It is to be something very different from the man of today. It is to have a spirit yet streaming from the waters of baptism; it is to believe in love, to believe in loveliness, to believe in belief; it is to be so little that the elves can reach to whisper in your ear; it is to turn pumpkins into coaches, and mice into horses, lowness into loftiness, and nothing into everything, for each child has its fairy godmother in its soul.

Shelley. In The Dublin Review [July 1908]

Sidney Webb, Lord Passfield
1859–1947
and
Beatrice Webb
1858–1943

2 The inevitability of gradualness.

Labor on the Threshold [1923][1]

Jane Addams
1860–1935

3 Private beneficence is totally inadequate to deal with the vast numbers of the city's disinherited.

Twenty Years at Hull House [1910]

4 The common stock of intellectual enjoyment should not be difficult of access because of the economic position of him who would approach it. *Ib.*

Sir James Matthew Barrie
1860–1937

5 Them that has china plates themsels is the maist careful no to break the china plates of others.

The Little Minister [1891], ch. 26

6 We never understand how little we need in this world until we know the loss of it.

Margaret Ogilvy [1896], ch. 8

7 Shall we make a new rule of life from tonight: always to try to be a little kinder than is necessary?

The Little White Bird [1902], ch. 4

8 His lordship may compel us to be equal upstairs, but there will never be equality in the servants' hall.

The Admirable Crichton [1903], act I

[1]Sidney Webb's opening address as president of the Labour Party Congress [June 28, 1923].

9 Do you believe in fairies? . . . If you believe, clap your hands!

Peter Pan [1904], act IV

10 It's a sort of bloom on a woman. If you have it [charm], you don't need to have anything else, and if you don't have it, it doesn't much matter what else you have. Some women, the few, have charm for all; and most have charm for one. But some have charm for none.[2]

What Every Woman Knows [1908], act I

11 The tragedy of a man who has found himself out. *Ib. IV*

12 One's religion is whatever he is most interested in, and yours is Success.

The Twelve-Pound Look [1910]

13 Peter and Wendy.

Title of novel [1911]

John Collins Bossidy
1860–1928

14 And this is good old Boston,
The home of the bean and the cod,
Where the Lowells talk to the Cabots
And the Cabots talk only to God.[3]

Toast, Holy Cross Alumni Dinner [1910]

William Jennings Bryan
1860–1925

15 The humblest citizen of all the land, when clad in the armor of a righteous cause, is stronger than all the hosts of Error.

Speech at the National Democratic Convention, Chicago [1896]

16 You shall not press down upon the brow of labor this crown of thorns. You shall not crucify mankind upon a cross of gold.[4]

Ib.

[2]What is charm? It is what the violet has and the camellia has not.—F. MARION CRAWFORD [1854–1909], *Children of the King, ch. 5*

"Charm"—which means the power to effect work without employing brute force—is indispensable to women. Charm is a woman's strength just as strength is a man's charm.—HAVELOCK ELLIS [1859–1939], *The Task of Social Hygiene, ch. 3*

[3]Patterned on the toast given at the twenty-fifth anniversary dinner of the Harvard Class of 1880, by a Westerner:

Here's to old Massachusetts, / The home of the sacred cod, / Where the Adamses vote for Douglas, / And the Cabots walk with God.

[4]I shall not help crucify mankind upon a cross of gold. I shall not aid in pressing down upon the bleeding brow of labor this crown of thorns.—WILLIAM JENNINGS BRYAN, *speech in the House of Representatives* [December 22, 1894]

Anton Pavlovich Chekhov
1860–1904

1 I feel more confident and more satisfied when I reflect that I have two professions and not one. Medicine is my lawful wife and literature is my mistress. When I get tired of one I spend the night with the other. Though it's disorderly it's not so dull, and besides, neither really loses anything through my infidelity.

Letter to A. S. Suvorin [September 11, 1888][1]

2 I would like to be a free artist and nothing else, and I regret God has not given me the strength to be one.

Letter to Alexei Pleshcheev [October 4, 1888][1]

3 My holy of holies is the human body, health, intelligence, talent, inspiration, love, and the most absolute freedom imaginable, freedom from violence and lies, no matter what form the latter two take. Such is the program I would adhere to if I were a major artist. *Ib.*

4 An artist must pass judgment only on what he understands; his range is limited as that of any other specialist—that's what I keep repeating and insisting upon. Anyone who says that the artist's field is all answers and no questions has never done any writing or had any dealings with imagery. An artist observes, selects, guesses and synthesizes.

Letter to A. S. Suvorin [October 27, 1888][1]

5 I try to catch every sentence, every word you and I say, and quickly lock all these sentences and words away in my literary storehouse because they might come in handy.

The Seagull [1896],[2] *act II*

6 People should be beautiful in every way — in their faces, in the way they dress, in their thoughts and in their innermost selves.

Uncle Vanya [1897],[2] *act I*

7 We shall find peace. We shall hear the angels, we shall see the sky sparkling with diamonds. *Ib. IV*

8 To Moscow, to Moscow, to Moscow!

Three Sisters [1901], act II

9 All Russia is our orchard.

The Cherry Orchard [1904],[2] *act II*

[1]Translated by SIMON KARLINSKY.
[2]Translated by RONALD HINGLY.

Charles Townsend Copeland
1860–1952

10 If I had not been there I should have been very much bored.[3]

Comment on a tea party. From WALTER LIPPMANN, *William Bolitho: A Memoir*

Harry Micajah Daugherty
1860–1941

11 In a smoke-filled room in some hotel.[4]

Attributed

Hamlin Garland
1860–1940

12 A Son of the Middle Border.

Title of autobiographical narrative [1917]

Charlotte Perkins Gilman
1860–1935

13 There is no female mind. The brain is not an organ of sex. As well speak of a female liver.

Woman and Economics [1898], ch. 8

14 Women are growing honester, braver, stronger, more healthful and skillful and able and free, more human in all ways.

Ib.

15 Cried all, "Before such things can come,
You idiotic child,
You must alter human nature!"
And they all sat back and smiled.

In This Our World [1899]. Similar Cases

16 "I do not want to be a fly!
I want to be a worm!"

Ib. A Conservative, st. 6

17 I ran against a Prejudice
That quite cut off the view.

Ib. An Obstacle, st. 1

[3]I quite agree with Alexander Dumas who, when asked how he had enjoyed a fearfully dull party, said, "I should not have enjoyed it if *I* had not been there."—LAURA TENNANT, *letter to Sidney Colvin* [December 1884]; from E. V. Lucas, *The Colvins and Their Friends*

[4]According to the *New York Times* [February 21, 1920], Daugherty, presidential campaign manager for Senator Warren G. Harding, predicted that the convention would be deadlocked and would be decided by a group of men who "will sit down about two o'clock in the morning around a table in a smoke-filled room." Daugherty maintained that he had not said "smoke-filled." The room was in the suite occupied by George Harvey, rooms 804–805 in the Blackstone Hotel.

1 The people people have for friends
Your common sense appall,
But the people people marry
Are the queerest folk of all.

Queer People

William Ralph Inge
1860–1954

2 A man may build himself a throne of bayonets, but he cannot sit on it.

From Wit and Wisdom of Dean Inge, edited by MARCHANT, *no. 108*

James Ball Naylor
1860–1945

3 King David and King Solomon
Led merry, merry lives,
With many, many lady friends
And many, many wives;
But when old age crept over them—
With many, many qualms,
King Solomon wrote the Proverbs
And King David wrote the Psalms.

Ancient Authors

Sir D'Arcy Wentworth Thompson
1860–1948

4 Numerical precision is the very soul of science.

On Growth and Form [1917], ch. 1

5 The harmony of the world is made manifest in Form and Number, and the heart and soul and all the poetry of Natural Philosophy are embodied in the concept of mathematical beauty. *Ib. 10*

6 The perfection of mathematical beauty is such . . . that whatsoever is most beautiful and regular is also found to be most useful and excellent. *Ib.*

Owen Wister
1860–1938

7 When you call me that, *smile!*

The Virginian [1902], ch. 2

William Bliss Carman
1861–1929

8 No fidget and no reformer, just
A calm observer of ought and must.

The Joys of the Road, st. 22

9 The scarlet of the maples can shake me like a cry
Of bugles going by.

A Vagabond Song, st. 2

10 There is something in October sets the gypsy blood astir. *Ib. st. 3*

11 I took a day to search for God,
And found Him not. But as I trod
By rocky ledge, through woods untamed,
Just where one scarlet lily flamed,
I saw His footprint in the sod.

Vestigia, st. 1

Pierre Maurice Marie Duhem
1861–1916

12 It is impossible to follow the march of one of the great theories of physics, to see it unroll majestically its regular deductions starting from initial hypotheses, to see its consequences represent a multitude of experimental laws, down to the smallest detail, without being charmed by the beauty of such a construction, without feeling keenly that such a creation of the human mind is truly a work of art.

The Aim and Structure of Physical Theory (La Théorie Physique: Son Objet, Sa Structure) [1906],[1] *pt. I, ch. 2*

Louise Imogen Guiney
1861–1920

13 He has done with roofs and men,
Open, Time, and let him pass.

Ballad of Kenelm

14 A short life in the saddle, Lord!
Not long life by the fire.

The Knight Errant, st. 2

John Luther Long
1861–1927

15 To die with honor when one can no longer live with honor.[2]

Madame Butterfly [1897]

Albert Bigelow Paine
1861–1937

16 The Great White Way.[3]

Title of novel [1901]

[1] Translated by PHILIP P. WIENER.
[2] Inscription on Samurai blade.
One should die proudly when it is no longer possible to live proudly.—NIETZSCHE [1844–1900], *The Twilight of the Idols, Skirmishes in a War with the Age, 36*
[3] Later a name for Broadway.

Sir Walter Raleigh
1861–1922

1 I wish I loved the human race;
I wish I loved its silly face;
I wish I liked the way it walks;
I wish I liked the way it talks;
And when I'm introduced to one
I wish I thought, *What jolly fun!*

Wishes of an Elderly Man; wished at a garden party [June 1914]

Rabindranath Tagore
1861–1941

2 When one knows thee, then alien there is none, then no door is shut. Oh, grant me my prayer that I may never lose the touch of the one in the play of the many.

Gitanjali [1913]

3 At my dying hour, and over my long life,
A clock strikes somewhere at the city's edge.

Poem [1941]

Alfred North Whitehead
1861–1947

4 The study of mathematics is apt to commence in disappointment. . . . We are told that by its aid the stars are weighed and the billions of molecules in a drop of water are counted. Yet, like the ghost of Hamlet's father, this great science eludes the efforts of our mental weapons to grasp it.

An Introduction to Mathematics [1911], ch. 1

5 Civilization advances by extending the number of important operations which we can perform without thinking about them.

Ib. 5

6 All the world over and at all times there have been practical men, absorbed in irreducible and stubborn facts; all the world over and at all times there have been men of philosophic temperament, who have been absorbed in the weaving of general principles.

Science and the Modern World [1925], ch. 1

7 The science of pure mathematics, in its modern developments, may claim to be the most original creation of the human spirit.

Ib. 2

8 The greatest invention of the nineteenth century was the invention of the method of invention. *Ib. 6*

9 Religion is the vision of something which stands beyond, behind and within the passing flux of immediate things; something which is real, and yet waiting to be realized; something which is a remote possibility, and yet the greatest of present facts; something that gives meaning to all that passes, and yet eludes apprehension; something whose possession is the final good, and yet is beyond all reach; something which is the ultimate ideal, and the hopeless quest. *Ib. 12*

10 The religious vision, and its history of persistent expansion, is our one ground for optimism. Apart from it, human life is a flash of occasional enjoyments lighting up a mass of pain and misery, a bagatelle of transient experience. *Ib.*

11 Rationalism is an adventure in the clarification of thought.

Process and Reality [1929], pt. I, ch. 1, sec. 3

12 The safest general characterization of the European philosophical tradition is that it consists of a series of footnotes to Plato.

Ib. II, 1, 1

13 The human body is an instrument for the production of art in the life of the human soul.

Adventures of Ideas [1933], ch. 18

14 A general definition of civilization: a civilized society is exhibiting the five qualities of truth, beauty, adventure, art, peace.

Ib. 19

15 The deliberate aim at Peace very easily passes into its bastard substitute, Anesthesia.

Ib. 20

16 There are no whole truths; all truths are half-truths. It is trying to treat them as whole truths that plays the devil.

Dialogues of Alfred North Whitehead [1953],[1] prologue

17 The vitality of thought is in adventure. *Ideas won't keep.* Something must be done about them. When the idea is new, its custodians have fervor, live for it, and, if need be, die for it. *Ib. ch. 12, April 28, 1938*

18 Intelligence is quickness to apprehend as distinct from ability, which is capacity to act wisely on the thing apprehended.

Ib. 17, December 15, 1939

[1] As recorded by Lucien Price.

1 Our minds are finite, and yet even in these circumstances of finitude we are surrounded by possibilities that are infinite, and the purpose of human life is to grasp as much as we can out of that infinitude.

Ib. 21, June 28, 1941

2 A culture is in its finest flower before it begins to analyze itself.

Ib. 22, August 17, 1941

3 What is morality in any given time or place? It is what the majority then and there happen to like, and immorality is what they dislike. *Ib. August 30, 1941*

4 The ideas of Freud[1] were popularized by people who only imperfectly understood them, who were incapable of the great effort required to grasp them in their relationship to larger truths, and who therefore assigned to them a prominence out of all proportion to their true importance.

Ib. 28, June 3, 1943

5 Art is the imposing of a pattern on experience, and our aesthetic enjoyment in recognition of the pattern.

Ib. 29, June 10, 1943

6 A philosopher of imposing stature doesn't think in a vacuum. Even his most abstract ideas are, to some extent, conditioned by what is or is not known in the time when he lives. *Ib.*

7 With the sense of sight, the idea communicates the emotion, whereas, with sound, the emotion communicates the idea, which is more direct and therefore more powerful.

Ib.

8 Intellect is to emotion as our clothes are to our bodies; we could not very well have civilized life without clothes, but we would be in a poor way if we had only clothes without bodies. *Ib.*

9 No period of history has ever been great or ever can be that does not act on some sort of high, idealistic motives, and idealism in our time has been shoved aside, and we are paying the penalty for it.

Ib. 32, January 13, 1944

10 The English never abolish anything. They put it in cold storage.

Ib. 36, January 19, 1945

11 Shakespeare wrote better poetry for not knowing too much; Milton, I think, knew too much finally for the good of his poetry.

Ib. 43, November 11, 1947

[1]See Freud, 678.

Arthur Christopher Benson

1862–1925

12 Land of hope and glory, mother of the free,
How shall we extol thee, who are born of thee?
Wider still and wider shall thy bounds be set;
God, who made thee mighty, make thee mightier yet.

Land of Hope and Glory [1902],[2] *chorus*

Albert Jeremiah Beveridge

1862–1927

13 This party comes from the grass roots. It has grown from the soil of the people's hard necessities.

Address at the Bull Moose Convention, Chicago [August 5, 1912]

James W. Blake

1862–1935

14 East Side, West Side, all around the town,
The tots sang "Ring-a-rosie," "London Bridge is falling down";
Boys and girls together, me and Mamie O'Rorke,
Tripped the light fantastic on the sidewalks of New York.

The Sidewalks of New York [1894][3]

Carrie Jacobs Bond

1862–1946

15 Well, this is the end of a perfect day,
Near the end of a journey, too.

A Perfect Day, st. 2

16 For memory has painted this perfect day
With colors that never fade,
And we find at the end of a perfect day
The soul of a friend we've made. *Ib.*

Nicholas Murray Butler

1862–1947

17 An expert is one who knows more and more about less and less.

Commencement address, Columbia University

[2]First *Pomp and Circumstance* march by SIR EDWARD ELGAR.

[3]Music by CHARLES B. LAWLOR.

John Jay Chapman
1862–1933

1 The New Testament, and to a very large extent the Old, *is* the soul of man. You cannot criticize it. It criticizes you.
Letter [March 26, 1898]

2 The present in New York is so powerful that the past is lost. *Ib. [1909]*

3 People who love soft words and hate iniquity forget this, that reform consists in taking a bone away from a dog. Philosophy will not do this. *Saying*

Goldsworthy Lowes Dickinson
1862–1932

4 Dissatisfaction with the world in which we live and determination to realize one that shall be better, are the prevailing characteristics of the modern spirit.
The Greek View of Life [1898], ch. 5

5 The United States of America—the greatest potential force, material, moral, and spiritual, in the world.
The Choice Before Us [1917], ch. 1

6 Government is everywhere to a great extent controlled by powerful minorities, with an interest distinct from that of the mass of the people. *Ib. 4*

Edward, Viscount Grey of Fallodon
1862–1933

7 The lamps are going out all over Europe; we shall not see them lit again in our lifetime.
Comment [August 3, 1914],[1] *standing at the windows of his room in the Foreign Office, London, as the lamplighters were turning on the lights in St. James Park*

O. Henry
[William Sydney Porter]
1862–1910

8 Perhaps there is no happiness in life so perfect as the martyr's.
The Trimmed Lamp [1907]. The Country of Elusion

9 It was beautiful and simple as all truly great swindles are.
The Gentle Grafter [1908]. The Octopus Marooned

[1]War was declared at 11 P.M. on August 4, 1914.

10 Busy as a one-armed man with the nettle-rash pasting on wallpaper.
Ib. The Ethics of Pig

11 Bagdad-on-the-Subway.[2]
Roads of Destiny [1909]. The Discounters of Money

12 History is bright and fiction dull with homely men who have charmed women.
Ib. Next to Reading Matter

13 You can't appreciate home till you've left it, money till it's spent, your wife till she's joined a woman's club, nor Old Glory till you see it hanging on a broomstick on the shanty of a consul in a foreign town.
Ib. The Fourth in Salvador

14 She plucked from my lapel the invisible strand of lint (the universal act of woman to proclaim ownership).
Strictly Business [1910]. A Ramble in Aphasia

15 East is East, and West is San Francisco,[3] according to Californians. Californians are a race of people; they are not merely inhabitants of a State.
Ib. A Municipal Report

16 Take of London fog 30 parts; malaria 10 parts; gas leaks 20 parts; dewdrops gathered in a brickyard at sunrise 25 parts; odor of honeysuckle 15 parts. Mix. The mixture will give you an approximate conception of a Nashville drizzle. *Ib.*

17 It couldn't have happened anywhere but in little old New York.[4]
Whirligigs [1910]. A Little Local Color

18 A straw vote only shows which way the hot air blows.
Rolling Stones [1913]. A Ruler of Men

19 Take it from me—he's got the goods.
The Unprofitable Servant

20 Turn up the lights—I don't want to go home in the dark.[5]
Last words [June 5, 1910]

[2]Also in *A Madison Square Arabian Night, A Night in New Arabia,* and *What You Want.*

[3]Make no mistake, stranger, San Francisco is West as all hell.—BERNARD DE VOTO; *quoted by* CURT GENTRY, *Dolphin Guide to San Francisco* [1962]

[4]Also in *A Midsummer Knight's Dream, Past One at Rooney's,* and *The Rubber Plant's Story.*

[5]I'm Afraid to Go Home in the Dark.—HARRY H. WILLIAMS [1879–1922], *title of song* [1907]

Charles Evans Hughes
1862–1948

1 We are under a Constitution, but the Constitution is what the judges say it is, and the judiciary is the safeguard of our liberty and of our property under the Constitution.
Speech at Elmira, New York [May 3, 1907]

2 How amazing it is that, in the midst of controversies on every conceivable subject, one should expect unanimity of opinion upon difficult legal questions! In the highest ranges of thought, in theology, philosophy and science, we find differences of view on the part of the most distinguished experts — theologians, philosophers and scientists. The history of scholarship is a record of disagreements. And when we deal with questions relating to principles of law and their applications, we do not suddenly rise into a stratosphere of icy certainty.
Speech to the American Law Institute [May 7, 1936]

3 The greater the importance of safeguarding the community from incitements to the overthrow of our institutions by force and violence, the more imperative is the need to preserve inviolate the constitutional rights of free speech, free press and free assembly in order to maintain the opportunity for free political discussion, to the end that government may be responsive to the will of the people and that changes, if desired, may be obtained by peaceful means. Therein lies the security of the Republic, the very foundation of constitutional government.
DeJonge v. Oregon, 299 U.S. 353, 365 [1937]

Maurice Maeterlinck
1862–1949

4 It is always a mistake not to close one's eyes, whether to forgive or to look better into oneself. *Pelléas et Mélisande [1892]*

5 There are no dead.
The Blue Bird [1909], act IV, sc. ii

Sir Henry Newbolt
1862–1938

6 To set the cause above renown,
To love the game beyond the prize,
To honor, while you strike him down,
The foe that comes with fearless eyes;
To count the life of battle good
And dear the land that gave you birth,
And dearer yet the brotherhood
That binds the brave of all the earth.
The Island Race. Clifton Chapel, st. 2

7 *Qui procul hinc,* the legend's writ,
The frontier grave is far away —
Qui ante diem periit:
Sed miles, sed pro patria.[1] *Ib. st. 4*

8 Take my drum to England, hang et by the shore,
Strike et when your powder's runnin' low;
If the Dons sight Devon, I'll quit the port o' Heaven,
An' drum them up the Channel as we drummed them long ago.
Drake's Drum, st. 2

9 Drake he's in his hammock till the great Armadas come.
(Capten, art tha sleepin' there below?)
Ib. st. 3

10 Now the sunset breezes shiver,
And she's fading down the river,
But in England's song forever
She's the Fighting Téméraire.
The Fighting Téméraire, st. 6

11 Play up! play up! and play the game![2]
Vitai Lampada

12 Keep the Nelson touch.
Minora Sidera

Robert Cameron Rogers
1862–1912

13 The hours I spent with thee, dear heart,
Are as a string of pearls to me;
I count them over, every one apart,
My rosary, my rosary. *My Rosary*

Edith Wharton[3]
1862–1937

14 There are two ways of spreading light: to be
The candle or the mirror that reflects it.
Vesalius in Zante

15 Mrs. Ballinger is one of the ladies who pursue Culture in bands, as though it were dangerous to meet it alone. *Xingu [1916]*

[1]Who died far away, before his time: but as a soldier, for his country.
[2]See Rice, 773:3.
[3]Traditionally, Henry James has been placed slightly higher up the slope of Parnassus than Edith Wharton. But now that the prejudice against the female writer is on the wane, they look to be exactly what they are: giants, equals, the tutelary and benign gods of our American literature. — Gore Vidal [1925–], *The Edith Wharton Omnibus* [1978], *introduction*

1 In the rotation of crops there was a recognized season for wild oats; but they were not sown more than once.

The Age of Innocence [1920], ch. 31

2 It was the old New York way of taking life "without effusion of blood": the way of people who dreaded scandal more than disease, who placed decency above courage, and who considered that nothing was more ill-bred than "scenes," except the behavior of those who gave rise to them. *Ib. 33*

3 The worst of doing one's duty was that it apparently unfitted one for doing anything else. *Ib. 34*

4 There's no such thing as old age; there is only sorrow.

A Backward Glance [1934].[1] *A First Word*

5 In spite of illness, in spite even of the archenemy sorrow, one *can* remain alive long past the usual date of disintegration if one is unafraid of change, insatiable in intellectual curiosity, interested in big things, and happy in small ways. *Ib.*

6 I was never allowed to read the popular American children's books of my day because, as my mother said, the children spoke bad English *without the author's knowing it.* *Ib. ch. 3*

7 To [Henry] James's intimates, however, these elaborate hesitancies, far from being an obstacle, were like a cobweb bridge flung from his mind to theirs, an invisible passage over which one knew that silver-footed ironies, veiled jokes, tiptoe malices, were stealing to explode a huge laugh at one's feet.[2] *Ib. 8*

Black Elk[3]

1863–1950

8 Everything an Indian does is in a circle,[4] and that is because the power of the world always works in circles, and everything tries to be round. In the old days when we were a strong and happy people, all our power came to us from the sacred hoop of the nation, and so long as the hoop was unbroken the people flourished.

Black Elk Speaks, Being the Life Story of a Holy Man of the Oglala Sioux, as told through JOHN G. NEIHARDT *[1961]*

9 Even the seasons form a great circle in their changing, and always come back again to where they were. The life of a man is a circle from childhood to childhood and so it is in everything where power moves. Our tepees were round like the nests of birds, and these were always set in a circle, the nation's hoop. *Ib.*

Constantine Peter Cavafy

1863–1933

10 But Argos can do without the sons of Atreus.
Ancient houses are not eternal.

When the Watchman Saw the Light[5] *[1900]*

11 We won't be deceived
by titles such as Indispensable and Unique and Great.
Someone else indispensable and unique and great
can always be found at a moment's notice.[6]

Ib.

12 He who longs to strengthen his spirit
must go beyond obedience and respect.
He will continue to honor some laws
but he will mostly violate
both law and custom.

Strengthening the Spirit [1903][7]

13 Pleasure will have much to teach him.
He will not be afraid of the destructive act;
one half of the house must be pulled down.
This way he will grow virtuously into knowledge. *Ib.*

14 What are we all waiting for
gathered together like this on the public square?
The Barbarians are coming today.

Waiting for the Barbarians [1904],[8] *l. 1*

15 Why are our two consuls and our praetors
all got up in their embroidered scarlet robes?
Why are they covered with bracelets and rings? . . .
The Barbarians are coming today.
And such things impress the Barbarians.

Ib. l. 16

[1] See Whitman, 577:10.
[2] See Henry James, 652.
[3] Hehaka Sapa.
[4] In this circle / O ye warriors / Lo, I tell you / Each his future. / All shall be / As I now reveal it / In this circle; / Hear ye! —*Song of the Seer*

[5] Translated by EDMUND KEELEY and GEORGE SAVIDIS. See Aeschylus, 71:3.
[6] See F. D. Roosevelt, 779:9.
[7] Translated by EDMUND KEELEY and GEORGE SAVIDIS.
[8] Translated by W. H. AUDEN and MARGUERITE YOURCENAR.

1 Why are the streets and the squares all emptying so quickly?
Why is everybody going home looking so blue?
Because night has fallen and the Barbarians have not come.
And some people have just come back from the frontiers
who say there are no more Barbarians.
And now, without the Barbarians, what is to become of us?
After all, they would have been a kind of solution. *Ib. l. 28*

2 You'll not find another place, you'll not find another sea.
This city is going to follow you.
The City [1910],[1] l. 9

3 Do not uselessly lament
your luck that is giving way, your work that has failed,
your life's plans that have all ended in despair.
Like a man long prepared, like a man of courage,
bid her farewell, the Alexandria that leaves you.
The God Abandons Antony [1911],[1] l. 4

4 Setting out on the voyage to Ithaca
you must pray that the way be long,
full of adventures and experiences.
Ithaca [1911],[2] l. 11

5 Body, remember not only how much you were loved,
not only the beds you lay on,
but also those desires glowing openly
in eyes that looked at you,
trembling for you in voices.
Body, Remember [1918][3]

6 And then he was the best of all things, Greek—
no quality more precious has mankind:
what lies beyond only the gods may find.
Epitaph of Antiochos King of Kommagene [1923],[2] l. 15

7 I created you while I was happy, while I was sad,
with so many incidents, so many details.

And, for me, the whole of you has been transformed into feeling.
In the Same Space [1929]

[1]Translated by Robert Liddell.
[2]Translated by John Mavrogordato.
[3]Translated by Edmund Keeley and Phillip Sherrard.

8 Whatever job they give me,
I'll try to be useful to the country. That's what I intend.
To Have Taken the Trouble [1930], l. 18

9 One of the three will want me anyway.
And my conscience is quiet
about my not caring which one I choose:
the three of them are equally bad for Syria.
Ib. l. 28

10 The almighty gods ought to have taken the trouble
to create a fourth, a decent man.
I would gladly have gone along with him.
Ib. l. 34

11 And from that wonderful expedition of all the Greeks[4]
The victorious, the renowned,
The illustrious, the famous,
As no expedition has ever been,
The incomparable, we have risen
A great new Hellenic world.
200 B.C. [1931][5]

William Randolph Hearst
1863–1951

12 You furnish the pictures and I'll furnish the war.
Cable to artist Frederic Remington in Cuba [March 1898]

Hugo Münsterberg
1863–1916

13 The results of experimental psychology will have to be introduced systematically into the study of the fitness of the personality from the lowest to the highest technical activity and from the simplest sensory function to the most complex mental achievement.
Psychology and Industrial Efficiency [1913]

Sir Arthur Thomas Quiller-Couch
1863–1944

14 Literature is not an abstract science, to which exact definitions can be applied. It is an art, the success of which depends on personal persuasiveness, on the author's skill to give as on ours to receive.
Inaugural Lecture at Cambridge University [1913]

[4]Alexander the Great's expedition.
[5]Translated by C. M. Bowra.

James Harvey Robinson
1863–1936

1 Political campaigns are designedly made into emotional orgies which endeavor to distract attention from the real issues involved, and they actually paralyze what slight powers of cerebration man can normally muster.
The Human Comedy [1937], ch. 9

2 With supreme irony, the war to "make the world safe for democracy"[1] ended by leaving democracy more unsafe in the world than at any time since the collapse of the revolutions of 1848. *Ib.*

George Santayana
1863–1952

3 O World, thou choosest not the better part!
It is not wisdom to be only wise,
And on the inward vision close the eyes,
But it is wisdom to believe the heart.
Columbus found a world, and had no chart,
Save one that faith deciphered in the skies;
To trust the soul's invincible surmise
Was all his science and his only art.
O World, Thou Choosest Not [1894]

4 The whole machinery of our intelligence, our general ideas and laws, fixed and external objects, principles, persons, and gods, are so many symbolic, algebraic expressions. They stand for experience; experience which we are incapable of retaining and surveying in its multitudinous immediacy. We should flounder hopelessly, like the animals, did we not keep ourselves afloat and direct our course by these intellectual devices. Theory helps us to bear our ignorance of fact.
The Sense of Beauty [1896], pt. III, Form

5 Beauty as we feel it is something indescribable: what it is or what it means can never be said. *Ib. IV, Expression*

6 Beauty is a pledge of the possible conformity between the soul and nature, and consequently a ground of faith in the supremacy of the good. *Ib.*

7 Even the most inspired verse, which boasts not without a relative justification to be immortal, becomes in the course of ages a scarcely legible hieroglyphic; the language it was written in dies, a learned education and an imaginative effort are requisite to catch even a vestige of its original force. Nothing is so irrevocable as mind.
The Life of Reason [1905–1906], vol. I, Reason in Common Sense

8 Happiness is the only sanction of life; where happiness fails, existence remains a mad and lamentable experiment. *Ib.*

9 That life is worth living is the most necessary of assumptions, and, were it not assumed, the most impossible of conclusions.[2] *Ib.*

10 Fanaticism consists in redoubling your efforts when you have forgotten your aim. *Ib.*

11 Those who cannot remember the past are condemned to repeat it.[3] *Ib.*

12 The highest form of vanity is love of fame.
Ib. II, Reason in Society

13 The human race, in its intellectual life, is organized like the bees: the masculine soul is a worker, sexually atrophied, and essentially dedicated to impersonal and universal arts; the feminine is a queen, infinitely fertile, omnipresent in its brooding industry, but passive and abounding in intuitions without method and passions without justice. *Ib.*

14 When Socrates and his two great disciples composed a system of rational ethics they were hardly proposing practical legislation for mankind . . . They were merely writing an eloquent epitaph for their country.
Ib. V, Reason in Science

15 Let a man once overcome his selfish terror at his own finitude, and his finitude is, in one sense, overcome.
The Ethics of Spinoza [1910], introduction

16 Perhaps the only true dignity of man is his capacity to despise himself. *Ib.*

17 Miracles are propitious accidents, the natural causes of which are too complicated to be readily understood. *Ib.*

18 The Bible is literature, not dogma. *Ib.*

19 American life is a powerful solvent. It seems to neutralize every intellectual element, however tough and alien it may be, and

[1]See Woodrow Wilson, 682:12.

[2]See Oliver Wendell Holmes, Jr., 644:6, and William James, 649:13.

[3]See Euripides, 77:22, and Thucydides, 80:15.

to fuse it in the native good will, complacency, thoughtlessness, and optimism.

Character and Opinion in the United States [1920]

1 All his life he [the American] jumps into the train after it has started and jumps out before it has stopped; and he never once gets left behind, or breaks a leg. *Ib.*

2 England is the paradise of individuality, eccentricity, heresy, anomalies, hobbies, and humors.

Soliloquies in England and Later Soliloquies [1922]. The British Character

3 The world is a perpetual caricature of itself; at every moment it is the mockery and the contradiction of what it is pretending to be. *Ib. Dickens*

4 There is no cure for birth and death save to enjoy the interval. *Ib. War Shrines*

5 I like to walk about amidst the beautiful things that adorn the world; but private wealth I should decline, or any sort of personal possessions, because they would take away my liberty.

Ib. The Irony of Liberalism

6 My atheism, like that of Spinoza, is true piety towards the universe and denies only gods fashioned by men in their own image, to be servants of their human interests.

Ib. On My Friendly Critics

7 The living have never shown me how to live. *Ib.*

8 Profound skepticism is favorable to conventions, because it doubts that the criticism of conventions is any truer than they are. *Ib.*

9 The young man who has not wept is a savage, and the old man who will not laugh is a fool. *Dialogues in Limbo [1926], ch. 3*

10 Religion in its humility restores man to his only dignity, the courage to live by grace. *Ib. 4*

11 There is nothing impossible in the existence of the supernatural: its existence seems to me decidedly probable.

The Genteel Tradition at Bay [1931]

12 They [the wise spirits of antiquity in the first circle of Dante's *Inferno*] are condemned, Dante tells us, to no other penalty than to live in desire without hope, a fate appropriate to noble souls with a clear vision of life. *Obiter Scripta [1936]*

Konstantin Sergeevich Alekseev Stanislavski
1863–1938

13 Our type of creativeness is the conception and birth of a new being—the person in the part. It is a natural act similar to the birth of a human being.

An Actor Prepares [1936],[1] *ch. 16*

14 In the creative process there is the father, the author of the play; the mother, the actor pregnant with the part; and the child, the role to be born. *Ib.*

Ernest Lawrence Thayer
1863–1940

15 There was ease in Casey's manner as he stepped into his place,
There was pride in Casey's bearing, and a smile on Casey's face,
And when, responding to the cheers, he lightly doffed his hat,
No stranger in the crowd could doubt 'twas Casey at the bat.

Casey at the Bat [1888],[2] *st. 6*

16 Oh! somewhere in this favored land the sun is shining bright;
The band is playing somewhere, and somewhere hearts are light;
And somewhere men are laughing and somewhere children shout,
But there is no joy in Mudville—mighty Casey has struck out. *Ib. st. 13*

Sir Roger Casement
1864–1916

17 Where all your rights become only an accumulated wrong; where men must beg with bated breath for leave to subsist in their own land, to think their own thoughts, to sing their own songs, to garner the fruits of their own labors . . . then surely it is braver, a saner and truer thing, to be a rebel in act and deed against such circumstances as these than tamely to accept it as the natural lot of men.

Statement from prison [June 29, 1916]

[1] Translated by Elizabeth Reynolds Hapgood.

[2] First printed in the *San Francisco Examiner* [June 3, 1888].

Yet I'd take my chance with fame, / Calmly let it go at that, / With the right to sign my name / Under "Casey at the Bat."—Grantland Rice [1880–1954], *The Masterpiece*

Joseph Hayden
fl. 1896

1 There'll be a hot time in the old town tonight.
A Hot Time in the Old Town [1896][1]

Richard Hovey
1864–1900

2 For it's always fair weather
When good fellows get together
With a stein on the table and a good song ringing clear.
A Stein Song [1898], st. 1

3 O, Eleazer Wheelock was a very pious man;
He went into the wilderness to teach the Indian. . . .
Eleazer was the faculty, and the whole curriculum
Was five hundred gallons of New England rum.
Eleazer Wheelock,[2] *st. 1*

Mark Antony De Wolfe Howe
1864–1960

4 Now, thieving Time, take what you must—
Quickness to hear, to move, to see;
When dust is drawing near to dust
Such diminutions needs must be.
Yet leave, O leave exempt from plunder
My curiosity, my wonder!
Thieving Time [1951]

Robert Loveman
1864–1923

5 It is not raining rain to me,
It's raining daffodils.
April Rain [1901], st. 1

6 It is not raining rain to me,
It's raining violets.
Ib. st. 4

Andrew Barton [Banjo] Paterson
1864–1941

7 Once a jolly swagman camped by a billabong,
Under the shade of a coolibar tree,
And he sang as he sat and waited for his billy-boil,
"You'll come a-waltzing, Matilda, with me."[3]
Waltzing Matilda[4]

Jules Renard
1864–1910

8 To succeed you must add water to your wine, until there is no more wine.
Journal

9 There are moments when everything goes well; don't be frightened, it won't last.
Ib.

10 I am not sincere even when I am saying that I am not sincere. *Journal*

11 We don't understand life any better at forty than at twenty, but we know it and admit it. *Ib.*

Miguel de Unamuno
1864–1936

12 The man of flesh and blood; the one who is born, suffers and dies—above all, who dies; the man who eats and drinks and plays and sleeps and thinks and wills; the man who is seen and is heard; the brother, the real brother.
The Tragic Sense of Life [1913], ch. 1

13 Consciousness is a disease. *Ib.*

14 Pantheism is said . . . to be merely atheism in disguise. *Ib. 5*

15 Science is a cemetery of dead ideas, even though life may issue from them. *Ib.*

16 True science teaches, above all, to doubt and be ignorant. *Ib.*

17 To believe in God is to yearn for His existence and, furthermore, it is to act as if He did exist. *Ib. 8*

18 Martyrs create faith, faith does not create martyrs.[5] *Ib. 9*

19 To fall into a habit is to begin to cease to be.
Ib.

20 The intellectual world is divided into two classes—dilettantes, on the one hand, and pedants, on the other. *Ib. 11*

21 Warmth, warmth, more warmth! for we are dying of cold and not of darkness. It is not the night that kills, but the frost.
Ib. Conclusion

[1] Hayden's text for a march, *A Hot Time in the Old Town Tonight* [1886], by THEODORE AUGUST METZ [1848–1936], later a favorite of Theodore Roosevelt's Rough Riders in Cuba, and still later Roosevelt's campaign song.
[2] Dartmouth College song.

[3] Swagman: tramp. Billabong: pool. Coolibar: gum tree. Billy: tin container used for brewing tea.
[4] Australian soldiers' marching song.
[5] See Tertullian, 126:3, and Suarès, 726:9.

1 The devil is an angel too.
Two Mothers

2 There are pretenses which are very sincere, and marriage is their school. *Ib.*

3 And killing time is perhaps the essence of comedy, just as the essence of tragedy is killing eternity.
San Manuel Bueno, prologue

4 I would say that teleology is theology, and that God is not a "because," but rather an "in order to." *Ib.*

5 Let us go on committing suicide by working among our people, and let them dream life just as the lake dreams the sky. *Ib.*

6 One of those leaders of what they call the social revolution has said that religion is the opiate of the people.[1] Opium . . . opium . . . opium, yes. Let us give them opium so that they can sleep and dream. *Ib.*

7 Use harms and even destroys beauty. The noblest function of an object is to be contemplated. *Mist [1914]*

8 Isolation is the worst possible counselor.
Civilization Is Civilism

9 Every peasant has a lawyer inside of him, just as every lawyer, no matter how urbane he may be, carries a peasant within himself.
Ib.

10 It is sad not to be loved, but it is much sadder not to be able to love.
To a Young Writer

11 These terrible sociologists, who are the astrologers and alchemists of our twentieth century. *Fanatical Skepticism*

12 Faith which does not doubt is dead faith.
The Agony of Christianity

13 We never know, believe me, when we have succeeded best. *Essays and Soliloquies*

Israel Zangwill
1864–1926

14 Scratch the Christian and you find the pagan—spoiled.
Children of the Ghetto [1892]

15 America is God's crucible, the great melting pot where all the races of Europe are melting and re-forming![2]
The Melting Pot [1908], act I

[1]See Marx, 562:15.
[2]See Crèvecoeur, 382:8.

Mrs. Patrick Campbell [Beatrice Stella Tanner Campbell]
1865–1940

16 My dear, I don't care what they do, so long as they don't do it in the street and frighten the horses. *Attributed*

Edith Cavell
1865–1915

17 I realize that patriotism is not enough. I must have no hatred or bitterness towards anyone.
Last words [October 12, 1915], before her execution by the Germans

Herbert Albert Laurens Fisher
1865–1940

18 All political decisions are taken under great pressure, and if a treaty serves its turn for ten or twenty years, the wisdom of its framers is sufficiently confirmed.[3]
Political Prophecies [1918]

19 It is easier for eight or nine elderly men to feel their way towards unanimity if they are not compelled to conduct their converging maneuvers under the microscopes and telescopes of the press, but are permitted to shuffle about a little in slippers.
An International Experiment[4] [1921]

20 Purity of race does not exist. Europe is a continent of energetic mongrels.
A History of Europe [1934], ch. 1

21 Politics is the art of human happiness.
Ib. 31

George V
1865–1936

22 How is the Empire?
Last words [January 21, 1936]

Frederic William Goudy
1865–1947

23 I am the voice of today, the herald of tomorrow. . . . I am the leaden army that conquers the world—I am TYPE.
The Type Speaks

[3]Thirty years is the life of most great treaties.—R. B. MOWAT, *A History of Great Britain* [1922]
[4]The League of Nations.

Laurence Hope
[Adela Florence Cory Nicolson]
1865–1904

1 To have — to hold — and — in time — let go!
Indian Love Lyrics. The Teak Forest

2 Pale hands I loved beside the Shalimar.
Ib. Kashmiri Song, st. 1

Rudyard Kipling
1865–1936

3 I have eaten your bread and salt.
I have drunk your water and wine.
The deaths ye died I have watched beside
And the lives ye led were mine.
Departmental Ditties [1886]. Prelude, st. 1

4 Little Tin Gods on Wheels.
Ib. Public Waste, st. 4

5 The toad beneath the harrow knows
Exactly where each tooth point goes;
The butterfly upon the road
Preaches contentment to that toad.
Ib. Pagett, M.P., prelude

6 And a woman is only a woman, but a good cigar is a smoke.
Ib. The Betrothed, st. 25

7 It takes a great deal of Christianity to wipe out uncivilized Eastern instincts, such as falling in love at first sight.
Plain Tales from the Hills [1888]. Lispeth

8 Never praise a sister to a sister, in the hope of your compliments reaching the proper ears. *Ib. False Dawn*

9 Many religious people are deeply suspicious. They seem — for purely religious purposes, of course — to know more about iniquity than the unregenerate.
Ib. Watches of the Night

10 Everyone is more or less mad on one point.[1]
Ib. On the Strength of a Likeness

11 The silliest woman can manage a clever man; but it needs a very clever woman to manage a fool!
Ib. Three and — an Extra

12 Lalah is a member of the most ancient profession in the world.
In Black and White [1888]. On the City Wall

[1]Semel insanivimus omnes [We have all once been mad]. — JOHANNES BAPTISTA MANTUANUS [1448–1516], *Eclogues, no. I*

13 Steady the Buffs.
Soldiers Three [1888]

14 Down to Gehenna or up to the Throne,
He travels the fastest who travels alone.[2]
Ib. The Winners (L' Envoi: What Is the Moral?), st. 1

15 More men are killed by overwork than the importance of the world justifies.
The Phantom 'Rickshaw [1888]

16 Oh, East is East, and West is West, and never the twain shall meet,
Till Earth and Sky stand presently at God's great Judgment Seat;
But there is neither East nor West, border, nor breed, nor birth,
When two strong men stand face to face, though they come from the ends of the earth!
The Ballad of East and West [1889]

17 For all we take we must pay, but the price is cruel high.
The Courting of Dinah Shadd [1890]

18 Bite on the bullet, old man, and don't let them think you're afraid.
The Light That Failed [1890–1891]

19 If I were damned of body and soul,
I know whose prayers would make me whole,
Mother o' mine, O mother o' mine.
Mother o' Mine [1891]

20 And the end of the fight is a tombstone white with the name of the late deceased,
And the epitaph drear: "A Fool lies here who tried to hustle the East."
The Naulahka [1892], ch. 5

21 When Earth's last picture is painted, and the tubes are twisted and dried,
When the oldest colors have faded, and the youngest critic has died,
We shall rest, and, faith, we shall need it — lie down for an eon or two,
Till the Master of All Good Workmen shall put us to work anew.
When Earth's Last Picture Is Painted [1892], st. 1

22 Ever the wide world over, lass,
Ever the trail held true,
Over the world and under the world,
And back at the last to you.
The Gipsy Trail [1892], st. 2

23 They rise to their feet as He passes by, gentlemen unafraid.
Ballads and Barrack Room Ballads [1892, 1893]. Dedication, st. 5

[2]He may well win the race that runs by himself. — BENJAMIN FRANKLIN, *Poor Richard's Almanac* [1757]

1 "What are the bugles blowin' for?" said Files-on-Parade.
"To turn you out, to turn you out," the Color-Sergeant said.
Ib. Danny Deever, st. 1

2 They've taken of his buttons off an' cut his stripes away,
An' they're hangin' Danny Deever in the mornin'. *Ib.*

3 We aren't no thin red 'eroes.[1]
Ib. Tommy, st. 4

4 For it's Tommy this, an' Tommy that, an' "Chuck 'im out, the brute!"
But it's "Savior of 'is country" when the guns begin to shoot. *Ib. st. 5*

5 So 'ere's *to* you, Fuzzy-Wuzzy, at your 'ome in the Soudan;
You're a pore benighted 'eathen but a first-class fightin' man.
Ib. Fuzzy-Wuzzy, st. 1

6 Though I've belted you an' flayed you,
By the livin' Gawd that made you,
You're a better man than I am, Gunga Din!
Ib. Gunga Din, st. 5

7 'Ave you 'eard o' the Widow at Windsor
With a hairy gold crown on 'er 'ead?
Ib. The Widow at Windsor, st. 1

8 By the old Moulmein Pagoda, lookin' eastward to the sea,
There's a Burma girl a-settin', and I know she thinks o' me;
For the wind is in the palm trees, and the temple bells they say:
"Come you back, you British soldier; come you back to Mandalay!"
Ib. Mandalay, st. 1

9 On the road to Mandalay,
Where the flyin' fishes play,
An' the dawn comes up like thunder outer China 'crost the Bay! *Ib.*

10 Ship me somewheres east of Suez, where the best is like the worst,
Where there aren't no Ten Commandments, an' a man can raise a thirst. *Ib. st. 6*

11 The Devil whispered behind the leaves, "It's pretty, but is it Art?"
Ib. The Conundrum of the Workshops, st. 1

12 But the Devil whoops, as he whooped of old:
"It's clever, but is it Art?" *Ib. st. 6*

[1] See Sir W. H. Russell, 578:14.

13 To the legion of the lost ones, to the cohort of the damned.
Ib. Gentlemen Rankers, st. 1

14 We're poor little lambs who've lost our way,
Baa! Baa! Baa!
We're little black sheep who've gone astray,
Baa—aa—aa!
Gentlemen rankers out on the spree,
Damned from here to Eternity,
God ha' mercy on such as we,
Baa! Yah! Baa! *Ib. refrain*

15 We have done with Hope and Honor, we are lost to Love and Truth,
We are dropping down the ladder rung by rung;
And the measure of our torment is the measure of our youth.
God help us, for we knew the worst too young!
Ib. st. 4

16 And what should they know of England who only England knows?
Ib. The English Flag, st. 1

17 And the naked soul of Tomlinson grew white as a rain-washed bone.
Ib. Tomlinson, l. 10

18 The sin ye do by two and two ye must pay for one by one. *Ib. l. 60*

19 There's a legion that never was 'listed,
That carries no colors or crest.
Ib. The Lost Legion, st. 1

20 To go and find out and be damned
(Dear boys!). *Ib.*

21 There are nine and sixty ways of constructing tribal lays,
And every single one of them is right.
Ib. In the Neolithic Age, st. 5

22 There be triple ways to take, of the eagle or the snake,
Or the way of a man with a maid;[2]
But the sweetest way to me is a ship's upon the sea
In the heel of the Northeast Trade.
Ib. The Long Trail, st. 5

23 He wrapped himself in quotations[3]—as a beggar would enfold himself in the purple of emperors.
Many Inventions [1893]. The Finest Story in the World

24 When 'Omer smote 'is bloomin' lyre,
He'd 'eard men sing by land an' sea;

[2] See *Proverbs 30:19*, 26:4.

[3] In literature quotation is good only when the writer whom I follow goes my way, and, being better mounted than I, gives me a cast.—Emerson, *Quotation and Originality* [1876]

An' what he thought 'e might require,
'E went an' took—the same as me!
When 'Omer Smote 'Is Bloomin' Lyre [1894], st. 1

1 Back to the Army again, sergeant,
Back to the Army again.
Out o' the cold an' the rain.
Back to the Army Again [1894], refrain

2 We be of one blood, ye and I.
The Jungle Book [1894]. Kaa's Hunting

3 Brother, thy tail hangs down behind.
Ib. Road Song of the Bandar-Log, refrain

4 Now this is the Law of the Jungle—as old and as true as the sky;
And the Wolf that shall keep it may prosper, but the Wolf that shall break it must die.
The Second Jungle Book [1895]. The Law of the Jungle, st. 1

5 When Pack meets with Pack in the Jungle, and neither will go from the trail,
Lie down till the leaders have spoken—it may be fair words shall prevail.
Ib. st. 6

6 Now these are the Laws of the Jungle, and many and mighty are they;
But the head and the hoof of the Law and the haunch and the hump is—Obey!
Ib. st. 19

7 They change their skies above them,
But not their hearts that roam.[1]
The Nativeborn [1895], st. 2

8 The Liner she's a lady, an' she never looks nor 'eeds—
The Man-o'-War's 'er 'usband, an' 'e gives 'er all she needs,
But, oh, the little cargo boats that sail the wet seas roun',
They're just the same as you an' me a-plyin' up and down!
The Liner She's a Lady [1895], st. 1

9 I've taken my fun where I've found it.
The Ladies [1895], st. 1

10 An' I learned about women from 'er.
Ib. refrain

11 For the Colonel's Lady an' Judy O'Grady
Are sisters under their skins! *Ib. st. 8*

12 Though there's never a wave of all her waves
But marks our English dead.
The Song of the Dead [1896], II, st. 1

[1] See Horace, 109:5.

13 'E's a sort of a bloomin' cosmopolouse—soldier an' sailor too.
Soldier an' Sailor Too [1896], st. 2

14 A fool there was and he made his prayer
(Even as you and I!)
To a rag and a bone and a hank of hair
(We called her the woman who did not care)
But the fool he called her his lady fair—
(Even as you and I!)
The Vampire [1897], st. 1

15 Daughter am I in my mother's house;
But mistress in my own.
Our Lady of the Snows[2] *[1898], st. 1*

16 God of our fathers, known of old,
Lord of our far-flung battle line,
Beneath whose awful Hand we hold
Dominion over palm and pine—
Lord God of Hosts, be with us yet,
Lest we forget—lest we forget!
Recessional [1899], st. 1

17 The tumult and the shouting dies;
The captains and the kings depart.
Ib. st. 2

18 Lo, all our pomp of yesterday
Is one with Nineveh and Tyre!
Ib. st. 3

19 Lesser breeds without the Law.
Ib. st. 4

20 For frantic boast and foolish word—
Thy mercy on Thy People, Lord!
Ib. st. 5

21 Take up the White Man's burden,[3]
Send forth the best ye breed—
Go, bind your sons to exile
To serve your captives' need.
The White Man's Burden [1899], st. 1

22 Little Friend of All the World.
Kim [1901], ch. 1

23 The flanneled fools at the wicket or the muddied oafs at the goals.
The Islanders [1902], l. 31

24 When the ship goes *wop* (with a wiggle between)
And the steward falls into the soup tureen . . .
Why, then you will know (if you haven't guessed)
You're "Fifty north and forty west!"
The Just-So Stories [1902]. How the Whale Got Its Throat

[2] The Dominion of Canada.

[3] Pile on the brown man's burden / To satisfy your greed.—*London Truth; reprinted in Middlebury (Vermont) Register* [March 17, 1899]

1 We get the hump—
Cameelious hump—
The hump that is black and blue!
Ib. How the Camel Got His Hump

2 I keep six honest serving men
(They taught me all I knew);
Their names are What and Why and When
And How and Where and Who.
Ib. The Elephant's Child

3 The great gray-green, greasy Limpopo River, all set about with fever-trees.
Ib.

4 Rolling down to Rio.
Ib. The Beginning of the Armadilloes, st. 4

5 The Cat. He walked by himself, and all places were alike to him.
Ib. The Cat That Walked By Himself

6 He went through the wet wild woods, waving his wild tail, and walking by his wild lone. But he never told anybody. *Ib.*

7 Who hath desired the sea?—the sight of salt water unbounded.
The Sea and the Hills [1903], st. 1

8 So and no otherwise—hillmen desire their hills! *Ib.*

9 Something hidden. Go and find it. Go and look behind the Ranges—
Something lost behind the Ranges. Lost and waiting for you. Go![1]
The Explorer [1903], st. 2

10 Boots—boots—boots—boots—movin' up and down again!
There's no discharge in the war![2]
Boots [1903], st. 1

11 'Tisn't beauty, so to speak, nor good talk necessarily. It's just It. Some women'll stay in a man's memory if they once walked down a street.
Traffics and Discoveries [1904]. Mrs. Bathurst

12 Of all the trees that grow so fair,
Old England to adorn,
Greater are none beneath the Sun,
Than oak, and ash, and thorn.[3]
Puck of Pook's Hill [1906]. A Tree Song, st. 1

[1] Because it is there.—George Leigh Mallory [1886–1924], *when asked why he wanted to climb Mount Everest*
[2] See *Ecclesiastes 8:8*, 27:13.
[3] See Anonymous: Ballads, 926:20.

13 Enough work to do, and strength enough to do the work.
A Doctor's Work. [October 1908][4]

14 Brothers and Sisters, I bid you beware
Of giving your heart to a dog to tear.
The Power of the Dog [1909]

15 Take of English earth as much
As either hand may rightly clutch.
In the taking of it breathe
Prayer for all who lie beneath.
Rewards and Fairies [1910].[5] *A Charm, st. 1*

16 If you can meet with Triumph and Disaster
And treat those two impostors just the same.[6] *Ib. If, st. 2*

17 If you can talk with crowds and keep your virtue,
Or walk with Kings—nor lose the common touch. *Ib. st. 4*

18 Yours is the Earth and everything that's in it,
And—which is more—you'll be a Man, my son! *Ib.*

19 One man in a thousand, Solomon says,
Will stick more close than a brother.[7]
Ib. The Thousandth Man, st. 1

20 But the Thousandth Man will stand by your side
To the gallows foot—and after!
Ib. st. 4

21 The female of the species is more deadly than the male.
The Female of the Species [1911], st. 1

22 Oh, Adam was a gardener,[8] and God who made him sees
That half a proper gardener's work is done upon his knees. *Ib. st. 8*

23 For all we have and are,
For all our children's fate,
Stand up and take the war.
The Hun is at the gate!
For All We Have and Are [1914], st. 1

24 What stands if Freedom fall?
Who dies if England live? *Ib. st. 4*

[4] Address at Middlesex Hospital, where Kipling died in 1936.
[5] See Corbet, 262:14.
[6] Inscribed over the doors to the center court at Wimbledon.
[7] See *Ecclesiastes 7:28*, 27:11.
[8] See Bacon, 181:10; Shakespeare, 185:26 and 224:5; and Tennyson, 528:10.

1 Hot and bothered.
Independence. Rectorial Address at St. Andrews [October 10, 1923]

2 Never again will I spend another winter in this accursed bucketshop of a refrigerator called England.
Letter to Sidney Colvin. From E. V. LUCAS, *The Colvins and Their Friends [1928], p. 294*

3 When your Daemon is in charge, do not try to think consciously. Drift, wait, and obey.
Something of Myself for My Friends Known and Unknown [1937], ch. 8

Logan Pearsall Smith[1]
1865–1946

4 There are two things to aim at in life: first, to get what you want; and, after that, to enjoy it. Only the wisest of mankind achieve the second. *Afterthoughts [1931]*

5 How awful to reflect that what people say of us is true! *Ib.*

6 Solvency is entirely a matter of temperament and not of income. *Ib.*

7 The indefatigable pursuit of an unattainable perfection, even though it consist in nothing more than in the pounding of an old piano, is what alone gives a meaning to our life on this unavailing star. *Ib.*

8 What I like in a good author is not what he says, but what he whispers. *Ib.*

9 Thank heavens, the sun has gone in, and I don't have to go out and enjoy it. *Ib.*

Arthur Symons
1865–1945

10 And I would have, now love is over,
An end to all, an end:
I cannot, having been your lover,
Stoop to become your friend!
After Love [1892], st. 3

11 The gray-green stretch of sandy grass,
Indefinitely desolate;
A sea of lead, a sky of slate;
Already autumn in the air, alas!
One stark monotony of stone,
The long hotel, acutely white,
Against the after-sunset light
Withers gray-green, and takes the grass's tone.
Color Studies [1895]. At Dieppe

12 My soul is like this cloudy, flaming opal ring.
Opals [1896]

13 Here in a little lonely room
I am master of earth and sea,
And the planets come to me.
The Loom of Dreams [1900], st. 1

14 He knew that the whole mystery of beauty can never be comprehended by the crowd, and that while clearness is a virtue of style, perfect explicitness is not a necessary virtue.
The Symbolist Movement in Literature [1899]. Gérard de Nerval

15 Without charm there can be no fine literature, as there can be no perfect flower without fragrance. *Ib. Stéphane Mallarmé*

16 The mystic too full of God to speak intelligibly to the world. *Ib. Arthur Rimbaud*

17 Criticism is properly the rod of divination: a hazel switch for the discovery of buried treasure, not a birch twig for the castigation of offenders.
An Introduction to the Study of Browning [1906], preface

Herbert Trench
1865–1923

18 A circumnavigator of the soul.
Shakespeare, st. 4

William Butler Yeats[2]
1865–1939

19 The woods of Arcady are dead,
And over is their antique joy;
Of old the world on dreaming fed;
Gray Truth is now her painted toy.
Crossways [1889]. The Song of the Happy Shepherd, st. 1

20 Words alone are certain good. *Ib.*

21 Dream, dream, for this is also sooth.
Ib. last line

22 Down by the salley gardens my love and I did meet;

[1] Two weeks before his death, a friend asked him half jokingly if he had discovered any meaning in life. "Yes," he replied, "there is a meaning; at least, for me, there is one thing that matters—to set a chime of words tinkling in the minds of a few fastidious people."—CYRIL CONNOLLY [1903–1974], *A Tribute to Logan Pearsall Smith*, in *The New Statesman*

[2] Yeats was the greatest poet of our times . . . certainly the greatest in this language, and so far as I am able to judge, in any language.—T. S. ELIOT
See W. H. Auden, 868:11.

She passed the salley gardens with little snow-white feet.
She bid me take love easy, as the leaves grow on the tree;
But I, being young and foolish, with her would not agree.
Ib. Down by the Salley Gardens

1 She bid me take life easy, as the grass grows on the weirs;
But I was young and foolish, and now am full of tears. *Ib.*

2 The years like great black oxen tread the world,
And God the herdsman goads them on behind,
And I am broken by their passing feet.
The Countess Cathleen [1892] last lines

3 Red Rose, proud Rose, sad Rose of all my days!
Come near me, while I sing the ancient ways.
The Rose [1893]. To the Rose Upon the Rood of Time, st. 1

4 I will arise and go now, and go to Innisfree,
And a small cabin build there, of clay and wattles made:
Nine bean-rows will I have there, a hive for the honeybee,
And live alone in the bee-loud glade.
Ib. The Lake Isle of Innisfree,[1] *st. 1*

5 I hear it in the deep heart's core.
Ib. st. 3

6 A pity beyond all telling
Is hid in the heart of love.
Ib. The Pity of Love

7 The brawling of a sparrow in the eaves,
The brilliant moon and all the milky sky,
And all that famous harmony of leaves,
Had blotted out man's image and his cry.
Ib. The Sorrow of Love, st. 1

8 When you are old and gray and full of sleep,
And nodding by the fire, take down this book.[2] *Ib. When You Are Old, st. 1*

9 How many loved your moments of glad grace,
And loved your beauty with love false or true,
But one man loved the pilgrim soul in you,
And loved the sorrows of your changing face.
Ib. st. 2

[1] I had still the ambition, formed in Sligo in my teens, of living in imitation of Thoreau on Innisfree, a little island in Lough Gill, and when walking through Fleet Street very homesick I heard a little tinkle of water and saw a fountain in a shop window which balanced a little ball upon its jet, and began to remember lake water. From the sudden remembrance came my poem Innisfree.— *The Trembling of the Veil* [1926]

[2] See Ronsard, 162:12.

10 The Land of Faery,
Where nobody gets old and godly and grave,
Where nobody gets old and crafty and wise,
Where nobody gets old and bitter of tongue.
The Land of Heart's Desire [1894], l. 48

11 Land of Heart's Desire,
Where beauty has no ebb, decay no flood,
But joy is wisdom, time an endless song.
Ib. l. 373

12 All things uncomely and broken, all things worn out and old,
The cry of a child by the roadway, the creak of a lumbering cart,
The heavy steps of the plowman, splashing the wintry mold,
Are wronging your image that blossoms a rose in the deeps of my heart.
The Wind Among the Reeds [1899]. The Lover Tells of the Rose in His Heart, st. 1

13 And God stands winding His lonely horn,
And time and the world are ever in flight.
Ib. Into the Twilight

14 And pluck till time and times are done
The silver apples of the moon,
The golden apples of the sun.
Ib. The Song of Wandering Aengus, st. 3

15 Had I the heavens' embroidered cloths,
Enwrought with gold and silver light.
Ib. He Wishes for the Cloths of Heaven

16 But I, being poor, have only my dreams;
I have spread my dreams under your feet;
Tread softly because you tread on my dreams. *Ib.*

17 When I play on my fiddle in Dooney,
Folk dance like a wave of the sea.
Ib. The Fiddler of Dooney, st. 1

18 O heart! O heart! if she'd but turn her head,
You'd know the folly of being comforted.
In the Seven Woods [1904]. The Folly of Being Comforted

19 Never give all the heart, for love
Will hardly seem worth thinking of
To passionate women if it seem
Certain, and they never dream
That it fades out from kiss to kiss;
For everything that's lovely is
But a brief, dreamy kind delight.
Ib. Never Give All the Heart

20 I said, "A line will take us hours maybe;
Yet if it does not seem a moment's thought,

Our stitching and unstitching has been naught.
Better go down upon your marrow-bones
And scrub a kitchen pavement, or break stones."
Ib. Adam's Curse, st. 1

1 For to articulate sweet sounds together
Is to work harder than all these, and yet
Be thought an idler by the noisy set
Of bankers, schoolmasters, and clergymen
The martyrs call the world. *Ib.*

2 It's certain there is no fine thing
Since Adam's fall but needs much laboring.
Ib. st. 3

3 I heard the old, old men say,
"All that's beautiful drifts away
Like the waters."
Ib. The Old Men Admiring Themselves in the Water

4 The friends that have it I do wrong
When ever I remake a song
Should know what issue is at stake,
It is myself that I remake.
The Collected Works in Verse and Prose of William Butler Yeats [1908], II, preliminary poem

5 Why, what could she have done, being what she is?
Was there another Troy for her to burn?
The Green Helmet and Other Poems [1910]. No Second Troy

6 The fascination of what's difficult
Has dried the sap out of my veins, and rent
Spontaneous joy and natural content
Out of my heart.
Ib. The Fascination of What's Difficult

7 Wine comes in at the mouth
And love comes in at the eye;
That's all we shall know for truth
Before we grow old and die.
Ib. A Drinking Song

8 Though leaves are many, the root is one;
Through all the lying days of my youth
I swayed my leaves and flowers in the sun;
Now I may wither into the truth.
Ib. The Coming of Wisdom with Time

9 In dreams begins responsibility.[1]
Responsibilities [1914], epigraph (from an old play)

10 Pardon, old fathers.
Ib. preliminary poem

[1] In Dreams Begin Responsibilities.—DELMORE SCHWARTZ, *title of book of poems* [1938]

11 Was it for this the wild geese spread
The gray wing upon every tide;
For this that all that blood was shed,
For this Edward Fitzgerald died,
And Robert Emmet and Wolfe Tone,
All that delirium of the brave?
Romantic Ireland's dead and gone,
It's with O'Leary in the grave.
Ib. September 1913, st. 3

12 Be secret and exult,
Because of all things known
That is most difficult.
Ib. To a Friend Whose Work Has Come to Nothing

13 The uncontrollable mystery on the bestial floor.
Ib. The Magi, last line

14 I made my song a coat
Covered with embroideries
Out of old mythologies
From heel to throat;
But the fools caught it,
Wore it in the world's eyes
As though they'd wrought it.
Song, let them take it,
For there's more enterprise
In walking naked. *Ib. A Coat*

15 Upon the brimming water among the stones
Are nine-and-fifty swans.
The Wild Swans at Coole [1919]. The Wild Swans at Coole, st. 1

16 Unwearied still, lover by lover,
They paddle in the cold
Companionable streams or climb the air;
Their hearts have not grown old.
Ib. st. 4

17 Some burn damp faggots, others may consume
The entire combustible world in one small room.
Ib. In Memory of Major Robert Gregory, st. 11

18 What made us dream that he could comb gray hair? *Ib.*

19 A thought
Of that late death took all my heart for speech. *Ib. st. 12*

20 I know that I shall meet my fate
Somewhere among the clouds above;
Those that I fight I do not hate,
Those that I guard I do not love;
My country is Kiltartan Cross,
My countrymen Kiltartan's poor.
Ib. An Irish Airman Foresees His Death, l. 1

1 Nor law, nor duty bade me fight,
Nor public men, nor cheering crowds,
A lonely impulse of delight
Drove to this tumult in the clouds.

Ib. l. 9

2 And I may dine at journey's end
With Landor and with Donne.

Ib. To a Young Beauty, st. 3

3 Lord, what would they say
Did their Catullus walk that way?

Ib. The Scholars, st. 2

4 All the wild witches, those most noble ladies,
For all their broomsticks and their tears,
Their angry tears, are gone.

Ib. Lines Written in Dejection l. 4

5 I knew a phoenix in my youth, so let them have their day.

Ib. His Phoenix, refrain

6 Hands, do what you're bid:
Bring the balloon of the mind
That bellies and drags in the wind
Into its narrow shed.

Ib. The Balloon of the Mind

7 We have lit upon the gentle, sensitive mind
And lost the old nonchalance of the hand;
Whether we have chosen chisel, pen or brush,
We are but critics, or but half create.

Ib. Ego Dominus Tuus

8 Minnaloushe creeps through the grass
Alone, important and wise,
And lifts to the changing moon
His changing eyes.

Ib. The Cat and the Moon

9 All changed, changed utterly:
A terrible beauty is born.

Michael Robartes and the Dancer [1921]. Easter 1916, st. 1

10 Too long a sacrifice
Can make a stone of the heart.
O when may it suffice? *Ib. st. 4*

11 Nothing that we love overmuch
Is ponderable to our touch.

Ib. Towards Break of Day, st. 3

12 Turning and turning in the widening gyre
The falcon cannot hear the falconer;
Things fall apart; the center cannot hold;
Mere anarchy is loosed upon the world,
The blood-dimmed tide is loosed, and everywhere
The ceremony of innocence is drowned;
The best lack all conviction, while the worst
Are full of passionate intensity.

Ib. The Second Coming, st. 1

13 Now I know
That twenty centuries of stony sleep
Were vexed to nightmare by a rocking cradle,
And what rough beast, its hour come round at last,
Slouches towards Bethlehem to be born?[1]

Ib. st. 2

14 Imagining in excited reverie
That the future years had come,
Dancing to a frenzied drum,
Out of the murderous innocence of the sea.

Ib. A Prayer for My Daughter, st. 2

15 For such,
Being made beautiful overmuch,
Consider beauty a sufficient end,
Lose natural kindness and maybe
The heart-revealing intimacy
That chooses right, and never find a friend.

Ib. st. 3

16 It's certain that fine women eat
A crazy salad with their meat.

Ib. st. 4

17 In courtesy I'd have her chiefly learned;
Hearts are not had as a gift but hearts are earned. *Ib. st. 5*

18 And many a poor man that has roved,
Loved and thought himself beloved,
From a glad kindness cannot take his eyes.

Ib.

19 If there's no hatred in a mind
Assault and battery of the wind
Can never tear the linnet from the leaf.

Ib. st. 7

20 An intellectual hatred is the worst,
So let her think opinions are accursed.
Have I not seen the loveliest woman born
Out of the mouth of Plenty's horn,
Because of her opinionated mind
Barter that horn and every good
By quiet natures understood
For an old bellows full of angry wind?

Ib. st. 8

21 All hatred driven hence,
The soul recovers radical innocence
And learns at last that it is self-delighting,
Self-appeasing, self-affrighting,
And that its own sweet will is Heaven's will.

Ib. st. 9

22 That is no country for old men. The young
In one another's arms, birds in the trees
—Those dying generations—at their song,
The salmon-falls, the mackerel-crowded seas,
Fish, flesh, or fowl, commend all summer long

[1] See Heine, 482:3.

Whatever is begotten, born, and dies.
Caught in that sensual music all neglect
Monuments of unaging intellect.

The Tower [1928]. Sailing to Byzantium, st. 1

1 An aged man is but a paltry thing,
A tattered coat upon a stick, unless
Soul clap its hands and sing, and louder sing
For every tatter in its mortal dress.

Ib. st. 2

2 Consume my heart away; sick with desire
And fastened to a dying animal
It knows not what it is; and gather me
Into the artifice of eternity. *Ib. st. 3*

3 Once out of nature I shall never take
My bodily form from any natural thing,
But such a form as Grecian goldsmiths make
Of hammered gold and gold enameling
To keep a drowsy Emperor awake;
Or set upon a golden bough to sing
To lords and ladies of Byzantium
Of what is past, or passing, or to come.[1]

Ib. st. 4

4 What shall I do with this absurdity—
O heart, O troubled heart—this caricature,
Decrepit age that has been tied to me
As to a dog's tail?
Never had I more
Excited, passionate, fantastical
Imagination, nor an ear and eye
That more expected the impossible.

Ib. The Tower, I

5 Does the imagination dwell the most
Upon a woman won or a woman lost?

Ib. II, st. 13

6 The night can sweat with terror as before
We pieced our thoughts into philosophy,
And planned to bring the world under a rule,
Who are but weasels fighting in a hole.

Ib. Nineteen Hundred and Nineteen, I, st. 4

7 But is there any comfort to be found?
Man is in love and loves what vanishes,
What more is there to say? *Ib. st. 6*

8 O but we dreamed to mend
Whatever mischief seemed
To afflict mankind, but now
That winds of winter blow
Learn that we were crack-pated when we dreamed. *Ib. III, st. 3*

9 Come let us mock at the great
That had such burdens on the mind
And toiled so hard and late
To leave some monument behind,
Nor thought of the leveling wind.

Ib. V, st. 1

10 Mock mockers after that
That would not lift a hand maybe
To help good, wise or great
To bar that foul storm out, for we
Traffic in mockery. *Ib. st. 4*

11 Much did I rage when young,
Being by the world oppressed,
But now with flattering tongue
It speeds the parting guest.

Ib. Youth and Age

12 Odor of blood when Christ was slain
Made all Platonic tolerance vain
And vain all Doric discipline.

Ib. Two Songs from a Play, II, st. 1

13 Everything that man esteems
Endures a moment or a day.
Love's pleasure drives his love away,
The painter's brush consumes his dreams.

Ib. st. 2

14 Whatever flames upon the night
Man's own resinous heart has fed. *Ib.*

15 Locke sank into a swoon;
The Garden died;
God took the spinning-jenny
Out of his side. *Ib. Fragments, I*

16 A shudder in the loins engenders there
The broken wall, the burning roof and tower
And Agamemnon dead.

Ib. Leda and the Swan, st. 3

17 Labor is blossoming or dancing where
The body is not bruised to pleasure soul,
Nor beauty born out of its own despair,
Nor blear-eyed wisdom out of midnight oil.
O chestnut tree, great-rooted blossomer,
Are you the leaf, the blossom or the bole?
O body swayed to music, O brightening glance,
How can we know the dancer from the dance?

Ib. Among School Children, st. 8

18 The true faith discovered was
When painted panel, statuary,
Glass-mosaic, window-glass,
Amended what was told awry
By some peasant gospeler. *Ib. Wisdom*

19 Never to have lived is best, ancient writers say;
Never to have drawn the breath of life, never to have looked into the eye of day;

[1] I have read somewhere that in the Emperor's palace at Byzantium was a tree made of gold and silver, and artificial birds that sang.—YEATS's *note*

The second best's a gay goodnight and quickly turn away.[1]
From "Oedipus at Colonus," st. 3

1 That toil of growing up;
The ignominy of boyhood; the distress
Of boyhood changing into man;
The unfinished man and his pain.
The Winding Stair and Other Poems [1933]. A Dialogue of Self and Soul, II, st. 1

2 I am content to live it all again
And yet again, if it be life to pitch
Into the frog-spawn of a blind man's ditch.
Ib. st. 3

3 When such as I cast out remorse
So great a sweetness flows into the breast
We must laugh and we must sing,
We are blest by everything,
Everything we look upon is blest.
Ib. st. 4

4 But what is Whiggery?
A leveling, rancorous, rational sort of mind
That never looked out of the eye of a saint
Or out of a drunkard's eye.
Ib. The Seven Sages

5 Only God, my dear,
Could love you for yourself alone
And not your yellow hair.
Ib. For Anne Gregory, st. 3

6 Swift has sailed into his rest;
Savage indignation there
Cannot lacerate his breast,
Imitate him if you dare,
World-besotted traveler; he
Served human liberty.
Ib. Swift's Epitaph[2]

7 The intellect of man is forced to choose
Perfection of the life, or of the work,
And if it take the second must refuse
A heavenly mansion, raging in the dark.
Ib. The Choice, st. 1

8 The unpurged images of day recede;
The Emperor's drunken soldiery are abed;
Night resonance recedes, night-walkers' song
After great cathedral gong.
Ib. Byzantium, st. 1

9 At midnight on the Emperor's pavement flit
Flames that no faggot feeds, nor steel has lit.
Ib. st. 4

10 An agony of flame that cannot singe a sleeve.
Ib.

[1]See Theognis, 67:5; Sophocles, 75:13; Bacon, 181:19; and Auden, 868:7.
[2]See Swift, 323:25.

11 That dolphin-torn, that gong-tormented sea.
Ib. st. 5

12 No man has ever lived that had enough
Of children's gratitude or woman's love.
Ib. Vacillation, III, st. 1

13 Things said or done long years ago,
Or things I did not do or say
But thought that I might say or do,
Weigh me down, and not a day
But something is recalled,
My conscience or my vanity appalled.
Ib. V, st. 2

14 Homer is my example and his unchristened heart. *Ib. VIII*

15 Somewhere beyond the curtain
Of distorting days
Lives that lonely thing
That shone before these eyes
Targeted, trod like Spring.
Ib. Quarrel in Old Age, st. 2

16 I had wild Jack for a lover.
Ib. Words for Music Perhaps, V, Crazy Jane on God, st. 4

17 "Fair and foul are near of kin,
And fair needs foul," I cried.
"My friends are gone, but that's a truth
Nor grave nor bed denied."
Ib. VI, Crazy Jane Talks with the Bishop, st. 2

18 But Love has pitched his mansion in
The place of excrement
For nothing can be sole or whole
That has not been rent. *Ib. st. 3*

19 What were all the world's alarms
To mighty Paris when he found
Sleep upon a golden bed
That first dawn in Helen's arms?
Ib. XVI, Lullaby, st. 1

20 Speech after long silence; it is right,
All other lovers being estranged or dead . . .
That we descant and yet again descant
Upon the supreme theme of Art and Song:
Bodily decrepitude is wisdom; young
We loved each other and were ignorant.
Ib. XVII, After Long Silence

21 I carry the sun in a golden cup,
The moon in a silver bag.[3]
Ib. XIX, Those Dancing Days Are Gone

[3]"The sun in a golden cup" . . . though not "the moon in a silver bag," is a quotation from the last of Mr. Ezra Pound's *Cantos.*—W. B. YEATS, note in *The Winding Stair and Other Poems*

1 I gave what other women gave
That stepped out of their clothes,
But when this soul, its body off,
Naked to naked goes,
He it has found shall find therein
What none other knows.
Ib. A Woman Young and Old, IX, A Last Confession, st. 3

2 He that sings a lasting song
Thinks in a marrowbone.
A Full Moon in March [1935]. A Prayer for Old Age, st. 1

3 I pray—for fashion's word is out
And prayer comes round again—
That I may seem, though I die old,
A foolish, passionate man. *Ib. st. 3*

4 Whence had they come,
The hand and lash that beat down frigid Rome?
What sacred drama through her body heaved
When world-transforming Charlemagne was conceived?
Ib. Supernatural Songs, VIII, Whence Had They Come?

5 All perform their tragic play,
There struts Hamlet, there is Lear.
Last Poems [1936–1939]. Lapis Lazuli, st. 2

6 Heaven blazing into the head:
Tragedy wrought to its uttermost.
Though Hamlet rambles and Lear rages,
And all the drop-scenes drop at once
Upon a hundred thousand stages,
It cannot grow by an inch or an ounce.
Ib.

7 Their eyes mid many wrinkles, their eyes,
Their ancient, glittering eyes, are gay.
Ib. st. 5

8 If soul may look and body touch,
Which is the more blest?
Ib. The Lady's Second Song, st. 3

9 My temptation is quiet.
Here at life's end
Neither loose imagination,
Nor the mill of the mind
Consuming its rag and bone,
Can make the truth known.
Ib. An Acre of Grass, st. 2

10 Grant me an old man's frenzy,
Myself must I remake
Till I am Timon and Lear
Or that William Blake
Who beat upon the wall
Till Truth obeyed his call. *Ib. st. 3*

11 An old man's eagle mind. *Ib. st. 4*

12 Hurrah for revolution and more cannon-shot!
A beggar upon horseback lashes a beggar on foot.
Hurrah for revolution and cannon come again!
The beggars have changed places, but the lash goes on. *Ib. The Great Day*

13 You think it horrible that lust and rage
Should dance attention upon my old age;
They were not such a plague when I was young;
What else have I to spur me into song?
Ib. The Spur

14 John Synge, I and Augusta Gregory, thought
All that we did, all that we said or sang
Must come from contact with the soil, from that
Contact everything Antaeus-like grew strong.
Ib. The Municipal Gallery Revisited, st. 6

15 Think where man's glory most begins and ends,
And say my glory was I had such friends.
Ib. st. 7

16 Down the mountain walls
From where Pan's cavern is
Intolerable music falls.
Foul goat-head, brutal arm appear,
Belly, shoulder, bum,
Flash fishlike; nymphs and satyrs
Copulate in the foam.
Ib. News for the Delphic Oracle, st. 3

17 Like a long-legged fly upon the stream
His mind moves upon silence.
Ib. Long-Legged Fly, refrain

18 What shall I do for pretty girls
Now my old bawd is dead?
Ib. John Kinsella's Lament for Mrs. Mary Moore, refrain

19 Fifteen apparitions have I seen;
The worst a coat upon a coat-hanger.
Ib. The Apparitions, refrain

20 Players and painted stage took all my love,
And not those things that they were emblems of.
Ib. The Circus Animals' Desertion, II, st. 3

21 Now that my ladder's gone,
I must lie down where all the ladders start,
In the foul rag-and-bone shop of the heart.
Ib. III

22 Irish poets, learn your trade,
Sing whatever is well made.
Ib. Under Ben Bulben, V

1 Under bare Ben Bulben's head
In Drumcliff churchyard Yeats is laid.
Ib. VI

2 On limestone quarried near the spot
By his command these words are cut:
Cast a cold eye
On life, on death.
Horseman, pass by![1] *Ib.*

3 I am still of opinion that only two topics can be of the least interest to a serious and studious mood—sex and the dead.
The Letters of W. B. Yeats

4 If a poet interprets a poem of his own he limits its suggestibility. *Ib.*

5 We poets would die of loneliness but for women, and we choose our men friends that we may have somebody to talk about women with.
Ib. Letter to Olivia Shakespeare [1936]

6 In life courtesy and self-possession, and in the arts style, are the sensible impressions of the free mind, for both arise out of a deliberate shaping of all things and from never being swept away, whatever the emotion, into confusion or dullness.
Essays and Introductions [1961]. Poetry and the Tradition

George W. Young
fl. 1900

7 The lips that touch liquor must never touch mine!
The Lips That Touch Liquor, st. 5

George Ade
1866–1944

8 In uplifting, get underneath.
Fables in Slang [1899]. The Good Fairy

9 Stay with the procession or you will never catch up.
Forty Modern Fables [1901]. The Old-Time Pedagogue

10 Draw your salary before spending it.
Ib. The People's Choice

11 Last night at twelve I felt immense,
But now I feel like thirty cents.
The Sultan of Sulu [1902]. Remorse

12 But, R-e-m-o-r-s-e!
The water-wagon is the place for me;
It is no time for mirth and laughter,
The cold, gray dawn of the morning after![2]
Ib.

Tristan Bernard
1866–1947

13 To live happily with other people one should ask of them only what they can give.
L'Enfant Prodigue du Vesinet [1921]

14 Men are always sincere. They change sincerities, that's all.[3]
Ce Que l'On Dit aux Femmes [1922], act III

Gelett Burgess
1866–1951

15 I never saw a purple cow,
I never hope to see one;
But I can tell you, anyhow,
I'd rather see than be one.
The Purple Cow [1895]

16 Ah, yes, I wrote the "Purple Cow"—
I'm sorry, now, I wrote it!
But I can tell you, anyhow,
I'll kill you if you quote it.
Cinq Ans Après [1914]

Edmund Vance Cooke
1866–1932

17 Oh, a trouble's a ton, or a trouble's an ounce,
Or a trouble is what you make it,
And it isn't the fact that you're hurt that counts,
But only how did you take it.[4]
How Did You Die? st. 1

Harry Dacre
d. 1922

18 Daisy, Daisy, give me your answer, do!
I'm half crazy, all for the love of you!
It won't be a stylish marriage,
I can't afford a carriage,
But you'll look sweet upon the seat
Of a bicycle built for two!
Daisy Bell [1892]

[1] The last three lines are inscribed on Yeats's grave.

[2] See Byron, 460:23, and Dickens, 547:23.

[3] Les hommes sont toujours sincères. Ils changent de sincérité, voilà tout.

[4] See Rice, 773:3.

Thomas Lansing Masson
1866–1934

1 A Safe and Sane Fourth. *Slogan*

Beatrix Potter
1866–1943

2 Once upon a time there were four little Rabbits, and their names were—Flopsy, Mopsy, Cottontail, and Peter.
The Tale of Peter Rabbit [1902]

3 But don't go into Mr. McGregor's garden.
Ib.

4 No more twist!
The Tailor of Gloucester [1903]

5 The water was all slippy-sloppy in the larder and the back passage. But Mr. Jeremy liked getting his feet wet; nobody ever scolded him, and he never caught a cold.
The Tale of Mr. Jeremy Fisher [1906]

Henry J. Sayers
d. 1932

6 Ta-ra-ra-boom-de-ay!
Title of minstrel show number [1891], made famous by Lottie Collins [1892]

Lincoln Steffens
1866–1936

7 "So you've been over into Russia?" said Bernard Baruch, and I answered very literally, "I have been over into the future, and it works."[1]
Autobiography [1931], ch. 18

Sun Yat-sen[2]
1866–1925

8 It is only after mature deliberation and thorough preparation that I have decided upon the Program of Revolution and defined the procedure of the revolution in three stages. The first is the period of military government; the second, the period of political tutelage; and the third, the period of constitutional government.
The Three Phases of National Reconstruction [1918]

[1] On Steffens's return from the Bullitt mission [1919].
[2] From *Sources of Chinese Tradition* [1960], edited by William Theodore de Bary.

9 The Chinese people have only family and clan solidarity; they do not have national spirit . . . they are just a heap of loose sand. . . . Other men are the carving knife and serving dish; we are the fish and the meat.
China as a Heap of Loose Sand [1924]

10 China is now suffering from poverty, not from unequal distribution of wealth. Where there are inequalities of wealth, the methods of Marx can, of course, be used; a class war can be advocated to destroy the inequalities. But in China, where industry is not yet developed, Marx's class war and dictatorship of the proletariat are impracticable.
Capital and the State [1924]

11 In the construction of a country it is not the practical workers but the idealists and planners that are difficult to find.
Chung-shan Ch'üan-shu [1936], vol. II

Bert Leston Taylor
1866–1921

12 A bore is a man who, when you ask him how he is, tells you.
The So-Called Human Race [1922]

Herbert George Wells
1866–1946

13 The Time Machine.
Title of book [1895]

14 The past is but the beginning of a beginning, and all that is and has been is but the twilight of the dawn.
The Discovery of the Future [1901]

15 Nothing could have been more obvious to the people of the early twentieth century than the rapidity with which war was becoming impossible. And as certainly they did not see it. They did not see it until the atomic bombs burst in their fumbling hands.
The World Set Free [1914]

16 The catastrophe of the atomic bombs which shook men out of cities and businesses and economic relations, shook them also out of their old-established habits of thought, and out of the lightly held beliefs and prejudices that came down to them from the past.
Ib.

17 The War That Will End War.
Title of book [1914]

18 The professional military mind is by necessity an inferior and unimaginative mind; no

man of high intellectual quality would willingly imprison his gifts in such a calling.

The Outline of History [1920], ch. 40

1 The Great War and the Petty Peace.

Ib.

2 Human history is in essence a history of ideas. *Ib.*

3 Every one of these hundreds of millions of human beings is in some form seeking happiness. . . . Not one is altogether noble nor altogether trustworthy nor altogether consistent; and not one is altogether vile. . . . Not a single one but has at some time wept.

Ib.

4 Our true nationality is mankind.

Ib. ch. 41

5 Human history becomes more and more a race between education and catastrophe.

Ib.

6 Life begins perpetually. Gathered together at last under the leadership of man . . . unified, disciplined, armed with the secret powers of the atom and with knowledge as yet beyond dreaming, Life, forever dying to be born afresh, forever young and eager, will presently stand upon this earth as upon a footstool, and stretch out its realm amidst the stars.[1] *Ib.*

7 An artist who theorizes about his work is no longer artist but critic.

The Temptation of Harringay [1929]

8 In England we have come to rely upon a comfortable time lag of fifty years or a century intervening between the perception that something ought to be done and a serious attempt to do it.

The Work, Wealth and Happiness of Mankind [1931], ch. 11

9 The Shape of Things to Come.[2]

Title of book [1933]

A.E.
[George William Russell]
1867–1935

10 Our hearts were drunk with a beauty
Our eyes could never see.

Homeward Songs by the Way [1894]. The Unknown God

[1]See *Matthew 5:34–35*, 37:9; Pope, 336:19; and Day, 746:20.

[2]See Cicero, 98:21; Shakespeare, 226:5; Campbell, 443:14; and Shelley, 470:5.

Stanley Baldwin
1867–1947

11 When you think about the defense of England you no longer think of the chalk cliffs of Dover. You think of the Rhine. That is where our frontier lies today.

Speech in the House of Commons [July 30, 1934]

Julien Benda
1867–1956

12 Le Trahison des Clercs [The Treason of the Intellectuals]. *Title of book [1927]*

Enoch Arnold Bennett
1867–1931

13 The Old Wives' Tale.[3]

Title of novel [1908]

14 Being a husband is a whole-time job.

The Title [1918], act I

15 Pessimism, when you get used to it, is just as agreeable as optimism.

Things That Have Interested Me [1918]

16 The price of justice is eternal publicity.

Ib. Second Series [1923]

Vicente Blasco-Ibáñez
1867–1928

17 It was the roar of the real, the only beast [the crowd in the arena].

Sangre y Arena (Blood and Sand) [1908]

18 Los Cuatro Jinetes del Apocalipsis [The Four Horsemen of the Apocalypse].[4]

Title of book [1916]

Rubén Darío[5]
[Félix Rubén García-Sarmiento]
1867–1916

19 I seek a form that my style cannot discover,
a bud of thought that wants to be a rose.

Prosas Profanas y Otros Poemas (Profane Hymns and Other Poems) [1896]. I Seek a Form

[3]See *I Timothy 4:7*, 50:29.

A fool he is to believe the tales of an old wife. — ALEXANDER BARCLAY, *The Ship of Fools* [1508]

Old wives' foolish tales of Robin Hood. — NICHOLAS UDALL [1542]

[4]Phrase derived from the four allegorical horses in the Bible (Revelation 6:1–8).

See Rice, 773:6.

[5]Translated by LYSANDER KEMP.

1 The tree is happy because it is scarcely sentient;
the hard rock is happier still, it feels nothing:
there is no pain as great as being alive,
no burden heavier than that of conscious life.

Los Cisnes y Otros Poemas (The Swans and Other Poems) [1905]. Fatalidad (Fatality)

2 Pity for him who one day looks upon
his inward sphinx and questions it. He is lost.

Ib. Pity for Him Who One Day

3 The America of Moctezuma and Atahualpa,
the aromatic America of Columbus,
Catholic America, Spanish America,
the America where noble Cuauhtémoc said:
"I am not on a bed of roses"[1] — our America,
trembling with hurricanes, trembling with Love:
O men with Saxon eyes and barbarous souls,
our America lives. And dreams. And loves.
And it is the daughter of the Sun. Be careful.

Cantos de Vida y Esperanza (Songs of Life and Hope) [1905]. A Roosevelt (To Roosevelt)

Ernest Dowson
1867–1900

4 Last night, ah, yesternight, betwixt her lips and mine
There fell thy shadow,[2] Cynara! thy breath was shed
Upon my soul between the kisses and the wine;
And I was desolate and sick of an old passion,
Yea, I was desolate and bowed my head:
I have been faithful to thee, Cynara! in my fashion.[3]

Non Sum Qualis Eram Bonae Sub Regno Cynarae [1896],[4] st. 1

5 I have forgot much, Cynara! gone with the wind,[5]
Flung roses, roses riotously with the throng.

Ib. st. 3

6 I cried for madder music and for stronger wine,
But when the feast is finished and the lamps expire,
Then falls thy shadow, Cynara! the night is thine.

Ib. st. 4

[1]Often quoted: Am I, then, upon a bed of roses? Words of encouragement from CUAUHTÉMOC [c. 1495–1525], last Aztec emperor, to the prince of Tlacopán. Both were under torture when the Spanish conquerors were trying to find the Aztec treasure [1521].

[2]See T. S. Eliot, 805:17.

[3]See Cole Porter, 820:8.

[4]See Horace, *Odes IV, i, 3*, 108:10.

[5]See Rutebeuf, 139:8.

7 They are not long, the weeping and the laughter,
Love and desire and hate:
I think they have no portion in us after
We pass the gate.

They are not long, the days of wine and roses;
Out of a misty dream
Our path emerges for a while, then closes
Within a dream.

Vitae Summa Brevis Spem Nos Vetat Incohare Longam[6] [1896]

8 From troublous sights and sounds set free;
In such a twilight hour of breath,
Shall one retrace his life, or see,
Through shadows, the true face of death?

Extreme Unction [1896], st. 3

Finley Peter Dunne
[Mr. Dooley]
1867–1936

9 Life'd not be worth livin' if we didn't keep our inimies.

Mr. Dooley in Peace and in War [1898]. On New Year's Resolutions

10 Th' dead ar-re always pop'lar. I knowed a society wanst to vote a monyment to a man an' refuse to help his fam'ly, all in wan night.

Ib. On Charity

11 "I think," said Mr. Dooley, "that if th' Christyan Scientists had some science an' th' doctors more Christianity, it wudden't make anny diff'rence which ye called in — if ye had a good nurse."

Mr. Dooley's Opinions [1900]. Christian Science

12 No matther whether th' constitution follows th' flag or not, th' supreme coort follows th' iliction returns.

Ib. The Supreme Court's Decisions

13 I think a lie with a purpose is wan iv th' worst kind an' th' mos' profitable.

Ib. On Lying

14 Th' dimmycratic party ain't on speakin' terms with itsilf.

Ib. Mr. Dooley Discusses Party Politics

15 Th' raypublican party broke ye, but now that ye're down we'll not turn a cold shoulder to ye. Come in an' we'll keep ye — broke.

Ib.

[6]See Horace, 107:2.

1 Hogan's r-right whin he says: "Justice is blind." Blind she is, an' deef an' dumb an' has a wooden leg.

Ib. Cross-Examinations

2 No wan cares to hear what Hogan calls "Th' short an' simple scandals iv th' poor."

Ib.

3 'Twas founded be th' Puritans to give thanks f'r bein' presarved fr'm th' Indyans, an' . . . we keep it to give thanks we are presarved fr'm th' Puritans.

Ib. Thanksgiving

4 Vice . . . is a creature of such heejous mien . . . that th' more ye see it th' betther ye like it.

Ib. The Crusade Against Vice

5 Glory be, whin business gets above sellin' tinpinny nails in a brown paper cornucopy, 't is hard to tell it fr'm murther.

Ib. On Wall Street

6 "D' ye think th' colledges has much to do with th' progress iv th' wurruld?" asked Mr. Hennessy.

"D' ye think," said Mr. Dooley, "'tis th' mill that makes th' wather run?" *Ib.*

7 If ye live enough befure thirty ye won't care to live at all afther fifty.

Ib. Casual Observations

8 Among men, Hinnissy, wet eye manes dhry heart. *Ib.*

9 A fanatic is a man that does what he thinks th' Lord wud do if He knew th' facts iv th' case. *Ib.*

10 'Tis as hard f'r a rich man to enther th' kingdom iv Hiven as it is f'r a poor man to get out iv Purgatory. *Ib.*

11 Thrust ivrybody, but cut th' ca-ards.

Ib.

12 A man that'd expict to thrain lobsters to fly in a year is called a loonytic; but a man that thinks men can be tu-rrned into angels be an iliction is called a rayformer an' remains at large. *Ib.*

13 Miracles are laughed at be a nation that r-reads thirty millyon newspapers a day an' supports Wall sthreet. *Ib.*

14 Th' flag[1] floats free an' well guarded over th' govermint offices, an' th' cheery people go an' come on their errands—go out alone an' come back with th' throops. Iverywhere happiness, contint, love iv th' shtep-mother counthry, excipt in places where there ar-re people.

Observations by Mr. Dooley [1902]. The Philippine Peace

[1]The American flag in the Philippines.

15 If a man is wise, he gets rich, an' if he gets rich, he gets foolish, or his wife does. That's what keeps the money movin' around.

Ib. Newport

16 "Oh, well," said Mr. Hennessy, "we are as th' Lord made us."

"No," said Mr. Dooley, "lave us be fair. Lave us take some iv th' blame oursilves."

Ib.

17 But th' best thing about a little judicyous swearin' is that it keeps th' temper. 'Twas intinded as a compromise between runnin' away an' fightin'. Befure it was invinted they was on'y th' two ways out iv an argymint.

Ib. Swearing

18 I don't think we injye other people's sufferin', Hinnissy. It isn't acshally injyement. But we feel betther f'r it.

Ib. Enjoyment

19 "Ye know a lot about [raising children]," said Mr. Hennessy.

"I do," said Mr. Dooley. "Not bein' an author, I'm a gr-reat critic."

Dissertations by Mr. Dooley [1906]. The Bringing Up of Children

20 Th' old story iv th' ant an' th' grasshopper —th' ant that ye can step on an' th' grasshopper ye can't catch.

Ib. The Labor Troubles

21 It is his jooty to rigorously enforce th' rules iv th' Sinit. There ar-re none. Th' Sinit is ruled be courtesy, like th' longshoreman's union. *Ib. The Vice-President*

22 "Spare th' rod an' spile th' child," said Mr. Hennessy.

"Yes," said Mr. Dooley, "but don't spare th' rod an' ye spile th' rod, th' child, an' th' child's father."

Ib. Corporal Punishment

23 This home iv opporchunity where ivry man is th' equal iv ivry other man befure th' law if he isn't careful.

Ib. The Food We Eat

24 "Ye ra-aly do think dhrink is a nicissry evil?" said Mr. Hennessy.

"Well," said Mr. Dooley, "if it's an evil to a man, it's not nicissry, an' if it's nicissry it's an evil." *Ib. The Bar*

25 "He made [money]," said Mr. Dooley, "because he honestly loved it with an innocint affiction. He was thrue to it. Th' reason ye

have no money is because ye don't love it f'r itsilf alone. Money won't iver surrinder to such a flirt."

Mr. Dooley on Making a Will and Other Evil Necessities [1919]. On Making a Will

John Galsworthy

1867–1933

1 Nobody tells me anything.

Repeatedly spoken by James Forsyte in The Man of Property [1906] and In Chancery [1920]

2 Justice is a machine that, when someone has once given it the starting push, rolls on of itself. *Justice [1910], act II*

3 Summer—summer—summer! The soundless footsteps on the grass!

Indian Summer of a Forsyte [1918]

4 Public opinion's always in advance of the law. *Windows [1922], act I*

5 The value of a sentiment is the amount of sacrifice you are prepared to make for it. *Ib. II*

6 If you do not think about the future, you cannot have one.

Swan Song [1928], pt. II, ch. 6

7 A man of action forced into a state of thought is unhappy until he can get out of it. *Maid in Waiting [1931], ch. 3*

8 There's just one rule for politicians all over the world: Don't say in Power what you say in Opposition; if you do, you only have to carry out what the other fellows have found impossible. *Ib. 7*

9 One's eyes are what one is, one's mouth what one becomes.

Flowering Wilderness [1932], ch. 2

10 The beginnings and endings of all human undertakings are untidy, the building of a house, the writing of a novel, the demolition of a bridge, and, eminently, the finish of a voyage. *Over the River [1933], ch. 1*

11 How to save the old that's worth saving, whether in landscape, houses, manners, institutions, or human types, is one of our greatest problems, and the one that we bother least about. *Ib. 39*

Edith Hamilton

1867–1963

12 Great literature, past or present, is the expression of great knowledge of the human heart; great art is the expression of a solution of the conflict between the demands of the world without and that within.

The Greek Way [1930], ch. 1

13 They [the Greeks] were the first Westerners; the spirit of the West, the modern spirit, is a Greek discovery and the place of the Greeks is in the modern world. *Ib.*

14 To rejoice in life, to find the world beautiful and delightful to live in, was a mark of the Greek spirit which distinguished it from all that had gone before. It is a vital distinction. *Ib.*

15 "All things are to be examined and called into question. There are no limits set to thought." *Ib.*

16 "All things are at odds when God lets a thinker loose on this planet." *Ib.*

Charles Edward Montague

1867–1928

17 I was born below par to th' extent of two whiskies. *Fiery Particles [1923]*

Luigi Pirandello

1867–1936

18 Right You Are If You Think You Are [Cosi è se vi pare].

Title of play [1917; English version, 1922]

19 Six Characters in Search of an Author [Sei personaggi in cerca d'autore].

Title of play [1921; English version, 1922]

20 Life is a very sad piece of buffoonery, because we have . . . the need to fool ourselves continuously by the spontaneous creation of a reality (one for each and never the same for everyone) which, from time to time, reveals itself to be vain and illusory.

Autobiographical Sketch in Le Lettere, Rome [October 15, 1924][1]

21 As You Desire Me [Come tu mi vuoi].

Title of play [1930; English version, 1931]

Henry Lewis Stimson

1867–1950

22 The only way to make a man trustworthy is to trust him; and the surest way to make

[1] Translated by William Murray.

him untrustworthy is to distrust him and show your distrust.

The Bomb and the Opportunity [March 1946]

1 The only deadly sin I know is cynicism.

On Active Service in Peace and War [1948], introduction

Edward Bradford Titchener
1867–1927

2 Common sense is the very antipodes of science.

Systematic Psychology: Prolegomena [1929]

Harry Leon Wilson
1867–1939

3 I can be pushed just so far.

Ruggles of Red Gap [1915]

Wilbur Wright
1867–1912
and
Orville Wright
1871–1948

4 Success. Four flights Thursday morning. All against twenty-one-mile wind. Started from level with engine power alone. Average speed through air thirty-one miles. Longest fifty-nine seconds. Inform press. Home Christmas.

Telegram to the Reverend Milton Wright, from Kitty Hawk, N.C. [December 17, 1903]

Émile Auguste Chartier [Alain]
1868–1951

5 To think is to say *no.*

Le Citoyen contre les Pouvoirs

6 We prove what we want to prove, and the real difficulty is to know what we want to prove. *Système des Beaux-Arts [1920]*

7 Nothing is more dangerous than an idea, when it's the only one we have.

Libres-propos

Paul Claudel
1868–1955

8 You explain nothing, O poet, but thanks to you all things become explicable.

La Ville [1897], act I

9 The words I use
Are everyday words and yet are not the same!
You will find no rhymes in my verse, no
magic.
There are your very own phrases.

La Muse Qui Est la Grace [1910]

10 When man tries to imagine Paradise on earth, the immediate result is a very respectable Hell.

Conversations dans le Loir-et-Cher [1929]

Norman Douglas
1868–1952

11 You can tell the ideals of a nation by its advertisements.

South Wind [1917], ch. 7

12 No one can expect a majority to be stirred by motives other than ignoble. *Ib. 10*

13 No great man is ever born too soon or too late. *Ib. 13*

14 Many a man who thinks to found a home discovers that he has merely opened a tavern for his friends. *Ib. 24*

William Edward Burghardt Du Bois
1868–1963

15 The problem of the twentieth century is the problem of the color line.[1]

To the Nations of the World; address to Pan-African conference, London [1900]

16 Herein lies the tragedy of the age: not that men are poor—all men know something of poverty; not that men are wicked—who is good? Not that men are ignorant—what is truth? Nay, but that men know so little of men. *The Souls of Black Folk [1903]*

17 It is a peculiar sensation, this double-consciousness, this sense of always looking at one's self through the eyes of others. . . . One feels his two-ness—an American, a Negro; two souls, two thoughts, two unreconciled strivings; two warring ideals in one dark body, whose dogged strength alone keeps it from being torn asunder. *Ib.*

18 The cost of liberty is less than the price of repression.

John Brown [1909]. The Legacy of John Brown

19 Liberty trains for liberty. Responsibility is the first step in responsibility. *Ib.*

[1] See Frederick Douglass, 556:8 and 556:9.

1 The dark world is going to submit to its present treatment just as long as it must and not one moment longer.

Darkwater [1920]. The Souls of White Folk

2 The return from your work must be the satisfaction which that work brings you and the world's need of that work. With this, life is heaven, or as near heaven as you can get. Without this—with work which you despise, which bores you, and which the world does not need—this life is hell.

To His Newborn Great-Grandson; address on his ninetieth birthday [1958]

3 Believe in life! Always human beings will live and progress to greater, broader, and fuller life.

Last message to the world [written 1957]. Read at his funeral [1963]

Maxim Gorki[1]
[Aleksei Maksimovich Peshkov]
1868–1936

4 Former People [Creatures That Once Were Men]. *Title of story [1897]*

5 Let the storm rage ever stronger![2]

Song of a Stormy Petrel [1901]

6 Lies—there you have the religion of slaves and taskmasters.[3]

The Lower Depths [1903]

7 How marvelous is Man! How proud the word rings—Man! *Ib.*

8 In time I came to understand that out of the misery and murk of their lives the Russian people had learned to make sorrow a diversion, to play with it like a child's toy; seldom are they diffident about showing their happiness. And so, through their tedious weekdays, they made a carnival of grief; a fire is entertainment; and on a vacant face a bruise becomes an adornment.

Autobiography [1913]. Childhood

9 The proletarian state must bring up thousands of excellent "mechanics of culture," "engineers of the soul."[4]

Speech at the Writers' Congress [1934]

[1]Gorki, "the bitter one," was the writer's pseudonym for his first sketch in a Tiflis newspaper [1892].
[2]This became a rallying cry of the revolutionaries.
[3]The censor forbade this line to be spoken on the stage.
[4]Attributed to Stalin in conversation with Gorki [October 26, 1934].

10 The basic hero of our books should be labor; that is, man organized by the processes of labor. *Ib.*

Frank McKinney "Kin" Hubbard
[Abe Martin]
1868–1930

11 It's no disgrace t' be poor, but it might as well be.

Abe Martin's Sayings and Sketches [1915]

12 When a fellow says it hain't the money but the principle o' the thing, it's th' money.

Hoss Sense and Nonsense [1926]

13 Nobuddy ever fergits where he buried a hatchet.

Abe Martin's Broadcast [1930]

14 If capital an' labor ever do git t'gether it's good night fer th' rest of us. *Saying*

15 Now and then an innocent man is sent to the legislature. *Ib.*

Edward Verrall Lucas
1868–1938

16 The French never allow a distinguished son of France to lack a statue.

Wanderings and Diversions [1926]. Zigzags in France

17 Americans are people who prefer the Continent to their own country, but refuse to learn its languages.

Ib. The Continental Dictionary

18 People in hotels strike no roots. The French phrase for chronic hotel guests even says so: they are called dwellers *sur la branche.* *Ib. To Be Let or Sold*

19 There can be no defense like elaborate courtesy.

Reading, Writing and Remembering [1932]

William Tyler Page
1868–1942

20 I believe in the United States of America as a Government of the people, by the people, for the people; whose just powers are derived from the consent of the governed; a democracy in a republic, a sovereign Nation of many sovereign States; a perfect Union one and inseparable; established upon those principles of freedom, equality, justice and humanity for which American patriots sac-

rificed their lives and fortunes. I therefore believe it is my duty to my country to love it, to support its Constitution, to obey its laws, to respect its flag, and to defend it against all enemies. *The American's Creed*[1]

Edmond Rostand
1868–1918

1 A great nose indicates a great man—
Genial, courteous, intellectual,
Virile, courageous.
Cyrano de Bergerac [1897],[2] *act I*

2 Free fighters, free lovers, free spenders—
The Cadets of Gascoyne—the defenders
Of old homes, old names, and old splendors.
Ib. act II

3 I fall back dazzled at beholding myself all rosy red,
At having, I myself, caused the sun to rise.
Chantecler [1907], act II, sc. iii

4 It is at night that faith in light is admirable.
Ib.

Robert Falcon Scott
1868–1912

5 Had we lived, I should have had a tale to tell of the hardihood, endurance, and courage of my companions which would have stirred the heart of every Englishman. These rough notes and our dead bodies must tell the tale.[3]
Diary of the Terra Nova Expedition to the Antarctic.[4] *Message to the Public*

6 Blizzard bad as ever—Wilson and Bowers unable to start—tomorrow last chance—no fuel and only one or two of food left—must be near the end. Have decided it shall be natural—we shall march for the depot with or without our effects and die in our tracks.
Ib. Thursday, March 22 and 23, 1912

7 Every day we have been ready to start for our depot *eleven miles* away, but outside the door of the tent it remains a scene of whirling drift. I do not think we can hope for any better things now. We shall stick it out to the end, but we are getting weaker, of course, and the end cannot be far.

It seems a pity, but I do not think I can write more.

R. Scott

For God's sake look after our people.
Ib. Thursday, March 29, 1912 (last entry)

Luther Standing Bear[5]
1868–1939

8 Only to the white man was nature a "wilderness" and only to him was the land "infested" with "wild" animals and "savage" people. To us it was tame. Earth was bountiful and we were surrounded with the blessings of the Great Mystery. Not until the hairy man from the east came and with brutal frenzy heaped injustices upon us and the families that we loved was it "wild" for us. When the very animals of the forest began fleeing from his approach, then it was that for us the "Wild West" began.
Land of the Spotted Eagle [1933]

André Suarès
1868–1948

9 Heresy is the lifeblood of religions. It is faith that begets heretics. There are no heresies in a dead religion.[6] *Péguy*

William Allen White
1868–1944

10 Tinhorn politicians.
Emporia Gazette [October 25, 1901]

11 All dressed up, with nowhere to go.
Of the Progressive party in 1916, after Theodore Roosevelt retired from presidential competition

12 Put fear out of your heart. This nation will survive, this state will prosper, the orderly business of life will go forward if only men can speak in whatever way given them to utter what their hearts hold—by voice, by posted card, by letter, or by press. Reason never has failed men. Only force and oppression have made the wrecks in the world.
Emporia Gazette [July 27, 1922]

13 The talent of a meat-packer, the morals of a moneychanger and the manners of an undertaker.
Obituary of Frank A. Munsey [December 23, 1925]

[1] Adopted by the House of Representatives [April 3, 1918].
[2] Translated by Brian Hooker.
[3] Inscribed on the memorial to Captain Scott and his companions, Waterloo Place, London.
[4] Found by searching party [November 1912]. First published [1913] as *Scott's Last Expedition: Journals.*
[5] Chief of the Oglala Tribe of the Sioux Nation.
[6] See Tertullian, 126:3, and Unamuno, 705:18.

Laurence Binyon
1869–1943

1 They shall grow not old, as we that are left grow old:
Age shall not weary them, nor the years condemn.
At the going down of the sun and in the morning
We will remember them.
For the Fallen, st. 4

Neville Chamberlain
1869–1940

2 For the second time in our history, a British Prime Minister has returned from Germany bringing peace with honor.[1] I believe it is peace for our time.[2] . . . Go home and get a nice quiet sleep.
Address from 10 Downing Street, London [September 30, 1938], after returning from the Munich Conference

3 Hitler has missed the bus.
Speech in the House of Commons [April 4, 1940]

Mohandas Karamchand [Mahatma] Gandhi[3]
1869–1948

4 Nonviolence is the first article of my faith. It is also the last article of my creed.
Defense against charge of sedition [March 23, 1922]

5 The term *Satyagraha* was coined by me . . . in order to distinguish it from the movement then going on . . . under the name of Passive Resistance.

Its root meaning is "holding on to truth," hence "force of righteousness." I have also called it love force or soul force. In the application of *Satyagraha*, I discovered in the earliest stages that pursuit of truth did not permit violence being inflicted on one's opponent, but that he must be weaned from error by patience and sympathy. For what appears truth to the one may appear to be error to the other. And patience means self-suffering. So the doctrine came to mean vindication of truth, not by the infliction of suffering on the opponent, but on one's self.[4]
Ib.

6 Nonviolence and truth *(Satya)* are inseparable and presuppose one another. There is no god higher than truth.
True Patriotism: Some Sayings of Mahatma Gandhi [1939][5]

André Gide
1869–1951

7 Families, I hate you! Shut-in homes, closed doors, jealous possessions of happiness.[6]
Les Nourritures Terrestres (Fruits of the Earth) [1897], bk. IV

8 What another would have done as well as you, do not do it. What another would have said as well as you, do not say it; written as well, do not write it. Be faithful to that which exists nowhere but in yourself—and thus make yourself indispensable.
Ib. Envoi

9 Sin is whatever obscures the soul.[7]
La Symphonie Pastorale [1919]

10 The most decisive actions of our life . . . are most often unconsidered actions.
Les Faux Monnayeurs (The Counterfeiters) [1926]

11 Art begins with resistance—at the point where resistance is overcome. No human masterpiece has ever been created without great labor. *Poétique*

12 It is with noble sentiments that bad literature gets written.[8]
Letter to François Mauriac [1928]

Strickland Gillilan
1869–1954

13 Bilin' down 's repoort, wuz Finnigin!
An' he writed this here: "Musther Flannigan—
Off agin, on agin,
Gone agin.—FINNIGIN."
Finnigin to Flannigan, st. 6

14 Adam
Had 'em.
Lines on the Antiquity of Microbes[9]

[1] While we endeavor to maintain peace, I certainly should be the last to forget that if peace cannot be maintained with honor, it is no longer peace.—LORD JOHN RUSSELL, *speech at Greenock, Scotland* [September 19, 1853]
See Russell, 466:3, and Disraeli, 502:18.
[2] See *The Book of Common Prayer (English)*, 56:15.
[3] Mahatma: Great Soul.

[4] See Martin Luther King, 909:11.
[5] Edited by S. HOBHOUSE.
[6] Familles, je vous hais! foyers clos; portes refermées; possessions jalouses du bonheur.
[7] Le péché, c'est ce qui obscurcit l'âme.
[8] C'est avec de beaux sentiments qu'on fait de la mauvaise littérature.
[9] Said to be the shortest poem in the language.

Stephen Butler Leacock
1869–1944

1 He flung himself from the room, flung himself upon his horse and rode madly off in all directions.
Gertrude the Governess [1911]

2 By American literature in the proper sense we ought to mean literature written in an American way, with an American turn of language and an American cast of thought. The test is that it couldn't have been written anywhere else.
Mark Twain as National Asset [1932]

Edgar Lee Masters
1869–1950

3 All, all, are sleeping on the hill.
Spoon River Anthology [1915]. The Hill, refrain

4 Seeds in a dry pod, tick, tick, tick,
Tick, tick, tick, what little iambics,
While Homer and Whitman roar in the pines! *Ib. Petit, the Poet*

5 Degenerate sons and daughters,
Life is too strong for you—
It takes life to love life.
Ib. Lucinda Matlock

6 Out of me unworthy and unknown
The vibrations of deathless music.
Ib. Anne Rutledge

7 I am Anne Rutledge who sleep beneath these weeds,
Beloved in life of Abraham Lincoln.
Ib.

8 Immortality is not a gift,
Immortality is an achievement;
And only those who strive mightily
Shall possess it.
Ib. The Village Atheist

Henri Matisse
1869–1954

9 I want to reach that state of condensation of sensations which constitutes a picture.
Notes d'un Peintre [1908]

10 What interests me most is neither still life nor landscape, but the human figure. It is through it that I best succeed in expressing the almost religious feeling I have towards life. *Ib.*

William Vaughn Moody
1869–1910

11 This earth is not the steadfast place
We landsmen build upon;
From deep to deep she varies pace,
And while she comes is gone.
Gloucester Moors [1901], st. 4

12 Gigantic, willful, young,
Chicago sitteth at the northwest gates.
An Ode in Time of Hesitation [1901], st. 3

13 The spring-laden breeze
Out of the gladdening west is sinister
With sounds of nameless battle overseas.[1]
Ib. st. 7

14 O ye who lead,
Take heed!
Blindness we may forgive, but baseness we will smite. *Ib. st. 9*

Edwin Arlington Robinson
1869–1935

15 I would have rid the earth of him
Once, in my pride. . . .
I never knew the worth of him
Until he died. *An Old Story*

16 Life is the game that must be played.
Ballade by the Fire. Envoy

17 Like dead, remembered footsteps on old floors. *The Pity of the Leaves*

18 The saddest among kings of earth,
Bowed with a galling crown, this man
Met rancor with a cryptic mirth,
Laconic—and Olympian.
The Master: Lincoln

19 Miniver Cheevy, child of scorn,
Grew lean while he assailed the seasons;
He wept that he was ever born,
And he had reasons.
Miniver Cheevy [1910], st. 1

20 Miniver Cheevy, born too late,
Scratched his head and kept on thinking;
Miniver coughed and called it fate,
And kept on drinking. *Ib. st. 8*

21 I shall have more to say when I am dead.
John Brown

22 Art's long hazard, where no man may choose
Whether he play to win, or toil to lose.
Caput Mortuum

[1] The war in the Philippines.

1 Love that's wise
Will not say all it means.
Tristram [1927], pt. VII

2 Here where the wind is always north-northeast
And children learn to walk on frozen toes.
New England

3 Are you to pay for all you have
With all you are? *Cassandra, st. 12*

4 He glittered when he walked.
Richard Cory, st. 2

5 So on we worked, and waited for the light,
And went without the meat, and cursed the bread;
And Richard Cory, one calm summer night,
Went home and put a bullet through his head. *Ib. st. 4*

George Sterling
1869–1926

6 Thou art the star for which all evening waits.
Aldebaran at Dusk

William Strunk, Jr.
1869–1946

7 Omit needless words.
Vigorous writing is concise. A sentence should contain no unnecessary words, a paragraph no unnecessary sentences, for the same reason that a drawing should have no unnecessary lines and a machine no unnecessary parts. This requires not that the writer make all his sentences short, or that he avoid all detail and treat his subjects only in outline, but that every word tell.
The Elements of Style [1918], ch. 2, sec. 13

Booth Tarkington
1869–1946

8 There are two things that will be believed of any man whatsoever, and one of them is that he has taken to drink.
Penrod [1914], ch. 10

9 They were upon their great theme: "When I get to be a man!" Being human, though boys, they considered their present estate too commonplace to be dwelt upon. So, when the old men gather, they say: "When I was a boy!" It really is the land of nowadays that we never discover. *Ib. 26*

Frank Lloyd Wright
1869–1959

10 No house should ever be *on* any hill or on anything. It should be *of* the hill, belonging to it, so hill and house could live together each the happier for the other.
An Autobiography [1932]

Bernard Mannes Baruch
1870–1965

11 America has never forgotten—and will never forget—the nobler things that brought her into being and that light her path—the path that was entered upon only one hundred and fifty years ago. . . . How young she is! It will be centuries before she will adopt that maturity of custom—the clothing of the grave—that some people believe she is already fitted for.
Address on accepting The Churchman Award, New York [May 23, 1944]

12 Behind the black portent of the new atomic age lies a hope which, seized upon with faith, can work out salvation. . . . Let us not deceive ourselves: we must elect world peace or world destruction.
Address to the United Nations Atomic Energy Commission [June 14, 1946]

13 We are in the midst of a cold war[1] which is getting warmer.
Speech before the Senate Committee [1948]

Hilaire Belloc
1870–1953

14 Child! do not throw this book about;
Refrain from the unholy pleasure
Of cutting all the pictures out!
Preserve it as your chiefest treasure.
A Bad Child's Book of Beasts [1896], dedication

15 When people call this beast to mind,
They marvel more and more
At such a little tail behind,
So large a trunk before.
Ib. The Elephant

16 A smell of burning fills the startled air—
The Electrician is no longer there!
Newdigate Poem

[1] The phrase was first used by Baruch in 1947.

1 How slow the shadow creeps: but when 'tis past
How fast the shadows fall. How fast! How fast! *For a Sundial*

2 Loss and Possession, death and life are one,
There falls no shadow where there shines no sun. *Ib.*

3 And the men that were boys when I was a boy
Shall sit and drink with me.
The South Country, st. 10

4 Of courtesy, it is much less
Than courage of heart or holiness,
Yet in my walks it seems to me
That the Grace of God is in courtesy.
Courtesy

5 Do you remember an inn,
Miranda? *Tarantella*

6 I said to Heart, "How goes it?" Heart replied:
"Right as a Ribstone Pippin!" But it lied.
The False Heart

7 The chief defect of Henry King
Was chewing little bits of string.
Cautionary Tales [1907]. Henry King

8 "Oh, my friends, be warned by me,
That breakfast, dinner, lunch and tea
Are all the human frame requires . . ."
With that the wretched child expires.
Ib.

9 Matilda told such dreadful lies,
It made one gasp and stretch one's eyes;
Her aunt, who, from her earliest youth,
Had kept a strict regard for truth,
Attempted to believe Matilda:
The effort very nearly killed her.
Ib. Matilda

10 It happened that a few weeks later
Her aunt was off to the theater
To see that interesting play
The Second Mrs. Tanqueray. *Ib.*

11 For every time she shouted "Fire!"
They only answered "Little liar!"
And therefore when her aunt returned,
Matilda, and the house, were burned.
Ib.

12 Pale Ebenezer thought it wrong to fight,
But Roaring Bill (who killed him) thought it right. *The Pacifist*

13 When I am dead, I hope it may be said:
"His sins were scarlet,[1] but his books were read." *On His Books*

[1]See *Isaiah 1:18*, 28:30.

Benjamin Nathan Cardozo
1870–1938

14 What has once been settled by a precedent will not be unsettled overnight, for certainty and uniformity are gains not lightly to be sacrificed. Above all is this true when honest men have shaped their conduct on the faith of the pronouncement.
The Paradoxes of Legal Science [1928]

15 As I search the archives of my memory, I seem to discern six types or methods [of judicial writing] which divide themselves from one another with measurable distinctness. There is the type magisterial or imperative; the type laconic or sententious; the type conversational or homely; the type refined or artificial, smelling of the lamp,[2] verging at times upon preciosity or euphuism; the type demonstrative or persuasive; and finally the type tonsorial or agglutinative, so called from the shears and the pastepot which are its implements and emblem.
Law and Literature [1931]

16 [The Constitution] was framed upon the theory that the peoples of the several states must sink or swim together, and that in the long run prosperity and salvation are in union and not division.
Baldwin v. Seelig, 294 U.S. 511, 523 [1935]

17 Freedom of expression is the matrix, the indispensable condition, of nearly every other form of freedom.
Palko v. Connecticut, 302 U.S. 319, 327 [1937]

Arthur J. Lamb
1870–1928

18 Her beauty was sold for an old man's gold,
She's a bird in a gilded cage.
A Bird in a Gilded Cage [1900]

Sir Harry Lauder
1870–1950

19 Oh, it's nice to get up in the mornin',
But it's nicer to lie in bed. *Song*

20 Just a wee doch-an'-dorris
Before we gang awa' . . .
If y' can say

[2]See Pytheas, 90:12.

It's a braw brecht moonlecht necht,
Yer a' recht, that's a'. *Song*

1 Roamin' in the gloamin'. *Song*

2 I Love a Lassie. *Title of song*

Vladimir Ilyich Lenin [Vladimir Ilyich Ulyanov]

1870–1924

3 Political institutions are a superstructure resting on an economic foundation.
The Three Sources and Three Constituent Parts of Marxism [1913][1]

4 Every cook has to learn how to govern the state.
Will the Bolsheviks Retain Government Power? [1917]

5 The war is relentless: it puts the alternative in a ruthless relief: either to perish, or to catch up with the advanced countries and outdistance them, too, in economic matters.
The Impending Catastrophe and How to Fight It [1917]

6 Communism is Soviet government plus the electrification of the whole country.
New External and Internal Position and the Problems of the Party [1920]

7 When we say "the state," the state it is we, it is the proletariat, it is the advanced guard of the working class.
Speech [May 27, 1922]

8 It is true that liberty is precious — so precious that it must be rationed.
Attributed. Quoted by SIDNEY AND BEATRICE WEBB, *Soviet Communism: A New Civilization? [1936], p. 1036*

Amado Nervo

1870–1919

9 The literary man has a circle of the chosen few who read him and become his only public. . . . What more natural than that he should write for those who, even if they do not pay him, at least understand him?
Nuestra Literatura (Our Literature) [1899][2]

[1]Translated by MAX EASTMAN.
[2]Our literature: Mexican literature.

Roscoe Pound

1870–1964

10 The law must be stable, but it must not stand still.
Introduction to the Philosophy of Law [1922]

Saki [Hector Hugh Munro]

1870–1916

11 The cook was a good cook, as cooks go; and as cooks go she went.
Reginald [1904]. Reginald on Besetting Sins

12 Women and elephants never forget an injury. *Ib.*

13 I might have been a goldfish in a glass bowl for all the privacy I got.
Ib. The Innocence of Reginald

14 The Western custom of one wife and hardly any mistresses.
Reginald in Russia [1910]. A Young Turkish Catastrophe

15 Poverty keeps together more homes than it breaks up.
The Chronicles of Clovis [1911]. Esmé

16 Sredni Vashtar went forth,
His thoughts were red thoughts and his teeth
were white.
His enemies called for peace, but he brought
them death.
Sredni Vashtar the Beautiful.
Ib. Sredni Vashtar

17 The sacrifices of friendship were beautiful in her eyes as long as she was not asked to make them.
Beasts and Super-Beasts [1914]. Fur

18 A little inaccuracy sometimes saves tons of explanation.
The Square Egg [1924]. The Comments of Moung Ka

T. Laurence Seibert

fl. 1900

19 Casey Jones! Orders in his hand.
Casey Jones! Mounted to the cabin,
Took his farewell journey to that promised
land.
Casey Jones [1909]. Adapted from verses by WALLACE SAUNDERS,[3] *set to music by* EDDIE NEWTON

[3]Of the many versions of this traditional ballad, the most familiar is printed in CARL SANDBURG, *The Ameri-*

Stephen Crane

1871–1900

1 They were going to look at war, the red animal—war, the blood-swollen god.

The Red Badge of Courage [1895], ch. 3

2 It was surprising that Nature had gone tranquilly on with her golden process in the midst of so much devilment. *Ib. 5*

3 At times he regarded the wounded soldiers in an envious way. He conceived persons with torn bodies to be peculiarly happy. He wished that he, too, had a wound, a red badge of courage. *Ib. 9*

4 The red sun was pasted in the sky like a wafer. *Ib.*

5 He had fought like a pagan who defends his religion. *Ib. 17*

6 He had been to touch the great death, and found that, after all, it was but the great death. He was a man. *Ib. 24*

7 When it came night, the white waves paced to and fro in the moonlight, and the wind brought the sound of the great sea's voice to the men on shore, and they felt that they could then be interpreters.

The Open Boat [1898], last line

8 A man said to the universe:
"Sir, I exist!"
"However," replied the universe,
"The fact has not created in me
A sense of obligation."

War Is Kind [1899]. Fragment

William Henry Davies

1871–1940

9 What is this life if, full of care,
We have no time to stand and stare?[1]

Leisure

can Songbag [1927]. It begins: Come all you rounders, for I want you to hear / The story of a brave engineer. / Casey Jones was the rounder's name, / On a big eight-wheeler of a mighty fame.

To the memory of the locomotive engineer whose name as "Casey Jones" became a part of folklore and the American language. "For I'm going to run till she leaves the rail—or make it on time with the southbound mail." —*Inscription on monument to* JOHN LUTHER JONES [1864–1900], *in Calvary Cemetery, Jackson, Tennessee*

[1] See Browning, 545:23.

Theodore Dreiser

1871–1945

10 Our civilization is still in a middle stage, scarcely beast, in that it is no longer wholly guided by instinct; scarcely human, in that it is not yet wholly guided by reason.

Sister Carrie [1900]

11 I acknowledge the Furies, I believe in them, I have heard the disastrous beating of their wings. *To Grant Richards [1911]*

12 An American Tragedy.

Title of novel [1925]

13 Oh, the moon is fair tonight along the Wabash,
From the fields there comes the breath of new-mown hay;
Through the sycamores the candle lights are gleaming
On the banks of the Wabash, far away.

On the Banks of the Wabash, chorus[2]

Arthur Guiterman

1871–1943

14 Amoebas at the start
Were not complex;
They tore themselves apart
And started Sex. *Sex, st. 1*

15 Of all cold words of tongue or pen
The worst are these: "I knew him when—"[3]

Prophets in Their Own Country

Ralph Hodgson

1871–1962

16 'Twould ring the bells of Heaven
The wildest peal for years,
If Parson lost his senses
And people came to theirs,
And he and they together
Knelt down with angry prayers
For tamed and shabby tigers
And dancing dogs and bears,
And wretched, blind pit ponies,
And little hunted hares.

The Bells of Heaven

17 Time, you old gypsy man,
Will you not stay,
Put up your caravan
Just for one day?

Time, You Old Gypsy Man, st. 1

[2] Dreiser's brother Paul is credited with writing the song, but according to H. L. Mencken, Dreiser wrote the chorus.

[3] See Whittier, 513:14.

1 Oh, had our simple Eve
Seen through the make-believe!
Had she but known the
Pretender he was!
Out of the boughs he came,
Whispering still her name,
Tumbling in twenty rings
Into the grass. *Eve, st. 5*

2 How they all pitied
Poor motherless Eve! *Ib.*

3 Reason has moons, but moons not hers
Lie mirrored on her sea,
Confounding her astronomers,
But O! delighting me. *Reason*

4 I saw in vision
The worm in the wheat,
And in the shops nothing
For people to eat;
Nothing for sale in
Stupidity Street. *Stupidity Street*

James Weldon Johnson

1871–1938

5 Lift every voice and sing
Till earth and heaven ring,
Ring with the harmonies of Liberty.
Lift Every Voice and Sing [1900], st. 1

6 We have come over a way that with tears has been watered,
We have come, treading our path through the blood of the slaughtered. *Ib. st. 2*

7 The colored people of this country know and understand the white people better than the white people know and understand them.
The Autobiography of an Ex-Colored Man [1912], ch. 2

8 Every race and every nation should be judged by the best it has been able to produce, not by the worst. *Ib. 10*

9 O black and unknown bards of long ago,
How came your lips to touch the sacred fire?
How, in your darkness, did you come to know
The power and beauty of the minstrels' lyre?
O Black and Unknown Bards [1917], st. 1

10 And God stepped out on space,
And He looked around and said,
"I'm lonely—
I'll make me a world."
God's Trombones [1927]. The Creation, st. 1

11 And God smiled again,
And the rainbow appeared,
And curled itself around his shoulder.
Ib. st. 7

12 With his head in his hands,
God thought and thought,
Till he thought: I'll make me a man!
Ib. st. 10

13 Find Sister Caroline . . .
And she's tired—
She's weary—
Go down, Death, and bring her to me.
Ib. Go Down, Death, st. 5

14 It is from the blues that all that may be called American music derives its most distinctive characteristic.
Black Manhattan [1930], ch. 11

William McDougall

1871–1938

15 Psychologists must cease to be content with the sterile and narrow conception of their science as the science of consciousness, and must boldly assert its claim to be the positive science of mind in all its aspects and modes of functioning, or, as I would prefer to say, the positive science of conduct or behavior.
An Introduction to Social Psychology [1908]

Herbert George Ponting

1871–1935

16 On the outside grows the furside, on the inside grows the skinside;
So the furside is the outside, and the skinside is the inside.[1] *The Sleeping Bag*[2]

Marcel Proust

1871–1922

17 When from a long distant past nothing subsists, after the people are dead, after the things are broken and scattered, still, alone, more fragile, but with more vitality, more unsubstantial, more persistent, more faithful, the smell and taste of things remain

[1] He, to get the cold side outside, / Put the warm side fur side inside. / That's why he put the fur side inside, / Why he put the skin side outside, / Why he turned them inside outside.—*Anonymous, The Modern Hiawatha*

[2] For the *South Polar Times*, Midwinter Day [June 22, 1911], prepared by the men of Captain Robert Falcon Scott's last Antarctic expedition. Ponting was the photographer for the Scott expedition.

poised a long time, like souls, ready to remind us, waiting and hoping for their moment, amid the ruins of all the rest; and bear unfaltering, in the tiny and almost impalpable drop of their essence, the vast structure of recollection.

Remembrance of Things Past [1913–1926].[1] *Swann's Way*

1 Once I had recognized the taste of the crumb of madeleine soaked in her decoction of lime flowers which my aunt used to give me . . . immediately the old gray house upon the street, where her room was, rose up like the scenery of a theater. *Ib.*

2 In his younger days a man dreams of possessing the heart of the woman whom he loves; later, the feeling that he possesses the heart of a woman may be enough to make him fall in love with her. *Ib.*

3 What artists call posterity is the posterity of the work of art.

Ib. Within a Budding Grove, pt. I

4 Not only does one not retain all at once the truly rare works, but even within such works it is the least precious parts that one perceives first. Less deceptive than life, these great masterpieces do not give us their best at the beginning.[2] *Ib.*

5 The time which we have at our disposal every day is elastic; the passions that we feel expand it, those that we inspire contract it; and habit fills up what remains. *Ib.*

6 Like everybody who is not in love, he imagined that one chose the person whom one loved after endless deliberations and on the strength of various qualities and advantages.

Ib. Cities of the Plain, pt. I

7 We passionately long that there may be another life in which we shall be similar to what we are here below. But we do not pause to reflect that, even without waiting for that other life, in this life, after a few years we are unfaithful to what we have been, to what we wished to remain immortally. *Ib. II*

8 The bonds that unite another person to ourself exist only in our mind. Memory as it grows fainter relaxes them, and notwithstanding the illusion by which we would fain be cheated and with which, out of love, friendship, politeness, deference, duty, we cheat other people, we exist alone. Man is the creature that cannot emerge from himself, that knows his fellows only in himself; when he asserts the contrary, he is lying.

Ib. The Sweet Cheat Gone

9 We do not succeed in changing things according to our desire, but gradually our desire changes. The situation that we hoped to change because it was intolerable becomes unimportant. We have not managed to surmount the obstacle, as we were absolutely determined to do, but life has taken us round it, led us past it, and then if we turn round to gaze at the remote past, we can barely catch sight of it, so imperceptible has it become. *Ib.*

10 There is not a woman in the world the possession of whom is as precious as that of the truths which she reveals to us by causing us to suffer. *Ib.*

11 We are healed of a suffering only by experiencing it to the full. *Ib.*

12 Happiness is beneficial for the body but it is grief that develops the powers of the mind.

Ib. The Past Recaptured

13 Only through art can we get outside of ourselves and know another's view of the universe which is not the same as ours and see landscapes which would otherwise have remained unknown to us like the landscapes of the moon. Thanks to art, instead of seeing a single world, our own, we see it multiply until we have before us as many worlds as there are original artists. . . . And many centuries after their core, whether we call it Rembrandt or Vermeer, is extinguished, they continue to send us their special rays.

The Maxims of Marcel Proust [1948][3]

Ernest Rutherford

1871–1937

14 We cannot control atomic energy to an extent which would be of any value commercially, and I believe we are not likely ever to be able to do so.

Speech to the British Association for the Advancement of Science [1933]

[1] *À la Recherche du Temps Perdu,* translated by C. K. Scott Moncrieff, except the last section, *The Past Recaptured,* which was translated by Frederick A. Blossom.

[2] See Daniel Gregory Mason, 740:14.

[3] Edited and translated by Justin O'Brien.

John Millington Synge
1871–1909

1 What is the price of a thousand horses against a son where there is one son only?
Riders to the Sea [1904]

2 When I was writing *The Shadow of the Glen* I got more aid than any learning could have given me from a chink in the floor of the old Wicklow house where I was staying, that let me hear what was being said by the servant girls in the kitchen.
The Playboy of the Western World [1907], preface

3 May I meet him with one tooth and it aching, and one eye to be seeing seven and seventy divils in the twists of the road, and one old timber leg on him to limp into the scalding grave. There he is now crossing the strands, and that the Lord God would send a high wave to wash him from the world.[1]
Ib. act II

4 They're cheering a young lad, the champion playboy of the Western World.
Ib. III

5 A man who is not afraid of the sea will soon be drowned, he said, for he will be going out on a day he shouldn't. But we do be afraid of the sea, and we do only be drowned now and again.
The Aran Islands [1907]

6 There is no language like the Irish for soothing and quieting. *Ib.*

7 A translation is no translation, he said, unless it will give you the music of a poem along with the words of it. *Ib.*

8 I knew the stars, the flowers, and the birds,
The gray and wintry sides of many glens,
And did but half remember human words,
In converse with the mountains, moors, and fens.
Prelude [1910]

Paul Valéry
1871–1945

9 The folly of mistaking a paradox for a discovery, a metaphor for a proof, a torrent of verbiage for a spring of capital truths, and oneself for an oracle, is inborn in us.
Introduction to the Method of Leonardo da Vinci [1895][2]

10 Collect all the facts that can be collected about the life of Racine and you will never learn from them the art of his verse. All criticism is dominated by the outworn theory that the man is the cause of the work as in the eyes of the law the criminal is the cause of the crime. Far rather are they both the effects.
Ib.

11 The sea, the ever renewing sea![3]
Charmes [1922]. Le Cimetière Marin

12 The wind is rising . . . we must attempt to live.[4] *Ib.*

13 Poetry is simply literature reduced to the essence of its active principle. It is purged of idols of every kind, of realistic illusions, of any conceivable equivocation between the language of "truth" and the language of "creation." *Littérature [1930]*

14 An intelligent woman is a woman with whom one can be as stupid as one wants.
Mauvaises Pensées et Autres [1941]

15 The painter should not paint what he sees, but what will be seen. *Ib.*

16 That which has always been accepted by everyone, everywhere, is almost certain to be false. *Tel Quel [1943]*

17 God created man, and finding him not sufficiently alone, gave him a female companion so that he might feel his solitude more acutely. *Ib.*

18 The purpose of psychology is to give us a completely different idea of the things we know best. *Ib.*

19 Politeness is organized indifference.[5]
Ib.

Sir Norman Angell
1872–1967

20 The Great Illusion.
Title of book [1910] on the futility of war

Sir Max Beerbohm
1872–1956

21 Most women are not so young as they are painted. *A Defense of Cosmetics*

[1] May the grass grow at your door and the fox build his nest on your hearthstone. May the light fade from your eyes, so you never see what you love. May your own blood rise against you, and the sweetest drink you take be the bitterest cup of sorrow. May you die without benefit of clergy; may there be none to shed a tear at your grave, and may the hearthstone of hell be your best bed forever. — *Traditional Wexford curse*

[2] Translated by THOMAS MCGREEVY.

[3] La mer, la mer toujours recommencée!

[4] Le vent se lève . . . il faut tenter de vivre.

[5] La politesse, c'est l'indifférence organisée.

1 Zuleika, on a desert island, would have spent most of her time in looking for a man's footprint. *Zuleika Dobson [1911], ch. 2*

2 She was one of the people who say "I don't know anything about music really, but I know what I like."[1] *Ib. 9*

3 Of all the objects of hatred, a woman once loved is the most hateful. *Ib. 13*

4 All fantasy should have a solid base in reality. *Ib. Note to 1946 edition*

5 I have known no man of genius who had not to pay, in some affliction or defect either physical or spiritual, for what the gods had given him. *No. 2. The Pines*

6 It seems to be a law of nature that no man ever is loth to sit for his portrait. *Quia Imperfectum*

7 To say that a man is vain means merely that he is pleased with the effect he produces on other people. A conceited man is satisfied with the effect he produces on himself. *Ib.*

8 Strange, when you come to think of it, that of all the countless folk who have lived before our time on this planet not one is known in history or in legend as having died of laughter. *Laughter*

9 The past is a work of art, free of irrelevancies and loose ends. *Comment*

Léon Blum

1872–1950

10 Life does not give itself to one who tries to keep all its advantages at once. I have often thought morality may perhaps consist solely in the courage of making a choice. *On Marriage*

11 No government can remain stable in an unstable society and an unstable world. *À l'Échelle Humaine [1945]*

Patrick Reginald Chalmers

1872–1942

12 What's lost upon the roundabouts we pulls up
on the swings!
Roundabouts and Swings, st. 2

[1] Bromide no. 1.—GELETT BURGESS, *Are You a Bromide?* [1906]
See Thurber, 831:3.

Calvin Coolidge

1872–1933

13 There is no right to strike against the public safety by anybody, anywhere, any time. *Telegram to Samuel Gompers, president of the American Federation of Labor, on the Boston police strike [September 14, 1919]*

14 One with the law is a majority. *Speech [July 27, 1920]*

15 Inflation is repudiation. *Speech at Chicago [January 11, 1922]*

16 The chief business of the American people is business. *Speech to the American Society of Newspaper Editors [January 17, 1925]*

17 They hired the money, didn't they? *Referring to the European war debts [1925]*

18 I do not choose to run for President in 1928.[2] *Statement to reporters [August 2, 1927]*

19 I love Vermont because of her hills and valleys, her scenery and invigorating climate, but most of all because of her indomitable people. *Address from train platform, Bennington, Vermont [September 21, 1928]*

20 If you don't say anything, you won't be called on to repeat it. *Saying*

21 He said he was against it. *On being asked what a clergyman preaching on sin had said*

Edward Gordon Craig

1872–1966

22 That is what the title of artist means: one who perceives more than his fellows, and who records more than he has seen. *On the Art of the Theatre [1911]*

Paul Laurence Dunbar

1872–1906

23 It is not a carol of joy or glee,
But a prayer that he sends from his heart's
deep core . . .
I know why the caged bird sings!
Sympathy, st. 3

[2] See Rogers, 766:3.

1 Since thou[1] and those who died with thee for right
Have died, the Present teaches, but in vain!
Robert Gould Shaw

2 It's easy 'nough to titter w'en de stew is smokin' hot,
But hit's mighty ha'd to giggle w'en dey's nuffin' in de pot. *Philosophy*

Learned Hand
1872–1961

3 You may ask what then will become of the fundamental principles of equity and fair play which our constitutions enshrine; and whether I seriously believe that unsupported they will serve merely as counsels of moderation. I do not think that anyone can say what will be left of those principles; I do not know whether they will serve only as counsels; but this much I think I do know — that a society so riven that the spirit of moderation is gone, no court *can* save; that a society where that spirit flourishes, no court *need* save; that in a society which evades its responsibility by thrusting upon the courts the nurture of that spirit, that spirit in the end will perish.
The Contribution of an Independent Judiciary to Civilization [1942]

4 Justice, I think, is the tolerable accommodation of the conflicting interests of society, and I don't believe there is any royal road to attain such accommodations concretely.
From PHILIP HAMBURGER, *The Great Judge [1946]*

5 "I beseech ye in the bowels of Christ, think that ye may be mistaken."[2] I should like to have that written over the portals of every church, every school, and every courthouse, and, may I say, of every legislative body in the United States. I should like to have every court begin, "I beseech ye in the bowels of Christ, think that we may be mistaken."
Morals in Public Life [1951]

6 I had rather take my chance that some traitors will escape detection than spread abroad a spirit of general suspicion and distrust, which accepts rumor and gossip in place of undismayed and unintimidated inquiry.
Speech to the Board of Regents, University of the State of New York [October 24, 1952]

7 That community is already in the process of dissolution where each man begins to eye his neighbor as a possible enemy, where nonconformity with the accepted creed, political as well as religious, is a mark of disaffection; where denunciation, without specification or backing, takes the place of evidence; where orthodoxy chokes freedom of dissent; where faith in the eventual supremacy of reason has become so timid that we dare not enter our convictions in the open lists, to win or lose. *Ib.*

8 The mutual confidence on which all else depends can be maintained only by an open mind and a brave reliance upon free discussion. *Ib.*

John McCrae
1872–1918

9 In Flanders fields the poppies blow
Between the crosses, row on row.
In Flanders Fields [1915], st. 1

10 To you from failing hands we throw
The torch; be yours to hold it high.
Ib. st. 3

José Enrique Rodó
1872–1917

11 To govern is to populate, assimilating in the beginning, then educating and selecting.
Ariel [1900]

12 If one could say of utilitarianism that it is the word of the English spirit, the United States may be considered the incarnation of that word. *Ib.*

Bertrand Russell, Earl Russell
1872–1970

13 Thus mathematics may be defined as the subject in which we never know what we are talking about, nor whether what we are saying is true.
Recent Work on the Principles of Mathematics [1901]. In International Monthly, vol. 4, p. 84

14 Mathematics, rightly viewed, possesses not only truth, but supreme beauty — a beauty cold and austere, like that of sculpture, without appeal to any part of our weaker nature,

[1]Colonel Robert Gould Shaw, white commander of the Fifty-fourth Massachusetts regiment (first enlisted black regiment in the Civil War) died with many others of the regiment at Fort Wagner [July 18, 1863].
See C. W. Eliot, 617:6; William James, 650:13; and Robert Lowell, 893:12.

[2]See Oliver Cromwell, 272:18.

without the gorgeous trappings of painting or music, yet sublimely pure, and capable of a stern perfection such as only the greatest art can show.[1]

The Study of Mathematics [1902]

1 Mathematics takes us still further from what is human, into the region of absolute necessity, to which not only the actual world, but every possible world, must conform.

Ib.

2 It is preoccupation with possession, more than anything else, that prevents men from living freely and nobly.

Principles of Social Reconstruction [1917]

3 The psychology of adultery has been falsified by conventional morals, which assume, in monogamous countries, that attraction to one person cannot coexist with a serious affection for another. Everybody knows that this is untrue.

Marriage and Morals [1929], ch. 16

4 To fear love is to fear life, and those who fear life are already three parts dead.

Ib.

5 Fear is the main source of superstition, and one of the main sources of cruelty. To conquer fear is the beginning of wisdom.

An Outline of Intellectual Rubbish [1950]

6 Three passions, simple but overwhelmingly strong, have governed my life: the longing for love, the search for knowledge, and unbearable pity for the suffering of mankind.

Autobiography [1967], prologue

Ellery Sedgwick
1872–1960

7 Autobiographies ought to begin with Chapter Two.

The Happy Profession [1946], ch. 1

8 In America, getting on in the world means getting out of the world we have known before. *Ib.*

Carl Lotus Becker
1873–1945

9 Economic distress will teach men, if anything can, that realities are less dangerous than fancies, that fact-finding is more effective than fault-finding.

Progress and Power [1935]

[1]See Millay, 823:8.

10 The significance of man is that he is that part of the universe that asks the question, What is the significance of Man? He alone can stand apart imaginatively and, regarding himself and the universe in their eternal aspects, pronounce a judgment: The significance of man is that he is insignificant and is aware of it. *Ib.*

George Bennard
1873–1958

11 I will cling to the old rugged cross,
And exchange it some day for a crown.[2]

The Old Rugged Cross [1913], refrain

Guy Wetmore Carryl
1873–1904

12 Thank God for peace! Thank God for peace,
when the great gray ships come in!

When the Great Gray Ships Come In [New York Harbor, August 20, 1898], st. 4

Willa Sibert Cather
1873–1947

13 No one can build his security upon the nobleness of another person.

Alexander's Bridge [1912], ch. 8

14 There are only two or three human stories, and they go on repeating themselves as fiercely as if they had never happened before.

O Pioneers! [1913], pt. II, ch. 4

15 The history of every country begins in the heart of a man or a woman. *Ib.*

16 I like trees because they seem more resigned to the way they have to live than other things do. *Ib. 8*

17 I tell you there is such a thing as creative hate!

The Song of the Lark [1915], pt. I

18 Artistic growth is, more than it is anything else, a refining of the sense of truthfulness. The stupid believe that to be truthful is easy; only the artist, the great artist, knows how difficult it is. *Ib. VI*

[2]See *Matthew 10:38*, 39:5; Quarles, 267:10; and Penn, 314:9.

1 That is happiness; to be dissolved into something complete and great.[1]

My Antonia[2] *[1918], bk. I, ch. 2*

2 Winter lies too long in country towns; hangs on until it is stale and shabby, old and sullen. *Ib. II, 7*

3 Art, it seems to me, should simplify. That, indeed, is very nearly the whole of the higher artistic process; finding what conventions of form and what detail one can do without and yet preserve the spirit of the whole—so that all that one has suppressed and cut away is there to the reader's consciousness as much as if it were in type on the page.[3]

On the Art of Fiction [1920]

4 That irregular and intimate quality of things made entirely by the human hand.

Death Comes for the Archbishop [1927], bk. I, ch. 3

5 In New Mexico he always awoke a young man. . . . He had noticed that this peculiar quality in the air of new countries vanished after they were tamed by man and made to bear harvests . . . that lightness, that dry aromatic odor . . . one could breathe that only on the bright edges of the world, on the great grass plains or the sagebrush desert. . . . Something soft and wild and free; something that whispered to the ear on the pillow, lightened the heart, softly, softly picked the lock, slid the bolts, and released the prisoned spirit of man into the wind, into the blue and gold, into the morning, into the morning![4]

Ib. IX, 3

6 Only solitary men know the full joys of friendship. Others have their family; but to a solitary and an exile his friends are everything.

Shadows on the Rock [1931], bk. III, ch. 5

Arthur Chapman
1873–1935

7 Out where the handclasp's a little stronger,
Out where the smile dwells a little longer,
That's where the West begins.

Out Where the West Begins, st. 1

8 Where there's more of singing and less of sighing,
Where there's more of giving and less of buying,
And a man makes friends without half trying. *Ib. st. 3*

Colette
[Sidonie Gabrielle Colette]
1873–1954

9 Those pleasures so lightly called physical.

Mélanges

10 Whether you are dealing with an animal or a child, to convince is to weaken.

Le Pur et l'Impur [1932]

11 By means of an image we are often able to hold on to our lost belongings. But it is the desperateness of losing which picks the flowers of memory, binds the bouquet.

Mes Apprentissages [1936]

12 The day after that wedding night I found that a distance of a thousand miles, abyss and discovery and irremediable metamorphosis, separated me from the day before.

Noces [1945]

Walter de la Mare
1873–1956

13 Slowly, silently, now the moon
Walks the night in her silver shoon.

Silver

14 Here lies a most beautiful lady,
Light of step and heart was she;
I think she was the most beautiful lady
That ever was in the West Country.

An Epitaph

15 "Is there anybody there?" said the Traveler,
Knocking on the moonlit door;
And his horse in the silence champed the grasses
Of the forest's ferny floor.

The Listeners

16 "Tell them that I came, and no one answered,
That I kept my word," he said. *Ib.*

17 Look thy last on all things lovely,
Every hour—let no night
Seal thy sense in deathly slumber
Till to delight
Thou hast paid thy utmost blessing.

Fare Well, st. 3

18 Nought but vast sorrow was there—
The sweet cheat gone. *The Ghost*

[1] Inscribed on Willa Cather's grave in Jaffrey, New Hampshire.

[2] It lifts me to all my superlatives.—OLIVER WENDELL HOLMES, JR., *letter to Ferris Greenslet*

[3] See Hemingway, 845:13.

[4] The moment I saw the brilliant proud morning shine high up over the deserts of Santa Fe, something stood still in my soul, and I started to attend. . . . In the magnificent fierce morning of New Mexico one sprang awake, a new part of the soul woke up suddenly, and the old world gave way to a new.—D. H. LAWRENCE, *New Mexico, in Survey Graphic* [1931]

1 Who said "Peacock Pie"?
The old king to the sparrow:
Who said "Crops are ripe"?
Rust to the harrow.
The Song of the Mad Prince

2 Who said, "Ay, mum's the word"? *Ib.*

3 Poor Jim Jay
Got stuck fast
In Yesterday. *Jim Jay*

4 It's a very odd thing—
As odd as can be—
That whatever Miss T. eats
Turns into Miss T. *Miss T.*

5 Three jolly gentlemen,
In coats of red,
Rode their horses
Up to bed. *The Huntsmen*

6 Bang! Now the animal
Is dead and dumb and done.
Nevermore to peep again, creep again, leap again,
Eat or sleep or drink again, oh, what fun!
Hi!

Mark Fenderson
1873–1944

7 What's the use? Yesterday an egg, tomorrow a feather duster.
Caption of cartoon: The Dejected Rooster

Ford Madox [Hueffer] Ford
1873–1939

8 This is the saddest story I have ever heard.[1]
The Good Soldier [1915], first line

9 Only two classes of books are of universal appeal: the very best and the very worst.
Joseph Conrad [1924]

10 No more hope, no more glory, not for the nation, not for the world I dare say, no more parades. *No More Parades [1925]*

Lena Guilbert Ford
d. 1918

11 Keep the home fires burning,[2]
While your hearts are yearning;
Though your lads are far away
They dream of home.
There's a silver lining[3]
Through the dark cloud shining;
Turn the dark cloud inside out,
Till the boys come home.
Keep the Home Fires Burning [1915]

[1]See Robert Lowell, 892:11.
[2]First line attributed to Ivar Novello [1893–1951], who composed the music.
[3]See Wodehouse, 775:10.

William Christopher Handy
1873–1958

12 I hate to see the evenin' sun go down.
The St. Louis Blues [1914]

Otto Harbach
1873–1963

13 When a lovely flame dies,
Smoke gets in your eyes.
Roberta [1933]. Smoke Gets In Your Eyes

Daniel Gregory Mason
1873–1953

14 Art of any profundity can be appreciated only slowly, gradually, in leisurely contemplation.[4] *Artistic Ideals [1927]*

George Edward Moore
1873–1958

15 It appears to me that in Ethics, as in all other philosophical studies, the difficulties and disagreements, of which history is full, are mainly due to a very simple cause: namely to the attempt to answer questions, without first discovering precisely *what* question it is which you desire to answer.
Principia Ethica [1903], preface

Albert Jay Nock
1873–1945

16 All Souls College, Oxford, planned better than it knew when it limited the number of its undergraduates to four; four is exactly the right number for any college which is really intent on getting results.
Memoirs of a Superfluous Man [1943], III, ch. 3

17 Money does not pay for anything, never has, never will. It is an economic axiom as old as the hills that goods and services can be paid for only with goods and services.
Ib. 13

18 As sheer casual reading matter, I still find the English dictionary the most interesting book in our language. *Ib. IV, ch. 1*

[4]See Proust, 734:4.

Charles Péguy
1873–1914

1 Surrender is essentially an operation by means of which we set about explaining instead of acting.
Les Cahiers de la Quinzaine [1905]

2 Homer is new and fresh this morning, and nothing, perhaps, is as old and tired as today's newspaper.[1]
Note sur M. Bergson et la Philosophie Bergsonienne [1914]

3 Freedom is a system based on courage.
From HALÉVY, *Life of Charles Péguy*

Sime Silverman[2]
1873–1933

4 Wall Street Lays an Egg.
Headline announcing stock market crash [October 1929]

5 Sticks Nix Hicks Pix.
Headline, meaning that rural audiences do not care for motion pictures dealing with country themes

Alfred Emanuel Smith[3]
1873–1944

6 The kiss of death.
Alluding to Hearst's support of Ogden Mills, Smith's unsuccessful opponent for governor of New York State [1926]

7 Let's look at the record.
Campaign speeches [1928]

8 The Governor of New York State does not have to be an acrobat.
Speech in behalf of Franklin D. Roosevelt [1928]

9 Nobody shoots at Santa Claus.
Campaign speeches [1936]

10 No matter how thin you slice it, it's still baloney. *Ib.*

[1]Homère est nouveau ce matin, et rien n'est peut-être aussi vieux que le journal d'aujourd-hui.

[2]Silverman, who founded and edited the famous theatrical trade paper *Variety* [1905], had perhaps more influence on American slang than any man of his time.

[3]He is the Happy Warrior of the political battlefield. — FRANKLIN D. ROOSEVELT, *nominating speech, Democratic National Convention* [June 26, 1924]. See Wordsworth, 427:21.

Al Smith knew as much as any living man of the art of democratic government. — ELLERY SEDGWICK, *The Happy Profession* [1946], *ch. 17*

Henry Major Tomlinson
1873–1958

11 The sea is at its best at London, near midnight, when you are within the arms of a capacious chair, before a glowing fire, selecting phases of the voyages you will never make. *The Sea and the Jungle [1912]*

12 As to the sea itself, love it you cannot. Why should you? I will never believe again the sea was ever loved by anyone whose life was married to it. It is the creation of Omnipotence, which is not of humankind and understandable, and so the springs of its behavior are hidden. *Ib.*

13 The reader who is illuminated is, in a real sense, the poem.
Between the Lines [1930]

Maurice Baring
1874–1945

14 All theories of what a good play is, or how a good play should be written, are futile. A good play is a play which when acted upon the boards makes an audience interested and pleased. A play that fails in this is a bad play.
Have You Anything to Declare?

Charles Austin Beard
1874–1948
and
Mary Ritter Beard
1876–1958

15 At no time, at no place, in solemn convention assembled, through no chosen agents, had the American people officially proclaimed the United States to be a democracy. The Constitution did not contain the word or any word lending countenance to it, except possibly the mention of "We, the people," in the preamble . . . When the Constitution was framed no respectable person called himself or herself a democrat.
America in Midpassage [1939], ch. 17

Gordon Bottomley
1874–1948

16 When you destroy a blade of grass
You poison England at her roots.
To Ironfounders and Others

Arthur Henry Reginald Buller

1874–1944

1 There was a young lady named Bright,
Whose speed was far faster than light;
She set out one day
In a relative way,
And returned home the previous night.

Limerick. In Punch [December 19, 1923]

Gilbert Keith Chesterton

1874–1936

2 "The Christian ideal," it is said, "has not been tried and found wanting; it has been found difficult and left untried."

What's Wrong with the World [1910], pt. I, ch. 5

3 Nothing sublimely artistic has ever arisen out of mere art, any more than anything essentially reasonable has ever arisen out of pure reason. There must always be a rich moral soil for any great aesthetic growth.

A Defense of Nonsense [1911]

4 For the great Gaels of Ireland
Are the men that God made mad,
For all their wars are merry,
And all their songs are sad.

The Ballad of the White Horse [1911], bk. II

5 Every great literature has always been allegorical—allegorical of some view of the whole universe. *Ib. V*

6 The whole difference between construction and creation is exactly this: that a thing constructed can only be loved after it is constructed; but a thing created is loved before it exists.

Preface to DICKENS*, Pickwick Papers*

7 A good joke is the one ultimate and sacred thing which cannot be criticized. Our relations with a good joke are direct and even divine relations. *Ib.*

8 The world will never starve for wonders; but only for want of wonder.

Inscription, General Motors Building, Century of Progress Exposition, Chicago

9 Strong gongs groaning as the guns boom far
(Don John of Austria is going to the war);
Stiff flags straining in the night blasts cold
In the gloom black-purple, in the glint old gold;
Torchlight crimson on the copper kettle-drums,
Then the tuckets, then the trumpets, then the cannon, and he comes.

Lepanto [1915]

10 Cervantes on his galley sets the sword back in the sheath
(Don John of Austria rides homeward with a wreath).
And he sees across a weary land a straggling road in Spain,
Up which a lean and foolish knight forever rides in vain. *Ib.*

11 To an open house in the evening
Home shall men come,
To an older place than Eden
And a taller town than Rome.

The House of Christmas

12 Burn from my brain and from my breast
Sloth, and the cowardice that clings,
And stiffness and the soul's arrest:
And feed my brain with better things.

A Ballade of a Book Reviewer

13 Don't ever take a fence down until you know the reason why it was put up.[1]

Ascribed to Chesterton by John F. Kennedy in a 1945 notebook

14 St. George he was for England,
And before he killed the dragon
He drank a pint of English ale
Out of an English flagon.

The Englishman

15 Step softly, under snow or rain,
To find the place where men can pray;
The way is all so very plain
That we may lose the way.

The Wise Men

16 And Noah he often said to his wife when he sat down to dine,
"I don't care where the water goes if it doesn't get into the wine."

Wine and Water

17 I also had my hour;
One far fierce hour and sweet:
There was a shout about my ears,
And palms before my feet.

The Donkey

Sir Winston Spencer Churchill[2]

1874–1965

18 I pass with relief from the tossing sea of Cause and Theory to the firm ground of Result and Fact.

The Malakand Field Force [1898]

[1] See Robert Frost, 747:6.

[2] He mobilized the English language and sent it into

1 It is better to be making the news than taking it; to be an actor rather than a critic. *Ib.*

2 Nothing in life is so exhilarating as to be shot at without result. *Ib.*

3 There are men in the world who derive as stern an exaltation from the proximity of disaster and ruin, as others from success. *Ib.*

4 Victory is the beautiful, bright-colored flower. Transport is the stem without which it could never have blossomed.

The River War [1899]

5 Terminological inexactitude.

Speech in the House of Commons [February 22, 1906]

6 The maxim of the British people is "Business as usual."

Speech at the Guildhall [November 9, 1914]

7 Politics are almost as exciting as war, and quite as dangerous. In war you can only be killed once, but in politics many times.

Remark [1920]

8 By being so long in the lowest form [at Harrow] I gained an immense advantage over the cleverer boys. . . . I got into my bones the essential structure of the ordinary British sentence—which is a noble thing. Naturally I am biased in favor of boys learning English; I would make them all learn English: and then I would let the clever ones learn Latin as an honor, and Greek as a treat.

Roving Commission: My Early Life [1930]

9 It is a good thing for an uneducated man to read books of quotations. Bartlett's *Familiar Quotations* is an admirable work, and I studied it intently. The quotations when engraved upon the memory give you good thoughts. They also make you anxious to read the authors and look for more. *Ib.*

10 Come on now, all you young men, all over the world. You are needed more than ever now to fill the gap of a generation shorn by the war. You have not an hour to lose. You must take your places in life's fighting line. Twenty to twenty-five! These are the years! Don't be content with things as they are. "The earth is yours and the fullness thereof." Enter upon your inheritance, accept your responsibilities. *Ib.*

11 You will make all kinds of mistakes; but as long as you are generous and true, and also fierce, you cannot hurt the world or even seriously distress her. She was made to be wooed and won by youth. *Ib.*

12 Decided only to be undecided, resolved to be irresolute, adamant for drift, solid for fluidity, all-powerful to be impotent.[1]

While England Slept [1936]

13 Dictators ride to and fro upon tigers which they dare not dismount. And the tigers are getting hungry.[2] *Ib.*

14 I have watched this famous island descending incontinently, fecklessly, the stairway which leads to a dark gulf. *Ib.*

15 The German dictator, instead of snatching the victuals from the table, has been content to have them served to him course by course.

Speech on the Munich agreement, House of Commons [October 5, 1938]

16 That long [Canadian] frontier from the Atlantic to the Pacific Oceans, guarded only by neighborly respect and honorable obligations, is an example to every country and a pattern for the future of the world.

Speech in honor of R. B. Bennett, Canada Club, London [April 20, 1939]

17 I cannot forecast to you the action of Russia. It is a riddle wrapped in a mystery inside an enigma.

Radio broadcast [October 1, 1939]

18 For each and for all, as for the Royal Navy, the watchword should be, "Carry on, and dread nought."

Speech on traffic at sea, House of Commons [December 6, 1939]

19 I have nothing to offer but blood, toil, tears and sweat.[3]

First Statement as Prime Minister, House of Commons [May 13, 1940]

---

battle.—EDWARD R. MURROW, *I Can Hear It Now* [1933–1945]

Quoted by John F. Kennedy on conferring honorary citizenship on Churchill [April 9, 1963].

See Roosevelt and Churchill, 781.

[1] Of Stanley Baldwin's policies.

[2] He who rides a tiger is afraid to dismount.—WILLIAM SCARBOROUGH, *Chinese Proverbs* [1875], *no. 2082*

[3] Mollify it with thy tears, or sweat, or blood.—JOHN DONNE, *An Anatomy of the World* [1611], *I, 430–431*

Year after year they voted cent per cent, / Blood, sweat, and tear-wrung millions—why? for rent!—BYRON, *The Age of Bronze* [1823], *XIV*

See Prescott, 481:2, and Garibaldi, 509:7.

Their sweat, their tears, their blood bedewed the endless plain.—WINSTON S. CHURCHILL, *The Unknown War* [1931], referring to the armies of the czar before the Russian Revolution

Churchill referred to his promise of blood, toil, tears,

1 Victory at all costs, victory in spite of all terror, victory however long and hard the road may be; for without victory there is no survival. *Ib.*

2 We shall not flag or fail. We shall go on to the end. We shall fight in France, we shall fight on the seas and oceans, we shall fight with growing confidence and growing strength in the air, we shall defend our island, whatever the cost may be, we shall fight on the beaches, we shall fight on the landing grounds, we shall fight in the fields and in the streets, we shall fight in the hills; we shall never surrender.

Speech on Dunkirk, House of Commons [June 4, 1940]

3 If we open a quarrel between the past and the present, we shall find that we have lost the future.

Speech in the House of Commons [June 18, 1940]

4 Let us . . . brace ourselves to our duties, and so bear ourselves that if the British Empire and its Commonwealth last for a thousand years, men will still say: "This was their finest hour." *Ib.*

5 We shall defend every village, every town and every city. The vast mass of London itself, fought street by street, could easily devour an entire hostile army; and we would rather see London laid in ruins and ashes than that it should be tamely and abjectly enslaved.

Radio broadcast [July 14, 1940]

6 Never in the field of human conflict was so much owed by so many to so few.

Tribute to the Royal Air Force, House of Commons [August 20, 1940]

7 The British Empire and the United States will have to be somewhat mixed up together in some of their affairs for mutual and general advantage. For my own part, looking out upon the future, I do not view the process with any misgivings. *Ib.*

8 This wicked man Hitler, the repository and embodiment of many forms of soul-destroying hatred, this monstrous product of former wrongs and shame.

Radio broadcast [September 11, 1940]

and sweat in subsequent speeches on October 8, 1940, May 7 and December 2, 1941, and January 27 and November 10, 1942.

9 Death and sorrow will be the companions of our journey; hardship our garment; constancy and valor our only shield. We must be united, we must be undaunted, we must be inflexible.

Report on the war, House of Commons [October 8, 1940]

10 We are waiting for the long-promised invasion. So are the fishes.

Radio broadcast to the French people [October 21, 1940]

11 History with its flickering lamp stumbles along the trail of the past, trying to reconstruct its scenes, to revive its echoes, and kindle with pale gleams the passion of former days. What is the worth of all this? The only guide to a man is his conscience; the only shield to his memory is the rectitude and sincerity of his actions. It is very imprudent to walk through life without this shield, because we are so often mocked by the failure of our hopes and the upsetting of our calculations; but with this shield, however the fates may play, we march always in the ranks of honor.

Tribute to Neville Chamberlain, House of Commons [November 12, 1940]

12 I do not resent criticism, even when, for the sake of emphasis, it parts for the time with reality.

Speech in the House of Commons [January 22, 1941]

13 Here is the answer which I will give to President Roosevelt. . . . Give us the tools, and we will finish the job.

Radio broadcast [February 9, 1941]

14 This is one of those cases in which the imagination is baffled by the facts.

Remark in the House of Commons following the parachute descent in Scotland of Rudolf Hess [May 13, 1941]

15 The British nation is unique in this respect. They are the only people who like to be told how bad things are, who like to be told the worst.

Report on the war, House of Commons [June 10, 1941]

16 A vile race of quislings[1]—to use the new word which will carry the scorn of mankind down the centuries.

Speech at St. James's Palace, London [June 12, 1941]

[1] Vidkun Quisling, head of the Nasjonal Samling party in Norway, who cooperated and collaborated with the Nazis when Germany invaded Norway [April 9, 1940]. Quisling was executed [October 23, 1945].

1 The destiny of mankind is not decided by material computation. When great causes are on the move in the world . . . we learn that we are spirits, not animals, and that something is going on in space and time, and beyond space and time, which, whether we like it or not, spells duty.

Radio broadcast to America on receiving the honorary degree of Doctor of Laws from the University of Rochester, New York [June 16, 1941]

2 Hitler is a monster of wickedness, insatiable in his lust for blood and plunder. Not content with having all Europe under his heel, or else terrorized into various forms of abject submission, he must now carry his work of butchery and desolation among the vast multitudes of Russia and of Asia. The terrible military machine, which we and the rest of the civilized world so foolishly, so supinely, so insensately allowed the Nazi gangsters to build up year by year from almost nothing, cannot stand idle lest it rust or fall to pieces. . . . So now this bloodthirsty guttersnipe must launch his mechanized armies upon new fields of slaughter, pillage and devastation.

Radio broadcast on the German invasion of Russia [June 22, 1941]

3 We will have no truce or parley with you [Hitler], or the grisly gang who work your wicked will. You do your worst—and we will do our best.

Speech to the London County Council [July 14, 1941]

4 The V sign is the symbol of the unconquerable will of the occupied territories, and a portent of the fate awaiting the Nazi tyranny.

Message to the people of Europe on launching the V for Victory propaganda campaign [July 20, 1941]

5 Nothing is more dangerous in wartime than to live in the temperamental atmosphere of a Gallup Poll,[1] always feeling one's pulse and taking one's temperature.

Report on the war, House of Commons [September 30, 1941]

6 Never give in, never give in, never, never, never, never—in nothing, great or small, large or petty—never give in except to convictions of honor and good sense.[2]

Address at Harrow School [October 29, 1941]

[1] Dr. George H. Gallup founded the British Institute of Public Opinion in 1936.

[2] See Shakespeare, 235:18, and William Pitt, 351:5.

7 Do not let us speak of darker days; let us speak rather of sterner days. These are not dark days: these are great days—the greatest days our country has ever lived; and we must all thank God that we have been allowed, each of us according to our stations, to play a part in making these days memorable in the history of our race. *Ib.*

8 In the past we have had a light which flickered, in the present we have a light which flames, and in the future there will be a light which shines over all the land and sea.

Speech on war with Japan, House of Commons [December 8, 1941]

9 What kind of people do they [the Japanese] think we are?

Speech to the U.S. Congress [December 26, 1941]

10 We have not journeyed all this way across the centuries, across the oceans, across the mountains, across the prairies, because we are made of sugar candy.

Speech to the Canadian Senate and House of Commons, Ottawa [December 30, 1941]

11 This is no time to speak of the hopes of the future, or the broader world which lies beyond our struggles and our victory. We have to win that world for our children. We have to win it by our sacrifices. We have not won it yet. The crisis is upon us. . . . In this strange, terrible world war there is a place for everyone, man and woman, old and young, hale and halt; service in a thousand forms is open. There is no room now for the dilettante, the weakling, for the shirker, or the sluggard. The mine, the factory, the dockyard, the salt sea waves, the fields to till, the home, the hospital, the chair of the scientist, the pulpit of the preacher—from the highest to the humblest tasks, all are of equal honor; all have their part to play. *Ib.*

12 When I warned [the French] that Britain would fight on alone whatever they did, their generals told their prime minister and his divided cabinet, "In three weeks England will have her neck wrung like a chicken." Some chicken; some neck. *Ib.*

13 The late M. Venizelos[3] observed that in all her wars England—he should have said Britain, of course—always wins one battle—the last.

Speech at the Lord Mayor's Day Luncheon, London [November 10, 1942]

[3] Eleutherios Venizelos [1864–1936], Greek statesman.

1 Now this is not the end. It is not even the beginning of the end.[1] But it is, perhaps, the end of the beginning. *Ib.*

2 I have not become the King's First Minister in order to preside over the liquidation of the British Empire. *Ib.*

3 The soft underbelly of the Axis.
Report on the war, House of Commons [November 11, 1942]

4 There was a man who sold a hyena skin while the beast still lived and who was killed in hunting it.
Speech on Allied war gains, House of Commons [August 2, 1944]

5 "Not in vain" may be the pride of those who survived and the epitaph of those who fell.[2]
Speech in the House of Commons [September 28, 1944]

6 The United States is a land of free speech. Nowhere is speech freer — not even here where we sedulously cultivate it even in its most repulsive form. *Ib.*

7 He [President Franklin D. Roosevelt] died in harness, and we may well say in battle harness, like his soldiers, sailors and airmen who died side by side with ours and carrying out their tasks to the end all over the world. What an enviable death was his.
Speech in the House of Commons [April 17, 1945]

8 I think "No comment" is a splendid expression. I am using it again and again. I got it from Sumner Welles.
To reporters at the Washington airport, after conferring with President Truman at the White House [February 12, 1946]

9 From Stettin in the Baltic to Trieste in the Adriatic an iron curtain[3] has descended across the Continent.
Address at Westminster College, Fulton, Missouri [March 5, 1946]

10 This address to which I have given the title, "The Sinews of Peace."[4] *Ib.*

11 In War: Resolution. In Defeat: Defiance. In Victory: Magnanimity. In Peace: Good Will.
The Second World War: Moral of the Work, vol. I, The Gathering Storm [1948]

12 No one can guarantee success in war, but only deserve it.
Ib. II, Their Finest Hour [1949]

13 When you have to kill a man it costs nothing to be polite.
Ib. III, The Grand Alliance [1950]

14 Everyone has his day and some days last longer than others.
Speech in the House of Commons [January 1952]

15 A fanatic is one who can't change his mind and won't change the subject. *Saying*

16 The inherent vice of capitalism is the unequal sharing of blessings; the inherent virtue of socialism is the equal sharing of miseries. *Ib.*

17 Short words are best and the old words when short are best of all. *Ib.*

18 It is hard, if not impossible, to snub a beautiful woman — they remain beautiful and the rebuke recoils. *Ib.*

19 This is the sort of English up with which I will not put. *Attributed*

Clarence Day

1874–1935

20 It is possible that our race may be an accident, in a meaningless universe, living its brief life uncared for, on this dark, cooling star: but even so — and all the more — what

[1] See Talleyrand, 400:17.

[2] The eight thousand paratroopers of the First British Airborne Division who landed in Arnhem, Holland, behind the German lines and held the area for nine days and nights, with a loss of six thousand [September 1944]. Major General R. E. Urquhart, the division commander, radioed to Field Marshal Bernard Montgomery: All will be ordered to break out rather than surrender.

[3] Between them [Germany] and me there is now a bloody iron curtain which has descended forever! — QUEEN ELIZABETH OF BELGIUM [1876–1965], *in 1914*. Though German-born, she stood staunchly by her adopted country in World War I.

France . . . a nation of forty millions with a deep-rooted grievance and an iron curtain at its frontier. — GEORGE WASHINGTON CRILE, *A Mechanistic View of War and Peace* [1915]

With a rumble and a roar, an iron curtain is descending on Russian history. — VASILI ROZANOV, *Apocalypse of Our Time* [1918]

We were behind the "iron curtain" at last. — ETHEL ANNAKIN SNOWDEN, *Through Bolshevik Russia* [1920]

The Nazi minister of enlightenment and propaganda, Dr. Josef Goebbels [1897–1945], used the phrase "iron curtain" in reference to the USSR in *Das Reich* [February 23, 1945].

Churchill used it — not publicly — in a top-secret telegram to President Truman [May 12, 1945].

[4] See Cicero, 99:11.

marvelous creatures we are! What fairy story, what tale from the Arabian Nights of the jinns, is a hundredth part as wonderful as this true fairy story of simians! It is so much more heartening, too, than the tales we invent. A universe capable of giving birth to many such accidents is—blind or not—a good world to live in, a promising universe. . . . We once thought we lived on God's footstool; it may be a throne.[1]

This Simian World [1920]. XIX

Robert Frost

1874–1963

1 They would not find me changed from him they knew—
Only more sure of all I thought was true.
Into My Own [1913], st. 4

2 Ah, when to the heart of man
Was it ever less than a treason
To go with the drift of things,
To yield with a grace to reason,
And bow and accept the end
Of a love or a season?[2]
Reluctance [1913], st. 4

3 I'm going out to clean the pasture spring;
I'll only stop to rake the leaves away
(And wait to watch the water clear, I may):
I shan't be gone long.—You come too.
The Pasture [1914], st. 1

4 Something there is that doesn't love a wall.
Mending Wall [1914]

5 My apple trees will never get across
And eat the cones under his pines, I tell him.
He only says, "Good fences make good neighbors."[3]
Ib.

6 Before I built a wall I'd ask to know
What I was walling in or walling out.[4]
Ib.

7 And nothing to look backward to with pride,
And nothing to look forward to with hope.
The Death of the Hired Man [1914]

8 Home is the place where, when you have to go there,
They have to take you in.
Ib.

9 The nearest friends can go
With anyone to death, comes so far short
They might as well not try to go at all.
Home Burial [1914]

[1] See *Matthew 5:34–35*, 37:9; Pope, 336:19; and H. G. Wells, 720:6.

[2] See Pope, 339:29.

[3] See Herbert, 269:19.

[4] See Chesterton, 742:13.

10 Most of the change we think we see in life
Is due to truths being in and out of favor.
The Black Cottage [1914]

11 The best way out is always through.
A Servant to Servants [1914]

12 Pressed into service means pressed out of shape.
The Self-Seeker [1914]

13 I shall be telling this with a sigh
Somewhere ages and ages hence:
Two roads diverged in a wood, and I—
I took the one less traveled by,
And that has made all the difference.
The Road Not Taken [1916], st. 4

14 The Hyla breed
That shouted in the mist a month ago,
Like ghost of sleighbells in a ghost of snow.
Hyla Brook [1916]

15 We love the things we love for what they are.
Ib.

16 I'd like to get away from earth awhile
And then come back to it and begin over.
May no fate willfully misunderstand me
And half grant what I wish and snatch me away
Not to return. Earth's the right place for love:
I don't know where it's likely to go better.
Birches [1916]

17 One could do worse than be a swinger of birches.
Ib.

18 I shall set forth for somewhere,
I shall make the reckless choice
Some say when they are in voice
And tossing so as to scare
The white clouds over them on,
I shall have less to say,
But I shall be gone.
The Sound of the Trees [1916]

19 Do you know,
Considering the market, there are more
Poems produced than any other thing?
No wonder poets sometimes have to *seem*
So much more businesslike than businessmen.
Their wares are so much harder to get rid of.
New Hampshire [1923]

20 The Vermont mountains stretch extended straight;
New Hampshire mountains curl up in a coil.
Ib.

21 The snake stood up for evil in the Garden.
The Ax-Helve [1923]

1 Why make so much of fragmentary blue
In here and there a bird, or butterfly,
Or flower, or wearing-stone, or open eye,
When heaven presents in sheets the solid hue?
Fragmentary Blue [1923], st. 1

2 Some say the world will end in fire,
Some say in ice.
From what I've tasted of desire
I hold with those who favor fire.
But if it had to perish twice,
I think I know enough of hate
To say that for destruction ice
Is also great
And would suffice.
Fire and Ice[1] *[1923]*

3 The way a crow
Shook down on me
The dust of snow
From a hemlock tree

Has given my heart
A change of mood
And saved some part
Of a day I had rued.
Dust of Snow [1923]

4 We heard the miniature thunder where he fled. *The Runaway [1923]*

5 Whose woods these are I think I know.
His house is in the village though;
He will not see me stopping here
To watch his woods fill up with snow.
Stopping by Woods on a Snowy Evening [1923], st. 1

6 My little horse must think it queer
To stop without a farmhouse near.
Ib. st. 2

7 The woods are lovely, dark and deep.
But I have promises to keep,
And miles to go before I sleep,[2]
And miles to go before I sleep.
Ib. st. 4

8 Love at the lips was touch
As sweet as I could bear;
And once that seemed too much;
I lived on air.
To Earthward [1923], st. 1

9 Now no joy but lacks salt
That is not dashed with pain
And weariness and fault;
I crave the stain

Of tears, the aftermark
Of almost too much love,
The sweet of bitter bark
And burning clove. *Ib. st. 5, 6*

10 Keep cold, young orchard. Goodbye and keep cold.
Dread fifty above more than fifty below.
Goodbye and Keep Cold [1923]

11 It looked as if a night of dark intent
Was coming, and not only a night, an age.
Someone had better be prepared for rage.
There would be more than ocean-water broken
Before God's last *Put out the Light* was spoken.
Once by the Pacific [1928]

12 Tree at my window, window tree,
My sash is lowered when night comes on;
But let there never be curtain drawn
Between you and me.
Tree at My Window [1928], st. 1

13 That day she put our heads together,
Fate had her imagination about her,
Your head so much concerned with outer,
Mine with inner, weather. *Ib. st. 4*

14 I have been one acquainted with the night.
Acquainted with the Night [1928]

15 If, as they say, some dust thrown in my eyes
Will keep my talk from getting overwise,
I'm not the one for putting off the proof.
Let it be overwhelming.
Dust in the Eyes [1928]

16 Don't join too many gangs. Join few if any.
Join the United States and join the family—
But not much in between unless a college.
Build Soil [1932]

17 The sun was warm but the wind was chill.
You know how it is with an April day
When the sun is out and the wind is still,
You're one month on in the middle of May.
But if you so much as dare to speak,
A cloud comes over the sunlit arch,
A wind comes off a frozen peak,
And you're two months back in the middle of March.
Two Tramps in Mud Time [1936], st. 3

18 But yield who will to their separation,
My object in living is to unite
My avocation and my vocation
As my two eyes make one in sight.
Only where love and need are one,
And the work is play for mortal stakes,
Is the deed ever really done
For Heaven and the future's sakes.
Ib. st. 9

[1]See Dante, 140:19, and Housman, 691:6.
[2]The stars look very cold about the sky, / And I have many miles on foot to fare.—KEATS, *Keen, Fitful Gusts Are Whispering Here and There* [1817]

1 No memory of having starred
Atones for later disregard,
Or keeps the end from being hard.

Better to go down dignified
With boughten friendship by your side
Than none at all. Provide, provide!
Provide, Provide [1936], st. 6, 7

2 The old dog barks backward without getting up.
I can remember when he was a pup.
The Span of Life [1936]

3 The land was ours before we were the land's.
She was our land more than a hundred years
Before we were her people.
The Gift Outright [1941][1]

4 She is as in a field a silken tent
At midday when a sunny summer breeze
Has dried the dew and all its ropes relent,
So that in guys it gently sways at ease.
The Silken Tent [1942]

5 But strictly held by none, is loosely bound
By countless silken ties of love and thought
To everything on earth the compass round,
And only by one's going slightly taut
In the capriciousness of summer air
Is of the slightest bondage made aware.
Ib.

6 Happiness Makes Up in Height for What It Lacks in Length. *Title of poem [1942]*

7 Far in the pillared dark
Thrush music went—
Almost like a call to come in
To the dark and lament.

But no, I was out for stars:
I would not come in.
I meant not even if asked,
And I hadn't been.
Come In [1942], st. 4, 5

8 And were an epitaph to be my story
I'd have a short one ready for my own.
I would have written of me on my stone:
I had a lover's quarrel with the world.
The Lesson for Today [1942]

9 We dance round in a ring and suppose,
But the Secret sits in the middle and knows.
The Secret Sits [1942]

10 Here are your waters and your watering place.
Drink and be whole again beyond confusion.
Directive [1947]

[1]Read first before the Phi Beta Kappa Society at William and Mary College [December 5, 1941], later at the inauguration of President John F. Kennedy [January 20, 1961].

11 Have I not walked without an upward look
Of caution under stars that very well
Might not have missed me when they shot and fell?
It was a risk I had to take—and took.
Bravado [1947]

12 Any eye is an evil eye
That looks in on to a mood apart.
A Mood Apart [1947]

13 All those who try to go it sole alone,
Too proud to be beholden for relief,
Are absolutely sure to come to grief.
Haec Fabula Docet [1947]

14 It asks a little of us here.
It asks of us a certain height,
So when at times the mob is swayed
To carry praise or blame too far,
We may take something like a star
To stay our minds on and be staid.
Take Something Like a Star [1949]

15 Forgive, O Lord, my little jokes on Thee
And I'll forgive Thy great big one on me.
From In the Clearing [1962]

16 I am assured at any rate
Man's practically inexterminate.
Someday I must go into that.
There's always been an Ararat
Where someone someone else begat
To start the world all over at.
A-Wishing Well [1962]

17 It takes all sorts of in and outdoor schooling
To get adapted to my kind of fooling.
It Takes All Sorts [1962]

18 Unless I'm wrong
I but obey
The urge of a song:
I'm—bound—away![2]

And I may return
If dissatisfied
With what I learn
From having died.
Away! [1962], st. 5, 6

19 A poem . . . begins as a lump in the throat, a sense of wrong, a homesickness, a lovesickness. . . . It finds the thought and the thought finds the words.
Letter to Louis Untermeyer [January 1, 1916]

20 It is absurd to think that the only way to tell if a poem is lasting is to wait and see if it lasts. The right reader of a good poem can tell the moment it strikes him that he has taken

[2]See Anonymous: Shanties, 934:20.

an immortal wound — that he will never get over it.[1]

The Poetry of Amy Lowell. From the Christian Science Monitor [May 16, 1925]

1 Everything written is as good as it is dramatic. It need not declare itself in form, but it is drama or nothing.
A Way Out [1929], preface

2 It should be of the pleasure of a poem itself to tell how it can. The figure a poem makes. It begins in delight and ends in wisdom. The figure is the same for love.
The Figure a Poem Makes. Preface to Collected Poems [1939]

3 No tears in the writer, no tears in the reader.[2] *Ib.*

4 Like a piece of ice on a hot stove the poem must ride on its own melting. . . . Read it a hundred times; it will forever keep its freshness as a metal keeps its fragrance. It can never lose its sense of a meaning that once unfolded by surprise as it went.[3] *Ib.*

5 How many times it thundered before Franklin took the hint! How many apples fell on Newton's head before he took the hint! Nature is always hinting at us. It hints over and over again. And suddenly we take the hint. *Comment*

6 It is only a moment here and a moment there that the greatest writer has. *Ib.*

7 Love is an irresistible desire to be irresistibly desired. *Ib.*

8 Poetry is a way of taking life by the throat. *Ib.*

9 Talking is a hydrant in the yard and writing is a faucet upstairs in the house. Opening the first takes all the pressure off the second. *Ib.*

10 The greatest thing in family life is to take a hint when a hint is intended — and not to take a hint when a hint isn't intended. *Ib.*

11 Always fall in with what you're asked to accept. Take what is given, and make it over your way. My aim in life has always been to hold my own with whatever's going. Not against: with. *Ib.*

[1]See Coleridge, 437:1, and Frost, 750:4.
[2]See Charles Churchill, 375:8.
[3]See Coleridge, 437:1, and Frost, 749:20.

12 There's absolutely no reason for being rushed along with the rush. Everybody should be free to go very slow. . . . What you want, what you're hanging around in the world waiting for, is for something to occur to you. *[March 21, 1954]*

13 Education is . . . hanging around until you've caught on. *[January 30, 1963]*

Ellen Glasgow

1874–1945

14 No idea is so antiquated that it was not once modern. No idea is so modern that it will not someday be antiquated.
Address to the Modern Language Association [1936]

15 Preserve, within a wild sanctuary, an inaccessible valley of reveries.
A Certain Measure [1943]

16 Tilling the fertile soil of man's vanity. *Ib.*

Herbert Clark Hoover

1874–1964

17 The American system of rugged individualism.[4]
Campaign speech, New York [October 22, 1928]

18 The grass will grow in the streets of a hundred cities. *Speech [October 31, 1932]*

19 A good many things go around in the dark besides Santa Claus.
Address to the John Marshall Republican Club, St. Louis, Missouri [December 16, 1935]

20 Older men declare war. But it is youth that must fight and die. And it is youth who must inherit the tribulation, the sorrow, and the triumphs that are the aftermath of war.[5]
Speech at the Republican National Convention, Chicago [June 27, 1944]

[4]While I can make no claim for having introduced the term "rugged individualism," I should be proud to have invented it. It has been used by American leaders for over a half-century in eulogy of those God-fearing men and women of honesty whose stamina and character and fearless assertion of rights led them to make their own way in life. — HOOVER, *The Challenge to Liberty* [1934], *ch. 5*
[5]See Grantland Rice, 773:4.

Harold L. Ickes
1874–1952

1 I am against government by crony.
On resigning as secretary of the interior [February 1946]

William Lyon Mackenzie King[1]
1874–1950

2 Government, in the last analysis, is organized opinion. Where there is little or no public opinion, there is likely to be bad government, which sooner or later becomes autocratic government.
Message of the Carillon [1927]

Karl Kraus[2]
1874–1936

3 There are women who are not beautiful but only look that way.
Sprüche und Wiedersprüche (Aphorisms and More Aphorisms) [1909]

4 What is the Ninth Symphony compared to a Tin Pan Alley hit played on a hurdy-gurdy and a memory? *Ib.*

5 An aphorism is never exactly truthful. It is either a half-truth or a truth and a half.
Ib.

Amy Lowell
1874–1925

6 A pattern called a war.
Christ! What are patterns for?
Patterns

7 Sappho would speak, I think, quite openly,
And Mrs. Browning guard a careful silence,
But Emily would set doors ajar and slam them
And love you for your speed of observation.
The Sisters

8 Heart-leaves of lilac all over New England,[3]
Roots of lilac under all the soil of New England,
Lilac in me because I am New England.
Lilacs

[1] See Truman, 787:15.
[2] Translated by RICHARD HANSER.
[3] Stands the lilac bush tall-growing with heart-shaped leaves of rich green. — WALT WHITMAN, *When Lilacs Last in the Dooryard Bloomed* [1865–1866]

William Somerset Maugham
1874–1965

9 Like all weak men he laid an exaggerated stress on not changing one's mind.
Of Human Bondage [1915], ch. 39

10 People ask you for criticism, but they only want praise. *Ib. 50*

11 There is nothing so degrading as the constant anxiety about one's means of livelihood. . . . Money is like a sixth sense without which you cannot make a complete use of the other five. *Ib. 51*

12 I forget who it was that recommended men for their soul's good to do each day two things they disliked[4] . . . it is a precept that I have followed scrupulously; for every day I have got up and I have gone to bed.
The Moon and Sixpence [1919], ch. 2

13 Impropriety is the soul of wit.[5]
Ib. 4

14 Conscience is the guardian in the individual of the rules which the community has evolved for its own preservation.
Ib. 14

15 Do you know that conversation is one of the greatest pleasures in life? But it wants leisure.
The Trembling of a Leaf [1921], ch. 3

16 The tragedy of love is indifference.
Ib. 4

17 I [Death] was astonished to see him in Baghdad, for I had an appointment with him tonight in Samarra.
Sheppy [1933], act III

18 She [Sadie Thompson] gathered herself together. No one could describe the scorn of her expression or the contemptuous hatred she put into her answer.
"You men! You filthy dirty pigs! You're all the same, all of you. Pigs! Pigs!"
Altogether [1934]. Rain

19 I would sooner read a timetable or a catalogue than nothing at all. They are much more entertaining than half the novels that are written. *The Summing Up [1938]*

20 If a nation values anything more than freedom, it will lose its freedom; and the irony of it is that if it is comfort or money that it values more, it will lose that too.
Strictly Personal [1941], ch. 31

[4] See T. H. Huxley, 596:5, and William James, 648:9.
[5] See Shakespeare, 220:10.

Alice Duer Miller
1874–1942

1 The white cliffs of Dover, I saw rising steeply
Out of the sea that once made her [England]
secure. *The White Cliffs [1940]*

2 But in a world where England is finished and
dead,
I do not wish to live. *Ib.*

John Davison Rockefeller, Jr.
1874–1960

3 I believe that every right implies a responsibility; every opportunity, an obligation; every possession, a duty.
Ten Principles: Address in behalf of United Service Organizations, New York [July 8, 1941]

Robert William Service
1874–1958

4 This is the Law of the Yukon, that only the
strong shall thrive;
That surely the weak shall perish, and only
the fit survive.
Dissolute, damned and despairful, crippled
and palsied and slain,
This is the Will of the Yukon—Lo, how she
makes it plain!
The Law of the Yukon

5 Back of the bar, in a solo game, sat Dangerous
Dan McGrew,
And watching his luck was his light-o'-love,
the lady that's known as Lou.
The Shooting of Dan McGrew, st. 1

6 The Northern Lights have seen queer sights,
But the queerest they ever did see
Was that night on the marge of Lake Lebarge
I cremated Sam McGee.
The Cremation of Sam McGee, st. 1

7 A promise made is a debt unpaid.
Ib. st. 8

Gertrude Stein
1874–1946

8 Rose is a rose is a rose is a rose.
Sacred Emily [written 1913]

9 You are all a lost generation.[1]
Used by Ernest Hemingway as an epigraph for The Sun Also Rises [1926]

10 Pigeons on the grass alas.
Four Saints in Three Acts [written 1927]

11 Before the Flowers of Friendship Faded Friendship Faded.
Title [written 1930]

12 Remarks are not literature [said to Hemingway].
The Autobiography of Alice B. Toklas [written 1930]

13 America is my country and Paris is my home town and it is as it has come to be. After all anybody is as their land and air is. Anybody is as the sky is low or high, the air heavy or clear and anybody is as there is wind or no wind there. It is that which makes them and the arts they make and the work they do and the way they eat and the way they drink and the way they learn and everything.

And so I am an American and I have lived half my life in Paris, not the half that made me but the half in which I made what I made.
An American and France [1936]

14 In the United States there is more space where nobody is than where anybody is.

This is what makes America what it is.
The Geographical History of America [1936]

15 What is the answer? [*I was silent.*] In that case, what is the question?
Last words. From ALICE B. TOKLAS, *What Is Remembered [1963]*

Trumbull Stickney
1874–1904

16 Be still. The Hanging Gardens were a dream.
Be Still [1905]

17 It's autumn in the country I remember.
Mnemosyne

Edward Lee Thorndike
1874–1949

18 The intellect, character and skill possessed by any man are the product of certain original tendencies and the training which they have received.
Educational Psychology: Briefer Course [1914]

[1] Hemingway states that the remark was originally made by a garage owner in the Midi to Gertrude Stein in reference to his young mechanics, who were "une génération perdue."

Harry Williams
1874–1924

1 It's a long way to Tipperary, it's a long way to go;
It's a long way to Tipperary, to the sweetest girl I know!
Goodbye, Piccadilly, farewell, Leicester Square,
It's a long, long way to Tipperary, but my heart's right there!

Tipperary [1908][1]

2 In the Shade of the Old Apple Tree.

Title of song[1]

Edmund Clerihew[2] Bentley
1875–1956

3 Sir Christopher Wren
Said "I am going to dine with some men.
If anybody calls
Say I am designing St. Paul's."

Biography for Beginners. Sir Christopher Wren

4 John Stuart Mill
By a mighty effort of will
Overcame his natural bonhomie
And wrote *Principles of Political Economy.*

Ib. John Stuart Mill

5 George the Third
Ought never to have occurred.
One can only wonder
At so grotesque a blunder.[3]

Ib. George III

Mary McLeod Bethune
1875–1955

6 What does the Negro want? His answer is very simple. He wants only what all other Americans want. He wants opportunity to make real what the Declaration of Independence and the Constitution and the Bill of Rights say, what the Four Freedoms establish. While he knows these ideals are open to no man completely, he wants only his equal chance to obtain them.[4]

"Certain Unalienable Rights." From What the Negro Wants [1944], edited by RAYFORD W. LOGAN

7 If we accept and acquiesce in the face of discrimination, we accept the responsibility ourselves and allow those responsible to salve their conscience by believing that they have our acceptance and concurrence. We should, therefore, protest openly everything . . . that smacks of discrimination or slander.

Ib.

John Buchan, Lord Tweedsmuir
1875–1940

8 We can only pay our debt to the past by putting the future in debt to ourselves.

Address to the people of Canada, on the coronation of George VI [May 12, 1937]

9 Public life is regarded as the crown of a career, and to young men it is the worthiest ambition. Politics is still the greatest and the most honorable adventure.

Pilgrim's Way [1940]

Edgar Rice Burroughs
1875–1950

10 As the body rolled to the ground Tarzan of the Apes placed his foot upon the neck of his lifelong enemy, and raising his eyes to the full moon threw back his fierce young head and voiced the wild and terrible cry of his people.

Tarzan of the Apes [1914], ch. 7

Carl Gustav Jung
1875–1961

11 Without this playing with fantasy no creative work has ever yet come to birth. The debt we owe to the play of imagination is incalculable.

Psychological Types [1923], ch. 1, p. 82

12 The great problems of life—sexuality, of course, among others—are always related to the primordial images of the collective unconscious. These images are really balancing or compensating factors which correspond with the problems life presents in actuality. This is not to be marveled at, since these images are deposits representing the accumulated experience of thousands of years of struggle for adaptation and existence.

Ib. 5, p. 271

13 We should not pretend to understand the world only by the intellect; we apprehend it just as much by feeling. Therefore the judg-

[1] Set to music by JACK JUDGE [1878–1938].
[2] A quatrain in the form Bentley popularized is known as a clerihew.
[3] George the First was always reckoned / Vile, but viler George the Second; / And what mortal ever heard / Any good of George the Third? / When from earth the Fourth descended / God be praised, the Georges ended!—WALTER SAVAGE LANDOR, *epigram after hearing Thackeray's lectures on the four Georges* [1855]
See Frazer, 673:1.
[4] See Jordan, 913:9.

ment of the intellect is, at best, only the half of truth, and must, if it be honest, also come to an understanding of its inadequacy.

Ib. conclusion, p. 628

1 The woman is increasingly aware that love alone can give her her full stature, just as the man begins to discern that spirit alone can endow his life with its highest meaning. Fundamentally, therefore, both seek a psychic relation one to the other, because love needs the spirit, and the spirit love, for their fulfillment.

Contributions to Analytical Psychology [1928], p. 185

2 Seldom, or perhaps never, does a marriage develop into an individual relationship smoothly and without crises; there is no coming to consciousness without pain.

Ib. p. 193

3 The growth of the mind is the widening of the range of consciousness, and . . . each step forward has been a most painful and laborious achievement. *Ib. p. 340*

4 The meeting of two personalities is like the contact of two chemical substances: if there is any reaction, both are transformed.

Modern Man in Search of a Soul [1933], p. 57

5 The great decisions of human life have as a rule far more to do with the instincts and other mysterious unconscious factors than with conscious will and well-meaning reasonableness. The shoe that fits one person pinches another; there is no recipe for living that suits all cases. Each of us carries his own life-form—an indeterminable form which cannot be superseded by any other.

Ib. p. 69

6 Aging people should know that their lives are not mounting and unfolding but that an inexorable inner process forces the contraction of life. For a young person it is almost a sin—and certainly a danger—to be too much occupied with himself; but for the aging person it is a duty and a necessity to give serious attention to himself.

Ib. p. 125

7 All ages before ours believed in gods in some form or other. Only an unparalleled impoverishment in symbolism could enable us to rediscover the gods as psychic factors, which is to say, as archetypes of the unconscious. No doubt this discovery is hardly credible as yet.

The Integration of the Personality [1939], p. 72

8 If there is anything that we wish to change in the child, we should first examine it and see whether it is not something that could better be changed in ourselves.

Ib. p. 285

9 The conscious mind allows itself to be trained like a parrot, but the unconscious does not—which is why St. Augustine thanked God for not making him responsible for his dreams.

Psychology and Alchemy [1953], p. 51

10 The unconscious is not just evil by nature, it is also the source of the highest good: not only dark but also light, not only bestial, semihuman, and demonic but superhuman, spiritual, and, in the classical sense of the word, "divine."

The Practice of Psychotherapy [1953], p. 364

11 The little world of childhood with its familiar surroundings is a model of the greater world. The more intensively the family has stamped its character upon the child, the more it will tend to feel and see its earlier miniature world again in the bigger world of adult life. Naturally this is not a conscious, intellectual process.

From Psychological Reflections: A Jung Anthology [1953],[1] *p. 83: Collected Works, vol. 4, The Theory of Psychoanalysis [1913]*

12 This whole creation is essentially subjective, and the dream is the theater where the dreamer is at once scene, actor, prompter, stage manager, author, audience, and critic.

Ib. p. 58: vol. 8, General Aspects of Dream Psychology [1928]

13 The dream is the small hidden door in the deepest and most intimate sanctum of the soul, which opens into that primeval cosmic night that was soul long before there was a conscious ego and will be soul far beyond what a conscious ego could ever reach.

Ib. p. 46: vol. 10, The Meaning of Psychology for Modern Man [1934]

14 Emotion is the chief source of all becoming-conscious. There can be no transforming of darkness into light and of apathy into movement without emotion.

Ib. p. 32: vol. 9, Psychological Aspects of the Modern Archetype [1938]

[1] Edited by Jolande Jacobi.

1 No one can flatter himself that he is immune to the spirit of his own epoch, or even that he possesses a full understanding of it. Irrespective of our conscious convictions, each one of us, without exception, being a particle of the general mass, is somewhere attached to, colored by, or even undermined by the spirit which goes through the mass. Freedom stretches only as far as the limits of our consciousness.

Ib. p. 143: vol. 15, Paracelsus the Physician [1942]

2 Where love rules, there is no will to power; and where power predominates, there love is lacking. The one is the shadow of the other.

Ib. p. 87: vol. 7, The Psychology of the Unconscious [1943]

3 The erotic instinct is something questionable, and will always be so whatever a future set of laws may have to say on the matter. It belongs, on the one hand, to the original animal nature of man, which will exist as long as man has an animal body. On the other hand, it is connected with the highest forms of the spirit. But it blooms only when spirit and instinct are in true harmony. If one or the other aspect is missing, then an injury occurs, or at least there is a one-sided lack of balance which easily slips into the pathological. Too much of the animal disfigures the civilized human being, too much culture makes a sick animal. *Ib. p. 93*

Thomas Mann

1875–1955

4 We are most likely to get angry and excited in our opposition to some idea when we ourselves are not quite certain of our own position, and are inwardly tempted to take the other side.

Buddenbrooks [1903], pt. VIII, ch. 2

5 Beauty can pierce one like a pain.

Ib. XI, 2

6 Space, like time, engenders forgetfulness; but it does so by setting us bodily free from our surroundings and giving us back our primitive, unattached state. . . . Time, we say, is Lethe; but change of air is a similar draught, and, if it works less thoroughly, does so more quickly.

The Magic Mountain [1924],[1] *ch. 1*

7 A man lives not only his personal life, as an individual, but also, consciously or unconsciously, the life of his epoch and his contemporaries. *Ib. 2*

[1]Translated by H. T. Lowe-Porter.

8 The only religious way to think of death is as part and parcel of life; to regard it, with the understanding and the emotions, as the inviolable condition of life. *Ib. 5*

9 Time has no divisions to mark its passage, there is never a thunderstorm or blare of trumpets to announce the beginning of a new month or year. Even when a new century begins it is only we mortals who ring bells and fire off pistols. *Ib.*

10 Order and simplification are the first steps toward the mastery of a subject — the actual enemy is the unknown. *Ib.*

11 Human reason needs only to will more strongly than fate, and she *is* fate. *Ib. 6*

12 Opinions cannot survive if one has no chance to fight for them. *Ib.*

13 All interest in disease and death is only another expression of interest in life. *Ib.*

14 The invention of printing and the Reformation are and remain the two outstanding services of central Europe to the cause of humanity. *Ib.*

15 Speech is civilization itself. The word, even the most contradictory word, preserves contact — it is silence which isolates. *Ib.*

16 A man's dying is more the survivors' affair than his own. *Ib.*

17 What we call mourning for our dead is perhaps not so much grief at not being able to call them back as it is grief at not being able to want to do so. *Ib. 7*

18 Time cools, time clarifies; no mood can be maintained quite unaltered through the course of hours. *Ib.*

19 Death in Venice.

Stories of Three Decades [1936], title of story

20 Disorder and Early Sorrow. *Ib.*

21 In the Word is involved the unity of humanity, the wholeness of the human problem, which permits nobody to separate the intellectual and artistic from the political and social, and to isolate himself within the ivory tower of the "cultural" proper.

Letter to the dean of the Philosophical Faculty, Bonn University [January 1937][2]

[2]Mann, who had left Germany [1933], wrote from Zurich after being informed that his name had been struck off the list of Honorary Doctors.

1 Hold fast the time! Guard it, watch over it, every hour, every minute! Unregarded it slips away, like a lizard, smooth, slippery, faithless, a pixy wife. Hold every moment sacred. Give each clarity and meaning, each the weight of thine awareness, each its true and due fulfillment.

The Beloved Returns [1939]

Hughes Mearns
1875–1965

2 As I was going up the stair
I met a man who wasn't there.
He wasn't there again today.
I wish, I wish he'd stay away.

The Psychoed

Hasegawa Nyozekan[1]
1875–1969

3 The war was started as the result of a mistaken intuitive "calculation" which transcended mathematics. We believed with a blind fervor that we could triumph over scientific weapons and tactics by means of our mystic will. . . . The characteristic reliance on intuition by Japanese had blocked the objective cognition of the modern world.

The Lost Japan [1952]

Frank Ward O'Malley
1875–1932

4 Life is just one damned thing after another.[2]

Attributed. (Also attributed to Elbert Hubbard)

Rainer Maria Rilke
1875–1926

5 He was a poet and hated the approximate.

The Journal of My Other Self[3]

6 Love consists in this, that two solitudes protect and touch and greet each other.

Letters to a Young Poet[4]

7 The future enters into us, in order to transform itself in us, long before it happens.

Ib.

[1] From *Sources of Japanese Tradition* [1960], edited by William Theodore de Bary.

[2] The phrase probably precedes both O'Malley and Hubbard.

[3] Translated by John Linton.

[4] Translated by M. D. Herter Norton.

8 We're never single-minded, unperplexed, like migratory birds.

The Duino Elegies, 4

9 The most visible joy can only reveal itself to us when we've transformed it, within.

Ib. 7

10 Death is the side of life which is turned away from us.

Letter to W. von Hulewicz

11 A good marriage is that in which each appoints the other guardian of his solitude.

Letters[5]

12 Once the realization is accepted that even between the *closest* human beings infinite distances continue to exist, a wonderful living side by side can grow up, if they succeed in loving the distance between them which makes it possible for each to see the other whole against the sky. *Ib.*

13 In the difficult are the friendly forces, the hands that work on us. *Ib.*

14 Works of art are indeed always products of having been in danger, of having gone to the very end in an experience, to where man can go no further. *Ib.*

Rafael Sabatini
1875–1950

15 Born with the gift of laughter and the sense that the world was mad,[6] and that was his only patrimony. *Scaramouche, ch. 1*

Albert Schweitzer
1875–1965

16 Late on the third day, at the very moment when, at sunset, we were making our way through a herd of hippopotamuses, there flashed upon my mind, unforeseen and unsought, the phrase, "Reverence for Life."[7]

Out of My Life and Thought [1949]

17 Affirmation of life is the spiritual act by which man ceases to live unreflectively and

[5] Translated by Jane Barnard Greene and M. D. Herter Norton.

[6] Inscribed over a door in the Hall of Graduate Studies, Yale University. The architect, John Donald Tuttle, explained in a letter in *The New Yorker* [December 8, 1934] his recoiling from collegiate Gothic, "a type of architecture that had been designed expressly . . . to enable yeomen to pour molten lead through slots on their enemies below. As a propitiatory gift to my gods . . . and to make them forget by appealing to their senses of humor, I carved the inscription over the door."

[7] See W. E. Channing, 448:3.

begins to devote himself to his life with reverence in order to raise it to its true value. To affirm life is to deepen, to make more inward, and to exalt the will to live. *Ib.*

1 Truth has no special time of its own. Its hour is now—always. *Ib.*

2 You don't live in a world all alone. Your brothers are here too.
On Receiving the Nobel Prize [1952]

Sherwood Anderson
1876–1941

3 Everyone in the world is Christ and they are all crucified.
Winesburg, Ohio [1919]. The Philosopher

4 I am a lover and have not found my thing to love. *Ib. Tandy*

Sarah Norcliffe Cleghorn
1876–1959

5 The golf links lie so near the mill
That almost every day
The laboring children can look out
And watch the men at play.
Quatrain [1915]

Irvin Shrewsbury Cobb
1876–1944

6 It smells like gangrene starting in a mildewed silo, it tastes like the wrath to come, and when you absorb a deep swig of it you have all the sensations of having swallowed a lighted kerosene lamp. A sudden, violent jolt of it has been known to stop the victim's watch, snap his suspenders and crack his glass eye right across.
Definition of "corn licker" given to the Distillers' Code Authority, NRA

Max Jacob
1876–1944

7 The poet's expression of joy conceals his despair at not having found the reality of joy.
La Défense de Tartufe [1919]

8 When you get to the point where you cheat for the sake of beauty, you're an artist.[1]
Art Poétique [1922]

[1] C'est au moment où l'on triche pour le beau que l'on est artiste.

9 What is called a sincere work is one that is endowed with enough strength to give reality to an illusion. *Ib.*

Charles Franklin Kettering
1876–1958

10 We should all be concerned about the future because we will have to spend the rest of our lives there.
Seed for Thought [1949]

Maxim Maximovich Litvinov
1876–1951

11 Peace is indivisible.[2]
Speech to the League of Nations, Geneva, condemning Italian aggression in Ethiopia [July 1, 1936]

Wilson Mizner
1876–1933

12 Life's a tough proposition, and the first hundred years are the hardest.
Saying

13 Be nice to people on your way up because you'll meet 'em on your way down.
Ib. (Also attributed to Jimmy Durante)

14 When you steal from one author, it's plagiarism; if you steal from many, it's research.
Ib.

15 You sparkle with larceny. *Remark*

16 You're a mouse studying to be a rat.
Ib.

Pope Pius XII
[Eugenio Pacelli]
1876–1958

17 Private property is a natural fruit of labor, a product of intense activity of man, acquired through his energetic determination to ensure and develop with his own strength his own existence and that of his family, and to create for himself and his own an existence of just freedom, not only economic, but also political, cultural and religious.
Radio broadcast [September 1, 1944]

[2] In an earlier speech at the League [September 5, 1935] during the Italian preparations for the invasion, Litvinov used a similar phrase: "The thesis of the indivisibility of peace. . . . It has now become clear to the whole world that each war is the creation of a preceding war and the generator of new present or future wars."
See Wendell Willkie, 824:10.

1 If a worker is deprived of hope to acquire some personal property, what other natural stimulus can be offered him that will inspire him to hard work, labor, saving and sobriety today, when so many nations and men have lost everything and all they have left is their capacity for work? *Ib.*

George Macaulay Trevelyan
1876–1962

2 A man and what he loves and builds have but a day and then disappear; nature cares not—and renews the annual round untired. It is the old law, sad but not bitter. Only when man destroys the life and beauty of nature, there is the outrage.
Grey of Fallodon [1937], bk. I, ch. 3

3 Disinterested intellectual curiosity is the lifeblood of real civilization.
English Social History [1942], preface

4 Education . . . has produced a vast population able to read but unable to distinguish what is worth reading. *Ib. ch. 18*

Anthony Henderson Euwer
1877–1955

5 As a beauty I'm not a great star.
There are others more handsome, by far,
But my face—I don't mind it
For I am behind it;
It's the people in front get the jar.
Limeratomy[1]

Rose Fyleman
1877–1957

6 There are fairies at the bottom of our garden!
The Fairies, st. 1

Godfrey Harold Hardy
1877–1947

7 A mathematician, like a painter or a poet, is a maker of patterns. If his patterns are more permanent than theirs, it is because they are made with ideas.
A Mathematician's Apology [1940]

Sir James Hopwood Jeans
1877–1946

8 Taking a very gloomy view of the future of the human race, let us suppose that it can only expect to survive for two thousand million years longer, a period about equal to the past age of the earth. Then, regarded as a being destined to live for threescore years and ten, humanity, although it has been born in a house seventy years old, is itself only three days old.
The Wilder Aspects of Cosmogony [1928]

[1]Often quoted by Woodrow Wilson.

9 All the pictures which science now draws of nature and which alone seem capable of according with observational fact are mathematical pictures. . . . From the intrinsic evidence of his creation, the Great Architect of the Universe now begins to appear as a pure mathematician.
The Mysterious Universe [1930]

10 Physics tries to discover the pattern of events which controls the phenomena we observe. But we can never know what this pattern means or how it originates; and even if some superior intelligence were to tell us, we should find the explanation unintelligible.
Physics and Philosophy [1942]

Lewis Madison Terman
1877–1956

11 One of the most serious problems confronting psychology is that of connecting itself with life. . . . Theory that does not someway affect life has no value.
Genius and Stupidity [1906]

McLandburgh Wilson
fl. 1915

12 'Twixt the optimist and pessimist
The difference is droll:
The optimist sees the doughnut
But the pessimist sees the hole.
Optimist and Pessimist

John Munro Woolsey
1877–1945

13 If Joyce[2] did not attempt to be honest in developing the technique which he has adopted in *Ulysses* the result would be psychologically misleading and thus unfaithful to his chosen technique. Such an attitude would be artistically inexcusable.
U.S. v. One Book Called "Ulysses," 5 Federal Supplement 182, 184 [1933], III

[2]See Joyce, 778:1–778:4.

1 I am quite aware that owing to some of its scenes *Ulysses* is a rather strong draught to ask some sensitive, though normal, persons to take. But my considered opinion, after long reflection, is that whilst in many places the effect of *Ulysses* on the reader is somewhat emetic, nowhere does it tend to be an aphrodisiac.

Ulysses may, therefore, be admitted into the United States.[1] *Ib.*

Emiliano Zapata
c. 1877–1919

2 Men of the South! It is better to die on your feet than to live on your knees![2]
Attributed

Yosano Akiko
1878–1942

3 Because my songs are brief,
People think I hoarded words.
I have spared nothing in my songs.
There is nothing I can add.
Unlike a fish, my soul swims without gills.
I sing on one breath. *My Songs*[3]

George Michael Cohan
1878–1942

4 Always Leave Them Laughing When You Say Goodbye.
Mother Goose [1903], title of song

5 Give my regards to Broadway,
Remember me to Herald Square,
Tell all the gang at Forty-second Street
That I will soon be there.
Little Johnny Jones [1904]. Give My Regards to Broadway

6 I'm a Yankee Doodle dandy,
A Yankee Doodle do or die;
A real live nephew of my Uncle Sam's
Born on the Fourth of July.
Ib. Yankee Doodle Dandy

7 The Yanks are coming,
The drums rum-tumming everywhere.
Over There [1917]

8 And we won't come back till it's over over there. *Ib.*

9 What's all the shootin' for?
The Tavern [1920]

Adelaide Crapsey
1878–1914

10 These be
Three silent things:
The falling snow . . . the hour
Before the dawn . . . the mouth of one
Just dead. *Cinquain: Triad*

Harry Emerson Fosdick
1878–1969

11 The Sea of Galilee and the Dead Sea are made of the same water. It flows down, clear and cool, from the heights of Hermon and the roots of the cedars of Lebanon. The Sea of Galilee makes beauty of it, for the Sea of Galilee has an outlet. It gets to give. It gathers in its riches that it may pour them out again to fertilize the Jordan plain. But the Dead Sea with the same water makes horror. For the Dead Sea has no outlet. It gets to keep.
The Meaning of Service [1920]

Oliver St. John Gogarty
1878–1957

12 If only gladiators died,
Or heroes, death would be his pride;
But have not little maidens gone,
And Lesbia's sparrow,[4] all alone?
Per Iter Tenebricosum

Donald Robert Perry Marquis
1878–1937

13 My heart hath followed all my days
Something I cannot name.
The Name, st. 1

14 I love you as New Englanders love pie!
Sonnets to a Red-Haired Lady [1922], XII

15 dedicated to babs
with babs knows what
and babs knows why
archy[5] and mehitabel [1927][6]

[1] See Joyce, 778:1.
[2] Mejor morir a pie que vivir en rodillas.
Later a Republican watchword in the Spanish Civil War [1936–1939], especially identified with a speech at Madrid [July 18, 1936] by LA PASIONARA [DOLORES IBARRURI], page 833.
See F. D. Roosevelt, 780:14.
[3] From *Modern Japanese Literature* [1960], edited by DONALD KEENE.

[4] See Catullus, 101:15.
[5] Archy, a cockroach, is unable to use the shift key on the typewriter for capitals and punctuation.
[6] Published later with other works by archy as *the lives and times of archy and mehitabel* [1943].

1 oh i should worry and fret
death and i will coquette
there s a dance in the old dame yet
toujours gai toujours gai
Ib. the song of mehitabel

2 procrastination is the
art of keeping
up with yesterday
Ib. certain maxims of archy

3 an optimist is a guy
that has never had
much experience *Ib.*

4 what in hell
have i done to deserve
all these kittens
Ib. mehitabel and her kittens

5 dance mehitabel dance
caper and shake a leg
what little blood is left
will fizz like wine in a keg
Ib. mehitabel dances with boreas

6 it wont be long now it wont be long
man is making deserts of the earth
it wont be long now
before man will have it used up
so that nothing but ants
and centipedes and scorpions
can find a living on it
Ib. what the ants are saying

7 what man calls civilization
always results in deserts *Ib.*

8 each generation wastes a little more
of the future with greed and lust for riches
Ib.

9 it wont be long now it wont be long
till earth is barren as the moon
and sapless as a mumbled bone *Ib.*

10 i have noticed that when chickens quit quarreling over their food they often find that there is enough for all of them i wonder if it might not be the same with the human race
archy's life of mehitabel [1933]. random thoughts by archy

11 it is a cheering thought to think
that god is on the side of the best digestion[1]
archy does his part [1935]. the big bad wolf

12 there is bound to be a certain amount of
trouble running any country
if you are president the trouble happens to you
but if you are a tyrant you can arrange things so
that most of the trouble happens to other people
Ib. archy's newest deal

13 there is always
a comforting thought
in time of trouble when
it is not our trouble
Ib. comforting thoughts

[1] Give me a good digestion, Lord, / And also something to digest. — ANONYMOUS, *A Pilgrim's Grace, st. 1*

John Masefield
1878–1967

14 I must down to the seas again, to the lonely sea and the sky,
And all I ask is a tall ship and a star to steer her by,
And the wheel's kick and the wind's song and the white sail's shaking,
And a gray mist on the sea's face and a gray dawn breaking.
Sea Fever [1902], st. 1

15 I must down to the seas again, for the call of the running tide
Is a wild call and a clear call that may not be denied. *Ib. st. 2*

16 I must down to the seas again, to the vagrant gypsy life,
To the gull's way and the whale's way where the wind's like a whetted knife;
And all I ask is a merry yarn from a laughing fellow rover,
And quiet sleep and a sweet dream when the long trick's over. *Ib. st. 3*

17 It's a warm wind, the west wind, full of birds' cries. *The West Wind [1902], st. 1*

18 The days that make us happy make us wise.
Biography

19 Quinquireme of Nineveh from distant Ophir,
Rowing home to haven in sunny Palestine,
With a cargo of ivory,
And apes and peacocks,[2]
Sandalwood, cedarwood, and sweet white wine. *Cargoes, st. 1*

20 Dirty British coaster with a salt-caked smokestack,
Butting through the Channel in the mad March days,
With a cargo of Tyne coal,
Road rail, pig lead,
Firewood, ironware, and cheap tin trays.
Ib. st. 3

21 What am I, Life? A thing of watery salt
Held in cohesion by unresting cells,

[2] See *I Kings 10:22, 13:36.*

Which work they know not why, which never halt,
Myself unwitting where their Master dwells?
Sonnets, 14

1 But he[1] has gone,
A nation's memory and veneration,
Among the radiant, ever venturing on,
Somewhere, with morning, as such spirits will.
On the Finish of the Sailing Ship Race Lisbon to Manhattan [July 1964]

Paul Reynaud
1878–1966

2 We shall win because we are the stronger.[2]
Radio Speech [September 10, 1939]

Carl Sandburg
1878–1967

3 I am the people—the mob—the crowd—the mass.
Do you know that all the great work of the world is done through me?
I Am the People, the Mob [1916]

4 Hog butcher for the world,
Tool maker, stacker of wheat,
Player with railroads and the nation's freight handler;
Stormy, husky, brawling,
City of the big shoulders.
Chicago [1916]

5 The fog comes
on little cat feet.
It sits looking
over the harbor and city
on silent haunches
and then moves on. *Fog [1916]*

6 Pile the bodies high at Austerlitz and Waterloo.
Shovel them under and let me work—
I am the grass; I cover all.

And pile them high at Gettysburg
And pile them high at Ypres and Verdun.

Two years, ten years, and passengers ask the conductor:
What place is this?
Where are we now? *Grass [1918]*

[1] John F. Kennedy.
See J. R. Lowell, 568:19.
[2] Nous vaincrons parceque nous sommes les plus forts. The phrase became a war slogan.

7 I tell you the past is a bucket of ashes.
Prairie [1918]

8 When Abraham Lincoln was shoveled into the tombs, he forgot the copperheads and the assassin . . . in the dust, in the cool tombs. *Cool Tombs [1918]*

9 Tell me if the lovers are losers . . . tell me if any get more than the lovers. *Ib.*

10 Lay me on an anvil, O God.
Beat me and hammer me into a crowbar.
Let me pry loose old walls.
Let me lift and loosen old foundations.
Prayers of Steel [1920]

11 Drum on your drums, batter on your banjos, sob on the long cool winding saxophones.
Go to it, O jazzmen.
Jazz Fantasia [1920]

12 The republic is a dream.
Nothing happens unless first a dream.
Washington Monument by Night [1922]

13 Look out how you use proud words.
When you let proud words go, it is not easy to call them back.
They wear long boots, hard boots.
Primer Lesson [1922]

14 Sometime they'll give a war and nobody will come.[3] *The People, Yes [1936]*

15 The people will live on.
The learning and blundering people will live on.
They will be tricked and sold and again sold
And go back to the nourishing earth for rootholds. *Ib.*

16 The people know the salt of the sea
and the strength of the winds
lashing the corners of the earth.
The people take the earth
as a tomb of rest and a cradle of hope.
Who else speaks for the Family of Man?
Ib.

17 Man is a long time coming.
Man will yet win.
Brother may yet line up with brother:

This old anvil laughs at many broken hammers.
There are men who can't be bought.
The People Will Live On [1936]

[3] Suppose They Gave a War, and No One Came?—CHARLOTTE KEYES [1914–], *article in McCall's* [October 1966]

Louis Edwin Thayer

1878–1956

1 I fancy when I go to rest someone will bring to light
Some kindly word or goodly act long buried out of sight;
But, if it's all the same to you, just give to me, instead,
The bouquets while I'm living and the knocking when I'm dead.[1]

Of Post-Mortem Praises, st. 1

John Broadus Watson

1878–1958

2 Give me a dozen healthy infants, well-formed, and my own specified world to bring them up in and I'll guarantee to take any one at random and train him to become any type of specialist I might select—doctor, lawyer, artist, merchant chief and, yes, even beggarman and thief, regardless of his talents, penchants, tendencies, abilities, vocations, and race of his ancestors. I am going beyond the facts and I admit it, but so have the advocates of the contrary and they have been doing it for many thousands of years.

Behaviorism [1925], ch. 5

3 If "mind" acts on body, then all physical laws are invalid. *Ib. 6*

4 The universe will change if you bring up your children, not in the freedom of the libertine, but in behavioristic freedom—a freedom which we cannot even picture in words, so little do we know of it. *Ib. 12*

Hans Zinsser

1878–1940

5 The scientist takes off from the manifold observations of predecessors, and shows his intelligence, if any, by his ability to discriminate between the important and the negligible, by selecting here and there the significant steppingstones that will lead across the difficulties to new understanding. The one who places the last stone and steps across to the terra firma of accomplished discovery gets all the credit. Only the initiated know and honor those whose patient integrity and devotion to exact observation have made the last step possible.[2]

As I Remember Him [1940], ch. 20

[1] See Martial, 119:13, and Hazlitt, 445:8.

[2] See Sir Francis Darwin, 662:3, and Sir Alexander Fleming, 774:2.

Ethel Barrymore

1879–1959

6 That's all there is, there isn't any more.

Added with the permission of author THOMAS RACEWARD, *as the curtain line of his play Sunday [1906], starring Miss Barrymore*

William Maxwell Aitken, Baron Beaverbrook

1879–1964

7 Who is responsible for this work of development [in the Aircraft Ministry] on which so much depends? To whom must the praise be given? To the boys in the back rooms. They do not sit in the limelight. But they are the men who do the work.

Broadcast when he was minister of aircraft production [1941]

Sir William Henry Beveridge

1879–1963

8 There is no inherent mechanism in our present system which can with certainty prevent competitive sectional bargaining for wages from setting up a vicious spiral of rising prices under full employment.

Full Employment in a Free Society [1945]

Louis Brownlow

1879–1963

9 They [the President's aides] should be possessed of high competence, great physical vigor, and a passion for anonymity.[3]

Administrative Management in the Government of the United States: Report of the President's Committee on Administrative Management [January 1937]

James Branch Cabell

1879–1958

10 The optimist proclaims that we live in the best of all possible worlds; and the pessimist fears this is true.

The Silver Stallion [1926], ch. 26

[3] Tell the President that the way to solve his problem is to find that one man who would turn out to be . . . possessed of high competence, great physical vigor, and a passion for anonymity.—TOM JONES (private secretary to Prime Minister Stanley Baldwin) to Brownlow [1936]

Ch'en Tu-hsiu[1]

1879–1942

1 The pulse of modern life is economic and the fundamental principle of economic production is individual independence.

The New Youth [December 1916]

2 All religions, laws, moral and political systems are but necessary means to preserve social order. *Ib. [February 1918]*

3 Man's happiness in life is the result of man's own effort and is neither the gift of God nor a spontaneous natural product.

Ib.

4 During his lifetime, an individual should devote his efforts to create happiness and to enjoy it, and also to keep it in store in society so that individuals of the future may also enjoy it. *Ib.*

Albert Einstein

1879–1955

5 $E=mc^2$.

Statement of the mass-energy equivalence relationship[2]

6 The most beautiful thing we can experience is the mysterious. It is the source of all true art and science.

What I Believe [1930]

7 To know that what is impenetrable to us really exists, manifesting itself as the highest wisdom and the most radiant beauty, which our dull facilities can comprehend only in the most primitive forms — this knowledge, this feeling, is at the center of true religiousness. In this sense, and in this sense only, I belong to the ranks of the devoutly religious men.

Ib.

8 Concern for man himself and his fate must always form the chief interest of all technical endeavors, concern for the great unsolved problems of the organization of labor and the distribution of goods — in order that the creations of our mind shall be a blessing and not a curse to mankind. Never forget this in the midst of your diagrams and equations.

Address, California Institute of Technology [1931]

[1]From *Sources of Chinese Tradition* [1960], edited by William Theodore de Bary. Ch'en was the founder [1921] of the Chinese Communist Party.

[2]Energy equals mass times the speed of light squared. The original statement is: If a body gives off the energy L in the form of radiation, its mass diminishes by L/c^2. — Einstein, *Ist die Tragheit eines Korpers von Seinem Energieghalt Abhangig?* [1905]

9 The whole of science is nothing more than a refinement of everyday thinking.

Physics and Reality [1936]

10 Physical concepts are free creations of the human mind, and are not, however it may seem, uniquely determined by the external world. *Evolution of Physics [1938]*

11 Some recent work by E. Fermi and L. Szilard, which has been communicated to me in manuscript, leads me to expect that the element uranium may be turned into a new and important source of energy in the immediate future. Certain aspects of the situation which has arisen seem to call for watchfulness and, if necessary, quick action on the part of the Administration.

Letter to President Franklin D. Roosevelt [August 2, 1939] (the letter that resulted in the assignment of government funds for developing the atom bomb)

12 This new phenomena [atomic energy] would also lead to the construction of bombs. . . . A single bomb of this type, carried by boat and exploded in a port, might very well destroy the whole port, together with some of the surrounding territory. However, such bombs might very well prove to be too heavy for transportation by air. *Ib.*

13 As long as there are sovereign nations possessing great power, war is inevitable.

Einstein on the Atomic Bomb. From the Atlantic Monthly [November 1945]

14 I do not believe that civilization will be wiped out in a war fought with the atomic bomb. Perhaps two thirds of the people of the earth might be killed, but enough men capable of thinking, and enough books, would be left to start again, and civilization could be restored. *Ib.*

15 Since I do not foresee that atomic energy is to be a great boon for a long time, I have to say that for the present it is a menace. Perhaps it is well that it should be. It may intimidate the human race into bringing order into its international affairs, which, without the pressure of fear, it would not do. *Ib.*

16 I shall never believe that God plays dice with the world.[3]

From Philipp Frank, Einstein, His Life and Times [1947]

[3]See Anatole France, 655:13.

1 The Lord God is subtle, but malicious he is not.[1]

Inscription in Fine Hall, Princeton University

2 Every intellectual who is called before one of the committees ought to refuse to testify, i.e., he must be prepared . . . for the sacrifice of his personal welfare in the interest of the cultural welfare of his country. . . . This kind of inquisition violates the spirit of the Constitution.

If enough people are ready to take this grave step they will be successful. If not, then the intellectuals of this country deserve nothing better than the slavery which is intended for them.

Letter to William Frauenglass[2] *[May 16, 1953]*

3 The unleashed power of the atom has changed everything save our modes of thinking, and we thus drift toward unparalleled catastrophes.

From Ralph E. Lapp, *The Einstein Letter That Started It All. In the New York Times Magazine [August 2, 1964]*

4 Our defense is not in armaments, nor in science, nor in going underground. Our defense is in law and order.[3] *Ib.*

5 Something deeply hidden had to be behind things.

Ib. [autobiographical handwritten note]

Dorothy Canfield Fisher

1879–1958

6 A mother is not a person to lean on, but a person to make leaning unnecessary.

Her Son's Wife [1926], ch. 37

Edward Morgan Forster

1879–1970

7 When the book of life is opening, our readings are secret.

The Longest Journey [1907]

8 Nonsense and beauty have close connections. *Ib.*

9 Only connect! That was the whole of her sermon. Only connect the prose and the passion, and both will be exalted, and human love will be seen at its height. Live in fragments no longer. Only connect, and the beast and the monk, robbed of the isolation that is life to either, will die.

Howards End [1910], ch. 22

10 The echo began in some indescribable way to undermine her hold on life. Coming at a moment when she chanced to be fatigued, it had managed to murmur, "Pathos, piety, courage—they exist, but are identical, and so is filth. Everything exists, nothing has value." If one had spoken vileness in that place, or quoted lofty poetry, the [echo's] comment would have been the same—"Ou-boum." *A Passage to India [1924]*

Edmund L. Gruber

1879–1941

11 Over hill, over dale,[4] we have hit the dusty
trail
And those caissons go rolling along.

The Caisson Song[5] *[1908]*

12 Oh, it's hi-hi-yee! for the field artilleree,
Shout out your numbers loud and strong,
And where'er we go, you will always know
That those caissons are rolling along.

Ib.

Joe Hill [Joseph Hillstrom]

1879–1915

13 Work and pray, live on hay,
You'll get pie in the sky when you die.

The Preacher and the Slave

John Haynes Holmes

1879–1964

14 If Christians were Christians, there would be no anti-Semitism. Jesus was a Jew. There is nothing that the ordinary Christian so dislikes to remember as this awkward historical fact.

The Sensible Man's View of Religion [1933]

15 Priests are no more necessary to religion than politicians to patriotism. *Ib.*

16 The universe is not hostile, nor yet is it friendly. It is simply indifferent. *Ib.*

[1] Raffiniert ist der Herr Gott, aber Boshaft ist er nicht. See Dostoevski, 581:20.

[2] Einstein's letter was published in the *New York Times* [June 12, 1953]. Mr. Frauenglass had been subpoenaed to testify before the Senate Internal Security Subcommittee.

[3] See Lincoln, 520:7.

[4] See Shakespeare, 196:10.

[5] The 1st Battalion of the 5th Field Artillery relieved the 2nd Battalion in the Philippines [April 1908]. Gruber, then a lieutenant in the 5th, was asked to write a song that would symbolize the spirit of the reunited regiment. There are many variant wordings.

1 The life of humanity upon this planet may yet come to an end, and a very terrible end. But I would have you notice that this end is threatened in our time not by anything that the universe may do to us, but only by what man may do to himself. *Ib.*

Vachel Lindsay

1879–1931

2 Booth died blind and still by faith he trod,
Eyes still dazzled by the ways of God.
General William Booth Enters into Heaven [1913]

3 Sleep softly . . . eagle forgotten . . . under the stone.
The Eagle That is Forgotten[1] *[1913], st. 5*

4 Factory windows are always broken.
Somebody's always throwing bricks,
Somebody's always heaving cinders,
Playing ugly Yahoo tricks.
Factory Windows, st. 1

5 Fat black bucks in a wine-barrel room,
Barrel-house kings; with feet unstable,
Sagged and reeled and pounded on the table,
Pounded on the table,
Beat an empty barrel with the handle of a broom. *The Congo [1914], pt. I*

6 Then I saw the Congo, creeping through the black,
Cutting through the forest with a golden track. *Ib.*

7 Be careful what you do,
Or Mumbo-Jumbo, God of the Congo,
And all of the other
Gods of the Congo,
Mumbo-Jumbo will hoo-doo you. *Ib.*

8 A bronzed, lank man! His suit of ancient black,
A famous high top-hat and plain worn shawl
Make him the quaint great figure that men love,
The prairie-lawyer, master of us all.
Abraham Lincoln Walks at Midnight [1914], st. 3

9 They spoke, I think, of perils past.
They spoke, I think, of peace at last.
One thing I remember:
Spring came on forever,
Spring came on forever,
Said the Chinese nightingale.
The Chinese Nightingale [1917], end

10 Planting the trees that would march and train
On, in his name to the great Pacific,
Like Birnam Wood to Dunsinane,[2]
Johnny Appleseed[3] swept on.
In Praise of Johnny Appleseed

11 The more probable chance for me will come in some little row where strikers are being shot down. . . . I would be with the fool strikers, right or wrong.
Letter to Eleanor Dougherty [October 12, 1918]

Dixon Lanier Merritt

1879–1972

12 A wonderful bird is the pelican,
His bill will hold more than his belican.
He can take in his beak
Food enough for a week,
But I'm damned if I see how the helican.
The Pelican [1910]

Jack Norworth

1879–1959

13 Take me out to the ball game,
Take me out with the crowd.
Buy me some peanuts and cracker-jack—
I don't care if I never get back.
Take Me Out to the Ball Game [1908]

14 For it's one, two, three strikes you're out
At the old ball game. *Ib.*

Will Rogers

1879–1935

15 All I know is just what I read in the papers.
Prefatory remark

16 I tell you folks, all politics is applesauce.
The Illiterate Digest [1924], p. 30

17 Everything is funny as long as it is happening to somebody else. *Ib. p. 131*

[1]John Peter Altgeld [1847–1902; governor of Illinois, 1893–1897], widely criticized for pardoning, in June 1893, the anarchists who had been serving life terms since the Haymarket riot in Chicago on May 4, 1886. In pardoning them, Altgeld declared that "the judge conducted the trial with malicious ferocity."

[2]See Shakespeare, 239:12.

[3]John Chapman [1774–1847].
Remember Johnny Appleseed, / All ye who love the apple; / He served his kind by word and deed, / In God's grand greenwood chapel.—WILLIAM HENRY VENABLE [1836–1920], *Johnny Appleseed, st. 25*

1 More men have been elected between sundown and sunup than ever were elected between sunup and sundown. *Ib. p. 152*

2 A comedian can only last till he either takes himself serious or his audience takes him serious.
Syndicated newspaper article [June 28, 1931]

3 I not only "don't choose to run"[1] [for President] but I don't even want to leave a loophole in case I am drafted, so I won't "choose." I will say "won't run" no matter how bad the country will need a comedian by that time.
Ib.

4 Politics has got so expensive that it takes lots of money to even get beat with.
Ib.

5 My forefathers didn't come over on the *Mayflower,* but they met the boat.[2]
Remark

6 I joked about every prominent man in my lifetime, but I never met one I didn't like.
Epitaph

Joseph Stalin
[Iosif Vissarionovich Dzhugashvili]
1879–1953

7 Print is the sharpest and the strongest weapon of our party.
Speech [April 19, 1923]

8 The most remarkable thing about socialist competition is that it creates a basic change in people's view of labor, since it changes the labor from a shameful and heavy burden into a matter of honor, matter of fame, matter of valor and heroism.
Speech [June 27, 1930]

9 The Hitlerite blackguards . . . have turned Europe into a prison of nations,[3] and this they call the new order in Europe.
Address to the Moscow Soviet [November 6, 1942]

10 You cannot make a revolution with silk gloves. *Attributed*

11 A single death is a tragedy, a million deaths is a statistic. *Attributed*

[1]See Calvin Coolidge, 736:18.
[2]Rogers was of Indian descent.
[3]. . . The saying that Russia is a prison of nations. — V. I. Lenin, *On the Question of National Policy* (and elsewhere)
See Custine, 464:9.

Wallace Stevens
1879–1955

12 I heard them cry — the peacocks.
Was it a cry against the twilight
Or against the leaves themselves
Turning in the wind,
Turning as the flames
Turned in the fire,
Turning as the tails of the peacocks
Turned in the loud fire,
Loud as the hemlocks
Full of the cry of the peacocks?
Or was it a cry against the hemlocks?
Domination of Black [1923]

13 Twenty men crossing a bridge,
Into a village,
Are twenty men crossing twenty bridges,
Into twenty villages,
Or one man
Crossing a single bridge into a village.
Metaphors of a Magnifico [1923]

14 Crispin, merest minuscule in the gales,
Dejected his manner to the turbulence.
The Comedian as the Letter C [1923], I, 3

15 Green barbarism turning paradigm.
Ib. II, 2

16 An annotator has his scruples, too.
Ib. II, 4

17 The book of moonlight is not written yet.
Ib. III, 1

18 And as he came he saw that it was spring,
A time abhorrent to the nihilist
Or searcher for the fecund minimum.
Ib. III, 4

19 The natives of the rain are rainy men.
Ib. IV, 1

20 The plum survives its poems. *Ib. V, 1*

21 Arointing his dreams with fugal requiems?
Ib. V, 2

22 Yet the quotidian saps philosophers.
Ib. V, 4

23 Green crammers of the green fruits of the world. *Ib. VI, 2*

24 Poetry is the supreme fiction, madame.
A High-toned Old Christian Woman [1923]

25 Let be be finale of seem.
The only emperor is the emperor of ice cream.
The Emperor of Ice Cream [1923]

1 Only, here and there, an old sailor,
Drunk and asleep in his boots,
Catches tigers
In red weather.
Disillusionment of Ten O'clock [1923]

2 Complacencies of the peignoir, and late
Coffee and oranges in a sunny chair.
Sunday Morning [1923], st. 1

3 She says, "But in contentment I still feel
The need of some imperishable bliss."
Death is the mother of Beauty; hence from her,
Alone, shall come fulfillment to our dreams
And our desires. *Ib. st. 5*

4 We live in an old chaos of the sun,
Or old dependency of day and night,
Or island solitude, unsponsored, free,
Of that wide water, inescapable.
Deer walk upon our mountains, and the quail
Whistle about us their spontaneous cries;
Sweet berries ripen in the wilderness;
And, in the isolation of the sky,
At evening, casual flocks of pigeons make
Ambiguous undulations as they sink,
Downward to darkness, on extended wings.
Ib. st. 8

5 Chieftain Iffucan of Azcan in caftan
Of tan with henna hackles, halt!
Bantams in Pine Woods [1923], st. 1

6 Damned universal cock, as if the sun
Was blackamoor to bear your blazing tail.
Ib. st. 2

7 I placed a jar in Tennessee,
And round it was, upon a hill.
It made the slovenly wilderness
Surround that hill.
Anecdote of the Jar [1923], st. 1

8 Frogs Eat Butterflies. Snakes Eat Frogs.
Hogs Eat Snakes. Men Eat Hogs.[1]
Title of poem [1923]

9 Just as my fingers on these keys
Make music, so the self-same sounds
On my spirit make a music, too.
Peter Quince at the Clavier [1923], I

10 Beauty is momentary in the mind—
The fitful tracing of a portal;
But in the flesh it is immortal.

The body dies; the body's beauty lives.
Ib. IV

11 Susanna's music touched the bawdy strings
Of those white elders; but, escaping,
Left only Death's ironic scraping.
Now, in its immortality, it plays
On the clear viol of her memory,
And makes a constant sacrament of praise.
Ib.

12 I do not know which to prefer,
The beauty of inflections
Or the beauty of innuendoes,
The blackbird whistling
Or just after.
Thirteen Ways of Looking at a Blackbird [1923], st. 5

13 The gongs rang loudly as the windy booms
Hoo-hooed it in the darkened ocean-blooms.
Sea Surface Full of Clouds [1923], II

14 Then the sea
And heaven rolled as one and from the two
Came fresh transfigurings of freshest blue.
Ib. V

15 She sang beyond the genius of the sea,
The water never formed to mind or voice,
Like a body wholly body, fluttering
Its empty sleeves; and yet its mimic motion
Made constant cry, caused constantly a cry,
That was not ours although we understood,
Inhuman, of the veritable ocean.
The Idea of Order at Key West [1936], st. 1

16 Oh! Blessed rage for order, pale Ramón,
The maker's rage to order words of the sea,
Words of the fragrant portals, dimly starred,
And of ourselves and of our origins,
In ghostlier demarcations, keener sounds.
Ib. st. 7

17 Poetry is the subject of the poem.
The Man with the Blue Guitar [1937], XXII

18 I am a native in this world
And think in it as a native thinks.
Ib. XXVIII

19 Light
Is the lion that comes down to drink.
The Glass of Water [1942], st. 2

20 A. A violent order is disorder; and
B. A great disorder is an order. These
Two things are one.
Connoisseur of Chaos [1942], st. 1

21 One's grand flights, one's Sunday baths,
One's tootings at the weddings of the soul
Occur as they occur.
The Sense of the Sleight-of-Hand Man [1942], st. 1

22 And, capable, created in his mind,
Eventual victor, out of the martyrs' bones
The ultimate elegance: the imagined land.
Mrs. Alfred Uruguay [1942], st. 4

[1] See Ambrose Bierce, 647:11.

1 The prologues are over. It is a question, now,
Of final belief. So, say that final belief
Must be in a fiction. It is time to choose.
Asides on the Oboe [1942], st. 1

2 The motive for metaphor, shrinking from
The weight of primary noon,
The ABC of being,

The ruddy temper, the hammer
Of red and blue, the hard sound—
Steel against intimation—the sharp flash,
The vital, arrogant, fatal, dominant X.
The Motive for Metaphor [1947], st. 4, 5

3 To get at the thing
Without gestures is to get at it as
Idea.
So-and-So Reclining on Her Couch [1947], st. 6

4 It was the last nostalgia: that he
Should understand.
Esthétique du Mal [1947], X

5 The greatest poverty is not to live
In a physical world, to feel that one's desire
Is too difficult to tell from despair.
Ib. XV

6 Thus the theory of description matters most.
It is the theory of the word for those

For whom the word is the making of the world,
The buzzing world and lisping firmament.

It is a world of words to the end of it,
In which nothing solid is its solid self.
Description Without Place [1947], VII

7 Torn by dreams,

By the terrible incantations of defeats
And by the fear that defeats and dreams are one.

The whole race is a poet that writes down
The eccentric propositions of its fate.
Men Made Out of Words [1947]

8 The inconceivable idea of the sun.

You must become an ignorant man again
And see the sun again with an ignorant eye
And see it clearly in the idea of it.
Notes Toward a Supreme Fiction [1947]. It Must Be Abstract, I

9 The death of one god is the death of all.
Ib.

10 There is a project for the sun. The sun
Must bear no name, gold flourisher, but be
In the difficulty of what it is to be. *Ib.*

11 It is the celestial ennui of apartments
That sends us back to the first idea.
Ib. II

12 And still the grossest iridescence of ocean
Howls hoo and rises and howls hoo and falls.
Ib. III

13 We are the mimics. Clouds are pedagogues.
Ib. IV

14 An abstraction blooded. *Ib. VI*

15 The President ordains the bee to be
Immortal. *Ib. It Must Change, II*

16 Booming and booming of the new-come bee.
Ib.

17 He chose to include the things
That in each other are included, the whole,
The complicate, the amassing harmony.
Ib. It Must Give Pleasure, VI

18 These external regions, what do we fill them with
Except reflections, the escapades of death,
Cinderella fulfilling herself beneath the roof.
Ib. VIII

19 Perhaps
The man-hero is not the exceptional monster,
But he that of repetition is most master.
Ib. IX

20 They will get it straight one day at the Sorbonne. *Ib. X*

21 Until flicked by feeling. *Ib.*

22 And one trembles to be so understood and, at last,
To understand, as if to know became
The fatality of seeing things too well.
The Novel [1950], st. 16

23 We keep coming back and coming back
To the real: to the hotel instead of the hymns
That fall upon it out of the wind.
An Ordinary Evening in New Haven [1950], IX

24 A more severe,

More harassing master would extemporize
Subtler, more urgent proof that the theory
Of poetry is the theory of life,

As it is, in the intricate evasions of as,
In things seen and unseen, created from nothingness,
The heavens, the hells, the worlds, the longed-for lands. *Ib. XXVIII*

25 Total grandeur of a total edifice,
Chosen by an inquisitor of structures
For himself. He stops upon this threshold

As if the design of all his words takes form
And frame from thinking and is realized.
To an Old Philosopher in Rome [1950], st. 16

1 A new scholar replacing an older one reflects
A moment on this fantasia. He seeks
For a human that can be accounted for.
Looking Across the Fields and Watching the Birds Fly [1950], st. 13

2 Light the first light of evening, as in a room
In which we rest and, for small reason, think
The world imagined is the ultimate good.
Final Soliloquy of the Interior Paramour [1950], st. 1

3 We say God and the imagination are one . . .
How high that highest candle lights the dark.
Ib. st. 5

4 There it was, word for word,
The poem that took the place of a mountain.
The Poem That Took the Place of a Mountain [1952], st. 1

5 Is it Ulysses that approaches from the east,
The interminable adventurer?
The World as Meditation [1952], st. 1

6 A form of fire approaches the cretonnes of Penelope. *Ib. st. 2*

7 She wanted nothing he could not bring her by coming alone. *Ib. st. 5*

8 But was it Ulysses? Or was it only the warmth of the sun
On her pillow? The thought kept beating in her like her heart.
The two kept beating together. It was only day. *Ib. st. 6*

9 The barbarous strength within her would never fail. *Ib. st. 7*

10 That scrawny cry—It was
A chorister whose *c* preceded the choir.
It was part of the colossal sun.
Not Ideas About the Thing but the Thing Itself [1954], st. 5

11 The palm at the end of the mind,
Beyond the last thought, rises . . .
A gold-feathered bird
Sings in the palm.
Of Mere Being [1957], st. 1, 2

12 The essential gaudiness of poetry.
Stevens's note to The Emperor of Ice Cream

13 The essential thing in form is to be free in whatever form is used. A free form does not assure freedom. As a form, it is just one more form. So that it comes to this, I suppose, that I believe in freedom regardless of form.
A Note on Poetry [1937]

14 What makes the poet the potent figure that he is, or was, or ought to be, is that he creates the world to which we turn incessantly and without knowing it and that he gives to life the supreme fictions without which we are unable to conceive of it.
The Noble Rider and the Sound of Words [1942]

15 The subject matter of poetry is not that "collection of solid, static objects extended in space" but the life that is lived in the scene that it composes; and so reality is not that external scene but the life that is lived in it. Reality is things as they are.
The Necessary Angel [1951]

16 His [the poet's] function is to make his imagination theirs [the people's] and he fulfills himself only as he sees his imagination become the light in the minds of others. His role, in short, is to help people to live their lives. *Ib.*

17 The humble are they that move about the world with the lure of the real in their hearts.
Ib. About One of Marianne Moore's Poems

18 The greatest truth we could hope to discover, in whatever field we discovered it, is that man's truth is the final resolution of everything.
Ib. The Relations Between Poetry and Painting

19 Poetry is poetry, and one's objective as a poet is to achieve poetry precisely as one's objective in music is to achieve music.
On selecting Domination of Black as his best poem

20 A poem is a meteor.
Opus Posthumous [1957]. Adagia

21 Sentimentality is a failure of feeling. *Ib.*

22 A poem should be part of one's sense of life. *Ib.*

23 A poet looks at the world as a man looks at a woman. *Ib.*

24 All history is modern history. *Ib.*

25 Poetry is a purging of the world's poverty and change and evil and death. It is a present perfecting, a satisfaction in the irremediable poverty of life. *Ib.*

26 In the world of words, the imagination is one of the forces of nature. *Ib.*

1 God is in me or else is not at all (does not exist). *Ib.*

2 The world is a force, not a presence. *Ib.*

3 Poetry is a search for the inexplicable. *Ib.*

Simeon Strunsky
1879–1948

4 Famous remarks are very seldom quoted correctly. *No Mean City [1944], ch. 38*

Leon Trotsky
1879–1940

5 The literary "fellow travelers" of the Revolution. *Literature and Revolution [1923], ch. 2*

6 The dictatorship of the Communist Party is maintained by recourse to every form of violence. *Terrorism and Communism [1924], p. 71*

7 Old age is the most unexpected of all the things that happen to a man. *Diary in Exile [1935]*[1]

8 The vengeance of history is more terrible than the vengeance of the most powerful General Secretary. *Stalin [1946], ch. 12*

Guillaume Apollinaire
[Wilhelm Apollinaris de Kostrowitsky]
1880–1918

9 Shepherdess, O Eiffel Tower, your flock of bridges is bleating this morning.[2] *Alcools [1913].*[3] *Zone*

10 Come night, strike hour.
Days go, I endure.[4]
Ib. Le Pont Mirabeau (Mirabeau Bridge), refrain

11 I hibernated in my past.[5] *Ib. La Chanson du Mal-Aimé (Song of the Poorly Loved), st. 10*

[1] Translated by E. Zarudnaya.
[2] Bergère ô tour Eiffel le troupeau des ponts bêle ce matin.
[3] Translated by William Meredith.
[4] Vienne la nuit sonne l'heure / Les jours s'en vont je demeure.
[5] J'ai hiverné dans mon passé.
Translated by Roger Shattuck.

12 O Milky Way, sister in whiteness
To Canaan's rivers and the bright
Bodies of lovers drowned,
Can we follow toilsomely
Your path to other nebulae?[6]
Ib. st. 13 (also st. 27)

13 Pass on, let us pass, all is passing,
And I will look back many times:

The sound of hunting horns, when it dies
On the wind, is like our memories.[7]
Ib. Cors de Chasse (Hunting Horns), st. 2, 3

George Asaf
[George H. Powell]
1880–1951

14 What's the use of worrying?
It never was worthwhile,
So, pack up your troubles in your old kit-bag,
And smile, smile, smile.
Pack Up Your Troubles in Your Old Kit-Bag [1915]

Alexander Blok
1880–1921

15 Black evening, white snow. *The Twelve [1918]*

16 With your whole body, with your whole heart, with your whole conscience, listen to the Revolution. . . . This is the music everyone who has ears should hear. *The Intelligentsia and the Revolution [1918]*

William Claude Fields
1880–1946

17 It ain't a fit night out for man or beast. *The Fatal Glass of Beer*

18 Anyone who hates children and dogs can't be all bad.[8] *Attributed*

19 On the whole, I'd rather be in Philadelphia. *His own epitaph*

[6] Voie lactée ô soeur lumineuse / Des blancs ruisseaux de Chanaan / Et des corps blancs des amoureuses / Nageurs morts suivrons-nous d'ahan / Ton cours vers d'autres nébuleuses.
[7] Passons passons puisque tout passe / Je me retournerai souvent / / Les souvenirs sont cors de chasse / Dont meurt le bruit parmi le vent.
See Anonymous: French, 928:3.
[8] Anyone who hates babies and dogs can't be all bad. — Leo C. Rosten [1908–], *in tribute to Fields at a banquet* [1939]
The quip has become most familiar with "children" (as attributed to Fields).
See Carlyle, 472:20.

Helen Keller
1880–1968

1 Literature is my Utopia. Here I am not disfranchised. No barrier of the senses shuts me out from the sweet, gracious discourse of my book friends. They talk to me without embarrassment or awkwardness.

The Story of My Life [1902]

Douglas MacArthur
1880–1964

2 The unfailing formula for production of morale is patriotism, self-respect, discipline, and self-confidence within a military unit, joined with fair treatment and merited appreciation from without. . . . It will quickly wither and die if soldiers come to believe themselves the victims of indifference or injustice on the part of their government, or of ignorance, personal ambition, or ineptitude on the part of their military leaders.

Annual Report of the Chief of Staff, U.S. Army, for the Fiscal Year Ending June 30, 1933

3 I shall return.

On leaving Corregidor for Australia [March 11, 1942]

4 I have returned. By the grace of Almighty God, our forces stand again on Philippine soil.

Upon landing on Leyte [October 20, 1944]

5 I see that the old flagpole still stands. Have your troops hoist the colors to its peak, and let no enemy ever haul them down.

To Colonel George M. Jones and 503rd Regimental Combat Team, who recaptured Corregidor [March 2, 1945]

6 In war there is no substitute for victory.

Address to a Joint Meeting of Congress [April 19, 1951]

7 I still remember the refrain of one of the most popular barracks ballads of that day, which proclaimed most proudly that old soldiers never die; they just fade away. I now close my military career and just fade away.[1]

Ib.

8 It is fatal to enter any war without the will to win it.

Speech at the Republican National Convention [July 7, 1952]

[1] See Anonymous, 924:9.

George Catlett Marshall
1880–1959

9 The refusal of the British and Russian peoples to accept what appeared to be inevitable defeat was the great factor in the salvage of our civilization.

Biennial Report of the Chief of Staff, United States Army [September 1, 1945]

10 If man does find the solution for world peace it will be the most revolutionary reversal of his record we have ever known.

Ib.

11 Our policy is directed not against any country or doctrine but against hunger, poverty, desperation and chaos. Its purpose should be the revival of a working economy in the world so as to permit the emergence of political and social conditions in which free institutions can exist.

Address at Harvard University [June 5, 1947], embodying the European Recovery Plan (Marshall Plan)

12 It is not enough to fight. It is the spirit which we bring to the fight that decides the issue. It is morale that wins the victory.

Military Review [October 1948]

13 Morale is the state of mind. It is steadfastness and courage and hope. It is confidence and zeal and loyalty. It is *élan, esprit de corps* and determination. *Ib.*

Henry Louis Mencken
1880–1956

14 The virulence of the national appetite for bogus revelation.

A Book of Prefaces [1917], ch. 1

15 To the man with an ear for verbal delicacies — the man who searches painfully for the perfect word, and puts the way of saying a thing above the thing said — there is in writing the constant joy of sudden discovery, of happy accident. *Ib. 2*

16 Poverty is a soft pedal upon all branches of human activity, not excepting the spiritual.

Ib. 4

17 Time is a great legalizer, even in the field of morals. *Ib.*

18 The public . . . demands certainties. . . . But there *are* no certainties.

Prejudices, First Series [1919], ch. 3

1 All successful newspapers are ceaselessly querulous and bellicose. They never defend anyone or anything if they can help it; if the job is forced upon them, they tackle it by denouncing someone or something else.
Ib. 13

2 The great artists of the world are never Puritans, and seldom even ordinarily respectable. *Ib. 16*

3 To be in love is merely to be in a state of perceptual anesthesia—to mistake an ordinary young man for a Greek god or an ordinary young woman for a goddess. *Ib.*

4 Philadelphia is the most pecksniffian of American cities, and thus probably leads the world.
The American Language [1919]

5 It is the dull man who is always sure, and the sure man who is always dull.
Prejudices, Second Series [1920], ch. 1

6 If, after I depart this vale, you ever remember me and have thought to please my ghost, forgive some sinner and wink your eye at some homely girl.
Epitaph. From Smart Set [December 1921]

7 There are no mute, inglorious Miltons,[1] save in the hallucinations of poets. The one sound test of a Milton is that he functions as a Milton.
Prejudices, Third Series [1922], ch. 3

8 Nine times out of ten, in the arts as in life, there is actually no truth to be discovered; there is only error to be exposed. *Ib.*

9 Injustice is relatively easy to bear; what stings is justice. *Ib.*

10 The older I grow the more I distrust the familiar doctrine that age brings wisdom.
Ib.

11 Faith may be defined briefly as an illogical belief in the occurrence of the improbable.
Ib. 14

12 To be happy one must be (*a*) well fed, unhounded by sordid cares, at ease in Zion,[2] (*b*) full of a comfortable feeling of superiority to the masses of one's fellow men, and (*c*) delicately and unceasingly amused according to one's taste. It is my contention that, if this definition be accepted, there is no country in the world wherein a man constituted as I am—a man of my peculiar weakness, vanities, appetites, and aversions—can be so happy as he can be in the United States.
On Being An American [1922]

13 The difference between a moral man and a man of honor is that the latter regrets a discreditable act, even when it has worked and he has not been caught.
Prejudices, Fourth Series [1924], ch. 11

14 Nothing can come out of an artist that is not in the man.
Ib. Fifth Series [1926], ch. 5

15 Of all escape mechanisms, death is the most efficient.
A Book of Burlesques [1928]

16 When A annoys or injures B on the pretense of saving or improving X, A is a scoundrel.
Newspaper Days: 1899–1906 [1941]

17 Conscience is the inner voice that warns us somebody may be looking.
A Mencken Chrestomathy [1949]

18 There are some people who read too much: the bibliobibuli. I know some who are constantly drunk on books, as other men are drunk on whiskey or religion. They wander through this most diverting and stimulating of worlds in a haze, seeing nothing and hearing nothing.
Minority Report: H. L. Mencken's Notebooks [1956]

19 The booboisie. *Passim*

20 No one ever went broke underestimating the intelligence [or taste] of the American people. *Attributed*

Alfred Noyes
1880–1958

21 Forty singing seamen, who was puzzled for to know
If the grog they dreamed they swallowed made them dream of all that followed.
Forty Singing Seamen

22 Go down to Kew in lilac time (it isn't far from London!)
And you shall wander hand in hand with love in summer's wonderland.
Barrel Organ, st. 5

23 The wind was a torrent of darkness among the gusty trees,

[1]See Gray, 362:9.
[2]See *Amos 6:1*, 33:21.

The moon was a ghostly galleon tossed upon cloudy seas,
The road was a ribbon of moonlight over the purple moor,
And the highwayman came riding—
Riding—riding—
The highwayman came riding, up to the old inn-door.
The Highwayman

1 I'll come to thee by moonlight, though hell should bar the way.
Ib.

2 Calling as he used to call, faint and far away,
In Sherwood, in Sherwood, about the break of day.
Sherwood

Grantland Rice
1880–1954

3 When the One Great Scorer comes to write against your name—
He marks—not that you won or lost—but how you played the game.[1]
Alumnus Football

4 All wars are planned by old men
In council rooms apart.[2]
Two Sides of War, st. 1

5 I've noticed nearly all the dead
Were hardly more than boys.
Ib. st. 4

6 Outlined against a blue-gray October sky, the Four Horsemen[3] rode again. In dramatic lore they were known as Famine, Pestilence, Destruction, and Death. These are only aliases. Their real names are Stuhldreher, Miller, Crowley, and Layden.[4]
Story on Notre Dame football victory over Army, New York Tribune [October 18, 1924]

Richard Henry Tawney
1880–1962

7 Industrialized communities neglect the very objects for which it is worth while to acquire riches in their feverish preoccupation with the means by which riches can be acquired.
The Acquisitive Society [1920]

8 It is not till it is discovered that high individual incomes will not purchase the mass of mankind immunity from cholera, typhus, and ignorance, still less secure them the positive advantages of educational opportunity and economic security, that slowly and reluctantly, amid prophecies of moral degeneration and economic disaster, society begins to make collective provision for needs which no ordinary individual, even if he works overtime all his life, can provide himself.
Equality [1931], ch. 4, sec. 2

Thomas Russell Ybarra
1880–

9 A Christian is a man who feels
Repentance on a Sunday
For what he did on Saturday
And is going to do on Monday.
The Christian

Franklin Pierce Adams [F.P.A.]
1881–1960

10 Christmas is over and Business is Business.
For the Other 364 Days

11 Up, to the office . . . and so to bed.
A Ballade of Mr. Samuel Pepys. Refrain

12 Ruthlessly pricking our gonfalon bubble,
Making a Giant hit into a double,
Words that are weighty with nothing but trouble:
"Tinker to Evers to Chance."
Baseball's Sad Lexicon

13 The best you get is an even break.[5]
Ballade of Schopenhauer's Philosophy

14 Of making many books there is no end—
So Sancho Panza said, and so say I.[6]
Thou wert my guide, philosopher and friend
When only one is shining in the sky.
Lines on and from Bartlett's Familiar Quotations

15 Go, lovely Rose that lives its little hour!
Go, little booke! and let who will be clever!
Roll on! From yonder ivy-mantled tower
The moon and I could keep this up forever.
Ib.

Joseph Campbell
1881–1944

16 As a white candle
In a holy place,
So is the beauty
Of an aged face.
The Old Woman, st. 1

[1] See Newbolt, 700:11, and Cooke, 718:17.
[2] See Hoover, 750:20.
[3] See Blasco-Ibáñez, 720:18.
[4] Thereafter known as the Four Horsemen of Notre Dame.
[5] See Albee, 683:1.
[6] See Saxe, 556:2.

Padraic Colum
1881–1972

1 A little house — a house of my own —
Out of the wind's and the rain's way.
An Old Woman of the Roads, st. 6

Sir Alexander Fleming
1881–1955

2 It is the lone worker who makes the first advance in a subject: the details may be worked out by a team, but the prime idea is due to the enterprise, thought and perception of an individual.[1]
Address at Edinburgh University [1951]

Edgar Albert Guest
1881–1959

3 Somebody said that it couldn't be done,
But he with a chuckle replied
That maybe it couldn't, but he would be one
Who wouldn't say so till he'd tried.
It Couldn't Be Done

4 It takes a heap o' livin' in a house t' make it home,
A heap o' sun an' shadder, an' ye sometimes have t' roam
Afore ye really 'preciate the things ye lef' behind,
An' hunger fer 'em somehow, with 'em allus on yer mind. *Home*

5 Let me be a little kinder,
Let me be a little blinder
To the faults of those around me,
Let me praise a little more. *A Creed*

Pope John XXIII
[Angelo Giuseppe Roncalli]
1881–1963

6 The social progress, order, security and peace of each country are necessarily connected with the social progress, order, security and peace of all other countries.
Pacem in Terris. Encyclical letter [April 11, 1963]

7 The moral order, which needs public authority in order to promote the common good in human society, requires also that the authority be effective in attaining that end. . . .

[1]See Darwin, 662:3, and Zinsser, 762:5.

Today the universal common good poses problems of world-wide dimensions, which cannot be adequately tackled or solved except by the efforts of public authorities endowed with a wideness of power, structure and means of the same proportions: that is, of public authorities which are in a position to operate in an effective manner on a world-wide basis. The moral order itself, therefore, demands that such a form of public authority be established. *Ib.*

8 An act of the highest importance performed by the United Nations Organization was the universal Declaration of Human Rights, approved in the General Assembly of December 10, 1948. . . . The document represents an important step on the path towards the juridical-political organization of the world community. For in it, in most solemn form, the dignity of a person is acknowledged to all human beings; and as a consequence there is proclaimed, as a fundamental right, the right of free movement in search for truth and in the attainment of moral good and of justice, and also the right to a dignified life. *Ib.*

9 The representative of the highest spiritual authority of the earth is glad, indeed boasts, of being the son of a humble but robust and honest laborer.
Remark to the mayor of Fleury-sur-Loire. From Wit and Wisdom of Good Pope John, collected by HENRI FESQUET *[1963]*

Pablo Picasso
1881–1973

10 For me, a painting is a dramatic action in the course of which reality finds itself split apart. For me, that dramatic action takes precedence over all other considerations. The pure plastic act is only secondary as far as I'm concerned. What counts is the drama of that plastic act, the moment at which the universe comes out of itself and meets its own destruction.
From FRANÇOISE GILOT AND CARLTON LAKE, *Life with Picasso [1964], pt. I*

11 Painting isn't an aesthetic operation; it's a form of magic designed as a mediator between this strange hostile world and us, a way of seizing the power by giving form to our terrors as well as our desires. *Ib. VI*

12 I am only a public entertainer who has understood his time. *Remark*

Pierre Teilhard de Chardin[1]

1881–1955

1 If there were no internal propensity to unite, even at a prodigiously rudimentary level—indeed in the molecule itself—it would be physically impossible for love to appear higher up.

The Phenomenon of Man [1955], bk. IV, ch. 2, sec. 2

2 Love alone is capable of uniting living beings in such a way as to complete and fulfill them, for it alone takes them and joins them by what is deepest in themselves. . . . Does not love every instant achieve all around us, in the couple or the team, the magic feat . . . of "personalizing" by totalizing?

Ib.

3 We have only to believe. And the more threatening and irreducible reality appears, the more firmly and desperately must we believe. Then, little by little, we shall see the universal horror unbend, and then smile upon us, and then take us in its more than human arms.

The Divine Milieu [1957], pt. III, ch. 3, sec. B

William Temple

1881–1944

4 There is no structural organization of society which can bring about the coming of the Kingdom of God on earth, since all systems can be perverted by the selfishness of man.

The Malvern Manifesto[2]

5 Human status ought not to depend upon the changing demands of the economic process. *Ib.*

Ludwig Edler von Mises

1881–1973

6 Unemployment as a mass phenomenon is the outcome of allegedly "pro-labor" policies of the governments and of labor union pressure and compulsion. This explanation is by no means peculiar to those economists whom the "progressives" call "reactionaries."

Bureaucracy [1944]

7 Millions are fascinated by the plan to transform the whole world into a bureau, to make everybody a bureaucrat, and to wipe out any private initiative. The paradise of the future is visualized as an all-embracing bureaucratic apparatus. . . . Streams of blood have been shed for the realization of this ideal. *Ib.*

8 There are in the fields of economics no constant relations, and consequently no measurement is possible.

Human Action [1949]

9 Statistical figures referring to economic events are historical data. They tell us what happened in a nonrepeatable historical case.

Ib.

Sir Pelham Grenville Wodehouse

1881–1975

10 Look for the silver lining[3]
Whene'er a cloud appears in the blue.
Remember somewhere the sun is shining
And so the right thing to do is make it shine
for you.

Sally [1920]. Look for the Silver Lining

11 So always look for the silver lining
And try to find the sunny side of life.

Ib.

12 The Inimitable Jeeves.

Title of book [1924]

Max Born

1882–1970

13 The human race has today the means for annihilating itself—either in a fit of complete lunacy, i.e., in a big war, by a brief fit of destruction, or by careless handling of atomic technology, through a slow process of poisoning and of deterioration in its genetic structure.

Bulletin of the Atomic Scientists [June 1957]

Berton Braley

1882–1966

14 And so they sailed away, these three,
Mencken, Nathan and God.[4]

Three Minus One, st. 1

15 Back of the job—the dreamer
Who's making the dream come true!

The Thinker, st. 4

[1] Translated by BERNARD WALL.

[2] Drawn up by a Conference of the Province of York, January 10, 1941; signed for the Conference by Temple, then Archbishop of York (later Archbishop of Canterbury).

[3] See Lena Ford, 740:11.

[4] See Field, 666:16.

Georges Braque
1882–1963

1 Art upsets, science reassures.
Pensées sur l'Art

2 Truth exists, only falsehood has to be invented. *Ib.*

Percy Williams Bridgman
1882–1961

3 The concept of length is . . . fixed when the operations by which length is measured are fixed . . . The concept is synonymous with the corresponding set of operations.
The Logic of Modern Physics [1927]

Edward Arthur Burroughs, Bishop of Ripon
1882–1934

4 After all we could get on very happily if aviation, wireless, television and the like advanced no further than at present. . . . The sum of human happiness would not necessarily be reduced if for ten years every physical and chemical laboratory were closed and the patient and resourceful energy displayed in them transferred to the lost art of getting on together and finding the formula for making both ends meet in the scale of human life. Much, of course, we should lose by this universal scientific holiday . . . but human happiness would not necessarily suffer.
Sermon to the British Association for the Advancement of Science, Leeds [September 4, 1927]

Father Divine [George Baker]
c. 1882–1965

5 Peace, it's wonderful.
Motto of the Peace Mission Movement

Sir Arthur Stanley Eddington
1882–1944

6 It is one thing for the human mind to extract from the phenomena of nature the laws which it has itself put into them; it may be a far harder thing to extract laws over which it has no control. It is even possible that laws which have not their origin in the mind may be irrational, and we can never succeed in formulating them.
Space, Time, and Gravitation [1920], ch. 12

7 We have found that where science has progressed the farthest, the mind has but regained from nature that which the mind put into nature.

We have found a strange footprint on the shores of the unknown. We have devised profound theories, one after another, to account for its origin. At last we have succeeded in reconstructing the creature that made the footprint. And lo! it is our own. *Ib.*

8 I am afraid of this word Reality, not connoting an ordinarily definable characteristic of the things it is applied to, but used as though it were some kind of celestial halo.
The Nature of the Physical World [1928], ch. 13

9 Man is slightly nearer to the atom than to the star. . . . From his central position man can survey the grandest works of Nature with the astronomer, or the minutest works with the physicist.
Stars and Atoms [1928], lecture 1

10 I ask you to look both ways. For the road to a knowledge of the stars leads through the atom; and important knowledge of the atom has been reached through the stars.
Ib.

Felix Frankfurter
1882–1965

11 The [Fifteenth] Amendment nullifies sophisticated as well as simple-minded modes of discrimination.
Lane v. Wilson, 307 U.S. 268, 275 [1939]

12 The history of liberty has largely been the history of the observance of procedural safeguards.
McNabb v. United States, 318 U.S. 332, 347 [1943]

13 One who belongs to the most vilified and persecuted minority in history is not likely to be insensible to the freedoms guaranteed by our Constitution. . . . But as judges we are neither Jew nor Gentile, neither Catholic nor agnostic.
Flag Salute Cases, 319 U.S. 624, 646 [1943]

14 Courts ought not to enter this political thicket.
Colegrove v. Green, 328 U.S. 549, 556 [1946]

1 After all, this is the Nation's ultimate judicial tribunal, not a super-legal-aid bureau.

Uveges v. Pennsylvania, 335 U.S. 437, 449 [1948]

2 In a democratic society like ours, relief must come through an aroused popular conscience that sears the conscience of the people's representatives.

Baker v. Carr, 369 U.S. 186, 270 [1962]

3 I know of no title that I deem more honorable than that of Professor of the Harvard Law School.

Of Law and Life and Other Things [1965]

Jean Giraudoux

1882–1944

4 There are truths which can kill a nation.

Electra

5 Faithful women are all alike, they think only of their fidelity, never of their husbands.

Amphitryon 38 [1929]

Samuel Goldwyn

1882–1974

6 Include me out. *Attributed*

7 In two words: im-possible.

From ALVA JOHNSTON, *The Great Goldwyn*

8 I read part of it all the way through.

Ib.

9 Anybody who goes to see a psychiatrist ought to have his head examined.

Attributed

Hermann Hagedorn

1882–1964

10 The bomb that fell on Hiroshima fell on America too.
It fell on no city, no munition plants, no docks.
It erased no church, vaporized no public buildings, reduced no man to his atomic elements.
But it fell, it fell.
It burst. It shook the land.
God have mercy on our children.
God have mercy on America.

The Bomb That Fell on America

William Frederick Halsey, Jr.

1882–1959

11 Attack — Repeat — Attack.

Dispatch [October 26, 1942] to the South Pacific Force before the battle of Santa Cruz Islands

12 Hit hard, hit fast, hit often.[1]

Formula for waging war

13 Send them our latitude and longitude.

Retort to the enemy's question: "Where is the American fleet?" [October 1944]

14 Our ships have been salvaged and are retiring at high speed toward the Japanese fleet.

Radio message [October 1944] after Japanese claims that most of the U.S. Third Fleet had either been sunk or had retired

James Joyce

1882–1941

15 He was outcast from life's feast.

Dubliners [1916]. A Painful Case

16 Snow was general all over Ireland. It was falling on every part of the dark central plain, on the treeless hills, falling softly upon the Bog of Allen and, farther westward, softly falling into the dark mutinous Shannon waves. It was falling, too, upon every part of the lonely churchyard on the hill where Michael Furey lay buried. It lay thickly drifted on the crooked crosses and headstones, on the spears of the little gate, on the barren thorns. His soul swooned slowly as he heard the snow falling faintly through the universe and faintly falling, like the descent of their last end, upon all the living and the dead.

Ib. The Dead

17 Pity is the feeling which arrests the mind in the presence of whatsoever is grave and constant in human sufferings and unites it with the human sufferer.

A Portrait of the Artist as a Young Man [1916], ch. 5

18 Welcome, O life! I go to encounter for the millionth time the reality of experience and to forge in the smithy of my soul the uncreated conscience of my race.

Old father, old artificer, stand me now and ever in good stead.

Ib. Concluding words of Stephen Dedalus

[1]See Grant, 589:15.

1 History, Stephen said, is a nightmare from which I am trying to awake.

Ulysses [1922][1]

2 My patience are exhausted [Martha Clifford]. *Ib.*

3 A man of genius makes no mistakes. His errors are volitional and are the portals of discovery. *Ib.*

4 And yes I said yes I will Yes.

Ib. Last words

5 Can't hear with bawk of bats, all thim liffeying waters of. Ho, talk save us! My foos won't moos. I feel as old as yonder elm. A tale told of Shaun or Shem? All Livia's daughter-sons. Dark hawks hear us. Night! Night! My ho head halls. I feel as heavy as yonder stone. Tell me of John or Shaun? Who were Shem and Shaun the living sons or daughters of? Night now! Tell me, tell me, tell me, elm! Night night! Telmetale of stem or stone. Beside the rivering waters of, hitherandthithering waters of. Night!

Finnegans Wake [1939], pt. I (end)

6 I am passing out. O bitter ending! I'll slip away before they're up. They'll never see. Nor know. Nor miss me. And it's old and old it's sad and old it's sad and weary I go back to you, my cold father, my cold mad father, my cold mad feary father, till the near sight of the mere size of him, the moyles and moyles of it, moananoaning, makes me seasilt saltsick and I rush, my only, into your arms, I see them rising! Save me from those therrble prongs! Two more. Onetwo moremens more. So. Avelaval. My leaves have drifted from me. All. But one clings still. I'll bear it on me. To remind me of. Lff! So soft this morning, ours. Yes. Carry me along, taddy, like you done through the toy fair! If I seen him bearing down on me now under whitespread wings like he'd come from Arkangels, I sink I'd die down over his feet, humbly dumbly, only to washup. Yes, tid. There's where. First. We pass through grass behush the bush to. Whish! A gull. Gulls. Far calls. Coming, far! End here. Us then. Finn, again! Take. Bussoftlhee, mememormee! Till thousendsthee. Lps. The keys to. Given! A way a lone a last a loved a long the *Ib. IV*

[1] See Woolsey, 758:13 and 759:1.

Philip Henry Kerr, Marquess of Lothian

1882–1940

7 A limitation of armaments by political appeasement.

Letter to The Times (London) [May 1934]

Fiorello Henry La Guardia

1882–1947

8 Ticker tape ain't spaghetti.

Speech to the United Nations Relief and Rehabilitation Administration [March 29, 1946]

9 When I make a mistake it's a beaut!

On an indefensible appointment

Winifred Mary Letts

1882–c. 1936

10 I saw the spires of Oxford
As I was passing by,
The gray spires of Oxford
Against a pearl-gray sky.
My heart was with the Oxford men
Who went abroad to die.

The Spires of Oxford, st. 1

Jacques Maritain

1882–1973

11 In the modern social order, the *person* is sacrificed to the *individual*. The individual is given universal suffrage, equality of rights, freedom of opinion; while the person, isolated, naked, with no social armor to sustain and protect him, is left to the mercy of all the devouring forces which threaten the life of the soul, exposed to relentless actions and reactions of conflicting interests and appetites. . . . It is a homicidal civilization.

Three Reformers [1925]

Alan Alexander Milne

1882–1956

12 I am a Bear of Very Little Brain, and long words Bother me.

Winnie-the-Pooh [1926], ch. 4

13 Time for a little something. *Ib. 6*

Sam Rayburn

1882–1961

1 I like to make running water walk.

On Conversation. From VALTON J. YOUNG, *The Speaker's Agent [1956]*

2 The greatest domestic problem facing our country is saving our soil and water. Our soil belongs also to unborn generations.

Ib.

3 The one thing besides people that I claim to know is land. *Ib.*

4 To get along, go along.[1] *Attributed*

Franklin Delano Roosevelt

1882–1945

5 There is nothing I love as much as a good fight.

Interview in the New York Times [January 22, 1911]

6 These unhappy times call for the building of plans . . . that build from the bottom up and not from the top down, that put their faith once more in the forgotten man[2] at the bottom of the economic pyramid.

Radio address [April 7, 1932]

7 The country needs and, unless I mistake its temper, the country demands bold, persistent experimentation. It is common sense to take a method and try it. If it fails, admit it frankly and try another. But above all, try something.

Address at Oglethorpe University, Atlanta, Georgia [May 22, 1932]

8 I pledge you, I pledge myself, to a new deal for the American people.

Speech accepting the Democratic nomination for the presidency, Chicago [July 2, 1932]

9 There is no indispensable man.[3]

Campaign speech, New York [November 3, 1932]

10 The only thing we have to fear is fear itself.[4]

First Inaugural Address [March 4, 1933]

11 In the field of world policy I would dedicate this nation to the policy of the good neighbor.[5] *Ib.*

12 If I were asked to state the great objective which Church and State are both demanding for the sake of every man and woman and child in this country, I would say that that great objective is "a more abundant life."

Address to the Federal Council of Churches of Christ [December 6, 1933]

13 We are moving forward to greater freedom, to greater security for the average man than he has ever known before in the history of America.

Fireside Chat [September 30, 1934]

14 We have earned the hatred of entrenched greed.

Message to Congress [January 3, 1936]

15 The truth is found when men are free to pursue it.

Address at Temple University, Philadelphia [February 22, 1936]

16 Out of this modern civilization economic royalists carved new dynasties. . . . The royalists of the economic order have conceded that political freedom was the business of the Government, but they have maintained that economic slavery was nobody's business.

Speech accepting renomination [June 27, 1936]

17 This generation of Americans has a rendezvous with destiny. *Ib.*

18 I have seen war. . . . I hate war.

Address at Chautauqua, New York [August 14, 1936]

19 I have not sought, I do not seek, I repudiate the support of any advocate of Communism or of any other alien "ism" which would by fair means or foul change our American democracy.

Address at Syracuse [September 29, 1936]

20 I should like to have it said of my first Administration that in it the forces of selfishness and of lust for power met their match. I should like to have it said of my second Administration that in it these forces met their master.

Speech at Madison Square Garden [October 31, 1936]

[1] Another version: The way to get along is to go along.

[2] See William Graham Sumner, 642:11.

All honor to the one that in this hour / Cries to the world as from a lighted tower — / Cries for the Man Forgotten. — EDWIN MARKHAM [1852–1940], *The Forgotten Man*

[3] Il n'y a point d'homme nécessaire. — *French proverb*

See Cavafy, 701:11.

[4] See *Proverbs 3:25*, 23:6; Montaigne, 164:7; Bacon, 179:13; Wellington, 421:10; and Thoreau, 557:9.

[5] I am as desirous of being a good neighbor as I am of being a bad subject. — THOREAU, *Civil Disobedience* [1849]

1 We have always known that heedless self-interest was bad morals; we know now that it is bad economics.

Second Inaugural Address [January 20, 1937]

2 I see one-third of a nation ill-housed, ill-clad, ill-nourished. *Ib.*

3 The test of our progress is not whether we add more to the abundance of those who have much; it is whether we provide enough for those who have too little. *Ib.*

4 The epidemic of world lawlessness is spreading. When an epidemic of physical disease starts to spread, the community approves and joins in a quarantine of the patients in order to protect the health of the community against the spread of the disease. . . . The will for peace on the part of peace-loving nations must express itself to the end that nations that may be tempted to violate their agreements and the rights of others will desist from such a course. There must be positive endeavors to preserve peace.

Speech at Chicago [October 5, 1937][1]

5 War is a contagion. *Ib.*

6 The only sure bulwark of continuing liberty is a government strong enough to protect the interests of the people, and a people strong enough and well enough informed to maintain its sovereign control over its government.

Fireside Chat [April 14, 1938]

7 A program whose basic thesis is not that the system of free private enterprise for profit has failed in this generation, but that it has not yet been tried.

Message on Concentration of Economic Power [April 29, 1938]

8 The Soviet Union, as everybody who has the courage to face the fact knows, is run by a dictatorship as absolute as any other dictatorship in the world.

Address to the American Youth Congress [February 10, 1940]

9 On this tenth day of June 1940 the hand that held the dagger has struck it into the back of its neighbor.[2]

Address at the University of Virginia, Charlottesville [June 10, 1940]

[1] The "Quarantine the Aggressors" speech.

[2] Italian Foreign Minister Count Galeazzo Ciano had just notified the French ambassador that Italy considered herself at war with France beginning June 11.

10 Eternal truths will be neither true nor eternal unless they have fresh meaning for every new social situation.

Address at the University of Pennsylvania [September 20, 1940]

11 And while I am talking to you mothers and fathers, I give you one more assurance. I have said this before, but I shall say it again and again and again: Your boys are not going to be sent into any foreign wars.

Campaign speech in Boston [October 30, 1940]

12 We must be the great arsenal of democracy.

Fireside Chat [December 29, 1940]

13 We look forward to a world founded upon four essential human freedoms. The first is freedom of speech and expression—everywhere in the world. The second is freedom of every person to worship God in his own way—everywhere in the world. The third is freedom from want . . . everywhere in the world. The fourth is freedom from fear . . . anywhere in the world.[3]

Message to Congress [January 6, 1941]

14 We, too, born to freedom, and believing in freedom, are willing to fight to maintain freedom. We, and all others who believe as deeply as we do, would rather die on our feet than live on our knees.[4]

On receiving the degree of Doctor of Civil Law from Oxford University [June 19, 1941]

15 Yesterday, December 7, 1941—a date which will live in infamy—the United States of America was suddenly and deliberately attacked by naval and air forces of the Empire of Japan.

War Message to Congress [December 8, 1941]

16 Never before have we had so little time in which to do so much.[5]

Fireside Chat [February 23, 1942]

17 Books cannot be killed by fire. People die, but books never die. No man and no force can abolish memory. . . . In this war, we know, books are weapons.

Message to the American Booksellers Association [April 23, 1942]

18 It is not a tax bill but a tax relief bill providing relief not for the needy but for the greedy.

Tax bill veto message [February 22, 1944]

[3] See Roosevelt and Churchill, 781:8.

[4] See Zapata, 759:2.

[5] See Churchill, 744:6.

1 I think I have a right to resent, to object to libelous statements about my dog.[1]

Speech at the Teamsters' Dinner, Washington [September 23, 1944]

2 All of our people all over the country—except the pure-blooded Indians—are immigrants or descendants of immigrants, including even those who came over here on the *Mayflower.*

Campaign speech in Boston [November 4, 1944]

3 The American people are quite competent to judge a political party that works both sides of a street. *Ib.*

4 Perfectionism, no less than isolationism or imperialism or power politics, may obstruct the paths to international peace.

State of the Union Message [January 6, 1945]

5 We have learned that we cannot live alone, at peace; that our own well-being is dependent on the well-being of other nations, far away. We have learned that we must live as men, and not as ostriches, nor as dogs in the manger. We have learned to be citizens of the world,[2] members of the human community.

Fourth Inaugural Address [January 20, 1945]

6 More than an end to war, we want an end to the beginnings of all wars.

Address written for Jefferson Day broadcast [April 13, 1945][3]

Franklin Delano Roosevelt and Winston Churchill

7 First, their countries seek no aggrandizement, territorial or other.

Second, they desire to see no territorial changes that do not accord with the freely expressed wishes of the peoples concerned.

Atlantic Charter, drawn up aboard the U.S.S. Augusta in Argentia Harbor, Newfoundland [issued August 14, 1941]

8 Sixth, after the final destruction of the Nazi tyranny, they hope to see established a peace which will afford to all nations the means of dwelling in safety within their own boundaries, and which will afford assurance that all the men in all the lands may live out their lives in freedom from fear and want.[4] *Ib.*

9 Eighth, they believe that all of the nations of the world, for realistic as well as spiritual reasons, must come to the abandonment of the use of force. Since no future peace can be maintained if land, sea or air armaments continue to be employed by nations which threaten, or may threaten, aggression outside of their frontiers, they believe, pending the establishment of a wider and permanent system of general security, that the disarmament of such nations is essential. *Ib.*

James Stephens
1882–1950

10 I hear a sudden cry of pain!
There is a rabbit in a snare.

The Snare

11 Forgive us all our trespasses,
Little creatures, everywhere!

Little Things, st. 5

12 In cloud and clod to sing
Of everything and anything.

The Pit of Bliss

13 They fell out over pigs, let them fall in over pigs. *In the Land of Youth [1924]*

14 Women are wiser than men because they know less and understand more.

The Crock of Gold [1930], ch. 2

Virginia Woolf[5]
1882–1941

15 In people's eyes, in the swing, tramp, and trudge; in the bellow and uproar; the carriages, motor cars, omnibuses, vans, sandwich men shuffling and swinging; brass bands; barrel organs; in the triumph and the jingle and the strange high singing of some aeroplane overhead was what she loved; life; London; this moment in June.

Mrs. Dalloway [1925]

16 Those comfortably padded lunatic asylums which are known, euphemistically, as the stately homes of England.[6]

The Common Reader [1925]. Lady Dorothy Nevill

17 Trivial personalities decomposing in the eternity of print.

Ib. The Modern Essay

[1] It had been charged that the President's Scottie, Fala, allegedly stranded in the Aleutian Islands, had been brought home by a destroyer at a cost of millions.

[2] See Socrates, 79:7; Bacon, 180:13; Paine, 385:2; and Garrison, 505:10.

[3] President Roosevelt died on April 12, at Warm Springs, Georgia.

[4] See Roosevelt, 780:13.

[5] The talent of this generation which is most certain of survival.—REBECCA WEST, *Ending in Earnest* [1931]

[6] See Felicia D. Hemans, 470:13.

1 There is no room for the impurities of literature in an essay. *Ib.*

2 That complete statement which is literature.
Ib. How It Strikes a Contemporary

3 The word-coining genius, as if thought plunged into a sea of words and came up dripping. *Ib. An Elizabethan Play*

4 The beauty of the world has two edges, one of laughter, one of anguish, cutting the heart asunder. *A Room of One's Own [1929]*

5 Women have served all these centuries as looking-glasses possessing the magic and delicious power of reflecting the figure of man at twice its natural size. *Ib.*

6 Death is the enemy. . . . Against you I will fling myself, unvanquished and unyielding, O Death. *The Waves [1931]*

7 Surely it was time someone invented a new plot, or that the author came out from the bushes. *Between the Acts [1941]*

Coco [Gabrielle] Chanel
1883–1970

8 How many cares one loses when one decides not to be something but to be someone.
Remark

9 There are people who have money and people who are rich. *Remark*

10 As long as you know that most men are like children you know everything.
Remark

11 Good taste ruins certain true spiritual values: such as taste itself. *Remark*

12 Adornment is never anything except a reflection of the heart. *Remark*

Sir Andrew Browne Cunningham
1883–1963

13 We are so outnumbered there's only one thing to do. We must attack.[1]
Before attacking the Italian fleet, Taranto [November 1940]

Kahlil Gibran
1883–1931

14 Let there be spaces in your togetherness.[2]
The Prophet [1923]. On Marriage

15 You may give them your love but not your thoughts,
For they have their own thoughts.
You may house their bodies but not their souls,
For their souls dwell in the house of tomorrow, which you cannot visit, not even in your dreams.
You may strive to be like them, but seek not to make them like you,
For life goes not backward nor tarries with yesterday.
You are the bows from which your children as living arrows are sent forth.[3]
Ib. On Children

16 You give but little when you give of your possessions. It is when you give of yourself that you truly give.[4] *Ib. On Giving*

17 Work is love made visible. And if you cannot work with love but only with distaste, it is better that you should leave your work and sit at the gate of the temple and take alms of those who work with joy. *Ib. On Work*

18 You pray in your distress and in your need; would that you might pray also in the fullness of your joy and in your days of abundance. *Ib. On Prayer*

19 He who wears his morality but as his best garment were better naked.
Ib. On Religion

20 I have learned silence from the talkative, toleration from the intolerant, and kindness from the unkind; yet strange, I am ungrateful to those teachers.
Sand and Foam [1926]

21 We shall never understand one another until we reduce the language to seven words.[5]
Ib.

Nikos Kazantzakis
1883–1957

22 To cleave that sea [the Aegean] in the gentle autumnal season, murmuring the name of each islet, is to my mind the joy most apt to transport the heart of man into paradise.
Zorba the Greek [1946], ch. 2

23 How simple and frugal a thing is happiness: a glass of wine, a roast chestnut, a wretched little brazier, the sound of the sea. . . . All that is required to feel that here

[1]Quoted in *British Commanders*, published by British Information Services [1945].
[2]See Rilke, 756:12.
[3]See Goethe, 395:16.
[4]See Emerson, 498:6; James Russell Lowell, 567:14; and Whitman, 574:26.
[5]If we go on explaining we shall cease to understand one another. — TALLEYRAND [1754–1838], *quoted by* BERNARD BERENSON, *Aesthetics and History*

and now is happiness is a simple, frugal heart. *Ib. 7*

1 As I watched the seagulls, I thought: "That's the road to take; find the absolute rhythm and follow it with absolute trust." *Ib. 21*

2 The highest point a man can attain is not Knowledge, or Virtue, or Goodness, or Victory, but something even greater, more heroic and more despairing: Sacred Awe! *Ib. 24*

John Maynard Keynes
1883–1946

3 He [Clemenceau] had one illusion—France; and one disillusion—mankind, including Frenchmen.
Economic Consequences of the Peace [1919], ch. 3

4 Watching the company, with six or seven senses not available to ordinary men, judging character, motive, and subconscious impulse, perceiving what each was thinking and even what each was going to say next, and compounding with telepathic instinct the argument or appeal best suited to the vanity, weakness, or self-interest of his immediate auditor.[1] *Ib.*

5 He [Woodrow Wilson] could write Notes from Sinai or Olympus; he could remain unapproachable in the White House or even in the Council of Ten and be safe. But if he once stepped down to the intimate quality of the Four, the game was evidently up. *Ib.*

6 To make the defeated Central Empires into good neighbors. *Ib. 6*

7 Marxian Socialism must always remain a portent to the historians of opinion—how a doctrine so illogical and so dull can have exercised so powerful and enduring an influence over the minds of men, and, through them, the events of history.
The End of Laissez-Faire [1925], ch. 3

8 The engine which drives Enterprise is not Thrift, but Profit.
A Treatise on Money [1930]

9 Lenin is said to have declared that the best way to destroy the capitalist system was to debauch the currency. By a continuing process of inflation, governments can confiscate, secretly and unobserved, an important part of the wealth of their citizens. . . . Lenin was certainly right.
Essay in Persuasion [1931], pt. II

[1] Lloyd George.

10 The love of money[2] as a possession—as distinguished from the love of money as a means to the enjoyments and realities of life—will be recognized for what it is, a somewhat disgusting morbidity, one of those semi-criminal, semi-pathological propensities which one hands over with a shudder to the specialists in mental disease. *Ib. V*

11 Words ought to be a little wild for they are the assault of thoughts on the unthinking.
In the New Statesman and Nation [July 15, 1933]

12 His [Newton's] peculiar gift was the power of holding continuously in his mind a purely mental problem until he had seen through it.
Essays in Biography [1933]

13 There is no harm in being sometimes wrong—especially if one is promptly found out. *Ib.*

14 Of the maxims of orthodox finance, none, surely, is more antisocial than the fetish of liquidity. . . . It forgets that there is no such thing as liquidity of investment for the community as a whole.
The General Theory of Employment, Interest and Money [1936], ch. 12

15 There are no intrinsic reasons for the scarcity of capital. *Ib. 24*

16 Practical men, who believe themselves to be quite exempt from any intellectual influences, are usually the slaves of some defunct economist. . . . It is ideas, not vested interests, which are dangerous for good or evil. *Ib. end*

Alfred Hart Miles
1883–1956

17 Anchors aweigh, my boys,
Anchors aweigh!
Farewell to college joys,
We sail at break of day.
Anchors Aweigh [1907]

Benito Mussolini
1883–1945

18 The Italian proletariat needs a blood bath for its force to be renewed.
Editorial, Popolo d'Italia [1920]

[2] See *I Timothy 6:10*, 51:2, and Bellamy, 665:18.

1 War alone brings up to its highest tension all human energy and puts the stamp of nobility upon the peoples who have the courage to face it.

Written for The Italian Encyclopedia. From GEORGE SELDES, *Sawdust Caesar [1935]*

2 We have buried the putrid corpse of liberty.

Speech. From MAURICE PARMELEE, *Bolshevism, Fascism and the Liberal-Democratic State [1934]*

José Ortega y Gasset
1883–1955

3 Rancor is an outpouring of a feeling of inferiority.

Meditations on Quixote [1911]

4 I am myself and what is around me, and if I do not save it, it shall not save me. *Ib.*

5 The Mediterraneans, who do not think clearly, do see clearly. *Ib.*

6 Culture is not life in its entirety, but just the moment of security, strength, and clarity. *Ib.*

7 Nations are formed and are kept alive by the fact that they have a program for tomorrow. *Invertebrate Spain [1922], ch. 2*

8 A society without an aristocracy, without an elite minority, is not a society. *Ib. 4*

9 Conversation is the socializing instrument par excellence, and in its style one can see reflected the capacities of a race. *Ib. 7*

10 Man was formed by his struggle with exterior forces and it is only easy for him to discern things which are outside of himself.

The Modern Theme [1923], ch. 2

11 Rationalism, in order to save truth, renounces life. *Ib. 3*

12 The choice of a point of view is the initial act of a culture. *Ib. 7*

13 To define is to exclude and negate. *Ib. appendix*

14 Order is not pressure which is imposed on society from without, but an equilibrium which is set up from within.

Mirabeau and Politics [1927]

15 Europe is really a swarm: many bees on a single course.

The Revolt of the Masses [1930], prologue

16 America, far from being the future, was in truth a remote past because it was primitivism. *Ib.*

17 Minorities are individuals or groups of individuals especially qualified. The masses are the collection of people not specially qualified. *Ib. ch. 1*

18 Physical space and time are the absolute stupidity of the universe. *Ib. 4*

19 Our life is at all times and before anything else the consciousness of what we can do. *Ib.*

20 A revolution only lasts fifteen years, a period which coincides with the effectiveness of a generation. *Ib. 10*

21 War is not an instinct but an invention. *Ib. epilogue*

22 It is not the material of life which makes up Dostoevski's "realism," but rather the shape of life.

Notes on the Novel [1948]

23 The person portrayed and the portrait are two entirely different things.

The Dehumanization of Art [1948]

24 The masses feel that it is easy to flee from reality, when it is the most difficult thing in the world. *Ib.*

25 The metaphor is probably the most fertile power possessed by man. *Ib.*

26 I am a Spaniard, that is to say, a man without imagination.

Esthetic Essays [1956]

27 Primitive man is by definition tactile man. *Ib.*

Joseph Alois Schumpeter
1883–1950

28 Entrepreneurial profit . . . is the expression of the value of what the entrepreneur contributes to production in exactly the same sense that wages are the value expression of what the worker "produces." It is not a profit of exploitation any more than are wages.

The Theory of Economic Development [1934], ch. 4

29 Without development there is no profit, without profit no development. For the capitalist system it must be added further that without profit there would be no accumulation of wealth. *Ib.*

1 Marxism *is* a religion. To the believer it presents, first, a system of ultimate ends that embody the meaning of life and are absolute standards by which to judge events and actions; and, secondly, a guide to those ends which implies a plan of salvation and the indication of the evil from which mankind, or a chosen section of mankind, is to be saved.
Capitalism, Socialism and Democracy [1942], ch. 1

2 Marxism is essentially a product of the bourgeois mind. *Ib.*

3 He who places his trust in the Marxian synthesis as a whole, in order to understand present situations and problems, is apt to be woefully wrong. *Ib. 4*

4 Capitalism inevitably and by virtue of the very logic of its civilization creates, educates and subsidizes a vested interest in social unrest. *Ib. 13*

5 There is inherent in the capitalist system a tendency toward self-destruction.
Ib. 14

6 As a matter of practical necessity, socialist democracy may eventually turn out to be more of a sham than capitalist democracy ever was. *Ib. 23*

7 There is little reason to believe that this socialism will mean the advent of the civilization of which orthodox socialists dream. It is much more likely to present fascist features. That would be a strange answer to Marx's prayer. But history sometimes indulges in jokes of questionable taste. *Ib. 27*

Howard Arnold Walter
1883–1918

8 I would be true, for there are those who trust me;
I would be pure, for there are those who care;
I would be strong, for there is much to suffer;
I would be brave, for there is much to dare.
My Creed

William Carlos Williams
1883–1963

9 No wreaths please—
especially no hothouse flowers.
Some common memento is better,
something he prized and is known by:
his old clothes—a few books perhaps.
Tract [1917]

10 Hell take curtains! Go with some show
of inconvenience; sit openly—
to the weather as to grief.
Or do you think you can shut grief in?
Ib.

11 so much depends
upon
a red wheel
barrow
glazed with rain
water
beside the white
chickens
Spring and All [1923], no. XXI

12 Mothlike in mists, scintillant in the minute
brilliance of cloudless days, with broad bellying sails
they glide to the wind tossing green water
from their sharp prows while over them the crew crawls.
The Yachts [1935], st. 1, 2

13 It's the anarchy of poverty
delights me. *The Poor [1938], st. 1*

14 THESE
are the desolate, dark weeks
when nature in its barrenness
equals the stupidity of man.[1]

The year plunges into night
and the heart plunges
lower than night.
These [1938], st. 1, 2

James Elroy Flecker
1884–1915

15 West of these out to seas colder than the Hebrides
I must go
Where the fleet of stars is anchored and the young
Star captains glow. *The Dying Patriot*

16 I have seen old ships sail like swans asleep.
The Old Ships [1915]

17 A ship, an isle, a sickle moon—
With few but with how splendid stars.[2]
A Ship, An Isle, A Sickle Moon

Texas [Mary Louise Cecilia] Guinan
1884–1933

18 Hello, sucker!
Greeting to night club patrons

[1] See William Cullen Bryant, 471:10.
[2] See Whitman, 574:19.

Franz Kafka[1]

1884–1924

1 "This village belongs to the Castle, and whoever lives here or passes the night here does so in a manner of speaking in the Castle itself. Nobody may do that without the Count's permission."

The Castle [1926][2]

2 The true way goes over a rope which is not stretched at any great height but just above the ground. It seems more designed to make people stumble than to be walked upon.

The Great Wall of China. Reflections

3 You do not need to leave your room. Remain sitting at your table and listen. Do not even listen, simply wait. Do not even wait, be quite still and solitary. The world will freely offer itself to you to be unmasked, it has no choice, it will roll in ecstasy at your feet.

Ib.

4 I think we ought to read only the kind of books that wound and stab us. . . . We need the books that affect us like a disaster, that grieve us deeply, like the death of someone we loved more than ourselves, like being banished into forests far from everyone, like a suicide. A book must be the axe for the frozen sea inside us.

Letter to Oskar Pollak [January 27, 1904]

5 Only our concept of time makes it possible for us to speak of the Day of Judgment by that name; in reality it is a summary court in perpetual session.

Letters. Quoted in MAX BROD, *Franz Kafka*

6 There are two cardinal sins from which all the others spring: impatience and laziness.

Ib.

Alice Lee Roosevelt Longworth

1884–1980

7 If you can't say anything good about someone, sit right here by me.

Embroidered on a pillow in her sitting room

[1]Had one to name the author who comes nearest to bearing the same kind of relation to our age as Dante, Shakespeare and Goethe bore to theirs, Kafka is the first one would think of. — W. H. AUDEN

[2]Translated by EDWIN and WILLA MUIR.

Bronislaw Malinowski

1884–1942

8 Is war a biological necessity? As regards the earliest cultures the answer is emphatically negative. The blow of the poisonous dart from behind a bush, to murder a woman or a child in their sleep, is not pugnacity. Nor is head-hunting, body-snatching, or killing for food instinctive or natural.

Phi Beta Kappa Address, Harvard University [September 17, 1936]

Sean O'Casey

1884–1964

9 The whole world is in a state of chassis.

Juno and the Paycock[3] *[1924]*

10 One minute with him is all I ask; one minute alone with him, while you're runnin' for th' priest an' th' doctor.

The Plow and the Stars [1926], act II

11 A few hundhred scrawls o' chaps with a couple o' guns and Rosary beads, again' a hundhred thousand thrained men with horse, fut an' artillery . . . an' he wants us to fight fair! *Ib. IV*

Anna Eleanor Roosevelt[4]

1884–1962

12 No one can make you feel inferior without your consent. *This Is My Story [1937]*

13 You gain strength, courage and confidence by every experience in which you really stop to look fear in the face. You are able to say to yourself, "I lived through this horror. I can take the next thing that comes along." . . . You must do the thing you think you cannot do.

You Learn by Living [1960]

14 Life was meant to be lived, and curiosity must be kept alive. One must never, for whatever reason, turn his back on life.

The Autobiography of Eleanor Roosevelt [1961]

[3]See Aesop, 66:12.

[4]I have lost more than a friend, I have lost an inspiration. She would rather light candles than curse the darkness and her glow has warmed the world. — ADLAI E. STEVENSON [November 7, 1962]

It is better to light one candle than curse the darkness. — *Motto of the Christopher Society*

Damon Runyon
1884–1946

1 Guys and Dolls.

Title of collection of stories [1931] and musical [1950]

2 My boy . . . always try to rub up against money, for if you rub up against money long enough, some of it may rub off on you.

Furthermore [1938]. A Very Honorable Guy

3 A freeloader is a confirmed guest. He is the man who is always willing to come to dinner.

Short Takes [1946]. Freeloading Ethics

George Sarton
1884–1956

4 Scientific activity is the only one which is obviously and undoubtedly cumulative and progressive.

The History of Science and the History of Civilization [1930]

Sara Teasdale
1884–1933

5 When I am dead and over me bright April
Shakes out her rain-drenched hair,
Though you should lean above me broken-hearted,
I shall not care.

I Shall Not Care, st. 1

6 Let it be forgotten, as a flower is forgotten,
Forgotten as a fire that once was singing gold,
Let it be forgotten forever and ever,
Time is a kind friend, he will make us old.

Let It Be Forgotten [1921], st. 1

7 O beauty, are you not enough?
Why am I crying after love?

Spring Night

Norman Mattoon Thomas
1884–1968

8 I'd rather see America save her soul than her face.

Speech before antiwar protest, Washington, D.C. [November 27, 1965]

Harry S. Truman
1884–1972

9 When they told me yesterday what had happened, I felt like the moon, the stars and all the planets had fallen on me.

To reporters the day after his accession to the presidency [April 13, 1945]

10 The responsibility of the great states is to serve and not to dominate the world.

First Message to Congress [April 16, 1945]

11 When Kansas and Colorado have a quarrel over the water in the Arkansas River they don't call out the National Guard in each state and go to war over it. They bring a suit in the Supreme Court of the United States and abide by the decision. There isn't a reason in the world why we cannot do that internationally.

Speech in Kansas City [April 1945]

12 We must build a new world, a far better world—one in which the eternal dignity of man is respected.

Radio address to delegates at the opening session of the United Nations conference, San Francisco [April 23, 1945]

13 Sixteen hours ago an American airplane dropped one bomb on Hiroshima. . . . The force from which the sun draws its power has been loosed against those who brought war to the Far East.

First announcement of the atomic bomb [August 6, 1945]

14 The release of atomic energy constitutes a new force too revolutionary to consider in the framework of old ideas.

Message to Congress on atomic energy [October 3, 1945]

15 Means of destruction hitherto unknown, against which there can be no adequate military defense, and in the employment of which no single nation can in fact have a monopoly.

Declaration on Atomic Energy by President Truman and Prime Ministers Clement Attlee (Britain) and W. L. Mackenzie King (Canada) [November 15, 1945]

16 Effective, reciprocal, and enforceable safeguards acceptable to all nations. *Ib.*

17 We must embark on a bold new program for making the benefits of our scientific advances and industrial progress available for

the improvement and growth of underdeveloped areas.
Inaugural Address (Point Four Program) [January 20, 1949]

1 If you can't stand the heat, get out of the kitchen. *Saying*[1]

2 There is enough in the world for everyone to have plenty to live on happily and to be at peace with his neighbors.
Memoirs [1955], vol. I, Year of Decisions, preface

3 A President either is constantly on top of events or, if he hesitates, events will soon be on top of him. I never felt that I could let up for a single moment.
Ib. II, Years of Trial and Hope, ch. 1

4 No one who has not had the responsibility can really understand what it is like to be President, not even his closest aides or members of his immediate family. There is no end to the chain of responsibility that binds him, and he is never allowed to forget that he is President. *Ib.*

5 Once a decision was made, I did not worry about it afterward. *Ib.*

6 Most of the problems a President has to face have their roots in the past. *Ib.*

7 The Marshall Plan will go down in history as one of America's greatest contributions to the peace of the world. *Ib. 8*

8 To me, party platforms are contracts with the people. *Ib. 13*

9 A President cannot always be popular.
Ib. 14

10 A President needs political understanding to *run* the government, but he may be *elected* without it. *Ib.*

11 The convention system has its faults, of course, but I do not know of a better method for choosing a presidential nominee.
Ib.

12 All my life I have fought against prejudice and intolerance. *Ib. 19*

[1] President Truman has used variations of the aphorism . . . for many years, both orally and in his writings. For instance, in his book *Mr. Citizen* [1960], in the chapter entitled "Some Thoughts on the Presidency," he states, "Some men can make decisions and some cannot. Some men fret and delay under criticism. I used to have a saying that applies here, and I note that some people have picked it up."—*Letter to editor from* PHILIP D. LAGERQUIST, *Harry S. Truman Library, Independence, Missouri* [February 11, 1966]

13 The Bill of Rights, contained in the first ten amendments to the Constitution, is every American's guarantee of freedom. *Ib.*

14 If there is one basic element in our Constitution, it is civilian control of the military.
Ib.

15 There is a right kind and wrong kind of victory, just as there are wars for the right thing and wars that are wrong from every standpoint. . . . The kind of victory MacArthur had in mind—victory by the bombing of Chinese cities, victory by expanding the conflict to all of China—would have been the wrong kind of victory. *Ib.*

16 The buck stops here.
Sign on Truman's desk when President. From ALFRED STEINBERG. *The Man from Missouri [1962]*

17 The only thing new in the world is the history you don't know.
From MERLE MILLER, *Plain Speaking: An Oral Biography of Harry S. Truman [1974], ch. 23*

18 Secrecy and a free, democratic government don't mix. *Ib. 35*

19 A leader has to lead, or otherwise he has no business in politics. *Ib. 38*

Charter of the United Nations

20 We, the peoples of the United Nations, determined to save succeeding generations from the scourge of war, which twice in our lifetime has brought untold sorrow to mankind, and to reaffirm faith in fundamental human rights, in the dignity and worth of the human person, in the equal right of men and women and of nations large and small . . .

And for these ends to practice tolerance and live together in peace with one another as good neighbors . . .

Have resolved to combine these efforts to accomplish our aims.
Charter of the United Nations [June 1945], preamble[2]

Sophie Tucker[3]
c. 1884–1966

21 From birth to age eighteen, a girl needs good parents. From eighteen to thirty-five, she needs good looks. From thirty-five to fifty-

[2] The preamble is based on a draft by JAN CHRISTIAN SMUTS [1870–1950].

[3] Known as "The Last of the Red-Hot Mamas" from the title of a song by JACK YELLEN [1892–1958], which she introduced in 1928.

five, she needs a good personality. From fifty-five on, she needs good cash.

Said at sixty-nine

1 I have been poor and I have been rich. Rich is better. *Attributed*

Niels Bohr

1885–1962

2 In our description of nature the purpose is not to disclose the real essence of the phenomena but only to track down, so far as it is possible, relations between the manifold aspects of our experience.

Atomic Theory and the Description of Nature [1934]

Arthur Wallace Calhoun

1885–

3 Gentlemen of the old régime in the South would say, "A woman's name should appear in print but twice—when she marries and when she dies."

Social History of the American Family [1918], citing MYRTA LOCKETT AVARY, *Dixie After the War [1906]*

Zechariah Chafee, Jr.

1885–1957

4 The press is a sort of wild animal in our midst—restless, gigantic, always seeking new ways to use its strength. . . . The sovereign press for the most part acknowledges accountability to no one except its owners and publishers.

The Press Under Pressure [Nieman Reports, April 1948]

5 Freedom from something is not enough. It should also be freedom for something. Freedom is not safety but opportunity. Freedom ought to be a means to enable the press to serve the proper functions of communication in a free society. *Ib.*

Isak Dinesen [Karen Blixen]

1885–1962

6 What is man, when you come to think upon him, but a minutely set, ingenious machine for turning with infinite artfulness, the red wine of Shiraz into urine?

Seven Gothic Tales [1934]

7 Out on the safaris, I had seen a herd of buffalo, one hundred and twenty-nine of them, come out of the morning mist under a copper sky, one by one, as if the dark and massive, iron-like animals with the mighty horizontally swung horns were not approaching, but were being created before my eyes and sent out as they were finished.

Out of Africa [1937], pt. I, ch. 1

8 I had seen a herd of elephant traveling through dense native forest . . . pacing along as if they had an appointment at the end of the world. *Ib.*

9 The giraffe, in their queer, inimitable, vegetative gracefulness, as if it were not a herd of animals but a family of rare, long-stemmed, speckled gigantic flowers slowly advancing. *Ib.*

10 If I know a song of Africa—I thought—of the giraffe, and the African new moon lying on her back, of the plows in the fields, and the sweaty faces of the coffee-pickers, does Africa know a song of me? Would the air over the plain quiver with a color that I had had on, or the children invent a game in which my name was, or the full moon throw a shadow over the gravel of the drive that was like me, or would the eagles of Ngong look out for me? *Ib. 4*

11 I have before seen other countries, in the same manner, give themselves to you when you are about to leave them. *Ib. V, 1*

Will Durant

1885–

12 A statesman cannot afford to be a moralist.

What Is Civilization?

13 The health of nations is more important than the wealth of nations. *Ib.*

Karen Horney

1885–1952

14 Fortunately [psycho]analysis is not the only way to resolve inner conflicts. Life itself still remains a very effective therapist.

Our Inner Conflicts [1945]

Ishikawa Takuboku

1885–1912

15 Like a kite
Cut from the string,
Lightly the soul of my youth
Has taken flight. *Song of My Youth*[1]

[1] From *Modern Japanese Literature* [1960], edited by DONALD KEENE.

Frank Hyneman Knight
1885–1974

1 If all properly economic problems were solved once for all . . . the social struggle and strife would . . . [not necessarily] be reduced in amount or intensity . . . in the absence of some moral revolution which could by no means be assumed to follow in consequence of this change itself.
Freedom and Reform [1947], ch. 4

2 The truth seems . . . to be that in the ultimate and essential problem the economic factor is relatively superficial and unimportant.
Ib. 5

3 Market competition is the only form of organization which can afford a large measure of freedom to the individual. *Ib. 13*

4 Large scale collective bargaining . . . is merely a seductive name for bilateral monopoly, and means either adjudication of conflicts in terms of power, or deadlock and stoppage, usually injuring outside people more than the immediate parties to the dispute.
Ib.

5 Conflicting economic interest is relatively unimportant as a cause of war. *Ib. 15*

Ring Lardner
1885–1933

6 A good many young writers make the mistake of enclosing a stamped, self-addressed envelope, big enough for the manuscript to come back in. This is too much of a temptation to the editor.
How to Write Short Stories [1924]

7 "Are you lost, daddy?" I asked tenderly.
"Shut up," he explained.
The Young Immigrunts

David Herbert Lawrence
1885–1930

8 You love me so much, you want to put me in your pocket. And I should die there smothered. *Sons and Lovers [1913], ch. 15*

9 Not I, not I, but the wind that blows through me!
A fine wind is blowing the new direction of Time.
Song of a Man Who Has Come Through [1920]

10 If only I am keen and hard like the sheer tip of a wedge
Driven by invisible blows,
The rock will split, we shall come at the wonder, we shall find the Hesperides.
Ib.

11 I never saw a wild thing
Sorry for itself. *Self-Pity [1923]*

12 A snake came to my water trough
On a hot, hot day, and I in pajamas for the heat,
To drink there. *Snake [1923]*

13 For he seemed to me again like a king,
Like a king in exile, uncrowned in the underworld,
Now due to be crowned again. *Ib.*

14 Necessary, forever necessary, to burn out false shames and smelt the heaviest ore of the body into purity.
Lady Chatterley's Lover [1928]

15 How beastly the bourgeois is
especially the male of the species.
How Beastly the Bourgeois Is [1929]

16 Now in November nearer comes the sun
down the abandoned heaven.
November by the Sea [1929]

17 Beauty is a mystery. You can neither eat it nor make flannel out of it.
Sex Versus Loveliness [1930]

18 Sex and beauty are inseparable, like life and consciousness. And the intelligence which goes with sex and beauty, and arises out of sex and beauty, is intuition. *Ib.*

19 How the horse dominated the mind of the early races, especially of the Mediterranean! You were a lord if you had a horse. Far back, far back in our dark soul the horse prances. . . . The horse, the horse! The symbol of surging potency and power of movement, of action, in man. *Apocalypse [1931]*

20 For man, as for flower and beast and bird, the supreme triumph is to be most vividly, most perfectly alive. *Ib.*

21 I am part of the sun as my eye is part of me. That I am part of the earth my feet know perfectly, and my blood is part of the sea. My soul knows that I am part of the human race, my soul is an organic part of the great human race, as my spirit is part of my nation. In my own very self, I am part of my family.
Ib.

22 Whales in mid-ocean, suspended in the waves of the sea
great heaven of whales in the waters, old hierarchies.
And enormous mother whales lie dreaming suckling their whale-tender young

and dreaming with strange whale eyes wide
open in the waters of the beginning and
the end.

Whales Weep Not! [1932]

1 Reach me a gentian, give me a torch!
Let me guide myself with the blue, forked
torch of a flower
down the darker and darker stairs, where
blue is darkened on blueness
even where Persephone goes, just now, from
the frosted September
to the sightless realm where darkness is
awake upon the dark.

Bavarian Gentians [1932]

2 Build then the ship of death, for you must
take
the longest journey, to oblivion.

The Ship of Death [1932], V

3 We are dying, we are dying, piecemeal our
bodies are dying
and our strength leaves us,
and our soul cowers naked in the dark rain
over the flood,
cowering in the last branches of the tree of
our life. *Ib. VI*

4 Oh build your ship of death. Oh build it!
For you will need it.
For the voyage of oblivion awaits you.

Ib. X

Sinclair Lewis

1885–1951

5 His name was George F. Babbitt, and . . . he was nimble in the calling of selling houses for more than people could afford to pay.

Babbitt [1922], ch. 1

6 A sensational event was changing from the brown suit to the gray the contents of his pockets. He was earnest about these objects. They were of eternal importance, like baseball or the Republican Party. *Ib.*

7 Every compulsion is put upon writers to become safe, polite, obedient, and sterile. In protest, I declined election to the National Institute of Arts and Letters some years ago, and now I must decline the Pulitzer Prize.[1]

Letter declining the Pulitzer Prize for his novel Arrowsmith [1926]

8 What is love? . . . It is the morning and the evening star.

Elmer Gantry [1927], ch. 20

[1]Lewis became a member of the National Institute in 1935.

9 Our American professors like their literature clear and cold and pure and very dead.

The American Fear of Literature. Address in Stockholm on receiving the Nobel Prize for Literature [December 12, 1930]

10 It Can't Happen Here.

Title of book [1935]

François Mauriac

1885–1970

11 There is no accident in our choice of reading. All our sources are related.

Mémoires Intérieures [1959]

André Maurois

1885–1967

12 The minds of different generations are as impenetrable one by the other as are the monads of Leibniz.

Ariel [1924],[2] ch. 12

13 Modesty and unselfishness — these are virtues which men praise — and pass by.

Ib. 24

Chester William Nimitz

1885–1966

14 Uncommon valor was a common virtue.

Of the Marines at Iwo Jima [February–May 1945]

George Smith Patton[3]

1885–1945

15 Wars may be fought with weapons, but they are won by men. It is the spirit of the men who follow and of the man who leads that gains the victory.

In the Cavalry Journal [September 1933]

16 To be a successful soldier you must know history. . . . What you must know is how man reacts. Weapons change but man who uses them changes not at all. To win battles you do not beat weapons — you beat the soul of man of the enemy man.

Letter to Cadet George S. Patton IV [June 6, 1944]

17 Take calculated risks. That is quite different from being rash. *Ib.*

[2]Translated by ELLA D'ARCY.
[3]Old Blood and Guts.

1 The most vital quality a soldier can possess is self-confidence, utter, complete and bumptious. *Ib.*

2 Never tell people *how* to do things. Tell them *what* to do and they will surprise you with their ingenuity.
War As I Knew It [1947], pt. III, ch. 1

3 In war nothing is impossible, provided you use audacity.[1] *Ib.*

4 A pint of sweat will save a gallon of blood.[2]
Ib. Appendix D, letter [April 3, 1944]

Ezra Pound
1885–1972

5 Your mind and you are our Sargasso Sea.
Portrait d'une Femme [1916]

6 Haie! Haie!
These were the swift to harry;
These the keen-scented;
These were the souls of blood.
Slow on the leash,
pallid the leash-men!
The Return [1916]

7 The apparition of these faces in the crowd;
Petals on a wet, black bough.
In a Station of the Metro [1916]

8 Winter is icumen in,
Lhude sing Goddamm,
Raineth drop and staineth slop,
And how the wind doth ramm!
Sing: Goddamm.[3] *Ancient Music*

9 The leaves fall early this autumn, in wind.
The paired butterflies are already yellow with August
Over the grass in the West garden;
They hurt me. I grow older.
The River Merchant's Wife: A Letter (After Rihaku)

10 For three years, out of key with his time,
He strove to resuscitate the dead art
Of poetry; to maintain "the sublime"
In the old sense. Wrong from the start—
No, hardly, but seeing he had been born
In a half savage country, out of date.
Hugh Selwyn Mauberley. E.P. Ode pour l'élection de son sepulchre [1920], I

11 His true Penelope was Flaubert,
He fished by obstinate isles. *Ib.*

12 The age demanded an image
Of its accelerated grimace,
Something for the modern stage,
Not, at any rate, an Attic grace. *Ib. II*

13 Better mendacities
Than the classics in paraphrase! *Ib.*

14 Some quick to arm,
some for adventure,
some from fear of weakness,
some from fear of censure,
some for love of slaughter, in imagination,
learning later . . .
some in fear, learning love of slaughter;
Died some, pro patria,
non "dulce" non "et decor" . . .
walked eye-deep in hell
believing in old men's lies, the unbelieving
came home, home to a lie. *Ib. IV*

15 hysterias, trench confessions,
laughter out of dead bellies. *Ib.*

16 There died a myriad,
And of the best, among them,
For an old bitch gone in the teeth,
For a botched civilization.

Charm, smiling at the good mouth,
Quick eyes gone under earth's lid,

For two gross of broken statues,
For a few thousand battered books. *Ib. V*

17 As for literature
It gives no man a sinecure.
And no one knows, at sight, a masterpiece.
And give up verse, my boy,
There's nothing in it. *Ib. IX. Mr. Nixon*[4]

18 Hang it all, Robert Browning,
there can be but the one "Sordello."
Cantos [1925–1959], II

19 And the betrayers of language
......n and the press gang
And those who had lied for hire;
The perverts, the perverters of language, the perverts, who have set money-lust
Before the pleasures of the senses;
howling, as of a hen-yard in a printing-house, the clatter of presses,
the blowing of dry dust and stray paper,
foetor, sweat, the stench of stale oranges.
Ib. XIV

20 With *Usura*
With usura hath no man a house of good stone
each block cut smooth and well fitting.
Ib. XLV

[1] See Spenser, 173:20; Danton, 412:2; and Channing, 448:4.
[2] A drop of sweat on the drill ground will save many drops of blood on the battlefield.—August Willich [1810–1878], *The Army: Standing Army or National Army?* [1866]
[3] See Vogelweide, 138:7, and Anonymous, 916:14.
[4] Arnold Bennett.

1 No picture is made to endure nor to live with
but it is made to sell and sell quickly
with usura, sin against nature,
is thy bread ever more of stale rags
is thy bread dry as paper. *Ib.*

2 Usura slayeth the child in the womb
It stayeth the young man's courting
It hath brought palsey to bed, lyeth
between the young bride and her bridegroom
CONTRA NATURAM *Ib.*

3 What thou lovest well remains, the rest is dross
What thou lov'st well shall not be reft from thee
What thou lov'st well is thy true heritage
Whose world, or mine or theirs or is it of none?
First came the seen, then thus the palpable
Elysium, though it were in the halls of hell.
What thou lovest well is thy true heritage.
Ib. LXXXI

4 The ant's a centaur in his dragon world.
Pull down thy vanity, it is not man
Made courage, or made order, or made grace,
Pull down thy vanity, I say pull down.
Learn of the green world what can be thy place
In scaled invention or true artistry,
Pull down thy vanity,
Paquin pull down!
The green casque has outdone your elegance.
Ib.

5 The history of an art is the history of masterwork, not of failures, or mediocrity.
The Spirit of Romance [1910]

6 Poetry must be as well written as prose.
Letter to Harriet Monroe [January 1915]

7 Objectivity and again objectivity, and expression: no hindside-before-ness, no straddled adjectives (as "addled mosses dank"), no Tennysonianness of speech; nothing—nothing that you couldn't, in some circumstance, in the stress of some emotion, actually say.
Ib.

8 Literature is language charged with meaning. *ABC of Reading [1934], ch. 2*

9 Literature is news that *stays* news.
Ib.

10 Genius . . . is the capacity to see ten things where the ordinary man sees one, and where the man of talent sees two or three, *plus* the ability to register that multiple perception in the material of his art.
Jefferson and/or Mussolini [1935]

11 America, my country, is almost a continent and hardly yet a nation. *Patria Mia*

Charles Seymour
1885–1963

12 We seek the truth, and will endure the consequences.
Statement made while president of Yale University [1937–1950]

Harold Tucker Webster
1885–1952

13 Caspar Milquetoast: The Timid Soul.
Character in series of cartoons

14 The Thrill that Comes Once in a Lifetime.
Title of series of cartoons

Humbert Wolfe
1885–1940

15 Like a small gray
coffee pot
sits the squirrel.
The Gray Squirrel [1924], st. 1

16 Listen! the wind is rising,
and the air is wild with leaves,
We have had our summer evenings,
now for October eves!
Autumn (Resignation) [1926], st. 2

Elinor Hoyt Wylie
1885–1928

17 We shall walk in velvet shoes:
Wherever we go
Silence will fall like dews
On white silence below.
Velvet Shoes [1921], st. 4

18 Avoid the reeking herd,
Shun the polluted flock,
Live like that stoic bird
The eagle of the rock.
The Eagle and the Mole [1921], st. 1

19 If you would keep your soul
From spotted sight or sound,
Live like the velvet mole;
Go burrow underground.

And there hold intercourse
With roots of trees and stones,
With rivers at their source,
And disembodied bones. *Ib. st. 5, 6*

20 Say not of Beauty she is good,
Or aught but beautiful. *Beauty [1921]*

1 Enshrine her and she dies, who had
The hard heart of a child. *Ib.*

2 Down to the Puritan marrow of my bones
There's something in this richness that I hate.
I love the look, austere, immaculate,
Of landscapes drawn in pearly monotones.
Wild Peaches [1921], st. 4

3 I was, being human, born alone;
I am, being woman, hard beset;
I live by squeezing from a stone
The little nourishment I get.
Let No Charitable Hope [1923], st. 2

4 My soul, be not disturbed
By planetary war;
Remain securely orbed
In this contracted star.
Address to My Soul [1928], st. 1

5 A subtle spirit has my path attended,
In likeness not a lion but a pard;
And when the arrows flew like hail, and hard,
He licked my wounds, and all my wounds were mended.
One Person [1928]. Sonnet 9

6 If any have a stone to throw
It is not I, ever or now. *The Pebble*

7 The worst and best are both inclined
To snap like vixens at the truth;
But, O, beware the middle mind
That purrs and never shows a tooth!
Nonsense Rhyme, st. 2

8 Honeyed words like bees,
Gilded and sticky, with a little sting.
Pretty Words

9 Hail, element of earth, receive thy own,
And cherish, at thy charitable breast,
This man, this mongrel beast:
He plows the sand, and, at his hardest need,
He sows himself for seed.
Hymn to Earth [1929], st. 6

Zoë Akins
1886–1958

10 The Greeks Had a Word for It.
Title of play [1930]

Karl Barth
1886–1968

11 Conscience is the perfect interpreter of life.
The Word of God and the Word of Man [1957]

12 We have before us the fiendishness of business competition and the world war, passion and wrongdoing, antagonism between classes and moral depravity within them, economic tyranny above and the slave spirit below.
Ib.

William Rose Benét
1886–1950

13 Rain, with a silver flail;
Sun, with a golden ball;
Ocean, wherein the whale
Swims minnow-small. *Whale, st. 1*

14 And now there is merely silence, silence, silence, saying
All we did not know. *Sagacity*

Hugo La Fayette Black
1886–1971

15 No higher duty, or more solemn responsibility, rests upon this Court than that of translating into living law and maintaining this constitutional shield deliberately planned and inscribed for the benefit of every human being subject to our Constitution — of whatever race, creed or persuasion.
Chambers v. Florida, 309 U.S. 227 [1938]

16 The First Amendment has erected a wall between church and state. That wall must be kept high and impregnable. We could not approve the slightest breach.
Everson v. Board of Education, 330 U.S. 1 [1947]

17 It is my belief that there *are* "absolutes" in our Bill of Rights, and that they were put there on purpose by men who knew what words meant and meant their prohibitions to be "absolutes."
Interview Before the American Jewish Congress [April 14, 1962]

18 My view is, without deviation, without exception, without any ifs, buts, or whereases, that freedom of speech means that you shall not do something to people either for the views they have or the views they express or the words they speak or write. *Ib.*

19 I am for the First Amendment from the first word to the last. I believe it means what it says. *Ib.*

20 An unconditional right to say what one pleases about public affairs is what I consider

to be the minimum guarantee of the First Amendment.

New York Times Company v. Sullivan, 376 U.S. 254 [1964]

Frances Cornford
1886–1960

1 Magnificently unprepared
For the long littleness of life.

Rupert Brooke[1] *[1915]*

2 O why do you walk through the fields in gloves,
Missing so much and so much?
O fat white woman whom nobody loves,
Why do you walk through the fields in gloves
When the grass is as soft as the breast of doves
And shivering-sweet to the touch?

To a Fat Lady Seen from the Train [1915]

Alain-Fournier [Henri Alban Fournier]
1886–1914

3 Le Grand Meaulnes (The Wanderer).

Title of novel [1913]

Al Jolson
1886–1950

4 You ain't heard nothin' yet, folks.

Ad lib remark introduced in the first talking motion picture, The Jazz Singer [July 1927]

Gus Kahn
1886–1941
and
Raymond B. Egan
1890–1952

5 There's nothing surer,
The rich get rich and the poor get poorer,[2]
In the meantime, in between time,
Ain't we got fun.

Ain't We Got Fun [1921]

Joyce Kilmer
1886–1918

6 I think that I shall never see
A poem lovely as a tree. *Trees*[3] *[1913]*

7 Poems are made by fools like me,
But only God can make a tree. *Ib.*

[1] See Rupert Brooke, 796.
[2] See Nehru, 814:7.
[3] See Broun, 803:1, and Nash, 855:15.

Aldo Leopold
1886–1948

8 There are some who can live without wild things, and some who cannot.

A Sand County Almanac [1949], foreword

9 We face the question whether a still higher "standard of living" is worth its cost in things natural, wild, and free. For us of the minority, the opportunity to see geese is more important than television, and the chance to find a pasqueflower is a right as inalienable as free speech. *Ib.*

10 We abuse land because we regard it as a commodity belonging to us. When we see land as a community to which we belong, we may begin to use it with love and respect. *Ib.*

11 Conservation is a state of harmony between men and land.

Ib. Part III, The Land Ethic

David Morton
1886–1957

12 The light falls the way the light fell,
And it is not clear,
In the elm-shadows, if it be ourselves, here,
Or others, who were before us.

Village Street

Siegfried Sassoon
1886–1967

13 Soldiers are citizens of death's gray land.

Dreamers [1918]

14 Soldiers are dreamers; when the guns begin
They think of firelit homes, clean beds, and wives. *Ib.*

15 And when the war is done and youth stone dead
I'd toddle safely home and die—in bed.

Base Details [1918]

16 Who will remember, passing through this gate,
The unheroic dead who fed the guns?
Who shall absolve the foulness of their fate—
Those doomed, conscripted, unvictorious ones?

On Passing the New Menin Gate [1918]

Tanizaki Junichiro
1886–1965

1 The Chinese love jade. That strange lump of stone with its faintly muddy light, like the crystallized air of the centuries, melting dimly, dully back, deeper and deeper—are not we Orientals the only ones who know its charm? We cannot say ourselves what it is that we find in this stone. It quite lacks the brightness of a ruby or an emerald or the glitter of a diamond. But this much we can say: when we see that shadowy surface, we think how Chinese it is, we seem to find in cloudiness the accumulated sediment of the long Chinese past, we think how appropriate it is that the Chinese should admire that surface and that shadow.
In Praise of Shadows [1934][1]

2 I would call back at least for literature this world of shadows we are losing. In the mansion called literature I would have the eaves deep and the walls dark, I would push back into the shadows the things that come forward too clearly, I would strip away the useless decoration. I do not ask that this be done everywhere, but perhaps we may be allowed at least one mansion where we can turn off the electric lights and see how it is without them. *Ib.*

Bruce Bairnsfather
1888–1959

3 Well, if you knows of a better 'ole,[2] go to it.
Fragments from France [1915]. Caption of cartoon

Ruth Fulton Benedict
1887–1948

4 From the moment of his birth the customs into which [an individual] is born shape his experience and behavior. By the time he can talk, he is the little creature of his culture.[3]
Patterns of Culture [1934], ch. 1

5 Our children are not individuals whose rights and tastes are casually respected from infancy, as they are in some primitive societies. . . . They are fundamentally extensions of our own egos and give a special opportunity for the display of authority.
Ib. 7

[1] From Edward Seidensticker's adaptation, *Atlantic Monthly* Supplement: *Perspective of Japan* [January 1955].

[2] A shell crater.

[3] See Boas, 685:6.

6 In world history, those who have helped to build the same culture are not necessarily of one race, and those of the same race have not all participated in one culture. In scientific language, culture is not a function of race.
Race: Science and Politics [1940], ch. 2

7 Racism is the dogma that one ethnic group is condemned by nature to congenital inferiority and another group is destined to congenital superiority. *Ib. 7*

8 The tough-minded . . . respect difference. Their goal is a world made safe for differences, where the United States may be American to the hilt without threatening the peace of the world, and France may be France, and Japan may be Japan on the same conditions.
The Chrysanthemum and the Sword [1946], ch. 1

Rupert Brooke[4]
1887–1915

9 Breathless, we flung us on the windy hill,
Laughed in the sun, and kissed the lovely
grass. *The Hill [1910]*

10 And then you suddenly cried, and turned
away. *Ib.*

11 Curates, long dust, will come and go
On lissom, clerical, printless toe.
The Old Vicarage, Grantchester [1912]

12 Oh! yet
Stands the church clock at ten to three?
And is there honey still for tea? *Ib.*

13 Fish say, they have their stream and pond;
But is there anything beyond?
Heaven [1913]

14 And in that Heaven of all their wish,
There shall be no more land, say fish.
Ib.

15 But there's wisdom in women, of more than
they have known,
And thoughts go blowing through them, are
wiser than their own.
There's Wisdom in Women [1913]

16 Then, the cool kindliness of sheets, that soon
Smooth away trouble; and the rough male
kiss
Of blankets; grainy wood; live hair that is
Shining and free; blue-massing clouds; the
keen

[4] See Frances Cornford, 795:1.

Unpassioned beauty of a great machine;
The benison of hot water; furs to touch;
The good smell of old clothes.
The Great Lover [1914]

1 If I should die, think only this of me:
That there's some corner of a foreign field
That is forever England.
The Soldier [1914]

2 Now, God be thanked, Who has matched us with His hour,
And caught our youth, and wakened us from sleeping. *Peace*

3 The worst friend and enemy is but Death.
Ib.

4 Blow out, you bugles, over the rich dead!
There's none of these so lonely and poor of old,
But, dying, has made us rarer gifts than gold.
The Dead [1914], I

5 Honor has come back, as a king, to earth.
Ib.

Marc Chagall
1887–

6 Do not leave my hand without light.
Interview [1977]

Marcus Garvey
1887–1940

7 We are not engaged in domestic politics, in church building or in social uplift work, but we are engaged in nation building.
Speech, The Principles of the Universal Negro Improvement Association, at New York [November 25, 1922]

Isaac Goldberg
1887–1938

8 Diplomacy is to do and say
The nastiest thing in the nicest way.
The Reflex

Martin Luis Guzmán
1887–

9 Here lay the dilemma: either Villa would submit to the idea of the revolution without understanding it, in which case he and the true revolution would succeed; or Villa would follow his instincts blindly, and the revolution and he would both fail.[1]
El Aguila y la Serpiente (The Eagle and the Serpent) [1928], pt. II, bk. I, ch. 1

Robinson Jeffers
1887–1962

10 You make haste on decay: not blameworthy; life is good, be it stubbornly long or suddenly
A mortal splendor; meteors are not needed less than mountains: shine, perishing republic.
Shine, Perishing Republic [1924], st. 3

11 Lend me the stone strength of the past and I will lend you
The wings of the future, for I have them.
To the Rock That Will be a Cornerstone [1924]

12 The deep dark-shining
Pacific leans on the land,
Feeling his cold strength
To the outmost margins. *Night [1925]*

13 Happy people die whole, they are all dissolved in a moment, they have had what they wanted,
No hard gifts; the unhappy
Linger a space, but pain is a thing that is glad to be forgotten; but one who has given
His heart to a cause or a country,
His ghost may spaniel it a while, disconsolate to watch it. *Post Mortem [1926]*

14 The world's God is treacherous and full of unreason. *Birth-Dues [1928]*

15 I'd sooner, except the penalties, kill a man than a hawk. *Hurt Hawks [1928]*

16 I have grown to believe
A stone is a better pillow than many visions.
Clouds of Evening [1930]

17 The strong lean upon death as on a rock.
Gale in April [1930]

18 Give Your Heart to the Hawks.
Title of poem [1933]

19 I hate my verses, every line, every word.
Love the Wild Swan

20 Does it matter whether you hate your . . . self? At least
Love your eyes that can see, your mind that can

[1]Translated by RACHEL PHILLIPS.

Hear the music, the thunder of the wings.
Love the wild swan. *Ib.*

1 Well: the day is a poem but too much
Like one of Jeffers's, crusted with blood and barbaric omens,
Painful to excess, inhuman as a hawk's cry.
The Day Is a Poem (September 19, 1939) [1941]

2 If millions are born millions must die.
May–June 1940, st. 3

3 As for me, I would rather
Be a worm in a wild apple than a son of man.
Original Sin [1948]

Le Corbusier [Charles Édouard Jeanneret]

1887–1965

4 A house is a machine for living in.[1]
Vers une Architecture [1923]

Emilio Mola

1887–1937

5 Fifth column.[2]
Phrase, Spanish Civil War [1936–1939]

Sir Bernard Montgomery, Viscount Montgomery of Alamein

1887–1976

6 To us is given the honor of striking a blow for freedom which will live in history, and in the better days that lie ahead men will speak with pride of our doings.
Message to his troops, on the eve of the Allied invasion of Europe [June 5, 1944]

Marianne Moore

1887–1972

7 Dürer would have seen a reason for living in a town like this.
The Steeple-Jack [1935], st. 1

8 The sweet air coming into your house on a
fine day, from water etched
with waves as formal as the scales on a fish.
Ib.

[1] Une maison est une machine-à-habiter.

[2] Mola, one of Franco's generals, boasted that he had four columns of troops to lead against Madrid and a fifth column of sympathizers inside Madrid.

9 Of the crow-blue mussel shells, one keeps
adjusting the ash heaps;
opening and shutting itself like

an
injured fan. *The Fish [1935], st. 1, 2*

10 I, too, dislike it.
Reading it, however, with a perfect contempt for it, one discovers in
it, after all, a place for the genuine.
Poetry [1935; revised 1967]

11 Nor till the poets among us can be "literalists of
the imagination"—above
insolence and triviality and can present

for inspection, "imaginary gardens with real toads in them," shall we have
it.
Ib. st. 4, 5 (excluded in 1967 revision)[3]

12 The wrinkles progress among themselves in a phalanx—beautiful under networks of foam,
and fade breathlessly while the sea rustles in and out of the seaweed.
A Grave [1935]

13 And the ocean, under the pulsation of lighthouses and noise of bell buoys,
advances as usual, looking as if it were not that ocean in which dropped things are bound to sink—
in which if they turn and twist, it is neither with volition nor consciousness.
Ib.

14 I wonder what Adam and Eve
think of it by this time.
Marriage [1935]

15 Ecstasy affords
the occasion and expediency determines the form.
The Past Is the Present [1935]

16 My father used to say,
"Superior people never make long visits,
have to be shown Longfellow's grave
or the glass flowers at Harvard."
Silence [1935][4]

17 "The deepest feeling always shows itself in silence;
not in silence, but restraint."

[3] Omissions are not accidents.—MARIANNE MOORE, *Complete Poems* [1967], *author's note*

[4] Author's note: My father used to say, "Superior people never make long visits. When I am visiting, I like to go about by myself. I never had to be shown Longfellow's grave or the glass flowers at Harvard."—MISS A. M. HOMANS

Nor was he insincere in saying, "Make my
house your inn."[1]
Inns are not residences. *Ib.*

1 There is a great amount of poetry in unconscious fastidiousness.

Critics and Connoisseurs [1935]

2 What is our innocence,
what is our guilt? All are
naked, none is safe.

What Are Years? [1941]

3 The power of the visible
is the invisible.

He "Digesteth Harde Yron" [1941], st. 8

4 I am troubled, I'm dissatisfied, I'm Irish.

Spenser's Ireland [1941], last line

5 Another armored animal—scale
lapping scale with spruce cone regularity
until they
form the uninterrupted central
tail row! *The Pangolin [1941], st. 1*

6 Bedizened or stark
naked, man, the self, the being we call
human, writing
master to this world. *Ib. st. 8*

7 Among animals, *one* has a sense of humor.
Humor saves a few steps, it saves years.

Ib.

8 The prey of fear, he, always
curtailed, extinguished, thwarted by the
dusk, work partly done,
says to the alternating blaze,
"Again the sun!
anew each day; and new and new and new,
that comes into and steadies my soul."

Ib. st. 9

9 What sap
went through that little thread
to make the cherry red!

Nevertheless [1944], st. 11

10 They say there is a sweeter air
where it was made, than we have here.

A Carriage from Sweden [1944]

11 The mind is an enchanting thing
is an enchanted thing,
like the glaze on a
katydid-wing
subdivided by sun
till the nettings are legion.

The Mind Is an Enchanting Thing [1944], st. 1

[1] Author's note: Edmund Burke, in *Burke's Life*, by Prior: "Throw yourself into a coach," said he. "Come down and make my house your inn."

12 I inwardly did nothing.
O Iscariot-like crime!

In Distrust of Merits [1941], st. 8

13 We don't like flowers that do
not wilt; they must die, and nine
she-camel hairs aid memory.

The Sycamore [1956], st. 2

14 O to be a dragon,
a symbol of the power of Heaven—of silkworm
size or immense; at times invisible.
Felicitous phenomenon!

O To Be a Dragon [1959]

15 To wear the arctic fox
you have to kill it.

The Arctic Ox (Or Goat) [1959], st. 1

16 Camels are snobbish
and sheep, unintelligent;
water buffaloes, neurasthenic—
even murderous.
Reindeer seem over-serious. *Ib. st. 9*

17 Why an inordinate interest in animals and athletes? They are subjects for art and exemplars of it, are they not? minding their own business. Pangolins, hornbills, pitchers, catchers, do not pry or prey—or prolong the conversation; do not make us self-conscious; look their best when caring least.

A Marianne Moore Reader [1961], foreword

Samuel Eliot Morison

1887–1976

18 A tough but nervous, tenacious but restless race [the Yankees]; materially ambitious, yet prone to introspection, and subject to waves of religious emotion. . . . A race whose typical member is eternally torn between a passion for righteousness and a desire to get on in the world.

Maritime History of Massachusetts [1921], ch. 2

19 On her first voyage, the *Columbia* had solved the riddle of the China trade. On her second, empire followed in the wake.

Ib. 4

20 He [Columbus] enjoyed long stretches of pure delight such as only a seaman may know, and moments of high, proud exultation that only a discoverer can experience.

Admiral of the Ocean Sea [1942], ch. 49

1 A few hints as to literary craftsmanship may be useful to budding historians. First and foremost, *get writing!*

History as a Literary Art. Old South Leaflets, ser. II, No. 1 [1946]

2 Franklin may . . . be considered one of the founding fathers of American democracy, since no democratic government can last long without conciliation and compromise.

The Wisdom of Benjamin Franklin [1961]

3 An historian should yield himself to his subject, become immersed in the place and period of his choice, standing apart from it now and then for a fresh view.

Vistas of History [1964]. The Experiences and Principles of an Historian

4 If the European discovery had been delayed for a century or two, it is possible that the Aztec in Mexico or the Iroquois in North America would have established strong native states capable of adopting European war tactics and maintaining their independence to this day, as Japan kept her independence from China.

The Oxford History of the American People [1965], ch. 1

5 America was discovered accidentally by a great seaman who was looking for something else; when discovered it was not wanted; and most of the exploration for the next fifty years was done in the hope of getting through or around it. America was named after a man who discovered no part of the New World. History is like that, very chancy. *Ib. 2*

6 But sea power has never led to despotism. The nations that have enjoyed sea power even for a brief period—Athens, Scandinavia, the Netherlands, England, the United States—are those that have preserved freedom for themselves and have given it to others. Of the despotism to which unrestrained military power leads we have plenty of examples from Alexander to Mao. *Ib. 3*

7 Make no mistake; the American Revolution was not fought to *obtain* freedom, but to *preserve* the liberties that Americans already had as colonials.[1] Independence was no conscious goal, secretly nurtured in cellar or jungle by bearded conspirators, but a reluctant last resort, to preserve "life, liberty and the pursuit of happiness." *Ib. 12*

8 If the American Revolution had produced nothing but the Declaration of Independence, it would have been worth while. . . . The beauty and cogency of the preamble,[2] reaching back to remotest antiquity and forward to an indefinite future, have lifted the hearts of millions of men and will continue to do. . . . These words are more revolutionary than anything written by Robespierre, Marx, or Lenin, more explosive than the atom, a continual challenge to ourselves as well as an inspiration to the oppressed of all the world. *Ib. 14*

9 The freedmen were not really free in 1865, nor are most of their descendants really free in 1965. Slavery was but one aspect of a race and color problem that is still far from solution here, or anywhere. In America particularly, the grapes of wrath have not yet yielded all their bitter vintage. *Ib. 33*

10 These clipper ships of the early 1850's were built of wood in shipyards from Rockland in Maine to Baltimore. These architects, like poets who transmute nature's message into song, obeyed what wind and wave had taught them, to create the noblest of all sailing vessels, and the most beautiful creations of man in America. With no extraneous ornament except a figurehead, a bit of carving and a few lines of gold leaf, their one purpose of speed over the great ocean routes was achieved by perfect balance of spars and sails to the curving lines of the smooth black hull; and this harmony of mass, form and color was practiced to the music of dancing waves and of brave winds whistling in the rigging. These were our Gothic cathedrals, our Parthenon; but monuments carved from snow. For a few brief years they flashed their splendor around the world, then disappeared with the finality of the wild pigeon.[3] *Ib. 36*

11 No big modern war has been won without preponderant sea power; and, conversely, very few rebellions of maritime provinces have succeeded without acquiring sea power.[4] *Ib. 40*

Georgia O'Keeffe

1887–

12 Where I was born and where and how I have lived is unimportant. It is what I have done with where I have been that should be of interest. *Georgia O'Keeffe [1976]*

[1] See Calhoun, 449:11.

[2] See Jefferson, 387:9.

[3] A shorter version of this passage appeared in *Maritime History of Massachusetts* [1921], *ch. 23*.

[4] See Themistocles, 70:19; Bacon, 181:11; Waller, 276:3; Washington, 379:5; and Mahan, 642:8.

1 I find that I have painted my life—things happening in my life—without knowing.

Ib.

2 I had to create an equivalent for what I felt about what I was looking at—not copy it.

Ib.

Fairfield Osborn
1887–1969

3 We do not live to extenuate the miseries of the past nor to accept as incurable those of the present.

The Limits of the Earth, ch. 10

John Reed
1887–1920

4 Ten Days That Shook the World.

Title of firsthand account of the outbreak of the Bolshevik Revolution [1919]

Dame Edith Sitwell
1887–1964

5 Remember only this of our hopeless love
That never till Time is done
Will the fire of the heart and the fire of the mind be one.

Heart and Mind

6 Still falls the Rain—
Dark as the world of man, black as our loss—
Blind as the nineteen hundred and forty nails
Upon the Cross.

Still Falls the Rain [1940]

7 My poems are hymns of praise to the glory of life.

Collected Poems [1957]. Some Notes on My Poetry

8 Rhythm is one of the principal translators between dream and reality. Rhythm might be described as, to the world of sound, what light is to the world of sight. It shapes and gives new meaning. Rhythm was described by Schopenhauer as melody deprived of its pitch.

Taken Care Of [1965], ch. 14

Alexander Woollcott
1887–1943

9 The two oldest professions in the world—ruined by amateurs.

The Knock at the Stage Door. The Actor and the Streetwalker

10 All the things I really like to do are either immoral, illegal, or fattening.

Remark

11 Germany was the cause of Hitler just as much as Chicago is responsible for the Chicago *Tribune.*

Last words before the microphone [January 23, 1943], on the People's Platform program

Sam M. Lewis
1885–1959
and
Joe Young
1889–1939

12 How You Gonna Keep 'Em Down on the Farm After They've Seen Paree?

Title and refrain of song [1919]

Anna Akhmatova[1]
1888–1966

13 Who will grieve for this woman? Does she not seem
too insignificant for our concern?
Yet in my heart I never will deny her,
Who suffered death because she chose to turn.

Lot's Wife [composed 1922–1924]

14 No foreign sky protected me,
no stranger's wing shielded my face.
I stand as witness to the common lot,
survivor of that time, that place.

Requiem [composed mainly 1935–1940]. Epigraph [composed 1961]

15 In the terrible years of the Yezhov terror I spent seventeen months waiting in line outside the prison in Leningrad. One day somebody in the crowd identified me . . . and asked me in a whisper . . . "Can you describe this?" And I said: "I can."

Ib. Instead of a Preface [composed 1957]

16 That was a time when only the dead
could smile.

Ib. Prologue [composed 1935–1940]

17 I should be proud to have my memory graced,
but only if the monument be placed . . .

here, where I endured three hundred hours
in line before the implacable iron bars.

Ib. Epilogue [composed 1940], II

18 And from my motionless bronze-lidded sockets

[1] Translated by STANLEY KUNITZ with MAX HAYWARD.

may the melting snow, like teardrops, slowly
trickle
and a prison dove coo somewhere, over and
over,
as the ships sail softly down the flowing Neva.
Ib.

1 Great Russian word,
fit for the songs of our children's children,
pure on their tongues, and free.
Courage [composed 1942]

Maxwell Anderson
1888–1959

2 Oh, it's a long, long while
From May to December,
But the days grow short,
When you reach September.
Knickerbocker Holiday [1938].[1] *September Song*

3 Oh, the days dwindle down
To a precious few . . .
And these few precious days
I'll spend with you. *Ib.*

Maxwell Anderson
1888–1959
and
Laurence Stallings
1894–1968

4 What Price Glory? *Title of play [1924]*

Irving Berlin
1888–

5 You've got to get up, you've got to get up,
You've got to get up this morning!
Oh! How I Hate to Get Up in the Morning [1918]

6 A Pretty Girl Is Like a Melody.
Ziegfeld Follies [1919], title of song

7 Say It with Music.
Music Box Revue [1921], title of song

8 Dancing cheek to cheek.
Top Hat [1935]. Cheek to Cheek

9 God bless America,
Land that I love.
God Bless America [1938]

10 From the mountains to the prairies,
To the oceans white with foam,
God bless America,
My home sweet home! *Ib.*

[1] Music by Kurt Weill.

11 I'm dreaming of a white Christmas.
Holiday Inn [1942]. White Christmas

12 There's No Business Like Show Business.
Annie Get Your Gun [1946], title of song

13 The Hostess with the Mostes' on the Ball.
Call Me Madam [1950], title of song

Georges Bernanos
1888–1948

14 Hell, Madame, is to love no longer.
Le Journal d'un Curé de Campagne (The Diary of a Country Priest) [1936]

15 Democracies cannot dispense with hypocrisy any more than dictatorships can with cynicism.
Nous Autres Français (We French)

16 The most dangerous of our calculations are those we call illusions.
Dialogue des Carmelites [1949]

Henry Beston
1888–1968

17 The world today is sick to its thin blood for lack of elemental things,[2] for fire before the hands, for water welling from the earth, for air, for the dear earth itself underfoot.
The Outermost House [1928], ch. 1

18 The animal shall not be measured by man. In a world older and more complete than ours they move finished and complete, gifted with extensions of the senses we have lost or never attained, living by voices we shall never hear. They are not brethren, they are not underlings; they are other nations, caught with ourselves in the net of life and time, fellow prisoners of the splendor and travail of the earth. *Ib. 2*

19 The three great elemental sounds in nature are the sound of rain, the sound of wind in a primeval wood, and the sound of outer ocean on a beach. *Ib. 3*

20 For a moment of night we have a glimpse of ourselves and of our world islanded in its stream of stars—pilgrims of mortality, voyaging between horizons across the eternal seas of space and time. *Ib.*

[2] See Markham, 671:2.

Heywood Broun
1888–1939

1 "Trees" maddens me, because it contains the most insincere line ever written by mortal man. Surely the Kilmer tongue must have been not far from the Kilmer cheek when he wrote, "Poems are made by fools like me."[1]

It Seems to Me [1935]. "Trees," "If," and "Invictus"

2 Life is a copycat and can be bullied into following the master artist who bids it come to heel. *Ib. Nature the Copycat*

3 The swaggering underemphasis of New England.

Heywood Broun: Collected Edition [1941]

Dale Carnegie
1888–1955

4 How to Win Friends and Influence People.
Title of book [1938]

Raymond Chandler
1888–1959

5 The Big Sleep.[2]
Title of novel [1939]

James Frank Dobie
1888–1964

6 Conform and be dull.
The Voice of the Coyote [1949], introduction

John Foster Dulles
1888–1959

7 Local defense will always be important. But there is no local defense which alone will contain the mighty land power of the Communist world. Local defense must be reinforced by the further deterrent of massive retaliatory power.

Address to the Council on Foreign Relations [January 12, 1954]

8 You have to take chances for peace, just as you must take chances in war. . . . The ability to get to the verge without getting into the war is the necessary art. If you try to run away from it, if you are scared to go to the brink,[3] you are lost.

From JAMES SHEPLEY, How Dulles Averted War, in Life [January 16, 1956]

[1]See Kilmer, 795:6.
[2]A synonym for death.

Thomas Stearns Eliot
1888–1965

9 Let us go then, you and I,
When the evening is spread out against the sky
Like a patient etherized upon a table.
The Love Song of J. Alfred Prufrock [1917]

10 In the room the women come and go
Talking of Michelangelo. *Ib.*

11 There will be time to murder and create. *Ib.*

12 And indeed there will be time
To wonder, "Do I dare?" and, "Do I dare?" *Ib.*

13 I have measured out my life with coffee spoons. *Ib.*

14 I should have been a pair of ragged claws
Scuttling across the floors of silent seas. *Ib.*

15 Should I, after tea and cakes and ices,
Have the strength to force the moment to its crisis? *Ib.*

16 I have seen the moment of my greatness flicker,
And I have seen the eternal Footman hold my coat, and snicker,
And in short, I was afraid. *Ib.*

17 No! I am not Prince Hamlet, nor was meant to be;
Am an attendant lord, one that will do
To swell a progress, start a scene or two,
Advise the prince; no doubt, an easy tool,
Deferential, glad to be of use,
Politic, cautious, and meticulous;
Full of high sentence, but a bit obtuse;
At times, indeed, almost ridiculous—
Almost, at times, the Fool. *Ib.*

18 I grow old . . . I grow old . . .
I shall wear the bottoms of my trousers rolled. *Ib.*

19 Shall I part my hair behind? Do I dare to eat a peach?
I shall wear white flannel trousers, and walk upon the beach.

[3]From the phrase "to the brink" developed "brinkmanship."

I have heard the mermaids singing,[1] each to each.
I do not think that they will sing to me.
Ib.

1 Till human voices wake us, and we drown.
Ib.

2 And I must borrow every changing shape
To find expression.
Portrait of a Lady [1917], III

3 One thinks of all the hands
That are raising dingy shades
In a thousand furnished rooms.
Preludes [1917], II

4 Twelve o'clock.
Along the reaches of the street
Held in a lunar synthesis.
Rhapsody on a Windy Night [1917]

5 I am aware of the damp souls of housemaids
Sprouting despondently at area gates.
Morning at the Window [1917]

6 The readers of the *Boston Evening Transcript*
Sway in the wind like a field of ripe corn.
The Boston Evening Transcript [1917]

7 Upon the glazen shelves kept watch
Matthew and Waldo, guardians of the faith,
The army of unalterable law.[2]
Cousin Nancy [1917]

8 His laughter tinkled among the teacups.
Mr. Apollinax [1917]

9 He laughed like an irresponsible foetus.
Ib.

10 Stand on the highest pavement of the stair—
Lean on a garden urn—
Weave, weave the sunlight in your hair.
La Figlia Che Piange [1917], st. 1

11 Simple and faithless as a smile and shake of the hand. *Ib. st. 2*

12 Sometimes these cogitations still amaze
The troubled midnight and the noon's repose.
Ib. st. 3

13 Here I am, an old man in a dry month,
Being read to by a boy, waiting for rain.
Gerontion [1920]

14 After such knowledge, what forgiveness? Think now
History has many cunning passages, contrived corridors
And issues, deceives with whispering ambitions,
Guides us by vanities. *Ib.*

[1]See Donne, 252:1.
[2]See Meredith, 600:28.

15 Neither fear nor courage saves us. Unnatural vices
Are fathered by our heroism. Virtues
Are forced upon us by our impudent crimes.
These tears are shaken from the wrath-bearing tree. *Ib.*

16 Paint me the bold anfractuous rocks
Faced by the snarled and yelping seas.
Sweeney Erect [1920], st. 1

17 This oval O cropped out with teeth.
Ib. st. 4

18 I shall not want Honor in Heaven
For I shall meet Sir Philip Sidney
And have talk with Coriolanus
And other heroes of that kidney.
A Cooking Egg [1920], st. 3

19 Over buttered scones and crumpets
Weeping, weeping multitudes
Droop in a hundred A.B.C.'s. *Ib. st. 8*

20 The hippopotamus's day
Is passed in sleep; at night he hunts;
God works in a mysterious way—
The Church can sleep and feed at once.
The Hippopotamus [1920], st. 6

21 Webster was much possessed by death
And saw the skull beneath the skin.
Whispers of Immortality [1920], st. 1

22 He knew the anguish of the marrow
The ague of the skeleton;
No contact possible to flesh
Allayed the fever of the bone.
Ib. st. 4 [of Donne]

23 Uncorseted, her friendly bust
Gives promise of pneumatic bliss.
Ib. st. 5

24 Reorganized upon the floor
She yawns and draws a stocking up.
Sweeney Among the Nightingales [1920], st. 4

25 The nightingales are singing near
The Convent of the Sacred Heart,

And sang within the bloody wood
When Agamemnon cried aloud,
And let their liquid siftings fall
To stain the stiff dishonored shroud.
Ib. st. 10

26 April is the cruelest month, breeding
Lilacs out of the dead land, mixing
Memory and desire, stirring
Dull roots with spring rain.
The Waste Land [1922]. I, The Burial of the Dead

1 You know only
A heap of broken images, where the sun beats,
And the dead tree gives no shelter, the cricket no relief,
And the dry stone no sound of water. Only
There is shadow under this red rock,
(Come in under the shadow of this red rock),
And I will show you something different from either
Your shadow at morning striding behind you
Or your shadow at evening rising to meet you;
I will show you fear in a handful of dust.
Ib.

2 I had not thought death had undone so many.[1]
Sighs, short and infrequent, were exhaled.[2]
Ib.

3 I think we are in rats' alley
Where the dead men lost their bones.
Ib. II, The Game of Chess

4 O O O O that Shakespeherian Rag—
It's so elegant
So intelligent. *Ib.*

5 Hurry up please its time. *Ib.*

6 But at my back from time to time I hear[3]
The sound of horns and motors, which shall bring
Sweeney to Mrs. Porter in the spring.
O the moon shone bright on Mrs. Porter
And on her daughter
They wash their feet in soda water.
Ib. III, The Fire Sermon

7 At the violet hour, when the eyes and back
Turn upward from the desk, when the human engine waits
Like a taxi throbbing waiting,
I Tiresias, though blind, throbbing between two lives.[4] *Ib.*

8 When lovely woman stoops to folly[5] and
Paces about her room again, alone,
She smooths her hair with automatic hand,
And puts a record on the gramophone.
Ib.

9 Phlebas the Phoenician, a fortnight dead,
Forgot the cry of gulls, and the deep sea swell
And the profit and loss.
Ib. IV, Death by Water

[1] DANTE, *Inferno, canto III, ll. 55–57.*
[2] DANTE, *Inferno, canto IV, ll. 25–27.*
[3] See Marvell, 296:28.
[4] See Arnold, 586:10.
[5] See Goldsmith, 369:20.

10 Here is no water but only rock.
Ib. V, What the Thunder Said

11 Who is the third who walks always beside you? *Ib.*

12 And voices singing out of empty cisterns and exhausted wells. *Ib.*

13 *Dayadhvam:* I have heard the key
Turn in the door once and turn once only
We think of the key, each in his prison
Thinking of the key, each confirms a prison.[6]
Ib.

14 These fragments I have shored against my ruins. *Ib.*

15 We are the hollow men
We are the stuffed men
Leaning together
Headpiece filled with straw. Alas!
The Hollow Men [1925], I

16 Shape without form, shade without color,
Paralyzed force, gesture without motion;

Those who have crossed
With direct eyes, to death's other Kingdom
Remember us—if at all—not as lost
Violent souls, but only
As the hollow men
The stuffed men. *Ib.*

17 Between the idea
And the reality
Between the motion
And the act
Falls the Shadow.[7] *Ib. V*

18 This is the way the world ends
Not with a bang but a whimper. *Ib.*

19 A cold coming we had of it,
Just the worst time of the year.
Journey of the Magi [1927]

20 Because I do not hope to turn again[8]
Because I do not hope
Because I do not hope to turn.
Ash-Wednesday [1930], I

21 Because these wings are no longer wings to fly
But merely vans to beat the air
The air which is now thoroughly small and dry
Smaller and dryer than the will
Teach us to care and not to care
Teach us to sit still. *Ib.*

22 Lady, three white leopards sat under a juniper tree. *Ib. II*

[6] See *The Upanishads,* 56:24.
[7] See Dowson, 721:4.
[8] GUIDO CAVALCANTI, *Perch' Io Non Spero.*

1 Terminate torment
Of love unsatisfied
The greater torment
Of love satisfied. *Ib.*

2 Blown hair is sweet, brown hair over the mouth blown,
Lilac and brown hair;
Distraction, music of the flute, stops and steps of the mind over the third stair,
Fading, fading; strength beyond hope and despair
Climbing the third stair. *Ib. III*

3 Redeem
The time. Redeem
The unread vision in the higher dream
While jeweled unicorns draw by the gilded hearse. *Ib. IV*

4 Against the Word the unstilled world still whirled
About the center of the silent Word.

O my people, what have I done unto thee.

Where shall the word be found, where will the word
Resound? Not here, there is not enough silence. *Ib. V*

5 Wavering between the profit and the loss
In this brief transit where the dreams cross
The dreamcrossed twilight between birth and dying. *Ib.*

6 The white sails still fly seaward, seaward flying
Unbroken wings.

And the lost heart stiffens and rejoices
In the lost lilac and the lost sea voices
And the weak spirit quickens to rebel
For the bent goldenrod and the lost sea smell. *Ib.*

7 Even among these rocks,
Our peace in His will.[1] *Ib.*

8 What seas what shores what gray rocks and what islands
What water lapping the bow
And scent of pine and the woodthrush singing through the fog
What images return
O my daughter. *Marina [1930]*

9 I'll convert *you!*
Into a stew.
A nice little, white little, missionary stew!
Sweeney Agonistes

10 Birth, and copulation, and death.
That's all the facts when you come to brass tacks. *Ib.*

[1]See Dante, 142:11.

11 Two live as one
One live as two
Two live as three
Under the bam
Under the boo
Under the bamboo tree. *Ib.*

12 Stone, bronze, stone, steel, stone, oakleaves, horses' heels
Over the paving.
Coriolan I. Triumphal March

13 O hidden under the dove's wing, hidden in the turtle's breast,
Under the palmtree at noon, under the running water
At the still point of the turning world. O hidden. *Ib.*

14 How unpleasant to meet Mr. Eliot![2]
With his features of clerical cut,
And his brow so grim
And his mouth so prim.
Five-Finger Exercises, V

15 All our knowledge brings us nearer to our ignorance,
All our ignorance brings us nearer to death,
But nearness to death no nearer to God.
Where is the Life we have lost in living?
Where is the wisdom we have lost in knowledge?
Where is the knowledge we have lost in information?
The cycles of Heaven in twenty centuries
Bring us farther from God and nearer to the Dust. *The Rock [1934], I*

16 Yet we have gone on living,
Living and partly living.
Murder in the Cathedral [1935], pt. I

17 They know and do not know, what it is to act or suffer.
They know and do not know, that acting is suffering. *Ib.*

18 Saint and Martyr rule from the tomb.
Ib.

19 The last temptation is the greatest treason:
To do the right deed for the wrong reason.
Ib.

20 Human kind cannot bear very much reality.[3]
Ib. II

21 Clear the air! clean the sky! wash the wind! take the stone from the stone, take the skin from the arm, take the muscle from bone, and wash them. *Ib.*

[2]See Lear, 550:5.
[3]Also in *Four Quartets, Burnt Norton*, pt. I.

1 Time present and time past
Are both perhaps present in time future,
And time future contained in time past.
Four Quartets. Burnt Norton [1935], I

2 Footfalls echo in the memory
Down the passage which we did not take
Towards the door we never opened
Into the rose garden. *Ib.*

3 Shall we follow
The deception of the thrush? Into our first world. *Ib.*

4 Garlic and sapphires in the mud
Clot the bedded axle-tree.
The trilling wire in the blood
Sings below inveterate scars
And reconciles forgotten wars. *Ib. II*

5 At the still point of the turning world.
Neither flesh nor fleshless. *Ib.*

6 Except for the point, the still point,
There would be no dance, and there is only the dance. *Ib.*

7 Only through time time is conquered. *Ib.*

8 Sudden in a shaft of sunlight
Even while the dust moves
There rises the hidden laughter
Of children in the foliage
Quick now, here, now, always—
Ridiculous the waste sad time
Stretching before and after. *Ib. V*

9 In my beginning is my end.
Ib. East Coker [1940], I

10 Keeping time,
Keeping the rhythm in their dancing
As in their living in the living seasons
The time of the seasons and the constellations
The time of milking and the time of harvest
The time of the coupling of man and woman
And that of beasts. Feet rising and falling.
Eating and drinking. Dung and death. *Ib.*

11 What is the late November doing
With the disturbance of the spring. *Ib. II*

12 A periphrastic study in a worn-out poetical fashion,
Leaving one still with the intolerable wrestle
With words and meanings. The poetry does not matter. *Ib.*

13 The only wisdom we can hope to acquire
Is the wisdom of humility: humility is endless. *Ib.*

14 The houses are all gone under the sea. *Ib.*

15 The dancers are all gone under the hill. *Ib.*

16 O dark dark dark.[1] They all go into the dark,
The vacant interstellar spaces, the vacant into the vacant. *Ib.*

17 And we all go with them, into the silent funeral,
Nobody's funeral, for there is no one to bury.
I said to my soul, be still,[2] and let the dark come upon you
Which shall be the darkness of God. *Ib.*

18 To arrive where you are, to get from where you are not,
You must go by a way wherein there is no ecstasy.
In order to arrive at what you do not know
You must go by the way which is the way of ignorance. *Ib.*

19 The whole earth is our hospital
Endowed by the ruined millionaire. *Ib.*

20 We call this Friday good. *Ib.*

21 And so each venture
Is a new beginning, a raid on the inarticulate
With shabby equipment always deteriorating
In the general mess of imprecision of feeling,
Undisciplined squads of emotion. *Ib. V*

22 For us, there is only the trying. The rest is not our business. *Ib.*

23 Home is where one starts from. As we grow older
The world becomes stranger, the pattern more complicated
Of dead and living. Not the intense moment
Isolated, with no before and after,
But a lifetime burning in every moment
And not the lifetime of one man only
But of old stones that cannot be deciphered. *Ib.*

24 Love is most nearly itself
When here and now cease to matter.
Old men ought to be explorers[3]
Here and there does not matter
We must be still and still moving
Into another intensity
For a further union, a deeper communion
Through the dark cold and the empty desolation,

[1] See Milton, 288:20.
[2] See *Psalm 46:10*, 19:12.
[3] See Roethke, 874:8.

The wave cry, the wind cry, the vast waters
Of the petrel and the porpoise. In my end is
my beginning.[1] *Ib.*

1 I do not know much about gods; but I think
that the river
Is a strong brown god—sullen, untamed and
intractable.
Ib. The Dry Salvages [1941], I

2 The sea is the land's edge also, the granite
Into which it reaches, the beaches where it
tosses
Its hints of earlier and other creation:
The starfish, the hermit crab, the whale's
backbone;
The pools where it offers to our curiosity
The more delicate algae and the sea anemone.
It tosses up our losses, the torn seine,
The shattered lobsterpot, the broken oar
And the gear of foreign dead men. The sea
has many voices.[2] *Ib.*

3 There is no end of it, the voiceless wailing,
No end to the withering of withered flowers.
Ib. II

4 Only the hardly, barely prayable
Prayer of the one Annunciation. *Ib.*

5 The backward look behind the assurance
Of recorded history, the backward halflook
Over the shoulder, towards the primitive terror. *Ib.*

6 Time the destroyer is time the preserver.[3]
Ib.

7 Not fare well,
But fare forward, voyagers. *Ib. III*

8 Music heard so deeply
That it is not heard at all, but you are the
music
While the music lasts. *Ib. V*

9 Only undefeated
Because we have gone on trying;
We, content at the last
If our temporal reversion nourish
(Not too far from the yew tree)
The life of significant soil. *Ib.*

10 What the dead had no speech for, when living,
They can tell you, being dead: the communication
Of the dead is tongued with fire beyond the
language of the living.
Ib. Little Gidding [1942], I

11 Ash on an old man's sleeve
Is all the ash the burnt roses leave.
Dust in the air suspended
Marks the place where a story ended.
Dust inbreathed was a house—
The wall, the wainscot and the mouse
The death of hope and despair,
This is the death of air. *Ib. II*

12 Water and fire shall rot
The marred foundations we forgot,
Of sanctuary and choir.
This is the death of water and fire.
Ib.

13 In the uncertain hour before the morning
Near the ending of interminable night
At the recurrent end of the unending
After the dark dove with the flickering
tongue
Had passed below the horizon of his homing.
Ib.

14 Since our concern was speech, and speech impelled us
To purify the dialect of the tribe.[4] *Ib.*

15 Who then devised the torment? Love.
Love is the unfamiliar Name
Behind the hands that wove
The intolerable shirt of flame
Which human power cannot remove.
We only live, only suspire
Consumed by either fire or fire.
Ib. IV

16 A people without history
Is not redeemed from time, for history is a
pattern
Of timeless moments. So, while the light
fails
On a winter's afternoon, in a secluded chapel
History is now and England. *Ib. V*

17 We shall not cease from exploration
And the end of all our exploring
Will be to arrive where we started
And know the place for the first time.
Ib.

18 A condition of complete simplicity
(Costing not less than everything)
And all shall be well and
All manner of thing shall be well
When the tongues of flame are infolded
Into the crowned knot of fire
And the fire and the rose are one. *Ib.*

19 By the delicate, invisible web you wove—
The inexplicable mystery of sound.
To Walter de la Mare [1948]

[1] See Mary, Queen of Scots, 167:2.
[2] See *Revelation 14:2*, 53:22, and Tennyson, 529:13.
[3] See Bruno, 171:11.
[4] Donner un sens plus pur aux mots de la tribu.—STÉPHANE MALLARMÉ [1842–1898], *Le Tombeau d'Edgar Poe*

1 What is hell? Hell is oneself,
Hell is alone, the other figures in it
Merely projections.[1]

The Cocktail Party [1950]

2 It [tradition] cannot be inherited, and if you want it you must obtain it by great labor.

Tradition and the Individual Talent [1919]

3 The progress of an artist is a continual self-sacrifice, a continual extinction of personality. *Ib.*

4 Poetry is not a turning loose of emotion, but an escape from emotion; it is not the expression of personality, but an escape from personality. But, of course, only those who have personality and emotions know what it means to want to escape from these things. *Ib.*

5 The only way of expressing emotion in the form of art is by finding an "objective correlative"; in other words, a set of objects, a situation, a chain of events which shall be the formula of that *particular* emotion.

Hamlet and His Problems [1919]

6 Immature poets imitate; mature poets steal. *Philip Massinger [1920]*

7 Every vital development in language is a development of feeling as well. *Ib.*

8 In the seventeenth century a dissociation of sensibility set in, from which we have never recovered; and this dissociation, as is natural, was aggravated by the influence of the two most powerful poets of the century, Milton and Dryden.

The Metaphysical Poets [1921]

9 Poets in our civilization, as it exists at present, must be *difficult*. . . . The poet must become more and more comprehensive, more allusive, more indirect, in order to force, to dislocate if necessary, language into its meaning. *Ib.*

10 Humility is the most difficult of all virtues to achieve; nothing dies harder than the desire to think well of oneself.

Shakespeare and the Stoicism of Seneca [1927]

11 The great poet, in writing himself, writes his time.[2] *Ib.*

[1]See Virgil, 105:23; Marlowe, 183:21 and 184:1; Browne, 274:15; Milton, 283:13 and 285:12; Sartre, 865:12; and Robert Lowell, 893:7.

[2]In a footnote, Eliot writes: "Rémy de Gourmont said much the same thing, in speaking of Flaubert."

12 We know too much, and are convinced of too little. Our literature is a substitute for religion, and so is our religion.

A Dialogue on Dramatic Poetry [1928]

13 The general point of view may be described as classicist in literature, royalist in politics, and Anglo-Catholic in religion.

For Lancelot Andrews [1928], preface

14 We fight for lost causes because we know that our defeat and dismay may be the preface to our successors' victory, though that victory itself will be temporary; we fight rather to keep something alive than in the expectation that anything will triumph.

Ib. Francis Herbert Bradley

15 Genuine poetry can communicate before it is understood. *Dante [1929]*

16 More can be learned about how to write poetry from Dante than from any English poet. . . . The language of each great English poet is his own language; the language of Dante is the perfection of a common language. *Ib.*

17 Shakespeare gives the greatest width of human passion; Dante the greatest altitude and greatest depth. *Ib.*

18 Sometimes, however, to be a "ruined man" is itself a vocation.

The Use of Poetry and the Use of Criticism [1933]. Wordsworth and Coleridge

19 As things are, and as fundamentally they must always be, poetry is not a career, but a mug's game. No honest poet can ever feel quite sure of the permanent value of what he has written: he may have wasted his time and messed up his life for nothing.

Ib. Conclusion

20 Tradition by itself is not enough; it must be perpetually criticized and brought up to date under the supervision of what I call orthodoxy. *After Strange Gods [1934]*

Joseph Patrick Kennedy

1888–1969

21 Don't get mad, get even. *Attributed*

William L. Laurence

1888–

22 A great ball of fire about a mile in diameter, changing colors as it kept shooting upward, from deep purple to orange, expanding,

growing bigger, rising as it was expanding, an elemental force freed from its bonds after being chained for billions of years.

On the first atom bomb explosion.[1] *In the New York Times [September 26, 1945]*

1 At first it was a giant column that soon took the shape of a supramundane mushroom. *Ib.*

T. E. Lawrence[2]

1888–1935

2 I loved you, so I drew these tides of men into my hands and wrote my will across the sky in stars.
To earn you Freedom, the seven-pillared worthy house, that your eyes might be shining for me
When we came.

Seven Pillars of Wisdom[3] *[1926], dedication*

3 There could be no honor in a sure success, but much might be wrested from a sure defeat.

Revolt in the Desert [1927], ch. 19

Katherine Mansfield

1888–1923

4 I want, by understanding myself, to understand others. I want to be all that I am capable of becoming. . . . This all sounds very strenuous and serious. But now that I have wrestled with it, it's no longer so. I feel happy—deep down. *All is well.*

Journal [1922], last entry

Eugene O'Neill

1888–1953

5 Dat ole davil, sea.

Anna Christie [1922], act I

6 We's all poor nuts and things happen, and we yust get mixed in wrong, that's all.

Ib. IV

7 For de little stealin' dey gits you in jail soon or late. For de big stealin' dey makes you emperor and puts you in de Hall o' Fame when you croaks. If dey's one thing I learns in ten years on de Pullman cars listenin' to de white quality talk, it's dat same fact.

The Emperor Jones [1920], sc. i

[1] At Alamogordo, New Mexico [July 16, 1945].
[2] Lawrence changed his name to T. E. Shaw in 1927.
[3] See *Proverbs 9:1*, 23:18.

8 *Yank:* Sure! Lock me up! Put me in a cage! Dat's de on'y answer yuh know. G'wan, lock me up!
Policeman: What you been doin'?
Yank: Enough to gimme life for! I was born, see? Sure, dat's de charge. Write it in de blotter. I was born, get me!

The Hairy Ape [1922], sc. vii

9 Desire Under the Elms.

Title of play [1924]

10 God is a Mother.[4]

Strange Interlude [1928], pt. I, act V

11 Strange interlude! Yes, our lives are merely strange dark interludes in the electrical display of God the Father!

Ib. II, IX

12 Mourning Becomes Electra.

Title of dramatic trilogy [1931]

13 The sea hates a coward.

Mourning Becomes Electra [1931]. The Hunted, act IV

14 The damned don't cry.

Ib. The Haunted, act III

15 The dead! Why can't the dead die!

Ib. IV

16 A Long Day's Journey into Night.

Title of play [1956]

John Crowe Ransom

1888–1974

17 Two evils, monstrous either one apart,
Possessed me, and were long and loath at going:
A cry of Absence, Absence, in the heart,
And in the wood the furious winter blowing.

Winter Remembered

18 Hands hold much of heat in little storage.

They Hail the Sunrise

19 The lazy geese, like a snow cloud
Dripping their snow on the green grass,
Tricking and stopping, sleepy and proud,
Who cried in goose, Alas.

Bells for John Whiteside's Daughter

20 Here lies a lady of beauty and high degree.
Of chills and fever she died, of fever and chills,
The delight of her husband, her aunts, an infant of three,
And of medicos marveling sweetly on her ills.

Here Lies a Lady

[4] See Suti and Hor, 5:3; Eddy, 583:1; and John Paul I, 881:6.

1 God have mercy on the sinner
Who must write with no dinner,
No gravy and no grub,
No pewter and no pub,
No belly and no bowels,
Only consonants and vowels.
Survey of Literature

2 Captain Carpenter rose up in his prime
Put on his pistols and went riding out.
Captain Carpenter, st. 1

Knute Kenneth Rockne
1888–1931

3 Show me a good and gracious loser and I'll show you a failure.[1]
Remark to Wisconsin basketball coach Walter Meanwell [1920s]

4 Win this one for the Gipper.
Attributed[2]

Alan Seeger
1888–1916

5 I have a rendezvous with Death
At some disputed barricade,
When spring comes back with rustling shade
And apple blossoms fill the air.
I Have a Rendezvous with Death

6 And I to my pledged word am true,
I shall not fail that rendezvous. *Ib.*

Bartolomeo Vanzetti
1888–1927

7 If it had not been for this thing, I might have lived out my life talking at street corners to scorning men. I might have died unmarked, unknown, a failure. Now we are not a failure. This is our career and our triumph. Never in our full life could we hope to do such work for tolerance, for justice, for man's understanding of man, as now we do by accident. *Letter to his son [April 1927]*

8 Our words—our lives—our pains: nothing! The taking of our lives—lives of a good shoemaker and a poor fish peddler—all! That last moment belongs to us—that agony is our triumph. *Ib.*

9 I found myself compelled to fight back from my eyes the tears, and quanch my heart trobling to my throat to not weep before him. But Sacco's name will live in the hearts of the people when your name, your laws, institutions and your false god are but a dim rememoring of a cursed past in which man was wolf to the man. *Last speech to the court*[3]

Henry Agard Wallace
1888–1965

10 Unemployed purchasing power means unemployed labor and unemployed labor means human want in the midst of plenty. This is the most challenging paradox of modern times. *Address [1934]*

11 The century on which we are entering can be and must be the century of the common man.
Address, The Price of Free World Victory [May 8, 1942]

Conrad Aiken
1889–1973

12 Music I heard with you was more than music,
And bread I broke with you was more than bread.
Now that I am without you, all is desolate;
All that was once so beautiful is dead.
Bread and Music [1914]

13 Stars in the purple dusk above the rooftops
Pale in a saffron mist and seem to die,
And I myself on a swiftly tilting planet
Stand before a glass and tie my tie.
Senlin. Morning Song

14 One by one in the moonlight there,
Neighing far off on the haunted air,
The unicorns come down to the sea.
Ib. Evening Song

15 Rock meeting rock can know love better
Than eyes that stare or lips that touch.
All that we know in love is bitter,
And it is not much.
Annihilation, st. 8

16 All lovely things will have an ending,
All lovely things will fade and die,
And youth, that's now so bravely spending,
Will beg a penny by and by.
All Lovely Things Will Have an Ending

17 The hiss was now becoming a roar—the whole world was a vast moving screen of

[1] More familiar version: Show me a good loser and I'll show you a loser.

[2] Derived from Rockne's quote from George Gipp at halftime of Army game [1928]: Rock, someday when things look real tough for Notre Dame, ask the boys to go out there and win one for me.

[3] Vanzetti and Nicola Sacco, Italian anarchists, were executed August 23, 1927, by the Commonwealth of Massachusetts on charges, never conclusively proved, of murder and robbery.

snow—but even now it said peace, it said remoteness, it said cold, it said sleep.

Silent Snow, Secret Snow [1932]

1 O Altitudo in the bloodstream swims.[1]

And in the Human Heart [1940]. Sonnet 6

2 Ice is the silent language of the peak;
and fire the silent language of the star.

Ib. 10

3 For brief as water falling will be death,
and brief as flower falling, or a leaf,
brief as the taking, and the giving, breath;
thus natural, thus brief, my love, is grief.

Ib. 18

Robert Charles Benchley
1889–1945

4 I must get out of these wet clothes and into a dry Martini. *Attributed*

5 Tell us your phobias and we will tell you what you are afraid of. *Phobias*

6 It took me fifteen years to discover that I had no talent for writing, but I couldn't give it up because by that time I was too famous.

Remark

Charlie [Sir Charles Spencer] Chaplin
1889–1977

7 [The tramp character] A tramp, a gentleman, a poet, a dreamer, a lonely fellow, always hopeful of romance and adventure.

My Autobiography [1964], ch. 10

8 There are more valid facts and details in works of art than there are in history books.

Ib. 20

9 [Beauty is] an omnipresence of death and loveliness, a smiling sadness that we discern in nature and all things, a mystic communion that the poet feels—an expression of it can be a dustbin with a shaft of sunlight across it, or it can be a rose in the gutter.[2]

Ib. 29

10 Man is an animal with primary instincts of survival. Consequently, his ingenuity has developed first and his soul afterwards. Thus the progress of science is far ahead of man's ethical behavior. *Ib.*

[1] See Sir Thomas Browne, 274:4.

[2] "Of all melancholy topics, what, according to the universal understanding of mankind, is the most melancholy?" Death—was the obvious reply. "And when," I said, "is this most melancholy of topics most poetical?" . . . The answer . . . is obvious—"When it most closely allies itself to beauty."—EDGAR ALLAN POE, *The Philosophy of Composition* [1846]

Christopher Dawson
1889–

11 As soon as men decide that all means are permitted to fight an evil, then their good becomes indistinguishable from the evil that they set out to destroy.

The Judgment of the Nations [1942]

Philip Guedalla
1889–1944

12 The work of Henry James has always seemed divisible by a simple dynastic arrangement into three reigns: James I, James II, and the Old Pretender.[3]

Supers and Supermen [1920]

Adolf Hitler
1889–1945

13 My adversaries . . . applied the one means that wins the easiest victory over reason: terror and force.

Mein Kampf (My Battle) [1933], vol. I, ch. 2

14 A majority can never replace the man. . . . Just as a hundred fools do not make one wise man, an heroic decision is not likely to come from a hundred cowards. *Ib. 3*

15 Strength lies not in defense but in attack.

Ib.

16 All propaganda has to be popular and has to adapt its spiritual level to the perception of the least intelligent of those towards whom it intends to direct itself. *Ib. 6*

17 The great masses of the people . . . will more easily fall victims to a big lie than to a small one. *Ib. 10*

18 Never tolerate the establishment of two continental powers in Europe.

Ib. II, 14

19 After fifteen years of work I have achieved, as a common German soldier and merely with my fanatical will power, the unity of the German nation, and have freed it from the death sentence of Versailles.[4]

Proclamation to the troops on taking over the leadership of the German armed forces [December 21, 1941]

[3] See Henry James, 652.

[4] The Allied and Associated Governments affirm and Germany accepts the responsibility of Germany and her Allies for causing all the loss and damage to which the Allied and Associated Governments and their nationals have been subjected as a consequence of the war imposed

1 This war no longer bears the characteristics of former inter-European conflicts. It is one of those elemental conflicts which usher in a new millennium and which shake the world once in a thousand years.

Speech to the Reichstag [April 26, 1942]

2 Is Paris burning?[1]

Asked at the Oberkommando der Wehrmacht, Rastenburg, Germany [August 25, 1944]

George S. Kaufman
1889–1961

3 Satire is what closes Saturday night.

Saying

George S. Kaufman
1889–1961
and
Moss Hart
1904–1961

4 You Can't Take It with You.[2]

Title of play [1936]

5 The Man Who Came to Dinner.

Title of play [1939]

6 George Washington Slept Here.

Title of play [1940]

Stoddard King
1889–1933

7 There's a long, long trail a-winding
Into the land of my dreams,
Where the nightingales are singing
And a white moon beams.

The Long, Long Trail [1913]

Walter Lippmann
1889–1974

8 Whether we wish it or not we are involved in the world's problems, and all the winds of heaven blow through our land.

A Preface to Politics [1913], ch. 4

9 The liberal philosophy holds that enduring governments must be accountable to someone beside themselves; that a government responsible only to its own conscience is not for long tolerable. It holds that since any government is liable to fail, there is needed a method of changing the governors without wrecking the state. It holds that unless there is a method, be it through elections or otherwise, by which the governed can make their views effective in some proportion to their weight, the nation is at the mercy of violence in the form of terrorism, assassination, conspiracy, mass compulsion, and civil war.

In Defense of Liberalism. From Vanity Fair [November 1934]

10 This law which is the spirit of law is the opposite of an accumulation of old precedents and new fiats. By this higher law, that men must not be arbitrary, the old law is continually tested and the new law reviewed.

The Good Society [1937], ch. 15

11 In foreign relations, as in all other relations, a policy has been formed only when commitments and power have been brought into balance.

U.S. Foreign Policy [1943]

12 The final test of a leader is that he leaves behind him in other men the conviction and the will to carry on. . . . The genius of a good leader is to leave behind him a situation which common sense, without the grace of genius, can deal with successfully.

Roosevelt Has Gone [April 14, 1945]

13 The world state is inherent in the United Nations as an oak tree is in an acorn.

One World or None [1946]

14 A regime, an established order, is rarely overthrown by a revolutionary movement; usually a regime collapses of its own weakness and corruption and then a revolutionary movement enters among the ruins and takes over the powers that have become vacant.

For Charles de Gaulle. From Today and Tomorrow [June 5, 1958]

15 We have neglected our own affairs. Our education is inadequate, our cities are badly built, our social arrangements are unsatisfactory. We can't wait another generation. Unless we can surmount this crisis, and work and get going onto the path of a settlement in Asia, and a settlement in Europe, all of these plans of the Great Society here at home, all the plans for the rebuilding of backward countries in other continents will all be put on the shelf, because war interrupts everything like that.

Conversations with Walter Lippmann [1965]. Lippmann and Eric Sevareid [February 22, 1965]

---

upon them by the aggression of Germany and her Allies. —*Article 231 (the "war guilt clause"), Treaty of Versailles* [June 28, 1919]

[1] Brennt Paris?

[2] See *The Song of the Harper*, 3:2; *Ecclesiastes 5:15*, 27:2; *I Timothy 6:7*, 51:1; and Theognis, 67:6.

1 A free press is not a privilege but an organic necessity in a great society. . . . A great society is simply a big and complicated urban society.[1]

Address at the International Press Institute Assembly, London [May 27, 1965]

2 Without criticism and reliable and intelligent reporting, the government cannot govern. *Ib.*

3 Responsible journalism is journalism responsible in the last analysis to the editor's own conviction of what, whether interesting or only important, is in the public interest. *Ib.*

4 As the free press develops, the paramount point is whether the journalist, like the scientist or scholar, puts truth in the first place or in the second. *Ib.*

Jawaharlal Nehru

1889–1964

5 The basic fact of today is the tremendous pace of change in human life.

Credo. Reprinted in the New York Times [September 7, 1958]

6 Democracy and socialism are means to an end, not the end itself. *Ib.*

7 The forces of a capitalist society, if left unchecked, tend to make the rich richer and the poor poorer.[2] *Ib.*

8 I want nothing to do with any religion concerned with keeping the masses satisfied to live in hunger, filth, and ignorance. I want nothing to do with any order, religious or otherwise, which does not teach people that they are capable of becoming happier and more civilized, on this earth, capable of becoming true *man,* master of his fate and captain of his soul.[3]

From EDGAR SNOW, *Journey to the Beginning [1958]*

Vannevar Bush

1890–1974

9 Science: The Endless Frontier.

Title of book [1945]

10 The scene changes but the aspirations of men of good will persist.

Modern Arms and Free Men [1949], foreword

11 If democracy loses its touch, then no great war will be needed to overwhelm it. If it keeps and enhances its strength, no great war need come again. *Ib. Conclusion*

12 It was through the Second World War that most of us suddenly appreciated for the first time the power of man's concentrated efforts to understand and control the forces of nature. We were appalled by what we saw.

Science Is Not Enough [1967]

13 Science is emphatically an important part of culture today, as scientific knowledge and its applications continue to transform the world, and condition every aspect of the relations between men and nations. *Ib.*

Karel Čapek

1890–1938

14 Rossum's Universal Robots.[4]

R.U.R. [1920]

Marcus Cook Connelly

1890–

15 Gangway for de Lawd God Jehovah!

The Green Pastures[5] *[1930]*

16 *God:* I'll jest r'ar back an' pass a miracle. *Ib.*

17 *Gabriel:* How about cleanin' up de whole mess of 'em and sta'tin' all over ag'in wid some new kind of animal?
God: An' admit I'm licked? *Ib.*

18 Even bein' Gawd ain't a bed of roses. *Ib.*

Elmer Davis

1890–1958

19 The republic was not established by cowards, and cowards will not preserve it.

Phi Beta Kappa Oration, Harvard [1953]

20 With a great price our ancestors obtained this freedom, but we were born free[6] . . . But that freedom can be retained only by the eternal vigilance which has always been its price.

But We Were Born Free [1954], ch. 1

[1] See Lyndon Johnson, 872:13.
[2] See Kahn and Egan, 795:5.
[3] See Sallust, 103:1 and 103:5; Bacon, 181:6; Shakespeare, 215:6; Tennyson, 534:7; and Henley, 663:11.
[4] The term "robot" came into English through Čapek's play.
[5] Suggested by Roark Bradford's stories, *Ol' Man Adam an' His Chillun.*
[6] See *Acts* 22:28, 46:26; Milton, 282:13; and Rousseau, 358:12.

1 The first and great commandment is, Don't let them scare you. *Ib.*

2 This will remain the land of the free only so long as it is the home of the brave. *Ib.*

3 What makes Western civilization worth saving is the freedom of the mind, now under heavy attack from the primitives . . . who have persisted among us. If we have not the courage to defend that faith, it won't matter much whether we are saved or not. *Ib. 6*

Charles André Joseph Marie de Gaulle

1890–1970

4 The sword is the axis of the world, and grandeur is indivisible. *Le Fil de l'Épée [1934]*

5 The perfection preached in the Gospels never yet built up an empire. Every man of action has a strong dose of egotism, pride, hardness, and cunning. But all those things will be forgiven him, indeed, they will be regarded as high qualities, if he can make of them the means to achieve great ends. *Ib.*

6 Nothing great will ever be achieved without great men, and men are great only if they are determined to be so. *Ib.*

7 France has lost a battle. But France has not lost the war. *Broadcast from London to the French people after the fall of France [June 18, 1940]*

8 Since those whose duty it was to hold the sword of France have let it fall, I have picked up its broken point. *Radio address [July 13, 1940]*

9 If I live, I will fight, wherever I must, as long as I must, until the enemy is defeated and the national stain washed clean. *Les Mémoires de Guerre, vol. I [1954]*

10 France cannot be France without greatness. *Ib.*

11 I always thought I was Jeanne d'Arc and Bonaparte. How little one knows oneself. *Reply to speaker who compared him to Robespierre. From Figaro Littéraire [1958]*

Dwight David Eisenhower

1890–1969

12 People of Western Europe: A landing was made this morning on the coast of France by troops of the Allied Expeditionary Force. This landing is part of the concerted United Nations plan for the liberation of Europe, made in conjunction with our great Russian allies. . . . I call upon all who love freedom to stand with us now. Together we shall achieve victory. *Broadcast on D-Day [June 6, 1944]*

13 Humility must always be the portion of any man who receives acclaim earned in the blood of his followers and the sacrifices of his friends. *Address at Guildhall, London [July 12, 1945]*

14 Nothing is easy in war. Mistakes are always paid for in casualties and troops are quick to sense any blunder made by their commanders. *Infantry School Quarterly [April 1953]*

15 This conjunction of an immense military establishment and a large arms industry is new in the American experience. . . . We recognize the imperative need for this development. Yet we must not fail to comprehend its grave implications. . . . In the councils of government, we must guard against the acquisition of unwarranted influence, whether sought or unsought, by the military-industrial complex. The potential for the disastrous rise of misplaced power exists and will persist. *Farewell Radio and Television Address to the American People [January 17, 1961]*

Sir Alan Patrick Herbert

1890–1971

16 Holy Deadlock.[1] *Title of novel [1934] satirizing the paradoxes of British divorce law*

17 The Common Law of England has been laboriously built upon a mythical figure—the figure of "The Reasonable Man." *Uncommon Law [1935], p. 1*

18 The critical period in matrimony is breakfast-time. *Ib. p. 98*

[1] Monagony—the state of being married to one person. —Brooks Beck [1963]

1 An Act of God was defined as something which no reasonable man could have expected. *Ib. p. 316*

Samuel Hoffenstein

1890–1947

2 Babies haven't any hair;
Old men's heads are just as bare;
Between the cradle and the grave[1]
Lies a haircut and a shave.
Songs of Faith in the Year After Next, VIII

3 The heart's dead
Are never buried. *Summer Day*

Gerald White Johnson

1890–

4 Nothing changes more constantly than the past; for the past that influences our lives does not consist of what actually happened, but of what men believe happened.
American Heroes and Hero-Worship [1943], ch. 1

5 In revolutionary times the rich are always the people who are most afraid.
American Freedom and the Press [1958]

Hanns Johst

1890–

6 When I hear the word "culture" . . . I reach for my revolver.[2]
Schlageter [1933]

Robert Ley

1890–1945

7 Strength through joy.[3]
Instruction for the German Labor Front [December 2, 1933]

Howard Phillips Lovecraft

1890–1937

8 The most merciful thing in the world, I think, is the inability of the human mind to correlate all its contents.
The Call of Cthulhu [1928], ch. 1

[1]See Dyer, 345:3; Shelley, 467:9; and Bellamy, 665:17.
[2]Wenn ich Kultur höre . . . entsichere ich meinen Browning.
Often attributed to Goering.
[3]Kraft durch Freude.

Christopher Morley

1890–1957

9 There is only one success — to be able to spend your life in your own way.
Where the Blue Begins [1922]

10 Life is a foreign language; all men mispronounce it.
Thunder on the Left [1925], ch. 14

11 April prepares her green traffic light and the world thinks Go.
John Mistletoe [1931], 8

12 A human being; an ingenious assembly of portable plumbing.
Human Being [1932], ch. 11

13 There was so much handwriting on the wall
That even the wall fell down.
Around the Clock [1943]

14 Chattering voltage like a broken wire
The wild cicada cried, Six weeks to frost!
End of August

15 Why do they put the Gideon Bibles only in the bedrooms, where it's usually too late, and not in the barroom downstairs?
Contribution to a Contribution

Allan Nevins

1890–1971

16 Too little and too late.
Current History [1935]

Boris Pasternak

1890–1960

17 Art is unthinkable without risk and spiritual self-sacrifice.
On Modesty and Bravery [1936]. Speech at Writers' Conference[4]

18 I am alone; all drowns in the Pharisees' hypocrisy.
To live your life is not as simple as to cross a field.[5] *Hamlet [1946]*[6]

19 You are eternity's hostage
A captive of time. *Night [1957]*[6]

20 But what are pity, conscience, or fear
To the brazen pair, compared
With the living sorcery
Of their hot embraces?
Bacchanalia [1957],[6] *st. 4*

[4]Translated by E. Levin.
[5]See Anonymous: Russian, 934:12.
[6]Translated by Max Hayward.

1 During the last years of Mayakovski's life,[1] when all poetry had ceased to exist . . . literature had stopped.

I Remember [1958][2]

2 It snowed and snowed, the whole world over,
Snow swept the world from end to end.
A candle burned on the table;
A candle burned.

Doctor Zhivago [1958]. The Poems of Yurii Zhivago, Winter Night, st. 1

3 A corner draft fluttered the flame
And the white fever of temptation
Upswept its angel wings that cast
A cruciform shadow. *Ib. st. 7*

4 And when the war broke out, its real horrors, its real dangers, its menace of real death were a blessing compared with the inhuman reign of the lie, and they brought relief because they broke the spell of the dead letter.

Ib. epilogue

5 Departure beyond the borders of my country is for me equivalent to death.

Letter to Khrushchev [1958][3]

6 I am caught like a beast at bay.
Somewhere are people, freedom, light,
But all I hear is the baying of the pack,
There is no way out for me.

The Nobel Prize [1959][4]

"Red" Rowley

fl. 1915

7 Mademoiselle from Armenteers,
Hasn't been kissed in forty years,
Hinky dinky, parley-voo.

Mademoiselle from Armentières[5]

8 Mademoiselle from St. Nazaire,
She never heard of underwear. *Ib.*

George Seldes

1890–1970

9 Sawdust Caesar.[6]

Title of book [1932]

[1] Vladimir Mayakovski [1893–1930].
[2] Translated by Manya Harari.
[3] Translated by E. Levin.
[4] Translated by Max Hayward.
[5] Soldiers' song of World War I, with innumerable versions. The tune and verse structure were based on a British Army song composed by Alfred James Walden ["Harry Wincott," 1867–1947].
[6] Mussolini.

Frederick Moore Vinson

1890–1953

10 Wars are not "acts of God." They are caused by man, by man-made institutions, by the way in which man has organized his society. What man has made, man can change.

Speech at Arlington National Cemetery [Memorial Day, 1945]

Charles Erwin Wilson

1890–1961

11 What is good for the country is good for General Motors, and what's good for General Motors is good for the country.

To the Senate Armed Forces Committee [1952]

Agatha Christie

1891–1976

12 "This affair must all be unraveled from within." He [Hercule Poirot] tapped his forehead. "These little gray cells. It is 'up to them'—as you say over here."

The Mysterious Affair at Styles [1920], ch. 10

13 Every murderer is probably somebody's old friend. *Ib. 11*

14 It is completely unimportant. That is why it is so interesting.

The Murder of Roger Ackroyd [1926]

15 I don't think necessity is the mother of invention[7]—invention, in my opinion, arises directly from idleness, possibly also from laziness. To save oneself trouble.

An Autobiography [1977]. Pt. III, Growing Up

16 If you love, you will suffer, and if you do not love, you do not know the meaning of a Christian life. *Ib.*

17 Trains are wonderful. . . . To travel by train is to see nature and human beings, towns and churches and rivers, in fact, to see life.

Ib. IV, Flirting, Courting, Banns Up, Marriage

18 One is left with the horrible feeling now that war settles nothing; that to win a war is as disastrous as to lose one! . . . We shall not survive war, but shall, as well as our adversaries, be destroyed by war.[8]

Ib. X, The Second War

[7] See Persius, 117:8, and Anonymous Latin, 134:9.
[8] See Pyrrhus, 92:10.

Jean Cocteau
1891–1963

1 Mirrors should reflect a little before throwing back images. *Des Beaux-Arts*

2 The worst tragedy for a poet is to be admired through being misunderstood.
Le Rappel à l'Ordre [1926]

3 The Blood of a Poet.
Title of film [1933]

4 The matters I relate
Are true lies.[1]
The Journals of Jean Cocteau [1956]. Quoted by WALLACE FOWLIE *in the introduction*

Ely Culbertson
1891–1955

5 The bizarre world of cards . . . a world of pure power politics where rewards and punishments were meted out immediately. A deck of cards was built like the purest of hierarchies, with every card a master to those below it, a lackey to those above it. And there were "masses"—long suits—which always asserted themselves in the end, triumphing over the kings and aces.
Total Peace [1943], ch. 1

6 Power politics is the diplomatic name for the law of the jungle.
Must We Fight Russia? [1946], ch. 2

7 We must conquer war, or war will conquer us. *Ib.*

8 God and the politicians willing, the United States can declare peace upon the world, and win it. *Ib. 5*

Karl Kelchner Darrow
1891–

9 One of the things which distinguishes ours from all earlier generations is this, that we have seen our atoms.
The Renaissance of Physics [1936]

Hu Shih[2]
1891–1962

10 Only when we realize that there is no eternal, unchanging truth or absolute truth can we arouse in ourselves a sense of intellectual responsibility.
La Jeunesse Nouvelle [April 1919]

11 The most outstanding characteristic of Eastern civilization is to know contentment, whereas that of Western civilization is not to know contentment.
Ib. Hu Shih wen ts'un

12 The civilization under which people are restricted and controlled by a material environment from which they cannot escape, and under which they cannot utilize human thought and intellectual power to change environment and improve conditions, is the civilization of a lazy and nonprogressive people. It is a truly materialistic civilization.
Ib.

Jomo Kenyatta [Kamau Wa Ngengi]
1891–1978

13 The question of land tenure . . . is the key to the [Kikuyu] people's life; it secures for them that peaceful tillage of the soil which supplies their material needs and enables them to perform their magic and traditional ceremonies in undisturbed serenity, facing Mount Kenya.
Facing Mount Kenya: The Tribal Life of the Gikuyu (Kikuyu) [1938], preface

14 The African is conditioned, by the cultural and social institutions of centuries, to a freedom of which Europe has little conception, and it is not in his nature to accept serfdom forever. He realizes that he must fight unceasingly for his own complete emancipation; for without this he is doomed to remain the prey of rival imperialisms.
Ib. Conclusion

15 We must try to trust one another. Stay and cooperate.[3]
Statement, as first president of the Republic of Kenya, to the white settlers [1964]

David Low
1891–1963

16 I have never met anybody who wasn't against war. Even Hitler and Mussolini were, according to themselves.
From the New York Times [February 10, 1946]

[1] Les choses que je conte / Sont des mensonges vrais.
[2] From *Sources of Chinese Tradition* [1960], edited by WILLIAM THEODORE DE BARY.
[3] Harambee [Swahili for "Let's pull together"].—*National motto of Kenya*

Osip Mandelstam
1891–1938

1 We live, deaf to the land beneath us,
Ten steps away no one hears our speeches,

But where there's so much as half a conversation
The Kremlin's mountaineer will get his mention.
Stalin [1934], st. 1, 2

2 One by one forging his laws, to be flung
Like horseshoes at the head, the eye, or the groin.

And every killing is a treat
For the broad-chested Ossete.
Ib. st. 7, 8

Claude McKay
1891–1948

3 Upon the clothes behind the tenement,
That hang like ghosts suspended from the lines,
Linking each flat to each indifferent,
Incongruous and strange the moonlight shines.
A Song of the Moon

4 Although she feeds me bread of bitterness,
And sinks into my throat her tiger's tooth,
Stealing my breath of life, I must confess
I love this cultured hell that tests my youth!
Her vigor flows like tides into my blood,
Giving me strength erect against her hate.
Her bigness sweeps my being like a flood.
America

5 If we must die, let it not be like hogs
Hunted and penned in an inglorious spot.
If We Must Die

6 If we must die, O let us nobly die. *Ib.*

7 What though before us lies the open grave?
Like men we'll face the murderous, cowardly pack,
Pressed to the wall, dying, but fighting back!
Ib.

Irene Rutherford McLeod
1891–1964

8 I'm a lean dog, a keen dog, a wild dog, and alone.
Songs to Save a Soul [1919]. Lone Dog

Henry Miller
1891–1980

9 It's good to be just plain happy; it's a little better to know that you're happy; but to understand that you're happy and to know why and how . . . and still be happy, be happy in the being and the knowing, well that is beyond happiness, that is bliss.
The Colossus of Maroussi [1941], pt. I

10 Greece is the home of the gods; they may have died but their presence still makes itself felt. The gods were of human proportion: they were created out of the human spirit.
Ib. III

11 If men cease to believe that they will one day become gods then they will surely become worms. *Ib.*

12 Until he [man] has become fully human, until he learns to conduct himself as a member of the earth, he will continue to create gods who will destroy him. The tragedy of Greece lies not in the destruction of a great culture but in the abortion of a great vision.
Ib.

Elliot Paul
1891–1958

13 The last time I see Paris will be on the day I die. The city was inexhaustible, and so is its memory.
The Last Time I Saw Paris [1942],[1] *pt. II, 23*

Michael Polanyi
1891–1976

14 An art which has fallen into disuse for the period of a generation is altogether lost. There are hundreds of examples of this to which the process of mechanization is continuously adding new ones. These losses are usually irretrievable. It is pathetic to watch the endless efforts—equipped with microscopy and chemistry, with mathematics and electronics—to reproduce a single violin of the kind the half-literate Stradivarius turned out as a matter of routine more than two hundred years ago.
Personal Knowledge [1958]

[1] See Hammerstein, 833:9.

Cole Albert Porter
1891–1964

1 You do something to me,
Something that simply mystifies me.
Fifty Million Frenchmen [1929]. You Do Something to Me

2 Night and day you are the one,
Only you beneath the moon and under the sun.
Gay Divorce [1932]. Night and Day

3 I get no kick from champagne.
Mere alcohol doesn't thrill me at all,
So tell me why should it be true
That I get a kick out of you.
Anything Goes [1934]. I Get a Kick Out of You

4 You're the Nile,
You're the Tower of Pisa,
You're the smile
On the Mona Lisa. . . .
But if, Baby, I'm the bottom you're the top!
Ib. You're the Top!

5 It was great fun,
But it was just one of those things.
Jubilee [1935]. Just One of Those Things

6 It's delightful, it's delicious, it's de-lovely.
Red, Hot and Blue [1936]. It's De-Lovely

7 My Heart Belongs to Daddy.
Leave It to Me [1938], title of song

8 But I'm always true to you, darlin', in my fashion,[1]
Yes, I'm always true to you, darlin', in my way.
Kiss Me, Kate [1948]. Always True to You in My Fashion

Nicola Sacco
1891–1927

9 Help the weak ones that cry for help, help the prosecuted and the victim . . . they are the comrades that fight and fall . . . for the conquest of the joy of freedom for all the poor workers. In this struggle for life you will find more love and you will be loved.
Letter to his son Dante

Haile Selassie
1891–1975

10 Outside the kingdom of the Lord there is no nation which is greater than any other. God and history will remember your judgment.
Speech, the League of Nations [1936][2]

Arthur Hays Sulzberger
1891–1968

11 Obviously, a man's judgment cannot be better than the information on which he has based it.
Address to the New York State Publishers Association [August 30, 1948]

12 Freedom cannot be trifled with. You cannot surrender it for security unless in a state of war, and then you must guard carefully the methods of so doing.
Upon receiving the Columbia College award for distinguished service [1952]

13 The vital measure of a newspaper is not its size but its spirit—that is its responsibility to report the news fully, accurately and fairly.
On accepting an award to the New York Times by Temple Israel, Boston [May 9, 1956]

Earl Warren
1891–1974

14 To separate [Negro children] from others of similar age and qualifications solely because of their race generates a feeling of inferiority as to their status in the community that may affect their hearts and minds in a way unlikely ever to be undone. . . . We conclude that in the field of public education the doctrine of "separate but equal"[3] has no place. Separate educational facilities are inherently unequal.
Brown v. Board of Education of Topeka, 347 U.S. 483 [1954][4]

15 When an individual is taken into custody or otherwise deprived of his freedom by the authorities and is subjected to questioning . . . he must be warned prior to any ques-

[1] See Dowson, 721:4.

[2] He sought sanctions against Italy, which had invaded Ethiopia.

[3] All railway companies carrying passengers in their coaches in the state shall provide equal but separate accommodations for the white and colored races.—*Louisiana Acts of 1890, no. III, p. 152;* quoted by Mr. Justice Henry B. Brown in *Plessy v. Ferguson, 163 U.S. 537* [1896]

[4] In a later implementation of the same case (*349 U.S. 294* [1955]), the Supreme Court asked that desegregation proceed "with all deliberate speed."

tioning that he has the right to remain silent, that anything he says can be used against him in a court of law, that he has the right to the presence of an attorney, and that if he cannot afford an attorney one will be appointed for him prior to any questioning if he so desires.

Miranda v. Arizona, 384 U.S. 436 [1965]

Herbert V. Wiley
1891–1954

1 Stand by to crash.

Last command to the crew of the falling U.S. Navy dirigible Akron [April 4, 1933]

Stella Benson
1892–1933

2 Call no man foe, but never love a stranger.

To the Unborn, st. 3

Pearl S. Buck
1892–1973

3 I feel no need for any other faith than my faith in human beings. Like Confucius of old, I am so absorbed in the wonder of earth and the life upon it that I cannot think of heaven and the angels. I have enough for this life. If there is no other life, then this one has been enough to make it worth being born, myself a human being. *I Believe [1939]*

Walter C. Hagen
1892–1969

4 Don't hurry, don't worry. You're only here for a short visit. So be sure to stop and smell the flowers.

From the New York Times [May 22, 1977]

John Burdon Sanderson Haldane
1892–1964

5 Now, my suspicion is that the universe is not only queerer than we suppose, but queerer than we *can* suppose. . . . I suspect that there are more things in heaven and earth than are dreamed of, in any philosophy.[1] That is the reason why I have no philosophy myself, and must be my excuse for dreaming. *Possible Worlds [1927]*

[1]See Shakespeare, 220:3.

Robert Houghwout Jackson
1892–1954

6 If there is any fixed star in our constitutional constellation, it is that no official, high or petty, can prescribe what shall be orthodox in politics, nationalism, religion, or other matters of opinion or force citizens to confess by word or act their faith therein.[2]

Minersville School District v. Gobitis, 319 U.S. 624, 642 [1940]

7 The first trial in history for crimes against the peace of the world imposes a grave responsibility. The wrongs which we seek to condemn and punish have been so calculated, so malignant and so devastating that civilization cannot tolerate their being ignored because it cannot survive their being repeated.

Opening address before the International Military Tribunal, Nuremberg [1945]

8 There is danger that, if the Court does not temper its doctrinaire logic with a little practical wisdom, it will convert the constitutional Bill of Rights into a suicide pact.

Terminiello v. Chicago, 337 U.S. 1, 37 [1949]

9 It is not the function of our Government to keep the citizen from falling into error; it is the function of the citizen to keep the Government from falling into error.

American Communications Association v. Douds, 339 U.S. 382, 442 [1950]

10 The day that this country ceases to be free for irreligion, it will cease to be free for religion.

Dissenting opinion, Zorach v. Clausor, 343 U.S. 306, 325 [1952]

Archibald MacLeish
1892–

11 Beauty is that Medusa's head
Which men go armed to seek and sever:
It is most deadly when most dead,
And dead will stare and sting forever.

The Happy Marriage [1924]

12 There with vast wings across the canceled skies,
There in the sudden blackness the black pall
Of nothing, nothing, nothing—nothing at all. *The End of the World [1926]*

13 A poem should not mean
But be. *Ars Poetica [1926]*

[2]See E. B. White, 846:17.

1 And here face downward in the sun
To feel how swift how secretly
The shadow of the night comes on.
You, Andrew Marvell [1930]

2 We were the first that found that famous country:
We marched by a king's name: we crossed the sierras:
Unknown hardships we suffered: hunger.
Conquistador [1932]. Bernál Díaz' Preface

3 We were the lords of it all. . . . *Ib.*

4 She lies on her left side her flank golden:
Her hair is burned black with the strong sun.
The scent of her hair is of rain in the dust on her shoulders:
She has brown breasts and the mouth of no other country.
Frescoes for Mr. Rockefeller's City [1933]. Landscape as a Nude, st. 1

5 And learn O voyager to walk
The roll of earth, the pitch and fall
That swings across these trees those stars:
That swings the sunlight up the wall.
Seafarer [1933], st. 1

6 The world was always yours: you would not take it. *Speech to a Crowd [1936]*

7 Christ but this earth goes over to the squall of time!
Hi but she heels to it—rail down: ribs down: rolling
Dakotas under her hull! And the night climbing
Sucking the green from the ferns by these Berkshire boulders!
The Sunset Piece [1936]

8 America was promises . . .
It was Man who had been promised.
America Was Promises [1939]

9 old age
level light
evening in the afternoon
love without the bitterness and so
good-night
Definitions of Old Age [1976]

10 Now, the fourth day evening, we descend,
make fast, set foot at last upon her beaches,
stand in her silence, lift our heads and see
above her, wanderer in her sky,
a wonder to us past the reach of wonder,
a light beyond our lights, our lives, the rising earth,
a meaning to us,
O, a meaning!
Voyage to the Moon [1976]

Edna St. Vincent Millay
1892–1950

11 All I could see from where I stood
Was three long mountains and a wood.
Renascence [1912], l. 1

12 The world stands out on either side
No wider than the heart is wide;
Above the world is stretched the sky,—
No higher than the soul is high.[1]
The heart can push the sea and land
Farther away on either hand;
The soul can split the sky in two,
And let the face of God shine through.
But East and West will pinch the heart
That cannot keep them pushed apart;
And he whose soul is flat—the sky
Will cave in on him by and by.
Ib. last lines

13 O world, I cannot hold thee close enough!
God's World [1917], st. 1

14 Lord, I do fear
Thou'st made the world too beautiful this year.
My soul is all but out of me—let fall
No burning leaf; prithee, let no bird call.
Ib. st. 2

15 I will be the gladdest thing under the sun!
I will touch a hundred flowers and not pick one.
Afternoon on a Hill [1917], st. 1

16 Life goes on forever like the gnawing of a mouse. *Ashes of Life [1917], st. 3*

17 My candle burns at both ends;
It will not last the night;
But, ah, my foes, and, oh, my friends—
It gives a lovely light.[2]
A Few Figs from Thistles [1920]. First Fig

18 Safe upon the solid rock the ugly houses stand:
Come and see my shining palace built upon the sand![3] *Ib. Second Fig*

19 We were very tired, we were very merry—
We had gone back and forth all night on the ferry. *Ib. Recuerdo*

20 I had a little sorrow,
Born of a little sin.
Ib. The Penitent, st. 1

[1] See Hartley Coleridge, 480:12.
[2] I burned my candle at both ends, / And now have neither foes nor friends.—SAMUEL HOFFENSTEIN [1890–1947], *Songs of Fairly Utter Despair, 8*
[3] See *Matthew 7:26*, 38:21.

1 Whether or not we find what we are seeking
Is idle, biologically speaking.
Ib. I Shall Forget You Presently, l. 13

2 Death devours all lovely things;
Lesbia with her sparrow
Shares the darkness — presently
Every bed is narrow.
Passer Mortuus Est [1921], st. 1

3 My heart is warm with the friends I make,
And better friends I'll not be knowing;
Yet there isn't a train I wouldn't take,
No matter where it's going.
Travel [1921], st. 3

4 I know I am but summer to your heart,
And not the full four seasons of the year.
I Know I Am But Summer [1923], l. 1

5 I drank at every vine.
The last was like the first.
I came upon no wine
So wonderful as thirst.
Feast [1923], st. 1

6 I only know that summer sang in me
A little while, that in me sings no more.
What Lips My Lips Have Kissed [1923], l. 13

7 Pity me that the heart is slow to learn
What the swift mind beholds at every turn.
Pity Me Not [1923], l. 13

8 Euclid alone
Has looked on Beauty bare.[1] Fortunate they
Who, though once only and then but far away,
Have heard her massive sandal set on stone.
Euclid Alone Has Looked on Beauty Bare [1923], l. 11

9 How strange a thing is death, bringing to his knees, bringing to his antlers
The buck in the snow . . .
Life, looking out attentive from the eyes of the doe.
The Buck in the Snow [1928]

10 If ever I said, in grief or pride,
I tired of honest things, I lied.
The Goose Girl [1923], l. 5

11 Music my rampart, and my only one.
On Hearing a Symphony of Beethoven [1928], l. 14

12 I am not resigned to the shutting away of loving hearts in the hard ground.
So it is, and so it will be, for so it has been, time out of mind:
Into the darkness they go, the wise and the lovely. Crowned
With lilies and with laurel they go; but I am not resigned.
Dirge Without Music [1928], st. 1

13 Love is not all: it is not meat nor drink
Nor slumber nor a roof against the rain;
Nor yet a floating spar to men that sink.
Love Is Not All [1931], l. 1

14 Time can make soft that iron wood.
Wine from These Grapes [1934]. The Leaf and the Tree

[1] See Russell, 737:14.

Reinhold Niebuhr

1892–1971

15 God, give us grace to accept with serenity the things that cannot be changed, courage to change the things which should be changed, and the wisdom to distinguish the one from the other. *The Serenity Prayer [1943]*[2]

16 Goodness, armed with power, is corrupted; and pure love without power is destroyed.
Beyond Tragedy [1938]

17 The prophet himself stands under the judgment which he preaches. If he does not know that, he is a false prophet. *Ib.*

18 Man's capacity for justice makes democracy possible, but man's inclination to injustice makes democracy necessary.
The Children of Light and the Children of Darkness [1944]

19 Humor is a prelude to faith and
Laughter is the beginning of prayer.
Discerning the Signs of the Times [1949]

20 Life has no meaning except in terms of responsibility. *Faith and History [1949]*

21 Nothing worth doing is completed in our lifetime; therefore, we must be saved by hope. Nothing true or beautiful or good makes complete sense in any immediate context of history; therefore, we must be saved by faith. Nothing we do, however virtuous, can be accomplished alone; therefore, we are saved by love.
The Irony of American History [1952]

[2] Written for a service in the Congregational church of Heath, Massachusetts, where Dr. Niebuhr spent many summers, the prayer was first printed in a monthly bulletin of the Federal Council of Churches. Enormously popular, it has been circulated in millions of copies.

Martin Niemoeller
1892–

1 In Germany they came first for the Communists, and I didn't speak up because I wasn't a Communist. Then they came for the Jews, and I didn't speak up because I wasn't a Jew. Then they came for the trade unionists, and I didn't speak up because I wasn't a trade unionist. Then they came for the Catholics, and I didn't speak up because I was a Protestant. Then they came for me, and by that time no one was left to speak up.[1]
Attributed

Harold Wallace Ross
1892–1951

2 *The New Yorker* will not be edited for the old lady from Dubuque.[2]
Upon founding The New Yorker [1925]

John Ronald Reuel Tolkien
1892–1973

3 In a hole in the ground there lived a hobbit. Not a nasty, dirty, wet hole, filled with the ends of worms and an oozy smell, nor yet a dry, bare, sandy hole with nothing in it to sit down on or to eat: it was a hobbit-hole, and that means comfort.
The Hobbit; or There and Back Again [1937], ch. 1

César Vallejo
1892–1938

4 I will die in Paris with hard dirty rain, on a day I now remember.
I will die in Paris — and I don't run — maybe a Thursday, like today, in autumn.
Human Poems (Poemas Humanos) [1939].[3] Black Stone on a White Stone (Piedra Negra Sobre una Piedra Blanca), st. 1

5 A man walks by with a loaf of bread on his shoulder.
I'm going to write, after that, about my double? *Ib. A Man Walks By, st. 1*

6 Another shakes from cold, hacks, spits blood.
Is it possible to even mention the profound I?

Another searches in the mud for bones, rinds.
How write after that about the infinite?
Ib. st. 5, 6

[1]See Lincoln, 520:2.
[2]Later this became: the little old lady from Dubuque.
[3]Translated by Clayton Eshleman.

7 Whatever may be the cause I have to defend before God, beyond death I have a defender: God.
Ib. Whatever May Be the Cause

Mae West
1892–

8 Come up and see me sometime.
Diamond Lil [1932]

9 Beulah, peel me a grape.
I'm No Angel [1933]

Wendell Lewis Willkie
1892–1944

10 Freedom is an indivisible word.[4] If we want to enjoy it, and fight for it, we must be prepared to extend it to everyone, whether they are rich or poor, whether they agree with us or not, no matter what their race or the color of their skin. *One World, ch. 13*

11 The Constitution does not provide for first and second class citizens.
An American Program [1944], ch. 2

12 I believe in America because in it we are free —
free to choose our government, to speak our minds,
to observe our different religions.
Because we are generous with our freedom, we share
our rights with those who disagree with us.
Because we hate no people and covet no people's lands.
Because we are blessed with a natural and varied abundance.
Because we have great dreams and because we have the
opportunity to make those dreams come true.
His creed, inscribed on a marker by his grave in Rushville, Indiana

Jack Yellen
1892–1958

13 Happy days are here again,
The skies above are clear again:
Let us sing a song of cheer again,
Happy days are here again!
Happy Days Are Here Again [1929][5]

[4]See Litvinov, 757:11.
[5]Composed by Milton Ager [1893–1979], it was played at the 1932 Democratic presidential convention and became a campaign song for Franklin D. Roosevelt.

Omar Bradley

1893–

1 We have grasped the mystery of the atom and rejected the Sermon on the Mount.

Address on Armistice Day [1948]

2 The world has achieved brilliance without conscience. Ours is a world of nuclear giants and ethical infants. *Ib.*

3 Our military forces are one team — in the game to win regardless of who carries the ball. This is no time for "fancy dans" who won't hit the line with all they have on every play, unless they can call the signals. Each player on this team — whether he shines in the spotlight of the backfield or eats dirt in the line — must be an All-American.

Testimony to the Committee on Armed Services, House of Representatives [October 19, 1949]

4 In war there is no second prize for the runner-up.

In the Military Review [February 1950]

5 Red China is not the powerful nation seeking to dominate the world. Frankly, in the opinion of the Joint Chiefs of Staff, this strategy would involve us in the wrong war, at the wrong place, at the wrong time, and with the wrong enemy.

Testimony to the Committee on Armed Services and Committee on Foreign Affairs, U.S. Senate [May 15, 1951]

6 Only one military organization can hold and gain ground in war — a ground army supported by tactical aviation with supply lines guarded by the navy.

In the Military Review [September 1951]

Lew Brown

1893–1958

and

Buddy [George Gard] De Sylva

1895–1950

7 And love can come to everyone,
The best things in life are free.

Good News [1927].[1] The Best Things in Life Are Free

8 Keep your sunny side up.

Sunny Side Up [1929].[1] Sunny Side Up

[1] Music by RAY HENDERSON.

James Bryant Conant

1893–1978

9 He who enters a university walks on hallowed ground.

Notes on the Harvard Tercentenary [1936]

10 Liberty like charity must begin at home.

Our Unique Heritage[2]

11 There is only one proved method of assisting the advancement of pure science — that of picking men of genius, backing them heavily, and leaving them to direct themselves.

Letter to the New York Times [August 13, 1945]

12 Diversity of opinion within the framework of loyalty to our free society is not only basic to a university but to the entire nation.

Education in a Divided World [1948]

13 The stumbling way in which even the ablest of the scientists in every generation have had to fight through thickets of erroneous observations, misleading generalizations, inadequate formulations, and unconscious prejudice is rarely appreciated by those who obtain their scientific knowledge from textbooks.

Science and Common Sense [1951]

Jimmy [James Francis] Durante

1893–1980

14 Goodnight, Mrs. Calabash, wherever you are. *Radio series sign-off [1942]*

15 Dese are de conditions dat prevail.

Saying

16 Stop da music! *Saying*

Hermann Goering

1893–1946

17 Shoot first and inquire afterwards, and if you make mistakes, I will protect you.

Instruction for the Prussian police [1933]

Harold Joseph Laski

1893–1950

18 We live under a system by which the many are exploited by the few, and war is the ultimate sanction of that exploitation.

Plan or Perish [1945]

[2] Address at the opening of the first wartime summer term, Harvard College [June 30, 1942].

1 We must plan our civilization or we must perish. *Ib.*

2 It would be madness to let the purposes or the methods of private enterprise set the habits of the age of atomic energy. *Ib.*

Anita Loos

1893–

3 Gentlemen always seem to remember blondes.
Gentlemen Prefer Blondes [1925], ch. 1

4 She always believed in the old adage, "Leave them while you're looking good."
Ib.

5 Kissing your hand may make you feel very, very good, but a diamond and sapphire bracelet lasts forever. *Ib. 4*

Mao Tse-tung

1893–1976

6 A revolution is not the same as inviting people to dinner, or writing an essay, or painting a picture . . . A revolution is an insurrection, an act of violence by which one class overthrows another.
Selected Works of Mao Tse-tung [1965], vol. I, p. 28

7 Every Communist must grasp the truth: "Political power grows out of the barrel of a gun." *Ib. II, 224*

8 The contradiction between imperialism and the Chinese nation, and the contradiction between feudalism and the great masses of the people, are the principal contradictions in modern Chinese society. . . . The great revolutions of modern and contemporary China have emerged and developed on the basis of these fundamental contradictions.
Ib. III, 81–82

9 Weapons are an important factor in war, but not the decisive one; it is man and not materials that counts.[1] *Lecture [1938]*

10 War cannot for a single minute be separated from politics.[2] *Ib.*

11 The people are like water and the army is like fish.
Aspects of China's Anti-Japanese Struggle [1948]

[1] There is still one absolute weapon. . . . That weapon is man himself. — MATTHEW B. RIDGWAY, *Address at Cleveland, Ohio* [November 10, 1953]

[2] See Clausewitz, 448:8.

12 The policy of letting a hundred flowers blossom and a hundred schools of thought contend is designed to promote the flourishing of the arts and the progress of science; it is designed to enable a socialist culture to thrive in our land. Different forms and styles in art can develop freely, and different schools in science can develop freely, and different schools in science can contend freely.
Speech at Peking [February 27, 1957]

John Phillips Marquand

1893–1960

13 It is worthwhile for anyone to have behind him a few generations of honest, hard-working ancestry.
The Late George Apley [1937], ch. 3

14 Marriage . . . is a damnably serious business, particularly around Boston.
Ib. 11

15 There is a certain phase in the life of the aged when the warmth of the heart seems to increase in direct proportion with the years. This is a time of life when a solicitous family does well to watch affectionately over the vagaries of its unattached relatives, particularly of those who are comfortably off.
Ib. 23

Vladimir Mayakovski

1893–1930

16 If you wish,
I shall grow irreproachably tender:
Not a man, but a cloud in trousers!
Cloud in Trousers [1915][3]

17 Citizen!
Consider my traveling expenses:
Poetry—
  all of it—
    is a journey to the unknown.
Conversation with a Tax Collector about Poetry [1926][4]

18 Then there's amortization,
    the deadliest of all,
Amortization
    of the heart and soul. *Ib.*

19 But I subdued myself,
    setting my heel
On the throat
    of my own song.
At the Top of My Voice[3]

[3] Translated by GEORGE REAVEY.

[4] Translated by MAX HAYWARD.

Wilfred Owen
1893–1918

1 Above all, this book is not concerned with Poetry,
The subject of it is War, and the pity of War.
The Poetry is in the pity.
All a poet can do is warn.[1]
Poems [1920], preface

2 What passing bells for these who die as cattle?
Only the monstrous anger of the guns.
Only the stuttering rifles' rapid rattle
Can patter out their hasty orisons.
The Anthem for Doomed Youth, st. 1

3 And bugles calling for them from sad shires.
Ib.

4 What candles may be held to speed them all?
Not in the hands of boys, but in their eyes
Shall shine the holy glimmers of goodbyes.
Ib.

5 And each slow dusk a drawing-down of blinds. *Ib.*

6 Red lips are not so red
As the stained stones kissed by the English dead. *Greater Love*

7 Courage was mine, and I had mystery,
Wisdom was mine, and I had mastery:
To miss the march of this retreating world
Into vain citadels that are not walled.
Strange Meeting

Dorothy Parker
1893–1967

8 Four be the things I am wiser to know:
Idleness, sorrow, a friend, and a foe.
Enough Rope [1927]. Inventory, st. 1

9 Four be the things I'd been better without:
Love, curiosity, freckles, and doubt.
Ib. st. 2

10 Scratch a lover, and find a foe.
Ib. Ballade of a Great Weariness, st. 1

11 Men seldom make passes
At girls who wear glasses.
Ib. News Item

12 Guns aren't lawful;
Nooses give;
Gas smells awful;
You might as well live. *Ib. Résumé*

13 Why is it no one ever sent me yet
One perfect limousine, do you suppose?
Ah no, it's always just my luck to get
One perfect rose.
Ib. One Perfect Rose, st. 3

14 He lies below, correct in cypress wood,
And entertains the most exclusive worms.
Death and Taxes [1931]. Epitaph for a Very Rich Man

15 There was nothing more fun than a man!
Ib. The Little Old Lady in Lavender Silk, st. 3

16 Runs the gamut of emotions from A to B.
Attributed theater review, comment on a player

17 Excuse my dust.
Epitaph, suggested by herself

18 Wit has truth in it; wisecracking is simply calisthenics with words.
In the Paris Review [Summer 1956]

Frederick Salomon Perls
1893–

19 I do my thing, and you do your thing . . .
You are you and I am I,
And if by chance we find each other, it's beautiful;
If not, it can't be helped.
Gestalt Therapy Verbatim [1969]

Sir Herbert Read
1893–1968

20 The no-man's-years between the wars [1919–1939].
Annals of Innocence and Experience [1940]

Robert Leroy Ripley
1893–1949

21 Believe It or Not.
Title of syndicated newspaper feature

Dorothy Leigh Sayers
1893–1957

22 The worst sin — perhaps the only sin — passion can commit, is to be joyless.
Gaudy Night [1936], ch. 23

[1] The last three lines serve as the motto for Benjamin Britten's *War Requiem (Op. 66)*, which uses the Latin text of the Mass for the Dead and some of the poems of Wilfred Owen.

Albert Szent-Györgyi von Nagyrapolt
1893–

1 The real scientist . . . is ready to bear privation and, if need be, starvation rather than let anyone dictate to him which direction his work must take.
Science Needs Freedom. From World Digest [1943]

Harold Clayton Urey
1893–

2 One World or None.
Title of book [1946]

Fred Allen
1894–1956

3 To a newspaperman a human being is an item with the skin wrapped around it.
Saying

Isaac Babel
1894–c. 1939

4 A phrase is born into the world both good and bad at the same time. The secret lies in a slight, an almost invisible twist. The lever should rest in your hand, getting warm, and you can only turn it once, not twice.
Guy de Maupassant [1924][1]

5 No steel can pierce the human heart so chillingly as a period at the right moment.[2]
Ib.

6 Speaking of silence, we can't help talking about me, the past master of this genre.
Speech at First Writers' Congress [1934]

7 The right to write badly was the privilege we widely used.
Ib.

Louis Ferdinand Céline [Louis Ferdinand Destouches]
1894–1961

8 Those who talk about the future are scoundrels. It is the present that matters. To evoke one's posterity is to make a speech to maggots.
Voyage au Bout de la Nuit (Journey to the End of the Night) [1932]

[1]Translated by Walter Morison.
[2]Translated by Max Hayward.

Edward Estlin Cummings[3]
1894–1962

9 All in green went my love riding
on a great horse of gold
into the silver dawn.
All in green went my love riding [1923]

10 four lean hounds crouched low and smiling
my heart fell dead before.
Ib.

11 in Just-
spring when the world is mud-
luscious the little
lame balloonman
whistles far and wee
Chansons Innocentes [1923], I

12 when the world is puddle-wonderful
Ib.

13 Buffalo Bill's
defunct
who used to
ride a watersmooth-silver
stallion
and break onetwothreefourfive pigeonsjustlikethat
Jesus
he was a handsome man
and what i want to know is
how do you like your blueeyed boy
Mister Death
Portraits [1923], 8

14 the Cambridge ladies who live in furnished souls
are unbeautiful and have comfortable minds.
Sonnets—Realities [1923], I

15 Humanity i love you because
when you're hard up you pawn your
intelligence to buy a drink.
Humanity i love you [1925]

16 i spill my bright incalculable soul.
Sonnets [1925], II

17 take it from me kiddo
believe me
my country, 'tis of

you, land of the Cluett
Shirt Boston Garter and Spearmint
Girl With The Wrigley Eyes (of you
land of the Arrow Ide
and Earl &
Wilson
Collars) of you i
sing: land of Abraham Lincoln and Lydia E. Pinkham,

[3]The terror of typesetters, an enigma to book reviewers, and the special target of all the world's literary philistines. —*Publisher's note, Modern Library edition of The Enormous Room*

land above all of Just Add Hot Water And Serve—
from every B.V.D.

let freedom ring

amen.

Poem, Or Beauty Hurts Mr. Vinal [1926]

1 Turn Your Shirttails Into Drawers and If It Isn't An Eastman It Isn't A Kodak *Ib.*

2 And there're a
hun-dred-mil-lion-oth-ers, like
all of you successfully if
delicately gelded (or spaded)
gentlemen (and ladies) *Ib.*

3 a tiny violetflavored nuisance *Ib.*

4 next to of course god america i
love you land of the pilgrims' and so forth
next to of course god america i [1926]

5 thy sons acclaim your glorious name by gorry
by jingo by gee by gosh by gum *Ib.*

6 for life's not a paragraph
And death i think is no parenthesis.
since feeling is first [1926]

7 lady through whose profound and fragile lips
the sweet small clumsy feet of April came
into the ragged meadow of my soul.
if i have made, my lady, intricate [1926]

8 i sing of Olaf glad and big
whose warmest heart recoiled at war
i sing of Olaf glad and big [1931]

9 "I will not kiss your f.ing flag" *Ib.*

10 "there is some s. I will not eat" *Ib.*

11 unless statistics lie he was
more brave than me:more blond than you. *Ib.*

12 somewhere i have never traveled, gladly beyond
any experience, your eyes have their silence.
somewhere I have never traveled [1931]

13 nobody, not even the rain, has such small hands *Ib.*

14 King Christ, this world is all aleak;
and lifepreservers there are none:
and waves which only He may walk
Who dares to call Himself a man.
Jehovah buried, Satan dead [1935]

15 Always the beautiful answer who asks a more beautiful question.
Collected Poems [1938], introduction

16 as freedom is a breakfastfood
or truth can live with right and wrong
or molehills are from mountains made
—long enough and just so long
will being pay the rent of seem
and genius please the talentgang
and water most encourage flame
as freedom is a breakfastfood [1940]

17 worms are the words but joy's the voice *Ib.*

18 anyone lived in a pretty how town
(with up so floating many bells down)
spring summer autumn winter
he sang his didn't he danced his did.
anyone lived in a pretty how town [1940]

19 my father moved through dooms of love
through sames of am through haves of give,
singing each morning out of each night
my father moved through depths of height
my father moved through dooms of love [1940]

20 though dull were all we taste as bright,
bitter all utterly things sweet,
maggoty minus and dumb death
all we inherit, all bequeath *Ib.*

21 and nothing quite so least as truth
—i say though hate were why men breathe—
because my father lived his soul
love is the whole and more than all *Ib.*

22 a politician is an arse upon
which everyone has sat except a man
One Times One [1944], 10

23 mr u will not be missed
who as an anthologist
sold the many on the few
not excluding mr u *Ib. 11*

24 pity this busy monster, manunkind,
not. Progress is a comfortable disease.
Ib. 14

25 A world of made
is not a world of born *Ib.*

26 We doctors know
a hopeless case if—listen: there's a hell
of a good universe next door; let's go
Ib.

1 what if a much of a which of a wind
gives the truth to summer's lie. *Ib. 20*

2 —when skies are hanged and oceans drowned,
the single secret will still be man *Ib.*

3 all ignorance toboggans into know
and trudges up to ignorance again
Ib. 39

Dashiell Hammett

1894–1961

4 That's the part of it I [Sam Spade] always liked. He [Flitcraft] adjusted himself to beams falling, and then no more of them fell, and he adjusted himself to their not falling.
The Maltese Falcon [1930], ch. 7

5 The Thin Man.
Title of novel [1934]

Herman Hupfeld

1894–1951

6 You must remember this, a kiss is still a kiss,
A sigh is just a sigh;
The fundamental things apply,
As time goes by.
Everybody's Welcome [1931].[1] *As Time Goes By*

7 It's still the same old story,
A fight for love and glory,
A case of do or die!
The world will always welcome lovers,
As time goes by. *Ib.*

Aldous Leonard Huxley

1894–1963

8 A bad book is as much of a labor to write as a good one; it comes as sincerely from the author's soul.
Point Counter Point [1928], ch. 13

9 There is no substitute for talent. Industry and all the virtues are of no avail. *Ib.*

10 Parodies and caricatures are the most penetrating of criticisms. *Ib. 28*

11 Blood of the world, time staunchless flows;
The wound is mortal and is mine.
Seasons

12 A poor degenerate from the ape,
Whose hands are four, whose tail's a limb,
I contemplate my flaccid shape
And know I may not rival him
Save with my mind.
First Philosopher's Song

[1] Also in the film *Casablanca* [1943].

Nikita Sergeyevich Khrushchev

1894–1971

13 Cult of personality.
Special Report to Twentieth Party Congress [February 1956]

14 About the capitalist states, it doesn't depend on you whether or not we exist. If you don't like us, don't accept our invitations, and don't invite us to come and see you. Whether you like it or not, history is on our side. We will bury you.[2]
Reported statement at reception for Wladyslaw Gomulka at the Polish Embassy, Moscow [November 18, 1956]

Westbrook Pegler

1894–1969

15 I am a reactionary, that is what I am, and I would like to see a political reaction get off to a good start in our largest city.
In the New York World-Telegram [October 31, 1941]

16 I am a member of the rabble in good standing. *The Lynching Story*

John Boynton Priestley

1894–

17 This country is geology by day and astronomy by night.
Midnight on the Desert [1937]

Genevieve Taggard

1894–1948

18 Try tropic for your balm,
Try storm,
And after storm, calm.
Try snow of heaven, heavy, soft, and slow,
Brilliant and warm.
Nothing will help, and nothing do much harm.
Of the Properties of Nature for Healing an Illness, st. 1

[2] Neither the original nor the translation of the last two sentences appeared in either *Pravda* or the *New York Times,* which carried the rest of the text. Another possible translation of the last sentence is: We shall be present at your funeral; i.e., we shall outlive you; but the above is the familiar version.

James Thurber
1894–1961

1 Well, if I called the wrong number, why did you answer the 'phone?
Caption for cartoon in The New Yorker

2 I love the idea of there being two sexes, don't you? *Ib.*

3 He knows all about art, but he doesn't know what he likes.[1] *Ib.*

4 It's a naive domestic Burgundy without any breeding, but I think you'll be amused by its presumption. *Ib.*

5 The War Between Men and Women.
Series of cartoons

6 Is Sex Necessary?
Title of book [1929] written with E. B. WHITE[2]

7 Let Your Mind Alone.
Title of book [1937]

8 Early to rise and early to bed makes a male healthy and wealthy and dead.
Fables for Our Time [1940]. The Shrike and the Chipmunks

9 You might as well fall flat on your face as lean over too far backward.
Ib. The Bear Who Let It Alone

10 Don't count your boobies until they're hatched.
Ib. The Unicorn in the Garden

11 Red Barber announces the Dodger games and he uses these expressions—picked them up down South. "Tearing up the pea patch" means going on a rampage, "sitting in the catbird seat" means sitting pretty, like a batter with three balls and no strikes on him.
The Thurber Carnival [1945]. The Catbird Seat

12 It is better to know some of the questions than all of the answers. *Saying*

Jean Toomer
1894–1967

13 O can't you see it, O can't you see it,
Her skin is like dusk on the eastern horizon
. . . When the sun goes down.
Cane [1923]. Karintha

14 Wind is in the cane. Come along.
Cane leaves swaying, rusty with talk,
Scratching choruses above the guinea's
squawk,
Wind is in the cane. Come along.
Ib. Carma

15 O land and soil, red soil and sweet-gum tree,
So scant of grass, so profligate of pines.
Ib. Song of the Son, st. 2

16 A feast of moon and men and barking
hounds,
An orgy for some genius of the South
With blood-hot eyes and cane-lipped scented
mouth,
Surprised in making folk songs from soul
sounds. *Ib. Georgia Dusk, st. 2*

17 Beyond plants are animals,
Beyond animals is man,
Beyond man is the universe.

The Big Light,
Let the Big Light in!
The Blue Meridian

18 What use bombs and antibombs,
Sovereign powers, brutal lives, ugly deaths?
Are men born to go down like this?
Ib.

19 Men,
Men and women—
Liberate! *Ib.*

20 Each new American—
To be taken as a golden grain
And lifted, as the wheat of our bodies,
To matter superbly human. *Ib.*

Mark Van Doren
1894–1972

21 Wit is the only wall
Between us and the dark. *Wit, st. 1*

Norbert Wiener
1894–1964

22 We have decided to call the entire field of control and communication theory, whether in the machine or in the animal, by the name of Cybernetics, which we form from the Greek [for] steersman.
Cybernetics [1948]

23 This new development [automation] has unbounded possibilities for good and for evil.
Ib.

24 The independent scientist who is worth the slightest consideration as a scientist has a

[1] See Beerbohm, 736:2.
[2] E. B. White entry, 846.

consecration which comes entirely from within himself: a vocation which demands the possibility of supreme self-sacrifice.

The Human Use of Human Beings [1950]

1 The future offers very little hope for those who expect that our new mechanical slaves will offer us a world in which we may rest from thinking. Help us they may, but at the cost of supreme demands upon our honesty and our intelligence. The world of the future will be an ever more demanding struggle against the limitations of our intelligence, not a comfortable hammock in which we can lie down to be waited upon by our robot slaves. *God and Golem, Inc. [1964]*

Edward, Duke of Windsor [Edward VIII]

1894–1972

2 At long last, I am able to say a few words of my own. . . . Until now it has not been constitutionally possible for me to speak. I have found it impossible to carry the heavy burden of responsibility and to discharge my duties as King as I would wish to do without the help and support of the woman I love.

Farewell broadcast after abdication [December 11, 1936]

Bud [William] Abbott

1895–1974

and

Lou Costello [Louis Francis Cristillo]

1906–1959

3 Who's on first, What's on second, I Don't Know is on third—

The Naughty Nineties [1945]

Paul Éluard

1895–1952

4 I was born to know you
To give you your name
Freedom.[1]

Poésie et Vérité [1942]. Liberté

5 Farewell sadness
Good morning sadness.[2]

Ib. La Vie Immédiate

[1]Je suis né pour te connaître / Pour te nommer / Liberté.

[2]Adieu tristesse / Bonjour tristesse.

Richard Buckminster Fuller

1895–

6 Don't fight forces; use them.

Shelter [1932]

7 God is a verb.

No More Secondhand God [1963]

8 For at least two million years men have been reproducing and multiplying on a little automated Spaceship Earth.

Prospect for Humanity [1964]

9 Nature has . . . some sort of arithmetical-geometrical coordinate system, because nature has all kinds of models. What we experience of nature is in models, and all of nature's models are so beautiful. It struck me that nature's system must be a real beauty, because in chemistry we find that the associations are always in beautiful whole numbers —there are no fractions.

From In the Outlaw Area; profile by CALVIN TOMKINS *in The New Yorker [January 8, 1966]*

10 Synergy means behavior of whole systems unpredicted by the behavior of their parts.

What I Have Learned [1966]. How Little I Know

11 Thinking is a momentary dismissal of irrelevancies. *Utopia or Oblivion [1969]*

12 Change the environment; do not try to change man.[3] *Design Science [1969]*

13 Either man is obsolete or war is.

I Seem to Be a Verb [1970]

14 I am the only guinea pig I have.

Address to Engineering Society at Tel Aviv [June 16, 1972]

15 Dare to be naive.

Synergetics [1975]. Moral of the Work

16 Synergetics is energetic geometry since it identifies energy with number.

Ib. sec. 200.03

17 Unity is plural and, at minimum, is two.

Ib. 224.12

18 Universe is the aggregate of all humanity's consciously apprehended and communicated nonsimultaneous and only partially overlapping experiences. *Ib. 301.10*

19 Nature is trying very hard to make us succeed, but nature does not depend on us. We are not the only experiment.

Interview in the Minneapolis Tribune [April 30, 1978]

[3]See Bronowski, 870:15.

1 Love is metaphysical gravity.
The Lord's Prayer, third version [written May 1978]

2 Universe to each must be
All that is, including me.
Environment in turn must be
All that is, excepting me.
Synergetics 2 [1979], sec. 100.12, Universal Requirements

Robert Graves
1895–

3 As you are woman, so be lovely:
As you are lovely, so be various,
Merciful as constant, constant as various,
So be mine, as I yours for ever.
Pygmalion to Galatea

4 Goodbye to All That.
Title of autobiography [1929]

5 A well-chosen anthology is a complete dispensary of medicine for the more common mental disorders, and may be used as much for prevention as cure.
On English Poetry, 29

6 The reason why the hairs stand on end, the eyes water, the throat is constricted, the skin crawls and a shiver runs down the spine when one writes or reads a true poem is that a true poem is necessarily an invocation of the White Goddess, or Muse, the Mother of All Living, the ancient power of fright and lust—the female spider or the queen bee whose embrace is death.[1]
The White Goddess [1948], ch. 1

Oscar Hammerstein II
1895–1960

7 Ol' Man River[2]
He just keeps rollin' along.
Show Boat [1927].[3] Ol' Man River

8 Can't help lovin' that man of mine.
Ib. Can't Help Lovin' That Man

9 The last time I saw Paris, her heart was warm and gay.
I heard the laughter of her heart in every street café.
The Last Time I Saw Paris [1940][4]

10 Oh, what a beautiful mornin'
Oh, what a beautiful day.
I got a beautiful feelin'
Everything's going my way.
Oklahoma! [1943].[5] Oh, What a Beautiful Mornin'

11 The corn is as high as an elephant's eye,
An' it looks like it's climbin' clear up to the sky. *Ib.*

12 June Is Bustin' Out All Over.
Carousel [1945], title of song

13 Some enchanted evening . . .
You may see a stranger
Across a crowded room.
South Pacific [1949].[6] Some Enchanted Evening

14 Younger than springtime are you.
Ib. Younger Than Springtime

15 I'm Gonna Wash That Man Right Outa My Hair. *Ib. Title of song*

16 There Is Nothing Like a Dame.
Ib. Title of song

17 The King and I.[7]
Title of musical [1951]

Lorenz Milton Hart
1895–1943

18 That's why the lady is a tramp.
Babes in Arms [1937].[5] The Lady Is a Tramp

19 Bewitched, Bothered and Bewildered.
Pal Joey [1940],[5] title of song

Lesley Poles Hartley
1895–

20 The past is a foreign country; they do things differently there.
The Go-Between [1953], prologue

Dolores Ibarruri [La Pasionara][8]
1895–

21 No pasarán [They shall not pass]![9]
Republican watchword in the Spanish Civil War [1936–1939]

[1] See Dickinson, 608:6, and Housman, 692:14.
[2] The Mississippi.
[3] Based on the novel *Show Boat* [1926], by EDNA FERBER. Music by JEROME KERN.
[4] Music by JEROME KERN.
See Paul, 819:13.
[5] Music by RICHARD RODGERS.
[6] Based on *Tales of the South Pacific*, by JAMES A. MICHENER. Music by RICHARD RODGERS.
[7] Based on *Anna and the King of Siam*, by MARGARET LANDON. Music by RICHARD RODGERS.
[8] See Zapata, 759:2 and 759:*n2*.
[9] End of radio speech [July 18, 1936] calling on the women of Spain to help defend the Republic.
See Pétain, 679:13.

Basil Henry Liddell Hart
1895–1970

1 Keep strong, if possible. In any case, keep cool. Have unlimited patience. Never corner an opponent, and always assist him to save his face. Put yourself in his shoes—so as to see things through his eyes. Avoid self-righteousness like the devil—nothing so self-blinding.

Deterrent or Defense [1960]. Advice to Statesmen

Groucho [Julius Henry] Marx
1895–1977

2 I never forget a face, but in your case I'll make an exception. *Saying*

3 I wouldn't want to belong to any club that would accept me as a member.

Attributed

Lewis Mumford
1895–

4 Layer upon layer, past times preserve themselves in the city until life itself is finally threatened with suffocation; then, in sheer defense, modern man invents the museum. *The Culture of Cities [1938]*

Edward E. Paramore, Jr.
1895–1956

5 Oh, the North Countree is a hard countree
That mothers a bloody brood;
And its icy arms hold hidden charms
For the greedy, the sinful and lewd.
And strong men rust, from the gold and the lust
That sears the Northland soul.

The Ballad of Yukon Jake [1921]

6 Oh, tough as a steak was Yukon Jake—
Hard-boiled as a picnic egg. *Ib.*

Edmund Wilson
1895–1972

7 As for the aims and ideals of Marxism, there is one feature of them that is now rightly suspect. The taking-over by the state of the means of production and the dictatorship in the interests of the proletariat can by themselves never guarantee the happiness of anybody but the dictators themselves. Marx and Engels, coming out of authoritarian Germany, tended to imagine socialism in authoritarian terms; and Lenin and Trotsky after them, forced as they were to make a beginning among a people who had known nothing but autocracy, also emphasized this side of socialism and founded a dictatorship which perpetuated itself as an autocracy.

To the Finland Station [1940]. Summary as of 1940

8 I have derived a good deal more benefit of the civilizing as well as of the inspirational kind [of tradition] from the admirable American bathroom than I have from the cathedrals of Europe. . . . I have had a good many more uplifting thoughts, creative and expansive visions—while soaking in comfortable baths or drying myself after bracing showers—in well-equipped American bathrooms than I have ever had in any cathedral.

A Piece of My Mind [1956], ch. 4

9 I attribute such success as I have had to the use of the periodic sentence.

An Interview with Edmund Wilson [1962]

Edmund Blunden
1896–1974

10 I am for the woods against the world,
But are the woods for me? *The Kiss*

11 Then is not Death at watch
Within those secret waters?
What wants he but to catch
Earth's heedless sons and daughters?

The Midnight Skaters

12 Court him, elude him, reel and pass,
And let him hate you through the glass.

Ib.

André Breton
1896–1966

13 Subjectivity and objectivity commit a series of assaults on each other during a human life out of which the first one suffers the worse beating.[1] *Nadja [1928], preface*

14 It is at the movies that the only absolutely modern mystery is celebrated.

From J. H. MATHEWS, Surrealism and Film

[1] Translated by CESAR ALBINI.

John Roderigo Dos Passos
1896–1970

1 The chilly December day[1]
two shivering bicycle mechanics from Dayton, Ohio,[2]
first felt their homemade contraption
whittled out of hickory sticks,
gummed together with Arnstein's bicycle cement,
stretched with muslin they'd sewn on their sister's sewingmachine in their own backyard on Hawthorn Street in Dayton, Ohio,
soar into the air
above the dunes and the wide beach
at Kitty Hawk.

The Big Money [1936]. The Campers at Kitty Hawk

[1]December 17, 1903.
[2]See Wilbur and Orville Wright, page 724.

Francis Scott Fitzgerald
1896–1940

2 The victor belongs to the spoils.
The Beautiful and Damned [1922]

3 Then wear the gold hat, if that will move her;
If you can bounce high, bounce for her too,
Till she cry "Lover, gold-hatted, high-bouncing lover,
I must have you!"
The Great Gatsby [1925], epigraph

4 Everyone suspects himself of at least one of the cardinal virtues, and this is mine: I am one of the few honest people that I have ever known. *Ib. ch. 3*

5 Her voice is full of money. *Ib. 7*

6 Thirty—the promise of a decade of loneliness, a thinning list of single men to know, a thinning briefcase of enthusiasm, thinning hair. *Ib.*

7 They were careless people, Tom and Daisy—they smashed up things and creatures and then retreated back into their money or their vast carelessness, or whatever it was that kept them together, and let other people clean up the mess they had made.
Ib. 9

8 So we beat on, boats against the current, borne back ceaselessly into the past.
Ib. last line

9 One writes of scars healed, a loose parallel to the pathology of the skin, but there is no such thing in the life of an individual. There are open wounds, shrunk sometimes to the size of a pinprick, but wounds still. The marks of suffering are more comparable to the loss of a finger, or of the sight of an eye. We may not miss them, either, for one minute in a year, but if we should there is nothing to be done about it.
Tender Is the Night [1933], bk. III, ch. 13

10 The test of a first-rate intelligence is the ability to hold two opposed ideas in the mind at the same time, and still retain the ability to function. *The Crack-up [1936]*

11 In a real dark night of the soul it is always three o'clock in the morning.[3] *Ib.*

12 It was about then [1920] that I wrote a line which certain people will not let me forget: "She was a faded but still lovely woman of twenty-seven." *Early Success [1937]*

13 Egyptian Proverb: The worst things:
To be in bed and sleep not,
To want for one who comes not.
To try to please and please not.
Notebooks[4]

14 Show me a hero and I will write you a tragedy. *Ib.*

15 Draw your chair up close to the edge of the precipice and I'll tell you a story. *Ib.*

16 It is in the thirties that we want friends. In the forties we know they won't save us any more than love did. *Ib.*

17 The hangover became a part of the day as well allowed-for as the Spanish siesta.
My Lost City[4]

18 All good writing is swimming under water and holding your breath.
Undated letter

Ira Gershwin[5]
1896–

19 Oh, lady be good
To me.
Lady Be Good [1924]. Oh, Lady Be Good

20 'S wonderful! 'S marvelous—
You should care for me!
Funny Face [1927]. 'S Wonderful

21 I got rhythm,
I got music,
I got my man—
Who could ask for anything more?
Girl Crazy [1930]. I Got Rhythm

[3]See St. John of the Cross, 167:1, and Napoleon, 421:1.
[4]In *The Crack-up,* edited by Edmund Wilson [1945].
[5]Music for all the lyrics is by George Gershwin.

1 Wintergreen for President.
Of Thee I Sing [1931],[1] *title of song*

2 Love Is Sweeping the Country.
Ib. title of song

3 Of thee I sing, baby,
You have got that certain thing, baby,
Shining star and inspiration
Worthy of a mighty nation,
Of thee I sing! *Ib. title song*

4 Summertime
And the livin' is easy.
Porgy and Bess [1935].[2] *Summertime*

5 A Woman Is a Sometime Thing.
Ib. title of song

6 I got plenty of nothin',
And nothin's plenty for me.
Ib. I Got Plenty of Nothin'

7 It ain't necessarily so—
The things that you're liable
To read in the Bible—
It ain't necessarily so.
Ib. It Ain't Necessarily So

8 Let's Call the Whole Thing Off!
Shall We Dance [1937], title of song

9 The memory of all that—
No, no! They can't take that away from me.
Ib. They Can't Take That Away from Me

Harold N. Gilbert
1896–1966

10 Keep 'em flying.
Slogan of the Air Force, poster caption, World War II

Joe Jacobs
1896–1940

11 We was robbed!
After the heavyweight title fight between Max Schmeling and Jack Sharkey [June 21, 1932], Jacobs, Schmeling's manager, shouted into the microphone this protest against the decision

12 I should of stood in bed.
After leaving a sickbed to attend the World Series in Detroit [October 1935] and betting on the loser

[1] First musical to receive the Pulitzer Prize.

[2] Porgy and Bess.—*Title of play* [1927] *by* DuBose Heyward [1885–1940] *and* Dorothy Heyward [1890–1961], *and of opera* [1935] *by* George Gershwin

Liam O'Flaherty
1896–

13 He [the informer] was a poor weak human being like themselves, a human soul, weak and helpless in suffering, shivering in the toils of the eternal struggle of the human soul with pain. *The Informer [1925]*

Robert Emmet Sherwood
1896–1955

14 The trouble with me is, I belong to a vanishing race. I'm one of the intellectuals.
The Petrified Forest [1934]

15 Poor, dear God. Playing Idiot's Delight. The game that never means anything, and never ends. *Idiot's Delight [1936]*

Luther W. Youngdahl
1896–

16 When public excitement runs high as to alien ideologies, is the time when we must be particularly alert not to impair the ancient landmarks[3] set up in the Bill of Rights.
United States v. Lattimore, 112 F. Supp. 507, 518 [May 2, 1953]

Joseph Auslander
1897–1965

17 So there are no more words and all is ended;
The timbrel is stilled, the clarion laid away;
And Love with streaming hair goes unattended
Back to the loneliness of yesterday.
So There Are No More Words [1924]

Louise Bogan
1897–1970

18 I burned my life, that I might find
A passion wholly of the mind,
Thought divorced from eye and bone,
Ecstasy come to breath alone.
The Alchemist, st. 1

19 I had found unmysterious flesh—
Not the mind's avid substance—still
Passionate beyond the will. *Ib. st. 2*

20 Women have no wilderness in them,
They are provident instead,
Content in the tight hot cell of their hearts
To eat dusty bread. *Women, st. 1*

[3] See *Proverbs 22:28, 25:3.*

1 Up from the bronze, I saw
Water without a flaw
Rush to its rest in air,
Reach to its rest, and fall.
Roman Fountain, st. 1

2 The cold remote islands
And the blue estuaries
Where what breathes, breathes
The restless wind of the inlets,
And what drinks, drinks
The incoming tide. *Night, st. 1*

3 — O remember
In your narrowing dark hours
That more things move
Than blood in the heart. *Ib. st. 4*

Bernard De Voto
1897–1955

4 New England is a finished place. Its destiny is that of Florence or Venice, not Milan, while the American empire careens onward toward its unpredicted end. . . . It is the first American section to be finished, to achieve stability in the conditions of its life. It is the first old civilization, the first permanent civilization in America.
New England: There She Stands. In Harper's Magazine [March 1932]

5 The West begins where the average annual rainfall drops below twenty inches. When you reach the line which marks that drop — for convenience, the one hundredth meridian — you have reached the West.
The Plundered Province. In Harper's Magazine [August 1934]

6 Pessimism is only the name that men of weak nerves give to wisdom.
Mark Twain: The Ink of History. Address at the University of Missouri [December 1935]

7 Art is the terms of an armistice signed with fate. *Mark Twain at Work [1942]*

8 The achieved West had given the United States something that no people had ever had before, an internal, domestic empire.
The Year of Decision [1943]

9 Between the amateur and the professional . . . there is a difference not only in degree but in kind. The skillful man is, within the function of his skill, a different integration, a different nervous and muscular and psychological organization. . . . A tennis player or a watchmaker or an airplane pilot is an automatism but he is also criticism and wisdom.
Across the Wide Missouri [1947]

10 You can no more keep a martini in the refrigerator than you can keep a kiss there. The proper union of gin and vermouth is a great and sudden glory; it is one of the happiest marriages on earth and one of the shortest-lived. *The Hour [1951]*

11 The water of life was given to us to make us see for a while that we are more nearly men and women, more nearly kind and gentle and generous, pleasanter and stronger, than without its vision there is any evidence we are. *Ib.*

12 History abhors determinism but cannot tolerate chance.
The Course of Empire [1952], preface

13 The dawn of knowledge is usually the false dawn. *Ib. ch. 2*

Sir Anthony Eden
1897–1977

14 Every succeeding scientific discovery makes greater nonsense of old-time conceptions of sovereignty.
Speech in the House of Commons [November 22, 1945]

William Faulkner
1897–1962

15 The Long Hot Summer.
Title of movie [1928]

16 Time is dead as long as it is being clicked off by little wheels; only when the clock stops does time come to life.
The Sound and the Fury [1929]. June Second 1910

17 I've seed de first en de last. . . . I seed de beginnin, en now I sees de endin.
Ib. April Eighth 1928

18 Because no battle is ever won he said. They are not even fought. The field only reveals to man his own folly and despair, and victory is an illusion of philosophers and fools.
Ib.

19 They[1] endured. *Ib. last line*

20 They [the Negroes] will endure. They are better than we are. Stronger than we are. Their vices are vices aped from white men or

[1] The black people in the novel.

that white men and bondage have taught them: improvidence and intemperance and evasion — not laziness: evasion: of what white men had set them to, not for their aggrandizement or even comfort but his own. . . . And their virtues. . . . Endurance . . . and pity and tolerance and forbearance and fidelity and love of children . . . whether their own or not or black or not.

The Bear [1932], pt. IV

1 Poor man. Poor mankind.

Light in August [1932], ch. 4

2 Too much happens. . . . Man performs, engenders, so much more than he can or should have to bear. That's how he finds that he can bear anything. . . . That's what's so terrible. *Ib. 13*

3 It's not when you realize that nothing can help you — religion, pride, anything — it's when you realize that you don't need any aid. *Ib.*

4 Gettysburg.[1] . . . You cant understand it. You would have to be born there.

Absalom, Absalom! [1936], ch. 9

5 Why do you hate the South?
I dont hate it. . . . I dont hate it. . . . I *dont hate it* he thought, panting in the cold air, the iron New England dark; *I dont. I dont! I dont hate it! I dont hate it!* *Ib.*

6 JEFFERSON, YOKNAPATAWPHA CO., Mississippi. Area, 2400 Square Miles. Population, Whites, 6298; Negroes, 9313. WILLIAM FAULKNER, Sole Owner & Proprietor.

Ib. Inscription on endpaper map drawn by author

7 Intruder in the Dust.

Title of novel [1948]

8 He [the writer] must teach himself that the basest of all things is to be afraid; and, teaching himself that, forget it forever, leaving no room in his workshop for anything but the old verities and truths of the heart, the old universal truths lacking which any story is ephemeral and doomed — love and honor and pity and pride and compassion and sacrifice.

Speech upon receiving the Nobel Prize [December 10, 1950]

9 I decline to accept the end of man. *Ib.*

10 I believe that man will not merely endure: he will prevail. *Ib.*

[1] Representing, in context, the South.

11 He is immortal, not because he alone among creatures has an inexhaustible voice, but because he has a soul, a spirit capable of compassion and sacrifice and endurance. *Ib.*

12 It is his [the poet's, the writer's] privilege to help man endure by lifting his heart, by reminding him of the courage and honor and hope and pride and compassion and pity and sacrifice which have been the glory of his past. The poet's voice need not merely be the record of man, it can be one of the props, the pillars to help him endure and prevail. *Ib.*

13 The writer's only responsibility is to his art. He will be completely ruthless if he is a good one. He has a dream. It anguishes him so much he must get rid of it. He has no peace until then. Everything goes by the board: honor, pride, decency, security, happiness, all, to get the book written. If a writer has to rob his mother, he will not hesitate; the "Ode on a Grecian Urn" is worth any number of old ladies.

From an interview with FAULKNER *in New York City [1956] by* JEAN STEIN. *From Writers at Work: The Paris Review Interviews [1959]*

14 Really the writer doesn't want success. . . . He knows he has a short span of life, that the day will come when he must pass through the wall of oblivion, and he wants to leave a scratch on that wall — Kilroy was here[2] — that somebody a hundred, or a thousand years later will see.

Faulkner in the University [1959], Session 8

Paul Joseph Goebbels

1897–1945

15 We can do without butter, but, despite all our love of peace, not without arms. One cannot shoot with butter but with guns.[3]

Address in Berlin [January 17, 1936]

David McCord

1897–

16 A handful of sand is an anthology of the universe.

Once and for All [1929], introduction

[2] See Anonymous, 924:20.
[3] Probably the origin of the slogan: Guns or butter.

1 March is outside the door
Flaming some old desire
As man turns uneasily from his fire.
The Crows [1934]

2 By and by
God caught his eye.
Epitaphs: The Waiter

3 The cricket's gone, we only hear machines;
In erg and atom they exact their pay.
And life is largely lived on silver screens.
Ballade of Time and Space [1935]

4 Still for us where Cottons mather
In the spring the Willas cather
As of yore.
And What's More: On Stopping at a New Hampshire Inn [1941]

5 The decent docent doesn't doze;
He teaches standing on his toes.
His student dassn't doze and does,
And that's what teaching is and was.
What Cheer [1945]

6 But man must light for man
The fires no other can,
And find in his own eye
Where the strange crossroads lie.
Communion [1950]

7 Life is the garment we continually alter, but which never seems to fit.
Whereas to Mr. Franklin [1956]

8 Your life will be rich for others only as it is rich for you.
On the Frontiers of Understanding [1959]

Erich Maria Remarque
1897–1970

9 Monotonously the lorries sway, monotonously come the calls, monotonously falls the rain. It falls on our heads and on the heads of the dead up the line, on the body of the little recruit with the wound that is so much too big for his hip; it falls on Kemmerich's grave; it falls in our hearts.
All Quiet on the Western Front (Im Westen Nichts Neues) [1929]

Thornton Niven Wilder
1897–1975

10 Even memory is not necessary for love. There is a land of the living and a land of the dead and the bridge is love, the only survival, the only meaning.
The Bridge of San Luis Rey [1927], last lines

11 George Brush is my name
America's my nation
Luddington's my dwelling place
And Heaven's my destination.
Heaven's My Destination [1934], title page poem[1]

12 A man looks pretty small at a wedding, George. All those good women standing shoulder to shoulder, making sure that the knot's tied in a mighty public way.
Our Town [1938], act II

13 The dead don't stay interested in us living people for very long. Gradually, gradually, they let go hold of the earth . . . and the ambitions they had . . . and the pleasures they had . . . and the things they suffered . . . and the people they loved. They get weaned away from earth—that's the way I put it—weaned away. *Ib. III*

14 That's what it was to be alive. To move about in a cloud of ignorance; to go up and down trampling on the feelings of those about you. To spend and waste time as though you had a million years. To be always at the mercy of one self-centered passion, or another. Now you know—that's the happy existence you wanted to go back to. Ignorance and blindness. *Ib.*

15 My advice to you is not to inquire why or whither, but just enjoy your ice cream while it's on your plate—that's my philosophy.
The Skin of Our Teeth [1942], act I

16 I hold that we cannot be said to be aware of our minds save under responsibility.
The Ides of March [1948]

17 Ninety-nine percent of the people in the world are fools and the rest of us are in great danger of contagion.
The Matchmaker [1954], act I

18 The best part of married life is the fights. The rest is merely so-so. *Ib. II*

Stephen Vincent Benét
1898–1943

19 I died in my boots like a pioneer
With the whole wide sky above me.
A Ballad of William Sycamore, 1790–1880 [1923], st. 16

20 Go play with the towns you have built of blocks,
The towns where you would have bound me!

[1] Labeled by Wilder: Doggerel verse which children of the Middle West were accustomed to write in their schoolbooks.

I sleep in my earth like a tired fox,
And my buffalo have found me.
Ib. st. 19

1 Oh, Georgia booze is mighty fine booze,
The best yuh ever poured yuh,
But it eats the soles right offen yore shoes,
For Hell's broke loose in Georgia.
The Mountain Whippoorwill [1923], st. 48

2 I have fallen in love with American names,
The sharp names that never get fat,
The snakeskin titles of mining claims,
The plumed war bonnet of Medicine Hat,
Tucson and Deadwood and Lost Mule Flat.
American Names [1927], st. 1

3 Bury my heart at Wounded Knee.
Ib. st. 7

4 American Muse, whose strong and diverse heart
So many men have tried to understand
But only made it smaller with their art,
Because you are as various as your land.
John Brown's Body [1928]. Invocation, st. 1

5 And Thames and all the rivers of the kings
Ran into Mississippi and were drowned.

They planted England with a stubborn trust,
But the cleft dust was never English dust.
Ib. st. 12, 13

6 Broad-streeted Richmond . . .
The trees in the streets are old trees used to living with people,
Family trees that remember your grandfather's name.
Ib. bk. IV

7 Stonewall Jackson, wrapped in his beard and his silence.
Ib.

8 Sherman's buzzin' along to de sea,
Like Moses ridin' on a bumblebee.
Ib. VIII

9 We thought we were done with these things but we were wrong.
We thought, because we had power, we had wisdom.
Litany for Dictatorships [1936]

10 Our fathers and ourselves sowed dragon's teeth.
Our children know and suffer the armed men.
Ib.

11 If two New Hampshiremen aren't a match for the devil, we might as well give the country back to the Indians.
The Devil and Daniel Webster [1936]

12 Even the damned may salute the eloquence of Mr. Webster.
Ib.

13 When Daniel Boone goes by at night
The phantom deer arise
And all lost, wild America
Is burning in their eyes.
Daniel Boone [1942]

14 They were half of the first families in Virginia.
Well, where do you start, when you start counting F.F.V.s?
Western Star [1943], bk. I

Bertolt Brecht
1898–1956

15 Oh, the shark has pretty teeth, dear—
And he shows them pearly white—
Just a jackknife has Macheath, dear—
And he keeps it out of sight.
The Threepenny Opera (Die Dreigroschenoper) [1928].[1] *The Ballad of Mack the Knife*[2] *(Moritat)*

16 Mackie's back in town.
Ib.

17 Who built the seven gates of Thebes?
In the books are listed the names of kings.
Did the kings heave up the building blocks?[3]
Question of a Literary Worker (Fragen Eines Lesenden Arbeiters)

18 Oh! Moon of Alabama
We now must say good-bye
We've lost our good old mama
And must have whiskey
Oh, you know why!
Rise and Fall of the City of Mahagonny (Aufstieg und Fall der Stadt Mahagonny) [1931].[4] *Alabama Song*

19 What they could do with round here is a good war. What else can you expect with peace running wild all over the place? You know what the trouble with peace is? No organization.
Mother Courage and Her Children [1941], act I

20 One can describe the world of today to the people of today only if one describes it as capable of alteration.
Can Today's World Become Restored Through Theater? [1955]

[1] Music by KURT WEILL. Translated by MARC BLITZSTEIN. Based on the libretto of *The Beggar's Opera* by JOHN GAY. See Gay, 331:20–332:7.
[2] Mackie Messer.
[3] Translated by BULLITT LOWRY.
[4] Music by KURT WEILL.

William Orville Douglas
1898–1980

1 The Fifth Amendment is an old friend and a good friend. It is one of the great landmarks in man's struggle to be free of tyranny, to be decent and civilized.

An Almanac of Liberty [1954]

2 A Wilderness Bill of Rights.

Title of book [1965]

3 The First Amendment makes confidence in the common sense of our people and in the maturity of their judgment the great postulate of our democracy.

Quoted in the New York Times [January 20, 1980]

4 My faith is that the only soul a man must save is his own. *Ib.*

Federico García Lorca
1898–1936

5 In the parched path
I have seen the good lizard
(one drop of crocodile)
meditating.

The Old Lizard (El Lagarto Viejo) [1921][1]

6 In the black moon
of the highwaymen,
the spurs sing.

Little black horse.
Whither with your dead rider?

Song of the Rider, 1860 (Cancion de Jinete, 1860) [1921–1924][2]

7 Tree, tree,
Dry and green.

The girl of beautiful face
goes gathering olives.
The wind, that suitor of towers,
grasps her round the waist.

Tree, Tree . . . (Arbole, Arbole . . .) [1921–1924][2]

8 Green, how much I want you green.
Green wind. Green branches.
The ship upon the sea
and the horse in the mountain.

Somnambule Ballad (Romance Sonámbulo) [1928][2]

9 But I am no more I,
nor is my house now my house. *Ib.*

[1]Translated by Lysander Kemp.
[2]Translated by Stephen Spender and J. L. Gili.

10 I touched her sleeping breasts,
and they opened to me suddenly
like spikes of hyacinth.

The Faithless Wife (La Casada Infiel) [1928][2]

11 Without silver light on their foliage
the trees had grown larger
and a horizon of dogs
barked very far from the river. *Ib.*

12 Black are the horses.
The horseshoes are black.
On the dark capes glisten
stains of ink and of wax.
Their skulls are leaden,
which is why they don't weep.
With their patent leather souls
they come down the street.

Ballad of the Spanish Civil Guard (Romance de la Guardia Civil Española) [1928][3]

13 They pass where they want,
and they hide in their skulls
a vague astronomy
of shapeless pistols. *Ib.*

14 They ride in ranks of two,
a double nocturne in serge.
The sky, so they fancy,
is a showcase of spurs. *Ib.*

15 At five in the afternoon.
Ah, that fatal five in the afternoon!
It was five by all the clocks!
It was five in the shade of the afternoon!

Lament for Ignacio Sanchez Mejias (Llanto por Ignacio Sanchez Mejias) [1935],[2] *I*

16 I will not see it!

Tell the moon to come
for I do not want to see the blood
of Ignacio on the sand. *Ib. II*

17 The New York dawn has
four columns of mud
and a hurricane of black doves
that paddle in putrescent waters.

The Poet in New York (Poeta en Nueva York) [1940]. The Dawn (La Aurora),[2] *st. 1*

18 The dawn comes and no one receives it in his mouth,
for there no morn or hope is possible.

Ib. st. 3

[3]Translated by A. L. Lloyd.

1 The light is buried under chains and noises
in impudent challenge of rootless science.
Through the suburbs sleepless people stagger,
as though just delivered from a shipwreck of blood.
Ib. st. 5

George Gershwin[1]

1898–1937

2 Rhapsody in Blue.
Title of composition [1924]

3 True music . . . must repeat the thought and inspirations of the people and the time. My people are Americans. My time is today.
From Edward Jablonski *and* Lawrence D. Stewart, *The Gershwin Years [1926]*

Horace Gregory

1898–

4 My boyhood saw
Greek islands floating over Harvard Square.[2]
Chorus for Survival [1935], 14

Edgar Y. Harburg

1898–

5 Once I built a railroad, now it's done.
Brother, can you spare a dime?
Americana [third edition, 1932].[3] Brother, Can You Spare a Dime?

6 Somewhere over the rainbow
Bluebirds fly.
Birds fly over the rainbow—
Why then, oh why can't I?
The Wizard of Oz [1939].[4] Over the Rainbow

7 We gotta be free—
The eagle and me.
Bloomer Girl [1944].[5] The Eagle and Me

8 How are things in Glocca Morra this fine day?
Finian's Rainbow [1947].[6] How Are Things in Glocca Morra?

[1]See Ira Gershwin, 835.
[2]The speaker in the poem is Emerson.
[3]Music by Jay Gorney.
[4]Music by Harold Arlen.
See Baum, 677:7.
[5]Music by Harold Arlen.
The emancipation of woman from intemperance, injustice, prejudice, and bigotry.—Amelia Jenks Bloomer [1818–1894], *masthead of her paper The Lily*
[6]Music by Burton Lane.

Clive Staples Lewis

1898–1963

9 The safest road to Hell is the gradual one—the gentle slope, soft underfoot, without sudden turnings, without milestones, without signposts.
The Screwtape Letters [1941], 12

10 The Future is something which everyone reaches at the rate of sixty minutes an hour, whatever he does, whoever he is.
Ib. 25

11 The long, dull, monotonous years of middle-aged prosperity or middle-aged adversity are excellent campaigning weather [for the Devil].
Ib. 28

Golda Meir

1898–1978

12 We only want that which is given naturally to all peoples of the world, to be masters of our own fate, only of our fate, not of others, and in cooperation and friendship with others.
Address to Anglo-American Committee of Inquiry [March 25, 1946]

Norman Vincent Peale

1898–

13 The Power of Positive Thinking.
Title of book [1952]

Amelia Earhart Putnam

1898–1937

14 Courage is the price that life exacts for granting peace.
The soul that knows it not, knows no release
From little things;
Knows not the livid loneliness of fear,
Nor mountain heights where bitter joy can hear
The sound of wings.
Courage

Lionel Charles Robbins, Lord Robbins

1898–

15 Economics is the science which studies human behavior as a relationship between ends and scarce means which have alternative uses.
An Essay on the Nature and Significance of Economic Science [1932], ch. 1, sec. 3

1 Economics is entirely neutral between ends. *Ib. 2, 2*

Ben Shahn
1898–1969

2 Ever since I could remember I'd wished I'd been lucky enough to be alive at that great time—when something big was going on, like the Crucifixion. And suddenly I realized I was. Here I was living through another crucifixion. Here was something to paint!
On painting a gouache: Bartolomeo Vanzetti and Nicola Sacco [1932]

Humphrey DeForest Bogart
1899–1957

3 Tennis anyone? *Attributed*

4 Here's looking at you, kid.
Spoken as Rick in the film Casablanca [1943][1]

Jorge Luis Borges
1899–

5 Patio, heaven's watercourse.
The patio is the slope
down which the sky flows into the house.
Serenely
eternity waits at the crossway of the stars.
Fervor of Buenos Aires (Fervor de Buenos Aires) [1923], Un Patio[2]

6 A man gradually identifies himself with the form of his fate; a man is, in the long run, his own circumstances.
El Aleph [1949]. La Escritura de Dios

7 It would be exaggerating to say that our relationship is hostile; I live, I let myself live, so that Borges can weave his literature and that literature justifies me. . . . I don't know which of us is writing this page.[3]
Personal Anthology (Antologia Personal) [1961]. Borges and Myself (Borges y Yo)

Noel Coward
1899–1973

8 Mad dogs and Englishmen go out in the midday sun.
Mad Dogs and Englishmen

9 I'll see you again,
Whenever spring breaks through again.
Bittersweet [1929], act I, sc. i

10 Extraordinary how potent cheap music is.
Private Lives [1930], act I

11 I've got those weary Twentieth-Century Blues.
Cavalcade [1931], pt. 3, sc. ii

12 Don't Let's Be Beastly to the Germans.
Title of song

Hart Crane
1899–1932

13 Compass, quadrant and sextant contrive
No farther tides . . . High in the azure steeps
Monody shall not wake the mariner.
This fabulous shadow only the sea keeps.
At Melville's Tomb [1926], st. 4

14 And yet this great wink of eternity,
Of rimless floods, unfettered leewardings.
Voyages [1926], II, st. 1

15 Adagios of islands, O my Prodigal.
Ib. st. 3

16 Bind us in time, O seasons clear, and awe.
O minstrel galleons of Carib fire,
Bequeath us to no earthly shore until
Is answered in the vortex of our grave
The seal's wide spindrift gaze toward paradise. *Ib. st. 5*

17 It was a kind and northern face
That mingled in such exile guise
The everlasting eyes of Pierrot
And, of Gargantua, the laughter.
Praise for an Urn: In Memoriam Ernest Nelson [1926]

18 And biased by full sails, meridians reel
Thy purpose—still one shore beyond desire!
The sea's green crying towers a-sway, Beyond. *The Bridge [1930]. Ave Maria*

19 Damp tonnage and alluvial march of days . . .
Tortured with history, its one will—flow.
Ib. The River (Mississippi)

20 The swift red flesh, a winter king—
Who squired the glacier woman down the sky?
She ran the neighing canyons all the spring;
She spouted arms; she rose with maize—to die. *Ib. The Dance*

[1]Screenplay by JULIUS EPSTEIN [1909–], PHILIP G. EPSTEIN [1912–], and HOWARD KOCH [1916–].
See Hupfeld, 830:6, and Woody Allen, 913:11.
[2]Translated by ROBERT FITZGERALD.
[3]Translated by RACHEL PHILLIPS.

1 Bunched in mutual glee
The bearings glint—O murmurless and shined
In oilrinsed circles of blind ecstasy!
Ib. Power: Cape Hatteras

2 And why do I often meet your visage here,
Your eyes like agate lanterns—on and on
Below the toothpaste and the dandruff ads?
And did their riding eyes right through your side,
And did their eyes like unwashed platters ride?
And Death, aloft—gigantically down[1]
Probing through you toward me, O evermore!
Ib. The Tunnel

Friedrich August von Hayek
1899–

3 The system of private property is the most important guaranty of freedom, not only for those who own property, but scarcely less for those who do not.
The Road to Serfdom [1944], ch. 8

4 The power which a multiple millionaire, who may be my neighbor and perhaps my employer, has over me is very much less than that which the smallest *fonctionnaire* possesses who wields the coercive power of the state, and on whose discretion it depends whether and how I am to be allowed to live or to work. *Ib.*

5 Competition means decentralized planning by many separate persons.
The Use of Knowledge in Society, in Individualism and Economic Order [1948], ch. 4

6 We must look at the price system as . . . a mechanism for communicating information if we want to understand its real function. *Ib.*

7 Many of the greatest things man has achieved are not the result of consciously directed thought, and still less the product of a deliberately coordinated effort of many individuals, but of a process in which the individual plays a part which he can never fully understand.
The Counterrevolution of Science [1952], ch. 8

8 The rationalist whose reason is not sufficient to teach him those limitations of the powers of conscious reason, and who despises all the institutions and customs which have not been consciously designed, would thus become the destroyer of the civilization built upon them. *Ib.*

9 I am certain that nothing has done so much to destroy the juridical safeguards of individual freedom as the striving after this mirage of social justice.
Economic Freedom and Representative Government [1973]

10 Inflation . . . sooner or later makes a more extensive unemployment inevitable than that which that policy was intended to prevent. It does so by drawing more and more workers into kinds of jobs which depend on continuing or even accelerating inflation.
From the New York Times [November 15, 1974]

Ernest Hemingway
1899–1961

11 You and me, we've made a separate peace.
In Our Time [1924]. A Very Short Story

12 It makes one feel rather good deciding not to be a bitch. . . . It's sort of what we have instead of God.
The Sun Also Rises [1926], ch. 19

13 "Oh, Jake," Brett said, "we could have had such a damned good time together." . . .
"Yes," I said. "Isn't it pretty to think so?"
Ib. last lines

14 I had seen nothing sacred, and the things that were glorious had no glory and the sacrifices were like the stockyards at Chicago if nothing was done with the meat except to bury it . . . Abstract words such as glory, honor, courage, or hallow were obscene.
A Farewell to Arms [1929], ch. 27

15 The world breaks everyone and afterward many are strong at the broken places. But those that will not break it kills. It kills the very good and the very gentle and the very brave impartially. If you are none of these you can be sure that it will kill you too but there will be no special hurry. *Ib. 34*

16 You never had time to learn. They threw you in and told you the rules and the first time they caught you off base they killed you. *Ib. 41*

17 It was like saying goodbye to a statue. After a while I went out and left the hospital and walked back to the hotel in the rain. *Ib. 47*

18 Grace under pressure.
Definition of "guts" in The New Yorker [November 30, 1929]

[1] See Poe, 525:13.

1 I know only that what is moral is what you feel good after and what is immoral is what you feel bad after.

Death in the Afternoon [1932], ch. 1

2 I was trying to write then and I found the greatest difficulty, aside from knowing truly what you really felt, rather than what you were supposed to feel, and had been taught to feel, was to put down what really happened in action; what the actual things were which produced the emotion that you experienced . . . the real thing, the sequence of motion and fact which made the emotion and which would be as valid in a year or in ten years or, with luck and if you stated it purely enough, always. *Ib.*

3 If he wrote it he could get rid of it. He had gotten rid of many things by writing them.

Winner Take Nothing [1933]. Fathers and Sons

4 All good books are alike in that they are truer than if they had really happened and after you are finished reading one you will feel that all that happened to you and afterwards it all belongs to you: the good and the bad, the ecstasy, the remorse and sorrow, the people and the places and how the weather was. If you can get so that you can give that to people, then you are a writer.

Old Newsman Writes. From Esquire [December 1934]

5 All modern American literature comes from one book by Mark Twain called *Huckleberry Finn.*

Green Hills of Africa [1935], ch. 1

6 Ezra [Pound] was right half the time, and when he was wrong, he was so wrong you were never in any doubt about it. Gertrude [Stein] was always right.

To John Peale Bishop; quoted in his Homage to Hemingway, New Republic [November 11, 1936]

7 The rich were dull and they drank too much. . . . He remembered poor Julian[1] and his romantic awe of them and how he had started a story once that began, "The very rich are different from you and me." And how someone had said to Julian, "Yes, they have more money."[2]

The Fifth Column and The First Forty-Nine Stories [1938]. The Snows of Kilimanjaro

8 Kilimanjaro is a snow-covered mountain 19,710 feet high, and is said to be the highest mountain in Africa. Its western summit is called the Masai "Ngàje Ngài," the House of God. Close to the western summit there is the dried and frozen carcass of a leopard. No one has explained what the leopard was seeking at that altitude. *Ib. epigraph*

9 If we win here we will win everywhere. The world is a fine place and worth the fighting for and I hate very much to leave it.

For Whom the Bell Tolls [1940], ch. 43

10 Cowardice, as distinguished from panic, is almost always simply a lack of ability to suspend the functioning of the imagination.

Men at War [1942], introduction

11 Time is the least thing we have of.

From The New Yorker profile by LILLIAN ROSS *[May 13, 1950]*[3]

12 A man can be destroyed but not defeated.

The Old Man and the Sea [1952]

13 If it is any use to know it, I always try to write on the principle of the iceberg. There is seven-eighths of it under water for every part that shows. Anything you know you can eliminate and it only strengthens your iceberg. It is the part that doesn't show. If a writer omits something because he does not know it then there is a hole in the story.[4]

Interview in the Paris Review [Spring 1958]

14 If you are lucky enough to have lived in Paris as a young man, then wherever you go for the rest of your life, it stays with you, for Paris is a movable feast.[5]

A Movable Feast [1964], epigraph

Robert Maynard Hutchins

1899–1977

15 Equality and justice, the two great distinguishing characteristics of democracy, follow inevitably from the conception of men, all men, as rational and spiritual beings.

Democracy and Human Nature

16 The death of democracy is not likely to be an assassination from ambush. It will be a

[1] In original publication, "poor Scott Fitzgerald" [*Esquire,* August 1936].

[2] In 1936 Maxwell Perkins, the legendary editor of Fitzgerald and Hemingway at Charles Scribner's Sons, lunched with Hemingway and the critic Mary Colum. When Hemingway announced, "I am getting to know the rich," Mary Colum replied, "The only difference between the rich and other people is that the rich have more money." — MATTHEW J. BRUCCOLI, *Scott and Ernest* [1978]

[3] Reprinted in book form: *Portrait of Hemingway* [1961].

[4] See Cather, 739:3.

[5] See *The Book of Common Prayer,* 54:9.

slow extinction from apathy, indifference, and undernourishment.

Great Books [1954]

Charles W. Morton

1899–1967

1 It was around two decades ago, in the city room of the Boston *Evening Transcript*, that I first became aware of the elongated-yellow-fruit school of writing. The phrase turned up in a story . . . about some fugitive monkeys and the efforts of police to recapture them by using bananas as bait.

The Elongated Yellow Fruit [1954]

Vladimir Nabokov

1899–1977

2 The cradle rocks above an abyss, and common sense tells us that our existence is but a brief crack of light between two eternities of darkness.[1]

Speak, Memory [1947], ch. 1

3 Between the age limits of nine and fourteen there occur maidens who, to certain bewitched travelers, twice or many times older than they, reveal their nature, which is not human, but nymphic (that is, demoniac); and these chosen creatures I propose to designate as "nymphets."

Lolita [1955], pt. I, ch. 5

4 Enchanted isle of time. *Ib.*

5 I am thinking of aurochs and angels, the secret of durable pigments, prophetic sonnets, the refuge of art. And this is the only immortality you and I may share, my Lolita.

Ib. last paragraph

Elwyn Brooks White[2]

1899–

6 All poets who, when reading from their own works, experience a choked feeling, are major. For that matter, all poets who read from their own works are major, whether they choke or not.

How to Tell a Major Poet from a Minor Poet

7 "It's broccoli, dear."

"I say it's spinach, and I say the hell with it."

Caption for cartoon by Carl Rose in The New Yorker [December 8, 1928]

[1]See *The Wisdom of Solomon 5:13*, 34:15; Hall, 257:12; and Beckett, 866:13.

[2]See Thoreau, 558:*n1*.

See James Thurber, 831:6.

8 Commuter—one who spends his life
In riding to and from his wife;
A man who shaves and takes a train
And then rides back to shave again.

Commuter [1929]

9 I have occasionally had the exquisite thrill of putting my finger on a little capsule of truth, and heard it give the faint squeak of mortality under my pressure.

Letter to Stanley Hart White [January 1929]

10 A writer is like a bean plant—he has his little day, and then gets stringy.

Letter to Harold Ross [September 19, 1938]

11 I don't know which is more discouraging, literature or chickens.

Letter to James Thurber [November 18, 1938]

12 It is easier for a man to be loyal to his club than to his planet; the bylaws are shorter, and he is personally acquainted with the other members.

One Man's Meat [1944]

13 The future . . . seems to me no unified dream but a mince pie, long in the baking, never quite done. *Ib.*

14 When Mrs. Frederick C. Little's second son was born, everybody noticed that he was not much bigger than a mouse. The truth of the matter was, the baby looked very much like a mouse in every way. He was only two inches high; and he had a mouse's sharp nose, a mouse's tail, a mouse's whiskers, and the pleasant, shy manner of a mouse. Before he was many days old he was not only looking like a mouse but acting like one, too—wearing a gray hat and carrying a small cane.

Stuart Little [1945], ch. 1

15 "My name is Margalo," said the bird, softly, in a musical voice. "I come from fields once tall with wheat, from pastures deep in fern and thistle; I come from vales of meadowsweet, and I love to whistle." *Ib. 8*

16 Democracy is the recurrent suspicion that more than half of the people are right more than half of the time.

The Wild Flag [1946]

17 I am a member of a party of one, and I live in an age of fear. Nothing lately has unsettled my party and raised my fears so much as your editorial, on Thanksgiving Day, suggesting that employees should be required to state their beliefs in order to hold their jobs.

The idea is inconsistent with our constitutional theory and has been stubbornly opposed by watchful men since the early days of the Republic.[1]

Letter to the New York Herald Tribune [November 29, 1947]

1 Security, for me, took a tumble not when I read that there were Communists in Hollywood but when I read your editorial in praise of loyalty testing and thought control. If a man is in health, he doesn't need to take anybody else's temperature to know where he is going. *Ib.*

2 When I get sick of what men do, I have only to walk a few steps in another direction to see what spiders do. Or what the weather does. This sustains me very well indeed.

Letter to Carrie A. Wilson [May 1, 1951]

3 It was the best place to be, thought Wilbur, this warm delicious cellar, with the garrulous geese, the changing seasons, the heat of the sun, the passage of swallows, the nearness of rats, the sameness of sheep, the love of spiders, the smell of manure, and the glory of everything.

Charlotte's Web [1952], ch. 22

4 We grow tyrannical fighting tyranny. . . . The most alarming spectacle today is not the spectacle of the atomic bomb in an unfederated world, it is the spectacle of the Americans beginning to accept the device of loyalty oaths and witchhunts, beginning to call anybody they don't like a Communist.

Letter to Janice White [April 27, 1952]

5 Life's meaning has always eluded me and I guess always will. But I love it just the same.

Letter to Mary Virginia Parrish [August 29, 1969]

6 An unhatched egg is to me the greatest challenge in life.

Letter to Reginald Allen [March 5, 1973]

7 As long as there is one upright man, as long as there is one compassionate woman, the contagion may spread and the scene is not desolate. Hope is the thing that is left us in a bad time.

Letter to Mr. Nadeau [March 30, 1973]

8 Sailors . . . say the weather is a great bluffer. I guess the same is true of our human society—things can look dark, then a break shows in the clouds, and all is changed.

Ib.

9 A man who publishes his letters becomes a nudist—nothing shields him from the world's gaze except his bare skin. A writer, writing away, can always fix things up to make himself more presentable, but a man who has written a letter is stuck with it for all time.

Letter to Corona Machemer [June 11, 1975]

10 The essayist . . . can pull on any sort of shirt, be any sort of person, according to his mood or his subject matter—philosopher, scold, jester, raconteur, confidant, pundit, devil's advocate, enthusiast.

Essays of E. B. White [1977], foreword

Louis Armstrong [Satchmo]

1900–1971

11 Man, if you gotta ask you'll never know.[2]

Reply when asked what jazz is

Denis William Brogan

1900–1974

12 A people that has licked a more formidable enemy than Germany or Japan, primitive North America . . . a country whose national motto has been "root, hog, or die."

The American Character [1944]

13 Any well-established village in New England or the northern Middle West could afford a town drunkard, a town atheist, and a few Democrats. *Ib.*

Herbert Butterfield

1900–

14 It [the scientific revolution] outshines everything since the rise of Christianity and reduces the Renaissance and Reformation to the rank of mere episodes, mere internal displacements, within the system of medieval Christendom. . . . It looms so large as the real origin of the modern world and of the modern mentality that our customary periodization of European history has become an anachronism and an encumbrance.

The Origins of Modern Science [1949]

[1] See Robert H. Jackson, 821:6.

[2] Lady, if you got to ask you ain't got it.—THOMAS [FATS] WALLER [1904–1943], *when asked to explain rhythm*

Theodosius Dobzhansky
1900–1975

1 Nature's stern discipline enjoins mutual help at least as often as warfare. The fittest may also be the gentlest.
Mankind Evolving [1962]

Elizabeth, Queen Mother of England
1900–

2 The children will not leave unless I do. I shall not leave unless their father does, and the King will not leave the country in any circumstances whatever.
Reported reply as to whether the princesses would leave England after the bombing of Buckingham Palace [1940]

Gilberto Freyre
1900–

3 Casa Grande e Senzala [The Masters and the Slaves]. *Title of book [1946]*[1]

Gottfried Haberler
1900–

4 There are compelling reasons for the proposition that the actual importance of business monopolies for inflation is quite small compared with that of labor unions.
Economic Growth and Stability [1974], ch. 6

5 No private business monopoly, producer organization or cartel wields the market (and physical) power or commands the discipline over its members which many unions have achieved. *Ib.*

James Hilton
1900–1954

6 Anno domini—that's the most fatal complaint of all in the end.
Goodbye, Mr. Chips [1934], ch. 1

7 The austere serenity of Shangri-La. Its forsaken courts and pale pavilions shimmered in repose from which all the fret of existence had ebbed away, leaving a hush as if moments hardly dared to pass.
Lost Horizon [1933], ch. 5

8 If you forgive people enough you belong to them, and they to you, whether either person likes it or not—squatter's rights of the heart.
Time and Time Again [1953]

[1]Translated by SAMUEL PUTNAM from the fourth and definitive Brazilian edition.

Margaret Mitchell
1900–1949

9 The usual masculine disillusionment in discovering that a woman has a brain.
Gone With the Wind [1936], pt. IV, ch. 36

10 Death and taxes[2] and childbirth! There's never any convenient time for any of them.
Ib. 38

11 My dear, I don't give a damn [Rhett Butler to Scarlett O'Hara].[3] *Ib. V, 63*

Wayne Lyman Morse
1900–1974

12 Liberalism in politics can best be defined in terms of specific issues. Political liberalism should also be defined in terms of objectives. A major objective is the protection of the economic weak and doing it within the framework of a private property economy. The liberal, emphasizing the civil and property rights of the individual, insists that the individual must remain so supreme as to make the state his servant.
Definition contributed to Nine Definitions of Liberalism. In the New Republic [July 22, 1946]

Stephen Potter
1900–1969

13 Gamesmanship: The Art of Winning Games Without Actually Cheating.
Title of book [1947]

14 One-Upmanship.
Title of book [1952]

Ernie Pyle
1900–1945

15 I write from the worm's-eye point of view.
Here Is Your War [1943]

Leo Robin
1900–

16 Diamonds Are a Girl's Best Friend.
Gentlemen Prefer Blondes [1949],[4] *title of song*

[2]See Franklin, 348:16.
[3]Frankly, my dear, I don't give a damn.—SIDNEY HOWARD, *screenplay for Gone With the Wind* [1939]
[4]See Loos, 826:3.
Music by JULE STYNE.

Antoine de Saint-Exupéry
1900–1944

1 Although human life is priceless, we always act as if something had an even greater price than life. . . . But what is that something?

Vol de Nuit (Night Flight) [1931], ch. 14

2 Grown-ups never understand anything for themselves, and it is tiresome for children to be always and forever explaining things to them. *The Little Prince [1943],*[1] *ch. 1*

3 It is much more difficult to judge oneself than to judge others. *Ib. 10*

4 It is only with the heart that one can see rightly; what is essential is invisible to the eye. *Ib. 21*

5 Freedom and constraint are two aspects of the same necessity, which is to be what one is and no other.

La Citadelle [1948], ch. 43

George Seferis [Giorgios Sefiriades]
1900–1971

6 Three years
we waited intently for the herald
closely watching
the pines the shore and the stars.

Mythistorema [1935],[2] *I*

7 We were searching to rediscover the first seed
so that the ancient drama could begin again.

Ib.

8 We brought back
these reliefs of a humble art. *Ib.*

9 I woke with this marble head in my hands;
it exhausts my elbows and I don't know where to put it down.
It was falling into the dream as I was coming out of the dream
so our life became one and it will be very difficult for it to separate again.

Ib. III

10 What are they after, our souls, traveling
on the decks of decayed ships . . . ?

Ib. VIII

11 Swimming in the waters of this sea
and of that sea . . .
in a country that is no longer ours
nor yours.

We knew that the islands were beautiful
somewhere round about here where we're groping—
a little nearer or a little farther,
the slightest distance. *Ib.*

12 We have no rivers, we have no wells, we have no springs,
only a few cisterns—and these empty—that echo, and we worship them.
A stagnant hollow sound, the same as our loneliness
the same as our love, the same as our bodies.

Ib. X

13 Give us, outside sleep, serenity.

Ib. XV

14 They were lovely, your eyes, but you didn't know where to look. *Ib. XVI*

15 They're a burden for us
the friends who no longer know how to die.

Ib. XIX

16 Sinks whoever raises the great stones;
I've raised these stones as long as I was able . . .
Wounded by my own soil
tortured by my own shirt
condemned by my own gods,
these stones.

Gymnopaidia II. Mycenae [1936]

17 Wherever I travel Greece wounds me.

In the Manner of G.S. [1936]

18 In the sea caves
there's a thirst there's a love
there's an ecstasy
all hard like shells
you can hold them in your palm.

From Book of Exercises [1937]

19 This sun was mine and yours; we shared it.
Who's suffering behind the golden silk, who's dying? *Our Sun [1937]*

20 It was ours, this sun, we saw nothing behind the gold embroidery
then the messengers came, dirty and breathless,
stuttering unintelligible words . . .
You told them to rest first and then to speak, the light had blinded you.
You'd forgotten that no one rests. *Ib.*

21 This sun was ours; you kept all of it, you didn't want to follow me.
And it was then I found out about those things behind the gold and the silk:
we don't have the time. The messengers were right. *Ib.*

22 Each of us earns his death, his own death, which belongs to no one else
and this game is life.

The Last Day [1939]

[1] Translated by Katherine Woods.

[2] Translated by Edmund Keeley and Philip Sherrard.

1 The angels are white flaming white and the eye that would confront them shrivels
and there's no other way you've got to become like stone if you want their company
and when you look for the miracle you've got to scatter your blood to the eight points of the wind
because the miracle is nowhere but circulating in the veins of man.
Les Anges Sont Blancs [1939]

2 Here where one meets the path of rain, wind, and ruin
does there exist the movement of the face, shape of the tenderness
of those who've shrunk so strangely in our lives,
those who remained the shadow of waves and thoughts with the sea's boundlessness
or perhaps no, nothing is left but the weight
the nostalgia for the weight of a living existence . . .
the poet a void.
The King of Asine [1940]

3 It's painful and difficult, the living are not enough for me.
Stratis Thalassinos Among the Agapanthi [1942]

4 The moment I fall asleep
the companions cut the silver strings
and the flask of the winds empties.
Ib.

5 I want no more than to speak simply, to be granted that grace . . .
and it's time to say our few words because tomorrow the soul sets sail.
An Old Man of the River Bank [1942]

6 Sometimes it crosses my mind that the things I write here are nothing
other than images that prisoners or sailors tattoo on their skin.
Logbook II [1944], epigraph

7 Horror
really can't be talked about because it's alive,
because it's mute and goes on growing:
memory-wounding pain
drips by day drips in sleep.
Last Stop [1944]

8 Countries of the sun, and yet you can't face the sun.
Countries of men, and yet you can't face man.
"Thrush" [1946], III

9 You see the sun with different eyes:
you know that those who stayed behind were deceiving you
the delirium of flesh, the lovely dance
that ends in nakedness. *Ib.*

10 The heart of the Scorpion has set,
the tyrant in man has fled,
and all the daughters of the sea, Nereids, Graeae,
hurry to the radiance of the rising goddess:
whoever has never loved will love,
in the light. . . . *Ib.*

11 Great suffering descended on Greece.
So many bodies thrown
into the jaws of the sea, the jaws of the earth . . .
all for a linen undulation, a bit of cloud,
a butterfly's flicker, a swan's down,
an empty tunic—all for a Helen.
Helen [1953]

12 It doesn't take much time
for evil to raise its head,
and the sick mind emptying
doesn't take much time
to fill with madness:
There is an island.
Salamis in Cyprus [1953]

13 He grew old between the fires of Troy
and the quarries of Sicily.
Euripides the Athenian [1953]

14 He saw man's veins
as a net the gods made to catch us in like wild beasts:
he tried to pierce it.
He was a sour man, his friends were few;
when the time came he was torn to pieces by dogs. *Ib.*

15 They are children of many men, our words.
On Stage [1966],[1] *6*

16 As pines
keep the shape of the wind
even when the wind has fled and is no longer there,
so words
guard the shape of man
even when man has fled and is no longer there. *Ib.*

17 The blank page, difficult mirror,
gives back only what you were.
Summer Solstice [1966], 6

18 Your music is this life
you wasted.
You could regain it if you wish,
if you fasten to this indifferent thing

[1] Translated by WALTER KAISER.

which casts you back
there where you set out. *Ib.*

1 All you have experienced falls in an unsubstantial heap
if you do not trust this void.
Perhaps you will find there what you thought lost:
the flowering of youth, the rightful sinking of age.
Your life is what you gave:
this void is what you gave:
the blank page. *Ib.*

2 I watched you with all the light and darkness I have. *Ib. 11*

3 When, on the road to Thebes, Oedipus met the Sphinx, who asked him her riddle, his answer was: *Man.*[1] This simple word destroyed the monster. We have many monsters to destroy. Let us think of Oedipus' answer.

Speech upon receiving the Nobel Prize [1963]

Ignazio Silone [Secondo Tranquilli]

1900–1978

4 Liberty is the possibility of doubting, the possibility of making a mistake, the possibility of searching and experimenting, the possibility of saying "No" to any authority — literary, artistic, philosophic, religious, social, and even political.

Essay in The God That Failed [1950][2]

Adlai Ewing Stevenson

1900–1965

5 The most American thing about America is the free common school system.

Address to Citizens' School Committee, Chicago [1948]

6 Government is more than the sum of all the interests; it is the paramount interest, the public interest. It must be the efficient, effective agent of a responsible citizenry, not the shelter of the incompetent and the corrupt.

Speech at Bloomington, Illinois [1948]

7 Communism is the corruption of a dream of justice.

Speech at Urbana, Illinois [1951]

8 More important than winning the election, is governing the nation. That is the test of a political party — the acid, final test.

Speech accepting the Democratic presidential nomination [July 26, 1952]

9 Let's talk sense to the American people. *Ib.*

10 When an American says that he loves his country, he . . . means that he loves an inner air, an inner light in which freedom lives and in which a man can draw the breath of self-respect.

Speech at New York City [August 27, 1952]

11 A hungry man is not a free man.[3]

Speech at Kasson, Minnesota [September 6, 1952]

12 The time to stop a revolution is at the beginning, not the end.

Speech at San Francisco [September 9, 1952]

13 Your public servants serve you right.

Speech at Los Angeles [September 11, 1952]

14 Those who corrupt the public mind are just as evil as those who steal from the public purse.

Speech at Albuquerque, New Mexico [September 12, 1952]

15 Nature is neutral. Man has wrested from nature the power to make the world a desert or to make the deserts bloom. There is no evil in the atom; only in men's souls.[4]

Speech at Hartford, Connecticut [September 18, 1952]

16 As citizens of this democracy, you are the rulers and the ruled, the lawgivers and the law-abiding, the beginning and the end.

Speech at Chicago [September 29, 1952]

17 Unreason and anti-intellectualism abominate thought. . . . But shouting is not a substitute for thinking and reason is not the subversion but the salvation of freedom.

Godkin Lectures, Harvard University [March 1954]

18 Democracy cannot be saved by supermen, but only by the unswerving devotion and goodness of millions of little men.

Speech [1955]

[1] See *The Riddle of the Sphinx*, 74:n5.
[2] Edited by Richard Crossman.
[3] See Cato, 95:9, and La Fontaine, 296:21.
[4] See J. Robert Oppenheimer, 861:6.

1 If total isolationism is no answer, total interventionism is no answer, either. In fact, the clear, quick, definable, measurable answers are ruled out. In this twilight of power, there is no quick path to a convenient light switch.[1]

Speech at Harvard University [June 17, 1965]

2 The art of government has grown from its seeds in the tiny city-states of Greece to become the political mode of half the world. So let us dream of a world in which all states, great and small, work together for the peaceful flowering of the republic of man.

Ib.

3 This must be the context of our thinking — the context of human interdependence in the face of the vast new dimensions of our science and our discovery . . . the awful majesty of outer space.

Speech in Geneva [July 9, 1965]

Spencer Tracy

1900–1967

4 Just know your lines and don't bump into the furniture. *Advice on acting*

William Lindsay White

1900–1973

5 They Were Expendable.

Title of book [1942]

Thomas Wolfe

1900–1938

6 A stone, a leaf, an unfound door.

Look Homeward, Angel![2] [1929], foreword

7 Which of us has known his brother? Which of us has looked into his father's heart? Which of us has not remained forever prison-pent? Which of us is not forever a stranger and alone? *Ib.*

8 O lost, and by the wind grieved, ghost, come back again. *Ib.*

9 Most of the time we think we're sick, it's all in the mind. *Ib. pt. I, ch. 1*

10 Making the world safe for hypocrisy.

Ib. III, 36

11 The young men of this land are not, as they are often called, a "lost" race — they are a race that never yet has been discovered. And the whole secret, power, and knowledge of their own discovery is locked within them — they know it, feel it, have the whole thing in them — and they cannot utter it.

The Web and the Rock [1939], ch. 13

[1] See John F. Kennedy, 890:11.
[2] See Milton, 281:3.

12 If a man has a talent and cannot use it, he has failed. If he has a talent and uses only half of it, he has partly failed. If he has a talent and learns somehow to use the whole of it, he has gloriously succeeded, and won a satisfaction and a triumph few men ever know. *Ib. 30*

13 You Can't Go Home Again.

Title of novel [1940]

Roy Campbell

1901–1957

14 The sap is the music, the stem is the flute,
And the leaves are the wings of the seraph I shape
Who dances, who springs in a golden escape,
Out of the dust and the drought of the plain,
To sing with the silver hosannas of rain.

The Palm [1928]

15 Pass world! : I am the dreamer that remains;
The man clear cut against the last horizon.

Epigraph for Laurens Van der Post, *The Lost World of the Kalahari*[3]

Margaret Craven

1901–

16 The Indian knows his village and feels for his village as no white man for his country, his town, or even for his own bit of land. His village is not the strip of land four miles long and three miles wide that is his as long as the sun rises and the moon sets. The myths are the village, and the winds and rains. The river is the village, and . . . the talking bird, the owl, who calls the name of the man who is going to die.

I Heard the Owl Call My Name [1973], pt. I

Werner Karl Heisenberg

1901–1976

17 Every tool carries with it the spirit by which it has been created.

Physics and Philosophy [1958]

[3] See Van der Post, 867:16.

1 Since the measuring device has been constructed by the observer . . . we have to remember that what we observe is not nature in itself but nature exposed to our method of questioning. *Ib.*

James Michael Kieran, Jr.

1901–1952

2 The brains trust.

In conversation with Franklin D. Roosevelt [August 1932], referring to the professors and other such advisers who served Roosevelt in his first campaign. The phrase later became "brain trust."

André Malraux

1901–1976

3 The great mystery is not that we should have been thrown down here at random between the profusion of matter and that of the stars; it is that from our very prison we should draw, from our own selves, images powerful enough to deny our nothingness.

Man's Fate (La Condition Humaine) [1933]

4 If man is not ready to risk his life, where is his dignity? *Ib.*

5 One cannot create an art that speaks to men when one has nothing to say.

Man's Hope (L'Espoir) [1938]

6 All art is a revolt against man's fate.

Voices of Silence (Les Voix du Silence) [1951]

7 The human mind invents its Puss-in-Boots and its coaches that change into pumpkins at midnight because neither the believer nor the atheist is completely satisfied with appearances.

Anti-Memoirs [1967], preface

8 The genius of Christianity is to have proclaimed that the path to the deepest mystery is the path of love.

Ib. Anti-Memoirs, sec. 6

9 The extermination camps, in endeavoring to turn man into a beast, intimated that it is not life alone which makes him man.

Ib. La Condition Humaine, sec. 2

10 The attempt to force human beings to despise themselves . . . is what I call hell.

Ib.

11 Nazism . . . aimed at making you lose your soul, in the sense in which one talks about "losing one's reason." *Ib.*

12 Our civilization . . . is not devaluing its awareness of the unknowable; nor is it deifying it. It is the first civilization that has severed it from religion and superstition. In order to question it.

Picasso's Mask [1976]

Margaret Mead

1901–1978

13 As the traveler who has once been from home is wiser than he who has never left his own doorstep, so a knowledge of one other culture should sharpen our ability to scrutinize more steadily, to appreciate more lovingly, our own.

Coming of Age in Samoa [1928], introduction

14 In this casual attitude towards life, in this avoidance of conflict, of poignant situations, Samoa contrasts strongly not only with America but also with most primitive civilizations. *Ib. ch. 13*

15 If we are to achieve a richer culture, rich in contrasting values, we must recognize the whole gamut of human potentialities, and so weave a less arbitrary social fabric, one in which each diverse human gift will find a fitting place.

Sex and Temperament in Three Primitive Societies [1935], conclusion

16 We know of no culture that has said, articulately, that there is no difference between men and women except in the way they contribute to the creation of the next generation.

Male and Female [1948]

17 The overwhelming importance of the atmosphere means that there are no longer any frontiers to defend against pollution, attack, or propaganda. It means, further, that only by a deep patriotic devotion to one's country can there be a hope of the kind of protection of the whole planet, which is necessary for the survival of the people of other countries.

Culture and Commitment [1970]

18 The mind is not sex-typed.

Blackberry Winter [1972], ch. 5

19 Because of their age-long training in human relations—for that is what feminine intuition really is—women have a special contribution to make to any group enterprise, and I feel it is up to them to contribute the kinds of awareness that relatively few men . . . have incorporated through their education. *Ib. 14*

Linus Carl Pauling

1901–

1 Science is the search for truth—it is not a game in which one tries to beat his opponent, to do harm to others. We need to have the spirit of science in international affairs, to make the conduct of international affairs the effort to find the right solution, the just solution of international problems, not the effort by each nation to get the better of other nations, to do harm to them when it is possible.

No More War! [1958]

Arna Bontemps

1902–

2 Yet what I sowed and what the orchard yields
My brother's sons are gathering stalk and root,
Small wonder then my children glean in fields
They have not sown, and feed on bitter fruit.

A Black Man Talks of Reaping [1963], st. 3

3 Yet would we die as some have done:
Beating a way for the rising sun.

The Daybreakers [1963]

Thomas Edmund Dewey

1902–1971

4 That's why it's time for a change.[1]

Campaign speech at San Francisco [September 21, 1944]

Erik Homburger Erikson

1902–

5 This sense of identity provides the ability to experience one's self as something that has continuity and sameness, and to act accordingly.[2] *Childhood and Society [1950]*

Stella Gibbons

1902–

6 The farm was crouched on a bleak hillside, whence its fields, fanged with flints, dropped steeply to the village of Howling a mile away.

Cold Comfort Farm [1932], ch. 3

7 Something nasty in the woodshed.

Ib. 8

Wolcott Gibbs

1902–1958

8 Backward ran sentences until reeled the mind.

More in Sorrow [1958]. Time . . . Fortune . . . Life . . . Luce

9 Where it will all end, knows God!

Ib.

10 Generally speaking, the American theater is the aspirin of the middle classes.[3]

Ib. Shakespeare, Here's Your Hat

Langston Hughes

1902–1967

11 It is the duty of the younger Negro artist . . . to change through the force of his art that old whispering "I want to be white," hidden in the aspirations of his people, to "Why should I want to be white? I am a Negro—and beautiful!"[4]

The Negro Artist and the Racial Mountain. In The Nation [June 23, 1926]

12 I've known rivers:
I've known rivers ancient as the world and older than the flow of human blood in human veins.
My soul has grown deep like the rivers.

The Negro Speaks of Rivers [1926]

13 I am a Negro:
Black as the night is black,
Black like the depths of my Africa.

Negro [1926]

14 Rest at pale evening . . .
A tall slim tree . . .
Night coming tenderly
Black like me.

Dream Variations [1926]

15 I got the Weary Blues
And I can't be satisfied.

The Weary Blues [1926]

16 Wear it
Like a banner
For the proud—
Not like a shroud. *Color [1943]*

17 Good morning, daddy!
Ain't you heard

[1] The phrase was used extensively in the campaigns of 1944, 1948, and 1952.

[2] "Identity crisis"—a term that Erikson dimly recalls having minted during World War II in connection with "shell-shocked" patients who had "lost a sense of personal sameness and historical continuity."—William Braden, *The Age of Aquarius* [1970]

[3] See Marx, 562:15.

[4] See Anonymous, 925:14.

The boogie-woogie rumble
Of a dream deferred?
Dream Boogie [1951]

1 You think
It's a happy beat? *Ib.*

2 What happens to a dream deferred?
Does it dry up
like a raisin in the sun? . . .
Or does it explode? *Harlem [1951]*

3 Negro blood is sure powerful — because just *one* drop of black blood makes a colored man. *One* drop — you are a Negro! . . . Black is powerful.[1]
Simple Takes a Wife [1953]

4 I am the American heartbreak —
The rock on which Freedom
Stumped its toe.
American Heartbreak [1951]

5 Quick, sunrise, come!
Sunrise out of Africa,
Quick, come!
Junior Addict [1967], st. 6

Harold Dwight Lasswell

1902–

6 Politics: Who Gets What, When, How.
Title of book [1936]

Carlo Levi

1902–1975

7 Christ Stopped at Eboli.[2]
Title of book [1945]

Charles Augustus Lindbergh[3]

1902–1974

8 We (that's my ship and I) took off rather suddenly. We had a report somewhere around 4 o'clock in the afternoon before that the weather would be fine, so we thought we would try it.
Lindbergh's Own Story. In the New York Times [May 23, 1927]

9 I saw a fleet of fishing boats. . . . I flew down almost touching the craft and yelled at them, asking if I was on the right road to Ireland. They just stared. Maybe they didn't hear me. Maybe I didn't hear them. Or maybe they thought I was just a crazy fool. An hour later I saw land. *Ib.*

[1] See Carmichael and Hamilton, 914:15.

[2] Cristo Si è Fermato a Eboli.

[3] In the spring of '27, something bright and alien flashed across the sky. A young Minnesotan [Lindbergh] who seemed to have had nothing to do with his generation did a heroic thing, and for a moment people set down their glasses in country clubs and speakeasies and thought of their old best dreams. — F. SCOTT FITZGERALD

Ogden Nash

1902–1971

10 Candy
Is dandy
But liquor
Is quicker.
Hard Lines [1931]. Reflections on Ice-Breaking

11 One would be in less danger
From the wiles of the stranger
If one's own kin and kith
Were more fun to be with.
Ib. Family Court

12 The turtle lives 'twixt plated decks
Which practically conceal its sex.
I think it clever of the turtle
In such a fix to be so fertile.
Ib. The Turtle

13 A bit of talcum
Is always walcum.
Free Wheeling [1931]. The Baby

14 Certainly there are lots of things in life that money won't buy, but it's very funny —
Have you ever tried to buy them without money?
Happy Days [1933]. The Terrible People

15 I think that I shall never see
A billboard lovely as a tree.
Indeed, unless the billboards fall
I'll never see a tree at all.[4]
Ib. Song of the Open Road

16 There is something about a Martini,
Ere the dining and dancing begin,
And to tell you the truth,
It is not the vermouth —
I think that perhaps it's the gin.
The Primrose Path [1935]. A Drink with Something in It

17 There are two kinds of people who blow through life like a breeze,
And one kind is gossipers, and the other kind is gossipees.
I'm a Stranger Here Myself [1938]. I Have It on Good Authority

18 Bankers Are Just Like Anybody Else, Except Richer. *Ib. Title of poem*

[4] See Joyce Kilmer, 795:6.

1 Dogs display reluctance and wrath
If you try to give them a bath.
They bury bones in hideaways
And half the time they trot sideaways.
Ib. An Introduction to Dogs, st. 4

2 There was a young belle of old Natchez
Whose garments were always in patchez.
When comment arose
On the state of her clothes,
She drawled, When Ah itchez, Ah scratchez!
Ib. Requiem

3 There is only one way to achieve happiness on this terrestrial ball,
And that is to have either a clear conscience, or none at all.
Ib. Interoffice Memorandum

4 I believe a little incompatibility is the spice of life, particularly if he has income and she is pattable.
Versus [1949]. I Do, I Will, I Have

5 He tells you when you've got on too much lipstick,
And helps you with your girdle when your hips stick.
Ib. The Perfect Husband

6 Ten years ago she split the air
To seize what she could spy;
Tonight she bumps against a chair,
Betrayed by milky eye.
She seems to pant, Time up, time up!
My little dog must die,
And lie in dust with Hector's pup;[1]
So, presently, must I.
Ib. For a Good Dog, st. 3

7 When I remember bygone days
I think how evening follows morn;
So many I loved were not yet dead,
So many I love were not yet born.
Ib. The Middle

8 A door is what a dog is perpetually on the wrong side of.
The Private Dining Room [1953]. A Dog's Best Friend Is His Illiteracy

9 How confusing the beams from memory's lamp are;
One day a bachelor, the next a grampa.
What is the secret of the trick?
How did I get so old so quick?
You Can't Get There from Here [1957]. Preface to the Past

10 Here lies my past. Good-bye I have kissed it;
Thank you, kids. I wouldn't have missed it.
Ib.

[1] See Anonymous, 921:18.

11 Maybe I couldn't be dafter,
But I keep wondering if this time we couldn't settle our differences before a war instead of after.
Everyone but Thee and Me [1962]. Is There an Oculist in the House?

12 I myself am more and more inclined to agree with Omar and Satchel Paige as I grow older:
Don't try to rewrite what the moving finger has writ, and don't ever look over your shoulder.[2]
There's Always Another Windmill [1968]. If a Boder Meet a Boder, Need a Boder Cry? Yes[3]

13 Discretion is the better part of virtue,
Commitments the voters don't know about can't hurt you.
The Old Dog Barks Backwards [1972]. Political Reflection

14 Linguistics becomes an ever eerier area, like I feel like I'm in Oz,
Just trying to tell it like it was.[4]
Ib. What Do You Want, A Meaningful Dialogue or a Satisfactory Talk?

Sir Karl Raimund Popper

1902–

15 Our belief in any particular natural law cannot have a safer basis than our unsuccessful critical attempts to refute it.
Conjectures and Refutations [1963]

Stevie [Margaret Florence] Smith

1902–1971

16 I was much too far out all my life
And not waving but drowning.
Not Waving but Drowning [1957]

17 Smile, smile, and get some work to do
Then you will be practically unconscious without positively having to go.
Thoughts About the Person from Porlock [1962]

18 Sin recognized—but that—may keep us humble,
But oh, it keeps us nasty.
Recognition Not Enough [1962]

19 He [Christ] did not love in the human way.
Was He Married? [1962]

[2] See FitzGerald, 517:2, and Paige, 867:9.
[3] See Anonymous, 919:17.
[4] Tell it like it is.—*Youth slogan* [1960s]

1 To choose a god of love, as he did and does,
Is a little move then? . . .

A larger one will be when men
Love love and hate hate but do not deify them?

It will be a larger one. *Ib.*

2 Why does my Muse only speak when she is unhappy?
She does not, I only listen when I am unhappy. *My Muse [1962]*

3 Yet a time may come when a poet or any person
Having a long life behind him, pleasure and sorrow . . .
May fancy life comes to him with love and says:
We are friends enough now for me to give you death;
Then he may commit suicide, then
He may go. *Exeat [1966]*

John Ernst Steinbeck

1902–1968

4 Man, unlike any other thing organic or inorganic in the universe, grows beyond his work, walks up the stairs of his concepts, emerges ahead of his accomplishments.
The Grapes of Wrath [1939], ch. 14

5 Okie use' ta mean you was from Oklahoma. Now it means you're scum. Don't mean nothing itself, it's the way they say it.
Ib. 18

Nathanael West

1902–1940

6 Are you in trouble?—Do-you-need-advice?—Write-to-Miss-Lonelyhearts-and-she-will-help-you. *Miss Lonelyhearts [1933]*

7 The Miss Lonelyhearts are the priests of twentieth-century America. *Ib.*

8 The Day of the Locust.
Title of novel [1939]

Tallulah Brockman Bankhead

1903–1968

9 There is less in this than meets the eye.
Remark to Alexander Woollcott at Aglavaine and Selysette by MAURICE MAETERLINCK *[January 3, 1922]*

Erskine Caldwell

1903–

10 Tobacco Road.
Title of novel [1932][1]

Count Galeazzo Ciano

1903–1944

11 As always, victory finds a hundred fathers but defeat is an orphan.[2]
The Ciano Diaries 1939–1943 [1946]. [September 9, 1942]

Cyril Vernon Connolly

1903–1974

12 Obesity is a mental state, a disease brought on by boredom and disappointment.
The Unquiet Grave [1945], pt. I

13 Imprisoned in every fat man a thin one is wildly signaling to be let out. *Ib. II*

Countee Cullen

1903–1946

14 One three centuries removed
From the scenes his fathers loved,
Spicy grove, cinnamon tree,
What is Africa to me?
Heritage [1925]

15 So I lie, who all day long
Want no sound except the song
Sung by wild barbaric birds
Goading massive jungle herds,
Juggernauts of flesh that pass
Trampling tall defiant grass. *Ib.*

16 Not yet has my heart or head
In the least way realized
They and I are civilized. *Ib.*

William Thomas Cummings[3]

1903–1944

17 There are no atheists in the foxholes.[4]
Field sermon, Bataan [1942]. From CARLOS P. ROMULO, *I Saw the Fall of the Philippines [1942]*

[1]The play [1933], adapted by JACK KIRKLAND [1903–1969], had one of the longest runs in American stage history.

[2]There's an old saying that victory has a hundred fathers and defeat is an orphan.—JOHN F. KENNEDY, *after the debacle at the Bay of Pigs, Cuba* [April 21, 1961]

[3]Father Cummings, a chaplain, was aboard an unmarked Japanese ship transporting prisoners from the Philippines to Japan which was sunk by an American submarine [December 15, 1944].

[4]See Young, 330:14.

Malcolm Muggeridge

1903–

1 As Man alone, Jesus could not have saved us; as God alone, he would not; Incarnate, he could and did. *Jesus [1975], pt. I*

Anaïs Nin

1903–1977

2 It's all right for a woman to be, above all, human. I am a woman first of all.
The Diary of Anaïs Nin, vol. I [1966], June 1933

3 There is not one big cosmic meaning for all, there is only the meaning we each give to our life. . . . To seek a total unity is wrong. To give as much meaning to one's life as possible is right to me.
Ib. II [1967], June 1935

4 People living deeply have no fear of death.
Ib. August 1935

5 Dreams are necessary to life.
Ib. June 1936 (letter to her mother)

6 Each friend represents a world in us, a world possibly not born until they arrive, and it is only by this meeting that a new world is born. *Ib. March 1937*

7 Poverty is the great reality. That is why the artist seeks it. *Ib. Summer 1937*

8 Every individual is representative of the whole . . . and should be intimately understood, and this would give a far greater understanding of mass movements and sociology. *Ib. III [1969], September 1940*

9 Life shrinks or expands in proportion to one's courage. *Ib. June 1941*

10 There are very few human beings who receive the truth, complete and staggering, by instant illumination. Most of them acquire it fragment by fragment, on a small scale, by successive developments, cellularly, like a laborious mosaic. *Ib. Fall 1943*

11 Beware of allowing a tactless word, a rebuttal, a rejection to obliterate the whole sky.
Ib. January 1944

George Orwell [Eric Blair]

1903–1950

12 All animals are equal, but some animals are more equal than others.
Animal Farm [1945], ch. 10

13 It was a bright cold day in April and the clock was striking thirteen.
1984 [1948], opening line

14 Big Brother is watching you. *Ib.*

Benjamin Spock

1903–

15 The more people have studied different methods of bringing up children the more they have come to the conclusion that what good mothers and fathers instinctively feel like doing for their babies is the best after all.
The Common Sense Book of Baby and Child Care [1946], ch. 1

Evelyn Waugh

1903–1966

16 *"What war?"* said the Prime Minister sharply. "No one has said anything to me about a war. I really think I should have been told. I'll be damned," he said defiantly, "if they shall have a war without consulting me. What's a cabinet for, if there's not more mutual confidence than that? What do they want a war for, anyway?"
Vile Bodies [1930], ch. 8

Peter Arno

1904–1968

17 I consider your conduct unethical and lousy. *Caption for cartoon*

18 Well, back to the old drawing board.
Caption for cartoon showing designer walking away from crashed plane

Richard Eberhart

1904–

19 But the year had lost its meaning,
And in intellectual chains
I lost both love and loathing,
Mured up in the wall of wisdom.
Collected Poems, 1930–1960 [1960]. The Groundhog

20 I stood there in the whirling summer,
My hand capped a withered heart,
And thought of China and of Greece,
Of Alexander in his tent;
Of Montaigne in his tower,
Of Saint Theresa in her wild lament.
Ib.

1 It is what man does not know of God
Composes the visible poem of the world.
Ib. On a Squirrel

2 This fevers me, this sun on green,
On green glowing, this young spring.
Ib. A Bravery of Earth

Bergen Evans
1904–1978

3 Freedom of speech and freedom of action are meaningless without freedom to think. And there is no freedom of thought without doubt.
The Natural History of Nonsense [1946], ch. 19

Clifton Fadiman
1904–

4 When you reread a classic you do not see more in the book than you did before; you see more in *you* than there was before.
Any Number Can Play [1957]

Graham Greene
1904–

5 This Gun for Hire.
Title of novel [1936]

6 There is always one moment in childhood when the door opens and lets the future in.
The Power and the Glory [1940], ch. 1

7 In human relations kindness and lies are worth a thousand truths.
The Heart of the Matter [1948], pt. I, ch. 2, sec. iv

8 No human being can really understand another, and no one can arrange another's happiness. *Ib. III, 1, i*

9 The Third Man.
Title of novel [1950]

10 If we had not been taught how to interpret the story of the Passion, would we have been able to say from their actions alone whether it was the jealous Judas or the cowardly Peter who loved Christ?
The End of the Affair [1951]

11 Have you seen a room from which faith has gone? . . . Like a marriage from which love has gone. . . . And patience, patience everywhere like a fog.
The Potting Shed [1957]

12 Our Man in Havana.
Title of novel [1958]

13 Catholics and Communists have committed great crimes, but at least they have not stood aside, like an established society, and been indifferent. I would rather have blood on my hands than water like Pilate . . . if you have abandoned one faith, do not abandon all faith. There is always an alternative to the faith we lose. Or is it the same faith under another name?
The Comedians [1966]

14 Our worst enemies here are not the ignorant and the simple, however cruel; our worst enemies are the intelligent and corrupt.
The Human Factor [1978], pt. III, ch. 3

Moss Hart[1]
1904–1961

15 Boredom is the keynote of poverty . . . for where there is no money there is no change of any kind, not of scene or of routine.
Act One [1959], pt. I

16 Poor people know poor people, and rich people know rich people. It is one of the few things La Rochefoucauld did not say, but then La Rochefoucauld never lived in the Bronx. *Ib.*

17 A too constant preoccupation with money may seem to indicate the lack of a proper sense of moral values, but [let] those who have always had money . . . be without it for a while, and they will soon discover how quickly it becomes their chief concern.
Ib. II

18 The self-hatred that destroys is the waste of unfulfilled promise. *Ib.*

19 Can success change the human mechanism so completely between one dawn and another? Can it make one feel taller, more alive, handsomer, uncommonly gifted and indomitably secure with the certainty that this is the way life will always be? It can and it does!
Ib.

20 The only credential the city [New York] asked was the boldness to dream. For those who did, it unlocked its gates and its treasures, not caring who they were or where they came from. *Ib.*

[1] See also Kaufman and Hart, page 813.

Christopher William Bradshaw Isherwood

1904–

1 I am a camera with its shutter open, quite passive, recording, not thinking. Recording the man shaving at the window opposite and the woman in the kimono washing her hair. Some day, all this will have to be developed, carefully printed, fixed.

The Berlin Stories [1945]. Goodbye to Berlin [1939], A Berlin Diary [Autumn 1930]

George Frost Kennan

1904–

2 Many of the present relationships of international life are only the eroded remnants of ones which, at one time, were relationships of uncompromising hostility. Every government is in some respects a problem for every other government, and it will always be this way so long as the sovereign state, with its supremely self-centered rationale, remains the basis of international life.

Russia and the West under Lenin and Stalin [1961], ch. 25

3 If we are to regard ourselves as a grown-up nation—and anything else will henceforth be mortally dangerous—then we must, as the Biblical phrase goes, put away childish things; and among these childish things the first to go, in my opinion, should be self-idealization and the search for absolutes in world affairs: for absolute security, absolute amity, absolute harmony. *Ib.*

4 There is no political or ideological difference between the Soviet Union and the United States—nothing which either side would like, or would hope, to achieve at the expense of the other—that would be worth the risks and sacrifices of a military encounter.

The Cloud of Danger [1977], ch. 11

5 A war regarded as inevitable or even probable, and therefore much prepared for, has a very good chance of eventually being fought. *Ib. 13*

6 The greatest danger inherent in the existing competition between the Soviet Union and the United States in the military field is . . . that the momentum of this tremendous and infinitely dangerous weapons race will get out of hand, will become wholly uncontrollable and will, either through proliferation or by accident, carry us all to destruction. *Ib.*

Cecil Day Lewis

1904–1972

7 Tempt me no more; for I
Have known the lightning's hour,
The poet's inward pride,
The certainty of power.

Tempt Me No More, st. 1

Pablo Neruda [Neftalí Ricardo Reyes y Basualto]

1904–1973

8 I could write the saddest poem tonight.
For example, "The night is starry bright
and the ice-blue orbs are shivering far above" . . .
I could write the saddest poem tonight.
I loved her, and sometimes she loved me too.

Twenty Love Poems and a Song of Despair (Veinte Poemas de Amor y una Canción Desesperada) [1924]. I Could Write (Puedo Escribir)[1]

9 I happen to be tired of being a man
I happen to enter tailor shops and movie houses
withered, impenetrable, like a felt swan
navigating in a water of sources and ashes.

Residencia en la Tierra (Residence on Earth), series II [1935]. Walking Around[2]

10 Treacherous
generals:
look at my dead house,
look at broken Spain.

Ib. series III [1947]. I Explain a Few Things (Explico Algunas Cosas)[2]

11 But from each hollow of Spain
Spain comes forth. *Ib.*

12 But from each crime are born bullets
that will one day seek out in you
where the heart lies. *Ib.*

13 All paths lead to the same goal: to convey to others what we are. And we must pass through solitude and difficulty, isolation and silence, in order to reach forth to the enchanted place where we can dance our clumsy dance and sing our sorrowful song—but in this dance or in this song there are fulfilled the most ancient rites of our con-

[1]Translated by RACHEL PHILLIPS.
[2]Translated by DONALD D. WALSH.

science in the awareness of being human and of believing in a common destiny.

Toward the Splendid City, upon receiving the Nobel Prize [1971]

1 What a great language I have, it's a fine language we inherited from the fierce Conquistadors . . . They carried everything off and left us everything . . . They left us the words.

Memoirs (Confieso Que He Vivido: Memorias) [1974],[1] *ch.* 2

2 Night in Valparaiso! . . . The immense deserted night set up its formation of colossal figures that seeded light far and wide. Aldebaran trembled, throbbing far above, Cassiopeia hung her dress on heaven's doors, while the noiseless chariot of the Southern Cross rolled over the night sperm of the Milky Way. *Ib.* 3

3 Poetry is an act of peace. Peace goes into the making of a poet as flour goes into the making of bread. *Ib.* 6

4 I continue to work with the materials I have, the materials I am made of. With feelings, beings, books, events, and battles, I am omnivorous. I would like to swallow the whole earth. I would like to drink the whole sea. *Ib.* 11

5 Poetry is a deep inner calling in man; from it came liturgy, the psalms, and also the content of religions. *Ib.*

J. Robert Oppenheimer[2]

1904–1967

6 In some sort of crude sense which no vulgarity, no humor, no overstatement can quite extinguish, the physicists have known sin; and this is a knowledge which they cannot lose.[3]

Physics in the Contemporary World, lecture at Massachusetts Institute of Technology [November 25, 1947]

7 The open society, the unrestricted access to knowledge, the unplanned and uninhibited association of men for its furtherance—these are what may make a vast, complex, ever growing, ever changing, ever more specialized and expert technological world, nevertheless a world of human community.

Science and the Common Understanding [1953]

Sidney Joseph Perelman

1904–1979

8 One Touch of Venus.

Title of play [1943] (with Ogden Nash*)*

9 Crazy Like a Fox.

Title of book [1944]

Isaac Bashevis Singer

1904–

10 When literature becomes overly erudite, it means that interest in the art has gone and curiosity about the artist is what's most important. It becomes a kind of idolatry.

Isaac Bashevis Singer Talks . . . About Everything, interview with Richard Burgin in the New York Times Magazine [November 26, 1978]

11 It seems that the analysis of character is the highest human entertainment. And literature does it, unlike gossip, without mentioning real names. *Ib.*

12 When the writer becomes the center of his attention, he becomes a nudnik. And a nudnik who believes he's profound is even worse than just a plain nudnik. *Ib.*

13 We know what a person thinks not when he tells us what he thinks, but by his actions. *Ib.*

14 The greatness of art is not to find what is common but what is unique. *Ib.*

15 Sometimes love is stronger than a man's convictions. *Ib.*

16 If you write about the things and the people you know best, you discover your roots. Even if they are new roots, fresh roots . . . they are better than . . . no roots. *Ib.*

17 What nature delivers to us is never stale. Because what nature creates has eternity in it. *Ib.*

18 The very essence of literature is the war between emotion and intellect, between life and death. When literature becomes too intellectual—when it begins to ignore the

[1] Translated by Hardie St. Martin.

[2] For the passage quoted by Oppenheimer at the explosion of the first atom bomb [Alamogordo, New Mexico, July 16, 1945], see *Bhagavad Gita,* 94:15. He also quoted Vishnu from the *Gita:* I am become death, the destroyer of worlds.

[3] See Adlai Stevenson, 851:15.

passions, the emotions — it becomes sterile, silly, and actually without substance.

Isaac Bashevis Singer's Universe, interview with Richard Burgin in the New York Times Magazine [December 3, 1978]

1 Man cannot live without self-control. *Ib.*

2 When you betray somebody else, you also betray yourself. *Ib.*

3 Doubt is part of all religion. All the religious thinkers were doubters. *Ib.*

4 I never say the universe was an accident. The word "accident" should be erased from the dictionary. *Ib.*

5 Our knowledge is a little island in a great ocean of non-knowledge. *Ib.*

6 Originality is not seen in single words or even sentences. Originality is the sum total of a man's thinking or his writing. *Ib.*

Burrhus Frederic Skinner

1904–

7 The one fact that I would cry from every housetop is this: the Good Life is waiting for us — here and now! . . . At this very moment we have the necessary techniques, both material and psychological, to create a full and satisfying life for everyone.

Walden Two [1948], ch. 23

8 I remember the rage I used to feel when a prediction went awry. I could have shouted at the subjects of my experiments, "Behave, damn you, behave as you ought!" Eventually I realized that the subjects were always right. It was I who was wrong. I had made a bad prediction. *Ib. 32*

9 We shouldn't teach great books; we should teach a love of reading.

From R. Evans, B. F. Skinner: The Man and His Ideas [1968]

10 The real problem is not whether machines think but whether men do.

Contingencies of Reinforcement [1969], ch. 9

11 We do not choose survival as a value; it chooses us.

Transcript of television program [October 17, 1971]

12 We are all controlled by the world in which we live, and part of that world has been and will be constructed by men. The question is this: are we to be controlled by accidents, by tyrants, or by ourselves in effective cultural design?

Cumulative Record [third edition, 1972], ch. 1

13 Physics does not change the nature of the world it studies, and no science of behavior can change the essential nature of man, even though both sciences yield technologies with a vast power to manipulate their subject matters. *Ib. 5*

Jane Ace

1905–1974

14 Time wounds all heels.[1]

From Goodman Ace, The Fine Art of Hypochondria; or, How Are You? [1966]

James William Fulbright

1905–

15 There is an inevitable divergence, attributable to the imperfections of the human mind, between the world as it is and the world as men perceive it.

Speech in the Senate [March 27, 1964]

16 We are handicapped by [foreign] policies based on old myths rather than current realities. *Ib.*

17 A policy that can be accurately, though perhaps not prudently, defined as one of "peaceful coexistence." *Ib.*

18 There is much cant in American moralism and not a little inconsistency. *Ib.*

19 We are inclined to confuse freedom and democracy, which we regard as moral principles, with the way in which these are practiced in America — with capitalism, federalism and the two-party system, which are not moral principles, but simply the accepted practices of the American people. *Ib.*

20 The master myth of the cold war is that the Communist bloc is a monolith, composed of governments which are not really governments at all, but organized conspiracies . . . all equally resolute and implacable in their determination to destroy the free world. *Ib.*

21 We must dare to think "unthinkable" thoughts. We must learn to explore all the options and possibilities that confront us in a complex and rapidly changing world. We must learn to welcome and not to fear the

[1] See Terence, 96:*n*11.

voices of dissent. We must dare to think about "unthinkable things" because when things become unthinkable, thinking stops and action becomes mindless. *Ib.*

1 The Arrogance of Power.
Title of book [1967]

Greta Garbo [Greta Gustafson]
1905–

2 I want to be alone.[1] *Attributed*

Dag Hammarskjöld
1905–1961

3 What gives life its value you can find—and lose. But never possess. This holds good above all for "the Truth about Life."
Markings

4 The longest journey[2]
Is the journey inwards
Of him who has chosen his destiny.
Ib.

5 He who has nothing can give nothing. The gift is God's—to God. *Ib.*

Lillian Hellman
1905–

6 There are people who eat the earth and eat all the people on it like in the Bible with the locusts. And other people who stand around and watch them eat it.
The Little Foxes [1939], act III

7 For every man who lives without freedom, the rest of us must face the guilt.
Watch on the Rhine [1941], act II

8 Lonely people talking to each other can make each other lonelier.
The Autumn Garden [1951], act I

9 I am most willing to answer all questions about myself . . . But . . . I am not willing, now or in the future, to bring bad trouble to people who, in my past association with them, were completely innocent of any talk or any action that was disloyal or subversive.
Letter to the House Committee on Un-American Activities [May 19, 1952]

10 I cannot and will not cut my conscience to fit this year's fashions. *Ib.*

[1] Garbo maintains that her most famous remark has always been misquoted. . . . "I only said, 'I want to be *let* alone!' "—John Bainbridge, *in Life* [January 24, 1955]

[2] See Shelley, 468:21.

11 A man should be jailed for telling lies to the young. *Candide [1956],*[3] *act II, sc. iii*

12 We will not think noble because we are not noble. We will not live in beautiful harmony because there is no such thing in this world, nor should there be. We promise only to do our best and live out our lives. Dear God, that's all we can promise in truth. *Ib.*

13 I do not believe in recovery. The past, with its pleasures, its rewards, its foolishness, its punishments, is there for each of us forever, and it should be.
Scoundrel Time [1976]

Stanley Kunitz
1905–

14 Now, while the antler of the eaves
Liquefies, drop by drop, I brood
On a Christian thing: unless the leaves
Perish, the tree is not renewed.

If all our perishable stuff
Be nourished to its rot, we clean
Our trunk of death, and in our tough
And final growth are evergreen.
Deciduous Branch [1930], st. 4, 5

15 I stand on the terrible threshold, and I see
The end and the beginning in each other's
arms. *Open the Gates [1944], st. 3*

16 Awake!
My whirling hands stay at the noon,
Each cell within my body holds a heart
And all my hearts in unison strike twelve.
The Science of the Night [1958]

17 Doomsday is the eighth day of the week.
Foreign Affairs [1958]

18 On the royal road to Thebes
I had my luck, I met a lovely monster,
And the story's this: I made the monster me.
The Approach to Thebes [1958]

19 We learn, as the thread plays out, that we
belong
Less to what flatters us than to what scars,
So, freshly turning, as the turn condones,
For her I killed the propitiatory bird,
Kissing her down. Peace to her bitter bones,
Who taught me the serpent's word, but yet
the word.
The Dark and the Fair [1958]

20 I recognize the gods' capricious hand
And write this poem for money, rage, and
love. *The Thief [1958]*

[3] A comic operetta based upon Voltaire's satire.
See Voltaire, 343:8–343:14, and Wilbur, 900:5.

1 An agitation of the air,
A perturbation of the light
Admonished me the unloved year
Would turn on its hinge that night.
End of Summer [1958], st. 1

2 Already the iron door of the north
Clangs open: birds, leaves, snows
Order their populations forth,
And a cruel wind blows. *Ib. st. 4*

3 The thing that eats the heart is mostly heart.
The Thing That Eats the Heart [1958], last line

4 I was a stranger on earth.
Stepping on the moon, I begin
the gay pilgrimage to new
Jerusalems
in foreign galaxies.
Heat. Cold. Craters of silence.
The Sea of Tranquillity
rolling on the shores of entropy.
And, beyond,
the intelligence of the stars.
The Flight of Apollo [1971], 2

5 Slime, in the grains of the State,
like smut in the corn,
from the top infected.
Hatred made law.
Around Pastor Bonhoeffer [1971]. Next to Last Things

6 He had heard the midnight bells
jangling: *if you permit
this evil, what is the good
of the good of your life?* *Ib.*

7 On the threshold
of the last mystery,
at the brute absolute hour,
you have looked into the eyes
of your creature self,
which are glazed with madness,
and you say
he is not broken but endures,
limber and firm
in the state of his shining,
forever inheriting his salt kingdom,
from which he is banished
forever. *King of the River*[1] *[1971]*

8 That pack of scoundrels
tumbling through the gate
emerges
as the Order of the State.
The System [1971]

9 I've a long way to go
Who never learned to pray.
The Game [1971], st. 4

[1]The Pacific salmon.

10 These relics on display . . .
make a noble, dissolving music
out of homely fife and drum,
and that's miraculous.
The Lincoln Relics [1979], 1

11 *Liebchen,*
with whom should I quarrel
except in the hiss of love,
that harsh, irregular flame?
The Quarrel [1979]

12 In every house of marriage
there's room for an interpreter.
Route Six [1979]

13 How shall the heart be reconciled
to its feast of losses?
In a rising wind
the manic dust of my friends,
those who fell along the way,
bitterly stings my face.
Yet I turn, I turn. *The Layers [1979]*

14 "Live in the layers,
not on the litter" . . .
No doubt the next chapter
in my book of transformations
is already written.
I am not done with my changes. *Ib.*

Phyllis McGinley

1905–1977

15 Meek-eyed parents hasten down the ramps
To greet their offspring, terrible from camps.
Ode to the End of Summer

16 Prince, I warn you, under the rose,
Time is the thief you cannot banish.
These are my daughters, I suppose.
But where in the world did the children vanish? *Ballade of Lost Objects [1954]*

17 Always on Monday morning the press reports
God as revealed to His vicars in various guises—
Benevolent, stormy, patient, or out of sorts.
God knows which God is the God God recognizes. *The Day After Sunday [1954]*

18 Ah! some love Paris,
And some Purdue.
But love is an archer with a low I.Q.
A bold, bad bowman, and innocent of pity.
So I'm in love with
New York City.
A Kind of Love Letter to New York [1954]

19 A mother's hardest to forgive.
Life is the fruit she longs to hand you,

Ripe on a plate. And while you live,
Relentlessly she understands you.

The Adversary

1 We who belong to that Profession [of housewife] hold the fate of the world in our hands.

Sixpence in Her Shoe [1964], ch. 3

John O'Hara

1905–1970

2 Hot lead can be almost as effective coming from a linotype as from a firearm.

The Portable F. Scott Fitzgerald [1945], introduction

3 An artist is his own fault. *Ib.*

Ayn Rand

1905–

4 Civilization is the progress toward a society of privacy. The savage's whole existence is public, ruled by the laws of his tribe. Civilization is the process of setting man free from men. *The Fountainhead [1943]*

5 Great men can't be ruled. *Ib.*

6 Kill reverence and you've killed the hero in man. *Ib.*

Jean Paul Sartre

1905–1980

7 Everything is gratuitous, this garden, this city and myself. When you suddenly realize it, it makes you feel sick and everything begins to drift . . . that's nausea.

La Nausée [1938]

8 Man is not the sum of what he has but the totality of what he does not yet have, of what he might have. *Situations [1939], I*

9 We do not do what we want and yet we are responsible for what we are — that is the fact. *Ib. II*

10 Because the Nazi venom worked its way even into our thoughts, every accurate thought was a conquest; because an all-powerful police sought to force us into silence, every word became as precious as a declaration of principle; because we were persecuted, each of our gestures carried the weight of a commitment.

Les Mouches (The Flies) [1943]

11 Man can will nothing unless he has first understood that he must count on no one but himself; that he is alone, abandoned on earth in the midst of his infinite responsibilities, without help, with no other aim than the one he sets himself, with no other destiny than the one he forges for himself on this earth.

L'Être et le Néant (Being and Nothingness) [1943]

12 Hell is — other people![1]

Huis-Clos (In Camera) [1945], sc. v

13 I was escaping from Nature and at last becoming myself, that Other whom I was aspiring to be in the eyes of others.

The Words (Les Mots) [1964][2]

14 All the same, they [books] do serve some purpose. Culture doesn't save anything or anyone, it doesn't justify. But it's a product of man: he projects himself into it, he recognizes himself in it; that critical mirror alone offers him his image. *Ib.*

15 Never have I thought that I was the happy possessor of a "talent"; my sole concern has been to save myself by work and faith.

Ib.

16 If I relegate impossible Salvation to the proproom, what remains? A whole man, composed of all men and as good as all of them and no better than any. *Ib.*

Sir Charles Percy Snow

1905–

17 Literary intellectuals at one pole — at the other scientists. . . . Between the two a gulf of mutual incomprehension.

The Two Cultures and the Scientific Revolution [1959]

18 No one is fit to be trusted with power. . . . No one. . . . Any man who has lived at all knows the follies and wickedness he's capable of. If he does not know it, he is not fit to govern others. And if he does know it, he knows also that neither he nor any man ought to be allowed to decide a single human fate. *The Light and the Dark [1961]*

19 Corridors of Power.

Title of novel [1965]

Lionel Trilling

1905–1976

20 The poet is in command of his fantasy, while it is exactly the mark of the neurotic that he is possessed by his fantasy.

The Liberal Imagination [1950]. Freud and Literature

[1] L'enfer, c'est les Autres.
See Virgil, 105:23; Marlowe, 183:21 and 184:1; Browne, 274:15; Milton, 283:13 and 285:12; Eliot, 809:1; and Robert Lowell, 893:7.

[2] Translated by Bernard Frechtman.

1 There is no connection between the political ideas of our educated class and the deep places of the imagination.
Ib. The Function of the Little Magazine

2 Occasions are rare when the best literature becomes, as it were, the folk literature, and generally speaking literature has always been carried on within small limits and under great difficulties. *Ib.*

3 We are all ill [i.e., neurotic]: but even a universal sickness implies an idea of health.
Ib. Art and Neurosis

4 The poet . . . may be used as the barometer, but let us not forget that he is also part of the weather.
Ib. The Sense of the Past

Harold Adamson
1906–

5 Comin' In on a Wing and a Prayer.
Title of song [1943]

Hannah Arendt
1906–1975

6 Aristotle explicitly assures us that man, insofar as he is a natural being and belongs to the species of mankind, possesses immortality; through the recurrent cycle of life, nature assures the same kind of being-forever to things that are born and die as to things that are and do not change.
Between Past and Future [1961], ch. 2

7 It was as though in those last minutes he [Eichmann] was summing up the lessons that this long course in human wickedness had taught us — the lesson of the fearsome, word-and-thought-defying *banality of evil.*
Eichmann in Jerusalem: A Report on the Banality of Evil [1963], ch. 15

8 No punishment has ever possessed enough power of deterrence to prevent the commission of crimes. On the contrary, whatever the punishment, once a specific crime has appeared for the first time, its reappearance is more likely than its initial emergence could have been. *Ib. epilogue*

9 In a constellation that poses the threat of total annihilation through war against the hope for the emancipation of all mankind through revolution . . . no cause is left but the most ancient of all, the one, in fact, that from the beginning of our history has determined the very existence of politics, the cause of freedom versus tyranny.
On Revolution [1963], introduction

10 As witnesses not of our intentions but of our conduct, we can be true or false, and the hypocrite's crime is that he bears false witness against himself. What makes it so plausible to assume that hypocrisy is the vice of vices is that integrity can indeed exist under the cover of all other vices except this one. Only crime and the criminal, it is true, confront us with the perplexity of radical evil; but only the hypocrite is really rotten to the core. *Ib. ch. 2*

Samuel Beckett
1906–

11 He can't think without his hat.
Waiting for Godot [1952], act I

12 We all are born mad. Some remain so.
Ib.

13 They give birth astride a grave, the light gleams an instant, then it's night once more.[1] *Ib. II*

14 Do you believe in the life to come? Mine was always that. *Endgame [1957]*

15 Krapp's Last Tape.
Title of play [1959]

John Betjeman
1906–

16 He rose, and he put down The Yellow Book.
He staggered — and, terrible-eyed,
He brushed past the palms on the staircase
And was helped to a hansom outside.
The Arrest of Oscar Wilde at the Cadogan Hotel [1937], st. 9

17 Gracious Lord, oh bomb the Germans.
Spare their women for Thy Sake,
And if that is not too easy
We will pardon Thy Mistake.
But, gracious Lord, whate'er shall be,
Don't let anyone bomb me.
In Westminster Abbey [1940]

18 The sort of girl I like to see
Smiles down from her great height at me.
The Olympic Girl [1954]

19 Oh! would I were her racket pressed
With hard excitement to her breast.
Ib.

20 Summoned by Bells.
Title of book [1960]

[1] See the *Wisdom of Solomon 5:13*, 34:15; Hall, 257:12; and Nabokov, 846:2.

Leo Durocher

1906–

1 Nice guys finish last. *Remark*

Dilys Laing

1906–1960

2 To be a woman and a writer
is double mischief, for
the world will slight her
who slights "the servile house," and who would rather
make odes than beds.

Sonnet to a Sister in Error [1957], st. 2

Curtis Emerson LeMay

1906–

3 My solution to the problem would be to tell [the North Vietnamese Communists] . . . they've got to draw in their horns and stop their aggression or we're going to bomb them into the Stone Age.

Mission with LeMay [1965]

Anne Morrow Lindbergh

1906–

4 The wave of the future is coming and there is no fighting it.

The Wave of the Future [1940]

5 I . . . understand why the saints were rarely married women. I am convinced it has nothing inherently to do, as I once supposed, with chastity or children. It has to do primarily with distractions. . . . Woman's normal occupations run counter to creative life, or contemplative life or saintly life.

Gift from the Sea [1955], ch. 2

6 The most exhausting thing in life . . . is being insincere. *Ib.*

7 When one is a stranger to oneself then one is estranged from others too. *Ib. 3*

8 By and large, mothers and housewives are the only workers who do not have regular time off. They are the great vacationless class. *Ib.*

Satchel [Leroy] Paige

c. 1906–

9 Don't look back. Something may be gaining on you. *How to Keep Young [1953]*

Roberto Rossellini

1906–1977

10 I am not a pessimist; to perceive evil where it exists is, in my opinion, a form of optimism.

Interview in Cahiers du Cinéma [1954]

Laurens Van der Post

1906–

11 Life is its own journey, presupposes its own change and movement, and one tries to arrest them at one's eternal peril.

Venture to the Interior [1951], pt. III

12 There is a way in which the collective knowledge of mankind expresses itself, for the finite individual, through mere daily living: a way in which life itself is sheer knowing. *Ib.*

13 Africa has always walked in my mind proudly upright, an African giant among the other continents, toes well dug into the final ocean of one hemisphere, rising to its full height in the graying skies of the other; head and shoulders broad, square and enduring, making light of the bagful of blue Mediterranean slung over its back as it marches patiently through time.

Flamingo Feather [1955], ch. 3

14 Of all man's inborn dispositions there is none more heroic than the love in him. Everything else accepts defeat and dies, but love will fight no-love every inch of the way.

Ib. 7

15 The buffalo's powerful head darkening the yellow grass, like the lion's imperative roar and the elephant's long, somnambulistic stride, has more of the quintessential Africa in it for me than any other manifestation of all the scores of animals that I know and love.

Ib. 10

16 Human beings are perhaps never more frightening than when they are convinced beyond doubt that they are right.

The Lost World of the Kalahari [1958], ch. 3

17 By chance (to use the only phrase we have for describing one of the most significant manifestations of life). *Ib. 8*

Wystan Hugh Auden

1907–1973

1 Let us honor if we can
The vertical man
Though we value none
But the horizontal one.
Epigraph for Poems [1930]

2 If we really want to live, we'd better start at once to try;
If we don't it doesn't matter, we'd better start to die.
If We Really Want to Live [1930]

3 Sir, no man's enemy, forgiving all
But will his negative inversion, be prodigal.
Sir, No Man's Enemy [1930]

4 Harrow the house of the dead; look shining at
New styles of architecture, a change of heart.
Ib.

5 Fish in the unruffled lakes
The swarming colors wear,
Swans in the winter air
A white perfection have,
And the great lion walks
Through his innocent grove
Lion, fish, and swan
Act, and are gone
Upon Time's toppling wave.
Fish in the Unruffled Lakes [1936], st. 1

6 We must lose our loves,
On each beast and bird that moves
Turn an envious look. *Ib. st. 2*

7 The greater the love, the more false to its object,
Not to be born is the best for man;[1]
After the kiss comes the impulse to throttle,
Break the embraces, dance while you can.
O Who Can Ever Gaze His Fill [1937]

8 The stars are dead. The animals will not look.
We are left alone with our day, and the time short, and History to the defeated
May say Alas but cannot help nor pardon.
Spain [1937]

9 About suffering they were never wrong,
The Old Masters.
Musée des Beaux Arts [1940]

10 O plunge your hands in water,
Plunge them in up to the wrist;
Stare, stare in the basin
And wonder what you've missed.

[1]See Theognis, 67:5; Sophocles, 75:13; Bacon, 181:19; and Yeats, 715:19.

The glacier knocks in the cupboard,
The desert sighs in the bed,
And the crack in the tea cup opens
A lane to the land of the dead.
As I Walked Out One Evening [1940], st. 10, 11

11 Earth, receive an honored guest;
William Yeats is laid to rest.
Let the Irish vessel lie
Emptied of its poetry.
In Memory of W. B. Yeats [1940],[2] III, st. 1

12 In the nightmare of the dark
All the dogs of Europe bark. *Ib. st. 2*

13 Intellectual disgrace
Stares from every human face,
And the seas of pity lie
Locked and frozen in each eye.
Ib. st. 3

14 To us he is no more a person
Now but a whole climate of opinion.
In Memory of Sigmund Freud[3] [1940]

15 One rational voice is dumb: over a grave
The household of Impulse mourns one dearly loved.
Sad is Eros, builder of cities,
And weeping anarchic Aphrodite.
Ib.

16 Lay your sleeping head, my love,
Human on my faithless arm.
Lullaby [1940], st. 1

17 Every farthing of the cost,
All the dreaded cards foretell,
Shall be paid, but from this night
Not a whisper, not a thought,
Not a kiss nor look be lost. *Ib. st. 3*

18 At Dirty Dick's and Sloppy Joe's
We drank our liquor straight,
Some went upstairs with Margery,
And some, alas, with Kate.
The Sea and the Mirror [1944]. Master and Boatswain

19 And children swarmed to him like settlers.
He became a land.
Edward Lear [1945]

20 Sob, heavy world,
Sob as you spin,
Mantled in mist, remote from the happy.
The Age of Anxiety [1947]

21 She looked over his shoulder
For vines and olive trees,

[2]See Yeats, 711.
[3]See Freud, 678.

Marble, well-governed cities
And ships upon wine-dark seas;
But there on the shining metal
His hands had put instead
An artificial wilderness
And a sky like lead.
The Shield of Achilles [1955], st. 1

1 The mass and majesty of this world, all
That carries weight and always weighs the same,
Lay in the hands of others; they were small
And could not hope for help, and no help came;
What their foes liked to do was done, their shame
Was all the worst could wish: they lost their pride
And died as men before their bodies died.
Ib. st. 6

2 Our researchers into Public Opinion are content
That he held the proper opinions for the time of year;
When there was peace, he was for peace; when there was war, he went.
The Unknown Citizen (To JS/07/M/378 This Marble Monument Is Erected by the State)

3 Was he free? Was he happy? The question is absurd:
Had anything been wrong, we should certainly have heard. *Ib.*

4 A culture is no better than its woods.
Bucolics. Woods

5 When a just man dies,
Lamentation and praise,
Sorrow and joy, are one.
Elegy for John F. Kennedy [1963]

6 Some thirty inches from my nose
The frontier of my Person goes,
And all the untilled air between
Is private *pagus* or demesne.
Stranger, unless with bedroom eyes
I beckon you to fraternize,
Beware of rudely crossing it:
I have no gun, but I can spit.[1]
About the House [1965]

7 Some books are undeservedly forgotten; none are undeservedly remembered.
The Dyer's Hand[2] *[1962]. Pt. I, Reading*

8 It takes little talent to see clearly what lies under one's nose, a good deal of it to know in which direction to point that organ.
Ib. Writing

9 The old lady, quoted by E. M. Forster—"How can I know what I think till I see what I say?" *Ib.*

10 Speaking for myself, the questions which interest me most when reading a poem are two. The first is technical: "Here is a verbal contraption. How does it work?" The second is, in the broadest sense, moral: "What kind of a guy inhabits this poem? What is his notion of the good life or the good place? His notion of the Evil One? What does he conceal from the reader? What does he conceal even from himself?"
Ib. II, Making, Knowing and Judging

11 Whatever its actual content and overt interest, every poem is rooted in imaginative awe. Poetry can do a hundred and one things, delight, sadden, disturb, amuse, instruct—it may express every possible shade of emotion, and describe every conceivable kind of event, but there is only one thing that all poetry must do; it must praise all it can for being and for happening. *Ib.*

Jacques Barzun
1907–

12 Whoever wants to know the heart and mind of America had better learn baseball, the rules and realities of the game—and do it by watching first some high school or small-town teams.
God's Country and Mine [1954]

Rachel Louise Carson
1907–1964

13 The sea lies all about us. The commerce of all lands must cross it. The very winds that move over the lands have been cradled on its broad expanse and seek ever to return to it. The continents themselves dissolve and pass to the sea, in grain after grain of eroded land. So the rains that rose from it return again in rivers. In its mysterious past it encompasses all the dim origins of life and receives in the end, after, it may be, many transmutations, the dead husks of that same life. For all at last returns to the sea—to Oceanus, the ocean river, like the ever-flowing stream of time, the beginning and the end.
The Sea Around Us [1951], ch. 14, ending

[1] See Sommer, 910:12.
[2] See Shakespeare, 245:17.

1 As crude a weapon as the cave man's club, the chemical barrage has been hurled against the fabric of life.

Silent Spring [1962]

Christopher Fry

1907–

2 I travel light; as light,
That is, as a man can travel who will
Still carry his body around because
Of its sentimental value.

The Lady's Not for Burning [1950], act I

3 Religion
Has made an honest woman of the supernatural.

Ib. II

4 Try thinking of love or something.
Amor vincit insomnia.[1]

A Sleep of Prisoners [1951]

Louis MacNeice

1907–1963

5 It's no go my honey love, it's no go my poppet;
Work your hands from day to day, the winds will blow the profit.
The glass is falling hour by hour, the glass will fall forever,
But if you break the bloody glass you won't hold up the weather.

Bagpipe Music, last stanza

6 The sunlight on the garden
Hardens and grows cold,
We cannot cage the minute
Within its net of gold,
When all is told
We cannot beg for pardon.

The Sunlight on the Garden, st. 1

John Wayne

1907–1979

7 Talk low, talk slow, and don't say too much.

Advice on acting

Simone de Beauvoir

1908–

8 I wish that every human life might be pure transparent freedom.

The Blood of Others (Le Sang des Autres) [1946]

[1]See Virgil, 103:*n*13.

9 This has always been a man's world, and none of the reasons hitherto brought forward in explanation of this fact has seemed adequate.

The Second Sex (Le Deuxième Sex) [1949–1950], pt. II, ch. 4

10 It is not in giving life but in risking life that man is raised above the animal; that is why superiority has been accorded in humanity not to the sex that brings forth but to that which kills.

Ib.

11 One is not born a woman, one becomes one.[2]

Ib. IV, 12

12 When we abolish the slavery of half of humanity, together with the whole system of hypocrisy that it implies, then the "division" of humanity will reveal its genuine significance and the human couple will find its true form.

Ib. VII. Conclusion

13 It is for man to establish the reign of liberty in the midst of the world of the given. To gain the supreme victory, it is necessary, for one thing, that by and through their natural differentiation men and women unequivocally affirm their brotherhood.

Ib.

Jacob Bronowski

1908–1974

14 Man is a singular creature. He has a set of gifts which make him unique among the animals: so that, unlike them, he is not a figure in the landscape — he is a shaper of the landscape. In body and in mind he is the explorer of nature, the ubiquitous animal, who did not find but has made his home in every continent.

The Ascent of Man [1973], ch. 1

15 Nature — that is, biological evolution — has not fitted man to any specific environment. . . . Among the multitude of animals which scamper, fly, burrow, and swim around us, man is the only one who is not locked into his environment. His imagination, his reason, his emotional subtlety and toughness, make it possible for him not to accept the environment but to change it.[3] And that series of inventions by which man from age to age has remade his environment is a different kind of evolution — not biological, but cultural evolution. I call that brilliant sequence of cultural peaks *The Ascent of Man.*

Ib.

[2]On ne naît pas femme, on le devient.
[3]See R. B. Fuller, 832:12.

Jacob Bronowski
1908–1974
and
Bruce Mazlish
1923–

1 Every thoughtful man who hopes for the creation of a contemporary culture knows that this hinges on one central problem: to find a coherent relation between science and the humanities.

The Western Intellectual Tradition [1960]

Howell M. Forgy
1908–

2 Praise the Lord and pass the ammunition.[1]

Said at Pearl Harbor [December 7, 1941]

John Kenneth Galbraith
1908–

3 One can relish the varied idiocy of human action during a panic to the full, for, while it is a time of great tragedy, nothing is being lost but money.

The Great Crash, 1929 [1955], ch. 1

4 The stock market is but a mirror which . . . provides an image of the underlying or *fundamental* economic situation. Cause and effect run from the economy to the stock market, never the reverse. In 1929 the economy was headed for trouble. Eventually that trouble was violently reflected in Wall Street.

Ib. 6

5 Men have been swindled by other men on many occasions. The autumn of 1929 was, perhaps, the first occasion when men succeeded on a large scale in swindling themselves. *Ib. 7*

6 When people are least sure, they are often most dogmatic. *Ib. 10*

7 It is a far, far better thing to have a firm anchor in nonsense than to put out on the troubled seas of thought.

The Affluent Society [1958], ch. 11

8 The myth that military power is a function of economic output. If peace and survival are to be achieved, the search must almost certainly go beyond the effort to find a balance in thermonuclear terror. *Ib. 12*

[1] Forgy was serving as chaplain on a cruiser at the time of the Japanese attack; the words were said to a chain of men handling ammunition. They were the basis of the song *Praise the Lord and Pass the Ammunition* [1942] by Frank Loesser [1910–1969].

9 Just as there must be balance in what a community produces, so there must also be balance in what the community consumes.

Ib. 17

10 The greater the wealth, the thicker will be the dirt. This indubitably describes a tendency of our time. *Ib.*

11 In a community where public services have failed to keep abreast of private consumption things are very different. Here, in an atmosphere of private opulence and public squalor, the private goods have full sway.

Ib. 18

12 Nothing so weakens government as persistent inflation. *Ib.*

13 Social imbalance reflects itself in inability to enforce laws, including significantly those which protect and advance basic social justice, and in failure to maintain and improve essential services. . . . Over much of the world, there is a rough and not accidental correlation between the strength of indigenous Communist parties or the frequency of revolutions and the persistence of inflation.

Ib.

14 The leisured class has been replaced by another and much larger class to which work has none of the older connotation of pain, fatigue, or other mental or physical discomfort. We have failed to observe the emergence of this New Class, as it may be simply called.

Ib. 24

15 People are the common denominator of progress. So . . . no improvement is possible with unimproved people, and advance is certain when people are liberated and educated. It would be wrong to dismiss the importance of roads, railroads, power plants, mills, and the other familiar furniture of economic development. . . . But we are coming to realize . . . that there is a certain sterility in economic monuments that stand alone in a sea of illiteracy. Conquest of illiteracy comes first.

Economic Development [1964], ch. 2

16 Affluence adds to the need for . . . stabilization of aggregate demand. A man who lives close to the margin of subsistence must spend to exist and what he spends is spent. A man with ample income can save . . . Moreover, a rich society owes its productivity and income, at least in part, to large-scale organization—to the corporation.

The New Industrial State [1967], ch. 1

1 The imperatives of technology and organization, not the images of ideology, are what determine the shape of economic society.

Ib.

2 We are becoming the servants in thought, as in action, of the machine we have created to serve us. *Ib.*

3 The enemy of the market is not ideology but the engineer. *Ib. 3*

4 The individual serves the industrial system not by supplying it with savings and the resulting capital; he serves it by consuming its products. *Ib. 4*

5 It was with Malthus and Ricardo that economics became the dismal science.[1]

The Age of Uncertainty [1977], ch. 1

Lyndon Baines Johnson
1908–1973

6 Come now, let us reason together.[2]

Saying

7 I am a free man, an American, a United States Senator, and a Democrat, in that order.

Quoted by Adlai Stevenson *in his introduction to* Johnson, *A Time for Action [1964]*

8 All I have I would have given gladly not to be standing here today.

First address to Congress as President [November 27, 1963]

9 We have talked long enough in this country about equal rights. We have talked for a hundred years or more. It is time now to write the next chapter—and to write in the books of law. *Ib.*

10 Unfortunately many Americans live on the outskirts of hope—some because of their poverty, some because of their color, and all too many because of both. Our task is to help replace their despair with opportunity.[3]

First State of the Union Message [January 8, 1964]

11 The challenge of the next half century is whether we have the wisdom to use [our] wealth to enrich and elevate our national life—and to advance the quality of American civilization.

Speech at the University of Michigan [May 22, 1964]

12 We still seek no wider war.

Radio/television speech [August 4, 1964] on the Gulf of Tonkin resolution

13 This nation, this generation, in this hour has man's first chance to build a Great Society,[4] a place where the meaning of man's life matches the marvels of man's labor.

Address, accepting the presidential nomination [August 1964]

Otto Kerner, Jr.
1908–1976

14 Our nation is moving toward two societies, one black, one white—separate and unequal.

Report of the National Advisory Commission on Civil Disorders [1968], p. 1

Abraham Harold Maslow
1908–1970

15 A musician must make music, an artist must paint, a poet must write, if he is to be ultimately at peace with himself. What a man can be, he must be.

Motivation and Personality [1954]

Edward Roscoe Murrow
1908–1965

16 This—is London.

Opening phrase for broadcasts from London during World War II [1939–1945]

17 We must not confuse dissent with disloyalty.

See It Now (broadcast). Report on Senator Joseph R. McCarthy [March 7, 1954]

18 We will not be driven by fear into an age of unreason if we . . . remember that we are not descended from fearful men, not from men who feared to write, to speak, to associate and to defend causes which were, for the moment unpopular. *Ib.*

19 I am entirely persuaded that the American public is more reasonable, restrained and mature than most of the broadcast industry's planners believe. Their fear of controversy is not warranted by the evidence.

Speech at the Radio and Television News Directors Convention, Chicago [October 15, 1958]

[1] See Carlyle, 474:11.
[2] See *Isaiah 1:18*, 28:30.
[3] See Michael Harrington, 908:5.
[4] See Lippmann, 814:1.

1 In order to progress, radio need only go backward, to the time when singing commercials were not allowed on news reports, when there was no middle commercial on a news report, when radio was rather proud, alert and fast. *Ib.*

Theodore Roethke

1908–1963

2 My secrets cry aloud.
I have no need for tongue.
My heart keeps open house,
My doors are widely flung.
Open House [1941], st. 1

3 Thought does not crush to stone.
The great sledge drops in vain.
Truth never is undone;
His shafts remain.
The Adamant [1941], st. 1

4 For something is amiss or out of place
When mice with wings can wear a human face. *The Bat [1941], st. 5*

5 This urge, wrestle, resurrection of dry sticks,
Cut stems struggling to put down feet,
What saint strained so much,
Rose on such lopped limbs to a new life?
Cuttings Later [1948]

6 Nothing would sleep in that cellar.
Root Cellar [1948]

7 Nothing would give up life:
Even the dirt kept breathing a small breath.
Ib.

8 Tugging all day at perverse life:
The indignity of it!
The Weed Puller [1948]

9 And afterwards I always felt mean, jogging back over the logging road,
As if I had broken the natural order of things in that swampland;
Disturbed some rhythm, old and of vast importance,
By pulling off flesh from the living planet;
As if I had committed, against the whole scheme of life, a desecration.
Moss Gathering [1948]

10 The whiskey on your breath
Could make a small boy dizzy;
But I hung on like death:
Such waltzing was not easy.
My Papa's Waltz [1948], st. 1

11 I study the lives on a leaf: the little
Sleepers, numb nudgers in cold dimensions,
Beetles in caves, newts, stone-deaf fishes,
Lice tethered to long limp subterranean weeds,
Squirmers in bogs,
And bacterial creepers.
The Minimal [1948]

12 At Woodlawn I heard the dead cry;
I was lulled by the slamming of iron,
A slow drip over stones,
Toads brooding in wells.
All the leaves stuck out their tongues;
I shook the softening chalk of my bones,
Saying,
Snail, snail, glister me forward,
Bird, soft-sigh me home.
Worm, be with me.
This is my hard time.
The Lost Son [1948], I

13 Fear was my father, Father Fear.
His look drained the stones. *Ib. III*

14 A lively understandable spirit
Once entertained you.
It will come again.
Be still.
Wait. *Ib. V*

15 And the new plants, still awkward in their soil,
The lovely diminutives.
I could watch! I could watch!
I saw the separateness of all things!
A Field of Light [1948], III

16 To follow the drops sliding from a lifted oar,
Head up, while the rower breathes, and the small boat drifts quietly shoreward;
To know that light falls and fills, often without our knowing.
The Shape of the Fire [1948], V

17 I remember the neckcurls, limp and damp as tendrils,
And her quick look a sidelong pickerel smile.
Elegy for Jane [1953]

18 I take this cadence from a man named Yeats;
I take it, and I give it back again.
Four for Sir John Davies [1953], I. The Dance

19 All lovers live by longing, and endure:
Summon a vision and declare it pure.
Ib. IV. The Vigil

20 Who rise from flesh to spirit know the fall:
The word outleaps the world, and light is all.
Ib. 4

21 I wake to sleep,[1] and take my waking slow.
I feel my fate in what I cannot fear.
I learn by going where I have to go.
The Waking [1953]

[1] See Montaigne, 165:9.

1 I knew a woman, lovely in her bones,
When small birds sighed, she would sigh back at them;
Ah, when she moved, she moved more ways than one:
The shapes a bright container can contain!
I Knew a Woman [1958]

2 I weep for what I'm like when I'm alone.
The Sententious Man [1958], st. 6

3 Each one's himself yet each one's everyone.
Ib.

4 When I was a lark, I sang;
When I was a worm, I devoured.
What Can I Tell My Bones? [1958]

5 I live in light's extreme; I stretch in all directions;
Sometimes I think I'm several. *Ib.*

6 The sun! The sun! And all we can become!
And the time ripe for running to the moon!
In the long fields, I leave my father's eye;
And shake the secrets from my deepest bones;
My spirit rises with the rising wind.
Ib.

7 I long for the imperishable quiet at the heart of form. *The Longing [1964]*

8 Old men should be explorers?[1]
I'll be an Indian.
Ogalala?
Iroquois. *Ib.*

9 Now, in this waning of light,
I rock with the motion of morning;
In the cradle of all that is,
I'm lulled into half-sleep
By the lapping of water,
Cries of the sandpiper.
Water's my will, and my way,
And the spirit runs, intermittently,
In and out of the small waves,
Runs with the intrepid shorebirds—
How graceful the small before danger!

In the first of the moon,
All's a scattering,
A shining.
Meditation at Oyster River [1964], IV

10 What I love is near at hand,
Always, in earth and air.
The Far Field [1964], III

11 All finite things reveal infinitude.
Ib. IV

[1] See T. S. Eliot, 807:24.

12 Light listened when she sang.
Light Listened [1964], st. 4

13 I am most immoderately married:
The Lord God has taken my heaviness away;
I have merged, like the bird, with the bright air,
And my thought flies to the place by the bo-tree.

Being, not doing, is my first joy.
The Abyss [1964], V

14 We end in joy.
The Moment [1964], last line

15 In a dark time, the eye begins to see.
In a Dark Time [1964], st. 1

16 A steady storm of correspondences!
A night flowing with birds, a ragged moon,
And in broad day the midnight come again!
Ib. st. 3

17 Was I too glib about eternal things,
An intimate of air and all its songs?
Pure aimlessness pursued and yet pursued
And all wild longings of the insatiate blood
Brought me down to my knees. O who can be
Both moth and flame? The weak moth blundering by.
Whom do we love? I thought I knew the truth;
Of grief I died, but no one knew my death.
The Sequel [1964], I

18 The soul has many motions, body one.
The Motion [1964], I

19 Love begets love. This torment is my joy.
Ib. II

20 Rising or falling's all one discipline!
The line of my horizon's growing thin!
Which is the way? I cry to the dread black,
The shifting shade, the cinders at my back.
Which is the way? I ask, and turn to go,
As a man turns to face on-coming snow.
The Decision [1964], II

21 What's the worst portion in this mortal life?
A pensive mistress, and a yelping wife.
The Marrow [1964], I

22 Brooding on God, I may become a man.
Pain wanders through my bones like a lost fire;
What burns me now? Desire, desire, desire.
Ib. II

23 Lord, hear me out, and hear me out this day:
From me to Thee's a long and terrible way.
Ib. III

1 Yea, I have slain my will, and still I live;
I would be near; I shut my eyes to see;
I bleed my bones, their marrow to bestow
Upon that God who knows what I would know.
Ib. IV

2 The present falls, the present falls away;
How pure the motion of the rising day,
The white sea widening on a farther shore.
The bird, the beating bird, extending wings—
Thus I endure this last pure stretch of joy,
The dire dimension of a final thing.
The Tree, the Bird [1964]

3 Let others probe the mystery if they can.
Time-harried prisoners of *Shall* and *Will*—
The right thing happens to the happy man.

The bird flies out, the bird flies back again;
The hill becomes the valley, and is still;
Let others delve that mystery if they can.
The Right Thing [1964], st. 1, 2

4 Now I adore my life
With the Bird, the abiding Leaf,
With the Fish, the questing Snail,
And the Eye altering all;
And I dance with William Blake
For love, for Love's sake.
Once More, the Round [1964]

William Saroyan

1908–

5 The Time of Your Life.
Title of play [1939]

6 If you give to a thief he cannot steal from you, and he is then no longer a thief.
The Human Comedy [1943], ch. 4

Victor Frederick Weisskopf

1908–

7 In man's brain the impressions from outside are not merely registered; they produce concepts and ideas. They are the imprint of the external world upon the human brain. Therefore, it is not surprising that, after a long period of searching and erring, some of the concepts and ideas in human thinking should have come gradually closer to the fundamental laws of this world, that some of our thinking should reveal the true structure of atoms and the true movements of the stars. Nature, in the form of man, begins to recognize itself.
Knowledge and Wonder [1962]

Richard Wright

1908–1960

8 Goddammit, look! We live here and they live there. We black and they white. They got things and we ain't. They do things and we can't. It's just like living in jail.
Native Son [1940]

9 Who knows when some slight shock, disturbing the delicate balance between social order and thirsty aspiration, shall send the skyscrapers in our cities toppling? *Ib.*

10 If we had been allowed to participate in the vital processes of America's national growth, what would have been the textures of our lives, the pattern of our traditions, the routine of our customs, the state of our arts, the code of our laws, the function of our government! . . . We black folk say that America would have been stronger and greater.
Twelve Million Black Voices [1941]

James Agee

1909–1955

11 Now is the night one blue dew.
A Death in the Family [1957], Knoxville: Summer 1915

12 Sleep, soft smiling, draws me unto her: and those receive me, who quietly treat me, as one familiar and well-beloved in that home: but will not, oh, will not, not now, not ever; but will not ever tell me who I am.
Ib.

Paul Brooks

1909–

13 We shall never understand the natural environment until we see it as a living organism. Land can be healthy or sick, fertile or barren, rich or poor, lovingly nurtured or bled white. Our present attitudes and laws governing the ownership and use of land represent an abuse of the concept of private property . . . In America today you can murder land for private profit. You can leave the corpse for all to see, and nobody calls the cops.
The Pursuit of Wilderness [1971], ch. 1

Dazai Osamu [Tsushima Shuji]

1909–1948

14 My unhappiness was the unhappiness of a person who could not say no.
No Longer Human

Edwin Herbert Land

1909–

1 The bottom line is in heaven.

Reply [1977] rejecting view that only the bottom line of the balance sheet shows the worth of a product

Stanislaw Jerzy Lec

1909–1966

2 One has to multiply thoughts to the point where there aren't enough policemen to control them. *Unkempt Thoughts [1962]*[1]

3 Proverbs contradict each other. That is the wisdom of a nation. *Ib.*

4 No snowflake in an avalanche ever feels responsible.

More Unkempt Thoughts [1968][1]

5 Get out of the way of Justice. She is blind. *Ib.*

6 Prolong human life only when you can shorten its miseries. *Ib.*

7 Most of the sighs we hear have been edited. *Ib.*

Malcolm Lowry

1909–1957

8 Malcolm Lowry
Late of the Bowery
His prose was flowery
And often glowery
He lived, nightly, and drank, daily,
And died playing the ukelele. *Epitaph*

9 Success is like some horrible disaster
Worse than your house burning.[2]

After publication of Under the Volcano [1962]

10 Fame like a drunkard consumes the house of
the soul. *Ib.*

11 Ah, that I had never suffered this treacherous kiss
And had been left in darkness forever to
founder and fail. *Ib.*

Elting Elmore Morison

1909–

12 The computer is no better than its program.

Men, Machines and Modern Times [1966]

[1]Translated by Jacek Galazka.
[2]See Cunninghame-Graham, 670:11.

13 From Knowhow to Nowhere.

Title of book [1975]

Cyril Northcote Parkinson

1909–

14 Work expands so as to fill the time available for its completion.

Parkinson's Law [1957], ch. 1

Stephen Spender

1909–

15 I think continually of those who were truly
great—
The names of those who in their lives fought
for life,
Who wore at their hearts the fire's center.

I Think Continually of Those

16 Born of the sun they traveled a short while
towards the sun,
And left the vivid air signed with their honor.

Ib.

Simone Weil

1909–1943

17 Attachment is the great fabricator of illusions; reality can be attained only by someone who is detached.

Gravity and Grace (La Pesanteur et la Grace) [1947]

18 Purity is the ability to contemplate defilement. *Ib.*

19 Man alone can enslave man.

Oppression and Liberty [1958]. Reflections Concerning the Causes of Liberty and Social Oppression

20 What a country calls its vital economic interests are not the things which enable its citizens to live, but the things which enable it to make war. Gasoline is much more likely than wheat to be a cause of international conflict.

The Need for Roots (L'Enracinement) [1949]

Eudora Welty

1909–

21 I haven't a literary life at all, not much of a confession, maybe. But I do feel that the people and things I love are of a true and human world, and there is no clutter about

them. . . . I would not understand a literary life.

Selected Stories of Eudora Welty [1943], introduction

1 The storm had rolled away to faintness like a wagon crossing a bridge.

A Curtain of Green [1941]. A Piece of News

2 The excursion is the same when you go looking for your sorrow as when you go looking for your joy.

The Wide Net [1943]. The Wide Net

3 Beauty is . . . associated with reticence, with stubbornness, of a number of kinds. It arises somehow from a desire not to comply with what may be expected, but to act inevitably, as long as some human truth is in sight, whatever that inevitability may call for. Beauty is not a means . . . it is a result; it belongs to ordering, to form, to aftereffect.

The Eye of the Story [1979]. On Writing. Looking at Short Stories

4 Relationship is a pervading and changing mystery; it is not words that make it so in life, but words have to make it so in a story. Brutal or lovely, the mystery waits for people wherever they go, whatever extreme they run to.

Ib. Writing and Analyzing a Story

Jean Anouilh

1910–

5 Orpheus — they've gone on now, the good as well as the bad. . . . They've done their little song and dance in your life. . . . They are that way in you now, forever.

Eurydice [1942]

6 This horror and all these useless gestures, this grotesque adventure is ours. We must live it. Death is absurd also.

Romeo and Jeannette [1946]

7 And under this carnival disguise the heart of an old youngster who is still waiting to give his all. But how to be recognized under this mask? This is what they call a fine career.

The Waltz of the Toreadors [1952]. English version

Jimmy Cannon

1910–1973

8 He's a credit to his race — the human race.

On Joe Louis

Tony [Two-Ton] Galento

1910–1979

9 I'll moider de bum.

Before his unsuccessful fight with Joe Louis for the heavyweight championship [June 28, 1939]

Jean Genet

1910–

10 To achieve harmony in bad taste is the height of elegance.

The Thief's Journal (Le Journal du Voleur) [1949]

11 I was already refusing to have taste. I forbade myself to have it. I knew that the cultivation of it would have not refined me but softened me. *Ib.*

12 I call saintliness not a state but the moral procedure leading to it.

Quoted by Jean Paul Sartre in Saint Genet [1952]

Thomas Anthony Harris

1910–

13 I'm OK — You're OK.[1]

Title of book [1969]

George Caspar Homans

1910–

14 Liberty is a beloved discipline.

The Human Group [1950], ch. 12

Wright Morris

1910–

15 In the dry places . . . towns, like weeds, spring up when it rains, dry up when it stops. But in a dry climate the husk of the plant remains. The stranger might find, as if preserved in amber, something of the green life that was once lived there, and the ghosts of men who have gone on to a better place. The withered towns are empty, but not uninhabited. *The Works of Love [1952], ch. 1*

David Morris Potter

1910–1971

16 Democracy is clearly most appropriate for countries which enjoy an economic surplus

[1] See Anonymous, 921:19.

and least appropriate for countries where there is an economic insufficiency.

People of Plenty: Economic Abundance and the American Character [1954]

Don K. Price

1910–

1 Science . . . cannot exist on the basis of a treaty of strict nonaggression with the rest of society; from either side, there is no defensible frontier.

Government and Science [1954]

Elizabeth Bishop

1911–1979

2 This iceberg cuts its facets from within.
Like jewelry from a grave
It saves itself perpetually and adorns
Only itself.

The Imaginary Iceberg [1946], st. 3

3 Icebergs behoove the soul
(Both being self-made from elements least visible)
To see them so: fleshed, fair, erected, indivisible. *Ib.*

4 Think of the storm roaming the sky uneasily
like a dog looking for a place to sleep in,
listen to it growling.

Little Exercise [1946], st. 1

5 Until everything
was rainbow, rainbow, rainbow!
And I let the fish go. *The Fish [1946]*

6 Cold dark deep and absolutely clear,
element bearable to no mortal,
to fish and to seals . . .

At the Fishhouses [1955]

7 It is like what we imagine knowledge to be:
dark, salt, clear, moving, utterly free,
drawn from the cold hard mouth
of the world, derived from the rocky breasts
forever, flowing and drawn, and since
our knowledge is historical, flowing, and flown. *Ib.*

8 From Brooklyn, over the Brooklyn Bridge, on
this fine morning, please come flying.

Invitation to Miss Marianne Moore [1955], st. 1

9 Should we have stayed at home,
wherever that may be?

Questions of Travel [1965]

10 *Time to plant tears,* says the almanac.
The grandmother sings to the marvelous stove
and the child draws another inscrutable house. *Sestina [1965]*

11 The staring sailor
that shakes his watch
that tells the time
of the poet, the man
that lies in the house of Bedlam.

Visits to St. Elizabeths [1965], st. 11

12 He was all white, like a doll
that hadn't been painted yet.

First Death in Nova Scotia [1965], st. 4

13 I knew that nothing stranger
had ever happened.

In the Waiting Room [1976]

14 How had I come to be here
like them, and overhear
a cry of pain that could have
got loud and worse but hadn't? *Ib.*

15 Homemade, homemade! But aren't we all?

Crusoe in England [1976]

16 Why didn't I know enough of something? *Ib.*

17 I'd have
nightmares of other islands
stretching away from mine, infinities
of islands, islands spawning islands
like frogs' eggs turning into polliwogs
of islands, knowing that I had to live
on each and every one, eventually,
for ages, registering their flora,
their fauna, their geography. *Ib.*

18 And Friday, my dear Friday, died of measles
seventeen years ago come March. *Ib.*

19 Life and the memory of it cramped,
dim, on a piece of Bristol board.

Poem [1976]

20 Yesterday brought to today so lightly!
(A yesterday I find almost impossible to lift.)

Five Flights Up [1976]

Max Frisch

1911–

21 Technology . . . the knack of so arranging the world that we don't have to experience it.

Homo Faber [1957]

William Golding

1911–

22 The Lord of the Flies.

Title of book [1954]

Hubert Horatio Humphrey
1911–1978

1 The politics of joy.
Presidential campaign slogan [1968]

2 Compassion is not weakness, and concern for the unfortunate is not socialism.
Remark

3 Some people look upon any setback as the end. They're always looking for the benediction rather than the invocation. . . . But you can't quit. That isn't the way our country was built. *Remark*

Clark Kerr
1911–

4 The university has become the multiversity and the nature of the presidency has followed this change. . . . The president of the multiversity is leader, educator, wielder of power, pump; he is also officeholder, caretaker, inheritor, consensus seeker, persuader, bottleneck. But he is mostly a mediator.
The Uses of the University. The Godkin lectures at Harvard University [1963]

Marshall Herbert McLuhan
1911–

5 The medium is the message.
Understanding Media [1964], title of first chapter

6 The new electronic interdependence re-creates the world in the image of a global village.
The Medium Is the Message [1967]

Kenneth Patchen
1911–1972

7 Let us have madness openly, O men
Of my generation. Let us follow
The footsteps of this slaughtered age.
Let Us Have Madness Openly [1936]

8 There is no betrayal in the human face.
Time's fin, hoof, wing, and fang struggle
there.
To Whom It May Concern [1939]

9 I'd like to die like this . . .
with the dark fingers of the water
closing and unclosing over these sleepy lights
and a sad bell somewhere murmuring good
night.
Crossing on Staten Island Ferry [1939]

10 Do I not deal with angels
When her lips I touch.
For Miriam [1942]

11 I am come to her wonder
Like a boy finding a star in a haymow
And there is nothing cruel or mad or evil
Anywhere. *Ib.*

12 Great mother of big apples it is a pretty
World!
I Feel Drunk All the Time [1945]

13 I don't know how the rest of you feel,
But I feel drunk all the time. *Ib.*

14 I am the magical mouse
I don't eat cheese
I eat sunsets
And the tops of trees.
The Magical Mouse [1952], st. 1

15 Oh lonesome's a bad place
To get crowded into.
Lonesome Boy Blues [1952]

Ernst Friedrich Schumacher
1911–1977

16 Small Is Beautiful: Economics As If People Mattered. *Title of book [1973]*

17 A census . . . treats people as if they were units, whereas they are not. Each is a universe. *Good Work [1979], ch. 6*

Jorge Amado
1912–

18 Color of cinnamon
Clove's sweet smell,
I've come a long way
To see Gabrielle.
Gabriela, Clove and Cinnamon (Gabriela, Cravo e Canela) [1958], epigraph

John Cheever
1912–

19 Fear tastes like a rusty knife and do not let her into your house. Courage tastes of blood. Stand up straight. Admire the world. Relish the love of a gentle woman. Trust in the Lord.
The Wapshot Chronicle [1957], ch. 36, end

20 This is a night when kings in golden mail ride their elephants over the mountains.
The Stories of John Cheever [1978], preface

1 The deep joy we take in the company of people with whom we have just recently fallen in love is undisguisable.
Ib. The Bus to St. James

2 For lovers, touch is metamorphosis. All the parts of their bodies seem to change, and they become something different and better.
Ib.

3 Homesickness is . . . absolutely nothing. Fifty percent of the people in the world are homesick all the time . . . You don't really long for another country. You long for something in yourself that you don't have, or haven't been able to find.
Ib. The Bella Lingua

Lawrence George Durrell

1912–

4 So the riders of the darkness pass
On their circuit: the luminous island
Of the self trembles and waits,
Waits for us all, my friends,
Where the sea's big brush recolors
The dying lives, and the unborn smiles.
Fangbrand [1946], last stanza

5 I felt once more the strange equivocal power of the city—its flat alluvial landscape and exhausted airs . . . Alexandria; which is neither Greek, Syrian nor Egyptian, but a hybrid: a joint. *Justine [1957], pt. I*

6 We are the children of our landscape; it dictates behavior and even thought in the measure to which we are responsive to it.
Ib.

Milton Friedman

1912–

7 Positive economics is in principle independent of any particular ethical position or normative judgments . . . In short, positive economics is or can be an "objective" science.
Essays in Positive Economics [1953], pt. I, ch. 1

8 Factual evidence can never "prove" a hypothesis; it can only fail to disprove it, which is what we generally mean when we say, somewhat inexactly, that the hypothesis is "confirmed" by experience. *Ib.*

9 Economics as a positive science is a body of tentatively accepted generalizations about economic phenomena that can be used to predict the consequences of changes in circumstances. *Ib.*

10 The construction of hypotheses is a creative act of inspiration, intuition, invention; its essence is the vision of something new in familiar material. *Ib.*

11 Freedom in economic arrangements is itself a component of freedom broadly understood, so economic freedom is an end in itself . . . Economic freedom is also an indispensable means toward the achievement of political freedom.
Capitalism and Freedom [1962], ch. 1

12 History suggests that capitalism is a necessary condition for political freedom. Clearly it is not a sufficient condition. *Ib.*

13 Fundamentally, there are only two ways of coordinating the economic activities of millions. One is central direction involving the use of coercion—the technique of the army and of the modern totalitarian state. The other is voluntary cooperation of individuals—the technique of the marketplace.
Ib.

14 The Great Depression, like most other periods of severe unemployment, was produced by government mismanagement rather than by any inherent instability of the private economy. *Ib.*

15 The long-range solution [to high unemployment] is to increase the incentive for ordinary people to save, invest, work and employ others. We make it costly for employers to employ people, and we subsidize people not to go to work. We have a system that increasingly taxes work and subsidizes nonwork.
In U.S. News & World Report [March 7, 1977]

16 I would cut the real taxes borne by the American people by cutting all government spending 10 percent across the board.
Ib.

17 There's only one place where inflation is made: that's in Washington . . . in response to pressures from the people at large . . . The voting public . . . ask their Congressmen to enact goodies in the form of spending, but they are unhappy about having taxes raised to pay for those goodies. *Ib.*

18 The government first provides very poor schooling, and then the harm is multiplied by the minimum wage law, which makes it difficult . . . to get on-the-job training. Without the minimum wage law, the least skilled could offer to work for low wages, which would provide an incentive for employers to hire and train them. *Ib.*

Woody [Woodrow Wilson] Guthrie

1912–1967

1 This land is your land, this land is my land,
From California to the New York island,
From the redwood forest to the Gulf Stream
waters,
This land was made for you and me.

This Land Is Your Land [1956]

Eugène Ionesco

1912–

2 Take a perfect circle, caress it and you'll have a vicious circle.

The Bald Soprano (La Cantatrice Chauve) [1950]

3 We haven't the time to take our time.

Exit the King (Le Roi Se Meurt) [1963]

4 Explanation separates us from astonishment, which is the only gateway to the incomprehensible. *Découvertes [1969]*

Pope John Paul I [Albino Luciani]

1912–1978

5 If all the sons and daughters of the Church would know how to be tireless missionaries of the Gospel, a new flowering of holiness and renewal would spring up in this world that thirsts for love and for truth.

Homily at the mass celebrating his installation [September 3, 1978]

6 He is Father. Even more, God is Mother, who does not want to harm us.[1]

At Sunday Angelus blessing, St. Peter's Square [September 17, 1978]

7 I am only a poor man, accustomed to small things and silence.

Illustrissimi [1978], epilogue

Mary McCarthy

1912–

8 The Man in the Brooks Brothers Shirt.

The Company She Keeps [1942]. Title of story

[1]See Suti and Hor, 5:3; Eddy, 583:1; and O'Neill, 810:10.

David Rousset

1912–

9 Concentration Camp Universe [L'Univers Concentrationnaire].

Title of book [1946][2]

Studs [Louis] Terkel

1912–

10 Perhaps it is this specter that most haunts working men and women: the planned obsolescence of people that is of a piece with the planned obsolescence of the things they make. Or sell.

Working [1972], introduction

George Barker

1913–

11 Fiend behind the fiend behind the fiend be-
hind the
Fiend. Mastodon with mastery, monster with
an ache
At the tooth of the ego, the dead drunk
judge:
Wheresoever Thou art our agony will find
Thee
Enthroned on the darkest altar of our heart-
break
Perfect. Beast, brute, bastard. O dog my God!

Sacred Elegy V [1943], iv

Menachem Begin

1913–

12 Who will condemn the hatred of evil that springs from the love of what is good and just? *The Revolt [1951],*[3] *introduction*

13 If you love freedom, you must hate slavery; if you love your people, you cannot but hate the enemies that compass their destruction; if you love your country, you cannot but hate those who seek to annex it. *Ib.*

14 The ancient Jewish people gave the New World a vision of eternal peace, of universal disarmament, of abolishing the teaching and learning of war.

On signing the Egyptian-Israeli peace treaty, Washington, D.C. [March 26, 1979][4]

15 A great day in the annals of two ancient nations, Egypt and Israel, whose sons met in battle five times, fighting and falling. . . . It is thanks to our fallen heroes that we could have reached this day. *Ib.*

[2]Translated as *The Other Kingdom* by Ramon Guthrie.
[3]Translated by Samuel Katz.
[4]See Sadat, 895:17.

1 No more wars, no more bloodshed. Peace unto you. Shalom, salaam, forever. *Ib.*

Albert Camus

1913–1960

2 Mother died today, or maybe it was yesterday.

The Stranger (L'Étranger) [1942], I

3 For the first time, the first, I laid my heart open to the benign indifference of the universe. To feel it so like myself, indeed, so brotherly, made me realize that I'd been happy, and that I was happy still.

Ib. IV

4 The absurd is essentially a divorce. It is in neither one nor the other of the compared elements. It is born of their confrontation.

Le Mythe de Sisyphe [1942]

5 The absurd is the essential concept and the first truth. *Ib.*

6 The struggle to reach the top is itself enough to fulfill the heart of man. One must believe that Sisyphus is happy. *Ib.*

7 It is not rebellion itself which is noble but the demands it makes upon us.

The Plague (La Peste) [1947]

8 Can one be a saint if God does not exist? That is the only concrete problem I know of today. *Ib.*

9 I shall tell you a great secret, my friend. Do not wait for the last judgment. It takes place every day. *The Fall (La Chute) [1956]*

10 Freedom of the press is perhaps the freedom that has suffered the most from the gradual degradation of the idea of liberty.

Resistance, Rebellion, and Death [1960] [1]

11 A free press can of course be good or bad, but, most certainly, without freedom it will never be anything but bad. . . . Freedom is nothing else but a chance to be better, whereas enslavement is a certainty of the worse. *Ib.*

12 Poe and the four conditions for happiness: (1) Life in the open air. (2) The love of another being. (3) Freedom from all ambition. (4) Creation.

Notebooks: 1935–1942 [1963], III, April 1939–February 1942

13 In the depth of winter, I finally learned that within me there lay an invincible summer.

Summer (L'Été) [1954]. Return to Tipasa

[1]Translated by JUSTIN O'BRIEN from selected essays in *Actuelles* [1950, 1953, 1958].

Gerald Rudolph Ford

1913–

14 I'm a Ford, not a Lincoln.

Comment after his nomination for the vice-presidency [October 12, 1973]

15 Our long national nightmare is over.

On being sworn in as President [August 9, 1974]

Donald Francis Mason

1913–

16 Sighted sub, sank same.

Radio message to U.S. Navy Base [January 28, 1942]

Richard Milhous Nixon

1913–

17 You won't have Nixon to kick around anymore, because, gentlemen, this is my last press conference.

To the press [November 7, 1962]

18 Bring us together again.

Speech in New York City [October 31, 1968]

19 The greatest honor history can bestow is the title of peacemaker. This honor now beckons America. . . . This is our summons to greatness.

Inaugural address [January 20, 1969]

20 Because of what you have done the heavens have become a part of man's world. And as you talk to us from the Sea of Tranquility, it inspires us to redouble our efforts to bring peace and tranquility to earth.

Phone call to the moon [July 20, 1969] [2]

21 The great silent majority.

Speech [November 3, 1969]

22 The Chinese are a great and vital people who should not remain isolated from the international community. . . . It is certainly in our interest, and in the interest of peace and stability in Asia and the world, that we take what steps we can toward improved practical relations with Peking.

First Foreign Policy Report to Congress [February 1970]

23 If when the chips are down, the world's most powerful nation . . . acts like a pitiful,

[2]See Armstrong, 910.

helpless giant, the forces of totalitarianism and anarchy will threaten free nations and free institutions throughout the world.

Televised speech [April 30, 1970] announcing major United States offensive into Cambodia

1 I want you all to stonewall it.

Presidential transcript [March 22, 1973]

2 I made my mistakes, but in all my years of public life I have never profited, *never* profited from public service. I have earned every cent. . . . I welcome this kind of examination because people have got to know whether or not their President is a crook. Well, I'm not a crook.

Press conference [November 11, 1973]

3 Always give your best, never get discouraged, never be petty; always remember, others may hate you. Those who hate you don't win unless you hate them. And then you destroy yourself.

Address to members of the administration on leaving office [August 9, 1974]

4 When the President does it, that means that it is not illegal.

Interview with David Frost [May 19, 1977]

Tillie Olsen

1913–

5 She would not exchange her solitude for anything. Never again to be forced to move to the rhythms of others.

Tell Me a Riddle [1960], title story, sec. 1

6 Women are traditionally trained to place others' needs first . . . their satisfaction to be in making it possible for others to use their abilities. *Silences [1978], pt. I*

7 Children need one *now* . . . The very fact that these are real needs, that one feels them as one's own (love, not duty); *that there is no one else responsible for these needs,* gives them primacy. It is distraction, not meditation, that becomes habitual; interruption, not continuity; spasmodic, not constant toil. . . . Unused capacities atrophy, cease to be.

Ib.

8 We are in a time of more and more hidden and foreground silences, women *and* men. Denied full writing life, more may try to "nurse through night" (that part-time, part-self night) "the ethereal spark," but it seems to me there would almost have had to be "flame on flame" first; and time as needed, afterwards; and enough of the self, the capacities, undamaged for the rebeginnings on the frightful task. *Ib.*

Muriel Rukeyser

1913–

9 Fly down, Death: Call me:
I have become a lost name.

Madboy's Song, refrain

Delmore Schwartz[1]

1913–1966

10 Time is the school in which we learn,
Time is the fire in which we burn.

For Rhoda [1938]

11 That inescapable animal walks with me.
Has followed me since the black womb held,
Moves where I move, distorting my gesture,
A caricature, a swollen shadow,
A stupid clown of the spirit's motive,
Perplexes and affronts with his own darkness,
The secret life of belly and bone.

The Heavy Bear Who Goes with Me, st. 3

Karl Shapiro

1913–

12 Haul up the flag, you mourners,
Not half-mast but all the way;
The funeral is done and disbanded;
The devil's had the final say.

Elegy for Two Banjos, st. 1, 14

Lewis Thomas

1913–

13 What is [the earth] *most* like? . . . It is *most* like a single cell.

The Lives of a Cell [1974]. The Lives of a Cell

14 There is really no such creature as a single individual; he has no more life of his own than a cast-off cell marooned from the surface of your skin.

Ib. Antaeus in Manhattan

15 An active field of science is like an immense anthill; the individual almost vanishes into the mass of minds tumbling

[1] See Robert Lowell, 892:15.

over each other, carrying information from place to place, passing it around at the speed of light. *Ib. Natural Science*

1 Viewed from the distance of the moon, the astonishing thing about the earth . . . is that it is alive. . . . Aloft, floating free beneath the moist, gleaming membrane of bright blue sky, is the rising earth, the only exuberant thing in this part of the cosmos. . . . It has the organized, self-contained look of a live creature, full of information, marvelously skilled in handling the sun.
Ib. The World's Biggest Membrane

2 We are a spectacular, splendid manifestation of life. We have language . . . We have affection. We have genes for usefulness, and usefulness is about as close to a "common goal" of nature as I can guess at. And finally, and perhaps best of all, we have music.
The Medusa and the Snail [1979]. The Youngest and Brightest Thing Around

3 We are, perhaps, uniquely among the earth's creatures, the worrying animal. We worry away our lives, fearing the future, discontent with the present, unable to take in the idea of dying, unable to sit still.
Ib.

4 Selfness is an essential fact of life. The thought of nonselfness, precise sameness, is terrifying.
Ib. On Cloning a Human Being

5 The only solid piece of scientific truth about which I feel totally confident is that we are profoundly ignorant about nature. . . . It is this sudden confrontation with the depth and scope of ignorance that represents the most significant contribution of twentieth-century science to the human intellect.
Ib.

6 We pass the word around; we ponder how the case is put by different people; we read the poetry; we meditate over the literature; we play the music; we change our minds; we reach an understanding. Society evolves this way, not by shouting each other down, but by the unique capacity of unique, individual human beings to comprehend each other.
Ib. On Committees

John Berryman

1914–1972

7 Huffy Henry hid the day,
Unappeasable Henry sulked.
77 Dream Songs [1964], poem no. 1

8 I don't see how Henry, pried
open for all the world to see, survived.
Ib.

9 Life, friends, is boring. We must not say so.
Ib. 14

10 Two daiquiris
withdrew into a corner of the gorgeous room
and one told the other a lie. *Ib. 16*

11 It's not a good position I am in.
If I had to do the whole thing over again
I wouldn't. *Ib. 28*

12 But never did Henry, as he thought he did,
end anyone and hacks her body up
and hide the pieces, where they may be found.
He knows: he went over everyone, & nobody's missing.
Often he reckons, in the dawn, them up.
Nobody is ever missing. *Ib. 29*

13 Something can (has) been said for sobriety
but very little. *Ib. 57*

14 But I do guess mos peoples gonna *lose.*
Ib. 60

15 The world is gradually becoming a place
where I do not care to be any more.
His Toy, His Dream, His Rest [1968], poem no. 149

16 I do this thrice a year; that is, I grope
a few sore hours among my actuals
for evidence of knighthood. *Ib. 163*

17 This world is a solemn place, with room for tennis. *Ib. 175*

18 It is a true error to marry with poets
or to be by them. *Ib. 187*

19 Decent fall the cloths
over a high income. *Ib. 196*

20 I saw in my dream
the great lost cities, Machu Picchu, Cambridge Mass., Angkor. *Ib. 197*

21 With shining strides hear his redeemer come,
in a hospital gown. *Ib. 202*

22 What was it missing, then, at the man's heart
so that he does not wound?
Ib. 219 (So Long? Stevens)

23 Perhaps God resembles one of the last etchings of Goya
& not Velasquez, never Rembrandt no.
Ib. 238 (Henry's Programme for God)

24 I always wanted to be old, I wanted to say
I haven't read that for fifteen years.
Ib. 264

1 Ingratitude is the necessary curse
of making things new. *Ib. 312*

2 I haven't lost a battle yet but I am tense
for the first losing. *Ib. 315*

3 Offering dragons quarter is no good,
they regrow all their parts & come on again,
they have to be killed. *Ib. 316*

4 When will indifference come. *Ib. 384*

Ralph Ellison

1914–

5 I am an invisible man. . . . I am a man of substance, of flesh and bone, fiber and liquids —and I might even be said to possess a mind. I am invisible, understand, simply because people refuse to see me.
The Invisible Man [1952], prologue

6 America is woven of many strands; I would recognize them and let it so remain. . . . Our fate is to become one, and yet many.
Ib. epilogue

John Hersey

1914–

7 There was no sound of planes. The morning was still; the place was cool and pleasant.

Then a tremendous flash of light cut across the sky. Mr. Tanimoto has a distinct recollection that it traveled from east to west, from the city toward the hills. It seemed a sheet of sun. Both he and Mr. Matsuo reacted in terror. . . . Under what seemed to be a local dust cloud, the day grew darker and darker.
Hiroshima [1946], ch. 1

8 There, in the tin factory, in the first moment of the atomic age, a human being was crushed by books. *Ib.*

Randall Jarrell

1914–1965

9 Nothing comes from nothing,
The darkness from the darkness. Pain comes
from the darkness
And we call it wisdom. It is pain.[1]
90 North [1955], st. 8

10 But I identify myself, as always,
With something that there's something
wrong with,
With something human.
The One Who Was Different [1965]

[1]See Aeschylus, 71:5.

Ross Parker

1914–

and

Hughie Charles

1907–

11 There'll Always Be an England.
Title of song [1939]

Nicanor Parra

1914–

12 Our Father who art where thou art
Surrounded by unfaithful Angels
Sincerely don't suffer any more for us
You must take into account
That the gods are not infallible
And that we have come to forgive everything.
Breathing Exercises (Ejercicios Respirato) [1966]. Our Father (Padre Nuestro),[2] st. 5

13 A little snow is starting to fall again.
Russian Songs (Canciones Rusas) [1967]. Snow[2]

Octavio Paz

1914–

14 Would it not be true to say that North Americans prefer to use reality rather than to know it?
The Labyrinth of Solitude (El Labrinto de la Soledad) [1950],[3] ch. 1

15 Love is an attempt at penetrating another being, but it can only succeed if the surrender is mutual. *Ib. ch. 2*

16 Contemporary man has rationalized the myths, but he has not been able to destroy them. *Ib. Appendix*

17 Solitude lies at the lowest depth of the human condition. Man is the only being who feels himself to be alone and the only one who is searching for the Other. *Ib.*

18 Touched by poetry, language is more fully language and at the same time is no longer language: it is a poem.
Claude Lévi-Strauss [1967],[3] ch. 3

19 Alienation, if such an overused word still has meaning, is not only the result of social systems, be they capitalist or socialist, but of the very nature of technology: the new means

[2]Translated by Miller Williams.
[3]Translated by Rachel Phillips.

of communication accentuate and strengthen noncommunication. *Ib. ch. 4*

1 We are condemned
to kill time:
Thus we die
bit by bit
Cuento de los Jardines [1968]

2 Political crises are moral crises.
Postscript (Posdata) [1970]

3 The supreme value is not the future but the present. The future is a deceitful time that always says to us, "Not yet," and thus denies us. The future is not the time of love: what man truly wants he wants *now.* Whoever builds a house for future happiness builds a prison for the present. *Ib.*

4 Criticism, the acid that dissolves images. . . . Criticism tells us that we should learn to dissolve the idols. *Ib.*

5 And the world is changed
if two people shaken by dizziness and enlaced
are fallen among the grass.
Configurations [1971]. Sun Stone (Piedra de Sol),[1] *l. 432*

6 My steps along this street
Resound
in another street
In which
I hear my steps
Passing along this street
In which

Only the mist is real. *Ib. Here (Aquí)*[2]

7 If man is dust
Those who go through the plain
Are men. *Ib. Apparition (Aparición)*[2]

8 The absolutes the eternities
Their outlying districts
Are not my theme
I am hungry for life and for death also
I know what I know and I write it.
Ib. Vrindaban,[3] *l. 152*

9 Western civilization should be feminized.
Seven Voices [1972], interview

10 There can be a "boom" in petroleum or wheat, but there can't be a boom in the novel and less still in poetry. *Ib.*

11 Modern art is modern because it is critical.
Children of the Mire (Los Hijos del Limo) [1974], ch. 6

[1]Translated by Muriel Rukeyser.
[2]Translated by Charles Tomlinson.
[3]Translated by Lysander Kemp.

Dylan Thomas

1914–1953

12 The force that through the green fuse drives the flower
Drives my green age; that blasts the roots of trees
Is my destroyer.
And I am dumb to tell the crooked rose
My youth is bent by the same wintry fever.
The Force That Through the Green Fuse Drives the Flower [1934]

13 Light breaks where no sun shines;
Where no sea runs, the waters of the heart
Push in their tides.
Light Breaks Where No Sun Shines [1934]

14 The hand that signed the paper felled a city;
Five sovereign fingers taxed the breath,
Doubled the globe of dead and halved a country;
These five kings did a king to death.
The Hand That Signed the Paper [1936]

15 When all my five and country senses see,
The fingers will forget green thumbs and mark
How, through the halfmoon's vegetable eye,
Husk of young stars and handfull zodiac,
Love in the frost is pared and wintered by.
When All My Five and Country Senses See [1939]

16 And death shall have no dominion.[4]
Refrain and title of poem [1943]

17 After the first death there is no other.
A Refusal to Mourn the Death, by Fire, of a Child in London [1946]

18 Forgotten mornings when he walked with his mother
Through the parables
Of sunlight
And the legend of the green chapels.
Poem in October [1946]

19 Now as I was young and easy under the apple boughs
About the lilting house and happy as the grass was green.
Fern Hill, st. 1 [1946]

20 And honored among wagons I was prince of the apple towns. *Ib.*

21 And the sabbath rang slowly
In the pebbles of the holy streams.
Ib. st. 2

[4]See *Romans 6:9, 47:3.*

1 In the sun that is young once only,
Time let me play and be
Golden in the mercy of his means. *Ib.*

2 And honored among foxes and pheasants by the gay house
Under the new-made clouds and happy as the heart was long,
In the sun born over and over,
I ran my heedless ways.
Ib. st. 5

3 Time held me green and dying
Though I sang in my chains like the sea.
Ib. st. 6

4 Do not go gentle into that good night,
Old age should burn and rave at close of day;
Rage, rage against the dying of the light.
Do Not Go Gentle into That Good Night [1952]

5 One Christmas was so much like another, in those years around the seatown corner now and out of all sound except the distant speaking of the voices I sometimes hear a moment before sleep, that I can never remember whether it snowed for six days and six nights when I was twelve or whether it snowed for twelve days and twelve nights when I was six.
Quite Early One Morning [1954]. A Child's Christmas in Wales

6 It is spring, moonless night in the small town, starless and bible-black.
Under Milk Wood [1954]

7 You can tear a poem apart to see what makes it technically tick. . . . You're back with the mystery of having been moved by words. The best craftsmanship always leaves holes and gaps in the works of the poem so that something that is *not* in the poem can creep, crawl, flash, or thunder in.

The joy and function of poetry is, and was, the celebration of man, which is also the celebration of man.
Dylan Thomas's Poetic Manifesto. In the Texas Quarterly [Winter 1961]

Tennessee Williams

1914–

8 Knowledge—Zzzzzp! Money—Zzzzzp!—Power! That's the cycle democracy is built on!
The Glass Menagerie [1945], sc. vii

9 A Streetcar Named Desire.
Title of play [1947]

10 Time rushes toward us with its hospital tray of infinitely varied narcotics, even while it is preparing us for its inevitably fatal operation.
The Rose Tattoo [1950]. Foreword, The Timeless World of a Play

11 Nothing's more determined than a cat on a tin roof—is there? Is there, baby?
Cat on a Hot Tin Roof[1] *[1955], act III, last line*

Saul Bellow

1915–

12 There was a disturbance in my heart, a voice that spoke there and said, *I want, I want, I want!* It happened every afternoon, and when I tried to suppress it it got even stronger. . . . It never said a thing except *I want, I want, I want!*
Henderson the Rain King [1959]

13 I am simply a human being, more or less.
Herzog [1964]

14 A novel is balanced between a few true impressions and the multitude of false ones that make up most of what we call life. It tells us that for every human being there is a diversity of existences, that the single existence is itself an illusion in part, that these many existences signify something, tend to something, fulfill something; it promises us meaning, harmony, and even justice. . . . Art attempts to find in the universe, in matter as well as in the facts of life, what is fundamental, enduring, essential.
Speech upon receiving the Nobel Prize [1976]

Jerome Seymour Bruner

1915–

15 The shrewd guess, the fertile hypothesis, the courageous leap to a tentative conclusion—these are the most valuable coin of the thinker at work.
The Process of Education [1960]

16 Any subject can be taught effectively in some intellectually honest form to any child at any stage of development. *Ib.*

Sir Peter Brian Medawar

1915–

17 The scientist values research by the size of its contribution to that huge, logically

[1]See John Ray, 301:17.

articulated structure of ideas which is already, though not yet half built, the most glorious accomplishment of mankind.
The Art of the Soluble [1967]

1 Among scientists are collectors, classifiers, and compulsive tidiers-up; many are detectives by temperament and many are explorers; some are artists and others artisans. There are poet-scientists and philosopher-scientists and even a few mystics. *Ib.*

Arthur Miller
1915–

2 I don't say he's a great man. Willy Loman never made a lot of money. His name was never in the paper. He's not the finest character that ever lived. But he's a human being, and a terrible thing is happening to him. So attention must be paid. He's not to be allowed to fall into his grave like an old dog. Attention, attention must be finally paid to such a person.
Death of a Salesman [1949], act I

3 Willy was a salesman. And for a salesman, there is no rock bottom to the life. He don't put a bolt to a nut, he don't tell you the law or give you medicine. He's a man way out there in the blue, riding on a smile and a shoeshine. And when they start not smiling back—that's an earthquake. And then you get yourself a couple of spots on your hat, and you're finished. Nobody dast blame this man. A salesman is got to dream, boy. It comes with the territory. *Ib. Requiem*

Jean Stafford
1915–

4 To her own heart, which was shaped exactly like a valentine, there came a winglike palpitation, a delicate exigency, and all the fragrance of all the flowery springtime love affairs that ever were seemed waiting for them in the whiskey bottle.
Children Are Bored on Sundays [1953], title story

Margaret Abigail Walker
1915–

5 For my people lending their strength to the years, the gone years and the now years and the maybe years.
For My People [1942], st. 2

6 Let a new earth rise. Let another world be born. . . . Let a beauty full of healing and a strength of final clenching be the pulsing in our spirits and our blood. Let the martial songs be written, let the dirges disappear. Let a race of men now rise and take control. *Ib. st. 10*

7 My grandmothers were strong.
They followed plows and bent to toil,
They moved through fields sowing seed.
They touched earth and grain grew.
Lineage [1942]

John Malcolm Brinnin
1916–

8 I seek a father who most need a son.
Oedipus: His Cradle Song [1963]

9 In their big peppermint hotels.
News from the Islands [1963]

10 Another hill town:
another dry Cinzano in the sun.
Hotel Paradiso è Commerciale [1963]

11 I start by the cats' corridors (Banco di Roma,
wineshops, gorgeous butcheries)
toward some mild angel of annunciation—
upstairs, most likely, badly lit,
speaking in rivets on a band of gold.
Ib.

12 We have all done this before; we're
bored and terrified.
Flight 539 [1963]

13 All of a sudden came the pelicans:
crazy old men in baseball caps, who flew
like jackknives and collapsed like fans.
Skin Diving in the Virgins [1970]

John Ciardi
1916–

14 It is by falling in and in we make
the all-bearing point, for one another's sake,
in faultless failing, raised by our own weight.
Most Like an Arch This Marriage [1958]

Walter Cronkite
1916–

15 And that's the way it is.
Sign-off sentence, CBS Evening News

Elizabeth Hardwick
1916–

1 Collaborating in the very private way of love or the highest kind of friendship . . . is the way for gifted, energetic wives of writers to a sort of composition of their own, this peculiar illusion of collaboration.
Seduction and Betrayal: Women in Literature [1974]. Amateurs

2 This is the unspoken contract of a wife and her works. In the long run wives are to be paid in a peculiar coin—consideration for their feelings. And it usually turns out this is an enormous, unthinkable inflation few men will remit, or if they will, only with a sense of being overcharged. *Ib.*

3 The raging productivity of the Victorians shattered nerves and punctured stomachs, but it was a thing noble, glorious, awesome in itself. *Ib.*

Walker Percy
1916–

4 The fact is I am quite happy in a movie, even a bad movie. Other people, so I have read, treasure memorable moments in their lives. *The Moviegoer [1961]*

Gwendolyn Brooks
1917–

5 Maud went to college.
Sadie stayed at home.
Sadie scraped life
With a fine-tooth comb.
A Street in Brownsville [1945]. Sadie and Maud, st. 1

6 People are so in need, in need of help.
People want so much that they do not know.
Ib. The Sundays of Satin-Legs Smith, st. 8

7 What shall I give my children? who are poor,
Who are adjudged the leastwise of the land.
Annie Allen [1949]. The Womanhood. The Children of the Poor, sonnet 2

8 And plenitude of plan shall not suffice
Nor grief nor love shall be enough alone
To ratify my little halves who bear
Across an autumn freezing everywhere.
Ib.

9 First fight. Then fiddle. *Ib. 4*

10 Win war. Rise bloody, maybe not too late
For having first to civilize a space
Wherein to play your violin with grace.
Ib.

11 Exhaust the little moment. Soon it dies.
And be it gash or gold it will not come
Again in this identical disguise.
Ib. Exhaust the Little Moment

12 And remembering . . .
Remembering, with twinklings and twinges,
As they lean over the beans in their rented back room that is full of beads and receipts and dolls and cloths, tobacco crumbs, vases and fringes.
The Bean Eaters [1960]. The Bean Eaters, st. 3

13 We real cool. We
Left school. *Ib. We Real Cool, st. 1*

14 When there were all those gods
administering to panthers,
jumping over mountains,
and lighting stars and comets and a moon,
what was their one Belief?
what was their joining thing?
In the Mecca [1968], st. 4

15 What else is there to say but everything?
Ib. st. 16

16 He opened us—
who was a key,
who was a man.
Ib. After Mecca. Malcolm X

17 Build with lithe love. With love like lion-eyes.
With love like morningrise,
With love like black, our black.
Ib. The Sermon on the Warpland

18 The time
cracks into furious flower. Lifts its face
all unashamed. And sways in wicked grace.
Ib. The Second Sermon on the Warpland, st. 4

19 Big Bessie's feet hurt like nobody's business,
but she stands—bigly—under the unruly scrutiny, stands in the wild weed.
In the wild weed
she is a citizen. *Ib.*

20 Conduct your blooming in the noise and whip of the whirlwind. *Ib.*

21 Beware the easy griefs
that fool and fuel nothing.
Beckonings [1975]. Boys. Black, st. 7

Joe Darion

1917–

1 To dream the impossible dream,
To reach the unreachable star!

The Impossible Dream [1965]

John Fitzgerald Kennedy

1917–1963

2 It was involuntary. They sank my boat.

Remark when asked how he became a hero. Quoted in ARTHUR M. SCHLESINGER, JR., *A Thousand Days [1965], ch. 4*

3 For without belittling the courage with which men have died, we should not forget those acts of courage with which men . . . have *lived*. . . . A man does what he must — in spite of personal consequences, in spite of obstacles and dangers and pressures — and that is the basis of all human morality.

Profiles in Courage [1956], ch. 11

4 It is time for a new generation of leadership, to cope with new problems and new opportunities. For there is a new world to be won. *Television address [July 4, 1960]*

5 The New Frontier of which I speak is not a set of promises — it is a set of challenges. It sums up not what I intend to offer the American people, but what I intend to ask of them.

Speech accepting the Democratic presidential nomination [July 15, 1960]

6 For of those to whom much is given, much is required.[1] And when at some future date the high court of history sits in judgment on each of us, recording whether in our brief span of service we fulfilled our responsibilities to the state, our success or failure, in whatever office we hold, will be measured by the answers to four questions: First, were we truly men of courage . . . Second, were we truly men of judgment . . . Third, were we truly men of integrity . . . Finally, were we truly men of dedication?

Speech to the Massachusetts State Legislature [January 9, 1961]

7 Let the word go forth from this time and place, to friend and foe alike, that the torch has been passed to a new generation of Americans, born in this century, tempered by war, disciplined by a hard and bitter peace, proud of our ancient heritage, and unwilling to witness or permit the slow undoing of those human rights to which this nation has always been committed, and to which we are committed today at home and around the world.

Let every nation know, whether it wishes us well or ill, that we shall pay any price, bear any burden, meet any hardship, support any friend, oppose any foe to assure the survival and the success of liberty.

Inaugural address [January 20, 1961]

8 If a free society cannot help the many who are poor, it cannot save the few who are rich.

Ib.

9 Let us never negotiate out of fear, but let us never fear to negotiate. *Ib.*

10 All this will not be finished in the first one hundred days. Nor will it be finished in the first one thousand days, nor in the life of this Administration, nor even perhaps in our lifetime on this planet. But let us begin.

Ib.

11 Now the trumpet summons us again — not as a call to bear arms, though arms we need; not as a call to battle, though embattled we are; but a call to bear the burden of a long twilight struggle,[2] year in and year out, "rejoicing in hope, patient in tribulation," a struggle against the common enemies of man: tyranny, poverty, disease and war itself. *Ib.*

12 And so, my fellow Americans, ask not what your country can do for you; ask what you can do for your country.[3] *Ib.*

13 It is our task in our time and in our generation to hand down undiminished to those who come after us, as was handed down to us by

[1] See *Luke 12:48*, 43:22.

[2] See Adlai Stevenson, 852:1.

[3] For, stripped of the temporary associations which gave rise to it, it is now the moment when by common consent we pause to become conscious of our national life and to rejoice in it, to recall what our country has done for each of us, and to ask ourselves what we can do for our country in return. — OLIVER WENDELL HOLMES, JR., *Address Before John Sedwick Post No. 4, Grand Army of the Republic* [May 30, 1884]

As has often been said, the youth who loves his Alma Mater will always ask, not "What can she do for me?" but "What can I do for her?" — LE BARON RUSSELL BRIGGS, *Routine and Ideals* [1904], *College Life*

In the great fulfillment we must have a citizenship less concerned about what the government can do for it and more anxious about what it can do for the nation. — WARREN GAMALIEL HARDING, *Republican National Convention, Chicago* [June 7, 1916]

This thought had lain in Kennedy's mind for a long time. As far back as 1945 he had noted down in a looseleaf notebook a quotation from Rousseau: "As soon as any man says of the affairs of the state, What does it matter to me? the state may be given up as lost." — ARTHUR M. SCHLESINGER, JR., *A Thousand Days* [1965], *prologue, footnote*

See Rousseau, 359:1.

those who went before, the natural wealth and beauty which is ours.

Address at the dedication ceremonies of the National Wildlife Federation Building [March 3, 1961]

1 Unconditional war can no longer lead to unconditional victory. It can no longer serve to settle disputes. It can no longer be of concern to great powers alone. For a nuclear disaster, spread by winds and waters and fear, could well engulf the great and the small, the rich and the poor, the committed and the uncommitted alike. Mankind must put an end to war or war will put an end to mankind.

Address to the United Nations [September 25, 1961]

2 If we all can persevere, if we can in every land and office look beyond our own shores and ambitions, then surely the age will dawn in which the strong are just and the weak secure and the peace preserved. *Ib.*

3 Those who make peaceful revolution impossible will make violent revolution inevitable.

Address to Latin American diplomats, the White House [March 12, 1962]

4 There is always inequity in life. Some men are killed in a war and some men are wounded, and some men never leave the country . . . Life is unfair.

Press conference [March 21, 1962]

5 The wave of the future is not the conquest of the world by a single dogmatic creed but the liberation of the diverse energies of free nations and free men.

Address at the University of California, Berkeley [March 23, 1962]

6 In a time of turbulence and change, it is more true than ever that knowledge is power.[1] *Ib.*

7 I think this is the most extraordinary collection of talent, of human knowledge, that has ever been gathered together at the White House, with the possible exception of when Thomas Jefferson dined alone.

Address at a White House dinner and reception honoring Nobel Prize winners [April 1962]

8 If . . . history . . . teaches us anything, it is that man, in his quest for knowledge and progress, is determined and cannot be deterred.

Address at Rice University, Houston [September 12, 1962]

[1]See Bacon, 178:17.

9 We don't see the end of the tunnel, but I must say I don't think it is darker than it was a year ago, and in some ways lighter.[2]

Press conference [December 12, 1962]

10 Liberty without learning is always in peril and learning without liberty is always in vain.

Remarks on the ninetieth anniversary of Vanderbilt University [March 18, 1963]

11 If we cannot end now our differences, at least we can help make the world safe for diversity.

Address at American University, Washington, D.C. [June 10, 1963]

12 Every American ought to have the right to be treated as he would wish to be treated, as one would wish his children to be treated. This is not the case.

Television address on civil rights, after the registration of two Negroes at the University of Alabama [June 11, 1963]

13 No one has been barred on account of his race from fighting or dying for America—there are no "white" or "colored" signs on the foxholes or graveyards of battle.

Message to Congress on proposed civil rights bill [June 19, 1963]

14 All free men, wherever they may live, are citizens of Berlin. And therefore, as a free man, I take pride in the words "Ich bin ein Berliner."

Address at City Hall, West Berlin [June 26, 1963]

15 Yesterday, a shaft of light cut into the darkness. . . . For the first time, an agreement has been reached on bringing the forces of nuclear destruction under international control.

Television address in Washington [July 26, 1963][3]

16 When power leads man toward arrogance, poetry reminds him of his limitations. When power narrows the areas of man's concern, poetry reminds him of the richness and diversity of his existence. When power corrupts,[4] poetry cleanses, for art establishes the basic human truths which must serve as the touchstone of our judgment.

Address at Amherst College [October 26, 1963]

[2]The light at the end of the tunnel.—*Current phrase*

[3]In Moscow on July 25, Averell Harriman, Lord Hailsham, and Chairman Khrushchev initialed the nuclear test ban treaty.

[4]See Pitt, 351:1; Shelley, 466:7; and Lord Acton, 615:15.

1 Leadership and learning are indispensable to each other.

Remarks prepared for delivery at the Trade Mart in Dallas [November 22, 1963]

2 Washington is a city of southern efficiency and northern charm.

Remark. Quoted in ARTHUR M. SCHLESINGER, JR., *A Thousand Days [1965], ch. 25*

Walter Lord

1917–

3 A Night to Remember.

Title of book [1955]

Robert Traill Spence Lowell

1917–1977

4 Christ walks on the black water. In Black Mud
Darts the kingfisher. On Corpus Christi, heart,
Over the drum-beat of St. Stephen's choir
I hear him, *Stupor Mundi,* and the mud
Flies from his hunching wings and beak—my heart,
The blue kingfisher dives on you in fire.

Colloquy in Black Rock [1946], st. 5

5 I will catch Christ with a greased worm.

The Drunken Fisherman [1946], st. 5

6 I saw the spiders marching through air,
Swimming from tree to tree that mildewed day
In latter August when the hay
Came creaking to the barn.[1]

Mr. Edwards and the Spider [1946], st. 1

7 On Windsor Marsh, I saw the spider die
When thrown into the bowels of fierce fire:
There's no long struggle, no desire
To get up on its feet and fly—
It stretches out its feet
And dies. This is the sinner's last retreat;
Yes, and no strength exerted on the heat
Then sinews the abolished will, when sick
And full of burning, it will whistle on a brick.

Ib. st. 4

8 This is the Black Widow, death.

Ib. st. 5

[1]Jonathan Edwards [1703–1758], the Calvinist theologian, wrote at the age of twelve a series of scientific observations on the spider. One of his most famous sermons was "Sinners in the Hands of an Angry God."

9 I saw the sky descending, black and white,
Not blue, on Boston.

Where the Rainbow Ends [1946], st. 1

10 Now Paris, our black classic, breaking up
like killer kings on an Etruscan cup.

Beyond the Alps [1959]

11 Your *Good Soldier*
the best French novel in the language.[2]

Ford Madox Ford [1959]

12 O divorced, divorced
from the whale-fat of postwar London! Boomed,
cut, plucked and booted! In Provence, New York . . .
marrying, blowing . . . nearly dying
at Boulder, when the altitude
pressed the world on your heart. *Ib.*

13 Fiction! I'm selling short
your lies that made the great your equals. Ford,
you were a kind man and you died in want.

Ib.

14 "There is no God and Mary is His Mother."

For George Santayana [1959]

15 You said:
"We poets in our youth begin in sadness;
thereof in the end come despondency and madness."[3]

To Delmore Schwartz (Cambridge 1946) [1959]

16 Who asks for me, the Shelley of my age,
must lay his heart out for my bed and board.

Words for Hart Crane [1959]

17 I doodle handlebar
moustaches on the last Russian Czar.

Grandparents [1959]

18 We are old-timers,
each of us holds a locked razor.

Waking in the Blue [1959]

19 I keep no rank nor station.
Cured, I am frizzled, stale and small.

Home After Three Months Away [1959]

20 Only teaching on Tuesdays, bookworming
in pajamas fresh from the washer each morning,
I hog a whole house on Boston's
"hardly passionate Marlborough Street."[4]

Memories of West Street and Lepke [1959]

[2]See Ford Madox Ford, 740:8.
[3]See Democritus, 79:*n*5; Robert Burton, 258:13; and Wordsworth, 425:10.
[4]The quotation is from Henry James.

1 These are the tranquillized *Fifties,*
and I am forty. Ought I to regret my seedtime?
I was a fire-breathing Catholic C.O.,
and made my manic statement,
telling off the state and president, and then
sat waiting sentence in the bull pen
beside a Negro boy with curlicues
of marijuana in his hair. *Ib.*

2 Flabby, bald, lobotomized,
he drifted in a sheepish calm,
where no agonizing reappraisal
jarred his concentration on the electric
chair—
hanging like an oasis in his air
of lost connections. *Ib.*

3 Tamed by *Miltown,* we lie on Mother's bed.
Man and Wife [1959]

4 Oh my *Petite,*
clearest of all God's creatures, still all air and
nerve. *Ib.*

5 your old-fashioned tirade—
loving, rapid, merciless—
breaks like the Atlantic Ocean on my head.
Ib.

6 Gored by the climacteric of his want,
he stalls above me like an elephant.
"To Speak of Woe That Is in Marriage" [1959]

7 My mind's not right.

A car radio bleats,
"Love, O careless Love. . . ." I hear
my ill-spirit sob in each blood cell,
as if my hand were at its throat. . . .
I myself am hell;[1]
nobody's here.
Skunk Hour [1959], st. 5, 6

8 My old flame, my wife!
Remember our lists of birds?
The Old Flame [1964], st. 1

9 Father, forgive me
my injuries,
as I forgive
those I
have injured!

You never climbed
Mount Sion, yet left
dinosaur
death-steps on the crust,
where I must walk.
Middle Age [1964], st. 3, 4

[1]See Virgil, 105:23; Marlowe, 183:21 and 184:1; Browne, 274:15; Milton, 283:13 and 285:12; Eliot, 809:1; and Sartre, 865:12.

10 We are like a lot of wild
spiders crying together,
but without tears.
Fall 1961 [1964], st. 4

11 I am tired. Everyone's tired of my turmoil.
Eye and Tooth [1964], st. 9

12 Two months after marching through Boston,
half the regiment was dead;
at the dedication,
William James could almost hear the bronze
Negroes[2] breathe.

Their monument sticks like a fishbone
in the city's throat.
Its Colonel is as lean
as a compass needle.

He has an angry wrenlike vigilance,
a greyhound's gentle tautness;
he seems to wince at pleasure,
and suffocate for privacy.
For the Union Dead [1964], st. 7–9

13 Some mote, some eye-flaw, wobbles in the
heat,
hair-thin, hair-dark, the fragment of a
hair—

a noose, a question?
The Flaw [1964], st. 1, 2

14 on Boylston Street, a commercial photograph
shows Hiroshima boiling. *Ib. st. 14*

15 When I crouch to my television set,
the drained faces of Negro school children rise like balloons. *Ib. st. 15*

16 The Aquarium is gone. Everywhere,
giant finned cars nose forward like fish;
a savage servility
slides by on grease. *Ib. st. 17*

17 We beg delinquents for our life.
Central Park. In the New York Review [October 1965]

18 Rome, if built at all, must be built in a day.
Marcus Cato 234–149 B.C. [1973]

19 Christ lost, our only king without a sword,
turning the word *forgiveness* to a sword.
Anne Dick 2. 1936 [1973]

20 No one like one's mother and father ever
lived. *Returning [1973]*

[2]On the Saint-Gaudens monument to Colonel Robert Gould Shaw and the 54th Massachusetts Regiment.

There on foot go the dark outcasts, so true to nature that one can almost hear them breathing as they march.
—WILLIAM JAMES, *Oration at Dedication of the Monument* [May 31, 1897]

See Charles W. Eliot, 617:6; William James, 650:13; and Paul Laurence Dunbar, 737:1.

1 The cliff drops; over it, the water drops,
and steams out the footprints that led us on.
Die Gold Orangen [1973]

2 Creature could face creator in this suit,
fishers of fish not men. *Seals [1973]*

3 After loving you so much, can I forget
you for eternity, and have no other choice?
Obit [1973]

4 The line must terminate.
Yet my heart rises, I know I've gladdened a lifetime
knotting, undoing a fishnet of tarred rope;
the net will hang on the wall when the fish are eaten,
nailed like illegible bronze on the futureless future. *Fishnet [1973]*

5 If I could go through it all again,
the slender iron rungs of growing up,
I would be as young as any,
a child lost
in unreality and loud music.
Realities [1977]

6 Still seeking a boy's license
to see the countryside without arrival.
The Withdrawal [1977]

7 Darling,
terror in happiness may not cure the hungry future,
the time when any illness is chronic,
and the years of discretion are spent on complaint—
until the wristwatch is taken from the wrist.
Ib.

8 It has taken me the time since you died
to discover you are as human as I am . . .
if I am. *To Mother [1977]*

9 I—
really I can do little,
as little now as then,
about the infernal fires—
I cannot blow out a match.
Grass Fires [1977]

10 How often have my antics
and insupportable, trespassing tongue
gone astray and led me to prison . . .
to lying . . . kneeling . . . standing.
The Downlook [1977]

11 We are poor passing facts,
warned by that to give
each figure in the photograph
his living name. *Epilogue [1977]*

Carson Smith McCullers
1917–1967

12 The Heart Is a Lonely Hunter.[1]
Title of novel [1940]

13 The Member of the Wedding.
Title of novel [1946] and play [1950]

14 If you walk along the main street on an August afternoon there is nothing whatsoever to do.
The Ballad of the Sad Cafe [1951]

Arthur Meier Schlesinger, Jr.
1917–

15 Above all he [John F. Kennedy] gave the world for an imperishable moment the vision of a leader who greatly understood the terror and the hope, the diversity and the possibility, of life on this planet and who made people look beyond nation and race to the future of humanity.
A Thousand Days [1965], ch. 37

Harlan Cleveland
1918–

16 The Revolution of Rising Expectations.[2]
Title of speech at Colgate University [1949]

Alan Jay Lerner
1918–

17 Oh, wouldn't it be loverly?
My Fair Lady [1956], act I, sc. i

18 They're always throwing goodness at you
But with a little bit of luck
A man can duck. *Ib. ii*

19 The rain in Spain stays mainly in the plain.
Ib. v

20 In Hertford, Hereford and Hampshire, hurricanes hardly ever happen. *Ib.*

21 I could have danced all night! *Ib.*

[1] See Sharp, 677:5.

[2] Almost fifteen years ago, when I was working for Paul Hoffman in the Marshall Plan, I had to substitute for him in making a speech at Colgate University. Remembering Edmund Burke's famous commentary on the turbulence of his time, I called this speech "Reflections on the Revolution of Rising Expectations." The phrase has since been attributed to nearly every literate American of our time, but I think this was the first time that phrase saw the light of day. — HARLAN CLEVELAND, *The Evolution of Rising Responsibility, address before the U.N.* [December 13, 1964]

1 Get me to the church on time!
Ib. II, iii

2 Why can't a woman be more like a man?
Ib. iv

3 I've grown accustomed . . . to her face.
Ib. vi

4 Don't let it be forgot
That once there was a spot
For one brief shining moment that was known
As Camelot. *Camelot [1960], end*

5 On a Clear Day You Can See Forever.
Title of musical [1965]

6 Pleasure without joy is as hollow as passion without tenderness.
The Street Where I Live [1978]. My Fair Lady

7 Coughing in the theater is not a respiratory ailment. It is a criticism. *Ib.*

8 Men die but an idea does not. *Ib.*

Edwin O'Connor
1918–1968

9 The Last Hurrah.
Title of novel [1956]

Anwar al-Sadat
1918–

10 Land is immortal, for it harbors the mysteries of creation.
In Search of Identity [1978], ch. 1

11 A man's village is his peace of mind.
Ib. 2

12 Most people seek after what they do not possess and are thus enslaved by the very things they want to acquire. *Ib.*

13 Without a vocation, man's existence would be meaningless. . . . [Each man] should first recognize and be loyal to his real entity within . . . for it is this alone which will enable him to belong and owe allegiance to that Entity which is greater, vaster, and more permanent than his individual self. *Ib. 3*

14 Only when he has ceased to need things can a man truly be his own master and so really exist. *Ib.*

15 There can be hope only for a society which acts as one big family, and not as many separate ones. *Ib.*

16 Peace is much more precious than a piece of land.
Speech in Cairo [March 8, 1978]

17 Let there be no more war or bloodshed between Arabs and Israelis. Let there be no more suffering or denial of rights. Let there be no more despair or loss of faith.
On signing the Egyptian–Israeli peace treaty, Washington, D.C. [March 26, 1979][1]

Alexander Solzhenitsyn
1918–

18 A great writer is, so to speak, a second government in his country. And for that reason no regime has ever loved great writers, only minor ones. *The First Circle [1964]*

19 The sole substitute for an experience which we have not ourselves lived through is art and literature. *Nobel Lecture [1972]*

20 Literature transmits incontrovertible condensed experience . . . from generation to generation. In this way literature becomes the living memory of a nation. *Ib.*

21 World literature is . . . a kind of collective body and a common spirit, a living unity of the heart which reflects the growing spiritual unity of mankind. *Ib.*

22 Violence does not and cannot exist by itself; it is invariably intertwined with *the lie.*
Ib.

23 The Kolyma was the greatest and most famous island, the pole of ferocity of that amazing country of Gulag, which, though scattered in an archipelago geographically, was, in the psychological sense, fused into a continent — an almost invisible, almost imperceptible country inhabited by the Zek people.
The Gulag Archipelago 1918–1956, [1974, in translation], I, preface

24 The Western world has lost its civil courage, both as a whole and separately, in each country, each government, each political party, and of course in the United Nations.
The Exhausted West. Commencement Address at Harvard University [June 8, 1978]

25 I have spent all my life under a Communist regime, and I will tell you that a society without any objective legal scale is a terrible one indeed. But a society with no other scale but the legal one is not quite worthy of man either. *Ib.*

[1] See Begin, 881:14.

Muriel Spark

1918–

1 I am putting old heads on your young shoulders . . . and all my pupils are the *crème de la crème.*

The Prime of Miss Brodie [1962], ch. 1

2 Give me a girl at an impressionable age, and she is mine for life. *Ib.*

3 One's prime is elusive. You little girls, when you grow up, must be on the alert to recognize your prime at whatever time of your life it may occur. *Ib.*

4 It is one of the secrets of Nature in its mood of mockery that fine weather lays a heavier weight on the mind and hearts of the depressed and the inwardly tormented than does a really bad day with dark rain sniveling continuously and sympathetically from a dirty sky.

Territorial Rights [1979], ch. 3

Doris Lessing

1919–

5 A woman without a man cannot meet a man, any man, of any age, without thinking, even if it's for a half-second, Perhaps this is *the* man.

The Golden Notebook [1962]. Free Women, 5

6 None of you [men] ask for anything—except everything, but just for so long as you need it. *Ib.*

Wladziu Valentino [Lee] Liberace

1919–

7 I cried all the way to the bank.

Liberace: An Autobiography [1973], ch. 2

Laurence Johnston Peter

1919–

8 In a hierarchy, every employee tends to rise to his level of incompetence.

The Peter Principle [1969]

Jerome David Salinger

1919–

9 I keep picturing all these little kids in this big field of rye. . . . If they're running and they don't look where they're going I have to come out from somewhere and catch them. That's all I'd do all day. I'd just be the catcher in the rye and all. I know it's crazy.

The Catcher in the Rye [1951]

10 There isn't anyone *any*where that isn't Seymour's Fat Lady. Don't you know that? Don't you know that goddam secret yet? And don't you know—*listen* to me, now—*don't you know who that Fat Lady really is? . . . Ah,* buddy. It's Christ Himself. Christ Himself, buddy.

Franny and Zooey [1961]

Pete [Peter] Seeger

1919–

11 Where have all the flowers gone?
The girls have picked them every one.
Oh, when will they ever learn?

Where Have All the Flowers Gone? [1961]

May Swenson

1919–

12 Body my house
my horse my hound
what will I do
when you are fallen

Question [1954], st. 1

13 Where can I go
without my mount
all eager and quick
How will I know
in thicket ahead
is danger or treasure
when Body my good
bright dog is dead *Ib. st. 3*

14 Is there anything I can do
or has everything been done
or do
you prefer somebody else to do
it or don't
you trust me to do
it right or is it hopeless.

The Key to Everything [1954]

15 Behind the wall of St. John's in the city
in the shade of the garden the Rector's wife
walks with her baby a girl and the first.

The Garden at St. John's [1954]

16 The summer that I was ten—
Can it be there was only one
summer that I was ten?

The Centaur [1958]

1 Youth is given. One must put it away
like a doll in a closet,
take it out and play with it only
on holidays. *How to Be Old [1963]*

2 The idea is to make a vehicle
out of it. *Out of My Head [1963]*

3 In the lobby (in a niche)
between two glass revolving doors
sluff sluff sluff sluff
(rubber bottoms of whirling doors)
flick flick click click
(women in women out) sits a nun.
A Fixture [1963]

4 My face
a negative in the slate
window,
I sit
in a lit
corridor that races
through a dark
one. *Riding the "A" [1963]*

5 But night is a fiction
hollowed at the back of our ball,
when from its obverse side
a cone of self-thrown shade
evades the shining.
Sleeping Overnight on the Shore [1967]

6 A bloody
egg yolk. A burnt hole
spreading in a sheet. An enraged rose threatening to bloom.
Out of the Sea, Early [1967]

Pope John Paul II [Karol Wojtyla]

1920–

7 The greatness of work is inside man.
Easter Vigil and Other Poems [1979]. The Quarry, I, Material

8 Hands are the heart's landscape. *Ib.*

9 Man matures through work
Which inspires him to difficult good.
Ib. II, Inspiration

10 We must ask ourselves whether there will continue to accumulate over the heads of this new generation of children the threat of common extermination . . . Are the children to receive the arms race from us as a necessary inheritance? How are we to explain this unbridled race?
Speech at the United Nations [October 2, 1979]

Timothy Leary

1920–

11 Turn On, Tune In, Drop Out.
Title of lecture [1967]

Howard Nemerov

1920–

12 But all that whalebone came from whales.
I Only Am Escaped Alone to Tell Thee [1955]

13 And he heard how once
a team and driver drowned in the break of spring:
the man's cry melting from the ice that summer
frightened the sherbet-eaters off the terrace.
The Icehouse in Summer [1960]

14 Flaubert wanted to write a novel
About nothing. *Style [1967]*

15 On this side of the tapestry
There sits the bearded king.
The Tapestry [1973]

16 When the gray stranger shows up in your dream. *Nightmare [1975], st. 1*

17 You know
That if you were for a time in mortal danger,
And are so still, it was not from a stranger.
Ib. st. 3

Mario Puzo

1920–

18 I'll make him an offer he can't refuse.
The Godfather [1969]

Stewart Lee Udall

1920–

19 The most common trait of all primitive peoples is a reverence for the lifegiving earth, and the native American shared this elemental ethic: the land was alive to his loving touch, and he, its son, was brother to all creatures. His feelings were made visible in medicine bundles and dance rhythms for rain, and all of his religious rites and land attitudes savored the inseparable world of nature and God, the master of Life. During the long Indian tenure the land remained undefiled save for scars no deeper than the scratches of

cornfield clearings or the farming canals of the Hohokams on the Arizona desert.

The Quiet Crisis[1] *[1963], ch. 1*

1 A land ethic for tomorrow should be as honest as Thoreau's *Walden*, and as comprehensive as the sensitive science of ecology. It should stress the oneness of our resources and the live-and-help-live logic of the great chain of life. If, in our haste to "progress," the economics of ecology are disregarded by citizens and policy makers alike, the result will be an ugly America. *Ib. 14*

Sloan Wilson

1920–

2 The Man in the Gray Flannel Suit.

Title of novel [1955]

Hal David

1921–

3 What the world needs now is love, sweet love,
It's the only thing that there's just too little of.

What the World Needs Now Is Love [1965]

Betty Naomi Friedan

1921–

4 When she stopped conforming to the conventional picture of femininity she finally began to enjoy being a woman.

The Feminine Mystique [1963], ch. 14

5 Girls must be encouraged to go on [after college], to make a life plan. It has been shown that girls with this kind of commitment are less eager to rush into early marriage. . . . Most of them marry, of course, but on a much more mature basis. Their marriages then are not an escape but a commitment shared by two people that becomes part of their commitment to themselves and society. *Ib.*

6 A girl should not expect special privileges because of her sex, but neither should she "adjust" to prejudice and discrimination. She must learn to compete . . . not as a woman, but as a human being.[2] *Ib.*

7 Who knows what women can be when they are finally free to become themselves? Who knows what women's intelligence will contribute when it can be nourished without denying love? . . . The time is at hand when the voices of the feminine mystique can no longer drown out the inner voice that is driving women on to become complete.[3]

Ib. end

Bill [William Henry] Mauldin

1921–

8 I feel like a fugitive from th' law of averages.

Up Front [1944]. Caption for cartoon

9 Look at an infantryman's eyes and you can tell how much war he has seen. *Ib.*

10 He's right, Joe, when we ain't fightin' we should ack like sojers. *Ib.*

Julius Kambarage Nyerere

1921–

11 The survival of our wildlife is a matter of grave concern to all of us in Africa. These wild creatures amid the wild places they inhabit are not only important as a source of wonder and inspiration but are an integral part of our natural resources and of our future livelihood and well-being.

The Arusha Declaration, Tanganyika [September 1961][4]

Peter Ustinov

1921–

12 The superpowers have the privilege of being able to destroy our planet several times in rapid succession, and yet there are still those who try to score political points by declaring that one or other of them is lagging dangerously behind the other in potential for obliteration. *Dear Me [1977], ch. 11*

13 I am convinced that it is of primordial importance to learn more every year than the year before. After all, what is education but a process by which a person begins to learn how to learn? *Ib. 13*

14 The young need old men. They need men who are not ashamed of age, not pathetic imitations of themselves. . . . Parents are the bones on which children sharpen their teeth.

Ib. 18

[1] The race between education and erosion, between wisdom and waste has not run its course. . . . The nation's battle to preserve the common estate is far from won. . . . The crisis may be quiet, but it is urgent.—JOHN F. KENNEDY, *introduction to The Quiet Crisis*

[2] See Anthony, 578:1 and 578:2.

[3] See Sheehy, 914:3.

[4] Conference on the conservation of nature and natural resources in modern African states.

Richard Purdy Wilbur

1921–

1 But up in his room by artificial light
My father paints the summer.
My Father Paints the Summer [1947]

2 The selfsame toothless voice for death or bridal.
Bell Speech [1947]

3 Great Paul, great pail of sound, still dip and draw
Dark speech from the deep and quiet steeple well.
Ib. st. 4

4 It is a graph of a theme that flings
The dancer kneeling on nothing into the wings.
Grace [1947], st. 3

5 We respect
Some scholars' stutters.
Ib. st. 5

6 The beautiful changes as a forest is changed
By a chameleon's tuning his skin to it.
The Beautiful Changes [1947], st. 2

7 I dreamt the past was never past redeeming:
But whether this was false or honest dreaming
I beg death's pardon now. And mourn the dead.
The Pardon [1950], last stanza

8 We milk the cow of the world, and as we do
We whisper in her ear, "You are not true."
Epistemology [1950], II

9 I never knew the road
From which the whole earth didn't call away,
With wild birds rounding the hill crowns,
Haling out of the heart an old dismay.
The Sirens [1950], st. 1

10 Forgive the hero, you who would have died
Gladly with all you knew; he rode that tide
To Ararat: all men are Noah's sons.
Still, Citizen Sparrow [1950], last stanza

11 Ho-hum. I am for wit and wakefulness,
And love this feigning lady by Bazille.
What's lightly hid is deepest understood,
And when with social smile and formal dress
She teaches leaves to curtsy and quadrille,
I think there are most tigers in the wood.
Ceremony [1950], st. 3

12 The eyes open to a cry of pulleys,
And spirited from sleep, the astounded soul
Hangs for a moment bodiless and simple.
as false dawn.
Outside the open window
The morning air is all awash with angels.
Love Calls Us to the Things of This World [1956]

13 The soul shrinks
From all that it is about to remember,
From the punctual rape of every blessèd day,
And cries,
"Oh, let there be nothing on earth but laundry,
Nothing but rosy hands in the rising steam
And clear dances done in the sight of heaven."
Ib.

14 Neither pale nor bright,
The turkey-cock parades
Through radiant squalors, darkly auspicious as
The ace of spades,

Himself his own cortège
And puffed with the pomp of death,
Rehearsing over and over with strangled râle
His latest breath.
A Black November Turkey [1956], st. 3, 4

15 Mind in its purest play is like some bat
That beats about in caverns all alone,
Contriving by a kind of senseless wit
Not to conclude against a wall of stone.

It has no need to falter or explore;
Darkly it knows what obstacles are there,
And so may weave and flitter, dip and soar
In perfect courses through the blackest air.

And has this simile a like perfection?
The mind is like a bat. Precisely. Save
That in the very happiest intellection
A graceful error may correct the cave.
Mind [1956]

16 Dear God, let it be with these donkeys that I come,
And let it be that angels lead us in peace
To leafy streams where cherries tremble in air,
Sleek as the laughing flesh of girls; and there
In that haven of souls let it be that, leaning above
Your divine waters, I shall resemble these donkeys,
Whose humble and sweet poverty will appear
Clear in the clearness of your eternal love.
Francis Jammes: A Prayer to Go to Paradise with the Donkeys [1956]

17 The werewolf's painful change. Turning his head away
On the sweaty bolster, he tries to remember
The mood of manhood,

But lies at last, as always,
Letting it happen, the fierce fur soft to his face,
Hearing with sharper ears.
Beasts [1956], st. 3, 4

1 What is our praise or pride
But to imagine excellence, and try to make it?
What does it say over the door of Heaven
But *homo fecit?*

For the New Railway Station in Rome [1956], last stanza

2 When you come, as you soon must, to the streets of our city,
Mad-eyed from stating the obvious,
Not proclaiming our fall but begging us
In God's name to have self-pity,

Spare us all word of the weapons, their force and range,
The long numbers that rocket the mind;
Our slow, unreckoning hearts will be left behind,
Unable to fear what is too strange.

Nor shall you scare us with talk of the death of the race.
How should we dream of this place without us?—
The sun mere fire, the leaves untroubled about us,
A stone look on the stone's face?

Advice to a Prophet [1961], st. 1–3

3 Ask us, prophet, how we shall call
Our natures forth when that live tongue is all
Dispelled, that glass obscured or broken

In which we have said the rose of our love and the clean
Horse of our courage, in which beheld
The singing locust of the soul unshelled,
And all we mean or wish to mean.

Ib. st. 7, 8

4 Duke, keep your coin. All men are born distraught,
And will not for the world be satisfied.
Whether we live in fact, or but in thought,
We die of thirst, here at the fountainside.

Ballade for the Duke of Orléans[1] *[1961], who offered a prize at Blois [c. 1457] for the best ballade employing the line "Je meurs de soif auprès de la fontaine."*

5 All bitter things conduce to sweet,
As this example shows;
Without the little spirochete
We'd have no chocolate to eat,
Nor would tobacco's fragrance greet
The European nose.

Pangloss's Song: A Comic Opera Lyric [1961][2]

[1]See Charles d'Orléans, 148:21.
[2]See Hellman, 863:11.

6 What can I do but move
From folly to defeat,
And call that sorrow sweet
That teaches us to see
The final face of love
In what we cannot be?

Someone Talking to Himself [1961], last stanza

7 All things shall be brought
To the full state and stature of their kind,
By what has found the manhood of this stone.
May that vast motive wash and wash our own.

On the Marginal Way [1969], st. 2

8 This plant would like to grow
And yet be embryo.

Seed Leaves [1969]

9 We could no doubt mistake
These flowers for some answer to that fright
We felt for all creation's sake
In our dark talk last night.

In the Field [1969]

10 But no one style, I think, is recommended.

A Wood [1969]

11 All that we do
Is touched with ocean, yet we remain
On the shore of what we know.

For Dudley [1969]

12 What you hope for
Is that at some point of the pointless journey,
Indoors or out, and when you least expect it,
Right in the middle of your stride, like that,
So neatly that you never feel a thing,
The kind assassin Sleep will draw a bead
And blow your brains out.

Walking to Sleep [1969]

13 Let us have music again when the light dies
(Sullenly, or in glory) and we can give it
Something to organize.

C Minor [1976]

Whitney Moore Young, Jr.

1921–1971

14 It is obvious that the urban crisis stems in large part from the failure to resolve the problems that confront the Negro.

Speech, The Crisis of the Cities [1967]

15 Black is beautiful when it is a slum kid studying to enter college, when it is a man learning new skills for a new job, or a slum mother battling to give her kids a chance for a better life. But white is beautiful, too, when

it helps change society to make our system work for black people also. White is ugly when it oppresses blacks—and so is black ugly when black people exploit other blacks. No race has a monopoly on vice or virtue, and the worth of an individual is not related to the color of his skin.

Beyond Racism: Building an Open Society [1969]

1 Together, blacks and whites can move our country beyond racism and create for the benefit of all of us an open society, one that assures freedom, justice, and full equality for all. *Ib.*

Jack Kerouac

1922–1969

2 The beat generation. *Remark*

3 But then they danced down the street like dingledodies, and I shambled after as I've been doing all my life after people who interest me, because the only people for me are the mad ones, the ones who are mad to live, mad to talk, mad to be saved, desirous of everything at the same time, the ones who never yawn or say a commonplace thing, but burn, burn, burn like fabulous yellow roman candles exploding like spiders across the stars and in the middle you see the blue centerlight pop and everybody goes "Awww!"

On the Road [1957]

Philip Larkin

1922–

4 Only one ship is seeking us, a black-
Sailed unfamiliar, towing at her back
A huge and birdless silence. In her wake
No waters breed or break.

Next, Please [1955]

Alain Robbe-Grillet

1922–

5 The true writer has nothing to say. What counts is the way he says it.[1]

For a New Novel [1963]

Charles Monroe Schultz

1922–

6 Happiness Is a Warm Puppy.

Title of book [1962]

[1] Le véritable écrivain n'a rien à dire, il a seulement une manière de le dire.

7 You're a Good Man, Charlie Brown.

Title of play [1967] based on the comic strip Peanuts

Kurt Vonnegut, Jr.

1922–

8 You know—we've had to imagine the war here, and we have imagined that it was being fought by aging men like ourselves. We had forgotten that wars were fought by babies. When I saw those freshly shaved faces, it was a shock. "My God, my God—" I said to myself, "it's the Children's Crusade."

Slaughterhouse-Five [1969],[2] *ch. 5*

9 High school is closer to the core of the American experience than anything else I can think of.

From his introduction to Our Time Is Now: Notes from the High School Underground, edited by JOHN BIRMINGHAM *[1970]*

Paddy Chayevsky

1923–

10 I'm mad as hell, and I'm not going to take it any more.

Network, screenplay [1976]

James Dickey

1923–

11 Inventing a story with grass,
I find a young horse deep inside it.

A Birth [1962]

12 A shudder of joy runs up
The trunk: the needles tingle;
One bird uncontrollably cries.
The wind changes round, and I stir
Within another's life. Whose life?

In the Tree House at Night [1962]

13 All families lie together, though some are
burned alive.
The others try to feel
For them. Some can, it is often said.

The Firebombing [1965]

14 There,
In the other wood,

The uncornered animal's, running off
Upon instinct. Sails spread, fox wings

[2] Their address was this: Schlachthof-Fünf. *Schlachthof* meant *slaughterhouse. Fünf* was good old *five.*—VONNEGUT, *Slaughterhouse-Five, ch. 6*

Lift him alive over gullies,
Hair tips all over him lightly

Touched with the moon's red silver,
Back-hearing around
The stream of his body the tongue of hounds
Feather him. In his own animal sun
Made of human moonlight,

He flies like a bolt running home.
Fox Blood [1965]

1 All day I climb myself
Bowlegged up those damned poles rooster-heeled in all
Kinds of weather.
Power and Light [1967]

2 And this is the house I pass through on my way
To power and light. *Ib.*

3 People are calling each other weeping with a hundred thousand
Volts making deals pleading laughing like fate,
Far off, invulnerable. *Ib.*

4 We have all been in rooms
We cannot die in. *Adultery [1967]*

5 Something has licked my heel
Like a surgeon
And I have a problem with
My right foot and my life.
Snakebite [1967]

6 The moon lying on the brain
as on the excited sea as on
The strength of fields. Lord, let me shake
With purpose.
The Strength of Fields [1977]

7 More kindness will do nothing less
Than save every sleeping one
And nightwalking one
Of us.
My life belongs to the world. I will do what I can. *Ib. last lines*

Joseph Heller

1923–

8 There was only one catch and that was Catch-22, which specified that a concern for one's own safety in the face of dangers that were real and immediate was the process of a rational mind. Orr was crazy and could be grounded. All he had to do was ask; and as soon as he did, he would no longer be crazy and would have to fly more missions. . . . If he flew them he was crazy and didn't have to; but if he didn't want to he was sane and had to. . . . "That's some catch, that Catch-22," he [Yossarian] observed. "It's the best there is," Doc Daneeka agreed.
Catch-22 [1955], ch. 5

Henry Alfred Kissinger

1923–

9 Power is the great aphrodisiac.[1]
From the New York Times [January 19, 1971]

10 History knows no resting places and no plateaus.
White House Years [1979], ch. 3

11 The management of a balance of power is a permanent undertaking, not an exertion that has a foreseeable end. *Ib. 5*

Denise Levertov

1923–

12 I like to find
what's not found
at once, but lies
within something of another nature
in repose, distinct. *Pleasures [1959]*

13 The butterfly glow

in the narrow flute from which the morning-glory
opens blue and cool on a hot morning.
Ib.

14 That's joy, it's always
a recognition, the known
appearing fully itself, and
more itself than one knew.
Matins [1962], II

15 Marvelous Truth, confront us
at every turn,
in every guise. *Ib. VII*

16 Dwell
in our crowded hearts
our steaming bathrooms, kitchens full of
things to be done, the
ordinary streets.

Thrust close your smile
that we know you, terrible joy. *Ib.*

17 Two by two in the ark of
the ache of it.
The Ache of Marriage [1964]

[1] Also quoted as: Power is the ultimate aphrodisiac.

Hank Williams

1923–1953

1 Hear that lonesome whippoorwill,
He sounds too blue to fly.
The midnight train is whining low,
I'm so lonesome, I could cry.

I'm So Lonesome I Could Cry [1942]

James Baldwin

1924–

2 [The Negro past] of rope, fire, torture, castration, infanticide, rape; death and humiliation; fear by day and night, fear as deep as the marrow of the bone; doubt that he was worthy of life, since everyone around him denied it; sorrow for his women, for his kinfolk, for his children, who needed his protection, and whom he could not protect; rage, hatred and murder, hatred for white men so deep that it often turned against him and his own, and made all love, all trust, all joy impossible.

The Fire Next Time [1963]

3 If we do not now dare everything, the fulfillment of that prophecy, re-created from the Bible in song by a slave, is upon us: *God gave Noah the rainbow sign, No more water, the fire next time!* *Ib. end*

Truman Capote

1924–

4 Other Voices, Other Rooms.

Title of book [1948]

5 I didn't want to harm the man. I thought he was a very nice gentleman. Soft-spoken. I thought so right up to the moment I cut his throat. *In Cold Blood [1966]*

Jimmy [James Earl, Jr.] Carter

1924–

6 No poor, rural, weak, or black person should ever again have to bear the additional burden of being deprived of the opportunity for an education, a job, or simple justice.

Inaugural address as governor, Atlanta [January 12, 1971]

7 We believe that the first time we're born, as children, it's human life given to us; and when we accept Jesus as our Savior, it's a new life. That's what "born again" means.[1]

In an interview with Robert L. Turner [March 16, 1976]

[1] See *John 3:3, 44:31*.

8 All I want is the same thing you want. To have a nation with a government that is as good and honest and decent and competent and compassionate and as filled with love as are the American people.

Speech to the California State Senate, Sacramento [May 20, 1976]

9 The first step in providing economic equality for women is to ensure a stable economy in which every person who wants to work can work.

Speech at Women's Agenda Conference, Washington, D.C. [October 2, 1976]

10 Within the stable economy it's necessary to eliminate all forms of sexual discrimination, and to provide women for the first time in our history with economic opportunities equal to those of men. *Ib.*

11 We are of course a nation of differences. Those differences don't make us weak. They're the source of our strength. . . . The question is not when we came here . . . but why our families came here. And what we did after we arrived.

Speech at Al Smith Dinner, New York City [October 21, 1976]

Arthur Charles Erickson

1924–

12 North American civilization is one of the ugliest to have emerged in human history, and it has engulfed the world. Asphalt and exhaust fumes clog the villages. . . . This great, though disastrous, culture can only change as we begin to stand off and see . . . the inveterate materialism which has become the model for cultures around the globe.

Speech at Simon Fraser University [1973]

13 What the West has thrown on the waters of the world drifts back to us on a tide of cultural pollution appalling to behold.

Speech at International Congress of Architecture in Iran [1974]

Yogi [Lawrence Peter] Berra

1925–

14 The game isn't over till it's over.

Attributed

John Daniel Ehrlichman

1925–

1 It'll play in Peoria. *Phrase*[1] *[1970]*

2 I think we ought to let him [Patrick Gray] hang there. Let him twist slowly, slowly in the wind.

Telephone conversation with John Dean [March 7/8, 1973]

Maxine Kumin

1925–

3 I took the lake between my legs.

Morning Swim [1965]

4 Something went crabwise
across the snow this morning.

The Presence [1970]

5 Love, we are a small pond.

We Are [1970]

6 Here on the drawing board
fingers and noses
leak from the air brush
maggots lie under
if i should die before
if i should die
in the back room
stacked up in smooth boxes
like soapflakes or tunafish
wait the undreamt of.

The Nightmare Factory [1970]

7 And the pond's stillness nippled as if
by rain instead is pocked with life.

Creatures [1972]

8 Meanwhile
let us cast one shadow
in air or water. *Turning To [1972]*

9 Our daughters and sons have burst
from the marionette show
leaving a tangle of strings
and gone into the unlit audience.

The Absent Ones [1972]

10 Can it be
I am the only Jew residing in Danville, Kentucky,
looking for matzoh in the Safeway and the A & P?

Living Alone with Jesus [1972]

11 It is said to begin with the father.

The Horsewoman [1975]

12 The time on either side of *now* stands fast.

July, Against Hunger [1978]

[1] Meaning politically acceptable to "middle America."

Malcolm X
[El-Hajj Malik El-Shabazz]

1925–1965

13 Speaking like this doesn't mean that we're anti-white, but it does mean we're anti-exploitation, we're anti-degradation, we're anti-oppression.

Speech, The Ballot or the Bullet [1964]

14 The political philosophy of black nationalism means that the black man should control the politics and the politicians in his own community; no more. *Ib.*

15 We are not fighting for integration, nor are we fighting for separation. We are fighting for recognition as human beings. We are fighting for . . . human rights.

Speech, Black Revolution, New York [1964]

16 I am a Muslim and . . . my religion makes me be against all forms of racism. It keeps me from judging any man by the color of his skin. It teaches me to judge him by his deeds and his conscious behavior. And it teaches me to be for the rights of all human beings, but especially the Afro-American human being, because my religion is a natural religion, and the first law of nature is self-preservation.

Speech, Prospects for Freedom, New York [1965]

17 Power in defense of freedom is greater than power in behalf of tyranny and oppression. *Ib.*

Zhores Aleksandrovich Medvedev

1925–

18 Science and technology, and the various forms of art, all unite humanity in a single and interconnected system. As science progresses, the worldwide cooperation of scientists and technologists becomes more and more of a special and distinct intellectual community of friendship, in which, in place of antagonism, there is growing up a mutually advantageous sharing of work, a coordination of efforts, a common language for the exchange of information, and a solidarity, which are in many cases independent of the social and political differences of individual states.

The Medvedev Papers [1970], preface

Mishima Yukio
[Kimitake Hiraoka]
1925–1970

1 My solitude grew more and more obese, like a pig.
Temple of the Golden Pavilion[1] *[1959]*

Flannery O'Connor
1925–1964

2 Does one's integrity ever lie in what he is not able to do? I think that usually it does, for free will does not mean one will, but many wills conflicting in one man. Freedom cannot be conceived simply.
Wise Blood [1952], foreword

3 "She would of been a good woman," The Misfit said, "if it had been somebody there to shoot her every minute of her life."
A Good Man Is Hard to Find [1955]

4 I doubt if the texture of Southern life is any more grotesque than that of the rest of the nation, but it does seem evident that the Southern writer is particularly adept at recognizing the grotesque; and to recognize the grotesque, you have to have some notion of what is not grotesque and why.
Talk at Notre Dame University [spring 1957]

5 Southern culture has fostered a type of imagination that has been influenced by Christianity of a not too unorthodox kind and by a strong devotion to the Bible, which has kept our minds attached to the concrete and the living symbol.
Ib.

A. R. Ammons
1926–

6 The wind said
You know I'm
the result of
forces beyond my control.
The Wide Land [1972]

7 The air's glass
jail seals each thing in its entity.
Gravelly Run, l. 21

8 The sunlight has never
heard of trees.
Ib. l. 27

9 Though I have looked everywhere
I can find nothing lowly
in the universe.
Still [1972]

10 In nature there are few sharp lines.
Corson's Inlet [1972], l. 31

11 No humbling of reality to precept.
Ib. l. 116

12 Counting my numberless fingers.
Mountain Talk [1972]

13 Not so much looking for the shape
as being available
to any shape that may be
summoning itself
through me
from the self not mine but ours.
Poetics [1972]

14 The stones are
prepared: they are round and ready.
Upland [1972]

15 A squash blossom dies, I feel withered as if a stained
zucchini.
Cut the Grass [1972]

Robert Bly
1926–

16 I have wandered in a face, for hours,
Passing through dark fires.
I have risen to a body
Not yet born,
Existing like a light around the body,
Through which the body moves like a sliding moon.
The Light Around the Body [1967]. Looking into a Face

17 What shall the world do with its children?
There are lives the executives
Know nothing of . . .
The other world is like a thorn
In the ear of a tiny beast!
Ib. Romans Angry About the Inner World

18 The sound of the rampaging Missouri,
Bending the reeds again and again—something inside us
Like a ghost train in the Rockies
About to be buried in snow!
Its long hoot
Making the owl in the Douglas fir turn his head.
Ib. Asian Peace Offers Rejected Without Publication

Fidel Castro
1926–

19 We are not only a Latin-American nation; we are an Afro-American nation also.
Speech in Havana [1977]

[1] Translated by IVAN MORRIS.

Allen Ginsberg
1926–

1 I saw the best minds of my generation destroyed by madness, starving hysterical naked,
dragging themselves through the negro streets at dawn looking for an angry fix
angelheaded hipsters burning for the ancient heavenly connection to the starry dynamo in the machinery of night.
Howl [1956]

James Ingram Merrill
1926–

2 Crossing the street,
I saw the parents and the child
At their window, gleaming like fruit
With evening's mild gold leaf.
The Broken Home [1966], st. 1

3 Again last night I dreamed the dream called Laundry. *The Mad Scene [1966]*

4 I yearned for the kind of unseasoned telling found
In legends, fairy tales, a tone licked clean
Over the centuries by mild old tongues,
Grandam to cub, serene, anonymous.
The Book of Ephraim [1976], sec. A

5 What we dream up must be lived down, I think. *Ib. I*

6 HE PREFERS
LIVE MUSIC TO A PATRON'S HUMDRUM SPHERES
Is this permitted? WHEN U ARE MOZART YES
He's living *now?* As what? A BLACK ROCK STAR
WHATEVER THAT IS. *Ib. P*

7 Jung says—or if he doesn't, all but does—
That God and the Unconscious are one. Hm.
Ib. U

8 The plants, the sorry few that linger, scatter
Leaflets advocating euthanasia. *Ib. Z*

William D. Snodgrass
1926–

9 It was the nature of the thing:
No moon outlives its leaving night,
No sun its day. And I went on
Rich in the loss of all I sing
To the threshold of waking light,
To larksong and the live, gray dawn.
So night by night, my life has gone.
Orpheus [1959]

10 Though trees turn bare and girls turn wives,
We shall afford our costly seasons;
There is a gentleness survives
That will outspeak and has its reasons.
There is a loveliness exists,
Preserves us, not for specialists.
April Inventory [1959]

John Ashbery
1927–

11 As I sit looking out of a window of the building
I wish I did not have to write the instruction manual on the uses of a new metal.
The Instruction Manual [1956]

12 Guadalajara! City of rose-colored flowers!
City I wanted most to see, and most did not see, in Mexico!
But I fancy I see, under the press of having to write the instruction manual,
Your public square, city, with its elaborate little bandstand! *Ib.*

13 Calling attention
Isn't the same thing as explaining.
Some Trees [1956]

14 The carnivorous
Way of these lines is to devour their own nature, leaving
Nothing but a bitter impression of absence, which as we know involves presence, but still,
Nevertheless these are fundamental absences, struggling to get up and be off themselves. *Ib.*

15 As Parmgianino did it, the right hand
Bigger than the head, thrust at the viewer
And swerving easily away, as though to protect
What it advertises.
Self-Portrait in a Convex Mirror [1975]

16 Something like living occurs, a movement
Out of the dream into its codification.
Ib.

Cesar Estrada Chavez
1927–

17 Viva la huelga [Long live the strike]!
Slogan of the United Farm Workers [the 1960s]

Ronald David Laing
1927–

18 We are born into a world where alienation awaits us.
The Politics of Experience [1967], introduction

1 Madness need not be all breakdown. It may also be breakthrough. It is potential liberation and renewal as well as enslavement and existential death. *Ib. ch. 6*

William Stanley Merwin

1927–

2 This is the black sea brute bulling through wave wrack,
Ancient as ocean's shifting hills, who in sea toils
Traveling, who furrowing the salt acres
Heavily, his wake hoary behind him,[1]
Shoulders spouting, the fist of his forehead
Over wastes gray-green crashing.
Leviathan [1956]

3 He is that curling serpent that in ocean is,
Sea fright he is, and the shadow under the earth. *Ib.*

4 It was never there and already it's vanishing.
Before That [1963]

5 Coming late, as always,
I try to remember what I almost heard.
The Poem [1963]

6 I live up here. *I Live Up Here [1967]*

7 You came back to us in a dream and we were not here. *Come Back [1967]*

8 The dead will think the living are worth it we will know
Who we are
And we will all enlist again.
When the War Is Over [1967]

9 Whatever I have to do has not yet begun
It is March
And from a corner the sounds of a small bird trying
From time to time to fly a few beats in the dark. *The Room [1967]*

10 Every year without knowing it I have passed the day.
For the Anniversary of My Death [1967]

11 Of course there is nothing the matter with the stars
It is my emptiness among them
While they drift farther away in the invisible morning.
In the Winter of My Thirty-eighth Year [1967]

[1] He maketh a path to shine after him; one would think the deep to be hoary. — *Job 41:32*

12 Whiteness came back to the paths after each footstep and the travelers
never met in the single files
who deepened the same
shadows. *The Prints [1971]*

13 In the quiver on Paris's back the head
of the arrow for Achilles' heel
smiled in its sleep.
The Judgment of Paris [1971]

14 Through the evening
the mountains approach over the desert
sails from a windless kingdom.
The Calling Under the Breath [1971]

15 At the day's end
all our footsteps are added up
to see how near. *Last People [1971]*

16 I think I was cold in the womb.
The Forebears [1971]

17 I am the son of the first fish who climbed ashore but the news has not yet reached my bowels.
Psalm: Our Fathers [1971]

18 Like shadows
of the plumbing
that is all that is left
of the great city.
The Plumbing [1971]

19 Some alien blessing
is on its way to us.
Midnight in Early Spring [1971]

20 All through the dark the wind looks
for the grief it belongs to.
Night Wind [1971]

21 Oh pile of white shirts who is coming
to breathe in your shapes.
The Night of the Shirts [1971]

22 Deliver me

From the ruth of the lair, which clings to me in the morning.
Lemuel's Blessing [1973], st. 2

23 From the ruth of kindness with its licked hands;
I have sniffed baited fingers and followed
Toward necessities which were not my own.
Ib. st. 3

24 From the ruth of prepared comforts, with its
Habitual dishes sporting my name and its collars and leashes of vanity.
Ib. st. 4

25 From the ruth of approval, with its nets, kennels, and taxidermists. *Ib. st. 5*

Andy Warhol

1927–

1 In the future everyone will be world-famous for fifteen minutes.

Catalogue of his photo exhibition in Stockholm [1968]

Edward Franklin Albee

1928–

2 *George:* Who's afraid of Virginia Woolf . . .

Martha: I . . . am . . . George . . . I am.

Who's Afraid of Virginia Woolf?[1] *[1962]. The Exorcism*

Gabriel García Márquez

1928–

3 It was foreseen that the city of mirrors (or mirages) would be wiped out by the wind and exiled from the memory of men at the precise moment when Aureliano Babilonia would finish deciphering the parchments, and that everything written on them was unrepeatable since time immemorial and forevermore, because races condemned to one hundred years of solitude did not have a second opportunity on earth.

One Hundred Years of Solitude (Cien Años de Soledad) [1967][2]

Larry Gelbart

1928–

and

Burt Shevelove

1915–

4 A Funny Thing Happened on the Way to the Forum.

Title of musical comedy [1962]

Michael Harrington

1928–

5 The other America, the America of poverty, is hidden today in a way that it never was before. Its millions are socially invisible to the rest of us. . . . The very development of American society is creating a new kind of blindness about poverty. The poor are increasingly slipping out of the very experience and consciousness of the nation.[3]

The Other America: Poverty in the United States [1962], ch. 1

6 For the urban poor the police are those who arrest you. In almost any slum there is a vast conspiracy against the forces of law and order. *Ib.*

Donn Pearce

1928–

7 What we've got here is a failure to communicate.

Cool Hand Luke, screenplay [1967]

Anne Sexton

1928–1974

8 You, Doctor Martin, walk
from breakfast to madness. Late August,
I speed through the antiseptic tunnel where
the moving dead still talk
of pushing their bones against the thrust
of cure. And I am queen of this summer hotel
or the laughing bee on a stalk
of death.

You, Doctor Martin [1960], st. 1

9 And we are magic talking to itself,
noisy and alone. I am queen of all my sins
forgotten. Am I still lost?
Once I was beautiful. Now I am myself,
counting this row and that row of moccasins
waiting on the silent shelf.

Ib. last stanza

10 I have gone out, a possessed witch,
haunting the black air, braver at night.

Her Kind [1960]

11 A woman like that is not a woman, quite.
I have been her kind. *Ib.*

12 Leaving the page of the book carelessly open,
something unsaid, the phone off the hook
and the love, whatever it was, an infection.

Wanting to Die [1966], last stanza

13 Little Girl, My Stringbean, My Lovely Woman. *Title of poem [1966]*

14 I say Live, Live, because of the sun,
The dream, the excitable gift.

Live [1966]

15 I would like a simple life
yet all night I am laying
poems away in a long box.

The Ambition Bird [1973], st. 4

[1] Who's Afraid of the Big, Bad Wolf? — *Title of song,* WALT DISNEY *film cartoon Three Little Pigs* [1933]

[2] Translated by GREGORY RABASSA.

[3] See Lyndon Johnson, 872:10.

Alvin Toffler

1928–

1 Future shock[1] . . . the shattering stress and disorientation that we induce in individuals by subjecting them to too much change in too short a time.

Future Shock [1970], ch. 1

Anne Frank[2]

1929–1945

2 Whoever is happy will make others happy too. He who has courage and faith will never perish in misery!

Anne Frank: The Diary of a Young Girl [1952].[3] *March 7, 1944*

3 What *one* Christian does is his own responsibility, what *one* Jew does is thrown back at all Jews. *Ib. May 22, 1944*

4 [Daddy] said: "All children must look after their own upbringing." Parents can only give good advice or put them on the right paths, but the final forming of a person's character lies in their own hands.

Ib. July 15, 1944

5 In spite of everything I still believe that people are really good at heart. *Ib.*

Martin Luther King, Jr.

1929–1968

6 If a man hasn't discovered something that he will die for, he isn't fit to live.

Speech in Detroit [June 23, 1963]

7 Injustice anywhere is a threat to justice everywhere.

Letter from the Birmingham jail. In the Atlantic Monthly [August 1963]

8 Unearned suffering is redemptive.

Ib.

9 I have a dream[4] that one day on the red hills of Georgia the sons of former slaves and the sons of former slaveowners will be able to sit down together at the table of brotherhood.

Speech at Civil Rights March on Washington [August 28, 1963]

[1] Future shock . . . the dizzying disorientation brought on by the premature arrival of the future.—TOFFLER, *article in Horizon* [1965]

[2] Two months before Holland was liberated, Anne died in the concentration camp at Bergen-Belsen.

[3] Translated by B. M. MOOYART.

[4] I see an America in which Martin Luther King's dream is our national dream.—JIMMY CARTER, *speech at Martin Luther King Hospital, Los Angeles* [June 1, 1976]

10 I have a dream that my four little children will one day live in a nation where they will not be judged by the color of their skin, but by the content of their character. *Ib.*

11 Nonviolence is the answer to the crucial political and moral questions of our time; the need for man to overcome oppression and violence without resorting to oppression and violence.

Man must evolve for all human conflict a method which rejects revenge, aggression and retaliation. The foundation of such a method is love.[5]

Speech accepting the Nobel Peace Prize [December 11, 1964]

12 The tortuous road which has led from Montgomery to Oslo is a road over which millions of Negroes are traveling to find a new sense of dignity. It will, I am convinced, be widened into a superhighway of justice.

Ib.

13 I refuse to accept the idea that the "isness" of man's present nature makes him morally incapable of reaching up for the "oughtness" that forever confronts him. *Ib.*

14 I refuse to accept the cynical notion that nation after nation must spiral down a militaristic stairway into the hell of nuclear destruction. I believe that unarmed truth and unconditional love will have the final word in reality. *Ib.*

15 Nonviolent action, the Negro saw, was the way to supplement, not replace, the process of change. It was the way to divest himself of passivity without arraying himself in vindictive force. *Why We Can't Wait [1964]*

16 The Negro was willing to risk martyrdom in order to move and stir the social conscience of his community and the nation . . . he would force his oppressor to commit his brutality openly, with the rest of the world looking on . . . Nonviolent resistance paralyzed and confused the power structures against which it was directed. *Ib.*

17 I just want to do God's will. And He's allowed me to go to the mountain. And I've looked over, and I've seen the promised land . . . So I'm happy tonight. I'm not worried about anything. I'm not fearing any man.

Speech at Birmingham, Alabama [April 3, 1968], the evening before his assassination

[5] See Gandhi, 727:5.

John James Osborne

1929–

1 Look Back in Anger.

Title of play [1956]

Dory Previn

c. 1929–

2 i was you baby
i was you too long

On My Way to Where [1971]. I Was You

3 i can't go on . . .
i really
can't go on
i swear
i can't go on
so
i guess
i'll get up
and go on

Ib. I Can't Go On

Adrienne Rich

1929–

4 I want this to be yours
in the sense that if you find it and read it
it will be there in you already
and the leaflet then merely something
to leave behind, a little leaf
in the drawer of a sublet room.

Leaflets [1971]

5 My visionary anger cleansing my sight.

The Stranger [1973]

6 I am the androgyne. *Ib.*

7 There is a ladder.
The ladder is always there
hanging innocently
close to the side of the schooner.

Diving into the Wreck [1973]

8 I came to explore the wreck. *Ib.*

9 I came to see the damage that was done
and the treasures that prevail. *Ib.*

10 I stroke the beam of my lamp
slowly along the flank
of something more permanent
than fish or weed. *Ib.*

11 There is a cop who is both prowler and father.

Rape [1973]

Robert Sommer

1929–

12 Personal space refers to an area with invisible boundaries surrounding a person's body into which intruders may not come.[1]

Personal Space: The Behavioral Basis of Design [1969]

Neil Alden Armstrong

1930–

13 Houston, Tranquility Base here. The Eagle has landed.

On reaching the moon [July 20, 1969][2]

14 That's one small step for a man, one giant leap for mankind.

On first stepping on the moon [July 20, 1969]

Wilfrid Sheed

1930–

15 If God had died in the blare of the twentieth century and in houses too new and cheap to be haunted, one must seek him in the old quiet places, where he might still live on in retirement.

The Good Word [1978], pt. I, ch. 12

16 Suicide . . . is about life, being in fact the sincerest form of criticism life gets.

Ib. 15

17 The odds on any intelligent person having an unhappy childhood are better than fair, and the odds on a sad ending are practically off the board. *Ib. 33*

18 [Published] letters by a living man are a bit like a stately home with the owner around —one isn't sure how much one can touch.

Ib. II, 12

Stephen Sondheim

1930–

19 Tonight, tonight, won't be just any night.
Tonight there will be no morning star.

West Side Story [1957].[3] *Tonight*

[1] See Auden, 869:6.

[2] Armstrong commanded the Apollo 11 mission, which resulted in the first known lunar landing.

[3] Music by LEONARD BERNSTEIN.

Derek Walcott

1930–

1 I who am poisoned with the blood of both,
Where shall I turn, divided to the vein?
I who have cursed
The drunken officer of British rule, how choose
Between this Africa and the English tongue I love?
A Far Cry from Africa [1962]

2 To change your language you must change your life. *Codicil [1965]*

John Le Carré [David John Moore Cornwell]

1931–

3 The Spy Who Came In from the Cold. *Title of novel [1963]*

Tom [Thomas Kennerly, Jr.] Wolfe

1931–

4 The Life—that *feeling*—The Life—the late 1940s early 1950s American Teenage Drive-In Life. *The Electric Kool-Aid Acid Test*[1] *[1968], ch. 4*

5 A glorious place, a glorious age, I tell you! A very Neon Renaissance—And the myths that actually touched you at that time—not Hercules, Orpheus, Ulysses and Aeneas—but Superman, Captain Marvel, Batman. *Ib.*

6 Radical Chic. *Title of book [1970]*

7 The Me Decade and the Third Great Awakening. *Title of essay [1976]*

Sylvia Plath

1932–1963

8 The silence drew off, baring the pebbles and shells and all the tatty wreckage of my life. Then, at the rim of vision, it gathered itself, and in one sweeping tide, rushed me to sleep. *The Bell Jar [1963]*

9 A living doll, everywhere you look.
It can sew, it can cook,
It can talk, talk, talk. . . .
My boy, it's your last resort.
Will you marry it, marry it, marry it.
The Applicant [1966]

10 I have done it again.
Lady Lazarus [1966], st. 1

11 Dying
Is an art, like everything else.
I do it exceptionally well. *Ib. st. 15*

12 Out of the ash
I rise with my red hair
And I eat men like air. *Ib. last stanza*

13 What a thrill—
My thumb instead of an onion.
Cut [1966]

14 White
Godiva, I unpeel—
Dead hands dead stringencies.
Ariel [1966]

15 And now I
Foam to wheat, a glitter of seas. *Ib.*

16 You do not do, you do not do
Any more, black shoe
In which I have lived like a foot
For thirty years, poor and white,
Barely daring to breathe or Achoo.
Daddy [1966], st. 1

17 I have always been scared of you,
With your Luftwaffe, your gobbledygoo.
And your neat moustache
And your Aryan eye, bright blue.
Panzer-man, panzer-man, O You—
Ib. st. 9

18 Every woman adores a Fascist,
The boot in the face, the brute
Brute heart of a brute like you.
Ib. st. 10

François Truffaut

1932–

19 Airing one's dirty linen never makes for a masterpiece.[2] *Bed and Board [1972]*

John Updike

1932–

20 You climb up through the little grades and then get to the top and everybody cheers; with the sweat in your eyebrows you can't see very well and the noise swirls around you and lifts you up, and then you're out, not forgotten at first, just out, and it feels good and cool and free. You're out, and sort of melt, and keep lifting, until you become like to these kids just one more piece of the sky of adults that hangs over them in the town, a piece that for some queer reason has clouded and visited them. *Rabbit, Run [1960]*

[1] See Kesey, 913:7.

[2] Les rendements de contes ne font jamais un chef d'oeuvre.

1 We walk through volumes of the unexpressed and like snails leave behind a faint thread excreted out of ourselves.
The Blessed Man of Boston

Vine Victor Deloria, Jr.[1]

1933–

2 Tribalism is the strongest force at work in the world today.
Custer Died for Your Sins [1969], ch. 11

3 Religion cannot be kept within the bounds of sermons and scriptures. It is a force in itself and it calls for the integration of lands and peoples in harmonious unity. The lands [of the planet] wait for those who can discern their rhythms. The peculiar genius of each continent, each river valley, the rugged mountains, the placid lakes, all call for relief from the constant burden of exploitation.
God Is Red [1973], ch. 16

4 The future of mankind lies waiting for those who will come to understand their lives and take up their responsibilities to all living things. *Ib.*

5 As the long-forgotten peoples of the respective continents rise and begin to reclaim their ancient heritage, they will discover the meaning of the lands of their ancestors.
Ib.

Theodore Roszak

1933–

6 The Making of a Counter Culture.
Title of book [1969]

Andrei Voznesenski

1933–

7 I am Goya
of the bare field, by the enemy's beak gouged
till the craters of my eyes gape
I am grief

I am the tongue
of war, the embers of cities
on the snows of the year 1941
I am hunger
I Am Goya [1960],[2] st. 1, 2

[1] A Standing Rock Sioux.
[2] A good example of his use of assonance: *Ya Goya . . . nagoye . . . ya gore . . . ya golos . . . goda . . . ya golod . . . ya gorlo . . . goloi.*—P. Blake and M. Hayward, *eds., Antiworlds: Poetry by Andrei Voznesensky* [1966]
Translated by Stanley Kunitz.

8 They carried him[3] not to bury him:
They carried him down to crown him. . . .
The poet flourished here, disheveled,
Who would not bow before votive lamps
But to the common spade.
Leaves and Roots [1960][4]

9 The urge to kill, like the urge to beget,
Is blind and sinister. Its craving is set
Today on the flesh of a hare: tomorrow it can
Howl the same way for the flesh of a man.
Hunting a Hare [1964],[5] st. 5

10 Along a parabola life like a rocket flies,
Mainly in darkness, now and then on a rainbow. *Parabolic Ballad [1960]*[5]

Yevgeny Alexandrovich Yevtushenko

1933–

11 There is no Jewish blood in my veins,
But I am hated with a scabby hatred
By all the anti-Semites,
like a Jew.
And therefore
I am a true Russian.
Babi Yar [1961]

Amiri Baraka [LeRoi Jones]

1934–

12 Lately, I've become accustomed to the way
The ground opens up and envelops me
Each time I go out to walk the dog.
Preface to a Twenty Volume Suicide Note [1961]

13 And then last night I tiptoed up
To my daughter's room and heard her
Talking to someone, and when I opened
The door, there was no one there . . .
Only she on her knees, peeking into

Her own clasped hands. *Ib.*

14 Saturday mornings we listened to *Red Lantern* & his undersea folk.
At 11, *Let's Pretend* / & we did / & I, the poet, still do, Thank God!
In Memory of Radio [1961]

15 Walk it slow
where you go
walk it slow . . .
We in the world
Poor as dirt
Don't get some rhythm
Somebody'll get hurt
the world is black

[3] Pasternak.
[4] Translated by Stanley Kunitz.
[5] Translated by W. H. Auden.

the world is green
the world is red, yellow, brown
the world is mean

3rd World Blues [1979]

James Brown

1934–

1 Say It Loud: "I'm Black and I'm Proud."

Title of song [1968]

Joan Didion

1934–

2 Writers are always selling somebody out.

Slouching Towards Bethlehem [1968], preface

Carl Sagan

1934–

3 We are an intelligent species and the use of our intelligence quite properly gives us pleasure. In this respect the brain is like a muscle. When it is in use we feel very good. Understanding is joyous.

Broca's Brain [1979], ch. 2

Mark Strand

1934–

4 Ink runs from the corners of my mouth.
There is no happiness like mine.
I have been eating poetry.

Eating Poetry [1968]

[Leroy] Eldridge Cleaver

1935–

5 You're either part of the solution or part of the problem. *Attributed [c. 1968]*

Ken Kesey

1935–

6 A sound of cornered-animal fear and hate and surrender and defiance . . . like the last sound the treed and shot and falling animal makes as the dogs get him, when he finally doesn't care any more about anything but himself and his dying.

One Flew over the Cuckoo's Nest [1962], pt. IV

7 There are going to be times when we can't wait for somebody. Now, you're either on the bus or off the bus. If you're on the bus, and you get left behind, then you'll find it again. If you're off the bus in the first place—then it won't make a damn.

Quoted by TOM WOLFE *in The Electric Kool-Aid Acid Test [1968],*[1] *ch. 6*

John McGahern

1935–

8 Anything that is given can be at once taken away. We have to learn never to expect anything, and when it comes it's no more than a gift on loan.

The Leavetaking [1974], pt. II

Barbara C. Jordan

1936–

9 "We, the people." It is a very eloquent beginning. But when that document[2] was completed on the seventeenth of September in 1787 I was not included in that "We, the people." I felt somehow for many years that George Washington and Alexander Hamilton, just left me out by mistake. But through the process of amendment, interpretation and court decision I have finally been included in "We, the people."

Statement at Debate on Articles of Impeachment, Committee on the Judiciary, House of Representatives, Ninety-third Congress [July 25, 1974]

Kris Kristofferson

1936–

and

Fred Foster

10 Freedom's just another word for nothin' left
to lose,
And nothin' ain't worth nothin' but it's free.

Me and Bobby McGee [1969]

Woody Allen

1937–

11 Play It Again, Sam.[3]

Title of film [1969]

[1] See Wolfe, 911:4 and 911:5.

[2] Preamble to the Constitution of the United States. See Bethune, 753:6.

[3] Play it, Sam.—JULIUS and PHILIP EPSTEIN and HOWARD KOCH, *Casablanca* [1943], screenplay, spoken by Ingrid Bergman
Play it!—*Ib.*, spoken by Humphrey Bogart

1 If my film makes one more person feel miserable I'll feel I've done my job.
Interview by Time [April 30, 1979]

Thomas Pynchon

1937–

2 Yet who can presume to say *what* the war wants, so vast and aloof it is . . . so *absentee*.
Gravity's Rainbow [1973]

Gail Sheehy

1937–

3 If women had wives to keep house for them, to stay home with vomiting children, to get the car fixed, fight with the painters, run to the supermarket, reconcile the bank statements, listen to everyone's problems, cater the dinner parties, and nourish the spirit each night, just imagine the possibilities for expansion—the number of books that would be written, companies started, professorships filled, political offices that would be held, by women.[1] *Passages [1976], ch. 11*

Tom Stoppard

1937–

4 I learned three things in Zurich during the war. I wrote them down. Firstly, you're either a revolutionary or you're not, and if you're not you might as well be an artist as anything else. Secondly, if you can't be an artist, you might as well be a revolutionary . . . I forget the third thing.
Travesties [1975], last lines

Liv Ullmann

1938–

5 To be a woman is to have the same needs and longings as a man.

We need love and we wish to give it.

If only we all could accept that there is no difference between us where human values are concerned. Whatever sex. Whatever the life we have chosen to live.
Changing [1976]. Twinkle, Twinkle, Little Star

6 The best thing that can come with success is the knowledge that it is nothing to long for.
Ib. Masks

[1]See Friedan, 898:7.

James Rado

1939–

and

Gerome Ragni

1942–

7 When the moon is in the seventh house
And Jupiter aligns with Mars,
Then peace will guide the planets,
And love will steer the stars;
This is the dawning of the age of Aquarius,
The age of Aquarius.
Hair [1966]. Aquarius

John Lennon

1940–

and

Paul McCartney

1942–

8 I'll tell you something
I think you'll understand,
Then I'll say that something,
I want to hold your hand.
I Want to Hold Your Hand [1963]

9 There's a shadow hanging over me,
Oh yesterday came suddenly.
Yesterday [1965]

10 All the lonely people, where do they all belong? *Eleanor Rigby [1966]*

11 I get by with a little help from my friends.
A Little Help from My Friends [1967]

12 How does it feel to be one of the beautiful people?[2]
Baby You're a Rich Man [1967]

13 Give Peace a Chance.
Title of song [1969]

14 Let It Be. *Title of song [1970]*

Stokely Carmichael [Kwame Toure]

1941–

and

Charles Vernon Hamilton

1929–

15 Black power[3] . . . is a call for black people in this country to unite, to recognize their

[2]I could have introduced you to some very beautiful people. Mrs. Langtry and Lady Lonsdale and a lot of clever beings who were at tea with me.—OSCAR WILDE, *letter to Harold Boulton* [December 1879]

[3]Carmichael had used the phrase "Black power" in a speech in Greenwood, Mississippi [June 17, 1966].

See Langston Hughes, 855:3.

To demand these God-given rights is to seek black

heritage, to build a sense of community. It is a call for black people to begin to define their own goals, to lead their own organizations and to support those organizations. It is a call to reject the racist institutions and values of this society.

Black Power! [1967], ch. 2

1 Before a group can enter the open society, it must first close ranks. *Ib.*

Bob Dylan
[Robert Zimmerman]

1941–

2 How many roads must a man walk down
Before you call him a man?
Blowin' in the Wind [1962]

3 The answer, my friend, is blowin' in the wind,
The answer is blowin' in the wind. *Ib.*

4 A Hard Rain's A-Gonna Fall.
Title of song [1963]

5 The order is
Rapidly fadin'.
And the first one now
Will later be last[1]
For the times they are a-changin'.
The Times They Are A-Changin' [1963]

6 How does it feel
To be on your own
With no direction home
Like a complete unknown
Like a rolling stone?
Like a Rolling Stone [1965]

7 You don't need a weatherman to know which way the wind blows.
Subterranean Homesick Blues [1965]

Robin Morgan

1941–

8 Sisterhood Is Powerful.
Title of book [1970]

power—what I call audacious power—the power to build black institutions of splendid achievement.—ADAM CLAYTON POWELL, JR., *Baccalaureate address at Howard University* [May 29, 1966]

[1]See *Matthew 19:30*, 40:8.

Helen Reddy

1941–

9 If I have to, I can do anything.
I am strong, I am invincible, I am woman.
I Am Woman [1972]

Muhammad Ali[2]

1942–

10 I am the greatest.
Slogan, inspired by wrestler Gorgeous George

11 Float like a butterfly, sting like a bee.
Boxing credo, devised by aide Drew "Bundini" Brown

12 Not only do I knock 'em out, I pick the round. *Statement [December 1962]*

13 Keep asking me no matter how long—
On the war in Vietnam I sing this song—
I ain't got no quarrel with the Viet Cong.
On the draft [February 1966]

Paul Simon

1942–

14 And here's to you, Mrs. Robinson,
Jesus loves you more than you will know.
God bless you, please, Mrs. Robinson,
Heaven holds a place for those who pray.
Mrs. Robinson [1968]

15 Like a bridge over troubled water
I will lay me down.
Bridge over Troubled Water [1969]

Rap [Hubert Gerold] Brown

1943–

16 Violence is necessary; it is as American as cherry pie. *Remark [c. 1966]*

Robert Crumb

1943–

17 Keep on truckin'.
Slogan of cartoon character

Nikki Giovanni

1943–

18 His headstone said
FREE AT LAST, FREE AT LAST
But death is a slave's freedom
We seek the freedom of free men
And the construction of a world

[2]Formerly Cassius Clay.

Where Martin Luther King could have lived
and preached nonviolence.
The Funeral of Martin Luther King, Jr. [1968]

1 show me someone not full of herself and i'll
show you a hungry person
Poem for a Lady Whose Voice I Like [1970], last line

2 I really hope no white person ever has cause
to write about me
because they never understand
Black love is Black wealth and they'll
probably talk about my hard childhood
and never understand that
all the while I was quite happy.
Nikki-Rosa [1970]

3 and if ever i touched a life i hope that life knows
that i know that touching was and still is and always will be the true
revolution *When I Die [1972]*

Janis Joplin

1943–1970

4 Down on me, down on me,
Looks like everybody in this whole round world
Is down on me. *Down on Me [1967]*

5 Lord, won't you buy me a Mercedes-Benz,
My friends all drive Porsches,
I must make amends.
Mercedes-Benz [1970]

Joni Mitchell

1943–

6 They paved paradise
And put up a parking lot.
Big Yellow Taxi [1969]

7 We are stardust,
We are golden,
And we've got to get ourselves
Back to the garden. *Woodstock [1969]*

Mick [Michael Philip] Jagger

1944–

and

Keith Richards

1944–

8 Please allow me to introduce myself,
I'm a man of wealth and taste.
I've been around for long, long years,
Stolen many a man's soul and faith.
Sympathy for the Devil [1968]

9 Well, we all need someone we can lean on,
And if you want it, well, you can lean on me.
Let It Bleed [1969]

10 War, children, is just a shot away, it's just a shot away. *Gimme Shelter [1969]*

Steve [Stephen Bantu] Biko

1946–1977

11 Even today, we are still accused of racism. This is a mistake. We know that all interracial groups in South Africa are relationships in which whites are superior, blacks inferior. So as a prelude whites must be made to realize that they are only human, not superior. Same with blacks. They must be made to realize that they are also human, not inferior.
Statement quoted in the Boston Globe [October 25, 1977]

12 The basic tenet of black consciousness is that the black man must reject all value systems that seek to make him a foreigner in the country of his birth and reduce his basic human dignity.
Statement as witness [May 3, 1976][1]

Stevie Wonder [Steveland Judkins Hardaway]

1950–

13 You are the sunshine of my life,
That's why I'll always stay around.
You Are the Sunshine of My Life [1972]

Anonymous

14 Summer is icumen in,
Lhude sing cuccu!
Groweth sed, and bloweth med,
And springth the wude nu—
Sing cuccu![2] *Cuckoo Song [c. 1250]*

15 A new broom sweeps clean.
Saying [13th century]

16 Ich am of Irlonde
Ant of the holy lande
Of Irlonde.
Gode sire, pray ich the,
For of saynte charite,
Come ant dance wyth me
In Irlonde.
Ich Am of Irlonde [14th century][3]

[1] From *Black Consciousness in South Africa* [1979], edited by MILLARD ARNOLD.

[2] See Vogelweide, 138:7, and Pound, 792:8.

[3] "I am of Ireland, / And the Holy Land of Ireland, / And time runs on," cried she. / "Come out of charity, / Come dance with me in Ireland."—WILLIAM BUTLER YEATS,

1 When Adam delved and Eve span
Who was then a gentleman?
Text used by JOHN BALL *for his speech at Blackheath to the men in Wat Tyler's Rebellion [1381]*

2 Hew not too high lest the chips fall in thine eye. *Proverb [14th century]*

3 I sing of a maiden
That is makeless;
King of all kings
To her son she ches.
Carol. I Sing of a Maiden [15th century]

4 For in my mind, of all mankind
I love but you alone.
The Nut-Brown Maid [15th century], refrain

5 For I must to the greenwood go,
Alone, a banished man. *Ib.*

6 No burial this pretty pair
Of any man receives,
Till Robin Redbreast piously
Did cover them with leaves.
The Children in the Wood, st. 16

7 Before you trust a man, eat a peck of salt with him. *Proverb*[1]

8 A fool's paradise.
Paston Letters [1462], no. 457

9 Everyman, I will go with thee, and be thy guide,
In thy most need to go by thy side.
Everyman [before 1500], act I, l. 522

10 O Western wind, when wilt thou blow,
That the small rain down can rain?
Christ, that my love were in my arms
And I in my bed again!
O Western Wind [c. 1530]

11 Crabbed age and youth cannot live together.
Youth is full of pleasance, age is full of care.
The Passionate Pilgrim[2] *[1599]*

12 Love me little, love me long,
Is the burden of my song.[3]
Love Me Little [1569–1570], refrain

13 Multiplication is vexation,
Division is as bad;
The rule of three doth puzzle me,
And practice drives me mad.
Elizabethan MS [1570]

14 Alas, my Love! ye do me wrong
To cast me off discourteously:
And I have loved you so long,
Delighting in your company.
From A Handful of Pleasant Delights [1584], st. 1

15 Greensleeves was all my joy,
Greensleeves was my delight;
Greensleeves was my heart of gold,
And who but Lady Greensleeves.
Ib. refrain

16 Shall I bid her go? What, and if I do?
Shall I bid her go, and spare not?
O no, no, no, I dare not.[4]
Corydon's Farewell to Phillis, st. 2

17 Where griping griefs the heart would wound
And doleful dumps the mind oppress,
There music with her silver sound
With speed is wont to send redress.[5]
A Song to the Lute in Musicke, st. 1

18 The blinded boy that shoots so trim,[6]
From heaven down did hie.
King Cophetua and the Beggar Maid, st. 2

19 It was a friar of orders gray[7]
Walked forth to tell his beads.
The Friar of Orders Gray,[8] *st. 1*

20 Our joys as wingèd dreams do fly;
Why then should sorrow last?
Since grief but aggravates thy loss,
Grieve not for what is past. *Ib. st. 13*

21 King Stephen was a worthy peer,
His breeches cost him but a crown.
Take Thy Old Cloak About Thee,[9] *st. 7*

22 It's pride that puts this country down;
Man, take thine old cloak about thee. *Ib.*

23 A fool and his money are soon parted.
English proverb

24 April is in my mistress' face,
And July in her eyes hath place,
Within her bosom is September,
But in her heart a cold December.
From THOMAS MORLEY, *Madrigals to Four Voices [1594]*

25 Hobson's choice.[10]
Phrase for no choice

The Winding Stair and Other Poems [1933], *Words for Music Perhaps, no. 20, "I Am of Ireland," refrain*

[1] An adage originating before Cicero, who quotes a version of it in *De Amicitia 19, 67*.

[2] Often attributed to Shakespeare.

[3] See Shakespeare, 193:1, and Herrick, 266:8.

[4] Paraphrased by Shakespeare in *Twelfth-Night* [1598–1600], *act II, sc. iii.*

[5] Another version is used by Shakespeare in *Romeo and Juliet* [1594–1595], *act IV, sc. v.*

[6] See Shakespeare, 192:1.

[7] See Shakespeare, 188:37.

[8] Composed by THOMAS PERCY [1728–1811] from fragments of ancient ballads in Shakespeare; published in his *Reliques of Ancient English Poetry* [1765].

[9] Quoted in Shakespeare, *Othello* [1604–1605], *act II, sc. iii, l. 93.*

[10] Liveryman Thomas Hobson [1544–1631] obliged customers "to take the horse which stood near the stable door" (RICHARD STEELE, *The Spectator*, no. 509, October 14, 1712).

1 Lo here a new Aurora!

From THOMAS MORLEY, *The First Book of Canzonets to Two Voices [1595]*

2 Kill then, and bliss me,
But first come kiss me.

From THOMAS MORLEY, *The First Book of Ballets to Five Voices [1595]*

3 Shoot, false Love, I care not.
Spend thy shafts and spare not. *Ib.*

4 I was more true to Love than Love to me.

From JOHN DOWLAND, *The First Book of Songs or Airs [1597]*

5 Jerusalem, my happy home,
When shall I come to thee?
When shall my sorrows have an end?
Thy joys when shall I see?

The Song of Mary [1601]

6 What poor astronomers are they
Take women's eyes for stars!

From JOHN DOWLAND, *The Third Book of Songs or Airs [1603]*

7 Oh, what a plague is love! How shall I bear it?
She will inconstant prove, I greatly fear it.

Phillida Flouts Me, st. 1

8 And let all women strive to be
As constant as Penelope.

Constant Penelope, st. 18

9 Fain would I change that note
To which fond Love hath charmed me.

From TOBIAS HUME, *Musical Humors [1605]*

10 Turn again, Whittington,
Lord Mayor of London.[1]

Refrain of Bow Bells heard by Dick Whittington [c. 1605]

11 From the hag and hungry goblin
That into rags would rend ye,
And the spirit that stands by the naked man
In the book of Moons defend ye!

Tom o' Bedlam [17th century], st. 1

12 With an host of furious fancies
Whereof I am commander,
With a burning spear, and a horse of air,
To the wilderness I wander.
By a knight of ghosts and shadows
I summoned am to tourney
Ten leagues beyond the wide world's end.
Methinks it is no journey. *Ib. st. 8*

13 The law locks up both man and woman
Who steals the goose from off the common,
But lets the greater felon loose
Who steals the common from the goose.

From EDWARD POTTS CHEYNEY, *Social and Industrial History of England [1901], introduction*

14 There is a lady sweet and kind,
Was never face so pleased my mind;
I did but see her passing by,
And yet I love her till I die.

From THOMAS FORD, *Music of Sundry Kinds [1607], st. 1*

15 Cupid is wingèd and doth range,
Her country so my love doth change;
But change she earth, or change she sky,
Yet will I love her till I die. *Ib. st. 6*

16 Love not me for comely grace,
For my pleasing eye or face,
Nor for any outward part,
No, nor for a constant heart.

From JOHN WILBYE, *Second Set of Madrigals [1609]*

17 The silver swan, who living had no note,
When death approached unlocked her silent throat;
Leaning her breast against the reedy shore,
Thus sung her first and last, and sung no more:[2]
Farewell, all joys; O death, come close mine eyes;
More geese than swans now live, more fools than wise.

From ORLANDO GIBBONS, *The First Set of Madrigals and Motets of Five Parts [1612], I*

18 Stay, O sweet, and do not rise!
The light that shines comes from thine eyes;
The day breaks not: it is my heart,
Because that you and I must part.
Stay, or else my joys will die,
And perish in their infancy.[3]

From JOHN DOWLAND, *A Pilgrim's Solace [1612]*

19 We gather together to ask the Lord's blessing;
He chastens and hastens his will to make known;
The wicked oppressing now cease from distressing:[4]
Sing praises to his Name; he forgets not his own. *Hymn [1625]*[5]

[1] Richard Whittington, son of a London mercer, rose to be mayor of London three times before his death [1423].

[2] See Plato, 83:18; Shakespeare, 199:22 and 202:16; and Byron, 461:9.

[3] Attributed also to JOHN DONNE, and included in a variant in the seventh edition of his poems [1669].

[4] See *Job 3:17, 15:9*.

[5] Translated by THEODORE BAKER.
Written by an unknown author in celebration of Dutch freedom from Spanish sovereignty at the end of the sixteenth century. — *The Hymnal 1940 Companion*

1 If there is a paradise on the face of the earth,
It is this, oh! it is this, oh! it is this.
Mogul Inscription in the Red Fort at Delhi [1640]

2 Hear no evil, see no evil, speak no evil.
Legend related to the "Three Wise Monkeys" carved over door of Sacred Stable, Nikko, Japan [17th century]

3 Over the mountains and over the waves,
Under the fountains and under the graves;
Under floods that are deepest, which Neptune obey,
Over rocks that are steepest, Love will find out the way.
Love Will Find Out the Way, st. 1

4 Begone, dull Care! I prithee begone from me!
Begone, dull Care! Thou and I shall never agree.
From JOHN PLAYFORD, *Musical Companion [1687]*

5 Though little, I'll work as hard as a Turk,
If you'll give me employ,
To plow and sow, and reap and mow,
And be a farmer's boy.
The Farmer's Boy [before 1689], st. 2

6 Carriages without horses shall go,
And accidents fill the world with woe.
Attributed to Mother Shipton [1]

7 Around the world thoughts shall fly
In the twinkling of an eye. *Ib.*

8 Under water men shall walk,
Shall ride, shall sleep, and talk;
In the air men shall be seen
In white, in black, and in green. *Ib.*

9 Iron in the water shall float
As easy as a wooden boat. *Ib.*

10 A swarm of bees in May
Is worth a load of hay;
A swarm of bees in June
Is worth a silver spoon;
A swarm of bees in July
Is not worth a fly. *Old English proverb*

11 When poverty comes in at the door, love flies out the window.
Saying [17th century]

12 Please to remember the fifth of November,
Gunpowder treason and plot.
Guy Fawkes rhyme [17th century]

[1] Prophecies of the reputed fifteenth-century Mother Shipton first appeared in 1641.

13 A zealous locksmith died of late,
And did arrive at heaven gate,
He stood without and would not knock,
Because he meant to pick the lock.
Epitaph upon a Puritanical Locksmith; from WILLIAM CAMDEN, *Remains Concerning Britain [1637]*

14 All the brothers were valiant, and all the sisters virtuous.
From the inscription on the tomb of the Duchess of Newcastle in Westminster Abbey [1673]

15 It is so soon that I am done for,
I wonder what I was begun for.
For a child aged three weeks, Cheltenham Churchyard

16 Live and let live. *Scottish proverb*

17 When I rest I rust [Rast ich, so rost ich].
German proverb

18 Coming through the rye.[2]
The Bob-tailed Lass, refrain

19 Sabina has a thousand charms
To captivate my heart;
Her lovely eyes are Cupid's arms,
And every look a dart:
But when the beauteous idiot speaks,
She cures me of my pain;
Her tongue the servile fetters breaks
And frees her slave again.
From Amphion Anglicus [1700]

20 God rest you merry, gentlemen,
Let nothing you dismay;
Remember Christ our Savior,
Was born on Christmas Day. *Carol*

21 The holly and the ivy,
When they are both full grown,
Of all the trees that are in the wood,
The holly bears the crown:
The rising of the sun
And the running of the deer,
The playing of the merry organ,
Sweet singing in the choir. *Carol*

22 Sister Anne, do you see anyone coming?
Bluebeard; the cry of Fatima

23 Rain cats and dogs. *Saying*

24 Who will change old lamps for new?
The Arabian Nights (A Thousand and One Nights).[3] *The History of Aladdin*

[2] Gin a body meet a body / Coming through the rye; / Gin a body kiss a body, / Need a body cry? — BURNS, *Coming Through the Rye, st. 1*
See Nash, 856:12.

[3] First European translation (GALLAND), 1704–1717.

1 Open sesame!
Ib. The History of Ali Baba

2 Drive a coach and six through an Act of Parliament.
Credited to Sir Stephen Rice [1637–1715], Chief Baron of the Exchequer, by MACAULAY *in History of England [1849–1861], ch. 12*

3 The Campbells are comin', oho, oho.
Song [c. 1715]

4 And when with envy Time, transported,
Shall think to rob us of our joys,
You'll in your girls again be courted,
And I'll go wooing in my boys.
Winifreda [1726], st. 8

5 Fools' names, like fools' faces,
Are often seen in public places.[1]
Saying

6 And this is law, I will maintain,
Unto my dying day, sir,
That whatsoever king shall reign,
I will be the Vicar of Bray, sir!
The Vicar of Bray [1734], chorus

7 The Girl I Left Behind Me.
Title of song [1759]

8 The united voice of all His Majesty's free and loyal subjects in America—liberty and property, and no stamps.
Motto of various American colonial newspapers [1765–1766]

9 Yankee Doodle came to town
Riding on a pony,
He stuck a feather in his hat
And called it macaroni.

Yankee Doodle, keep it up,
Yankee Doodle dandy,
Mind the music and the step,
And with the girls be handy.
Yankee Doodle,[2] st. 1 and chorus

10 It's all in the day's work.
Current since the 18th century

11 Man may work from sun to sun,
But woman's work is never done.
Saying

12 Count that day lost whose low descending sun
Views from thy hand no worthy action done.[3]
Saying

13 Don't tread on me.
Motto of the first official American flag; first raised by Lieutenant John Paul Jones in Commodore Esek Hopkins's flagship Alfred [December 3, 1775]

14 Rebellion to tyrants is obedience to God.[4]
Motto on Thomas Jefferson's seal [c. 1776]

15 Lost is our old simplicity of times,
The world abounds with laws, and teems with crimes.
On the Proceedings Against America,[5] st. 1

16 Our cargoes of meat, drink, and clothes beat the Dutch.
Siege of Boston [1775]

17 There were three gypsies a-come to my door,
And downstairs ran this lady, O!
One sang high and another sang low,
And the other sang bonny, bonny Biscay, O!
The Wraggle-Taggle Gypsies, O! st. 1

18 She's gone with the wraggle-taggle gypsies, O!
Ib. st. 2

19 Down in the valley, the valley so low,
Hang your head over, hear the wind blow.
Down in the Valley

20 The goose hangs high.[6]
Saying

21 O Paddy dear, an' did ye hear the news that's goin' round?
The shamrock is by law forbid to grow on Irish ground!
No more St. Patrick's Day we'll keep, his color can't be seen,
For there's a cruel law agin the wearin' o' the Green!
The Wearing o' the Green; or, The Shan-von-Voght [c. 1795]

22 For they're hangin' men an' women there for wearin' o' the Green.
Ib.

[1] Collected by THOMAS FULLER [1654–1734], in *Gnomologia* [1732].

[2] This version was sufficiently popular in America in 1767 to be used in the ballad opera *The Disappointment; or, The Force of Credulity* by ANDREW BARTON.

Father and I went up to camp, / Along with Captain Goodwin; / And there we saw the men and boys, / As thick as hasty pudding. / Yankee doodle do.—*Version used by* ROYALL TYLER, *in The Contrast* [1790]

[3] An earlier version, signed by JAMES BOBART [December 8, 1697], begins "Think" rather than "Count."

[4] The motto of one, I believe, of the regicides of Charles I.—*Letter from Jefferson to Edward Everett* [February 24, 1823]

Jefferson's reference probably is to John Bradshaw [1602–1659].

[5] In the *Pennsylvania Gazette* [February 8, 1775], "from a late London Magazine."

[6] Originally, perhaps, "the goose *honks* high"—it cries and flies high. Wild geese fly higher when the weather is fine or promises to be fine. Hence, the prospects are bright; everything is favorable.—*Century Dictionary*

1 With drums and guns, and guns and drums
The enemy nearly slew ye.
My darling dear, you look so queer,
Oh, Johnny, I hardly knew ye.
Irish folk song, st. 1

2 Here we are on Tom Tiddler's ground
Picking up gold and silver.
Children's game

3 Christmas is coming, the geese are getting fat,
Please to put a penny in the old man's hat;
If you haven't got a penny, a ha'penny will do,
If you haven't got a ha'penny, God bless you!
Beggar's rhyme

4 From ghoulies and ghosties and long-leggety beasties
And things that go bump in the night, Good Lord, deliver us! *Cornish prayer*

5 Rest and be thankful.
Inscription on stone seat in the Scottish Highlands, and title of one of Wordsworth's poems

6 The wisdom of many and the wit of one.
Definition of a proverb[1]

7 Don't cross the bridge until you come to it.
Proverb

8 It's gude to be merry and wise,
It's gude to be honest and true;
It's gude to be off with the old love,
Before you are on with the new.[2]
Rhyme

9 Oh, ye'll tak' the high road an' I'll tak' the low road,
An' I'll be in Scotland before ye;
But me and my true love will never meet again,
On the bonnie, bonnie banks o' Loch Lomond.
Loch Lomond, refrain

10 The woods are full of them.
Quoted by ALEXANDER WILSON, *American Ornithology [1808], preface*

11 I wooed her in the wintertime
And in the summer too;
And the only, only thing I did that was wrong
Was to keep her from the foggy, foggy dew.
The Foggy, Foggy Dew, st. 1

12 Turkey in the straw, turkey in the hay,
Roll 'em up and twist 'em up a high tuck-ahaw,
And hit 'em up a tune called Turkey in the Straw.
Turkey in the Straw,[3] *st. 1 and refrain*

13 Sugar in the gourd and honey in the horn,
I never was so happy since the hour I was born. *Ib. st. 6*

14 Jimmie crack corn and I don't care,
Old Massa's gone away.
The Blue-tail Fly, chorus

15 Give me that old-time religion,
It's good enough for me. *Hymn*

16 It was good for Paul and Silas
And it's good enough for me. *Ib.*

17 I've been working on the railroad
All the livelong day,
I've been working on the railroad
To pass the time away.
Don't you hear the whistle blowing?
Rise up so early in the morn.
Don't you hear the captain shouting,
"Dinah blow your horn."
I've Been Working on the Railroad

18 When [or Since] Hector was a pup.[4]
American saying

19 OK.
Secret name for New York Democratic clubs in the 1840 presidential campaign; derived from Old Kinderhook, the home of Martin Van Buren[5]

20 Buffalo gals, won't you come out tonight,
And dance by the light of the moon?
Buffalo Gals

21 Women and children first.
The Birkenhead Drill[6] *[February 26, 1852]*

[1] Probably based on the definition of a proverb which LORD JOHN RUSSELL gave one morning at breakfast at Mardock's: "One man's wit, and all men's wisdom."—*Memoirs of Sir James Mackintosh* [1765–1832], *vol. I, p. 473*

[2] Quoted as an old song by ANTHONY TROLLOPE in *Barchester Towers* [1857], *ch. 46.*
See G. B. Shaw, 680:2.

[3] The classical American rural tune . . . steps around like an apple-faced farmhand . . . as American as Andrew Jackson, Johnny Appleseed, and Corn on the Cob. —CARL SANDBURG, *The American Songbag* [1927]

[4] See Ogden Nash, 856:6.

[5] The Whigs, unable to penetrate the meaning of O.K., put it about that President Andrew Jackson wrote O.K. as an abbreviation for "all correct."
Everything is A-OK.—JOHN A. POWERS [1922–1979], *in radio/TV reports of early manned space flights*

[6] The women and children were the first to be removed from the sinking ship *Birkenhead.*

1 Up and down the City Road,
In and out the Eagle,
That's the way the money goes—
Pop goes the weasel!
Pop Goes the Weasel[1] *[c. 1853]*

2 Free soil, free men, free speech, Frémont.[2]
Republican party rallying cry [1856]

3 Muscular Christianity.[3]
Popular term for Christian social reform in England

4 It is a newspaper's duty to print the news and raise hell.
The Chicago Times [1861]

5 Dirty work at the crossroads.
Attributed[4] *to* WALTER MELVILLE'S *melodrama The Girl Who Took the Wrong Turning; or, No Wedding Bells for Him*

6 The man on horseback.
Popular term for General Georges Ernest Boulanger [1837–1891]

7 All I want of you is a little seevility, and that of the commonest goddamnedest kind.[5]
The New Bedford Classic, as reported in ZEPHANIAH W. PEASE, *The History of New Bedford [1918]. Supposed to be said by the mate of a whaler to his ill-humored captain*

8 John Henry told his captain,
Says, "A man ain't nothin' but a man,
And before I'd let your steam drill beat me down, Lord,
I'd die with this hammer in my hand.
John Henry

9 You-all means a race or section,
Family, party, tribe, or clan;
You-all means the whole connection
Of the individual man.
You-All; from the Richmond Times-Dispatch

10 Some talk of Alexander, and some of Hercules;
Of Hector, and Lysander, and such great names as these;
But of all the world's brave heroes, there's none that can compare
With a tow, row, row, row, row, row for the British Grenadier.
The British Grenadiers

11 From the halls of Montezuma,
To the shores of Tripoli,
We fight our country's battles
On the land as on the sea.
The Marines' Hymn [1847],[6] *st. 1*

12 There is a tavern in the town,
And there my true love sits him down,
And drinks his wine with laughter and with glee,
And never, never thinks of me.
There Is a Tavern in the Town, st. 1

13 Adieu, adieu, kind friends, adieu, adieu, adieu,
I can no longer stay with you.
I'll hang my harp on a weeping willow-tree,[7]
And may the world go well with thee.
Ib. refrain

14 I belong to that highly respectable tribe
Which is known as the Shabby Genteel . . .
Too proud to beg, too honest to steal.[8]
The Shabby Genteel; sung by Sol Smith Russell [1848–1901] in A Poor Relation

15 The sons of the prophet are brave men and bold,
And quite unaccustomed to fear,
But the bravest by far in the ranks of the Shah
Was Abdullah Bulbul Amir.
Abdullah Bulbul Amir, st. 1

16 Now the heroes were plenty and well known to fame
In the troops that were led by the Czar,
And the bravest of these was a man by the name
Of Ivan Petrofski Skevar. *Ib. st. 3*

17 Is that Mr. Reilly, can anyone tell?
Is that Mr. Reilly that owns the hotel?
Well, if that's Mr. Reilly, they speak of so highly,
Upon me soul, Reilly, you're doin' quite well.
Is That Mr. Reilly?[9] *[1882], chorus*

18 Sow a thought, and you reap an act;
Sow an act, and you reap a habit;

[1] The weasel was a hatter's tool, and "pop" was a term meaning to pawn or "hock." The Eagle was a music hall in the City Road. The song is attributed to W. R. MANDALE.

[2] John Charles Frémont [1813–1890] was the party's candidate for President.

[3] A term applied (from about 1857) to the ideal of religious character exhibited in the writings of Charles Kingsley.—*Oxford English Dictionary*

His Christianity was muscular.—DISRAELI, *Endymion* [1880], *ch. 14*

[4] In *Notes and Queries* (London).

[5] Another traditional version, repudiated by a New Bedford authority, is that the skipper said: "All I want out of you is silence, and damn little of that."

[6] See Anonymous, 925:1.

[7] See *Psalm 137:2*, 22:15.

[8] See *Luke 16:3*, 43:30.

[9] Assumed origin of "the life of Riley" (an easy life).

Sow a habit, and you reap a character;
Sow a character, and you reap a destiny.
Quoted by SAMUEL SMILES *[1812–1904], in Life and Labor [1887]*

1 Now is the time for all good men to come to the aid of the party.
Practice sentence used in typewriting[1]

2 The quick brown fox jumps over the lazy dog. *Ib. (using whole alphabet)*

3 As Maine goes, so goes the nation.[2]
American political maxim [c. 1888]

4 Slide, Kelly, Slide.
Title of song by J. W. KELLY *[1889]*

5 Lizzie Borden took an ax
And gave her mother forty whacks;
When she saw what she had done
She gave her father forty-one!
Rhyme popular after the murder trial of Lizzie Borden, Fall River, Massachusetts [June 1893]

6 Out in the fields with God!
Out in the Fields

7 Remember the Maine![3]
Slogan in the Spanish-American War [1898]

8 Frankie and Johnny were lovers, my gawd, how they could love,
Swore to be true to each other, true as the stars above;
He was her man, but he done her wrong.
Frankie and Johnny,[4] *st. 1*

9 The halls of fame are open wide
And they are always full;
Some go in by the door called "push,"
And some by the door called "pull."
Quoted by STANLEY BALDWIN *[1867–1947] in a speech in the House of Commons*

10 The codfish lays ten thousand eggs,
The homely hen lays one.
The codfish never cackles
To tell you what she's done.
And so we scorn the codfish,
While the humble hen we prize,
Which only goes to show you
That it pays to advertise.
It Pays to Advertise

11 One white foot—try him,
Two white feet—buy him,
Three white feet—look well about him;
Four white feet—go without him.[5]
Rhyme for a horse-buyer

12 An apple a day keeps the doctor away.
Current since the 19th century

13 Time is of the essence. *Saying*

14 All the world is queer save me and thee; and sometimes I think thee is a little queer.
Attributed to a Quaker, speaking to his wife

15 Everyone has at least one sermon in him.
Saying

16 You can always tell a Harvard man, but you can't tell him much.
Attributed to JAMES BARNES *[1866–1936]*

17 I seen my duty and I done it.
Current since the 19th century

18 Keeping up with the Joneses.
Popular saying

19 Paying through the nose.[6]
Popular phrase for excessive payment

20 Doesn't amount to Hannah Cook.[7]
Saying common in Maine and on Cape Cod

21 Hit's a lot worse to be soul-hungry than to be body-hungry.
A Kentucky mountain woman asking for her granddaughter to be admitted to Berea College high school [c. 1900]. Quoted by CARL R. WOODWARD *in The Wonderful World of Books, edited by Alfred Stefferud [1953]*

22 Anyone who has to ask the cost can't afford it.[8] *Saying [1900s]*

[1] Charles Weller, a court reporter, originated this expression in . . . 1867 to test the efficiency of the first practical typewriter which his friend Christopher Sholes had constructed.—*Life* [April 11, 1955]

[2] As Maine goes, so goes Vermont.—JAMES FARLEY, *statement to press* [November 4, 1936] *after predicting that Roosevelt would carry all but two states in the presidential election*

[3] On February 15, 1898, the American battleship *Maine* was blown up in Havana harbor, Cuba.

[4] Traditional ballad; there are innumerable versions and verses.
See Shakespeare, 189:27.

[5] Three white feet and a white nose, / Rip off his skin and throw him to the crows.—*New Hampshire version of last two lines*

[6] Grimm says that Odin had a poll tax which was called in Sweden a nose tax; it was a penny per nose, or poll. —*Deutsche Rechts Alterthümer*

[7] Variously explained as a character who once lived on Campobello Island; a corruption of a phrase in Indian dialect; and a comparison with the worthlessness (for navigation) of a cook on board ship.

[8] Any man who has to ask about the annual upkeep of a yacht can't afford one.—*Attributed to* JOHN PIERPONT MORGAN [1837–1913]

1 There ain't no such animal.

Caption for cartoon of a farmer at the circus looking at a dromedary. From Life [November 7, 1907], credited to Everybody's Magazine

2 How old is Ann?

Popular phrase for "who knows?" [early 20th century][1]

3 The Pyramids first, which in Egypt were laid;
Next Babylon's Garden, for Amytis made;
Then Mausolos' Tomb of affection and guilt;
Fourth, the Temple of Dian in Ephesus built;
The Colossus of Rhodes, cast in brass, to the
Sun;
Sixth, Jupiter's Statue, by Phidias done;
The Pharos of Egypt comes last, we are told,
Or the Palace of Cyrus, cemented with gold.

Seven Wonders of the Ancient World

4 Use it up, wear it out;
Make it do, or do without.

New England maxim

5 Earned a precarious living by taking in one another's washing. *Saying*

6 Something old, something new,
Something borrowed, something blue,
And a lucky sixpence in her shoe.[2]

Wedding rhyme

7 God looks after fools, drunkards, and the United States. *Epigram*

8 Oh, why don't you work
Like other men do?
How the hell can I work
When there's no work to do?

Hallelujah, I'm a Bum [c. 1907]

9 Old soldiers never die;
They only fade away![3]

British Army song [c. 1915]

10 She was poor but she was honest,[4]
And her parents was the same,
Till she met a city feller,
And she lost her honest name.

Song [c. 1915]

11 It's the same the whole world over,
It's the poor wot gets the blame,
It's the rich wot gets the pleasure,
Ain't it all a bloomin' shame?

Ib. chorus

[1]"Mary is 24 years old. She is twice as old as Ann was when Mary was as old as Ann is now. How old is Ann?"—*Braintwister in the New York Press* [October 16, 1903]

Answer: Ann is 18.

[2]There are variants for the less familiar last line, such as: And a silver sixpence in each shoe.

[3]See MacArthur, 771:7.

[4]See Shakespeare, 227:12.

12 Fifty million Frenchmen can't be wrong.[5]

Saying popular with American soldiers during World War I [1917–1918]

13 Say it ain't so, Joe.

Small boy to "Shoeless Joe" Jackson of the Chicago White Sox, as he emerged from a grand jury session [1920] on corruption in the 1919 World Series

14 Don't sell America short.[6]

Saying [c. 1925]

15 Lord, through this hour
Be Thou our Guide,
So by Thy power
No foot shall slide.

Westminster Chimes

16 Climb high
Climb far
Your goal the sky
Your aim the star.

Inscription on Hopkins Memorial Steps, Williams College, Williamstown, Massachusetts

17 Mother, may I go out to swim?
Yes, my darling daughter:
Hang your clothes on a hickory limb
And don't go near the water. *Rhyme*

18 See the happy moron,
He doesn't give a damn.
I wish I were a moron—
My God, perhaps I am! *Rhyme*

19 The difficult we do immediately. The impossible takes a little longer.

Slogan of United States Army Service Forces

20 Kilroy was here.[7]

Army saying, World War II

21 SNAFU (Situation Normal All Fouled Up).

Ib.

22 G.I. Joe.

World War II term for infantryman[8]

[5]Sometimes "forty" or "thirty" is heard instead of "fifty." When Texas Guinan and her troupe were refused entry into France [1931], she was quoted as saying: "It goes to show that fifty million Frenchmen *can* be wrong." She promptly renamed her show *Too Hot for Paris,* and toured the United States with it.

[6]The phrase may have stemmed from "Never be a bear on the United States," attributed variously to JUNIUS S. MORGAN [1813–1890] and J. P. MORGAN [1837–1913].

[7]See Faulkner, 838:14.

[8]This name, chosen for the soldier in Lieutenant DAVE BREGER'S comic strip for *Yank,* the Army weekly, first appeared in the issue of June 17, 1942. Writing in *Time* [February 26, 1945], Lieutenant Breger said: "I decided

1 And when he goes to heaven
To Saint Peter he will tell:
Another Marine reporting, sir;
I've served my time in hell![1]

Epitaph on grave of Pfc. Cameron of the Marine Corps, Guadalcanal [1942]

2 Stay with me, God. The night is dark,
The night is cold: my little spark
Of courage dies. The night is long;
Be with me, God, and make me strong.

A Soldier—His Prayer,[2] *st. 1*

3 We sure liberated the hell out of this place.

American soldier in the ruins of a French village [1944]; quoted by MAX MILLER, *The Far Shore [1945]*

4 Spartan simplicity must be observed. Nothing will be done merely because it contributes to beauty, convenience, comfort, or prestige.

From the Office of the Chief Signal Officer, U.S. Army [May 29, 1945]

5 Education is what you have left over after you have forgotten everything you have learned. *Saying*

6 Time is a river without banks.[3]

Saying

7 Till Hell freezes over. *Saying*

8 One man, one vote.

Civil rights slogan

9 We shall overcome, we shall overcome,
We shall overcome some day
Oh, deep in my heart I do believe
We shall overcome some day.

Adapted [1960s] for the civil rights movement from an old religious song[4]

10 This is the grave of Mike O'Day
Who died maintaining his right of way.
His right was clear, his will was strong,
But he's just as dead as if he'd been wrong.

Rhyme [20th century]

11 Do not fold, spindle, or mutilate.

Instructions on punch cards and computer cards [c. 1930s]

12 That's the way the cookie crumbles.

Saying [1950s]

13 Garbage in, garbage out (gigo).

Computerists' aphorism [1950s]

14 Black is beautiful.[5] *Slogan [1960s]*

15 Winning isn't everything, it's the only thing.

Saying, often attributed to Vince Lombardi[6]

16 Eyeball to eyeball.[7]

Common expression

17 America, love it or leave it.

Slogan [1960s]

18 It became necessary to destroy the town in order to save it.

Attributed to an American officer firing on Ben Tre, Vietnam [February 8, 1968]

19 Today is the first day of the rest of your life.

Wall slogan [1970s]

20 Expletive deleted.

White House transcripts [published 1974]

Anonymous: African

21 In the time when Dendid created all things,
He created the sun,
And the sun is born, and dies, and comes
again. *Old Song (Dinka)*

22 He created man,
And man is born, and dies, and does not come
again. *Ib.*

23 Somewhere the Sky touches the Earth, and the name of that place is the End.

Saying (Wakamba)

24 All animals of the forest are alike, though we eat some and not others, because we the Dorobo and the animals all live side by side in the forest. *From a Dorobo*

25 Everything has an end.

Saying (Masai)

26 When elephants fight it is the grass that suffers. *Proverb (Kikuyu)*

27 Haste, haste, has no blessing.

Proverb (Swahili)

on 'G.I. Joe,' the 'G.I.' [Government Issue] because of its prevalence in Army talk, and the 'Joe' for the alliterative effect."

[1]From *The Marines' Hymn;* see Anonymous, 922:11.

[2]This poem, found on a scrap of paper in a slit trench in Tunisia during the battle of El Agheila, was printed in *Poems from the Desert,* by members of the British Eighth Army [1944].

[3]Title of a painting by Marc Chagall.
See Marcus Aurelius, 124:25, and Watts, 328:12.

[4]Originating in pre-Civil War days, this song was adapted [c. 1900] by C. ALBERT TINDLEY as a Baptist hymn called "I'll Overcome Some Day." It became famous as a protest theme when sung by black workers on picket lines in Charleston, S.C. [1946].

[5]See Hughes, 854:13.

[6]Winning isn't everything, but wanting to win is.—VINCE [VINCENT THOMAS] LOMBARDI [1913–1970], *interview* [1962]

[7]We're eyeball to eyeball, and I think the other fellow just blinked.—DEAN RUSK [1909–], *Conversation* [October 24, 1962] *during the Cuban missile crisis*

1 To the person who seizes two things, one always slips from his grasp!
Proverb (Swahili)

2 The lie has seven endings.
Proverb (Swahili)

3 Goodness sold itself, badness flaunted itself about. *Proverb (Swahili)*

4 Speak silver, reply gold.
Proverb (Swahili)

5 The prayer of the chicken hawk does not get him the chicken.
Proverb (Swahili)

6 Wisdom is not bought.
Proverb (Akan)

7 Not even God is wise enough.
Proverb (Yoruba)

8 Leave a log in the water as long as you like: it will never be a crocodile.
Proverb (Guinea-Bissau)

Anonymous: Ballads

9 The king sits in Dunfermline town
Drinking the blude-red wine.
Sir Patrick Spens, st. 1

10 To Noroway, to Noroway,
To Noroway o'er the faem;
The king's daughter o' Noroway,
'Tis thou must bring her hame.
Ib. st. 4

11 I saw the new moon late yestreen
Wi' the auld moon in her arm;
And if we gang to sea, master,
I fear we'll come to harm. *Ib. st. 10*

12 O laith, laith were our gude Scots lords
To wet their cork-heel'd shoon;
But lang or a' the play was play'd
They wat their hats aboon. *Ib. st. 15*

13 Half owre, half owre to Aberdour,
'Tis fifty fathoms deep;
And there lies gude Sir Patrick Spens,
Wi' the Scots lords at his feet!
Ib. st. 19

14 "And what will ye leave to your ain mither dear,
Edward, Edward?"
Edward, Edward, st. 7

15 "The curse of hell frae me sall ye bear,
Sic counsels ye give to me, O!" *Ib.*

16 Fight on, my merry men all;
For why, my life is at an end.[1]
Chevy Chase

17 A fairer lady there never was seen
Than the blind beggar's daughter of Bethnal Green.
The Beggar's Daughter of Bethnal Green,[2] st. 33

18 When captains courageous, whom death could not daunt,
Did march to the siege of the city of Gaunt,
They mustered their soldiers by two and by three,
And the foremost in battle was Mary Ambree. *Mary Ambree,[3] st. 1*

19 "I'll rest," said he, "but thou shalt walk";
So doth this wandering Jew
From place to place, but cannot rest
For seeing countries new.
The Wandering Jew, st. 9

20 Glasgerion swore a full great oath,
By oak, and ash and thorn.[4]
Glasgerion, st. 19

21 In Scarlet town, where I was born,
There was a fair maid dwellin',
Made every youth cry Well-a-way!
Her name was Barbara Allen.

All in the merry month of May,
When green buds they were swellin',
Young Jemmy Grove on his deathbed lay,
For love of Barbara Allen.
Barbara Allen's Cruelty, st. 1, 2

22 So slowly, slowly rase she up,
And slowly she came nigh him,
And when she drew the curtain by—
"Young man, I think you're dyin'."
Ib. st. 4

23 True Thomas lay on Huntlie Bank;
A ferlie he spied wi' his e'e;
And there he saw a lady bright
Come riding down by the Eildon Tree.
Thomas the Rhymer, st. 1

24 "A bed, a bed," Clerk Saunders said,
"A bed for you and me!"
"Fye na, fye na," said may Margaret,
"Till anes we married be!"
Clerk Saunders, st. 2

---

[1] Says Johnnie, "Fight on, my merry men all, / I'm a little wounded, but I am not slain; / I will lay me down for to bleed a while, / Then I'll rise and fight with you again."—*Johnnie Armstrong's Last Goodnight, st. 18; from* DRYDEN'S *Miscellanies* [1702]

[2] This very house was built by the blind beggar of Bednall Green, so much talked of and sung in ballads.—SAMUEL PEPYS, *Diary* [June 26, 1663]

[3] BEN JONSON calls any virago Mary Ambree, and JOHN FLETCHER alludes to Mary Ambree in *The Scornful Lady* [1616].

[4] See Kipling, 710:12.

1 There were twa sisters sat in a bour;
Binnorie, O Binnorie!
There came a knight to be their wooer,
By the bonnie milldams o' Binnorie.
Binnorie, st. 1

2 There were three ravens sat on a tree,
They were as black as they might be.

The one of them said to his mate,
"Where shall we our breakfast take?"
The Three Ravens, st. 1, 2

3 Down there came a fallow doe
As great with young as she might go.
Ib. st. 6

4 She buried him before the prime,
She was dead herself ere evensong time.

God send every gentleman
Such hounds, such hawks, and such leman.
Ib. st. 9, 10

5 Mony a one for him maks mane,
But nane sall ken where he is gane:
O'er his white banes, when they are bare,
The wind sall blaw for evermair.
The Twa Corbies, st. 5

6 Ye Highlands and ye Lawlands,
O where hae ye been?
They hae slain the Earl of Murray,
And laid him on the green.
The Bonny Earl of Murray, st. 1

7 O waly, waly, up the bank,
And waly, waly, doun the brae,
And waly, waly, yon burnside,
Where I and my Love wont to gae!
Waly, Waly, st. 1

8 "What gat ye to your dinner, Lord Randal, my son?
What gat ye to your dinner, my handsome young man?"
"I gat eels boil'd in broo'; mother, make my bed soon,
For I'm weary wi' hunting, and fain wald lie down."
Lord Randal

Anonymous: Cowboy Songs

9 As I was a-walking one morning for pleasure,
I spied a cowpuncher a-riding along.
Whoopee Ti Yi Yo, Git Along, Little Dogies

10 Whoopee ti yi yo, git along, little dogies,
It's your misfortune and none of my own,
Whoopee ti yi yo, git along, little dogies,
For you know Wyoming will be your new home.
Ib.

11 My foot in the stirrup, my pony won't stand,
Good-bye, Old Paint, I'm a-leavin' Cheyenne.
Good-bye Old Paint

12 Foot in the stirrup and hand on the horn,
Best damned cowboy ever was born.
Come-a ti yi youpy, youpy yea, youpy yea,
Come-a ti yi youpy, youpy yea.
The Old Chisholm Trail[1]

13 Last night as I lay on the prairie,
And looked at the stars in the sky,
I wondered if ever a cowboy
Would drift to that sweet bye-and-bye.
The Cowboy's Dream

14 As I walked out in the streets of Laredo,
As I walked out in Laredo one day,
I spied a poor cowboy wrapped up in white linen,
Wrapped up in white linen as cold as the clay.
The Cowboy's Lament, st. 1

15 Oh, beat the drum slowly[2] and play the fife lowly,
Play the Dead March as you carry me along;
Take me to the green valley, there lay the sod o'er me,
For I'm a young cowboy and I know I've done wrong.
Ib. refrain

16 Oh bury me not on the lone prairie
Where the wild coyotes will howl o'er me.
The Dying Cowboy

17 Oh, bury me out on the prairie,
Where the coyotes may howl o'er my grave.
Bury Me Out on the Prairie

18 Remember the Red River Valley
And the cowboy that loves you so true.
Red River Valley

19 Oh, give me a home where the buffalo roam,
Where the deer and the antelope play,
Where seldom is heard a discouraging word
And the skies are not cloudy all day.
Home on the Range [1873][3]

Anonymous: French

20 Revenons à nos moutons [Let us return to our sheep—i.e., subject].
Maître Pathelin (15th-century farce)

21 Il ne faut pas être plus royaliste que le roi [One must not be more royalist than the king].
Saying from the time of Louis XVI

[1] Of all songs, the most universally sung by the cowboys. —J. A. LOMAX, *Cowboy Songs and Other Frontier Ballads* [1910]
[2] Also familiar as: Oh, bang the drum slowly.
[3] Possibly written by BREWSTER HIGLEY.

1 Ça ira, ça tiendra [That will be, that will last].

Revolutionary song, based on a phrase of Benjamin Franklin's

2 Liberté! Égalité! Fraternité! [Liberty! Equality! Fraternity!]

Phrase from before the French Revolution, officially adopted in 1793

3 Tout passe, tout casse, tout lasse [Everything passes, everything perishes, everything palls]. *Proverb*

4 Ah, les bons vieux temps où nous étions si malheureux! [Oh, the good old times when we were so unhappy!] *Saying*

5 L'amour, l'amour fait tourner le monde [It's love, it's love that makes the world go round].[1] *Song*

6 On ne saurait faire une omelette sans casser des oeufs [You can't make an omelet without breaking eggs]. *Proverb*

7 Ami, entends-tu
Le vol noir—des corbeaux—sur nos
plaines . . .
Ami, entends-tu
Les cris sourds—du pays—qu'on enchaine.[2]

Song of the Partisans [1940s]

8 Au clair de la lune,
Mon ami Pierrot,
Prête-moi ta plume
Pour écrire un mot.

Au Clair de la Lune[3]

Anonymous: North American Indian

9 Screaming the night away
With his great wing feathers
Swooping the darkness up;
I hear the Eagle bird
Pulling the blanket back
Off from the eastern sky.

Invitation Song (Iroquois)

10 Holy Mother Earth, the trees and all nature, are witnesses of your thoughts and deeds. *Saying (Winnebago)*

11 A people without history is like the wind on the buffalo grass. *Saying (Sioux)*

12 Out of the earth
I sing for them

[1] See Gilbert, 629:2.

[2] Friend, do you hear / The black flight—of our crows—on our plains . . . / Friend, do you hear / The faint cries—of the country—in chains.

[3] By the light of the moon, / My friend Pierrot, / Lend me your pen / To write a word.
Popular since the time of Louis XVI [1638–1715]. Composed by Jean Baptiste Lully [1632–1687].

a Horse nation . . .
I sing for them
the animals.

I Sing for the Animals (Teton Sioux)

13 O our Mother the Earth, O our Father the Sky,
Your children are we, and with tired backs
We bring you gifts.

Song of the Sky Loom (Tewa)

14 May the warp be the white light of morning,
May the weft be the red light of evening,
May the fringes be the falling rain,
May the border be the standing rainbow.
Thus weave for us a garment of brightness.

Ib.

15 Lovely! See the cloud, the cloud appear!
Lovely! See the rain, the rain draw near!
Who spoke?
It was the little corn ear
High on the tip of the stalk.

Corn-grinding Song (Zuñi)

16 Big Blue Mountain Spirit,
The home made of blue clouds . . .
I am grateful for that mode of goodness there.

Chant (Apache)[4]

17 The black turkey gobbler, the tips of his beautiful tail; above us the dawn becomes yellow.
The sunbeams stream forward.

Black Turkey Gobbler Chant (Apache)[5]

18 House made of dawn,
House made of evening light,
House made of the dark cloud. . . .
Dark cloud is at the house's door,
The trail out of it is dark cloud,
The zigzag lightning stands high upon it.

Night Chant (Navaho)[6]

19 Happily may I walk.
May it be beautiful before me.
May it be beautiful behind me.
May it be beautiful below me.
May it be beautiful above me.
May it be beautiful all around me.
In beauty it is finished. *Ib.*

20 Lo, the Turquoise Horse of Johano-ai . . .
There he spurneth dust of glittering grains—
How joyous his neigh.

Song of the Horse (Navaho)

21 Hi! ni! ya! Behold the man of flint, that's me!
Four lightnings zigzag from me, strike and return. *War Chant (Navaho)*

[4] Translated by Harry Hoijer.

[5] Translated by Pliny E. Goddard.

[6] Translated by Washington Matthews.

1 The ancient folk with evil spells, dashed to earth, plowed under! *Ib.*

2 Quarry mine, blessed am I
In the luck of the chase.
Comes the deer to my singing.
Hunting Song (Navaho)

3 Idlers and cowards are here at home now,
But the youth I love is gone to war, far hence.
Weary, lonely, for me he longs.
Wind Song (Kiowa)

4 In the beginning God gave to every people a cup of clay, and from this cup they drank their life. *Proverb (Northern Paiute)*

5 As long as the moon shall rise,
As long as the rivers shall flow,
As long as the sun shall shine,
As long as the grass shall grow.
Expression for term of a treaty

6 It ended . . .
With his body changed to light,
A star that burns forever in that sky.
The Flight of Quetzalcoatl (Aztec)[1]

7 I was out in my kayak . . .
and the seal came gently toward me.
Why didn't I harpoon him?
Was I sorry for him?
Was it the day, the spring day, the seal
playing in the sun
like me? *Spring Fjord (Eskimo)*[2]

Anonymous: Nursery Rhymes[3]

8 A man of words and not of deeds
Is like a garden full of weeds.
A Man of Words and Not of Deeds

9 It's like a lion at the door;
And when the door begins to crack,
It's like a stick across your back;
And when your back begins to smart,
It's like a penknife in your heart;
And when your heart begins to bleed,
You're dead, and dead, and dead, indeed.
Ib.

10 Cock a doodle doo!
My dame has lost her shoe;
My master's lost his fiddle stick,
And knows not what to do.
Cock a Doodle Doo

[1]Translated by JEROME ROTHENBERG.

[2]Translated by ARMAND SCHWERNER.

[3]The title *Mother Goose Tales* originated with CHARLES PERRAULT [1628–1703], who published *Contes de Ma Mère l'Oye* [1697], a collection of traditional tales. JOHN NEWBURY [1713–1767], who originated the publication of children's books, first published the rhymes [1765].

11 Three blind mice, see how they run!
They all ran after the farmer's wife,
She cut off their tails with a carving knife,
Did you ever see such a sight in your life,
As three blind mice?
Three Blind Mice

12 A frog he would a-wooing go.
Sing heigh-ho says Rowley.
A Frog He Would A-Wooing Go

13 With a rowley powley gammon and spinach,
Heigh-ho says Anthony Rowley.
Ib. chorus

14 Old King Cole
Was a merry old soul,
And a merry old soul was he,
He called for his pipe,
And he called for his bowl,
And he called for his fiddlers three.
Old King Cole

15 The King of France went up the hill
With forty thousand men;
The King of France came down the hill
And ne'er went up again.
The King of France

16 Jack Sprat could eat no fat,
His wife could eat no lean;
And so betwixt them both,
They licked the platter clean.
Jack Sprat

17 Rain, rain, go away,
Come again another day. *Rain, Rain*

18 Pat-a-cake, pat-a-cake, baker's man,
Bake me a cake as fast as you can;
Pat it and prick it, and mark it with B,
Put it in the oven for baby and me.
Pat-a-Cake

19 The lion and the unicorn
Were fighting for the crown;
The lion beat the unicorn
All round about the town.
Some gave them white bread,
And some gave them brown;
Some gave them plum cake,
And sent them out of town.
The Lion and the Unicorn

20 Little Jack Horner sat in the corner,
Eating a Christmas pie.
He put in his thumb, and pulled out a plum,
And said, "What a good boy am I!"
Little Jack Horner

21 London Bridge is broken down,
My fair lady. *London Bridge*

22 Tell tale tit,
Your tongue shall be slit,

And all the dogs in our town
Shall have a bit. *Tell Tale Tit*

1 As I was going to St. Ives,
I met a man with seven wives,
Each wife had seven sacks,
Each sack had seven cats,
Each cat had seven kits:
Kits, cats, sacks, and wives,
How many were there going to St. Ives?
As I Was Going to St. Ives

2 The man in the wilderness asked of me
How many strawberries grew in the sea.
I answered him as I thought good,
"As many as red herrings grow in the wood."
The Man in the Wilderness

3 Ladybug, ladybug, fly away home,
Your house is on fire, and your children will burn. *Ladybug, Ladybug*

4 Hickory dickory dock,
The mouse ran up the clock,
The clock struck one,
The mouse ran down;
Hickory dickory dock.
Hickory Dickory Dock

5 Baa, baa, black sheep,
Have you any wool?
Yes, sir, yes, sir,
Three bags full:
One for my master,
And one for my dame,
And one for the little boy
Who lives down the lane.
Baa, Baa, Black Sheep

6 Mary, Mary, quite contrary,
How does your garden grow?
With silver bells, and cockleshells,
And pretty maids all in a row.
Mary, Mary, Quite Contrary

7 Oranges and lemons,
Say the bells of St. Clement's.
You owe me five farthings,
Say the bells of St. Martin's.
When will you pay me?
Say the bells of Old Bailey.
When I grow rich,
Say the bells of Shoreditch.
Oranges and Lemons

8 Here comes a candle to light you to bed,
Here comes a chopper to chop off your head.
Ib.

9 "Who killed Cock Robin?"
"I," said the sparrow,
"With my bow and arrow,
I killed Cock Robin."[1]
Who Killed Cock Robin?

[1] See Byron, 462:11.

10 "Who saw him die?"
"I," said the fly,
"With my little eye,
I saw him die." *Ib.*

11 This little pig went to market;
This little pig stayed home;
This little pig had roast beef;
This little pig had none;
And this little pig cried, Wee, wee, wee!
All the way home. *This Little Pig*

12 Little boy blue, come blow your horn,
The sheep's in the meadow, the cow's in the corn;
But where is the boy who looks after the sheep?
He's under the haystack fast asleep.
Will you wake him? No, not I,
For if I do, he'll be sure to cry.
Little Boy Blue

13 Simple Simon met a pieman
Going to the fair:
Says Simple Simon to the pieman,
"Let me taste your ware."
Simple Simon

14 Ding dong bell,
Pussy's in the well.
Who put her in?
Little Johnny Green. *Ding Dong Bell*

15 Little Tom Tucker
Sings for his supper;
What shall he eat?
White bread and butter.
How will he cut it
Without e'er a knife?
How will he be married
Without e'er a wife?
Little Tom Tucker

16 Crosspatch, draw the latch,
Set by the fire and spin:
Take a cup and drink it up,
Then call your neighbors in.
Crosspatch

17 High diddle diddle
The cat and the fiddle,
The cow jumped over the moon;
The little dog laughed
To see such craft
And the dish ran away with the spoon.
High Diddle Diddle

18 Three wise men of Gotham
Went to sea in a bowl:
And if the bowl had been stronger,
My song had been longer.
Three Wise Men of Gotham

1 Jack and Jill went up the hill
To fetch a pail of water;
Jack fell down and broke his crown,
And Jill came tumbling after.
Jack and Jill

2 Seesaw, Margery Daw,
Jacky shall have a new master;
Jacky must have but a penny a day,
Because he can work no faster.
Seesaw, Margery Daw

3 Taffy was a Welshman, Taffy was a thief;
Taffy came to my house and stole a piece of beef.
I went to Taffy's house, Taffy wasn't in;
Taffy came to my house and stole a marrow-bone.
Taffy Was a Welshman

4 The Queen of Hearts
She made some tarts,
All on a summer's day;
The Knave of Hearts
He stole the tarts,
And took them clean away.
The Queen of Hearts

5 Bye baby bunting,
Daddy's gone a-hunting.
Gone to get a rabbit skin
To wrap the baby bunting in.
Bye Baby Bunting

6 Come, let's to bed,
Says Sleepyhead;
Tarry awhile, says Slow;
Put on the pot,
Says Greedy-gut,
We'll sup before we go.
Let's to Bed

7 Four and twenty tailors went to kill a snail,
The best man among them durst not touch her tail.
She put out her horns like a little Kyloe cow,
Run, tailors, run, or she'll kill you all e'en now.
Four and Twenty Tailors

8 Goosey goosey gander,
Whither shall I wander?
Upstairs and downstairs,
And in my lady's chamber;
There I met an old man who wouldn't say his prayers;
I took him by the left leg
And threw him down the stairs.
Goosey Goosey Gander

9 Sing a song of sixpence,
A pocket full of rye,
Four and twenty blackbirds,
Baked in a pie;
When the pie was opened,
The birds began to sing;
Wasn't that a dainty dish
To set before a king?

The king was in his countinghouse
Counting out his money;
The queen was in the parlor
Eating bread-and honey;
The maid was in the garden
Hanging out the clothes,
Along came a blackbird,
And snipped off her nose.
Sing a Song of Sixpence

10 There was an old woman who lived in a shoe,
She had so many children she didn't know what to do;
She gave them some broth without any bread,
She whipped them all soundly and put them to bed.
There Was an Old Woman

11 Ride a cockhorse to Banbury Cross,
To see a fine lady upon a white horse;
Rings on her fingers and bells on her toes,
She shall have music wherever she goes.
Ride a Cockhorse

12 Tom, Tom, the piper's son,
He learned to play when he was young.
But all the tune that he could play
Was "Over the hills and far away."[1]
Tom, Tom, the Piper's Son

13 Tom, Tom, the piper's son,
Stole a pig, and away he run;
The pig was eat, and Tom was beat,
And Tom went howling down the street.
Ib.

14 "Where are you going to, my pretty maid?"
"I'm going a-milking, sir," she said.
Where Are You Going To, My Pretty Maid?

15 "My face is my fortune, sir," she said.
Ib.

16 "Nobody asked you, sir," she said.
Ib.

17 One a penny, two a penny, hot cross buns;
If you have no daughters, give them to your sons.
Hot Cross Buns

18 Pease-porridge hot, pease-porridge cold,
Pease-porridge in the pot, nine days old.
Pease-Porridge Hot

19 Curlylocks, Curlylocks,
Wilt thou be mine?
Thou shalt not wash dishes
Nor yet feed the swine,
But sit on a cushion
And sew a fine seam,
And feed upon strawberries,
Sugar and cream.
Curlylocks

[1]See Gay, 332:1, and Tennyson, 530:13.

1 I had a little nut tree, nothing would it bear
But a silver nutmeg and a golden pear;
The king of Spain's daughter came to visit me,
And all for the sake of my little nut tree.
I Had a Little Nut Tree

2 Humpty Dumpty sat on a wall,
Humpty Dumpty had a great fall;
All the king's horses
And all the king's men
Couldn't put Humpty Dumpty together again. *Humpty Dumpty*

3 Little Bo-peep has lost her sheep,
And cannot tell where to find them;
Leave them alone, and they'll come home,
And bring their tails behind them.
Little Bo-peep

4 Little Polly Flinders
Sat among the cinders,
Warming her pretty little toes.
Her mother came and caught her,
And whipped her little daughter
For spoiling her nice new clothes.
Little Polly Flinders

5 There was an old woman tossed in a blanket,
Seventeen times as high as the moon;
But where she was going no mortal could tell,
For under her arm she carried a broom.
Old woman, old woman, old woman, said I,
Whither, ah whither, ah whither so high?
To sweep the cobwebs from the sky,
And I'll be with you by and by.
There Was an Old Woman

6 The north wind doth blow,
And we shall have snow,
And what will poor robin do then,
Poor thing?
He'll sit in a barn,
To keep himself warm,
And hide his head under his wing,
Poor thing!
The North Wind Doth Blow

7 Old mother Hubbard
Went to the cupboard,
To fetch her poor dog a bone;
But when she came there
The cupboard was bare,
And so the poor dog had none.
Old Mother Hubbard

8 Pussy cat, pussy cat, where have you been?
I've been to London to look at the queen.
Pussy cat, pussy cat, what did you there?
I frightened a little mouse under the chair.
Pussy Cat

9 Peter Piper picked a peck of pickled peppers;
A peck of pickled peppers Peter Piper picked.
If Peter Piper picked a peck of pickled peppers,
Where's the peck of pickled peppers Peter Piper picked? *Peter Piper*

10 Monday's child is fair of face,
Tuesday's child is full of grace,
Wednesday's child is full of woe,
Thursday's child has far to go,
Friday's child is loving and giving,
Saturday's child has to work for its living,
But a child that's born on the Sabbath day
Is fair and wise and good and gay.
Monday's Child Is Fair of Face

11 Solomon Grundy,
Born on a Monday,
Christened on Tuesday,
Married on Wednesday,
Took ill on Thursday,
Worse on Friday,
Died on Saturday,
Buried on Sunday:
This is the end
Of Solomon Grundy. *Solomon Grundy*

12 What are little boys made of?
Snips and snails, and puppy dogs' tails;
That's what little boys are made of.
What Are Little Boys Made Of?

13 What are little girls made of?
Sugar and spice, and everything nice;
That's what little girls are made of.
Ib.

14 Hickety pickety, my black hen,
She lays eggs for gentlemen.
Gentlemen come every day
To see what my black hen doth lay.
Hickety Pickety

15 Little Miss Muffet
Sat on a tuffet,
Eating some curds and whey.
Along came a spider,
And sat down beside her,
And frightened Miss Muffet away.
Little Miss Muffet

16 Peter, Peter Pumpkin-Eater,
Had a wife and couldn't keep her.
He put her in a pumpkin shell,
And there he kept her very well.
Peter, Peter Pumpkin-Eater

17 Jack, be nimble,
Jack, be quick,
Jack, jump over the candlestick.
Jack Be Nimble

18 There was a crooked man, and he went a crooked mile,

He found a crooked sixpence against a crooked stile;
He bought a crooked cat, which caught a crooked mouse,
And they all lived together in a little crooked house.
There Was a Crooked Man

1 Diddle diddle dumpling, my son John,
He went to bed with his stockings on;
One shoe off, one shoe on;
Diddle diddle dumpling, my son John.
Diddle Diddle Dumpling

2 Rub-a-dub-dub,
Three men in a tub,
And who do you think they be?
The butcher, the baker,
The candlestick-maker;
Turn 'em out, knaves all three!
Rub-a-Dub-Dub

3 I saw three ships come sailing by,
Come sailing by, come sailing by,
I saw three ships come sailing by,
On New Year's Day in the morning.
I Saw Three Ships

4 In fir tar is,
In oak none is.
In mud eel is,
In clay none is.
Goats eat ivy.
Mares eat oats.
In Fir Tar Is

5 Lucy Locket lost her pocket,
Kitty Fisher found it;
There was not a penny in it,
But a ribbon round it.
Lucy Locket

6 There were three jolly huntsmen,
As I have heard them say,
And they would go a-hunting
Upon St. David's Day.
There Were Three Jolly Huntsmen

7 All day they hunted,
And nothing did they find,
But a ship a-sailing,
A-sailing with the wind.
Ib.

8 O do you know the muffin man,
The muffin man, the muffin man,
O do you know the muffin man,
That lives in Drury Lane?
The Muffin Man

9 To market, to market, to buy a fat pig,
Home again, home again, jiggety-jig.
To Market, To Market

10 Doctor Foster went to Gloucester
In a shower of rain;
He stepped in a puddle, up to his middle,
And never went there again.
Doctor Foster

11 There was an old woman
Lived under a hill;
And if she's not gone,
She lives there still.
There Was an Old Woman

12 There was a little man, and he had a little gun,
And his bullets were made of lead, lead, lead;
He went to the brook, and saw a little duck,
And shot it through the head, head, head.
There Was a Little Man

13 Lavender's blue, dilly dilly, lavender's green;
When I am king, dilly dilly, you shall be queen.
Lavender's Blue

14 A dillar, a dollar,
A ten o'clock scholar,
What makes you come so soon?
You used to come at ten o'clock,
And now you come at noon.
A Dillar, a Dollar

15 One flew east, one flew west,
One flew over the cuckoo's nest.
One Flew East

16 I had a little pony,
His name was Dapple Gray;
I lent him to a lady
To ride a mile away.
She whipped him, she slashed him,
She rode him through the mire;
I would not lend my pony now
For all the lady's hire.
I Had a Little Pony

17 Polly, put the kettle on,
We'll all have tea.
Polly, Put the Kettle On, st. 1

18 Sukey, take it off again,
They've all gone away.
Ib.

19 Little Tommy Tittlemouse
Lived in a little house;
He caught fishes
In other men's ditches.
Little Tommy Tittlemouse

20 The farmer in the dell, the farmer in the dell,
Heigho! the derry oh, the farmer in the dell.
The Farmer in the Dell

21 Hark! Hark! The dogs do bark,
The beggars are coming to town;
Some in rags, some in tags,
And some in velvet gowns.
Hark! Hark!

22 Ten little Indians standing in a line—
One went home, and then there were nine.
Ten Little Indians

1 When good King Arthur ruled this land,
He was a goodly king,
He bought three pecks of barley meal,
To make a bag pudding.
Good King Arthur

2 One misty, moisty morning,
When cloudy was the weather,
I chanced to meet an old man
Clothed all in leather;
He began to compliment,
And I began to grin—
"How do you do?" and "How do you do?"
And "How do you do?" again!
One Misty, Moisty Morning

3 Bobby Shaftoe's gone to sea,
Silver buckles on his knee;
He'll come back and marry me,
Pretty Bobby Shaftoe. *Bobby Shaftoe*

4 Fe fi fo fum!
I smell the blood of an Englishman;
Be he alive or be he dead,
I'll grind his bones to make my bread.
Fe Fi Fo Fum

5 Sing, sing! What shall I sing?
The cat's run away with the pudding-bag string.
Sing, Sing! What Shall I Sing?

6 Shoe the horse, shoe the mare,
But let the little colt go bare.
Shoe the Horse

7 There was a man in our town,
And he was wondrous wise;
He jumped into a bramble bush
And scratched out both his eyes.
There Was a Man in Our Town

8 There were two blackbirds,
Sitting on a hill,
The one named Jack,
The other named Jill;
Fly away, Jack! Fly away, Jill!
Come again, Jack! Come again, Jill!
Two Blackbirds

9 This is the farmer sowing the corn,
That kept the cock that crowed in the morn,
That waked the priest all shaven and shorn,
That married the man all tattered and torn,
That kissed the maiden all forlorn,
That milked the cow with the crumpled horn,
That tossed the dog
That worried the cat
That killed the rat
That ate the malt
That lay in the house that Jack built.
The House That Jack Built

Anonymous: Russian

10 Let the woman into Paradise, she'll bring her cow along. *Proverb*

11 An egg is dear on Easter Day. *Proverb*

12 To live a life through is not like crossing a field.[1] *Proverb*

13 The eggs do not teach the hen. *Proverb*

14 Without a shepherd sheep are not a flock. *Proverb*

15 Live with wolves, howl like a wolf. *Proverb*

Anonymous: Shanties

16 Whiskey is the life of man,
Whiskey, Johnny!
Oh, I'll drink whiskey while I can,
Whiskey for my Johnny!
Whiskey Johnny

17 Oh, blow the man down, bullies, blow the man down!
To me way-aye, blow the man down.
Oh, blow the man down, bullies, blow him right down!
Give me some time to blow the man down!
Blow the Man Down

18 What shall we do with the drunken sailor,
Early in the morning?
The Drunken Sailor

19 Hooray and up she rises
Early in the morning. *Ib. chorus*

20 Oh, Shenandoah, I long to hear you,
Way-hay, you rolling river!
Oh, Shenandoah, I long to hear you,
Ha-ha, we're bound away,
'Cross the wide Missouri! *Shenandoah*

21 A-roving, a-roving,
Since roving's been my ru-i-in,
I'll go no more a-roving
With you, fair maid! *A-Roving*

22 Glos'ter girls they have no combs,
Heave away, heave away!
They comb their hair with codfish bones.
The Codfish Shanty

23 Oh, you New York girls, can't you dance the polka?
Can't You Dance the Polka?

[1] See Pasternak, 816:18.

1 Good-bye, fare you well!
We're homeward bound for New York town,
Hurrah, my boys, we're homeward bound!
Good-bye, Fare You Well

2 Oh, the times are hard and the wages low;
Leave her, Johnny, leave her!
I'll pack my bag and go below.
It's time for us to leave her!
Leave Her, Johnny

3 There were two lofty ships, from old England they set sail,
Blow high, blow low, and so sailed we! . . .
Cruising down along the shores of High Barbaree!
High Barbaree

4 There was a ship came from the north country,
And the name of the ship was the *Golden Vanity.*
And they feared she might be taken by the Turkish enemy,
That sails upon the Lowland, Lowland, Lowland,
That sails upon the Lowland sea.
The Golden Vanity

5 Then blow ye winds, heigh-ho!
A-roving I will go,
I'll stay no more on England's shore,
To hear the music play.
I'm off on the morning train
To cross the raging main,
I'm taking a trip on a Government ship,
Ten thousand miles away!
Ten Thousand Miles Away

6 There is a flash packet, flash packet of fame,
She hails from New York and the *Dreadnought*'s her name.
The Dreadnought

7 She's the Liverpool packet—O Lord, let her go!
Ib.

Anonymous: Spanish

8 A enemigo que huye puente de plata [If your enemy turns to flee, give him a silver bridge].
Proverb

9 Al que madruga Dios le ayuda [God helps those who get up early].
Proverb

10 Con pan y vino se anda el camino [With bread and wine you can walk your road].
Proverb

11 El pez muere por la boca [The fish dies because he opens his mouth].
Proverb

12 El que se sienta en la puerta de su casa vera pasar el cadaver de su enemigo [He who sits at the door of his house will watch his enemy's corpse go by].
Proverb

13 En boca cerrada no entran moscas [The close mouth swallows no flies].
Proverb

14 En casa del lenero cuchillo de palo [In the woodsman's house the knives are of wood].
Proverb

15 No por mucho madrugar amanece mas temprano [Dawn comes no sooner for the early riser].
Proverb

16 Quien bien te quiere te hara llorar [Whoever really loves you will make you cry].
Proverb

17 El oro y amores eran malos de encubrir [Gold and love affairs are difficult to hide].[1]
Proverb

18 Dios te tenga en su santa mano [God keep you in his holy hand].
A farewell

Anonymous: Spirituals

19 Nobody knows the trouble I've seen,
Nobody knows but Jesus.
Nobody Knows the Trouble I've Seen

20 Joshua fit the battle of Jericho,
And the walls come tumbling down.[2]
Joshua Fit the Battle of Jericho

21 Go down, Moses,
Way down in Egypt land,
Tell old Pharaoh,
Let my people go.[3]
Go Down, Moses

22 Free at last, free at last,
Thank God Almighty, we're free at last.
Free at Last

23 I looked over Jordan, and what did I see? . . .
A band of angels coming after me,
Coming for to carry me home.
Swing Low, Sweet Chariot, st. 1

24 Swing low, sweet chariot,
Coming for to carry me home.
Ib. refrain

25 Michael row the boat ashore,
Hallelujah!
Michael Row the Boat Ashore

26 Rise and shine[4] and give God the glory
For the year of Jubilee.[5]
Rise and Shine

[1] See George Herbert, 269:12.
[2] See *Joshua 6:20*, 11:31.
[3] See *Exodus 5:1*, 9:16.
[4] See *Isaiah 60:1*, 31:23.
[5] See *Leviticus 25:10*, 10:22.

1 My Lord, what a morning,[1]
When the stars begin to fall.
My Lord, What a Morning

2 You'll hear the trumpet sound,
To wake the nations underground,
Look in my God's right hand,
When the stars begin to fall. *Ib.*

3 One more river,
And that's the river of Jordan,
One more river,
There's one more river to cross.
One More River

4 Oh, freedom! Oh, freedom!
Oh, freedom over me!
And before I'd be a slave, I'll be buried in my grave,
And go home to my Lord and be free.
Oh, Freedom!

[1] Also written as: mourning.

5 Get on board, little children,
There's room for many a more.
Get on Board, Little Children

6 The Gospel train's a-coming. *Ib.*

7 Just like a tree that's standing by the water,[2]
We shall not be moved.[3]
We Shall Not Be Moved[4]

8 O Lord, I want to be in that number
When the saints go marching in.
When the Saints Go Marching In

[2] See *Psalm 1:3*, 17:12.
[3] See *Psalm 46:5*, 19:11.
[4] Later adapted as a labor and civil rights song.

Index

Index

Please see the Index section of the Guide to the Use of Familiar Quotations, page xv.

A

A, black A white E, 673 : 20
emotions from A to B, 827 : 16
first write a crowned A, 145 : 20
injures B to improve X, 772 : 16
on gown letter A, 503 : 5
A', for a. that and a. that, 411 : 19
A-angling, be quiet and go a., 271 : 14
Aaron's, like A. serpent, 337 : 4
rod, 9 : 19
Ab Iove principium, 103 : *n* 7
ovo, 109 : *n* 12
urbe condita, 133 : 3
Abandon, all hope a. who enter here, 140 : 13
basely a. noble struggle, 383 : 4
do not fear to a. faults, 68 : 7
government which kept free, 388 : 17
learning and no sorrow, 64 : 9
nation never a. fate, 616 : 1
to cries and lamentations, 116 : 7
Abandoned, down the a. heaven, 790 : 16
God a. these defended, 692 : 4
man a. on earth, 865 : 11
Abandonment of force, 781 : 9
Abased, whoso exalt himself be a., 40 : 17
Abashed the Devil stood, 286 : 8
Abatement and low price, 213 : 8
Abbot of Aberbrothok, 439 : 17
Abbots purple as their wines, 340 : 26
ABC, learn ABC of science, 665 : 5
of being, 768 : 2
of woman's rights, 577 : 18
A.B.C.'s, droop in a hundred A., 804 : 19
Abdullah Bulbul Amir, 922 : 15
Abednego, Shadrach Meshach and A., 32 : 33
A-begging, truth goes a., 156 : 4
Abel was keeper of sheep, 7 : 14
Aberbrothok, Abbot of A., 439 : 17
Aberdour, half owre to A., 926 : 13
Abhor and detest Sabbath, 624 : 8
makers and laws approve, 305 : 26
Abhorred in my imagination, 224 : 14
shears, 280 : 15
that senseless tribe, 322 : 19
Abhors, nature a. a vacuum, 308 : 4
Abide, fates impose that men a., 186 : 16
nowhere did a., 434 : 27
others a. our question, 584 : 9
something in him we cannot a., 263 : 16
time nyl no man a., 147 : 17

Abide (*continued*)
under the shadow of the Almighty, 20 : 16
who shall a. in thy tabernacle, 17 : 22
with me, 470 : 23
Abides, in mystery soul a., 584 : 18
there a. peace of thine, 585 : 1
Abideth, earth a. forever, 26 : 11
faith hope charity, 48 : 25
Abiding leaf, 875 : 4
shepherds a. in field, 42 : 28
Abiezer, vintage of A., 12 : 11
Abiit ad plures, 117 : *n* 9
excessit evasit erupit, 98 : *n* 3
Abilities, common opinions uncommon a., 597 : 9
from each according to a., 563 : 1
possible for others to use a., 883 : 6
splendid a. but utterly corrupt, 439 : 7
Ability alone insufficient, 313 : 5
capacity to act wisely, 697 : 18
charge not soul save to its a., 131 : 15
distressed by want of a., 69 : 12
laughter a. and sighing, 606 : 7
lean and low a., 214 : 25
retain a. to function, 835 : 10
they never perform, 226 : 13
to get to verge, 803 : 8
to register multiple perception, 793 : 10
Abject are usually ambitious, 308 : 18
submission, 379 : 2
Abjure my so much loved variety, 253 : 21
Able and willing to pull weight, 687 : 7
at least as far as a., 668 : 10
be a. for thine enemy, 227 : 9
rather a. than learned, 164 : 13
Ablest navigators, 383 : 13
Ablution round earth's shores, 478 : 20
Abner a prince and a great man, 13 : 13
smote him under the fifth rib, 13 : 12
Aboard at a ship's helm, 575 : 19
Abode, brightly as from rich a., 560 : 18
destined hour, 516 : 10
dread a., 362 : 19
Last A. is Life, 132 : 1
Olympus a. of the gods, 59 : 27
untented Kosmos my a., 669 : 3
Abodes, aiming at blessed a., 336 : 18
august a., 442 : 16
peaceful a. of the gods, 59 : *n* 5
sprung from blessed a., 335 : 9
Abolish, English never a., 698 : 10
right to alter or a. it, 387 : 9
serfdom from above, 561 : 7

Abolish (*continued*)
slavery of half of humanity, 870 : 12
tyranny and vice, 380 : 6
vice destroy virtue, 274 : 18
Abolished will, 892 : 7
Abolition of private property, 563 : 7
Abolitionists yet to learn woman's rights, 577 : 18
Abominable, newspapers the most a., 399 : 5
Abominably, imitated humanity so a., 222 : 3
Abomination, Mass an a., 156 : 6
of desolation, 40 : 23
Abora, singing of Mount A., 433 : 26
Aboriginal nature, 557 : 18
Aborigines, fell on knees then on a., 562 : 14
A-borrowing, goeth a., 163 : 5
Abou Ben Adhem, 454 : 4
Abound, grace a., 47 : 2
joys a. as seasons fleet, 185 : 14
Abounded, where sin a., 47 : 2
About about in reel and rout, 434 : 17
it and about but evermore, 516 : 16
Above, at once a. beneath around, 365 : 6
economic tyranny a., 794 : 12
every good gift is from a., 51 : 29
insolence and triviality, 798 : 11
may it be beautiful a. me, 928 : 19
no stander a. or apart, 574 : 20
world stretched the sky, 822 : 12
Abra ready ere I called, 320 : 25
Abraham, God of A. not of philosophers, 300 : 15
of scientific men, 580 : 7
that which has been sent down on A., 130 : 11
thy name shall be A., 8 : 10
we are coming Father A., 537 : 2
Abraham's, beggar in A. bosom, 43 : 33
liest in A. bosom, 425 : 17
sleep in A. bosom, 187 : 17
Abram dwelled in Canaan, 8 : 7
O father A., 198 : 27
Abreast, into midnight galloped a., 541 : 12
of truth, 567 : 8
one but goes a., 226 : 18
Abreuve nos sillons, 415 : 1
Abridging freedom of speech, 391 : 14
Abridgment of all pleasant in man, 371 : 16
of freedom, 398 : 4
Abroad for good of my country, 329 : 10

Abroad (*continued*)
  know own country before goes a., 360:18
  lie a. for commonwealth, 251:4
  obsequious a., 452:16
  purchase great alliance, 186:12
  schoolmaster is a., 444:14
  what should not be published a., 79:13
  when he next doth ride a., 376:16
Absalom my son my son, 13:23
Absence, bitter impression of a., 906:14
  conspicuous by a., 466:4
  courage not a. of fear, 624:21
  cry of a. in heart, 810:17
  cure of love, 169:15
  darkness death, 253:1
  diminishes mediocre passions, 293:31
  dote on his very a., 198:15
  doth breed continual remembrance, 148:*n* 8
  involves presence, 906:14
  like a winter my a., 245:8
  love cannot admit a., 253:3
  love renewed by a., 352:13
  makes heart fonder, 112:25
  of mind we have borne, 442:11
  of occupation not rest, 376:8
  of romance in my history, 80:15
  opens springs of love, 555:6
  peace not a. of war, 308:3
  re-begot of a., 253:1
  seemed my flame to qualify, 245:14
  Ulysses' a., 242:10
Absences, fundamental a. struggling, 906:14
Absent, friends a. speak, 254:4
  from Him I roam, 429:17
  if to be a. were to be away, 296:5
  in body present in spirit, 48:8
  in the spring, 245:9
  let no one speak ill of a. 112:23
  one from another, 8:23
  or dead friend dear, 334:20
  room of a. child, 201:26
  thee from felicity, 225:1
Absentee, war vast aloof a., 914:2
Absentes, in a. felicior aestus amantes, 112:*n* 12
Absenti nemo non nocuisse velit, 112:*n* 10
Absents, presents endear a., 441:25
Absit omen, 133:4
Absolute and in herself complete, 287:8
  atoms preserved by a. solidity, 100:9
  be a. for death, 228:14
  built a. trust, 236:15
  dictatorship a. as any other, 780:8
  find a. rhythm, 783:1
  foreknowledge a., 284:19
  freedom of navigation, 682:14
  how a. the knave is, 224:12
  idea of knowledge, 85:12
  Johannes fac totum, 178:12
  mark you his a. shall, 242:18
  natures or kinds, 85:12
  notion of a. beauty, 83:9
  power corrupts absolutely, 615:15
  power in majority, 382:4
  power over wives, 392:9
  security, 860:3
Absolute (*continued*)
  truth forever a., 538:17
Absolutely, corrupts a., 615:15
  line a. straight, 471:*n* 3
Absolutes in Bill of Rights, 794:17
  in world affairs, 860:3
  meant prohibitions to be a., 794:17
  the a. the eternities, 886:8
Absolutism tempered by assassination, 417:4
Absolve, compensate bad in man a. him so, 545:12
  foulness of their fate, 795:16
  pray God a. us all, 150:10
Absolved from allegiance, 378:12
  judge condemned when criminal a., 111:10
Absorb as parallax a flame, 607:5
Absorbing, reflects images without a., 635:6
Absorbs, country a. him affectionately, 573:20
  tinged by what a. it, 650:10
Abstain from fleshly lusts, 52:10
  from ignorance, 552:1
  from intentional wrongdoing, 79:13
Abstains from words, 565:30
Abstinence easy to me, 353:19
  lean and sallow a., 279:30
  lend easiness to next a., 223:11
  sows sand all over, 404:16
Abstinete, a fabis a., 258:15
Abstract concepts, 390:7
  ideas conditioned by time, 698:6
  liberty not found, 372:18
  love of beauty in a., 479:13
  man in the a., 602:11
  science knowledge of reasons, 465:12
  words obscene, 844:14
Abstracted, take high a. man alone, 571:2
Abstraction, an a. blooded, 768:14
Abstracts and brief chronicles, 221:4
Absurd, death a. also, 877:6
  essentially a divorce, 882:4
  is essential concept, 882:5
  lick a. pomp, 222:4
  logic of heart a., 378:13
  man never changes, 451:*n* 4
  poets creatures most a., 339:29
  proving a. all written, 543:25
  question is a., 869:3
  the a. not the improbable, 552:12
  to be believed because a., 126:8
Absurdities of next age, 664:12
Absurdity, dull without a single a., 369:6
  man only subject to a., 264:14
  privilege of a., 264:14
  what to do with this a., 715:4
Abundance, add more to a., 780:3
  full sharers in a., 666:22
  if thou hast a., 34:7
  in a. lack, 80:1
  natural and varied a., 824:12
  out of a. mouth speaketh, 39:11
  possesses virtue in a., 64:18
  pray in days of a., 782:18
  result of brain and brawn, 666:22
  will not suffer him to sleep, 27:1
Abundant, blueness a., 546:1
  good communicated more a., 286:14
  more a. life, 779:12
Abundant (*continued*)
  shower of curates, 555:20
  wretched and a. Russia, 584:3
Abundantly, have life more a., 45:10
Abuse, cry out loudest its a., 309:3
  drug it's fashion to a., 630:10
  how long Catiline a. our patience, 98:1
  land as commodity, 795:10
  of greatness, 215:15
  wicked dreams a., 237:14
  you cause what you a., 316:1
Abused, better to be much a., 231:9
  or disabused, 337:2
Abuses, evils exist only in a., 419:4
  excites hatred to conceal a., 444:4
Abusing, abstain from a. bodies, 79:13
  of God's patience, 225:12
  power without a. it, 488:18
  stop a. my verses or publish, 119:4
Abydos, Sestos and A. of her breasts, 253:23
Abysm of time, 247:10
Abysmal dark of center, 480:12
Abyss, cradle rocks above a., 846:2
  discovery metamorphosis, 739:12
  look long into a., 657:22
  looks into you, 657:22
  man is rope over a., 657:12
  nameless a., 593:11
Abysses, dread a. unknown tides, 651:3
Abyssinia, Rasselas Prince of A., 352:15
Abyssinian maid, 433:26
Academe, groves of A., 109:14
  olive grove of A., 288:14
Academes, they are the books the a., 191:5
Academi, inter silvas A., 109:*n* 6
Academic life, 257:11
Academy, Frenchman in A., 354:*n* 4
Accelerated grimace, 792:12
Acceleration proportional to applied force, 313:*n* 5
Accent, Greek a. slanting wrong, 560:21
Accents, aged a. untimely words, 182:6
  caught his clear a., 541:6
  yet unknown, 216:7
Accept, bow and a. end, 747:2
  decline to a. end of man, 838:9
  fall in with what asked to a., 750:11
  God a. him, 533:6
  if nominated not a., 579:4
  learn to a. in silence, 664:18
  never a. thing as true, 272:8
  not a beggar would a., 607:8
  not God I don't a., 582:4
  our thanksgiving a., 631:15
  place providence found, 496:21
  tamely a., 704:17
  things that cannot be changed, 823:15
  universe, 536:13
  what cannot be changed, 823:15
  will for deed a., 158:*n* 3
Acceptable, be a. in thy sight, 18:3
  more a. the straightforward man, 4:3
  offices a. here, 388:14
  safeguards a. to all nations, 787:16
Acceptation, news worthy of a., 319:15

Accepted, fellow mortals a. as they are, 565 : 3
now is a. time, 49 : 15
that which a. false, 735 : 16
Accepting, charms by a., 335 : 23
not by a. favors, 81 : 3
Access and passage to remorse, 236 : 17
Accident, by a. got its liberty, 154 : 8
counts for much, 634 : 16
found out by a., 442 : 15
happy a., 261 : 18, 771 : 15
never say universe a., 862 : 4
of sentiment, 619 : 7
our race may be a., 746 : 20
progress not a. but necessity, 579 : 5
proliferation or a. in weapons race, 860 : 6
shot of a., 231 : 26
what seems a. springs from destiny, 413 : 12
Accidentally, America discovered a., 800 : 5
only a. am I French, 341 : 10
Accidents, chapter of a. very long, 342 : 14
controlled by a. or by ourselves, 862 : 12
fill world, 919 : 6
in best-regulated families, 548 : 35
miracles propitious a., 703 : 17
moving a. by flood, 229 : 28
omissions are not a., 798 : *n* 3
shackles a., 241 : 24
Acclaim earned in blood, 815 : 13
your glorious name, 829 : 5
Accommodating vice, 298 : 3
Accommodation, tolerable a. of interests, 737 : 4
Accommodations, equal but separate a., 820 : *n* 3
Accompany old age, 239 : 31
Accomplice, art a. of love, 686 : 2
evening comes like a., 581 : 2
Accomplish little, 413 : 32
you must a. as you may, 188 : 20
Accomplished, desire a. is sweet, 23 : 33
her warfare is a., 30 : 30
nothing a. alone, 823 : 21
nothing great a. without passion, 422 : 13
plan of Zeus was being a., 57 : 4
Accomplisher, Zeus a., 71 : 27
Accomplishes without any action, 64 : 17
Accomplishing, armorers a. the knights, 208 : 1
their appointed courses, 78 : 19
Accomplishments, emerges ahead of a., 857 : 4
give luster, 342 : 10
Accord, someone whom we a. with, 395 : 6
Accordance, activity in a. with excellence, 87 : 23
According as man is must you humor him, 97 : 5
to every man a. to his work, 19 : 28
Account, closing your a. and mine, 516 : 21
of her life to clod, 209 : 6
sent to my a., 219 : 24
whatever you lose no a., 110 : 23
Accountability to no one, 789 : 4
Accountable, governments a., 813 : 9
Accounting, death the final a., 134 : 10
no a. for tastes, 133 : 17
Accumulate, horrors a., 231 : 14
sage does not a., 65 : 10
Accumulated experience, 753 : 12
wrong, 704 : 17
Accumulates, where wealth a., 369 : 30
Accumulation, law of a., 621 : 10
Accuracy tried by severe tests, 80 : 15
Accurate in his judgment, 380 : *n* 2
thought a conquest, 865 : 10
Accurately, report news a., 820 : 13
Accursed bucketshop 711 : 2
craving for gold, 105 : 6
fear most a. of base passions, 185 : 5
he that first invented war, 183 : 4
night she bore me, 76 : 10
opinions are a., 714 : 20
what blessed prove a., 544 : 29
Accuse, not a. me before the God, 4 : 9
j'a., 643 : 9
justice enough to a., 369 : 15
not Nature, 287 : 9
not servant to his master, 26 : 2
Accuser, no a. so terrible, 95 : 19
Accuses, excuses himself a. himself, 163 : 8
Accusing Spirit, 360 : 17
Accustomed to deliberate when drunk, 78 : 6
to her face, 895 : 3
to way ground opens up, 912 : 12
Ace, auspicious as a. of spades, 899 : 14
Aces, Christian with four a., 626 : 20
triumphing over kings and a., 818 : 5
Achaeans, brought upon the A. myriad woes, 57 : 3
well-greaved A., 57 : 24
A-changin', times they are a., 915 : 5
Achates, faithful A., 105 : 16
fidus A., 105 : *n* 8
Ache, age a. penury, 228 : 21
ark of the a. of it, 902 : 17
at tooth of the ego, 881 : 11
charm a. with air, 210 : 4
Ached, never a. with heart, 632 : 13
Acheron, fear of A. be sent packing, 100 : 20
Aches, my heart a., 476 : 21
sense a. at thee, 232 : 5
when the head a., 169 : 38
Achieve and cherish peace, 524 : 7
cannot as you would a., 188 : 20
some a. greatness, 214 : 9
the a. of the mastery, 656 : 2
Achieved by others' death, 202 : 8
matchless deed's a., 365 : 9
the a. West, 837 : 8
Achievement, bring it to a., 76 : 19
consciousness painful a., 754 : 3
death of endeavor, 647 : 7
immortality an a., 728 : 8
quality of man of a., 479 : 5
sum of human a., 664 : 19
talent in every branch of a., 80 : 17
today's a. tomorrow's confusion, 631 : 18
wealth opportunity for a., 81 : 1
Achievements of intellect everlasting, 103 : 2
Achieveth, naught n' assaieth naught n' a., 145 : 1
Achieving, still a. still pursuing, 509 : 16
Achilles exists only through Homer, 419 : 8
not even A. will bring all to fulfillment, 59 : 4
O fortunate youth A., 90 : 13
see the great A., 529 : 13
what name A. assumed, 275 : 5
wrath of A., 57 : 3
Achilles', Paris's back A. heel, 907 : 13
stood upon A. tomb, 461 : 12
wrath, 334 : *n* 4
Aching, bring my a. heart to rest, 97 : 10
ease one life the a., 606 : 12
one tooth and it a., 735 : 3
spare my a. sight, 363 : 7
they have left a. void, 375 : 15
Achitophel, false A. was first, 303 : 20
Achoo, barely daring to A., 911 : 16
Acid final test, 851 : 8
Acknowledge and bewail our sins, 55 : 17
and confess our sins, 54 : 11
I a. the Furies, 732 : 11
restraint of reverence, 80 : 17
Acknowledged, governments whose independence a., 408 : 3
Acknowledgment, transcribed without a., 116 : 4
A-clickin' like tickin' of a clock, 665 : 14
A-cold, owl a., 476 : 8
poor Tom's a., 234 : 12
A-coming, Gospel train's a., 936 : 6
Acorn, inherent as oak in a., 813 : 13
Acorns, hogs eat a., 290 : *n* 3
oaks from little a., 134 : 15
Acquaintance, creditable a., 321 : 20
in which no new a., 357 : 4
promoter of mutual a., 617 : 7
should auld a., 410 : 11
slight a. with numbers, 417 : 3
visiting a., 398 : 14
Acquaintances, make new a., 354 : 4
Acquainted, she and I long a., 692 : 5
with grief, 31 : 14
with the night, 748 : 14
Acquaints, misery a. with strange bedfellows, 247 : 30
Acquent, when we were first a., 410 : 7
Acquiesce, if we a. in discrimination, 753 : 7
Acquire and beget a temperance, 221 : 23
Acquired, fortune has a. him, 92 : 8
knowledge a. under compulsion, 84 : 21
Acquiring and possessing property, 367 : 4
Acquisition, desire increases with a., 360 : 4
Acquisitions or losses by nature, 393 : 7
Acre, God's a., 510 : 12
in Middlesex, 488 : 5
of barren ground, 247 : 8
Acres, a few paternal a. bound, 332 : 10
happy man works ancestral a., 106 : 23
over whose a. blessed feet, 202 : 22
Acrobat, governor of New York not a., 741 : 8
Act against Constitution, 367 : 9
against natural equity, 367 : 9
and are gone, 868 : 5
as if God did exist, 705 : 17

Act (*continued*)
as if there were God, 650 : 4
beauty and valor and a., 656 : 3
between motion and a., 805 : 17
both a. and know, 296 : 25
bring to light goodly a., 762 : 1
but not rely on own ability, 64 : 4
capacity to a. wisely, 697 : 18
condemn fault and not a., 228 : 5
frankly listen to stars, 536 : 6
has no ethical quality unless chosen, 648 : 16
heaven helps not men who will not a., 66 : *n* 7
in doubt to a. or rest, 337 : 2
in the noon, 404 : 5
initial a. of culture, 784 : 12
last a. crowns play, 267 : 18
lover's or Roman's part, 335 : 8
no a. of kindness ever wasted, 66 : 2
not afraid of destructive a., 701 : 13
not criminal unless intent criminal, 133 : 6
of fear, 218 : 20
of God defined, 816 : 1
of life, 654 : 8
old age play's last a., 99 : 10
only on that maxim, 366 : 14
our Antipodes, 275 : 14
perform every a. as though your last, 124 : 6
poem of a. of mind, 437 : *n* 4
power to live and a., 429 : 1
prologues to swelling a., 236 : 10
promptly, 679 : 10
reap an a., 922 : 18
sins they love to a., 243 : 11
sleep an a. or two, 249 : 19
think himself a. of God, 555 : 12
two witnesses to overt a., 391 : 12
virtue and prudent a., 373 : 4
vote and a. to bring good, 649 : 18
Way of sage is to a., 65 : 10
what it is to a. or suffer, 806 : 17
Acta est fabula, 133 : 5
Actaeon ego sum dominum cognoscite, 113 : *n* 12
I am A., 113 : 18
Acted, lofty scene be a. o'er, 216 : 7
Acting is suffering, 806 : 17
of dreadful thing, 215 : 18
only when off stage he was a., 371 : 18
surrender explaining not a., 741 : 1
Action, accomplishes without any a., 64 : 17
advantage of taking no a., 64 : 15
brave in a. patient in labors, 617 : 6
crowded with glorious a., 432 : 16
faithful honor clear, 336 : 5
feeling for single good a., 395 : 25
fruit of a. not be motive, 94 : 10
give a. its character, 83 : 1
great end of life a., 596 : 6
horse symbol of a., 790 : 19
imitate a. of the tiger, 207 : 16
imitation of a. that is serious, 88 : 16
impartial in thought and a., 682 : 1
in a. how like an angel, 220 : 28
in a. soar as high, 557 : 20
in bondage to history, 602 : 3
in thought as in a., 872 : 2
initial cause of a., 603 : 6
knowledge must come through a., 75 : 6
Action (*continued*)
life a. and passion, 643 : 16
lose the name of a., 221 : 12
lust in a., 245 : 23
made to follow path of a., 68 : 25
makes the a. fine, 269 : 8
man is origin of his a., 87 : 19
man of a., 815 : 5
man of a. forced to thought, 723 : 7
mindless a., 862 : 21
moment not of a. or inaction, 94 : *n* 9
no worthy a. done, 920 : 12
nor utterance nor speech, 216 : 28
nothing more terrible than ignorance in a., 397 : 11
of masses of men, 558 : 3
on a. alone be thy interest, 94 : 10
painting dramatic a., 774 : 10
pious a. sugar o'er, 221 : 11
pious fraud as with bad a., 385 : 6
proud men of a., 481 : 16
Puritans gave world a., 538 : 13
science guide of a., 660 : 6
sense of honor in a., 81 : 5
sentiments weigh less than a., 569 : 12
spectator of a. he describes, 592 : 7
suit a. to the word, 222 : 1
Tao takes no a., 64 : 13
test lies in a., 71 : 25
thought child of a., 501 : 3
thought too much for a., 638 : 2
to every a. equal reaction, 313 : 15
truth in a., 502 : 2
vice by a. dignified, 192 : 20
Actions, decisive a. unconsidered, 727 : 10
emanate from personality, 688 : 7
exceeds in his a., 69 : 8
extreme a. ascribed to vanity, 657 : 9
know what person thinks by a., 861 : 13
less conscious a. mold lives, 620 : 7
morality of his a., 359 : 1
must be his spirit, 88 : 23
mutual a. of two bodies, 313 : 15
my a. are my ministers', 302 : 21
not always a. show man, 335 : 14
not always true sons, 291 : 10
of the just, 272 : 13
predestined from eternity, 602 : 3
rectitude and sincerity of a., 744 : 11
society exists for noble a., 88 : 5
speaks according to his a., 68 : 9
speech is image of a., 62 : 15
think beforehand that a. be resolute, 89 : 15
thousand a. once afoot, 207 : 8
what a. most excellent, 585 : 19
when our a. do not, 239 : 16
work good of agent, 308 : 15
Active, deeply and intensely a., 647 : 23
experimentation a. science, 551 : 14
free a. individuals, 586 : 17
through form and figure, 438 : 1
to the vigilant a. brave, 383 : 3
walked with step so a., 442 : 24
Activest, his a. part, 292 : 14
Activity in accordance with excellence, 87 : 23
property product of a., 757 : 17
scientific a. cumulative and progressive, 787 : 4
Actor, better be a. than critic, 743 : 1
Actor (*continued*)
dreamer is a., 754 : 12
pregnant with part, 704 : 14
well-graced a. leaves, 195 : 15
Actors, like a. in ancient plays, 673 : 17
these our a. were spirits, 248 : 13
Acts before he speaks, 68 : 9
four a. already past, 330 : 25
his a. being seven ages, 211 : 15
let a play have five a., 109 : 29
nameless unremembered a., 423 : 9
our angels are, 260 : 17
our lives in a. exemplary, 178 : 3
psychical a. develop by reflex, 603 : 5
to keep good a. refresh with new, 179 : 20
with such a. fill a pen, 182 : 15
Actual, dig deep into a., 654 : 13
solid earth a. world, 557 : 21
true account of a. is poetry, 558 : 18
Actuality of thought is life, 87 : 11
Actuals, grope among a. for knighthood, 884 : 16
Actus non facit reum, 133 : 6
Acute inquisitive dexterous, 372 : 20
Acutely, companion so feel solitude a., 735 : 17
A.D., the war what A.D. is elsewhere, 623 : 15
Ad astra per aspera, 133 : 7
maiorem Dei gloriam, 161 : *n* 11
unguem factus homo, 106 : *n* 12
Ad infinitum, so proceed a., 322 : 21
Adage, poor cat i' the a., 237 : 2
Adagios of islands, 843 : 15
Adam and his wife, 528 : 10
brought death into world, 624 : 13
called his wife's name Eve, 7 : 12
deep sleep upon A., 7 : 2
had 'em, 727 : 14
in A. all die, 48 : 29
offending A., 207 : 3
old A., 56 : 16
rage and hate from A. down, 570 : 13
son of A. and Eve, 321 : 2
the goodliest man, 285 : 20
was a gardener, 185 : 26, 710 : 22
was but human, 624 : 12
when A. delved, 917 : 1
wonder what A. and Eve think, 798 : 14
young A. Cupid, 192 : 1
Adamant for drift, 743 : 12
frame of a., 351 : 18
Adamantine chains, 283 : 4
Adam's dream, 479 : 2
fall, 713 : 2
hold up A. profession, 224 : 5
in A. ear left voice, 287 : 2
in A. fall sinned, 320 : 4
sons conceived in sin, 259 : 9
Adamses vote for Douglas, 694 : *n* 3
Adaptation, struggle for a., 753 : 12
Adapted, means plainly a. to end, 402 : 6
to my kind of fooling, 749 : 17
Adazzle dim, 656 : 5
Add hue to rainbow, 202 : 5
more to abundance, 780 : 3
one cubit to stature, 38 : 3
power to a. or detract, 523 : 4
to these retired leisure, 278 : 16
to those with too much, 780 : 3
what we can to life, 664 : 15

Added, all these things a. unto
you, 38 : 6
Adder, like the deaf a., 19 : 23
stingeth like an a., 25 : 11
tread upon the lion and a., 20 : 17
Addicted, really a. artist, 653 : 12
Adding insult to injury, 358 : 7
Addison, volumes of A., 352 : 23
Addled mosses dank, 793 : 7
Addressed her winged words, 57 : 8
Addressing popular audiences, 88 : 15
Adds precious seeing to the eye, 191 : 3
Adelante adelante, 646 : *n* 3
Adequate, no a. military
defense, 787 : 15
strength not a. to resist, 89 : 1
Adeste fideles, 133 : 8
Adhere, time nor place did then
a., 237 : 4
Adherence to Monroe Doctrine, 687 : 10
Adieu, bid you welcome a., 616 : 9
chers tableaux, 273 : *n* 3
fair day a., 201 : 22
forevermore my dear, 410 : 6
kind friends, 922 : 13
she cries and waved, 331 : 10
tristesse, 832 : *n* 2
Adjectives, American without
qualifying a., 667 : 1
straddled a., 793 : 7
Adjoining, lain in a. room, 605 : 13
Adjunct, learning an a. to
ourself, 191 : 1
Adjusted in the tomb, 605 : 13
Adjustment of colonial claims, 682 : 14
Adjusts tumbled head, 607 : 12
Administered, whate'er best a.
best, 337 : 9
Administration, conduct affairs of
a., 524 : 3
during my a. no blood shed, 389 : 13
economical a., 631 : 9
life of this a., 890 : 10
proper a. of wealth, 621 : 5
said of first a., 779 : 20
said of second a., 779 : 20
Administrator of universal
law, 566 : 18
Admirable, express and a., 220 : 28
Admirably, those which most a.
flourish, 245 : *n* 1
Admiral cheered them holding out
hope, 150 : 14
Dewey was the A., 647 : 2
kill a. from time to time, 343 : 11
Admirals have died of gout, 301 : 2
Admiration, as great in a. as
herself, 249 : 17
from fastidious, 487 : 18
greatness worthy to excite a., 588 : 16
jumps from a. to love, 440 : 18
of the poet, 437 : 17
only of weak minds, 288 : 7
season your a., 218 : 17
Victorians turned a. into hero
worship, 663 : 6
Admirations, culture lives by a., 651 : 2
Admire, fools a., 333 : 11
many a. few know, 80 : 11
most men a. virtue, 288 : 5
that riches grow in hell, 284 : 1
to a. we should not
understand, 324 : 13
too simple to a. it, 487 : 18
Admire (*continued*)
we like those who a. us, 293 : 32
where none a., 357 : 10
Admired, celerity never more a., 241 : 7
few a. by own domestics, 165 : 17
that she might a. be, 190 : 4
through being misunderstood, 818 : 2
Admires, coral lip a., 272 : 1
meanly a. mean things, 539 : 11
Admiring bog, 604 : 19
in gloomy shade, 276 : 4
Senate a. its members, 634 : 20
Admit I'm licked, 814 : 17
impediments, 245 : 18
never a. them in sight, 440 : 22
no kind of traffic, 247 : 26
some faults men readily a., 121 : 17
Admitted, good pun may be a., 386 : 1
Admonished me the unloved
year, 864 : 1
Adolescence' doubt, 571 : 4
Adonais, soul of A. like star, 469 : 17
weep for A., 468 : 22
Adonis, my A. hath a sweet
tooth, 175 : 21
this A. in loveliness, 453 : 22
Adoo, welcome a., 616 : 9
Adopt character of octopus, 67 : 4
Adopting European war tactics, 800 : 4
Adoption, their a. tried, 218 : 30
Adoration, breathless with a., 425 : 16
down in a. falling, 139 : 10
for a. all the ranks, 365 : 7
Adorations, Desires and A., 469 : 3
Adore, command where I a., 214 : 8
I a. thee implore thee, 167 : 3
Jews kiss and infidels a., 334 : 1
my gifts instead of me, 269 : 1
now I a. my life, 875 : 4
Adored first wife, 675 : 5
I have still a., 435 : 13
in every clime a., 340 : 1
spirit of Liberty, 435 : 13
still be a., 446 : 11
Adores, rapt seraph a. and
burns, 336 : 22
Adoring, I die a. God, 344 : 12
Adorn, Greece Italy and England did
a., 306 : 1
manners must a. knowledge, 342 : 2
modest looks cottage a., 370 : 17
nothing he did not a., 355 : 23
old England to a., 710 : 12
point moral or a. tale, 351 : 19
Adorned, holy city a. for
husband, 53 : 29
humble grave a., 335 : 10
in naked beauty more a., 286 : 3
when unadorned a. most, 345 : 14
Adornin', bride in rich a., 661 : 10
Adornment is reflection of
heart, 782 : 12
some women handsome without
a., 98 : 13
Adorns and cheers our way, 368 : 12
only itself, 878 : 2
subject, 342 : 8
Adult, world of a. life, 754 : 11
Adulterers, drunkards liars and
a., 233 : 5
Adulteries of art, 255 : 18
Adultery, committed a. in his
heart, 37 : 8
gods call a., 460 : 13
Adultery (*continued*)
psychology of a., 738 : 3
thou shalt not commit a., 10 : 7
Adults, sky of a. over kids, 911 : 20
Advance, mark out your doings in
a., 481 : 16
not to go back to a., 339 : 17
of science an evolution, 673 : 10
quality of American
civilization, 872 : 11
retrograde if not a., 383 : 15
twice set to partners, 612 : 6
Advanced, death's pale flag not
a., 193 : 27
guard of working class, 731 : 7
other world by which faith a., 151 : 8
outdistance a. countries, 731 : 5
true friends, 585 : 11
work they who fought a., 523 : 4
Advancement, from whom a.
befall, 564 : 19
of pure science, 825 : 11
Advances, Chief who in triumph
a., 431 : 9
in direction of dreams, 560 : 16
scientific a. available, 787 : 17
Advancing, flowers slowly a., 789 : 9
Advantage in the past judged, 88 : 21
mixed up for mutual a., 744 : 7
nailed for our a., 202 : 22
nature to a. dressed, 333 : 3
no way of taking a., 655 : 9
ocean gain a. on shore, 244 : 22
of taking no action, 64 : 15
over cleverer boys, 743 : 8
them that take a. get a., 565 : 8
to whose a., 98 : 6
Advantages, in hope of fair a., 199 : 9
little a. every day, 348 : 20
tries to keep a. of life, 736 : 10
various qualities and a., 734 : 6
Adventure art peace, 697 : 14
death beautiful a., 574 : *n* 1
fair a. of tomorrow, 202 : 15
most unto itself, 606 : 8
politics greatest a., 753 : 9
some for a., 792 : 14
this grotesque a. ours, 877 : 6
vitality of thought in a., 697 : 17
Adventurer, no lover and no a., 683 : 8
Ulysses interminable a., 769 : 5
well-wishing a., 243 : *n* 4
Adventures come into harbor, 663 : 15
embellish a., 385 : 10
of Tom Sawyer, 623 : 20
way full of a. and experiences, 702 : 4
Adventuring, by a. both, 198 : 6
Adverbs only qualifications I
respect, 654 : 6
Adversaries, do as a. do in law, 188 : 29
Adversary, sallies out and sees
a., 282 : 1
that mine a. had written a
book, 16 : 20
your a. the devil, 52 : 16
Adverse to rights of other
citizens, 398 : 1
Adversity best discover virtue, 180 : 7
blessing of New Testament, 180 : 5
bread of a., 30 : 18
contending with a., 259 : 7
dark hour of a., 452 : 15
enemy not hidden in a., 35 : 23
faint in the day of a., 25 : 13

Adversity (*continued*)
good things which belong to a., 180 : 4
if not taste of a., 290 : 11
in a. difficult to find friend, 88 : *n* 4
in a. keep even mind, 107 : 18
in a. mask is off, 100 : 21
in day of a. consider, 27 : 7
middle-aged a., 842 : 11
more supportable, 620 : 6
not without comforts, 180 : 6
of sharpe a. worste kynde, 144 : 24
remorse wakes up in a., 359 : 3
sometimes hard, 474 : 1
studies a refuge in a., 98 : 7
sweet are uses of a., 210 : 24
test of strong men, 115 : 2
tries friends, 112 : 10
Adversity's sweet milk philosophy, 193 : 12
Adverting to dignity of high calling, 373 : 9
Advertise, don't tell they'd a., 604 : 19
it pays to a., 923 : 10
Advertisements, tell ideals by a., 724 : 11
Advertises, protect what it a., 906 : 15
Advice, few profit by a., 110 : 21
given so profusely as a., 293 : 20
is seldom welcome, 341 : 22
old like to give good a., 293 : 17
smallest current coin, 647 : 8
tea and comfortable a., 479 : 14
to persons about to marry, 660 : 11
to persons about to write history, 615 : 16
unwise to be heedless while giving a., 114 : 5
we may give a., 294 : 5
Advices, lengthened sage a., 411 : 5
Advise, Death whom none could a., 173 : 4
the prince, 803 : 17
Advisedly, entered into a., 56 : 6
Advisement, take wyf without a., 147 : 22
Advocate, good have no need of a., 86 : 8
is Christ thy a., 315 : 2
we have a. with the Father, 52 : 21
Aegean, booming surge of A., 83 : 6
heard it on A., 587 : 15
to cleave the A., 782 : 22
Aegritudinem, diem adimere a. hominibus, 96 : *n* 10
Aeneas, mother of A. and his race, 100 : 1
Aequam memento rebus in arduis, 107 : *n* 16
Aeschylus, thundering A., 256 : 14
Aesculapius of our age, 166 : *n* 9
Aeson, herbs that did renew A., 200 : 22
Aesop's fly, 472 : 15
fox, 258 : 12
Aesthetic intellectual wants, 649 : 16
moral soil for a. growth, 742 : 3
painting not a. operation, 774 : 11
recognition of pattern, 698 : 5
Aestheticism, aiming toward art or a., 577 : 12
Afar and asunder, 627 : 5
from a. to view flight, 320 : 14
what sought they thus a., 561 : 1
Afeard, a soldier and a., 239 : 24
A-feelin' blue, 684 : 18
Affability, man of lowliness and a., 155 : 11
Affair, world is a strange a., 297 : 14
Affaires, les a. l'argent des autres, 594 : *n* 2
Affairs, absolutes in world a., 860 : 3
crisis of human a., 402 : 5
debate of commonwealth a., 207 : 4
office and a. of love, 209 : 9
political a., 517 : 24
tide in a. of men, 217 : 5
wealth the sinews of a., 92 : 6
Affamé, ventre a., 296 : *n* 8
Affect, learned pedants much a., 290 : 20
study what you most a., 188 : 25
Affectation of affectation, 349 : 13
spruce a., 191 : 9
Affected, zealously a. in good, 49 : 27
Affecting charity and devotion, 90 : 6
natural simple a., 371 : 18
to seem unaffected, 324 : 22
Affection and guilt, 924 : 3
attraction and a., 738 : 3
beaming in one eye, 547 : 30
bear a. without pride, 665 : 1
cannot hold bent, 214 : 2
hath unknown bottom, 212 : 26
let falling out be renewing of a., 96 : *n* 6
neither heat a. limb, 228 : 16
never wasted, 511 : 4
not break bonds of a., 521 : 14
on things above, 50 : 11
slave to animosity or a., 379 : 12
thy intention stabs, 246 : 12
two qualities inspire a., 87 : 29
we have a., 884 : 2
Affectionately, country absorbs him a., 573 : 20
Affectioned, be kindly a., 47 : 20
Affection's, to me-wards your a. strong, 266 : 8
Affections dark as Erebus, 201 : 3
great primary human a., 585 : 19
great strain on a., 565 : 27
hath not a Jew a., 199 : 17
holiness of heart's a., 479 : 1
life history of a., 452 : 19
of a. mild, 305 : *n* 2
old offenses of a. new, 245 : 16
run to waste, 458 : 18
sensible a. of flesh, 274 : 13
t' a. and to faculties, 253 : 7
which attend human life, 327 : 14
Affects to nod, 306 : 13
to renounce principles, 391 : 5
Affirm life, 756 : 17
uprising unveiling a., 526 : 5
what seems to be truth, 85 : 15
Affirmation of individual, 643 : 7
of life, 756 : 17
Affirmative, minds naturally a., 631 : 1
speak the a., 500 : 8
Affixed, thou deemest mountains a., 131 : 18
Afflict, coward conscience a. me, 187 : 27
the best, 361 : 13
Afflicted, commend those who are a., 55 : 6
neither oppress the a., 25 : 2
Affliction alters, 247 : 3
bread of a., 14 : 11
Affliction (*continued*)
consoling in depths of a., 521 : 3
day of a., 35 : 21
enamored of thy parts, 193 : 11
forgetfulness of a., 35 : 21
furnace of a., 31 : 6
one day smile again, 190 : 17
pay in a. or defect, 736 : 5
remembering mine a. and misery, 32 : 23
saveth in time of a., 34 : 23
water of a., 14 : 11, 30 : 18
Affluence adds to need for stabilization, 871 : 16
rising from a. to poverty, 624 : 7
Afford, ask cost can't a. yacht, 923 : *n* 8
cannot a. indignation, 437 : 4
our costly seasons, 906 : 10
purest treasure mortal times a., 193 : 32
selling houses for more than people could a., 791 : 5
statesman cannot a. to be moralist, 789 : 12
Affright air at Agincourt, 207 : 2
the bad a., 361 : 13
Affrighted, rend the a. skies, 334 : 10
Affront, sensible man not a. me, 376 : 2
Affronts with his own darkness, 883 : 11
Afire, Ucalegon's a. next door, 104 : 36
A-fishing, east wind never blow when he goes a., 270 : 32
gone a., 270 : 29
time is stream I go a. in, 559 : 28
Afloat, golden lilies a., 507 : 23
A-flying, old Time is still a., 266 : 11
Afoot and light-hearted, 575 : 9
game is a., 689 : 12
game's a., 207 : 18
swiftest traveler goes a., 559 : 13
thousand actions once a., 207 : 8
Afraid, be not a. neither dismayed, 11 : 28
be not a. of greatness, 214 : 9
be not a. of life, 649 : 15
be not a. of sudden fear, 23 : 6
be not a. to give that little, 34 : 7
because we tremble, 649 : 7
contempt for governor who is a., 74 : 10
death is a. of him, 132 : 27
don't let them think you're a., 707 : 18
dying to be a. of thee, 606 : 9
for the terror by night, 20 : 16
happiness makes heart a., 485 : 6
in short I was a., 803 : 16
it is I be not a., 39 : 27
man not a. of sea, 735 : 5
more a. than hurt, 159 : 12
neither let it be a., 45 : 24
not a. to die for friends, 108 : 14
not a. to follow truth, 389 : 16
not a. to go, 379 : 15
not so much a. as ashamed of Death, 274 : 12
of fear, 421 : 10
of the light, 599 : 15
of whom shall I be a., 18 : 11
of word Reality, 776 : 8
public a. of itself, 445 : 7
rich people most a., 816 : 5
small men a. of writings, 378 : 10
so I was a., 540 : 31

Afraid (*continued*)
sore a., 42 : 28
stranger and a., 691 : 23
teach himself to be a., 838 : 8
tell you what a. of, 812 : 5
to do if last hour, 346 : 2
to go home in dark, 699 : *n* 5
to look upon God, 9 : 12
to stand ridicule, 325 : 4
to strike, 338 : 14
whistling to keep from being a., 306 : 4
who's a. of Virginia Woolf, 908 : 2
wife and children stand a., 274 : 12
yet not a. to blame, 333 : 22
Afresh, kiss a., 266 : 10
Africa, all A. and her prodigies, 274 : 6
always something new out of A., 117 : 1
Asia and A. expelled freedom, 384 : 12
black like depths of my A., 854 : 13
choose between A. and English tongue, 911 : 1
does A. know song of me, 789 : 10
ex A. semper aliquid novi, 117 : *n* 1
giant among continents, 867 : 13
Kilimanjaro highest in A., 845 : 8
quintessential A. in it, 867 : 15
song of A., 789 : 10
sunrise out of A., 855 : 5
survival of wildlife in A., 898 : 11
what A. to me, 857 : 14
African, Americans of A. descent, 617 : 6
conditioned to freedom, 818 : 14
new moon lying on back, 789 : 10
where still A. complains, 399 : 18
Afric's burning shore, 438 : 12
sunny fountains, 452 : 8
Afro-American, not only Latin-American nation but A., 905 : 19
rights of A., 904 : 16
After, before war instead of a., 856 : 11
blackbird whistling or just a., 767 : 12
man a. his own heart, 12 : 35
old man looks before and a., 57 : 22
that out of all whooping, 212 : 6
this therefore because of this, 134 : 18
After-dinner talk, 528 : 3
After-dinner's sleep, 228 : 16
Aftereffect, to ordering to form to a., 877 : 3
Aftermark of too much love, 748 : 9
Aftermath of war, 750 : 20
Aftermaths of soft September, 692 : 5
Afternoon, all in golden a., 611 : 1
evening in a., 822 : 9
fatal five in a., 841 : 15
land in which always a., 528 : 13
rude multitude call a., 191 : 8
summer a. most beautiful words, 654 : 12
winter's a. in chapel, 808 : 16
Afternoons, winter a., 604 : 18
After-sunset light, 711 : 11
Afterthoughts, stronger than all a., 76 : 18
After-times, leave something to a., 281 : 12
Afterwards day, 604 : 5
Afton, flow gently sweet A., 410 : 13
Again, off a. on a., 727 : 13
play it a. Sam, 913 : 11
Again (*continued*)
thing which has been never is a., 619 : 2
Against, every sword a. his fellow, 12 : 36
he not with me a. me, 39 : 9
hope believed in hope, 47 : 1
kick a. the pricks, 71 : 12
not a. with, 750 : 11
who can be a. us, 47 : 12
Agamemnon, brave men before A., 108 : 13
cried aloud, 804 : 25
dead, 715 : 16
gazed on face of A., 591 : 5
Agape, who are you cried one a., 626 : 21
Agate, eyes like a. lanterns, 844 : 2
no bigger than a. stone, 191 : 23
Age, accompany old a., 239 : 31
ache penury, 228 : 21
Aesculapius of our a., 166 : *n* 9
and body of the time, 222 : 2
at your a. heyday in blood, 223 : 4
atomic a., 729 : 12, 885 : 8
Augustan a., 363 : 21
beats off louring old a., 153 : 8
belongs only to own a., 472 : 16
best in four things, 179 : 18
born empty into modern a., 312 : 20
cannot wither her, 241 : 1
carefulness bringeth a., 36 : 1
cast me not off in the time of old a., 19 : 34
centuries roll back to a. of gold, 108 : 11
childhood manhood and decrepit a., 267 : 19
come to thy grave in full a., 15 : 18
comfort to my a., 210 : 28
contribution according to a., 563 : *n* 1
crabbed a. and youth, 917 : 11
dance attention on old a., 717 : 13
decrepit a. tied to me, 715 : 4
demanded an image, 792 : 12
disease or sorrows strike, 564 : 14
distrust that a. brings wisdom, 772 : 10
does not make us childish, 396 : 8
drives my green a., 886 : 12
each a. a lens, 606 : 10
education best provision for old a., 87 : 4
employed in edging steel, 399 : 16
enchantments of the Middle A., 587 : 1
every a. has its pleasures, 311 : 5
face to occupy a., 544 : 26
father of all in every a., 340 : 1
first moment of atomic a., 885 : 8
folly in all of every a., 311 : 9
fool in every a., 339 : 12
forehead of the a. to come, 475 : 8
foreign nations and the next a., 181 : 16
fortify thy name against old a., 182 : 7
freethinking of one a. common sense of next, 589 : 1
full of care, 917 : 11
gods have neither a. nor death, 75 : 11
Golden A., 103 : 14
golden a. before us, 108 : *n* 10
Age (*continued*)
golden a. in imagination, 489 : 4
good God what an a., 309 : 17
green old a., 303 : 15
grow virtuous in old a., 340 : 12
habits of a. of atomic energy, 826 : 2
hardly feel pressure of a., 84 : 4
he hath not forgotten my a., 439 : 16
how tasteless and ill-bred, 102 : 2
if youth but knew if old a. but could, 163 : 11
ill layer-up of beauty, 208 : 19
in a good old a., 8 : 8
in a. I bud again, 269 : 5
in old a. intent upon our interests, 97 : 6
in the flower of their a., 12 : 28
in which strong just, 891 : 2
in wintry a. no chill, 377 : 20
in year of his a., 133 : 9
infirmity of his a., 233 : 2
is grown so picked, 224 : 13
is opportunity, 512 : 17
is sorrow, 72 : 23
known in any land or a., 576 : 8
labor of an a., 277 : 13
lady of certain a., 461 : 19
leaves friends and wine, 447 : 9
lee shore of a., 664 : 1
make a. to come my own, 295 : 1
master spirits of this a., 216 : 9
middle a. time of improving, 290 : 9
mind torpid in old a., 355 : 27
miracle of our a. Sir Philip Sidney, 176 : *n* 4
my a. lusty winter, 210 : 30
no falsehood lingers to old a., 75 : 20
no old a. only sorrow, 701 : 4
no other difference than a., 414 : 21
nor sword nor a. destroy, 113 : 24
not by a. is wisdom acquired, 93 : 9
not numbered by years, 168 : 1
not of an a. but for all time, 256 : 15
not one continued faithful until old a., 86 : 5
not only a night an a., 748 : 11
not profited so much as lost, 559 : 7
not so well qualified as youth, 559 : 7
not to be tuneless in old a., 107 : *n* 11
not weary them, 727 : 1
of antiquity youth of world, 178 : *n* 11
of Aquarius, 914 : 7
of chivalry gone, 373 : 22
of discord and strife, 185 : 7
of ease, 370 : 2
of fear, 846 : 17
of gold, 108 : 11, 277 : 9
of iron, 342 : 22
of miracles, 473 : 27
of revolution and reformation, 389 : 2
of unreason, 872 : 18
old a. a regret, 501 : 15
old a. and experience, 315 : 21
old a. come after you, 575 : 13
old a. coming bolt door, 133 : 2
old a. crown of life, 99 : 10
old a. in universal man, 178 : *n* 12
old a. is woman's hell, 296 : 6
old a. island, 614 : 10
old a. lacking neither honor nor lyre, 107 : 13
old a. level light, 822 : 9
old a. most unexpected, 770 : 7
old a. not yet arrived, 564 : 4

Age (*continued*)
old a. only disease, 497 : 27
old a. play's last act, 99 : 10
old a. serene and bright, 427 : 20
old a. should burn, 887 : 4
old a. time of spending, 290 : 9
olives of endless a., 245 : 13
or grief or sickness, 267 : 6
outworn buried a., 244 : 21
pays us with a. and dust, 173 : 5
peaceful as old a., 543 : 2
perform promises of youth, 352 : 15
philosophies of one a., 664 : 12
physician of Iron A., 585 : 3
poets' work to represent the a., 507 : 20
prayers which are a. his alms, 177 : 9
preferable to youth, 327 : 15
regret in chilled a., 654 : 7
restored of the Antonines, 383 : *n* 7
returns the Golden A., 103 : 14
shakes rooted folly of a., 311 : 13
shall be clearer than noonday, 15 : 26
Shelley of my a., 892 : 16
sign of old a., 433 : 16
smack of a. in you, 205 : 24
soon comes a., 173 : 14
soul of the a., 256 : 11
spirit of a., 344 : 7
tested to extreme old a., 584 : 8
the a. is dull and mean, 513 : 12
the harbor of all ills, 92 : 5
therefore summon a., 544 : 12
think at your a. it is right, 611 : 9
thinks better of gilded fool, 251 : 9
this slaughtered a., 879 : 7
thou hast nor youth nor a., 228 : 16
'tis well an old a. is out, 307 : 1
to age succeeds, 527 : 22
too late or cold climate, 287 : 13
toys of a., 337 : 7
tragedy of the a., 724 : 16
vastness and a., 525 : 16
veracity with old a., 294 : 6
very staff of my a., 199 : 2
view a. of poverty, 200 : 15
war dearth a. agues, 254 : 9
weak evils a. and hunger, 211 : 14
what was done in remote a., 496 : 14
when a. in wit out, 209 : 28
when old a. crept over, 696 : 3
when Thule no more ultimate, 115 : 13
with stealing steps, 162 : 6
without a name, 375 : 1
wives companions for middle a., 180 : 10
world's great a. begins, 468 : 17
worst of woes wait on a., 457 : 10
young men of new a., 406 : 20
young whom a. doth chill, 290 : 6
youth and a. equally a burden, 84 : 4
youth passed a. not arrived, 564 : 4
Aged, beauty of a. face, 773 : 16
certain age means a., 461 : 19
later times more a. than earlier, 178 : *n* 12
man paltry thing, 715 : 1
matched with a. wife, 529 : 6
thrush frail gaunt, 641 : 12
youth becomes as a., 228 : 16
Agent, actions work good of a., 308 : 15
free a. you were before, 125 : 12
imagination a. of perception, 437 : 11
Agent (*continued*)
Nature a. and patient at once, 87 : 5
thus the poor a. despised, 227 : 8
trust no a., 209 : 9
Agents of men of thought, 481 : 16
public officers a., 631 : 6
Age's, poison for a. tooth, 201 : 10
Ages, all a. believed in gods, 754 : 7
and ages hence, 747 : 13
before history, 378 : 1
cycle of the a. renewed, 103 : 14
emptiness of a. in face, 670 : 14
famous to all a., 281 : 19
God our help in a. past, 328 : 10
gone a. long ago, 476 : 20
heir of all a., 530 : 7
how many a. hence, 216 : 7
now he belongs to the a., 553 : 5
rock of A., 386 : 3
seven a., 211 : 15
thousand a. in Thy sight, 328 : 11
three poets in three a., 306 : 1
through a. one purpose, 530 : 3
trace events of a., 482 : 11
value from esteem of a., 302 : 18
what thing not thought of a. long ago, 396 : 22
ye unborn a., 363 : 7
Agglomeration called Holy Roman Empire, 343 : 7
Agglutinative, tonsorial or a. type, 730 : 15
Aggrandizement, no a. territorial or other, 781 : 7
Aggravate, I will a. my voice, 196 : 8
Aggravation of self, 634 : 23
Aggravations, accept minor a., 664 : 18
Aggregate efforts of busy multitude, 592 : 5
interests of community, 398 : 1
of humanity's experiences, 832 : 18
stabilization of a. demand, 871 : 16
Aggression of Germany, 812 : *n* 3
threaten a., 781 : 9
Aggressions, when a. require war, 389 : 3
Aggressors, quarantine the a., 780 : *n* 1
Agin, off a. on a., 727 : 13
Agincourt, affright air at A., 207 : 2
Aging people in contraction of life, 754 : 6
person give attention to self, 754 : 6
Agir, j'ai trop pensé pour a., 638 : *n* 2
Agitation of the air, 864 : 1
those who deprecate a., 556 : 4
A-gley, gang aft a., 408 : 14
Aglow, all a. is the work, 104 : 11
Agnes, world dear A. is strange, 297 : 14
Agnes', St. A. Eve, 476 : 8
Agnosco veteris vestigia flammae, 105 : *n* 4
Agnostic, compliment to be called a., 684 : 10
judges neither Catholic nor a., 776 : 13
Agnosticism, that's all a. means, 684 : 10
Agnus Dei, 54 : 5
A-going out with tide, 549 : 3
Agonies, exultations a., 425 : 21
small talk dies in a., 468 : 3
Agonizing, most a. spy, 606 : 3
reappraisal, 893 : 2
Agony, charm a. with words, 210 : 4
Agony (*continued*)
leave off a., 661 : 12
of flame that cannot singe, 716 : 10
strong swimmer in a., 460 : 21
that a. our triumph, 811 : 8
will find Thee, 881 : 11
Agree, agreed we can't never a., 660 : 3
all things differ all a., 334 : 15
birds in little nests a., 328 : 4
how a. kettle and pot, 35 : 25
let mankind a., 306 : 28
music and poetry a., 257 : 9
not free thought for those who a., 645 : 11
people have good sense a. with us, 294 : 1
two of a trade never a., 331 : 18, 600 : 14
whether they a. or not, 824 : 10
with her would not a., 711 : 22
Agreeable, do not want people a., 441 : 2
haint one a. feetur, 567 : 22
impressions of American manners, 449 : 1
in conversation, 326 : 17
person agrees with me, 502 : 13
what is more a. than home, 98 : 19
Agreeably, affect you a. in reading, 386 : 12
Agreed, except they be a., 33 : 20
to differ, 440 : 9
together we can't agree, 660 : 3
Agreement, living in a. with nature, 91 : 19
love is a., 182 : 12
on nuclear control, 891 : 15
who does not forget old a., 69 : 6
with hell, 505 : 14
with hell are we at a., 30 : 14
Agreements, nations tempted to violate a., 780 : 4
Agrees, agreeable person a., 502 : 13
large style a. not with purse, 185 : 8
what a. disagrees, 70 : 5
Agricultural population produces bravest men, 117 : 4
Agriculture, navigation commerce a., 381 : 14
Ague of skeleton, 804 : 22
Ague's privilege, 194 : 16
Agues, praise doth nourish a., 204 : 33
war dearth age a., 254 : 9
Ahab, all evil to crazy A., 570 : 13
flag of A., 571 : 9
he ran before A., 14 : 4
Ahead, far far a. lies land, 564 : 13
of the world, 65 : 3
sure you're right go a., 455 : 9
Ahkoond of Swat, 550 : *n* 3
A-hunting, daddy's gone a., 931 : 5
daren't go a., 594 : 2
upon St. David's Day, 933 : 6
we will go, 349 : 10
Aid, alliteration's artful a., 375 : 9
and comfort, 391 : 12
come to a. of party, 923 : 1
expletives feeble a. join, 333 : 7
foreign a. of ornament, 345 : 14
lend us thine a., 452 : 5
mutual a. law of animal life, 651 : 7
realize you don't need a., 838 : 3
saints a. if men call, 434 : 2
small a. is wealth, 77 : 3

Aid (*continued*)
super legal a. bureau, 777 : 1
thine a. supply strength bestow, 139 : 12
to interpretation of future, 80 : 15
to worker God lends a., 66 : *n* 7
vanity give no hollow a., 458 : 8
Wisdom's a., 364 : 16
wit hope flock to a., 496 : 13
Ail, what can a. thee, 478 : 10
Ailed, what a. us O gods, 632 : 16
Ailes de géant l'empêchent, 580 : *n* 5
Ailest here and here, 585 : 3
Ailments, our a. are the same, 321 : 19
selfish clod of a., 680 : 15
Aim at the infinite, 645 : 15
being's end and a., 337 : 10
fixed as an a. or butt, 207 : 6
forgotten a., 703 : 10
hit only what a. at, 559 : 12
malice never was his a., 322 : 19
man sets himself, 865 : 11
mind thine own a., 494 : 1
prince have no a. but war, 153 : 21
rivalry of a., 635 : 9
thought to a. at some good, 87 : 13
two things a. at in life, 711 : 4
who a. at great deeds must suffer, 97 : 15
your a. the star, 924 : 16
Aime, je ne vous a. pas Hylas, 319 : *n* 9
qui m'a. me suive, 143 : *n* 1
Aimest, all the ends thou a. at, 249 : 8
Aiming at blessed abodes, 336 : 18
slight not what's near by a. far, 76 : 14
Aimless rhetoric, 596 : 11
Aimlessness pursued, 874 : 17
Aims, above man's a. his nature, 610 : 8
and ideals of Marxism, 834 : 7
death a. with fouler spite, 267 : 11
Ain't heard nothing yet, 795 : 4
necessarily so, 836 : 7
we got fun, 795 : 5
Air, affright a. at Agincourt, 207 : 2
agitation of a., 864 : 1
all a. and nerve, 893 : 4
allaying both with its sweet a., 247 : 20
always in earth and a., 874 : 10
an a. and peculiar grace, 328 : 17
anybody as a. heavy or clear, 752 : 13
autumn in a. alas, 711 : 11
awash with angels, 899 : 12
babbling gossip of the a., 213 : 19
bites shrewdly, 219 : 8
blackest a., 899 : 15
breathe his native a., 332 : 10
breathe the a. again, 578 : 12
brightness falls from the a., 250 : 10
cast shadow in a. or water, 904 : 8
Cervantes' serious a., 340 : 14
change of a., 755 : 6
charm ache with a., 210 : 4
chartered libertine, 207 : 5
clear a., 806 : 21
common sun a. skies, 362 : 20
crows that wing midway a., 234 : 28
crystallized a. of centuries, 796 : 1
dance upon the a., 676 : 9
death of a., 808 : 11
diviner a., 428 : 22
drew in New England's a., 567 : 9
Air (*continued*)
drinks water her keel plows a., 178 : 6
dust in a. suspended, 808 : 11
earth and fire and sea and a. 643 : 2
earth or a., 217 : 25
eat men like a., 911 : 12
eating a. on promise of supply, 206 : 6
emptier ever dancing in a., 195 : 11
fairer than evening a., 184 : 5
false as a. as water, 226 : 15
fields of a., 377 : 26
fight with strength in a., 744 : 2
flies through a. with ease, 636 : 12
fog and filthy a., 235 : 22
fowls of the a. shall tell, 15 : 29
fowls of the a. sow not, 38 : 2
fresh a. sunshine good water, 670 : 13
happy good-night a., 641 : 13
haunting the black a., 908 : 10
he says with solemn a., 408 : 17
highest honors a. give, 570 : 12
honor is a., 205 : 5
horse of a., 918 : 12
hurtles in darkened a., 363 : 10
I drew in the common a., 34 : 18
I eat the a., 222 : 8
I lived on a., 748 : 8
if lungs receive our a., 376 : 20
image of spirituality, 679 : 5
in a. men seen, 919 : 8
in new countries, 739 : 5
inebriate of a., 604 : 14
inner a. inner light, 851 : 10
intimate of a., 874 : 17
is delicate, 236 : 21
leave little lives in a., 334 : 16
let out to warm a., 322 : 13
melted into a., 248 : 13
merged with bright a., 874 : 13
meteor of ocean a., 518 : 12
might wash leaves cover me, 632 : 18
mock a. with idle state, 363 : 4
most excellent canopy a., 220 : 28
neighing in haunted a., 811 : 14
nimbly and sweetly recommends itself, 236 : 21
now a. is hushed, 364 : 12
now in happier a., 587 : 11
now thoroughly small, 805 : 21
of delightful studies, 281 : 13
of Seven Dials, 628 : 20
on a. bird stamped, 605 : 7
other passions fleet to a., 199 : 28
over the plain quiver, 789 : 10
prison a., 676 : 13
retrace steps to upper a., 105 : 15
round ocean and living a., 423 : 13
saw the a. with hand, 221 : 23
sea and a. common to all, 163 : 13
shakes fires in burdened a., 403 : 18
sightless couriers of a., 236 : 24
signed with their honor, 876 : 16
smells as if from meadow, 571 : 7
smiles and languished a., 402 : 14
so fragrant, 150 : 13
soar into a. above dunes, 835 : 1
soft summer a., 598 : 6
solemn stillness holds, 361 : 21
speech in substaunce ys but a., 143 : 18
speed through a. thirty-one, 724 : 4
spiders marching through a., 892 : 6
sweet a. coming into house, 798 : 8
Air (*continued*)
sweet as English a., 530 : 22
sweeter a. where it was made, 799 : 10
take into a. my breath, 476 : 28
ten years ago split a., 856 : 6
that kills, 691 : 9
thin a., 248 : 13
tremble even at a. pump, 379 : 16
trifles light as a., 231 : 7
troubled a., 283 : *n* 4
underneath him steady a., 656 : 1
untilled a. between, 869 : 6
vans to beat a., 805 : 21
walking in a. of glory, 299 : 8
wanton in the a., 296 : 2
waste sweetness on desert a., 362 : 8
water rush to rest in a., 837 : 1
way of eagle in a., 26 : 4
web of sunny a., 555 : 16
whether in earth or a., 217 : 25
which way hot a. blows, 699 : 18
wild, 656 : 14
wild with leaves, 793 : 16
word honor is a., 205 : 5
world sick for a., 802 : 17
world-mothering a., 656 : 14
wound with mercy as if a., 656 : 13
Aircraft Ministry on which so much depends, 762 : 7
Air-drawn dagger, 238 : 26
Airly, git up a. to take in God, 567 : 21
Airmen, soldiers sailors a., 746 : 7
Airplane, strange high singing of a., 781 : 15
Air's glass jail, 905 : 7
Airs, all a. make one country, 274 : 17
don't give yourself a., 611 : 11
melting a., 377 : 13
naiad a., 525 : 9
soft Lydian a., 278 : 6
sounds and sweet a., 248 : 10
Airy distance with majestic motion, 458 : 7
ever so a. tread, 533 : 25
gold to a. thinness beat, 253 : 4
in a. rings skim heath, 334 : 16
navies, 529 : 24
nothing, 197 : 12
objects in an a. height, 320 : 14
reveries so a., 376 : 27
servitors, 281 : 15
subtleties in religion, 274 : 3
tongues that syllable, 279 : 16
unseen within thy a. shell, 279 : 18
Aisle, long-drawn a., 362 : 4
Aisles, monastic a., 493 : 16
of Christian Rome, 493 : 18
Ajalon, valley of A., 11 : 34
Akond of Swat, 550 : 14
Alabama, come from A., 598 : 1
moon of A., 840 : 18
Alabaster box of ointment, 41 : 2
grandsire cut in a., 197 : 29
smooth as monumental a., 232 : 13
Alacrity, kind of a. in sinking, 225 : 23
Aladdin's lamp, 461 : 25, 568 : 20
Alamo, remember the A., 506 : 1
Alarm, give moderate a., 505 : 12
ride and spread a., 512 : 7
Alarming, serious and a. consequences, 379 : 6
Alarms, confused a. of struggle, 587 : 16
look of love a., 404 : 19

Alarms (*continued*)
sighs his a., 177 : 12
world's a. to Paris, 716 : 19
Alarums, wars and a. unto nations, 174 : 7
Alas, cried in goose A., 810 : 19
how love can trifle, 190 : 5
I loved you best, 316 : 7
my love, 917 : 14
our young affections, 458 : 18
poor Yorick, 224 : 14
Postumus fleeting years slip by, 107 : 23
say A. but cannot help, 868 : 8
Albatross, shot the a., 434 : 12
thought he saw a., 614 : 8
Albion, perfidious A., 421 : 6
Alcestis, like A. from the grave, 282 : 20
Alchemists, sociologists a., 706 : 11
Alchemized and free of space, 475 : 20
shine full a., 475 : 20
Alchemy, courtesy true a., 600 : 13
happy a. of mind, 344 : 15
hide her a., 494 : 6
love wrought new a., 253 : 1
of the word, 674 : 7
richest a., 215 : 14
Alcides, none equal A. except himself, 115 : 11
Alcohol, narcotics a. and Christianity, 658 : 9
Alcoran, rather believe fables in A., 180 : 16
Alcuin my name learning I loved, 135 : 8
Aldebaran and Betelgueux, 640 : 6
trembled, 861 : 2
Alderman, agate on forefinger of a., 191 : 23
Ale, belly God send thee good a., 163 : 10
cakes and a., 213 : 26
Christmas broached mightiest a., 430 : 22
fame for pot of a., 207 : 19
fed purely upon a., 329 : 7
man ale's the stuff, 691 : 17
news older than a., 370 : 12
nut-brown a., 278 : 2
of myghty a. a large quart, 146 : 31
pint of English a., 742 : 14
shoulder sky and drink a., 691 : 20
sleep upon a., 329 : 7
take size of pots of a., 290 : 21
Alea, iacta a. est, 99 : *n* 14
Aleak, world is all a., 829 : 14
Alehouse, an honest a., 271 : 3
Aleppo, in A. once, 232 : 21
Alert not to impair landmarks, 836 : 16
radio was rather a., 873 : 1
Ale's the stuff to drink, 691 : 17
Alexander, Diogenes asked by A., 86 : 9
examples from A. to Mao, 800 : 6
if I were not A., 90 : 14
in his tent, 858 : 20
of course A. the Great was hero, 518 : 2
some talk of A., 922 : 10
trace noble dust of A., 224 : 15
Alexandria, strange power of A., 880 : 5
the A. that leaves you, 702 : 3
Alexandrine, needless A. ends song, 333 : 8
Algae, delicate a. and sea anemone, 808 : 2
Algebra, clock doth strike by a., 291 : 1
Algiers, dying in A., 514 : 10
Ali cibus aliis venenum, 101 : *n* 6
Alibi, stick to the a., 546 : 25
Alice, can't explain myself said A., 611 : 8
grave A., 512 : 5
replied offended, 611 : 21
what use of book thought A., 611 : 2
Alien blessing on its way, 907 : 19
corn, 477 : 1
excitement as to a. ideologies, 836 : 16
ism, 779 : 19
nothing human is a., 96 : 7
something bright and a., 855 : *n* 3
there is none, 697 : 2
Alienation not only result of social system, 885 : 19
world where a. awaits, 906 : 18
Alieni appetens sui profusus, 102 : *n* 10
Alienum, humani nil a me a. puto, 96 : *n* 8
Alike, all animals of forest a., 925 : 24
all places distant from heaven a., 259 : 12
by nature all a., 259 : 9
by nature men nearly a., 69 : 18
darkness and light a. to thee, 22 : 18
destiny waits a., 71 : 15
equals and unequals a., 85 : 3
glory and danger a., 81 : 2
looks on a., 247 : 1
to suffer all a., 241 : 10
Alive and so bold O earth, 468 : 19
and wagging tail in mud, 90 : 11
astonishing earth is a., 884 : 1
attitude in which most a., 647 : 23
be a. at great time, 843 : 2
bricks a. to testify, 185 : 27
curiosity must be kept a., 786 : 14
deeply and intensely a., 647 : 23
hardly a man now a., 512 : 6
how possible that dead be brought a., 131 : 12
I am a. forevermore, 52 : 32
in Christ all made a., 48 : 29
in that dawn to be a., 424 : 5
keep a. hoary establishment, 414 : 16
keep a. rather than triumph, 809 : 14
looking as if a., 540 : 22
more come through a., 58 : 24
no pain as great as being a., 721 : 1
officiously to keep a., 564 : 19
remain a. past usual date, 701 : 5
since none returned a. I answer, 141 : 15
some burned a., 901 : 13
still while thy book live, 256 : 11
supreme triumph to be most a., 790 : 20
the most a. is wildest, 560 : 28
to be awake to be a., 559 : 23
was dead and is a., 43 : 28
what it was to be a., 839 : 14
All a green willow, 158 : 15
aglow is the work, 104 : 11
all alone, 434 : 26
all are gone, 441 : 5
all of a piece throughout, 307 : 1
all sleeping on hill, 728 : 3
and a. that tribe, 106 : 14
All (*continued*)
are but ministers of love, 435 : 20
be as before love, 541 : 21
bedtime Hal and a. well, 205 : 4
best of dark and bright, 459 : 13
blind and ignorant in a., 251 : 6
bound as befitting each, 576 : 22
changed changed utterly, 714 : 9
charity for a., 524 : 7
Christ is a. and in a., 50 : 12
come out of Gogol's Overcoat, 582 : 16
comes from the mind, 72 : 15
contains a. nothing lacking, 575 : 6
cry and no wool, 149 : *n* 2
death closes a., 529 : 12
deliberate speed, 820 : *n* 4
did you say a., 239 : 21
died to save us a., 561 : 9
do a. bravely, 536 : 6
down come baby and a., 660 : 19
driven into same fold, 107 : 19
eggs in one basket, 169 : 11
else confusion, 531 : 7
end crowns a., 227 : 5
enough for a., 760 : 10
except sun is set, 461 : 3
fish that cometh to net, 160 : 14
flesh is grass, 30 : 32
for a. that and a' that, 411 : 19
for love, 173 : 13
for one, 491 : 5
for our rightfu' king, 410 : 4
from a. things one and from one a. things, 70 : 5
gas and gaiters, 547 : 17
Gaul divided into three parts, 99 : 14
give a. to love, 494 : 10
God for us a., 161 : 14
God's above a., 230 : 19
harm to one harm to a., 618 : 10
have not gift of martyrdom, 305 : 21
having nothing yet hath a., 250 : 16
hell broke loose, 286 : 9
his faults observed, 217 : 4
homemade but aren't we a., 878 : 15
honorable men, 216 : 18
hope abandon who enter here, 140 : 13
I and you and a. of us, 216 : 25
I could see from where I stood, 822 : 11
I dare do a., 237 : 3
I have is thine, 43 : 29
I know you a., 203 : 5
I want out of you, 922 : *n* 5
I write poets a., 605 : 17
in all, 218 : 16, 535 : 10
in a. things charity, 294 : 18
in all to one another, 628 : 14
in blue unclouded weather, 528 : 25
in day's work, 920 : 10
in green went my love, 828 : 9
in the Downs, 331 : 9
in valley of death, 533 : 9
is beauty, 540 : 30
is best though we doubt, 289 : 10
is but toys, 238 : 7
is done that men can do, 410 : 5
is ephemeral, 124 : 23
is flux, 69 : 24
is for the best, 343 : 8
is love yet law, 543 : 18
is mended, 197 : 23
is not lost, 283 : 8

All (*continued*)
is not well, 218 : 25
is passing, 770 : 13
is vanity, 26 : 11
is well, 810 : 4
know a. except myself, 150 : 11
learned all drunk, 377 : 9
liberty justice for a., 677 : 10
lord of a. yet prey to a., 337 : 2
lose thy love lose a., 335 : 3
lost save honor, 157 : 6
mankind love lover, 497 : 14
men created equal, 387 : 9, 523 : 4
men have need of gods, 59 : 21
men my compatriots, 166 : 2
moderation in a. things, 96 : 1
my days are trances, 525 : 18
my pretty ones, 239 : 21
news fit to print, 686 : 6
noblest Roman of them a., 217 : 13
not a. capable of everything, 103 : 16
ocean the source of a., 58 : 21
of a piece throughout, 307 : 1
on our meat and on us a., 267 : 1
once so beautiful is dead, 811 : 12
one for a. a. for one, 189 : 19
one from a., 126 : 19
one law for a., 373 : 18
or nothing, 599 : 6
our yesterdays have lighted fools, 240 : 4
our youth our joys our a., 173 : 5
passes, 640 : 1
passion spent, 289 : 11
perform tragic play, 717 : 5
persons share in government, 88 : 6
quiet along Potomac, 598 : 10
quiet on Western front, 839 : 9
readiness is a., 224 : 28
ripeness is a., 235 : 11
root and a., 535 : 10
round the town, 929 : 19
safely gathered in, 536 : 2
sees Me in a., 94 : 13
shall be well, 808 : 18
shall die, 206 : 22
sharing government who assist it, 519 : 21
should cry Beware, 433 : 27
silence an' all glisten, 568 : 4
Souls College limited undergraduates, 740 : 16
take him for a. in a., 218 : 16
that is and shall be, 74 : 18
that live must die, 218 : 1
that makes a man, 534 : 23
that most maddens, 570 : 13
that we see or seem, 525 : 3
that's a. there is, 762 : 6
that's beautiful drifts, 713 : 3
the brothers too, 214 : 6
the brothers valiant, 919 : 14
the lonely people, 914 : 10
the perfumes of Arabia, 239 : 27
the way home, 930 : 11
the winds of doctrine, 282 : 5
the world and his wife, 323 : 21
the world's a stage, 211 : 15
things are as they were, 125 : 18
things are momentary, 125 : 18
things are one, 69 : 26
things bright and beautiful, 561 : 8
things come of you Nature, 124 : 19
things come to who wait, 496 : *n* 4

All (*continued*)
things full of signs, 126 : 18
things how small soever, 307 : 12
things to all men, 48 : 14
things work together, 47 : 10
this above a., 219 : 2
this and heaven too, 319 : 17
this the world well knows, 245 : 23
time takes a. gives a., 171 : 11
to a. to each, 576 : 4
unkindest cut of a., 216 : 24
waiting to give his a., 877 : 7
warts and a., 272 : *n* 7
was light, 340 : 6
was lost, 287 : 19
we are sinners a., 185 : 19
we have and are, 710 : 23
we hope in heaven, 525 : 2
we know for truth, 713 : 7
we know in love bitter, 811 : 15
we know of love, 608 : 5
we need of hell, 607 : 18
well that ends well, 159 : 28
which will not pass, 457 : 21
who love freedom, 815 : 12
with one voice, 46 : 22
with thee all with thee, 511 : 9
word over a., 576 : 1
work and no play, 271 : 17
world queer, 923 : 14
ye know on earth, 477 : 11
ye that pass by, 32 : 22
All-American, each player must be A., 825 : 3
Allay, glowing axle doth a., 279 : 10
Allayed fever of bone, 804 : 22
Allaying fury and my passion, 247 : 20
no a. Thames, 296 : 3
not a drop of a. Tiber, 242 : 12
Allegiance, not bound to swear a., 108 : 16
pledge a. to flag, 677 : 10
to British, 378 : 12
to the South, 444 : 6
Allegorical, great literature a., 742 : 5
Allegory, life continual a., 479 : 19
on banks of Nile, 398 : 12
Allegra, laughing A., 512 : 5
Alleluia, Jesus Christ risen today A., 317 : 8
Allemand, je parle a. à mon cheval, 143 : *n* 10
Allen, for love of Barbara A., 926 : 21
humble A., 339 : 14
name was Barbara A., 926 : 21
snow on Bog of A., 777 : 16
Alleviates, legacy a. sorrow, 171 : 7
Alley, in bowling a. bowled sun, 314 : 20
lives in our a., 331 : 5
rats' a., 805 : 3
Sally in our a., 331 : 5
titanic of cypress, 527 : 1
Alleys, lowest and vilest a., 689 : 6
All-form only form, 650 : 12
All-good, must a. too follow, 462 : 10
All-Great were All-loving too, 543 : 28
All-harmonious, Father-Mother God a., 583 : 1
Alliance, holy a. to exorcise specter, 563 : 2
unless abroad purchase a., 186 : 12
Alliances, entangling a., 389 : 2
permanent a., 379 : 13
Allied Expeditionary Force, 815 : 12

Allied (*continued*)
great wits to madness a., 303 : 20
remembrance and reflection how a., 303 : *n* 1
Allies, great Russian a., 815 : 12
no eternal a., 454 : 12
thou hast great a., 425 : 21
All-in-all, intellectual A., 424 : 16
Alliteration, sentiment and a., 619 : 7
Alliteration's artful aid, 375 : 9
All-night vigil in soft face of girl, 74 : 23
Allons enfants de la patrie, 415 : 1
Allotment, corner of God's a., 640 : 19
Allow not nature more than needs, 233 : 21
that you do not know it, 68 : 11
Allowance, no a. for ignorance, 595 : 12
Allowed, have merit handsomely a., 356 : 22
on every hand a. be, 409 : 3
Alloy, base a. of hypocrisy, 520 : 2
so strange an a., 653 : 15
All-pervasiveness, infallible impeccable a., 651 : 3
All-powerful must all-good follow, 462 : 10
should fear everything, 275 : 22
to be impotent, 743 : 12
All's a scattering, 874 : 9
blue, 545 : 23
fair in love and war, 564 : 2
love yet law, 543 : 18
right with world, 540 : 15
well for happy warrior sleeps, 427 : *n* 2
well that ends well, 227 : 18
All-shaking, thou a. thunder, 233 : 24
All-softening overpowering knell, 461 : 16
Allure, to a. by denying, 555 : 7
Allure si vagabonde, 164 : *n* 15
Allured to brighter worlds, 370 : 7
Allures, war where wealth a., 305 : 22
Alluring, sea shows false a. smile, 100 : 18
Allusive, poet become more a., 809 : 9
Alluvial march of days, 843 : 19
Alma, noche oscura del a., 167 : *n* 1
Alma mater, youth who loves a., 890 : *n* 3
Almanac, look in a. find out moonshine, 196 : 25
plant tears says a., 878 : 10
Almighty dollar, 453 : 6
gave dog, 432 : 12
gold, 256 : 7
has own purposes, 524 : 6
shadow of the A., 20 : 16
that the A. would answer me, 16 : 20
gold, 256 : *n* 1
Almighty's, arrow from A. bow, 406 : 7
form glasses itself, 458 : 28
God A. gentlemen, 304 : 12
orders to perform, 325 : 7
Almond, peach once bitter a., 624 : 14
tree shall flourish, 27 : 25
Almoner, best a. keeps nothing, 128 : 4
Almost thou persuadest me, 46 : 36
Alms, beg a. of palsied eld, 228 : 16
for a. a pilgrim's wallet, 314 : 2
for oblivion, 226 : 16
give a. accordingly, 34 : 7
of those who work with joy, 782 : 17
when thou doest a., 37 : 14

Alms (*continued*)
who gives self with a., 567 : 14
Alms-basket of words, 191 : 7
Almshouse, sun reflected from a., 560 : 18
Almsman's gown, 195 : 6
Aloft, Death a., 844 : 2
invisible in night, 683 : 5
Aloha oe, 636 : 13
Alone a banished man, 917 : 5
alone all all alone, 434 : 26
and palely loitering, 478 : 10
art should stand a., 619 : 8
as sparrow a. upon housetop, 21 : 5
be a. on earth, 457 : 10
being human born a., 794 : 3
better to live a., 72 : 18
beweep my outcast state, 244 : 8
born unto himself a., 267 : 9
Britain fight on a., 745 : 12
cannot live a. at peace, 781 : 5
clouded you will be a., 113 : 28
don't live in world a., 757 : 2
dwell kings of sea, 584 : 14
go it a., 556 : 1
go it sole a., 749 : 13
grief mine a., 462 : 18
heaven a. given away, 567 : 12
hell is a., 809 : 1
here at gate a., 533 : 20
how said I am a., 196 : 17
I a. sit lingering here, 299 : 7
I am a., 816 : 18
I did it, 242 : 26
I lie down a., 692 : 8
I sleep a., 63 : 8
I want to be a., 863 : 2
I weep for what I'm like a., 874 : 2
in bee-loud glade, 712 : 4
in the midst of the earth, 29 : 4
Jacob was left a., 8 : 24
learn to stand a., 599 : 11
leaving me never a., 641 : 22
Lesbia's sparrow all a., 759 : 12
let her a. she will court you, 256 : 6
let me a., 15 : 22
let us a., 528 : 17
long way I tread a., 471 : 7
love but you a., 917 : 4
love lives not a. in brain, 191 : 2
loved him for himself a., 398 : 24
man a. at moment of birth, 116 : 7
man a. start today, 559 : 15
man is a., 560 : 3, 865 : 11
man not sufficiently a., 735 : 17
man only feels a., 885 : 17
man thinking or working is a., 560 : 3
man with God strive, 458 : 8
Minnaloushe a. important wise, 714 : 8
never a. accompanied with noble thoughts, 176 : 5
never a. with poet in pocket, 381 : 15
never less a. than when a., 416 : 2
never less a. than wholly a., 99 : 1
not a. God is within, 121 : 2
not good that man be a., 7 : 1
not live by bread a., 11 : *n* 6
nothing accomplished a., 823 : 21
on wide wide sea, 434 : 26
one minute a. with him, 786 : 10
paces about room a., 805 : 8
right to be let a., 677 : 14

Alone (*continued*)
she wanted nothing he could not bring a., 769 : 7
sometimes be a., 268 : 5
soon find himself a., 354 : 4
strange city lying a., 525 : 11
stranger and a., 852 : 7
strongest stands a., 599 : 21
though in wilderness never a., 121 : *n* 2
through dreary tract, 525 : 19
through seas of thought a., 424 : 2
travels fastest a., 707 : 14
trodden the winepress a., 31 : 26
virtue not left to stand a., 68 : 18
we exist a., 734 : 8
we live as we dream a., 683 : 15
we millions live a., 585 : 13
we shall die a., 300 : 3
weep and you weep a., 670 : 3
wild dog and a., 819 : 8
with conscience, 660 : 9
withouten compaignye, 146 : 28
you a. are you, 244 : 29
Along came a spider, 932 : 15
to get a. go a., 779 : 4
Aloof in order to gain reputation, 85 : 17
with hermit eye, 435 : 21
Aloud, all a. wind doth blow, 191 : 15
not winced nor cried a., 663 : 10
secrets cry a., 873 : 2
think a., 497 : 18
to fight a. very brave, 604 : 7
vaunting a., 283 : 9
Alpes, au delà des A. l'Italie, 110 : *n* 8
in conspectu A. alterum latus Italiae, 110 : *n* 8
Alph the sacred river, 433 : 21
Alpha, I am A. and Omega, 53 : 33
Alphabet, cunning a., 571 : 13
of flowers, 253 : 18
Alpine mountains cold, 282 : 18
Alps, beyond A. lies Italy, 110 : 13
on Alps arise, 332 : 21
Already with thee, 476 : 25
Altar, family a., 590 : 2
learning's a. vanish, 562 : 10
of freedom, 524 : 4
of our heartbreak, 881 : 11
what green a., 477 : 9
with this inscription, 46 : 15
Altars, priests a. victims, 335 : *n* 1
strike for a. and fires, 464 : 12
their a. their hearths, 102 : 28
to unknown gods, 648 : 6
Altar-stairs, great world's a., 532 : 12
Alter human nature, 695 : 14
life garment we a., 839 : 7
make and a. constitutions, 379 : 10
right to a. or abolish it, 387 : 9
when hills do, 606 : 5
Alter ego, 91 : *n* 10
Alteration, alters when it a. finds, 245 : 18
world capable of a., 840 : 20
Altereth, law of the Medes and Persians which a. not, 33 : 2
Alteri seculo, 95 : *n* 10
Altering, Eye a. all, 875 : 4
Alters, affliction a., 247 : 3
love a. not, 245 : 18
when it alteration finds, 245 : 18

Altitude pressed world on heart, 892 : 12
what leopard seeking at a., 845 : 8
Altitudo in bloodstream, 812 : 1
Alway, I would not live a., 15 : 22
Lo I am with you a., 41 : 31
Always, believed a. everywhere by all, 129 : 16
fair weather, 705 : 2
I am with you a., 41 : 31
in earth and air, 874 : 10
poor a. with you, 41 : 4
suspect everybody, 547 : 25
the beautiful answer, 829 : 15
three o'clock, 835 : 11
Alyosha, not God I don't accept A., 582 : 4
Am, I a. not what I was, 321 : 1
I a. that I a., 9 : 14
I a. what I a., 48 : 28
I think therefore I a., 272 : 10
my God perhaps I a., 924 : 18
not I a fly, 405 : 6
sames of a., 829 : 19
tell them I A., 365 : 6
what I a. so shall thou be, 135 : 7
Amanece no mas temprano, 935 : 15
Amantium irae amoris integratio est, 96 : *n* 6
Amaranth, no fields of a., 442 : 19
Amaryllis, anger of A. a sad thing, 103 : 11
sport with A., 280 : 15
Amassing harmony, 768 : 17
Amateur, between a. and professional, 837 : 9
whine of a. for three, 619 : 3
Amateurs, hell full of musical a., 680 : 19
ruined by a., 801 : 9
Amaze the unlearned, 333 : 5
Amazed and curious, 411 : 11
gazing rustics, 370 : 11
I am a. methinks, 202 : 13
silent and a., 575 : 23
wise a. temperate furious, 238 : 8
Amazing grace how sweet the sound, 367 : 7
Ambassador from Britain's crown, 536 : 7
is an honest man, 251 : 4
Ambassadors in every quarter, 539 : 15
Amber, bee preserved in a., 119 : 7
flies preserved in a., 119 : *n* 2
pretty in a. to observe, 338 : 12
scent of odorous perfume, 288 : 30
waves of grain, 688 : 5
Amber-dropping hair, 280 : 3
Ambiguities, smile vehicle for a., 571 : 12
Ambiguous undulations, 767 : 4
Ambition a species of madness, 308 : 22
all the pride cruelty and a., 173 : 4
bookish a., 258 : 2
Caesar without a., 591 : 11
choked with a. of meaner sort, 185 : 3
distraction uglification, 612 : 5
drove men to become false, 102 : 24
first sprung, 335 : 9
fling away a., 249 : 7
forego even a., 540 : 1
heart's supreme a., 357 : 8
ignorance a. or ineptitude, 771 : 2
let not a. mock, 362 : 2

Ambition (continued)
low a. and pride of kings, 336 : 10
low a. and thirst of praise, 375 : 21
made of sterner stuff, 216 : 19
of living like Thoreau, 712 : n 1
pen instrument to inflame a., 380 : 7
public life worthiest a., 753 : 9
soldier's virtue, 241 : 6
thick-sighted, 475 : 15
to be fair, 357 : 8
to grasp continent, 592 : 5
to reign is worth a., 283 : 14
vain the a. of kings, 262 : 11
vaulting a., 236 : 24
wars that make a. virtue, 231 : 11
when not with a. joined, 324 : 17
who doth a. shun, 211 : 3
Ambition's, young a. ladder, 215 : 16
Ambitions, let go hold of a., 839 : 13
look beyond own a., 891 : 2
weakens their a., 63 : 14
which climb on miseries, 684 : 5
whispering a., 804 : 14
Ambitious, abject usually a., 308 : 18
as a. I slew him, 216 : 15
finger, 248 : 20
man have no satisfaction, 255 : 5
materially a., 799 : 18
not a. to appear man of letters, 301 : 11
picturesque liar, 624 : 6
we live in a. poverty, 122 : 7
Ambitiously, leaders a. contending, 398 : 2
Ambles, who Time a. withal, 212 : 11
Ambree, foremost in battle Mary A., 926 : 18
Ambrosia, streams flow with a., 76 : 25
Âme, l'â. d'un emploi, 667 : n 1
péché c'est obscurcit l'â., 727 : n 7
quelle â. est sans défauts, 674 : n 2
Amebas at start not complex, 732 : 14
Amelette Ronsardelette, 123 : n 13
Amelioration, machinery for reducing a., 640 : 15
Amemus, vivamus atque a., 101 : n 15
Amen, sound of great A., 596 : 14
stuck in my throat, 237 : 20
will no man say a., 195 : 10
Amend your ways, 32 : 1
Amended, little said soon a., 169 : 17
Amending, constitutional right of a., 521 : 11
Amendment, Fifth A. old friend, 841 : 1
First A. has erected wall, 794 : 16
First A. makes common sense, 841 : 3
Fourteenth A. not enact Spencer, 644 : 10
guarantee of First A., 794 : 20
I am for First A., 794 : 19
Amends, I must make a., 916 : 5
no making a. in world, 565 : 4
America, all lost wild A., 840 : 13
America, 688 : 5
attitude towards life, 853 : 14
bad Americans die go to A., 675 : 14
bomb on Hiroshima on A. too, 777 : 10
breach with A. calamity, 673 : 1
cannot be ostrich, 682 : 7
destiny of A., 556 : 8
destiny of republics of A., 569 : 10
discovered accidentally, 800 : 5
don't sell A. short, 924 : 14

America (continued)
for me, 671 : 10
furnished Washington, 451 : 7
getting on in A., 738 : 8
glorious morning for A., 365 : 4
God bless A., 802 : 9, 802 : 10
God have mercy on A., 777 : 10
God's crucible, 706 : 15
gone to degeneration, 643 : 12
greatest question debated in A., 381 : 6
half brother of world, 555 : 15
heart and mind of A., 869 : 12
hope of the world, 368 : n 3
huntsmen are up in A., 275 : 14
I believe in A., 824 : 12
I hear A. singing, 574 : 2
i love you, 829 : 4
I see an A., 909 : n 4
is just ourselves, 588 : 13
land of unlimited possibilities, 662 : 4
land of wonders, 506 : 7
love it or leave it, 925 : 17
melting pot, 706 : 15
middle class in A. the nation, 589 : 8
most American thing in A., 851 : 5
my country hardly a nation, 793 : 11
my country Paris home town, 752 : 13
my new-found land, 254 : 2
named after man, 800 : 5
never forget nobler things, 729 : 11
new regions A. we call New World, 152 : 17
nothing less than whole A., 372 : 17
of dreams at an end, 599 : 1
of Moctezuma, 721 : 3
of poverty, 908 : 5
one yet many, 885 : 6
only idealistic nation, 682 : 16
our A. lives, 721 : 3
political democracy in A., 577 : 1
proclaimed rights of human nature, 418 : 1
rejoice that A. resisted, 350 : 17
remote from wrangling world, 384 : 15
save soul rather than face, 787 : 8
settlement of A. a grand scene, 380 : 8
so happy as A., 384 : 15
Spain not ruler of A., 416 : 18
spend blood and might, 682 : 13
such is state of A., 372 : 8
the other A., 908 : 5
this honor beckons A., 882 : 19
true original native of A., 348 : 13
ugly A., 898 : 1
war in which A. engaged, 384 : 20
was primitivism, 784 : 16
was promises, 822 : 8
what is left of A., 491 : n 1
would be no longer ruler of own spirit, 418 : 2
you cannot conquer A., 351 : 5
you have it better, 397 : 14
youth of A. tradition, 675 : 15
American, advance A. civilization, 872 : 11
as filled with love as A. people, 903 : 8
bathrooms, 834 : 8
bills of rights, 367 : n 4
born live and die an A., 451 : 14
cast of thought, 728 : 2

American (continued)
chief business of A. people, 736 : 16
children's books, 701 : 6
complex fate being A., 652 : 5
continents not subjects for colonization, 408 : 1
cradle of A. liberty, 451 : 15
credit card good in Europe, 666 : 1
destiny of colored A., 556 : 8
each new A. as grain, 831 : 20
empire careens onward, 837 : 4
experiment of A. people, 379 : 7
flag floats from hill, 371 : 26
from blues A. music, 733 : 14
government devolved on A. nation, 416 : 17
great patriot man and A., 667 : 3
has no sense of privacy, 681 : 20
high school closer to core of A. experience, 901 : 9
how behave toward A. government, 558 : 1
hundred percent A. idiot, 681 : 19
I also am an A., 451 : 8
I am an A., 752 : 13, 872 : 7
I am the A. heartbreak, 855 : 4
if I were A., 351 : 5
imitate Europe not A. literature, 536 : 10
impressions of A. manners, 449 : 1
intelligence of A. people, 772 : 20
jumps into train, 704 : 1
life powerful solvent, 703 : 19
literature from one book, 845 : 5
literature in proper sense, 728 : 2
love mankind except A., 356 : 4
moralism, 862 : 18
most A. of Americans, 418 : n 8
most A. thing school, 851 : 5
most pecksniffian of A. cities, 772 : 4
Muse, 840 : 4
names, 840 : 2
new deal for A. people, 779 : 8
North A. civilization engulfed world, 903 : 12
not Virginian but A., 382 : 14
pass to A. strand, 269 : 11
Philistine livelier, 589 : 9
point of view, 574 : 6
professors like literature dead, 791 : 9
public more reasonable, 872 : 19
Revolution not to obtain freedom, 800 : 7
Revolution produced Declaration of Independence, 800 : 8
right A. stuff, 632 : 1
right to be treated as wish, 891 : 12
rugged individualism, 750 : 17
says he loves country, 851 : 10
sense to A. people, 851 : 9
subtleties of A. joke, 622 : 7
Teenage Drive-In Life, 911 : 4
theater aspirin, 854 : 10
tragedy, 732 : 12
turn of language, 728 : 2
violence A. as cherry pie, 915 : 16
what dissatisfies in A. civilization, 589 : 10
without qualifying adjectives, 667 : 1
write well of A. things, 652 : 4
written in A. way, 728 : 2
Americanism, hyphenated A., 688 : 1
Americanos conquerors, 574 : 5

American's guarantee of
freedom, 788 : 13
Americans, brave A. all, 378 : 11
disdain to be instruments, 401 : 14
educated A. go to Europe, 498 : 26
freemen or slaves, 379 : 2
good A. die go to Paris, 675 : 14
good at long shot, 455 : 12
hope of world, 368 : 3
hyphenated A., 688 : 1
I love the A., 351 : 3
in A. spark of idealism, 678 : 4
let us all be A., 667 : 1
love of wealth in all A. do, 506 : 11
must look outward, 642 : 9
my people are A., 842 : 3
new generation of A., 890 : 7
North A. use reality, 885 : 14
of African descent, 617 : 6
prefer Continent, 725 : 17
refuse to learn languages, 725 : 17
strength of A., 506 : 10
this generation of A., 779 : 17
America's my nation, 839 : 11
participate in A. growth, 875 : 10
read in A. signs, 383 : *n* 7
Âmes, par de pareils objects les â.
blessées, 297 : *n* 5
Ami entends-tu, 928 : 7
Amiability, brimstone behind
beautiful a., 489 : 17
Amiable, good a. or sweet, 287 : 22
good nature more a. than
beauty, 326 : 17
how a. are thy tabernacles, 20 : 6
lovely death, 201 : 25
virtue not always a., 381 : 12
weakness, 349 : 22
words, 534 : 23
Amicable, candor and a.
relations, 408 : 3
Amicably if they can, 438 : 11
Amice gray, 288 : 18
Amici diem perdidi, 119 : *n* 10
Amicus Plato sed magis amica
veritas, 87 : *n* 6
A-milking sir she said, 931 : 14
Amis, le choix fait les a., 385 : *n* 6
Amiss, nothing comes a. so money
comes, 188 : 28
or out of place, 873 : 4
thou shalt never do a., 35 : 12
Amittuntur, non a. sed
praemittuntur, 114 : *n* 8
Amity, absolute a., 860 : 3
'Ammer along 'ard 'igh road, 660 : 14
Ammiral, mast of some great a., 283 : 15
Ammunition, pass a., 871 : 2
Amo amas, 394 : 6
odi et a., 102 : *n* 6
Amoebas at start not complex, 732 : 14
Among them but not of them, 458 : 4
Amor, and after A. vincit
omnia, 145 : 20
omnia vincit a., 103 : *n* 13
vincit insomnia, 870 : 4
Amor, batallas de a. campo de
pluma, 113 : *n* 3
l'a. che muove il sole e l'altre
stelle, 142 : *n* 7
Amores, el oro y a. malos de
encubrir, 935 : 17
Amorous descant sung, 285 : 25
excite my a. propensities, 353 : 23
Amorous (*continued*)
from a. causes springs, 333 : 24
nightingale a., 632 : 7
of their strokes, 240 : 29
sweet reluctant a. delay, 285 : 19
tangled in a. nets, 288 : 6
Amorphous, all was vague and
a., 97 : 7
Amortization of heart and soul, 826 : 18
Amount to Hannah Cook, 923 : 20
Amour, beginning of an A., 312 : 19
Amour, doux comme l'a., 400 : *n* 3
l'a. l'histoire de la vie des
femmes, 417 : *n* 3
on ne badine pas avec l'a., 537 : *n* 3
un peu d'a., 617 : *n* 1
Amphibious ill-born mob, 318 : 6
Amphitrite, O sweet A., 569 : 20
Amphitryon, I am the true A., 306 : 5
true A. gives dinners, 298 : 5
Ample, knowledge her a. page, 362 : 7
room and verge enough, 363 : 5
Ampler ether, 428 : 22
Amplified, hand prosperity down
a., 687 : 14
Amuck, too discreet to run a., 339 : 6
Amun give me what I found, 4 : 12
obelisks for my father A., 5 : 1
Amurath, not A. an A.
succeeds, 206 : 35
Amuse his riper stage, 337 : 7
you with stories, 372 : 12
Amused according to taste, 772 : 12
by its presumption, 831 : 4
delicately and unceasingly a., 772 : 12
we are not a., 573 : 17
Amusement, let early education be
a., 85 : 1
Amusements, great friend to public
a., 355 : 1
Amusing with numerous errors, 369 : 6
Amyntas, what if A. is dark, 103 : 23
Amytis, for A. made, 924 : 3
Anachronism, periodization of
history a., 847 : 14
Analogies, linked a., 570 : 15
make one more at home, 678 : 13
prove nothing, 678 : 13
Analogy least misleading thing, 620 : 18
Analysis, last point reached by
a., 390 : 8
subject men to a., 665 : 4
submit data to a., 397 : 17
Analyze, culture a. itself, 698 : 2
Ananda, since A. women received
permission, 73 : 5
the Tathagata, 72 : 19
Anarch, thy hand great A., 340 : 28
Anarchic, weeping a.
Aphrodite, 868 : 15
Anarchy, digest of a., 373 : 19
freedom cure of a., 373 : 3
of poverty, 785 : 13
show me greater evil, 74 : 20
threaten free nations, 882 : 23
wild a. of drink, 256 : 19
Anathema Maranatha, 49 : 10
Anatomizing of motives, 499 : 6
Anatomy, learn a. from
dissections, 260 : 9
Pinch a mere a., 188 : 15
Ancestor, I am my own a., 86 : *n* 1
I feel shame in recalling, 596 : 11
Ancestors, democracy makes man
forget a., 506 : 9
glory belongs to our a., 120 : 8
Great Spirit gave a. lands we
possess, 419 : 14
insult to spirits of a., 591 : 4
look backward to a., 373 : 20
meaning of lands of a., 912 : 5
no need of a., 343 : 4
of honorable gentleman, 501 : 9
owe it to a., 390 : 13
part of self, 648 : 17
true picture of a., 489 : 5
turned savage wilderness, 373 : 9
very good kind of folks, 398 : 14
wisdom of our a., 372 : 3
Ancestral, amidst tall a. trees, 470 : 13
happy man works a. acres, 106 : 23
in a. Jove Troy's sons rejoice, 105 : 28
voices prophesying war, 433 : 24
Ancestry and cultural
environment, 685 : 6
heirs to polish of a., 592 : 6
honest hard-working a., 826 : 13
Anchor, all sail no a., 489 : 9
firm a. in nonsense, 871 : 7
free that a. and chain, 93 : 3
heaves ship swings free, 492 : 14
hoist instantly a., 576 : 16
holding a. lost, 186 : 23
it is time raise a., 581 : 4
that a. holds, 535 : 3
Anchorage, long a. we leave, 576 : 20
Anchored, fleet of stars a., 785 : 15
Anchoring, yond tall a. bark, 234 : 28
Anchorite, saintship of an a., 456 : 23
Anchors aweigh, 783 : 17
moor bark with two a., 110 : 20
sons a. of mother's life, 75 : 18
Ancient, according to a. custom, 324 : 7
account a. ordine retrogrado, 178 : 21
and fish-like smell, 247 : 29
and honorable, 29 : 17
and natural strength, 365 : 16
angels keep a. places, 693 : 18
around a. track, 600 : 28
cause of freedom, 866 : 9
claim a. heritage, 912 : 5
close her from a. walls, 407 : 7
curse, 404 : 21
drama begin again, 849 : 7
Europe of a. parapets, 673 : 18
fear thee a. mariner, 434 : 25
feed fat the a. grudge, 198 : 20
feel spark of that a. flame, 105 : 8
feet in a. time, 406 : 21
folk with evil spells, 929 : 1
gentlemen, 224 : 5
glittering eyes, 717 : 7
good uncouth, 567 : 8
heavenly connection, 906 : 1
heavens fresh and strong, 427 : 16
hills a. as sun, 471 : 4
houses not eternal, 701 : 10
how left the a. love, 403 : 1
landmark, 25 : 3
landmarks in Bill of Rights, 836 : 16
like actors in a. plays, 673 : 17
mariner, 434 : 4, 434 : 25
Mariner called Old Sailor, 621 : 2
marry a. people, 277 : 2
models perpetuated, 129 : 20
most a. profession, 707 : 12
of a. race by birth, 304 : 15

Ancient (*continued*)
of days, 33 : 5, 614 : 9
of Days, 445 : 21
power of fright, 833 : 6
praise of a. authors, 264 : 19
raven, 526 : 15
recognize signals of a. flame, 142 : 6
remove not the a. landmark, 25 : 3
rites of our conscience, 860 : 13
rivers a. as world, 854 : 12
sanity in a. literature, 586 : 8
simplicity is gone, 312 : 24
sing a. ways, 712 : 3
suit of a. black, 765 : 8
these times are a. times, 178 : 21
trusty drouthy crony, 411 : 6
walked among a. trees, 405 : 1
with the a. is wisdom, 15 : 30
writers say, 715 : 19
Ancients, speak of a. without idolatry, 341 : 23
we are a. of the earth, 178 : *n* 12
wisdom of the a., 372 : *n* 3
Anderson, John A. my jo John, 410 : 7
Andes, making hay under A., 571 : 7
Andragathos my soul's half, 87 : *n* 1
Andrew with brindled hair, 668 : 19
Andrey, Prince A. went to tomb, 602 : 2
Androgyne, I am a., 910 : 6
Ane, I've lost but a., 411 : 20
Anecdotage, fell into a., 502 : 10
Anemone, delicate algae and sea a., 808 : 2
Anesthesia bastard substitute, 697 : 15
perceptual a., 772 : 3
Anew, ruined love when built a., 245 : 21
think a. act a., 522 : 12
Anfractuous rocks, 804 : 16
Ange, pur comme un a., 400 : *n* 3
Angel and archangel join, 339 : 22
ape or a., 502 : 4
appear to each lover, 329 : 14
as messenger, 131 : 9
as you are insect in you, 581 : 20
beautiful ineffectual a., 589 : 13
came soon as I went, 404 : 11
consideration like a. came, 207 : 3
curse his better a., 232 : 17
devil an a. too, 706 : 1
drew one a., 544 : 2
ended and in Adam's ear, 287 : 2
golden hours on a. wings, 410 : 18
good and bad a., 258 : 14
half a. half bird, 545 : 1
he is a. of light, 560 : 26
hold the fleet a. fast, 346 : 14
how like a. came I down, 311 : 22
I who fashioned myself a., 674 : 8
in action how like an a., 220 : 28
Israfel, 525 : *n* 3
like an a. sings, 201 : 1
like patriarch's a., 513 : 5
look homeward A., 281 : 3
lost a. of ruined paradise, 469 : 2
loud uplifted a. trumpets, 281 : 10
man neither a. nor beast, 300 : 8
man no a., 484 : 14
mild a. of annunciation, 888 : 11
ministering a. thou, 431 : 2
of backward look, 513 : 23
of death spread wings, 459 : 15
of Lord smote Assyrians, 14 : 20
of the Lord came down, 317 : 4
Angel (*continued*)
of the Lord came upon them, 42 : 28
on the outward side, 228 : 27
or earthly paragon, 243 : 24
pure as an a., 400 : 15
Recording A., 360 : 17
send an A. before thee, 10 : 11
shall my sister be, 224 : 18
she drew an a. down, 306 : 23
shined in my a. infancy, 299 : 2
sigh sword of A. King, 406 : 7
strength like fallen a., 475 : 13
that presided o'er birth, 407 : 3
time is man's a., 413 : 14
to radiant a. linked, 219 : 22
visits few and far between, 443 : 8
white as a. English child, 403 : 6
whose heartstrings lute, 525 : *n* 3
wings cast shadow, 817 : 3
woman yet think man a., 539 : 17
would act a. acts beast, 300 : 8
wrestled as a. with Jacob, 270 : 28
writing in book, 454 : 5
wrote like an a., 363 : 17
Angelheaded hipsters, 906 : 1
Angelic host proclaim, 350 : 15
songs swelling, 552 : 22
sprite, 254 : 7
to love for sake of loving, 464 : 19
Angel's, dropped from a. wing, 429 : 4
her a. face, 173 : 10
philosophy clip a. wings, 476 : 6
quill from a. wing, 429 : *n* 1
tear, 475 : 5
wit and singular learning, 155 : 11
Angels, air awash with a., 899 : 12
all pallid and wan, 526 : 5
alone that soar above, 296 : 4
and ministers of grace, 219 : 10
are bright still, 239 : 18
are painted fair, 317 : 2
ascending and descending, 8 : 19, 44 : 25
aspiring to be a., 336 : 18
aurochs and a., 846 : 5
band of a. coming, 935 : 23
beggar carried by a., 43 : 33
bending near earth, 537 : 16
better a. of our nature, 521 : 14
blow your trumpets a., 254 : 8
by good a. tenanted, 526 : 1
by that sin fell the a., 249 : 7
coming after me, 935 : 23
death nor life nor a., 47 : 15
desire of power caused a. to fall, 180 : 14
do I not deal with a., 879 : 10
entertained a. unawares, 51 : 22
fear to tread, 333 : 20
food too fine for a., 314 : 23
forget-me-nots of a., 511 : 3
four a. on corners of earth, 53 : 12
four a. to my bed, 294 : 16
give a. charge over thee, 43 : 1
give his a. charge over thee, 20 : 17
glorious fault of a., 335 : 9
go with me like good a., 248 : 25
God and a. as surety, 131 : 9
guardian a. sung this strain, 345 : 19
hark the herald a. sing, 350 : 15
hear a. sing, 537 : 16
holy a. guard thy bed, 328 : 8
if a. fell, 336 : 18
in forms of kings, 388 : 18
Angels (*continued*)
in heaven above, 527 : 9
invite God and his a., 255 : 2
keep ancient places, 693 : 18
lead us in peace, 899 : 16
made him a little lower than the a., 17 : 17
made spectacle to a., 48 : 7
maiden a. name Lenore, 526 : 12
make the a. weep, 228 : 10
maketh his a. spirits, 51 : 13
men tu-rrned into a., 722 : 12
men would be a., 180 : *n* 6, 336 : 18
Michael and a. fought, 53 : 19
ne'er like a. till passion dies, 251 : 12
on side of a., 502 : 4
only God and a. lookers-on, 179 : 4
our acts our a. are, 260 : 17
pass in a. say, 494 : 15
preventing a. met it, 305 : 29
progeny of light, 286 : 22
sad as a., 360 : *n* 2
send his a. with trumpet, 40 : 25
sing thee to thy rest, 225 : 3
sons of men and a. say, 350 : 11
sorrow for a., 541 : 8
surrounded by unfaithful a., 885 : 12
swearing I was right, 524 : 11
tears such as a. weep, 283 : 26
they have the faces of a., 130 : 7
tongues of a., 48 : 22
trumpet-tongued, 236 : 24
twice descending, 604 : 3
walking in peace, 131 : 9
walking like a. white, 654 : 18
we shall hear a., 695 : 7
where a. fear to tread, 333 : 20
where a. tremble, 363 : 2
white flaming white, 850 : 1
with a. and archangels, 55 : 18
with cashboxes for hearts, 484 : 17
women are a. wooing, 225 : 34
would be gods, 336 : 18
wrote of A. and God, 403 : 19
yield eternal thanks, 365 : 7
Angels', as far as a. ken, 283 : 5
bread made bread of man, 139 : 11
man did eat a. food, 20 : 4
visits short and bright, 318 : 4
Anger, a God slow to a., 14 : 31
at clog of his body, 276 : 15
contempt and a. of lip, 214 : 16
forget a. before sleep, 454 : 17
furious a., 35 : 18
he that is slow to a., 24 : 8
is a short madness, 109 : 2
is a weed, 129 : 11
look back in a., 910 : 1
monstrous a. of guns, 827 : 2
more in sorrow than a., 218 : 21
of Amaryllis, 103 : 11
of Lord kindled, 13 : 15
of lovers renews love, 96 : *n* 6
one of sinews of soul, 277 : 4
provoke not children to a., 50 : 13
slow to a., 24 : 13
take care you strike in a., 680 : 25
these you but a., 339 : 13
tread them in mine a., 31 : 26
visionary a. cleansing sight, 910 : 5
words of pain tones of a., 140 : 15
Angkor, Machu Picchu Cambridge A., 884 : 20
Angle, brother of the A., 270 : 33

Angle (*continued*)
in every a. greet, 297 : 7
Angler, honest a., 270 : 32
no man born an a., 270 : 31
now with God, 271 : 6
Anglers, too good for any but a., 271 : 12
Angles, that they were called A., 130 : 7
Angli, non A. sed Angeli, 130 : *n* 2
Angling, be quiet and go a., 271 : 14
frequent practicer of a., 270 : 34
like mathematics, 270 : 30
like virtue of humility, 271 : 1
never fully learned, 270 : 30
of a. as of strawberries, 271 : 10
produce gentleness, 271 : *n* 1
reward to itself, 270 : 34
Anglo-Catholic in religion, 809 : 13
Angry, be ye a., 49 : 36
bellows full of a. wind, 714 : 20
feel a. because we strike, 649 : 7
feigned an a. look, 316 : 7
God, 892 : *n* 1
I was a. with my foe, 405 : 13
I was a. with my friend, 405 : 13
in hands of a. God, 892 : *n* 1
like an a. ape, 228 : 10
looking for a. fix, 906 : 1
opposition to idea, 755 : 4
passions rise, 328 : 3
prayers, 732 : 16
proud and a. dust, 691 : 20
tears gone, 714 : 4
when a. count four, 624 : 20
when a. count ten, 390 : 4
when a. it thunders, 609 : 6
when very a. swear, 624 : 20
wrenlike vigilance, 893 : 12
Anguis, latet a. in herba, 103 : *n* 8
Anguish, divinest a., 562 : 2
edges of laughter and a., 782 : 4
in a. uplift new song, 684 : 13
lessened by another's a., 191 : 19
must an a. pay, 604 : 6
of bereavement, 524 : 4
of the marrow, 804 : 22
pain and a. wring brow, 431 : 2
pale A. keeps gate, 676 : 13
whatever a. of spirit, 383 : 1
Anguishes, dream a. writer, 838 : 13
Angularity of facts, 496 : 15
Anima, dum a. est spes est, 98 : *n* 12
Animae dimidium meae, 106 : *n* 20
Animal, aid law of a. life, 651 : 7
ancient a. symbols of St. John, 482 : 3
another armored a., 799 : 5
bang now the a., 740 : 6
cow a good a. in field, 355 : 4
dead and dumb and done, 740 : 6
erotic instinct a., 755 : 3
fastened to dying a., 715 : 2
inescapable a. walks with me, 883 : 11
man a noble a., 275 : 11
man a political a., 87 : 26
man a poor bare forked a., 234 : 7
man a reasoning a., 114 : 20
man a social a., 308 : 20
man a successful a., 686 : 3
man a tool-using a., 472 : 22
man is raised above a., 870 : 10
man only a. devours own
kind, 388 : 5
man the ubiquitous a., 870 : 14
no a. more invincible than
woman, 82 : 13
Animal (*continued*)
no such a., 924 : 1
not measured by man, 802 : 18
poor bare forked a., 234 : 7
press a wild a., 789 : 4
public is a mean a., 445 : 7
red a. war, 732 : 1
relation of reaction of a. to
world, 665 : 3
rope between a. and
Superman, 657 : 12
sta'tin' wid new kind of a., 814 : 17
sun, 901 : 14
too much culture makes sick
a., 755 : 3
too much of a. disfigures, 755 : 3
we are worrying a., 884 : 3
Animality, endued with a., 378 : 1
Animal's, uncornered a., 901 : 14
Animals, all a. equal, 858 : 12
all a. of forest alike, 925 : 24
among a., 799 : 7
beyond a. is man, 831 : 17
boy most unmanageable of a., 86 : 2
confront as trees and a. do, 574 : 1
experiment on a., 515 : 12
first a. then intelligences, 600 : 17
heart of a., 260 : 7
I sing for them the a., 928 : 12
infuse themselves, 200 : 7
interest in a. and athletes, 799 : 17
iron-like a. with mighty
horns, 789 : 7
medicine distinguishes man from
a., 664 : 14
merely passage for food, 152 : 2
placid and self-contained, 574 : 24
production of higher a., 515 : 3
tomb for other a., 152 : 2
turn and live with a., 574 : 24
warm-blooded a., 378 : 1
will not look, 868 : 8
Animate and encourage each
other, 379 : 1
onion atoms a. whole, 433 : 11
Animated bust, 362 : 5
forces by which nature a., 397 : 17
only by faith and hope, 352 : 24
Animosity, inflamed with mutual
a., 398 : 2
slave to a. or affection, 379 : 12
Animula vagula blandula, 123 : *n* 13
Animus, dux et imperator a.
est, 103 : *n* 1
spiritus, 679 : 5
Anise, tithe of mint and a., 40 : 18
Ankle, down-gyved to his a., 220 : 8
Ann, how old is A., 924 : 2
marry A., 680 : 18
Anna whom three realms obey, 334 : 4
Annabel, I and my A. Lee, 527 : 8
Annals of the poor, 362 : 2
war's a. cloud into night, 642 : 2
writ your a. true, 242 : 26
Anne Donne Un-Done, 251 : *n* 7
mother of Mary, 638 : 11
Sister A. do you see, 919 : 22
yes by Saint A., 213 : 26
Anne's, tell 'em Queen A. dead, 415 : 7
Annette, good night A., 625 : *n* 3
Annie, witch tales A. tells, 665 : 11
Annie Laurie, all sang A., 596 : 17
Annihilate but space and time, 336 : 8
Annihilating all that's made, 297 : 3
Annihilating (*continued*)
means for a. itself, 775 : 13
Annihilation, beings doomed to
a., 515 : 15
through war, 866 : 9
Anniversaries, secret a. of
heart, 512 : 22
Anno aetatis suae, 133 : 9
domini fatal complaint, 848 : 6
Annotator has scruples too, 766 : 16
Announced by trumpets of sky, 493 : 21
Announcer, victor or a. of victor, 70 : 20
Annoy, only does it to a., 611 : 15
Annoyance of good example, 624 : 25
Annoying to be honest to no
purpose, 114 : 1
Annoys, buzz witty and fair a., 338 : 19
scent the fair a., 376 : 3
Annual upkeep of yacht, 923 : *n* 8
Annuities, enrage those paying your
a., 344 : 8
Annuity, buy a. cheap, 547 : 34
Annunciation, prayer of one A., 808 : 4
Anointed, I am your a. Queen, 163 : 16
Lord's a. temple, 238 : 5
sovereign of sighs, 190 : 26
wash balm from an a. king, 194 : 26
Anointest my head with oil, 18 : 7
Anomalies hobbies and humors, 704 : 2
Anonymity, passion for a., 762 : 9
Another, absent one from a., 8 : 23
and better world, 415 : 3
called a. Abra came, 320 : 25
I, 91 : 18
love one a., 45 : 19, 47 : 27
one good turn deserves a., 117 : 14
such victory and we are
undone, 92 : 10
Another's, burns out a. burning, 191 : 19
can I see a. woe, 403 : 16
make point for one a. sake, 888 : 14
semblance in a. case, 377 : 25
Answer a fool according to his
folly, 25 : 18
always the beautiful a., 829 : 15
but is that an a., 482 : 7
came there none, 613 : *n* 1, 613 : 9
Daisy give me a., 718 : 18
dat's on'y a. yuh know, 810 : 8
dusty a., 600 : 20
echoes, 530 : 26
gratified to a. promptly, 623 : 7
I will give Roosevelt, 744 : 13
is blowin' in the wind, 915 : 3
me in one word, 212 : 7
not every question deserves
a., 111 : 25
Pilate would not stay for a., 179 : 22
silver a. rang, 507 : 8
since none returned alive I a., 141 : 15
soft a. turneth away wrath, 24 : 5
that the Almighty would a.
me, 16 : 20
the words of truth, 25 : 1
think of Oedipus' a., 851 : 3
to Hi or loud cry, 613 : 21
to punish they a. prayers, 66 : *n* 8
trickled through head, 613 : 18
what is the a. what is the
question, 752 : 15
what shall I a. thee, 17 : 2
why did you a. phone, 831 : 1
without knowing what
question, 740 : 15

Answer (*continued*)
woods a. and Echo ring, 174 : 17
Answered as I thought good, 930 : 2
calumnies a. best with silence, 255 : 15
I came no one a., 739 : 16
jealous souls not a., 231 : 20
Lord a. Job out of the whirlwind, 16 : 27
prayer a. who rises a better man, 600 : 9
slowly a. Arthur, 534 : 31
three questions, 611 : 11
Answering, whereto a. the sea, 575 : 18
Answers, better to know questions than a., 831 : 12
clear quick a. ruled out, 852 : 1
she who ne'er a., 335 : 23
Ant and the grasshopper, 66 : 11
go to the a., 23 : 11
not so much as weight of a., 130 : 18
to ant is dear, 92 : 14
ye can step on, 722 : 20
Antaeus-like grew strong, 717 : 14
Antagonism between classes, 563 : 8, 794 : 12
Antagonist is our helper, 374 : 2
Antediluvian tone, 614 : 2
Antelope, deer and a. play, 927 : 19
Anthem, pealing a. swells, 362 : 4
Anthems, hollaing and singing of a., 206 : 2
service high and a. clear, 278 : 26
Anthill, active field of science like a., 883 : 15
Anthologist, who as an a., 829 : 23
Anthology dispensary of medicine, 833 : 5
of universe, 838 : 16
well-chosen a., 833 : 5
Anthropology, familiar facts of a., 673 : 4
Anthropophagi 229 : 30
Antibombs, what use bombs and a., 831 : 18
Antic, dance the a. hay, 183 : 16
disposition, 220 : 4
old father a. the law, 202 : 28
Antichrist that denieth the Father, 52 : 22
Anticipate, what we a. seldom occurs, 501 : 10
Antics, how often have my a., 894 : 10
Anti-degradation, we're a., 904 : 13
Antidote, she is a. to desire, 324 : 21
sweet oblivious a., 239 : 32
Anti-exploitation, we're a., 904 : 13
Anti-oppression, we're a., 904 : 13
Antipodes, act our A., 275 : 14
common sense a. of science, 724 : 2
conquests even to A., 181 : *n* 5
Antiquas, stare super vias a., 31 : *n* 4
Antiquated, idea a. once modern, 750 : 14
Antiquates, time which a. antiquities, 275 : 4
Antique joy, 711 : 19
learning, 592 : 6
mask and a. pageantry, 278 : 6
more a. Roman than Dane, 224 : 32
pen would have expressed, 245 : 12
Persians taught, 462 : 4
traveler from a. land, 466 : 12
ye a. towers, 361 : 8
Antiquitas saeculi juventus mundi, 178 : 21
Antiquities, even living men were a., 274 : 26
time which antiquates a., 275 : 4
Antiquity, a little skill in a., 180 : *n* 7
age of a. youth of world, 178 : *n* 11
beautiful women of a., 638 : 10
blasted with a., 206 : 1
country with no a., 504 : 2
farther from beginning, 178 : *n* 12
history brings tidings of a., 98 : 9
night shrouds remote a., 324 : 2
one who is fond of a., 68 : 22
preamble reaching remotest a., 800 : 8
Anti-Semites, hated by a., 912 : 11
Antiseptic tunnel, 908 : 8
Antisocial, buying and selling a., 665 : 16
Antithesis, himself one vile a., 339 : 2
Anti-white, doesn't mean we're a., 904 : 13
Antler of the eaves, 863 : 14
Antlers, bringing to his a., 823 : 9
Antonines, Age restored of the A., 383 : *n* 7
united reigns of A., 383 : 9
Antonio, Stradivari's violins without A., 564 : 21
Antony brought drunken forth, 241 : 27
catch another A., 242 : 7
happy horse to bear A., 240 : 21
much A. of Hamlet most, 663 : 8
my A. is away, 240 : 20
my oblivion is a very A., 240 : 19
that revels long o' nights, 216 : 1
who lost A. the world, 316 : 16
Ant's centaur in dragon world, 793 : 4
Ants, belligerent a. claimed boundaries, 419 : *n* 5
nothing but a. find living, 760 : 6
preserved in amber, 119 : *n* 2
upon this hummock's crown, 558 : 19
Anulus in digito tenuatur, 100 : *n* 4
Anvil laughs at hammers, 761 : 17
lay me on a., 761 : 10
sword out of stone and a., 149 : 6
what the a., 405 : 8
when an a. hold still, 269 : 30
when you are a. bear, 269 : *n* 5
Anxiety about livelihood, 751 : 11
banquet partaken in a., 66 : 6
born with a. about weather, 630 : 22
state of man a., 299 : 19
tabooed by a., 628 : 26
Anxious, pleasing a. being, 362 : 14
Anybody anywhere any time, 736 : 13
can make history, 676 : 5
else I knew as well, 558 : 26
is as their land is, 752 : 13
more space where nobody than a., 752 : 14
no one's a., 630 : 8
there said Traveler, 739 : 15
who goes to psychiatrist, 777 : 9
Anyone lived in pretty how town, 829 : 18
tennis a., 843 : 3
who has to ask the cost, 923 : 22
who hates children, 770 : 18
Anythin' for quiet life, 546 : 28
Anything, courage not to believe in a., 564 : 6
Anything (*continued*)
everything and a., 781 : 12
for a quiet life, 261 : 19, 546 : 28
for good of country, 329 : 10
he hasn't got a. on, 505 : 6
is there a. beyond, 796 : 13
is there a. I can do, 896 : 14
never expect a., 913 : 8
not a. to show more fair, 425 : 13
nothing done while a. remained, 118 : 9
possible except fair play, 640 : 12
A-OK, everything is A., 921 : *n* 5
Apart, get to be wide a., 69 : 18
man's love a thing a., 460 : 19
mood a., 749 : 12
no stander above or a., 574 : 20
standing a. from it, 800 : 3
through hatred borne a., 75 : 23
Apartments, celestial ennui of a., 768 : 11
Apathetic end, 529 : 3
Apathy, extinction from a., 845 : 16
no a. into movement without emotion, 754 : 14
Ape, Devil is ever God's a., 156 : 5
for his grandfather, 596 : 11
how like to us, 95 : 3
like an angry a., 228 : 10
or angel, 502 : 4
poor degenerate from a., 830 : 12
sedulous a., 668 : 23
Aped, vices a. from white men, 837 : 20
Apennine, folding of A., 587 : 11
mists the A., 604 : 12
Apes, ivory a. and peacocks, 13 : 36, 760 : 19
lead a. in hell, 188 : 30
leave Now for dogs and a., 542 : 17
Tarzan of the A., 753 : 10
Aphorism never truthful, 751 : 5
Aphorisms, interline a., 386 : 12
Aphrodisiac, power the great a., 902 : 9
Ulysses nowhere a., 759 : 1
Aphrodite on your rich-wrought throne, 63 : 4
sleep with golden A., 60 : 6
spoke and loosened girdle, 58 : 19
stronger bolts than A., 76 : 22
weeping anarchic A., 868 : 15
what delight without A., 62 : 3
with intricate charms, 63 : *n* 5
work of soft A., 63 : 9
Apish, tardy a. nation, 194 : 11
Aplomb, before presidents with a., 577 : 2
A-plyin' up and down, 709 : 8
Apocalypse, four horsemen of A., 720 : 18
new a., 482 : 3
Apollo, bards in fealty to A., 475 : 6
harsh after songs of A., 191 : 16
I swear by A. Physician, 79 : 13
imbecile, 495 : 13
nor does A. always stretch bow, 107 : 22
Apollo's, burned is A. laurel bough, 184 : 11
first, 271 : 18
musical as A. lute, 191 : 4, 279 : 25
Apollos watered, 48 : 3
Apollyon, foul fiend A., 302 : 3
Apologists, northern a. tremble, 505 : 11
Apology for Devil, 620 : 23

Apology (*continued*)
too prompt, 287 : 21
Apostle, by the a. Paul, 187 : 29
of Philistines Macaulay, 587 : 5
Apostles, I am least of a., 48 : 28
true a. of equality, 588 : 19
would have done as they, 460 : 14
Apostolic blows and knocks, 291 : 5
Apothecary never out of spirits, 398 : 21
ounce of civet good a., 235 : 1
true a. thy drugs quick, 193 : 29
Appall, common sense a., 696 : 1
Appalled by what we saw, 814 : 12
conscience or vanity a., 716 : 13
property was thus a., 225 : 30
Appalling ocean surrounds land, 570 : 14
Apparel, every true man's a., 229 : 2
fashion wears out more a., 209 : 27
gay a., 195 : 6
oft proclaims the man, 219 : 1
Appareled in celestial light, 426 : 10
like the spring, 243 : 10
Apparent queen unveiled her light, 285 : 25
Apparition, lovely a. sent, 427 : 3
of these faces, 792 : 7
that a. sole of men he saw, 466 : 16
wall confronting a., 582 : 12
who enjoys not life an a., 274 : 13
Apparitions, fifteen a. seen, 717 : 19
seen and gone, 318 : 4
Appeal best suited to auditor, 783 : 4
books of universal a., 740 : 9
hark to exiled son's a., 639 : 15
I a. to any white man, 367 : 3
I a. unto Caesar, 46 : 32
to arms and God of hosts, 383 : 4
Appeals to religious prejudice, 596 : 11
Appear, fishermen a. like mice, 234 : 28
small vices do a., 235 : 3
things not what a. to be, 121 : 10
to be and appear not to be, 85 : 15
while these visions did a., 197 : 23
Appearance, in a. at friendship, 310 : 15
judge not according to a., 44 : 43
looketh on the outward a., 12 : 38
never attain reality, 413 : 22
never wears mean a., 496 : 3
takes on a. of nearby rock, 67 : 4
Appearances, judging people by a., 296 : 16
keep up a., 547 : 32
neither satisfied with a., 853 : 7
often are deceiving, 65 : 18
to mind are four kinds, 121 : 10
Appeared, there a. a chariot of fire, 14 : 12
Appears, thine in mine a., 251 : 16
Appeasement, political a., 778 : 7
Appeaseth strife, 24 : 8
Appendix, idleness an a. to nobility, 258 : 18
Appetite a feeling and a love, 423 : 12
an universal wolf, 226 : 3
breakfast with a., 248 : 32
cloy hungry edge of a., 194 : 7
comes with eating, 157 : 9
for bogus revelation, 771 : 14
good digestion wait on a., 238 : 24
humble pie with a., 549 : 4
increase of a., 218 : 8
loss of a. for mediocrities, 651 : 1
makes eating a delight, 290 : 3
Appetite (*continued*)
man given to a., 25 : 5
may sicken, 213 : 7
not meat but a., 290 : 3
quench a. keep reason under control, 125 : 17
sharpen with cloyless sauce his a., 240 : 27
will into a., 226 : 3
with keen a. he sits down, 199 : 5
Appetites, cloy a. they feed, 241 : 1
conflicting interests and a., 778 : 11
man of my a., 772 : 12
not their a., 231 : 6
subdue a. my dears, 547 : 8
Appius, that which A. says, 103 : 5
Applaud hollow ghost, 587 : 17
old people a. it, 169 : 39
thee to the very echo, 240 : 1
world forever a., 522 : 12
Applause, deference and a. deserve, 385 : 10
delight wonder of our stage, 256 : 11
from none but self a., 581 : 14
ignominy of popular a., 670 : 11
joy pleasance revel and a., 230 : 26
not least in honor or a., 174 : *n* 3
of single human being, 356 : 17
sit attentive to own a., 338 : 14
Apple a day, 923 : 12
as an a. reddens, 63 : 10
blossoms fill air, 811 : 5
cleft through core, 414 : 1
easy under the a. boughs, 886 : 19
for apple's sake, 624 : 12
my a. trees never eat cones, 747 : 5
of the eye, 17 : 25
pickers passed it by, 63 : 10
pie and cheese, 666 : 13
prince of a. towns, 886 : 20
rotten at the heart, 198 : 23
round as a. was his face, 144 : 5
shade of Old A. Tree, 753 : 2
to eat with a. tart, 668 : 13
tree among the trees, 28 : 5
undigested a. dumpling, 570 : 9
where a. reddens, 541 : 22
worm in wild a., 798 : 3
ye who love a., 765 : *n* 3
you are a. of my eye, 916 : 13
Apple-bearing Hesperian coast, 76 : 25
Apple-faced farmhand, 921 : *n* 3
Apple's, apple for a. sake, 624 : 12
cleft through core, 414 : 1
Apples, comfort me with a., 28 : 6
golden a. of sun, 712 : 14
great mother of big a., 879 : 12
of gold in pictures of silver, 25 : 14
on Dead Sea's shore, 457 : 20
on Newton's head, 750 : 5
silver a. of moon, 712 : 14
since Eve ate a., 461 : 29
small choice in rotten a., 188 : 26
sweeter than a., 673 : 15
Applesauce, politics is a., 765 : 16
Appleseed, Johnny A., 765 : 10
Appliance, by desperate a. relieved, 223 : 14
Appliances, with all a. to boot, 206 : 18
Application, lays in a. on it, 548 : 20
Applied, acceleration proportional to a. force, 313 : *n* 5
science not exist, 591 : 1
Apply its polished lips, 442 : 16
Apply (*continued*)
our hearts unto wisdom, 20 : 14
thine heart unto my knowledge, 24 : 37
Applying thought one finds, 499 : *n* 2
Appointed, their a. courses, 78 : 19
for my second race, 299 : 2
house a. for all living, 16 : 18
limits keep, 596 : 18
Appointeth the moon for seasons, 21 : 11
Appointment at end of world, 789 : 8
in Samarra, 751 : 17
never yields by a., 453 : 9
Appoints, man a., 148 : *n* 7
Appreciate, not a. home till left, 699 : 13
things left behind, 774 : 4
to criticize is to a., 653 : 17
Appreciated, art a. only slowly, 740 : 14
Appreciates what others comprehend, 154 : 3
Appreciation, merited a., 771 : 2
Apprehend, quickness to a., 697 : 18
some joy, 197 : 12
we a. good clearly, 76 : 19
Apprehended, next world as closely a., 275 : 2
Apprehension, death most in a., 228 : 17
in a. how like a god, 220 : 28
of the good, 194 : 7
Apprenticehood, serve long a., 194 : 4
Appris, rien a. ni rien oublié, 400 : *n* 4
Approach like rugged bear, 238 : 28
near a. a bed may show, 290 : 8
see a. proud Edward's, 411 : 15
snuff a. of tyranny, 372 : 20
sweet a. of even or morn, 285 : 5
Approbation, cold a., 351 : 11
from Sir Hubert Stanley, 416 : 9
Appropriate, all means which are a., 402 : 6
to criticize is to a., 653 : 17
Approval, own a. worth a hundred, 625 : 6
ruth of a., 907 : 25
Approve, abhor makers and laws a., 305 : 26
by his loved mansionry, 236 : 21
gods a. the depth, 428 : 21
men of sense a., 333 : 11
not a. slightest breach, 794 : 16
Approved as beautiful, 685 : 4
Approximate, hated the a., 756 : 5
Après nous le déluge, 364 : 17
April, bright cold day in A., 858 : 13
eighteenth of A., 512 : 6
he smells A. and May, 225 : 20
hoarfrost spread, 434 : 28
how it is with A. day, 748 : 17
in mistress' face, 917 : 24
is the cruelest month, 804 : 26
laugh thy girlish laughter, 688 : 4
love resembleth A. day, 189 : 32
lovely A. of her prime, 244 : 2
men A. when they woo, 212 : 25
of A. May of June, 265 : 17
prepares green light, 816 : 11
proud-pied A., 245 : 9
shakes out her hair, 787 : 5
showers May flowers, 163 : 4
so sweet that A. morn, 654 : 17
sweet small feet of A., 829 : 7
thirty days hath A., 162 : 7
those that A. wears, 229 : *n* 1
uncertain glory of A. day, 189 : 32

April (*continued*)
with his shoures soote, 145 : 12
April's breeze unfurled, 494 : 13
if you were A. lady, 633 : 12
now that A. there, 541 : 16
Aprons, sewed fig leaves and made a., 7 : 7
Apt alliteration's aid, 375 : 9
words have power, 288 : 24
Aptitude, genius a. for patience, 349 : 3
Aptitudes, produce according to a., 563 : *n* 1
Aquarium is gone, 893 : 16
Aquarius, age of A., 914 : 7
A-quarreling, set them a., 357 : 17
Aquitaine, Prince of A., 514 : 9
Arab in desert, 354 : *n* 4
Arabia, all the perfumes of A., 239 : 27
Arabian, as fast as A. trees, 232 : 20
Arabs, fold tents like A., 510 : 22
no more war between A. and Israelis, 895 : 17
of the desert, 132 : 9
Arahat Buddhas who appear in world, 72 : 21
Ararat, always been an A., 749 : 16
rode tide to A., 899 : 10
Arbiter is taste, 527 : 14
of everyone's fortune, 103 : *n* 5
of taste, 122 : 23
Arbitrary, deliberative forces over a., 677 : 12
Arbitrator, old common a. Time, 227 : 5
Arboreal, hairy quadruped probably a., 515 : 8
Arbores, serit a. quae alteri seculo, 95 : *n* 10
Arcadia, et in A. ego, 133 : 23
I too am in A., 133 : 23
Arcady, woods of A. dead, 711 : 19
Arch, broken a. of London Bridge, 488 : 7
experience a. to build upon, 634 : 18
experience is an a., 529 : 8
night's black a., 411 : 9
of ranged empire fall, 240 : 14
sunlit a., 748 : 17
Archangel a little damaged, 441 : 14
angel and a. join, 339 : 22
ruined, 283 : 23
Archangelic shrieks, 571 : 9
Archangels, whitespread wings like A., 778 : 6
with angels and a., 55 : 18
Arched flood, 494 : 13
heaven gates not so a., 262 : 9
Archer, feat of Tell the a., 414 : 1
laughs at a., 580 : 17
mark a. little meant, 431 : 19
Arches, fled Him down a. of years, 693 : 10
Archetypes of unconscious, 754 : 7
Archipelago, Gulag a., 895 : 23
Archipelagoes, starry a. and islands, 673 : 19
Archipels sidéraux et des îles, 673 : *n* 12
Architect, every man a. of his fortune, 103 : 5
fate of a., 395 : 22
man his own a., 545 : 19
of Universe a mathematician, 758 : 9
venture to call himself a., 431 : 21
Architects like poets, 800 : 10
Architecture adaptation of form, 573 : 9
beginning of arts, 690 : 1
dancing and a., 690 : 1
frolic a. of snow, 493 : 23
frozen music, 396 : 6
give children right to study a., 381 : 14
love's a. is his own, 292 : 18
man that has taste of a., 326 : 12
music in space, 396 : *n* 1
new styles of a., 868 : 4
sculpture painting, 579 : 11
sons study naval a., 381 : 14
test of civilization, 481 : 1
wondrous a. of world, 183 : 6
Archives, language the a. of history, 498 : 3
of memory, 730 : 15
Archy a cockroach, 759 : *n* 5
Arcs, on earth broken a., 544 : 4
Arctic, to wear a. fox, 799 : 15
Arcturus, guide A. with his sons, 16 : 34
Arden, now am I in A., 210 : 32
Ardent, love of glory most a., 327 : 14
marigolds, 474 : 22
Ardeur dans mes veines cachée, 312 : *n* 5
Ardor gives the charge, 223 : 5
learning must be sought with a., 393 : 2
Are and are not, 85 : 15
I will tell you what you a., 401 : 6
judge you as you a., 228 : 7
right you a., 723 : 18
we know what we a., 223 : 23
what you a. stands over you, 499 : 24
Area, he who controls a. controls religion, 133 : 16
Arena, only beast in a. the crowd, 720 : 17
Aren't I a woman, 482 : 17
Areopagus to watch over education, 452 : 2
Arethusa grant me this labor, 103 : 22
Argent, les affaires l'a. des autres, 594 : *n* 2
Argos do without sons of Atreus, 701 : 10
dying dreams of his A., 106 : 5
Argos, dulces moriens reminiscitur A., 106 : *n* 3
Argosies of magic sails, 529 : 24
Argue, good man does not a., 65 : 10
hard to a. with belly, 95 : 9
liberty to a. freely, 282 : 4
not against Heaven's hand, 282 : 19
point with him, 570 : 8
though vanquished a. still, 370 : 11
Argued each case with wife, 611 : 10
Argues, heart a. not mind, 586 : 13
not to know me a. yourselves unknown, 286 : 7
who a. is not a good man, 65 : 10
Arguing, in a. parson owned skill, 370 : 11
much a. much writing, 282 : 2
no a. with Johnson, 371 : 23
not a. I am telling, 619 : 11
with inevitable, 568 : 27
Arguit, stilus virum a., 258 : 8
Argument and intellects too, 369 : 11
best suited to auditor, 783 : 4
blood is their a., 208 : 4
Argument (*continued*)
conduct right a. wrong, 371 : 15
exact and priggish a., 504 : 16
finer than staple of his a., 191 : 6
for a week, 203 : 20
force instead of a., 391 : 7
good symbol best a., 500 : 3
heard great a., 516 : 16
height of this great a., 283 : 2
I have found a., 357 : 1
in a. with men, 289 : 1
in fire and brimstone, 622 : 13
knockdown a., 306 : 3, 613 : 16
knowest not what a., 493 : 14
maintain his a., 207 : 21
makes thee beat wings, 100 : *n* 8
meter-making a., 498 : 1
necessity a. of tyrants, 412 : 4
needs no reason, 65 : 16
not stir without great a., 223 : 19
overrefines a. brings self to grief, 143 : 3
sheathed swords for lack of a., 207 : 17
with east wind, 568 : 27
Arguments, no time for catch a., 522 : 11
sure experiments and demonstrated a., 166 : 15
Argus, dark death seized A., 60 : 24
A-riding, cowpuncher a. along, 927 : 9
Ariel, deal of A., 663 : 8
I A. will be correspondent, 247 : 17
Ariosto of north, 458 : 9
A-ripening, greatness is a., 249 : 3
Aris, pro a. atque focis, 102 : *n* 15
Arise, ah for man to a., 533 : 18
arise from death, 254 : 8
avenger of wrongs, 105 : 11
awake a., 283 : 17
Barak and lead captivity captive, 12 : 4
from dreams of thee, 468 : 1
how shall the dead a., 274 : 14
I will a. and go, 712 : 4
my lady sweet a., 243 : 16
Phoebus 'gins a., 243 : 16
prisoners of starvation, 555 : 24
shine for thy light is come, 31 : 23
soldiers of Christ a., 350 : 14
take up thy bed, 41 : 33
thoughts that a. in me, 530 : 19
wretched of earth, 555 : 24
Arises, democracy a. out of notion, 88 : 8
Ariseth a little cloud like a man's hand, 14 : 3
sun also a., 26 : 11
sun a. they gather themselves, 21 : 11
Aristocracy always cruel, 538 : 20
authors a natural a., 559 : 31
clover any time a., 607 : 13
government by a., 687 : 20
natural a. among men, 389 : 8
not society without a., 784 : 8
of moneybag, 473 : 21
untitled a., 519 : 17
Aristocratic, beast of prey in a. races, 658 : 5
Aristotle and all you philosophers, 462 : *n* 6
assures us man possesses immortality, 866 : 6
books of A. and his philosophie, 145 : 27

Aristotle (*continued*)
is it A. Pliny Buffon, 358 : 23
Plato A. Socrates secretaries of Nature, 271 : 16
Aristotle's, live and die in A. works, 183 : 19
Arithmetic, branches of a., 612 : 5
wealth a. cannot number, 262 : 21
Arithmetical, subsistence in a. ratio, 417 : 3
Arizona, Hohokams on A. desert, 897 : 19
is my land, 603 : 1
Ark, into Noah's a., 376 : 10
lay hand upon the a., 376 : 21
make thee an a., 7 : 28
of bulrushes, 9 : 8
of God is taken, 12 : 32
of the ache of it, 902 : 17
straight out of a., 432 : 22
Uzzah put hand to a., 13 : 15
Arks, these are the a., 182 : 7
Arm and burgonet of men, 240 : 22
brutal a. appear, 717 : 16
can honor set to a., 205 : 5
clothed in white samite, 149 : 8
doth bind restless wave, 596 : 18
faithless a., 868 : 16
I bit my a., 434 : 18
is very long, 78 : 20
it in rags, 235 : 3
it is the cannon's roar, 457 : 16
maketh flesh his a., 32 : 11
mortal a. and nerve feel, 431 : 24
my bended a. for pillow, 68 : 21
on bended a. doglike, 71 : 3
on lover's a. she leant, 530 : 11
reared a. crested world, 241 : 25
seal upon thine a., 28 : 23
short a. to reach heaven, 693 : 20
slumbering on own right a., 475 : 12
some quick to a., 792 : 14
soon shall thy a., 377 : 26
the obdured breast, 284 : 21
under a. carried broom, 932 : 5
wreath of hair which crowns my a., 253 : 11
Arma, cedant a. togae, 98 : *n* 18
virumque cano, 104 : *n* 8
Armadas, till great A. come, 700 : 9
Armageddon, place called A., 53 : 25
we stand at A., 687 : 17
Armament not decisive factor, 826 : 9
Armaments, defense not in a., 764 : 4
limitation of a., 778 : 7
Armchair, old a., 562 : 11
Armed at points exactly, 218 : 19
goeth on to meet the a. men, 16 : 37
goodness a. with power, 823 : 16
neutrality, 682 : 11
peace, 273 : 12
rhinoceros, 238 : 28
so strong in honesty, 217 : 2
suffer the a. men, 840 : 10
thrice a. that hath quarrel just, 185 : 17
thy want as an a. man, 23 : 12
to seek and sever, 821 : 11
without innocent within, 339 : 18
Armentières, mademoiselle from A., 817 : 7
Armes, aux a. citoyens, 415 : 1
Armies, anarchy scatters a., 74 : 20
disbanding hired a., 472 : 21
Armies (*continued*)
embattled a. clad in iron, 288 : 23
ignorant a. clash by night, 587 : 16
mechanized a., 745 : 2
of ransomed saints, 536 : 3
resisted but not an idea, 491 : 11
swore in Flanders, 360 : 10
when a. are mobilized, 65 : 4
Arming me from fear, 562 : 4
Armistice signed with fate, 837 : 7
Armor is his honest thought, 250 : 14
man in a. slave, 545 : 16
no a. against fate, 272 : 15
not boast who puts a. on, 512 : 13
of light, 47 : 29
of righteous cause, 694 : 15
person with no social a., 778 : 11
put your a. on, 350 : 14
whole a. of God, 49 : 38
Armored, another a. animal, 799 : 5
Armorers accomplishing knights, 208 : 1
Arms against a sea of troubles, 221 : 12
and God of hosts, 383 : 4
and the man I sing, 104 : 15, 306 : 11
blow trumpet to a., 384 : 8
bring to our ears clash of a., 383 : 5
by little a. plied, 611 : 1
children receive a. race from us, 897 : 10
come to my a., 612 : 18
Cupid's a., 919 : 19
defy Omnipotent to a., 283 : 4
end and beginning in each other's a., 863 : 15
everlasting a., 11 : 26
excites us to a., 305 : 11
fall into a. not hands, 647 : 18
field his a., 177 : 12
foes will provide with a., 105 : 3
fury provides a., 104 : 20
glorious in a., 190 : 20
haughty nation proud in a., 279 : 5
Helen's a., 716 : 19
hold hidden charms, 834 : 5
hug it in my a., 228 : 18
I never would lay down a., 351 : 5
imparadised in one another's a., 285 : 22
industry, 815 : 15
Infinite Goodness has wide a., 141 : 21
law stands mute in midst of a., 98 : 5
laws and a. foundations of states, 153 : 20
let a. yield to toga, 98 : 27
lord of folded a., 190 : 26
made a. ridiculous, 288 : 23
man in a. wish to be, 427 : 21
mewling in nurse's a., 211 : 15
might do what this has done, 276 : 5
mightier than they in a., 286 : 26
more than human a., 775 : 3
more towns with words than a., 259 : *n* 2
muscles of brawny a., 510 : 7
nurse of a., 369 : 2
of chambermaid, 356 : 8
of seeming a. short essay, 307 : 8
people in a., 483 : 9
right to keep and bear a., 391 : 15
rush my only into your a., 778 : 6
seek it in My a., 693 : 15
spouted a., 843 : 20
sure enwinding a., 576 : 5
Arms (*continued*)
take your last embrace, 193 : 28
takes vigor from a., 373 : 10
that my love were in my a., 917 : 10
though a. we need, 890 : 11
three corners of world in a., 202 : 20
thrice thrown a. about her neck, 105 : 5
to a. citizens, 415 : *n* 1
to war and a. I fly, 295 : 22
tries everything before a., 96 : 20
with his a. outstretched, 226 : 19
young in one another's a., 714 : 22
Army, back to the a. again, 709 : 1
Chief of the A., 421 : 7
composed of scum, 421 : 11
courage and conduct of a., 379 : 2
discipline soul of a., 378 : 14
each a. hath a hand, 201 : 22
feel a. in my fist, 412 : 5
gives you a. and navy, 373 : 7
hum of either a., 208 : 1
is like fish, 826 : 11
leaden a. that conquers world, 706 : 23
London devour entire a., 744 : 5
marches on stomach, 421 : 4
noble a. of Martyrs, 55 : 1
not halted by eloquence, 553 : 11
not reliance against tyranny, 520 : 7
of cranks, 676 : 16
of pointed firs, 664 : 2
of six hundred syllogisms, 153 : 9
of the Potomac, 522 : 4
of unalterable law, 600 : 28, 804 : 7
ours is invading a., 558 : 2
Prussian a., 483 : 9
supported by aviation, 825 : 6
technique of a., 880 : 13
terrible as an a. with banners, 28 : 17
Wellington's a., 359 : *n* 4
would be base rabble, 373 : 7
Arnica, better for bruise than a., 544 : 28
Arnstein's bicycle cement, 835 : 1
Aroint thee witch, 236 : 1
Arointing dreams with fugal requiems, 766 : 21
Aromatic, as a. plants bestow, 180 : *n* 2
die of rose in a. pain, 336 : 20
dry a. odor, 739 : 5
Arose a mother in Israel, 12 : 3
from out azure main, 345 : 19
people a. as one man, 12 : 23
up a new king over Egypt, 9 : 7
Around, at once above beneath a., 365 : 6
how they do get a. us, 82 : 14
ice was all a., 434 : 11
may it be beautiful a. me, 928 : 19
Arouse, happier in passion we feel than a., 293 : 30
Aroused popular conscience, 777 : 2
A-roving, go no more a., 460 : 5
I will go, 935 : 5
I'll go no more a., 934 : 21
Arques, we fought at A., 175 : 2
Arrant jade on a journey, 369 : 22
knave, 220 : 2
knaves all, 221 : 16
thankless a., 172 : 14
Array, battle's stern a., 457 : 19
my silks and fine a., 402 : 14
summon his a., 488 : 13

Array (*continued*)
trim a., 428 : 2
Arrayed, not a. like one of these, 38 : 5
Arrears, pay glad life's a., 544 : 22
Arrest, death strict in his a., 224 : 30
I'm under God's a., 315 : 3
police those who a. you, 908 : 6
stiffness and soul's a., 742 : 12
Arrests, pity a. the mind, 777 : 17
Arrêter tant de menus de ses agitations, 164 : *n* 15
Arrival, see countryside without a., 894 : 6
Arrive at what you do not know, 807 : 18
gods a., 494 : 11
to a. where you are, 807 : 18
travel better than to a., 668 : 1
where we started, 808 : 17
Arrivé, le jour de gloire est a., 415 : 1
Arrived at island called Guanahaní, 150 : 15
evils which never a., 495 : 18
hour of departure has a., 83 : 15
in good harbor, 265 : 7
openly a. at, 682 : 14
Arrives the snow, 493 : 21
too swift a. as tardy, 193 : 1
Arriving, serenely a., 576 : 4
Arrogance of power, 863 : 1
power leads to a., 891 : 16
Arrogancy of the proud, 29 : 21
Arrogant fatal X, 768 : 2
made a. by consideration, 81 : 7
not a. because of knowledge, 3 : 4
Arrow, barb in a. of childhood, 677 : 3
falls in flames, 645 : 15
feathered with eagle's plumes, 66 : 24
for heart like voice, 462 : 3
from Almighty's bow, 406 : 7
land of the A. Ide, 828 : 17
my bow and a., 930 : 9
often recoils upon sender, 128 : 2
shot a. into air, 510 : 24
smiled in its sleep, 907 : 13
sped a. comes not back, 109 : *n* 5
that flieth by day, 20 : 16
thine old a., 606 : 9
Arrows, as a. in the hand, 22 : 10
bow he bar and a. bright, 146 : 23
children living a., 782 : 15
envy slays itself by own a., 132 : 21
flew like hail, 794 : 5
loosed several ways, 207 : 8
love's keen a., 212 : 15
of desire, 406 : 21
of outrageous fortune, 221 : 12
thine a. stick fast in me, 18 : 28
which speak to the wise, 71 : 24
Arrowy Rhone, 457 : 27
shower, 363 : 10
Ars est celare artem, 619 : *n* 2
humana aedificayit urbes, 97 : *n* 10
vita brevis a. longa, 80 : *n* 2
Arse, politician is an a., 829 : 22
Arsenal of democracy, 780 : 12
Art accomplice of love, 686 : 2
adulteries of a., 255 : 18
adventure a. peace, 697 : 14
all a. quite useless, 674 : 23
all the gloss of a., 370 : 15
alone enduring stays, 640 : 1
alone eternal, 538 : 7
an a. fallen into disuse is lost, 819 : 14

Art (*continued*)
and science in particulars, 407 : 6
appreciated only slowly, 740 : 14
attempts to find essential, 887 : 14
begins with resistance, 727 : 11
book of deeds words and a., 573 : 11
Central Park single work of a., 590 : 13
clever but is it a., 708 : 12
comes from a. not chance, 333 : 9
comes proposing frankly, 638 : 15
cookery become an a., 258 : 16
criticism easy a. difficult, 329 : 18
dead a. of poetry, 792 : 10
desiring this man's a., 244 : 9
discrimination and selection, 653 : 13
dying is a. I do it well, 911 : 11
each a. to please, 338 : 14
each exercise a. he knows, 82 : 3
emotions foreign to a., 619 : 8
errors not in a., 313 : 12
establishes human truths, 891 : 16
expressing emotion in a., 809 : 5
finish which is almost a., 684 : 1
first and second best a., 648 : 2
flies in face of presumptions, 652 : 15
for art's sake, 465 : 11
for art's sake empty phrase, 504 : 18
given for that, 543 : 29
gives quality to moments, 638 : 15
glib and oily a., 232 : 29
great a. expression of solution, 723 : 12
great a. to saunter, 557 : 5
great is a. of beginning, 512 : 23
greatness of a. to find unique, 861 : 14
has reason for being, 499 : 11
hateful a. how to forget, 267 : 8
hath an enemy Ignorance, 255 : 9
he tried each a., 370 : 7
his science and only a., 703 : 3
history of an a., 793 : 5
imagination master of a., 684 : 6
imitates Nature, 117 : *n* 6
imitation of nature, 114 : 26
in a. best is good enough, 395 : 13
in a. economy is beauty, 654 : 3
in a. truth means to end, 471 : 16
independent of claptrap, 619 : 8
individuality of expression beginning and end of a., 397 : 4
industry in a. necessity, 619 : 6
industry without a. brutality, 573 : 7
is a habit, 260 : 11
is armistice with fate, 837 : 7
is I science is we, 552 : 4
jealous mistress, 498 : 25
keep pure both life and a., 79 : 13
knows all about a., 831 : 3
last and greatest a., 339 : 27
lies in concealing art, 619 : *n* 2
life earnest a. gay, 413 : 6
life is short a. long, 80 : 9
live without a., 609 : 13
long life short, 395 : 7
long Time fleeting, 509 : 14
made poetry mechanic a., 375 : 22
made tongue-tied by authority, 244 : 24
madness of a., 653 : 5
makes life, 654 : 10
may err, 307 : 4
mediatress, 437 : 22

Art (*continued*)
modern a. modern because critical, 886 : 11
moral sense of work of a., 653 : 11
more matter with less a., 220 : 11
more valid facts in a. than in history books, 812 : 8
most cherishes, 542 : 5
most intense individualism, 676 : 2
my a. negation of society, 643 : 7
my trade and a. is living, 165 : 1
mysterious is source of a. and science, 763 : 6
nature is but a. unknown, 337 : 1
nature is the a. of God, 274 : 7
nature not dull a., 490 : 9
nature's above a., 234 : 29
Nature's handmaid A., 303 : 4
never try to be popular, 676 : 3
next to nature a., 443 : 1
not learned much by a., 262 : 12
not thou man, 405 : 6
nothing without form, 583 : 6
of angling, 270 : 34
of being wise, 649 : 6
of dancing source of arts, 690 : 1
of democratic government, 741 : *n* 3
of ending, 512 : 23
of getting on together, 776 : 4
of government, 852 : 2
of knowing what to overlook, 649 : 6
of necessities strange, 233 : 30
of Racine's verse, 735 : 10
of seeing things invisible, 322 : 6
of teaching is awakening, 655 : 10
of telling you nothing, 297 : 26
of war simple, 589 : 15
of winning games, 848 : 13
only clean thing, 662 : 19
only through a. get outside selves, 734 : 13
past is work of a., 736 : 9
pattern on experience, 698 : 5
personality of a., 552 : 4
politics a. of possible, 553 : *n* 3
politics not science but a., 553 : *n* 3
posterity of work of a., 734 : 3
practice and thought forge a., 103 : 28
pretty but is it a., 708 : 11
production of a. in soul, 697 : 13
professor of a. of puffing, 399 : 7
purpose inherent in a. so in nature, 87 : 5
refuge of a., 846 : 5
register multiple perception in a., 793 : 10
reliefs of a humble a., 849 : 8
respect for a., 645 : 8
revolt against fate, 853 : 6
romantic character in a., 639 : 4
schoolman's subtle a., 339 : 4
science and a. unite humanity, 904 : 18
selfish and perverse, 421 : 20
shield from existence, 674 : 19
should simplify, 739 : 3
smaller with their a., 840 : 4
stylization makes a., 317 : 11
subjects for a. and exemplars, 799 : 17
subordinates a. to nature, 437 : 17
substitute for experience, 895 : 19
take away a. of writing, 419 : 8
take love away no a., 686 : 2

Art (*continued*)
tell thee what thou a., 170 : 25
tender strokes of a., 334 : 12
thanks to a. see world multiply, 734 : 13
that speaks, 853 : 5
theme of a. and song, 716 : 20
then must a. retire, 413 : 22
theory of physics 696 : 12
through a. perfection, 674 : 19
'tis all thou a., 335 : 11
to blot, 339 : 27
to find mind's construction, 236 : 15
to make dust of all things, 275 : 4
to please, 338 : 14
too precise in every part, 266 : 7
transmission of highest feelings, 602 : 14
unpremeditated a., 468 : 11
unthinkable without risk, 816 : 17
upsets, 776 : 1
useless, 674 : 23
vaunted works of a., 495 : 14
war only a. necessary, 153 : 21
war's glorious a., 330 : 1
what a. wash guilt away, 369 : 20
where love of man love of a., 79 : 16
which is almost a. which is a., 684 : 1
who comprehends a., 421 : 19
work of a. corner of creation, 643 : 6
work of a. resembles artist, 688 : 7
work of body and soul, 572 : 15
work that aspires to a., 683 : 2
works of a. products of danger, 756 : 14
works of a. turned to wall, 595 : 6
wrestle with the angel A., 572 : 5
writer's responsibility to a., 838 : 13
Arteries, man as old as his a., 301 : 3
Artery, makes each petty a., 219 : 15
Artful, alliteration's a. aid, 375 : 9
careless with a. care, 324 : 22
Dodger, 546 : 31
Arthur, good King A., 934 : 1
knightly endured pain, 149 : 9
most renowned Christian king, 149 : 4
slowly answered A., 534 : 31
Arthur's bosom, 207 : 13
Article, fundamental a. of political creed, 382 : 4
snuffed out by a., 461 : 24
Articles, Christians agree in a., 354 : 9
Articulate, bleats a. monotony, 428 : *n* 2
sweet sounds together, 713 : 1
Artifice of eternity, 715 : 2
Artificer, great a. made my mate, 669 : 8
in brass and iron, 7 : 23
lean unwashed a., 202 : 10
old father old a., 777 : 18
Artificers, errors not in art but in a., 313 : 12
Artificial, all things are a., 274 : 7
kill in a. manner, 473 : 17
natural and a., 437 : 17
objects especially tools, 688 : 10
refined or a. type, 730 : 15
speech lacking in a. graces, 98 : 13
wilderness, 868 : 21
Artillery, hi-hi-yee for field a., 764 : 12
to thine a. left a friend, 606 : 9
Artilleryman, red-haired a., 602 : 1
struggle with a., 602 : 1
Artist, allow a. freedom of choice, 652 : 15
be free a. and nothing else, 695 : 2
be more of an a., 480 : 5
cheat for sake of beauty, 757 : 8
create do not talk, 397 : 2
critic helper of a., 653 : 3
critic when cannot be a., 583 : 8
curiosity about a., 861 : 10
do something beyond surface, 619 : 9
find more than a. expressed, 504 : 3
grant a. his subject, 652 : 15
greatest a. greatest ideas, 572 : 8
has masters in eye, 504 : *n* 1
if not a. be revolutionary, 914 : 4
imitate that within, 438 : 1
is his own fault, 865 : 3
keep work to himself, 396 : 7
knows how difficult truth is, 738 : 18
master a. who bids come to heel, 803 : 2
masterpiece joy to a., 619 : 7
must paint, 872 : 15
no home save Paris, 658 : 23
no man born an a., 270 : 31
nothing come out of a. not in man, 772 : 14
perceives more than fellows, 736 : 22
progress of a. self-sacrifice, 809 : 3
range limited as specialist, 695 : 4
records more than has seen, 736 : 22
search for subject, 483 : 14
selects guesses synthesizes, 695 : 4
speaks to our capacity, 683 : 3
that queer monster the a., 654 : 8
what an a. dies with me, 118 : 4
who theorizes, 720 : 7
why a. seeks poverty, 858 : 7
work of art resembles a., 688 : 7
writes own autobiography, 689 : 20
Artiste triche pour le beau, 757 : *n* 1
Artistic growth refining of truthfulness, 738 : 18
moral personality, 577 : 4
nature's a. skill, 125 : 22
not separate a. from social, 755 : 21
nothing a. from mere art, 742 : 3
public make itself a., 676 : 3
undeveloped a. nature, 597 : 8
Artistries in circumstance, 641 : 17
Artistry, scaled invention or true a., 793 : 4
Artists, as many worlds as a., 734 : 13
great a. never puritans, 772 : 2
scientists a. and mystics, 888 : 1
what a. call posterity, 734 : 3
Artless and free with all they possess, 151 : 4
full of a. jealousy, 223 : 20
Art's, art for a. sake, 465 : 11
long hazard, 728 : 22
long time short, 80 : *n* 2
Arts, Athens mother of a., 288 : 13
babblative and scribblative, 440 : 11
dancing source of a., 690 : 1
degrade first the a., 405 : 15
fashion's brightest a., 370 : 16
flourishing of the a., 826 : 12
Imagination with Reason mother of a., 394 : *n* 1
impersonal universal a., 703 : 13
in the a. style, 718 : 6
in which wise excel, 316 : 5
inglorious a. of peace, 296 : 22
Arts (*continued*)
liberal a. study humanizes, 114 : 2
medicine most distinguished of a., 80 : 4
mother of a. and eloquence, 288 : 13
music highest of fine a., 579 : 15
no a. no letters no society, 264 : 17
no relish of those a., 326 : 12
nurse of a. plenties, 208 : 16
of war and peace, 617 : 8
stomach teacher of a., 117 : 8
that caused to rise, 338 : 14
that lie outside person, 690 : 1
they are the books the a., 191 : 5
three a. with all things, 85 : 8
well fitted in a., 190 : 20
what state of our a., 875 : 10
Aryan, neat moustache and A. eye, 911 : 17
As if, 650 : 4
intricate evasions of a., 768 : 24
you desire me, 723 : 21
A-sailing with the wind, 933 : 7
Ascend above restrictions, 621 : 15
base degrees by which a., 215 : 16
if I a. up into heaven, 22 : 17
into the hill of the Lord, 18 : 8
muse of fire a., 207 : 1
Ascendancy, capital in a. system of plunder, 562 : 20
Ascended, bright pomp a. jubilant, 287 : 1
into heaven, 55 : 2
morning hymns a., 597 : 17
Ascending, angels a. and descending, 8 : 19, 44 : 25
Ascends to mountaintops, 457 : 22
Ascent, no a. too steep for mortals, 106 : 27
of Man, 870 : 15
Ascetic in unnecessary points, 648 : 9
systematically a., 648 : 9
Asclepius cured the body, 83 : *n* 3
I swear by A., 79 : 13
owe a cock to A., 79 : 8
Ash, oak a. and thorn, 710 : 12, 926 : 20
on old man's sleeve, 808 : 11
one adjusting a. heaps, 798 : 9
out of a. I rise, 911 : 12
Ashamed, epitaph of which not a., 669 : 15
more a. more respectable, 680 : 17
naked and were not a., 7 : 4
never a. to own wrong, 340 : 10
no reason to be a. of ape, 596 : 11
nor ever a. so we be named, 610 : 11
not a. to defend a friend, 35 : 35
not a. to fail, 351 : 15
of death, 274 : 12
of divine idea, 496 : 20
of having been in love, 293 : 11
shame is a. to sit, 193 : 10
to be seen with him, 310 : 12
to die, 480 : 14
to look upon one another, 271 : 8
with noble shame, 567 : 1
workman that needeth not to be a., 51 : 7
Ashen, skies a. and sober, 526 : 22
Ashes, all a. to taste, 457 : 20
am I and dust, 135 : 7
beauty for a., 31 : 25
cinders a. dust, 476 : 5
e'en in our a. live, 362 : 15

Ashes (*continued*)
from his a. made, 531 : 22
handful of gray a. at rest, 591 : 9
heaven and earth in a., 139 : 4
in a. olde is fyr yreke, 147 : 1
in a. rather than enslaved, 744 : 5
into a. all my lust, 297 : 1
new-create another heir, 249 : 17
of his fathers, 488 : 14
of Napoleon Bonaparte, 421 : 15
out of a. life again, 660 : 10
past a bucket of a., 761 : 7
put on sackcloth with a., 14 : 32
speak to your silent a., 102 : 18
splendid in a., 275 : 11
to ashes, 56 : 13
turn to a. on lips, 447 : 15
turns a. or prospers, 516 : 9
water of sources and a., 860 : 9
well-wrought urn becomes greatest a., 252 : 12
yesterday embryo tomorrow a., 124 : 27
Ashore, till last galoot's a., 636 : 3
Asia and Africa expelled freedom, 384 : 12
peace and stability in A., 882 : 22
settlement in A., 813 : 15
seven churches in A., 52 : 28
vast multitudes of A., 745 : 2
Aside, in life many things draw us a., 121 : 9
not idly stand a., 81 : 5
to step a. is human, 409 : 21
Asinorum, pons a., 92 : *n* 2
Ask, all I a. is merry yarn, 760 : 16
all I a. is tall ship, 760 : 14
and it shall be given, 38 : 12
and ye shall receive, 45 : 28
cease to a. what morrow will bring, 107 : 7
don't a. me to take none, 547 : 35
dost thou a. proof, 587 : 12
drink divine, 256 : 8
for anything except time, 420 : 7
for me tomorrow, 193 : 5
for no meaner pelf, 557 : 20
for the old paths, 31 : 37
how he is he tells you, 719 : 12
I do not a. you much, 202 : 18
if you got to a. you ain't got it, 847 : *n* 2
me blessing, 235 : 12
me no more, 531 : 10
me no more where Jove bestows, 271 : 19
me no questions, 371 : 12
never a. refuse resign office, 348 : 19
not a dinner to a. a man to, 354 : 17
not a. for what you wish you had not, 114 : 31
not offer to people but a., 890 : 5
not what country can do for you, 890 : 12
not whom sleep beside, 690 : 19
nothing want nothing, 138 : 3
of him will they a. more, 43 : 22
of thee forgiveness, 235 : 12
only what they can give, 718 : 13
the beasts, 15 : 29
the Lord's blessing, 918 : 19
the young, 400 : 12
us prophet, 900 : 3
we a. and a., 584 : 9
Ask (*continued*)
wealth I a. not, 669 : 2
what you can do for country, 890 : 12
where a. is have, 365 : 8
who could a. for more, 835 : 21
why I have no statue, 95 : 11
wilt thou go a. the mole, 403 : 17
Asked a lithe lady, 404 : 11
are you lost I a., 790 : 7
for it Georges Dandin, 298 : 7
how pearls did grow, 266 : 5
no other thing, 605 : 20
not come even if a., 749 : 7
Oliver a. for more, 546 : 30
one another the reason, 212 : 31
thief to steal me peach, 404 : 11
to be where no storms, 655 : 17
Askelon, publish it not in the streets of A., 13 : 8
Asking, keep a. over and over, 482 : 7
only God had for a., 567 : 12
too much, 422 : 6
Asks a little of us here, 749 : 14
if this be joy, 370 : 16
of us certain height, 749 : 14
Asleep, athwart noses as they lie a., 191 : 23
awake and a. the same, 70 : 8
birds are a. in trees, 397 : 3
devil is a., 679 : 12
drunk and a. in boots, 767 : 1
half a. as they stalk, 642 : 2
in lap of legends, 476 : 12
is in world of his own, 120 : 13
keep it quiet till it falls a., 302 : 19
lips of those that are a. to speak, 28 : 21
moment I fall a., 850 : 4
my Mary's a., 410 : 13
on furrow sound a., 477 : 18
sail like swans a., 785 : 16
sucks the nurse a., 242 : 4
tide moving seems a., 535 : 19
under haystack a., 930 : 12
very houses seem a., 425 : 14
where winds all a., 584 : 12
A-sorrowing, goeth a., 163 : 5
Aspect, lend the eye terrible a., 207 : 16
meet in her a. and eyes, 459 : 13
sweet a. of princes, 249 : 3
Aspects, relations between a. of experience, 789 : 2
Aspen, as a. leef gan to quake, 144 : 23
light quivering a., 431 : 2
Aspens quiver, 528 : 24
Asphalt and exhaust fumes, 903 : 12
Aspics' tongues, 231 : 17
Aspiration, cannot prove an a., 637 : 3
social order and thirsty a., 875 : 9
Aspirations of men of good will, 814 : 10
right a., 73 : 2
Aspire, by due steps a., 279 : 4
light and will a., 189 : 8
mind a. to higher things, 176 : 9
on what wings dare he a., 405 : 7
smile we would a. to, 249 : 3
there bade me a., 586 : 9
to what greater character can mortal a., 380 : 6
Aspired to be and was not, 544 : 11
Aspires, each of us a. to goodness, 171 : 19
Aspirin of middle classes, 854 : 10
Aspiring, all to have a. minds, 183 : 6
Aspiring (*continued*)
to be gods, 336 : 18
youth that fired Ephesian dome, 275 : *n* 1
Ass, egregiously an a., 230 : 16
enamored of an a., 197 : 7
idle to play lyre for a., 127 : 17
jawbone of an a., 12 : 17
knoweth his master's crib, 28 : 26
law a., 547 : 6
not covet neighbor's a., 10 : 7
opened the mouth of the a., 11 : 2
recover and prove an a., 197 : 20
riding upon an a., 33 : 32
sinned against my brother the a., 139 : 1
wild a. stamps o'er head, 516 : 11
will carry load, 171 : 2
write me down an a., 210 : 2
Assail, ills scholar's life a., 351 : 17
Assailed, everything hard to attain easily a., 124 : 1
seasons, 728 : 19
Assails, all he reads a., 333 : 19
Assassin, forgot copperheads and a., 761 : 8
kind a. Sleep, 900 : 12
Assassinated, rather be a. than surrender, 521 : 8
Assassination, absolutism tempered by a., 417 : 4
extreme censorship, 681 : 16
trammel up consequence, 236 : 22
Assault and battery of wind, 714 : 19
of thoughts on unthinking, 783 : 11
Assaults, defend in a. of our enemies, 55 : 4
Assay so hard, 144 : 8
Assayed, thrice he a., 283 : 26
Assayeth, naught n' a. naught n' acheveth, 145 : 1
Assays of bias, 220 : 7
Assemblage of sloth sleep and littleness, 381 : 13
Assemble, peaceably to a., 391 : 14
Assemblies, nails fastened by masters of a., 27 : 26
Assembling, slow in a., 80 : 16
Assembly, club a. of good fellows, 352 : 7
free speech press a., 700 : 3
of portable plumbing, 816 : 12
power in majority of popular a., 382 : 4
proper office of representative a., 508 : 17
suppression of free a., 677 : 13
Assent and you are sane, 605 : 11
with civil leer, 338 : 14
Assert eternal Providence, 283 : 2
Assertions, convince hearers of own a., 84 : 1
Asses made to bear and you, 188 : 31
mankind a. that pull, 462 : 9
Asses' bridge, 92 : *n* 2
Assimilating educating selecting, 737 : 11
Assist him to save face, 834 : 1
Assistance, gives persecution no a., 379 : 8
of Thee do we beg a., 130 : 9
Assisting advancement of science, 825 : 11
Associate, the good must a., 372 : 4

Associated, cannot be a. with government, 558 : 1
Association, quotations touch a., 685 : 15
unplanned uninhibited a., 861 : 7
Ass's, white curd of a. milk, 338 : 18
Assuage anguish of bereavement, 524 : 4
Assuaged, half a. for Itylus, 632 : 7
Assume a virtue, 223 : 10
honorable style of Christian, 273 : 15
spirits either sex a., 283 : 18
what I a. you a., 574 : 11
Assumes, no vice but a. some virtue, 199 : 25
the god affects to nod, 306 : 13
Assuming, start a. that men are bad, 154 : 7
Assumptions, most necessary of a., 703 : 9
not admit a. of superiority, 89 : 17
Assurance given by looks, 184 : 13
make a. double sure, 239 : 11
of a man, 223 : 3
of recorded history, 808 : 5
Assure survival of liberty, 890 : 7
Assured, crown themselves a., 245 : 13
ignorant of what he's most a., 228 : 10
Assyria, Sennacherib king of A., 14 : 20
Assyrian came down like wolf, 459 : 14
Asterisk of death, 512 : 14
Astern, look a. row ahead, 120 : 18
Astolat, lily maid of A., 534 : 11
Astonish, gratify some a. rest, 626 : 1
things that would a. you, 628 : 23
Astonished at my own moderation, 367 : 2
Astonishing thing about earth, 884 : 1
Astonishment, curse a. hissing and reproach, 32 : 16
gateway to incomprehensible, 881 : 4
thou shalt become an a., 11 : 19
wine of a., 19 : 24
Astra, ad a. per aspera, 133 : 7
sic itur ad a., 106 : *n* 1
Astray, all likely to go a., 74 : 22
black sheep gone a., 708 : 14
if world go a., 142 : 3
light that led a., 409 : 5
light which cannot lead a., 324 : 2
one that had been led a., 278 : 18
we like sheep have gone a., 31 : 16
Astrologers, sociologists a., 706 : 11
Astronomer, survey grandest with a., 776 : 9
undevout a. is mad, 330 : 19
Astronomers, confounding a., 733 : 3
what poor a., 918 : 6
Astronomy compels soul to look upwards, 84 : 18
geology by day a. night, 830 : 17
of shapeless pistols, 841 : 13
Astrophil, who knew not A., 184 : 12
Asunder, afar and a., 627 : 5
half a life a., 612 : 15
let no man put a., 56 : 11
let not man put a., 40 : 5
put this rogue and whore a., 323 : 2
villain and he many miles a., 193 : 16
We clave them a., 131 : 13
whirl a. and dismember me, 201 : 22
Asylum among mob, 569 : 19
Jesus Christ in a., 690 : 11
lunatic a. in Jerusalem, 690 : 11
Asylum (*continued*)
optimism in lunatic a., 690 : 3
prepare a. for mankind, 384 : 12
their last a., 365 : 5
Asylums, comfortably padded a., 781 : 16
Atahualpa, America of A., 721 : 3
Ataualpa, who strangled A., 488 : 6
Ate cheeses out of vats, 541 : 1
the malt, 934 : 9
when we were not hungry, 322 : 15
with runcible spoon, 550 : 10
Aten, O living A., 5 : 4
shine as A. of daytime, 5 : 6
Athanasian Creed splendid lyric, 502 : 22
Atheism like that of Spinoza, 704 : 6
little philosophy inclineth to a., 180 : 17
owlet A., 435 : 16
pantheism a. in disguise, 705 : 14
religion and not a., 373 : 3
Atheist half believes God, 330 : 14
not satisfied with appearances, 853 : 7
superstitious a., 543 : 7
town a., 847 : 13
Atheist-laugh's a poor exchange, 409 : 13
Atheists, no a. in foxholes, 857 : 17
Athena, gray-eyed A., 59 : 19
Athenian, Thucydides an A., 80 : 14
Athenians commanded by myself, 70 : 15
crushed gold-bearing Medes, 67 : 18
quality of A. lucidity, 589 : 6
war between Peloponnesians and A., 80 : 14
Athens, bringing owls to A., 82 : 6
divine city, 72 : 9
Euripides' land, 75 : *n* 13
fix eyes on greatness of A., 81 : 5
maid of A., 456 : 19
nigh to Euboea, 83 : 6
nurse of men, 75 : 12
the eye of Greece, 288 : 13
to A. sent ships, 461 : *n* 1
weeds of A. he doth wear, 196 : 22
ye men of A., 46 : 15
Athirst, man a. supposes mirage to be water, 131 : 17
Athis, loved you once long ago A., 63 : 7
Athlete crowned in sweat of brow, 127 : 14
Athletes, interest in animals and a., 799 : 17
stronger than backers, 128 : 16
Athwart men's noses as asleep, 191 : 23
A-tiptoe, stand a. when day named, 208 : 10
Atlanta to the sea, 614 : 14
Atlantic, dawn on other side of A., 363 : 21
drag A. for whales, 623 : 5
frontier from A. to Pacific, 743 : 16
Ocean on my head, 893 : 5
steep A. stream, 279 : 10
Thule and A. surge, 345 : 15
Atlas, Teneriff or A. unremoved, 286 : 10
Atmosphere, clear brown twilight a., 503 : 15
of Gallup Poll, 745 : 5
Atmosphere (*continued*)
overwhelming importance of a., 853 : 17
Atom changed everything save thinking, 764 : 3
intense a. glows, 469 : 5
knowledge of stars through a., 776 : 10
man nearer a. than star, 776 : 9
movements of lightest a., 397 : 17
mystery of the a., 825 : 1
no evil in a., 851 : 15
on matter duplicate in mind, 570 : 15
secret powers of a., 720 : 6
Atomic age, 729 : 12
bomb in unfederated world, 847 : 4
bombs burst in hands, 719 : 15
cannot control a. energy, 734 : 14
careless handling of a. technology, 775 : 13
energy a menace, 763 : 15
energy lead to bombs, 763 : 12
first moment of a. age, 885 : 8
habits of age of a. energy, 826 : 2
reduced no man to a. elements, 777 : 10
reduced to a. mechanics, 617 : 11
release of a. energy, 787 : 14
war fought with a. bomb, 763 : 14
Atomies, crumbled out again to his a., 254 : 5
team of little a., 191 : 23
Atom's weight of good, 132 : 18
Atoms and compounds of atoms, 100 : 9
cannot be swamped by force, 100 : 9
in reality a. and space, 79 : 11
onion a. lurk in bowl, 433 : 11
or systems, 336 : 14
reduction to motions of a., 636 : 16
true structure of a., 875 : 7
we have seen our a., 818 : 9
Atone, pictures for page a., 340 : 18
Atoned, microcosm and macrocosm a., 595 : 3
not a. too dearly by death, 412 : 17
Atones for later disregard, 749 : 1
Atreus, Argos do without sons of A., 701 : 10
son of A., 57 : 27
Atrocious crime of being young man, 350 : 16
Atrophied, sexually a., 703 : 13
Atrophy, unused capacities a., 883 : 7
Attach golden chain from heaven, 58 : 6
Attachée, à sa proie a., 312 : *n* 5
Attachment fabricator of illusions, 876 : 17
to government, 373 : 7
Attack all the more boldly, 105 : 14
first to a. neighbors, 297 : 16
is the reaction, 355 : 12
lawless a. upon liberty, 365 : 3
no frontiers against a., 853 : 17
prompt in a., 372 : 20
repeat attack, 777 : 11
so outnumbered we a., 782 : 13
strength in a., 812 : 15
Attacked, rather a. than unnoticed, 356 : 9
United States a., 780 : 15
Attacking and getting hammered, 681 : 3
situation excellent I am a., 670 : 6

Attacks, try to answer a., 524 : 11
Attain, everything hard to a. easily assailed, 124 : 1
old experience do a., 279 : 1
Attainable, is uniformity of opinion a., 387 : 15
Attainment, Zeus grant a. of sweet delight, 71 : 27
Attains upmost round, 215 : 16
Attempt and not the deed, 237 : 18
fearing to a., 227 : 29
literary a. unfortunate, 357 : 18
no limit to what novelist a., 652 : 13
perception and a., 720 : 8
the end, 266 : 18
wind rising a. to live, 735 : 12
Attempted, not done is not a., 506 : 7
something a. done, 510 : 9
Attend men and not women, 85 : 16
shooting stars a. thee, 266 : 14
to history of Rasselas, 352 : 15
Attendance, dance a., 249 : 16
Attendant, am an a. lord, 803 : 17
bark a. sail, 338 : 2
Attended, is on his way a., 426 : 15
Attending, captive good a. captain ill, 244 : 25
softest music to a. ears, 192 : 17
Attendre, j'ai failli a., 312 : *n* 3
Attention, calling a. not same as explaining, 906 : 13
dance a. on old age, 717 : 13
like deep harmony, 194 : 9
must be paid, 888 : 2
pen instrument to fix a., 380 : 7
Attentions, trivial a. men think manly, 414 : 10
Attentive eyes, 353 : 10
sit a. to own applause, 338 : 14
Attic, beauty crieth in a., 620 : 3
bird, 288 : 14
not an A. grace, 792 : 12
seasoned with A. salt, 298 : 14
shape, 477 : 10
Atticus, if A. were he, 338 : 15
Attire comely not costly, 175 : 9
in halls in gay a., 430 : 6
man's a., 35 : 33
rich a. creeps rustling, 476 : 17
Attitude artistically inexcusable, 758 : 13
fair a., 477 : 10
in which most alive, 647 : 23
Attitudenize, don't a., 357 : 3
Attorney, Hocus an old cunning a., 344 : *n* 7
right to a., 820 : 15
Attorney's, go to a. office pay for it, 555 : 3
office boy to a. firm, 627 : 14
Attract silver churn, 628 : 9
Attracted, those far off are a., 69 : 3
Attraction and affection, 738 : 3
Attractive, sweet a. grace, 184 : 13, 285 : 18
Attracts envy of world, 372 : 12
Attribute, no a. of superior man greater, 89 : 2
to awe and majesty, 200 : 9
Attributes characteristics of living creature, 572 : 10
God and a. of God eternal, 308 : 5
Attunement, from things that differ comes a., 70 : 4
Auber, dank tarn of A., 526 : 23
Auburn, sweet A., 369 : 28
Audace, de l'a. encore de l'a., 412 : *n* 1
Audacia certe laus erit, 112 : *n* 9
Audacibus annue coeptis, 103 : *n* 15
Audacious power, 914 : *n* 2
Audacity more audacity always audacity, 412 : 2
nothing impossible provided you use a., 792 : 3
Audentes fortuna iuvat, 106 : *n* 2
Audi partem alteram, 129 : *n* 2
Audible, ill-bred as a. laughter, 370 : *n* 1
Audience, Boston a. critics, 622 : 3
dreamer a. of dream, 754 : 12
for sake of crowded a., 80 : 2
gone into unlit a., 904 : 9
good play a. pleased, 741 : 14
how long a. sits, 442 : 22
never fail to laugh, 82 : 17
takes him serious, 766 : 2
Audiences, addressing popular a., 88 : 15
great poets great a., 577 : 9
Auditor, appeal best suited to a., 783 : 4
Auf Flügeln des Gesanges, 481 : *n* 9
Aught that I could ever read, 195 : 22
Augur misgovernment, 372 : 20
Augurs mock their own presage, 245 : 13
Augury, defy a., 224 : 28
his powers of a., 57 : 20
single best a. is to fight, 58 : 14
August, day in latter A., 892 : 6
winter recommence in A., 461 : 27
yellow with A., 792 : 9
Augustan, next A. age will dawn, 363 : 21
Augustine, Saint A. well said, 511 : 22
why St. A. thanked God, 754 : 9
Auld lang syne, 410 : 11, 410 : 12
moon in her arm, 926 : 11
should a. acquaintance, 410 : 11
Aunt kept regard for truth, 730 : 9
Aunts, delight of husband a. infant, 810 : 20
sisters cousins and a., 627 : 13
Auream quisquis mediocritatem diliget, 107 : *n* 18
Aureliano Babilonia finish deciphering, 908 : 3
Aurochs and angels, 846 : 5
Aurora Leighs, no more A. thank God, 517 : 16
new A., 918 : 1
Aurora Borealis, bounded on north by A. , 535 : *n* 6
Aurore, Belle A., 545 : 15
Auspicious as ace of spades, 899 : 14
one a. eye, 217 : 29
Austere beauty of mathematics, 737 : 14
look a. of landscapes, 794 : 2
Austerlitz, pile bodies at A., 761 : 6
Austria, Don John of A., 742 : 10
outlive eagle of A., 383 : 16
Authentic, when a. watch is shown, 289 : 19
Author acquainted with authors, 597 : 7
and finisher of our faith, 51 : 19
choose a. as choose friend, 309 : 8
dreamer a. of dream, 754 : 12
Author (*continued*)
he was the a., 114 : 4
Holy A. of that religion, 319 : 22
leaves of any a., 274 : 10
not bein' a. gr-reat critic, 722 : 19
of peace, 55 : 4
ourselves a. and finisher, 519 : 22
out from bushes, 782 : 7
read by five hundred, 635 : 7
relationship of a. to works, 683 : 6
revised and corrected by A., 346 : 15
same steps as a., 479 : 10
select five hundred readers, 635 : 7
sent by a. with autograph, 442 : 13
shrimp of an a., 363 : 12
six characters in search of a., 723 : 19
steal from one a. plagiarism, 757 : 14
thou Virgil art my master and a., 140 : 12
time the a. of authors, 178 : 19
unsuccessful a. turns critic, 436 : *n* 1
what good a. whispers, 711 : 8
what I like in good a., 711 : 8
when man of rank an a., 356 : 22
where any a. teaches such beauty, 191 : 1
worst thing do to a., 356 : 9
Authoritarian Germany, 834 : 7
socialism in a. terms, 834 : 7
Authorities, destruction shows activity of a., 518 : 3
nihilist not bow to a., 564 : 3
world-wide public a., 774 : 7
Authority, adduces a. uses not intellect, 152 : 7
age in virtuous carries a., 327 : 15
and place try tempers of men, 120 : 4
and show of truth, 209 : 30
base a. from others' books, 190 : 12
by whose a. do you act, 385 : 11
children opportunity for display of a., 796 : 5
common good and public a., 774 : 7
compass of national a., 402 : 1
every shadow of a., 373 : 10
fit for public a., 74 : 19
forgets a dying king, 534 : 30
highest spiritual a., 774 : 9
little brief a., 228 : 10
miracle mystery a., 582 : 7
nation cannot control, 616 : 1
not majority, 492 : 12
obedient to whomsoever in a., 80 : 17
of Church moved me, 129 : 8
precepts backed by a., 679 : 1
saying No to a., 851 : 4
sovereign a. of our partners, 393 : 3
throw your a. at our feet, 392 : 9
Tolstoi a. tremendous, 601 : *n* 2
tongue-tied by a., 244 : 24
truth basis of moral a., 580 : 12
without wisdom, 290 : 10
Author's life a vacuum, 597 : 7
sincerely from a. soul, 830 : 8
skill to give, 702 : 14
without a. knowing it, 701 : 6
Authors, acquainted with best a., 597 : 7
among good a. accounted Plagiarè, 282 : 11
are a natural aristocracy, 559 : 31
books like men their a., 321 : 10
damn a. they never read, 375 : 12
established it as rule, 326 : 15

Authors (*continued*)
old a. to read, 179 : 18
praise of ancient a., 264 : 19
proof against mutability, 453 : 1
steal from many a. research, 757 : 14
time the author of a., 178 : 19
when a. talk of sublime, 385 : 7
who flourished allotted time, 452 : 20
Authors', judge of a. names, 333 : 12
Autobiographies begin Chapter Two, 738 : 7
nations write a., 573 : 11
Autobiography, artist writes own a., 689 : 20
Autocracy, communism a. upside down, 550 : 2
dictatorship perpetuated as a., 834 : 7
Autocratic government, 751 : 2
Autograph, foolish a. at beginning, 442 : 13
Automatic hand, 805 : 8
Automation has unbounded possibilities, 831 : 23
mechanized a., 466 : 7
Automatism but also criticism, 837 : 9
Automne violons de l'a., 659 : *n* 6
Autres, l'enfer c'est les A., 865 : *n* 1
pour encourager les a., 343 : *n* 4
Autumn, descends a. evening, 588 : 5
dull dark day in a., 525 : 19
fell like a. fruit, 303 : 16
freezing everywhere, 889 : 8
happy a. fields, 531 : 3
I saw old A., 485 : 9
in air alas, 711 : 11
in everything, 542 : 22
in misty morn, 485 : 9
it's a. in the country, 752 : 17
leaves fall early this a., 792 : 9
no season such delight as a., 265 : 16
nodding o'er yellow plain, 345 : 13
of 1929, 871 : 5
rose more exquisite, 171 : 20
that grew by reaping, 241 : 25
Thursday like today in a., 824 : 4
violins of a., 659 : 12
Autumnal, deep a. tone, 467 : 21
face, 253 : 20
sea in gentle a. season, 782 : 22
thick as a. leaves, 283 : 16
Autumn's, breath of a. being, 467 : 17
Auxiliary, suffering an a. of creation, 661 : 1
Available to any shape, 905 : 13
Availeth, struggle naught a., 564 : 16
Avalanche, snowflake in a., 876 : 4
Avarice a species of madness, 308 : 22
an incurable disease, 3 : 7
and happiness, 347 : 7
disease of old men, 261 : 11
good old-gentlemanly vice, 261 : *n* 8
melancholy who has dismissed a., 386 : 11
Pride Envy A. three sparks, 141 : 5
prudery a kind of a., 453 : 11
rich beyond dreams of a., 356 : 20, 358 : 8
seems not so much a vice, 308 : *n* 5
spur of industry, 357 : 13
take up with a., 261 : *n* 8
Ave atque vale, 102 : *n* 7
Caesar morituri te salutamus, 123 : *n* 12
Avelaval, so a., 778 : 6
Avenge O Lord thy slaughtered saints, 282 : 18
wish of some is to a., 80 : 16
Avenged of Philistines, 12 : 20
South is a., 635 : 23
1440 times a day, 647 : 19
Avenger, mightest still the enemy and a., 17 : 17
of these wrongs, 105 : 11
time the a., 458 : 20
Avenues of ill, 495 : 3
Average man, 779 : 13
of all the virtues, 630 : 16
type hear Tao, 64 : 14
Averages, fugitive from law of a., 898 : 8
Averni, facilis descensus A., 105 : *n* 7
Averse alike to flatter or offend, 333 : 22
what cat's a. to fish, 361 : 15
Aversion, in matrimony begin with a., 398 : 6
world outlasts a., 584 : 16
Aversions, man of my a., 772 : 12
Aviary, mind is an a., 85 : 19
Aviation, if a. no further advanced, 776 : 4
supported by tactical a., 825 : 6
Avid, mind's a. substance, 836 : 19
Avocation, my a. and my vocation, 748 : 18
Avoid citations from poets, 80 : 2
evil do good, 72 : 17
fall into Scylla to a. Charybdis, 200 : *n* 1
perils by united forces, 308 : 21
ready for war to a. it, 316 : 12
reeking herd, 793 : 18
self-righteousness, 834 : 1
what is to come, 223 : 8
Avon, swan of A., 256 : 18
Avowed erect and manly foe, 422 : 5
Await occasions, 536 : 6
wanderer a. it too, 585 : 22
Awaits alike inevitable hour, 362 : 3
Awake, all shall a. again, 275 : 14
and asleep the same, 70 : 8
and sing, 30 : 10
arise, 283 : 17
Deborah and utter a song, 12 : 4
England a., 407 : 7
for morning, 516 : 1
for night is flying, 176 : 20
keep drowsy emperor a., 715 : 3
lying a. with headache, 628 : 26
my lute a., 161 : 24
my soul, 346 : 1
my soul and with the sun, 311 : 18
my St. John, 336 : 10
my whirling hands, 863 : 16
O north wind, 28 : 14
thy Nightingales a., 591 : 9
to be a. to be alive, 559 : 23
wide a. moon and I, 629 : 9
Awaken, friends for when we a., 273 : 3
Awakened, the A. One (Buddha), 72 : 17
Awakening, near a. when dream that we dream, 438 : 10
Third Great A., 911 : 7
A-walking, as I was a., 927 : 9
Devil is gone, 440 : 13
A-waltzing Matilda, 705 : 7
Awards, friendships won by a. not real, 153 : 24
Aware, mind a. of own rectitude, 104 : 28
of damp souls, 804 : 5
of minds under responsibility, 839 : 16
of slightest bondage mad a., 749 : 5
valet not a. of this, 88 : 26
Awareness, give each moment a., 756 : 1
of the unknowable, 853 : 12
quickens mental demand, 654 : 9
women contribute a., 853 : 19
A-watering last year's crops, 565 : 5
Away and mock the time, 237 : 8
bound a., 934 : 20
can't take that a. from me, 836 : 9
from men and towns, 470 : 3
look a., 554 : 1
O soul, 576 : 16
o'er hills and far a., 530 : 13
over hills and far a., 332 : 1, 931 : 12
pass not a., 8 : 11
round the world a., 566 : 14
you rolling river, 934 : 20
you scullion, 206 : 10
Awe, attribute to a. and majesty, 200 : 9
devised to keep strong in a., 187 : 30
ever-increasing wonder and a., 366 : 12
imaginative a., 869 : 11
lifted hand in a., 330 : 1
man from career of humor, 209 : 19
of such thing as myself, 215 : 4
romantic a. of rich, 845 : 7
Sacred A., 783 : 2
strike a. into beholders, 322 : 10
tradition inspires a., 657 : 10
Aweary of the sun, 240 : 5
she said I am a., 527 : 18
A-wearyin', jest a. fer you, 684 : 18
Awed by firmness, 81 : 7
Awful, anything a. makes me laugh, 441 : 13
beneath a. Hand we hold, 709 : 16
face some a. moment, 427 : 24
felt how a. goodness is, 286 : 8
magnificent and a. cause, 376 : 21
pause prophetic of end, 330 : 6
phantom of hungry poor, 621 : 16
reg'lar, 622 : 16
shadow of unseen Power, 466 : 8
still and a. red, 434 : 28
stirrings speak of soul, 571 : 3
warmth about heart, 479 : 12
within a. volume lies, 432 : 5
A-whining, born naked and falls a., 116 : *n* 4
A-winding into land of dreams, 813 : 7
Awkward, Allen with a. shame, 339 : 14
always made a. bow, 480 : 6
historical fact, 764 : 14
in their soil, 873 : 15
to play with souls, 543 : 13
Awkwardness has no forgiveness, 499 : 7
Awoke and behold it was dream, 302 : 11
and found it truth, 479 : 2
and found myself famous, 459 : 1
one night from dream, 454 : 4
A-wooing, frog a. go, 929 : 12
Awry, amended what told a., 715 : 18
currents turn a., 221 : 12
leaning all a., 517 : 8

Awww, everybody goes A., 901 : 3
Ax fitter to bruise, 290 : 10
laid unto the root, 36 : 29
Lizzie Borden took a., 923 : 5
neither hammer nor a., 13 : 32
to grind, 448 : 12
Axe, book a. for frozen sea inside us, 786 : 4
Axe's edge did try, 296 : 23
Axes, no a. rung, 377 : *n* 5
sharp-edged a., 575 : 14
talking of a., 611 : 14
Axiom hatred of bourgeois, 583 : 17
old as hills, 740 : 17
Axioms, derives a. from particulars, 179 : 7
flies from particulars to a., 179 : 7
of mathematics, 643 : 15
proved upon our pulses, 479 : 10
Axis of earth sticks out, 519 : 12
soft underbelly of A., 746 : 3
sword a. of world, 815 : 4
Axle, glowing a. doth allay, 279 : 10
Axletree, clot bedded a., 807 : 4
Aye, have profferer construe A., 189 : 31
Aylmer, Rose A. whom these eyes, 442 : 18
Ayuda, al que madruga Dios a., 935 : 9
Azcan, Chieftain Iffucan of A., 767 : 5
Azores, behind lay gray A., 646 : 6
Flores in the A., 535 : 11
Aztec would have had strong states, 800 : 4
Aztecs by no means would give up, 156 : 13
Azure, arose from out a. main, 345 : 19
far in a. deeps, 510 : 15
pellucid in a. depths, 577 : 7
riding o'er a. realm, 363 : 6
ringed with a. world, 532 : 28
steeps, 843 : 13
Azure-lidded sleep, 476 : 18
Azures, devouring green a., 673 : 16
Azurs, dévorant les a. verts, 673 : *n* 9

B

B, emotions from A to B, 827 : 16
mark it with B, 929 : 18
Baa baa baa, 708 : 14
baa black sheep, 930 : 5
Baalim, Peor and B., 277 : 12
Babbitt, his name was B., 791 : 5
Babblative, arts b. and scribblative, 440 : 11
Babbled of green fields, 207 : 13
Babbling drunkenness, 214 : 26
gossip of the air, 213 : 19
Babblings, profane and vain b., 51 : 5
Babe, becomes a b. in eternity, 406 : 14
birth-strangled b., 239 : 6
let mighty b. alone, 292 : 18
love b. that milks me, 237 : 5
pity like newborn b., 236 : 24
pretty B. all burning bright, 182 : 2
whose birth embraves morn, 292 : 18
Babel, name of it called B., 8 : 5
stir of the great B., 377 : 4
Babes around thee cling, 427 : 19
out of the mouth of b., 17 : 17
Babies, anyone who hates b., 770 : *n* 8
Babies (*continued*)
bit b. in cradles, 541 : 1
feel like doing for b., 858 : 15
haven't hair, 816 : 2
toast works down to b., 622 : 21
wars fought by b., 901 : 8
Bablock-hithe, Thames at B., 585 : 21
Baboon who saved comrade, 515 : 9
Babs knows what and babs knows why, 759 : 15
Baby a girl and the first, 896 : 15
and me, 929 : 18
blessing and bother, 622 : 17
bunting, 931 : 5
down come b. and all, 660 : 19
figure of giant mass, 226 : 5
I was you b., 910 : 2
inestimable blessing and bother, 622 : 17
looked like mouse, 846 : 14
Mother laid her B., 561 : 10
my b. at my breast, 242 : 4
of thee I sing b., 836 : 3
rockabye b., 660 : 19
Tar-b. ain't sayin' nuthin', 662 : 6
Babylon, ere B. was dust, 466 : 16
I was king in B., 663 : 13
is fallen, 29 : 27, 53 : 23
king of B. stood at the parting, 32 : 27
Babylonish dialect, 290 : 20
Babylon's gardens, 924 : 3
Bacchus ever fair and ever young, 306 : 15
that first, 279 : 7
with pink eyne, 241 : 5
Bachelor, die a b., 209 : 19
got acquainted with a b., 441 : 11
one day b. next grampa, 856 : 9
see b. of threescore, 209 : 1
Back, African moon lying on b., 789 : 10
all roads new going b., 664 : 7
and side go bare, 163 : 10
at b. from time to time hear, 805 : 6
at last to you, 707 : 22
at my b. I always hear, 296 : 28
begins to smart, 929 : 9
borne me on his b., 224 : 14
boys in the b. rooms, 762 : 7
care not who sees your b., 203 : 29
carries sky on b., 557 : 10
cast-iron b. with hinge, 603 : 9
dagger into b. of neighbor, 780 : 9
die with harness on our b., 240 : 6
eyes and b. turn upward, 805 : 7
far b. in soul horse prances, 790 : 19
follow and not see its b., 64 : 7
got over Devil's b., 261 : 7
I turn my b. to the east, 402 : 15
look forward not b., 590 : 8
mermaid on dolphin's b., 196 : 14
never came b. to me, 550 : 12
never turn b. on life, 786 : 14
nowhere to come but b., 684 : 15
on b. burden of world, 670 : 14
on bat's b. I do fly, 248 : 16
shop entirely free, 164 : 17
showed his b. above element, 241 : 25
so much upon his b., 257 : 10
speed today put b. tomorrow, 174 : 10
those before cried B., 488 : 15
to army again, 709 : 1
to loneliness of yesterday, 836 : 17
to the old drawing board, 858 : 18
to you cold father, 778 : 6
Back (*continued*)
unto ladder turns his b., 215 : 16
wallet at his b., 226 : 16
what we b. ourselves to be, 649 : 1
where you set out, 850 : 18
Backbone, whale's b., 808 : 2
Backed like a weasel, 222 : 20
with God and seas, 186 : 15
Backfield, spotlight of the b., 825 : 3
Back-friend a shoulder-clapper, 188 : 11
Background, if people keep me in b., 519 : 20
slumbers in b. of the times, 412 : 14
Back-hearing around, 901 : 14
Backing men of genius, 825 : 11
plague upon such b., 203 : 29
Backs, birthrights proudly on b., 201 : 11
making beast with two b., 229 : 20
not sit on others' b., 657 : 17
Backslidings, our b. are many, 32 : 7
Backward, angel of b. look, 513 : 23
dark b. and abysm of time, 247 : 10
Glance o'er Traveled Roads, 577 : 10
goes who toils most, 141 : 27
half-look over shoulder, 808 : 5
I by b. steps move, 299 : 4
lean over too far b., 831 : 9
life goes not b., 782 : 15
life understood b., 552 : 10
look b. to ancestors, 373 : 20
look b. to with pride, 747 : 7
look behind assurance, 808 : 5
old dog barks b., 749 : 2
radio need only go b., 873 : 1
ran sentences, 854 : 8
revolutions never go b., 538 : 19
turn b. O time, 610 : 10
Backwards, memory that only works b., 613 : 12
Bacon, celebrities such as B., 615 : 14
not written Hamlet, 474 : 17
secretary of Nature and learning, 271 : 15
taking b. was stealing, 622 : 14
think how B. shined, 337 : 15
Bacterial creepers, 873 : 11
Bad Americans die go to America, 675 : 14
as for b. all theirs dies, 77 : 18
beginning makes bad ending, 77 : 13
better b. epitaph, 221 : 4
better for being a little b., 229 : 9
bold b. man, 173 : 9, 248 : 26
book as much labor, 830 : 8
breeding, 81 : 13
by b. women been deceived, 288 : 25
can't be all b., 770 : *n* 8
cause supported by bad means, 384 : 16
charm to make b. good, 229 : 1
circumstance makes action good or b., 83 : 1
free press good or b., 882 : 11
from b. beginning great friendships, 96 : 23
fustian's so sublimely b., 338 : 13
good and b. angel, 258 : 14
good and b. of every land, 555 : 15
good b. indifferent, 308 : 19, 360 : 9
good b. worst best, 525 : 11
good die early b. late, 318 : 12
good or b. for humankind, 427 : 24
great cases make b. law, 644 : 9
grow into likeness of b. men, 86 : 1

Bad (*continued*)
hates children can't be all b., 770 : 18
he is writing b. stuff, 685 : 14
herdsmen ruin flocks, 60 : 22
I have b. dreams, 220 : 26
immoral what you feel b. after, 845 : 1
keep no b. company, 370 : *n* 3
laws bring about worse, 358 : 17
leaves aside good and b., 375 : 3
mad b. and dangerous, 454 : 22
man who brings b. news, 74 : 11
man's good knowing he is b., 545 : 2
man's refuge, 64 : 22
meaning good or b., 304 : 17
means and bad men, 384 : 16
men as b. and as good, 524 : 2
men live that they may eat, 79 : 6
moral character, 348 : 13
neighbor is misfortune, 61 : 18
never b. man good service, 373 : 14
never good to bring b. news, 241 : 4
never good war or b. peace, 348 : 6
news travels fast, 120 : 14
no benefit in gifts of b. man, 76 : 15
no man who laughed b., 472 : 20
no to everything b., 650 : 1
nothing either good or b., 220 : 25
obstinacy in b. cause, 274 : 8, 359 : 24
or obnoxious laws, 589 : 21
persecution b. way to plant religion, 274 : 9
pious fraud as with b. action, 385 : 6
play not please audience, 741 : 14
prosperity comes to a b. man, 67 : 3
provide b. examples, 293 : 17
rhyming a disease, 339 : 30
sad and b. and mad, 544 : 20
sad b. brother's name, 634 : 11
so much b. in best of us, 646 : *n* 2
start assuming that men are b., 154 : 7
streak of b. luck, 630 : 12
the b. affright, 361 : 13
the three equally b. for Syria, 702 : 9
things ill got had b. success, 186 : 5
truth told with b. intent, 406 : 12
two nations good b., 297 : 5
war never slays b. man, 75 : 8
when b. men combine, 372 : 4
when b. she was horrid, 513 : 1
wiser being good than b., 544 : 29
work follers ye, 568 : 10
world is grown so b., 187 : 5
Badge, mercy nobility's true b., 188 : 16
of all our tribe, 198 : 24
red b. of courage, 732 : 3
Badine, on ne b. pas avec l'amour, 537 : *n* 3
Badly, right to write b., 828 : 7
when things going b., 343 : 10
Badness flaunted itself, 926 : 3
you can get easily, 61 : 17
Baffled get up begin again, 542 : 12
imagination b. by facts, 744 : 14
to fight better, 546 : 7
Baffling, beat down b. foes, 585 : 11
Bag and baggage, 212 : 5
bagworm separated from b., 314 : 2
empty b. cannot stand, 347 : 21
given us b. to hold, 407 : 14
moon in silver b., 716 : 21
pack b. and go below, 935 : 2
Bag (*continued*)
sealed b. of ducats, 199 : 11
to make b. pudding, 934 : 1
your old kit b., 770 : 14
Bagatelle of transient experience, 697 : 10
Bagdad-on-the-Subway 699 : 11
Bagful of blue Mediterranean, 867 : 13
Baggage, bag and b., 212 : 5
Bags, three b. full, 930 : 5
two sealed b. of ducats, 199 : 11
Bagworm separated from bag, 314 : 2
Bah humbug, 548 : 5
to you ha ha to you, 628 : 10
Bahamas, arrived at island of B., 150 : 15
Bahram that great hunter, 516 : 11
Bail, excessive b. nor excessive fines, 392 : 3
no b. no demurrer, 398 : 22
Bailey, bells of Old B., 930 : 7
unfortunate Miss B., 415 : 13
Bait, as a swallowed b., 245 : 23
hook well, 209 : 18
hook without b., 499 : 4
melancholy b., 198 : 4
your b. of falsehood, 220 : 7
Baited like eagles, 204 : 30
Baits, good news b., 289 : 7
Bake me a cake, 929 : 18
Baked, funeral b. meats, 218 : 14
in a pie, 931 : 9
me too brown, 612 : 10
Baker, butcher b. candlestickmaker, 933 : 2
Street irregulars, 689 : 4
Baker's man, 929 : 18
Bakestone, cat upon hot b., 301 : 17
Baking, long b. never done, 846 : 13
Balaam, ass said unto B., 11 : 2
Balance between order and aspiration, 875 : 9
between what acquire and use, 464 : 1
civilization in b., 682 : 13
commitments and power b., 813 : 11
in thermonuclear terror, 871 : 8
in what community produces, 871 : 9
not weigh faith in b., 665 : 2
of power, 328 : 20, 682 : 8, 902 : 11
or reconciliation of opposite, 437 : 17
redress b. of the Old, 422 : 7
small dust of the b., 30 : 36
uncertain b. of proud time, 178 : 13
Balanced and Miltonic style, 656 : 22
film with film, 607 : 17
Balances, weighed in the b., 33 : 1
Balbec, editions of B. and Palmyra, 363 : 21
Bald, old b. cheater Time, 255 : 13
wish b. eagle not chosen, 348 : 13
Baldheaded, go into it b., 568 : 3
Baldness abundant, 546 : *n* 1
Baldric, milky b. of skies, 474 : 18
Bale, bliss and b., 653 : 15
Bales, down with costly b., 529 : 24
Ball, balm scepter and b., 208 : 7
earthly b. a peopled garden, 395 : 6
great b. of fire, 809 : 22
hostess with mostes' on the b., 802 : 13
one fish b., 592 : 4
regardless who carries b., 825 : 3
sun with golden b., 794 : 13
Ball (*continued*)
take me out to b. game, 765 : 13
terrestrial b., 856 : 3
Ballad, I love a b. in print, 246 : 30
in street, 496 : 11
to mistress' eyebrow, 211 : 15
Balladmongers, meter b., 204 : 13
Ballads, better than all b., 512 : 2
permitted to make all b., 317 : 17
songs and snatches, 629 : 4
stuck about wall, 271 : 3
Ballast, more sail than b., 314 : 16
no better b. than business, 569 : 8
Balloon of the mind, 714 : 6
philosopher man in b., 610 : 9
Balloonman, little lame b., 828 : 11
Balloons, faces rise like b., 893 : 15
Ballot, natural right to b., 578 : 5
paper you drop in b. box, 558 : 25
pathway to b. box, 554 : 8
rap on b. box, 491 : 1
stronger than bullet, 520 : 3
Balls, elliptical billiard b., 629 : 13
Balm in Gilead, 32 : 3
not the b. the scepter, 208 : 7
of hurt minds, 237 : 21
the hydroptic earth hath drunk, 252 : 25
tropic for your b., 830 : 18
wash b. from anointed king, 194 : 26
Balmy sleep, 330 : 4
spring brings back b. warmth, 102 : 3
Baloney, it's still b., 741 : 10
Bam, under the b., 806 : 11
Bamboo, under the b. tree, 806 : 11
'Ban 'Ban Ca-Caliban, 248 : 2
Ban, in every voice every b., 405 : 9
spreading ruin scattering b., 507 : 23
Banal Eldorado of old bachelors, 581 : 3
Banality of evil, 866 : 7
Bananas as bait, 846 : 1
Banbury Cross, 931 : 11
Banco di Roma wineshops, 888 : 11
Band, heaven-born b., 422 : 21
no soldier in gallant b., 630 : 2
of angels, 935 : 23
of brothers, 208 : 11
pilgrim b., 616 : 8
playing somewhere, 704 : 16
speckled b., 689 : 5
Bandersnatch, frumious B., 612 : 17
Bandits, kingdoms destroyed by b., 312 : 25
Bands, brass b. and barrel organs, 781 : 15
dissolve political b., 387 : 9
drew them with b. of love, 33 : 14
end of life cancels b., 204 : 23
her hands as b., 27 : 10
iron b., 510 : 7
loose the b. of Orion, 16 : 33
pursue culture in b., 700 : 15
Bandusian, O fount B., 108 : 4
Bane of all genius, 466 : 7
precious b., 284 : 1
suspicion b. of good society, 384 : 10
Baneful, luxury that b. poison, 392 : 15
spirit of party, 379 : 11
Banes, o'er his white b., 927 : 5
Bang, not with b. but whimper, 805 : 18
now animal is dead, 740 : 6
the drum slowly, 927 : *n* 2
these dogs of Seville, 535 : 13
Banish all the world, 204 : 7

Banish (*continued*)
pleasures b. pain, 328 : 15
plump Jack, 204 : 7
thief you cannot b., 864 : 16
think not king did b. thee, 194 : 5
understanding from his mind, 78 : *n* 1
wisdom, 90 : 8
with night we b. sorrow, 257 : 18
Banished, alone a b. man, 917 : 5
find moral in narrative b., 623 : 19
for my willful crime b., 288 : 3
salt kingdom from which b., 864 : 7
yet true-born Englishman, 194 : 8
Banishing for hours, 376 : 3
Banishment, bitter bread of b., 194 : 25
Banjo on my knee, 598 : 1
Banjos, batter on your b., 761 : 11
Bank and shoal of time, 236 : 22
breathes upon b. of violets, 213 : 7
broke b. at Monte Carlo, 666 : 21
contemplate entangled b., 515 : 1
cried all the way to b., 896 : 7
curls done up with b. notes, 554 : 11
grass b. beyond, 594 : 3
moonlight sleeps upon this b., 201 : 1
waly up the b., 927 : 7
whereon wild thyme blows, 196 : 18
Banker, Burglar B. Father, 604 : 3
Bankers just like anybody, 855 : 18
schoolmasters clergymen, 713 : 1
Bankrupt of life, 304 : 1
Banks, allegory on b. of Nile, 398 : 12
and braes o' bonny Doon, 409 : 24
Brignall b., 431 : 18
o' Loch Lomond, 921 : 9
of Wabash far away, 732 : 13
Tiber trembled underneath b., 215 : 1
time river without b., 925 : 6
vast surplus in b., 449 : 9
Banner, blood-red b. streams, 452 : 7
over me was love, 28 : 6
royal b. and all quality, 231 : 11
that b. in sky, 518 : 12
torn but flying, 458 : 17
wear it like b. for proud, 854 : 16
with strange device, 510 : 14
yet freedom yet thy b., 458 : 17
Banners, all thy b. wave, 443 : 15
confusion on thy b. wait, 363 : 4
flout the sky, 235 : 23
hang b. on outward walls, 240 : 2
terrible as an army with b., 28 : 17
unfurled o'er world, 535 : *n* 4
Banquet, behave in life as at b., 121 : 20
hall deserted, 447 : 8
partaken in anxiety, 66 : 6
sated with b. of life, 101 : 4
Banqueting upon borrowing, 35 : 30
Baptism enslaved me, 674 : 5
spirit streaming from b., 694 : 1
suffering may be b., 565 : 10
Baptist's, John B. head in a charger, 39 : 23
Baptizing in name of Father, 41 : 30
Bar against tyranny resolute men, 577 : 15
back of b. in solo game, 752 : 5
crossed the b., 535 : 21
foul storm out, 715 : 10
gold b. of heaven, 601 : 13
harbor b. moaning, 566 : 9
judge himself dragged to b., 571 : 6
no moaning of b., 535 : 19
to b. as very young man, 628 : 22
Barabbas a publisher, 462 : 20
stock of B., 200 : 16
was a robber, 45 : 31
Barak, arise B. and lead captivity captive, 12 : 4
Barb in arrow of childhood, 677 : 3
Barbara, for love of B. Allen, 926 : 21
name was B. Allen, 926 : 21
Barbaree, shores of High B., 935 : 3
Barbarian Scythian bond nor free, 50 : 12
weeping above dead, 615 : 7
Barbarians Philistines Populace, 588 : 13
such things impress B., 701 : 15
the B. are coming, 701 : 14
without B. what to become of us, 702 : 1
Barbaric omens, 798 : 1
pearl and gold, 284 : 3
sung by wild b. birds, 857 : 15
tribes brought to faith, 156 : 12
yawp, 575 : 3
Barbarism and despotism, 390 : 1
fanaticism to b. one step, 359 : 15
fastnesses of ancient b., 592 : 6
from b. to degeneration, 643 : 12
green b. turning paradigm, 766 : 15
my native land prey to b., 127 : 12
theater flourish in b., 654 : 5
war is at best b., 579 : 3
Barbarous dissonance, 279 : 26
in beauty stooks arise, 656 : 6
multitude, 199 : 13
races however b., 154 : 12
strength within her, 769 : 9
triumph o'er her b. foes, 351 : 10
woman more b. than man, 657 : 21
Barber, imprudently married b., 364 : 5
Barchester Towers not die quite at once, 555 : 9
Bard and people who inspire him, 672 : 8
hear voice of the B., 405 : 1
here dwelt, 345 : 21
is envious of bard, 61 : 13
music sent up by lover and b., 544 : 5
old or modern b., 279 : 6
whom none to praise, 424 : *n* 2
Bardolph's face, 204 : 26
Bards, black and unknown b., 733 : 9
eighth commandment not for b., 436 : 6
have a share of honor, 60 : 7
in fealty to Apollo, 475 : 6
name me among lyric b., 106 : 25
of old enjoyed in you, 403 : 1
of passion, 477 : 15
Olympian b., 494 : 9
saints heroes, 584 : 10
sublime, 510 : 20
Bare, back and side go b., 163 : 10
Ben Bulben's head, 718 : 1
bodkin, 221 : 12
cupboard was b., 932 : 7
gift without giver b., 567 : 14
Goya of the b. field, 912 : 7
imagination of feast, 194 : 7
let little colt go b., 934 : 6
looked on Beauty b., 823 : 8
old men's heads b., 816 : 2
on b. earth he lies, 306 : 18
poor b. forked animal, 234 : 7
ruined choirs, 244 : 27
Bare (*continued*)
to the buff, 669 : 5
trees turn b., 906 : 10
Bare-bosomed night, 574 : 19
Barefaced poverty drove me to verses, 109 : 15
Barefoot boy, 513 : 10
dance b. on wedding day, 188 : 30
dervishes, 495 : 5
him that makes shoes go b., 160 : *n* 10
Barère's, not read B. Memoirs, 489 : 1
Bares, foeman b. steel tarantara, 628 : 2
Bargain catch cold and starve, 243 : 14
in the way of b., 204 : 15
necessity never good b., 347 : 9
never better b. driven, 176 : 7
Bargaining, collective b. bilateral monopoly, 790 : 4
for wages, 762 : 8
Barge, Arthur from the b., 534 : 31
drag the slow b., 377 : 26
like burnished throne, 240 : 29
Bark, all dogs of Europe b., 868 : 12
and bite, 328 : 2
attendant sail, 338 : 2
band of exiles moored b., 470 : 15
bitter b. burning clove, 748 : 9
cynic b., 494 : 1
fatal and perfidious b., 280 : 18
hark dogs do b., 933 : 21
if my b. sinks, 562 : 9
is on the sea, 460 : 4
let no dog b., 198 : 2
moor b. with two anchors, 110 : 20
off shot the specter b., 434 : 21
puts from native bay, 199 : 6
see they b. at me, 234 : 15
star to every wandering b., 245 : 18
watchdog's honest b., 460 : 16
worse than bite, 270 : 25
yond tall anchoring b., 234 : 28
Barked, dogs b. far from river, 841 : 11
Barking, crowing of cocks and b. of dogs, 65 : 9
Barkis is willin', 548 : 23
Barks, Hylax b. in doorway, 103 : 18
Nicean b. of yore, 525 : 9
old dog b. backward, 749 : 2
Barley, land of wheat and b., 11 : 14
Barleycorn, inspiring bold John B., 411 : 10
John B. got up again, 409 : 18
Barn, hay creaking to b., 892 : 6
sit in a b., 932 : 6
stack or the b. door, 277 : 23
Barnaby, like B. Rudge, 567 : 18
Barns, cockerels in Hubbard's b., 557 : 8
neither reap nor gather into b., 38 : 2
Barometer, high and low b., 622 : 19
poet b. but also weather, 866 : 4
sweeping around, 622 : 19
Baron, Sir Leoline the b. rich, 433 : 28
Barrage, chemical b. against life, 870 : 1
Barred on account of race, 891 : 13
recognize good but be b., 72 : 1
Barrel, beat an empty b., 765 : 5
of meal wasted not, 13 : 43
organs, 781 : 15
Barrel-house kings, 765 : 5
Barren, acre of b. ground, 247 : 8
after summer b. winter, 185 : 14
among b. crags, 529 : 6

Barren (*continued*)
bosom starves birth, 361 : 17
bride, 335 : 18
buds of b. flowers, 633 : 20
earth b. as moon, 760 : 9
imagination cold and b., 372 : 13
leave this b. spot, 443 : 19
live a b. sister all your life, 195 : 20
small model of b. earth, 195 : 2
superfluity of words, 318 : 16
sword sung on b. heath, 404 : 15
'tis all b., 360 : 22
weep b. tears, 466 : 17
Barrenness, nature in its b., 785 : 14
Barricade, disputed b., 811 : 5
Barrier between day and day, 428 : 3
escaped b. of your teeth, 57 : 27
of senses, 771 : 1
Barriers against tyranny of political, 506 : 3
Barroom floor, 652 : 3
Gideon Bibles in b., 816 : 15
Barrow, crowbar hoe and b., 455 : 8
Bars, contentions are like b. of a castle, 24 : 21
implacable iron b., 801 : 17
nor iron b. a cage, 296 : 4
Barter, government founded on b., 373 : 4
that horn, 714 : 20
Bartlett's Familiar Quotations, 743 : 9
Base, army would be b. rabble, 373 : 7
authority from others' books, 190 : 12
beetles o'er his b., 219 : 14
contagious clouds, 203 : 5
fall to the b. earth, 194 : 24
first time caught off b., 844 : 16
fly from firm b., 431 : 13
keep down b. in man, 534 : 23
laws of servitude began, 303 : 8
like the b. Indian, 232 : 20
limps after in b. imitation, 194 : 11
men being in love, 230 : 15
of b. passions fear most accursed, 185 : 5
sale of chapmen's tongues, 190 : 19
scorning the b. degrees, 215 : 16
small things made b. men proud, 185 : 21
to what b. uses return, 224 : 15
Baseball, chalk mark b. score, 652 : 3
eternal importance like b., 791 : 6
pelicans old men in b. caps, 888 : 13
to know America learn b., 869 : 12
Baseless fabric of this vision, 248 : 13
Basely, spend that shortness b., 205 : 8
Baseness to write fair, 224 : 26
we will smite, 728 : 14
Baser, fellows of b. sort, 46 : 14
Basest, our b. beggars, 233 : 21
Bashful, maiden of b. fifteen, 399 : 1
stream hath seen God, 292 : *n* 3
virgin's sidelong looks, 369 : 29
Basic element in Constitution, 788 : 14
hero of books labor, 725 : 10
Basilisk is sure to kill, 332 : 5
Basil-pot, steal my B., 476 : 7
Basin, stare in b., 868 : 10
Basis of democratic state, 88 : 12
Basket, eggs in one b., 169 : 11, 624 : 23
watch that b., 624 : 23
Basks at the fire, 278 : 3
Bassarid, blatant B. of Boston, 634 : 9
Bassoon, flute violin b., 533 : 22
Bassoon (*continued*)
heard the loud b., 434 : 8
Bastard, anesthesia b. substitute, 697 : 15
beast brute b., 881 : 11
soft b. Latin, 460 : 8
truth comes like b., 281 : 16
Bat, black b. night, 533 : 20
Casey at the b., 704 : 15
ere b. hath flown, 238 : 20
mind is like b., 899 : 15
that beats in caverns, 899 : 15
twinkle little b., 611 : 20
weak-eyed b., 364 : 12
wool of b. tongue of dog, 239 : 5
Bataillons, formez vos b., 415 : 1
Bate, nor b. one jot of heart, 282 : 19
Bated breath and whispering humbleness, 198 : 25
Bath, blood b., 783 : 18
sore labor's b., 237 : 21
try to give dog b., 856 : 1
Bathe in fiery floods, 228 : 20
Bathed in poem of sea, 673 : 16
like eagles lately b., 204 : 30
Bathing, caught Whigs b., 501 : 22
large b. machine, 629 : 1
Bathroom, more benefit from b., 834 : 8
Bathrooms, dwell in our steaming b., 902 : 16
well-equipped American b., 834 : 8
Baths, grand flights Sunday b., 767 : 21
of all western stars, 529 : 13
uplifting thoughts in b., 834 : 8
Batman, not Hercules but B., 911 : 5
Baton, French soldier carries marshal's b., 421 : 5
Bat's, on b. back I do fly, 248 : 16
Bats, bawk of b., 778 : 5
cast idols to moles and b., 28 : 32
do b. eat cats, 611 : 3
Battalions, God for big b., 294 : *n* 9
God with strongest b., 358 : 4
sorrows come in b., 223 : 25
Battening our flocks, 280 : 10
Batter my heart, 254 : 15
on your banjos, 761 : 11
Battered caravanserai, 516 : 10
cottage b. and decayed, 276 : 12
few thousand b. books, 792 : 16
Battering sandal, 656 : 8
Battery, assault and b. of wind, 714 : 19
Battiades, tomb of B., 92 : 18
Battle and the breeze, 443 : 10
borne the b., 524 : 7
Britain wins last b., 745 : 13
common perils of b., 617 : 6
cry of freedom, 578 : 13
day is past, 597 : 15
delight of b., 529 : 8
each b. sees other's face, 208 : 1
far-flung b. line, 709 : 16
first blow half the b., 371 : 9
flags were furled, 530 : 1
foremost in b. Mary Ambree, 926 : 18
France has lost b., 815 : 7
from b. and murder, 55 : 12
harness like soldiers, 746 : 7
haven't lost b. yet, 885 : 2
in b. fighting and falling, 881 : 15
is to strong, 684 : 13
life a b. and sojourning, 124 : 10
life of b. good, 700 : 6
marriage field of b., 667 : 13
Battle (*continued*)
nameless b. overseas, 728 : 13
no b. ever won, 837 : 18
noise of b. rolled, 534 : 29
not to the strong, 27 : 17, 383 : 3
nothing except b. lost, 421 : 8
of first rank, 491 : 18
of Jericho, 935 : 20
of Waterloo won on fields, 421 : 16
one b. or by degrees, 384 : 18
or business, 556 : 1
puts armor off b. done, 512 : 13
rages loud and long, 443 : 11
see b. from castle, 100 : *n* 7
see front o' b. lower, 411 : 15
sent English language into b., 742 : *n* 1
set Uriah in forefront of b., 13 : 18
shout, 518 : 12
sing tongue the glorious b., 139 : *n* 6
smelleth the b. afar off, 16 : 38
so melancholy as b. won, 421 : 8
Te Deum before b. begun, 490 : 2
through b. through defeat, 575 : 16
Troy walls famed in b., 104 : 35
was on once more, 591 : 3
we b. for the Lord, 687 : 17
who prepare himself to b., 48 : 26
with my peers, 529 : 8
Battled, dream of b. fields, 431 : 8
Battlefield and patriot grave, 521 : 14
happy warrior of political b., 741 : *n* 3
heart of man, 582 : 1
is holy ground, 461 : 20
met on great b., 523 : 4
Battlements, entrance under my b., 236 : 17
fate sits on dark b., 416 : 11
frowning b., 520 : 7
towers and b. it sees, 277 : 25
Battle's magnificently stern array, 457 : 19
no war or b. sound, 277 : 8
when b. lost and won, 235 : 21
Battles, feelings beings books events b., 861 : 4
fight our country's b., 922 : 11
fought his b. o'er again, 306 : 17
he lives not long who b. immortals, 57 : 29
juster b. enacted now, 558 : 19
long ago, 426 : 5
O God of b., 208 : 8
sieges fortunes, 229 : 27
transacted by mechanism, 473 : 17
when someone b. hard, 58 : 9
witness I have fought b., 302 : 15
Bauble, pleased with b. still, 337 : 7
shallow b. boats, 225 : 36
Baudelaire foremost seer, 580 : *n* 3
sedulous ape to B., 668 : 23
Bawd, call b. a b., 91 : *n* 4
now my old b. is dead, 717 : 18
opportunity is great b., 347 : 11
Bawds, clocks the tongues of b., 202 : 23
Bawdy strings of elders, 767 : 11
Bawk of bats, 778 : 5
Bawn, bred en b. in brier patch, 662 : 8
Bay, bark puts from native b., 199 : 6
brothers call from b., 584 : 11
China 'crost the b., 708 : 9
cliffs vast in tranquil b., 587 : 13
deep-mouthed welcome, 460 : 16
in the B. of Biscay O, 415 : 6

Bay (*continued*)
like b. of Portugal, 212 : 26
nightcap instead of b., 368 : 8
no fetters in B. State, 513 : 3
rather be dog and b. moon, 216 : 32
reeking into Cadiz B., 541 : 18
sings in boat on b., 530 : 19
somebody bet on b., 598 : 2
spreading himself like a green b. tree, 18 : 26
Bayed the whispering wind, 370 : 4
Baying, hear b. of pack, 817 : 6
Bayonets, by push of b., 358 : 1
leave at point of b., 397 : 20
throne of b., 696 : 2
Bays, lingering b., 351 : 11
no b. to crown it, 268 : 21
Bazille, feigning lady by B., 899 : 11
Be, appear to b. and appear not to b., 85 : 15
better not to b., 527 : 19
bold, 173 : 20
business of life is to b., 637 : 7
cheerful while you are alive, 3 : 11
first say what you would b., 121 : 19
he is or was or has to b., 344 : 10
let it b., 914 : 14
merciful to me a fool, 646 : 13
near me when light low, 532 : 5
not the first, 333 : 6
not to seem but b. best, 71 : 18
not too bold, 173 : 21
off depart, 98 : *n* 3
off or I'll kick you, 611 : 11
one must b. to do, 396 : 4
poem should not mean but b., 821 : 13
powers that b., 47 : 26
say B. and it is, 131 : 4
shalt b. what thou art promised, 236 : 16
still and know that I am God, 19 : 12
strong, 49 : 9
such things to b., 532 : 15
tell what and where b., 533 : 26
that will b. that will last, 928 : 1
the serpent under it, 236 : 20
there ye may b. also, 45 : 21
thing that hath been is that which shall b., 26 : 14
to b. or not to b., 221 : 12
to b. what we are, 668 : 2
to her virtues very kind, 320 : 17
want to b. happy b., 561 : 6
what it is to be, 768 : 10
what man can b. he must b., 872 : 15
what one is, 849 : 5
what we are, 668 : 2
what we cannot b., 900 : 6
with us yet, 709 : 16
Beach, across narrow b. we flit, 621 : 17
along briny b., 613 : 3
at Kitty Hawk, 835 : 1
fishermen that walk b., 234 : 28
life like stroll on b., 558 : 8
rugged and without a b., 311 : 14
sound of outer ocean on b., 802 : 19
walk upon the b., 803 : 19
warm sea-scented b., 541 : 14
Beaches, fight on b., 744 : 2
set foot upon her b., 822 : 10
where it tosses, 808 : 2
Beacon of the wise, 226 : 7
Beacons from where Eternal are, 469 : 17
Beacons (*continued*)
of wise men, 596 : 3
Beaded bubbles winking, 476 : 23
Beadle on Boxin' Day, 546 : 23
very b. to humorous sigh, 190 : 25
Beadroll, Fame's eternal b., 173 : 22
Beads and prayerbooks, 337 : 7
couple o' guns and rosary b., 786 : 11
give jewels for set of b., 195 : 6
receipts dolls vases, 889 : 12
tell his b., 917 : 19
Beak, by enemy's b. gouged, 912 : 7
from out my heart, 526 : 18
hunching wings and b., 892 : 4
in b. enough for week, 765 : 12
Beaker, bring me b. of wine, 81 : 12
O for a b., 476 : 23
Beaks, hold on with b. to the weeds, 600 : 1
Be-all and end-all, 236 : 22
Beam, cast b. out of own eye, 38 : 10
in thine own eye, 38 : 9
midday b., 282 : 3
on starboard b. Charybdis, 200 : *n* 1
Beamish boy, 612 : 18
Beams, adjusted to b. falling, 830 : 4
all his b. full dazzling, 575 : 24
and blazes in adversity, 452 : 15
athwart the sea, 529 : 5
bemocked sultry main, 434 : 28
best not to see b. of sun, 67 : 5
how far candle throws b., 201 : 4
in sunny b. did glide, 402 : 12
layeth the b. of his chambers, 21 : 8
learn to bear b. of love, 403 : 7
of wit on other souls, 304 : 25
white moon b., 813 : 7
Bean, home of b. and cod, 694 : 14
nine b. rows have, 712 : 4
writer like b. plant, 846 : 10
Bean-fed horse beguile, 196 : 12
Beans and brown bread, 676 : 16
determined to know b., 560 : 6
eat no b., 258 : 15
full o' b., 500 : 20
over b. in their back room, 889 : 12
Bear all cheerfully, 536 : 6
all naked truths, 478 : 5
any burden, 890 : 7
asses made to b. and you, 188 : 31
beams of love, 403 : 7
blazing tail, 767 : 6
bonds that gall, 633 : 9
brunt pay arrears, 544 : 22
bush supposed a b., 197 : 12
cannot b. mother's tears, 106 : 2
care borne and yet must b., 466 : 15
caves of ocean b., 362 : 8
charmed life, 240 : 8
cow and b. shall feed, 29 : 19
exit pursued by a b., 246 : 19
false witness, 10 : 7
finds he can b. anything, 838 : 2
flying chariot, 377 : 26
for which we b. to live, 337 : 10
his friend's infirmities, 217 : 3
his mild yoke, 282 : 17
his own burden, 49 : 31
ills we ought to b., 585 : 10
infirmities of weak, 47 : 34
it that the opposed beware thee, 219 : 1
like the Turk, 338 : 14
melancholy as lugged b., 202 : 29
Bear (*continued*)
more than he can b., 838 : 2
my tavern the Big B., 673 : 12
never be b. on United States, 924 : *n* 6
never could b. but did, 481 : 9
not b. much reality, 806 : 20
not every soil can b. all, 104 : 2
nothing he not fitted to b., 125 : 3
nothing would it b., 932 : 1
of very little brain, 778 : 12
one clings I'll b. it, 778 : 6
pain to the b., 489 : 6
pleasing punishment women b., 187 : 33
punishment greater than I can b., 7 : 18
results of own example, 114 : 8
right to keep and b. arms, 391 : 15
rugged Russian b., 238 : 28
shade him till he can b., 403 : 8
sing savageness out of b., 231 : 24
sweet as I could b., 748 : 8
sword of heaven will b., 228 : 26
them we can, 691 : 20
they shall b. thee up, 20 : 17, 43 : 1
those ills we have, 221 : 12
too tender heart, 335 : 8
up and steer right onward, 282 : 19
vapor like b. or lion, 241 : 17
virgin shall b. a son, 29 : 13
whatever you stuff men with they b., 561 : 5
when you are anvil b., 269 : *n* 5
whips and scorns of time, 221 : 12
who would fardels b., 221 : 12
with all the faults of man, 250 : 4
wounded spirit who can b., 24 : 20
yoke in his youth, 32 : 24
Bear-baiting, Puritan hated b., 489 : 6
Beard, built nests in b., 550 : 4
hath not offended king, 155 : 10
his b. was grizzled, 218 : 23
husband with b., 209 : 4
icicle on Dutchman's b., 214 : 18
lion in his den, 430 : 23
long gray b., 434 : 4
of formal cut, 211 : 15
old man with b., 550 : 4
plucks dead lions by b., 201 : 13
plucks off my b., 221 : 8
white b. decreasing leg, 205 : 28
wrapped in b. and silence, 840 : 7
Bearded conspirators, 800 : 7
like the pard, 211 : 15
sits the b. king, 897 : 15
Beards, tarry until b. be grown, 13 : 17
where b. wag all, 163 : 6
Bearing birthrights proudly, 201 : 11
burdens of government, 519 : 21
on excellence of character, 87 : 22
precious seed, 22 : 7
seen him b. down on me, 778 : 6
Bearings glint, 844 : 1
lays in application, 548 : 20
Bears all its sons away, 328 : 12
dancing dogs and b., 732 : 16
each b. his own Hell, 105 : 23
first born are shapeless, 117 : 3
greatest names, 289 : 2
his blushing honors, 249 : 3
in itself causes of destruction, 358 : 16
it out to edge of doom, 245 : 18

Bears (*continued*)
rhythms for b. to dance to, 583 : 11
sorrows with steadfast spirit, 60 : 26
stamp of human condition, 165 : 18
strongly it b. us, 435 : 18
time b. away all things, 103 : 20
Beast, a very gentle b., 197 : 16
blond b., 658 : 5
brute bastard, 881 : 11
call this b. to mind, 729 : 15
caught like b. at bay, 817 : 6
civilization scarcely b., 732 : 10
cursed above every b., 7 : 9
deem himself god or b., 337 : 2
ear of tiny b., 905 : 17
either a b. or god, 87 : 28
endeavoring to turn man into b., 853 : 9
every b. of the forest is mine, 19 : 13
first b. like a lion, 53 : 7
fourth b. like a flying eagle, 53 : 7
in view, 307 : 1
like wild b. guards way, 406 : 1
little better than b., 198 : 14
making b. with two backs, 229 : 20
man and bird and b., 435 : 10
man neither angel nor b., 300 : 8
mark or name of the b., 53 : 21
maw-crammed b., 544 : 9
more subtile than any b., 7 : 5
multitude b. of many heads, 108 : *n* 14
no b. so fierce but knows pity, 187 : 1
no more, 223 : 17
of prey in aristocratic races, 658 : 5
on b. turn envious look, 868 : 6
only b. in arena the crowd, 720 : 17
only connect b. and monk, 764 : 9
owest b. no hide, 234 : 7
Pellinore followed questing b., 149 : 7
people a many-headed b., 108 : 19
people resemble wild b., 154 : 8
righteous man regardeth the life of his b., 23 : 29
second b. like a calf, 53 : 7
serpent subtlest b., 287 : 14
strangest b. ever he saw, 149 : 7
that wants discourse of reason, 218 : 11
third b. had a face as a man, 53 : 7
what rough b., 714 : 13
with many heads butts me, 242 : 21
would act angel acts b., 300 : 8
Beastie, tim'rous b., 408 : 12
Beasties, long-leggety b., 921 : 4
Beastly, how b. bourgeois is, 790 : 15
to the Germans, 843 : 12
Beast's, man's life cheap as b., 233 : 21
Beasts, ape vilest of b., 95 : 3
ask the b., 15 : 29
browse on their herbs, 5 : 7
coupling of b., 807 : 10
fly to wilderness, 89 : 9
four b. had six wings, 53 : 7
invent new b. so terrible, 482 : 3
judgment fled to b., 216 : 20
man lived with birds and b., 90 : 7
nature teaches b. to know friends, 242 : 11
of all wild b. preserve me from tyrant, 255 : 14
of the forest creep forth, 21 : 11
pair of very strange b., 213 : 1
shall be at peace with thee, 15 : 17
Beasts (*continued*)
small and great b., 21 : 11
transform ourselves into b., 230 : 26
upon earth draw us to kingdom, 126 : 15
what is man without b., 456 : 1
whatever happens to b. happens to man, 456 : 1
Beasts', not God's not b., 544 : 16
Beat an empty barrel, 765 : 5
Blake b. on wall, 717 : 10
down baffling foes, 585 : 11
downward b. thy wings, 100 : *n* 8
earth with unfettered foot, 107 : 15
generation, 901 : 2
gold to airy thinness b., 253 : 4
heart hear her and b., 533 : 25
him when he sneezes, 611 : 15
his breast, 434 : 8
in Belgrave Square, 628 : 20
me and hammer me, 761 : 10
my people to pieces, 28 : 35
on wall till Truth obeyed, 717 : 10
so we b. on, 835 : 8
soul of enemy man, 791 : 16
sound trumpet b. drums, 346 : 7
sound trumpets b. drums, 306 : 14
swords into plowshares, 28 : 31
the bush, 159 : 5, 265 : 1
the drum slowly, 927 : 15
the Dutch, 920 : 16
the ground, 279 : 14
they b. and Voice b., 693 : 11
to win not b. weapons, 791 : 16
Turk b. a Venetian, 232 : 21
upon whorled ear, 655 : 18
water they b., 240 : 29
waves of science b. in vain, 580 : 9
with fist instead of stick, 290 : 14
you b. your pate, 336 : 7
you think it's a happy b., 855 : 1
Beaten at all points, 81 : 10
genius disdains b. path, 519 : 24
poop was b. gold, 240 : 29
till they know, 291 : 16
with his own rod, 158 : 20
Beatific, enjoyed in vision b., 283 : 28
Beating bird extending wings, 875 : 2
disastrous b. of wings, 732 : 11
in void luminous wings, 589 : 13
thinking living, 571 : 5
way for rising sun, 854 : 3
Beatitude, ninth b., 336 : 6
Beatrice a light between truth and intellect, 141 : 25
Beats about in caverns, 899 : 15
all lies you can invent, 406 : 12
at clay-shuttered doors, 693 : 17
back envious siege, 194 : 14
fly a few b. in dark, 907 : 9
light b. on throne, 534 : 1
upon high shore of world, 208 : 7
with his blood, 531 : 14
Beaumont, not bid B. lie, 256 : 11
rare B., 265 : 14
Beaut, when I make mistake it's a b., 778 : 9
Beauteous bright creation, 135 : 2
commands the b. files, 299 : 10
dear b. death, 299 : 9
evening calm and free, 425 : 16
eye of heaven to garnish, 202 : 5
idiot speaks, 919 : 19
kindness not b. looks, 189 : 1
Beauteous (*continued*)
pearls in b. ladies' eyes, 190 : 6
prove a b. flower, 192 : 14
Beauties, glory of honors b. wits, 252 : 22
in small proportions b. see, 256 : 20
meaner b. of the night, 251 : 1
not his own, 340 : 18
unripened b. of north, 325 : 15
Beautifier, rank great b., 493 : 4
Beautiful a fairy's child, 478 : 11
all b. drifts away, 713 : 3
all b. sentiments in world, 569 : 12
all once so b. is dead, 811 : 12
all things bright and b., 561 : 8
always the b. answer, 829 : 15
and ineffectual angel, 589 : 13
and therefore to be wooed, 185 : 6
art for sake of b., 504 : 18
as the sky, 576 : 1
be b. and be sad, 581 : 5
beauty making b. old rhyme, 245 : 12
beauty not good or aught but b., 793 : 20
black is b., 925 : 14
changes as forest, 899 : 6
childish but divinely b., 412 : 15
dancing most b. art, 690 : 2
death b. adventure, 574 : *n* 1
dreamer, 598 : 8
Evelyn Hope, 542 : 1
evermore, 568 : 19
face candid brow, 683 : 12
find b. human soul, 393 : 4
find each other it's b., 827 : 19
for spacious skies, 688 : 5
from perceived harmony, 436 : 19
how b. they are, 435 : 25
how b. they stand, 470 : 13
how b. they stood, 470 : *n* 4
I am Negro and b., 854 : 11
in faces dress thoughts, 695 : 6
introduced you to b. people, 914 : *n* 2
islands b. where we're groping, 849 : 11
joyous b. and free, 467 : 10
life b. or reverse, 689 : 23
may it be b. before me, 928 : 19
most b. among gods, 61 : 10
most b. lady, 739 : 14
most b. most useful, 696 : 6
most b. most useless, 572 : 14
most b. mouth in world, 342 : 15
most b. thing is mysterious, 763 : 6
nature's models b., 832 : 9
not b. but look b., 751 : 3
nothing b. makes complete sense, 823 : 21
nothing in house not b., 618 : 9
nothing more b. than death, 574 : 10
oh what a b. mornin', 833 : 10
once I was b., 908 : 9
overmuch, 714 : 15
palace B., 302 : 1
passionate body, 632 : 13
pea-green boat, 550 : 7
people, 914 : 12
poetry most b. mode, 587 : 2
pussy you are, 550 : 7
quarto page, 398 : 29
question, 829 : 15
sacrifices of friendship b., 731 : 17
scorn looks b., 214 : 16
small is b., 879 : 16

Beautiful (*continued*)
so various so b. so new, 587 : 16
soup, 612 : 11
Sredni Vashtar the B., 731 : 16
swindles b. and simple, 699 : 9
that war must be lost, 576 : 1
thing raises man, 154 : 15
things adorn world, 704 : 5
this is b. country, 487 : 1
time of young love, 413 : 21
too b. to live, 547 : 10
true words are not b., 65 : 10
uncut hair of graves, 574 : 17
upon the mountains, 31 : 12
what is b. is moral, 583 : 19
what may be approved as b., 685 : 4
when I was b., 162 : 12
whole numbers, 832 : 9
wise and b., 584 : 10
woman with one eye, 401 : 7
women indisputably b. or ugly, 342 : 4
wonderful world, 593 : 7
words are not true, 65 : 10
world too b. this year, 822 : 14
Beautifully blue, 440 : 2, 461 : 13
Beautify, to b. life give it object, 671 : 21
Beauty, addition of strangeness to b., 639 : 4
adventure art, 697 : 14
all is b., 540 : 30
all that b. all that wealth, 362 : 3
and high degree, 810 : 20
and virtue rarely together, 143 : 6
and wisdom rarely conjoined, 117 : 18
are you not enough, 787 : 7
as b. not great star, 758 : 5
as much b. as could die, 256 : 5
as we feel it, 703 : 5
barbarous in b. stooks, 656 : 6
beholding b. with eye of mind, 83 : 10
bereft of b., 189 : 5
best of all we know, 654 : 14
body's b. lives 767 : 10
born of own despair, 715 : 17
bought by judgment of eye, 190 : 19
brute b. and valor, 656 : 3
by b. and by fear, 423 : 17
calls, 317 : 14
carves bow of b., 494 : 6
cheat for sake of b., 757 : 8
clad in b. of thousand stars, 184 : 5
cold and austere, 737 : 14
come near your b. with nails, 185 : 10
concept of mathematical b., 696 : 5
convenience comfort, 925 : 4
creation of b., 527 : 14
crieth in attic, 620 : 3
crowds me till I die, 607 : 15
daily b. in his life, 232 : 11
dead black chaos, 189 : 14
Death mother of B., 767 : 3
definition of b., 436 : 18
die for b., 495 : 2
doth of itself persuade, 189 : 16
draws with single hair, 334 : 3
dreamed life b., 555 : 23
ease and speed not give work b., 147 : *n* 11
elevation and b., 589 : 10
ever ancient and ever new, 129 : 5
exists in mind, 357 : 14
extent of b. and power, 487 : 14
facts in naked simple b., 183 : 2

Beauty (*continued*)
fatal gift of b., 458 : 10
flattered upon b., 342 : 4
for ashes, 31 : 25
for confiding youth, 428 : 23
fruits of life and b., 404 : 16
full of healing, 888 : 6
gift of God, 86 : 18
give b. in the inward soul, 83 : 7
good nature more amiable than b., 326 : 17
grows familiar to lover, 325 : 16
half mad with b., 618 : 3
half the b. you possess, 417 : 16
has not been fathomed, 581 : 20
Helen's b. in brow of Egypt, 197 : 12
her b. and her chivalry, 457 : 14
I died for b., 605 : 13
ill layer-up of b., 208 : 19
images of b., 83 : 10
in all things, 480 : 4
in art economy is b., 654 : 3
in b. it is finished, 928 : 19
in eye of beholder, 676 : 20
in naked b. more adorned, 286 : 3
indescribable, 703 : 5
is a mystery, 790 : 17
is there b. in Sodom, 582 : 1
is there in truth no b., 268 : 14
is truth, 477 : 11
is vain, 26 : 10
keep back b., 656 : 12
know b. as b., 63 : 13
left b. on shore, 493 : 15
light from her own b., 468 : 7
like hers is genius, 601 : 18
little concerned with b., 643 : 5
looked on B. bare, 823 : 8
love b. truth we seek, 467 : 13
love built on b., 253 : 16
loved your b., 712 : 9
lust not after her b., 23 : 13
makes b. because outlet, 759 : 11
making beautiful old rhyme, 245 : 12
mathematics supreme b., 737 : 14
mercy have on me, 607 : 15
momentary in mind, 767 : 10
must be truth, 479 : 1
mystery of b., 711 : 14
Nature's coin, 279 : 31
nature's system a real b., 832 : 9
ne'er enjoys, 338 : 19
neither heat limb nor b., 228 : 16
no excellent b., 181 : 9
no spring nor summer b., 253 : 20
nonsense and b. close connections, 764 : 8
not lip or eye b. call, 333 : 1
not means but result, 877 : 3
notion of absolute b., 83 : 9
of aged face, 773 : 16
of good old cause, 425 : 15
of great machine, 796 : 16
of holiness, 18 : 14
of inflections, 767 : 12
of innuendoes, 767 : 12
of minstrel's lyre, 733 : 9
of own b. mind diseased, 458 : 19
of the lilies, 566 : 5
of true manliness, 609 : 6
of world has edges, 782 : 4
omnipresence of death and loveliness, 812 : 9
one's b. another's ugliness, 497 : 26

Beauty (*continued*)
orators dumb when b. pleadeth, 189 : 22
our eyes never see, 720 : 10
own excuse for being, 494 : 5
perception of b. moral, 557 : 11
perfection of mathematical b., 696 : 6
pierce like pain, 755 : 5
pledge of conformity, 703 : 6
power of b. I remember, 307 : 5
power of Greek in b., 588 : 11
principal b. in a building, 276 : 18
provoketh thieves, 210 : 21
renown which riches or b. confer, 102 : 22
sat B. in my lap, 674 : 3
say not of B., 793 : 20
sense of pity b. pain, 683 : 3
sex and b. inseparable, 790 : 18
she walks in b., 459 : 13
skin deep, 250 : *n* 1
sleep sleep b. bright, 404 : 12
smother up his b., 203 : 5
so long as b. shall be, 127 : 1
sold for old man's gold, 730 : 18
source of b. is in itself, 124 : 18
stone to b. grew, 493 : 18
sublimely pure, 737 : 14
such b. as you master, 245 : 12
such seems your b. still, 245 : 11
sufficient end, 714 : 15
take winds of March with b., 246 : 26
teaches such b. as woman's eye, 191 : 1
terrible and awful, 581 : 20
terrible b. is born, 714 : 9
that comes from happiness, 583 : 12
that dost consecrate, 466 : 9
that Medusa's head, 821 : 11
that must die, 477 : 23
thing of b. joy, 475 : 16
though injurious, 289 : 3
thy b. is to me, 525 : 9
'tisn't b. nor good talk, 710 : 11
to mind shameful to heart b., 582 : 1
too rich for use, 191 : 26
troubled by this b., 638 : 10
truly blent, 213 : 17
unadorned, 312 : 17
undiminished natural b., 890 : 13
unmask her b. to moon, 218 : 27
use harms b., 706 : 7
what b. is cannot be said, 703 : 5
when death allies to b., 812 : *n* 2
where b. has no ebb, 712 : 11
where perhaps some b. lies, 277 : 25
whole mystery of b., 711 : 14
whose b. past change, 656 : 5
will come unannounced, 497 : 30
wit high birth, 226 : 20
with him b. slain, 189 : 14
withdraws mind from love of b., 68 : 4
without extravagance, 81 : 1
without grace, 499 : 4
without vanity, 456 : 9
witty b. a power, 601 : 4
worship in b. of holiness, 18 : 14
wrought out from within, 638 : 10
your b. will wither, 163 : 1
Beauty's, blazon of sweet b. best, 245 : 12
but skin deep, 250 : 2
ensign yet is crimson, 193 : 27

Beauty's (*continued*)
none of B. daughters, 460 : 1
orient deep, 271 : 19
parallels in b. brow, 244 : 20
rose might never die, 243 : 31
thy b. field, 244 : 1
Beaux, where none are b., 357 : 10
Beaver, on account of his b. hat, 550 : 15
young Harry with b. on, 204 : 31
Became, nothing b. him like leaving, 236 : 14
Because, God not a "b.," 706 : 4
I do not hope, 805 : 20
it is there, 710 : *n* 1
Beckon you to fraternize, 869 : 6
Beckoning shadows dire, 279 : 16
what b. ghost, 335 : 7
Beckons, Longing leans and b., 569 : 4
Becks, nods and b., 277 : 19
our minds to fellowship, 475 : 20
Become, all that may b. a man, 237 : 3
I have b. lost name, 883 : 9
ignorant man again, 768 : 8
let each b. all capable of, 472 : 4
man to behave toward government, 558 : 1
not b. king's first minister, 746 : 2
them with half so good grace, 228 : 6
vilest things b. themselves, 241 : 1
what capable of, 668 : 2
Becomes, blessed youth b. as aged, 228 : 16
nothing b. him ill, 190 : 20
that which is not b., 125 : 25
throned monarch better, 200 : 9
Becoming father easy enough, 610 : 12
growing and a b., 588 : 17
limit of b. mirth, 190 : 21
present gone in b., 649 : 3
Becoming-conscious, emotion source of b., 754 : 14
Bed, a b. Clerk Saunders said, 926 : 24
am I on b. of roses, 721 : *n* 1
and so to b., 309 : 14, 773 : 11
angels guard thy b., 328 : 8
be blest that I lie on, 294 : 16
be in b. and sleep not, 835 : 13
book took him out of b., 258 : *n* 2
brimstone b., 440 : 13
by night, 370 : 13
by night on my b. I sought him, 28 : 10
candle to light to b., 930 : 8
celestial b., 219 : 22
creep into narrow b., 588 : 1
desert sighs in b., 868 : 10
die in b., 795 : 15
dull stale tired b., 233 : 3
early to b. early to rise, 347 : 12
early to rise early to b., 831 : 8
earth in earthy b., 533 : 25
every b. is narrow, 823 : 2
every day got up and gone to b., 751 : 12
for this huge birth, 292 : 17
four angels to my b., 294 : 16
go to b. by day, 668 : 9
go to b. with lamb, 175 : 17
goes to b. and does not pray, 268 : 18
goes to b. by bell, 622 : 16
gravity out of his b., 204 : 2
has found out thy b., 405 : 5
heaped for beloved's b., 469 : 18
heart for my b. and board, 892 : 16
Bed (*continued*)
holy angels guard thy b., 328 : 8
horn brought me from b., 474 : 19
I go to b. with ideas, 672 : 6
I in my b. again, 917 : 10
I their map lie flat on this b., 254 : 18
in b. laugh in b. cry, 290 : 8
in thy cold b., 267 : 6
laid in b. majestical, 208 : 7
let's to b. says Sleepyhead, 931 : 6
lie down on bloody b., 572 : 4
lie on Mother's b., 893 : 3
lies in his b. walks with me, 201 : 26
lovers to b., 197 : 22
made his own b. ere born, 292 : 18
made his pendent b., 236 : 21
make my b. in hell, 22 : 17
make my b. soon, 927 : 8
manger for his b., 561 : 10
marriage not b. of roses, 667 : 13
mourn upon thy b., 633 : 17
near approach b. may show, 290 : 8
nicer to lie in b., 730 : 19
nor grave nor b. denied, 716 : 17
not on b. of roses, 721 : 3
O b. O delicious b., 485 : 14
of daffodil sky, 533 : 21
on my grave as now my b., 274 : 23
outcries call me from naked b., 176 : 21
put them to b., 931 : 10
rode horses up to b., 740 : 5
run into it as to lover's b., 241 : 19
sate itself in celestial b., 219 : 22
should of stood in b., 836 : 12
sleep upon golden b., 716 : 19
take up thy b., 41 : 33
to b. go sober, 260 : 14
toddle home die in b., 795 : 15
warm weather in b., 321 : 17
welcome to your gory b., 411 : 15
went to b. with stockings on, 933 : 1
what torment not a marriage b., 254 : 23
when I jump into my b., 668 : 12
Zeus's b. of love, 76 : 25
Bedecked, so b. ornate and gay, 288 : 30
Bedeuten, ich weiss nicht was soll es b., 481 : *n* 7
Bedevilment, man's b. and God's, 691 : 23
Bedewed with liquid odors, 107 : 3
Bedfellows, strange b., 247 : 30, 603 : 11
Bedizened or stark naked, 799 : 6
Bedlam, lies in house of B., 878 : 11
mad as B., 548 : 28
Tom o' B., 233 : 6
Bedroom eyes, 869 : 6
Beds, bliss not b. of down, 267 : 10
housewives in your b., 230 : 8
make thee b. of roses, 183 : 10
not only b. you lay on, 702 : 5
rather make odes than b., 867 : 2
think of clean b., 795 : 14
Bed's-feet, as to b. life is shrunk, 252 : 25
Bedtime, would it were b. Hal, 205 : 4
Bee, booming of new-come b., 768 : 16
brisk as a b., 353 : 22
busy as a b., 175 : 18
busy b. improve each hour, 328 : 5
busy b. no time for sorrow, 404 : 1
clover and one b., 608 : 3
had stung it newly, 290 : 1
how doth the busy b., 328 : 5
Bee (*continued*)
laughing b. on stalk, 908 : 8
love in my bosom like a b., 177 : 4
making money like b., 73 : 3
not good for swarm not good for b., 125 : 8
pedigree not concern b., 607 : 13
preserved in amber, 119 : 7
where the b. sucks, 248 : 16
with honeyed thigh, 278 : 25
Beech, sang beneath spreading b., 104 : 14
Beechen green and shadows, 476 : 22
spare the b. tree, 443 : 19
Beef, great eater of b., 213 : 12
meals of b. iron steel, 207 : 26
old England's roast b., 349 : 7
pig had roast b., 930 : 11
roast b. of old England, 349 : *n* 3
stole piece of b., 931 : 3
without mustard, 655 : 16
Beef-faced boys, 547 : 4
Bee-loud glade, 712 : 4
Beelzebub, early morning B. arose, 466 : 5
Been, it might have b., 513 : 14
what has b. has b., 305 : 2
what never has b. may have when, 619 : 2
Beer and skittles, 546 : *n* 2, 590 : 10
chronicle small b., 230 : 12
come my lad and drink b., 353 : 11
corrodes copper, 623 : 12
felony to drink small b., 185 : 23
questionable superfluity small b., 185 : *n* 6
show vilely to desire small b., 185 : *n* 6
teetotaler, 680 : 9
Beersheba, Dan to B., 12 : 22, 360 : 22
Bee's collected treasures, 363 : 13
kiss now, 540 : 29
Bees black with gilt surcingles, 607 : 11
excel the b. for government, 167 : 9
for flies and hornets for bees, 155 : 14
helmet now hive for b., 177 : 9
honeyed words like b., 794 : 8
if b. are few, 608 : 3
innumerable b., 531 : 13
intellectual life like b., 703 : 13
many b. on single course, 784 : 15
rob the Hybla b., 217 : 8
stirring birds on wing, 436 : 9
swarm of b. and honey in the carcass, 12 : 13
swarm of b. in May, 919 : 10
Beetle booms adown glooms, 665 : 7
nor death-moth, 477 : 21
poor b. we tread upon, 228 : 17
shard-borne b., 238 : 20
wheels droning flight, 361 : 21
winds sullen horn, 364 : 12
Beetles in caves, 873 : 11
o'er his base, 219 : 14
scarce so gross as b., 234 : 28
Befall, may opposite b. me, 79 : 13
whatever b. you preordained, 125 : 19
Befallen, that which hath b. thee, 34 : 5
Befell, these that twice b., 607 : 18
Befits proud birth, 73 : 10
Befitting, bound as b. each, 576 : 22
Before a joy proposed, 245 : 23
all be as b. love, 541 : 21
clearest vision of what is b., 81 : 2

Before (*continued*)
he is b. all things, 50 : 9
may it be beautiful b. me, 928 : 19
not lost but gone b., 114 : 25
old man looks b. and after, 57 : 22
reaching forth unto things b., 50 : 4
war instead of after, 856 : 11
Beforehand, not think b. of his words, 89 : 15
Befriend, good b. themselves, 75 : 10
like sparks of fire b. thee, 266 : 14
Beg alms of palsied eld, 228 : 16
cannot b. for pardon, 870 : 6
cold comfort, 202 : 18
death's pardon now, 899 : 7
delinquents for our life, 893 : 17
leave to subsist, 704 : 17
often our own harms, 240 : 26
penny by and by, 811 : 16
sleep under bridges b. and steal, 655 : 14
to b. I am ashamed, 43 : 30
too proud to b., 922 : 14
virtue of vice pardon b., 223 : 9
Began best can't end worst, 544 : 29
I am that which b., 634 : 4
this universal frame b., 305 : 9
twilight of things that b., 634 : 7
violence and injury return on him who b., 101 : 10
Begat, fathers that b. us, 36 : 10
someone someone else b., 749 : 16
Beget, acquire and b. temperance, 221 : 23
get and b., 664 : 13
urge to b., 912 : 9
Begets, kindness b. kindness, 73 : 12
love b. love, 874 : 19
money b. money, 301 : 14
Begetter, onlie b. of insuing sonnets, 243 : *n* 4
Beggar, be not made a b., 35 : 30
carried by angels, 43 : 33
crawl at his side, 517 : 15
in purple of emperors, 708 : 23
is envious of beggar, 61 : 13
King Cophetua loved b. maid, 192 : 1
maid be queen, 530 : 17
not a b. would accept, 607 : 8
on foot, 717 : 12
set a b. on horseback, 186 : *n* 1
that I am, 220 : 27
that is dumb, 172 : 13
true b. true king, 374 : 16
twice stood a b., 604 : 3
upon horseback, 717 : 12
Beggared all description, 240 : 29
by strumpet wind, 199 : 6
Beggarly Scotchman, 354 : 2
weak and b. elements, 49 : 26
when I was b. boy, 568 : 20
Beggar's daughter of Bethnal Green, 926 : 17
Beggars are from Zeus, 60 : 1
changed places, 717 : 12
coming to town, 933 : 21
might ride, 301 : 13
mounted run horse to death, 186 : 1
our basest b., 233 : 21
should be no choosers, 160 : 2
when b. die, 215 : 25
Beggary in love that can be reckoned, 240 : 13
poverty is sister of b., 82 : 24
Begged, living Homer b. bread, 257 : *n* 5
Begging, nor his seed b. bread, 18 : 25
truth goes a-b., 156 : 4
us to have self-pity, 900 : 2
Begin and cease, 587 : 14
at the beginning, 612 : 13
better never to b. than to stop, 135 : 4
come back b. over, 747 : 16
dare to be wise b., 108 : 20
from Zeus let us b., 92 : 11
get up b. again, 542 : 12
hard thing's to b., 567 : 15
in creating hard to b., 567 : 15
in gladness, 425 : 10
in sadness, 892 : 15
it is said to b. with father, 904 : 11
let it b. here, 374 : 19
let us b., 890 : 10
liberty must b. at home, 825 : 10
must b. with single step, 65 : 1
time to b. a new, 307 : 1
to cease to be, 705 : 19
winking Mary-buds b., 243 : 16
with certainties end in doubts, 178 : 20
with Jove I b., 103 : 10
Beginnin, seed de b., 837 : 17
Beginning, always best in their b., 299 : 12
and end of all art, 397 : 4
and end of political education, 635 : 1
art of b., 512 : 23
as it was in the b., 54 : 18
bad b. makes bad ending, 77 : 13
before b. of years, 632 : 9
begin at b., 612 : 13
better is the end than the b., 27 : 6
blessed latter end of Job more than b., 17 : 11
each venture new b., 807 : 21
easier to resist at b., 152 : 10
end and b., 863 : 15
end consequent upon our b., 115 : 18
end of the b., 746 : 1
fear of the Lord b. of wisdom, 21 : 19
from bad b. great friendships, 96 : 23
good b. a good end, 159 : 29
Great B. produced emptiness, 97 : 7
hard b. good ending, 159 : 9
hatred of bourgeois b. of wisdom, 583 : 17
in my b. is my end, 807 : 9
in my end my b., 167 : 2, 807 : 24
in the b. God created, 6 : 10
in the b. was the Word, 44 : 17
long choosing and b. late, 287 : 12
look with favor on bold b., 103 : 26
masterpieces not best at b., 734 : 4
never ending still b., 306 : 19
no vestige of a b., 367 : 12
not even b. of end, 746 : 1
of a feast, 204 : 36
of an Amour, 312 : 19
of the end, 400 : 17, 746 : 1
of wisdom desire of discipline, 34 : 17
of work most important part, 84 : 8
of years, 634 : 7
past b. of b., 719 : 14
pleasure the b. and end, 91 : 15
rid of folly b. of wisdom, 108 : 17
stop revolution at b., 851 : 12
take fill at b. of cask, 61 : 21
the b. and the end, 53 : 33
Beginning (*continued*)
to faint in light, 533 : 21
to flee vice b. of virtue, 108 : 17
told you from the b., 31 : 1
true b. of our end, 197 : 14
whole has b. middle and end, 88 : 17
you are b. and end, 851 : 16
Beginnings and endings untidy, 723 : 10
end to b. of wars, 781 : 6
mighty things from small b. grow, 303 : 4
of things not distinguished by eye, 100 : 6
out of small b., 265 : 13
resist b., 113 : 25
Begins, blossom by blossom spring b., 632 : 8
charity b. at home, 96 : 6
elections end slavery b., 381 : 10
family history b. with me, 86 : 6
in delight ends in wisdom, 750 : 2
in dreams b. responsibility, 713 : 9
law ends tyranny b., 307 : 17
laws end tyranny b., 351 : 1
life b. perpetually, 720 : 6
life closed life b., 576 : 20
one ends other b., 526 : 7
pack when it b. to rain, 233 : 18
when love b. to sicken, 216 : 30
where West b., 739 : 7
world's great age b., 468 : 17
Begone dull Care, 919 : 4
Begot, how b. how nourished, 199 : 23
in ventricle of memory, 190 : 30
monster b. upon itself, 231 : 20
of nothing but vain fantasy, 191 : 24
to whom related by whom b., 335 : 11
when they b. me, 359 : 18
Begotten born and dies, 714 : 22
by despair, 297 : 6
drops of dew, 16 : 32
flowers b., 632 : 8
has not b. and not been b., 132 : 19
not made, 55 : 3
of his Father before all worlds, 55 : 3
only b. Son, 44 : 34
Beguile, bean-fed horse b., 196 : 12
light of light b., 190 : 11
many be beguiled by one, 231 : 21
Satan that waiteth to b., 147 : 7
the thing I am, 230 : 10
you from grief, 524 : 4
Beguiled, be b. by one, 231 : 21
serpent b. me, 7 : 9
Beguiles, history of wound b. pain, 360 : 3
Beguiling, smiling of Fortune b., 359 : 10
Begun, end just where you b., 372 : 8
kiss afresh as when we first b., 266 : 10
not yet b. to fight, 394 : 4
war has actually b., 383 : 5
well b. is half done, 88 : 11
what I was b. for, 919 : 15
who has b. has half done, 108 : 20
Behave as we wish friends to behave, 87 : 3
damn you, 862 : 8
how they b. in quarrel, 680 : 4
how well I b., 691 : 2
in life as at banquet, 121 : 20
learn to b. by being, 645 : 6
mannerly at table, 668 : 10

Behavior, control over human b., 665 : 4
customs shape b., 796 : 4
determined not by racial affiliation, 685 : 6
human b. as relationship, 842 : 15
of silk-sack clouds, 656 : 6
positive science of b., 733 : 15
put on good b., 461 : 15
science of b. not change nature of man, 862 : 13
springs of sea b. hidden, 741 : 12
surfeit of our own b., 233 : 5
synergy b. of whole systems, 832 : 10
Behavioristic, children in b. freedom, 762 : 4
Beheld, till I prince of love b., 402 : 12
Behemoth, behold now b., 17 : 3
Behind a dream, 245 : 23
bit by him that comes b., 322 : 21
creeds one Spirit, 657 : 5
forgetting those things b., 50 : 4
get thee b. me, 39 : 37
him lay gray Azores, 646 : 6
leave not a rack b., 248 : 13
may it be beautiful b. me, 928 : 19
never gets left b., 704 : 1
part my hair b., 803 : 19
those he leaves b., 593 : 5
turn thee b. me, 14 : 17
you're on bus and get left b., 913 : 7
Behold, be what they b., 334 : 12
her judge for yourselves, 450 : 13
home return who him b., 692 : 2
human beings in underground den, 84 : 17
I am vile, 17 : 2
I come quickly, 53 : 32
I do not give lectures, 574 : 26
I will build me a nest, 651 : 9
mad if they b. a cat, 200 : 2
my head, 269 : 6
now another providence, 265 : 12
now behemoth, 17 : 3
power to say B., 195 : 23
rainbow in the sky, 425 : 7
the child, 337 : 7
the Lamb of God, 44 : 23
the man, 45 : 32
the upright, 18 : 27
this dreamer cometh, 8 : 27
thou mayest in me b., 244 : 27
upon night's starred face, 478 : 18
you again in dying, 669 : 9
your God, 30 : 34
Beholden, much b. to Machiavel, 179 : 5
Beholder, beauty in eye of b., 676 : 20
Beholders, strike awe into b., 322 : 10
Beholding beauty with eye of mind, 83 : 10
desire and dream, 683 : 8
myself rosy red, 726 : 3
Beholds, swift mind b., 823 : 7
Behoove, icebergs b. the soul, 878 : 3
Behooves, hardly b. any to talk, 646 : *n* 2
Behove, requires for my b., 162 : 5
Behoving and unbehoving, 507 : 7
Being a little flesh a little breath, 124 : 5
ABC of b., 768 : 2
all things come from b., 64 : 13
and happening, 869 : 11
applause of single human b., 356 : 17

Being (*continued*)
art has reason for b., 499 : 11
beauty own excuse for b., 494 : 5
chain of b., 499 : 12
changes control our b., 529 : 4
circle of potential b., 648 : 3
civilized human b., 755 : 3
contending against some b., 575 : 23
currents of Universal B., 496 : 4
ends of b., 507 : 14
ennobled by own exertions, 414 : 9
father can be rough, 610 : 12
human b. more or less, 887 : 13
human b. portable plumbing, 816 : 12
human b. through descent from group, 685 : 7
if God were not necessary B., 303 : 1
intellectual b., 284 : 9
let there always be b., 63 : 12
move and have our b., 46 : 17
no creature whose inward b., 565 : 25
not doing, 874 : 13
offered B. for it, 605 : 20
organic b. striving to increase, 515 : 2
perfected b. survives after death, 73 : 4
place in chain of b., 499 : 12
pleasing anxious b., 362 : 14
receives reproach of b., 245 : 22
things come into b., 324 : 1
Being-forever, nature assures b., 866 : 6
Being's, my b. worth, 607 : 17
Beings, all b. thou shouldst not mourn, 94 : 9
are honey of this Self, 56 : 22
burn books burn human b., 481 : 11
capacity of human b. to comprehend, 884 : 6
distances between human b., 756 : 12
faith in human b., 821 : 3
human b. into machines, 562 : 18
human b. living in den, 84 : 17
millions of human b., 720 : 3
noble happy human b., 572 : 19
rights over human b., 395 : 21
sentient b. doomed, 515 : 15
three b. worthy respect, 581 : 8
which compose nature, 397 : 17
Belched, Nobodaddy farted b. and coughed, 404 : 22
Beld, now your brow is b. John, 410 : 7
Belfry, clock in b. strikes one, 614 : 12
Belgium's capital gathered then, 457 : 14
Belgrave, hearts beat in B. Square, 628 : 20
Belial, sons of B., 283 : 19
thus B. counseled, 284 : 13
Belican, bill hold more than b., 765 : 12
Belie all corners of world, 243 : 21
state fact b. another, 496 : 18
Belief, final b. in fiction, 768 : 1
help create fact, 649 : 15
illogical b. in improbable, 772 : 11
in particular natural law, 856 : 15
not within prospect of b., 236 : 6
ripened into faith, 428 : 16
to believe in b., 694 : 1
what was their one B., 889 : 14
Beliefs, bombs shook men out of b., 719 : 16
dead ideas and b., 599 : 15

Beliefs (*continued*)
employees required to state b., 846 : 17
forsaken b., 587 : 1
keep as many old b. as we can, 650 : 10
less than chaff, 683 : 18
more b. than can digest, 690 : 7
Believe a lie, 407 : *n* 1
also in me, 45 : 20
an expert, 106 : 6
as it is convenient let us b., 113 : 10
attempted to b. Matilda, 730 : 9
because it is impossible, 126 : *n* 6
courage not to b., 564 : 6
deep in heart b., 925 : 9
do you b. in life to come, 866 : 14
don't b. no sich person, 548 : 2
easier to b. than deny, 631 : 1
good tidings to people who b., 130 : 14
her though I know she lies, 246 : 2
I b. and take it, 164 : 4
I b. in America, 824 : 12
I b. in God the Father, 55 : 2
if you b. clap hands, 694 : 9
in freedom regardless of form, 769 : 13
in God yearn for God, 705 : 17
in life, 725 : 3
in United States of America, 725 : 20
It or Not, 827 : 21
know what he ought to b., 139 : 14
leads you to b. a lie, 407 : 10
Lord I b., 42 : 10
man ready to b. what is told, 117 : 13
me if all those endearing young charms, 446 : 11
me my country 'tis of you, 828 : 17
men b. what they wish, 99 : 15
more firmly as reality more threatening, 775 : 3
my own stories, 453 : 5
ne'er b. do what you please, 406 : 17
never b. God plays dice, 763 : 16
no evil till evil's done, 296 : 7
not know what safely b., 644 : 18
oft repeating they b. 'em, 320 : 24
only possibilities, 274 : 14
own thought genius, 496 : 19
rather b. fables in legends, 180 : 16
rather b. God not exist, 504 : 19
Robert who has tried it, 106 : *n* 4
sailors won't b. it, 432 : 10
Sisyphus happy, 882 : 6
that which they desire, 303 : *n* 3
they half b. in it, 64 : 14
thy will my power to b., 543 : 21
to doubt or b. everything, 673 : 7
we have only to b., 775 : 3
we what we wish, 303 : 14
wisdom to b. heart, 703 : 3
with all my soul, 568 : 1
woman or epitaph, 456 : 15
ye b. in God, 45 : 20
ye do by no means b., 132 : 9
Believed, against hope b. in hope, 47 : 1
always everywhere by all, 129 : 16
because he b. in his God, 33 : 4
I wept and I b., 419 : 6
juggling fiends no more b., 240 : 9
not seen yet b., 45 : 37
to be b. because absurd, 126 : 8
truth never understood and not b., 404 : 8

Believed (*continued*)
what we least know, 164 : 15
Believer, above all a b. in culture, 588 : 14
not satisfied with appearances, 853 : 7
Believers, half b. of casual creeds, 585 : 22
O true b., 132 : 8
Believes, atheist half b. God, 330 : 14
each b. his own, 332 : 15
he who b. nothing, 387 : 12
what each wishes he b., 88 : 22
Believeth, he that b. shall live, 45 : 13
liveth and b., 45 : 13
neither b. that it is sound of the trumpet, 16 : 38
whosoever b. in him, 44 : 34
Believing, be not faithless but b., 45 : 36
in old men's lies, 792 : 14
slave better than idolater, 130 : 12
to b. souls gives light, 185 : 12
where cannot prove, 531 : 16
Bell book and candle, 201 : 23
book b. and candle, 149 : 16
ding dong b., 930 : 14
eats and goes to bed by b., 622 : 16
fancy from flower b., 543 : 5
foam b. no consequence, 587 : 4
for whom the b. tolls, 254 : 22
hear the surly sullen b., 244 : 26
heart sound as b., 209 : 21
in cowslip's b. I lie, 248 : 16
invites me, 237 : 16
merry as marriage b., 457 : 14
middle b. trills out, 518 : 9
noise of b. buoys, 798 : 13
sad b. murmuring good night, 879 : 9
sexton tolled b., 485 : 3
silence that dreadful b., 230 : 20
some cost passing b., 492 : 15
strikes one, 330 : 7
swung to and fro, 669 : 20
the cat, 66 : 16, 143 : 15
tocsin the dinner b., 461 : 16
tongue sounds as sullen b., 205 : 20
twilight and evening b., 535 : 20
very word like b., 477 : 2
who will b. cat, 66 : 16, 143 : 15
Belle Aurore, 545 : 15
of old Natchez, 856 : 2
vain to be a b., 357 : 10
where none beaux vain be a b., 357 : 10
Belle dame sans merci, 478 : 13
sois b. et sois triste, (AG) 581 : *n* 4
Bellicose, newspapers querulous and b., 772 : 1
Bellies and drags in wind, 714 : 6
cold comfort to fill hungry b., 265 : 11
fills their b., 63 : 14
laughter out of dead b., 792 : 15
Bellies', for b. sake creep, 280 : 20
Belligerent ants, 419 : *n* 5
Bellman, fatal b., 237 : 17
would cry crew reply, 613 : 22
Bellow, in b. and uproar, 781 : 15
Bellows full of angry wind, 714 : 20
like sea combated by winds, 140 : 21
Bells and bonfires, 381 : 7
bells bells bells, 527 : 11
cap and b., 567 : 12
floating many b. down, 829 : 18
for these who die, 827 : 2
Bells (*continued*)
heard midnight b. jangling, 864 : 6
I hear, 576 : 6
in your parlors, 230 : 8
knolled to church, 211 : 12
merits of B. and Fudges, 488 : *n* 3
noisy b. be dumb, 691 : 4
of Old Bailey, 930 : 7
of Shoreditch, 930 : 7
of St. Clement's, 930 : 7
of St. Martin's, 930 : 7
on her toes, 931 : 11
ring b. for new century, 755 : 9
ring b. of heaven, 732 : 16
ring O b., 576 : 7
ring out wild b., 532 : 21
ring out your b., 176 : 8
silver b. cockleshells, 930 : 6
sound on Bredon, 691 : 4
summoned by b., 866 : 20
sweet b. jangled, 221 : 21
temple b. they say, 708 : 8
Bells', to b. cheerful sound, 403 : 4
Belly, eye bigger than b., 270 : 24
fill his b. with east wind, 15 : 36
God send thee good ale, 163 : 10
hard to argue with b., 95 : 9
has no ears, 95 : 9
he who does not mind his b., 354 : 16
if it is well with your b., 109 : 6
increasing b., 205 : 28
injured by hunger, 89 : 27
Jonah was in the b. of the fish, 33 : 22
justice in fair round b., 211 : 15
like a heap of wheat, 28 : 19
men's only God their b., 127 : 12
no b. no bowels, 811 : 1
noise in the beast's b., 149 : 7
secret life of b., 883 : 11
shoulder bum, 717 : 16
spent under b., 261 : 7
upon thy b. shalt thou go, 7 : 9
wears his wit in his b., 226 : 6
whose God is their b., 50 : 5
Bellyful of fighting, 243 : 15
Bellying, broad b. sails, 785 : 12
Belong, idea does not b. to soul, 639 : 6
land to which we b., 795 : 10
less to what flatters, 863 : 19
secret things b. unto the Lord, 11 : 21
suffice for who b. to them, 575 : 11
to Company G, 619 : 15
to oneself, 164 : 18
to vanishing race, 836 : 14
where do they all b., 914 : 10
wouldn't want to b., 834 : 3
Belongings, hold on to lost b., 739 : 11
Belongs, now he b. to ages, 553 : 5
Beloved, ah my b. fill cup, 516 : 13
creature that is b., 213 : 29
escape me never b., 542 : 11
from pole to pole, 434 : 30
he giveth his b. sleep, 22 : 9
let my b. come into his garden, 28 : 14
liberty a b. discipline, 877 : 14
never be b. by men, 406 : 11
of Abraham Lincoln, 728 : 7
our own b. home, 578 : 12
Pan, 83 : 7
perfection in b., 453 : 8
physician, 50 : 15
so is my b. among the sons, 28 : 5
Son, 36 : 31
this is my b., 28 : 16
Beloved (*continued*)
thought himself b., 714 : 18
Beloved's, heaped for b. bed, 469 : 18
I am my b., 28 : 22
Below, down and away b., 584 : 11
joy to pass to world b., 105 : 12
may it be beautiful b. me, 928 : 19
my thoughts remain b., 222 : 28
no safety here b., 156 : 1
serfdom abolish itself from b., 561 : 7
slave spirit b., 794 : 12
thy element's b., 233 : 17
what we are here b., 734 : 7
Belshazzar made a great feast, 32 : 35
Belted, prince can make b. knight, 411 : 18
you and flayed you, 708 : 6
Belua multorum es capitum, 108 : *n* 14
Bemocked, beams b. sultry main, 434 : 28
Ben Adhem's name led rest, 454 : 7
Bolt, 566 : 1
Bulben's head, 718 : 1
Jonson his best poetry, 256 : 4
O rare B. Jonson, 255 : *n* 3
Bench, log hut with simple b., 609 : 10
Bend, grass must b. when wind blows, 69 : 2
I b. but do not break, 296 : 12
if I cannot b. Heaven, 105 : 29
shall I b. low, 198 : 25
soften rocks or b. oak, 324 : 14
Bended, on b. arm doglike, 71 : 3
Bendemeer's stream, 447 : 12
Bending sickle's compass, 245 : 18
to your wool, 162 : 12
Bends, blue sky b. over all, 434 : 2
gallant mast, 453 : 19
though she b. him, 511 : 18
to the grave, 370 : 3
with remover to remove, 245 : 18
Beneath, at once above b. around, 365 : 6
rung battle shout, 518 : 12
Benedick the married man, 209 : 3
Benediction, face like a b., 168 : 17
looking for b. rather than invocation, 879 : 3
Benefaction, calling to mind previous b., 79 : 16
Benefactor, less to blame than b., 293 : 18
Beneficence, private b. inadequate, 694 : 3
Beneficent mother of gods and men, 5 : 3
Beneficial, the opposite is b., 70 : 4
Beneficient, belief in b. power, 641 : 1
Benefit, find man to b. kingdom, 89 : 4
from illnesses, 80 : 8
from literary accomplishments in women, 392 : 11
God made for b. of men, 303 : 1
government for common b., 367 : 5
he receives hope who recognizes b., 130 : 5
human b. and enjoyment, 373 : 4
if men stop work at sixty, 664 : 20
means of acquiring knowledge greatest b., 418 : 10
no b. in gifts of bad man, 76 : 15
of clergy, 735 : *n* 1
of ill, 245 : 20
practical b. in failures, 595 : 17

Benefit (*continued*)
trees to b. another generation, 95 : 15
Way of Heaven to b. others, 65 : 10
written in water, 155 : *n* 4
Benefits, caution in refusing b., 308 : 24
disable b. of your country, 212 : 20
doubly b. who gives quickly, 110 : 15
gratitude a desire for b., 293 : 33
memory of b. fades, 73 : 12
of scientific advances available, 787 : 17
water b. all things, 64 : 3
Benevolence, beans and b., 500 : 20
calls his trusting b., 369 : 23
decrees of farseeing b., 579 : 7
is man's mind, 89 : 21
not infused from without, 89 : 20
peace a disposition for b., 308 : 3
tranquil habitation of man, 89 : 10
whether b. does good, 597 : 5
Benevolent, heart b. and kind, 409 : 19
people turn to b. rule, 89 : 9
stormy patient, 864 : 17
Benighted, pore b. 'eathen, 708 : 5
Benign indifference of universe, 882 : 3
is solitude, 424 : 3
Benison of hot water, 796 : 16
to fall, 267 : 1
Benjamin's, fell upon B. neck and wept, 8 : 37
mess five times theirs, 8 : 33
Bennet called us Quakers, 300 : 22
Mrs. B. stirring fire, 440 : 19
Bent, affection cannot hold b., 214 : 2
as twig b. tree's inclined, 335 : 15
bow cannot stand b., 169 : 36
find out natural b., 85 : 1
fool me to top of my b., 222 : 21
goldenrod, 806 : 6
idly b. on him that enters next, 195 : 15
man who has b. himself, 89 : 5
natural b. in accordance with nature's, 639 : 13
thoughts downward b., 283 : 28
to be b. is to become straight, 64 : 10
Bentham and Coleridge seminal minds, 508 : 2
Benumbs all his faculties, 353 : 22
care's a canker that b., 630 : 4
Bequeath my soul to God, 181 : 16
myself to dirt, 575 : 4
us to no shore, 843 : 16
Bereaved, black as if b. of light, 403 : 6
Bereavement, anguish of b., 524 : 4
Bereft, muddy ill-seeming b. of beauty, 189 : 5
Bergère ô tour Eiffel, 770 : *n* 2
Bergson you are a magician, 688 : *n* 2
Berkeley, Bishop B. said no matter, 461 : 22
Berkshire, ferns by B. boulders, 822 : 7
Berlin, citizens of B., 891 : 14
Berliner, ich bin ein B., 891 : 14
Bermoothes, still-vexed B., 247 : 16
Bermudas, remote B. ride, 297 : 8
Berries harsh and crude, 280 : 6
I come to pluck your b., 280 : 6
sweet b. ripen in wilderness, 767 : 4
two b. on one stem, 197 : 2
Berry, could have made better b., 271 : 10
Beseech, lighten our darkness we b., 55 : 9
Beseech (*continued*)
thee for all sorts of men, 55 : 5
Walrus did b., 613 : 3
ye in bowels of Christ, 737 : 5
you brethren, 47 : 18
you in bowels of Christ, 272 : 18
you of your pardon, 231 : 3
Beset, being woman hard b., 794 : 3
Besetting errors, 464 : 5
Beside, leadeth me b. still waters, 18 : 7
thou art b. thyself, 46 : 33
Besiege, forty winters b. thy brow, 244 : 1
Besieged, by flatterers b., 338 : 14
Bespangling, dew b. herb and tree, 266 : 19
Best, a little wise b. fools be, 252 : 14
afflict the b., 361 : 13
all b. though we doubt, 289 : 10
all is for the b., 343 : 8
always b. in beginning, 299 : 12
always give your b., 883 : 3
and brightest come away, 470 : 2
and the brightest, 452 : *n* 1
and worst of this is, 634 : 3
are but shadows, 197 : 15
beauty b. of all we know, 654 : 14
began b. can't end worst, 544 : 29
blazon of sweet beauty's b., 245 : 12
butter, 611 : 19
common-looking people b., 523 : 5
country is at home, 368 : 15
damned cowboy born, 927 : 12
did it for the b., 693 : 5
discretion b. part of valor, 205 : *n* 2
do b. I can, 524 : 11
do your worst we our b., 745 : 3
done his b. for his time, 413 : 5
forward b. foot, 202 : *n* 4
good bad worst b., 525 : 11
he gives the b., 352 : 2
he made the b. of this, 411 : 22
he was b. of all Greek, 702 : 6
hope for the b., 432 : 21
how much the b., 394 : 10
is enemy of good, 343 : 21
is good enough, 395 : 13
is yet to be, 544 : 8
known and thought in world, 586 : 24
lack all conviction, 714 : 12
last b. hope of earth, 522 : 12
last commonly b., 258 : 6
laughs b. who laughs last, 321 : 6
look b. when caring least, 799 : 17
love is b., 542 : 4
man worst-natured muse, 315 : 15
masterpieces not give b. at beginning, 734 : 4
men molded of faults, 229 : 9
men of few words b., 207 : 20
men take b. they can get, 356 : 2
minds of my generation, 906 : 1
never lived is b., 715 : 19
no b. in kind but degree, 511 : 14
no worse a husband than b. of men, 240 : 28
not expected to go true, 353 : 16
not to be born, 67 : 5, 868 : 7
not to seem but be b., 71 : 18
of all God's works, 287 : 22
of all patrons, 102 : 4
of all ways, 447 : 1
of me is diligence, 233 : 7
of men that e'er wore earth, 251 : 11
Best (*continued*)
of possible worlds, 343 : 8, 762 : 10
of times worst of times, 549 : 22
old friends are b., 179 : *n* 4
part of married life fights, 839 : 18
past and to come seem b., 206 : 8
pianist doing his b., 675 : 6
political community, 88 : 7
promise only to do our b., 863 : 12
race and nation judged by b., 733 : 8
second b. to go back quickly, 75 : 13
second thoughts are b., 76 : 21
seen the b. of our time, 233 : 4
should rule who rule b., 88 : 4
so much bad in b. of us, 646 : *n* 2
sometimes forget, 230 : 21
steed was the b., 430 : 17
stolen sweets are b., 325 : 3
that is in one, 658 : 2
things confused with ill, 466 : 17
things in life free, 825 : 7
thought his who says it b., 568 : 21
to forget, 545 : 24
water is b., 71 : 20
way of doing everything, 498 : 28
way out is through, 747 : 11
when b. a little worse than man, 198 : 14
where b. like worst, 708 : 10
wisest discreetest b., 287 : 8
worst and b. inclined to snap, 794 : 7
you get is even break, 773 : 13
Bestia, simia turpissima b., 95 : *n* 3
Bestial, mystery on b. floor, 713 : 13
semihuman and demonic, 754 : 10
what remains is b., 230 : 23
Best-laid schemes, 408 : 14
Bestow, fee b. upon foul disease, 232 : 28
goods to poor, 48 : 23
Bestowed, favor well b., 327 : 18
Bestowing, warmth of love's b., 617 : 3
Bestows, where Jove b., 271 : 19
Best-regulated families, 548 : 35
Bestrid, his legs b. the ocean, 241 : 25
Bestride the narrow world, 215 : 6
Best's, second b. gay goodnight, 715 : 19
Bet my money on bobtail nag, 598 : 2
Beteem, not b. winds of heaven, 218 : 7
Betelgueux, Aldebaran and B., 640 : 6
Bethlehem, Christ born in B., 350 : 15
come ye to B., 133 : 8
Jesus was born in B., 36 : 20
little town of B., 619 : 16
slouches toward B., 714 : 13
venite in B., 133 : 8
Bethnal Green, 926 : 17
Bethumped with words, 201 : 17
Betokened, red morn that b., 189 : 10
Betray, all things b. thee, 693 : 11
emptiness b., 339 : 1
finds too late men b., 369 : 20
Fortune flatters to b., 111 : 1
Nature never did b., 423 : 15
one of you b. me, 41 : 7
somebody else betray yourself, 862 : 2
tender happiness b., 427 : 26
thee who betrayest Me, 693 : 11
to promote commerce and not b. it, 310 : *n* 1
us in deepest consequence, 236 : 9
Betrayal, no b. in human face, 879 : 8
Betrayed and baffled still, 631 : 15
by false within, 600 : 18
by fancy into metaphor, 444 : 15

Betrayed (*continued*)
by his manners, 174 : 4
guilt by silence b., 305 : 27
mistress that b. man, 635 : 19
Son of man is b., 41 : 14
Betrayers of language, 792 : 19
Betrayest, betray thee who b. Me, 693 : 11
Betrays instead of serving, 372 : 9
our style b. us, 258 : 8
Betsey and I are out, 660 : 2
Bette, auf seinem B., 395 : *n* 2
Better a little chiding, 225 : 29
all shall be b. than well, 618 : 11
another and b. world, 415 : 3
approve b. but follow worse, 113 : 21
be ignorant than half know, 112 : 9
be prepared for rage, 748 : 11
boundless b. worse, 527 : 20
by God she'd b., 536 : *n* 3
curse his b. angel, 232 : 17
damned than not mentioned, 385 : 13
does it with b. grace, 213 : 24
don't know where go b., 747 : 16
envied than pitied, 78 : 10
far far b. thing, 549 : 24
feed brain with b. things, 742 : 12
few are b. than their fathers, 59 : 18
fifty years of Europe, 530 : 9
for being a little bad, 229 : 9
for b. for worse, 56 : 9
for him a millstone, 43 : 35
four things b. without, 827 : 9
freedom the chance to be b., 882 : 11
friends not be knowing, 823 : 3
from b. selves too long parted, 424 : 3
getting b. and b., 684 : 9
give place to b. men, 272 : 19
go down dignified, 749 : 1
go down on marrowbones, 712 : 20
good as all no b. than any, 865 : 16
good b. made by ill, 180 : *n* 2
good laws lead to b., 358 : 17
got the b. of himself, 171 : 4
grow wiser and b., 302 : 24
half a loaf, 160 : 11
is a dinner of herbs, 24 : 7
is a neighbor that is near, 25 : 25
is a poor and wise child, 26 : 25
is an handful with quietness, 26 : 23
is life of a poor man, 35 : 39
is little with the fear of the Lord, 24 : 7
is the end of a thing, 27 : 6
is thy love than wine, 28 : 13
know useless things than nothing, 114 : 30
known a b. day, 429 : 20
last smile, 321 : *n* 3
late than never, 110 : 12
make b. chairs or knives, 495 : 29
make worse appear b. reason, 81 : 14
man than I am Gunga Din, 708 : 6
minds made b. by presence, 564 : 22
my dear my b. half, 176 : 6
nae b. than he should be, 409 : 3
ne'er been born, 432 : 6
Negroes are b. than we, 837 : 20
no b. than should be, 168 : 30
no b. thing under the sun, 27 : 14
not to be, 527 : 19
one's own duty, 94 : 11
part, 703 : 3
part of valor, 205 : 14
Better (*continued*)
punishment not make man b., 658 : 6
rich is b., 789 : 1
seen b. days, 211 : 13, 243 : 6
selves, 424 : 3
spared better man, 205 : 13
striving to b. oft mar, 233 : 12
than the vintage of Abiezer, 12 : 11
that thou not vow, 26 : 27
the day better the deed, 261 : 5
three hours too soon, 225 : 18
to be fool than dead, 667 : 18
to be lowly born, 248 : 27
to be vile than vile esteemed, 245 : 22
to bow than break, 159 : 21
to die on feet than live on knees, 759 : 2
to dwell in a corner, 24 : 33
to go to house of mourning, 27 : 4
to have loved and lost, 532 : 3
to hide ignorance, 70 : 10
to incur loss, 93 : 12
to know some questions, 831 : 12
to light one candle, 786 : *n* 4
to live alone, 72 : 18
to marry than burn, 48 : 11
which is b. God only knows, 83 : 15
word b. than gift, 35 : 29
world than this, 210 : 18
world's in birth, 555 : 24
Bettered, better b. expectation, 208 : 21
Betters what is done, 246 : 27
Between acting of dreadful thing, 215 : 18
dark and daylight, 512 : 3
few and far b., 443 : 8
how long halt ye b. two opinions, 14 : 1
idea and reality, 805 : 17
Lord watch b. me and thee, 8 : 23
motion and act, 805 : 17
no hate lost b. us, 261 : 21
no strife b. me and thee, 8 : 6
Betwixt stirrup and ground, 171 : 18
Beulah peel me a grape, 824 : 9
Bevy of fair women, 287 : 31
Bewail, acknowledge and b. our sins, 55 : 17
Beware, all should cry B., 433 : 27
an act of avarice, 3 : 7
brothers and sisters b., 710 : 14
fury of a patient man, 304 : 16
Hieronymo b., 177 : 2
ides of March, 215 : 2
Jabberwock, 612 : 17
Jubjub bird, 612 : 17
let buyer b., 133 : 13
man of one book, 133 : 11
my fangs, 199 : 31
my lord of jealousy, 230 : 34
of desperate steps, 377 : 21
of dog, 133 : 12
of enterprises that require new clothes, 559 : 10
of entrance to quarrel, 219 : 1
of false prophets, 38 : 16
of judging by appearances, 296 : 16
of language, 463 : 20
of punishing wrongfully, 4 : 2
of rashness, 523 : 1
of robbing a wretch, 6 : 3
the middle mind, 794 : 7
when thinker loose, 497 : 25
Beweep my outcast state, 244 : 8
Bewildered, bewitched bothered b., 833 : 19
in maze of schools, 332 : 17
Bewitch, more b. me than when art, 266 : 7
prosperity doth b. men, 262 : 5
Bewitched bothered bewildered, 833 : 19
Bewitching, love brings b. grace, 76 : 22
wine, 60 : 18
Bewrayed by his manners, 174 : 4
Bewrayeth, thy speech b. thee, 41 : 17
Beyond Alps lies Italy, 110 : 13
far b. my depth, 249 : 3
is there anything b., 796 : 13
plants are animals, 831 : 17
religion vision of something b., 697 : 9
sea's towers a-sway B., 843 : 18
this nothing but sandy deserts, 119 : 21
to go b. is wrong, 68 : 27
utmost bound of thought, 529 : 10
Bharata, son of B., 94 : 9
Bias, assays of b., 220 : 7
Commodity b. of the world, 201 : 19
strongest b. rules, 332 : 19
Biased with compassion or favor, 289 : 14
Bibendum, nunc est b., 107 : *n* 13
Bibi-mus vivi-mus oremus, 365 : 12
Bible, both read the B., 407 : 9
Christianity and devotion to B., 905 : 5
English B., 487 : 14
for the B. tells me so, 599 : 4
like in B. with locusts, 863 : 6
literature not dogma, 703 : 18
paintings the B. of laity, 137 : 2
pessimistic utterances in B., 649 : 11
study but litel on B., 146 : 5
text of B. symbol, 689 : 18
things you're liable to read in B., 836 : 7
this B. for government by people, 143 : 12
Bible-black, starless and b., 887 : 6
Biblical, Homeric or B. canticles, 577 : 13
Bibliobibuli read too much, 772 : 18
Bicker down a valley, 533 : 15
reason we b. creates war, 165 : 4
Bickering brattle, 408 : 12
Bickerings, such b. to recount, 289 : 12
Bicycle built for two, 718 : 18
mechanics from Dayton, 835 : 1
Bid, come between b. us part, 345 : 18
farewell to every fear, 328 : 14
gave thee life b. thee feed, 403 : 5
me discourse, 189 : 7
me Good morning, 387 : 3
me to live, 266 : 2
not serve God if devil b., 229 : 19
shall I b. her go, 917 : 16
soul of Orpheus sing, 278 : 22
them wash their faces, 242 : 15
time return, 194 : 27
you a welcome adoo, 616 : 9
you top o' the mornin', 661 : 10
Bidding, thousands at his b. speed, 282 : 17
Bide by the buff and the blue, 411 : 24
Bids, do what manhood b., 581 : 14
expectation rise, 368 : 11

Bids (*continued*)
it break, 239 : 20
it come to heel, 803 : 2
remembrance rise, 368 : 9
Bien sûr, il me pardonnera, 482 : 8
Big Bessie's feet hurt, 889 : 19
big D, 627 : 12
Blue Mountain Spirit, 928 : 16
Brother watching you, 858 : 14
business give square deal, 687 : 19
carry b. stick, 687 : 6
city of b. shoulders, 761 : 4
lie, 812 : 17
Light, 831 : 17
monstrous b. river, 624 : 2
my tavern the B. Bear, 673 : 12
sleep, 803 : 5
stealin' makes you emperor, 810 : 7
this too would become b., 61 : 20
words always punished, 75 : 2
Big-boned and hardy-handsome, 656 : 7
Bigger, eye b. than belly, 270 : 24
no b. than agate stone, 191 : 23
seems no b. than his head, 234 : 28
they come harder fall, 78 : *n* 7
Biggest fish got away, 666 : 14
Bigness, her b. sweeps my being, 819 : 4
world in b. as star, 285 : 3
Bigotry, emancipation of woman from b., 842 : *n* 5
gives b. no sanction, 379 : 8
Big-Sea-Water, shining B., 511 : 16
Bilateral, collective bargaining b. monopoly, 790 : 4
Bile, sentences that stir b., 693 : 5
Bill, as if God wrote b., 495 : 3
cool dew in b., 514 : 3
fellers call me B., 666 : 19
hold more than belican, 765 : 12
larger b. for darker ill, 562 : *n* 2
make real the B. of Rights, 753 : 6
Roaring B. who killed him, 730 : 12
tax relief b., 780 : 18
unpaid b. Despair, 470 : 4
wilderness b. of rights, 841 : 2
Bill of Rights, absolutes in B., 794 : 17
guarantee of freedom, 788 : 13
into suicide pact, 821 : 8
landmarks in B., 836 : 16
Billabong, camped by b., 705 : 7
Billboard lovely as tree, 855 : 15
Billboards, unless b. fall, 855 : 15
Billet, bullet has its b., 316 : 10
Billiard, elliptical b. balls, 629 : 13
Billions, chained for b. of years, 809 : 22
Billow above which is a billow, 131 : 17
what a b. be, 606 : 17
Billows, rocked to sleep between b., 570 : 7
smooth and bright, 613 : 1
swelling and limitless b., 435 : 18
thy b. far and near, 458 : 31
Bill's, Buffalo B. defunct, 828 : 13
Bills of rights, 367 : *n* 4
Billy-boil, waited for b., 705 : 7
Bind another to its delight, 405 : 4
arm b. restless wave, 596 : 18
fast b. fast find, 159 : 4
in body and in soul b., 430 : 9
safe b. safe find, 159 : *n* 2
shall my joyful temples b., 276 : 5
the sweet influences of Pleiades, 16 : 33
up my wounds, 187 : 26
Bind (*continued*)
up nation's wounds, 524 : 7
us in time, 843 : 16
Binding Nature fast in fate, 340 : 2
Binds brave of all earth, 700 : 6
he who b. to himself a joy, 404 : 18
so dear a head, 468 : 22
the bouquet, 739 : 11
vow b. too strictly, 534 : 19
Binnorie, milldams o' B., 927 : 1
Biographers, Boswell first of b., 353 : *n* 4
reviewers would have been b., 436 : 15
Biographies clothes and buttons, 626 : 9
geniuses shortest b., 498 : 15
history innumerable b., 473 : *n* 5
Biography, heroic poem a b., 472 : 9
history of world b., 473 : 24
no history only b., 496 : 16
of man cannot be written, 626 : 9
written by acute enemy, 661 : 15
Biological, is war b. necessity, 786 : 8
not b. but cultural evolution, 870 : 15
Biologically, idle b. speaking, 823 : 1
Biped, divide b. class, 86 : *n* 4
Birch most shy ladylike, 567 : 10
Tom B. brisk as a bee, 353 : 22
twig for castigation, 711 : 17
Birches, swinger of b., 747 : 17
Bird, a very few a b. or two, 604 : 9
as b. endearment tries, 370 : 7
Attic b., 288 : 14
beat bush another take b., 159 : *n* 3
beating b. extending wings, 875 : 2
change me to winged b., 76 : 24
clumsy dirty gray b., 505 : 8
crop-full b., 544 : 9
cuckoo shall I call thee b., 427 : 1
day after day b. flies, 514 : *n* 2
divine b. of Zeus, 71 : 24
flee as a b., 17 : 19
flies out, 875 : 3
forgets dying b., 385 : 1
gold-feathered b. sings in palm, 769 : 11
guides me and b., 540 : 7
half angel half b., 545 : 1
heart like singing b., 608 : 11
here and there b. or butterfly, 748 : 1
I sing as b. sings, 395 : 1
if men like wise b., 660 : 15
immortal b., 477 : 1
in gilded cage, 730 : 18
in hand worth two in bush, 120 : *n* 3
is in the sky, 300 : 19
is on the wing, 516 : 4
it was carol of b., 459 : 23
Jubjub b., 612 : 17
know why caged b. sings, 736 : 23
let no b. call, 822 : 14
like b. on wing, 688 : 12
live like stoic b., 793 : 18
loaf to every b., 606 : 6
man and b. and beast, 435 : 10
merged like the b., 874 : 13
night's sweet b., 469 : 14
no b. but invisible thing, 427 : 2
no b. soars too high, 404 : 2
no further than wanton's b., 192 : 18
O comfortable b., 475 : 18
of bad moral character, 348 : 13
of dawning, 217 : 26
of night did sit, 215 : 12
Bird (*continued*)
of wonder dies, 249 : 17
on b. turn envious look, 868 : 6
or devil, 526 : 17
perhaps singing b. come, 132 : 25
pinnace like fluttered b., 535 : 11
propitiatory b., 863 : 19
rare b. on earth, 122 : 8
rise up at the voice of the b., 27 : 24
said b. in musical voice, 846 : 15
sees white man come, 557 : 18
shall carry the voice, 27 : 19
silence with waking b., 533 : 22
small hot b., 666 : 15
soft-sigh me home, 873 : 12
soul of grandam inhabit b., 200 : *n* 3
sounds of small b. trying, 907 : 9
stamped foot, 605 : 7
swift as b. or thought, 60 : 2
that filleth own nest, 153 : 2
that shunnest noise of folly, 278 : 17
this her solemn b., 286 : 1
thou never wert, 468 : 11
thou warbling b., 409 : 24
to nest from wandering, 692 : 2
to others flew, 265 : 1
turkey a more respectable b., 348 : 13
uncontrollably cries, 901 : 12
with b. the abiding leaf, 875 : 4
wonderful b. is pelican, 765 : 12
Birdcage, like summer b. in garden, 165 : *n* 10
Birdless silence, 901 : 4
Bird's, consciousness like b. life, 648 : 13
night b. wail, 629 : 20
sweet b. throat, 211 : 1
Birds, all the tribes of b. sang, 138 : 7
are asleep in trees, 397 : 3
as b. caught in snare, 27 : 17
babes and sages, 536 : 6
bees stirring b. on wing, 436 : 9
began to sing, 931 : 9
blossoms b. and bowers, 265 : 17
chant ye little b., 409 : 24
charm of earliest b., 285 : 27
days when b. come back, 604 : 9
do sing, 250 : 8
eagle suffers little b. to sing, 188 : 21
fear b. of prey, 227 : 30
flowers fruits and many b., 150 : 16
flowing with b., 874 : 16
fly from their nests, 5 : 7
fly over the rainbow, 842 : 6
fly to calico tree, 550 : 12
if b. confabulate or no, 377 : 23
in little nests agree, 328 : 4
in the trees, 714 : 22
kinds of knowledge, 85 : 19
knew stars flowers b., 735 : 8
leaves snows, 864 : 2
little b. that fly, 329 : 13
man lived with b. and beasts, 90 : 7
melodious b. sing madrigals, 183 : 9
million golden b., 673 : 19
mind an aviary of b., 85 : 19
named b. without gun, 494 : 14
no b. happy as we, 551 : 7
no b. in last year's nest, 171 : 6
no b. sing, 478 : 10
not know too much about b., 577 : 8
not only fine feathers make fine b., 66 : 8
of a feather, 259 : 17

Birds (*continued*)
of air have nests, 38 : 23
other men catch b., 159 : 5
our lists of b., 893 : 8
sing like b. i' the cage, 235 : 12
sit brooding in snow, 191 : 15
their trackless way, 540 : 6
these are days b. come back, 604 : 9
time of the singing of b., 28 : 7
trees flowers watercraft, 577 : 8
unperplexed like migratory b., 756 : 8
warble sweet in springtime, 672 : 19
we are nest of singing b., 353 : 21
when b. do sing, 212 : 33
when small b. sighed, 874 : 1
where late sweet b. sang, 244 : 27
wild barbaric b., 857 : 15
wild b. rounding hill, 899 : 9
without despair to get in, 165 : 19
Birds', wind full of b. cries, 760 : 17
Birdsong at morning, 669 : 4
Birnam wood to Dunsinane, 239 : 12, 765 : 10
Birth and copulation and death, 806 : 10
Angel that presided o'er b., 407 : 3
as if b. sundered, 558 : 20
at b. our death sealed, 115 : 18
bed for this huge b., 292 : 17
befits proud b., 73 : 10
begins to die from b., 358 : 16
better world's in b., 555 : 24
between b. and dying, 806 : 5
boasts his b., 462 : 15
border nor breed nor b., 707 : 16
certain is b. for the dead, 94 : 8
creativeness conception and b., 704 : 13
day of one's b., 27 : 3
death borders upon our b., 257 : 12
dew of thy b., 173 : *n* 6
distinction of b. or fortune, 420 : 19
embraves this morn, 292 : 18
false idol or noble true b., 85 : 16
famous by their b., 194 : 13
fashion b. intellect, 593 : 1
foreigner in country of b., 916 : 12
from b. to age eighteen, 788 : 21
frowned not on humble b., 362 : 17
give b. astride grave, 866 : 13
grievous burden was thy b., 187 : 18
high b. vigor of bone, 226 : 20
honor land of b., 667 : 1
inquiries about events following b., 124 : 2
is sorrow, 72 : 23
land that gave you b., 700 : 6
life and death, 315 : 9
mourned at b. not death, 341 : 6
my love of b. as rare, 297 : 6
new b. of freedom, 523 : 4
no cure for b., 704 : 4
of ancient race by b., 304 : 15
of morning dew, 173 : 15
rejoice at b., 624 : 18
repeats story of her b., 325 : 9
Saviour's b. celebrated, 217 : 26
sleep and a forgetting, 426 : 14
starves her generous b., 361 : 17
sunshine a glorious b., 426 : 12
their b. weeping, 262 : 7
training rather than b., 312 : 23
Birthday of my life, 608 : 12
Birthplace of valor, 410 : 8
Birthplace (*continued*)
sell picturs of b., 616 : 22
Birthright, Esau sold his b., 8 : 16
Birthrights, bearing b. proudly, 201 : 11
Births, joyful b., 208 : 16
latent b. of vowels, 673 : 20
Birth-strangled babe, 239 : 6
Bis dat qui cito dat, 133 : 10
Biscay, bonny bonny B. O, 920 : 17
in the Bay of B. O, 415 : 6
Bishop, church without b., 484 : 20
hypocrisy of b., 391 : 2
Bit babies in cradles, 541 : 1
by him that comes behind, 322 : 21
dogs have a b., 929 : 22
hair of dog that b. us, 160 : 18
I b. my arm sucked blood, 434 : 18
though he had b. me, 235 : 7
went mad and b. the man, 369 : 18
Bitch, deciding not to be b., 844 : 12
gone in the teeth, 792 : 16
son of mongrel b., 233 : 13
toothless mastiff b., 433 : 28
Bitch-goddess Success, 648 : 4
Bite, bark and b., 328 : 2
bark worse than b., 270 : 25
bullet, 707 : 18
dead man cannot b., 99 : 13
dog prosperous will not b., 624 : 24
hand that fed them, 374 : 11
jaws that b., 612 : 17
man recovered of the b., 369 : 19
smaller still to b. 'em, 322 : 21
sorrow hath less power to b., 194 : 6
this fish will b., 209 : 18
Bites, air b. shrewdly, 219 : 8
Biteth like a serpent, 25 : 11
Biting, eager soul b. for anger, 276 : 15
Bitter all utterly things sweet, 829 : 20
all we know in love b., 811 : 15
as coloquintida, 230 : 4
as wormwood, 23 : 10
bark and burning clove, 748 : 9
bones, 863 : 19
bread of banishment, 194 : 25
chill it was, 476 : 8
do it with b. look, 676 : 8
every b. thing is sweet, 25 : 24
feed on b. fruit, 854 : 2
feel by turns b. change, 284 : 23
found Beauty b., 674 : 3
from fountain wells up b. taste, 101 : 7
groan of martyr's woe, 406 : 7
herbs, 9 : 24
if life b. pardon, 634 : 13
joy hear wings, 842 : 14
laugh my b. laugh, 518 : 11
love b. with treason, 633 : 6
make oppression b., 221 : 9
more b. than death, 27 : 10
mortals make earth b., 473 : 16
most b. is scornful jest, 351 : 8
nailed on b. cross, 202 : 22
news to hear, 591 : 9
O b. ending, 778 : 6
old and b. of tongue, 712 : 10
old law sad not b., 758 : 2
peaches, 314 : 2
read in the b. letter, 229 : 23
shed b. tear, 613 : 2
some b. o'er flowers, 457 : 2
sweet and b. fancy, 212 : 28
things conduce to sweet, 900 : 5
Bitter (*continued*)
'tis b. cold, 217 : 15
to have known love, 632 : 20
to look into happiness, 212 : 32
truth always b., 127 : 19
vintage of race problem, 800 : 9
Bitterest, this lot is b., 72 : 1
Bitterness, by convention b., 79 : 11
feeds me bread of b., 819 : 4
gall of b., 46 : 3
heart knoweth his own b., 23 : 36
I must have no b., 706 : 17
love without b., 822 : 9
mingles sweet b. with her cares, 102 : 10
of life, 614 : 6
of my soul, 30 : 28
of things, 429 : 7
rose's scent b., 693 : 6
Bitterns, London habitation of b., 488 : *n* 3
Bitters, mawkishness and b., 475 : 15
Bivouac of the dead, 578 : 10
Bizarre world of cards, 818 : 5
Blabbing eastern scout, 279 : 13
gaudy b. and remorseful day, 185 : 20
Blabs, when my tongue b., 213 : 9
Black A white E red I, 673 : 20
and midnight hags, 239 : 8
and unknown bards, 733 : 9
and white not blue, 892 : 9
and white separate as fingers, 681 : 24
as hell, 246 : 7
as if bereaved of light, 403 : 6
as night is black, 854 : 13
as our loss, 801 : 6
as pit from pole to pole, 663 : 10
as the devil, 400 : 15
as they might be, 927 : 2
bat night flown, 533 : 20
beautiful when, 900 : 15
black's not so b., 422 : 4
burn out to b., 691 : 15
burned b. with sun, 822 : 4
but comely, 28 : 2
consciousness, 916 : 12
control politics in own community, 904 : 14
creeping through the b., 765 : 6
devil damn thee b., 239 : 29
drop of b. blood, 855 : 3
evening white snow, 770 : 15
eyes and lemonade, 447 : 6
fat b. bucks, 765 : 5
folk say America would have been stronger, 875 : 10
Hecate's summons, 238 : 20
horseshoes are b., 841 : 12
hump b. and blue, 710 : 1
hung be heavens with b., 184 : 15
I am b. but O my soul is white, 403 : 6
I'm b. and I'm proud, 913 : 1
in B. Mud kingfisher, 892 : 4
institutions of splendid achievement, 914 : *n* 2
is beautiful, 925 : 14
let b. flower blossom, 503 : 9
let the devil wear b., 222 : 9
like me, 854 : 14
little b. sheep, 708 : 14
long b. land, 541 : 13
love is Black wealth, 916 : 2
love like b. our b., 889 : 17

Black (*continued*)
love of children whether b. or not, 837 : 20
men are pearls, 190 : 6
men fought on Coromandel, 488 : 11
my b. hen, 932 : 14
nationalism, 904 : 14
night's b. arch, 411 : 9
no b. person be deprived, 903 : 6
no b. raiment when I am gone, 95 : *n* 2
not so b. as painted, 177 : 5
Old B. Joe, 598 : 7
pall of nothing, 821 : 12
people unite, 914 : 15
played b. or white, 489 : 10
portent of atomic age, 729 : 12
pot calls kettle b., 170 : 36
power, 914 : 15
powerful, 855 : 3
ram tupping your ewe, 229 : 18
rank and file, 617 : 6
rock star, 906 : 6
secret b. midnight hags, 239 : 8
seek b. power, 914 : *n* 2
since b. womb held, 883 : 11
spirits and white, 261 : 22
spot to keep concealed, 599 : 7
star-studded lute wears b. sun, 514 : 9
suit of ancient b., 765 : 8
suits of solemn b., 218 : 2
swan rare bird, 122 : 8
these b. bodies, 403 : 7
thou readest b., 407 : 9
turkey gobbler, 928 : 17
two societies one b. one white, 872 : 14
ugly when black exploit blacks, 900 : 15
we b. and they white, 875 : 8
wet b. bough, 792 : 7
what is B. Spot, 668 : 6
white not neutralize b., 545 : 12
Widow death, 892 : 8
wings one b. other white, 289 : 2
wires grow on her head, 246 : 1
with gilt surcingles, 607 : 11
world b. green red yellow, 912 : 15
years like great b. oxen, 712 : 2
yellow b. pale hectic red, 467 : 17
Black Hawk fought for countrymen, 418 : 13
last sun shone on B., 418 : 12
Blackamoor, as if sun b., 767 : 6
Blackberries, reasons as plenty as b., 203 : 31
Blackbird snipped off nose, 931 : 9
than b. 'tis to whistle, 290 : 15
whistling or just after, 767 : 12
Blackbirds, four and twenty b., 931 : 9
sitting on a hill, 934 : 8
Blackens every blot, 534 : 1
skuttle fish b. water, 327 : 1
Blackest, Cerberus and b. Midnight, 277 : 17
perfect through b. air, 899 : 15
Blackguard whose faulty vision, 647 : 10
Blackguards, Hitlerite b., 766 : 9
Blackness, faces all gather b., 33 : 24
faces as b. of a kettle, 33 : *n* 2
in sudden b. the pall, 821 : 12
of darkness, 52 : 26
of death, 100 : 20
Blackness (*continued*)
power of b. in Hawthorne, 569 : 16
Black-purple, in gloom b., 742 : 9
Black's not so black, 422 : 4
Blacks, enemies of persecuted b., 505 : 11
human not inferior, 916 : 11
move beyond racism, 901 : 1
Black-sailed unfamiliar, 901 : 4
Bladder, blows man up like a b., 204 : 3
Bladders, boys that swim on b., 249 : 3
of philosophy, 315 : 20
Blade, destroy b. of grass, 741 : 16
first b. then ear, 42 : 1
grasp by b. or handle, 569 : 5
knife without a b., 386 : 16
of grass always blade of grass, 259 : *n* 3
trenchant b. Toledo trusty, 291 : 7
upper or under b. of scissors, 652 : 2
vorpal b., 612 : 18
Blade's, grass b. no easier than oak, 567 : 15
Blades, two b. of grass grow, 322 : 12
which b. bears better temper, 184 : 20
Blade-straight, steel-true and b., 669 : 8
Blaine marched down halls, 615 : 4
Blaize, lament for Madame B., 368 : 7
Blake, dance with William B., 875 : 4
William B. beat on wall, 717 : 10
Blame, alike reserved to b., 338 : 14
bloody full of b., 245 : 23
needless to b. things past, 68 : 12
neither is most to b., 634 : 3
no dispraise or b., 289 : 9
no reason to b. Trojans, 57 : 24
or b. it too much, 371 : 14
poor wot gets b., 924 : 11
praise at morning b. at night, 333 : 14
praise nor b. writings, 333 : 12
praise or b. momentary, 479 : 13
praise or b. too far, 749 : 14
secret thoughts without b., 264 : 16
take some iv th' b. oursilves, 722 : 16
ungrateful man less to b., 293 : 18
yet not afraid to b., 333 : 22
Blame-all and Praise-all blockheads, 347 : 5
Blamed living man, 587 : 17
Blameless life, 534 : 1
vestal's lot, 335 : 4
Blameworthy, least b. was Confucius, 375 : 2
the other strife is b., 61 : 12
Blaming, always b. circumstances, 680 : 5
mortals are b. the gods, 59 : 15
Blanch, Tray B. and Sweetheart, 234 : 15
without owner's crime, 428 : 23
Blanching, under b. mays, 692 : 5
Bland as a Jesuit, 663 : 7
cruel composed b., 588 : 4
Blandishing persuasion, 58 : 19
Blandishments not fascinate us, 393 : 9
Blank, a b. my lord, 214 : 5
bumbast out b. verse, 178 : 12
our b. in bliss to fill, 604 : 5
page difficult mirror, 850 : 17
pain has element of b., 606 : 2
this void the b. page, 851 : 1
universal b., 285 : 5
Blanket of the dark, 236 : 18
old woman tossed in b., 932 : 5
Blanket (*continued*)
pulling b. from eastern sky, 928 : 9
sleeping is a wool b., 82 : 21
Blankets, people have no b., 642 : 7
rough male kiss of b., 796 : 16
Blare of bugles ruffle of drums, 676 : *n* 5
Blaspheme what they do not know, 300 : 13
Blasphemies, great truths begin as b., 681 : 10
Blasphemy, in soldier is flat b., 228 : 11
Mass the greatest b., 156 : 6
middle-class b., 681 : 9
Blast, contrary b. proclaims, 289 : 2
drives wicked spirits, 140 : 22
midnight b., 462 : 1
of no b. he died, 303 : 16
of war blows in our ears, 207 : 16
one b. upon bugle horn, 431 : 15
spread wings on b., 459 : 15
stormy b., 328 : 10
striding the b., 236 : 24
Blast-beruffled plume, 641 : 12
Blasted with antiquity, 206 : 1
with excess of light, 363 : 2
with the east wind, 8 : 31
Blastments, contagious b. imminent, 218 : 27
Blasts, hollow b. of wind, 331 : 7
icy b. blow on love, 583 : 15
newborn infant's tear, 405 : 10
night b. cold, 742 : 9
roots of trees, 886 : 12
Blatant Bassarid of Boston, 634 : 9
Blaze, burst out into sudden b., 280 : 15
dark amid b. of noon, 288 : 20
heavens b. forth, 215 : 25
the sapphire b., 363 : 2
Blazing evidence of immortality, 496 : 1
heaven b. into head, 717 : 6
in gold quenching in purple. 604 : 16
no more b. hearth, 362 : 1
potentates b. in the heavens, 71 : 3
tail, 767 : 6
Blazon of sweet beauty's best, 245 : 12
Blazoning, quirks of b. pens, 230 : 7
Bleached, driftwood b. and dry, 621 : 17
Bleak December, 526 : 11
in b. midwinter frosty wind, 608 : 17
Bleakness, country of b., 518 : 8
Blear-eyed wisdom, 715 : 17
Bleat the one at the other, 246 : 10
Bleats articulate monotony, 428 : *n* 2
Bled, buried Caesar b., 516 : 12
in freedom's cause, 422 : 21
Scots wha hae wi' Wallace b., 411 : 15
Bleed awhile, 926 : *n* 7
carcasses b. at sight of murderer, 148 : *n* 1
heart begins to b., 929 : 9
I fall upon thorns I b., 467 : 20
if you prick us do we not b., 199 : 18
my bones, 875 : 1
Bleeding brow of labor, 694 : *n* 4
from Roman rods, 377 : 22
piece of earth, 216 : 11
purple testament of b. war, 195 : 4
Blemish, Christianity immortal b., 658 : 17
evidence of industry b., 619 : 6
formed without b., 67 : 16
lamb shall be without b., 9 : 23
Blendings of death and life, 637 : 17

Blent, beauty truly b., 213 : 17
Bless bed I lie on, 294 : *n* 5
except thou b. me, 8 : 25
God b. the Pretender, 341 : 12
God b. us every one, 548 : 11
God b. you, 921 : 3
God b. you my dear, 357 : 5
hand that gave blow, 304 : 20
her when she is riggish, 241 : 1
his name, 21 : 3
hold angel until he b. thee, 346 : 14
house from wikked wight, 146 : 30
I b. God in libraries, 365 : 10
Lord b. and keep thee, 10 : 23
man who invented sleep, 556 : 2
squire and relations, 548 : 15
thee Bottom, 196 : 26
them that curse you, 37 : 11
turf that wraps clay, 364 : 9
ye the Lord, 36 : 14
Blessed Abbot of Aberbrothok, 439 : 17
abodes, 335 : 9, 336 : 18
all generations call me b., 42 : 21
always to be b., 336 : 15
are the dead, 53 : 24
are the forgetful, 657 : 24
are the meek, 37 : 4
are the merciful, 37 : 4
are the peacemakers, 37 : 4, 185 : 11
are the poor in spirit, 37 : 4
are the pure in heart, 37 : 4
are they that mourn, 37 : 4
are they that put their trust in him, 17 : 14
are they which are persecuted, 37 : 4
are they which hunger and thirst, 37 : 4
are ye when men revile you, 37 : 4
art thou among women, 42 : 17
barrier between day and day, 428 : 3
be he that cometh, 22 : 1
be Lord God of Israel, 42 : 24
be man that spares these stones, 250 : 1
be the name of the Lord, 15 : 4
bed be b. that I lie on, 294 : 16
by country's wishes b., 364 : 8
by everything, 716 : 3
by yonder b. moon, 192 : 11
candles of night, 201 : 8
children call her b., 26 : 9
come what may been b., 459 : 4
damozel, 601 : 13
endless sabbaths b. ones see, 136 : 7
fell upon knees and b. God, 265 : 7
green groves of the b., 105 : 21
half part of b. man, 201 : 16
he who has found his work, 474 : 6
hope whereof he knew, 641 : 13
horny hands of toil, 567 : 2
I had lived a b. time, 238 : 7
is man who expects nothing, 336 : 6
is the fruit of thy womb, 42 : 19
is the man that trusteth, 32 : 11
is the man that walketh not in counsel of ungodly, 17 : 12
judge none b., 35 : 22
kings may be b., 411 : 7
little b. with soft phrase, 229 : 24
Lord b. the latter end of Job, 17 : 11
love of God had b., 454 : 7
man who expects nothing, 336 : 6
man who possesses keen mind, 82 : 22
memory of the just is b., 23 : 22
Blessed (*continued*)
mood, 423 : 10
more b. to give, 46 : 23
mother of us all, 390 : 5
mutter of Mass, 541 : 20
nor what b. prove accursed, 544 : 29
over whose acres b. feet, 202 : 22
part to heaven, 249 : 11
plot this earth, 194 : 13
quarry mine b. am I, 929 : 2
rage for order, 767 : 16
seeming b. they grow, 368 : 19
soul or body more b., 717 : 8
sprung from b. abodes, 335 : 9
them unaware, 434 : 29
they that have not seen, 45 : 37
thou fallest a b. martyr, 249 : 8
thrice and four times b., 104 : 19
to put cares away, 101 : 23
twice b., 200 : 9
were but as b. as I, 329 : 13
who have no talent, 495 : 27
who having nothing to say, 565 : 30
whom thou blessest is b., 11 : 1
with milk and honey b., 563 : 13
with natural abundance, 824 : 12
youth becomes as aged, 228 : 16
Blessedness, perfect b. vision of God, 140 : 2
single b., 195 : 21
Blesses stars and thinks it luxury, 325 : 13
Blessest, whom thou b. is blessed, 11 : 1
Blesseth him that gives and him that takes, 200 : 9
Blessing, alien b. on its way, 907 : 19
and cursing, 11 : 22
ask me b., 235 : 12
baby b. and bother, 622 : 17
brother hath taken away thy b., 8 : 18
good neighbor is great b., 61 : 18
haste haste has no b., 925 : 27
hold fast till gives b., 513 : 5
I had most need of b., 237 : 20
makes a b. dear, 290 : 5
money cannot buy, 271 : 13
national debt b., 401 : 10, 450 : 12
no harm in b., 341 : 12
of St. Peter's Master, 271 : 14
out of God's b. into sun, 160 : 32
paid thy utmost b., 739 : 17
public debt a public b., 401 : *n* 6
science be b. not curse, 763 : 8
society is a b., 384 : 9
unqualified b., 419 : 4
war b. compared with reign of lie, 817 : 4
Blessings, free trade one of b., 487 : 5
God from whom all b. flow, 311 : 19
health and intellect the two b., 91 : 11
health greatest of b., 80 : 8
of civilization, 625 : 25
on him who invented sleep, 171 : 1
on thee little man, 513 : 10
on this house, 382 : 1
on your frosty pow, 410 : 7
one of evils and another of b., 59 : 12
reap b. of freedom, 384 : 17
secure b. of liberty, 391 : 10
two supreme b., 77 : 6
unequal sharing of b., 746 : 16
upon head of the just, 23 : 22
use b. of gods with wisdom, 108 : 14
without number, 328 : 8
Blessings-of-civilization trust, 625 : 25
Blew, fair breeze b., 434 : 13
great guns, 549 : 11
slughorn to my lips and b., 234 : *n* 3
Blicke nicht trauernd, 510 : *n* 2
Blight man was born for, 656 : 10
Blighted, seared and b. heart, 525 : 4
Blights with plagues, 405 : 10
Blind and ignorant in all, 251 : 6
and naked ignorance, 534 : 10
as nails upon Cross, 801 : 6
beggar's daughter, 926 : 17
Booth died b., 765 : 2
causes conspire to b., 332 : 19
ecstasy, 844 : 1
eyes for the b., 615 : 6
eyes of the b. shall be opened, 30 : 24
eyes to the b., 16 : 17
for being b. God prepare me, 310 : 17
Fortune painted b. with muffler, 181 : *n* 2
Fortune though b. not invisible, 181 : 5
Fury with abhorred shears, 280 : 15
guides, 40 : 19
halt and b., 43 : 23
he was as often seene, 146 : 23
Homer sing to me, 184 : 3
I was b., 45 : 8
justice b. deef and dumb, 722 : 1
Justice is b., 876 : 5
leaders of the blind, 39 : 31
leading blind to pit, 127 : 13
love is b., 147 : 23, 199 : 7
love needs be b., 196 : *n* 1
love to faults always b., 404 : 14
man's ditch, 716 : 2
mouths, 280 : 21
none so b., 319 : 11
O b. hearts, 100 : 13
obedience to command, 690 : 9
oblivion swallowed cities, 226 : 15
old mad b. despised king, 468 : 4
right to be b. sometimes, 408 : 5
three b. mice, 929 : 11
till some b. hand, 405 : 6
Tiresias though b., 805 : 7
to faults a little b., 320 : 17
urge to kill b., 912 : 9
was b. but now I see, 367 : 7
winged Cupid painted b., 196 : 1
wretched b. pit ponies, 732 : 16
Blinded boy, 917 : 18
Blinder, be a little b., 774 : 5
Blindly, had we never loved sae b., 410 : 3
Blindness about poverty, 908 : 5
heathen in his b., 452 : 10
ignorance and b., 839 : 14
we may forgive, 728 : 14
Blinds, drawing-down of b., 827 : 5
too much light often b., 380 : 4
Blindworms, newts and b. do no wrong, 196 : 21
Blink facts not to our taste, 580 : 6
Blinked, other fellow b., 925 : *n* 7
Bliss and bale, 653 : 15
beyond happiness is b., 819 : 9
bought by years, 561 : 21
contrary bringeth b., 185 : 7
cuckold lives in b., 230 : 34
deprived of everlasting b., 183 : 21
happy be and have immortal b., 173 : 17

Bliss (*continued*)
he lives in b., 411 : 22
heart intoxicated with b., 413 : 21
hours of b., 443 : 8
in our brows bent, 240 : 18
in proof, 245 : 23
kill and b. me, 918 : 2
like thine, 561 : 21
mutual and partaken b., 279 : 31
need of imperishable b., 767 : 3
never parted b. or woe, 287 : 23
no right to b., 585 : 7
not beds of down, 267 : 10
O b. O poop-poop, 690 : 15
of dying, 333 : 23
of human b. to human woe, 290 : 8
of solitude, 427 : 11
our blank in b., 604 : 5
perfect b. and sole felicity, 183 : 6
pneumatic b., 804 : 23
shadow's b., 199 : 15
soul in b., 235 : 8
source of all my b., 371 : 1
sum of earthly b., 287 : 7
waking b., 279 : 20
was it in that dawn, 424 : 5
where ignorance is b., 361 : 12
which centers in mind, 369 : 5
Blisses about my pilgrimage, 640 : 3
Blissful dreams of long ago, 636 : 2
Blister, never had b. in hand, 82 : 2
thirst b. easier, 605 : 1
Blithe, buxom b. and debonair, 277 : 18
Irish lad, 443 : 9
newcomer, 427 : 1
no lark more b. than he, 382 : 6
spirit, 468 : 11
Blizzard bad as ever, 726 : 6
Bloc, Communist b., 862 : 20
Block, chip of old b., 373 : 11
do not b. way of inquiry, 639 : 5
each b. cut smooth, 792 : 20
mind a b. of wax, 85 : 18
Blockhead, bookful b., 333 : 19
no man but a b., 355 : 20
Blockheads, Blame-all Praise-all b., 347 : 5
read what blockheads write, 342 : 11
Blocks, towns you built of b., 839 : 20
Blond beast, 658 : 5
more b. than you, 829 : 11
Blondes, gentlemen prefer b., 826 : 3
Blood, all nations one b., 46 : 16
and fire, 680 : 30
bath, 783 : 18
be on your own heads, 46 : 18
bit arm sucked b., 434 : 18
blow in cold b., 680 : 25
burns in veins, 576 : 16
by man shall his b. be shed, 8 : 2
Christ's b. streams, 184 : 8
created man of b. clot, 132 : 17
created you of b. clot, 131 : 14
crusted with b., 798 : 1
cry aloud for b., 579 : 3
devise laws for b., 198 : 10
drenched in fraternal b., 450 : 15
drop of manly b., 495 : 19
earth one mighty b. spot, 503 : 2
effusion of b., 701 : 2
every drop of b. drawn, 524 : 7
faith beats with b., 531 : 14
felt in the b., 423 : 8
fizz like wine, 760 : 5

Blood (*continued*)
flesh and b. so cheap, 485 : 20
for this all that b. shed, 713 : 11
freeze thy young b., 219 : 18
future smells of b., 482 : 4
glories of our b. and state, 272 : 15
good enough to shed b., 687 : 8
good honest fighting b., 661 : 4
guiltless of country's b., 362 : 9
hand raised to shed b., 336 : 13
harbors I by sweating b. won, 151 : 10
heart dry of b., 478 : 8
her young suck up b., 17 : 1
heyday in the b. is tame, 223 : 4
his b. be on us, 41 : 23
impetuous b., 425 : 1
impure b. drench field, 415 : *n* 1
in b. stepped in so far, 239 : 3
in torrents pour, 684 : 14
inhabits our frail b., 214 : 26
insatiate b., 874 : 17
iron and b., 553 : 6
is nipped and ways be foul, 191 : 14
is their argument, 208 : 4
is their thinking, 75 : 24
it will have b. they say, 239 : 1
liquors in my b., 210 : 29
lust for b. and plunder, 745 : 2
magic to stir men's b., 661 : 3
make thick my b., 236 : 17
man of flesh and b., 705 : 12
man whose b. is snow-broth, 227 : 28
man whose b. is warm, 197 : 29
meditate on b., 208 : 17
mingle b. with b. of children, 486 : 16
more stirs to rouse lion, 203 : 14
more things move than b. in heart, 837 : 3
Negro b. sure powerful, 855 : 3
new testament in my b., 48 : 21
no Jewish b. in my veins, 912 : 11
no sure foundation on b., 202 : 8
nor can b. be in sticks, 101 : 1
Norman b., 528 : 11
not a drop of b. shed, 389 : 13
not against flesh and b., 49 : 39
not see b. of Ignacio, 841 : 16
odor of b. Christ slain, 715 : 12
of a poet, 818 : 3
of an Englishman, 934 : 4
of Christians is seed, 126 : 3
of followers, 815 : 13
of martyrs seed of Church, 126 : *n* 2
of nation never be shed, 316 : 14
of our heroes, 389 : 2
of patriots and tyrants, 388 : 7
of the lamb, 53 : 15
of the new testament, 41 : 10
of the slaughtered, 733 : 6
of the world, 830 : 11
of this just person, 41 : 22
oh b. that freezes b. that burns, 542 : 4
old man had so much b., 239 : 25
one b. ye and I, 709 : 2
own b. rise against you, 735 : *n* 1
part of the sea, 790 : 21
pint of sweat save gallon of b., 792 : 4
poet's feverish b., 585 : 18
poisoned with b. of both, 911 : 1
present joys more to flesh and b., 305 : 25
pulsing in our spirits and b., 888 : 6
pure and eloquent b., 254 : 6

Blood (*continued*)
rather than water on hands, 859 : 13
rivers older that flow of b., 854 : 12
scatter b. to eight points of wind, 850 : 1
sets gypsy b. astir, 696 : 10
shakes hacks spits b., 824 : 6
shed by immortal King, 139 : 9
shed for bureaucratic ideal, 775 : 7
shed for you and for many, 54 : 7
sheds his b. with me, 208 : 11
sign to know gentle b., 174 : 20
smell b. of British man, 234 : 13
souls of b., 792 : 6
spend her b. and might, 682 : 13
spill no drop of b., 643 : 2
sprinkled upon garments, 31 : 26
still b. is strong, 483 : 20
stir men's b., 216 : 28
strong as flesh and b., 428 : 4
strong wyn reed as b., 146 : 13
such impetuous b., 425 : 1
summon up the b., 207 : 16
sun's o'ercast with b., 201 : 22
sweat and tear-wrung millions, 743 : *n* 2
sweat on drill ground save b. on battlefield, 792 : *n* 2
sweating b., 151 : 10
tears sweat or b., 743 : *n* 2
thick water's thin, 629 : 2
thicker than water, 301 : 15
thicks man's b. with cold, 434 : 19
this is my b., 41 : 10
to drink, 503 : 17
toil tears sweat, 743 : 19
trade of b. and guile, 435 : 21
tree of liberty refreshed with b., 388 : 7
trilling wire in b., 807 : 4
up to eyes in b., 372 : 8
vigor flows into my b., 819 : 4
voice of thy brother's b., 7 : 16
wash this b. from hand, 238 : 1
watered by b. of tyrants, 401 : 4
weltering in his b., 306 : 18
what little b. is left, 760 : 5
when the b. burns, 219 : 6
whoso sheddeth man's b., 8 : 2
will have blood, 239 : 1
without shedding of b., 51 : 17
young b. have its course, 566 : 14
young b. not obey old decree, 190 : 33
Blood-dimmed tide loosed, 714 : 12
Blooded, an abstraction b., 768 : 14
Bloodless sportsman I, 685 : 10
substitute for life, 667 : 21
week of repose, 82 : *n* 6
Blood-red banner, 452 : 7
sunset glorious b., 541 : 18
wine, 926 : 9
Blood's a rover, 690 : 18
Bloodshed, fear and b., 427 : 22
no more b., 882 : 1
no more war or b., 895 : 17
Bloodstream, O Altitudo in b. swims, 812 : 1
Blood-swollen, war b. god, 732 : 1
Bloodthirsty guttersnipe, 745 : 2
Blood-tinctured of humanity, 506 : 14
Bloody and invisible hand, 238 : 21
be b. bold and resolute, 239 : 10
book of law, 229 : 23
but unbowed, 663 : 10

Bloody (*continued*)
dark and b. ground, 578 : 11
egg yolk, 897 : 6
even so my b. thoughts, 231 : 18
full of blame, 245 : 23
iron curtain, 746 : *n* 2
mothers a b. brood, 834 : 5
often wipe b. nose, 331 : 15
sang within the b. wood, 804 : 25
sweats, 676 : 11
treason flourished, 216 : 25
win war rise b., 889 : 10
Bloom along the bough, 690 : 16
flower b. another year, 478 : 9
flowers that b. in spring, 629 : 15
full on thy b., 409 : 10
how can ye b., 409 : 24
is gone, 587 : 9
its b. is shed, 411 : 8
kill b. before its time, 428 : 23
lemon trees b., 395 : 3
look at things in b., 690 : 17
make deserts b., 851 : 15
meadow flower b. unfold, 429 : 12
now withering in my b., 334 : 27
o'er folded b., 665 : 7
of young Desire, 362 : 21
perfect in bud as in b., 619 : 7
sight of vernal b., 285 : 5
sort of b. on woman, 694 : 10
spoiling b. of memory, 684 : 7
water lily b., 528 : 27
well in prison air, 676 : 13
with the b. go I, 587 : 9
Bloomed, when lilacs in dooryard b., 576 : 2
Bloomin' cosmopolouse, 709 : 13
lyre, 708 : 24
shame, 924 : 11
Blooming, conduct b. in whirlwind, 889 : 20
left b. alone, 446 : 14
Blooms each thing, 250 : 8
o'er folded b., 665 : 7
Bloomy, nightingale on b. spray, 281 : 8
Blossom by blossom spring begins, 632 : 8
desert b. as the rose, 30 : 23
every b. on bush, 607 : 12
in purple and red, 533 : 25
in the dust, 272 : 13
leaf b. or bole, 715 : 17
let black flower b., 503 : 9
May when lusty heart b., 149 : 13
squash b. dies, 905 : 15
that hangs on bough, 248 : 16
Blossomed lovely stars, 511 : 3
Blossomer, great rooted b., 715 : 17
Blossoming, labor b. or dancing, 715 : 17
Blossoms, apple b. fill air, 811 : 5
birds and bowers, 265 : 17
new life b. in ruins, 414 : 2
of my sin, 219 : 24
rose in my heart, 712 : 12
tomorrow b., 249 : 3
Blot, art to b., 339 : 27
blackens every b., 534 : 1
discreetly b., 276 : 11
in thy scutcheon, 170 : 31
Lord b. out his name, 308 : *n* 2
on escutcheon of Common Law, 638 : 8
out his name, 53 : 4
sin and b., 646 : 5
Blot (*continued*)
where is the b., 546 : 1
Blotted from life's page, 457 : 10
out man's image, 712 : 7
Shakespeare never b. line, 256 : 21
unpleasantest words that b. paper, 199 : 30
word out forever, 360 : 17
would he had b. a thousand, 256 : 21
Blotter, write in b. I was born, 810 : 8
Blow, all aloud wind doth b., 191 : 15
and swallow at same moment, 94 : 5
as straws that b., 663 : 9
bless hand that gave b., 304 : 20
breathe and b., 530 : 25
buds forgot to b., 637 : 22
bugle blow, 530 : 26
but a word and a b., 306 : 3
come from moon and b., 530 : 25
death loves signal b., 330 : 16
east wind never b., 270 : 32
first b. half battle, 371 : 9
for freedom, 798 : 6
genius gave final b., 456 : 17
great winds shorewards b., 584 : 11
high blow low and so sailed we, 935 : 3
him again to me, 530 : 25
horrid deed in every eye, 236 : 24
hot and cold, 66 : 17
I the b. and cheek, 581 : 1
I will b. you out, 594 : 13
in cold blood not forgiven, 680 : 25
know what wood by the b., 291 : 16
liberty's in every b., 411 : 16
might be the be-all, 236 : 22
north wind doth b., 932 : 6
on whom I please, 211 : 10
out you bugles, 797 : 4
pay with a deadly b., 71 : 16
pealing organ b., 278 : 26
perhaps return the b., 422 : 5
selfsame winds that b., 669 : 21
stormy winds do b., 273 : 7, 443 : 11
struck a deep mortal b., 71 : 9
the man down, 934 : 17
thou winter wind, 211 : 16
through life like breeze, 855 : 17
trumpet to arms, 384 : 8
up an' gie them a b., 417 : 7
upon my garden, 28 : 14
when wilt thou b., 917 : 10
who would be free strike b., 457 : 8
wind come wrack, 240 : 6
wind sall b., 927 : 5
winds crack your cheeks, 233 : 24
word and a b., 193 : 4
wreathed horn, 428 : 1
ye winds heigh ho, 935 : 5
your trumpets angels, 254 : 8
Bloweth med, 916 : 14
spirit b. and is still, 584 : 18
wind b. where it listeth, 44 : 32
Blowin' in the wind, 915 : 3
what bugles b. for, 708 : 1
Blowing, Elfland faintly b., 531 : 1
furious winter b., 810 : 17
new direction of Time, 790 : 9
noise of tongues, 527 : 22
of dry dust, 792 : 19
strong nor'wester's b. Bill, 429 : 19
thoughts go b. through them, 796 : 15
what are bugles b. for, 708 : 1
Blown buds of barren flowers, 633 : 20
Blown (*continued*)
by wind of criticism, 357 : 2
crimes broad b., 222 : 27
dust that is b. away, 34 : 16
hair is sweet, 806 : 2
pipe b. by surmises, 205 : 18
what though mast b. overboard, 186 : 23
with restless violence, 228 : 20
Blows, apostolic b. and knocks, 291 : 5
blast of war b. in ears, 207 : 16
cruel wind b., 864 : 2
Dick the shepherd b. his nail, 191 : 14
driven by invisible b., 790 : 10
dust b. in your face, 234 : 22
feather for each wind that b., 246 : 17
from yon far country b., 691 : 9
grass must bend when wind b., 69 : 2
ill wind b. no man good, 161 : 11
it in my face, 221 : 8
man up like a bladder, 204 : 3
meanest flower that b., 426 : 23
never b. so red, 516 : 12
soft zephyr b., 363 : 6
taught by rod and b., 156 : 1
to know which way the wind b., 915 : 7
vile b. and buffets, 238 : 15
which way hot air b., 699 : 18
wild thyme b., 196 : 18
wind b. cradle rock, 660 : 19
wind b. it back again, 406 : 3
wind from blue heaven b., 395 : 3
wind that b. through me, 790 : 9
Blude-red wine, 926 : 9
Bludgeoning, democracy means b., 675 : 24
Bludgeonings of chance, 663 : 10
Blue, against b. a pine tree, 317 : 16
all the time a-feelin' b., 684 : 18
all's b., 545 : 23
and gold mistake, 604 : 9
Aryan eye bright b., 911 : 17
beneath b. of day, 691 : 1
Big B. Mountain Spirit, 928 : 16
breeches b., 440 : 14
buff and the b., 411 : 24
color source of delight, 572 : 16
daisies pied and violets b., 191 : 13
darkened on blueness, 791 : 1
darkly deeply b., 440 : 2, 461 : 13
estuaries, 837 : 2
ethereal sky, 325 : 8
forked torch of flower, 791 : 1
fragmentary b., 748 : 1
fresh ever free, 456 : 3
freshest b., 767 : 14
going home looking b., 702 : 1
grappling in central b., 529 : 24
hammer of red and b., 768 : 2
hands b., 550 : 11
home made of b. clouds, 928 : 16
hump black and b., 710 : 1
inns of molten b., 604 : 14
into b. and gold into morning, 739 : 5
kingfisher dives, 892 : 4
lavender's b., 933 : 13
little boy b. blow horn, 930 : 12
Little Boy B. kissed them, 666 : 17
little tent of b., 676 : 6
living air and b. sky, 423 : 13
morning-glory b. and cool, 902 : 13
night one b. dew, 875 : 11
not b. on Boston, 892 : 9

Blue (*continued*)
O, 673 : 20
ocean b. as cornflower, 505 : 3
October's bright b. weather, 609 : 11
old books old Nankin b., 179 : *n* 4
pine needles, 314 : 6
Presbyterian true b., 291 : 3
promontory with trees, 241 : 17
remembered hills, 691 : 9
rest of heaven b., 525 : 6
rhapsody in b., 842 : 2
rushing of arrowy Rhone, 457 : 27
sky bends over all, 434 : 2
sky of spring, 594 : 3
something b., 924 : 6
true b., 291 : 3
twitched his mantle b., 281 : 6
unclouded weather, 528 : 25
unholy b., 446 : 13
wave rolls nightly, 459 : 14
wings were b., 550 : 12
Bluebeard's chaplain said, 546 : 19
Bluebird carries sky, 557 : 10
Bluebirds, over rainbow b. fly, 842 : 6
Blue-eyed boy, 828 : 13
Blue-fringed lids, 435 : 16
Blue-massing clouds, 796 : 16
Blueness abundant, 546 : 1
blue darkened on b., 791 : 1
Blues, from b. American music, 733 : 14
I got the Weary B., 854 : 15
Twentieth-Century b., 843 : 11
Bluestocking, sagacious b., 488 : 12
Bluffer, weather a great b., 847 : 8
Blume, du bist wie eine B., 481 : *n* 8
Blunder, frae monie a b. free us, 409 : 8
made by commanders, 815 : 14
man b. of God or God of man, 658 : 10
so grotesque a b., 753 : 5
worse than crime it is b., 415 : 3
youth a b., 501 : 15
Blunderbuss against religion, 354 : 2
Blundered, someone had b., 533 : 11
Blundering kind of melody, 304 : 17
learning b. people live on, 761 : 15
moth b. by, 874 : 17
Blunders, forgetful get better of b., 657 : 24
like ropes, 491 : 21
nature never makes b., 561 : 15
round meaning, 338 : 13
Blunt monster with uncounted heads, 205 : 18
plain b. man, 216 : 27
Blush, born to b. unseen, 362 : 8
fair regions raise our b., 399 : 18
nymphs b. not he, 601 : 3
shame where is thy b., 223 : 5
to find it fame, 339 : 14
to give it in, 360 : *n* 2
to make man b., 459 : 11
truth does not b., 126 : 7
Blushed at herself, 229 : 26
saw its God and b., 292 : 5
Blushes at the name, 592 : 2
into wine, 292 : *n* 3
man only animal that b., 625 : 11
who b. at name, 592 : 2
Blushful Hippocrene, 476 : 23
Blushing, bears his b. honors, 249 : 3
flowers shall rise, 332 : 12
religion b. veils fires, 340 : 28
Blustering, pity from b. wind, 296 : 5
Blut, Eisen und B., 553 : *n* 2
Blut (*continued*)
O Haupt vol B. und Wunden, 276 : *n* 4
Blynken, Wynken B. and Nod, 666 : 16
Boanerges, neigh like B., 605 : 19
Board, back to the old drawing b., 858 : 18
dim on Bristol b., 878 : 19
get on b. little children, 936 : 5
heart for bed and b., 892 : 16
here on drawing b. fingers, 904 : 6
money in ginger jar, 618 : 16
struck the b., 268 : 21
well-benched ships, 62 : 18
Boards, ships are but b., 198 : 17
Boast, frantic b., 709 : 20
having my freedom b. of nothing, 194 : 4
let not him that girdeth on his harness b., 14 : 6
not b. who puts armor on, 512 : 13
not of what thou wouldst have done, 289 : 5
not thyself of tomorrow, 25 : 21
now b. thee death, 242 : 5
of heraldry, 362 : 3
of this I can, 194 : 8
such is the patriot's b., 368 : 15
Boasters, great nations not b., 498 : 21
Boasteth, when he is gone his way then he b., 24 : 30
Boastful, high and b. neighs, 208 : 1
in war daring b., 463 : 13
Boasting, strength without b., 388 : 12
Boasts, that which b. his birth, 462 : 15
Boat, carry Caesar in your b., 99 : 20
drifts quietly, 873 : 16
forefathers met the b., 766 : 5
is on the shore, 460 : 4
Michael row b. ashore, 935 : 25
news of the b., 496 : 11
of life be light, 692 : 15
pea-green b., 550 : 7
sings in b. on bay, 530 : 19
speed bonny b., 688 : 12
they sank my b., 890 : 2
Boats against the current, 835 : 8
messing about in b., 690 : 14
oh the little cargo b., 709 : 8
shallow bauble b., 225 : 36
that are not steered, 243 : 29
Boatswain, memory of B. a dog, 456 : 9
tight and midshipmite, 627 : 7
Bobolink for chorister, 605 : 4
Bobtail nag, 598 : 2
Boca, el pez muere por la b., 935 : 11
en b. cerrada no entran moscas, 935 : 13
Bodes some strange eruption, 217 : 18
Bodice, loosens fragrant b., 476 : 17
Bodies a living sacrifice, 47 : 18
abstain from abusing b., 79 : 13
are buried in peace, 36 : 12
as clothes to b., 698 : 8
as imagination b. forth, 197 : 12
clothes without b., 698 : 8
died before b. died, 869 : 1
elements or principles of b., 390 : 8
freedom of living b., 551 : 18
gave b. to commonwealth, 81 : 5
ghosts of defunct b. fly, 291 : 2
house b. but not souls, 782 : 15
loneliness love b., 849 : 12
molecules that compose b., 390 : 8
Bodies (*continued*)
movements of largest b., 397 : 17
mutual actions of two b., 313 : 15
nature works by b. unseen, 100 : 8
of unburied men, 262 : 3
our b. are our gardens, 230 : 2
our selves our souls and b., 55 : 19
persons with torn b. happy, 732 : 3
piecemeal our b. are dying, 791 : 3
pile b. at Austerlitz, 761 : 6
princes like to heavenly b., 180 : 19
rough notes and dead b., 726 : 5
single soul in two b., 87 : 1
soldiers bore dead b. by, 203 : 8
these black b., 403 : 7
thrown into sea, 850 : 11
unclothed, 254 : 3
wavy b. 'gainst streams, 475 : 1
we have seen dead b., 486 : 13
Bodiless and simple, 899 : 12
Bodily decrepitude wisdom, 716 : 20
exercise when compulsory, 84 : 21
form from natural thing, 715 : 3
form of them b., 634 : 4
states following perception, 649 : 7
Boding tremblers, 370 : 10
Bodkin, bare b., 221 : 12
Body, absent in b. present in spirit, 48 : 8
age and b. of the time, 222 : 2
and spirit twins, 634 : 14
art work of b. and soul, 572 : 15
Asclepius cured the b., 83 : *n* 3
beautiful passionate b., 632 : 13
book makes b. cold, 608 : 6
carry b. for sentimental value, 870 : 2
changed to light, 929 : 6
clog of his b., 276 : 15
collective b. and common spirit, 895 : 21
continues in state of rest, 313 : 13
damned of b. and soul, 707 : 19
demd damp b., 547 : 15
dies body's beauty lives, 767 : 10
distressed in mind b. or estate, 55 : 6
droops debarred from air, 448 : 6
dungeon yet palaces, 668 : 21
each cell within b., 863 : 16
each petty artery in b., 219 : 15
employ b. to serve, 102 : 21
filled and vacant mind, 208 : 7
find thy b. by wall, 588 : 3
gave b. to country's earth, 195 : 8
gin b. meet b., 919 : *n* 2
give b. to be burned, 48 : 23
happiness beneficial for b., 734 : 12
health intelligence talent, 695 : 3
her b. thought, 254 : 6
here in the b. pent, 429 : 17
human b. sacred, 575 : 5
I have risen to a b., 905 : 16
ideals in one dark b., 724 : 17
if b. meet b., 919 : *n* 2
if mind acts on b., 762 : 3
in b. and in soul bind, 430 : 9
infirm and exhausted, 151 : 11
instrument for art, 697 : 13
is haven for b. possible, 138 : 1
is his book, 253 : 8
is Nature God is soul, 336 : 21
is not b. more than raiment, 38 : 2
its b. brevity, 435 : 24
John Brown's b., 619 : 14
joint and motive of b., 227 : 3

Body (*continued*)
lean b. and visage, 276 : 15
lifeless b. little valued, 503 : 22
light around the b., 905 : 16
light of the b., 37 : 18
like b. wholly b., 767 : 15
little b. mighty heart, 207 : 11
loves world as his b., 64 : 5
marry my b. to that dust, 267 : 6
material fortune associated with b., 124 : 3
mind or b. to prefer, 337 : 2
my b. my dungeon is, 668 : 21
my b. now an old tree, 314 : 2
my good bright dog, 896 : 13
my house, 896 : 12
naught cared b. for wind, 436 : 7
no riches above sound b., 35 : 40
not b. enough to cover mind, 432 : 24
not bruised to pleasure soul, 715 : 17
not more than soul, 574 : 27
of Benjamin Franklin Printer, 346 : 15
of each creature different, 80 : 12
of little recruit, 839 : 9
of this death, 47 : 7
old in b. but never mind, 99 : 8
one motion, 874 : 18
oppressions of b. and mind, 389 : 12
part of man's self, 648 : 17
pass from colder to hotter b., 589 : 14
perfectly spherical, 550 : 6
politic like human body, 358 : 16
power lies in mind and b., 102 : 21
presence of b. in question, 442 : 11
pygmy b., 303 : 20
reading to mind as exercise to b., 327 : 12
remember, 702 : 5
Resurrection of the b., 55 : 2
ruler having human b. as subject, 84 : 5
sex woven into whole b., 689 : 19
ship of the b., 575 : 20
sickness-broken b., 276 : 14
so young b. with so old head, 200 : 8
soul gentle companion of b., 123 : 15
soul is form and doth b. make, 174 : 19
soul its b. off, 717 : 1
soul look b. touch, 717 : 8
sound mind in sound b., 122 : 17
sound of b. and mind, 107 : 13
swayed to music, 715 : 17
swung gently, 647 : 5
this is my b., 41 : 10, 48 : 20
this is My B., 54 : 6
'tis mind makes b. rich, 189 : 2
to be buried obscurely, 181 : 16
whole b. not be cast into hell, 37 : 8
with whole b. listen, 770 : 16
without spirit dead, 51 : 33
woman's b. the woman, 647 : 6
worms destroy this b., 16 : 4
Bodyguard, army is McClellan's b., 522 : 4
Body-hungry, soul-hungry worse than b., 923 : 22
Body's beauty lives, 767 : 10
casting b. vest aside, 297 : 4
go Soul the b. quest, 172 : 14
hardly in a b. power, 409 : 4
Body-snatching not natural, 786 : 8
Boffin the Golden Dustman, 549 : 31
Bog, snow falling on B. of Allen, 777 : 16
to an admiring b., 604 : 19
Bogus revelation, 771 : 14
Boil, maketh the deep b. like a pot, 17 : 7
we b. at different degrees, 499 : 13
Boilers, parcel of b. and vats, 356 : 20
Boiling, Hiroshima b., 893 : 14
why sea b. hot, 613 : 5
Boils, day b. at last, 540 : 14
round naked isles, 345 : 15
Bois, n'irons plus aux b., 591 : *n* 3
Boisterously, as b. maintained as gained, 202 : 3
Bold, alive and so b. O earth, 468 : 19
and turbulent of wit, 303 : 20
anfractuous rocks, 804 : 16
bad man, 173 : 9, 248 : 26
be bloody b. and resolute, 239 : 10
be b., 173 : 20
be not too b., 173 : 21
brave men and b., 922 : 15
cook and captain b., 627 : 7
in conscious virtue b., 334 : 12
in that freedom b., 429 : 12
inspiring b. John Barleycorn, 411 : 10
jockey of Norfolk not too b., 173 : *n* 8
let our minds be b., 678 : 2
look with favor on b. beginning, 103 : 26
maiden never b., 229 : 26
man first eat oyster, 323 : 10
peasantry, 369 : 30
persistent experimentation, 779 : 7
righteous are b. as a lion, 25 : 27
story of Cambuscan b., 278 : 23
too b. to imagine, 378 : 1
virtue is b., 228 : 23
what makes robbers b. but lenity, 186 : 7
Bolder and stronger peoples, 687 : 4
knits a b. one, 605 : 8
note than this swell, 525 : 10
Boldest held his breath, 443 : 16
painters cannot trace, 328 : 17
sons of toil, 592 : 6
Boldly, attack all the more b., 105 : 14
ride, 527 : 5
tells disagreeable truth b., 386 : 8
Boldness certain to win praise, 112 : 22
lends hand to honest b., 91 : 8
to dream, 859 : 20
Bole, elm tree b., 541 : 16
leaf blossom or b., 715 : 17
Bolingbroke adorns subject, 342 : 8
this canker B., 203 : 12
Bolívar, speak of B. amidst thunder, 451 : *n* 7
Bolster, head on sweaty b., 899 : 17
Bolt, Ben B., 566 : 1
fool's b. soon shot, 160 : 23
of Cupid fell, 196 : 15
old age coming b. door, 133 : 2
running home, 901 : 14
Bolts, something picked lock slid b., 739 : 5
stronger b. than Aphrodite, 76 : 22
up change, 241 : 24
wresting from Jupiter his b., 115 : 16
Bomb, atomic b. in unfederated world, 847 : 4
don't let anyone b. me, 866 : 17
Lord b. Germans, 866 : 17
might destroy whole port, 763 : 12
Bomb (*continued*)
on Hiroshima, 777 : 10, 787 : 13
severity path to b., 637 : 14
them into Stone Age, 867 : 3
war fought with atomic b., 763 : 14
Bombast out blank verse, 178 : 12
second sublime third b., 118 : 15
Bombastiloquent 82 : 19
Bombing of Chinese cities, 788 : 15
Bombs, atomic b. burst in hands, 719 : 15
atomic energy lead to b., 763 : 12
bursting in air, 446 : 1
what use b. and antibombs, 831 : 18
Bonaparte, ashes of Napoleon B., 421 : 15
Jeanne d'Arc and B., 815 : 11
Bond, break that sole b., 373 : 6
happy whom unbroken b. unites, 107 : 9
I'll seal to such a b., 198 : 26
let him look to his b., 199 : 16
neither b. nor free, 50 : 12
of iniquity, 46 : 3
of one immortal look, 544 : 23
of scattered family, 617 : *n* 3
prosperity's very b. of love, 247 : 3
scatter and unloose from b., 189 : 18
so nominated in the b., 200 : 13
take a b. of fate, 239 : 11
tied by chance b., 557 : 2
'tis not in the b., 200 : 14
trust man on oath or b., 243 : 1
universal and common b., 166 : 2
which keeps me pale, 238 : 21
word as good as b., 170 : 30
Bondage, hold fellow men in b., 418 : 6
of irrational fears, 677 : 13
out of the house of b., 9 : 29
slightest b. mad aware, 749 : 5
to previous history, 602 : 3
Bondman in hand bears power, 215 : 13
Bondman's, in a b. key, 198 : 25
Bonds, bear b. that gall, 633 : 9
man frees himself from b., 504 : 9
no b. attached him to life, 142 : 23
of Union dissolved, 438 : 11
that unite only in mind, 734 : 8
Bondsman's unrequited toil, 524 : 7
Bone, behind mortal b., 605 : 8
break b. suck out marrow, 157 : 7
bright hair about the b., 253 : 12
consuming rag and b., 717 : 9
divorced from eye and b., 836 : 18
every part of b. Nature makes b., 125 : 24
fetch poor dog a b., 932 : 7
fever of the b., 804 : 22
flesh of flesh b. of b., 287 : 23
life near b. sweetest, 560 : 19
of manhood, 372 : 14
of my bones, 7 : 3
of thy bone, 168 : 4
rag and b. and hair, 709 : 14
reform taking b. from dog, 699 : 3
secret life of b., 883 : 11
take muscle from b., 806 : 21
vigor of b., 226 : 20
white as rain-washed b., 708 : 17
zero at the b., 606 : 14
Boneless gums, 237 : 5
Bones are dust, 436 : 4
arise from my b., 105 : 11
bitter b., 863 : 19

Bones (*continued*)
bleed my b., 875 : 1
bone of my b., 7 : 3
bound b. and veins in me, 655 : 19
bury b. in hideaways, 856 : 1
can these b. live, 32 : 29
chalk of my b., 873 : 12
cursed be he that moves my b., 250 : 1
dead men lost b., 805 : 3
dice human b., 462 : 14
disembodied b., 793 : 19
dry b., 32 : 30
England keep my b., 202 : 12
exercises b. with toil, 89 : 25
full of dead men's b., 40 : 20
good oft interred with b., 216 : 17
grind b. to make bread, 934 : 4
have quietly rested, 275 : 3
honored b., 277 : 13
jest breaks no b., 356 : 23
lay his weary b. among ye, 249 : 10
let us have tongs and b., 197 : 4
lie scattered on the Alpine mountains, 282 : 18
lovely in her b., 874 : 1
martyrs' b., 767 : 22
mutine in matron's b., 223 : 5
of his b. coral made, 247 : 21
pain wanders through b., 874 : 22
paste and cover to our b., 195 : 2
Puritan marrow of my b., 794 : 2
pushing their b., 908 : 8
rattle his b. over stones, 486 : 1
searches in mud for b., 824 : 6
shake secrets from my b., 874 : 6
strengthens their b., 63 : 14
valley of dry b., 32 : 28
weave their thread with b., 214 : 3
Bonfire, everlasting b., 238 : 2
Bonfires and illuminations, 381 : 7
Bong, land where B. tree grows, 550 : 8
Bonhomie, overcame natural b., 753 : 4
Bonjour, et puis b., 617 : *n* 1
tristesse, 832 : *n* 2
Bonnet, in her latest new b., 639 : 20
war b. of Medicine Hat, 840 : 2
Bonnets of Bonny Dundee, 432 : 15
Bonny, am I no a b. fighter, 668 : 16
banks and braes o' b. Doon, 409 : 24
banks o' Loch Lomond, 921 : 9
bonnets of B. Dundee, 432 : 15
bonny Biscay O, 920 : 17
brow was brent, 410 : 7
milldams o' Binnorie, 927 : 1
speed b. boat, 688 : 12
thou b. gem, 409 : 9
Bono, cui b. fuerit, 98 : *n* 6
pro b. publico, 134 : 20
Bononcini, some say Signor B., 341 : 13
Bons mots, laboring to produce b., 297 : 28
Bonsoir, et puis b., 617 : *n* 1
Bonum, summum b., 98 : *n* 17, 101 : *n* 9
Boo, under the b., 806 : 11
Boobies, don't count your b., 831 : 10
Booboisie 772 : 19
Booby, give her b. for another, 331 : 13
Boogie-woogie rumble of dream deferred, 854 : 17
Boojum, Snark was a B., 614 : 5
Book, alive while thy b. live, 256 : 11
American literature from one b., 845 : 5

Book (*continued*)
and heart never part, 320 : 5
and volume of my brain, 219 : 28
angel writing in b., 454 : 5
another damned thick b., 387 : 6
axe for frozen sea inside us, 786 : 4
bad b. as much labor, 830 : 8
bell b. and candle, 201 : 23
beware man of one b., 133 : 11
big b. big bore, 92 : 17
bloody b. of law, 229 : 23
blot out of b. of life, 53 : 4
body is his b., 253 : 8
camerado this no b., 576 : 21
chief need is be readable, 555 : 11
curse with b. bell and candle, 149 : 16
dainties bred of a b., 190 : 27
destroys b. kills reason, 281 : 23
do not throw b. about, 729 : 14
doings of mankind subject of my b., 122 : 1
English dictionary best b., 740 : 18
face is as a b., 236 : 19
farewell my b. and my devocioun, 145 : 10
furnishes no quotations, 455 : 4
genius when I wrote that b., 323 : 24
go b. and wish to all, 145 : *n* 4
go forth my b., 145 : *n* 4
go litel b. litel myn tragedye, 145 : 7
go little b., 773 : 15
go now b. to every place, 145 : *n* 4
good b. best of friends, 538 : 2
good b. happened to you, 845 : 4
good puts in working mood, 495 : 13
good reader makes good b., 499 : 17
I am myself matter of my b., 164 : 5
I'll drown my b., 248 : 15
in b. of my memory a rubric, 140 : 7
in his hand, 301 : 20
kill man as kill b., 281 : 23
leaves of Judgment B. unfold, 596 : 16
lifeblood of spirit, 281 : 24
like cover of old b., 346 : 15
like person has fortunes, 639 : 1
liked the b. the better, 371 : 11
little b. go without me, 145 : *n* 4
little b. I cast thee on waters, 145 : *n* 4
Macaulay a b. in breeches, 433 : 10
made by Mr. Mark Twain, 623 : 20
makes my body cold, 608 : 6
may be very amusing, 369 : 6
mighty b. mighty theme, 571 : 1
mine adversary had written a b., 16 : 20
moral or immoral b., 674 : 22
my b. friends talk to me, 771 : 1
nature's infinite b. of secrecy, 240 : 15
new era in life from b., 559 : 34
no b. so bad but some good, 123 : 9
no frigate like b., 607 : 4
not at his picture but his b., 256 : 10
not concerned with poetry, 827 : 1
not more in b. than before, 859 : 4
note it in a b., 30 : 17
note you in b. of memory, 185 : 1
of a certain Cicero, 129 : 2
of deeds words and art, 573 : 11
of egoism, 600 : 24
of female logic, 539 : 21
of knowledge fair, 285 : 5
of Life begins, 675 : 16

Book (*continued*)
of life was opened, 53 : 28
of moonlight not written, 766 : 17
of moons defend ye, 918 : 11
of Nature, 168 : *n* 3
of nature, 301 : 11
of Songs and Sonnets, 225 : 8
of transformations, 864 : 14
of verses underneath bough, 516 : 7
oh for b. and shady nook, 643 : 3
one b. furnishes treatise, 358 : 23
only one b. in them, 433 : 8
page of b. carelessly open, 908 : 12
people praise don't read, 625 : 10
present new b. to Cornelius, 101 : 13
read b. not year old, 499 : 5
read b. of fate, 206 : 20
reads but one b., 270 : 27
recognizes me in my b., 165 : 20
same today and forever, 538 : 2
say in sentences what others in b., 658 : 13
sealed with seven seals, 53 : 9
sour misfortune's b., 193 : 25
take down this b., 712 : 8
that they were printed in a b., 16 : 3
that took him out of bed, 258 : *n* 2
that wonderful b., 487 : 18
the world the b. of God, 250 : 12
this grand b. the universe, 182 : 20
thou art the b., 267 : 4
though nothing in 't, 456 : 12
throw whole b. in fire, 504 : 10
Time criticized for us, 569 : 6
to be read in twilight, 503 : 15
turn over library make b., 355 : 14
well-chosen b. or friend, 250 : 15
what is this marvelous b., 358 : 23
what is use of b., 611 : 2
what thou seest write in a b., 52 : 28
what you don't know make b., 433 : 13
when b. of life opening, 764 : 7
when nobleman writes b., 356 : *n* 5
which does not sell, 442 : 13
without pictures or conversations, 611 : 2
works at body of b., 368 : 5
written in God's b., 130 : 18
you read from duty, 354 : *n* 5
Bookful blockhead, 333 : 19
Bookish ambition, 258 : 2
theoric, 229 : 13
Bookmen, you two are b., 190 : 29
Book's a book though nothing in 't, 456 : 12
Books about books, 166 : 7
all b. else so poor, 316 : 6
all b. he reads, 333 : 19
all good b. alike, 845 : 4
ambition to be stored with b., 258 : 2
are not absolutely dead, 281 : 22
as schoolboys from b., 192 : 15
authority from others' b., 190 : 12
bear him up, 315 : 20
belong to eyes, 498 : 4
best b. universal appeal, 740 : 9
bloodless substitute, 667 : 21
borrowers of b., 441 : 18
burn b. burn human beings, 481 : 11
by persons in America, 536 : 10
by which printers have lost, 276 : 19
cannot learn men from b., 501 : 3
children of brain, 321 : 11

Books (*continued*)
clad in blak or reed, 145 : 27
consumed midnight oil, 331 : 12
cover country in b., 657 : 2
crushed by b., 885 : 8
deep versed in b., 288 : 17
do serve some purpose, 865 : 14
do with friends as b., 497 : 22
do you read b. through, 355 : 7
dreams b. each a world, 428 : 4
drunk on b., 772 : 18
feelings beings b. events battles, 861 : 4
few friends and many b., 295 : 4
few thousand battered b., 792 : 16
from b. of honor razed, 244 : 7
gentleman not in your b., 208 : 26
God be thanked for b., 448 : 5
God written all the b., 620 : 23
good b. truer than real, 845 : 4
historical b. with no lies, 655 : 3
Homer all b. you need, 316 : 6
I cannot live without b., 389 : 10
I have read all the b., 651 : 13
I'll burn my b., 184 : 10
in b. soul of past, 473 : 28
in running brooks, 210 : 24
intercourse with superior minds, 448 : 5
knowing I loved my b., 247 : 15
lard their lean b., 258 : 5
learn anatomy not from b., 260 : 9
learning wiser without b., 377 : 14
legacies genius leaves, 326 : 16
like men their authors, 321 : 10
lineaments of Gospel b., 184 : 13
listed names of Kings, 840 : 17
live without b., 609 : 13
magic preservation in b., 473 : 29
many b. and never use them, 258 : 2
men read as b. too much, 335 : 12
more in woods than in b., 136 : 9
must follow sciences, 181 : 20
never die, 780 : 17
never read children's b., 701 : 6
new French b., 543 : 7
next o'er his b., 340 : 17
no b. but score and tally, 185 : 28
no furniture charming as b., 432 : 23
not all b. dull as readers, 559 : 33
not in your b., 208 : 26
not killed by fire, 780 : 17
of all time, 573 : 2
of making many b., 27 : 27, 773 : 14
of quotations, 743 : 9
of the hour, 573 : 2
old b. manners wine, 371 : 3
old b. old Nankin blue, 179 : *n* 4
old clothes a few b., 785 : 9
only b. woman's looks, 447 : 5
out of olde b. newe science, 144 : 9
read deliberately as written, 559 : 29
read only b. that wound us, 786 : 4
read what b. I please, 338 : 16
readers like my b., 181 : 22
reading valueless b., 573 : 1
real war never in b., 577 : 5
receive value from esteem, 302 : 18
rural quiet friendship b., 345 : 12
shouldn't teach great b., 862 : 9
sins scarlet b. read, 730 : 13
some b. not adequately reviewed, 637 : 10
some b. to be tasted, 181 : 12

Books (*continued*)
spectacles of b., 303 : 6
start life with good b., 689 : 14
sweet serenity of b., 512 : 15
they are the b. the arts, 191 : 5
think for me, 442 : 8
three b. on soul, 543 : 25
treasured wealth of world, 559 : 31
trees shall be my b., 211 : 17
true levelers, 448 : 5
truest of b. Solomon's, 570 : 16
twenty b. at his beddes heed, 145 : 27
two classes of b., 573 : 2
undeservedly forgotten, 869 : 7
university collection of b., 473 : 30
weapons, 780 : 17
well or badly written, 674 : 22
why so few good b., 597 : 7
with b. the same, 570 : 16
worst b. universal appeal, 740 : 9
you may carry to fire, 353 : 17
Books', things in b.' clothing, 442 : 9
Booksellers, for all b. in world, 365 : 10
Bookstore, human nature weak in b., 551 : 12
Bookworming in pajamas, 892 : 20
Boom, guns b. far, 742 : 9
in petroleum but not poetry, 886 : 10
Boomed cut plucked booted, 892 : 12
Booming of new-come bee, 768 : 16
surge of Aegean, 83 : 6
Booms, beetle b. adown glooms, 665 : 7
windy b. hoo-hooed it, 767 : 13
Boon, is life a b., 629 : 23
sordid b., 427 : 29
southern country, 587 : 11
Boone, when Daniel B. goes by, 840 : 13
Boot, hey for b. and horse, 566 : 14
look for me under b. soles, 575 : 4
saddle to horse, 540 : 26
Booted, boomed cut plucked b., 892 : 12
ready b. and spurred, 298 : 18
Booth died blind, 765 : 2
Bootless cries, 244 : 8
Boots boots boots, 710 : 10
died in b. like pioneer, 839 : 19
drunk and asleep in b., 767 : 1
gunpowder ran out heels of b., 364 : 5
long b. hard b., 761 : 13
not to resist wind and tide, 186 : 16
what b. it at one gate to make defense, 288 : 28
what b. with incessant care, 280 : 15
Booze, Georgia b., 840 : 1
Bo-peep, as if they played at b., 266 : 13
little B., 932 : 3
Borden, Lizzie B. took ax, 923 : 5
Border, Germany's river but not b., 420 : 2
nor breed nor birth, 707 : 16
not move markers on b., 6 : 5
son of Middle B., 695 : 12
through all wide b., 430 : 17
Borders, departure beyond b. death, 817 : 5
invade b. of my realm, 163 : 15
Bore, accursed the night she b. me, 76 : 10
art of never appearing b., 667 : 5
big book big b., 92 : 17
bored more contemptible than b., 620 : 1
Chankly B., 551 : 4

Bore (*continued*)
every hero becomes b., 498 : 14
first lion thought last a b., 438 : 12
forgive those who b. us, 293 : 34
me in southern wild, 403 : 6
no b. we dread as own minds, 569 : 7
not only as sin but b., 461 : 18
secret of being a b., 343 : 1
soldiers b. dead bodies by, 203 : 8
talks, 647 : 9
tells you how he is, 719 : 12
to be in society a b., 675 : 17
too short to b. ourselves, 657 : 25
Bored and terrified, 888 : 12
Bores and B., 461 : 28
if I had not been there, 695 : 10
mankind by thee less b., 270 : *n* 7
more contemptible than bore, 620 : 1
with good wine, 501 : 17
Boredom, against b. gods struggle, 413 : *n* 4
at core of life, 301 : 10
foe of happiness, 463 : 8
God created woman b. ceased, 658 : 15
keynote of poverty, 859 : 15
obesity brought on by b., 857 : 12
state of man b., 299 : 19
vice and need, 343 : 13
Bores and Bored, 461 : 28
through his castle wall, 195 : 3
Borges, I live so B. can weave literature, 843 : 7
Boring, life is b., 884 : 9
Born, a man be b. again, 44 : 31
again, 903 : 7
all men b. free, 282 : 13
another world be b., 888 : 6
are men b. to go down like this, 831 : 18
as one b. out of time, 48 : 28
as soon as we were b., 34 : 15
begotten b. and dies, 714 : 22
being b. to die, 181 : 19
being human b. alone, 794 : 3
best not to be b., 67 : 5, 868 : 7
better ne'er been b., 432 : 6
better to be lowly b., 248 : 27
blight man b. for, 656 : 10
bred en b. in brier patch, 662 : 8
but I was free b., 46 : 26
but to die, 337 : 2
certain is death for the b., 94 : 8
Christ b. across sea, 566 : 5
Christ b. in Bethlehem, 350 : 15
cross cause why we were b., 190 : 33
cry for being b., 181 : 19
day perish wherein I was b., 15 : 7
died before god of love was b., 253 : 9
else wherefore b., 534 : 5
empty into modern age, 312 : 20
envy b. from the start, 78 : 11
first b. as children, 903 : 7
free, 282 : 13, 358 : 12, 814 : 20
free and equal, 387 : *n* 4
friends b. not made, 634 : 21
genius must be b., 306 : 8
glad not b. before tea, 433 : 15
good if he had not been b., 41 : 9
happy is he b. and taught, 250 : 14
have to be b. there, 838 : 4
he was not b. to shame, 193 : 10
hour I was b., 921 : 13
house where I was b., 485 : 4

Born (*continued*)
human race b. to fly upward, 142 : 2
I was b. dat's de charge, 810 : 8
I was b. to know you, 832 : 4
if millions b. millions must die, 798 : 2
ignorance in which b., 360 : 26
in a cellar, 364 : 3
in bed in bed we die, 290 : 8
in days when wits were fresh, 586 : 1
in half savage country, 792 : 10
in my b. days, 168 : 14
in other's pain, 693 : 7
in soft regions b. soft men, 78 : 22
in this century, 890 : 7
into world where alienation awaits, 906 : 18
jealousy b. with love, 294 : 2
life worth being b., 821 : 3
live die an American, 451 : 14
loveliest woman b., 714 : 20
lucky to be b., 574 : 18
made his own bed ere b., 292 : 18
man b. and dies, 925 : 22
man b. in chains, 413 : 2
man b. suffers dies, 705 : 12
man is b. for uprightness, 68 : 19
man is b. free, 358 : 12
man is b. unto trouble, 15 : 15
man that is b. of a woman, 15 : 33
Miniver Cheevy b. too late, 728 : 20
monster b. on itself, 231 : 20
naked and falls a-whining, 116 : *n* 4
no man b. an angler, 270 : 31
no man b. unto himself, 267 : 9
nobly b. must nobly meet fate, 77 : 16
none of woman b., 239 : 10
not a world of b., 829 : 25
not b. for death, 477 : 1
not b. under rhyming planet, 210 : 8
not b. woman becomes one, 870 : 11
not conscious of being b., 315 : 9
not to be b., 181 : *n* 9
not to be b. best, 67 : 5, 868 : 7
not to be b. surpasses thought, 75 : 13
of a little Sin, 822 : 20
of blackest Midnight b., 277 : 17
of the Spirit, 44 : 32
of the sun, 876 : 16
of their confrontation, 882 : 4
of Virgin Mary, 55 : 2
of virgin mother b., 277 : 6
old and ugly, 547 : 28
on a Monday, 932 : 11
on Christmas Day, 919 : 20
on Fourth of July, 759 : 6
One b. in a manger, 299 : 10
out of my due time, 618 : 7
poet's made as well as b., 256 : 17
posthumously, 658 : 25
powerless to be b., 586 : 10
risen to body not yet b., 905 : 16
so many not yet b., 856 : 7
soil good to be b. on, 568 : 26
some are b. great, 214 : 9
some b. to endless night, 406 : 19
some b. to sweet delight, 406 : 19
strength though of muses b., 475 : 13
sucker b. every minute, 536 : 4
sun b. and dies, 925 : 21
sun b. over and over, 887 : 2
terrible beauty b., 714 : 9
they had never been b., 36 : 11
thing I was b. to do, 182 : 9

Born (*continued*)
things that are b. and die, 866 : 6
time to be b., 26 : 21
to be king, 688 : 12
to be nobly b. now crime, 262 : 20
to blush unseen, 362 : 8
to set it right, 220 : 6
to the manner b., 219 : 9
to write, 338 : 14
too soon or too late, 724 : 13
toward Bethlehem to be b., 714 : 13
under one law to another bound, 175 : 5
under that was I b., 209 : 13
unto us a child is b., 29 : 16
unto you is b., 42 : 28
we are all b. mad, 866 : 12
we were not b. to sue, 193 : 34
went to trouble to be b., 378 : 9
wept that he was b., 728 : 19
when we are b. we cry, 235 : 5
where I was b. unimportant, 800 : 12
with anxiety about weather, 630 : 22
with gift of laughter, 756 : 15
with silver spoon, 171 : 5
would thou hadst ne'er been b., 232 : 5
Borne and yet must bear, 466 : 15
angel b. on my bosom, 544 : 2
back into past, 835 : 8
his faculties so meek, 236 : 24
like thy bubbles, 458 : 30
me on his back, 224 : 14
not b. this in my hot youth, 108 : 5
oldest hath b. most, 235 : 20
the burden, 40 : 9
through hatred b. apart, 75 : 23
well b. without defeat, 207 : 8
Borogoves, mimsy were b., 612 : 17
Borrow army for a while, 522 : 4
every changing shape, 804 : 2
good and truth to b., 495 : 16
men who b. men who lend, 441 : 17
to live within means, 616 : 20
Borrowed plumes, 66 : 7
something b., 924 : 6
wit, 265 : 2
Borrower is servant to the lender, 24 : 36
neither b. nor lender be, 219 : 2
of the night, 238 : 12
Borrowers always ill-spenders, 573 : 3
of books, 441 : 18
Borrowing accounted Plagiarè, 282 : 11
banqueting upon b., 35 : 30
dulls edge of husbandry, 219 : 2
everything of neighbors, 310 : 11
goeth a-b., 163 : 5
life that depends on b., 599 : 9
only lingers it out, 206 : 5
Boshaft ist er nicht, 764 : *n* 1
Bosom, Abraham's b., 43 : 33, 187 : 17, 425 : 17
angel borne on my b., 544 : 2
Arthur's b., 207 : 13
barren b. starves birth, 361 : 17
beggar in Abraham's b., 43 : 33
can a man take fire in his b., 23 : 14
carry them in his b., 30 : 35
crept into b. of the sea, 185 : 20
friend of sun, 477 : 17
glory in His b., 566 : 5
heart out of b., 690 : 21
her hand on her b., 232 : 8

Bosom (*continued*)
heroic b. beats no more, 461 : 5
I must not see, 297 : 20
in ocean's b. unespied, 297 : 8
in your fragrant b. dies, 271 : 21
let me to Thy b. fly, 350 : 12
liest in Abraham's b., 425 : 17
loosened from her b. the girdle, 58 : 19
of his Father and his God, 362 : 19
of urgent west, 654 : 15
pearl in b. of sea, 257 : 13
sleep in Abraham's b., 187 : 17
stuffed b. of perilous stuff, 239 : 32
swell b. with thy fraught, 231 : 17
third in your b., 192 : 23
thorns that in b. lodge, 219 : 25
warm cheek and rising b., 362 : 21
which thy frozen b. bears, 229 : *n* 1
wife of thy b., 11 : 16
within b. is September, 917 : 24
within b. of rose, 530 : 14
wring his b., 369 : 21
write sorrow on b. of the earth, 195 : 1
Bosomed deep in vines, 340 : 26
high in tufted trees, 277 : 25
Bosoms, hair hang and brush b., 543 : 12
men's business and b., 179 : 21
waters lift their b., 226 : 2
white b. of actresses, 353 : 23
Bossuet, celebrities such as B., 615 : 14
Boston, a Thucydides at B., 363 : 21
audience four thousand critics, 622 : 3
blatant Bassarid of B., 634 : 9
Cluett Shirt B. Garter, 828 : 17
Concord Lexington, 450 : 13
Evening Transcript, 804 : 6, 846 : 1
good old B., 694 : 14
hub of solar system, 519 : 11
in B. ask how much does he know, 625 : 23
marching through B., 893 : 12
marriage serious around B., 826 : 14
not blue on B., 892 : 9
runs to brains, 676 : 16
Boston's Marlborough Street, 892 : 20
Bo'sun tight and midshipmite, 627 : 7
Boswell first of biographers, 353 : *n* 4
Botanist, puzzle to b., 619 : 7
Botanize, peep and b., 424 : 15
Botany, all their b. Latin, 494 : 12
Botch of it trying to swap, 523 : 8
Botched civilization, 792 : 16
Boteler, Dr. B. said of strawberries, 271 : 10
Both, by adventuring b., 198 : 6
I am with b., 201 : 22
plague o' b. houses, 193 : 6
wear b. for b. are thine, 187 : 2
Bother, baby blessing and b., 622 : 17
long words b. me, 778 : 12
Bothered, bewitched b. bewildered, 833 : 19
hot and b., 711 : 1
Bo-tree, place by the b., 874 : 13
Bottle, a little for the b., 393 : 10
empires changed by b., 398 : *n* 1
fragrance in whiskey b., 888 : 4
friend in need nor b., 548 : 18
large cold b., 666 : 15
leave b. on chimleypiece, 547 : 35

Bottle (*continued*)
my b. of salvation, 172 : 15
of hay, 197 : 5
Bottled lightning, 547 : 16
Bottleneck, president is b., 879 : 4
Bottles, narrow-necked b., 340 : 11
new wine in old b., 38 : 30
stay the b. of heaven, 16 : 35
Bottom, bless thee B., 196 : 26
build from b. up, 779 : 6
dive into b. of deep, 203 : 15
I see not the b. of it, 226 : 22
line is in heaven, 876 : 1
not in one b. trusted, 197 : 25
of the monstrous world, 281 : 2
of the worst, 226 : 7
of woe deep, 570 : 5
sees into b. of my grief, 193 : 18
sees sea b. from shore, 142 : 15
sit on our own b., 166 : 9
strike rock and go to b., 407 : 16
unknown b. like bay of Portugal, 212 : 26
Bottomless, consciousness as b. lake, 639 : 12
gulf of civil pensions, 449 : 6
in b. nights you sleep, 673 : 19
perdition, 283 : 4
some ponds thought b., 560 : 11
Bouchon, plus léger qu'un b., 673 : *n* 7
Bough, apple reddens on high b., 63 : 10
bloom along b., 690 : 16
blossom that hangs on b., 248 : 16
book of verses underneath b., 516 : 7
breaks cradle fall, 660 : 19
golden b., 715 : 3
here beneath walnut b., 558 : 19
here by baring b., 641 : 14
old forsaken b., 519 : 19
sings on orchard b., 541 : 16
touch not single b., 492 : 10
wet black b., 792 : 7
Boughs, bird that lives in the b., 395 : 1
cedar green with b., 671 : 3
easy under the apple b., 886 : 19
incense hangs upon b., 476 : 26
lowest b. brushwood sheaf, 541 : 16
off many a tree, 268 : 13
out of b. he came, 733 : 1
shade of melancholy b., 211 : 12
shadows of pine b., 319 : 1
soul into b. does glide, 297 : 4
which shake against cold, 244 : 27
Bought, beauty b. by judgment of eye, 190 : 19
bliss b. by years, 561 : 21
crooked cat, 932 : 18
Dickon thy master b., 173 : *n* 8
golden opinions, 237 : 1
good names to be b., 202 : 30
Hudibras again, 309 : 22
knowledge b. in market, 564 : 10
men who can't be b., 761 : 17
three pecks of meal, 934 : 1
wisdom is not b., 926 : 6
Boughten friendship by side, 749 : 1
Bouillabaisse noble dish is, 539 : 19
Boulder, nearly dying at B., 892 : 12
Boulders, build house of b., 497 : 31
ferns by Berkshire b., 822 : 7
Bounce for her too, 835 : 3
Bound as befitting each, 576 : 22
bones and veins in me, 655 : 19
Bound (*continued*)
born under one law to another b., 175 : 5
bourn b. of land, 247 : 26
by countless ties, 749 : 5
by own definition of criticism, 586 : 24
each to each, 425 : 7
heaven not at single b., 566 : 2
I'm b. away, 749 : 18
in icy chains by thee, 229 : *n* 1
in shallows and miseries, 217 : 5
in to saucy doubts, 238 : 23
in with triumphant sea, 194 : 14
nothing but hath his b., 188 : 1
of the everlasting hills, 9 : 6
though my wing closely b., 296 : *n* 3
towns where you would have b. me, 839 : 20
upon wheel of fire, 235 : 8
utmost b. of thought, 529 : 10
we're b. away, 934 : 20
with red tape, 549 : 6
Boundaries, geographical b. or race, 579 : 9
Great Spirit knows no b., 419 : 9
here b. meet, 581 : 20
in safety within b., 781 : 8
which divide life, 526 : 7
without war because no b., 419 : *n* 5
Boundary, no b. to efforts of man, 506 : 7
Bounded in a nutshell, 220 : 26
our country however b., 535 : 22
waters lift bosoms, 226 : 2
Boundless as we wish our souls, 467 : 11
contiguity of shade, 376 : 18
drew from b. deep, 535 : 19
endless sublime, 458 : 29
his wealth, 430 : 10
is b. better b. worse, 527 : 20
power without abusing, 488 : 18
universe, 527 : 20
vision grows, 592 : 6
Bounds, he fills he b., 336 : 22
living know no b., 272 : 11
mind power has no b., 115 : 19
of place and time, 363 : 2
wider b. be set, 698 : 12
Bountiful, Lady B., 329 : 8
Bounty, few great b. he may show, 315 : 17
for his b. no winter, 241 : 25
large was his b., 362 : 18
lust of goat b. of God, 404 : 3
those his former b. fed, 306 : 18
Bouquet, binds the b., 739 : 11
Bouquets while I'm living, 762 : 1
Bourbon or Nassau claim higher, 321 : 2
Bourgeois anyone whose thinking vulgar, 583 : 18
hatred of b. beginning of wisdom, 583 : 17
horrible invention the b., 583 : 7
how beastly b. is, 790 : 15
in ferment of youth, 583 : 14
Marxism product of b. mind, 785 : 2
you must shock b., 581 : 11
Bourgeois, épater le b., 581 : *n* 6
quelle atroce invention b., 583 : *n* 2
Bourgeoisie class of modern capitalists, 563 : *n* 3
Bourgeoisie (*continued*)
draws nations into civilization, 563 : 5
face to face with b., 563 : 6
played revolutionary role, 563 : 4
Bourn bound of land, 247 : 26
country from whose b., 221 : 12
Bout, notes with many a winding b., 278 : 6
with love, 67 : 8
Bovary, Madame B. had beauty, 583 : 12
Bow, always made awkward b., 480 : 6
and accept end, 747 : 2
arrow from Almighty's b., 406 : 7
as unto b. cord is, 511 : 18
better to b. than break, 159 : 21
bow lower middle classes, 628 : 15
cannot stand bent, 169 : 36
down thine ear, 24 : 37
draw b. ride and speak truth, 462 : 4
he bar and arwes bright, 146 : 23
many strings to b., 160 : 9
nor does Apollo always stretch b., 107 : 22
of burning gold, 406 : 21
or brooch or braid, 656 : 12
set my b. in the cloud, 8 : 3
strong men shall b. themselves, 27 : 24
tensely strung easily broken, 111 : 7
themselves when he did sing, 248 : 29
to that whose course run, 363 : 15
was made in England, 689 : 16
what water lapping b., 806 : 8
when trees b. heads, 608 : 19
with my b. and arrow, 930 : 9
Bowed, at her feet he b., 12 : 7
by weight of centuries, 670 : 14
he fell where he b., 12 : 7
his comely head down, 296 : 24
to idolatries patient knee, 458 : 3
with galling crown, 728 : 18
with grief and shame b. down, 276 : 13
Bowels, fatal b. of deep, 187 : 15
news not yet reached my b., 907 : 17
no belly no b., 811 : 1
of Christ, 272 : 18, 737 : 5
of compassion, 52 : 23
of fierce fire, 892 : 7
of the land, 187 : 23
were moved for him, 28 : 15
Bower, in hall or b., 279 : 6
in heaven's high b., 403 : 12
keep b. quiet for us, 475 : 16
lime tree b. my prison, 433 : 20
of roses by Bendemeer's, 447 : 12
Bowers, blossoms birds and b., 265 : 17
unable to start, 726 : 6
Bowery, Malcolm Lowry of B., 876 : 8
Bowl, called for his b., 929 : 14
capacious salad b., 668 : 18
fill b. with Samian wine, 461 : 8
golden b. be broken, 27 : 25
goldfish in glass b., 731 : 13
inverted b. we call sky, 517 : 3
love in a golden b., 403 : 17
lurk I in gossip's b., 196 : 12
of night, 516 : 1
onion atoms lurk in b., 433 : 11
roasted crabs hiss in b., 191 : 15
went to sea in b., 930 : 18
Bowled, in bowling alley b. sun, 314 : 20

Bowlegged, climb myself b. up poles, 902 : 1
Bowling, poor Tom B., 393 : 11
Bows down to wood and stone, 452 : 10
from which children sent, 782 : 15
wood of English b., 689 : 16
Bowwow, big B. strain, 440 : *n* 4
rather have a b., 677 : 6
Bowwows, demnition b., 547 : 19
Box, alabaster b. of ointment, 41 : 2
laying poems away in long b., 908 : 15
paper you drop in ballot b., 558 : 25
pathway to ballot b., 554 : 8
pouncet b., 203 : 7
twelve good men into b., 444 : 15
where sweets compacted lie, 268 : 16
Boxin' Day, beadle on B., 546 : 23
Boy, barefoot b., 513 : 10
be a farmer's b., 919 : 5
beamish b., 612 : 18
beggarly b., 568 : 20
blue-eyed b., 828 : 13
Chatterton marvelous b., 425 : 10
close upon the growing b., 426 : 14
eternal, 246 : 9
even when little b., 575 : 23
every b. and every gal, 628 : 23
finding star in haymow, 879 : 11
from sandhills of Nantucket, 571 : 8
good b. am I, 929 : 20
harshness for good of b., 313 : 9
if b. have not woman's gift, 188 : 24
imagination of b. healthy, 475 : 15
is most powerful of Hellenes, 70 : 15
lad of mettle a good b., 203 : 25
let b. win his spurs, 143 : 8
like b. playing on seashore, 313 : 17
lily-livered b., 239 : 30
little b. blue, 930 : 12
Little B. Blue kissed them, 666 : 17
little tiny b., 214 : 29
love is a b., 291 : 19
make a small b. dizzy, 873 : 10
Minstrel B., 446 : 15
most unmanageable of all animals, 86 : 2
my b. always rub up against money, 787 : 2
my greatness, 241 : 27
my lovely living b., 168 : 2
office b. to attorney's firm, 627 : 14
only way to make b. sharp, 546 : 17
parlous b., 187 : 12
purblind wayward b., 190 : 26
read to by a b., 804 : 13
schoolrooms for b., 562 : 12
smiling b. fell dead, 540 : 21
speak roughly to little b., 611 : 15
stood on burning deck, 470 : 17
sun errand b., 571 : 5
than when I was b., 485 : 5
that shoots so trim, 917 : 18
too much hope of thee loved b., 256 : 3
well for fisherman's b., 530 : 19
what good b. am I, 929 : 20
when I was a b., 485 : 5, 729 : 9, 730 : 3
who lives down lane, 930 : 5
who looks after sheep, 930 : 12
will you marry it, 911 : 9
wine dear b. and truth, 62 : 19
Boyhood changing into man, 716 : 1
ignominy of b., 716 : 1
Boyhood's thoughtless faith, 571 : 4
years, 447 : 7
Boylston Street, on B. photograph, 893 : 14
Boy's love, 234 : 14
still seeking b. license, 894 : 6
will wind's will, 511 : 25
Boys and girls level with men, 241 : 22
and girls together, 698 : 14
are marching, 578 : 12
as b. do sparrows, 321 : 12
as flies to wanton b., 234 : 21
be damned dear b., 708 : 20
being human though b., 729 : 9
claret the liquor for b., 356 : 11
dead hardly more than b., 773 : 5
few b. late at play, 588 : 5
generous b. in happiness bred, 572 : 4
in the back rooms, 762 : 7
infants b. men Ifs eternally, 571 : 4
lightfoot b., 691 : 14
little b. made of, 932 : 12
mealy b. beef-faced b., 547 : 4
not in hands of b., 827 : 4
not sent into foreign wars, 780 : 11
rally round flag b., 578 : 13
say b. another whiskey, 652 : 3
steady b. steady, 363 : 16
that swim on bladders, 249 : 3
there we saw men and b., 920 : *n* 2
three merry b. are we, 260 : 15
throw stones at frogs, 92 : 9
till b. come home, 740 : 11
we are the b., 371 : 10
when I was a boy, 730 : 3
wooing in my b., 920 : 4
Bozzy, come to me my dear B., 356 : 18
Brace lace latch or catch, 656 : 12
ourselves to duties, 744 : 4
Bracelet of bright hair, 253 : 12
Bracelets, covered with b. and rings, 701 : 15
Braces oneself to risk declaration, 653 : 4
Brach, Lady the b., 233 : 8
rather hear Lady my b., 204 : 18
Bracing, drying after b. showers, 834 : 8
Bradford, there goes John B., 162 : 3
Brae, waly doun the b., 927 : 7
Braes, banks and b. o' bonny Doon, 409 : 24
green b., 410 : 13
Brag, beauty is Nature's b., 280 : 1
left this vault to b. of, 238 : 7
one went to b., 292 : 6
Bragg, more grape Captain B., 454 : 14
Bragging, bray of b. tongues, 74 : 8
Brahmin caste of New England, 519 : 17
hymn B. sings, 495 : 12
Braid, bow or brooch or b., 656 : 12
Braids, twisted b. of lilies, 280 : 3
Brain, all that cakes b., 570 : 13
bear of very little b., 778 : 12
book and volume of my b., 219 : 28
books children of b., 321 : 11
brainsick b. workers, 618 : 10
burn from b. and breast, 742 : 12
changes continuous, 648 : 14
children of an idle b., 191 : 24
disillusionment that woman has b., 848 : 9
feed b. with better things, 742 : 12
gladness thy b. know, 468 : 15
Brain (*continued*)
heat-oppressed b., 237 : 13
him with lady's fan, 203 : 23
how this small b. think, 571 : 5
imprint of external world on b., 875 : 7
in what furnace thy b., 405 : 8
intoxicate the b., 332 : 20
is like a muscle, 913 : 3
light broke upon b., 459 : 23
light doth seize my b., 402 : 15
love not alone immured in b., 191 : 2
may devise laws, 198 : 10
memory warder of b., 237 : 7
moon lying on b., 902 : 6
more b. O Lord, 600 : 19
not an organ of sex, 695 : 13
of feathers heart of lead, 340 : 20
paper bullets of the b., 209 : 19
pen gleaned teeming b., 478 : 17
Plato's b., 495 : 15
possess a poet's b., 182 : 19
schoolmasters puzzle b., 371 : 5
superior have best b., 615 : 5
unquiet heart and b., 531 : 21
weeds of mine own b., 274 : 10
where heart lies b. also, 544 : 1
wider than sky, 605 : 21
work like madness in b., 434 : 3
work of the b. and fancy, 311 : 1
written troubles of the b., 239 : 32
Brains as well as beans, 676 : 16
Boston runs to b., 676 : 16
cudgel thy b. no more, 224 : 6
dashed the b. out, 237 : 5
hair not curl less if b. within, 595 : 9
kind assassin blow b. out, 900 : 12
of better heads, 274 : 3
steal away their b., 230 : 26
to make fool of self, 667 : 19
trust, 853 : 2
unhappy b. for drinking, 230 : 17
Brainsick brain workers, 618 : 10
Bramble, gold and b. dew, 669 : 8
jumped into b. bush, 934 : 7
Brambles pale with mist, 587 : 11
Branch, not hang b. over wine, 112 : 12
shall grow out of his roots, 29 : 18
that might have grown straight, 184 : 11
Branch-charmed by earnest stars, 478 : 4
Branche, sur la b., 725 : 18
Branches, fruit of my b., 634 : 5
giant b. tossed, 470 : 14
green wind green b., 841 : 8
last b. of tree of life, 791 : 3
ne'er remember, 478 : 14
of evil, 559 : 19
tree whose b. overspread whole land, 408 : 11
Brand Excalibur, 528 : 29
Brandy, glass of b. and water, 416 : 6
hero must drink b., 356 : 11
music b. of the damned, 680 : 19
Branksome Hall, custom of B., 430 : 2
Brass, artificer in b. and iron, 7 : 23
bands and barrel organs, 781 : 15
bound with fetters of b., 12 : 19
braw b. collar, 409 : 6
come to b. tacks, 806 : 10
evil manners live in b., 249 : 14
feet like unto fine b., 52 : 30
sounding b., 48 : 22

Brass (*continued*)
thou mayest dig b., 11 : 14
vessels of b. oft handled, 183 : 18
voice of iron chest of b., 105 : 20
Brattle, bickering b., 408 : 12
Brave Americans all, 378 : 11
and earnest men, 497 : 30
binds b. of all earth, 700 : 6
both coward and b. held in same honor, 58 : 9
clime of unforgotten b., 459 : 2
delirium of b., 713 : 11
fair women and b. men, 457 : 14
fortune favors the b., 97 : *n* 1, 106 : 4
fortune helps the b., 97 : 1
home of the b., 446 : 1, 815 : 2
how sleep the b., 364 : 8
I would be b., 785 : 8
in action patient in labors, 617 : 6
just friends and b. enemies, 389 : 3
know how to forgive, 359 : 16
man braver less daring, 569 : 21
man inattentive to duty, 419 : 1
man struggling, 334 : 13
man with a sword, 676 : 8
man's choice is danger, 77 : 4
men and bold, 922 : 15
men and worthy patriots, 281 : 19
men brave from first, 275 : 17
men lived before Agamemnon, 108 : 13
men living and dead, 523 : 4
more b. than me, 829 : 11
new world, 248 : 17
none but b. deserves fair, 306 : 12
on ye b., 443 : 15
outrage b. man dead, 73 : 16
overhanging firmament, 220 : 28
passing b. to be a king, 183 : 5
resistance or submission, 379 : 2
secret of freedom a b. heart, 81 : 5
so true so b., 423 : 1
that are no more, 377 : 19
then I was clean and b., 691 : 2
they shall be gentle b. strong, 643 : 2
to fight aloud b., 604 : 7
to the vigilant active b., 383 : 3
toll for the b., 377 : 19
translunary things, 182 : 18
war spares not the b., 67 : 10
when were b. in majority, 560 : 22
world kills the b., 844 : 15
world sir, 312 : 13
world's b. heroes, 922 : 10
Braved, deep difficulty b., 653 : 12
Bravely, do all b., 536 : 6
fleshed maiden sword, 205 : 15
greatly think or b. die, 335 : 8
Braver at night, 908 : 10
brave man b. less daring, 569 : 21
I have done one b. thing, 252 : 4
to be rebel, 704 : 17
women growing b., 695 : 14
Bravery never out of fashion, 540 : 2
on and tackle trim, 288 : 30
Bravest, agricultural population produces b. men, 117 : 4
always to be b., 58 : 2
by far, 922 : 15
who have clearest vision, 81 : 2
Braw brass collar, 409 : 6
brecht moonlecht necht, 730 : 20
Brawling courts, 532 : 18
judgments unashamed, 534 : 10
of sparrow in eaves, 712 : 7

Brawling (*continued*)
stormy husky b., 761 : 4
woman in a wide house, 24 : 33
Brawn, abundance result of b., 666 : 22
Brawny, lean rats b. rats, 541 : 2
muscles of b. arms, 510 : 7
Bray of bragging tongues, 74 : 8
Vicar of B., 920 : 6
Brazen forehead of every traitor, 615 : 4
Stentor with b. voice, 57 : 31
throat of war, 287 : 33
Brazil he twirled a button, 605 : 20
Breach, could not approve slightest b., 794 : 16
imminent deadly b., 229 : 28
more honored in b., 219 : 9
not a b. but an expansion, 253 : 4
once more unto the b., 207 : 16
with America calamity, 673 : 1
Bread and circuses, 122 : 15
angels' b. made b. of man, 139 : 11
beans and brown b., 676 : 16
better b. with happy heart, 6 : 6
bitter b. of banishment, 194 : 25
broken life up for b., 632 : 21
broth without b., 931 : 10
brown b. and the Gospel, 319 : 10
cast thy b. upon the waters, 27 : 20
consecrated b. to take, 604 : 10
country people had no b., 359 : 6
crust of b. and liberty, 339 : 11
cursed the b., 729 : 5
daily b., 37 : 15
daily b. of the eyes, 495 : 24
dear flesh cheap, 485 : 20
distressful b., 208 : 7
dry as paper, 793 : 1
eat b. in sweat of thy face, 7 : 12
eat b. without scarceness, 11 : 14
eat dusty b., 836 : 20
eaten in secret, 23 : 20
eaten your b. and salt, 707 : 3
ever more stale rags, 793 : 1
feeds me b. of bitterness, 819 : 4
first necessity of life, 666 : 3
from mouth of labor, 389 : 1
gave Esau b. and pottage, 8 : 16
give thine enemy b., 25 : 15
give us our daily b., 37 : 15
giver of breath and b., 655 : 19
grind bones to make b., 934 : 4
halfpennyworth of b., 204 : 9
how salt is another's b., 142 : 13
I am the b. of life, 44 : 41
I broke with you, 811 : 12
if son ask b., 38 : 13
in sorrow ate, 395 : 2
live for b., 495 : 2
living b. from heaven, 139 : 11
living Homer begged b., 257 : *n* 5
loaf of b. and thou, 516 : 7
looked to government for b., 374 : 11
man with b. on shoulder, 824 : 5
neither yet b. to wise, 27 : 17
nor his seed begging b., 18 : 25
not live by b. only, 11 : 12
of adversity, 30 : 18
of affliction, 14 : 11
of deceit is sweet, 24 : 31
of heaven, 21 : 12
of idleness, 26 : 9
of life, 44 : 41
of life dropped in mouth, 315 : 1

Bread (*continued*)
on which side b. buttered, 161 : 9
peace into poet as flour into b., 861 : 3
quarrel with b. and butter, 323 : 7
ravens brought him b., 13 : 41
sauce of happy ending, 653 : 6
sell b. buy hyacinth, 133 : 1
seven days shall ye eat unleavened b., 9 : 27
shows b. in other hand, 93 : 11
sky daily b. of eyes, 495 : 24
some gave white b., 929 : 19
staff of life, 319 : 8
strengthens man's heart, 319 : 8
struggle for b., 684 : 1
took b. and blessed it, 41 : 10
took b. and brake it, 164 : 4
unleavened b. and bitter herbs, 9 : 24
white b. and butter, 930 : 15
who ne'er b. in sorrow ate, 395 : 2
whole stay of b., 28 : 34
with bitter herbs, 565 : 16
with b. and wine walk road, 935 : 10
with one fish ball, 592 : 4
with you more than bread, 811 : 12
wringing b. from sweat, 524 : 5
you earn b. I'll eat, 520 : 8
Breadth, taller by b. of nail, 322 : 10
Break, bend but do not b., 296 : 12
best you get is even b., 773 : 13
better to bow than b., 159 : 21
bids it b., 239 : 20
bloody glass, 870 : 5
break break, 530 : 19
bruised reed shall he not b., 31 : 4
embraces, 868 : 7
eternal Sabbath, 304 : 23
even b., 683 : 1
frame of Nature b., 325 : 11
given thee till b. of day, 405 : 2
heart b. piecemeal, 557 : 1
hugest hearts that b., 607 : 10
I'll b. my staff, 248 : 15
into hundred thousand flaws, 233 : 23
it to our hope, 240 : 9
mounting at b. of day, 428 : 2
never doubted clouds b., 546 : 7
never give sucker even b., 683 : 1
never knew piece of land to run away or b., 382 : 2
no waters breed or b., 901 : 4
oath he never made, 291 : 22
off last lamenting kiss, 253 : 14
onetwothreefourfive pigeons, 828 : 13
out rather than surrender, 746 : *n* 2
shins against wit, 210 : 36
that sole bond, 373 : 6
those eyes the b. of day, 228 : 28
thou'll b. my heart, 409 : 24
time to b. down, 26 : 21
until the day b., 28 : 9
up by b. of day, 268 : 13
you may b. you may shatter, 447 : 2
Breakdown, madness need not be all b., 907 : 1
Breaker recede tide come in, 487 : 17
Breakers, more dangerous b., 461 : 14
wandering by lone sea b., 659 : 9
wantoned with b., 458 : 30
Breakfast dinner lunch tea, 730 : 8
for her own b. a scheme, 329 : 23
from b. to madness, 908 : 8
hope is good b. bad supper, 179 : 15

Breakfast (*continued*)
kills seven dozen Scots at b., 203 : 26
Michelangelo for b., 622 : 5
six impossible things before b., 613 : 14
where our b. take, 927 : 2
with appetite, 248 : 32
Breakfastfood, freedom is a b., 829 : 16
Breakfasts at five-o'clock tea, 614 : 1
Breakfast-time critical period, 815 : 18
Breaking, cheerfulness always b. in, 357 : 12
gray dawn b., 487 : 2, 760 : 14
sleep that knows not b., 431 : 8
stop heart from b., 606 : 12
through foul and ugly mists, 203 : 5
tired waves vainly b., 564 : 17
waves dashed high, 470 : 14
wrestled until b. of day, 8 : 24
Breaks, bough b. cradle fall, 660 : 19
butterfly upon wheel, 338 : 18
chains from every mind, 404 : 14
jest b. no bones, 356 : 23
lance of justice b., 235 : 3
light through yonder window b., 192 : 2
like Atlantic Ocean, 893 : 5
my pate across, 221 : 8
rider that b. youth, 270 : 9
sorrow b. seasons, 187 : 11
sun b. through darkest clouds, 189 : 2
world b. everyone, 844 : 15
Breakthrough, madness may be b., 907 : 1
Breast, arm the obdured b., 284 : 21
burn from brain and b., 742 : 12
cherish at charitable b., 794 : 9
crude Orson-like b., 652 : *n* 3
deep in her b. like silent wound, 105 : 9
from her hardy b., 567 : 9
Hampden with dauntless b., 362 : 9
heart at rest within b., 403 : 15
hope springs in human b., 336 : 15
in thy b. stars of fate, 413 : 17
lacerate his b., 716 : 6
love lodged in woman's b., 250 : 13
Madeline's fair b., 476 : 16
marched b. forward, 546 : 7
mark on red b., 514 : 3
master passion in b., 337 : 4
my baby at my b., 242 : 4
Nature's learned b., 168 : 3
nunnery of thy chaste b., 295 : 22
of huge Mississippi, 587 : 4
one thought in b. another on tongue, 102 : 24
pressed with excitement to b., 866 : 19
sail upon her patient b., 225 : 36
soft as b. of doves, 795 : 2
soothe a savage b., 324 : 14
soul wears out b., 460 : 5
sweetness flows into b., 716 : 3
tamer of human b., 361 : 13
that gives rose, 600 : 21
that's fallen on my b., 481 : 7
thy b. encloseth my heart, 187 : 2
trembles in the b., 429 : 18
truth hath a quiet b., 194 : 1
turtle's b., 806 : 13
two souls dwell in my b., 396 : 12
wail or knock the b., 289 : 9
weariness toss him to my b., 269 : 2
Breast (*continued*)
Wedding Guest beat b., 434 : 8
what his b. forges, 242 : 20
Breast-burned, named B., 514 : *n* 2
Breastie, panic's in thy b., 408 : 12
Breastplate of faith, 50 : 20
what stronger b. than heart, 185 : 17
Breasts, brown b., 822 : 4
come to my woman's b., 236 : 17
from rocky b. forever flowing, 878 : 7
her b. are dun, 246 : 1
like two young roes, 28 : 11
Sestos and Abydos of her b., 253 : 23
that feed France, 178 : 9
touched her sleeping b., 841 : 10
Breath, a b. thou art, 228 : 15
a little flesh a little b., 124 : 5
bated b. and whispering humbleness, 198 : 25
boldest held his b., 443 : 16
breathes with human b., 528 : 2
brief as giving b., 812 : 3
by the gate of b., 633 : 1
call the fleeting b., 362 : 5
Chaucer whose sweet b., 528 : 21
dirt breathing a small b., 873 : 7
draw thy b. in pain, 225 : 1
dulcet and harmonious b., 196 : 14
ecstasy come to b., 836 : 18
everything that hath b., 22 : 25
fancied life in others' b., 337 : 12
flattered its rank b., 458 : 3
fly away b., 214 : 4
from one mother both draw b., 72 : 6
give hautboys b. he comes, 306 : 14
giver of b. and bread, 655 : 19
he giveth b., 46 : 16
healthy b. of morn, 478 : 2
hearest hardly a b., 397 : 3
heaven's b. smells wooingly, 236 : 21
hot and cold with same b., 66 : 17
I sing on one b., 759 : 3
if b. terrible as terminations, 209 : 10
is in his nostrils, 28 : 33
kept b. to cool his pottage, 62 : 5
last b. most valued, 625 : 15
life of mortal b., 511 : 11
lightly draws its b., 423 : 3
love endures for b., 632 : 9
make them as breath made, 369 : 30
mouth-honor b., 239 : 31
my quiet b., 476 : 28
never drawn b. of life, 715 : 19
no b. at all, 235 : 18
of autumn's being, 467 : 17
of life, 6 : 17, 715 : 19
of new-mown hay, 732 : 13
of self-respect, 851 : 10
of the night wind, 587 : 16
of vernal shower, 363 : 13
poetry b. of knowledge, 424 : 7
princes but b. of kings, 408 : 18
rehearsing latest b., 899 : 14
rides on posting winds, 243 : 21
say with final b., 570 : 6
some of us out of b., 613 : 6
stealing my b. of life, 819 : 4
summer's ripening b., 192 : 14
sweet is the b.of morn, 285 : 27
thought takes b. away, 591 : 10
thy b. was shed, 721 : 4
to last moment of b., 368 : 11
toil of b., 438 : 9
twilight hour of b., 721 : 8
Breath (*continued*)
utter sweet b., 197 : 11
want of words lack of b., 289 : 1
weary of b., 485 : 21
when b. blew back, 604 : 11
whiskey on your b., 873 : 10
world gray from thy b., 633 : 6
writing is holding your b., 835 : 18
Breathe air again, 578 : 12
and blow, 530 : 25
as though to b. life, 529 : 9
daring to b. or Achoo, 911 : 16
hate were why men b., 829 : 21
hear bronze Negroes b., 893 : 12
heart pause to b., 460 : 5
his native air, 332 : 10
if such there b., 430 : 10
not his name, 446 : 7
prayer for all beneath, 710 : 15
slaves cannot b. in England, 376 : 20
thou thereon didst only b., 256 : 9
thoughts that b., 363 : 3
yearning to b. free, 664 : 10
you but knock b. shine, 254 : 15
Breathed, first true gentleman that b., 251 : 11
still b. in sighs, 334 : 26
Breathes, hell itself b. out, 222 : 23
of nations saved, 461 : 20
restless wind of inlets, 837 : 2
there the man, 430 : 10
upon bank of violets, 213 : 7
with human breath, 528 : 2
Breathing, almost hear them b. as they march, 893 : *n* 2
and sighing round it, 652 : *n* 3
closer He than b., 535 : 9
health and quiet b., 475 : 16
household laws, 425 : 15
music b. from her face, 295 : *n* 11
revenge, 561 : 2
talking coeval with b., 323 : 30
whether b. is eating, 82 : 21
without a tighter b., 606 : 14
Breathless, hanging b. on fate, 511 : 8
we flung us on hill, 796 : 9
with adoration, 425 : 16
Breath's a ware that will not keep, 690 : 18
Bred, dainties b. of a book, 190 : 27
en bawn in brier patch, 662 : 8
me long ago, 691 : 11
where is fancy b., 199 : 23
Bredon, bells sound on B., 691 : 4
Breeches, coat red b. blue, 440 : 14
cost a crown, 917 : 21
hand in b. pocket, 479 : 6
Macaulay a book in b., 433 : 10
women wear the b., 258 : 11
Breed and haunt, 236 : 21
border nor b. nor birth, 707 : 16
careful of b. of horses, 314 : 14
feared by their b., 194 : 13
happy b. of men, 194 : 13
Hyla b., 747 : 14
if sun b. maggots, 220 : 17
no waters b. nor break, 901 : 4
or England b. again, 182 : 15
resolute b. of men, 577 : 15
use doth b. habit, 190 : 7
Breeding, bad b. and vulgar manner, 81 : 13
Burgundy without b., 831 : 4
eating drinking b., 574 : 20

Breeding (*continued*)
lilacs out of dead land, 804 : 26
test of man's or woman's b., 680 : 4
write with ease to show b., 399 : 11
Breeds, familiarity b. contempt, 66 : 4, 626 : 14
lesser b. without Law, 709 : 19
Breeze, Athena sent favorable b., 59 : 19
battle and the b., 443 : 10
blow through life like b., 855 : 17
fair b. blew, 434 : 13
flag to April's b., 494 : 13
folds rippling in b., 539 : 3
free as the b., 429 : 16
ghost fled like fluttering b., 105 : 5
midday summer b., 749 : 4
of morning moves, 533 : 21
snuff thee up sea b., 569 : 20
spring-laden b. sinister, 728 : 13
tyranny in tainted b., 372 : 20
Breezes dusk and shiver, 528 : 24
sunset b. shiver, 700 : 10
Breezy call of morn, 361 : 24
Brekekekex 82 : 18
Brennt Paris, 813 : *n* 1
Brent, bonny brow was b., 410 : 7
Brer Fox he lay low, 662 : 6
Brethren, firstborn among many b., 47 : 11
for b. to dwell together, 22 : 14
forget love to friends and b., 34 : 2
least of these my b., 41 : 1
our b. already in field, 383 : 5
we be b., 8 : 6
Brève, la vie est b., 617 : *n* 1
Brevis, vita b. est, 80 : *n* 2
Brevity, its body b., 435 : 24
soul of wit, 220 : 10
Brew, soup or broth or b., 539 : 19
Brewed, taste liquor never b., 604 : 13
Brewer's, I am a b. horse, 204 : 24
Brews, as he b. so shall he drink, 255 : 7
livelier liquor than Muse, 691 : 17
Bribe, too poor for b., 363 : 11
Bribery, treason b. or other high crimes, 391 : 11
Bribes, tell everyone I take b., 518 : 4
Brick, no more straw to make b., 9 : 17
whistle on a b., 892 : 7
Yellow B. Road, 677 : 8
Bricks alive to testify, 185 : 27
and sermons, 625 : 24
lie to throw b. at, 625 : 24
Rome a city of b., 110 : 8
somebody's always throwing b., 765 : 4
Brickyard, dewdrops gathered in b., 699 : 16
Bridal, bridegrooms brides and b. cakes, 265 : 17
of earth and sky, 268 : 15
same voice for death or b., 899 : 2
Bride, barren b., 335 : 18
bridegroom seek your b., 692 : 2
encounter darkness as a b., 228 : 18
holy city as a b., 53 : 29
in her rich adornin', 661 : 10
lyeth between b. and bridegroom, 793 : 2
never turns to b., 690 : 19
of quietness, 477 : 4
paced into the hall, 434 : 9

Bride (*continued*)
society my glittering b., 428 : 13
Bride-bed, thought b. to have decked, 224 : 20
Bridechamber, can children of b. mourn, 38 : 29
Bridegroom all night through, 690 : 19
coming out of his chamber, 17 : 28
fresh as a b., 203 : 7
happy b. Hesper brings, 692 : 2
in my death, 241 : 19
lyeth between bride and b., 793 : 2
mourn as b. with them, 38 : 29
went forth to meet b., 40 : 28
Bridegrooms brides and bridal cakes, 265 : 17
Brides, as lion woos his b., 366 : 9
bridegrooms b. and bridal cakes, 265 : 17
Bridge, asses' b., 92 : *n* 2
body swung beneath b., 647 : 5
broken arch of London B., 488 : 7
by rude b., 494 : 13
cobweb b. from mind, 701 : 7
don't cross b. until come to it, 921 : 7
give him silver b., 935 : 8
grave a covered b., 512 : 12
London B. broken down, 929 : 21
London B. falling down, 698 : 14
of Sighs, 458 : 5
of time, 581 : 12
over troubled water, 915 : 15
stood on b. at midnight, 510 : 16
that arched the flood, 494 : 13
twenty men crossing b., 766 : 13
youth build b. to moon, 557 : 12
Bridges, crossing twenty b., 766 : 13
flock of b. bleating, 770 : 9
forbids to sleep under b., 655 : 14
Bridle, between spur and b., 270 : 12
gae his b. reins a shake, 410 : 6
Bridled, millions saddled and b., 298 : 18
Brief as lightning in collied night, 195 : 23
as water falling, 812 : 3
as woman's love, 222 : 12
chronicles of the time, 221 : 4
December day, 513 : 20
dreamy kind of delight, 712 : 19
hours and weeks, 245 : 18
life here our portion, 563 : 12
little b. authority, 228 : 10
out out b. candle, 240 : 4
rude b. recitative, 575 : 21
thanksgiving, 633 : 22
thus b. is grief, 812 : 3
transit where dreams cross, 806 : 5
when b. I become obscure, 109 : 20
when our b. light has set, 101 : 18
Briefcase of enthusiasm, 835 : 6
Brier, bred en bawn in b. patch, 662 : 8
thorough bush thorough b., 196 : 10
Briers, full of b. is working-day world, 210 : 20
Brig, mate of Nancy b., 627 : 7
transom of merchant b., 498 : 20
Brigade, Light B., 533 : 10
thy b. with cold cascade, 628 : 25
Bright, all calm all b., 466 : 2
all calm as it was b., 299 : 6
all things b. beautiful, 561 : 8
and battering sandal, 656 : 8
and violet-crowned, 72 : 9

Bright (*continued*)
angels are b. still, 239 : 18
angels' visits short and b., 318 : 4
Apollo's lute, 191 : 4
April shakes out her hair, 787 : 5
beauteous b. creation, 135 : 2
best of dark and b., 459 : 13
billows smooth and b., 613 : 1
bodies of lovers drowned, 770 : 12
bracelet of b. hair, 253 : 12
container can contain, 874 : 1
countenance of truth, 281 : 13
creature scorn not one, 429 : 11
dark with excessive b., 285 : 7
day is done, 241 : 26
day so cool so calm so b., 268 : 15
early b. transient chaste, 307 : *n* 3
edges of world, 739 : 5
exhalation in the evening, 249 : 1
eye of heaven shined b., 173 : 10
eyes of danger, 669 : 3
girdle furled, 587 : 16
gleam of noble deeds, 72 : 7
glories afar shine b., 262 : 6
goddess excellently b., 255 : 12
hard medal, 653 : 15
harmony in her b. eye, 295 : 21
he saw lady b., 926 : 23
honor b., 226 : 17
incalculable soul, 828 : 16
is the ring of words, 669 : 6
jewels of the mine, 561 : *n* 1
keep up your b. swords, 229 : 21
ladies whose b. eyes, 278 : 5
lamps shone o'er, 457 : 14
land is b., 564 : 17
little tight little, 629 : 19
merged with b. air, 874 : 13
moon shines b., 200 : 22
moon still as b., 460 : 5
more b. than Mayday morn, 399 : 20
musical as b. Apollo's lute, 191 : 4
my b. mane forever, 403 : 14
neither pale nor b., 899 : 14
no b. reversion in sky, 335 : 8
not gold that showeth b., 137 : *n* 8
October's b. blue weather, 609 : 11
old age serene and b., 427 : 20
orange b., 297 : 9
particular star, 227 : 10
patines of b. gold, 201 : 1
pearl and crystal shining b., 406 : 6
perseverance keeps honor b., 226 : 17
pluck b. honor from moon, 203 : 15
pomp ascended jubilant, 287 : 1
pretty Babe all burning b., 182 : 2
reversion in sky, 335 : 8
seraphim in burning row, 281 : 10
shoots of everlastingness, 299 : 3
sleep sleep beauty b., 404 : 12
softest clothing wooly b., 403 : 5
spouse so b. and clear, 254 : 16
star would I were steadfast, 478 : 20
their memory fair and b., 299 : 7
things come to confusion, 195 : 23
thought thee b., 246 : 7
Tiger Tiger burning b., 405 : 7
torch and casement, 477 : 13
used key always b., 347 : 24
wherever b. sun shall shine, 249 : 18
with freedom's light, 514 : 13
young lady named B., 742 : 1
youth passes swiftly, 67 : 7
Bright-colored, victory b. flower, 743 : 4

Brightened, countenance soon
b., 428 : 15
Brightening, all his prospects b., 370 : 3
O b. glance, 715 : 17
Brightens, how the wit b., 333 : 13
Brighter, allured to b. worlds, 370 : 7
emits a b. ray, 368 : 12
in some b. clime, 387 : 3
look b. when we come, 460 : 16
Brightest and best of sons of
morning, 452 : 5
best and b., 452 : *n* 1
best and b. come away, 470 : 2
fashion's b. arts, 370 : 16
flashes of thought, 580 : 5
heaven of invention, 207 : 1
old wood burn b., 262 : 1
sometimes hath b. day a
cloud, 185 : 14
though the b. fell, 239 : 18
wisest b. meanest, 337 : 15
Brightness falls from the air, 250 : 10
not lost original b., 283 : 23
weave garment of b., 928 : 14
when god-given b. comes, 72 : 2
Brignall banks wild and fair, 431 : 18
Brilliance, minute b., 785 : 12
without conscience, 825 : 2
Brilliant and warm, 830 : 18
moon milky sky, 712 : 7
Brillig and slithy toves, 612 : 17
Brim, bubbles winking at b., 476 : 23
filled to b. with glee, 629 : 8
o'er night's b. day, 540 : 14
primrose by river's b., 423 : 16
sparkles near the b., 457 : 12
Brimstone bed at break of day, 440 : 13
fire and b., 622 : 13
of a creature I am, 489 : 17
Brindled, dear Andrew with b.
hair, 668 : 19
Bring all Heaven before mine
eyes, 278 : 26
balloon of mind, 714 : 6
can I b. him back, 13 : 21
cease to ask what morrow will
b., 107 : 7
chance b. us through, 585 : 8
down my gray hairs, 8 : 32
eternal note of sadness, 587 : 14
fear Greeks even when they b.
gifts, 104 : 32
forth a son, 36 : 19
forth children in sorrow, 7 : 11
fresh showers, 468 : 9
go Death b. her, 733 : 13
good old bugle, 614 : 13
in lion among ladies, 196 : 24
it to achievement, 76 : 19
me a beaker of wine, 81 : 12
me arrows of desire, 406 : 21
me my bow, 406 : 21
me my chariot of fire, 406 : 21
me my spear, 406 : 21
men to match mountains, 671 : *n* 1
much money as 'twill b., 291 : 17
my kisses b. again, 228 : 28
never good to b. bad news, 241 : 4
redemption from above did b., 277 : 6
slovenly unhandsome corpse, 203 : 8
suit in Supreme Court, 787 : 11
Sweeney to Mrs. Porter, 805 : 6
the rathe primrose, 281 : 1
us together again, 882 : 18
Bring (*continued*)
with thee jest, 277 : 19
Bringer of good tidings, 130 : 14
of that joy, 197 : 12
of unwelcome news, 205 : 20
Bringeth forth his fruit in
season, 17 : 12
thee into a good land, 11 : 13
to light the shadow of death, 15 : 31
Bringing his sheaves with him, 22 : 7
in secret her whom thou takest
away, 97 : 16
owls to Athens, 82 : 6
Brings desired timely things, 692 : 2
fortune b. in some boats, 243 : 29
loathing to stomach b., 196 : 23
love remembered such wealth
b., 244 : 10
to pass every word, 71 : 1
wretchedness that glory b., 243 : 7
yew to deck my grave, 402 : 14
Brink, scared to go to b., 803 : 8
tread upon b. of meaning, 352 : 26
Brinkmanship 803 : *n* 3
Briny, along b. beach, 613 : 3
Brioche, qu'ils mangent de la
b., 359 : *n* 2
Brisk, airs martial b. or grave, 377 : 13
and giddy-paced times, 213 : 28
as bee in conversation, 353 : 22
Brisking about the life, 365 : 14
Bristles, Wax and B. three sheets in
wind, 553 : *n* 4
Bristol, dim on piece of B.
board, 878 : 19
fashion, 553 : 19
Britain, connection between them
and B., 378 : 12
fight on alone, 745 : 12
first at Heaven's command, 345 : 19
limits of B. laid bare, 123 : 2
spleen that scourge of B., 486 : 6
that once was B., 340 : 21
wins last battle, 745 : 13
Britain's, ambassador from B.
crown, 536 : 7
forgot was B. glory, 596 : 17
Britannia needs no bulwarks, 443 : 12
rule B., 345 : 19
Brither, Tam lo'ed him like a b., 411 : 6
British, allegiance to B., 378 : 12
come back B. soldier, 708 : 8
dirty B. coaster, 760 : 20
Empire and United States, 744 : 7
government best model, 401 : 11
greatness of B. nation, 326 : 22
Grenadier, 922 : 10
hold B. as rest of mankind, 387 : 10
I smell blood of a B. man, 234 : 13
if B. Empire last thousand
years, 744 : 4
if B. went by water, 382 : 12
liquidation of B. Empire, 746 : 2
maxim of B., 743 : 6
Museum of infirmities, 626 : 18
people like to be told worst, 744 : 15
piece of B. manhood, 472 : 13
prime minister returned, 727 : 2
public in fit of morality, 487 : 19
refusal to accept defeat, 771 : 9
rule, 911 : 1
shadow of B. oak, 373 : 28
stony B. stare, 533 : 19
structure of B. sentence, 743 : 8
British (*continued*)
warrior queen, 377 : 22
British-Americans, have done with
B., 667 : 1
Britons never will be slaves, 345 : 19
Brittle, dream bonds were b., 633 : 9
glass of years is b., 633 : 7
Broached, Christmas b. mightiest
ale, 430 : 22
death has b. him to, 393 : 11
Broad, brooks too b. for
leaping, 691 : 14
crimes b. blown, 222 : 27
famous English poet, 261 : 15
is the way, 38 : 15
limbo large and b., 285 : 8
margin to my life, 560 : 1
passage b. to hell, 92 : *n* 5
where b. ocean leans, 368 : 20
with b. flat nails, 86 : 10
Broadcast doings of day and
night, 573 : 19
industry's planners, 872 : 19
Broadcloth without, 377 : 17
Broad-streeted Richmond, 840 : 6
Broadway, give regards to B., 759 : 5
Broccoli, it's b. dear, 846 : 7
Brod, wer nie sein b., 395 : *n* 2
Broke, all hell b. loose, 286 : 9
bank at Monte Carlo, 666 : 21
cable b. anchor lost, 186 : 23
chancel window-squares, 642 : 1
come in we'll keep ye b., 721 : 15
die in molding Sheridan, 459 : 20
made him and then b. mold, 154 : 11
my high-blown pride b. under
me, 249 : 3
no one ever went b., 772 : 20
no promise served no end, 336 : 5
when time is b., 195 : 16
Broken and a contrite heart, 19 : 19
arch of London Bridge, 488 : 7
be merciful to b. reed, 179 : 11
bow tensely strung easily b., 111 : 7
by sorrow spirit b., 24 : 6
by their passing feet, 712 : 2
cheerful hearts now b., 447 : 7
factory windows always b., 765 : 4
fortune like glass easily b., 111 : 2
glass obscured or b., 900 : 3
golden bowl be b., 27 : 25
he has departed withdrawn b.
out, 98 : 3
heap of b. images, 805 : 1
heart lies here, 489 : 3
hell's b. loose, 178 : 14
how but through b. heart, 676 : 14
I am like a b. vessel, 18 : 16
it up for daily bread, 632 : 21
laughs at b. hammers, 761 : 17
more than ocean water b., 748 : 11
Nature's social union, 408 : 13
not with club heart b., 607 : 7
oar and gear of dead men, 808 : 2
on earth b. arcs, 544 : 4
picked up b. point, 815 : 8
pitcher b. at the fountain, 27 : 25
renewal of b. relations, 635 : 5
resting upon b. staff, 379 : 4
staff of this b. reed, 30 : 26
things b. and scattered, 733 : 17
things uncomely and b., 712 : 12
two gross b. statues, 792 : 16
unto the ground, 29 : 27

Broken (*continued*)
wall burning tower, 715 : 16
wheel b. at the cistern, 27 : 25
with storms of state, 249 : 10
wound heart that's b., 431 : 19
Brokenhearted, half b., 456 : 8
hoped we were b., 634 : 2
lean above b., 787 : 5
we had ne'er been b., 410 : 3
Bromide number one, 736 : *n* 1
Bronx, La Rochefoucauld never lived in B., 859 : 16
Bronze, hear b. Negroes breathe, 893 : 12
heart of b., 57 : 19
mangled by the b. spear, 59 : 6
monument more lasting than b., 108 : 8
nailed like illegible b., 894 : 4
stone b. stone steel, 806 : 12
up from b. I saw, 837 : 1
work with breathing b., 105 : 24
Bronzed lank man, 765 : 8
Brooch, bow or b. or braid, 656 : 12
of gold ful sheene, 145 : 20
Brooches, make you b. and toys, 669 : 4
Brood, mothers a bloody b., 834 : 5
of Folly, 278 : 9
on Christian thing, 863 : 14
Broodest o'er troubled sea, 475 : 18
Brooding, birds sit b. in snow, 191 : 15
on country's fate, 564 : 9
on God, 874 : 22
toads b. in wells, 873 : 12
Brook, dwelt by the b. Cherith, 13 : 40
many can b. the weather, 190 : 28
noise like hidden b., 435 : 1
smooth water where b. deep, 172 : *n* 7
went to the b., 933 : 12
where b. and river meet, 510 : 13
Brookland, far in western b., 691 : 11
Brooklyn, from B. over B. Bridge, 878 : 8
Brooks, as b. make rivers, 307 : 2
as hart panteth after water b., 19 : 5
books in running b., 210 : 24
for fishers of song, 685 : 11
golden sands crystal b., 253 : 2
I sing of b., 265 : 17
shallow b. and rivers wide, 277 : 25
strow b. in Vallombrosa, 283 : 16
too broad for leaping, 691 : 14
Brooks Brothers, man in B. shirt, 881 : 8
Broom, beat barrel with b., 765 : 5
new b. sweeps clean, 916 : 15
under arm carried b., 932 : 5
Broomstick, Old Glory on b., 699 : 13
write finely upon b., 322 : *n* 2
Broomsticks, all their b. and tears, 714 : 4
Broth without any bread, 931 : 10
Brother, am I not man and b., 375 : 5
and companion in tribulation, 52 : 27
be my b. or I kill you, 386 : 6
Big B. watching, 858 : 14
came with subtilty, 8 : 18
can you spare dime, 842 : 5
critic b. of artist, 653 : 3
Death and b. Sleep, 466 : 6
Death's b. Sleep, 105 : 17
devil to Despair, 659 : 5
every one said to his b., 31 : 3
every sword against his b., 32 : 31
Brother (*continued*)
far off, 25 : 25
fight against his b., 29 : 25
gently scan b. man, 409 : 21
half b. of world, 555 : 15
hypocrite reader my b., 580 : 16
I am that insect b., 581 : 20
lawless linsey-woolsey b., 291 : 15
life sweet b., 492 : 16
loved him like a b., 411 : 6
man and b., 375 : 5
more close than b., 710 : 19
my double my b., 580 : 16
no b. near the throne, 338 : 14
now must I depart from b., 4 : 12
of the Angle, 270 : 33
offended is harder to be won, 24 : 21
Remus and his b. knew this life, 104 : 7
safety for my son b. shipmates, 151 : 10
shall be my b., 208 : 11
sinned against my b. the ass, 139 : 1
sleep death's twin b., 58 : *n* 3
sleep the b. of death, 58 : 20, 182 : 4
sticketh closer than a b., 24 : 23
still to my b. turns, 368 : 14
Sun who brings us day, 138 : 12
the b. the real b., 705 : 12
thy tail hangs down, 709 : 3
to all creatures, 897 : 19
to dragons, 16 : 19
which of us known b., 852 : 7
would brother cheat, 138 : 9
yet line up with brother, 761 : 17
Brotherhood bind rich and poor, 621 : 5
crown good with b., 688 : 5
intellect triumphed over b., 503 : 4
love the b., 52 : 11
men and women affirm b., 870 : 13
of venerable trees, 426 : 8
sit down at table of b., 909 : 9
that binds brave, 700 : 6
Brotherly, feel it so b., 882 : 3
love, 47 : 20, 51 : 22
Brother's, called b. father dad, 201 : 17
keeper, 7 : 15
mote in b. eye, 38 : 9
murder, 222 : 25
sad mad b. name, 634 : 11
voice of thy b. blood, 7 : 16
what I sowed b. sons gathering, 854 : 2
Brothers above arch of stars, 412 : 10
all in honor, 424 : 4
all the b. too, 214 : 6
and sisters beware, 710 : 14
are evil, 4 : 5
as b. live together, 511 : 15
band of b., 208 : 11
call from bay, 584 : 11
forty thousand b., 224 : 22
good-bye b., 683 : 5
linsey-woolsey b., 340 : 21
men become b., 412 : 9
shall b. be for a' that, 411 : 19
sons kindred slain, 338 : *n* 8
valiant sisters virtuous, 919 : 14
ye are b. ye are men, 443 : 17
Brought, Antony b. drunken forth, 241 : 27
before the mountains were b. forth, 20 : 11
daughters of music b. low, 27 : 24
Brought (*continued*)
death into the world, 282 : 22
forth on this continent, 523 : 4
me down to knees, 874 : 17
me home to glory, 525 : 9
mouse will be b. forth, 109 : 25
never b. to mind, 410 : 11
nothing into this world, 51 : 1
over vast and furious ocean, 265 : 7
palsy to bed, 793 : 2
up in this city, 46 : 25
which b. us hither, 426 : 20
Brow, athlete crowned in sweat of b., 127 : 14
bonny b. was brent, 410 : 7
candid b., 683 : 12
dangerous b. by night, 215 : 19
flushing his b., 476 : 13
forty winters besiege thy b., 244 : 1
grace seated on this b., 223 : 3
Helen's beauty in b. of Egypt, 197 : 12
no wrinkle on azure b., 458 : 27
now your b. is beld John, 410 : 7
of labor, 694 : 16
of lip of eye of b., 245 : 12
pain and anguish wring b., 431 : 2
parallels in beauty's b., 244 : 20
pure unclouded b., 612 : 15
shine upon b. today, 662 : 22
so grim mouth so prim, 806 : 14
sweat of b., 559 : 14
upon his b. shame ashamed, 193 : 10
view with wrinkled b., 200 : 15
wet with honest sweat, 510 : 8
where he got that high b., 121 : 21
wrinkle deeper on b., 457 : 10
Brown, baked me too b., 612 : 10
bread and the Gospel, 319 : 10
breasts, 822 : 4
bright nightingale, 632 : 7
changing from b. suit to gray, 791 : 6
good man Charlie B., 901 : 7
hair and speaks small, 225 : 6
hair over mouth, 806 : 2
heath and shaggy wood, 430 : 11
hills melted into spring, 562 : 1
in b. study, 175 : 12
Jeanie with light b. hair, 598 : 6
long and lank and b., 434 : 25
long b. path before me, 575 : 9
man's burden, 709 : *n* 3
meadows b. and sere, 471 : 10
myrtles b., 280 : 6
not Old B. any longer, 560 : 26
prefer philanthropy of Captain B., 560 : 24
quick b. fox, 923 : 2
some gave them b., 929 : 19
strong b. god, 808 : 1
world black red yellow b., 912 : 15
Browne, sedulous ape to Sir Thomas B., 668 : 23
Browning, find B. plain, 542 : *n* 3
from B. some Pomegranate, 506 : 14
hang it all Robert B., 792 : 18
is what, 546 : *n* 1
Meredith prose B., 674 : 18
Mrs. B. guard silence, 751 : 7
since Chaucer was alive, 442 : 24
Browning, entsichere meinen B., 816 : *n* 2
Browning's, Mrs. B. death relief, 517 : 16
Brown's, John B. body, 619 : 14

Brows, bliss in our b. bent, 240 : 18
earned with sweat of b., 168 : 9
like gathering storm, 411 : 4
nightcap decked his b., 368 : 8
nodded with his darkish b., 57 : 12
not seen in either of our b., 182 : 16
of dauntless courage, 283 : 25
Bruce has aften led, 411 : 15
Brüder, alle Menschen werden B., 412 : *n* 3
Bruise, ax fitter to b., 290 : 10
better for b. than arnica, 544 : 28
it shall b. thy head, 7 : 10
thou shalt b. his heel, 7 : 10
Bruised, not b. to pleasure soul, 715 : 17
reed shall he not break, 31 : 4
together crushed and b., 334 : 15
Brunswick, Hamelin town's in B., 540 : 32
Brunt, bear b. pay arrears, 544 : 22
stands b. of life, 76 : 20
Brush, blind hand b. my wing, 405 : 6
essential in painting, 135 : 11
George B. is my name, 839 : 11
painter's b. consumes dreams, 715 : 13
whether chisel pen b., 714 : 7
whitewash and long-handled b., 622 : 11
work with so fine a b., 441 : 3
Brushed, hand has b. away, 405 : 6
past palms on staircase, 866 : 16
Brushwood sheaf, 541 : 16
Brutal arm appear, 717 : 16
Brutality, industry without art b., 573 : 7
oppressor commit b. openly, 909 : 16
that special b., 583 : 9
Brutalizing lower class, 589 : 4
Brute absolute hour, 864 : 7
beast b. bastard, 881 : 11
beauty and valor, 656 : 3
black sea b. bulling, 907 : 2
chuck 'im out the b., 708 : 4
heart of brute like you, 911 : 18
love of a b., 526 : 6
Brute, et tu B., 99 : *n* 17, 216 : 5
Brutes, as we to b. poets to us, 601 : 8
eating and drinking like b., 576 : 16
exterminate b., 683 : 19
man's difference from b., 649 : 16
nation of b., 683 : *n* 5
not born to live like b., 141 : 14
without you, 317 : 2
Brutish, nasty b. and short, 264 : 17
Brutus and Cassius not displayed, 122 : 20
Caesar had his B., 382 : 13
dear B., 215 : 6
is an honorable man, 216 : 18
makes mine greater, 217 : 3
no orator as B. is, 216 : 27
you also B., 99 : 24
Bubble, fire burn caldron b., 239 : 4
gonfalon b., 773 : 12
honor but an empty b., 306 : 19
life a b., 181 : *n* 7
like b. on fountain, 431 : 11
now a b. burst, 336 : 14
reputation, 211 : 15
world's a b., 181 : 17
Bubbles, borne like thy b. onward, 458 : 30
earth hath b., 236 : 7
Bubbles (*continued*)
man and his dwellings as b., 137 : 13
millions of b. like us, 516 : 21
we buy, 567 : 12
winking at brim, 476 : 23
Bubbling and loud-hissing urn, 377 : 3
cry of swimmer, 460 : 21
sinks with b. groan, 458 : 26
venom flings, 457 : 2
wellspring, 601 : 2
Buccaneers of buzz, 607 : 11
Buck in the snow, 823 : 9
stops here, 788 : 16
Bucket down and full of tears am I, 195 : 11
drop of a b., 30 : 36
of whitewash, 622 : 11
old oaken b., 455 : 7
past a b. of ashes, 761 : 7
up down as b. in a welle, 146 : 21
Buckets into empty wells, 376 : 27, 432 : 25
two b. filling one another, 195 : 11
Bucketshop of refrigerator, 711 : 2
Buckhurst, I would B. choose, 315 : 15
Buckingham, so much for B., 324 : 27
Buckle, pride plume here b., 656 : 3
Buckler, his truth thy shield and b., 20 : 16
Buckles, silver b. on knee, 934 : 3
Bucks, fat black b., 765 : 5
Bud, canker lives in sweetest b., 244 : 14
in age I b. again, 269 : 5
not as in b. of spring, 255 : 1
of thought wants to be rose, 720 : 19
rose is sweeter in b., 175 : 22
this b. of love, 192 : 14
worm in the b., 214 : 5
Buddha, go for refuge to B., 73 : 6
the Awakened One, 72 : 17
Buddhas, Arahat B. who appear in world, 72 : 21
Budding historians, 800 : 1
Buddy, Christ Himself b., 896 : 10
Budge, I'll not b. an inch, 188 : 23
Ten Commandments not b., 569 : 1
Buds, cankers in musk rose b., 196 : 19
darling b. of May, 244 : 5
forgot to blow, 637 : 22
green b. they were swellin', 926 : 21
of barren flowers, 633 : 20
sleep in root's white core, 478 : 9
young b. sleep in root, 478 : 9
Buff and the blue, 411 : 24
bare to the b., 669 : 5
Buffalo Bill's defunct, 828 : 13
created before my eyes, 789 : 7
gals come out tonight, 921 : 20
home where b. roam, 927 : 19
life breath of b. in wintertime, 581 : 15
my b. have found me, 839 : 20
thought he saw b., 614 : 7
wind on b. grass, 928 : 11
Buffaloes, water b. neurasthenic, 799 : 16
Buffalo's powerful head, 867 : 15
Buffet, not wise who b. against love, 75 : 5
Buffets, blows and b. of world, 238 : 15
fortune's b. and rewards, 222 : 5
Buffon, is it Aristotle Pliny B., 358 : 23
Buffoon and poet, 663 : 8
chemist fiddler and b., 304 : 10
Buffoonery, life piece of b., 723 : 20
Buffoons, great men not b., 498 : 21
Buffs, private of B., 536 : 7
steady the B., 707 : 13
Bug, flap b. with gilded wings, 338 : 19
snug as a b. in rug, 348 : 5
Bugle, blow b. blow, 530 : 26
bring good old b. boys, 614 : 13
one blast upon b. horn, 431 : 15
sound upon b. horn, 529 : 15
Bugles, blare of b., 676 : *n* 5
blow out you b., 797 : 4
calling for them, 827 : 3
cry of b. going by, 696 : 9
what are b. blowin' for, 708 : 1
Build a new world, 787 : 12
beneath stars, 330 : 17
except the Lord b. the house, 22 : 8
experience arch to b. upon, 634 : 18
from bottom up, 779 : 6
Great Society, 872 : 13
houses and inhabit them, 31 : 31
intending to b. tower, 43 : 24
lofty rhyme, 280 : 7
me nest on greatness of God, 651 : 9
me straight, 511 : 6
middle-aged b. woodshed, 557 : 12
on fortune build on sand, 265 : 4
on human heart, 540 : 12
pair nor b. nor sing, 436 : 9
schoolrooms for boy, 562 : 12
ship of death, 791 : 2
small cabin b. there, 712 : 4
thee more stately mansions, 519 : 7
they labor in vain that b. it, 22 : 8
throne of bayonets, 696 : 2
time to b. up, 26 : 21
upon this rock b. my church, 39 : 36
with lithe love, 889 : 17
your ship of death, 791 : 4
youth b. bridge to moon, 557 : 12
Builded better than knew, 493 : 18
was Jerusalem b. here, 406 : 21
wisdom hath b. her house, 23 : 18
Builders, stone which the b. refused, 21 : 25
Buildeth on vulgar heart, 206 : 7
Building beginning of arts, 690 : 1
castles in Spain, 149 : 1
principal beauty in a b., 276 : 18
roofs of gold, 207 : 7
stole life o' the b., 238 : 5
three things in b., 395 : 18
we are nation b., 797 : 7
Buildings he may never enter, 395 : 22
you may have all the b., 609 : 10
Builds, Devil b. chapel there, 318 : 5
heaven in hell's despair, 405 : 3
hell in heaven's despite, 405 : 4
marsh hen secretly b., 651 : 9
phoenix b. phoenix' nest, 292 : 18
phoenix b. spicy nest, 271 : 21
though he b. glorious temples, 567 : 16
what man b. has but a day, 758 : 2
Built absolute trust, 236 : 15
against will of gods, 58 : 13
almost lost that b. it, 275 : 8
before I b. wall, 747 : 6
bicycle b. for two, 718 : 18
fortress b. by Nature for herself, 194 : 13
God a church, 376 : 9
house that Jack b., 934 : 9

Built (*continued*)
in such logical way, 519 : 15
in the eclipse, 280 : 18
love b. on beauty, 253 : 16
my soul pleasure-house, 528 : 6
nests in beard, 550 : 4
of just a syllable, 607 : 10
Rome not b. in one day, 160 : 8
ruined love when b. anew, 245 : 21
science b. with facts, 673 : 8
till we have b. Jerusalem, 406 : 21
which b. desolate places, 15 : 8
who b. seven gates of Thebes, 840 : 17
Bulben's, bare Ben B. head, 718 : 1
Bull, a Cock and a B., 360 : 20
cloud that looked like b., 81 : 15
greatest of all is John B., 462 : 9
handsome as b. that kidnapped Europa, 98 : 20
John B. or Englishman's Fireside, 415 : 11
moose, 687 : 2
savage b. bear yoke, 209 : 2
Bullen's, dawned from B. eyes, 361 : 19
Bullet, ballot stronger than b., 520 : 3
bite b., 707 : 18
has its billet, 316 : 10
that will kill me not cast, 420 : 13
through his head, 729 : 5
Bullets made of lead, 933 : 12
paper b. of the brain, 209 : 19
seek out where heart lies, 860 : 12
word as b. flying, 683 : 7
Bullied into following master artist, 803 : 2
out of vice, 500 : 22
Bullocks, whose talk is of b., 36 : 9
Bullpen, waiting sentence in b., 893 : 1
Bulls, plowman's story of b., 112 : 20
Bulrush, seeking knot in a b., 93 : 10
Bulrushes, ark of b., 9 : 8
Bulwark, civic genius b. of democracy, 650 : 15
floating b. of our island, 365 : 16
never failing, 155 : 15
of continuing liberty, 780 : 6
of Greece famous Athens, 72 : 9
of our liberty, 520 : 7
Bulwarks, Britannia needs no b., 443 : 12
great b. of liberty, 367 : 6
Bum, belly shoulder b., 717 : 16
I'll moider the b., 877 : 9
Bumbast out blank verse, 178 : 12
Bumble, the law is a ass said Mr. B., 547 : 6
Bumblebee, Moses on b., 840 : 8
Bump, don't b. into furniture, 852 : 4
go b. in the night, 921 : 4
Bumper of good liquor, 398 : 26
Bumping, love b. against obstacles of civilization, 504 : 7
Bumps along the dusk, 665 : 7
miss many hard b., 320 : 1
Bumptious, self-confidence complete and b., 792 : 1
Bunbury, invaluable invalid B., 675 : 19
Bunched in mutual glee, 844 : 1
Buncombe and millions mostly fools, 474 : 12
Bunghole, stopping a b., 224 : 15
Bunk, been in his b. below, 647 : 21
history more or less b., 587 : *n* 2
Bunker Hill, there is Boston and B., 450 : 13
Buns, hot cross b., 931 : 17
Bunting, baby b., 931 : 5
Bunyan, swart convict B., 570 : 11
Buoy too small for sight, 234 : 28
Buoys, noise of bell b., 798 : 13
Burbled as it came, 612 : 18
Burden, bear any b., 890 : 7
bear his own b., 49 : 31
borne the b., 40 : 9
brown man's b., 709 : *n* 3
changes labor from b. to honor, 766 : 8
grasshopper shall be a b., 27 : 25
great b. upon his back, 301 : 20
grievous b. was thy birth, 187 : 18
life hollow existence b., 622 : 11
my b. is light, 39 : 8
not b. our remembrances, 248 : 18
of his song, 382 : 7
of incommunicable, 454 : 16
of long living, 633 : 17
of my song, 917 : 12
of nothing to do, 311 : 17
of the desert of the sea, 29 : 26
of the mystery, 423 : 10
of the world, 670 : 14
of them is intolerable, 55 : 17
on back b. of world, 670 : 14
they're a b. for us, 849 : 15
vapors weep their b., 533 : 27
weight of another's b., 270 : 18
white man's b., 709 : 21
with superfluous b. loads day, 282 : 10
years are still a b., 76 : 5
youth and age equally a b., 84 : 4
Burdened, shakes fires in b. air, 403 : 18
Burdens, bearing b. of government, 519 : 21
had such b. on mind, 715 : 9
they that bare b., 14 : 29
Burdensome, school in which nothing b., 129 : 21
when life is b., 78 : 16
Bureau, super legal aid b., 777 : 1
transform world into b., 775 : 7
Bureaucrat, make everybody b., 775 : 7
Burgeoning wood brings forth, 58 : 1
Burglar Banker Father, 604 : 3
Burglaree, with a little b., 628 : 4
Burglary, flat b. as ever committed, 209 : 33
vary piracy with b., 628 : 4
Burgonet, arm and b. of men, 240 : 22
Burgundy, naive domestic B., 831 : 4
treat wretch with B., 319 : 20
Burial, no b. this pretty pair, 917 : 6
Buried, bodies are b. in peace, 36 : 12
body to be b. obscurely, 181 : 16
Caesar bled, 516 : 12
dies and is b. with them, 77 : 18
Evangelist Saint John, 571 : 3
hatchet, 725 : 13
heart's dead never b., 816 : 3
here children born one b., 521 : 6
him before prime, 927 : 4
lie deep b., 67 : 5
life, 585 : 15
not b. in consecrated ground, 640 : 16
old Adam b., 56 : 16
on Sunday, 932 : 11
outworn b. age, 244 : 21
putrid corpse of liberty, 784 : 2
Buried (*continued*)
soil good to be b. in, 568 : 26
want to be b. among mountains, 603 : 1
was crucified dead and b., 55 : 2
where Michael Furey b., 777 : 16
Buries, day one b. her, 67 : 11
empires in common grave, 383 : 14
universal darkness b. all, 340 : 28
Burke great because brings thought, 586 : 22
Kelly and B. and Shea, 661 : 4
said Reporters' Gallery fourth estate, 472 : *n* 2
Burma girl a-settin', 708 : 8
Burn and rave, 887 : 4
another Troy to b., 713 : 5
better to marry than b., 48 : 11
books burn human beings, 481 : 11
children will b., 930 : 3
everything or throw into water, 156 : 13
fire b. caldron bubble, 239 : 4
flag yet terrific b., 443 : 13
from brain and breast, 742 : 12
frost itself doth b., 223 : 5
great sphere thou movest in, 241 : 20
heart b. within us, 44 : 15
I'll b. my books, 184 : 10
like fabulous candles, 901 : 3
no blazing hearth b., 362 : 1
old wood b. brightest, 262 : 1
old wood to b., 179 : 18
out false shames, 790 : 14
out to black, 691 : 15
some b. damp faggots, 713 : 17
stars that round her b., 325 : 9
time the fire in which we b., 883 : 10
to the socket, 428 : 11
violent fires soon b. out, 194 : 12
we b. daylight, 191 : 22
what thou hast worshipped, 129 : 18
with hard gemlike flame, 638 : 13
words that b., 363 : 3
you bid me b. letters, 381 : 4
Burned, and his feet not be b., 23 : 14
black with sun, 822 : 4
bush b. with fire, 9 : 10
candle b. on the table, 817 : 2
charmed water b. alway, 434 : 28
child fire dreadeth, 160 : 20
Christians b. each other, 460 : 14
feared witches and b. women, 677 : 13
feet as if b. in a furnace, 52 : 30
fire of thine eyes, 405 : 7
give my body to be b., 48 : 23
half his Troy was b., 205 : 19
heart ne'er within b., 430 : 10
is Apollo's laurel bough, 184 : 11
Matilda and house b., 730 : 11
money b. out his purse, 155 : 6
my life, 836 : 18
night's candles are b. out, 193 : 15
on the water, 240 : 29
some b. alive, 901 : 13
take fire and his clothes not be b., 23 : 14
temple of Diana, 275 : 8
topless towers of Ilium, 184 : 4
while I was musing the fire b., 18 : 30
word b. like a lamp, 36 : 13
worship what thou hast b., 129 : 18
Burning and shining light, 44 : 37

Burning (*continued*)
bow of b. gold, 406 : 21
boy stood on b. deck, 470 : 17
burns out another's b., 191 : 19
candle b. while sleeping, 258 : 2
clove, 748 : 9
fire in mind ever b., 172 : 9
for ancient connection, 906 : 1
heaven and earth in ashes b., 139 : 4
is Paris b., 813 : 2
keep home fires b., 740 : 11
let fall no b. leaf, 822 : 14
lifetime b. in moment, 807 : 23
marle, 283 : 15
pretty Babe all b. bright, 182 : 2
roof and tower, 715 : 16
Sappho, 461 : 2
seraphim in b. row, 281 : 10
sick and full of b., 892 : 7
smell of b. fills air, 729 : 16
spear horse of air, 918 : 12
success worse than house b., 876 : 9
three words as with b. pen, 412 : 11
Tiger Tiger b. bright, 405 : 7
your lights b., 43 : 21
Burnished, barge like b. throne, 240 : 29
livery of b. sun, 198 : 29
Burns, adores and b., 336 : 22
blood b. in veins, 576 : 16
blood that freezes blood that b., 542 : 4
candle b. at both ends, 822 : 17
it b. your clothes, 401 : 3
not she which b. in 't, 246 : 16
one fire b. out another's, 191 : 19
Shelley with us, 541 : 7
smell fire whose gown b., 269 : 18
wasted oil unprofitably b., 376 : 6
what b. me now, 874 : 22
when the blood b., 219 : 6
Burnside, waly yon b., 927 : 7
Burnt, millions of innocent b., 387 : 15
offering, 8 : 13
offerings, 33 : 11
Burr, I am a kind of b., 229 : 3
Burro, no laurel crown for outrunning b., 119 : 16
Burrow, go b. underground, 793 : 19
Burrs and thorns of life, 475 : 13
Burst cannon's roar, 518 : 12
first that ever b., 434 : 13
hot heart's shell, 570 : 13
joy's grape, 478 : 1
now a bubble b., 336 : 14
Bursts, melodious b., 528 : 21
Burthen of the mystery, 423 : 10
vapors weep their b., 533 : 27
weight of another's b., 270 : 18
Burton, great direction B. left, 356 : *n* 3
Bury bones in hideaways, 856 : 1
for nothing, 547 : 37
Great Duke, 533 : 1
heart at Wounded Knee, 840 : 3
I come to b. Caesar, 216 : 17
it fathoms in earth, 248 : 15
let dead b. their dead, 38 : 24
living scarce able to b. dead, 265 : 10
marry ancient people to b. them, 277 : 2
me in their buryingplace, 9 : 3
me not on lone prairie, 927 : 16
me out on prairie, 927 : 17
no one to b., 807 : 17
we will b. you, 830 : 14
Buryingplace, bury me in their b., 9 : 3
Bus, either on b. or off b., 913 : 7
Hitler missed b., 727 : 3
Bush afire with God, 507 : 22
beat the b., 159 : 5, 265 : 1
bird in hand worth two in b., 120 : *n* 3
burned with fire, 9 : 10
every blossom on b., 607 : 12
fear each b. an officer, 186 : 27
good wine needs no b., 112 : *n* 5
jumped into bramble b., 934 : 7
man in b. God meet, 493 : 13
supposed a bear, 197 : 12
thorough b. thorough brier, 196 : 10
through grass behind b., 778 : 6
was not consumed, 9 : 10
Bushel, put candle under a b., 37 : 6
words won't fill b., 347 : 32
Bushels, wheat in two b. of chaff, 198 : 5
Bushes, author out from b., 782 : 7
Busied with crowded hour, 495 : 4
Busier, yet semed b. than he was, 146 : 1
Busily all the night, 568 : 15
Business above sellin' tinpinny nails, 722 : 5
as usual, 743 : 6
best b. father's farm, 538 : 8
big b. give square deal, 687 : 19
could not make dull, 584 : 8
crises at intervals, 666 : 4
derned sight better b., 636 : 5
diligent in his b., 25 : 4
dinner lubricates b., 393 : 15
dirty b., 645 : 10
dispatch b. quickly, 150 : 12
dispatch the soul of b., 342 : 9
do b. in great waters, 21 : 14
do b. of day in day, 421 : 12
economic slavery nobody's b., 779 : 16
end of this day's b., 217 : 10
everybody's b. nobody's b., 271 : 2
fiendishness of b. competition, 794 : 12
fitter for new than settled b., 181 : 7
great b. of life, 637 : 7
he had talents equal to b., 122 : 21
hell where mind own b., 616 : *n* 4
if everybody minded b., 611 : 13
in battle or b., 556 : 1
in hands of a few, 621 : 6
is business, 773 : 10
laid aside b., 270 : 29
life's b. choice, 545 : 12
love only b. in life, 453 : 18
love yields to b., 113 : 26
marriage damnably serious b., 826 : 14
may bring money, 440 : 28
men ought to mind b., 616 : 1
men some to b. take, 335 : 22
men's b. and bosoms, 179 : 21
mind b. and spend less, 309 : 20
mind his own b., 169 : 8
monopolies and inflation, 848 : 4
monopoly market power, 848 : 5
my Father's b., 42 : 32
no better ballast than b., 569 : 8
no b. carried on at all, 342 : 5
no b. like show b., 802 : 12
no feeling of his b., 224 : 7
no foreigner do b. here, 151 : 1
Business (*continued*)
of American people is business, 736 : 16
of comic poet, 324 : 6
of the samurai, 299 : 11
one hundred and fifty lawyers do b. together, 389 : 17
other people's money, 594 : 8
overwise in doing thy b., 35 : 19
perpetual devotion to b., 667 : 22
politics conviviality, 577 : 6
sick of its b., 424 : 3
study to do your own b., 50 : 17
talk of nothing but b., 150 : 12
that we love, 241 : 14
that's his b., 482 : 8
that's true b. precept, 547 : 33
the rest not our b., 807 : 22
to be drunk the b. of day, 307 : 8
weather attending to b., 622 : 18
what a deal of b., 310 : 6
what b. is it of yours, 395 : 4
with income at heels, 376 : 7
without some dissimulation no b., 342 : 5
woman enter active b. of life, 471 : 1
Businesslike, more b. than businessmen, 747 : 19
Businessmen, more businesslike than b., 747 : 19
Bussoftlhee mememormee, 778 : 6
Bust, animated b., 362 : 5
friendly b., 804 : 23
outlasts citadel, 538 : 7
outlasts throne, 640 : 1
pallid b. of Pallas, 526 : 19
Busting, June b. out all over, 833 : 12
Bustle, love of b. not industry, 114 : 15
so illustrious, 607 : 8
Busts, picture placed the b. between, 330 : 26
Busy as a bee, 175 : 18
as one-armed man, 699 : 10
bee has no time for sorrow, 404 : 1
bee improve each hour, 328 : 5
curious thirsty fly, 344 : 16
hammers closing rivets, 208 : 1
haunts of men, 470 : 21
housewife ply evening care, 362 : 1
how doth the b. bee, 328 : 5
hum of men, 278 : 4
monster manunkind, 829 : 24
old fool unruly Sun, 252 : 7
riches make one b., 153 : 14
the stop to b. fools, 298 : 21
till night, 310 : 6
whisper circling round, 370 : 10
Busybodies, tattlers and b., 50 : 32
Butcher baker candlestick-maker, 933 : 2
his father was a b., 301 : 6
hog b. for world, 761 : 4
Butchered to make Roman holiday, 458 : 21
Butcheries, wineshops gorgeous b., 888 : 11
Butchers, gentle with these b., 216 : 11
Butchery, work of b. and desolation, 745 : 2
Butt and very sea-mark, 232 : 18
fixed as an aim or b., 207 : 6
knocks you with b. end, 371 : 23
Butter, guns or b., 838 : *n* 3
in a lordly dish, 12 : 6

Butter (continued)
it was the best b., 611 : 19
not melt in her mouth, 159 : 31
quarrel with bread and b., 323 : 7
white bread and b., 930 : 15
words b. no parsnips, 432 : 2
words smoother than b., 19 : 22
Buttercup, called Little B., 627 : 9
Buttered, on which side bread b., 161 : 9
scones and crumpets, 804 : 19
Butterflies are already yellow, 792 : 9
frogs eat b., 767 : 8
laugh at gilded b., 235 : 12
no b. no bees, 485 : 12
Butterfly, blue in b., 748 : 1
breaks b. upon wheel, 338 : 18
dreaming I was a b., 90 : 3
float like a b., 915 : 11
glow in narrow flute, 902 : 13
in eternity as b. in air, 662 : 20
upon road, 707 : 5
Butterfly's flicker swan's down, 850 : 11
Butter's spread too thick, 613 : 7
Butting through the Channel, 760 : 20
Button, Brazil he twirled b., 605 : 20
little b. at top, 364 : 5
pray you undo this b., 235 : 18
Buttoned-up and white-chokered, 651 : 3
Buttonhole, take you a b. lower, 191 : 10
Buttons be disclosed, 218 : 27
biographies clothes and b., 626 : 9
soul above b., 415 : 15
taken of b. off, 708 : 2
Buttress nor coign of vantage, 236 : 21
Butts, beast with many heads b. me, 242 : 21
Buxom blithe and debonair, 277 : 18
Buy a fat pig, 933 : 9
a world of happy days, 187 : 8
annuity cheap, 547 : 34
bubbles we b., 567 : 12
cherries which none may b., 250 : 5
costly as purse can b., 219 : 1
decline to b. repentance, 88 : 24
dispraise thing you desire to b., 226 : 23
ever tried to b. without money, 855 : 14
full and fair ones come and b., 266 : 3
hyacinths to feed soul, 133 : *n* 1
I will b. with you, 198 : 18
lose it that b. it with care, 197 : 27
lots of things money won't b., 855 : 14
no man might b. or sell, 53 : 21
nor can b. tomorrow, 251 : 13
pawn intelligence to b. drink, 828 : 15
spoils of office not b., 566 : 3
two white feet b. him, 923 : 11
what would you b., 492 : 15
what you do not want, 390 : 3
Buyer, city to perish if it finds b., 103 : 3
it is naught saith the b., 24 : 30
let b. beware, 133 : 13
needs a hundred eyes, 270 : 1
Buying and selling, 560 : 7
is antisocial, 665 : 16
it's no fish ye're b., 431 : 22
more giving less b., 739 : 8
Buys, who b. a minute's mirth, 189 : 20
Buzz, buccaneers of b., 607 : 11
crowd b. and murmurings, 295 : 3
Buzz (continued)
the witty and fair annoys, 338 : 19
Buzzing world lisping firmament, 768 : 6
B.V.D., from every B., 828 : 17
By and by easily said, 222 : 22
and by God caught eye, 839 : 2
Bye baby bunting, 931 : 5
Bye-and-bye, sweet b., 927 : 13
Bygone days, 856 : 7
Byproduct more valuable than product, 689 : 25
Byron, close thy B., 472 : 27
cuts a figure, 479 : 19
from poetry of B. ethics, 487 : 20
mad bad dangerous to know, 454 : 22
Byron's struggle cease, 585 : 2
Byway to heaven, 318 : 8
Byword, proverb and a b., 13 : 33
story and b. through world, 264 : 22
thou shalt become a b., 11 : 19
Byzantium, lords and ladies of B., 715 : 3

C

C Major of this life, 544 : 7
Caballero de la Triste Figura, 168 : *n* 15
Cabbage, cut a c. leaf, 364 : 5
with college education, 624 : 14
Cabbages and kings, 613 : 5
death find me planting c., 164 : 8
happy those who plant c., 158 : 4
no c. sprouting out, 520 : 5
Cabin, enter Logan's c. hungry, 367 : 3
mounted to the c., 731 : 19
small c. build there, 712 : 4
willow c. at gate, 213 : 18
Cabined cribbed confined, 238 : 23
from her c. loophole peep, 279 : 13
Cabinet is formed of gold, 406 : 6
post offices and c. appointments, 520 : *n* 3
Cabinets, make parties as ministers c., 565 : 26
Cable broke anchor lost, 186 : 23
no c. draw forcibly as love, 259 : 18
on seventh day scrape c., 553 : 17
Cabots talk only to God, 694 : 14
Cackle, don't c., w'en fine wum, 662 : 14
Cackles, codfish never c., 923 : 10
groans and dies, 470 : 11
Cadence from man named Yeats, 873 : 18
harsh c. of rugged line, 304 : 27
to his verse a smooth c., 311 : 3
tremulous c. slow, 587 : 14
Cadets of Gascoyne, 726 : 2
Cadiz, reeking into C. Bay, 541 : 18
Cadmean victory, 78 : 7
Cadmus, letters C. gave, 461 : 7
Caelum, quid si nunc c. ruat, 96 : *n* 12
Caesar, appeal unto C., 46 : 32
buried C. bled, 516 : 12
carry C. in your boat, 99 : 20
every wound of C., 216 : 29
great C. fell, 216 : 25
had his Brutus, 382 : 13
I come to bury C., 216 : 17
imperious C. dead, 224 : 16
not that I loved C. less, 216 : 14
O mighty C., 216 : 8
poor cried C. wept 216 : 19
Caesar (continued)
render unto C., 40 : 15
sawdust C., 817 : 9
thou art mighty yet, 217 : 11
upon what meat C. feed, 215 : 7
with senate at heels, 337 : 14
without ambition, 591 : 11
word of C. stood, 216 : 21
Caesar's, all is C., 292 : 12
dead C. trencher, 241 : 11
hand Plato's brain, 495 : 15
poison from C. crown, 406 : 16
self is God's, 292 : 12
wife must be above suspicion, 99 : *n* 13
Caesars, madness of the C., 555 : 22
Café, every street c., 833 : 9
Caftan of tan with henna, 767 : 5
Cage, gilded c., 730 : 18
minute within net of gold, 870 : 6
nor iron bars a c., 296 : 4
put me in a c., 810 : 8
robin redbreast in c., 406 : 9
sing like birds i' the c., 235 : 12
Caged, know why c. bird sings, 736 : 23
Cages, marriage as with c., 165 : 19
Cain, eye stared at C., 491 : 13
land God gave to C., 157 : 2
set a mark upon C., 7 : 19
was tiller of the ground, 7 : 14
went out from presence of the Lord, 7 : 20
Caïn, terre Dieu donna à C., 157 : *n* 2
Caius is a man, 602 : 11
Cake, bake c. fast as can, 929 : 18
eat c. and have it, 161 : 13
heaven's sugar c., 314 : 23
let them eat c., 359 : 6
see to substance of c., 685 : 14
some gave plum c., 929 : 19
Cakes, all that c. brain, 570 : 13
and ale, 213 : 26
bridegrooms brides and bridal c., 265 : 17
Calabash goodnight Mrs. C., 825 : 14
Calais, find C. lying in my heart, 162 : 8
Calamities of life, 318 : 13
rather be notorious for c., 118 : 20
Calamitous in drawn-out witticism, 442 : 20
necessity of going on, 385 : 6
to the conquered, 81 : 10
Calamity, child of c., 623 : 6
fortune not satisfied with one c., 110 : 28
in English history, 673 : 1
in power of no c., 657 : *n* 7
makes c. of so long life, 221 : 12
man's true touchstone, 263 : 10
no c. greater than lavish desires, 64 : 16
wedded to c., 193 : 11
Calamus, hinc quam sic c. saevior ense patet, 259 : 3
Calaveras County, 621 : 18
Calcaria, de c. in carbonarium, 126 : *n* 7
Calculate, no wisdom can c. end, 384 : 22
Calculated, nicely c. less or more, 429 : 6
so c. so malignant, 821 : 7
take c. risks, 791 : 17
Calculating average of virtues, 630 : 16

Calculation shining out of
other, 547 : 30
sum defies c., 395 : 19
Calculations, most dangerous c. we
call illusions, 802 : 16
upset most careful c., 313 : 1
Calculators, age of c., 373 : 22
Calculus, common sense reduced to
c., 397 : 18
Caldron, fire burn c. bubble, 239 : 4
of dissolute loves, 128 : 28
Caledonia stern and wild, 430 : 11
Caledonia's, support C. cause, 411 : 24
Calendar, a c. look in almanac, 196 : 25
striking from c., 517 : 1
Calf and young lion together, 29 : 19
bring fatted c., 43 : 27
false as wolf to c., 226 : 15
killed c. in high style, 301 : 6
second beast like a c., 53 : 7
trod in footsteps of c., 685 : 9
Calf's skin on recreant limbs, 201 : 21
Caliban, 'Ban 'Ban Ca-C., 248 : 2
Calico cat replied Meeow, 666 : 18
pie, 550 : 12
tree, 550 : 12
California, from C. to New York
island, 881 : 1
Californians race of people, 699 : 15
Calisthenics with words, 827 : 18
Call, almost like c. to come, 749 : 7
back world of shadows, 796 : 2
back yesterday, 194 : 27, 257 : 17
bawd a bawd, 91 : *n* 4
brothers c. from bay, 584 : 11
cattle home, 566 : 7
death c. too soon, 629 : 23
delicate creatures ours, 231 : 6
don't c. out National Guard, 787 : 11
dunno what to c. him, 685 : 1
fig a fig, 91 : 7
for robin redbreast, 262 : 3
forth thundering Aeschylus, 256 : 14
gods to witness, 242 : 30
grief at not wanting to c. dead
back, 755 : 17
heaven and earth to witness, 11 : 8
her blessed, 26 : 9
Himself a man, 829 : 14
how you c. to me c. to me, 641 : 24
in and invite God, 255 : 2
in thy death's head, 268 : 22
it not vain, 430 : 8
let no bird c., 822 : 14
let us c. thee devil, 230 : 25
let's c. whole thing off, 836 : 8
me early mother dear, 528 : 12
me horse, 203 : 30
me Ishmael, 570 : 3
neighbors in, 930 : 16
nigh unto them that c., 22 : 22
no man foe, 821 : 2
none dare c. it treason, 181 : 21
not easy to c. back, 761 : 13
nothing c. our own but death, 195 : 2
obey the important c., 377 : 10
of running tide, 760 : 15
one clear c. for me, 535 : 19
philosophy down from
heavens, 98 : 25
please to c. it rush candle, 189 : 3
saints aid if men c., 434 : 2
spade a spade, 91 : 7
spirits from vasty deep, 204 : 12
Call (*continued*)
that backing your friends, 203 : 29
that which we c. a rose, 192 : 6
the fleeting breath, 362 : 5
things by right names, 416 : 6
through curtains c. on us, 252 : 7
to the earth and sea, 574 : 19
today his own, 305 : 1
truth obeyed c., 717 : 10
try first thyself and after c.
God, 66 : *n* 7
unless they c. signals, 825 : 3
up your men, 432 : 15
upon all who love freedom, 815 : 12
upon my soul, 213 : 18
when you c. me that smile, 696 : 7
wild c. and clear c., 760 : 15
will they come when you c., 204 : 12
you back dear love, 76 : 3
you c. for faith, 543 : 8
you c. me misbeliever, 198 : 24
you Shepherd from hill, 585 : 20
Called back Emily, 608 : 7
brother's father dad, 201 : 17
fool c. her lady fair, 709 : 14
for his pipe, 929 : 14
him soft names, 476 : 28
if shape it might be c., 284 : 24
it macaroni, 920 : 9
many are c., 40 : 14
neither two nor one c., 225 : 30
New World into existence, 422 : 7
out of Egypt c. my son, 36 : 22
them untaught knaves, 203 : 8
till we are c. to rise, 607 : 2
whom he did predestinate he
c., 47 : 11
Calleth, deep c. unto deep, 19 : 7
them all by their names, 22 : 24
Callimachus, tomb of C., 92 : 18
Calling, bugles c. for them, 827 : 3
dignity of high c., 373 : 9
faint and far away, 773 : 2
followed mercenary c., 692 : 3
Callooh callay, 612 : 18
Calls back lovely April, 244 : 2
beauty c., 317 : 14
death c. ye to the crowd, 272 : 14
far c. coming far, 778 : 6
fool c. you foolish, 77 : 7
if anybody c., 753 : 3
Jerusalem thy sister c., 407 : 7
me Tom, 257 : 19
stated c. to worship, 352 : 24
who c. me villain, 221 : 8
Calm, after storm c., 830 : 18
after storm comes c., 319 : 13
all c. all bright, 466 : 2
all c. as it was bright, 299 : 6
cankers of c. world, 204 : 35
contending kings, 189 : 23
day so cool so c., 268 : 15
drifted in sheepish c., 893 : 2
envisage circumstance c., 478 : 5
escape into c. regions, 357 : 17
evening c. and free, 425 : 16
for a c. unfit, 303 : 20
gloomy c. of idle vacancy, 354 : 18
great events make me c., 573 : 15
he of c. and happy nature, 84 : 4
in c. sea every man pilot, 301 : 12
my soul's c. retreat, 298 : 21
no joy but c., 528 : 15
peace and public c., 586 : 12
Calm (*continued*)
Peace and Quiet, 278 : 15
quiet innocent recreation, 271 : 10
quiet interchange, 355 : 16
region where no night, 267 : 5
sea is c. tonight, 587 : 13
so deep, 425 : 14
Soul of all things, 585 : 1
stars in their c., 585 : 12
thou mayst smile, 394 : 3
Calme, luxe c. et volupté, 580 : *n* 8
Calmer of thoughts, 270 : 34
Calmness, law in c. made, 427 : 25
to remember, 597 : 1
Calumniating, envious and c.
time, 226 : 20
Calumnies answered best with
silence, 255 : 15
Calumnious strokes, 218 : 27
Calumny, envy c. hate pain, 469 : 12
thou shalt not escape c., 221 : 17
Calvary, place called C., 44 : 6
Calvin oatcakes and sulphur, 432 : 18
Calvinistic sense of innate
depravity, 569 : 16
Cambridge ladies, 828 : 14
Machu Picchu C. Angkor, 884 : 20
ye fields of C., 295 : 13
Cambuscan, story of C. bold, 278 : 23
Cambyses', King C. vein, 204 : 4
Came, fear c. upon me, 15 : 11
forth to see again stars, 141 : 16
gave a war nobody c., 761 : *n* 3
I c. I saw I conquered, 99 : 23
I c. like water, 516 : 17
I c. saw and overcame, 206 : 28
into woods Master c., 651 : 11
naked c. I out, 15 : 4
once a world, 605 : 1
out from Egypt, 9 : 29
Satan c. also, 15 : 1
tell them I c., 739 : 16
three thousand miles and
died, 568 : 14
to dark tower c., 234 : 13
to making of man, 632 : 9
to scoff, 370 : 8
upon midnight clear, 537 : 16
upon no wine, 823 : 5
Cameelious hump, 710 : 1
Camel, cloud in shape of a c., 222 : 20
easier for c. to go, 40 : 7
nine she-c. hairs aid memory, 799 : 13
swallow a c., 40 : 19
Camellia, what violet has c.
not, 694 : *n* 2
Camelot, brief shining moment
C., 895 : 4
looked down to C., 528 : 27
many-towered C., 528 : 23
Camels are snobbish, 799 : 16
rich folk on c., 547 : 36
Camera, I am a c., 860 : 1
Camerado this is no book, 576 : 21
Camino, con pan y vino se anda
c., 935 : 10
Camlet, my fine c. cloak, 309 : 13
Camp, concentration c.
universe, 881 : 9
court the c. the grove, 430 : 6
every c. has firmament for
roof, 637 : 21
father and I to c., 920 : *n* 2
Campaigning weather, 842 : 11

Campaigns are emotional orgies, 703 : 1
Campaspe, Cupid and my C., 175 : 23
Campbells are comin', 920 : 3
Camped by billabong, 705 : 7
Campground, tenting on old c., 618 : 1
Camping, Fame's eternal c. ground, 578 : 10
Camps, terrible from c., 864 : 15
Campus habet lumen auris acumen, 146 : *n* 5
Can, come fill up my c., 432 : 15
cry I c. no more, 656 : 15
guess if you c., 275 : 27
he who c. does, 680 : 23
I will do what I c., 902 : 7
if poor whenever you c., 86 : 11
if we c. we must, 691 : 20
live as we c., 90 : 17
live we how we c., 186 : 21
make us do what we c., 499 : 2
pass me the c. lad, 691 : 19
something hope wish, 656 : 15
youth replies I c., 494 : 21
Cana, miracles in C., 44 : 28
Canaan, Abram dwelled in C., 8 : 7
Canadian frontier pattern for world, 743 : 16
Canary wine, 477 : 16
Cancel all our vows, 182 : 16
and tear to pieces, 238 : 21
half a line, 517 : 2
power to c. captivity, 215 : 13
Canceled, across c. skies, 821 : 12
Cancels, end of life c. bands, 204 : 23
time c. young pain, 76 : 13
Candid, be c. where we can, 336 : 11
brow, 683 : 12
save me from c. friend, 422 : 5
ye marshes how c., 651 : 8
Candied, let c. tongue lick pomp, 222 : 4
Candle, bell book and c., 201 : 23
better to light one c., 786 : *n* 4
book bell and c., 149 : 16
burned on table, 817 : 2
burning while sleeping, 258 : 2
burns at both ends, 822 : 17
extinguishes natural c., 314 : 19
feel steady c. flame, 541 : 20
highest c. lights dark, 769 : 3
hold c. to my shames, 199 : 8
hold farthing c. to sun, 259 : *n* 9
how far c. throws beams, 201 : 4
if you please to call it a rush c., 189 : 3
light c. to the sun, 298 : 20
lights gleaming, 732 : 13
not care a farthing c., 442 : 4
of understanding, 34 : 6
one small c. light a thousand, 265 : 13
out out brief c., 240 : 4
put c. under a bushel, 37 : 6
scarcely fit to hold c., 341 : 13
set a c. in the sun, 259 : 19
this day light such a c., 156 : 14
to be c. or mirror, 700 : 14
to light you to bed, 930 : 8
two chairs half c., 550 : 16
white c. in holy place, 773 : 16
Candlelight, colors by c., 507 : 5
dress by yellow c., 668 : 9
Candlelit, old at evening c., 162 : 12
Candles are all out, 237 : 10
blessed c. of night, 201 : 8
Candles (*continued*)
burn like fabulous c., 901 : 3
held to speed them, 827 : 4
night's c. burnt out, 193 : 15
rather light c., 786 : *n* 4
when c. out all women fair, 120 : 17
Candlestick, jump over c., 932 : 17
put candle on a c., 37 : 6
Candlestick-maker, butcher baker c., 933 : 2
Candlesticks, seven golden c., 52 : 29
Candor and amicable relations, 408 : 3
Candy deal of courtesy, 203 : 16
is dandy, 855 : 10
not made of sugar c., 745 : 10
Cane, carrying a small c., 846 : 14
wind is in the c., 831 : 14
Canem, cave c., 133 : 12
Canker, as killing as c. to rose, 280 : 13
galls infants of spring, 218 : 27
loathesome c., 244 : 14
that benumbs, 630 : 4
this c. Bolingbroke, 203 : 12
worm c. and grief, 462 : 18
Cankers in musk rose buds, 196 : 19
of calm world, 204 : 35
Cannibals that each other eat, 229 : 30
Cannikin, why clink c., 541 : 3
Cannon come again, 717 : 12
his name c. his voice, 601 : 12
revolution more c. shot, 717 : 12
then c. and he comes, 742 : 9
to right of them, 533 : 13
Cannon's, burst c. roar, 518 : 12
mouth, 211 : 15
opening roar, 457 : 16
Cannons taken or saved, 602 : 1
thundering c. roar, 371 : 10
Cannot, he who c. teaches, 680 : 23
Canoe, paddle own c., 112 : *n* 11, 466 : 1
Canon 'gainst self-slaughter, 218 : 5
Canopy, most excellent c. the air, 220 : 28
my c. the skies, 336 : 19
who spread its c., 314 : 20
Canst, give all thou c., 429 : 6
Cant, clear your mind of c., 356 : 29
in American moralism, 862 : 18
nothing but c., 455 : 3
of criticism, 360 : 11
of hypocrites the worst, 360 : 11
of not men but measures, 372 : 5
Cantankerous, small speech c., 90 : 1
Canted in this canting world, 360 : 11
Canter, little finishing c., 645 : 12
Canters, as they c. awaäy, 535 : 7
Canticles, Homeric or Biblical c., 577 : 13
Cantie wi' mair, 409 : 23
Canting, canted in this c. world, 360 : 11
Cants, clear myself of c., 473 : 10
which are canted, 360 : 11
Canvas of heavy foresail, 683 : 5
sail even with c. rent, 114 : 19
set your full c. flying, 93 : 3
to our imaginations, 558 : 14
Canyons, neighing c., 843 : 20
Cap and bells, 567 : 12
by night, 368 : 8
feather in his c., 360 : 14
for c. and bells lives pay, 567 : 12
riband in c. of youth, 224 : 3
Capability and godlike reason, 223 : 17
negative c., 479 : 5
Capable, all I am c. of becoming, 810 : 4
and wide revenge, 231 : 18
become all c. of, 472 : 4
created in his mind, 767 : 22
hand now warm and c., 478 : 8
mathematician c. of reasoning, 84 : 19
mind c. of anything, 683 : 17
not all c. of everything, 103 : 16
of being in uncertainties, 479 : 5
of every wickedness, 684 : 4
of greatest vices, 272 : 7
of nothing but dumbshows, 221 : 23
Capacious salad bowl, 668 : 18
Capacities, unused c. atrophy, 883 : 7
Capacity, all men have is c. for work, 758 : 1
by c. is wisdom acquired, 93 : 9
contribution according to c., 563 : *n* 1
for delight and wonder, 683 : 3
for taking pains, 630 : 17
for taking trouble, 349 : *n* 2, 474 : 14, 620 : 21
functional c., 393 : 7
genius is c. to see, 793 : 10
man's c. for justice, 823 : 18
naught enters thy c., 213 : 8
to despise himself, 703 : 16
Cap-a-pe 218 : 19
Caparisons, no c. if you please, 398 : 15
Cape, nobly C. St. Vincent, 541 : 18
oftenest round C. Horn, 569 : 21
round c. of a sudden, 541 : 15
Capella, star called C. yellow, 640 : 6
Caper and shake a leg, 760 : 5
Capers, he c. he dances, 225 : 20
nimbly in lady's chamber, 186 : 31
strange c., 210 : 34
Capes, ink and wax on dark c., 841 : 12
Capital and labor get together, 725 : 14
Belgium's c. gathered, 457 : 14
bring c. into competition, 366 : 8
fruit of labor, 522 : 3
has its rights, 522 : 3
in ascendancy system of plunder, 562 : 20
labor not ask patronage of c., 450 : 4
labor prior to c., 522 : 3
not by savings and c., 872 : 4
reasons for scarcity of c., 783 : 15
ship for ocean trip, 647 : 21
where kingly Death, 469 : 1
Capitalism condition for political freedom, 880 : 12
creates social unrest, 785 : 4
inherent vice of c., 746 : 16
practice not principle, 862 : 19
Capitalist, more sham than c. democracy, 785 : 6
production begets own negation, 562 : 19
society unchecked, 814 : 7
tendency toward self-destruction, 785 : 5
way to destroy c. system, 783 : 9
Capitalists owners of means of production, 563 : *n* 3
Capitol, musing amidst ruins of C., 384 : 7
woman betrayed the C., 316 : 16
Capon, belly with good c. lined, 211 : 15
Capons, unless minutes c., 202 : 23
you cannot feed c. so, 222 : 8
Caprice and lifelong passion, 675 : 2

Caprice (*continued*)
lasts a little longer, 675 : 2
of minutest event, 571 : 10
Capricious, gods' c. hand, 863 : 20
Capriciousness of summer air, 749 : 5
Caps, threw their c., 242 : 9
Capsule, finger on c. of truth, 846 : 9
Captain art tha sleepin', 700 : 9
captive good attending c. ill, 244 : 25
Carpenter rose up, 811 : 2
chief c. answered, 46 : 26
cook and c. bold, 627 : 7
Death old c., 581 : 4
don't you hear c. shouting, 921 : 17
his c. Christ, 195 : 8
my Captain, 576 : 6
no c. do very wrong, 408 : 7
O C. my C., 576 : 6
of all these men of death, 302 : 17
of Hampshire Grenadiers, 384 : 6
of his soul, 814 : 8
of my soul, 663 : 11
of second rank, 491 : 18
of the Pinafore, 627 : 10
of thine own fate, 103 : *n* 1
right good c. too, 627 : 10
should be judged as a c., 151 : 9
soul the c. of life, 103 : 1
walk deck my C. lies, 576 : 7
Captain's choleric word, 228 : 11
crew of c. gig, 627 : 7
troubled c. mind, 647 : 21
Captains and kings depart, 709 : 17
courageous, 926 : 18
of industry, 474 : 8
sea c. young or old, 575 : 22
star c. glow, 785 : 15
thunder of the c., 16 : 38
Capten art tha sleepin', 700 : 9
Captivating as new knowledge, 463 : 18
Captive, carried us away c., 22 : 15
good attending captain ill, 244 : 25
Israel, 563 : 14
jailer another kind of c., 514 : 8
lead captivity c., 12 : 4
of time, 816 : 19
today unbind c., 494 : 17
weak minds led c., 288 : 7
Captivity, home after years in c., 4 : 8
is consciousness, 605 : 9
lead c. captive, 12 : 4
not Jews of c., 649 : 11
power to cancel his c., 215 : 13
spent many years in c., 4 : 8
Capture of men by women, 539 : *n* 2
Captured, faced enslavement if c., 617 : 6
Capulet, I'll no longer be a C., 192 : 5
Car, drive the rapid c., 377 : 26
gilded c. of day, 279 : 10
radio bleats, 893 : 7
rattling o'er stony street, 457 : 15
Caravan, innumerable c. which moves, 471 : 6
put up your c., 732 : 17
Caravanserai, battered c., 516 : 10
Carcass fit for hounds, 215 : 20
honey in the c. of the lion, 12 : 13
of leopard, 845 : 8
where c. is eagles gather, 40 : 24
Carcasses bleed at sight of murderer, 148 : *n* 1
Card, by c. by letter by press, 726 : 12
clear conscience is sure c., 175 : 16

Card (*continued*)
he's a sure c., 304 : 21
insipid as queen on c., 535 : 4
master to those below, 818 : 5
speak by the c., 224 : 12
Cardinal, two c. sins, 786 : 6
Cards, cheat at c. genteelly, 355 : 13
dreaded c. foretell, 868 : 17
luck not holding best c., 636 : 7
nothing but pack of c., 612 : 14
patience and shuffle c., 170 : 24
played c. for kisses, 175 : 23
thrust ivrybody but cut c., 722 : 11
world of c., 818 : 5
Care a farthing candle, 442 : 4
age full of c., 917 : 11
and not to care, 805 : 21
begone dull C., 919 : 4
beyond His love and c., 513 : 24
careless with artful c., 324 : 22
cast away c., 169 : 6, 251 : 13
dark C. sits enthroned, 107 : 26
deliberation and public c., 284 : 14
driveth away sleep, 36 : 2
earliest latest c., 357 : 8
fig for c. fig for woe, 158 : 17
for who shall have borne battle, 524 : 7
full of c. no time, 732 : 9
golden c., 206 : 29
happy man void of c., 328 : 19
happy whose wish and c., 332 : 10
housewife ply evening c., 362 : 1
I c. for nobody, 382 : 7
I don't c. one straw, 96 : 18
I don't c. what they do, 706 : 16
I prayed and did God c., 605 : 7
I sae weary fu' o' c., 409 : 24
I shall not c., 787 : 5
insensate c. of mortals, 100 : *n* 8
irks c. the crop-full bird, 544 : 9
Jimmie crack corn I don't c., 921 : 14
keeps his watch, 192 : 21
killed a cat, 210 : 7
least feel c. of law, 175 : 7
lose it that buy it with much c., 197 : 27
my c. like my shadow, 163 : 14
naught but c. on ev'ry han', 409 : 14
nor c. beyond today, 361 : 10
nor for itself hath c., 405 : 3
not who sees your back, 203 : 29
of discipline is love, 34 : 17
of heaven, 337 : 6
of life and happiness, 389 : 4
of the poor, 309 : 1
of this world, 39 : 16
punch with c., 614 : 16
raveled sleave of c., 237 : 21
reason is past c., 246 : 6
rest that knows no c., 101 : 4
sat on his faded cheek, 283 : 25
so wan with c., 202 : 21
sought it with c., 614 : 4
sounds take c. of themselves, 612 : 3
steering with c., 575 : 19
there are those who c., 785 : 8
things past redress past c., 194 : 23
tiresome verse-reciter C., 470 : 4
weep away life of c., 466 : 15
what boots it with incessant c., 280 : 15
what c. I how fair she be, 264 : 23
what is life if full of c., 732 : 9

Care (*continued*)
where c. lodges sleep never lie, 192 : 21
windy side of c., 209 : 12
woman who did not c., 709 : 14
wrinkled C. derides, 277 : 20
your sex's earliest c., 357 : 8
Care-charmer Sleep, 182 : 4
Cared as much as bird, 605 : 7
not to be at all, 284 : 5
Careens, American empire c. onward, 837 : 4
Career, awe man from c. of his humor, 209 : 19
now close my military c., 771 : 7
poetry not c., 809 : 19
public life crown of c., 753 : 9
this is our c., 811 : 7
what they call fine c., 877 : 7
Careful, be c. what you do, 765 : 7
ivry man equal if not c., 722 : 23
not c. what they mean, 188 : 21
o' vidders, 546 : 18
so c. of type, 532 : 11
surgeons must be c., 604 : 4
Carefulness bringeth age, 36 : 1
Careless, be not c. in deeds, 125 : 14
desolation, 212 : 13
ease from tree to tree, 329 : 13
first fine c. rapture, 541 : 17
I tasted c. then, 605 : 1
love, 893 : 7
merits or faults to scan, 370 : 6
of censure, 333 : 22
of mankind, 528 : 19
of single life, 532 : 11
on granary floor, 477 : 18
people Tom and Daisy, 835 : 7
shoestring, 266 : 7
trifle, 236 : 14
with artful care, 324 : 22
Carelessly, fleet the time c., 210 : 11
Carelessness, lose both parents c., 675 : 21
Care's an enemy to life, 213 : 10
canker that benumbs, 630 : 4
check and curb, 298 : 21
Cares and joys abound, 185 : 14
blessed to put c. away, 101 : 23
cast all c. on God, 535 : 3
eating c., 278 : 6
heart depressed with c., 332 : 3
humble c. delicate fears, 425 : 5
kingdoms are but c., 150 : 1
no one c. for me, 382 : 7
now all ended, 206 : 34
partisan c. nothing about rights, 84 : 1
prime of youth a frost of c., 177 : 10
soothe c. lift thoughts, 475 : 13
that infest day, 510 : 22
to fret thy soul with c., 174 : 11
unhounded by sordid c., 772 : 12
who c. or knows, 470 : 8
Caress, take perfect circle and c. it, 881 : 2
Caretaker, president is c., 879 : 4
Cargo, little c. boats, 709 : 8
of ivory, 760 : 19
of Tyne coal, 760 : 20
Cargoes of meat drink clothes, 920 : 16
Carian, dear old C. guest, 591 : 9
Carib fire, 843 : 16
Caricature a swollen shadow, 883 : 11

Caricature (*continued*)
decrepit age, 715 : 4
world c. of itself, 704 : 3
Caricatures most penetrating of criticisms, 830 : 10
Caritas, in omniis c., 294 : *n* 6
Carlyle loves silence platonically, 473 : *n* 1
Carnage and conquests cease, 459 : 7
war and c. be lost, 576 : 1
Carnal, pearl for c. swine, 291 : 21
Carnegie, Johnnie C. lais heer, 321 : *n* 2
Carnival, make c. of grief, 725 : 8
Carol, it was c. of bird, 459 : 23
not c. of joy or glee, 736 : 23
Caroline, find Sister C., 733 : 13
Carolings, so little cause for c., 641 : 13
Carols, varied c. I hear, 574 : 2
Carp at weakness of human mind, 308 : 9
of truth, 220 : 7
Carpe diem, 107 : *n* 8
Carpent tua poma nepotes, 103 : *n* 12
Carpenter, Captain C. rose up, 811 : 2
hewing wood for master c., 65 : 7
said nothing but, 613 : 7
Walrus and the C., 613 : 2
Carpenter's, is not this the c. son, 39 : 20
Carpet, figure in the c., 653 : 7
Carpets, long c. rose, 476 : 19
Carriage, can't afford c., 718 : 18
held just ourselves, 606 : 4
king in c. ride, 517 : 15
small second class c., 629 : 1
Carriages motorcars omnibuses, 781 : 15
without horses go, 919 : 6
women helped into c., 482 : 17
Carried, beggar c. by angels, 43 : 33
not get self c. aloft, 657 : 17
pardon slowly c., 227 : 22
though the mountains be c. into the sea, 19 : 10
us away captive, 22 : 15
with every wind of doctrine, 49 : 35
Carrier of news and knowledge, 617 : 7
Carrière ouverte aux talents, 420 : 19
Carries no colors or crest, 708 : 19
regardless who c. ball, 825 : 3
Carriest, thou c. them away as with a flood, 20 : 11
Carrion comfort despair, 656 : 15
god kissing c., 220 : 17
Carrot, single c. freshly observed, 638 : 5
Carry all he knew, 370 : 11
big stick, 687 : 6
Caesar in your boat, 99 : 20
gentle peace, 249 : 8
in traveling c. knowledge, 356 : 6
lad born to be king, 688 : 12
lesson seems to c., 377 : 24
me along taddy, 778 : 6
me back to old Virginny, 672 : 19
me home, 935 : 23
me out of Egypt, 9 : 3
message to Garcia, 679 : 10
on dread naught, 743 : 18
praise or blame too far, 749 : 14
sun in golden cup, 716 : 21
them in his bosom, 30 : 35
we can c. nothing out, 51 : 1
wealth of Indies, 356 : 6
with us wonders we seek, 274 : 6
Carrying coals to Newcastle, 106 : *n* 13
you into fields of light, 76 : 3
Cars, giant finned c., 893 : 16
ten years on Pullman c., 810 : 7
Cart, creak of lumbering c., 712 : 12
draw sin with a c. rope, 29 : 6
set c. before horse, 161 : 4
Cartel market power, 848 : 5
Carthage, come again to C., 200 : 22
must be destroyed, 95 : 12
to C. I came, 128 : 28
Carthago, delenda est C., 95 : *n* 8
Carve him as dish, 215 : 20
let neighbor c. for you, 323 : 1
to all but just enough, 323 : 1
Carved beforn his fader at table, 145 : 17
monuments c. from snow, 800 : 10
new dynasties, 779 : 16
not a line, 465 : 9
Carves bow of beauty, 494 : 6
Carving, conversation is but c., 323 : 1
Casa, en c. del lenero, 935 : 14
sienta en la perta de c., 935 : 12
Casca, envious C., 216 : 23
Cascade, brigade with cold c., 628 : 25
Cascades, clear c., 314 : 6
Case, argued each c. with wife, 611 : 10
as the c. stands, 261 : 13
He never lost his c., 315 : 2
heard only one side of c., 620 : 23
her nominative c., 394 : 6
in c. anything turned up, 548 : 25
is closed, 129 : 13
lady's in the c., 331 : 17
medicine for c. like mine, 577 : 7
no one should judge own c., 111 : 19
nothing to do with c., 629 : 15
semblance in another's c., 377 : 25
still before courts, 109 : 21
we doctors know hopeless c., 829 : 26
who knows only his side of c., 508 : 6
Casement jessamine stirred, 533 : 22
on c. shone wintry moon, 476 : 16
Casements, magic c., 477 : 1
Cases, circumstances alter c., 481 : 4
concrete c., 644 : 11
great c. make bad law, 644 : 9
hard c. make bad law, 644 : 9
his quillets his c., 224 : 10
Casey at the bat, 704 : 15
Jones, 731 : 19
mighty C. struck out, 704 : 16
Casey's, ease in C. manner, 704 : 15
tabble dote, 666 : 11
Cash, from fifty-five needs c., 788 : 21
squalid c. interpretation, 648 : 4
take c. let credit go, 516 : 8
to have no c. means powerlessness, 504 : 14
Cashboxes for hearts, 484 : 17
Cashiered, when he's old c., 229 : 15
Cashiering kings and senates, 472 : 21
Cask, take fill at beginning of c., 61 : 21
Caspar Milquetoast, 793 : 13
Caspian fact, 607 : 6
Casque has outdone elegance, 793 : 4
Casques that did affright air at Agincourt, 207 : 2
Cassiopeia dress on heaven's doors, 861 : 2
Cassius, Brutus and C. not displayed, 122 : 20
forever farewell C., 217 : 9
Cassius (*continued*)
has lean hungry look, 215 : 8
no terror C., 217 : 2
Cast a stone at her, 45 : 2
all cares on God, 535 : 3
away care, 169 : 6, 251 : 13
beam out of own eye, 38 : 10
better c. into sea, 43 : 35
bullet to kill me not c., 420 : 13
cold eye, 718 : 2
die is c., 99 : 19
forth no more, 692 : 10
gifts of the gods not to be c. aside, 57 : 21
into outer darkness, 38 : 22
it from thee, 37 : 8
longing eye on offices, 388 : 14
lots upon my vesture, 18 : 6
me not off in the time of old age, 19 : 34
me off discourteously, 917 : 14
mine eyes and see, 266 : 22
off his friends, 371 : 19
off works of darkness, 47 : 29
one longing look, 362 : 14
one's eyes so low, 234 : 28
over Edom will I c. out my shoe, 19 : 25
pale c. of thought, 221 : 12
pearls before swine, 38 : 11
set exact wealth at one c., 204 : 29
set my life upon c., 187 : 32
thy bread upon the waters, 27 : 20
time to c. away stones, 26 : 21
tree is c. into the fire, 36 : 29
unprofitable servant into darkness, 40 : 31
why art thou c. down, 19 : 6
wilt c. forth no more, 692 : 10
Caste, Brahmin c. of New England, 519 : 17
regard for thine own c. duty, 94 : 9
Castest, why c. thou off my soul, 20 : 10
Casteth, perfect love c. out fear, 52 : 25
Castigation, birch twig for c., 711 : 17
Castilian, choose what becomes C., 481 : 2
Casting body's vest aside, 297 : 4
dim religious light, 278 : 26
Cast-iron back with hinge, 603 : 9
Castle, bores through his c. wall, 195 : 3
contentions like bars of c., 24 : 21
Doubting C., 302 : 8
habitant of c. gray, 562 : 8
hath pleasant seat, 236 : 21
man's house his c., 172 : 2
splendor falls on c. walls, 530 : 26
stand in window of c., 100 : *n* 7
village belongs to C., 786 : 1
Castled crag of Drachenfels, 457 : 25
Castlereagh, mask like C., 468 : 5
Castle's strength will laugh, 240 : 2
Castles, building c. in Spain, 149 : 1
Castration, Negro past of c., 903 : 2
Casts, shadow that it c., 429 : 11
to write a living line, 256 : 16
Casual attitude towards life, 853 : 14
creeds, 585 : 22
flocks of pigeons, 767 : 4
Casualties, mistakes paid in c., 815 : 14
Cat and fiddle, 930 : 17
bell the c., 66 : 16, 143 : 15
bought crooked c., 932 : 18
calico c. replied Meeow, 666 : 18

Cat (*continued*)
care killed a c., 210 : 7
cat's a c. Rolet a knave, 311 : 7
Cheshire C. vanished slowly, 611 : 17
consider my c. Jeoffrey, 365 : 13
differences between c. and lie, 624 : 16
dog pipe or two, 692 : 15
endow college or c., 336 : 1
fog comes on c. feet, 761 : 5
had seven kits, 930 : 1
had Tiberius been c., 588 : 4
harmless necessary c., 200 : 3
has only nine lives, 624 : 16
in gloves catches no mice, 347 : 30
I've got a little c., 677 : 6
mad if they behold a c., 200 : 2
made a c. laugh, 480 : 15
may look on king, 160 : 34
melancholy as gib c., 202 : 29
mew and dog have day, 224 : 24
my c. Jeoffrey, 365 : 13
nine lives like a c., 160 : 24
not room enough to swing c., 365 : 2
on hot bakestone, 301 : 17
on hot tin roof, 301 : *n* 3
on tin roof, 887 : 11
owest c. no perfume, 234 : 7
pastime to c. more than she to me, 165 : 3
poor c. i' the adage, 237 : 2
that sits on hot stove lid, 625 : 5
walked by himself, 710 : 5
watch mouse, 323 : 19
who shall bell the c., 66 : 16
who will bell c., 143 : 15
worried the c., 934 : 9
would eat fish, 160 : 7
Catalogue, in c. ye go for men, 238 : 14
no reading more fascinating than c., 655 : 2
of things necessary, 310 : 18
read c. sooner than nothing, 751 : 19
Cataract, faint idea of c., 489 : 1
leaps in glory, 530 : 26
sounding c. haunted me, 423 : 12
Cataracts and hurricanoes, 233 : 24
Catastrophe, education and c., 720 : 5
of old comedy, 233 : 6
tickle your c., 206 : 10
Catastrophes, unparalleled c., 764 : 3
Catastrophist constructs theories, 471 : 17
Catbird, sitting in c. seat, 831 : 11
Catch a falling star, 252 : 1
another Antony, 242 : 7
as catch can, 364 : 5
bargain c. cold and starve, 243 : 14
Christ with worm, 892 : 5
claws that c., 612 : 17
conscience of the king, 221 : 10
earth's heedless sons, 834 : 11
ere she change, 335 : 17
hard to c. and conquer, 601 : 1
him once upon hip, 198 : 20
nets to c. the wind, 262 : 11
only one c. Catch-22, 902 : 8
perdition c. my soul, 230 : 30
perish or c. up, 731 : 5
springes to c. woodcocks, 219 : 5
the driving gale, 337 : 8
the manners living, 336 : 11
the nearest way, 236 : 16
up with advanced countries, 731 : 5
Catch (*continued*)
when pleasure can be had c. it, 355 : 24
with his surcease success, 236 : 22
you will never c. up, 718 : 9
Catch-22, some catch that C., 902 : 8
Catched fish and talked, 623 : 22
swallow gudgeons ere they're c., 65 : *n* 10
Catcher in the rye, 896 : 9
Catches, slow man c. up with swift, 60 : 5
Catching, poverty's c., 312 : 15
Catchwords, man lives by c., 667 : 15
Catechism, so ends my c., 205 : 5
Catechist, something of Shorter C., 663 : 8
Categorical imperative, 366 : 14
order c., 628 : 1
Caterpillar, I don't see said C., 611 : 8
Caterpillars of the commonwealth, 194 : 22
Caters for the sparrow, 210 : 28
Catharsis, tragedy a c., 88 : 16
Cathay, cycle of C., 530 : 9
Cathedral, after great c. gong, 716 : 8
in vast c. leave him, 533 : 6
mankind inspired made c., 667 : 10
needs more than opinion to erect c., 482 : 1
tunes, 604 : 18
Cathedrals, more benefit from bathroom than c., 834 : 8
our Gothic c., 800 : 10
Cather, Willas c., 839 : 4
Catholic America Spanish American, 721 : 3
C.O., 893 : 1
holy C. Church, 55 : 2
judges neither C. nor agnostic, 776 : 13
Catholicism minus Christianity, 595 : 13
Catholics, all equal except C., 520 : 2
and Communists, 859 : 13
they came for C., 824 : 1
Catiline, how long C., 98 : 1
prodigal of own possessions, 102 : 23
Catins, mes pensées sont mes c., 359 : *n* 6
Cato, like C. give laws, 338 : 14
vanquished had C., 118 : 5
Cat's a cat and Rolet a knave, 311 : 7
pull chestnuts with c. paw, 297 : 11
run away with string, 934 : 5
what c. averse to fish, 361 : 15
Cats, all c. gray when candles out, 120 : *n* 7
and monkeys monkeys and cats, 652 : 8
do c. eat bats, 611 : 3
fought dogs killed c., 541 : 1
have two holes in coat, 387 : 2
rain c. and dogs, 919 : 23
seven c., 930 : 1
those who play with c., 169 : 9
Cats', start by c. corridors, 888 : 11
Cattle beneath shadow of oak, 373 : 28
call c. home, 566 : 7
cursed above all c., 7 : 9
die as c., 827 : 2
if c. and horses had hands, 67 : 13
lowly c. shed, 561 : 10
men the c. of God, 4 : 3
Cattle (*continued*)
upon a thousand hills, 19 : 13
would draw gods like cattle, 67 : 13
Catullus be resolved and firm, 101 : 20
walk that way, 714 : 3
worst of all poets, 102 : 4
you should cease folly, 101 : 19
Caucasus, thinking on frosty C., 194 : 7
Caught at God's skirts, 540 : 31
God c. his eye, 839 : 2
hanging around till you've c. on, 750 : 13
him yes I held him, 653 : 8
his clear accents, 541 : 6
in that sensual music, 714 : 22
like beast at bay, 817 : 6
moral man regrets even if not c., 772 : 13
morning's minion, 656 : 1
mother came and c. her, 932 : 4
my heavenly jewel, 176 : 15
our youth, 797 : 2
she c. him by his garment, 8 : 30
trout c. with tickling, 214 : 7
with his sweet perfections c., 184 : 14
without diadem, 606 : 19
Cauliflower cabbage with education, 624 : 14
Causa latet vis notissima, 113 : *n* 13
Causation, law of c., 617 : 11
Cause and effect from economy, 871 : 4
armor of righteous c., 694 : 15
bad c. bad means, 384 : 16
be c. strong or weak, 567 : 17
beauty of good old c., 425 : 15
calledst me dog before c., 199 : 31
cannot cross c. why born, 190 : 33
common c. decays, 80 : 16
common c. to save Union, 521 : 7
died in virtue's c., 188 : 18
effect defective comes by c., 220 : 13
effect whose c. is God, 377 : 16
evolution not c. but law, 637 : 1
final c. produces motion, 87 : 10
found spiritual c., 583 : 2
full c. of weeping, 233 : 23
Germany the c. of Hitler, 801 : 11
given his heart to c., 797 : 13
good old c. is gone, 425 : 15
Great First C., 378 : 1
griefs we c. ourselves, 74 : 4
hear me for my c., 216 : 13
hidden but result well known, 113 : 19
idea of oneself as c., 308 : 13
if any man show just c., 56 : 7
if astray c. is in you, 142 : 3
is there any c. in nature, 234 : 16
it is just, 446 : 2
just c. overwhelming power, 689 : 1
laws or kings c. or cure, 352 : 21
little grace my c., 229 : 25
magnificent and awful c., 376 : 21
no warrants but upon probable c., 391 : 16
not a field but a c., 384 : 18
not be judge in own c., 111 : *n* 11
not jealous for the c., 231 : 20
nothing comes without c., 346 : 5
obstinacy in bad c., 274 : 8, 359 : 24
of freedom cause of God, 415 : 4
of freedom versus tyranny, 866 : 9
of this effect, 220 : 13
or men of Emerald Isle, 400 : 10
perseverance in good c., 359 : 24

Cause (*continued*)
produces more than one effect, 579 : 12
report me and my c., 224 : 31
sea of c. and theory, 742 : 18
set c. above renown, 700 : 6
spreads over land and sea, 618 : 13
support Caledonia's c., 411 : 24
tenacious of purpose in rightful c., 107 : 28
try c. condemn to death, 611 : 6
turn him to c. of policy, 207 : 5
watercolors to impaint c., 205 : 3
what in effect already in c., 688 : 9
whatever c. I defend, 824 : 7
when just c. reaches flood tide, 689 : 1
wherein tongue confuted, 276 : 17
wit in other men, 205 : 21
you c. what you abuse, 316 : 1
Zeus first c., 71 : 11
Caused the widow's heart to sing, 16 : 16
Causes célèbres, 327 : 19
defend c. which were unpopular, 872 : 18
flowers as in c. sleep, 271 : 19
from amorous c. springs, 333 : 24
great c. on move, 745 : 1
happy man who could search out c., 104 : 5
hidden c. of things, 251 : 8
home of lost c., 587 : 1
investigation of hidden c., 166 : 15
lost c. preface victory, 809 : 14
of destruction, 358 : 16
which impel separation, 387 : 9
why and wherefore, 208 : 13
Caution in refusing benefits, 308 : 24
scars of others teach c., 128 : 9
upward look of c., 749 : 11
Cautious people never bring reform, 577 : 17
politic c. and meticulous, 803 : 17
seldom err, 68 : 17
statistical Christ, 659 : 8
under whose c. hand, 576 : 8
Cavalry of woe, 604 : 7
Cave, courts thee in some pleasant c., 107 : 3
error correct c., 899 : 15
idols of the c., 179 : 8
shadows on opposite wall of c., 84 : 17
sky will c. in on him, 822 : 12
Stygian c. forlorn, 277 : 17
vacant interlunar c., 288 : 21
Cave ab homine unius libri, 133 : 11
canem, 133 : 12
Caveat emptor, 133 : 13
Cavern, mossy c., 477 : 16
Pan's c., 717 : 16
Caverns cool and deep, 584 : 12
in c. all alone, 899 : 15
measureless to man, 433 : 21
sand-strewn c., 584 : 12
twice ten thousand c., 478 : 16
Caves, beetles in c., 873 : 11
dark unfathomed c., 362 : 8
in sea c. a thirst, 849 : 18
of ice, 433 : 25
Caviar to the general, 221 : 3
Cavil on ninth part of hair, 204 : 15
Cawdor, Glamis thou art and C., 236 : 16
Cawdor (*continued*)
I am Thane of C., 236 : 11
shall sleep no more, 237 : 22
Cease and then again begin, 587 : 14
Byron's struggle c., 585 : 2
Catullus you should c. folly, 101 : 19
day and night shall not c., 8 : 1
efforts to find where last rose lingers, 107 : 17
every joy, 443 : 8
fears that I may c., 478 : 17
from mental fight, 406 : 21
from thine own wisdom, 25 : 6
long contention c., 588 : 2
man I am c. to be, 533 : 18
not c. from exploration, 808 : 17
poor shall never c., 11 : 17
sing or c. to sing, 339 : 29
the wicked c. from troubling, 15 : 9
time c. and midnight never come, 184 : 7
to ask what morrow will bring, 107 : 7
to be free for religion, 821 : 10
upon the midnight, 476 : 28
weeping without c., 659 : 15
wonders never c., 393 : 12
ye from man, 28 : 33
Ceased, God created woman boredom c., 658 : 15
only when c. to need things, 895 : 14
when Lucy c. to be, 424 : 12
Ceaseless devouring of weak by strong, 579 : 19
thoughts of roaming, 313 : 23
turns with c. pain, 368 : 14
Ceases, forbearance c. to be virtue, 372 : 2
happiness c. like dream, 273 : 5
to be free for irreligion, 821 : 10
Ceasing, O swiftness never c., 177 : 8
of exquisite music, 511 : 2
pray without c., 50 : 21
Cedant arma togae, 98 : *n* 18
Cedar, as c. tall and slender, 394 : 6
grow like a c. in Lebanon, 20 : 18
lordly c. green with boughs, 671 : 3
Cedars of Lebanon, 21 : 10
roots of c. of Lebanon, 759 : 11
Cedarwood, sandalwood c., 760 : 19
Célébrait, Ronsard me c., 162 : *n* 8
Celebrate, I c. myself, 574 : 11
not c. funeral with weeping, 95 : 2
Celebrated cultivated Duke of Plaza Toro, 630 : 1
Saviour's birth c., 217 : 26
Celebrates his obsequies, 430 : 8
pale Hecate's offerings, 237 : 14
Celebration of man, 887 : 7
Célèbres, causes c., 327 : 19
Celebrities, congress of c., 615 : 14
Celeriter, sat c. fieri satis bene, 110 : *n* 5
Celerity never more admired, 241 : 7
Celestial, appareled in c. light, 426 : 10
ennui of apartments, 768 : 11
pattern of c. peace, 185 : 7
sailing c. spaces, 637 : 21
sate itself in c. bed, 219 : 22
so c. article as freedom, 384 : 13
wisdom calms the mind, 352 : 3
Celia, come my C., 255 : 16
has undone me, 361 : 6
Celibacy has no pleasures, 352 : 18
Cell, deposit little c. by c., 638 : 10
Cell (*continued*)
dwell on rock or in c., 172 : 17
earth most like single c., 883 : 13
ill-spirit sob in each c., 893 : 7
in body holds heart, 863 : 16
in narrow c. forever laid, 361 : 23
thine eternal c., 225 : 4
tight hot c., 836 : 20
Cellar, born in a c., 364 : 3
lived in c. damp, 568 : 20
nothing sleep in that c., 873 : 6
secretly nurtured in c., 800 : 7
warm delicious c., 847 : 3
Cells, all c. from pre-existing c., 584 : *n* 2
better schoolrooms than c., 562 : 12
condemned c. of Newgate, 620 : 9
held in cohesion by c., 760 : 21
little gray c., 817 : 12
unresting c., 760 : 21
Cellula, omnis c. a c., 584 : 5
Celts certainly have style, 588 : 10
Cement glue and lime of love, 266 : 1
gummed with bicycle c., 835 : 1
Cemetery of dead ideas, 705 : 15
Censorship, assassination extreme c., 681 : 16
if c. reigns, 378 : 10
Censure, careless of c., 333 : 22
durst not c., 351 : 11
every trade save c., 456 : 13
fear of c., 792 : 14
freely who have written well, 332 : 16
mankind c. injustice, 84 : 7
pardons raven, 122 : 2
take each man's c., 219 : 1
tax for being eminent, 322 : 3
Census, test of civilization not c., 499 : 10
treats people as units, 879 : 17
Cent, not one c. for tribute, 416 : 12
Centaur, cloud that looked like c., 81 : 15
in dragon world, 793 : 4
Center cannot hold, 714 : 12
in universe neither c. nor circumference, 171 : 15
intention stabs the c., 246 : 12
man c. of circle, 615 : 2
many lines in dial's c., 207 : 8
my c. giving way, 670 : 6
of my sinful earth, 246 : 4
of silent Word, 806 : 4
unfathomed c., 480 : 12
wore fire's c., 876 : 15
Centerlight, blue c. pop, 901 : 3
Centipedes, ants c. and scorpions, 760 : 6
Central stream of what we feel, 588 : 22
Central Park, one great purpose of C., 590 : 14
single work of art, 590 : 13
Cents, feel like thirty c., 718 : 11
hours and minutes dollars and c., 348 : *n* 1
Centuries, across c. across oceans, 745 : 10
all c. but this, 629 : 7
bowed by weight of c., 670 : 14
crystallized air of c., 796 : 1
cycles of heaven in c., 806 : 15
don't care for great c., 643 : 5
forty c. look down, 420 : 6
joked over fifty c., 630 : 9

Centuries (*continued*)
lie through c., 541 : 20
of folly noise sin, 542 : 4
of stony sleep, 714 : 13
prior work of past c., 673 : 10
roll back to age of gold, 108 : 11
sequent c., 494 : 22
three c. removed, 857 : 14
wish days to be as c., 499 : 1
wit lasts two c., 453 : 16
years roll into c., 534 : 25
Century, born in this c., 890 : 7
challenge of next half c., 872 : 11
fantastic c. move, 399 : 16
grain of poetry season c., 672 : 4
lain for c. dead, 533 : 25
live for more than one c., 101 : 14
of common man, 811 : 11
of sonnets, 543 : 30
problem of twentieth c. color line, 724 : 15
ring bells for new c., 755 : 9
seventeenth c. dissociation, 809 : 8
Cerberus and blackest Midnight, 277 : 17
give sop to C., 132 : 22
like C. three gentlemen, 398 : 16
Cerebration, slight powers of c., 703 : 1
Ceremonies, hampering with c. 90 : 6
Ceremony, idol c., 208 : 6
love useth enforced c., 216 : 30
of innocence drowned, 714 : 12
save c. save general c., 208 : 6
that to great ones 'longs, 228 : 6
thrice gorgeous c., 208 : 7
Certain am I of the spot, 606 : 17
because impossible, 126 : 9
is birth for the dead, 94 : 8
is death for the born, 94 : 8
no c. life achieved, 202 : 8
nothing c. but death and taxes, 348 : 16
of his fate, 230 : 34
of nothing but affection, 479 : 1
permanent and c. characteristics, 352 : 4
signs should prefigure events, 98 : 21
there is no fine thing, 713 : 2
Certainties, begin with c. end in doubts, 178 : 20
begin with doubts end in c., 178 : 20
hot for c., 600 : 20
public demands c., 771 : 18
there are no c., 771 : 18
Certainty, certitude not test of c., 644 : 22
enslavement c. of worse, 882 : 11
generally illusion, 644 : 3
no such thing as absolute c., 508 : 5
not lightly sacrificed, 730 : 14
of power, 860 : 7
of the words of truth, 25 : 1
pass from suspicion to c., 293 : 6
principles of icy c., 700 : 2
quit c. for uncertainty, 352 : 14
sober c. of waking bliss, 279 : 20
without doubt, 139 : 5
Certitude nor peace nor help, 587 : 16
not test of certainty, 644 : 22
Certum est quia impossible est, 126 : *n* 6
Cervantes, arm of old C., 570 : 11
on his galley, 742 : 10
smiled chivalry away, 461 : 26
Cervantes' serious air, 340 : 14
Cesspool, London great c., 689 : 2
Cetera quis nescit, 113 : *n* 2
Chacun au bien aspire, 171 : *n* 9
Chaeronea, dishonest victory at C., 282 : 6
Chafe, champ and c. and toss, 584 : 11
reason c., 495 : 9
Chafed, high blood c., 461 : *n* 1
Chafes, on unnumbered pebbles c., 234 : 28
Chaff, hope corn in c., 456 : 15
principles less than c., 683 : 18
wheat hid in bushels of c., 198 : 5
which the wind driveth away, 17 : 12
Chaffinch sings on bough, 541 : 16
Chagrined, not be very much c., 519 : 20
Chain about ankle of fellow man, 556 : 12
as with an iron c., 485 : 24
drags lengthening c., 368 : 14
fastened about own neck, 556 : 12
free that anchor and c., 93 : 3
golden c. from heaven, 58 : 6
handled with a c., 605 : 11
hanging in a golden c., 285 : 3
love c. to bind child to parents 524 : 12
never broke c. freed soul, 626 : 19
of life, 898 : 1
of responsibility, 788 : 4
on oppressor's head break c., 418 : 4
pearl c. of all virtues, 257 : 14
wear c. I forged, 548 : 6
what the c., 405 : 8
winds th' exhausted c., 410 : 14
Chained for billions of years, 809 : 22
Chainless soul, 562 : 3
Chains, adamantine c. and fire, 283 : 4
and slavery, 383 : 5, 411 : 15
bound in icy c., 229 : *n* 1
breaks c. from every mind, 404 : 14
cries of country in c., 928 : *n* 2
everywhere he is in c., 358 : 12
familiarize with c., 520 : 7
in c. or in laurels, 538 : 16
intellectual c., 858 : 19
man born in c., 413 : 2
mourns his yet unbroken c., 399 : 18
not all free who scorn c., 374 : 17
nothing to lose but c., 563 : 10
ocean loose c. of things, 115 : 13
prayer for deliverance from c., 556 : 3
sang in my c., 887 : 3
untwisting c. that tie, 278 : 7
Chair, draw c. up close to edge, 835 : 15
electric c. like oasis, 893 : 2
give Dayrolles a c., 342 : 18
is the c. empty, 187 : 22
one c. for solitude, 560 : 4
oranges in sunny c., 767 : 2
Rabelais' easy c., 340 : 14
sea best in c. before fire, 741 : 11
seated in thy silver c., 255 : 12
tonight bumps against c., 856 : 6
vacant c., 511 : 10, 552 : 18
Chair, la c. triste hélas, 651 : *n* 2
Chairman, by God Mr. C., 367 : 2
Chairs, three c. for society, 560 : 4
two c. for friendship, 560 : 4
two old c. half candle, 550 : 16
why smash the c., 518 : 2
Chalice of my blood, 54 : 7
that is Grail, 535 : *n* 4
Chaliced, on c. flowers that lies, 243 : 16
Chalk cliffs of Dover, 720 : 11
give me piece of c., 652 : 3
of my bones, 873 : 12
Challenge of next half century, 872 : 11
send c. to his end, 292 : 9
unhatched egg greatest c., 847 : 6
Challenges, New Frontier is c., 890 : 5
not in calm that great c. are formed, 392 : 16
Chamber, bridegroom coming out of his c., 17 : 28
get you to my lady's c., 224 : 14
he capers nimbly in lady's c., 186 : 31
hear in c. above me, 512 : 4
I throw myself down in my c., 255 : 2
in my lady's c., 931 : 8
in silent halls, 471 : 6
rapping at c. door, 526 : 10
Star C. matter, 225 : 5
with naked foot stalking my c., 161 : 25
Chambering and wantonness, 47 : 29
Chambermaid, as happy in arms of c., 356 : 8
Chambers, layeth the beams of his c., 21 : 8
Chameleon's dish, 222 : 8
tuning skin to it, 899 : 6
Chameleons feed on light, 467 : 16
Champ and chafe and toss, 584 : 11
Champagne and chicken at last, 341 : 1
no kick from c., 820 : 3
teetotaler, 680 : 9
Champed grasses, 739 : 15
Champion, Gray C., 503 : 1
people have always some c., 85 : 5
playboy, 735 : 4
Champions, cullest thy selectest c., 570 : 11
four c. fierce strive, 284 : 27
Chance, afford all fair c., 522 : 2
all have equal c., 521 : 8
all whom c. hath slain, 254 : 9
at hands of Time and C., 640 : 12
bludgeonings of c., 663 : 10
by c. only phrase we have, 867 : 17
comes from art not c., 333 : 9
dart of c., 231 : 26
dice never abolish c., 651 : 15
direction thou canst not see, 337 : 1
favors mind prepared, 591 : 2
fool right by c., 375 : 25
give peace a c., 914 : 13
give them a c., 562 : *n* 2
history cannot tolerate c., 837 : 12
hour before this c., 238 : 7
if c. will have me king, 236 : 12
learning not attained by c., 393 : 2
main c., 291 : 23
may crown me, 236 : 12
nativity c. or death, 225 : 28
nickname for Providence, 386 : 5
no gifts from C., 584 : 17
no such thing as c., 413 : 12
not leave right to c., 558 : 3
not yet exempt from c., 467 : 7
of war, 225 : 32
power erring men call C., 279 : 28
pseudonym of God, 655 : 13
set my life on any c., 238 : 16
shall not control, 584 : 15
slave to fate c. kings, 254 : 12
something left to c., 408 : 6

Chance (*continued*)
stand to the main c., 175:14
take c. that traitors escape, 737:6
time and c. happeneth to all, 27:17
Tinker to Evers to C., 773:12
to find yourself, 683:16
to talk a little wild, 248:23
weight of c. desires, 427:14
will bring us through, 585:8
wisdom and deliberation follow c., 166:1
Chanced to meet old man, 934:2
Chancel, broke c. window-squares, 642:1
Chancellor, conscience of C., 263:13
susceptible c., 628:18
Chancellor's foot, 263:13
Chancery, wards in C., 628:17
Chances change by course, 182:1
like sunbeams pass, 347:*n* 5
spake of disastrous c., 229:28
take c. for peace, 803:8
Chancy, history very c., 800:5
Change, all that is not true c. in future, 504:11
and migration of the soul, 83:13
anything we c. in child, 754:8
bolts up c., 241:24
but cannot die, 468:10
by tomorrow and fleet, 446:11
can't c. mind won't c. subject, 746:15
catch ere she c., 335:17
chances c. by course, 182:1
clime not disposition, 109:5
courage to c., 823:15
environment not man, 832:12
ever-whirling wheel of c., 174:6
everything except loves, 344:3
extremes by c. more fierce, 284:23
fear of c., 283:24
feel by turns bitter c., 284:23
given heart c. of mood, 748:3
hands and still confute, 290:16
heavy c. now thou art gone, 280:11
hopes no more c. name, 427:14
human nature not c., 524:2
I would not c. for thine, 256:8
language change life, 911:2
life presupposes its c. and movement, 867:11
lobsters and retire, 612:6
man c. environment, 870:15
me to winged bird, 76:24
my state with kings, 244:10
never c. when love has found home, 112:19
no money no c. of routine, 859:15
nonviolent action supplement c., 909:15
nothing endures but c., 69:25
nothing lasts save eternal c., 265:3
of air, 755:6
of heart, 868:4
of motion proportional, 313:14
old lamps for new, 919:24
one quality we predicate, 676:4
pace of c., 814:5
people c. what is in themselves, 131:1
places and which is thief, 235:2
religion knavery and c., 312:13
ringing grooves of c., 530:8
secure from c., 568:19
she earth or sky, 918:15
Change (*continued*)
skies above them, 709:7
speech small c. of Silence, 600:12
stamp of nature, 223:11
success c. human mechanism, 859:19
the many c. and pass, 469:16
the more things c., 514:5
them when we will, 531:15
things that are and do not c., 866:6
thought love never c., 654:17
time for a c., 854:4
time will c. your opinions, 86:3
times c. and move continually, 174:8
times c. and we c. with them, 134:30
to c. language c. life, 911:2
to virtue and worthiness, 215:14
too much c. too short time, 909:1
unafraid of c., 701:5
universe is c., 124:14
we think we see, 747:10
weapons c. but not man, 791:16
werewolf's painful c., 899:17
what man made man can c., 817:10
what should be changed, 823:15
when worse it must c., 155:14
Changé, nous avons c. tout cela, 297:*n* 6
Changeable, young men's minds are c., 57:22
Changed, accept what cannot be c., 823:15
all c. sometimes suddenly, 847:8
changed utterly, 714:9
eternity has c. him, 651:14
from the one all to me, 641:24
innocence for innocence, 246:10
like change in my face, 665:13
mind not to be c., 283:13
minds of gods not c. suddenly, 59:22
not c. a wink, 571:8
not c. from him they knew, 747:1
sea c. Egdon remained, 640:11
something better c. in ourselves, 754:8
things that cannot be c., 823:15
we have c. all that, 297:24
we shall be c., 49:7
whole world have been c., 300:1
ye too c. ye hills, 587:6
Changeful mind of mortals, 72:13
presuming on c. potency, 227:1
Changes, absurd man never c., 451:*n* 4
control our being, 529:4
desire c., 734:9
follow c. of the moon, 231:2
God c. and man and form, 634:4
God c. not people until they change, 131:1
human nature c., 676:4
man c. not at all, 791:16
monthly c. in circled orb, 192:11
not done with my c., 864:14
past c. constantly, 816:4
sea never c., 683:14
sky c. when wives, 212:25
woman often c., 105:*n* 5
world's a scene of c., 295:6
Changeth, old order c., 534:31
sweareth to his own hurt and c. not, 17:23
Changin' times they are a-c., 915:5
Changing, borrow every c. shape, 804:2
Changing (*continued*)
method of c. governors, 813:9
moon changing eyes, 714:8
scenes of life, 317:6
shallow c. woman, 187:21
stress on not c. mind, 751:9
things according to desire, 734:9
Chankly Bore, 551:4
Channel, butting through the C., 760:20
crossing C. and tossing, 629:1
drum them up C., 700:8
man merely c. for food, 152:2
Chant, do use to c. it, 214:3
how can ye c., 409:24
Chanticleer, lungs crow like c., 211:7
Chanting, exaltation in c. of Muses, 76:12
faint hymns to moon, 195:20
Chants doleful hymn, 202:16
Chaos and old Night, 283:21
beauty dead black c., 189:14
bounded by primeval c., 535:*n* 6
breeds life, 635:4
is come again, 230:30
of the sun, 767:4
of thought and passion, 337:2
our policy against c., 771:11
rough unordered mass, 113:15
this is why there is c., 90:9
thy dread empire C., 340:28
what a c. is man, 300:11
Chaos-like together crushed, 334:15
Chap, intellectual c., 628:23
Chapel, afternoon in secluded c., 808:16
Devil builds c. there, 318:5
Devil would build c., 156:5
God's greenwood c., 765:*n* 3
Chapels had been churches, 198:9
legend of green c., 886:18
Chapfallen, quite c., 224:14
Chaplain, Bluebeard's c., 546:19
Chapmen, you do as c. do, 226:23
Chapmen's, not uttered by c. tongues, 190:19
Chaps with couple o' guns, 786:11
Chapter, autobiographies begin C. Two, 738:7
in my book of transformations, 864:14
of accidents very long, 342:14
of knowledge very short, 342:14
said he could repeat c., 356:1
write the next c., 872:9
Chapters in art of living, 580:10
of lives to natural end, 664:8
these thirty c., 6:8
Character, accommodatin' c., 616:10
acquire everything but c., 453:10
adopt c. of octopus, 67:4
analysis of c. highest entertainment, 861:11
bearing on excellence of c., 87:22
best way to define c., 647:23
bird of bad moral c., 348:13
easier kept than recovered, 384:21
education for c., 579:6
energy of c., 414:18
family stamped c. on child, 754:11
formed in world's torrent, 395:15
give action its c., 83:1
good c. remembered, 4:4
habits and manners, 592:7

Character (*continued*)
his c. arbiter of everyone's fortune, 103 : *n* 5
influence of c. in infancy, 498 : 8
judging c. motive impulse, 783 : 4
liberal arts humanizes c., 114 : 2
lies in own hands, 909 : 4
limitations of own c., 637 : 9
man that makes c., 330 : 2
man's c. is his fate, 70 : 11
men of contrary c., 68 : 16
no talent but c., 482 : 5
of mistress from dress of maids, 128 : 7
of perfection, 588 : 17
poetical c., 479 : 17
politics ruins c., 553 : 15
power of Latin in c., 588 : 11
product of tendencies and training, 752 : 18
reap a c., 922 : 18
Scott hand in Southern c., 623 : 17
simplicity of c., 637 : 8
society wholesome for c., 569 : 14
Characteristic artistic personality, 577 : 4
reality definable c., 776 : 8
Characteristics, attributes c. of living creature, 572 : 10
not have certain mental c., 685 : 7
of democracy, 845 : 15
of modern spirit, 699 : 4
of popular politician, 81 : 13
of vigorous mind, 352 : 4
Characterless, mighty states c., 226 : 15
Characters, dreams touchstones of c., 558 : 15
fashioning our c. wrong, 648 : 10
high c. cries one, 289 : 20
knowledge of c. of rulers, 380 : 9
most women have no c., 335 : 16
of hell to trace, 363 : 5
six c. in search of author, 723 : 19
venerate four c., 386 : 11
Charge Chester charge, 431 : 3
compulsive ardor gives c., 223 : 5
Cromwell I c. thee, 249 : 7
give his angels c. over thee, 20 : 17
give lie to slander c., 455 : 12
not soul save to its ability, 131 : 15
once more be dumb, 588 : 3
prepared lawyers met, 332 : 7
such is the c., 83 : 11
take thou in c., 488 : 16
with all thy chivalry, 443 : 15
within the bosom, 604 : 7
Charged, hear it c. against me, 575 : 7
language c. with meaning, 793 : 8
troops of error, 274 : 1
Charger, John Baptist's head in c., 39 : 23
Charges against others come home, 128 : 19
die to save c., 258 : 23
Chariest maid prodigal enough, 218 : 27
Charing Cross, heaven and C., 693 : 19
Chariot, appeared a c. of fire, 14 : 12
flying c. through air, 377 : 26
maketh clouds his c., 21 : 8
of fire, 406 : 21
of Israel, 14 : 13
sweet c., 935 : 24
swing low sweet c., 935 : 24
that bears human soul, 607 : 4
Chariot (*continued*)
Time's winged c., 296 : 28
why is his c. so long in coming, 12 : 8
Chariots, why tarry the wheels of his c., 12 : 8
Charitable, cherish at c. breast, 794 : 9
intents wicked or c., 219 : 11
men's c. speeches, 181 : 16
Charite, of saynte c., 916 : 16
Charities of kiss or smile, 438 : 8
Charity, affecting c. and devotion, 90 : 6
and have not c., 48 : 22
anticipate c. by preventing poverty, 137 : 10
beareth all things, 48 : 24
begins at home, 96 : 6, 274 : 19
believeth all things, 48 : 24
come out of c., 916 : *n* 3
crawling for c., 90 : 7
creates multitude of sins, 676 : 1
degrades, 504 : 11
edifieth, 48 : 13
endureth all things, 48 : 24
envieth not, 48 : 23
Faith Hope C., 443 : 2
for all, 524 : 7
frozen as c., 439 : 9
greatest is c., 48 : 25
hopeth all things, 48 : 24
I am in c. with world, 323 : 5
in all things c., 294 : 18
in c. no excess, 180 : 12
in c. to all mankind, 418 : 6
in love and c. with neighbors, 55 : 16
indiscriminate c., 621 : 9
is kind, 48 : 23
justice not c. wanting in world, 414 : 12
lectures or a little c., 574 : 26
liberty like c., 825 : 10
little earth for c., 249 : 10
love friendship c., 226 : 20
mankind's concern is c., 337 : 9
never faileth, 48 : 24
not puffed up, 48 : 23
now abideth c., 48 : 25
of saynte c., 916 : 16
pity gave ere c. began, 370 : 6
rarity of Christian c., 485 : 22
scrimped and iced, 659 : 8
shall cover multitude of sins, 52 : 14
suffereth long, 48 : 23
towards each other, 383 : 6
towards others, 274 : 19
vaunteth not, 48 : 23
weep for me who has c., 152 : 1
where c. neither fear nor ignorance, 138 : 14
Charity's golden ladder, 137 : 10
Charlemagne, world-transforming C., 717 : 4
Charlemagne's, their age not C., 507 : 20
Charles, gentlehearted C., 441 : *n* 1
immense empire of C. the Fifth, 412 : *n* 6
navy of C. the Second, 489 : 7
successors of C. the Fifth, 383 : 16
the First his Cromwell, 382 : 13
Charles's, King C. head, 548 : 31
Charlie is my darling, 417 : 6
live and die wi' C., 422 : 19
o'er the water to C., 422 : 19
Charlie Brown, good man C., 901 : 7
Charm ache with air, 210 : 4
by thoughts supplied, 423 : 12
in melancholy, 416 : 4
indispensable to women, 694 : *n* 2
music oft hath such a c., 229 : 1
no c. against tyranny, 577 : 15
northern c., 892 : 2
object in possession seldom retains c., 123 : 8
of all the Muses, 535 : 15
of earliest birds, 285 : 27
one native c., 370 : 15
quality in others, 580 : 13
simplicity and c., 106 : 19
smiling at good mouth, 792 : 16
some have c. for none, 694 : 10
some women c. all, 694 : 10
strength man's c., 694 : *n* 2
strengthen and teach, 511 : 14
to stay morning star, 435 : 22
touching all the muses' c., 100 : 10
wasted on sky, 494 : 5
what c. soothe melancholy, 369 : 20
what is c., 694 : *n* 2
witch hath power to c., 217 : 26
without c. no literature, 711 : 15
woman's strength, 694 : *n* 2
Charmed, bear a c. life, 240 : 8
fond love c. me, 918 : 9
it with smiles and soap, 614 : 4
magic casements, 477 : 1
water burnt away, 434 : 28
with foolish whistling, 295 : 16
Charmer, were t'other c. away, 332 : 6
Charmers, will not hearken to voice of c., 19 : 23
Charmian is this well done, 242 : 6
Charming, be c. with nothing, 667 : 5
evening criminal's friend, 581 : 2
form of government, 85 : 3
friendly and c. relationship, 156 : 7
how c. divine philosophy, 279 : 25
left his voice, 287 : 2
never so wisely, 19 : 23
no furniture c. as books, 432 : 23
to totter into vogue, 363 : 20
Charms, Aphrodite with intricate c., 63 : *n* 5
by accepting, 335 : 23
endearing young c., 446 : 11
freedom has thousand c., 375 : 19
icy arms hold c., 834 : 5
music has c. to soothe, 324 : 14
O Solitude where are c., 376 : 13
or ear or sight, 436 : 1
other maids' surpass, 399 : 20
power obtained by c., 414 : 11
Sabina has thousand c., 919 : 19
strike the sight, 334 : 11
Charon could not prevent me, 76 : 3
Chart that faith deciphered, 703 : 3
Charter, large a c. as wind, 211 : 10
this was c. of land, 345 : 19
Chartered libertine, 207 : 5
Charybdis, I fall into C., 200 : 1
implacable C. guards left, 200 : *n* 1
on starboard beam C., 200 : *n* 1
Chase, blessed in luck of c., 929 : 2
glowing hours, 457 : 15
had a beast in view, 307 : 1
lead a wild-goose c., 169 : 3
my gloom away, 416 : 4
panting syllable, 376 : 10
piteous c., 210 : 25

Chase (*continued*)
the sport of kings, 328 : 18
unhurrying c., 693 : 11
when heated in the c., 317 : 7
Chased, more c. than enjoyed, 199 : 6
Chassis, state of c., 786 : 9
Chaste and fair, 255 : 12
as ice, 221 : 17
as the icicle, 242 : 23
as unsunned snow, 243 : 17
early bright transient c., 307 : *n* 3
fair c. unexpressive she, 211 : 18
modest and commonly c., 463 : 13
nunnery of thy c. breast, 295 : 22
to her husband, 335 : 18
was she not c., 119 : 23
Chasten, power to c. and subdue, 423 : 13
Chasteneth, he that loveth c. him, 23 : 34
whom the Lord loveth he c., 51 : 20
Chastening in hour of pride, 521 : 3
Chastise, I will c. with scorpions, 13 : 38
Chastised, father hath c. you, 13 : 38
having been a little c., 34 : 13
Chastity, give me c. but not now, 129 : 3
my brother Chastity, 279 : 24
of honor, 373 : 24
Chat, before we have our c., 613 : 6
Chat, la patte du c., 297 : *n* 3
Châteaux, O seasons O c., 674 : 2
Chatter against bird of Zeus, 71 : 24
and love and hate, 588 : 7
harebrained c., 502 : 21
insignificant c. of world, 555 : 1
of transcendental kind, 628 : 6
those who have learned art c., 71 : 24
Chattering voltage, 816 : 14
Chatterton marvelous boy, 425 : 10
Chaucer, Dan C. first warbler, 528 : 21
nigh to learned C., 265 : 14
not lodge thee by C., 256 : 11
since C. was alive, 442 : 24
that broad famous English poet, 261 : 15
well of English, 173 : 22
whose sweet breath, 528 : 21
Chaucer's, corruption since C. days, 261 : 17
Chaud comme l'enfer, 400 : *n* 3
Chaudron, parole humaine comme un c. fêlé, 583 : *n* 5
Chavender or Chub, 271 : 5
Cheap defense of nations, 373 : 23
flesh and blood so c., 485 : 20
good counsel c., 259 : 10
greet c. holde at litel prys, 147 : 10
hold c. the strain, 544 : 10
how potent c. music is, 843 : 10
ill ware is never c., 269 : 13
life not c. but sacred, 499 : 1
man's life c. as beast's, 233 : 21
never buy because c., 390 : 3
sitting as standing, 323 : 4
sleep a c. pleasure, 171 : 1
sold c. what is most dear, 245 : 16
tin trays, 760 : 20
what we obtain too c., 384 : 13
Cheapens, possession c., 631 : 18
Cheaper than keep cow, 621 : 3
Cheapest, man richest whose pleasures c., 557 : 17
Cheat against cheat, 120 : *n* 1
at cards genteelly, 355 : 13
Cheat (*continued*)
for sake of beauty, 757 : 8
language often c., 463 : 20
life 'tis all a c., 303 : 10
out of love c. others, 734 : 8
pleasure as great as to c., 291 : 24
sweet c. gone, 739 : 18
Cheated by anyone but himself, 497 : 13
illusion by which c., 734 : 8
pleasure of being c., 291 : 24
Cheater, old bald c. Time, 255 : 13
Cheating, winning games without c., 848 : 13
Check, care's c. and curb, 298 : 21
judicial power a c., 381 : 11
rod to c. the erring, 427 : 13
Checked, be c. for silence, 227 : 9
Checkerboard of nights and days, 516 : 22
Checkered shade, 278 : 1
Checks, as if c. given, 606 : 17
handed in his c., 630 : 12
Cheek, care sat on his faded c., 283 : 25
dancing c. to c., 802 : 8
feed on her damask c., 214 : 5
he that loves a rosy c., 272 : 1
I the blow and c., 581 : 1
iron tears down Pluto's c., 278 : 22
language in her eye her c., 227 : 3
leans her c. upon her hand, 192 : 4
of tan, 513 : 10
she hangs on c. of night, 191 : 26
that I might touch that c., 192 : 4
tongue not far from Kilmer c., 803 : 1
turn the other c., 37 : 10
warm c. and rising bosom, 362 : 21
withered c. tresses gray, 429 : 20
yellow c. white beard, 205 : 28
Cheekbone, short a c. and ear, 579 : *n* 1
Cheeks, blood spoke in her c., 254 : 6
blow winds and crack c., 233 : 24
crimson in lips and c., 193 : 27
make pale my c. with care, 264 : 23
of sorry grain, 280 : 1
rosy lips and c., 245 : 18
stain my man's c., 233 : 22
tears are on her c., 32 : 21
wind on our c., 557 : 21
Cheer, all his c. as in his herte, 146 : 27
at Christmas make good c., 163 : 2
be of good c., 39 : 27, 45 : 29
but not inebriate, 330 : 22, 377 : 3
is best physician, 72 : 3
our weary hearts, 618 : 1
piped with merry c., 403 : 2
poor man's heart, 430 : 22
scarce forbear to c., 488 : 17
sing song of c. again, 824 : 13
small c. and great welcome, 188 : 5
three cheers one c. more, 627 : 11
unite with a c., 384 : 8
up comrades they come, 578 : 12
Cheered, Admiral c. them holding out hope, 150 : 14
ship was c., 434 : 7
up with ends of verse, 291 : 14
Cheerer of spirits, 270 : 34
Cheerful, be c. while you are alive, 3 : 11
giver, 49 : 18
godliness, 425 : 23
man of c. yesterdays, 428 : 18
merry heart maketh a c. countenance, 24 : 6
Cheerful (*continued*)
to bells' c. sound, 403 : 4
warm precincts of c. day, 362 : 14
ways of men cut off, 285 : 5
when God sends c. hour, 282 : 10
Cheerfully, bear all c., 536 : 6
do evil so c., 300 : 14
he seems to grin, 611 : 5
part with life c., 124 : 27
support government, 631 : 11
Cheerfulness always breaking in, 357 : 12
keeps daylight in mind, 326 : 21
Cheering, public men nor c. crowds, 714 : 1
young lad, 735 : 4
Cheerless over hills of gray, 513 : 20
Cheerly rouse the slumbering morn, 277 : 23
she loves me dearly, 476 : 4
Cheers, adorns and c. our way, 368 : 12
responding to the c., 704 : 15
silence no worse than c., 691 : 3
tar's labor, 462 : 16
three c. one cheer more, 627 : 11
Cheese, apple pie and c., 666 : 13
dessert without c., 401 : 7
dreamed of toasted c., 668 : 8
moon made of green c., 161 : 8
Cheeses, ate c. out of vats, 541 : 1
Cheevy, Miniver C., 728 : 19
Chef d'oeuvre, les rendements de contes ne font jamais c., 911 : *n* 2
Chemical barrage against life, 870 : 1
personalities like c. contact, 754 : 4
Chemist fiddler and buffoon, 304 : 10
Chemistry, microscopy c. mathematics, 819 : 14
Cherchez la femme, 491 : *n* 4
Cherish, achieve and c. peace, 524 : 7
at charitable breast, 794 : 9
means of knowledge, 380 : 10
those hearts that hate thee, 249 : 8
to love and to c., 56 : 9
to love c. and obey, 56 : 17
Cherished, country c. in hearts, 535 : 22
memory of loved and lost, 524 : 4
Cherishes, art most c., 542 : 5
love of comfort, 69 : 5
Cherishin', prof'tible c. mem'ry, 616 : 22
Cherishing enemy in disguise, 379 : 16
Cherith, dwelt by the brook C., 13 : 40
Cherries fairly do enclose, 250 : 6
grow which none may buy, 250 : 5
tremble in air, 899 : 16
Cherry, grew like a double c., 197 : 2
hung with snow, 690 : 17
I did cut c. tree, 378 : *n* 9
isle, 266 : 3
now hung with bloom, 690 : 16
ripe I cry, 266 : 3
sap make c. red, 799 : 9
violence American as c. pie, 915 : 16
Cherry-ripe themselves do cry, 250 : 5
Cherub, he rode upon a c., 17 : 26
Cherubims east of the garden, 7 : 13
Cherubin, heaven's c. horsed, 236 : 24
young and rose-lipped c., 232 : 4
Cherubin's, fire-red c. face, 146 : 12
Cherubins, young-eyed c., 201 : 1
Ches, to her son she c., 917 : 3
Cheshire Cat vanished slowly, 611 : 17
Chess board is the world, 595 : 12

Chess (*continued*)
pieces phenomena of universe, 595 : 12
Chest, as if c. a mortar, 570 : 13
contrived double debt, 370 : 13
Dead Man's C., 668 : 4
if it is well with your c., 109 : 6
of drawers by day, 370 : 13
voice of iron c. of brass, 105 : 20
Chester, charge C. charge, 431 : 3
Chestnut, O c. tree, 715 : 17
roast c. happiness, 782 : 23
spreading c. tree, 510 : 7
Chestnuts, pull c. out of fire, 297 : 11
sailor's wife had c., 236 : 1
Chevalier, the young c., 417 : 6
Chew cud and are silent, 373 : 28
Chewed, few books to be c., 181 : 12
Cheweth, whatsoever c. the cud, 10 : 16
Chewing food of fancy, 212 : 28
little bits of string, 730 : 7
Cheyenne, I'm a-leavin' C., 927 : 11
Chic, radical c., 911 : 6
Chicago at northwest gates, 728 : 12
responsible for Tribune, 801 : 11
Chicken, champagne and c. at last, 341 : 1
in pot every Sunday, 174 : 25
prayer of hawk not get c., 926 : 5
she's no c., 323 : 8
some c. some neck, 745 : 12
Chickens, all my pretty c., 239 : 21
as hen gathereth c., 40 : 21
beside white c., 785 : 11
count c. before hatched, 65 : 19
literature or c., 846 : 11
quit quarreling over food, 760 : 10
Chide, fall out and c. and fight, 328 : 4
God for countenance, 212 : 20
me for loving armchair, 562 : 11
trumpets 'gan to c., 476 : 9
Chides, at fifty c. delay, 330 : 10
Chiding, better a little c., 225 : 29
Chief, a c. a rod, 337 : 13
defect of Henry King, 730 : 7
good and market, 223 : 17
hail to the C., 431 : 9
his c. beside, 540 : 21
Justice was rich quiet, 488 : 9
nourisher in life's feast, 237 : 21
of the Army, 421 : 7
sinners of whom I am c., 50 : 24
society's c. joys, 376 : 3
Chiefest treasure, 729 : 14
Chief's, vain the c. pride, 339 : 32
Chiefs, our c. are killed, 642 : 7
Chieftain Iffucan of Azcan, 767 : 5
Chield's amang you takin' notes, 410 : 20
Child, a simple c., 423 : 3
again just for tonight, 610 : 10
always say what's true, 668 : 10
and the child's father, 722 : 22
any c. at any stage, 887 : 16
anything we change in c., 754 : 8
around c. bend all three, 443 : 2
as yet a c., 338 : 10
beautiful a fairy's c., 478 : 11
behold the c., 337 : 7
better is a poor and wise c., 26 : 25
burnt c. fire dreadeth, 160 : 20
christom c., 207 : 13
cry of c. by roadway, 712 : 12
dear C. of Nature, 427 : 18
Child (*continued*)
do not throw book, 729 : 14
draws inscrutable house, 878 : 10
duty's faithful c., 484 : 9
Eros Zeus's c., 76 : 22
every c. may joy to hear, 403 : 3
family stamped character on c., 754 : 11
fast fold thy c., 656 : 14
father of the man, 425 : 7
foster c. of silence, 477 : 4
get with c. mandrake root, 252 : 1
give a little love to c., 573 : 4
great with c. longing for prunes, 228 : 2
hard heart of c., 794 : 1
has fairy godmother, 694 : 1
hasn't got anything on little c. said, 505 : 6
heard one calling C., 268 : 23
Heaven-born c., 277 : 7
her innocence a c., 305 : 8
here a little c. I stand, 267 : 1
I spake as a c., 48 : 25
I was a c., 527 : 8
idiotic c., 695 : 14
if you strike a c., 680 : 25
in simplicity a c., 336 : 9
in the name of this C., 56 : 4
infirm, 495 : 1
is father of the man, 425 : 7
is known by his doings, 24 : 29
Jesus Christ her little C., 561 : 10
keeps secret well, 491 : 24
know what it is to be c., 694 : 1
lie down like tired c., 466 : 15
life like froward c., 302 : 19
like three years' c., 434 : 6
little c. shall lead them, 29 : 19
look upon a little c., 350 : 13
lost in unreality, 894 : 5
love chain to bind c. to parents, 524 : 12
Magus Zoroaster my dead c., 466 : 16
make c. able man, 164 : 13
meet nurse for poetic c., 430 : 11
Monday's c. fair, 932 : 10
more hideous in a c., 233 : 10
my c. wife, 549 : 7
ne'er spend fury on c., 186 : 25
of calamity, 623 : 6
of my right hand, 256 : 3
of our grandmother Eve, 190 : 16
of pure unclouded brow, 612 : 15
of scorn, 728 : 19
old man twice a c., 220 : 32
on a cloud I saw a c., 403 : 2
on parent knees newborn c., 394 : 3
painted c. of dirt, 338 : 19
parents and c. at window, 906 : 2
permit c. to join, 604 : 10
role to be born, 704 : 14
room of absent c., 201 : 26
Rowland to dark tower, 234 : 13
said What is grass, 574 : 15
saving little c., 636 : 5
seemed a small ungainly c., 63 : 7
seen a curious c., 428 : 15
Shakespeare Fancy's c., 278 : 6
shall play on hole of the asp, 29 : 19
she was a c., 527 : *n* 2
slayeth c. in womb, 793 : 2
spare rod and spoil c., 91 : *n* 3, 291 : 19
Child (*continued*)
teach c. to doubt, 406 : 15
thankless c., 233 : 11
there is a man c. conceived, 15 : 7
this c. to myself take, 424 : 13
thought as a c., 48 : 25
to mother sheep to fold, 692 : 2
train up a c. in the way, 24 : 35
tyrant is c. of pride, 74 : 3
understood as a c., 48 : 25
unto us a c. is born, 29 : 16
virgin shall be with c., 36 : 19
warble c., 190 : 23
what will c. learn sooner, 339 : 26
when I was a c., 48 : 25
white as angel English c., 403 : 6
wise father knows own c., 199 : 3
would have made ugly c., 611 : 16
wretched c. expires, 730 : 8
young c. with Mary, 36 : 21
Childbirth, death taxes c., 848 : 10
Childhood, barb in arrow of c., 677 : 3
eye of c., 237 : 23
eye of c. fears painted devil, 237 : 23
in my days of c., 441 : 5
life a circle from c. to c., 701 : 9
little world of c., 754 : 11
make glad heart of c., 638 : 6
manhood and decrepit age, 267 : 19
model of greater world, 754 : 11
odds on unhappy c., 910 : 17
one moment in c., 859 : 6
scenes of my c., 455 : 6
shows the man, 288 : 12
talk about my hard c., 916 : 2
wove web in c., 555 : 16
Childhood's hour, 447 : 14, 525 : 5
Childish but divinely beautiful, 412 : 15
inconstant c. proud, 475 : 3
practice c. ways, 59 : 17
put away c. things, 860 : 3
religion but a c. toy, 183 : 11
sweet c. days, 425 : 8
things, 48 : 25
treble, 211 : 15
Childishly, sucked on pleasures c., 251 : 14
Childishness, second c., 211 : 15
Childless and crownless, 458 : 16
Children, age finds us true c. still, 396 : 8
an' all us other c., 665 : 11
and fools cannot lie, 160 : 13
and fools want everything, 310 : 18
as c. fear in darkness, 100 : 22
as he would wish c. treated, 891 : 12
become as little c., 40 : 1
begin by loving parents, 675 : 3
belonged to man I didn't know, 623 : 23
blood on us and on our c., 41 : 23
bones on which c. sharpen teeth, 898 : 14
books c. of brain, 321 : 11
breed of horses dogs c., 314 : 14
bring forth c. in sorrow, 7 : 11
bringing up c., 858 : 15
can c. of bridechamber mourn, 38 : 29
can't form c. on own concepts, 395 : 16
come dear c. let us away, 584 : 11
dream that my four c., 909 : 10
drinkest tears of c., 454 : 18
even c. followed, 370 : 9

Children (*continued*)
extensions of our egos, 796:5
familiarity breeds c., 626:14
fear death as c. fear dark, 180:2
forever explaining to grown-ups, 849:2
freezing to death, 642:7
get on board little c., 936:5
give c. right to study painting, 381:14
God have mercy on c., 777:10
Great Spirit make them all for his c., 419:13
had so many c., 931:10
hates c. and dogs can't be all bad, 770:18
her c. arise up, 26:9
herd c. home to mothers, 63:11
here my c. born, 521:6
in behavioristic freedom, 762:4
in days of our c., 687:14
in peace c. inter parents, 78:5
in the foliage, 807:8
in the wood, 917:6
indifferent c. of earth, 220:23
iniquity of the fathers upon the c., 10:5
invent a game, 789:10
king over c. of pride, 17:9
know and suffer, 840:10
laboring c. look out, 757:5
let c. walk with nature, 637:17
listen my c., 512:6
living arrows, 782:15
look after own upbringing, 909:4
love of c. whether black or not, 837:20
most men are like c., 782:10
my c. glean, 854:2
nature fits c., 567:19
Nature's c. given into slavery, 152:15
need one now, 883:7
Negro school c., 893:15
nigger saying he would steal his c., 623:23
no longer any c., 298:16
nor do c. prattle about his knees, 57:29
not leave unless I do, 848:2
of an idle brain, 191:24
of kingdom cast out, 38:22
of larger growth, 342:3
of light, 43:31, 587:3
of light and day, 50:19
of men full of wiles, 82:8
of the day, 50:19
of the devil, 535:13
of this world wiser, 43:31
old men are c., 82:1
parents bore their c., 681:6
provoke not c. to anger, 50:13
Rachel weeping for her c., 36:23
receive arms race from us, 897:10
red c. acknowledge no boundaries, 419:9
return ye c. of men, 20:11
Revolution eats own c., 552:8
second wife hateful to c., 76:1
shall wander in the wilderness, 10:25
sins of fathers upon c., 77:23
so act toward c. so toward wife, 121:20
so are c. of the youth, 22:10
songs of children's c., 802:1

Children (*continued*)
suffer armed men, 840:10
suffer little c., 42:11
swarmed like settlers, 868:19
sweeter than apples to c., 673:15
tale which holdeth c. from play, 176:11
tan-faced c., 575:14
teach them diligently unto thy c., 11:9
terrible c., 502:24
their country their c., 102:28
they shall be called c. of God, 37:4
walk on frozen toes, 729:2
war c. is just a shot away, 916:10
we are c. of our landscape, 880:6
wealth and c. adornment of life, 131:11
weeping O brothers, 507:2
were all thy c. kind, 207:11
what give my c., 889:7
what shall world do with c., 905:17
when voices of c., 403:15
where did c. vanish, 864:16
who needed his protection, 903:2
wife and c. impediments, 180:9
wife and c. stand afraid, 274:12
will burn, 930:3
win war for c., 745:11
wisdom exalteth her c., 35:1
wisdom justified of c., 39:7
women and c. first, 921:21
words c. of many men, 850:15
your c. are we, 928:13
Children's, all our c. fate, 710:23
books of my day, 701:6
gratitude woman's love, 716:12
Hour, 512:3
lips shall echo, 457:21
my God the C. Crusade, 901:8
songs of c. children, 802:1
teeth set on edge, 32:17
Child's amang you takin' notes, 410:20
credulity c. strength, 441:22
no c. pley to take wyf, 147:22
not lose his c. heart, 89:16
Child's-heart, not lose his c., 89:16
Chill and drear, 430:13
bitter c. it was, 476:8
in wintry age feel no c., 377:20
mantle of wind and c. and rain, 148:22
penury, 362:7
sun was warm wind c., 748:17
thy dreaming nights, 478:8
wind is c., 430:21
young whom age doth c., 290:6
Chilling, on love request for money c., 583:15
Chillingly, no steel pierce so c., 828:5
Chills, of c. and fever died, 810:20
winter lingering c. May, 368:18
Chilly December day, 835:1
I feel c. and old, 543:12
Chime, faintly as tolls evening c., 446:5
higher than the sphery c., 280:5
hours to which heaven c., 298:21
set c. of words tinkling, 711:*n* 1
to guide their c., 297:10
Chimera, what a c. is man, 300:11
Chimeras, how many vain c. have you created, 152:14
nothing great without c., 593:13

Chimerical, reduction to atoms c. ideal, 636:16
Chimes at midnight, 206:24
little jingle little c., 331:4
Chimleypiece, bottle on c., 547:35
Chimney, as c. sweepers come to dust, 243:27
hung by c. with care, 446:3
little c. hot in moment, 188:*n* 4
made c. in my father's house, 185:27
makes c. of your nose, 401:3
old men from c. corner, 176:11
Chimneypiece, buffalo upon c., 614:7
Chimney's, stretched out c. length, 278:3
Chimneys, your c. I sweep, 403:9
Chin, close-buttoned to the c., 377:17
dogs shame the gray c., 59:6
new-reaped, 203:7
China, break c. plates of others, 694:5
crost the bay, 708:9
great revolutions of C., 826:8
mankind from C. to Peru, 351:16
not seeking to dominate world, 825:5
riddle of C. trade, 799:19
suffering poverty, 719:10
though c. fall, 335:24
thought of C. and Greece, 858:20
twine wine and C. teas, 558:10
Chinese, bombing of C. cities, 788:15
contradiction between imperialism and C., 826:8
contradictions in C. society, 826:8
great and vital people, 882:22
love jade, 796:1
nightingale, 765:9
people have solidarity, 719:9
sediment of long C. past, 796:1
Chink, importunate c., 373:28
in floor of Wicklow house, 735:2
Chinks of her sickness-broken body, 276:14
that Time has made, 276:12
Chip of old block, 373:11
Chips down nation acts helpless, 882:23
lest c. fall in eye, 917:2
let c. fall where may, 602:15
Chirurgery, what c. relieve conscience, 260:5
Chisel, whether c. pen or brush, 714:7
Chiseled, down c. names raindrop, 642:4
Chivalrous, proud and c. spirit, 88:23
quixotic sense of c., 527:4
Chivalry, age of c. gone, 373:22
charge with all thy c., 443:15
her beauty and her c., 457:14
herein c. courtesy humanity, 149:5
smiled c. away, 461:26
Chloe, what can C. want, 335:20
Chocolate, no c. to eat, 900:5
Choice and master spirits, 216:9
brave man's c. is danger, 77:4
can I have no other c., 894:3
careful in c. of enemies, 674:26
courage of making c., 736:10
difficulty in life is c., 671:6
government of our own c., 381:5
grain into this wilderness, 307:11
hidden handful of Inert, 570:12
Hobson's c., 917:25
in the worth and c., 255:11

Choice (*continued*)
life's business c., 545 : 12
of horse and wife, 584 : 6
of point of view, 784 : 12
pays money takes c., 660 : 12
reckless c., 747 : 18
small c. in rotten apples, 188 : 26
word measured phrase, 425 : 11
Choir, chorister whose c preceded c., 769 : 10
full-voiced c. below, 278 : 26
invisible, 564 : 22
of saints, 254 : 17
sanctuary and c., 808 : 12
singing in the c., 919 : 21
St. Stephen's c., 892 : 4
wailful c., 477 : 19
Choirs, bare ruined c., 244 : 27
Choix, le c. fait les amis, 385 : *n* 6
Choke fountain of industry, 451 : 5
them amid flowers, 101 : 7
Choked with ambition of meaner sort, 185 : 3
Cholera typhus ignorance, 773 : 8
Choleric, captain's c. word, 228 : 11
who subdued passion, 386 : 11
Chondria, Russia's c. for short, 486 : 6
Choose, any language you c., 628 : 26
author as you c. friend, 309 : 8
between Africa and English tongue, 911 : 1
do not c. to run, 736 : 18
don't c. to run, 766 : 3
equality, 589 : 2
firm cloud, 335 : 17
fool multitude c. by show, 199 : 12
free to c. government, 824 : 12
ground and take thy rest, 462 : 19
if you dare, 275 : 27
intellect forced to c., 716 : 7
it is time to c., 768 : 1
let's c. executors, 195 : 1
likely man in preference to rich, 70 : 16
multitude that c. by show, 199 : 12
not alone proper mate, 377 : 24
not c. not to be, 656 : 15
on'y wut Guv'ment c., 568 : 12
path leading where I c., 575 : 9
slavery or death, 325 : 17
the irregular, 659 : 16
therefore c. life, 11 : 22
to live without friends, 87 : 20
Venus here c. dwelling, 306 : 6
we c. our friends, 385 : 12
we do not c. survival, 862 : 11
what becomes Castilian, 481 : 2
Choosers, beggars should be no c., 160 : 2
Chooses, consciousness c. object, 648 : 15
intimacy that c. right, 714 : 15
no man c. evil, 414 : 5
survival c. us, 862 : 11
Choosest not better part, 703 : 3
Choosing, long c. and beginning late, 287 : 12
presidential nominee, 788 : 11
Chop off her head, 611 : 14
off your head, 930 : 8
Chopper to chop off your head, 930 : 8
Chord in melancholy, 485 : 7
in unison is touched, 377 : 13
mirth has c. in melancholy, 258 : *n* 1
Chord (*continued*)
struck c. of music, 596 : 14
Chords of memory, 521 : 14
that vibrate pleasure, 410 : 1
Chorister, bobolink for c., 605 : 4
whose c preceded choir, 769 : 10
Chortled in his joy, 612 : 18
Chorus ending from Euripides, 543 : 5
from Atlanta to sea, 614 : 14
of Union, 521 : 14
what a c., 442 : 22
Choruses above guinea's squawk, 831 : 14
Chose, David c. him five smooth stones, 13 : 2
Chosen, few are c., 40 : 14
I have c. you, 45 : 26
Lord hath c. thee, 11 : 11
old ocean c. by thee, 575 : 22
people of God, 388 : 2
vessel, 46 : 7
Choses que je conte, 818 : *n* 1
Choughs that wing air, 234 : 28
Choux, que la mort me trouve plantant mes c., 164 : *n* 7
Christ ain't going to be too hard, 636 : 4
all at once what C. is, 656 : 21
blood when C. slain, 715 : 12
born across the sea, 566 : 5
born in Bethlehem, 350 : 15
bowels of C., 272 : 18, 737 : 5
but this earth goes over, 822 : 7
came from God and woman, 483 : 1
came to save sinners, 50 : 24
catch C. with worm, 892 : 5
cautious statistical C., 659 : 8
deep did rot O C., 434 : 16
Don Quixote and I, 452 : 4
everyone in world is C., 757 : 3
half a drop ah my C., 184 : 8
Himself buddy, 896 : 10
his captain C., 195 : 8
I believe in Jesus C., 55 : 2
in C. all made alive, 48 : 29
is all and in all, 50 : 12
is C. thy advocate, 315 : 2
it is the Inchcape Rock, 440 : 1
Jesus C. her little Child, 561 : 10
Jesus C. the righteous, 52 : 21
Jesus C. the same yesterday, 51 : 24
joint heirs with C., 47 : 8
Judas or Peter who loved C., 859 : 10
keep your hearts through C. Jesus, 50 : 6
kingdom and patience of Jesus C., 52 : 27
kingdoms of his C., 53 : 18
Lord C. enter in, 676 : 14
lost turning forgiveness to sword, 893 : 19
not love in human way, 856 : 19
our Lord, 56 : 1
our Passover sacrificed, 48 : 10
our Savior, 919 : 20
receive him, 533 : 6
redemption by Jesus C., 55 : 7
risen from dead, 48 : 29
rule given by C., 602 : 6
save us all, 510 : 6
Savior which is C., 42 : 28
see the C. stand, 543 : 23
show me dear C. Thy spouse, 254 : 16
shut up in asylum, 690 : 11
Christ (*continued*)
so Judas did to C., 195 : 10
soldiers of C. arise, 350 : 14
stopped at Eboli, 855 : 7
testimony of Jesus C., 52 : 27
that it were possible, 533 : 26
that my love in my arms, 917 : 10
the Lord risen today, 350 : 11
the Son in Father's stead, 679 : 4
thief said last word to C., 545 : 3
this world all aleak, 829 : 14
thou art the C., 39 : 35
to live is C., 50 : 1
took the kindness, 545 : 3
vision of C. thou see, 407 : 8
walks on black water, 892 : 4
what are patterns for, 751 : 6
Christendom, christianize C., 570 : 2
eager to get stake, 625 : 25
in C. where Christian, 497 : 8
live in any place in C., 163 : 16
wisest fool in C., 175 : 3
Christened on Tuesday, 932 : 11
Christes loore and his apostles, 146 : 10
Christian, any husband rather than C., 200 : 16
bear other's misfortunes like C., 340 : 9
charity, 485 : 22
darkness fell upon C., 302 : 10
enterprise for glory of C. religion, 151 : 1
feels repentance on Sunday, 773 : 9
fled with a C., 199 : 11
forgive them as C., 440 : 22
ground, 340 : 27
hate him for a C., 198 : 19
honorable style of C., 273 : 15
I am a C. faithful man, 187 : 8
ideal difficult, 742 : 2
if victory I shall become C., 129 : 19
in what peace a C. can die, 327 : 5
inconsistent with C. religion, 364 : 7
meaning of C. life, 817 : 16
not so good C. as thinks, 669 : 10
O my C. ducats, 199 : 11
only C. come to these parts, 151 : 1
pagan spoiled, 706 : 14
persuadest me to be C., 46 : 36
practice C. forbearance, 383 : 6
principle of suffering, 504 : 9
richest in C. world, 412 : 18
Science, 583 : 5
Scientists some science, 721 : 11
scratch C. find pagan, 706 : 14
soldiers, 616 : 6
thing, 863 : 14
what one C. does, 909 : 3
where C. in Christendom, 497 : 8
with four aces, 626 : 20
without hypocrisy, 591 : 11
witness of soul naturally C., 126 : 1
wonders of C. religion, 319 : 22
word of gentleman and C., 169 : 26
you are Ciceronian not C., 127 : 16
you were a C. slave, 663 : 13
Christianity a son religion, 679 : 4
and devotion to Bible, 905 : 5
blemish of mankind, 658 : 17
Catholicism minus C., 595 : 13
cult called C., 641 : 18
doctors more C., 721 : 11
enormous perversion, 658 : 17
genius of C., 853 : 8

Christianity (*continued*)
is an idea, 481 : 15
Muscular C., 922 : 3
narcotics alcohol and C., 658 : 9
one great curse, 658 : 17
since introduction of C., 387 : 15
takes great deal of C., 707 : 7
Christianize Christendom, 570 : 2
Christians, all C. agree, 354 : 9
blood of C. is seed, 126 : 3
good C. good citizens, 450 : 3
have burnt each other, 460 : 14
have comfortable creed, 460 : 22
have little difference, 354 : 24
lord believing C. from sky, 151 : 2
see how C. love one another, 126 : 2
want something for nothing, 681 : 17
what these C. are, 198 : 27
Christmas, at C. no more desire rose, 190 : 13
at C. play, 163 : 2
born on C. Day, 919 : 20
broached mightiest ale, 430 : 22
brought sports again, 430 : 22
comes but once a year, 163 : 2
Day in workhouse, 661 : 14
dreaming of white C., 802 : 11
gambol, 430 : 22
Ghost of C. Past, 548 : 7
Ghost of C. Present, 548 : 9
Ghost of C. Yet to Come, 548 : 12
happy C. to all, 446 : 4
home C., 724 : 4
is coming, 921 : 3
it was C. Day, 182 : 3
jest 'fore C., 666 : 20
keep C. all the year, 548 : 13
keep our C. merry still, 430 : 21
night before C., 446 : 3
one C. much like another, 887 : 5
over and business is business, 773 : 10
pie, 929 : 20
told merriest tale, 430 : 22
won't be Christmas, 610 : 6
Christom child, 207 : 13
Christ's blood streams, 184 : 8
in C. coach, 314 : 21
lady of C. College, 301 : 5
Lord C. heart, 495 : 15
lore and his apostles twelve, 146 : 10
progress and His prayer time, 298 : 21
stamp, 268 : 9
Chromis did not save himself, 57 : 20
Chronic anxiety about weather, 630 : 22
do not weep it's c., 547 : 31
hotel guests, 725 : 18
melancholy of civilized, 641 : 1
time when illness c., 894 : 7
Chronicle of wasted time, 245 : 12
pride his own c., 226 : 9
small beer, 230 : 12
wars of kites, 289 : 12
Chronicles, brief c. of the time, 221 : 4
transcribe my c., 486 : 10
Chrysanthemum, white c. remains immaculate, 314 : 5
Chuang-tzu, Begone cried C., 90 : 11
Chub, Chavender or C., 271 : 5
Chuck 'im out the brute, 708 : 4
Chuckle, he with c. replied, 774 : 3
little kind of low c., 623 : 22
Chuds, the C. Slavs and Krivchians, 136 : 2
Church and state demand for country, 779 : 12
and state separate, 590 : 2
authority of C. moved me, 129 : 8
bells knolled to c., 211 : 12
blood of martyrs seed of C., 126 : *n* 2
built God a c., 376 : 9
come to c. good people, 691 : 4
erased no c., 777 : 10
get me to c. on time, 895 : 1
holy Catholic C., 55 : 2
I like a c., 493 : 16
I like silent c., 497 : 5
keep Sabbath going to c., 605 : 4
Mother C., 126 : 5
nearer to c. further from God, 159 : 19
no other c. understood, 488 : 8
nobody at c. except hog, 623 : 25
not forgotten inside of c., 204 : 24
not God for father if not C. for mother, 126 : 16
persecuted c. of God, 48 : 28
plain as way to parish c., 211 : 11
prayers of c. to preserve travel, 323 : 17
saw a wedding in the c., 310 : 1
see a c. by daylight, 209 : 7
sleep and feed at once, 804 : 20
some to c. repair, 333 : 7
sons and daughters of C., 881 : 5
stands c. clock at ten to three, 796 : 12
take care of the c., 50 : 25
to be of no c. dangerous, 352 : 24
to c. and with my mourning very handsome, 310 : 10
two lanterns in North C., 382 : 12
upon this rock build my c., 39 : 36
wall between c. and state, 794 : 16
where God built c., 156 : 5
wide as a c. door, 193 : 5
without bishop, 484 : 20
world or c. or state, 568 : 23
Churches, chapels had been c., 198 : 9
in flat countries, 428 : *n* 6
scab of c., 251 : 5
seven c. in Asia, 52 : 28
Churchman, I that cowled c. be, 493 : 16
Churchyard abounds with images, 352 : 27
Drumcliff c., 718 : 1
thing, 476 : 14
where Michael Furey buried, 777 : 16
Churchyards yawn, 222 : 23
Churlish, reply c., 213 : 4
Churn, silver c., 628 : 9
Cibus, ali c. aliis venenum, 101 : *n* 6
Cicada, wild c. cried, 816 : 14
Cicadas, cries of c., 314 : 1
like c. so leaders of Trojans, 57 : 23
pour out their piping voices, 57 : 23
Cicala to cicala is dear, 92 : 14
Cicero, book of a certain C., 129 : 2
Ciceronian, you are C. not Christian, 127 : 16
Ciel, j'allais sous le c. Muse, 673 : *n* 4
Cigar, good c. is a smoke, 707 : 6
good five-cent c., 673 : 6
sometimes c. is just c., 679 : 8
Cilicia, Tarsus in C., 46 : 24
Cinara, reign of the good C., 108 : 10
Cincinnatus of the West, 459 : 11
Cinderella fulfilling herself, 768 : 18
Cinders ashes dust, 476 : 5
sat among the c., 932 : 4
Cinders (*continued*)
somebody's always heaving c., 765 : 4
Cinnamon, color of c., 879 : 18
nutmegs ginger c. cloves, 268 : 1
tree, 857 : 14
Cinzano, another dry C. in sun, 888 : 10
Cipher, write and c. too, 370 : 10
Circle, all within this c. move, 276 : 6
close c. of felicities, 389 : 1
drew c. shut me out, 671 : 4
ever-nearing c. weaves shade, 587 : 10
everything Indian does is in a c., 701 : 8
glory like a c. in water, 184 : 18
if you have formed a c., 407 : 2
in this c. O ye warriors, 701 : *n* 4
in which relations appear to stop, 653 : 10
life self-evolving c., 501 : *n* 7
live too much in c., 501 : 21
man center of c., 615 : 2
of potential being, 648 : 3
of the golden year, 529 : 5
of wedding ring, 325 : 2
perfect c. and vicious c., 881 : 2
restricted c. of potential, 648 : 3
seasons form great c., 701 : 9
shock of recognition whole c. round, 569 : 18
small c. as we will, 395 : 23
that took him in, 671 : 4
vicious c., 617 : 1
weave c. round him, 433 : 27
wheel is come full c., 235 : 15
Circled, darkly c., 513 : 20
monthly changes in c. orb, 192 : 11
Circles of blind ecstasy, 844 : 1
power of w. works in c., 701 : 8
produce perfect c., 89 : 7
triangles c. and other geometrical figures, 182 : 20
Circling, busy whisper c. round, 370 : 10
morn waked by c. hours, 286 : 25
Circuit, his c. unto the ends of it, 17 : 28
Circumcised, took by throat the c. dog, 232 : 21
Circumcision, neither c. nor uncircumcision, 50 : 12
Circumference, disseminating their c., 606 : 10
fatal c., 615 : 2
in universe neither center nor c., 171 : 15
Circumlocution Office, 549 : 19
Circumnavigator of soul, 711 : 18
Circumscribed, not c. in one self place, 184 : 1
Circumspection deliberation fortitude, 365 : 3
Circumspections, truth has c. and limits, 166 : 8
Circumspectly, goes most c., 569 : 21
Circumstance and proper timing, 83 : 1
artistries in c., 641 : 17
envisage c. calm, 478 : 5
fell clutch of c., 663 : 10
of glorious war, 231 : 11
some c. to please us, 294 : *n* 4
unsifted in perilous c., 219 : 4
Circumstances, all classes times c., 553 : 20
alter cases, 481 : 4
concatenation of c., 450 : 19

Circumstances (*continued*)
creatures of men, 501 : 7
fortuitous c., 432 : 3
harmony of temperament and c., 583 : 12
man is his own c., 843 : 6
man not creature of c., 501 : 7
people always blaming c., 680 : 5
rule men, 78 : 17
same c. same phenomena, 324 : 1
war train of c., 384 : 22
Circumstantial, lie c., 213 : 4
some c. evidence strong, 557 : 14
things essential or things c., 302 : 4
Circumvent God, 224 : 9
Circuses, bread and c., 122 : 15
Cistern contains. 104 : 4
wheel broken at the c., 27 : 25
Cisterns, empty c. exhausted wells, 805 : 12
we have c. and worship them, 849 : 12
Citadel, did not go to c. of Troy, 62 : 18
sacked the holy c. of Troy, 59 : 13
towered c. pendant rock, 241 : 17
Citadels, vain c. not walled, 827 : 7
Citations, avoid c. from poets, 80 : 2
Cite, devil can c. Scripture, 198 : 22
Cité, le buste survit à la c., 538 : *n* 2
Cities, anarchy why c. tumble, 74 : 20
buries c. in common grave, 383 : 14
embers of c., 912 : 7
Eros builder of c., 868 : 15
grass in a hundred c., 750 : 18
great lost c., 884 : 20
hum of c. torture, 457 : 28
London flower of c. all, 153 : 4
man's skill built c., 97 : 14
marble well-governed c., 868 : 21
most pecksniffian of c., 772 : 4
never have rest from evils, 84 : 15
oblivion swallowed c. up, 226 : 15
of men and manners, 529 : 8
of the plain, 8 : 7
our c. badly built, 813 : 15
place philosophy in c., 98 : 25
say unto the c. of Judah, 30 : 34
towered c. please us then, 278 : 4
warred for Homer dead, 257 : 20
Citizen consider traveling expenses, 826 : 17
first requisite of good c., 687 : 7
free nation great, 491 : 25
good c. not silent, 598 : 15
humblest c. of land, 694 : 15
I am a Roman c., 98 : 4
in wild weed she is c., 889 : 19
keep c. from error, 821 : 9
nation guarantees maintenance of c., 665 : 17
obliged to be c., 584 : 2
of no mean city, 46 : 24
of the world, 79 : 7, 180 : 13
private c. without wrong, 591 : 11
Citizenry, government agent of c., 851 : 6
Citizens clamoring for what is wrong, 107 : 28
demean selves as good c., 379 : 8
equal before law, 615 : 1
faction is number of c., 398 : 1
fat and greasy c., 210 : 27
force c. to confess, 821 : 6
frenzy of his fellow c., 107 : 28
good Christians good c., 450 : 3
Citizens (*continued*)
no ruling class of c., 615 : 1
not women or Negroes but c., 554 : 8
of Berlin, 891 : 14
of death's land, 795 : 13
of middle class, 88 : 7
of the world, 781 : 5
people born in U.S. are c., 392 : 4
rights of other c., 398 : 1
rulers and ruled, 851 : 16
second class c., 824 : 11
to arms c., 415 : *n* 1
welfare of good c., 687 : 15
Citizenship anxious about what do for nation, 890 : *n* 3
science education for c., 684 : 16
Citoyens, aux armes c., 415 : 1
City and proud seat of Lucifer, 287 : 26
Athens divine c., 72 : 9
Babylon that great c., 53 : 23
bomb fell on no c., 777 : 10
bust survives c., 538 : 7
defend village town c., 744 : 5
education to Greece, 81 : 4
entire c. has suffered, 61 : 15
except the Lord keep the c., 22 : 8
failing that the rest of the c., 84 : 11
famous Hanover c., 540 : 32
for sale, 103 : 3
God made first c., 295 : 14
great c. greatest men, 575 : 12
harder to be won than a strong c., 24 : 21
he that taketh a c., 24 : 13
hell c. like London, 468 : 2
honor once at home in c., 264 : 8
how doth the c. sit solitary, 32 : 20
in country you praise c., 106 : 22
in the c. of David, 42 : 28
is teacher of the man, 67 : 17
land raises taxes, 603 : 14
like rain falling on c., 659 : 13
long in populous c. pent, 287 : 17
looking over harbor and c., 761 : 5
make glad the c. of God, 19 : 11
men make the c., 81 : 8
most glorious c. of God, 129 : 15
no continuing c., 51 : 25
no mean c., 46 : 24
obedient to his will, 84 : 16
of big shoulders, 761 : 4
of mirrors, 908 : 3
of night perchance death, 618 : 18
of the soul, 458 : 15
one long in c. pent, 475 : 4
Rome a c. of bricks, 110 : 8
room of Transcript, 846 : 1
rose-red c., 552 : 9
royal David's c., 561 : 10
set on an hill, 37 : 6
since the founding of the c., 133 : 3
speck of light below, 669 : 20
sweet c. dreaming spires, 587 : 7
taking in hand a c., 70 : 12
this c. going to follow you, 702 : 2
this great hive the c., 295 : 3
throne in a strange c., 525 : 11
to the c. and the world, 134 : 33
up and down C. Road, 922 : 1
upon a hill, 264 : 22
what is the c. but people, 242 : 19
without a c. wall, 561 : 9
Zion c. of our God, 367 : 8
City's disinherited, 694 : 3
City's (*continued*)
feel amid c. jar, 585 : 1
City-states of Greece, 852 : 2
Civet, give me an ounce of c., 235 : 1
in the room, 376 : 4
Civic genius of people, 650 : 14
some c. manhood, 531 : 15
Civil, assent with c. leer, 338 : 14
discord, 326 : 5
engaged in great c. war, 523 : 4
founder of c. society, 358 : 9
fury first grew high, 290 : 13
in respect of c. rights, 615 : 1
limitation daunts utterance, 601 : 3
over violent or over c., 304 : 11
rights of Englishman, 390 : 11
sea grew c. at her song, 196 : 14
text of c. instruction, 389 : 2
too c. by half, 398 : 13
Civil War rebirth of Union, 682 : 4
Civilian control of military, 788 : 14
Civility, a little c., 922 : 7
wild c., 266 : 7
Civilization, advance American c., 872 : 11
advances by operations we perform without thinking, 697 : 5
advances poetry declines, 487 : 9
architecture test of c., 481 : 1
at cock-crowing, 498 : 8
blessings-of-c. trust, 625 : 25
botched c., 792 : 16
bourgeoisie draws nations into c., 563 : 5
cannot survive wrongs, 821 : 7
civilize c., 570 : 2
could be restored, 763 : 14
curiosity lifeblood of c., 758 : 3
definition of c., 697 : 14
drama only develop in c., 654 : 5
elements of modern c., 472 : 5
English c. humanizing, 589 : 7
farmers founders of c., 451 : 6
first permanent c. in America, 837 : 4
France conquered for c., 592 : 6
homicidal c., 778 : 11
in middle stage, 732 : 10
in the balance, 682 : 13
its awareness of unknowable, 853 : 12
nature and c. literary field, 652 : 4
not exhausted, 517 : 22
not wiped out by atomic war, 763 : 14
obstacles of c., 504 : 7
of which orthodox socialists dream, 785 : 7
plan c. or perish, 826 : 1
poets in our c. difficult, 809 : 9
progress toward privacy, 865 : 4
provision for poor is test of c., 354 : 23
rationalist become destroyer of c., 844 : 8
requires slaves, 675 : 25
results in deserts, 760 : 7
safety enlightenment c., 582 : 12
salvage of our c., 771 : 9
speech is c., 755 : 15
theory of true c., 581 : 10
thin crust over revolution, 689 : 26
true test of c. is man, 499 : 10
usual interval of c., 643 : 12
western c. be feminized, 886 : 9
Western c. worth saving, 815 : 3
what dissatisfies in c., 589 : 10
workers mainstay of c., 666 : 22

Civilize a space, 889 : 10
civilization, 570 : 2
Civilized, efflorescence of c. life, 579 : 11
human being, 755 : 3
in Japan c. nation, 617 : 8
law as soon as c., 644 : 19
man has habits of house, 557 : 4
man not live without cooks, 609 : 13
no c. life without clothes, 698 : 8
society five qualities, 697 : 14
they and I are c., 857 : 16
valued by c. men, 677 : 14
woman last thing c., 600 : 8
Civilizer, comedy the ultimate c., 600 : 22
Civilizers, two c. of man, 502 : 14
Civilizes, sex whose presence c., 376 : 3
Civis Romanus sum, 98 : *n* 4
Clad in beauty of thousand stars, 184 : 5
in complete steel, 279 : 24
in sober livery c., 285 : 24
morn in russet mantle c., 217 : 27
naked every day he c., 369 : 16
with native honor c., 285 : 17
Claim that our city is education, 81 : 4
woman takes off c. to respect, 78 : 4
Claims, adjustment of colonial c., 682 : 14
of long descent, 528 : 10
snakeskin titles of c., 840 : 2
Clamor, not in c. of street, 512 : 18
of crowded street, 512 : 18
persons who constantly c., 451 : 5
Clamoring, citizens c. for what is wrong, 107 : 28
Clamorous lapwings, 334 : 16
owl that nightly hoots, 196 : 20
Clamors, immortal Jove's dread c., 231 : 11
venom c. of jealous woman, 188 : 13
Clan, family party tribe c., 922 : 9
leaf last of its c., 433 : 30
Clanging rookery home, 529 : 18
Clangor, trumpet's loud c., 305 : 11
Clangs, iron door c. open, 864 : 2
Clap, if you believe c. hands, 694 : 9
padlock on her mind, 320 : 17
soul c. hands and sing, 715 : 1
Clapper, his tongue the c., 209 : 21
Claps, at heaven's gates c. wings, 176 : 1
Claptrap, art independent of c., 619 : 8
Claret liquor for boys, 356 : 11
Clarification, adventure in c. of thought, 697 : 11
Clarifies, time cools time c., 755 : 18
Clarion laid away, 836 : 17
Clarity, culture moment of c., 784 : 6
give each moment c., 756 : 1
Clarum et venerabile nomen, 118 : *n* 11
Clash, bring to our ears c. of arms, 383 : 5
ignorant armies c., 587 : 16
Clasp, dare deadly terrors c., 405 : 8
thrice tried to c. her image, 60 : 8
Clasps crag with crooked hands, 532 : 28
Class, advanced guard of working c., 731 : 7
brutalizing lower c., 589 : 4
equal wealth made us one c., 666 : 2
ideas of ruling c., 563 : 9
Class (*continued*)
leisured c. replaced by New C., 871 : 14
materializing upper c., 589 : 4
middle c. best political community, 88 : 7
middle c. in America the nation, 589 : 8
middle c. safety of England, 540 : 3
no criminal c. except Congress, 625 : 3
no superior ruling c., 615 : 1
one c. overthrows another, 826 : 6
proletariat revolutionary c., 563 : 6
second c. citizens, 824 : 11
struggles, 563 : 3
taking from one c., 343 : 19
vulgarizing middle c., 589 : 4
war destroy inequalities, 719 : 10
while lower c. I am in it, 676 : 18
worst enemy in middling c., 492 : 20
Classes, all c. times circumstances, 553 : 20
antagonism between c., 563 : 8, 794 : 12
aspirin of middle c., 854 : 10
back masses against c., 517 : 23
bow lower middle c., 628 : 15
cultivated c., 580 : 14
draw powers into higher c., 390 : 2
four c. of idols, 179 : 8
let ruling c. tremble, 563 : 10
noblest work she c. O, 409 : 15
other c. decay disappear, 563 : 6
ruin of contending c., 563 : 3
tempt upper c., 684 : 17
Classic book people praise don't read, 625 : 10
face, 525 : 9
Paris our black c., 892 : 10
reread c., 859 : 4
tread on c. ground, 325 : 6
Classical quotation, 356 : 21
Classicist in literature, 809 : 13
royalist Anglo-Catholic, 809 : 13
Classics at home drowsily read, 498 : 20
charm in country inn, 498 : 20
in paraphrase, 792 : 13
Classified, objects c., 395 : 25
Clatter of hailstones on icebergs, 569 : 20
of presses, 792 : 19
they make with his coach, 310 : 11
Clause, servant with this c., 269 : 8
two kinds of relative c., 686 : 1
Clavichord, stately at the c., 543 : 10
Claw, from c. can tell a lion, 133 : 24
red in tooth and c., 532 : 13
Clawed, age c. me in his clutch, 162 : 6
Claws, neatly spreads c., 611 : 5
pair of ragged c., 803 : 14
that catch, 612 : 17
Clay, bless turf that wraps c., 364 : 9
dead and turned to c., 224 : 16
feet of c., 32 : 32
in c. none is, 933 : 4
kingdoms are c., 240 : 14
lies still, 690 : 18
man mass of thawing c., 560 : 12
of c. and wattles made, 712 : 4
porcelain c. of humankind, 306 : 2
potter thunping his wet c., 516 : 20
power over the c., 47 : 16
say to him that fashioneth it, 31 : 5
Clay (*continued*)
tenement of c., 303 : 20
to every people cup of c., 929 : 4
weak creatures of c., 82 : 9
white linen cold as c., 927 : 14
Clay-shuttered doors, 693 : 17
Clean, art only c. thing, 662 : 19
bid them keep teeth c., 242 : 15
create in me a c. heart, 19 : 16
cry that it isn't c., 316 : 2
he that hath c. hands, 18 : 8
hearth, 441 : 19
horse of courage, 900 : 3
let other people c. up mess, 835 : 7
our trunk of death, 863 : 14
passed c. over Jordan, 11 : 29
pasture spring, 747 : 3
purge me and I shall be c., 19 : 15
starved for a look, 244 : 28
the sky 806 : 21
then c. and brave, 691 : 2
things holy profane c. obscene, 264 : 16
think of c. beds, 795 : 14
tumbler and corkscrew, 547 : 16
wash blood c. from hand, 238 : 1
Cleaned windows swept floor, 627 : 14
Cleanliest shift is to kiss, 212 : 22
Cleanliness next to godliness, 346 : 11
who of late for c., 262 : 15
Cleanly, leave sack and live c., 205 : 17
not too c. manger, 292 : 17
room lavender in windows, 271 : 3
thus so c. I myself can free, 182 : 16
Cleanse stuffed bosom of perilous stuff, 239 : 32
thou me from secret faults, 18 : 2
thoughts of our hearts, 55 : 15
Cleansed, what God hath c., 46 : 9
Cleanses, poetry c., 891 : 16
Clean-shaven, buttoned-up and c., 651 : 3
Clean-winged hearth, 513 : 21
Clear, action faithful honor c., 336 : 5
and cool clear and cool, 566 : 13
and present danger, 644 : 23
as a whistle, 341 : 14
as crystal, 550 : 1
as nose in face, 158 : *n* 5
as the sun, 28 : 17
as you go, 627 : 4
brown twilight atmosphere, 503 : 15
but one rule to be c., 453 : 15
coast was c., 182 : 17
conscience is sure card, 175 : 16
conscience or none, 856 : 3
deep and absolutely c., 878 : 6
doctrines plain and c., 291 : 27
fire clean hearth, 441 : 19
for life six hundred pounds, 339 : 10
honor c., 336 : 5
honor purchased by merit, 199 : 14
in clearness of love, 899 : 16
in cool September morn, 513 : 16
in his great office, 236 : 24
literature c. and cold, 791 : 9
my sad thoughts doth c., 299 : 7
one c. call for me, 535 : 19
read my title c., 328 : 14
religion of heaven, 475 : 20
ship c. she leaps, 576 : 20
spouse so bright and c., 254 : 16
stained the water c., 403 : 3
summers wet and winters c., 103 : 27

Clear (*continued*)
the air, 806 : 21
they could get it c., 613 : 2
though deep yet c., 294 : 19
viol of her memory, 767 : 11
what is not c. is not French, 400 : 4
wild call and c. call, 760 : 15
your mind of cant, 356 : 29
Cleared, if this were only c., 613 : 2
ship cheered harbor c., 434 : 7
Clearer, age c. than noonday, 15 : 26
view ourselves with c. eyes, 267 : 5
Clearest of God's creatures, 893 : 4
way into universe through forest, 637 : 18
who have c. vision, 81 : 2
Clearly, I see so c., 396 : 11
well conceived c. said, 311 : 4
Clearness, chief merit of language c., 125 : 20
of eternal love, 899 : 16
virtue of style, 711 : 14
Clears today of past regrets, 516 : 13
Cleave, man c. to his like, 35 : 26
that sea in gentle autumnal season, 782 : 22
thou canst not c. the earth, 131 : 7
to her, 534 : 22
to sunnier side of doubt, 535 : 16
tongue c. to the roof of my mouth, 22 : 15
unto his wife, 7 : 4
wood there am I, 126 : 14, 671 : 9
Cleft, apple's c. through core, 414 : 1
Rock of Ages c. for me, 386 : 3
who c. Devil's foot, 252 : 1
Clemenceau had one illusion, 783 : 3
Clemency a species of nobility, 308 : 15
Clemens Lincoln of literature, 632 : 2
Clement's, bells of St. C., 930 : 7
Cleopatra, every man's C., 303 : 13
squeaking C., 241 : 27
Cleopatra's nose, 300 : 1
Clercs, le trahison des c., 720 : 12
Clergy, without benefit of c., 735 : *n* 1
Clergyman, avoid c. who is man of business, 127 : 22
proud c., 350 : 3
so much at home, 620 : 11
who never refuses dinner, 128 : 3
Clergymen, bankers schoolmasters c., 713 : 1
men women and c., 433 : 2
Clergymen's households unhappy, 620 : 11
Cleric before and Lay behind, 291 : 15
Clerical, features of c. cut, 806 : 14
printless toe, 796 : 11
Clerk, a bed C. Saunders said, 926 : 24
no difference 'twixt Priest and C., 266 : 9
send c. to province, 313 : 2
there was of Oxenford, 145 : 25
Clerks, greatest c. noght wisest men, 147 : 2
Clever but is it art, 708 : 12
encouraging c. pupil, 350 : 8
if all c. people good, 643 : 4
let who will be c., 566 : 12, 773 : 15
of the turtle, 855 : 12
silliest woman manage c. man, 707 : 11
think oneself more c., 293 : 21
Clever (*continued*)
wet mind and say something c., 81 : 12
woman manage fool, 707 : 11
young poets, 438 : 4
Cleverer, advantage over c. boys, 743 : 8
Cleverness, sages superior only in c., 375 : 2
Clicked behind the door, 370 : 13
off by little wheels, 837 : 16
Clickin' like tickin' of clock, 665 : 14
Client, art thou his c., 315 : 2
Clients, good counselors lack no c., 227 : 25
Cliff between lowland and highland, 634 : 12
dreadful summit of the c., 219 : 14
the c. drops the water drops, 894 : 1
Cliffs of Dover, 720 : 11
of England stand, 587 : 13
of fall frightful sheer, 656 : 18
white c. of Dover, 752 : 1
would I were under the c., 76 : 24
Climacteric of his want, 893 : 6
Climate, age too late or cold c., 287 : 13
coal portable c., 498 : 23
difference of soil and c., 424 : 8
fell upon ungenial c., 590 : 4
whole c. of opinion, 868 : 14
Climate's sultry, 460 : 13
Climates councils governments, 529 : 8
Climb, all day c. myself bowlegged, 902 : 1
back to upper air, 105 : 15
but I must c. the tree, 268 : 12
fain c. yet fear to fall, 172 : 11
high climb far, 924 : 16
if heart fails c. not, 172 : *n* 6
into the fold, 280 : 20
no man c. beyond limitations, 637 : 9
Sinais c. and know it not, 567 : 11
teach ye how to c., 280 : 5
up get to top, 911 : 20
Climbed, never c. Mount Sion, 893 : 9
to top of greasy pole, 502 : 9
Climber upward turns face, 215 : 16
Climbest, moon c. skies, 176 : 14
Climbing, down thou c. sorrow, 233 : 17
night c., 822 : 7
shakes his dewy wings, 275 : 30
still c. after knowledge infinite, 183 : 6
third stair, 806 : 2
Climbs, sun c. slow how slowly, 564 : 17
Clime, change c. not disposition, 109 : 5
deeds done in their c., 459 : 5
in some brighter c., 387 : 3
love no season knows nor c., 252 : 8
of unforgotten brave, 459 : 2
that lieth sublime, 526 : 8
Climes, cloudless c. starry skies, 459 : 13
Cling, babes around thee c., 427 : 19
bough where I c., 519 : 19
kiss and c., 614 : *n* 3
to old rugged cross, 738 : 11
together in one society, 423 : 18
Clings, cowardice that c., 742 : 12
desire for glory c., 122 : 26
leaves drifted one c., 778 : 6
pain c. cruelly, 476 : 2
Clink, why c. cannikin, 541 : 3
Clip, philosophy c. wings, 476 : 6
Clipper ships of 1850's, 800 : 10
Cliques, worst c. one man, 681 : 15
Cloak, covers man like c., 171 : 1
martial c. around him, 465 : 8
my fine camlet c., 309 : 13
not alone my inky c., 218 : 2
old c. about thee, 917 : 22
smiler with knyf under c., 146 : 24
sold even to c. I wore, 151 : 11
Cloaked, firs darkly c., 664 : 2
Clock, a-clickin' like tickin' of c., 665 : 14
collected in tower, 692 : 1
doth strike by algebra, 291 : 1
forgot to wind c., 359 : 19
in belfry strikes one, 614 : 12
stands c. at ten to three, 796 : 12
stops time come to life, 837 : 16
strikes at city's edge, 697 : 3
striking thirteen, 858 : 13
struck one, 930 : 4
time made me numbering c., 195 : 17
turned into a c., 595 : 16
varnished c., 370 : 13
will strike Devil will come, 184 : 8
worn out with eating time, 303 : 16
Clocks tongues of bawds, 202 : 23
were striking hour, 510 : 16
Clod, a kneaded c., 228 : 20
feverish selfish little c., 680 : 15
if c. washed away, 254 : 22
in cloud and c., 781 : 12
in the soul in the c., 543 : 19
no dull c. on my coffin, 569 : 20
of wayward marl, 209 : 6
Clods, only a man harrowing c., 642 : 2
Clog, anger at c. of his body, 276 : 15
three generations between c. and c., 621 : *n* 2
Clogged, if drainpipes of house c., 583 : 10
Clogs which else might overscar, 467 : 7
Cloister, pale with breath of c., 592 : 6
Cloistered, flown his c. flight, 238 : 20
virtue, 282 : 1
Close bare-bosomed night, 574 : 19
behind him tread, 435 : 3
cannot hold thee c. enough, 822 : 13
circle of felicities, 389 : 1
decay grossly c. it in, 201 : 1
designs crooked counsels, 303 : 20
draw the curtain c., 185 : 19
eyes with holy dread, 433 : 27
her from ancient walls, 407 : 7
instantly c. with offer, 595 : 16
life closed before its c., 607 : 18
little garden c., 618 : 5
mistake not to c. eyes, 700 : 4
more c. than brother, 710 : 19
mouth swallows no flies, 935 : 13
not a friend to c. eyes, 306 : 18
ranks, 915 : 1
rave at c. of day, 887 : 4
scent survives c., 693 : 6
setting sun and music at c., 194 : 10
shutters fast, 377 : 3
to edge of precipice, 835 : 15
up his eyes and draw curtain, 185 : 19
upon the growing boy, 426 : 14
wall up with English dead, 207 : 16
weary lips I c., 363 : 9
Close-buttoned to the chin, 377 : 17
Closed, dust hath c. Helen's eye, 250 : 10

Closed (*continued*)
eyes in endless night, 363 : 2
in death attentive eyes, 353 : 10
life c. life begins, 576 : 20
twice before its close, 607 : 18
Closer is He than breathing, 535 : 9
sticketh c. than a brother, 24 : 23
walk with God, 375 : 14
Closes, life as it c., 632 : 15
one door c. another open, 153 : 17
path emerges then c., 721 : 7
Closet, back in c. lays, 516 : 22
do very well in a c., 342 : 2
knowledge not in c., 341 : 17
Closing, busy hammers c. rivets, 208 : 1
diapason c. full in Man, 305 : 9
Clot bedded axletree, 807 : 4
created man of blood c., 132 : 17
created you of blood c., 131 : 14
Cloth, cut my coat after my c., 159 : 18
green c., 625 : 25
meat drink and c. to us, 158 : 13
untrue with twisted cue, 629 : 13
Clothe my naked villainy, 187 : 6
with hammered gold, 570 : 11
with rags, 25 : 9
Clothed all in leather, 934 : 2
and in right mind, 42 : 6
his neck with thunder, 16 : 36
in white samite held sword, 149 : 8
in white samite mystic, 534 : 4
man c. with rags, 301 : 20
naked and he c. him, 367 : 3
naked and ye c. me, 40 : 33
with heavens, 311 : 20
with integrity, 298 : 1
Clothes, as c. to bodies, 698 : 8
biographies c. and buttons, 626 : 9
Emperor's New C., 505 : 5
enterprises that require new c., 559 : 10
food fuel and c., 573 : 10
hanging out c., 931 : 9
his old c. a few books, 785 : 9
it burns your c., 401 : 3
kindles in c. a wantonness, 266 : 6
liquefaction of her c., 266 : 22
loves but their oldest c., 252 : 5
Mordecai rent his c., 14 : 32
nothing wears c. but Man, 268 : 19
on hickory limb, 924 : 17
out of wet c., 812 : 4
part of man's self, 648 : 17
put on his Sunday c., 466 : 5
smell of old c., 796 : 16
spoiling nice new c., 932 : 4
stepped out of c., 717 : 1
swaddling c., 42 : 27
take fire and his c. not be burned, 23 : 14
through tattered c., 235 : 3
thrown on with pitchfork, 323 : 9
upon c. behind tenement, 819 : 3
walked away with c., 501 : 22
wear our c. and what difference, 259 : 9
when he put on his c., 369 : 16
Clothing, come in sheep's c., 38 : 16
of delight, 403 : 5
of the grave, 729 : 11
softest c. wooly bright, 403 : 5
strength and honor are her c., 26 : 8
things in books' c., 442 : 9
wolf in sheep's c., 65 : 17
Cloths, heavens' embroidered c., 712 : 15
Clotilda, God of C. grant victory, 129 : 19
Cloud, are as a floating c., 68 : 21
brightest day hath c., 185 : 14
but c. and like shady grove, 403 : 7
choose a firm c., 335 : 17
comes over sunlit arch, 748 : 17
every c. engenders not storm, 186 : 22
fair luminous c., 435 : 27
geese like snow c., 810 : 19
house made of dark c., 928 : 18
in c. and clod to sing, 781 : 12
in shape of a camel, 222 : 20
in trousers, 826 : 16
joy the luminous c., 436 : 1
lift me as wave leaf c., 467 : 20
lightning out of dark c., 657 : 13
like a fiend in a c., 402 : 15, 405 : 12
like a man's hand, 14 : 3
lovely see c. appear, 928 : 15
nature mutable c., 496 : 17
not a c. in heart, 609 : 6
of barbarism and despotism, 390 : 1
of ignorance, 839 : 14
of witnesses, 51 : 19
on a c. I saw a child, 403 : 2
pillar of c., 9 : 30
sable c., 279 : 17
scowl of c., 545 : 25
seemed to be local dust c., 885 : 7
set my bow in the c., 8 : 3
Son of man coming in c., 44 : 2
stirred by solitary c., 313 : 23
stooping through a fleecy c., 278 : 18
that looked like centaur, 81 : 15
that's dragonish, 241 : 17
thickest c. stretched, 544 : 29
through dark c. shining, 740 : 11
took form of demon, 525 : 6
wandered lonely as c., 427 : 7
when c. is scattered, 470 : 1
will turn to rain, 512 : 19
Cloud-capped towers, 248 : 13
Cloud-Cuckoo-Land 82 : 10
Clouded, moon rising in c. majesty, 285 : 25
shine forth upon c. hills, 406 : 21
Cloud-kissing Ilion, 189 : 26
Cloudless climes starry skies, 459 : 13
fill sky with c. sunshine, 108 : 7
scintillant in c. days, 785 : 12
Clouds and eclipses stain, 244 : 14
are pedagogues, 768 : 13
ascribing to c. the flame, 115 : 16
base contagious c., 203 : 5
blue-massing c., 796 : 16
cannot be in deep sea, 101 : 1
color that paints morning evening c., 142 : 19
creeping quietly over it, 602 : 1
fill sky with black c., 108 : 7
he that regardeth the c., 27 : 21
her life filled with c. of goodness, 392 : *n* 1
home made of blue c., 928 : 16
hung oppressively, 525 : 19
hungry c. swag, 403 : 18
looks in the c., 215 : 16
maketh the c. his chariot, 21 : 8
mountains fleeting as c., 131 : 18
never doubted c. break, 546 : 7
new-made c., 887 : 2
Clouds (*continued*)
no pity sitting in c., 193 : 18
nor c. soak with showers, 59 : *n* 5
now here now there, 470 : 10
number the c. in wisdom, 16 : 35
O c. unfold, 406 : 21
of June, 609 : 11
out of c. silence, 660 : 10
pack c. away, 257 : 18
prince of c., 580 : 17
return after the rain, 27 : 24
robe of c., 460 : 6
round setting sun, 426 : 23
scare white c. on, 747 : 18
sees God in c., 336 : 16
ships dim-discovered from c., 345 : 8
silk-sack c., 656 : 6
somewhere among c. above, 713 : 20
spirits of wise sit in c., 206 : 13
storm c. brood on heights, 551 : 4
sun breaks through darkest c., 189 : 2
sweep c. no more, 518 : 12
to soar again, 456 : 17
trailing c. of glory, 426 : 14
tumult in the c., 714 : 1
what with all these c., 82 : 10
white c. on wing, 594 : 3
wrapped in c. and snow, 457 : 22
Cloud-topped hill, 336 : 16
Cloudy, among c. trophies hung, 478 : 1
flaming opal ring, 711 : 12
huge c. symbols, 478 : 18
skies not c. all day, 927 : 19
tabernacle parted, 480 : 16
was the weather, 934 : 2
Clove, burning c., 748 : 9
Cloven tongues as of fire, 45 : 39
Clovenfooted, whatsoever is c., 10 : 16
Clover and one bee, 608 : 3
any time aristocracy, 607 : 13
daisies and c., 578 : 9
Clove's sweet smell, 879 : 18
Cloves, nutmegs ginger cinnamon c., 268 : 1
Clown, be you c. or be you king, 667 : 7
emperor and c., 477 : 1
of spirit's motive, 883 : 11
Cloy appetites they feed, 241 : 1
hungry edge of appetite, 194 : 7
of all meats soonest c., 295 : 3
Cloyless sauce, 240 : 27
Club, any c. that would accept me, 834 : 3
assembly of good fellows, 352 : 7
loyal to c. rather than planet, 846 : 12
not with c. heart broken, 607 : 7
spear to thrust c. to strike, 157 : 5
swamp elm c., 676 : 16
wife joined woman's c., 699 : 13
Clubs typical of strife, 377 : 6
Cluett, land of the C. Shirt, 828 : 17
Clumsy feet of April, 829 : 7
Clusium, Lars Porsena of C., 488 : 13
Cluster of gifts constitute experience, 652 : 14
woes c., 223 : *n* 5
Clustered spires of Frederick, 513 : 17
Clutch, age clawed me in his c., 162 : 6
come let me c. thee, 237 : 13
either hand rightly c., 710 : 15
fell c. of circumstance, 663 : 10
Clutching inviolable shade, 586 : 2
C.O., Catholic C.O., 893 : 1
Coach, Christ's c., 314 : 21

Coach (*continued*)
clatter they make with c., 310 : 11
come my c., 223 : 24
rascals in c., 567 : *n* 1
rattling of a c., 255 : 2
through act of Parliament, 920 : 2
Coaches, turn pumpkins into c., 694 : 1
Coal, cargo of Tyne c., 760 : 20
portable climate, 498 : 23
Coals, can one go upon hot c., 23 : 14
carrying c. to Newcastle, 106 : *n* 13
heap c. of fire, 25 : 15
Coarse complexions and cheeks, 280 : 1
style familiar but not c., 352 : 23
Coast, apple-bearing Hesperian c., 76 : 25
stern and rockbound c., 470 : 14
was clear, 182 : 17
Coaster, dirty British c., 760 : 20
Coasts, bristling sea c., 520 : 7
Coat, cats have two holes in c., 387 : 2
cut my c. after my cloth, 159 : 18
eternal Footman hold my c., 803 : 16
her c. so warm, 449 : 14
made song a c., 713 : 14
of many colors, 8 : 28
passion for a scarlet c., 322 : 16
red breeches blue, 440 : 14
riband to stick in c., 541 : 5
upon a coat-hanger, 717 : 19
upon a stick, 715 : 1
Coat-hanger, coat upon a c., 717 : 19
Coats, if hole in a' your c., 410 : 20
in c. of red, 740 : 5
make my small elves c., 196 : 19
Coats-of-arms, worth hundred c., 528 : 8
Coaxed, habit c. downstairs, 624 : 15
Cobbett a kind of fourth estate, 445 : 3
Cobbler should not judge above last, 90 : 16
stick to your last, 90 : *n* 6
Cobblers, souls of emperors and c., 165 : 4
Cobweb bridge flung from mind, 701 : 7
Cobweb-covered, dusty c. maimed, 620 : 3
Cobwebs, laws are like c., 321 : 15
sweep c. from sky, 932 : 5
Cochineal, rush of c., 607 : 12
Cock, a C. and a Bull, 360 : 20
a doodle doo, 929 : 10
before the c. crow, 41 : 18
crow louder in own farmyard, 555 : 2
crowing of the c., 217 : 26
damned universal c., 767 : 6
diminished to her c., 234 : 28
Diogenes plucked a c., 86 : 10
has great influence on own dunghill, 111 : 5
her c. a buoy, 234 : 28
immediately the c. crew, 41 : 18
that crowed in morn, 934 : 9
thought sun risen to hear him, 565 : 9
trumpet to the morn, 217 : 24
with lively din, 277 : 23
Cock Robin, who killed C., 930 : 9
Cockatoo, cage not natural to c., 680 : 31
Cockatrice' den, 29 : 19
Cock-crowing, civilization at c., 498 : 8
Cockerels crow in Hubbard's barns, 557 : 8
Cockhorse, ride a c., 931 : 11
Cockle hat and staff, 223 : 21
Cockleburs, corn cotton and c., 674 : 13
Cockleshells, silver bells c., 930 : 6
Cockney impudence, 619 : *n* 1
Cockroach, archy a c., 759 : *n* 5
Cocks and lions jocund be, 253 : 15
crowing of c. and barking of dogs, 65 : 9
drowned the c., 233 : 24
ere barn c. say, 641 : 25
Cocksure, wish I was c. of anything, 487 : *n* 1
Cocktail, stiffish c., 544 : 28
stonefence cobbler, 452 : 14
Cod, home of bean and c., 694 : 14
home of sacred c., 694 : *n* 3
Code of modern morals, 468 : 21
Codfish, comb hair with c. bones, 934 : 22
lays ten thousand eggs, 923 : 10
Codification, out of dream into c., 906 : 16
Coeli, fiat justitia et ruant c., 133 : *n* 11
Coelum, fiat justitia ruat c., 133 : 25
quid si c. ruat, 96 : *n* 12
ruat c. fiat voluntas tua, 134 : 24
Coercion, effect of c. to make fools and hypocrites, 387 : 15
or voluntary cooperation, 880 : 13
subject opinion to c., 387 : 14
Coeur, blessent mon c. d'une langueur, 659 : *n* 6
il pleure dans mon c., 659 : *n* 7
le c. a ses raisons, 300 : *n* 3
triste c. bave à la poupe, 673 : *n* 6
Coexistence, peaceful c., 862 : 17
Coffee and oranges in sunny chair, 767 : 2
government decided over c., 398 : *n* 1
makes politician wise, 334 : 8
measured life with c. spoons, 803 : 13
Racine will go out of style like c., 301 : 8
Coffee-pickers, sweaty faces of c., 789 : 10
Coffeepot, small gray c., 793 : 15
Coffer, man c. full of corruption, 152 : 2
Coffin asks whither, 615 : 7
even in c. face the same, 602 : 2
no dull clod on my c., 569 : 20
Coffins, shook all our c., 642 : 1
Cogitations, sometimes c. still amaze, 804 : 12
Cogito ergo sum, 272 : 10
Cognition of modern world, 756 : 3
Cognitive, perception would be c., 649 : 7
Cognosce, occasionem c., 62 : *n* 7
Coherence, all in pieces all c. gone, 254 : 5
Cohesion, held in c. by cells, 760 : 21
Cohesive power of vast surplus, 449 : 9
Cohort of the damned, 708 : 13
Cohorts gleaming in purple, 459 : 14
Coign of cliff, 634 : 12
of vantage, 236 : 21
Coil, mortal c., 221 : 12
mountains curl up in c., 747 : 20
Coin, advice smallest c., 647 : 8
beauty is Nature's c., 279 : 31
Duke keep your c., 900 : 4
far as c. would stretch, 202 : 27
is sinews of war, 157 : 10
outlasts Tiberius, 640 : 1
Coin (*continued*)
paid in his own c., 168 : 25
pays him in own c., 323 : 20
valuable c. of thinker, 887 : 15
Coincide, men c. with epoch or differ, 672 : 3
Coincidence, want of c. between accounts, 80 : 15
Cold accretion called world, 640 : 18
age or c. climate, 287 : 13
and heat, 8 : 1
and hot moist and dry, 305 : 9
and naked and he clothed him, 367 : 3
and not cleanly manger, 292 : 17
and to temptation slow, 245 : 4
and unhonored his relics, 446 : 7
and white sleeping at last, 608 : 20
approbation, 351 : 11
as any stone, 207 : 14
as cucumbers, 263 : 4
as paddocks, 267 : 1
at summit c. increases, 658 : 16
bargain catch c. and starve, 243 : 14
blow hot and c., 66 : 17
blow in c. blood, 680 : 25
book makes body c., 608 : 6
boughs which shake against c., 244 : 27
calculating average of virtues, 630 : 16
cast c. eye, 718 : 2
comfort, 202 : 18
comfort like c. porridge, 247 : 25
comfort to fill hungry bellies, 265 : 11
coming we had of it, 805 : 19
companionable streams, 713 : 16
dark deep clear, 878 : 6
dined upon c. meat, 310 : 4
doth not sting, 250 : 8
dull c. ear of death, 362 : 5
every drop of ink ran c., 363 : 19
fallen c. and dead, 576 : 7
feeling his c. strength, 797 : 12
foot and hand go c., 163 : 10
friendship sounds too c., 447 : 11
fruitless moon, 195 : 20
good-bye and keep c., 748 : 10
gray dawn of morning after, 718 : 12
gray stones O sea, 530 : 19
hand of death, 205 : 10
hardens and grows c., 870 : 6
he makes c. as he wishes, 5 : 3
heart grown c. in vain, 469 : 12
heat c. craters of silence, 864 : 4
heat flow from hot to c. object, 589 : *n* 1
her empty room is c., 97 : 10
his limbs c. in death, 106 : 7
hot c. moist and dry, 284 : 27
imagination c. and barren, 372 : 13
in c. blood, 680 : 25
in the earth, 562 : 1
in the womb, 907 : 16
in thy c. bed, 267 : 6
iron, 455 : 12
it grew wondrous c., 434 : 10
keep c. young orchard, 748 : 10
large c. bottle, 666 : 15
lie in c. obstruction, 228 : 20
light and hot shade, 405 : 15
literature clear and c., 791 : 9
mad father, 778 : 6
meddles with c. iron, 173 : *n* 3

Cold (*continued*)
more c. to you than I, 528 : 9
morn and c. indifference, 327 : 21
my lodging on c. ground, 331 : 11
neither c. nor care John, 417 : 11
neither c. nor hot, 53 : 5
neutrality, 374 : 6
never caught a c., 719 : 5
night blasts c., 742 : 9
night is c., 925 : 2
no such c. thing, 269 : 3
out o' c. and rain, 709 : 1
out of dead c. ashes life, 660 : 10
owl a-c., 476 : 8
pain darkness and c., 544 : 22
pease-porridge c., 931 : 18
poor Tom's a-c., 234 : 12
principle, 270 : *n* 7
put it in c. storage, 698 : 10
remote islands, 837 : 2
shakes from c., 824 : 6
side outside, 733 : *n* 1
sleep in dull c. marble, 249 : 6
sleep is heat for c., 171 : 1
snow said c. said sleep, 811 : 17
so c. no fire warm, 608 : 6
spy who came in from c., 911 : 3
stars look c. about sky, 748 : *n* 2
sweat bathes me, 63 : 5
temper leaps over c. decree, 198 : 10
thicks man's blood with c., 434 : 19
three months of c. weather, 590 : 4
through dark c. and desolation, 807 : 24
till sun grows c., 596 : 16
'tis bitter c., 217 : 15
to distant misery, 383 : 12
trembling c. in ghastly fears, 404 : 10
upon dead Caesar's trencher, 241 : 11
war getting warmer, 729 : 13
waters to a thirsty soul, 25 : 16
way long wind c., 429 : 20
we are dying of c., 705 : 21
winter with wrathful nipping c., 185 : 14
words of tongue or pen, 732 : 15
years grow c. to love, 104 : 9
Colder, heat cannot pass from c., 589 : 14
than the Hebrides, 785 : 15
Coldly furnish forth marriage tables, 218 : 14
sadly descends autumn, 588 : 5
Coldness of my dear, 331 : 11
Cold-shouldered, nothing harder than being c., 643 : 13
Cole, old King C., 929 : 14
Coleridge, Bentham and C. seminal minds, 508 : 2
poet and philosopher, 589 : 12
Coliseum, while stands C. Rome stand, 458 : 22
Collaboration, peculiar illusion of c., 889 : 1
Collapsed, then all c. sea rolled, 571 : 9
Collapses, what's old c., 414 : 2
Collar, braw brass c., 409 : 6
Collars and leashes of vanity, 907 : 24
Earl & Wilson C., 828 : 17
Collateral, with intellect only c. relations, 527 : 14
Collected, bee's c. treasures, 363 : 13
Collection of facts not science, 673 : 8
Collections, mutilators of c., 441 : 18
Collections (*continued*)
not c. of pictures but of fruit, 97 : 12
Collective bargaining is bilateral monopoly, 790 : 4
knowledge of mankind, 867 : 12
monism thinks c. only form, 650 : 12
provision for needs, 773 : 8
unconscious, 753 : 12
unit form, 650 : 12
Collectors, scientists c. classifiers, 888 : 1
College, cabbage with c. education, 624 : 14
endow c. or cat, 336 : 1
farewell to c. joys, 783 : 17
intent on getting results, 740 : 16
it is a small c., 450 : 2
lady of Christ's C., 301 : 5
not much between unless c., 748 : 16
whaleship my Yale C., 570 : 10
Colleges lit up relish, 651 : 1
to do with progress, 722 : 6
Collied night, 195 : 23
Collins Mr. C. had only to change, 440 : 19
Collision, avoid foreign c., 444 : 2
Collop cut of own flesh, 160 : 1
Cologne, Rhine wash city of C., 436 : 13
Colonel lean as needle, 893 : 12
Colonel's lady an' Judy O'Grady, 709 : 11
Colonels full of corn, 693 : 2
Colonial, adjustment of c. claims, 682 : 14
Colonies are and ought to be free, 381 : 6
commerce with our c., 372 : 13
religion prevalent in c., 372 : 19
these united c., 378 : 12
Colonization, American continents not subjects for c., 408 : 1
Colony, dissenting c., 381 : 6
Coloquintida, bitter as c., 230 : 4
Color, air quiver with c., 789 : 10
blue c. delight, 572 : 16
by convention there is c., 79 : 11
flash of c. beneath sky, 676 : *n* 5
free from judging by c. of skin, 904 : 16
her c. comes and goes, 640 : 2
his c. can't be seen, 920 : 21
horse of different c., 213 : *n* 4
horse of that c., 213 : 27
in the cup, 25 : 11
line, 724 : 15
loves and skin, 252 : 5
met by c. line, 556 : 11
no matter c. of skin, 824 : 10
not judged by c. of skin, 909 : 10
not superior by c., 615 : 5
of ground in him, 671 : 2
prejudice against c., 554 : 6
prison for c. of hair, 692 : 12
problem of c. line, 724 : 15
race and c. problem, 800 : 9
right to vote not denied on account of c., 392 : 5
sergeant said, 708 : 1
shade without c., 805 : 16
some because of c., 872 : 10
that paints morning and evening clouds, 142 : 19
till heart tinged with c., 438 : 2
white is their c., 269 : 6
Colorado, Kansas and C. have quarrel, 787 : 11
Color-blind, Constitution is c., 615 : 1
Colored, destiny of c. American, 556 : 8
ground c. man occupies, 556 : 7
people understand white people, 733 : 7
relation between white and c. people, 556 : 9
skins not c. like your own, 556 : 6
twopence c., 669 : 1
white or c. signs, 891 : 13
Coloring, sober c. from eye, 426 : 23
Colors, all c. suffusion from light, 436 : 1
changing c. shooting upward, 809 : 22
coat of many c., 8 : 28
embroidered girdle of many c., 58 : 19
hoist c. to peak, 771 : 5
nailed c. to the mast, 430 : 14
no c. or crest, 708 : 19
of imagination, 437 : 14
oldest c. have faded, 707 : 21
perfumes c. sounds echo, 580 : 18
seen by candlelight, 507 : 5
that are but skin deep, 250 : *n* 1
that never fade, 698 : 16
their c. and their forms, 423 : 12
under whose c. he fought so long, 195 : 8
Colossal figures seeded light, 861 : 2
silent c. national lie, 625 : 24
symmetrical complete c., 623 : 18
Colossus, bestride world like C., 215 : 6
of Rhodes, 924 : 3
Colt, let little c. go bare, 934 : 6
Columbia, hail C., 422 : 21
solved riddle of China trade, 799 : 19
Columbus, aromatic America of C., 721 : 3
enjoyed pure delight, 799 : 20
found world had no chart, 703 : 3
Column, fifth c., 798 : 5
fountain's silvery c., 435 : 19
rising toward heaven, 450 : 5
throws up a steamy c., 377 : 3
Comb gray hair, 713 : 18
hair with codfish bones, 934 : 22
me all to thunder, 622 : 16
scraped life with fine-tooth c., 889 : 5
Combat ceased for want of combatants, 275 : 18
deepens, 443 : 15
life c. between love and hate, 671 : 17
obstacles to get repose, 635 : 18
reason left free to c. it, 388 : 16, 389 : 16
Combatants, dust involves the c., 376 : 26
want of c., 275 : 18
Combination and a form indeed, 223 : 3
human c. or society, 273 : 11
no powers of c., 374 : 10
of fortuitous circumstances, 432 : 3
Combine, when bad men c., 372 : 4
Combined, knotted and c. locks part, 219 : 18
Combs, Glos'ter girls they have no c., 934 : 22
Combustible, entire c. world, 713 : 17
Combustion, hideous ruin and c., 283 : 4
Come again another day, 929 : 17
again Jack, 934 : 8
again to Carthage, 200 : 22

Come (*continued*)
again with rejoicing, 22 : 7
all things c. of thee, 14 : 26
all to church good people, 691 : 4
all you rounders, 731 : *n* 2
and trip it as you go, 277 : 20
as chimney sweepers c. to dust, 243 : 27
as the winds come, 431 : 23
as you soon must, 900 : 2
avoid what is to c., 223 : 8
a-waltzing Matilda, 705 : 7
away death, 214 : 4
back to earth begin over, 747 : 16
back to Mandalay, 708 : 8
before his presence with singing, 21 : 3
before the swallow dares, 246 : 26
believe in life to c., 866 : 14
between bid us part, 345 : 18
blow wind c. wrack, 240 : 6
blow your horn, 930 : 12
cannot c. again, 691 : 9
cannot c. to good, 218 : 12
cheer up they c., 578 : 12
children shut up box, 539 : 10
consider where you c. out, 112 : 4
cry is still They c., 240 : 2
curates will c. and go, 796 : 11
cut and c. again, 400 : 8
dance wyth me, 916 : 16
days to c. are wisest witnesses, 71 : 21
dear children let us away, 584 : 11
death c. when it will c., 215 : 26
down redeem us, 632 : 16
dreaming on things to c., 245 : 13
ethereal mildness c., 345 : 10
fill the cup, 516 : 4
fill up my cup, 432 : 15
first c. first served, 138 : *n* 8
first c. kiss me, 918 : 2
flee from wrath to c., 36 : 28
for the life to c., 246 : 23
forth into light of things, 423 : 6
friends who plow sea, 628 : 4
from dying moon, 530 : 25
from ends of earth, 707 : 16
from haunts, 533 : 15
gentle Spring, 345 : 10
ghost c. back again, 852 : 8
Ghost of Christmas Yet to C., 548 : 12
give a war and nobody c., 761 : 14
give us taste of quality, 221 : 2
he slow, 430 : 16
here I want you, 661 : 7
hither, 211 : 1
home to roost, 440 : 3
home with me now, 614 : 12
honor has c. back, 797 : 5
hour is not yet c., 44 : 26
I c. quickly, 53 : 32
I c. to bury Caesar, 216 : 17
I hear you I will c., 691 : 4
I will c. again, 45 : 21
I would not c. in, 749 : 7
idea whose time c., 491 : 11
if not to c. will be now, 224 : 28
if now 'tis not to c., 224 : 28
in the evening, 552 : 19
in the rearward of woe, 245 : 3
in under shadow, 805 : 1
in we'll keep ye broke, 721 : 15
into the garden Maud, 533 : 20
it shall not c. nigh thee, 20 : 16

Come (*continued*)
jump the life to c., 236 : 22
King of glory shall c. in, 18 : 9
kiss me sweet and twenty, 213 : 23
knit hands, 279 : 14
know end ere it c., 217 : 10
knowledge must c. through action, 75 : 6
let me clutch thee, 237 : 13
let us kiss and part, 182 : 16
let us mock at great, 715 : 9
let us sing unto Lord, 20 : 20
let's away to prison, 235 : 12
like shadows so depart, 239 : 13
live with me and be my love, 183 : 8, 253 : 2
Lord is c., 328 : 13
lovely soothing death, 576 : 4
men may c. and go, 533 : 16
Mr. Watson c. here, 661 : 7
my Celia let us prove, 255 : 16
my coach, 223 : 24
my lad and drink beer, 353 : 11
my own c. to me, 630 : 21
my tan-faced children, 575 : 14
near me while I sing, 712 : 3
never c. back to me, 530 : 20
never c. back to us, 541 : 9
night strike hour, 770 : 10
not between dragon and wrath, 232 : 27
not near our fairy queen, 196 : 21
not to steal away hearts, 216 : 27
nothing will c. of nothing, 232 : 24
now and let us reason, 28 : 30
nowhere to c. but back, 684 : 15
O come Emmanuel, 563 : 14
on now young men, 743 : 10
one come all, 431 : 13
over into Macedonia, 46 : 13
over way with tears watered, 733 : 6
past and to c. seem best, 206 : 8
past passing or to c., 715 : 3
perhaps singing bird c., 132 : 25
Romeo c. forth, 193 : 11
season to c. and go, 339 : 29
see my shining palace, 822 : 18
seeling night, 238 : 21
shan't be gone long you c. too, 747 : 3
shape of things to c., 720 : 9
soon soon, 469 : 22
that it should c. to this, 218 : 6
that it will never c. again, 608 : 1
that they might have life, 45 : 10
the foe they c., 457 : 18
things past or things to c., 302 : 4
things to c., 226 : 5
thou monarch of the vine, 241 : 5
thou'lt c. no more, 235 : 18
three corners of world, 202 : 20
thy kingdom c., 37 : 15
till boys c. home, 740 : 11
to aid of party, 923 : 1
to dedicate field, 523 : 4
to lay weary bones among ye, 249 : 10
to me my dear Bozzy, 356 : 18
to my arms, 612 : 18
to my woman's breasts, 236 : 17
to pluck your berries, 280 : 6
to see and be seen, 113 : 9
to take their ease, 249 : 19
to thee by moonlight, 773 : 1
to this favor she must c., 224 : 14
to this stage of fools, 235 : 5

Come (*continued*)
treading path through blood, 733 : 6
unbutton here, 234 : 7
until I c. in peace, 14 : 11
unto me ye that labor, 39 : 8
unto my love, 174 : 18
unto these yellow sands, 247 : 19
up and see me, 824 : 8
weal come woe, 422 : 19
what come may, 236 : 13
what dreams may c., 221 : 12
what is to c. I know not, 34 : 4
what may I have been blessed, 459 : 4
what may Sinon said, 114 : 9
wheel is c. full circle, 235 : 15
when shall I c. to thee, 918 : 5
whence had they c., 717 : 4
whistle and I'll c. to you, 410 : 10
whistle and she'll c. to you, 263 : 9
will they c. when you call, 204 : 12
will ye no c. back again, 417 : 5
with singing unto Zion, 31 : 9
within a pint of wine, 327 : 8
within bending sickle's compass c., 245 : 18
without warning, 552 : 19
women c. and go, 803 : 10
won't c. back till it's over, 759 : 8
worst yet to c., 535 : 5
ye thankful people, 536 : 2
ye to the waters, 31 : 18
you back British soldier, 708 : 8
you spirits that tend, 236 : 17
Come del morire, 255 : *n* 4
Come-a ti yi youpy youpy yea, 927 : 12
Comedian can last till he takes himself serious, 766 : 2
no matter if country need c., 766 : 3
Comedy, catastrophe of the old c., 233 : 6
dressed for this short c., 173 : 1
killing time essence of c., 706 : 3
most lamentable c., 196 : 2
the c. is finished, 686 : 4
the ultimate civilizer, 600 : 22
world is a c., 363 : 22
Comely, attire c. not costly, 175 : 9
black but c., 28 : 2
bowed his c. head down, 296 : 24
grace, 918 : 16
Comer, grasps in the c., 226 : 19
Comers, entertain all c., 57 : 32
Comes appareled like spring, 243 : 10
at one stride c. the dark, 434 : 21
at the last, 195 : 3
Autumn c. jovial on, 345 : 13
conquering hero c., 346 : 7
Death who c. at last, 430 : 16
effect defective c. by cause, 220 : 13
ever 'gainst that season c., 217 : 26
fog c. on cat feet, 761 : 5
God behind them, 544 : 27
God c. as sun at noon, 255 : 1
he c. he c., 306 : 14
here c. the lady, 193 : 2
hope never c., 283 : 7
in the sweet o' the year, 246 : 21
knowledge c. wisdom lingers, 530 : 4
look who c. here, 201 : 24
love that c. too late, 227 : 22
moment to decide, 567 : 6
nearer c. the sun, 790 : 16
pat he c., 233 : 6

Comes (*continued*)
rainbow c. and goes, 426 : 11
silent flooding in the main, 564 : 17
something wicked this way c., 239 : 7
take it as it c., 630 : 4
then cannon and he c., 742 : 9
thrill that c. once in lifetime, 793 : 14
to me o'er and o'er, 594 : 6
unlooked for if c. at all, 332 : 13
want for one who c. not, 835 : 13
wear day out before it c., 664 : 6
while she c. is gone, 728 : 11
wine c. in at mouth, 713 : 7
Comest in such questionable
shape, 219 : 11
whence c. thou, 15 : 2
Cometh, another generation c., 26 : 11
behold the day c. that shall
burn, 33 : 38
forth like a flower, 15 : 33
from afar, 426 : 14
from whence c. my help, 22 : 4
hour c. and now is, 44 : 36
in the name of the Lord, 22 : 1
joy c. in the morning, 18 : 15
my help c. from the Lord, 22 : 4
the night c., 45 : 7
this dreamer c., 8 : 27
whence it c., 44 : 32
Comets, discoverers as c., 350 : 8
when beggars die no c., 215 : 25
Comfort and despair, 246 : 3
carrion c., 656 : 15
cold c. I beg, 202 : 18
cold c. to fill hungry bellies, 265 : 11
conceited carry c., 565 : 17
continual c. in a face, 184 : 13
gives c. in despair, 185 : 12
giving enemies aid and c., 391 : 12
hobbit-hole and that means c., 824 : 3
is any c. to be found, 715 : 7
like cold porridge, 247 : 25
me with apples, 28 : 6
nightingale sing of c., 505 : 7
no c. to one not sociable, 243 : 25
of c. no man speak, 195 : 1
old poets c. to man, 663 : 17
scholar who cherishes love of
c., 69 : 5
she hath none to c. her, 32 : 21
so will I c. you, 31 : 32
thy rod and thy staff c. me, 18 : 7
to my age, 210 : 28
values c. or money more, 751 : 20
warn to c. and command, 427 : 6
what gnashing is not a c., 254 : 23
ye my people, 30 : 29
Comfortable advice, 479 : 14
creed, 460 : 22
easy and c. on raft, 624 : 1
feeling of superiority, 772 : 12
minds, 828 : 14
no c. feel, 485 : 12
O c. bird, 475 : 18
progress a c. disease, 829 : 24
words, 534 : 3
Comfortably in debt, 539 : 7
padded lunatic asylums, 781 : 16
speak c. to Jerusalem, 30 : 30
Comforted, be c. for him, 36 : 8
folly of being c., 712 : 18
they shall be c., 37 : 4
would not be c., 36 : 23
Comforters, miserable c. are ye
all, 15 : 37
Comforteth, love c. like
sunshine, 189 : 12
one whom his mother c., 31 : 32
Comforting thought when not our
trouble, 760 : 13
Comfortless, grim-visaged c.
Despair, 361 : 11
not leave you c., 45 : 23
through c. despairs, 174 : 11
Comforts, adversity not without
c., 180 : 6
creature c., 319 : 5
essential c. of life, 481 : 1
flee, 470 : 23
from whence c. increased, 402 : 15
of life not indispensable, 559 : 8
of weary pilgrimage, 356 : 25
ruth of prepared c., 907 : 24
what I aspired c. me, 544 : 11
Comic, perception of c. tie, 500 : 5
poet paint follies, 324 : 6
Comical how nature contrive, 628 : 23
Comin' for to carry me home, 935 : 24
in on a wing, 866 : 5
Campbells are c., 920 : 3
Coming back and coming back, 768 : 23
Campbells are c., 920 : 3
cold c. we had of it, 805 : 19
events cast shadows, 443 : 14
far calls c. far, 778 : 6
far off his c. shone, 286 : 27
for to carry me home, 935 : 24
good time c., 431 : 26, 553 : 4
Gospel train's a-c., 936 : 6
hither, 235 : 11
hold fort I am c., 579 : 1, 635 : 22
I am c. says Death, 106 : 9
I'm c., 598 : 7
in on a wing, 866 : 5
it's c. yet for a' that, 411 : 19
man a long time c., 761 : 17
my own my sweet, 533 : 25
night of dark intent c., 748 : 11
of the Lord, 52 : 4, 566 : 4
patient unto c. of Lord, 52 : 4
preserve thy going out and c.
in, 22 : 4
see anyone c., 919 : 22
sometimes c. sometimes coy, 312 : 12
through the rye, 919 : 18
to the sacrifice, 477 : 9
together foretaste of
resurrection, 463 : 5
way of c. into world, 321 : 10
we are c. Father Abraham, 537 : 2
Yanks are c., 759 : 7
Comings-in, what are thy c., 208 : 6
Command against stealing in
Bible, 622 : 14
best fitted to c., 570 : 1
by his c. words cut, 718 : 2
correspondent to c., 247 : 17
eagle mount at thy c., 17 : 1
ensigns of c., 418 : 8
fit for c., 379 : 3
give what you c., 129 : 6
Heaven's c., 345 : 19
iron fist to c. them, 421 : 13
justice peace and sobriety, 273 : 11
man to c., 531 : 7
morals simply obedience to words
of c., 690 : 9
Command (*continued*)
more invitation than c., 327 : 11
move only in c., 239 : 28
my heart and me, 292 : 7
not born to sue but to c., 193 : 34
not full c. of myself, 157 : 11
obedient to c. of God, 580 : 7
prize of general is c., 644 : 15
she might c. him tasks, 231 : 23
sneer of cold c., 466 : 12
success, 325 : 12
take c. of troops, 420 : 12
threaten and c., 223 : 3
warn to comfort and c., 427 : 6
where I adore, 214 : 8
who commands sea has c., 70 : 19
Commanded, do without being c., 87 : 2
God so c., 287 : 18
Hellenes c. by Athenians, 70 : 15
nature to be c. must be
obeyed, 179 : 10
rain shower of c. tears, 188 : 24
Commander to the people, 31 : 19
whereof I am c., 918 : 12
Commanders, blunder made by
c., 815 : 14
Commandment, a new c., 45 : 19
eighth c. not for bards, 436 : 6
first and great c., 40 : 16, 815 : 1
one unconditional c., 649 : 18
Commandments, aren't no ten
c., 708 : 10
fear God and keep his c., 27 : 27
hearkened to my c., 31 : 7
love me and keep my c., 10 : 5
on these two c. hang law and
prophets, 40 : 16
public opinion and Ten C., 603 : 13
set my ten c. in your face, 185 : 10
ten c., 10 : 15
Ten C. not budge, 569 : 1
Commands, he that c. sea is at
liberty, 181 : 11
the beauteous files, 299 : 10
those he c. move in command, 239 : 28
war necessary to one who c., 153 : 21
who c. the sea has command, 70 : 19
Commedia è finita, 686 : *n* 3
Commemorated as day of
deliverance, 381 : 7
Commencement of history, 378 : 1
Commences, heaven c. ere world
past, 370 : 3
Commend, all our swains c. her, 190 : 4
all summer long, 714 : 22
blame or to c., 338 : 14
my spirit, 44 : 10
those who are afflicted, 55 : 6
to cold oblivion, 468 : 21
to write to to c., 253 : 10
Commendable, humility a thing
c., 159 : *n* 11
Commendations, paltry c. of
man, 526 : 9
Commended yellow stockings, 214 : 10
Comment, no c. splendid
expression, 746 : 8
Commerce and honest
friendship, 389 : 2
between equals, 369 : 25
equal to whole of that c., 372 : 12
heavens fill with c., 529 : 24
in matters of c., 422 : 6
instrument of trade and c., 617 : 7

Commerce (*continued*)
navigation c. agriculture, 381 : 14
promote c. not betray it, 310 : *n* 1
where c. long prevails, 368 : 16
with our colonies, 372 : 13
Commercial, no middle c., 873 : 1
Commercials, singing c. not allowed, 873 : 1
Commercing, looks c. with the skies, 278 : 13
Commission, dropped his warm c., 650 : 13
sins of c. mortal, 357 : 11
Commit, follies that themselves c., 199 : 7
oldest sins newest ways, 206 : 33
thou shalt not c. adultery, 10 : 7
Commitment, each gesture a c., 865 : 10
shared by two people, 898 : 5
Commitments and power in balance, 813 : 11
voters don't know can't hurt you, 856 : 13
Committed, crimes c. in thy name, 400 : 14
flat burglary as ever c., 209 : 33
sins most grievously c., 55 : 17
themselves to God, 265 : 6
to whom men have c. much, 43 : 22
vices c. genteelly, 355 : 13
Committee for affairs of bourgeoisie, 563 : 4
inquisition, 764 : 2
Committees, intellectual before c., 764 : 2
Committing suicide by working, 706 : 5
Commodities, hateful tax on c., 352 : 9
sell c. above natural price, 366 : 1
Commodity bias of the world, 201 : 19
of good names, 202 : 30
regard land as c., 795 : 10
smooth-faced gentleman C., 201 : 19
tickling C., 201 : 19
Commodores, proud gods and c., 570 : 5
Common affairs of life, 445 : 6
as light is love, 467 : 5
blot on escutcheon of C. Law, 638 : 8
buries empires in c. grave, 383 : 14
bush afire with God, 507 : 22
call not thou c., 46 : 9
cause decays, 80 : 16
cause to save Union, 521 : 7
century of c. man, 811 : 11
crowd of c. men, 272 : 14
crude material, 632 : 1
denominator of progress, 871 : 15
dictate of c. sense, 346 : 6
earth and every c. sight, 426 : 10
education forms c. mind, 335 : 15
faction united by c. impulse, 398 : 1
fade into light of c. day, 426 : 15
friends have all in c., 83 : 8
government for c. benefit, 367 : 5
grayness silvers everything, 542 : 21
greatness of art not to find c., 861 : 14
hate the c. herd, 107 : 25
I drew in the c. air, 34 : 18
law not omnipresence, 644 : 21
law nothing but reason, 171 : 21
law of England, 815 : 17
life in c. ideal, 504 : 13
life's c. way, 425 : 23
make good thing too c., 206 : 3
man, 658 : 4, 811 : 11
Common (*continued*)
not jump with c. spirits, 199 : 13
nothing c. did or mean, 296 : 23
old c. arbitrator Time, 227 : 5
opinions uncommon abilities, 597 : 9
people of the skies, 251 : 1
provide for c. defense, 391 : 10
rich in c. sense, 533 : 3
right of humanity, 520 : 8
roll of c. men, 204 : 11
sense and plain dealing, 497 : 29
sense antipodes of science, 724 : 2
sense appall, 696 : 1
sense hasty superficial, 558 : 18
sense master workman, 464 : 2
sense not so common, 343 : 18
sense of next age, 589 : 1
sense of our people, 841 : 3
sense on ground floor, 519 : 18
sense reduced to calculus, 397 : 18
sense without genius, 813 : 12
something else than c. land, 571 : 8
steals c. from goose, 918 : 13
sun air skies, 362 : 20
sweets grown c., 245 : 10
talk of the town, 309 : 18
the actual world the c. sense, 557 : 21
thou knowest 'tis c., 218 : 1
touch, 710 : 17
uncommon valor c. virtue, 791 : 14
universal and c. bond, 166 : 2
weal and woe is c., 273 : 11
where climate's sultry, 460 : 13
witness to c. lot, 801 : 14
Commonest, see-vility of the c. goddamnedest kind, 922 : 7
Common-looking people best, 523 : 5
Commonplace, never yawn or say c., 901 : 3
unassuming c. of Nature, 426 : 2
Commons faithful to system, 416 : 14
kingly c., 570 : 11
Commonwealth, caterpillars of the c., 194 : 22
debate of c. affairs, 207 : 4
gave bodies to c., 81 : 5
in c. by contraries execute, 247 : 26
last thousand years, 744 : 4
lie abroad for the c., 251 : 4
or human combination, 273 : 11
realization of c., 618 : 10
wise men refrain to meddle in c., 155 : 5
Commonwealths, raise c., 303 : 19
Communicate, failure to c., 908 : 7
poetry can c. before understood, 809 : 15
speech given to c., 310 : 22
to do good and to c., 51 : 26
Communicated, good the more c., 286 : 14
Communicatest with dreams, 246 : 12
Communicating, price system mechanism for c., 844 : 6
Communication, facilitated means of c., 563 : 5
in free society, 789 : 5
monk's state transcends c., 73 : 4
of the dead, 808 : 10
poetry c. of pleasure, 436 : 14
science c. of truth, 436 : 14
strengthen noncommunication, 885 : 19
theory, 831 : 22
Communications, evil c., 49 : 2
Communion, further union deeper c., 807 : 24
good marriage a c., 156 : 7
last c. in haze, 604 : 10
of Holy Ghost, 49 : 24
of Saints, 55 : 2
with her visible forms, 471 : 2
Communism autocracy upside down, 550 : 2
corruption of dream, 851 : 7
government plus electrification, 731 : 6
repudiate support of c., 779 : 19
specter of C., 563 : 2
Communist, because I wasn't C., 824 : 1
bloc, 862 : 20
call anybody they don't like a C., 847 : 4
dictatorship of C. Party, 770 : 6
every C. grasp truth, 826 : 7
indigenous C. parties, 871 : 13
spent life under C. regime, 895 : 25
what is a c., 449 : 4
world, 803 : 7
Communists, Catholics and C., 859 : 13
disdain to conceal views, 563 : 10
read there were C. in Hollywood, 847 : 1
theory of C., 563 : 7
Communities divide into few and the many, 401 : 12
industrialized c., 773 : 7
overlook one another, 65 : 9
Community, aim at c. of goods, 414 : 22
best political c., 88 : 7
brothers as in one c., 424 : 4
control politics in own c., 904 : 14
human c., 781 : 5, 861 : 7
in dissolution, 737 : 7
investment for c. as whole, 783 : 14
like a ship, 599 : 18
of power, 682 : 8
permanent interests of c., 398 : 1
power of c. mass of powers, 418 : 3
property subject to c., 687 : 16
quarantine to protect c., 780 : 4
rules c. evolved, 751 : 14
safeguarding c., 700 : 3
see land as c., 795 : 10
standing in the c., 671 : 15
what c. produces, 871 : 9
world c., 774 : 8
Commuter one who spends life, 846 : 8
Compact, highest c. we can make, 498 : 30
of imagination all c., 197 : 12
spirit all c. of fire, 189 : 8
Compacted, sweets c. lie, 268 : 16
Compacts between lions and men, 59 : 8
Compagnon Roland sonnez, 136 : *n* 9
Companion, brother and c. in tribulation, 52 : 27
companionable as solitude, 560 : 3
God gave man female c., 735 : 17
no better c. than oar, 592 : 8
none like unto mind, 162 : 4
of pleasures and toils, 432 : 12
peaceful and sweet c., 314 : *n* 5
sad c. dull-eyed melancholy, 243 : 12
so man feel solitude, 735 : 17
suspicion c. of mean souls, 384 : 10
to owls, 16 : 19
Companionable as solitude, 560 : 3

Companionable (*continued*)
cold c. streams, 713 : 16
Companion's words of persuasion, 58 : 12
Companions, a few select c., 326 : 10
all her lovely c., 446 : 14
cut silver strings, 850 : 4
disparity in those they intend for c., 392 : 12
I have had c., 441 : 5
in misery, 112 : 13
innocence and health, 370 : 1
many c. for food and drink, 67 : 1
not keep pace with c., 560 : 17
of our journey, 744 : 9
such c. thou'dst unfold, 232 : 6
think of c. true, 422 : 2
while their c. slept, 511 : 23
Companionship, accident counts in c., 634 : 16
with fool no c., 72 : 18
Company, belong to C. G, 619 : 15
best c. when you read, 433 : 6
crowds without c., 384 : 5
delighting in your c., 917 : 14
doomed to c. with pain, 427 : 22
except the present c., 394 : 7
fool yet he keeps much c., 309 : 18
good c. good discourse, 271 : 4
he is wont to keep, 77 : 20
high-lived c., 369 : 14
keep no bad c., 370 : *n* 3
love and good c., 329 : 11
love to be worst of c., 321 : 20
misery loves c., 301 : 16
of just and righteous, 77 : 12
poverty parts good c., 432 : 8
separate from pleasure of c., 441 : 7
so small hardly worth saving, 622 : 13
such a jocund c., 427 : 10
take tone of c., 341 : 20
tell me thy c., 170 : 25
thou keepest, 209 : *n* 5
time lost in idle c., 309 : 20
to bear him c., 510 : 4
villainous c. spoil of me, 204 : 25
what c. good poets are, 671 : 19
with the c. of heaven, 55 : 18
Compare great with small, 103 : 7, 285 : 1
learn c. collect facts, 665 : 6
thee to summer's day, 244 : 5
with me ye women, 290 : 12
Compared, not fit that men be c. with gods, 102 : 11
nothing c. with tobacco, 462 : *n* 6
to an infant, 64 : 18
Comparison, no c. no judgment, 374 : 10
Comparisons are odious, 149 : 3
make no c., 370 : *n* 3
she and c. are odious, 253 : 19
Compartments of the floors, 494 : 15
Compass, bending sickle's c., 245 : 18
lean as c. needle, 893 : 12
of national authority, 402 : 1
produces perfect circles, 89 : 7
quadrant and sextant, 843 : 13
through all c. of notes, 305 : 9
truth within little c., 329 : 2
wide c. round fetched, 544 : 29
Compassed about with cloud of witnesses, 51 : 19
with dangers c. round, 286 : 28
Compasses, stiff twin c., 253 : 5
Compassion, bowels of c., 52 : 23
full of c. and mercy, 34 : 23
not weakness, 879 : 2
sacrifice and endurance, 838 : 11
Samaritan had c., 43 : 14
to poor or favor to rich, 289 : 14
Compassionate, one c. woman, 847 : 7
Compassionating, in charity even c., 418 : 6
Compatriots, all men my c., 166 : 2
Compeer, without c. among swindles, 623 : 18
Compel us to be equal upstairs, 694 : 8
Compelled from their own worship, 273 : 11
say nothin' without c., 568 : 13
to fight back tears, 811 : 9
to keep on guard, 658 : 24
Compels, astronomy c. soul to look upwards, 84 : 18
you or me to get up, 359 : 20
Compensate bad in man, 545 : 12
Compensation, world of c., 521 : 1
Compensations, paltry c. of man, 526 : 9
Compete, act but not to c., 65 : 10
not as woman but as human being, 898 : 6
Competency lives longer, 198 : 8
Competition and mutual envy, 264 : 19
best for race, 621 : 6
every man free to pursue c., 366 : 8
fiendishness of business c., 794 : 12
happiest conversation no c., 355 : 16
hard for individual, 621 : 6
market c. afford freedom, 790 : 3
means decentralized planning, 844 : 5
socialist c., 766 : 8
tradition approves c., 564 : 20
Complacencies of peignoir, 767 : 2
Complacency and thoughtlessness, 703 : 19
Complain, fail me I'll c., 545 : 22
I heard him c., 328 : 9
moping owl to moon c., 361 : 22
of injustice of government, 419 : 3
Complaining, soft c. flute, 305 : 12
Complaint, anno domini fatal c., 848 : 6
strange c., 624 : 19
years of discretion spent on c., 894 : 7
young man's heart's c., 574 : 22
Complaints, dust and soot of c., 664 : 18
Complete, clad in c. steel, 279 : 24
dead corse in c. steel, 219 : 12
in herself c., 287 : 8
just my vengeance c., 540 : 31
man, 69 : 6
saved and hold c., 545 : 22
self-confidence c. and bumptious, 792 : 1
simplicity, 808 : 18
something c. and great, 739 : 1
statement literature, 782 : 2
symmetrical c. colossal, 623 : 18
Thy spinning-wheel c., 314 : 22
women to become c., 898 : 7
Completed, melancholia of everything c., 658 : 3
nothing c. in lifetime, 823 : 21
Completely, men never do evil so c., 300 : 14
Completeness, unities sir a c., 547 : 13
Completing, in c. one discovery, 380 : 1
Completion of their appointed rounds, 78 : *n* 8
time available for c., 876 : 14
Complex, amoebas not c., 732 : 14
military-industrial c., 815 : 15
Complexion, fresh c. and heart, 247 : 3
is perfect gallows, 247 : 7
mislike me not for c., 198 : 29
of what c. soever, 225 : 26
Complexions, coarse c. and cheeks, 280 : 1
Complicate amassing harmony, 768 : 17
Complicated, pattern c. of dead and living, 807 : 23
state of mind, 628 : 6
Complice, il vient comme un c., 581 : *n* 2
Complies against his will, 291 : 30
Compliment, he began to c., 934 : 2
kiss through veil, 492 : 3
to be called agnostic, 684 : 10
Compliments only things we can pay, 675 : 7
reaching proper ears, 707 : 8
Comply, not c. with what expected, 877 : 3
Component, decay inherent in all c. things, 72 : 22
Components of individuality are sorrow, 72 : 23
Composed and bland, 588 : 4
superior man satisfied and c., 68 : 24
thy decent limbs c., 335 : 10
to be everlasting possession, 80 : 15
Composes visible poem, 859 : 1
Composition and fierce quality, 233 : 3
mad c., 201 : 18
regular orderly c., 352 : 8
way to c. of their own, 889 : 1
Compositions, read over your c., 355 : 8
Compound for sins they are inclined to, 291 : 6
Compounded of many simples, 212 : 18
Comprehend, capacity of human beings to c., 884 : 6
first seems to c. whole, 605 : 17
intelligence which could c., 397 : 17
whose faculties can c., 183 : 6
Comprehended, darkness c. it not, 44 : 18
mystery of beauty not c., 711 : 14
Comprehends, intellect which c. by itself, 154 : 3
some bringer of joy, 197 : 12
who c. art, 421 : 19
Comprehensive, most c. of rights, 677 : 14
most c. soul, 303 : 5
poet become more c., 809 : 9
Comprendre, tout c. tout pardonner, 417 : *n* 5
Compromise, government founded on c., 373 : 4
no government without c., 800 : 2
Compulsion, fools by heavenly c., 233 : 5
give reason on c., 203 : 31
knowledge acquired under c., 84 : 21
put upon writers, 791 : 7
sweet c. in music lie, 277 : 16
two gods Persuasion and C., 70 : 17
Compulsive ardor gives charge, 223 : 5
icy current and c. course, 231 : 18

Compulsory, bodily exercise when c., 84 : 21
education c. on all, 569 : 10
Compunctious visitings of nature, 236 : 17
Computation backward from ourselves, 178 : 21
material c., 745 : 1
Computer no better than its program, 876 : 12
Comrades, cheer up c. they come, 578 : 12
leave me here a little, 529 : 15
that fight and fall, 820 : 9
Comradeship, capable of genuine c., 689 : 21
Comte's philosophy, 595 : 13
Concatenation of circumstances, 450 : 19
Concave, hell's c., 283 : 21
shores, 215 : 1
Conceal dreary morals like vice, 669 : 14
half c. soul within, 531 : 20
its sex, 855 : 12
knowing how to c. skill, 293 : 29
no disguise can c. love, 293 : 10
reveal love it would c., 436 : 11
speech given to c. mind, 310 : 22
speech to c. thoughts, 343 : 24
speech to c. wants, 310 : *n* 1
what c. from reader, 869 : 10
Concealed beauties of writer, 326 : 19
lay c. throughout war, 630 : 2
Concealing, hazard of c., 409 : 12
Concealment like worm in bud, 214 : 5
Conceit, all in high c., 493 : 13
lies in his hamstring, 226 : 4
man wise in his own c., 25 : 19
pride and c. original sin, 323 : 28
Conceited carry their comfort, 565 : 17
man satisfied with effect on himself, 736 : 7
throw away love on c., 565 : *n* 2
Conceits, wise in your c., 47 : 22
Conceive, heart to c., 391 : 4
in sin did my mother c. me, 19 : 14
many without the one, 85 : 14
so hopeless to c., 607 : 18
tongue not able to c., 197 : 10
virgin shall c., 29 : 13
wise or stupid thing can man c., 396 : 22
Conceived by the Holy Ghost, 55 : 2
greater than God cannot be c., 136 : 5
in liberty, 523 : 4
nation so c., 523 : 4
there is a man child c., 15 : 7
well c. is clearly said, 311 : 4
when Charlemagne was c., 717 : 4
Concentered, wretch c. all in self, 430 : 10
Concentrate their energies, 679 : 10
Concentrates his mind wonderfully, 355 : 25
Concentration camp universe, 881 : 9
of business, 621 : 6
on electric chair, 893 : 2
Concept, essential c. and first truth, 882 : 5
of length, 776 : 3
of time makes possible Day of Judgment, 786 : 5
Concept (*continued*)
portray phenomenon c. needed, 390 : 7
to call forth c., 390 : 7
Conception, creativeness c. and birth, 704 : 13
low intellect have c., 649 : 2
sin their c., 262 : 7
Conceptions, nonsense of c. of sovereignty, 837 : 14
Concepts, abstract c., 390 : 7
can't form children on own c., 395 : 16
physical c. free creations, 763 : 10
stairs of c., 857 : 4
Conceptual, polyp would be c., 649 : 2
Concern, conduct largest c. of life, 588 : 23
for man and his fate, 763 : 8
mankind's c. is charity, 337 : 9
our c. be peace of mind, 92 : 13
your c. Roman to rule under law, 105 : 24
your c. when neighbor's wall on fire, 109 : 11
Concerns, entrusted with great c., 69 : 16
Concert of free peoples, 682 : 13
Concessions born of earnest struggle, 556 : 4
of the weak, 372 : 11
Conciliate with dignity, 358 : 6
Conciliation, no government without c., 800 : 2
religion c. of powers, 673 : 2
Concise, vigorous writing c., 729 : 7
Conclave of the night's stars, 71 : 3
Conclude against wall of stone, 899 : 15
grant before we c. prayer, 305 : 29
only on edge of grave, 634 : 19
Concludes with Cupid's curse, 177 : 7
Conclusion, foregone c., 231 : 16
lame and impotent c., 230 : 12
leap to c., 887 : 15
of the whole matter, 27 : 27
Conclusions from insufficient premises, 620 : 16
most impossible of c., 703 : 9
necessary c., 525 : 1
Concord and Lexington, 450 : 13
give to all nations c., 55 : 13
give you home and gracious c., 59 : 28
love quarrels in c. end, 289 : 4
lover of c., 55 : 4
of sweet sounds, 201 : 3
sweet milk of c., 239 : 19
traveled a good deal in C., 559 : 1
wolves and lambs have no c., 59 : 8
Concordant is discordant, 70 : 5
Concordia discors, 109 : *n* 3
Concrete cases, 644 : 11
general with c., 437 : 17
man has one interest, 648 : 5
Condemn, conscience makes us c. ourselves, 260 : 4
fault and not act, 228 : 5
innocent person, 343 : 5
men whom men c. as ill, 646 : 5
neither do I c., 45 : 3
nor years c., 727 : 1
these men because few, 560 : 22
try cause c. to death, 611 : 6
wrongs we seek to c., 821 : 7
Condemnation, justice thunders c., 555 : 24
Condemned alike to groan, 361 : 12
by my own gods, 849 : 16
cells of Newgate, 620 : 9
into everlasting redemption, 210 : 1
judge c. when criminal absolved, 111 : 10
soul c. to be, 606 : 8
to kill time, 886 : 1
to repeat past, 703 : 11
Condemnest, thou c. thyself, 46 : 37
Condemns, every tale c. me, 187 : 28
Condensation of sensations, 728 : 9
Condescend to take a bit, 322 : 7
Condescending, not c. to anything within reach, 85 : 17
Condition, abnormal exhausting c., 681 : 1
bears stamp of human c., 165 : 18
confronts us not theory, 631 : 10
death inviolable c. of life, 755 : 8
decoyed into our c., 310 : 1
ideal c. to be right by instinct, 74 : 22
indispensable c. of freedom, 730 : 17
live in equality of c., 618 : 10
of complete simplicity, 808 : 18
of man condition of war, 264 : 12
on which God given liberty, 397 : 21
sweat and whine about c., 574 : 24
world in good c., 310 : 7
Conditions, all sorts and c. of men, 55 : 5
dat prevail, 825 : 15
four c. for happiness, 882 : 12
stars govern our c., 234 : 26
Condolement, obstinate c., 218 : 4
Condones, as the turn c., 863 : 19
Condor's quill, 571 : 1
Conduct, characters and c. of rulers, 380 : 9
courage and c. of army, 379 : 2
if c. mean and paltry, 88 : 23
life teaches c., 645 : 6
positive science of c., 733 : 15
right argument wrong, 371 : 15
right c., 73 : 2
rottenness begins in c., 388 : 14
shaped c. on faith, 730 : 14
three-fourths of life, 588 : 23
unethical and lousy, 858 : 17
we do not inspire c., 294 : 5
your blooming in whirlwind, 889 : 20
Conductor, passengers ask c., 761 : 6
when you receive fare, 614 : 16
Conductors, truths of which symbols c., 436 : 20
Cone, country an inverted c., 356 : 3
nature in terms of c., 638 : 3
of self-thrown shade, 897 : 5
Cones, eat c. under pines, 747 : 5
Confabulate, if birds c. or no, 377 : 23
Confederacy, principle kept C. together, 521 : 8
Confer, heaven about to c. great office, 89 : 25
nothing to c., 429 : 13
Conference maketh a ready man, 181 : 13
my last press c., 882 : 17
Conferring rather than accepting favors, 81 : *n* 1
Confers, honor to him who c. it, 327 : 18
Confess faith therein, 821 : 6
man knows how to c., 347 : 20
our sins, 54 : 11

Confess (*continued*)
to little faults, 293 : 37
yourself to heaven, 223 : 8
Confession in open court, 391 : 12
next thing to innocence, 112 : 15
no refuge from c., 450 : 17
Confessions, trench c., 792 : 15
Confessor, deceive not thy c., 269 : 15
Confide in strength without boasting, 388 : 12
Confided, secret not secret if c., 561 : 11
Confidence and strength in air, 744 : 2
by experience with fear, 786 : 13
forfeit c. of citizens, 524 : 10
have c. in the people, 390 : 2
in justice of people, 521 : 12
of Christian with four aces, 626 : 20
of twenty-one, 354 : 5
on which all else depends, 737 : 8
peace a disposition for c., 308 : 3
plant of slow growth, 350 : 18
zeal loyalty, 771 : 13
Confidences, passages seem c., 499 : 17
Confident, glad c. morning, 541 : 9
in this will I be c., 18 : 12
tomorrows, 428 : 18
with vine leaves in hair, 600 : 5
Confides, England c. every man do duty, 408 : *n* 5
Confiding, beauty for c. youth, 428 : 23
Confine, hies to his c., 217 : 25
on very verge of her c., 233 : 19
Confined, cabined cribbed c., 238 : 23
forfeit to a c. doom, 245 : 13
slender waist c., 276 : 5
Confirm, experiments not to c. ideas, 552 : 6
tidings as they roll, 325 : 9
Confirmations, to jealous c. strong, 231 : 7
Confirmed, hypothesis c. by experience, 880 : 8
Confirms, each c. a prison, 805 : 13
Conflict, avoidance of c., 853 : 14
field of human c., 744 : 6
heat of c., 427 : 25
laws c. courts decide, 402 : 3
the harder the c., 384 : 13
victory by expanding c., 788 : 15
Conflicting economic interest, 790 : 5
interests and appetites, 778 : 11
interests of society, 737 : 4
Conflicts, elemental c., 813 : 1
resolve inner c., 789 : 14
Confluent, design of all parts c., 590 : 13
Conform and be dull, 803 : 6
to tyrant custom, 167 : 14
world c. to mathematics, 738 : 1
Conformable, governments c. to nature of governed, 324 : 3
Conformation of his mind, 488 : 2
Conforming, when she stopped c., 898 : 4
Conformity between soul and nature, 703 : 6
knowledge c. of object and intellect, 137 : 8
most in request, 496 : 22
Confound all unity on earth, 239 : 19
foolish things to c. wise, 48 : 1
the language of all earth, 8 : 5
Confounded, confusion worse c., 285 : 2
Hellas, 81 : 11
reason in itself c., 225 : 31
Confounding her astronomers, 733 : 3
Confounds, attempt and not deed c., 237 : 18
Confront night storms hunger, 574 : 1
Confrontation, born of their c., 882 : 4
Confronts, condition c. us not theory, 631 : 10
Confucius least blameworthy, 375 : 2
Confuse, not c. dissent with disloyalty, 872 : 17
Confused alarms of struggle, 587 : 16
be not c. in words, 125 : 14
thought and passion all c., 337 : 2
world harmoniously c., 334 : 15
Confusing beams from memory's lamp, 856 : 9
dreams are c., 61 : 2
Confusion, all else c., 531 : 7
all is c. beyond it, 372 : 8
be whole again beyond c., 749 : 10
bright things come to c., 195 : 23
in ruin and c. hurled, 325 : 11
life inclusion and c., 653 : 13
never swept into c., 718 : 6
now made masterpiece, 238 : 5
on thy banners wait, 363 : 4
today's achievement tomorrow's c., 631 : 18
worse confounded, 285 : 2
Confute change hands and still confute, 290 : 16
Confuted, tongue c. by conscience, 276 : 17
Congealed, depths c. in heart of sea, 9 : 35
Congenial horrors hail, 345 : 5
to my heart, 370 : 15
Congo, Gods of the C., 765 : 7
Congratulate, to c. friends made haste, 305 : 5
Congratulatory regrets, 502 : 19
Congregation, latter has largest c., 318 : 5
of vapors, 220 : 28
Congrès, le C. ne marche pas, 382 : *n* 6
Congress doesn't run it waltzes, 382 : 9
halls of American C., 615 : 4
Jehovah and Continental C., 385 : 11
no criminal class except C., 625 : 3
of eminent celebrities, 615 : 14
power to declare Act of C. void, 644 : 17
shall make no law, 391 : 14
Congruity of reason and will, 436 : 19
Congs, kinquering c. titles take, 659 : 10
Conjecture, though puzzling not beyond c., 275 : 5
withhold finding or c., 396 : 7
Conjectures, surmises jealousies c., 205 : 18
Conjured, Nazarite c. the devil, 198 : 18
Conjures up most evil demons, 678 : 6
Connect, only c., 764 : 9
Connection, ancient heavenly c., 906 : 1
between them and Britain, 378 : 12
no c. between political ideas and imagination, 866 : 1
of individual man, 922 : 9
Connections, air of lost c., 893 : 2
Connects and equals all, 336 : 22
Conned, learned and c. by rote, 217 : 4
Connubiality, wictim o' c., 546 : 19
Conquer but to save, 443 : 17
England wont to c. others, 194 : 15
Conquer (*continued*)
every day c. them anew, 396 : 25
fight and c. again, 363 : 16
hard to catch and c., 601 : 1
he went forth to c., 53 : 10
in the end truth will c., 143 : 10
in this sign c., 127 : 3
like Douglas c., 366 : 11
love that run away, 272 : 3
resolve to c. or die, 379 : 2
war or war conquer us, 818 : 7
we must, 446 : 2
who every day must c. them anew, 396 : 25
without risk, 275 : 16
you cannot c. America, 351 : 5
Conquered, establish peace spare c., 105 : 24
fame of heroes, 575 : 8
fever called living c. at last, 527 : 6
human natur, 547 : 8
I came I saw I c., 99 : 23
most calamitous to c., 81 : 10
nation perpetually to be c., 372 : 16
O pale Galilean, 633 : 6
through his honor I c. him, 264 : 8
through time time c., 807 : 7
tyranny not easily c., 384 : 13
woe, 245 : 3
woe to the c., 134 : 35
women like to be c., 539 : 22
you have c. Galilean, 127 : 5
Conquering army on border, 553 : 11
he went forth c., 53 : 10
hero comes, 346 : 7
Conqueror creates a muse, 276 : 2
favorite of mother a c., 679 : 6
lie at proud foot of c., 202 : 19
Worm, 526 : 5
Conquerors, Americanos c., 574 : 5
Conquers, if nature c., 413 : 22
love c. all things, 103 : 24
no one c. who doesn't fight, 150 : 4
ruling passion c. reason, 336 : 2
wherever Roman c. he dwells, 115 : 8
Conquest, every thought a c., 865 : 10
horse noblest c. of man, 349 : 1
of illiteracy first, 871 : 15
of joy of freedom, 820 : 9
of world by creed, 891 : 5
right of c., 358 : 14
shameful c. of itself, 194 : 15
Conquest's crimson wing, 363 : 4
Conquests, carnage and c. cease, 459 : 7
even to Antipodes, 181 : *n* 5
honorable c., 373 : 9
shrunk to this, 216 : 8
through legislation, 483 : 8
tramplings of three c., 275 : 3
Conquistadors, language inherited from C., 861 : 1
Con's, from pro's and c. they fell, 169 : 16
Conscience ae thing I cannae bear, 668 : 22
alone with c., 660 : 9
ancient rites of c., 860 : 13
and cowardice the same, 674 : 25
argue according to c., 282 : 4
aroused popular c., 777 : 2
bend c. to dealing, 569 : 1
beyond physicians, 517 : 19
brilliance without c., 825 : 2

Conscience (*continued*)
but word cowards use, 187 : 30
catch c. of the king, 221 : 10
clear c. is sure card, 175 : 16
clear c. or none, 856 : 3
confides in c., 391 : 7
courage of c., 484 : 18
coward c. dost afflict, 187 : 27
dictates of c., 383 : 6
does make cowards, 221 : 12
excused from it as against c., 364 : 7
freedom of c., 625 : 9
gentle beast of good c., 197 : 16
god to all mortals, 91 : 13
good c. continual feast, 260 : 3
guardian of community rules, 751 : 14
hath thousand tongues, 187 : 28
Hebraism strictness of c., 588 : 21
in everything, 360 : 8
is a coward, 369 : 15
is great ledger book, 260 : 4
judgment enough, 660 : 9
justice temporary but c. eternal, 156 : 3
liberty of c., 273 : 11
little grain of c., 530 : 18
live without c., 609 : 13
love gets better of c., 641 : 7
makes egotists, 675 : 4
matters of c., 365 : 5
money in jar c. clear, 618 : 16
my c. is quiet, 702 : 9
no more to do with gallantry, 398 : 27
no witness so dreadful as c., 95 : 19
not cut c. to fit fashions, 863 : 10
of Chancellor, 263 : 13
of her worth, 287 : 6
of people's representatives, 777 : 2
only guide c., 744 : 11
or vanity appalled, 716 : 13
perception of rejection, 678 : 7
perfect interpreter of life, 794 : 11
private c. for guide, 305 : 20
quiet c. stands brunt of life, 76 : 20
salve c. by our concurrence, 753 : 7
science without c. ruin of soul, 157 : 13
seared with hot iron, 50 : 27
sit alone with c., 660 : 9
social c. of nation, 909 : 16
still and quiet c., 249 : 4
strict regard to c., 382 : 11
tongue confuted by c., 276 : 17
uncreated c. of race, 777 : 18
upright and stainless, 141 : 19
value it next to good c., 271 : 13
void of offense, 46 : 30
warns somebody looking, 772 : 17
what can assuage c., 260 : 5
with injustice corrupted, 185 : 17
with intellect or with c., 527 : 14
with whole c. listen, 770 : 16
Conscience-calmed, thou be c., 478 : 8
Consciences, historian of fine c., 684 : 8
Conscientious, sensible and c. men, 354 : *n* 4
Conscious, beyond what c. ego can reach, 754 : 13
elevate life by c. endeavor, 559 : 24
in c. virtue bold, 334 : 12
less c. actions mold lives, 620 : 7
life burden, 721 : 1
mind c. of rectitude, 104 : *n* 14
Conscious (*continued*)
mind trained like parrot, 754 : 9
movements reflex, 603 : 5
of our own existence, 87 : 21
that we are perceiving, 87 : 21
water saw its God, 292 : 5
Consciously, greatest things achieved not c. directed, 844 : 7
institutions and customs not c. designed, 844 : 8
not try to think c., 711 : 3
Consciousness, all in reader's c., 739 : 3
black c., 916 : 12
captivity is c., 605 : 9
existence determines c., 562 : 16
freedom stretches to limits of c., 755 : 1
growth of mind widening c., 754 : 3
Hellenism spirit of c., 588 : 21
inseparable like life and c., 790 : 18
is disease, 705 : 13
life c. of what we can do, 784 : 19
like bird's life, 648 : 13
national c., 682 : 4
neither with volition nor c., 798 : 13
no c. without pain, 754 : 2
not c. that determines existence, 562 : 16
of freedom, 422 : 12
one unbroken stream, 648 : 14
pace of parts of c., 648 : 13
painful achievement, 754 : 3
poor slipping out of c., 908 : 5
religious feeling in c., 580 : 9
science of c., 733 : 15
stream of c., 648 : 13
use small portion of c., 648 : 3
welcomes or rejects, 648 : 15
whole past experience in c., 639 : 12
Consciousnesses melt into each other, 648 : 14
Conscripted unvictorious ones, 795 : 16
Consecrate to thee, 442 : 18
we cannot c., 523 : 4
with thine own hues, 466 : 9
Consecrated bread to take, 604 : 10
it above our power, 523 : 4
not buried in c. ground, 640 : 16
Consecration and poet's dream, 427 : 17
from within himself, 831 : 24
what we did had c., 503 : 11
Consecutive, two c. moments, 580 : 3
Consensus, President is c. seeker, 879 : 4
Consent, deriving powers from c., 387 : 9
if sinners entice thee c. not, 23 : 2
not govern without c., 520 : 1
not inferior without your c., 786 : 12
of governed, 387 : 9, 725 : 20
of governors and governed, 381 : 2
of the governed, 578 : 5
reference to one c., 207 : 8
silence gives c., 369 : 26
taxed without c., 367 : *n* 9
whispering I will ne'er c. consented, 460 : 15
Consents, no injustice to person who c., 135 : 1
poverty but not my will c., 193 : 21
Consequence, applause of great c., 356 : 17
deepest c., 236 : 9
repentance is fear of c., 293 : 24
Consequence (*continued*)
servitude c. of crime, 397 : 21
'tis almost c., 607 : 8
trammel up the c., 236 : 22
Consequences, endure the c., 793 : 12
I note and enjoy noting, 654 : 8
in nature c., 615 : 11
logical c. are beacons, 596 : 3
looking toward c., 650 : 8
pernicious c., 553 : 20
serious and alarming c., 379 : 6
will be the same, 384 : 18
Conservation harmony between men and land, 795 : 11
principle of c. of force, 583 : 21
Conservatism adherence to old and tried, 521 : 4
meanness in argument of c., 497 : 34
Conservative government hypocrisy, 501 : 23
habit c. agent of society, 648 : 7
little Liberal or C., 628 : 23
Consider anything don't cry, 613 : 13
beauty sufficient end, 714 : 15
her ways and be wise, 23 : 11
him well, 234 : 7
how my light is spent, 282 : 15
in day of adversity c., 27 : 7
let every man c. last day, 74 : 7
lilies of field, 38 : 4
my cat Jeoffrey, 365 : 13
my traveling expenses, 826 : 17
one must c. the end, 296 : 15
where you come out, 112 : 4
wise what they cleave to, 124 : 24
Consideration, first c. earning living, 312 : 21
like an angel came, 207 : 3
made arrogant by c., 81 : 7
of public object, 80 : 16
wives to be paid in c., 889 : 2
Considers, no physician c. own good, 84 : 5
Consimility, wonderful c. of fancy, 263 : *n* 2
Consist, by him all things c., 50 : 9
Consistency, foolish c., 497 : 2
with c. great soul has nothing to do, 497 : 2
Consistent, not one altogether c., 720 : 3
with letter and spirit, 402 : 6
Consolation, companions c. to wretched, 112 : 13
in thanks of Republic, 524 : 4
thought of suicide c., 657 : 23
Console, not to be consoled but to c., 138 : 15
physical science not c. me, 299 : 16
Consoler of lonely, 617 : 7
Consoling in depths of affliction, 521 : 3
Consonants, only c. and vowels, 811 : 1
Consort, such c. as they keep, 278 : 25
Conspicuous by absence, 466 : 4
consumption, 685 : 2
wastefulness, 685 : 4
Conspiracies, organized c., 862 : 20
Conspiracy against law and order, 908 : 6
against manhood, 496 : 22
against the public, 366 : 2
O.C., 215 : 19
open-eyed C., 247 : 28
to oppress rob degrade, 556 : 14
Conspirators, bearded c., 800 : 7

Conspire, causes which c. to blind, 332 : 19
you and I with Him c., 517 : 13
Conspired against God with Lucifer, 183 : 20
Constabulary duty's to be done, 628 : 3
Constancy and valor our shield, 744 : 9
hope c. in wind, 456 : 15
in realms above, 434 : 3
let him in c., 302 : *n* 4
obstinacy in bad cause c. in good, 274 : 8
of purpose, 502 : 15
of women who love me, 680 : 3
Constant as northern star, 216 : 3
as Penelope, 918 : 8
as various, 833 : 3
but yet woman, 203 : 24
friendship c. save in love, 209 : 9
heart, 918 : 16
image of the creature, 213 : 29
in nature inconstancy, 295 : 6
nothing c. but inconstancy, 321 : 16
one here will c. be, 302 : 14
sacrament of praise, 767 : 11
so c. to me and so kind, 476 : 4
to one thing c. never, 209 : 16
Constellation, constitutional c., 821 : 6
poses war against revolution, 866 : 9
principles bright c., 389 : 2
Constellations, not want c. nearer, 575 : 11
seasons and c., 807 : 10
when they wane, 71 : 3
Constituted for practice of good, 89 : 19
Constitution, act against C. void, 367 : 9
and laws of U.S., 391 : 13
basic element in C., 788 : 14
by my physical c. I am ordinary, 381 : 13
cases involving Federal C., 678 : 3
color-blind, 615 : 1
difficulties from C., 506 : 4
does not provide for second class, 824 : 11
end within scope of C., 402 : 6
follows flag, 721 : 12
forbidden by C., 402 : 1
freedoms guaranteed by C., 776 : 13
genius of C., 351 : 6
in view of C., 615 : 1
intended to endure, 402 : 5
it is a c. we are expounding, 402 : 4
law for rulers and people, 553 : 20
laws and c., 391 : 4
letter and spirit of C., 402 : 6
like British C., 640 : 7
looks to indestructible Union, 514 : 4
make real the C., 753 : 6
most remarkable work, 517 : 24
named a democracy, 80 : 17
not contain word democracy, 741 : 15
not merely for generation, 444 : 7
of United States a shield, 553 : 20
one country one c., 451 : 4
openly invaded, 390 : 14
ordain and establish C., 391 : 10
our C. is in operation, 348 : 16
people made the C., 402 : 8
principle of English c., 365 : 18
principles of free c. lost, 383 : 8
proportioned to human c., 330 : 22
sail no anchor, 489 : 9
support C. obey laws, 725 : 20
Constitution (*continued*)
venerable parts of c., 373 : 10
what judges say it is, 700 : 1
what's C. between friends, 639 : 18
Constitutional constellation, 821 : 6
exercise c. right, 521 : 11
government, 700 : 3, 719 : 8
inconsistent with c. theory, 846 : 17
means which are c., 402 : 6
period of c. government, 719 : 8
rights, 700 : 3
shield, 794 : 15
statesman, 597 : 9
symptom of c. liberty, 383 : 11
Constitutions, equity our c. enshrine, 737 : 3
make and alter c., 379 : 10
Constraineth, spirit within me c. me, 16 : 22
Constraining norm selectively shaping, 685 : 4
Constraint, freedom and c., 849 : 5
Constructed, thing c. loved after c., 742 : 6
Constructing tribal lays, 708 : 21
Construction and creation, 742 : 6
find the mind's c., 236 : 15
Constructive, superstition c. religion, 580 : 8
Construe, have profferer c. Aye, 189 : 31
Consul, my youth when Plancus was c., 108 : 5
shanty of c., 699 : 13
Consule, fortunatam natam me c. Roman, 99 : *n* 2
Consuls, each year new c., 123 : 17
our c. and our praetors, 701 : 15
Consulship, Rome natal neath my c., 99 : 2
Consult concerning great goddess, 421 : 19
first c. our private ends, 294 : *n* 4
Consume according to need, 563 : *n* 1
engines of despotism, 390 : 1
entire combustible world, 713 : 17
my heart away, 715 : 2
time c. strongest cord, 431 : 24
without producing, 680 : 8
your own smoke, 664 : 18
Consumed, bush was not c., 9 : 10
by either fire or fire, 808 : 15
days are c. like smoke, 21 : 4
them as stubble, 9 : 35
Consumedly, they laughed c., 329 : 9
Consumer, promoting interest of c., 366 : 7
Consumes, delight that c. desire, 632 : 14
painter's brush c. dreams, 715 : 13
what community c., 871 : 9
Consumeth, watching for riches c. flesh, 36 : 2
Consuming rag and bone, 717 : 9
serves industrial system by c., 872 : 4
Consummated, marriages c. on earth, 176 : 3
Consummation devoutly to be wished, 221 : 12
quiet c. have, 243 : 28
Consumption, captain of men of death was C., 302 : 17
conspicuous c., 685 : 2
of the purse, 206 : 5
Consumption (*continued*)
private c., 871 : 11
sole purpose of production, 366 : 7
Contact contact, 557 : 21
possible to flesh, 804 : 22
with the soil, 717 : 14
word preserves c., 755 : 15
Contagion, foul c. spread, 280 : 22
of world's slow stain, 469 : 12
rest of us in danger of c., 839 : 17
to this world, 222 : 23
war is a c., 780 : 5
Contagious, base c. clouds, 203 : 5
blastments imminent, 218 : 27
Contain, I c. multitudes, 575 : 2
one the other will c., 605 : 21
show c. and nourish all world, 191 : 5
Contained nothing but itself, 635 : 6
Container, bright c. can contain, 874 : 1
Contains all nothing lacking, 575 : 6
the cistern c., 404 : 4
what fortitude soul c., 608 : 4
Contemneth small things, 35 : 31
Contemplate entangled bank, 515 : 1
my flaccid shape, 830 : 12
our forefathers, 365 : 3
Contemplated, object is to be c., 706 : 7
Contemplation, beneath thy c., 563 : 13
everything object of c., 437 : 22
he for c. formed, 285 : 18
her best nurse C., 279 : 22
leisurely c. of art, 740 : 14
mind serene for c., 326 : *n* 2
more than reading, 301 : 4
right c., 73 : 2
sundry c. of my travels, 212 : 18
Contemplative or saintly life, 867 : 5
Contemporaries, man lives life of c., 755 : 7
society of c., 496 : 21
Contemporary, both c. and hereditary, 571 : 2
creation of c. culture, 871 : 1
man rationalized myths, 885 : 16
Contempt against majesty of heaven, 346 : 4
and anger of lip, 214 : 16
comes from head, 463 : 3
familiarity breeds c., 66 : 4, 626 : 14
for c. too high, 295 : 2
for governor who is afraid, 74 : 10
for wildest blow, 647 : 21
no weakness no c., 289 : 9
reading it with perfect c., 798 : 10
silence is c., 504 : 6
speak of moderns without c., 341 : 23
treating with c. all from God, 156 : 9
Contemptible, bored more c. than bore, 620 : 1
rendered United States c., 682 : 10
ridiculous c. animal, 350 : 3
struggle, 372 : 4
Contemptuous, discerning reader c., 685 : 15
Contend, different schools c. freely, 826 : 12
gods c. in vain, 413 : 26
no more love, 541 : 21
seven towns c. for Homer, 257 : *n* 5
ye powers of heaven, 292 : 17
Contending against some being, 575 : 23
calm c. kings, 189 : 23
fierce c. nations, 326 : 5

Contending (*continued*)
for liberty, 379 : 1
leaders ambitiously c., 398 : 2
with adversity, 259 : 7
Content at the last, 808 : 9
be c. with your lot, 66 : 12
don't be c., 743 : 10
farewell c., 231 : 11
good pleasure ease c., 337 : 10
humble livers in c., 248 : 27
I am c., 418 : 11
if reversion nourish, 808 : 9
in health and mind's c., 310 : 8
in tight hot cell, 836 : 20
in whatsoever state to be c., 50 : 8
land of lost c., 691 : 9
majority of men c., 154 : 2
make c. with fortunes fit, 234 : 1
mind c. both crown and kingdom, 178 : 11
money means and c., 212 : 1
my crown is called c., 186 : 8
natural c., 713 : 6
nothing less will c. me, 372 : 17
poor and c. is rich, 231 : 1
shut up in measureless c., 237 : 12
thoughts that savor of c., 178 : 10
to breathe his native air, 332 : 10
to entertain lag-end of my life, 205 : 1
to live it all again, 716 : 2
travelers must be c., 210 : 32
wisdom of just c., 610 : 8
with life retire from world, 106 : 13
with my harm, 212 : 2
with small means, 536 : 6
with vegetable love, 628 : 7
with your lot, 66 : 12
Contented, always c. with his life, 486 : 4
I'm c. you should stay, 560 : 30
live on little with c. mind, 101 : 8
men employed best c., 348 : 21
most enjoy c. least, 244 : 9
slaves howe'er c., 375 : 19
white people never c., 419 : 12
wi' little, 409 : 23
Contentedness, procurer of c., 270 : 34
Contention, let long c. cease, 588 : 2
man of strife and c., 32 : 9
Contentions are like bars of a castle, 24 : 21
fat c., 281 : 18
of a wife, 24 : 25
Contentious, petty wisdom c., 90 : 1
Contentment characteristic of East, 818 : 11
fails, 368 : 16
in c. still feel need, 767 : 3
nor poorest receive c., 255 : 5
preaches c. to toad, 707 : 5
recover through c. with physician, 79 : 16
Western not to know c., 818 : 11
Contents, inability of mind to correlate all c., 816 : 8
torn out and stripped, 346 : 15
Contest, end a c. quicker, 398 : 26
great c. follows, 376 : 26
let fools c., 337 : 9
this is a people's c., 522 : 2
Contests, hard c. men must win, 687 : 4
what mighty c. rise, 333 : 24
Context, immediate c. of history, 823 : 21
Context (*continued*)
our c. majesty of space, 852 : 3
Contiguity, boundless c. of shade, 376 : 18
Continence, give me c. but not now, 129 : 3
Continent allotted by Providence, 552 : 13
almost a c. hardly a nation, 793 : 11
Americans prefer C., 725 : 17
brought forth on c., 523 : 4
disappoint a c., 619 : 10
heart no island but c., 180 : 13
iron curtain across C., 746 : 9
man home in every c., 870 : 14
man is a piece of the c., 254 : 22
mighty c. hitherto unknown, 151 : 6
most momentous question on c., 592 : 9
one small spot a c., 610 : 8
our c. the old one, 397 : 14
peculiar genius of each c., 912 : 3
striving to grasp c., 592 : 5
untamed c., 592 : 6
Continental, Jehovah and C. Congress, 385 : 11
never tolerate two c. powers, 812 : 18
Continents, Africa giant among c., 867 : 13
American c. not subjects for colonization, 408 : 1
dissolve into sea, 869 : 13
long-forgotten peoples of c., 912 : 5
potters' fields of four c., 571 : 3
Contingencies, O to be self-balanced for c., 574 : 1
Continual comfort in a face, 184 : 13
contentions of wife are c. dropping, 24 : 25
endeavor in c. motion, 207 : 6
feast, 24 : 7
live in c. mortification, 346 : 3
small have c. plodders won, 190 : 12
Continually, think c. of truly great, 876 : 15
times change and move c., 174 : 8
Continue, stealing will c. stealing, 569 : 1
Continued, not one c. faithful until old age, 86 : 5
Continueth, he fleeth and c. not, 15 : 33
Continuing, faculty of c. to improve, 378 : 1
no c. city, 51 : 25
Continuity, self has c. and sameness, 854 : 5
Continuous and seems always existing, 64 : 2
and stationary music, 417 : 14
as stars that shine, 427 : 8
brain changes c., 648 : 14
nature one and c., 558 : 20
use of any organ, 393 : 7
Contra naturam, 793 : 2
Contract, passions we inspire c. time, 734 : 5
permanent c. on temporary feeling, 641 : 6
succession bourn none, 247 : 26
'twixt Hannah God and me, 615 : 13
unspoken c. of wife and her works, 889 : 2
Contracted, orbed in this c. star, 794 : 4
Contraction of life, 754 : 6
Contracts with the people, 788 : 8
Contradict, do I c. myself, 575 : 2
proverbs c. each other, 876 : 3
speak though it c. everything you said, 497 : 2
Contradiction between imperialism and Chinese, 826 : 8
phrase long poem c., 527 : 12
what a c. is man, 300 : 11
when we risk no c., 331 : 14
woman's a c. still, 335 : 25
world a c., 704 : 3
Contradictions exist side by side, 581 : 20
in Chinese society, 826 : 8
Contraption, homemade c., 835 : 1
verbal c., 869 : 10
Contraries, by c. execute all things, 247 : 26
life of one another, 274 : 18
Contrariously, work c., 207 : 8
Contrariwise 612 : 24
Contrary blast proclaims, 289 : 2
bringeth bliss, 185 : 7
everythink c. with me, 548 : 22
hear what you say to c., 499 : 24
Mary quite c., 930 : 6
men of c. character, 68 : 16
not state things c. to fact, 95 : 18
runneth not to the c., 365 : 17
Spirit and flesh c., 49 : 29
to the c. notwithstanding, 391 : 13
Contribute to diversion or improvement of country, 326 : 7
Contribution according to capacity, 563 : *n* 1
to current literature, 620 : 19
Contributions to peace of world, 788 : 7
Contrite, broken and c. heart, 19 : 19
Contrivance of human wisdom, 373 : 21
Contrivances, wisdom of human c., 372 : 15
Contrive, head to c., 289 : 16
no farther tides, 843 : 13
our fees to pilfer, 82 : 2
Contrived corridors, 804 : 14
double debt to pay, 370 : 13
Contriving, life a jest of Fate's c., 332 : *n* 2
Control and communication theory, 831 : 22
atomic energy, 734 : 14
authority nation cannot c., 616 : 1
chance shall not c., 584 : 15
civilian c. of military, 788 : 14
experiments to c. ideas, 552 : 6
forces beyond my c., 905 : 6
forces of nature, 814 : 12
grammar c. even kings, 298 : 13
lease of my true love c., 245 : 13
man c. the wind, 585 : 9
nothing short of club c., 676 : 16
nuclear c., 891 : 15
ought to c. thoughts, 515 : 4
over human behavior, 665 : 4
prison walls cannot c., 296 : *n* 3
stops at the shore, 458 : 25
without c. over ourselves, 397 : 13
Controlled by world constructed by men, 862 : 12
events c. me, 523 : 6
Controlling intelligence understands, 125 : 6
Controls, love of other sights c., 251 : 15

Controversy, fear of c. not
warranted, 872 : 19
hearts of c., 215 : 5
Contumely, proud man's c., 221 : 12
Conturbat, timor mortis c. me, 153 : 6
Convenience comfort prestige, 925 : 4
he that for c. takes oath, 291 : 22
Convenient, a c. season, 46 : 31
light switch, 852 : 1
never c. time for childbirth, 848 : 10
that there be gods, 113 : 10
Convent of the Sacred Heart, 804 : 25
Convention, by c. there is color, 79 : 11
is ruler of all, 72 : 12
system has faults, 788 : 11
Conventional, ground in mill of
c., 652 : 10
merely c. signs, 613 : 22
picture of femininity, 898 : 4
Conventionalities, punctilious in
c., 620 : 20
Conventionality not morality, 555 : 18
Conventions, profound skepticism
favorable to c., 704 : 8
restrictions and c. of world, 621 : 15
Convent's narrow room, 427 : 28
solitary gloom, 334 : 27
Convents, happy c., 340 : 26
Conversation art of never appearing
a bore, 667 : 5
brisk as bee in c., 353 : 22
for c. well endued, 322 : 17
good nature agreeable in c., 326 : 17
happiest c. no competition, 355 : 16
hinges in French c., 360 : 23
improved for literary c., 258 : *n* 2
is but carving, 323 : 1
Johnson's c. was mustard, 386 : 13
of most searching sort, 497 : 20
of select companions, 326 : 10
one of greatest pleasures, 751 : 15
preaching word for dull c., 432 : 19
smaller excellences of c., 386 : 1
socializing instrument, 784 : 9
three cannot take part in c., 497 : 20
unforced as c. passed, 486 : 3
wants leisure, 751 : 15
when you fall into a man's c., 327 : 13
where there's half a c., 819 : 1
writing name for c., 360 : 5
Conversational or homely type, 730 : 15
Conversations, without pictures or
c., 611 : 2
Converse and live with ease, 338 : 14
formed by thy c., 338 : 1
high c. with mighty dead, 345 : 7
Hispanic for c. with God, 357 : 19
with men of unseen
generations, 142 : 22
with mountains and fens, 735 : 8
Conversing I forget all time, 285 : 27
Conversion, goal of Providence c. of
souls, 154 : 13
refuse till c. of Jews, 296 : 27
Convert Bill of Rights, 821 : 8
you into stew, 806 : 9
Converted and become as
children, 40 : 1
love c. from thing it was, 244 : 17
silenced man not c., 637 : 5
Converting human beings to
machines, 562 : 18
Convex, organ too c. or concave, 498 : 5
Convey the wise it call, 225 : 9
Convey (*continued*)
to others what we are, 860 : 13
Convict, swart c. Bunyan, 570 : 11
Convicted, Daniel had c. them, 36 : 15
Conviction, do evil from religious
c., 300 : 14
editor's c., 814 : 3
faithful to c. to old age, 86 : 5
impeachment for and c. of high
crimes, 391 : 11
sadness of c., 643 : 19
the best lack all c., 714 : 12
we are loved, 491 : 15
Convictions, enter c. in open
lists, 737 : 7
love sometimes stronger than
c., 861 : 15
opposition that has c., 480 : 9
people in old times had c., 482 : 1
transcend own c., 644 : 16
Convince hearers of own
assertions, 84 : 1
to c. is to weaken, 739 : 10
Convinced of too little, 809 : 12
Convinces, man who c. the
world, 662 : 3
Convincing while they thought of
dining, 371 : 14
Conviviality, taper of c., 547 : 20
Convolutions of smooth-lipped
shell, 428 : 15
Convulsions, system liable to c., 666 : 4
Conwiviality, taper of c., 547 : 20
Cook, amount to Hannah C., 923 : 20
and captain bold, 627 : 7
every c. learn to govern, 731 : 4
good c. as cooks go, 731 : 11
ill c. that cannot lick fingers, 193 : 20
makes his c. his merit, 297 : 27
Cookery is an art a noble
science, 258 : 16
kissing don't last c. do, 600 : 11
Cookie, the way c. crumbles, 925 : 12
Cooking, ruling like c. small fish, 64 : 21
Cooks are gentlemen, 258 : 16
as c. go she went, 731 : 11
Epicurean c., 240 : 27
God sends meat Devil sends
c., 159 : *n* 6
guests praise it not c., 181 : 22
not live without c., 609 : 13
Cooks' own ladles, 541 : 1
Cool, caverns c. and deep, 584 : 12
clear and c. clear and c., 566 : 13
day so c. so calm, 268 : 15
glassy c. translucent wave, 280 : 3
in any case keep c., 834 : 1
in dust in c. tombs, 761 : 8
in gardens when eve c., 604 : 1
keep c. it will be all one, 498 : 17
kept breath to c. pottage, 62 : 5
kindliness of sheets, 796 : 16
Negro c. strong
imperturbable, 556 : 10
of the day, 7 : 7
one pain, 606 : 12
place was c. and pleasant, 885 : 7
sequestered vale of life, 362 : 12
Siloam's shady rill, 452 : 6
we real c., 889 : 13
winding saxophones, 761 : 11
Cooled a long age, 476 : 23
Cool-enfolding death, 576 : 5
Coolibar tree, 705 : 7
Cooling, dark c. star, 746 : 20
streams, 317 : 7
Coolness, wind to bring c. to
men, 59 : 26
Cools, till husband c., 335 : 23
time c. time clarifies, 755 : 18
Coon, gone c., 455 : 10
Cooped we live and die, 517 : 3
Cooperate stay and co., 818 : 15
Cooperation, coercion or voluntary
c., 880 : 13
spontaneous c. of free people, 682 : 17
Coordinate, nature has c.
system, 832 : 9
Coordinated effort of many, 844 : 7
Coort, supreme c. follows
iliction, 721 : 12
Coot, haunts of c., 533 : 15
Cop both prowler and father, 910 : 11
Cope, starry c. of heaven, 286 : 11
Co-perception, intellectual c., 500 : 10
Cophetua loved the beggarmaid, 192 : 1
sware oath, 530 : 17
Copious Dryden, 339 : 27
Copper, beneath her c. a worm, 558 : 9
Irishman lined with c., 623 : 12
kettledrums, 742 : 9
whiskey polishes c., 623 : 12
Copperheads, forgot c. and
assassin, 761 : 8
Coppice, leant upon c. gate, 641 : 11
Copulate in the foam, 717 : 16
Copulation, birth c. and death, 806 : 10
let c. thrive, 234 : 31
Copy, create equivalent not c., 801 : 2
leave the world no c., 213 : 17
show c. to whom you please, 386 : 12
your forefathers, 3 : 13
Copycat, life is a c., 803 : 2
Copying, by c. ancient models
perpetuated, 129 : 20
Copyists, shortened labor of c., 472 : 21
Coquette, death and i c., 760 : 1
Cor lacerare nequit, 323 : 25
Coral is far more red, 246 : 1
lip admires, 272 : 1
of his bones c. made, 247 : 21
Corals, maple puts c. on, 568 : 25
Corbeaux, le vol noir des c., 928 : 7
Cord, as unto bow c. is, 511 : 18
no c. draw forcibly as love, 259 : 18
silver c. be loosed, 27 : 25
stretch c. however fine, 471 : 14
threefold c. not quickly
broken, 26 : 24
time consume strongest c., 431 : 24
Cordelia, such sacrifices my C., 235 : 13
Cordial, gold in phisik is a c., 146 : 6
restore with c. fruit, 268 : 21
speech, 495 : 17
Cords, draw iniquity with c. of
vanity, 29 : 6
scourge of small c., 44 : 29
Core, apple's cleft through c., 414 : 1
boredom at c. of life, 301 : 10
deep heart's c., 712 : 5
hypocrite rotten to the c., 866 : 10
pounces on human c., 651 : 2
wear him in heart's c., 222 : 6
Corinth, not everyone can get to
C., 109 : 9
Corinthian a lad of mettle, 203 : 25
Coriolanus, have talk with C., 804 : 18
Corioli, Volscians in C., 242 : 26

Cork, drunkard cannot meet c., 607 : 14
lighter than c. on waves, 673 : 14
Cork-heeled shoon, 926 : 12
Corkscrew, clean tumbler and c., 547 : 16
Cormorant devouring Time, 190 : 8
sat like a c., 285 : 14
Corn, alien c., 477 : 1
before my tears did drown it, 268 : 21
colonels full of c., 693 : 2
cotton c. and taters, 672 : 19
cow's in the c., 930 : 12
crop of c. a field of tares, 177 : 10
ear on tip of stalk, 928 : 15
farmer sowing the c., 934 : 9
field of ripe c., 804 : 6
fields of c. where Troy was, 113 : 14
full c. in the ear, 42 : 1
full of kernels, 693 : 2
high as elephant's eye, 833 : 11
hope c. in chaff, 456 : 15
Jimmie crack c., 921 : 14
licker stop victim's watch, 757 : 6
like smut in c., 864 : 5
meadows rich with c., 513 : 16
never thrust sickle in another's c., 111 : 27
no use of metal c. or wine, 247 : 26
not move sickle unto neighbor's c., 11 : 18
out of olde feldes newe c., 144 : 9
rain on c. a sad thing, 103 : 11
sent not c. for rich men only, 242 : 8
shock of c. cometh in season, 15 : 18
staff of life, 319 : *n* 4
state that raises c., 674 : 13
two ears of c. grow, 322 : 12
was orient, 311 : 21
whar man gits c. pone, 626 : 12
Cornelia said These are my jewels, 259 : 20
Cornelius, my new book to you C., 101 : 13
Corner, better to dwell in a c., 24 : 33
draft fluttered flame, 817 : 3
driven from every other c., 365 : 5
head stone of the c., 21 : 25
in deepest heart, 649 : 10
in the thing I love, 231 : 6
never c. opponent, 834 : 1
of foreign field, 797 : 1
of nonsense, 438 : 7
old men from chimney c., 176 : 11
sits wind in that c., 209 : 17
thing not done in c., 46 : 35
work of art c. of creation, 643 : 6
years around seatown c., 887 : 5
Cornered-animal fear, 913 : 6
Corners, belie all c. of world, 243 : 21
come three c. of world, 202 : 20
four angels on c. of earth, 53 : 12
four c. to my bed, 294 : *n* 5
in his hand are c. of earth, 54 : 17
not wholly reap the c., 10 : 19
round earth's imagined c., 254 : 8
Cornets, played before Lord on c., 13 : 14
Cornfield, o'er green c. did pass, 212 : 33
Cornflower, ocean as blue as c., 505 : 3
Cornish, twenty thousand C. men, 500 : 13
Corollaries, axioms and c., 643 : 15
Coromandel, black men fought on C., 488 : 11
Coromandel (*continued*)
coast of C., 550 : 16
Coronation, kind as kings upon c. day, 305 : 19
Coronets, kind hearts more than c., 528 : 11
Corporal, in c. sufferance, 228 : 17
Corporation of the Goosequill, 539 : 15
rich society owes productivity to c., 871 : 16
Corporations cannot commit treason, 172 : 4
cry out against c., 451 : 5
have no souls, 172 : 4
Corpse, frozen c. was he, 510 : 5
make a lovely c., 547 : 38
of public credit, 451 : 1
putrid c. of liberty, 784 : 2
slovenly unhandsome c., 203 : 8
watch enemy's c. go by, 935 : 12
Corpse-gazings, no c. when I am gone, 95 : *n* 2
Corpses, behold they were dead c., 14 : 20
Corpulent man of fifty, 453 : 22
Corpus, habeas c., 134 : 4, 389 : 2
hoc est c., 344 : *n* 7
hoc est enim C. meum, 54 : 6
Corpus Christi, on C. heart, 892 : 4
Correct, easier critical than c., 502 : 3
in cypress wood, 827 : 14
what all mortals may c., 322 : 19
Corrected, revised and c. by Author, 346 : 15
Corrections, error bursting with c., 662 : 21
Correctness, passion with c., 651 : 4
Correggios and stuff, 371 : 21
Correlate, inability of mind to c. all contents, 816 : 8
Correlative, objective c., 809 : 5
Correspondences, storm of c., 874 : 16
Correspondent to command, 247 : 17
Corridor, lit c. races through dark c., 897 : 4
Corridors, contrived c., 804 : 14
of power, 865 : 19
of Time, 510 : 20
start by cats' c., 888 : 11
Corrupt a saint, 203 : 1
abilities utterly c., 439 : 7
enemies intelligent and c., 859 : 14
evil communications c., 49 : 2
government not shelter of c., 851 : 6
influence, 373 : 10
judge no king can c., 248 : 30
moth and rust doth c., 37 : 16
one good custom c. world, 534 : 31
peace c., 288 : 1
plea tainted and c., 199 : 24
power tends to c., 615 : 15
progeny yet more c., 107 : 30
public mind, 851 : 14
unlimited power apt to c., 351 : 1
word like corrupt tree, 131 : 3
Corrupted, conscience with injustice c., 185 : 17
goodness with power c., 823 : 16
sun not c., 86 : *n* 7
traitorously c. youth, 185 : 28
Corruptible put on incorruption, 49 : 7
Corruption and pernicious example, 452 : 2
Corruption (*continued*)
guilty of c. and renounce defense, 179 : 11
honest words suffered c., 261 : 17
I have said to c., 15 : 39
man coffer full of c., 152 : 2
smiting c. swiftly, 650 : 14
sown in c., 49 : 5
strong c. inhabits blood, 214 : 26
symptom of liberty, 383 : 11
wins not more than honesty, 249 : 8
Corruptly, offices not derived c., 199 : 14
Corrupts, absolute power c. absolutely, 615 : 15
power c. poetry cleanses, 891 : 16
Socrates c. the youth, 83 : 11
Corsair's, left c. name, 459 : 10
Corse, dead c. in complete steel, 219 : 12
to rampart we hurried, 465 : 7
Cortège, himself his own c., 899 : 14
Cortez, stout C., 475 : 7
Cory, Richard C. one summer night, 729 : 5
Corydon what madness has caught you, 103 : 9
Cosi è se vi pare, 723 : 18
Cosmic and ethical process, 596 : 10
night, 754 : 13
not one big c. meaning, 858 : 3
Cosmographers, physicians by their love grown c., 254 : 18
Cosmopolite, best c. loves country, 535 : 17
Cosmopolouse, bloomin' c., 709 : 13
Cosmos, push and pressure of c., 650 : 7
Cost, anyone who has to ask the c., 923 : 22
every farthing of c., 868 : 17
give and not count c., 157 : 3
good words c. little, 269 : 22
is labor to produce thing, 572 : 20
little less than new, 325 : 1
loved and c. me so much, 273 : 8
of outworn buried age, 244 : 21
sitteth and counteth c., 43 : 24
utility or c. of production, 652 : 2
Costing not less than everything, 808 : 18
Costly, attire comely not c., 175 : 9
morality private c. luxury, 635 : 12
seasons, 906 : 10
so c. a sacrifice, 524 : 4
thy habit, 219 : 1
Costs, good counsel c. nothing, 259 : 10
nothing to be polite, 746 : 13
Cottage, hides not visage from our c., 247 : 1
modest looks c. adorn, 370 : 17
poor man in mean c., 35 : 39
poorest man in his c., 351 : 7
soul's dark c., 276 : 12
Cottages, poor men's c. palaces, 198 : 9
Cotton, corn and c. and cockleburs, 674 : 13
is king, 491 : 4
land of c., 554 : 1
spinning noble, 474 : 4
where c. and taters grow, 672 : 19
Cottons mather, 839 : 4
Cotton-spinners, we are not c. all, 533 : 8
Cottontail and Peter, 719 : 2
Couch, frowsy c. in sorrow steep, 411 : 23

Couch (*continued*)
when owls do cry, 248 : 16
wraps drapery of c., 471 : 6
Cough, love and a c., 269 : 12
Coughed and called it fate, 728 : 20
Nobodaddy farted belched and c., 404 : 22
Coughing drowns parson's saw, 191 : 15
in theater is criticism, 895 : 7
Could, if youth but knew if old age but c., 163 : 11
nor even thing I c. be, 411 : 21
Couleurs, les parfums les c., 580 : *n* 6
Council, before ashes of c. fire cold, 591 : 4
outcome of words is in the c., 58 : 25
power in aristocratical c., 382 : 4
unapproachable in C. of Ten, 783 : 5
Zeus god of c., 57 : 16
Councilor ought not to sleep, 57 : 15
Councils, takes wisdom from c., 373 : 10
Counsel, fitter for execution than c., 181 : 7
good c. cheap, 259 : 10
how hard for women to keep c., 216 : 2
if this c. be of men, 46 : 1
love overwhelms wise c., 61 : 10
man who c. can bestow, 333 : 21
of thine own heart, 36 : 6
princely c. in his face, 284 : 14
sometimes c. take, 334 : 4
spirit of c. and might, 29 : 18
three keep c. if two away, 160 : 29
took sweet c. together, 19 : 21
two may keep c., 160 : *n* 17
walketh not in c. of ungodly, 17 : 12
who darkeneth c. by words, 16 : 27
Counseled ignoble ease, 284 : 13
Counselor, isolation worst c., 706 : 8
name shall be called C., 29 : 16
Counselors, good c. lack no clients, 227 : 25
kings and c. of the earth, 15 : 8
multitude of c., 23 : 24
wisest of c. Time, 73 : 7
Counsels, close designs crooked c., 303 : 20
excellent things in c., 25 : 1
hate c. not in such quality, 199 : 21
how monie c. sweet, 411 : 5
of moderation, 737 : 3
principles serve as c., 737 : 3
sic c. ye give, 926 : 15
Count, as long as I c. votes, 594 : 1
as naught in world, 568 : 23
chickens before hatched, 65 : 19
don't c. your boobies, 831 : 10
let me c. the ways, 507 : 14
let us c. our spoons, 354 : 12
milestones till haze dances, 518 : 9
myself in nothing else so happy, 194 : 19
myself king of space, 220 : 26
only sunny hours, 445 : *n* 3
that day lost, 920 : 12
them over every one apart, 700 : 13
until nothing else to c., 499 : 18
when angry c. ten, 390 : 4
Counted as the small dust, 30 : 36
them and cursed luck, 692 : 1
two and seventy stenches, 436 : 12
Countenance, bright c. of truth, 281 : 13
cannot lie, 184 : 13
Countenance (*continued*)
chide God for c., 212 : 20
damned disinheriting c., 399 : 2
did the c. divine, 406 : 21
heart changeth his c., 35 : 28
his c. like richest alchemy, 215 : 14
human c. composed of ten parts, 116 : 12
Knight of the Sorrowful C., 168 : 26
lift up his c. upon thee, 10 : 23
lift up the light of thy c., 17 : 15
like lightning, 41 : 29
merry heart maketh a cheerful c., 24 : 6
more in sorrow than anger, 218 : 21
of all science, 424 : 7
soon brightened, 428 : 15
tyrant's threatening c., 107 : 28
Counter original spare strange, 656 : 5
stake c. boldly, 543 : 14
Counteracts Devil who is Death, 365 : 14
Countercheck quarrelsome, 213 : 4
Counterculture, making of c., 912 : 6
Counterfeit a gloom, 278 : 20
Jove's dread clamors c., 231 : 11
sleep death's c., 238 : 6
Counterfeited, laughed with c. glee, 370 : 10
Counterparts in world of fact, 580 : 5
Counters, wise men's c., 264 : 13
Countesses had no outlines, 547 : 14
Counteth, sitteth and c. cost, 43 : 24
Counting my numberless fingers, 905 : 12
this row, 908 : 9
Countinghouse, king in c., 931 : 9
Countless infinitesimals of feeling, 438 : 8
thousands mourn, 408 : 16
Countree, hame to my ain c., 453 : 21
is this mine own c., 435 : 4
North C. hard c., 834 : 5
Countries, air in new c., 739 : 5
churches in flat c., 428 : *n* 6
give themselves to you, 789 : 11
of sun, 850 : 8
outdistance advanced c., 731 : 5
peace of all c. connected, 774 : 6
preferreth all c. before his own, 262 : 13
seek no aggrandizement, 781 : 7
tamed and made to bear, 739 : 5
wandering through many c., 102 : 18
Country, abroad for good of c., 329 : 10
absorbs poet, 573 : 20
all places all airs one c., 274 : 17
America my c., 752 : 13, 793 : 11
American says he loves c., 851 : 10
anything for good of c., 329 : 10
as soldier for c., 700 : *n* 1
ask not what c. do for you, 890 : 12
be useful to c. what I intend, 702 : 8
behind people your c., 590 : 6
belongs to people, 521 : 11
best c. is at home, 368 : 15
best service for c., 644 : 14
boon southern c., 587 : 11
but from my c.'s will, 418 : 8
cannot ask success even for c., 417 : 17
ceases to be free for irreligion, 821 : 10
cherished in hearts, 535 : 22
Country (*continued*)
construction of c., 719 : 11
cover c. in books, 657 : 2
cries of c. in chains, 928 : *n* 2
defended by our hands, 535 : 22
departed into their own c., 36 : 21
die but once to serve c., 326 : 1
die in defense of his c., 58 : 23
disable benefits of your c., 212 : 20
disenthrall selves save c., 522 : 12
diversion, 324 : 18
divine nature gave us c., 97 : 14
dreary tract of c., 525 : 19
duty to c. love it, 725 : 20
epitaph for their c., 703 : 14
essential service to c., 322 : 12
every c. but his own, 629 : 7
every c. hath its Machiavel, 153 : *n* 5
fame noised throughout c., 11 : 32
fate of c. not in ballot, 558 : 25
father of your c., 378 : *n* 9
fight for one's c., 58 : 14
fight to set c. free, 384 : 19
five and c. senses, 886 : 15
Flora and c. green, 476 : 23
foreign troop in my c., 351 : 5
fornication but in another c., 183 : 15
fortunes of my c., 419 : 11
found that famous c., 822 : 2
friend of every c. but own, 422 : 3
from yon far c. blows, 691 : 9
genius is of no c., 375 : 6
give c. back to Indians, 840 : 11
given heart to cause or c., 797 : 13
God made the c., 376 : 17
good for c. good for General Motors, 817 : 11
good news from a far c., 25 : 16
governed by despot, 356 : 3
government spirit of c., 672 : 14
grow up with c., 554 : *n* 2
half savage c., 792 : 10
hame to my ain c., 453 : 21
his ruling passion, 667 : 3
history of c. begins in heart, 738 : 15
honorable to die for one's c., 107 : 27
I loathe the c., 324 : 18
I tremble for my c., 388 : 1
if you love your c., 881 : 13
in c. you praise city, 106 : 22
in highlands in c. places, 669 : 7
in town, 119 : 18
is this mine own c., 435 : 4
it's autumn in c., 752 : 17
king will not leave c., 848 : 2
know something of own c., 360 : 18
leaving c. for country's sake, 329 : *n* 2
love c. and be poor, 340 : 7
love home love c., 547 : 22
love sweeping c., 836 : 2
loved c. as no other man, 590 : 7
loves native c. best, 535 : 17
man to all c. dear, 370 : 5
master of sea master of every c., 181 : *n* 5
merchants have no c., 389 : 9
most beautiful in West C., 739 : 14
mouth of no other c., 822 : 4
my c. is Kiltartan Cross, 713 : 20
my c. is the world, 385 : 2
my c. right or wrong, 445 : *n* 4
my c. 'tis of thee, 514 : 12
my c. 'tis of you, 828 : 17
my soul there is a c., 299 : 10

Country (*continued*)
needs good five-cent cigar, 673 : 6
never so virtuous, 689 : 22
no c. for old men, 714 : 22
no longer ours nor yours, 849 : 11
no matter if c. need comedian, 766 : 3
North C. hard c., 834 : 5
nothing old about c., 623 : 3
of the Gadarenes, 42 : 3
of worth, 410 : 8
one c. one constitution, 451 : 4
one life to lose for my c., 401 : 9
our c. however bounded, 535 : 22
our c. right or wrong, 445 : 19, 603 : 4
our c. the world, 505 : 10
peace of each c., 774 : 6
pride of c., 539 : 3
pride puts c. down, 917 : 22
prophet in his own c., 39 : 21
punished as enemy of c., 418 : 14
relinquish life for good of c., 420 : 14
richest which nourishes happy beings, 572 : 19
right or wrong, 445 : 19, 603 : 4
saved from itself, 689 : 22
savior of 'is c., 708 : 4
sell a c., 419 : 13
serve c. and mankind, 617 : 5
serves party best serves c., 590 : 9
she is my c. still, 375 : 13
shed blood for his c., 687 : 8
shrink from service of c., 384 : 13
slow sort of c., 612 : 21
small c. with few people, 65 : 9
spirit of resistance in c., 390 : 12
spread over globe, 518 : 9
stand by c. as mother, 590 : 6
stranger in strange c., 75 : 9
stroll a gallery, 595 : 6
sucked on c. pleasures, 251 : 14
the past a foreign c., 833 : 20
their c. their children, 102 : 28
they've undone his c., 325 : 19
this c. to preserve liberty, 390 : 1
this c. with its institutions, 521 : 11
this happy c., 365 : 5
this is a beautiful c., 487 : 1
this slave c., 486 : 16
touch our c. shackles fall, 376 : 20
trouble running any c., 760 : 12
Union is my c., 444 : 6
unjustly overrun, 558 : 2
vegetate like the c., 445 : 10
way our c. built, 879 : 3
what c. has done for us, 890 : *n* 3
where art thou my c., 461 : 5
where liberty is there is my c., 367 : 11
where no pretense of liberty, 520 : 2
who serves c. well, 343 : 4
whole c. nothing but c., 450 : 8
with no antiquity, 504 : 2
word new with our c., 623 : 3
Countrymen, all one c. now, 177 : 16
are mankind, 505 : 10
first in hearts of c., 402 : 10
friends Romans c., 216 : 17
Kiltartan's poor, 713 : 20
rebels our c. again, 589 : 19
Romans c. and lovers, 216 : 13
warring on that day, 457 : 21
what a fall was there my c., 216 : 25
Country's, all the ends be thy c., 249 : 8
Country's (*continued*)
bold peasantry c. pride, 369 : 30
brooding on c. fate, 564 : 9
by all c. wishes blessed, 364 : 8
fight our c. battles, 922 : 11
for c. glory fast, 430 : 14
guiltless of c. blood, 362 : 9
leaving country for c. sake, 329 : *n* 2
never to see my c. ruin, 316 : 9
pleasant c. earth, 195 : 8
spare c. flag, 513 : 18
Countryside, may c. content me, 104 : 4
smiling beautiful c., 689 : 6
Count's, nobody without C. permission, 786 : 1
Counts, isn't hurt that c., 718 : 17
who c. wampum of night, 604 : 8
County Guy hour is nigh, 432 : 9
Couple, human c. find true form, 870 : 12
Coupled for a common flight, 156 : *n* 5
Couples are wholes and not wholes, 70 : 5
Coupling of man and woman, 807 : 10
Courage and conduct of this army, 379 : 2
and devotion of patriot, 617 : 6
be of good c., 31 : 3
bear his share with c., 595 : 5
bear with a good c., 34 : 5
befitting a man, 665 : 1
brows of dauntless c., 283 : 25
by experience with fear, 786 : 13
civic c., 650 : 13
fear nor c. saves us, 804 : 15
fires us with c. love joy, 332 : 2
freedom based on c., 741 : 3
gaiety and quiet mind, 669 : 17
his c. foes proclaim, 304 : 6
horse of our c., 900 : 3
if one only had c., 600 : 4
life expands in proportion to c., 858 : 9
like a man of c., 702 : 3
lonely c., 650 : 13
mastiffs of unmatchable c., 207 : 25
May giveth unto lovers c., 149 : 13
moral c. physical timidity, 641 : 3
mounteth with occasion, 201 : 12
my spark of c., 925 : 2
never to submit or yield, 283 : 8
not to believe in anything, 564 : 6
of conscience, 484 : 18
of heart or holiness, 730 : 4
of making choice, 736 : 10
of my companions, 726 : 5
of New England, 484 : 18
one man with c. a majority, 419 : 5
pathos piety c., 764 : 10
placed decency above c., 701 : 2
price life exacts, 842 : 14
red badge of c., 732 : 3
resistance to fear, 624 : 21
Robert Shaw showed, 650 : 13
screw your c., 237 : 6
secret of liberty, 677 : 12
spark of c., 925 : 2
species of c., 308 : 15
steadfastness c. hope, 771 : 13
strong and of good c., 11 : 28
tastes of blood, 879 : 19
to change what should be, 823 : 15
to endure, 562 : 3
to forget, 597 : 1
Courage (*continued*)
to him that can get it, 302 : 15
to live, 472 : 19
to live by grace, 704 : 10
two o'clock in morning c., 421 : 1
unprepared c., 421 : 1
was mine, 827 : 7
were we men of c., 890 : 6
Western world lost civil c., 895 : 24
who has c. never perish in misery, 909 : 2
with which men died, 890 : 3
with which men lived, 890 : 3
without ferocity, 456 : 9
without justice c. weak, 347 : 4
won by men with c., 81 : 5
words such as c. obscene, 844 : 14
Courageous because of deep love, 65 : 3
captains c., 926 : 18
intellectual virile c., 726 : 1
Couriers, sightless c. of the air, 236 : 24
stays these c., 78 : *n* 8
Course, bow to that whose c. run, 363 : 15
chances change by c., 182 : 1
earth's diurnal c., 424 : 14
finished my c., 51 : 9
great nature's second c., 237 : 21
I must stand the c., 234 : 17
icy current compulsive c., 231 : 18
impediments in fancy's c., 227 : 23
insisture c. proportion, 225 : 37
many bees on single c., 784 : 15
my whole c. of love, 229 : 25
of empire, 330 : 25
of impious stubbornness, 218 : 4
of true love, 195 : 22
preudunt c. steadied, 568 : 3
straight c. to highest good, 101 : 11
turned from one's c. by opinions, 93 : 6
westward the c. of empire, 330 : 25
what c. others may take, 383 : 5
whate'er the c., 227 : 18
when in c. of human events, 387 : 9
young blood have c., 566 : 14
Coursers, nor c. like a page, 607 : 4
Courses, accomplishing their appointed c., 78 : 19
stars in their c. fought, 12 : 5
Court a mistress she denies you, 256 : 6
attacks upon the C., 644 : 18
bring suit in Supreme C., 787 : 11
confession in open c., 391 : 12
English not Turkish c., 206 : 35
envious c., 210 : 23
for owls, 30 : 22
hear rogues talk of c. news, 235 : 12
him elude him, 834 : 12
in beauty and decay, 469 : 1
in perpetual session, 786 : 5
keeps Death his c., 195 : 2
let her alone she will c. you, 256 : 6
moderation gone no c. save, 737 : 3
no justice in or out of c., 684 : 12
overruled earlier decisions, 678 : 3
starry threshold of Jove's C., 279 : 2
sun that shines upon his c., 247 : 1
supreme c. follows iliction, 721 : 12
temper doctrinaire logic, 821 : 8
the camp the grove, 430 : 6
though lewdness c. it, 219 : 22
world history is world's c., 412 : 12

Courte, n'ai pas loisir de la faire plus c., 299 : *n* 3
Courted by all the winds, 288 : 30
in girls again c., 920 : 4
Courteous, gracious and c. to strangers, 180 : 13
intellectual virile, 726 : 1
lowly and servysable, 145 : 17
retort c., 213 : 4
Courtesan, word love in mouth of c., 495 : 28
Courtesies, sweet c. of life, 360 : 24
Courtesy, always time for c., 499 : 22
and self-possession, 718 : 6
candy deal of c., 203 : 16
grace of God in c., 730 : 4
greater man greater c., 534 : 18
herein chivalry c. humanity, 149 : 5
high-erected thoughts in heart of c., 176 : 4
in c. have her learned, 714 : 17
like longshoreman's union, 722 : 21
mirror of all c., 147 : 5, 248 : 24
no defense like c., 725 : 19
pink of c., 170 : 14, 192 : 25
true alchemy, 600 : 13
wins as valor, 534 : 20
Courthouse, portals of every c., 737 : 5
Courtier, heel of c., 224 : 13
Courtier's soldier's scholar's, 221 : 19
Courtiers upon every road, 539 : 15
Courting, stayeth young man's c., 793 : 2
Courtliness and desire of fame, 534 : 23
Courtly nurture, 592 : 6
Courts, brawling c., 532 : 18
case still before c., 109 : 21
day in thy c., 20 : 8
forsaken c. pale pavilions, 848 : 7
hollow murmurs through c., 416 : 11
into his c. with praise, 21 : 3
laws conflict c. decide, 402 : 3
not enter political thicket, 776 : 14
prophecies of what c. do, 644 : 2
shown in c. at feasts, 280 : 1
thee on roses, 107 : 3
thrusting on c. nurture of spirit, 737 : 3
where Jamshyd gloried, 516 : 11
Cousins, little c. called back, 608 : 7
sisters c. and aunts, 627 : 13
Coûte, il n'y a que le premier pas qui c., 344 : *n* 6
Couvrez ce sein que je ne saurais voir, 297 : *n* 5
Covenant of reconciliation, 565 : 29
token of a c., 8 : 3
with death, 30 : 14, 505 : 14
words of the c., 10 : 15
Covenanted with him for silver, 41 : 5
Covenants, open c. of peace, 682 : 14
Cover country in books, 657 : 2
cunning sin c. itself, 209 : 30
her face, 262 : 10
I c. all, 761 : 6
like c. of old book, 346 : 15
only art guilt to c., 369 : 21
paste and c. to our bones, 195 : 2
that bosom I must not see, 297 : 20
thee with his feathers, 20 : 16
them with leaves, 917 : 6
Covered, death a c. way, 512 : *n* 4
up our names, 605 : 14
Covers, out of night that c., 663 : 10
Covers (*continued*)
who c. faults, 233 : 1
Covert from the tempest, 30 : 21
Covet no people's lands, 824 : 12
sin to c. honor, 208 : 9
those that c. with gain fond, 189 : 18
thou shalt not c., 10 : 7, 564 : 20
Coveted her and me, 527 : 8
Covetous desires of the world, 56 : 4
man ever in want, 109 : 1
of others' possessions, 102 : 23
sordid fellow, 341 : 21
Covetousness, wealth cause of c., 183 : 13
when he is old c., 69 : 20
Cow and bear shall feed, 29 : 19
cheaper than keep c., 621 : 3
good animal in field, 355 : 4
jumped over moon, 930 : 17
little Kyloe c., 931 : 7
milk c. of world, 899 : 8
purple c., 718 : 15
red and white, 668 : 13
she'll bring her c. along, 934 : 10
till the c. comes home, 263 : 5
with crumpled horn, 934 : 9
you do de pullin' Sis C., 662 : 9
Coward and brave held in same honor, 58 : 9
conscience dost afflict, 187 : 27
conscience is a c., 369 : 15
count myself the c., 535 : 12
does it with kiss, 676 : 8
fight when sure of winning, 565 : 1
had not resolution to fire it, 354 : 2
never forgave, 359 : 16
no c. soul mine, 562 : 4
sea hates c., 810 : 13
so great c. as he thinks, 669 : 10
turns away, 77 : 4
worth little more than c., 419 : 1
Cowardice, conscience and c. same, 674 : 25
distinguished from panic, 845 : 10
here all c. be ended, 140 : 14
herein friendship c. murder, 149 : 5
peace with disgrace and c., 95 : 16
protection against temptation, 625 : 13
that clings, 742 : 12
Cowardly, fatal as it is c., 580 : 6
war spares the c., 67 : 10
Cowards, conscience but word c. use, 187 : 30
conscience does make c., 221 : 12
die many times, 215 : 26
hundred c., 812 : 14
idlers and c. at home, 929 : 3
in reasoning, 325 : 4
mannish c., 210 : 22
not preserve republic, 814 : 19
plague of all c., 203 : 27
public greatest of c., 445 : 7
when c. mock patriot's fate, 592 : 2
Cowboy, best damned c., 927 : 12
I wondered if ever a c., 927 : 13
I'm a young c., 927 : 15
that loves you so true, 927 : 18
wrapped in white linen, 927 : 14
Cowl does not make monk, 133 : 15
I like a c., 493 : 16
take wife or c., 168 : *n* 12
Cowled, I that c. churchman be, 493 : 16
Cowley had fanciful mind, 437 : 5
Cowpuncher a-riding along, 927 : 9
Cow'rin', wee sleekit c., 408 : 12
Cow's in the corn, 930 : 12
Cows are my passion, 548 : 19
till the c. come home, 263 : *n* 4
Cowslip's, hang pearl in c. ear, 196 : 11
in c. bell I lie, 248 : 16
sweet c. grace, 394 : 6
Coxcombs, some made c. nature meant fools, 332 : 17
Coy and hard to please, 431 : 2
denial vain and c. excuse, 280 : 9
sometimes coming sometimes c., 312 : 12
yielded with c. submission, 285 : 19
Coyness, this c. were no crime, 296 : 26
Coyotes howl o'er grave, 927 : 17
wild c. howl over me, 927 : 16
Crab, hermit c. whale's backbone, 808 : 2
teach c. to walk straight, 82 : 4
very likeness of roasted c., 196 : 12
Crabbed age and youth, 917 : 11
philosophy not harsh and c., 279 : 25
talk of c. old men, 101 : 18
Crabs, roasted c. hiss in bowl, 191 : 15
Crabwise, womething c. across snow, 904 : 4
Crack any of those old jokes, 82 : 17
blow winds c. cheeks, 233 : 24
door begins to c., 929 : 9
glass eye across, 757 : 6
hear the mighty c., 325 : 11
heaven's vaults should c., 235 : 16
in teacup opens, 868 : 10
nature's molds, 233 : 24
sail-yards tremble masts c., 178 : 6
she discovered c. in wall, 583 : 10
stretch out to c. of doom, 239 : 14
Cracked growled roared howled, 434 : 11
the mirror c., 528 : 27
Cracker-jack, buy peanuts and c., 765 : 13
Crackled and gone up in smoke, 693 : 14
Crackling of thorns under a pot, 27 : 5
Crack-pated when we dreamed, 715 : 8
Cracks, now c. a noble heart, 225 : 3
sinews cakes brain, 570 : 13
Cradle asks whence, 615 : 7
between c. and grave, 345 : 3, 816 : 2
bough breaks c. fall, 660 : 19
earth c. of hope, 761 : 16
endlessly rocking, 575 : 17
from c. to grave, 467 : 9, 665 : 17
hand that rocks c., 573 : 18
of all that is, 874 : 9
of every science, 595 : 7
of liberty, 451 : 15
of the deep, 456 : 5
procreant c., 236 : 21
rocks above abyss, 846 : 2
stands in the grave, 257 : 12
vexed to nightmare by c., 714 : 13
will rock, 660 : 19
Cradled into poetry by wrong, 467 : 15
Cradles, bit babies in c., 541 : 1
plodding from c. to graves, 569 : 20
some c. preserve as sacred, 623 : 1
to graves, 569 : 20
Craft, life so short c. so long, 144 : 8
neat little sweet little c., 629 : 19

Craft (*continued*)
to seme fle fro thyng men hunte, 144 : 16
Craftiness, taketh wise in their c., 15 : 16
Craftsman against craftsman, 61 : 13
Craftsmanship, criticism easier than c., 83 : 5
leaves holes, 887 : 7
literary c., 800 : 1
Crafty afraid to act, 63 : 14
old and c. and wise, 712 : 10
Crag, castled c. of Drachenfels, 457 : 25
clasps c. with crooked hands, 532 : 28
of rock and strong place, 17 : 1
Crags, among these barren c., 529 : 6
Cram within this wooden O, 207 : 2
Crammed with distressful bread, 208 : 7
Crammers, green c. of green fruits, 766 : 23
Cramped, life and memory c., 878 : 19
up and smothery, 624 : 1
Cranes of Ibycus, 65 : *n* 8
Crankiness, saving mind from c., 569 : 8
Cranks, cursed with army of c., 676 : 16
quips and c., 277 : 19
Crannied wall, 535 : 10
Crannies, pluck you out of c., 535 : 10
Crannying wind, 457 : 23
Cras amet qui nunquam amavit, 133 : 14
ingens iterabimus aequor, 107 : *n* 5
Crash, stand by to c., 821 : 1
Crater, Vesuvius' c. for inkstand, 571 : 1
Craters of my eyes gape, 912 : 7
of silence, 864 : 4
Crave, my mind forbids to c., 167 : 5
no pelf, 243 : 1
stain of tears, 748 : 9
then Lucasta might I c., 296 : 5
thing we may not have, 147 : 9
too much still do c., 167 : 6
we crie al day and c., 147 : 9
Craved no crumb, 629 : 22
Craven, some c. scruple, 223 : 18
Craves a kind of wit, 214 : 12
Craving, accurst c. for gold, 105 : 6
sorrow arises from c., 72 : 23
to go to law, 630 : 20
Crawl, felt siroccos c., 605 : 16
flash or thunder in, 887 : 7
upon earth, 322 : 11
with legs, 434 : 16
Crawling between heaven and earth, 221 : 16
cooped we live die, 517 : 3
cruel c. foam, 566 : 8
for charity, 90 : 7
on all fours, 343 : 16
Crawls, crew c., 785 : 12
sea beneath him c., 532 : 28
Crazy and didn't have to fly, 902 : 8
as hauling timber into woods, 106 : 18
half c. for love of you, 718 : 18
like a fox, 861 : 9
man is certainly c., 165 : 7
salad with their meat, 714 : 16
Creak of lumbering cart, 712 : 12
Creaking, hay c. to barn, 892 : 6
Cream and mantle like standing pond, 198 : 1
Cream (*continued*)
emperor of ice c., 766 : 25
gives c. with all might, 668 : 13
masquerades as c., 627 : 16
Cream-faced loon, 239 : 29
Create a fourth a decent man, 702 : 10
belief help c. fact, 649 : 15
cannot c. when nothing to say, 853 : 5
creative c. itself, 479 : 14
critics or but half c., 714 : 7
do not talk, 397 : 2
equivalent for what I felt, 801 : 2
in me a clean heart, 19 : 16
martyrs c. faith, 705 : 18
new heavens and a new earth, 31 : 30
noblest of sailing vessels, 800 : 10
strains that might c. a soul, 279 : 27
taste by which relished, 428 : 8
those who love and c., 672 : 9
time to murder and c., 803 : 11
to know to kill to c., 581 : 8
what half c. what perceive, 423 : 14
Created, all men c. equal, 387 : 9, 523 : 4
by him all things c., 50 : 9
by him and for him, 50 : 9
God c. heaven and earth, 6 : 10
half to rise, 337 : 2
hath not one God c. us, 33 : 36
I c. you while happy, 702 : 7
in mind imagined land, 767 : 22
male and female c. he, 6 : 14
man is c. free, 413 : 2
man to be immortal, 34 : 12
Medici c. and destroyed me, 152 : 16
monster I had c., 482 : 14
new thrill, 491 : 14
not c. sense of obligation, 732 : 8
nothing can be c. from nothing, 100 : 5
nothing great c. suddenly, 121 : 3
remember We have c. man, 131 : 12
signs in what God has c., 130 : 16
something of nothing, 277 : 3
thing c. loved before it exists, 742 : 6
thou hast c. all things, 53 : 8
time when Dendid c. all things, 925 : 21
tool carries spirit by which c., 852 : 17
We c. Man, 132 : 10
world but small parenthesis, 275 : 15
you of dust, 131 : 14
Creates, poet c. world, 769 : 14
state which c. revolutions, 88 : 9
what nature c. has eternity, 861 : 17
Creating, in c. begin, 567 : 15
new doubts, 380 : 1
whole tribe of fops, 233 : 3
Creation, beauteous bright c., 135 : 2
condition for happiness, 882 : 12
construction and c., 742 : 6
did ever woman since c., 359 : 19
division same as c., 90 : 2
drives plowshare o'er c., 330 : 18
earlier and other c., 808 : 2
essentially subjective, 754 : 12
false c. from brain, 237 : 13
in infinite I Am, 437 : 11
initial of c., 606 : 11
kelson of c. love, 574 : 14
land harbors mysteries of c., 895 : 10
language of c., 735 : 13
life is c., 552 : 3
lords o' the c., 409 : 7
Creation (*continued*)
O fairest of c., 287 : 22
of next generation, 853 : 16
one thing in c. to demonstrate Providence, 121 : 4
rhythmical c. of beauty, 527 : 14
same as destruction, 90 : 2
sea c. of Omnipotence, 741 : 12
sleeps, 330 : 6
suffering an auxiliary of c., 661 : 1
the tire of all c., 519 : 11
to which whole c. moves, 532 : 27
tremendous object of c., 371 : 7
we bless thee for our c., 55 : 7
whole c. groaneth, 47 : 9
work of art corner of c., 643 : 6
Creation's dawn beheld, 458 : 27
fright we felt for c. sake, 900 : 9
Creations, impose on c. of thought, 636 : 17
of mind blessing not curse, 763 : 8
Creative contemplative or saintly life, 867 : 5
create itself, 479 : 14
critical power c. power, 586 : 20
hate, 738 : 17
hypothesis c. act, 880 : 10
in c. process father mother child, 704 : 14
without playing no c. work, 753 : 11
woman's normal occupations counter c. life, 867 : 5
Creativeness conception and birth, 704 : 13
Creator and Preserver, 55 : 5
creature could face c., 894 : 2
duty we owe C., 383 : 6
endowed by their c., 387 : 9
from his work returned, 287 : 1
glorify C. of universe, 307 : 12
good when it leaves C., 358 : 18
great C. drew his spirit, 307 : 9
law of our C., 373 : 18
life breathed by C., 515 : 3
made Italy from designs by Michelangelo, 622 : 6
pity C. had not taken advice, 139 : *n* 4
remember now thy C., 27 : 24
uncreated, 5 : 2
Creators of odd volumes, 441 : 18
realities and c., 496 : 22
Creature, bright c. scorn not one, 429 : 11
comforts, 319 : 5
constant image of the c., 213 : 29
Constitution c. of people, 402 : 8
could face creator, 894 : 2
drink pretty c., 425 : 3
every c. drink but I, 295 : 8
every c. mystery to other, 549 : 23
every c. of God is good, 50 : 28
every c. purified, 184 : 2
eyes of c. self, 864 : 7
God's first c. light, 285 : *n* 1
Hobbes proves every c., 322 : 20
kindness to fellow c., 439 : 2
lash magic c., 607 : 7
little c. formed of joy, 407 : 3
lone lorn c., 548 : 22
man is singular c., 870 : 14
man most detestable c., 626 : 10
man not c. of circumstances, 501 : 7
no human c. give orders to love, 504 : 8

Creature (*continued*)
nor any other c., 47 : 15
not a c. stirring, 446 : 3
of circumstances, 501 : 7
preach to every c., 42 : 16
quite separate from others, 602 : 11
sets man apart from every other c., 394 : 16
that made footprint, 776 : 7
that thou madest, 692 : 10
torture one tiny c., 582 : 5
universe a single complex creature, 126 : 19
what c. walks in morning, 74 : *n* 5
what more felicity to c., 174 : 12
wine a good familiar c., 230 : 27
world hath not a sweeter c., 231 : 23
wretched despicable c., 346 : 4
Creatures, all c. here below, 311 : 19
brother to all c., 897 : 19
by rule in nature teach, 207 : 6
clearest of God's c., 893 : 4
delicate c. ours, 231 : 6
England breeds valiant c., 207 : 25
essences of seasons became myriad c., 97 : 7
from fairest c. desire increase, 243 : 31
generations of living c. changed, 100 : 15
God's c., 525 : *n* 3
great and small, 561 : 8
Leviathan hugest of c., 286 : 30
little c. everywhere, 781 : 11
love my fellow c., 629 : 3
make fellow c. happy, 385 : 5
makes meaner c. kings, 187 : 24
of a day, 72 : 2
of all c. man most detestable, 626 : 10
poets c. most absurd, 339 : 29
praise for all thy c., 138 : 12
smashed up c., 835 : 7
soul same in all c., 80 : 12
spiritual c. walk unseen, 286 : 2
that creep swim or fly, 311 : 12
that once were men, 725 : 4
till all c. own thy sway, 597 : 18
weak c. of clay, 82 : 9
what marvelous c. we are, 746 : 20
widows most perverse c., 326 : 20
wild c. and places are natural resources, 898 : 11
you dissect, 335 : 13
Creatures', human c. lives, 485 : 19
Credential, only c. New York asked, 859 : 20
Credit, an't much c. in that, 547 : 29
card as good as gold, 666 : 1
dead corpse of Public C., 451 : 1
done my c. much wrong, 517 : 10
gradual growth of c., 502 : 8
greatly to his c. that he is Englishman, 627 : 17
having more c. than money, 394 : 15
his own lie, 247 : 11
let the c. go, 516 : 8
not to whom idea occurs, 662 : 3
places last stone gets c., 762 : 5
plans c. and Muse, 494 : 10
shadow of authority and c., 373 : 10
to human race, 877 : 8
to man who convinces, 662 : 3
used my c., 202 : 27
Creditable acquaintance, 321 : 20
Creditors, executors or c., 570 : 10
we are debtors or c., 395 : 23
Credo quia impossibile, 126 : *n* 6
Credulities, ambitions climb on c., 684 : 5
Credulity, a little c. helps, 536 : 15
helps enjoyment, 577 : 8
listen with c. to fancy, 352 : 15
man's weakness, 441 : 22
youth the season of c., 350 : 18
Credulous, hatred renders votaries c., 359 : 5
Creed, Athanasian C. lyric, 502 : 22
comfortable c., 460 : 22
fundamental article of political c., 382 : 4
is a rod, 634 : 6
life to neighbor's c., 493 : 14
most authentic c., 615 : 7
necessity the c. of slaves, 412 : 4
nonviolence article of c., 727 : 4
of our political faith, 389 : 2
put c. into your deed, 494 : 19
sapping solemn c., 458 : 1
single dogmatic c., 891 : 5
suckled in c. outworn, 428 : 1
theory matter of policy not c., 681 : 23
whatever race c. or persuasion, 794 : 15
Creeds, behind c. one Spirit, 657 : 5
casual c., 585 : 22
dust of c. outworn, 467 : 2
dust of systems and c., 527 : 22
human hopes and c., 647 : 1
new names for mystery, 646 : 4
so many gods so many c., 670 : 4
than in half the c., 532 : 19
that refuse and restrain, 632 : 16
Creeks, through c. and inlets, 564 : 17
Creep and let no more be said, 588 : 1
beasts of the forest c. forth, 21 : 11
dwarfed and abased, 671 : *n* 1
feet like snails did c., 266 : 13
flesh c., 546 : 13
for bellies' sake c., 280 : 20
in one dull line, 333 : 7
into narrow bed, 588 : 1
learn to c. ere learn to go, 160 : 10
let music c. in our ears, 201 : 1
love will c. in service, 160 : *n* 4
men c. not walk, 513 : 12
nevermore to c. again, 740 : 6
something not in poem c. in, 887 : 7
swim or fly, 311 : 12
where it may not go, 160 : 6
wit that can c., 339 : 3
Creepers, bacterial c., 873 : 11
Creeping, gray clouds c. quietly, 602 : 1
hours of time, 211 : 12
like snail to school, 211 : 15
thing in sober way, 562 : 8
things c. innumerable, 21 : 11
through the black, 765 : 6
Creeps, how slow shadow c., 730 : 1
in this petty pace, 240 : 4
Creetur, lone lorn c., 548 : 22
Cremated Sam McGee, 752 : 6
Crème, my pupils c. de la c., 896 : 1
Crepidam, ne supra c. sutor iudicaret, 90 : *n* 6
Crept into bosom of the sea, 185 : 20
like frightened girl, 674 : 15
music c. by upon waters, 247 : 20
night c. upon our talk, 217 : 7
Crepuscular time, 564 : 4
Cressid, as false as C., 226 : 15
where C. lay that night, 200 : 22
Crest, no colors or c., 708 : 19
Crested, reared arm c. the world, 241 : 25
Cretan, played C. against C., 120 : 1
Cretonnes of Penelope, 769 : 6
Crew, Bellman cry c. reply, 613 : 22
crawls, 785 : 12
darling of our c., 393 : 11
dismayed her c., 647 : 21
ghastly c., 434 : 31
immediately the cock c., 41 : 18
Mirth admit me of thy c. 277 : 22
of captain's gig, 627 : 7
Crib, ass knoweth his master's c., 28 : 26
Cribbed, cabined c. confined, 238 : 23
Cricket, merry as c., 160 : 3
no relief, 805 : 1
on the hearth, 278 : 20
Cricket's, the c. gone, 839 : 3
Cried A sail a sail, 434 : 18
Agamemnon c. aloud, 804 : 25
all the way to bank, 896 : 7
for madder music, 721 : 6
Give me, 605 : 7
in goose Alas, 810 : 19
mercy to myself I c., 424 : 11
No more, 268 : 21
not winced nor c. aloud, 663 : 10
out of the depths have I c., 22 : 11
Peter denied Lord c., 320 : 7
poor c. Caesar wept, 216 : 19
you suddenly c., 796 : 10
Crier, good c. of green sauce, 158 : 2
town c. spoke my lines, 221 : 23
Cries, bootless c., 244 : 8
damned that c. Hold enough, 240 : 11
fisted with wild c., 683 : 5
holy and meek she c., 404 : 11
man who turnips c., 353 : 12
my fate c. out, 219 : 15
of cicadas, 314 : 1
of country in chains, 928 : *n* 2
of sandpiper, 874 : 9
out Where is it, 435 : 16
pitying the tender c., 403 : 13
rump-fed ronyon c., 236 : 1
that which world c. up, 309 : 22
to world from tower, 779 : *n* 2
voice of Nature loudly c., 410 : 15
whistle spontaneous c., 767 : 4
wind full of birds' c., 760 : 17
Crieth, brother's blood c., 7 : 16
in the wilderness, 30 : 30
wisdom c. without, 23 : 3
Crillon, hang yourself brave C., 175 : 2
Crime, blanch without owner's c., 428 : 23
could not tell all forms of c., 105 : 20
criminal not cause of c., 735 : 10
curious c. wickedness, 545 : 9
fear of death never deterred c., 414 : 17
foulest c. in history, 576 : 8
from c. born bullets, 860 : 12
from single c. know nation, 104 : 33
hypocrite's c. bear false witness against self, 866 : 10
Iscariot-like c., 799 : 12
like virtue has degrees, 312 : 10
medicine for c. is wisdom, 595 : 15
now madden to c., 459 : 5

Crime (*continued*)
of being young man, 350 : 16
once appeared reappearance likely, 866 : 8
popularity a c., 310 : 19
prevention of mutual c., 88 : 5
punishment fit c., 629 : 11
servitude consequence of c., 397 : 21
successful c. called virtue, 115 : 12
this coyness were no c., 296 : 26
to be nobly born now c., 262 : 20
to love too well, 335 : 8
who for my willful c., 288 : 3
with us poverty a c., 493 : 3
worse than c. it is blunder, 415 : 3
Crimes against peace, 821 : 7
and misfortunes, 343 : 26
broad blown, 222 : 27
committed c. but not stood aside, 859 : 13
committed in thy name, 400 : 14
high c. and misdemeanors, 391 : 11
history register of c., 383 : 10
no punishment prevent c., 866 : 8
one virtue thousand c., 459 : 10
reach the dignity of c., 393 : 14
teems with c., 920 : 15
virtues forced upon us by c., 804 : 15
worst of c. is poverty, 680 : 28
Criminal element I am of it, 676 : 18
judge condemned when c. absolved, 111 : 10
no c. class except Congress, 625 : 3
not cause of crime, 735 : 10
not c. unless intent c., 133 : 6
Criminal's, evening c. friend, 581 : 2
Criminals, less evil that some c. escape, 645 : 10
Criminel, le soir charmant ami du c., 581 : *n* 2
Crimson, beauty's ensign c., 193 : 27
conquest's c. wing, 363 : 4
of c. joy, 405 : 5
petal, 531 : 11
torchlight c. on kettledrums, 742 : 9
with fury, 612 : 1
Crimson-tipped flower, 409 : 9
Crines ingenio suo flexi, 117 : *n* 12
Cringe, souls that c. plot, 567 : 11
Cripple, beware of attacking c., 6 : 3
Crippled palsied and slain, 752 : 4
Crises, business c. wrecked industries, 666 : 4
Constitution adapted to c., 402 : 5
great c. show resources, 648 : 3
marriage seldom develop without c., 754 : 2
political c. moral c., 886 : 2
Crisis, force moment to its c., 803 : 15
identity c., 854 : *n* 2
moulting season c., 559 : 11
quiet but urgent, 898 : *n* 1
Crisp, deep and c. and even, 563 : 11
Crisped, leaves c. and sere, 526 : 22
Crispian, feast of C., 208 : 10
Crispin merest minuscule in gales, 766 : 14
Cristo si è fermato a Eboli, 855 : *n* 2
Critic, better be actor than c., 743 : 1
cry of c. for five, 619 : 3
dreamer c. of dream, 754 : 12
dwell upon excellencies, 326 : 19
good c. tells of masterpieces, 655 : 11
helper of artist, 653 : 3
Critic (*continued*)
most degraded of trades, 626 : 11
no longer artist but c., 720 : 7
not bein' author gr-reat c., 722 : 19
peep or cynic bark, 494 : 1
severe c. on own works, 479 : 13
unsuccessful author turns c., 436 : *n* 1
valuable instrument, 653 : 3
when cannot be artist, 583 : 8
wise skepticism is good c., 569 : 15
you have frowned, 429 : 10
youngest c. died, 707 : 21
Critical, easier c. than correct, 502 : 3
effort, 586 : 15
generous sternly c., 663 : 8
mirror of culture, 865 : 14
modern art c., 886 : 11
nothing if not c., 230 : 9
power creative power, 586 : 20
readers should be c. of historians, 95 : 18
sense rare, 653 : 3
Criticism acid that dissolves images, 886 : 4
ask c. want praise, 751 : 10
automatism but also c., 837 : 9
blown by wind of c., 357 : 2
cant of c., 360 : 11
coughing in theater c., 895 : 7
definition of c., 586 : 24
dominated by outworn theory, 735 : 10
easier than craftsmanship, 83 : 5
easy art difficult, 329 : 18
father of English c., 352 : 25
not govern without c., 814 : 2
reviewing not c., 653 : 2
rod of divination, 711 : 17
stealthy school of c., 601 : 22
to make enjoyment aware, 654 : 9
when c. parts with reality, 744 : 12
work of c. shaped by geometry, 318 : 3
Criticisms, parodies penetrating c., 830 : 10
Criticize, cannot c. Testament, 699 : 1
to c. is to appreciate, 653 : 17
Criticized, book Time c. for us, 569 : 6
good joke not c., 742 : 7
relation with c. thing, 653 : 17
tradition perpetually c., 809 : 20
Criticizes, Testament c. you, 699 : 1
Critics, before you trust in c., 456 : 15
Boston audience c., 622 : 3
failed therefore turn c., 436 : 15
go hang yourselves, 158 : 11
in peace ye c. dwell, 334 : 24
men who have failed, 502 : 12
modest dress true c. please, 319 : 18
or but half create, 714 : 7
ready made, 456 : 13
shouting He's unknown, 647 : 4
when c. talk of sublime, 385 : 7
Crito I owe a cock, 79 : 8
Croaks fatal entrance of Duncan, 236 : 17
Hall o' Fame when you c., 810 : 7
Crocodile, how doth little c., 611 : 5
log never be c., 926 : 8
not move underjaw, 268 : 20
one drop of c., 841 : 5
tears, 177 : *n* 6
Crocodiles, not be seized by c., 114 : 7
Cromwell, celebrities such as C., 615 : 14
Charles the First his C., 382 : 13
damned to fame, 337 : 15
guiltless of country's blood, 362 : 9
I charge thee, 249 : 7
if thou fallest O C., 249 : 8
Crone, some old c. let us seek, 92 : 13
Crony, ancient trusty drouthy c., 411 : 6
government by c., 751 : 1
Crook, by hook or by c., 143 : 11
I am not a c., 883 : 2
pregnant hinges of knees, 222 : 4
shepherd's c. beside scepter, 493 : 5
Crooked cannot be made straight, 26 : 16
close designs c. counsels, 303 : 20
hands, 532 : 28
house, 932 : 18
lane, 485 : 10
Leviathan that c. serpent, 30 : 12
man went crooked mile, 932 : 18
roads are roads of genius, 404 : 7
set c. straight, 618 : 7
shall be made straight, 30 : 31
slim and c. genius, 652 : 7
tell the c. rose, 886 : 12
Crookedest river in world, 623 : 2
Crop, familiar as c. in summer, 124 : 26
fungus c. of sentiment, 631 : 19
of corn a field of tares, 177 : 10
Crop-full bird, 544 : 9
Crops are ripe, 740 : 1
flowery food, 336 : 13
men want c. without plowing, 556 : 4
watering last year's c., 565 : 5
Cross, a sparkling c. she wore, 334 : 1
blind as nails upon C., 801 : 6
cannot c. cause why born, 190 : 33
don't c. bridge until come to it, 921 : 7
he that taketh not his c., 39 : 5
hot c. buns, 931 : 17
nailed on bitter c., 202 : 22
no c. no crown, 267 : 10, 314 : 9
of gold,, 694 : 16
of Jesus, 616 : 6
old rugged c., 738 : 11
one more river to c., 936 : 3
over river and rest, 594 : 10
transit where dreams c., 806 : 5
Crossbow, with my c., 434 : 12
Crossed, oyster may be c. in love, 399 : 12
the Sierras, 822 : 2
when I have c. bar, 535 : 21
with direct eyes, 805 : 16
Crosses, crooked c. and headstones, 777 : 16
row on row, 737 : 9
to fret thy soul with c., 174 : 11
Cross-gartered, see thee c., 214 : 10
Crossing Channel and tossing, 629 : 1
death is but c. world, 314 : 13
street saw parents and child, 906 : 2
stripling Thames, 585 : 21
Crosspatch draw latch, 930 : 16
Crossroads, dirty work at c., 922 : 5
strange c. lie, 839 : 6
Crossway of the stars, 843 : 5
Crossways, things at home c., 660 : 2
Crotchets in thy head, 225 : 14
Crouch, to fawn to c. to wait, 174 : 11
to television set, 893 : 15

Crow beautified with our
feathers, 178 : 12
before the cock c., 41 : 18
louder in own farmyard, 555 : 2
lungs c. like chanticleer, 211 : 7
makes wing to rooky wood, 238 : 21
many-wintered c., 529 : 18
safer 'n to c., 568 : 6
sees white man come, 557 : 18
shook down on me, 748 : 3
sun risen to hear him c., 565 : 9
think thy swan a c., 191 : 20
we'll pluck c. together, 188 : 7
Crowbar, creation for c., 519 : 11
hammer me into c., 761 : 10
hoe and barrow, 455 : 8
Crow-blue mussel shells, 798 : 9
Crowd, after night I do c., 402 : 15
all at once I saw a c., 427 : 7
and buzz and murmurings, 295 : 3
beauty not comprehended by
c., 711 : 14
faces in the c., 792 : 7
firm against c., 531 : 15
for c. they need interpreters, 71 : 24
great man in c., 497 : 1
I am the c., 761 : 3
into a shade, 332 : 12
not feel the c., 377 : 4
not on my soul, 363 : 7
of common men, 272 : 14
only beast in arena the c., 720 : 17
out of the c. a mistress or
friend, 468 : 21
will support itself, 602 : *n* 4
you were a good c., 683 : 5
Crowded, for sake of c. audience, 80 : 2
hour of glorious life, 375 : 1
too busied with c. hour, 495 : 4
with glorious action, 432 : 16
world's most c. streets, 585 : 15
Crowd's, madding c. ignoble
strife, 362 : 12
Crowds, beauty c. me till I die, 607 : 15
noise c. beloved smoke, 441 : 9
public men nor cheering c., 714 : 1
talk with c. keep virtue, 710 : 17
without company, 384 : 5
Crowed, cock that c. in morn, 934 : 9
Crowing, faded on c. of the cock, 217 : 26
of cocks and barking of dogs, 65 : 9
Crowley, Stuhldreher Miller C.
Layden, 773 : 6
Crown, allegiance to c., 378 : 12
ambassador from Britain's c., 536 : 7
becomes monarch better than
c., 200 : 9
bowed with galling c., 728 : 18
breeches cost a c., 917 : 21
Caesar's laurel c., 406 : 16
carried him c. him, 912 : 8
chance may c. me, 236 : 12
contrary to c. built paper
mill, 185 : 28
cross for c., 738 : 11
defiance to forces of C., 351 : 7
every noble c. is of thorns, 474 : 5
fell down broke c., 931 : 1
fighting for c., 929 : 19
fill me from c. to toe, 236 : 17
from c. of head to sole, 209 : 20
golden c. like a deep well, 195 : 11
good with brotherhood, 688 : 5
Greece with freedom, 67 : 20
Crown (*continued*)
hairy gold c. on 'ead, 708 : 7
hath worn the c., 35 : 20
have I no bays to c. it, 268 : 21
head that wears a c., 206 : 19
hoary head a c. of glory, 24 : 13
hollow c., 195 : 2
holly bears the c., 919 : 21
immortal c., 346 : 1
is called content, 186 : 8
is in my heart, 186 : 8
is love and friendship, 475 : 21
is of night, 634 : 6
jewel in c. of Social Republic, 638 : 8
kingly c. to gain, 452 : 7
laurel c. yield to praise, 98 : 27
many a c. spotless now, 413 : 11
mind content both c. and
kingdom, 178 : 11
no cross no c., 267 : 10, 314 : 9
nor c. nor scepter would I ask, 418 : 8
not the king's c. nor sword, 228 : 6
of glory, 52 : 15
of life, 51 : 28, 53 : 1
of life as it closes, 632 : 15
of Monomakh, 486 : 12
of thorns, 474 : 5
of thorns on brow of labor, 694 : 16
old age c. of life, 99 : 10
old Winter's head, 292 : 10
ourselves with rosebuds, 34 : 11
quiet mind richer than c., 178 : 10
sorrow's c. of sorrow, 529 : 20
still the fine's the c., 227 : 18
sullied in the winning, 413 : 11
sweet fruition of earthly c., 183 : 6
sword mace c. imperial, 208 : 7
that seldom kings enjoy, 186 : 8
the watery glade, 361 : 8
themselves assured, 245 : 13
thorns thy only c., 276 : 13
though they possess c., 318 : 10
virtuous woman is a c., 23 : 28
Crowned, due to be c. again, 790 : 13
ghost sitting c. upon grave, 264 : 18
him long ago, 460 : 6
knot of fire, 808 : 18
Peace c. with smiles, 299 : 10
with lilies, 823 : 12
with stars, 311 : 20
with the sickle, 345 : 13
Crownest year with thy
goodness, 19 : 30
Crownets, walked crowns and
c., 241 : 25
Crowning, reason God's c. gift, 74 : 21
Crownless in voiceless woe, 458 : 16
Crowns and pounds and
guineas, 690 : 20
are empty things, 318 : 10
birds rounding hill c., 899 : 9
end c. all, 227 : 5
end c. the work, 133 : 26
end c. us not fight, 266 : 4
if store of c. be scant, 257 : 8
in shades like these, 370 : 2
last act c. play, 267 : 18
not c. but men, 449 : 2
walked c. and crownets, 241 : 25
Crows and choughs that wing
air, 234 : 28
black flight of c., 928 : *n* 2
throw him to c., 923 : *n* 5
wars of kites or c., 289 : 12
Crow's-feet, til c. be growen, 144 : 19
Cru, j'ai pleuré et j'ai c., 419 : *n* 1
Crucible, God's c., 706 : 15
not test faith in c., 665 : 2
Crucified dead and buried, 55 : 2
everyone Christ and all c., 757 : 3
if this woman must be c., 554 : 9
let him be c., 41 : 21
where dear Lord c., 561 : 9
Crucifixion, living through another
C., 843 : 2
Cruciform shadow, 817 : 3
Crucify mankind on cross of
gold, 694 : 16
Son of God afresh, 51 : 16
Crude, berries harsh and c., 280 : 6
no c. surfeit reigns, 279 : 25
Cruel and unrelenting enemy, 379 : 2
and unusual punishment, 392 : 3
aristocracy always c., 538 : 20
as death, 345 : 6
but composed and bland, 588 : 4
crawling foam, 566 : 8
death of Pyramus, 196 : 2
doubts more c. than truths, 297 : 30
foam is not c., 572 : 10
I must be c. to be kind, 223 : 12
jealousy is c. as the grave, 28 : 23
mother of sweet loves, 108 : 10
never be c., 548 : 29
nothing c. or evil anywhere, 879 : 11
price c. high, 707 : 17
savage extreme rude c., 245 : 23
say we are c. to each other, 554 : 9
slain by fair c. maid, 214 : 4
tender mercies of the wicked are
c., 23 : 29
'tis said she, 476 : 7
wind blows, 864 : 2
Cruelest, April c. month, 804 : 26
lies told in silence, 667 : 16
she alive, 213 : 17
Cruelly, Fortune c. scratched, 227 : 19
pain clings c. to us, 476 : 2
Cruelty, all the pride c. and
ambition, 173 : 4
farewell fair c., 213 : 20
fear source of c., 738 : 5
full of direst c., 236 : 17
has human heart, 405 : 14
Mr. C., 302 : 6
of pirates, 568 : 16
soldier without c., 591 : 11
to load falling man, 249 : *n* 1
war is c., 578 : 15
Cruise, all on our last c., 667 : 17
Cruising down shores of High
Barbaree, 935 : 3
Crumb, craved no c., 629 : 22
just a c. to me, 606 : 6
of madeleine, 734 : 1
Crumbled out again to his
atomies, 254 : 5
Crumbles, the way cookie c., 925 : 12
Time c. things, 87 : 6
Crumbs, dogs eat of c., 39 : 32
Crumpets, buttered scones and
c., 804 : 19
Crumpetty tree, 550 : 15
Crumpled, cow with c. horn, 934 : 9
Crusade, my God the Children's
C., 901 : 8
Cruse, little oil in a c., 13 : 42
Crush amang the stoure, 409 : 9

Crush (*continued*)
man shall man no longer c., 399 : 18
the infamous thing, 343 : 17
thought not c. to stone, 873 : 3
Crushed, human being c. by books, 885 : 8
in winepress of passion, 150 : 2
most fragrant when c., 180 : 8
odors c. sweeter still, 180 : *n* 2
the sweet poison, 279 : 7
to ground diffuse sweets, 180 : *n* 2
together c. and bruised, 334 : 15
truth c. to earth, 471 : 12
Crushes, friend supports whom Fortune c., 118 : 11
Crusoe, Robinson C., 318 : 13, 358 : 23
Crust, dinosaur death-steps on c., 893 : 9
eaten in peace, 66 : 6
of bread and liberty, 339 : 11
over volcano of revolution, 689 : 26
upper c., 463 : 15, 481 : 3
water and c., 476 : 5
Crusted with blood, 798 : 1
Cry against hemlocks, 766 : 12
all should c. Beware, 433 : 27
at a play to laugh or c., 322 : 16
battle c. of freedom, 578 : 13
Bellman c. crew reply, 613 : 22
bubbling c. of swimmer, 460 : 21
but behold a c., 29 : 4
caused constantly a c., 767 : 15
cherry-ripe themselves do c., 250 : 5
consider anything don't c., 613 : 13
couch when owls do c., 248 : 16
damned don't c., 810 : 14
don't you c. for me, 598 : 1
every infant's c. of fear, 405 : 9
feel sorry because c., 649 : 7
for being born, 181 : 19
for restful death I c., 244 : 23
forgot c. of gulls, 805 : 9
God for Harry, 207 : 18
great c. in Egypt, 9 : 28
harlot's c. from street, 406 : 18
Havoc, 216 : 12
hear us when we c., 596 : 18
heard the dead c., 873 : 12
heard them c. the peacocks, 766 : 12
he'll be sure to c., 930 : 12
hi or any loud c., 613 : 21
Hold hold, 236 : 18
hounds join in glorious c., 349 : 10
I can no more, 656 : 15
in bed laugh in bed c., 290 : 8
in every c. of every man, 405 : 9
inhuman as hawk's c., 798 : 1
is still They come, 240 : 2
kitten and c. mew, 204 : 13
laugh for fear of having to c., 378 : 6
man's image and his c., 712 : 7
melting from ice, 897 : 13
much c. no wool, 149 : 2
mum, 170 : *n* 11
my eyes out, 169 : 23
need a body c., 919 : *n* 2
nor swooned nor uttered c., 531 : 8
not when father dies, 353 : 12
of Absence Absence in heart, 810 : 17
of bugles going by, 696 : 9
of child by roadway, 712 : 12
of pulleys, 899 : 12
onward sailors c., 688 : 12
out liberty freedom, 216 : 6
Cry (*continued*)
out loudest its abuse, 309 : 3
out Olivia, 213 : 19
raise a hue and c., 169 : 10
scarcely c. weep, 403 : 9
scrawny c. chorister, 769 : 10
secrets c. aloud, 873 : 2
shake me like a c., 696 : 9
so lonesome I could c., 903 : 1
stone shall c. out of wall, 33 : 26
stones c. out, 43 : 42
sudden c. of pain, 781 : 10
that was not ours, 767 : 15
the more it made them c., 371 : 11
there little girl don't c., 665 : 9
too big to c., 522 : 9
truth c. of all, 330 : 23
voice c. Sleep no more, 237 : 21
war war still the c., 457 : 3
wave c. wind c., 807 : 24
we c. that we are come, 235 : 5
we still should c., 181 : 19
what shall I c., 30 : 32
whoever loves you make you c., 935 : 16
Cryin' at the lock, 537 : 6
Crying, first voice was c., 34 : 18
in the wilderness, 36 : 26
infant c. in night, 532 : 10
no more c., 53 : 30
spiders c. together, 893 : 10
watchmen on the heights are c., 176 : 20
why c. after love, 787 : 7
with sighing and c., 167 : 3
Cryptic, met rancor with c. mirth, 728 : 18
Crystal, golden sands c. brooks, 253 : 2
pearl and c. shining bright, 406 : 6
river of c. light, 666 : 16
soul pure as c., 550 : 1
Crystallization action of mind, 453 : 8
Crystallized air of centuries, 796 : 1
Cuauhtémoc, noble C., 721 : 3
Cub, grandam to c., 906 : 4
Cubic inch of space miracle, 576 : 14
Cubit, add one c. to stature, 38 : 3
Cuccu, lhude sing c., 916 : 14
Cuckold lives in bliss, 230 : 34
Cuckoo, as c. is in June, 204 : 21
Cloud-C.-Land, 82 : 10
jug-jug pu-we, 250 : 8
lhude sing c., 916 : 14
shall I call thee bird, 427 : 1
then on every tree, 191 : 13
thus sings he C., 191 : 13
Cuckoo-buds of yellow hue, 191 : 13
Cuckoo's, one flew over c. nest, 933 : 15
Cucullus non facit monachum, 133 : 15
Cucumbers, cold as c., 263 : 4
lodge in garden of c., 28 : 28
sunbeams out of c., 322 : 13
Cud, chew c. and are silent, 373 : 28
whatsoever cheweth the c., 10 : 16
Cudgel thy brains no more, 224 : 6
Cudgel's, know what wood a c. of, 291 : 16
Cue is villainous melancholy, 233 : 6
twisted c., 629 : 13
Cueillez les roses de la vie, 162 : *n* 9
Cuff, the roses get it says Sergeant C., 594 : 7
Cui bono fuerit, 98 : *n* 6
Culled, nosegay of c. flowers, 166 : 6
Cullest race in time, 575 : 22
selectest champions, 570 : 11
Culpa, mea c., 54 : 2
O felix c., 54 : 8
Culprit, stirs c. life, 604 : 4
Cult called Christianity, 641 : 18
of personality, 830 : 13
Cultivate peace and harmony, 379 : 12
sedulously c. free speech, 746 : 6
we must c. our garden, 343 : 14
Cultivated, celebrated c. Duke, 630 : 1
classes, 580 : 14
Cultivates the golden mean, 107 : 20
Cultiver, il faut c. notre jardin, 343 : *n* 6
Cultural, character of c. environment, 685 : 6
effective c. design, 862 : 12
evolution, 870 : 15
ivory tower of c., 755 : 21
tide of c. pollution, 903 : 13
Culture, above all believer in c., 588 : 14
appreciate our own c., 853 : 13
believe only in French c., 658 : 21
creation of contemporary c., 871 : 1
destruction of great c., 819 : 12
equal opportunities of c., 666 : 2
European c. a misunderstanding, 658 : 21
Germany ruins c., 658 : 22
great law of c., 472 : 4
great though disasterous c., 903 : 12
Greek essential to c., 598 : 13
hear word c. reach for revolver, 816 : 6
highest moral c., 515 : 4
in finest flower, 698 : 2
individual creature of his c., 796 : 4
initial act of c., 784 : 12
lives by sympathies, 651 : 2
making of counter c., 912 : 6
mechanics of c., 725 : 9
men of c. true apostles, 588 : 19
moment of clarity, 784 : 6
no better than its woods, 869 : 4
not c. but personality, 577 : 2
not even German c., 658 : 21
not function of race, 796 : 6
product of man, 865 : 14
pursue c. in bands, 700 : 15
pursuit of perfection, 588 : 12
science important part of c., 814 : 13
socialist c. to thrive, 826 : 12
soul takes nothing but education and c., 84 : 3
study of perfection, 588 : 15
to achieve richer c., 853 : 15
too much c. sick animal, 755 : 3
Cultures, materialism model for c., 903 : 12
Cum grano salis, 117 : *n* 4
Cumbered with much serving, 43 : 16
Cumin, tithe of anise and c., 40 : 18
Cumulative, scientific activity c., 787 : 4
Cunard's liners and telegraph, 566 : 6
Cunning alphabet, 571 : 13
duplicate in mind, 570 : 15
Esau was a c. hunter, 8 : 15
history has c. passages, 804 : 14
Hocus old c. attorney, 344 : *n* 7
in war boastful c., 463 : 13
livery of hell, 228 : 19
men pass for wise, 180 : 21

Cunning (*continued*)
more c. to be strange, 192 : 10
nature's sweet c. hand, 213 : 17
old Fury, 611 : 6
punishment sharpens c., 658 : 6
right hand forget her c., 22 : 15
sin cover itself, 209 : 30
strong dose of c., 815 : 5
truth which c. times put on, 199 : 27
what plighted c. hides, 233 : 1
Cunningly, little world made c., 254 : 7
Cunning'st pattern, 232 : 14
Cup, between c. and lip, 259 : 11
come fill the c., 516 : 4
come fill up my c., 432 : 15
dash down yon c., 461 : 9
drained c. of Lethe, 106 : 24
drowned glory in c., 517 : 10
Etruscan c., 892 : 10
fear at heart as at c., 434 : 22
giveth his color in the c., 25 : 11
he took the c., 41 : 10
is new testament in my blood, 48 : 21
leave a kiss but in the c., 256 : 8
let this c. pass, 41 : 12
life's enchanted c., 457 : 12
man in whose hand the c. is found, 8 : 36
my c. runneth over, 18 : 7
o' kindness yet, 410 : 12
of hot wine, 242 : 12
of Samian wine, 461 : 9
of trembling, 31 : 10
sun in golden c., 716 : 21
take c. drink it up, 930 : 16
that clears today, 516 : 13
to every people c. of clay, 929 : 4
valley his golden c., 600 : 25
woodspurge has c. of three, 601 : 15
Cupboard, glacier knocks in c., 868 : 10
was bare, 932 : 7
went to the c., 932 : 7
Cupboards, keys took and c. opened, 640 : 13
Cupid and my Campaspe, 175 : 23
bolt of C. fell, 196 : 15
has his camps, 113 : 5
it has long stood void, 267 : 14
paid, 175 : 23
senior-junior Dan C., 190 : 26
silent note C. strikes, 274 : 20
winged and doth range, 918 : 15
winged C. painted blind, 196 : 1
young Adam C., 192 : 1
Cupiditas, radix malorum est c., 51 : *n* 2
Cupido upon his shuldres wynges, 146 : 23
Cupid's arms, 919 : 19
concludes with C. curse, 177 : 7
Cups, flowing c. pass swiftly, 296 : 3
that cheer, 377 : 3
when they are in their c., 34 : 2
Cur, ears of the old c., 291 : 11
Cur ergo haec ipse non facis, 127 : *n* 12
Curable, presume disease c., 463 : 22
Curates long dust, 796 : 11
shower of c., 555 : 20
will come and go, 796 : 11
Curb, care's check and c., 298 : 21
your magnanimity, 480 : 5
Curd, white c. of ass's milk, 338 : 18
Curdied by frost from snow, 242 : 23
Curds and whey, 932 : 15
Cure, absence c. of love, 169 : 15
Cure (*continued*)
disease kill patient, 180 : 25
freedom c. of anarchy, 373 : 3
laws or kings cause or c., 352 : 21
no c. for birth and death, 704 : 4
not worth the pain, 111 : *n* 2
on exercise depend, 306 : 26
one illness one c., 380 : 5
past c. I am, 246 : 6
past hope past c. past help, 193 : 19
tale would c. deafness, 247 : 12
the c. is freedom, 487 : 11
thrust of c., 908 : 8
Cured, Asclepius c. the body, 83 : *n* 3
I am frizzled stale, 892 : 19
I treated him God c. him, 162 : 9
more than Galen c., 269 : 26
of every folly but vanity, 358 : 25
some hurts you c., 495 : 18
Cures, endure neither evils nor c., 110 : 11
me of my pain, 919 : 19
opposites c. for opposites, 80 : 3
to fear worst c. worse, 226 : 12
Cureth, quiet mind c. all, 260 : 5
Curfew, far-off c. sound, 278 : 19
must not ring tonight, 669 : 19
tolls knell, 361 : 20
Curiosity becomes idolatry, 861 : 10
culture origin not in c., 588 : 15
damnable detestable c., 515 : 12
do well in closet by way of c., 342 : 2
insatiable intellectual c., 701 : 5
intellectual c., 758 : 3
love c. freckles doubt, 827 : 9
must be kept alive, 786 : 14
my c. my wonder, 705 : 4
natural c. of young, 655 : 10
offers to our c., 808 : 2
order awakened c., 496 : 2
permanent and certain, 352 : 4
Curious, amazed and c., 411 : 11
busy c. thirsty fly, 344 : 16
crime, 545 : 9
in unnecessary matters, 34 : 27
incident of dog, 689 : 8
objects and knowledge c., 576 : 5
quaint and c. war is, 641 : 15
seen a c. child, 428 : 15
volume of forgotten lore, 526 : 10
Curiouser and curiouser, 611 : 4
Curl, had a little c., 513 : 1
make your hair c., 629 : 18
New Hampshire mountains c., 747 : 20
not c. less gracefully, 595 : 9
Curled, rainbow c. around shoulder, 733 : 11
up on the floor, 630 : 14
wealthy c. darlings, 229 : 22
wonderful waters c., 593 : 7
Curlicues of marijuana, 893 : 1
Curls done up with bank notes, 554 : 11
frocks and c., 606 : 7
Hyperion's c., 223 : 3
natural c., 117 : 20
Curlylocks wilt be mine, 931 : 19
Currency, debauch c., 783 : 9
no images except c., 564 : 18
Current, azure c. floweth, 553 : 3
genial c. of soul, 362 : 7
icy c. compulsive course, 231 : 18
noiseless c. strong, 588 : 22
swollen c. masses of ice, 538 : 21
Current (*continued*)
take c. when it serves, 217 : 6
time a river of strong c., 124 : 25
Currents, fresh c. of life, 536 : 10
turn awry, 221 : 12
Curriculum was rum, 705 : 3
Curried, short horse soon c., 159 : 24
Currite, lente c. noctis equi, 113 : *n* 4, 184 : 8
Curs of low degree, 369 : 17
Curse astonishment hissing and reproach, 32 : 16
began to c., 41 : 18
bless them that c. you, 37 : 11
Christianity one great c., 658 : 17
creations of mind blessing not c., 763 : 8
God and die, 15 : 6
has come upon me, 528 : 27
his better angel, 232 : 17
I know how to c., 247 : 18
much knowledge a c., 90 : 10
O c. of marriage, 231 : 6
of hell frae me, 926 : 15
on his virtues, 325 : 19
primal eldest c., 222 : 25
remove ancient c., 404 : 21
selfishness greatest c., 517 : 25
the darkness, 786 : *n* 4
with book bell and candle, 149 : 16
youthful harlot's c., 405 : 10
Cursed above all cattle, 7 : 9
be he that moves my bones, 250 : 1
be man that trusteth in man, 32 : 11
be my tribe, 198 : 21
be the verse, 338 : 17
Beauty in lap and c. her, 674 : 3
Boston c. with cranks, 676 : 16
bread, 729 : 5
counted and c. luck, 692 : 1
drunken officer, 911 : 1
Fate has c. you, 76 : 11
floundered enjoyed, 654 : 7
hard reading, 399 : 11
me with his eye, 434 : 24
name to all ages c., 303 : 20
O c. spite, 220 : 6
past, 811 : 9
plagues with which mankind c., 318 : 9
sat Beauty and I c. her, 674 : 3
thoughts, 237 : 11
Curses all Eve's daughters, 225 : 26
like young chickens, 440 : 3
not loud but deep, 239 : 31
of the firmament, 308 : *n* 2
rigged with c. dark, 280 : 18
Cursing, blessing and c., 11 : 22
Cursores vitae lampada tradunt, 100 : *n* 9
Curtailed, always c. thwarted, 799 : 8
Curtain, Anarch lets c. fall, 340 : 28
close his eyes and draw c., 185 : 19
iron c., 746 : 9
never c. between you and me, 748 : 12
never outward swings, 513 : 22
Priam's c., 205 : 19
purple c., 526 : 13
somewhere beyond c., 716 : 15
when she drew c. by, 926 : 22
Curtained, dreams abuse c. sleep, 237 : 14
Curtains, for whom your c. drawn, 265 : 14

Curtains (*continued*)
fringed c. of thine eye, 247 : 22
hell take c., 785 : 10
let fall the c., 377 : 3
of Solomon, 28 : 2
spread canopy or c. spun, 314 : 20
through c. call on us, 252 : 7
Curtius Rufus seems descended from himself, 86 : *n* 1
Curtsied when you have, 247 : 19
Curtsy, leaves c. and quadrille, 899 : 11
nice customs c. to great kings, 208 : 20
while you're thinking, 612 : 19
Cushion, sit on a c., 931 : 19
Custodians of new ideas have fervor, 697 : 17
Custody, individual taken into c., 820 : 15
Custom, age cannot wither nor c. stale, 241 : 1
almost second nature, 190 : *n* 1
conform to tyrant c., 167 : 14
despot of mankind, 486 : 5
follow c. of church where you are, 127 : *n* 5
Fortune more kind than her c., 200 : 15
gods' c. to bring low greatness, 78 : 14
guide of human life, 357 : 15
in all line of order, 225 : 37
made property of easiness, 224 : 8
make it their perch, 227 : 30
maturity of c., 729 : 11
more honored in breach, 219 : 9
nature her c. holds, 224 : 4
no law more binding than c., 688 : 13
of Branksome Hall, 430 : 2
old c. made life sweet, 210 : 23
one good c. corrupt, 534 : 31
public use and c., 163 : 13
reconciles to everything, 372 : 1
sitting at receipt of c., 38 : 26
stern C. spreads afar, 412 : 9
to whom c. due, 47 : 27
violate law and c., 701 : 12
whereof memory of man, 365 : *n* 7
Customary fate of new truths, 596 : 9
suits of solemn black, 218 : 2
Customer, tough c., 547 : 26
Customers, empire for raising c., 366 : 6
sign brings c., 296 : 18
Customs have to be obeyed, 626 : 5
language manners laws c., 424 : 8
laws sand c. rock, 626 : 6
nice c. curtsy to great kings, 208 : 20
oh the times the c., 98 : 2
politics and tongue, 593 : 3
shape experience and behavior, 796 : 4
Cut, all one c. away in reader's consciousness, 739 : 3
and come again, 400 : 8
anyone introduced to, 613 : 20
diamond c. diamond, 264 : 9
features of clerical c., 806 : 14
hawsers haul out, 576 : 16
him out in little stars, 193 : 9
if thy hand offend thee c. it off, 37 : 8
in the evening it is c. down, 20 : 11
is branch that might have grown, 184 : 11
it is soon c. off and we fly away, 20 : 13
Cut (*continued*)
it without any knife, 930 : 15
kite c. from string, 789 : 15
knives that serve or c., 569 : 5
laurels all c., 591 : 6
like a flower and is c. down, 15 : 33
moment I c. his throat, 903 : 5
my coat after my cloth, 159 : 18
not c. conscience to fit fashions, 863 : 10
off in blossoms of sin, 219 : 24
off tails, 929 : 11
short c. to everything, 353 : 8
stems struggling, 873 : 5
stripes away, 708 : 2
unkindest c. of all, 216 : 24
ways of men c. off, 285 : 5
where were the righteous c. off, 15 : 10
with beard of formal c., 211 : 15
Cuts, psychology c. both ways, 582 : 14
Cutthroat dog, 198 : 24
Cutting all pictures out, 729 : 14
corner of nonsense, 438 : 7
through the forest, 765 : 6
Cutty sark o' Paisley harn, 411 : 12
weel done C. Sark, 411 : 13
Cybele, sea C. fresh from ocean, 458 : 7
Cybernetics from Greek steersman, 831 : 22
Cycle of Cathay, 530 : 9
of the ages renewed, 103 : 14
Cycles of heaven, 806 : 15
Cygnet to this pale swan, 202 : 16
Cylinder, nature in terms of c., 638 : 3
Cymbal, tinkling c., 48 : 22
Cymbals, high sounding c., 22 : 25
played before Lord on c., 13 : 14
Cynara, faithful to thee C., 721 : 4
falls thy shadow C., 721 : 6
fell thy shadow C., 721 : 4
Cynic bark, 494 : 1
knows price of everything, 675 : 11
sees things as they are, 647 : 10
Cynicism deadly sin, 724 : 1
dictatorships cannot dispense with c., 802 : 15
intellectual dandyism, 600 : 23
Cynosure of neighboring eyes, 277 : 25
Cynthia of this minute, 335 : 17
regent of night, 331 : 8
Cypress, alley of c., 527 : 1
and myrtle, 459 : 5
correct in c. wood, 827 : 14
in palace walk, 531 : 11
sad c., 214 : 4
shady c. tree, 608 : 13
Cyprian, forsake her C. groves, 306 : 6
Cyrus, Palace of C., 924 : 3
Cythera famous in song, 581 : 3
Czar, I am a c. a slave, 387 : 5
last Russian C., 892 : 17
long live c., 486 : 13
troops led by the C., 922 : 16

D

D, never use big big D, 627 : 12
Da da da iti, 56 : *n* 8
Da mi basia mille, 101 : *n* 15
Dab at an index, 368 : 5
Dad, called brother's father d., 201 : 17
Daddy, are you lost d., 790 : 7
my heart belongs to d., 820 : 7
Daddy's gone a-hunting, 931 : 5
Daemon, when your d. in charge, 711 : 3
Daffodil doth of the dew, 606 : 5
sky, 533 : 21
surfeit when d., 606 : 5
Daffodils, fair d. we weep to see, 266 : 12
host of golden d., 427 : 7
raining d., 705 : 5
that come before swallow, 246 : 26
Dafter, maybe I couldn't be d., 856 : 11
Dagger, air-drawn d., 238 : 26
into back of neighbor, 780 : 9
is this a d. which I see, 237 : 13
of the mind, 237 : 13
wear not my d. in my mouth, 243 : 26
Daggers, give me the d., 237 : 23
speak d. to her, 222 : 24
Daily beauty in his life, 232 : 11
before us lies in d. life, 287 : 3
die d., 274 : 13
duly and d. serving him, 365 : 13
give us our d. bread, 37 : 15
wealth small aid for d. gladness, 77 : 3
with souls that cringe, 567 : 11
Dainties bred of a book, 190 : 27
such d. to them, 371 : 22
Daintiest last to make end sweet, 193 : 35
Dainty dish, 931 : 9
Daiquiris, two d. withdrew, 884 : 10
Daisies and clover, 578 : 9
lie upon the d., 628 : 6
meadows trim with d. pied, 277 : 25
pied and violets blue, 191 : 13
she can hear d. grow, 674 : 14
such as men callen d., 145 : 11
Daisy, blessings-of-civilization trust a d., 625 : 25
by shadow it casts, 429 : 11
give me answer do, 718 : 18
there's a d., 224 : 2
Dakotas I am for war, 591 : 4
under her hull, 822 : 7
Dale, haunted spring and d., 277 : 11
hawthorn in the d., 277 : 24
over hill over d., 196 : 10
Dales, hills and valleys d. and fields, 183 : *n* 5
Dalliance, not give d. rein, 248 : 12
primrose path of d., 218 : 28
silken d., 207 : 10
Dallies with innocence of love, 214 : 3
Dam, all my chickens and their d., 239 : 21
Damage, came to see d. done, 910 : 9
Damaged, archangel a little d., 441 : 14
Damaging, nothing more d. than old error, 397 : 5
Damask, feed on her d. cheek, 214 : 5
Dam'd by earthquake, 623 : 4
Dame, dance in old d. yet, 760 : 1
has lost shoe, 929 : 10
la belle d. sans merci, 478 : 13
nothing like a d., 833 : 16
one for my d., 930 : 5
our sulky sullen d., 411 : 4
smiled at the d., 404 : 11
Dames, ah gentle d., 411 : 5
struts his d. before, 277 : 23
that squire of d., 173 : 18

Damn authors they never read, 375 : 12
devil d. thee black, 239 : 29
doesn't give a d., 924 : 18
don't care twopenny d., 421 : 15
don't give a d., 632 : 6
my dear I don't give a d., 848 : 11
no general proposition worth d., 645 : 2
such, 386 : *n* 3
the torpedoes, 490 : 4
with faint praise, 338 : 14
Damnable deceitful woman, 316 : 16
detestable curiosity, 515 : 12
iteration, 203 : 1
Damnably, marriage d. serious business, 826 : 14
Damnation, deal d. round land, 340 : 3
deep d. of his taking off, 236 : 24
distilled d., 416 : 6
marriage bed to this d., 254 : 23
two fingers' breadth of d., 63 : *n* 1
Damned, another d. thick book, 387 : 6
at certain revolutions all the d., 284 : 23
be d. dear boys, 708 : 20
be him that first cries Hold, 240 : 11
better d. than not mentioned, 385 : 13
born by dying and being d., 156 : 8
cohort of the d., 708 : 13
conjecturally d., 640 : 19
could have had d. good time, 844 : 13
darkness of d., 520 : 7
dear d. distracting town, 334 : 24
devilish and d. tobacco, 259 : 15
disinheriting countenance, 399 : 2
dissolute d. despairful, 752 : 4
don't cry, 810 : 14
drama whether d. or not, 398 : 20
Faustus must be d., 184 : 8
forever d. with Lucifer, 183 : 20
from here to eternity, 708 : 14
I will see thee d. first, 422 : 1
if goats cannot be d., 254 : 10
if I see how helican, 765 : 12
if you do or don't, 444 : 9
in fair wife, 229 : 12
many an old host d., 204 : 6
music brandy of the d., 680 : 19
of body and soul, 707 : 19
one d. thing after another, 756 : 4
one hour then d. perpetually, 184 : 7
out d. spot, 239 : 23
perpetually, 184 : 7
public be d., 584 : 4
publish and be d., 421 : 17
salute eloquence, 840 : 12
smiling d. villain, 220 : 1
to everlasting fame, 337 : 15
universal cock, 767 : 6
vacillating state, 527 : 16
what d. minutes tells he, 230 : 34
Damning those they have no mind to, 291 : 6
Damozel, blessed d., 601 : 13
Damp, demd d. moist unpleasant body, 547 : 15
lived in cellar d., 568 : 20
nights are very d., 614 : 8
souls of housemaids, 804 : 5
tonnage, 843 : 19
years d. my intended wing, 287 : 13
Damsel lay deploring, 331 : 7
to every man a d. or two, 12 : 9
with dulcimer, 433 : 26
Damyata (Control), 56 : *n* 8
datta dayadhvamiti, 56 : *n* 8
Dan, Dangerous D. McGrew, 752 : 5
from D. to Beersheba, 12 : 22
senior-junior D. Cupid, 190 : 26
Danaë to the stars, 531 : 12
Danaos, timeo D. et dona ferentis, 104 : *n* 15
Dance, a god has given the d., 58 : 17
and drink and sing, 405 : 6
and Provençal song, 476 : 23
antic hay, 183 : 16
as often as d. it can, 433 : 30
attendance, 249 : 16
attention on old age, 717 : 13
barefoot on wedding day, 188 : 30
by light of moon, 921 : 20
can't you d. polka, 934 : 23
change lobsters and d., 612 : *n* 2
dancer from d., 715 : 17
in old dame yet, 760 : 1
join the d., 612 : 8, 612 : 9
like wave of sea, 712 : 17
maids d. in a ring, 250 : 8
mehitabel dance, 760 : 5
move easiest who learned to d., 333 : 9
on with the d., 457 : 15
our clumsy dance, 860 : 13
praise him with d., 22 : 25
Pyrrhic d. as yet, 461 : 7
rhythms for rain, 897 : 19
round in ring and suppose, 749 : 9
rouses him up to d., 60 : 18
sweet d. to violins, 676 : 9
that ends in nakedness, 850 : 9
the antic hay, 183 : 16
there is only the d., 807 : 6
time to d., 26 : 21
tipsy d. and jollity, 279 : 11
to flutes dance to lutes, 676 : 9
tossing heads in sprightly d., 427 : 9
upon the air, 676 : 9
walk before they d., 339 : 17
when you do d., 246 : 28
while you can, 868 : 7
with me in Ireland, 916 : *n* 3
with William Blake, 875 : 4
wyth me in Irlonde, 916 : 16
Danced by light of moon, 550 : 10
daughter of Herodias Salome d., 39 : 22
David d. before the Lord, 13 : 16
death-fires d., 434 : 17
his did, 829 : 18
I could have d. all night, 894 : 21
lighter than cork, 673 : 14
like dinglebodies, 901 : 3
moon on Monan's rill, 431 : 5
Salome d., 39 : 22
star d., 209 : 13
till doomsday, 324 : 11
to see that banner, 518 : 12
Dancer from the dance, 715 : 17
kneeling on nothing, 899 : 4
Dancers all gone under hill, 807 : 15
dancing in tune, 533 : 22
Dances as often as dance it can, 433 : 30
he capers he d., 225 : 20
in golden escape, 852 : 14
in hamlets d. on green, 430 : 6
in sight of heaven, 899 : 13
in what ethereal d., 525 : 18
lulled with d. and delight, 196 : 18
Dances (*continued*)
oh she d. such a way, 289 : 21
when she d. in the wind, 305 : 3
Dancing and architecture, 690 : 1
cheek to cheek, 802 : 8
dancers d. in tune, 533 : 22
days are done, 191 : *n* 3
dining and d. begin, 855 : 16
dogs and bears, 732 : 16
emptier ever d. in air, 195 : 11
in the checkered shade, 278 : 1
is life itself, 690 : 2
keeping rhythm in d., 807 : 10
labor blossoming or d., 715 : 17
loftiest of arts, 690 : 2
music of d. waves, 800 : 10
on volcano, 472 : 2
past our d. days, 191 : 25
source of arts, 690 : 1
to frenzied drum, 714 : 14
very merry d. drinking, 306 : 27
Dandin, asked for it Georges D., 298 : 7
Dandruff, toothpaste and d. ads, 844 : 2
Dandy, candy is d., 855 : 10
I'm a Yankee Doodle d., 759 : 6
Yankee Doodle d., 920 : 9
Dandyism, intellectual d., 600 : 23
Dane, more antique Roman than D., 224 : 32
Danger, above noise and d., 299 : 10
bear the brunt of d., 575 : 15
brave man's choice is d., 77 : 4
bright eyes of d., 669 : 3
clear and present d., 644 : 23
days of d., 431 : 8
dear Fatherland no d. thine, 573 : 12
difficulty and d., 391 : 1
familiarity with d., 569 : 21
feared no d. knew no sin, 305 : 14
foretold that d. lurks within, 186 : 18
glory and d. alike, 81 : 2
graceful the small before d., 874 : 9
hackneyed phrases d. signals, 685 : 14
in view of d. give up life, 69 : 6
inherent in weapons race, 860 : 6
is in discord, 511 : 15
less d. from stranger, 855 : 11
neither shape of d. dismay, 427 : 26
nettle d., 203 : 22
not from a stranger, 897 : 17
of faction, 398 : 3
of violent death, 264 : 17
or treasure, 896 : 13
pleased with d., 303 : 20
she suspected no d., 583 : 10
spur of all great minds, 178 : 7
there is d. from all men, 380 : 13
when fatherland in d., 412 : 1
where is man out of d., 596 : 7
Dangerous, delays d. in war, 175 : *n* 5
delays have d. ends, 185 : 4
demur you're d., 605 : 11
edge of things, 543 : 7
guiled shore to d. sea, 199 : 26
have in me something d., 224 : 21
idea d. when only one, 724 : 7
ideas d. for good or evil, 783 : 16
if a little knowledge d., 596 : 7
into d. world I leaped, 405 : 12
little learning d., 332 : 20
mad bad d. to know, 454 : 22
most d. calculations we call illusions, 802 : 16

Dangerous (*continued*)
politics as d. as war, 743 : 7
realities less d. than fancies, 738 : 9
say nothing in d. times, 264 : 4
show thy d. brow by night, 215 : 19
such men are d., 215 : 8
temptation in gay colors, 250 : *n* 1
thirst d. thing, 692 : 15
to be of no church d., 352 : 24
to meet culture alone, 700 : 15
to our peace and safety, 408 : 3
who make no noise are d., 296 : 19
Danger's troubled night, 443 : 13
Dangers, concern for safety in face of d., 902 : 8
defend us from d. of night, 55 : 9
delays breed d., 175 : 11
greatest d. to liberty, 677 : 15
in what great d. ye spend little span, 100 : 13
no d. fright him, 351 : 18
of the seas, 273 : 6
she loved me for the d., 229 : 31
thorns and d. of world, 202 : 13
what d. thou make us scorn, 411 : 10
with d. compassed round, 286 : 28
Daniel, cast D. into the den of lions, 33 : 3
come to judgment, 200 : 11
had convicted them, 36 : 15
second D., 200 : 19
Dank, addled mosses d., 793 : 7
tarn of Auber, 526 : 23
Danny, hangin' D. Deever, 708 : 2
Dans, no time for fancy d., 825 : 3
Dante greatest depth of passion, 809 : 17
language of D. common language, 809 : 16
more learned from D., 809 : 16
of dread Inferno, 544 : 2
Daphnis, my songs draw D. home, 103 : 17
Dapple, name was D. Gray, 933 : 16
Dappled things, 656 : 4
turf at ease, 426 : 3
Dapple-dawn-drawn Falcon, 656 : 1
Darbies, ease d. at wrist, 572 : 7
Darby, always same D. my own, 663 : 1
Dare all that may plant man's lordship, 643 : 2
ask just God's assistance, 524 : 5
bear to live or d. to die, 337 : 10
call soul my own, 507 : 17
choose if you d., 275 : 27
deadly terrors clasp, 405 : 8
do duty as understand it, 521 : 5
endure greater than d., 540 : 1
enter you who d., 600 : 29
first ponder then d., 489 : 11
heart would deny and d. not, 239 : 31
I d. do all, 237 : 3
I d. yet may not, 167 : 7
imitate him if you d., 716 : 6
is highest wisdom, 448 : 4
letting I d. not, 237 : 2
love that and say so too, 252 : 6
mighty things, 686 : 13
never d. utter untruth, 98 : 10
never grudge throe, 544 : 10
no no no I d. not, 917 : 16
none d. call it treason, 181 : 21
O what men d. do, 209 : 29
on what wings d. he aspire, 405 : 7
Dare (*continued*)
slaves who d. not be, 567 : 4
soul to d., 431 : 7
speak truth as much as I d., 165 : 16
there is much to d., 785 : 8
think unthinkable, 862 : 21
to be ahead of the world, 65 : 3
to be naive, 832 : 15
to be true, 268 : 4
to be wise, 108 : 20
to eat a peach, 803 : 19
to love country and be poor, 340 : 7
what hand d. seize fire, 405 : 7
what man d. I d., 238 : 28
wonder Do I d., 803 : 12
Dared, determined d. and done, 365 : 9
none d. thou hast, 173 : 4
Daren't go a-hunting, 594 : 2
Dares, come before swallow d., 246 : 26
life d. send challenge, 292 : 9
to call Himself a man, 829 : 14
who d. do more is none, 237 : 3
Darest thou now O soul, 576 : 17
thou then, 430 : 23
Darien, peak in D., 475 : 7
Daring, brave man braver less d., 569 : 21
in war d. boastful, 463 : 13
pilot in extremity, 303 : 20
well-doing and d., 354 : *n* 4
young man on trapeze, 636 : 12
Dark, abysmal d. of center, 480 : 12
afraid to go home in d., 699 : *n* 5
after that the d., 535 : 20
all night in d. and wet, 668 : 11
amid blaze of noon, 288 : 20
and bloody ground, 578 : 11
and his d. secret love, 405 : 5
and lonely hiding place, 435 : 16
as Erebus, 201 : 3
as good in the d., 266 : 9
as world of man, 801 : 6
at one stride comes the d., 434 : 21
backward and abysm of time, 247 : 10
best of d. and bright, 459 : 13
between d. and daylight, 512 : 3
bird fly few beats in d., 907 : 9
blanket of the d., 236 : 18
blue ocean roll, 458 : 25
Care sits enthroned, 107 : 26
Chromis did not save himself from d. death, 57 : 20
clear moving utterly free, 878 : 7
cloud at house's door, 928 : 18
cold and empty desolation, 807 : 24
come to d. and lament, 749 : 7
cooling star, 746 : 20
dark dark amid blaze, 288 : 20
dark dark spaces, 807 : 16
days d. and dreary, 510 : 11
dove with flickering tongue, 808 : 13
dull d. soundless day, 525 : 19
ever-during d., 285 : 5
every hour of light d., 576 : 14
fate sits on d. battlements, 416 : 11
fear death as children fear d., 180 : 2
fell of d. not day, 656 : 19
go home in d., 699 : 20
great leap in the d., 264 : 21
hawks hear us, 778 : 5
highest candle lights d., 769 : 3
horse, 501 : 8
hour or twain, 238 : 12
hunt it in the d., 376 : 10
Dark (*continued*)
in d. time eye begins to see, 874 : 15
in nightmare of the d., 868 : 12
in the d. and silent grave, 173 : 5
inscrutable workmanship, 423 : 18
iron New England d., 838 : 5
irrecoverably d., 288 : 20
let d. come upon you, 807 : 17
lie awake in d. weep for sins, 574 : 24
life one long struggle in d., 100 : 14
Maid and her lord, 76 : 3
mutinous Shannon waves, 777 : 16
narrowing d. hours, 837 : 3
night is d., 490 : 6, 925 : 2
night of d. intent, 748 : 11
night of the soul, 167 : 1, 835 : 11
not d. days great days, 745 : 7
o'er d. her mantle threw, 285 : 25
on d. theme trace verses of light, 100 : 10
pillared d., 749 : 7
raging in the d., 716 : 7
road whence no one returns, 101 : 16
Satanic mills, 406 : 21
some days d. and dreary, 510 : 11
soul's d. cottage, 276 : 12
sun to me is d., 288 : 21
they all go into d., 807 : 16
things in d. besides Santa Claus, 750 : 19
to d. tower came, 234 : 13
'twill soon be d., 494 : 1
unconscious not only d. but light, 754 : 10
unfathomed caves, 362 : 8
violets are d. too, 103 : 23
wall between us and d., 831 : 21
wandering in d. labyrinth, 182 : 20
we are for the d., 241 : 26
we work in d., 653 : 5
what if Amyntas is d., 103 : 23
what in me is d. illumine, 283 : 2
whistles in d., 678 : 10
who art d. as night, 246 : 7
with excessive bright, 285 : 7
with torment and tears, 561 : 21
wood where straight way lost, 140 : 10
woods lovely d. deep, 748 : 7
world and wide, 282 : 15
world present treatment, 725 : 1
Darkened, blue d. on blueness, 791 : 1
hurtles in d. air, 363 : 10
ocean-booms, 767 : 13
sun or light be not d., 27 : 24
windows be d., 27 : 24
Darkeneth, who d. counsel by words, 16 : 27
Darker and darker stairs, 791 : 1
as d. grows the night, 368 : 12
grows the valley, 601 : 2
larger bill for d. ill, 562 : *n* 2
the tinge that saddens, 503 : 7
Darkest altar of heartbreak, 881 : 11
before day dawneth, 277 : 5
day will have passed, 377 : 21
sun breaks through d. clouds, 189 : 2
Dark-heaving boundless, 458 : 29
Darkies how heart grows weary, 598 : 4
Darkling I listen, 476 : 28
plain, 587 : 16
roll d. down torrent, 352 : 1
stand varying shore, 241 : 20

Darkly deeply beautifully blue, 440 : 2, 461 : 13
it knows obstacles, 899 : 15
see through glass d., 48 : 25
wise and rudely great, 337 : 2
Darkness, absence d. death, 253 : 1
affronts with his own d., 883 : 11
again and silence, 512 : 10
all the d. I have, 851 : 2
and light alike to thee, 22 : 18
and shadow of death, 15 : 24, 21 : 13, 42 : 26
as children fear in d., 100 : 22
awake upon dark, 791 : 1
awful d. silence reign, 551 : 3
blackness of d., 52 : 26
cast into outer d., 38 : 22
comprehended it not, 44 : 18
crown of our life is d., 632 : 15
curse the d., 786 : *n* 4
dawn on our d., 452 : 5
deep but dazzling d., 299 : 1
deep things out of d., 15 : 31
deepens, 470 : 23
distant voice in d., 512 : 10
downward to d. on wings, 767 : 4
dying of cold not d., 705 : 21
eagle swooping d. up, 928 : 9
embalmed d., 476 : 26
encounter d. as a bride, 228 : 18
falls at thy behest, 597 : 17
falls from wings, 510 : 17
fell upon Christian, 302 : 10
from the darkness, 885 : 9
gives light in d., 185 : 12
good kind d., 647 : *n* 2
horror of outer d., 614 : 17
hovers earth is silent, 5 : 6
how great that d., 37 : 19
how in your d. know, 733 : 9
if light in thee be d., 37 : 19
in d. and with dangers, 286 : 28
in him is no d., 52 : 19
in what d. of life spend little span, 100 : 13
instruments of d., 236 : 9
into d. peering, 526 : 14
into d. they go, 823 : 12
into eternal d. fire and ice, 140 : 19
jaws of d. do devour it, 195 : 23
land of d. and shadow, 15 : 24
lead me from d. to light, 56 : 20
leaves world to d., 361 : 20
lest d. come, 45 : 17
light excelleth d., 26 : 18
light shineth in d., 44 : 18
lighten our d., 55 : 9
love in spite of d., 252 : 21
mainly in d., 912 : 10
man ever in d., 132 : 4
man in unsearchable d., 654 : 19
no d. into light without emotion, 754 : 14
no light but d. visible, 283 : 6
not walk in d., 45 : 4
of God, 807 : 17
of the damned, 520 : 7
outer d., 38 : 22, 40 : 31, 614 : 17
pain d. and cold, 544 : 22
peace and d., 692 : 10
people that walked in d., 29 : 15
people which sat in d., 37 : 2
pestilence that walketh in d., 20 : 16
prince of d. a gentleman, 234 : 11
Darkness (*continued*)
raven down of d., 279 : 19
rulers of the d., 49 : 39
scatters rear of d. thin, 277 : 23
shaft of light in d., 891 : 15
shares the d., 823 : 2
sit in d. here, 284 : 15
such as sit in d., 21 : 13
them that sit in d., 42 : 26
thou makest d., 21 : 11
through a brief d., 512 : 12
through d. up to God, 532 : 12
to d. and to me, 361 : 20
two eternities of d., 846 : 2
universal d. buries all, 340 : 28
upon face of the deep, 6 : 10
we are not of d., 50 : 19
where d. let me sow light, 138 : 15
which may be felt, 9 : 21
wind torrent of d., 772 : 23
works of d., 47 : 29
worms and shrouds, 475 : 13
year of now done d., 656 : 16
Dark-shining Pacific, 797 : 12
Darky's heart longed to go, 672 : 19
Darling buds of May, 244 : 5
Charlie is my d., 417 : 6
daughter, 924 : 17
I am growing old, 662 : 22
my d. dear, 921 : 1
my d. from the lions, 18 : 22
Nature's d., 362 : 22
of men and gods, 100 : 1
of my heart, 331 : 5
of our crew, 393 : 11
old man's d., 161 : 6
sin, 435 : 17
Darlings, we must march my d., 575 : 15
wealthy curled d., 229 : 22
Dart, every look a d., 919 : 19
feather on fatal d., 456 : 17
poisonous d. not pugnacity, 786 : 8
time throw a d. at thee, 265 : 15
Darwin Abraham of scientific men, 580 : 7
Darwin's theory conjectural, 509 : 6
Dash down yon cup, 461 : 9
thy foot against a stone, 20 : 17
thy foot against stone, 43 : 1
Dashed, breaking waves d. high, 470 : 14
in pieces the enemy, 9 : 34
the brains out, 237 : 5
through thick and thin, 304 : 17
Dastard in war, 430 : 19
Dastardly pitiful Public, 445 : 7
Dat veniam corvis vexat censura columbas, 122 : *n* 1
Data, submit d. to analysis, 397 : 17
Date, in South d. from war, 623 : 15
out of d., 792 : 10
will live in infamy, 780 : 15
Dates of wars deaths of kings, 627 : 2
Datta (Give), 56 : *n* 8
Daubed with slime and pitch, 9 : 8
Daughter all her life, 597 : 14
am I in mother's house, 709 : 15
as mother so her d., 32 : 26
at point of death, 42 : 7
beggar's d. of Bethnal Green, 926 : 17
fairer d. of fair mother, 107 : 10
harping on my d., 220 : 18
have you a d., 220 : 17
Daughter (*continued*)
I have a d., 200 : 16
images return O my d., 806 : 8
king of Spain's d., 932 : 1
light God's eldest d., 276 : 18
little d. whispered, 556 : 15
marry d. when you can, 269 : 20
Mrs. Porter and d., 805 : 6
my d. O my ducats, 199 : 11
of a hundred earls, 528 : 7
of debate, 163 : 18
of earth and water, 468 : 10
of Elysium, 412 : 9
of Herodias Salome danced, 39 : 22
of Jove, 361 : 13
of Moon Nokomis, 511 : 16
of the gods, 528 : 22
one fair d., 221 : 1
sole d. of his voice, 287 : 18
stern d. of voice of God, 427 : 12
still harping on my d., 220 : 18
taken his little d., 510 : 4
undaunted d. of desires, 292 : 15
whipped her little d., 932 : 4
yes my darling d., 924 : 17
your d. and the Moor, 229 : 20
Daughter's a daughter all her life, 597 : 14
preaching down d. heart, 529 : 22
tiptoed to d. room, 912 : 13
Daughters and sons gone, 904 : 9
curses all Eve's d., 225 : 26
degenerate sons and d., 728 : 5
earth's heedless sons and d., 834 : 11
fairest of her d. Eve, 285 : 20
have done virtuously, 26 : 10
horseleach hath two d., 26 : 3
if you have no d., 931 : 17
my d. I suppose, 864 : 16
none of Beauty's d., 460 : 1
O d. of Jerusalem, 28 : 2, 28 : 16
of music brought low, 27 : 24
of my father's house, 214 : 6
of sea, 850 : 10
of time, 495 : 5
prayers are d. of Zeus, 58 : 11
sage d. of Muses, 72 : 3
tigers not d., 234 : 25
who Shem and Shaun d. of, 778 : 5
words are d. of earth, 352 : 6
Daughter-sons, all Livia's d., 778 : 5
Daunt, death could not d., 926 : 18
Dauntless, brows of d. courage, 283 : 25
Hampden with d. breast, 362 : 9
in war, 430 : 18
slughorn to my lips, 234 : *n* 3
Dauphin, daylight's d., 656 : 1
David, and D. his ten thousands, 13 : 4
danced before the Lord, 13 : 16
died full of days, 14 : 28
in the city of D., 42 : 28
in the midst, 365 : 7
Josias, 320 : 6
King D. and King Solomon, 696 : 3
my sling the sling of D., 672 : 15
no more behind your scenes D., 353 : 23
played before the Lord, 13 : 14
prevailed over the Philistine, 13 : 3
the son of Jesse, 13 : 25
David's, once in royal D. city, 561 : 10
upon St. D. Day, 933 : 6
Davil, ole d. sea, 810 : 5
Davos, I am D. not Oedipus, 96 : 4

Daw, Margery D., 931 : 2
no wiser than a d., 184 : 20
Dawn becomes yellow, 928 : 17
before d. of day, 368 : 2
bodiless as false d., 899 : 12
comes no one receives it, 841 : 18
comes no sooner for early riser, 935 : 15
comes up like thunder, 708 : 9
creation's d. beheld, 458 : 27
embraced summer d., 674 : 10
gray d. breaking, 487 : 2, 760 : 14
house made of d., 928 : 18
in Helen's arms, 716 : 19
in that d. to be alive, 424 : 5
into silver d., 828 : 9
live gray d., 906 : 9
Morning Star herald of d., 97 : 16
of knowledge false dawn, 837 : 13
of morning after, 718 : 12
on other side of Atlantic, 363 : 21
on our darkness, 452 : 5
past is twilight of d., 719 : 14
rosy-fingered d., 57 : 11
said to d. Be sudden, 693 : 13
speeds a man, 61 : 22
will dispel night, 464 : 15
with silver-sandaled feet, 674 : 15
Dawned from Bullen's eyes, 361 : 19
Dawneth, darkest before day d. 277 : 5
Dawning, bird of d., 217 : 26
here hath been d., 474 : 16
not as d. of day, 255 : 1
Dawn's early light, 446 : 1
light dispersed, 63 : 11
Daws, for d. to peck at, 229 : 17
Day, a little work and good d., 617 : 3
a summer's d. and with the setting sun, 284 : 2
after wedding night, 739 : 12
afterwards d., 604 : 5
all days as marriage d., 267 : 20
all on summer's d., 931 : 4
all the livelong d., 921 : 17
all things all d. long, 534 : 10
alternation of night and d., 130 : 16
and night shall not cease, 8 : 1
and way we met, 634 : 2
another blue d., 474 : 16
apple a d., 923 : 12
April d., 748 : 17
as it fell upon a d., 257 : 6
as morning shows the d., 288 : 12
a-tiptoe when d. named, 208 : 10
aye fair in land o' leal, 417 : 11
barrier between d. and d., 428 : 3
battle d. past, 597 : 15
be d. never so long, 161 : 7
be she fairer than the d., 264 : 23
beneath blue of d., 691 : 1
best d. first to flee, 104 : 8
better d. better deed, 261 : 5
beyond night across d. 530 : 13
boils at last, 540 : 14
bounded by D. of Judgment, 535 : *n* 6
breaks not it is heart, 918 : 18
brief December d., 513 : 20
bright cold d. in April, 858 : 13
bright d. is done, 241 : 26
bright d. not for aye, 561 : 21
broadcast doings of d., 573 : 19
brought back my night, 282 : 21
burden and heat of d., 40 : 9
by d. in a pillar of cloud, 9 : 30

Day (*continued*)
called feast of Crispian, 208 : 10
cares that infest d., 510 : 22
chest of drawers by d., 370 : 13
children of the d., 50 : 19
Christmas D. in workhouse, 661 : 14
clear d. see forever, 895 : 5
close eye of d., 281 : 9
come another d., 929 : 17
cometh that shall burn as oven, 33 : 38
compare thee to summer's d., 244 : 5
cool of the d., 7 : 7
count that d. lost, 920 : 12
country geology by d., 830 : 17
creatures of a d., 72 : 2
dance barefoot on wedding d., 188 : 30
darkest before d. dawneth, 277 : 5
darkest d., 377 : 21
death will have his d., 194 : 28
dependency of d. and night, 767 : 4
dies at the opening d., 328 : 12
dim light of immortal d., 467 : 9
dines on following d., 614 : 1
do business of d. in d., 421 : 12
do each d. two things disliked, 751 : 12
dog hath a d., 160 : 17
dog will have his d., 224 : 24
doomsday eighth d., 863 : 17
dreadful d., 430 : 12
drink oblivion of d., 600 : 16
dying d. sir, 920 : 6
each d. like a year, 676 : 12
eighth d. of week, 863 : 17
end of perfect d., 698 : 15
endures moment or d., 715 : 13
entertains the harmless d., 250 : 15
ere I had seen that d., 218 : 14
evening and morning were first d., 6 : 11
every d. got up and gone to bed, 751 : 12
every d. hidden growth, 565 : 20
every d. in every way, 684 : 9
every d. passed as if our last, 111 : 29
every dog has his d., 492 : 18
every dog his d., 566 : 14
every year passed d., 907 : 10
everyone has his d., 746 : 14
exact d. labor light denied, 282 : 16
faint in the d. of adversity, 25 : 13
fair d. adieu, 201 : 22
famous d. and year, 512 : 6
faster and more fast, 540 : 14
fate put heads together, 748 : 13
fell of dark not d., 656 : 19
first last everlasting d., 252 : 22
first spring d., 671 : 14
fogs prevail upon the d., 304 : 25
follow as night the d., 219 : 2
forever and a d., 212 : 24
fourth d. evening we descend, 822 : 10
frabjous d., 612 : 18
friends I have lost a d., 119 : 20
from our immortal d., 403 : 13
from this d. forward, 56 : 9
gaudy blabbing remorseful d., 185 : 20
gilded car of d., 279 : 10
given thee till break of d., 405 : 2
go to bed by d., 668 : 9
God is d. night winter summer, 70 : 2
got tired of me, 605 : 10

Day (*continued*)
great and dreadful d. of the Lord, 34 : 1
guest that tarrieth but a d., 34 : 16
gwine to run all d., 598 : 2
happiest d. happiest hour, 525 : 4
hath brightest d. a cloud, 185 : 14
he that outlives this d., 208 : 10
health and a d., 496 : 5
hippopotamus's d., 804 : 20
home being washing d., 310 : 4
how it is with April d., 748 : 17
I had rued, 748 : 3
I hate the d., 174 : 13
I have lived my d., 108 : *n* 7
I will move into d., 171 : 12
idle singer of empty d., 618 : 6
if she be a d., 323 : 8
in d. of adversity consider, 27 : 7
in d. of prosperity be joyful, 27 : 7
in its hotness, 585 : 12
in the d. in the night, 576 : 4
in the d. of vengeance, 23 : 15
in the posteriors of this d., 191 : 8
in thy courts, 20 : 8
in which ye came out, 9 : 29
infinite d. excludes the night, 328 : 15
is a poem, 798 : 1
is at hand, 47 : 29
is done and darkness, 510 : 17
is for honest men, 77 : 5
is past and gone, 470 : 19
it is his d., 149 : 12
it was Christmas D., 182 : 3
it was only d., 769 : 8
jocund d. stands tiptoe, 193 : 15
joint-laborer with d., 217 : 20
journey take whole long d., 608 : 10
July's d. short as December, 246 : 13
just for one d., 732 : 17
kings upon coronation d., 305 : 19
knell of parting d., 361 : 20
known a better d., 429 : 20
left alone with our d., 868 : 8
lengthens not a d., 251 : 13
let every man consider last d., 74 : 7
let the d. perish, 15 : 7
let them have their d., 714 : 5
life but a d., 475 : 10
light of common d., 426 : 15
light of fuller d., 566 : 11
light through the word named d., 135 : 2
like d. without sunshine, 401 : 8
long weary d. have end, 174 : 18
looked into eye of d., 715 : 19
love o' life's young d., 482 : 13
love resembleth April d., 189 : 32
maddest merriest d., 528 : 12
makes d. seep into night, 132 : 5
meditate d. and night, 17 : 12
merry as d. is long, 209 : 5
merry heart goes all d., 246 : 24
mildewed d. in August, 892 : 6
most wasted d. of all, 386 : 4
motion of rising d., 875 : 2
mounting at break of d., 428 : 2
night and d. you are the one, 820 : 2
night mother of d., 513 : 6
night of time surpasseth d., 275 : 10
night thousand eyes d. one, 670 : 8
no d. without a line, 555 : *n* 2
not a d. without a line, 90 : 15
not as dawning of d., 255 : 1

Day (*continued*)
not look same by d., 507 : 5
not to me returns d., 285 : 5
not up soon as I, 202 : 15
now d. over, 616 : 7
now's the d., 411 : 15
of adversity, 27 : 7
of affliction, 35 : 21
of death better than birth, 27 : 3
of deliverance, 381 : 7
of empires come, 627 : 6
of glory has come, 415 : *n* 1
of my destiny's over, 460 : 3
of one's birth, 27 : 3
of prosperity, 35 : 21
of small things, 33 : 31
of spirits, 298 : 21
of the great reckoning, 4 : 9
of the locust, 857 : 8
of the Lord, 50 : 18
of vengeance, 23 : 15
of wrath, 139 : 4, 430 : 12
on seventh d. God ended his work, 6 : 16
on that d. no soul wronged, 132 : 6
one buries her, 67 : 11
one marries her, 67 : 11
pack clouds away and welcome d., 257 : 18
past and yet I saw no sun, 177 : 10
perfect d., 698 : 15
perpetual morning, 559 : 22
petty pace from d. to d., 240 : 4
precincts of cheerful d., 362 : 14
proper man as see in summer's d., 196 : 9
rain it raineth every d., 214 : 29, 234 : 1
rape of every blessed d., 899 : 13
rare as d. in June, 567 : 13
red-letter d., 170 : *n* 4
remember the sabbath d., 10 : 6
returns too soon, 460 : 5
Rome must be built in d., 893 : 18
Rome not built in one d., 160 : 8
rose with delight to us, 267 : 8
runs through roughest d., 236 : 13
Saint Patrick's d., 920 : 21
saw my evil d., 418 : 12
seize the d., 107 : 8
set down as gain each d., 107 : 7
seventh d. thou shalt not work, 10 : 6
shall declare it, 48 : 5
shall stand at the latter d., 16 : 4
she set out one d., 742 : 1
shineth unto perfect d., 23 : 8
sleep neither night nor d., 236 : 2
so cool so calm, 268 : 15
so foul and fair a d., 236 : 4
soundless d. in autumn, 525 : 19
specter night and d., 406 : 1
stocking all the d., 368 : 8
sufficient unto d. is evil, 38 : 7
sun anew each d., 799 : 8
sun gone down while it was d., 32 : 8
sun shall not smite thee by d., 22 : 4
sunbeam in winter's d., 345 : 3
superfluous to demand time of d., 202 : 23
support us all d. long, 490 : 10
take yourself away any d., 560 : 30
tender eye of pitiful d., 238 : 21
tenderly haughty d., 494 : 18

Day (*continued*)
thanks to heroes reached this d., 881 : 15
that d. read no more, 454 : 2
that is dead, 530 : 20
that shall burn as oven, 33 : 38
think every d. your last, 109 : 3
third d. comes a frost, 249 : 3
third d. he rose again, 55 : 2
third d. he will raise us up, 33 : 9
this d. for a memorial, 9 : 26
this d. we must part, 487 : 3
this January d., 607 : 14
those eyes the break of d., 228 : 28
those who dream by d., 526 : 3
thou d. I hour, 628 : 14
thou gavest Lord is ended, 597 : 17
thought it Judgment D., 642 : 1
time makes possible D. of Judgment, 786 : 5
tire the d. in toil, 267 : 12
'tis true 'tis d., 252 : 21
today first d. of rest of life, 925 : 19
today isn't any other d., 613 : 11
tomorrow a new d., 170 : 26
tomorrow as today, 246 : 9
took d. to search for God, 696 : 11
trysting d., 488 : 13
turn by night or d., 426 : 10
two nights to every d., 268 : 18
unpurged images of d., 716 : 8
until the d. break, 28 : 9
unto day uttereth speech, 17 : 27
up by break of d., 268 : 13
vulgarize d. of judgment, 500 : 16
was it the spring d., 929 : 7
weakening eye of d., 641 : 11
wear d. out before comes, 664 : 6
wedding d. fixed, 350 : 2
well-spent d. happy sleep, 152 : 4
what a d. may bring, 25 : 21
when heaven was falling, 692 : 3
which the Lord hath made, 21 : 26
while it is d., 45 : 7
with superfluous burden loads d., 282 : 10
without all hope of d., 288 : 20
withstand in the evil d., 49 : 39
would God d. were dead, 633 : 17
wrestled until breaking of d., 8 : 24
year and a d., 550 : 8
yield d. to night, 184 : 15
Dayadhvam 805 : 13
(Sympathize), 56 : *n* 8
Daybreak, it is d. everywhere, 513 : 2
very plainly before d., 575 : 18
Daylight, between dark and d., 512 : 3
in death d. finish, 545 : 22
in the mind, 326 : 21
night but d. sick, 201 : 6
see a church by d., 209 : 7
we burn d., 191 : 22
you love the d., 76 : 6
Daylight's dauphin, 656 : 1
Dayrolles, give D. a chair, 342 : 18
Day's, all in d. work, 920 : 10
at d. end footsteps added, 907 : 15
at the morn, 540 : 15
death of each d. life, 237 : 21
disasters, 370 : 10
end of this d. business, 217 : 10
every d. news, 228 : 25
garish eye, 278 : 25
good d. work, 348 : 21

Day's (*continued*)
journey take whole day, 608 : 10
long d. journey, 810 : 16
long d. task is done, 241 : 18
march nearer home, 429 : 17
wages for day's work, 474 : 2
year's midnight and the d., 252 : 24
Days about which I never worry, 655 : 1
after three d. weary of guest, 347 : 2
age not numbered by d., 168 : 1
all d. as marriage day, 267 : 20
all my d. are trances, 525 : 18
alluvial march of d., 843 : 19
among dead are past, 440 : 6
Ancient of d., 33 : 5
Ancient of D., 445 : 21
Ancient of d., 614 : 9
and nights to Addison, 352 : 23
are consumed like smoke, 21 : 4
are swifter than shuttle, 15 : 20
as thy d. so thy strength, 11 : 25
at best dull and hoary, 299 : 8
begin with trouble, 320 : 11
checkerboard of nights and d., 516 : 22
curtain of distorting d., 716 : 15
dark and dreary, 510 : 11
David died full of d., 14 : 28
dead-letter d., 441 : 16
decrease autumn grows, 542 : 22
dividing lover and lover, 632 : 8
dwindle down, 802 : 3
evil d. come not, 27 : 24
expect halcyon d., 184 : 17
fallen on evil d., 286 : 28
fasted forty d. and nights, 37 : 1
fled Him down d., 693 : 10
flight of future d., 284 : 12
flowers withered while I spent my d., 135 : 9
forty d. and forty nights, 7 : 30
go I endure, 770 : 10
golden d. of golden deeds, 285 : 6
greatest d. country lived, 745 : 7
halcyon d., 82 : 11, 184 : 17
happy d. here again, 824 : 13
happy those early d., 299 : 2
have been wondrous free, 329 : 13
heart followed all my d., 759 : 13
heavenly d. that cannot die, 424 : 10
his d. are as grass, 21 : 7
humanity only three d. old, 758 : 8
hypocritic d., 495 : 5
in length of d. understanding, 15 : 30
in my born d., 168 : 14
in my school d., 198 : 6
in the d. of my youth, 439 : 16
in yellow leaf, 462 : 18
joyfulness prolongeth his d., 35 : 41
leave them in midst of his d., 32 : 13
length of d. in her right hand, 23 : 4
light of other d., 447 : 7
live all d. of your life, 323 : 16
live laborious d., 280 : 15
long as twenty d. now, 425 : 8
looked on better d., 211 : 12
lying d. of my youth, 713 : 8
mad March d., 760 : 20
man born of a woman is of few d., 15 : 33
may come days may go, 636 : 2
measure of my d., 19 : 1
melancholy d. are come, 471 : 10

Days (*continued*)
Moses was there forty d., 10 : 15
multitude of d., 351 : 20
my dancing d. are done, 191 : *n* 3
my d. are past, 15 : 38
my d. are vanity, 15 : 22
my d. have crackled, 693 : 14
my d. of endless doubt, 172 : 7
my salad d., 240 : 25
nine d. old, 931 : 18
no d. like good old d., 519 : *n* 1
no guest welcome after three d., 94 : 1
nor hours d. months, 252 : 8
not dark d. great d., 745 : 7
number the d. of eternity, 34 : 21
of danger, 431 : 8
of Herod the king, 36 : 20
of Methuselah, 7 : 25
of our years, 20 : 13
of our youth are days of glory, 462 : 6
of wine and roses, 721 : 7
often often in old d., 587 : 6
on the earth are as a shadow, 14 : 27
our d. are scored against us, 119 : 10
past our dancing d., 191 : 25
precious d. spend with you, 802 : 3
red-letter d., 441 : 16
remember bygone d., 856 : 7
remember thy Creator in d. of thy youth, 27 : 24
sacrament of summer d., 604 : 10
sad Rose of all my d., 712 : 3
salad d., 240 : 25
seemed but a few d., 8 : 22
seen better d., 211 : 13, 243 : 6, 462 : 12
short when you reach September, 802 : 2
shortly see better d., 312 : 13
shuts up story of our d., 173 : 5
six d. shalt labor, 10 : 6, 553 : 17
slow drag of d., 76 : 5
so haunt thy d., 478 : 8
sober studious d., 334 : 25
some d. dark and dreary, 510 : 11
some d. longer than others, 746 : 14
spring full of sweet d., 268 : 16
sterner d. not darker d., 745 : 7
stink in three d., 94 : *n* 1
sweet childish d., 425 : 8
swift d. near their goal, 562 : 3
teach us to number our d., 20 : 14
ten d. that shook world, 801 : 4
that are gone Maggie, 636 : 9
that are no more, 531 : 3
that are yet to come, 618 : 12
that make us happy, 760 : 18
that might be better spent, 174 : 10
that thy d. may be long, 10 : 7
that wove your doom, 633 : 14
then if ever perfect d., 567 : 13
thousand d., 890 : 10
three whole d. together, 290 : 4
Time in hours d. years, 299 : 6
to come are wisest witnesses, 71 : 21
to Indian all d. are God's, 686 : 7
travelers of eternity, 313 : 23
two d. when woman is pleasure, 67 : 11
unalterable d., 494 : 23
untell the d., 257 : 17
virtue extends our d., 119 : 14

Days (*continued*)
ways to lengthen our d., 447 : 1
weary of d. and hours, 633 : 20
when birds come back, 604 : 9
will grow to weeks, 534 : 25
wish d. to be as centuries, 499 : 1
wish my d. to be, 425 : 7
wonderful d. a-coming, 618 : 11
world of happy d., 187 : 8
year whose d. long, 676 : 12
Days', his six d. work a world, 287 : 1
Dayspring from on high, 42 : 26
Daystar arise in your hearts, 52 : 17
in ocean bed, 281 : 4
Dayton, bicycle mechanics from D., 835 : 1
Dazzle, mine eyes d., 262 : 10
my eyes d., 643 : 18
Dazzled at beholding myself, 726 : 3
by ways of God, 765 : 2
Dazzles at it as at eternity, 299 : 5
Dazzling, all beams full d., 575 : 24
deep but d. darkness, 299 : 1
taught her d. fence, 280 : 2
De gustibus non disputandum, 133 : 17
te fabula, 106 : *n* 7
Deacon, enough to make d. swear, 568 : 7
Dead, absent or d. friend, 334 : 20
Adonais is d., 468 : 22
after people are d., 733 : 17
Agamemnon d., 715 : 16
all once so beautiful d., 811 : 12
all the d. lie down, 605 : 15
all the rest are d., 512 : 2
always popular, 721 : 10
and dumb and done, 740 : 6
and gone lady, 223 : 22
and rotten, 347 : 18
and turned to clay, 224 : 16
are but as pictures, 237 : 23
art of poetry, 792 : 10
barbarian weeping above d., 615 : 7
beautiful Evelyn Hope d., 542 : 1
beauty d. chaos comes, 189 : 14
become lumber of world, 315 : 22
being d. with him beauty slain, 189 : 14
besides the wench is d., 183 : 15
better to be fool than d., 667 : 18
bivouac of the d., 578 : 10
blow bugles over rich d., 797 : 4
Body good dog d., 896 : 13
body without spirit is d., 51 : 33
books not absolutely d., 281 : 22
brave men living and d., 523 : 4
breed maggots in d. dog, 220 : 17
broke spell of d. letter, 817 : 4
by ships lies a d. man, 59 : 9
Caesar's trencher, 241 : 11
can tell you being dead, 808 : 10
cemetery of d. ideas, 705 : 15
certain is birth for the d., 94 : 8
Christ risen from d., 48 : 29
close wall with English d., 207 : 16
communication of d., 808 : 10
corpse of Public Credit, 451 : 1
corse in complete steel, 219 : 12
crucified d. buried, 55 : 2
day that is d., 530 : 20
days among d. past, 440 : 6
dead and dead indeed, 929 : 9
deadly when most d., 821 : 11
dear d. women, 543 : 12

Dead (*continued*)
Death once d., 246 : 5
deathless hour, 601 : 17
descent of last end on d., 777 : 16
desire d. be near us, 532 : 7
dirge for doubly d., 525 : *n* 5
dishonor not trouble once I am d., 76 : 7
dooms imagined for d., 475 : 17
doubled globe of d., 886 : 14
drunk judge, 881 : 11
earth that bears thee d., 205 : 11
earth to living not d., 389 : 7
England finished and d., 752 : 2
envy for d., 625 : 8
envy of the d., 76 : 10
faith d. which does not doubt, 706 : 12
faith without works is d., 51 : 33
fallen cold and d., 576 : 7
fame sun of d., 484 : 12
fell at his feet as d., 52 : 31
for a ducat dead, 222 : 29
for Love is d., 176 : 8
for Lycidas sorrow not d., 281 : 4
forgotten as a d. man out of mind, 18 : 16
full of d. men's bones, 40 : 20
gear of foreign d. men, 808 : 2
God is d., 657 : 11
govern living, 483 : 13
great god Pan is d., 120 : 19
greatest service or injury to d. man, 84 : 3
half d. a living death, 288 : 22
half regiment d., 893 : 12
hands dead stringencies, 911 : 14
happier to be d., 495 : 2
hardly more than boys, 773 : 5
harrow house of d., 868 : 4
he is d., 587 : 8
heads of d. up line, 839 : 9
healthy wealthy and d., 831 : 8
heard the d. cry, 873 : 12
heart fell d., 828 : 10
heart's d. never buried, 816 : 3
Hector is d., 227 : 7
help for living hope for d., 615 : 8
her warrior d., 531 : 8
herself ere evensong, 927 : 4
high converse with mighty d., 345 : 7
honor dies man d., 513 : 8
how fares it with happy d., 532 : 4
how possible that d. be brought alive, 131 : 12
how shall the d. arise, 274 : 14
I am every d. thing, 253 : 1
ideas and dead beliefs, 599 : 15
if Lucy should be d., 424 : 11
immortal d. who live again, 564 : 22
in praise of ladies d., 245 : 12
is at rest, 36 : 8
is God d., 482 : 16
is he d. then, 656 : 7
is the king d., 187 : 22
just as d. as if wrong, 925 : 10
King Pandion he is d., 257 : 7
kissed by English d., 827 : 6
knocking when I'm d., 762 : 1
know not any thing, 27 : 15
lain for century d., 533 : 25
land of d., 839 : 10, 868 : 10
laughter out of d. bellies, 792 : 15
law hath not been d., 228 : 8
left it d. and with head, 612 : 18

Dead (*continued*)
let d. bury their d., 38 : 24
level of mass, 570 : 12
life is shrunk d. and interred, 252 : 25
light in dust lies d., 470 : 1
like vampire d. many times, 638 : 11
lilacs out of d. land, 804 : 26
living and d. are same, 70 : 8
living dog better than d. lion, 27 : 15
living scarce able to bury d., 265 : 10
look at my d. house, 860 : 10
Lord of living and d., 655 : 19
loses past and d. for future, 77 : 22
love never sick old d., 172 : 9
Magus Zoroaster my d. child, 466 : 16
maid not d. but sleepeth, 38 : 31
man cannot bite, 99 : 13
man divine as myself d., 576 : 1
man held on end, 641 : 23
Man's Chest, 668 : 4
men rise up never, 633 : 22
mie love ys d., 399 : 15
mighty d., 345 : 7
mindful of unhonored d., 362 : 16
Mistah Kurtz he d., 683 : 21
more to say when d., 728 : 21
most lovely d., 525 : 15
mourn the d., 899 : 7
mouth of one just d., 759 : 10
my enemy is d., 576 : 1
my lady's sparrow is d., 101 : 15
nature seems d., 237 : 14
ne'er said till friend d., 660 : 7
no longer mourn when I am d., 244 : 26
noble living and noble d., 424 : 6
not a house where not one d., 9 : 28
not d. but gone before, 114 : *n* 8
not God of d., 43 : 43
not interested in living, 839 : 13
not know we are d., 83 : *n* 7
not make war on d., 161 : 20
not reverence of d. but envy of living, 264 : 19
now he is d. should I fast, 13 : 21
objects essentially d., 437 : 12
of d. nothing but good, 62 : *n* 5
old bawd is d., 717 : 18
old men are all d., 642 : 7
once d. never return, 516 : 19
one d. other powerless, 586 : 10
only d. who do not return, 401 : 5
only good Indians d., 610 : 4
our English d., 709 : 12
out of d. cold ashes life, 660 : 10
outrage brave man d., 73 : 16
pattern of d. and living, 807 : 23
people so d. to liberty, 350 : 17
perfection, 533 : 17
Phlebas a fortnight d., 805 : 9
plucks d. lions by beard, 201 : 13
poetry of earth never d., 475 : 9
poets d. and gone, 477 : 16
poets in misery d., 425 : 12
praised the d. already d., 26 : 22
professors like literature d., 791 : 9
quick and the d., 55 : 2
remembered footsteps, 728 : 17
renown and grace is d., 238 : 7
respite to be d., 606 : 15
rest for the d., 616 : 5
rest her soul she's d., 224 : 11
resurrection of the d., 48 : 29
revisit in dreams the dear d., 76 : 2

Dead (*continued*)
romantic Ireland's d., 713 : 11
rough notes and d. bodies, 726 : 5
rule over the departed d., 60 : 15
say I'm sick I'm d., 338 : 5
Sea and Sea of Galilee, 759 : 11
Sea fruits, 447 : 15
Sea's shore, 457 : 20
seek living among d., 44 : 13
shall be raised, 49 : 7
shall live living die, 305 : 13
sheeted d., 217 : 21
smiling the boy fell d., 540 : 21
so dull so d. in look, 205 : 19
so long as refuse to die, 595 : 2
so many not yet d., 856 : 7
soldiers bore d. bodies by, 203 : 8
something d. in each of us, 676 : 10
soul so d., 430 : 10
Spartan d., 461 : 6
speak ill of the d., 62 : 8
stare and sting forever, 821 : 11
stars are d., 868 : 8
steppingstones of d. selves, 531 : 19
still talk of pushing bones, 908 : 8
tell 'em Queen Anne's d., 415 : 7
there are no d., 700 : 5
there he fell down d., 12 : 7
these d. not died in vain, 523 : 4
these honored d., 523 : 4
think living worth it, 907 : 8
thirty is as good as d., 396 : 21
those who fear life part d., 738 : 4
though d. shall he live, 45 : 13
three keep secret if two d., 347 : 10
thy greatest enemy d., 35 : 13
time is d., 837 : 16
time you have to spend d., 164 : 10
told me Heraclitus d., 591 : 9
took wages and are d., 692 : 3
topics of sex and the d., 718 : 3
travel to home among d., 468 : 21
tree gives no shelter, 805 : 1
trophies and d. things, 262 : 11
truth never fell d. 537 : 11
unhonored d., 362 : 16
until he is d. do not call man happy, 62 : 17
vast and middle of night, 218 : 18
wake the d., 530 : 12
warred for Homer being d., 257 : 20
was d. and is alive, 43 : 28
what d. had no speech for, 808 : 10
what was d. was hope, 676 : 10
when I am d., 787 : 5
when I am d. my dearest, 608 : 13
when living might exceed d., 274 : 26
when only d. could smile, 801 : 16
where d. men lost bones, 805 : 3
which die in the Lord, 53 : 24
which he slew at his death, 12 : 21
who fed the guns, 795 : 16
why can't d. die, 810 : 15
winds' riot, 633 : 19
with d. desire not die, 430 : 9
word d. when said, 607 : 3
working for d. horse, 171 : 3
would God day were d., 633 : 17
would that I were d., 527 : 18
youth stone d., 795 : 15
Dead March, play D. as you carry me, 927 : 15
Dead-born, fell d. from the press, 357 : 18

Dead-letter days, 441 : 16
Deadliest enemies within borders, 650 : 14
Deadlock, holy d., 815 : 16
Deadly, dare d. terrors clasp, 405 : 8
forfeit should release, 277 : 6
imminent d. breach, 229 : 28
more d. than mad dog's tooth, 188 : 13
more d. than male, 710 : 21
pay with a d. blow, 71 : 16
soap and education d., 622 : 2
when most dead, 821 : 11
wither and come to d. use, 234 : 23
Deadwood and Lost Mule Flat, 840 : 2
Deaf and dumb has wooden leg, 722 : 1
ears of the d. shall be unstopped, 30 : 24
justice blind d. and dumb, 722 : 1
law d. as adder to clamors of populace, 380 : 12
like the d. adder, 19 : 23
live d. to land beneath us, 819 : 1
music good nor bad to d., 308 : 19
trouble d. heaven, 244 : 8
Deafness, tale would cure d., 247 : 12
Deal, candy d. of courtesy, 203 : 16
damnation round land, 340 : 3
falsely with God, 264 : 22
in remnants of remnants, 324 : 20
infinite d. of nothing, 198 : 5
intolerable d. of sack, 204 : 9
new d., 779 : 8
of scorn looks beautiful, 214 : 16
square d., 687 : 8
to d. plainly, 235 : 9
what a d. of business, 310 : 6
Dealing, bend conscience to d., 569 : 1
common sense plain d., 497 : 29
hard d. teaches them suspect, 198 : 27
Deals, making d. pleading laughing, 902 : 3
Dean could write finely upon broomstick, 322 : *n* 2
Dear, absent friend d., 334 : 20
all they hold d., 687 : 4
as light and life, 410 : 18
as remembered kisses, 531 : 4
beauty for earth too d., 191 : 26
Brutus, 215 : 6
coldness of my d. 331 : 11
damned distracting town, 334 : 24
dead women, 543 : 12
experience keeps d. school, 347 : 23
Fatherland, 573 : 12
friends we love so d., 618 : 1
God bless you my d., 357 : 5
how d. to this heart, 455 : 6
I die, 252 : 18
is life so d., 383 : 5
jesses my d. heartstrings, 231 : 4
land that gave you birth, 700 : 6
Lord and Father, 514 : 1
lose their d. delight, 245 : 10
makes a blessing d., 290 : 5
makes remembrance d., 227 : 20
man to all country d., 370 : 5
my d. times' waste, 244 : 11
name forever sad forever d., 334 : 26
nurse of arts, 208 : 16
old Carian guest, 591 : 9
pay too d. for what's given freely, 246 : 8
Plato and truth are d., 87 : 14
so d. I love him, 287 : 20

Dear (*continued*)
sold cheap what is most d., 245 : 16
son of memory, 277 : 13
think on thee d. friend, 244 : 12
thoughts to memory d., 431 : 16
to God famous to all ages, 281 : 19
to me as ruddy drops, 215 : 23
to me more d., 370 : 15
too d. for my possessing, 245 : 1
what restraint to grief for one so d., 107 : 12
wisdom never d. if genuine, 538 : 10
Wotton a most d. lover, 270 : 34
Dearer, honor d. than life, 169 : 25
yet the brotherhood, 700 : 6
Dearest, met my d. foe in heaven, 218 : 14
nearest and d. enemy, 204 : 22
throw away d. thing owed, 236 : 14
when I am dead my d., 608 : 13
Dearly let or let alone, 267 : 14
Dearness only gives value, 384 : 13
Dears, Nature swears the lovely d., 409 : 15
Dearth, war d. age agues, 254 : 9
Deary, flew o'er me and my d., 410 : 18
in short my d. kiss me, 341 : 2
Death a necessary end, 215 : 26
a secret of Nature, 124 : 15
absence darkness d., 253 : 1
absurd also, 877 : 6
Adam brought d. into world, 624 : 13
after d. better bad epitaph, 221 : 4
after first d. no other, 886 : 17
after life does please, 173 : 12
after life is d., 633 : 18
aims with fouler spite, 267 : 11
all seasons thine O D., 470 : 20
aloft gigantically down, 844 : 2
always a tragedy, 687 : 1
amiable lovely d., 201 : 25
and all is vain, 601 : 21
and brother Sleep, 466 : 6
and i coquette, 760 : 1
and life one, 730 : 2
and Night wash world, 576 : 1
and sorrow our companions, 744 : 9
and taxes, 348 : 16
angel of d. spread wings, 459 : 15
any man's d. diminishes me, 254 : 22
anyone's d. releases stupefaction, 583 : 16
arise arise from d., 254 : 8
ashamed of d., 274 : 12
asterisk of d., 512 : 14
at birth our d. sealed, 115 : 18
be absolute for d., 228 : 14
be not proud, 254 : 11
beautiful adventure, 574 : *n* 1
beautiful blendings of d. and life, 637 : 17
beauty d. and loveliness, 812 : 9
because chose to turn, 801 : 13
become sought-after refuge, 78 : 16
beggars mounted run horse to d., 186 : 1
belongs to no one else, 849 : 22
better than day of birth, 27 : 3
beyond us even before d., 337 : 12
birth copulation and d., 806 : 10
birth life and d., 315 : 9
Black Widow d., 892 : 8
blackness of d., 100 : 20
blaze forth d. of princes, 215 : 25

Death (*continued*)
body of this d., 47 : 7
borders upon our birth, 257 : 12
bridegroom in my d., 241 : 19
brief as water falling d., 812 : 3
bring d. to a friend, 74 : 15
bringeth to light the shadow of d., 15 : 31
brought d. into world, 282 : 22
build your ship of d., 791 : 4
by inches, 242 : 25
by man came d., 48 : 29
by the shadow of d., 623 : 9
calls ye to the crowd, 272 : 14
came d. into the world, 34 : 12
captain of men of d., 302 : 17
certain is d. for the born, 94 : 8
certain to all, 206 : 22
chance d. and mutability, 467 : 7
chants doleful hymn to d., 202 : 16
Chromis did not save himself from dark d., 57 : 20
city of night perchance d., 618 : 18
clean trunk of d., 863 : 14
closed in d. attentive eyes, 353 : 10
closes all, 529 : 12
cold hand of d., 205 : 10
come away d., 214 : 4
come close eyes, 918 : 17
cometh soon or late, 488 : 14
cool-enfolding d., 576 : 5
could not daunt, 926 : 18
counteracts Devil who is D., 365 : 14
covenant with d., 30 : 14, 505 : 14
crossing the world, 314 : 13
cruel as d., 345 : 6
cruel d. always near, 320 : 11
cruel d. of Pyramus, 196 : 2
darkness and shadow of d., 15 : 24, 21 : 13, 42 : 26
daughter at point of d., 42 : 7
dear beauteous d., 299 : 9
defend to d. your right to say it, 344 : 11
delicate d., 576 : 4
departure beyond borders d., 817 : 5
desire father's d., 582 : 11
desireth not d. of sinner, 54 : 15
destroyer of worlds, 861 : *n* 2
devours lovely things, 823 : 2
die a dry d., 247 : 9
die not poor d., 254 : 11
die the d. of the righteous, 11 : 3
direst shapes of d., 592 : 6
does not end all, 112 : 26
done to d. by slanderous tongues, 210 : 10
doomed to d. though fated not to die, 305 : 15
draw trigger at his d., 354 : 2
dread d., 59 : 7
dread of something after d., 221 : 12
dry d., 247 : 9
dull cold ear of d., 362 : 5
dumb d., 829 : 20
dung and d., 807 : 10
dusty d., 240 : 4
each earns his d., 849 : 22
easeful d., 476 : 28
eaten to d. with rust, 206 : 4
éclat of d., 607 : 8
Elizabeth-Jane not told of my d., 640 : 16
eloquent just and mighty D., 173 : 4

Death (*continued*)
embrace is d., 833 : 6
end of worldly soore, 146 : 29
enviable d. was his, 746 : 7
equal in presence of d., 110 : 14
equal piece of justice D., 274 : 11
ere thou hast slain another, 265 : 15
escapades of d., 768 : 18
eternal sleep, 415 : 17
even D. listened, 505 : 7
even in Arcadia there am I D., 133 : *n* 9
everybody's looks of d., 309 : 24
exodus of d., 511 : 24
face of d., 721 : 8
face to meet d. with, 544 : 26
faithful unto d., 53 : 1
Falstaff sweats to d., 203 : 21
Famine Pestilence Destruction D., 773 : 6
fear and danger of violent d., 264 : 17
fear d. as children fear dark, 180 : 2
fear d. feel fog, 544 : 21
fear of d. more dread than d., 111 : 16
fear of d. troubles me, 153 : *n* 3
fear of ignominious d., 414 : 17
fed on fullness of d., 633 : 6
feed on D., 246 : 5
fell sergeant d., 224 : 30
final accounting, 134 : 10
find me planting cabbages, 164 : 8
fly down D., 883 : 9
for restful d. I cry, 244 : 23
for thirty pence my d., 268 : 11
foretaste of d., 463 : 5
fortune favored him in moment of d., 123 : 5
found d. in life, 438 : 9
fraternity or d., 386 : *n* 2
friends enough now for d., 857 : 3
from d. to immortality, 56 : 20
from sudden d., 55 : 12
fruit threw d., 254 : 10
functions which resist d., 429 : 14
gallop Pegasus to d., 339 : 15
gates of dark D. stand wide, 105 : 15
give me liberty or d., 383 : 5
giving life by d. of others, 152 : 2
go down D. bring her, 733 : 13
go with anyone to d., 747 : 9
gods have neither age nor d., 75 : 11
gone to her d., 485 : 21
good d. does honor to whole life, 143 : 4
good thing to escape d., 74 : 15
great d., 732 : 6
grim d., 262 : 22
grim D. my son and foe, 284 : 26
had appointment in Samarra, 751 : 17
had undone so many, 805 : 2
half dead a living d., 288 : 22
halls of d., 471 : 6
has broached him to, 393 : 11
hath no more dominion, 47 : 3
hath ten thousand doors, 262 : 8
he also to d. must fall, 300 : 17
he brought them d., 731 : 16
he taketh all away, 591 : 9
heaven gives favorites early d., 91 : *n* 1
here find life in d., 438 : 9
hideous storm of terror, 262 : 7
his d. eclipsed gaiety, 353 : 1

Death (*continued*)
how can you know about d., 68 : 26
how little room we take in d., 272 : 11
how strange a thing is d., 823 : 9
how they pray for d., 76 : 5
how wonderful is D., 466 : 6
hungry for life and d., 886 : 8
I am near to d., 63 : 5
I here importune d., 241 : 21
I hung on like d., 873 : 10
idle and who has done much meet d. alike, 58 : 9
if D. knew how to forgive, 104 : 12
immortal D. has taken mortal life, 101 : 3
in d. daylight finish, 545 : 22
in d. they were not divided, 13 : 9
in his d. all things appear fair, 59 : 6
in itself is nothing, 303 : 9
in our own power, 657 : *n* 7
in ranks of d. find him, 446 : 15
in stars written d. of every man, 147 : 6
in the midst of life d., 56 : 12
in the pot, 14 : 15
in the shadow of d., 21 : 13, 42 : 26
in vain to wish for d., 75 : 3
in Venice, 755 : 19
interest in d. interest in life, 755 : 13
intricate as d., 255 : 3
is a debt, 398 : 22
is a sleep, 633 : 8
is afraid of him, 132 : 27
is as lover's pinch, 242 : 3
is dead not he, 469 : 13
is in my sight today, 4 : 8
is knowledge, 413 : 23
is most efficient, 772 : 15
is not D. at watch, 834 : 11
is nothing to us, 91 : 14, 101 : 2
is only a horizon, 642 : 10
is slave's freedom, 915 : 18
is slumber, 466 : 10
is sorrow, 72 : 23
is swallowed up, 49 : 8
is the enemy, 782 : 6
island surrounded by d., 614 : 10
jaws of d., 167 : 13, 533 : 14
judge none blessed before his d., 35 : 22
just d. kind umpire, 185 : 2
just that distance from d., 63 : 1
keeps D. his court, 195 : 2
keys of hell and d., 52 : 32
kingly D. keeps court, 469 : 1
kings did king to d., 886 : 14
kiss of d., 741 : 6
land of darkness and shadow of d., 15 : 24
land of the shadow of d., 29 : 15
last enemy is d., 49 : 1
last guerdon of d., 102 : 18
laugh myself to d., 248 : 1
lays icy hand on kings, 272 : 15
leaden d., 334 : 16
leaves body at d., 94 : 14
life d. and that forever, 566 : 12
life perfected by d., 507 : 1
life shadow of d., 275 : 13, 632 : 9
life that which men call d., 77 : 21
life well used brings happy d., 152 : 4
like sleep steal on me, 466 : 15
like this, 510 : 6
limbs cold in d., 106 : 7

Death (*continued*)
literature war between life and d., 861 : 18
lively form of d., 177 : 1
long since D. had majority, 274 : *n* 11
looks gigantically, 525 : 13
love better after d., 507 : 15
love is strong as d., 28 : 23
love posterior to d., 606 : 11
love to woman life or d., 670 : 2
lovely and soothing d., 576 : 4
loves shining mark, 330 : 16
low delicious word d., 575 : 18
made d. his ladder, 174 : 14
make d. proud to take us, 241 : 23
makes equal high and low, 158 : 17
makes life live, 545 : 14
men at point of d., 193 : 26
men of d., 302 : 17
milder fate than tyranny, 71 : 10
Mister D., 828 : 13
more bitter than d., 27 : 10
mother of Beauty, 767 : 3
mourned at birth not d., 341 : 6
must call too soon, 629 : 23
naked in d. on unknown shore, 105 : 13
nativity chance or d., 225 : 28
nearness to d. no nearer God, 806 : 15
Negro past of d., 903 : 2
neither fear nor long for d., 119 : 15
never taste of d. but once, 215 : 26
newspaper d., 635 : 11
no cure for d., 704 : 4
no God stronger than d., 633 : 8
no life by others' d., 202 : 8
no more d., 53 : 30
no one knew my d., 874 : 17
no parenthesis, 829 : 6
no work pause for d., 545 : 5
none hath joy of d., 633 : 10
nor life nor angels, 47 : 15
not atoned too dearly by d., 412 : 17
not born for d., 477 : 1
not d. but dying terrible, 349 : 26
not D. but Love, 507 : 8
not d. for I stood up, 605 : 15
not room for D., 562 : 5
not stop for d., 606 : 4
not the worst, 75 : 3
nothing call our own but d., 195 : 2
nothing more beautiful than d., 574 : 10
nothing to look forward to but d., 151 : 10
nothing to us, 91 : 14, 101 : 2
now boast thee d., 242 : 5
now to D. devote, 287 : 22
O d. I will be thy plagues, 33 : 16
O d. in life, 531 : 4
O proud d., 225 : 4
of a dear friend, 197 : 19
of air, 808 : 11
of democracy, 845 : 16
of each day's life, 237 : 21
of endeavor birth of disgust, 647 : 7
of friends inspire us, 558 : 13
of hope and despair, 808 : 11
of one god death of all, 768 : 9
of the most noblest knights, 149 : 17
of the race, 900 : 2
of water and fire, 808 : 12
old captain, 581 : 4
on else immortal us, 254 : 10

Death (*continued*)
on his pale horse, 287 : 28
on life on d., 718 : 2
once dead, 246 : 5
one in life and d. are we, 628 : 14
one of things Nature wills, 125 : 15
one studied in his d., 236 : 14
one talent d. to hide, 282 : 15
only a horizon, 642 : 10
or dreamful ease, 528 : 18
our souls survive d., 112 : *n* 13
out of jaws of d., 167 : *n* 10
owe God a d., 206 : 25
pale horse and on him was D., 53 : 11
pang preceding d., 368 : 11
part and parcel of life, 755 : 8
parting foretaste of d., 463 : 5
past so he waited, 543 : 17
people given over to d., 101 : 12
people living deeply no fear of d., 858 : 4
perfected being survives after d., 73 : 4
play to you d. to us, 294 : 20
pomp of d., 899 : 14
portal we call d., 511 : 11
posterior to d., 606 : 11
precious is the d. of his saints, 21 : 24
protracting life not deduct from d., 101 : 5
proud d., 225 : 4
proud to take us, 241 : 23
quick even in d., 171 : 13
quiet us in d. so noble, 289 : 9
ranks of d., 446 : 15
Reaper whose name D., 510 : 1
reared himself throne, 525 : 11
reasonable moderator D., 274 : 11
redeem them from d., 33 : 16
remain until d. do part, 681 : 1
remembered kisses after d., 531 : 4
rendezvous with d., 811 : 5
reports of d. exaggerated, 625 : 21
ribs of D., 279 : 27
ride not free horse to d., 171 : 2
right to d. or liberty, 593 : 16
sad stories of d. of kings, 195 : 2
same voice for d. or bridal, 899 : 2
sane and sacred d., 576 : 3
seems covered way, 512 : *n* 4
seized Argus, 60 : 24
sense of d. in apprehension, 228 : 17
sentence of Versailles, 812 : 19
set before you life and d., 11 : 22
set d. i' the other, 215 : 3
setter up and plucker down of kings, 186 : 6
shall be no more, 254 : 13
shall be surely put to d., 10 : 9
shall have no dominion, 886 : 16
ship of d., 791 : 2, 791 : 4
sickness sin d., 583 : 4
side of life away from us, 756 : 10
silent halls of d., 471 : 6
single d. tragedy, 766 : 11
sit in shadow of d., 21 : 13, 42 : 26
slavery or d., 325 : 17
sleep brother of d., 58 : 20
Sleep brother to D., 182 : 4
sleep is a d., 274 : 23
sleep of d., 221 : 12
sleep the sleep of d., 407 : 7
slew at d. more than in life, 12 : 21
slew not him, 174 : 14

Death (*continued*)
someone's d., 543 : 5
song attain full purport after d. of singer, 577 : 14
soul sorrowful unto d., 41 : 11
stalk of d., 908 : 8
state of nothingness, 83 : 13
storm desertion d., 481 : 2
strange that d. should sing, 202 : 16
strict in his arrest, 224 : 30
strong lean upon d., 797 : 17
struck sharp on d., 507 : 16
sudden d. best, 99 : 22
suffuses all with blackness of d., 100 : 20
sure as d., 255 : 6
swallow up d. in victory, 30 : 8
swallowed up in d., 83 : 17
sweet is d., 534 : 15
sword sung song of d., 404 : 15
taste of d. but once, 215 : 26
taxes childbirth, 848 : 10
there is no d., 511 : 11
think not disdainfully of d., 125 : 15
this fell sergeant d., 224 : 30
those who died so cruel a d., 157 : 4
thou not born for d., 477 : 1
thou shalt die, 254 : 13
thou wilt bring me to d., 16 : 18
thought of that late d., 713 : 19
till d. us do part, 56 : 9
time of d. every moment, 94 : *n* 9
touch the great d., 732 : 6
tramples it to fragments, 469 : 16
treats us all alike, 626 : 16
true to thee till d., 552 : 21
truly longed for d., 528 : 2
try cause condemn to d., 611 : 6
twitches my ear, 106 : 9
two fates of dread d., 59 : 7
ugly fact nature hides, 609 : 3
unknown song sounded by D., 464 : 17
useless life is early d., 395 : 9
valley of d., 533 : 9
valley of shadow of d., 18 : 7
vasty hall of d., 586 : 4
veil called life, 467 : 6
violent d. of slaveholder, 560 : 23
visit us with d., 265 : 10
wages of sin is d., 47 : 5
way to dusty d., 240 : 4
Webster possessed by d., 804 : 21
what should it know of d., 423 : 3
what ugly sights of d., 187 : 9
what we fear of d., 228 : 21
when d. allies to beauty, 812 : *n* 2
when is d. not within ourselves, 70 : 8
where is thy sting, 49 : 8
who comes at last, 430 : 16
who longs for d., 267 : 2
who puts end to pain, 534 : 15
will have his day, 194 : 28
with impartial tread, 107 : 1
world easily reconciled to d., 503 : 20
worse things than d., 633 : 1
worst friend and enemy D., 797 : 3
worst is d., 194 : 28
would be his pride, 759 : 12
your d. Heraclitus, 93 : 1
your loveliness and my d., 480 : 3
Deathbed, Jemmy Grove on d. lay, 926 : 21
Death-bedde, gon to hys d., 399 : 15
Death-fires danced at night, 434 : 17
Deathless Aphrodite on your throne, 63 : 4
dead d. hour, 601 : 17
his mansions are d., 59 : 24
music, 728 : 6
Deathly slumber, 739 : 17
Death-moth, beetle nor d., 477 : 21
Death's a debt, 398 : 22
beg d. pardon now, 899 : 7
brother Sleep, 105 : 17
call in thy d. head, 268 : 22
fell d. untimely frost, 410 : 19
gray land, 795 : 13
head or a memento mori, 204 : 26
ironic scraping, 767 : 11
life's old d. new, 546 : 4
other kingdom, 805 : 16
pale flag not advanced, 193 : 27
sleep d. counterfeit, 238 : 6
sleep D. twin brother, 58 : *n* 3
Deaths, after so many d., 269 : 5
all d. could endure, 287 : 20
brutal lives ugly d., 831 : 18
by feigned d. to die, 252 : 15
die many times before d., 215 : 26
glorious in thy defense, 325 : *n* 9
happen at ebb tide, 672 : 20
million d. statistic, 766 : 11
more d. than one, 676 : 11
of kings, 627 : 2
ye died watched beside, 707 : 3
Death-steps, dinosaur d., 893 : 9
Death-world claws at everything, 93 : 1
Debases, virtue d. in justifying, 342 : 21
Debate, daughter of d., 163 : 18
of commonwealth affairs, 207 : 4
Roman senate long d., 325 : 17
Debated, greatest question ever d., 381 : 6
Debauch currency, 783 : 9
friend's wife genteelly, 355 : 13
Debauchee of dew, 604 : 14
Debonair, buxom blithe and d., 277 : 18
Deborah arose, 12 : 3
awake D. and utter a song, 12 : 4
Deboshed, thou d. fish thou, 248 : 6
Debt, by no means run in d., 268 : 6
comfortably in d., 539 : 7
death's a d., 398 : 22
discharged through eternity, 395 : 19
double d. to pay, 370 : 13
gratitude repays installment on d., 115 : 9
how well live in d., 539 : 7
life that depends on d., 599 : 9
millions of d., 373 : 10
national d. blessing, 401 : 10, 450 : 12
pay every d., 495 : 3
promise is d. unpaid, 752 : 7
public d. public blessing, 401 : *n* 6
put future in d. to ourselves, 753 : 8
remember to pay the d., 79 : 8
run in d. by disputation, 290 : 17
to die a d. we must discharge, 267 : *n* 5
to imagination, 753 : 11
to Nature's quickly paid, 267 : 15
which cancels all others, 448 : 11
Debtors, as we forgive our d., 37 : 15
we are d. or creditors, 395 : 23
Debts, forgive us our d., 37 : 15
he that dies pays all d., 248 : 9
new way to pay old d., 263 : 1
Debts (*continued*)
words pay no d., 226 : 11
Decade, Me D., 911 : 7
promise of d. of loneliness, 835 : 6
Decay, by gentle d., 302 : 24
court in beauty and d., 469 : 1
degeneracy and d., 489 : 4
fondest hope d., 447 : 14
found its d., 359 : 10
fretted the pygmy body to d., 303 : 20
human things subject to d., 304 : 24
inherent in all component things, 72 : 22
love sicken and d., 216 : 30
make haste on d., 797 : 10
man dupe deceiver d., 467 : 9
muddy vesture of d., 201 : 1
no flood, 712 : 11
of that colossal wreck, 466 : 13
on d. greenest mosses cling, 513 : 6
our love hath no d., 252 : 22
riches hasten to d., 150 : 1
state falls into d., 451 : 18
thoughts of men d., 174 : 9
Time makes these d., 272 : 1
unperceived d., 370 : 3
wealth accumulates and men d., 369 : 30
while great and wise d., 636 : 11
woods d. and fall, 533 : 27
Decayed, cottage battered and d., 276 : 12
think sufficiently d., 629 : 17
Decays, common cause d., 80 : 16
mere glimmering and d., 299 : 8
unconscious of d., 303 : *n* 5
Deceased, ghost of d. Roman Empire, 264 : 18
he first d., 251 : 2
name of late d., 707 : 20
Deceit, bread of d. is sweet, 24 : 31
hug the dear d., 346 : 13
look of soft d., 404 : 19
men creatures of d., 312 : 20
men favor d., 303 : 10
noble and incapable of d., 432 : 12
not up to small d., 630 : 13
rumor of oppression and d., 376 : 18
small d. or sinful games, 630 : 13
smile of d., 406 : 5
threshold high to turn d., 671 : 12
Deceitful, damnable d. woman, 316 : 16
favor is d., 26 : 10
heart is d., 32 : 12
kisses of enemy d., 25 : 23
simplicity d. mistress, 635 : 19
Deceitfully, who hath not sworn d., 18 : 8
Deceitfulness of riches, 39 : 16
Deceits, from all d. of the world, 55 : 11
Deceive, dreams at length d. 'em, 320 : 24
falsehood no longer d., 391 : 1
not thy physician, 269 : 15
one's own self, 493 : 2
pleasure to d. deceiver, 296 : 13
practice to d., 431 : 1
we d. ourselves, 52 : 20, 358 : 22
Deceived, be not d., 49 : 32
by bad women been d., 288 : 25
good sense not d., 390 : 12
more ignominious to mistrust than be d., 293 : 15
the mother of mankind, 283 : 3

Deceived (*continued*)
true way to be d., 293 : 21
world wants to be d., 152 : 18
Deceiver, gay d., 415 : 14
man dupe d. decay, 467 : 9
man's d. never mine, 692 : 7
memory thou fond d., 368 : 10
pleasure to deceive d., 296 : 13
Deceivers, men were d. ever, 209 : 16
Deceives, everything that d. enchants, 84 : 10
nature never d. us, 358 : 22
springtime d., 641 : 14
with whispering ambitions, 804 : 14
Deceiveth, serpent d. whole world, 53 : 20
Deceiving, appearances often are d., 65 : 18
December, brief D. day, 513 : 20
chilly D. day, 835 : 1
drear-nighted D., 478 : 14
from May to D., 802 : 2
in heart cold D., 917 : 24
in the bleak D., 526 : 11
July's day short as D., 246 : 13
love you in D., 651 : 6
seek roses in D., 456 : 15
wallow naked in D. snow, 194 : 7
when they wed, 212 : 25
Decembers, fifteen wild D., 562 : 1
Decency, placed d. above courage, 701 : 2
want of d. want of sense, 309 : 9
Decent and manly examination, 439 : 5
cloths over high income, 884 : 19
create a fourth a d. man, 702 : 10
docent, 839 : 5
easy men, 384 : 1
provision for poor, 354 : 23
respect to opinions, 387 : 9
thy d. limbs composed, 335 : 10
Decently and in order, 48 : 27
Decentralized, competition means d. planning, 844 : 5
Deception, lying is d. not words, 572 : 12
of thrush, 807 : 3
Deceptive, masterpieces less d. than life, 734 : 4
Decide, comes moment to d., 567 : 6
forever betwixt two things, 624 : 5
law conflict courts d., 402 : 3
wise men speak fools d., 63 : 3
Decided, matter d. considered true, 134 : 23
on what they will not do., 89 : 14
only to be undecided, 743 : 12
Decides, doctors differ who d., 335 : *n* 2
Deciding not to be bitch, 844 : 12
Deciphered, faith d. in skies, 703 : 3
stones that cannot be d., 807 : 23
Decision by majorities expedient, 517 : 17
heroic d. not from cowards, 812 : 14
once a d. made, 788 : 5
valley of d., 33 : 18
Decisions, careful resolutions unerring d., 121 : 13
court overruled earlier d., 678 : 3
great d. of life, 754 : 5
more of instincts than will, 754 : 5
political d. under pressure, 706 : 18
Deck, boy stood on burning d., 470 : 17
of cards hierarchies, 818 : 5
soul with gladness, 295 : 20
Deck (*continued*)
walk d. my Captain lies, 576 : 7
yew to d. my grave, 402 : 14
Decked, bride-bed to have d., 224 : 20
crown not d. with diamonds, 186 : 8
nightcap d. his brows, 368 : 8
Decks, holystone d., 553 : 17
on d. of decayed ships, 849 : 10
turtle 'twixt plated d., 855 : 12
Declamation, New World favorable to d., 683 : 22
roared Passion slept, 351 : 12
Declaration, for support of this d., 387 : 11
make real D. of Independence, 753 : 6
of Human Rights, 774 : 8
of Independence generalities, 485 : 2
Revolution produced D. of Independence, 800 : 8
sentiments in D. of Independence, 521 : 8
Declare, day shall d. it, 48 : 5
fishes shall d. unto thee, 15 : 29
heavens d. glory of God, 17 : 27
if thou hast understanding, 16 : 28
older men d. war, 750 : 20
seen what she could not d., 422 : 20
we all d. for liberty, 523 : 7
Decline and fall of Rome 384 : 7
of belief, 641 : 1
to accept end of man, 838 : 9
to buy repentance, 88 : 24
Declined election some years ago, 791 : 7
into vale of years, 231 : 5
star of fate d., 460 : 3
Declines and falls, 549 : 30
Declineth, shadow when it d., 21 : 17
Declining, without d. west, 251 : 16
Decompose, not yet been able to d., 390 : 8
Decomposing in eternity of print, 781 : 17
Decoration, strip away useless d., 796 : 2
Decorum, observances of paltry d., 432 : 16
Decorum, dulce et d. est, 107 : *n* 23
Découvrir saint Pierre pour couvrir saint Paul, 160 : *n* 2
Decoy, fashion's brightest arts d., 370 : 16
Decoyed into our condition, 310 : 1
Decreasing leg increasing belly, 205 : 28
Decree, God and man d., 691 : 22
stately pleasure dome d., 433 : 21
temper leaps over cold d., 198 : 10
young blood not obey old d., 190 : 33
Decreed, my own soul has d., 475 : 11
Decrees of farseeing benevolence, 579 : 7
Decrepit age tied to me, 715 : 4
childhood manhood and d. age, 267 : 19
Decrepitude, bodily d. wisdom, 716 : 20
Dedde, mie love ys d., 399 : 15
Dedicate our lives and fortunes, 682 : 13
we cannot d., 523 : 4
Dedicated here to unfinished work, 523 : 4
nation so d., 523 : 4
to babs, 759 : 15
Dedicated (*continued*)
to great task remaining, 523 : 4
to proposition men equal, 523 : 4
Dedication, were we men of d., 890 : 6
Deduced, not d. from phenomena, 313 : 11
Deductions, theory unroll majestically its d., 696 : 12
Dee, diddle we take it is d., 634 : 15
lived on River D., 382 : 6
sands of D., 566 : 7
Deed, attempt and not the d., 237 : 18
better day better d., 261 : 5
by thought word and d., 55 : 17
do a d. without God's knowledge, 71 : 22
everything glory nothing, 396 : 24
foul d. which she plotted, 60 : 11
good d. in naughty world, 201 : 4
good d. to say well, 248 : 31
him who has done d. to suffer, 71 : 16
horrid d. in every eye, 236 : 24
is d. really done for heaven, 748 : 18
look for d. soul performed, 132 : 14
makes no noise over good d., 125 : 2
nameless d., 416 : 11
no evil d. live on, 647 : 3
of dreadful note, 238 : 20
put creed into d., 494 : 19
right d. wrong reason, 806 : 19
so I may do d., 475 : 11
unsung noblest d. will die, 72 : 10
whereat valor will weep, 242 : 27
without a name, 239 : 9
word shadow of d., 79 : 12
Deed's, matchless d. achieved, 365 : 9
Deeds, a god has given d. of war, 58 : 17
bright gleam of noble d., 72 : 7
die however nobly done, 174 : 9
done in their clime, 459 : 5
evil d. do not prosper, 60 : 5
excused his devilish d., 285 : 21
foul d. will rise, 218 : 26
fruitful of golden d., 285 : 6
gentle mind by gentle d., 174 : 4
gentle that dooth gentil d., 147 : 16
golden d., 534 : 22
great d. wrought at great risks, 78 : 18
how many are your d., 5 : 8
ill d. doubled with evil word, 188 : 10
like poison weeds, 676 : 13
little d. of kindness, 591 : 8
live in d. not years, 555 : 13
looks quite through d. of men, 215 : 9
man of words not d., 929 : 8
man witness unto his d., 132 : 16
matter for virtuous d., 178 : 3
means to do ill d., 202 : 11
necessity excused devilish d., 285 : 21
noise of tongues and d., 527 : 22
not let d. belie words, 127 : 21
pinions of great d., 395 : 11
privy to do gentil d., 147 : 15
render the d. of mercy, 200 : 9
sager sort our d. reprove, 250 : 3
speaker of words and doer of d., 58 : 10
thing that ends other d., 241 : 24
unlucky d. relate, 232 : 20
war and d. of carnage, 576 : 1
who aim at great d. must suffer, 97 : 15
whosoever performs good d., 132 : 2

Deeds (*continued*)
words are no d., 248 : 31
words are women d. men, 270 : 16
words have longer life than d., 72 : 4
Deef, justice blind d. and dumb, 722 : 1
Deem himself god or beast, 337 : 2
this which you d. of no moment, 86 : 4
Deep and crisp and even, 563 : 11
and dark blue ocean, 458 : 25
and dreamless sleep, 619 : 16
and gloomy wood, 423 : 12
as first love, 531 : 4
attention like d. harmony, 194 : 9
autumnal tone, 467 : 21
beauty's but skin d., 250 : 2
beauty's orient d., 271 : 19
both may be called d., 63 : 12
but dazzling darkness, 299 : 1
calleth unto deep, 19 : 7
caverns cool and d., 584 : 12
clouds swag on the d., 403 : 18
curses not loud but d., 239 : 31
damnation of his taking off, 236 : 24
darkness upon face of the d., 6 : 10
dark-shining Pacific, 797 : 12
dive into bottom of d., 203 : 15
drew from boundless d., 535 : 19
drop me d. fathoms down, 572 : 7
fatal bowels of d., 187 : 15
felt calm so d., 425 : 14
from d. to d. varies pace, 728 : 11
golden crown like a d. well, 195 : 11
great d. to great d., 535 : 2
ground four thousand miles d., 603 : 8
he discovereth d. things, 15 : 31
heart's core, 712 : 5
home is on the d., 443 : 12
in lowest d. lower d., 285 : 12
in shady sadness, 478 : 2
into darkness peering, 526 : 14
lie d. buried, 67 : 5
maketh the d. boil like a pot, 17 : 7
midnight lair made, 431 : 5
moans round, 529 : 13
natural philosophy d. moral grave, 181 : 14
night lies upon the d., 104 : 18
not so d. as a well, 193 : 5
of night is crept, 217 : 7
on his front engraven, 284 : 14
one is of the d., 428 : *n* 2
places of the earth, 20 : 20
potations pottle d., 230 : 18
rocked in cradle of d., 456 : 5
shallow murmur but d. are dumb, 172 : 12
silence d. and white, 568 : 15
skin d., 250 : *n* 1
smooth water where brook d., 172 : *n* 7
sound strikes, 457 : 14
spirits from vasty d., 204 : 12
strong obscure and d., 588 : 22
surmise pierces and scatters, 558 : 21
terms too d. for me, 628 : 6
there rolls the d., 532 : 24
thicket's gloom, 395 : 3
think d. to be hoary, 907 : *n* 1
though d. yet clear, 294 : 19
thoughts too d. for tears, 426 : 23
too d. for his hearers, 371 : 14
trenches in beauty's field, 244 : 1

Deep (*continued*)
versed in books, 288 : 17
very d. did rot O Christ, 434 : 16
woods lovely dark d., 748 : 7
young man, 628 : 6
Deep-contemplative, fools so d., 211 : 7
Deep-delved earth, 476 : 23
Deepening fidelity with friends, 299 : 11
Deeper, eyes d. than depth, 601 : 13
than plummet sound, 248 : 15
Deepest consequence, 236 : 9
feeling in silence, 798 : 17
loathing to stomach, 196 : 23
rivers least sound, 172 : *n* 7
stream smoothest water d., 172 : *n* 7
thrill d. notes of woe, 410 : 1
Deeply, I d. sympathize, 613 : 8
music heard so d., 808 : 8
Deep-mouthed welcome, 460 : 16
Deeps, distant d. or skies, 405 : 7
far in yon azure d., 510 : 15
Deep-searched, not d. with saucy looks, 190 : 12
Deer and antelope play, 927 : 19
comes d. to my singing, 929 : 2
I was a stricken d., 376 : 25
in Highlands a-chasing d., 410 : 9
mice and such small d., 234 : 10
phantom d. arise, 840 : 13
poor d. thou makest testament, 210 : 26
running of the d., 919 : 21
stricken d. go weep, 222 : 17
stricken d. that left herd, 376 : 25
walk upon our mountains, 767 : 4
Deever, hangin' Danny D., 708 : 2
Deface, no rude hand d., 425 : 4
Defaced, by Time's fell hand d., 244 : 21
lost d. deflowered, 287 : 22
Défauts, quelle âme sans d., 674 : *n* 2
Defeat enemy in one battle, 384 : 18
from folly to d., 900 : 6
in d. defiance, 746 : 11
in ourselves triumph and d., 512 : 18
is orphan, 857 : 11
much wrested from sure d., 810 : 3
night this world's d., 298 : 21
not interested in d., 573 : 16
not victory nor d., 686 : 13
preface to successors' victory, 809 : 14
refusal to accept d., 771 : 9
through battle through d., 575 : 16
unkindness may d. my life, 232 : 7
victories worse than d., 565 : 1
well borne without d., 207 : 8
Defeated, destroyed but not d., 845 : 12
history to the d., 868 : 8
make d. empires good neighbors, 783 : 6
principles never d., 505 : 17
Defeats, terrible incantations of d., 768 : 7
Defect, cause of this d., 220 : 13
chief d. of Henry King, 730 : 7
of modern literature, 586 : 8
pay in affliction or d., 736 : 5
satire points at no d., 322 : 19
Defective, effect d. comes by cause, 220 : 13
Defects, faith for all d. supplying, 139 : 10
Defend, book of moons d. ye, 918 : 11
country against enemies, 725 : 20

Defend (*continued*)
dog foremost to d., 456 : 10
every village town city, 744 : 5
from all perils, 55 : 9
God d. the right, 185 : 13
me from friends, 422 : *n* 2
ministers of grace d. us, 219 : 10
neighbor he promised to d., 488 : 11
newspapers not d. if can help it, 772 : 1
not ashamed to d. a friend, 35 : 35
our island whatever cost, 744 : 2
ourselves and henroosts, 560 : 25
ready to d. liberty, 451 : 3
refuses to d. rights, 418 : 14
to death your right to say it, 344 : 11
us thy humble servants, 55 : 4
whatever cause I d., 824 : 7
will d. what's mine, 172 : *n* 2
with their helps only d., 186 : 15
you from seasons, 234 : 3
your departed friend, 306 : 9
Defended, country d. by hands 535 : 22
God abandoned these d., 692 : 4
Defender, beyond death I have d., 824 : 7
Faith's D., 341 : 12
shield and d. Ancient of Days, 445 : 21
Defenders, no error fails to find d., 615 : 14
of old homes, 726 : 2
truth suffers by heat of d., 314 : 11
Defending not field but cause, 384 : 18
Defense, as well for d. as repose, 172 : 3
at one gate to make d., 288 : 28
cheap d. of nations, 373 : 23
deaths glorious in thy d., 325 : *n* 9
die in d. of his country, 58 : 23
friend is strong d., 35 : 9
guilty of corruption and renounce d., 179 : 11
he is my d., 19 : 27
immodest words admit no d., 309 : 9
is in law and order, 764 : 4
local d. important, 803 : 7
millions for d., 416 : 12
navy its greatest d., 365 : 16
no adequate military d., 787 : 15
no d. against reproach, 326 : 13
no d. like courtesy, 725 : 19
not in armaments, 764 : 4
of England on Rhine, 720 : 11
of more importance than opulence, 366 : 5
of our Liberty Tree, 384 : 8
provide for common d., 391 : 10
ready in d., 372 : 20
vain to look for d. against lightning, 112 : 7
Defenseless, shield for d., 615 : 6
Defensible, no d. frontier, 878 : 1
Defensive, moat d. to a house, 194 : 13
Defer, not d. kindness, 439 : 2
not to be wise, 324 : 23
'tis madness to d., 330 : 8
Deference, out of d. cheat others, 734 : 8
Deferential glad to be of use, 803 : 17
Deferred, dream d., 854 : 17
hope d. maketh the heart sick, 23 : 31
Defiance, fear hate surrender d., 913 : 6
in defeat d., 746 : 11
in their eye, 369 : 1
spirit of d., 577 : 15

Defiance (*continued*)
to all forces of Crown, 351 : 7
Deficiency, easier discover d. than see value, 422 : 14
Defile, vengeance presume to d., 400 : 10
Defiled, he that toucheth pitch d., 35 : 24
his father's grave, 110 : 4
they that touch pitch d., 209 : 26
Defilement, purity ability to contemplate d., 876 : 18
Defileth, not that which goeth into mouth d., 39 : 30
that which cometh out of mouth d., 39 : 30
Define, hold good d. it well, 532 : 8
life in a word, 552 : 3
to d. is to exclude, 784 : 13
Defined, liberalism d. in terms of objectives, 848 : 12
Definite, evolution from vague to d., 639 : 10
Definition, difference escapes d., 648 : 2
of a philosopher, 610 : 9
of criticism, 586 : 24
of oats meant to vex, 352 : *n* 3
of style, 322 : 8
of word liberty, 523 : 7
Definitions, I hate d., 501 : 2
Deflower, age that will pride d., 173 : 14
Deflowered and now to Death devote, 287 : 22
Defoe, sedulous ape to D., 668 : 23
Defraud not the poor, 34 : 29
Defunct, Buffalo Bill's d., 828 : 13
economist, 783 : 16
ghosts of d. bodies fly, 291 : 2
Defy augury, 224 : 28
man know to d. opinion, 417 : 13
the Omnipotent to arms, 283 : 4
tooth of time, 330 : 3
Degeneracy and decay, 489 : 4
progress in d. rapid, 520 : 2
Degenerate into hands like mine, 461 : 5
poor d. from ape, 830 : 12
sons and daughters, 728 : 5
Degenerates, extensive state d., 451 : 18
in hands of man, 358 : 18
Degeneration, from barbarism to d., 643 : 12
Degradation, does mean we're anti-d., 904 : 13
not to overcome poverty, 81 : 1
of idea of liberty, 882 : 10
Degrade first the arts, 405 : 15
Degraded, critic most d. of trades, 626 : 11
women d. by trivial attentions, 414 : 10
Degrades, charity d., 504 : 11
Degrading anxiety about livelihood, 751 : 11
classes of white people, 520 : 2
Degree, beauty and high d., 810 : 20
curs of low d., 369 : 17
exalted them of low d., 42 : 22
law depends on differences of d., 644 : 19
no best in kind but d., 511 : 14
only difference lies in d., 311 : 9
priority and place, 225 : 37
stand each in our d., 641 : 21
Degree (*continued*)
take but d. away, 226 : 2
unless d. preserved place not safe, 112 : 14
when d. is shaked, 226 : 1
Degrees, boil at different d., 499 : 13
crime like virtue has d., 312 : 10
estates d. and offices, 199 : 14
grows up by d., 263 : 6
ill habits gather by unseen d., 307 : 2
one battle or by d., 384 : 18
scorning the base d., 215 : 16
set down to adversity by d., 620 : 6
things through all d., 426 : 3
what wound heal but by d., 230 : 29
Dehumanizing Negro, 520 : 7
Dei, Agnus D., 54 : 5
Deified, by our own spirits d., 425 : 10
Deign on passing world, 351 : 17
Deity, design of D. preservation of species, 414 : 20
ever vindictively, 527 : 3
everlastingly appointed by D., 572 : 16
Greeks give sea separate d., 570 : 4
offended, 409 : 13
Dejected Mariana, 228 : 24
most d. thing of fortune, 234 : 19
Dejectedly, takes d. his seat, 585 : 23
Delacroix, recipe for making D., 646 : 9
Delay, in d. no plenty, 213 : 23
in me is no d., 288 : 3
infamous d., 330 : 10
law's d., 221 : 12
preferable to error, 388 : 11
reproved each dull d., 370 : 7
sweet reluctant amorous d., 285 : 19
Delayed till I am indifferent, 353 : 26
Delaying, by d. preserved state, 95 : 1
make gift rich by d., 555 : 7
not hurrying not, 575 : 18
Delays breed dangers, 175 : 11
dangerous in war, 175 : *n* 5
disease gained strength by d., 113 : 25
have dangerous ends, 185 : 4
life admits not of d., 355 : 24
Delectable mountains, 302 : 9
not because troubles are d. joy, 100 : 12
Delenda est Carthago, 95 : *n* 8
Deleted, expletive d., 925 : 20
Deliberate, accustomed to d. when drunk, 78 : 6
derangement of senses, 674 : 12
shaping of things, 718 : 6
speed, 693 : 11, 820 : *n* 4
Deliberately, live d., 559 : 25
read as d. as written, 559 : 29
shield d. planned, 794 : 15
Deliberates, woman that d. is lost, 325 : 18
Deliberation fortitude perseverance, 365 : 3
sat and public care, 284 : 14
Deliberations, chose after endless d., 734 : 6
Deliberative forces over arbitrary, 677 : 12
Delicate, air is d., 236 : 21
algae and sea anemone, 808 : 2
and rare, 676 : 9
creatures ours, 231 : 6
death, 576 : 4
fare in another's house, 35 : 39
Delicate (*continued*)
fears, 425 : 5
invisible web, 808 : 19
relationship of author to works, 683 : 6
Delicate-filmed as new-spun silk, 642 : 3
Delicately gelded, 829 : 2
Delicious, low d. word death, 575 : 18
moan, 477 : 12
torment, 497 : 15
Deliciousness, eternal delight and d., 570 : 6
Delight, aim of oratory to d., 98 : 16
all love all liking all d., 266 : 21
and deliciousness, 570 : 6
and wonder of our stage, 256 : 11
appetite makes eating d., 290 : 3
begins in d. ends in wisdom, 750 : 2
bind another to its d., 405 : 4
blue color d., 572 : 16
brief dreamy d., 712 : 19
capacity for d. and wonder, 683 : 3
clothing of d., 403 : 5
commonest d. of race, 603 : 7
desire that outruns d., 632 : 14
dogs d. to bark and bite, 328 : 2
enjoy d. with liberty, 174 : 12
far upward and inward d., 570 : 5
followed d. with heart unsatisfied, 135 : 7
give d. and hurt not, 248 : 10
go to it with d., 241 : 14
Greensleeves my d., 917 : 15
hear thy shrill d., 468 : 13
higher top of d., 570 : 5
impulse of d., 714 : 1
in conceiving Iago, 479 : 17
in singing, 442 : 23
intellectual d. and freedom, 420 : 3
is in law of the Lord, 17 : 12
labor we d. in physics pain, 238 : 4
lady of my d., 661 : 11
land of pure d., 328 : 15
lo she that was world's d., 632 : 17
love with d. discourses, 140 : 9
lulled with dances and d., 196 : 18
moon of my d., 517 : 4
my d. and thy d., 654 : 18
my ever new d., 286 : 13
never d. in another's misfortune, 111 : 13
no season such d. can bring, 265 : 16
of battle, 529 : 8
of husband aunts infant, 810 : 20
on starboard of woe sure d., 570 : 5
paint the meadows with d., 191 : 13
phantom of d., 427 : 3
playing Idiot's D., 836 : 15
plaything gives youth d., 337 : 7
rebirth brings d., 72 : 23
some born to sweet d., 406 : 19
spirit of D., 469 : 23
stars gave the first d., 276 : 4
stretches of pure d., 799 : 20
strongest tower of d., 571 : 10
studies a d. to the old, 98 : 7
sweets grown common lose d., 245 : 10
temple of d., 478 : 1
that consumes desire, 632 : 14
these virtues of d., 403 : 10
to d. paid blessing, 739 : 17
to do things I ought, 449 : 15
toys for your d., 669 : 4

Delight (*continued*)
unrest men miscall d., 469 : 12
weighing d. and dole, 217 : 29
what d. without Aphrodite, 62 : 3
with silent d., 403 : 12
Zeus grant sweet d., 71 : 27
Delighted spirit, 228 : 20
us long enough, 440 : 20
Delighteth, speech finely framed d., 36 : 18
whom the king d. to honor, 14 : 33
Delightful, both wise both d., 295 : 4
delicious de-lovely, 820 : 6
in this d. garden grows, 173 : 17
still air of d. studies, 281 : 13
task rear tender thought, 345 : 11
Delighting and instructing at the same time, 110 : 1
best poetry d. us, 589 : 11
in your company, 917 : 14
O d. me, 733 : 3
Delights, all d. are vain, 190 : 10
all thoughts passions d., 435 : 20
anarchy of poverty d. me, 785 : 13
fleeting d. of days, 464 : 14
from heart of fountain of d., 101 : 7
hence all you vain d., 261 : 4
joy d. in joy, 244 : 3
man d. not me, 220 : 29
misery still d. to trace, 377 : 25
reader and instructs too, 311 : 13
scorn d., 280 : 15
stylization d. minds, 317 : 11
these d. if thou canst give, 278 : 8
violent d. have violent ends, 192 : 27
were dolphin-like, 241 : 25
winter his d., 250 : 7
Delineation, happiest d., 440 : 29
Delinquents, beg d. for life, 893 : 17
Delirium, all that d. of brave, 713 : 11
of flesh, 850 : 9
Deliver, from winter plague Lord d. us, 250 : 9
good Lord d. us, 55 : 10, 921 : 4
I will d. him to you, 41 : 5
me from body of death, 47 : 7
me from errors of wise, 290 : 7
me from phlegmatic preachers, 392 : 10
me from ruth of lair, 907 : 22
no human efforts d. them, 379 : 2
round unvarnished tale d., 229 : 25
thee from the snare, 20 : 16
us from evil, 37 : 15
Deliverance, day of d., 381 : 7
Delivered from perils and miseries, 265 : 7
upon mellowing of occasion, 190 : 30
Deliverer, Lord is my d., 13 : 24
Delivering improvements by generation, 378 : 1
Dell, heart-stifled in d., 476 : 15
De-lovely, delightful delicious d., 820 : 6
Deluding, vain d. Joys, 278 : 9
Deluge, after us the d., 364 : 17
pedigree far as D., 539 : 20
rain a d. showered, 415 : 5
Déluge, après nous le d., 364 : 17
Delusion, give up liberties under d., 373 : 13
Solon was under a d., 84 : 20
to be paid before work, 171 : *n* 2
to the philanthropist, 619 : 7
trial by jury a d., 445 : 20
Delusions, sovereign exposed to innumerable d., 366 : 8
Delusive, most d. of passions, 681 : 1
Delve, let other d. mystery, 875 : 3
Delved, Adam d., 917 : 1
Delves parallels in beauty's brow, 244 : 20
Delving in patient industry, 642 : 11
Demand, never fully supplying d., 366 : 1
superflous to d. time of day, 202 : 23
Demanded an image, 792 : 12
Demands, heavenly race d. zeal, 346 : 1
rebellion makes upon us, 882 : 7
time like this d., 566 : 3
Demarcations, ghostlier d., 767 : 16
Demd damp moist unpleasant body, 547 : 15
dowager's a d. outline, 547 : 14
horrid grind, 547 : 18
Demean themselves as good citizens, 379 : 8
Demented with owning things, 574 : 24
Demesne, private pagus or d., 869 : 6
Demeter, goddess D. or Earth, 77 : 6
Demi-Atlas of this earth, 240 : 22
Demi-paradise, this other Eden d., 194 : 13
Demirep that loves, 543 : 7
Demitasses, villainous d., 684 : 17
Demnition bowwows, 547 : 19
Democracies cannot dispense with hypocrisy, 802 : 15
security to d. against despots, 397 : *n* 8
Democracy and socialism have word equality, 506 : 12
appropriate for economic surplus, 877 : 16
arises out of notion, 88 : 8
arsenal of d., 780 : 12
bludgeoning of people, 675 : 24
characteristics of d., 845 : 15
charming form of government, 85 : 3
citizens of this d., 851 : 16
constitution named a d., 80 : 17
cycle d. built on, 887 : 8
death of d., 845 : 16
direct self-government, 537 : *n* 4
egg of d., 569 : 9
equality and justice in d., 845 : 15
freedom and d. principles, 862 : 19
government of people, 537 : 15
if d. loses touch, 814 : 11
if liberty and equality found in d., 88 : 6
in a republic, 725 : 20
injustice makes d. necessary, 823 : 18
ism change American d., 779 : 19
justice makes d. possible, 823 : 18
means to end, 814 : 6
more unsafe than ever, 703 : 2
my idea of d., 520 : 6
neither despotism nor d., 401 : 13
not saved by supermen, 851 : 18
passes into despotism, 85 : 4
pervading evil of d., 616 : 2
political d. gymnasium, 577 : 1
recurrent suspicion, 846 : 16
self-canceling business, 473 : 22
shuts past opens future, 506 : 8
socialist d. may be sham, 785 : 6
still upon trial, 650 : 15
true d. never existed, 358 : 15
Democracy (*continued*)
United States not proclaimed d., 741 : 15
whatever differs from this no d., 520 : 6
world safe for d., 682 : 12, 703 : 2
Democrat, I am a D., 872 : 7
no person called self d., 741 : 15
Democratic, basis of d. state, 88 : 12
God, 570 : 11
nations not care for past, 506 : 8
party ain't on speakin' terms, 721 : 14
public men, 681 : 12
secrecy and d. government, 788 : 18
society like ours, 777 : 2
Democrats, afford a few D., 847 : 13
raises corn and D., 674 : 13
Demon in my view, 525 : 6
when your d. in charge, 711 : 3
you have roused, 520 : 7
Demoniac frenzy, 287 : 29
Demonic, semihuman and d., 754 : 10
Demonisms, subtle d. of life, 570 : 13
Demon-lover, wailing for her d., 433 : 22
Demons down under sea, 527 : 9
half-tamed d. in breast, 678 : 6
Demonstrandum, quod erat d., 92 : 3
Demonstrate, cannot d. an emotion, 637 : 3
Demonstrating careless desolation, 212 : 13
Demonstration, full monstrous d., 654 : 11
Demonstrative or persuasive type, 730 : 15
Demoralizing, human slavery d., 675 : 25
nothing so d. as money, 74 : 12
Demosthenes first of orators, 353 : *n* 4
Demur you're dangerous, 605 : 11
Demure, sober steadfast and d., 278 : 12
Demurrer, no bail no d., 398 : 22
Den, beard lion in his d., 430 : 23
cast Daniel into the d. of lions, 33 : 3
cockatrice' d., 29 : 19
living in underground d., 84 : 17
made it a d. of thieves, 40 : 12
seven sleepers' d., 251 : 14
Dendid, when D. created all things, 925 : 21
Denial vain and coy excuse, 280 : 9
Denied, call may not be d., 760 : 15
exact day labor light d., 282 : 16
no other was d., 605 : 20
Peter d. Lord, 320 : 7
the faith, 50 : 31
this only d. to God, 82 : 27
Denies, court a mistress she d. you, 256 : 6
heaven to gaudy day d., 459 : 13
spirit that always d., 396 : 13
voyager further sailing, 76 : 25
Denieth, antichrist d. the Father, 52 : 22
Denmark, ne'er villain in D., 220 : 2
something rotten in D., 219 : 17
sure it may be so in D., 220 : 1
Denominator, common d. of progress, 871 : 15
Denoted foregone conclusion, 231 : 16
Denouncing someone or something else, 772 : 1
Dens and fastnesses of barbarism, 592 : 6
lay them down in their d., 21 : 11

Denunciation in place of
evidence, 737 : 7
Deny, easier to believe than d., 631 : 1
me thrice, 41 : 18
O was no d., 404 : 10
participation of freedom, 373 : 6
poor heart would fain d., 239 : 31
themselves nothing, 539 : 7
thy father, 192 : 5
us for our good, 240 : 26
Denying, to allure by d., 555 : 7
Deo, gloria in excelsis D., 54 : 4
Deos fortoribus adesse, 123 : *n* 1
Depart, ah she doth d., 404 : 10
be off, 98 : *n* 3
better to serve, 617 : 5
captains and kings d., 709 : 17
come like shadows so d., 239 : 13
from evil, 18 : 21
loth to d., 320 : 21
ready to d., 443 : 1
servant d. in peace, 42 : 30
this vale, 772 : 6
to be to do to d., 637 : 7
to d. from evil is
understanding, 16 : 15
when old he will not d. from it, 24 : 35
when ye d. shake off dust, 38 : 35
Departed, all but he d., 447 : 8
defend your d. friend, 306 : 9
ghosts of d. quantities, 330 : 21
glory is d. from Israel, 12 : 32
he has d. withdrawn gone
away, 98 : 3
his spirit is d., 36 : 8
into their own country, 36 : 21
mind me o' d. joys, 409 : 24
never to return, 409 : 24
rule over the d. dead, 60 : 15
sacred to d. spirit, 133 : 20
souls d. shadows of living, 275 : 13
took man's life when he d., 472 : 13
Departeth, heart d. from the
Lord, 32 : 11
Departing, knolling d. friend, 205 : 20
leave behind us, 509 : 15
Department, duty of judicial d., 402 : 3
fair sex your d., 689 : 13
Departure beyond borders
death, 817 : 5
hour of d. has arrived, 83 : 15
is taken for misery, 34 : 13
Depend, all the rest on us d., 575 : 15
on fleeting things, 413 : 29
Dependence, in marriage d.
mutual, 471 : 1
of art on felt life, 653 : 11
upon militia, 379 : 4
women educated for d., 414 : 8
Dependency, old d. of day and
night, 767 : 4
Dependent, all d. every soul of
us, 681 : 9
mortals live d. upon another, 100 : 15
Depends, happiness d. as Nature
shows, 375 : 18
so much d. upon, 785 : 11
Deploring, damsel lay d., 331 : 7
Deportment, model of d., 549 : 15
Depose my state but not my
griefs, 195 : 12
Deposed, ghosts they have d., 195 : 2
some have been d., 195 : 2
Deposit for substantial virtue, 388 : 2
Deposit (*continued*)
little cell by cell, 638 : 10
Deposited, near this spot d., 456 : 9
Depository of public interests, 390 : 2
of truth, 300 : 11
safe d. of ultimate powers, 389 : 15
Deposits of accumulated
experience, 753 : 12
Depot eleven miles away, 726 : 7
Depravations of Europe, 319 : 22
Depraved, no one becomes d. in
moment, 122 : 3
Depraves all good dispositions, 388 : 3
Depravity, Calvinistic sense of innate
d., 569 : 16
perverse d. of nature, 316 : 15
within classes, 794 : 12
Depressed, fine weather heavier on
d., 896 : 4
heart d. with cares, 332 : 3
Depression, Great D. produced by
government mismanagement,
880 : 14
Deprive or divest posterity, 367 : 4
Deprived, melody d. of pitch, 801 : 8
of everlasting bliss, 183 : 21
of voice in legislation, 393 : 3
poor man d. of power, 85 : 2
without due process of law, 391 : 17
Depth, far beyond my d., 249 : 3
gods approve d. not tumult, 428 : 21
height nor d., 47 : 15
in philosophy bringeth to
religion, 180 : 17
of divine despair, 531 : 3
to weep make less d. of grief, 186 : 3
truth lies in the d., 79 : 10
walked in the search of the d., 16 : 31
Depths, cannot fathom their d., 658 : 27
congealed in heart of sea, 9 : 35
Germans and women have no
d., 658 : 27
go down again to the d., 21 : 15
of height, 829 : 19
out of the d. have I cried, 22 : 11
pellucid in azure d., 577 : 7
Deputed sword, 228 : 6
Deputies, not d. but despoilers, 422 : 18
Derangement, immense d. of
senses, 674 : 12
nice d. of epitaphs, 398 : 11
of all senses, 674 : 12
Derby, Justice Bennet of D., 300 : 22
Dérèglement de tous les sens, 674 : *n* 4
Derides, shame them d., 233 : 1
wrinkled Care d., 277 : 20
Derision, uglification and d., 612 : 5
Derive from women's eyes this
doctrine, 191 : 5
Derives axioms from
particulars, 179 : 7
Deriving just powers from
consent, 387 : 9
Derned sight better business, 636 : 5
Dervishes, barefoot d., 495 : 5
Descant, amorous d. sung, 285 : 25
Descartes, seen further than D., 313 : 10
Descend make fast set foot, 822 : 10
ready to d. throne, 420 : 14
to meet, 497 : 16
we d. from Jove, 105 : 28
we too into dust d., 516 : 15
Descendants, democracy hides
d., 506 : 9
Descendants (*continued*)
shall gather your fruits, 103 : 19
Descended, Curtius Rufus seems d.
from himself, 86 : *n* 1
desirable to be well d., 120 : 8
from a god, 452 : 12
from heroic monkey, 515 : 9
into hell, 55 : 2
of so many kings, 242 : 6
Descending, angels ascending and
d., 8 : 19, 44 : 25
angels twice d., 604 : 3
black and white, 892 : 9
like a dove, 36 : 30
low d. sun, 920 : 12
Descends autumn evening, 588 : 5
new generation d. from on
high, 103 : 14
Descent, Americans of African
d., 617 : 6
claims of long d., 528 : 10
from certain group of people, 685 : 7
if d. from heroic sires, 311 : 11
of last end on living, 777 : 16
to Hades is same, 72 : 14
Describe undescribable, 458 : 11
world of today, 840 : 20
Description, beggared all d., 240 : 29
of nature, 789 : 2
short d. of happy state, 307 : 18
theory of d. matters most, 768 : 6
Descriptions of the fairest
wights, 245 : 12
Dese are conditions dat prevail, 825 : 15
Desecration, committed d. against
whole scheme of life, 873 : 9
Desert, Arab in d., 354 : *n* 4
from d. I come to thee, 596 : 15
heath in the d., 32 : 11
Hohokams on Arizona d., 897 : 19
in service, 226 : 20
inaccessible, 211 : 12
legs of stone in d., 466 : 12
make a d. call it peace, 123 : 3
make straight in the d. a
highway, 30 : 30
make world d., 851 : 15
mice d. building about to fall, 117 : 2
mountains approach over d., 907 : 14
my dwelling place, 458 : 23
never d. Mr. Micawber, 548 : 26
of a thousand lines, 339 : 24
of the sea, 29 : 26
rats d. sinking ship, 117 : *n* 2
sagebrush d., 739 : 5
shall rejoice, 30 : 23
sighs in bed, 868 : 10
these gardens of d., 471 : 11
until d. knows water grows, 607 : 6
use every man after d., 221 : 5
waste sweetness on d. air, 362 : 8
water but the d., 458 : 18
wildernesses, 279 : 16
you for creeds that refuse, 632 : 16
Deserted at his utmost need, 306 : 18
banquet hall d., 447 : 8
Desertion, storm d. death, 481 : 2
Desert's dusty face, 516 : 9
Deserts, beyond this nothing but
sandy d., 119 : 21
civilization results in d., 760 : 7
make d. bloom, 851 : 15
man making d., 760 : 6
of vast eternity, 296 : 28

Deserts (*continued*)
or his d. are small, 292 : 3
when she d. the night, 288 : 21
Deserve all these kittens, 760 : 4
better of mankind, 322 : 12
neither liberty nor safety, 348 : 2
Sempronius we'll d. it, 325 : 12
Deserved, least d. such a fate, 81 : 9
less at country's hands, 590 : 7
so mighty a Redeemer, 54 : 8
Deserves, government it d., 400 : 2
love and thanks, 384 : 13
none but brave d. fair, 306 : 12
one good turn d. another, 117 : 14
to be a slave, 418 : 14
Deserving, lost without d., 230 : 24
of freedom he only is d., 396 : 25
Design, grand d. in providence, 380 : 8
of all his words, 768 : 25
of all parts helpful to motive, 590 : 13
to make haste to be gone, 273 : 1
Designed, great masterpiece d., 410 : 16
to make people stumble, 786 : 2
Designing Saint Paul's, 753 : 3
Designs, close d. crooked counsels, 303 : 20
ladder to all high d., 226 : 1
nature full of d., 650 : 4
were strictly honorable, 349 : 23
Desirable, more d. than fortunate hour, 102 : 9
Desire, a' the learning I d., 409 : 1
accomplished is sweet, 23 : 33
antidote to d., 324 : 21
arrows of d., 406 : 21
as you d. me, 723 : 21
beholding face of d., 683 : 8
believe that which they d., 303 : *n* 3
bloom of young D., 362 : 21
changes, 734 : 9
dead be near us, 532 : 7
death end of man's d., 633 : 18
delight that consumes d., 632 : 14
difficult to tell from despair, 768 : 5
dispraise thing you d., 226 : 23
drink provokes d., 238 : 3
father's death, 582 : 11
flaming some old d., 839 : 1
follow your d., 3 : 6
from fairest creatures d. increase, 243 : 31
gain heart's d., 680 : 21
gratified plants fruits, 404 : 16
hast given him his heart's d., 18 : 4
heart's d., 517 : 13, 712 : 11
his d. is toward me, 28 : 22
in it was love and d., 58 : 19
kindle soft d., 306 : 22
know what he ought to d., 139 : 14
lineaments of gratified d., 404 : 20
liveth not in fierce d., 430 : 9
love and d. and hate, 721 : 7
love distills d., 76 : 22
men by nature d. knowledge, 87 : 9
men d. the good, 88 : 3
mixing memory and d., 804 : 26
more love and knowledge, 210 : 18
my d. is that the Almighty answer me, 16 : 20
nature of d. not to be satisfied, 88 : 1
no more d. rose, 190 : 13
not mortal what you d., 113 : 16
of discipline, 34 : 17
of fame, 534 : 23
Desire (*continued*)
of knowledge increases, 360 : 4
of moth for star, 469 : 20
of power in excess, 180 : 14
one shore beyond d., 843 : 18
outlive performance, 206 : 16
perpetual rack, 258 : 21
prayer soul's sincere d., 429 : 18
pure and just d. of man, 154 : 15
remold it nearer to d., 517 : 13
satisfiest the d. of every living thing, 22 : 21
second silence of d., 512 : 20
shall fail, 27 : 25
sick with d., 715 : 2
so hillmen d. hills, 710 : 8
speed of my d., 596 : 15
streetcar named D., 887 : 9
that outruns delight, 632 : 14
those who d. slavery, 524 : 8
to a bottle of hay, 197 : 5
to appear natural, 294 : 8
to be immortal, 537 : 14
to be irresistibly desired, 750 : 7
to get on in world, 799 : 18
to live again, 658 : 18
to live beyond income, 620 : 17
to think well of oneself, 809 : 10
train noble natures not to d. more, 88 : 1
under the elms, 810 : 9
unspeakable d., 585 : 15
vain d. vain regret, 601 : 21
vanquished by d., 63 : 9
we may be better strangers, 212 : 9
what I've tasted of d., 748 : 2
what we ought not to have, 111 : 22
which of us has his d., 539 : 10
with dead d. not die, 430 : 9
without hope, 704 : 12
without hope we live in d., 140 : 20
without knowledge or d., 63 : 14
wonder and wild d., 545 : 1
yearning in d., 529 : 10
Desired and timely things, 692 : 2
irresistibly d., 750 : 7
more to be d. than gold, 18 : 1
not one to be d., 528 : 7
pinch which hurts and is d., 242 : 3
that which most d., 316 : 15
who hath d. sea, 710 : 7
Desires and Adorations, 469 : 3
and dreams and powers, 633 : 20
and petitions of thy servants, 55 : 8
be for what is good, 69 : 2
covetous d. of the world, 56 : 4
each of us d. the good, 171 : 19
from Death fulfillment to d., 767 : 3
grant all things your heart d., 59 : 28
have few d., 64 : 8
heart's d. be with you, 210 : 15
liberty doing what one d., 508 : 15
limited nature infinite d., 464 : 16
mastery of d., 658 : 6
no calamity greater than lavish d., 64 : 16
painting gives form to d., 774 : 11
religion falls in with d., 679 : 3
reviving old d., 516 : 2
sinful d. of the flesh, 56 : 4
submitting things to d. of mind, 179 : 2
those d. glowing openly, 702 : 5
two d. toss about, 585 : 18
Desires (*continued*)
undaunted daughter of d., 292 : 15
unto whom all d. known, 55 : 15
weaned heart from low d., 155 : 1
weight of chance d., 427 : 14
Desireth not death of sinner, 54 : 15
Desiring this man's art, 244 : 9
Desirous, aught else on earth d., 332 : 2
Desist, I shall ask leave to d., 275 : 32
Desk, but a d. to write upon, 291 : 18
student glued to d., 592 : 8
turn upward from d., 805 : 7
Desolate amid sad forest, 503 : 3
and sick of old passion, 721 : 4
dark weeks, 785 : 14
home of mirth made d., 503 : 3
indefinitely d., 711 : 11
no one so d., 510 : 10
shores, 478 : 16
which built d. places, 15 : 8
windswept space, 626 : 21
winter's dregs made d., 641 : 11
without you all is d., 811 : 12
Desolation, abomination of d., 40 : 23
and dim night, 525 : 16
blood vengeance d., 579 : 3
butchery and d., 745 : 2
careless d., 212 : 13
dark cold and empty d., 807 : 24
intellectual d., 562 : 18
seat of d. void of light, 283 : 12
Despair, almost about to d., 481 : 9
at not having found joy, 757 : 7
beauty born of own d., 715 : 17
begotten by d., 297 : 6
beyond hope and d., 806 : 2
carrion comfort d., 656 : 15
comfort and d., 246 : 3
comfortless D., 361 : 11
death of hope and d., 808 : 11
desire difficult to tell from d., 768 : 5
divine d., 531 : 3
Doubt brother devil to D., 659 : 5
dying and in d., 602 : 11
endure my own d., 320 : 3
fiercer by d., 284 : 4
from d. high uplifted, 284 : 3
Giant D., 302 : 8
gives comfort in d., 185 : 12
hell's d., 405 : 3
in d. comes wisdom, 71 : 5
infinite wrath and d., 285 : 12
law chance hath slain, 254 : 9
melancholy and d., 260 : 2
mournful lean D., 402 : 14
my ending is d., 248 : 19
my only hope lies in d., 312 : 6
never d., 107 : 4
plans all ended in d., 702 : 3
procures extremity of bitterness, 260 : 2
racked with deep d., 283 : 9
rash-embraced d., 199 : 28
replace d. with opportunity, 872 : 10
result of fatal situations, 514 : 7
reveals own folly and d., 837 : 18
seraphs might d., 456 : 22
shall I wasting in d., 264 : 23
shame d. her teachers, 503 : 12
toils d. to reach, 320 : 23
warder is D., 676 : 13
where d. let me sow hope, 138 : 15
white sustenance d., 606 : 1
ye mighty and d., 466 : 13

Despair (*continued*)
you with unpaid bill D., 470 : 4
Despairful, dissolute damned d., 752 : 4
Despairing songs loveliest, 537 : 9
Despairs, leaden-eyed d., 476 : 24
through comfortless d., 174 : 11
Desperandum, nil d., 107 : *n* 4
Desperate, beware of d. steps, 377 : 21
by d. appliance relieved, 223 : 14
diseases d. grown, 223 : 14
marriage a d. thing, 263 : 23
seas long wont to roam, 525 : 9
slave to d. men, 254 : 12
tempt not d. man, 193 : 24
the joy, 454 : 2
wisdom not to do d. things, 559 : 5
Desperately, deceitful and d. wicked, 32 : 12
Desperateness of losing binds bouquet, 739 : 11
Desperation, our policy against d., 771 : 11
quiet d., 559 : 4
Despicable, wretched d. creature, 346 : 4
Despise, a contrite heart thou wilt not d., 19 : 19
capacity to d. himself, 703 : 16
force human beings to d. themselves, 853 : 10
hold to one d. other, 38 : 1
ignorant d. education, 111 : 23
not thy mother, 25 : 10
pity and d. him, 547 : 11
what female heart gold d., 361 : 15
with work you d., 725 : 2
Despised and dying king, 468 : 4
and rejected of men, 31 : 14
being unarmed be d., 153 : 22
day of small things, 33 : 31
poor infirm d. old man, 233 : 26
race, 617 : 6
straight, 245 : 23
thus the poor agent d., 227 : 8
Despises, husband frae wife d., 411 : 5
Despising, myself almost d., 244 : 9
Despite, heaven's d., 405 : 4
Despitefully, them which d. use you, 37 : 11
Despoilers, not deputies but d., 422 : 18
Despond, slough was D., 301 : 22
Despondency and madness, 425 : 10, 892 : 15
Despondently, sprouting d. at gates, 804 : 5
Desponding view of present, 489 : 4
Despot, country governed by d., 356 : 3
custom d. of mankind, 486 : 5
man once d. and slave, 467 : 9
Despotism, cloud of barbarism and d., 390 : 1
degenerates into d., 451 : 18
democracy passes into d., 85 : 4
feeble engines of d., 390 : 1
France d. tempered by epigrams, 473 : 11
in majority of popular assembly, 382 : 4
neither d. nor democracy, 401 : 13
sea power never led to d., 800 : 6
seeds of d. at doors, 520 : 7
to liberty in featherbed, 388 : 9
whatever crushes individuality is d., 508 : 11
Despotism (*continued*)
where d. taken pure, 520 : 2
will destroy all good, 550 : 3
Despots, security against d., 397 : *n* 8
Dessert without cheese, 401 : 7
Destination, heaven's my d., 839 : 11
Destined, his d. hour, 516 : 10
Destinies, veiled D., 469 : 3
Destiny, believing in common d., 860 : 13
chosen his d., 863 : 4
day of d. is over, 460 : 3
exercises influence, 657 : 7
follow ideals reach d., 603 : 2
hanging and wiving go by d., 159 : *n* 4
heavenly d., 426 : 4
man forges for himself, 865 : 11
manifest d., 552 : 13
not by material computation, 745 : 1
obscure, 362 : 2
of colored American, 556 : 8
of New England, 837 : 4
one country one d., 451 : 4
reap a d., 922 : 18
rendezvous with d., 779 : 17
repose not d. of man, 644 : 3
riddle of d., 442 : 3
shady leaves of d., 292 : 8
waits alike, 71 : 15
wedding is d., 159 : 6
what seems accident springs from d., 413 : 12
with men for pieces plays, 516 : 22
Destitute of emotional warmth, 649 : 7
Destroy, abolish vice d. virtue, 274 : 18
blade of grass, 741 : 16
does thy life d., 405 : 5
evil they set out to d., 812 : 11
fib or sophistry, 338 : 9
for one grape vine d., 189 : 20
free world, 862 : 20
many monsters to d., 851 : 3
natural resources, 687 : 14
nor sword nor age d., 113 : 24
not come to d. law, 37 : 6
not to d. but fulfill, 37 : 6
one to d. is murder, 330 : 1
power of reasoning, 85 : 13
power to tax involves power to d., 402 : 7
power to tax not power to d., 645 : 9
sought to d. institutions, 575 : 7
surely not in wrath d., 517 : 7
they shall not hurt nor d., 29 : 19
those who hate and d., 672 : 9
thought would d. paradise, 361 : 12
town to save it, 925 : 18
whom God wishes to d., 78 : 1, 134 : 21
winged life d., 404 : 18
worms d. this body, 16 : 4
Destroyed but not defeated, 845 : 12
by each other, 316 : 11
by madness, 906 : 1
Carthage must be d., 95 : 12
flower of kings and knights d., 149 : 18
if men are d., 73 : 8
last enemy d. is death, 49 : 1
love without power d., 823 : 16
Medici created and d. me, 152 : 16
nations are d. or flourish, 407 : 5
poetry painting music d., 407 : 5
Destroyed (*continued*)
the very ruins d., 118 : 14
things violently d., 424 : 8
when once d., 369 : 30
Destroyer and preserver hear, 467 : 18
death d. of worlds, 861 : *n* 2
force that blasts trees is my d., 886 : 12
time d. time preserver, 808 : 6
Destroying, fighting still still d., 306 : 19
not by d. but promoting, 373 : 9
Destroys good book kills reason, 281 : 23
habit d. first nature, 393 : *n* 2
nothing d. us but time, 132 : 7
outrage when man d. nature, 758 : 2
saliva d. serpents, 116 : 13
use d. beauty, 706 : 7
Destruction, all other to d. draw, 252 : 22
brought her dowry d., 71 : 6
causes of d., 358 : 16
creation same as d., 90 : 2
Famine Pestilence D. Death, 773 : 6
flight perhaps to d., 582 : 12
fool's mouth is his d., 24 : 19
for d. ice suffice, 748 : 2
forces of nuclear d., 891 : 15
give enemies means of our d., 66 : 24
hell of nuclear d., 909 : 14
I will be thy d., 33 : 16
if d. be our lot, 519 : 22
means of d. hitherto unknown, 787 : 15
of life and happiness, 389 : 4
of Nazi tyranny, 781 : 8
of Tao and virtue, 90 : 7
of tea so bold, 380 : 14
of world not dreadful, 515 : 15
pride goeth before d., 24 : 12
proliferation or accident carry us to d., 860 : 6
set him apart for d., 308 : *n* 2
shows activity of authorities, 518 : 3
that wasteth at noonday, 20 : 16
their going seemed utter d., 34 : 13
thou turnest man to d., 20 : 11
universe meets own d., 774 : 10
way that leadeth to d., 38 : 15
whose end is d., 50 : 5
word deals d., 683 : 7
world peace or world d., 729 : 12
Destructions, rescue my soul from their d., 18 : 22
Destructive damnable woman, 316 : 16
not afraid of d. act, 701 : 13
smiling d. man, 317 : 15
Desuetude, innocuous d., 631 : 8
Detached, reality attained only by d., 876 : 17
Detail, feel forces behind d., 644 : 14
finding what d. to do without, 739 : 3
frittered away by d., 559 : 26
Details, so many incidents so many d., 702 : 7
Detect, lose it in moment you d., 335 : 13
Detection, traitors escape d., 737 : 6
Detectives, scientists d. and explorers, 888 : 1
Deteriorating, shabby equipment d., 807 : 21
Determinate, every thing has d. idea, 85 : 13

Determination enough in mighty enterprises, 112 : 22
esprit de corps and d., 771 : 13
for better world, 699 : 4
Determine, education will d. future life, 84 : 13
men d. gods dispose, 259 : n 4
people seldom d. right, 401 : 12
Determined by what lies outside it, 565 : 25
dared and done, 365 : 9
so long d. not to do it, 308 : 17
to know beans, 560 : 6
Determinism, history abhors d., 837 : 12
otherwise no d. in science, 551 : 17
Deterred, man cannot be d., 891 : 8
Deterrent of massive retaliatory power, 803 : 7
Detest, begin to d. him, 391 : 5
I d. what you write, 344 : n 5
love offender d. offense, 307 : n 2
pageantry of king, 391 : 2
phrases I d., 693 : 5
Sabbath day, 624 : 8
Detested first husband, 675 : 5
Detesting, die d. superstition, 344 : 12
Dethroned bereft of reason, 496 : 7
Detract, power to add or d., 523 : 4
Detraction will not suffer it, 205 : 5
Deus, Domine D. Agnus Dei, 54 : 5
ex machina, 91 : 6
homo proponet D. disponit, 148 : n 7
vult, 133 : 19
Deutschland über alles, 483 : 17
Devastation, slaughter pillage d., 745 : 2
Develop, men free to d. faculties, 677 : 12
Development, great unital continuous d., 617 : 11
in language development in feeling, 809 : 7
psychic d. of individual, 678 : 9
without d. no profit, 784 : 29
Develops and enlarges organ, 393 : 7
Deviates, Shadwell never d. into sense, 304 : 25
Deviation from truth is multiplied, 87 : 7
Device, banner with strange d., 510 : 14
miracle of rare d., 433 : 25
no work nor d. nor knowledge, 27 : 16
that is our d., 491 : 5
Devil, abashed the D. stood, 286 : 8
an angel too, 706 : 1
apology for D., 620 : 23
a-walking the D. is gone, 440 : 13
became woman, 491 : 9
beggar will outride the D., 186 : n 1
bird or d., 526 : 17
black as the d., 400 : 15
brother d. to Despair, 659 : 5
builds a chapel there, 318 : 5
can cite Scripture, 198 : 22
children of d., 535 : 13
come and Faustus damned, 184 : 8
counteracts D. who is Death, 365 : 14
created in man's image, 582 : 3
damn thee black, 239 : 29
did grin, 435 : 17
Don or d. 535 : 13
drink and d. had done, 668 : 4
eat with d. have long spoon, 147 : n 12
Devil (*continued*)
envy of the d., 34 : 12
every man God or D., 304 : 11
fears a painted d., 237 : 23
from deceits of the d., 55 : 11
from d. does proceed, 401 : 3
give d. his due, 168 : 23
go poor d., 360 : 6
God and d. fighting, 582 : 1
God sends meat D. sends cooks, 159 : n 6
had final say, 883 : 12
hath not arrow, 462 : 3
having trouble with wife, 679 : 12
he's a very d., 214 : 24
how the d. they got there, 338 : 12
if d. doesn't exist, 582 : 3
if the d. dress her not, 242 : 1
is a gentleman, 234 : n 2
is asleep, 679 : 12
is ever God's ape, 156 : 5
Jim having seen d., 623 : 21
knows how to row, 435 : 7
let the d. wear black, 222 : 9
let us call thee d., 230 : 25
love a mischievous d., 620 : 24
man for himself d. for all, 161 : n 8
match for d., 840 : 11
Nazarite conjured the d., 198 : 18
needs go whom d. drive, 161 : 3
not serve God if d. bid, 229 : 19
old serpent called the D., 53 : 20
ole d. sea, 810 : 5
renounce the d., 56 : 4
resist the d., 52 : 2
sarcasm language of d., 473 : 3
seem saint when most play d., 187 : 6
showed him kingdoms, 42 : 34
speak truth and shame D., 158 : 8
sugar o'er d. himself, 221 : 11
take her, 289 : 18
take the hindmost, 263 : 8
thou wast made d., 260 : 16
to pay, 169 : 31
walketh about as roaring lion, 52 : 16
what the d. was he doing in that galley, 298 : 12
whispered behind leaves, 708 : 11
whoops, 708 : 12
why d. have all good tunes, 393 : 6
wi' usquebae face the d., 411 : 10
would build chapel, 156 : 5
your father the d., 45 : 6
Devil-and-all to pay, 169 : 31
Devildoms of Spain, 535 : 12
Devilish and damned tobacco, 259 : 15
excused his d. deeds, 285 : 21
sly, 548 : 16
this wisdom is d., 52 : 1
Devilment, midst of so much d., 732 : 2
Devil's, got over D. back, 261 : 7
had final say, 883 : 12
leavings, 340 : 12
pundit d. advocate enthusiast, 847 : 10
true poet and of D. party, 403 : 19
who cleft the D. foot, 252 : 1
Devils, as many d. in Worms as tiles, 156 : 10
being offended, 230 : 8
fight like d., 207 : 26
heart place d. dwell in, 274 : 15
in twists of road, 735 : 3
Lord transformed them to d., 135 : 3
Devils (*continued*)
more d. than hell hold, 197 : 12
not so black as painted, 177 : 5
seven and seventy d., 735 : 3
to ourselves, 227 : 1
wrote at liberty when of D., 403 : 19
Devils', one more d. triumph, 541 : 8
Devise, for thirty pence my death d., 268 : 11
laws for blood, 198 : 10
wit write pen, 190 : 18
Devised to keep strong in awe, 187 : 30
who d. torment, 808 : 15
Deviseth, man's heart d. his way, 24 : 11
Devoid of sense and motion, 284 : 9
Devon, if Dons sight D., 700 : 8
Devote himself to life, 756 : 17
not to Death d., 287 : 22
Devoting himself to duty, 299 : 11
Devotion, affecting charity and d., 90 : 6
farewell my book and my d., 145 : 10
give me man capable of d., 630 : 16
ignorance mother of d., 259 : 23
increased d. to cause, 523 : 4
last full measure of d., 523 : 4
no concern with art, 619 : 8
of patriot soldier, 617 : 6
to something afar, 469 : 20
Devotion's visage, 221 : 11
Devotions, I beheld your d., 46 : 15
Devour entire hostile army, 744 : 5
jaws of darkness do d. it, 195 : 23
seeking whom he may d., 52 : 16
which d. widows' houses, 42 : 12
Devoured, great ones d. the small, 243 : n 1
when I was a worm I d., 874 : 4
Devourer, time d. of all things, 113 : 23
Devouring, cormorant d. Time, 190 : 8
green azures, 673 : 16
of weak by strong, 579 : 19
Devours, animal which d. own kind, 388 : 5
death d. lovely things, 823 : 2
Devoutly to be wished, 221 : 12
Dew, as sun the morning d., 307 : 9
begotten drops of d., 16 : 32
bespangling herb and tree, 266 : 19
breeze dried the d., 749 : 4
cool d. in little bill, 514 : 3
daffodil doth of d., 606 : 5
debauchee of d., 604 : 14
fearfully o'ertrip the d., 200 : 22
ghastly d., 529 : 24
gold and bramble d., 669 : 8
honey-heavy d. of slumber, 215 : 22
into a sea of d., 666 : 16
like d. on mountain, 431 : 11
liquid d. of youth, 218 : 27
night one blue d., 875 : 11
no d. on daisies and clover, 578 : 9
not think we Dew, 647 : 2
of thy birth, 173 : n 6
of yon high eastern hill, 217 : 27
of youth, 21 : 18, 218 : 27
on face of dead, 598 : n 3
pour sweet d. on his tongue, 61 : 9
smell d. and rain, 269 : 5
thaw and resolve into a d., 218 : 5
timely d. of sleep, 285 : 26
will rust them, 229 : 21
womb of morning d., 173 : 15
Dewdrop, lingering d., 429 : 11

Dewdrop (*continued*)
on perilous way, 475 : 10
starlight and d., 598 : 8
Dewdrops gathered in brickyard, 699 : 16
seek some d. here, 196 : 11
with showers and d. wet, 608 : 13
Dewey feel discouraged, 647 : 2
was the morning, 647 : 2
Dew-pearled, hillside's d., 540 : 15
Dews, fresh d. of night, 280 : 10
of evening shun, 342 : 17
silence fall like d., 793 : 17
Dewy, from noon to d. eve, 284 : 2
morn to dewy night, 618 : 5
shakes his d. wings, 275 : 30
William D. Tranter Reuben, 641 : 10
Dewy-feathered sleep, 278 : 25
Dexterous, acute inquisitive d., 372 : 20
Dhamma, hold fast to d. as a lamp, 72 : 20
Dhrink, is d. necessary evil, 722 : 24
Dhry, wet eye d. heart, 722 : 8
Diable, noir comme le d., 400 : *n* 3
que d. allait-il faire dans cette galère, 298 : *n* 5
Diadem, caught without d., 606 : 19
of snow, 460 : 6
Diadems and fagots, 495 : 5
Diagnosis often impossible, 463 : 21
Diagrams, in midst of d. and equations, 763 : 8
Dial, drew d. from his poke, 211 : 5
laugh an hour by his d., 211 : 7
not figures on d., 555 : 13
true as d. to sun, 291 : 29
Dialect, Babylonish d., 290 : 20
purify d. of tribe, 808 : 14
Dialogue, wooden d. and sound, 226 : 4
Dial's, many lines in d. center, 207 : 8
Dials signs of leaping houses, 202 : 23
Diamond cut diamond, 264 : 9
immortal d. is immortal d., 656 : 21
in the sky, 449 : 13
lacks glitter of d., 796 : 1
lasts forever, 826 : 5
O D. thou little knowest the mischief done, 313 : 18
point of a d., 32 : 10
rough d., 342 : 2
sixty d. minutes, 480 : 13
spots of d. form, 377 : 6
Diamonds, crown not decked with d., 186 : 8
girl's best friend, 848 : 16
sky sparkling with d., 695 : 7
Dian, Temple of D., 924 : 3
Diana, burned temple of D., 275 : 8
of the Ephesians, 46 : 22
Diana's foresters, 202 : 24
Dian's, hangs on D. temple, 242 : 23
Diapason closing full in Man, 305 : 9
Diary, never travel without d., 675 : 23
Dice, God plays d. with world, 763 : 16
Hercules and Lichas play at d., 198 : 30
human bones, 462 : 14
never abolish chance, 651 : 15
Dicers', false as d. oaths, 223 : 1
Dick the shepherd blows his nail, 191 : 14
Dickens, what the d. his name is, 225 : 19
Dickon thy master bought and sold, 173 : *n* 8
Dick's, Dirty D., 868 : 18
Dickybird why do you sit, 629 : 16
Dictate of common sense, 346 : 6
terms between old and new world, 401 : 14
what direction work must take, 828 : 1
Dictates of conscience, 383 : 6
of the heart, 413 : 20
Dictator, German d., 743 : 15
Dictators ride on tigers, 743 : 13
Dictatorship as absolute as any other, 780 : 8
of Communist Party, 770 : 6
of proletariat, 719 : 10
perpetuated as autocracy, 834 : 7
Soviet Union run by d., 780 : 8
Dictatorships cannot dispense with cynicism, 802 : 15
Dictatress, might become d. of world, 418 : 2
Dictionaries and temporary poems, 352 : 10
are like watches, 353 : 16
writer of d., 352 : 11
Dictionary, English d. best reading, 740 : 18
not grammar, 490 : 14
Did, danced his d., 829 : 18
it for the best, 693 : 5
Lucrece swears he d. her wrong, 189 : 27
till we loved, 251 : 14
Diddle diddle, 930 : 17
diddle dumpling, 933 : 1
we take it is dee, 634 : 15
Didn't, sang his d., 829 : 18
Dido with willow in her hand, 200 : 22
Die a bachelor, 209 : 19
adoring God loving friends, 344 : 12
all die merrily, 204 : 34
all shall d., 206 : 22
all that live must d., 218 : 1
Americans d. go to Paris, 675 : 14
and endow college, 336 : 1
and go we know not where, 228 : 20
and rise the same, 252 : 11
anything but d. for tobacco, 442 : 5
appetite sicken and d., 213 : 7
as cattle, 827 : 2
as much beauty as could d., 256 : 5
as my fathers died, 633 : 7
as some have done, 854 : 3
at the top, 323 : 23
be ashamed to d., 480 : 14
beast and monk d., 764 : 9
beauty crowds till I d., 607 : 15
beauty that must d., 477 : 23
beauty's rose never d., 243 : 31
because a woman's fair, 264 : 23
been in rooms we cannot d. in, 902 : 4
before grow old and d., 713 : 7
before I wake, 320 : 12
before our own eyes, 664 : 8
before we laugh, 315 : 7
begins to d. from birth, 358 : 16
being born to d., 181 : 19
better start to d., 868 : 2
better to suffer than d., 296 : 10
bit by bit, 886 : 1
books never d., 780 : 17
born but to d., 337 : 2
Die (*continued*)
born in bed in bed we d., 290 : 8
broke d. in molding Sheridan, 459 : 20
but once to d., 267 : 17
but once to serve country, 326 : 1
by famine die by inches, 319 : 6
by feigned deaths to d., 252 : 15
change but cannot d., 468 : 10
cooped we live and d., 517 : 3
cowards d. many times, 215 : 26
curse God and d., 15 : 6
daily, 274 : 13
dare to d., 337 : 10
dead live the living d., 305 : 13
dead so long as refuse to d., 595 : 2
dead which d. in the Lord, 53 : 24
dear I d., 252 : 18
death thou shalt d., 254 : 13
deeds d. however nobly done, 174 : 9
do or d., 261 : 3, 411 : 16, 830 : 7
down over feet humbly, 778 : 6
dry death, 247 : 9
easy live quiet d., 432 : 1
ere their story d., 642 : 2
face man might d. for, 544 : *n* 3
fated not to d., 305 : 15
fighting in defense of his country, 58 : 23
flowers must d., 799 : 13
for friends or fatherland, 108 : 14
for love, 227 : 11
for my people my country, 610 : 5
for such a long time, 297 : 12
for the people, 45 : 15
for truth ought to d., 495 : 9
friends who no longer know how to d., 849 : 15
frogs do not d. in sport, 92 : 9
from loneliness of spirit, 456 : 1
gladly d., 668 : 20
go since I needs must d., 172 : 14
good d. early bad late, 318 : 12
good d. first, 428 : 11
greatly think or bravely d., 335 : 8
gross flesh sinks here to d., 195 : 19
Guards d. never surrender, 421 : 21
hang there till tree d., 243 : 30
happy people d. whole, 797 : 13
hazard of the d., 187 : 32
hearken ere I d., 528 : 4
heart-stifled in dell, 476 : 15
heavenly days that cannot d., 424 : 10
here in rage, 322 : 18
honorable to d. for one's country, 107 : 27
how can man d. better, 488 : 14
how to d. harder lesson, 164 : *n* 8
I am sick I must d., 250 : 10
I d. but have possessed, 459 : 4
I d. hard, 379 : 15
I shall not wholly d., 108 : 9
I to d. and you to live, 83 : 15
I will d. in Paris, 824 : 4
I will show you how to d., 164 : *n* 8
I'd like to d. like this, 879 : 9
if I must d., 228 : 18
if I should d., 797 : 1
if I should d. before, 904 : 6
if it were now to d., 230 : 14
if man d. shall he live, 15 : 35
if millions born millions must d., 798 : 2
if we must d., 819 : 5

Die (*continued*)
if you poison us do we not d., 199 : 18
in Adam all d., 48 : 29
in bed, 795 : 15
in evening without regret, 68 : 14
in last dike, 373 : 17
in lowly pomp ride to d., 465 : 3
in music, 83 : *n* 1
in our tracks, 726 : 6
in the last ditch, 316 : 9
in this faith I will live and d., 150 : 8
in what peace a Christian can d., 327 : 5
is cast, 99 : 19
jealousy not d. with love, 294 : 2
joys will d., 918 : 18
king tomorrow shall d., 35 : 17
lads that d. in glory, 691 : 5
lest we d., 10 : 8
let friendship d., 356 : 25
let me d. in a tavern, 137 : 1
let us d. like men, 514 : 11
let us do or d., 411 : 16
like Douglas d., 366 : 11
little dog must d., 856 : 6
live and d. all I have to do, 338 : 16
live and d. for idea, 697 : 17
live and d. in Aristotle's works, 183 : 19
live and d. in Dixie, 554 : 2
live and d. r-r-rich, 549 : 35
live and d. wi' Charlie, 422 : 19
live like a wretch and d. rich, 258 : 24
live through time or d. by suicide, 519 : 22
lives on hope d. fasting, 347 : 33
living know they shall d., 27 : 15
look about us and to d., 336 : 10
love her till I d., 918 : 15
love me sure to d., 447 : 14
lovely things fade and d., 811 : 16
lucky to d. and I know it, 574 : 18
man can d. but once, 206 : 25
men d. fast enough, 316 : 11
men d. idea does not, 895 : 8
more deaths than one must d., 676 : 11
mortal or immortal here I d., 570 : 6
music when soft voices d., 469 : 18
must d. at last, 252 : 15
names not born to d., 464 : 13
never know life till d., 545 : 14
no one so young he cannot d., 153 : 15
no young man ever thinks he shall d., 445 : 13
nobly to d., 73 : 10
not d. before we have explained ourselves, 382 : 3
not know when to d., 675 : 22
not poor death, 254 : 11
not quickened except it d., 49 : 3
not willingly let it d., 281 : 12
novels which do not d. at once, 555 : 9
O let us nobly d., 819 : 6
of nothing but rage to live, 335 : 19
of remedies, 298 : 17
of rose in aromatic pain, 336 : 20
of that roar, 565 : 23
of thirst at fountainside, 900 : 4
oh do not d., 252 : 19
oh might it d. or rest, 468 : 18
old soldiers never d., 771 : 7, 924 : 9
on feet not live on knees, 780 : 14

Die (*continued*)
on feet than live on knees, 759 : 2
on gallows or of pox, 368 : 4
on mine own sword, 240 : 7
only art is to d., 369 : 21
or let me d., 425 : 7
or rest at last, 468 : 18
Owen why did you d., 552 : 20
owl calls name of man to d., 852 : 16
pale in mist seem to d., 811 : 13
pattern to live and d., 541 : 6
perceives it d. away, 426 : 15
pie in sky when you d., 764 : 13
poets d. of loneliness, 718 : 5
praise that will never d., 81 : 5
pray as if to d. tomorrow, 347 : 31
proudly, 696 : *n* 2
regret can d., 532 : 16
remember that we d. all, 35 : 13
resolve to conquer or d., 379 : 2
reverences age d. with it, 472 : 16
rich, 356 : 7
root hog or d., 847 : 12
rose with maize to d., 843 : 20
sail until I d., 529 : 13
saw spider d., 892 : 7
seem though I d. old, 717 : 3
seems rich to d., 476 : 28
shall never d., 45 : 13
shall Trelawny d., 500 : 13
sink or swim live or d., 450 : 9
soil good to d. for, 568 : 26
something he will d. for, 909 : 6
spirit d. of inanition, 586 : 23
swanlike sing and d., 461 : 9
Tamburlaine must d., 183 : 7
taught us how to d., 325 : *n* 5
teach men to d., 164 : 9
teach us how to d., 458 : 8
tells me I must d., 478 : 7
the death of the righteous, 11 : 3
theirs but to do and d., 533 : 12
there smothered, 790 : 8
they seemed to d., 34 : 13
things that are born and d., 866 : 6
thou shalt surely d., 6 : 20
time to d., 26 : 21
to d. honorably greatest virtue, 67 : 20
to d. is debt we must discharge, 267 : *n* 5
to d. is gain, 50 : 1, 83 : 13
to d. to sleep, 221 : 12
to itself it live and d., 245 : 5
to leave to d. a little, 679 : 9
to make men free, 566 : 5
to part is to d. a little, 463 : *n* 3
to save charges, 258 : 23
toddle home d. in bed, 795 : 15
trust that when we d., 617 : 3
unlamented let me d., 332 : 11
unsung noblest deed will d., 72 : 10
unto the Lord, 47 : 32
we about to d. salute you, 123 : 14
we d. and we live, 132 : 7
we d. only once, 297 : 12
we must, 186 : 21
we must be free or d., 426 : 1
we must needs d., 13 : 22
we shall d. alone, 300 : 3
we will d. free men, 393 : 9
weep or she will d., 531 : 8
went abroad to d., 778 : 10
what it is to d., 274 : 23

Die (*continued*)
when beggars d., 215 : 25
when dream is past, 507 : 7
when good men d., 77 : 18
when he shall d. cut him in stars, 193 : 9
when I came to d., 559 : 25
who saw him d., 930 : 10
who would wish to d., 492 : 16
why can't dead d., 810 : 15
wisdom shall d. with you, 15 : 27
with dead desire not d., 430 : 9
with face to sun, 672 : 11
with hammer in hand, 922 : 8
with harness on our back, 240 : 6
with honor, 696 : 15
with you be ready to d., 108 : 2
without benefit of clergy, 735 : *n* 1
without visiting one another, 65 : 9
wolf that break it d., 709 : 4
world a place to d. in, 274 : 21
Xerxes did d., 320 : 9
ye shall d. like men, 20 : 5
youth fight and d., 750 : 20
Died as one studied in death, 236 : 14
as soldier for his country, 700 : *n* 1
before bodies died, 869 : 1
before god of love born, 253 : 9
Booth d. blind, 765 : 2
came three thousand miles d., 568 : 14
courage with which men d., 890 : 3
David d. full of days, 14 : 28
deaths ye d., 707 : 3
die as my fathers d., 633 : 7
dog it was that d., 369 : 19
far away before his time, 700 : *n* 1
for beauty, 605 : 13
for God and to procure wealth, 157 : 4
for this Fitzgerald d., 713 : 11
gloriously on field, 524 : 4
had I d. hour before, 238 : 7
had no poet and d., 339 : 32
he that d. o' Wednesday, 205 : 5
I only d. last night, 626 : 21
if only gladiators d., 759 : 12
in bitter pains, 609 : 12
in boots like pioneer, 839 : 19
in harness, 746 : 7
in hollow murmurs d., 364 : 15
in virtue's cause, 188 : 18
in want, 892 : 13
land where fathers d., 514 : 12
last night of my physician, 320 : 20
learn from having d., 749 : 18
like wise one d., 171 : 8
liked it not and d., 251 : 2
maintaining right of way, 925 : 10
man that d. for men, 636 : 4
men d. but not for love, 212 : 23
Mithridates he d. old, 691 : 18
Mother d. today, 882 : 2
never knew worth till he d., 728 : 15
no one d. of laughter, 736 : 8
of chills and fever d., 810 : 20
of grief I d., 874 : 17
of no blast he d., 303 : 16
on Saturday, 932 : 11
one who d. for truth, 605 : 13
playing ukelele, 876 : 8
queens have d. young and fair, 250 : 10
she d. so young, 525 : *n* 5

Died (*continued*)
she d. young, 262 : 10
she should have d. hereafter, 240 : 4
some pro patria, 792 : 14
that ever d. so young, 525 : 15
there d. a myriad, 792 : 16
these dead not d. in vain, 523 : 4
those who d. with thee for right, 737 : 1
to have d. once enough, 106 : 1
to make men holy, 566 : 5
to northwest d. away, 541 : 18
to save us all, 561 : 9
unmarked unknown, 811 : 7
wandered till I d., 587 : 12
when I d. last, 252 : 18
when my mother d., 403 : 9
withered when my father d., 224 : 2
would I had d. for thee, 13 : 23
would we had d. in the land of Egypt, 10 : 1
you who would have d., 899 : 10
youngest critic d., 707 : 21
zealous locksmith d., 919 : 13
Diem adimere aegritudinem hominibus, 96 : *n* 10
carpe d., 107 : *n* 8
Dies, above all man who d., 705 : 12
after many a summer d. swan, 533 : 27
all that was theirs d., 77 : 18
an honest fellow, 260 : *n* 5
as when a giant d., 228 : 17
at the opening day, 328 : 12
begotten born and d., 714 : 22
bird of wonder d., 249 : 17
body d. body's beauty lives, 767 : 10
cackles groans and d., 470 : 11
cry not when father d., 353 : 12
enshrine her and she d., 794 : 1
ere he knows it, 542 : 19
fish d. because he opens mouth, 935 : 11
fling stone giant d., 344 : 14
he d. and makes no sign, 185 : 18
he that d. pays all debts, 248 : 9
if tree d. plant another, 350 : 10
in single blessedness, 195 : 21
in your fragrant bosom d., 271 : 21
kicks the dust, 559 : 16
language d., 703 : 7
light d. before thy word, 340 : 28
light d. with dying sun, 670 : 8
like a dog, 513 : 19
love built on beauty d., 253 : 16
man born suffers d., 705 : 12
man d. in pain, 315 : 9
ne'er like angels till passion d., 251 : 12
no gossip ever d. away, 61 : 24
noblest lives and d., 581 : 14
not how man d. but lives, 354 : 20
on wind like memories, 770 : 13
primrose that forsaken d., 281 : 1
reputation d., 334 : 5
reputation d. quickly, 308 : 23
re-resolves then d., 330 : 10
rich dies disgraced, 621 : 11
Sahara d., 607 : 6
something in us never d., 410 : 15
stretches out feet and d., 892 : 7
swan, 533 : 27
tumult and shouting d., 709 : 17
what an artist d. with me, 118 : 4
Dies (*continued*)
when just man d., 869 : 5
when lovely flame d., 740 : 13
when the Poet d., 430 : 8
who d. if England live, 710 : 24
whom gods love d. young, 91 : 1
youth grows pale and d., 476 : 24
Dies irae dies illa, 139 : *n* 1
nulla d. sine linea, 90 : *n* 5, 555 : *n* 2
optima d. prima fugit, 104 : *n* 3
Diet, Doctor D., 323 : 15
oft with gods doth d., 278 : 15
praise best d. for us, 433 : 4
scrip of joy immortal d., 172 : 15
sober in d., 341 : 2
Dieth, how d. the wise man, 26 : 20
man d. and wasteth away, 15 : 34
no man d. to himself, 47 : 32
Dieu a donc oublié, 312 : *n* 2
mesure le froid à la brebis tondue, 163 : *n* 6
Dieux, l'homme forge d. à douzaines, 165 : *n* 4
Differ, agreed to d., 440 : 9
all things d. all agree, 334 : 15
from things that d. comes attunement, 70 : 4
when doctors d., 335 : *n* 2
Difference, distinction without d., 349 : 20
extent of d. no democracy, 520 : 6
is important, 649 : 19
makes d. whose ox gored, 156 : 11
night makes no d., 266 : 9
no other d. than age and sex, 414 : 21
of opinion divide, 273 : 16
of opinion makes horse races, 624 : 26
of religion breeds quarrels, 538 : 18
of taste in jokes, 565 : 27
oh the d. to me, 424 : 12
only d. lies in degree, 311 : 9
sameness with d., 437 : 17
that made all the d., 747 : 13
the d. to him, 424 : *n* 2
they wear our clothes and what d., 259 : 9
wear rue with a d., 224 : 2
Differences among experts, 700 : 2
settle d. before war, 856 : 11
source of strength, 903 : 11
trivial and political, 354 : 9
world make safe for d., 796 : 8
Different drummer, 560 : 17
forms and styles, 826 : 12
from being rash, 791 : 17
from ordinary men, 609 : 5
hatched o'er and hatched d., 565 : 6
hog is d., 623 : 25
integration, 837 : 9
like but oh how d., 427 : 27
mob not ask better only d., 155 : 14
names after they are produced, 63 : 12
schools in science, 826 : 12
something d. from either, 805 : 1
to d. minds, 495 : 20
trees beautiful and d., 150 : 16
zeal for d. opinions, 398 : 2
Differentiation, through natural d. affirm brotherhood, 870 : 13
Differently, they do things d. there, 833 : 20
Differeth, one star d., 49 : 4
Differs, whatever d. from this is no democracy, 520 : 6
Difficile, Latin was no more d., 290 : 15
Difficilis facilis fucundus acerbus, 119 : *n* 7
Difficult and left untried, 742 : 2
as easy as temperance d., 353 : 19
Christian ideal d., 742 : 2
criticism easy art d., 329 : 18
diagnosis often d., 463 : 21
do immediately, 924 : 19
dreams surely are d., 61 : 2
even those d. to please, 272 : 5
excellent things d. as rare, 309 : 5
fascination of what's d., 713 : 6
in d. are friendly forces, 756 : 13
judgment d., 80 : 9, 395 : 7
living up to it d., 539 : 16
nothing so d. but may be found, 96 : 10
of things known most d., 713 : 12
Olympian is a d. foe, 57 : 13
people d. to govern, 65 : 2
poetry d. to read, 545 : 4
poets must be d., 809 : 9
to flee from reality, 784 : 24
to lay aside long-cherished love, 102 : 15
too d. to think nobly, 359 : 4
when you do it reluctantly, 96 : 13
Difficulties show what men are, 121 : 7
willingness great d. not great, 154 : 5
Difficulty and danger, 391 : 1
daunted by no d., 540 : 1
deep d. braved, 653 : 12
friend long sought with d. kept, 127 : 7
govern tongues with d., 308 : 10
in life is choice, 671 : 6
makes d. his first business, 68 : 20
most worth tackling, 653 : 12
of what it is to be, 768 : 10
Diffused knowledge immortalizes, 416 : 13
Diffuses, dissolves d. dissipates, 437 : 12
numbness d. my senses, 106 : 24
Diffusion, increase and d. of knowledge, 417 : 1
Dig deep into actual, 654 : 13
deep trenches in beauty's field, 244 : 1
forbear to d. dust enclosed here, 250 : 1
grave and let me lie, 668 : 20
I cannot d., 43 : 30
them up again, 262 : 4
Digest, edible wholesome to d., 647 : 11
inwardly d. the Scriptures, 56 : 3
more beliefs than can d., 690 : 7
no more than able to d., 323 : 1
of anarchy, 373 : 19
some writers cannot them d., 181 : 22
something to d., 760 : *n* 1
Digested, few books to be d., 181 : 12
Digestion, give me good d. Lord, 760 : *n* 1
god on side of best d., 760 : 11
good d. wait on appetite, 238 : 24
prove in d. sour, 194 : 3
sleep from pure d. bred, 286 : 12
with sound d. man may front much, 473 : 4
Digestions, unquiet meals make ill d., 188 : 14

Digests experiences as digests meats, 658 : 8
Diggeth a pit, 25 : 20
Dight, storied windows richly d., 278 : 26
Dignified, better go down d., 749 : 1
right to d. life, 774 : 8
vice by action d., 192 : 20
Dignitate, otium cum d., 98 : *n* 7
Dignities, earthly d., 249 : 4
Dignity and worth of person, 788 : 20
conciliate with d., 358 : 6
contrary to d. built paper mill, 185 : 28
human d., 916 : 12
in effort of patriots, 380 : 14
in tilling field, 681 : 25
leisure with d., 98 : 8
Negroes find new sense of d., 909 : 12
of high calling, 373 : 9
of history, 329 : 4, 489 : 5
of man respected, 787 : 12
of person acknowledged, 774 : 8
of truth lost with protesting, 255 : 19
poet's d. and ease, 338 : 16
proper d. and proportion, 124 : 22
reach the d. of crimes, 393 : 14
wear undeserved d., 199 : 14
where is his d., 853 : 4
Digression, began a lang d., 409 : 7
Digressions, eloquent d., 596 : 11
sunshine of reading, 360 : 2
Digressively, said I rather d., 570 : 9
Dike, last d. of prevarication, 373 : 17
Dilemma, here lay the d., 797 : 9
horns of my d., 360 : 13
Dilettante, no room for d., 745 : 11
Dilettantes and pedants, 705 : 20
Diligence, best of me is d., 233 : 7
keep thy heart with all d., 23 : 9
learning must be attended to with d., 393 : 2
mother of good fortune, 170 : 34
observe physician with same d., 254 : 19
work out salvation with d., 72 : 22
Diligent dispensation of pleasure, 453 : 2
in his business, 25 : 4
Diligently, teach them d. unto thy children, 11 : 9
they d. practice it, 64 : 14
Dillar, a d. a dollar, 933 : 14
Dim and joyless if not shared, 447 : 16
behind d. unknown, 567 : 7
desolation and d. night, 525 : 16
forsake their temples d., 277 : 12
in intense inane, 467 : 7
on Bristol board, 878 : 19
religious light, 278 : 26
spot which men call earth, 279 : 3
sun in d. eclipse, 283 : 24
upland d., 587 : 11
windows of the soul, 407 : 10
Dim-discovered, ships d., 345 : 8
Dime, brother can you spare d., 842 : 5
Dimension of final thing, 875 : 2
Dimensions, hath not a Jew d., 199 : 17
Diminish, joys with age d., 545 : 22
some nations increase others d., 100 : 15
Diminished, force in nature not d., 583 : 21
hide your d. rays, 285 : *n* 3
Diminished (*continued*)
stars hide their d. heads, 285 : 10
to her cock, 234 : 28
Diminishes, any man's death d. me, 254 : 22
functional capacity, 393 : 7
Diminution of original sin, 581 : 10
without increase or d., 438 : 13
Diminutions needs must be, 705 : 4
Diminutives, lovely d., 873 : 15
Dimitri, long live D. Ivanovich, 486 : 13
Dimmycratic party ain't on speakin' terms, 721 : 14
Dimness, elms fade into d., 588 : 5
most experience sunk to d., 639 : 12
Dimpling, shallow streams run d., 339 : 1
Din, cock with lively d., 277 : 23
hear the merry d., 434 : 5
of strife, 585 : 15
when my d. done, 632 : 1
Dinah blow your horn, 921 : 17
Dine at journey's end, 714 : 2
at ten sup at six, 492 : 6
going to d. with men, 753 : 3
hang that jurymen d., 334 : 6
when Noah sat down to d., 742 : 16
with some men, 753 : 3
Dined, I have d. today, 433 : 12
on mince, 550 : 10
upon cold meat, 310 : 4
when Jefferson d. alone, 891 : 7
Diners-out from whom we guard spoons, 488 : 1
Dines on following day, 614 : 1
Ding dong bell, 930 : 14
hey d. a d. d., 212 : 33
Dinginess, country of d., 518 : 8
Dingledodies, danced like d., 901 : 3
Dingy, raising d. shades, 804 : 3
Dining and dancing begin, 855 : 16
while they thought of d., 371 : 14
Dinner, after d. is after d., 322 : 1
among old soakers, 309 : 23
better is a d. of herbs, 24 : 7
breakfast d. lunch tea, 730 : 8
good d. and feasting, 309 : 25
his life d. wife, 486 : 4
lubricates business, 393 : 15
man always willing to come to d., 787 : 3
man who came to d., 813 : 5
Michelangelo for d., 622 : 5
much depends on d., 461 : 29
not a d. to ask a man to, 354 : 17
revolution not same as inviting to d., 826 : 6
seldom thinks more than of d., 461 : *n* 6
three hours' march to d., 445 : 12
tocsin the d. bell, 461 : 16
what gat ye to d., 927 : 8
write with no d., 811 : 1
Dinner's, over glass when d. done, 543 : 3
Dinners, true Amphitryon gives d., 298 : 5
visits his d. not him, 297 : 27
Dinosaur death-steps, 893 : 9
Diogenes, if not Alexander would be D., 90 : 14
plucked a cock, 86 : 10
struck father when son swore, 259 : 21
Diomede, this sodeyn D., 145 : 4
Dios te tenga en su mano, 935 : 18
Diplomacy is to do and say, 797 : 8
Diplomats, pens of d. not ruin, 386 : 15
Dipped into the future, 529 : 24
Jonathan d. rod in honeycomb, 12 : 37
Dirck galloped, 541 : 11
Dire, beckoning shadows d., 279 : 16
dimension of final thing, 875 : 2
effects from civil discord, 326 : 5
gorge of salt sea tide, 200 : *n* 1
offense from amorous causes, 333 : 24
Dire, une manière de le d., 901 : *n* 1
Direct and honest not safe, 231 : 15
eminently plain and d., 586 : 14
him where to look for it, 254 : 5
leaving to d. themselves, 825 : 11
lie d., 213 : 4
relations with good joke, 742 : 7
understanding to d., 391 : 4
Directed unerringly to you, 576 : 10
Direction, advances in d. of dreams, 560 : 16
dictate d. work must take, 828 : 1
great thing is what d., 519 : 6
guide horse in d. it wants, 678 : 14
in which education starts, 84 : 13
new d. of Time, 790 : 9
of right line, 313 : 14
which thou canst not see, 337 : 1
Directions, by indirections find d., 220 : 7
rode off in all d., 728 : 1
Directs the storm, 325 : 7, 340 : 22
Direful spring of Grecian woes, 334 : 18
Direst, full of d. cruelty, 236 : 17
shapes of death, 592 : 6
Dirge, by forms unseen d. sung, 364 : 9
for her doubly dead, 525 : *n* 5
for most lovely dead, 525 : 15
in marriage, 217 : 29
of dying year, 467 : 19
Dirges, let d. disappear, 888 : 6
Dirt, bequeathe myself to d., 575 : 4
breathing a small breath, 873 : 7
eats d. in the line, 825 : 3
greater wealth thicker d., 871 : 10
hairs or straws or d., 338 : 12
instead of d. and poison, 321 : 14
loss of wealth loss of d., 158 : 16
matter out of place, 638 : 8
painted child of d., 338 : 19
Dirty, airing d. linen never masterpiece, 911 : 19
all d. and wet, 323 : 22
at his d. work again, 338 : 9
British coaster, 760 : 20
business, 645 : 10
Dick's and Sloppy Joe's, 868 : 18
wash d. linen at home, 420 : 11
work again, 338 : 9
work at crossroads, 922 : 5
Dis aliter visum, 105 : *n* 1
manibus sacrum, 133 : 20
Disable benefits of your country, 212 : 20
Disabused, by himself abused or d., 337 : 2
Disaffection, nonconformity mark of d., 737 : 7
Disagree, doctors d., 335 : 26
in faith and hope world d., 337 : 9
share rights with those who d., 824 : 12
Disagreeable, such a d. man, 629 : 3

Disagreeable (*continued*)
  tells d. truth boldly, 386 : 8
Disagreements, scholarship record of d., 700 : 2
Disagrees, what agrees d., 70 : 5
Disappearance, law master after my d., 73 : 1
Disappeared, sun would have d., 690 : 10
  with finality of pigeon, 800 : 10
Disappoint continent, 619 : 10
  not d. hoping soul, 412 : 19
  that I may not d. myself, 557 : 20
Disappointed, woman, 324 : *n* 7
  he shall never be d., 336 : 6
  in monkey, 626 : 17
  tide, 604 : 11
  who expects nothing never d., 336 : 6
Disappointment, boredom and d., 857 : 12
  mathematics commence in d., 697 : 4
Disappointments, too familiar with d., 519 : 20
Disappoints, man appoints God d., 148 : *n* 7
Disapprove of what you say, 344 : 11
Disarmament is essential, 781 : 9
  vision of universal d., 881 : 14
Disaster clouded Union cause, 617 : 6
  evil gains equivalent of d., 61 : 19
  exaltation from d. and ruin, 743 : 3
  'gainst all d., 302 : *n* 4
  no greater d. than greed, 64 : 16
  noble spirit raises itself in d., 120 : 3
  nuclear d. engulf all, 891 : 1
  success like d., 876 : 9
  triumph and d., 710 : 16
  unmerciful d., 526 : 16
Disasters, day's d. in morning face, 370 : 10
  make guilty of our d., 233 : 5
  middle station fewest d., 318 : 13
  weary with d., 238 : 16
Disastrous beating of wings, 732 : 11
  born to d. end, 174 : 11
  spake of d. chances, 229 : 28
  twilight sheds, 283 : 24
Disbanded, funeral done and d., 883 : 12
Disbelief in great men, 473 : 23
  suspension of d., 437 : 15
  then skepticism then d., 571 : 4
Disbranch, sliver and d., 234 : 23
Discard knowledge, 90 : 8
Discarded, welcome home d. faith, 202 : 14
Discern, as I can now d., 557 : 20
  infinite passion, 542 : 10
  innocence of neighbors, 560 : 13
  with this clear eye, 557 : 20
Discerner of the thoughts, 51 : 14
Discerning, gives genius better d., 371 : 5
  to a d. eye, 605 : 11
Discharge, no d. in war, 27 : 13, 710 : 10
  to die a debt we must d., 267 : *n* 5
Discharged, at once indebted and d., 285 : 11
  debt d. through eternity, 395 : 19
  with greater ease, 267 : 15
Discharging less than tenth, 226 : 13
Disciple not above master, 39 : 2
  true teacher has no d., 484 : 5
Disciples, gave bread to d., 41 : 10
Disciples (*continued*)
  masters ashamed to become d., 250 : 11
  threatening against d., 46 : 4
Discipline, care of d. is love, 34 : 17
  desire of d., 34 : 17
  Doric d. vain, 715 : 12
  in military unit, 771 : 2
  liberty a beloved d., 877 : 14
  organization and d. of war, 153 : 21
  rising or falling's one d., 874 : 20
  soul of army, 378 : 14
  that I have established, 73 : 1
Disciplined by peace, 890 : 7
  inaction, 416 : 16
Disciplines, I know d. of wars, 207 : 22
Disclose, merits to d., 362 : 19
  not d. essence of phenomena, 789 : 2
Disclosed, before buttons be d., 218 : 27
Discobolus standeth face to wall, 620 : 3
Discomforts accompany my being blind, 310 : 17
Disconsolate to watch it, 797 : 13
Discontent, but only want and d., 292 : 2
  divine d., 567 : 1
  want of self-reliance, 497 : 6
  waste nights in d., 174 : 10
  wealth and poverty parents of d., 84 : 12
  winter of our d., 186 : 29
  yields nothing but d., 372 : 8
Discontented, stirs of d. strife, 257 : 11
Discontentment, no greater guilt than d., 64 : 16
Discord, age of d. and strife, 185 : 7
  civil d., 326 : 5
  danger in d., 511 : 15
  eke d. doth sow, 163 : 18
  harmony in d., 109 : 7
  harmony not understood, 337 : 1
  music must investigate d., 120 : 5
  so musical a d., 197 : 8
  what d. follows, 226 : 2
Discordant, concordant is d., 70 : 5
  drum's d. sound, 375 : 4
  reconciles d. elements, 423 : 18
  reconciliation of d. qualities, 437 : 17
  wavering multitude, 205 : 18
Discourage and abolish tyranny and vice, 380 : 6
Discouraged, Dewey feel d., 647 : 2
  lest they be d., 50 : 13
  never get d., 883 : 3
Discouragement, there's no d., 302 : 14
Discouraging, which more d. literature or chickens, 846 : 11
Discourse according to learning, 206 : *n* 4
  bid me d., 189 : 7
  everybody's d. of death, 309 : 24
  excellent dumb d., 248 : 11
  good company good d., 271 : 4
  in novel phrases, 628 : 6
  made us with large d., 223 : 17
  of book-friends, 771 : 1
  of fools is irksome, 35 : 37
  of reason, 218 : 11
  of the elders, 35 : 14
  rather thy d. than play, 259 : 16
  showers of sweet d., 292 : 10
Discourteously, cast me off d., 917 : 14
Discover everybody's face but own, 321 : 13
Discover (*continued*)
  I had no talent, 812 : 6
  I had not lived, 559 : 25
  never d. land of nowadays, 729 : 9
  who could d. God, 115 : 17
  you are human as I, 894 : 8
Discovered, America d. accidentally, 800 : 5
  I was not God, 645 : 13
  plant whose virtues not d., 500 : 6
  race never yet d., 852 : 11
  unconscious before me, 678 : 11
  when d. not wanted, 800 : 5
Discoverer, exultation only d. can experience, 799 : 20
Discoverers among them as comets, 350 : 8
  ill d. think there is no land, 179 : 3
  sea d. to new worlds, 251 : 15
Discovereth, he d. deep things, 15 : 31
Discovering, only two ways of d. truth, 179 : 7
Discovers, flute in dying notes d., 305 : 12
  fresh perfection, 453 : 8
Discovery, abyss d. metamorphosis, 739 : 12
  errors portals of d., 778 : 3
  if European d. delayed, 800 : 4
  in completing one d., 380 : 1
  joy of sudden d., 771 : 15
  mistaking paradox for d., 735 : 9
  separated me from before, 739 : 12
  terra firma of accomplished d., 762 : 5
Discredit what they do not excel in, 90 : 9
Discreditable, regrets d. act, 772 : 13
Discreet, too d. to run amuck, 339 : 6
Discreetest, virtuousest d. best, 287 : 8
Discreetly blot, 276 : 11
  entered into reverently d. advisedly, 56 : 6
Discretion, better part of valor d., 205 : 14
  better part of virtue, 856 : 13
  drunkenness sepulture of his d. 148 : 1
  fair woman without d., 23 : 25
  in man not too young, 116 : 2
  inform their d., 389 : 15
  philosophy nothing but d., 263 : 22
  should be thrown aside, 91 : 2
  to the young man knowledge and d., 23 : 1
  years of d. spent on complaint, 894 : 7
Discriminate between important and negligible, 762 : 5
Discriminating, keen d. sight, 422 : 4
Discrimination, art d. and selection, 653 : 13
  eliminate sexual d., 903 : 10
  exactness and d., 354 : *n* 11
  not adjust to d., 898 : 6
  protest d. and slander, 753 : 7
  sophisticated modes of d., 776 : 11
Discuss freely settle question, 487 : 16
Discussing duty to God, 574 : 24
Discussion, free political d., 700 : 3
  open mind free d., 737 : 8
Disdain, for thee to d. it, 469 : 19
  give me more love or more d., 271 : 22
  Lady D., 208 : 27
  to be instruments, 401 : 14

Disdained, one feeling d., 469 : 19
Disdainful smile, 362 : 2
Disdainfully, think not d. of death, 125 : 15
Disdaining littlenesses, 85 : 17
Disdains all things above his reach, 262 : 13
culture not live by d., 651 : 2
Disease, as physician observes d., 254 : 19
bad rhyming a d., 339 : 30
brought on by boredom, 857 : 12
called lack of money, 157 : 14
consciousness d., 705 : 13
cure d. kill patient, 180 : 25
cured yesterday of my d., 320 : 20
dreaded scandal more than d., 701 : 2
fee bestow upon foul d., 232 : 28
gained strength by delays, 113 : 25
interest in d. interest in life, 755 : 13
is sorrow, 72 : 23
life is an incurable d., 295 : 12
long d. my life, 338 : 11
medicine has to examine d., 120 : 5
meet d. at first stage, 117 : 11
of evil conscience, 517 : 19
of modern life, 586 : 1
of not listening, 205 : 25
of old men avarice, 261 : 11
old age only d., 497 : 27
or sorrows strike him, 564 : 14
part in developing man, 631 : 5
people given over to d., 101 : 12
physician hath favorite d., 349 : 17
presume d. curable, 463 : 22
quarrels sedition, 316 : 13
remedies worse than d., 111 : 4
remedy too strong for d., 75 : 16
shapes of foul d., 532 : 23
specialists in mental d., 783 : 10
success our national d., 648 : 4
the d. is incurable, 206 : 5
to pretend to know is a d., 65 : 5
tyranny poverty d. war, 890 : 11
tyranny's d., 70 : 24
wine cause of d., 316 : 13
writing a contagious d., 136 : 8
Diseased, mind d. always illusion. 552 : 7
minister to mind d., 239 : 32
nature breaks forth, 204 : 10
of own beauty mind d., 458 : 19
words are physicians of mind d., 70 : 25
Diseases desperate grown, 223 : 14
of physical frame, 503 : 8
Disembodied bones, 793 : 19
emotion nonentity, 649 : 8
Disenthrall ourselves save country, 522 : 12
Disfigure, in a moment so d. us, 274 : 12
Disfranchised, in literature not d., 771 : 1
Disgrace and ignominy of natures, 274 : 12
impatient of d., 303 : 20
in d. with fortune and men's eyes, 244 : 8
intellectual d., 868 : 13
lived without d. without praise, 140 : 16
might as well be d. to be poor, 725 : 11
not without d. associated, 558 : 1
peace with d., 95 : 16
Disgraced, dies rich dies d., 621 : 11
Disgraces, labor d. no man, 590 : 3
Disguise, again in this identical d., 889 : 11
cherishing enemy in d., 379 : 16
fair nature with rage, 207 : 16
no d. can conceal love, 293 : 10
pantheism atheism in d., 705 : 14
profession is to d., 155 : 4
to go naked best d., 324 : 9
virtues but vices in d., 292 : 21
Disguises, gods go in various d., 60 : 25
troublesome d. we wear, 286 : 4
Disgust, achievement birth of d., 647 : 7
carry work without d., 639 : 3
not exist where hunger is, 683 : 18
Dish, as a man wipeth a d., 14 : 22
butter in a lordly d., 12 : 6
chameleon's d., 222 : 8
dainty d., 931 : 9
feast of joy a d. of pain, 177 : 10
fit for gods, 215 : 20
of meat too good, 271 : 12
other men serving d., 719 : 9
ran away with spoon, 930 : 17
thirty-two religions one d., 400 : 18
woman a d. for the gods, 242 : 1
Dishes, shalt not wash d., 931 : 19
sporting my name, 907 : 24
Disheveled, poet flourished here d., 912 : 8
Dishonest victory at Chaeronea, 282 : 6
Dishonor, by honor and d., 49 : 16
fears d. worse than death, 108 : 14
honor rooted in d., 534 : 14
no d. to halt at second place, 98 : 12
vessel unto d., 47 : 16
ways to d. Sabbath, 624 : 8
will not trouble me, 76 : 7
Dishonorable graves, 215 : 6
Dishonorably, to speak d. is pardonable, 75 : 17
Dishonored fragments of Union, 450 : 15
shroud, 804 : 25
Disiecti membra poetae, 106 : *n* 11
Disillusion, one d. mankind, 783 : 3
Disillusionment that woman has brain, 848 : 9
Disingenuousness of years, 489 : 2
Disinherited, city's d., 694 : 3
Disinheriting, damned d. countenance, 399 : 2
Disinterested as being who made him, 380 : *n* 2
commerce between equals, 369 : 25
endeavor to learn, 586 : 24
intellectual curiosity, 758 : 3
patriotism in female most d. of virtues, 393 : 3
Disinterestedness, self-interest plays d., 293 : 7
Disjoins remorse from power, 215 : 15
Dislike, hesitate d., 338 : 14
I too d. it, 798 : 10
same things is friendship, 102 : 26
Disliked, each day do two things d., 751 : 12
person who d. gravy, 298 : *n* 4
Dislikes, culture not live by d., 651 : 2
Dislocate language into meaning, 809 : 9
Disloyal or subversive, 863 : 9
Disloyalty, not confuse dissent with d., 872 : 17
Dismal, at d. treatise rouse, 240 : 3
economics d. science, 872 : 5
headache, 628 : 26
science, 474 : 11
tidings when he frowned, 370 : 10
universal hiss, 287 : 27
Waterloo d. plain, 491 : 12
Dismay, neither shape of danger d., 427 : 26
nothing you d., 919 : 20
old d., 899 : 9
Dismayed her crew, 647 : 21
neither be d., 11 : 28
ran d. away, 200 : 22
was there man d., 533 : 10
Dismember or overthrow it, 521 : 11
whirl asunder and d. me, 201 : 22
Dismembered poet, 106 : 15
Dismissed, at length d. from thee, 454 : 18
Dismount, rides tiger afraid to d., 743 : *n* 2
Disobedience, discontent disorder d., 372 : 8
of man's first d., 282 : 22
Disobedient, even if d. I shall follow, 92 : 2
Disorder, all prodigality and d., 373 : 10
and early sorrow, 755 : 20
democracy full of d., 85 : 3
discontent d. disobedience, 372 : 8
domestic d., 316 : 13
great d. is order, 767 : 20
order and d., 344 : 19
sweet d. in the dress, 266 : 6
violent order d., 767 : 20
Disordered, men d. like you, 356 : *n* 3
Disorders, all ruinous d., 233 : 4
medicine for mental d., 833 : 5
Disorientation, shattering stress and d., 909 : 1
Dispatch in putting end to it, 89 : 6
the soul of business, 342 : 9
Dispatchful looks, 286 : 18
Dispelled, live tongue all d., 900 : 3
mist d. when woman appears, 332 : 3
Dispelling, gleams through fog without d., 360 : 29
Dispensary, anthology a d., 833 : 5
Dispensation of pleasure, 453 : 2
Dispense with necessaries, 519 : 10
with trifles, 225 : 13
Dispensing equality, 85 : 3
Disperse, by spreading d. to naught, 184 : 18
Dispersed, Scots d. over whole earth, 177 : 16
Display, electrical d. of God, 810 : 11
extended to d. its patterns, 70 : 18
Displayed, flower d. doth fall, 214 : 2
Displeasing, misfortune of our friends not d., 294 : 11
Dispoged, lips to it when d., 547 : 35
Dispose, men determine gods d., 259 : *n* 4
unsearchable d., 289 : 10
Disposed, tyrant has d. of foreign enemies, 85 : 7
Disposer of other men's stuff, 166 : *n* 6
Disposes, man proposes God d., 148 : 15
Disposition, antic d., 220 : 4
horridly to shake our d., 219 : 12

Disposition (*continued*)
I know d. of women, 96 : 21
patronizing d., 565 : 7
to be pleased, 355 : 24
truant d., 218 : 13
unfriendly d. towards U.S., 408 : 3
Dispossessed, his little heart d., 653 : 8
Dispraise, no d. or blame, 289 : 9
thing you desire to buy, 226 : 23
Dispraised no small praise, 288 : 9
Dispraises, praising most d., 338 : *n* 9
Disprized, pangs of d. love, 221 : 12
Disputable, dispute upon everything d., 314 : 15
Disputandi pruritus ecclesiarum scabies, 251 : *n* 3
Disputants put me in mind of skuttle fish, 327 : 1
Disputation, feeling d., 204 : 17
run in debt by d., 290 : 17
Disputations, doubtful d., 47 : 30
Dispute confute change hands, 290 : 16
it like a man, 239 : 22
my right none to d., 376 : 12
scholars d. and case still before courts, 109 : 21
'twixt Tweedledum and Tweedledee, 341 : 13
upon everything disputable, 314 : 15
will you d. with Muhammad, 132 : 11
Disputed barricade, 811 : 5
Disputes, equal justice in private d., 80 : 17
Disputing, itch of d., 251 : 5
warmer way of d., 169 : 16
Disquieted, never to be d., 267 : 6
they are d. in vain, 19 : 3
why art thou d. in me, 19 : 6
Disquietly, follow d. to our graves, 233 : 4
Disquiets, almighty time d., 75 : 11
Disregard, atones for later d., 749 : 1
Disruption, noise d. of thought, 463 : 7
Dissatisfaction with world, 699 : 4
Dissatisfied, I am troubled I'm d., 799 : 4
not one is d., 574 : 24
Socrates d., 508 : 19
with what I learn, 749 : 18
Dissatisfies, what d. in American civilization, 589 : 10
Dissect, creatures you d., 335 : 13
Dissections, learn anatomy from d., 260 : 9
Dissemble, right to d. your love, 407 : 13
Disseminating their circumference, 606 : 10
Dissension, in d. never judge, 77 : 1
Dissent, dissidence of d., 372 : 19
in few days I should d., 273 : 16
not confuse d. with disloyalty, 872 : 17
orthodoxy chokes d., 737 : 7
voices of d., 862 : 21
Dissenting, passed without one d. colony, 381 : 6
Dissever my soul from the soul, 527 : 9
sacred hair d., 334 : 10
Dissevered discordant belligerent, 450 : 15
Dissidence of dissent, 372 : 19
Dissimulation innate in woman, 463 : 6
love without d., 47 : 19
playing the knave and d., 309 : 17
Dissimulation (*continued*)
without d. no business, 342 : 5
Dissipates to re-create, 437 : 12
to shining ether, 496 : 15
Dissipation without pleasure, 384 : 5
Dissociate language from science, 390 : 7
Dissociation of sensibility, 809 : 8
Dissolute, caldron of d. loves, 128 : 28
damned despairful, 752 : 4
Dissolutely spent Tuesday morning, 202 : 25
Dissolution, community in d., 737 : 7
keep these limbs from d., 253 : 11
Dissolve, all which it inherit d., 248 : 13
and quite forget, 476 : 24
me into ecstasies, 278 : 26
political bands, 387 : 9
wish to d. Union, 388 : 16
Dissolved in a moment, 797 : 13
into something great, 739 : 1
ought to be totally d., 378 : 12
Union not to be d., 520 : 4
Union virtually d., 438 : 11
Dissolves diffuses dissipates, 437 : 12
when all the world d., 184 : 2
Dissonance, barbarous d., 279 : 26
Dissonant, no sound d., 441 : *n* 1
Distance, airy d., 458 : 7
augur misgovernment at d., 372 : 20
just that d. from death, 63 : 1
lends enchantment, 443 : 4
the slightest d., 849 : 11
Distances, infinite d. between humans, 756 : 12
Distant deeps or skies, 405 : 7
dull prospect of d. good, 305 : 25
from heaven alike, 259 : 12
in what d. deeps, 405 : 7
misery, 383 : 12
Ophir, 760 : 19
religion of which rewards d., 352 : 24
speaking of voices, 887 : 5
ye d. spires, 361 : 8
Distasteful, found life d., 545 : 22
Distastes, prosperity not without d., 180 : 6
Distemper, of no d. died, 303 : 16
Distill, would men d. goodness out, 208 : 3
Distillation, history d. of rumor, 473 : 18
Distilled almost to jelly, 218 : 20
damnation, 416 : 6
earthlier happy is rose d., 195 : 21
from limbecks foul, 245 : 19
Distills, love d. desire, 76 : 22
Distinct, in repose d., 902 : 12
Distinction between virtue and vice, 354 : 12
make no d. between Trojan and Tyrian, 104 : 27
of rich and poor, 414 : 21
without difference, 349 : 20
Distinctions of race, 579 : 9
Distinctive, man's d. mark, 544 : 16
Distinctiveness, vice of d. to become queer, 656 : 22
Distinctly I remember, 526 : 11
Distinguish, he could d. and divide, 290 : 16
read but not d. what worth it, 758 : 4
true from false, 308 : 7
wisdom to d., 823 : 15
Distinguished, beginnings of things not d. by eye, 100 : 6
no two men who cannot be d., 116 : 12
Distorting, curtain of d. days, 716 : 15
my gesture, 883 : 11
Distorts, human understanding d., 179 : 9
the heavens, 407 : 10
Distract attention from issues, 703 : 1
Distracted, seat in this d. globe, 219 : 27
Distracting, dear damned d. town, 334 : 24
Distraction music of flute, 806 : 2
not meditation, 883 : 7
to mankind, 260 : 16
uglification, 612 : 5
Distraught, all men born d., 900 : 4
with dreams visions, 512 : 20
Distress, all pray in their d., 403 : 10
economic d. will teach, 738 : 9
exposed to suffering and d., 427 : 23
greatest d. is poverty, 313 : 4
mean man always full of d., 68 : 24
needy in d., 30 : 6
of boyhood into man, 716 : 1
pray in your d. and need, 782 : 18
reality of d., 385 : 1
time removes d., 96 : 9
Distressed by his want of ability, 69 : 12
town like place d., 309 : 24
vacant mind d., 376 : 8
we recommend those who are d., 55 : 6
Distresses of our friends, 294 : *n* 4
Distressful bread, 208 : 7
Distributed, good sense equally d., 272 : 5
Distribution according to need, 45 : 41
laws of d., 621 : 10
unequal d. of property, 398 : 2
Distributive, economy d. virtue, 374 : 10
Distributively, pluralism lets exist d., 650 : 12
Distrust all in whom impulse to punish, 657 : 15
doctrine that age brings wisdom, 772 : 10
fear and d. the people, 390 : 2
here all d. left behind, 140 : 14
is safeguard, 397 : *n* 8
spirit of suspicion and d., 737 : 6
to make man untrustworthy d. him, 723 : 22
Distrusting, heart d. asks, 370 : 16
Distrusts, him who d. self, 293 : 14
Disturb not her dream, 410 : 13
Disturbance of the spring, 807 : 11
Disturbed by planetary war, 794 : 4
Disturbing delicate balance, 875 : 9
Disturbs, presence that d. me, 423 : 13
Disuse, iron rusts from d., 152 : 8
of any organ, 393 : 7
Ditch, blind man's d., 716 : 2
both fall into d., 39 : 31
die in the last d., 316 : 9
Ditch-delivered by a drab, 239 : 6
Ditchers, gardeners d. and gravemakers, 224 : 5
Ditches, other men's d., 933 : 19
women lifted over d., 482 : 17
Ditty, mournful d., 469 : 24
Diurnal, earth's d. course, 424 : 14
Dive, heaven's great lamps d., 250 : 3

Dive (*continued*)
into bottom of deep, 203 : 15
Diver in deep seas, 638 : 11
Omar plucked them, 569 : 2
Diverb, as the d. goes, 259 : 22
Diverged, two roads d., 747 : 13
Divers, state of man in d. functions, 207 : 6
why d. send out oil, 116 : 5
Diverse, man vain d. undulating, 164 : 6
strong and d. heart, 840 : 4
Diversion or improvement of country, 326 : 7
present life a d., 132 : 1
walking 'tis a country d., 324 : 18
Diversity of opinion basic to nation, 825 : 12
universal quality is d., 165 : 14
world safe for d., 891 : 11
Diverter of sadness, 270 : 34
Divest, deprive or d. posterity, 367 : 4
Divide and rule, 133 : 21
biped class, 86 : *n* 4
distinguish and d., 290 : 16
great scramble and big d., 642 : 11
life from death, 526 : 7
mountains d. us, 483 : 20
never d. upon opinion, 273 : 16
not d. Sunday from week, 217 : 19
sense from thought d., 303 : *n* 1
therefore doth heaven d., 207 : 6
thin partitions their bounds d., 303 : 20
two almost d. the kind, 335 : 21
words d. and rend, 632 : 10
Divide et impera, 133 : 21
Divided an inheritance with him, 386 : 7
duty, 229 : 32
fair d. excellence, 201 : 16
Gaul d. into three parts, 99 : 14
have they not d. the prey, 12 : 9
house d. against itself, 41 : 35, 520 : 4
in death they were not d., 13 : 9
mankind into parties, 398 : 2
thy kingdom is d., 33 : 1
we fall, 378 : *n* 7
with but half a heart, 267 : 7
Dividends, literature pays d., 630 : 23
Dividing asunder of soul and spirit, 51 : 14
by d. we fall, 378 : 11
lover and lover, 632 : 8
your sweet d. throat, 271 : 20
Divination, criticism rod of d., 711 : 17
Divine, against thy D. Majesty, 55 : 17
all is d. harmony, 637 : 17
all save man d., 459 : 6
all things by law d., 467 : 24
and terrible radiance, 491 : 16
ask a drink d., 256 : 8
Athens d. city, 72 : 9
bird of Zeus, 71 : 24
comfortable words, 534 : 3
countenance d. shine forth, 406 : 21
despair, 531 : 3
discontent, 567 : 1
discovery of d. truths, 329 : 5
drink d., 256 : 8
event, 532 : 27
fear of some d. powers, 259 : 24
fellowship d., 475 : 20
Divine (*continued*)
God the Father a school d., 339 : 22
good amiable or sweet, 287 : 22
Hand that made us is d., 325 : 10
how d. a thing woman, 427 : 19
human face d., 285 : 5
human form d., 403 : 11, 405 : 14
I myself more d., 536 : 9
idea which each represents, 496 : 20
ideas below, 494 : 9
illusion, 589 : 5
Inert, 570 : 12
Love the human form d., 403 : 11
love which graybeards call d., 186 : 28
lyre so long d., 461 : 5
majority, 605 : 2
makes drudgery d., 269 : 8
man d. as myself dead, 576 : 1
men whom men pronounce d., 646 : 5
nature gave us country, 97 : 14
no government by d. right, 439 : 3
nor glimpse d., 340 : 28
one who shares in the d., 115 : 17
philosophy, 279 : 25, 532 : 8
plain face, 441 : 15
principle and rule of harmony, 583 : 5
profane no d. ordinances, 370 : *n* 3
relations with good joke, 742 : 7
reliance on d. providence, 387 : 11
right d. of kings, 340 : 24
right of kings, 520 : 8
sign indicates future, 79 : 4
superhuman spiritual and d., 754 : 10
tale of Troy d., 278 : 21
Terror human form d., 405 : 14
thought thinks of itself, 87 : 12
to forgive d., 333 : 15
tobacco d. rare, 259 : 15
train d., 587 : 11
truth is precious and d., 291 : 21
utterance, 601 : 8
what the form d., 442 : 17
whatever poet writes with d. inspiration, 79 : 9
Divinely, childish but d. beautiful, 412 : 15
in the wrong, 329 : 22
tall, 528 : 22
Divineness, in poesy participation of d., 179 : 2
Diviner air, 428 : 22
Diviner's, glad d. theme, 304 : 5
Divinest anguish, 562 : 2
madness d. sense, 605 : 11
Melancholy, 278 : 11
Divining, takes d. rod to find, 678 : 4
Divinities, new d. of his own, 83 : 11
Divinity, all the d. I understand, 170 : 19
doth hedge a king, 223 : 27
dry volumes of d., 387 : 7
gives wealth even to wicked man, 67 : 2
gossip a kind of d., 61 : 24
in odd numbers, 225 : 28
lectures of ethics or d., 316 : 8
man own doctor of d., 667 : 11
nature full of d., 557 : 15
piece of d. in us, 274 : 22
stirs within us, 326 : 3
that shapes our ends, 224 : 25
wingy mysteries in d., 274 : 3
Divisa, Gallia est omnis d. in partes tres, 99 : *n* 10
Division, equal d. of unequal earnings, 449 : 4
is as bad, 917 : 13
mirth the music of d., 173 : 1
salvation not in d., 730 : 16
same as creation, 90 : 2
saw d. grow together, 225 : 31
Divorce, absurd essentially a d., 882 : 4
long d. of steel, 248 : 25
Divorced divorced, 892 : 12
from eye and bone, 836 : 18
from whale-fat, 892 : 12
sorrow from which not d., 453 : 3
Divulge, I will never d. such things, 79 : 13
Dixie Land, 554 : 1
live and die in D., 554 : 2
Dixit, ipse d., 134 : 7
Dizziness, two people shaken by d., 886 : 5
Dizzy, how fearful and d., 234 : 28
make a small boy d., 873 : 10
Do, a' is done that men can d., 410 : 5
all the good you can, 346 : 12
as chapmen do, 226 : 23
as I say not as I do, 264 : 6
as you would be done by, 38 : *n* 1, 341 : 19
boys do, 662 : 17
damned if you d., 444 : 9
decided on what they will not d., 89 : 14
don't d. it in street, 706 : 16
duty which lies nearest, 473 : 8
each day two things disliked, 751 : 12
enough work to d., 710 : 13
go and d. likewise, 43 : 15
great right little wrong, 200 : 10
his arms might d. what this has done, 276 : 5
how not to d. it, 549 : 19
I dare d. all, 237 : 3
I d. it more natural, 213 : 24
I will d. what I can, 902 : 7
if I had to d. over I wouldn't, 884 : 11
if to d. as easy as to know, 198 : 9
it after high Roman fashion, 241 : 23
it as for thee, 269 : 7
it with thy might, 27 : 16
just as one pleases, 445 : 11
justice, 4 : 2
justly and love mercy, 33 : 23
know not what they d., 44 : 7
know what he ought to d., 139 : 14
let us d. or die, 411 : 16
make it d. or d. without, 924 : 4
nastiest thing in nicest way, 797 : 8
never d. today what can put off, 593 : 6
never tell how to d. things, 792 : 2
no one knows what he can d., 112 : 6
noble things not dream, 566 : 12
not as some pastors, 218 : 28
not choose to run, 736 : 18
not do thing they most do show, 245 : 4
not do to others, 69 : 14
not do what we want, 865 : 9
not go gentle, 887 : 4
not kill, 4 : 2
not we wanderer await, 585 : 22
not what we ought, 585 : 8

Do (*continued*)
nothing we d. wiped out, 648 : 11
now I'll d. it, 222 : 26
O what men dare d., 209 : 29
one must be to d., 396 : 4
or die, 261 : 3, 411 : 16, 830 : 7
other men for they do you, 547 : 33
reckless what I d., 238 : 15
seeks little thing to d., 542 : 19
she can d. no other, 682 : 13
so much to d., 532 : 15, 672 : 18
that thou doest d. quickly, 45 : 18
the evil I d., 47 : 6
the very best I can, 524 : 11
theirs but to d. and die, 533 : 12
they d. things we can't, 875 : 8
they know not what they d., 44 : 7
thing I was born to d., 182 : 9
thing that ends other deeds, 241 : 24
thing think you cannot, 786 : 13
thing you have to, 596 : 5
things I did not d., 716 : 13
things worth the writing, 347 : 18
this in remembrance, 44 : 3
this one thing I d., 50 : 4
this will never d., 428 : *n* 3
thou but thine, 287 : 9
to be to d. to d. without, 637 : 7
to will and to d. his pleasure, 50 : 3
trust me to d. it right, 896 : 14
two things is to do neither, 110 : 16
we d. what we can, 653 : 5
what country d. for you, 890 : 12
what d. about it, 594 : 1
what d. when you fallen, 896 : 12
what d. you mean to d., 641 : 21
what have you or I to d. with it, 359 : 20
what he may, 224 : 24
what I will with mine, 40 : 10
what man may d. to himself, 765 : 1
what man would d. exalts, 543 : 22
what manhood bids, 581 : 14
what then thou would'st, 289 : 5
what thou wilt, 157 : 12
what we back ourselves to d., 649 : 1
what you can d. for country, 890 : 12
what you d. still betters what is done, 246 : 27
what you have to d., 121 : 19
whatsoever thy hand findeth to d., 27 : 16
will to d., 431 : 7
without being commanded, 87 : 2
write what men d., 179 : 5
ye even so unto them, 38 : 14
you d. not d., 911 : 16
Doasyouwouldbedoneby, Mrs. D., 566 : 16
Docent, decent d., 839 : 5
Doch-an'-dorris, wee d., 730 : 20
Docile and omnipotent, 605 : 19
Dockyard, mine factory d., 745 : 11
Doctor and saint, 516 : 16
apple keeps d. away, 923 : 12
Diet Quiet Merryman, 323 : 15
every man own d. of divinity, 667 : 11
fee d. for nauseous draught, 306 : 26
Foster went to Gloucester, 933 : 10
kills more than general, 315 : 12
Livingstone I presume, 646 : 15
while runnin' for d., 786 : 10
Doctor's, outlived the d. pill, 332 : 5
Doctors, believe d. nothing wholesome, 609 : 1
best d. in the world, 323 : 15
if d. had more Christianity, 721 : 11
is all swabs, 668 : 5
we d. know hopeless case, 829 : 26
when d. disagree, 335 : 26
Doctrinaire logic, 821 : 8
Doctrine, all the winds of d., 282 : 5
every wind of d., 49 : 35
from women's eyes this d., 191 : 5
go for refuge to D., 73 : 6
hidden under strange verses, 141 : 7
involving pernicious consequences, 553 : 20
little difference in d., 354 : 24
not for d. but music, 333 : 7
of pathological generation, 584 : 5
of separate but equal, 820 : 14
of strenuous life, 686 : 12
or practice or interpretation, 125 : 13
peculiar d., 560 : 23
prove their d. orthodox, 291 : 5
so illogical and dull, 783 : 7
that each one select, 468 : 21
yesterday fact today d., 390 : 10
Doctrines, makes d. plain and clear, 291 : 27
Documents, historian wants d., 654 : 1
Dodger, artful D., 546 : 31
Doe, came a fallow d., 927 : 3
life looking out from eyes of d., 823 : 9
Doer, speaker of words and d. of deeds, 58 : 10
Doers of the word, 51 : 31
talkers no good d., 187 : 7
Does, dogged as d. it, 555 : 5
he who can d., 680 : 23
sees it and d. it, 542 : 19
Doeth, what thy right hand d., 37 : 14
whatsoever he d. shall prosper, 17 : 12
Doff it for shame, 201 : 21
Doffed, lightly d. hat, 704 : 15
Dog, absolutely unselfish friend is d., 609 : 4
Almighty gave d., 432 : 12
better than his d., 529 : 17
beware of d., 133 : 12
bites man not news, 659 : 19
Boatswain a d., 456 : 9
Body my good bright d., 896 : 13
breed maggots in dead d., 220 : 17
cat d. pipe or two, 692 : 15
circumcised d., 232 : 21
cutthroat d., 198 : 24
did nothing in nighttime, 689 : 8
dies like a d., 513 : 19
difference between d. and man, 624 : 24
door what d. on wrong side of, 856 : 8
drunken d. ragged head, 441 : 6
each time I walk the d., 912 : 12
empty house like stray d., 620 : 14
every d. his day, 566 : 14
faithful d. bear him company, 336 : 17
fetch poor d. a bone, 932 : 7
gingham d. went Bowwow, 666 : 18
grim king's d., 76 : 3
hair of d. that bit us, 160 : 18
has his day, 492 : 18
hath a day, 160 : 17
Dog (*continued*)
have his day, 224 : 24, 566 : 14
heart to d. to tear, 710 : 14
hold-fast the only d., 207 : 15
I am his Highness' d., 340 : 5
I'm a lean d. keen d., 819 : 8
in grave like old d., 888 : 2
in life firmest friend, 456 : 10
in the manger, 66 : 10
is thy servant a d., 14 : 16
it was that died, 369 : 19
jumps over lazy d., 923 : 2
let no d. bark, 198 : 2
like d. hunts in dreams, 529 : 21
little d. laughed, 930 : 17
little d. must die, 856 : 6
living d. better than dead lion, 27 : 15
looking for place to sleep, 878 : 4
make starving d. prosperous, 624 : 24
man bites d., 659 : 19
man's best friend d., 609 : *n* 1
mine enemy's d., 235 : 7
O d. my God, 881 : 11
offers drowning d. drink, 269 : 14
old d. barks backward, 749 : 2
old d. Tray, 443 : *n* 4
old wife old d. ready money, 347 : 17
poor d. Tray, 443 : 9
rather be d. and bay the moon, 216 : 32
reform taking bone from d., 699 : 3
returneth to his vomit, 25 : 19
since I am a d. beware, 199 : 31
so poor he could not keep a d., 127 : 2
starved at master's gate, 406 : 10
suspicious of buried bone, 653 : 13
this d. my d., 197 : 17
thou calledst me d., 199 : 31
to gain private ends, 369 : 18
to this d. praise, 507 : 4
tossed d. that worried cat, 934 : 9
toy d. covered with dust, 666 : 17
truth's a d. must to kennel, 233 : 8
turned to his own vomit, 52 : 18
whose d. are you, 340 : 5
why should a d. have life, 235 : 18
will have his day, 224 : 24
wool of bat tongue of d., 239 : 5
Dogged as does it, 555 : 5
strength, 724 : 17
strong d. unenlightened, 587 : 3
Doggedly, set himself d. to it, 353 : 24
Doggerel, rhymed d., 148 : 3
Dogies, git along little d., 927 : 10
Doglike, on bended arm d., 71 : 3
Dogma, Bible literature not d., 703 : 18
Dogmas of past inadequate, 522 : 12
Dogmatic, least sure most d., 871 : 6
Dogmatism, greater ignorance greater d., 664 : 11
puppyism at full growth, 500 : 15
Dogmatisms, narrow d., 653 : 4
Dog's, more deadly than mad d. tooth, 188 : 13
walking, 354 : 15
Dogs, all d. of Europe bark, 868 : 12
all the d. in town, 929 : 22
as many d. there be, 369 : 17
black d. bay moon, 629 : 20
careful of breed of d., 314 : 14
crowing of cocks and barking of d., 65 : 9
dancing d. and bears, 732 : 16
delight to bark and bite, 328 : 2

Dogs (*continued*)
display reluctance, 856 : 1
drink running at the Nile, 114 : 7
eat of crumbs, 39 : 32
fought d. killed cats, 541 : 1
hark d. do bark, 933 : 21
hates babies and d., 770 : *n* 8
hates children and d., 770 : 18
horizon of d., 841 : 11
Inquisition d., 535 : 12
leave Now for d. and apes, 542 : 17
let slip d. of war, 216 : 12
lies with d. riseth with fleas, 269 : 31
little d. and all, 234 : 15
mad d. and Englishmen, 843 : 8
more I admire my d., 464 : 20
not live as d. in manger, 781 : 5
of Seville, 535 : 13
rain cats and d., 919 : 23
shall eat Jezebel, 14 : 8
shame the gray head, 59 : 6
sleeping d. lie, 549 : 5
straw d., 64 : 1
throw physic to the d., 239 : 32
torn to pieces by d., 850 : 14
which hath deeper mouth, 184 : 20
Dogs', puppy d. tails, 932 : 12
Dog-star rages, 338 : 5
Doing, being not d., 874 : 13
cease to think about d., 445 : 16
good one of professions which are full, 559 : 17
is another thing, 165 : 13
it all takes d. and I do, 654 : 8
joy's soul lies in d., 225 : 34
learn by d., 87 : 16
manners happy ways of d., 498 : 28
miserable d. or suffering, 283 : 10
secure friends by d. favors, 81 : 3
the great god Pan, 507 : 23
up and d., 509 : 16
Doings, amend your ways and your d., 32 : 1
broadcast d. of day night, 573 : 19
child known by his d., 24 : 29
mark out your d. in advance, 481 : 16
of mankind subject of my book, 122 : 1
something in d. of man, 573 : 19
Dolabella's Cleopatra, 303 : 13
Dolce far niente, 123 : *n* 10
vita, 142 : *n* 6
Dole, happy man be his d., 159 : *n* 5
happy man happy d., 159 : 7
unequal laws, 529 : 6
weighing delight and d., 217 : 29
Doleful, chants d. hymn, 202 : 16
dumps, 188 : *n* 2, 917 : 17
shades, 283 : 7
Doll in the doll's house, 549 : 33
living d. can sew cook, 911 : 9
put youth away like d., 897 : 1
that hadn't been painted, 878 : 12
your d. wife, 599 : 10
Dollar, a dillar a d., 933 : 14
almighty d., 453 : 6
broken never dollar again, 561 : 11
Dollars, hours and minutes d. and cents, 348 : *n* 1
Dolls cloths tobacco fringes, 889 : 12
guys and d., 787 : 1
the children my d., 599 : 10
Dolores, splendid and sterile D., 632 : 12
Dolphin-like, his delights were d., 241 : 25
Dolphin's, mermaid on d. back, 196 : 14
Dolphin-torn gong-tormented sea, 716 : 11
Dolts, three greatest d., 452 : 4
Domain, such d. France conquered, 592 : 6
Dome, fired Ephesian d., 275 : *n* 1
of many-colored glass, 469 : 16
of thought palace of soul, 457 : 6
of vast sepulcher, 467 : 19
orchard for a d., 605 : 4
rounded Peter's d., 493 : 18
stately pleasure d., 433 : 21
sunny pleasure d., 433 : 25, 433 : 27
Domestic disorder, 316 : 13
insure d. tranquility, 391 : 10
internal d. empire, 837 : 8
malice d. foreign levy, 238 : 19
naive d. Burgundy, 831 : 4
races made d. mild tractable, 154 : 12
sentiment of mankind, 502 : 5
Domestica, quae est d. sede iucundior, 98 : *n* 13
Domestics, few admired by own d., 165 : 17
Domina mater ecclesia, 126 : *n* 3
Dominant X, 768 : 2
Dominate, China not seeking to d. world, 825 : 5
serve and not d. world, 787 : 10
Dominated, horse d. mind of early races, 790 : 19
Domination of the world, 687 : 4
Dominations, Thrones D. Princedoms, 286 : 22
Domine Deus Agnus Dei, 54 : 5
speravi in te, 167 : *n* 3
Dominion, between Grand Army and d. of world, 642 : 8
death hath no more d., 47 : 3
death shall have no d., 886 : 16
good old D., 390 : 5
no such strange d., 470 : 10
over every living thing, 6 : 15
over palm and pine, 709 : 16
tired of dark d., 600 : 27
truly sorry man's d., 408 : 13
Dominions, sun in d. never sets, 412 : 18
Dominus illuminatio mea, 18 : *n* 3
vobiscum, 54 : 1
Domus tutissimum refugium, 172 : 2
Don John of Austria, 742 : 10
or devil, 535 : 13
Quixote and I, 452 : 4
Done, a' is d. that men can do, 410 : 5
ah what have you d. to me, 602 : 2
because we are too many, 641 : 8
bright day is d., 241 : 26
by the rule, 241 : 2
Charmian is this well d., 242 : 6
dared and d., 365 : 9
dead and dumb and d., 740 : 6
do as you would be d. by, 38 : *n* 1, 341 : 19
fearful trip d., 576 : 6
foolish thing well d., 355 : 6
game is d. I've won, 434 : 20
God's will be d., 385 : 14
her wrong, 923 : 8
him who has d. deed to suffer, 71 : 16
his best for his time, 413 : 5
I have d. it again, 911 : 10
Done (*continued*)
I have d. the state service, 232 : 20
if d. when 'tis d., 236 : 22
it couldn't be d., 774 : 3
it unto the least, 41 : 1
I've d. it from my youth, 400 : 6
knowing when to have d., 474 : 9
let what will be d., 388 : 10
long day's task is d., 241 : 18
much to be d., 353 : 6
my dancing days are d., 191 : *n* 3
my story being d., 229 : 31
my task is smoothly d., 280 : 4
nay I have d., 182 : 16
no sooner said than d., 94 : 16
no worthy action d., 920 : 12
not my will be d., 44 : 4
one braver thing, 252 : 4
servant of God well d., 286 : 26
sight of means makes ill deeds d., 202 : 11
so little d., 532 : 15, 672 : 18
some villain hath d. me wrong, 189 : *n* 3
still betters what is d., 246 : 27
surprised to find it d. at all, 354 : 15
take honor and my life is d., 193 : 33
that which is d. is that which shall be d., 26 : 14
there shall be d. a deed, 238 : 20
things that are d., 68 : 12
things we ought not to, 54 : 13
things won are d., 225 : 34
to deserve kittens, 760 : 4
to have loved thought d., 585 : 11
treason has d. his worst, 238 : 19
'twere well d. quickly, 236 : 22
we have d. this before, 888 : 12
well begun is half d., 88 : 11
well d. is quickly d., 110 : 7
what another would have d. as well, 727 : 8
what have I d. unto thee, 11 : 2
what have you d. to me, 602 : 2
what have you d. with your youth, 659 : 15
what without Zeus is d., 71 : 11
what you do not want d. to yourself, 69 : 14
what's d. is d., 238 : 17
when the hurlyburly's d., 235 : 21
who has begun has half d., 108 : 20
work may yet be d., 529 : 12
worldly task hast d., 243 : 27
Donkeys, I shall resemble d., 899 : 16
let it be with d., 899 : 16
Donna è mobile, 105 : *n* 5
Donne, John D. Anne D. Undone, 251 : *n* 7
whose muse on dromedary trots, 436 : 5
with Landor and with D., 714 : 2
Donnée, subject idea d., 652 : 15
Donner un sens plus pur, 808 : *n* 4
Dons, if D. sight Devon, 700 : 8
Don't, advice to persons about to marry D., 660 : 11
advice to persons about to write history D., 615 : 16
be gentle to your wife, 60 : 13
damned if you d., 444 : 9
fire until you see whites of eyes, 368 : 1
give up the ship, 449 : *n* 1

Don't (*continued*)
go near water, 924 : 17
look back, 867 : 9
sell America short, 924 : 14
tell her everything, 60 : 13
tread on me, 920 : 13
Doodle handlebar moustaches, 892 : 17
Dooley, I think said Mr. D., 721 : 11
Doom, adolescence' doubt common d., 571 : 4
edge of d., 245 : 18
feeling inevitable as d., 503 : 7
felicity or d., 608 : 4
forfeit to a confined d., 245 : 13
involve others in our d., 365 : 3
regardless of their d., 361 : 10
stretch out to crack of d., 239 : 14
who's to d., 571 : 6
your d. Faustine, 633 : 14
Doomed conscripted ones, 795 : 16
sentient beings d., 515 : 15
story ephemeral and d., 838 : 8
to company with pain, 427 : 22
to death though fated not, 305 : 15
Dooms imagined for mighty dead, 475 : 17
of love, 829 : 19
Doomsday, danced till d., 324 : 11
eighth day, 863 : 17
is near, 204 : 34
sick almost to d., 217 : 22
Doomsters, purblind d., 640 : 3
Doon, banks and braes o' bonny D., 409 : 24
Dooney, play on fiddle in D., 712 : 17
Door, at its own stable d., 605 : 19
at the d. of life, 633 : 1
at this d. England sentry, 639 : 16
before d. of God, 604 : 3
before his cottage d., 439 : 10
begins to crack, 929 : 9
beside a human d., 424 : 19
big front d., 627 : 14
called push, 923 : 9
came out by same d., 516 : 16
clicked behind d., 370 : 13
dark cloud at house's d., 928 : 18
dream hidden d. of soul, 754 : 13
ever-open d., 57 : *n* 8
foot wear steps of his d., 35 : 11
form from off d., 526 : 18
golden d., 664 : 10
handle of big front d., 627 : 14
he who sits at d. of house, 935 : 12
I am the d., 45 : 9
iron d. of north, 864 : 2
know grass beyond d., 601 : 23
leave world by natural d., 672 : 11
lion at the d., 929 : 9
March is outside d., 839 : 1
moonlit d., 739 : 15
no d. is shut, 697 : 2
no right to open d., 83 : 16
nor so wide as church d., 193 : 5
of all subtleties, 63 : 12
old age coming bolt d., 133 : 2
one d. closes another open, 153 : 17
open d., 636 : 8
open to remedy, 168 : 20
opening of a d., 608 : 4
opens and lets future in, 859 : 6
over that same d. was writ, 173 : 20
Pity stands before the d., 406 : 4
Door (*continued*)
put in his hand by the hole of the d., 28 : 15
rapping at chamber d., 526 : 10
say over d. of heaven, 900 : 1
shut shut the d., 338 : 5
sits on horse at hostess' d., 201 : 15
stack or the barn d., 277 : 23
stand at the d. and knock, 53 : 6
steed stolen shut stable d., 159 : 30
stone leaf unfound d., 852 : 6
then shuts the d., 605 : 2
three gypsies a-come to d., 920 : 17
through the pale d., 526 : 2
to which no key, 516 : 18
turn in d. once only, 805 : 13
unfound d., 852 : 6
up to old inn d., 772 : 23
we never opened, 807 : 2
what dog on wrong side of, 856 : 8
what is wind in that d., 149 : 10
whining of a d., 255 : 2
wide as a church d., 193 : 5
wolf at d., 695 : 17
wolf from d., 153 : 1
world make path to d., 496 : *n* 1
younger generation knocking at d., 600 : 7
Doorkeeper in the house of my God, 20 : 8
Doors are widely flung, 873 : 2
as yet shut upon me, 479 : 11
be ye lift up ye everlasting d., 18 : 9
clay-shuttered d., 693 : 17
Emily set d. ajar, 751 : 7
for men to take their exits, 262 : 8
from keep of well-closed d., 576 : 18
in to the upper d., 494 : 15
open d. of his face, 17 : 5
open your living d., 287 : 1
pictures out of d., 230 : 8
shut d. against setting sun, 243 : 2
shut in the streets, 27 : 24
shut-in homes closed d., 727 : 7
ten thousand several d., 262 : 8
two glass revolving d., 897 : 3
Doorway, Hylax barks in d., 103 : 18
to get in a god, 567 : 16
Dooryard, when lilacs last in d., 576 : 2
Dorian mood of flutes, 283 : 22
Doric discipline, 715 : 12
lay, 281 : 5
Dorking, hens of D., 551 : 1
Dormons, veillons dormants et veillants d., 165 : *n* 5
Dorobo and animals live side by side, 925 : 24
Dorure en reste aux mains, 583 : *n* 6
Dostoevski's realism, 784 : 22
Dotages, plagues and d. of humankind, 258 : 25
Dote, Casey's tabble d., 666 : 11
on his very absence, 198 : 15
on myself, 574 : 21
on scraps of learning d., 329 : 20
Dotes yet doubts, 230 : 34
Double debt to pay, 370 : 13
double toil and trouble, 239 : 4
ducats stolen by daughter, 199 : 11
eyes upon d. string, 253 : 6
for all her sins, 30 : 30
Giant hit into d., 773 : 12
grew like a d. cherry, 197 : 2
halve rights d. duties, 463 : 2
Double (*continued*)
health to thee, 460 : 4
hypocrite reader my d., 580 : 16
life's fading space, 119 : *n* 5
make assurance d. sure, 239 : 11
nocturne in serge, 841 : 14
of orient pearl a d. row, 250 : 6
palter with us in d. sense, 240 : 9
pleasure to deceive deceiver, 296 : 13
single nature's d. name, 225 : 30
snakes with d. tongue, 196 : 21
tongue, 494 : 19
write about my d., 824 : 5
Double-consciousness peculiar sensation, 724 : 17
Doubled globe of dead, 886 : 14
Double-faced, fame if not d., 289 : 2
Double-mouthed, fame is d., 289 : 2
Doubly benefits who gives quickly, 110 : 15
dead, 525 : *n* 5
dying, 430 : 10
hammered leaves of gold, 570 : 11
seconded with will and power, 226 : 3
Doubt, adolescence' d., 571 : 4
all best thought oft d., 289 : 10
brother devil to Despair, 659 : 5
doubter and d., 495 : 12
explain till all men d., 340 : 25
faith dead which does not d., 706 : 12
faith in honest d., 532 : 19
frets d. maw-crammed beast, 544 : 9
grows with knowledge, 397 : 6
he was worthy of life, 903 : 2
hesitation and pain, 541 : 9
I d. it said Carpenter, 613 : 2
I d. some foul play, 218 : 25
I show you d., 543 : 8
ignorant taught to d., 644 : 18
in d. to act or rest, 337 : 2
iron time of d., 585 : 4
let us not pretend to d., 639 : 9
loop to hang d. on, 231 : 13
love curiosity freckles d., 827 : 9
modest d. called beacon, 226 : 7
more d. stronger faith, 543 : 8
my days of endless d., 172 : 7
never d. I love, 220 : 14
never stand to d., 266 : 18
new philosophy calls all in d., 254 : 5
night of d. and sorrow, 616 : 8
no freedom of thought without d., 859 : 3
no manner of d., 630 : 3
one may prove a fool, 503 : 21
our d. is our passion, 653 : 5
part of all religion, 862 : 3
read to d., 432 : 6
road to resolution lies by d., 267 : 16
science teaches d., 552 : 1
solve one d., 380 : 1
sun and moon should d., 406 : 17
sunnier side of d., 535 : 16
teach child to d., 406 : 15
that sun doth move, 220 : 14
thou stars are fire, 220 : 14
time d. of Rome, 461 : 12
to be once in d., 231 : 2
to d. or believe 673 : 7
true science teaches d., 705 : 16
truth to be liar, 220 : 14
when in d. tell truth, 625 : 1
when in d. win trick, 327 : 6
where d. let me sow faith, 138 : 15

Doubt (*continued*)
where d. there truth, 532 : *n* 6
wherefore didst thou d., 39 : 28
who dares d. poet wise, 275 : 31
Doubted, never d. clouds break, 546 : 7
who never d. never believed, 532 : *n* 6
Doubter and the doubt, 495 : 12
Doubters, religious thinkers d., 862 : 3
Doubtful disputations, 47 : 30
dreams of dreams, 633 : 19
in d. things liberty, 294 : 18
nice hazard of d. hour, 204 : 29
thinking about thing no longer d., 508 : 7
thoughts, 199 : 28
Doubting Castle, 302 : 8
dreaming dreams, 526 : 14
liberty is possibility of d., 851 : 4
Doubtless come again with rejoicing, 22 : 7
God never did, 271 : 10
Doubts are traitors, 227 : 29
begin with certainties end in d., 178 : 20
begin with d. end in certainties, 178 : 20
creating new d., 380 : 1
dotes yet d., 230 : 34
from what he sees, 406 : 17
littlest d. are fear, 222 : 13
more cruel than truths, 297 : 30
saucy d. and fears, 238 : 23
Doughnut, optimist sees d., 758 : 12
Douglas, Adamses vote for D., 694 : *n* 3
in his hall, 430 : 23
like D. conquer, 366 : 11
old song of Percy and D., 176 : 12
owl in D. fir turn head, 905 : 18
tender and true, 597 : 13
tongues of D. and myself, 520 : 8
Douglass superb in love and logic, 556 : *n* 3
Doux comme l'amour, 400 : *n* 3
Dove, all eagle in thee all d., 292 : 16
beside the springs of D., 424 : 12
descending like a d., 36 : 30
found no rest, 7 : 31
harmless as d., 38 : *n* 3
loves when it quarrels, 129 : 12
more serpent than d., 183 : 14
prison d. coo over and over, 801 : 18
roar you gently as sucking d., 196 : 8
that I had wings like a d., 19 : 20
visited upon d., 122 : 2
white rose a d., 659 : 6
wings of the d., 459 : 18
with flickering tongue, 808 : 13
Dovecote, like eagle in a d., 242 : 26
Dover, chalk cliffs of D., 720 : 11
white cliffs of D., 752 : 1
Dove's, hidden under d. wing, 806 : 13
Doves, be harmless as d., 38 : 36
hurricane of black d., 841 : 17
in immemorial elms, 531 : 13
soft as breast of d., 795 : 2
Dovetailedness, universal d., 547 : 13
Dowager's a demd outline, 547 : 14
Down and away below, 584 : 11
bliss not beds of d., 267 : 10
blow the man d., 934 : 17
by salley gardens, 711 : 22
can't hold man d. without staying d. with him, 681 : 26
come baby cradle and all, 660 : 19
Down (*continued*)
coming d. I can shift, 155 : 9
down that town settle hence, 525 : 14
drink it d., 630 : 15
from rising of the sun unto going d., 21 : 20
gigantically d., 525 : 13, 844 : 2
go d. again to the depths, 21 : 15
go d. to the sea in ships, 21 : 14
go up and d. as a talebearer, 10 : 20
gone d. drain of eternity, 76 : 8
he that is d., 302 : 13
in the valley, 920 : 19
keep 'em d. on farm, 801 : 12
lay me d. in peace, 17 : 16
lay them d. in their dens, 21 : 11
levelers wish to level d., 354 : 13
look not d. but up, 544 : 13
look up not d., 590 : 8
maketh me to lie d., 18 : 7
moon is d., 237 : 9
on me down on me, 916 : 4
on your knees, 212 : 16
road up and road d. one and same, 70 : 6
Satan walking up and d., 15 : 2
sloth finds d. pillow hard, 243 : 23
smoothing the raven d., 279 : 19
the abandoned heaven, 790 : 16
the darker stairs, 791 : 1
the way Persephone goes, 791 : 1
thou climbing sorrow, 233 : 17
to Gehenna up to throne, 707 : 14
to Puritan marrow, 794 : 2
to sea again, 760 : 14
unseen full of water, 195 : 11
vast edges drear, 587 : 16
when chips d. nation acts helpless, 882 : 23
who pulls me d., 184 : 8
why art thou cast d., 19 : 6
world turned upside d., 258 : 11
you'll meet 'em on way d., 757 : 13
Down-gyved to his ankle, 220 : 8
Down's, sea d. edge, 634 : 12
Downs, all in the D., 331 : 9
Downsitting, thou knowest my d., 22 : 16
Downstairs, habit coaxed d., 624 : 15
kick you d., 611 : 11
threw him d., 931 : 8
why kick me d., 407 : 13
Downward beat thy wings, 100 : *n* 8
face d. in sun, 822 : 1
thoughts always d. bent, 283 : 28
to darkness, 767 : 4
world turned upside d., 258 : 11
Downwards, look no way but d., 302 : 12
Downy, shake off this d. sleep, 238 : 6
Dowry, brought her d. destruction, 71 : 6
Doxy, heterodoxy another man's d., 345 : 2
orthodoxy is my d., 345 : 2, 473 : 19
Doze, docent doesn't d., 839 : 5
student dassn't d., 839 : 5
Dozen, kills seven d. Scots, 203 : 26
Dozens, reckons up by d., 627 : 13
Drab, ditch-delivered by a d., 239 : 6
Drachenfels, crag of D., 457 : 25
Drachmas, buy repentance at ten thousand d., 88 : 24
Draft, corner d. fluttered flame, 817 : 3
Drafted, no loophole in case d., 766 : 3
Drag Atlantic for whales, 623 : 5
slow d. of days, 76 : 5
the slow barge, 377 : 26
Zeus from heaven to earth, 58 : 6
Dragged, idleness d. toward evil, 80 : 7
Dragging themselves through negro streets, 906 : 1
Dragon, before he killed d., 742 : 14
between d. and wrath, 232 : 27
great d. was cast out, 53 : 20
Michael fought against d., 53 : 19
O to be a d., 799 : 14
Saint George that swinged d., 201 : 15
that is in the sea, 30 : 12
world, 793 : 4
young lion and the d., 20 : 17
Dragonflies draw flame, 656 : 11
Dragonfly on the river, 507 : 23
Dragonish, cloud that's d., 241 : 17
Dragon's teeth, 840 : 10
Dragons, brother to d., 16 : 19
habitation of d., 30 : 22
offering d. quarter no good, 885 : 3
Drags at each remove, 368 : 14
bellies and d. in wind, 714 : 6
its slow length along, 333 : 8
verity d. me to ground, 380 : 3
Drain, leave by town d., 659 : 11
of eternity, 76 : 8
Drained cup of Lethe, 106 : 24
faces of Negro children, 893 : 15
loungers of Empire d., 689 : 2
Drainless shower of light, 475 : 12
Drainpipes, if d. of house clogged, 583 : 10
Drains, it d. your purse, 401 : 3
opiate to d., 476 : 21
Drake he's in his hammock, 700 : 9
let me lie down with D., 569 : 20
Drakes, ducks and d. with shillings, 177 : 15
Dram, single d. of heaven, 607 : 17
Drama, ancient d. begin again, 849 : 7
close d. with the day, 330 : 25
episode in d. of pain, 640 : 17
of plastic act, 774 : 10
only develop in civilization, 654 : 5
through her body heaved, 717 : 4
whether damned or not, 398 : 20
writing is d. or nothing, 750 : 1
Dramatic, writing as good as it is d., 750 : 1
Dramatist wants more liberties, 654 : 1
Dramatists, Shakespeare first of d., 353 : *n* 4
Dramatize it dramatize it, 654 : 2
Drang, Sturm und D., 399 : 19
Drank at every vine, 823 : 5
lived nightly d. daily, 876 : 8
our liquor straight, 868 : 18
pint of English ale, 742 : 14
rich d. too much, 845 : 7
without thirst, 322 : 15
Drapery, one that wraps d. of couch, 471 : 6
Draught, fee doctor for nauseous d., 306 : 26
of life, 607 : 17
of vintage, 476 : 23
one d. above heat, 213 : 16
Draughts, shallow d., 332 : 20
Draw, able to d. with their feet, 67 : 13
all other things to destruction d., 252 : 22

Draw (*continued*)
as love with thread, 259 : 18
began to d. to our end, 34 : 15
bow ride and speak truth, 462 : 4
chair up close to edge, 835 : 15
close his eyes and d. curtain, 185 : 19
evils d. men together, 88 : 14
from one mother both d. breath, 72 : 6
from others lesson, 96 : 8
inward quality after, 241 : 10
line where God has not, 646 : 5
living faces from marble, 105 : 24
my songs d. Daphnis home, 103 : 17
new mischief on, 229 : 33
not d. out more than already know, 658 : 26
out leviathan with a hook, 17 : 4
powers into higher classes, 390 : 2
right here a picture, 652 : 3
salary before spending, 718 : 10
thy breath in pain, 225 : 1
up the papers lawyer, 660 : 2
you with single hair, 259 : *n* 8
Drawers, chest of d. by day, 370 : 13
of water, 11 : 33
Shirttails Into D., 829 : 1
Draweth out thread of his verbosity, 191 : 6
Drawing, back to the old d. board, 858 : 18
down of blinds, 827 : 5
from no less kindled earth, 462 : 15
here on d. board fingers, 904 : 6
love hanging and d. and quartering, 404 : 22
no unnecessary lines, 729 : 7
nothing up, 376 : 27
Drawing-down of blinds, 827 : 5
Drawn in pearly monotones, 794 : 2
linked sweetness long d. out, 278 : 6
never curtain d., 748 : 12
never d. breath of life, 715 : 19
wine of life is d., 238 : 7
with team of atomies, 191 : 23
yet were they d. swords, 19 : 22
Draws, beauty d. with single hair, 334 : 3
lightly d. its breath, 423 : 3
Drayhorse, great gray d., 656 : 8
Dread abode, 362 : 19
and fear of kings, 200 : 9
back from the d. fray, 57 : 29
close eyes with holy d., 433 : 27
empire chaos, 340 : 28
fifty above, 748 : 10
Inferno, 544 : 2
innocence has nothing to d., 312 : 9
Jove's d. clamors, 231 : 11
nothing more d. and shameless, 60 : 11
of mother-in-law, 673 : 4
of something after death, 221 : 12
two fates of d. death, 59 : 7
walk in fear and d., 435 : 3
what d. grasp, 405 : 8
whence this secret d., 326 : 3
Dreadeth, burnt child fire d., 160 : 20
Dreadful, acting of d. thing, 215 : 18
called thee mighty and d., 254 : 11
day, 430 : 12
deed of d. note, 238 : 20
done a thousand d. things, 188 : 22
endured something more d., 61 : 3
Dreadful (*continued*)
gathers samphire d. trade, 234 : 28
knowledge of truth, 74 : 2
lion among ladies d., 196 : 24
loud roared d. thunder, 415 : 5
no witness so d., 95 : 19
noise of waters, 187 : 9
note of preparation, 208 : 1
past, 528 : 17
pleasing d. thought, 326 : 3
silence that d. bell, 230 : 20
summit of the cliff, 219 : 14
Dreading e'en fools, 338 : 14
Dreadnought's her name, 935 : 6
Dream, Adam's d., 479 : 2
all night without stir, 478 : 4
anguishes writer, 838 : 13
awakened from d. of life, 469 : 11
behind a d., 245 : 23
behold it was a d., 302 : 11
beholding shape of d., 683 : 8
beneath tamarind tree, 525 : 7
boldness to d., 859 : 20
bonds were brittle, 633 : 9
but I love thee still, 534 : 24
came back in d. and we not here, 907 : 7
closes within d., 721 : 7
compared life to a d., 165 : 9
deep d. of peace, 454 : 4
deferred, 854 : 17
deferred dry up like raisin, 855 : 2
disturb not her d., 410 : 13
dream this also sooth, 711 : 21
dreamed d. called laundry, 906 : 3
dreamer making d. true, 775 : 15
eye hath not heard what my d. was, 197 : 10
falling into d. as coming out of d., 849 : 9
fly forgotten as a d., 328 : 12
ghost fled like d., 105 : 5
glory and freshness of a d., 426 : 10
glory and the d., 426 : 13
grandeur is a d., 377 : 1
Greeks have dreamt d. of life best, 397 : 12
Hanging Gardens a d., 752 : 16
happiness ceases like d., 273 : 5
hidden door of soul, 754 : 13
hope a waking d., 86 : 16
hope beyond shadow of d., 476 : 1
horrid dreams, 571 : 11
how d. of place without us, 900 : 2
how I'll d. fast asleep, 572 : 7
I d. and say Why not, 681 : 11
I have a d., 909 : 9, 909 : 10
impossible dream, 890 : 1
iridescent d., 615 : 3
is a theater, 754 : 12
King's d. our national d., 909 : *n* 4
let no man d., 534 : 24
life an empty d., 332 : *n* 2
life as lake dreams sky, 706 : 5
life but empty d., 509 : 13
life is a d., 273 : 2
like a shadow like a d., 60 : 8
lost cities in my d., 884 : 20
love's young d 446 : 12
mankind is d. of a shadow, 72 : 2
might be all we d. of, 467 : 13
movement out of d. into codification, 906 : 16
Dream (*continued*)
near awakening when d. that we d., 438 : 10
no mortal dared d. before, 526 : 14
nor Homer nods but we d., 332 : 18
not all a dream, 460 : 2
not d. all day long, 566 : 12
not so wild a d., 503 : 6
nothing happens unless first d., 761 : 12
of battled fields, 431 : 8
of home, 740 : 11
of Jeanie, 598 : 6
of joy all but in vain, 149 : *n* 1
of spring, 436 : 9
of things that were, 457 : 4
old men shall d. dreams, 33 : 17
old men's d., 304 : 5
opium so they can d., 706 : 6
out of misty d., 721 : 7
past the wit of man, 197 : 9
past vanished like d., 473 : 28
phantasma or hideous d., 215 : 18
poet's d., 427 : 17
President had d., 523 : 5
republic is a d., 761 : 12
salesman got to d., 888 : 3
short as any d., 195 : 23
sight to d. of not tell, 434 : 1
silently as a d., 377 : 11
sits as new-risen from d., 188 : 38
sleep not d. not, 561 : 21
somnambulist of vanished d., 491 : 17
stranger in your d., 897 : 16
summer d. beneath tree, 525 : 7
sweet d. when trick's over, 760 : 16
taught me this wisdom, 273 : 5
that I forget, 633 : 16
that it fades from kiss to kiss, 712 : 19
that we dream, 438 : 10
the d. is one, 8 : 31
the d. the excitable gift, 908 : 14
theater, 754 : 12
those who d. by day, 526 : 3
to sleep perchance to d., 221 : 12
too is from Zeus, 57 : 5
translators between d. and reality, 801 : 8
vision in higher d., 806 : 3
vision or waking d., 477 : 3
warned in a d., 36 : 21
we live as we d. alone, 683 : 15
what we d. up, 906 : 5
with d. of meet death with, 544 : 26
within dream, 525 : 3
you are crossing Channel, 629 : 1
youthful poets d., 278 : 6
Dreamcrossed twilight, 806 : 5
Dreamed, crack-pated when we d., 715 : 8
dream called laundry, 906 : 3
Greece might be free, 461 : 4
he d. and behold a ladder, 8 : 19
I dwelt in marble halls, 480 : 11
life was beauty, 555 : 23
never d. wrong triumph, 546 : 7
of in any philosophy, 821 : 5
of in your philosophy, 220 : 3
of toasted cheese, 668 : 8
past never past redeeming, 899 : 7
Dreamer, beautiful d., 598 : 8
behold this d. cometh, 8 : 27
I am d. that remains, 852 : 15
making dream come true, 775 : 15

Dreamer (*continued*)
of dreams, 11 : 15, 618 : 7
scene actor prompter, 754 : 12
Dreamers of dreams, 659 : 9
soldiers are d., 795 : 14
Dreamful ease, 528 : 18
Dreaming, butterfly d. I am a man, 90 : 3
dreams no mortal dared, 526 : 14
eyes of wonder, 612 : 15
false or honest d., 899 : 7
I was a butterfly, 90 : 3
lives and souls d. d., 571 : 3
my excuse for d., 821 : 5
o'er joys of night, 404 : 12
of white Christmas, 802 : 11
on both, 228 : 16
on things to come, 245 : 13
pool, 566 : 13
spires, 587 : 7
with strange whale eyes, 790 : 22
world on d. fed, 711 : 19
Dreamless, deep and d. sleep, 619 : 16
Dreamlike trade of blood, 435 : 21
Dreams abuse curtained sleep, 237 : 14
advances in direction of d., 560 : 16
all my nightly d., 525 : 18
arise from d. of thee, 468 : 1
arointing d. with requiems, 766 : 21
at length deceive 'em, 320 : 24
before us like land of d., 587 : 16
being poor have only d., 712 : 16
blissful d. of long ago, 636 : 2
books each a world, 428 : 4
communicatest with d., 246 : 12
desires d. and powers, 633 : 20
doubtful d. of d., 633 : 19
dream horrid d., 571 : 11
dreamer of d., 11 : 15, 618 : 7
dying d. of his Argos, 106 : 5
forgotten d., 528 : 1
from Death fulfillment to d., 767 : 3
gate of ivory for false d., 105 : 26
have two gates, 61 : 2
hunters of d., 685 : 11
hunts in d., 529 : 21
I have bad d., 220 : 26
in d. begins responsibility, 713 : 9
in d. behold Hebrides, 483 : 20
in my d. I'd be, 505 : 1
jailer envious of prisoner's d., 514 : 8
joys as d. do fly, 917 : 20
land of d., 587 : 16
land of my d., 813 : 7
lies down to pleasant d., 471 : 6
make d. come true, 824 : 12
man's best d. to shame, 507 : 13
men in exile feed on d., 71 : 13
necessary to life, 858 : 5
night full of ghastly d., 187 : 8
no mortal dared before, 526 : 14
not responsible for d., 754 : 9
old men shall dream d., 33 : 17
painter's brush consumes d., 715 : 13
pleasing d. slumbers light, 431 : 4
revisit in d. the dear dead, 76 : 2
rich beyond d. of avarice, 356 : 20, 358 : 8
sighed for Agnes' d., 476 : 11
sleep full of sweet d., 475 : 16
somnambulisms reveries, 571 : 3
spread d. under your feet, 712 : 16
stuff as d. are made on, 248 : 13
Dreams (*continued*)
surely are difficult, 61 : 2
than this world d. of, 535 : 1
themselves are only dreams, 273 : 2
thought of old best d., 855 : *n* 3
to sell, 492 : 15
torn by d., 768 : 7
touchstones of characters, 558 : 15
transit where d. cross, 806 : 5
tread softly on d., 712 : 16
true I talk of d., 191 : 24
vain hopes like d. of those who wake, 118 : 1
we are dreamers of d., 659 : 9
we have great d., 824 : 12
what d. may come, 221 : 12
Dreamy, brief d. delight, 712 : 19
lullaby, 629 : 4
Drear, chill and d., 430 : 13
epitaph d., 707 : 20
vast edges d., 587 : 16
Dreariest and longest journey, 468 : 21
Drear-nighted December, 478 : 14
Dreary, all world sad d., 598 : 4
if morals make you d., 669 : 14
midnight d., 526 : 10
some days dark and d., 510 : 11
these d. dumps, 188 : 19
to be somebody, 604 : 19
tract of country, 525 : 19
Dregs, drunken the d., 31 : 10
of life, 303 : 11
of Romulus, 98 : 17
Drenched in fraternal blood, 450 : 15
our steeples, 233 : 24
Dress, all this fleshly d., 299 : 3
as nation don't d. well, 680 : 10
by yellow candlelight, 668 : 9
if the devil d. her not, 242 : 1
Peace the human d., 403 : 11
plain in d. sober in diet, 341 : 2
Secrecy the human d., 405 : 14
style the d. of thoughts, 342 : 7
sweet disorder in the d., 266 : 6
tatter in mortal d., 715 : 1
Dressed, all d. up nowhere to go, 726 : 11
April d. in all his trim, 245 : 9
fine as I will, 328 : 7
for this short comedy, 173 : 1
good spirits when well d., 547 : 29
in brief authority, 228 : 10
lord neat trimly d., 203 : 7
nature to advantage d., 333 : 3
out in all her finery, 371 : 7
still to be d., 255 : 17
world beautifully d., 593 : 7
Drew circle shut me out, 671 : 4
Creator d. his spirit, 307 : 9
everything that begins with M, 611 : 22
from out boundless deep, 535 : 19
Jew that Shakespeare d., 340 : 8
many-colored life he d., 351 : 10
men as they ought to be, 73 : *n* 10
one angel, 544 : 2
she d. an angel down, 306 : 23
them with bands of love, 33 : 14
Dried carcass of leopard, 845 : 8
sap out of veins, 713 : 6
tubes twisted and d., 707 : 21
Drift, adamant for d., 743 : 12
cannot d. beyond His love, 513 : 24
everything begins to d., 865 : 7
Drift (*continued*)
go with d. of things, 747 : 2
not d. or lie at anchor, 519 : 6
of pinions, 693 : 17
outside tent whirling d., 726 : 7
tell you my d., 209 : 14
toward unparalleled catastrophes, 764 : 3
wait and obey, 711 : 3
we know your d., 209 : *n* 3
Drifted in sheepish calm, 893 : 2
leaves d. from me, 778 : 6
on crooked crosses, 777 : 16
Drifting down big still river, 623 : 22
Drifts, all beautiful d. away, 713 : 3
dank yellow d. of leaves, 588 : 5
life at ease d., 601 : 11
Driftwood, scattered d. bleached, 621 : 17
Drill, before steam d. beat me down, 922 : 8
drop of seat on d. ground, 792 : *n* 2
Drink, a little in d., 327 : 9
ale's stuff to d., 691 : 17
and be whole again, 749 : 10
and devil done for rest, 668 : 4
and forget poverty, 26 : 5
as he brews so shall he d., 255 : 7
as oft as ye d. it, 48 : 21
ask a d. divine, 256 : 8
blood to d., 503 : 17
come my lad and d. beer, 353 : 11
dance and d. and sing, 405 : 6
deep or taste not, 332 : 20
divine, 256 : 8
eat d. be merry, 27 : 14, 43 : 19
every creature d. but I, 295 : 8
felony to d. small beer, 185 : 23
five reasons we should d., 315 : 13
follow strong d., 29 : 5
for tomorrow we die, 30 : 2
for your lips to d., 632 : 21
give me to d. mandragora, 240 : 20
goes in wit goes out, 269 : 24
good men eat and d. to live, 79 : 6
herbs to d. smoke thereof, 150 : 17
here and there eat and d., 588 : 7
is d. necessary evil, 722 : 24
it down, 630 : 15
it up, 930 : 16
it with pleasure, 35 : 15
Jesus saith give me to d., 44 : 35
let him d. merrily, 251 : 13
life to the lees, 529 : 7
light is lion comes to d., 767 : 19
man takes d. d. takes man, 646 : 12
many companions for food and d., 67 : 1
meat d. and cloth to us, 158 : 13
more than enough to d., 692 : 15
never taste who always d., 256 : *n* 6
nevermore to d. again, 740 : 6
no longer water, 50 : 33
nor any drop to d., 434 : 15
not d. fruit of the vine, 41 : 10
not meat nor d., 823 : 13
not my design to d., 273 : 1
not the third glass, 268 : 3
not to elevation, 348 : 18
oblivion of a day, 600 : 16
offers drowning dog d., 269 : 14
old wine to d., 179 : 18
one can d. too much, 374 : 18
pawn intelligence to buy d., 828 : 15

Drink (*continued*)
pretty creature, 425 : 3
provokes desire, 238 : 3
Russians' joy to d., 136 : 4
shoulder sky d. ale, 691 : 20
sit and d. with me, 730 : 3
sleep is d. to thirsty, 171 : 1
snake came to d. there, 790 : 12
snowed of mete and d., 146 : 3
stagger but not with strong d., 30 : 16
strive mightily d. as friends, 188 : 29
strong d. is raging, 24 : 27
sweetest d. be sorrow, 735 : *n* 1
taken to d., 729 : 8
think that I can d., 163 : 9
thirsty and ye gave d., 40 : 33
tippled d. more fine, 477 : 16
to general joy of table, 238 : 27
to me only with thine eyes, 256 : 8
to the lass, 399 : 1
today and drown sorrow, 260 : 13
unto him that is ready to perish, 26 : 5
water of gall, 32 : *n* 3
way they eat d. and everything, 752 : 13
when men d. they are rich, 81 : 12
while you live d., 516 : 19
wild anarchy of d., 256 : 19
will not d. with you, 198 : 18
wine of astonishment, 19 : 24
with me and drink as I, 344 : 16
with you in my Father's kingdom, 41 : 10
ye all of it, 41 : 10
Drinker, God be merciful to this d., 137 : 11
Drinkest tears of children, 454 : 18
Drinking, and kept on d., 728 : 20
and Sabbath-breaking, 454 : 21
blude-red wine, 926 : 9
deep of divinest anguish, 562 : 2
eating and d. like brutes, 576 : 16
eating d. breeding, 574 : 20
eating d. dung death, 807 : 10
largely sobers us again, 332 : 20
laws which ran like d. songs, 81 : 11
merry dancing d. time, 306 : 27
much d. little thinking, 322 : 1
my griefs, 195 : 11
not d. but excess, 263 : 15
now is time for d., 107 : 15
poor brains for d., 230 : 17
prescribe rule for d., 326 : 18
since leaving d. of wine, 309 : 20
Son of man came d., 39 : 7
what's d., 462 : 17
with d. fresh and fair, 295 : 7
Drinks and gapes for drink again, 295 : 7
eats d. and plays, 705 : 12
incoming tide, 837 : 2
long time between d., 669 : 12
one never d. enough, 374 : 18
she d. water her keel plows air, 178 : 6
willingly d. their wines, 396 : 16
wine with laughter, 922 : 12
Dripped, from eyelids d. love, 61 : 11
Dripping snow on green grass, 810 : 19
thought came up d., 782 : 3
water hollows stone, 100 : 7
Drips, pain d. by day d. in sleep, 850 : 7
Drive, needs go whom devil d., 161 : 3
Drive (*continued*)
one heat d. out another, 177 : 18
out Nature with a pitchfork, 109 : 4
people difficult to d., 445 : 1
the rapid car, 377 : 26
Drive-In, American Teenage D. Life, 911 : 4
Driven, all d. into same fold, 107 : 19
by love are d. away, 402 : 14
by passion d., 409 : 5
by the spheres, 299 : 6
from every other corner, 365 : 5
leaves dead d. like ghosts, 467 : 17
sickness is d. away, 403 : 13
white as d. snow, 246 : 29
Drives, final Ruin fiercely d., 330 : 18
horses of sun, 661 : 16
my green age, 886 : 12
night along with stars from heaven, 515 : 16
Ruin's plowshare d. elate, 409 : 10
through green fuse d. flower, 886 : 12
where storm d. me I take shelter, 108 : 16
who d. fat oxen, 356 : 30
Driveth, care d. away sleep, 36 : 2
chaff which wind d. away, 17 : 12
Jehu d. furiously, 14 : 18
time d. onward, 528 : 17
Driving, catch the d. gale, 337 : 8
is like the d. of Jehu, 14 : 18
Drizzle, Nashville d., 699 : 16
Dromedary, muse on d. trots, 436 : 5
Drone, frogs d. their lament, 104 : 1
Droned, minister d. monotonously, 622 : 13
Droning, beetle wheels d. flight, 361 : 21
Droop, parted by world and d., 424 : 3
Drooped, great star early d., 576 : 2
Drop but not be dropped by, 356 : 19
created you of sperm d., 131 : 14
drop-scenes d. at once, 717 : 6
every d. drawn by lash, 524 : 7
flood of words d. of reason, 347 : 13
lips of a strange woman d. as honeycomb, 23 : 10
makes it run over, 385 : 17
me deep fathoms down, 572 : 7
merrily did we d., 434 : 7
never d. retourne may, 144 : 3
nor any d. to drink, 434 : 15
not a d. of blood shed, 389 : 13
of a bucket, 30 : 36
of allaying Tiber, 242 : 12
of black blood, 855 : 3
of manly blood, 495 : 19
of sweat on drill ground, 792 : *n* 2
one d. would save my soul, 184 : 8
raineth d. staineth slop, 792 : 8
tears as fast, 232 : 20
tiny d. of thing's essence, 733 : 17
turn on tune in d. out, 897 : 11
Dropped from angel's wing, 429 : 4
from zenith like star, 284 : 2
his tongue d. manna, 284 : 8
my love d. like a flower, 101 : 21
not wish to be d. by, 356 : 19
plates d. from his pocket, 241 : 25
Recording Angel d. tear, 360 : 17
things bound to sink, 798 : 13
Droppeth as gentle rain, 200 : 9
Dropping buckets into empty wells, 376 : 27
Dropping (*continued*)
contentions of a wife are continual d., 24 : 25
down ladder rung by rung, 708 : 15
down with bales, 529 : 24
one d. eye, 217 : 29
pearls and vermin, 489 : 8
ships d. from clouds, 345 : 8
Drops, begotten d. of dew, 16 : 32
blue-fringed lids, 435 : 16
earliest to ground, 200 : 6
into poetry, 549 : 30
kindred d. been mingled, 376 : 19
little d. of light, 276 : 4
little d. of water, 591 : 7
number the d. of rain, 34 : 21
of water hollow out stone, 100 : *n* 4
on gate bars hang in row, 642 : 6
sliding from oar, 873 : 16
that visit heart, 215 : 23
Drop-scenes, all d. drop at once, 717 : 6
Dropsical, he's d. she sore-eyed, 663 : *n* 1
Dross, rest is d., 793 : 3
stoops not to show of d., 199 : 9
what gods call d., 568 : 18
Drought, careful in the year of d., 32 : 11
dust and d. of plain, 852 : 14
of March perced to roote, 145 : 12
rain snow hail d., 622 : 19
Drouthy, ancient trusty d. crony, 411 : 6
Drove out the man, 7 : 13
them out of temple, 44 : 29
to tumult in clouds, 714 : 1
Drown, before my tears did d. it, 268 : 21
drink today and d. sorrow, 260 : 13
I'll d. my book, 248 : 15
neither can floods d. it, 28 : 24
tears shall d. the wind, 236 : 24
wake us and we d., 804 : 1
what pain it was to d., 187 : 9
Drownded now and again, 735 : 5
Drowned, bodies of lovers d., 770 : 12
ceremony of innocence d., 714 : 12
dreams, 571 : 3
glory in shallow cup, 517 : 10
in break of spring, 897 : 13
into Mississippi and d., 840 : 5
jail with chance of being d., 354 : 6
not afraid of sea will be d., 735 : 5
now and again, 735 : 5
oceans d., 830 : 2
pluck up d. honor, 203 : 15
plunged into fountain and d., 570 : 4
the cocks, 233 : 24
with us in endless night, 266 : 21
Drowning, no d. mark upon him, 247 : 7
not waving but d., 856 : 16
offers d. dog drink, 269 : 14
Drowns, coughing d. parson's saw, 191 : 15
in Pharisees' hypocrisy, 816 : 18
third d. him, 213 : 16
Drowsed with fume of poppies, 477 : 18
Drowsiness shall clothe a man with rags, 25 : 9
Drowsy, beetle with his d. hums, 238 : 20
dull ear of d. man, 202 : 1
ear of night, 456 : 20
keep d. emperor awake, 715 : 3
makes heaven d. with harmony, 191 : 4

Drowsy (*continued*)
numbness pains, 476 : 21
syrups of world, 231 : 8
tinklings lull, 361 : 21
who d. at that hour, 275 : 14
Drowsyhead, land of d., 345 : 20
Drudge, harmless d., 352 : 11
Drudgery, makes d. divine, 269 : 8
Drug it's the fashion to abuse, 630 : 10
which takes away grief and passion, 59 : 25
Drugs, true apothecary thy d. quick, 193 : 29
Druids, stand like D. of old, 510 : 26
Drum, bang the d. slowly, 927 : *n* 2
beat d. slowly, 927 : 15
clamor of fife and d., 598 : 15
dumb as d. vith hole, 546 : 20
frenzied d., 714 : 14
homely fife and d., 864 : 10
not a d. was heard, 465 : 7
on your drums, 761 : 11
pulpit d. ecclesiastic, 290 : 14
rumble of distant d., 516 : 8
spirit-stirring d., 231 : 11
take my d. to England, 700 : 8
them up the Channel, 700 : 8
war d. throbbed no longer, 530 : 1
Drumbeat, morning d. circles earth, 451 : 2
of St. Stephen's, 892 : 4
Drumcliff churchyard, 718 : 1
Drummed, as we d. them long ago, 700 : 8
Drummer, different d., 560 : 17
Drum's discordant sound, 375 : 4
Drums and tramplings of three conquests, 275 : 3
drum on your d., 761 : 11
hearts like muffled d., 509 : 14
ruffle of d., 676 : *n* 5
rum-tumming everywhere, 759 : 7
sound trumpet beat d., 346 : 7
sound trumpets beat d., 306 : 14
with d. and guns, 921 : 1
Drunk, accustomed to deliberate when d., 78 : 6
all learned all d., 377 : 9
and asleep in boots, 767 : 1
dead d. judge, 881 : 11
delight of battle, 529 : 8
gloriously d., 377 : 10
hasten to be d., 307 : 8
hath not d. ink, 190 : 27
hearts d. with beauty, 720 : 10
hemlock I had d., 476 : 21
hydroptic earth hath d., 252 : 25
I feel d. all the time, 879 : 13
is he who prostrate lies, 455 : 1
milk of Paradise, 433 : 27
not d. who can rise, 455 : 1
pleasure to be d., 349 : 5
queen be d. as we, 349 : 5
stag d. his fill, 431 : 5
what potions have I d., 245 : 19
with fire, 412 : 9
your water and wine, 707 : 3
Drunkard and glutton shall come to poverty, 25 : 9
cannot meet cork, 607 : 14
fame like a d., 876 : 10
town d., 847 : 13
Drunkard's eye, 716 : 4
Drunkards, fools d. and United States, 924 : 7
liars and adulterers, 233 : 5
where notorious d. laid, 640 : 19
Drunken, Antony brought d. forth, 241 : 27
but not with wine, 30 : 16
dog ragged head, 441 : 6
of things Lethean, 633 : 6
private of Buffs, 536 : 7
sailor on a mast, 187 : 15
stagger like a d. man, 21 : 16
the dregs, 31 : 10
what shall we do with d. sailor, 934 : 18
Drunkenness, babbling d., 214 : 26
degrees of d., 491 : 22
is sepulture of wit, 148 : 1
not in rioting and d., 47 : 29
Drury, lives in D. Lane, 933 : 8
Dry, air thoroughly small and d., 805 : 21
aromatic odor, 739 : 5
before my sighs did d. it, 268 : 21
blowing of d. dust, 792 : 19
bones hear word of Lord, 32 : 30
bread d. as paper, 793 : 1
cold hot moist and d., 305 : 9
desert of a thousand lines, 339 : 24
die a d. death, 247 : 9
driftwood bleached and d., 621 : 17
eyes and laugh at fall, 542 : 12
good wine a friend or being d., 315 : 13
hand yellow cheek, 205 : 28
heart d. of blood, 478 : 8
hearts d. as summer dust, 428 : 11
his hands formed the d. land, 20 : 20
hot cold moist and d., 284 : 27
in a d. and thirsty land, 19 : 29
in the d. places, 877 : 15
into d. Martini, 812 : 4
into the sea upon d. ground, 9 : 31
keep powder d., 444 : 12
never miss water till well d., 347 : *n* 5
O ye d. bones, 32 : 30
old man in d. month, 804 : 13
prepared the d. land, 54 : 17
rivers of water in a d. place, 30 : 21
smooth-shaven green, 278 : 18
stone no sound of water, 805 : 1
stood firm on d. ground, 11 : 29
sun dry wind, 159 : *n* 2
valley of d. bones, 32 : 28
volumes of ethics, 387 : 7
wet eye d. heart, 722 : 8
what shall be done in the d., 44 : 5
when the well's d., 347 : 25
wrung life d., 632 : 21
Dryad, light-winged d., 476 : 22
Dryden aggravated dissociation, 809 : 8
copious D., 339 : 27
Dryer, smaller and d. than will, 805 : 21
Drying after bracing showers, 834 : 8
Du bist wie eine Blume, 481 : *n* 8
Dubuque, old lady from D., 824 : 2
Ducat, dead for a d. dead, 222 : 29
Ducats, my daughter O my d., 199 : 11
Duchess, arms of chambermaid as d., 356 : 8
my last D., 540 : 22
said D. in hoarse growl, 611 : 13
tut tut said D., 612 : 2
Duck, born in d. yard, 505 : 8
hold-fast the only dog my d., 207 : 15
saw a little d., 933 : 12
Ducks and drakes with shillings, 177 : 15
four d. on pond, 594 : 3
wild d. plunging to bottom, 600 : 1
Due, custom to whom custom d., 47 : 27
fear to whom fear d., 47 : 27
give devil his d., 168 : 23
honor to whom honor d., 47 : 27
meat in d. season, 21 : 11
process of law, 391 : 17, 392 : 4
see that none is d., 604 : 8
that you may have d., 323 : 1
to be crowned again, 790 : 13
tribute to whom tribute d., 47 : 27
word spoken in d. season, 24 : 9
Dues, render to all their d., 47 : 27
Duke, bury the Great D., 533 : 1
everybody praised the d., 439 : 14
keep your coin, 900 : 4
marquis d. and a' that, 411 : 18
of Plaza Toro, 630 : 1
Dukedom, library d. large enough, 247 : 13
prize above my d., 247 : 15
Dulce et decorum est, 107 : *n* 23
non d. non et decor, 792 : 14
Dulces moriens reminiscitur Argos, 106 : *n* 3
Dulcet and harmonious breath, 196 : 14
Dulcimer, damsel with d., 433 : 26
Dulcis, me d. alebat Parthenope, 104 : *n* 6
Dull, age d. and mean, 513 : 12
business not make d., 584 : 8
care, 919 : 4
cold ear of death, 362 : 5
conform and be d., 803 : 6
creep in one d. line, 333 : 7
dark soundless day, 525 : 19
ear of drowsy man, 202 : 1
fighter and keen guest, 204 : 36
how d. to pause, 529 : 9
in Fleet Street, 441 : 8
man always sure, 772 : 5
moon talk d., 623 : 16
motions of his spirit d., 201 : 3
my days d. and hoary, 299 : 8
narcotics numbing pain, 531 : 21
not all books d. as readers, 559 : 33
not only d. himself, 356 : 28
opiate to drains, 476 : 21
ought to be d. sometimes, 326 : 15
piercing night's d. ear, 208 : 1
privations and lean emptiness, 253 : 1
prospect of distant good, 305 : 25
rich d. and drank, 845 : 7
roots with spring rain, 804 : 26
sherry is d., 354 : 14
sleep in d. cold marble, 249 : 6
so d. so dead in look, 205 : 19
spur my d. revenge, 223 : 17
stale tired bed, 233 : 3
stirring d. roots, 804 : 26
sublunary lovers' love, 253 : 3
though gentle yet not d., 294 : 19
venerably d., 375 : 7
were all we taste, 829 : 20
without single absurdity, 369 : 6
would he be of soul, 425 : 13
Dullard, George Third honest d., 673 : 1
Duller than fat weed, 219 : 19

Dull-eyed melancholy, 243 : 12
Dullness, cause of d. in others, 356 : 28
correcting of d. and rawness, 600 : 22
eat not to d., 348 : 18
gentle D. loves joke, 340 : 19
never swept into d., 718 : 6
of fool whetstone of wits, 210 : 12
Dulls edge of husbandry, 219 : 2
Duly and daily serving him, 365 : 13
Dum anima est spes est, 98 : *n* 12
Dumb and silent be led, 379 : 6
as drum vith hole, 546 : 20
beggar that is d., 172 : 13
charge once more be d., 588 : 3
dead and d. and done, 740 : 6
death, 829 : 20
excellent d. discourse, 248 : 11
great griefs d., 115 : 15
in havens d., 655 : 17
inscrutable grand, 588 : 4
justice blind deaf d., 722 : 1
lips are d., 528 : 17
listen ye nations be d., 475 : 8
muffled and d., 495 : 5
noisy bells be d., 691 : 4
one rational voice d., 868 : 15
Oracles are d., 277 : 10
orators d. when beauty pleadeth, 189 : 22
sense of what life means, 650 : 7
shallow murmur but deep are d., 172 : 12
to d. forgetfulness a prey, 362 : 14
to tell crooked rose, 886 : 12
tongue of the d. shall sing, 30 : 24
Dumbly, humbly d., 778 : 6
Dumbshows, inexplicable d., 221 : 23
Dumpling, diddle diddle d., 933 : 1
hell idea born on undigested d., 570 : 9
Dumps, doleful d. mind oppress, 188 : *n* 2, 917 : 17
these dreary d., 188 : 19
Dumpy, hate a d. woman, 460 : 12
Dun, her breasts are d., 246 : 1
Duncan, fatal entrance of D., 236 : 17
hath borne his faculties, 236 : 24
hear it not D., 237 : 16
is in his grave, 238 : 19
Dunce kept at home, 375 : 24
sent to roam, 375 : 24
with wits, 340 : 23
Dunces, wit with d., 340 : 23
Dundee, bonnets of Bonny D., 432 : 15
single hour of that D., 426 : 9
Dunes, soar into air above d., 835 : 1
Dunfermline town, 926 : 9
Dung and death, 807 : 10
Dungeon, live upon vapor of d., 231 : 6
my body my d. is, 668 : 21
scourged to his d., 471 : 6
so dark as own heart, 503 : 19
Dunghill, cock has great influence on own d., 111 : 5
sun shineth upon d., 86 : *n* 7
Dunsinane, Birnam wood to D., 239 : 12, 765 : 10
Dunstable, Miss D. curls pass muster, 554 : 11
Dupe, man d. deceiver decay, 467 : 9
mind is d. of heart, 293 : 19
Duplicate, atom on matter d. in mind, 570 : 15
Duplicates, mob of unnecessary d., 571 : 2
Durability, territory of certain d., 522 : 10
Durable, make recollection d., 348 : 17
northern thought slow d., 542 : 20
odors of ointments more d., 180 : 11
true love a d. fire, 172 : 9
Durance vile, 411 : 23
Duration, not deduct from d. of death, 101 : 5
Dürer in a town like this, 798 : 7
Durst defy the Omnipotent, 283 : 4
Dusk, breezes d. and shiver, 528 : 24
bumps along the d., 665 : 7
each slow d., 827 : 5
faces with silken turbans, 288 : 11
out of d. shadow, 660 : 10
skin like d. on horizon, 831 : 13
stars in purple d., 811 : 13
thwarted by d., 799 : 8
Dusky night rides down sky, 349 : 10
rear my d. race, 530 : 6
trusty d. vivid true, 669 : 8
Dust and drought of plain, 852 : 14
and reek of towns, 569 : 20
and silence of shelf, 487 : 8
and soot of complaints, 664 : 18
as chimney sweepers come to d., 243 : 27
as d. that drives, 663 : 9
as we are, 423 : 18
ashes am I and d., 135 : 7
blossom in the d., 272 : 13
blowing of dry d., 792 : 19
bones are d., 436 : 4
cinders ashes d., 476 : 5
cleft d. never English d., 840 : 5
created you of d., 131 : 14
darkness fruit there of d., 632 : 15
drawing near to dust, 705 : 4
earth and grave and d., 173 : 5
equal but in d., 255 : 5
even while d. moves, 807 : 8
excuse my d., 827 : 17
farther from God nearer d., 806 : 15
forbear to dig d. enclosed here, 250 : 1
formed man of d. of the ground, 6 : 17
guilty of d. and sin, 269 : 9
handful of d., 805 : 1
hath closed Helen's eye, 250 : 10
heap called history, 666 : 8
heap of d. alone remains, 335 : 11
hear her and beat, 533 : 25
hearts dry as summer d., 428 : 11
I shall lie in the d., 59 : 1
if as they say some d., 748 : 15
if man is d., 886 : 7
in air suspended, 808 : 11
in the d. the cool tombs, 761 : 8
into d. and under d., 516 : 15
intruder in d., 838 : 7
kicks d., 559 : 16
lay mightily in whirl of d., 58 : 26
lick the d., 20 : 1
light in d. lies, 470 : 1
limns on water writes in d., 181 : 18
love reachest but to d., 176 : 9
make d. of all things, 275 : 4
make d. our paper, 195 : 1
maniac scattering d., 532 : 6
manic d. of my friends, 864 : 13
marry my body to that d., 267 : 6
Dust (*continued*)
mouth filled with d., 255 : 5
much learned d., 376 : 26
mysteries beyond thy d., 299 : 9
name not perish in d., 440 : 7
noble d. of Alexander, 224 : 15
not without d. and heat, 282 : 1
of creeds outworn, 467 : 2
of glittering grains, 928 : 20
of snow, 748 : 3
of systems and creeds, 527 : 22
on marble pavement d. grows, 97 : 10
pays us with age and d., 173 : 5
plummets to d. of hope, 74 : 3
pride that licks the d., 339 : 3
proud and angry d., 691 : 20
quaint honor turn to d., 297 : 1
quintessence of d., 220 : 29
rain in d. on her shoulders, 822 : 4
return to the earth, 27 : 25
returneth to d. again, 614 : 17
seemed to be local d. cloud, 885 : 7
shake off d. of your feet, 38 : 35
shalt thou eat, 7 : 9
silent d., 362 : 5
small d. of the balance, 30 : 36
so nigh grandeur to d., 494 : 21
tear o'er English d., 489 : 3
that is a little gilt, 226 : 21
that is blown away, 34 : 16
this d. once the man, 576 : 8
this quiet d., 606 : 7
thou art to dust returneth, 509 : 13
thou art unto dust return, 7 : 12
thrown in my eyes, 748 : 15
to dust, 56 : 13
toy dog covered with d., 666 : 17
unto d. return, 7 : 12
valiant d., 209 : 6
vile d. whence he sprung, 430 : 10
was gentlemen and ladies, 606 : 7
we are but d. and shadow, 108 : 12
we too into d. descend, 516 : 15
weighed me d. by d., 607 : 17
what a d. I raise, 472 : 15
what is pomp but earth and d., 186 : 21
with d. is dark and dim, 424 : *n* 2
write good in d., 155 : 8
you are not worth the d., 234 : 22
you've long been d., 93 : 1
Dustbin with sunlight, 812 : 9
Duster, tomorrow feather d., 740 : 7
Dustman, Golden D., 549 : 31
Dusty answer, 600 : 20
cobweb-covered maimed, 620 : 3
eat d. bread, 836 : 20
grated to d. nothing, 226 : 15
hit the d. trail, 764 : 11
purlieus of law, 532 : 18
road long and d. to grave, 667 : 14
way to d. death, 240 : 4
Dutch, beat the D., 920 : 16
fault of the D., 422 : 6
Dutchman in Eden would plant it, 561 : 13
see Flying D., 659 : 4
Dutchman's, icicle on D. beard, 214 : 18
Duties, brace ourselves to d., 744 : 4
halve rights double d., 463 : 2
live without d. obscene, 500 : 7
new occasions new d., 567 : 8
property has d., 501 : 19

Duty, astray from d. and
interest, 379 : 12
better one's own d., 94 : 11
book you read from d., 354 : *n* 5
brave man inattentive to d., 419 : 1
cannot exist without faith, 501 : 24
daily stage of d. run, 311 : 18
dare do d. as we understand
it, 521 : 5
dead then my d. ended, 656 : 7
devoting himself to d., 299 : 11
discussing d. to God, 574 : 24
divided d., 229 : 32
do d. in all things, 509 : 9
do your d., 275 : 19
doing d. unfitted one for anything
else, 701 : 3
done my d. and no more, 349 : 6
essence of judicial d., 402 : 3
expects every man to do d., 408 : 8
fight required of d., 94 : 9
gratifying d. done, 630 : 6
knowledge of their d., 81 : 5
laid on me a sinner, 486 : 10
lies in what is near, 89 : 11
limping with d., 90 : 7
lively sense of filial d., 387 : 7
love is then our d., 332 : 4
my d. to obey orders, 594 : 9
neatness a d., 346 : 11
no concern with d. or truth, 527 : 14
nor law nor d. bade fight, 714 : 1
not to be silent, 598 : 15
of being happy, 667 : 23
of judicial department, 402 : 3
of younger Negro artist, 854 : 11
out of d. cheat others, 734 : 8
path of d. way to glory, 533 : 5
performed or duty violated, 450 : 20
picket's off d. forever, 598 : *n* 3
possession implies d., 752 : 3
public d., 590 : 1
rule of joy and d. one, 644 : 5
sacred d. to myself, 599 : 12
seen d. and done it, 923 : 17
sense of d. pursues us, 450 : 20
some sense of d., 531 : 15
stern daughter of voice of
God, 427 : 12
subject's d. is king's, 208 : 5
sublimest word, 509 : 9
such d. as subject owes, 189 : 6
thank God I have done d., 408 : 9
to love those who wrong him, 125 : 10
to my country to love it, 725 : 20
transforms obedience into d., 358 : 13
trespasses against d., 372 : 7
we owe Creator, 383 : 6
which lies nearest, 473 : 8
whispers low, 494 : 21
whole d. of man, 27 : 27
woke found life d., 555 : 23
Duty's, constabulary d. to be
done, 628 : 3
faithful child, 484 : 9
Dux femina facti, 104 : *n* 12
O vitae philosophia d., 98 : *n* 16
vitae animus est, 103 : *n* 1
Dwarf on shoulders of giant, 258 : 7
sees farther than giant, 118 : *n* 6
Dwarfed and abased below, 671 : *n* 1
Dwarfish thief, 239 : 28
whole, 435 : 24
Dwell a weeping hermit, 364 : 9
Dwell (*continued*)
at ease for aye d., 528 : 6
better to d. in a corner, 24 : 33
critic d. on excellencies, 326 : 19
heart place devils d. in, 274 : 15
house we d. in every day, 607 : 16
in house of the Lord, 18 : 7
in midst of people of unclean
lips, 29 : 10
in our crowded hearts, 902 : 16
in the tents of wickedness, 20 : 8
in the uttermost parts of the
sea, 22 : 17
not d. in temples, 300 : 20
nothing ill d. in such a
temple, 247 : 24
on heights of mankind, 413 : 25
peace and rest never d., 283 : 7
shall I like a hermit d., 172 : 17
such as d. in tents, 7 : 21
to perdition there to d., 283 : 4
together in unity, 22 : 14
two souls d. in my breast, 396 : 12
where Israfel, 525 : 10
who shall d. in thy holy hill, 17 : 22
with vilest worms to d., 244 : 26
world and they that d. therein, 18 : 8
Dwelled, Abram d. in Canaan, 8 : 7
Lot d. in the cities, 8 : 7
Dwellers by the sea, 672 : 20
sur la branche, 725 : 18
Dwelleth in the secret place, 20 : 16
not in temples, 46 : 16
Dwellin', fair maid d., 926 : 21
Dwelling, desert my d. place, 458 : 23
much on right, 311 : 15
of the blest, 105 : 21
single soul d. in two bodies, 87 : 1
thou hast been our d. place, 20 : 11
Venus here choose d., 306 : 6
whose d. is light of suns, 423 : 13
Dwells, in me d. no greatness, 534 : 13
loving Father surely d., 412 : 10
unwitting where Master d., 760 : 21
water d. in lowly places, 64 : 3
wherever Roman conquers he
d., 115 : 8
with beauty, 477 : 23
with gods above, 226 : 14
Dwelt among untrodden ways, 424 : 12
by the brook Cherith, 13 : 40
child who d. upon tract, 428 : 15
in marble halls, 480 : 11
Judah and Israel d. safely, 13 : 29
like star and d. apart, 425 : 23
too long have d. on thee, 252 : 23
unerring wisdom never d., 311 : 9
where Israfel d., 525 : 10
Word d. among us, 44 : 21
Dwindle, days d. down, 802 : 3
peak and pine, 236 : 3
Dwindles, man only growth that
d., 368 : 17
Dyer's hand, 245 : 17
Dyes, mingled with gorgeous
d., 474 : 18
Dyin', young man you're d., 926 : 22
Dying and in despair, 602 : 11
at my d. hour, 697 : 3
behold you again in d., 669 : 9
between birth and d., 806 : 5
bless hand that gave blow, 304 : 20
bliss of d., 333 : 23
born by d. and being damned, 156 : 8
Dying (*continued*)
but fighting back, 819 : 7
come from d. moon, 530 : 25
day sir, 920 : 6
despised and d. king, 468 : 4
dirge of d. year, 467 : 19
doubly d., 430 : 10
dreams of his Argos, 106 : 5
echoes d. d. d., 530 : 26
Egypt d., 241 : 21
eyes were closed, 335 : 10
fall, 213 : 7
fastened to d. animal, 715 : 2
flute in d. notes, 305 : 12
forgets d. bird, 385 : 1
generations, 714 : 22
green and d., 887 : 3
has made us rarer gifts, 797 : 4
himself and his d., 913 : 6
I am d. Egypt d., 241 : 21
in Algiers, 514 : 10
in d. we are born, 138 : 15
is a trifle, 606 : 15
is art I do it well, 911 : 11
light dies with d. sun, 670 : 8
live as you will wish when d., 360 : 28
lives and unborn smiles, 880 : 4
living indisposeth for d., 275 : 6
man to dying men, 294 : 17
men enforce attention, 194 : 9
more survivors' affair, 755 : 16
multifold, 606 : 15
nearly d. at Boulder, 892 : 12
no more d. then, 246 : 5
not death but d. is terrible, 349 : 26
not d. for faith hard, 539 : 16
not grasp thought of d., 602 : 11
of cold, 705 : 21
of thirst by the fountain, 148 : 21
on log expiring frog, 546 : 14
rage against d. of light, 887 : 4
separate d. ember, 526 : 11
so great an experiment as d., 275 : 32
stay d. here all night, 399 : 10
to be afraid of thee, 606 : 9
tomorrow will be d., 266 : 11
truth on lips of d., 586 : 7
unconscionable time d., 302 : 23
we are d. we are d., 791 : 3
we live, 545 : 24
whether living is d., 82 : 21
who's d., 849 : 19
wine near my d. mouth, 137 : 1
yet fancy ourselves eternal, 128 : 13
young man you're d., 926 : 22
Dynamo, starry d., 906 : 1
Dynasties, carved new d., 779 : 16
go onward though d. pass, 642 : 2
Dyspepsias, hereditary d., 570 : 9
Dyspepsy ruin of most things, 454 : 20

E

E equals mc², 763 : 5
white E red I, 673 : 20
E pur si muove, 183 : *n* 3
Each bears his own Hell, 105 : 23
from e. according to abilities, 563 : 1
hath one and is one, 251 : 15
is a universe, 879 : 17
man for hymself, 146 : 17
of us aspires to goodness, 171 : 19

Each (*continued*)
one's himself yet everyone, 874 : 3
singing e. to e., 803 : 19
slow dusk, 827 : 5
to e. according to needs, 563 : 1
Each-form, pluralism lets exist in e., 650 : 12
Eager, don't be e., 401 : 1
keep guest back who is e., 60 : 19
mount e. and quick, 896 : 13
soul biting for anger, 276 : 15
Eagle and me, 842 : 7
bald e. not chosen, 348 : 13
by all the e. in thee, 292 : 16
called e. bearer down, 474 : 18
does the e. know, 403 : 17
fly as e. toward heaven, 25 : 7
fly like e. wings of wren, 646 : 3
forgotten, 765 : 3
fourth beast like flying e., 53 : 7
from e. in his flight, 510 : 17
has landed, 910 : 13
I hear E. bird, 928 : 9
in a dovecote, 242 : 26
in and out the E., 922 : 1
like sick e., 478 : 7
looking at the sky, 478 : 7
mewing her mighty youth, 282 : 3
mount up at thy command, 17 : 1
of house of Austria, 383 : 16
of the rock, 793 : 18
old man's e. mind, 717 : 11
or the snake, 708 : 22
stretched on plain, 456 : 17
suffers little birds to sing, 188 : 21
Tom Jones outlive imperial e., 383 : 16
way of an e. in the air, 26 : 4
with e. eyes, 475 : 7
Eagle's fate and mine are one, 66 : *n* 10
feathered with e. plumes, 66 : 24
Eagles, baited like e., 204 : 30
mount up with wings as e., 31 : 2
of Ngong look out, 789 : 10
prey where e. dare not perch, 187 : 5
swifter than e., 13 : 9
where carcass is e. gather, 40 : 24
Ear and eye expected impossible, 715 : 4
and to my listening e., 428 : *n* 5
as mind pitched e. pleased, 377 : 13
bow down thine e., 24 : 37
came o'er my e. like sweet sound, 213 : 7
charms or e. or sight, 436 : 1
deaf adder that stoppeth her e., 19 : 23
death twitches my e., 106 : 9
drowsy e. of night, 456 : 20
dull cold e. of death, 362 : 5
dull e. of drowsy man, 202 : 1
first blade then e., 42 : 1
flattery lost on poet's e., 430 : 7
flea in mine e., 158 : 3
for verbal delicacies, 771 : 15
give every man thy e., 219 : 1
hang pearl in cowslip's e., 196 : 11
heard of thee by hearing of the e., 17 : 10
hearing e. seeing eye, 24 : 29
I have no e., 441 : 20
I was all e., 279 : 27
I will enchant thine e., 189 : 7
in Adam's e. left voice, 287 : 2
Ear (*continued*)
in one e. out other, 144 : *n* 10
incline thine e., 30 : 27
jest's prosperity lies in e., 191 : 12
keep word of promise to our e., 240 : 9
mighty world of eye and e., 423 : 14
more meant than meets e., 278 : 24
never e. did hear that tongue, 184 : 14
nor e. heard, 48 : 2
nor the e. filled with hearing, 26 : 13
of jealousy heareth all, 34 : 9
of man hath not seen, 197 : 10
one e. herde at tothir out, 144 : 25
open vowels tire, 333 : 7
piercing night's dull e., 208 : 1
reasonable good e. in music, 197 : 4
rich jewel in Ethiop's e., 191 : 26
short a cheekbone and e., 579 : *n* 1
soothe thine e., 364 : 11
sweetness through mine e., 278 : 26
to my e. morning brings, 494 : 16
toad at e. of Eve, 286 : 6
unpleasing to a married e., 191 : 13
whorled e. 655 : 18
won the e. of Pluto, 278 : 8
wood has a sharp e., 146 : *n* 5
wrong sow by e., 161 : 10
'Ear my 'erse's legs, 535 : 7
Earl, slain E. of Murray, 927 : 6
Earlier and other creation, 808 : 2
later times more aged than e., 178 : *n* 12
Earliest, charm of e. birds, 285 : 27
drop e. to ground, 200 : 6
Earls, daughter of hundred e., 528 : 7
Early and latter rain, 52 : 4
bright transient chaste, 307 : *n* 3
call me e. mother, 528 : 12
falls e. or too late, 260 : 17
git up e. to take in God, 567 : 21
God helps those who get up e., 935 : 9
good die e. bad late, 318 : 12
had it been e. had been kind, 353 : 26
happy those e. days, 299 : 2
in the morning, 934 : 18
late and e. pray, 250 : 15
leaves fall e., 792 : 9
let e. education be amusement, 85 : 1
nipped my flower sae e., 410 : 19
not rise e. never do good, 353 : 7
those that seek me e., 23 : 17
to bed early to rise, 347 : 12
to rise early to bed, 831 : 8
too e. seen unknown, 191 : 27
vote e. and often, 590 : 12
Early-born, dawn the e., 57 : 11
Earn, I e. that I eat, 212 : 2
little to e., 566 : 9
living by sweat, 559 : 14
set to e. livings, 690 : 13
you e. bread I'll eat, 520 : 8
Earned, hearts are e., 714 : 17
night's repose, 510 : 9
with sweat of brows, 168 : 9
Earnest about these objects, 791 : 6
between jest and e., 169 : 19
frogs die in e., 92 : 9
in seeking knowledge, 68 : 22
intermingle jest with e., 181 : 3
life e. art gay, 413 : 6
life real life e., 509 : 13
stars, 478 : 4
Earnest (*continued*)
those who are really in e., 577 : 17
'twixt e. and joke, 404 : *n* 4
Earnestness, sincerity e. and kindness, 69 : 19
Earning, first consideration e. living, 312 : 21
Earnings, division of unequal e., 449 : 4
labor of F. poured e., 592 : 10
Earns, each e. his death, 849 : 22
whate'er he can, 510 : 8
Ear-piercing fife, 231 : 11
Ears, belly has no e., 95 : 9
blast of war in e., 207 : 16
bring to our e. clash of arms, 383 : 5
compliments reaching proper e., 707 : 8
earth has stopped e., 691 : 3
give your e., 6 : 2
got a wolf by the e., 97 : 3
have e. and hear not, 31 : 34
have e. but hear not, 21 : 22
have heard Holy Word, 405 : 1
having e. hear not, 383 : 1
he that hath e., 39 : 6
hearing with sharper e., 899 : 17
hum about mine e., 248 : 10
I have e. in vain, 476 : 28
lend me your e., 216 : 17
let music creep in our e., 201 : 1
look with thine e., 235 : 2
my e. hum, 63 : 5
noise of waters in my e., 187 : 9
of people attentive unto law, 14 : 30
of the deaf shall be unstopped, 30 : 24
of the old cur, 291 : 11
only for what experience gives access, 658 : 26
porches of mine e., 219 : 23
seven empty e., 8 : 31
seven good e., 8 : 31
she gave me e., 425 : 5
shout about my e., 742 : 17
small pitchers have wide e., 160 : 30
softest music to attending e., 192 : 17
sound lifts me by e., 557 : 6
speech delighteth the e., 36 : 18
split e. of groundlings, 221 : 23
tail and pointed e., 515 : 8
to hear, 39 : 6
trust e. less than eyes, 78 : 3
walls have e., 146 : *n* 5
with ravished e., 306 : 13
wode hath e., 146 : 20
woods have e., 146 : *n* 5
word of earth in e. of world, 634 : 7
Earth, a little e. whereon to grow, 408 : 11
a meaning to us, 822 : 10
abideth forever, 26 : 11
after e. stopped ears, 691 : 3
all Danaë to stars, 531 : 12
all e. forgot, 447 : 3
all e. o'erwhelm them, 218 : 26
all the corners of e., 54 : 17
all things in e., 50 : 9
all ye know on e., 477 : 11
alone on e. as I am now, 457 : 10
always in e. and air, 874 : 10
and every common sight, 426 : 10
and fire and sea and air, 643 : 2
and grave and dust, 173 : 5
and heaven ring, 733 : 5
and high heaven, 691 : 10

Earth (*continued*)
and water strive again, 334 : 15
angels bending near e., 537 : 16
as showers that water the e., 19 : 35
astonishing thing about e., 884 : 1
axis of e. sticks out, 519 : 12
barren as moon, 760 : 9
beat e. with unfettered foot, 107 : 15
beauty for e. too dear, 191 : 26
belongs to living, 389 : 7
best of men that e'er wore e., 251 : 11
bleeding piece of e., 216 : 11
blessed are peacemakers on e., 185 : 11
bodies thrown into e., 850 : 11
brave of all the e., 700 : 6
bridal of e. and sky, 268 : 15
brightens when you dawn, 5 : 6
bringeth forth fruit, 42 : 1
by me created, 641 : 16
call heaven and e. to witness, 11 : 8
call to e. and sea, 574 : 19
center of my sinful e., 246 : 4
change she e. or sky, 918 : 15
cloud enveloping the e., 435 : 27
cold in the e., 562 : 1
combined essences of heaven and e., 97 : 7
confound all unity on e., 239 : 19
confound the language of all e., 8 : 5
covenant between me and the e., 8 : 3
cradle of hope, 761 : 16
crawling between heaven and e., 221 : 16
dashed to e. plowed under, 929 : 1
daughter of E. and Water, 468 : 10
days on the e. are as a shadow, 14 : 27
deep places of the e., 20 : 20
deep-delved e., 476 : 23
demi-Atlas of this e., 240 : 22
did quake, 41 : 28
dim spot men call e., 279 : 3
dust shall return to e., 27 : 25
element of e., 794 : 9
embroil e. about line, 311 : 15
ends of the e., 707 : 16
English e. as much, 710 : 15
every living thing that moveth upon e., 6 : 15
every other creature on e., 394 : 16
exponent of e., 606 : 11
fall to the base e., 194 : 24
false as sandy e., 226 : 15
fell to e. knew not where, 510 : 24
fell upon the e., 34 : 18
felt the wound, 287 : 19
get away from e. awhile, 747 : 16
giants in the e., 7 : 27
girdle round about e., 196 : 16
glance from heaven to e., 197 : 12
glory from the e., 426 : 12
God created heaven and e., 6 : 10
God light of heavens and e., 131 : 16
goddess Demeter or E., 77 : 6
goes over to squall of time, 822 : 7
going the way of all the e., 11 : 36
going to and fro in the e., 15 : 2
great society on e., 424 : 6
handful of e. stops mouths, 482 : 7
has not anything to show, 425 : 13
hath bubbles, 236 : 7
hear word of the Lord, 32 : 15
heard in dread, 365 : 6

Earth (*continued*)
heaven and e. pass away, 40 : 26, 430 : 12
heaven and e. to witness, 11 : 8
heaven like egg e. like yolk, 123 : 16
heaven on e., 285 : 15
hell on e., 680 : 16
help of any thing on e., 407 : 3
holy E. giver of life, 76 : 25
holy Mother E., 71 : 2
Holy Mother E., 928 : 10
hurt not the e., 53 : 13
hydroptic e. hath drunk, 252 : 25
I am part of e., 790 : 21
I have come back to e., 674 : 8
I will move the e., 93 : 5
if e. be shadow of heaven, 286 : 21
in ashes burning, 139 : 4
in darkness as if in death, 5 : 5
in earthy bed, 533 : 25
in universal law, 530 : 2
indifferent children of e., 220 : 23
introduction into e. of life, 482 : 12
is full of his glory, 29 : 9
is full of thy riches, 21 : 11
is my mother, 419 : 10
is the Lord's, 18 : 8, 48 : 18
kindly e. slumber, 530 : 2
kindly fruits of the e., 55 : 14
kings and counselors of e., 15 : 8
kiss heaven gives the e., 273 : 13
ladder set up on the e., 8 : 19
lap of e., 362 : 17
lards the lean e., 203 : 21
last best hope of e., 522 : 12
lay her in the e., 224 : 17
learned on e. practice in heaven, 542 : 5
left souls on e., 477 : 15
less of e. than heaven, 431 : 10
let all the e. keep silence, 33 : 27
let go hold of e., 839 : 13
let loose to play upon e., 282 : 5
let new e. rise, 888 : 6
let the e. rejoice, 21 : 2
lie lightly gentle e., 263 : 7
light be the e., 76 : 4
like snake renew, 468 : 17
like to swallow whole e., 861 : 4
little e. for charity, 249 : 10
Lord of heaven and e., 46 : 16
love of e. he instills, 600 : 25
lovelier flower on e., 424 : 13
made heaven and e., 4 : 3
made the e. to tremble, 29 : 23
make e. happy, 591 : 8
Maker of Heaven and e., 55 : 2
man making deserts of e., 760 : 6
man marks e. with ruin, 458 : 25
marriages consummated on e., 176 : 3
master of e. and sea, 711 : 13
measuring e. and heaven, 85 : 17
meek shall inherit the e., 18 : 24
more near e. than wont, 232 : 15
more things in heaven and e., 220 : 3, 821 : 5
most like single cell, 883 : 13
my footstool e., 336 : 19
new heaven and new e., 53 : 29
new heavens and a new e., 31 : 30
niggard e., 361 : 17
nigher heaven than now, 540 : 18
nightly to listening e., 325 : 9

Earth (*continued*)
no less kindled e., 462 : 15
no more a mother, 116 : *n* 3
not gray but rosy, 545 : 23
not resound on e. again, 486 : *n* 1
not steadfast place, 728 : 11
nothing but hath bound in e., 188 : 1
nothing on e. but laundry, 899 : 13
of the e. earthy, 49 : 6
offered this trust to e., 132 : 4
on bare e. he lies, 306 : 18
on e. broken arcs, 544 : 4
on e. no sure happiness, 174 : 5
on e. peace and good will, 42 : 29
on e. peace to men, 54 : 4
one mighty blood spot, 503 : 2
only when we are half e., 600 : 15
or air, 217 : 25
or ever thou hadst formed the e., 20 : 11
our Mother the E., 928 : 13
out of e. I sing, 928 : 12
paradise on e., 724 : 10
parameters of skies and e., 132 : 12
peace and tranquility to e., 882 : 20
peace on e. good will, 537 : 16
peace on e. mercy mild, 350 : 15
peasants born kings of e., 504 : 12
people who eat the e., 863 : 6
peopling e. waters and sky, 311 : 12
pleasant country's e., 195 : 8
poetry of e. never dead, 475 : 9
power passing from the e., 428 : 5
proudly wears Parthenon, 493 : 19
put on e. a little space, 403 : 7
puts forth sweet flowers, 100 : 2
rain was upon the e., 7 : 30
raises man from e. to God, 154 : 15
receive her King, 328 : 13
receive honored guest, 868 : 11
render back from breast, 461 : 6
replenish the e., 6 : 15
rest lightly on you, 134 : 28
reverence for e., 897 : 19
rich stone in bowels of e., 257 : 13
rid e. of him in my pride, 728 : 15
room on e. for honest men, 384 : 19
sad its lot, 641 : 16
saddest among kings of e., 728 : 18
salt of the e., 37 : 5
scum of the e., 421 : 11
second opportunity on e., 908 : 3
sepulcher of famous men, 81 : 5
shadow under the e., 907 : 3
shall be full of knowledge, 29 : 19
shall not perish from e., 523 : 4
since e. began to exist, 378 : 1
sing ye heavens e. reply, 350 : 11
skies and e. a solid mass, 131 : 13
sleepers in quiet e., 562 : 7
small model of barren e., 195 : 2
so much of e., 425 : 1
solid e. actual world, 557 : 21
somewhere sky touches E., 925 : 23
Spaceship E., 832 : 8
speak to the e., 15 : 29
spirit given on e., 525 : 2
splendor and travail of e., 802 : 18
sprung from e. sinks back to e., 100 : 19
stand at Judgment Seat, 707 : 16
stand on e. as footstool, 720 : 6
stood hard as iron, 608 : 17
stranger on e., 864 : 4

Earth (*continued*)
suffered to crawl upon e., 322 : 11
sufficient, 575 : 11
sun is lost and the e., 254 : 5
sure and firm-set e., 237 : 15
swear not by heaven nor e., 37 : 9
table e. dice human bones, 462 : 14
that bears thee dead, 205 : 11
the e. that is sufficient, 575 : 11
their proper element, 265 : 7
they shall inherit the e., 37 : 4
they touched e. and grain grew, 888 : 7
thirsty e. soaks up rain, 295 : 7
this blessed plot this e., 194 : 13
this e. of majesty, 194 : 13
this goodly frame the e., 220 : 28
this is the last of e., 418 : 11
those who labor in e., 388 : 2
though the e. be removed, 19 : 10
thy will be done in e., 37 : 15
till heaven and e. pass, 37 : 7
to earth, 56 : 13
to e. and thee restore, 692 : 10
tomb of rest, 761 : 16
touch of e., 534 : 12
truth crushed to e., 471 : 12
two kinds of people on e., 670 : 1
unfolds both heaven and e., 195 : 23
until man a member of e., 819 : 12
upon e. there is not his like, 17 : 8
walk not on e. exultantly, 131 : 7
walk the e. unseen, 286 : 2
walk the roll of e., 822 : 5
was bountiful, 726 : 8
was without form, 6 : 10
weaned away from e., 839 : 13
what e. and its interests, 558 : 21
what is pomp but e. and dust, 186 : 21
when I am laid in e., 317 : 3
when I laid the foundations of the e., 16 : 28
when religion makes e. uncomfortable, 570 : 8
whether in e. or air, 217 : 25
which made heaven and e., 22 : 4
while the e. remaineth, 8 : 1
whole e. and all time, 424 : 8
whole e. for religion's sake, 574 : 7
whole e. grows rich, 312 : 20
whole e. our hospital, 807 : 19
why on e. except to grow, 543 : 26
winds lashing e., 761 : 16
with her thousand voices, 435 : 23
wonder of e. and life, 821 : 3
word of e. in ears of world, 634 : 7
words are daughters of e., 352 : 6
would know no adventurer, 683 : 8
wretched of e., 555 : 24
write sorrow on bosom of the e., 195 : 1
you made e. as you wished, 5 : 8
yours and fullness thereof, 743 : 10
yours is the e., 710 : 18
Earthen, kettle and e. pot, 35 : 25
Earthlier happy is rose distilled, 195 : 21
Earthly ball a peopled garden, 395 : 6
dignities, 249 : 4
fancies, 533 : 6
godfathers of heaven's lights, 190 : 12
mighty e. marchings, 570 : 11
nothing e. surpass her, 460 : 10
paragon, 243 : 24
Earthly (*continued*)
power then likest God's, 200 : 9
sum of e. bliss, 287 : 7
sweet fruition of e. crown, 183 : 6
things heavenly or things e., 302 : 4
this wisdom is e., 52 : 1
thoughts of e. men, 60 : 26
touch of e. years, 424 : 14
very honey of all e. joy, 295 : 3
who mind e. things, 50 : 5
Earthquake, dam'd by e., 623 : 4
gloom of e. and eclipse, 466 : 14
Lord was not in the e., 14 : 5
when not smiling back, 888 : 3
Earthquakes with thunder lightning, 622 : 19
Earth's, ablution round e. shores, 478 : 20
crammed with heaven, 507 : 22
diurnal course, 424 : 14
foundations fled, 692 : 3
foundations stand, 692 : 11
green fields, 552 : 22
heedless sons, 834 : 11
human shores, 478 : 20
last picture painted, 707 : 21
lid, 792 : 16
like e. empires pass away, 597 : 18
returns, 542 : 4
right place for love, 747 : 16
round e. imagined corners, 254 : 8
round e. shore, 587 : 16
shadows fly, 469 : 16
smoothness rough, 544 : 10
Earth-star and snow-star, 557 : 16
Earthworm, feeble e., 300 : 11
Earthworms, land plowed by e., 515 : 11
Earthy and cold hand of death, 205 : 10
earth in e. bed, 533 : 25
of the earth e., 49 : 6
Ease after war, 173 : 12
an age of e., 370 : 2
and speed not give work beauty, 147 : *n* 11
at e. for aye dwell, 528 : 6
at e. in my generation, 643 : 5
at e. in nature, 573 : 21
at e. in Zion, 33 : 21
but for another gives e., 405 : 3
careless e., 329 : 13
dappled turf at e., 426 : 3
darbies at wrist, 572 : 7
death or dreamful e., 528 : 18
done with so much e., 303 : 18
equal e. unto my pain, 271 : 22
for e. from heaven, 407 : 4
full-throated e., 476 : 22
gently sways at e., 749 : 4
gives happiness or leaves e., 339 : 30
good pleasure e. content, 337 : 10
greater e. than hogs eat, 290 : *n* 3
ignoble e., 104 : 13, 686 : 12
ignoble e. and peaceful sloth, 284 : 13
joys in another's loss of e., 405 : 4
lest we rest in e., 529 : 4
life at e. drifts, 601 : 11
life of e. not for man, 474 : 4
live at home at e., 273 : 6
live with e., 338 : 14
Nature bent to e. us, 294 : *n* 4
never desire worldly e., 346 : 3
no healthful e., 485 : 12
one life the aching, 606 : 12
poet's dignity and e., 338 : 16
Ease (*continued*)
prodigal of e., 304 : 1
rots in e. on Lethe wharf, 219 : 19
slothful e., 687 : 4
some come to take their e., 249 : 19
somebody's right and e., 653 : 15
take mine e. in mine inn, 159 : 14
take thine e., 43 : 19
true e. in writing, 333 : 9
Truth one side E. other, 537 : 12
with e. and you beside, 605 : 21
with the greatest of e., 636 : 12
woman in hours of e., 431 : 2
words flow with e., 311 : 4
write with e. to show breeding, 399 : 11
Easeful death, 476 : 28
Eases, time e. all things, 74 : 5
Easier go through eye of needle, 40 : 7
grass blade's no e. than oak, 567 : 15
nothing e. than rest, 635 : 11
nothing e. than self-deceit, 88 : 22
played on than pipe, 222 : 19
swallowed than flap-dragon, 191 : 7
sweats e. than I., 559 : 14
thirst blister e., 605 : 1
to be critical than correct, 502 : 3
to believe than deny, 631 : 1
to get favor from Fortune, 111 : 3
to get into enemy's toils, 66 : 23
to resist at beginning, 152 : 10
to stay out than get out, 625 : 7
Easiest, move e. who learned to dance, 333 : 9
Easily, by and by e. said, 222 : 22
never have come back so e., 679 : 12
Easiness, lend a kind of e., 223 : 11
property of e., 224 : 8
East and West will pinch heart, 822 : 12
argument with e. wind, 568 : 27
blasted with the e. wind, 8 : 31
cherubims e. of the garden, 7 : 13
fill his belly with e. wind, 15 : 36
from e. to western Ind, 212 : 3
good is good from e. to e., 646 : 4
gorgeous e. in fee, 425 : 18
gorgeous E. with richest hand, 284 : 3
I turn my back to the e., 402 : 15
is East and West is San Francisco, 699 : 15
is East and West is West, 707 : 16
it is the e. Juliet the sun, 192 : 2
new Judea between E. and West, 565 : 29
of Suez, 708 : 10
one flew e., 933 : 15
one ship e. another west, 669 : 21
or west Phoenix builds, 271 : 21
Side West Side, 698 : 14
somewheres e. of Suez, 708 : 10
star in the e., 36 : 20
tried to hustle the E., 707 : 20
west south north, 488 : 13
wind never blow, 270 : 32
youth who from e. travel, 426 : 15
Eastard and points between, 622 : 19
Easter, egg dear on E. Day, 934 : 11
no sun upon an E. day, 289 : 21
Eastern, blabbing e. scout, 279 : 13
civilization know contentment, 818 : 11
dew of yon high e. hill, 217 : 27
dusk on e. horizon, 831 : 13
pulling blanket off e. sky, 928 : 9

Eastern (*continued*)
wipe out E. instincts, 707 : 7
Eastman, If It Isn't An E., 829 : 1
East's, feeling E. gift, 542 : 20
Eastward, a garden e. in Eden, 6 : 18
roll of world e., 640 : 6
to the sea, 708 : 8
Easy, abstinence e. to me, 353 : 19
all zeal Mr. E., 465 : 14
and comfortable on raft, 624 : 1
as e. to marry rich woman, 539 : 14
as grass grows on weirs, 712 : 1
as leaves grow on tree, 711 : 22
bid me take love e., 711 : 22
criticism e. art difficult, 329 : 18
decent e. men, 384 : 1
diagnosis often e., 463 : 21
evil is e., 300 : 9
false man does e., 238 : 10
give throne would be e., 89 : 4
how e. bush supposed a bear, 197 : 12
if to do as e. as to know, 198 : 9
jolly and e. in minds, 539 : 7
leap to pluck bright honor, 203 : 15
live quiet die, 432 : 1
morning's ride, 607 : 12
my yoke is e., 39 : 8
not e. to call back, 761 : 13
not pray for e. lives, 619 : 18
nothing e. in war, 815 : 14
nothing so e. but becomes difficult, 96 : 13
poetry e. to write, 618 : 2
Rabelais' e. chair, 340 : 14
road to Hades e. to travel, 92 : 7
smooth e. inoffensive down to Hell, 92 : *n* 5
so e. and so plain a stop, 205 : 18
summertime and livin' e., 836 : 4
there life is supremely e., 59 : 26
to blow and swallow not e., 94 : 5
to go down into hell, 105 : 15
words are e. like the wind, 257 : 8
writing's cursed hard reading, 399 : 11
young and e., 886 : 19
Eat bread in sweat of thy face, 7 : 12
bread without scarceness, 11 : 14
cake and have it, 161 : 13
cannibals that each other e., 229 : 30
cannot e. but little meat, 163 : 9
cones under his pines, 747 : 5
dare to e. a peach, 803 : 19
did e. and were filled, 39 : 25
dogs shall e. Jezebel, 14 : 8
don't e. your heart, 65 : 12
drink be merry, 27 : 14, 43 : 19
drink for tomorrow we die, 30 : 2
dust shalt thou e., 7 : 9
dusty bread, 836 : 20
eat me soul, 315 : 1
enough to e. and wear, 692 : 15
fine women e. crazy salad, 714 : 16
frogs e. butterflies, 767 : 8
great ones e. up little ones, 243 : 13
he hath not e. paper, 190 : 27
heart, 65 : 12
his pleasant fruits, 28 : 14
I earn that I e., 212 : 2
I e. and e. I swear, 208 : 14
I e. the air, 222 : 8
I e. what I see, 611 : 18
I want to e. you up, 420 : 4
I'll e. my head, 547 : 3
Eat (*continued*)
in orchard enough to e., 331 : 2
in the evening, 404 : 5
it in haste, 9 : 25
let them e. cake, 359 : 6
like wolves fight like devils, 207 : 26
men like air, 911 : 12
Nebuchadnezzar did e. grass, 32 : 34
neither e. it nor make flannel, 790 : 17
nevermore to e. again, 740 : 6
no beans, 258 : 15
no fat, 929 : 16
no onions nor garlic, 197 : 11
not to dullness, 348 : 18
not to e. not for love, 495 : 21
of fish that fed of worm, 223 : 15
of the habitation, 198 : 18
of the tree I did e., 7 : 8
peck of salt with him, 917 : 7
people who e. the earth, 863 : 6
plant vineyards and e. the fruit, 31 : 31
poor when anything to e., 86 : *n* 5
so I did sit and e., 269 : 10
some hae meat canna e., 411 : 1
some s. I will not e., 829 : 10
strive mightily e. as friends, 188 : 29
take e. this is my body, 41 : 10, 48 : 20
tell me what you e., 401 : 6
that shall ye e., 10 : 16
that they may live, 79 : 6
the fat of the land, 9 : 1
their flesh shall ye not e., 10 : 17
they shall e. the flesh, 9 : 24
thou shalt not e. of it, 6 : 20
to e. thy heart, 174 : 11
to e. with apple tart, 668 : 13
to live not live to eat, 298 : 4, 347 : 1
up himself, 226 : 3
wad e. that want it, 411 : 1
way they e. drink and everything, 752 : 13
we hae meat we can e., 411 : 1
will not e. with you, 198 : 18
worm that e. of a king, 223 : 15
you earn bread I'll e., 520 : 8
Eaten a sour grape, 32 : 17
crust e. in peace, 66 : 6
God made and e., 541 : 20
have we e. on insane root, 236 : 8
me out of house and home, 206 : 11
thee for a word, 191 : 7
they'd e. every one, 613 : 9
to death with rust, 206 : 4
worms have e. them, 212 : 23
your bread and salt, 707 : 3
Eater, great e. of beef, 213 : 12
out of the e. came meat, 12 : 14
Eateth grass as an ox, 17 : 3
'Eathen pore benighted 'e., 708 : 5
Eating air on promise of supply, 206 : 6
and drinking like brutes, 576 : 16
appetite comes with e., 157 : 9
appetite makes e. delight, 290 : 3
bitter bread of banishment, 194 : 25
bread and honey, 931 : 9
cares, 278 : 6
Christmas pie, 929 : 20
curds and whey, 932 : 15
drinking breeding, 574 : 20
drinking dung death, 807 : 10
poetry, 913 : 4
produce of the land, 59 : 5
Eating (*continued*)
proof of pudding in e., 169 : 33
Son of man came e., 39 : 7
whether breathing is e., 82 : 21
worn out with e. time, 303 : 16
Eats, believes he e. God, 361 : 2
dirt in the line, 825 : 3
drinks and plays, 705 : 12
proud e. up himself, 226 : 9
Revolution e. own children, 552 : 8
seeking the food he e., 211 : 3
she-wolf's young, 435 : 6
soles offen shoes, 840 : 1
thing that e. heart, 864 : 3
whatever Miss T. e., 740 : 4
Eau verte pénétra ma coque de sapin, 673 : *n* 8
Eaves, antler of e., 863 : 14
brawling of sparrow in e., 712 : 7
gilded e., 531 : 5
Ebb and flow by the moon, 235 : 12
ceaseless e. and flow, 672 : 20
deaths at e. tide, 672 : 20
ne'er e. to humble love, 231 : 18
ne'er feels retiring e., 231 : 18
where beauty has no e., 712 : 11
Ebenezer, pale E., 730 : 12
Eboli, Christ stopped at E., 855 : 7
Ebon throne in rayless majesty, 330 : 5
Ecbatana, here in mid-plain of E., 83 : 6
Ecce homo, 45 : *n* 4
Eccentric propositions of its fate, 768 : 7
Eccentricities of genius, 546 : 21
Eccentricity heresy anomalies, 704 : 2
Ecclesiarum, disputandi pruritus e. scabies, 251 : *n* 3
Ecclesiastes fine steel of woe, 570 : 16
Ecclesiastic, pulpit drum e., 290 : 14
tyranny's worst, 318 : 9
Échasses, sur des é. marcher de nos jambes, 166 : *n* 7
Echo and light unto eternity, 468 : 23
applaud thee to the very e., 240 : 1
began to undermine, 764 : 10
catch e. of infinite, 644 : 4
children's lips e., 457 : 21
distant footsteps e., 510 : 20
footfalls e. in memory, 807 : 2
my speech to a T, 158 : *n* 2
name of which e. faint, 442 : 19
ne'er sink while e. left, 462 : 15
of your mournful song, 518 : 8
perfumes colors sounds e., 580 : 18
sound an e. to sense, 333 : 9
sounds that e. still, 528 : 21
sublimity the e. of noble mind, 118 : 16
sweet E. sweetest nymph, 279 : 18
virtue no empty e., 413 : 3
where is E., 601 : 16
woods answer and E. ring, 174 : 17
Echoes, answer e., 530 : 26
of that voice, 436 : 1
roll from soul to soul, 531 : 2
wild e. flying, 530 : 26
Echoing, on the e. green, 403 : 4
Éclat of death, 607 : 8
Eclipse, built in the e., 280 : 18
earthquake and e., 466 : 14
first the rest nowhere, 364 : 6
irrecoverably dark total e., 288 : 20
moon hath her e. endured, 245 : 13

Eclipse (*continued*)
sick almost to doomsday with e., 217 : 22
sun in dim e., 283 : 24
Eclipsed gaiety of nations, 353 : 1
Eclipses, clouds and e. stain, 244 : 14
of moon and other experiments, 151 : 7
Ecology, sensitive science of e., 898 : 1
Economic, coordinating e. activities of millions, 880 : 13
democracy appropriate for e. surplus, 877 : 16
distress teach men, 738 : 9
equality for women, 903 : 9
existence of e. freedom, 757 : 17
factor relatively unimportant, 790 : 2
figures referring to e. events, 775 : 9
freedom, 757 : 17
freedom means to political freedom, 880 : 11
fundamental e. situation, 871 : 4
if e. problems solved, 790 : 1
interest as cause of war, 790 : 5
military power and e. output, 871 : 8
monuments, 871 : 15
position, 694 : 4
principle of e. production, 763 : 1
progress in e. world slow, 652 : 1
prophecies of e. disaster, 773 : 8
provide women with e. opportunities, 903 : 10
pulse of modern life e., 763 : 1
pyramid, 779 : 6
royalists, 779 : 16
shape e. society, 872 : 1
slavery nobody's business, 779 : 16
status not depend on e. process, 775 : 5
strongest of e. motives, 685 : 3
superstructure on e. foundation, 731 : 3
tyranny above, 794 : 12
vital e. interests, 876 : 20
Economical, experience in e. order, 636 : 14
Economics as if people mattered, 879 : 16
can be objective science, 880 : 7
dismal science, 872 : 5
generalizations about economic phenomena, 880 : 9
heedless self-interest bad e., 780 : 1
in e. no constant relations, 775 : 8
neutral as between ends, 843 : 1
studies human behavior, 842 : 15
Economist, give me political e., 566 : 6
slaves of defunct e., 783 : 16
Economists, age of e., 373 : 22
progressives call reactionaries, 775 : 6
Economize, let us e. truth, 625 : 2
Economy distributive virtue, 374 : 10
ensure stable e., 903 : 9
from e. to stock market, 871 : 4
is beauty, 654 : 3
kings pretend to watch over e., 366 : 3
not saving but selection, 374 : 10
parsimony not e., 374 : 9
Principles of Political E., 753 : 4
revival of working e., 771 : 11
within stable e., 903 : 10
Écrasez l'infâme, 343 : *n* 7
Écrivain n'a rien a dire, 901 : *n* 1
original celui que personne ne peut imiter, 419 : *n* 2
Ecstasies, dissolve me into e., 278 : 26
Ecstasy affords occasion, 798 : 15
blind e., 844 : 1
come to breath, 836 : 18
in sea caves e., 849 : 18
in such an e., 476 : 28
maintain e. success, 638 : 13
roll in e. at your feet, 786 : 3
rung upon rein in his e., 656 : 1
very e. of love, 220 : 9
waked to e. living lyre, 362 : 6
way wherein no e., 807 : 18
what wild e., 477 : 5
Ecstatic, carolings of e. sound, 641 : 13
each e. instant, 604 : 6
Eddy, most men e. about, 588 : 7
Eden, a garden eastward in E., 6 : 18
east of the garden of E., 7 : 13
find fault in E., 561 : 13
flow'rets of E. inherit, 447 : 13
older place than E., 742 : 11
our woe with loss of E., 282 : 22
still his E. keeps, 484 : 6
that old-fashioned house, 607 : 16
this other E., 194 : 13
through E. took solitary way, 288 : 4
voice that breathed o'er E., 465 : 13
Edens, lest we lose E., 541 : 22
Edge, as near e. as I can, 558 : 8
axe's e. did try, 296 : 23
children's teeth set on e., 32 : 17
cloy hungry e. of appetite, 194 : 7
dangerous e. of things, 543 : 7
dulls e. of husbandry, 219 : 2
finest e. with blunt whetstone, 175 : 10
knife ill-used lose e., 245 : 7
no jesting with e. tools, 261 : 2
of doom, 245 : 18
sea land's e. also, 808 : 2
slander whose e. sharper than sword, 243 : 21
Edged with poplar pale, 277 : 11
Edges, bright e. of world, 739 : 5
two e. one of laughter, 782 : 4
vast e. drear, 587 : 16
Edging, age employed in e. steel, 399 : 16
Edible good to eat wholesome, 647 : 11
Edifice, total grandeur of total e., 768 : 25
Edifices where Greeks worship God, 136 : 3
Edifies his ears, 333 : 19
Edifieth, charity e., 48 : 13
Edi-mus bibi-mus vivi-mus ore-mus, 365 : 12
Edited, dead sinner revised and e., 647 : 17
for old lady from Dubuque, 824 : 2
most sighs e., 876 : 7
Edith with golden hair, 512 : 5
Edition, if life had second e., 470 : 12
in new more elegant e., 346 : 15
mollusk cheap e. of man, 499 : 19
Editions of Balbec and Palmyra, 363 : 21
Editor, temptation to the e., 790 : 6
Editor's conviction, 814 : 3
Edmund, here lies our good E., 371 : 14
Edom, over E. will I cast out my shoe, 19 : 25
Educated Americans go to Europe, 498 : 26
beyond intellect, 632 : 4
men superior, 86 : 19
only e. are free, 121 : 11
till women more rationally e., 414 : 7
women e. for dependence, 414 : 8
Educating, assimilating e. selecting, 737 : 11
in e. the young, 307 : *n* 8
Education a process, 898 : 13
accumulates inert facts, 635 : 14
and catastrophe, 720 : 5
beer and skittles part of e., 590 : 10
beginning and end of political e., 635 : 1
best provision for old age, 87 : 4
by e. I mean goodness, 307 : *n* 8
cabbage with college e., 624 : 14
city is e. to Greece, 81 : 4
contact with manners is e., 112 : 18
deal o' pains with his e., 546 : 17
difference of e. between male and female, 392 : 12
direction in which e. starts, 84 : 13
first part of politics, 483 : 19
for character, 579 : 6
forms common mind, 335 : 15
hanging around till caught on, 750 : 13
in field of public e., 820 : 14
in laws of Nature, 595 : 14
in the obvious, 644 : 16
is making men, 609 : *n* 3
let early e. be amusement, 85 : 1
liberal e., 319 : 14
makes people easy to lead, 445 : 1
moral and intellectual e., 573 : 10
most valuable result of e., 596 : 5
much depends upon early e., 392 : 11
no person deprived of e., 903 : 6
not only common but compulsory, 569 : 10
of a liberal e., 169 : 7
of imaginative life, 654 : 9
of itself to look upon, 463 : 14
one e. for all, 414 : 21
only ignorant despise e., 111 : 23
our e. inadequate, 813 : 15
produced population able to read, 758 : 4
respect poets by e., 499 : 21
root of honesty in good e., 120 : 7
science e. for citizenship, 684 : 16
seek e. in paths of duty, 635 : 16
soap and e. deadly, 622 : 2
soul takes nothing but e. and culture, 84 : 3
supervise national e., 452 : 2
to love her is liberal e., 327 : 11
travel part of e., 180 : 18
treatise of natural e., 358 : 23
trifling narrow e. of females, 392 : 13
what left over, 925 : 5
women given deplorable e., 504 : 9
youth sacred to e., 665 : 15
Educational relations strongest tie, 672 : 17
separate e. facilities, 820 : 14
Educator wielder of power, 879 : 4
Edward Edward, 926 : 14
sons of E. sleep, 187 : 17

Edward's, proud E. power, 411 : 15
winding-sheet of E. race, 363 : 5
Eel, in mud e. is, 933 : 4
Eels boiled in broo', 927 : 8
Eerier, linguistics an ever e. area, 856 : 14
Effaced, forget when image e., 85 : 18
Effect, cause and e. from economy, 871 : 4
cause of this e., 220 : 13
cause produces more than one e., 579 : 12
defective comes by cause, 220 : 13
ek gret e. write in place lite, 145 : 6
little e. much labor, 441 : 3
man e. of work, 735 : 10
nature but name for e., 377 : 16
nothing exists without e., 308 : 6
peace between e. and it, 236 : 17
what in e. already in cause, 688 : 9
Effective, governed make views e., 813 : 9
life a very e. therapist, 789 : 14
poetry most wisely e. mode, 587 : 2
reciprocal safeguards, 787 : 16
simplicity makes uneducated e., 88 : 15
Effects, baneful e. of party, 379 : 11
dire e. from civil discord, 326 : 5
no e., 473 : 12
Effectual fervent prayer, 52 : 6
Efficiency, highest best form of e., 682 : 17
in struggle for bread, 684 : 1
southern e., 892 : 2
Efficient, death most e., 772 : 15
Efflorescence of civilized life, 579 : 11
Effort, critical e., 586 : 15
dignity in e. of patriots, 380 : 14
happiness result of man's e., 763 : 3
keep faculty of e. alive, 648 : 9
nearly killed her, 730 : 9
right e., 73 : 2
supposes resistance, 639 : 7
to get up, 560 : 29
to see and represent, 653 : 16
Efforts, no human e. deliver them, 379 : 2
noble e. in last war, 351 : 3
of busy multitude, 592 : 5
redoubling e., 703 : 10
to create happiness, 763 : 4
Effusion, foils foe by e. of ink, 365 : 11
of blood, 701 : 2
Effusions, liveliest e. of wit, 440 : 29
Égalité, liberté é. fraternité, 928 : 2
Egdon, glory of E. waste, 640 : 9
Egg, as one e. like another, 158 : *n* 8
best way to boil e., 498 : 28
bloody e. yolk, 897 : 6
egg's way of making e., 620 : 2
from the e., 109 : 26
full of quarrels as e. full of meat, 193 : 3
good to keep nest e., 170 : 9
hard-boiled as picnic e., 834 : 6
heaven like e. earth like yolk, 123 : 16
innocent as new-laid e., 627 : 8
is dear on Easter, 934 : 11
of democracy, 569 : 9
puritanism laid e. of democracy, 569 : 9
serpent's e., 215 : 17
Egg (*continued*)
unhatched e. greatest challenge, 847 : 6
Wall Street lays e., 741 : 4
yesterday e. tomorrow duster, 740 : 7
you've got a bad e., 660 : 18
Egg's way of making egg, 620 : 2
Eggs, all e. in one basket, 169 : 11, 624 : 23
as like as e., 158 : *n* 8
as the partridge sitteth on e., 32 : 13
as weasel sucks e., 211 : 2
can't make omelet without breaking e., 928 : 6
codfish ten thousand e., 923 : 10
do not teach hen, 934 : 13
goose with golden e., 66 : 18
lays e. for gentlemen, 932 : 14
set house on fire to roast e., 180 : 23
silent when e. hatched, 277 : 1
walk on e., 257 : 16
Eglantine, sweet musk roses and e., 196 : 18
Ego serves three masters, 678 : 15
soul beyond e. reach, 754 : 13
to id as rider to horse, 678 : 14
tooth of the e., 881 : 11
where id was there e. be, 678 : 16
Ego, alter e., 91 : *n* 10
non flocci pendere, 96 : *n* 18
sum rex Romanus, 298 : *n* 6
Egoism, book of e., 600 : 24
Egos, children extensions of our e., 796 : 5
Egotism sloth idleness, 452 : 2
strong dose of e., 815 : 5
Egotists, conscience makes e., 675 : 4
Egregiously an ass, 230 : 16
Egypt, ancient nations E. and Israel, 881 : 15
came out from E., 9 : 29
carry me out of E., 9 : 3
great cry in E., 9 : 28
Helen's beauty in brow of E., 197 : 12
I am dying E. dying, 241 : 21
I will pass through the land of E., 9 : 25
in E. pyramids laid, 924 : 3
one more plague upon E., 9 : 22
out of E. called my son, 36 : 22
Pharos of E., 924 : 3
way down in E. land, 935 : 21
Egypt's dark sea, 447 : 10
Eheu fugaces Postume Postume, 107 : *n* 20
Eichmann lessons in wickedness, 866 : 7
Eiffel Tower your flock of bridges, 770 : 9
Eigentlich, wie es e. gewesen, 480 : *n* 2
Eight or nine elderly men, 706 : 19
pieces of e., 668 : 7
victories over Syracusans, 78 : 2
Eighteen, from birth to age e., 788 : 21
from e. to thirty-five, 788 : 21
Eighteenth of April, 512 : 6
Eightfold, noble e. path, 72 : 23
path, 73 : 2
Eighth commandment not for bards, 436 : 6
day of week, 863 : 17
Eight-wheeler of mighty fame, 731 : *n* 2
Eighty, if only one were e., 645 : *n* 4
Eildon, riding by E. Tree, 926 : 23
Ein' feste burg, 156 : *n* 1
Eisen und Blut, 553 : *n* 2
Elaborately constructed forms, 515 : 1
Elaine the fair, 534 : 11
Élan and determination, 771 : 13
vital, 688 : 11
Elastic and vigorous thought, 559 : 22
time is e., 734 : 5
Elate, Ruin's plowshare drives e., 409 : 10
Elbow, soul hath e. room, 202 : 17
through world, 472 : 10
Elbows, our horizon never at our e., 560 : 2
Eld, beg alms of palsied e., 228 : 16
memories of e., 525 : 16
Elder, more e. than thy looks, 200 : 12
sun is e. by a year, 252 : 22
take e. than herself, 214 : 1
Elderly, eight or nine e. men, 706 : 19
Elders, discourse of the e., 35 : 14
regarding e. as senile, 634 : 24
strings of white e., 767 : 11
when he sitteth among e., 26 : 7
Eldest, primal e. curse, 222 : 25
Eldorado of all old bachelors, 581 : 3
seek for E., 527 : 5
Eleazer faculty, 705 : 3
Elect, God's e., 47 : 13
predestined e. thinned down, 622 : 13
Elected between sundown and sunup, 766 : 1
if e. I will not serve, 579 : *n* 3
silence sing to me, 655 : 18
without political understanding, 788 : 10
Election, declined e. some years ago, 791 : 7
supreme court follows e., 721 : 12
tub told of his e., 155 : 7
turned into angels by e., 722 : 12
Elections end slavery begins, 381 : 10
succeeds in carrying e., 616 : 2
Elective, women to secure e. franchise, 554 : 5
Electra, mourning becomes E., 810 : 12
Electric chair hanging like oasis, 893 : 2
Electrical, air pump or e. machine, 379 : 16
display of God, 810 : 11
Electrically prompt, 626 : 2
Electrician no longer there, 729 : 16
Electrification of whole country, 731 : 6
Electronic interdependence re-creates world, 879 : 6
Electronics, chemistry mathematics e., 819 : 14
Electrum, obelisks wrought with e., 5 : 1
Elegance, harmony in bad taste e., 877 : 10
of female friendship, 352 : 20
rather than luxury, 536 : 6
ultimate e. imagined land, 767 : 22
Elegant but not ostentatious, 352 : 23
in new more e. edition, 346 : 15
simplicity of three percents, 394 : 1
so e. so intelligent, 805 : 4
sufficiency, 345 : 12
Elegantiae arbiter, 122 : *n* 17
Element, back above e. they lived in, 241 : 25
basic e. in Constitution, 788 : 14

Element (*continued*)
bearable to no mortal, 878 : 6
criminal e. I am of it, 676 : 18
earth their proper e., 265 : 7
of blank, 606 : 2
of earth, 794 : 9
of fire quite put out, 254 : 5
one God law e., 532 : 27
people most important e., 89 : 28
uranium new source, 763 : 11
Elemental force freed, 809 : 22
lack of e. things, 802 : 17
things, 671 : 2
this war e. conflict, 813 : 1
three great e. sounds, 802 : 19
Elementary feelings permanently in race, 585 : 19
said Holmes, 689 : 10
Elemented, things which e. it, 253 : 3
Element's, thy e. below, 233 : 17
Elements and angelic sprite, 254 : 7
by term e. we mean, 390 : 8
essential provider of e., 586 : 23
framed us of four e., 183 : 6
government balance of e., 672 : 14
heaven earth and all the e., 148 : 16
I tax you not you e., 233 : 25
least visible, 878 : 3
reconciles discordant e., 423 : 18
so mixed in him, 217 : 14
something in us before e., 274 : 22
weak and beggarly e., 49 : 26
Elephant leans or stands, 268 : 20
like e. roaming at will, 72 : 18
stalls above like e., 893 : 6
that practiced on fife, 614 : 6
traveling through dense forest, 789 : 8
tried to use telephant, 667 : 9
Elephant's, corn high as e. eye, 833 : 11
somnambulistic stride, 867 : 15
Elephants endorsed with towers, 288 : 10
kings ride e. over mountains, 879 : 20
place e. for want of towns, 119 : *n* 11
when e. fight grass suffers, 925 : 26
women and e., 731 : 12
Elephone tried to use telephone, 667 : 9
Elevate condition of men, 522 : 2
life by conscious endeavor, 559 : 24
Elevated, joy of e. thoughts, 423 : 13
Elevation and beauty, 589 : 10
drink not to e., 348 : 18
removal of hindrances to her e., 471 : 1
Eleven, possession e. points, 324 : 25
Elfin from green grass, 525 : 7
Elfland, horns of E., 531 : 1
Elginbrodde, here lie I Martin E., 594 : 14
Martin E., 594 : 14
Elgin's, stands in E. place, 536 : 7
Eli Eli lama sabachthani, 41 : 27
Elijah, mantle of E., 14 : 14
the prophet, 34 : 1
went up by a whirlwind, 14 : 12
Eliminated impossible, 689 : 3
Eliot meet Mr. E., 806 : 14
Elisha took up mantle of Elijah, 14 : 14
Elite minority, 784 : 8
Eliza, at last Elizabeth E. said, 578 : 8
made desperate retreat, 538 : 21
Elizabeth, at last E. Eliza said, 578 : 8
from Jane to E., 440 : 19
Elizabeth (*continued*)
great E., 528 : 21
servant to Queen E., 175 : 6
Elizabeth-Jane Farfrae not told of my death, 640 : 16
Ell, give an inch take an e., 161 : 12
Ellen, wed fair E., 430 : 19
Elliptical billiard balls, 629 : 13
Elm, expect pears from an e., 111 : *n* 18
old as yonder e., 778 : 5
round e. tree bole, 541 : 16
tell me tell me e., 778 : 5
Elms, desire under the e., 810 : 9
fade into dimness apace, 588 : 5
immemorial e., 531 : 13
Elm-shadows, not clear in e., 795 : 12
Elocution, wherefore waste e., 630 : 4
Elongated-yellow-fruit school of writing, 846 : 1
Eloquence, army not halted by e., 553 : 11
fill winepress of e., 128 : 17
frothy e. not convince me, 674 : 13
gods do not give all men e., 60 : 4
in forum rhetoric in study, 559 : 30
mother of arts and e., 288 : 13
of Mr. Webster, 840 : 12
silence more e., 538 : 1
splendid e., 342 : 8
take e. wring neck, 659 : 17
talking and e. not same, 257 : 4
thou has inspired with, 136 : 6
true e. takes no heed of e., 299 : 14
truth secret of e., 580 : 12
turned scale, 493 : *n* 1
Éloquence prends l'é. tords-lui son cou, 659 : *n* 11
Eloquent but 'tis not true, 585 : 16
digressions, 596 : 11
epitaph for country, 703 : 14
feeling and imagination make us e., 118 : 2
just and mighty Death, 173 : 4
old man e., 282 : 6
pure and e. blood, 254 : 6
to be not as e. more e., 380 : 2
what an e. manikin, 102 : 6
Else, leave all e. to the gods, 107 : 6
Elude him reel and pass, 834 : 12
Eluded, life's meaning e. me, 847 : 5
Elusive, The Vague and E., 64 : 7
Elves, make my small e. coats, 196 : 19
whisper in your ear, 694 : 1
whose little eyes glow, 266 : 14
Elysian, life e., 511 : 11
send you to E. plain, 59 : 26
Elysium as far as nearest room, 608 : 4
daughter of E., 412 : 9
palpable E., 793 : 3
what E. known, 477 : 16
Emanation, my e. far within, 406 : 1
Emancipates, everything that e. spirit, 397 : 13
Emancipating all nations, 392 : 9
Emancipation, African fight for e., 818 : 14
of individual, 550 : 3
of slavish part of mankind, 380 : 8
of woman, 842 : *n* 5
through revolution, 866 : 9
Emasculate, pallid and e. scholarship, 592 : 8
Embalmed and treasured up to life, 281 : 24
Embalmed (*continued*)
darkness, 476 : 26
Embalms, precedent e. principle, 502 : 1
Embark, firs cloaked as if to e., 664 : 2
on bold new program, 787 : 17
Embarras des richesses, 344 : *n* 2
Embarrassment of riches, 344 : 5
Embattled armies clad in iron, 288 : 23
farmers stood, 494 : 13
we are, 890 : 11
Embellish adventures, 385 : 10
Embellished, no part Nature has not e., 125 : 24
Embellit tout ce qu'il touche, 342 : *n* 2
Ember, each separate dying e., 526 : 11
Embers, glowing e. through the room, 278 : 20
O joy that in our e., 426 : 17
of cities, 912 : 7
Emblem, shears and pastepot e., 730 : 15
Emblems of deeds done in clime, 459 : 5
of untimely graves, 377 : 6
sacred e. to partake, 604 : 10
those things they were e. of, 717 : 20
Embodiment, flag e. of history, 682 : 5
of everything excellent, 628 : 16
of hatred, 744 : 8
Embody the law, 628 : 16
Embodying thee untamed as thee, 575 : 22
Emboldens, nothing e. sin as mercy, 243 : 4
Embosomed in the deep, 368 : 20
Embrace, arms take your last e., 193 : 28
as to e. me she inclined, 282 : 21
endure then pity then e., 337 : 5
is death, 833 : 6
my dead mother's ghost, 60 : 8
none do there e., 297 : 1
Pole as Frenchman, 166 : 2
possibilities I didn't e., 654 : 7
principles or mistresses, 368 : 4
rest that knows no care, 101 : 4
simplicity, 64 : 8
time to e., 26 : 21
Embraced, be e. ye millions, 412 : 10
by strumpet wind, 199 : 6
ghost e. fled, 105 : 5
summer dawn, 674 : 10
Embraces, break e., 868 : 7
sorcery of hot e., 816 : 20
your e. give life, 4 : 12
Embraves this morn, 292 : 18
Embroidered, heavens' e. cloths, 712 : 15
loosened the e. girdle, 58 : 19
speech like e. tapestries, 70 : 18
Embroideries, coat covered with e., 713 : 14
Embroidery, nothing behind gold e., 849 : 20
Embroil earth about fancied line, 311 : 15
Embryo, plant grow yet be e., 900 : 8
yesterday e. tomorrow ashes, 124 : 27
Emerald, cause or men of E. Isle, 400 : 10
green as e., 434 : 10
resonance of e., 607 : 12
Emergencies, government in e., 524 : 1
great e. show resources, 648 : 3

Emergencies (*continued*)
presence of mind in e., 568 : 17
Emerges ahead of accomplishments, 857 : 4
path e. then closes, 721 : 7
with verb in mouth, 624 : 9
Emetic, Ulysses somewhat e., 759 : 1
Emigrated to another star, 609 : 12
Emily, called back E., 608 : 7
set doors ajar, 751 : 7
Eminence, raised to that bad e., 284 : 3
Eminent, censure is tax for being e., 322 : 3
Eminently noble, 586 : 14
plain and direct, 586 : 14
Emits a brighter ray, 368 : 12
Emmanuel, call his name E., 36 : 19
O come O come E., 563 : 14
Emmet, Robert E. and Wolfe Tone, 713 : 11
Emotion, cannot demonstrate an e., 637 : 3
communicates idea, 698 : 7
disembodied e. a nonentity, 649 : 8
expressing e. in art, 809 : 5
formula of that particular e., 809 : 5
idea communicates e., 698 : 7
intellect is to e. as clothes, 698 : 8
more than usual e., 437 : 17
no transforming without e., 754 : 14
poetry escape from e., 809 : 4
poetry express every e., 869 : 11
real thing that made e., 845 : 2
recollected in tranquillity, 424 : 9
source of becoming-conscious, 754 : 14
undisciplined squads of e., 807 : 21
war between e. and intellect, 861 : 18
weave e. thought sound, 486 : 8
Emotional, destitute of e. warmth, 649 : 7
orgies, 703 : 1
subtlety and toughness, 870 : 15
Emotions, escape from e., 809 : 4
expression of e., 138 : 4
foreign to art, 619 : 8
from A to B, 827 : 16
of the Spaniards, 480 : 16
Empêchent, ailes de géant l'e., 580 : *n* 5
Emperor and clown, 477 : 1
big stealin' makes you e., 810 : 7
hasn't anything on, 505 : 6
in mine own house, 172 : *n* 2
keep drowsy e. awake, 715 : 3
of ice cream, 766 : 25
pope and e., 491 : 8
power in single e., 382 : 4
subject to no one but God, 137 : 7
you are E. yet you weep, 312 : 5
Emperor's, at midnight on E. pavement, 716 : 9
drunken soldiery abed, 716 : 8
New Clothes, 505 : 5
she might lie by e. side, 231 : 23
Emperors have died of gout, 301 : 2
pomp of e. ridiculous, 496 : 5
purple of e., 708 : 23
souls of e. and cobblers, 165 : 4
Emphasis of passionate love, 442 : 19
Empire, American e. careens onward, 837 : 4
British E. and United States, 744 : 7
course of e., 330 : 25
England an e., 483 : 18
Empire (*continued*)
entrusted with e., 64 : 5
followed in wake, 799 : 19
for raising customers, 366 : 6
God's princes of e., 570 : 12
great e. and little minds, 373 : 8
Holy Roman E., 343 : 7
how is the E., 706 : 22
internal domestic e., 837 : 8
is e. unpossessed, 187 : 22
last thousand years, 744 : 4
liquidation of British E., 746 : 2
loungers of E. drained, 689 : 2
neither holy nor e., 343 : 7
Neptune's e., 217 : 22
perfection never built e., 815 : 5
power in trust, 304 : 7
preserve unity of e., 373 : 6
rod of e., 362 : 6
sun never sets on e., 412 : *n* 6
this alone e. and victory, 467 : 10
thy dread e. Chaos, 340 : 28
vast e. of human society, 424 : 8
westward the course of e., 330 : 25
wide arch of ranged e. fall, 240 : 14
wilderness into e., 373 : 9
Empire's lamentation, 533 : 1
Empires, buries e. in common grave, 383 : 14
changed by bottle, 398 : *n* 1
day of e. come, 627 : 6
dyspepsy ruin of e., 454 : 20
game was e., 462 : 14
hatching vain e., 284 : 15
like earth's e. pass away, 597 : 18
make central e. good neighbors, 783 : 6
vaster than e. and more slow, 296 : 27
Emploi, le physique d'un e., 667 : *n* 1
Employ, how fit to e., 543 : 16
means requisite to ends, 401 : 17
Employed, age e. in edging steel, 399 : 16
men e. best contented, 348 : 21
Employee rise to level of incompetence, 896 : 8
Employees required to state beliefs, 846 : 17
Employment, rising prices full e., 762 : 8
Emptied some dull opiate, 476 : 21
Emptier ever dancing in air, 195 : 11
Emptiness, dull privations and lean e., 253 : 1
eternal smiles e. betray, 339 : 1
my e. among stars, 907 : 11
of ages in face, 670 : 14
produced the universe, 97 : 7
Emptor, caveat e., 133 : 13
Empty, a little louder but as e., 337 : 7
bag cannot stand, 347 : 21
beat an e. barrel, 765 : 5
born e. into modern age, 312 : 20
buckets into e. wells, 376 : 27
buckets into wells, 432 : 25
cisterns exhausted wells, 805 : 12
crowns are e. things, 318 : 10
fame nothing but e. name, 375 : 10
go not e. unto thy mother-in-law, 12 : 27
her e. room is cold, 97 : 10
honor but an e. bubble, 306 : 19
house like stray dog, 620 : 14
idle singer of e. day, 618 : 6
Empty (*continued*)
is the chair e., 187 : 22
life an e. dream, 332 : *n* 2, 509 : 13
mirrors on e. space, 652 : *n* 3
no life moves in e. passageways, 74 : 1
no patriot on e. stomach, 421 : *n* 3
quacks, 650 : 14
rich sent e. away, 42 : 23
room my heart keeps e., 267 : 6
seek e. world again, 562 : 2
seven e. ears, 8 : 31
solid pudding e. praise, 340 : 15
tigers or roaring sea, 193 : 23
to be e. is to be full, 64 : 10
turn down e. glass, 517 : 14
vessel greatest sound, 208 : 12
virtue no e. echo, 413 : 3
words are e. thanks, 324 : 26
Empty-vaulted night, 279 : 19
Emulation, propensity for e., 685 : 3
shouting their e., 242 : 9
Enable press to serve functions, 789 : 5
socialist culture to thrive, 826 : 12
Enacting laws like drinking songs, 81 : 11
Enactments, wicked cruel e., 486 : 16
Enameled, makes music with e. stones, 189 : 34
quaint e. eyes, 281 : 1
snake throws e. skin, 196 : 18
Enameling, hammered gold and gold e., 715 : 3
Enamored, affliction e. of thy parts, 193 : 11
of an ass, 197 : 7
Encamp, though an host should e., 18 : 12
Enchafed flood, 230 : 6
Enchains us to permitted ill, 467 : 13
Enchant, I will e. thine ear, 189 : 7
unity doth e. me, 171 : 13
what deceives may be said to e., 84 : 10
Enchanted, enter e. woods, 600 : 29
holy and e., 433 : 22
isle of time, 846 : 4
life's e. cup, 457 : 12
Medea gathered e. herbs, 200 : 22
mind is e. thing, 799 : 11
place where we can dance, 860 : 13
some e. evening, 833 : 13
Enchanter, ghosts from e. fleeing, 467 : 17
Enchanting, mind is e. thing, 799 : 11
Enchantment, distance lends e., 443 : 4
Enchantments, last e. of Middle Age, 587 : 1
Enchantress, tune e. plays, 692 : 5
Enchants my sense, 226 : 10
Enclose, cherries fairly do e., 250 : 6
Enclosed, forbear to dig dust e. here, 250 : 1
Encloseth, thy breast e. my heart, 187 : 2
Enclosing, mistake of e. envelope, 790 : 6
Encompass, poetic fields e. me, 325 : 6
unencompassable, 561 : 3
Encompassed by horrors, 570 : 14
Encompasseth, my ring e. thy finger, 187 : 2
Encounter darkness as a bride, 228 : 18
truth in free and open e., 282 : 5

Encountering fly this January
day, 607 : 14
Encourage, animate and e., 379 : 1
no vice, 370 : *n* 3
to e. the others, 343 : 11
water most e. flame, 829 : 16
Encouraged, examination of
government e., 439 : 5
he ought to be e., 356 : *n* 5
Encouragement for cultivation of her
powers, 471 : 1
Encourager, pour e. les
autres, 343 : *n* 4
Encouraging clever pupil, 350 : 8
Encroach, habit will e., 433 : 7
Encroaching, white people always
e., 419 : 12
Encroachment, insidious e. by men of
zeal, 677 : 15
Encroachments, gradual and silent
e., 398 : 4
Encumbers him with help, 353 : 26
Encumbrance, periodization of
history e., 847 : 14
Encyclopedia of Error, 615 : 14
End a contest quicker, 398 : 26
apathetic e., 529 : 3
appointment at e. of world, 789 : 8
at his e. shall be a fool, 32 : 13
at the e. take your fill, 61 : 21
at their wit's e., 21 : 16
attempt the e., 266 : 18
beauty sufficient e., 714 : 15
began to draw to our e., 34 : 15
begin with certainties e. in
doubts, 178 : 20
beginning and the e., 53 : 33
beginning of the e., 400 : 17
being's e. and aim, 337 : 10
better is the e. of a thing, 27 : 6
blessed the latter e. of Job, 17 : 11
born to disastrous e., 174 : 11
bow and accept e., 747 : 2
by opposing e. them, 221 : 12
by sleep we e. heartache, 221 : 12
chapters of lives to natural e., 664 : 8
consequent upon our
beginning, 115 : 18
crowns all, 227 : 5
crowns the work, 133 : 26
crowns us not the fight, 266 : 4
death a necessary e., 215 : 26
decline to accept e. of man, 838 : 9
democracy means to e., 814 : 6
despondency and madness, 425 : 10
dine at journey's e., 714 : 2
dispatch in putting e. to it, 89 : 6
easier to resist at beginning than
e., 152 : 10
even unto e. of world, 41 : 31
everything has e., 925 : 25
experience itself the e., 638 : 12
fairest things fleetest e., 693 : 6
go till the e., 612 : 13
go with me to my e., 248 : 25
God will put an e. to these, 104 : 21
going forth is from the e. of the
heaven, 17 : 28
good beginning good e., 159 : 29
good of subjects e. of kings, 318 : 10
great e. of learning, 89 : 22
guide original and e., 130 : 3
hair to stand an e., 219 : 18
heartache, 221 : 12
End (*continued*)
here, 778 : 6
here at life's e., 717 : 9
hope to the e., 52 : 7
humanity come to terrible e., 765 : 1
if e. brings me out, 524 : 11
in e. despondency and
madness, 892 : 15
in joy, 874 : 14
in my beginning is my e., 807 : 9
in my e. my beginning, 167 : 2,
807 : 24
in one purpose, 207 : 8
in science truth only e., 471 : 16
in the e. truth will conquer, 143 : 10
is bitter as wormwood, 23 : 10
is not yet, 40 : 22
is the renown, 227 : 18
journey's e., 232 : 18, 714 : 2
journeys e. in lovers meeting, 213 : 22
justifying means by the e., 127 : 20
keep e. in view, 118 : 8
keeps e. from being hard, 749 : 1
knocks you with butt e., 371 : 23
last e. be like his, 11 : 3
latter e. of a fray, 204 : 36
laws e. tyranny begins, 351 : 1
let e. try the man, 206 : 12
let the e. be legitimate, 402 : 6
let there be e., 540 : 10
liberty as e. and means, 677 : 12
long weary day have e., 174 : 18
losses restored and sorrows
e., 244 : 12
love hath an e., 633 : 5
made finer e. and went away, 207 : 13
make me to know mine e., 19 : 1
makes a swanlike e., 199 : 22
mankind put e. to war, 891 : 1
minutes hasten to their e., 244 : 19
must be near e., 726 : 6
must justify the means, 320 : 15
my wrath did e., 405 : 13
no e. in wandering mazes, 284 : 19
no e. of it the voiceless
wailing, 808 : 3
no e. to chain of
responsibility, 788 : 4
no e. to withering, 808 : 3
no prospect of an e., 367 : 12
not even beginning of e., 746 : 1
not forsake me in my e., 309 : 11
of every man's desire, 633 : 18
of exploring to arrive, 808 : 17
of fight tombstone white, 707 : 20
of journey too, 698 : 15
of life cancels bands, 204 : 23
of life is action, 596 : 6
of love or season, 747 : 2
of making many books there is no
e., 27 : 27, 773 : 14
of my tether, 407 : 15
of perfect day, 698 : 15
of that man is peace, 18 : 27
of the beginning, 746 : 1
of the tunnel, 891 : 9
of the unending, 808 : 13
of the world, 41 : 31
of this day's business, 217 : 10
one must consider the e., 296 : 15
only when life comes to e., 71 : 8
pleasure the beginning and e., 91 : 15
pursue the unknown e., 645 : 3
quiet-colored e. of evening, 542 : 3
End (*continued*)
recurrent e. of unending, 808 : 13
remember the e., 35 : 12
right true e. of love, 253 : 22
sans e., 516 : 15
see the e. and beginning, 863 : 15
served no private e., 336 : 5
sleep itself must e., 275 : 14
snow swept world e. to e., 817 : 2
socialism means to e., 814 : 6
some say world e. in fire, 748 : 2
something ere the e., 529 : 12
stay awhile e. the sooner, 179 : 17
stick it out to e., 726 : 7
such e. true lovers have, 402 : 14
their words to the e. of the
world, 17 : 28
there's an e. of May, 691 : 19
there's an e. on 't, 355 : 10
this is not the e., 746 : 1
till I e. my song, 174 : 21
Time will one day e. it, 227 : 5
to all an e., 711 : 10
to beginnings of wars, 781 : 6
to make the e. most sweet, 193 : 35
to pause to make e., 529 : 9
to war, 781 : 6
true beginning of our e., 197 : 14
true lover therefore had good
e., 149 : 14
truth to the e. of reckoning, 229 : 6
war put e. to mankind, 891 : 1
war that will e. war, 719 : 17
we shall go on to e., 744 : 2
where e. knows God, 854 : 9
where sky touches Earth is
E., 925 : 23
where you begun, 372 : 8
whole has beginning middle and
e., 88 : 17
whose e. is destruction, 50 : 5
world without e., 54 : 18, 378 : 1
yes to the very e., 608 : 10
you are beginning and e., 851 : 16
End-all, be-all and e., 236 : 22
Endanger, power to e. public
liberty, 380 : 13
Endearing elegance of female
friendship, 352 : 20
with e. wile, 370 : 9
young charms, 446 : 11
Endearment, each fond e. tries, 370 : 7
Endeavor, achievement death of
e., 647 : 7
by no e. can magnet, 628 : 9
disinterested e. to learn, 586 : 24
elevate life by e., 559 : 24
in continual motion, 207 : 6
Endeavors to live life imagined, 560 : 16
to preserve peace, 780 : 4
Ended, God be praised Georges
e., 753 : *n* 3
his cares now all e., 206 : 34
our revels now are e., 248 : 13
so e. Sicilian expedition, 81 : 10
with his body changed to
light, 929 : 6
Endin, now sees de e., 837 : 17
Ending, all lovely things have
e., 811 : 16
art of e., 512 : 23
bad beginning makes bad e., 77 : 13
bread sauce of happy e., 653 : 6
hard beginning good e., 159 : 9

Ending (*continued*)
is despair, 248 : 19
never e. still beginning, 306 : 19
O bitter e., 778 : 6
odds on sad e., 910 : 17
of interminable night, 808 : 13
Endings, beginnings and e. untidy, 723 : 10
lie has seven e., 926 : 2
Endless, absence which is e., 555 : 6
extinction of unhappy hates, 586 : 12
frontier, 814 : 9
humility is e., 807 : 13
in e. error hurled, 337 : 2
my days of e. doubt, 172 : 7
night, 266 : 21, 363 : 2
olives of e. age, 245 : 13
perpetual posterity, 444 : 7
pure and e. light, 299 : 6
regret or happiness, 664 : 5
road you tread, 691 : 16
some born to e. night, 406 : 19
summer days, 604 : 14
time an e. song, 712 : 11
whole vocation e. imitation, 426 : 16
Endlessly, cradle e. rocking, 575 : 17
Endorsed, elephants e. with towers, 288 : 10
Endow college or cat, 336 : 1
with all my goods I thee e., 56 : 18
Endowed by ruined millionaire, 807 : 19
by their creator, 387 : 9
Endows, native personality e. man, 577 : 2
Ends, all well that e. well, 159 : 28
all's well that e. well, 227 : 18
and scarce means 842 : 15
candle burns at both e., 822 : 17
come from e. of earth, 707 : 16
consult our private e., 294 : *n* 4
delays have dangerous e., 185 : 4
dog to gain private e., 369 : 18
economics neutral as between e., 843 : 1
filled with e. of worms, 824 : 3
formula for making e. meet, 776 : 4
game that never e., 836 : 15
his circuit unto the e. of it, 17 : 28
in wisdom, 750 : 2
irrelevancies and loose e., 736 : 9
law e. tyranny begins, 307 : 17
man's glory most begins and e., 717 : 15
means requisite to e., 401 : 17
means to achieve great e., 815 : 5
needless Alexandrine e. song, 333 : 8
of being and ideal grace, 507 : 14
of world come, 638 : 10
one e. other begins, 526 : 7
past free of loose e., 736 : 9
smile upon fingers' e., 207 : 13
strange eventful history, 211 : 15
thing that e. other deeds, 241 : 24
thou aimest at, 249 : 8
violent delights have violent e., 192 : 27
watch that e. night, 328 : 11
way the world e., 805 : 18
with Revelations, 675 : 16
your family history e. with you, 86 : 6
Endurance and courage, 726 : 5
for one moment more, 660 : 8
Endure accent of coming foot, 608 : 4
all deaths I could e., 287 : 20
all that human hearts e., 352 : 21
days go I e., 770 : 10
for ages to come, 402 : 5
greater than dare, 540 : 1
his name shall e. forever, 20 : 2
knows how to e. poverty, 108 : 14
last pure stretch, 875 : 2
live by longing and e., 873 : 19
man will not merely e., 838 : 10
men must e. their going, 235 : 11
misfortunes of others, 293 : 2
more able to e., 427 : 23
my heart, 61 : 3
my own despair, 320 : 3
naught e. but mutability, 466 : 11
Negroes will e., 837 : 20
neither evils nor cures, 110 : 11
no picture made to e., 793 : 1
not e. husband with beard, 209 : 4
not yet a breach, 253 : 4
philosopher e. toothache, 210 : 5
poet's privilege to help man e., 838 : 12
so long shall your honor e., 104 : 29
testing whether nation e., 523 : 4
the consequences, 793 : 12
then pity then embrace, 337 : 5
weeping may e. for a night, 18 : 15
what Malherbe writes will e., 176 : 19
would you have songs e., 540 : 12
youth's a stuff will not e., 213 : 23
Endured, moon hath her eclipse e., 245 : 13
much e. little enjoyed, 352 : 17
remembers all that he wrought and e., 60 : 20
something more dreadful, 61 : 3
they e., 837 : 19
torments of grief e., 495 : 18
Endures, heaven e., 692 : 11
man in love e. more, 658 : 14
moment or day, 715 : 13
nothing e. but change, 69 : 25
Endureth, blessed the man that e. temptation, 51 : 28
his mercy e. for ever, 14 : 23
his truth e., 21 : 3
word of the Lord e., 52 : 9
Enduring monument, 469 : 8
the e. are near to virtue, 69 : 4
Endymion, in E. leaped headlong, 479 : 14
Enemies called for peace, 731 : 16
careful in choice of e., 674 : 26
defend country against e., 725 : 20
defend in assaults of our e., 55 : 4
die not hating e., 344 : 12
disposed of foreign e., 85 : 7
fourth glass for mine e., 326 : 18
German for converse with e., 357 : 19
give e. means of our destruction, 66 : 24
giving e. aid and comfort, 391 : 12
giving e. the slip, 359 : 22
governments set example of killing e., 679 : 11
great woe to their e., 59 : 28
his e. shall lick the dust, 20 : 1
humanity has three e., 664 : 16
I can defend myself from e., 422 : *n* 2
in the presence of mine e., 18 : 7
in war in peace friends, 387 : 10
Enemies (*continued*)
intelligent and corrupt, 859 : 14
internal e., 650 : 14
just friends and brave e., 389 : 3
learn from our e., 113 : 20
look e. in face, 309 : 17
love him for e., 598 : 11
love your e., 37 : 11
make e. of nations, 376 : 19
make my e. ridiculous, 343 : 25
naked to mine e., 249 : 9
no perpetual e., 454 : 12
not worth living without e., 721 : 9
of man, 890 : 11
of persecuted blacks, 505 : 11
old friends become bitter e., 258 : 9
saved from our e., 42 : 25
secret history of e., 511 : 19
soften to us our e., 669 : 17
ten jokes a hundred e., 359 : 21
trophies to e. of truth, 274 : 1
unhappy lot finds no e., 111 : 15
we are not e. but friends, 521 : 14
wise learn from e., 82 : 7
Enemigo, el cavader de us e., 935 : 12
que huye, 935 : 8
Enemy and friend together hurt, 625 : 16
art hath e. Ignorance, 255 : 9
be able for thy e., 227 : 9
be taken by Turkish e., 935 : 4
beat soul of e. man, 791 : 16
best is e. of good, 343 : 21
biography written by e., 661 : 15
cannot be hidden, 35 : 23
care's an e. to life, 213 : 10
cherishing e. in disguise, 379 : 16
cruel and unrelenting e., 379 : 2
dashed in pieces the e., 9 : 34
death is the e., 782 : 6
defeat e. in one battle, 384 : 18
drive e. beyond frontier, 420 : 12
English laborer finds worst e., 492 : 20
every man his greatest e., 274 : 19
eye neighbor as e., 737 : 7
faints not nor faileth, 564 : 16
find out where e. is, 589 : 15
goes over to e., 372 : 7
happiness e. to pomp, 326 : 10
hast thou found me O mine e., 14 : 7
here shall he see no e., 211 : 1
if thine e. be hungry, 25 : 15
in their mouths, 230 : 26
is the unknown, 755 : 10
kisses of e. deceitful, 25 : 23
last e. is death, 49 : 1
met e. and it is us, 455 : *n* 1
met e. they are ours, 455 : 5
mightest still the e., 17 : 17
more formidable e. than Germany, 847 : 12
my e. is dead, 576 : 1
my vision's greatest e., 407 : 8
nearest and dearest e., 204 : 22
nearly slew ye, 921 : 1
no e. ever haul colors, 771 : 5
no man's e., 868 : 3
nobody's e. but own, 548 : 34
not how many e. are but where, 78 : 25
of market not ideology, 872 : 3
one e. is too much, 270 : 7
place ship alongside e., 408 : 7
punished as e. of country, 418 : 14

Enemy (*continued*)
reason greatest e. faith has, 156 : 9
rejoice not over thy e., 35 : 13
spy e. could send, 606 : 3
there is no little e., 347 : 3
thyself may be thine e., 605 : 9
to slander you, 625 : 16
treat friend as if he might become e., 111 : 8
turns to flee, 935 : 8
weak man better e. than friend, 561 : 14
wherever e. goes troops go, 589 : 18
will meet one e. everywhere, 130 : 8
worst friend and e. Death, 797 : 3
you my e. and I yours, 348 : 7
Enemy's, by e. beak gouged, 912 : 7
easier to get into e. toils, 66 : 23
mine e. dog, 235 : 7
stand aside from e. onset, 81 : 5
watch e. corpse go by, 935 : 12
Energetic mongrels, 706 : 20
synergetics e. geometry, 832 : 16
Energies, best e. of men and women, 590 : 4
diverse e. of free men, 891 : 5
self-circling e., 436 : 20
Energy and sleepless vigilance, 523 : 1
atomic e., 734 : 14
atomic e. lead to bombs, 763 : 12
atomic e. menace, 763 : 15
child of hell, 572 : 6
equals mass times speed of light squared, 763 : *n* 2
government want e. to preserve itself, 388 : 17
horse provides locomotor e., 678 : 14
of character, 414 : 18
of thought, 490 : 8
power wielded by abnormal e., 635 : 15
public life situation of e., 372 : 7
release of atomic e., 787 : 14
silent e. of nature, 490 : 3
small quantities of e., 678 : 17
synergetics identifies e. with number, 832 : 16
uranium new source of e., 763 : 11
Enfant terrible of literature, 620 : 22
Enfants de la patrie, 415 : 1
terribles, 502 : 24
Enfer, chaud comme l'e., 400 : *n* 3
l'e. c'est les Autres, 865 : *n* 1
l'e. des femmes, 296 : *n* 4
Enfold, how many perils do e., 173 : 11
Enforce, tongues of dying e. attention, 194 : 9
with temper, 358 : 6
Enforceable safeguards, 787 : 16
Enforced from our quiet sphere, 206 : 26
it useth e. ceremony, 216 : 30
obedience, 233 : 5
Enforcement, gentleness my strong e., 211 : 12
Enfranchisement, liberty freedom e., 216 : 6
Engaged in great civil war, 523 : 4
struggle in which so long e., 383 : 4
Engagement, get loose from honorable e., 372 : 5
positive e. to marry, 489 : 15
Engarlanded, with mist e., 587 : 11
Engenders, every cloud e. not storm, 186 : 22
not white hair that e. wisdom, 91 : 10
shudder in loins e., 715 : 16
so much more, 838 : 2
Engine, great e. never sleeps, 539 : 15
human e. waits, 805 : 7
power alone, 724 : 4
steam e. in trousers, 433 : 5
two-handed e. at door, 280 : 22
which drives enterprise, 783 : 8
wit's an unruly e., 268 : 7
Engineer, enemy of market is e., 872 : 3
give me the e., 566 : 6
hoist with own petar, 223 : 13
sometimes striking the e., 268 : 7
story of brave e., 731 : *n* 2
Engineers of soul, 725 : 9
Enginer hoist with own petar, 223 : 13
Engines, feeble e. of despotism, 390 : 1
O you mortal e., 231 : 11
England, always be an E., 885 : 11
an empire, 483 : 18
and Saint George, 207 : 18
awake, 407 : 7
be E. what she will, 375 : 13
bound with triumphant sea, 194 : 14
bow made in E., 689 : 16
breeds valiant creatures, 207 : 25
cliffs of E. stand, 587 : 13
common law of E., 815 : 17
corner of field forever E., 797 : 1
dress in E., 680 : 10
expects, 408 : 8
from old E. they set sail, 935 : 3
frontier of E. on Rhine, 720 : 11
further off from E., 612 : 9
gentlemen of E., 273 : 6
Greece Italy and E. did adorn, 306 : 1
has no name for prairies, 471 : 11
hath given warning, 384 : 12
hath need of thee, 425 : 22
highroad to E., 354 : 10
history is now and E., 808 : 16
I am in E. everywhere, 274 : 17
if E. to itself true, 202 : 20
in E. I've mate, 551 : 2
in E. now, 541 : 16
in E. time lag, 720 : 8
Ireland gives E. generals, 601 : 7
keep my bones, 202 : 12
know kings of E., 628 : 1
knuckle-end of E., 432 : 18
let not E. forget precedence, 281 : 17
light candle in E., 156 : 14
many a peer of E. brews, 691 : 17
mariners of E., 443 : 10
martial airs of E., 451 : 2
men of E. wherefore plow, 467 : 23
meteor flag of E., 443 : 13
middle class in E., 589 : 8
middle class safety of E., 540 : 3
model to inward greatness, 207 : 11
my England, 663 : 14
navy of E., 365 : 16
neck wrung like chicken, 745 : 12
never at foot of conqueror, 202 : 19
nor E. did I know, 425 : 6
of a king of E. too, 163 : 15
oh to be in E., 541 : 16
old E. to adorn, 710 : 12
or E. breed again, 182 : 15
paradise for women, 259 : 22
paradise of individuality, 704 : 2
England (*continued*)
paradise of women, 174 : 23
planted E. with stubborn trust, 840 : 5
poison E. at roots, 741 : 16
poorest he in E., 264 : 11
refrigerator called E., 711 : 2
reversed system succeeded, 593 : 2
rightwise king of E., 149 : 6
roast beef of E., 349 : 7
roast beef of old E., 349 : *n* 3
Saint George for E., 742 : 14
Scots friends to E., 177 : 16
sea once made E. secure, 752 : 1
shower of curates on E., 555 : 20
slaves cannot breathe in E., 376 : 20
stands sentry, 639 : 16
stately homes of E., 470 : 13, 781 : 16
such night in E., 488 : 3
take my drum to E., 700 : 8
there I find flag of E., 420 : 16
this realm this E., 194 : 13
was merry England, 430 : 22
what have I done for E., 663 : 14
what is left of E., 491 : *n* 1
what would I not do E., 663 : 14
who dies if E. live, 710 : 24
who only E. knows, 708 : 16
whoever wakes in E., 541 : 16
wins last battle, 745 : 13
with all thy faults, 375 : *n* 6
wont to conquer others, 194 : 15
world where E. dead, 752 : 2
youth of E. are on fire, 207 : 10
England's green and pleasant land, 406 : 21
mountains green, 406 : 21
old E. winding sheet, 406 : 18
pleasant pastures, 406 : 21
song forever, 700 : 10
stay no more on E. shore, 935 : 5
English, among E. poets after death, 479 : 16
attain E. style, 352 : 23
can't think of E., 612 : 22
Chaucer well of E., 173 : 22
civilization humanizing, 589 : 7
cleft dust never E. dust, 840 : 5
close wall with E. dead, 207 : 16
dictionary best reading, 740 : 18
father of E. criticism, 352 : 25
fields upland dim, 587 : 11
for suppressing other, 586 : 21
hierarchy tremble, 379 : 16
his E. sweete upon his tonge, 145 : 24
in an E. lane, 542 : 6
in favor of boys learning E., 743 : 8
king's E., 225 : 12
kissed by E. dead, 827 : 6
laborer finds worst enemy, 492 : 20
language of E. poet, 809 : 16
majority of E. snobs, 681 : 2
marks our E. dead, 709 : 12
most beautiful words in E. language, 654 : 12
mother made moan, 568 : 14
never abolish anything, 698 : 10
not Turkish court, 206 : 35
one pair of E. legs, 207 : 23
pint of E. ale, 742 : 14
principle of E. constitution, 365 : 18
spoke bad E. in children's books, 701 : 6
strung on E. thread, 569 : 2

English (*continued*)
sweet as E. air, 530 : 22
take of E. earth, 710 : 15
tear, 489 : 3
tongue I love, 911 : 1
trick of our E. nation, 206 : 3
up with which not put, 746 : 19
utilitarianism word of E. spirit, 737 : 12
we E. nation of brutes, 683 : *n* 5
white as angel E. child, 403 : 6
winter ending in July, 461 : 27
wood of E. bows, 689 : 16
Englishman beat three Frenchmen, 326 : 22
blood of an E., 934 : 4
content to say nothing, 356 : 14
either for E. or Jew, 407 : 11
he is an E., 627 : 17
if I were American as I am E., 351 : 5
in Eden find fault, 561 : 13
in Wellington's army, 359 : *n* 4
last great E., 533 : 2
moral when uncomfortable, 680 : 20
prejudices of true E., 326 : 22
rights of E., 390 : 11
stirred heart of E., 726 : 5
true-born E., 194 : 8
vain ill-natured E., 318 : 6
Englishman's, part of every E. education, 590 : 10
thoughts, 586 : 23
Englishmen, mad dogs and E., 843 : 8
O when shall E., 182 : 15
our fathers were E., 265 : 8
English-speaking, union of E. peoples, 672 : 16
Engraven, deep on his front e., 284 : 14
Enhance, rubs e. value of favors, 369 : 8
Enigma, riddle in mystery an e., 743 : 17
Enisled, in sea of life e., 585 : 13
Enjoy, crown that seldom kings e., 186 : 8
delight with liberty, 174 : 12
don't have to go e. it, 711 : 9
get what want and e. it, 711 : 4
grudge what they cannot e., 66 : 10
her while she's kind, 305 : 3
honey-heavy dew of slumber, 215 : 22
ice cream while it's on plate, 839 : 15
indifferent and cannot e. it, 353 : 26
interval, 704 : 4
most e. contented least, 244 : 9
neither e. nor suffer, 686 : 13
other people's sufferin', 722 : 18
private men e., 208 : 6
prize not while we e. it, 209 : 31
resources within thy reach, 71 : 28
things we ought, 87 : 22
too late to e. it, 310 : 3
your dear wit, 280 : 2
Enjoyed, bards of old e. in you, 403 : 1
hours I once e., 375 : 15
in vision beatific, 283 : 28
more chased than e., 199 : 6
much endured little e., 352 : 17
no sooner but despised, 245 : 23
not e. if not been there, 695 : *n* 3
supinely e. gifts of founder, 384 : 1
the lady, 404 : 11
to have e. sun, 585 : 11
Enjoying, oh think it worth e., 306 : 19
Enjoyment, communal e. of fruits of earth, 414 : 22
credulity helps e., 577 : 8
human benefit and e., 373 : 4
intellectual e., 694 : 4
life not from e. to e., 355 : 21
of life and liberty, 367 : 4
variety mother of e., 501 : 4
Enjoyments, occasional e. lighting pain, 697 : 10
seasoning of all e., 298 : 2
Enjoys, beauty ne'er e., 338 : 19
who e. not life, 274 : 13
Enlaced and fallen among grass, 886 : 5
Enlarge, circle never ceaseth to e., 184 : 18
my life, 351 : 20
Enlarger of public life, 617 : 7
Enlarges, develops and e. organ, 393 : 7
Enlighten people generally, 389 : 12
Enlightened enough to exercise control, 389 : 15
his eyes were e., 12 : 37
who knows himself is e., 64 : 11
Enlightenment, safety e. civilization, 582 : 12
Enlist, we will all e. again, 907 : 8
Enmity between thee and the woman, 7 : 10
three classes of friendship and e., 124 : 4
Ennoble, we must e. our works, 140 : 6
Ennobled by own exertions, 414 : 9
Ennui, celestial e. of apartments, 768 : 11
Enoch walked with God, 7 : 24
Enormous, knowledge e., 478 : 6
Enough as good as feast, 161 : 17
beauty are you not e., 787 : 7
damned that cries Hold e., 240 : 11
for all, 760 : 10
for my life, 35 : 4
for this life, 821 : 3
freedom from something not e., 789 : 5
God if this were e., 669 : 5
Gods have e., 561 : 1
if something, 429 : 1
in world for everyone, 788 : 2
know e. of something, 878 : 16
know what is more than e., 404 : 6
long e. and just so long, 829 : 16
love is e., 618 : 8
never know what is e., 404 : 6
not e. to fight, 771 : 12
not e. to help feeble up, 242 : 29
of children's gratitude, 716 : 12
or too much, 404 : 9
the living are not e., 850 : 3
time e. for that, 247 : 6
'tis e. 'twill serve, 193 : 5
to have died once e., 106 : 1
tradition not e., 809 : 20
word to wise e., 170 : 33
work to do, 710 : 13
Enrage those paying your annuities, 344 : 8
Enraged rose threatening, 897 : 6
Enrich yourselves, 456 : 4
Enriched, pension never e. young man, 270 : 5
Enriches, that which not e. him, 230 : 33
Ensanguined hearts, 377 : 6
Enshrine her and she dies, 794 : 1
Ensign, beauty's e. yet is crimson, 193 : 27
full high advanced, 283 : 20
tear tattered e., 518 : 12
Ensigns of command, 418 : 8
Enskyed, thing e. and sainted, 227 : 27
Enslave, man alone e. man, 876 : 19
people impossible to e., 445 : 1
we fight not to e., 384 : 19
Enslaved, baptism e. me, 674 : 5
by things they want, 895 : 12
destiny alike for free and e., 71 : 15
London in ruins rather than e., 744 : 5
tamely and abjectly e., 744 : 5
to sects, 125 : 21
Enslavement and existential death, 907 : 1
certainty of worse, 882 : 11
faced e. if captured, 617 : 6
Ensnare, man's imperial race e., 334 : 3
Ensured release, 692 : 11
Entails, when truth e. ruin, 75 : 17
Entangling alliances, 389 : 2
what so e. as death, 255 : 3
Enter, all hope abandon who e. here, 140 : 13
enchanted woods, 600 : 29
into his gates with thanksgiving, 21 : 3
into joy, 40 : 29
into kingdom of heaven, 38 : 19
Lord Christ e. in, 676 : 14
nation which keepeth truth may e., 30 : 9
not into temptation, 41 : 13
they that e. must go on knees, 262 : 9
to grow in wisdom, 617 : 5
wind storm rain may e., 351 : 7
ye shall not e. into heaven, 40 : 1
Entered, I have e. on enterprise, 359 : 2
into springs of sea, 16 : 31
into unadvisedly, 56 : 6
Entergraft our hands, 253 : 6
Enterprise for glory of Christian, 151 : 1
heroic e. gone, 373 : 23
is sick, 226 : 1
lifeblood of our e., 204 : 28
more e. in walking naked, 713 : 14
private e. not yet tried, 780 : 7
profit engine of e., 783 : 8
set habits of age, 826 : 2
want of e. and faith, 560 : 7
without precedent, 359 : 2
Enterprises, in mighty e. determination enough, 112 : 22
of great pith, 221 : 12
that require new clothes, 559 : 10
Enters, idly bent on him that e. next, 195 : 15
naught e. there, 213 : 8
war seldom e. but where wealth allures, 305 : 22
Entertain all comers, 57 : 32
lag-end of my life, 205 : 1
strangers, 51 : 22
this starry stranger, 292 : 17
Entertained angels unawares, 51 : 22
spirit once e. you, 873 : 14
Entertainer who understood his time, 774 : 12
Entertaining, more e. than half the novels, 751 : 19

Entertainment, analysis of character e., 861:11
Entertains exclusive worms, 827:14
harmless day, 250:15
Enthroned, dark Care sits e., 107:26
mercy e. in hearts of kings, 200:9
on darkest altar, 881:11
Enthusiasm, briefcase of e., 835:6
faith an excitement and e., 504:16
nothing great without e., 497:28
whatever poet writes with e., 79:9
Enthusiasts, how to deal with e., 488:8
Entice dewy-feathered sleep, 278:25
if sinners e. thee, 23:2
Entière, Vénus toute e., 312:*n* 5
Entire, that ye may be perfect and e., 51:27
Entities not multiplied unnecessarily, 143:2
Entitled, more no man e. to, 687:8
Entity, air's jail seals each e., 905:7
and quiddity, 291:2
be loyal to e. within, 895:13
greater than self, 895:13
Entrails, in our own proper e., 217:11
webs from e. spin, 167:*n* 9
Entrance, all men have one e. into life, 34:19
beware e. to quarrel, 219:1
fatal e. of Duncan, 236:17
give God e. ticket, 582:4
Entrances, exits and their e., 211:15
Entrap, seeming truth to e. wisest, 199:27
Entrapped, love of you e. me, 4:11
Entreats, Hesperus e. thy light, 255:12
Entrenched greed, 779:14
Entrepreneur, what e. contributes, 784:28
Entrepreneurial profit, 784:28
Entreprise, c'est une épineuse e., 164:*n* 15
Entropy, shores of e., 864:4
Entrusted, man to whom populace is e., 57:15
with great concerns, 69:16
Entrusts life to one hole only, 93:14
Entwine itself verdantly, 446:11
Envelope, mistake of enclosing e., 790:6
Enveloping earth, 435:27
Envelops, ground opens and e. me, 912:12
Enviable death was his, 746:7
Envied, better e. than pitied, 78:10
Envieth, charity e. not, 48:23
love e. not, 48:23
Envious and calumniating time, 226:20
beggar is e. of beggar, 61:13
Casca, 216:23
humble are usually e., 308:18
more free than e. court, 210:23
of wounded soldiers, 732:3
serpents e., 254:10
siege of watery Neptune, 194:14
silence e. tongues, 249:8
turn e. look, 868:6
ungrateful Public, 445:7
Environ, what perils do e., 173:*n* 3
Environment, ancestry and cultural e., 685:6
change e., 818:12
change e. not man, 832:12
controlled by e., 818:12
Environment (*continued*)
freedom in e., 551:18
inequality of e., 621:6
internal e., 551:19
is all excepting me, 833:2
man not locked into e., 870:15
natural e. living organism, 875:13
Envisage circumstance all calm, 478:5
Envoys, her e. ubiquitous, 539:15
two punctilious e. Thine and Mine, 311:15
Envy and wrath shorten life, 36:1
attracts e. of world, 372:12
born from the start, 78:11
calumny hate pain, 469:12
coal hissing hot, 555:14
dared not hate, 459:11
for the dead, 625:8
from e. hatred and malice, 55:10
golden mean avoids e. of palace, 107:20
honor without e. friend who prospered, 71:7
no man's happiness, 212:2
not e. generals, 575:8
not reverence of dead but e. of living, 264:19
of less happier lands, 194:13
of the dead, 76:10
of the devil, 34:12
pain successful men cause neighbors, 116:3
Pride E. Avarice three sparks, 141:5
Pride E. Malice, 443:2
slayeth the silly, 15:14
slays itself by own arrows, 132:21
stirred up with e., 283:3
strongly rooted as e., 399:4
toil e. want, 351:17
too low for e., 295:2
vice of republics, 511:1
void of e. guile lust, 345:21
whim e. or resentment, 375:12
with e. Time transported, 920:4
Envying, strife and e., 47:29
Envy's a coal comes hissing, 555:14
Enwrought with gold and silver, 712:15
Eon, lie down for e. or two, 707:21
Epater le bourgeois, 581:*n* 6
Ephemeral, fame is e., 124:23
story e. and doomed, 838:8
Ephesian sod, 571:3
youth that fired E. dome, 275:*n* 1
Ephesus, temple in E. built, 924:3
Ephraim, gleaning of grapes of E., 12:11
Epicure, serenely full e. say, 433:12
Epicurean cooks sharpen his appetite, 240:27
paradox, 519:10
Epicurus, he was E. owene sone, 146:2
set forth highest good, 101:11
Epicurus', hog of E. herd, 109:3
Epidemic of world lawlessness, 780:4
Epidemical love of flattery, 327:16
Epigram, what is an e., 435:24
Epigrams, France despotism tempered by e., 473:11
your e. are shorter, 119:5
Epigram-surprise, or with e., 486:3
Epilogue, no e. I pray you, 197:21
Episode in drama of pain, 640:17
love an e. in man's life, 417:12
Episodes, Renaissance and Reformation e., 847:14
Epitaph, believe woman or e., 456:15
better bad e., 221:4
drear, 707:20
for their country, 703:14
me who am their e., 252:25
not remembered in thy e., 205:12
of those who fell, 746:5
of which not ashamed, 669:15
to be my story, 749:8
Epitaphs, let's talk of e., 195:1
nice derangement of e., 398:11
Epithet belongs to gentleman, 441:6
his surname e. for knave, 153:*n* 5
Epithets, stuffed with e. of war, 229:11
Epitome, all mankind's e., 304:10
Epoch, coincide with e. or differ, 672:3
man lives life of e., 755:7
no one immune to spirit of e., 755:1
spirit of e., 755:1
Epocha in history, 380:14
Equal, admitted to that e. sky, 336:17
all animals e., 858:12
all e. except Negroes, 520:2
all evils e. when extreme, 275:20
all men and women created e., 554:4
all men created e., 387:9, 523:4
and exact justice, 389:2
before the law, 615:1
born free and e., 387:*n* 4
but in dust, 255:5
chance to obtain rights, 753:6
division of unequal earnings, 449:4
I am e. and whole, 634:4
in e. scale weighing, 217:29
in marriage independence e., 471:1
in presence of death, 110:14
inferiors revolt to be e., 88:9
ivry man e. if not careful, 722:23
justice for all, 80:17
male and female e., 574:9
male cannot tolerate living with e., 508:22
more e. than others, 858:12
mutual actions e., 313:15
nature with e. mind, 585:9
none e. Alcides except himself, 115:11
pay for equal work, 578:2
piece of justice Death, 274:11
protection of laws, 392:4
rate with unequal weights, 100:17
sees with e. eye as God, 336:14
separate and e. station, 387:9
separate but e., 820:14
sharing of miseries, 746:16
some more e., 858:12
syllables require, 333:7
taken with e. thanks, 222:5
talked long enough about e. rights, 872:9
those e. in any respect, 88:8
to a god sitting opposite you, 102:5
to all things, 371:14
to Him is not anyone, 132:19
to whole of that commerce, 372:12
upstairs, 694:8
wealth and opportunities, 666:2
when favor of gods was e., 78:2
Equaling, think of e. men of worth, 68:16
Equality, apostles of e., 588:19

Equality (*continued*)
  believe in e. of man, 385:5
  characteristic of democracy, 845:15
  choose e., 589:2
  democracy and socialism have word e., 506:12
  dispensing e., 85:3
  economic e. for women, 903:9
  if e. found in democracy, 88:6
  justice humanity, 725:20
  law in majestic e., 655:14
  liberty e. fraternity, 928:2
  live in e., 618:10
  never e. in servants' hall, 694:8
  of property, 506:2
Equalizer, work great e., 664:17
Equally, because e. free absolutely equal, 88:8
  entitled to protection, 419:3
  youth and age e. a burden, 84:4
Equals and unequals alike, 85:3
  commerce between e., 369:25
  connects and e. all, 336:22
  energy e. mass times speed of light squared, 763:*n* 2
  first among e., 134:19
  peace between e., 682:9
  revolt to be superior, 88:9
  virtue only flourish amongst e., 414:6
Equanimity, cultivate e., 665:1
Equations, in midst of diagrams and e., 763:8
Equators, north poles and e., 613:22
Equi et poetae alendi, 171:*n* 8
  lente currite noctis e., 113:*n* 4, 184:8
  noli e. dentes inspicere donati, 128:*n* 8
Equilibrium from within, 784:14
Equinox, who knows when was the e., 275:10
Equinoxes, precession of e., 535:*n* 6
Equipment, shabby e. deteriorating, 807:21
Equitable, aim at something more e., 414:22
Equity according to conscience of Chancellor, 263:13
  act against natural e., 367:9
  and fair play, 737:3
  is a roguish thing, 263:13
  law of humanity justice e., 373:18
Equivalent, create e. for what I felt, 801:2
  evil gains e. of disaster, 61:19
  mechanical e. of heat, 650:16
  moral e. of war, 650:16
Equivocate, I will not e., 505:13
Equivocation, poetry purged of e., 735:13
  will undo us, 224:12
Era, new e. in life from reading, 559:34
Eradicated, savage in man never e., 557:19
Ercles' vein, 196:4
Erebus, dark as E., 201:3
Erect, avowed e. and manly foe, 422:5
  by bending above fallen, 615:6
  godlike e., 285:17
  sprang to feet stood e., 540:31
  two souls e. and strong, 507:11
Erected, fleshed fair e., 878:3
Erected (*continued*)
  least e. spirit, 283:28
  with e. look, 305:5
Erecting, corrupted youth in e. grammar school, 185:28
Eremite, nature's patient E., 478:20
Eretria, farewell renowned E., 83:6
Erg, in e. and atom, 839:3
Erinyes who exact punishment underground, 59:3
Eripuit coelo fulmen, 346:*n* 5
Ernährt, Krieg e. den Krieg, 413:*n* 3
'Eroes thin red 'e., 708:3
  thin red line of 'e., 578:*n* 4
Eros builder of cities, 868:15
  unarm E., 241:18
  Zeus's child, 76:22
Erotic instinct questionable, 755:3
Err, Art may e., 307:4
  better e. with Pope, 456:16
  cautious seldom e., 68:17
  fifty times to one does e., 315:19
  grossly as few, 304:13
  mortal and may e., 272:12
  reasoning but to e., 337:2
  they do not e., 430:8
  to e. human forgive divine, 333:15
  to e. is human, 120:21, 133:22
Errand, fool's e., 359:23
  joyous e., 517:14
  sleeveless e., 159:16
  sun e. boy, 571:5
  thy e. here below, 442:3
Errare humanum est, 133:22
Erred, we have e. and strayed, 54:12
  wisest men have e., 288:25
Erring, blind man's e. judgment, 332:19
  extravagant and e. spirit, 217:25
  Lord for the e. thought, 631:15
  power e. men call Chance, 279:28
  reason's spite, 337:1
  rod to check the e., 427:13
  sister's shame, 459:3
Erroneous, thickets of e. observations, 825:13
  truth in things e., 579:16
Error, all men liable to e., 307:16
  charged the troops of e., 274:1
  correct cave, 899:15
  delay preferable to e., 388:11
  Encyclopedia of E., 615:14
  fled before reason and experiment, 387:13
  fruitful e., 662:21
  guilty of no e., 444:15
  hardy plant, 537:17
  hosts of e., 694:15
  if this be e., 245:18
  ignorance preferable to e., 387:12
  in endless e. hurled, 337:2
  in pride our e. lies, 336:18
  is immense, 329:2
  keep citizen from e., 821:9
  keep Government from e., 821:9
  life a mist of e., 262:7
  life is only e., 413:23
  love truth pardon e., 343:2
  more dangerous the more truth, 580:11
  no e. not find defenders, 615:14
  not afraid to tolerate e., 389:16
  nothing more damaging than old e., 397:5
Error (*continued*)
  of opinion tolerated, 388:16
  of 1848 and 1849, 553:6
  old and gray-headed e., 274:25
  only e. to be exposed, 772:8
  opponent weaned from e., 727:5
  prophecy gratuitous e., 565:22
  reformers of e., 389:5
  religion not popular e., 593:10
  show a man he is in e., 307:15
  sink of uncertainty and e., 300:11
  to expect favors, 379:14
  to marry with poets, 884:18
  trial and e., 678:3
  truth to one e. to other, 727:5
  very e. of the moon, 232:15
Errors, amusing with numerous e., 369:6
  besetting e., 464:5
  correct e. when shown e., 522:7
  deliver from e. of wise, 290:7
  if to her female e. fall, 334:2
  not in art but in artificers, 313:12
  reasoned e., 596:8
  stratagems which e. seem, 332:18
  volitional, 778:3
  wanderings mists and tempests, 100:*n* 7
Errs if he hopes to do deed without God's knowledge, 71:22
  man e. as long as he strives, 396:9
'Erse's., 'ear 'e. legs, 535:7
Erump, evade e., 98:*n* 3
Erupit, abiit excessit evasit e., 98:*n* 3
Eruption, strange e. to our state, 217:18
Eruptions, strange e., 204:10
Esau, hands are hands of E., 8:17
  sold his birthright, 8:16
  was a cunning hunter, 8:15
Escalier, l'esprit de l'e., 359:14
Escapades of death, 768:18
Escape, better ten guilty e., 365:19
  cannot e. history, 522:12
  golden e., 852:14
  good thing to e. death, 74:15
  how will you e. it, 582:8
  immortals cannot e. love, 74:23
  into calm regions, 357:17
  less evil that some e., 645:10
  let no guilty e., 590:1
  marriages are not e., 898:5
  me never, 542:11
  not e. my iambics, 102:20
  of all e. mechanisms, 772:15
  poetry e. from emotion, 809:4
  shifts to e. thinking, 569:7
  those who dream at night, 526:3
  thou shalt not e. calumny, 221:17
  what struggle to e., 477:5
  whipping, 221:5
Escaped from the deep, 140:11
  what speech e. your teeth, 57:27
  with skin of my teeth, 16:2
Escapes, hair-breadth e., 229:28
  rarely e. injuring own hands, 65:7
  virtue e. not calumnious strokes, 218:27
Escaping left Death's scraping, 767:11
Eschewed, one that e. evil, 14:35
Escurial, thou art to me E., 270:2
  Tom Jones will outlive E., 383:16
Escutcheon, blot on e. of Common Law, 638:8

Eskimo Ootah had explanation, 679 : 12
Esoteric, exoteric and e. doctrine, 72 : 19
Espaces infinis, 300 : *n* 1
Espagnol, je parle e. à Dieu, 143 : *n* 10
Espoir, un peu d'e., 617 : *n* 1
Espouse everlasting sea, 425 : 19
Espoused, saw my late e. saint, 282 : 20
Esprit de corps, 771 : 13
 l'e. de l'escalier, 359 : 14
 l'e. de son âge, 344 : *n* 3
 une allure de notre e., 164 : *n* 15
Essay loose sally of mind, 352 : 8
 no room for impurities in e., 782 : 1
 of arms make short e., 307 : 8
Essayist philosopher scold jester, 847 : 10
Essays, my e. come home, 179 : 21
Essence, drop of thing's e., 733 : 17
 fellowship with e., 475 : 20
 his glassy e., 228 : 10
 knows e. of beauty, 83 : 9
 look to e. of thing, 125 : 13
 not disclose e. of phenomena, 789 : 2
 time is of e., 923 : 13
Essences, combined e. of heaven and earth, 97 : 7
Essential, art find e., 887 : 14
 assistance from fate e., 313 : 5
 concept and first truth, 882 : 5
 disarmament is e., 781 : 9
 economic factor in e. problem, 790 : 2
 facts of life, 559 : 25
 four e. freedoms, 780 : 13
 gaudiness of poetry, 769 : 12
 give up e. liberty, 348 : 2
 great expense may be e., 374 : 9
 is invisible to eye, 849 : 4
 knowledge, 552 : 11
 natural e. rights, 387 : *n* 4
 poetry, 437 : 1
 provider of elements, 586 : 23
 relationship to existence, 552 : 11
 service to country, 322 : 12
 thing in form, 769 : 13
 things e. or things circumstantial, 302 : 4
Essentially, objects e. fixed and dead, 437 : 12
Essentials, six e. in painting, 135 : 11
Establish justice, 391 : 10
 ordain and e. Constitution, 391 : 10
 peace spare conquered, 105 : 24
 thou the work of our hands, 20 : 15
Established for prevention of crime, 88 : 5
 he hath e. it upon the floods, 18 : 8
 hope to see peace e., 781 : 8
 liberal institutions cease when e., 658 : 12
 name is estate, 525 : 8
 order rarely overthrown, 813 : 14
 society, 859 : 13
Establishment, immense military e., 815 : 15
 keep alive hoary e., 414 : 16
 military e., 815 : 15
 of religion, 391 : 14
 of system of security, 781 : 9
Estate, distressed in mind body or e., 55 : 6
 fallen from his high e., 306 : 18
 fourth e., 472 : 17, 539 : 15
 fourth e. in politics, 445 : 3
Estate (*continued*)
 Fourth E. more important than all, 472 : *n* 2
 good fame, 494 : 10
 how fleeting the e. of man, 124 : 27
 low e. of his handmaiden, 42 : 21
 name an e. in tenure, 525 : 8
 pleasure during getting e., 310 : 3
 who not offended with his e., 130 : 1
 wish e. of world undone, 240 : 5
Estates degrees and offices, 199 : 14
Esteem everything esteem nothing, 297 : 25
 give to get e., 368 : 19
 lightly what obtain cheap, 384 : 13
 nothing above virtue, 68 : 13
 to all, 378 : 14
 value from e. of ages, 302 : 18
Esteemed, better vile than vile e., 245 : 22
 man of sovereign parts, 190 : 20
 medicine least e. of arts, 80 : 4
 wonder that gold e., 155 : 3
Esteems, everything man e., 715 : 13
 man worth as he e. himself, 158 : 1
Estimate, thou knowest thy e., 245 : 1
Estimation, nothing in world's e., 577 : 17
Estranged faces, 693 : 18
 lovers e. or dead, 716 : 20
 stranger to oneself e. from others, 867 : 7
Estranging, unplumbed e. sea, 585 : 14
Estuaries, blue e., 837 : 2
Et cum spiritu tuo, 54 : 1
 in Arcadia ego, 133 : 23
 tu Brute, 99 : *n* 17, 216 : 5
État l'é. c'est moi, 312 : *n* 1
Etched by tonight's moon, 317 : 16
Etching, an e. a mezzotint, 544 : 25
Eternal, abode where E. are, 469 : 17
 ancient houses not e., 701 : 10
 art alone e., 538 : 7
 assert e. Providence, 283 : 2
 attributes of God are e., 308 : 5
 boy e., 246 : 9
 death an e. sleep, 415 : 17
 delight and deliciousness, 570 : 6
 dignity of man, 787 : 12
 dying yet fancy ourselves e., 128 : 13
 Fame's e. beadroll, 173 : 22
 Fame's e. camping ground, 578 : 10
 Father strong to save, 596 : 18
 feast in thine e. cell, 225 : 4
 feel and know we are e., 309 : 4
 feminine draws us on, 396 : 27
 fitness of things, 349 : 19
 Footman snicker, 803 : 16
 gift of God e. life, 47 : 5
 glib about e. things, 874 : 17
 God is thy refuge, 11 : 26
 gone to e. rest, 525 : 11
 heaven's e. year, 305 : 6
 hope springs e., 336 : 15
 hostility against tyranny, 388 : 15
 importance like baseball, 791 : 6
 in whom standeth e. life, 55 : 4
 justice temporary but conscience e., 156 : 3
 lack of pence, 530 : 16
 law, 72 : 16
 lay hold on e. life, 51 : 3
 lids apart, 478 : 20
 life e. love immortal, 642 : 10
Eternal (*continued*)
 live as if e., 83 : *n* 7
 misery together, 317 : 1
 no e. truth, 818 : 10
 note of sadness, 587 : 14
 nothing lasts save e. change, 265 : 3
 now does always last, 295 : 11
 our e. home, 328 : 10
 pain short joy e., 413 : 27
 passion e. pain, 586 : 6
 prompts e. sigh, 337 : 10
 quantity of force e., 583 : 21
 Sabbath of his rest, 304 : 23
 Saki from bowl poured, 516 : 21
 seas of space and time, 802 : 20
 sigh, 337 : 10
 silence of infinite spaces, 300 : 2
 smiles emptiness betray, 339 : 1
 Son of Heaven's e. King, 277 : 6
 spirit real and e., 583 : 3
 summer gilds them, 461 : 3
 swear an e. friendship, 298 : 10
 tasted e. joys of Heaven, 183 : 21
 things not seen e., 49 : 13
 thy e. summer not fade, 244 : 6
 tracings of e. light, 412 : 11
 truths have fresh meaning, 780 : 10
 unwept in e. night, 108 : 13
 vigilance, 397 : 21, 814 : 20
 what e. streams, 525 : 18
 whisperings around, 478 : 16
Eternally, secluded e. from God, 254 : 23
Éternel, le silence é., 300 : *n* 1
Eternities, the absolutes the e., 886 : 8
 two e. of darkness, 846 : 2
Eternity and I are one, 631 : 16
 artifice of e., 715 : 2
 becomes a babe in e., 406 : 14
 can I forget you for e., 894 : 3
 contract for e., 615 : 13
 dazzles at it as at e., 299 : 5
 debt through e., 395 : 19
 deserts of vast e., 296 : 28
 drain of e., 76 : 8
 from e. shall not fail, 691 : 20
 from here to e., 708 : 14
 heirs of all e., 190 : 9
 horologe of E., 510 : 23
 I saw E., 299 : 6
 image of E., 458 : 29
 image of his own e., 34 : 12
 in an hour, 406 : 8
 instant made e., 542 : 16
 intimates e. to man, 326 : 3
 into himself e. changed him, 651 : 14
 is the sea, 674 : 1
 it is e. now, 662 : 20
 kill time injuring e., 559 : 3
 killing e. essence of tragedy, 706 : 3
 leave e. to Thee, 570 : 6
 memorial to soul's e., 601 : 17
 no e. will return, 412 : 13
 not use again until e., 607 : 1
 nothing but e. triumphed, 173 : 2
 now is e., 662 : 20
 number the days of e., 34 : 21
 only a single night, 83 : 13
 onset with e., 604 : 11
 palace of e., 279 : 4
 passing through nature to e., 218 : 1
 Pilgrim of E., 469 : 8
 pleasing dreadful thought, 326 : 3
 positive e. of pain, 619 : 1

Eternity (*continued*)
predestined from all e., 602 : 3
responsible through e., 522 : 11
sea gone with sun, 674 : 1
sells e. to get toy, 189 : 20
shut in a span, 292 : 19
small parenthesis in e., 275 : 15
sole one who traverses e., 5 : 2
teacher affects e., 635 : 8
tears of e., 692 : 6
thoughts that wander through e., 284 : 9
throughout all e., 406 : 2
time the image of e., 125 : 27
travelers of e., 313 : 23
waits at crossway of stars, 843 : 5
wants nothing but e., 242 : 24
was in our lips and eyes, 240 : 18
was in that moment, 324 : 4
what nature creates has e., 861 : 17
white radiance of e., 469 : 16
wink of e., 843 : 14
Eternity's, lives in e. sunrise, 404 : 18
you are e. hostage, 816 : 19
Ether, ampler e., 428 : 22
falls through clear e., 475 : 5
shining e., 496 : 15
Ethereal, blue e. sky, 325 : 8
mildness come, 345 : 10
minstrel, 429 : 8
sky, 283 : 4
what e. dances, 525 : 18
Etherized upon a table, 803 : 9
Ethic, land e. for tomorrow, 898 : 1
Ethical, cosmic and e. process, 596 : 10
man's e. behavior, 812 : 10
not e. unless chosen, 648 : 16
nuclear giants e. infants, 825 : 2
Ethics, difficulties in e., 740 : 15
dry volumes of e., 387 : 7
flower read us lectures of e., 316 : 8
of misanthropy and voluptuousness, 487 : 20
system of rational e., 703 : 14
Ethiopian change his skin, 32 : 6
Ethiop's, rich jewel in E. ear, 191 : 26
Ethnic, dogma of e. superiority, 796 : 7
Etiam periere ruinae, 118 : *n* 12
Etiquette, isn't e. to cut anyone, 613 : 20
Étoiles, on voudrait attendrir les é., 583 : *n* 5
Eton, Waterloo won on fields of E., 421 : 16
Êtres, n'existe que trois ê. respectables, 581 : *n* 5
Etruscan cup, 892 : 10
Étude, la vraie é. de l'homme, 337 : *n* 2
Étudié, hé Dieu si j'eusse é., 150 : *n* 2
Euboea, Athens nigh to E., 83 : 6
Euclid looked on Beauty bare, 823 : 8
Euphemistically, asylums known e., 781 : 16
Euphuism, preciosity or e., 730 : 15
Eureka I have found it, 93 : 4
Euripides, all Greece the monument of E., 75 : *n* 13
chorus ending from E., 543 : 5
drew men as they were, 73 : *n* 10, 75 : *n* 13
Europa, bull that kidnapped E., 98 : 20
Europe a precious graveyard, 582 : 2
all dogs of E. bark, 868 : 12
artist no home in E. save Paris, 658 : 23

Europe (*continued*)
continent of energetic mongrels, 706 : 20
depravations of E., 319 : 22
educated Americans to E., 498 : 26
fifty years of E., 530 : 9
glory of E. extinguished, 373 : 22
governments of E., 388 : 5
if clod washed away E. less, 254 : 22
lamps going out over E., 699 : 7
liberation of E., 815 : 12
libraries of E., 390 : 1
longest kingly line in E., 343 : *n* 1
new order in E., 766 : 9
noblest river in E., 326 : 22
of ancient parapets, 673 : 18
people of Western E., 815 : 12
powers of old E., 563 : 2
prison of nations, 766 : 9
races of E. melting, 706 : 15
really a swarm, 784 : 15
regards her as stranger, 384 : 12
Russia's future danger for E., 550 : 3
sauntered E. round, 340 : 27
settlement in E., 813 : 15
specter haunting E., 563 : 2
superstitious valuation of E., 652 : 5
two continental powers in E., 812 : 18
under his heel, 745 : 2
United States and E., 408 : 3
United States of E., 492 : 7
window on E., 486 : 14
European, adopting E. war tactics, 800 : 4
colonization by E. powers, 408 : 1
if E. discovery delayed, 800 : 4
instruments of E. greatness, 401 : 14
Mozart last of great E. taste, 658 : 1
narcotics, 658 : 9
no E. in governance of nation, 416 : 17
nose, 900 : 5
periodization of E. history, 847 : 14
philosophical tradition footnotes to Plato, 697 : 12
wars of E. powers, 408 : 2
Eurydice, half-regained E., 278 : 8
Euthanasia, leaflets advocating e., 906 : 8
Eutrapelia happy flexibility, 589 : 6
Euxine, more dangerous breakers than E., 461 : 14
Evade erump, 98 : *n* 3
Evanescence, route of e., 607 : 12
Evanescent, velocities of e. increments, 330 : 21
Evangelical, things moral or things e., 302 : 4
Evangelist Saint John, 571 : 3
Evasion of what white men set them, 837 : 20
Evasions, intricate e. of as, 768 : 24
Evasit, abiit excessit e. erupit, 98 : *n* 3
Eve and I, 541 : 22
called his wife's name E., 7 : 12
child of our grandmother E., 190 : 16
fairest of daughters E., 285 : 20
from noon to dewy e., 284 : 2
like toad at ear of E., 286 : 6
motherless E., 733 : 2
obey voice at e., 495 : 8
oh had simple E., 733 : 1
pensive E., 364 : 11
said to e. Be soon, 693 : 13
since E. ate apples, 461 : 29

Eve (*continued*)
son of Adam and E., 321 : 2
span, 917 : 1
stag at e., 431 : 5
St. Agnes' E., 476 : 8
warblest at e., 281 : 8
wonder what Adam and E. think, 798 : 14
Evelyn, beautiful E. Hope, 542 : 1
Even, approach of e. or morn, 285 : 5
as you and I, 709 : 14
break, 683 : 1, 773 : 13
deep and crisp and e., 563 : 11
don't get mad get e., 809 : 21
gray-hooded E., 279 : 15
such is time, 173 : 5
waters stilled at e., 601 : 13
would God it were e., 11 : 20
Even-balanced soul, 584 : 8
Even-handed justice, 236 : 23
Evening and morning were first day, 6 : 11
beauteous e. calm free, 425 : 16
black e. white snow, 770 : 15
Boston E. Transcript, 804 : 6, 846 : 1
bright exhalation in the e., 249 : 1
charming e. criminal's friend, 581 : 2
come in the e., 552 : 19
descends autumn e., 588 : 5
dews of e. carefully shun, 342 : 17
die in e. without regret, 68 : 14
eat in the e., 404 : 5
expects his e. prey, 363 : 6
fairer than e. air, 184 : 5
follows morn, 856 : 7
gracious e. star, 552 : 14
grateful e. mild, 286 : 1
hate to see e. sun go down, 740 : 12
house made of e. light, 928 : 18
housewife ply e. care, 362 : 1
in afternoon, 822 : 9
in the e. it is cut down, 20 : 11
is come rise up, 102 : 8
isolation of sky at e., 767 : 4
it was a summer e., 439 : 10
light first light of e., 769 : 2
like an e. gone, 328 : 11
love morning and e. star, 791 : 8
man that was in e. made, 276 : 4
morning incense e. meal, 400 : 5
must usher night, 469 : 7
now came still e. on, 285 : 24
of their lives, 592 : 6
open house in e., 742 : 11
quickly come as the E. Star, 97 : 16
quiet-colored end of e., 542 : 3
rainy e. to read this discourse, 270 : 32
red light of e., 928 : 14
rest at pale e., 854 : 14
shades of e. drew on, 525 : 19
shades prevail, 325 : 9
shadow at e. rising, 805 : 1
shadows of the e., 616 : 7
shut of e. flowers, 287 : 16
slight sound at e., 557 : 6
some enchanted e., 833 : 13
soup of the e., 612 : 11
spread out against sky, 803 : 9
star for which e. waits, 729 : 6
star love's harbinger, 287 : 32
star you shine on dead, 468 : *n* 5
sunset and e. star, 535 : 19
to his labor until e., 21 : 11

Evening (*continued*)
twilight and e. bell, 535 : 20
until e. comes, 490 : 10
walks at e. on three feet, 74 : *n* 5
welcome peaceful e. in, 377 : 3
when it is e. fair weather, 39 : 33
withhold not thine hand in the e., 27 : 22
Evening's gold leaf, 906 : 2
Evenings, we had had summer e., 793 : 16
Evensong, at last ring to e., 161 : 7
at length ringeth to e., 161 : *n* 3
dead ere e., 927 : 4
Event, caprice of minutest e., 571 : 10
divine e., 532 : 27
greatest e. in war, 81 : 10
haunt spot of great e., 503 : 7
how much the greatest e., 394 : 10
men labels that name e., 602 : 3
one e. happeneth to all, 26 : 19
prophets make sure of e., 364 : 1
thinking too precisely on e., 223 : 18
third e. to me, 607 : 18
unveil third e. to me, 607 : 18
verity is an e., 650 : 11
Eventful, strange e. history, 211 : 15
Eventide, fast falls e., 470 : 23
Events cast shadows before, 443 : 14
controlled me, 523 : 6
course of human e., 387 : 9
great e. make me calm, 573 : 15
not lead e. but follow them, 121 : 18
President on top of e., 788 : 3
signs should prefigure e., 98 : 21
some great e. some mean hypocrisies, 381 : 13
soon on top of him, 788 : 3
spirits of great e., 443 : *n* 6
study e. in bearings, 592 : 7
three e. in life, 315 : 9
Ever-during dark surrounds me, 285 : 5
sleep one e. night, 250 : 3
Ever-fixed mark, 245 : 18
Evergreen, final growth e., 863 : 14
Ever-increasing wonder and awe, 366 : 12
Everlasting, achievements of intellect e., 103 : 2
an e. now, 295 : *n* 1
bonfire, 238 : 2
composed to be e. possession, 80 : 15
condemned into e. redemption, 210 : 1
damned to e. fame, 337 : 15
deprived of e. bliss, 183 : 21
doors, 18 : 9
espouse e. sea, 425 : 19
eyes of Pierrot, 843 : 17
farewells, 454 : 19
Father, 29 : 16
first last e. day, 252 : 22
flint, 193 : 2
from e. to e. thou art God, 20 : 11
God the E. Refuge, 132 : 19
had not fixed canon, 218 : 5
here set up my e. rest, 193 : 28
hills, 9 : 6
his mercy is e., 21 : 3
life, 44 : 34
no, 472 : 23
open ye e. gates, 287 : 1
stood from e. to e., 311 : 21
the e. arms, 11 : 26
yea, 472 : 25
Everlastingness, bright shoots of e., 299 : 3
Ever-living, our e. poet, 243 : *n* 4
Evermore, probing through you O e., 844 : 2
Ever-nearing circle weaves shade, 587 : 10
Ever-returning spring, 576 : 2
Ever-rolling, time like e. stream, 328 : 12
Evers, Tinker to E. to Chance, 773 : 12
Ever-whirling wheel, 174 : 6
Every day in every way, 684 : 9
day's news, 228 : 25
inch a king, 234 : 30
man architect of his fortune, 103 : 5
man for himself, 161 : 14
Everybody, everything happens to e., 681 : 13
goes Awww, 901 : 3
hard to please e., 112 : 1
he who praises e., 385 : 16
if e. minded business, 611 : 13
looks like e. is down on me, 916 : 4
suspect e., 547 : 25
Everybody's business nobody's business, 271 : 2
Everyday, refinement of e. thinking, 763 : 9
Everyman I will go with thee, 917 : 9
Everyone, each one's himself yet e., 874 : 3
enough in world for e., 788 : 2
has one sermon, 923 : 15
in world is Christ, 757 : 3
is a moon, 625 : 19
love come to e., 825 : 7
mad on one point, 707 : 10
not e. can get to Corinth, 109 : 9
reaches Future, 842 : 10
satisfying life for e., 862 : 7
to his own, 300 : 19
upon which e. has sat, 829 : 22
war of e. against e., 264 : 12
went over e. nobody's missing, 884 : 12
when e. is somebody, 630 : 8
will say, 628 : 7
world breaks e., 844 : 15
Everyone's tired of turmoil, 893 : 11
true worship, 83 : 2
Everything, a bore to tell e., 343 : 1
and anything, 781 : 12
autumn in e., 542 : 22
belongs to fatherland, 412 : 1
cannot do e. but something, 590 : 5
comes if man wait, 501 : 26
conscience in e., 360 : 8
costing not less than e., 808 : 18
custom reconciles to e., 372 : 1
deed e. glory nothing, 396 : 24
don't tell her e., 60 : 13
else is still, 403 : 15
esteem e. esteem nothing, 297 : 25
exists nothing has value, 764 : 10
feeling not always e., 583 : 6
for e. missed gained something, 497 : 11
for poetry idea e., 589 : 5
for security of future e., 609 : 9
glory of e., 847 : 3
God not willing to do e., 154 : 6
good for something, 304 : 22
good in e., 210 : 24
Everything (*continued*)
grayness silvers e., 542 : 21
grows old under power of Time, 87 : 6
happens to everybody, 681 : 13
hard to attain easily assailed, 124 : 1
has an end, 925 : 25
has e. been done, 896 : 14
has two handles, 121 : 22
he is above e. he possesses, 343 : 12
he wants nothing you want, 590 : 11
I have e. yet nothing, 96 : 16
I touch mean and farcical, 600 : 6
in its place, 627 : 3
in relation to nothing, 299 : 17
includes itself in power, 226 : 3
is gratuitous, 865 : 7
is in mind of man, 683 : 17
is lawful, 582 : 8
know e. forgive e., 417 : *n* 5
lived in me, 595 : 3
made of one stuff, 497 : 12
man esteems, 715 : 13
man grows used to e., 581 : 18
man's truth is resolution of e., 769 : 18
mean between nothing and e., 299 : 17
men ask for e., 896 : 6
moments when e. goes well, 705 : 9
not all capable of e., 103 : 16
now dare e., 903 : 3
passes, 538 : 7, 928 : 3
passes art alone eternal, 928 : 3
practice is e., 111 : *n* 8
public opinion e., 521 : 2
sans e., 211 : 15
smattering of e., 546 : 9
spirit of youth in e., 245 : 9
that emancipates spirit, 397 : 13
that pretty is, 243 : 16
that's lovely is, 712 : 19
training is e., 624 : 14
tries e. before arms, 96 : 20
turn nothing into e., 694 : 1
understand e. makes tolerant, 417 : 15
was rainbow, 878 : 5
way they eat drink learn and e., 752 : 13
we look on blessed, 716 : 3
what else to say but e., 889 : 15
what is God e., 72 : 11
winning isn't e., 925 : 15
worth what purchaser will pay, 112 : 8
written as good as dramatic, 750 : 1
young know e., 400 : 12
Everything's got a moral, 612 : 2
so reg'lar can't stand it, 622 : 16
Everywhere, daybreak e., 513 : 2
he is in chains, 358 : 12
his place, 295 : 10
I roam, 598 : 4
one little room an e., 251 : 15
the same as e., 394 : 13
water water e., 434 : 15
we have need of Zeus, 92 : 11
who lives e. lives nowhere, 119 : 12
Eve's, curses all E. daughters, 225 : 26
one star, 478 : 2
Eves, flies on summer e., 476 : 27
now for October e., 793 : 16
summer e. by haunted stream, 278 : 6

Evidence, denunciation in place of e., 737 : 7
for God, 650 : 9
growth e. of life, 490 : 7
never prove hypothesis, 880 : 8
no notion of e., 464 : 8
of immortality, 496 : 1
of things not seen, 51 : 18
of truth but only evidence, 444 : 5
passions cannot alter e., 380 : 11
some circumstantial e. strong, 557 : 14
take everything on e., 549 : 28
Evil, agricultural population least given to e., 117 : 4
all e. to crazy Ahab, 570 : 13
ancient folk with e. spells, 929 : 1
atom's weight of e., 132 : 18
avoid e. do good, 72 : 17
banality of e., 866 : 7
be not overcome of e., 47 : 25
be thou my good, 285 : 13
believe no e. till done, 296 : 7
bent on e. never want occasion, 111 : 12
brothers are e., 4 : 5
by e. and good report, 49 : 16
communications, 49 : 2
days and evil tongues, 286 : 28
days come not, 27 : 24
deeds do not prosper, 60 : 5
deeds religion prompt, 100 : 4
deliver us from e., 37 : 15
depart from e., 18 : 21
do after good leave e., 149 : 5
do e. so completely, 300 : 14
do not seek e. gains, 61 : 19
entire city suffered because of e. man, 61 : 15
every e. has good, 497 : 10
extravagance of her e., 60 : 12
eye that looks to mood apart, 749 : 12
fallen on e. days, 286 : 28
find means of e., 283 : 11
generation, 43 : 18
good becomes indistinguishable from e., 812 : 11
good comes out of e., 631 : 5
good e. reward punishment, 307 : 19
good or e. side, 567 : 6
goodness in things e., 208 : 3
government necessary e., 384 : 9
hacking at branches of e., 559 : 19
hear no e. see no e., 919 : 2
hope in the day of e., 32 : 14
I will fear no e., 18 : 7
idleness dragged toward e., 80 : 7
if all means permitted to fight e., 812 : 11
if dhrink e. not nicissry, 722 : 24
if you permit e., 864 : 6
ill deeds doubled with e. word, 188 : 10
imagination of man's heart is e., 7 : 33
in life of worms, 595 : 5
inadvertently said some e. thing, 86 : 7
infect the soul with e., 84 : 2
is easy, 300 : 9
judge should have learned to know e., 84 : 9
keep thy tongue from e., 18 : 21
knowing good and e., 7 : 6
Evil (*continued*)
lack of money root of e., 680 : 27
Lord shall preserve thee from all e., 22 : 4
maketh sun rise on e. and good, 37 : 12
manners live in brass, 249 : 14
many e. men are rich, 62 : 12
marriage a necessary e., 91 : 9
marriage an e. most men welcome, 91 : *n* 6
met me in e. hour, 409 : 9
most e. of half-tamed demons, 678 : 6
necessary for triumph of e., 374 : 12
never suffer e. in future, 60 : 26
news fly faster than good, 120 : *n* 5
news rides post, 289 : 7
no e. can happen to good man, 83 : 14
no e. deed live on, 647 : 3
no e. in atom, 851 : 15
no man chooses e., 414 : 5
not into e. wrought, 631 : 15
notion of E. One, 869 : 10
obscures the show of e., 199 : 24
of moral e. and of good, 423 : 7
on ground of expediency, 687 : 3
one e. ignorance, 79 : 3
one that eschewed e., 14 : 35
overcome e. with good, 47 : 25
partial e. universal good, 337 : 1
perceive e. where exists, 867 : 10
perplexity of radical e., 866 : 10
pervading e. of democracy, 616 : 2
plan is most harmful to planner, 61 : 16
please his e. neighbor, 414 : 3
political good carried to extreme productive of e., 414 : 15
possibilities for good and e., 831 : 23
punish world for their e., 29 : 21
raise its head, 850 : 12
rash hand in e. hour, 287 : 19
recognition of e., 63 : 13
recompense no e. for e., 47 : 22
resist not e., 37 : 10
return good for e., 321 : 5
rewarded e. for good, 8 : 34
rewardeth e. for good, 24 : 16
root of all e., 51 : 2
saw my e. day, 418 : 12
say e. against you, 37 : 4
show me a greater e., 74 : 20
snake stood for e. in Garden, 747 : 21
Socrates a doer of e., 83 : 11
spinning fates good or e., 648 : 11
stifling opinion is e., 508 : 8
stubborn heart shall fare e., 34 : 28
submit to present e., 114 : 3
sufficient unto day is e., 38 : 7
supernatural source of e., 684 : 4
that men do lives after them, 216 : 17
the e. I do, 47 : 6
them that call e. good, 29 : 7
thing of e., 526 : 17
to depart from e. is understanding, 16 : 15
to him who evil thinks, 143 : 7
tongue an unruly e., 51 : 35
tree of knowledge of good and e., 6 : 20
unconscious not only e. but good, 754 : 10
vanish like e. spirits, 389 : 12
vice lost half its e., 373 : 25
Evil (*continued*)
what e. I intend to do, 76 : 18
whether it be good or e., 27 : 27
who condemn hatred of e., 881 : 12
wi' tippenny fear nae e., 411 : 10
winning soul to good or e., 65 : 14
with indifference notes e., 486 : 11
with lent money e. done, 573 : 3
withstand in the e. day, 49 : 39
write e. in marble, 155 : 8
wrought by want of thought, 485 : 8
Evildoers, seeing e. taken to execution, 162 : 3
Evildoing, greatest penalty of e., 86 : 1
pleasantness waits upon e., 127 : 19
Evil's, believe no evil till e. done, 296 : 7
Evils, all e. equal when extreme, 275 : 20
avoided powers exercised, 121 : 13
cities no rest from e., 84 : 15
compel philosophy to inquire about e., 98 : 25
Congress has right to prevent, 644 : 23
draw men together, 88 : 14
endure neither e. nor cures, 110 : 11
greatest of e. is poverty, 680 : 28
he must expect new e., 180 : 24
knowledgeable of e., 70 : 21
least of the e., 87 : 18
least of two e., 58 : *n* 5
most preferable of e., 58 : 28
newly acquired freedom produces, 487 : 11
no necessary e. in government, 419 : 4
one of e. and another of blessings, 59 : 12
philosophy triumphs over past e., 293 : 3
present e. triumph over philosophy, 293 : 3
suffering e. of long peace, 122 : 10
they say e. come from us, 59 : 15
three great e., 343 : 13
two e. monstrous either one, 810 : 17
weak e. age and hunger, 211 : 14
when e. most free, 215 : 19
which never arrived, 495 : 18
yield not to e., 105 : 14
Evolution, advance of science an e., 673 : 10
cultural e., 870 : 15
from vague to definite, 639 : 10
general theory of e., 617 : 11
not a force but a process, 637 : 1
of thought, 586 : 14
some call it e., 545 : *n* 2
Evolved, endless beautiful forms e., 515 : 3
Ewe, lilting at e. milking, 368 : 2
tupping your white e., 229 : 18
Ewes, milk my e. and weep, 247 : 2
Ewig-Weibliche, das E. zieht uns hinan, 396 : *n* 11
Ex pede Herculem, 78 : *n* 6
ungue leonem, 133 : 24
Exact, aim of e. science, 610 : 1
devotion to e. observation, 762 : 5
equal and e. justice, 389 : 2
knowledge of the past, 80 : 15
set e. wealth of states, 204 : 29
writing maketh an e. man, 181 : 13

Exaction becomes extortion, 631 : 9
Exactitude, judgment and e. enter him, 3 : 3
Exactitude, l'e. la politesse des rois, 402 : *n* 1
Exactness, facts detailed with e., 592 : 7
write life with e., 354 : *n* 11
Exaggerated, reports of death e., 625 : 21
stress on not changing mind, 751 : 9
Exaggeration, chargeable with no e., 444 : 15
Exalt him above all, 36 : 14
himself shall be abased, 40 : 17
will to live, 756 : 17
Exaltation from proximity of disaster, 743 : 3
in chanting of Muses, 76 : 12
Exalted, both will be e., 764 : 9
every valley shall be e., 30 : 31
God an e. father, 678 : 8
no very e. opinion, 372 : 10
Satan e. sat, 284 : 3
them of low degree, 42 : 22
whoso humble himself be e., 40 : 17
Exalteth, righteousness e. a nation, 24 : 4
wisdom e. her children, 35 : 1
Exalts, not what man does e., 543 : 22
Examination, decent and manly e., 439 : 5
of acts of government, 439 : 5
Examine, turn inwards and e., 68 : 16
Examined, all things are to be e., 723 : 15
ought to have head e., 777 : 9
Example, annoyance of good e., 624 : 25
bear patiently results of own e., 114 : 8
from others take e., 97 : 4
government teaches by e., 678 : 1
is school of mankind, 374 : 8
lower orders set e., 675 : 18
more efficacious than precept, 352 : 19
profit by their e., 382 : 13
salutary influence of e., 352 : 24
Examples from Alexander to Mao, 800 : 6
no longer able to provide bad e., 293 : 17
Excalibur, so fell the brand E., 528 : 29
Exceed, flies worms e. me still, 328 : 7
never e. your rights, 358 : 10
reach e. grasp, 543 : 1
Exceedeth, thy wisdom and prosperity e. the fame, 13 : 35
Exceeding, grind e. small, 273 : 14
honest e. poor man, 199 : 1
wise fair-spoken, 249 : 15
Exceeds, far e. all earthly bliss, 167 : *n* 5
man's might, 226 : 14
Excel, arts in which wise e., 316 : 5
bees for government, 167 : 9
discredit what they do not e. in, 90 : 9
not e. because they labor, 445 : 17
teach who themselves e., 332 : 16
thou shalt not e., 9 : 4
useless to e., 357 : 10
Excellence, activity in accordance with e., 87 : 23
bearing on e. of character, 87 : 22
Excellence (*continued*)
fair divided e., 201 : 16
fame of her e., 61 : 5
imagine e., 900 : 1
in front of e. gods put sweat, 61 : 17
long time to bring e. to maturity, 112 : 5
mental e. a splendid possession, 102 : 22
not exchange e. for riches, 62 : 12
not only know e. but use it, 87 : 25
stewards of their e., 245 : 5
to few men comes e., 67 : 2
Excellencies, smaller e. of conversation, 386 : 1
true critic dwell on e., 326 : 19
Excellent angler now with God, 271 : 6
dumb discourse, 248 : 11
everything that's e., 628 : 16
fancy, 224 : 14
first e. second good, 154 : 3
foppery of the world, 233 : 5
hard to be truly e., 67 : 16
how e. is thy lovingkindness, 18 : 23
how e. is thy name, 17 : 18
I cried, 689 : 10
man of understanding is of e. spirit, 24 : 18
most e. canopy the air, 220 : 28
most regular most e., 696 : 6
parts of it are e., 660 : 18
situation e. I am attacking, 670 : 6
so e. a king, 218 : 7
so-so is e. good, 212 : 29
the e. lies before us, 417 : 2
thing in woman, 235 : 17
things difficult as rare, 309 : 5
things in counsels, 25 : 1
things that are more e., 46 : 39
to have giant's strength, 228 : 9
to make a poet e., 292 : 2
well a fishmonger, 220 : 15
what actions most e., 585 : 19
wretch, 230 : 30
Excellently, goddess e. bright, 255 : 12
Excellest, thou e. them all, 26 : 10
Excelleth, light e. darkness, 26 : 18
wisdom e. folly, 26 : 18
Excelling, cunningest pattern of e. nature, 232 : 14
Isle all isles e., 306 : 6
Excels dunce kept at home, 375 : 24
quirks of blazoning pens, 230 : 7
Excelsior 510 : 14
Excelsis, gloria in e. Deo, 54 : 4
Except a man be born again, 44 : 31
it die, 49 : 3
the Lord build the house, 22 : 8
the Lord keep the city, 22 : 8
the present company, 394 : 7
thou bless me, 8 : 25
Exception, in your case make e., 834 : 2
no rule admits not some e., 258 : 17
proves rule, 258 : *n* 10
Exceptional, glorious to be e., 537 : 10
Exceptions, science admits no e., 551 : 17
Excess, blasted with e. of light, 363 : 2
desire of power in e., 180 : 14
don't regret a single e., 654 : 7
give me e. of it, 213 : 7
in charity no e., 180 : 12
moderation even in e., 501 : 5
not drinking but e., 263 : 15
Excess (*continued*)
nothing in e., 134 : 12
of glory obscured, 283 : 23
of severity not order, 637 : 14
of subjective propensities, 649 : 16
of wealth cause of covetousness, 183 : 13
reform carried to e. needs reforming, 437 : 2
reproach to religion, 314 : 12
such e. of stupidity, 354 : 14
surprise by fine e., 479 : 7
wasteful and ridiculous e., 202 : 5
when love is in e., 76 : 16
Excessit, abiit e. evasit erupit, 98 : *n* 3
Excessive, bail nor e. fines, 392 : 3
dark with e. bright, 285 : 7
good fortune, 599 : 2
if national debt not e., 401 : 10
laughter, 35 : 33
Exchange, atheist-laugh's a poor e., 409 : 13
by just e. one for other, 176 : 7
cross for crown, 738 : 11
excellence for riches, 62 : 12
Exchequer of the poor, 194 : 20
Excise hateful tax, 352 : 9
those to whom e. paid, 352 : 9
Excitabat enim fluctus in simpulo, 99 : *n* 4
Excitable gift, 908 : 14
Excite my amorous propensities, 353 : 23
Excited abnormal condition, 681 : 1
passionate fantastical, 715 : 4
passions not at will e., 526 : 9
reverie, 714 : 14
Excitement, faith an e. and enthusiasm, 504 : 16
public e. runs high, 836 : 16
spiritual e., 588 : 9
Excites us to arms, 305 : 11
Exciting, found it less e., 629 : 25
politics almost e. as war, 743 : 7
Exclude, not till sun do I e. you, 576 : 13
to define is to e., 784 : 13
Excludes, not till sun e. you, 576 : 13
Exclusion, principle of e., 593 : 2
Exclusive, entertains e. worms, 827 : 14
Excommunicate, corporations cannot be e., 172 : 4
Excrement, place of e., 716 : 18
Excursion same for sorrow as joy, 877 : 2
Excuse, any e. will serve tyrant, 66 : 14
came prologue, 287 : 21
denial vain and coy e., 280 : 9
fault worse by e., 202 : 6
for the glass, 399 : 1
I will not e., 505 : 13
my dust, 827 : 17
never e., 197 : 21
play needs no e., 197 : 21
Excused from it as against my conscience, 364 : 7
his devilish deeds, 285 : 21
Excuses himself accuses himself, 163 : 8
ignorance e. no man, 263 : 17
Excusing, love shows by e. nothing, 297 : 29
make fault worse, 202 : 6
Execrable shape, 284 : 25
sum of all villainies, 346 : 9
Execute, by contraries e., 247 : 26

Execute (*continued*)
hand to e., 289 : 16, 391 : 4
orders, 374 : 3
to e. laws royal office, 374 : 3
villainy you teach me, 199 : 19
Executed, successfully e., 395 : 18
Execution, fitter for e. than counsel, 181 : 7
seeing evildoers taken to e., 162 : 3
stringent e. of bad laws, 589 : 21
Executioner, I victim and e., 581 : 1
man his own e., 274 : 19
mine own e., 254 : 20
the master e., 65 : 7
Executioners would be most learned, 155 : 12
Executions far from useful examples, 414 : 17
for the master executioner, 65 : 7
Executive, judicial distinct from e., 381 : 11
legislative nominated by e., 383 : 8
of modern state, 563 : 4
pliant instrument of E., 439 : 4
political e. magistracy, 374 : 3
Executives, lives e. know nothing of, 905 : 17
Executors, let's choose e., 195 : 1
or more properly creditors, 570 : 10
Exemplary, our lives in acts e., 178 : 3
Exempt from public haunt, 210 : 24
true nobility e. from fear, 185 : 22
Exercise, being honest good e., 678 : 5
bodily e. when compulsory, 84 : 21
each e. art he knows, 82 : 3
free e. of religion, 383 : 6
gratuitous e. every day, 648 : 9
prohibiting free e. thereof, 391 : 14
reading to mind as e. to body, 327 : 12
sad mechanic e., 531 : 21
their constitutional right, 521 : 11
wise for cure on e. depend, 306 : 26
Exercises his mind with suffering, 89 : 25
Exertions, ennobled by own e., 414 : 9
what people attained with e., 386 : 15
Exhalation, bright e. in evening, 249 : 1
Exhaled, he was e., 307 : 9
sighs infrequent e., 805 : 2
Exhaust the little moment, 889 : 11
Exhausted business politics, 577 : 6
my body infirm and e., 151 : 11
my patience are e., 778 : 2
resources of civilization not e., 517 : 22
Time winds th' e. chain, 410 : 14
wells, 805 : 12
worlds imagined new, 351 : 10
Exhausting thing is being insincere, 867 : 6
Exhibited, human relations perfectly e., 89 : 7
Exhilarating to be shot at without result, 743 : 2
Exigencies, great e. of government, 553 : 20
Exile guise, 843 : 17
king in e., 790 : 13
kiss long as my e., 242 : 22
men in e. feed on dreams, 71 : 13
sleep in e., 673 : 19
to e. friends everything, 739 : 6
Exiled, joy Marcellus e. feels, 337 : 14
on ground in jeers, 580 : 17
Exiled (*continued*)
son's appeal, 639 : 15
Exile's life is no life, 93 : 2
Exiles, band of e. moored bark, 470 : 15
paradise of e. Italy, 467 : 12
woe none save e. feel, 551 : 10
Exist, be own master really e., 895 : 14
God is in me or does not e., 770 : 1
if God did not e., 344 : 2
must spend to e., 871 : 16
pathos piety courage e., 764 : 10
rather believe God not e., 504 : 19
saint if God does not e., 882 : 8
since earth began to e., 378 : 1
sir I e., 732 : 8
true democracy never will e., 358 : 15
we e. alone, 734 : 8
Existed, true democracy never e., 358 : 15
Existence, art shield from e., 674 : 19
brief crack of light, 846 : 2
called New World into e., 422 : 7
closing your account, 516 : 21
conscious of our own e., 87 : 21
consecutive moments of e., 580 : 3
determination to develop own e., 757 : 17
determines consciousness, 562 : 16
essential relationship to e., 552 : 11
fret of e., 848 : 7
human e. girt with mystery, 508 : 24
knowledge enlarges sphere of e., 418 : 10
life hollow e. burden, 622 : 11
nature owes me another e., 396 : 5
of supernatural probable, 704 : 11
precisely an e., 607 : 17
saw him spurn reign, 351 : 10
single e. illusion, 887 : 14
sordid perils of actual e., 674 : 19
sorrow of human e., 375 : 3
spoke herself into e. as nation, 418 : 1
struggle for e., 514 : 16, 753 : 12
teach men sense of e., 657 : 13
truth find e., 684 : 6
without vocation e. meaningless, 895 : 13
woman's whole e., 460 : 19
you wanted to go back to, 839 : 14
Existential, enslavement and e. death, 907 : 1
Existing like light around body, 905 : 16
Exists, everything e. nothing has value, 764 : 10
nowhere but in yourself, 727 : 8
Exit pursued by a bear, 246 : 19
wheresoever called to make e., 393 : 9
Exits and their entrances, 211 : 15
doors for men to take their e., 262 : 8
Exodus, mysterious e. of death, 511 : 24
Exoteric and esoteric doctrine, 72 : 19
Expanding conflict to all China, 788 : 15
Expands, life shrinks or e., 858 : 9
Expansion, not a breach but an e., 253 : 4
Expatiate free o'er scene of man, 336 : 10
Expect, never e. anything, 913 : 8
Saint Martin's summer, 184 : 17
something for nothing, 671 : 16
Expectation, better bettered e., 208 : 21
makes a blessing dear, 290 : 5
oft e. fails, 227 : 13
Expectation (*continued*)
rise, 368 : 11
Shields of E., 568 : 19
songs of e., 616 : 8
whirls me round, 226 : 10
Expectations, Revolution of Rising E., 894 : 16
Expected, least e. happens, 501 : 10
no reasonable man e., 816 : 1
Expects, blessed man who e. nothing, 336 : 6
England e., 408 : 8
Expediency determines form, 798 : 15
evil on ground of e., 687 : 3
Expedient, all things not e., 48 : 17
as lighting by gas, 517 : 17
free trade e., 501 : 12
that one die, 45 : 15
Expedition, so ended Sicilian e., 81 : 10
wonderful e. of all Greeks, 702 : 11
Expeditionary, Allied E. Force, 815 : 12
Expeditions, dyspepsy ruin of e., 454 : 20
Expelled, Asia and Africa e. freedom, 384 : 12
Expendable, they were e., 852 : 5
Expende Hannibalem, 122 : *n* 12
Expenditures, book of public e., 449 : 6
Expense, great e. may be essential, 374 : 9
of spirit in waste of shame, 245 : 23
pretend to restrain e., 366 : 3
Expenses, consider my traveling e., 826 : 17
work stops e. run on, 95 : 8
Expensive, nothing so e. as glory, 432 : 20
politics e., 766 : 4
Experience, accumulated e., 753 : 12
an arch wherethrough, 529 : 8
arch to build upon, 634 : 18
arranged in order, 636 : 14
art pattern on e., 698 : 5
believe one who has e., 106 : *n* 4
causes of future e., 649 : 17
child of thought, 501 : 3
cluster of gifts e., 652 : 14
court bows to e., 678 : 3
customs shape e., 796 : 4
effects of past e., 649 : 17
encounter reality of e., 777 : 18
essential to great e., 597 : 6
get out of e. only wisdom in it, 625 : 5
gladly beyond any e., 829 : 12
gone to end in e., 756 : 14
has given no access, 658 : 26
home where small e. grows, 188 : 27
ideas stand for e., 703 : 4
ignorant in spite of e., 350 : 16
keeps dear school, 347 : 23
knowledge not personal e., 84 : 9
lamp of e., 383 : 2
Liberal tempered by e., 588 : 14
life of law, 643 : 14
make me sad, 212 : 19
mother of sciences, 169 : 4
name for mistakes, 675 : 12
no knowledge beyond e., 307 : 14
not fruit of e. but e., 638 : 12
of this sweet life, 142 : 16
Old Age and E., 315 : 21
old e. do attain, 279 : 1
optimist never had much e., 760 : 3

Experience (*continued*)
prophecy of wise men, 464 : 18
pushed beyond facts, 683 : *n* 3
recognize same e., 649 : 2
relations between aspects of e., 789 : 2
substitute for e. is art and literature, 895 : 19
tells in every soil, 369 : 3
transmits e. from generation to generation, 895 : 20
travel part of e., 180 : 18
treacherous, 80 : 9
triumph of hope over e., 354 : 22
what e. and history teach, 422 : 9
whole past e. in consciousness, 639 : 12
wisdom acting upon e., 353 : 14
write only from e., 652 : 14
Experienced, all you e. unsubstantial heap, 851 : 1
industrious liar, 624 : 6
not real till e., 479 : 20
Experiences, aggregate of humanity's e., 832 : 18
evidence for God in inner e., 650 : 9
flag represents e., 682 : 5
in solitude, 650 : 2
shared e., 420 : 8
strong man digests e., 658 : 8
way full of adventures and e., 702 : 4
Experiencing nature, 597 : 6
suffering to full, 734 : 11
Experientia docet, 548 : *n* 2
does it, 548 : 24
Experiment, as all life is e., 645 : 1
convinced of imbecility by e., 353 : 5
entrusted to American people, 379 : 7
every e. like weapon, 157 : 5
mad and lamentable e., 703 : 8
on animals, 515 : 12
psychology cannot e. with men, 443 : 3
reason and e. indulged, 387 : 13
so great an e. as dying, 275 : 32
stimulate and direct e., 681 : 23
to me every one I meet, 606 : 18
we are not the only e., 832 : 19
Experimental, consequences represent multitude of e. laws, 696 : 12
philosophy, 313 : 11
results of e. psychology, 702 : 13
thinking is e. dealing, 678 : 17
youth is wholly e., 669 : 18
Experimentation active science, 551 : 14
bold persistent e., 779 : 7
Experiments, eclipses of moon and other e., 151 : 7
I love fools' e., 515 : 14
sure e. and demonstrated arguments, 166 : 15
to control ideas, 552 : 6
Expert, believe an e., 106 : 6
knows more about less, 698 : 17
Experto credite, 106 : *n* 4
Experts, differences among e., 700 : 2
Expire, if I e. today, 607 : 15
lamps e., 721 : 6
Expires, last armed foe e., 464 : 12
unawares Morality e., 340 : 28
wretched child e., 730 : 8
Expiring frog, 546 : 14
Explain, can't e. myself said Alice, 611 : 8
his explanation, 460 : 9
spoil it by trying to e., 398 : 17
till all men doubt, 340 : 25
time will e. all, 77 : 14
you e. nothing O poet, 724 : 8
Explained, not die before we have e. ourselves, 382 : 3
shut up he e., 790 : 7
Explaining, calling attention not same as e., 906 : 13
go on e. cease to understand, 782 : *n* 5
surrender e. not acting, 741 : 1
Explanation, explain his e., 460 : 9
inaccuracy saves e., 731 : 18
unintelligible, 758 : 10
Expletive deleted, 925 : 20
Expletives their feeble aid do join, 333 : 7
Explicable, thanks to poet things e., 724 : 8
Explicitness not necessary virtue, 711 : 14
Explode, dream dry up or e., 855 : 2
huge laugh at feet, 701 : 7
Exploitation, does mean we're anti-e., 904 : 13
relief from constant e., 912 : 3
ultimate sanction of e., 825 : 18
Exploited, many e. by few, 825 : 18
Exploits, capable of noble e., 583 : 14
fond of relating own e., 308 : 14
Exploration, not cease from e., 808 : 17
Explore all options, 862 : 21
came to e. wreck, 910 : 8
falter or e., 899 : 15
happy Nature to e., 337 : 6
unconscious, 688 : 8
Explorer, man e. of nature, 870 : 14
Explorers, old men ought to be e., 807 : 24
old men should be e., 874 : 8
scientists detectives and e., 888 : 1
Exploring, end of e. to arrive, 808 : 17
Exponent of earth, 606 : 11
Exposed, intellect improperly e., 432 : 24
left e. a friend, 606 : 9
more e. to suffering, 427 : 23
on bare earth e. he lies, 306 : 18
Exposition of sleep upon me, 197 : 6
Expounding, it is a constitution we are e., 402 : 4
Express flowery tale, 477 : 4
it in numbers, 594 : 11
speech not to e. but conceal, 310 : *n* 1
we half e. ourselves, 496 : 20
Expressed even such a beauty, 245 : 12
find more than poet e., 504 : 3
ideas that can be e. in words, 688 : 6
monitor e., 428 : 15
ne'er so well e., 333 : 3
not e. in fancy, 219 : 1
that which cannot be e., 573 : 13
whatever is felicitously e., 417 : 2
Expresses, this young man e. himself, 628 : 6
Expressing emotion in art, 809 : 5
itself beyond expression, 256 : 2
Expression, borrow shape to find e., 804 : 2
expressing itself beyond e., 256 : 2
freedom of e. matrix, 730 : 17
Expression (*continued*)
freedom of speech and e., 780 : 13
impassioned e., 424 : 7
individuality of e. end of art, 397 : 4
monk's state transcends e., 73 : 4
natural e. of villainy, 622 : 9
of all e. not expressed, 573 : 13
of working of mind, 595 : 8
paleness of symbolic e., 610 : 2
Expressive silence, 345 : 16
Expunge, fool enough to e., 356 : 10
Expunged, Nature's works to me e., 285 : 5
Exquisite, autumn rose more e., 171 : 20
ceasing of e. music, 511 : 2
most e. and strong, 318 : 4
passions, 638 : 10
pleasure so e. almost pain, 454 : 11
Extemporize subtler more urgent proof, 768 : 24
Extend freedom to everyone, 824 : 10
system to this hemisphere, 408 : 3
Extended, eye like mind sought e. view, 387 : *n* 2
to display its patterns, 70 : 18
Extensive and honorable conquests, 373 : 9
Extenuate, it is vain sir to e., 383 : 5
miseries of past, 801 : 3
nothing e., 232 : 20
Exterior, fair e. silent recommendation, 110 : 27
less on e. things, 375 : 18
struggle with e. forces, 784 : 10
Exterminate all the brutes, 683 : 19
Extermination camps intimated, 853 : 9
threat of common e., 897 : 10
External artistries in circumstance, 641 : 17
differ in e. forms, 354 : 24
falseness in impressions of e., 572 : 10
reimpressed by e. ordinances, 352 : 24
sensory stimulation, 603 : 6
these e. regions, 768 : 18
Extinct, our name not become e., 603 : 1
Extinction, continual e. of personality, 809 : 3
from apathy, 845 : 16
of unhappy hates, 586 : 12
slavery in course of e., 520 : 4
Extinguish hope from soul, 674 : 4
Extinguished, centuries after core e., 734 : 13
fire which seems e., 275 : 26
his soul, 520 : 7
nature seldom e., 181 : 4
prey of fear he e., 799 : 8
theologians, 595 : 7
Extinguishes natural candle, 314 : 19
Extol, how shall we e. thee, 698 : 12
Extolling past, 433 : 16
Extortion, exaction becomes e., 631 : 9
Extract laws from nature, 776 : 6
Extracted from many objects, 212 : 18
Extracting sunbeams of cucumbers, 322 : 13
Extraction of living intellect, 281 : 22
Extraordinary results of idealism, 678 : 4
youth the time for e. toil, 84 : 20
Extravagance, beauty without e., 81 : 1
calls his e. generosity, 369 : 23

Extravagance (*continued*)
if e. but little is left, 95 : 7
of her evil, 60 : 12
science throws treasures with lavish e., 636 : 15
Extravagant and erring spirit, 217 : 25
flaunting e. quean, 399 : 1
Extreme actions ascribed to vanity, 657 : 9
all evils equal when e., 275 : 20
fear neither fight nor fly, 189 : 21
for e. illnesses e. treatments, 80 : 10
I live in light's e., 874 : 5
in quest to have e., 245 : 23
justice extreme injustice, 134 : 29
justice often injustice, 96 : *n* 13
law often extreme injustice, 96 : 12
of wickedness or folly, 521 : 13
perplexed in the e., 232 : 20
political good carried to e., 414 : 15
savage e. rude cruel, 245 : 23
Extremes, change of fierce e., 284 : 23
fate of all e., 335 : 12
meet, 386 : 2
women run to e., 315 : 11
Extremism in defense of liberty, 385 : *n* 2
Extremity, daring pilot in e., 303 : 20
Exult, be secret and e., 713 : 12
O shores, 576 : 7
Exultantly, walk not on earth e., 131 : 7
Exultation only discoverer can experience, 799 : 20
Exultations agonies, 425 : 21
Exulting, people all e., 576 : 6
Eye, adds precious seeing to the e., 191 : 3
affection beaming in one e., 547 : 30
aloof with hermit e., 435 : 21
altering all, 875 : 4
an unforgiving e., 399 : 2
apple of the e., 17 : 25
Athens the e. of Greece, 288 : 13
beam in thine own e., 38 : 9
beauty bought by judgment of e., 190 : 19
beauty in e. of beholder, 676 : 20
beginnings of things not distinguished by e., 100 : 6
begins to see, 874 : 15
beholding beauty with e. of mind, 83 : 10
betrayed by milky e., 856 : 6
bigger than belly, 270 : 24
cast cold e., 718 : 2
cast longing e. on offices, 388 : 14
casts a sheep's e., 170 : 3
chips fall in e., 917 : 2
close e. of day, 281 : 9
corn high as elephant's e., 833 : 11
crack glass e. across, 757 : 6
cursed me with his e., 434 : 24
day's garish e., 278 : 25
defiance in their e., 369 : 1
discern with clear e., 557 : 20
divorced from e. and bone, 836 : 18
drunkard's e., 716 : 4
dust hath closed Helen's e., 250 : 10
ear and e. expected impossible, 715 : 4
easier to go through e. of needle, 40 : 7
equal e. as God, 336 : 14
essential is invisible to e., 849 : 4

Eye (*continued*)
every old man's e., 192 : 21
every tear from every e., 406 : 14
evil e. that looks to mood apart, 749 : 12
expert e. finds prior work, 673 : 10
far as human e. see, 529 : 24
fettered to her e., 296 : 2
find in his own e., 839 : 6
fire in each e., 338 : 6
for eye, 10 : 10
fringed curtains of thine e., 247 : 22
glad me with soft e., 447 : 14
glittering e., 434 : 4
God caught e., 839 : 2
gray e. glances, 525 : 18
great e. of heaven, 173 : 10
had but one e., 547 : 7
half hidden from the e., 424 : 12
halfmoon's vegetable e., 886 : 15
harmony in her bright e., 295 : 21
harvest of a quiet e., 424 : 18
hath not seen, 48 : 2
hearing ear seeing e., 24 : 29
heavenly rhetoric of thine e., 190 : 32
I have good e. uncle, 209 : 7
I have only one e., 408 : 5
I leave my father's e., 874 : 6
if thy right e. offend, 37 : 8
ignorant e., 768 : 8
in my mind's e. Horatio, 218 : 15
in tomb stared at Cain, 491 : 13
inquiring e. or tongue, 442 : 24
intent on wondrous plan, 410 : 16
interest unborrowed from e., 423 : 12
inward e., 427 : 11
is not satisfied with seeing, 26 : 13
is part of me, 790 : 21
jaundiced e., 333 : 16
king's e. made horse fat, 120 : 9
lackluster e., 211 : 5
language in her e., 227 : 3
lend e. terrible aspect, 207 : 16
less than meets e., 857 : 9
lifting up a fearful e., 182 : 2
light of the body is e., 37 : 18
like Mars, 223 : 3
like mind sought extended view, 387 : *n* 2
locked and frozen in e., 868 : 13
locked up from mortal e., 292 : 8
looked into e. of day, 715 : 19
looks with threatening e., 202 : 2
love comes in at e., 713 : 7
made quiet by power, 423 : 11
many an e. danced, 518 : 12
mighty world of e. and ear, 423 : 14
mild and magnificent e., 541 : 6
moist e. dry hand, 205 : 28
mote in brother's e., 38 : 9
my face in thine e., 251 : 16
my great Taskmaster's e., 277 : 15
my striving e. dazzles, 299 : 5
Nature's walks, 336 : 11
negotiate for itself, 209 : 9
neighbor as possible enemy, 737 : 7
never e. did see that face, 184 : 14
no e. to watch, 447 : 3
not lip or e. beauty call, 333 : 1
nothing situate under heaven's e., 188 : 1
now mine e. seeth thee, 17 : 10
of childhood, 237 : 23
of heaven shined bright, 173 : 10

Eye (*continued*)
of heaven to garnish, 202 : 5
of lip of e. of brow, 245 : 12
of man hath not heard, 197 : 10
of newt toe of frog, 239 : 5
of saint, 716 : 4
of the law, 615 : 1
of trilobite, 509 : 4
one auspicious e., 217 : 29
places e. of heaven visits, 194 : 5
poet have sensuous e., 500 : 10
poet's e. in fine frenzy, 197 : 12
rude e. of rebellion, 202 : 14
sail with unshut e., 584 : 13
see e. to e., 31 : 13
see for hand not mind, 558 : 23
see out of needle's e., 547 : 36
see with e. serene, 427 : 5
see with half an e., 170 : 27
see with not through e., 407 : 10
seeing seven and seventy devils, 735 : 3
sees open heaven, 413 : 21
seller needs not one e., 270 : 1
set honor in one e., 215 : 3
smile in her e., 482 : 9
smile on lips tear in e., 430 : 20
sober coloring from e., 426 : 23
soul fix intellectual e., 482 : 15
still soliciting e., 232 : 30
such a wistful e., 676 : 6
such beauty as woman's e., 191 : 1
tender e. of pitiful day, 238 : 21
that sun thine e., 244 : 17
thoughts legible in the e., 184 : 13
to a discerning e., 605 : 11
tongue sword, 221 : 19
twinkling of e., 49 : 7
unshut e., 584 : 13
vacant heart hand e., 432 : 1
vanquished by space, 171 : 14
view with hollow e., 200 : 15
wearing-stone or open e., 748 : 1
went with frightened e., 593 : 4
wet e. dhry heart, 722 : 8
what immortal hand or e., 405 : 7
when first your e. I eyed, 245 : 11
which girls hath merriest e., 184 : 20
wishing his foot equal with e., 186 : 10
with my little e., 930 : 10
woman with one e., 401 : 7
you are apple of my e., 916 : 13
Eyeball, I become transparent e., 496 : 4
to eyeball, 925 : 16
we're e. to e., 925 : *n* 7
Eye-beams, our e. twisted, 253 : 6
Eyebrow, mistress' e., 211 : 15
Eyed, when first your eye I e., 245 : 11
Eye-deep in hell, 792 : 14
Eye-flaw, some mote some e., 893 : 13
Eyeless in Gaza, 288 : 19
Eyelids a little weary, 638 : 10
from e. dripped love, 61 : 11
from e. wiped tear, 211 : 12
heavy and red, 485 : 16
of the morn, 280 : 10
slumber to mine e., 22 : 13
take thee with her e., 23 : 13
tinged e. and hands, 638 : 11
tired e. on tired eyes, 528 : 14
weigh e. down, 206 : 17
Eyes, all things flourish where you turn e., 332 : 12

Eyes (*continued*)
ancient glittering e., 717 : 7
and back turn upward, 805 : 7
and see not, 31 : 34
are what one is, 723 : 9
as in a theater e. of men, 195 : 15
attentive e., 353 : 10
avenged for my two e., 12 : 20
beauty e. never see, 720 : 10
bedroom e., 869 : 6
before streaming e., 613 : 8
begin to roll, 340 : 17
black e. and lemonade, 447 : 6
bright e. of danger, 669 : 3
Bullen's e., 361 : 19
burnt fire of thine e., 405 : 7
buyer needs a hundred e., 270 : 1
candid brow pure e., 683 : 12
cast mine e. and see, 266 : 22
cast one's e. so low, 234 : 28
changing moon changing e., 714 : 8
close e. with holy dread, 433 : 27
close up his e. and draw curtain, 185 : 19
closed e. in endless night, 363 : 2
confess secrets of heart, 128 : 8
craters of my e. gape, 912 : 7
crossed with direct e., 805 : 16
cry my e. out, 169 : 23
cynosure of neighboring e., 277 : 25
dazzle, 643 : 18
death come close e., 918 : 17
deeper than depth, 601 : 13
desires in e. that looked at you, 702 : 5
die before our own e., 664 : 8
do not set e. on things far off, 71 : *n* 9
dreaming e. of wonder, 612 : 15
drink to me only with thine e., 256 : 8
dry e. laugh at fall, 542 : 12
dust thrown in my e., 748 : 15
dying e. were closed, 335 : 10
eagle e., 475 : 7
elves whose little e. glow, 266 : 14
eternity was in our e., 240 : 18
everlasting e. of Pierrot, 843 : 17
eyelids upon tired e., 528 : 14
face facts with both e. open, 154 : 10
fearless e., 700 : 6
fields have e. woods have ears, 146 : 20
fix e. on greatness of Athens, 81 : 5
foe with fearless e., 700 : 6
for the blind, 615 : 6
fortune and men's e., 244 : 8
fountains fraught with tears, 177 : 1
from kindness cannot take e., 714 : 18
from starlike e. seek, 272 : 1
from those great e., 513 : 8
from women's e. this doctrine, 191 : 5
full of e. within, 53 : 7
gasp and stretch e., 730 : 9
gather to the e., 531 : 3
get thee glass e., 235 : 4
gone under earth's lid, 792 : 16
good for sore e., 323 : 3
had I your tongues and e., 235 : 16
hands and e. and heart, 458 : 20
hands only serve e., 557 : 3
hath not a Jew e., 199 : 17
have seen glory, 566 : 4
have their silence, 829 : 12
have they but see not, 21 : 22
having e. see not, 383 : 1

Eyes (*continued*)
he turned up his e., 404 : 11
heaven before mine e., 278 : 26
heaven to look with many e., 670 : *n* 3
her aspect and her e., 459 : 13
her e. were wild, 478 : 11
him who has e. to see, 595 : 11
his e. are in his mind, 196 : *n* 1
his e. were enlightened, 12 : 37
his flashing e., 433 : 27
I will lift up mine e., 22 : 4
I will not give sleep to mine e., 22 : 13
infantryman's e., 898 : 9
is burning in their e., 840 : 13
July in her e., 917 : 24
kindling her undazzled e., 282 : 3
ladies whose bright e., 278 : 5
learning how to use e., 504 : 17
let mine e. not see, 213 : 9
light comes from thine e., 918 : 18
light fade from e., 735 : *n* 1
light of knowledge in e., 643 : 1
light that lies in woman's e., 447 : 4
like agate lanterns, 844 : 2
like unwashed platters, 844 : 2
living lightning from e., 334 : 10
long-strayed e., 252 : 23
look into happiness through another's e., 212 : 32
look your last, 193 : 28
love learned in lady's e., 191 : 2
love looks not with e., 196 : 1
love-darting e., 280 : 1
lovely e. Cupid's arms, 919 : 19
lovely your e., 849 : 14
made for seeing, 494 : 5
make thy two e. like stars, 219 : 18
mind has thousand e., 670 : 8
mine e. dazzle, 262 : 10
mine e. have seen the King, 29 : 10
mistake not to close e., 700 : 4
my mistress' e., 246 : 1
needy e., 34 : 29
night has thousand e., 670 : 8
night hath a thousand e., 176 : 2
no eyes but fountains, 177 : 1
not a friend to close e., 306 : 18
not only in my e. is Paradise, 142 : 14
of all people upon us, 264 : 22
of flame, 612 : 18
of gold and bramble dew, 669 : 8
of the blind shall be opened, 30 : 24
of unholy blue, 446 : 13
of your creature self, 864 : 7
of youth, 225 : 20
on inward vision close e., 703 : 3
on world to turn thine e., 351 : 17
ope their golden e., 243 : 16
open before marriage, 347 : 19
open to cry of pulleys, 899 : 12
painted to the e., 640 : 2
painting feast for e., 483 : 15
pair of sparkling e., 630 : 7
Paradise stood formed in her e., 145 : 2
pearls in beauteous ladies' e., 190 : 6
pearls that were his e., 247 : 21
persuade e. without orator, 189 : 16
pictures in our e. to get, 253 : 6
poorly satisfy our e., 251 : 1
quaint enameled e., 281 : 1
rainy e., 195 : 1
rapt soul in thine e., 278 : 13

Eyes (*continued*)
ravished e., 325 : 6
read history in nation's e., 362 : 10
riding e. through side, 844 : 2
right in his own e., 12 : 24
sans teeth sans e., 211 : 15
saw him with my own e., 297 : 23
scales fell from e., 46 : 8
scornful yet jealous e., 338 : 14
scratched out both e., 934 : 7
see sun with different e., 850 : 9
see things through his e., 834 : 1
see whites of e., 358 : 1
see with no e., 235 : 2
severe and beard, 211 : 15
she gave me e., 425 : 5
shining for me, 810 : 2
show his e., 239 : 13
shut my e. to see, 875 : 1
sight for sore e., 323 : *n* 1
silent tongues of love, 168 : 16
sky daily bread of e., 495 : 24
smoke gets in your e., 740 : 13
so long as e. can see, 127 : 1
soft e. looked love, 457 : 14
Spearmint Girl With Wrigley E., 828 : 17
still dazzled by God, 765 : 2
stretched forth necks and wanton e., 29 : 1
strike mine e. but not my heart, 255 : 18
suspicion stuck full of e., 205 : 6
tear each other's e., 328 : 3
that can see, 797 : 20
that shone now dimmed, 447 : 7
that stare lips that touch, 811 : 15
that would not look on me, 398 : 23
the glowworm lend thee, 266 : 14
their ancient glittering e., 717 : 7
there the lion's ruddy e., 403 : 13
these wakeful e. weep, 442 : 18
those e. the break of day, 228 : 28
to keep our e. open longer, 275 : 14
to the blind, 16 : 17
trust ears less than e., 78 : 3
two e. make one in sight, 748 : 18
two holes in coat where e. are, 387 : 2
ugly sights of death in e., 187 : 9
unused to melting mood, 232 : 20
up to e. in blood, 372 : 8
upon double string, 253 : 6
upraised as inspired, 364 : 14
view ourselves with clearer e., 267 : 5
whale e. wide open in waters, 790 : 22
where 'er casual e. cast, 440 : 6
which spake again, 457 : 14
whites of their e., 368 : 1
wipe my weeping e., 328 : 14
women's e. for stars, 918 : 6
world's e., 713 : 14
young maidens quiet e., 669 : 7
your e. my witness, 260 : 12
your e. shall be opened, 7 : 6
Eyewitnesses, accounts of different e., 80 : 15
Eyne, Bacchus with pink e., 241 : 5
Ezra read from morning to midday, 14 : 30
right half the time, 845 : 6

F

Fabian policy, 95 : *n* 1
Fabis, a f. abstinete, 258 : 15
Fable, old old f. haunts me, 481 : 7
  song or fleeting shade, 266 : 21
Fabled undulations, 571 : 3
Fables, old wives' f., 50 : 29
  rather believe f. in legends, 180 : 16
Fabric, mystic f. sprung, 377 : *n* 5
  of life, 870 : 1
  of this vision, 248 : 13
  silently f. rose, 377 : 11
Fabula, acta est f., 133 : 5
  de te f., 106 : *n* 7
Fabulous shadow only sea keeps, 843 : 13
Fac animo haec praesenti dicas, 96 : *n* 19
Face, a spirit passed before my f., 15 : 12
  accustomed to her f., 895 : 3
  America save soul rather than f., 787 : 8
  angel's f., 173 : 10
  April in her f., 917 : 24
  assert nose on f. his own, 376 : 1
  assist him to save f., 834 : 1
  autumnal f., 253 : 20
  beautiful f. candid brow, 683 : 12
  beauty of aged f., 773 : 16
  blows it in my f., 221 : 8
  but then f. to f., 48 : 25
  change in my f., 665 : 13
  climber upward turns f., 215 : 16
  continual comfort in a f., 184 : 13
  cover her f., 262 : 10
  darkness upon f. of the deep, 6 : 10
  desert's dusty f., 516 : 9
  divine plain f., 441 : 15
  downward in sun, 822 : 1
  dust blows in your f., 234 : 22
  dust of friends stings f., 864 : 13
  emptiness of ages in f., 670 : 14
  everybody's f. but own, 321 : 13
  fall flat on your f., 831 : 9
  false f. must hide, 237 : 8
  fierce fur soft to f., 899 : 17
  final f. of love, 900 : 6
  find one f. there, 566 : 15
  garden in her f., 250 : 5
  gazed on f. of Agamemnon, 591 : 5
  give me a f., 255 : 18
  God f. to f., 8 : 26
  God has given you one f., 221 : 18
  God moved upon f. of the waters, 6 : 10
  grace and music of her f., 295 : 21
  hides smiling f., 375 : 17
  honest labor bears a lovely f., 251 : 10
  how am I to f. the odds, 691 : 23
  how silently with how wan f., 176 : 14
  human f. divine, 285 : 5
  husband with beard on f., 209 : 4
  I have wandered in a f., 905 : 16
  I never forget a f., 834 : 2
  if I lie spit in my f., 203 : 30
  in sweat of thy f., 7 : 12
  in thy f. see map of honor, 185 : 16
  is as a book, 236 : 19
  is my fortune, 931 : 15
  Jealousy a human f., 405 : 14
  Jezebel painted her f., 14 : 19
  kind and northern f., 843 : 17
Face (*continued*)
  knew thy f. or name, 252 : 20
  languid patience of thy f., 433 : 18
  lifts f. all unashamed, 889 : 18
  like a benediction, 168 : 17
  look fear in the f., 786 : 13
  look on her f., 334 : 2
  magic of a f., 272 : 4
  make f. of heaven so fine, 193 : 9
  man die for, 544 : *n* 3
  mice wear human f., 873 : 4
  mind's construction in f., 236 : 15
  mirror of mind, 128 : 8
  mist in my f., 544 : 21
  morning f., 370 : 10
  Moses hid his f., 9 : 12
  most loved happy human f., 454 : 1
  music breathing from her f., 295 : *n* 11
  my f. I don't mind it, 758 : 5
  my f. in thine eye, 251 : 16
  negative in slave window, 897 : 4
  never eye did see that f., 184 : 14
  night's starred f., 478 : 18
  no betrayal in human f., 879 : 8
  no more spoil upon my f., 208 : 19
  no stranger's wing shielded my f., 801 : 14
  nose on man's f., 189 : 33
  of God shine through, 822 : 12
  on barroom floor, 652 : *n* 2
  on-coming snow, 874 : 20
  one f. is somebody's ease, 653 : 15
  open doors of his f., 17 : 5
  open f. of heaven, 475 : 4
  pardoned all except f., 461 : 17
  Pity has a human f., 403 : 11
  plain as nose in f., 158 : 9
  poor lean lank f., 520 : 5
  prism and silent f., 424 : 2
  round jolly fruitful f., 520 : *n* 3
  sages have seen in thy f., 376 : 13
  saw manners in f., 353 : 10
  sea's f. and gray dawn, 760 : 14
  sees other's umbered f., 208 : 1
  set my ten commandments in your f., 185 : 10
  she has a lovely f., 528 : 28
  shining morning f., 211 : 15
  smiling f. dream of spring, 436 : 9
  smiling in my f., 237 : 5
  so pleased my mind, 918 : 14
  soft f. of a girl, 74 : 23
  some awful moment, 427 : 24
  something in a f., 328 : 17
  sorrows of changing f., 712 : 9
  strong men f. to f., 707 : 16
  surrenders his f. to God, 132 : 2
  that drove me mad, 652 : 3
  that launched a thousand ships, 184 : 4
  this fair f. the cause, 184 : *n* 2
  this sunburnt f., 403 : 7
  thou canst not see my f., 10 : 14
  thy classic f., 525 : 9
  to face silent, 507 : 11
  to lose youth for, 544 : 26
  true f. of death, 721 : 8
  truth has such f. and mien, 305 : 16
  truth showing its f. undisguised, 72 : 5
  turned f. with ghastly pang, 434 : 24
  visit her f. too roughly, 218 : 7
  wear one f. to himself, 503 : 13
Face (*continued*)
  whole f. of world changed, 300 : 1
  why hidest thou thy f. from me, 20 : 10
  wish I loved silly f., 697 : 1
  with twain he covered his f., 29 : 8
  worst thing about him, 228 : 4
  you could not see, 550 : 15
  you loved when all was young, 566 : 15
Faced by snarled seas, 804 : 16
Face's, viewed in her fair f. field, 189 : 17
Faces all gather blackness, 33 : 24
  bid them wash their f., 242 : 15
  draw living f. from marble, 105 : 24
  dusk f. with silken turbans, 288 : 11
  estranged f., 693 : 18
  fools' names like fools' f., 920 : 5
  grind the f. of the poor, 28 : 35
  hearts do in the f. rest, 251 : 16
  in f. I see God, 575 : 1
  in the crowd, 792 : 7
  lords and owners of their f., 245 : 5
  millions of f. none alike, 116 : *n* 9
  of coffee-pickers, 789 : 10
  of men and women, 575 : 1
  of Negro children, 893 : 15
  old familiar f., 441 : 5
  old men have rosy f., 669 : 7
  put on two several f., 309 : 17
  sea of upturned f., 431 : 25
  strange with f. new, 569 : 3
  sweat of other men's f., 524 : 5
  Thracian ships foreign f., 632 : 7
Facets, iceberg cuts f. from within, 878 : 2
Facias ipse quod faciamus suades, 94 : *n* 4
Facilis descensus Averni, 105 : *n* 7
Facility of octosyllabic verse, 459 : 8
Facing fearful odds, 488 : 14
  man who sits f. you, 63 : 5
Façon, je veux qu'on m'y voit en ma f., 164 : *n* 3
Fact, awkward historical f., 764 : 14
  bear our ignorance of f., 703 : 4
  belief help create f., 649 : 15
  Caspian f., 607 : 6
  death ugly f. nature hides, 609 : 3
  falsehood more miraculous than f., 357 : 16
  fatal futility of f., 653 : 14
  firm ground of f., 742 : 18
  frontiers where man fronts f., 558 : 17
  grown-ups correct on f., 690 : 12
  idea is the f., 589 : 5
  irritable reaching after f., 479 : 5
  live in f. or thought, 900 : 4
  natural f. spiritual f., 496 : 6
  not state things contrary to f., 95 : 18
  simplest matter of f., 464 : 8
  spiritual f., 496 : 6
  state one f. belie another, 496 : 18
  superiority in f. of conservatism, 497 : 34
  thought counterparts in f., 580 : 5
  yesterday f. today doctrine, 390 : 10
Fact-finding more effective than fault-finding, 738 : 9
Faction, danger of f., 398 : 3
  is number of citizens, 398 : 1
Factions, old religious f., 374 : 5

Factor, timing is most important f., 61 : 23
Factors, gods as psychic f., 754 : 7
Factory, mine f. dockyard, 745 : 11
windows always broken, 765 : 4
Facts alarm more than principles, 391 : 6
all f. when come to brass tacks, 806 : 10
alone wanted in life, 549 : 16
angularity of f., 496 : 15
are sacred, 661 : 5
are stubborn things, 323 : 31, 380 : 11
at first seem improbable, 183 : 2
blink f. not to our taste, 580 : 6
collection of f. not science, 673 : 8
detailed with exactness, 592 : 7
drop cloak stand forth naked, 183 : 2
front essential f. of life, 559 : 25
I admit going beyond f., 762 : 2
if Lord knew f. iv case, 722 : 9
ignorance inert f., 635 : 14
imagination baffled by f., 744 : 14
imagination for f., 399 : 13
impartial analysis of f., 684 : 16
in joruri describe f., 317 : 9
inert f., 635 : 14
irreducible stubborn f., 697 : 6
judges of f. not laws, 330 : 20
learn compare collect f., 665 : 6
looking toward f., 650 : 8
men absorbed in f., 697 : 6
more valid f. in art than in history books, 812 : 8
passions cannot alter f., 380 : 11
politics is ignoring f., 635 : 13
power most serious of f., 635 : 15
science built with f., 673 : 8
test all theories, 509 : 5
we poor passing f., 894 : 11
what I want is f., 549 : 16
Faculties, benumbs all his f., 353 : 22
borne his f. so meek, 236 : 24
men free to develop f., 677 : 12
t' affections and to f., 253 : 7
whose f. can comprehend, 183 : 6
Faculty, Eleazer was f., 705 : 3
infinite in f., 220 : 28
of continuing to improve, 378 : 1
unshackled exercise of every f., 491 : 3
Fade as a leaf, 31 : 27
breathlessly while sea rustles, 798 : 12
colors that never f., 698 : 16
far away, 476 : 24
first to f. away, 447 : 14
into light of common day, 426 : 15
loved flowers that f., 654 : 16
lovely things f. and die, 811 : 16
loveliness f., 446 : 11
may flourish or may f., 369 : 30
nothing of him that doth f., 247 : 21
old soldiers f. away, 771 : 7, 924 : 9
thy eternal summer not f., 244 : 6
Faded and gone, 446 : 14
but still lovely woman, 835 : 12
care sat on his f. cheek, 283 : 25
Flowers of Friendship F., 752 : 11
Friendship F., 752 : 11
insubstantial pageant f., 248 : 13
oldest colors f., 707 : 21
on crowing of the cock, 217 : 26
Fades glimmering landscape, 361 : 21
Fades (*continued*)
out from kiss to kiss, 712 : 19
Fadeth, crown of glory that f. not, 52 : 15
flower f., 30 : 33
Fadin', order is rapidly f., 915 : 5
Fading, bestows the f. rose, 271 : 19
down the river, 700 : 10
fading, 806 : 2
in music, 199 : 22
joys we dote upon, 318 : 4
life f. fast away, 662 : 22
Faery, land of f., 712 : 10
lands forlorn, 477 : 1
Faggot, flames no f. feeds, 716 : 9
Faggots, some burn damp f., 713 : 17
Fagots, diadems and f., 495 : 5
Fail, audience never f. to laugh, 82 : 17
desire shall f., 27 : 25
forever to founder and f., 876 : 11
from eternity shall not f., 691 : 20
if freedom f., 495 : 10
if we should f., 237 : 6
let no man's heart f., 12 : 40
many f. one succeeds, 530 : 10
no such word as f., 493 : 7
not ashamed to f., 351 : 15
not f. that rendezvous, 811 : 6
not flag or f., 744 : 2
possible to f. in many ways, 87 : 17
sooner f. than not be greatest, 479 : 15
strength within her never f., 769 : 9
this could not f., 522 : 12
we'll not f., 237 : 6
Failed if cannot use talent, 852 : 12
principle of exclusion f., 593 : 2
therefore turn critics, 436 : 15
tried a little f. much, 669 : 15
Faileth, faints not nor f., 564 : 16
forsake me not when strength f., 19 : 34
Failing, bulwark never f., 155 : 15
every f. but their own, 459 : 3
from f. hands throw, 737 : 10
tell aloud greatest f., 322 : 17
that the rest of the city, 84 : 11
Failings, conspicuous f. of mankind, 597 : 4
leaned to virtue's side, 370 : 6
Fails, contentment f., 368 : 16
goodness investment that never f., 560 : 8
if heart f. climb not, 172 : *n* 6
my voice f. me, 372 : 8
oft expectation f., 227 : 13
persuades when speaking f., 246 : 15
Failure, heaven's success or earth's f., 542 : 18
hell f. in great object, 475 : 14
I'll show you f., 811 : 3
is impossible, 578 : 7
might have died a f., 811 : 7
minute's success pays f., 546 : 6
most progress most f., 543 : 27
to communicate, 908 : 7
Failures, benefit in f. early, 595 : 17
haste brings f., 78 : 15
history of masterwork not f., 793 : 5
of all f. witticism worst, 442 : 20
practical benefit in f., 595 : 17
Fain climb yet fear to fall, 172 : 11
wald lie down, 927 : 8
would I but dare not, 167 : 7
Faint, chanting f. hymns to moon, 195 : 20
cygnet to pale f. swan, 202 : 16
damn with f. praise, 338 : 14
heart ne'er won fair lady, 170 : 10
heart never won fair lady, 629 : 2
in light she loves, 533 : 21
in the day of adversity, 25 : 13
man so f. so spiritless, 205 : 19
to some f. meaning make pretense, 304 : 25
walk and not f., 31 : 2
whole heart is f., 28 : 27
with envy of the dead, 76 : 10
Faintest, water hears thy f. word, 292 : *n* 3
why f. thou, 587 : 12
Fainting robin, 606 : 12
Faintly then he praises, 338 : *n* 9
Faints not nor faileth, 564 : 16
Fair adventure of tomorrow, 202 : 15
all f. is good, 174 : 20
all's f. in love and war, 564 : 2
always f. weather, 705 : 2
ambition to be f., 357 : 8
and f. and twice so f., 177 : 6
and flagrant things, 292 : 13
and foul near kin, 716 : 17
and learned and good as she, 265 : 15
and softly goes far, 144 : *n* 12
and stately palace, 526 : 1
and unpolluted flesh, 224 : 17
and wise good and gay, 932 : 10
angels are painted f., 317 : 2
anything possible except f. play, 640 : 12
anything to show more f., 425 : 13
as a star, 424 : 12
as f. as any may be, 177 : 6
as the moon, 28 : 17
at first when our day f., 641 : 24
attitude, 477 : 10
Bacchus ever f. and young, 306 : 15
baseness to write f., 224 : 26
bevy of f. women, 287 : 31
book of knowledge f., 285 : 5
breeze blew, 434 : 13
buzz witty and f. annoys, 338 : 19
chaste and f., 255 : 12
chaste unexpressive she, 211 : 18
daffodils we weep to see, 266 : 12
damned in a f. wife, 229 : 12
day adieu, 201 : 22
day aye f. in land o' leal, 417 : 11
day's wages for work, 474 : 2
die because a woman's f., 264 : 23
disguise f. nature, 207 : 16
divided excellence, 201 : 16
Elaine the f., 534 : 11
Ellen of brave Lochinvar, 430 : 19
equity and f. play, 737 : 3
exterior a silent recommendation, 110 : 27
fairer daughter of f. mother, 107 : 10
fallen unto me in a f. ground, 17 : *n* 3
farewell f. cruelty, 213 : 20
fat f. and forty, 394 : 8
find how to make it f., 543 : 4
fleshed f. erected, 878 : 3
fool called her lady f., 709 : 14
forever love and she f., 477 : 7
forfeit f. renown, 430 : 10
from foul to f., 182 : 1
going to f., 930 : 13

Fair (*continued*)
Greece sad relic, 457 : 7
guerdon we hope to find, 280 : 15
hand that made you f., 228 : 22
Harvard, 465 : 1
holy f. and wise is she, 190 : 4
hot wench in taffeta, 202 : 23
house upon another man's ground, 225 : 17
how sweet and f. she seems, 276 : 7
I have sworn thee f., 246 : 7
I was also, 396 : 19
if it prove f. weather, 290 : 4
if ladies but young and f., 211 : 9
in hope of f. advantages, 199 : 9
is foul and foul is fair, 235 : 22
it will be f. weather, 39 : 33
justice in f. round belly, 211 : 15
laughs morn, 363 : 6
like through toy f., 778 : 6
luminous cloud, 435 : 27
Madeline's f. breast, 476 : 16
maid dwellin', 926 : 21
maidens commonly fortunate, 175 : 19
means or foul, 779 : 19
mistress moderately f., 295 : 5
Montague I am too fond, 192 : 9
most divinely f., 528 : 22
my f. lady, 929 : 21
my own f. hands, 321 : 18
none but brave deserves f., 306 : 12
not to fancy what f. in life, 543 : 4
nothing f. alone, 493 : 14
one f. daughter, 221 : 1
open face of heaven, 475 : 4
play f. just and patient, 595 : 12
power of one f. face, 155 : 1
practices to fair notions, 83 : 9
queens have died young and f., 250 : 10
rise up my f. one, 28 : 7
Sabrina f., 280 : 3
sae fresh and f., 409 : 24
scent the f. annoys, 376 : 3
Science frowned not, 362 : 17
seedtime had my soul, 423 : 17
sex, 170 : 8
sex your department, 689 : 13
she a f. divided excellence, 201 : 16
she that was ever f., 230 : 11
slain by f. cruel maid, 214 : 4
so f. a house, 247 : 24
so foul and f. a day, 236 : 4
so lovely f., 232 : 5
so pure and f. to see, 481 : 8
stood wind for France, 182 : 14
tale of a tub, 155 : 7
terms and villain's mind, 198 : 28
their very memory is f., 299 : 7
thou art all f., 28 : 12
though f. and wise, 468 : 21
tide full moon lies f., 587 : 13
to me f. friend never old, 245 : 11
treatment and appreciation, 771 : 2
trees that grow so f., 710 : 12
tresses race ensnare, 334 : 3
view f. Melrose, 430 : 4
viewed in her f. face's field, 189 : 17
wants us to fight f., 786 : 11
was she not f., 119 : 23
weather cometh out of the north, 16 : 26
what care I how f. she be, 264 : 23

Fair (*continued*)
what's right and f., 590 : 11
when love and life f., 676 : 9
wild and f., 431 : 18
wisely f. and softe, 144 : 28
woman true and f., 252 : 2
women and brave men, 457 : 14
words shall prevail, 709 : 5
young and so f., 485 : 21
young f. maidens quiet eyes, 669 : 7
Faire, laissez f. laissez passer, 342 : 20
Fairer, be she f. than the day, 264 : 23
daughter of fair mother, 107 : 10
grows f. than at first, 245 : 21
lady never seen, 926 : 17
marks, 267 : 11
than evening air, 184 : 5
when we look back, 569 : 4
Fairest, descriptions of f. wights, 245 : 12
from f. creatures desire increase, 243 : 31
Isle all isles excelling, 306 : 6
joys give most unrest, 476 : 3
mock time with f. show, 237 : 8
of creation, 287 : 22
of her daughters Eve, 285 : 20
things fleetest end, 693 : 6
thou f. among women, 28 : 3
Fair-haired Rhadamanthys, 59 : 26
Fairies at bottom of garden, 758 : 6
rewards and f., 262 : 14
Fairies' midwife, 191 : 23
Fairing, ah Tam thou'll get thy f., 411 : 14
Fairly, report news f., 820 : 13
Fair-spoken and persuading, 249 : 15
Fairy, by f. fiction dressed, 363 : 8
by f. hands knell rung, 364 : 9
come not near our f. queen, 196 : 21
fruits and flowers, 525 : 17
gifts fading away, 446 : 11
godmother in soul, 694 : 1
gold, 246 : 20
love-gift of f. tale, 612 : 15
loveliest f. in world, 566 : 16
no f. takes, 217 : 26
queen, 196 : 21
story of simians, 746 : 20
'tis almost f. time, 197 : 22
wide enough to wrap a f., 196 : 18
Fairy's child, 478 : 11
Fais ce que voudras, 157 : *n* 14
Faith, alternative to f. we lose, 859 : 13
an excitement and enthusiasm, 504 : 16
and fire within us, 641 : 25
and justice to nations, 379 : 12
and knowledge in medicine, 464 : 4
and morals hold, 426 : 1
animated by f. and hope, 352 : 24
barbaric tribes brought to f., 156 : 12
be alone and f. renew, 646 : 11
become intuition, 428 : 16
begets heretics, 726 : 9
blind f. unpardonable sin, 595 : 10
boyhood's thoughtless f., 571 : 4
breastplate of f., 50 : 20
cannot dispense with f., 686 : 10
confess f. therein, 821 : 6
conquers unbelief, 564 : 12
creed of our political f., 389 : 2
dead which does not doubt, 706 : 12
deciphered in skies, 703 : 3

Faith (*continued*)
denied the f., 50 : 31
dream his f. is fast, 507 : 7
duty cannot exist without f., 501 : 24
dying for f. not hard, 539 : 16
for all defects supplying, 139 : 10
fresh and full of f., 501 : 25
fruit of Spirit is f., 49 : 30
good fight of f., 51 : 3
great act of f., 644 : 12
guardians of the f., 804 : 7
have f. and pursue end, 645 : 3
he mauna fa' that, 411 : 18
he who has courage and f., 909 : 2
holy f., 552 : 21
Hope Charity, 443 : 2
humor prelude to f., 823 : 19
if f. o'ercomes doubt, 543 : 8
if scholar have not f., 89 : 24
if strong f. indulge in skepticism, 658 : 11
illogical belief in improbable, 772 : 11
in f. and hope world disagree, 337 : 9
in human beings, 821 : 3
in light admirable, 726 : 4
in result makes result, 649 : 12
in some nice tenets, 295 : 19
in supremacy of good, 703 : 6
in the might of f., 156 : *n* 5
in this f. I will live and die, 150 : 8
in womankind, 531 : 14
is her own scourge, 118 : *n* 9
is sight and knowledge, 557 : 3
is the substance of things hoped for, 51 : 18
kept the f., 51 : 9
magicians do more by f., 171 : 16
many a man's soul and f., 916 : 8
martyrs create f., 705 : 18
modes of f., 337 : 9
more f. in honest doubt, 532 : 19
no f. held with him, 167 : 15
no f. in immortality, 514 : 7
nonviolence article of f., 727 : 4
nor love nor law, 467 : 4
not create martyrs, 705 : 18
not f. but philosophy, 274 : 14
not for all his f. see, 493 : 16
not yet entered your hearts, 132 : 9
nothing more wonderful than f., 665 : 2
now abideth f., 48 : 25
O thou of little f., 39 : 28
O ye of little f., 38 : 25
of our fathers, 552 : 21
of the pronouncement, 730 : 14
other world by which f. advanced, 151 : 8
passive or hereditary f., 448 : 7
pin f. in things not seen, 125 : 23
pity their want of f., 385 : 9
plain and simple f., 216 : 30
Punic f., 103 : 4
reaffirm f. in human rights, 788 : 20
reason greatest enemy f. has, 156 : 9
room from which f. gone, 859 : 11
save myself by work and f., 865 : 15
saved by f., 823 : 21
sea of f., 587 : 16
shines equal arming me, 562 : 4
show doubt prove f., 543 : 8
simple f. than Norman blood, 528 : 11
something of a f., 531 : 15
staff of f. to walk upon, 172 : 15

Faith (*continued*)
stand fast in f., 49 : 9
still by f. he trod, 765 : 2
that could remove mountains, 48 : 23
that yields to none, 113 : 3
thy f. hath saved thee, 43 : 5
triumphant o'er fears, 511 : 9
true f. discovered was, 715 : 18
true f. ready hands, 566 : 3
under another name, 859 : 13
unfaithful, 534 : 14
walk by f. not sight, 49 : 14
want of enterprise and f., 560 : 7
wears f. as fashion of hat, 208 : 25
welcome home discarded f., 202 : 14
when f. lost honor dies, 513 : 8
where f. in reason timid, 737 : 7
who breaks his f., 167 : 15
without works, 51 : 33
ye must have f., 686 : 10
you call for f., 543 : 8
Faithful Achates, 105 : 16
action f. honor clear, 336 : 5
among the faithless f., 286 : 24
are the wounds of a friend, 25 : 23
at all times f. husband, 327 : 9
Christian f. man, 187 : 8
dog bear him company, 336 : 17
duty's f. child, 484 : 9
ever f., 134 : 26
falling out of f. friends, 96 : *n* 6
fierce wars and f. loves, 173 : 7
friend is medicine, 35 : 10
friend is strong defense, 35 : 9
friends hard to find, 257 : 8
Gêlert roam, 423 : 1
good and f. servant, 40 : 29
in least faithful in much, 43 : 32
in love, 430 : 18
love is f., 148 : 20
O come all ye f., 133 : 8
O f. shepherd, 588 : 8
Penelope, 61 : 5
three f. friends, 347 : 17
to conviction to old age, 86 : 5
to thee Cynara, 721 : 4
to what exists only in you, 727 : 8
unsubstantial persistent f., 733 : 17
unto death, 53 : 1
women all alike, 777 : 5
Faithfully to serve State, 272 : 17
Faithfulness, His infinite f., 319 : 22
hold f. and sincerity, 68 : 5
to truth of history, 592 : 7
Faithless, among the f. faithful, 286 : 24
arm, 868 : 16
as a smile, 804 : 11
as winds or seas, 312 : 12
be not f., 45 : 36
but f. was she, 584 : 14
in friendship but f. haven, 73 : 14
Faith's Defender, 341 : 12
sought f. pure shrine, 561 : 1
Faiths, fighting f., 645 : 1
men's f. wafer-cakes, 207 : 15
old f. loosen and fall, 633 : 6
Falcon, dapple-dawn-drawn F., 656 : 1
Indian of f. glance, 465 : 6
like a f. swooping, 4 : 10
not hear falconer, 714 : 12
red rose a f., 659 : 6
towering in her pride, 238 : 11
Falconer, falcon not hear f., 714 : 12
Falconer's, O for a f. voice, 192 : 16
Falcons, hopes like towering f., 320 : 14
Fall, a little snow f. again, 885 : 13
a thousand shall f. at thy side, 20 : 16
Anarch lets curtain f., 340 : 28
and leave little lives, 334 : 16
as wrong as to f. short, 68 : 27
benison to f., 267 : 1
bigger they come harder f., 78 : *n* 7
both f. into ditch, 39 : 31
by dividing we f., 378 : 11
choose cloud before it f., 335 : 17
cradle will f., 660 : 19
decline and f. of Rome, 384 : 7
desire of power caused angels to f., 180 : 14
divided we f., 378 : *n* 7
down can f. no lower, 291 : 13
dying f., 213 : 7
fain climb yet fear to f., 172 : 11
fear no f., 302 : 13
flat on your face, 831 : 9
flower displayed doth f., 214 : 2
forts of folly f., 588 : 3
fruit that can f. without shaking, 341 : 4
glass f. forever, 870 : 5
half to rise half to f., 337 : 2
hard rain's a-gonna f., 915 : 4
haughty spirit before a f., 24 : 12
he also to death must f., 300 : 17
he that trusteth in riches shall f., 23 : 26
hero perish or sparrow f., 336 : 14
Humpty Dumpty had f., 932 : 2
I f. into Charybdis, 200 : 1
I with shuddering f., 600 : 21
if freedom f., 710 : 24
if you stay price will f., 180 : 20
in love with Athens, 81 : 5
in over pigs, 781 : 13
in with what asked to accept, 750 : 11
into a habit, 705 : 19
into arms not hands, 647 : 18
into Scylla to avoid Charybdis, 200 : *n* 1
leaves f. early, 792 : 9
let chips f. where may, 602 : 15
let f. no burning leaf, 822 : 14
let f. the curtains, 377 : 3
let sword of France f., 815 : 8
lie talking of f. of man, 560 : 29
like a bright exhalation, 249 : 1
like one of the princes, 20 : 5
liquid siftings f., 804 : 25
not a sparrow f., 39 : 3
O what a f. was there, 216 : 25
of a sparrow, 224 : 28
one by one, 372 : 4
out and chide and fight, 328 : 4
pride will have a f., 74 : *n* 3
Satan as lightning f., 43 : 11
silence f. like dews, 793 : 17
since Adam's f., 713 : 2
soar not too high to f., 262 : 18
some by virtue f., 228 : 1
some rain must f., 510 : 11
stars begin to f., 936 : 1
sweet music's melting f., 363 : 13
take heed lest he f., 48 : 16
things f. apart, 714 : 12
though china f., 335 : 24
though heaven f. thy will be done, 134 : 24
to reprobation, 232 : 17
Fall (*continued*)
to the base earth, 194 : 24
tyrants f. in every foe, 411 : 16
unless billboards f., 855 : 15
upon gilded eaves, 531 : 5
upon thorns of life, 467 : 20
water reach rest and f., 837 : 1
we f. to rise, 546 : 7
what if sky were to f., 96 : 11
wide arch of ranged empire f., 240 : 14
wit on other souls may f., 304 : 25
woods decay and f., 533 : 27
Fallacy, pathetic f., 572 : 10
Fallen at length that tower, 533 : 4
Babylon is f., 29 : 27, 53 : 23
be forever f., 283 : 17
by the edge of the sword, 35 : 38
by the tongue, 35 : 38
cold and dead, 576 : 7
fallen fallen fallen, 306 : 18
from grace, 49 : 28
from his high estate, 306 : 18
god who remembers heavens, 464 : 16
how are mighty f., 13 : 10
how art thou f., 29 : 22
into the sere, 239 : 31
lines are f. unto me, 17 : 24
lot is f. unto me, 17 : *n* 3
moon stars f. on me, 787 : 9
on evil days, 286 : 28
prince and great man f., 13 : 13
so f. so lost, 513 : 7
soldier's pole is f., 241 : 22
speak for f. and weak, 567 : 3
splendid tear, 533 : 24
strength like f. angel, 475 : 13
though f. great, 457 : 7
what do when body f., 896 : 12
Fallest a blessed martyr, 249 : 8
if thou f. O Cromwell, 249 : 8
Fallible men governed by bad passions, 387 : 14
will of another f. being, 414 : 8
Falling, adjusted to beams f., 830 : 4
brief as water f., 812 : 3
by f. in and in, 888 : 14
catch a f. star, 252 : 1
cruelty to load f. man, 249 : *n* 1
gently f. on thy head, 328 : 8
greatly f. with f. state, 334 : 13
horror of f. into naught, 326 : 3
in love at first sight, 707 : 7
in melody back, 435 : 19
into dream as I was coming out, 849 : 9
London Bridge f. down, 698 : 14
of a leaf, 571 : 10
on dark central plain, 777 : 16
out of faithful friends, 96 : *n* 6
press not f. man, 249 : 2
righted up f. man, 560 : 21
secure amidst f. world, 325 : 11
softly on Bog of Allen, 777 : 16
star, 284 : 2
what's this am I f., 602 : 1
when heaven f., 692 : 3
with f. oars kept time, 297 : 10
Falling-off, what a f. was there, 219 : 21
Fallow, came a f. doe, 927 : 3
Falls, as long divorce of steel f., 248 : 25
brightness f. from the air, 250 : 10
Coliseum Rome fall, 458 : 22

Falls (*continued*)
commonly we say judgment f., 263 : 16
declines and f., 549 : 30
force without wisdom f. of own weight, 107 : 29
howls hoo and f., 768 : 12
into abatement, 213 : 8
light f. the way light fell, 795 : 12
like Lucifer, 249 : 3
monotonously f. rain, 839 : 9
nature f. into revolt, 206 : 30
nips his root then he f., 249 : 3
no shadow where no sun, 730 : 2
ripest fruit first f., 194 : 17
salmon f., 714 : 22
splendor f. on castle, 530 : 26
the Shadow, 805 : 17
thy shadow Cynara, 721 : 6
with leaf in October, 260 : 14
False Achitophel was first, 303 : 20
ambition drove men to become f., 102 : 24
and hollow, 284 : 8
as air as water, 226 : 15
as common fame, 315 : 18
as Cressid, 226 : 15
as dicers' oaths, 223 : 1
as tears of crocodiles, 177 : *n* 6
as water, 232 : 16
betrayed by f. within, 600 : 18
burn out f. shames, 790 : 14
by philosopher equally f., 383 : 7
creation from brain, 237 : 13
distinguish true from f., 308 : 7
face must hide, 237 : 8
fictions only and f. hair, 268 : 14
framed to make women f., 230 : 5
from f. to f., 226 : 15
gallop of verses, 212 : 4
history must be f., 329 : 1
how f. the argument, 100 : *n* 8
idea of what true and f., 308 : 7
idle and f. imposition, 230 : 24
idol or noble true birth, 85 : 16
if I be f. or swerve, 226 : 15
in friendship f., 304 : 3
knowingly write what is f., 95 : 18
little better than f. knaves, 209 : 32
maids in love, 226 : 15
man does easy, 238 : 10
man f. man, 317 : 15
never be f., 548 : 29
never say I was f., 245 : 14
not f. to others, 180 : 22
novel true and f., 887 : 14
of heart, 245 : 14
or honest dreaming, 899 : 7
philosophy, 284 : 20
pilots true or f. necessary, 303 : 19
prophet, 823 : 17
prophets, 38 : 16
proved true before prove f., 291 : 27
punishment if one swears f. oath, 59 : 3
ring out the f., 532 : 22
sea shows f. alluring smile, 100 : 18
shoot f. love, 918 : 3
that which accepted f., 735 : 16
to any man, 219 : 2
to object, 868 : 7
to two or three, 252 : 3
understanding is f. mirror, 179 : 9
what f. heart doth know, 237 : 8
False (*continued*)
wit, 325 : *n* 3
witness against thy neighbor, 10 : 7
witness by their own mouth, 36 : 15
words infect the soul, 84 : 2
Falsehood, flattery and f., 391 : 1
God's mouth knows not f., 71 : 1
goodly outside f. hath, 198 : 23
has to be invented, 776 : 2
let her and F. grapple, 282 : 5
Mississippi of f., 587 : 4
more miraculous than fact, 357 : 16
no f. lingers to old age, 75 : 20
no word to express lying and f., 322 : 14
not veil truth with f., 130 : 10
of the tongue, 388 : 3
stick the heart of f., 226 : 15
strife of Truth F., 567 : 6
time's glory to unmask f., 189 : 23
trouble to pull down f., 464 : 3
truth f. to world beyond, 165 : 8
upbraid my f., 226 : 15
your bait of f., 220 : 7
Falsehoods, we know how to speak f., 61 : 8
Falsely, deal f. with God, 264 : 22
science f. so called, 51 : 5
true, 534 : 14
Falseness in impressions of external, 572 : 10
Falser than vows made in wine, 212 : 17
tomorrow's f. than former day, 303 : 10
Falstaff in Arthur's bosom, 207 : 13
sweats to death, 203 : 21
Falter life away, 585 : 22
or explore, 899 : 15
when the sun, 606 : 5
Fama volat, 105 : *n* 3
Fame, all Greek all Roman f., 339 : 20
blush to find it f., 339 : 14
conquered f. of heroes, 575 : 8
consumes house of soul, 876 : 10
created something of nothing, 277 : 3
damned to everlasting f., 337 : 15
desire of f., 534 : 23
enjoying timeless f., 67 : 20
estate good f., 494 : 10
fair F. inspires, 338 : 14
flash packet of f., 935 : 6
fool to f., 338 : 10
foolish and false as f., 315 : 18
for his f. the ocean sea, 257 : 5
for pot of ale, 207 : 19
from zone to zone, 647 : 4
great heir of f., 277 : 13
Hall o' F. when you croaks, 810 : 7
halls of f., 923 : 9
heard of the f. of Solomon, 13 : 34
heroes as well as F., 413 : 10
if not double-faced, 289 : 2
is ephemeral, 124 : 23
is no plant, 280 : 16
is the spur, 280 : 15
lives in f. died in virtue's cause, 188 : 18
lost to f., 104 : 4
love and f. to nothingness, 478 : 19
love of f. vanity, 703 : 12
nor F. I slight, 332 : 13
nor too fond of f., 333 : 22
nor yet fool to f., 338 : 10
nothing but empty name, 375 : 10
Fame (*continued*)
of her excellence, 61 : 5
only to myself, 275 : 29
outlives in f. pious fool, 275 : *n* 1
over living head bent, 469 : 8
poets' food love and f., 467 : 16
pursues f. at risk of losing self, 90 : 5
rage for f., 385 : 13
rather than love money f., 560 : 20
Riches F. and Pleasure, 309 : 6
ruins of another's f., 331 : 16
sang of love not of f., 596 : 17
sun of dead, 484 : 12
take my chance with f., 704 : *n* 2
temple of f., 391 : 9
thirst of youth, 458 : 2
to fortune and f. unknown, 362 : 17
trust to common f., 495 : 29
was noised throughout the country, 11 : 32
well known to f., 922 : 16
what's F., 337 : 12
while f. elates thee, 446 : 6
wisdom and prosperity exceedeth the f., 13 : 35
Famed in song famous Athens, 72 : 9
Troy walls f. in battle, 104 : 35
Fame's eternal beadroll, 173 : 22
eternal camping ground, 578 : 10
Familiar acts beautiful, 467 : 8
and well-beloved in home, 875 : 12
as his garter, 207 : 5
as rose in spring, 124 : 26
be thou f., 218 : 30
beauty grows f. to lover, 325 : 16
new things are made f., 353 : 2
old and f. objects, 437 : 17
old f. faces, 441 : 5
style f. but not coarse, 352 : 23
things are made new, 353 : 2
wine a good f. creature, 230 : 27
Familiarity breeds contempt, 66 : 4
breeds contempt and children, 626 : 14
with danger, 569 : 21
Familiarize yourselves with chains, 520 : 7
Families, best-regulated f., 548 : 35
first f. in Virginia, 840 : 14
God setteth the solitary in f., 19 : 33
great f. of yesterday, 318 : 7
happy f. alike, 602 : 9
I hate you, 727 : 7
lie together, 901 : 13
rooks in f. go, 642 : 6
Familles je vous hais, 727 : *n* 6
Family, children of one f., 328 : 4
church and private school, 590 : 2
father of a f., 123 : 10
greatest thing in f. life, 750 : 10
history begins with me, 86 : 6
holding the ropes, 610 : 9
I am part of my f., 790 : 21
join the f., 748 : 16
nobody not in f., 440 : 27
of Man, 761 : 16
of rare long-stemmed flowers, 789 : 9
party tribe or clan, 922 : 9
refuse to help f., 721 : 10
relationship, 689 : 23
represents one aspect, 689 : 23
root of the state, 89 : 8
servant of scattered f., 617 : 7
society which acts as f., 895 : 15

Family (*continued*)
stamped character on child, 754 : 11
supporting f. paying taxes, 642 : 11
trees remember name, 840 : 6
unhappy f. unhappy in own way, 602 : 9
world like great f., 315 : 17
Famine, die by f. die by inches, 319 : 6
fever f. and war, 664 : 16
Pestilence Destruction Death, 773 : 6
seven years of f., 8 : 31
Fam'ly, refuse to help f., 721 : 10
Famous Athens divine city, 72 : 9
awoke and found myself f., 459 : 1
by my pen, 292 : *n* 2
by my sword, 292 : 4
by their birth, 194 : 13
Chaucer broad f. poet, 261 : 15
day and year, 512 : 6
earth sepulcher of f. men, 81 : 5
forgotten for want of writers, 108 : *n* 11
found that f. country, 822 : 2
Hanover city, 540 : 32
harmony of leaves, 712 : 7
high top-hat, 765 : 8
island descending, 743 : 14
let us praise f. men, 36 : 10
maiden f. to all time, 108 : 3
make thee f. by my pen, 292 : *n* 2
not give up writing too f., 812 : 6
remarks seldom quoted correctly, 770 : 4
through infinite inferiority, 570 : 12
to all ages, 281 : 19
victory, 439 : 14
world-f. for fifteen minutes, 908 : 1
Famoused, painful warrior f. for fight, 244 : 7
Fan, brain him with lady's f., 203 : 23
cool gales f. the glade, 332 : 12
like an injured f., 798 : 9
Fanatic can't change mind, 746 : 15
does what Lord wud do, 722 : 9
Fanatical, my f. will power, 812 : 19
Fanaticism redoubling efforts, 703 : 10
to barbarism one step, 359 : 15
Fancied, can it be f. that Deity, 527 : 3
Fancies, high reason of f., 281 : 11
host of furious f., 918 : 12
lay earthly f. down, 533 : 6
our f. are more giddy, 214 : 1
proud and full of f., 475 : 3
realities less dangerous than f., 738 : 9
Fanciful, no test which is not f., 75 : 6
Fancy, ever let f. roam, 477 : 14
excellent f., 224 : 14
from flower bell, 543 : 5
full of shapes is f., 213 : 8
hopeless f. feigned, 531 : 4
is mode of memory, 437 : 13
motives of more f., 227 : 23
my f. flies, 368 : 20
no time for f. dans, 825 : 3
not expressed in f., 219 : 1
not to f. what fair in life, 543 : 4
now f. passes by, 691 : 2
sweet and bitter f., 212 : 28
when I go to rest, 762 : 1
where is f. bred, 199 : 23
whispers of f., 352 : 15
work of the brain and f., 311 : 1
young man's f., 529 : 16
Fancy-free, maiden meditation f., 196 : 15
Fancy's, impediments in f. course, 227 : 23
misled by f. meteor ray, 409 : 5
Shakespeare F. child, 278 : 6
Faneuil Hall cradle of liberty, 451 : 15
Fang, hoof wing and f., 879 : 8
Fanged, fields f. with flints, 854 : 6
Fangs, beware my f., 199 : 31
Fanny's, pretty F. way, 329 : 15
Fans, pelicans collapsed like f., 888 : 13
Fantasia, reflects on this f., 769 : 1
Fantasies, thousand f. begin to throng, 279 : 16
twilight f., 469 : 3
Fantastic century move, 399 : 16
light f. round, 279 : 14
light f. toe, 277 : 20
plays such f. tricks, 228 : 10
reveries, 638 : 10
summer's heat, 194 : 7
tripped light f., 698 : 14
Fantastical, high f., 213 : 8
imagination, 715 : 4
Fantasy, begot of vain f., 191 : 24
have base in reality, 736 : 4
master of f., 674 : 6
neurotic possessed by f., 865 : 20
poet in command of f., 865 : 20
should have base in reality, 736 : 4
Fantasy's, not f. hot fire, 430 : 9
Far and few, 550 : 11
and near unite, 384 : 8
as angels' ken, 283 : 5
as coin would stretch, 202 : 27
bad news travels f., 120 : 14
be it from God, 16 : 24
brother f. off, 25 : 25
calls coming far, 778 : 6
do not peer too f., 71 : 23
do not set eyes on things f. off, 71 : *n* 9
down among dim West, 525 : 11
fair and softly goes f., 144 : *n* 12
fierce hour and sweet, 742 : 17
forward since we have come so f., 189 : 3
from fiery noon, 478 : 2
from madding crowd, 362 : 12
from old folks at home, 598 : 4
from the sun, 362 : 22
green hill f. away, 561 : 9
how f. candle throws beams, 201 : 4
in pillared dark, 749 : 7
in western brookland, 691 : 11
much too f. out all my life, 856 : 16
not too f. from yew, 808 : 9
o'er hills and f. away, 530 : 13
on ringing plains of Troy, 529 : 8
one near one too f., 542 : 9
over hills and f. away, 332 : 1, 931 : 12
peace to him that is f. off, 31 : 22
pushed just so f., 724 : 3
slight not what's near by aiming f., 76 : 14
so f. only should we hate, 73 : 14
so f. trust thee Kate, 203 : 24
so near yet so f., 532 : 20
those f. off are attracted, 69 : 3
whistles f. and wee, 828 : 11
why art thou so f. from helping me, 18 : 5
Far East, those who brought war to F., 787 : 13
Far West, seek gold in F., 591 : 4
Farce is played, 158 : 14
Farced title 'fore king, 208 : 7
Farcical, everything I touch f., 600 : 6
Fardels, who would f. bear, 221 : 12
Fare, bread and Gospel good f., 319 : 10
delicate f. in another's house, 35 : 39
forward, 94 : *n* 9
forward voyagers, 808 : 7
good-bye f. you well, 935 : 1
hard very hard is my f., 331 : 11
I have eaten traveler's f., 314 : 2
last of Romans f. thee well, 217 : 12
like my peers, 544 : 22
miles on foot to f., 748 : *n* 2
thee well if forever, 459 : 19
when you receive f., 614 : 16
Fared forth far beyond heavens, 100 : 3
Fares, how f. it with happy dead, 532 : 4
ill f. the land, 369 : 30
Farewell all joys, 918 : 17
also called F., 601 : 20
and then forever, 410 : 2
bid Alexandria f., 702 : 3
bid f. to every fear, 328 : 14
content, 231 : 11
dear paintings, 273 : 8
distracting town f., 334 : 24
fair cruelty, 213 : 20
forever f. Cassius, 217 : 9
goes out sighing, 226 : 19
hail and f. my brother, 102 : 19
hope, 285 : 13
Horace whom I hated, 458 : 14
king, 195 : 3
Leicester Square, 753 : 1
lobster-nights f., 334 : 25
Monsieur Traveler, 212 : 20
Morning Star, 97 : 16
my bok and my devocioun, 145 : 10
neighing steed, 231 : 11
only feel f., 456 : 7
Othello's occupation's gone, 231 : 11
plumed troop, 231 : 11
remorse, 285 : 13
renowned Eretria, 83 : 6
rewards and fairies, 262 : 14
sadness, 832 : 5
sweets to the sweet f., 224 : 19
the tranquil mind, 231 : 11
thou art too dear, 245 : 1
thou child of my right hand, 256 : 3
to all my greatness, 249 : 3
to college joys, 783 : 17
to Lochaber, 331 : 3
to the Highlands, 410 : 8
to thee farewell, 636 : 13
Farewells, as many f. as stars, 226 : 24
everlasting f., 454 : 19
should be sudden, 462 : 7
Far-flung battle line, 709 : 16
Farfrae, Elizabeth-Jane F. not told of my death, 640 : 16
Farm, best business father's f., 538 : 8
crouched on hillside, 854 : 6
is like a man, 95 : 7
keep 'em down on f., 801 : 12
snug little f. the world, 440 : 13
village and f., 512 : 7
Farmer in the dell, 933 : 20
sowing the corn, 934 : 9

Farmer's boy, 919 : 5
on f. land may fall, 660 : 1
wife, 929 : 11
Farmers, ah too fortunate f., 104 : 3
embattled f., 494 : 13
founders of civilization, 451 : 6
gentlemen f., 461 : 21
mechanics and laborers, 419 : 3
pray that summers be wet, 103 : 27
Farmhand, apple-faced f., 921 : *n* 3
Farmhouse, stop without f. near, 748 : 6
Farms, houses and f. pillaged, 379 : 2
what spires what f., 691 : 9
Farmsteads, when people inspect f., 97 : 12
Farmyard, cock louder in own f., 555 : 2
Far-off curfew sound, 278 : 19
divine event, 532 : 27
old unhappy f. things, 426 : 5
spies a f. shore, 186 : 10
touch of greatness, 534 : 13
Farquhar, Peyton F. was dead, 647 : 5
Far-reaching ancestry, 592 : 6
Farrier, Felix Randal the f., 656 : 7
Far-stretched, all the f. greatness, 173 : 4
Farted, Nobodaddy f. belched and coughed, 404 : 22
Farther away on either hand, 822 : 12
off from heaven, 485 : 5
Farthest Thule, 103 : 25, 345 : 15
way home's the f. way, 267 : 16
Farthing, do not care a f. candle, 442 : 4
every f. of cost, 868 : 17
hold f. candle to sun, 259 : *n* 9
two sparrows sold for f., 39 : 3
Farthings, Latin word for three f., 190 : 24
owe me five f., 930 : 7
Fas est et ab hoste doceri, 113 : *n* 14
Fascinate, blandishments not f. us, 393 : 9
Fascination frantic, 629 : 17
grace force f., 575 : 13
of war when regarded as wicked, 674 : 20
of what's difficult, 713 : 6
Fascist, socialism present f. features, 785 : 7
woman adores F., 911 : 18
Fashion birth intellect, 593 : 1
bravery never out of f., 540 : 2
Bristol f., 553 : 19
drug it's f. to abuse, 630 : 10
faithful in my f., 721 : 4
glass of f. mold of form, 221 : 20
high Roman f., 241 : 23
like rusty mail, 226 : 17
literature out of life, 632 : 1
of these times, 210 : 31
of this world passeth, 48 : 12
out of world out of f., 324 : 24
refinement rather than f., 536 : 6
seen in my natural f., 164 : 5
shipshape and Bristol f., 553 : 19
true to you in my f., 820 : 8
wears faith as f. of hat, 208 : 25
wears out more apparel, 209 : 27
worn-out poetical f., 807 : 12
Fashionable, other f. topics, 369 : 14
supersede f. novel, 488 : 10
time like f. host, 226 : 19
Fashioned, gods f. by men, 704 : 6
Providence f. us holler, 567 : 23
so slenderly, 485 : 21
such world I f. not, 641 : 16
Fashion's brightest arts, 370 : 16
word is out, 717 : 3
Fashions in proud Italy, 194 : 11
not cut conscience to fit f., 863 : 10
old f. please best, 188 : 33
Fast and furious, 411 : 11
bind fast find, 159 : 4
driveth onward f., 528 : 17
drop tears as f., 232 : 20
faster and more f., 540 : 14
followed f. and faster, 526 : 16
hit f. hit often, 777 : 12
how f. shadows fall, 730 : 1
ill weed groweth f., 159 : 32
men die f. enough, 316 : 11
now he is dead should I f., 13 : 21
or come he f., 430 : 16
spare F., 278 : 15
stumble that run f., 192 : 22
they follow, 223 : *n* 5
thick and f. came at last, 613 : 4
thine arrows stick f. in me, 18 : 28
wit speeds too f., 190 : 22
Fasted forty days and nights, 37 : 1
Fasten hands upon their hearts, 691 : 21
him as a nail, 30 : 3
to indifferent thing, 850 : 18
Fastened me flesh, 655 : 19
to dying animal, 715 : 2
Venus f. to prey, 312 : 8
Faster and more fast, 540 : 14
beat to follow f., 240 : 29
faster, 612 : 20
followed fast and f., 526 : 16
speed far f. than light, 742 : 1
travel f. than stagecoach, 371 : 2
walk a little f., 612 : 7
world would go round f., 611 : 13
Fastest, travels f. alone, 707 : 14
Fastidious, a few f. people, 711 : *n* 1
most f. critics, 487 : 18
Fastidiousness, unconscious f., 799 : 1
Fasting, lives on hope die f., 347 : 33
thank heaven f., 212 : 16
when full talk of f. easy, 128 : 10
Fat, all of us are f., 613 : 6
and bean-fed horse, 196 : 12
and greasy citizens, 210 : 27
and sleek a true hog, 109 : 3
black bucks, 765 : 5
contentions, 281 : 18
duller than f. weed, 219 : 19
eat the f. of the land, 9 : 1
fair and forty, 394 : 8
feast of f. things, 30 : 7
feed f. the ancient grudge, 198 : 20
geese are getting f., 921 : 3
if to be f. be hated, 204 : 6
is in the fire, 159 : 1
Jack Sprat eat no f., 929 : 16
Jeshurun waxed f., 11 : 24
king's eye made horse f., 120 : 9
laugh and grow f., 210 : *n* 1
men about me that are f., 215 : 8
more f. than bard beseems, 345 : 21
of others' works, 258 : 5
oily man of God, 345 : 22
one is f. and grows old, 203 : 28
resolved to grow f., 394 : *n* 3
Seymour's F. Lady, 896 : 10
Fat (*continued*)
sharp names never f., 840 : 2
should himself be f., 356 : 30
take f. with lean, 549 : 9
thin man in every f. one, 857 : 13
Venus grown f., 454 : 9
whale f. of postwar London, 892 : 12
white woman, 795 : 2
who drives f. oxen, 356 : 30
Fatal and perfidious bark, 280 : 18
as it is cowardly, 580 : 6
asterisk of death, 512 : 14
bellman, 237 : 17
bowels of deep, 187 : 15
circumference, 615 : 2
complaint, 848 : 6
dominant X, 768 : 2
entrance of Duncan, 236 : 17
facility of octosyllabic, 459 : 8
futility of fact, 653 : 14
gift of beaty, 458 : 10
shadows walk by us, 260 : 17
to have no will to win, 771 : 8
troika dashes on, 582 : 12
vision, 237 : 13
Waterloo, 457 : 21
yes, I am f. man, 539 : 13
Fatality of seeing things too well, 768 : 22
Fate, all our children's f., 710 : 23
assistance from f. essential, 313 : 5
cannot harm me, 433 : 12
certain of his f., 230 : 34
chooses our relatives, 385 : 12
commands all f., 260 : 17
complex f. being American, 652 : 5
coughed and called it f., 728 : 20
death milder f. than tyranny, 71 : 10
determines or indicates f., 559 : 2
did f. begin weaving, 633 : 14
eagle's f. and mine are one, 66 : *n* 10
eccentric propositions of its f., 768 : 7
far off invulnerable, 902 : 3
fears his f. too much, 292 : 3
fixed f. free will, 284 : 19
forced by f., 306 : 11
foulness of their f., 795 : 16
gave his sad lucidity, 584 : 15
gave whate'er denied, 568 : 24
had imagination about, 748 : 13
hanging breathless on f., 511 : 8
has cursed you, 76 : 11
have conquered F., 584 : 17
heart for any f., 509 : 16
heart for every f., 460 : 4
hold f. of world in hands, 865 : 1
human reason is f., 755 : 11
hung on razor's edge, 67 : 21
I feel my f., 873 : 21
I thy f. shall overtake, 267 : 6
is the handspike, 571 : 5
lead me Zeus and F., 92 : 2
man identifies with his f., 843 : 6
man's character is his f., 70 : 11
man's f., 853 : 6
master of f., 534 : 7, 814 : 8
master of my f., 663 : 11
masters of our f., 842 : 12
meet f. among clouds, 713 : 20
men cannot suspend f., 318 : 12
my f. cries out, 219 : 15
no armor against f., 272 : 15
no f. misunderstand me. 747 : 16
no one so accursed by f., 510 : 10

Fate (*continued*)
nobly born must nobly meet f., 77 : 16
not decide single human f., 865 : 18
of all extremes, 335 : 12
of architect, 395 : 22
of empires, 398 : *n* 1
of nation in own power, 489 : 12
of nation riding, 512 : 8
of new truths, 596 : 9
of unborn millions, 379 : 2
proud captain of thine own f., 103 : *n* 1
Providence will and f., 284 : 19
rave no more 'gainst f., 630 : 21
read book of f., 206 : 20
reason is f., 755 : 11
seemed to wind him up, 303 : 16
seize f. by the throat, 421 : 18
sits on dark battlements, 416 : 11
slave to f., 254 : 12
stars of thy f., 413 : 17
stronger than anything 76 : 12
struggling in storms of f., 334 : 13
summons monarchs obey, 304 : 24
take a bond of f. 239 : 11
take F. by throat. 610 : 7
thy f. and mine sealed, 531 : 10
torrent of his f., 352 : 1
voice of f., 413 : 20
what f. predestined, 420 : 20
why know their f., 361 : 12
wisest ask no more of F., 568 : 23
Fated, though f. not to die, 305 : 15
Fateful lightning, 566 : 4
Fate's, jest of F. contriving, 332 : *n* 2
Fates have given a patient soul, 59 : 11
impose that men abide, 186 : 16
masters of their f., 215 : 6
of dread death, 59 : 7
spinning our own f., 648 : 11
Father Abraham, 537 : 2
alone is God, 448 : 1
and I went to camp, 920 : *n* 2
and mither gae mad, 410 : 10
answered never word, 510 : 5
antichrist denieth the F., 52 : 22
author of play, 704 : 14
baptizing in the name of F., 41 : 30
becoming f. easy enough, 610 : 12
bosom of his F., 362 : 19
Burgler Banker F., 604 : 3
called brother's f. dad, 201 : 17
calls me William, 666 : 19
chiefly known by rod, 570 : 6
child f. of man, 425 : 7
cold mad f., 778 : 6
cop both prowler and f., 910 : 11
dear f. come home, 614 : 12
deny thy f., 192 : 5
eternal F. strong to save, 596 : 18
far greater than his f., 58 : 4
fear was my f., 873 : 13
foolish son calamity of f., 24 : 25
for hoarding went to hell, 186 : 5
forgive my injuries, 893 : 9
full fathom five thy f. lies, 247 : 21
gave f. forty-one, 923 : 5
ghost of Hamlet's f., 697 : 4
glorify your F. in heaven, 37 : 6
glory be to the F., 54 : 18
God an exalted f., 678 : 8
God F. even more Mother, 881 : 6
Great F. building forts among us, 591 : 4
Father (*continued*)
Great Spirit is my f., 419 : 10
greatness in f. overwhelms son, 257 : 2
happy to be f. to many sons, 186 : 9
hath chastised you, 13 : 38
have we not all one f., 33 : 36
heard my f. say, 382 : 2
held out golden scales, 59 : 7
honor thy f. and thy mother, 10 : 7
I cannot tell a lie, 378 : *n* 9
in my youth said f., 611 : 10
in Thy gracious keeping, 597 : 16
into thy hands, 44 : 10
it is said to begin with f., 904 : 11
liar and f. of it, 45 : 6
lived his soul, 829 : 21
loving F. surely dwells, 412 : 10
mad feary f., 778 : 6
man shall leave f. and mother, 7 : 4
many talks from great f., 374 : 21
more than hundred schoolmasters, 270 : 11
moved through dooms, 829 : 19
my f. feeds flocks, 366 : 10
my f. paints summer, 899 : 1
my f. sold me 403 : 9
my f. wept, 405 : 12
my God my F. and Friend, 309 : 11
name called everlasting F., 29 : 16
no one like one's f. ever lived, 893 : 20
not God for f. if not Church for mother, 126 : 16
of a family, 123 : 10
of all in every age, 340 : 1
of English criticism, 352 : 25
of Jealousy, 404 : 13
of lights, 51 : 29
of mankind, 514 : 1
of many nations, 8 : 10
of such as dwell in tents, 7 : 21
of such as handle harp, 7 : 22
of Waters unvexed to sea, 523 : 2
of your country, 378 : *n* 9
old f. antic the law, 202 : 28
old f. old artificer, 777 : 18
old F. William, 439 : 15, 611 : 9
omnipotent F. with his thunder, 60 : *n* 3
our F. the Sky, 928 : 13
Our F. who art where, 885 : 12
please world and f., 296 : 14
prince subject F. Son, 254 : 5
rather have turnip than f., 353 : 12
religion, 679 : 4
resembled my f. as he slept, 237 : 19
ruffian, 204 : 5
Scylla your f., 200 : 1
seek f. who need son, 888 : 8
smile at his f., 102 : 7
Son and Holy Ghost, 41 : 30, 311 : 19
struck f. when son swore, 259 : 21
Tiber, 488 : 16
to corruption thou art my f., 15 : 39
took second place, 679 : 4
true-begotten f., 198 : 31
used to say, 798 : 16
was a butcher, 301 : 6
which art in heaven, 37 : 15
who art in heaven, 37 : *n* 4
will of my F., 38 : 19
wise son maketh a glad f., 23 : 21
wish f. to thought, 206 : 31
withered when my f. died, 224 : 2
Father (*continued*)
without f. bred, 278 : 9
you think your f. does not, 76 : 6
your f. the devil, 45 : 6
Fathered, so f. and so husbanded, 215 : 24
Fatherland, dear F. no danger thine, 573 : 12
die for friends or f., 108 : 14
everything belongs to f., 412 : 1
German F., 420 : 1
no danger thine, 573 : 12
O f. O Ilium, 104 : 35
Fatherless, judge the f., 28 : 30
Father-Mother God, 583 : 1
Father's, about my F. business, 42 : 32
daughters of my f. house, 214 : 6
desire f. death, 582 : 11
drink in my F. kingdom, 41 : 10
grave, 110 : 4
house not house of merchandise, 44 : 30
I leave my f. eye, 874 : 6
in my f. house, 45 : 20
joy mother's pride, 431 : 17
lean in joy upon f. knee, 403 : 8
looked into f. heart, 852 : 7
made chimney in my f. house, 185 : 27
my f. theory, 663 : 5
my land my f. land, 603 : 1
sword girded on, 446 : 15
without f. word, 470 : 18
Fathers, ashes of his f., 488 : 14
brought forth nation, 523 : 4
desire not merely what f. had, 88 : 3
faith of our f., 552 : 21
Franklin one of founding f., 800 : 2
God of f. known of old, 709 : 16
good mothers and f., 858 : 15
have eaten a sour grape, 32 : 17
iniquity of the f., 10 : 5
land where f. died, 514 : 12
lie with my f., 9 : 3
our f. were Englishmen, 265 : 8
pardon old f., 713 : 10
provoke not your children, 50 : 13
scenes f. loved, 857 : 14
sins of f. upon children, 77 : 23
sojourner as all my f. were, 19 : 4
sons similar to their f., 59 : 18
sowed dragon's teeth, 840 : 10
talking to you mothers and f., 780 : 11
that begat us, 36 : 10
victory hundred f., 857 : 11
worshiped stocks and stones, 282 : 18
your f. where are they, 33 : 28
Fathers-forth whose beauty past change, 656 : 5
Fathom, cannot f. their depths, 658 : 27
full f. five, 247 : 21
line could never touch, 203 : 15
Fathomed, beauty not been f., 581 : 20
the fathomable, 397 : 7
Fathomless universe, 576 : 5
Fathoms, down f. down, 572 : 7
fifty f. deep, 926 : 13
Fatigue of judging for themselves, 399 : 8
of supporting freedom, 384 : 17
without f. of traveling, 170 : 6
Fatiguing as uncompleted task, 648 : 1
Fatling, lion and f. together, 29 : 19
Fatness of these pursy times, 223 : 9
Fatted calf, 43 : 27

Fattenin' hogs ain't in luck, 662:16
Fattening, immoral illegal or f., 801:10
Fatter, valley sheep f., 455:2
Fatti maschii parole femine, 270:n5
Fatuus, ignis f. of mind, 315:19
Faucet, writing f. upstairs, 750:9
Faulkner sole owner, 838:6
Fault, all f. who hath no f., 534:12
artist is his own f., 865:3
by her f. dropped like flower, 101:21
condemn f. and not act, 228:5
every man has his f., 243:3
faultless to f., 545:8
feed on for f. not mine, 462:10
fellow f. came to match, 212:12
glorious f. of angels, 335:9
grows two thereby, 268:4
hide the f. I see, 340:4
if f. only on one side, 294:10
if sack and sugar be f., 204:6
just hint a f., 338:14
knows how to confess f., 347:20
no f. or flaw, 628:16
not in our stars, 215:6
O happy f., 54:8
of penetrating wit, 294:4
of the Dutch, 422:6
of wit to go beyond mark, 294:4
one f. at first, 268:n4
only f. that he has no f., 123:13
seeming monstrous, 212:12
subordinate who never finds f., 662:2
talk and find f., 168:18
through my f., 54:2
weariness and f., 748:9
worse by excuse, 202:6
Fault-finding, fact-finding more effective than f., 738:9
Faultily faultless, 533:17
Faultless falling raised by own weight, 888:14
monster world ne'er saw, 289:n6
piece to see, 333:2
to a fault, 545:8
Faults, all his f. observed, 217:4
all men make f., 244:14
bear with all the f. of man, 250:4
best men molded of f., 229:9
cleanse me from secret f., 18:2
do not fear to abandon f., 68:7
greatest of f. to be conscious of none, 123:n11
if no f. of our own, 293:5
it has not strength to prevent, 369:15
lie gently on him, 249:12
love to f. always blind, 404:14
loves him better for f., 369:24
man must have f., 117:15
not for thy f. but mine, 458:14
not free from f., 333:22
of those around me, 774:5
persuade ourselves we have no great f., 293:37
pleasure in f. of others, 293:5
some f. men readily admit, 121:17
to f. a little blind, 320:17
to scan, 370:6
vile ill-favored f., 225:21
who covers f., 233:1
with all her f., 375:13
with all thy f. I love thee, 375:n6
Fauna flora geography, 878:17
Faustine, your doom F., 633:14
Faustus must be damned, 184:8
Faut, il f. cultiver notre jardin, 343:n6
Faute, pire qu'un crime c'est une f., 415:3
Favor, flattery in return for f., 421:20
found f. in thy sight, 8:11
from Fortune easier to get, 111:3
in that same way grant f., 94:12
increased in f., 42:33
is deceitful, 26:10
look with f. on bold beginning, 103:26
men f. deceit, 303:10
nor f. to men of skill, 27:17
obedience to law right not f., 687:9
render praise and f., 507:4
those who f. fire, 748:2
to rich, 289:14
to this f. she must come, 224:14
truths in and out of f., 747:10
well bestowed, 327:18
when f. of gods was equal, 78:2
with God and man, 42:33
Favorite has no friend, 361:16
man f. of mother, 679:6
physician hath f. disease, 349:17
that f. subject myself, 385:15
Favorites, all kings and their f., 252:22
heaven gives its f., 91:n1
Way has no f., 65:8
Favoritism in public life, 683:6
Favors, conferring rather than accepting f., 81:n1
error to expect f., 379:14
felt all its f., 359:10
fortune f. the brave, 97:n1, 106:4
hangs on princes' f., 249:3
lively sense of future f., 293:n6
nor for her f. call, 332:13
not by accepting f., 81:3
not won by trifling f., 447:18
rhyme into ladies' f., 208:18
rubs enhance value of f., 369:8
shower f. alike, 419:4
Fawn, to f. to crouch to wait, 174:11
Fawning greyhound proffer, 203:16
publican, 198:19
thrift may follow f., 222:4
Fawns, when lion f. upon lamb, 186:20
Fe fi fo fum, 934:4
Fear, act of f., 218:20
actions ascribed to f., 657:9
afraid of f., 421:10
age of f., 846:17
all-powerful should f., 275:22
and bloodshed, 427:22
and danger of violent death, 264:17
and distrust the people, 390:2
angels f. to tread, 333:20
arming me from f., 562:4
as children f. in darkness, 100:22
at my heart as at cup, 434:22
be just and f. not, 249:8
be not afraid of sudden f., 23:6
better is little with the f. of the Lord, 24:7
bid farewell to every f., 328:14
birds of prey, 227:30
boys that f. no noise, 371:10
by beauty and by f., 423:17
by day and night, 903:2
came upon me, 15:11
cannot be without hope, 308:16
Fear (*continued*)
concessions of f., 372:11
conquer f. beginning of wisdom, 738:5
cornered-animal f., 913:6
courage resistance to f., 624:21
death as children fear dark, 180:2
death feel fog, 544:21
deep as marrow, 903:2
do not f. to abandon faults, 68:7
doth Job f. God for nought, 15:3
every infant's cry of f., 405:9
extreme f. neither fight nor fly, 189:21
fain climb yet f. to fall, 172:11
farewell f., 285:13
Father F., 873:13
feel fate in what I cannot f., 873:21
for f. very stones prate, 237:15
foundation of governments, 381:9
freedom from f., 780:13, 781:8
frightened out of f., 241:13
from hope and f. set free, 633:22
God and keep his commandments, 27:27
God and take own part, 492:17
God honor the king, 52:11
Greeks even when they bring gifts, 104:32
hair stand up in panic f., 75:15
I am not in perfect mind, 235:9
I cannot taint with f., 239:n2
I will f. no evil, 18:7
imagining some f., 197:12
in handful of dust, 805:1
is sharp-sighted, 168:28
keeps men in obedience, 259:24
let them hate so long they f., 97:9
littlest doubts are f., 222:13
loneliness of f., 842:14
look f. in the face, 786:13
love and f. hardly together, 153:19
love fear life, 738:4
made without f., 17:8
mean actions ascribed to f., 657:9
mercy toward them that f. him, 21:6
my heart shall not f., 18:12
natural f. increased with tales, 180:2
never f. to negotiate, 890:9
never negotiate out of f., 890:9
no fall, 302:13
no f. stand up to hunger, 683:18
no more heat o' the sun, 243:27
nor courage saves us, 804:15
not I bring good tidings, 42:28
not lest existence, 516:21
not these well-fed long-haired men I f., 99:25
not thou child infirm, 495:1
not to touch the best, 172:14
nothing terrible except f. itself, 179:13
nothing to be feared as f., 557:9
nothing you carry Caesar, 99:20
O word of f., 191:13
of Acheron be sent packing, 100:20
of censure, 792:14
of change, 283:24
of controversy, 872:19
of death more dread than death, 111:16
of having to cry, 378:6
of hell's a hangman's whip, 259:n11
of ignominious death, 414:17

Fear (*continued*)
of kings, 200 : 9
of little men, 594 : 2
of some divine powers, 259 : 24
of suffering injustice, 293 : 13
of the Lord, 29 : 18
of the Lord is beginning of wisdom, 21 : 19
of the Lord is wisdom, 16 : 15
of weakness, 792 : 14
only thing to f. is f., 779 : 10
pale hungry-looking men, 99 : 25
perfect love casteth out f., 52 : 25
pine with f. and sorrow, 174 : 10
possess them not with f., 208 : 8
prey of f., 799 : 8
punishment increases f., 658 : 6
put f. out of heart, 726 : 12
quite unaccustomed to f., 922 : 15
repentance is f. of consequence, 293 : 24
shuddering f. green-eyed jealousy, 199 : 28
so artless after f. lost, 151 : 4
source of cruelty, 738 : 5
source of superstition, 738 : 5
spirit of f., 51 : 6
strange that men f., 215 : 26
tastes like rusty knife, 879 : 19
that defeats and dreams are one, 768 : 7
that reigns with tyrants, 511 : 1
thee ancient Mariner, 434 : 25
theoretic and visionary f., 388 : 17
therefore will we not f., 19 : 10
thief doth f. each bush, 186 : 27
thing I f. most is f., 164 : 7
thou shalt f. waking, 633 : 17
thy nature, 236 : 16
thy skinny hand, 434 : 25
to appear weak, 301 : 9
to be we know not what, 303 : 9
to f. worst cures worse, 226 : 12
to him in f. everything rustles, 75 : 19
to live or die, 495 : 4
to prevent war not f. it, 439 : 6
to speak for fallen, 567 : 3
to whom f. due, 47 : 27
true nobility exempt from f., 185 : 22
walk in f. and dread, 435 : 3
was my father, 873 : 13
watch not one another out of f., 251 : 15
we f. in the light, 100 : 22
we must get rid of f., 473 : 25
we will not be driven by f., 872 : 18
what is too strange, 900 : 2
what others do from f. of law, 87 : 2
what we f. of death, 228 : 21
where angels f. to tread, 333 : 20
whom shall I f., 18 : 11
whom they f. they hate, 95 : 6
work out salvation with f., 50 : 2
world too beautiful, 822 : 14
yet do I f. thy nature, 236 : 16
Feared, better to be loved than f., 153 : 19
by their breed, 194 : 13
just as I f., 550 : 4
no danger knew no sin, 305 : 14
nothing to be f. as fear, 557 : 9
one that f. God, 14 : 35
safer to be f. than loved, 153 : 19
Feared (*continued*)
tread underfoot what too much f., 101 : 9
witches, 677 : 13
Fearest nor sea rising, 654 : 15
Feareth, woman that f. the Lord, 26 : 10
Fearful, come forth thou f. man, 193 : 11
concatenation of circumstances, 450 : 19
frame thy f. symmetry, 405 : 7
goodness never f., 228 : 23
how f. and dizzy, 234 : 28
innocence, 425 : 15
lifting up a f. eye, 182 : 2
not a more f. wildfowl, 196 : 24
odds, 488 : 14
saw a thousand f. wracks, 187 : 9
snatch a f. joy, 361 : 9
summons, 217 : 23
thing see soul take wing, 459 : 22
to lead people into war, 682 : 13
trip is done, 576 : 6
why are ye f., 38 : 25
Fearfully and wonderfully made, 22 : 19
o'ertrip the dew, 200 : 22
Fearing, respect strength without f., 388 : 12
stood there f., 526 : 14
to attempt, 227 : 29
to be spilt, 223 : 20
Fearless, foe with f. eyes, 700 : 6
for unknown shores, 576 : 15
Fears a painted devil, 237 : 23
bondage of irrational f., 677 : 13
dishonor worse than death, 108 : 14
do make us traitors, 239 : 16
doubt disputes distractions f., 585 : 4
faith triumphant o'er f., 511 : 9
grown from sudden f., 459 : 21
his fate too much, 292 : 3
hopes and f. of all years, 619 : 16
humanity with all f., 511 : 8
humble cares delicate f., 425 : 5
I had no human f., 424 : 14
less than imaginings, 236 : 11
miserable he who f. death, 267 : 2
more pangs and f., 249 : 3
not mine own f., 245 : 13
past regrets future f., 516 : 13
prosperity not without f., 180 : 6
saucy doubts and f., 238 : 23
tenderness its joys and f., 426 : 23
that I may cease to be, 478 : 17
tie up thy f., 268 : 22
to speak of Ninety-eight, 592 : 2
trembling cold in ghastly f., 404 : 10
when little f. grow great, 222 : 13
Fearsome banality of evil, 866 : 7
Feary, mad f. father, 778 : 6
Feast, bare imagination of f., 194 : 7
beginning of a f., 204 : 36
Belshazzar made a great f., 32 : 35
despair not f. on thee, 656 : 15
dressed as going to a f., 255 : 17
enough as good as f., 161 : 17
for eyes, 483 : 15
good conscience continual f., 260 : 3
great f. of languages, 191 : 7
is made for laughter, 27 : 18
is set, 434 : 5
movable f., 845 : 14
nourisher in life's f., 237 : 21
of Crispian, 208 : 10
of fat things, 30 : 7
Feast (*continued*)
of joy a dish of pain, 177 : 10
of losses, 864 : 13
of moon and men, 831 : 16
of nectared sweets, 279 : 25
of reason flow of soul, 339 : 8
of Stephen, 563 : 11
of wines on the lees, 30 : 7
outcast from life's f., 777 : 15
pomp and f. and revelry, 278 : 6
riseth from f. with keen appetite, 199 : 5
sat at good man's f., 211 : 12
small cheer makes merry f., 188 : 5
to spleen a grateful f., 428 : 14
to the Lord, 9 : 26
what f. is toward, 225 : 4
when f. finished, 721 : 6
when I make a f., 181 : 22
Feasting, good dinner and f., 309 : 25
house of f., 27 : 4
Feasts, movable f., 54 : 9
O nights and f. of gods, 106 : 21
shown in courts at f., 280 : 1
Feat of Tell the archer, 414 : 1
Feather, a wit's a f., 337 : 13
as f. wafted downward, 510 : 17
birds of a f., 259 : 17
for each wind, 246 : 17
his own f. on dart, 456 : 17
in hand better than bird in air, 120 : *n* 3
in his cap, 360 : 14
never moults f., 547 : 20
pluck out flying f., 633 : 13
pun pistol not f., 442 : 12
sharpened f., 571 : 10
stuck f. in hat, 920 : 9
tomorrow f. duster, 740 : 7
whence pen was shaped, 429 : 4
Featherbed, depotism to liberty in f., 388 : 9
Feathered, divide into featherless and f., 86 : *n* 4
his nest well, 261 : 10
wakeful thought, 557 : 8
with eagle's plumes, 66 : 24
Featherless, divide into f. and feathered, 86 : *n* 4
Feathers, beat f. flat as pancakes, 261 : 12
brain of f., 340 : 20
cover thee with his f., 20 : 16
crow beautified with our f., 178 : 12
field of f. for strife of love, 113 : *n* 3
great wing f. swooping darkness, 928 : 9
not only fine f. make fine birds, 66 : 8
Old Fuss n' F., 455 : *n* 4
owl for all f., 476 : 8
plumes her f., 279 : 22
thing with f., 604 : 17
twitter and f. sleek, 475 : 2
with our own f., 66 : *n* 10
Featly, foot it f., 247 : 19
Feats, 'twas one of my f., 462 : 11
Feature, haint one agreeable f., 567 : 22
show virtue her own f., 222 : 2
Features, homely f. to keep home, 280 : 1
human f. composed of ten parts, 116 : 12
of clerical cut, 806 : 14
paint man as well as f., 619 : 9

Feblit, and f. with infermite, 153 : 6
February, excepting F. alone, 162 : *n* 3
Fecit, homo f., 900 : 1
Fecund, searcher for f. minimum, 766 : 18
Fed, bite hand that f., 374 : 11
dead who f. the guns, 795 : 16
fish that hath f. of worm, 223 : 15
grown by what it f. on, 218 : 8
look up and are not f., 280 : 22
man's resinous heart f., 715 : 14
of dainties bred of a book, 190 : 27
on fullness of death, 633 : 6
on honeydew hath f., 433 : 27
purely upon ale, 329 : 7
those former bounty f., 306 : 18
to be happy be well f., 772 : 12
world on dreaming f., 711 : 19
Federal, not approve of f. system, 452 : 1
our F. Union, 419 : 2
Federalism practice not principle, 862 : 19
Federalists, we are all F., 388 : 16
Federation of the world, 530 : 1
Fee bestow upon foul disease, 232 : 28
doctor for nauseous draught, 306 : 26
gorgeous east in f., 425 : 18
set life at pin's f., 219 : 13
Feeble, and f. with infirmity, 153 : 6
assist f. and friendless, 380 : 6
earthworm, 300 : 11
engines of despotism, 390 : 1
expletives f. aid join, 333 : 7
help f. up, 242 : 29
if Virtue f. were, 280 : 5
most forcible F., 206 : 23
religion of f. minds, 374 : 1
to quote argues f. industry, 80 : 2
we have become f. plant, 408 : 11
Feebler, nothing f. than a man, 60 : 26
Feed among the lilies, 28 : 11
brain with better things, 742 : 12
Church sleep and f. at once, 804 : 20
cloy appetites they f., 241 : 1
cow and bear shall f., 29 : 19
fat the ancient grudge, 198 : 20
gave thee life bid thee f., 403 : 5
He that doth ravens f., 210 : 28
him with bread of affliction, 14 : 11
his flock like a shepherd, 30 : 35
his sacred flame, 435 : 20
men in exile f. on dreams, 71 : 13
nor f. the swine, 931 : 19
on bitter fruit, 854 : 2
on Death, 246 : 5
on for fault not mine, 462 : 10
on her damask cheek, 214 : 5
on hope, 174 : 10
sleep and f., 223 : 17
this mind of ours, 423 : 5
upon strawberries, 931 : 19
upon what meat Caesar f., 215 : 7
worm shall f. sweetly, 16 : 10
you cannot f. capons so, 222 : 8
Feeds, Death that f. on men, 246 : 5
mock meat it f. on, 230 : 34
my father f. flocks, 366 : 10
three, 567 : 14
upon burrs of life, 475 : 13
who gives himself f. three, 567 : 14
Feel amid city's jar, 585 : 1
and know we are eternal, 309 : 4
as if top of head off, 608 : 6
Feel (*continued*)
as if we were free, 650 : 4
beauty as we f., 703 : 5
by turns bitter change, 284 : 23
can Sporus f., 338 : 18
fog in throat, 544 : 21
great forces behind detail, 644 : 14
happier in passion we f., 293 : 30
heavy as yonder stone, 778 : 5
hell within myself, 274 : 15
how swift how secretly, 822 : 1
I must f. it as a man, 239 : 22
in wintry age f. no chill, 377 : 20
it and am in torment, 102 : 17
it cannot utter it, 852 : 11
it so like myself, 882 : 3
let me f. your pulse, 188 : 12
like doing for babies, 858 : 15
like morning star, 619 : 15
like thirty cents, 718 : 11
mighty free on a raft, 624 : 1
more to do than f., 441 : 4
my fate, 873 : 21
my heart new opened, 249 : 3
not f. the crowd, 377 : 4
now does he f. his title, 239 : 28
old as yonder elm, 778 : 5
only f. farewell, 456 : 7
paint best who f. most, 335 : 6
passions we f. expand time, 734 : 5
rather to f. than reason, 414 : 11
see not f. how beautiful, 435 : 25
speak what we f., 235 : 20
steady candle flame, 541 : 20
thee again old sea, 569 : 20
thing that could not f., 424 : 14
those who would make us f., 375 : 8
thy finger and find thee, 655 : 19
tragedy to those that f., 363 : 22
we are greater, 429 : 2
we reason deeply when we f., 414 : 19
what we f. indeed, 588 : 22
what we think we f., 588 : 22
what wretches feel, 234 : 4
Feeling, a f. and a love, 423 : 12
apprehend by f. as by intellect, 753 : 13
blue, 684 : 18
comfortable f. of superiority, 772 : 12
deepest f. in silence, 798 : 17
development of f. in language, 809 : 7
disputation, 204 : 17
fellow f., 258 : 4
flicked by f., 768 : 21
for single good action, 395 : 25
formal f. comes, 605 : 6
gives greater f. to the worse, 194 : 7
gratifying f. duty done, 630 : 6
high mountains a f., 457 : 28
his cold strength, 797 : 12
I got beautiful f., 833 : 10
imprecision of f., 807 : 21
in all its nakedness, 484 : 13
makes us eloquent, 118 : 2
no f. not in every heart, 595 : 1
no f. of his business, 224 : 7
not always everything, 583 : 6
of sadness and longing, 510 : 18
one f. falsely disdained, 469 : 19
permanent contract on temporary f., 641 : 6
petrifies the f., 409 : 12
profound or vehement, 437 : 17
push of cosmos, 650 : 7
Feeling (*continued*)
religious f. part of consciousness, 580 : 9
religious f. toward life, 728 : 10
sensible to f. as to sight, 237 : 13
sentimentality failure of f., 769 : 21
taste f. inheritance, 635 : 2
the East's gift, 542 : 20
whole of you transformed into f., 702 : 7
Feelings, art transmission of highest f., 602 : 14
beings books events battles, 861 : 4
consideration for wives' f., 889 : 2
not figures on dial, 555 : 13
opinion determined by f., 579 : 8
overflow of powerful f., 424 : 9
permanently in race, 585 : 19
some f. to mortals given, 431 : 10
trampling on f., 839 : 14
violent f. produce falseness, 572 : 10
Feels, heroism f. never reasons, 497 : 24
it with great sensibility, 354 : 7
ne'er f. retiring ebb, 231 : 18
never f. wanton stings, 227 : 28
Fees, contrive our f. to pilfer, 82 : 2
flowing f., 281 : 18
Feet, able to draw with their f., 67 : 13
and did those f., 406 : 21
and his f. not be burned, 23 : 14
are always in water, 407 : 16
at her f. he bowed, 12 : 7
at the f. of Gamaliel, 46 : 25
beneath her petticoat, 289 : 21
broken by passing f., 712 : 2
cat would not wet f., 160 : 7
chase hours with flying f., 457 : 15
die on f. not live on knees, 759 : 2, 780 : 14
die over f. to washup, 778 : 6
dreams under your f., 712 : 16
dust of your f., 38 : 35
earth my f. know, 790 : 21
fell at his f. as dead, 52 : 31
fog comes on cat f., 761 : 5
four white f. go without him, 923 : 11
get up on f. and fly, 892 : 7
heaven under our f., 560 : 10
if it is well with your f., 109 : 6
in ancient time, 406 : 21
keep thou my f., 490 : 6
lamp by which f. guided, 383 : 2
lamp unto my f., 22 : 2
leave but not hearts, 518 : 16
like unto fine brass, 52 : 30
liked getting f. wet, 719 : 5
little snow-white f., 711 : 22
making a tinkling with their f., 29 : 1
more instant than F., 693 : 11
nearer than hands f., 535 : 9
neither ground for f., 576 : 17
nimble f. dance on air, 676 : 9
of clay, 32 : 32
of him that bringeth good tidings, 31 : 12
old shoes easiest for f., 179 : *n* 4
over whose acres blessed f., 202 : 22
palms before my f., 742 : 17
patter of little f., 512 : 4
pleasures lie about f., 425 : 9
pretty f. like snails, 266 : 13
regards what is before his f., 95 : 4
rising and falling, 807 : 10
roll in ecstasy at your f., 786 : 3

Feet (*continued*)
Scots lords at his f., 926 : 13
shalt thou trample under f., 20 : 17
silver-sandaled f., 674 : 15
six f. of land, 602 : 12
standing with reluctant f., 510 : 13
stretches out f. and dies, 892 : 7
teach f. a measure, 633 : 13
to the lame, 16 : 17
tremble under her f., 533 : 25
unstable, 765 : 5
walks in morning on four f., 74 : *n* 5
washed f. in soda water, 805 : 6
what flowers at my f., 476 : 26
wind's f. shine along sea, 632 : 18
with goat f. dance antic hay, 183 : 16
with twain he covered his f., 29 : 8
with your shoes on your f., 9 : 25
Feetur, haint one agreeable f., 567 : 22
Feign thing or fynde wordes
new, 146 : 15
Feigned an angry look, 316 : 7
by f. deaths to die, 252 : 15
necessities, 272 : 20
Feigning lady by Bazille, 899 : 11
Feigned, hopeless fancy f., 531 : 4
Felicities, close circle of f., 389 : 1
poet with so many f., 423 : *n* 1
Felicitous phenomenon, 799 : 14
Felicitously, whatever is f.
expressed, 417 : 2
Felicity, absent thee from f., 225 : 1
and flower of wickedness, 545 : 9
green f., 478 : 14
human f., 348 : 20
or doom, 608 : 4
perfect bliss and sole f., 183 : 6
possession without
obligation, 600 : 24
we make or find, 352 : 21
what more f. to creature, 174 : 12
Felix culpa, 54 : 8
qui potuit cognoscere
causas, 104 : *n* 1
Fell, all of us f. down, 216 : 25
among thieves, 43 : 13
at his feet as dead, 52 : 31
at one f. swoop, 239 : 21
bolt of Cupid f., 196 : 15
by that sin f. the angels, 249 : 7
clutch of circumstance, 663 : 10
epitaph of those who f., 746 : 5
fiend f. from heaven, 135 : 3
from morn to noon he f., 284 : 2
Great Caesar f., 216 : 25
heart f. dead, 828 : 10
help me when I f., 449 : 12
house f. not, 38 : 20
I do not love thee Doctor F., 319 : 19
I f. as a dead body, 141 : 4
if angels f., 336 : 18
in the great victory, 439 : 12
it f. it burst it shook land, 777 : 10
lash magic creature till it f., 607 : 7
like autumn fruit, 303 : 16
men f. out knew not why, 290 : 13
mightiest Julius f., 217 : 21
my f. of hair, 240 : 3
of dark not day, 656 : 19
out over pigs, 781 : 13
scales f. from eyes, 46 : 8
seeds f. by wayside, 39 : 13
sergeant death, 224 : 30
shake my f. purpose, 236 : 17
Fell (*continued*)
so f. the brand Excalibur, 528 : 29
some f. into good ground, 39 : 15
spirits that f. with Lucifer, 183 : 20
the wall f. down flat, 11 : 31
there he f. down dead, 12 : 7
thy shadow Cynara, 721 : 4
thy tempests f. all night, 269 : 5
Time's f. hand, 244 : 21
to earth knew not where, 510 : 24
upon his brother Benjamin's
neck, 8 : 37
upon knees blessed God, 265 : 7
we f. out I know not why, 530 : 23
when stars shot and f., 749 : 11
Felled, hand that signed f. city, 886 : 14
Feller, met a city f., 924 : 10
sweetes' little f., 685 : 1
Fellers call me Bill, 666 : 19
Fellow, covetous sordid f., 341 : 21
damned in fair wife, 229 : 12
dies an honest f., 260 : *n* 5
every sword against his f., 12 : 36
fault came to match, 212 : 12
feeling, 258 : 4
folly has not f., 691 : 1
good hay hath no f., 197 : 5
hail f. well met, 323 : 22
has this f. no feeling, 224 : 7
have such a f. whipped, 221 : 23
he was a good f., 146 : 4
hook-nosed f. of Rome, 206 : 28
I shot his f., 198 : 6
laughing f. rover, 760 : 16
love my f. creatures, 629 : 3
loves his f. men, 454 : 6
make f. creatures happy, 385 : 5
met a city f., 924 : 10
narrow f. in the grass, 606 : 13
never met this f., 606 : 14
no f. in firmament, 216 : 3
of infinite jest, 224 : 14
robustious periwig-pated f., 221 : 23
savage-creating f., 82 : 19
sweetest little f., 685 : 1
travelers of revolution, 770 : 5
want of it the f., 337 : 11
with best king, 146 : *n* 2
Fellowman, assist reduced f., 137 : 10
Fellow's got to swing, 676 : 7
wise enough to play fool, 214 : 12
Fellows call me Bill, 666 : 19
club assembly of good f., 352 : 7
good f. get together, 705 : 2
it hurts to think, 691 : 17
lewd f., 46 : 14
man knows f. in himself, 734 : 8
of infinite tongue, 208 : 18
such f. as I crawling, 221 : 16
Fellows', other f. brindled
hair, 668 : *n* 4
Fellowship divine, 475 : 20
neither honesty nor good f., 203 : 4
right hands of f., 49 : 25
such a f. of good knights, 149 : 15
with essence, 475 : 20
Felon, lets greater f. loose, 918 : 13
Felony to drink small beer, 185 : 23
Felt, darkness which may be f., 9 : 21
how awful goodness is, 286 : 8
I like watcher of skies, 475 : 7
in the blood, 423 : 8
jests that never f. wound, 192 : 2
knowing what really f., 845 : 2
Felt (*continued*)
like planets fallen on me, 787 : 9
ne'er saw I never f., 425 : 14
never deeply f. nor willed, 585 : 22
through all this fleshy dress, 299 : 3
touch scarcely f. or seen, 341 : 3
world go by, 604 : 11
Felt-life in work of art, 653 : 11
Female, child of Eve a f., 190 : 16
difference of education between
male and f., 392 : 12
elegance of f. friendship, 352 : 20
God gave man f. companion, 735 : 17
if to her f. errors fall, 334 : 2
male and f. created he, 6 : 14
male and f. equal, 574 : 9
male and f. fuse into one solid, 80 : 12
of sex it seems, 288 : 30
of the species, 710 : 21
patriotism in f. most disinterested
of virtues, 393 : 3
subtle and profound f., 64 : 2
there is no f. mind, 695 : 13
warriors, 343 : 22
what f. heart gold despise, 361 : 15
woman, 616 : 12
Females, trifling narrow education of
f., 392 : 13
Femina, varium et mutabile f., 105 : *n* 5
Feminine, eternal f. draws us
on, 396 : 27
intuition, 853 : 19
Italian for converse with f.
sex, 357 : 19
mystique, 898 : 7
research into f. soul, 679 : 7
she's of f. gender, 394 : 6
soul a queen, 703 : 13
Femininity, conventional picture of
f., 898 : 4
Feminized, western civilization be
f., 886 : 9
Femme, cherchez la f., 491 : *n* 4
ne naît pas f. le devient, 870 : *n* 2
Femmes, l'enfer des f., 296 : *n* 4
Fen of stagnant waters, 425 : 22
Fence, don't take f. down, 742 : 13
only f. against the world, 308 : 2
reason why f. put up, 742 : 13
seas for f. impregnable, 186 : 15
taught her dazzling f., 280 : 2
thirty yards of board f., 622 : 11
Tom surveyed the f., 622 : 11
Fenced in piece of land, 358 : 9
Fences, come to look after f., 593 : 14
good f. good neighbors, 747 : 5
mend f., 593 : *n* 2
there by starlit f., 691 : 12
Fens, mountains moors f., 735 : 8
Fere libenter homines, 99 : *n* 11
Ferlie he spied wi' hise'e, 926 : 23
Ferment, bourgeois in f. of
youth, 583 : 14
space in which soul in f., 475 : 15
Fermi, work by F. and Szilard, 763 : 11
Fern, grasshoppers under f., 373 : 28
pastures deep in f., 846 : 15
sparkle out among f., 533 : 15
Ferns, sucking green from f., 822 : 7
Ferocity, courage without f., 456 : 9
malicious f., 765 : *n* 1
Ferry, back and forth all night on
f., 822 : 19
Fertile hypothesis, 887 : 15

Fertile (*continued*)
metaphor f. power, 784 : 25
miles of f. ground, 433 : 21
soil of vanity, 750 : 16
soul infinitely f., 703 : 13
to be so f., 855 : 12
Fertilize Jordan plain, 759 : 11
Fervent, effectual f. prayer, 52 : 6
Fervet opus, 104 : *n* 5
Fervor, stranger moral f., 316 : 2
with measure, 651 : 4
Fester, lilies that f., 245 : 6
Festina lente, 110 : *n* 4
Festive, gay and f. scene, 549 : 32
Festively she puts forth, 428 : 2
Festivity, Two Lands are in f., 5 : 6
Fetch pail of water, 931 : 1
poor dog a bone, 932 : 7
the Age of Gold, 277 : 9
Fetched, wide compass round f., 544 : 29
Fetching it with full hands, 574 : 15
Fetter in shackles of historian, 276 : 1
Fettered, poetry f. fetters race, 407 : 5
so free we seem so f. are, 542 : 23
to her eye, 296 : 2
Fetters, no f. in Bay State, 513 : 3
poetry fettered f. race, 407 : 5
reason Milton wrote in f., 403 : 19
servile f. breaks, 919 : 19
Fettle for great gray drayhorse, 656 : 8
Feudalism, contradiction between f. and masses, 826 : 8
Feuds, forget all f., 489 : 3
rent with civil f., 450 : 15
Fever called living, 527 : 6
famine and war, 664 : 16
is Nature's instrument, 301 : 1
life's fitful f., 238 : 19
most terrible enemy, 664 : 16
of chills and f. died, 810 : 20
of life over, 490 : 10
of temptation, 817 : 3
of the bone, 804 : 22
passion a f. in mind, 314 : 17
set about with f. trees, 710 : 3
weariness f. fret, 476 : 24
youth bent by wintry f., 886 : 12
Feverish preoccupation with riches, 773 : 7
selfish little clod, 680 : 15
Fevers, this f. me, 859 : 2
Fever-trees, set about with f., 710 : 3
Few admired by own domestics, 165 : 17
and far between, 443 : 8
and far between are the Tathagatas, 72 : 21
are chosen, 40 : 14
business in hands of a f., 621 : 6
but how splendid stars, 785 : 17
companions f. in serious business, 67 : 1
condemn men because f., 560 : 22
could know when Lucy ceased, 424 : 12
days precious f., 802 : 3
err grossly as the f., 304 : 13
far and f., 550 : 11
give but f. thy voice, 219 : 1
happy f., 208 : 11
honored by the f., 568 : 23
how f. know own good, 306 : 10
if bees are f., 608 : 3
Few (*continued*)
immortal names, 464 : 13
in hands not of f. but many, 80 : 17
in science the f. dictate, 493 : 10
join f. if any, 748 : 16
know how to be old, 294 : 7
laborers are f., 38 : 32
let thy words be f., 26 : 26
many admire f. know, 80 : 11
many exploited by f., 825 : 18
men of f. words best, 207 : 20
much in f. words, 36 : 3
my people are f., 455 : 14
philosophy is for the f., 166 : 14
scientific truth property of f., 509 : 3
small country with f. people, 65 : 9
so much owed to so f., 744 : 6
sold the many on the f., 829 : 23
some f. books to be chewed, 181 : 12
that f. is all the world, 182 : 8
the f. and the many, 401 : 12
the f. despoilers of the many, 422 : 18
the notes are f., 403 : 1
there be that find, 38 : 15
to f. men comes excellence, 67 : 2
very f. to love 424 : 12
yellow leaves or none or f., 244 : 27
Fewest, having f. wants, 79 : 2
Fezziwig, Mrs. F. one vast smile, 548 : 8
F.F.V.'s, counting F., 840 : 14
Fiat justitia pereat coelum, 417 : 17
justitia ruat coelum, 133 : 25
lux, 6 : *n* 14
ruat coelum f. voluntas tua, 134 : 24
Fiats, old precedents and new f., 813 : 10
Fib, destroy f. or sophistry, 338 : 9
Fiber, show food in minutest f., 438 : 2
Fibers, made of multitude of f., 491 : 21
Fibs, I'll tell you no f., 371 : 12
Fickle, whatever is f. freckled, 656 : 5
woman always a f. thing, 105 : 10
Fickleness of women I love, 680 : 3
Fico, a f. for the phrase, 225 : 9
Fiction, by fairy f. dressed, 363 : 8
final belief in f., 768 : 1
I'm selling short, 892 : 13
lags after truth, 372 : 13
night is f., 897 : 5
poetry supreme f., 766 : 24
tongue to deal in f., 331 : 14
truth stranger than f., 462 : 2
Fictions only and false hair, 268 : 14
supreme f. of life, 769 : 14
Fiddle, cat and f., 930 : 17
de-dee, 551 : 5
first fight then f., 889 : 9
master's lost f. stick, 929 : 10
play on f. in Dooney, 712 : 17
robes riche or f., 145 : 27
we know is diddle, 634 : 15
Fiddle-de-dee, French for f., 613 : 19
Fiddler, in came a f., 548 : 8
statesman and buffoon, 304 : 10
Fiddlers three, 929 : 14
Fide, Punica f., 103 : *n* 3
Fidelity, deepening f., with friends, 299 : 11
gossamer f. of man, 526 : 6
think of f. not husbands, 777 : 5
Fidget, no f. and no reformer, 696 : 8
Fidus Achates, 105 : *n* 8
Fie fie upon her, 227 : 3
foh and fum, 234 : 13
Fie (*continued*)
my lord fie, 239 : 24
upon this quiet life, 203 : 26
Field accidents by flood and field, 229 : 28
as a flower of the f., 21 : 7
betokened tempest to f., 189 : 10
consider lilies of f., 38 : 4
cow a good animal in f., 355 : 4
crop of corn a f. of tares, 177 : 10
dedicate portion of f., 523 : 4
dignity in tilling f., 681 : 25
Esau was a man of the f., 8 : 15
goodliness as the flower of the f., 30 : 32
Goya of the bare f., 912 : 7
happy f. mossy cavern, 477 : 16
has sight 146 : *n* 5
hath eyen wode eres, 146 : 20
heaping f. and highway, 568 : 15
hi-hi-yee for f. artillery, 764 : 12
his arms, 177 : 12
in league with stones of f., 15 : 17
lay f. to f., 29 : 4
life is not like crossing f., 934 : 12
little f. well tilled, 347 : 8
man for the f., 531 : 7
man tills f. lies beneath, 533 : 27
not a f. but a cause, 384 : 18
not simple as to cross f., 816 : 18
not wholly reap corners of f., 10 : 19
of human conflict, 744 : 6
of ripe corn, 804 : 6
potter's f., 41 : 19
Prussia hurried to the f., 399 : *n* 7
ring with importunate chink, 373 : 28
roamed from f. to f., 402 : 12
she is as in a f., 749 : 4
shepherds abiding in f., 42 : 28
sickle in fruitful f., 404 : 15
six Richmonds in the f., 187 : 32
so truth be in the f., 282 : 5
strewn with dank drifts, 588 : 5
thy beauty's f., 244 : 1
viewed in her fair face's f., 189 : 17
what though f. be lost, 283 : 8
Fields, as long as f. green, 469 : 7
as on strength of f., 902 : 6
babbled of green f., 207 : 13
battle won on playing f., 421 : 16
carrying you into f. of light, 76 : 3
dream of battled f., 431 : 8
earth's green f., 552 : 22
English f. upland dim, 587 : 11
fanged with flints, 854 : 6
fight in f. and streets, 744 : 2
flowering of His f., 534 : 27
gone into the f., 470 : 4
happy autumn f., 531 : 3
have eyes woods have ears, 146 : *n* 5
hills and valleys dales and f., 183 : *n* 5
hunt in f. for health, 306 : 26
in Flanders f., 737 : 9
in those holy f., 202 : 22
little tyrant of his f., 362 : 9
no f. of amaranth, 442 : 19
of air, 377 : 26
of corn where Troy was, 113 : 14
of immortality, 468 : 20
once tall with wheat, 846 : 15
out in f. with God, 923 : 6
out of olde f. newe corn, 144 : 9
plows in the f., 789 : 10
poetic f. encompass me, 325 : 6

Fields (*continued*)
potters' f. of continents, 571 : 3
they have not sown, 854 : 2
they moved through f. sowing seed, 888 : 7
unshorn f. boundless, 471 : 11
valleys groves hills f., 183 : 8
walk through f. in gloves, 795 : 2
Fiend behind the fiend, 881 : 11
fell from heaven, 135 : 3
foul F. Apollyon, 302 : 3
frightful f., 435 : 3
like a f. in a cloud, 402 : 15, 405 : 12
long spoon eat with f., 147 : 26
lubber f., 278 : 3
marble-hearted f., 233 : 10
so spake the F., 285 : 21
swung the f., 600 : 27
Fiendishness of business competition, 794 : 12
Fiends, juggling f., 240 : 9
that plague thee thus, 434 : 12
Fierce and accustomed to woods, 154 : 8
bowels of f. fire, 892 : 7
change of f. extremes, 284 : 23
composition and f. quality, 233 : 3
contending nations know, 326 : 5
extremes by change more f., 284 : 23
far f. hour, 742 : 17
four champions f. strive, 284 : 27
fur soft to face, 899 : 17
generous true and f., 743 : 11
grew more f. and wild, 268 : 23
light beats on throne, 534 : 1
lion not so f. as they paint him, 269 : 27
liveth not in f. desire, 430 : 9
look not so f. on me, 184 : 9
more f. and inexorable far, 193 : 23
no beast so f. but knows pity, 187 : 1
safer meek than f., 544 : 29
spirit f., 467 : 21
though little she is f., 197 : 3
wars and faithful loves, 173 : 7
wretchedness that glory brings, 243 : 7
Fierceness, swalloweth the ground with f., 16 : 38
Fiercer, now f. by despair, 284 : 4
Fiercest, strongest and f. spirit, 284 : 4
Fiery, bathe in f. floods, 228 : 20
far from f. noon, 478 : 2
furnace, 32 : 33
mind very f. particle, 461 : 24
Pegasus, 204 : 32
soul, 303 : 20
Fiery-footed steeds, 193 : 8
Fife, clamor of f. and drum, 598 : 15
ear-piercing f., 231 : 11
elephant practiced on f., 614 : 6
homely f. and drum, 864 : 10
play f. lowly, 927 : 15
Thane of F. had a wife, 239 : 26
wry-necked f., 199 : 4
Fifteen apparitions seen, 717 : 19
maiden of bashful f., 399 : 1
men on Dead Man's Chest, 668 : 4
minutes of hell, 660 : 4
wild Decembers, 562 : 1
Fifth Amendment old friend, 841 : 1
column, 798 : 5
no place for f. wheel, 138 : 10
of November, 919 : 12
shall close drama, 330 : 25
Fifth (*continued*)
smote him under the f. rib, 13 : 12
Fifths, three f. genius, 567 : 18
Fifties, tranquilized F., 893 : 1
Fiftieth, hallow f. year, 10 : 22
Fifty, at f. chides delay, 330 : 10
corpulent man of f., 453 : 22
dread f. above more than f. below, 748 : 10
forty till f. stoic or satyr, 677 : 2
here's to the widow of f., 399 : 1
million Frenchmen, 924 : 12
north forty west, 709 : 24
not care to live after f., 722 : 7
only leaves me f. more, 690 : 17
score strong, 540 : 25
springs little room, 690 : 17
wise at f., 269 : 32
years of Europe, 530 : 9
Fifty-four forty or fight, 492 : 13
Fifty-fourth, Negroes of the F., 650 : 13
Regiment, 617 : 6
Fifty-three, we have sighted f., 535 : 11
Fig bear fruit then ripen, 121 : 3
call f. a f., 91 : 7
every man under his f. tree, 13 : 29
for care fig for woe, 158 : 17
land of vines and f. trees, 11 : 14
sewed f. leaves together, 7 : 7
Figements, de longs f. violets, 673 : *n* 10
Fight against his brother, 29 : 25
aloud very brave, 604 : 7
and conquer again, 363 : 16
and not heed wounds, 157 : 3
back from eyes tears, 811 : 9
baffled to f. better, 546 : 7
beyond your strength, 58 : 18
cannot f. future, 517 : 18
don't f. forces use them, 832 : 6
don't want to f., 598 : 9
Duke great f. did win, 439 : 14
end crowns us not f., 266 : 4
end of f. tombstone white, 707 : 20
extreme fear neither f. nor fly, 189 : 21
fall out and chide and f., 328 : 4
fifty-four forty or f., 492 : 13
fire and ice within me f., 691 : 6
first f. then fiddle, 889 : 9
for lost causes, 809 : 14
for love and glory, 830 : 7
for one's country, 58 : 14
fought a good f., 51 : 9
fought the better f., 286 : 26
gods f. against necessity, 62 : 9
gone to f. French, 415 : 16
good fight of faith, 51 : 3
government for which men f., 381 : 5
graceless zealots f., 337 : 9
harder matter to f., 535 : 6
her till she sinks, 449 : 5
I give the f. up, 540 : 10
I will f. no more forever, 642 : 7
if all means permitted to f. evil, 812 : 11
if life not real f., 649 : 14
in fields and streets, 744 : 2
in France and on seas, 744 : 2
it out on this line, 589 : 17
like devils, 207 : 26
love as much as good f., 779 : 5
man who runs may f. again, 91 : 12
mental f., 406 : 21
Fight (*continued*)
no one conquers who doesn't f., 150 : 4
not law nor duty bade f., 714 : 1
not to strong the f., 671 : 11
not wear best trousers to f., 599 : 20
not yet begun to f., 394 : 4
nothing sure in sea f., 408 : 6
on beaches fields streets, 744 : 2
on merry men all, 926 : 16
opinions not survive without f., 755 : 12
our country's battles, 922 : 11
painful warrior famoused for f., 244 : 7
people f. for their law, 70 : 9
perish in the f., 514 : 11
required of duty, 94 : 9
rise and f. again, 926 : *n* 7
the good fight, 51 : 3
those I f. I do not hate, 713 : 20
through perilous f., 446 : 1
till last gasp, 184 : 16
to keep something alive, 809 : 14
to maintain freedom, 780 : 14
too proud to f., 682 : 3
undivulged pretense I f., 238 : 9
wants us to f. fair, 786 : 11
we f. not to enslave, 384 : 19
we must f., 383 : 4
when f. begins within, 543 : 9
when sure of winning, 565 : 1
whenever I must, 815 : 9
why f. what's decisive, 486 : 5
wrong to f., 730 : 12
youth f. and die, 750 : 20
Fighter, am I no a bonny f., 668 : 16
dull f. and keen guest, 204 : 36
that means to have been a f., 396 : 3
Fighters, free f. free lovers, 726 : 2
Fightin', first-class f. man, 708 : 5
like sojers when not f., 898 : 10
runnin' away and f., 722 : 17
show you're up to f., 568 : 9
Fighting, Aztecs would die f., 156 : 13
bellyful of f., 243 : 15
dying but f. back, 819 : 7
faiths, 645 : 1
first-class f. man, 708 : 5
for human rights, 904 : 15
for the crown, 929 : 19
God and devil f., 582 : 1
in forefront of the Greeks, 67 : 18
life's f. line, 743 : 10
like soldiers when not f., 898 : 10
runnin' away and f., 722 : 17
show you're up to f., 568 : 9
still still destroying, 306 : 19
Téméraire, 700 : 10
words braver than f., 3 : 12
world worth f. for, 845 : 9
Fights, best part of married life f., 839 : 18
historical, 628 : 1
Figs, long life better than f., 240 : 16
of thistles, 38 : 17, 534 : 17
Figurative, figure not f., 479 : 19
Figure, baby f. of giant mass, 226 : 5
but not figurative, 479 : 19
his f. is handsome, 636 : 12
human f. interests me most, 728 : 10
in the carpet, 653 : 7
in the landscape, 870 : 14
make me a fixed f., 232 : 3

Figure (*continued*)
of a nut, 606 : 18
poem makes, 750 : 2
quaint great f., 765 : 8
same for love, 750 : 2
Figures, other f. merely projections, 809 : 1
pedantical, 191 : 9
universe in geometrical f., 182 : 20
Filament, one living f., 378 : 1
Filches my good name, 230 : 33
File, black rank and f., 617 : 6
marching in endless f., 495 : 5
Files, beauteous f., 299 : 10
foremost f. of time, 530 : 7
on Parade, 708 : 1
single f. who deepened same shadows, 907 : 12
Filial, lively sense of f. duty, 387 : 7
piety is the root of man, 289 : 13
youth should be f., 68 : 3
Filius Patris, 54 : 5
Fill all penuries, 255 : 1
all the glasses there, 295 : 8
at beginning of cask take your f., 61 : 21
cup that clears, 516 : 13
high the bowl with Samian wine, 461 : 8
his belly with east wind, 15 : 36
Ithaca full of moths, 242 : 10
me from crown to toe, 236 : 17
stag drunk his f., 431 : 5
void world never f., 375 : 15
woods f. up with snow, 748 : 5
world with fools, 579 : 22
Filled, because 'tis f. with fire, 404 : 19
body f. and vacant mind, 208 : 7
did eat and were f., 39 : 25
little house well f., 347 : 8
mouth f. with dust, 255 : 5
rosebuds f. with snow, 250 : 6
sails f. streamers waving, 288 : 30
source that keeps it f., 601 : 2
the hungry, 42 : 23
they shall be f., 37 : 4
thicket with honeyed song, 82 : 5
with ends of worms, 824 : 3
with Holy Ghost, 45 : 39
Fillet, solemn f., 495 : 6
Filleth, bird that f. own nest, 153 : 2
Filling, two buckets f. one another, 195 : 11
Fillip, giving f. to passage, 685 : 14
Fills, grief f. room of absent child, 201 : 26
he f. he bounds, 336 : 22
shadows and windy places, 632 : 7
white rustling sail, 453 : 19
Filly, likeness of f. foal, 196 : 12
Film, balanced f. with f., 607 : 17
if f. makes person miserable, 914 : 1
thought beneath slight f., 604 : 12
Filtered, opinion truth f., 538 : 17
Filth, hunger f. and ignorance, 814 : 8
identical and so is f., 764 : 10
Filths savor but themselves, 234 : 24
Filthy, fog and f. air, 235 : 22
let him be f. still, 53 : 32
lucre, 50 : 26
righteousnesses are as f. rags, 31 : 27
so f. nobody touched, 489 : 8
tobacco f. weed, 401 : 3
Fin, commencement de la f., 400 : *n* 5
Fin, gold f. in porphyry, 531 : 11
hoof wing fang, 879 : 8
Final belief in fiction, 768 : 1
cause produces motion, 87 : 10
dire dimension of f. thing, 875 : 2
face of love, 900 : 6
growth evergreen, 863 : 14
harbor, 571 : 4
judged in light of f. issue, 88 : 21
resting place, 523 : 4
Ruin fiercely drives, 330 : 18
word in reality, 909 : 14
Finale of seem, 766 : 25
Finance, maxims of orthodox f., 783 : 14
Financial, stranger in f. straits, 79 : 16
Find at end of perfect day, 698 : 16
beautiful human soul, 393 : 4
but seldom use them, 497 : 22
by searching f. out God, 15 : 25
chance to f. yourself, 683 : 16
directions out, 220 : 7
faithful friends hard to f., 257 : 8
fast bind fast f., 159 : 4
felicity we make or f., 352 : 21
few there be that f., 38 : 15
go and f. it, 710 : 9
happiness she does not f., 352 : 3
happy could he f. it, 270 : 26
hard to f. one just suited, 443 : 18
he f. you sleeping, 42 : 14
he it found shall f., 717 : 1
he that loseth life shall f. it, 39 : 5
his mouth a rein, 633 : 13
if we f. each other, 827 : 19
if you f. it and read it, 910 : 4
in his own eye, 839 : 6
in His ways f. Him not, 534 : 27
like again, 430 : 15
little to perceive, 429 : 13
look for truth not f. it, 359 : 13
love f. way, 919 : 3
man to benefit kingdom difficult, 89 : 4
moral if you can f. it, 612 : 2
next morning it was someone else, 416 : 5
none but love f. me out, 172 : 7
our agony will f. Thee, 881 : 11
ourselves dishonorable graves, 215 : 6
out be damned dear boys, 708 : 20
out cause of this effect, 220 : 13
out moonshine, 196 : 25
out of good f. evil, 283 : 11
out where enemy is, 589 : 15
place where men pray, 742 : 15
raise stone and f. me, 671 : 9
safe bind safe f., 159 : *n* 2
search will f. it out, 266 : 18
seek all day ere you f. them, 198 : 5
seek and ye shall f., 38 : 12
seeking shall f. Him, 542 : 19
so much of goodness, 646 : 5
so much of sin, 646 : 5
sure to f. use for it, 432 : 14
sure your sin will f. you out, 11 : 7
talk and f. fault, 168 : 18
the mind's construction, 236 : 15
thee sitting careless, 477 : 18
there is enough, 760 : 10
thy body by wall, 588 : 3
to strive seek f., 529 : 14
touch and do not f. it, 64 : 6
Find (*continued*)
trout in milk, 557 : 14
turn to pleasure all they f., 344 : 15
two better hemispheres, 251 : 16
vain my weary search to f., 369 : 5
virtue possession would not show, 209 : 31
we profit by losing prayers, 240 : 26
what gives life value, 863 : 3
what lies beyond only gods f., 702 : 6
what we are seeking, 823 : 1
what's not found at once, 902 : 12
where last rose lingers, 107 : 17
where seek is f., 365 : 8
you shall f. me grave man, 193 : 5
Findeth, he that f. his life, 39 : 5
Finding smoother pebble, 313 : 17
withhold f. or conjecture, 396 : 7
Finds, alters when it alteration f., 245 : 18
he can bear anything, 838 : 2
mark archer little meant, 431 : 19
pang as great, 228 : 17
sixpence in her shoe, 262 : 15
tongues in trees, 210 : 24
too late men betray, 369 : 20
young keeps young, 290 : 6
Fine camlet cloak, 309 : 13
eye in f. frenzy rolling, 197 : 12
first f. careless rapture, 541 : 17
grave's f. private place, 297 : 1
issues, 227 : 24
lady on white horse, 931 : 11
make face of heaven so f., 193 : 9
makes the action f., 269 : 8
mine has been a f. one, 492 : 18
music highest of f. arts, 579 : 15
not only f. feathers make f. birds, 66 : 8
passage particularly f., 355 : 8
poetry less subtle and f., 281 : 20
puss-gentleman, 376 : 4
put too f. a point, 171 : 9
that f. madness, 182 : 19
thing needs laboring, 713 : 2
too f. point on it, 549 : 14
wind blowing new direction, 790 : 9
women eat crazy salad, 714 : 16
words butter no parsnips, 432 : 2
Finely, spirits not f. touched, 227 : 24
Finemque tenere, 118 : *n* 7
Finer than staple of his argument, 191 : 6
Finery, dressed out in all her f., 371 : 7
Fine's, still the f. the crown, 227 : 18
Fines, nor excessive f. imposed, 392 : 3
Finest hour, 744 : 4
spectacles in nature, 348 : 4
woman in nature, 327 : 10
Finger, ambitious f., 248 : 20
don't rewrite what moving f. writ, 856 : 12
feel thy f. and find thee, 655 : 19
God's f. touched, 532 : 17
goodness in little f., 323 : 13
his slow and moving f., 232 : 3
in every pie, 168 : 29
let our f. ache, 169 : *n* 6
moving f. writes 517 : 2
moving only little f., 648 : 3
my ring encompasseth thy f., 187 : 2
of birth-strangled babe, 239 : 6
of God, 9 : 20
on capsule of truth, 846 : 9

Finger (*continued*)
pipe for fortune's f., 222 : 6
silent f. points to heaven, 428 : 17
struck f. on the place, 585 : 3
Fingering slave, 424 : 15
Fingers and noses leak from air brush, 904 : 6
counting my numberless f., 905 : 12
five sovereign f., 886 : 14
heavens the work of thy f., 17 : 17
ill cook cannot lick own f., 193 : 20
just as my f. on keys, 767 : 9
made before forks 323 : 12
on keys make music, 767 : 9
paddling palms and pinching f., 246 : 11
separate as f. one as hand, 681 : 24
trailing f. wet, 585 : 21
twirled f. madly, 551 : 2
wandered idly, 596 : 13
weary and worn, 485 : 16
will forget green thumbs, 886 : 15
with forced f. rude, 280 : 6
Fingers', smile upon f. ends, 207 : 13
two f. breadth of damnation, 63 : *n* 1
Finis bonus totum bonum, 159 : *n* 13
coronat opus, 133 : 26
Finish, give tools f. job, 744 : 13
nice guys f. last, 867 : 1
strive on to f., 524 : 7
whether sufficient to f., 43 : 24
which is almost art, 684 : 1
Finished all is finished, 536 : 3
by such a she, 201 : 16
it is f., 45 : 34
my course, 51 : 9
New England a f. place, 837 : 4
our hand f. it, 114 : 4
the comedy is f., 686 : 4
when feast f., 721 : 6
Finisher, author and f. of our faith, 51 : 19
ourselves author and f., 519 : 22
Finite, cannot bury infinite under f., 472 : 26
hearts that yearn, 542 : 10
minds are f., 698 : 1
things reveal infinitude, 874 : 11
Finitude overcome, 703 : 15
Finn again, 778 : 6
Finned cars nose forward, 893 : 16
Finnigin, gone again F., 727 : 13
Fir, in f. tar is, 933 : 4
Fire and brimstone, 622 : 13
and ice within me fight, 691 : 6
and rose are one, 808 : 18
and water, 225 : 22
answers fire, 208 : 1
appeared a chariot of f., 14 : 12
as kingfishers catch f., 656 : 11
basks at the f. 278 : 3
because 'tis filled with f., 404 : 19
before ashes of council f. cold, 591 : 4
beside the f. bending, 162 : 12
best of servants, 474 : 3
blood and f., 680 : 30
books not killed by f., 780 : 17
books you may carry to f., 353 : 17
bound upon wheel of f., 235 : 8
bowels of fierce f., 892 : 7
burn caldron bubble, 239 : 4
burnt child f. dreadeth, 160 : 20
burnt f. of thine eyes, 405 : 7
bush burned with f., 9 : 10
Fire (*continued*)
can a man take f. in his bosom, 23 : 14
Carib f., 843 : 16
chains and penal f., 283 : 4
chariot of f., 406 : 21
clear f. clean hearth, 441 : 19
consumed by either f. or f., 808 : 15
death of water and f., 808 : 12
dives on you in f., 892 : 4
don't f. unless fired upon, 374 : 19
don't f. until you see whites of eyes 368 : 1
doubt thou stars are f., 220 : 14
drunk with f., 412 : 9
dying in the grate, 600 : 15
earth and f. and sea and air, 643 : 2
element of f. put out, 254 : 5
ever-living f. being kindled and going out, 70 : 1
every time she shouted F., 730 : 11
falsely shouting f. in theater 644 : 23
faster and not give up ship, 449 : 5
fat is in the f., 159 : 1
fills blue urn with f., 494 : 18
flowers of f., 451 : *n* 7
follow good side to f., 165 : 15
form of f. approaches, 769 : 6
fretted with golden f., 220 : 28
gold shines like f., 71 : 20
great ball of f., 809 : 22
heap coals of f., 25 : 15
hearts touched with f., 643 : 17
heretic that makes the f., 246 : 16
hide f. but w'at do wid smoke, 662 : 15
hold f. in his hand, 194 : 7
house on f. children burn, 930 : 3
if his pistol misses f., 371 : 23
in asshen olde is f. yreke, 147 : 1
in each eye, 338 : 6
in mind ever burning, 172 : 9
in the f. of spring, 516 : 4
in the lake, 5 : 9
into eternal darkness f. and ice, 140 : 19
is test of gold, 115 : 2
knot of f., 808 : 18
like sparks of f. befriend thee, 266 : 14
lips touch sacred f., 733 : 9
liquid f., 416 : 6
little f. kindleth great matter, 51 : 34
little f. quickly trodden out, 186 : 19
Lord was not in the f., 14 : 5
maketh ministers flame of f., 51 : 13
melt in her own f., 223 : 5
Milton Proteus of f., 437 : 19
moral man shines like f., 73 : 3
most tolerable third party, 557 : 13
motion of hidden f., 429 : 18
Mrs. Bennet stirring f., 440 : 19
muse of f., 207 : 1
my heart consumed in f., 135 : 10
Negro past of f., 903 : 2
neither wrath of love nor f., 113 : 24
next time, 903 : 3
no f. without smoke, 160 : 33
not fantasy's hot f., 430 : 9
not f. nor stars, 76 : 22
not long life by f., 696 : 14
not resolution to f. it, 354 : 2
now stir the f., 377 : 3
of life, 443 : 1
of soul kindled, 547 : 20
of the heart, 801 : 5
of the mind, 801 : 5
Fire (*continued*)
old and nodding by f., 712 : 8
one f. burns out another's, 191 : 19
out of frying pan into f., 126 : 10
overcome heresy with f., 155 : 12
pain like lost f., 874 : 22
pale his uneffectual f., 219 : 26
pillar of f., 9 : 30
pull chestnuts out of f., 297 : 11
revealed by f., 48 : 5
run through f. and water, 225 : 22
sacred f. of liberty, 379 : 7
sea or f., 217 : 25
set around kitchen f., 665 : 11
set by f. and spin, 930 : 16
set f. to Thames, 364 : 4
set house on f. to roast eggs, 180 : 23
shadows which f. throws, 84 : 17
shall try man's work, 48 : 5
silent language of star, 812 : 2
sit beside lonely f., 597 : 1
smell f. whose gown burns, 269 : 18
some say world end in f., 748 : 2
soul of f. 351 : 18
spark o' Nature's f., 409 : 1
sparkle right Promethean f., 191 : 5
spirit all compact of f., 189 : 8
stallion shod with f., 596 : 15
stand by the f. and stink, 233 : 8
stood against my f., 235 : 7
sun mere f., 900 : 2
that in heart resides, 584 : 18
that once was gold, 787 : 6
thorough flood thorough f., 196 : 10
those who favor f., 748 : 2
three removes as bad as f., 347 : 34
through f. and through water, 19 : 32
throw whole book in f., 504 : 10
time the f. in which we burn, 883 : 10
tongued with f. beyond living, 808 : 10
tongues of f., 45 : 39
tree is cast into f., 36 : 29
true love a durable f., 172 : 9
turning as flames in f., 766 : 12
turns uneasily from f., 839 : 1
two irons in the f., 263 : 3
view what f. was near, 182 : 2
virtue more than water or f., 69 : 17
water and f. rot, 808 : 12
what hand dare seize f., 405 : 7
what of faith and f., 641 : 25
when ready Gridley, 631 : 13
whether in sea or f., 217 : 25
which seems extinguished, 275 : 26
while I was musing the f. burned, 18 : 30
world is ever-living f., 70 : 1
years steal f. from mind, 457 : 12
youth of England on f., 207 : 10
Firebell, like f. in the night, 389 : 14
Firebrand to smoke, 150 : 17
Fire-breathing Catholic C.O., 893 : 1
Fired another Troy, 306 : 21
don't fire unless f. upon, 374 : 19
Ephesian dome, 275 : *n* 1
shot heard round world, 494 : 13
that house reject him, 338 : 7
Fireflies and nightingales, 507 : 25
Firefly, life flash of f. in night, 581 : 15
wakens, 531 : 11
Fire-folk sitting in the air, 655 : 21
Firelit, think of f. homes, 795 : 14
Fire-red cherubin's face, 146 : 12

Fire's, wore f. center, 876 : 15
Fires, death f. danced, 434 : 17
do little about infernal f., 894 : 9
fuel to maintain his f., 272 : 1
hollow f. burn to black, 691 : 15
keep home f. burning, 740 : 11
late when the f. out 668 : 11
live their wonted f., 362 : 15
no other can, 839 : 6
of Troy, 850 : 13
passing through dark f., 905 : 16
roars and shakes his f., 403 : 18
show remnant of their f., 311 : 11
that scorch, 514 : 3
thought-executing f., 233 : 24
true genius kindles, 338 : 14
veils her sacred f., 340 : 28
violent f. soon burn out, 194 : 12
wine inspires and f. us, 332 : 2
Fireside, king by your own f., 168 : 5
no f. howsoe'er defended, 511 : 10
sit by f. with sorrow, 470 : 4
Firesides, protect health homes f., 666 : 22
Firewood ironware and trays, 760 : 20
Firing, no f. till you see whites of eyes, 358 : 1
Firkin, meal in f., 496 : 11
Firm against the crowd, 531 : 15
and stable earth, 265 : 7
Catullus be resolved and f., 101 : 20
choose a f. cloud, 335 : 17
fly from f. base, 431 : 13
ground of result, 742 : 18
heart f. as stone, 17 : 6
how take f. hold, 89 : 24
my f. nerves never tremble, 238 : 28
priests stood f. on dry ground, 11 : 29
office boy to attorney's f., 627 : 14
soil win of watery main, 244 : 22
stands watch along Rhine, 573 : 12
the f. are near to virtue, 69 : 4
too f. a heart, 335 : 8
Firmament, brave overhanging f., 220 : 28
buzzing world lisping f., 768 : 6
Christ's blood streams in f., 184 : 8
curses of the f., 308 : *n* 2
fall to base earth from f., 194 : 24
no fellow in f., 216 : 3
now glowed the f., 285 : 25
planets and the f., 254 : 5
showeth his handiwork, 17 : 27
spacious f. on high, 325 : 8
starry f. for roof, 637 : 21
Firmer, tired ox treads with f. step, 128 : 15
Firm-footed by sea unchanging, 486 : 14
Firmness, awed by f., 81 : 7
in the right, 524 : 7
Firm-set earth, 237 : 15
Firs, pointed f. darkly cloaked, 664 : 2
First, absurd is the f. truth, 882 : 5
after f. death no other, 886 : 17
after last returns f., 544 : 29
Amendment has erected wall, 794 : 16
Amendment makes common sense, 841 : 3
among equals, 134 : 19
and foremost I am individual, 599 : 13
First (*continued*)
and great commandment, 40 : 16, 815 : 1
and second class citizens, 824 : 11
as a wit if not f., 371 : 17
best country is at home, 368 : 15
between acting and f. motion, 215 : 18
blow half battle, 371 : 9
born as children, 903 : 7
came the seen, 793 : 3
cannot be f. in everything, 66 : 12
cast a stone, 45 : 2
chance to build Great Society, 872 : 13
come first served, 138 : *n* 8
comes f. eats f., 138 : 11
evening and morning were f. day, 6 : 11
families in Virginia, 840 : 14
fight then fiddle, 889 : 9
fine careless rapture, 541 : 17
for which f. made, 544 : 8
get there f., 583 : 20
God f. planted garden, 181 : 10
golden time of f. love, 413 : 21
good die f., 428 : 11
Great F. Cause, 378 : 1
guarantee of F. Amendment, 794 : 20
He is the f. and the last, 132 : 13
him f. last midst, 286 : 16
hundred days, 890 : 10
I am for F. Amendment, 794 : 19
in hearts of countrymen, 402 : 10
in the f. is the last, 543 : 21
in the f. of moon, 874 : 9
in the very f. line, 371 : 17
in war first in peace, 402 : 10
is deep love, 65 : 3
last everlasting day, 252 : 22
last shall be f., 40 : 8
last was like the f., 823 : 5
light of evening, 769 : 2
looking away from f. things, 650 : 8
loved at f. sight, 183 : 17
man among these than second in Rome, 99 : 18
man who said This is mine, 358 : 9
men f. subjects afterward, 557 : 22
moment of atomic age, 885 : 8
office of government splendid misery, 388 : 13
one now later last, 915 : 5
pay for it f. or last, 555 : 3
say what you would be, 121 : 19
seed de f. en last, 837 : 17
seems to comprehend whole, 605 : 17
shall be last, 40 : 8
shoot f. inquire afterwards, 825 : 17
step is hardest, 344 : 18
sweet sleep of night, 468 : 1
that ever burst, 434 : 13
that found famous country, 822 : 2
the f. and the last, 53 : 33
there is no last or f., 540 : 19
thing let's kill lawyers, 185 : 24
things the f. poets had, 182 : 18
thy f. love, 52 : 33
true gentleman, 251 : 11
try to make it f. rate, 644 : 14
we pass through grass, 778 : 6
we practice to deceive, 431 : 1
what are we f., 600 : 17
who's on f., 832 : 3
women and children f., 921 : 21
First (*continued*)
youth tested to old age, 584 : 8
Zeus f. cause, 71 : 11
Firstborn among many brethren, 47 : 11
brought forth f. son, 42 : 27
offspring of heaven f., 285 : 4
smite all the f., 9 : 25
First-class fightin' man, 708 : 5
Firstfruits of them that slept, 48 : 29
Firstling of the infant year, 272 : 2
First-rate, test of f. intelligence, 835 : 10
Fish, a poor f. peddler, 811 : 8
all f. that cometh to net, 160 : 14
and guests in three days, 94 : *n* 1
army is like f., 826 : 11
biggest f. got away, 666 : 14
cannot live in fields, 101 : 1
cars nose forward like f., 893 : 16
cat would eat f., 160 : 7
catched f. and talked, 623 : 22
dart before you, 5 : 7
dies because he opens mouth, 935 : 11
disputants put me in mind of skuttle f., 327 : 1
dominion over f. of the sea, 6 : 15
eat f. that fed of worm, 223 : 15
fiddle de-dee, 551 : 5
fishers of f. not men, 894 : 2
flesh or fowl, 714 : 22
formal as scales on f., 798 : 8
I let f. go, 878 : 5
in troubled waters, 319 : 7
in unruffled lakes, 868 : 5
in water lives the f., 300 : 19
it's no f. ye're buying, 431 : 22
Jonah was in the belly of the f., 33 : 22
kettle of f., 628 : 21
little f. swam, 550 : 13
no more land say f., 796 : 14
nor flesh nor good red herring, 159 : 27
not with melancholy bait, 198 : 4
one f. ball, 592 : 4
out of water, 313 : 21
ruling like cooking small f., 64 : 21
say they have stream, 796 : 13
sensible f. swims down, 686 : *n* 4
son of first f. ashore, 907 : 17
teaching a f. to swim, 134 : 17
this f. will bite, 209 : 18
thou deboshed f. thou, 248 : 6
to f. and to seals, 878 : 6
we are f. and meat, 719 : 9
what cat's averse to f., 361 : 15
when you tadpole and I f., 688 : 3
with f. questing snail, 875 : 4
with worm that eat king, 223 : 15
Fishbone in city's throat, 893 : 12
Fished by obstinate isles, 792 : 11
Fisher, Kitty F. found it, 933 : 5
Fisherman's, well for f. boy, 530 : 19
Fishermen that walk upon the beach, 234 : 28
Fishers of fish not men, 894 : 2
of men, 37 : 3
of song, 685 : 11
Fishes, as f. taken in evil net, 27 : 17
five loaves and two f., 39 : 24
flyin' f. play, 708 : 9
in other men's ditches, 933 : 19
marvel how f. live in sea, 243 : 13
men lived like f., 243 : *n* 1

Fishes (*continued*)
of sea draw us to kingdom, 126 : 15
shall declare unto thee, 15 : 29
stone-deaf f., 873 : 11
talk like whales, 371 : 24
thousand men that f. gnaw, 187 : 9
waiting for invasion so are f., 744 : 10
welcomes little f. in, 611 : 5
Fishified, flesh how art thou f., 192 : 24
Fishing, east wind never blow when he goes a-f., 270 : 32
gone a-f., 270 : 29
time is stream I go a-f. in, 559 : 28
Fishlike, ancient and f. smell, 247 : 29
flash f., 717 : 16
Fishmonger, you are a f., 220 : 15
Fishnet, undoing f. of tarred rope, 894 : 4
Fish-shape Paumanok, 574 : 3
Fist, closed f. of teacher, 72 : 19
feel army in my f., 412 : 5
iron f., 421 : 13
with f. instead of stick, 290 : 14
Fisted canvas, 683 : 5
Fit, be f. for work, 572 : 13
bed for this huge birth, 292 : 17
content with fortunes f., 234 : 1
dish f. for gods, 215 : 20
for business entrusted with, 319 : 16
for crooked counsels f., 303 : 20
for public authority, 74 : 19
for the kingdom of God, 43 : 7
for treasons strategems, 201 : 3
instruments of ill, 334 : 9
life never seems to f., 839 : 7
night for man or beast, 770 : 17
not f. that men be compared with gods, 102 : 11
not f. that you sit here longer, 272 : 19
only the f. survive, 752 : 4
public trusts in hands of f., 319 : 16
to one neutral thing both sexes f., 252 : 11
which ordinary men f. for, 233 : 7
why then I'll f. you, 177 : 3
Fitful, life's f. fever, 238 : 19
tracing of portal, 767 : 10
Fitness, eternal f. of things, 349 : 19
of the personality, 702 : 13
Fits dull fighter, 204 : 36
periodical f. of mortality, 487 : 19
shoe f. one pinches another, 754 : 5
think by f. and starts, 691 : 21
'twas sad by f., 364 : 13
your thief, 229 : 2
Fitted, best f. to command, 570 : 1
him to a T, 158 : *n* 2
in thy lips, 24 : 37
nothing he not f. to bear, 125 : 3
well f. in arts, 190 : 20
Fitter being sane than mad, 544 : 29
love for me, 252 : 15
young men f. to invent, 181 : 7
Fittest may also be gentlest, 848 : 1
survival of f., 514 : 15, 579 : 20, 621 : 6
Fitting and proper we do this, 523 : 4
for princess descended of kings, 242 : 6
Fitzgerald, for this F. died, 713 : 11
strung on English thread, 569 : 2
Five and country senses, 886 : 15
Benjamin's mess was f. times as much, 8 : 33
chose him f. smooth stones, 13 : 2
Five (*continued*)
cry of critic for f., 619 : 3
fatal f. in the afternoon, 841 : 15
full fathom f., 247 : 21
kings did king to death, 886 : 14
reasons we should drink, 315 : 13
sons who died gloriously, 524 : 4
sovereign fingers, 886 : 14
were wise five foolish, 40 : 28
Five-cent, good f. cigar, 673 : 6
good f. nickel, 673 : *n* 2
Five-pound note, 550 : 7
Fix eyes on greatness of Athens, 81 : 5
in such f. be fertile, 855 : 12
looking for angry f., 906 : 1
Fixed as an aim or butt, 207 : 6
Everlasting had not f., 218 : 5
fate free will, 284 : 19
give name to every f. star, 190 : 12
great gulf f., 43 : 34
like a plant, 337 : 3
make me a f. figure, 232 : 3
objects f. and dead, 437 : 12
of old founded strong, 691 : 10
sentinels almost receive, 208 : 1
star in constitutional constellation 821 : 6
still stood f. to hear, 287 : 2
thy soul the f. foot, 253 : 5
wedding day f., 350 : 2
Fizz, blood f. like wine, 760 : 5
Flabbiness, moral f., 648 : 4
Flabby bald lobotomized, 893 : 2
Flaccid, contemplate my f. shape, 830 : 12
Flag, American f. floats, 371 : 26
beneath starry f., 578 : 12
braved a thousand years, 443 : 10
companionship and country, 539 : 3
death's pale f., 193 : 27
embodiment of history, 682 : 5
floats free and guarded, 722 : 14
goes by, 676 : 17
haul up the f., 883 : 12
in f. government and truths, 551 : 11
is passing by, 676 : *n* 5
meteor f. of England, 443 : 13
not f. only but nation, 551 : 11
not f. or fail, 744 : 2
not kiss your f.ing f., 829 : 9
obey laws respect f., 725 : 20
of our union 492 : 11
one f. land heart hand, 518 : 15
passing by, 676 : *n* 5
pledge allegiance to f., 677 : 10
rally round f. boys, 578 : 13
represents experiences, 682 : 5
spare country's f., 513 : 18
special f. or ship signal, 575 : 21
that makes you free, 614 : 14
there I find f. of England, 420 : 16
there is national f., 539 : 3
to April's breeze, 494 : 13
was still there, 446 : 1
Flagon, out of English f., 742 : 14
Flagons, stay me with f., 28 : 6
Flagpole, old f. still stands, 771 : 5
Flagrant cases of wrongdoing, 687 : 10
fair and f. things, 292 : 13
Flagrante delicto, 134 : 1
Flags, battle f. furled, 530 : 1
stiff f. straining, 742 : 9
Flail, rain with silver f., 794 : 13
Flame, adding fuel to the f., 289 : 6
Flame (*continued*)
as parallax a f., 607 : 5
Bolivar lived among flames was f., 451 : *n* 7
both moth and f., 874 : 17
courses beneath my skin, 63 : 5
draft fluttered f., 817 : 3
dragonflies draw f., 656 : 11
feel spark of that ancient f., 105 : 8
feel steady candle f., 541 : 20
fury slinging f., 532 : 6
great f. follows little spark, 142 : 10
hard gemlike f., 638 : 13
idealism fanned into f., 678 : 4
Jabberwock with eyes of f., 612 : 18
love harsh irregular f., 864 : 11
maketh ministers f. of fire, 51 : 13
miserable mortals f. with life, 59 : 5
my f. to qualify, 245 : 14
nor public f. nor private, 340 : 28
of freedom in souls, 643 : 1
old f. my wife, 893 : 8
on flame, 883 : 8
recognize signals of ancient f., 142 : 6
sacred f., 435 : 20
shirt of f., 808 : 15
that cannot singe sleeve, 716 : 10
thin smoke without f., 642 : 2
tongues of f. infolded, 808 : 18
vital spark of heavenly f., 333 : 23
water most encourage f., 829 : 16
when lovely f. dies, 740 : 13
words full of subtle f., 263 : 2
Flame-colored, hot wench in f., taffeta, 202 : 23
Flamed, scarlet lily f., 696 : 11
Flamens, here lies two f., 271 : 18
Flames, arrow falls in f., 645 : 15
have spread over globe, 390 : 1
in forehead of sky, 281 : 4
in present light f., 745 : 8
must waste away, 272 : 1
no faggot feeds, 716 : 9
paly f., 208 : 1
rich f. and hired tears, 275 : 1
rolled on, 470 : 18
turning as f. in fire, 766 : 12
went by her like thin f., 601 : 14
whatever f. upon night, 715 : 14
Flaming bounds of place and time, 363 : 2
hurled headlong f., 283 : 4
ruddy limbs f. hair, 404 : 16
some old desire, 839 : 1
sword which turned, 7 : 13
thou f. minister, 232 : 14
youth, 223 : 5
Flanders, armies swore in F., 360 : 10
in F. fields, 737 : 9
Flank golden, 822 : 4
of something more permanent, 910 : 10
Flanks, silken f., 477 : 9
Flannel, neither eat it nor make f., 790 : 17
wear white f. trousers, 803 : 19
Flanneled fools at wicket, 709 : 23
Flap bug with gilded wings, 338 : 19
Flap-dragon, easier swallowed than f., 191 : 7
Flaps glad green leaves, 642 : 3
Flare, quick to f. up, 60 : 3
Flash, crawl f. or thunder in, 887 : 7
fishlike, 717 : 16

Flash (*continued*)
mirth like f. of lightning, 326 : 21
of color beneath sky, 676 : *n* 5
of light cut across sky, 885 : 7
one f. of it within tavern, 517 : 5
packet of fame, 935 : 6
sharp f., 768 : 2
Flashed the living lightning, 334 : 10
Flashes, brightest f. of thought, 580 : 5
occasional f. of silence, 433 : 10
of merriment, 224 : 14
Flashing eyes, 433 : 27
Flask of winds empties, 850 : 4
Flat as pancakes, 261 : 12
blasphemy, 228 : 11
burglary as ever committed, 209 : 33
churches in f. countries, 428 : *n* 6
clothes lines linking each f. to each, 819 : 3
he whose soul is f., 822 : 12
hev it plain and f., 567 : 20
how weary stale f., 218 : 5
I their map lie f., 254 : 18
in f. sea sunk, 279 : 22
on your face, 831 : 9
strike f. thick rotundity, 233 : 24
the wall fell down f., 11 : 31
with broad f. nails, 86 : 10
Flatter, averse to f. or offend, 333 : 22
more we love less we f., 297 : 29
Neptune for his trident, 242 : 20
not f. me at all, 272 : 22
Flattered, being then most f., 215 : 21
himself on being without prejudices, 655 : 6
into virtue, 500 : 22
not f. its rank breath, 458 : 3
upon understandings, 342 : 4
Flatterer can risk everything, 323 : 27
of all tame a f., 255 : 14
scoundrel hypocrite f., 407 : 6
Flatterers, by f. besieged, 338 : 14
self-love greatest of f., 293 : 1
solitude hath no f., 458 : 8
tell him he hates f., 215 : 21
Flattereth, meddle not with him that f., 24 : 32
Flattering mighty gold, 256 : *n* 1
now with f. tongue, 715 : 11
some with f. word, 676 : 8
unction, 223 : 7
Flatters, everyone that f., 257 : 8
Fortune f. to betray, 111 : 1
less to what f. us, 863 : 19
wolf hates when it f., 129 : 12
Flattery and falsehood, 391 : 1
art not submit to f., 421 : 20
guarding oneself against f., 154 : 4
imitation sincerest f., 448 : 10
in return for favor, 421 : 20
lost on poet's ear, 430 : 7
love of f., 327 : 16
proud taken in by f., 309 : 2
sincere f., 378 : 10
soothe ear of death, 362 : 5
woman gained by f., 342 : 13
Flattery's the food of fools, 322 : 7
Flaubert, true Penelope was F., 792 : 11
write novel about nothing, 897 : 14
Flaunted, badness f. itself, 926 : 3
Flaunting extravagant quean, 399 : 1
Flavor absorbed remains, 447 : *n* 1
you f. everything, 433 : 1
Flaw, conceal f. world will imagine worst, 119 : 6
man without a f., 106 : 16
no kind of fault or f., 628 : 16
Flaws, heart break into f., 233 : 23
what soul without f., 674 : 2
Flax, smoking f. shall he not quench, 31 : 4
Flayed, belted you and f. you, 708 : 6
Flea in mine ear, 158 : 3
naturalists observe f., 322 : 21
though he kill none, 254 : 21
Fleas, riseth with f., 269 : 31
smaller f. on him prey, 322 : 21
Fled, a life which has f., 65 : 15
across margent of world f., 693 : 12
as if that soul were f., 446 : 9
earth's foundations f., 692 : 3
from this vile world, 244 : 26
ghost f. from grasp, 105 : 5
Him down the nights, 693 : 10
I waked she f., 282 : 21
is that music, 477 : 3
judgment f. to beasts, 216 : 20
soul has f., 513 : 8
to boon southern country f., 587 : 11
visionary gleam, 426 : 13
whence all but he f., 470 : 17
with a Christian, 199 : 11
Flee as a bird, 17 : 19
best day first to f., 104 : 8
from me that did me seek, 161 : 25
from reality, 784 : 24
from those who f. no glory, 58 : 24
from wrath to come, 36 : 28
if your enemy f., 935 : 8
let sound of it f., 384 : 8
resist devil and he will f., 52 : 2
shadows f. away, 28 : 9
sorrow and sighing shall f. away, 30 : 25
to f. vice is beginning of virtue, 108 : 17
whither shall I f. from thy presence, 22 : 17
wicked f. when no man pursueth, 25 : 27
Fleece white as snow, 463 : 1
white but 'tis too cold, 173 : *n* 8
Fleecy, stooping through a f., cloud, 278 : 18
Fleeing, such swift f., 641 : 23
Flees, who f. will fight again, 91 : *n* 7
Fleet, all in Downs f. moored, 331 : 9
away with wings, 459 : 18
dull in F. Street, 441 : 8
in my arms, 446 : 11
joys abound as seasons f., 185 : 14
of life like tree leaves, 82 : 9
of stars anchored, 785 : 15
other passions f. to air, 199 : 28
retiring toward Japanese f., 777 : 14
say to the f., 408 : *n* 5
such sweet things f., 634 : 1
the time carelessly, 210 : 11
though time be f., 612 : 15
Fleetest, fairest things f. end, 693 : 6
Fleeth as a shadow, 15 : 33
Fleeting, art long time f., 509 : 14
call the f. breath, 362 : 5
fable song or f. shade, 266 : 21
ghost fled like f. dream, 105 : 5
how f. the estate of man, 124 : 27
mountains f. as clouds, 131 : 18
Fleeting (*continued*)
opportunity f., 80 : 9
ornament life in f. way, 413 : 29
renown is f. and frail, 102 : 22
years slip by, 107 : 23
Fleets, ten thousand f. sweep, 458 : 25
Flere, si vis me f., 109 : *n* 10
Flesh, all f. is as grass, 52 : 9
all f. is grass, 30 : 32
and blood so cheap, 485 : 20
brought him bread and f., 13 : 41
collop cut of own f., 160 : 1
consorteth according to kind, 35 : 26
contact possible to f., 804 : 22
delirium of f., 850 : 9
every living thing of all f., 7 : 29
every part of f. Nature makes f., 125 : 24
fair and unpolluted f., 224 : 17
fastened me f., 655 : 19
fish f. or fowl, 714 : 22
fish nor f. nor good red herring, 159 : 27
from deceits of the f., 55 : 11
from living planet, 873 : 9
gross f. sinks downward, 195 : 19
hair of my f. stood up, 15 : 12
how art thou fishified, 192 : 24
howl for f. of man, 912 : 9
in f. beauty immortal, 767 : 10
in my f. shall I see God, 16 : 4
is sad alas, 651 : 13
is weak, 41 : 13
juggernauts of f. that pass, 857 : 15
laughing f. of girls, 899 : 16
little f. little breath, 124 : 5
lusteth against Spirit, 49 : 29
make not provision for f., 47 : 29
maketh f. his arm, 32 : 11
man of f. and blood, 705 : 12
marriage makes one f., 324 : 8
more f. than another man, 204 : 27
much study is weariness of the f., 27 : 27
my f. longeth for thee, 19 : 29
neither f. nor fleshless, 807 : 5
of flesh bone of bone, 287 : 23
of my flesh, 7 : 3
of thy flesh, 168 : 4
on f. siroccos crawl, 605 : 16
present joys more to f. and blood, 305 : 25
profiteth nothing, 44 : 42
rise from f. to spirit, 873 : 20
sensible affections of f., 274 : 13
set today on f. of hare, 912 : 9
sinful desires of the f., 56 : 4
star stone f. soul, 543 : 19
strong as f. and blood, 428 : 4
strong is your hold O mortal f., 576 : 19
swift red f., 843 : 20
that f. is heir to, 221 : 12
their f. shall ye not eat, 10 : 17
these set our f. upright, 254 : 1
they shall be one f., 7 : 4
they shall eat the f., 9 : 24
this f. of mine might be, 632 : 18
this too too solid f., 218 : 5
thorn in f., 49 : 22
unmysterious f., 836 : 19
wants to make f. creep, 546 : 13
watching for riches consumeth f., 36 : 2

Flesh (*continued*)
way of all f., 262 : 2
we are one f., 287 : 24
we wrestle not against f., 49 : 39
World was made f., 44 : 21
world-wearied f., 193 : 28
Flesh-colored fruit of my branches, 634 : 5
Fleshed fair erected, 878 : 3
maiden sword, 205 : 15
Fleshless, neither flesh nor f., 807 : 5
Fleshly, all this f. dress, 299 : 3
lusts, 52 : 10
school of poetry, 643 : 10
Fleshpots, sat by the f., 10 : 1
Fleshy, turbulent f. sensual, 574 : 20
Flew, arrows f. like hail, 794 : 5
bird to others f., 265 : 1
down yelled at craft, 855 : 9
o'er me and my deary, 410 : 18
one f. over cuckoo's nest, 933 : 15
screaming over gulf, 571 : 9
white foam f., 434 : 13
Flexibility, happy gracious f., 589 : 6
Flicked by feeling, 768 : 21
Flicker, moment of greatness f., 803 : 16
Flickered, in past our light f., 745 : 8
Flickering, dove with f. tongue, 808 : 13
history with f. lamp, 744 : 11
Flies, ain't no f. on me, 666 : 20
as f. to wanton boys, 234 : 21
bees for f. hornets for bees, 155 : 14
bird f. out, 875 : 3
care f. when I pursue, 163 : 14
close mouth swallows no f., 935 : 13
follow shadow it f. you, 256 : 6
from particulars to axioms, 179 : 7
happiness too swiftly f., 361 : 12
hope f. with swallow's wings, 187 : 24
in night in howling storm, 405 : 5
kisses joy as it f., 404 : 18
laws catch small f., 321 : 15
like bolt running, 901 : 14
lord of the f., 878 : 22
my fancy f., 368 : 20
on summer eves, 476 : 27
preserved in amber, 119 : *n* 2
rumor f., 105 : 7
see where it f., 184 : 4
shoot folly as it f., 336 : 11
thought f. to bo-tree, 874 : 13
through air with ease, 636 : 12
time's f., 243 : 5
unto you at last she f., 271 : 21
verse find who sermon f., 268 : 2
who f. can fight anew, 91 : *n* 7
wings of Time grief f., 296 : 17
worms and flowers, 328 : 7
Flieth, arrow that f. by day, 20 : 16
Flight, beetle wheels droning f., 361 : 21
black f. of crows, 928 : *n* 2
cannot control the f., 296 : *n* 3
fellow of selfsame f., 198 : 6
flown his cloistered f., 238 : 20
from afar to view f., 320 : 14
his wild airy f., 289 : 2
joys soonest take f., 318 : 4
never-ending f. of days, 284 : 12
not attained by sudden f., 511 : 23
puts all pomp to f., 335 : 5
puts stars to f., 516 : 1
soul of youth taken f., 789 : 15
struggle and f., 587 : 16
sun scattered into f., 515 : 16

Flight (*continued*)
swift be thy f., 469 : 22
through sky thy certain f., 471 : 7
time and world in f., 712 : 13
time arrest f., 464 : 14
time in your f., 610 : 10
troika f. to destruction, 582 : 12
Flights and perchings, 648 : 13
four f. Thursday, 724 : 4
grand f. Sunday baths, 767 : 21
of angels sing thee, 225 : 3
Flinch, we did not f., 67 : 21
Flinders, little Polly F., 932 : 4
Fling away ambition, 249 : 7
garment of repentance f., 516 : 4
stone giant dies, 344 : 14
Flinging pot of paint at public, 619 : *n* 1
Flings, bubbling venom f., 457 : 2
Flint, behold man of f., 928 : 21
everlasting f., 193 : 2
weariness snore upon f., 243 : 23
Flints, fields fanged with f., 854 : 6
Flippant, behold thee f. vain, 475 : 3
Flirt, money won't surrender to f., 722 : 25
Flirtation, significant word f., 342 : 15
Flit, across narrow beach we f., 621 : 17
on wings of borrowed wit, 265 : 2
Flits by on leathern wing, 364 : 12
Flitter dip and soar, 899 : 15
Flitting, Raven never f., 526 : 19
Float, how sweetly did they f., 279 : 19
iron in water f., 919 : 9
like a butterfly, 915 : 11
Floated, web f. wide, 528 : 27
Floating bulwark of our island, 365 : 16
hair, 433 : 27
ice mast-high came f. by, 434 : 10
like vapor on air, 598 : 6
many bells down, 829 : 18
on the floor, 526 : 20
over Harvard Square, 842 : 4
spar to men that sink, 823 : 13
Floats above wrecks of time, 636 : 11
on high o'er vales, 427 : 7
though unseen among us, 466 : 8
Flock, birds of a feather f. together, 259 : *n* 7
feed his f. like a shepherd, 30 : 35
keeping watch over their f., 42 : 28
of bridges bleating, 770 : 9
shun the polluted f., 793 : 18
silent f. in fold, 476 : 8
without shepherd sheep not f., 934 : 14
Flocks, bad herdsmen ruin their f., 60 : 22
battening our f., 280 : 10
casual f. of pigeons, 767 : 4
my father feeds f., 366 : 10
or herds or human face, 285 : 5
while shepherds watched f., 317 : 4
Flogged, man never f. never taught, 91 : 3
she f. herself, 518 : 5
Flood, accidents by f. and field, 229 : 28
arched the f., 494 : 13
carriest them away as with a f., 20 : 11
dark rain over f., 791 : 3
decay no f., 712 : 11
enchafed f., 230 : 6
giant race before the f., 306 : 7
half our sailors swallowed in f., 186 : 23

Flood (*continued*)
land of mountain and f., 430 : 11
Milton Proteus of f., 437 : 19
of mortal ills, 155 : 15
of words drop of reason, 347 : 13
taken at the f., 217 : 5
ten years before the F., 296 : 27
thorough f. thorough fire, 196 : 10
torn Naiad from f., 525 : 7
when just cause reaches f. tide, 689 : 1
Flooding in the main, 564 : 17
Floods, bathe in fiery f., 228 : 20
haystack in f., 618 : 4
he hath established it upon the f., 18 : 8
neither can f. drown it, 28 : 24
passions like f. and streams, 172 : 12
rimless f., 843 : 14
stood upright as an heap, 9 : 35
that are deepest, 919 : 3
Floor, along gusty f., 476 : 19
barroom f., 652 : 3
careless on granary f., 477 : 18
cleaned windows swept f., 627 : 14
common sense on ground f., 519 : 18
curled up on f., 630 : 14
forest's ferny f., 739 : 15
front of this small f., 292 : 20
mystery on bestial f., 713 : 13
nicely sanded f., 370 : 13
of heaven is inlaid, 201 : 1
puncheon f. in summertime, 623 : 25
reorganized upon f., 804 : 24
scratching at f., 695 : 17
starry f., 405 : 2
sunk beneath watery f., 281 : 4
two jars on f. of Zeus, 59 : 12
wrought ghost upon f., 526 : 11
Floors, dead footsteps on old f., 728 : 17
of silent seas, 803 : 14
Flopsy Mopsy Cottontail Peter, 719 : 2
Flora and country green, 476 : 23
Lady F. lovely Roman, 601 : 16
Flores in the Azores, 535 : 11
Flots, léger j'ai dansé sur les f., 673 : *n* 7
Floundered enjoyed suffered, 654 : 7
Flour, peace into poet as f. into bread, 861 : 3
Flourish, almond tree shall f., 27 : 25
first onion f. there, 668 : 18
may f. or may fade, 369 : 30
men f. only for a moment, 61 : 1
nations are destroyed or f., 407 : 5
poetry painting music f., 407 : 5
righteous shall f., 20 : 18
set on youth, 244 : 20
those which most admirably f., 245 : *n* 1
where you turn eyes, 332 : 12
Flourished, bloody treason f., 216 : 25
hoop unbroken people f., 701 : 8
Flourisher, gold f., 768 : 10
Flourishes, society where moderation f., 737 : 3
Flourisheth as flower of the field, 21 : 7
in the morning it f., 20 : 11
Flourishing like a green bay tree, 18 : *n* 4
of the arts, 826 : 12
Flours, no f. on grave, 640 : 16
Flout, banners f. the sky, 235 : 23
'em and scout 'em, 248 : 8

Flout (*continued*)
thing to f., 671 : 4
Flow, all pleasant fruits do f., 250 : 5
ceaseless ebb and f., 672 : 20
ebb and f. by the moon, 235 : 12
from discord f., 326 : 5
from my lips would f., 468 : 15
from whom all blessings f., 311 : 19
gently sweet Afton, 410 : 13
how well soe'er it f., 338 : 17
I within did f., 311 : 23
its one will f., 843 : 19
of soul, 339 : 8
oh could I f. like thee, 294 : 19
salt tides seawards f., 584 : 11
streams f. with ambrosia, 76 : 25
with tears of gold, 403 : 13
words to say it f., 311 : 4
Flower, as a f. of the field, 21 : 7
bee does not hurt f., 73 : 3
bloom another year, 478 : 9
blue forked torch of f., 791 : 1
brief as f. falling, 812 : 3
can read us lectures, 316 : 8
crimson-tipped f., 409 : 9
culture in finest f., 698 : 2
displayed doth fall, 214 : 2
fadeth, 30 : 33
fancy from f. bell, 543 : 5
first f. of wilderness, 465 : 2
forgotten as f. forgotten, 787 : 6
from every opening f., 328 : 5
full many a f., 362 : 8
glory in the f., 426 : 21
glory of man as f. of grass, 52 : 9
goodliness as the f. of the field, 30 : 32
he cometh forth like a f., 15 : 33
heaven in wild f., 406 : 8
in crannied wall, 535 : 10
in the f. of their age, 12 : 28
let black f. blossom, 503 : 9
little f. if I understand, 535 : 10
little western f., 196 : 15
London f. of cities all, 153 : 4
look like innocent f., 236 : 20
loved tree or f., 447 : 14
lovelier f. on earth, 424 : 13
lovely little f. is free, 429 : 12
maiden in her f., 528 : 8
masterpiece appear as f., 619 : 7
meadow f. bloom unfold, 429 : 12
meanest f. that blows, 426 : 23
moon like a f., 403 : 12
my love dropped like a f., 101 : 21
nipped my f. sae early, 410 : 19
of all his race, 423 : 1
of kings and knights destroyed, 149 : 18
of knyghthod and of fredom f., 148 : 5
of wickedness, 545 : 9
of wyfly pacience, 147 : 19
or wearing-stone, 748 : 1
prized beyond sculptured f., 471 : 9
prove a beauteous f., 192 : 14
safety, 203 : 22
seize the f., 411 : 8
summer's f. to summer sweet, 245 : 5
that smiles today, 266 : 11
thou tree I f., 628 : 14
through green fuse drives f., 886 : 12
time cracks in furious f., 889 : 18
torch of a f., 791 : 1
victory bright-colored f., 743 : 4
wearing learning like f., 532 : 26
Flower (*continued*)
weed f. in disguise, 500 : *n* 1
white f. blameless life, 534 : 1
winds creep from f. to f., 466 : 8
without fragrance, 711 : 15
you're lovely as a f., 481 : 8
Floweret, meanest f. of vale, 362 : 20
Flowering in lonely word, 535 : 15
of His fields, 534 : 27
of republic of man, 852 : 2
wantons through f. thorn, 409 : 24
Flowerlike, love is f., 436 : 8
Flowers, all its twined f., 477 : 18
all the f. were mine, 525 : 17
alphabet of f., 253 : 18
and fruits of love, 462 : 18
and that f. gynnen sprynge, 145 : 10
appear on the earth, 28 : 7
April showers May f., 163 : 4
are lovely, 436 : 8
as in causes sleep, 271 : 19
begotten, 632 : 8
buds of barren f., 633 : 20
choke them amid f., 101 : 7
cover with leaves and f., 262 : 3
fairy fruits and f., 525 : 17
flies worms and f., 328 : 7
foam of f., 632 : 18
for thee earth puts forth f., 100 : 2
fruits and many birds, 150 : 16
fruits f. leaves branches, 659 : 14
fruits outdo what f. promised, 176 : 18
glass f. at Harvard, 798 : 16
hollows where f. grew, 646 : 11
in garden meat in hall, 145 : *n* 4
in the fields appear, 93 : 3
knew stars f. birds, 735 : 8
leaves and f. in sun, 713 : 8
love I most f. white and rede, 145 : 11
loved f. that fade, 654 : 16
lulled in these f., 196 : 18
madeleine soaked in lime f., 734 : 1
mistake f. for answer, 900 : 9
no f. on grave, 640 : 16
no hothouse f., 785 : 9
nosegay of culled f., 166 : 6
o'er f. venom flings, 457 : 2
of all hue, 285 : 16
of fire, 451 : *n* 7
of forest a' wede away, 368 : 2
of forest withered, 359 : 11
of Friendship Faded, 752 : 11
of June together, 609 : 11
on chaliced f. that lies, 243 : 16
picks f. of memory, 739 : 11
play with f. and smile, 207 : 13
rare long-stemmed f., 789 : 9
reaps f. that grow, 510 : 1
shown glass f., 798 : 16
shut of evening f., 287 : 16
slowly advancing, 789 : 9
stop and smell f., 821 : 4
summer with f. that fell, 632 : 9
sweetest f. in forest, 173 : 16
that bloom in spring, 629 : 15
that do not wilt, 799 : 13
through grass, 138 : 7
to strew Thy way, 268 : 13
touch a hundred f., 822 : 15
trees f. watercraft, 577 : 8
vernal f., 281 : 1
what f. are at feet, 476 : 26
where have all the f. gone, 896 : 11
Flowers (*continued*)
where'er you tread f. rise, 332 : 12
Winter's head with f., 292 : 10
withered while I spent my days, 135 : 9
withering of withered f., 808 : 3
Flowery, at her f. work doth sing, 278 : 25
crops f. food, 336 : 13
meads in May, 264 : 23
tale more sweetly, 477 : 4
walk f. way, 628 : 7
Floweth, sea itself f. in veins, 311 : 20
Flowing cups pass swiftly round, 296 : 3
fees, 281 : 18
from rocky breasts forever f., 878 : 7
land f. with milk and honey, 9 : 13
robes loosely f., 255 : 18
with birds, 874 : 16
Flown, black bat night f., 533 : 20
forever flowing and f., 878 : 7
his cloistered flight, 238 : 20
with insolence and wine, 283 : 19
Flows, as water f. downwards, 89 : 9
methinks how sweetly f., 266 : 22
thence f. all that charms, 436 : 1
time staunchless f., 830 : 11
Fluctuat nec mergitur, 134 : 2
Flügeln, auf F. des Gesanges, 481 : *n* 9
Fluidity of self-revelation, 654 : 4
solid for f., 743 : 12
Flumina, altissima f. minimo sono, 172 : *n* 7
Flung, doors are widely f., 873 : 2
roses roses riotously, 721 : 5
us on windy hill, 796 : 9
Flush as May, 222 : 27
roses for f. of youth, 608 : 18
Flushing his brow, 476 : 13
Flute, distraction music of f., 806 : 2
soft complaining f., 305 : 12
stem is the f., 852 : 14
violin bassoon, 533 : 22
Flutes, dance to f., 676 : 9
Dorian mood of f., 283 : 22
sound of lyres and f., 638 : 11
tune of f. kept stroke, 240 : 29
Fluttered, draft f. flame, 817 : 3
pinnace like f. bird, 535 : 11
round the lamp, 614 : 8
your Volscians, 242 : 26
Fluttering empty sleeves, 767 : 15
ghost fled like f. breeze, 105 : 5
sets my heart to f., 63 : 5
Flutterings, innumerable f. agitate mind, 164 : 19
yellow f., 475 : 2
Flux, all is f., 69 : 24
of the senses, 436 : 20
passing f. of immediate things, 697 : 9
Fluxions, what are these f., 330 : 21
Fly a few beats in dark, 907 : 9
a f. like thee, 405 : 6
Aesop's f., 472 : 15
all things on earth f., 518 : 9
as arrows f. to one mark, 207 : 8
as the sparks f. upward, 15 : 15
away breath, 214 : 4
away home, 930 : 3
away Jack, 934 : 8
beasts f. to wilderness, 89 : 9
busy curious thirsty f., 344 : 16
but little way to f., 516 : 4

Fly (*continued*)
creep swim or f., 311 : 12
do not want to be f., 695 : 15
down Death, 883 : 9
encountering a f., 607 : 14
extreme fear neither fight nor f., 189 : 21
forgotten as a dream, 328 : 12
from not hate mankind, 457 : 26
get up on feet and f., 892 : 7
ghosts of defunct bodies f., 291 : 2
gilded f. does lecher, 234 : 31
have to f. more missions, 902 : 8
human race born to f. upward, 142 : 2
I can f. or I can run, 280 : 4
I said the f., 930 : 10
in greatness of God, 651 : 9
joys as dreams f., 917 : 20
land can't f. away, 555 : 4
laughed at for exclaiming, 472 : 15
let me to Thy bosom f., 350 : 12
like eagle wings of wren, 646 : 3
little birds f., 550 : 12
little birds that f., 329 : 13
little f., 405 : 6
long-legged f. upon stream, 717 : 17
make fur f., 291 : 11
my words f. up, 222 : 28
neglect God for noise of a f., 255 : 2
no longer wings to f., 805 : 21
on bat's back I do f., 248 : 16
riches f. away as an eagle, 25 : 7
rode upon a cherub and did f., 17 : 26
seem to f. it, 256 : 6
shoo f., 619 : 15
soon cut off and we f. away, 20 : 13
sounds too blue to f., 903 : 1
spider to f., 485 : 23
stir her lawn canapie, 167 : 11
that sips treacle, 332 : 5
then f. betimes, 272 : 3
this rock shall f., 431 : 13
thrain lobsters to f., 722 : 12
Timothy learned sin to f., 320 : 8
to her, 531 : 5
to one mark, 207 : 8
to others we know not of, 221 : 12
to war and arms I f., 295 : 22
up above world you f., 611 : 20
upon the wings of the wind, 17 : 26
way I f. is hell, 285 : 12
when me they f., 495 : 12
which way shall I f., 285 : 12
white sails f. seaward, 806 : 6
willingly as kill a f., 188 : 22
wishes soon as granted f., 430 : 9
with arms outstretched would f., 226 : 19
with twain he did f., 29 : 8
Flyin' fishes play, 708 : 9
Flying, banner torn but f., 458 : 17
care follows me f., 163 : 14
chariot through air, 377 : 26
Dutchman, 659 : 4
fishes play, 708 : 9
from Brooklyn please come f., 878 : 8
hoping lingering f., 333 : 23
keep 'em f., 836 : 10
mind f. abroad, 85 : 17
old Time still a-f., 266 : 11
pluck out f. feather, 633 : 13
seaward f., 806 : 6
time f. never to return, 104 : 10
trapeze, 636 : 12
Flying (*continued*)
wild echoes f., 530 : 26
Foal, likeness of filly f., 196 : 12
poor little f., 433 : 18
Foam bell no consequence, 587 : 4
born and die like f., 137 : 13
copulate in f., 717 : 16
cruel crawling f., 566 : 8
is not cruel, 572 : 10
like f. on river, 431 : 11
networks of f., 798 : 12
now I f. to wheat, 911 : 15
oceans white with f., 802 : 10
of flowers, 632 : 18
opening on the f., 477 : 1
poetry new as f., 495 : 25
sea folk turn into f. on sea, 505 : 4
too full for sound and f., 535 : 19
weeds and f., 493 : 15
white f. flew, 434 : 13
Foaming out their own shame, 52 : 26
Foams, my sad heart f. at stern, 673 : 13
Focis, pro aris atque f., 102 : *n* 15
Fodder's in the shock, 665 : 14
Foe, angry with my f., 405 : 13
at another gate let in the f., 288 : 28
avowed erect manly f., 422 : 5
call no man f., 821 : 2
comes with fearless eyes, 700 : 6
foils f. by effusion of ink, 365 : 11
friend to her f., 418 : 14
grim Death my son and f., 284 : 26
heat not furnace for f., 248 : 22
his f. was folly, 627 : *n* 2
idleness sorrow friend f., 827 : 8
last armed f. expires, 464 : 12
make one worthy man f., 338 : 17
meet insulting f., 399 : 17
met dearest f. in heaven, 218 : 14
never made a f., 534 : 16
of favoritism, 683 : 6
officious fool worse than f., 420 : 5
Olympian a difficult f., 57 : 13
overcome but half his f., 283 : 27
perhaps a jealous f., 468 : 21
scratch lover find f., 827 : 10
sheer into heart of f., 535 : 14
someday to prove our f., 73 : 14
sternest knight of f., 149 : 20
support friend oppose f., 890 : 7
the f. they come, 457 : 18
thou that seemest f., 156 : 1
timorous f., 338 : 14
tyrants fall in every f., 411 : 16
unrelenting f. to love, 345 : 18
without hate, 591 : 11
wolf that's f. to men, 262 : 4
Foeman bares steel tarantara, 628 : 2
Foeman's, beneath f. frown, 536 : 7
Foemen worthy of steel, 431 : 14
Foes, ah my f., 822 : 17
beat down baffling f., 585 : 11
fools or f., 339 : 13
his courage f. proclaim, 304 : 6
inveterate f. saluted, 305 : 5
judge man by f., 683 : 9
learning's barbarous f., 351 : 10
man that makes character makes f., 330 : 2
not know friends from f., 558 : 7
our f. press on, 139 : 12
so far only hate our f., 73 : 14
thrice he routed f., 306 : 17
what their f. liked was done, 869 : 1
Foes (*continued*)
will provide with arms, 105 : 3
Foetus, irresponsible f., 804 : 9
Fog and filthy air, 235 : 22
comes on cat feet, 761 : 5
feel f. in throat, 544 : 21
gleams through f., 360 : 29
London f. thirty parts, 699 : 16
London particular a f., 549 : 13
patience everywhere like f., 859 : 11
woodthrush singing through f., 806 : 8
Foggy foggy dew, 921 : 11
Fogs, his rising f. prevail, 304 : 25
Foh a fico for the phrase, 225 : 9
fie f. and fum, 234 : 13
Foibles, half our misery from f., 393 : 13
Foiled, after thousand victories f., 244 : 7
Foils foe by effusion of ink, 365 : 11
Fold, all driven into same f., 107 : 19
as I guard o'er the f., 403 : 14
climb into the f., 280 : 20
do not f. spindle or mutilate, 925 : 11
flock in wooly f., 476 : 8
hands and wait, 630 : 21
home fast f. thy child, 656 : 14
sheep not of this f., 45 : 12
sheep to f., 692 : 2
star that bids shepherd f., 279 : 9
tents like Arabs, 510 : 22
walking round the f., 403 : 13
wolf in f. sad thing, 103 : 11
Folded, lord of f. arms, 190 : 26
Folding of the Apennine, 587 : 11
of the hands to sleep, 23 : 12
Folds, lull distant f., 361 : 21
of bright girdle furled, 587 : 16
rippling in breeze, 539 : 3
wings and is rocked to sleep, 570 : 7
Foliage, children in f., 807 : 8
silver light on f., 841 : 11
Folio, whole volumes in f., 190 : 18
Folk, ancient f. with evil spells, 929 : 1
black f. say American would have been stronger, 875 : 10
dance like wave of sea, 712 : 17
down there sea f. live, 505 : 3
messenger with language of his f., 131 : 2
O yonge fresshe f., 145 : 8
queerest f. of all, 696 : 1
rare when best literature become f. literature, 866 : 2
songs from soul sounds, 831 : 16
Folks go to church when got to, 623 : 25
never understand f. they hate, 568 : 8
rail against other folks, 349 : 15
there's where old f. stay, 598 : 3
unhappy f. on shore now, 429 : 19
Folks', lazy f. stummucks, 662 : 11
Follies and misfortunes of mankind, 383 : 10
and wickedness, 865 : 18
cease with youth, 350 : 16
of town crept slowly, 371 : 2
perished by their own f., 59 : 14
that themselves commit, 199 : 7
vices and f. of humankind, 324 : 6
woes because of their own f., 59 : 15
Follow a shadow, 256 : 6
admire virtue f. not her lore, 288 : 5
after peace, 47 : 33
and will not see its back, 64 : 7

Follow (*continued*)
as night the day, 219 : 2
beat to f. faster, 240 : 29
deception of thrush, 807 : 3
do not f. in footsteps, 314 : 4
drops sliding from oar, 873 : 16
even if disobedient I shall f., 92 : 2
good to fire but not into it, 165 : 15
goodness and mercy shall f. me, 18 : 7
grasp subject words will f., 95 : 13
him who sets you right, 125 : 12
I f. but myself, 229 : 16
if thou f. thy star, 141 : 10
king, 534 : 5
knowledge like star, 529 : 10
lamb will never cease to f., 186 : 20
let who loves country f., 509 : 7
loves me let him f. me, 143 : 1
me fishers of men, 37 : 3
me let dead bury dead, 38 : 24
nature, 118 : 8
nor path to f., 576 : 17
so fast they f., 223 : *n* 5
spirit of men who f., 791 : 15
still changes of the moon, 231 : 2
the Gleam, 535 : 18
the king, 534 : 5
the Master, 302 : *n* 4
things which make for peace, 47 : 33
this city going to f. you, 702 : 2
thrift may f. fawning, 222 : 4
to f. lead of others, 313 : 3
truth wherever it may lead, 389 : 16
us disquietly to graves, 233 : 4
well in order, 575 : 14
what is right he will f., 68 : 15
you didn't want to f. me, 849 : 21
your desire 3 : 6
your spirit, 207 : 18
Followed fast and faster, 526 : 16
first f. it hymselve, 146 : 10
him honored him, 541 : 6
me since black womb held, 883 : 11
mercenary calling, 692 : 3
through all world she f. him, 530 : 13
Followeth, he that f. me, 45 : 4
not after me, 39 : 5
Following, in f. him I follow myself, 229 : 16
plow along mountainside, 425 : 10
the master artist, 803 : 2
the roe, 410 : 9
Follows but for form, 233 : 18
care f. me flying, 163 : 14
God in his works, 329 : 5
in His train, 452 : 7
Folly, according to his f., 684 : 3
alone stays fugue of Youth, 153 : 8
answer a fool according to his f., 25 : 18
brood of F., 278 : 9
call it madness f., 416 : 4
cannot remedy f. of people, 155 : 5
Catullus you should cease f., 101 : 19
centuries of f. noise sin, 542 : 4
every f. but vanity, 358 : 25
fool returneth to his f., 25 : 19
forts of f., 588 : 3
from f. to defeat, 900 : 6
genius goes f. stays, 494 : 23
has not fellow, 691 : 1
Heaven itself we seek in our f., 106 : 27
his foe was f., 627 : *n* 2
Folly (*continued*)
in all of every age, 311 : 9
joys to this are f., 258 : 3
lovely woman stoops to f., 369 : 20, 805 : 8
nights wherein you spend f., 261 : 4
noise of f., 278 : 17
of being comforted, 712 : 18
one's wisdom another's f., 497 : 26
profit by f. of others, 117 : 5
rememberest not slightest f., 210 : 33
reveals to man own f., 837 : 18
rid of f. beginning of wisdom, 108 : 17
shakes rooted f. of age, 311 : 13
shielding from effects of f., 579 : 22
shoot f. as it flies, 336 : 11
stoops to f., 805 : 8
to be wise, 361 : 12
uses f. like stalking-horse, 213 : 6
who lives without f., 293 : 25
wickedness or f., 521 : 13
wisdom excelleth f., 26 : 18
Folly's all they taught me, 447 : 5
at full length, 330 : 26
Fonctionnaire wields power of state, 844 : 4
Fond, ae f. kiss, 410 : 2
and wayward thoughts, 424 : 11
foolish f. old man, 235 : 9
got cat f. of that, 677 : 6
lover, 289 : 17
memory thou f. deceiver, 368 : 10
more f. than mistress, 335 : 2
nor too f. of fame, 333 : 22
prove so f., 243 : 1
those that covet with gain f., 189 : 18
too f. to rule alone, 338 : 14
trivial f. records, 219 : 27
Fonder, absence makes heart grow f., 112 : 25
Fondest hope decay, 447 : 14
Fondness, habitual hatred or f., 379 : 12
Fons Bandusiae splendidior vitro, 108 : *n* 4
Font, porphyry f., 531 : 11
Food as luscious as locusts, 230 : 4
chickens quit quarreling over f., 760 : 10
crops the flowery f., 336 : 13
for worms, 346 : 15
gathereth her f. in the harvest, 23 : 11
government see that people have f., 573 : 10
homely was their f., 318 : 17
if music f. of love, 213 : 7
man merely a passage for f., 152 : 2
many companions for f. and drink, 67 : 1
moody f. of love, 241 : 3
music f. of love, 213 : *n* 2
my life my joy my f., 168 : *n* 1
near tables wanted f., 423 : 2
of fancy, 212 : 28
of fools, 322 : 7
of love, 213 : *n* 2, 213 : 7
one f. for all, 414 : 21
people have no f., 642 : 7
poets' f. love and fame, 467 : 16
seeking the f. he eats, 211 : 3
struggle for f., 514 : *n* 7
sweet f. of knowledge, 176 : 10
to one poison to others, 101 : 6
Tom's f. for seven year, 234 : 10
too fine for angels, 314 : 23
Fool all people all the time, 524 : 10
almost at times the f., 803 : 17
and his money, 917 : 23
answer a f. according to his folly, 25 : 18
at forty fool indeed, 329 : 21
at his end shall be a f., 32 : 13
better to be f. than dead, 667 : 18
brains to make f. of self, 667 : 19
busy old f. unruly Sun, 252 : 7
called her his lady fair, 709 : 14
cannot be stille, 144 : 11
clever woman manage f., 707 : 11
dullness of f. whetstone of wits, 210 : 12
enough to expunge, 356 : 10
every f. will be meddling, 24 : 28
every inch not f. is rogue, 304 : 18
gilded f., 251 : 9
greatest f. is man, 311 : 12
gret f. bothe riche and nygard, 144 : 7
griefs that f., 889 : 21
happy he knows no more, 337 : 6
has feathered his nest, 261 : 10
haste of f. slowest thing, 313 : 20
hath said in his heart, 17 : 21
he that trusteth in his own heart is a f., 25 : 29
he's Don Quixote a muddled f., 170 : 16
hold tongue and pass for sage, 112 : 11
how ill white hairs become f., 206 : 36
I am fortune's f., 193 : 7
I have played the f., 13 : 7
in four letters, 297 : 17
invented kissing, 323 : 14
is he who is greedy, 4 : 1
laughter of the f., 27 : 5
learned f. more foolish, 298 : 15
lies here, 707 : 20
life time's f., 205 : 10
love's not time's f., 245 : 18
lunatic lean-witted f., 194 : 16
may prove self a f., 503 : 21
may talk wise man speaks, 257 : 4
may wys-man ofte gide, 144 : 15
me to top of my bent, 222 : 21
merciful to me a f., 646 : 13
met a f. in the forest, 211 : 4
more hope of a f., 25 : 19
more knave than f., 169 : 30, 183 : 14
motley f., 211 : 4
multitude choose by show, 199 : 12
my poor f. is hanged, 235 : 18
nature makes f. she means it, 561 : 15
need to f. ourselves, 723 : 20
no f. like old f., 160 : 21
nor yet f. to fame, 338 : 10
now and then right, 375 : 25
O f. I shall go mad, 233 : 23
officious f., 420 : 5
old doting f., 120 : 11
old man who will not laugh is f., 704 : 9
once harm done even f. understands, 58 : 27
one draught above heat makes him f., 213 : 16
patriot a f. in every age, 339 : 12
pious f. that raised it, 275 : *n* 1
play the Roman f., 240 : 7
poor f. with all my lore, 396 : 10
pure f., 552 : 17

Fool (*continued*)
rather have f. make me merry, 212 : 19
relenting f., 187 : 21
remains f. his life long, 399 : 14
resolved to live a f., 263 : 2
returneth to his folly, 25 : 19
said my muse to me, 176 : 13
serviceable, 684 : 3
smarts so little as f., 338 : 8
some people all the time, 524 : 10
strumpet's f., 240 : 12
suspects himself a f., 330 : 10
talk sense to a f., 77 : 7
the more f. I, 210 : 32
there was made his prayer, 709 : 14
think he is wise, 212 : 30
thinks himself wise is great f., 344 : 6
this night thy soul, 43 : 20
though he be a f., 309 : 18
to fame, 338 : 10
uttereth all his mind, 25 : 31
way of a f., 23 : 30
when he holdeth his peace, 24 : 18
when we play the f., 442 : 22
wise enough to play f., 214 : 12
wise man dieth as the f., 26 : 20
wise man knows himself f., 212 : 30
wisest f. in Christendom, 175 : 3
with f. no companionship, 72 : 18
with f. strikers right or wrong, 765 : 11
with foolish play the f., 91 : 2
with judges, 118 : *n* 2
Fooled with hope, 303 : 10
Foolery governs world, 263 : 24
that wise men have, 210 : 13
walk about like sun, 214 : 11
Fool-gudgeon opinion, 198 : 4
Fooling, adapted to my f., 749 : 17
Foolish, an' f. notion, 409 : 8
and false as fame, 315 : 18
consistency, 497 : 2
fond old man, 235 : 9
fool calls you f., 77 : 7
forgive f. ways, 514 : 1
frantic boast f. word, 709 : 20
gets f. or wife does, 722 : 15
God hath chosen f. things, 48 : 1
heaven save from f. friend, 420 : 5
hold that mortal f., 77 : 11
I being young and f., 711 : 22
idleness best thing to ruin f., 118 : 19
lean and f. knight, 742 : 10
learned fool more f., 298 : 15
man built house on sand, 38 : 21
man who trusts woman, 105 : *n* 5
men who accuse a woman, 316 : 1
never said a f. thing, 315 : 14
old and f. king, 26 : 25
passionate man, 717 : 3
penny wise pound f., 258 : 10
people without understanding, 31 : 34
seem f. among wise, 118 : 3
son is calamity of his father, 24 : 25
son the heaviness of his mother, 23 : 21
studied in my f. youth, 150 : 6
thing but a toy, 214 : 29
thing well done, 355 : 6
things to confound wise, 48 : 1
to make long prologue, 36 : 16
too f. for tear, 435 : 21
Foolish (*continued*)
virgins, 40 : 28
when he had not pen, 356 : 16
whistling of a name, 295 : 16
with f. play the fool, 91 : 2
women f. to match men, 565 : 12
wrath killeth the f., 15 : 14
young and f., 711 : 22
Foolishness, not fools but f., 262 : 17
of yesterday, 664 : 12
the past with its f., 863 : 13
Fool's bolt soon shot, 160 : 23
errand, 359 : 23
mouth is his destruction, 24 : 19
paradise, 497 : 7, 917 : 8
Fools, a little wise best f. be, 252 : 14
admire but men of sense approve, 333 : 11
amongst f. a judge, 118 : *n* 2
are my theme, 456 : 11
be thankful for f., 625 : 12
but f. caught it, 713 : 14
by follies they perished the f., 59 : 14
by heavenly compulsion, 233 : 5
children and f. cannot lie, 160 : 13
children and f. want everything, 310 : 18
crabbed as dull f. suppose, 279 : 25
discourse of f. is irksome, 35 : 37
do not imitate successes, 95 : 10
do not know how much more is half than whole, 61 : 14
dreading e'en f., 338 : 14
effect of coercion to make f., 387 : 15
fill world with f., 579 : 22
flanneled f. at wicket, 709 : 23
food of f., 322 : 7
God protects f. and United States, 924 : 7
great stage of f., 235 : 5
greatest f. most satisfied, 311 : 10
have always mocked wise, 138 : 8
hundred f. not make wise man, 812 : 14
I am two f. I know, 252 : 13
illusion of f., 837 : 18
in all tongues called f., 213 : 1
in idle wishes f. stay, 400 : 7
in town on our side, 624 : 3
laugh at men of sense, 315 : 8
learn in no other, 347 : 23
leaves 'em still two f., 324 : 8
let f. contest, 337 : 9
let f. use talents, 213 : 15
lighted f. way to dusty death, 240 : 4
make a mock at sin, 23 : 35
make such vain keeping, 262 : 7
millions mostly f., 474 : 12
more f. than wise, 918 : 17
ninety-nine percent of people f., 839 : 17
no more I'll tease, 334 : 24
not f. but foolishness, 262 : 17
of fortune, 243 : 5
of nature, 219 : 12
old men know young men f., 177 : 13
or foes, 339 : 13
Paradise of F., 285 : 8
play the f. with time, 206 : 13
poems made by f. like me, 795 : 7
poor f. decoyed, 310 : 1
pride vice of f., 332 : 19
print it and shame f., 338 : 7
rush in, 333 : 20
Fools (*continued*)
say man has or has not principles, 484 : 14
scarecrows of f., 596 : 3
so deep-contemplative, 211 : 7
some made coxcombs nature meant f., 332 : 17
suckle f., 230 : 12
suffer f. gladly, 49 : 20
tedious old f., 220 : 22
the stop to busy f., 298 : 21
too green and only good for f., 66 : *n* 1
we f. of nature, 219 : 12
what f. call nature, 545 : 10
what f. these mortals be, 114 : 13, 197 : 1
who came to scoff, 370 : 8
wise men profit more from f., 95 : 10
wise men speak f. decide, 63 : 3
wish to appear wise among f., 118 : 3
words are money of f., 264 : 13
young men think old men f., 177 : 13
Fools' experiments, 515 : 14
names like fools' faces, 920 : 5
outweighs all the f., 543 : 6
Foos, my f. won't moos, 778 : 5
Foot, accent of coming f., 608 : 4
and hand go cold, 163 : 10
beat earth with unfettered f., 107 : 15
beggar on f., 717 : 12
better f. before, 202 : 9
cannot put shoe on every f., 111 : 28
Chancellor's f., 263 : 13
crow to sole of f., 209 : 20
dash f. against stone, 43 : 1
dash thy f. against a stone, 20 : 17
for foot, 10 : 10
from the f. Hercules, 78 : 13
her f. speaks, 227 : 3
her f. was light, 478 : 11
in the stirrup, 927 : 11, 927 : 12
it featly, 247 : 19
lived like f. for thirty years, 911 : 16
miles on f. to fare, 748 : *n* 2
my f. on my native heath, 431 : 27
no f. of unfamiliar men, 587 : 6
no f. slide, 924 : 15
noiseless f. of time, 227 : 21
of hand of f. of lip, 245 : 12
one f. already in grave, 120 : 11
one f. in sea one on shore, 209 : 16
one white f. try him, 923 : 11
print of naked f., 318 : 14
problem with right f. and life, 902 : 5
proud f. of conqueror, 202 : 19
put forward best f., 202 : *n* 4
rest for the sole of her f., 7 : 31
so light a f., 193 : 2
stamped f. and cried, 605 : 7
suffer thy f. to be moved, 22 : 4
thy soul the fixed f., 253 : 5
to gallows f. and after, 710 : 20
wear steps of his door, 35 : 11
who cleft Devil's f., 252 : 1
wishing his f. equal with eye, 186 : 10
with naked f. stalking my chamber 161 : 25
worth on f., 567 : *n* 1
Foot-and-a-half-long words, 109 : 22
Football, in life as in f., 687 : 5
Footfalls echo in memory, 807 : 2
Footing, 'twixt his stretched f., 226 : 4
Foot-in-the-grave young man, 628 : 12

Footman, eternal F. snicker, 803 : 16
Footpads, when f. quail, 629 : 20
Footpath, jog on the f. way, 246 : 24
Footprint is our own, 776 : 7
on shores of unknown, 776 : 7
saw His f. in sod, 696 : 11
Zuleika looking for man's f., 736 : 1
Footprints in the sands of time, 509 : 15
of gigantic hound, 689 : 11
steams out f. that led us, 894 : 1
Footstep, where thy f. gleams, 525 : 18
Footsteps added up to see how near, 907 : 15
dead remembered f., 728 : 17
distant f. echo, 510 : 20
do not follow in f., 314 : 4
home his f. turned, 430 : 10
plants his f. in the sea, 375 : 16
soundless f. on grass, 723 : 3
trod in f. of calf, 685 : 9
Footstool, earth as f., 720 : 6
earth is his f., 37 : 9
God's f. may be throne, 746 : 20
my f. earth, 336 : 19
Foppery, excellent f. of the world, 233 : 5
Fops, whole tribe of f., 233 : 3
Forbade me to put off my hat, 300 : 21
to wade through slaughter, 362 : 11
Forbear and persevere, 669 : 17
be not too bold, 173 : *n* 8
cruel mother, 108 : 10
scarce f. to cheer, 488 : 17
to dig dust enclosed here, 250 : 1
to judge, 185 : 19
Forbearance ceases to be virtue, 372 : 2
practice Christian f., 383 : 6
Forbid, God f., 8 : 35, 8 : 35
it Almighty God, 383 : 5
it sea gods, 569 : 20
them not, 42 : 11
Forbidden by Constitution, 402 : 1
not f. is permitted, 413 : 7
tree whose mortal taste, 282 : 22
wanted apple because f., 624 : 12
Forbids, my mind f. to crave, 167 : 5
rich as well as poor, 655 : 14
Force, abandonment of f., 781 : 9
acceleration proportional to applied f., 313 : *n* 5
adaptation of form to resist f., 573 : 9
Allied Expeditionary F., 815 : 12
and beauty of process, 654 : 10
and oppression made wrecks, 726 : 12
change from liberty to f., 418 : 2
citizens to confess faith, 821 : 6
conservation of f., 583 : 21
constant f. for muddlement, 653 : 16
elemental f. freed, 809 : 22
evolution not a f., 637 : 1
from which sun draws power, 787 : 13
government is f., 615 : 3
grace f. fascination, 575 : 13
had not f. to shape, 534 : 28
has no place for skill, 78 : 12
impostor employs f., 391 : 7
in nature not increased, 583 : 21
interfere by f. with slaveholder, 560 : 23
joint f. and full result, 333 : 1
knowing f. of words, 69 : 23
knowledge more than f., 178 : *n* 10
language into meaning, 809 : 9
Force (*continued*)
love f., 727 : 5
material moral spiritual f., 699 : 5
moment to its crisis, 803 : 15
no f. however great, 471 : 14
no motion has she no f., 424 : 14
not by f. or violence, 383 : 6
not remedy, 538 : 4
of heaven-bred poesy, 190 : 3
of his own merit, 248 : 21
of righteousness, 727 : 5
of temporal power, 200 : 9
oppressor to commit brutality openly, 909 : 16
or fraud, 616 : 2
overthrow by f., 700 : 3
paralyzed f., 805 : 16
passion spent novel f., 529 : 17
produce according to f., 563 : *n* 1
proportional to motive f., 313 : 14
secret f. driving me, 518 : 8
some patient f., 531 : 15
soul f., 727 : 5
spiritual f. stronger, 499 : 26
surely not left vain, 588 : 6
terror and f., 812 : 13
that through green fuse, 886 : 12
them in spite of Nature, 291 : 9
them to write, 291 : 9
too revolutionary for old ideas, 787 : 14
tribalism strongest f. in world, 912 : 2
uncomprehended which was his life, 602 : 5
U.S. greatest potential f., 699 : 5
use of f. but temporary, 372 : 16
vivid f. of mind prevailed, 100 : 3
when one by f. subdues, 89 : 1
who overcomes by f., 283 : 27
wins easiest victory, 812 : 13
without wisdom falls of own weight, 107 : 29
world f. not presence, 770 : 2
Forced by fate, 306 : 11
gait of shuffling nag, 204 : 14
praise on our part, 541 : 9
the sound is f., 403 : 1
to surrender truth, 274 : 2
wedlock f. a hell, 185 : 7
Forces, avoid perils by united f., 308 : 21
beyond my control, 905 : 6
by which nature animated, 397 : 17
deliberative f., 677 : 12
determination of f., 594 : 12
don't fight f. use them, 832 : 6
feel f. behind detail, 644 : 14
imagination one of f. of nature, 769 : 26
impressed upon it, 313 : 13
in the difficult are friendly f., 756 : 13
man who f. opportunity, 400 : 19
military f. are one team, 825 : 3
natural and moral f., 584 : 1
one to repeat no, 659 : 2
our f. on Philippine soil, 771 : 4
politics struggle of f., 635 : 17
spiritual f., 679 : 5
these f. met master, 779 : 20
which theaten soul, 778 : 11
Forcible, how f. are right words, 15 : 19
most f. Feeble, 206 : 23
Forcibly if we must, 438 : *n* 1
Ford, I'm a F. not a Lincoln, 882 : 14
you were kind man, 892 : 13
Fordoes, makes me or f. me quite, 232 : 12
Forearmed, forewarned f., 170 : 11
Forecast, others f. the rising stars, 105 : 24
Forefathers, contemplate our f., 365 : 3
copy your f., 3 : 13
had no books but score, 185 : 28
met the boat, 766 : 5
rude f. of hamlet, 361 : 23
were warriors, 419 : 11
Forefinger, agate on f. of alderman, 191 : 23
of all time, 530 : 24
Forefront, fighting in f. of the Greeks, 67 : 18
set Uriah in f. of battle, 13 : 18
Forego, propensity to f., 647 : 20
Foregone conclusion, 231 : 16
Forehead, fist of f. over wastes, 907 : 2
of every traitor, 615 : 4
of frowning skies, 167 : 8
of humanity, 475 : 21
of the age to come, 475 : 8
of the morning sky, 281 : 4
right in middle of her f., 513 : 1
Foreheads villainous low, 248 : 14
Foreign aid of ornament, 345 : 14
apprenticehood to f. passages, 194 : 4
avoid f. collision, 444 : 2
banners of f. independence, 418 : 2
boys not sent into f. wars, 780 : 11
by f. hands eyes closed, 335 : 10
corner of f. field, 797 : 1
disposed of f. enemies, 85 : 7
gear of f. dead men, 808 : 2
intercourse with f. nations, 445 : 19
levy, 238 : 19
life is a f. language, 816 : 10
nations and the next age, 181 : 16
no f. sky protected me, 801 : 14
policies based on myths, 862 : 16
relations policy, 813 : 11
the past a f. country, 833 : 20
things f. or things at home, 302 : 4
troop in my country, 351 : 5
wandering on f. strand, 430 : 10
Foreigner in country of birth, 916 : 12
no f. do business here, 151 : 1
Foreigners, all equal except f., 520 : 2
spell better than pronounce, 622 : 4
Foreknow, for whom he did f., 47 : 11
Foreknowledge absolute, 284 : 19
Forelock, by f. take time, 174 : 16
Foremost files of time, 530 : 7
Forensic, aim of f. oratory, 98 : 16
Forepangs, pangs schooled at f., 656 : 17
Foresaw, sees what he f., 427 : 25
Foreseeing, no soul f., 641 : 23
Forest, beasts of the f. creep forth, 21 : 11
beautiful changes as f., 899 : 6
cannot see f. for trees, 380 : 4
cutting through the f., 765 : 6
every beast of the f. is mine, 19 : 13
flowers of the f., 359 : 11, 368 : 2
lyre even as f. is, 467 : 21
met a fool in the f., 211 : 4
primeval, 510 : 26
vast wastes of f. verdure, 592 : 6
way into universe through f., 637 : 18
wild f. green mansions, 646 : 1
Foresters, Diana's f., 202 : 24

Forest's ferny floor, 739 : 15
Forests are rended, 431 : 23
helmets gleamed in f., 592 : 6
in the f. of the night, 405 : 7
Pelion with its leafy f., 60 : 9
Foretold that danger lurks within, 186 : 18
Forever, ae farewell and then f., 410 : 2
and a day, 212 : 24
clear day see f., 895 : 5
corner of field f. England, 797 : 1
diamond lasts f., 826 : 5
fare thee well, 459 : 19
farewell Cassius, 217 : 9
Fortune wilt thou prove, 345 : 18
good jest f., 203 : 20
he is mine f., 580 : 15
his time is f., 295 : 10
I go on f., 533 : 16
life death and that f., 566 : 12
life goes on f., 822 : 16
man has F., 542 : 17
may be f., 487 : 3
never, 510 : 23
piping songs, 477 : 8
same yesterday today and f., 51 : 24
stranger and alone, 852 : 7
the past there for us f., 863 : 13
time will not be ours f., 255 : 16
would you live f., 358 : 2
Forevermore, adieu f., 410 : 6
glory gone f., 513 : 7
Forewarned forearmed, 170 : 11
Forfeit, all souls were f., 228 : 7
confidence of citizens, 524 : 10
fair renown, 430 : 10
to a confined doom, 245 : 13
Forgave, coward never f., 359 : 16
hugged offender f. offense, 307 : 7
took kindness f., theft, 545 : 3
Forge in smithy of soul, 777 : 18
practice and thought f. art, 103 : 28
random grim f., 656 : 8
Forged, chain I f. in life, 548 : 6
Forges, what his breast f., 242 : 20
Forget all feuds, 489 : 3
and forgive, 169 : 28, 235 : 10
and if thou wilt f., 608 : 13
and smile, 608 : 15
because we must, 586 : 11
best to f., 545 : 24
better by far f. and smile, 608 : 15
better to f., 492 : 9
can I f. you for eternity, 894 : 3
courage to f., 597 : 1
dissolve and f., 476 : 24
don't f. Virginia, 596 : 12
dream that I f., 633 : 16
green thumbs, 886 : 15
how long wilt thou f. me, 17 : 20
I must f. you first, 381 : 4
I never f. a face, 834 : 2
if I f. thee O Jerusalem, 22 : 15
knew we should both f., 634 : 2
learn hateful art how to f., 267 : 8
lest we f., 709 : 16
love to friends and brethren, 34 : 2
my own name, 169 : 22
my prince you'd soon f., 325 : 15
never f. he is President, 788 : 4
never f. horror of moment, 612 : 16
never f. it is a constitution, 402 : 4
never f. nobler things, 729 : 11
never f. what they did, 523 : 4
Forget (*continued*)
new-made honor doth f. men's names, 201 : 9
nor worms f., 548 : 3
not to do good and communicate, 51 : 26
not yet tried intent, 161 : 22
politician knows what to f., 637 : 11
source that keeps it filled, 601 : 2
teach unforgetful to f., 601 : 21
that I remember, 633 : 16
the best sometimes f., 230 : 21
the he and she, 252 : 6
thyself to marble, 278 : 14
till future dares f. past, 468 : 23
to take pleasure, 310 : 3
what I have been, 195 : 5
when image is effaced, 85 : 18
womb shall f. him, 16 : 10
women and elephants never f., 731 : 12
Forgetful, blessed are f., 657 : 24
of his horsemanship, 58 : 26
Forgetfulness, not in entire f., 426 : 14
of affliction, 35 : 21
of all ills, 59 : 25
space engenders f., 755 : 6
steep senses in f., 206 : 17
to dumb f. a prey, 362 : 14
Forget-me-nots of angels, 511 : 3
Forgets dying bird, 385 : 1
he f. not his own, 918 : 19
man f. to live, 315 : 9
Forgetting, if f. could be willed, 601 : 2
sleep and a f., 426 : 14
those things behind, 50 : 4
valley more and more f., 601 : 2
world f. by world forgot, 335 : 4
Forgive, as we f. our debtors, 37 : 15
as we f. those who trespass, 37 : *n* 5
being with the right to f., 582 : 4
blindness we may f., 728 : 14
children f. parents, 675 : 3
close eyes to f., 700 : 4
cursed be tribe if I f., 198 : 21
Father f. them, 44 : 7
forget and f., 169 : 28, 235 : 10
give thanks and f., 634 : 13
God f. you but I never, 163 : 19
good to f., 545 : 24
he will never f. you, 413 : 33
hero, 899 : 10
I f. you you f. me, 406 : 2
if Death knew how to f., 104 : 12
if you f. people you belong to them, 848 : 8
jealous readiest to f., 582 : 10
know everything f. everything, 417 : *n* 5
lambs not f., 548 : 3
man who forces opportunity, 400 : 19
me my injuries, 893 : 9
mercy to f., 305 : 18
mother's hardest to f., 864 : 19
O Lord my little jokes, 749 : 15
of course God will f. me, 482 : 8
only brave know how to f., 359 : 16
our foolish ways, 514 : 1
person displaying feeling, 484 : 13
public seldom f. twice, 386 : 10
some sinner, 772 : 6
them as a Christian, 440 : 22
those I have injured, 893 : 9
those who bore us, 293 : 34
Forgive (*continued*)
Thy great big one on me, 749 : 15
to f. divine, 333 : 15
us all our trespasses little creatures, 781 : 11
us our debts, 37 : 15
us our trespasses, 37 : *n* 5
we come to f. everything, 885 : 12
Forgiven and forgotten, 235 : *n* 1
her sins are f., 43 : 4
Forgiveness, after knowledge what f., 804 : 14
ask of thee f., 235 : 12
awkwardness has no f., 499 : 7
of sins, 54 : 7, 55 : 2
to injured does belong, 115 : *n* 3
turning word f. to sword, 893 : 19
Forgiving, enemy f. all, 868 : 3
Forgot, auld acquaintance be f., 410 : 11
by the world f., 335 : 4
copperheads and assassin, 761 : 8
cry of gulls, 805 : 9
don't let it be f., 895 : 4
Father Son are things f., 254 : 5
for which he toiled, 244 : 7
foundations we f., 808 : 12
much Cynara, 721 : 5
proposed as things f., 333 : 18
time hath f. itself, 226 : 15
to wind clock, 359 : 19
was Britain's glory, 596 : 17
world was all f., 454 : 2
Forgotten aim, 703 : 10
all I have done for him, 312 : 2
as a dead man out of mind, 18 : 16
as a fire, 787 : 6
as flower is forgotten, 787 : 6
eagle f., 765 : 3
even by God, 540 : 10
everything learned, 925 : 5
fly f. as a dream, 328 : 12
for want of writers, 108 : *n* 11
forgiven and f., 235 : *n* 1
glimpses of f. dreams, 528 : 1
grief f., 632 : 8
I am all f., 240 : 19
I have f. your name, 634 : 3
if you would not be f., 347 : 18
learned nothing f. nothing, 400 : 16
let it be f., 787 : 6
man, 642 : 11, 779 : 6
memory of them is f., 27 : 15
mornings, 886 : 18
not f. inside of church, 204 : 24
old times not f., 554 : 1
pain glad to be f., 797 : 13
through lapse of Time, 87 : 6
undeservedly f., 869 : 7
volume of f. lore, 526 : 10
wars, 807 : 4
you have f. my kisses, 634 : 3
Forked mountain or blue promontory, 241 : 17
poor bare f. animal, 234 : 7
torch of a flower, 791 : 1
Forks and hope, 614 : 4
fingers made before f., 323 : 12
Forlorn, faery lands f., 477 : 1
glimpses make me less f., 428 : 1
hic jacet, 425 : 4
Stygian cave f., 277 : 17
Form, all-f. only rational f., 650 : 12
and frame from thinking, 768 : 25
and pressure, 222 : 2

Form (*continued*)
architecture f. to resist force, 573 : 9
art nothing without f., 583 : 6
as goldsmiths make, 715 : 3
before heaven and earth had taken f., 97 : 7
bodily f. from natural thing, 715 : 3
can't f. children on own concepts, 395 : 16
charming f. of government, 85 : 3
collective unit f., 650 : 12
combination and f. indeed, 223 : 3
divine, 442 : 17
each carries own life f., 754 : 5
each of like f. from everlasting, 124 : 8
earth was without f., 6 : 10
essential thing in f., 769 : 13
ever follows function, 681 : 22
expediency determines f., 798 : 15
finding what f. to do without, 739 : 3
follows but for f., 233 : 18
follows function, 681 : 22
free f. not assure freedom, 769 : 13
free in whatever f. used, 769 : 13
freedom regardless of f., 769 : 13
from off my door, 526 : 18
harmony manifest in f., 696 : 5
human couple find true f., 870 : 12
human thought or f., 466 : 9
identifies with f. of his fate, 843 : 6
in f. in moving, 220 : 28
Love the human f. divine, 403 : 11
matter indifferent to f., 273 : 10
mold of f., 221 : 20
of popular government, 398 : 3
proportion season f., 225 : 37
quiet at heart of f., 874 : 7
shape without f., 805 : 16
soul is f. and doth body make, 174 : 19
spots of diamond f., 377 : 6
Terror the human f. divine, 405 : 14
Formal, beard of f. cut, 211 : 15
feeling comes, 605 : 6
Formalities, get f. right, 625 : 18
Formed but one such man, 459 : 20
by thy converse, 338 : 1
for ruin of our sex, 365 : 1
his hands f. the dry land, 20 : 20
if you have f. a circle, 407 : 2
man was f. for society, 365 : 15
moment when friendship f., 385 : 17
of joy and mirth, 407 : 3
of various stuff, 410 : 16
or ever thou hadst f. the earth, 20 : 11
Former, get rid of f. bear latter, 348 : 3
latter and f. rain, 33 : 10
no remembrance of f. things, 26 : 15
one jot of f. love retain, 182 : 16
people, 725 : 4
things grow old, 266 : 15
thy f. light restore, 232 : 14
Formez vos bataillons, 415 : 1
Formidable, makes small numbers, f., 378 : 14
tendency to lapidary style, 497 : 31
Formless ruin of oblivion, 227 : 4
Forms all produced by laws, 515 : 1
and styles develop freely, 826 : 12
by f. unseen dirge sung, 364 : 9
differ in external f., 354 : 24
endless f. most beautiful, 515 : 3
evil has infinite f., 300 : 9
for f. of government, 337 : 9
Forms (*continued*)
more real than living, 467 : 3
of things unknown, 197 : 12
their colors and their f., 423 : 12
truth in different f., 610 : 2
waves with purple f., 673 : 17
Formula for making ends meet, 776 : 4
for morale is patriotism, 771 : 2
in same f. largest and lightest, 397 : 17
of that particular emotion, 809 : 5
Formulas, clear myself of f., 473 : 10
Formulations, inadequate f., 825 : 13
Fornication but in another country, 183 : 15
Forsake, do not f. me in my end, 309 : 11
her Cyprian groves, 306 : 6
let the wicked f. his way, 31 : 20
me like memory lost, 470 : 8
me not when my strength faileth, 19 : 34
not an old friend, 35 : 15
their temples dim, 277 : 12
Forsaken beliefs, 587 : 1
courts pale pavilions, 848 : 7
have not seen the righteous f., 18 : 25
my God why hast thou f. me, 18 : 5, 41 : 27
old f. bough, 519 : 19
town like place f., 309 : 24
Forsakes, air in music wing f., 637 : 15
Forsaking all others, 56 : 8
Forsan et haec olim meminisse iuvabit, 104 : *n* 11
Forsitan et nomen miscebitur istis, 113 : *n* 9
Forspent, clean f., 651 : 11
Forster, old lady quoted by F., 869 : 9
Forswear, if I transgress and f., 79 : 13
Forsworn, that so sweetly were f., 228 : 28
Fort, hold f. I am coming, 579 : 1, 635 : 22
Forted residence, 229 : 5
Forties, in f. know won't save us, 835 : 16
Fortieth, laugh never granted before f. day, 116 : 8
Fortify thy name against old age, 182 : 7
Fortitude and perseverance, 365 : 3
great f. of mind, 353 : 20
what f. soul contains, 608 : 4
Fortnight, to be hanged in a f., 355 : 25
Fortress built by Nature for herself, 194 : 13
he is my refuge and my f., 20 : 16
house is as f., 172 : 3
Lord is my f., 13 : 24
mighty f. is our God, 155 : 15
thou art my f., 156 : 1
Forts, Great Father building f. among us, 591 : 4
of folly, 588 : 3
Fortuitous circumstances, 432 : 3
Fortunatam natam me consule Romam, 99 : *n* 2
Fortunate, fair maidens commonly f., 175 : 19
farmers, 104 : 3
first king f. soldier, 343 : 4
man takes measure of self, 464 : 1
more desirable than f. hour, 102 : 9
who is f. learn pain, 413 : 29
Fortunate (*continued*)
youth to have found Homer, 90 : 13
Fortunate senex, 103 : *n* 6
Fortunatus et ille deos, 104 : *n* 2
Fortune and men's eyes, 244 : 8
arbiter of everyone's f., 103 : *n* 5
brings in some boats, 243 : 29
carry Caesar and his f., 99 : 20
charge f. with partiality, 444 : 1
diligence mother of good f., 170 : 34
distinction of birth or f., 420 : 19
each day that F. grants, 107 : 7
every man architect of his f., 103 : 5
excessive good f., 599 : 2
face is my f., 931 : 15
favor from F. easier to get, 111 : 3
favored him in moment of death, 123 : 5
favors the brave, 97 : *n* 1, 106 : 4
flatters to betray, 111 : 1
fools of f., 243 : 5
friend supports whom F. crushes, 118 : 11
good f. elevate petty minds, 120 : 3
good f. is god among men, 71 : 14
good f. may be short-lived, 265 : 4
good f. to be born human, 313 : 6
good f. to be ladies, 622 : 21
good night, 233 : 16
great f. great slavery, 115 : 7
grow out at heels, 233 : 15
has acquired him, 92 : 8
he has not acquired a f., 92 : 8
helps the brave, 97 : 1
heroes as well as Fame and F., 413 : 10
hostages to f., 180 : 9
I am maker of my own f., 419 : 11
I myself good f., 575 : 10
if farmers knew own f., 104 : 3
if thou of f. bereft, 133 : *n* 1
in disgrace with f., 244 : 8
in home of man without f., 60 : 15
in west build f., 538 : 8
insults of F., 349 : 24
judge men by good f., 293 : 26
leads on to f., 217 : 5
leaves door to remedy, 168 : 20
like glass easily broken, 111 : 2
like the market, 180 : 20
made f. send for friends, 82 : 23
man in possession of f., 440 : 16
man whom F. scratched, 227 : 19
man's f. in own hand, 181 : 6
may turn by f. from weaker, 198 : 30
melted to water, 313 : 7
method of making f., 363 : 11
most dejected thing of f., 234 : 19
not satisfied with one calamity, 110 : 28
out of suits with f., 210 : 16
outrageous f., 221 : 12
painted blind with muffler, 181 : *n* 2
popular when F. on our side, 110 : 29
prey at f., 231 : 4
ready for F. as she wills, 141 : 11
rob lady of f. by marriage, 349 : 23
seize good f., 396 : 28
shifts of F. test friends, 99 : 6
shows herself more kind, 200 : 15
sick in f., 233 : 5
smiling of F. beguiling, 359 : 10
sustain good f., 293 : 4
though blind not invisible, 181 : 5

Fortune (*continued*)
tire out hostile f., 540 : 1
to be well-favored gift of f., 209 : 24
to f. and fame unknown, 362 : 17
to make f. fate is essential, 313 : 5
too wooed is farther off, 161 : 18
tugged with f., 238 : 16
vicissitudes of f., 383 : 14
when F. means most good, 202 : 2
whom F. wishes to destroy, 78 : *n* 1
will send it, 251 : 13
wilt thou prove, 345 : 18
Fortune's buffets and rewards, 222 : 5
I am F. fool, 193 : 7
not now in f. power, 291 : 13
pipe for f. finger, 222 : 6
wayward tyranny, 73 : 11
Fortunes, build up great f., 638 : 7
dedicate lives and f., 682 : 13
dubious f., 650 : 13
hazard of new f., 201 : 11
make content with f. fit, 234 : 1
mar your f., 232 : 25
parcel of their f., 241 : 10
pledge our lives our f., 387 : 11
pride fell with my f., 210 : 17
sacrificed lives and f., 725 : 20
seek f. further than home, 188 : 27
that I have passed, 229 : 27
try f. to last man, 206 : 27
Fortuneteller, threadbare juggler f., 188 : 15
Forty, at f. reforms plan, 330 : 10
cannot live on f. pound, 268 : 6
centuries look down, 420 : 6
days and forty nights, 7 : 30
difference of f. thousand men, 421 : 9
fasted f. days and f. nights, 37 : 1
fat fair and f., 394 : 8
fifty north f. west, 709 : 24
fool at f. fool indeed, 329 : 21
I am f., 893 : 1
look young till f., 394 : *n* 3
Moses was there f. days, 10 : 15
nor rich at f., 269 : 32
pounds a year, 370 : 5
rather than f. shillings, 225 : 8
round earth in f. minutes, 196 : 16
singing seamen, 772 : 21
stripes save one, 49 : 21
thousand brothers, 224 : 22
thousand men, 929 : 15
till fifty stoic or satyr, 677 : 2
understand life at f., 705 : 11
wander in the wilderness f. years, 10 : 25
whacks, 923 : 5
winters besiege brow, 244 : 1
work of men above f., 664 : 19
years on, 627 : 5
Forty-second, gang at F. Street, 759 : 5
Forum, eloquence in f., 559 : 30
funny thing happened on way to f., 908 : 4
Forward, ever f. but slowly, 386 : 14
fare f., 94 : *n* 9
fare f. voyagers, 808 : 7
Germany in the world f., 663 : 3
life lived f., 552 : 10
look f. not back, 590 : 8
look f. to posterity, 373 : 20
nothing to look f. to, 747 : 7
put f. best foot, 202 : *n* 4
since we have come so far, 189 : 3
Forward (*continued*)
some a f. motion love, 299 : 4
sons of France, 415 : *n* 1
the Light Brigade, 533 : 10
those behind cried F., 488 : 15
Forwards, life lived f., 552 : 10
Fossil, language is f. poetry, 498 : 3
Fossils, God hid f. in rocks, 663 : 5
Foster child of silence, 477 : 4
went to Gloucester, 933 : 10
Fostered alike by beauty and fear, 423 : 17
Foster-nurse of nature is repose, 234 : 27
Fotching him to his own, 636 : 5
Fou for weeks thegither, 411 : 6
wasna f., 409 : 17
Fought a good fight, 51 : 9
against prejudice, 788 : 12
and bled in freedom's cause, 422 : 21
battle not even f., 837 : 18
battles o'er again, 306 : 17
better to have f. and lost, 532 : *n* 2
Black Hawk f. against white men, 418 : 13
dogs killed cats, 541 : 1
each other for, 439 : 13
for life, 876 : 15
lie f. with outright, 535 : 6
like pagan, 732 : 5
man who never f. pilfers, 82 : 2
Michael and angels f., 53 : 19
spirit that f. in heaven, 284 : 4
stars f. against Sisera, 12 : 5
street by street, 744 : 5
the better fight, 286 : 26
to crown Greece with freedom, 67 : 20
under whose colors he f. so long, 195 : 8
war prepared for eventually f., 860 : 5
we f. at Arques, 175 : 2
witness that I have f., 302 : 15
work they who f. advanced, 523 : 4
Foul and pestilent, 220 : 28
and ugly mists, 203 : 5
as Vulcan's stithy, 222 : 7
bar f. storm out, 715 : 10
bird that filleth own nest, 153 : *n* 2
blood nipped and ways be f., 191 : 14
contagion spread, 280 : 22
deed which she plotted, 60 : 11
deeds will rise, 218 : 26
fair and f. near kin, 716 : 17
fair is f. and f. is fair, 235 : 22
fair means or f., 779 : 19
fee bestow upon f. disease, 232 : 28
fiend Apollyon, 302 : 3
from f. to fair, 182 : 1
goat-head, 717 : 16
I doubt some f. play, 218 : 25
limbecks f. as hell, 245 : 19
pearl in your f. oyster, 213 : 3
play, 218 : 25
rag-and-bone shop, 717 : 21
shapes of f. disease, 532 : 23
so f. and fair a day, 236 : 4
Fouler, death aims with f. spite, 267 : 11
Foulest crime in history, 576 : 8
Foulness of their fate, 795 : 16
Found, came to ask what he had f., 439 : 11
crooked sixpense, 932 : 18
death in life, 438 : 9
Found (*continued*)
dove f. no rest, 7 : 31
empire for raising customers, 366 : 6
favor in thy sight, 8 : 11
fresh rhodora, 494 : 4
fun where I f. it, 709 : 9
has f. out thy bed, 405 : 5
hast thou f. me O mine enemy, 14 : 7
Him in shining of stars, 534 : 27
I could extinguish hope, 674 : 4
I have f. it, 93 : 4
I oft f. both, 198 : 6
I once was lost now am f., 367 : 7
in heart of friend, 510 : 25
in that town dog was f., 369 : 17
in whose hand the cup is f., 8 : 36
it is f. again, 674 : 1
left unstained what f., 470 : 16
looked inwards f. Nature, 303 : 6
lost time never f., 347 : 27
man who has f. himself out, 694 : 11
one man among a thousand, 27 : 11
out the remedy, 228 : 7
promptly f. out, 783 : 13
rebellion in way he f. it, 205 : 2
Rome city of bricks, 110 : 8
sense beneath rarely f., 333 : 4
sheep which was lost, 43 : 25
someone else can always be f., 701 : 11
sought but f. him not, 28 : 10
struggle to f. Roman state, 104 : 17
that famous country, 822 : 2
unmysterious flesh, 836 : 19
was lost and is f., 43 : 28
weighed in the balances and f. wanting, 33 : 1
when f. make note, 548 : 18
where shall wisdom be f., 16 : 12
where word be f., 806 : 4
who loveliness within hath f., 252 : 5
woman have I not f., 27 : 11
you as a morsel, 241 : 11
Foundation, fear f. of governments, 381 : 9
is love, 909 : 11
laid in youth, 689 : 21
new government laying f., 387 : 9
no sure f. on blood, 202 : 8
of constitutional government, 700 : 3
Foundations, earth's f. fled, 692 : 3
earth's f. stand, 692 : 11
loosen old f., 761 : 10
marred f. we forgot, 808 : 12
of knowledge in mathematics, 139 : 5
of states laws and arms, 153 : 20
order our f. 483 : 11
when I laid f. of earth, 16 : 28
Founded, earth and heaven f. strong, 691 : 10
government f. on compromise, 373 : 4
he hath f. it upon the seas, 18 : 8
principle on which society not f., 361 : 1
securely f., 395 : 18
upon a rock, 38 : 20
Founder, supinely enjoyed gifts of f., 384 : 1
true f. of civil society, 358 : 9
Foundest me poor, 371 : 1
Founding, Franklin one of f. fathers, 800 : 2
since the f. of the city, 133 : 3
Fount Bandusian more sparkling than glass, 108 : 4

Fount (*continued*)
of joy's delicious springs, 457:2
still from the f., 457:2
Fountain and a shrine, 525:17
choke f. of industry, 451:5
dying of thirst by the f., 148:21
even f. have rest, 561:4
from f. wells up bitter taste, 101:7
like bubble on f., 431:11
of sweet tears, 425:5
pitcher broken at the f., 27:25
returns again to f., 511:4
rise like f. for me, 535:1
that which f. sends forth, 511:4
the f. overflows, 404:4
tormenting image in f., 570:4
troubled like f. stirred, 226:22
woman moved like f. troubled, 189:5
Fountain's silvery column, 435:19
Fountains, Afric's sunny f., 452:8
fraught with tears, 177:1
mountains are f. of men, 637:19
silver f. have mud, 244:14
under f. and graves, 919:3
Fountainside, die of thirst at f., 900:4
Four, age best in f. things, 179:18
and twenty tailors, 931:7
angels to my bed, 294:16
ducks on a pond, 594:3
freedoms, 780:13
grant that twice two not f., 564:8
hands are f., 830:12
horsemen of Apocalypse, 720:18
Horsemen rode again, 773:6
intimate quality of the F., 783:5
lean hounds, 828:10
not f. friends in world, 299:18
snakes gliding, 495:21
spend in prayer, 172:6
things better without, 827:9
things wiser to know, 827:8
two and two make f., 619:3
undergraduates right number, 740:16
venerate f. characters, 386:11
what F. Freedoms establish, 753:6
when angry count f., 624:20
winds of the heaven, 33:29
Fourfold, threefold f. tomb, 265:14
Four-in-hand, fiery f., 438:7
Fours, crawling on all f., 343:16
Fourscore and seven years ago, 523:4
and upward, 235:9
if by reason of strength they be f., 20:13
wind him up for f. years, 303:16
Foursquare in hand and foot, 67:16
to winds that blew, 533:4
Fourteen hundred years ago nailed, 202:22
Fourteenth Amendment not enact Spencer, 644:10
Fourth, born on F. of July, 759:6
create a f. a decent man, 702:10
estate, 472:17, 487:13, 539:15
estate in politics, 445:3
Estate more important than all, 472:*n* 2
generation of them that hate me, 10:5
safe and sane F., 719:1
this is the F., 382:*n* 3, 390:6
what to slave your F. of July, 556:5
Fowl, dominion over f. of the air, 6:15
Fowl (*continued*)
elegant f., 550:8
fish flesh or f., 714:22
Fowler, snare of the f., 20:16
Fowls, May comen I here f. synge, 145:10
of air draw us to kingdom, 126:15
of the air shall tell, 15:29
of the air sow not, 38:2
small f. flew screaming, 571:9
Fox, Aesop's f., 258:12
be f. to recognize traps, 154:1
Brer F. he lay low, 662:6
crazy like a f., 861:9
false as f. to lamb, 226:15
from lair in morning, 474:19
has many tricks, 62:*n* 1
knows many things, 62:2
may f. build on hearthstone, 735:*n* 1
prince imitate f. and lion, 154:1
prince must know how to play f., 119:*n* 13
quick brown f., 923:2
says they are not ripe, 66:*n* 1
sleep in earth like tired f., 839:20
to wear arctic f., 799:15
treason trusted like f., 205:6
wings lift him, 901:14
Foxes have holes, 38:23
honored among f., 887:2
little f. that spoil vines, 28:8
Foxey, maxim with F., 547:25
Foxholes, no atheists in f., 857:17
no white or colored signs in f., 891:13
Fox's, patch lion's skin with f., 119:24
Frabjous day, 612:18
Fractions, happiness made of f., 438:8
there are no f., 832:9
Fragile but with more vitality, 733:17
dewdrop on perilous way, 475:10
profound and f. lips, 829:7
Fragment, ship f. detached, 683:4
truth f. by f., 858:10
Fragmentary blue, 748:1
Fragments, broken dishonored f., 450:15
death tramples it to f., 469:16
gather up f., 44:40
live in f. no longer, 764:9
of the f. twelve baskets, 39:25
shored against ruins, 805:14
Fragrance, as metal keeps f., 750:4
jar will keep f., 447:*n* 1
no spicy f. while they grow, 180:*n* 2
perfect flower without f., 711:15
tobacco's f. greet, 900:5
Fragrant, air so f., 150:13
bodice, 476:17
centuries loaded f., 499:1
in your f. bosom dies, 271:21
most f. when crushed, 180:8
portals, 767:16
thousand f. posies, 183:10
Frail gaunt and small, 641:12
inhabits our f. blood, 214:26
may be f. its roof shake, 351:7
renown is fleeting and f., 102:22
so f. a thing man, 320:11
that I may know how f. I am, 19:1
to f. mortality trust, 181:18
Frailties from dread abode, 362:19
Frailty, in f. consider last day, 74:7
more flesh therefore more f., 204:27
noblest f. of mind, 313:19
Frailty (*continued*)
of the mind, 324:17
tempt f. of our powers, 227:1
thy name is woman, 218:9
Frame, all human f. requires, 730:8
heavens a shining f., 325:8
I f. no hypotheses, 313:11
mind mingles with whole f., 105:22
of adamant, 351:18
of Nature break, 325:11
out of three sounds f. star, 544:3
quit this mortal f., 333:23
stirs this mortal f., 435:20
this goodly f. earth, 220:28
this universal f. began, 305:9
thy fearful symmetry, 405:7
universal f. without mind, 180:16
Framed her last best work, 410:16
in prodigality of nature, 187:4
Nature hath f. strange fellows, 197:26
nature that f. us, 183:6
speech finely f., 36:18
to make women false, 230:5
Framers, wisdom of f. of treaty, 706:18
Français, je parle f. aux hommes, 143:*n* 10
France a person, 483:18
best colony of F., 593:2
breasts that feed F., 178:9
conquered for civilization, 592:6
despotism tempered by epigrams, 473:11
fair stood wind for F., 182:14
fight in F. and on seas, 744:2
forward sons of F., 415:*n* 1
get out of F. quickly, 360:*n* 5
has more need of me, 420:11
has not lost the war, 815:7
is invaded, 420:12
King of F. went up hill, 929:15
labor of F. poured earnings into Versailles, 592:10
landing on coast of F., 815:12
let sword of F. fall, 815:8
nearer is to F., 612:9
never go to F., 485:11
not France without greatness, 815:10
one illusion F., 783:3
one of radiant splendors of F., 504:*n* 4
order matter better in F., 360:21
Puritan born in F., 597:12
respect for art in F., 645:8
save squadron honor F., 545:15
shall F. remain here, 592:9
son of F. lack statue, 725:16
Francesca di Rimini miminy piminy, 628:11
Franchise, women to secure elective f., 554:5
Frank, friendly and f., 538:3
if heart just f. kindly, 298:1
to all beside, 335:18
Frankie and Johnny, 923:8
Frankincense, gold and f., 36:21
Franklin, before F. took hint, 750:5
Benjamin F. Printer, 346:15
one of founding fathers, 800:2
Franklin's quiet memory, 462:15
Frankly I don't give a damn, 848:*n* 3
Frantic among thy servants, 35:3
boast foolish word, 709:20

Frantic (*continued*)
fascination f., 629:17
lover all as f., 197:12
when religion f., 570:8
with f. pain, 402:15
Frantic-mad with evermore unrest, 246:6
Fraternity, liberty equality f., 928:2
of henpecked, 327:2
of strangers, 492:4
or death, 386:*n* 2
Fraternize, beckon you to f., 869:6
Fraud, force or f., 616:2
pious f., 385:6
Frauds, pious f. of friendship, 350:1
Fraught, swell bosom with thy f., 231:17
Fray, all our great f. forgiven, 235:*n* 1
back from the dread f., 57:29
latter end of f., 204:36
Frayed, poor wings so f., 634:10
Freak, wanton f., 475:2
Freakish youth, 376:23
Freckled, whatever is fickle, f., 656:5
Freckles, love curiosity f. doubt, 827:9
Frederick, spires of F. stand, 513:17
without tyranny, 591:11
Free active individuals, 586:17
agent you were before, 125:12
alchemized and f. of space, 475:20
all men born f., 282:13
all men should be f., 524:8
and easy on raft, 624:1
and independent states, 378:12, 381:6
and loyal subjects, 920:8
artless and f. with all they possess, 151:4
as inalienable as f. speech, 795:9
as Nature first made man, 303:8
as the breeze, 429:16
as the road, 268:21
assure freedom to f., 522:12
at last, 935:22
be f. all worthy spirits, 178:5
be f. artist and nothing else, 695:2
beautiful and f. is life, 467:10
because equally f. absolutely equal, 88:8
best things in life f., 825:7
born f., 282:13, 814:20
born f. and equal, 387:*n* 4
but I was f. born, 46:26
colonies are and ought to be f., 381:6
communication in f. society, 789:5
dark clear moving f., 878:7
days have been wondrous f., 329:13
destiny alike for f. and enslaved, 71:15
die to make men f., 566:5
encounter, 282:5
evening calm and f., 425:16
exercise of religion, 383:6, 391:14
feel as if f., 650:4
fight to set country f., 384:19
fighters free lovers, 726:2
fixed fate f. will, 284:19
flag that makes you f., 614:14
for irreligion, 821:10
for religion, 821:10
form not assure freedom, 769:13
frae monie a blunder f. us, 409:8
Free (*continued*)
freedmen not really f., 800:9
from all meaning, 304:17
from hope and fear set f., 633:22
from troublous sights f., 721:8
furrows followed f., 434:13
go home to my Lord and be f., 936:4
God wills us f., 385:14
government f. to people, 314:10
government which kept us f., 388:17
habit shackle for f., 647:12
hair as f., 255:18
half slave half f., 520:4
headstone said f. at last, 915:18
healthy f. world before me, 575:9
her looks were f., 434:19
himself from God not f., 493:18
his half-regained Eurydice, 278:8
holiday-rejoicing spirit, 442:2
hungry man not f., 851:11
I am f. man, 872:7
if there be name more f., 335:2
if we wish to be f., 383:4
in historical sense not f., 602:3
in my soul am f., 296:4
in whatever form used, 769:13
Indian f. in Nature, 557:4
Jesu set me f., 167:3
land in beloved home, 578:12
land of the f., 446:1, 815:2
let me gang f., 432:15
like spirit animating universe, 482:11
live hair shining and f., 796:16
love Virtue she alone is f., 280:5
lovely little flower is f., 429:12
maids that weave thread, 214:3
majestic f., 425:23
man abide with honor, 558:6
man f. to do evil as good, 631:5
man is born f., 358:12
man is created f., 413:2
me from this turbulent priest, 137:9
men by nature equally f., 367:4
men citizens of Berlin, 891:14
monk with heart set f., 73:4
mother of the f., 698:12
my lines and life are f., 268:21
nation ignorant and f., 389:11
nations and free men, 891:5
neither bond nor f., 50:12
no one f. till all f., 579:10
not all f. who scorn chains, 374:17
not f. from faults, 333:22
not happy unless f., 464:10
nothin' ain't worth nothin' but it's f., 913:10
nothing-withholding and f., 651:8
now f. I once more weave, 486:8
only educated are f., 121:11
open mind f. discussion, 737:8
open-minded adjustment, 682:14
ourselves subdue our masters, 392:9
play of mind a pleasure, 586:23
political discussion, 700:3
press good or bad, 882:11
press necessity, 814:1
principle of f. thought, 645:11
principles of f. constitution lost, 383:8
private enterprise, 780:7
protection of f. speech, 644:23
pure in life f. from sin, 107:11
reason left f. to combat, 388:16
Free (*continued*)
Russian speech, 564:9
search for truth, 774:8
set bodily f. from surroundings, 755:6
set my poor heart f., 229:*n* 1
should himself be f., 356:*n* 9
so f. we seem so fettered are, 542:23
society, 890:8
soil free men, 922:2
solitude unsponsored f., 767:4
soul in prison I am not f., 676:18
speech in repulsive form, 746:6
speech press assembly, 700:3
spontaneous cooperation of f., people, 682:17
suppression of f. speech, 677:13
take away our f. will and glory, 154:6
that anchor and chain, 93:3
that moment they are f., 376:20
the human will, 340:2
thenceforward and forever f., 522:8
think they ought to be f., 372:8
thou art f., 584:9
though thrall, 171:13
thought, 645:11
thought is f., 248:8
thus so cleanly I myself can f., 182:16
to become themselves, 898:7
to choose government, 824:12
to go very slow, 750:12
to regulate industry, 389:1
to think speak write, 390:2
trade in ideas, 645:1
trade not a principle, 501:12
trade unpopular, 487:5
truth shall make you f., 45:5
unreproved pleasures f., 277:22
walk f., 576:12
was he f. was he happy, 869:3
we gotta be f., 842:7
we must be f. or die, 426:1
we were born f., 814:20
we will die f. men, 393:9
when actions are from personality, 688:7
when evils most f., 215:19
who would be f. strike blow, 457:8
wish all men everywhere f., 522:7
women growing more f., 695:14
woods more f. from peril, 210:23
world, 862:20
yearning to breathe f., 664:10
Freed, elemental force f., 809:22
no man's pie f. from his finger, 248:20
Freedmen not really free, 800:9
Freedom, abridging f. of speech, 391:14
abridgment of f., 398:4
African conditioned to f., 818:14
all solace to man gives, 143:9
all who love f., 815:12
altar of f., 524:4
and constraint, 849:5
and democracy as principles, 862:19
and not servitude, 373:3
assure f. to the free, 522:12
based on courage, 741:3
battle cry of f., 578:13
behavioristic f., 762:4
Bill of Rights guarantee of f., 788:13
born to f., 780:14

Freedom (*continued*)
born to give you your name F., 832 : 4
cannot surrender f., 820 : 12
capitalism condition for political f., 880 : 12
cause of f. cause of God, 415 : 4
chance to be better, 882 : 11
competition afford f. to individual, 790 : 3
crown Greece with f., 67 : 20
cultural f., 757 : 17
cure is f., 487 : 11
death is slave's f., 915 : 18
deny f. to others, 521 : 1
deny participation of f., 373 : 6
deprived of f. by authorities, 820 : 15
deserving of f. and life, 396 : 25
drawing f. and peace, 462 : 15
economic f., 757 : 17
equality justice, 725 : 20
every man who lives without f., 863 : 7
fight for f. and truth, 599 : 20
fight to maintain f., 780 : 14
fills space 'twixt marsh, 651 : 9
flame of f. in souls, 643 : 1
for all poor workers, 820 : 9
for something, 789 : 5
for thought we hate, 645 : 11
free form not assure f., 769 : 13
free press without f. bad, 882 : 11
from ambition condition for happiness, 882 : 12
from every B.V.D. f. ring, 828 : 17
from fear, 780 : 13, 781 : 8
from mountain height, 474 : 18
from prejudice, 589 : 6
from something not enough, 789 : 5
from violence and lies, 695 : 3
from want, 780 : 13, 781 : 8
generous with our f., 824 : 12
greater f. for average man, 779 : 13
greatest gift f. of will, 142 : 12
gret Press's f., 568 : 1
has a thousand charms, 375 : 19
having my f. boast of nothing, 194 : 4
history progress of f., 422 : 12
hunted round the globe, 384 : 12
idea of f., 537 : 15
if f. fail, 495 : 10
if f. fall, 710 : 24
if I have f. in my love, 296 : 4
in economic arrangements, 880 : 11
in highest position least f., 102 : 27
in that f. bold, 429 : 12
indispensable condition of f., 730 : 17
indivisible word, 824 : 10
infringement of human f., 412 : 4
intellectual delight and f., 420 : 3
is a breakfastfood, 829 : 16
is the prize, 418 : 4
law can only bring f., 397 : 1
let f. ring, 514 : 12
liberal institutions enemies of f., 658 : 12
liberty f. enfranchisement, 216 : 6
light in which f. lives, 851 : 10
lose f. if value something more, 751 : 20
love f. hate slavery, 881 : 13
love not f. but license, 282 : 12
means to enable press, 789 : 5
nation which enjoys most f., 418 : 3

Freedom (*continued*)
new birth of f., 523 : 4
no f. of thought without doubt, 859 : 3
none love f. but good men, 282 : 12
not conceived simply, 905 : 2
not safety but opportunity, 789 : 5
not trifled with, 820 : 12
obedience bane of f., 466 : 7
obtained with price, 814 : 20
of expression matrix, 730 : 17
of free men, 915 : 18
of f. he only is deserving, 396 : 25
of knyghthod and of f. flour, 148 : 5
of my mind, 279 : 29
of navigation, 682 : 14
of person, 389 : 2
of press, 389 : 2
of press bulwark of liberty, 367 : 6
of press has suffered most, 882 : 10
of religion, 389 : 2
of speech and conscience, 625 : 9
of speech and expression, 780 : 13
of speech may be taken, 379 : 6
of speech means, 794 : 18
of the mind, 815 : 3
of the soul, 296 : *n* 3
of thought, 365 : 5
of worship, 780 : 13
oh f. over me, 936 : 4
on mountains is f., 413 : 30
only to limits of consciousness, 755 : 1
people f. light, 817 : 6
political f., 757 : 17
political f. business of government, 779 : 16
power in defense of f., 904 : 17
preserved f. for themselves, 800 : 6
reap blessings of f., 384 : 17
regardless of form, 769 : 13
religious f., 757 : 17
Revolution not to obtain f., 800 : 7
rhymes suggest wildest f., 495 : 22
safeguards of individual f., 844 : 9
secret of f. a brave heart, 81 : 5
secret of happiness, 81 : 5
seven-pillared house, 810 : 2
shall awhile repair, 364 : 9
shrieked as Kosciusko fell, 443 : 5
slaves fought for f., 490 : 18
so celestial article as f., 384 : 13
spirit of truth and f., 599 : 8
striking blow for f., 798 : 6
stumped toe, 855 : 4
system based on courage, 741 : 3
system of private property guaranty of f., 844 : 3
those who profess to favor f., 556 : 4
to speak, 567 : 17
to think, 567 : 17
to worship God, 470 : 16
unchartered f. tires, 427 : 14
values anything more than f., 751 : 20
versus tyranny, 866 : 9
wars which usurp standard of f., 418 : 2
wealth and f. reign, 368 : 16
whose service is perfect f., 55 : 4
wish life be pure f., 870 : 8
with great sum obtained f., 46 : 26
without f. press bad, 882 : 11
yet F. yet thy banner, 458 : 17
Freedom's, bled in f. cause, 422 : 21

Freedom's (*continued*)
holy light, 514 : 13
just another word, 913 : 10
Freedoms, four f., 780 : 13
insensible to f. of Constitution, 776 : 13
what Four F. establish, 753 : 6
Freeloader confirmed guest, 787 : 3
Freely, different schools contend f., 826 : 12
give, 38 : 34
lives at ease that f. lives, 143 : 9
offer itself to you, 786 : 3
possession prevents living f., 738 : 2
serve because we freely love, 286 : 20
show f. your worst trait, 503 : 14
too dear for what's given f., 246 : 8
ye have received, 38 : 34
Freeman contending for liberty, 379 : 1
no f. taken except by legal judgment, 139 : 2
slave patrician plebeian, 563 : 3
Freemen, Americans f. or slaves, 379 : 2
nation of f., 519 : 22
who rules o'er f., 356 : *n* 9
Freer, nowhere is speech f., 746 : 6
Frees her slave again, 919 : 19
one word f. us, 75 : 14
Freethinking of one age, 589 : 1
Freeze, mountaintops that f., 248 : 29
thy young blood, 219 : 18
Freezes, till hell f. over, 925 : 7
Freight, nation's f. handler, 761 : 4
proportioned to groove, 608 : 5
Freiheit, nur der verdient sich F., 396 : *n* 9
Frémont, free speech F., 922 : 2
French, believe only in F. culture, 658 : 21
best F. novel in language, 892 : 11
for converse with friends, 357 : 19
for fiddle-de-dee, 613 : 19
for suppressing one, 586 : 21
gone to fight the F., 415 : 16
hinges in F. conversation, 360 : 23
I speak F. to men, 143 : 16
new F. books, 543 : 7
of Parys to hir unknowe, 145 : 18
on F. coast light gleams, 587 : 13
only accidentally F., 341 : 10
or Turk or Proosian, 627 : 18
phrase for hotel guests, 725 : 18
Radicals and German police spies, 563 : 2
Revolution began at top, 593 : 1
soldier carries marshal's baton, 421 : 5
spake ful faire and fetisly, 145 : 18
speak F. when can't think of English, 612 : 22
sprightliness of F., 357 : 19
stormed Ratisbon, 540 : 20
struggle of F. soldiers, 602 : 1
true German can't stand F., 396 : 16
what is not clear is not F., 400 : 4
word impossible not F., 420 : 10
Frenchman, embrace Pole as F., 166 : 2
first man then a F., 341 : 10
I praise the F., 376 : 11
in Academy, 354 : *n* 4
must be always talking, 356 : 14
Frenchmen, did march three F., 207 : 23
Englishman beat three F., 326 : 22

Frenchmen (*continued*)
fifty million F., 924 : 12
mankind including F., 783 : 3
Frenzied drum, 714 : 14
rush of our lawlessness, 582 : 12
Frenzy, demoniac f., 287 : 29
eye in fine f. rolling, 197 : 12
not shaken from resolve by f., 107 : 28
of his fellow citizens, 107 : 28
old man's f., 717 : 10
Frequent, eagerly f. doctor, 516 : 16
more f. use of any organ, 393 : 7
practicer of angling, 270 : 34
Frère, hypocrite lecteur mon f., 580 : 16
mon semblable mon f., 580 : *n* 4
sois mon f. ou je te tue, 386 : *n* 2
Fresh as a bridegroom, 203 : 7
as a lark, 428 : 2
as month of May, 145 : 15
as paint, 564 : 1
complexion and heart together, 247 : 3
dews of night, 280 : 10
from brawling courts, 532 : 18
heavens f. and strong, 427 : 16
how quick and f. art thou, 213 : 8
makes not f. again, 260 : 19
perfection in beloved, 453 : 8
sae f. and fair, 409 : 24
streams meet in salt sea, 207 : 8
suspicions, 231 : 2
transfigurings of blue, 767 : 14
waste not f. tears, 77 : 15
welcome faire f. May, 146 : 19
woods and pastures new, 281 : 6
world as f. as at first day, 595 : 11
Freshest blue, 767 : 14
Freshness, glory and f. of a dream, 426 : 10
poem forever keep f., 750 : 4
Fret, I should worry and f., 760 : 1
living we f., 545 : 24
nuns f. not, 427 : 28
of existence, 848 : 7
passage through it, 276 : 15
thy soul with crosses, 174 : 11
weariness fever f., 476 : 24
Fretful, quills upon f. porpentine, 219 : 18
Frets doubt maw-crammed beast, 544 : 9
struts and f. his hour, 240 : 4
Fretted the pygmy body to decay, 303 : 20
vault, 362 : 4
with golden fire, 220 : 28
your impatience so much f., 355 : 3
Freud, ideas of F., 698 : 4
Freude, Kraft durch F., 816 : *n* 3
Friar of orders gray, 188 : 37, 917 : 19
there was wantowne and merye, 145 : 22
Friars, barefoot f. singing vespers, 384 : 7
Fribsbi, fatal man Madame F., 539 : 13
Friday, call this F. good, 807 : 20
my dear Friday, 878 : 18
my man F., 318 : 15
worse on F., 932 : 11
Friday's child, 932 : 10
Friend, absolutely unselfish f. is dog, 609 : 4
all he wished a f., 362 : 18
ascend prosperity not meet f., 625 : 14
Friend (*continued*)
at least one f. left, 524 : 3
await felicity or doom, 608 : 4
be a f. of man, 685 : 12
best mirror an old f. 269 : 29
bosom f. of sun, 477 : 17
bring death to a f., 74 : 15
cannot be known, 35 : 23
choose author as choose f., 309 : 8
death of f. make man look sad, 197 : 19
defend your departed f., 306 : 9
diamonds girl's best f., 848 : 16
do a f. service, 73 : 14
do you hear, 928 : *n* 2
dog the firmest f., 456 : 10
down inside me, 524 : 3
each f. a world, 858 : 6
evening criminal's f., 581 : 2
every man will be thy f., 257 : 8
faithful are wounds of f., 25 : 23
favorite has no f., 361 : 16
forsake not old f., 35 : 15
found song in heart of f., 510 : 25
from morn to night my f., 608 : 10
good f. for Jesus' sake, 250 : 1
good wine a f. or being dry, 315 : 13
grant f. in my retreat, 376 : 11
guide philosopher and f., 338 : 3, 773 : 14
had not f. nor toy, 568 : 20
happy house shelters f., 497 : 17
heaven save from foolish f., 420 : 5
honor f. who prospered, 71 : 7
house to lodge f., 339 : 10
I was angry with my f., 405 : 13
idleness sorrow f. foe, 827 : 8
if I had a f. that loved her, 229 : 31
if thou wouldest get a f., 35 : 8
imperial f., 606 : 3
in need, 94 : 3
in need nor bottle, 548 : 18
in power friend lost, 634 : 22
is a second self, 99 : 7
is medicine of life, 35 : 10
is strong defense, 35 : 9
keep thy f. under own key, 227 : 9
keep tonge and keep f., 148 : 7
knolling departing f., 205 : 20
lack of intimate f., 4 : 7
left exposed a f., 606 : 9
little f. of all world, 709 : 22
loan loses itself and f., 219 : 2
long sought with difficulty kept, 127 : 7
lost every other f., 524 : 3
lost more than a f., 786 : *n* 4
lost no f., 336 : 5
makes no f. never made foe, 534 : 16
man's best f. dog, 609 : *n* 1
masterpiece of nature, 497 : 19
murderer somebody's old f., 817 : 13
my f. judge not me, 171 : 18
my God my Father and F., 309 : 11
'neath every one a f., 569 : 3
ne'er said till f. dead, 660 : 7
never find a f., 714 : 15
never known till need, 160 : 19
never want f. in need, 548 : 18
new f. fit to make old, 664 : 4
new f. is as new wine, 35 : 15
no f. in misery, 257 : 8
no f. like sister, 608 : 16
no man useless who has f., 669 : 13
Friend (*continued*)
nor f. to know me, 669 : 2
not a f. to close eyes, 306 : 18
not ashamed to defend a f., 35 : 35
of every country but own, 422 : 3
of friendless name the f., 356 : 24
of my better days, 464 : 11
of Pleasure, 364 : 16
one chained f., 468 : 21
one f. in lifetime much, 635 : 9
person with whom sincere, 497 : 18
poesy should be f., 475 : 13
save me from candid f., 422 : 5
say Welcome f., 292 : 9
sharpeneth countenance of his f., 25 : 26
should bear friend's infirmities, 217 : 3
single soul in two bodies, 87 : 1
so great poet so good f., 306 : 24
soul of f. we've made, 698 : 16
statesman yet f. to truth, 336 : 5
stoop to become f., 711 : 10
support f. oppose foe, 890 : 7
supports whom Fortune crushes, 118 : 11
suspicious f., 338 : 14
that sticketh closer than a brother, 24 : 23
think on thee dear f., 244 : 12
this is my f., 28 : 16
thou not my f., 493 : 12
time a kind f., 787 : 6
to get news to you, 625 : 16
to have f. be one, 497 : 21
to her foe, 418 : 14
to human race, 57 : *n* 8
to me fair f. never old, 245 : 11
to public amusements, 355 : 1
treat f. as if he might become enemy, 111 : 8
truest f. that bestrad horse, 149 : 20
weak man better enemy than f., 561 : 14
well-chosen book or f., 250 : 15
what is a f., 91 : 18
wildly striking sometimes a f., 268 : 7
without treachery, 591 : 11
worst f. and enemy Death, 797 : 3
Friendless, assist feeble and f., 380 : 6
bodies of unburied men, 262 : 3
of every f. name friend, 356 : 24
omnipotent but f., 467 : 4
Friendliness, herein f. hardiness love, 149 : 5
Friendly and charming relationship, 156 : 7
and frank, 538 : 3
bust, 804 : 23
cow red and white, 668 : 13
hath friends must show himself f., 24 : 23
in difficult are f. forces, 756 : 13
mingles with f. bowl, 339 : 8
open and f. in private, 80 : 17
social f. honest man, 409 : 2
universe not hostile nor f., 764 : 16
Friend's, bear his f. infirmities, 217 : 3
debauch f. wife genteelly, 355 : 13
Friends absent speak, 254 : 4
adieu kind f., 922 : 13
adversity tries f., 112 : 10
age leaves f. and wine, 447 : 9
all thy f. lapped in lead, 257 : 7

Friends (*continued*)
are exultations, 425 : 21
be warned by me, 730 : 8
become bitter enemies, 258 : 9
behave as we wish f. to behave, 87 : 3
better f. not be knowing, 823 : 3
book f. talk to me, 771 : 1
born not made, 634 : 21
call that backing your f., 203 : 29
death of f. inspire us, 558 : 13
deepening fidelity with f., 299 : 11
defend me from f., 422 : *n* 2
die adoring God loving f., 344 : 12
distresses of our f., 294 : *n* 4
do with f. as books, 497 : 22
enemies in war in peace f., 387 : 10
enough now for death, 857 : 3
ever best of f., 549 : 26
faithful f. hard to find, 257 : 8
falling out of faithful f., 96 : *n* 6
few f. and many books, 295 : 4
forget love to f. and brethren, 34 : 2
forsake me like memory, 470 : 8
French for converse with f., 357 : 19
gain f. for when we awaken, 273 : 3
get by with help from f., 914 : 11
golden f. I had, 691 : 13
good book best of f., 538 : 2
has thousand f. not friend to spare, 130 : 8
have all in common, 83 : 8
have no place in graveyard, 558 : 13
he cast off his f., 371 : 19
he that repeateth a matter separateth f., 24 : 15
held up of his f., 35 : 27
his truth proclaim, 304 : 6
honor truth above f., 87 : 14
humblest f., 429 : 11
if your f. are sore, 339 : 13
in thirties want f., 835 : 16
joy to their f., 59 : 28
just f. and brave enemies, 389 : 3
kindred days, 494 : 10
laugh at your f., 339 : 13
lay down life for f., 45 : 25
leave f. and go, 691 : 15
live without f., 609 : 13
look with love as f., 309 : 17
made fortune send for f., 82 : 23
make your world, 649 : 20
makes f. without trying, 739 : 8
man that hath f., 24 : 23
manic dust of f., 864 : 13
misfortune of our f., 294 : 11
misfortune shows who really f., 88 : 20
multitude of f., 255 : 11
my glory was I had such f., 717 : 15
nature teaches beasts to know f., 242 : 11
nearest f. can go, 747 : 9
never f. with roses, 633 : 3
no one would choose to live without f., 87 : 20
not be four f. in world, 299 : 18
not equal to yourself, 68 : 6
obsequiousness begets f., 96 : 2
of my youth where are they, 132 : 28
of today unlovable, 4 : 5
old f. always best, 664 : 4
old f. are best, 179 : *n* 4
old f. times manners, 371 : 3

Friends (*continued*)
old f. to trust, 179 : 18
ornament of house f., 499 : 15
ought to forgive our f., 179 : 19
part of self, 648 : 17
people people have for f., 696 : 1
power in hands of f., 635 : 16
preachers politicians f., 392 : 10
precious all things from f., 92 : 16
prosperity makes f., 112 : 10
Romans countrymen, 216 : 17
Scots f. to England, 177 : 16
second glass for my f., 326 : 18
secure f. by doing favors, 81 : 3
secure you count many f., 113 : 28
see f. and read books, 338 : 16
servant of parted f., 617 : *n* 3
share all things, 65 : 11
shifts of fortune test f., 99 : 6
soul remembering my good f., 194 : 19
spare to us our f., 669 : 17
state not know f. from foes, 558 : 7
strive mightily eat as f., 188 : 29
that have it I do wrong, 713 : 4
those f. thou hast, 218 : 30
three faithful f., 347 : 17
three f. hardly possible, 635 : 9
thrust away by his f., 35 : 27
to congratulate made haste, 305 : 5
to have advanced f., 585 : 11
trencher f., 243 : 5
troops of f., 239 : 31
two f. in lifetime many, 635 : 9
tyranny's disease to trust no f., 70 : 24
warm with f. I make, 823 : 3
we are not enemies but f., 521 : 14
we choose our f., 385 : 12
we love so dear, 618 : 1
wealth maketh many f., 24 : 24
were poor but honest, 227 : 12
what became of f. I loved so, 139 : 7
who go with the wind, 139 : 8
who no longer know how to die, 849 : 15
who plow sea, 628 : 4
wife and children afraid, 274 : 12
win f. and influence people, 803 : 4
without three good f., 212 : 1
women find few f., 357 : 7
wounded in house of my f., 33 : 35
wretched have no f., 303 : 12
you and I long f., 348 : 7
Friendship, author demands your f., 442 : 13
boughten f., 749 : 1
commerce between equals, 369 : 25
constant save in love, 209 : 9
crown is love and f., 475 : 21
elegance of female f., 352 : 20
Faded, 752 : 11
from wine sudden f., 331 : 19
hardly ever brings money, 440 : 28
herein f. cowardice murder, 149 : 5
highest kind of f., 889 : 1
holy passion of f., 624 : 17
in appearance at f. with me, 310 : 15
in f. but faithless haven, 73 : 14
in f. false, 304 : 3
is the strongest, 657 : 6
keep f. in repair, 354 : 4
last lifetime unless asked for money, 624 : 17
let f. die, 356 : 25

Friendship (*continued*)
like and dislike same things is f., 102 : 26
love f. charity, 226 : 20
love without wings, 456 : 6
moment when f. formed, 385 : 17
needs no reason, 65 : 16
needs parallelism of life, 635 : 9
of the many, 619 : 4
only solitary know joys of f., 739 : 6
out of f. cheat others, 734 : 8
paltry f. of man, 526 : 6
peace and honest f., 389 : 2
pious frauds of f., 350 : 1
rural quiet f. books, 345 : 12
sacrifices of f., 731 : 17
sets f. above public welfare, 74 : 10
sheltering tree, 436 : 8
sounds too cold, 447 : 11
swear an eternal f., 298 : 10
that can cease never real, 127 : 9
three classes of f. and enmity, 124 : 4
time strengthens f., 315 : 6
true f. never serene, 301 : 7
two chairs for f., 560 : 4
wing of f. never moults, 547 : 20
with a man, 89 : 17
Friendship's, true f. laws, 334 : 23
Friendships, for f. won by awards not real, 153 : 24
from bad beginning great f., 96 : 23
invalidated by marriage, 620 : 15
keep f. in repair, 354 : *n* 3
Frieze, no jutty f. buttress, 236 : 21
Frigate, no f. like book, 607 : 4
Fright, power of f. and lust, 833 : 6
we felt for creation's sake, 900 : 9
Frighted, sleep I have f. thee, 206 : 17
the reign of Chaos, 283 : 21
Frighten, don't do it and f. horses, 706 : 16
mountain cannot f. one born on it, 413 : 31
Frightened, crept like f. girl, 674 : 15
don't be f. it won't last, 705 : 9
little mouse under chair, 932 : 8
Miss Muffet away, 932 : 15
out of fear, 241 : 13
to death, 500 : 23
went with f. eye, 593 : 4
Frightening when convinced they are right, 867 : 16
Frightful fiend, 435 : 3
vice a monster of f. mien, 337 : 5
Frights, it f. the isle, 230 : 20
Frigid, beat down f. Rome, 717 : 4
Fringe, lunatic f., 687 : 18
Fringed curtains of thine eye, 247 : 22
Fringes be falling rain, 928 : 14
Frippery, a little f. necessary, 393 : 1
Frisk i' the sun, 246 : 10
Frisson nouveau, 491 : *n* 8
Fritter my wig, 613 : 21
Frittered away by detail, 559 : 26
Frittering away his age, 432 : 25
Frivolous, one who is f. all day, 3 : 10
work of polished idleness, 416 : 15
Frizzled stale and small, 892 : 19
Fro, going to and f. in the earth, 15 : 2
many shall run to and f., 33 : 6
reel to and f., 21 : 16
Frocks and curls, 606 : 7
Frog, better'n any other f., 622 : 1
eye of newt toe of f., 239 : 5

Frog (*continued*)
has drink enough to spare, 92 : 15
how public like a f., 604 : 19
leaping in, 314 : 7
on log expiring f., 546 : 14
outjump any f., 621 : 18
thus use your f., 271 : 11
would a-wooing go, 929 : 12
Frog's life is most jolly, 92 : 15
spawning islands like f. eggs, 878 : 17
Frogs die in earnest, 92 : 9
drone their lament, 104 : 1
eat butterflies, 767 : 8
in the marsh mud, 104 : 1
Frog-spawn of ditch, 716 : 2
Frolic architecture of snow, 493 : 23
wine, 266 : 17
Front, all quiet on Western f., 839 : 9
cannon in f., 533 : 13
of Jove himself, 223 : 3
of this small floor, 292 : 20
only essential facts, 559 : 25
see f. o' battle lower, 411 : 15
smoothed his wrinkled f., 186 : 30
Frontier from Atlantic to Pacific, 743 : 16
grave far away, 700 : 7
New F., 890 : 5
no defensible f., 878 : 1
of my Person goes, 869 : 6
science endless f., 814 : 9
Frontiers, aggression outside f., 781 : 9
wherever man fronts fact, 558 : 17
Frost, curdied by f. from snow, 242 : 23
fell death's untimely f., 410 : 19
is on the punkin, 665 : 14
it was not f., 605 : 16
itself doth burn, 223 : 5
love in the f., 886 : 15
not night kills but f., 705 : 21
performs secret ministry, 435 : 14
prime of youth a f. of cares, 177 : 10
six weeks to f., 816 : 14
snow congealed with biting f., 59 : *n* 5
third day comes a f., 249 : 3
was specter-gray, 641 : 11
which binds so dear head, 468 : 22
Frosted September, 791 : 1
Frosts are slain, 632 : 8
Frosty, blessings on your f. pow, 410 : 7
but kindly, 210 : 30
Caucasus, 194 : 7
wind made moan, 608 : 17
Frothy, hopping through f. waves, 613 : 4
Froward, life like a f. child, 302 : 19
Frowned, critic you have f., 429 : 10
dismal tidings when he f., 370 : 10
fair Science f. not, 362 : 17
Frowning, behind f. providence, 375 : 17
forehead of f. skies, 167 : 8
Frowns o'er wide Rhine, 457 : 25
sits on battlements and f., 416 : 11
Frowsy couch in sorrow steep, 411 : 23
Froze genial current, 362 : 7
me to hear such talk, 623 : 23
Frozen as charity, 439 : 9
carcass of leopard, 845 : 8
children walk on f. toes, 729 : 2
corpse was he, 510 : 5
grass, 476 : 8
milk comes f. home in pail, 191 : 14
music, 396 : 6
Frozen (*continued*)
sea inside us, 786 : 4
toes, 729 : 2
torrid or f. zone, 271 : 22
tunes f. up in horn, 385 : 8
when we are f. within, 587 : 17
which thy f. bosom bears, 229 : *n* 1
wind off f. peak, 748 : 17
Fructify in lives of others, 94 : *n* 9
Frugal, how f. the chariot, 607 : 4
mind, 376 : 14
swain, 366 : 10
wise and f. government, 389 : 1
Frugality, industry and f., 590 : 4
second is f., 65 : 3
Fruit, bound as f. to tree, 591 : 1
bringeth forth his f. in season, 17 : 12
brought forth f., 39 : 15
cease from yielding f., 32 : 11
collections of f., 97 : 12
earth bringeth forth f., 42 : 1
feed on bitter f., 854 : 2
fell like autumn f., 303 : 16
forth reaching to the f. she plucked, 287 : 19
gleaming like f. with evening's gold leaf, 906 : 2
hang like f. my soul, 243 : 30
husbandman waiteth for precious f., 52 : 4
I bore was sun, 120 : *n* 10
its f. sweet its shade delightful, 6 : 4
life f. ripe on plate, 864 : 19
man stole the f., 268 : 12
no f. but untimely grave, 271 : 23
of action not be motive, 94 : 10
of experience, 638 : 12
of her hands, 26 : 10
of loyal nature, 534 : 21
of my branches, 634 : 5
of sense beneath, 333 : 4
of Spirit, 49 : 30
of that forbidden tree, 282 : 22
of the vine, 41 : 10
of thy womb, 42 : 19
plant vineyards and eat the f., 31 : 31
plucking f. of memory, 684 : 7
reach ripest f. of all, 183 : 6
restore with cordial f., 268 : 21
ripest f. first falls, 194 : 17
that can fall without shaking, 341 : 4
that your seasons bring, 124 : 19
tree bringeth not forth f., 36 : 29
tree known by f., 39 : 10
tree whose f. threw death, 254 : 10
weakest f. drops earliest, 200 : 6
Fruited, above f. plain, 688 : 5
Fruitful, be f. and multiply, 6 : 15
error full of seeds, 662 : 21
of golden deeds, 285 : 6
sickle in f. field, 404 : 15
vineyard in a very f. hill, 29 : 3
was she not f., 119 : 23
Fruition, prospects more pleasing than f., 123 : *n* 7
sweet f. of earthly crown, 183 : 6
Fruitless, cold f. moon, 195 : 20
weak and f. words, 524 : 4
wishes, 316 : 15
Fruits, all pleasant f. do flow, 250 : 5
by their f. know them, 38 : 18
Dead Sea f., 447 : 15
descendants shall gather your f., 103 : 19
Fruits (*continued*)
eat his pleasant f., 28 : 14
fairy f. and flowers, 525 : 17
flowers f. and many birds, 150 : 16
green f. of world, 766 : 23
here are f. flowers leaves, 659 : 14
judge but by f., 462 : 10
kindly f. of the earth, 55 : 14
know them by f., 38 : 17
let not f. of action be motive, 94 : 10
no f. no flowers, 485 : 12
of earth are for everyone, 414 : 22
of life and beauty, 404 : 16
of love gone, 462 : 18
outdo what flowers promised, 176 : 18
Fruit-tree, tips with silver f. tops, 192 : 11
Frumious Bandersnatch, 612 : 17
Frustrate ghost, 543 : 15
not f. of his hope, 281 : 14
Fry in own grece, 147 : 8
me or fritter my wig, 613 : 21
Frying, out of f. pan into fire, 126 : 10
Fudge, call old notions f., 569 : 1
two fifths sheer f., 567 : 18
Fudges, merits of Bells and F., 488 : *n* 3
Fuel, adding f. to the flame, 289 : 6
to maintain his fires, 272 : 1
Fugal requiems, 766 : 21
Fugit inreparabile tempus, 104 : *n* 4
Fugitive and cloistered virtue, 282 : 1
from law of averages, 898 : 8
receive the f., 384 : 12
shalt thou be, 7 : 17
what was so f., 426 : 17
Fugue, folly alone stays f. of youth, 153 : 8
Fulfill desires of thy servants, 55 : 8
not to destroy but f., 37 : 6
to f. lusts, 47 : 29
Fulfilled, see f. prophets' warning, 139 : 4
till all be f., 37 : 7
Fulfilling, love is f. of law, 47 : 28
Fulfillment, all men's plans to f., 59 : 2
bring all his words to f., 59 : 4
give each moment f., 756 : 1
Fulfills, God f. in many ways, 534 : 31
great Nature's plan, 409 : 2
Full, age f. of care, 917 : 11
all his beams f. dazzling, 575 : 24
bloody f. of blame, 245 : 23
cause of weeping, 233 : 23
earth is f. of his glory, 29 : 9
earth is f. of thy riches, 21 : 11
fathom five, 247 : 21
hell f. of good intentions, 136 : 11
I am f. of matter, 16 : 22
isle is f. of noises, 248 : 10
little knowest that hast not tried, 174 : 10
man that hath quiver f., 22 : 10
meridian of my glory, 249 : 1
moon throw shadow, 789 : 10
night f. of ugly sights, 187 : 8
not the f. four seasons, 823 : 4
o' beans and benevolence, 500 : 20
o' milk of human kindness, 236 : 16
of artless jealousy, 223 : 20
of direst cruelty, 236 : 17
of few days and f. of trouble, 15 : 33
of grace and truth, 44 : 21
of high sentence, 803 : 17
of number of things, 668 : 14

Full (*continued*)
of quarrels as egg of meat, 193 : 3
of shapes is fancy, 213 : 8
of smiles in early days, 85 : 6
of sound and fury, 240 : 4
of spirit as month of May, 204 : 30
of strange oaths, 211 : 15
of wiles full of guile, 82 : 8
of wise saws, 211 : 15
reading maketh a f. man, 181 : 13
sea is not f., 26 : 12
sea of faith at f., 587 : 16
someone not f. of herself, 916 : 1
speed ahead, 490 : 4
supped f. with horrors, 240 : 3
that your joy may be f., 45 : 28
to be empty is to be f., 64 : 10
too f. for sound or foam, 535 : 19
wasna f. but had plenty, 409 : 17
wheel is come f. circle, 235 : 15
woods are f. of them, 921 : 10
youth f. of pleasance, 917 : 11
Full-blown rose, 476 : 13
Full-dazzling, all his beams f., 575 : 24
Fullness, earth and f. thereof, 18 : 8, 48 : 18
of all things, 58 : 16
of perfection in him, 201 : 16
Full-throated ease, 476 : 22
Full-voiced choir below, 278 : 26
Fully, report news f., 820 : 13
Fulmen, eripuit coelo f., 346 : *n* 5
eripuitque Jovi f., 115 : *n* 12
Fum, fie foh and f., 234 : 13
Fumble with the sheets, 207 : 13
Fume of poppies, 477 : 18
Fun, ain't we got f., 795 : 5
allowed himself f. and relaxation, 78 : 9
animal dead what f., 740 : 6
has the mostest f., 665 : 11
mirth and f. fast furious, 411 : 11
more f. to be with, 855 : 11
nothing more f. than a man, 827 : 15
taken f. where found it, 709 : 9
to match sorrow, 617 : 3
what jolly f., 697 : 1
Function, form follows f., 681 : 22
joy and f. of poetry, 887 : 7
judicial f., 678 : 3
not f. of government, 821 : 9
of citizen, 821 : 9
retain ability to f., 835 : 10
simplest sensory f., 702 : 13
to live is to f., 645 : 12
Functional capacity, 393 : 7
Functions, man in divers f., 207 : 6
which resist death, 429 : 14
Fund of good sense, 390 : 12
Fundamental, art find f., 887 : 14
article of political creed, 382 : 4
human rights, 788 : 20
principle of constitution, 365 : 18
principles of equity, 737 : 3
things apply, 830 : 6
Funeral baked meats, 218 : 14
done and disbanded, 883 : 12
grieve at f., 624 : 18
into silent f., 807 : 17
marches to grave, 509 : 14
mirth in f., 217 : 29
misbehaved once at f., 441 : 13
no f. gloom when I am gone, 95 : *n* 2
nobody's f., 807 : 17
Funeral (*continued*)
not a f. note, 465 : 7
not celebrate f. with weeping, 95 : 2
present at your f., 830 : *n* 2
Fünf was good old five, 901 : *n* 2
Fungus crop of sentiment, 631 : 19
Funny if happening to somebody else, 765 : 17
thing happened on way to forum, 908 : 4
Fur, fierce f. soft to face, 899 : 17
make f. fly, 291 : 11
oh my f. and whiskers, 611 : 7
Furey, churchyard where Michael F. buried, 777 : 16
Furies, I acknowledge the F., 732 : 11
Furious anger, 35 : 18
fancies, 918 : 12
fast and f., 411 : 11
to be frightened out of fear, 241 : 13
vast and f. ocean, 265 : 7
winter blowing, 810 : 17
winter's rages, 243 : 27
wise amazed temperate f., 238 : 8
Furiously, Jehu driveth f., 14 : 18
Furled, battle flags were f., 530 : 1
bright girdle f., 587 : 16
Furlongs, thousand f. of sea, 247 : 8
Furls sails lays him to rest, 570 : 7
Furnace, burning fiery f., 32 : 33
feet as if burned in a f., 52 : 30
heat not f. for foe, 248 : 22
in what f. thy brain, 405 : 8
lover sighing like f., 211 : 15
of affliction, 31 : 6
Furnish forth marriage tables, 218 : 14
means of acquiring knowledge, 418 : 10
you f. pictures I f. war, 702 : 12
you with argument and intellects, 369 : 11
Furnished, live in f. souls, 828 : 14
me from mine own library, 247 : 15
thousand f. rooms, 804 : 3
Furnishes oil for own wheels, 376 : 7
Furniture, don't bump into f., 852 : 4
for man's upper chamber, 519 : 18
no f. charming as books, 432 : 23
science first-rate f., 519 : 18
Furrow, half-reaped f., 477 : 18
Furrowing salt acres heavily, 907 : 2
Furrows followed free, 434 : 13
smite sounding f., 529 : 13
Furs to touch, 796 : 16
Furside is outside, 733 : 16
Further, get a little f. you are too near, 374 : 21
hitherto shalt thou come but no f., 16 : 30
nearer to church f. from God, 159 : 19
Fury, allaying their f., 247 : 20
blind F. with abhorred shears, 280 : 15
civil f. first grew high, 290 : 13
cunning old F., 611 : 6
full of sound and f., 240 : 4
in your words, 232 : 1
like woman scorned, 324 : 16
ne'er spend f. on child, 186 : 25
of disappointed woman, 324 : *n* 7
of patient man, 304 : 16
provides arms, 104 : 20
Queen crimson with f., 612 : 1
slinging flame, 532 : 6
Fury (*continued*)
stronger than afterthoughts, 76 : 18
trample them in my f., 31 : 26
Fuse, through green f. drives flower, 886 : 12
with Jacob's mystic heart, 572 : 5
Fuss, Old F. 'n Feathers, 455 : *n* 4
Fust in us unused, 223 : 17
Fustest, git thar f. with mostest, 583 : *n* 7
Fustian's so sublimely bad, 338 : 13
Fustilarian, you rampallian you f., 206 : 10
Futility, fatal f. of fact, 653 : 14
utility of f., 90 : 4
Future a mince pie, 846 : 13
aid to interpretation of f., 80 : 15
all concerned about f., 757 : 10
all f. in mind of man, 683 : 17
always says Not yet, 886 : 3
America was past not f., 784 : 16
as past would be present, 397 : 17
been into f. and it works, 719 : 7
cannot fight f., 517 : 18
cure the hungry f., 894 : 7
democracy shuts past opens f., 506 : 8
dipped into the f., 529 : 24
divine sign indicates f., 79 : 4
door opens and lets f. in, 859 : 6
education will determine f. life, 84 : 13
enters into us, 756 : 7
find we have lost f., 744 : 3
flight of f. days, 284 : 12
hope to world for f., 521 : 8
hopes of the f., 745 : 11
imagining f. years come, 714 : 14
in f. everyone world-famous, 908 : 1
in f. light will shine, 745 : 8
instruct as to f., 480 : 8
lays down law of today, 657 : 7
lively sense of f. favors, 293 : *n* 6
loses past and dead for f., 77 : 22
meet f. without fear, 510 : 2
most in league with f., 599 : 17
net nailed on futureless f., 894 : 4
never plan f. by past, 374 : 4
no way of judging f., 383 : 2
not think about f., 723 : 6
O f. Vigor, 673 : 19
of human race, 758 : 8
of mankind waiting, 912 : 4
optimistic f. of mankind, 678 : 12
paradise of f. is bureaucratic apparatus, 775 : 7
philosophy triumphs over f. evils, 293 : 3
preamble reaching indefinite f., 800 : 8
premature arrival of f., 909 : *n* 1
Present Past F. sees, 405 : 1
put f. in debt, 753 : 8
scaffold sways f., 567 : 7
security for the f., 351 : *n* 3
security of f., 609 : 9
serve the f. hour, 429 : 1
shock, 909 : 1
smells of Russian leather, 482 : 4
something everyone reaches, 842 : 10
spend rest of lives in f., 757 : 10
those who talk about f., 828 : 8
till f. dares forget past, 468 : 23
time f. in time past, 807 : 1
transforms self in us, 756 : 7

Future (*continued*)
true change in f. society, 504 : 11
wastes more of f., 760 : 8
wave of f. is coming, 867 : 4
wave of f. not conquest, 891 : 5
wings of the f., 797 : 11
world of f. a struggle, 832 : 1
Future's, heaven and f. sakes, 748 : 18
poor old Past the F. slave, 572 : 2
Futurity, shadows f. casts on present, 470 : 5
Fuzzy-Wuzzy, 'ere's to you F., 708 : 5

G

G, belong to company G, 619 : 15
Gab, gift of g., 465 : 15
Gaberdine, Jewish g., 198 : 24
Gabrielle, long way to see G., 879 : 18
Gadarenes, country of the G., 42 : 3
Gadding vine, 280 : 12
Gadire, bound for Javan or G., 288 : 30
Gaels of Ireland, 742 : 4
Gage, one for all we g., 189 : 19
Gai, toujours g., 760 : 1
Gaiety, courage g. and quiet mind, 669 : 17
eclipsed g. of nations, 353 : 1
Gain advantage on kingdom of shore, 244 : 22
better to incur loss than g., 93 : 12
every joy is g., 540 : 9
every way makes my g., 232 : 10
for everything g. lose something, 497 : 11
guile and lust of g., 345 : 21
individual intends his own g., 366 : 4
is gain however small, 540 : 9
little patch of ground, 223 : 16
madness of many for g. of few, 334 : 17, 340 : 13
man who in view of g., 69 : 6
my good vain hope of g., 177 : 10
necessity to glorious g., 427 : 22
painful inch to g., 564 : 17
serves and seeks for g., 233 : 18
set down as g. each day, 107 : 7
strength by experience, 786 : 13
the whole world, 39 : 38
those that covet with g. fond, 189 : 18
timely inn, 238 : 22
to die is g., 50 : 1, 83 : 13
to find beautiful soul, 393 : 4
tragedy to g. heart's desire, 680 : 21
voyage not for g. honor wealth, 152 : 1
Gained, boisterously maintained as g., 202 : 3
for everything missed g. something, 497 : 11
from heaven all he wished, 362 : 18
how little g., 532 : *n* 5
no title lost no friend, 336 : 5
something g. for universe, 649 : 14
this by philosophy, 87 : 2
whatever he may have g., 69 : 15
Gaining, something g. on you, 867 : 9
Gains, do not seek evil g., 61 : 19
evil g. equivalent of disaster, 61 : 19
light g. make heavy purses, 177 : 14
spirit that g. victory, 791 : 15
'Gainst all disaster, 302 : *n* 4
Gait, excessive laughter and g., 35 : 33
forced g. of shuffling nag, 204 : 14
Gaiters, gas and g., 547 : 17
Gal, every g. born into world, 628 : 23
Galaxies, new Jerusalems in foreign g., 864 : 4
Gale, catch the driving g., 337 : 8
no g. that blew, 647 : 21
note that swells g., 362 : 20
of life blew high, 691 : 7
partake g., 338 : 2
sun and summer g., 362 : 22
that sweeps from north, 383 : 5
yell for yell to g., 683 : 5
Galeed, name of it called G., 8 : 23
Galen, more than G. cured, 269 : 26
Galeotto was the book, 141 : 3
Galère, dans la g. d'un Turc, 298 : *n* 5
que diable allait-il faire dans cette g., 298 : *n* 5
Gales, cool g. fan the glade, 332 : 12
merest minuscule in g., 766 : 14
set of sails not g., 669 : 21
Galilean, O pale G., 633 : 6
Pilot of the G. lake, 280 : 19
you have conquered G., 127 : 5
Galilee, miracles in Cana of G. 44 : 28
Sea of G. and Dead Sea, 759 : 11
wave rolls nightly on deep G., 459 : 14
Galileo with his woes, 458 : 12
Gall, bear bonds that g., 633 : 9
drink the water of g., 32 : *n* 3
enough in thy ink, 214 : 19
I am g. I am heartburn, 656 : 20
lack g., 221 : 9
of bitterness, 46 : 3
take my milk for g., 236 : 17
wormwood and the g., 32 : 23
Gallant, in g. trim vessel goes, 363 : 6
Gallanter I know, 604 : 7
Gallantly streaming, 446 : 1
Gallantry, conscience no more to do with g., 398 : 27
what men call g., 460 : 13
Galled, let g. jade wince, 222 : 16
Galleon, moon ghostly g., 772 : 23
Galleons of Carib fire, 843 : 16
Gallery of works turned to wall, 595 : 6
what the devil do you do in that g., 298 : *n* 5
Galley, Cervantes on g., 742 : 10
on board a Turk's g., 298 : *n* 5
slave to pen, 484 : 11
what doing in that g., 298 : 12
Gallia est omnis divisa in partes tres, 99 : *n* 10
Galling, bowed with g. crown, 728 : 18
Gallio cared for none of those things, 46 : 19
Gallon, pint of sweat save g. of blood, 792 : 4
Gallop and gallop about, 668 : 11
apace fiery-footed steeds, 193 : 8
beggar will ride a g., 186 : *n* 1
false g. of verses, 212 : 4
go sir g., 420 : 7
Pegasus to death, 339 : 15
why does he g. and g., 668 : 11
Galloped, I g. Dirck g., 541 : 11
Gallops, who Time g. withal, 212 : 11
Gallows, complexion is perfect g., 247 : 7
die on g. or of pox, 368 : 4
hanged Haman on the g., 14 : 34
Gallows (*continued*)
to g. foot and after, 710 : 20
under the g. tree, 260 : 15
Galls, canker g. infants of spring, 218 : 27
his kibe, 224 : 13
Gallup Poll feeling pulse, 745 : 5
Galoot's, till last g. ashore, 636 : 3
Gals, buffalo g. come out tonight, 921 : 20
Galumphing back, 612 : 18
Gamaliel, at feet of G., 46 : 25
Gambol, Christmas g., 430 : 22
Gambols, your g. your songs, 224 : 14
Game, back of bar in solo g., 752 : 5
gunless g., 685 : 11
how you played g., 773 : 3
in the g. to win, 825 : 3
in which my name was, 789 : 10
is afoot, 207 : 18, 689 : 12
is done I've won I've won, 434 : 20
is up, 243 : 20
isn't over till it's over, 903 : 14
little pleasure of g., 320 : 14
lost or won g., 489 : 10
love g. beyond prize, 700 : 6
play up and play g., 700 : 11
played the g., 773 : 3
poetry mug's g., 809 : 19
rigor of the g., 441 : 19
royal g. of goose, 370 : 14
rules of g. laws of nature, 595 : 12
science not g., 854 : 1
start g. on lone heaths, 445 : 12
take me out to ball g., 765 : 13
that must be played, 728 : 16
that never means anything, 836 : 15
this g. is life, 849 : 22
truth the g. of few, 330 : 23
war's a g., 377 : 12
was empires, 462 : 14
whatever the g., 556 : 1
woman is his g., 531 : 6
Gamefish, only g. swims upstream, 686 : 5
Game's afoot, 207 : 18, 689 : 12
Games, shows g. sports guns, 381 : 7
sinful g., 630 : 13
victor in Olympic g. or announcer, 70 : 20
winning g. without cheating, 848 : 13
Gamesmanship art of winning games, 848 : 13
Gammon and spinach, 548 : 33, 929 : 13
Gamp my name and Gamp my nater, 547 : 39
Gamut of emotions, 827 : 16
Gander, goosey g., 931 : 8
Gane, nane sall ken where he is g., 927 : 5
Gang aft a-gley, 408 : 14
before we g. awa', 730 : 20
grisly g., 745 : 3
tell g. at Forty-second Street, 759 : 5
Ganglion in nerves of society, 644 : 7
Gangrene in mildewed silo, 757 : 6
Gang's, hail hail g. all here, 628 : *n* 1
Gangs, don't join too many g., 748 : 16
Gangsters, Nazi g., 745 : 2
will stop, 90 : 8
Gangway for de Lawd, 814 : 15
Gaol, all we know who lie in g., 676 : 12
Gap appeared in the mountain, 66 : 13

Gap (*continued*)
fill g. of a generation, 743 : 10
this great g. of time, 240 : 20
Gape, craters of my eyes g., 912 : 7
Gapes for drink again, 295 : 7
Gaping, love not a g. pig, 200 : 2
Garb, words in reason's g., 284 : 13
Garbage in garbage out, 925 : 13
prey on g., 219 : 22
Garcia, message to G., 679 : 10
Garde, la G. meurt mais ne se rend pas, 421 : *n* 8
Garden, blow upon my g., 28 : 14
cherubims east of the g., 7 : 13
come into g. Maud, 533 : 20
cultivate our g., 343 : 14
died, 715 : 15
earthly ball a peopled g., 395 : 6
fair g. we might win, 600 : 19
fairies at bottom of g., 758 : 6
flowers in g. meat in hall, 145 : *n* 4
full of weeds, 929 : 8
ghost of g. fronts sea, 634 : 12
God first planted g., 181 : 10
God the first g. made, 295 : 14
his own image walking in g., 466 : 16
how does g. grow, 930 : 6
hyacinth g. wears, 516 : 12
I know little g. close, 618 : 5
in her face, 250 : 5
in this delightful g. grows, 173 : 17
into the rose g., 807 : 2
its end comes in the g., 6 : 4
lean on g. urn, 804 : 10
let my beloved come into his g., 28 : 14
lodge in a g. of cucumbers, 28 : 28
Lord God planted a g., 6 : 18
lovesome thing, 603 : 17
maid in g., 931 : 9
man and woman in g., 675 : 16
mind attached like g., 652 : 9
Mr. McGregor's g., 719 : 3
no g. complete without toad, 603 : 10
of cucumbers, 28 : 28
of girls, 533 : 23
over grass in West g., 792 : 9
piece of land with a g., 106 : 20
rosebud g. of girls, 533 : 23
she went into the g., 364 : 5
show me your g., 170 : *n* 8
small house and large g., 295 : 4
snake stood up for evil in G., 747 : 21
suffer them and they'll overgrow g., 185 : 15
this g. city and myself, 865 : 7
tree of life in midst of the g., 6 : 19
turn her out of a g., 355 : 4
voice of Lord God walking in g., 7 : 7
we must cultivate our g., 343 : 14
we've got to get back to g., 916 : 7
who loves a g., 377 : 2, 484 : 6
Gardener Adam and his wife, 528 : 10
Adam was a g., 185 : 26, 710 : 22
though old man young g., 389 : 6
Gardener's, half proper g. work, 710 : 22
Gardeners ditchers and gravemakers, 224 : 5
gardens were before g., 181 : *n* 4
our wills are g., 230 : 2
Gardening, what man needs in g., 603 : 9
Garden's, river at my g. end, 339 : 10
Gardens, Babylon's g., 924 : 3
Gardens (*continued*)
down by salley g., 711 : 22
Hanging G. were a dream, 752 : 16
imaginary g. with real toads, 798 : 11
not God in g., 604 : 1
our bodies are our g., 230 : 2
these g. of desert, 471 : 11
trim g., 278 : 16
were before gardeners, 181 : *n* 4
Garfield, James G. sat on other, 609 : *n* 3
Gargantua, of G. the laughter, 843 : 17
Garish, day's g. eye, 278 : 25
pay no worship to g. sun, 193 : 9
Garland and singing robes, 281 : 11
green willow my g., 158 : 15
race where immortal g., 282 : 1
withered is the g. of war, 241 : 22
Garlands, bring flowering g. to me, 67 : 8
dead, 447 : 8
flanks with g., 477 : 9
gather g. there, 431 : 18
no g. for imitators, 413 : 4
Garlic and sapphires in mud, 807 : 4
eat no onions nor g., 197 : 11
wel loved he g. oynons lekes, 146 : 13
Garment, hardship our g., 744 : 9
left his g. in her hand, 8 : 30
life g. we alter, 839 : 7
morality as g., 782 : 19
of praise, 31 : 25
of repentance fling, 516 : 4
she caught him by his g., 8 : 30
weave g. of brightness, 928 : 14
Garments always in patchez, 856 : 2
blood sprinkled upon g., 31 : 26
of gladness, 34 : 8
part my g. among them, 18 : 6
purses proud g. poor, 189 : 2
stuffs out vacant g., 201 : 26
takes off respect with g., 78 : 4
trailing g. of Night, 509 : 12
Garnish, eye of heaven to g., 202 : 5
Garret, born in g., 364 : *n* 1
living in a g., 364 : 3
speech I wrote in a g., 350 : *n* 5
Garrick, here lies David G., 371 : 16
Garrick's a salad, 371 : 13
Garrulous geese, 847 : 3
old men g. by nature, 99 : 9
Garter, Cluett Shirt Boston G., 828 : 17
familiar as his g., 207 : 5
Garters, scarfs g. gold, 337 : 7
Garyalies, Joblillies and G., 364 : 5
Gas and gaiters, 547 : 17
expedient as lighting by g., 517 : 17
leaks twenty parts, 699 : 16
or steam or table turning, 581 : 10
smells awful, 827 : 12
Gascoyne, Cadets of G., 726 : 2
Gash, be it g. or gold, 889 : 11
Gasoline more cause of conflict that wheat, 876 : 20
Gasp and stretch eyes, 730 : 9
at the last g., 36 : 17
fight till last g., 184 : 16
Quintilian stare and g., 282 : 8
Gate, at one g. to make defense, 288 : 28
by the g. of breath, 633 : 1
drops on g. hang in row, 642 : 6
here at g. alone, 533 : 20
Hun is at g., 710 : 23
lark at heaven's g. sings, 243 : 16
Gate (*continued*)
leant upon coppice g., 641 : 11
longest part of journey passing of g., 97 : 11
of horn and of ivory, 61 : 2
of subtle and profound female, 64 : 2
pale Anguish keeps g., 676 : 13
passionflower at g., 533 : 24
spears of little g., 777 : 16
starved at master's g., 406 : 10
strait is the g., 38 : 15
street before the water g., 14 : 30
this is the g. of heaven, 8 : 21
we pass the g., 721 : 7
wide is the g., 38 : 15
willow cabin at your g., 213 : 18
Gatepost, you me and g., 545 : 20
Gates, at heaven's g. claps wings, 176 : 1
Chicago at northwest g., 728 : 12
dreams have two g., 61 : 2
enter into his g. with thanksgiving, 21 : 3
fling open golden g., 536 : 3
hateful as g. of Hades, 58 : 8
heaven g. not so arched, 262 : 9
her own works praise her in the g., 26 : 10
husband is known in the g., 26 : 7
lift up your heads O ye g., 18 : 9
lion on old stone g., 528 : 9
of dark Death stand wide, 105 : 15
of hell shall not prevail, 39 : 36
of Hercules, 646 : 6
of horn and of ivory, 61 : 2, 105 : 26
of temple of science, 686 : 10
open ye everlasting g., 287 : 1
open ye the g., 30 : 9
seven g. of Thebes, 840 : 17
shut g. of mercy, 362 : 11
sprouting at area g., 804 : 5
unbarred the g. of light, 286 : 25
Gateways of the stars, 693 : 12
Gath, tell it not in G., 13 : 8
Gather and squander, 588 : 7
descendants shall g. your fruits, 103 : 19
fast I g. bit by bit, 621 : 17
garlands there, 431 : 18
honey all the day, 328 : 5
ill habits g. by degrees, 307 : 2
knoweth not who shall g. them, 19 : 3
let me g. after the reapers, 12 : 26
me into artifice of eternity, 715 : 2
rose whilst prime, 173 : 14
roses of life today, 162 : 13
shalt not g. every grape, 10 : 19
shalt not g. the gleanings, 10 : 19
tears g. to the eyes, 531 : 3
the lambs with his arm, 30 : 35
themselves together, 21 : 11
time to g. stones together, 26 : 21
up the fragments, 44 : 40
we g. together, 918 : 19
we'll g. and go, 422 : 19
ye rosebuds, 266 : 11
Gathered, all safely g. in, 536 : 2
cannot be g. up again, 13 : 22
into Armageddon, 53 : 25
Medea g. enchanted herbs, 200 : 22
nations g. before him, 40 : 32
together in my name, 40 : 3
together in thy name, 55 : 8
Gatherer of other men's stuff, 166 : *n* 6

Gathereth her food in the
harvest, 23 : 11
Gathering brows like storm, 411 : 4
Gathers, one that g. samphire, 234 : 28
rolling stone g. no moss, 111 : 17
Gat-toothed I was, 147 : 11
Gaudeamus igitur, 134 : 3
Gaudiness of poetry, 769 : 12
Gaudy blabbing and remorseful
day, 185 : 20
day denies, 459 : 13
neat but not g., 319 : 18
night, 241 : 12
rich not g., 219 : 1
Gaul divided into three parts, 99 : 14
to G. to Greece, 376 : 10
Gaunt, city of G., 926 : 18
Gauntlet of mobs, 499 : 14
with gift in 't, 507 : 18
Gave bodies to commonwealth, 81 : 5
his honors to the world, 249 : 11
me for my pains, 229 : 31
more she g. awey the more she
hadde, 144 : 6
only begotten Son, 44 : 34
proof through the night, 446 : 1
she g. me of the tree, 7 : 8
the Lord g., 15 : 4
thee clothing of delight, 403 : 5
thee life bid thee feed, 403 : 5
to misery all he had, 362 : 18
up the ghost, 44 : 11
what chance shall not
control, 584 : 15
what other women gave, 717 : 1
Gavest, day thou g. Lord is
ended, 597 : 17
woman whom thou g., 7 : 8
Gawd, bein' G. ain't bed of
roses, 814 : 18
livin' G. that made you, 708 : 6
Gay and festive scene, 549 : 32
apparel, 195 : 6
bedecked ornate and g., 288 : 30
deceiver, 415 : 14
gilded scenes, 325 : 6
goodnight and quickly turn
away, 715 : 19
in halls in g. attire, 430 : 6
life earnest art g., 413 : 6
Lothario, 327 : 22
motes that people sunbeams, 278 : 10
poet could not but be g., 427 : 10
steer from grave to g., 338 : 1
their ancient eyes are g., 717 : 7
wit and g. rhetoric, 280 : 2
would not if I could be g., 416 : 4
Gaza, brought Samson to G., 12 : 19
eyeless in G., 288 : 19
Gaze, glass wherein we g., 633 : 7
on so fondly, 446 : 11
show and g. o' the time, 240 : 10
spindrift g., 843 : 16
there bade me g., 586 : 9
tremble while they g., 363 : 2
universe open to our g., 182 : 20
we all g. at stars, 95 : 4
Gazed on face of Agamemnon, 591 : 5
still they g., 370 : 11
Gazelle, nursed dear g., 447 : 14
Gazes on the ground, 670 : 14
Gazing rustics ranged around, 370 : 11
Géant, ailes de g. l'empêchent, 580 : *n* 5
Gear is Greek to me, 215 : *n* 4

Gear (*continued*)
of foreign dead men, 808 : 2
Gee, by jingo by g., 829 : 5
Geese, all his g. are swans, 364 : 2
all our g. are swans, 258 : 26
are getting fat, 921 : 3
are swans and swans geese, 588 : 2
did not claim boundaries, 419 : *n* 5
garrulous g., 847 : 3
lazy g. like snow cloud, 810 : 19
more g. than swans, 918 : 17
opportunity to see g., 795 : 9
riches made wings like g., 6 : 7
swans of others are g., 364 : 2
was it for this wild g. spread
wing, 713 : 11
Gehenna, down to G. up to
throne, 707 : 14
Geist, der G. der stets
verneint, 396 : *n* 4
Gelded, delicately g., 829 : 2
Gêlert, faithful G. roam, 423 : 1
Gem, best g. on her zone, 493 : 19
of all joy, 153 : 5
of purest ray serene, 362 : 8
thou bonny g., 409 : 9
Gemlike, hard g. flame, 638 : 13
Gems of heaven starry train, 286 : 1
phrase a string of g., 362 : *n* 4
rich and rare were g., 446 : 10
Gender, she's of feminine g., 394 : 6
General, caviar to the g., 221 : 3
ceremony, 208 : 6
doctor kills more than g., 315 : 12
drink to g. joy of table, 238 : 27
good is plea of scoundrel, 407 : 6
knowledges idiots possess, 405 : 16
mess of imprecision, 807 : 21
model of modern major g., 627 : 20
moves figures on map, 678 : 17
principle gives no help, 422 : 10
promote g. welfare, 391 : 10
with concrete, 437 : 17
General Motors, good for country
good for G., 817 : 11
General Secretary, vengeance of
most powerful G., 770 : 8
Generalities, glittering g., 485 : 2,
598 : 12
Generalizations, misleading g., 825 : 13
Generalize, to g. is to be idiot, 405 : 16
Generally, I g. had to give in, 420 : 18
Generals, before g. with aplomb, 577 : 2
have died of gout, 301 : 2
haven't all been g., 622 : 21
I do not envy g., 575 : 8
Ireland gives England g., 601 : 7
treacherous g., 860 : 10
victories of mighty g., 575 : 8
war too serious for g., 401 : *n* 2
Generation, an evil g., 43 : 18
another g. cometh, 26 : 11
at ease in my g., 643 : 5
beat g., 901 : 2
best minds of my g., 906 : 1
can't wait another g., 813 : 15
creation of next g., 853 : 16
each g. wastes more, 760 : 8
effectiveness of a g., 784 : 20
honor or dishonor to last g., 522 : 12
improvements by g., 378 : 1
lost g., 752 : 9
men of my g., 879 : 7
new g. descends from on high, 103 : 14

Generation (*continued*)
new g. of Americans, 890 : 7
new g. of leadership, 890 : 4
of men like leaves, 58 : 1
of vipers, 36 : 28
one g. passeth away, 26 : 11
pathological g., 584 : 5
shorn by war, 743 : 10
stubborn and rebellious g., 20 : 3
third and fourth g. of them that
hate me, 10 : 5
this g. of Americans, 779 : 17
transmits experience from g. to
g., 895 : 20
trees to benefit another g., 95 : 15
vices of our g., 553 : 1
wiser in their g., 43 : 31
wrongdoing of one g., 503 : 16
younger g. knocking at door, 600 : 7
Generations, converse with men of
unseen g., 142 : 22
dying g., 714 : 22
feast throughout your g., 9 : 26
honored in their g., 36 : 11
hungry g., 477 : 1
minds of different g., 791 : 12
of honest ancestry, 826 : 13
our dwelling place in all g., 20 : 11
save succeeding g., 788 : 20
shall call me blessed, 42 : 21
three g. of imbeciles, 645 : 7
three g. shirtsleeves to
shirtsleeves, 621 : 13
truth endureth to all g., 21 : 3
unborn g., 779 : 2
Generosity, calls his extravagance
g., 369 : 23
of soul, 69 : 19
Generous, be just before you're
g., 399 : 3
because of frugality, 65 : 3
boys in happiness bred, 572 : 4
great wisdom is g., 90 : 1
in peace just and g., 463 : 13
most vain most g., 663 : 8
nature take own way, 372 : 15
starves her g. birth, 361 : 17
thy Lord the most g., 132 : 17
true and fierce, 743 : 11
way plain peaceful g., 522 : 12
with our freedom, 824 : 12
Genes, we have g. for
usefulness, 884 : 2
Genetic, deterioration in g.
structure, 775 : 13
Genevieve, sweet G., 636 : 2
Genial courteous intellectual, 726 : 1
current of the soul, 362 : 7
Geniality, prefer g. to
grammar, 685 : 13
Génie, le g. n'est qu'une grande
aptitude, 349 : *n* 2
Genius and mortal instruments, 215 : 18
aptitude for patience, 349 : 3
bane of all g., 466 : 7
beauty like hers g., 601 : 18
behind poetry, 608 : 8
believe own thought g., 496 : 19
beyond g. of sea, 767 : 15
books legacies g. leaves, 326 : 16
capacity for getting into
trouble, 620 : 21
capacity for taking pains, 630 : 17

Genius (*continued*)
capacity for taking trouble, 349 : *n* 2, 474 : 14, 620 : 21
capacity to see, 793 : 10
civic g. of people, 650 : 14
crooked roads are of g., 404 : 7
does what it must, 609 : 14
eccentricities of g., 546 : 21
Edmund whose g. was such, 371 : 14
fires true g. kindles, 338 : 14
for not being ruled, 489 : 19
gives g. better discerning, 371 : 5
goes folly stays, 494 : 23
hand in hand, 569 : 18
imaginative g. of west, 577 : 13
investment of g. pays, 630 : 23
is of no country, 375 : 6
is patience, 349 : *n* 2
is that in whose power man is, 569 : 11
lost g. of independence, 520 : 7
love is the soul of g., 402 : 11
love of truth demanded of g., 397 : 8
man of g. had to pay, 736 : 5
man of g. makes no mistakes, 778 : 3
man of g. ruined by himself, 354 : 8
men of g. not excel, 445 : 17
must be born, 306 : 8
nature full of g., 557 : 15
ninety-nine percent perspiration, 661 : 9
no g. without touch of madness, 115 : 6
no taste for weaving sand, 500 : 9
obedience bane of g., 466 : 7
of Christianity, 853 : 8
of Constitution, 351 : 6
of leader, 813 : 12
one percent inspiration, 661 : 9
parting g. with sighing sent, 277 : 11
patience ingredient of g., 349 : *n* 2
perceiving in unhabitual way, 649 : 4
picking men of g., 825 : 11
please the talentgang, 829 : 16
poverty stepmother of g., 561 : 18
prayed to g. of the place, 105 : 27
raise the g., 334 : 12
since when g. respectable, 507 : 21
single g. equivalent to hundred mediocrities, 630 : 19
slim and crooked g., 652 : 7
solitude to g. stern friend, 498 : 27
some g. of the South, 831 : 16
substitute for g., 375 : 20
talent recognizes g., 689 : 15
thine own g. gave blow, 456 : 17
Thoreau's g., 652 : 7
three fifths of him g., 567 : 18
times in which g. would live. 392 : 16
towering g. disdains beaten path, 519 : 24
vessel of my g. now hoists sails, 141 : 17
what g. I had, 323 : 24
what use g. if no focus, 498 : 5
when my g. calls, 496 : 24
will live without training, 536 : 12
word-coining g., 782 : 3
work out own salvation, 479 : 14
Geniuses shortest biographies, 498 : 15
Genji, The Tale of G., 375 : 3
Genre of silence, 828 : 6
Genteel, Shabby G., 922 : 14
Genteelly, cheat at cards g., 355 : 13
Genteelly (*continued*)
debauch friend's wife g., 355 : 13
Gentian, reach me a g., 791 : 1
Gentile, judges neither Jew nor G., 776 : 13
might of the G., 459 : 16
Gentiles, light to lighten G., 42 : 31
Gentle, a very g. beast, 197 : 16
ah g. dames, 411 : 5
by g. decay, 302 : 24
carry g. peace, 249 : 8
come g. Spring, 345 : 10
do not go g., 887 : 4
don't be g. to your wife, 60 : 13
droppeth as g. rain, 200 : 9
from mouth flow g. words, 61 : 9
his life was g., 217 : 14
Jesus meek and mild, 350 : 13
knight pricking on plain, 173 : 8
lie lightly g. earth, 263 : 7
limbs did she undress, 433 : 31
love is g., 148 : 20
mind by gentle deeds, 174 : 4
more nearly kind and g., 837 : 11
most g. sleep, 206 : *n* 2
of manners g., 305 : *n* 2
our g. senses, 236 : 21
plain just resolute, 576 : 8
sensitive mind, 714 : 7
sign to know g. blood, 174 : 20
sleep it is a g. thing, 434 : 30
sleep O g. sleep, 206 : 17
that dooth gentil dedis, 147 : 16
they shall be g. brave strong, 643 : 2
though g. yet not dull, 294 : 19
trust thee g. Kate, 203 : 24
voice was g. and low, 235 : 17
wind does move, 404 : 10
with these butchers, 216 : 11
world kills the g., 844 : 15
Gentle-hearted, terming me g. in print, 441 : 6
Gentleman, ancestors of honorable g., 501 : 9
and scholar, 409 : 6
be g. be idle, 177 : 15
devil is a g., 234 : *n* 2
first true g., 251 : 11
God send every g., 927 : 4
not in your books, 208 : 26
on whom I built trust, 236 : 15
once g. always g., 549 : 21
prince of darkness a g., 234 : 11
showed him g. an' scholar, 409 : 6
smooth-faced g. Commodity, 201 : 19
so stout a g., 205 : 11
take hym for grettest g., 147 : 15
that loves to hear himself talk, 192 : 26
very nice g., 903 : 5
who was then a g., 917 : 1
word of g. and Christian, 169 : 26
writes well for a g., 328 : *n* 4
Gentleman-like, lovely g. man, 196 : 9
Gentlemen and seamen in navy, 489 : 7
cooks are g., 258 : 16
dust was g. and ladies, 606 : 7
farmers, 461 : 21
God Almighty's g., 304 : 12
God rest you merry g., 919 : 20
great-hearted g., 540 : 25
lays eggs for g., 932 : 14
like Cerberus three g., 398 : 16
may cry Peace, 383 : 5
Gentlemen (*continued*)
no ancient g., 224 : 5
not to forget we are g., 372 : 6
of England, 273 : 6
of old regime, 789 : 3
of the shade, 202 : 24
prefer blondes, 826 : 3
rankers, 708 : 14
scholars and g., 424 : 4
three jolly g., 740 : 5
two g. rolled into one, 415 : 9
unafraid, 707 : 23
unhand me g., 219 : 16
were not seamen, 489 : 7
what is it the g. wish, 383 : 5
who wrote with ease, 339 : 23
Gentleness, angling produce g., 271 : *n* 1
fruit of Spirit is g., 49 : 30
has perished, 4 : 6
let g. my strong enforcement be, 211 : 12
man of g., 155 : 11
method is love and g., 154 : 12
survives, 906 : 10
Gentler, still g. sister woman, 409 : 21
Gentlest, fittest may also be g., 848 : 1
Gentlier on spirit lies, 528 : 14
Gently brother gently pray, 516 : 20
do my spiriting g., 247 : 17
faults lie g. on him, 249 : 12
flow g. sweet Afton, 410 : 13
o'er perfumed sea, 525 : 9
roar you g. as sucking dove, 196 : 8
scan brother man, 409 : 21
smiling jaws, 611 : 5
speak g. she can hear, 674 : 14
thou and nature so g. part, 242 : 3
use all g., 221 : 23
Genuine, discovers place for the g., 798 : 10
night admits no ray, 304 : 25
substantial and g. virtue, 388 : 2
wisdom never dear if g., 538 : 10
Genus, hoc g. omne, 106 : *n* 10
irritabile vatum, 109 : *n* 7
Geographers crowd edges of maps, 119 : 21
Geographical boundaries or distinctions of race, 579 : 9
Geography, my sons ought to study g., 381 : 14
Geological, introduction into earth at g. periods, 482 : 12
Geologists, tempt g. into infidelity, 663 : 5
Geology by day astronomy night, 830 : 17
Geometric, he by g. scale, 290 : 21
Geometrical, increases in g. ratio, 417 : 3
mind, 318 : 3
universe in g. figures, 182 : 20
Geometrician, grammarian rhetorician g., 122 : 4
Geometry, geometrical mind not bound to g., 318 : 3
no royal road to g., 92 : 4
of artist's own, 653 : 10
shaped by hand of g., 318 : 3
synergetics energetic g., 832 : 16
George be a king, 540 : 4
England and Saint G., 207 : 18
for King G. upon throne, 415 : 16
Saint G. for England, 742 : 14

George (*continued*)
Saint G. that swinged dragon, 201 : 15
the First vile, 753 : *n* 3
the Second viler, 753 : *n* 3
the Third honest dullard, 673 : 1
the Third ought never to have occurred, 753 : 5
the Third profit by example, 382 : 13
when G. the Third was king, 108 : *n* 5
George's, St. G. Hanover Square, 620 : 9
Georges, God be praised G. ended, 753 : *n* 3
Georgia booze mighty fine, 840 : 1
Hell's broke loose in G., 840 : 1
marching through G., 614 : 14
on red hills of G., 909 : 9
Germ of all virtue, 567 : 1
German, achieved as G. soldier, 812 : 19
dictator, 743 : 15
dives into sentence, 624 : 9
Fatherland, 420 : 1
for converse with enemies, 357 : 19
I speak G. to my horse, 143 : 16
not even G. culture, 658 : 21
statecraft, 553 : 8
sturdiness of G. tongue, 357 : 19
to be G. means, 552 : 15
true G. can't stand French, 396 : 16
unity of G. nation, 812 : 19
wherever G. tongue heard, 420 : 1
German-Americans, have done with G., 667 : 1
Germans and women have no depths, 658 : 27
are like women, 658 : 27
beastly to the G., 843 : 12
fear God nothing else, 553 : 16
Lord bomb G., 866 : 17
Germany, aggression of G., 812 : *n* 3
authoritarian G., 834 : 7
in G. they came for Communists, 824 : 1
in the world forward, 663 : 3
is a nation, 483 : 18
Prussia part of G., 480 : 10
put G. in saddle, 553 : 10
ruins culture, 658 : 22
the cause of Hitler, 801 : 11
Germany's, Rhine G. river, 420 : 2
Germens, all g. spill at once, 233 : 24
Gertrude always right, 845 : 6
Gesang, Wein Weib und G., 399 : *n* 3
Gesanges, auf Flügeln des G., 481 : *n* 9
Gesture, distorting my g., 883 : 11
each g. a commitment, 865 : 10
without motion, 805 : 16
Gestures, get at thing without g., 768 : 3
Get and beget, 664 : 13
at enemy as soon as you can, 589 : 15
at thing without gestures, 768 : 3
by with help from friends, 914 : 11
desire to g. on in world, 799 : 18
easier stay out than g. out, 625 : 7
from where you are not, 807 : 18
men take best they can g., 356 : 2
money still get money, 108 : *n* 13
on board little children, 936 : 5
out of kitchen, 788 : 1
that I wear, 212 : 2
the trick, 624 : 11
thee behind me, 39 : 37
thee glass eyes, 235 : 4
Get (*continued*)
thee to a nunnery, 221 : 15
there first with most, 583 : 20
time to g., 26 : 21
to g. along go along, 779 : 4
understanding, 23 : 7
up begin again, 542 : 12
up sweet slug-a-bed, 266 : 19
what you want, 711 : 4
with child mandrake root, 252 : 1
writing, 800 : 1
you g. no more of me, 182 : 16
you to my lady's chamber, 224 : 14
you've got to g. up, 802 : 5
Gets, Dead Sea g. to keep, 759 : 11
Galilee g. to give, 759 : 11
him to rest, 208 : 7
pleased with what he g., 211 : 3
them that has g., 661 : 6
up by bell, 622 : 16
Getting along with women, 394 : 15
and spending, 427 : 29
better and better, 684 : 9
Gospel of G. On, 680 : 7
not g. what one wants, 675 : 10
on in world, 738 : 8
on together, 776 : 4
out of world known before, 738 : 8
prevent lower from g. more, 88 : 1
to heaven at last, 605 : 5
what one wants, 675 : 10
with all thy g. get understanding, 23 : 7
youth is the time of g., 290 : 9
Gettysburg can't understand it, 838 : 4
pile high at G., 761 : 6
Gewesen, wie es eigentlich g., 480 : *n* 2
Ghastly crew, 434 : 31
dew, 529 : 24
grim ancient Raven, 526 : 15
long and g. kitchen, 551 : 15
night full of g. dreams, 187 : 8
rapid river, 526 : 2
trembling cold in g. fears, 404 : 10
turned face with g. pang, 434 : 24
Ghost, beckoning g., 335 : 7
before not g. of shores, 646 : 6
come back again, 852 : 8
embrace my mother's g., 60 : 8
escapes from vanquished pyre, 112 : 26
frustrate g., 543 : 15
guessed, 656 : 10
he gave up g., 44 : 11
hollow g., 587 : 17
lost and by wind grieved g., 852 : 8
make g. of him that lets me, 219 : 16
man giveth up the g., 15 : 34
may spaniel it, 797 : 13
of Christmas Past, 548 : 7
of Christmas Present, 548 : 9
of Christmas Yet to Come, 548 : 12
of deceased Roman Empire, 264 : 18
of garden fronts sea, 634 : 12
of Hamlet's father, 697 : 4
of sleighbells, 747 : 14
of snow, 747 : 14
please my g., 772 : 6
some old lover's g., 253 : 9
thrice the g. fled, 105 : 5
vex not his g., 235 : 19
what beckoning g., 335 : 7
wrought g. upon floor, 526 : 11
your g. will walk, 542 : 6
Ghosties, ghoulies and g., 921 : 4
Ghostlier demarcations, 767 : 16
Ghostlike, haunt g. the spot, 503 : 7
Ghostly galleon, 772 : 23
Ghosts, clothes hang like g. from lines, 819 : 3
driven like g., 467 : 17
from enchanter fleeing, 467 : 17
haunted by g. deposed, 195 : 2
knight of g. and shadows, 918 : 12
of defunct bodies fly, 291 : 2
of departed quantities, 330 : 21
true love is like g., 293 : 12
we are all g., 599 : 15
Ghosts' high noon, 629 : 20
Ghoul-haunted woodland of Weir, 526 : 23
Ghoulies and ghosties, 921 : 4
G.I. Joe, 924 : 22
Giant, as when a g. dies, 228 : 17
Atlas upholds, 76 : 25
baby figure of g. mass, 226 : 5
branches tossed, 470 : 14
Despair, 302 : 8
dwarf on shoulders of g., 258 : 7
fling stone g. dies, 344 : 14
making G. hit into double, 773 : 12
my g. goes with me, 497 : 7
nation acts like helpless g., 882 : 23
pitiful helpless g., 882 : 23
race before the flood, 306 : 7
tyrannous to use it like g., 228 : 9
wings prevent walking, 580 : 17
Giant-dwarf, senior-junior g., 190 : 26
Giant's robe, 239 : 28
strength, 228 : 9
Giants in the earth, 7 : 27
pygmies on shoulders of g., 118 : 7
standing upon shoulders of g., 313 : 10
strength of the ancient g., 60 : *n* 3
Gib, melancholy as g. cat, 202 : 29
Gibber, squeak and g., 217 : 21
Gibbets, better schoolrooms than g., 562 : 12
keep lifted hand in awe, 330 : 1
Gibbon eh Mr. G., 387 : 6
Gibe, call it humor when they g., 322 : 19
Gibeon, sun stand still upon G., 11 : 34
Gibes, where be your g. now, 224 : 14
Giddy, fancies are more g., 214 : 1
habitation g. and unsure, 206 : 7
I am g., 226 : 10
thinks world turns round, 189 : 4
Giddy-paced, brisk and g. times, 213 : 28
Gideon Bibles only in bedrooms, 816 : 15
sword of Lord and of G., 12 : 10
Gie me ae spark, 409 : 1
Gift, beauty the g. of God, 86 : 18
crave of thee g., 458 : 20
dream the excitable g., 908 : 14
every good g. and perfect g., 51 : 29
every woman g. of world to me, 481 : 12
fatal g. of beauty, 458 : 10
feeling the East's g., 542 : 20
gauntlet with g., 507 : 18
God's to God, 863 : 5
great grace with little g., 92 : 16
greatest g. freedom of will, 142 : 12
have the g. to know it, 211 : 9
hearts not had as g., 714 : 17

Gift (*continued*)
heavenly g. of poesy, 305 : 7
heaven's last best g., 286 : 13
immortality not g., 728 : 8
it is a god who gave you this g., 57 : 7
love g. of fairy tale, 612 : 15
love God's ultimate g., 543 : 20
make g. rich by delaying, 555 : 7
manner of giving worth more than g., 275 : 24
Muses gave me honeyed g., 93 : 2
never look g. horse in mouth, 128 : 22
not so much nature of g., 668 : 3
of excellence to few men, 67 : 2
of God eternal life, 47 : 5
of laughter, 756 : 15
of martyrdom, 305 : 21
of sleep, 663 : 12
of the gab, 465 : 15
of tongues, 396 : 17
only g. portion of thyself, 498 : 6
reason God's crowning g., 74 : 21
skilled poet through natural g., 71 : 24
spirit in which g. offered, 668 : 3
tablet a g. of Memory, 85 : 18
terrible g. lifted from hearts, 582 : 7
though small is precious, 60 : 1
time with g. of tears, 632 : 9
to be well-favored g. of fortune, 209 : 24
true love's the g., 430 : 9
various g. to each, 511 : 14
who know heaven save by heaven's g., 115 : 17
without giver bare, 567 : 14
woman's g. to rain shower, 188 : 24
word better than g., 35 : 29
Gifted, poetically g., 586 : 16
Giftie, some power g. gie us, 409 : 8
Gifts, adore my g. instead of me, 269 : 1
benefit in g. of bad man, 76 : 15
cluster of g. experience, 652 : 14
enjoyed g. of founder, 384 : 1
fairy g. fading away, 446 : 11
fear Greeks even when they bring g., 104 : 32
glorious g. of the gods, 57 : 21
gods do not give all men g., 60 : 4
liberality in g., 315 : 5
more of his grace than g., 250 : 15
my lady's admirable g., 140 : 9
no g. from Chance, 584 : 17
no hard g., 797 : 13
people I cannot win with g., 300 : 23
presented unto him g., 36 : 21
rarer g. than gold, 797 : 4
rich g. wax poor, 221 : 14
riches to make g. to friends, 77 : 3
seven hundred pounds goot g., 225 : 7
spend not then his g. in vain, 255 : 16
two jars of the g. he gives, 59 : 12
with tired back we bring g., 928 : 13
Gig, crew of captain's g., 627 : 7
Gigantic hound, 689 : 11
press restless g., 789 : 4
speckled g. flowers, 789 : 9
willful young, 728 : 12
Gigantically down, 525 : 13, 844 : 2
Giggle, ha'd to g. w'en nuffin' in pot, 737 : 2
Gigo garbage in garbage out, 925 : 13
Gild refined gold, 202 : 5
Gilded and sticky, 794 : 8
cage, 730 : 18
car of day, 279 : 10
eaves, 531 : 5
flap bug with g. wings, 338 : 19
fly does lecher, 234 : 31
fool, 251 : 9
gay g. scenes, 325 : 6
hearse, 806 : 3
laugh at g. butterflies, 235 : 12
not marble nor g. monuments, 244 : 18
throne is bit of wood g., 420 : 11
vessel goes, 363 : 6
Gilding, stripped of lettering and g., 346 : 15
Gilds, eternal summer g. them, 461 : 3
love g. the scene, 398 : 20
Gilead, no balm in G., 32 : 3
Gills, soul swims without g., 759 : 3
Gilpin long live he, 376 : 16
Gilt comes off on our hands, 583 : 13
dust that is a little g., 226 : 21
more laud than g. o'erdusted, 226 : 21
surcingles, 607 : 11
Gimble, gyre and g., 612 : 17
Gin, perhaps it's the g., 855 : 16
union of g. and vermouth, 837 : 10
Ginger, board money in g. jar, 618 : 16
hot i' the mouth, 213 : 26
nutmegs g. cinnamon cloves, 268 : 1
Gingham, bits of g. and calico, 666 : 18
dog went Bowwow, 666 : 18
Gins, snares traps g. pitfalls, 539 : *n* 2
Gipper, win for G., 811 : 4
Giraffe in queer gracefulness, 789 : 9
Gird up thy loins like a man, 16 : 27
Girded, father's sword g. on, 446 : 15
he g. up his loins, 14 : 4
let loins be g., 43 : 21
with praise, 445 : 21
with your loins g., 9 : 25
Girdeth, him that g. on his harness, 14 : 6
Girdle, bright g. furled, 587 : 16
helps with g., 856 : 5
loosened the embroidered g., 58 : 19
round about earth, 196 : 16
round about world, 178 : 1
Girdled, walls and towers g. round, 433 : 21
Girl at impressionable age, 896 : 2
Burma g. a-settin', 708 : 8
crept like frightened g., 674 : 15
green g., 219 : 4
heaven protect working g., 684 : 17
I left behind me, 920 : 7
I like to see, 866 : 18
little g. my stringbean, 908 : 13
Little Match G., 505 : 9
needs good parents, 788 : 21
nice g. won't give an inch, 119 : 9
not expect special privileges, 898 : 6
of beautiful face, 841 : 7
soft face of a g., 74 : 23
speak like a green g., 219 : 4
Spearmint G., 828 : 17
sweet g. graduates, 530 : 21
sweetest g. I know, 753 : 1
then spoke I to my g., 266 : 5
there little g. don't cry, 665 : 9
there was a little g., 513 : 1
unlessoned g. unschooled, 199 : 29
wild solitary g. Rima, 646 : 2
Girl (*continued*)
wink at homely g., 772 : 6
Girlish glee, 629 : 8
laughter, 688 : 4
Girl's, diamonds g. best friend, 848 : 16
Girls, all g. he can please, 636 : 12
boys and g. level with men, 241 : 22
boys and g. together, 698 : 14
dust was lads and g., 606 : 7
encouraged to make life plan, 898 : 5
garden of g., 533 : 23
Glos'ter g. they have no combs, 934 : 22
golden lads and g., 243 : 27
hear what servant g. said, 735 : 2
in g. again courted, 920 : 4
laughing flesh of g., 899 : 16
little g. made of, 932 : 13
little g. recognize your prime, 896 : 3
of all g. so smart, 331 : 5
oh you New York g., 934 : 23
turn wives, 906 : 10
what shall I do for pretty g., 717 : 18
which g. hath merriest eye, 184 : 20
who wear glasses, 827 : 11
with g. be handy, 920 : 9
wretched un-ideaed g., 353 : 25
Girt, just g. me for onset, 604 : 11
Git thar fustest with mostest, 583 : *n* 7
Gitche Gumee, shores of G., 511 : 16
Gits, them that has g., 661 : 6
Give a little love to child, 573 : 4
a man enough rope, 158 : *n* 7
a new commandment, 45 : 19
all that a man hath will he g., 15 : 5
all thou canst, 429 : 6
all to love, 494 : 10
an inch take an ell, 161 : *n* 6
and not count cost, 157 : 3
ask only what they can g., 718 : 13
author's skill to g., 702 : 14
Aztecs by no means would g. up, 156 : 13
bouquets while I'm living, 762 : 1
countries g. themselves to you, 789 : 11
country back to Indians, 840 : 11
cried G. me, 605 : 7
crowns pounds guineas, 690 : 20
Dayrolles a chair, 342 : 18
delight and hurt not, 248 : 10
enemies means of our destruction, 66 : 24
every man thy ear, 219 : 1
fame for pot of ale, 207 : 19
freely received freely g., 38 : 34
Gods above should g., 561 : 1
great meals of beef, 207 : 26
hand and heart, 450 : 9
has nothing g. nothing, 863 : 5
hautboys breath he comes, 306 : 14
haves of g., 829 : 19
him a little earth, 249 : 10
him death by inches, 242 : 25
his angels charge, 20 : 17
I generally had to g. in, 420 : 18
I will g. you rest, 39 : 8
I will not g. sleep to mine eyes, 22 : 13
if you can g. that you're a writer, 845 : 4
in life did harbor g., 256 : 5
it an understanding, 218 : 24
it gets to g., 759 : 11
kiss better than you g., 227 : 2

Give (*continued*)
me a kiss, 266 : 10
me a look, 255 : 18
me a thousand kisses, 101 : 18
me a torch, 791 : 1
me ae spark, 409 : 1
me again my hollow tree, 339 : 11
me an ounce of civet, 235 : 1
me another horse, 187 : 26
me back my heart, 456 : 19
me back my legions, 110 : 5
me but that, 169 : 5
me excess of it, 213 : 7
me good digestion Lord, 760 : *n* 1
me hand that is honest, 429 : 16
me handfuls of lilies, 105 : 25
me health and a day, 496 : 5
me John Baptist's head, 39 : 23
me liberty or death, 383 : 5
me liberty to know, 282 : 4
me more love or more disdain, 271 : 22
me my scallop shell, 172 : 15
me ocular proof, 231 : 12
me quoth I, 236 : 1
me splendid silent sun, 575 : 24
me that man, 222 : 6
me that old-time religion, 921 : 15
me the daggers, 237 : 23
me to drink mandragora, 240 : 20
me today take tomorrow, 132 : 23
me truth, 560 : 20
me Vesuvius' crater, 571 : 1
me where to stand, 93 : 5
me your answer do, 718 : 18
me your hand, 188 : 12
me your tired your poor, 664 : 10
meanest flower can g., 426 : 23
more blessed to g., 46 : 23
mother g. me sun, 599 : 16
my regards to Broadway, 759 : 5
name to every fixed star, 190 : 12
Nature a chance, 166 : 10
never g. all heart, 712 : 19
never g. in never, 745 : 6
no more g. the people straw, 9 : 17
no more to every guest, 323 : 1
not a windy night rainy morrow, 245 : 3
not what we g. but share, 567 : 14
O g. me a home, 927 : 19
of possessions is little, 782 : 16
of yourself truly g., 782 : 16
peace a chance, 914 : 13
peace I g. unto you, 45 : 24
peace in our time, 56 : 15
place to better men, 272 : 19
reason on compulsion, 203 : 31
sop to Cerberus, 132 : 22
sorrow words, 239 : 20
thee peace, 10 : 23
them meat in due season, 21 : 11
these delights if thou canst g., 278 : 8
throne would be easy, 89 : 4
thy thoughts no tongue, 218 : 29
thy worst of thoughts, 230 : 32
to a thief, 875 : 6
to get esteem, 368 : 19
to spend to g. to want, 174 : 11
to the poor, 40 : 6
two daughters crying g. g., 26 : 3
up verse my boy, 792 : 17
us a song to cheer, 618 : 1
us grace and strength, 669 : 17

Give (*continued*)
us luxuries, 519 : 10
us our daily bread, 37 : 15
us rest or death, 528 : 18
us serenity, 823 : 15
us taste of your quality, 221 : 2
us the tools, 744 : 13
warning to world, 244 : 26
we g. what we have, 653 : 5
we receive but what we g., 435 : 26
what shall I g. my children, 889 : 7
what we g. and preserve, 522 : 12
what you command, 129 : 6
what you have, 511 : 5
when I g. I g. myself, 574 : 26
while we have praise to g., 256 : 11
world assurance of a man, 223 : 3
world the lie, 172 : 14
you some violets, 224 : 2
your heart to hawks, 797 : 18
Given, anything g. can be taken away, 913 : 8
as if checks g., 606 : 17
ask and it shall be g., 38 : 12
gladly not to be standing here, 872 : 8
God has g. you one face, 221 : 18
hast thou g. the horse strength, 16 : 36
heart change of mood, 748 : 3
heaven alone g. away, 567 : 12
his heart to cause, 797 : 13
I have g. suck and know, 237 : 5
in vain in vain, 534 : 15
more g. less work, 602 : 13
much g. much required, 43 : 22
not have g. it for monkeys, 199 : 20
nothing g. nothing required, 349 : 11
of thine own have we g. thee, 14 : 26
our hearts away, 427 : 29
pay for what gods g., 736 : 5
take what is g., 750 : 11
thee till break of day, 405 : 2
them the slip, 319 : 12
thou hast g. him his heart's desire, 18 : 4
too dear for what's g. freely, 246 : 8
unto everyone that hath be g., 40 : 30
what scanted in hair g. in wit, 188 : 4
youth to whom was g., 425 : 1
Giver, cheerful g., 49 : 18
gift without g. bare, 567 : 14
keep modest as g., 657 : 14
Givers, when g. prove unkind, 221 : 14
Gives, blesseth him that g., 200 : 9
but for another g. ease, 405 : 3
but greater feeling to worse, 194 : 7
doubly benefits who g. quickly, 110 : 15
'er all she needs, 709 : 8
he that lends g., 270 : 15
heart and soul away, 691 : 1
himself with alms, 567 : 14
lovely light, 822 : 17
new meaning, 801 : 8
no man a sinecure, 792 : 17
secure whate'er he g., 352 : 2
sternest good-night, 237 : 17
the more he g. to others, 65 : 10
thoughts nature g. way to, 237 : 11
time takes all g. all, 171 : 11
to airy nothing, 197 : 12
truth to summer's lie, 830 : 1
twice who gives promptly, 133 : 10
Giveth his beloved sleep, 22 : 9

Giveth (*continued*)
land the Lord g. thee, 10 : 7
life and breath, 46 : 16
man g. up the ghost, 15 : 34
not as world g., 45 : 24
unto the poor, 25 : 30
Giving, brief as the g. breath, 812 : 3
enemies the slip, 359 : 22
heart to dog to tear, 710 : 14
in g. we receive, 138 : 15
know nothing of g., 689 : 24
manner of g. worth more, 275 : 24
more g. less buying, 739 : 8
not g. life but risking life, 870 : 10
not in g. vein today, 187 : 16
stealing and g. odor, 213 : 7
Gizzard, something in her g., 310 : 14
Glacier knocks in cupboard, 868 : 10
woman, 843 : 20
Glad did I live gladly die, 668 : 20
diviner's theme, 304 : 5
green leaves like wings, 642 : 3
heart too soon g., 540 : 23
kindness, 714 : 18
let us live and be g., 134 : 3
make g. heart of childhood, 638 : 6
make g. the city of God, 19 : 11
me with soft black eye, 447 : 14
moments of g. grace, 712 : 9
never g. confident morning, 541 : 9
New Year, 528 : 12
not born before tea, 433 : 15
of other men's good, 212 : 2
Olaf g. and big, 829 : 8
pain g. to be forgotten, 797 : 13
sad g. brother's name, 634 : 11
show ourselves g., 54 : 16
some have what others would be g. of, 349 : 15
tidings of great joy, 317 : 5
to be of use, 803 : 17
to sleep with Aphrodite, 60 : 6
when they said unto me, 22 : 5
while he lives be g., 633 : 10
wine that maketh g. the heart, 21 : 9
wise son maketh a g. father, 23 : 21
with all my heart, 182 : 16
you like adverbs, 654 : 6
Gladdening west, 728 : 13
Gladdest thing under sun, 822 : 15
Glade, bee-loud g., 712 : 4
cool gales fan the g., 332 : 12
crown the watery g., 361 : 8
points to yonder g., 335 : 7
Gladiators, if only g. died, 759 : 12
Gladly, be your wife g., 551 : 2
beyond any experience, 829 : 12
die, 668 : 20
died g. with all you knew, 899 : 10
gone along with decent man, 702 : 10
lerne and gladly teche, 145 : 28
suffer fools g., 49 : 20
Gladness, begin in g., 425 : 10
deck soul with g., 295 : 20
garments of g., 34 : 8
I that in heill wes and g., 153 : 6
notes of g., 443 : 21
of the heart, 35 : 41
serve the Lord with g., 21 : 3
teach me half g., 468 : 15
wealth small aid for daily g., 77 : 3
Gladsome light of jurisprudence, 172 : 1
Glamis hath murdered sleep, 237 : 22
thou art and Cawdor, 236 : 16

Glamour, moment of romance of g., 683 : 11
Glance, Backward G. o'er Traveled Roads, 577 : 10
from heaven to earth, 197 : 12
glum, 629 : 22
matron's g. reprove, 369 : 29
O brightening g., 715 : 17
of the Lord, 459 : 16
ten thousand saw I at a g., 427 : 9
without a g. my way, 605 : 20
Glances, gray eye g., 525 : 18
Glare, moths caught by g., 456 : 22
rockets' red g., 446 : 1
sunburnt by g. of life, 507 : 19
surrounds king hides him, 165 : 21
Glareth, not all gold that g., 137 : *n* 8
Glasgerion swore great oath, 926 : 20
Glass, air's g. jail, 905 : 7
break bloody g., 870 : 5
dome of many-colored g., 469 : 16
drink not the third g., 268 : 3
excuse for the g., 399 : 1
falling hour by hour, 870 : 5
fill every g., 332 : 2
first g. for myself, 326 : 18
Fortune like g. easily broken, 111 : 2
fount more sparkling than g., 108 : 4
get thee g. eyes, 235 : 4
grief with g. that ran, 632 : 9
hate you through g., 834 : 12
house is g., 269 : 25
house of German statecraft, 553 : 8
if your windows g., 347 : 16
made mouths in a g., 233 : 27
mosaic window glass, 715 : 18
obscured or broken, 900 : 3
of brandy and water, 416 : 6
of fashion mold of form, 221 : 20
of years is brittle, 633 : 7
people in g. houses, 269 : *n* 3
pride is his own g., 226 : 9
satire a sort of g., 321 : 13
see through g. darkly, 48 : 25
shown g. flowers, 798 : 16
stand before g. tie my tie, 811 : 13
swift sandy g., 257 : 17
thou art thy mother's g., 244 : 2
thou canst not tame, 268 : 3
Time turn up his g., 257 : 17
turn down empty g., 517 : 14
Venus take my votive g., 321 : 1
wherein noble youth dress, 206 : 14
whose house is g., 269 : 25
Glasses, fill all the g. there, 295 : 8
girls who wear g., 827 : 11
itself in tempests, 458 : 28
Shakespeare and the musical g., 369 : 14
Glass's, over g. edge dinner done, 543 : 3
Glassy cool translucent wave, 280 : 3
his g. essence, 228 : 10
Glaze on katydid-wing, 799 : 11
Glazed with rainwater, 785 : 11
Glazen, upon the g. shelves, 804 : 7
Gleam, bright g. of noble deeds, 72 : 7
fled visionary g., 426 : 13
follow the G., 535 : 18
of her own dying smile, 469 : 3
Gleamed upon my sight, 427 : 3
Gleaming, like g. taper's light, 368 : 12
twilight's last g., 446 : 1
Gleams, light g. an instant, 866 : 13
Gleams (*continued*)
light g. and is gone, 587 : 13
of remoter world, 466 : 10
on whom pale moon g., 659 : 9
through fog, 360 : 29
thy footstep g., 525 : 18
untraveled world, 529 : 8
Glean, let me g. after the reapers, 12 : 26
shalt not g. thy vineyard, 10 : 19
Gleaned my teeming brain, 478 : 17
Gleaning of grapes of Ephraim, 12 : 11
Gleanings, shalt not gather the g., 10 : 19
Glee, counterfeited g., 370 : 10
girlish g., 629 : 8
mutual g., 844 : 1
piping songs of pleasant g., 403 : 2
Glen, down the rushy g., 594 : 2
Glenartney's, lone G. hazel shade, 431 : 5
Glens, gray and wintry g., 735 : 8
Glib about eternal things, 874 : 17
and oily art, 232 : 29
Glide, in sunny beams did g., 402 : 12
leisurely we g., 611 : 1
safe into haven g., 350 : 12
soul into boughs does g., 297 : 4
to wind tossing water, 785 : 12
Glideth at own sweet will, 425 : 14
Gliding, snakes g. up hollow, 495 : 21
Glimmer of twilight, 541 : 9
on my mind, 443 : 8
Glimmering, gone g., 457 : 4
hold g. tapers to sun, 259 : *n* 9
incarnations of hopes, 469 : 3
mere g. and decays, 299 : 8
now fades g. landscape, 361 : 21
river lake g. pool, 592 : 6
weirs, 691 : 12
Glimmers, holy g. of goodbyes, 827 : 4
Glimpse, nor g. divine, 340 : 28
same old g. of Paradise, 693 : 1
Glimpses make me less forlorn, 428 : 1
of forgotten dreams, 528 : 1
revisitest g. of the moon, 219 : 12
thousand g. wins, 585 : 5
Glint, bearings g., 844 : 1
in g. old gold, 742 : 9
Glisten, all silence an' g., 568 : 4
Glister me forward, 873 : 12
Glistering grief, 248 : 27
Glisters, all that g. not gold, 137 : *n* 8
Glitter of seas, 911 : 15
Glittered when he walked, 729 : 4
Glittering, ancient g. eyes, 717 : 7
eye, 434 : 4
generalities, 485 : 2, 598 : 12
how that g. taketh me, 266 : 22
society my g. bride, 428 : 13
Glitters, all that g. is not gold, 137 : *n* 8
Gloamin', roamin' in the g., 731 : 1
Gloaming, shuddering in g. light, 626 : 21
snow had begun in g., 568 : 15
Global village, 879 : 6
Globe, country spread over half g., 518 : 9
distracted g., 219 : 27
doubled g. of dead, 886 : 14
flames have spread over g., 390 : 1
freedom hunted round the g., 384 : 12
great g. itself, 248 : 13
interior of solid g., 482 : 11
power dotted over g., 451 : 2
Globe (*continued*)
sop of all this solid g., 226 : 2
Glocca Morra, how are things in G., 842 : 8
Gloire, le jour de g. est arrivé, 415 : 1
Gloom, chase my g. away, 416 : 4
convent's solitary g., 334 : 27
counterfeit a g., 278 : 20
deep thicket's g., 395 : 3
encircling g., 490 : 6
in g. black-purple, 742 : 9
moral g. of world, 503 : 3
no funeral g. when I am gone, 95 : *n* 2
nor g. of night, 78 : *n* 8
of earthquake and eclipse, 466 : 14
tempted her out of g., 527 : 2
Glooms, beetle booms adown g., 665 : 7
Splendors and G., 469 : 3
welcome kindred g., 345 : 5
Gloomy calm of idle vacancy, 354 : 18
deep and g. wood, 423 : 12
view of future, 758 : 8
Gloria in excelsis Deo, 54 : 4
mundi, 148 : 13
Gloriam, ad maiorem Dei g., 161 : *n* 11
Gloried and drank deep, 516 : 11
Glories, conquests g. triumphs spoils, 216 : 8
heaven's g. shine, 562 : 4
like glowworms, 262 : 6
my g. and state depose, 195 : 12
of our blood and state, 272 : 15
of the winter moon, 529 : 1
with their triumphs and their g., 542 : 4
Glorieth, let him that g. glory in me, 32 : 5
Glorified pawnbrokers, 687 : 20
whom he justified he g., 47 : 11
Glorify Father in heaven, 37 : 6
Glorious, acclaim your g. name, 829 : 5
blood-red, 541 : 18
builds g. temples, 567 : 16
by my sword, 292 : *n* 2
circumstance of g. war, 231 : 11
crowded hour of g. life, 375 : 1
crowded with g. action, 432 : 16
deaths g. in thy defense, 325 : *n* 9
fault of angels, 335 : 9
full many a g. morning, 244 : 13
gifts of the gods, 57 : 21
heaven's g. sun, 190 : 12
honorable and g., 379 : 5
hours even in poorhouse, 560 : 18
how g. and painful, 537 : 10
in arms, 190 : 20
institution, 373 : 7
king's daughter all g. within, 19 : 9
made g. summer by sun of York, 186 : 29
make thee g. by my pen, 292 : 4
making city g. and great, 70 : 12
mirror, 458 : 28
mission of trade unions, 666 : 22
morning for America, 365 : 4
most g. city of God, 129 : 15
most g. to victors, 81 : 10
necessity to g. gain, 427 : 22
place glorious age, 911 : 5
right hand is become g., 9 : 34
shadow of g. name, 118 : 6
song of old, 537 : 16
stirring sight, 690 : 15

Glorious (*continued*)
sun in heaven, 435 : 16
sunshine a g. birth, 426 : 12
Tam was g., 411 : 7
the g. Ninety-two, 382 : 11
the more g. the triumph, 384 : 13
thing to be pirate king, 627 : 19
things had no glory, 844 : 14
things of thee are spoken, 367 : 8
war's g. art, 330 : 1
Gloriously drunk, 377 : 10
he hath triumphed g., 9 : 32
perjured, 108 : 3
succeeded, 852 : 12
Glory, a light a g., 435 : 27
and danger alike, 81 : 2
and freshness of a dream, 426 : 10
and nothing of a name, 459 : 17
and shame of universe, 300 : 11
and the dream, 426 : 13
be the perfect one, 606 : 5
be to the Father, 54 : 18
belongs to our ancestors, 120 : 8
cataract leaps in g., 530 : 26
crown of g., 52 : 15
day of g. has come, 415 : *n* 1
days of youth days of g., 462 : 6
deed everything g. nothing, 396 : 24
desire for g. clings, 122 : 26
desirous of honor and g., 309 : 3
die in g. never old, 691 : 5
doesn't mean argument, 613 : 16
drowned g. in cup, 517 : 10
excess of g. obscured, 283 : 23
fight for love and g., 830 : 7
for country's g. fast, 430 : 14
forgot was Britain's g., 596 : 17
from gray hairs gone, 513 : 7
from the earth, 426 : 12
full meridian of my g., 249 : 1
George Sand unequaled in g., 504 : *n* 4
glorious had no g., 844 : 14
go where g. waits thee, 446 : 6
guards bivouac of dead, 578 : 10
heavens declare the g. of God, 17 : 27
hoary head a crown of g., 24 : 13
Homer herald of your g., 90 : 13
hope of g., 55 : 7
hymns to g. of life, 801 : 7
in His bosom, 566 : 5
in one day fill stage, 267 : 19
in the flower, 426 : 21
is departed from Israel, 12 : 32
is in their shame, 50 : 5
jest and riddle of world, 337 : 2
King of g. shall come in, 18 : 9
land of hope and g., 698 : 12
left him alone with g., 465 : 9
let him that glorieth g. in me, 32 : 5
like a circle in water, 184 : 18
like a shooting star, 194 : 24
long hair g. to woman, 48 : 19
love of g. most ardent, 327 : 14
mine the travaille thyn the g., 146 : 26
my gown of g., 172 : 15
no more g., 740 : 10
nothing so expensive as g., 432 : 20
O what joy and g. must be, 136 : 7
of Christian religion, 151 : 1
of coming of Lord, 566 : 4
of Europe extinguished, 373 : 22
of everything, 847 : 3
of Him who moves everything, 142 : 9

Glory (*continued*)
of his country, 450 : 5
of honors beauties wits, 252 : 22
of Lord shone, 42 : 28
of old story is forever, 105 : 30
of the Lord is risen, 31 : 23
of their times, 36 : 11
of thy people Israel, 42 : 31
of war moonshine, 579 : 3
of winning were she won, 601 : 1
of woman who occasions least talk, 81 : 6
Old G., 493 : 11
Old G. on broomstick, 699 : 13
one star differeth in g., 49 : 4
or grave, 443 : 15
pacing alone, 484 : 2
path of duty way to g., 533 : 5
paths of g., 362 : 3
pomp and g. of this world, 249 : 3
power and g., 44 : 2
power and the g., 14 : 25
precious forever, 77 : 9
pride of peacock g. of God, 404 : 3
pursuit of human g., 271 : 23
race of g. run, 288 : 29
rainbow's g. is shed, 470 : 1
search their own g., 25 : 17
set stars of g. there, 474 : 18
shone around, 317 : 4
shows the way, 317 : 14
sing tongue the Savior's g., 139 : 9
sittest throned in g., 614 : 9
so passes g. of world, 148 : 13
Solomon in all his g., 38 : 5
such g. over everything, 593 : 15
sudden g. maketh laughter, 264 : 15
summers in a sea of g., 249 : 3
take away our free will and g., 154 : 6
that was Greece, 525 : 9
they to g. ride therein, 314 : 21
thine is the g., 37 : 15
this goin' ware g. waits, 567 : 22
time's g. calm contending kings, 189 : 23
to God for dappled things, 656 : 4
to God in highest, 42 : 29, 54 : 4
to Man in highest, 634 : 8
to newborn King, 350 : 15
to some extent already, 151 : 3
to the greater g. of God, 161 : 21
trailing clouds of g., 426 : 14
trembles before your g., 74 : 23
triumph without g., 275 : 16
'twas my one g., 606 : 16
uncertain g. of April day, 189 : 32
vain pomp and g., 56 : 4
visions of g., 363 : 7
walked in g. and joy, 425 : 10
walking in an air of g., 299 : 8
was I had such friends, 717 : 15
what price g., 802 : 4
who is this King of g., 18 : 10
wonder and g. of universe, 515 : 7
words such as g. obscene, 844 : 14
wretchedness that g. brings, 243 : 7
you probably take away g., 419 : 8
Glory's small change, 491 : 10
Gloss, all the g. of art, 370 : 15
Glosses, write g. about each other, 166 : 7
Glossy, not for fine g. surface, 369 : 7

Gloucester, Doctor Foster went to G., 933 : 10
girls they have no combs, 934 : 22
Glove, hand in g., 323 : 18
iron hand in velvet g., 161 : 19
O that I were a g., 192 : 4
Gloves, cat in g. catches no mice, 347 : 30
not make revolution with silk g., 766 : 10
walk through fields in g., 795 : 2
Glow has warmed the world, 786 : *n* 4
star captains g., 785 : 15
Glowed, now g. the firmament, 285 : 25
Glowered, as Tammie g., 411 : 11
Glowing axle doth allay, 279 : 10
chase g. hours, 457 : 15
desires g. openly, 702 : 5
embers through the room, 278 : 20
green g., 859 : 2
Glows, gold orange g., 395 : 3
in every heart, 329 : 19
intense atom g., 469 : 5
Glowworm, eyes the g. lend thee, 266 : 14
shows matin to be near, 219 : 26
Glowworms, glories like g., 262 : 6
Glue and lime of love, 266 : 1
Glued, student g. to desk, 592 : 8
Glum, glance g., 629 : 22
Glut sorrow on rose, 477 : 22
Gluts twice ten thousand caverns, 478 : 16
Glutton, drunkard and g. shall come to poverty, 25 : 9
Gluttonous, behold a man g., 39 : 7
Glynn, marshes of G., 651 : 9
Gnarling sorrow hath less power, 194 : 6
Gnashing, weeping and g. of teeth, 38 : 22
what g. is not a comfort, 254 : 23
Gnat, strain at g., 40 : 19
Gnats, small g. mourn, 477 : 19
Gnaw, thousand men that fishes g., 187 : 9
Gnawing, like g. of mouse, 822 : 16
what g. of worm not tickling, 254 : 23
Go a-angling, 271 : 14
about woodlands I g., 690 : 17
a-fishing, 559 : 28
a-hunting we will g., 349 : 10
all right then I'll g. to hell, 624 : 5
alone come back with throops, 722 : 14
and catch a falling star, 252 : 1
and do thou likewise, 43 : 15
and listen as thou goest, 141 : 24
and look behind Ranges, 710 : 9
and sin no more, 45 : 3
and the Lord be with thee, 13 : 1
as cooks g. she went, 731 : 11
at once, 238 : 30
back to great sweet mother, 633 : 2
burrow underground, 793 : 19
by go by, 177 : 2
by way wherein no ecstasy, 807 : 18
clear as you g., 627 : 4
come and trip it as you g., 277 : 20
don't want to g. no furder, 567 : 20
down again to the depths, 21 : 15
down Death, 733 : 13
down Moses, 935 : 21
down to Kew, 772 : 22

Go (*continued*)
down to the sea in ships, 21:14
dressed up nowhere to g., 726:11
easy to g. down into Hell, 105:15
find out be damned, 708:20
for refuge to Buddha, 73:6
for they call you, 585:20
forth under open sky, 471:3
forward give us victories, 523:1
from me, 507:9
from strength to strength, 20:7
gentle into that good night, 887:4
hang yourselves critics, 158:11
home and get sleep, 727:2
home in dark, 699:20
I can't g. on, 910:3
I die as often as from thee I g., 252:18
I g. on forever, 533:16
I g. to prepare a place, 45:20
I will arise and g. now, 712:4
if g. high use own legs, 657:17
if I could g. through all again, 894:5
in peace, 43:5, 134:34
into it baldheaded, 568:3
into it yourself, 407:2
into night g. one and all, 663:9
into the house of the Lord, 22:5
it alone, 556:1
know where'er I g., 426:12
learn to creep ere learn to g., 160:10
leave friends and g., 691:15
let my people g., 9:16
let us g. then, 803:9
let world g., 158:17
like wind I g., 516:17
little bok litel myn tragedye, 145:7
little book, 773:15
long way to g., 753:1
love without the help, 407:3
lovely rose, 276:7, 773:15
mark him well, 430:10
men may come and g., 533:16
miles to g. before I sleep, 748:7
needs g. whom devil drive, 161:3
no g. my honey love, 870:5
no more a-roving, 460:5
nor sit nor stand but g., 544:10
not for every grief to physician, 269:28
not into every way, 35:5
not like quarry slave, 471:6
not to Lethe, 477:20
not try to g. at all, 747:9
O Lord let her g., 935:7
off with you where you want to g., 145:*n* 4
once let ripe moment g., 404:17
out see Nature's riches, 281:21
out to swim, 924:17
over rolling waters g., 530:25
poor devil, 360:6
season to come and g., 339:29
second best to g. back quickly, 75:13
shall I bid her g., 917:16
side that I must g. withal, 201:22
since I needs must die, 172:14
sir gallop, 420:7
softly all my years, 30:28
Soul the body's quest, 172:14
sweetest love I do not g., 252:15
tedious as g. o'er, 239:3
tell the Spartans, 67:19
tell those who sent you, 397:20

Go (*continued*)
then he may g., 857:3
they all g. into dark, 807:16
they'd immediately g. out, 406:17
through world safely g., 406:13
till the end, 612:13
time stays we g., 639:19
to bed by day, 668:9
to encounter reality, 777:18
to get along g. along, 779:4
to g. beyond is wrong, 68:27
to grandfather's house we g., 490:20
to grass, 261:1
to it O jazzmen, 761:11
to it with delight, 241:14
to lost sheep of Israel, 38:33
to pot, 371:25
to the ant, 23:11
travel to g., 667:12
try to g. it sole alone, 749:13
up and down as a talebearer, 10:20
waiting for you g., 710:9
walk it slow where you g., 912:15
we know not where, 228:20
we shall g. on to end, 744:2
we'll gather and g., 422:19
west young man, 554:3
when half-gods g., 494:11
where glory waits thee, 446:6
where money is, 535:8
where we will on surface, 558:16
who will g. for us, 29:11
will not let thee g., 8:25
with anyone to death, 747:9
with drift of things, 747:2
with me like good angels, 248:25
with night will g., 402:15
with show of inconvenience, 785:10
with thee to g. is to stay, 288:3
women come and g., 803:10
world thinks G., 816:11
would not g. without father's word, 470:18
write it before them, 30:17
ye and teach, 41:30
ye into all the world, 42:16
year going let him g., 532:22
you may call it madness, 416:4
Goä wheer munny is, 535:8
Goads them on behind, 712:2
words of wise are as g., 27:26
Goal, do not turn back at g., 111:24
good final g. of ill, 532:9
grave not life's g., 509:13
independence no conscious g., 800:7
is living in agreement with nature, 91:19
not g. that matters, 690:5
paths lead to same g., 860:13
pint people to the g., 568:1
progress our g., 483:11
rider determining g., 678:14
riders not stop at g., 645:12
the sky, 924:16
Goals, black people define g., 914:15
muddied oafs at g., 709:23
Goat, lust of g. bounty of God, 404:3
splashing with hoofs of g., 507:23
with g. feet dance antic hay, 183:16
Goat-head, foul g., 717:16
Goats, divideth sheep from g., 40:32
eat ivy, 933:4
lecherous g., 254:10
you herd g., 63:11

Gobbledygoo, your Luftwaffe your g., 911:17
Gobbler, black turkey g., 928:17
Gobble-uns 'at gits you, 665:11
Goblet, upon first g., 491:22
Goblin, hag and hungry g., 918:11
Goblins 'at gits you, 665:11
sprits and g., 246:14
God, a G. ready to pardon, 14:31
abandoned these defended, 692:4
accept him, 533:6
act as if G. exist, 705:17
act as if there were G., 650:4
act of G., 555:12
act of G. defined, 816:1
afraid to look upon G., 9:12
all mercy is God unjust, 330:13
all service same with G., 540:19
allowed lands to be discovered, 156:12
Almighty has hung sign, 451:16
Almighty's gentlemen, 304:12
alone knows, 630:18
am I a g. I see so clearly, 396:11
and angels as surety, 131:9
and attributes eternal, 308:5
and devil fighting, 582:1
and history remember, 820:10
and I knew once, 630:18
and imagination one, 769:3
and man decree, 691:22
and nature do nothing uselessly, 87:*n* 12
and politicians, 818:8
and sinners reconciled, 350:15
and Unconscious are one, 906:7
and your native land, 464:12
angler now with G., 271:6
angry G., 892:*n* 1
announced selves descended from a g., 452:12
answers sharp, 507:18
appeal to arms and G., 383:4
as G. alone Jesus not saved us, 858:1
as G. gives us to see right, 524:7
as I would do were I Lord G., 594:14
as if G. wrote bill, 495:3
as revealed to vicars, 864:17
assumes the g., 306:13
atheist half believes G., 330:14
attribute to G. himself, 200:9
backed with G. and seas, 186:15
be merciful, 43:40
be praised Georges ended, 753:*n* 3
be still and know that I am G., 19:12
be thanked, 797:2
be thanked for books, 448:5
beauty the gift of G., 86:18
became man devil woman, 491:9
beggar before door of G., 604:3
behold your G., 30:34
bein' G. ain't bed of roses, 814:18
being with thee, 425:17
believe in one G. and no more, 385:5
believes he eats G., 361:2
bequeath my soul to G., 181:16
bless America, 802:9, 802:10
bless man who invented sleep, 556:2
bless the Pretender, 341:12
bless us every one, 548:11
bless you, 921:3
bless you my dear, 357:5

God (*continued*)
body Nature G. soul, 336 : 21
brooding on G., 874 : 22
built G. a church, 376 : 9
bush afire with G., 507 : 22
but for grace of G., 162 : 3
by G. Mr. Chairman, 367 : 2
by G. she'd better, 536 : *n* 3
by grace of G. our forces in Philippines, 771 : 4
Cabots talk only to G., 694 : 14
Cabots walk with G., 694 : *n* 3
cast all cares on G., 535 : 3
caught his eye, 839 : 2
cause of freedom cause of G., 415 : 4
caused a deep sleep, 7 : 2
changes and man and form, 634 : 4
changes not people until they change, 131 : 1
charged with grandeur of G., 655 : 20
chide G. for countenance, 212 : 20
chosen people of G., 388 : 2
Christ came from G. and woman, 483 : 1
circumvent G., 224 : 9
city of G., 129 : 15
closer walk with G., 375 : 14
comes as sun at noon, 255 : 1
comes G. behind them, 544 : 27
committed themselves to G., 265 : 6
conscience a g. to all mortals, 91 : 13
could have made a better berry, 271 : 10
course of Nature art of G., 274 : *n* 3
created heaven and earth, 6 : 10
created woman and boredom ceased, 658 : 15
curse G. and die, 15 : 6
darkness of G., 807 : 17
dazzled by ways of G., 765 : 2
dear G. the very houses, 425 : 14
dear G. who loveth us, 435 : 11
dear to G. famous to all ages, 281 : 19
death not originate in G., 583 : 4
death of one g. death of all, 768 : 9
decides he is not G., 644 : 12
deem himself g. or beast, 337 : 2
defend the right, 185 : 13
did G. care, 605 : 7
didn't want to sign, 655 : 13
die adoring G. loving friends, 344 : 12
died before g. of love was born, 253 : 9
discovered I was not G., 645 : 13
discussing duty to G., 574 : 24
doorway to get in g., 567 : 16
doth G. exact day labor, 282 : 16
draw line where G. has not, 646 : 5
dwells there among men, 136 : 3
ef you want to take in G., 567 : 21
effect whose cause is G., 377 : 16
either a beast or a g., 87 : 28
electrical display of G., 810 : 11
Enoch walked with G., 7 : 24
enter into kingdom of G., 40 : 7
equal to a g. sitting opposite you, 102 : 5
erects house of prayer, 318 : 5
eternal G. is thy refuge, 11 : 26
every g. set his seal, 223 : 3
every man G. or Devil, 304 : 11
evidence for G. in inner experiences, 650 : 9
exalt man into a g., 488 : 4

God (*continued*)
except for G. our only lord, 182 : 13
face of G. shine through, 822 : 12
far be it from G., 16 : 24
farther from G. nearer dust, 806 : 15
favor with G. and man, 42 : 33
fear G. and keep commandments, 27 : 27
fear G. and take own part, 492 : 17
fear G. honor the king, 52 : 11
fear G. nothing else, 553 : 16
fell upon knees and blessed G., 265 : 7
finding man not sufficiently alone, 735 : 17
finger of G., 9 : 20
first planted garden, 181 : 10
for G. sake hold your tongue, 252 : 10
for Harry, 207 : 18
for us all, 161 : 14
forbid it Almighty G., 383 : 5
forgive you but I never, 163 : 19
forgotten all I have done, 312 : 2
forgotten even by G., 540 : 10
formed matter, 313 : 16
freedom to worship G., 470 : 16
from the machine, 91 : 6
from whom blessings flow, 311 : 19
fulfills in many ways, 534 : 31
gave every people cup of clay, 929 : 4
gave loaf to bird, 606 : 6
gave Noah rainbow sign, 903 : 3
gave the increase, 48 : 3
gift is God's to G., 863 : 5
give him blood to drink, 503 : 17
give them wisdom, 213 : 15
give us grace to accept, 823 : 15
give us men, 566 : 3
give us serenity, 823 : 15
giver of breath and bread, 655 : 19
giveth both mouth and meat, 159 : *n* 6
glory to G., 42 : 29, 54 : 4
good fortune is g. among men, 71 : 14
good G. prepare me, 310 : 17
grace is given of G., 564 : 10
grace of G. in courtesy, 730 : 4
grant you find one face, 566 : 15
granted it, 343 : 25
grants liberty, 451 : 3
great democratic G., 570 : 11
great G. I ask thee, 557 : 20
great G. I'd rather be, 428 : 1
great G. our King, 514 : 13
great g. Pan, 507 : 23
great G. to thee we tend, 130 : 3
greater than G. cannot be conceived, 136 : 5
greatness of G., 651 : 9
guideth whom He will, 131 : 19
ha' mercy on such as we, 708 : 14
had I but studied, 150 : 6
handiwork you give G., 670 : 15
Hannah G. and me, 615 : 13
happiness not gift of G., 763 : 3
has brought us this peace, 103 : 6
has given you one face, 221 : 18
has G. sent a mortal as messenger, 131 : 9
has written all the books, 620 : 23
hates bray of bragging, 74 : 8
hath chosen foolish things, 48 : 1
hath given liberty, 397 : 21
hath made man upright, 27 : 12

God (*continued*)
hath made them so, 328 : 2
hath not given spirit of fear, 51 : 6
hath not one G. created us, 33 : 36
hath numbered thy kingdom, 33 : 1
hath said there is no G., 17 : 21
hath sifted a nation, 307 : 11
have mercy on America, 777 : 10
have mercy on sinner, 811 : 1
have mercy on such as we, 708 : 14
he for G. only, 285 : 18
heirs of G., 47 : 8
help us we knew worst too young, 708 : 15
helping her, 682 : 13
helps them that help selves, 347 : 15
helps those who get up early, 935 : 9
herdsman goads, 712 : 2
here I stand G. help me, 155 : 13
hid fossils in rocks, 663 : 5
Himself can't kill words, 109 : *n* 5
himself from G. not free, 493 : 18
himself scarce seemed to be, 435 : 9
his Father and his G., 362 : 19
honest G. noblest work, 615 : 10
honest man noblest work of G., 337 : 13, 408 : 18
I am a g., 467 : 1
I am a jealous G., 10 : 5
I am a worm a g., 387 : 5
I am like G., 300 : 18
I am part and parcel of G., 496 : 4
I am the Lord thy G., 10 : 3
I bless G. in libraries, 365 : 10
I have defender G., 824 : 7
I treated him G. cured him, 162 : 9
I who saw face of G., 183 : 21
I wretch wrestling with G., 656 : 16
if G. be for us, 47 : 12
if G. did not exist, 344 : 2
if G. died, 910 : 15
if G. were not necessary, 303 : 1
if G. will, 131 : 10
if it be of G., 46 : 1
if this were enough, 669 : 5
if triangles had g., 341 : 7
if you want to take in G., 567 : 21
I'll leap up to my G., 184 : 8
in apprehension like a g., 220 : 28
in faces I see G., 575 : 1
in G. dazzling darkness, 299 : 1
in G. is our trust, 446 : 2
in hand of G. I stand, 238 : 9
in mercy lend grace, 528 : 28
in name of most merciful G., 130 : 9
in the image of G., 8 : 2
in three Persons, 452 : 11
in works and in word, 329 : 5
in youth remembered my G., 439 : 16
inclines to think there is G., 564 : 14
incomprehensibility of G., 484 : 16
insult to G., 541 : 8
invite G. and his angels, 255 : 2
is a Mother, 810 : 10
is a verb, 832 : 7
is an exalted father, 678 : 8
is an "in order to," 706 : 4
is and all well, 514 : 2
is and is not voice of G., 339 : 21
is day night winter summer, 70 : 2
is dead, 657 : 11
is G. blunder of man, 658 : 10
is G. dead, 482 : 16
is here, 350 : 9

God (*continued*)
is in heaven, 26 : 26
is in me or does not exist, 770 : 1
is in the midst of her, 19 : 11
is light, 52 : 19
is love, 52 : 24
is man blunder of G., 658 : 10
is no respecter of persons, 46 : 10
is not a "because," 706 : 4
is not a man, 11 : 4
is not mocked, 49 : 32
is our refuge and strength, 19 : 10
is seen God, 543 : 19
is swift at the reckoning, 131 : 17
is their belly, 50 : 5
is they are, 544 : 16
isn't G. upon ocean, 556 : 15
it is a g. who gave you this gift, 57 : 7
it is fearful thing, 459 : 22
it's not G. I don't accept, 582 : 4
jealous G., 10 : 5
just are the ways of G., 288 : 26
keep you in his holy hand, 935 : 18
keeps thee from G., 490 : 8
Kingdom of G. within you, 43 : 36
kissing carrion, 220 : 17
know what G. and man is, 535 : 10
know ye that the Lord he is G., 21 : 3
knowledge and love of G., 56 : 1
knowledge makes g. of me, 478 : 6
knows which God God recognizes, 864 : 17
land G. gave to Cain, 157 : 2
law of G. law of good, 583 : 5
laws of G. are forever, 74 : 16
laws of G. laws of man, 691 : 22
laws of nature and nature's G., 387 : 9
lay me ahold on greatness of G., 651 : 9
lay me on anvil O G., 761 : 10
let it be with donkeys, 899 : 16
let not G. speak with us, 10 : 8
let us worship G., 408 : 17
life of ease not for a g., 474 : 4
light is shadow of G., 275 : 13
light of heavens and earth, 131 : 16
light prime work of G., 285 : *n* 1
live innocently G. here, 350 : 9
live out lifetime of G., 570 : 6
lives not without me, 300 : 17
livin' G. that made you, 708 : 6
living G., 19 : 5
looks after fools, 924 : 7
Lord G. Almighty, 452 : 11
Lord G. formed man, 6 : 17
Lord G. is subtle, 764 : 1
Lord G. made them all, 561 : 8
Lord G. of Hosts, 709 : 16
Lord G. planted a garden, 6 : 18
Lord G. send high wave, 735 : 3
Lord G. walking in garden, 7 : 7
love I dare say, 620 : 24
love not Pleasure love G., 473 : 7
love of G. had blessed, 454 : 7
loveth cheerful giver, 49 : 18
lust of goat bounty of G., 404 : 3
made him let him pass for man, 198 : 13
made integers, 592 : 3
made the country, 376 : 17
made the world, 46 : 16
make me strong, 925 : 2

God (*continued*)
make straight a highway for our G., 30 : 30
makes sech nights, 568 : 4
makes those who believe stand firm, 131 : 3
man appoints G. disappoints, 148 : *n* 7
man fallen g., 464 : 16
man g. in ruins, 496 : 8
man in bush G. meet, 493 : 13
man proposes G. disposes, 148 : 15
man sent from G., 44 : 19
man with G. always in majority, 162 : 2
man with G. strive, 458 : 8
man's word G. in man, 534 : 2
Masai House of G., 845 : 8
men G. made mad, 742 : 4
men the cattle of G., 4 : 3
Mencken Nathan and G., 775 : 14
mighty fortress is our G., 155 : 15
mills of G. grind slowly, 273 : 14
mistake young man for g., 772 : 3
most glorious city of G., 129 : 15
moved upon face of the waters, 6 : 10
moves in mysterious way, 375 : 16
music sent up to G., 544 : 5
my G. and King, 269 : 7
my G. Father and Friend, 309 : 11
my G. have mercy, 166 : 11
my G. look not so fierce, 184 : 9
my G. why hast thou forsaken me, 18 : 5, 41 : 27
my soul thirsteth for G., 19 : 5
nakedness work of G., 404 : 3
name called the mighty G., 29 : 16
name of G. upon lips, 358 : 19
Nature and Nature's G., 329 : 5
nature is the art of G., 274 : 7
Nature's G., 337 : 16
nature's G. commands slave to rise, 418 : 4
nearer my G. to thee, 505 : 1
nearer to church further from G., 159 : 19
nest on greatness of G., 651 : 9
never made work for man to mend, 306 : 26
never spoke with G., 606 : 17
next to of course g., 829 : 4
no G. and Mary His Mother, 892 : 14
no g. higher than truth, 727 : 6
no G. stronger than death, 633 : 8
no g. wrong worm, 495 : 1
no man hath seen G., 44 : 22
no more Aurora Leighs thank G., 517 : 16
no nearer to G., 806 : 15
no society bring kingdom of G., 775 : 4
noblest work of G., 337 : 13, 408 : 18
none other but the house of G., 8 : 21
nor what G. blessed prove accursed, 544 : 29
not alone G. is within, 121 : 2
not even G. is wise enough, 926 : 7
not G. for father if not Church for mother, 126 : 16
not G. in gardens, 604 : 1
not G. of dead, 43 : 43
not pay Saturdays, 545 : *n* 3
not serve G. if devil bid, 229 : 19
not willing to do everything, 154 : 6

God (*continued*)
nothing not G. greater than self, 574 : 27
now G. alone knows, 630 : 18
O dog my G., 881 : 11
O G. O Montreal, 620 : 3
O G. that bread so dear, 485 : 20
O G. that it were possible, 257 : 17
O Lamb of G., 54 : 5
of battles, 208 : 8
of Clotilda grant victory, 129 : 19
of fathers known of old, 709 : 16
of God, 55 : 3
of my idolatry, 192 : 12
of Nature, 269 : 1
of Nature placed in power, 383 : 3
of such is kingdom of G., 42 : 11
of the Congo, 765 : 7
of truth, 11 : 23
of universal laws, 650 : 6
on right hand of G., 55 : 2
on seventh day G. ended his work, 6 : 16
on side of best digestion, 760 : 11
on side of big squadrons, 294 : 21
one G. even the Father, 448 : 1
one g. greatest among gods, 67 : 14
one G. law element, 532 : 27
one G. one principle of being, 125 : 9
One God the Everlasting Refuge, 132 : 19
one nation under G., 677 : 10
one that feared G., 14 : 35
only G. and angels lookers-on, 179 : 4
only G. can make tree, 795 : 7
only G. had for asking, 567 : 12
only G. my dear, 716 : 5
only knows which is which, 634 : 14
or Mother Goose, 684 : 11
others call it G., 545 : *n* 2
our help in ages past, 328 : 10
out in fields with G., 923 : 6
out of me G. and man, 634 : 4
owe G. a death, 206 : 25
pairs off like with like, 60 : 21
patriarch obedient to G., 580 : 7
peace of G. passeth understanding, 50 : 6
Peace of G. which passeth all understanding, 56 : 1
perfect blessedness vision of G., 140 : 2
perhaps G. resembles etchings of Goya, 884 : 23
plays dice with world, 763 : 16
pleased G. to visit us with death, 265 : 10
poor dear G., 836 : 15
praise be to G., 130 : 9
presume not G. to scan, 337 : 2
pride of peacock glory of G., 404 : 3
pseudonym of G., 655 : 13
purlieu of g. of love, 253 : 10
put G. in his statements, 575 : 23
put hand to ark of G., 13 : 15
rather believe G. not exist, 504 : 19
reason in man like G. in world, 140 : 3
rebellion obedience to G., 920 : 14
reflect that G. is just, 388 : 1
register of G., 275 : 9
reigns government lives, 609 : 8
remains dead, 657 : *n* 3
render unto G., 40 : 15

God (*continued*)
rest you merry, 919 : 20
rib which Lord G. had taken, 7 : 2
rise and shine give G. glory, 935 : 26
round fat oily man of G., 345 : 22
sacrifice to G. of devil's leavings, 340 : 12
said I am tired, 494 : 16
said Let Newton be, 340 : 6
said Let there be light, 6 : 10
said Let us make man, 6 : 13
saint if G. does not exist, 882 : 8
save the king, 12 : 34, 331 : 6
save the king say amen, 195 : 10
save the mark, 203 : 10
save the people, 449 : 3
save thee Ancient Mariner, 434 : 12
saw that it was good, 6 : 12
say first of G. above, 336 : 12
says there is no G., 358 : 19
Scourge of G., 183 : 7
sea of infinite substance, 135 : 5
secluded from sight of G., 254 : 23
see G. made and eaten, 541 : 20
seek G. in old quiet places, 910 : 15
seen G. face to face, 8 : 26
sees G. in clouds, 336 : 16
self-reliance is reliance on G., 498 : 19
send every gentleman, 927 : 4
sends meat Devil sends cooks, 159 : *n* 6
servant of G. well done, 286 : 26
servant of living G., 365 : 13
served my G. with half the zeal, 249 : 9
service greater than the g., 226 : 8
sets nothing but riddles, 581 : 20
setteth the solitary in families, 19 : 33
shall any teach G., 16 : 8
shall smite thee, 46 : 27
shall wipe away tears, 53 : 30
she for G. in him, 285 : 18
shed grace on thee, 688 : 5
shield us, 196 : 24
shows sufficient light, 545 : 7
smiled again, 733 : 11
so commanded, 287 : 18
so loved the world, 44 : 34
so near G. to man, 494 : 21
sole G. beside whom is none, 5 : 8
some lesser g. made world, 534 : 28
Son of G. goes forth, 452 : 7
Son of the living G., 39 : 35
sons of G. shouted for joy, 16 : 29
sons of the living G., 33 : 7
souls are in the hand of G., 34 : 13
souls mounting up to G., 601 : 14
speed the mark, 494 : 1
Spirit of G. descending, 36 : 30
spirit shall return unto G., 27 : 25
standeth G. within shadow, 567 : 7
stands winding horn, 712 : 13
stay with me G., 925 : 2
stepped out on space, 733 : 10
stern daughter of voice of G., 427 : 12
strong brown g., 808 : 1
subject to G. and Justice, 137 : 7
sufficeth me, 130 : 15
surrenders his face to G., 132 : 2
take in G., 567 : 21
tempers wind, 163 : 12, 360 : 25
temple of G. is holy, 48 : 6
thank G. Almighty, 935 : 22
thank G. for peace, 738 : 12

God (*continued*)
thank G. for tea, 433 : 15
thank G. I have done duty, 408 : 9
the Father a school divine, 339 : 22
the Father in second place, 679 : 4
the first garden made, 295 : 14
the herdsman goads, 712 : 2
the most resembles G., 409 : 19
the unknown g., 46 : 15
the word spake it, 164 : 4
the world the book of G., 250 : 12
there is no G. but He, 130 : 15
these old men, 76 : 5
they shall be called children of G., 37 : 4
they shall see G., 37 : 4
think himself act of G., 555 : 12
think not G. at all, 288 : 26
think public opinion voice of G., 626 : 13
this nation under G., 523 : 4
this only is denied to G., 82 : 27
this thing is G., 634 : 6
those G. loves do not live long, 91 : *n* 1
those G. wishes to destroy, 78 : 1
those whom G. hath joined together, 56 : 11
thou art the Son of G., 39 : 29
thought and thought, 733 : 12
three-personed G., 254 : 15
through darkness up to G., 532 : 12
throws himself on G., 542 : 19
thy G. shall be my G., 12 : 25
'tis G. gives skill, 564 : 21
to choose a g. of love, 857 : 1
to kirk nearer from G. more far, 173 : 6
to the greater glory of G., 161 : 21
to whom G. assigns no light, 131 : 17
too full of G. to speak, 711 : 16
took day to search for G., 696 : 11
took spinning-jenny, 715 : 15
towards G. the other towards Satan, 581 : 7
trust in G. hope for best, 432 : 21
trust in G. keep powder dry, 444 : 12
two halves of G., 491 : 8
two not without G., 126 : 14
unchanging law of G., 537 : 15
universe language of G., 447 : 17
unless G. does that beating thinking living, 571 : 5
unto G. is the sequel, 132 : 2
up to Nature's G., 337 : 16
very G. of very G., 55 : 3
voice of people is voice of G., 135 : 6
walk humbly with thy G., 33 : 23
wants nothing of a g. but eternity, 242 : 24
war blood-swollen g., 732 : 1
was it G. was it man, 634 : 7
was the holy Lamb of G., 406 : 21
ways of G. justifiable, 288 : 26
ways of G. to man, 336 : 11
ways of G. to men, 283 : 2
we believe in G., 130 : 11
we praise thee O G., 54 : 19
what G. hath joined, 40 : 5
what hath G. wrought, 11 : 5
what I call G., 545 : 10
what is G. everything, 72 : 11
what kind of g. art thou, 208 : 6
what man not know of G., 859 : 1

God (*continued*)
what we have instead of G., 844 : 12
when you ask G. to send trials, 661 : 2
where end knows G., 854 : 9
where G. built church, 156 : 5
who brought over ocean, 265 : 7
who could discover G., 115 : 17
who gave life gave liberty, 387 : 8
who G. doth late and early pray, 250 : 15
who is able to prevail, 270 : 28
who is not we see, 634 : 15
who is our home, 426 : 14
who knows what I would, 875 : 1
who made him sees, 710 : 22
who made rich make poor, 507 : 12
who made thee mighty, 698 : 12
whole armor of G., 49 : 38
whom G. wishes to destroy, 134 : 21
whom science recognizes, 650 : 6
whom we see not is, 634 : 15
whose puppets are we, 540 : 19
why St. Augustine thanked G., 754 : 9
will not let us fall, 261 : 23
will of G. prevail, 588 : 18
will provide himself a lamb, 8 : 13
will put an end to these, 104 : 21
will take you to task for your hearts, 130 : 13
wills it, 133 : 19
wills us free, 385 : 14
wisdom by awful grace of G., 71 : 5
with G. nothing impossible, 42 : 18
with strongest battalions, 358 : 4
with thousand voices praises G., 435 : 23
with us, 36 : 19
without me G. cannot live, 300 : 17
word of G. is quick, 51 : 14
word of our G. shall stand, 30 : 33
Word was with G., 44 : 17
Words of G. not exhausted, 132 : 3
worketh in you, 50 : 3
works in mysterious way, 804 : 20
world as G. made it beauty, 540 : 30
world of nature and G., 897 : 19
world's G. is treacherous, 797 : 14
worship G. in own way, 780 : 13
would G. this flesh might be, 632 : 18
would have three sides, 341 : 7
wrath of G., 53 : 27
wrath of lion wisdom of G., 404 : 3
wrongs not men, 130 : 17
wrote of Angels and G., 403 : 19
yearning like g., 476 : 10
your false g. dim rememoring, 811 : 9
Zion city of our G., 367 : 8
Goddamm, Lhude sing G., 792 : 8
Goddamnedest, seevility of commonest g. kind, 922 : 7
Goddess, bitch g. Success, 648 : 4
consult concerning great g., 421 : 19
Demeter or Earth, 77 : 6
excellently bright, 255 : 12
mistake young woman for g., 772 : 3
moves a g., 334 : 19
night sable g., 330 : 5
of Grecian woes O g. sing, 334 : 18
of the silver lake, 280 : 3
radiance of rising g., 850 : 10
to thy shrine we come, 412 : 9
walk revealed her as true g., 104 : 24

Goddess (*continued*)
White G., 833 : 6
write about it G., 340 : 25
Goddesses, even if g. too should be looking, 60 : 6
take hold ye gods and g., 58 : 6
Godfathers of heaven's lights, 190 : 12
God-fearing, signs for a g. people, 130 : 16
God-given rights, 505 : 18
God-intoxicated man, 308 : *n* 2
Godiva, white G. I unpeel, 911 : 14
Godlessness, future smells of g., 482 : 4
Godlike, capability and g. reason, 223 : 17
erect, 285 : 17
man with g. intellect, 515 : 10
Godliness, cheerful g., 425 : 23
cleanliness next to g., 346 : 11
Godly, old and g. and grave, 712 : 10
Godmother, fairy g. in soul, 694 : 1
God's above all, 230 : 19
abusing of G. patience, 225 : 12
acre, 510 : 12
allotment, 640 : 19
arrest, 315 : 3
blessing said Sancho Panza, 171 : *n* 1
Caesar's self is G., 292 : 12
capricious hand, 863 : 20
crucible, 706 : 15
custom to bring low greatness, 78 : 14
dare ask just G. assistance, 524 : 5
Devil is ever G. ape, 156 : 5
do deed without G. knowledge, 71 : 22
earthly power then likest G., 200 : 9
elect, 47 : 13
finger touched, 532 : 17
first creature light, 285 : *n* 1
first temples, 471 : 8
footstool may be throne, 746 : 20
for G. sake sit upon ground, 195 : 2
gift is G. to God, 863 : 5
gifts put dreams to shame, 507 : 13
great Judgment Seat, 707 : 16
greenwood chapel, 765 : *n* 3
hand folks over to G. mercy, 565 : 11
heaven is G. throne, 37 : 9
help and their valor, 420 : 12
here is G. plenty, 307 : 3
I'm under G. arrest, 315 : 3
in G. wildness hope of world, 637 : 16
in his heaven, 540 : 15
instant men call years, 545 : 6
issue is in G. hands, 71 : 26
justify G. ways to man, 691 : 17
last Put out the light, 748 : 11
light G. eldest daughter, 276 : 18
look in my G. right hand, 936 : 2
love G. ultimate gift, 543 : 20
man's bedevilment and G., 691 : 23
mill grinds slow, 270 : 14
mouth knows not falsehood, 71 : 1
my spirit in G. hand, 300 : 19
not G. not beasts', 544 : 16
one on G. side majority, 538 : 14
Park specimen of G. handiwork, 590 : 14
reason G. crowning gift, 74 : 21
skirts, 540 : 31
spies, 235 : 12
things which are G., 40 : 15
thy country's thy G. and truth's, 249 : 8
to Indian all days are G., 686 : 7
God's (*continued*)
true princes of empire, 570 : 12
voice of G. creatures, 525 : *n* 3
ways to man, 691 : 17
we are in G. hand, 207 : 24
will be done, 385 : 14
woman G. second mistake, 658 : 15
word Be, 131 : 4
written in G. book, 130 : 18
ye are G. husbandry, 48 : 4
Gods above should give, 561 : 1
administering to panthers, 889 : 14
all ages believed in g., 754 : 7
all men have need of g., 59 : 21
altars to unknown g., 648 : 6
angels would be g., 180 : *n* 6, 336 : 18
approve the depth, 428 : 21
are just, 235 : 14
are on side of stronger, 123 : 1
arrive, 494 : 11
as flies to boys we to g., 234 : 21
as psychic factors, 754 : 7
aspiring to be g., 336 : 18
believe in g. of state, 83 : 11
believe they will become g., 819 : 11
built against will of g., 58 : 13
by Nine G. he swore, 488 : 13
call the g. to witness, 242 : 30
calling on the g., 80 : 13
contend in vain, 413 : 26
convenient that there be g., 113 : 10
created of human spirit, 819 : 10
darling of men and g., 100 : 1
daughter of g., 528 : 22
dish fit for g., 215 : 20
do not give all men gifts, 60 : 4
dwells with g. above, 226 : 14
even if g. should be looking, 60 : 6
execute judgment against g. of Egypt, 9 : 25
fashioned by men, 704 : 6
fault of angels and g., 335 : 9
fight against necessity, 62 : 9
forbid it sea g., 569 : 20
glorious gifts of the g., 57 : 21
go in various disguises, 60 : 25
good g. how he will talk, 317 : 12
grant me this, 102 : 16
graven images of her g., 29 : 27
hail to you g., 4 : 9
happy who knows rural g., 104 : 6
have neither age nor death, 75 : 11
have their own rules, 113 : 22
help them that help themselves, 66 : 20
immortal g. I crave no pelf, 243 : 1
in lap of the g., 59 : *n* 3
in likeness of men, 46 : 11
kings it makes g., 187 : 24
knees of the g., 59 : 16
laughter among the g., 57 : 14
leave all else to the g., 107 : 6
little tin g. on wheels, 707 : 4
live with the g., 125 : 4
love rules the g., 75 : 5
make G. to whom to impute ills, 585 : 10
makes g. by the dozen, 165 : 7
man create g. who destroy him, 819 : 12
may g. grant you all things, 59 : 28
men determine g. dispose, 259 : *n* 4
men that strove with g., 529 : 12
might of g. slow but sure, 77 : 8
Gods (*continued*)
minds of g. not changed, 59 : 22
mortals are blaming the g., 59 : 15
most beautiful among the immortal g., 61 : 10
mother of g. and men, 5 : 3
my own g. these stones, 849 : 16
nearest to g., 79 : 2
no other g. before me, 10 : 4
not fit that men be compared with g., 102 : 11
not infallible, 885 : 12
not know much about g., 808 : 1
not similar are immortal g. and men, 57 : 30
O nights and feasts of g., 106 : 21
of the Congo, 765 : 7
oft with g. doth diet, 278 : 15
Olympus abode of the g., 59 : 27
on hills like G. together, 528 : 19
opinion that there are no g., 86 : 5
ought to create decent man, 702 : 10
pay for what g. given, 736 : 5
proud g. and commodores, 570 : 5
right idea of the g., 86 : 4
search out purposes of g., 72 : 8
sent not corn for rich men only, 242 : 8
so many g. so many creeds, 670 : 4
spun the thread for mortals, 59 : 12
take good the g. provide, 306 : 19
take hold ye g. and goddesses, 58 : 6
temples of his g., 488 : 14
that wanton in the air, 296 : 2
themselves throw incense, 235 : 13
thought otherwise, 105 : 4
two g. Persuasion and Compulsion, 70 : 17
utterance of early g., 478 : 3
veins net g. made, 850 : 14
victor had g. the vanquished had Cato, 118 : 5
visit sins of fathers upon children, 77 : 23
voice of g. makes heaven drowsy, 191 : 4
what ailed us O g., 632 : 16
what g. call dross, 568 : 18
what lies beyond only g. find, 702 : 6
what men or g. are these, 477 : 5
whatever g. may be, 633 : 22, 663 : 10
when favor of g. was equal, 78 : 2
whoever obeys the g., 57 : 9
whom the g. love, 91 : 1
whom the g. would destroy, 78 : *n* 1
woman a dish for g., 242 : 1
would draw g. like horses, 67 : 13
would g. made thee poetical, 212 : 14
ye shall be as g., 7 : 6
Godunov, Maria G. and son poisoned, 486 : 13
Goes down with great shout, 671 : 3
from great deep he g., 535 : 2
in and out with me, 668 : 12
life g. on forever, 822 : 16
much against my stomach, 211 : 19
naked to naked g., 717 : 1
no one g. and comes back, 3 : 2
oftenest round Horn goes circumspectly, 569 : 21
one but g. abreast, 226 : 18
one never g. so far, 396 : 1
rainbow comes and g., 426 : 11

Goes (*continued*)
see how world g., 235 : 2
the further one g. the less one knows, 64 : 17
where tooth point g., 707 : 5
Goest, whither g. thou, 45 : 27
whither thou g. I will go, 12 : 25
with thee whithersoever thou g., 11 : 28
Goeth forth and weepeth, 22 : 7
he g. after her straightway, 23 : 16
light from wisdom never g. out, 34 : 20
man g. forth unto his work, 21 : 11
on to meet the armed men, 16 : 37
pride g. before a fall, 74 : *n* 3
whither it g., 44 : 32
Goethe has done pilgrimage, 585 : 3
in Weimar sleeps, 585 : 2
open thy G., 472 : 27
what Herder taught to G., 577 : 13
Gogol's Overcoat, 582 : 16
Going a journey, 445 : 9
all along, 605 : 5
all surely g. somewhere, 576 : 22
a-milking sir, 931 : 14
defense not in g. underground, 764 : 4
down the wind, 309 : 15
endure their g. hence, 235 : 11
from g. to and fro, 15 : 2
from rising of the sun unto g. down, 21 : 20
his g. forth is from end of the heaven, 17 : 28
I'm g. all along, 605 : 5
know world without g. outdoors, 64 : 17
learn by g., 873 : 21
long and loath at g., 810 : 17
no matter where it's g., 823 : 3
order of your g., 238 : 30
out to clean spring, 747 : 3
out with tide, 549 : 3
preserve thy g. out and coming in, 22 : 4
sage knows without g. about, 64 : 17
speed the g. guest, 339 : 9
sun knoweth his g. down, 21 : 11
the way of all the earth, 11 : 36
to St. Ives, 930 : 1
to the fair, 930 : 13
true order of g., 83 : 9
way of all flesh, 262 : 2
year is g. let him go, 532 : 22
Gold, accurst craving for g., 105 : 6
Age of G., 277 : 9
all g. goose could give, 66 : 18
all that glisters not g., 137 : *n* 8
all that glitters not g., 137 : *n* 8
almighty g., 256 : 7
and frankincense, 36 : 21
and love affairs difficult to hide, 935 : 17
and silver ivory and apes, 13 : 36
and silver light, 712 : 15
and the lust, 834 : 5
apples of g. in pictures of silver, 25 : 14
bar of heaven, 601 : 13
barbaric pearl and g., 284 : 3
be it gash or g., 889 : 11
beauty provoketh sooner than g., 210 : 21

Gold (*continued*)
becomes her object, 206 : 30
blazing in g., 604 : 16
blue and g. mistake, 604 : 9
bow of burning g., 406 : 21
bright g. ring on wand, 446 : 10
cabinet is formed of g., 406 : 6
cemented with g., 924 : 3
centuries roll back to age of g., 108 : 11
credit card as good as g., 666 : 1
cross of g., 694 : 16
doubly hammered g., 570 : 11
eyes of g. and bramble dew, 669 : 8
fairy g., 246 : 20
fin in porphyry font, 531 : 11
fire is test of g., 115 : 2
flattering g., 256 : *n* 1
flourisher, 768 : 10
flow with tears of g., 403 : 13
gateways of stars, 693 : 12
gild refined g., 202 : 5
gleaming in purple and g., 459 : 14
good as g., 548 : 10
great horse of g., 828 : 9
hairy g. crown on 'ead, 708 : 7
hammered g., 715 : 3
harps of g., 537 : 16
if g. ruste what shal iren do, 146 : 9
in glint old g., 742 : 9
in itself useless, 155 : 3
in physic is a cordial, 146 : 6
into blue and g. into morning, 739 : 5
jewel of g. in swine's snout, 23 : 25
leaves of finest g., 570 : 11
locks yellow as g., 434 : 19
lust of g., 532 : 23
man's the g. for all that, 411 : 17
more to be desired than g., 18 : 1
names written in letters of g., 157 : 4
net of g., 870 : 6
not all that shines as g., 137 : 12
nothing behind g. embroidery, 849 : 20
old man's g., 730 : 18
orange glows, 395 : 3
path of g. for him, 541 : 15
patines of bright g., 201 : 1
penetrable to shower of g., 473 : 13
picking up g. and silver, 921 : 2
plate sin with g., 235 : 3
poop was beaten g., 240 : 29
potable g., 259 : 15
purer than purest g., 256 : 1
purse of g. resolutely snatched, 202 : 25
quantity of g. temperate carry, 83 : 7
rarer gifts than g., 797 : 4
realms of g., 475 : 6
robe of g. and pearl, 208 : 7
roofs of g., 207 : 7
saint-seducing g., 191 : 18
scarfs garters g., 337 : 7
shall shine like the g., 403 : 14
shines like fire, 71 : 20
shower of g., 473 : 13
silver and g. have I none, 45 : 40
silver threads among g., 662 : 22
singing g., 787 : 6
so thin so pale yet g., 400 : 9
speak silver reply g., 926 : 4
that I never see, 691 : 8
therefore lovede g. in special, 146 : 6
things behind g. and silk, 849 : 21

Gold (*continued*)
thumb of g., 146 : 11
to airy thinness beat, 253 : 4
trodden g., 283 : 28
troops pass through seek g., 591 : 4
truth with g. she weighs, 340 : 15
turning to g. all it touches, 600 : 13
wear the g. hat, 835 : 3
what female heart g. despise, 361 : 15
what is g. doing in holy place, 117 : 9
what's become of g., 543 : 12
wisdom never comes g., 600 : 15
wonder that g. esteemed, 155 : 3
work transmutes humanity into g., 664 : 17
Gold-bearing, crushed the g. Medes, 67 : 18
Golden age before us not behind, 666 : 6
age exists in imagination, 489 : 4
age is before us, 108 : *n* 10
all in g. afternoon, 611 : 1
Aphrodite, 60 : 6, 62 : 3
apples of sun, 712 : 14
as they did in g. world, 210 : 11
bindest in wreaths thy g. hair, 107 : 3
bough, 715 : 3
bought g. opinions, 237 : 1
bowl be broken, 27 : 25
care, 206 : 29
chain from heaven, 58 : 6
circle of g. year, 529 : 5
crown like a deep well, 195 : 11
days fruitful of golden deeds, 285 : 6
deeds, 285 : 6, 534 : 22
door, 664 : 10
Dustman, 549 : 31
every g. scale, 611 : 5
father held out g. scales, 59 : 7
fretted with g. fire, 220 : 28
friends I had, 691 : 13
goose with g. eggs, 66 : 18
graduates in g. hair, 530 : 21
hair curl gracefully, 595 : 9
hanging in a g. chain, 285 : 3
her flank g., 822 : 4
host of g. daffodils, 427 : 7
hours on angel wings, 410 : 18
in mercy of his means, 887 : 1
Jerusalem the g., 563 : 13
keep g. mean, 107 : *n* 18
key, 279 : 4
kings in g. mail, 879 : 20
lads and girls, 243 : 27
lamps in a green light, 297 : 9
like untuned g. strings women are, 183 : 18
locks to silver turned, 177 : 8
love in a g. bowl, 403 : 17
mean, 107 : 20
miller hath g. thumb, 146 : *n* 3
million g. birds, 673 : 19
mind stoops not, 199 : 9
mottoes in the mouth, 572 : 4
nature with g. process, 732 : 2
ope their g. eyes, 243 : 16
opes the iron shuts, 280 : 19
pear, 932 : 1
returns the G. Age, 103 : 14
Rule, 38 : *n* 1
rule is no golden rule, 680 : 22
rule to fit everybody, 618 : 9
rule toward patients, 665 : 1
sands and crystal brooks, 253 : 2

Golden (*continued*)
seven g. candlesticks, 52 : 29
silence g., 473 : 9
sleep with g. Aphrodite, 60 : 6
stretches out my g. wing, 402 : 13
sun in g. cup, 716 : 21
sun with g. ball, 794 : 13
taken as g. grain, 831 : 20
time of first love, 413 : 21
track, 765 : 6
tree of life, 396 : 14
two g. hours, 480 : 13
Vanity, 935 : 4
we are g., 916 : 7
wear a g. sorrow, 248 : 27
what delight without g. Aphrodite, 62 : 3
years of g. deeds, 534 : 22
years return, 468 : 17
Goldengrove unleaving, 656 : 9
Goldenrod, bent g., 806 : 6
Gold-feathered bird sings in palm, 769 : 11
Goldfinches one by one drop, 475 : 2
Goldfish in glass bowl, 731 : 13
Gold-hatted high-bouncing lover, 835 : 3
Goldsmith, here lies Nolly G., 363 : 17
poet naturalist historian, 355 : 23
Goldsmiths, Grecian g. make, 715 : 3
Golf links lie so near mill, 757 : 5
Golgotha, place called G., 41 : 24
Gondola, swam in a g., 212 : 20
Gone agin Finnigin, 727 : 13
all all are g., 441 : 5
and never must return, 280 : 11
and past help, 246 : 18
aye ages long ago, 476 : 20
before to unknown shore, 441 : 10
before you know me g., 631 : 16
coon, 455 : 10
dead and g. lady, 223 : 22
down drain of eternity, 76 : 8
far away into silent land, 608 : 14
glimmering, 457 : 4
good old cause g., 425 : 15
goodness lives though they are g., 77 : 18
he has departed withdrawn g. away, 98 : 3
heaviness that's g., 248 : 18
heavy change now thou art g., 280 : 11
here and there, 245 : 16
here today g. tomorrow, 312 : 18
heroic enterprise g., 373 : 23
home art g., 243 : 27
I am g. like the shadow, 21 : 17
I shall be g., 747 : 18
I shan't be g. long, 747 : 3
I would have thee g., 192 : 18
if she's not g., 933 : 11
into world of light, 299 : 7
like snow on desert g., 516 : 9
line is g. out through all the earth, 17 : 28
mischief past and g., 229 : 33
my life has g., 906 : 9
not lost but g. before, 114 : 25
odds is g., 241 : 22
Othello's occupation's g., 231 : 11
poets dead and g., 477 : 16
romantic Ireland's dead and g., 713 : 11
room from which faith g., 859 : 11

Gone (*continued*)
sea discoverers to new worlds have g., 251 : 15
she's g. forever, 235 : 16
soon as she was g. from me, 404 : 10
sweet cheat g., 739 : 18
these things are past and g., 101 : 17
thou art g. and forever, 431 : 11
Thursday come and week g., 270 : 8
to her death, 485 : 21
under earth's lid, 792 : 16
while she comes is g., 728 : 11
wind passeth over it and it is g., 21 : 7
with all his rose, 516 : 3
with the wind, 721 : 5
years now years maybe years, 888 : 5
yes thou art g., 587 : 10
Gonfalon bubble, 773 : 12
Gong, after great cathedral g., 716 : 8
Gongs rang loudly, 767 : 13
strong g. groaning, 742 : 9
Gong-tormented sea, 716 : 11
Good, a little fun and g. morrow, 617 : 3
a little work and g. day, 617 : 3
a thing moderately g., 385 : 4
abroad for g. of country, 329 : 10
all g. men, 923 : 1
all g. to me is lost, 285 : 13
Americans die go to Paris, 675 : 14
amiable or sweet, 287 : 22
ancient g. uncouth, 567 : 8
and bad angel, 258 : 14
and bad of every land, 555 : 15
and faithful servant, 40 : 29
and truth borrow, 495 : 16
annoyance of g. example, 624 : 25
any g. thing I can do, 439 : 2
any g. thing out of Nazareth, 44 : 24
apothecary, 235 : 1
apprehension of the g., 194 : 7
arrived in a g. harbor, 265 : 7
art for sake of g., 504 : 18
as all no better than any, 865 : 16
as gold, 548 : 10
as g. almost kill man as g. book, 281 : 23
as g. be out of world, 324 : 24
as g. in the dark, 266 : 9
as g. luck would have it, 225 : 24
as I can be, 666 : 20
as seems beforehand, 565 : 19
ask not g. fortune, 575 : 10
atom's weight of g., 132 : 18
bad book as much labor as g., 830 : 8
bad indifferent, 308 : 19, 360 : 9
bad worst best, 525 : 11
be g. and happy today, 433 : 17
be g. be lonesome, 624 : 27
be g. sweet maid, 566 : 12
be of g. cheer, 39 : 27, 45 : 29
becomes indistinguishable from evil, 812 : 11
befriend themselves, 75 : 10
best is enemy of g., 343 : 21
best is g. enough, 395 : 13
better made by ill, 180 : *n* 2
bid me g. morning, 387 : 3
book best of friends, 538 : 2
book lifeblood of spirit, 281 : 24
boy am I, 929 : 20
bringer of g. tidings, 130 : 14
bringeth thee into a g. land, 11 : 13

Good (*continued*)
but not religious-good, 640 : 5
by evil and g. report, 49 : 16
by quiet natures understood, 714 : 20
call this Friday g., 807 : 20
cannot come to g., 218 : 12
can't say anything g., 786 : 7
captive g. attending captain ill, 244 : 25
character remembered, 4 : 4
charm to make bad g., 229 : 1
cheer is best physician, 72 : 3
chief g. and market, 223 : 17
cigar is a smoke, 707 : 6
circumstance makes action g. or bad, 83 : 1
club assembly of g. fellows, 352 : 7
comes out of evil, 631 : 5
commodity of g. names, 202 : 30
communicated more abundant, 286 : 14
company good discourse, 271 : 4
constituted for practice of g., 89 : 19
corn wood boards to sell, 495 : 29
counselors lack no clients, 227 : 25
crown g. with brotherhood, 688 : 5
day's work, 348 : 21
deed in naughty world, 201 : 4
deed to say well, 248 : 31
demean selves as g. citizens, 379 : 8
deny us for our g., 240 : 26
depart from evil and do g., 18 : 21
desires be for what is g., 69 : 2
devil have all g. tunes, 393 : 6
die early bad late, 318 : 12
die first, 428 : 11
die like a g. thing, 672 : 11
digestion wait on appetite, 238 : 24
dinner and feasting, 309 : 25
do after g. leave evil, 149 : 5
do all the g. I can, 629 : 3
do all the g. you can, 346 : 12
do g. purify mind, 72 : 17
do g. the right way, 637 : 4
do g. to them that hate you, 37 : 11
doing g. one of professions full, 559 : 17
each of us desires the g., 171 : 19
end of government to do g., 484 : 19
enough for me, 921 : 15
enough to shed blood, 687 : 8
Epicurus set forth highest g., 101 : 11
errors of g. men, 290 : 7
every creature of God is g., 50 : 28
every evil has g., 497 : 10
every g. gift, 51 : 29
everything in world g. for something, 304 : 22
evil be thou my g., 285 : 13
evil reward punishment, 307 : 19
fair and learned and g. as she, 265 : 15
fair is by nature g., 174 : 20
faith toward nations, 379 : 12
familiar creature, 230 : 27
fell into g. ground, 39 : 15
fellows get together, 705 : 2
fences make good neighbors, 747 : 5
fight of faith, 51 : 3
filches my g. name, 230 : 33
final g. yet beyond reach, 697 : 9
finds g. in everything, 210 : 24
five-cent cigar, 673 : 6
follow g. side to fire, 165 : 15

Good (*continued*)
for a man that he bear the yoke, 32 : 24
for country good for General Motors, 817 : 11
for sore eyes, 323 : 3
fortune is god among men, 71 : 14
fortune may be short-lived, 265 : 4
fortune to be born human, 313 : 6
fought a g. fight, 51 : 9
free press g. or bad, 882 : 11
friend for Jesus' sake, 250 : 1
full of g. nature as egg of meat, 193 : *n* 2
general g. is plea of scoundrel, 407 : 6
gentle beast of a g. conscience, 197 : 16
glad of other men's g., 212 : 2
go gentle into that g. night, 887 : 4
go with me like g. angels, 248 : 25
God saw that it was g., 6 : 12
gods do not give all men g. looks, 60 : 4
gods how he will talk, 317 : 12
government g. and honest, 903 : 8
gray head all knew, 533 : 3
great and joyous, 467 : 10
great man inherits, 436 : 2
great poet so g. friend, 306 : 24
half so g. a grace, 228 : 6
hand that made you g., 228 : 22
hanging too g. for him, 302 : 6
happiness the only g., 615 : 12
hard beginning g. ending, 159 : 9
have no need of advocate, 86 : 8
hay sweet hay, 197 : 5
he our g. will sever, 255 : 16
he who would do g., 407 : 6
hearkeners seldom hear g., 319 : 9
hell full of g. intentions, 136 : 11
hell full of g. meanings, 269 : 23
hell paved with g. intentions, 136 : *n* 8, 269 : *n* 2
help g. wise great, 715 : 10
highest g., 98 : 26, 101 : *n* 9
him that bringeth g. tidings, 31 : 12
hold fast that which is g., 50 : 22
hold thou the g., 532 : 8
honest painful sermon, 309 : 16
how few know own g., 306 : 10
how g. and how pleasant, 22 : 14
how g. man's life, 543 : 16
I am the g. shepherd, 45 : 11
I have g. eye uncle, 209 : 7
I will be g., 573 : 14
if all g. people clever, 643 : 4
if g. why do I yield, 236 : 11
if he had not been born, 41 : 9
ill wind blows no man g., 161 : 11
in everything, 210 : 24
in which mind at rest, 142 : 4
is good east to east, 646 : 4
it is not nor cannot come to g., 218 : 12
jest forever, 203 : 20
joke cannot be criticized, 742 : 7
judge men by g. fortune, 293 : 26
keep g. tongue in head, 248 : 7
King Arthur, 934 : 1
King Wenceslas, 563 : 11
kissing carrion, 220 : *n* 1
know g. as g., 63 : 13
know what were g. to do, 198 : 9
knowing g. and evil, 7 : 6
lad of mettle a g. boy, 203 : 25

Good (*continued*)
lady be g. to me, 835 : 19
largest universe of g., 649 : 18
law is g., 50 : 23
law is good order, 88 : 13
law of God law of g., 583 : 5
laws lead to better, 358 : 17
laws where state armed, 153 : 20
leave while looking g., 826 : 4
leaves aside g. and bad, 375 : 3
left country for country's g., 329 : *n* 2
life is g., 797 : 10
life of battle g., 700 : 6
life or good place, 869 : 10
Life waiting for us, 862 : 7
literature must do good, 692 : 13
live in world g. or bad, 558 : 4
Lord deliver us, 55 : 10, 921 : 4
Lord is g., 21 : 3
lose g. we oft might win, 227 : 29
loser, 811 : 3
love as much as g. fight, 779 : 5
love g. pursue the worst, 113 : *n* 15
love of what is g. and just, 881 : 12
love sought is g., 214 : 17
loves what he is g. at, 313 : 22
luck in odd numbers, 225 : 28
luxury was doing g., 318 : 17
maintain g. government, 401 : 12
make g. thing too common, 206 : 3
maketh sun rise on evil and g., 37 : 12
man and a just, 44 : 12
man does not argue, 65 : 10
Man pouring from pitcher, 572 : 6
man's fortune, 233 : 15
man's g. knowing he is bad, 545 : 2
man's love, 212 : 16
man's sin, 360 : *n* 2
man's treasure, 64 : 22
many g. men are poor, 62 : 12
marriage, 756 : 11
Master of All G. Workmen, 707 : 21
meaning g. or bad, 304 : 17
meaning in saying he is a g. man, 198 : 16
men and true, 209 : 23
men desire the g., 88 : 3
men eat that they may live, 79 : 6
men of g. will, 42 : *n* 3, 54 : 4, 814 : 10
men of ill judgment ignore g., 73 : 15
men to do nothing, 374 : 12
mingled yarn g. and ill, 227 : 16
moral what you feel g. after, 845 : 1
morning Midnight coming home, 605 : 10
morning sadness, 832 : 5
morrow to our waking souls, 251 : 15
mothers and fathers, 858 : 15
mouth-filling oath, 204 : 19
music g. to melancholy, 308 : 19
must associate, 372 : 4
my g. vain hope of gain, 177 : 10
my religion is to do g., 385 : 2
name better than precious ointment, 27 : 3
name better than riches, 110 : *n* 14
name in man and woman, 230 : 33
name is rather to be chosen, 24 : 34
name like precious ointment, 180 : 11
nature in conversation, 326 : 17
neighbor is great blessing, 61 : 18
neighbor policy, 779 : 11
neighbors, 788 : 20

Good (*continued*)
neither honesty nor g. fellowship, 203 : 4
never bad man g. service, 373 : 14
never g. to bring bad news, 241 : 4
never g. war or bad peace, 348 : 6
news baits, 289 : 7
news worthy of acceptation, 319 : 15
no evil can happen to g. man, 83 : 14
no physician considers own g., 84 : 5
noble be man helpful and g., 394 : 16
noble to be g., 528 : 11
noble type of g., 512 : 1
not enough to do g., 637 : 4
not enough to have g. mind, 272 : 6
not g. for swarm not g. for bee, 125 : 8
not g. that man should be alone, 7 : 1
not g. to be without temptations, 597 : 11
not three g. men unhanged, 203 : 28
not to make world g., 558 : 4
not too g. to be true, 319 : 15
nothing either g. or bad, 220 : 25
nothing g. alone, 493 : 14
nothing g. makes complete sense, 823 : 21
obstinacy in bad cause constancy in g., 274 : 8
of moral evil and of g., 423 : 7
of subjects end of kings, 318 : 10
of the good of your life, 864 : 6
oft interred with bones, 216 : 17
old age, 8 : 8
old Boston, 694 : 14
old paths where is the g. way, 31 : 37
old times are gone, 462 : 13
old times grand old times, 519 : *n* 1
old times when unhappy, 928 : 4
one g. custom corrupt, 534 : 31
one g. knowledge, 79 : 3
one g. turn deserves another, 117 : 14
only g. discerns g., 507 : 24
only what is g. in man, 676 : 13
or bad for humankind, 427 : 24
or evil side, 567 : 6
orator a g. man skilled in speaking, 95 : 14
out of g. find evil, 283 : 11
overcome evil with g., 47 : 25
panics produce as much g., 384 : 14
Parent of g., 286 : 15
partial evil universal g., 337 : 1
people all with one accord, 368 : 7
people really g. at heart, 909 : 5
people's g. the highest law, 99 : 3
perseverance in g. cause, 359 : 24
philosophy a g. horse, 369 : 22
phrase g. and bad at same time, 828 : 4
play audience pleased, 741 : 14
pleasure ease content, 337 : 10
poet's made as well as born, 256 : 17
political g. carried to extreme, 414 : 15
portion of g. man's life, 423 : 9
possibilities for g. and evil, 831 : 23
poverty parts g. company, 432 : 8
prospect of distant g., 305 : 25
provoke to harm, 229 : 1
public g., 134 : 20
public g. and private rights, 398 : 3
pun may be admitted, 386 : 1
put on g. behavior, 461 : 15

Good (*continued*)
quiet wise and g., 469 : 25
recognize g. but be barred, 72 : 1
religion g. that teaches g., 385 : 3
relinquish life for g. of country, 420 : 14
reputation valuable, 110 : 19
return g. for evil, 321 : 5
rewarded evil for g., 8 : 34
rewardeth evil for g., 24 : 16
rich in g. works, 51 : 4
right reader of g. poem, 749 : 20
ripe and g. scholar, 249 : 15
sat at g. man's feast, 211 : 12
say not of Beauty she is g., 793 : 20
Scots lords, 926 : 12
second class of intellect g., 154 : 3
see your g. works, 37 : 6
seize g. fortune, 396 : 28
sense equally distributed, 272 : 5
sense gift of Heaven, 336 : 4
sense in country, 390 : 12
seven g. kine, 8 : 31
seven hundred pounds g. gifts, 225 : 7
shall not see when g. cometh, 32 : 11
share the g. man's smile, 370 : 9
shepherd, 45 : 11
smell of old clothes, 796 : 16
so absolutely g. is truth, 545 : 18
so much g. in worst of us, 646 : *n* 2
Soldier best novel, 892 : 11
some g. some so-so, 119 : 2
some said It might do g., 301 : 18
so-so is g., 212 : 29
soul remembering my g. friends, 194 : 19
speech more hidden than malachite, 3 : 4
speed to your youthful valor, 106 : 3
spinning fates g. or evil, 648 : 11
strong and of g. courage, 11 : 28
strong thick stupefying, 541 : 20
substantial world pure and g., 428 : 4
sum of g. government, 389 : 1
supremacy of g., 703 : 6
sustain g. fortune, 293 : 4
taste and see that the Lord is g., 18 : 20
taste ruins certain spiritual values, 782 : 11
tendency to g. like water, 89 : 18
that horn and every g., 714 : 20
the gods provide thee, 306 : 19
the g. I do not, 47 : 6
the G. lies so near, 396 : 28
them that call evil g., 29 : 7
thing when an't woman's, 546 : 15
things fruits of originality, 508 : 10
things not had singly, 442 : 14
things strive to dwell, 247 : 24
things which belong to prosperity, 180 : 4
third glass for g. humor, 326 : 18
this world's g., 52 : 23
thought to aim at some g., 87 : 13
time coming, 431 : 26, 553 : 4
to be born on, 568 : 26
to be merry and wise, 158 : 19, 411 : 24, 921 : 8
to do g. and to communicate, 51 : 26
to forgive, 545 : 24
to love the unknown, 441 : 24
today better tomorrow, 506 : 6
too g. for any but anglers, 271 : 12

Good (*continued*)
too much of g. thing, 168 : 12
traced lives of g. men, 429 : 4
tree of knowledge of g. and evil, 6 : 20
trust that somehow g., 532 : 9
two nations g. bad, 297 : 5
unconscious the source of g., 754 : 10
undefined g. thirsted for, 448 : 4
universal common g., 774 : 7
value it next to g. conscience, 271 : 13
vote and act to bring g., 649 : 18
want power, 466 : 17
war slays g. man always, 75 : 8
wastes and withers there, 676 : 13
we know the g., 76 : 19
week's labor, 261 : 20
what a g. boy am I, 929 : 20
what do I care you are g., 581 : 5
what g. came of it, 439 : 14
whatsoever things are of g. report, 50 : 7
when all men's g., 529 : 5
when Fortune means most g., 202 : 2
when g. men die, 77 : 18
when she was g., 513 : 1
when were g. in majority, 560 : 22
whether benevolence g., 597 : 5
whether it be g. or evil, 27 : 27
whosoever performs g. deeds, 132 : 2
why g. words ne'er said, 660 : 7
wine a good creature, 230 : 27
wine needs no bush, 112 : *n* 5
winning soul to g. or evil, 65 : 14
wiser being g. than bad, 544 : 29
without three g. friends, 212 : 1
wits jump, 170 : 33
woman if five thousand a year, 539 : 9
word like good tree, 131 : 3
words alone certain g., 711 : 20
words worth much, 269 : 22
work inspires man to difficult g., 897 : 9
work together for g., 47 : 10
works better in sight of Lord, 131 : 11
world imagined ultimate g., 769 : 2
world kills the g., 844 : 15
write g. in dust, 155 : 8
writing as g. as it is dramatic, 750 : 1
yes to everything g., 650 : 1
Good-bye and keep cold, 748 : 10
brothers, 683 : 5
can scarcely bid g., 480 : 6
fare you well, 935 : 1
I have kissed it, 856 : 10
leave them laughing when say g., 759 : 4
like g. to statue, 844 : 17
night goodbye, 683 : 11
Old Paint, 927 : 11
Piccadilly, 753 : 1
proud world, 493 : 12
reap sowing and so g., 617 : 3
To All That, 833 : 4
to bar and moaning, 566 : 10
we now must say g., 840 : 18
without single kiss or g., 593 : 4
Goodbyes, holy glimmers of g., 827 : 4
Goodfellowship, nauseous sham g., 681 : 12
Good-humored stomach, 115 : 1
Goodies in form of spending, 880 : 17
Goodliest, Adam the g. man, 285 : 20
among press of knights, 149 : 20

Goodliness is as the flower of the field, 30 : 32
Goodly apple rotten at heart, 198 : 23
how g. are thy tents, 11 : 6
I have a g. heritage, 17 : 24
outside falsehood hath, 198 : 23
states and kingdoms, 475 : 6
this g. frame earth, 220 : 28
Good-morrow to our waking souls, 251 : 15
to sorrow bade g., 476 : 4
Good-natured woman, 441 : 11
Goodness and mercy shall follow me, 18 : 7
armed with power, 823 : 16
believe source of g. is sky, 151 : 5
crownest the year with thy g., 19 : 30
does not perish, 77 : 18
dwells only upon g., 375 : 3
each of us aspires to g., 171 : 19
felt how awful g. is, 286 : 8
find so much of g., 646 : 5
first acquired by child, 307 : *n* 8
fruit of Spirit is g., 49 : 30
grateful for mode of g., 928 : 16
her life filled with clouds of g., 392 : *n* 1
highest point not g., 783 : 2
how sad our Russia, 518 : 10
if g. lead him not, 269 : 2
in things evil, 208 : 3
Infinite G. has wide arms, 141 : 21
infinite power wisdom g., 319 : 22
investment that never fails, 560 : 8
more g. in little finger, 323 : 13
never fearful, 228 : 23
no g. dies, 472 : 14
no greatness where no g., 602 : 6
powerful g. want, 466 : 17
result of one's own merits, 136 : 14
sold itself, 926 : 3
tainted, 559 : 18
thanks for all thy g., 55 : 7
throw away g. on conceited, 565 : *n* 2
thy fatherly g., 55 : 6
wisdom and g. to vile, 234 : 24
Good-night, a little warmth and g., 617 : 3
and joy, 417 : 8
and so g., 822 : 9
Annette, 625 : *n* 3
dear heart, 625 : 20
ensured release, 692 : 11
for the rest of us, 725 : 14
fortune g., 233 : 16
gay g. and turn away, 715 : 19
gives sternest g., 237 : 17
Mrs. Calabash, 825 : 14
my last g., 267 : 6
my native land g., 457 : 1
sad bell murmuring g., 879 : 9
say not G., 387 : 3
sweet ladies, 223 : 24
sweet prince, 225 : 3
till it be morrow, 192 : 19
to all a g., 446 : 4
to each a fair g., 431 : 4
Goods, all his worldy g., 550 : 16
and services paid with goods and services, 740 : 17
compel philosophy to inquire about g., 98 : 25
consumption of valuable g., 685 : 2

Goods (*continued*)
distribution of g., 763 : 8
got the g., 699 : 19
not shared not goods, 153 : 11
not take g. with him, 3 : 2
set not heart upon g., 35 : 4
soul thou hast much g., 43 : 19
with all my worldly g., 56 : 18
Goodwill and complacency, 703 : 19
in peace g., 746 : 11
men of g., 42 : *n* 3, 54 : 4, 814 : 10
promoter of peace and g., 617 : 7
to men, 537 : 16
toward men, 42 : 29
Goodwin, along with Captain G., 920 : *n* 2
Goose, all gold the g. could give, 66 : 18
cried in g. Alas, 810 : 19
every g. a swan lad, 566 : 14
hangs high, 920 : 20
lead a wild-g. chase, 169 : 3
look, 239 : 29
royal game of g., 370 : 14
steals common from g., 918 : 13
voice of wild g., 4 : 11
wild-g. chase, 169 : 3
with golden eggs, 66 : 18
Goosequill, Corporation of G., 539 : 15
Goosey gander, 931 : 8
Goot, seven hundred pounds g. gifts, 225 : 7
Gopher, an ark of g. wood, 7 : 28
Gorboduc, niece of King G., 214 : 27
Gordian knot he will unloose, 207 : 5
Gore, preserved his g. O, 630 : 2
Gored by climacteric of want, 893 : 6
makes difference whose ox g., 156 : 11
mine own thoughts, 245 : 16
Gorge, dire g. of salt sea tide, 200 : *n* 1
my g. rises at it, 224 : 14
Gorgeous as sun at midsummer, 204 : 30
east in fee, 425 : 18
East with richest hand, 284 : 3
palaces, 248 : 13
so g. all London stared, 489 : 8
thrice g. ceremony, 208 : 7
Tragedy, 278 : 21
Gorges, torrents down g. go, 572 : 1
Gorgonized me, 533 : 19
Gorilla, distinguishable from g., 539 : *n* 2
Gory, shake thy g. locks at me, 238 : 25
welcome to your g. bed, 411 : 15
Gosh, by g. by gum, 829 : 5
Goshen, land of G., 9 : 2
Gospel, brown bread and the G., 319 : 10
go and preach g., 42 : 16
light first dawned, 361 : 19
lineaments of G. books, 184 : 13
not g. that thou speak, 160 : 22
of Getting On, 680 : 7
tireless missionaries of G., 881 : 5
train's a-comin', 936 : 6
true g. concerning wealth, 621 : 12
Gospeler, told by peasant g., 715 : 18
Gospels, perfection preached in G., 815 : 5
Gossamer fidelity of man, 526 : 6
Gossip, babbling g. of the air, 213 : 19
in place of inquiry, 737 : 6
is mischievous, 61 : 24
most knowing of persons, 114 : 21
no g. ever dies away, 61 : 24
Gossipers and gossipees, 855 : 17
Gossip's, lurk I in g. bowl, 196 : 12
Got the better of himself, 171 : 4
they g. thing we ain't, 875 : 8
you've g. to get up, 802 : 5
Goth and Moor bequeathed us, 639 : 16
Gotham, wise men of G., 930 : 18
Gothic, erect a G. cathedral, 482 : 1
more than G. ignorance, 349 : 21
our G. cathedrals, 800 : 10
Gottbetrunkener, ein G. Mensch, 308 : *n* 2
Göttingen, University of G., 422 : 2
Gouged, by enemy's beak g., 912 : 7
Gourd, sugar in the g., 921 : 13
Gout kills more rich than poor, 301 : 2
without g. or stone, 302 : 24
Govern, angels to g., 388 : 18
another without consent, 520 : 1
easy to g. not to enslave, 445 : 1
every cook learn to g., 731 : 4
how can tyrants safely g., 186 : 12
legitimate right to g., 439 : 3
most make least noise, 264 : 1
my passions with absolute sway, 302 : 24
no man g. another, 520 : 1
not g. without criticism, 814 : 2
others first master himself, 262 : 19
people difficult to g., 65 : 2
reflect how you are to g., 372 : 8
reigns but does not g., 167 : 4
right of kings to g. wrong, 340 : 24
stars g. our conditions, 234 : 26
syllables g. the world, 264 : 2
those that think must g., 369 : 3
to g. is to populate, 737 : 11
tongues with difficulty, 308 : 10
Governed, consent of g., 381 : 2
consent of the g., 387 : 9, 578 : 5, 725 : 20
governments result of nature of g., 324 : 3
grant of power from g., 439 : 3
make views effective, 813 : 9
with how little wisdom world g., 263 : *n* 10
Governing governor, 452 : 13
more important than winning, 851 : 8
Government a thousand leagues off, 381 : 5
all persons share in g., 88 : 6
art of g., 852 : 2
at Washington lives, 609 : 8
attachment to g., 373 : 7
attempting to make life livable, 645 : 8
bad g. becomes autocratic g., 751 : 2
balance of natural elements, 672 : 14
basis of g. opinion, 388 : 4
bearing burdens of g., 519 : 21
behave toward g. today, 558 : 1
behind g. and people, 590 : 6
best g. makes people happy, 487 : 4
British g. best model, 401 : 11
by aristocracy, 687 : 20
by crony, 751 : 1
by means of his virtue, 68 : 8
by mob, 687 : 20
by plutocracy, 687 : 20
charming form of g., 85 : 3
cheerfully support g., 631 : 11
complain of injustice of g., 419 : 3
conservative g. hypocrisy, 501 : 23
Government (*continued*)
consists in taking money, 343 : 19
constitutional g., 700 : 3, 719 : 8
contrivance of wisdom, 373 : 21
controlled by minorities, 699 : 6
cut taxes by cutting g. spending, 880 : 16
decided over coffee, 398 : *n* 1
deliberative forces in g., 677 : 12
draw me into pretensions, 617 : 9
end of g. to do good, 484 : 19
excel the bees for g., 167 : 9
excess reproach to g., 314 : 12
exigencies of g., 553 : 20
first duty of g., 573 : 10
first office of g. splendid misery, 388 : 13
for common benefit, 367 : 5
for forms of g. contest, 337 : 9
form of g. never take root, 420 : 8
forming a republican g., 401 : 13
founded on compromise, 373 : 4
free to choose g., 824 : 12
free to people, 314 : 10
gives bigotry no sanction, 379 : 8
good g. obtains, 69 : 3
great writer second g., 895 : 18
happiness end of g., 381 : 8
happiness sole object of g., 383 : 9
honest as American people, 903 : 8
in carrying on your g., 69 : 2
in flag g. and truths, 551 : 11
in which all have part, 677 : 1
include all people, 505 : 19
increase of his g., 29 : 16
inflation weakens g., 871 : 12
influenced by shopkeepers, 366 : 6
institute new g., 387 : 9
is a trust, 444 : 3
is force, 615 : 3
is organized opinion, 751 : 2
it deserves, 400 : 2
just obligations of g., 631 : 9
keep G. from error, 821 : 9
kept sheep rather than undertaken g., 272 : 21
lawful foundations of g., 418 : 1
legitimate object of g., 389 : 4
looked to g. for bread, 374 : 11
luxury of liberal g., 553 : 9
made for people, 450 : 14
maintain good g., 401 : 12
maintain in emergencies, 524 : 1
make it an article of faith, 387 : 13
more than sum of interests, 851 : 6
necessary evil, 384 : 9
never take root, 420 : 8
newspapers without g., 388 : 4
no administration injure g., 521 : 13
no g. by divine right, 439 : 3
no g. provides for termination, 521 : 9
no g. stable in unstable world, 736 : 11
no necessary evils in g., 419 : 4
not at war with rights, 388 : 8
not belong to God's g., 583 : 4
not endure half slave, 520 : 4
not function of g., 821 : 9
not to confer happiness, 448 : 2
not too strong for liberties, 524 : 1
object of British g., 401 : 11
object of g. welfare, 687 : 15
of all the people, 505 : 19
of by and for people, 523 : 4, 537 : 15, 725 : 20

Government (*continued*)
of eternal justice, 537 : 15
of laws not men, 381 : 1
of others, 388 : 18
of our own choice, 381 : 5
of statesmen or clerks, 501 : 14
of the sage, 63 : 14
old forms of g. oppressive, 579 : 14
only maxim of free g., 380 : 13
organize civil g. of community, 418 : 9
period of military g., 719 : 8
petition g. for redress, 391 : 14
petticoat g., 452 : 13
play ignoble part, 645 : 10
political freedom business of g., 779 : 16
political understanding to run g., 788 : 10
potent omnipresent teacher, 678 : 1
poverty a reproach to g., 314 : 12
power in g. sovereign, 401 : 17
power of making laws, 401 : 15
problem for other governments, 860 : 2
properly natives of country, 416 : 17
republican highest g., 579 : 21
republican model of g., 379 : 7
responsive to people, 700 : 3
resting on property, 85 : 2
result of shared experiences, 420 : 8
secrecy and free g., 788 : 18
shall be upon his shoulder, 29 : 16
sharing privileges of g., 519 : 21
sovereign control over g., 780 : 6
Soviet g. plus electrification, 731 : 6
spirit and form of popular g., 398 : 3
spirit of country, 672 : 14
strong enough to protect, 780 : 6
sum of good g., 389 : 1
teaches by example, 678 : 1
the less g. the better, 498 : 7
thing better than good g., 677 : 1
this Bible for g. by people, 143 : 12
this g. best hope, 388 : 17
to first class share in g., 401 : 12
trip on G. ship, 935 : 5
virtue of paper g., 372 : 10
watch and control g., 508 : 17
weary of existing g., 521 : 11
which imprisons unjustly, 558 : 6
which kept us free, 388 : 17
whose object is to elevate, 522 : 2
why g. at all, 401 : 16
will ever maintain good g., 401 : 12
wise and frugal g., 389 : 1
wise g. enforce conciliate, 358 : 6
without king, 484 : *n* 6
without newspapers, 388 : 4
women without share in g., 414 : 13
Governments accountable, 813 : 9
climates councils g., 529 : 8
confiscate wealth, 783 : 9
fear foundation of g., 381 : 9
government problem for other g., 860 : 2
instituted among men, 387 : 9
liberty is in moderate g., 401 : 13
never learned from history, 422 : 9
pro-labor policies of g., 775 : 6
result of nature of governed, 324 : 3
set example of killing enemies, 679 : 11
Governments (*continued*)
whose independence acknowledged, 408 : 3
Governor, contempt for g. who is afraid, 74 : 10
governing g., 452 : 13
of New York not acrobat, 741 : 8
of South Carolina said, 669 : 12
Governors, consent of g. and governed, 381 : 2
method of changing g., 813 : 9
supreme g. the mob, 363 : 18
Governs, foolery g. world, 263 : 24
law which g. all law, 373 : 18
like a king, 359 : 8
opinion g. world, 682 : 2
Gowd, man's g. for a' that, 411 : 17
Gower, O moral G., 145 : 9
Gown, chose wife as she wedding g., 369 : 7
my g. of glory, 172 : 15
plucked his g., 370 : 9
smell fire whose g. burns, 269 : 18
Gowns, furred g. hide all, 235 : 3
some in velvet g., 933 : 21
Goya of the bare field, 912 : 7
perhaps God resembles etchings of G., 884 : 23
Grace a summer's queen, 431 : 18
abound, 47 : 2
amazing g. how sweet the sound, 367 : 7
an air and peculiar g., 328 : 17
and music of her face, 295 : 21
and strength to forbear, 669 : 17
awful g. of God, 71 : 5
beauty without g., 499 : 4
but for g. of God, 162 : 3
comely g., 918 : 16
courage to live by g., 704 : 10
does it with better g., 213 : 24
fallen from g., 49 : 28
force fascination, 575 : 13
full of g. and truth, 44 : 21
get wealth with g., 339 : 19
given of God, 564 : 10
God in mercy lend g., 528 : 28
God shed g. on thee, 688 : 5
gods do not give all men gifts of g., 60 : 4
great g. with little gift, 92 : 16
half so good a g., 228 : 6
heaven such g. did lend her, 190 : 4
her strong toil of g., 242 : 7
ideal G., 507 : 14
inward and spiritual g., 56 : 5
little g. my cause, 229 : 25
love brings bewitching g., 76 : 22
makes simplicity a g., 255 : 18
me no grace, 194 : 21
ministers of g. defend us, 219 : 10
moments of glad g., 712 : 9
more of his g. than gifts, 250 : 15
never mind did mind his g., 184 : 14
no spring beauty hath such g., 253 : 20
not an Attic g., 792 : 12
not to the righteous g., 671 : 11
of day that is dead, 530 : 20
of God in courtesy, 730 : 4
of Lord Jesus Christ, 49 : 24
power of g., 443 : 6
renown and g. is dead, 238 : 7
seated on this brow, 223 : 3
Grace (*continued*)
silence gives proper g. to women, 73 : 9
speech be alway with g., 50 : 14
sways in wicked g., 889 : 18
sweet attractive g., 184 : 13, 285 : 18
sweet cowslip's g., 394 : 6
tender g. of day dead, 530 : 20
thanks for means of g., 55 : 7
unbought g. of life, 373 : 23
under pressure, 844 : 18
wherein play violin with g., 889 : 10
will to g. as horse to rider, 128 : 26
yield with g. to reason, 747 : 2
youth full of g., 575 : 13
Graced, proud to have memory g., 801 : 17
Graceful the small before danger, 874 : 9
Gracefulness, vegetative g., 789 : 9
Graceless, let g. zealots fight, 337 : 9
Graces, all other g. will follow, 300 : 16
beauty or g., 342 : 4
lead these g. to grave, 213 : 17
mourn ye G. and Loves, 101 : 15
Pride Envy Malice his G., 443 : 2
speech lacking in artificial g., 98 : 13
three sweet G., 443 : 2
Gracious, a God g. and merciful, 14 : 31
and be g. unto thee, 10 : 23
and courteous to strangers, 180 : 13
evening star, 552 : 14
God save our g. king, 331 : 6
happy g. flexibility, 589 : 6
heaven's all g. King, 537 : 16
how g. how benign, 424 : 3
keeping, 597 : 16
Lord bomb Germans, 866 : 17
my g. silence hail, 242 : 13
remembers me his g. parts, 201 : 26
seasoned with g. voice, 199 : 24
so hallowed and so g., 217 : 26
swear by thy g. self, 192 : 12
this is our g. will, 154 : 9
your great and g. ways, 593 : 4
Gradations, fixed g., 571 : 4
Gradual and silent encroachments, 398 : 4
degradation of idea of liberty, 882 : 10
road to hell g., 842 : 9
Gradually extricate babe from fire, 505 : 12
let go earth, 839 : 13
Gradualness, inevitability of g., 694 : 2
Graduates, sweet girl g., 530 : 21
Graeae, daughters of sea G., 850 : 10
Grail, chalice that is G., 535 : *n* 4
Grain, amber waves of g., 688 : 5
cheeks of sorry g., 280 : 1
Demeter gave nourishment of g., 77 : 6
of manhood, 288 : 27
of mustard seed, 39 : 17
of poetry season a century, 672 : 4
reaps bearded g., 510 : 1
say which g. will grow, 236 : 5
see world in g. of sand, 406 : 8
send g. into wilderness, 307 : 11
spirits of land and g., 89 : 28
taken as golden g., 831 : 20
they touched earth and g. grew, 888 : 7
with a g. of salt, 117 : 6
Grains, little g. of sand, 591 : 7

Grains (*continued*)
two g. of wheat in chaff, 198 : 5
Grainy wood, 796 : 16
Grammar control even kings, 298 : 13
corrupted youth in erecting g. school, 185 : 28
dictionary not g., 490 : 14
I am above g., 298 : *n* 6
lesson on g. impertinence, 591 : 10
nonsense and learning, 371 : 5
prefer geniality to g., 685 : 13
Grammarian rhetorician geometrician, 122 : 4
Grammaticam, rex et supra g., 298 : *n* 6
Grammatici certant sub iudice lis est, 109 : *n* 8
Gramophone, puts record on g., 805 : 8
Grampa, one day bachelor next g., 856 : 9
Grampian, on the G. hills, 366 : 10
Granary, sitting on g. floor, 477 : 18
Grand, dumb inscrutable g., 588 : 4
Meaulnes the wanderer, 795 : 3
O Ireland g. you look, 661 : 10
old times, 519 : *n* 1
Panjandrum, 364 : 5
seek a g. perhaps, 158 : 14
statues and pictures g., 618 : 17
style, 586 : 16
sweet song, 566 : 12
they said it would be g., 613 : 2
this g. book the universe, 182 : 20
'tis g. 'tis solemn, 463 : 14
Grand Army, between G. and dominion, 642 : 8
Grandam, soul of g. inhabit a bird, 200 : *n* 3
to cub, 906 : 4
Grandchild heir of the first, 257 : 2
Grandchildren come into world with thick skin, 482 : 4
Grande, casa g. e senzala, 848 : 3
Grande Ourse, mon auberge à la G., 673 : *n* 5
Grandest lesson On sail on, 646 : 7
of all sepulchers, 81 : 5
Grandeur, feel every kind of g., 484 : 3
hear with disdainful smile, 362 : 2
in this view of life, 515 : 3
indivisible, 815 : 4
is a dream, 377 : 1
of God, 655 : 20
of the dooms, 475 : 17
of these States religion, 574 : 8
remains without intensity, 118 : 17
Scotia's g. springs, 408 : 18
size is not g., 596 : 4
so nigh g. to dust, 494 : 21
that was Rome, 525 : 9
wonder g. woe, 571 : 2
Grandfather, ape for his g., 596 : 11
Grandfather's house, 490 : 20
remember g. name, 840 : 6
rule was safer, 568 : 6
Grandly, how g. it had rung, 646 : 14
Grandmother, ape as his g., 596 : *n* 3
child of our g. Eve, 190 : 16
sings to stove, 878 : 10
Grandmothers, my g. were strong, 888 : 7
Grandsire cut in alabaster, 197 : 29
proverbed with g. phrase, 191 : 21
Grandsires', sires' age worse than g., 107 : 30
Grange, moated g., 228 : 24, 527 : 17
Granite into which it reaches, 808 : 2
one block of hard g., 5 : 1
Grant before we conclude prayer, 305 : 29
half g. what I wish, 747 : 16
I may never prove so fond, 243 : 1
may gods g. you all things, 59 : 28
me old man's frenzy, 717 : 10
me this last labor, 103 : 22
O gods g. me this, 102 : 16
of power from governed, 439 : 3
that twice two not four, 564 : 8
us safe lodging, 490 : 10
youth's heritage, 544 : 12
Granted, and God g. it, 343 : 25
to behold you again, 669 : 9
Gran'ther's rule safer, 568 : 6
Granting our wish one of Fate's jokes, 66 : *n* 8
Grants, each day that Fortune g., 107 : 7
Grape, a little more g., 454 : 14
eaten a sour g., 32 : 17
first from out the purple g., 279 : 7
for one g. the vine destroy, 189 : 20
joy's g., 478 : 1
peel me a g., 824 : 9
rich g. juice of good sense, 128 : 17
shalt not gather every g., 10 : 19
Grapes are sour, 66 : 1
gleaning of the g. of Ephraim, 12 : 11
of thorns, 38 : 17
of wrath not yielded all, 800 : 9
where g. of wrath stored, 566 : 4
Grapeshot, whiff of g., 473 : 15
Grapple, let her and Falsehood g., 282 : 5
them to thy soul, 218 : 30
Grappling in central blue, 529 : 24
Grasp as much out of infinitude, 698 : 1
it like a man of mettle, 331 : 1
mathematics eludes our g., 697 : 4
reach should exceed g., 543 : 1
subject words will follow, 95 : 13
this sorry scheme, 517 : 13
what dread g., 405 : 8
what they do not know, 90 : 9
Grasped mystery of atom, 825 : 1
Grasping, a really g. imagination, 652 : 4
by g. at the shadow, 66 : 15
capable of earnest g., 478 : 8
Scrooge g. covetous, 548 : 4
Grasps in the comer, 226 : 19
Grass, all flesh is as g., 52 : 9
all flesh is g., 30 : 32
as long as g. grow, 929 : 5
as soft as breast of doves, 795 : 2
bank beyond, 594 : 3
below above vaulted sky, 470 : 9
between wind and the g., 69 : 2
blade of g. is blade of g., 259 : *n* 3
blade's no easier than oak, 567 : 15
destroy blade of g., 741 : 16
dripping snow on g., 810 : 19
eateth g. as an ox, 17 : 3
eating g. like ox, 496 : 7
elfin from green g., 525 : 7
enlaced and fallen among g., 886 : 5
from heaps of couch g., 642 : 2
go to g., 261 : 1
gray-green sandy g., 711 : 11
great g. plains, 739 : 5
Grass (*continued*)
green g. above me, 608 : 13
grow from g. I love, 575 : 4
grow in streets, 750 : 18
grows on weirs, 712 : 1
guests star-scattered on g., 517 : 14
happy as g. was green, 886 : 19
hearing g. grow, 565 : 23
his days are as g., 21 : 7
I am the g., 761 : 6
inventing story with g., 901 : 11
kissed the lovely g., 796 : 9
know g. beyond the door, 601 : 23
Leaves of G. a person on record 577 : 11
like g. which groweth up, 20 : 11
like rain upon mown g., 19 : 35
may g. grow at door, 735 : *n* 1
must bend when wind blows, 69 : 2
narrow fellow in the g., 606 : 13
Nebuchadnezzar did eat g., 32 : 34
no less than stars, 574 : 23
over g. in West garden, 792 : 9
paler than g., 63 : 5
people may eat g., 473 : 14
pigeons on g. alas, 752 : 10
roots, 698 : 13
roots marsh g. sends, 651 : 9
scant of g. profligate of pines, 831 : 15
snake in the g., 103 : 12
soft hair of the g., 634 : 5
soundless footsteps on g., 723 : 3
splendor in the g., 426 : 21
stoops not, 189 : 15
through frozen g., 476 : 8
through g. behind bush, 778 : 6
tides of g., 632 : 18
trampling tall defiant g., 857 : 15
tumbling in rings into g., 733 : 1
two blades of g. grow, 322 : 12
vaulter in sunny g., 454 : 3
what is the g., 574 : 15
when elephants fight g. suffers, 925 : 26
wind on buffalo g., 928 : 11
withereth flower fadeth, 30 : 33
withereth flower falleth, 52 : 9
wonderful g. on breast, 593 : 7
Grasses of forest's floor, 739 : 15
the spare few g., 484 : 2
Grass-green turf, 223 : 22
Grasshopper, ant and the g., 66 : 11
mouse lizard g. sing together, 637 : 15
shall be a burden, 27 : 25
ye can't catch, 722 : 20
Grasshoppers under fern, 373 : 28
Grass-roots heroes, 609 : 7
Grass's, takes g. tone, 711 : 11
Grassy, tell the g. hollow, 601 : 2
Grate, fire dying in g., 600 : 15
Grated to dusty nothing, 226 : 15
Grateful, elderly mistress so g., 347 : 36
evening mild, 286 : 1
mind by owing owes not, 285 : 11
to spleen a g. feast, 428 : 14
Gratiano, but as the world G., 197 : 28
speaks infinite deal of nothing, 198 : 5
Gratification of every passion, 583 : 9
Gratified, desire g. plants fruits, 404 : 16
lineaments of g. desire, 404 : 20
sorry if wishes were g., 66 : 21
to answer promptly, 623 : 7
with mediocrity, 417 : 2

Gratify some astonish rest, 626 : 1
Gratifying feeling duty done, 630 : 6
Grating, nor harsh nor g., 423 : 13
roar of pebbles, 587 : 14
Gratitude, children's g. woman's love, 716 : 12
deep debt of g. to Adam, 624 : 13
desire for benefits, 293 : 33
fruit of great cultivation, 353 : 9
repays first installment, 115 : 9
shall our g. sleep, 421 : 22
soon grows old, 86 : 17
still small voice of g., 363 : 13
Gratuities and privileges, 419 : 3
pensions and family g., 449 : 6
Gratuitous, everything is g., 865 : 7
exercise every day, 648 : 9
Grave, airs martial brisk or g., 377 : 13
Alcestis from the g., 282 : 20
Alice, 512 : 5
almost as go into g., 310 : 17
a-moldering in the g., 619 : 14
approach thy g., 471 : 6
before us lies open g., 819 : 7
bends to the g., 370 : 3
between cradle and g., 345 : 3, 816 : 2
botanize upon mother's g., 424 : 15
buries empires in common g., 383 : 14
but she is in her g., 424 : 12
clothing of g., 729 : 11
come to thy g. in full age, 15 : 18
conclude on edge of g., 634 : 19
coyotes how o'er g., 927 : 17
cradle stands in the g., 257 : 12
cradle to g., 665 : 17
defiled his father's g., 110 : 4
dig g. and let me lie, 668 : 20
Duncan is in his g., 238 : 19
earth and g. and dust, 173 : 5
expect of man this side g., 545 : 2
fall in g. like old dog, 888 : 2
fine and private place, 297 : 1
from cradle to g., 467 : 9
from g. to gay, 338 : 1
from g. to light, 311 : 2
frontier g. far, 700 : 7
funeral marches to g., 509 : 14
ghost sitting crowned upon g., 264 : 18
give birth astride g., 866 : 13
glory or g., 443 : 15
gone with old world to g., 663 : 13
has no victory, 637 : 17
hides things beautiful, 467 : 1
humble g. adorned, 335 : 10
hungry as the g., 345 : 6
I will pay you in g., 470 : 4
ignominy sleep with thee in g., 205 : 12
I'll be buried in g., 936 : 4
in law's g. study six, 172 : 6
in the dark and silent g., 173 : 5
is but a covered bridge, 512 : 12
is not life's goal, 509 : 13
jealousy is cruel as the g., 28 : 23
Kemmerich's g., 839 : 9
lead but to g., 362 : 3
lead thee to thy g., 427 : 20
lead these graces to g., 213 : 17
learned secrets of g., 638 : 11
little g. an obscure g., 195 : 7
mummers, 340 : 21
Grave (*continued*)
natural philosophy deep moral g., 181 : 14
nature a g., 483 : 5
no flowers on g., 640 : 16
no wisdom in the g., 27 : 16
none shed tear at g., 735 : *n* 1
nor g. nor bed denied, 716 : 17
not life's goal, 509 : 13
now with love now in colde g., 146 : 28
O g. I will be thy destruction, 33 : 16
of Mike O'Day, 925 : 10
old and godly and g., 712 : 10
on my g. as now my bed, 274 : 23
one foot already in the g., 120 : 11
our lives marches to g., 509 : *n* 5
peace is in g., 467 : 1
pompous in the g., 275 : 11
ransom them from the power of the g., 33 : 16
renowned be thy g., 243 : 28
rest profound as g., 635 : 11
road long and dusty to g., 667 : 14
rotting g. ne'er get out, 406 : 15
scalding g., 735 : 3
secret as the g., 170 : 38
secrets of the g., 638 : 11
shown Longfellow's g., 798 : 16
sinks without a g., 458 : 26
soldier's g. for thee best, 462 : 19
something beyond the g., 112 : 26
strewed thy g., 224 : 20
things holy profane g. and light, 264 : 16
this side of the g., 442 : 19
this verse g. for me, 668 : 20
untimely g., 271 : 23
unto a soul, 201 : 24
vortex of our g., 843 : 16
where is thy victory, 49 : 8
where Laura lay, 172 : 16
with O'Leary in g., 713 : 11
with sorrow to the g., 8 : 32
yew to deck my g., 402 : 14
you shall find me g. man, 193 : 5
Zeus grant g. restraint, 71 : 27
Graved inside of it Italy, 542 : 7
Gravel, mouth filled with g., 24 : 31
pick about g., 479 : 4
shadow over g. of drive, 789 : 10
Grave-makers, gardeners ditchers and g., 224 : 5
Grave-making, he sings at g., 224 : 7
Graven image, 10 : 4
images of her gods, 29 : 27
Grave's a fine and private place, 297 : 1
Graves, cradles to g., 569 : 20
dishonorable g., 215 : 6
follow disquietly to g., 233 : 4
from g. of our slain, 484 : 1
green g. of sires, 464 : 12
hair of g., 574 : 17
let's talk of g., 195 : 1
sacred g. plowed for corn, 591 : 4
stood tenantless, 217 : 21
under fountains and g., 919 : 3
untimely g., 377 : 6
watch from their g., 541 : 7
Graveyard, Europe a precious g., 582 : 2
friends have no place in g., 558 : 13
no g. grimness when I am gone, 95 : *n* 2
Graveyards, white or colored in g., 891 : 13
Gravitation, Newtonian principle of g., 387 : 13
Gravity, humor only test of g., 325 : *n* 3
love is metaphysical g., 833 : 1
out of his bed, 204 : 2
settled g., 244 : 17
sometimes man of g., 155 : 11
to practice g., 69 : 19
Gravy, no g. no grub, 811 : 1
person who disliked g., 298 : *n* 4
Gray, all cats g. when candles out, 120 : *n* 7
all theory is g., 396 : 14
amice g., 288 : 18
and melancholy waste, 471 : 5
and wintry glens, 735 : 8
beginning of years, 634 : 7
behind lay g. Azores, 646 : 6
bring down my g. hairs, 8 : 32
but not with years, 459 : 21
Champion, 503 : 1
changing from brown suit to g., 791 : 6
cheerless over hills of g., 513 : 20
cold g. stones O sea, 530 : 19
comb g. hair, 713 : 18
dawn breaking, 487 : 2, 760 : 14
dawn of morning after, 718 : 12
death's g. land, 795 : 13
dogs shame the g. head, 59 : 6
earth not g. but rosy, 545 : 23
flannel suit, 898 : 2
friar of orders g., 188 : 37, 917 : 19
glory from g. hairs gone, 513 : 7
good g. head all knew, 533 : 3
great g. drayhorse, 656 : 8
great g. ships come in, 738 : 12
habitant of castle g., 562 : 8
handful of g. ashes at rest, 591 : 9
head grown g. in vain, 469 : 12
iniquity, 204 : 5
little g. cells, 817 : 12
locks left are g., 439 : 15
long g. beard, 434 : 4
mist on sea's face, 760 : 14
name was Dapple G., 933 : 16
night is growing g., 641 : 25
old and g. full of sleep, 712 : 8
pilgrim g., 364 : 9
red spirits and g., 261 : 22
sad last g. hairs, 476 : 24
sea long black land, 541 : 13
set g. life, 529 : 3
spires of Oxford, 778 : 10
spirit yearning, 529 : 10
still evening and twilight g., 285 : 24
stranger in dream, 897 : 16
truth her painted toy, 711 : 19
where thy g. eye glances, 525 : 18
wing upon every tide, 713 : 11
withered cheek tresses g., 429 : 20
world g. from thy breath, 633 : 6
Graybeards, love which g. call divine, 186 : 28
Gray-eyed Athena, 59 : 19
Gray-fly winds her sultry horn, 280 : 10
Gray-green greasy Limpopo, 710 : 3
stretch of grass, 711 : 11
withers g., 711 : 11
Gray-haired Saturn, 478 : 2
Gray-headed, old and g. error, 274 : 25
Gray-hooded Even, 279 : 15

Grayness silvers everything, 542:21
Graze, as long as stars g., 104:29
 neither g. nor pierce, 231:26
Grazing, men like satyrs g., 183:16
 tilling and g. feed France, 178:9
Grease, fry in own g., 147:8
 lust melted him in own g., 147:*n* 5
 servility slides by on g., 893:16
 wheel that squeaks gets g., 561:19
Greased worm, 892:5
Greasy, fat and g. citizens, 210:27
 gray-green g. Limpopo, 710:3
 Joan doth keel pot, 191:14
 top of g. pole, 502:9
Great age begins anew, 468:17
 Amen, 596:14
 and mighty resolutions, 291:10
 and original writer, 428:8
 and wide sea, 21:11
 apostle of Philistines, 587:5
 Architect of Universe mathematician, 758:9
 army of pointed firs, 664:2
 artificer made my mate, 669:8
 Babel, 377:4
 ball of fire, 809:22
 be g. be misunderstood, 497:3
 because we have g. dreams, 824:12
 Beginning produced emptiness, 97:7
 Birnam wood, 239:12
 blew g. guns, 549:11
 Britain going to war, 677:11
 build a G. Society, 872:13
 burden upon his back, 301:20
 Caesar fell, 216:25
 ceremony that to g. ones 'longs, 228:6
 city greatest men and women, 575:12
 compare g. things with small, 103:7, 285:1
 creatures g. and small, 561:8
 death, 732:6
 deeds wrought at great risks, 78:18
 deep to great deep, 535:2
 democratic God, 570:11
 Depression produced by government mismanagement, 880:14
 desire to bottle of hay, 197:5
 dissolved into something g., 739:1
 do business in g. waters, 21:14
 do g. right little wrong, 200:10
 duration of g. sentiments makes g. men, 657:20
 Elizabeth, 528:21
 empire and little minds, 373:8
 engaged in g. civil war, 523:4
 Father building forts among us, 591:4
 feast of languages, 191:7
 fell g. oaks, 347:29
 finds pang as g., 228:17
 First Cause, 378:1
 fortune great slavery, 115:7
 Gaels of Ireland, 742:4
 globe itself, 248:13
 God our King, 514:13
 god Pan, 120:19, 507:23
 gray ships come in, 738:12
 gray-green greasy Limpopo, 710:3
 Gromboolian plain, 551:3
 gulf fixed, 43:34
Great (*continued*)
 hand of God, 238:9
 have seen the wicked in g. power, 18:26
 he is a g. observer, 215:9
 hedgehog knows one g. thing, 62:2
 heir of fame, 277:13
 help good wise g., 715:10
 horse of gold, 828:9
 how g. that darkness, 37:19
 ice also g. would suffice, 748:2
 ill can he rule the g., 174:2
 illusion, 735:20
 impotently g., 334:14
 in admiration as herself, 249:17
 in g. hand of God I stand, 238:9
 indispensable unique g., 701:11
 interests at stake, 88:10
 inwardly in secret g., 568:23
 is Diana, 46:22
 is glory of the woman, 81:6
 is truth, 34:3
 is truth and shall prevail, 34:*n* 2
 know well I am not g., 534:13
 leap in the dark, 264:21
 let us mock at g., 715:9
 live at level of g. men, 673:5
 lives of g. men remind us, 509:15
 making city glorious and g., 70:12
 malefactors of g. wealth, 687:12
 man does not lose child's-heart, 89:16
 man does not think beforehand, 89:15
 man's memory, 222:10
 many small make a g., 148:9
 many talks from G. father, 374:21
 mast of some g. ammiral, 283:15
 matter or small, 35:7
 meals of beef iron steel, 207:26
 men are not always wise, 16:21
 men can't be ruled, 865:5
 men contending with adversity, 259:7
 men great nations not boasters, 498:21
 men not scholars, 519:13
 men texts of Revelation, 473:6
 mother of big apples, 879:12
 names as these, 922:10
 nature's second course, 237:21
 Neptune's ocean wash, 238:1
 nice customs curtsy to g. kings, 208:20
 no g. man born too soon, 724:13
 no g. no small, 336:22
 none unhappy but g., 327:20
 nose great man, 726:1
 not g. pleasure to bring death, 74:15
 nothing g. accomplished without passion, 422:13
 nothing g. created suddenly, 121:3
 nothing g. without g. men, 815:6
 O that I were as g., 195:5
 old times, 519:*n* 1
 ones eat up little ones, 243:13
 only g. man write history, 676:5
 only g. poets can read g. poets, 559:32
 Original proclaim, 325:8
 our hearts are g., 534:6
 packs and sets of g. ones, 235:12
 patriot great man, 667:3
 pay g. deal too dear, 246:8
Great (*continued*)
 pearl of g. price, 39:18
 persons great kindnesses, 170:28
 pith and moment, 221:12
 poet writes his time, 809:11
 poetry result of national spirit, 577:13
 poets great audiences, 577:9
 prince and a g. man fallen, 13:13
 Prince in prison lies, 253:7
 quaint g. figure, 765:8
 rats small rats, 541:2
 redemption from above, 277:6
 responsibility of g. states, 787:10
 rightly to be g., 223:19
 rooted blossomer, 715:17
 rough diamond, 342:2
 rudely g., 337:2
 seekest thou g. things, 32:19
 shade of that once g., 425:20
 silence alone g., 483:7
 sleep out this g. gap, 240:20
 small and g. beasts, 21:11
 small thing analogy of g. things, 100:16
 so clear in his g. office, 236:24
 so g. a poet and friend, 306:24
 so g. is his mercy, 21:6
 society here at home, 813:15
 society on earth, 424:6
 some are born g., 214:9
 song after death of singer, 577:14
 souls suffer in silence, 412:16
 sphere thou movest in, 241:20
 stage of fools, 235:5
 star early drooped, 576:2
 sweet mother, 633:2
 that he is grown so g., 215:7
 thereby the g. is achieved, 64:12
 things are done, 407:1
 things both g. and small, 435:11
 things made of little, 544:27
 those who were truly g., 876:15
 though fallen g., 457:7
 thoughts come from heart, 361:3
 to be a g. man, 581:9
 to do thing that ends all other, 241:24
 too g. for revenge, 609:9
 truth is g. and endures, 3:5
 war and petty peace, 720:1
 whales sailing by, 584:13
 whatever little seemed g., 488:2
 when little fears grow g., 222:13
 when nature removes g. man, 498:13
 where love is g., 222:13
 White Way, 696:16
 who is from nature, 498:12
 wide beautiful world, 593:7
 winds shorewards blow, 584:11
 wink of eternity, 843:14
 with child and longing for prunes, 228:2
 with young, 927:3
 your g. and gracious ways, 593:4
Great Spirit appointed place for us, 419:9
 gave ancestors lands we possess, 419:14
 is my father, 419:10
 make them all for his children, 419:13
Greater, Brutus makes mine g., 217:3
 far g. than his father, 58:4

Greater (*continued*)
ignorance greater dogmatism, 664 : 11
love false to object, 868 : 7
love hath no man, 45 : 25
man greater courtesy, 534 : 18
more strong far g., 245 : 21
none beneath sun, 710 : 12
nothing g. than self, 574 : 27
out of small beginnings g. things, 265 : 13
prey upon less, 344 : 13
punishment g. than I can bear, 7 : 18
service g. than the god, 226 : 8
than God cannot be conceived, 136 : 5
than Solomon, 39 : 12
than we know, 429 : 2
the g. the more humble, 34 : 24
the wealth thicker the dirt, 871 : 10
thy necessity g. than mine, 176 : 16
to the g. glory of God, 161 : 21
Greatest, artist embodied g. ideas, 572 : 8
bears g. names, 289 : 2
best personality, 577 : 4
empty vessel g. sound, 208 : 12
event in war, 81 : 10
fool is man, 311 : 12
griefs those we cause, 74 : 4
happiness for greatest numbers, 342 : 19
how much the g. event, 394 : 10
I am the g., 915 : 10
man ever seen, 372 : *n* 1
minds capable of g. vices, 272 : 7
my vision's g. enemy, 407 : 8
of these is charity, 48 : 25
pass days in that where skill g., 112 : 21
politics g. adventure, 753 : 9
question ever debated, 381 : 6
scandal waits on greatest state, 189 : 24
service or greatest injury, 84 : 3
sooner fail than not g., 479 : 15
tell aloud g. failing, 322 : 17
things achieved not consciously directed, 844 : 7
vicissitude of things, 181 : 15
well-wrought urn becomes g. ashes, 252 : 12
Great-grandfather was but a waterman, 302 : 7
Greathearted gentlemen, 540 : 25
Stentor, 57 : 31
Greatly falling with falling state, 334 : 13
they shall be g. rewarded, 34 : 13
think or bravely die, 335 : 8
to find quarrel in straw, 223 : 19
Greatness, abuse of g., 215 : 15
all g. unconscious, 472 : 11
all the far-stretched g., 173 : 4
be not afraid of g., 214 : 9
boy my g., 241 : 27
changed to empty name, 488 : *n* 3
farewell to all my g., 249 : 3
far-off touch of g., 534 : 13
France not France without g., 815 : 10
gods' custom to bring low all things of g., 78 : 14
highest point of my g., 249 : 1
honor and g. of his name, 249 : 18
instruments of European g., 401 : 14
Greatness (*continued*)
inward g., 207 : 11
is a-ripening, 249 : 3
is spiritual condition, 588 : 16
knows itself, 204 : 37
moment of g. flicker, 803 : 16
no g. where no simplicity, 602 : 6
not size but quality, 619 : 19
nurse into g., 85 : 5
of Athens, 81 : 5
of British nation, 326 : 22
of God, 651 : 9
of name in the father, 257 : 2
political g. and wisdom meet, 84 : 15
rough road leads to g., 114 : 27
some achieve g., 214 : 9
summons to g., 882 : 19
thine O Lord is the g., 14 : 25
who say this not g., 540 : 1
within range of marshes, 651 : 9
won by men with courage, 81 : 5
Grecian goldsmiths make, 715 : 3
sighed soul toward G. tents, 200 : 22
Urn worth old ladies, 838 : 13
woes O goddess sing, 334 : 18
Greece, all G. Euripides' monument, 75 : *n* 13
Athens the eye of G., 288 : 13
beauty not repeat G., 497 : 30
bulwark of G. famous Athens, 72 : 9
city is education to G., 81 : 4
city-states of G., 852 : 2
enclose G. in soul, 484 : 3
fair G. sad relic, 457 : 7
gave our lives to save G., 67 : 21
glory that was G., 525 : 9
great suffering on G., 850 : 11
home of gods, 819 : 10
isles of G., 461 : 2
Italy England did adorn, 306 : 1
might still be free, 461 : 4
of China and of G., 858 : 20
saw Byron's struggle cease, 585 : 2
to Gaul to G., 376 : 10
to G. direful spring, 334 : *n* 4
tragedy of G., 819 : 12
wounds me, 849 : 17
Greed and lust for riches, 760 : 8
entrenched g., 779 : 14
no greater disaster than g., 64 : 16
satisfy your g., 709 : *n* 3
Greedy, fool is he who is g., 4 : 1
hands, 520 : *n* 3
not for needy but g., 780 : 18
of filthy lucre, 50 : 26
the sinful and lewd, 834 : 5
Greedy-gut, put on pot says G., 931 : 6
Greek accent slanting wrong, 560 : 21
all G. all Roman fame, 339 : 20
best of all things G., 702 : 6
come in Latin or in G., 276 : 9
he G. and Latin speaks, 290 : *n* 3
hungry little G., 122 : 4
imagery of G. and Latin, 357 : 19
is like lace, 356 : 15
islands over Harvard Square, 842 : 4
learn G. as treat, 743 : 8
mark of G. spirit, 723 : 14
neither G. nor Jew, 50 : 12
small Latin and less G., 256 : 13
speak G. naturally as pigs squeak, 290 : 15
thought and life, 598 : 13
to me, 215 : 11
Greek (*continued*)
turn pages of G. models, 109 : 30
Greeks, fear G. even when they bring gifts, 104 : 32
first westerners, 723 : 13
for G. or for Troy town, 558 : 19
give sea deity, 570 : 4
had modesty we have cant, 455 : 3
had word for it, 794 : 10
have dreamt dream of life best, 397 : 12
led us to where they worship, 136 : 3
seeking land of G., 395 : 8
when G. joined G., 317 : 13
wonderful expedition of all G., 702 : 11
Green, all a g. willow, 158 : 15, 232 : 8
all in g. went my love, 828 : 9
among thy g. braes, 410 : 13
and dying, 887 : 3
and pleasant land, 406 : 21
and yellow melancholy, 214 : 5
as emerald, 434 : 10
azures, 673 : 16
babbled of g. fields, 207 : 13
banks of Shannon, 443 : 9
barbarism turning paradigm, 766 : 15
bay tree, 18 : 26
be the g. grass above me, 608 : 13
be turf above thee, 464 : 11
beechen g., 476 : 22
casque has outdone elegance, 793 : 4
crammers of green fruits, 766 : 23
devouring g. azures, 673 : 16
do these things in g. tree, 44 : 5
drives my g. age, 886 : 12
dry smooth-shaven g., 278 : 18
elfin from g. grass, 525 : 7
England's mountains g., 406 : 21
felicity, 478 : 14
Flora and country g., 476 : 23
forget g. thumbs, 886 : 15
girl, 219 : 4
glowing young spring, 859 : 2
golden lamps in g. light, 297 : 9
good crier of g. sauce, 158 : 2
graves of your sires, 464 : 12
Greta woods are g., 431 : 18
groves of the blest, 105 : 21
grow the rashes O, 409 : 16
happy as grass was g., 886 : 19
heads g. hands blue, 550 : 11
heard on the g., 403 : 15
hill far away, 561 : 9
how much I want you g., 841 : 8
in hamlets dances on g., 430 : 6
in judgment, 240 : 25
in thy g. lap, 362 : 22
isle in sea love, 525 : 17
keep g. tree in heart, 132 : 25
keep memory g., 446 : 8
laid him on the g., 927 : 6
laurel g. for season, 633 : 6
lavender's g., 933 : 13
leaf shall be g., 32 : 11
learn of g. world, 793 : 4
legend of g. chapels, 886 : 18
lie down in g. pastures, 18 : 7
life once lived there, 877 : 15
light, 816 : 11
little Johnny G., 930 : 14
little vaulter, 454 : 3
making the g. one red, 238 : 1

Green (*continued*)
mansions, 646 : 1
mantle of standing pool, 234 : 9
Meander's margent g., 279 : 18
memory be g., 217 : 28
moon made of g. cheese, 161 : 8
o'er g. cornfield did pass, 212 : 33
old age, 303 : 15
on g. turf suck showers, 281 : 1
on ilka g. loaning, 368 : 2
on the echoing g., 403 : 4
pastures, 18 : 7
remain g. forever, 413 : 21
sea's g. crying towers, 843 : 18
sing all a g. willow, 232 : 8
snow on g. grass, 810 : 19
sod above, 625 : *n* 3, 625 : 20
soul bright invisible g., 558 : 11
speak like a g. girl, 219 : 4
sucking g. from ferns, 822 : 7
swell in havens dumb, 655 : 17
text old orator too g., 189 : 13
the golden tree of life, 396 : 14
thought in a green shade, 297 : 3
through g. fuse drives flower, 886 : 12
to what g. altar, 477 : 9
too g. and only good for fools, 66 : *n* 1
tossing g. water, 785 : 12
U blue O, 673 : 20
underwood and cover, 632 : 8
water spurted through hull, 673 : 15
wearin' o' the G., 920 : 21, 920 : 22
when all trees g., 566 : 14
with boughs, 671 : 3
Greenery yallery, 628 : 12
Greenest of our valleys, 526 : 1
Green-eyed jealousy, 199 : 28
monster, 230 : 34
Greenhouse, loves a g. too, 377 : 2
Greenland's icy mountains, 452 : 8
Greenly, we have done but g., 223 : 26
Greenness, heart recovered g., 269 : 4
Green-robed senators, 478 : 4
Greensleeves all my joy, 917 : 15
Green-walled by hills of Maryland, 513 : 17
Greenwood chapel, 765 : *n* 3
must to g. go, 917 : 5
under the g. tree, 211 : 1
Greet, in every angle g., 297 : 7
it gars me g., 411 : 5
me with that sun thine eye, 244 : 17
offspring from camps, 864 : 15
two solitudes g., 756 : 6
Greeting, 'change one g. and part, 581 : 12
Gregory, John Synge and Augusta G., 717 : 14
Grenadier, British G., 922 : 10
she strode like g., 683 : 12
Grenadiers, captain of Hampshire g., 384 : 6
Grenville, Sir Richard G. lay, 535 : 11
Greta woods are green, 431 : 18
Greville servant to Queen Elizabeth, 175 : 6
Grew, autumn that g. by reaping, 241 : 25
lean assailed seasons, 728 : 19
miles around wonder g., 691 : 2
still the wonder g., 370 : 11
sweetest thing that ever g., 424 : 19
three years she g., 424 : 13
together like double cherry, 197 : 2
Grew (*continued*)
up fostered by beauty, 423 : 17
where one g. before, 322 : 12
within this learned man, 184 : 11
Greyhound, fawning g. did proffer, 203 : 16
puppies, 518 : 4
Greyhound's gentle tautness, 893 : 12
Greyhounds, stand like g. in slips, 207 : 18
Gridley, fire when ready G., 631 : 13
Grief, acquainted with g., 31 : 14
age or g. or sickness, 267 : 6
aggravates loss, 917 : 20
at not wanting to call dead back, 755 : 17
beguile you from g., 524 : 4
but for g. as if not been, 469 : 6
can honor take away g., 205 : 5
can I see another's g., 403 : 16
can take care of itself, 625 : 17
develops mind, 734 : 12
divine radiance, 491 : 16
drug which takes away g., 59 : 25
each substance of a g., 194 : 18
everyone can master g., 209 : 22
fills room of absent child, 201 : 26
for every g. to physician, 269 : 28
forgotten, 632 : 8
glistering g., 248 : 27
great as my g., 195 : 5
hopeless g. passionless, 507 : 3
I am g., 912 : 7
in much wisdom is much g., 26 : 17
is proud, 201 : 20
itself be mortal, 469 : 6
journeyman to g., 194 : 4
joy misunderstood, 507 : 24
make carnival of g., 725 : 8
makes owner stoop, 201 : 20
melts away, 269 : 3
mortals live in g., 59 : 12
my joy my g., 276 : 6
nor g. nor love enough alone, 889 : 8
of g. I died, 874 : 17
past help should be past g., 246 : 18
pitched past pitch of g., 656 : 17
plague of sighing and g., 204 : 3
put in words g., 531 : 20
reason unhinged by g., 572 : 10
returns with revolving year, 469 : 4
sees into bottom of my g., 193 : 18
silent manliness of g., 370 : 18
smiling at g., 214 : 5
sure to come to g., 749 : 13
teaches to waver, 74 : 17
that does not speak, 239 : 20
think you can shut g. in, 785 : 10
thus brief my love is g., 812 : 3
to weather as to g., 785 : 10
to weep make less depth of g., 186 : 3
torments of g. endured, 495 : 18
unmanly g., 218 : 4
was ever g. like mine, 268 : 10
what greater g., 76 : 17
what restraint to g. for one so dear, 107 : 12
wind looks for g. it belongs to, 907 : 20
wings of Time g. flies, 296 : 17
with glass that ran, 632 : 9
with g. and shame bowed down, 276 : 13
worm canker and g., 462 : 18
you must first feel g., 109 : 23
Griefs, all my g. are gone, 182 : 5
beware the easy g., 889 : 21
drinking my g., 195 : 11
even his g. are a joy, 60 : 20
fresh tears over old g., 77 : 15
great g. dumb, 115 : 15
griping g., 917 : 17
he hath borne our g., 31 : 15
light g. loquacious, 115 : 15
my state depose but not my g., 195 : 12
patch g. with proverbs, 210 : 3
private g., 216 : 26
purify and prepare man, 671 : 22
some g. are medicinable, 243 : 18
sufferest mortal g., 208 : 6
that harass distressed, 351 : 8
we cause ourselves, 74 : 4
Grievance, no g. redress by mob law, 519 : 23
Grievances, clod of ailments and g., 680 : 15
inferior g. lose force, 390 : 14
redress of g., 391 : 14
repeat no g., 370 : *n* 3
Grieve at funeral, 624 : 18
his heart, 239 : 13
men are we and g., 425 : 20
not for what past, 917 : 20
not g. over inevitable, 94 : 8
one suffer than nation g., 304 : 8
who g. for this woman, 801 : 13
woman to be overmastered, 209 : 6
Grieved, by wind g. ghost, 852 : 8
Grieves, that which g. me more, 331 : 11
Grieving, Margaret are you g., 656 : 9
Grievous burden was thy birth, 187 : 18
gossip is g. to bear, 61 : 24
my most g. fault, 54 : 2
remembrance of them is g., 55 : 17
roar, 438 : 12
Grievously, sins most g. committed, 55 : 17
Griffith met by Mr. G., 327 : 8
Grim and ancient Raven, 526 : 15
brow g. mouth prim, 806 : 14
death, 262 : 22
Death my son and foe, 284 : 26
heaven not g., 545 : 23
hushed in g. repose, 363 : 6
king's dog, 76 : 3
shape towered up, 424 : 1
wolf with privy paw, 280 : 22
Grimace, accelerated g., 792 : 12
Grimaces called laughter, 264 : 15
Grimness, no graveyard g. when I am gone, 95 : *n* 2
Grim-visaged comfortless Despair, 361 : 11
war smoothed his front, 186 : 30
Grin, all Nature wears one g., 349 : 4
devil did g., 435 : 17
ending with the g., 611 : 17
how cheerfully seems to g., 611 : 5
owned with a g., 440 : 15
remained after rest gone, 611 : 17
universal g., 349 : 4
Grind, ax to g., 448 : 12
bones to make bread, 934 : 4
demd horrid g., 547 : 18
exceeding small, 273 : 14
faces of the poor, 28 : 35
in mill of truism, 496 : 13
in the prison house, 12 : 19

Grind (*continued*)
laws g. the poor, 369 : 4
mills of God g. slowly, 273 : 14
with water that's past, 269 : 21
Grinders cease, 27 : 24
Grinding, sound of the g. is low, 27 : 24
Grinds, God's mill g. slow, 270 : 14
Grindstone, hold noses to g., 159 : 15
tightfisted hand at g., 548 : 4
Grinning, mock your own g., 224 : 14
Griping griefs heart wound, 917 : 17
Grisilda, in trust to fynde G., 147 : 21
Grisly gang, 745 : 3
Gristle, a people still in the g., 372 : 14
Grizzled, his beard was g., 218 : 23
his hair just g., 303 : 15
Groan, condemned alike to g., 361 : 12
hear each other g., 476 : 24
of martyr's woe, 406 : 7
scarcely howl or g., 614 : 2
sinks with bubbling g., 458 : 26
spirit fled with g., 106 : 7
weep no more nor g., 260 : 19
Groaned, my mother g., 405 : 12
Groaneth, whole creation g., 47 : 9
Groaning, strong gongs g., 742 : 9
Groans, cackles g. and dies, 470 : 11
shrieks and g. of wounded, 579 : 3
sovereign of sighs and g., 190 : 26
Grog they dreamed they swallowed, 772 : 21
Groined aisles of Rome, 493 : 18
Gromboolian, great G. plain, 551 : 3
Groove, freight proportioned to g., 608 : 5
Grooves, ringing g. of change, 530 : 8
Grope for evidence of knighthood, 884 : 16
Gross and scope of my opinion, 217 : 18
flesh sinks downward, 195 : 19
gratitude not among g. people, 353 : 9
not g. to sink but light, 189 : 8
population violent and g., 596 : 2
scarce so g. as beetles, 234 : 28
things rank and g., 218 : 6
two g. broken statues, 792 : 16
Grossest iridescence of ocean, 768 : 12
superstitions, 515 : 9
Grossly, decay doth g. close it in, 201 : 1
err as g. as the few, 304 : 13
Grossness, lost evil by losing g., 373 : 25
Grosvenor Gallery young man, 628 : 12
Grotesque, so striking and g., 488 : 12
what is not g. and why, 905 : 4
Grotius, celebrities such as G., 615 : 14
Ground, accustomed to way g. opens up, 912 : 12
acre of barren g., 247 : 8
all seated on the g., 317 : 4
another man's g., 225 : 17
army supported by aviation, 825 : 6
as water spilt on the g., 13 : 22
beat the g., 279 : 14
betwixt stirrup and g., 171 : 18
bit of g. to call own, 603 : 8
Cain was tiller of g., 7 : 14
call it holy g., 470 : 16
cannot dedicate this g., 523 : 4
choose g. take thy rest, 462 : 19
Christian g., 340 : 27
colored man occupies, 556 : 7
crushed to g. diffuse sweets, 180 : *n* 2
dark and bloody g., 578 : 11

Ground (*continued*)
drops earliest to g., 200 : 6
exiled on g. in jeers, 580 : 17
fallen unto me in a fair g., 17 : *n* 3
Fame's camping g., 578 : 10
fell into good g., 39 : 15
four thousand miles deep, 603 : 8
gain little patch of g., 223 : 16
gazes on the g., 670 : 14
grow on Irish g., 920 : 21
hallowed g., 825 : 9
haunted holy g., 457 : 9
holy g. where they trod, 470 : 16
in mill of conventional, 652 : 10
into the sea upon dry g., 9 : 31
kings sat down upon the g., 35 : 20
lose g. won today, 585 : 22
miles of fertile g., 433 : 21
more malign with bad seed, 142 : 7
my lodging is on cold g., 331 : 11
my tail go to the g., 158 : 22
neither g. for feet, 576 : 17
not buried in consecrated g., 640 : 16
on g. between two stools, 158 : *n* 16
passion that left g., 544 : 5
place whereon thou standest is holy g., 9 : 11
plat of rising g., 278 : 19
rage outside happy g., 587 : 8
rope just above g., 786 : 2
sorrow holy g., 676 : 15
stand on own g., 555 : 4
stand your g., 374 : 19
stood firm on dry g., 11 : 29
stood like trees in g., 576 : 16
swalloweth g. with fierceness, 16 : 38
till thou return unto the g., 7 : 12
to own a bit of g., 603 : 7
Tom Tiddler's g., 921 : 2
tract of inland g., 428 : 15
tread on classic g., 325 : 6
vantage g. of truth, 100 : *n* 7
vapors weep burthen to g., 533 : 27
Groundlings, split ears of g., 221 : 23
Grounds, fight on landing g., 744 : 2
Group, before g. enter open society, 915 : 1
of willful men, 682 : 10
Grove, but cloud and like shady g., 403 : 7
court the camp the g., 430 : 6
Jemmy G. on deathbed lay, 926 : 21
lion walks innocent g., 868 : 5
meadow g. and stream, 426 : 10
no quiet g., 399 : 16
olive g. of Academe, 288 : 14
shade which g. of myrtles made, 257 : 6
spicy g. cinnamon tree, 857 : 14
Grovel, mediocre and you g., 378 : 8
Groveled here long enough, 576 : 16
Groveling, he who goeth g., 132 : 15
Groves are of laurel, 395 : 3
forsake her Cyprian g., 306 : 6
God's first temples, 471 : 8
green g. of the blest, 105 : 21
o'er shady g. they hover, 262 : 3
of Academe, 109 : 14
valleys g. hills fields, 183 : 8
Grow, asked how pearls did g., 266 : 5
cannot g. by inch, 717 : 6
consider lilies how they g., 38 : 4
corn and taters g., 672 : 19
enter to g. in wisdom, 617 : 5

Grow (*continued*)
forever and forever, 531 : 2
from grass I love, 575 : 4
grass will g. in streets, 750 : 18
green g. the rashes O, 409 : 16
hatched would g. mischievous, 215 : 17
heads g. beneath shoulders, 229 : 30
in place of one, 322 : *n* 3
into likeness of bad men, 86 : 1
learn but not wiser g., 321 : 9
liberties not made but g., 666 : 7
like a cedar in Lebanon, 20 : 18
like savages, 208 : 17
lopped tree may g. again, 73 : *n* 9
love's mysteries in souls g., 253 : 8
makes not fresh nor g. again, 260 : 19
my wrath did g., 405 : 13
oaks from acorns g., 134 : 15
old along with me, 544 : 8
on Irish ground, 920 : 21
out at heels, 233 : 15
pastime and happiness g., 428 : 4
pinks that g., 229 : *n* 1
poets by sufferings g., 292 : 2
riches g. in hell, 284 : 1
roses and white lilies g., 250 : 5
ruin to make them g., 504 : 2
say which grain will g., 236 : 5
she can hear daisies g., 674 : 14
so be it when I g. old, 425 : 7
straight in strength of spirit, 634 : 6
to what they seem, 368 : 19
trees g. up again quickly, 73 : 8
trees that g. fair, 710 : 12
two blades of grass g., 322 : 12
up with the country, 554 : *n* 2
vegetable love g. vaster, 296 : 27
virtuously into knowledge, 701 : 13
why on earth except to g., 543 : 26
Growed, I 'spect I g., 539 : 1
Groweth, like grass which g. up, 20 : 11
sed, 916 : 14
Growing and a becoming, 588 : 17
close upon the g. boy, 426 : 14
darling I am g. old, 662 : 22
iron rungs of g. up, 894 : 5
loves life like him g. old, 75 : 21
old in drawing nothing, 376 : 27
sorrow of day's g., 617 : 3
tender and g. night, 574 : 19
toil of g. up, 716 : 1
tree g. when ye're sleeping, 431 : 28
Growled, cracked g. roared howled, 434 : 11
Growling, listen to it g., 878 : 4
Grown, age g. so picked, 224 : 13
both full g., 919 : 21
by what it fed on, 218 : 8
diseases desperate g., 223 : 14
from sudden fears, 459 : 21
if it had g. up, 611 : 16
old before my time, 608 : 18
old in love, 407 : 4
sweets g. common, 245 : 10
that he is g. so great, 215 : 7
Grown-up nation, 860 : 3
people correct on fact, 690 : 12
Grown-ups never understand anything, 849 : 2
Grows, each thing that in season g., 190 : 13
everything that g., 244 : 4
fairer than at first, 245 : 21

Grows (*continued*)
great love g. there, 222 : 13
home where small experience g., 188 : 27
immortal spirit g., 423 : 18
in this delightful garden g., 173 : 17
lives in single blessedness, 195 : 21
marble wastes statue g., 154 : 14
no profit g. where no pleasure, 188 : 25
nodding violet g., 196 : 18
one is fat and g. old, 203 : 28
since when it g. and smells, 256 : 9
that which is g., 125 : 25
up by degrees, 263 : 6
weed that g. in every soil, 373 : 5
what soon g. old, 86 : 17
when watered by blood, 401 : 4
Growth, children of larger g., 342 : 3
confidence plant of slow g., 350 : 18
every day hidden g., 565 : 20
evidence of life, 490 : 7
final g. evergreen, 863 : 14
ideas have rate of g., 620 : 20
moral soil for aesthetic g., 742 : 3
of underdeveloped areas, 787 : 17
participate in America's g., 875 : 10
self-help root of g., 551 : 8
shadow kills the g., 257 : 2
Grub, no gravy no g., 811 : 1
Grubs, dirt or g. or worms, 338 : 12
Grubstreet inhabited by writers, 352 : 10
Grudge, dare never g. throe, 544 : 10
feed fat the ancient g., 198 : 20
potter bears g. against potter, 61 : 13
what they cannot enjoy, 66 : 10
Grudging worshipper of the gods, 107 : 14
Grumble, terrible g. rumble roar, 591 : 3
Grundy, Solomon G., 932 : 11
tyranny of Mrs. G., 579 : 13
what will Mrs. G. say, 416 : 10
Grunt and sweat under weary life, 221 : 12
Gruntin', I'll do de g., 662 : 9
Guadalajara city of rose-colored flowers, 906 : 12
Guadalupe, Our Lady of G., 400 : 1
Guanahani, called G. in Indians' tongue, 150 : 15
Guarantee, Bill of Rights g. of freedom, 788 : 13
happiness only of dictators, 834 : 7
no one g. success in war, 746 : 12
of First Amendment, 794 : 20
of freedom, 788 : 13
Guarantees, mutual g. of independence, 682 : 15
not worth paper, 509 : 1
Guard, advanced g. of working class, 731 : 7
and keep them, 65 : 3
as I g. o'er the fold, 403 : 14
careful silence, 751 : 7
don't call out National G., 787 : 11
grow weak keeping on g., 658 : 24
historians should be on g., 95 : 18
holy angels g. thy bed, 328 : 8
our native seas, 443 : 10
ready to g. liberty, 451 : 3
those I g. I do not love, 713 : 20
time every minute, 756 : 1
Guard (*continued*)
who is to g. the guards, 122 : 11
Guarded by neighborly respect, 743 : 16
virtue which requires to be g., 369 : 10
with ships, 276 : 3
Guardian angels sung this strain, 345 : 19
conscience g. of community rules, 751 : 14
Naiad of strand, 431 : 6
necessity g. of nature, 152 : 11
need a guardian, 122 : *n* 8
of other's solitude, 756 : 11
Guardians of the faith, 804 : 7
Guards bivouac of dead, 578 : 10
die never surrender, 421 : 21
like wild beast g. way, 406 : 1
Scylla g. right side, 200 : *n* 1
who is to guard the g., 122 : 11
Gude nicht and joy, 417 : 8
Scots lords, 926 : 12
to be merry and wise, 921 : 8
Gudeman's, when our g. awa, 382 : 10
Gudgeons, swallow g. ere they're catch'd, 65 : *n* 10
Guenever for whom I make mention, 149 : 14
Guerdon, fair g. we hope to find, 280 : 15
last g. of death, 102 : 18
Guérit, je le soignay Dieu le g., 162 : *n* 6
Guerre, magnifique mais pas la g., 536 : *n* 1
needed a nom de g., 621 : *n* 2
trop grave pour la confier à des militaries, 401 : *n* 2
Guess each sweet, 476 : 26
if you can, 275 : 27
now who holds thee, 507 : 8
shrewd g. valuable, 887 : 15
Guessed, ghost g., 656 : 10
will know if haven't g., 709 : 24
Guesses, secrets everybody g., 680 : 6
Guessing, pleasure of poem g., 651 : 16
Guest, after three days weary of g., 347 : 2
dear old Carian g., 591 : 9
dull fighter and keen g., 204 : 36
earth receive honored g., 868 : 11
freeloader confirmed g., 787 : 3
give no more to every g., 323 : 1
love is but a g., 250 : 13
make welcome the present g., 60 : 19
no g. welcome after three days, 94 : 1
remembrance of a g., 34 : 16
retire like g. sated, 101 : 4
retire like satisfied g., 106 : 13
shakes parting g. by hand, 226 : 19
soul g. of body, 123 : 15
speed the going g., 339 : 9
speed the parting g., 334 : 23
speeds parting g., 715 : 11
this g. of summer, 236 : 21
tie of host and g., 71 : 17
Wedding G. stood still, 434 : 6
welcome the coming g., 334 : 23
wrong to speed a g., 60 : 19
Guests are met feast set, 434 : 5
chronic hotel g., 725 : 18
fish and g. in three days, 94 : *n* 1
praise it not cooks, 181 : 22
star-scattered on grass, 517 : 14
Guests (*continued*)
unbidden g. welcomest when gone, 184 : 19
Guid to be merry and wise, 411 : 24
Guidance, history provides g. in daily life, 98 : 9
Guide Arcturus with his sons, 16 : 34
be Thou our G., 924 : 15
by light of reason, 678 : 2
canst not g. whom thou lovest, 131 : 19
custom g. of human life, 357 : 15
knowledge should be his g., 84 : 9
light to g., 427 : 13
love of wisdom g. of life, 407 : 17
myself with blue flower, 791 : 1
myself with torch of flower, 791 : 1
no g. overseer or ruler, 23 : 11
only g. conscience, 744 : 11
original and end, 130 : 3
our wanderings to g., 611 : 1
path motive g., 130 : 3
philosopher and friend, 338 : 3, 773 : 14
private conscience for g., 305 : 20
Providence their g., 288 : 4
science g. of action, 660 : 6
to g. their chime, 297 : 10
women g. the plot, 398 : 20
Guided, lamp by which feet g., 383 : 2
Guides, blind g., 40 : 19
cannot master joke, 622 : 7
choose ideals as g., 603 : 2
hope which g. changeful mind, 72 : 13
me and the bird, 540 : 7
through sky thy flight, 471 : 7
us by vanities, 804 : 14
Guideth, God g. whom He will, 131 : 19
Guild master and journeyman, 563 : 3
Guile, full of wiles full of g., 82 : 8
keep thy lips from speaking g., 18 : 21
serpent whose g. deceived, 283 : 3
trade of blood and g., 435 : 21
void of envy g. lust, 345 : 21
Guiled shore to dangerous sea, 199 : 26
Guilt, affection and g., 924 : 3
by silence betrayed, 305 : 27
earth one stain of g., 503 : 2
image of war without g., 328 : 18
life without industry g., 573 : 7
no greater g. than discontentment, 64 : 16
rest of us must face g., 863 : 7
so full of jealousy is g., 223 : 20
what art can wash g. away, 369 : 20
what is our g., 799 : 2
your g. consists in this, 420 : 4
Guiltier than him they try, 227 : 31
Guiltless of country's blood, 362 : 9
though g. must suffer, 77 : *n* 12
Guilty, better ten g. escape, 365 : 19
better to risk saving g., 343 : 5
make g. of our disasters, 233 : 5
no g. man escape, 590 : 1
of corruption and renounce defense, 179 : 11
of dust and sin, 269 : 9
splendor, 376 : 24
started like a g. thing, 217 : 23
suspicion haunts g. mind, 186 : 27
thing surprised, 426 : 18
Guinea, first g. more difficult, 358 : 11
I only g. pig I have, 832 : 14
jingling of g., 529 : 23

Guinea's, choruses above g. squawk, 831 : 14
rank but g. stamp, 411 : 17
Guineas, crowns pounds and g., 690 : 20
Guinevere for whom I make mention, 149 : 14
Guise, mingled in exile g., 843 : 17
truth in every g., 902 : 15
Guises, revealed in various g., 864 : 17
Guitar, sang to small g., 550 : 7
Gulag archipelago, 895 : 23
Gules, warm g., 476 : 16
Gulf, bottomless g., 449 : 6
famous island descending to a dark g., 743 : 14
great g. fixed, 43 : 34
of mutual incomprehension, 865 : 17
Versailles was a g., 592 : 10
yawning g., 571 : 9
Gulf Stream, from redwood forest to G. waters, 881 : 1
Gulfs, Persian g., 569 : 2
will wash us down, 529 : 13
Gull, landless g., 570 : 7
Gull's way and whale's way, 760 : 16
Gulls and deep sea swell, 805 : 9
far calls, 778 : 6
Gum, by gosh by g., 829 : 5
med'cinable g., 232 : 20
Gummed with Arnstein's cement, 835 : 1
Gums, boneless g., 237 : 5
Gun, escape from rope and g., 332 : 5
holy text of pike and g., 291 : 4
little man had little g., 933 : 12
named birds without g., 494 : 14
no g. but I can spit, 869 : 6
political power out of barrel of g., 826 : 7
this g. for hire, 859 : 5
Gunga Din, better man than I G., 708 : 6
Gunless game, 685 : 11
Gunpowder printing and religion, 472 : 5
ran out at heels, 364 : 5
treason and plot, 919 : 12
Guns aren't lawful, 827 : 12
begin to shoot, 708 : 4
blew great g., 549 : 11
boom far, 742 : 9
chaps with couple o' g., 786 : 11
dead who fed the g., 795 : 16
great g. unawares shook our coffins, 642 : 1
monstrous anger of g., 827 : 2
or butter, 838 : *n* 3
shows games sports g., 381 : 7
vile g., 203 : 11
with drums and g., 921 : 1
Gush, makest a spring to g. forth, 131 : 9
Gushed, love g. from my heart, 434 : 29
Gustibus, de g. non disputandum, 133 : 17
Gusts of clear-blowing west wind, 59 : 26
Gusty, carpets along g. floor, 476 : 19
Guts in his head, 226 : 6
Guttas in saxa cadentis, 100 : *n* 4
Gutter, rose in g., 812 : 9
we all in the g., 675 : 9
Guttering, lights g. low, 691 : 15
Guttersnipe, bloodthirsty g., 745 : 2
Guy, County G. hour is nigh, 432 : 9
what g. inhabits poem, 869 : 10
Guys and dolls, 787 : 1
in g. gently sways, 749 : 4
nice g. finish last, 867 : 1
Gymnasium, democracy life's g., 577 : 1
Gypsies, three g. a-come to door, 920 : 17
wraggle-taggle g. O, 920 : 18
Gypsy, sets g. blood astir, 696 : 10
Time you old g. man, 732 : 17
vagrant g. life, 760 : 16
Gyre and gimble in wabe, 612 : 17
turning in widening g., 714 : 12
Gyves, prisoner in his twisted g., 192 : 18

H

Ha ha quoth he, 435 : 7
saith among the trumpets H., 16 : 38
Habeas corpus, 134 : 4
protection of h., 389 : 2
Habersham, hills of H., 651 : 10
Habit, art h. science h., 260 : 11
costly thy h., 219 : 1
discontinued labor h. lost, 491 : 26
easy to abandon, 491 : 26
fall into h. cease to be, 705 : 19
fills up time, 734 : 5
flywheel of society, 648 : 7
honor peereth in meanest h., 189 : 2
is his nurse, 413 : 8
not to be flung out window, 624 : 15
nothing stronger than h., 113 : 12
of living, 275 : 6
of making history proof, 616 : 4
of moving little finger, 648 : 3
order breeds h., 635 : 4
ordinary actions ascribed to h., 657 : 9
reap a h., 922 : 18
rules unreflecting herd, 429 : 3
second nature, 393 : *n* 2
shackle for free, 647 : 12
takes place of happiness, 486 : 7
tyrannical h. of reading, 569 : 7
use doth breed a h., 190 : 7
will encroach, 433 : 7
with him test of truth, 400 : 6
Habitable, look round the h. world, 306 : 10
Habitant of castle gray, 562 : 8
Habitation, benevolence the tranquil h., 89 : 10
eat of the h., 198 : 18
giddy and unsure, 206 : 7
local h. and name, 197 : 12
of dragons, 30 : 22
Habits, character h. and manners, 592 : 7
civilized man has h. of house, 557 : 4
follow other men's h., 597 : 10
form second nature, 393 : 8
ill h. gather by degrees, 307 : 2
moral h. induced by public practices, 119 : 25
my other h. are good, 616 : 13
of age of atomic energy, 826 : 2
of peace and patience, 270 : 34
reforming other people's h., 624 : 22
well pursued betimes, 393 : 14
Habitual hatred or fondness, 379 : 12
lie becomes h., 388 : 3
nothing h. but indecision, 648 : 8
what you make h. practice, 121 : 15
Hack, somebody to hew and h., 291 : 7
Hacking at branches of evil, 559 : 19
Hackles, henna h. halt, 767 : 5
Hackney, starved h. sonneteer, 333 : 13
Hackneyed phrases, 685 : 14
Hack-writers, what difference from h., 95 : 18
Had having and in quest to have, 245 : 23
Hades, descent to H. is same, 72 : 14
hateful as gates of H., 58 : 8
is relentless, 58 : 7
no man takes wealth to H., 67 : 6
pass gates of H., 67 : 5
road to H. easy to travel, 92 : 7
sent to H. many valiant souls, 57 : 3
Hag and hungry goblin, 918 : 11
Haggard, if I do prove her h., 231 : 4
Haggards ride no more, 693 : 4
Hags, secret black midnight h., 239 : 8
Ha-ha we're bound away, 934 : 20
Hail and farewell my brother, 102 : 19
arrows flew like h., 794 : 5
Columbia, 422 : 21
congenial horrors h., 345 : 5
divinest Melancholy, 278 : 11
element of earth, 794 : 9
Emperor we who are about to die, 123 : 14
fellow well met, 323 : 22
hail gang's all here, 628 : *n* 1
holy light, 285 : 4
let others h. rising sun, 363 : 15
Liberty hail, 484 : 1
love-gift of fairy tale, 612 : 15
Master, 41 : 15
Our Lady of Guadalupe, 400 : 1
rain snow h. drought, 622 : 19
thou highly favored, 42 : 17
to the Chief, 431 : 9
to thee blithe spirit, 468 : 11
to you gods, 4 : 9
wedded love, 286 : 5
ye small sweet courtesies, 360 : 24
Hailed, so proudly we h., 446 : 1
Hailstones on icebergs, 569 : 20
Haine, un peu de h., 617 : *n* 1
Hair, amber-dropping h., 280 : 3
Andrew with brindled h., 668 : 19
as free, 255 : 18
babies haven't h., 816 : 2
beauty draws with single h., 334 : 3
bindest in wreaths thy golden h., 107 : 3
blown h. sweet, 806 : 2
bracelet of bright h., 253 : 12
brown h. and speaks small, 225 : 6
burned black with sun, 822 : 4
comb gray h., 713 : 18
difference matter of a h., 648 : 2
divide a h., 290 : 16
draw you with single h., 259 : *n* 8
draws us with single h., 334 : 3
Edith with golden h., 512 : 5
fictions only and false h., 268 : 14
girl graduates in golden h., 530 : 21
golden h. curl gracefully, 595 : 9
gray but not with years, 459 : 21
hair-dark fragment of h., 893 : 13
hank of h., 709 : 14

Hair (*continued*)
has become very white, 611 : 9
his floating h., 433 : 27
horrid image unfix h., 236 : 11
hyacinth h., 525 : 9
Jeanie with light brown h., 598 : 6
lie tangled in her h., 296 : 2
lilac and brown h., 806 : 2
live h. shining and free, 796 : 16
long h. glory, 48 : 19
Love with streaming h., 836 : 17
lute strung with his h., 191 : 4
make your h. curl, 629 : 18
most resplendent h., 428 : 23
my fell of h., 240 : 3
ninth part of a h., 204 : 15
not white h. that engenders wisdom, 91 : 10
not your yellow h., 716 : 5
of dog that bit us, 160 : 18
of my flesh stood up, 15 : 12
of yon gray head, 513 : 19
part my h. behind, 803 : 19
prison for color of h., 692 : 12
rain-drenched h., 787 : 5
recover h. that grows bald, 188 : 3
rise with my red h., 911 : 12
ruddy limbs flaming h., 404 : 16
sacred h. dissever, 334 : 10
scent of her h., 822 : 4
smooths h. with automatic hand, 805 : 8
soft h. of the grass, 634 : 5
soft-lifted, 477 : 18
stand up, 75 : 15
stars in h. seven, 601 : 13
stroke his silver h., 403 : 8
subtle wreath of h., 253 : 11
sugar my h., 612 : 10
swerve a h. from truth, 226 : 15
tangles of Neaera's h., 280 : 15
tips all over him, 901 : 14
to stand on end, 219 : 18
uncut h. of graves, 574 : 17
vine leaves in h., 600 : 5
was long, 478 : 11
wash that man outa my h., 833 : 15
weave sunlight in h., 804 : 10
what scanted in h. given in wit, 188 : 4
with such h. too, 543 : 12
Hairbreadth missings of happiness, 349 : 24
'scapes, 229 : 28
Haircut and a shave, 816 : 2
Hairs, bring down my gray h., 8 : 32
glory from gray h. gone, 513 : 7
how ill white h. become fool, 206 : 36
if h. be wires, 246 : 1
nine she-camel h. aid memory, 799 : 13
of your head numbered, 39 : 3
or straws or dirt, 338 : 12
sad last gray h., 476 : 24
she-camel h. aid memory, 799 : 13
stand on end, 833 : 6
superfluity sooner by white h., 198 : 8
those set our h. upright, 254 : 1
Hairy gold crown on 'ead, 708 : 7
man from east, 726 : 8
strength, 278 : 3
Hal, 'tis my vocation H., 203 : 3
would it were bedtime H., 205 : 4
Halcyon days, 82 : 11
Halcyon (*continued*)
expect h. days, 184 : 17
Hale Father William, 439 : 15
Half a drop ah my Christ, 184 : 8
a league, 533 : 9
a life asunder, 612 : 15
a loaf of, 160 : 11
angel half bird, 545 : 1
as old as Time, 416 : 3, 552 : 9
better be ignorant than h. know, 112 : 9
better h., 176 : 6
brother of world, 555 : 15
dead a living death, 288 : 22
grant what I wish, 747 : 16
his Troy was burned, 205 : 19
how much more is h. than whole, 61 : 14
how the other h. lives, 270 : 21
in love with death, 476 : 28
light half shade, 529 : 2
more than h. people right, 846 : 16
my life in Paris, 752 : 13
not the h. that made me, 752 : 13
of my own soul, 106 : 26
of one order half another, 291 : 15
one h. of the world, 440 : 25
overcome but h. his foe, 283 : 27
owre to Aberdour, 926 : 13
part of blessed man, 201 : 16
proper gardener's work, 710 : 22
reveal half conceal, 531 : 20
savage country, 792 : 10
seas over, 323 : 6
see with h. an eye, 170 : 27
served God with h. the zeal, 249 : 9
the wit for half the beauty, 417 : 16
they h. believe in it, 64 : 14
to rise and half to fall, 337 : 2
truth blackest lie, 535 : 6
use h. talent, 852 : 12
was not told me, 13 : 35
well begun is h. done, 88 : 11
who has begun has h. done, 108 : 20
with but h. a heart, 267 : 7
Half-acre tombs, 252 : 12
Half-a-crown, help to h., 641 : 15
Half-believers of casual creeds, 585 : 22
Half-dozen, six of one h. of other, 465 : 16
Half-gods, when h. go, 494 : 11
Half-held, sea h. by night, 574 : 19
Half-know, better know nothing than h., 561 : *n* 4
Half-known, horrors of h. life, 570 : 14
Half-look, backward h. over shoulder, 808 : 5
Half-moon, yellow h. large low, 541 : 13
Halfmoon's vegetable eye, 886 : 15
Half-reaped furrow, 477 : 18
Half-regained Eurydice, 278 : 8
Half-sleep, lulled into h., 874 : 9
Half-truth or truth and a half, 751 : 5
Half-truths, all truths are h., 697 : 16
Nature hints and h., 630 : 24
Half-witted, old h. sheep, 428 : *n* 2
saw state was h., 558 : 7
Half-world, o'er one h. nature dead, 237 : 14
Halicarnassian, my H. friend, 93 : 1
Haling out of heart old dismay, 899 : 9
Hall, bride paced into the h., 434 : 9
dazzlingly lighted h., 551 : 15
Douglas in his h., 430 : 23
Hall (*continued*)
equality in servants' h., 694 : 8
flowers in garden meat in h., 145 : *n* 4
in h. or bower, 279 : 6
Liberty H., 371 : 8
o' Fame when you croaks, 810 : 7
'tis merry in h., 163 : 6
Tom bears logs into the h., 191 : 14
vasty h. of death, 586 : 4
waiter roars through h., 592 : 4
Hallelujah, Michael row boat ashore H., 935 : 25
Halloo halloo loo loo, 234 : 5
Hallow the fiftieth year, 10 : 22
we cannot h., 523 : 4
words such as h. obscene, 844 : 14
Hallowed be thy name, 37 : 15
ground, 825 : 9
quiets of past, 568 : 22
relics should be hid, 277 : 13
so h. and so gracious, 217 : 26
Halls, in h. in gay attire, 430 : 6
marble h., 480 : 11
my ho head h., 778 : 5
of fame, 923 : 9
of hell, 793 : 3
of Montezuma, 922 : 11
Hallucinations of poets, 772 : 7
Halt and blind, 43 : 23
cells never h., 760 : 21
henna hackles h., 767 : 5
how long h. ye between opinions, 14 : 1
I pray you make a little stay, 135 : 7
no dishonor to h. at second place, 98 : 12
Halted, army not h. by eloquence, 553 : 11
Halter, hope one will cut h., 277 : 2
threats of h., 393 : 9
Halters, ill talking of h., 169 : 21
Halts, wanderer h. and hears, 691 : 12
Halve rights double duties, 463 : 2
Halves, ratify my little h., 889 : 8
two h. of God, 491 : 8
Ham, Noah begat H., 7 : 26
Haman, they hanged H., 14 : 34
Hame to my ain countree, 453 : 21
Hamelin town's in Brunswick, 540 : 32
Hamlet, Bacon not written H., 474 : 17
I am not Prince H., 803 : 17
much Antony of H. most, 663 : 8
O H. what a falling-off, 219 : 21
rambles Lear rages, 717 : 6
rude forefathers of h. 361 : 23
there struts H., 717 : 5
Hamlet's, ghost of H. father, 697 : 4
Hamlets, in h. dances on green, 430 : 6
they have H. we Karamazovs, 582 : 13
Hammer along 'ard 'igh road, 660 : 14
die with h. in hand, 922 : 8
iron when hot, 110 : 25
me into crowbar, 761 : 10
neither h. nor ax, 13 : 32
no sound of h., 377 : 11
of red and blue, 768 : 2
out solid piece of work, 644 : 14
what the h., 405 : 8
when you are a h. strike, 269 : 30
Hammered, attacking and getting h., 681 : 3
doubly h. gold, 570 : 11
fine h. steel of woe, 570 : 16

Hammered (*continued*)
gold and gold enameling, 715 : 3
Hammers, busy h. closing rivets, 208 : 1
laughs at broken h., 761 : 17
no h. fell, 377 : *n* 5
Hammock, Drake he's in his h., 700 : 9
future not a comfortable h., 832 : 1
me they'll lash in h., 572 : 7
Hampden, some village H., 362 : 9
Hampering with ceremonies and music, 90 : 6
Hampshire, captain of H. grenadiers, 384 : 6
Hams, taking h. was stealing, 622 : 14
Hamstring, conceit lies in his h., 226 : 4
Han', prentice h. tried on man, 409 : 15
Hand against every man, 8 : 9
against Heaven's h., 282 : 19
and heart to this vote, 450 : 9
and lash that beat Rome, 717 : 4
as arrows in the h., 22 : 10
automatic h., 805 : 8
beneath awful H. we hold, 709 : 16
bird in h. worth two in bush, 120 : *n* 3
bite h. that fed, 374 : 11
bless h. that gave blow, 304 : 20
bloody and invisible h., 238 : 21
bondman in h. bears power, 215 : 13
book in his h., 301 : 20
books you hold in h., 353 : 17
Caesar's h., 495 : 15
capped withered heart, 858 : 20
child of my right h., 256 : 3
close h. out of love, 657 : 14
cloud like a man's h., 14 : 3
cold h. of death, 205 : 10
death lays icy h. on kings, 272 : 15
died by the h. of the Lord, 10 : 1
do not saw air with h., 221 : 23
dry h. yellow cheek, 205 : 28
dyer's h., 245 : 17
each army hath a h., 201 : 22
East with richest h., 284 : 3
either h. rightly clutch, 710 : 15
even I be in Somebody's h., 640 : 14
every man's h. against him, 8 : 9
eye see for h. not mind, 558 : 23
farther away on either h., 822 : 12
fear thy skinny h., 434 : 25
findeth to do, 27 : 16
foot and h. go cold, 163 : 10
for hand, 10 : 10
from h. no worthy action, 920 : 12
gave into his mighty h., 474 : 18
give me your h., 188 : 12
God keep you in his h., 935 : 18
gods' capricious h., 863 : 20
great h. of God, 238 : 9
handle toward my h., 237 : 13
having put h. to plow, 43 : 7
heart in h., 538 : 3
heaving up my either h., 267 : 1
her h. on her bosom, 232 : 8
here's my h., 248 : 4
his hat in his h., 353 : 18
hold fire in his h., 194 : 7
hold infinity in palm of h., 406 : 8
hold your h. victorious, 77 : 9
hop a little from her h., 192 : 18
hour is at h., 41 : 14
hurts my h., 231 : 23
I want to hold your h., 914 : 8
if thy right h. offend thee, 37 : 8
in every honest h. a whip, 232 : 6

Hand (*continued*)
in glove, 323 : 18
in hand Americans all, 378 : 11
in hand on edge of sand, 550 : 10
in hand with wandering, 288 : 4
in her left h. riches and honor, 23 : 4
in his h. are the deep places, 20 : 20
in one h. a stone, 93 : 11
individual led by invisible h., 366 : 4
infection and h. of war, 194 : 13
iron h. in velvet glove, 161 : 19
kingdom of heaven is at h., 36 : 25
kissing h. may feel good, 826 : 5
lay h. upon the ark, 376 : 21
leans her cheek upon her h., 192 : 4
left h. know what right h. doeth, 37 : 14
left his garment in her h., 8 : 30
lend a h., 590 : 8
lends h. to honest boldness, 91 : 8
length of days in her right h., 23 : 4
lifted h. in awe, 330 : 1
like base Indian, 232 : 20
like this hand, 543 : 23
living from h. to mouth, 167 : 12
made all to prosper in his h., 8 : 29
man himself lend a h., 80 : 13
man's h. not able to taste, 197 : 10
may turn from weaker h., 198 : 30
medieval h., 628 : 7
mortality's strong h., 202 : 7
my spirit in God's h., 300 : 19
my thoughtless h., 405 : 6
my times are in thy h., 18 : 17
nature's sweet cunning h., 213 : 17
never had blister in h., 82 : 2
no rude h. deface it, 425 : 4
nonchalance of h., 714 : 7
not h. but understanding, 169 : 37
not leave my h. without light, 797 : 6
not lift h. to help, 715 : 10
of all that hate us, 42 : 25
of h. of foot of lip, 245 : 12
of potter shake, 517 : 8
Old Age and Experience h. in h., 315 : 21
on the horn, 927 : 12
orders in his h., 731 : 19
our h. finished it, 114 : 4
our times in his h., 544 : 8
papers in each h., 338 : 6
prentice h. tried on man, 409 : 15
put in his h. by the hole of the door, 28 : 15
raised to shed blood, 336 : 13
rash h. in evil hour, 287 : 19
red right h., 284 : 10
right h. bigger than head, 906 : 15
right h. forget her cunning, 22 : 15
right h. is become glorious, 9 : 34
right h. of God, 55 : 2
scepter snatched with unruly h., 202 : 3
separate as fingers one as h., 681 : 24
shake of the h., 804 : 11
shakes parting guest by h., 226 : 19
sheep of his h., 20 : 20
shut when thou shouldest repay, 35 : 3
souls of righteous in h. of God, 34 : 13
stout of h., 430 : 3
stretched out to receive, 35 : 3
sweet Roman h., 214 : 21
sweeten this little h., 239 : 27

Hand (*continued*)
sword sleep in my h., 406 : 21
take h. part with laughter, 633 : 15
taking in h. a city, 70 : 12
ten thousand at thy right h., 20 : 16
that held dagger struck, 780 : 9
that I were glove upon that h., 192 : 4
that is honest and hearty, 429 : 16
that made us is divine, 325 : 10
that made you fair, 228 : 22
that rocks cradle, 573 : 18
that rounded Peter's dome, 493 : 18
that signed the paper, 886 : 14
there shall thy h. lead me, 22 : 17
things made by human h., 739 : 4
this living h., 478 : 8
thou openest thine h., 22 : 21
three lilies in her h., 601 : 13
thy h. great Anarch, 340 : 28
thy h. presseth me sore, 18 : 28
thy right h. shall hold me, 22 : 17
till some blind h., 405 : 6
time hath taming h., 490 : 5
Time's fell h., 244 : 21
to execute, 289 : 16, 391 : 4
took his icy h., 556 : 15
touch of vanished h., 530 : 19
tricks by sleight of h., 324 : 13
under whose cautious h., 576 : 8
unfriendly to tyrants, 298 : 19
Uzzah put forth his h., 13 : 15
vacant heart h. eye, 432 : 1
wash blood from my h., 238 : 1
waved her lily h., 331 : 10
we are in God's h., 207 : 24
what h. dare seize fire, 405 : 7
what immortal h. or eye, 405 : 7
what thy right h. doeth, 37 : 14
whatsoever thou takest in h., 35 : 12
with other h. held weapon, 14 : 29
with your staff in your h., 9 : 25
withhold not thine h. in the evening, 27 : 22
work of thy h., 31 : 28
Handclasp's a little stronger, 739 : 7
Handed in his checks, 630 : 12
me my being's worth, 607 : 17
Handel, not care candle for H., 442 : 4
scarcely fit to hold candle, 341 : 13
Handful of Divine Inert, 570 : 12
of dust, 805 : 1
of gray ashes, 591 : 9
of meal in a barrel, 13 : 42
of sand, 838 : 16
of silver, 541 : 5
until h. of earth stops mouths, 482 : 7
with quietness, 26 : 23
zodiac, 886 : 15
Handfuls, give me h. of lilies, 105 : 25
Handiwork, firmament showeth his h., 17 : 27
Park specimen of God's h., 590 : 14
you give to God, 670 : 15
Handkerchief, holding pocket h., 613 : 8
of the Lord, 574 : 16
Handle, grasp by blade or h., 569 : 5
grasped the surest h., 132 : 2
jug without h., 550 : 16
knife for which h. missing, 386 : 16
lie a h. fits all tools, 519 : 9
of big front door, 627 : 14
right and wrong h. to everything, 121 : *n* 3

Handle (*continued*)
such as h. harp and organ, 7 : 22
touch not h. not, 50 : 10
toward my hand, 237 : 13
Handlebar moustaches on Czar, 892 : 17
Handled, vessels oft h. brightly shine, 183 : 18
with a chain, 605 : 11
Handler, nation's freight h., 761 : 4
Handles, everything has two h., 121 : 22
Handling, tuning lyre and h. harp, 70 : 12
Handmaid, Nature's h. Art, 303 : 4
philosophy h. to religion, 179 : 6
riches good h. worst mistress, 179 : 14
Handmaiden, low estate of his h., 42 : 21
Hands and eyes and heart, 458 : 20
and hearts, 186 : 17
and then take h., 247 : 19
are four, 830 : 12
are heart's landscape, 897 : 8
as bands, 27 : 10
bear thee up in their h., 20 : 17
believe in fairies clap h., 694 : 9
blue, 550 : 11
by fairy h. knell rung, 364 : 9
by foreign h. eyes closed, 335 : 10
clasps with crooked h., 532 : 28
clean h. and pure heart, 18 : 8
come knit h., 279 : 14
country defended by h., 535 : 22
dead h. dead stringencies, 911 : 14
degenerate into h. like mine, 461 : 5
diadems and fagots in h., 495 : 5
do what you're bid, 714 : 6
entergraft our h., 253 : 6
establish the work of our h., 20 : 15
failing h., 737 : 10
fasten h. upon hearts, 691 : 21
fate of world in h., 865 : 1
Father into thy h., 44 : 10
fetching with full h., 574 : 15
fold h. and wait, 630 : 21
folding of the h. to sleep, 23 : 12
fruit of her h., 26 : 10
gilt comes off on our h., 583 : 13
greedy h., 520 : *n* 3
had put instead, 868 : 21
hath not a Jew h., 199 : 17
his h. formed the dry land, 20 : 20
hold much of heat, 810 : 18
horny h. of toil, 567 : 2
idle h., 328 : 6
in h. not of few but many, 80 : 17
into thy h. I commend my spirit, 44 : 10
issue is in God's h., 71 : 26
kills Scots washes his h., 203 : 26
large and sinewy h., 510 : 7
little h. make pretense, 611 : 1
little h. never made, 328 : 3
made before knives, 323 : 12
man's fortune in own h., 181 : 6
many h. make light work, 160 : 31
marble head in my h., 849 : 9
musket molds in his h., 666 : 17
my own fair h., 321 : 18
nearer than h. and feet, 535 : 9
nobody has such small h., 829 : 13
not hearts, 231 : 19
not in h. of boys, 827 : 4
not without men's h., 564 : 21
of Esau, 8 : 17
Hands (*continued*)
of memory weave, 636 : 2
of sisters Death and Night, 576 : 1
one thinks of all the h., 804 : 3
only serve eyes, 557 : 3
oozing out at palm of h., 398 : 18
pale h. I loved, 707 : 2
peeking into her own clasped h., 912 : 13
Pilate washed h., 41 : 22
plunge h. in water, 868 : 10
predatory human h., 690 : 10
pure of h., 4 : 9
rarely escapes injuring own h., 65 : 7
right h. of fellowship, 49 : 25
rosy h. in steam, 899 : 13
savings in h. of one, 676 : 19
shake h. forever, 182 : 16
something from our h., 429 : 1
soul clap h. and sing, 715 : 1
speak h. for me, 216 : 4
strength without h. to smite, 632 : 9
temples made with h., 46 : 16
that rod of empire, 362 : 6
that work on us, 756 : 13
that wove shirt of flame, 808 : 15
true faith ready h., 566 : 3
union of h., 492 : 11
union of h. and hearts, 294 : 14
whirling h. at noon, 863 : 16
with Pilate wash your h., 195 : 13
work h. from day to day, 870 : 5
wounds in thine h., 33 : 35
Handsaw, know hawk from h., 220 : 31
Handsome as bull that kidnapped Europa, 98 : 20
big-boned and hardy-h., 656 : 7
his figure is h., 636 : 12
house to lodge friend, 339 : 10
in three hundred pounds, 225 : 21
is that handsome does, 369 : 9
Jesus he was a h. man, 828 : 13
man but gay deceiver, 415 : 14
not h. at twenty, 269 : 32
others more h. by far, 758 : 5
property, 603 : 8
rather a h. pig, 611 : 16
some women h. without adornment, 98 : 13
strong rich or wise, 269 : 32
ugly thinks herself h., 342 : 4
wee thing, 410 : 17
with my mourning very h., 310 : 10
Handsomely, have merit h. allowed, 356 : 22
Handsomer, success makes one feel h., 859 : 19
Handspike, Fate is the h., 571 : 5
Handwriting on the wall, 816 : 13
Handy, with girls be h., 920 : 9
Handy-dandy which is the justice, 235 : 2
Hang calf's skin on limbs, 201 : 21
caps on horns of the moon, 242 : 9
clothes on hickory limb, 924 : 17
enough rope h. himself, 158 : *n* 7
feel his title h. loose, 239 : 28
go h. yourselves critics, 158 : 11
in their own straps, 213 : 11
it all Robert Browning, 792 : 18
let him h. there, 904 : 2
like icicle on beard, 214 : 18
loop to h. doubt on, 231 : 13
my harp on willow-tree, 922 : 13
Hang (*continued*)
out our banners, 240 : 2
pearl in cowslip's ear, 196 : 11
she would h. on him, 218 : 8
so fretted you would h. yourself, 355 : 3
sorrow, 210 : *n* 1
that jurymen may dine, 334 : 6
them up in silent icicles, 435 : 15
themselves in hope one will cut halter, 277 : 2
there like fruit my soul, 243 : 30
together or hang separately, 348 : 8
up philosophy, 193 : 13
upon his penthouse lid, 236 : 2
us every mother's son, 196 : 7
when icicles h. by the wall, 191 : 14
yellow leaves do h., 244 : 27
your head over, 920 : 19
yourself brave Crillon, 175 : 2
Hanged, house of a man h., 169 : 21
I'll be h., 203 : 18
knows he is to be h., 355 : 25
men h. that horses not be stolen, 310 : 21
millstone h. about neck, 43 : 35
my poor fool is h., 235 : 18
our harps upon willows, 22 : 15
they h. Haman, 14 : 34
when skies are h., 830 : 2
Hangin' Danny Deever, 708 : 2
men and women there, 920 : 22
Hanging and wiving by destiny, 159 : *n* 4
around in world, 750 : 12
around till you've caught on, 750 : 13
breathless on thy fate, 511 : 8
Danny Deever, 708 : 2
Gardens were dream, 752 : 16
in a golden chain, 285 : 3
likewise destiny, 159 : 6
love h. and drawing and quartering, 404 : 22
men and women there, 920 : 22
no man not deserve h., 166 : 3
shadow h. over me, 914 : 9
too good for him, 302 : 6
worst use for man, 251 : 3
Hangman's, fear of hell's a h. whip, 259 : *n* 11
Hangover became part of day, 835 : 17
Hangs as mute on Tara's walls, 446 : 9
blossom that h. on bough, 248 : 16
bodiless as false dawn, 899 : 12
goose h. high, 920 : 20
he h. between in doubt, 337 : 2
head for shame, 592 : 2
in uncertain balance, 178 : 13
on Dian's temple, 242 : 23
on princes' favors, 249 : 3
tail h. down behind, 709 : 3
thereby h. a tale, 211 : 6
upon cheek of night, 191 : 26
Hank of hair, 709 : 14
Hannah, amount to H. Cook, 923 : 20
God and me, 615 : 13
Hannibal is at the gates, 134 : 5
know how to win victory H., 94 : 7
put H. in the scales, 122 : 16
Hanover, famous H. city, 540 : 32
St. George's H. Square, 620 : 9
Hansom, helped to h. outside, 866 : 16
Hap, from better h. to worse, 182 : 1
my hope my h. my love, 168 : 2

Ha'penny will do, 921 : 3
Haply I think on thee, 244 : 9
Happen, it can't h. here, 791 : 10
lies at last letting it h., 899 : 17
things you do not hope h., 94 : 4
we's nuts and things h., 810 : 6
Happened, good book h. to you, 845 : 4
nothing ever h. at all, 623 : 22
put down what really h., 845 : 2
this could have h. once 544 : 24
what men believe h., 816 : 4
Happening, being and h., 869 : 11
funny if h. to somebody else, 765 : 17
Happens, future in us before it h., 756 : 7
nothing h. unless first a dream, 761 : 12
too much h., 838 : 2
trouble h. to others, 760 : 12
trouble h. to you, 760 : 12
truth h. to idea, 650 : 11
unexpected always h., 94 : *n* 3
whatever h. h. as it should, 124 : 16
Happier air, 587 : 11
envy of less h. lands, 194 : 13
I am h. than I know, 287 : 5
in passion we feel, 293 : 30
people capable of being h., 814 : 8
Pobbles h. without toes, 551 : 6
remembering h. things, 529 : 20
the one who goes is h., 593 : 5
those who feel love most are h., 467 : 5
to be dead, 495 : 2
Happiest conversation no competition, 355 : 16
day happiest hour, 525 : 4
intellection, 899 : 15
martini one of h. marriages, 837 : 10
nations no history, 565 : 18
of mortals, 343 : 12
time of New Year, 528 : 12
treatise of natural education, 358 : 23
women have no history, 565 : 18
Happily may I walk, 928 : 19
plenty to live on h., 788 : 2
Happiness activity in accordance with excellence, 87 : 23
avarice and h., 347 : 7
beauty that comes from h., 583 : 12
being's end and aim, 337 : 10
beneficial for body, 734 : 12
beyond h. is bliss, 819 : 9
care of life and h., 389 : 4
ceases like dream, 273 : 5
consume h., 680 : 8
counting upon h., 479 : 4
depends less on exterior things, 375 : 18
efforts to create h., 763 : 4
envy no man's h., 212 : 2
episode in drama of pain, 640 : 17
every human seeking h., 720 : 3
four conditions for h., 882 : 12
freedom secret of h., 81 : 5
great step towards h., 453 : 7
greatest degree of h., 367 : 5
greatest h. for greatest numbers, 342 : 19
greatest h. for thinking man, 397 : 7
Greatest H. Principle, 508 : 18
habit takes place of h., 486 : 7
hairbreadth missings of h., 349 : 24
health foundation of h., 502 : 17

Happiness (*continued*)
hope for h. beyond life, 385 : 5
how simple and frugal is h., 782 : 23
ideal of h., 504 : 13
in hands of others, 445 : 6
in married estate, 277 : 1
is of retired nature, 326 : 10
is warm puppy, 901 : 6
ivrywhere excipt where people, 722 : 14
jealous possessions of h., 727 : 7
keep h. in store for society, 763 : 4
liberty secret of h., 677 : 12
lifetime of h. hell, 680 : 16
look into h. through another's eyes, 212 : 32
made of minute fractions, 438 : 8
make ourselves worthy of h., 366 : 13
makes up in height, 749 : 6
man mistakes evil for h., 414 : 5
mistaken path to h., 463 : 11
no h. like mine, 913 : 4
no h. perfect as martyr's, 699 : 8
no h. where no wisdom, 75 : 2
no man bear lifetime of h., 680 : 16
no one can arrange another's h., 859 : 8
not in multitude of friends, 255 : 11
not suffer from scientific holiday, 776 : 4
not write down h., 655 : 4
of anybody but dictators, 834 : 7
of human race, 373 : 9
of peoples, 655 : 7
of society end of government, 381 : 8
on earth no sure h., 174 : 5
on terrestrial ball, 856 : 3
only one h. in life, 504 : 15
pastime and our h., 428 : 4
politics art of human h., 706 : 21
principles to effect h., 387 : 9
produced by good tavern, 355 : 19
pursuing and obtaining h., 367 : 4
pursuit of h., 387 : 9
regret or secret h., 664 : 5
religion assures final h., 679 : 1
result h., 548 : 27
result of man's effort, 763 : 3
rhyming gives men h., 339 : 30
secret of h. freedom, 81 : 5
she does not find, 352 : 3
sole object of government, 383 : 9
sum of human h., 776 : 4
supreme h. of life, 491 : 15
take life-lie away take h., 600 : 2
tender h. betray, 427 : 26
terror in h., 894 : 7
that makes heart afraid, 485 : 6
the only good, 615 : 12
the only sanction of life, 703 : 8
thirst after h., 359 : 7
to be dissolved into something great, 739 : 1
to crave h. is revolt, 599 : 14
too swiftly flies, 361 : 12
two foes of human h., 463 : 8
what right have we to h., 599 : 14
wherein lies h., 475 : 20
work out h. for selves, 448 : 2
Happy a man as any in world, 309 : 21
accident, 261 : 18, 771 : 15
age when idle with impunity, 452 : 18
alchemy of mind, 344 : 15
all the while I was h., 916 : 2

Happy (*continued*)
and I wrote my h. songs, 403 : 3
as a lover, 427 : 24
as grass was green, 886 : 19
as heart was long, 887 : 2
as kings, 668 : 14
as we imagine, 293 : 8
ask yourself whether h., 508 : 23
autumn fields, 531 : 3
be and have immortal bliss, 173 : 17
be good and h. today, 433 : 17
beat, 855 : 1
best government desires to make people h., 487 : 4
bread sauce of h. ending, 653 : 6
breed of men, 194 : 13
bridegroom Hesper brings, 692 : 2
call that man h., 71 : 8
Christmas to all, 446 : 4
combination of circumstances, 432 : 3
convents, 340 : 26
created you while h., 702 : 7
days here again, 824 : 13
days that make us h., 760 : 18
deep down, 810 : 4
description of h. state, 307 : 18
duty of being h., 667 : 23
earthlier h. is rose distilled, 195 : 21
ending, 653 : 6
families alike, 602 : 9
fault, 54 : 8
few, 208 : 11
field mossy cavern, 477 : 16
fool h. he knows no more, 337 : 6
for son whose father went to hell, 186 : 5
good government when those near made h., 69 : 3
good to be just plain h., 819 : 9
good-night air, 641 : 13
hail Columbia h. land, 422 : 21
he of calm and h. nature, 84 : 4
he with such mother, 531 : 14
heart that sighed, 182 : 5
high majestical, 467 : 13
highways where I went, 691 : 9
horse to bear Antony, 240 : 21
hour wherein man might be h., 270 : 26
house shelters friend, 497 : 17
how h. he who crowns, 370 : 2
how h. vestal's lot, 335 : 4
how h. with either, 332 : 6
how we make ourselves h., 366 : 13
if all h. as we, 405 : 11
if ever wife h. in man, 290 : 12
if you want to be h. be, 561 : 6
illusion which makes me h., 380 : 3
in arms of chambermaid, 356 : 8
in being and knowing, 819 : 9
in even bad movie, 889 : 4
in nothing else so h., 194 : 19
in small ways, 701 : 5
in sorrow, 171 : 13
in work three things needed, 572 : 13
is he born and taught, 250 : 14
Isles, 529 : 13
Jerusalem h. home, 918 : 5
laugh before we are h., 315 : 7
let a lord once own the h. lines, 333 : 13
let us be h. as we can, 356 : 18
liking what they do, 361 : 1
little h. if say how much, 209 : 11

Happy (*continued*)
little needed to make h. life, 125 : 11
lucid intervals and h. pauses, 179 : 12
make earth h., 591 : 8
make fellow creatures h., 385 : 5
make two lovers h., 336 : 8
make wife h. while you are alive, 3 : 8
man be his dole, 159 : *n* 5
man happy dole, 159 : 7
man that hath his quiver full, 22 : 10
man who could search out causes, 104 : 5
man who works ancestral acres, 106 : 23
man's without a shirt, 158 : 16
master of himself a h. man, 108 : 7
mindful of h. time in misery, 141 : 2
moron, 924 : 18
Nature to explore, 337 : 6
never was so h., 921 : 13
no lad so h. as I, 443 : 9
no lot is altogether h., 107 : 24
no man h. who does not think so, 111 : 26
no one h. till all h., 579 : 10
noble h. human beings, 572 : 19
not h. unless free, 464 : 10
not to seem too h., 544 : 19
object of making men h., 582 : 5
old man, 103 : 8
pair, 285 : 23
people die whole, 797 : 13
people whose annals blank, 474 : 15
persons with torn bodies h., 732 : 3
place green groves of blest, 105 : 21
place to be h. here, 615 : 12
place with me, 562 : 9
policeman's lot not h., 628 : 3
ports and h. havens, 194 : 5
possessor of talent, 865 : 15
prologues to swelling act, 236 : 10
prospects more pleasing than fruition, 123 : *n* 7
rage outside h. ground, 587 : 8
rarely find a h. life, 106 : 13
realize I'd been h., 882 : 3
remote from the h., 868 : 20
rich h. in plenty, 337 : 6
right happens to h. man, 875 : 3
ring h. bells, 532 : 22
so h. as America, 384 : 15
that we are not over happy, 220 : 24
the h. that have called thee so, 440 : 5
the man and happy he alone, 305 : 1
the man who void of care, 328 : 19
the man whose wish, 332 : 10
they h. are and love, 276 : 8
thing to be father to many sons, 186 : 9
this h. country, 365 : 5
this the h. morn, 277 : 6
those early days when I, 299 : 2
those who plant cabbages, 158 : 4
those whose walls already rise, 104 : 25
time to be h. is now, 615 : 12
to be h. be well fed, 772 : 12
to be h. make others so, 615 : 12
to have been h. most unhappy, 129 : 22
too h. tree, 478 : 14
tree h. scarcely sentient, 721 : 1

Happy (*continued*)
'twere now to be most h., 230 : 14
until dead not call man h., 62 : 17
Warrior, 427 : 21
warrior of politics, 741 : *n* 3
warrior sleeps, 427 : *n* 2
was he free was he h., 869 : 3
where h. wing-beats are, 412 : 9
where one is h. there's homeland, 134 : 32
which of us h. in world, 539 : 10
who hath this only, 62 : 6
who in verse steer, 311 : 2
who knows rural gods, 104 : 6
who uses blessings with wisdom, 108 : 14
whoever h. make others h., 909 : 2
whom unbroken bond unites, 107 : 9
world not making you h., 680 : 15
world of h. days, 187 : 8
yet h. pair, 285 : 23
Harangue, telling nothing in great h., 297 : 26
Harbinger, evening star love's h., 287 : 32
Harbingers are come, 269 : 6
to heaven, 276 : 14
Harbor, age the h. of all ills, 92 : 5
arrived in a good h., 265 : 7
bar be moaning, 566 : 9
cleared, 434 : 7
even a little h. is good, 663 : 15
final h., 571 : 4
in life did h. give, 256 : 5
looking over h. and city, 761 : 5
run into a safe h., 62 : 21
ship comes into the h., 265 : 12
ship of state safely to h., 74 : 9
takes and gives something, 663 : 15
whence unmoor no more, 571 : 4
Harbors I by sweating blood won, 151 : 10
Hard as a piece of nether millstone, 17 : 6
as nails, 547 : 1
beginning good ending, 159 : 9
cause that makes these h. hearts, 234 : 16
Christ ain't going to be too h., 636 : 4
cursed h. reading, 399 : 11
dealing teaches them suspect, 198 : 27
doubtful dangerous times, 471 : 13
for women to keep counsel, 216 : 2
gemlike flame, 638 : 13
heart of child, 794 : 1
heroic for earth too h., 544 : 5
hit h. fast often, 777 : 12
hit the line h., 687 : 5
it is well I die h., 379 : 15
it shall go h., 199 : 19
keeps end from being h., 749 : 1
latent value, 653 : 13
like tip of wedge, 790 : 10
long boots h. boots, 761 : 13
no h. gifts, 797 : 13
not think what is h. is impossible, 125 : 7
nothing's so h. but search will find, 266 : 18
prove him with h. questions, 13 : 34
rain's a-gonna fall, 915 : 4
sloth finds down pillow h., 243 : 23
solid massy h. particles, 313 : 16

Hard (*continued*)
stairs, 142 : 13
things that are too h. for thee, 34 : 26
this is my h. time, 873 : 12
times h. and wages low, 935 : 2
to argue with belly, 95 : 9
to catch and conquer, 601 : 1
to kick against pricks, 46 : 6
to please everybody, 112 : 1
very hard is my fare, 331 : 11
was their lodging, 318 : 17
way of transgressors is h., 23 : 32
when h. up pawn intelligence, 828 : 15
Hard-boiled as picnic egg, 834 : 6
Hardened, he h. Pharaoh's heart, 9 : 19
Hardens and grows cold, 870 : 6
it h. a' within, 409 : 12
Harder, heart h. than stone, 61 : 4
nothing h. than indifference, 614 : 11
Hardest, first hundred years h., 757 : 12
first step is h., 344 : 18
knife ill-used, 245 : 7
of all to close hand, 657 : 14
softest things overcome h., 64 : 15
Hard-favored rage, 207 : 16
Hardihood, dauntless h., 592 : 6
endurance courage, 726 : 5
Hardiness, herein friendliness h. love, 149 : 5
Hardship, godlike h., 478 : 7
meet any h., 890 : 7
our garment, 744 : 9
Hardships, to stars through h., 133 : 7
unknown h. we suffered, 822 : 2
Hard-working ancestry, 826 : 13
Hardy as Nemean lion's nerve, 219 : 15
breast, 567 : 9
kiss me H., 408 : 10
Hardy-handsome, big-boned and h., 656 : 7
Hare and tortoise, 66 : 3
hold with h. run with hound, 159 : 26
limped trembling, 476 : 8
mad March h., 152 : 19
March H. went on, 611 : 18
of whom proverb goes, 201 : 13
rouse lion than start h., 203 : 14
today on the flesh of a h., 912 : 9
Harebells, health and h., 562 : 7
Harebrained chatter, 502 : 21
Hares, little hunted h., 732 : 16
pull dead lions by beard, 201 : *n* 2
Hark ah the nightingale, 586 : 5
deep sound strikes, 457 : 14
do you hear sea, 478 : *n* 3
don't ye hear it, 429 : 19
hark dogs do bark, 933 : 21
hark my soul, 552 : 22
hark the lark, 243 : 16
the herald angels sing, 350 : 15
to exiled son's appeal, 639 : 15
Harlot's cry, 406 : 18
youthful h. curse, 405 : 10
Harlots, ye h. sleep at ease, 334 : 24
Harm, content with my h., 212 : 2
didn't want to h. the man, 903 : 5
do h. to other nations, 854 : 1
do me no h., 449 : 14
do not h. subtle wreath of hair, 253 : 11
does h. to another, 61 : 16
does h. to my wit, 213 : 12
fate cannot h. me, 433 : 12
flea does all h. he can, 254 : 21

Harm (*continued*)
good provoke to h., 229 : 1
I abstain from intentional h., 79 : 13
no h. in being wrong, 783 : 13
no one h. man who does self no wrong, 128 : 24
none shall h. Macbeth, 239 : 10
nothing do much h., 830 : 18
once h. has been done, 58 : 27
to one harm to all, 618 : 10
whether benevolence good or h., 597 : 5
win us to our h., 236 : 9
Harmful, emancipation h. without control over ourselves, 397 : 13
more h. than reasoned errors, 596 : 8
Harmless as doves, 38 : 36
drudge, 352 : 11
entertains the h. day, 250 : 15
inoffensive aristocracy, 519 : 17
necessary cat, 200 : 3
pleasure, 353 : 1
Harmonies of Liberty, 733 : 5
tumult of mighty h., 467 : 21
Harmonious and humane life, 589 : 7
dulcet and h. breath, 196 : 14
Father-Mother God all-h., 583 : 1
madness from my lips, 468 : 15
Harmoniously confused, 334 : 15
Harmonizes natural and artificial, 437 : 17
Harmony, absolute h., 860 : 3
all is divine h., 637 : 17
attention like deep h., 194 : 9
between men and land, 795 : 11
between tides and life, 672 : 20
cultivate peace and h., 379 : 12
disposed to h., 441 : 21
famous h. of leaves, 712 : 7
for you my Universe, 124 : 19
from h. from heavenly h., 305 : 9
hidden soul of h., 278 : 7
I don't want h., 582 : 4
in bad taste elegance, 877 : 10
in discord, 109 : 7
in h. with universe, 566 : 6
is pure love, 182 : 12
like h. in music, 423 : 18
makes heaven drowsy with h., 191 : 4
manifest in form and number, 696 : 5
more h. in her bright eye, 295 : 21
music wherever there is h., 274 : 20
not live in h., 863 : 12
not understood, 337 : 1
of leaves, 712 : 7
of temperament and circumstances, 583 : 12
of the whole universe, 154 : 10
order proportion, 274 : 20
perceived h. of object, 436 : 19
power of h., 423 : 11
spirit and instinct in h., 755 : 3
such h. in immortal souls, 201 : 1
too high a price for h., 582 : 4
touches of sweet h., 201 : 1
universal h., 583 : 5
whole complicate amassing h., 768 : 17
with laws of Nature, 595 : 14
Harms, beg often our own h., 240 : 26
himself who does harm, 61 : 16
lesse of two h., 58 : *n* 5
took not for thy h., 693 : 15
Harness, battle h., 746 : 7
Harness (*continued*)
die with h. on our back, 240 : 6
died in h., 746 : 7
him that girdeth on his h., 14 : 6
Harold stands on place of skulls, 457 : 13
Harp, as harper lays palm on h., 512 : 11
hang h. on willow-tree, 922 : 13
no h. like my own, 443 : 9
not all who own h. are harpers, 97 : 13
not on that string, 187 : 20
once the h. of Innisfail, 443 : 21
praise him with h., 22 : 25
such as handle h., 7 : 22
that once through Tara's halls, 446 : 9
tuning lyre and handling h., 70 : 12
wild h. slung behind him, 446 : 15
Harper, as h. lays palm on harp, 512 : 11
Harpers, not all who own harp are h., 97 : 13
Harping, still h. on my daughter, 220 : 18
Harpoon, why didn't I h. him, 929 : 7
Harps, hanged h. upon willows, 22 : 15
of gold, 537 : 16
played before the Lord on h., 13 : 14
Harris, words she spoke of Mrs. H., 548 : 3
Harrow house of dead, 868 : 4
rust to the h., 740 : 1
toad beneath h., 707 : 5
up thy soul, 219 : 18
Harrowing clods, 642 : 2
Harry, cry God for H., 207 : 18
Harry succeeds, 206 : 35
little touch of H., 208 : 2
such a King H., 182 : 15
these were swift to h., 792 : 6
young H. with beaver on, 204 : 31
Harsh as truth, 505 : 12
berries h. and crude, 280 : 6
cadence of a rugged line, 304 : 27
ego serves three h. masters, 678 : 15
in this h. world, 225 : 1
life teaches us to be less h., 395 : 12
nor h. nor grating, 423 : 13
out of tune and h., 221 : 21
philosophy not h., 279 : 25
school in which nothing h., 129 : 21
words of Mercury are h., 191 : 16
Harsher, qualify war in h. terms, 578 : 15
Harshly, strings untouched will h. jar, 183 : 18
Harshness is for good of boy, 313 : 9
no h. gives offense, 333 : 9
Hart, as h. panteth after water brooks, 19 : 5
as pants the h., 317 : 7
be thou like to a young h., 28 : 25
lame man leap as an h., 30 : 24
ungalled play, 222 : 17
Harvard, always tell H. man, 923 : 16
fair H., 465 : 1
Greek islands over H. Square, 842 : 4
Law School, 777 : 3
whaleship my H., 570 : 10
Harvest, gathereth her food in the h., 23 : 11
God comes as sheaves in h., 255 : 1
home, 203 : 7, 536 : 2
is past, 32 : 2
Harvest (*continued*)
moon, 319 : 1
no h. but a thorn, 268 : 21
of a quiet eye, 424 : 18
reap the h. of your land, 10 : 19
seedtime and h., 8 : 1
shalt not gather the gleanings of h., 10 : 19
this was all the h. I reaped, 516 : 17
time of h., 807 : 10
truly is plenteous, 38 : 32
Harvests, countries made to bear h., 739 : 5
wholesome h. reaps, 484 : 6
Harwich, steamer from H., 629 : 1
Has, what man h. he's sure of, 170 : 35
Hasard, coup de dés n'abolira le h., 651 : *n* 4
Haste, always in h., 346 : 10
away so soon, 266 : 12
brings failures, 78 : 15
come time and h. day, 399 : 18
eat it in h., 9 : 25
haste has no blessing, 925 : 27
I said in my h., 21 : 23
in paying obligation, 293 : 28
in wicked h. no profit, 158 : *n* 14
make h. better foot before, 202 : 9
make h. my beloved, 28 : 25
make h. on decay, 797 : 10
maketh waste, 158 : 18
married in h. repent at leisure, 324 : 5
more h. less speed, 110 : 6
mounting in hot h., 457 : 17
now to my setting, 249 : 1
of fool slowest thing, 313 : 20
still pays haste, 229 : 8
thee Nymph, 277 : 19
this sweaty h., 217 : 20
while one with moderate h., 218 : 22
without h. but without rest, 397 : 15
wooed in h. wed at leisure, 188 : 34
Hasten, minutes h. to their end, 244 : 19
to be drunk, 307 : 8
Hastening, to h. ills a prey, 369 : 30
Hastens, midnight strikes and h., 692 : 8
Hastily, no workman may work well and h., 147 : 25
nothing can be done h. and prudently, 111 : 21
Hasty, common sense takes h. view, 558 : 18
marriage seldom proveth well, 186 : 14
orisons, 827 : 2
pudding, 400 : 5, 920 : *n* 2
start awa sae h., 408 : 12
Hat, cockle h. and staff, 223 : 21
he can't think without h., 866 : 11
his h. in his hand, 353 : 18
lightly doffed h., 704 : 15
Lord forbade me to put off my h., 300 : 21
my h. upon my head, 353 : 18
not worse for wear, 376 : 15
off with your h, 676 : 17
on account of beaver h., 550 : 15
penny in old man's h., 921 : 3
runcible h., 550 : 6
stuck feather in h., 920 : 9
wear the gold h., 835 : 3
wears faith as fashion of h., 208 : 25

Hat (*continued*)
word to lift h. to, 608 : 8
Hatched, count chickens before h., 65 : 19
don't count boobies until h., 831 : 10
o'er and hatched different, 565 : 6
silent when eggs h., 277 : 1
would grow mischievous, 215 : 17
Hatchet, buried h., 725 : 13
I did it with my h., 378 : *n* 9
I did it with my little h., 378 : *n* 9
Hatching vain empires, 284 : 15
Hate, because we h. no people, 824 : 12
chatter love and h., 588 : 7
cherish hearts that h. thee, 249 : 8
combat between love and h., 671 : 17
common herd, 107 : 25
counsels not in such quality, 199 : 21
creative h., 738 : 17
do good to them that h. you, 37 : 11
drum's discordant sound, 375 : 4
dumpy woman, 460 : 12
enough religion to make us h., 322 : 2
envy calumny h. pain, 469 : 12
envy dared not h., 459 : 11
families I h. you, 727 : 7
fear h. surrender defiance, 913 : 6
fly from not h. mankind, 457 : 26
foe without h., 591 : 11
for arts, 338 : 14
found only on stage, 461 : 11
freedom for thought we h., 645 : 11
gods h. the obvious, 56 : 23
hand of all that h. us, 42 : 25
herein h. viurtue sin, 149 : 5
him for a Christian, 198 : 19
I don't h. it, 838 : 5
I h. and I love, 102 : 17
I h. definitions, 501 : 2
I h. nobody, 323 : 5
I h. quotations, 495 : 26
I h. the day, 174 : 13
I h. war, 779 : 18
I h. ye all, 295 : 15
I know enough of h., 748 : 2
I shall h. all women, 252 : 19
immortal h., 283 : 8
implacable in h., 304 : 3
inaccuracy, 621 : 4
ingratitude, 214 : 26
Juno's unrelenting h., 306 : 11
let them h. so long they fear, 97 : 9
love and desire and h., 721 : 7
love freedom h. slavery, 881 : 13
love love and h. h., 857 : 1
love treason but h. traitor, 99 : 16
loved him too much not to h., 312 : 4
mankind, 243 : 8
matter whether you h. self, 797 : 20
my verses, 797 : 19
naught I did in h., 232 : 19
no h. lost between us, 261 : 21
no sport in h., 469 : 26
nor love thy life nor h., 287 : 30
of those below, 457 : 22
one and love other, 38 : 1
one another and know it, 310 : 15
only love sprung from only h., 191 : 27
only those who h. Negro, 672 : 13
owe no man h., 212 : 2
Persian luxury I h., 107 : 16
rage and h. from Adam down, 570 : 13
scourge laid upon your h., 193 : 30
Hate (*continued*)
skins not like your own, 556 : 6
smile to those that h., 460 : 4
so far only should we h., 73 : 14
something in this richness that I h., 794 : 2
strength against her h., 819 : 4
the tree, 129 : 11
things we ought, 87 : 22
those I fight I do not h., 713 : 20
those who h. and destroy, 672 : 9
those who h. you don't win, 883 : 3
time to h., 26 : 21
to be unquiet at home, 310 : 16
to leave world, 845 : 9
to see evenin' sun go down, 740 : 12
traitors and treason love, 305 : 26
understand folks they h., 568 : 8
war, 779 : 18
were why men breathe, 829 : 21
whom they fear they h., 95 : 6
whom they have injured they h., 115 : 4
why do you h. the South, 838 : 5
you through the glass, 834 : 12
Hated for my name's sake, 39 : 1
if to be fat be h., 204 : 6
past reason h., 245 : 23
the approximate, 756 : 5
to be h. needs but be seen, 337 : 5
with hate found on stage, 461 : 11
with scabby hatred, 912 : 11
Hateful art how to forget, 267 : 8
as the gates of Hades, 58 : 8
pride is h. before God, 35 : 16
second wife h. to children, 76 : 1
self is h., 300 : 12
woman once loved h., 736 : 3
Hater, very good h., 353 : 13
Hates, anyone who h. babies, 770 : *n* 8
children can't be all bad, 770 : 18
God h. bray of bragging, 74 : 8
him that would stretch him, 235 : 19
tell him he h. flatterers, 215 : 21
thing he would not kill, 200 : 4
unhappy h., 586 : 12
Hath, unto everyone that h., 40 : 30
Hating, die not h. enemies, 344 : 12
Hatred, all h. driven hence, 714 : 21
ceases by love, 72 : 16
comes from heart, 463 : 3
envy h. and malice, 55 : 10
excites h. to conceal abuses, 444 : 4
for white men, 903 : 2
habitual h. or fondness, 379 : 12
hate Negro see h. in him, 672 : 13
hated with scabby h., 912 : 11
healthy h. of scoundrels, 474 : 13
I must have no h., 706 : 17
intellectual h. worst, 714 : 20
love to h. turned, 324 : 16
made law, 864 : 5
must be preached, 496 : 24
not cease by hatred, 72 : 16
of bourgeois beginning of wisdom, 583 : 17
of entrenched greed, 779 : 14
rage h. and murder, 903 : 2
renders votaries credulous, 359 : 5
slavery's aftermath, 672 : 5
soul-destroying h., 744 : 8
stalled ox and h. therewith, 24 : 7
stirreth up strifes, 23 : 23
through h. borne apart, 75 : 23
Hatred (*continued*)
truth begets h., 96 : 2
where h. let me sow love, 138 : 15
who condemn h. of evil, 881 : 12
Hats off 676 : *n* 5
seraphs swing snowy h., 604 : 15
wat their h. aboon, 926 : 12
Hatter, can't take less said H., 611 : 21
Haughtiness of soul, 325 : 14
of the terrible, 29 : 21
Haughty day, 494 : 18
discountenance h. and lawless, 380 : 6
Juno's unrelenting hate, 306 : 11
nation proud in arms, 279 : 5
spirit before a fall, 24 : 12
vigilant resolute, 488 : 12
Haul, cut hawsers h. out, 576 : 16
up the flag, 883 : 12
Hauling, crazy as h. timber into woods, 106 : 18
Haunch and hump is Obey, 709 : 6
Haunches, sits on silent h., 761 : 5
Haunt, breed and h., 236 : 21
exempt from public h., 210 : 24
ghostlike the spot, 503 : 7
murmurous h. of flies, 476 : 27
so h. thy days, 478 : 8
Haunted air, 811 : 14
beneath waning moon h., 433 : 22
by ghosts, 195 : 2
holy ground, 457 : 9
me like a passion, 423 : 12
passage in Lear h. me, 478 : *n* 3
spring and dale, 277 : 11
summer eves by h. stream, 278 : 6
Haunting black air, 908 : 10
Haunts about thy shape, 477 : 4
busy h. of men, 470 : 21
of coot and hern, 533 : 15
old old fable h. me, 481 : 7
suspicion h. guilty mind, 186 : 27
tempest laughs at archer, 580 : 17
Haupt, O H. vol Blut und Wunden, 276 : *n* 4
Hautboys, give h. breath he comes, 306 : 14
Havana, our man in H., 859 : 12
Have, all I h. given gladly, 872 : 8
all we h. and are, 710 : 23
by hoping more h. but less, 189 : 18
curtsied when you h., 247 : 19
desire what we ought not to h., 111 : 22
everything yet nothing, 96 : 16
House of H., 638 : 7
in quest to h. extreme, 245 : 23
little h. and seek no more, 167 : 6
more than thou showest, 233 : 9
pay for all you h., 729 : 3
thee not yet see thee still, 237 : 13
these for yours, 692 : 11
to h. and to hold, 56 : 9
to h. to hold and let go, 707 : 1
to h. what we would h., 228 : 12
try to h. and use it, 87 : 25
what others would be glad of, 349 : 15
what we h. we prize not, 209 : 31
where ask is h., 365 : 8
Haven, in friendship but faithless h., 73 : 14
in sunny Palestine, 760 : 19
safe into h. glide, 350 : 12
under the hill, 530 : 19

Have-nots, haves and h., 170 : 18
Havens, in h. dumb, 655 : 17
ports and happy h., 194 : 5
Haves and have-nots, 170 : 18
of give, 829 : 19
Having fewest wants, 79 : 2
had h. and in quest to have, 245 : 23
not a h. and resting, 588 : 17
nothing possessing all, 49 : 17
Havoc, cry H., 216 : 12
Hawk, know h. from handsaw, 220 : 31
prayer of h. does not get chicken, 926 : 5
sooner kill man than h., 797 : 15
which h. flies higher pitch, 184 : 20
Hawked, by mousing owl h. at, 238 : 11
Hawk's, inhuman as h. cry, 798 : 1
Hawks, dark h. hear us, 778 : 5
give your heart to h., 797 : 18
such hounds such h., 927 : 4
Hawsers, cut h. haul out, 576 : 16
Hawthorn in the dale, 277 : 24
Hawthorne, power of clackness in H., 569 : 16
sedulous ape to H., 668 : 23
Hay, antic h., 183 : 16
bottle of h., 197 : 5
came creaking to barn, 892 : 6
good h. sweet h., 197 : 5
make h. when sun shineth, 159 : 2
mowers sleeping among new-mown h., 571 : 7
needle in bottle of h., 170 : 12
new-mown h., 732 : 13
work and pray live on h., 764 : 13
world bundle of h., 462 : 9
Haydn, some cry up H., 442 : 4
Haystack in the floods, 618 : 4
needle in h., 170 : *n* 3
under h. asleep, 930 : 12
Hazard, art's long h., 728 : 22
men that h. all, 199 : 9
nice h. of doubtful hour, 204 : 29
of concealing, 409 : 12
of new fortunes, 201 : 11
of the die, 187 : 32
of their lives, 687 : 4
Haze, last communion in h., 604 : 10
Hazel, lone Glenartney's h. shade, 431 : 5
switch for discovery, 711 : 17
Hazlitt, sedulous ape to H., 668 : 23
Hé Dieu si j'eusse étudié, 150 : *n* 2
He for God only, 285 : 18
forget the h. and she, 252 : 6
is risen, 42 : 15, 54 : 10
is the Rock, 11 : 23
poorest h. in England, 264 : 11
was he and I was I, 164 : 14
Head, adjusts tumbled h., 607 : 12
and hoof of Law, 709 : 6
anointest my h. with oil, 18 : 7
apples on Newton's h., 750 : 5
at his h. a grass-green turf, 223 : 22
bare Ben Bulben's h., 718 : 1
behold my h., 269 : 6
bending low, 598 : 7
binds so dear a h., 468 : 22
black wires grow on her h., 246 : 1
blessings upon the h. of the just, 23 : 22
bloody but unbowed, 663 : 10
bowed comely h. down, 296 : 24
buffalo's powerful h., 867 : 15
Head (*continued*)
bullet through his h., 729 : 5
call in thy death's h., 268 : 22
chop off her h., 611 : 14
chop off your h., 930 : 8
crotchets in thy h., 225 : 14
crown in my heart not on h., 186 : 8
crown of h. to sole, 209 : 20
desolate and bowed h., 721 : 4
dogs shame the gray h., 59 : 6
drunken dog ragged h., 441 : 6
eat my h., 547 : 3
feel as if top of h. off, 608 : 6
four angels round my h., 294 : 16
from heels up to h., 668 : 12
from the fair h. forever, 334 : 10
full of quarrels, 193 : 3
gently falling on thy h., 328 : 8
good gray h. all knew, 533 : 3
grown gray in vain, 469 : 12
guts in his h., 226 : 6
hairs of h. numbered, 39 : 3
hang your h. over, 920 : 19
heap coals of fire upon his h., 25 : 15
heart runs away with h., 415 : 12
heaven to weary h., 485 : 14
her h. on her knee, 232 : 8
here rests his h., 362 : 17
hers is the h., 638 : 10
hide h. under his wing, 932 : 6
hit nail on h., 161 : 16
hoary h. a crown of glory, 24 : 13
if she'd but turn her h., 712 : 18
imperfections on my h., 219 : 24
in heart or in h., 199 : 23
incessantly stand on h., 611 : 9
it shall bruise thy h., 7 : 10
Jezebel tired her h., 14 : 19
John Baptist's h., 39 : 23
keep good tongue in h., 248 : 7
King Charles's h., 548 : 31
lay sleeping h. my love, 868 : 16
make you shorter by the h., 163 : 17
man with the h., 531 : 7
Medusa's h., 821 : 11
meet and not see its h., 64 : 7
my hat upon my h., 353 : 18
my ho h. halls, 778 : 5
no bigger than his h., 234 : 28
no roof to shroud his h., 257 : 20
not sound the rest not well, 169 : *n* 6
not yet has heart or h., 857 : 16
not yet silvered, 376 : 23
O sacred h. now wounded, 276 : 13
off with her h., 612 : 1
off with his h., 187 : 14, 324 : 27
on horror's h. horrors, 231 : 14
one small h. could carry, 370 : 11
ought to have h. examined, 777 : 9
over h. and heels, 101 : 22
precious jewel in his h., 210 : 24
right hand bigger than h., 906 : 15
root of family is person of its h., 89 : 8
sacred h. of thine, 280 : 18
scratch h. with lightning, 623 : 5
shake of his poor little h., 629 : 16
shot it through the h., 933 : 12
show my h. to the people, 412 : 3
singe my white h., 233 : 24
slide into lover's h., 424 : 11
so young body with so old h., 200 : 8
some once lovely h., 516 : 12
Son of man nowhere to lay h., 38 : 23
Head (*continued*)
stone of the corner, 21 : 25
strike stars with my exalted h., 106 : 25
stuff the h. with reading, 340 : 25
sudden if thing comes in his h., 186 : 26
that wears crown, 206 : 19
this old gray h., 513 : 18
to contrive, 289 : 16
trickled through h., 613 : 18
turns no more his h., 435 : 3
up while rower breathes, 873 : 16
useful lesson to h., 377 : 14
very staid h., 200 : *n* 4
well-made rather than well-filled h., 164 : 13
when the h. aches, 169 : 38
whole h. is sick, 28 : 27
with its h. is went galumphing, 612 : 18
your h. concerned with outer weather, 748 : 13
Headache, dismal h., 628 : 26
Headhunting not natural, 786 : 8
Headings, good reduced to three h., 309 : 6
Headlong, hurled h. flaming, 283 : 4
Headpiece filled with straw, 805 : 15
Heads, beast of many h., 108 : *n* 14
beast with many h., 242 : 21
blood be on your h., 46 : 18
brains of better h., 274 : 3
day fate put h. together, 748 : 13
diminished h., 285 : 10
erect instead of bowing necks, 128 : 12
green hands blue, 550 : 11
grow beneath shoulders, 229 : 30
heart better than h., 493 : 1
heaven over our h., 560 : 10
hills whose h. touch heaven, 229 : 29
houseless h., 234 : 3
lift h. and see above her, 822 : 10
lift up your h. O ye gates, 18 : 9
monster with uncounted h., 205 : 18
not sit on others' h., 657 : 17
o'ertaxed, 586 : 1
old h. on young shoulders, 896 : 1
old men's h. bare, 816 : 2
so many h. so many wits, 97 : *n* 2
tossing h. in sprightly dance, 427 : 9
two h. better than one, 159 : 23
when trees bow h., 608 : 19
Headstone said free at last, 915 : 18
Headstones, crooked crosses and h., 777 : 16
milestones into h., 569 : 3
Headstrong as an allegory, 398 : 12
liberty lashed with woe, 188 : 1
Heal blows of sound, 518 : 13
physician h. thyself, 43 : 2
time to h., 26 : 21
wound h. by degrees, 230 : 29
Healed of suffering by experiencing it, 734 : 11
writes of scars h., 835 : 9
Healer, Plato h. of soul, 83 : *n* 3
Healing, beauty full of h., 888 : 6
in his wings, 33 : 39
matter of time, 79 : 14
Heals, time h. all wounds, 96 : *n* 10
Health and a day, 496 : 5
and intellect the two blessings, 91 : 11
and quiet breathing, 475 : 16
and wealth missed me, 454 : 8

Health (*continued*)
best physic to preserve h., 181 : 2
blessing money cannot buy, 271 : 13
by his h. sickness, 403 : 13
double h. to thee, 460 : 4
foundation of happiness, 502 : 17
greatest of blessings, 80 : 8
I swear by H., 79 : 13
I that in h. was and gladness, 153 : 6
in h. and mind's content, 310 : 8
in sickness and in h., 56 : 9
innocence and h., 370 : 1
intelligence talent, 695 : 3
more important than wealth, 789 : 13
nobody in good h. if not fresh air, 670 : 13
protect h. homes firesides, 666 : 22
recover h. through contentment 79 : 16
that mocks doctor's rules, 513 : 11
their h. it might hurt, 371 : 22
trust in horse's h., 234 : 14
unbought, 306 : 26
universal sickness implies idea of h., 866 : 3
unto all nations, 55 : 5
wait on both, 238 : 24
Healthful, sober h. with his wits, 294 : 15
Healths, urge no h., 370 : *n* 3
Healthy and wealthy and dead, 831 : 8
breath of morn, 478 : 2
free the world before me, 575 : 9
sick danger for h., 658 : 7
wealthy wise, 347 : 12
Heap coals of fire, 25 : 15
dust h. called history, 666 : 8
o' livin', 774 : 4
of broken images, 805 : 1
of dust alone remains, 335 : 11
of loose sand, 719 : 9
of stones not a house, 673 : 8
on more wood, 430 : 21
struck all of a h., 398 : 25
worn out before thrown on scrap h., 680 : 15
Heapeth, he h. up riches, 19 : 3
Heaping field and highway, 568 : 15
Heaps of miser's treasure, 279 : 23
Hear a little song, 395 : 5
all ye angels, 286 : 22
America singing, 574 : 2
angels sing, 537 : 16
at back from time to time h., 805 : 6
at my back I always h., 296 : 28
author has nothing to h., 597 : 7
be silent that you may h., 216 : 13
bells I h., 576 : 6
bronze Negroes breathe, 893 : 12
by tale or history, 195 : 22
can't h. with bawk of bats, 778 : 5
conclusion of the whole matter, 27 : 27
destroyer and preserver h., 467 : 18
did ye not h. it, 457 : 15
dust h. her and beat, 533 : 25
each other groan, 476 : 24
'erse's legs, 535 : 7
every child may joy to h., 403 : 3
falcon cannot h. falconer, 714 : 12
far-off curfew sound, 278 : 19
few love to h. sins they act, 243 : 11
friend do you h., 928 : *n* 2
Hear (*continued*)
hate enough to h. your prayers, 66 : *n* 8
have ears and h. not, 31 : 34
have ears but h. not, 21 : 22
having ears h. not, 383 : 1
he wept to h., 403 : 2
heart h. her and beat, 533 : 25
him prate, 601 : 9
hungry stomach cannot h., 296 : 21
I h. you I will come, 691 : 4
in chamber above me, 512 : 4
incline thine ear and h., 30 : 27
it in deep heart's core, 712 : 5
it not Duncan, 237 : 16
it O Thyrsis, 587 : 11
it roar now, 429 : 19
lady sing in Welsh, 204 : 18
let him h., 39 : 6
listen and do not h. it, 64 : 6
listen and you shall h., 512 : 6
Lord h. me out, 874 : 23
me for my cause, 216 : 13
mermaids singing, 252 : 1
mind-forged manacles I h., 405 : 9
music everyone should h., 770 : 16
never merry when I h. sweet music, 201 : 2
no evil, 919 : 2
none h. beside the singer, 442 : 23
not my steps, 237 : 15
now this, 31 : 11
now this foolish people, 31 : 34
old Triton, 428 : 1
one to speak another h., 558 : 12
other side, 129 : 7
quickness to h. move see, 705 : 4
replication of your sounds, 215 : 1
right way in the morning, 68 : 14
rogues talk of court news, 235 : 12
Shenandoah I long to h. you, 934 : 20
still stood fixed to h., 287 : 2
strike but h. me, 70 : 14
sudden cry of pain, 781 : 10
surly sullen bell, 244 : 26
swift to h., 51 : 30
that lonesome whippoorwill, 903 : 1
the word of the Lord, 32 : 15
the words of the wise, 24 : 37
thee and rejoice, 427 : 1
therefore h. now this, 31 : 11
those things ye h., 43 : 12
through midnight steets I h., 405 : 10
thy shrill delight, 468 : 13
Time's winged chariot, 296 : 28
to see moves more than to h., 189 : 25
us when we cry to Thee, 596 : 18
voice in every wind, 361 : 9
voice of the Bard, 405 : 1
whatsoever I shall see or h., 79 : 13
wind blow, 920 : 19
wooden dialogue and sound, 226 : 4
word culture reach for revolver, 816 : 6
world applaud ghost, 587 : 17
you this Triton, 242 : 18
Heard, ain't h. nothing yet, 795 : 4
by each let this be h., 676 : 8
cannot be h. so high, 234 : 28
chimes at midnight, 206 : 24
ears have h. Holy Word, 405 : 1
eye of man hath not h., 197 : 10
have ye not h., 31 : 1
heavens fill with shouting, 529 : 24
Heard (*continued*)
her massive sandal, 823 : 8
I have h. the key turn, 805 : 13
I will be h., 505 : 13
in ancient days, 477 : 1
it on the Aegean, 587 : 15
laughing h. on hill, 403 : 15
long after h. no more, 426 : 6
loud bassoon, 434 : 8
man who is seen and h., 705 : 12
melodies are sweet, 477 : 6
more he h. less he spoke, 660 : 15
music h. so deeply, 808 : 8
music I h. with you, 811 : 12
never h. so musical discord, 197 : 8
nor ear h., 48 : 2
not regarded, 204 : 21
of thee by hearing of the ear, 17 : 10
of wonderful one-hoss shay, 519 : 15
of your paintings, 221 : 18
old old men say, 713 : 3
other side, 77 : 1
recede disappointed tide, 604 : 11
remember what I almost h., 907 : 5
shot h. round the world, 494 : 13
sing songs not h. before, 107 : 25
stood and h. steeple, 691 : 24
sweetest song ever h., 459 : 23
the dead cry, 873 : 12
the mermaids singing, 803 : 19
them cry the peacocks, 766 : 12
then is h. no more, 240 : 4
trumpet be h. on high, 305 : 13
voice cry Sleep no more, 237 : 21
voices of children h. on the green, 403 : 15
we should certainly have h., 869 : 3
whether there be Holy Ghost, 46 : 21
wise man say, 690 : 20
wished she had not h. it, 229 : 31
Hearers, convince h. of own assertions, 84 : 1
not h. only, 51 : 31
readers and h. like my books, 181 : 22
too deep for his h., 371 : 14
Hearest thou hardly a breadth, 397 : 3
why h. thou music sadly, 244 : 3
Heareth, thy servant h., 12 : 30
Hearing ear and the seeing eye, 24 : 29
grass grow, 565 : 23
heard of thee by h. of the ear, 17 : 10
intellect gained h., 678 : 12
make passionate my h., 190 : 23
mentioned in your h., 440 : 22
nor ear filled with h., 26 : 13
of a voice, 571 : 10
Hearken ere I die, 528 : 4
will not h. to voice of charmers, 19 : 23
Hearkened, old men h. when he was young, 110 : 10
to my commandments, 31 : 7
Hearkeners seldom hear good, 319 : 9
Hears different drummer, 560 : 17
ear of him that h., 191 : 12
him in the wind, 336 : 16
monarch h., 306 : 13
neither h. nor sees, 424 : 14
other mainly h. the No, 395 : 10
step to music he h., 560 : 17
sun which h. all things, 57 : 26
wanderer halts and h., 691 : 12
you nearby sweetly speaking, 63 : 5
Hearse, gilded h., 806 : 3

Hearse (*continued*)
marriage h., 405 : 10
underneath this sable h., 265 : 15
Heart, a man's h. deviseth his way, 24 : 11
absence makes h. grow fonder, 112 : 25
abundance of the h., 39 : 11
adornment is reflection of h., 782 : 12
all that mighty h., 425 : 14
all the h. soul senses, 543 : 16
all thy h. open, 531 : 12
altitude pressed world on h., 892 : 12
amortization of h. and soul, 826 : 18
and mind of America, 869 : 12
and voice oppressed, 563 : 13
apple rotten at the h., 198 : 23
apply h. unto my knowledge, 24 : 37
argues not mind, 586 : 13
as he thinketh in his h., 25 : 8
awful warmth about h., 479 : 12
batter my h., 254 : 15
battlefield h. of man, 582 : 1
beat strong and cheerfully, 667 : 20
because my h. is pure, 530 : 15
begins to bleed, 929 : 9
benevolent and kind, 409 : 19
betray h. that loved her, 423 : 15
better than all heads, 493 : 1
black spot in any h., 599 : 7
blessed are the pure in h., 37 : 4
blood around men's h., 75 : 24
book and h. never part, 320 : 5
bread strengthens man's h., 319 : 8
break into flaws, 233 : 23
bring my aching h. to rest, 97 : 10
broken and contrite h., 19 : 19
broken h. lies here, 489 : 3
brute h. of brute like you, 911 : 18
build on human h., 540 : 12
buildeth on vulgar h., 206 : 7
bullets seek out where h. lies, 860 : 12
burn within us, 44 : 15
bury h. at Wounded Knee, 840 : 3
by sorrow of the h. the spirit is broken, 24 : 6
can push sea and land, 822 : 12
candle of understanding in thine h., 34 : 6
captivate my h., 919 : 19
caused the widow's h. to sing, 16 : 16
change of h., 868 : 4
cheer poor man's h., 430 : 22
clean hands and a pure h., 18 : 8
command my h. and me, 292 : 7
committed adultery in his h., 37 : 8
congenial to my h., 370 : 15
consume my h. away, 715 : 2
counsel of thine own h., 36 : 6
courage of h., 730 : 4
create in me a clean h., 19 : 16
Cruelty has human h., 405 : 14
cry of Absence in h., 810 : 17
cutting the h. asunder, 782 : 4
darling of my h., 331 : 5
day breaks not it is my h., 918 : 18
deep in h. believe, 925 : 9
departeth from the Lord, 32 : 11
dictates of h., 413 : 20
dispossessed had stopped, 653 : 8
distrusting asks, 370 : 16
do not submit in h., 89 : 1
don't eat your h., 65 : 12
don't let h. depend, 413 : 29

Heart (*continued*)
each cell holds h., 863 : 16
East and West will pinch h., 822 : 12
eat h., 65 : 12
eat thy h., 174 : 11
endure my h., 61 : 3
even in laughter the h. is sorrowful, 24 : 1
every h. prepare room, 328 : 13
executions hardening the h., 414 : 17
faint h. never won fair lady, 170 : 10, 629 : 2
false of h., 245 : 14
falsehood of the h., 388 : 3
fear at my h. as at cup, 434 : 22
fed on truth, 438 : 2
fell dead, 828 : 10
felt along the h., 423 : 8
find Calais lying in my h., 162 : 8
fire of the h., 801 : 5
fire that in h. resides, 584 : 18
firm as stone, 17 : 6
followed delight with h. unsatisfied, 135 : 7
fool hath said in his h., 17 : 21
for any fate, 509 : 16
for every fate, 460 : 4
for h. from itself kept, 631 : 15
forever you'll be in h., 916 : 13
foul rag-and-bone shop of h., 717 : 21
fountain of sweet tears, 425 : 5
fresh complexion and h., 247 : 3
full h. reveal, 436 : 11
give a loving h. to thee, 266 : 2
give h. to understand, 6 : 2
give lesson to head, 377 : 14
give me back my h., 456 : 19
give not your h. away, 690 : 20
give world another h., 475 : 8
give your h. to hawks, 797 : 18
given h. change of mood, 748 : 3
given h. to cause, 797 : 13
gives h. and soul away, 691 : 1
giving h. to dog to tear, 710 : 14
glad with all my h., 182 : 16
gladness of the h., 35 : 41
glows in every h., 329 : 19
good night dear h., 625 : 20
grant all things your h. desires, 59 : 28
great literature expression of h., 723 : 12
great thoughts come from h., 361 : 3
Greensleeves my h. of gold, 917 : 15
grieve his h., 239 : 13
grown cold in vain, 469 : 12
haling out of h. old dismay, 899 : 9
hands and eyes and h., 458 : 20
happiness makes h. afraid, 485 : 6
happy as h. was long, 887 : 2
happy the h. that sighed, 182 : 5
hard h. of child, 794 : 1
hardened Pharaoh's h., 9 : 19
has followed all my days, 759 : 13
has hidden treasures, 555 : 17
has its reasons, 300 : 4
he that is of a merry h., 24 : 7
hear her and beat, 533 : 25
heard of ghost guessed, 656 : 10
help by lifting his h., 838 : 12
here is my h., 659 : 14
hid in h. of love, 712 : 6
hide what false h. know, 237 : 8
high as my h., 212 : 10

Heart (*continued*)
high-erected thoughts in h. of courtesy, 176 : 4
history begins in h. of man or woman, 738 : 15
hold me in thy h., 225 : 1
hope deferred maketh h. sick, 23 : 31
hot within me, 18 : 30
how but through broken h., 676 : 14
how dear to this h., 455 : 6
how h. grows weary, 598 : 4
how shall h be reconciled, 864 : 13
how this small h. beat, 571 : 5
human h. by which we live, 426 : 23
I am sick at h., 217 : 15
I have h. of a king, 163 : 15
I told her all my h., 404 : 10
if h. fails climb not, 172 : *n* 6
if h. just frank kindly, 298 : 1
if one has no h., 482 : 2
imagination of man's h., 7 : 33
in h. a little heaven, 320 : 16
in h. cold December, 917 : 24
in h. voice said I want, 887 : 12
in his pained h., 476 : 13
in my h. of h., 222 : 6
in peril truth drawn from h., 100 : 21
in the h. or in the head, 199 : 23
into h. air that kills, 691 : 9
intoxicated with bliss, 413 : 21
is a lonely hunter, 677 : 5
is a treasury, 484 : 13
is deceitful, 32 : 12
is harder than stone, 61 : 4
is Highland, 483 : 20
is in Highlands, 410 : 9
is lying still, 425 : 14
is slow to learn, 823 : 7
is wounded within me, 21 : 17
keep green tree in h., 132 : 25
keep h. when all lost, 540 : 1
keep thy h. with all diligence, 23 : 9
keeps open house, 873 : 2
kep' goin' pity-pat, 568 : 5
kindness makes h. run over, 385 : 17
knock at my ribs, 236 : 11
know truth by the h., 300 : 5
knoweth own bitterness, 23 : 36
laid h. open to indifference, 882 : 3
language of the h., 339 : 4
large wealth larger h., 304 : 14
lay h. out for my board, 892 : 16
leaps up, 425 : 7
lent out h. with usury, 441 : 9
let no man's h. fail, 12 : 40
let not h. be troubled, 45 : 20, 45 : 24
level in her husband's h., 214 : 1
lies open unto me, 531 : 12
light of step and h., 739 : 14
like music on my h., 435 : 5
like singing bird, 608 : 11
little body mighty h., 207 : 11
live without h., 609 : 13
logic of h. absurd, 378 : 13
lonely hunter, 677 : 5, 894 : 12
look in thy h. and write, 176 : 13
look into your h., 413 : 1
looked into father's h., 852 : 7
Lord Christ's h., 495 : 15
Lord looketh on the h., 12 : 38
lost h. stiffens, 806 : 6
love cow with all my h., 668 : 13
love gushed from my h., 434 : 29

Heart (*continued*)
love Lord with h. soul and mind, 40 : 16
love the Lord with all thine h., 11 : 9
make a stone of h., 714 : 10
make glad h. of childhood, 638 : 6
man after his own h., 12 : 35
man's own resinous h. fed, 715 : 14
May when lusty h. blossom, 149 : 13
meditation of my h., 18 : 3
meet mutual h., 345 : 18
mend the h., 334 : 12
Mercy has a human h., 403 : 11
merry h. doeth good, 24 : 17
merry h. goes all day, 246 : 24
merry h. maketh cheerful countenance, 24 : 6
mind is dupe of the h., 293 : 19
mind lives on the h., 293 : *n* 4
mind thousand eyes h. one, 670 : 8
mine with my h. in it, 248 : 4
more knowledge of h. in Richardson, 355 : 2
mortality touches the h., 104 : 26
moved more than with trumpet, 176 : 12
music in h. I bore, 426 : 6
must break piecemeal, 557 : 1
must pause to breathe, 460 : 5
my crown is in my h., 186 : 8
my h. aches, 476 : 21
my h. belongs to daddy, 820 : 7
my h. consumed in fire, 135 : 10
my h. in my mouth, 117 : 17
my h. is at rest, 403 : 15
my h. is heavy, 396 : 18
my h. is not here, 410 : 9
my h. is pure, 530 : 15
my h. is sick and sad, 642 : 7
my h. is wax, 171 : 10
my h. leaps up, 425 : 7
my h. shall not fear, 18 : 12
my h. with Oxford men, 778 : 10
my sad h. foams at stern, 673 : 13
my true-love hath my h., 176 : 7
naughtiness of thine h., 12 : 39
ne'er within him burned, 430 : 10
never ached with h., 632 : 13
never give all h., 712 : 19
never given in vain, 690 : 21
never say I was false of h., 245 : 14
new-opened, 249 : 3
no feeling in h. not in every h., 595 : 1
no island but continent, 180 : 13
no matter from the h., 227 : 6
no nor for constant h., 918 : 16
no steel pierce h. so chillingly, 828 : 5
no wider than h. wide, 822 : 12
nor h. to report, 197 : 10
not a cloud in h., 609 : 6
not lose his child's h., 89 : 16
not with club h. broken, 607 : 7
not yet has h. or head, 857 : 16
not your h. away, 690 : 20
now cracks a noble h., 225 : 3
nowhere beats so kindly, 551 : 9
O h. if she'd but turn, 712 : 18
O h. O troubled h., 715 : 4
obey thy h., 494 : 10
o'erfraught h., 239 : 20
of a king, 163 : 15
of a lion, 132 : 27
of an old youngster, 877 : 7

Heart (*continued*)
of animals, 260 : 7
of bronze, 57 : 19
of form, 874 : 7
of hearts, 222 : 6
of lead, 340 : 20
of man changeth countenance, 35 : 28
of man depressed, 332 : 3
of man place devils dwell, 274 : 15
of Muhammad, 132 : 11
of my mystery, 222 : 18
of oak our ships, 363 : 16
of Russia not forget, 500 : 25
of scorpion set, 850 : 10
oh h. oh blood that freezes, 542 : 4
old darky's h., 672 : 19
once woman has given h., 321 : 3
one jot of h. or hope, 282 : 19
only with h. one can see, 849 : 4
open my h. and see, 542 : 7
open unto me, 531 : 12
out of h. rapture, 660 : 10
penknife in your h., 929 : 9
pent-up love of h., 661 : 10
people really good at h., 909 : 5
Pharaoh's h., 9 : 19
physical tinged with h., 503 : 8
pierce h. with languor, 659 : 12
plunges lower than night, 785 : 14
poor h. would fain deny, 239 : 31
possessing h. of woman, 734 : 2
pourest thy full h., 468 : 11
preaching down daughter's h., 529 : 22
press thee to my h., 484 : 9
prithee send back my h., 290 : 2
put fear out of h., 726 : 12
put the sayings in your h., 6 : 2
quanch my h. trobling, 811 : 9
razors to my wounded h., 188 : 17
recoiled at war, 829 : 8
records of h. in pain, 486 : 2
recovered greenness, 269 : 4
red-leaved table of my h., 257 : 15
replies, 377 : 13
revolting and rebellious h., 31 : 35
rise in the h., 531 : 3
rises I've gladdened lifetime, 894 : 4
room my h. keeps empty, 267 : 6
rose in deeps of h., 712 : 12
rule my h., 490 : 9
runs away with head, 415 : 12
sad h. of Ruth, 477 : 1
said to h. How goes it, 730 : 6
savage indignation lacerate h., 323 : 25
seal upon thine h., 28 : 23
search thine own h., 513 : 9
seared and blighted h., 525 : 4
season priketh every gentil h., 146 : 16
secret anniversaries of h., 512 : 22
secret of freedom a brave h., 81 : 5
set my poor h. free, 229 : *n* 1
set not h. upon goods, 35 : 4
sets my h. a-clickin', 665 : 14
sets my h. to fluttering, 63 : 5
shaft that quivered in h., 456 : 17
Shakespeare unlocked h., 429 : 10
shaped like valentine, 888 : 4
she wants a h., 335 : 20
sheer into h. of foe, 535 : 14
shot straighter to h., 606 : 9
sick at h., 217 : 15

Heart (*continued*)
simple frugal h., 782 : 23
some h. responds, 510 : 10
sound as bell, 209 : 21
soured kindness in my h., 236 : *n* 1
squatter's rights of h., 848 : 8
squirrel's h. beat, 565 : 23
steady of h., 430 : 3
stick the h. of falsehood, 226 : 15
stirred h. of Englishman, 726 : 5
stop h. from breaking, 606 : 12
strike mine eyes but not my h., 255 : 18
strong and diverse h., 840 : 4
stubborn h. shall fare evil, 34 : 28
stuff which weighs upon h., 239 : 32
subject of Japanese poetry, 344 : 19
summer to your h., 823 : 4
superior have best h., 615 : 5
sweeping up the h., 607 : 1
sweet to excess, 4 : 13
take beak from out my h., 526 : 18
that loveth nought in May, 144 : 2
there will your h. be also, 37 : 17
there's where h. turning, 598 : 3
thing that eats h., 864 : 3
thinks tongue speaks, 209 : 21
though h. still as loving, 460 : 5
thought kept beating like h., 769 : 8
thou'll break my h., 409 : 24
through fire for kind h., 225 : 22
thy breast encloseth my h., 187 : 2
tiger's h. in player's hide, 178 : 12
tiger's h. in woman's hide, 186 : 2
Time laid hand on my h., 512 : 11
tired h. cease to palpitate, 512 : 16
to conceive, 391 : 4
to dog to tear, 710 : 14
to heart, 430 : 9
to mind shameful to h. beauty, 582 : 1
too soon made glad, 540 : 23
too tender or too firm h., 335 : 8
took all h. for speech, 713 : 19
trusteth in his own h., 25 : 29
turned to stone, 231 : 23
turning home again, 671 : 10
unchristened h., 716 : 14
unfortified, 218 : 4
unity of h. unity of mankind, 895 : 21
unquiet h. and brain, 531 : 21
untraveled turns to thee, 368 : 14
vacant h. hand eye, 432 : 1
veracity h. of morality, 596 : 1
verities and truths of h., 838 : 8
visit my sad h., 215 : 23
want of thought and h., 485 : 8
war in his h., 19 : 22
warm and gay, 833 : 9
warm h. within, 377 : 17
warm with friends, 823 : 3
was one which most enamor, 460 : 7
waters of the h., 886 : 13
way to h. through stomach, 538 : 6
weaned h. from low desires, 155 : 1
wear h. upon my sleeve, 229 : 17
weeping in my h., 659 : 13
wet eye dhry h., 722 : 8
what dungeon dark as h., 503 : 19
what female h. gold despise, 361 : 15
what h. taught me I taught, 545 : 13
what missing at the man's h., 884 : 22
what stronger breastplate than h., 185 : 17

Heart (*continued*)
when my h. hath 'scaped, 245 : 3
when to h. of man, 747 : 2
where h. lies brain lie, 544 : 1
which beats only for you, 659 : 14
whole h. is faint, 28 : 27
wine that maketh glad the h., 21 : 9
wisdom of head and h., 549 : 17
wisdom to believe h., 703 : 3
wise and understanding h., 13 : 27
with but half a h., 267 : 7
with h. in hand, 538 : 3
with my whole h., 32 : 18
with rue h. laden, 691 : 13
with whole h. listen, 770 : 16
withered h., 858 : 20
within blood-tinctured, 506 : 14
woman whose h. is snares, 27 : 10
woman with the h., 531 : 7
words shall be in thine h., 11 : 9
world no wider than h., 822 : 12
wound h. that's broken, 431 : 19
wounded is wounding h., 292 : 14
Heartache, by sleep we end h., 221 : 12
Heartbreak, altar of our h., 881 : 11
American h., 855 : 4
better chiding than h., 225 : 29
Heartburn, I am h., 656 : 20
Heartfelt, simple and h. lay, 510 : 19
Hearth, by this still h., 529 : 6
clean-winged h., 513 : 21
clear fire clean h., 441 : 19
cricket on the h., 278 : 20
no more blazing h., 362 : 1
woman for the h., 531 : 7
Hearths, their country their h., 102 : 28
Hearthstone, every h. over land, 521 : 14
fox build on h., 735 : *n* 1
of hell best bed, 735 : *n* 1
Heartiest, purest h. tenderness, 577 : 3
Heartily know when half-gods go, 494 : 11
Heart-leaves of lilac, 751 : 8
Heart-revealing intimacy, 714 : 15
Heart's affections, 479 : 1
at liberty, 296 : *n* 3
dead never buried, 816 : 3
deep h. core, 712 : 5
desire, 18 : 4, 517 : 13, 712 : 11
desires be with you, 210 : 15
hands are h. landscape, 897 : 8
his h. his mouth, 242 : 20
hot h. shell, 570 : 13
lose h. desire, 680 : 21
my h. in the Highlands, 410 : 9
my h. right there, 753 : 1
my h. undoing, 447 : 4
supreme ambition, 357 : 8
wear him in my h. core, 222 : 6
young man's h. complaint, 574 : 22
Hearts, affect h. and minds, 820 : 14
all that human h. endure, 352 : 21
and minds, 56 : 1
apply our h. unto wisdom, 20 : 14
are earned, 714 : 17
as much love as if giving h., 151 : 4
as pure and fair, 628 : 20
blind h., 100 : 13
cashboxes for h., 484 : 17
cause that makes hard h., 234 : 16
cheerful h. now broken, 447 : 7
cherish h. that hate thee, 249 : 8
cleanse thoughts of our h., 55 : 15
Hearts (*continued*)
come not to steal away h., 216 : 27
country cherished in h., 535 : 22
daystar arise in your h., 52 : 17
drunk with beauty, 720 : 10
dry as summer dust, 428 : 11
dwell in our crowded h., 902 : 16
ensanguined h., 377 : 6
fasten hands upon h., 691 : 21
feet leave but not h., 518 : 16
finite h. that yearn, 542 : 10
first in h. of countrymen, 402 : 10
given our h. away, 427 : 29
high in people's h., 215 : 14
hoard little h. great, 534 : 6
hope men set h. upon, 516 : 9
hugest h. that break, 607 : 10
human h. to chew, 468 : 6
in imagination of their h., 42 : 22
in love use own tongues, 209 : 9
in retiring draw h., 288 : 6
in unison strike twelve, 863 : 16
itch grows old in sick h., 122 : 12
keep your h. and minds, 50 : 6
keeps their h. vacuous, 63 : 14
kind h. more than coronets, 528 : 11
Knave of H., 931 : 4
Lord dwelt in people's h., 300 : 20
Lord searcheth all h., 14 : 24
mercy enthroned in h. of kings, 200 : 9
minds and h. of depressed, 896 : 4
neither have h. to stay, 292 : 1
new heraldry hands not h., 231 : 19
not had as gift, 714 : 17
not their h. that roam, 709 : 7
O blind h., 100 : 13
of controversy, 215 : 5
of oak, 158 : 10
of the noble may be turned, 58 : 22
our h. all with thee, 511 : 9
palsied h., 586 : 1
pluck their h. from them, 208 : 8
Queen of H., 931 : 4
rain falls in h., 839 : 9
shutting away of loving h., 823 : 12
slow unreckoning h., 900 : 2
somewhere h. are light, 704 : 16
steel my soldiers' h., 208 : 8
strong minds great h., 566 : 3
that beat as one, 508 : 1
that roam, 709 : 7
their h. not grown old, 713 : 16
though stout and brave, 509 : 14
thousand h. beat happily, 457 : 14
tight hot cell of h., 836 : 20
touched with fire, 643 : 17
true plain h., 251 : 16
union of hands and h., 294 : 14
union of h., 492 : 11
unto whom all h. are open, 55 : 15
utter what h. hold, 726 : 12
what we do not doubt in h., 639 : 9
what your h. have amassed, 130 : 13
while your h. are yearning, 740 : 11
wine unto those of heavy h., 26 : 5
with your hands your h., 186 : 17
wore at h. the fire's center, 876 : 15
write upon h. of men, 412 : 11
Heartsease, infinite h., 208 : 6
Heart-shaped leaves of green, 751 : *n* 3
Heartsick hand workers, 618 : 10
Heart-stifled, die h., 476 : 15
Heartstrings are a lute, 525 : *n* 3
Heartstrings (*continued*)
though jesses my dear h., 231 : 4
Heart-whole, warrant him h., 212 : 21
Hearty, hand that is honest and h., 429 : 16
humble and h. thanks, 55 : 7
old man, 439 : 15
Heat as Mode of Motion, 580 : 2
burden and h. of day, 40 : 9
cannot pass from colder, 589 : 14
cold and h., 8 : 1
cold craters of silence, 864 : 4
fantastic summer's h., 194 : 7
fear no more h. o' the sun, 243 : 27
flow from hot to cold object, 589 : *n* 1
hands hold much of h., 810 : 18
he makes h. as he wishes, 5 : 3
if you can't stand h., 788 : 1
I'll shade him from h., 403 : 8
mechanical equivalent of h., 650 : 16
mote wobbles in h., 893 : 13
neither h. affection limb, 228 : 16
neither h. nor light, 262 : 6
neither sun light on them nor h., 53 : 16
no strength exerted on h., 892 : 7
not furnace for foe, 248 : 22
not see when h. cometh, 32 : 11
not snow nor rain nor h., 78 : 19
of conflict, 427 : 25
one draught above h., 213 : 16
one h. drive out another, 177 : 18
Promethean h., 232 : 14
race not without h., 282 : 1
surprised was I with sudden h., 182 : 2
there is nothing hid from the h., 17 : 28
which made my heart to glow, 182 : 2
Heated in the chase, 317 : 7
Heath and harebells, 562 : 7
best felt not clearly seen, 640 : 9
brown h. and shaggy wood, 430 : 11
foot on my native h., 431 : 27
in airy rings skim h., 334 : 16
in the desert, 32 : 11
sword sung on barren h., 404 : 15
Heathcliff, I am H., 562 : 6
Heathen in his blindness, 452 : 10
pore benighted h., 708 : 5
why do the h. rage, 17 : 13
Heather, know how h. looks, 606 : 17
Heaths, game on these lone h., 445 : 12
Heating, warm without h., 330 : 22
Heat-oppressed brain, 237 : 13
Heave away heave away, 934 : 22
Heaven about to confer great office, 89 : 25
above road below, 669 : 2
all h. around us, 447 : 3
all h. before mine eyes, 278 : 26
all hell that is not h., 184 : 2
all I ask h. above, 669 : 2
all places distant from h. alike, 259 : 12
all things in h., 50 : 9
all this and h. too, 319 : 17
all we hope in h., 525 : 2
alone given away, 567 : 12
and Charing Cross, 693 : 19
and earth in ashes, 139 : 4
and earth pass away, 40 : 26, 430 : 12
and earth to witness, 11 : 8
and future's sakes, 748 : 18

Heaven (*continued*)
and home, 429 : 9
and nature sing, 328 : 13
angels in H. above, 527 : 9
as it is in h., 37 : 15
as the h. is high, 21 : 6
ascended into h., 55 : 2
blazing into head, 717 : 6
bottom line is in h., 876 : 1
bread of h., 21 : 12
brightest h. of invention, 207 : 1
by h. I do love, 190 : 31
call h. and earth to witness, 11 : 8
care of h., 337 : 6
clear religion of h., 475 : 20
combined essences of h. and earth, 97 : 7
commences ere world past, 370 : 3
confess yourself to h., 223 : 8
court it in shape of h., 219 : 22
crawling between h. and earth, 221 : 16
dances in sight of h., 899 : 13
did recompense send, 362 : 18
down the abandoned h., 790 : 16
dragged h. with her, 571 : 9
each goes own byway to h., 318 : 8
earth and h. ring, 733 : 5
earth and high h., 691 : 10
earth nigher h. than now, 540 : 18
earth's crammed with h., 507 : 22
endures, 692 : 11
enter into kingdom of h., 38 : 19, 40 : 1
eye of h. to garnish, 202 : 5
eye sees open h., 413 : 21
farewells as stars in h., 226 : 24
finds means to kill joys, 193 : 30
floor of h. is inlaid, 201 : 1
four winds of the h., 33 : 29
from h. did hie, 917 : 18
gained from h., 362 : 18
gate of h., 8 : 21
gates not so arched, 262 : 9
gems of h. starry train, 286 : 1
gentle rain from h., 200 : 9
getting to h. at last, 605 : 5
gives its favorites, 91 : *n* 1
glance from h. to earth, 197 : 12
God created h. and earth, 6 : 10
God is in h., 26 : 26
God's in his h., 540 : 15
going forth is from the end of the h., 17 : 28
gold bar of h., 601 : 13
great eye of h., 173 : 10
had made her such a man, 229 : 31
harbingers to h., 276 : 14
has joined great issues, 427 : 24
have ye souls in h., 477 : 15
hell I suffer seems a h., 285 : 12
helps not men who will not act, 66 : *n* 7
hills whose heads touch h., 229 : 29
his blessed part to h., 249 : 11
holds place for those who pray, 915 : 14
hours to which h. chime, 298 : 21
how long permit to h., 287 : 30
humbler h., 336 : 16
husbandry in h., 237 : 10
if earth be shadow of h., 286 : 21
if h. looked on riches, 322 : 9
if I ascend up into h., 22 : 17

Heaven (*continued*)
if I cannot bend H., 105 : 29
in heart a little h., 320 : 16
in h. perfect round, 544 : 4
in hell's despair, 405 : 3
in which no horses, 670 : 12
is above all yet, 248 : 30
is love, 430 : 6
it smells to h., 222 : 25
itself points out hereafter, 326 : 3
itself we seek in our folly, 106 : 27
itself would stoop to her, 280 : 5
keys of kingdom of h., 39 : 36
kingdom of h. is at hand, 36 : 25
kingdom of h. like a net, 39 : 19
kingdom of h. like mustard seed, 39 : 17
kingdom of H. within you, 126 : 15
kiss h. gives earth, 273 : 13
knows how to put price, 384 : 13
lay up treasures in h., 37 : 16
leave her to h., 219 : 25
leave the rest to h., 275 : 19
leaving mercy to h., 349 : 18
less of earth than h., 431 : 10
let justice be done though h. fall, 133 : 25
lies about us in infancy, 426 : 14
lift my soul to h., 248 : 25
light from h., 409 : 5
like egg earth like yolk, 123 : 16
like the h. above, 591 : 8
Lord of h. and earth, 46 : 16
love is h., 430 : 6
made h. and earth, 4 : 3, 22 : 4
majesty of H., 346 : 4
make a h. of hell, 283 : 13
make face of h. so fine, 193 : 9
Maker of h. and earth, 55 : 2
makes h. drowsy with harmony, 191 : 4
man alone beneath h., 430 : 9
man is as H. made him, 170 : 1
marriages made in h., 176 : 3
matches made in h., 159 : *n* 4
meadows of h., 511 : 3
measuring earth and h., 85 : 17
met my dearest foe in h., 218 : 14
mild h. a time ordains, 282 : 10
mind of superior man like h., 609 : 6
more things in h. and earth, 220 : 3, 821 : 5
mount up to h., 21 : 15
near h. by sea as by land, 166 : 13
needs such men more than h. does, 386 : 19
never to h. go, 222 : 28
new h. and new earth, 53 : 29
no humor in h., 625 : 4
no rain left in h., 578 : 9
not at single bound, 566 : 2
not beteem winds of h., 218 : 7
not enter into kingdom of h., 40 : 1
not grim but fair, 545 : 23
not h. if we knew what it were, 290 : 5
not h. itself upon past has power, 305 : 2
not want honor in H., 804 : 18
nurseries of h., 693 : 8
of all their wish, 796 : 14
of whales in waters, 790 : 22
offspring of h. firstborn, 285 : 4
on earth, 285 : 15

Heaven (*continued*)
open face of h., 475 : 4
or near it, 468 : 11
ordinances of h., 69 : 21
our Father which art in h., 37 : 15
parting all we know of h., 607 : 18
peep through blanket, 236 : 18
Persian's h. easily made, 447 : 6
places eye of h. visits, 194 : 5
plays such tricks before h., 228 : 10
practice in h., 542 : 5
presents the solid hue, 748 : 1
prove that I and she ride together, 542 : 16
puts all h. in rage, 406 : 9
quit port o' h., 700 : 8
reach port of h., 519 : 6
rejects the lore, 429 : 6
remembrance fallen from h., 632 : 9
rest of h. blue, 525 : 6
rich man enter h., 722 : 10
ring bells of h., 732 : 16
same world hell h., 495 : 20
save from foolish friend, 420 : 5
say over door of h., 900 : 1
says nothing, 312 : 20
sea and h. as one, 767 : 14
see h. in wildflower, 406 : 8
see h. open, 44 : 25
sends love of her, 4 : 10
serve in h., 283 : 14
short arm to reach h., 693 : 20
silent finger points to h., 428 : 17
sincerity the way of h., 89 : 12
single dram of h., 607 : 17
smells to h., 222 : 25
so he goes to h., 222 : 26
so much of h., 425 : 1
spark from h., 585 : 22
spark from H. immortal, 412 : 9
spirit that fought in h., 284 : 4
star of unascended h., 467 : 7
starry cope of h., 286 : 11
stay the bottles of h., 16 : 35
steep and thorny way to h., 218 : 28
such grace did lend her, 190 : 4
summons thee to h. or hell, 237 : 16
sun drives night from h., 515 : 16
swear neither by h. nor earth, 37 : 9
symbol of power of H., 799 : 14
take my soul, 202 : 12
tasted eternal joys of H., 183 : 21
tell little Greek to go to h., 122 : 4
thank h. fasting, 212 : 16
that leads men to hell, 245 : 23
theirs is the kingdom of h., 37 : 4
then summer then h. of God, 605 : 17
therefore doth h. divide, 207 : 6
things are sons of h., 352 : 6
though h. fall thy will be done, 134 : 24
till h. and earth pass, 37 : 7
to appreciate h. well, 660 : 4
to be young was very h., 424 : 5
to gaudy day denies, 459 : 13
to h. being gone, 253 : 11
to throne in, 242 : 24
toward H. advancing, 412 : 9
treasure in h., 40 : 6
treasures in h., 37 : 16
trouble deaf h., 244 : 8
under feet as well as over heads, 560 : 10
unextinguishable laugh in h., 275 : 12

Heaven (*continued*)
unfolds both h. and earth, 195 : 23
vain war with h., 284 : 3
visited in h., 606 : 17
wanted one immortal song, 304 : 4
war in h., 53 : 19
watered h. with tears, 405 : 8
way to h. of like length, 166 : *n* 10
what's a h. for, 543 : 1
when h. was falling, 692 : 3
wherever bright sun of h., 249 : 18
which giant Atlas upholds, 76 : 25
who know h. save by heaven's gift, 115 : 17
who sword of h. will bear, 228 : 26
will most incorrect to h., 218 : 4
will protect working girl, 684 : 17
wind from blue h. blows, 395 : 3
winds of h. in our land, 813 : 8
winds of h. visit face roughly, 218 : 7
winged seraphs of H., 527 : 8
wished Hell for ease from H., 407 : 4
with all splendors lie, 567 : 11
with the company of h., 55 : 18
would I were h., 670 : *n* 3
Heaven-born band, 422 : 21
child, 277 : 7
Heaven-bred poesy, 190 : 3
Heaven-kissing hill, 223 : 3
Heavenly blessings without number, 328 : 8
can h. minds yield, 104 : 16
caught my h. jewel, 176 : 15
connection, 906 : 1
days that cannot die, 424 : 10
destiny, 426 : 4
fools by h. compulsion, 233 : 5
gift of poesy, 305 : 7
harmony, 305 : 9
mansion, 716 : 7
paradise is that place, 250 : 5
pen wherewith thou h. sing, 429 : *n* 1
Powers, 395 : 2
princes like to h. bodies, 180 : 19
race demands zeal, 346 : 1
rhetoric of thine eye, 190 : 32
Rosalind, 210 : 19
things h. or things earthly, 302 : 4
Heaven-rescued land, 446 : 2
Heaven's, against h. hand, 282 : 19
all gracious King, 537 : 16
at h. gates claps wings, 176 : 1
breath smells wooingly, 236 : 21
cherubin horsed, 236 : 24
command, 345 : 19
despite, 405 : 4
eternal King, 277 : 6
eternal year is thine, 305 : 6
glories shine, 562 : 4
godfathers of h. lights, 190 : 12
great lamps do dive, 250 : 3
in h. high bower, 403 : 12
lark at h. gate sings, 243 : 16
last best gift, 286 : 13
light forever shines, 469 : 16
men touched by h. virtue, 312 : 20
my destination, 839 : 11
net is indeed vast, 65 : 6
nothing situate under h. eye, 188 : 1
own sweet will h. will, 714 : 21
patio h. watercourse, 843 : 5
riches of h. pavement, 283 : 28
spangles sweeping of h. floor, 557 : 16
study like h. glorious sun, 190 : 12
Heaven's (*continued*)
success found, 542 : 18
sugar cake, 314 : 23
vaults should crack, 235 : 16
wide pathless way, 278 : 18
Heavens, ancient h., 427 : 16
clothed with h., 311 : 20
declare glory of God, 17 : 27
distorts the h., 407 : 10
fill with commerce, 529 : 24
fill with shouting, 529 : 24
flaming ramparts of h., 100 : 3
God light of h. and earth, 131 : 16
hells worlds longed-for lands, 768 : 24
hung be h. with black, 184 : 15
let justice be done though h. fall, 133 : *n* 11
new h. and a new earth, 31 : 30
offered this trust to h., 132 : 4
part of man's world, 882 : 20
potentates blazing in h., 71 : 3
pure as naked h., 425 : 23
rejoice in motion, 253 : 21
sing ye h. earth reply, 350 : 11
spangled h., 325 : 8
starry h. above me, 366 : 12
thank h. sun gone in, 711 : 9
themselves blaze forth, 215 : 25
themselves the planets, 225 : 37
when I consider thy h., 17 : 17
Heavens' embroidered cloths, 712 : 15
Heaviest ore of the body, 790 : 14
Heaviness, foolish son the h. of his mother, 23 : 21
garment of praise for spirit of h., 31 : 25
God taken h. away, 874 : 13
that's gone, 248 : 18
Heaving up my either hand, 267 : 1
Heavy as yonder stone, 778 : 5
change now thou art gone, 280 : 11
crown of Monomakh, 486 : 12
eyelids h. and red, 485 : 16
laden, 39 : 8
light gains make h. purses, 177 : 14
light wife h. husband, 201 : 7
my heart is h., 396 : 18
plummet's pace, 281 : 7
steps of plowman, 712 : 12
toward school with h. looks, 192 : 15
weight of world, 423 : 10
wine unto those of h. hearts, 26 : 5
Heavy-laden, I am h. with trouble, 4 : 7
Hebraism strictness of conscience, 588 : 21
Hebrew, called in H. Armageddon, 53 : 25
Hebrides, in dreams behold H., 483 : 20
seas colder than H., 785 : 15
stormy H., 281 : 2, 345 : 15
Hecate's, black H. summons, 238 : 20
pale H. offerings, 237 : 14
Hector is dead, 227 : 7
when H. was pup, 921 : 18
Hector's, in dust with H. pup, 856 : 6
Hecuba, what's H. to him, 221 : 7
Hedge, divinity doth h. a king, 223 : 27
over h. before stile, 168 : 24
pull not down your h., 269 : 19
Hedgehog knows one great thing, 62 : 2
Hedgehogs, thorny h., 196 : 21
Heed, I will take h. to my ways, 18 : 29
rumble of distant drum, 516 : 8
take h. lest he fall, 48 : 16
Heed (*continued*)
take h. of loving me, 253 : 13
ye who lead take h., 728 : 14
Heedless, earth's h. sons, 834 : 11
ran my h. ways, 887 : 2
self-interest bad economics, 780 : 1
unwise to be h. while giving advice, 114 : 5
Heejous, creature of h. mien, 722 : 4
Heel, bids it come to h., 803 : 2
coat from h. to throat, 713 : 14
Europe under his h., 745 : 2
of courtier, 224 : 13
of Northeast Trade, 708 : 22
on throat of my song, 826 : 19
something licked my h., 902 : 5
thou shalt bruise his h., 7 : 10
tread each other's h., 223 : *n* 5
Heels, at his h. a stone, 223 : 22
follow truth too near h., 173 : 3
fortune grow out at h., 233 : 15
from h. up to head, 668 : 12
gunpowder out at h., 364 : 5
hi but she h. to it, 822 : 7
horses' h. over paving, 806 : 12
out at h., 225 : 10
over head and h., 101 : 22
time wounds all h., 862 : 14
took to my h., 96 : 22
Heft of cathedral tunes, 604 : 18
Heifer, if ye had not plowed with my h., 12 : 15
lowing at skies, 477 : 9
Heifer's, false as wolf to h. calf, 226 : 15
Height, asks of us certain h., 749 : 14
depths of h., 829 : 19
happiness makes up in h., 749 : 6
measure h. by shade, 540 : 8
my soul can reach, 507 : 14
none can usurp h., 478 : 21
nor depth, 47 : 15
objects in an airy h., 320 : 14
of man equal to tips of hands, 116 : 14
smiles from h. at me, 866 : 18
stretch for greatness and h., 178 : 5
worth's unknown though h. taken, 245 : 18
Heights by great men reached, 511 : 23
dwell on h. of mankind, 413 : 25
towering h. of hills, 551 : 4
Heill, I that in h. wes and gladness, 153 : 6
Heir as great in admiration as herself, 249 : 17
grandchild h. of the first, 257 : 2
great h. of fame, 277 : 13
of all the ages, 530 : 7
of mongrel bitch, 233 : 13
that flesh is h. to, 221 : 12
yourself sole h. of world, 311 : 20
Heirs, joint h. with Christ, 47 : 8
of all eternity, 190 : 9
of God, 47 : 8
of spiritual life, 448 : 5
Helen brought her dowry destruction, 71 : 6
did not board the ships, 62 : 18
great suffering all for H., 850 : 11
Leda mother of H., 638 : 11
like another H., 306 : 21
sweet H. make me immortal, 184 : 4
threw into wine a drug, 59 : 25
thy beauty is to me, 525 : 9

Helen's beauty in brow of
  Egypt, 197 : 12
  dawn in H. arms, 716 : 19
  dust hath closed H. eye, 250 : 10
Helican, damned if I see how h., 765 : 12
Helicon, muses of H., 61 : 6
  shepherding below holy H., 61 : 7
  watered our horses in H., 178 : 8
Hell, agreement with h., 505 : 14
  all h. broke loose, 286 : 9
  all h. stir for this, 208 : 15
  all right then I'll go to h., 624 : 5
  all we need of h., 607 : 18
  better to reign in h., 283 : 14
  black as h., 246 : 7
  born on undigested dumpling, 570 : 9
  characters of h. to trace, 363 : 5
  city much like London, 468 : 2
  cunning livery of h., 228 : 19
  curse of h. frae me, 926 : 15
  each bears his own H., 105 : 23
  easy to go down into H., 105 : 15
  energy child of H., 572 : 6
  England h. for horses, 259 : 22
  England h. of horses, 174 : 23
  entertained great scorn of h., 141 : 8
  failure in great object, 475 : 14
  father for hoarding went to h., 186 : 5
  fifteen minutes of h., 660 : 4
  followed with him, 53 : 11
  full of good intentions, 136 : 11
  full of good meanings, 269 : 23
  full of musical amateurs, 680 : 19
  gates of h. not prevail, 39 : 36
  give 'em h., 454 : 13
  halls of h., 793 : 3
  has no fury, 324 : 16
  hath no limits, 184 : 1
  hearthstone of h. best bed, 735 : *n* 1
  heaven that leads men to h., 245 : 23
  hissing hot from h., 555 : 14
  hot as h., 400 : 15
  I love this cultured h., 819 : 4
  I myself am h., 893 : 7
  I oft wished for H., 407 : 4
  I shall move H., 105 : 29
  I suffer seems a heaven, 285 : 12
  I'm mad as h., 901 : 10
  in heaven's despite, 405 : 4
  in h. roast like herrin, 411 : 14
  injured lover's h., 286 : 19
  into mouth of h., 533 : 14
  is alone, 809 : 1
  is oneself, 809 : 1
  is other people, 865 : 12
  is to love no longer, 802 : 14
  Italy h. for women, 259 : 22
  itself breathes out, 222 : 23
  keys of h. and death, 52 : 32
  lead apes in h., 188 : 30
  liberated the h. out of place, 925 : 3
  limbecks foul as h., 245 : 19
  madness risen from h., 632 : 9
  make a heaven of h., 283 : 13
  make my bed in h., 22 : 17
  milk of concord into h., 239 : 19
  more devils than h. hold, 197 : 12
  myself am h., 285 : 12, 893 : 7
  never married that's his h., 259 : 5
  nor h. a fury like woman
    scorned, 324 : 16
  of a good universe, 829 : 26
  of nuclear destruction, 909 : 14
  old age is woman's h., 296 : 6
Hell (*continued*)
  on earth, 680 : 16
  out of h. leads to light, 284 : 17
  passage broad to h., 92 : *n* 5
  paved with good
    intentions, 136 : *n* 8, 269 : *n* 2
  paved with priests' skulls, 128 : 23
  Presbyterian in h., 626 : 8
  print news and raise h., 922 : 4
  procuress to lords of h., 532 : 8
  Puritan's idea of h., 616 : *n* 4
  rebellious h., 223 : 5
  reign in h., 283 : 14
  riches grow in h., 284 : 1
  rising from thousand
    thrones, 525 : 14
  road to H. gradual, 842 : 9
  same world h. heaven, 495 : 20
  San Francisco West as all h., 699 : *n* 3
  served my time in h., 925 : 1
  spinach and the h. with it, 846 : 7
  summons thee to heaven or
    h., 237 : 16
  take curtains, 785 : 10
  tell him to go to h., 454 : 15
  this is h. nor am I out, 183 : 21
  though h. bar way, 773 : 1
  till h. freezes, 925 : 7
  tyranny like h., 384 : 13
  very respectable h., 724 : 10
  walked eye-deep in h., 792 : 14
  war is h., 579 : 3
  way I fly is h., 285 : 12
  we make ourselves, 648 : 10
  wedlock forced a h., 185 : 7
  what h. in suing long, 174 : 10
  what I call h., 853 : 10
  what in h. have i done, 760 : 4
  what is h., 809 : 1
  where h. is there must we be, 184 : 1
  where we are is h., 184 : 1
  whip all h. yet, 579 : *n* 1
  whole body not be cast into h., 37 : 8
  with h. are we at agreement, 30 : 14
  with work which bores you life
    h., 725 : 2
  within him, 285 : 9
  within myself, 274 : 15
  wrote of Devils and H., 403 : 19
Hellas, confounded H., 81 : 11
  of Hellas, 75 : *n* 13
Hellenes, boy is most powerful of
  H., 70 : 15
Hellenic, great new H. world, 702 : 11
Hellenism, governing idea of
  H., 588 : 21
  spirit of consciousness, 588 : 21
Hellespont, Propontic and H., 231 : 18
Hell-kite, O h., 239 : 21
Hello sucker, 785 : 18
  thingumbob again, 649 : 2
Hell's broke loose in Georgia, 840 : 1
  broken loose, 178 : 14
  concave, 283 : 21
  despair, 405 : 3
  fear of h. a hangman's
    whip, 259 : *n* 11
Hells, tormented with ten thousand
  h., 183 : 21
Helm, aboard at ship's h., 575 : 19
  everyone prepared to take
    h., 599 : 18
  hold h. when sea calm, 111 : 6
  Pleasure at the h., 363 : 6
Helmet and the plume, 528 : 27
  for h. the hope of salvation, 50 : 20
  now hive for bees, 177 : 9
  of Navarre, 487 : 6
Helmets gleamed in forests, 592 : 6
Help, a little h. from friends, 914 : 11
  a very present h. in trouble, 19 : 10
  between hindrance and h., 425 : 2
  cannot h. nor pardon, 868 : 8
  could not hope for h., 869 : 1
  encumbers him with h., 353 : 26
  feeble up, 242 : 29
  for living hope for dead, 615 : 8
  from whence cometh my h., 22 : 4
  go love without the h., 407 : 3
  God our h. in ages past, 328 : 10
  God's h. and their valor, 420 : 12
  good wise great, 715 : 10
  her and that right early, 19 : 11
  here I stand God h. me, 155 : 13
  into Macedonia and h. us, 46 : 13
  Lord h. 'em how I pities all, 429 : 19
  make earth happy, 591 : 8
  man endure, 838 : 12
  man is without h., 865 : 11
  me with knowledge, 546 : 4
  my h. cometh from the Lord, 22 : 4
  not hope and no h. came, 869 : 1
  nothing will h., 830 : 18
  of the helpless, 470 : 23
  one fainting robin, 606 : 12
  others out of fellow feeling, 258 : 4
  past hope past cure past h., 193 : 19
  since there's no h., 182 : 16
  them that help themselves, 66 : 20
  things that h. with things that
    hurt, 653 : 15
  thou mine unbelief, 42 : 10
  to half-a-crown, 641 : 15
  use treatment to h. sick, 79 : 13
  what's gone past h., 246 : 18
  when no h. in truth, 74 : 2
  with h. of surgeon recover, 197 : 20
Helped every one his neighbor, 31 : 3
  to hansom outside, 866 : 16
Helper, antagonist our h., 374 : 2
  Lord is my h., 51 : 23
Helpers fail and comforts flee, 470 : 23
Helpful, noble be man h. and
  good, 394 : 16
Helping, God h. her, 682 : 13
  God h. me I can do no other, 155 : *n* 6
  men to practice virtue, 89 : 2
  so far from h. me, 18 : 5
Helpless, justice without strength is
  h., 300 : 6
  man in ignorance sedate, 352 : 1
  naked piping loud, 405 : 12
  rendered United States h., 682 : 10
Helpmeet, make him an h., 7 : 1
Helps, fortune h. the brave, 97 : 1
  God h. them that help selves, 347 : 15
  God h. those who get up
    early, 935 : 9
  who h. others saves himself, 138 : 6
  with their h. only defend, 186 : 15
Hemisphere, extend system to this
  h., 408 : 3
Hemispheres, where find two better
  h., 251 : 16
Hemlock I had drunk, 476 : 21
  shakes in the rafter, 572 : 1
  snow from h. tree, 748 : 3
Hemlocks, cry against the h., 766 : 12

Hemlocks (*continued*)
murmuring pines and h., 510 : 26
Hemp, molders h. and steel, 431 : 24
Hempen, sing in a h. string, 260 : 15
Hen, as h. gathereth chickens, 40 : 21
egg's way of making egg, 620 : 2
eggs do not teach h., 934 : 13
has right to set, 616 : 21
homely h. lays one, 923 : 10
marsh h. secretly builds, 651 : 9
my black h., 932 : 14
two owls and h., 550 : 4
yard in printing house, 792 : 19
Hence all you vain delights, 261 : 4
endure their going h., 235 : 11
horrible shadow, 238 : 29
loathed Melancholy, 277 : 17
stay far h. you prudes, 113 : 7
these tears, 96 : 3
vain deluding Joys, 278 : 9
with denial vain, 280 : 9
ye profane, 295 : 15
Henna hackles halt, 767 : 5
Hennessy, Oh well said Mr. H., 722 : 16
Henpecked, fraternity of h., 327 : 2
you all, 460 : 11
Henroosts, defend ourselves and h., 560 : 25
Henry, never did H. end anyone, 884 : 12
pried open for all to see, 884 : 8
unappeasable H. sulked, 884 : 7
Hens, milk-white h. of Dorking, 551 : 1
Hent, merrily h. the stile-a, 246 : 24
Heraclitus, told me H. dead, 591 : 9
your death H., 93 : 1
Herald, hark the h. angels sing, 350 : 15
Homer h. of your glory, 90 : 13
lark h. of the morn, 193 : 14
Morning Star h. of dawn, 97 : 16
of tomorrow, 706 : 23
owl night's h., 189 : 11
silence perfectest h. of joy, 209 : 11
station like h. Mercury, 223 : 3
three years we waited for h., 849 : 6
Herald Square, remember me to H., 759 : 5
Heraldry, boast of h., 362 : 3
new h. hands not hearts, 231 : 19
Herb, dew bespangling h. and tree, 266 : 19
Herba, latet anguis in h., 103 : *n* 8
Herbs and trees flourish in May, 149 : 13
better is a dinner of h., 24 : 7
bitter h., 9 : 24
bread with bitter h., 565 : 16
Medea gathered enchanted h., 200 : 22
men with h. to smoke, 150 : 17
of every joyous kind, 131 : 14
Hercules and Goth bequeathed us, 639 : 16
and Lichas play at dice, 198 : 30
behind Gates of H., 646 : 6
from the foot H., 78 : 13
labors of spasmodic H., 555 : 10
let H. do what he may, 224 : 24
not H. but Superman, 911 : 5
snakes beside cradle of H., 595 : 7
Theseus a second H., 119 : 22
Herd, avoid reeking h., 793 : 18
deer that left the h., 376 : 25
hate the common h., 107 : 25
Herd (*continued*)
Hesperus you h. homeward, 63 : 11
imitators you slavish h., 109 : 13
lowing h. wind slowly, 361 : 20
of elephant traveling, 789 : 8
ran into sea, 42 : 5
that only sleep and feed, 223 : *n* 3
unreflecting h., 429 : 3
Herder, what H. taught to Goethe, 577 : 13
Herds, flocks or h. or human, 285 : 5
massive jungle h., 857 : 15
of walruses and whales, 570 : 7
Herdsman, God the h. goads, 712 : 2
Herdsmen, bad h. ruin flocks, 60 : 22
Here a little child I stand, 267 : 1
a little there a little, 30 : 13
a sheer hulk, 393 : 11
am I, 12 : 29
am I send me, 29 : 11
and now cease to matter, 807 : 24
and now is happiness, 782 : 23
and there eat and drink, 588 : 7
comes the lady, 193 : 2
comes the trout, 214 : 7
from h. to eternity, 708 : 14
gone h. and there, 245 : 16
he lies where he longed, 668 : 20
I am and here I stay, 514 : 6
I have been h. before, 601 : 23
I stand, 155 : 13
in the body pent, 429 : 17
is God's plenty, 307 : 3
is my space, 240 : 14
is no water, 805 : 10
it can't happen h., 791 : 10
Kilroy was h., 838 : 14, 924 : 20
Lafayette we are h., 693 : 3
lies a King that ruled, 271 : 18
lies a truly honest man, 292 : 20
lies lady of beauty, 810 : 20
lies Matthew Prior, 321 : 2
lies my wife let her lie, 307 : 10
rests his head, 362 : 17
thou ailest h. and h., 585 : 3
today gone tomorrow, 312 : 18
where sword nations drew, 457 : 21
where wind north-northeast, 729 : 2
where world is quiet, 633 : 19
Hereafter, heaven points out h., 326 : 3
she should have died h., 240 : 4
what is love 'tis not h., 213 : 23
what may come h., 633 : 20
Hereditary, contemporary and h., 571 : 2
dyspepsias, 570 : 9
virtue is not h., 384 : 11
Here's looking at you kid, 843 : 4
Heresies, no h. in dead religion, 726 : 9
truths begin as h., 596 : 9
Heresy anomalies hobbies, 704 : 2
lifeblood of religions, 726 : 9
overcome h. with fire, 155 : 12
Heretic rebel thing to flout, 671 : 4
that makes the fire, 246 : 16
they will proclaim me h., 153 : 9
Heretics, faith begets h., 726 : 9
Heritage, claim ancient h., 912 : 5
I have a goodly h., 17 : 24
liberty h. of all, 520 : 7
of woe, 459 : 12
our h. the sea, 453 : 20
proud of ancient h., 890 : 7
what thou lovest thy true h., 793 : 3
Heritage (*continued*)
youth's h., 544 : 12
Hermit, aloof with h. eye, 435 : 21
crab whale's backbone, 808 : 2
dwell a weeping h., 364 : 9
old h. of Prague, 214 : 27
poor in place obscure, 172 : 7
shall I like a h. dwell, 172 : 17
Hermitage, give palace for h., 195 : 6
take that for h., 296 : 4
Hermon, heights of H., 759 : 11
Hern, coot and h., 533 : 15
Hero, A H. of Our Time, 553 : 1
basic h. of books labor, 725 : 10
conquering h. comes, 346 : 7
conqueror Worm, 526 : 5
every h. becomes bore, 498 : 14
forgive the h., 899 : 10
killed h. in man, 865 : 6
millions a h., 378 : 3
must drink brandy, 356 : 11
of course Alexander h., 518 : 2
perish or sparrow fall, 336 : 14
show me a h., 835 : 14
to his valet, 88 : *n* 8
Truth h. of my tale, 601 : 24
worship, 663 : 6
Herod, born in the days of H., 36 : 20
out-herods H., 221 : 23
Salome pleased H., 39 : 22
should not return to H., 36 : 21
Herodias, daughter of H. danced, 39 : 22
Heroes as well as idealists, 643 : 19
blood of our h., 389 : 2
broods on her shining h., 484 : 2
conquered fame of h., 575 : 8
gladiators died or h., 759 : 12
grass-roots h., 609 : 7
hail ye h., 422 : 21
hand in hand with my h., 518 : 7
if we will, 584 : 10
many valiant souls of h., 57 : 3
of that kidney, 804 : 18
peers h. of old, 544 : 22
seeds of patriots and h., 367 : *n* 8
statesmen philosophers, 392 : 11
thanks to fallen h., 881 : 15
thin red h., 708 : 3
thin red line of h., 578 : *n* 4
to think great thoughts be h., 643 : 19
virtue has h. too, 413 : 10
were plenty, 922 : 16
world's brave h., 922 : 10
Heroic decision not from cowards, 812 : 14
enterprise is gone, 373 : 23
for earth too hard, 544 : 5
giving man h. fiber, 631 : 5
lay tuneless now, 461 : 5
little monkey, 515 : 9
obstacle to being h., 503 : 21
pleasures of h. poesy, 276 : 1
poem a biography, 472 : 9
sires, 311 : 11
systematically h., 648 : 9
womanhood, 512 : 1
Heroically mad, 304 : 17
Heroism endurance for moment more, 660 : 8
feels never reasons, 497 : 24
labor matter of h., 766 : 8
truest h. to resist doubt, 503 : 21
upon land and sea, 574 : 6

Heroism (*continued*)
vices fathered by h., 804 : 15
with you is h., 574 : 6
Herostratus lives that burned temple, 275 : 8
Herring, in hell roast like h., 411 : 14
fish nor flesh nor good red h., 159 : 27
Herrings, red h., 930 : 2
Herself, show me someone not full of h., 916 : 1
Hertford Hereford Hampshire, 894 : 20
Herz, mein H. ist schwer, 396 : *n* 6
Hesiod, Homer and H. attributed to gods, 67 : 12
might have kept his breath, 62 : 5
taught H. beauteous song, 61 : 7
Hesitancies, elaborate h., 701 : 7
Hesitate and falter life away, 585 : 22
dislike, 338 : 14
Hesitates, if President h., 788 : 3
Hesitating so long at a word, 392 : 8
Hesitation, doubt h. pain, 541 : 9
Hesper loves to lead home, 692 : 2
Hesperian, apple-bearing H. coast, 76 : 25
Hesperides, we shall find H., 790 : 10
Hesperus entreats thy light, 255 : 12
it was schooner H., 510 : 4
that led the starry host, 285 : 25
you herd homeward, 63 : 11
Hessians, yonder are the H., 371 : 26
Heterodoxy another man's doxy, 345 : 2
thy-doxy, 473 : 19
Hew, not h. as carcass, 215 : 20
somebody to h. and hack, 291 : 7
to line of right, 602 : 15
Hewers of wood, 11 : 33
Hewing wood for master carpenter, 65 : 7
Hewn on Norwegian hills, 283 : 15
tree is h. down, 36 : 29
wisdom hath h. out her seven pillars, 23 : 18
Hexameter, in the h. rises, 435 : 19
Hey for boot and horse, 566 : 14
ho the wind and the rain, 214 : 29, 234 : 1
nonino, 212 : 33
to you good day to you, 628 : 10
Heyday in the blood is tame, 223 : 4
Hi, answer to h. or loud cry, 613 : 21
but she heels to it, 822 : 7
diddle diddle, 930 : 17
ni ya behold man of flint, 928 : 21
Hibernated in my past, 770 : 11
Hic est enim Calix Sanguinis mei, 54 : 7
Hic jacet, forlorn h., 425 : 4
narrow words H., 173 : 4
Hickety pickety, 932 : 14
Hickory, clothes on h. limb, 924 : 17
dickory dock, 930 : 4
whittled out of h., 835 : 1
Hicks, sticks nix h. pix, 741 : 5
Hid, city set on hill cannot be h., 37 : 6
fiend h. in a cloud, 405 : 12
half as well as he did, 630 : 2
hallowed relics h., 277 : 13
himself among women, 275 : 5
I h. from Him, 693 : 10
in heart of love, 712 : 6
in her interlunar cave, 288 : 21
lightly h. deepest understood, 899 : 11
Hid (*continued*)
love and a cough cannot be h., 269 : 12
Moses h. his face, 9 : 12
Nature and Nature's laws h., 340 : 6
there is nothing h. from the heat, 17 : 28
wheat h. in two bushels of chaff, 198 : 5
wherefore these things h., 213 : 13
which is to keep that h., 252 : 4
Hidden, America of poverty is h., 908 : 5
cause h. result well known, 113 : 19
growth in mind, 565 : 20
half h. from the eye, 424 : 12
handful of Divine Inert, 570 : 12
investigation of h. causes, 166 : 15
like h. lamps, 376 : 6
motion of h. fire, 429 : 18
nature often h., 181 : 4
noise like h. brook, 435 : 1
O h. under dove's wing, 806 : 13
player on other side h., 595 : 12
something h. behind things, 764 : 5
something h. go and find, 710 : 9
soul of harmony, 278 : 7
the manifest and the h., 132 : 13
treasures, 555 : 17
try to speak h. self, 585 : 16
under dove's wing, 806 : 13
Hide, furred gowns h. all, 235 : 3
head under his wing, 932 : 6
it under his tongue, 16 : 6
let me h. myself in thee, 386 : 3
lies to h. it, 268 : *n* 4
me from day's garish eye, 278 : 25
me O my Savior, 350 : 12
me under the shadow of thy wings, 17 : 25
nature wont to h. herself, 69 : 27
one talent death to h., 282 : 15
owest beast no h., 234 : 7
rude stream that must forever h. me, 249 : 3
shame from every eye, 369 : 21
stars h. their diminished heads, 285 : 10
the fault I see, 340 : 4
their diminished heads, 285 : 10
they h. in their skulls, 841 : 13
those hills of snow, 229 : *n* 1
thou wear lion's h., 201 : 21
thyself for a little moment, 30 : 11
tiger's heart in player's h., 178 : 12
tiger's heart in woman's h., 186 : 2
underground alchemy, 494 : 6
us from each other's sight, 267 : 5
what false heart know, 237 : 8
what may man within h., 228 : 27
world to h. virtues in, 213 : 14
your diminished rays, 285 : *n* 3
Hideaways, bones in h., 856 : 1
Hideous, making night h., 219 : 12
more h. in a child, 233 : 10
notes of woe, 462 : 1
phantasma or h. dream, 215 : 18
ruin and combustion, 283 : 4
storm of terror, 262 : 7
throng rush out forever, 526 : 2
vice a creature of h. mien, 722 : 4
Hides, death fact nature h., 609 : 3
glare surrounds king h. him, 165 : 21
night that h. things from us, 142 : 18
not visage from cottage, 247 : 1
Hides (*continued*)
one thing speaks another, 58 : 8
smiling face, 375 : 17
what plighted cunning h., 233 : 1
Hidest, why h. thou thy face from me, 20 : 10
Hiding, dark and lonely h. place, 435 : 16
place from the wind, 30 : 21
Hier stehe ich ich kann nicht anders, 155 : *n* 6
Hierarchies, deck of cards h., 818 : 5
old h. of whales, 790 : 22
Hierarchy, English h. tremble, 379 : 16
in h. employee tends to rise, 896 : 8
Hieroglyphic, immortal verse becomes h., 703 : 7
Hieronymo beware, 177 : 2
Hieronymo's mad againe, 177 : *n* 1
Hierophants of inspiration, 470 : 5
Hies to his confine, 217 : 25
High and boastful neighs, 208 : 1
and low rich and poor, 419 : 4
and palmy state of Rome, 217 : 21
as my heart, 212 : 10
as the heaven is h., 21 : 6
banished from h. life, 569 : 19
birth vigor of bone, 226 : 20
cannot be heard so h., 234 : 28
characters cries one, 289 : 20
corn h. as elephant's eye, 833 : 11
crimes and misdemeanors, 391 : 11
death makes equal h. and low, 158 : 17
diddle diddle, 930 : 17
earth and h. heaven, 691 : 10
for contempt too h., 295 : 2
full of h. sentence, 803 : 17
gale of life h., 691 : 7
hew not too h., 917 : 2
how h. that highest candle, 769 : 3
in action soar as h., 557 : 20
in azure steeps, 843 : 13
in heavens' h. bower, 403 : 12
in people's hearts, 215 : 14
instincts, 426 : 18
killed calf in h. style, 301 : 6
know how h. we are, 607 : 2
life, 369 : 14, 463 : 11, 569 : 19
man aiming at million, 542 : 19
mountains are a feeling, 457 : 28
no bird soars too h., 404 : 2
no h. no low, 336 : 22
no higher than soul h., 822 : 12
object strange and h., 297 : 6
on throne of royal state, 284 : 3
pile h. at Gettysburg, 761 : 6
price cruel h., 707 : 17
proud exultation of discoverer, 799 : 20
Roman fashion, 241 : 23
school closer to core of American experience, 901 : 9
shore of world, 208 : 7
shores of H. Barbaree, 935 : 3
soar not too h. to fall, 262 : 18
spacious firmament on h., 325 : 8
spiritual wickedness in h. places, 49 : 39
that proved too high, 544 : 5
thinking, 425 : 15
thoughts must have high language, 82 : 20
wall must be kept h., 794 : 16

High (*continued*)
where he got that h. brow, 121 : 21
ye'll take the h. road, 921 : 9
High-blown pride broke under me, 249 : 3
High-bouncing lover, 835 : 3
Higher, draw powers into h. classes, 390 : 2
law, 533 : 7
no h. than soul high, 822 : 12
rock that is h. than I, 19 : 26
see h. than himself, 537 : 13
standard of living, 795 : 9
steps h. that they took, 305 : 5
than the sphery chime, 280 : 5
High-erected thoughts, 176 : 4
Highest, dispose of h. wisdom, 289 : 10
Epicurus set forth h. good, 101 : 11
glory to God in h., 42 : 29, 54 : 4
good, 98 : 26, 101 : *n* 9
in h. position least freedom, 102 : 27
people's good the h. law, 99 : 3
point not knowledge, 783 : 2
point of my greatness, 249 : 1
rung on ladder of thought, 690 : 6
stand on h. pavement, 804 : 10
this is the very h. of all, 86 : 4
to humblest tasks, 745 : 11
type of men hear Tao, 64 : 14
High-hearted ways, 568 : 19
Highland, between lowland and h., 634 : 12
heart is H., 483 : 20
my sweet H. Mary, 410 : 18
your H. laddie gone, 415 : 16
Highlands, farewell to the H., 410 : 8
hills of H., 410 : 8
in h. in country places, 669 : 7
my heart's in the H., 410 : 9
ye H. and Lawlands, 927 : 6
High-lived, high life and h. company, 369 : 14
Highly, they speak of so h., 922 : 17
Highness', I am his H. dog, 340 : 5
Highroad that leads to England, 354 : 10
Highway, broad h. of world, 468 : 21
heaping field and h., 568 : 15
make straight a h. for our God, 30 : 30
novel a mirror that strolls along h., 453 : 13
quietly along king's h., 359 : 20
Highwayman, black moon of h., 841 : 6
came riding, 772 : 23
Highways, happy h. where I went, 691 : 9
Hi-hi-yee 764 : 12
Hill, all all sleeping on h., 728 : 3
alone on h. in midnight, 640 : 6
and house live together, 729 : 10
ascend into the h. of the Lord, 18 : 8
becomes the valley, 875 : 3
below the kirk below the h., 434 : 7
city set on an h., 37 : 6
city upon a h., 264 : 22
cloud-topped h., 336 : 16
dancers all gone under h., 807 : 15
flung us on windy h., 796 : 9
green h. far away, 561 : 9
haven under h., 530 : 19
heaven-kissing h., 223 : 3
high Dunsinane h., 239 : 12
house should be of h., 729 : 10

Hill (*continued*)
hunter home from h., 668 : 20
hunts on lonely h., 677 : 5
is this the h., 435 : 4
Jack and Jill went up h., 931 : 1
King of France up h., 929 : 15
laughing heard on h., 403 : 15
lived under a h., 933 : 11
on Richmond H. a lass, 399 : 20
over h. over dale, 196 : 10
over h. to poorhouse, 660 : 5
Pillicock h., 234 : 5
round it was upon a h., 767 : 7
shall be made low, 30 : 31
they call you Shepherd from the h., 585 : 20
tiptoe upon little h., 474 : 20
tree yet crowns h., 587 : 12
vineyard in a very fruitful h., 29 : 3
who shall dwell in thy holy h., 17 : 22
wild birds rounding h., 899 : 9
yon high eastern h., 217 : 27
Hillmen desire hills, 710 : 8
Hills, alter when h. do, 606 : 5
and valleys dales and fields, 183 : *n* 5
as old as h., 432 : 4
blue remembered h., 691 : 9
brown h. melted into spring, 562 : 1
cattle upon thousand h., 19 : 13
everlasting h., 9 : 6
far across h. went, 530 : 11
fight in the h., 744 : 2
Grampian h., 366 : 10
great shout upon h., 671 : 3
hewn on Norwegian h., 283 : 15
hide h. of snow, 229 : *n* 1
hillmen desire h., 710 : 8
Israel scattered upon the h., 14 : 10
lift up mine eyes unto the h., 22 : 4
little h. like lambs, 21 : 21
look down on mountains, 672 : 12
ocean of h. and hollows, 93 : 3
o'er h. and far away, 530 : 13
o'er vales and h., 427 : 7
of Chankly Bore, 551 : 4
of Habersham, 651 : 10
of Highlands, 410 : 8
of home, 669 : 9
of Maryland, 513 : 17
old as h., 740 : 17
on h. like Gods together, 528 : 19
out of h. thou mayest dig brass, 11 : 14
over h. and far away, 332 : 1, 931 : 12
peep o'er hills, 332 : 21
reared in vain, 562 : 10
reverberate h., 213 : 19
rock-ribbed and ancient, 471 : 4
shine forth upon clouded h., 406 : 21
sleep among lonely h., 428 : 7
snow on treeless h., 777 : 16
strength of h. is his, 20 : 20, 54 : 17
vales woodland plain, 334 : 15
valleys groves h. fields, 183 : 8
Vermont h. and valleys, 736 : 19
whose heads touch heaven, 229 : 29
ye too changed ye h., 587 : 6
Hillside, crouched on bleak h., 854 : 6
scholar travels loved h., 587 : 12
Hillside's dew-pearled, 540 : 15
Hilltops, o'er all the h. is quiet, 397 : 3
Him first him last, 286 : 16
Himself, above h. erect h., 182 : 10
each man for h., 146 : 17
every man for h., 161 : 14

Himself (*continued*)
go outside h. to find h., 672 : 7
got the better of h., 171 : 4
he h. said it, 134 : 7
his hungering neighbor, 567 : 14
his own cortège, 899 : 14
into h. at last Eternity changed him, 651 : 14
knows universe not h., 296 : 20
lives unto h., 267 : 9
lord of h., 250 : 16, 459 : 12
loved him for h. alone, 398 : 24
man count on no one but h., 865 : 11
man lost nothing if he has h., 164 : 16
master of h., 262 : 19
no man born unto h., 267 : 9
no man dieth to h., 47 : 32
no man wise by h., 94 : 2
none liveth to h., 47 : 32
out of reputation by h., 319 : 2
savage he who saves h., 152 : 9
seldom ruined but by h., 354 : 8
sows h. for seed, 794 : 9
special people unto h., 11 : 11
who helps others saves h., 138 : 6
witness against h., 391 : 17
yet everyone, 874 : 3
Hinc illae lacrymae, 96 : *n* 4
quam sic calamus saevior ense patet, 259 : 3
Hind, false as pard to h., 226 : 15
that would be mated, 227 : 11
Hindmost, devil take the h., 263 : 8
wheels of Phoebus' wain, 279 : 15
Hindrance, between h. and help, 425 : 2
Hindrances, luxuries h., 559 : 8
Hindside-before-ness 793 : 7
Hinge, cast-iron back with h., 603 : 9
no h. nor loop, 231 : 13
turn on h. that night, 864 : 1
Hinges in French conversation, 360 : 23
liberty of conscience upon two h., 273 : 11
pregnant h. of the knee, 222 : 4
Hinky dinky parley-voo, 817 : 7
Hint, before Franklin took h., 750 : 5
beholding at a h., 683 : 8
just h. a fault, 338 : 14
take h. when h. intended, 750 : 10
take nature's h., 750 : 5
upon this h. I spake, 229 : 31
Hinting, nature always h., 750 : 5
Hints for better ordering of universe, 139 : 6
Nature h. and half-truths, 630 : 24
nature h. over and over, 750 : 5
of earlier creation, 808 : 2
to literary craftsmanship, 800 : 1
Hip, catch him once upon h., 198 : 20
have him on the h., 161 : 1
I have thee on the h., 200 : 18
smote them h. and thigh, 12 : 16
Hipparchia, where is H., 601 : 16
Hippocrene, blushful H., 476 : 23
Hippopotamus's day, 804 : 20
Hips, when your h. stick, 856 : 5
Hipsters, angelheaded h., 906 : 1
Hire, for all lady's h., 933 : 16
idiots to paint, 405 : 15
laborer worthy of h., 43 : 10
shall win lover's h., 404 : 19
this gun for h., 859 : 5
those who lied for h., 792 : 19
Hired money didn't they, 736 : 17

Hired (*continued*)
oblivion not to be h., 275 : 9
tears, 275 : 1
wretches h., 352 : 9
Hirelings in camp and court, 406 : 20
Hiroshima boiling, 893 : 14
bomb on H., 787 : 13
bomb that fell on H., 777 : 10
Hispanic for converse with God, 357 : 19
magnificence of H., 357 : 19
Hiss, dismal universal h., 287 : 27
now becoming a roar, 811 : 17
of love, 864 : 11
roasted crabs h. in bowl, 191 : 15
Hissing, curse astonishment h. and reproach, 32 : 16
hot from hell, 555 : 14
Histoire vieille dame exaltée, 667 : *n* 2
Historian, first law for h., 98 : 10
Goldsmith poet h., 355 : 23
of fine consciences, 684 : 8
of the Roman Empire, 384 : 6
prophet in reverse, 438 : 15
shackles of a h., 276 : 1
sylvan h., 477 : 4
wants more documents, 654 : 1
yield self to subject, 800 : 3
Historians give own country a break, 95 : 18
hints to budding h., 800 : 1
of opinion, 783 : 7
readers should be critical of h., 95 : 18
reviewers would have been h., 436 : 15
their tyrants their h., 490 : 18
Historical books tedious, 655 : 3
fights h., 628 : 1
statistical figures are h. data, 775 : 9
Histories make men wise, 181 : 14
writers of small h., 352 : 10
History a nightmare, 778 : 1
abhors determinism, 837 : 12
absence of romance in my h., 80 : 15
action in bondage to h., 602 : 3
ages before commencement of h., 378 : 1
all h. modern h., 769 : 24
anybody can make h., 676 : 5
assurance of recorded h., 808 : 5
attests happiness depends on dinner, 461 : 29
bear witness to his patriotism, 418 : 5
biography of great men, 473 : 24
cannot escape h., 522 : 12
cannot tolerate chance, 837 : 12
completed chapter of Revelation named H., 473 : 6
consider an epocha in h., 380 : 14
court of h. in judgment, 890 : 6
dignity of h., 329 : 4, 489 : 5
distillation of rumor, 473 : 18
dust heap called h., 666 : 8
excitable lying old lady, 667 : 6
experience and h. teach, 422 : 9
faithfulness to truth of h., 592 : 7
family h. begins with me, 86 : 6
flag embodiment of h., 682 : 5
foulest crime in h., 576 : 8
God and h. remember, 820 : 10
greatest honor h. bestow, 882 : 19
happiest nations no h., 565 : 18
happiest women no h., 565 : 18
happy people whose h. blank, 474 : 15

History (*continued*)
has cunning passages, 804 : 14
hear by tale or h., 195 : 22
if h. teaches anything, 891 : 8
immediate context of h., 823 : 21
in all men's lives, 206 : 21
incomprehensible without Jesus, 593 : 8
indulges in jokes, 785 : 7
influence of sea power on h., 642 : 8
invented h., 344 : 17
is a race, 720 : 5
is more or less bunk, 587 : *n* 2
is now and England, 808 : 16
is on our side, 830 : 14
is philosophy learned from examples, 112 : 18
knows no plateaus, 902 : 10
language the archives of h., 498 : 3
lawyer without h. a mechanic, 431 : 21
let h. answer question, 388 : 18
life of peoples, 602 : 8
love the h. of woman's life, 417 : 12
Mississippi of falsehood, 587 : 4
more valid facts in art than in h. books, 812 : 8
must be false, 329 : 1
never embraces reality, 587 : *n* 2
no h. only biography, 496 : 16
no law of h., 572 : 21
of an art, 793 : 5
of country begins in heart, 738 : 15
of ideas, 720 : 2
of liberty history of safeguards, 776 : 12
of masterwork not failures, 793 : 5
of our race, 745 : 7
of progress of human liberty, 556 : 4
of society history of class struggles, 563 : 3
of soldier's wound, 360 : 3
only great man write h., 676 : 5
ought to judge past, 480 : 8
page of h. worth volume of logic, 645 : 4
pattern of timeless moments, 808 : 16
people never learned from h., 422 : 9
people without h., 808 : 16, 928 : 11
periodization of European h., 847 : 14
persons about to write h., 615 : 16
poetry more philosophic than h., 88 : 18
portrayal of crimes and misfortunes, 343 : 26
progress of freedom, 422 : 12
proof of theories, 616 : 4
psychology long past short h., 666 : 10
read h. aright, 496 : 14
read h. in nation's eyes, 362 : 10
register of crimes, 383 : 10
sacred thing, 169 : 40
second time in our h., 727 : 2
sons study natural h., 381 : 14
stage of h., 666 : 5
statements of h. are singulars, 88 : 18
strange eventful h., 211 : 15
takes a great deal of h., 652 : 6
Thucydides wrote h. of war, 80 : 14
to be soldier know h., 791 : 16
to the defeated, 868 : 8
tortured with h., 843 : 19
triumphed over time, 173 : 2
truth of h., 592 : 7

History (*continued*)
truth only merit to h., 616 : 3
uninstructed in natural h., 595 : 6
vengeance of h. terrible, 770 : 8
very chancy, 800 : 5
war makes good h., 641 : 20
what's her h., 214 : 5
with its flickering lamp, 744 : 11
witness to passing time, 98 : 9
world h. is world's court, 412 : 12
you don't know, 788 : 17
History's purchased page, 457 : 24
Hit, a very palpable h., 224 : 29
dusty trail, 764 : 11
hard hit fast hit often, 777 : 12
hard it rebounds, 355 : 12
nail on head, 161 : 16
only what aim at, 559 : 12
the line hard, 687 : 5
Hitch wagon to star, 499 : 9
Hither and thither moves, 516 : 22
and thither spins, 585 : 5
come h., 211 : 1
even as their coming h., 235 : 11
let him come h., 302 : 14
thither downward upward, 140 : 22
Hitherandthithering waters, 778 : 5
Hitherto shalt thou come but no further, 16 : 30
Hitler, even H. against war, 818 : 16
Germany the cause of H., 801 : 11
missed bus, 727 : 3
monster, 745 : 2
wicked man H., 744 : 8
Hitlerite blackguards, 766 : 9
Hive for the honeybee, 712 : 4
helmet now h. for bees, 177 : 9
this great h. the city, 295 : 3
Hiven, rich man enther H., 722 : 10
Hiverné dans mon passé, 770 : *n* 5
Hives, fill h. with honey and wax, 321 : 14
Ho everyone that thirsteth, 31 : 18
man they called H., 614 : 2
my h. head halls, 778 : 5
talk save us, 778 : 5
with a hey and a h., 212 : 33
Hoard little hearts great, 534 : 6
little h. of maxims, 529 : 22
Hoarded, beauty must not be h., 279 : 31
people think I h. words, 759 : 3
Hoarding, father for h. went to hell, 186 : 5
Hoarfrost, like April h. spread, 434 : 28
Hoarse, raven himself is h., 236 : 17
unchanged to h. or mute, 286 : 28
Hoary, as I in h. winter night, 182 : 2
deep be h., 907 : *n* 1
establishment, 414 : 16
head a crown of glory, 24 : 13
my days dull and h., 299 : 8
sage replied, 353 : 11
wake h. shoulders spouting, 907 : 2
Hobbes clearly proves, 322 : 20
Hobbies and humors, 704 : 2
Hobbit, in hole in ground lived h., 824 : 3
Hobbyhorse, rides h. peaceably, 359 : 20
Hobgoblin of little minds, 497 : 2
Hobson's choice, 917 : 25
Hoc erat in votis, 106 : *n* 15
est enim Corpus meum, 54 : 6

Hoc (*continued*)
genus omne, 106 : *n* 10
volo sic iubeo, 122 : *n* 6
Hockcarts, maypoles h. wassails, 265 : 17
Hocus an old cunning attorney, 344 : *n* 7
Hocus-pocus, law a h. science, 344 : 20
Hoe, crowbar h. and barrow, 455 : 8
leans upon h. and gazes, 670 : 14
scratch it with a h., 603 : 7
Hog butcher for world, 761 : 4
is different, 623 : 25
of Epicurus' herd, 109 : 3
root h. or die, 847 : 12
whole house, 892 : 20
Hogan's right, 722 : 1
Hogs eat acorns, 290 : *n* 3
eat snakes, 767 : 8
fattenin' h. ain't in luck, 662 : 16
let it not be like h., 819 : 5
like puncheon floor, 623 : 25
men eat h., 767 : 8
Hohokams on Arizona desert, 897 : 19
Ho-hum I am for wit, 899 : 11
Hoist colors to peak, 771 : 5
instantly anchor, 576 : 16
with his own petar, 223 : 13
Hold, affection cannot h. bent, 214 : 2
aloof to gain reputation, 85 : 17
bag, 407 : 14
candle to my shames, 199 : 8
cannot h. mortality's hand, 202 : 7
cannot h. thee close enough, 822 : 13
center cannot h., 714 : 12
cry H. h., 236 : 18
damned that cries H. enough, 240 : 11
dominion over palm and pine, 709 : 16
each thing his turn does h., 266 : 15
eternal Footman h. my coat, 803 : 16
faith h. which Milton held, 426 : 1
farthing candle to sun, 259 : *n* 9
fast that which is good, 50 : 22
fast the time, 756 : 1
fast till gives blessing, 513 : 5
fire in his hand, 194 : 7
fleet angel fast, 346 : 14
fort I am coming, 579 : 1, 635 : 22
given us bag to h., 407 : 14
glimmering tapers to sun, 259 : *n* 9
gorgeous east in fee, 425 : 18
how take firm h., 89 : 24
I h. it toward you, 478 : 8
I want to h. your hand, 914 : 8
infinity in palm of hand, 406 : 8
makes nice of no vile h., 202 : 3
me but safe again, 544 : 23
me in thy heart, 225 : 1
mirror up to nature, 222 : 2
more devils than hell can h., 197 : 12
net to h. the wind, 262 : *n* 4
nozzle agin the bank, 636 : 3
opinion with Pythagoras, 200 : 7
out relief is coming, 579 : *n* 1
own with whatever's going, 750 : 11
so h. und schön und rein, 481 : *n* 8
speak or forever h. his peace, 56 : 7
that you know it, 68 : 11
thou the good, 532 : 8
thy right hand shall h. me, 22 : 17
to have and to h., 56 : 9
to have to h. and let go, 707 : 1
to one despise other, 38 : 1
Hold (*continued*)
up Adam's profession, 224 : 5
water, 324 : 29
with hare run with hound, 159 : 26
world but as world, 197 : 28
world wide enough to h. both, 360 : 6
you as thing enskyed, 227 : 27
you here root and all, 535 : 10
your hand victorious, 77 : 9
your own by attacking, 681 : 3
your tongue and let me love, 252 : 10
yours to h. it high, 737 : 10
Hold-fast the only dog, 207 : 15
Holding mental problem in mind, 783 : 12
pocket handkerchief, 613 : 8
writing is h. your breath, 835 : 18
Holds, guess now who h. thee, 507 : 8
him with glittering eye, 434 : 6
in perfection but moment, 244 : 4
nature her custom h., 224 : 4
that anchor h., 535 : 3
Hole, better h., 796 : 3
child shall play on h. of the asp, 29 : 19
entrusts life to one h., 93 : 14
hobbit h., 824 : 3
in a' your coats, 410 : 20
in the story, 845 : 13
mouse that hath one h., 93 : *n* 11
not a nasty dirty wet h., 824 : 3
old swimmin' h., 665 : 13
pessimist sees h., 758 : 12
poisoned rat in h., 322 : 18
put in his hand by the h. of the door, 28 : 15
round man in square h., 625 : 22
stop h. to keep wind away, 224 : 16
weasels fighting in h., 715 : 6
where tail came through, 440 : 14
Holes, cats have two h. in coat, 387 : 2
foxes have h., 38 : 23
of different shapes, 432 : 17
Holiday, he speaks h., 225 : 20
regular h. to them, 546 : 27
Roman h., 458 : 21
specters' h., 629 : 20
sunshine h., 278 : 1
universal scientific h., 776 : 4
Holiday-rejoicing spirit, 442 : 2
Holidays, holiest of all h., 512 : 22
if year playing h., 203 : 5
put away youth take out on h., 897 : 1
Holier laws, 566 : 11
richer man held to be h., 127 : 12
than thou, 31 : 29
Holies, my holy of h., 695 : 3
Holiest of all holidays, 512 : 22
Holiness, art only clean thing except h., 662 : 19
courage or h., 730 : 4
in the beauty of h., 18 : 14
of heart's affections, 479 : 1
Holla your name to hills, 213 : 19
Hollaing and singing of anthems, 206 : 2
Holland, where H. lies, 368 : 20
Holler, Providence fashioned us h., 567 : 23
Hollow, all was false and h., 284 : 8
applaud h. ghost, 587 : 17
as passion without tenderness, 895 : 6
Hollow (*continued*)
blasts of wind, 331 : 7
crown, 195 : 2
fires burn to black, 691 : 15
give me again my h. tree, 339 : 11
in h. murmurs died, 364 : 15
life h. existence burden, 622 : 11
meet thee in h. vale, 267 : 6
men, 805 : 15, 805 : 16
snakes up and down h., 495 : 21
tell the grassy h., 601 : 2
view with h. eye, 200 : 15
voice in h. murmurs, 416 : 11
Hollow-eyed sharp-looking wretch, 188 : 15
Hollowness, machinations h. treachery, 233 : 4
Hollows, dripping water h. stone, 100 : 7
ocean of hills and h., 93 : 3
where flowers grew, 646 : 11
Holly and the ivy, 919 : 21
Hollywood, read there were Communists in H., 847 : 1
Holmes, Sherlock H., 689 : 7, 689 : 8
Holy alliance to exorcise specter, 563 : 2
and enchanted, 433 : 22
and meek she cries, 404 : 11
angels guard thy bed, 328 : 8
as h. as severe, 228 : 26
Author of that religion, 319 : 22
call it h. ground, 470 : 16
Catholic Church, 55 : 2
citadel of Troy, 59 : 13
city new Jerusalem, 53 : 29
close eyes with h. dread, 433 : 27
coming to that h. room, 254 : 17
deadlock, 815 : 16
died to make men h., 566 : 5
divine good or sweet, 287 : 22
ears have heard H. Word, 405 : 1
fair and wise is she, 190 : 4
glimmers of goodbyes, 827 : 4
ground, 9 : 11, 457 : 9, 470 : 16
hail h. light, 285 : 4
holding such things to be h. secrets, 79 : 13
holy holy, 29 : 9, 53 : 7, 452 : 11
I will keep pure and h., 79 : 13
in those h. fields, 202 : 22
knight of h. spirit, 481 : 10
Lamb of God, 406 : 21
Land of Ireland, 916 : *n* 3
land of Irlonde, 916 : 16
land of Walsinghame, 172 : 8
let him be h. still, 53 : 32
Mother Earth, 71 : 2, 928 : 10
mouth of h. prophets, 42 : 25
my h. mountain, 29 : 19
my h. of holies, 695 : 3
neither h. nor Roman, 343 : 7
odd old ends stolen of h. writ, 187 : 6
pebbles of h. streams, 886 : 21
Persians hold sea h., 570 : 4
place whereon thou standest is h. ground, 9 : 11
proofs of h. writ, 231 : 7
remember sabbath to keep it h., 10 : 6
Roman Empire, 343 : 7
sages once did sing, 277 : 6
shrieve me h. man, 435 : 8
silent night h. night, 466 : 2

Holy (*continued*)
simplicity, 148 : 12
sorrow h. ground, 676 : 15
stand in his h. place, 18 : 8
take not thy h. spirit from me, 19 : 17
temple of God is h., 48 : 6
text of pike and gun, 291 : 4
things h. profane clean obscene, 264 : 16
things h. revealed only to men h., 80 : 6
time quiet as nun, 425 : 16
tradition becomes h., 657 : 10
what is gold doing in h. place, 117 : 9
who shall dwell in thy h. hill, 17 : 22
writ, 231 : 7
Holy Ghost, conceived by the H., 55 : 2
communion of H., 49 : 24
Father Son and H., 41 : 30, 311 : 19
filled with H., 45 : 39
glory be to the H., 54 : 18
I believe in the H., 55 : 2
incarnate by the H., 55 : 3
sedentary life sin against H., 659 : 1
whether there be any H., 46 : 21
sin against H., 637 : 12
Holystone decks scrape cable, 553 : 17
Homage, owes no h. unto sun, 274 : 22
vice pays to virtue, 293 : 27
won by lavish h., 447 : 18
Home, afraid to go h. in dark, 699 : *n* 5
after years in captivity, 4 : 8
again America for me, 671 : 10
again jiggety-jig, 933 : 9
all the way h., 930 : 11
and being washing-day, 310 : 4
any more at h. like you, 685 : 8
art gone and ta'en wages, 243 : 27
artist no h. save Paris, 658 : 23
best be getting h. he said, 614 : 8
best country is at h., 368 : 15
call cattle h., 566 : 7
can't go h. again, 852 : 13
charity begins at h., 96 : 6, 274 : 19
Christmas, 724 : 4
come h. to roost, 440 : 3
comin' for to carry me h., 935 : 24
day's march nearer h., 429 : 17
dunce kept at h., 375 : 24
eaten out of house and h., 206 : 11
father come h. with me, 614 : 12
fly away h., 930 : 3
give you husband and h., 59 : 28
go h. in dark, 699 : 20
God who is our h., 426 : 14
good morning Midnight coming h., 605 : 10
harvest h., 203 : 7, 536 : 2
hate to be unquiet at h., 310 : 16
heaven and h., 429 : 9
Hesper loves to lead h., 692 : 2
hills of h., 669 : 9
his footsteps turned, 430 : 10
homely features to keep h., 280 : 1
homely h. simple pleasures, 692 : 15
hotel refuge from h. life, 680 : 11
how can tyrants govern h., 186 : 12
hunter h. from hill, 668 : 20
I am far from h., 490 : 6
I came h. forever, 442 : 1
I keep it staying at h., 605 : 4
I'm going h., 493 : 12
in minds of men, 81 : 5
in our own beloved h., 578 : 12

Home (*continued*)
is home, 465 : *n* 1
is on the deep, 443 : 12
is safest refuge, 172 : *n* 2
is the sailor, 668 : 20
is where one starts from, 807 : 23
Jerusalem happy h., 918 : 5
joy of the ancient h., 618 : 12
keep h. fires burning, 740 : 11
keep only son at h., 366 : 10
knock as you please nobody h., 336 : 7
knows when to go h., 636 : 7
liberty must begin at h., 825 : 10
life depends on borrowing, 599 : 9
life not natural, 680 : 31
longest way round shortest h., 267 : *n* 6
love h. love country, 547 : 22
made of blue clouds, 928 : 16
make house h., 774 : 4
man desires to see h., 4 : 8
man goeth to his long h., 27 : 25
merriest when from h., 207 : 9
my heart turning h. again, 671 : 10
my h. sweet h., 802 : 10
my songs draw Daphnis h., 103 : 17
naiad airs brought h., 525 : 9
nearer h. today, 594 : 6
never change when love has found h., 112 : 19
no h. like a raft, 624 : 1
no place like h., 465 : 4
not appreciated till left, 699 : 13
of bean and cod, 694 : 14
of lost causes, 587 : 1
of love, 245 : 15
of the brave, 446 : 1, 815 : 2
of wild mirth, 503 : 3
old Kentucky h., 598 : 5
our eternal h., 328 : 10
outlives day and comes safe h., 208 : 10
Paris my h. town, 752 : 13
place they have to take you in, 747 : 8
pleasure never at h., 477 : 14
returned h. previous night, 742 : 1
returns h. to find needs, 671 : 8
seek fortunes further than h., 188 : 27
send h. my long-strayed eyes, 252 : 23
shall men come, 742 : 11
show piety at h., 50 : 30
sick for h., 477 : 1
song of h. and friends, 618 : 1
tavern for friends, 724 : 14
they brought warrior, 531 : 8
they dream of h., 740 : 11
they'll come h., 932 : 3
things at h. crossways, 660 : 2
things foreign or things at h., 302 : 4
this pig stayed h., 930 : 11
till boys come h., 740 : 11
till the cow comes h., 263 : 5
to a lie, 792 : 14
to my ain countree, 453 : 21
to my Lord and be free, 936 : 4
toddle safely h., 795 : 15
turns again h., 535 : 19
welcome h. discarded faith, 202 : 14
well-beloved in that h., 875 : 12
what does it leave at h., 553 : 2
what is more agreeable than h., 98 : 19

Home (*continued*)
when you knock it never is h., 376 : 5
where buffalo roam, 927 : 19
where we love is h., 518 : 16
wherever that may be, 878 : 9
why everybody going h., 702 : 1
wish him safe at h., 415 : 16
with no direction h., 915 : 6
Wyoming will be your new h., 927 : 10
Home-keeping youth homely wits, 189 : 28
Homeland of patience, 500 : 26
where happy there's h., 134 : 32
wherever he prospers, 82 : 26
Homeless near thousand homes, 423 : 2
permission to enter h. state, 73 : 5
tempest-tossed, 664 : 10
Homely beauty of good old cause, 425 : 15
conversational or h. type, 730 : 15
definitions, 438 : 4
features to keep home, 280 : 1
hen lays one, 923 : 10
home be it never so h., 465 : *n* 1
home simple pleasures, 692 : 15
home-keeping youth h. wits, 189 : 28
joys, 362 : 2
men who charmed women, 699 : 12
slighted shepherd's trade, 280 : 15
something h. and innocent, 502 : 5
was their food, 318 : 17
wink at h. girl, 772 : 6
Homemade but aren't we all, 878 : 15
contraption, 835 : 1
Homer, Achilles exists only through H., 419 : 8
all the books you need, 316 : 6
and Hesiod attributed to the gods, 67 : 12
and Whitman roar in pines, 728 : 4
even good old H. nods, 110 : 2
first of heroic poets, 353 : *n* 4
found H. herald of your glory, 90 : 13
is my example, 716 : 14
learned root of H., 257 : *n* 5
liken H. to setting sun, 118 : 17
living H. begged bread, 257 : *n* 5
made blind H. sing to me, 184 : 3
new and fresh, 741 : 2
nods, 110 : 2, 332 : 18
our poets steal from H., 258 : 6
read H. once, 316 : 6
smote bloomin' lyre, 708 : 24
there were poets before H., 98 : 15
translator of H., 586 : 14
warred for H. being dead, 257 : 20
you must not call it H., 319 : 3
Homère noveau ce matin, 741 : *n* 1
Homeric or Biblical canticles, 577 : 13
Homer's rule best, 339 : 9
Homerus, quandoque dormitat H., 110 : *n* 1
Home's, way h. the farthest way, 267 : 16
Homes, homeless near thousand h., 423 : 2
introduce philosophy into h., 98 : 25
old h. old names, 726 : 2
poverty keeps h. together, 731 : 15
protect health h. firesides, 666 : 22
shut-in h. closed doors, 727 : 7
stately h. of England, 470 : 13, 781 : 16
think of firelit h., 795 : 14

Homesickness is nothing, 880 : 3
poem begins as h., 749 : 19
Homeward bound for New York town, 935 : 1
Hesperus you herd h., 63 : 11
look h. Angel, 281 : 3
plowman h. plods, 361 : 20
rooks in families h. go, 642 : 6
Homicidal civilization, 778 : 11
Homines, quot h. tot sententiae, 97 : n 2
Homing, horizon of his h., 808 : 13
Hominy, white man filled with Indians' h., 374 : 20
Homme avec Dieu dans la majorité, 162 : n 1
chaque h. porte la forme de l'humaîne condition, 165 : n 9
d'entendement n'a rien perdu, 164 : n 12
la vraie étude de l'h., 337 : n 2
le style c'est l'h. même, 349 : n 1
l'h. c'est un roseau pensant, 300 : n 4
l'h. est né libre, 358 : n 7
ne saurait forger un ciron, 165 : n 4
n'y a point h. nécessaire, 779 : n 3
qu'est-ce que l'h. dans la nature, 299 : n 4
vain divers et ondoyant, 164 : n 5
Hommes sont toujours sincères, 718 : n 3
Homo, ad unguem factus h., 106 : n 12
ecce h., 45 : n 4
fecit, 900 : 1
proponet Deus disponit, 148 : n 7
sum humani nil a me alienum puto, 96 : n 8
Honest, a few h. men, 272 : 16
alehouse, 271 : 3
and industrious men's lives, 265 : 9
and perfect man, 260 : 17
and wise men rule, 382 : 1
angler, 270 : 32
anglers or very h. men, 271 : 12
armor is his h. thought, 250 : 14
as world goes, 220 : 16
being h. good exercise, 678 : 5
day is for h. men, 77 : 5
depository of public interests, 390 : 2
dies an h. fellow, 260 : n 5
direct and h. not safe, 231 : 15
doubt, 532 : 19
dullard, 673 : 1
exceeding poor man, 199 : 1
George Third h. dullard, 673 : 1
God noblest work of man, 615 : 10
good h. painful sermon, 309 : 16
good to be h. and true, 411 : 24
government good and h., 903 : 8
gude to be h. and true, 921 : 8
hand that is h. and hearty, 429 : 16
hard-working ancestry, 826 : 13
here lies a truly h. man, 292 : 20
I one of few h. people, 835 : 4
in every h. hand a whip, 232 : 6
labor bears lovely face, 251 : 10
looking for h. man, 86 : 12
man appeals to understanding, 391 : 7
man close-buttoned, 377 : 17
man looked h. enough, 622 : 9
man sent to lie abroad, 251 : 4
man's aboon his might, 411 : 18
man's the noblest work of God, 337 : 13, 408 : 18
Honest (*continued*)
men rebel and revolutionize, 558 : 2
men shaped conduct, 730 : 14
merry and yet h. too, 225 : 27
nation secure only while h., 556 : 13
no such thing as h. man, 330 : 24
not h. that filleth own nest, 153 : 2
not so h. more h., 542 : n 4
peace and h. friendship, 389 : 2
poor but h., 227 : 12, 924 : 10
prejudices of Englishman, 326 : 22
religion made h. woman of the supernatural, 870 : 3
room for h. men, 384 : 19
six h. servingmen, 710 : 2
social friendly h. man, 409 : 2
soul that can be h., 260 : 18
tale speeds plainly told, 187 : 19
taught in intellectually h. form, 887 : 16
thief tender murderer, 543 : 7
tired of h. things, 823 : 10
to no purpose, 114 : 1
too h. to steal, 922 : 14
twelve h. men, 330 : 20
water, 242 : 32
whatsoever things are h., 50 : 7
win us with h. trifles, 236 : 9
words suffered corruption, 261 : 17
Honesta turpitudo est pro causa bona, 110 : n 15
Honester, women growing h., 695 : 14
Honestly, let us walk h., 47 : 29
Honesty, armed so strong in h., 217 : 2
best policy, 170 : 29
corruption wins not more than h., 249 : 8
is his fault, 243 : 3
is praised and starves, 121 : 23
love paradox without losing h., 497 : 32
manhood nor fellowship, 203 : 4
rich h. dwells like miser, 213 : 3
root of h. in good education, 120 : 7
thy h. and love, 230 : 22
Honey and plenty of money, 550 : 7
eating bread and h., 931 : 9
fill hives with h. and wax, 321 : 14
gather h. all the day, 328 : 5
in the carcass of the lion, 12 : 13
in the horn, 921 : 13
land flowing with milk and h., 9 : 13
land of h., 11 : 14
locusts and wild h., 36 : 27
milk and h., 9 : 13, 563 : 13
no go my h. love, 870 : 5
nor h. make nor pair, 436 : 9
pedigree of h., 607 : 13
speech sweeter than h., 57 : 10
still for tea, 796 : 12
surfeited with h., 204 : 20
sweeter than h. and honeycomb, 18 : 1
this Self is h. of all beings, 56 : 22
touch h. of romance, 674 : 16
very h. of earthly joy, 295 : 3
with milk and h. blessed, 563 : 13
Honeybee, hive for the h., 712 : 4
Honeybees, so work the h., 207 : 6
Honeycomb, dipped rod in h., 12 : 37
lips of a strange woman drop as h., 23 : 10
sweeter than honey and the h., 18 : 1
Will H. calls ladies, 327 : 17
Honeycomb (*continued*)
wrath sweeter than h., 58 : 30
Honeydew, on h. hath fed, 433 : 27
Honeyed, bee with h. thigh, 278 : 25
filled thicket with h. song, 82 : 5
Muses gave me h. gift, 93 : 2
suck the h. showers, 281 : 1
words like bees, 794 : 8
Honey-heavy dew of slumber, 215 : 22
Honeyless, leave them h., 217 : 8
Honeysuckle, odor of h. fifteen parts, 699 : 16
Honi soit qui mal y pense, 143 : 7
Honks, goose h. high, 920 : n 6
Honor, accompany old age as h., 239 : 31
action faithful h. clear, 336 : 5
all lost save h., 157 : 6
all men, 52 : 11
all tasks of equal h., 745 : 11
and greatness of his name, 249 : 18
as valiant I h. him, 216 : 15
bards have a share of h., 60 : 7
before h. is humility, 24 : 10
belongs to soul, 124 : 3
bright, 226 : 17
brothers all in h., 424 : 4
but an empty bubble, 306 : 19
by h. and dishonor, 49 : 16
can h. set a leg, 205 : 5
changes labor from burden to h., 766 : 8
chastity of h., 373 : 24
clear, 336 : 5
comes a pilgrim gray, 364 : 9
comes from Zeus, 57 : 16
dearer than life, 169 : 25
depends on opinion of mob, 308 : 23
desirous of h. and glory, 309 : 3
die with h., 696 : 15
done with hope and h., 708 : 15
favor well bestowed an h., 327 : 18
foe while you strike, 700 : 6
free man abide with h., 558 : 6
friend who prospered, 71 : 7
from books of h. razed, 244 : 7
full of days riches and h., 14 : 28
giving h. unto the wife, 52 : 13
good death does h. to whole life, 143 : 4
has come back, 797 : 5
his memory, 257 : 1
hurt that H. feels, 529 : 23
if peace not with h., 727 : n 1
if we can vertical man, 868 : 1
in her left hand riches and h., 23 : 4
inherits h. or wealth, 436 : 2
is a mere scutcheon, 205 : 5
jealous in h., 211 : 15
lacking neither h. nor lyre, 107 : 13
life and h. in hands, 617 : 6
like an island, 311 : 14
louder talked of h., 488 : n 1
love in excess brings nor h., 76 : 16
loved I not h. more, 296 : 1
make one vessel unto h., 47 : 16
man of h. regrets discreditable act, 772 : 13
man willing to sink, 567 : 17
map of h. in thy face, 185 : 16
march in ranks of h., 744 : 11
may we h. law, 451 : 12
men who have a sense of h., 58 : 24
men who have h., 566 : 3

Honor (*continued*)
mine h. is my life, 193 : 33
national h. national property, 407 : 18
naught in hate all in h., 232 : 19
neither property nor h. touched, 154 : 2
new-made h. doth forget, 201 : 9
no h. in sure success, 810 : 3
no longer live with h., 696 : 15
not least in h. or applause, 174 : *n* 3
not pay h. with tears, 95 : 2
of striking blow for freedom, 798 : 6
or dishonor to last generation, 522 : 12
our sacred h., 387 : 11
peace with h., 502 : 18, 727 : 2
peace with justice and h., 95 : 16
peace without h. not peace, 466 : 3
peasants carry h. in their hands, 264 : 8
peereth in meanest habit, 189 : 2
perseverance keeps h. bright, 226 : 17
physician, 36 : 7
pluck bright h. from moon, 203 : 15
pluck up drowned h., 203 : 15
post of h. is private station, 326 : 2
pricks me on, 205 : 5
prophet not without h., 39 : 21
purchased by merit, 199 : 14
quaint h. turn to dust, 297 : 1
Republic's roll of h., 603 : 3
rooted in dishonor, 534 : 14
sacred h., 387 : 11
sense of h. in action, 81 : 5
set h. in one eye, 215 : 3
shall uphold the humble, 25 : 33
signed with their h., 876 : 16
sin to covet h., 208 : 9
sin to prefer life to h., 122 : 14
sinks, 368 : 16
so long shall your h. endure, 104 : 29
stain in thine h., 36 : 5
strength and h. are her clothing, 26 : 8
subject of my story, 215 : 4
take h. from me and life done, 193 : 33
that h. would thee do, 207 : 11
the king, 52 : 11
those they have slain, 582 : 9
through his h. I conquered him, 264 : 8
thy father and mother, 10 : 7
to whom honor due, 47 : 27
travels in strait so narrow, 226 : 18
truth above friends, 87 : 14
voyage not for gain h. wealth, 152 : 1
what is h. a word, 205 : 5
what is left when h. lost, 110 : 26
when faith lost h. dies, 513 : 8
whom king delighteth to h., 14 : 33
with native h. clad, 285 : 17
words such as h. obscene, 844 : 14
Honorable, all h. men, 216 : 18
ancient and h., 29 : 17
and glorious, 379 : 5
Brutus is an h. man, 216 : 18
conquests, 373 : 9
designs were strictly h., 349 : 23
get loose from h. engagement, 372 : 5
have that which is truly h., 89 : 23
intentions h., 378 : 7
murderer, 232 : 19
no title more h., 777 : 3
not h. to tell lies, 75 : 17

Honorable (*continued*)
object only of war h., 384 : 20
obstinate truthful man, 549 : 12
politics most h. adventure, 753 : 9
quixotic sense of h., 527 : 4
retreat, 212 : 5
style of Christian, 273 : 15
to die for one's country, 107 : 27
true and h. wife, 215 : 23
yet write verse badly, 297 : 31
Honorably, to die h. greatest virtue, 67 : 20
Honored among foxes, 887 : 2
among wagons, 886 : 20
bones, 277 : 13
by strangers h., 335 : 10
by the few, 568 : 23
custom more h. in breach, 219 : 9
followed him h. him, 541 : 6
how loved how h. once, 335 : 11
in their generations, 36 : 11
of them all, 529 : 8
these h. dead, 523 : 4
Honorificabilitudinitatibus 191 : 7
Honoring, not so much h. thee, 256 : 9
Honor's, can h. voice provoke, 362 : 5
listen for dear h. sake, 280 : 3
when h. at the stake, 223 : 19
Honors acquired by unrighteousness, 68 : 21
bears his blushing h., 249 : 3
beauties wits, 252 : 22
female sex excluded from h. and offices, 393 : 3
gave his h. to the world, 249 : 11
highest h. this air give, 570 : 12
mindless of its just h., 429 : 10
people I cannot win with h., 300 : 23
Hood, him that wears a h., 163 : 9
more than a h. to make monk, 133 : *n* 6
Hoodoo, Mumbo-Jumbo will h. you, 765 : 7
Hoof, head and h. of Law, 709 : 6
whatsoever parteth the h., 10 : 16
wing fang struggle, 879 : 8
Hoofs of swinish multitude, 373 : 27
Hoohooed it in ocean-booms, 767 : 13
Hook, bait the h. well, 209 : 18
by h. or by crook, 143 : 11
draw out leviathan with a h., 17 : 4
spares next swath, 477 : 18
without bait, 499 : 4
Hooking, taking sweetmeats only h., 622 : 14
Hook-nosed fellow of Rome, 206 : 28
Hooks, silver h., 253 : 2
Hoop of the nation, 701 : 8
tepees in circle nation's h., 701 : 9
Hoops, grapple with h. of steel, 218 : 30
Hooray and up she rises, 934 : 19
Hooting and shrieking, 215 : 12
at glorious sun, 435 : 16
Hoots, owl that nightly h., 196 : 20
Hop, lets it h. a little, 192 : 18
light ladies, 662 : 17
Hope a waking dream, 86 : 16
Admiral cheered them holding out h., 150 : 14
against h. believed in h., 47 : 1
all h. abandon who enter here, 140 : 13
all we h. in heaven, 525 : 2
all will yet be well, 521 : 6

Hope (*continued*)
Americans h. of world, 368 : 3
animated by faith and h., 352 : 24
beautiful Evelyn H., 542 : 1
because I do not h., 805 : 20
beyond h. and despair, 806 : 2
beyond shadow of dream, 476 : 1
blessed h. whereof he knew, 641 : 13
break it to our h., 240 : 9
certain h. of Resurrection, 56 : 13
confidently h. all well, 521 : 6
conquers cowardice, 564 : 12
cradle of h., 761 : 16
days are spent without h., 15 : 20
death of h. and despair, 808 : 11
deferred maketh the heart sick, 23 : 31
desire without h., 704 : 12
done with h. and honor, 708 : 15
extinguish h. from soul, 674 : 4
Faith H. Charity, 443 : 2
farewell h., 285 : 13
fear cannot be without h., 308 : 16
feed on h., 174 : 10
fondest h. decay, 447 : 14
fooled with h., 303 : 10
for a season, 443 : 5
for helmet the h. of salvation, 50 : 20
for the best, 432 : 21
for years to come, 328 : 10
forks and h., 614 : 4
from h. and fear set free, 633 : 22
frustrate of his h., 281 : 14
full of immortality, 34 : 13
good breakfast bad supper, 179 : 15
hath happy place, 562 : 9
he receives h. who recognizes benefit, 130 : 5
help for living h. for dead, 615 : 8
if youth season of h., 565 : 24
illusions of h., 383 : 1
in faith and h. world disagree, 337 : 9
in grass-roots heroes, 609 : 7
in the day of evil, 32 : 14
in trembling h. repose, 362 : 19
is the thing left us in bad time, 847 : 7
is the thing with feathers, 604 : 17
is there any better h., 521 : 12
is to expect something for nothing, 671 : 16
land of h. and glory, 698 : 12
last best h. of earth, 522 : 12
leave light of h. behind, 443 : 8
lies to mortals, 692 : 7
like taper's light, 368 : 12
lined himself with h., 206 : 6
lives on h. die fasting, 347 : 33
look forward with h., 747 : 7
memory outlive his life, 222 : 10
men in exile feed on h., 71 : 13
men set hearts upon, 516 : 9
my good vain h. of gain, 177 : 10
my h. is sun will pierce, 544 : 29
my h. my hap my love, 168 : 2
my h. my love, 276 : 6
never comes, 283 : 7
never to h. again, 249 : 3
no more h., 740 : 10
no morn or h. possible, 841 : 18
no other medicine but h., 228 : 13
nor love nor friend, 669 : 2
not endure another's h., 320 : 3
not h. and no help came, 869 : 1

Hope (*continued*)
now abideth h., 48 : 25
nursing unconquerable h., 586 : 2
of fair advantages, 199 : 9
of glory, 55 : 7
of pride and power, 525 : 4
of the morrow, 618 : 12
of the ungodly, 34 : 16
on h. wretch relies, 368 : 11
one jot of heart or h., 282 : 19
one will cut halter, 277 : 2
only h. lies in despair, 312 : 6
outskirts of h., 872 : 10
past h. past cure past help, 193 : 19
phantoms of h., 352 : 15
pleasure in what yet remain, 303 : 11
plummets to dust of h., 74 : 3
prisoners of h., 33 : 33
ray of h. blown out, 520 : 7
rejoicing in h., 890 : 11
safety to h. not safety, 105 : 2
saved by h., 823 : 21
sin was too much h., 256 : 3
springs eternal, 336 : 15
that there it not withered be, 256 : 9
thing with feathers, 604 : 17
things you do not h. happen, 94 : 4
this government best h., 388 : 17
to see Pilot, 535 : 21
to the end, 52 : 7
to turn again, 805 : 20
to world for future, 521 : 8
transform h. to desire, 639 : 3
triumph of h. over experience, 354 : 22
true h. is swift, 187 : 24
understood terror and h., 894 : 15
virtue flock to their aid, 496 : 13
what was dead was h., 676 : 10
whence this pleasing h., 326 : 3
which guides changeful mind, 72 : 13
while life there's h., 96 : 14, 98 : 18
whose h. the Lord is, 32 : 11
without all h. of day, 288 : 20
without h. we live in desire, 140 : 20
without object cannot live, 436 : 10
work without h., 436 : 10
Hoped, substance of things h. for, 51 : 18
we were brokenhearted, 634 : 2
Hopeful, elders h. about us, 565 : 24
hey but I'm h., 628 : 8
Hopeless fancy feigned, 531 : 4
grief passionless, 507 : 3
or is it h., 896 : 14
our h. love, 801 : 5
passion, 539 : 13
so huge so h., 607 : 18
we doctors know h. case, 829 : 26
woes of h. lovers, 305 : 12
Hopelessness of early youth, 565 : 14
Hope's true gage, 172 : 15
Hopes, adversity not without h., 180 : 6
and fears of all years, 619 : 16
hearts h. prayers tears, 511 : 9
life's span forbids us enter on h., 107 : 2
like towering falcons, 320 : 14
no more change name, 427 : 14
of future years, 511 : 8
stirred up with high h., 281 : 19
tender leaves of h., 249 : 3
that resemble regrets, 564 : 4
that St. Nicholas, 446 : 3
Hopes (*continued*)
vain h. like dreams of those who wake, 118 : 1
vanity of human h., 352 : 5
what are h., 413 : 28
wholly h. to be, 544 : 16
Hoping, by h. more have but less, 189 : 18
not disappoint h. soul, 412 : 19
tender yearning sweet h., 413 : 21
trembling h. lingering, 333 : 23
Hopkins, Mark H. on one end, 609 : 10
Hopping, meager shriveled h., 373 : 28
through frothy waves, 613 : 4
Horace, studied spontaneity of H., 117 : 19
whom I hated so, 458 : 14
Horatii curiosa felicitas, 117 : *n* 11
Horatio, I knew him H., 224 : 14
in my mind's eye H., 218 : 15
more things in heaven H., 220 : 3
speak to it H., 217 : 17
thrift thrift H., 218 : 14
to what base uses we may return H., 224 : 15
Horde, society one polished h., 461 : 28
Horizon, dusk on eastern h., 831 : 13
last h., 852 : 15
limit of sight, 642 : 10
of dogs, 841 : 11
of his homing, 808 : 13
of human life, 498 : 5
our h. never at our elbows, 560 : 2
Horizon's, line of h. growing thin, 874 : 20
Horizontal, cord into h. line, 471 : 14
man, 868 : 1
Horn, barter that h., 714 : 20
beetle winds sullen h., 364 : 12
blow wreathed h., 428 : 1
come blow h., 930 : 12
cow with crumpled h., 934 : 9
Dinah blow your h., 921 : 17
gate of h., 61 : 2, 105 : 26
God winding lonely h., 712 : 13
gray-fly winds sultry h., 280 : 10
hand on h., 927 : 12
honey in the h., 921 : 13
hounds and h., 277 : 23
huntsman winds his h., 349 : 10
lusty h., 212 : 27
mouth of Plenty's h., 714 : 20
of hunter on hill, 487 : 2
one blast upon bugle h., 431 : 15
poured through mellow h., 364 : 14
Roland sound your h., 136 : 12
sound of h. at night, 483 : 3
sound upon bugle h., 529 : 15
tunes frozen up in h., 385 : 8
with his hounds and h., 474 : 19
Horned moon with one bright star, 434 : 23
Horner, little Jack H., 929 : 20
Hornets, bees for flies and h. for bees, 155 : 14
cobwebs let h. through, 321 : 15
Horns, hang caps on h. of the moon, 242 : 9
like Kyloe cow, 931 : 7
of Elfland, 531 : 1
of my dilemma, 360 : 13
sound of h. and motors, 805 : 6
sound of hunting h., 770 : 13
Horny hands of toil, 567 : 2
Horologe of eternity, 510 : 23
Horresco referens, 104 : *n* 16
Horrible, hence h. shadow, 238 : 29
imaginings, 236 : 11
invention the bourgeois, 583 : 7
that lust and rage, 717 : 13
voice, 81 : 13
Horribly, I will h. revenge, 208 : 14
live by medicine live h., 350 : 5
stuffed with epithets, 229 : 11
Horrid, blow h. deed in every eye, 236 : 24
dream h. dreams, 571 : 11
hideous notes of woe, 462 : 1
image doth unfix hair, 236 : 11
life demd h. grind, 547 : 18
shapes and shrieks, 277 : 17
when bad she was h., 513 : 1
Horridly to shake our disposition, 219 : 12
Horror can't be talked about, 850 : 7
Dead Sea makes h., 759 : 11
fell upon Christian, 302 : 10
lived through this h., 786 : 13
of falling into naught, 326 : 3
of outer darkness, 614 : 17
of that moment, 612 : 16
screams of h. rend, 334 : 10
soul of plot, 526 : 4
the h. the h., 683 : 20
this h. is ours, 877 : 6
universal h. unbend, 775 : 3
Horror's, on h. head horrors, 231 : 14
Horrors accumulate, 231 : 14
congenial h. hail, 345 : 5
of half-known life, 570 : 14
sunset stained with h., 673 : 17
supped full with h., 240 : 3
Horse, a dog a h. a rat, 235 : 18
and his rider hath he thrown, 9 : 32
bean-fed h. beguile, 196 : 12
beggars mounted run h. to death, 186 : 1
boot saddle to h., 540 : 26
brewer's h., 204 : 24
bring h. to water, 160 : 5
call me h., 203 : 30
cart before h., 161 : 4
choice of h. and wife, 584 : 6
dark h., 501 : 8
dearer than his h., 529 : 17
death on his pale h., 287 : 28
difference of opinion makes h. races, 624 : 26
dominated mind of early races, 790 : 19
ego to id as rider to h., 678 : 14
far back in soul h. prances, 790 : 19
fine lady on h., 931 : 11
flung himself on h., 728 : 1
foot an' artillery, 786 : 11
for want of h. rider lost, 270 : 4, 347 : 35
for want of shoe h. lost, 270 : 4, 347 : 35
give me another h., 187 : 26
great h. of gold, 828 : 9
guide h. in direction it wants, 678 : 14
happy h. to bear Antony, 240 : 21
hast thou given the h. strength, 16 : 36
hey for boot and h., 566 : 14
I am not so poor a h., 523 : 8
in silence champed, 739 : 15

Horse (*continued*)
king's eye made h. fat, 120 : 9
knows the way, 490 : 20
lean as is a rake, 145 : 26
little black h., 841 : 6
lord if you had h., 790 : 19
must think it queer, 748 : 6
my h. my hound, 896 : 12
my h. my wife my name, 500 : 21
my kingdom for a h., 187 : 31
nation, 928 : 12
never look gift h. in mouth, 128 : 22
noblest conquest of man, 349 : 1
nothing but talk of his h., 198 : 11
O for a h. with wings, 243 : 19
of air, 918 : 12
of different color 213 : *n* 4
of our courage, 900 : 3
of that color, 213 : 27
old h. stumbles and nods, 642 : 2
pale h., 53 : 11, 287 : 28
philosophy a good h., 369 : 22
shoe the h., 934 : 6
short h. soon curried, 159 : 24
shut door when h. stolen, 159 : *n* 15
sits on h. at hostess' door, 201 : 15
spur not unbroken h., 432 : 7
to h. and away, 540 : 26
truest friend that bestrad h., 149 : 20
Turquoise H. of Johano-ai, 928 : 20
uses folly like stalking-h., 213 : 6
with wings, 243 : 19
working for dead h., 171 : 3
young h. deep inside it, 901 : 11
Horseback, beggar on h., 186 : *n* 1, 717 : 12
man on h., 922 : 6
on h. through dreary tract, 525 : 19
Horsed upon sightless couriers, 236 : 24
Horseleach hath two daughters, 26 : 3
Horseman pass by, 718 : 2
Horsemanship, forgetful of his h., 58 : 26
witch world with noble h., 204 : 32
Horsemen, chariot and h. of Israel, 14 : 13
four h. of Apocalypse, 720 : 18
Four H. of Notre Dame, 773 : *n* 4
Horsemill, desire is a h., 258 : 21
Horse's, 'ear h. legs, 535 : 7
trusts in h. health, 234 : 14
Horses, all the king's h., 932 : 2
and poets not overfed, 171 : 17
as fed h. in the morning, 31 : 33
black are the h., 841 : 12
carriages without h., 919 : 6
chariot and h. of fire, 14 : 12
come saddle your h., 432 : 15
don't do it and frighten h., 706 : 16
England hell for h., 259 : 22
England hell of h., 174 : 23
handling of blooded h., 583 : 9
heaven in which no h., 670 : 12
if cattle and h. had hands, 67 : 13
if wishes were h., 301 : 13
Italy paradise for h., 259 : 22
men hanged that h. not be stolen, 310 : 21
more careful of breed of h. than children, 314 : 14
not swap h., 523 : 8
oats in England given to h., 352 : 12
price of thousand h., 735 : 1
rode h. up to bed, 740 : 5

Horses (*continued*)
run slowly h. of night, 113 : 6, 184 : *n* 4
turn mice into h., 694 : 1
watered our h. in Helicon, 178 : 8
which h. bear him best, 184 : 20
who drives h. of sun, 661 : 16
wild white h. play, 584 : 11
would draw gods like horses, 67 : 13
Horses' heels over paving, 806 : 12
Horseshoes, laws flung like h., 819 : 2
Horus non numero nisi serenas, 445 : 14
Hosannas, silver h. of rain, 852 : 14
Hose, youthful h. well saved, 211 : 15
Hospitable, in peace generous h., 463 : 13
on h. thoughts intent, 286 : 18
Hospital, redeemer in h. gown, 884 : 21
tray of narcotics, 887 : 10
whole earth our h., 807 : 19
world not inn but h., 274 : 21
Hospitality, given to h., 47 : 21
Host, Hesperus led starry h., 285 : 25
many an old h. damned, 204 : 6
of furious fancies, 918 : 12
of golden daffodils, 427 : 7
praise Him heavenly h., 311 : 19
though an h. should encamp, 18 : 12
tie of h. and guest, 71 : 17
time like fashionable h., 226 : 19
with angelic h. proclaim, 350 : 15
Hostage, you are eternity's h., 816 : 19
Hostages to fortune, 180 : 9
Hostess, reckoneth without his h., 159 : *n* 9
with mostes' on the ball, 802 : 13
Hostess', sits on horse at h. door, 201 : 15
Hostesses make parties as cabinets, 565 : 26
Hostile, universe not h. nor friendly, 764 : 16
Hostility, eternal h. against tyranny, 388 : 15
mad h. against institutions, 451 : 5
sorrow to disarm h., 511 : 19
uncompromising h., 860 : 2
Host's Canary wine, 477 : 16
Hosts, arms and God of h., 383 : 4
holy is the Lord of h., 29 : 9
Lord God of h., 709 : 16
Lord of h. King of glory, 18 : 10
of error, 694 : 15
Hot and bothered, 711 : 1
and cold and moist and dry, 284 : *n* 8
and rebellious liquors, 210 : 29
as hell, 400 : 15
blow h. and cold, 66 : 17
can one go upon h. coals, 23 : 14
cat on h. tin roof, 301 : *n* 3
cold and h. moist and dry, 284 : 27, 305 : 9
cold light and h. shade, 405 : 15
conscience seared with h. iron, 50 : 27
cross buns, 931 : 17
fair h. wench in taffeta, 202 : 23
for certainties, 600 : 20
ginger h. i' the mouth, 213 : 26
hammer iron when h., 110 : 25
haste, 457 : 17
heart's shell, 570 : 13
heat flow from h. to cold object, 589 : *n* 1

Hot (*continued*)
hissing h. from hell, 555 : 14
I would thou wert cold or h., 53 : 5
in my h. youth, 108 : 5
Just Add H. Water, 828 : 17
lead effective from linotype, 865 : 2
little pot and soon h., 188 : 36
long h. summer, 837 : 15
my heart was h. within me, 18 : 30
neither cold nor h., 53 : 5
pease-porridge h., 931 : 18
sleep is cold for the h., 171 : 1
small h. bird, 666 : 15
snake came on h. h. day, 790 : 12
so h. that it singe yourself, 248 : 22
temper leaps over, 198 : 10
time in old town tonight, 705 : 1
water to remain upon tea, 273 : 9
w'en stew smokin' h., 737 : 2
when iron is h. strike, 110 : *n* 16
which way h. air blows, 699 : 18
why sea boiling h., 613 : 5
your wit's too h., 190 : 22
Hotel, back to h. in rain, 844 : 17
great advantage of h., 680 : 11
instead of hymns, 768 : 23
long h. acutely white, 711 : 11
queen of this summer h., 908 : 8
refuge from home life, 680 : 11
smoke-filled room in h., 695 : 11
Hotels, big peppermint h., 888 : 9
people in h., 725 : 18
Hothouse, no h. flowers, 785 : 9
Hotness, day in its h., 585 : 12
Hotspur of the North, 203 : 26
Hotter, pass from colder to h., 589 : 14
Hound, footprints of gigantic h., 689 : 11
hold with hare run with h., 159 : 26
mongrel puppy whelp h., 369 : 17
my horse my h., 896 : 12
single h., 606 : 8
sleeping h. to wake, 144 : 21
Hounds and horn, 277 : 23
carcass fit for h., 215 : 20
four lean h., 828 : 10
join in glorious cry, 349 : 10
moon men and barking h., 831 : 16
noise like questing of thirty h., 149 : 7
of spring, 632 : 7
such h. such hawks, 927 : 4
with his h. and horn, 474 : 19
Hour before dawn silent, 759 : 10
books of the h., 573 : 2
childhood's h., 447 : 14, 525 : 5
Children's H., 512 : 3
cometh and now is, 44 : 36
County Guy h. is nigh, 432 : 9
crowded h., 495 : 4
crowded h. of glorious life, 375 : 1
dark h. or twain, 238 : 12
destined h., 516 : 10
eternity in an h., 406 : 8
every h. a miracle, 576 : 14
every h. that passes O, 409 : 14
fall that very h., 214 : 2
far fierce h. and sweet, 742 : 17
for one short h. see, 533 : 26
from h. to h. we ripe, 211 : 6
had I died h. before, 238 : 7
happiest day happiest h., 525 : 4
hazard of doubtful h., 204 : 29
I also had my h., 742 : 17

Hour (*continued*)
I have had my h., 305 : 2
I was born, 921 : 13
improve each shining h., 328 : 5
inevitable h., 362 : 3
is at hand, 41 : 14
is not yet come, 44 : 26
its h. come round at last, 714 : 13
last h. of my life, 346 : 2
laugh an h. by his dial, 211 : 7
lightning's h., 860 : 7
lives its little h., 471 : 9, 773 : 15
living at this h., 425 : 22
look on you when last h. comes, 112 : 27
look thy last every h., 739 : 17
Lord through this h., 924 : 15
matched us with His h., 797 : 2
met me in evil h., 409 : 9
more desirable than fortunate h., 102 : 9
nighing his h., 692 : 1
not an h. more or less, 235 : 9
not showpiece of an h., 80 : 15
nothing can bring back h., 426 : 21
now's the h., 411 : 15
o' night's black arch, 411 : 9
of adversity, 452 : 15
of departure has arrived, 83 : 15
of thoughtless youth, 423 : 13
of truth now always, 757 : 1
offspring of idle h., 636 : 10
one bare h. to live, 184 : 7
one dead deathless h., 601 : 17
one h. of life, 432 : 16
our h. is marked, 420 : 20
rash hand in evil h., 287 : 19
ripe, 206 : 32
self-approving h., 337 : 14
serve the future h., 429 : 1
single h. of that Dundee, 426 : 9
stay longer in h., 632 : 3
struts and frets his h., 240 : 4
takes away things, 355 : 24
that turns back longing of seafarers, 141 : 26
the wished the trysted h., 411 : 2
this was their finest h., 744 : 4
thou the day I the h., 628 : 14
time and the h., 236 : 13
torturing h., 361 : 13
uncertain h. before morning, 808 : 13
violet h., 805 : 7
watch with me one h., 41 : 13
what sweet h. yields, 470 : 4
when God sends cheerful h., 282 : 10
wherein man might be happy, 270 : 26
who drowsy at that h., 275 : 14
wonder of an h., 457 : 5
Hour's, never spent h. talk withal, 190 : 21
sleep before midnight, 270 : 19
Hours, age not numbered by h., 168 : 1
and minutes dollars and cents, 348 : *n* 1
arrest your course, 464 : 14
banishing for h., 376 : 3
better three h. too soon, 225 : 18
count only sunny h., 445 : *n* 3
creeping h. of time, 211 : 12
entertain lag-end with quiet h., 205 : 1

Hours (*continued*)
glorious h. even in poorhouse, 560 : 18
golden h. on angel wings, 410 : 18
his brief h. and weeks, 245 : 18
I once enjoyed, 375 : 15
I spent with thee, 700 : 13
lazy leaden-stepping H., 281 : 7
life short quiet h. few, 573 : 1
mournful midnight h., 395 : 2
narrowing dark h., 837 : 3
nor h. days months, 252 : 8
redeem these h., 257 : 17
seven h. to law, 172 : *n* 3
six h. in sleep, 172 : 6
sixteen h. ago Hiroshima, 787 : 13
sorrow breaks reposing h., 187 : 11
steal h. from night, 447 : 1
success unexpected in common h., 560 : 16
sweetest h. e'er I spend, 409 : 16
Time in h. days years, 299 : 6
to which heaven doth chime, 298 : 21
two golden h., 480 : 13
unless h. cups of sack, 202 : 23
waked by circling h., 286 : 25
weary of days and h., 633 : 20
what h. O what black h., 656 : 19
winged h. of bliss, 443 : 8
woman in our h. of ease, 431 : 2
House, all the h. of Israel played, 13 : 14
all through the h., 446 : 3
appointed for all living, 16 : 18
bear witness to his piety, 418 : 5
blessings on this h., 382 : 1
bodies but not souls, 782 : 15
built on sand, 38 : 21
built soul pleasure h., 528 : 6
by the side of the road, 57 : 32, 685 : 12
call upon my soul within the h., 213 : 18
child draws inscrutable h., 878 : 10
civilized man's h. prison, 557 : 4
clergyman so much about h., 620 : 11
covet thy neighbor's h., 10 : 7
crooked h., 932 : 18
daughter in mother's h., 709 : 15
daughters of my father's h., 214 : 6
divided against itself, 41 : 35, 520 : 4
doll in the doll's h., 549 : 33
doorkeeper in h. of my God, 20 : 8
dust inbreathed was h., 808 : 11
dwell in h. of the Lord, 18 : 7
eaten out of h. and home, 206 : 11
Eden old-fashioned h., 607 : 16
emperor in mine own h., 172 : *n* 2
empty h. like stray dog, 620 : 14
evil shall not depart from his h., 24 : 16
except the Lord build the h., 22 : 8
fell not, 38 : 20
fired that h. reject him, 338 : 7
for future prison for present, 886 : 3
from powerful fortressed h., 576 : 18
glass h. of German statecraft, 553 : 8
God erects h. of prayer, 318 : 5
great h. of Tarquin, 488 : 13
half of h. be pulled down, 701 : 13
harrow h. of dead, 868 : 4
he that troubleth own h., 23 : 27
he who sits at door of h., 935 : 12
heap of stones not h., 673 : 8
heart keeps open h., 873 : 2

House (*continued*)
hill and h. live together, 729 : 10
hog whole h., 892 : 20
I pass through on way, 902 : 2
in my Father's h., 45 : 20
in woodsman's h. knives wood, 935 : 14
is as fortress, 172 : 3
is in village though, 748 : 5
is of glass, 269 : 25
keepers of the h. shall tremble, 27 : 24
keeps his h. in hand, 74 : 19
kept h. the past and I, 641 : 22
let us go into the h. of the Lord, 22 : 5
lilting h., 886 : 19
lion in thy h., 35 : 3
little h. of my own, 774 : 1
little h. well filled, 347 : 8
lived in little h., 933 : 19
look at my dead h., 860 : 10
machine for living in, 798 : 4
made chimney in my father's h., 185 : 27
made of dawn, 928 : 18
make h. home, 774 : 4
make my h. your inn, 798 : 17
man so in way in h., 536 : 14
man's h. his castle, 172 : 2
master of the h. cometh, 42 : 14
Matilda and h. burned, 730 : 11
moat defensive to a h., 194 : 13
moon in seventh h., 914 : 7
must be a h. at least, 438 : 6
my Father's h. not h. of merchandise, 44 : 30
my h. called h. of prayer, 40 : 12
my h. horse hound, 896 : 12
my h. though small, 270 : 2
nae luck about the h., 382 : 10
no tool heard in h., 13 : 32
nor my h. now my h., 841 : 9
not a h. where there was not one dead, 9 : 28
of bondage, 9 : 29
of feasting, 27 : 4
of God, 8 : 21
of good stone, 792 : 20
of Have, 638 : 7
of marriage, 864 : 12
of mourning, 27 : 4
of Peers throughout war, 628 : 24
of prayer, 40 : 12, 318 : 5
of Representatives, 382 : 11
of the Lord, 22 : 5
of Usher, 525 : 19
of Want, 638 : 7
on fire children burn, 930 : 3
open h. in evening, 742 : 11
ornament of h. friends, 499 : 15
our h. a playroom, 599 : 10
out of the h. of bondage, 9 : 29
part of man's self, 648 : 17
peace to this h., 43 : 9
return no more to his h., 15 : 21
rich honesty in poor h., 213 : 3
rule his own h., 50 : 25
set h. on fire to roast eggs, 180 : 23
set thine h. in order, 14 : 21
seven-pillared worthy h., 810 : 2
shelters friend, 497 : 17
should be of hill, 729 : 10
sky flows into h., 843 : 5
small h. and large garden, 295 : 4

House (*continued*)
so fair a h., 247 : 24
sweet air coming into h., 798 : 8
Terror in h. does roar, 406 : 4
that Jack built, 934 : 9
them that join h. to h., 29 : 4
to be let for life, 267 : 14
to lodge friend, 339 : 10
upon another man's ground, 225 : 17
wandering about from h. to h., 50 : 32
we all dwell in h. of world, 637 : 21
we dwell in every day, 607 : 16
where I was born, 485 : 4
whose h. is glass, 269 : 25
wisdom hath builded her h., 23 : 18
with nobody in it, 620 : *n* 2
wounded in h. of my friends, 33 : 35
you take my h., 200 : 20
Housed where it gets possession, 188 : 8
Household, breathing h. laws, 425 : 15
keep h. in oneness, 59 : 28
of Impulse mourns, 868 : 15
permission to go out from h., 73 : 5
she looketh well to ways of her h., 26 : 9
Households, clergymen's h. unhappy, 620 : 11
Houseless heads and unfed sides, 234 : 3
Housemaids, damp souls of h., 804 : 5
Houses all gone under sea, 807 : 14
and farms pillaged, 379 : 2
build h. and inhabit them, 31 : 31
destroyed by rats, 312 : 25
devour widows' h., 42 : 12
great h. rain down, 74 : 20
mothers' wombs the tiring h., 173 : 1
nimble in selling h., 791 : 5
old h. mended, 325 : 1
people in glass h., 269 : *n* 3
plague o' both h., 193 : 6
signs of leaping h., 202 : 23
too new to be haunted, 910 : 15
ugly h. stand, 822 : 18
useful and beautiful in h., 618 : 9
very h. seem asleep, 425 : 14
Housetop, as a sparrow alone upon the h., 21 : 5
Housewife, here's to the h. that's thrifty, 399 : 1
holds fate of world in hands, 865 : 1
ply evening care, 362 : 1
Housewifery, players in your h., 230 : 8
Housewife's, tease the h. wool, 280 : 1
Housewives, good h. now may say, 262 : 14
in your beds, 230 : 8
mothers and h. vacationless, 867 : 8
Houston Tranquility Base here, 910 : 13
Hovel, golden mean avoids poverty of h., 107 : 20
Hover, o'er shady groves they h., 262 : 3
through fog and filthy air, 235 : 22
Hovered, tended while it h. nigh, 641 : 22
How and Where and Who, 710 : 2
can these things be, 44 : 33
do you do again, 934 : 2
feel to be on your own, 915 : 6
had I come to be here, 878 : 14
long Catiline, 98 : 1
many ages hence, 216 : 7
much more is half than whole, 61 : 14
How (*continued*)
never tell h. to do things, 792 : 2
not to do it, 549 : 19
question remains h., 481 : 9
should man be just, 15 : 23
Howard, left them my Lord H., 535 : 12
How-de-do, pretty h., 629 : 10
Howl howl howl howl, 235 : 16
Lady h. in Irish, 204 : 18
live with wolves h. like wolf, 934 : 15
same way for flesh of man, 912 : 9
scarcely a h. or groan, 614 : 2
Howled, cracked growled roared h., 434 : 11
Howling as of a hen-yard, 792 : 19
down the street, 931 : 13
flies in night in h. storm, 405 : 5
neither yield to h. of wolf, 177 : 17
no more hear tempest h., 393 : 11
village of H., 854 : 6
woe, 402 : 15
Howls hoo and rises, 768 : 12
Hub, Boston State-House h., 519 : 11
Hubbard, old mother H., 932 : 7
Hubbard's, cockerels in H. barns, 557 : 8
Huckleberry Finn, 845 : 5
Huddled masses, 664 : 10
Hudibras, bought H. again, 309 : 22
Hue, add another h. to rainbow, 202 : 5
cuckoo-buds of yellow h., 191 : 13
flowers of all h., 285 : 16
heaven presents solid h., 748 : 1
like when great painter dips, 466 : 14
native h. of resolution, 221 : 12
now turn different h., 67 : 4
raise a h. and cry, 169 : 10
shells of pearly h., 442 : 16
Huelga, viva la h., 906 : 17
Hues, rich h. marriage made, 654 : 16
Huffy Henry hid, 884 : 7
Hug dear deceit, 346 : 13
it in my arms, 228 : 18
Huge and birdless silence, 901 : 4
bed for this h. birth, 292 : 17
cloudy symbols, 478 : 18
ship's h. shadow, 434 : 28
so h. so hopeless, 607 : 18
walk under his h. legs, 215 : 6
Hugest hearts that break, 607 : 10
Leviathan h. of living, 286 : 30
Hugged and embraced by strumpet wind, 199 : 6
offender forgave offense, 307 : 7
Hugger-mugger to inter him, 223 : 26
Hulk, here a sheer h., 393 : 11
worm her h. shall bore, 558 : 10
Hull, Dakotas under her h., 822 : 7
water spurted through my h., 673 : 15
Hulls, ships are only h., 74 : 1
Hum, busy h. of men, 278 : 4
my ears h., 63 : 5
of either army, 208 : 1
of human cities torture, 457 : 28
of mighty workings, 475 : 8
still steeples h., 691 : 4
thousand instruments h., 248 : 10
Human, Adam was but h., 624 : 12
all h. life in monkeys and cats, 652 : 8
all h. must retrograde, 383 : 15
all right for woman to be h., 858 : 2
all that h. hearts endure, 352 : 21
alter h. nature, 695 : 14
Human (*continued*)
applause of single h. being, 356 : 17
as I am if I am, 894 : 8
awareness of being h., 860 : 13
bears stamp of h. condition, 165 : 18
behavior as relationship, 842 : 15
being crushed by books, 885 : 8
being h. born alone, 794 : 3
being h. though boys, 729 : 9
being item with skin wrapped around, 828 : 3
being more or less, 887 : 13
being portable plumbing, 816 : 12
being through descent from group, 685 : 7
beings in underground den, 84 : 17
beings into machines, 562 : 18
beings live and progress, 725 : 3
beings never more frightening, 867 : 16
benefit and enjoyment, 373 : 4
beside a h. door, 424 : 19
best work the h. mind, 410 : 16
bit of h. nature revolting, 597 : 8
body is sacred, 575 : 5
body politic like h. body, 358 : 16
build on h. heart, 540 : 12
burn books burn h. beings, 481 : 11
capacity of h. beings to comprehend, 884 : 6
chariot that bears h. soul, 607 : 4
civilization scarcely h., 732 : 10
civilized h. being, 755 : 3
combination or society, 273 : 11
community, 781 : 5, 861 : 7
compete not as woman but as h. being, 898 : 6
condition, 165 : 18
constant in h. sufferings, 777 : 17
contrivance of h. wisdom, 373 : 21
couple find true form, 870 : 12
course of h. events, 387 : 9
creatures' lives, 485 : 19
credit to h. race, 877 : 8
creeds root in human needs, 647 : 1
crises of h. affairs, 402 : 5
Cruelty has h. heart, 405 : 14
custom guide of h. life, 357 : 15
Declaration of H. Rights, 774 : 8
dignity, 916 : 12
distances between h. beings, 756 : 12
each h. gift find place, 853 : 15
earth's h. shores, 478 : 20
engine waits, 805 : 7
everything h. pathetic, 625 : 4
existence girt with mystery, 508 : 24
face divine, 285 : 5
faith in h. beings, 821 : 3
features composed of ten parts, 116 : 12
felicity produced by little advantages, 348 : 20
field of h. conflict, 744 : 6
fighting for h. rights, 904 : 15
figure interests me most, 728 : 10
find beautiful h. soul, 393 : 4
force h. beings to despise themselves, 853 : 10
four essential h. freedoms, 780 : 13
free the h. will, 340 : 2
functions and activities, 689 : 23
fundamental h. rights, 788 : 20
future of h. race, 758 : 8
gods created of h. spirit, 819 : 10

Human (*continued*)
good fortune to be born h., 313 : 6
happiness of h. race, 373 : 9
he served h. liberty, 716 : 6
heart break piecemeal, 557 : 1
heart by which we live, 426 : 23
heart has treasures, 555 : 17
hearts to chew, 468 : 6
highest type of h. nature, 579 : 21
hope springs in h. breast, 336 : 15
hopes and human creeds, 647 : 1
hum of h. cities, 457 : 28
I had no h. fears, 424 : 14
identify myself with something h., 885 : 10
in h. life much endured, 352 : 17
inextinguishable rights of h. nature, 418 : 1
informer poor weak h. being, 836 : 13
infringement of h. freedom, 412 : 4
Jealousy has a h. face, 405 : 14
kind not bear much reality, 806 : 20
king's might greater than h., 78 : 20
knowledge of h. nature, 440 : 29, 635 : 1
life a mansion, 479 : 11
life might be pure freedom, 870 : 8
life transient, 697 : 10
Love the h. form divine, 403 : 11
march of h. mind slow, 373 : 2
matter superbly h., 831 : 20
Mercy has a h. heart, 403 : 11
mice with wings wear h. face, 873 : 4
milk of h. kindness, 236 : 16
millions of h. beings, 720 : 3
moonlight, 901 : 14
more than h. arms, 775 : 3
music ministers to h. welfare, 579 : 15
my Treatise of H. Nature, 357 : 18
nature changes, 676 : 4
nature made arrogant by consideration, 81 : 7
nature not change, 524 : 2
nature weak in bookstore, 551 : 12
no h. being understand another, 859 : 8
no h. creature give orders to love, 504 : 8
no h. thing of importance, 85 : 9
no other difference between h. beings, 414 : 21
no themes so h., 653 : 15
noble happy h. beings, 572 : 19
nor h. spark is left, 340 : 28
nothing h. is alien, 96 : 7
O h. love, 525 : 2
observation of h. life, 565 : 15
observer of h. nature, 546 : 11
of h. bliss to h. woe, 290 : 8
on my faithless arm, 868 : 16
part of the h. race, 790 : 21
Peace the h. dress, 403 : 11
Pity has a h. face, 403 : 11
politics art of h. happiness, 706 : 21
pounces on h. core, 651 : 2
power cannot remove, 808 : 15
predatory h. hands, 690 : 10
primary h. affections, 585 : 19
principles of h. nature, 453 : 1
provide for h. wants, 373 : 21
pursuit of h. glory, 271 : 23
race born to fly upward, 142 : 2
race has means for annihilating itself, 775 : 13

Human (*continued*)
race never have rest from evils, 84 : 15
race organized like bees, 703 : 13
recognition as h. beings, 904 : 15
relations perfectly exhibited, 89 : 7
reverence h. nature, 448 : 3
rights, 788 : 20
rights over h. beings or monuments, 395 : 21
rights to which committed, 890 : 7
ruler having h. body as subject, 84 : 5
same with h. race, 760 : 10
scientific thought h. progress, 660 : 6
Secrecy the h. dress, 405 : 14
see h. soul take wing, 459 : 22
solitude at depth of h. condition, 885 : 17
sorrow of h. existence, 375 : 3
species of two races, 441 : 17
speech like cracked kettle, 583 : 11
stares from every h. face, 868 : 13
stars of h. race, 375 : 23
status not depend on economics, 775 : 5
stories repeat themselves, 738 : 14
subtlety never devise more than Nature, 152 : 12
success change h. mechanism, 859 : 19
suffering h. race, 585 : 3
sum of h. things, 393 : 13
tale of h. life, 375 : 3
tamer of h. breast, 361 : 13
Terror the h. form divine, 405 : 14
that can be accounted for, 769 : 1
the earth the h. race, 641 : 16
things subject to decay, 304 : 24
thought or form, 466 : 9
three words for h. race, 677 : 4
till h. nature came, 607 : 5
to err is h., 120 : 21, 133 : 22, 333 : 15
to love for being loved, 464 : 19
to step aside is h., 409 : 21
understanding is false mirror, 179 : 9
until man fully h., 819 : 12
vanity of h. hopes, 352 : 5
vast empire of h. society, 424 : 8
voices wake us, 804 : 1
weakness of h. mind, 308 : 9
wholeness of h. problem, 755 : 21
wisdom of h. contrivances, 372 : 15
women's training in h. relations, 853 : 19
Humane, harmonious and h. life, 589 : 7
heaven and earth are not h., 64 : 1
Humani nil a me alienum puto, 96 : *n* 8
Humanitarian, marches h., 574 : 5
Humanities, science and h., 871 : 1
Humanity, base metal of h., 664 : 17
common right of h., 520 : 8
exalts delights adorns h., 455 : 3
forehead of h., 475 : 21
has three enemies, 664 : 16
herein chivalry courtesy h., 149 : 5
history life of h., 602 : 8
i love you, 828 : 15
imitated h. so abominably, 222 : 3
justice and h., 725 : 20
justice equity, 373 : 18
law of h., 373 : 18
may come to end, 765 : 1
nothing real but h., 483 : 12

Humanity (*continued*)
one race, 671 : 5
only three days old, 758 : 8
reason and justice, 373 : 1
Religion of H., 508 : 26
science and art unite h., 904 : 18
slavery of half of h., 870 : 12
still sad music of h., 423 : 13
veined h., 506 : 14
victory for h., 480 : 14
wearisome condition of h., 175 : 5
with all its fears, 511 : 8
Humanity's, aggregate of h. experiences, 832 : 18
Humanizes, liberal arts study h., 114 : 2
Humanizing, power of h. nature, 437 : 22
whole body of society, 589 : 7
Humankind, good or bad for h., 427 : 24
lords of h. pass by, 369 : 1
not bear much reality, 806 : 20
of all tyrannies on h., 305 : 17
porcelain clay of h., 306 : 2
vices and follies of h., 324 : 6
Humble Allen, 339 : 14
and hearty thanks, 55 : 7
and sweet poverty, 899 : 16
appearance of telephone, 610 : 3
are usually envious, 308 : 18
as if pride not h., 545 : 26
be it ever so h., 465 : 4
cares delicate fears, 425 : 5
frowned not on h. birth, 362 : 17
grave adorned, 335 : 10
heyday in blood is h., 223 : 4
himself shall be exalted, 40 : 17
honor shall uphold the h., 25 : 33
livers in content, 248 : 27
members of society, 419 : 3
ne'er ebb to h. love, 231 : 18
pie, 549 : 4
reliefs of a h. art, 849 : 8
sin recognized keep us h., 856 : 18
soft meek patient h., 251 : 11
son of h. laborer, 774 : 9
the greater the more h., 34 : 24
through vainglory, 165 : 11
very h. person, 548 : 30
wisdom is h., 377 : 15
with lure of the real, 769 : 17
Humbleness, whispering h., 198 : 25
Humbler heaven, 336 : 16
read from some h. poet, 510 : 21
Humblest citizen of land, 694 : 15
friends, 429 : 11
highest to h. tasks, 745 : 11
peer of powerful, 615 : 1
Humbling, no h. of reality to precept, 905 : 11
Humbly beseech you of pardon, 231 : 3
dumbly, 778 : 6
walk h. with thy God, 33 : 23
Humbug, bah h., 548 : 5
government of H. or Humdrum, 501 : 14
Humdrum, government of Humbug or H., 501 : 14
passage might be h., 685 : 14
Humiliation, Negro past of h., 903 : 2
peace accepted in h., 682 : 9
valley of H., 302 : 2
Humility a thing commendable, 159 : *n* 11
a virtue all preach, 263 : 14

Humility (*continued*)
angling like virtue of h., 271 : 1
bear success with h., 665 : 1
before honor is h., 24 : 10
for acclaim earned in blood, 815 : 13
is endless, 807 : 13
modest stillness and h., 207 : 16
most difficult virtue, 809 : 10
pride that apes h., 435 : 17, 440 : 15
proud in h., 259 : 1
sense of reverence, 77 : 10
where there is h., 138 : 14
Hummock's, ants upon h. crown, 558 : 19
Humor, according as man is you must h. him, 97 : 5
awe man from career of his h., 209 : 19
call it h. when they gibe, 322 : 19
is a drug, 630 : 10
liveliest effusions of h., 440 : 29
most when she obeys, 335 : 23
no h. in heaven, 625 : 4
one has sense of h., 799 : 7
only test of gravity, 325 : *n* 3
prelude to faith, 823 : 19
saves a few steps, 799 : 7
source of h. sorrow, 625 : 4
that's the h. of it, 207 : 12
third glass for good h., 326 : 18
unconscious h., 620 : 19
unyoked h. of idleness, 203 : 5
woman in this h. wooed, 187 : 3
Humored, played with and h., 302 : 19
Humorous sadness, 212 : 18
very beadle to h. sigh, 190 : 25
Humors, gather h. of men daily, 301 : 6
hobbies and h., 704 : 2
Hump, cameelious h., 710 : 1
haunch and h. is Obey, 709 : 6
that is black and blue, 710 : 1
whale's white h., 570 : 13
without a positive h., 539 : 5
Humpty Dumpty, 932 : 2
when I use word said H., 613 : 16
Hums, beetle with drowsy h., 238 : 20
Hun is at the gate, 710 : 23
Huncamunca O, 345 : *n* 7
Hunching wings and beak, 892 : 4
Hundred, a few h. scrawls, 786 : 11
at three h. pence ointment prize, 268 : 11
buyer needs a h. eyes, 270 : 1
daughter of h. earls, 528 : 7
father more than h. schoolmasters, 270 : 11
first h. days, 890 : 10
first h. years hardest, 757 : 12
fourteen h. years ago nailed, 202 : 22
had I a h. tongues, 105 : 20
if very angry count h., 390 : 4
of three h. grant three, 461 : 6
one h. years hence, 498 : 17
percent American, 681 : 19
ran a h. years to a day, 519 : 15
rode the six h., 533 : 9
ten jokes a h. enemies, 359 : 21
thousand thrained men, 786 : 11
thousand to that h., 266 : 10
to that twenty add h. more, 266 : 10
touch a h. flowers, 822 : 15
victory finds a h. fathers, 857 : 11
while one might tell a h., 218 : 22
wi' a h. pipers an' a', 417 : 7
Hundredfold, brought forth fruit h., 39 : 15
Hun-dred-mil-lion-oth-ers 829 : 2
Hundred's soon hit, 542 : 19
Hung aloft the night, 478 : 20
among cloudy trophies h., 478 : 1
be heavens with black, 184 : 15
here h. those lips, 224 : 14
with bloom along bough, 690 : 16
Hunger and thirst after righteousness, 37 : 4
bodily h. in eyes, 680 : 29
fer 'em somehow, 774 : 4
filth and ignorance, 814 : 8
for self-approval, 626 : 3
God is war peace surfeit h., 70 : 2
he that cometh to me shall never h., 44 : 41
I am h., 912 : 7
I offer h. thirst battles, 509 : 7
mouth and belly injured by h., 89 : 27
no fear stand up to h., 683 : 18
no patience wear h. out, 683 : 18
no sauce like h., 170 : 2
they shall h. no more, 53 : 16
toil h. nakedness, 481 : 2
weak evils age and h., 211 : 14
when done with h. rich and poor as one, 77 : 3
Hungered and ye gave meat, 40 : 33
Hungering neighbor and me, 567 : 14
Hungry and he gave him meat, 367 : 3
as grave, 345 : 6
ate when we were not h., 322 : 15
clouds swag, 403 : 18
cloy h. edge of appetite, 194 : 7
cold comfort to fill h. bellies, 265 : 11
for life and death, 886 : 8
generations, 477 : 1
hag and h. goblin, 918 : 11
he hath filled h., 42 : 23
if thine enemy be h., 25 : 15
judges the sentence sign, 334 : 6
lean and h. look, 215 : 8
makes h. where most satisfies, 241 : 1
man not free, 851 : 11
ocean gain advantage, 244 : 22
Pinch a h. lean-faced villain, 188 : 15
poor, 621 : 16
rich when he is h., 86 : *n* 5
sheep look up, 280 : 22
show you h. person, 916 : 1
sleep is meat to h., 171 : 1
soul, 25 : 24
squalid population, 596 : 2
stomach cannot hear, 296 : 21
tigers getting h., 743 : 13
Hungry-looking, fear pale and h. men, 99 : 25
Hunt gunless game, 685 : 11
in fields for health, 306 : 26
it in the dark, 376 : 10
love down together, 633 : 13
Hunted and penned in inglorious spot, 819 : 5
freedom h. round globe, 384 : 12
little h. hares, 732 : 16
past reason h., 245 : 23
Hunter, Bahram that great h., 516 : 11
Esau was a cunning h., 8 : 15
heart lonely h., 677 : 5, 894 : 12
home from hill, 668 : 20
lo h. of east caught, 516 : 1
man is the h., 531 : 6
Hunter (*continued*)
Nimrod the mighty h., 8 : 4
Hunters who hunt gunless game, 685 : 11
woods for h. of dreams, 685 : 11
Hunting, ain't 'unting as 'urts 'un, 660 : 14
daddy's gone a-h., 931 : 5
daren't go a-h., 594 : 2
passion for h. something, 547 : 2
upon St. David's Day, 933 : 6
we will go, 349 : 10
weary wi' h., 927 : 8
Huntlie, true Thomas on H. Bank, 926 : 23
Huntress, queen and h., 255 : 12
Hunts, at night hippopotamus h., 804 : 20
in dreams, 529 : 21
on a lonely hill, 677 : 5
Huntsman, as h. his pack, 371 : 19
winds his horn, 349 : 10
Huntsmen are up in America, 275 : 14
three jolly h., 933 : 6
three jovial h., 349 : *n* 4
Hurdygurdies make tune their own, 662 : 18
Hurdy-gurdy and a memory, 751 : 4
Hurled headlong flaming, 283 : 4
in ruin and confusion h., 325 : 11
into ruin h., 336 : 14
world and her train h., 299 : 6
Hurlyburly's, when the h. done, 235 : 21
Hurrah for old Kentuck, 454 : 13
for revolution, 717 : 12
Last H., 895 : 9
my boys we're homeward bound, 935 : 1
we bring the Jubilee, 614 : 14
Hurricane of black doves, 841 : 17
sired by h., 623 : 4
Hurricanes hardly ever happen, 894 : 20
trembling with h., 721 : 3
Hurricanoes, cataracts and h., 233 : 24
Hurry, always in haste never in h., 346 : 10
don't h. don't worry, 821 : 4
Nature will h. back, 109 : 4
sick h. divided aims, 586 : 1
to see your lady, 4 : 10
up please its time, 805 : 5
Hurrying, delaying not h. not, 575 : 18
parted by h. world, 424 : 3
shapes met face to face, 626 : 21
Hurt, balm of h. minds, 237 : 21
enemy and friend h. you, 625 : 16
give delight and h. not, 248 : 10
he who shall h. wren, 406 : 11
if I don't h. her, 449 : 14
isn't h. that counts, 718 : 17
man keenest in self-love, 599 : 3
more afraid than h., 159 : 12
no h. found upon Daniel, 33 : 4
not the earth, 53 : 13
panics produce as much good as h., 384 : 14
power to h., 245 : 4
somebody'll get h., 912 : 15
sweareth to his own h., 17 : 23
that Honor feels, 529 : 23
the little wren, 406 : 11
their health it might h., 371 : 22
they h. me I grow older, 792 : 9

Hurt (*continued*)
they shall not h. nor destroy, 29 : 19
things that help with things that h., 653 : 15
too badly h. to laugh, 522 : 9
why should I h. thee, 360 : 6
Hurtles in darkened air, 363 : 10
Hurtless breaks, 235 : 3
Hurts, fellows it h. to think, 691 : 17
it h. my hand, 231 : 23
pinch which h. and is desired, 242 : 3
some h. you cured, 495 : 18
truth never h. teller, 545 : 18
Husband and wife keep a household, 59 : 28
any her h. rather than Christian, 200 : 16
at all times faithful h., 327 : 9
being h. whole-time job, 720 : 14
chaste to her h., 335 : 18
delight of h. aunts infant, 810 : 20
detested first h., 675 : 5
doth safely trust in her, 26 : 6
easier to be lover than h., 484 : 10
frae wife despises, 411 : 5
give you h. and home, 59 : 28
holy city adorned for h., 53 : 29
is known in the gates, 26 : 7
light wife heavy h., 201 : 7
lover in h. lost, 357 : 9
man-o'-war's 'er h., 709 : 8
no worse a h. than best of men, 240 : 28
shape a h. out of, 539 : *n* 2
sovereignty over h., 147 : 14
till h. cools, 335 : 23
virtuous woman a crown to her h., 23 : 28
with beard, 209 : 4
woman oweth duty to h., 189 : 6
Husbanded, so fathered and so h., 215 : 24
Husbandman waiteth for precious fruit, 52 : 4
Husbandry, edge of h., 219 : 2
in heaven, 237 : 10
ye are God's h., 48 : 4
Husband's, level in her h. heart, 214 : 1
Husbands at chirche dore hadde fyve, 146 : 7
friends lovers h., 392 : 10
think of fidelity not h., 777 : 5
unlimited power into hands of h., 392 : 7
Hush hark deep sound strikes, 457 : 14
my dear, 328 : 8
with setting moon, 533 : 22
Hushed be every thought, 429 : 7
in grim repose, 363 : 6
in silence h. his soul, 428 : 15
now air is h., 364 : 12
till it is h. and smooth, 475 : 18
Husk of young stars, 886 : 15
Husks, dead h. of life, 869 : 13
strewed with h., 227 : 4
Husky, old h. nurse, 575 : 22
stormy h. brawling, 761 : 4
Hustings, world's h., 570 : 12
Hustle, tried to h. the East, 707 : 20
Hustled, Indian summer never h., 635 : 21
Hut, love in h., 476 : 5
only in h. live without fears, 138 : 2
Huzzas, loud h., 337 : 14
Hyacinth, breasts like h., 841 : 10
hair, 525 : 9
sell bread and buy h., 133 : 1
the garden wears, 516 : 12
Hyacinths are dark too, 103 : 23
to feed thy soul, 133 : *n* 1
Hybla, words rob H. bees, 217 : 8
Hybrid, Alexandria a h., 880 : 5
Hyde, Dr. Jekyll and Mr. H., 668 : 15
Hydra, monstrosity more prodigious than H., 108 : *n* 14
Hydrant, talking is a h. in the yard, 750 : 9
Hydroptic earth hath drunk, 252 : 25
Hyena, man who sold h. skin, 746 : 4
song of siren nor voice of h., 177 : 17
Hyla breed shouted in mist, 747 : 14
Hylas, je ne vous aime pas H., 319 : *n* 9
Hylax barks in doorway, 103 : 18
Hymn Brahmin sings, 495 : 12
chants doleful h., 202 : 16
sober as a h., 663 : 7
Hymns, chanting faint h. to moon, 195 : 20
hotel instead of h., 768 : 23
of praise to life, 801 : 7
psalms h. and spiritual songs, 49 : 37
that fall out of wind, 768 : 23
to thee morning h. ascended, 597 : 17
Hyperboles, three-piled h., 191 : 9
Hyperion to a satyr, 218 : 7
Hyperion's curls, 223 : 3
Hyphenated Americanism, 688 : 1
Americans, 688 : 1
Hypocrisies, some great events some mean h., 381 : 13
Hypocrisy, base alloy of h., 520 : 2
Christian without h., 591 : 11
democracies cannot dispense with h., 802 : 15
drowns in Pharisees' h., 816 : 18
from pride vainglory and h., 55 : 10
has ample wages, 156 : 4
homage vice pays to virtue, 293 : 27
of bishop, 391 : 2
organized h., 501 : 23
panics touchstone of h., 384 : 14
speaking lies in h., 50 : 27
vice of vices, 866 : 10
world safe for h., 852 : 10
Hypocrite falls into sin, 128 : 18
lecteur, 580 : *n* 4, 580 : 16
reader, 580 : 16
rotten to the core, 866 : 10
scoundrel h. flatterer, 407 : 6
sometimes more sometimes less, 484 : 14
thou h., 38 : 10
Hypocrites, cant of h. the worst, 360 : 11
effect of coercion to make h., 387 : 15
not h. in sleep, 445 : 18
scribes and Pharisees h., 40 : 18
Hypocritic days, 495 : 5
Hypotheses, I frame no h., 313 : 11
starting from initial h., 696 : 12
Hypothesis, evidence never prove h., 880 : 8
fertile h., 887 : 15
no need of that h., 397 : 19
vision of something new, 880 : 10
whatever not deduced is h., 313 : 11
Hyrcan tiger, 238 : 28
Hyssop, purge me with h., 19 : 15
Hysterias trench confessions, 792 : 15
Hysterica passio, 233 : 17
Hysterical, starving h. naked, 906 : 1

I

I accept the universe, 536 : 13
am, 9 : 14, 437 : 11
am a Jew, 199 : 17
am a Liberal, 588 : 14
am a Roman citizen, 98 : 4
am Actaeon, 113 : 18
am Alpha and Omega, 53 : 33
am become death, 861 : *n* 2
am Davos not Oedipus, 96 : 4
am dying Egypt dying, 241 : 21
am Fortune's fool, 193 : 7
am from Missouri, 674 : 13
am guilty of corruption, 179 : 11
am he that liveth, 52 : 32
am I you are you, 542 : 11
am innocent of the blood, 41 : 22
Am Jehovah said, 365 : 6
am master of my fate, 663 : 11
am no more I, 841 : 9
am not as other men, 43 : 39
am not what I was, 108 : 10
am only guinea pig I have, 832 : 14
am only one, 590 : 5
am quite myself again, 691 : 2
am rising to a man's work, 125 : 1
am Sir Oracle, 198 : 2
am that I am, 9 : 14
am that which began, 634 : 4
am the androgyne, 910 : 6
am the bread of life, 44 : 41
am the door, 45 : 9
am the good shepherd, 45 : 11
am the grass, 761 : 6
am the greatest, 915 : 10
am the light of the world, 45 : 4
am the Lord thy God, 10 : 3
am the people, 761 : 3
am the resurrection, 45 : 13
am the state, 312 : 1, 420 : 11
am the way, 45 : 22
am what I am, 48 : 28
am whatever was or is, 120 : 20
am with both, 201 : 22
am with you always, 41 : 31
am woman, 915 : 9
am yet what who cares, 470 : 8
and my Annabel Lee, 527 : 8
and so do I, 642 : 6
and you and all of us, 216 : 25
another I, 91 : 18
art is I science is we, 552 : 4
become transparent eyeball, 496 : 4
believe and take it, 164 : 4
bring you good tidings, 42 : 28
bucket full of tears am I, 195 : 11
but what am I, 532 : 10
came I saw I conquered, 99 : 23
came saw and overcame, 206 : 28
can no more, 656 : 15
cannot explain the sadness, 481 : 7
can't go on, 910 : 3
cleave wood there am I, 126 : 14
did it with hatchet, 378 : *n* 9
do my thing, 827 : 19
don't know is on third, 832 : 3
Eve and I, 541 : 22
even as you and I, 709 : 14

I (*continued*)
fashioned myself sorcerer, 674 : 8
feel it and am in torment, 102 : 17
get a kick out of you, 820 : 3
have a dream, 909 : 9, 909 : 10
have found it, 93 : 4
have liberated my soul, 136 : 10
have lived my day, 108 : *n* 7
have not begun to fight, 394 : 4
have somewhat against thee, 52 : 33
he was he and I was I, 164 : 14
hear America singing, 574 : 2
heir of all ages, 530 : 7
here am I, 12 : 29
hid from Him, 693 : 10
in twelve thousand none, 195 : 10
infinite I am, 437 : 11
it is I, 39 : 27
John, 52 : 27
King and I, 833 : 17
knew him when, 732 : 15
know not the man, 41 : 18
know thee not old man, 206 : 36
letting I dare not, 237 : 2
live I let myself live, 843 : 7
Lord is it I, 41 : 8
man in the moon, 197 : 17
Muses' priest sing, 107 : 25
myself am hell, 893 : 7
myself on tilting planet, 811 : 13
once utter the I, 636 : 6
one alone I am with him, 126 : 14
profound I, 824 : 6
reader I married him, 555 : 19
red I green U, 673 : 20
rock fly as soon as I, 431 : 13
said the sparrow, 930 : 9
says the Quarterly, 462 : 11
see an America, 909 : *n* 4
shall return, 771 : 3
sing of brooks, 265 : 17
sleep alone, 63 : 8
so presently must I, 856 : 6
stand at the door and knock, 53 : 6
stranger and afraid, 691 : 23
struck the board, 268 : 21
survived, 394 : 9
the more fool I, 210 : 32
the sole unbusy thing, 436 : 9
then Roman now I, 691 : 7
think therefore I am, 272 : 10
Tiresias, 805 : 7
to die and you to live, 83 : 15
told you so, 462 : 1
too have lived in Arcadia, 133 : *n* 9
treated him God cured him, 162 : 9
want to be alone, 863 : 2
was you baby, 910 : 2
wasted time now doth time waste me, 195 : 17
went to the woods, 559 : 25
What am I Life, 760 : 21
who saw face of God, 183 : 21
will be good, 573 : 14
will be heard, 505 : 13
will move the earth, 93 : 5
Iacta alea est, 99 : *n* 14
Iago, delight in conceiving I., 479 : 17
pity of it I., 231 : 25
Iam ver egelidos refert tepores, 102 : *n* 1
Iambics, not escape my i., 102 : 20
what little i., 728 : 4
Ibycus, cranes of I., 65 : *n* 8
Ice and iron not be welded, 669 : 16
beneath sun's rays, 313 : 7
between Eliza and pursuer, 538 : 21
caves of i., 433 : 25
chaste as i., 221 : 17
emperor of i. cream, 766 : 25
fire and i. within fight, 691 : 6
for destruction would suffice, 748 : 2
into eternal darkness fire and i., 140 : 19
mast-high, 434 : 10
on hot stove, 750 : 4
seek i. in June, 456 : 15
silent language of peak, 812 : 2
skating over thin i., 497 : 23
smooth the i., 202 : 5
thick-ribbed i., 228 : 20
trust not one night's i., 270 : 3
was here ice was there, 434 : 11
Ice cream, enjoy i. while it's on plate, 839 : 15
Iceberg cuts facets from within, 878 : 2
write on principle of i., 845 : 13
Icebergs behoove the soul, 878 : 3
hailstones on i., 569 : 20
Ice-blue orbs shivering above, 860 : 8
Iced, charity scrimped and i., 659 : 8
Iceland, from Rome to I., 311 : 12
Ich am of Irlonde, 916 : 16
weiss nicht was soll es bedeuten, 481 : *n* 7
Ichabod, named the child I., 12 : 32
Icicle, chaste as the i., 242 : 23
on Dutchman's beard, 214 : 18
Icicles, silent i., 435 : 15
when i. hang by the wall, 191 : 14
Icily regular, 533 : 17
Icumen, sumer is i. in, 916 : 14
winter is i. in, 792 : 8
Icy arms hold hidden charms, 834 : 5
bound in i. chains, 229 : *n* 1
current compulsive course, 231 : 18
death lays i. hand on kings, 272 : 15
principles of i. certainty, 700 : 2
reason's i. intimations, 486 : 2
silence of tomb, 478 : 8
took his i. hand, 556 : 15
Id, ego to i. as rider to horse, 678 : 14
where i. was there ego be, 678 : 16
world superego and i., 678 : 15
Ida, mother many-fountained I., 528 : 4
Idea, absolute i. of knowledge, 85 : 12
angry opposition to i., 755 : 4
antiquated was once modern, 750 : 14
ashamed of divine i., 496 : 20
between i. and reality, 805 : 17
Christianity is an i., 481 : 15
communicates emotion, 698 : 7
conveyed but by symbol, 437 : 6
dangerous when only one, 724 : 7
different i. of things we know, 735 : 18
does not belong to soul, 639 : 6
due to individual, 774 : 2
emotion communicates i., 698 : 7
every i. an incitement, 645 : 5
every thing has determinate i., 85 : 13
for poetry i. everything, 589 : 5
get at it as i., 768 : 3
governing i. of Hellenism, 588 : 21
grant artist his i., 652 : 15
is the fact, 589 : 5
made true by events, 650 : 11
Idea (*continued*)
man to whom i. occurs, 662 : 3
men die i. does not, 895 : 8
nothing more dangerous than i., 724 : 7
O the i. was childish, 412 : 15
of freedom, 537 : 15
of sun, 768 : 8
of what true and false, 308 : 7
one i. and that wrong, 354 : 21
original i. animate nation, 536 : 10
pain of a new i., 597 : 3
psychology give different i., 735 : 18
right i. of the gods, 86 : 4
see clearly in i. of it, 768 : 8
sends us back to first i., 768 : 11
teach young i. to shoot, 345 : 11
truth happens to i., 650 : 11
when i. new its custodians have fervor, 697 : 17
whose time come, 491 : 11
with image, 437 : 17
Ideal, Christian i. difficult, 742 : 2
direction toward i. object, 508 : 26
higher than ordinary man, 586 : 17
life i. or reverse, 689 : 23
Milton attracts into his i., 437 : 19
of happiness, 504 : 13
polity, 84 : 16
reduction to atoms chimerical i., 636 : 16
to be right by instinct, 74 : 22
ultimate i., yet hopeless, 697 : 9
union fervor with measure, 651 : 4
Idealism shoved aside, 698 : 9
spark of i. fanned, 678 : 4
Idealist, people call me i., 682 : 16
Idealistic, America only i. nation, 682 : 16
motives, 698 : 9
Idealists and planners, 719 : 11
difficult to find, 719 : 11
heroes as well as i., 643 : 19
Idealize, imagination struggles to i., 437 : 12
Ideals, higher i. revolutionary, 649 : 17
I have three i., 665 : 1
like stars, 603 : 2
of Marxism, 834 : 7
tell i. by advertisements, 724 : 11
two warring i. in body, 724 : 17
Ideas, best i. common property, 114 : 17
burst forth, 616 : 1
cemetery of dead i., 705 : 15
conditioned by time, 698 : 6
dangerous for good or evil, 783 : 16
dead i. and beliefs, 599 : 15
divine i. below, 494 : 9
does away with i. of things, 85 : 13
experiments to control i., 552 : 6
free trade in i., 645 : 1
from America plain i., 616 : 1
greatest artist greatest i., 572 : 8
have rate of growth, 620 : 20
history of i., 720 : 2
I go to bed with i., 672 : 6
make best i. prevail, 586 : 20
man of nasty i., 322 : 5
matter and i., 586 : 14
patterns made with i., 758 : 7
poem words not i., 651 : 17
realize i. of intellect, 436 : 17
ruling i. of each age, 563 : 9
stand for experience, 703 : 4

Ideas (*continued*)
structure of i. not half built, 887 : 17
that are least truly ours, 688 : 6
to literature what light is to painting, 670 : 9
too revolutionary for old i., 787 : 14
two opposed i. at same time, 835 : 10
won't keep, 697 : 17
world of i. world of practice, 586 : 21
Idelogy, enemy of market not i., 872 : 3
Idem velle atque idem nolle, 102 : *n* 13
Identify myself with something human, 885 : 10
themselves with the people, 390 : 2
Identity crisis, 854 : *n* 2
poet has no i., 479 : 18
preserve and cultivate i., 489 : 18
provides ability to experience self, 854 : 5
single hound its own i., 606 : 8
Ideologies, excitement as to alien i., 836 : 16
Ideology, technology not i., 872 : 1
Ides are on fifteenth day, 162 : *n* 3
of March, 99 : 21, 215 : 2
Idiocy during panic, 871 : 3
Idiot, beauteous i. speaks, 919 : 19
law ass i., 547 : 6
nature's lay i., 253 : 17
ninety-nine percent i., 681 : 19
tale told by an i., 240 : 4
to generalize is to be i., 405 : 16
who praises, 629 : 7
Idiotic child, 695 : 14
Idiot's, playing I. Delight, 836 : 15
Idiots, general knowledges i. possess, 405 : 16
hire i. to paint, 405 : 15
Idle and false imposition, 230 : 24
as painted ship, 434 : 14
be a gentleman be i., 177 : 15
be not solitary be not i., 260 : 6
biologically speaking, 823 : 1
ceremony, 208 : *n* 1
chatter, 628 : 6
children of an i. brain, 191 : 24
gloomy calm of i. vacancy, 354 : 18
hands, 328 : 6
if i. be not solitary, 356 : 13
if solitary be not i., 356 : 13
in i. wishes fools stay, 400 : 7
little profits i. king, 529 : 6
man and he who has done much, 58 : 9
manners not i., 534 : 21
mind knows not what it wants, 95 : 5
mock air with i. state, 363 : 4
neither i. nor overworked, 618 : 10
never less i. than wholly i., 99 : 1
no occupation all men i., 247 : 26
not i. because absorbed, 491 : 23
on i. days mutinous and quarrelsome, 348 : 21
pass by me as i. wind, 217 : 2
singer of empty day, 618 : 6
spear and shield, 277 : 8
starvation of the i., 579 : 7
tears, 531 : 3
they learn to be i., 50 : 32
time lost in i. company, 309 : 20
unnumbered i. pebbles, 234 : 28
why stand we here i., 383 : 5
with impunity, 452 : 18
words as i. tales, 44 : 14
Idleness and lack of occupation, 80 : 7
and pride tax heavier, 348 : 3
appendix to nobility, 258 : 18
best thing to ruin foolish, 118 : 19
bread of i., 26 : 9
egotism sloth i., 452 : 2
evils of i. shaken off by work, 114 : 24
invention arises from i., 817 : 15
no i. no procrastination, 593 : *n* 1
polished i., 416 : 15
refuge of weak minds, 342 : 6
sorrow friend foe, 827 : 8
unyoked humor of i., 203 : 5
wine cause of i., 316 : 13
Idler, work harder yet thought i., 713 : 1
Idlers and cowards at home, 929 : 3
Idling, enjoy i. if work to do, 692 : 16
Idly bent on him that enters next, 195 : 15
fingers wandered i., 596 : 13
not i. stand aside, 81 : 5
Idol ceremony, 208 : 6
or noble true birth, 85 : 16
superannuated i., 326 : 11
thou the i. I the throng, 628 : 14
Idolater, believing slave better than i., 130 : 12
Idolatries, bowed to its i., 458 : 3
Idolatry, curiosity becomes i., 861 : 10
god of my i., 192 : 12
has ample wages, 156 : 4
know neither sect nor i., 151 : 5
mad i., 226 : 8
Mass the highest i., 156 : 6
on this side i., 257 : 1
speak of ancients without i., 341 : 23
Idols, cast his i. to the moles, 28 : 32
four classes of i., 179 : 8
I have loved so long, 517 : 10
learn to dissolve i., 886 : 4
of the tribe, 179 : 8
poetry purged of i., 735 : 13
shouldn't maltreat our i., 583 : 13
which beset men's minds, 179 : 8
If is the only peacemaker, 213 : 5
pondering repose of I., 571 : 4
Iffucan, Chieftain I. of Azcan, 767 : 5
Ifs eternally, 571 : 4
Ignacio, not see blood of I., 841 : 16
Ignem, nubibus i., 115 : *n* 12
Ignis fatuus of mind, 315 : 19
Ignobilis otii, 104 : *n* 6
Ignoble ease, 104 : 13, 686 : 12
ease and peaceful sloth, 284 : 13
government play i. part, 645 : 10
peace, 687 : 4
strife, 362 : 12
Ignobly vain and impotently great, 334 : 14
Ignominious, fear of i. death, 414 : 17
more i. to mistrust, 293 : 15
Ignominy of boyhood, 716 : 1
of our natures, 274 : 12
of popular applause, 670 : 11
sleep with thee, 205 : 12
Ignorance, abstain from i., 552 : 1
alike in i., 337 : 2
ambition or ineptitude, 771 : 2
and blindness, 839 : 14
and passion foes of morality, 580 : 14
art hath enemy called I., 255 : 9
best riches i. of wealth, 370 : 1
better to hide i., 70 : 10
Ignorance (*continued*)
blind and naked i., 534 : 10
brings nearer death, 806 : 15
cholera typhus i., 773 : 8
cloud of i., 839 : 14
depth of i. about nature, 884 : 5
Gothic i., 349 : 21
greater i. greater dogmatism, 664 : 11
hunger filth and i., 814 : 8
ignorant of i., 128 : 5, 484 : 8
in form of inert facts, 635 : 14
in which born, 360 : 26
intense loneliness and i., 677 : 3
know nothing except my i., 79 : 5
knowledge brings nearer i., 806 : 15
madame pure ignorance, 354 : 3
man ever in darkness of i., 132 : 4
mistakes made by writers from i., 95 : 18
mother I. lives, 251 : 8
mother of devotion, 259 : 23
never makes allowance for i., 595 : 12
never settles question, 502 : 6
no sin but i., 183 : 11
not innocence, 545 : 21
nothing more terrible than i. 397 : 11
of the law, 263 : 17
of those who practice medicine, 80 : 4
one evil i., 79 : 3
opinion begets i., 80 : 5
pity his i., 547 : 11
plays chief part, 125 : 26
preferable to error, 387 : 12
profound sense of i., 572 : 9
putting us to i. again, 543 : 25
sedate, 352 : 1
the only slavery, 615 : 12
theory helps bear i., 703 : 4
toboggans into know, 830 : 3
understand writer's i., 437 : 9
vagueness perhaps i., 577 : 8
way of i., 807 : 18
where i. is bliss, 361 : 12
where i. prevails, 556 : 14
Ignorant armies clash by night, 587 : 16
be not i. of anything, 35 : 7
become i. man again, 768 : 8
better i. than half know, 112 : 9
blind and i. in all, 251 : 6
eye, 768 : 8
far rather be i., 70 : 21
illumination of i., 380 : 8
in spite of experience, 350 : 16
learned fool more foolish than i. one, 298 : 15
loved and were i., 716 : 20
malady of i., 484 : 8
many i. men are sure, 684 : 10
nation i. and free, 389 : 11
not that men are i., 724 : 16
of his understanding, 437 : 9
of ignorance, 128 : 5, 484 : 8
of ourselves, 240 : 26
of what he's most assured, 228 : 10
only i. despise education, 111 : 23
science teaches to be i., 705 : 16
taught to doubt, 644 : 18
we are i. about nature, 884 : 5
Ignorantly read, 333 : 19
Ignore, men of ill judgment i. good, 73 : 15
Ignoring all you reject, 500 : 8
I-ity, annihilate my I., 489 : 16
Île triste et noire, 581 : *n* 3

Iliction, supreme coort follows i., 721 : 12
tu-rrned into angels be i., 722 : 12
Ilion, cloud-kissing I., 189 : 26
Ilium, O fatherland O I., 104 : 35
topless towers of I., 184 : 4
I'll not budge an inch, 188 : 23
Ill, as i. luck would have it, 225 : *n* 2
avenues of i., 495 : 3
benefit of i., 245 : 20
best things confused with i., 466 : 17
can he rule the great, 174 : 2
captive good attending captain i., 244 : 25
cook that cannot lick fingers, 193 : 20
deeds doubled with evil word 188 : 10
fares the land, 369 : 30
fit instruments of i., 334 : 9
good better made by i., 180 : *n* 2
good final goal of i., 532 : 9
habits gather by degrees, 307 : 2
how i. white hairs become fool, 206 : 36
larger bill for darker i., 562 : *n* 2
layer-up of beauty, 208 : 19
love pressed with i., 377 : 20
luck seldom alone, 169 : 2
maintain no i. opinions, 370 : *n* 3
malice or i. will, 418 : 6
means to do i. deeds, 202 : 11
men of i. judgment ignore good, 73 : 15
men whom men condemn as i., 646 : 5
met by moonlight, 196 : 13
mingled yarn good and i., 227 : 16
ne'er wants occasion, 269 : 16
not lived i. who passed unknown, 109 : 8
not speak i. of another, 132 : 8
nothing becomes him i., 190 : 20
nothing i. can dwell in such temple, 247 : 24
policy in Leo the Tenth, 379 : 16
power to do me i., 249 : *n* 4
rather calamities than suffer no i., 118 : 20
rather speak i. of ourselves than not talk, 293 : 22
report while you live, 221 : 4
run to meet i. luck, 500 : 17
speak i. of the dead, 62 : 8
spirit have so fair a house, 247 : 24
spirit sob in blood cell, 893 : 7
things i. got had bad success, 186 : 5
took i. on Thursday, 932 : 11
unquiet meals make i. digestions, 188 : 14
ware is never cheap, 269 : 13
weary and i. at ease, 596 : 13
weed groweth fast, 159 : 32
wind blows no man good, 161 : 11
Ill-advised, some quotations i., 685 : 15
Ill-born, amphibious i. mob, 318 : 6
Ill-bred as audible laughter, 370 : *n* 1
scenes, 701 : 2
this age how i., 102 : 2
Ill-clad, ill-housed i., 780 : 2
Illegal, immoral i. or fattening, 801 : 10
when President does it not i., 883 : 4
Ill-favored thing but mine own, 213 : 2
vile i. faults, 225 : 21
Ill-housed ill-clad ill-nourished, 780 : 2
Illiberal as audible laughter, 370 : *n* 1
Illiteracy, conquest of i. first, 871 : 15
sea of i., 871 : 15
Illiterate him from your memory, 398 : 5
Ill-natured, vain i. Englishman, 318 : 6
Illness, one i. one cure, 380 : 5
with which smitten, 486 : 6
Illnesses, benefit from i., 80 : 8
for extreme i. extreme treatments, 80 : 10
Ill-nourished, ill-housed ill-clad i., 780 : 2
Illogical belief in improbable, 772 : 11
doctrine so i. and dull, 783 : 7
Ills, age the harbor of all i., 92 : 5
bear those i. we have, 221 : 12
flood of mortal i. prevailing, 155 : 15
forgetfulness of all i., 59 : 25
from what i. you are free, 100 : 12
medicos marveling on i., 810 : 20
mighty i. done by woman, 316 : 16
no sense of i. to come, 361 : 10
o'er i. o' life victorious, 411 : 7
scholar's life assail, 351 : 17
to hastening i. a prey, 369 : 30
we ought to bear, 585 : 10
Ill-seeming, muddy i. thick, 189 : 5
Ill-spenders, borrowers i., 573 : 3
Ill-tempered and queer, 550 : 5
Ill-timed truth, 646 : 14
Illuminated reader is the poem, 741 : 13
Illuminatio, dominus i. mea, 18 : *n* 3
Illumination of ignorant, 380 : 8
truth by instant i., 858 : 10
Illuminations, bonfires and i., 381 : 7
Illumine, sunset i. rolling waves, 673 : 17
what in me is dark i., 283 : 2
Illumines, history i. reality, 98 : 9
Ill-used, hardest knife i., 245 : 7
Illusion by which cheated, 734 : 8
certainty generally i., 644 : 3
Clemenceau had one i., 783 : 3
give reality to i., 757 : 9
great i., 735 : 20
in love i. reaches zenith, 658 : 14
life is an i., 273 : 2
mind diseased always i., 552 : 7
of philosophers, 837 : 18
of power of friends, 635 : 16
religion an i., 679 : 3
that times were better, 538 : 9
which makes me happy, 380 : 3
world of divine i., 589 : 5
Illusions, attachment fabricator of i., 876 : 17
most dangerous calculations we call i., 802 : 16
natural to indulge in i., 383 : 1
poetry purged of i., 735 : 13
Illusory, reality reveals itself to be i., 723 : 20
Illustrate all shadows, 255 : 1
Illustration, vivid physical i., 610 : 2
Illustrious acts high raptures infuse, 276 : 2
bustle so i., 607 : 8
famous expedition, 702 : 11
name i. and revered, 118 : 12
predecessors, 350 : 4
Ill-will, no malice or i., 418 : 6
I'm mad as hell, 901 : 10
OK you're OK, 877 : 13
Image, age demanded an i., 792 : 12
Image (*continued*)
by means of i. hold belongings, 739 : 11
by means of i. we hold on, 739 : 11
constant i. of the creature, 213 : 29
culture offers man i., 865 : 14
graven i., 10 : 4
his own i. walking in garden, 466 : 16
horrid i. doth unfix hair, 236 : 11
idea with i., 437 : 17
in rivers and oceans, 570 : 4
in the i. of God, 8 : 2
made in i. mannikin, 527 : 3
make man in our i., 6 : 13
man is God's i., 268 : 9
man's i. and his cry, 712 : 7
of eternity, 458 : 29
of his own eternity, 34 : 12
of phantom of life, 570 : 4
of revolution, 5 : 9
of war without guilt, 328 : 18
of what we actually see, 638 : 4
scorn her own i., 222 : 2
speech is i. of actions, 62 : 15
that blossoms a rose, 712 : 12
thrice tried to clasp her i., 60 : 8
time the i. of eternity, 125 : 27
tormenting i. in fountain, 570 : 4
Imagery of Greek and Latin, 357 : 19
Images, both i. regard, 268 : 9
criticism dissolves i., 886 : 4
deposits of accumulated experience, 753 : 12
draw from ourselves i., 853 : 3
elevate i. of senses, 436 : 17
find mirror in every mind, 352 : 27
graven i. of her gods, 29 : 27
heap of broken i., 805 : 1
no graven i. worshipped, 564 : 18
of beauty, 83 : 10
of collective unconscious, 753 : 12
prisoners tattoo, 850 : 6
receives i. without absorbing, 635 : 6
reflect before throwing i., 818 : 1
what i. return O my daughter, 806 : 8
Imaginary gardens with real toads, 798 : 11
necessities, 272 : 20
relish is so sweet, 226 : 10
Imagination, a really grasping i., 652 : 4
abandoned by Reason, 394 : *n* 1
abhorred in my i., 224 : 14
Adam's dream, 479 : 2
as i. bodies forth, 197 : 12
baffled by facts, 744 : 14
bare i. of feast, 194 : 7
cold and barren, 372 : 13
colors of i., 437 : 14
dissolves diffuses, 437 : 12
dwell most on woman won or lost, 715 : 5
fantastical i., 715 : 4
fate had i. about her, 748 : 13
gifted with egotistical i., 502 : 20
God and i. one, 769 : 3
higher gift of i., 690 : 12
in balance or reconciliation, 437 : 17
in i. of their hearts, 42 : 22
incalculable debt to i., 753 : 11
indebted to i. for facts, 399 : 13
judgment and i., 436 : 19
lady's i. rapid, 440 : 18
literalists of the i., 798 : 11
living power prime agent, 437 : 11

Imagination (*continued*)
loose i., 717 : 9
makes us eloquent, 118 : 2
man without i., 784 : 26
master of art, 684 : 6
no i. is mere, 639 : 11
of boy healthy, 475 : 15
of i. all compact, 197 : 12
of man's heart, 7 : 33
one of forces of nature, 769 : 26
poet make his i. the people's, 769 : 16
political ideas and i., 866 : 1
primary i. living power, 437 : 11
reconciling mediatory power, 436 : 20
regulate i. by reality, 353 : 15
resemblance striking i., 385 : 1
solitude needful to i., 569 : 14
Southern culture fostered, 905 : 5
such tricks hath strong i., 197 : 12
suspend i., 845 : 10
sweeten my i., 235 : 1
synthetical and magical, 437 : 16
trace dust of Alexander, 224 : 15
truth of i., 479 : 1
truth only in i., 684 : 6
were it not for i., 356 : 8
wings of ostrich, 487 : 15
Imaginations and wanton tempers, 380 : 12
Lord understandeth all the i., 14 : 24
my i. are as foul, 222 : 7
world canvas to i., 558 : 14
Imaginative awe, 869 : 11
education of i. life, 654 : 9
genius of west, 577 : 13
Imagine excellence, 900 : 1
himself pleasing to all, 308 : 12
people i. a vain thing, 17 : 13
to i. is everything, 655 : 5
too bold to i., 378 : 1
you are creating human destiny, 582 : 5
Imagined, each i. pinnacle, 478 : 7
exhausted worlds i. new, 351 : 10
land, 767 : 22
live life he has i., 560 : 16
one chose person one loved, 734 : 6
republics and principalities, 153 : 23
round earth's i. corners, 254 : 8
world i. ultimate good, 769 : 2
Imagines he cannot do this or that, 308 : 17
Imagining in excited reverie, 714 : 14
some fear, 197 : 12
Imaginings, horrible i., 236 : 11
Imbalance, social i. reflects itself, 871 : 13
Imbecile, Apollo i., 495 : 13
Imbeciles, three generations of i., 645 : 7
Imbecility, convinced of i., 353 : 5
Imbres, cur i. ruerent, 115 : *n* 12
Imitate action of the tiger, 207 : 16
fools do not i. successes, 95 : 10
him if you dare, 716 : 6
immature poets .i, 809 : 6
original writer one nobody can i., 419 : 7
the sun, 203 : 5
Imitated humanity so abominably, 222 : 3
Imitates, art i. nature, 117 : *n* 6
third art i. them, 85 : 8
Imitation, art i. of nature, 114 : 26
Imitation (*continued*)
limps after in base i., 194 : 11
of action that is serious, 88 : 16
sincerest flattery, 448 : 10
to do opposite is form of i., 386 : 18
whole vocation endless i., 426 : 16
Imitator, without precedent and i., 359 : 2
Imitators, no garlands for i., 413 : 4
you slavish herd, 109 : 13
Imiter, celui que personne ne peut i., 419 : *n* 2
Immaculate, look i. of landscapes, 794 : 2
white chrysanthemum remains i., 314 : 5
Immanent Will and its designs, 641 : 17
Immanuel, call his name I., 29 : 13
Immature poets imitate, 809 : 6
Immediate context of history, 823 : 21
jewel of souls, 230 : 33
passage i. passage, 576 : 16
Immediately, difficult do i., 924 : 19
they'd i. go out, 406 : 17
Immemorial elms, 531 : 13
most i. year, 526 : 22
Immense, at twelve I felt i., 718 : 11
error is i., 329 : 2
long derangement, 674 : 12
river of oblivion, 593 : 11
silkworm size or i., 799 : 14
Immensity of first power, 417 : 3
of life, 518 : 7
Immersed in place and period, 800 : 3
Immigrants, all i. except Indians, 781 : 2
Imminent, contagious blastments i., 218 : 27
deadly breach, 229 : 28
Immoderate, unseasonable and i. sleep, 353 : 4
Immoderately married, 874 : 13
Immodest, no more modest than i., 574 : 20
words admit no defense, 309 : 9
Immoral illegal or fattening, 801 : 10
moral or i. book, 674 : 22
thing for moral reasons, 641 : 9
what you feel bad after, 845 : 1
Immorality, schools nurseries of i., 349 : 14
what majority dislike, 698 : 3
Immortal, bee to be i., 768 : 15
bird, 477 : 1
Christianity indestructible and i., 481 : 15
crown, 346 : 1
dead who live again, 564 : 22
death has taken mortal life, 101 : 3
Death the only i., 626 : 16
desire to be i., 537 : 14
diamond is immortal diamond, 656 : 21
dim light of this i. day, 467 : 9
driven away from i. day, 403 : 13
either soul i. or perishes, 83 : *n* 7
else i. us, 254 : 10
God created man to be i., 34 : 12
gods I crave no pelf, 243 : 1
grow i. as they quote, 329 : 20
happy be and have i. bliss, 173 : 17
hate, 283 : 8
he is i., 838 : 11
in flesh beauty i., 767 : 10
Immortal (*continued*)
Jove's dread clamors, 231 : 11
land is i., 895 : 10
lay plans as if i., 650 : 4
life eternal love i., 642 : 10
locks fell forward, 57 : 12
longings in me, 242 : 2
look, 544 : 23
make me i. with a kiss, 184 : 4
married to i. verse, 278 : 6
mortal or i. here I die, 570 : 6
names not born to die, 464 : 13
no i. work behind, 480 : 4
not similar are i. gods and men, 57 : 30
now is i. life, 662 : 20
one i. song, 304 : 4
part of myself, 230 : 23
reason i. all else mortal, 65 : 13
scrip of joy i. diet, 172 : 15
Shakespeare rose, 351 : 10
ship, 575 : 20
sight of i. sea, 426 : 20
songs composed of tears, 537 : 9
soul of man i., 85 : 10
spark from Heaven i., 412 : 9
spirit grows, 423 : 18
such harmony in i. souls, 201 : 1
thine i. wine, 604 : 10
though no more, 457 : 7
unrecorded laws of God, 74 : 16
verse becomes hieroglyphic, 703 : 7
way to be i. is die daily, 274 : 13
what i. hand or eye, 405 : 7
wheat, 311 : 21
where saints i. reign, 328 : 15
wound, 749 : 20
youth to mortal maids, 442 : 21
Immortality, evidence of i., 496 : 1
fields of i., 468 : 20
from death to i., 56 : 20
hope full of i., 34 : 13
if you destroy belief in i., 581 : 19
is an achievement, 728 : 8
labor at eternal task, 593 : 12
load of i., 479 : 12
longing after i., 326 : 3
man possesses i., 866 : 6
mortal put on i., 49 : 7
no faith in i., 514 : 7
not a gift, 728 : 8
nurslings of i., 467 : 3
only secret is I., 608 : 2
ourselves and i., 606 : 4
unveil third event, 607 : 18
you and I share Lolita, 846 : 5
Immortalizes, diffused knowledge i., 416 : 13
Immortally, wished to remain i., 734 : 7
Immortals cannot escape love, 74 : 23
he lives not long who battles i., 57 : 29
President of the I., 641 : 4
seek not life of i., 71 : 28
send you to Elysian plain, 59 : 26
Immune to spirit of own epoch, 755 : 1
Immunities, privileges or i. of citizens, 392 : 4
Immunity, incomes not purchase i., 773 : 8
Immured, love not alone i. in brain, 191 : 2
Imogen, as much Iago as I., 479 : 17
Imp of the perverse, 526 : 21
Impaint, watercolors to i. cause, 205 : 3

Imparadised in one another's arms, 285 : 22
Impart, solitary and cannot i. it, 353 : 26
Impartial adjustment of claims, 682 : 14
Death with i. tread, 107 : 1
in thought and action, 682 : 1
judge, 374 : 6
Impartiality, considers i. as his treasure, 97 : 8
of Nature best, 631 : 5
Impassioned expression in countenance, 424 : 7
great speech i., 90 : 1
Impatience and laziness, 786 : 6
so much fretted, 355 : 3
Impatient as the wind, 428 : 20
mind i., 218 : 4
of disgrace, 303 : 20
tenderly be not i., 576 : 19
Impeachment, removed from office on i., 391 : 11
soft i., 398 : 19
Impeccable all-pervasiveness, 651 : 3
Impediment, we marched without i., 187 : 23
Impediments, admit i., 245 : 18
in fancy's course, 227 : 23
to great enterprises, 180 : 9
wife and children are i., 180 : 9
Impel, causes which i. separation, 387 : 9
Impelled, speech i. us, 808 : 14
Impels all thinking things, 423 : 13
Impenetrable as monads of Leibniz, 791 : 12
know i. really exists, 763 : 7
movable particles, 313 : 16
Impera, divide et i., 133 : 21
Imperative, categorical i., 366 : 14
magisterial or i. type, 730 : 15
to preserve rights, 700 : 3
Imperator vitae animus est, 103 : *n* 1
Imperceptible, obstacle become i., 734 : 9
water, 485 : 13
Imperfect offices of prayer, 428 : 10
Imperfections, dwell on excellencies not i., 326 : 19
of human mind, 862 : 15
on my head, 219 : 24
Imperial, act of the i. theme, 236 : 10
ensign full high advanced, 283 : 20
friend, 606 : 3
man's i. race ensnare, 334 : 3
sword mace crown i., 208 : 7
Tom Jones outlive i. eagle, 383 : 16
votaress passed on, 196 : 15
Imperialism and Chinese, 826 : 8
obstruct peace, 781 : 4
Imperialisms, prey of rival i., 818 : 14
Imperiled, Union would be i., 644 : 17
Imperious Caesar dead, 224 : 16
Imperishable, need of i. bliss, 767 : 3
peace, 692 : 11
quiet, 874 : 7
soul of man i., 85 : 10
Impersonality of science, 552 : 4
Impertinence in kings and ministers, 366 : 3
lesson on grammar i., 591 : 10
Imperturbe, me i., 573 : 21
Impetuous, be thou me i. one, 467 : 21
such i. blood, 425 : 1
Impiety of pious, 579 : 18
Impious, course of i. stubbornness, 218 : 4
men bear sway, 326 : 2
Implacable Charybdis guards left, 200 : *n* 1
in hate, 304 : 3
Implausible already said by philosopher, 272 : 9
Implications, trace i. of things, 652 : 14
Implore, I adore thee i. thee, 167 : 3
Implores passing tribute of sigh, 362 : 13
Importance, art makes life and i., 654 : 10
eternal i. like baseball, 791 : 6
hence i. of poetry, 587 : 2
no human thing of i., 85 : 9
Important, beginning most i. part, 84 : 8
discriminate between i. and negligible, 762 : 5
if anyone think it important, 649 : 9
people most i. element, 89 : 28
principles inflexible, 524 : 9
question is what you think, 586 : 18
timing is most i. factor, 61 : 23
Importunate chink, 373 : 28
rashly i., 485 : 21
Importune, I here i. death, 241 : 21
too proud to i., 363 : 11
Impose, fates i. that men abide, 186 : 16
Imposition, reputation a false i., 230 : 24
Impossibility, begotten upon i., 297 : 6
likely i. preferable, 88 : 19
physical and metaphysical i., 472 : 8
Im-possible, in two words i., 777 : 7
Impossible, can't believe i. things, 613 : 14
carry out the i., 723 : 8
certain because i., 126 : 9
dream i. dream, 890 : 1
ear and eye expected i., 715 : 4
eliminate i. truth remains, 689 : 3
failure is i., 578 : 7
in two words i., 777 : 7
in war nothing i., 792 : 3
looked on as i. until effected, 116 : 11
love those who yearn for i., 396 : 23
loyalties, 587 : 1
most i. of conclusions, 703 : 9
not think what is hard is i., 125 : 7
nothing i. in supernatural, 704 : 11
nothing i. to willing heart, 159 : 13
nothing unnatural that is not i., 399 : 9
pure and complete sorrow i., 602 : 7
takes longer, 924 : 19
that not i. she, 292 : 7
these i. women, 82 : 14
to be cheated, 497 : 13
to be silent, 373 : 16
to live pleasurably without living wisely, 91 : 16
to love and be wise, 110 : *n* 12
to please all the world, 296 : 14
to reduce society to level, 537 : 4
to write history i., 602 : 8
with God nothing i., 42 : 18
word i. not French, 420 : 10
Impostor employs force, 391 : 7
Impostors, sages all i., 375 : 2
treat two i. same, 710 : 16
Impotent, all-powerful to be i., 743 : 12
Impotent (*continued*)
lame and i. conclusion, 230 : 12
Impotently great, 334 : 14
Impoverished stock of harmless pleasure, 353 : 1
Impoverishment in symbolism, 754 : 7
Imprecision of feeling, 807 : 21
Impregnable, seas for fence i., 186 : 15
Impress, themselves our minds i., 423 : 5
Impressed, line in which force i., 313 : 14
Impression as from seal of ring, 85 : 18
be not swept off feet by i., 121 : 16
Impressionable, girl at i. age, 896 : 2
Impressions, did not trust my own i., 80 : 15
early i. hard to eradicate, 128 : 14
falseness in i. of external, 572 : 10
forever courting new i., 638 : 14
of American manners, 449 : 1
of free mind, 718 : 6
Impressive, poetry most i. mode, 587 : 2
thunder i., 626 : 7
Imprinted, remember what is i., 85 : 18
Imprison gifts in such calling, 719 : 18
Imprisoned in every fat man, 857 : 13
in viewless winds, 228 : 20
millions of innocent i., 387 : 15
Montezuma, 488 : 6
Imprisonment, age ache penury and i., 228 : 21
Improbable, absurd not the i., 552 : 12
facts at first seem i., 183 : 2
truth sometimes i., 462 : *n* 1
what remains however i., 689 : 3
Impropriety, indulge in without i., 628 : 26
soul of wit, 751 : 13
Improve each shining hour, 328 : 5
shining tail, 611 : 5
Improved for literary conversation, 258 : *n* 2
Improvement, diversion or i. of country, 326 : 7
makes straight roads, 404 : 7
of underdeveloped areas, 787 : 17
Improvements by generation, 378 : 1
Improver of natural knowledge, 595 : 10
Improves, love i. a woman, 329 : 11
Improving, middle age time of i., 290 : 9
Improviste le courage de l'i., 421 : *n* 1
Imprudently married barber, 364 : 5
Impudence, Cockney i., 619 : *n* 1
Impulse, blot out pomp check i., 125 : 17
faction united by common i., 398 : 1
household of I. mourns, 868 : 15
lonely i. of delight, 714 : 1
natural i. God gave me, 316 : 4
one i. from vernal wood, 423 : 7
to see it tried, 524 : 8
to take life strivingly, 649 : 5
Impulses, primitive i. of heart, 526 : *n* 1
Impunity, no one provokes me with i., 134 : 11
ravage with i. rose, 540 : 13
Impure, although it passes among i., 86 : *n* 7
Impurities, no room for i. in essay, 782 : 1
Impute, sin I i. to ghost, 543 : 15
In and out the Eagle, 922 : 1

In (*continued*)
birds without despair to get i., 165 : 19
look out not i., 590 : 8
those i. wish to get out, 498 : 18
when age i. wit out, 209 : 28
who's i. who's out, 235 : 12
Inability of mind to correlate all contents, 816 : 8
to enforce laws, 871 : 13
to stay quiet, 597 : 4
Inaccessible, desert i., 211 : 12
tower of past, 569 : 4
valley of reveries, 750 : 15
Inaccuracy, not mind lying hate i., 621 : 4
saves explanation, 731 : 18
Inaction, disciplined i., 416 : 16
moment not of action or i., 94 : *n* 9
nor be thy attachment to i., 94 : 10
saps vigor of mind, 152 : 8
Inactivity, wise and masterly i., 416 : 14
Inadequacy, intellect understand its i., 753 : 13
Inadequate formulations, 825 : 13
Inadvertently said some evil thing, 86 : 7
Inane, insufferable i., 619 : 1
intense i., 467 : 7
Inanimate, mortality of i. things, 631 : 20
Inanition, spirit die of i., 586 : 23
Inarticulate, raid on i., 807 : 21
Inartistic, Thoreau i., 652 : 7
Inattention, patient i., 601 : 9
Inattentive, brave man i. to duty, 419 : 1
Inaudible and noiseless foot, 227 : 21
its name is The I., 64 : 6
Inauspicious stars, 193 : 28
Incalculable soul, 828 : 16
Incantations of defeats, 768 : 7
Incapable, noble and i. of deceit, 432 : 12
Incarnadine, seas i., 238 : 1
Incarnate by the Holy Ghost, 55 : 3
Fourth of July i., 418 : *n* 8
Well I told you so, 512 : 9
Incarnations of hopes and fears, 469 : 3
Incense, gods themselves throw i., 235 : 13
my morning i., 400 : 5
soft i. hangs, 476 : 26
stupefying i. smoke, 541 : 20
Incense-breathing morn, 361 : 24
Incensed, blows and buffets have i., 238 : 15
most fragrant when i., 180 : 8
Incentive, feel beautiful i. as pang, 653 : 12
to save invest work, 880 : 15
Incertainties now crown themselves, 245 : 13
Incessant, what boots it with i. care, 280 : 15
Incessantly stand on head, 611 : 9
weeps i. for my sin, 406 : 1
work i. to the last, 396 : 5
world joked i., 630 : 9
Inch, cannot grow by i., 717 : 6
cubic i. of space miracle, 576 : 14
every i. a king, 234 : 30
every i. not fool is rogue, 304 : 18
give an i. take an ell, 161 : 12
I'll not budge an i., 188 : 23
Inch (*continued*)
no painful i. to gain, 564 : 17
paint an i. thick, 224 : 14
queen it no i. further, 247 : 2
rule of taste, 635 : 2
Inchcape Rock, 440 : 1
Inches, death by i., 242 : 25
die by famine die by i., 319 : 6
thirty i. from nose, 869 : 6
Incident, curious i. of dog in nighttime, 689 : 8
Incidents, so many i. so many details, 702 : 7
Incidis in Scyllam cupiens, 200 : *n* 1
Incipit vita nova, 140 : 7
Incisions, underneath fine i., 604 : 4
Incitement, every idea an i., 645 : 5
Incitements, safeguarding from i., 700 : 3
Inciters of servile insurrection, 617 : 6
Incivility and procrastination, 454 : 21
Inclement, raw i. summers, 322 : 13
Inclination, read as i. leads, 354 : 11
thoughts according to i., 206 : *n* 4
to hear you, 327 : 13
to injustice, 823 : 18
Inclinations cannot alter evidence, 380 : 11
Incline thine ear O Lord, 30 : 27
Inclined, always to joy i., 404 : 14
as to embrace me she i., 282 : 21
as twig bent tree's i., 335 : 15
sins they are i. to, 291 : 6
to snap like vixens, 794 : 7
Inclines to think there is God, 564 : 14
Include me out, 777 : 6
things that included whole, 768 : 17
Included in We the people, 913 : 9
Includes itself in power, 226 : 3
Inclusion, life i. and confusion, 653 : 13
Income, annual i. twenty pounds, 548 : 27
business with i. at heels, 376 : 7
decent cloths over high i., 884 : 19
he has i. she pattable, 856 : 4
however great i., 95 : 7
just man will pay more i. tax, 84 : 6
live beyond i., 620 : 17
rent is sorrow i. tears, 267 : 14
solvency not matter of i., 711 : 6
twenty expenditure nineteen, 548 : 27
Incomes, high i. not purchase immunity, 773 : 8
not purchase immunity, 773 : 8
Incommunicable, burden of i., 454 : 16
Incomparable, Clemens sole i., 632 : 2
oil Macassar, 460 : 10
Incompatibility spice of life, 856 : 4
Incompatible things by same name, 523 : 7
Incompetence, rise to level of i., 896 : 8
Incomplete and unfit for view, 619 : 5
Incomprehensibility of God, 484 : 16
Incomprehensible, astonishment gateway to i., 881 : 4
history i. without Jesus, 593 : 8
Incomprehension, mutual i., 865 : 17
Inconceivable idea of sun, 768 : 8
Incongruous moonlight shines, 819 : 3
with intelligence, 580 : 8
Inconsistencies in principle, 640 : 7
of opinion justifiable, 451 : 10
Inconsistency in American moralism, 862 : 18
Inconsolé je suis le veuf l'i., 514 : *n* 5
Inconstancy, constant in Nature i., 295 : 6
nothing constant but i., 321 : 16
state of man i., 299 : 19
Inconstant childish proud, 475 : 3
mob is varied and i., 308 : 23
moon, 192 : 11
she will i. prove, 918 : 7
Inconvenience, go with show of i., 785 : 10
Inconveniences, modern i., 623 : 13
Incorrect, will most i. to heaven, 218 : 4
Incorruptible, dead raised i., 49 : 7
sea-green i., 473 : 20
Incorruption, corruptible put on i., 49 : 7
raised in i., 49 : 5
Increase and diffusion of knowledge, 417 : 1
as if i. of appetite, 218 : 8
from fairest creatures desire i., 243 : 31
God gave i., 48 : 3
his tribe i., 454 : 4
in proportion with years, 826 : 15
of his government, 29 : 16
some nations i. other diminish, 100 : 15
without i. or diminution, 438 : 13
Increased devotion to cause, 523 : 4
force in nature not i., 583 : 21
from whence comforts i., 402 : 15
Jesus i. in wisdom, 42 : 33
knowledge shall be i., 33 : 6
means and leisure, 502 : 14
Increases, absence i. great passions, 293 : 31
in geometrical ratio, 417 : 3
necessity of being ready i., 522 : 1
Increaseth, he that i. knowledge i. sorrow, 26 : 17
Increasing belly, 205 : 28
purpose runs, 530 : 3
store with loss, 244 : 22
youth waneth by i., 177 : 8
Increment, unearned i., 508 : 16
Increments, velocities of evanescent i., 330 : 21
Incumbent, care of poor i. on society, 309 : 1
Incurable, accept as i. the present, 801 : 3
disease is i., 206 : 5
life is an i. disease, 295 : 12
old age is an i. disease, 497 : *n* 3
Ind, from east to western I., 212 : 3
wealth of Ormus and I., 284 : 3
Indebted, at once i. and discharged, 285 : 11
to memory for his jests, 399 : 13
Indecency, prejudicial as public i., 170 : 21
Indecision, nothing habitual but i., 648 : 8
Indeed, friend in need friend i., 94 : *n* 2
Indefatigable pursuit of unattainable, 711 : 7
Indefinite, science repulses i., 551 : 16
Indefinitely desolate, 711 : 11
Indemnify, literature effort to i., 497 : 33

Indemnity for the past, 351 : n 3
Indenture, this oath and this i., 79 : 13
Independence, as Japan kept i., 800 : 4
  banners of foreign i., 418 : 2
  bulwark of our i., 520 : 7
  forever, 450 : n 5
  glittering generalities of Declaration of I., 485 : 2
  governments whose i. acknowledged, 408 : 3
  in marriage i. will be equal, 471 : 1
  individual i. economic principle, 763 : 1
  long live I., 400 : 1
  lost genius of i., 520 : 7
  magnanimity trust, 559 : 9
  make real Declaration of I., 753 : 6
  middle-class blasphemy, 681 : 9
  mutual guarantees of i., 682 : 15
  no conscious goal, 800 : 7
  now and independence forever, 450 : 10
  of solitude, 497 : 1
  reluctant last resort, 800 : 7
  Revolution produced Declaration of I., 800 : 8
  sentiments in Declaration of I., 521 : 8
  to this day, 800 : 4
Independent and have inherent rights, 367 : 4
  free and i. states, 378 : 12, 381 : 6
  scientist, 831 : 24
  support renders i., 379 : 3
Indescribable, beauty i., 703 : 5
Indestructible, Christianity i. and immortal, 481 : 15
  Union indestructible states, 514 : 4
Indeterminable, life-form i., 754 : 5
Index, a dab at an i., 368 : 5
  marble i. of a mind, 424 : 2
Indexes baby figure of giant mass, 226 : 5
Indian, I'll be an I., 874 : 8
  knows his village, 852 : 16
  land undefiled, 897 : 19
  like the base I., 232 : 20
  lo the poor I., 336 : 16
  morn on the I. steep, 279 : 13
  not decked with I. stones, 186 : 8
  of falcon glance lion bearing, 465 : 6
  stands free in Nature, 557 : 4
  summer of life, 635 : 21
  to I. all days are God's, 686 : 7
  to wilderness to teach I., 705 : 3
  white man come I. withdraw, 557 : 18
  wilderness, 319 : 22
Indians, all immigrants except I., 781 : 2
  give country back to I., 840 : 11
  know better how to live, 670 : 13
  only good I. dead, 610 : 4
  ten little I., 933 : 22
  thanks f'r bein' presarved fr'm I., 722 : 3
Indians', called Guanahaní in I. tongue, 150 : 15
India's coral strand, 452 : 8
Indicates, determines or i. man's fate, 559 : 2
Indictment against whole people, 372 : 21
Indies, had come to the I., 150 : 14
  wealth of I., 356 : 6
  went to I. to conquer a people, 151 : 9
Indifference, benign i. of universe, 882 : 3
  extinction from i., 845 : 16
  moral i. of cultivated, 580 : 14
  morn and cold i., 327 : 21
  on part of government, 771 : 2
  politeness organized i., 735 : 19
  softness of i., 614 : 11
  tragedy of love i., 751 : 16
  when will i. come, 885 : 4
Indifferent, all matter i. to form, 273 : 10
  and cannot enjoy it, 353 : 26
  children of earth, 220 : 23
  delayed till I am i., 353 : 26
  good bad i., 308 : 19, 360 : 9
  rather than believe God i., 504 : 19
  stood aside been i., 859 : 13
  this i. thing, 850 : 18
  to be i. essence of inhumanity, 680 : 14
  universe is i., 764 : 16
Indifferently, look on both i., 215 : 3
Indigested, irregular i. piece, 352 : 8
Indignant, no one such liar as i. man, 657 : 19
  spirit fled i. to shades, 106 : 7
Indignatio, ubi saeva i., 323 : 25
Indignation at literary wrongs, 437 : 4
  provoking thy wrath and i., 55 : 17
  savage i., 323 : 25, 716 : 6
  unsatisfied i., 582 : 4
  until the i. be overpast, 30 : 11
  will produce verses, 121 : 24
Indignity, the i. of it, 873 : 8
Indirect, persecution i. way to plant religion, 274 : 9
  poet become more i., 809 : 9
Indirections, by i. find directions, 220 : 7
Indiscretion, lover without i., 640 : 8
Indiscriminate charity, 621 : 9
Indispensable, as loved we are i., 669 : 13
  charm i. to women, 694 : n 2
  comforts not i., 559 : 8
  condition of freedom, 730 : 17
  make yourself i., 727 : 8
  no i. man, 779 : 9
  titles such as I., 701 : 11
Indisposeth, living i. for dying, 275 : 6
Indisputable, nothing more i. than senses, 363 : 14
Individual, affirmation of i., 643 : 7
  argue point with i., 570 : 8
  balance of i. with representative, 437 : 17
  competition afford freedom to i., 790 : 3
  competition hard for i., 621 : 6
  connection of i. man, 922 : 9
  development repetition of race, 678 : 9
  difficulties of i. of family, 440 : 27
  emancipation of i., 550 : 3
  first and foremost I am i., 599 : 13
  idea due to i., 774 : 2
  independence economic principle, 763 : 1
  labors to render annual revenue, 366 : 4
  liberty individual power, 418 : 3
  liberty of i., 508 : 9
  monopoly granted to i., 366 : 1
  must remain supreme, 848 : 12
Individual (*continued*)
  needs no i. can provide himself, 773 : 8
  no i. could resent, 322 : 19
  no progress except in i., 581 : 6
  no such creature as i., 883 : 14
  not accountable to society 508 : 13
  not i. but species, 349 : 12
  ontogenesis development of i., 617 : 10
  part he can never understand, 844 : 7
  person sacrificed to i., 778 : 11
  public strength i. security, 401 : 11
  representative of whole, 858 : 8
  serves industrial system, 872 : 4
  taken into custody, 820 : 15
  universe directed to one i., 576 : 10
  way of seeing, 650 : 7
  who refuses to defend, 418 : 14
Individualism, art most intense i., 676 : 2
  rugged i., 750 : 17
Individuality, components of i. are sorrow, 72 : 23
  draw chalk circle round i., 489 : 18
  England paradise of i., 704 : 2
  of expression beginning of art, 397 : 4
  whatever crushes i. is despotism, 508 : 11
Individuals, if i. have no virtues, 391 : 8
  not accommodate to conveniences of i., 650 : 6
  nothing good that ignores i., 576 : 9
  numerous free active, 586 : 17
  of all nations melted into new race, 382 : 8
  preservation of species not i., 414 : 20
  private i. occasionally kill enemies, 679 : 11
  reproduction to new i., 393 : 7
Indivisibility of peace, 757 : n 2
Indivisible, fleshed fair erected i., 878 : 3
  freedom i. word, 824 : 10
  grandeur i., 815 : 4
  nation under God i., 677 : 10
  peace i., 757 : 11
Indolence heaven's ally here, 572 : 6
  phlegmatic emerged from i., 386 : 11
  wealth the parent of i., 84 : 12
Indolent but agreeable doing nothing, 123 : 11
  readers become more i., 368 : 6
  vacuity of thought, 377 : 7
Indomitable people of Vermont, 736 : 19
  untamed as thee, 575 : 22
Indomitably on his instincts, 496 : 12
Indulge in luxury of skepticism, 658 : 11
  myself a little the more, 310 : 3
  never i. in poetics, 94 : 17
Indulged, reason and experiment i., 387 : 13
Indulgence of propensity to forego, 647 : 20
Indus, from I. to Pole, 335 : 1
Industrial progress available, 787 : 17
  serves i. system by consuming, 872 : 4
Industrialized communities, 773 : 7
Industries, business crises wrecked i., 666 : 4
Industrious ambitious liar, 624 : 6
  honest and i. men's lives, 265 : 9
  only a few i. Scots, 177 : 16

Industry, arms i., 815 : 15
avarice spur of i., 357 : 13
bring i. into competition, 366 : 8
captains of i., 474 : 8
choke fountain of i., 451 : 5
cultivated i. and frugality, 590 : 4
free to regulate i., 389 : 1
in art a necessity, 619 : 6
life without i. guilt, 573 : 7
love of bustle not i., 114 : 15
not i. only but judgment, 372 : 9
of no avail, 830 : 9
omnipresent in brooding i., 703 : 13
proletariat product of i., 563 : 6
superintending i. of private people, 366 : 8
to quote argues feeble i., 80 : 2
without art brutality, 573 : 7
Inebriate, cheer but not i., 330 : 22, 377 : 3
of air am I, 604 : 14
Inebriated with verbosity, 502 : 20
Ineffectual angel, 589 : 13
armed neutrality i., 682 : 11
Ineptitude, ignorance ambition or i., 771 : 2
Inequalities and unfairnesses, 625 : 24
Inequality effect of brutalizing, 589 : 4
of environment, 621 : 6
religion of i., 589 : 3
Inert, Divine I., 570 : 12
facts, 635 : 14
Inescapable animal walks with me, 883 : 11
wide water i., 767 : 4
Inestimable, thine i. love, 55 : 7
Inevitability of gradualness, 694 : 2
Inevitable, arguing with i., 568 : 27
awaits alike i. hour, 362 : 3
not grieve over i., 94 : 8
war is i., 763 : 13
war regarded as i. probable, 860 : 5
Inevitably, act i. if truth in sight, 877 : 3
Inexactitude, terminological i., 743 : 5
Inexcusable, attitude artistically i., 758 : 13
Inexhaustible, Paris i., 819 : 13
Inexorability of law of nature, 562 : 19
Inexorable boredom at core of life, 301 : 10
his own i. self, 570 : 5
law i. to cries of prisoners, 380 : 12
more fierce and i. far, 193 : 23
Inexplicable dumbshows, 221 : 23
mystery of sound, 808 : 19
poetry search for i., 770 : 3
Inexpugnably in the necessary, 649 : 16
Inexterminate, man's practically i., 749 : 16
Inextinguishable passion of woman, 323 : 30
rights of human nature, 418 : 1
Infallible all-pervasiveness, 651 : 3
gods not i., 885 : 12
symptom of liberty, 383 : 11
Infallibly gained by flattery, 342 : 13
Infâme écrasez l'i., 343 : *n* 7
Infamous, crush the i. thing, 343 : 17
delay, 330 : 10
rich quiet and i., 488 : 9
Infamy, date live in i., 780 : 15
Infancy, heaven about us in i., 426 : 14
nations like men have i., 329 : 3
Infancy (*continued*)
not only around our i., 567 : 11
perish in their i., 918 : 18
shined in my angel i., 299 : 2
tetchy and wayward thy i., 187 : 18
Infancy's unconscious spell, 571 : 4
Infant, compared to an i., 64 : 18
crying in night, 532 : 10
firstling of the i. year, 272 : 2
mewling and puking, 211 : 15
of three, 810 : 20
phenomenon, 547 : 12
Infanticide rape death humiliation, 903 : 2
Infantryman's, look at i. eyes, 898 : 9
Infant's, in every i. cry of fear, 405 : 9
newborn i. tear, 405 : 10
Infants boys men and Ifs eternally, 571 : 4
canker galls i. of spring, 218 : 27
nuclear giants ethical i., 825 : 2
where unbaptized i. are laid, 640 : 19
Infect, false words i. the soul, 84 : 2
to north star, 209 : 10
Infected, all seems i. that i. spy, 333 : 16
from the top i., 864 : 5
Infection and hand of war, 194 : 13
love whatever it was i., 908 : 12
Infelicity, her i. years too many, 262 : 10
sense of constant i., 294 : 12
Inferior grievances, 390 : 14
no one make you feel i., 786 : 12
of man whose rights I trample, 615 : 5
superior providence of i., 615 : 6
Inferiority, acknowledgment of i., 449 : 10
dogma of ethnic i., 796 : 7
feeling of i., 820 : 14
infinite i., 570 : 12
moral i. of man, 626 : 4
rancor feeling of i., 784 : 3
Senator seldom proclaims i., 634 : 20
Inferiors, between superiors and i., 69 : 2
revolt to be equal, 88 : 9
Infernal constancy, 680 : 3
newspapers the most i., 399 : 5
serpent whose guile, 283 : 3
Inferno, Dante of dread I., 544 : 2
wise spirits in Dante's I., 704 : 12
Infidel I have thee on the hip, 200 : 18
worse than an i., 50 : 31
Infidelity, neither loses through i., 695 : 1
tempt geologists into i., 663 : 5
Infidels, Jews kiss and i. adore, 334 : 1
sleep with Turks and i., 195 : 9
Infinite, aim at the i., 645 : 15
climbing after knowledge i., 183 : 6
day excludes the night, 328 : 15
deal of nothing, 198 : 5
debt through eternity, 395 : 19
echo of i., 644 : 4
evil has i. forms, 300 : 9
fellow of i. jest, 224 : 14
fellows of i. tongue, 208 : 18
genius i. capacity for taking pains, 630 : 17
God a sea of i. substance, 135 : 5
goodness has wide arms, 141 : 21
he cannot bury under finite, 472 : 26
heartsease, 208 : 6
how write after that about i., 824 : 6
Infinite (*continued*)
in faculty, 220 : 28
inferiority, 570 : 12
king of i. space, 220 : 26
marvelous mercies i. love, 633 : 4
meadows of heaven, 511 : 3
nature's i. book of secrecy, 240 : 15
nothing in relation to i., 299 : 17
passion and the pain, 542 : 10
possibilities are i., 698 : 1
power wisdom goodness, 319 : 22
riches in little room, 183 : 12
silence of i. spaces, 300 : 2
though i. can never meet, 297 : 7
variety, 241 : 1
virtue comest smiling, 241 : 15
what cannot see over is i., 473 : 2
what is that to I., 491 : 20
while men believe in i., 560 : 11
wrath and infinite despair, 285 : 12
Infinitesimals, countless i. of feeling, 438 : 8
Infinities, numberless i. of souls, 254 : 8
of islands, 878 : 17
Infinitude, finite reveal i., 874 : 11
grasp as much out of i., 698 : 1
of silence, 580 : 4
Infinity, hold i. in palm of hand, 406 : 8
Infirm, child i., 495 : 1
minstrel i. and old, 429 : 20
my body i. and exhausted, 151 : 11
of purpose, 237 : 23
poor i. weak old man, 233 : 26
Infirmities, bear his friend's i., 217 : 3
bear i. of weak, 47 : 34
man British Museum of i., 626 : 18
Infirmity, feblit with i., 153 : 6
first i. of weak minds, 280 : *n* 2
last i. of noble mind, 280 : 15
of his age, 233 : 2
of will, 497 : 6
Inflamed with mutual animosity, 398 : 2
with study of learning, 281 : 19
Inflation, continuing process of i., 783 : 9
is repudiation, 736 : 15
made in Washington, 880 : 17
makes unemployment inevitable, 844 : 10
monopolies unions and i., 848 : 4
persistence of i., 871 : 13
weakens government, 871 : 12
Inflections, beauty of i., 767 : 12
Inflexible, important principles i., 524 : 9
we must be i., 744 : 9
Influence, authors exert i. on mankind, 559 : 31
cock has great i. on own dunghill, 111 : 5
commands all light all i., 260 : 17
corrupt i., 373 : 10
planetary i., 233 : 5
rain i. and judge prize, 278 : 5
salutary i. of example, 352 : 24
some being or i., 575 : 23
teacher's i. never stops, 635 : 8
unwarranted i., 815 : 15
win friends i. people, 803 : 4
Influences, servile to all skyey i., 228 : 15
sweet i. of Pleiades, 16 : 33
wide world-embracing i., 472 : 17

Infolded, tongues of flame i., 808:18
Inform, occasions i. against me, 223:17
  press home Christmas, 724:4
  their discretion, 389:15
Information, can find i., 355:17
  judgment not better than i., 820:11
  knowledge lost in i., 806:15
  price system mechanism for communicating i., 844:6
  woman of little i., 440:17
Informed, correctly i. as to past, 489:4
  people well enough i., 780:6
Informer poor weak human being, 836:13
Infrequent, sighs short and i., 805:2
  worshipper of gods, 107:14
Infringement of human freedom, 412:4
Infuse, illustrious acs high raptures, i., 276:2
  souls of animals i. into men, 200:7
Infuses that liberal obedience, 373:7
Infusing thoughts and passions, 437:22
Ingenious machinery for reducing amelioration, 640:15
  portable plumbing, 816:12
Ingenuity developed first soul afterwards, 812:10
  surprise you with i., 792:2
Ingiuria, chi fa i. non perdona, 115:*n* 3
Inglorious arts of peace, 296:22
  mute i. Milton, 362:9
Ingrateful man, 233:24
Ingratitude, denounce i. coldness, 452:2
  haste in paying is i., 293:28
  hate i. more than lying, 214:26
  man's i., 211:16
  necessary curse, 885:1
  thou marble-hearted fiend, 233:10
Inhabit, build houses and i. them, 31:31
  country belongs to people who i. it, 521:11
  house and all that i. it, 382:1
  parched places, 32:11
  soul of grandam i. bird, 200:*n* 3
  we are symbols and i. symbols, 498:2
Inhabitant, Indian is Nature's i., 557:4
Inhabitants, Californians a race not i., 699:15
  not only i. of field, 373:28
  proclaim liberty to all i., 10:22
Inhabits our frail blood, 214:26
  poem, 869:10
Inharmonious, sickness sin death i., 583:4
Inhere as do the suns, 606:10
Inherent as oak tree in acorn, 813:13
  capitalist tendency toward self-destruction, 785:5
  decay i. in all component things, 72:22
  purpose i. in art so in nature, 87:5
  rights, 367:4
Inherit, all which it i. dissolve, 248:13
  flow'rets of Eden i., 447:13
  meek shall i. the earth, 18:24, 37:4
  the wind, 23:27
  with pain purchased i. pain, 190:10
Inheritance, divided an i. with him, 386:7
Inheritance (*continued*)
  enter upon your i., 743:10
  must I lose soul's i., 674:16
  not be destroyed, 390:13
  questions of i., 635:2
Inherited, tradition not i., 809:2
Inheritor, president is i., 879:4
Inherits honor or wealth, 436:2
Inhuman as hawk's cry, 798:1
  of the veritable ocean, 767:15
  reign of lie, 817:4
Inhumanity, indifferent is essence of i., 680:14
  man's i. to man, 408:16
Inimies, livin' without i., 721:9
Inimitable Jeeves, 775:12
  vegetagive gracefulness, 789:9
Iniquities, judge allow i., 645:10
Iniquity, bond of i., 46:3
  draw i. with cords of vanity, 29:6
  gray i., 204:5
  I was shapen in i., 19:14
  is pardoned, 30:30
  love soft words hate i., 699:3
  of oblivion, 275:7
  of the fathers, 10:5
  punish wicked for their i., 29:21
  reaped i., 33:13
  religious know more about i., 707:9
Initial of creation, 606:11
Initiative, wipe out private i., 775:7
Iniuria, volenti non fit i., 135:1
Injure, to benefit and not i., 65:10
Injured, forgiveness to i. does belong, 115:*n* 3
  like i. fan, 798:9
  lover's hell, 286:19
  minds i. by hunger and thirst, 89:27
  no one i. save by himself, 128:*n* 9
  party, 630:20
  those I have i., 893:9
  whom they have i. they hate, 115:4
Injures, never pardons those he i., 115:*n* 3
Injuries, forgive me my i., 893:9
  saints in your i., 230:8
Injuring, at expense of i. their virtue, 69:10
  kill time without i. eternity, 559:3
  rarely escapes i. own hands, 65:7
  restrain men from i., 389:1
Injurious, beauty though i., 289:3
Injury, add insult to i., 114:11, 358:7
  engraved in metal, 155:*n* 3
  fear of i., 677:13
  greatest service or greatest i., 84:3
  never forget i., 731:12
  never use treatment with view to i., 79:13
  recompense i. with justice, 69:9
  returns on him who began, 101:10
  sooner forgotten than insult, 341:18
  such i. vex a saint, 188:35
  where i. let me sow pardon, 138:15
Injustice, bear with patience i., 298:1
  complain of i. of government, 419:3
  conscience with i. corrupted, 185:17
  easy to bear, 772:9
  extreme justice extreme i., 134:29
  extreme justice often i., 96:*n* 13
  extreme law often extreme i., 96:12
  fear of suffering i., 293:13
  inclination to i., 823:18
  makes democracy necessary, 823:18
Injustice (*continued*)
  man ever in darkness of i., 132:4
  mankind censure i., 84:7
  no i. to person who consents, 135:1
  nothing so felt as i., 549:25
  on part of government, 771:2
  one man's justice another's i., 497:26
  road to downfall, 517:20
  sometimes public service, 391:6
  threat to justice, 909:7
Injustices, heaped i. upon us, 726:8
Injye other people's sufferin', 722:18
Ink, effusion of i., 365:11
  essential in painting, 135:11
  every drop of i. ran cold, 363:19
  gall enough in thy i., 214:19
  galley slave to i., 484:11
  hath not drunk i., 190:27
  never saw pen and i., 214:27
  runs from mouth, 913:4
  seven seas of i., 132:3
Inkstand, Vesuvius' crater for i., 571:1
Inky, not alone my i. cloak, 218:2
Inlaid with patines of bright gold, 201:1
Inland island, 634:12
  though i. far we be, 426:20
  tract of i. ground, 428:15
Inlets, restless wind of i., 837:2
  through creeks and i. making, 564:17
Inn, classics have charm in i., 498:20
  gain timely i., 238:22
  happiness produced by i., 355:19
  make my house your i., 798:17
  no room in the i., 42:27
  remember i. Miranda, 730:5
  take mine ease in mine i., 159:14
  up to old i. door, 772:23
  warmest welcome at an i., 355:*n* 8
  world not i. but hospital, 274:21
Inner air inner light, 851:10
  light will shine forth, 397:*n* 6
  man, 49:34
  mine with i. weather, 748:13
  resolve i. conflicts, 789:14
  temple's i. shrine, 425:17
  weather, 748:13
  what i. voice says, 412:19
Innisfail, harp of I., 443:21
Innisfree, go to I., 712:4
Innocence and health, 370:1
  ceremony of i., 714:12
  changed i. for i., 246:10
  confession next thing to i., 112:15
  fearful i., 425:15
  has nothing to dread, 312:9
  her i. a child, 305:8
  ignorance not i., 545:21
  murderous i. of sea, 714:14
  never blossom into license, 312:10
  of love, 214:3
  of our neighbors, 560:13
  our peace our i., 425:15
  recovered i., 560:13
  silence often of pure i., 246:15
  soul recovers i., 714:21
  what is our i., 799:2
Innocent, armed without i. within, 339:18
  as new-laid egg, 627:8
  believe theologians nothing i., 609:1
  calm quiet i. recreation, 271:10
  children's souls not i., 128:27

Innocent (*continued*)
condemn an i. person, 343 : 5
coursed down his i. nose, 210 : 25
he that maketh haste to be rich not i., 25 : 28
look like i. flower, 236 : 20
man sent to legislature, 725 : 15
merriment, 629 : 12
millions of i. burnt tortured, 387 : 15
minds i. and quiet, 296 : 4
moon, 693 : 9
no i. wit be suppressed, 386 : 1
of the blood, 41 : 22
officious i. sincere, 356 : 24
skin of i. lamb parchment, 185 : 25
sleep, 237 : 21
than one i. suffer, 365 : 19
who perished being i., 15 : 10
women i. and pure, 247 : 26
Innocently, live i. God here, 350 : 9
Innocuous desuetude, 631 : 8
Innovation, opponents of i. die out, 686 : 11
scientific i. rarely converts opponents, 686 : 11
Innovator, time the greatest i., 180 : 24
Inns not residences, 798 : 17
of molten blue, 604 : 14
Innuendoes, beauty of i., 767 : 12
Innumerable bees, 531 : 13
caravan which moves, 471 : 6
things creeping i., 21 : 11
Inoffensive, smooth easy i. down to Hell, 92 : *n* 5
untitled aristocracy, 519 : 17
Inordinate interest in animals and athletes, 799 : 17
Inquire, shoot first i. afterwards, 825 : 17
Inquirer, workshop of serious i., 636 : 16
Inquiries about events following birth, 124 : 2
suspended religious i., 384 : 2
Inquiring eye or tongue, 442 : 24
Inquiry, do not block way of i., 639 : 5
thought to aim at some good, 87 : 13
undismayed unintimidated i., 737 : 6
Inquisition, committee i., 764 : 2
dogs, 535 : 12
Inquisitive, acute i. dexterous, 372 : 20
Inquisitor of structures, 768 : 25
Inquisitors, whom will you make your i., 387 : 14
Insane, most i. of passions, 681 : 1
ordinarily he is i., 482 : 6
root, 236 : 8
Insanity often logic, 519 : 3
Insatiable intellectual curiosity, 701 : 5
Insatiate blood, 874 : 17
to pursue war with heaven, 284 : 3
Inscape is what I aim at, 656 : 22
Inscription, altar with i., 46 : 15
Inscriptions, lapidary i., 355 : 18
Inscrutable, dark i. workmanship, 423 : 18
dumb i. grand, 588 : 4
jest unseen i., 189 : 33
Insect carries impress of Maker, 316 : 8
I am that i. brother, 581 : 20
scraping on surface of life, 632 : 1
vile i. that has risen up, 346 : 4
Insects, get meaning for other i., 632 : 1
loud and troublesome i., 373 : 28
Insects (*continued*)
of the hour, 373 : 28
to whom God gave lust, 581 : 20
Insensate care of mortals, 100 : *n* 8
Insensibility, stark i., 353 : 20
Insensible, honor i. then, 205 : 5
to freedoms of Constitution, 776 : 13
Inseparable, nonviolence and truth i., 727 : 6
one and i., 450 : 16, 725 : 20
sex and beauty i., 790 : 18
Inshallah, say only I., 131 : 10
Inside, not forgotten i. of church, 204 : 24
Insidious encroachment by men of zeal, 677 : 15
Insight into universal nature, 420 : 3
Insignificant chatter of the world, 555 : 1
man i. and aware of it, 738 : 10
too i. for our concern, 801 : 13
vice-presidency most i. office, 381 : 16
Insincere, exhausting thing is being i., 867 : 6
most i. line written, 803 : 1
Insinuating appearance, 68 : 2
Insipid as queen on card, 535 : 4
tale without love i., 655 : 16
Insisture course proportion, 225 : 37
Insolence, above i. and triviality, 798 : 11
flown with i. and wine, 283 : 19
of office, 221 : 12
strength without i., 456 : 9
surfeit begets i., 67 : 3
Insolent menaces of villains, 382 : 11
Insomnia, amor vincit i., 870 : 4
Inspector of snowstorms rainstorms, 557 : 7
Inspiration, cleanse by the i. of thy Holy Spirit, 55 : 15
genius one percent i., 661 : 9
hierophants of i., 470 : 5
lost an i., 786 : *n* 4
love and freedom, 695 : 3
no more i. than muffins, 680 : 18
shining star and i., 836 : 3
whatever poet writes with divine i., 79 : 9
Inspirations of people and time, 842 : 3
Inspire hopeless passion, 539 : 13
two qualities i. affection, 87 : 29
we do not i. conduct, 294 : 5
who i. love most fortunate, 467 : 5
Inspired, eyes upraised as i., 364 : 14
Inspires, fair fame i., 338 : 14
wine i. us and fires us, 332 : 2
Inspiring bold John Barleycorn, 411 : 10
Installment, gratitude repays first i., 115 : 9
Instances, wise saws and modern i., 211 : 15
Instancy, majestic i., 693 : 11
Instant, for each ecstatic i., 604 : 6
in season, 51 : 8
made eternity, 542 : 16
more i. than Feet, 693 : 11
Instant's truce between virtue and vice, 560 : 8
Instinct, erotic i. questionable, 755 : 3
men should be right by i., 74 : 22
no longer guided by i., 732 : 10
of self-preservation, 685 : 3
reason against it i. for it, 621 : 1
Instinct (*continued*)
running off upon i., 901 : 14
sensation i. intelligence, 482 : 12
spirit and i. in harmony, 755 : 3
telepathic i., 783 : 4
volcanic political i., 681 : 21
war not an i., 784 : 21
Instinctive, killing for food not i., 786 : 8
pursuing i. course, 480 : 1
Instinctively, rats i. have quit it, 247 : 14
Instincts, a few strong i., 428 : 19
decisions more of i. than will, 754 : 5
heed no i. but our own, 296 : 8
high i., 426 : 18
plant himself on i., 496 : 12
uncivilized Eastern i., 707 : 7
Institooshuns, greatest i. of land, 616 : 12
Institute and digest of anarchy, 373 : 19
Instituted, governments i. among men, 387 : 9
Institution, glorious i., 373 : 7
lengthened shadow of one man, 497 : 4
life's a pleasant i., 630 : 4
Institutions and customs not consciously designed, 844 : 8
cease being liberal, 658 : 12
create nation, 502 : 7
greatest i. of land, 616 : 12
hostility against i., 451 : 5
liberal i. enemies of freedom, 658 : 12
neither for nor against i., 575 : 7
overthrow of i. by force, 700 : 3
political i. superstructure, 731 : 3
sought to destroy i., 575 : 7
this country with its i., 521 : 11
Instruct sorrows to be proud, 201 : 20
Instructing, delighting and i. at same time, 110 : 1
Instruction, I will better the i., 199 : 19
text of civil i., 389 : 2
Instructions for well-being, 6 : 1
Instructor, age not qualified as i., 559 : 7
Instructors, practice best of i., 111 : 11
Instructs, delights reader i. too, 311 : 13
Instrument, fever is Nature's i., 301 : 1
little i. appeared, 610 : 3
made i. to know, 291 : 25
mind like musical i., 580 : 4
of slavery, 364 : 7
of trade and commerce, 617 : 7
of your peace, 138 : 15
pen excellent i., 380 : 7
pliant i. of Executive, 439 : 4
sweeter than sound of i., 274 : 20
tune the i. here at the door, 254 : 17
Instruments, find fit i. of ill, 334 : 9
fit i. to make slaves, 350 : 17
genius and mortal i., 215 : 18
of darkness, 236 : 9
of European greatness, 401 : 14
played before the Lord on i., 13 : 14
stringed i. and organs, 22 : 25
thousand twangling i., 248 : 10
to plague us, 235 : 14
Insubstantial pageant faded, 248 : 13
Insufferable inane, 619 : 1
Insufficient, ability alone is i., 313 : 5
Insular Tahiti full of peace, 570 : 14
Insult, add i. to injury, 114 : 11, 358 : 7

Insult (*continued*)
injury sooner forgotten than i., 341 : 18
to God, 541 : 8
Insulting, rushed to meet i. foe, 399 : 17
Insults of Fortune, 349 : 24
unavenged, 428 : 12
Insure domestic tranquillity, 391 : 10
Insures us to git best o' noose, 568 : 12
Insurrection, never did i. want such watercolors, 205 : 3
revolution is i., 826 : 6
servile i., 617 : 6
suffers nature of an i., 215 : 18
Intangible, world i. we touch, 693 : 16
Integer vitae scelerisque purus, 107 : *n* 10
Integers, God made i., 592 : 3
Integration, different i., 837 : 9
not fighting for i., 904 : 15
of lands and peoples, 912 : 3
Integrity, clothed with i., 298 : 1
does one's i. lie, 905 : 2
in silence preserve i., 140 : 4
state of natural i., 90 : 7
territorial i., 682 : 15
were we men of i., 890 : 6
Intellect, achievements of i. everlasting, 103 : 2
adduces authority uses not i., 152 : 7
conformity of object and i., 137 : 8
extraction of living i., 281 : 22
fashion birth i., 593 : 1
feather to tickle i., 442 : 12
forced to choose, 716 : 7
health and i. the two blessings, 91 : 11
improperly exposed, 432 : 24
invisible to man who has none, 463 : 10
is to emotion as clothes, 698 : 8
judgment of i. half truth, 753 : 13
light between truth and i., 141 : 25
man with godlike i., 515 : 10
march of I., 440 : 12
marks of God in liberal i., 448 : 3
mugwump educated beyond i., 632 : 4
not i. but personality, 577 : 2
not understand only by i., 753 : 13
opinion from feelings not i., 579 : 8
physical tinged with i., 503 : 8
product of tendencies and training, 752 : 18
restless versatile i., 596 : 11
sin of i. that triumphed, 503 : 4
subtlety of i., 637 : 8
taste connects i. with senses, 436 : 17
thought labor of i., 492 : 1
unaging i., 714 : 22
understand its inadequacy, 753 : 13
voice of i. soft, 678 : 12
war between emotion and i., 861 : 18
weakness of i., 629 : 16
will and i. the same, 308 : 8
with i. or with conscience, 527 : 14
Intellection, happiest i., 899 : 15
Intellects, argument and i. too, 369 : 11
three classes of i., 154 : 3
Intellectual, a tear an i. thing, 406 : 7
All-in-all, 424 : 16
before committees, 764 : 2
being, 284 : 9
chains, 858 : 19
chap, 628 : 23
co-perception, 500 : 10
Intellectual (*continued*)
curiosity, 758 : 3
dandyism, 600 : 23
delight and freedom, 420 : 3
desolation, 562 : 18
disgrace, 868 : 13
enjoyment, 694 : 4
hatred worst, 714 : 20
life like bees, 703 : 13
material progress depends on i., 515 : 5
neutralize i. element, 703 : 19
Northwest Passage to i. world, 360 : 16
not separate i. from social, 755 : 21
ought to refuse to testify, 764 : 2
passion drives out sensuality, 152 : 3
product judged from age produced in, 638 : 9
responsibility, 818 : 10
rights and powers, 448 : 7
superiority of man, 626 : 4
take i. possession, 653 : 17
throne, 585 : 23
undeveloped i. nature, 597 : 8
virile courageous, 726 : 1
wants, 649 : 16
world divided, 705 : 20
Intellectuals at one pole, 865 : 17
deserve intended slavery, 764 : 2
I'm one of the i., 836 : 14
treason of the i., 720 : 12
Intelligence, controlling i. understands, 125 : 6
even if superior i. tell us, 758 : 10
gods do not give all men i., 60 : 4
incongruous with i., 580 : 8
machinery of our i., 703 : 4
making artificial objects, 688 : 10
of American people, 772 : 20
overwhelms i. of all gods, 61 : 10
pawn your i., 828 : 15
quickness to apprehend, 697 : 18
sensation instinct i., 482 : 12
struggle against limitations of i., 832 : 1
talent inspiration, 695 : 3
test of first-rate i., 835 : 10
use of i. pleasure, 913 : 3
vast enough to comprehend all forces, 397 : 17
which goes with sex, 790 : 18
women's i. nourished, 898 : 7
Intelligences, first animals then i., 600 : 17
Intelligent, all i. thoughts already thought, 397 : 10
enemies i. and corrupt, 859 : 14
may be called i. indeed, 69 : 1
perception of least i., 812 : 16
possesses keen i. mind, 82 : 22
reporting, 814 : 2
so elegant so i., 805 : 4
woman, 735 : 14
Intelligibly, speak i. to world, 711 : 16
Intemperance, no tyrant like i., 505 : 16
Intend, what evil I i. to do, 76 : 18
Intended an ode, 639 : 20
take hint when i., 750 : 10
years damp my i. wing, 287 : 13
Intending to build tower, 43 : 24
Intense loneliness intense ignorance, 677 : 3
moment isolated, 807 : 23
Intensely, soul listened i., 428 : 15
Intensity, all I care about is i., 643 : 5
full of passionate i., 714 : 12
grandeur remains without i., 118 : 17
moving into another i., 807 : 24
Intent, eye i. on wondrous plan, 410 : 16
forget not yet tried i., 161 : 22
his first avowed i., 302 : 14
is all, 145 : 6
love come with murderous i., 76 : 22
night of dark i., 748 : 11
not criminal unless i. criminal, 133 : 6
on hospitable thoughts i., 286 : 18
prick sides of my i., 236 : 24
truth told with bad i., 406 : 12
upon our interests in old age, 97 : 6
Intention of communicating truth, 437 : 7
stabs the center, 246 : 12
Intentional, abstain from i. wrongdoing, 79 : 13
Petersburg most i. town, 581 : 16
Intentions, hell full of good i., 136 : 11
hell paved with good i., 136 : *n* 8, 269 : *n* 2
honorable, 378 : 7
Intents are savage-wild, 193 : 23
discerner of thoughts and i., 51 : 14
wicked or charitable, 219 : 11
Inter, in hugger-mugger i. him, 223 : 26
in peace children i. parents, 78 : 5
Intercede with Neptune, 569 : 20
Interchange, quiet i. of sentiments, 355 : 16
Intercourse between tyrants and slaves, 369 : 25
hold i. with roots of trees, 793 : 19
lived in social i., 354 : 25
open and friendly in private i., 80 : 17
speed the soft i., 335 : 1
with foreign nations, 445 : 19
Interdependence, context of human i., 852 : 3
Interest, art makes life and i., 654 : 10
duty and i., 379 : 12
exceed in i. knock at door, 441 : 23
I du believe in i., 568 : 2
impulse of passion or i., 398 : 1
of the producer, 366 : 7
promote public i., 366 : 4
public i., 814 : 3
pursue his own i. his own way, 366 : 8
unborrowed from the eye, 423 : 12
Interested, not i. in defeat, 573 : 16
self interest other people, 639 : 2
Interesting because unimportant, 817 : 14
but tough, 623 : 24
only obligation of novel to be i., 652 : 12
want of the i., 589 : 10
war talk i., 623 : 16
Interest's on dangerous edge, 543 : 7
Interests, conflicting i. of society, 737 : 4
eternal and perpetual i., 454 : 12
exposed to conflicting i., 778 : 11
great i. at stake, 88 : 10
human figure i. me most, 728 : 10
of community, 398 : 1
various powerful i., 449 : 9
Interfere by force with slaveholder, 560 : 23

Interfered in behalf of rich, 486 : 15
Interfused, something far more
i., 423 : 13
Intergraft our hands, 253 : 6
Interim like a phantasma, 215 : 18
Interline aphorisms in reading, 386 : 12
Interlude, strange i., 810 : 11
Interludes, strange i., 810 : 11
Interlunar, vacant i. cave, 288 : 21
Intermeddle, stranger doth not
i., 23 : 36
Interminable night, 808 : 13
Ulysses i. adventurer, 769 : 5
Intermingle jest with earnest, 181 : 3
Intermission, laugh sans i., 211 : 7
pleasure is i. of pain, 264 : 5
Internal domestic empire, 837 : 8
environment, 551 : 19
medium, 551 : 18
International, bring order to i.
affairs, 763 : 15
nuclear control, 891 : 15
police power, 687 : 10
spirit of science in i. affairs, 854 : 1
Internationally, bring suit in court
i., 787 : 11
Interpose, who in quarrels i., 331 : 15
Interposed, mountains i., 376 : 19
Interpret interpretatons, 166 : 7
Interpretation, aid to i. of future, 80 : 15
doctrine or practice or i., 125 : 13
interpreter not need i., 637 : 6
science right i. of nature, 471 : 15
this is the i. of the thing, 33 : 1
Interpreter, critic i. of artist, 653 : 3
in marriage room for i., 864 : 12
is the hardest of the two, 399 : 6
man i. of nature, 471 : 15
nature not own i., 571 : 13
not need interpretation, 637 : 6
perfect i. of life, 794 : 11
Interpreters, for crowd they need
i., 71 : 24
men on shore i., 732 : 7
Interpreting divine Principle, 583 : 5
Interprets, poet i. poem, 718 : 4
Interred, good oft i. with bones, 216 : 17
life is shrunk dead and i., 252 : 25
Interrupt with such silly
question, 359 : 19
Interrupted by dying, 275 : 32
Interruption, noise impertinent
i., 463 : 7
not continuity, 883 : 7
Interstellar, vacant i. spaces, 807 : 16
Interstitially, judges legislate i., 644 : 20
Intertissued robe of gold, 208 : 7
Interval, enjoy i., 704 : 4
lucid i., 304 : 25
Intervals, full of lucid i., 170 : 16
lucid i. and happy pauses, 179 : 12
Interventionism, total i. no
answer, 852 : 1
Interview with Satan, 690 : 11
Intestines, prejudices traced to
i., 659 : 1
Intimacy, heart-revealing i., 714 : 15
Intimate of air, 874 : 17
quality of handmade things, 739 : 4
quality of the Four, 783 : 5
Intimates are predestined, 635 : 3
eternity to man, 326 : 3
Intimation, steel against i., 768 : 2
Intimations, reason's icy i., 486 : 2
Intimidate human race into
order, 763 : 15
threats of halter i., 393 : 9
Intolerable, burden of them is i., 55 : 17
deal of sack, 204 : 9
in worst state i., 384 : 9
music falls, 717 : 16
shirt of flame, 808 : 15
situation becomes
unimportant, 734 : 9
that beings doomed, 515 : 15
was i. becomes unimportant, 734 : 9
wrestle with words and
meanings, 807 : 12
Intolerance, fought against i., 788 : 12
Intolerant, learned toleration from
i., 782 : 20
Intoxicate the brain, 332 : 20
Intoxicated, heart i. with bliss, 413 : 21
Intractable, sullen untamed i., 808 : 1
Intrepid sailors, 575 : 22
shorebirds, 874 : 9
Intricate as death, 255 : 3
Intricated, poor i. soul, 255 : 4
Intrigue, spotless through i., 540 : 1
Intrinsic value of knowledge, 342 : 2
Introduce philosophy into
homes, 98 : 25
please allow me to i. myself, 916 : 8
Introduced, cut anyone i. to, 613 : 20
when I'm i. to one, 697 : 1
Introspection, prone to i., 799 : 18
Introversion, tendency to i., 499 : 6
Intrude, for bellies' sake i., 280 : 20
Intruder in dust, 838 : 7
Intruders, into which i. not
come, 910 : 12
Intrudes, society where none i., 458 : 24
Intuition, feminine i., 853 : 19
intelligence which goes with sex is
i., 790 : 18
more subtle than premise, 644 : 11
passionate i., 428 : 16
reliance on i., 756 : 3
Intuitions without method, 703 : 13
Intuitive, beautiful always i., 436 : 19
calculation transcended
mathematics, 756 : 3
Inurned, weep a people i., 488 : *n* 3
Invade, better not i., 455 : 8
Invaded, France is i., 420 : 12
Invading, ours is the i. army, 558 : 2
Invalid, invaluable permanent i.
Bunbury, 675 : 19
physical laws i., 762 : 3
Invalidated, friendships i. by
marriage, 620 : 15
Invasion can be resisted, 491 : 11
waiting for i. so are fishes, 744 : 10
Invent, lies you can i., 406 : 12
necessary to i. him, 344 : 2
would children i. game, 789 : 10
young men fitter to i., 181 : 7
Invented an invaluable invalid, 675 : 19
disappointed in monkey i.
man, 626 : 17
falsehood i., 776 : 2
first i. sleep, 171 : 1, 556 : 2
first i. war, 183 : 4
first i. work, 442 : 2
fool i. kissing, 323 : 14
history, 344 : 17
time someone i. plot, 782 : 7
Invention arises from idleness, 817 : 15
Invention (*continued*)
brightest heaven of i., 207 : 1
equal license in bold i., 109 : 18
greatest i. of century, 697 : 8
horrible i. the bourgeois, 583 : 7
if not true it is happy i., 387 : *n* 1
is unfruitful, 372 : 13
necessity mother of i., 117 : *n* 6,
134 : 9
necessity not mother of i., 817 : 15
noble i., 387 : 1
of method of invention, 697 : 8
scaled i., 793 : 4
stomach dispenser of i., 117 : 8
war is an i., 784 : 21
Inventions by which man remade
environment, 870 : 15
in Nature's i. nothing lacking, 152 : 12
sought out many i., 27 : 12
Inventories, statistics and history
i., 498 : 16
Inventors, seldom or never i., 343 : 22
Invents, modern man i.
museum, 834 : 4
Inversion, negative i., 868 : 3
Inverted, country an i. cone, 356 : 3
winter ruler of i. year, 377 : 5
Investigation of hidden causes, 166 : 15
scientific i., 595 : 8
Investment, goodness i. never
fails, 560 : 8
liquidity of i., 783 : 14
of genius pays dividends, 630 : 23
Inveterate, long i. foes saluted, 305 : 5
scars, 807 : 4
Invigorated and reimpressed, 352 : 24
Invincible, I am i. I am woman, 915 : 9
no animal more i. than
woman, 82 : 13
shaking her i. locks, 282 : 3
soul's i. surmise, 703 : 3
summer, 882 : 13
Inviolable shade, 586 : 2
Inviolate constitutional rights, 700 : 3
Invisible, all things visible and i., 50 : 9
aloft i. in night, 683 : 5
at times i., 799 : 14
bloody and i. hand, 238 : 21
choir i., 564 : 22
essential is i. to eye, 849 : 4
Fortune though blind not i., 181 : 5
individual led by i. hand, 366 : 4
its name is The I., 64 : 6
jest unseen inscrutable i., 189 : 33
labor, 491 : 23
man, 885 : 5
no bird but i. thing, 427 : 2
O world i., 693 : 16
power of visible is i., 799 : 3
skuttle fish becomes i., 327 : 1
soap, 485 : 13
soul bright i. green, 558 : 11
spirit of wine, 230 : 25
vision art of seeing i., 322 : 6
web you wove, 808 : 19
why art silent and i., 404 : 13
worm, 405 : 5
wounds i., 212 : 15
Invisibly, silently i., 404 : 10
Invitation, more i. than
command, 327 : 11
Invite, all occasions i. his
mercies, 255 : 1
God and his angels, 255 : 2

Invite (*continued*)
my soul, 574 : 12
Invites, bell i. me, 237 : 16
his wit i. you, 336 : *n* 2
my steps and points, 335 : 7
Invocation, true poem an i., 833 : 6
Invoke genius of Constitution, 351 : 6
Involuntary, it was i., 890 : 2
Involve us in wrong war, 825 : 5
Involved in mankind, 254 : 22
we are not person i., 624 : 18
Invulnerable, fate far off i., 902 : 3
Inward and spiritual grace, 56 : 5
as men of i. light are wont, 291 : 26
beauty in i. soul, 83 : 7
draw i. quality after, 241 : 10
eye, 427 : 11
greatness, 207 : 11
horror, 326 : 3
no creature whose i. being, 565 : 25
on i. vision close eyes, 703 : 3
outward and i. at one, 83 : 7
self-disparagement, 428 : 14
sphinx, 721 : 2
to read Nature he looked i., 303 : 6
upward and i. delight, 570 : 5
vision, 703 : 3
Inwardly in secret great, 568 : 23
Inwardness of the situation, 650 : 16
Inwards, journey i., 863 : 4
turn i. and examine, 68 : 16
Iona, ruins of I., 352 : 22
Ipse dixit, 134 : 7
I.Q., love archer with low I.Q., 864 : 18
Ira, ça i, ça tiendra, 928 : 1
Iram indeed is gone, 516 : 3
Ire, best way to escape His i., 544 : 19
Ireland, dance wyth me in I., 916 : 16
gives England generals, 601 : 7
grand you look, 661 : 10
great Gaels of I., 742 : 4
holy lande of I., 916 : 16
I am of I., 916 : *n* 3
ich am of I., 916 : 16
snow all over I., 777 : 16
was I on road to I., 855 : 9
Ireland's, romantic I. dead and gone, 713 : 11
Iridescence, grossest i. of ocean, 768 : 12
Iridescent dream, 615 : 3
Iris' woof, 279 : 8
Irish, blithe I. lad, 443 : 9
grow on I. ground, 920 : 21
I am troubled I'm I., 799 : 4
Lady howl in I., 204 : 18
let I vessel lie, 868 : 11
no language like I., 735 : 6
poets learn trade, 717 : 22
upon the I. shore, 410 : 6
Irish-Americans, have done with I., 667 : 1
Irishman, give I. lager for month, 623 : 12
in Eden boss it, 561 : 13
Irks care crop-full bird, 544 : 9
Irksome, discourse of fools is i., 35 : 37
Irlonde, dance wyth me in I., 916 : 16
holy lande of I., 916 : 16
ich am of I., 916 : 16
Iron, age of i., 342 : 22
and blood, 553 : 6
armies clad in i., 288 : 23
artificer in brass and i., 7 : 23
Iron (*continued*)
cold i., 173 : *n* 3, 455 : 12
conscience seared with hot i., 50 : 27
curtain, 746 : 9
door of north, 864 : 2
earth hard as i., 608 : 17
entered into his soul, 56 : 14
fist, 421 : 13
golden opes the i. shuts, 280 : 19
hammer i. when hot, 110 : 25
hand in velvet glove, 161 : 19
ice and i. not welded, 669 : 16
if gold ruste what shall i. do, 146 : 9
implacable i. bars, 801 : 17
in water float, 919 : 9
legs of i., 32 : 32
meals of beef i. steel, 207 : 26
meddles with cold i., 173 : *n* 3
nerve, 533 : 4
New England dark, 838 : 5
nor any tool of i., 13 : 32
nor i. bars a cage, 296 : 4
physician of I. Age, 585 : 3
rod of i., 53 : 2
rusts from disuse, 152 : 8
scourge, 361 : 13
sharpeneth iron, 25 : 26
slamming of i., 873 : 12
sleet of arrowy shower, 363 : 10
stones are i., 11 : 14
strike when i. hot, 110 : *n* 16
strong as i. bands, 510 : 7
tears down Pluto's cheek, 278 : 22
time make soft i. wood, 823 : 14
time of doubt, 585 : 4
tongue of midnight, 197 : 22
voice of i. chest of brass, 105 : 20
when i. hot strike, 110 : *n* 16
written with a pen of i., 32 : 10
Iron-bound bucket, 455 : 7
Ironic, Death's i. scraping, 767 : 11
Ironies, silver-footed i., 701 : 7
Irons, two i. in the fire, 263 : 3
Ironware, firewood i. and trays, 760 : 20
Iroquois, I'll be Indian I., 874 : 8
would have had strong states, 800 : 4
Irradiated an Indian wilderness, 319 : 22
Irradiating word, 609 : 2
Irrational fears, 677 : 13
laws of nature may be i., 776 : 6
to rational being i. unendurable, 121 : 1
Irrationally held truths, 596 : 8
Irrecoverably dark total eclipse, 288 : 20
Irregular and intimate quality, 739 : 4
choose the i., 659 : 16
indigested piece, 352 : 8
Irregulars, Baker Street i., 689 : 4
Irrelevancies, past free of i., 736 : 9
thinking is dismissal of i., 832 : 11
Irrelevant, most i. thing in nature, 442 : 6
Irreligion, free for i., 821 : 10
Irremediable poverty of life, 769 : 25
Irreparable ravages of time, 312 : 11
Irreproachably tender, 826 : 16
Irresistible desire to be irresistibly desired, 750 : 7
Irresistibly desired, 750 : 7
Irresolute, resolved to be i., 743 : 12
Irresponsible foetus, 804 : 9
Irritable reaching after fact, 479 : 5
Irrt, es i. der Mensch, 396 : *n* 2
Irruption, death i. of nothingness, 583 : 16
Is, all that i. and shall be, 74 : 18
as he i. so was he made, 654 : 19
he i. or was or has to be, 344 : 10
one i. or i. not, 85 : 15
seems madam Nay it i., 218 : 2
that that i. i., 214 : 27
which was and i., 53 : 7
Isaac, God of I. not philosophers, 300 : 15
that which has been sent down on I., 130 : 11
Iscariot-like crime, 799 : 12
Ishmael, call me I., 570 : 3
that which has been sent down on I., 130 : 11
Ishmael's hand against every man, 8 : 9
Islam, we have embraced I., 132 : 9
Island, arrived at i. of Bahamas, 150 : 15
defend our i. whatever cost, 744 : 2
entire of itself, 254 : 22
floating bulwark of our i., 365 : 16
heart no i. but continent, 180 : 13
honor is like an i., 311 : 14
in ocean of non-knowledge, 862 : 5
inland i., 634 : 12
luminous i. of self, 880 : 4
misty i., 483 : 20
no man is an i., 254 : 22
no owls in whole i., 356 : *n* 1
of England, 207 : 25
old age an i., 614 : 10
rough i. story, 533 : 5
sad dark i. Cythera, 581 : 3
savages in unknown i., 501 : 9
snug little i., 429 : 15
solitude unsponsored, 767 : 4
there is an i., 850 : 12
tight little i., 429 : 15
watched famous i. descending, 743 : 14
Islanded in stream of stars, 802 : 20
place remote and i., 664 : 5
Islands, adagios of i., 843 : 15
beautiful where we're groping, 849 : 11
cold remote i., 837 : 2
Greek i. over Harvard Square, 842 : 4
looked seaward among i., 664 : 2
nightmares of other i., 878 : 17
realms and i. as plates, 241 : 25
round many western i., 475 : 6
what gray rocks what i., 806 : 8
whose raving skies opened, 673 : 19
Isle, a ship an i., 785 : 17
all isles excelling, 306 : 6
cause or men of Emerald I., 400 : 10
cherry i., 266 : 3
enchanted i. of time, 846 : 4
green i. in sea, 525 : 17
in far-off seas, 540 : 17
is full of noises, 248 : 10
it frights the i., 230 : 20
sceptered i., 194 : 13
that is called Patmos, 52 : 27
Isled, wound with thee in thee i., 656 : 14
Isles, fished by obstinate i., 792 : 11
Isle all i. excelling, 306 : 6
moving i. of winter, 528 : 29
naked melancholy i., 345 : 15

Isles (*continued*)
of Greece, 461 : 2
sprinkled i., 543 : 24
throned on her hundred i., 458 : 6
touch Happy I., 529 : 13
Islet, murmuring name of each i., 782 : 22
Ism, alien i., 779 : 19
Isness of man's nature, 909 : 13
Isn't, as it i. it ain't, 612 : 24
Isolated, Chinese not remain i., 882 : 22
with no before and after, 807 : 23
Isolates, silence i., 755 : 15
Isolation of sky at evening, 767 : 4
pass through i. and silence, 860 : 13
robbed of i. that is life, 764 : 9
worst counselor, 706 : 8
Isolationism may obstruct peace, 781 : 4
total i. no answer, 852 : 1
Israel, ancient nations Egypt and I., 881 : 15
arose a mother in I., 12 : 3
blessed be Lord God of I., 42 : 24
captive I., 563 : 14
chariot of I., 14 : 13
glory departed from I., 12 : 32
glory of thy people I., 42 : 31
he that keepeth I., 22 : 4
Judah and I. dwelt safely, 13 : 29
lost sheep of house of I., 38 : 33
no king in I., 12 : 24
scattered upon the hills, 14 : 10
sweet psalmist of I., 13 : 25
thy tabernacles O I., 11 : 6
to your tents O I., 13 : 39
Israelis, no more war between Arabs and I., 895 : 17
Israfel, dwell where I. dwelt, 525 : 10
Issue is in God's hands, 71 : 26
judged in light of final i., 88 : 21
Issues, contrived corridors and i., 804 : 14
distract attention from i., 703 : 1
fine i., 227 : 24
heaven has joined great i., 427 : 24
out of it are the i. of life, 23 : 9
when i. are joined, 65 : 4
Isthmus of a middle state, 337 : 2
It can't happen here, 791 : 10
is finished, 45 : 34
it's just I., 710 : 11
Italia who hast fatal gift, 458 : 10
Italian for converse with feminine sex, 357 : 19
I speak I. to women, 143 : 16
perhaps I., 627 : 18
proletariat, 783 : 18
tenderness of I. tongue, 357 : 19
Italien, je parle i. aux femmes, 143 : *n* 10
Italy, beyond Alps lies I., 110 : 13
far from I. I lie, 93 : 2
fashions in proud I., 194 : 11
graved inside of it I., 542 : 7
Greece I. and England did adorn, 306 : 1
made from designs by Michelangelo, 622 : 6
paradise for horses, 259 : 22
paradise of exiles, 467 : 12
Itch, incurable i. for writing, 122 : 12
of disputing, 251 : 5
Itchez, Ah i. Ah scratchez, 856 : 2
Itching palm, 216 : 31
Item with skin wrapped around, 828 : 3
Items for imaginative genius of west, 577 : 13
Iteration, damnable i., 203 : 1
Ithaca, fill I. full of moths, 242 : 10
setting out on voyage to I., 702 : 4
Itself, is it true in and for i., 422 : 17
love is most nearly i., 807 : 24
more i. than one knew, 902 : 14
thou art the thing i., 234 : 7
Itylus, half assuaged for I., 632 : 7
Iucundior, quae est domestica sede i., 98 : *n* 13
Iudex damnatur ubi nocens absolvitur, 111 : *n* 7
Iudicaret, ne supra crepidam sutor i., 90 : *n* 6
Iura, sunt superis sua i., 113 : *n* 16
Ius est ars boni et aequi, 134 : 8
summum saepe summa est malitia, 96 : *n* 13
Ivan Ilych's life most simple, 602 : 10
Petrofski Skevar, 922 : 16
Ives, going to St. I., 930 : 1
Ivory apes and peacocks, 13 : 36, 760 : 19
bit of i. on which I work, 441 : 3
gate of i., 61 : 2, 105 : 26
neck is as a tower of i., 28 : 20
tower, 504 : 5, 755 : 21
Ivy, goats eat i., 933 : 4
holly and the i., 919 : 21
myrtle and i., 462 : 6
not hang i. over wine, 112 : 12
pluck i. branch for me, 608 : 18
with i. never sere, 280 : 6
Ivy-mantled tower, 361 : 22, 773 : 15

J

Jabal father of such as dwell in tents, 7 : 21
Jabberwock, beware J., 612 : 17
J'accuse 643 : 9
Jack and Jill, 931 : 1
banish plump J., 204 : 7
be nimble, 932 : 17
fly away J., 934 : 8
house that J. built, 934 : 9
joke poor potsherd, 656 : 21
little J. Horner, 929 : 20
makes J. a dull boy, 271 : 17
one named J., 934 : 8
Sprat eat no fat, 929 : 16
wild J. for a lover, 716 : 16
Jackknife, just a j. has Macheath, 840 : 15
Jackknives, pelicans flew like j., 888 : 13
Jackson, pick Andrew J. from pebbles, 570 : 11
standing like stone wall, 594 : 4
Stonewall J. wrapped in beard, 840 : 7
Jacky have new master, 931 : 2
Jacob called the place Peniel, 8 : 26
gave Esau bread and pottage, 8 : 16
God of J. not philosophers, 300 : 15
served seven years, 8 : 22
sold his birthright unto J., 8 : 16
Jacob (*continued*)
that which has been sent down on J., 130 : 11
thy tents O J., 11 : 6
was a plain man, 8 : 15
was left alone, 8 : 24
wrestled as angel with J., 270 : 28
Jacob's ladder, 693 : 19
mystic heart, 572 : 5
talk of J. ladder, 500 : 18
voice is J. voice, 8 : 17
Jade, arrant j. on a journey, 369 : 22
Chinese love j., 796 : 1
let galled j. wince, 222 : 16
Jael brought forth butter, 12 : 6
took a nail, 12 : 2
J'ai vécu, 394 : 9
Jail, air's glass j., 905 : 7
all we know who lie in j., 676 : 12
like living in j., 875 : 8
little stealin' gets you in j., 810 : 7
patron and the j., 351 : 17
with chance of being drowned, 354 : 6
Jailed for telling lies to young, 863 : 11
Jailer another kind of captive, 514 : 8
inexorable as self, 503 : 19
Jake, Yukon J., 834 : 6
Jam, calico j., 550 : 13
every other day, 613 : 10
tomorrow j. yesterday, 613 : 11
Jamaicas of remembrance, 607 : 14
James could almost hear the bronze Negroes, 893 : 12
councillor to King J., 175 : 6
First Second and Old Pretender, 812 : 12
let J. rejoice, 365 : 11
Truthful J., 630 : 13
work of Henry J., 812 : 12
James's elaborate hesitancies, 701 : 7
ladies of St. J., 640 : 2
Jamshyd gloried drank deep, 516 : 11
Jane, from J. to Elizabeth, 440 : 19
Jangled, sweet bells j., 221 : 21
January, a fly this J. day, 607 : 14
Japan, as J. kept her independence, 800 : 4
create in J. civilized nation, 617 : 8
forces of Empire of J., 780 : 15
from Paris to J., 311 : 12
what they say in J., 646 : 12
Japanese, heart subject of J. poetry, 344 : 19
life like J. picture, 645 : 15
reliance on intuition, 756 : 3
Japheth, Noah begat J., 7 : 26
Jar, feel amid city's j., 585 : 1
in Tennessee, 767 : 7
people in front get j., 758 : 5
strings untouched will harshly j., 183 : 18
wine j. when molding began, 109 : 19
Jardin, il faut cultiver notre j., 343 : *n* 6
Jargon of the schools, 320 : 13
Jars, two j. on floor of Zeus, 59 : 12
Jasper of jocundity, 153 : 5
Jaundice, jealousy j. of the soul, 305 : 24
Jaundiced eye, 333 : 16
Jaunts, Jorrocks' J. and Jollities, 500 : 19
Javan, bound for J. or Gadire, 288 : 30
Jaw, muscular strength to j., 611 : 10
Jawbone of an ass, 12 : 17
Jaws, gently smiling j., 611 : 5

Jaws (*continued*)
of darkness do devour it, 195 : 23
of death, 167 : 13, 533 : 14
of sea and earth, 850 : 11
that bite, 612 : 17
Jay, poor Jim J., 740 : 3
Jaybird don't rob own nes', 662 : 12
Jazz, ask what j. is, 847 : 11
Jazzmen, go to it O j., 761 : 11
Je connais tout fors moi-même, 150 : *n* 6
Jealous, art j. mistress, 498 : 25
confirmations, 231 : 7
for they are jealous, 231 : 20
I am a j. God, 10 : 5
in honor, 211 : 15
law a j. mistress, 447 : 18
not j. for the cause, 231 : 20
one not easily j., 232 : 20
possessions of happiness, 727 : 7
readiest to forgive, 582 : 10
scornful yet j. eyes, 338 : 14
souls not answered, 231 : 20
venom clamors of j. woman, 188 : 13
Jealousies, surmises j. conjectures, 205 : 18
Jealousy, beware my lord of j., 230 : 34
born with love, 294 : 2
ear of j. heareth all, 34 : 9
Father of J., 404 : 13
feeds upon suspicion, 293 : 6
full of artless j., 223 : 20
green-eyed j., 199 : 28
has a human face, 405 : 14
in j. more self-love, 293 : 36
injured lover's hell, 286 : 19
is cruel as the grave, 28 : 23
is the rage of a man, 23 : 15
jaundice of the soul, 305 : 24
life of j., 231 : 2
of rivals near throne, 392 : 12
Jean, farewell to my J., 331 : 3
Jeanie with light brown hair, 598 : 6
Jeanne d'Arc and Bonaparte, 815 : 11
Jeers, exiled on ground in j., 580 : 17
Jeeves, inimitable J., 775 : 12
Jefferson, celebrities such as J., 615 : 14
Thomas J. still lives, 382 : 5
when J. dined alone, 891 : 7
Yoknapatawpha County, 838 : 5
Jeffers's, too much like one of J., 798 : 1
Jehovah has triumphed, 447 : 10
in name of great J., 385 : 11
is my strength, 29 : 20
Jove or Lord, 340 : 1
Lawd God J., 814 : 15
tell them I Am J. said, 365 : 6
Jehu, the driving of J., 14 : 18
Jekyll, Dr. J. and Mr. Hyde, 668 : 15
Jelly, distilled almost to j., 218 : 20
out vile j., 234 : 18
Je-ne-sais-quoi young man, 628 : 11
Jenny kissed me, 454 : 8
Jeoffrey, consider my cat J., 365 : 13
Jeopardy, nor be twice put in j., 391 : 17
went in j. of their lives, 13 : 26
Jeremy, Mr. J. liked feet wet, 719 : 5
Jericho, from Jerusalem to J., 43 : 13
Joshua fit battle of J., 935 : 20
tarry at J. until beards be grown, 13 : 17
Jerusalem, daughters of J., 28 : 2
from J. to Jericho, 43 : 13
Jerusalem (*continued*)
I saw the new J., 53 : 29
I will wipe J., 14 : 22
if I forget thee O J., 22 : 15
meet in sweet J., 186 : 24
my happy home, 918 : 5
speak comfortably to J., 30 : 30
temple of J., 131 : 5
that killest prophets, 40 : 21
the golden, 563 : 13
thy sister calls, 407 : 7
was J. builded here, 406 : 21
wise men came to J., 36 : 20
Jerusalems in foreign galaxies, 864 : 4
Jeshurun waxed fat, 11 : 24
Jessamine, casement j. stirred, 533 : 22
Jesse, David the son of J., 13 : 25
rod out of the stem of J., 29 : 18
Jesses my dear heartstrings, 231 : 4
Jessica, sit J. look, 201 : 1
Jest and youthful jollity, 277 : 19
best to use myself in j., 252 : 15
between j. and earnest, 169 : 19
breaks no bones, 356 : 23
fellow of infinite j., 224 : 14
glory j. and riddle, 337 : 2
good j. forever, 203 : 20
I j. to Oberon, 196 : 12
intermingle j. with earnest, 181 : 3
life is a j., 332 : 8
most bitter is scornful j., 351 : 8
not bear serious examination, 325 : *n* 3
put his whole wit in a j., 263 : 2
unseen inscrutable, 189 : 33
Jested quaffed and swore, 536 : 7
Jester, fool and j., 206 : 36
Jester raconteur confidant pundit, 847 : 10
Jesting, no j. with edge tools, 261 : 2
what is truth said j. Pilate, 179 : 22
Jest's prosperity lies in ear, 191 : 12
Jests, he j. at scars, 192 : 2
indebted to memory for j., 399 : 13
Jesu Christ and seiynte Benedight, 146 : 30
Lord J. blessed Pelican, 139 : 13
my dearest one, 167 : 3
Jesuit, bland as a J., 663 : 7
Jesus, accept J. as Savior, 903 : 7
as J. sat at meat, 41 : 2
author and finisher, 51 : 19
came to save sinners, 50 : 24
Christ Don Quixote and I, 452 : 4
Cross of J., 616 : 6
gentle J. meek and mild, 350 : 13
her little Child, 561 : 10
history incomprehensible without J., 593 : 8
incarnate saved us, 858 : 1
increased in wisdom, 42 : 33
keep your hearts through Christ J., 50 : 6
king of Jews, 41 : 25
lover of my soul, 350 : 12
loves me this I know, 599 : 4
loves you Mrs. Robinson, 915 : 14
man who says he is J., 361 : 2
miracles did J. in Cana, 44 : 28
most scientific man, 583 : 2
nobody know but J., 935 : 19
none but J. heard, 482 : 17
saith give me to drink, 44 : 35
shut up in asylum, 690 : 11
Jesus (*continued*)
stand up stand up for J., 562 : 13
sure this J. will not do, 407 : 11
that which was given to J., 130 : 11
took bread, 41 : 10
was a Jew, 764 : 14
was born in Bethlehem, 36 : 20
went to them walking on the sea, 39 : 26
wept, 45 : 14
with J. we worship Father, 448 : 1
Jesus', good friend for J. sake, 250 : 1
Jesus Christ advocate with the Father, 52 : 21
I believe in J., 55 : 2
kingdom and patience of J., 52 : 27
our Lord, 56 : 1
redemption by our Lord J., 55 : 7
risen today, 317 : 8
testimony of J., 52 : 27
the same yesterday today and forever, 51 : 24
Jeunesse, au temps de ma j. folle, 150 : *n* 2
cueillez cueillez votre j., 163 : *n* 1
qu'as-tu fait de ta j., 659 : *n* 9
si j. savait, 163 : 11
Jew, because I wasn't J., 824 : 1
either for Englishman or J., 407 : 11
hated like a J., 912 : 11
hath not a J. eyes, 199 : 17
Jesus was a J., 764 : 14
judges neither J. nor Gentile, 776 : 13
much kindness in the J., 198 : 26
neither Greek nor J., 50 : 12
of Tarsus, 46 : 24
only J. in Danville looking for matzoh, 904 : 10
that Shakespeare drew, 340 : 8
wandering J., 926 : 19
what one J. does, 909 : 3
yes I am a J., 501 : 9
Jewel, caught my heavenly j., 176 : 15
immediate j. of souls, 230 : 33
in crown of Social Republic, 638 : 8
no j. like Rosalind, 212 : 3
of gold in swine's snout, 23 : 25
of the just, 299 : 9
precious j. in his head, 210 : 24
rich j. in Ethiop's ear, 191 : 26
Jeweled unicorns, 806 : 3
Jewelry, like j. from a grave, 878 : 2
Jewels, bright j. of the mine, 561 : *n* 1
five-words-long, 530 : 24
give j. for set of beads, 195 : 6
these are my j., 259 : 20
unclasps warmed j., 476 : 17
Jewish, ancient J. people gave New World, 881 : 14
gaberdine, 198 : 24
no J. blood in my veins, 912 : 11
Jews generally give value, 681 : 17
Jesus king of J., 41 : 25
King of the J., 36 : 20
kiss and infidels adore, 334 : 1
of Solomon's glory, 649 : 11
Papists Protestants J. Turks in one ship, 273 : 11
refuse till conversion of J., 296 : 27
thrown back at all J., 909 : 3
Jezebel, dogs shall eat J., 14 : 8
painted her face, 14 : 19
Jiggety-jig, home again j., 933 : 9
Jill, fly away J., 934 : 8

Jill (*continued*)
  Jack and J., 931:1
  other named J., 934:8
Jim most ruined for servant, 623:21
  poor J. Jay, 740:3
  simple child dear brother J., 423:*n* 3
Jimmie crack corn, 921:14
Jingle, little j. little chimes, 331:4
  triumph and the j., 781:15
Jingling of guinea, 529:23
Jingly, Lady J. Jones, 551:1
Jingo, by j. by gee, 829:5
  by j. if we do, 598:9
  repent by j., 485:11
Joan as my lady, 266:9
  Darby always the same to old wife J., 663:1
  greasy J. keel pot, 191:14
Job, back of j. the dreamer, 775:15
  blessed the latter end of J., 17:11
  doth J. fear God for nought, 15:3
  film makes person miserable done my j., 914:1
  give tools finish j., 744:13
  no person deprived of j., 903:6
  patience of J., 52:5
  poor as J., 205:26
  whatever j. they give me, 702:8
Joblillies, Picninnies and the J., 364:5
Jobs, right people in right j., 553:14
Jockey of Norfolk not too bold, 173:*n* 8
Jocund, cocks and lions j. be, 253:15
  day stands tiptoe, 193:15
  rebecks sound, 278:1
  such a j. company, 427:10
  then be thou j., 238:20
Jocundity, jasper of j., 153:5
Joe, G.I. Joe, 924:22
  Old Black J., 598:7
  say it ain't so J., 924:13
Joe's, Sloppy J., 868:18
Jog on the footpath way, 246:24
Johannes, absolute J. fac totum, 178:12
Johannisberg, extra bottle of J., 398:*n* 1
Johano-ai, Turquoise Horse of J., 928:20
John and I are quit, 320:26
  Anderson my jo, 410:7
  awake my St. J., 336:10
  Baptist's head, 39:23
  Barleycorn got up again, 409:18
  Brown's body, 619:14
  Bull or Englishman's Fireside, 415:11
  buried Evangelist Saint J., 571:3
  Don J. of Austria, 742:10
  Donne Anne Donne Undone, 251:*n* 7
  greatest of all is J. Bull, 462:9
  I J., 52:27
  I J. saw the holy city, 53:29
  inspiring bold J. Barleycorn, 411:10
  Matthew Mark Luke and J., 294:16
  my son J., 933:1
  or Shaun, 778:5
  outglittering J. Keats, 493:8
  Peel with coat so gay, 474:19
  shut the door good J., 338:5
  some said J. print it, 301:18
  speak for yourself J., 511:21
  Stuart Mill, 753:4
John (*continued*)
  there St. J. mingles, 339:8
  who killed J. Keats, 462:11
  whose name was J., 44:19
John Henry told his captain, 922:8
Johnny, Frankie and J., 923:8
  I hardly knew ye, 921:1
  leave her J. leave her, 935:2
  little J. Green, 930:14
  whiskey J., 934:16
John's, bounded by St. J., 535:22
Johnson, no arguing with J., 371:23
Join choir invisible, 564:22
  don't j. too many gangs, 748:16
  family, 748:16
  few gangs if any, 748:16
  hand in hand Americans, 378:11
  now j. your hands and hearts, 186:17
  them that j. house to house, 29:4
  triumph of skies, 350:15
  two lives j. oft scar, 542:9
  union and say equal pay, 578:2
  United States, 748:16
  will you j. dance, 612:8
Joined great issues, 427:24
  he has j. great majority, 117:12
  lawfully j. together, 56:7
  make third j. former two, 306:1
  my name j. to theirs, 113:13
  rogue and whore together, 323:2
  what God hath j., 40:5
  when issues are j., 65:4
  whom God hath j., 56:11
Joint, every j. and motive, 227:3
  force and full result, 333:1
  heirs with Christ, 47:8
  remove the j., 613:20
  time is out of j., 220:6
Joint-laborer, night j. with day, 217:20
Joints, dividing j. and marrow, 51:14
Joke, every j. long ago made, 630:9
  forgive Thy j. on me, 749:15
  gentle Dullness loves j., 340:19
  good j. not criticized, 742:7
  Jack j. poor potsherd, 656:21
  loses everything when joker laughs, 412:7
  many a j. had he, 370:10
  subtleties of American j., 622:7
  'twixt earnest and j., 404:*n* 4
Joked about every prominent man, 766:6
  world j. incessantly, 630:9
Joker, joke loses everything when j. laughs, 412:7
Jokes, crack any of these old j., 82:17
  difference of taste in j., 565:27
  Fate's saddest j., 66:*n* 8
  history indulges in j., 785:7
  little j. on Thee, 749:15
  standing j., 326:6
  ten j. a hundred enemies, 359:21
  veiled j., 701:7
Jollities, Jorrocks' Jaunts and J., 500:19
Jollity, jest and youthful j., 277:19
  tipsy dance and j., 279:11
Jolly and easy in minds, 539:7
  miller, 382:6
  red nose, 268:1
  swagman, 705:7
  three j. gentlemen, 740:5
  three j. huntsmen, 933:6
  what j. fun, 697:1
Jonah was in the belly of the fish, 33:22
Jonathan heard not his father's oath, 12:37
  loved him as his own soul, 13:5
Jones, Casey J., 731:19
  Lady Jingly J., 551:1
Joneses, keeping up with J., 923:18
Jonson and he did gather humors, 301:6
  Ben J. his best poetry, 256:4
  O rare Ben J., 255:*n* 3
Jonson's learned sock, 278:6
Jordan, fertilize J. plain, 759:11
  I looked over J., 935:23
  stood in midst of J., 11:29
  that's the river of J., 936:3
Joris and he, 541:11
Jorrocks' Jaunts and Jollities, 500:19
Joruri, writing j., 317:9
Joseph, king which knew not J., 9:7
  stript J. of his coat, 8:28
Joshua fit battle of Jericho, 935:20
  like J. commanded sun, 348:11
Jostling, no man lives without j., 472:10
  not done by j. in street, 407:1
Jot, one j. of former love retain, 182:16
  one j. of heart or hope, 282:19
  or tittle, 37:7
Jour, le j. de gloire est arrivé, 415:1
Journal, aussi vieux que le j. d'aujourdhui, 741:*n* 1
Journalism, responsible j., 814:3
Journalist, I was a fresh new j., 621:*n* 2
  whether j. puts truth first, 814:4
Journey, arrant jade on a j., 369:22
  begin j. on Sundays, 323:17
  dawn speeds a man on j., 61:22
  day's j. take whole day, 608:10
  death and sorrow on our j., 744:9
  end of j. too, 698:15
  going a j., 445:9
  he is in a j. or sleepeth, 14:2
  in middle of j. of life, 140:10
  life is its own j., 867:11
  long day's j. into night, 810:16
  longest j. go, 468:21
  longest j. inwards, 863:4
  longest part of j., 97:11
  methinks it is no j., 918:12
  of a thousand miles, 65:1
  some point of pointless j., 900:12
  soul of j. liberty, 445:11
  to oblivion, 791:2
  to promised land, 731:19
  to unknown, 826:17
  universe in map, 170:6
  with my strange heroes, 518:7
  your j. of so many days, 593:4
Journeyed across centuries, 745:10
Journeyman to grief, 194:4
Journeymen, nature's j., 222:3
Journey's, dine at j. end, 714:2
  here is my j. end, 232:18
  when j. over, 690:18
Journeys end in lovers meeting, 213:22
Journeywork of stars, 574:23
Jours s'en vont je demeure, 770:*n* 4
Jove, awful J. Phidias brought, 493:17
  daughter of J., 361:13
  deity own brother of J., 570:4
  for his power to thunder, 242:20

Jove (*continued*)
front of J. himself, 223 : 3
in ancestral J. Troy's sons rejoice, 105 : 28
Jehovah J. or Lord, 340 : 1
laughs at lovers' perjuries, 192 : 8
Rain-giver, 113 : 2
we descend from J., 105 : 28
where J. bestows, 271 : 19
with J. I begin, 103 : 10
Jove's, immortal J. dread clamors, 231 : 11
of J. nectar sup, 256 : 8
starry threshold of J. court, 279 : 2
Jovi, eripuitque J. fulmen, 115 : *n* 12
Jovial, Autumn comes j. on, 345 : 13
three j. huntsmen, 349 : *n* 4
Joy, all j. impossible, 903 : 2
all that j. can give, 335 : 19
although our last, 232 : 23
always a recognition, 902 : 14
always to j. inclined, 404 : 14
and function of poetry, 887 : 7
and love triumphing, 285 : 6
antique j., 711 : 19
apprehend some j., 197 : 12
asks if this be j., 370 : 16
at weeping, 208 : 22
be unconfined, 457 : 15
be wi' you a', 417 : 8
before a j. proposed, 245 : 23
being my first j., 874 : 13
being used for purpose, 680 : 15
bitter j., 842 : 14
brightened with j., 428 : 15
bringer of that j., 197 : 12
cease every j., 443 : 8
chortled in his j., 612 : 18
cometh in the morning, 18 : 15
conquers grief, 564 : 12
courage love j., 332 : 2
deep j. indisguisable, 880 : 1
deep power of j., 423 : 11
delights in joy, 244 : 3
desperate the j., 454 : 2
dream of j. all but in vain, 149 : *n* 1
enter into j., 40 : 29
even his griefs are a j., 60 : 20
every child may j. to hear, 403 : 3
every j. gain, 540 : 9
excursion same for sorrow as j., 877 : 2
father's j. mother's pride, 431 : 17
feast of j. a dish of pain, 177 : 10
for life and j. and objects, 576 : 5
for thee and me, 618 : 13
formed of j. and mirth, 407 : 3
fruit of Spirit is j., 49 : 30
full of peace and j., 570 : 14
gem of all j., 153 : 5
general j. of whole table, 238 : 27
glad tidings of great j., 317 : 5
good tidings of great j., 42 : 28
Greensleeves all my j., 917 : 15
grief j. misunderstood, 507 : 24
have j. or power, 495 : 23
he who binds to himself a j., 404 : 18
honey of all earthly j., 295 : 3
in trouble and in j., 317 : 6
is the sweet voice, 436 : 1
is wisdom, 712 : 11
kisses j. as it flies, 404 : 18
last pure stretch of j., 875 : 2
lean in j. upon father's knee, 403 : 8
Joy (*continued*)
love and thought and j., 425 : 5
man made for j. and woe, 406 : 13
Marcellus exiled feels, 337 : 14
marriage has more j. than pain, 75 : 25
masterpiece j. to artist, 619 : 7
meet with j. in sweet Jerusalem, 186 : 24
more of j. than sorrow, 570 : 16
my j. my grief, 276 : 6
my life my j., 168 : 2
no j. but calm, 528 : 15
no j. but lacks salt, 748 : 9
no j. in Mudville, 704 : 16
none hath j. of death, 633 : 10
nor love nor light, 587 : 16
not because troubles are delectable j., 100 : 12
not carol of j. or glee, 736 : 23
not intermeddle with his j., 23 : 36
now 'tis little j., 485 : 5
O j. that in our embers, 426 : 17
O what j. and glory must be, 136 : 7
ocean and my j., 458 : 30
of crimson j., 405 : 5
of elevated thoughts, 423 : 13
of life is variety, 352 : 13
of love too short, 149 : 11
of the ancient home, 618 : 12
oil of j. for mourning, 31 : 25
pain short j. eternal, 413 : 27
perfect j. therein I find, 167 : *n* 5
Phyllis is my only j., 312 : 12
pleasance revel, 230 : 26
pleasure without j. hollow, 895 : 6
poet's j. conceals despair, 757 : 7
politics of j., 879 : 1
pray in j. and abundance, 782 : 18
pure and complete j. impossible, 602 : 7
reveal itself when transformed in us, 756 : 9
riding's a j., 542 : 15
rule of j. and duty one, 644 : 5
scrip of j. immortal diet, 172 : 15
secret j. of thinker, 644 : 1
senses forever in j., 543 : 16
shall reap in j., 22 : 7
shipmate joy, 576 : 20
shudder of j. runs up, 901 : 12
silence perfectest herald of j., 209 : 11
silly j. at silly things, 370 : *n* 1
snatch a fearful j., 361 : 9
somebody to divide j. with, 625 : 17
sons of God shouted for j., 16 : 29
sorrow and j. are one, 869 : 5
source of humor not j., 625 : 4
spontaneous j., 713 : 6
stern j. warriors feel, 431 : 14
strength through j., 816 : 7
surprised by j., 428 : 20
that your j. be full, 45 : 28
the luminous cloud, 436 : 1
the thrill the whirl, 569 : 20
thing of beauty j. forever, 475 : 16
this alone life j. empire, 467 : 10
this torment my j., 874 : 19
thou spark from heaven, 412 : 9
to pass to world below, 105 : 12
to the world, 328 : 13
to their friends, 59 : 28
walked in glory and j., 425 : 10
was never sure, 633 : 21
Joy (*continued*)
we end in j., 874 : 14
we know you terrible j., 902 : 16
weep at j., 208 : 22
where poverty and j., 138 : 14
with j. and love triumphing, 285 : 6
work with j., 782 : 17
writhed not at passing j., 478 : 15
Joyce honest in technique in Ulysses, 758 : 13
Joyful all ye nations rise, 350 : 15
births, 208 : 16
in day of prosperity be j., 27 : 7
make a j. noise, 19 : 31, 20 : 20, 21 : 3
shall my j. temples bind, 276 : 5
Joyfulness prolongeth his days, 35 : 41
Joyless, sin to be j., 827 : 22
Joyous, good great and j., 467 : 10
how j. his neigh, 928 : 20
understanding is j., 913 : 3
we too launch out, 576 : 15
Joyously, flowers through grass j. sprang, 138 : 7
Joyousness, lends j. to a wall, 646 : 8
Joy's delicious springs, 457 : 2
grape, 478 : 1
soul lies in doing, 225 : 34
the voice, 829 : 17
Joys abound as seasons fleet, 185 : 14
and sorrows song aroused, 577 : 14
as winged dreams, 917 : 20
be j. three parts pain, 544 : 10
dreaming o'er j. of night, 404 : 12
fading j. we dote upon, 318 : 4
fairest j. give unrest, 476 : 3
fall not to rich alone, 109 : 8
homely j., 362 : 2
in another's loss of ease, 405 : 4
kill your j. with love, 193 : 30
let j. be as May, 267 : 20
minds me o' departed j., 409 : 24
mingle j. with occupation, 350 : 7
nakedness all j. are due to thee, 254 : 3
only solitary know j. of friendship, 739 : 6
our youth our j. our all, 173 : 5
perish in infancy, 918 : 18
present j. more to flesh and blood, 305 : 25
raise j. and triumphs high, 350 : 11
rob us of our j., 920 : 4
society's chief j., 376 : 3
summer hath his j., 250 : 7
taste whole j., 254 : 3
tasted eternal j. of Heaven, 183 : 21
tenderness its j. and fears, 426 : 23
thy j. when shall I see, 918 : 5
to this are folly, 258 : 3
vain deluding j., 278 : 9
with age diminish, 545 : 22
youth's season for j., 332 : 4
Jubal father of such as handle harp, 7 : 22
Jubilant, bright pomp ascended j., 287 : 1
Jubilee, bring the J., 614 : 14
fiftieth year j., 10 : 22
sons to thy j. throng, 465 : 1
year of J., 935 : 26
Jubjub bird, 612 : 17
Judah and Israel dwelt safely, 13 : 29
say unto the cities of J., 30 : 34
sin of J., 32 : 10

Judas had given them the slip, 319 : 12
  if J. had not been born, 41 : 9
  jealous J. cowardly Peter, 859 : 10
  saith Why is ointment not sold, 45 : 16
  so J. did to Christ, 195 : 10
Judea, a new J., 565 : 29
  Bethlehem of J., 36 : 20
Judge above his last, 90 : 16
  allow iniquities, 645 : 10
  amongst fools a j., 118 : *n* 2
  by deeds, 904 : 16
  by sample we j. whole, 168 : 10
  children j. parents, 675 : 3
  condemned when criminal absolved, 111 : 10
  dead drunk j., 881 : 11
  fitter to invent than j., 181 : 7
  forbear to j., 185 : 19
  himself dragged to bar, 571 : 6
  I j. not thee, 171 : 18
  I'll be j. I'll be jury, 611 : 6
  impartial j., 374 : 6
  justice j. or vicar, 398 : 26
  listening like j. supreme, 486 : 3
  man by foes, 683 : 9
  mind proper j. of man, 115 : 5
  more difficult to j. oneself, 849 : 3
  my friend j. not me, 171 : 18
  my witness and my j., 260 : 12
  never j. until other side heard, 77 : 1
  no king can corrupt, 248 : 30
  no one should j. own case, 111 : 19
  none blessed, 35 : 22
  not according to appearance, 44 : 43
  not play before done, 267 : 18
  not that we be not judged, 524 : 5
  not that ye be not judged, 38 : 8
  of all things, 300 : 11
  of authors' names, 333 : 12
  out of thy mouth will I j., 43 : 41
  people j. men by success, 293 : 26
  people seldom j. right, 401 : 12
  quick and the dead, 55 : 2
  rain influence and j. prize, 278 : 5
  right j. judges wrong, 74 : 13
  setting yourself up as j., 86 : 3
  should not be young, 84 : 9
  sober as j., 349 : 8
  sole j. of truth, 337 : 2
  the fatherless, 28 : 30
  to j. events sanely, 453 : 7
  upright j. learned j., 200 : 17
  whole piece by pattern, 652 : 14
  you as you are, 228 : 7
Judged according to lies, 138 : 8
  in light of final issue, 88 : 21
  intellectual product j. by age, 638 : 9
  judge not that we be not j., 524 : 5
  judge not that ye be not j., 38 : 8
  not to have lived, 643 : 16
  should be j. as a captain, 151 : 9
Judge's robe, 228 : 6
Judges, a fool with j., 118 : *n* 2
  all ranged, 332 : 7
  as j. neither Jew nor Gentile, 776 : 13
  common j. of property, 352 : 9
  constitution what j. say, 700 : 1
  do and must legislate, 644 : 20
  hungry j. sentence sign, 334 : 6
  in every state bound thereby, 391 : 13
  naïf simple-minded, 644 : 16
  of facts not laws, 330 : 20
  right judge j. wrong, 74 : 13
Judgest, thou j. another, 46 : 37
Judging character motive impulse, 783 : 4
  for themselves, 399 : 8
  no way of j. future, 383 : 2
  people by appearances, 296 : 16
Judgment, accurate in his j., 380 : *n* 2
  and exactitude enter him, 3 : 3
  and imagination, 436 : 19
  beauty bought by j. of eye, 190 : 19
  bounded by Day of J., 535 : *n* 6
  bring every work into j., 27 : 27
  commonly we say j. falls, 263 : 16
  complains of his j., 293 : 16
  Daniel come to j., 200 : 11
  defend against your j., 306 : 9
  difficult, 80 : 9, 395 : 7
  do not wait for last j., 882 : 9
  enough for me, 660 : 9
  ever awake, 437 : 17
  execute j. against gods of Egypt, 9 : 25
  fled to brutish beasts, 216 : 20
  God and history remember j., 820 : 10
  God's great J. Seat, 707 : 16
  green in j., 240 : 25
  hard to found j. on man, 164 : 6
  he looked for j., 29 : 4
  He which is top of j., 228 : 7
  his ways are j., 11 : 23
  I suspend my j., 165 : 5
  leaves of J. Book unfold, 596 : 16
  man's erring j., 332 : 19
  men of ill j. ignore good, 73 : 15
  no comparison no j., 374 : 10
  nor people's j. always true, 304 : 13
  not better than information, 820 : 11
  not industry only but j., 372 : 9
  of intellect half truth, 753 : 13
  or intuition more subtle, 644 : 11
  practical j. of Americans, 506 : 4
  private j., 365 : 5
  prophet under j. he preaches, 823 : 17
  reserve thy j., 219 : 1
  seek j., 28 : 30
  shallow spirit of j., 184 : 20
  time makes possible Day of J., 786 : 5
  vulgarize Day of J., 500 : 16
  we thought it J. Day, 642 : 1
  were we men of j., 890 : 6
  young in limbs in j. old, 199 : 10
Judgments, brawling j., 534 : 10
  men's j. parcel of their fortunes, 241 : 10
  of Lord righteous, 18 : 1, 524 : 7
  so in our very j., 289 : 19
  with j. as watches, 332 : 15
Judicial, duty of j. department, 402 : 3
  essence of j. duty, 402 : 3
  function, 678 : 3
  power distinct from legislative, 381 : 11
  writing, 730 : 15
Judiciary safeguard of liberty, 700 : 1
Judicious, a little j. levity, 669 : 11
  swearin' keeps temper, 722 : 17
  wales portion with j. care, 408 : 17
Jug of wine loaf of bread, 516 : 7
  one old j. without handle, 550 : 16
  w'en it gits loose fum j., 662 : 13
Jugement, je suspends mon j., 165 : *n* 2
Juggernauts of flesh that pass, 857 : 15
Juggler of Day is gone, 604 : 16
Juggler (*continued*)
  threadbare j. fortuneteller, 188 : 15
Juggling fiends no more believed, 240 : 9
Jug-jug, cuckoo j. pu-we, 250 : 8
Jugular, nearer unto him than his j. vein, 132 : 10
Julia, in silks my J. goes, 266 : 22
Julian, remembered poor J., 845 : 7
Julia's, where my J. lips smile, 266 : 3
Juliet and her Romeo, 193 : 31
  is the sun, 192 : 2
  unless philosophy make a J., 193 : 13
Julius Caesar thou art mighty yet, 217 : 11
  mightiest J. fell, 217 : 21
July, born on Fourth of J., 759 : 6
  English winter ending in J., 461 : 27
  in her eyes, 917 : 24
  June and J. flowers, 265 : 17
  March J. October May, 162 : *n* 3
  second day of J. 1776, 381 : 7
  swarm of bees in J., 919 : 10
  what to slave your Fourth of J., 556 : 5
July's day short as December, 246 : 13
Jumblies, lands where J. live, 550 : 11
Jump, good wits j., 170 : 33
  I see him j. before me, 668 : 12
  not j. with common spirits, 199 : 13
  over the candlestick, 932 : 17
  thought j. sea and land, 244 : 16
  we'd j. life to come, 236 : 22
Jumped into bramble bush, 934 : 7
Jumping from chair she sat in, 454 : 8
Jumps in after train started, 704 : 1
  over lazy dog, 923 : 2
June and July flowers, 265 : 17
  as cuckoo is in J., 204 : 21
  bustin' out all over, 833 : 12
  knee-deep in J., 665 : 12
  leafy month of J., 435 : 1
  newly sprung in J., 409 : 22
  rare as day in J., 567 : 13
  seek ice in J., 456 : 15
  sophistries of J., 604 : 9
  suns skies clouds of J., 609 : 11
  swarm of bees in J., 919 : 10
  tell one's name livelong J., 604 : 19
  tenth day of J. 1940, 780 : 9
  thirty days hath J., 162 : 7
  this moment in J., 781 : 15
  when J. is past the fading rose, 271 : 19
Jung says God and Unconscious are one, 906 : 7
Jungle, law of the j., 709 : 4
  laws of the j., 709 : 6
  massive j. herds, 857 : 15
  pack meets pack in j., 709 : 5
  power politics law of j., 818 : 6
Juniper, leopards under j. tree, 805 : 22
Juno's unrelenting hate, 306 : 11
Junto, power in oligarchical j., 382 : 4
Jupiter aligns with Mars, 914 : 7
  knows how to sugarcoat, 298 : 6
  laughs at perjuries of lovers, 113 : 1
  not bring back opportunity, 114 : 12
  singing vespers in Temple of J., 384 : 7
  what you see and touch, 118 : 13
  wresting from J. his thunder, 115 : 16
Jupiter's statue by Phidias, 924 : 3

Juridical safeguards of individual freedom, 844 : 9
Juridical-political organization, 774 : 8
Juries, trial by j., 389 : 2
Jurisprudence, gladsome light of j., 172 : 1
Jury, facts only impartial j., 509 : 5
 I'll be judge I'll be j., 611 : 6
 passing on prisoner's life, 227 : 31
 trial by impartial j., 392 : 1
 trial by j., 392 : 2
Jurymen, that j. may dine, 334 : 6
Just, a j. war, 348 : *n* 2, 384 : 20
 actions of the j., 272 : 13
 Add Hot Water, 828 : 17
 and lasting peace, 524 : 7
 are the ways of God, 288 : 26
 be j. and fear not, 249 : 8
 be j. before you're generous, 399 : 3
 blessing upon head of j., 23 : 22
 blood of this j. person, 41 : 22
 cause it is j., 446 : 2
 company of j. and righteous, 77 : 12
 contemplates j. and unjust, 486 : 11
 friends and brave enemies, 389 : 3
 gentle plain j. resolute, 576 : 8
 gods are j., 235 : 14
 good man and j., 44 : 12
 how should man be j., 15 : 23
 if all men were j., 82 : 28
 if heart j. frank kindly, 298 : 1
 in J.-spring, 828 : 11
 jewel of the j., 299 : 9
 made what is strong j., 300 : 6
 man will pay more income tax, 84 : 6
 memory of the j. is blessed, 23 : 22
 merely j. is severe, 343 : 3
 not a j. man upon earth, 27 : 9
 nothing to do with that j. man, 41 : 20
 path of the j. as shining light, 23 : 8
 place for j. man prison, 558 : 6
 play fair j. and patient, 595 : 12
 rain on j. and unjust, 37 : 12
 reflect that God is j., 388 : 1
 shall man be more j. than God, 15 : 13
 spirits of j. men, 51 : 21
 strong j. weak secure, 891 : 2
 thrice armed that hath quarrel j., 185 : 17
 unjust peace before j. war, 348 : *n* 2
 upright man laughed to scorn, 15 : 28
 way is plain peaceful j., 522 : 12
 whatever is is j., 303 : 14
 whatsoever things are j., 50 : 7
Juste, le j. milieu, 343 : *n* 9
Justice accommodation of interests, 737 : 4
 and humanity, 725 : 20
 art of good and fair, 134 : 8
 biased in point of j., 289 : 14
 blind deef and dumb, 722 : 1
 characteristic of democracy, 845 : 15
 Chief J. rich quiet infamous, 488 : 9
 confidence in j. of people, 521 : 12
 corruption of dream of j., 851 : 7
 do j., 4 : 2
 doing j. loving mercy, 385 : 5
 enough to accuse, 369 : 15
 equal and exact j., 389 : 2
 equal j. for all, 80 : 17
 equal piece of j. Death, 274 : 11
 establish j., 391 : 10
 even-handed j., 236 : 23
 extreme j. extreme injustice, 134 : 29
Justice (*continued*)
 extreme j. often injustice, 96 : *n* 13
 forever in passion, 539 : 21
 get out of way of J., 876 : 5
 government of eternal j., 537 : 15
 great interest of man, 451 : 9
 humanity reason and j., 373 : 1
 in fair round belly, 211 : 15
 in j. none should see salvation, 200 : 9
 is the only worship, 615 : 12
 judge or vicar, 398 : 26
 lance of j. hurtless breaks, 235 : 3
 law consistent with liberty and j., 366 : 2
 law of humanity j. equity, 373 : 18
 laws which advance social j., 871 : 13
 let j. be done though heaven fall, 133 : 25
 liberty and j. for all, 677 : 10
 liberty plucks j., 227 : 26
 love of j. simply fear, 293 : 13
 machine rolls of itself, 723 : 2
 made for sake of peace, 156 : 2
 makes democracy possible, 823 : 18
 man's capacity for j., 823 : 18
 mercy seasons j., 200 : 9
 mirage of social j., 844 : 9
 moderation in j., 385 : *n* 2
 no person deprived of j., 903 : 6
 no such thing as j., 684 : 12
 not charity wanting in world, 414 : 12
 not violate laws of j., 366 : 8
 one man's j. another's injustice, 497 : 26
 passions without j., 703 : 13
 peace a disposition for j., 308 : 3
 peace and sobriety, 273 : 11
 peace more important than j., 156 : 2
 penetrates Eternal J. as eye into sea, 142 : 15
 poetic j., 340 : 15
 price of j. publicity, 720 : 16
 rails upon thief, 235 : 2
 reason and j., 401 : 16
 recompense injury with j., 69 : 9
 returns, 103 : 14
 revenge a wild j., 180 : 3
 strength without j., 300 : 6
 strong lance of j., 235 : 3
 subject to God and j., 137 : 7
 superhighway of j., 909 : 12
 sword of j. has no scabbard, 400 : 3
 sword of j. lay down, 318 : 10
 temper j. with mercy, 287 : 25
 temporary but conscience eternal, 156 : 3
 the law my ducats, 199 : 11
 though j. be thy plea, 200 : 9
 threat to j. everywhere, 909 : 7
 thunders condemnation, 555 : 24
 Thwackum was for doing j., 349 : 18
 to none sell j., 139 : 3
 toward all nations, 379 : 12
 truth in action, 502 : 2
 uncompromising as j., 505 : 12
 waiting j. sleeps, 567 : *n* 1
 was done, 641 : 4
 weep for me who has j., 152 : 1
 what stings is j., 772 : 9
 where j. denied, 556 : 14
 which is the j., 235 : 2
 without j. courage weak, 347 : 4
 without strength, 300 : 6
 work for tolerance for j., 811 : 7
Justifiable, inconsistencies often j., 451 : 10
 ways of God j. to men, 288 : 26
Justification, work of art carry j., 683 : 2
Justified, evil not j. for expediency, 687 : 3
 whom he called he j., 47 : 11
 wisdom j. of her children, 39 : 7
Justifieth, it is God that j., 47 : 13
Justify, culture doesn't j., 865 : 14
 end must j. the means, 320 : 15
 God's ways to man, 691 : 17
 he will not j. you without you, 129 : 14
 thought to j. wrongdoings, 343 : 24
 ways of God to men, 283 : 2
Justifying means by the end, 127 : 20
 virtue debases in j., 342 : 21
Justitia, fiat j. ruat coelum 133 : 25
Justly, do j. and love mercy, 33 : 23
Just-spring, in J., 828 : 11
Jutty, no j. frieze buttress, 236 : 21
J'y suis j'y reste, 514 : *n* 4

K

Kaleidoscope, no more law of history than of k., 572 : 21
Kansas and Colorado have quarrel, 787 : 11
Karamazov way, 582 : 8
Karamazovs, all we K. such insects, 581 : 20
 they have Hamlets we K., 582 : 13
Kaspar's, old K. work was done, 439 : 10
Kate, kiss me K., 188 : 32
 O K. nice customs curtsy to great kings, 208 : 20
 some alas with K., 868 : 18
 trust thee gentle K., 203 : 24
Kathleen Mavourneen, 487 : 2
Katie, no music in rest K., 573 : 6
Katydid, glaze on k.-wing, 799 : 11
Kayak, I was out in my k., 929 : 7
Keats, out-glittering K., 493 : 8
 who killed John K., 462 : 11
Kedar, tents of K., 28 : 2
Keel, drinks water her k. plows air, 178 : 6
 greasy Joan doth k. pot, 191 : 14
 keep mind steady on k., 569 : 8
 ship sink on even k., 114 : 28
 thrill of life along k., 511 : 7
Keelson, main-truck higher than k. low, 570 : 5
 of creation is love, 574 : 14
Keen and hard like wedge, 790 : 10
 and quivering ratio, 604 : 6
 blessed man who possesses k. mind, 82 : 22
 discriminating sight, 422 : 4
 dull fighter and k. guest, 204 : 36
 love's k. arrows, 212 : 15
 polished razor k., 341 : 3
 with k. appetite he sits down, 199 : 5
Keener sounds, 767 : 16
 with constant use, 452 : 17
 with his k. eye, 296 : 23
Keen-scented, these the k., 792 : 6
Keep abreast of truth, 567 : 8
 and pass and turn again, 495 : 11

Keep (*continued*)
another thing hidden, 60 : 13
at times frae being sour, 409 : 4
bid them k. teeth clean, 242 : 15
breath's a ware will not k., 690 : 18
citizen from falling in error, 821 : 9
cold young orchard, 748 : 10
coming back and coming back, 768 : 23
company he is wont to k., 77 : 20
cool, 498 : 17
corner in thing I love, 231 : 6
down base in man, 534 : 23
drowsy emperor awake, 715 : 3
easier to get than k. Fortune, 111 : 3
'em down on the farm, 801 : 12
'em flying, 836 : 10
England k. my bones, 202 : 12
except the Lord k. the city, 22 : 8
eyes open before marriage, 347 : 19
fear God and k. his commandments, 27 : 27
golden mean, 107 : *n* 18
good tongue in head, 248 : 7
good-bye and k. cold, 748 : 10
Government from error, 821 : 9
green tree in heart, 132 : 25
guard and k. them, 65 : 3
he may k. that will and can, 691 : 22
home fires burning, 740 : 11
how to k. is there any, 656 : 12
ideas won't k., 697 : 17
in adversity k. an even mind, 107 : 18
in any case k. cool, 834 : 1
in despite of light k. us together, 252 : 21
it gets to k., 759 : 11
keeping men off k. them on, 331 : 20
let it k. one shape, 227 : 30
Lord bless thee and k. thee, 10 : 23
many to k., 566 : 9
me as the apple of the eye, 17 : 25
moving on, 589 : 15
Nelson touch, 700 : 12
no bad company, 370 : *n* 3
on truckin', 915 : 17
our Christmas merry still, 430 : 21
own appointed limits k., 596 : 18
Past upon throne, 568 : 14
promises to k., 748 : 7
push on k. moving, 416 : 8
republic if you can k. it, 348 : 15
right to k. and bear arms, 391 : 15
Sabbath going to church, 605 : 4
shop and shop keep thee, 177 : 14
six honest servingmen, 710 : 2
state in wonted manner k., 255 : 12
stiff upper lip, 594 : 5
stop hole to k. wind away, 224 : 16
strong if possible, 834 : 1
such consort as they k., 278 : 25
sunny side up, 825 : 8
sword within scabbard k., 306 : 28
talk from getting overwise, 748 : 15
thee in all thy ways, 20 : 17
thee in the way, 10 : 11
thee only unto her, 56 : 8
them within thee, 24 : 37
thing seven years, 432 : 14
this up forever, 773 : 15
thou my feet, 490 : 6
thy friend under own key, 227 : 9
thy heart with all diligence, 23 : 9
thy tongue from evil, 18 : 21

Keep (*continued*)
time to k., 26 : 21
to moderation, 118 : 8
up appearances, 547 : 32
up your bright swords, 229 : 21
who can, 426 : 7
wolf from door, 153 : *n* 1
word of promise to our ear, 240 : 9
wrong to k. guest back, 60 : 19
you shall k. the key, 219 : 3
your hearts and minds, 50 : 6
your powder dry, 444 : 12
yourself to yourself, 546 : 22
Keeper, Abel was k. of sheep, 7 : 14
brother's k., 7 : 15
of warm lights, 74 : 23
the Lord is thy k., 22 : 4
Keepers of the house shall tremble, 27 : 24
Keepest, company thou k., 209 : *n* 5
ports of slumber open, 206 : 29
Keepeth, he that k. Israel, 22 : 4
he that k. thee will not slumber, 22 : 4
Keeping, fools make such vain k., 262 : 7
in thy gracious k., 597 : 16
men off keep them on, 331 : 20
time keeping rhythm, 807 : 10
time time time, 527 : 11
up with Joneses, 923 : 18
up with yesterday, 760 : 2
Keeps, bond which k. me pale, 238 : 21
end from being hard, 749 : 1
finds young k. young, 290 : 6
his house in hand, 74 : 19
known by company he k., 77 : *n* 9
money movin' around, 722 : 15
on windy side of care, 209 : 12
perseverance k. honor bright, 226 : 17
self-made laws, 581 : 14
thee from thy God, 490 : 8
truly k. his first last day, 252 : 22
warm her note, 271 : 20
Keg, fizz like wine in k., 760 : 5
Kelly and Burke and Shea, 661 : 4
slide K. slide, 923 : 4
Kelly's, Fanny K. divine plain face, 441 : 15
Kelson, main-truck higher than k. low, 570 : 5
of creation is love, 574 : 14
Kemmerich's grave, 839 : 9
Ken, as far as angels' k., 283 : 5
nane sall k. where he is gane, 927 : 5
swims into his k., 475 : 7
Kennedy gave world vision, 894 : 15
Kennel, truth's a dog must to k., 233 : 8
Kennels, nets k. taxidermists, 907 : 25
Kennin', gang a k. wrang, 409 : 21
Kentuck, hurrah for old K., 454 : 13
Kentucky, moonlight softest in K., 657 : 6
old K. home, 598 : 5
Kenya, facing Mount K., 818 : 13
Kept breath to cool his pottage, 62 : 5
by transgressing k. law, 282 : 7
easier k. than recovered, 384 : 21
falling oars k. time, 297 : 10
I have not k. my square, 241 : 2
I k. my word he said, 739 : 16
the faith, 51 : 9
watch Matthew and Waldo, 804 : 7
when no proportion k., 195 : 16

Kernel, if it contain k., 606 : 18
Kernels, corn full of k., 693 : 2
Kestrels dear to kestrels, 92 : 14
Kettle, faces as blackness of a k., 33 : *n* 2
how agree the k. and pot, 35 : 25
of fish, 628 : 21
Polly put k. on, 933 : 17
pot calls k. black, 170 : 36
speech like cracked k., 583 : 11
Kettledrums, copper k., 742 : 9
Kew, his Highness' dog at K., 340 : 5
in lilac time, 772 : 22
Key, door to which no k., 516 : 18
golden k., 279 : 4
I have heard k., 805 : 13
in a bondman's k., 198 : 25
out of k. with his time, 792 : 10
think of k. each in prison, 805 : 13
this is the k. to it all, 570 : 4
to keep back beauty, 656 : 12
under thy own life's k., 227 : 9
used k. always bright, 347 : 24
who was a k. a man, 889 : 16
with this k. Shakespeare, 429 : 10
you shall keep the k., 219 : 3
Keys, fingers on these k., 767 : 9
of hell and death, 52 : 32
of kingdom of heaven, 39 : 36
over the noisy k., 596 : 13
shining k. took from her, 640 : 13
the k. to, 778 : 6
two massy k. he bore, 280 : 19
Keystone, night's black arch the k., 411 : 9
Kibe, galls his k., 224 : 13
Kick against pricks, 46 : 6, 71 : 12
I get k. out of you, 820 : 3
wheel's k., 760 : 14
why k. me downstairs, 407 : 13
won't have Nixon to k., 882 : 17
you downstairs, 611 : 11
Kicked and torn and beaten out, 470 : 11
until they can feel, 291 : 16
waxed fat and k., 11 : 24
Kicks dust, 559 : 16
Kid, here's looking at you k., 843 : 4
leopard shall lie down with the k., 29 : 19
Kiddo, take it from me k., 828 : 17
Kidney, heroes of that k., 804 : 18
man of my k., 225 : 25
Kids in big field of rye, 896 : 9
sky of adults over k., 911 : 20
thank you k., 856 : 10
Kikuyu, land tenure key to K. life, 818 : 13
Kilimanjaro highest mountain, 845 : 8
Kill admiral from time to time, 343 : 11
almost k. man as k. book, 281 : 23
and bliss me, 918 : 2
basilisk is sure to k., 332 : 5
be my brother or I k. you, 386 : 6
best to k. him right away, 396 : 21
bloom before its time, 428 : 23
bullet that will k. me, 420 : 13
cankers in musk rose buds, 196 : 19
care k. a cat, 210 : *n* 1
cure disease k. patient, 180 : 25
do not k., 4 : 2
flea though he k. none, 254 : 21
hates thing he would not k., 200 : 4
him in the shell, 215 : 17

Kill (*continued*)
in artificial manner, 473 : 17
joys with love, 193 : 30
kill kill kill kill, 235 : 6
learn him or k. him, 623 : 11
let's k. all the lawyers, 185 : 24
lust of office not k., 566 : 3
nor yet canst thou k. me, 254 : 11
not k. but needst not keep alive, 564 : 19
private individuals occasionally k., 679 : 11
reverence you've killed hero, 865 : 6
sooner k. man than hawk, 797 : 15
strike at king k. him, 500 : 12
things they do not love, 200 : 4
thou shalt not k., 10 : 7
thy physician, 232 : 28
time to k., 26 : 21
time which man trying to k., 580 : 1
time without injuring eternity, 559 : 3
to know to k. to create, 581 : 8
to wear fox have to k. it, 799 : 15
truths which can k. nation, 777 : 4
urge to k., 912 : 9
us for their sport, 234 : 21
when you have to k., 746 : 13
wife with kindness, 188 : 39
willingly as k. a fly, 188 : 22
you if you quote it, 718 : 16
Killed, before he k. dragon, 742 : 14
books not k. by fire, 780 : 17
by overwork, 707 : 15
calf in high style, 301 : 6
care k. a cat, 210 : 7
dragons have to be k., 885 : 3
effort nearly k. her, 730 : 9
fought dogs k. cats, 541 : 1
hawked at and k., 238 : 11
hunting hyena, 746 : 4
I'm k. sire, 540 : 21
many times in politics, 743 : 7
more k. by suppers, 269 : 26
only once in war, 743 : 7
propitiatory bird, 863 : 19
Roaring Bill who k. him, 730 : 12
scotched snake not k. it, 238 : 18
some sleeping k., 195 : 2
than frightened to death, 500 : 23
the rat, 934 : 9
two thirds of people k., 763 : 14
we have k. God, 657 : *n* 3
who k. Cock Robin, 930 : 9
who k. John Keats, 462 : 11
with report that old man eloquent, 282 : 6
you first time off base, 844 : 16
Killer kings on Etruscan cup, 892 : 10
Killeth, letter k., 49 : 11
wrath k. the foolish man, 15 : 14
Killing as canker to rose, 280 : 13
by simply exerting will, 582 : *n* 2
eternity essence of tragedy, 706 : 3
for food not natural, 786 : 8
frost, 249 : 3
time ends in k. man, 580 : 1
time essence of comedy, 706 : 3
treat for Ossete, 819 : 2
why use k. at all, 69 : 2
Kills, air that k., 691 : 9
destroys book k. reason, 281 : 23
doctor k. more, 315 : 12
gout k. more rich than poor, 301 : 2
Kills (*continued*)
not night that k., 705 : 21
shadow k. the growth, 257 : 2
six or seven dozen Scots, 203 : 26
superiority to sex that k., 870 : 10
the very good, 844 : 15
thing he loves, 676 : 8
world k. the good, 844 : 15
Kilmeny been she knew not where, 422 : 20
Kilmer tongue not far from cheek, 803 : 1
Kilroy was here, 838 : 14, 924 : 20
Kiltartan, my country K. Cross, 713 : 20
Kiltartan's poor, 713 : 20
Kimono, woman in k., 860 : 1
Kin, fair and foul k., 716 : 17
little more than k., 217 : 31
makes whole world k., 226 : 20
one's own k. and kith, 855 : 11
Kind, adieu k. friends, 922 : 13
and northern face, 843 : 17
art of being k., 670 : 4
as kings upon coronation, 305 : 19
be k. to my remains, 306 : 9
be to her virtues k., 320 : 17
blundering k. of melody, 304 : 17
charity is k., 48 : 23
consorteth according to k., 35 : 26
cruel only to be k., 223 : 12
enjoy her while she's k., 305 : 3
Fortune more k. than her custom, 200 : 15
had it been early had been k., 353 : 26
heart benevolent and k., 409 : 19
hearts more than coronets, 528 : 11
human k. not bear much reality, 806 : 20
I am a k. of burr, 229 : 3
I have been her k., 908 : 11
kindness not therefore k., 335 : 14
lady sweet and k., 918 : 14
less than k., 217 : 31
love is k., 48 : 23
man and died in want, 892 : 13
more nearly k. and gentle, 837 : 11
no best in k. but degree, 511 : 14
not seek for k. relief, 403 : 16
plenty of the k., 527 : 21
so constant and so k., 476 : 4
thief said last k. word, 545 : 3
through fire for k. heart, 225 : 22
time is a k. friend, 787 : 6
too k. to be k. enough, 332 : 9
two almost divide the k., 335 : 21
were all thy children k., 207 : 11
yet he was k., 370 : 10
Kinder, a little k. than necessary, 694 : 7
let me be a little k., 774 : 5
Kindle, cannot k. when will, 584 : 18
passion of former days, 744 : 11
soft desire, 306 : 22
truths k. light for t., 100 : 11
Kindled, anger of Lord k., 13 : 15
at taper of conwiviality, 547 : 20
earth, 462 : 15
light here k., 265 : 13
man like light k. and put out, 70 : 7
world fire k., 70 : 1
Kindles, fires true genius k., 338 : 14
in clothes a wantonness, 266 : 6
love kindled by virtue k. another, 142 : 5
Kindleth, how great a little fire k., 51 : 34
Kindliness of sheets, 796 : 16
Kindling her undazzled eyes, 282 : 3
Kindly, be k. affectioned, 47 : 20
earth slumber, 530 : 2
frosty but k., 210 : 30
fruits of the earth, 55 : 14
had we never loved sae k., 410 : 3
if heart just frank k., 298 : 1
Light, 490 : 6
Nature's k. law, 337 : 7
stopped for me, 606 : 4
to his fellow men, 57 : 32
word goodly act, 762 : 1
words do not enter so deeply, 89 : 26
Kindness, a God of great k., 14 : 31
acts of k. and of love, 423 : 9
and lies, 859 : 7
begets kindness, 73 : 12
Christ took k., 545 : 3
cup o' k. yet, 410 : 12
glad k., 714 : 18
have you had k. shown, 639 : 17
in women not looks, 189 : 1
kill wife with k., 188 : 39
learned k. from unkind, 782 : 20
lose natural k., 714 : 15
method is love and k., 154 : 12
milk of human k., 236 : 16
much k. in the Jew, 198 : 26
no act of k. ever wasted, 66 : 2
not free from ridicule, 523 : 3
not therefore kind, 335 : 14
recompense k. with k., 69 : 9
reputation for k. enters deeply, 89 : 26
ruth of k. with licked hands, 907 : 23
save every one of us, 902 : 7
show k. to parents, 131 : 6
sincerity earnestness and k., 69 : 19
to fellow creatures, 439 : 2
tongue is the law of k., 26 : 9
what wisdom greater than k., 358 : 21
Kindnesses, great persons great k., 170 : 28
one kindness among k., 385 : 17
thought of k. done, 102 : 14
Kindred, brothers sons k. slain, 338 : *n* 8
friends k. days, 494 : 10
like k. drops been mingled, 376 : 19
to God who made him, 522 : 5
true to k. points, 429 : 9
welcome k. glooms, 345 : 5
Kindreds, all nations and k., 53 : 14
Kinds, absolute natures or k., 85 : 12
birds are k. of knowledge, 85 : 19
material objects of two k., 100 : 9
Kine, learn from k. ruminating, 657 : 16
Pharaoh's lean k. loved, 204 : 6
seven good k., 8 : 31
seven thin k., 8 : 31
King, a' for our rightfu' k., 410 : 4
a new k. over Egypt, 9 : 7
and I, 833 : 17
authority forgets dying k., 534 : 30
balm from an anointed k., 194 : 26
be you clown or k., 667 : 7
best k. of good fellows, 146 : *n* 2
born to be k., 688 : 12
but thou the k. did banish, 194 : 5
by your own fireside, 168 : 5
Cambyses' vein, 204 : 4

King (*continued*)
can do no wrong, 365 : 18
cat may look on k., 160 : 34
catch conscience of k., 221 : 10
Charles's head, 548 : 31
chief defect of Henry K., 730 : 7
Christ this world all aleak, 829 : 14
come back as k., 797 : 5
cometh unto thee lowly, 33 : 32
contrary to k. built paper mill, 185 : 28
Cophetua loved beggarmaid, 192 : 1
cotton is k., 491 : 4
David and King Solomon, 696 : 3
divinity doth hedge a k., 223 : 27
earth receive her K., 328 : 13
every inch a k., 234 : 30
exists only as such, 165 : 21
farced title 'fore k., 208 : 7
farewell k., 195 : 3
first k. fortunate soldier, 343 : 4
follow the K., 534 : 5
George be a k., 540 : 4
glare surrounds k. hides him, 165 : 21
glorious to be pirate k., 627 : 19
glory to newborn K., 350 : 15
God bless the k., 341 : 12
God save the k., 12 : 34, 331 : 6
God save the k. say amen, 195 : 10
good K. Wenceslas, 563 : 11
governs like a k., 359 : 8
great God our K., 514 : 13
great K. above all gods, 20 : 20
greater than k. himself, 351 : 2
grew vain, 306 : 17
half the zeal I served my k., 249 : 9
heart and stomach of a k., 163 : 15
heaven's all gracious k., 537 : 16
here lies a k. that ruled, 271 : 18
here lies the k., 315 : 14
honor the k., 52 : 11
I am the Roman k., 298 : *n* 6
I was a k. in Babylon, 663 : 13
if chance will have me k., 236 : 12
in carriage may ride, 517 : 15
in exile, 790 : 13
in Prussia forward, 663 : 3
in sleep a k., 245 : 2
is the k. dead, 187 : 22
Jesus K. of Jews, 41 : 25
kings did k. to death, 886 : 14
let there be one k., 57 : 17
little profits idle k., 529 : 6
long live the k., 376 : 16
love is my lord and k., 532 : 25
made for quietness' sake, 264 : 7
mine eyes have seen the K., 29 : 10
mockery k. of snow, 195 : 14
Moloch sceptered k., 284 : 4
more royalist than k., 927 : 21
mortal temples of k., 195 : 2
my God and K., 269 : 7
niece of K. Gorboduc, 214 : 27
no k. in Israel, 12 : 24
not every year a k. born, 123 : 17
of a k. of England too, 163 : 15
of all kings, 917 : 3
of Babylon stood at the parting, 32 : 27
of France went up hill, 929 : 15
of glory shall come in, 18 : 9
of infinite space, 220 : 26
of kings, 53 : 26, 350 : *n* 4, 466 : 13
of love my shepherd is, 580 : 15

King (*continued*)
of pain, 633 : 13
of shreds and patches, 223 : 6
of Spain's daughter, 932 : 1
of terrors, 16 : 1
of the Jews, 36 : 20
offends no law is k. indeed, 178 : 4
old and foolish k., 26 : 25
old k. to sparrow, 740 : 1
old mad blind despised k., 468 : 4
on tapestry sits k., 897 : 15
only k. without sword, 893 : 19
over children of pride, 17 : 9
Ozymandias k. of kings, 466 : 13
pageantry of k., 391 : 2
Pandion he is dead, 257 : 7
passing brave to be a k., 183 : 5
pirate k., 627 : 19
reigns but not govern, 167 : 4
rightwise k. of England, 149 : 6
ruthless k., 363 : 4
seemed to me like k., 790 : 13
shall reign in righteousness, 30 : 20
sigh sword of Angel K., 406 : 7
sing Long live the k., 376 : 16
singer accompany the k., 413 : 25
sits in Dunfermline, 926 : 9
so excellent a k., 218 : 7
Son of Heaven's eternal K., 277 : 6
state without k., 484 : 20
still I am k. of those, 195 : 12
stomach of a k., 163 : 15
strike at k. kill him, 500 : 12
such a K. Harry, 182 : 15
the K. went on, 612 : 16
think not k. did banish thee, 194 : 5
this hath not offended k., 155 : 10
to be k. not within prospect, 236 : 6
to execute orders not to be k., 374 : 3
tomorrow shall die, 35 : 17
true beggar true k., 374 : 16
was in countinghouse, 931 : 9
wash balm from an anointed k., 194 : 26
whatsoever k. reign, 920 : 6
where Martin Luther K. could have lived, 915 : 18
who is this K. of glory, 18 : 10
who Pretender or who K., 341 : 12
wholesome even for k., 607 : 9
whom the k. delighteth to honor, 14 : 33
will not leave country, 848 : 2
winter k., 843 : 20
without woman I love, 832 : 2
world is a k., 421 : 20
worm that eat of a k., 223 : 15
year's pleasant k., 250 : 8
King Lear, impressed by reading K., 387 : 7
Kingdom, advantage on k. of shore, 244 : 22
and patience of Jesus Christ, 52 : 27
by the sea, 527 : 8
death's other k., 805 : 16
drink in my Father's k., 41 : 10
enter into k. of heaven, 38 : 19
fit for k. of God, 43 : 7
God hath numbered thy k., 33 : 1
good mind possesses k., 115 : 14
is divided, 33 : 1
keys of k. of heaven, 39 : 36
large k. for little grave, 195 : 7
man like little k., 215 : 18

Kingdom (*continued*)
mind content both crown and k. is, 178 : 11
my k. for a horse, 187 : 31
my mind to me a k. is, 167 : 5
no society bring k. of God, 775 : 4
not enter into k. of heaven, 40 : 1
of daylight's dauphin, 656 : 1
of God within you, 43 : 36
of heaven is at hand, 36 : 25
of heaven like a net, 39 : 19
of heaven like mustard seed, 39 : 17
of Heaven within you, 126 : 15
of perpetual night, 187 : 10
of such is k. of God, 42 : 11
of the shore, 244 : 22
remember me when in thy k., 44 : 8
rich man enter into k., 40 : 7
root of the k., 89 : 8
salt k. from which banished, 864 : 7
stands and grows forever, 597 : 18
teach order to peopled k., 207 : 6
theirs is the k. of heaven, 37 : 4
thine is the k., 14 : 25, 37 : 15
thy k. come, 37 : 15
to find man to benefit k., 89 : 4
who draw us to k., 126 : 15
Kingdoms, all the k. of world, 42 : 34
are but cares, 150 : 1
are clay, 240 : 14
destroyed by bandits, 312 : 25
did shake k., 29 : 23
goodly states and k., 475 : 6
kissed away k., 241 : 8
of this world, 53 : 18
sifted three k., 307 : *n* 4
Kingfisher, blue k. dives, 892 : 4
in Black Mud k., 892 : 4
Kingfishers, as k. catch fire, 656 : 11
Kingly commons, 570 : 11
crown to gain, 452 : 7
his state is k., 282 : 17
King's, all the k. horses, 932 : 2
daughter is all glorious within, 19 : 9
daughter o' Noroway, 926 : 10
English, 225 : 12
first minister, 746 : 2
grim k. dog, 76 : 3
marched by k. name, 822 : 2
Martin Luther K. dream, 909 : *n* 4
might greater than human, 78 : 20
name a tower of strength, 187 : 25
not the k. crown nor sword, 228 : 6
our only lord, 182 : 13
rides hobbyhorse along k. highway, 359 : 20
subject's duty is k., 208 : 5
Kings, all be happy as k., 668 : 14
all k. and their favorites, 252 : 22
alone dwell k. of sea, 584 : 14
and counselors of the earth, 15 : 8
and princes have philosophy, 84 : 15
angels in forms of k., 388 : 18
barrel-house k., 765 : 5
cabbages and k., 613 : 5
calm contending k., 189 : 23
captains and k. depart, 709 : 17
change state with k., 244 : 10
crown that seldom k. enjoy, 186 : 8
death beats at palaces of k., 107 : 1
death lays icy hand on k., 272 : 15
deaths of k., 627 : 2
descended of so many k., 242 : 6
did king to death, 886 : 14

Kings (*continued*)
did K. heave up building blocks, 840 : 17
divine right of k., 520 : 8
dread and fear of k., 200 : 9
flower of k. and knights, 149 : 18
glory to King of k., 350 : *n* 4
good of subjects end of k., 318 : 10
grammar control k., 298 : 13
have died of gout, 301 : 2
have sat down, 35 : 20
he shall stand before k., 25 : 4
heartsease must k. neglect, 208 : 6
in golden mail, 879 : 20
it makes gods, 187 : 24
kind as k. upon coronation day, 305 : 19
king of all k., 917 : 3
King of k., 53 : 26, 350 : *n* 4
know k. of England, 628 : 1
laws or k. cause or cure, 352 : 21
like stars, 468 : 16
listed names of K., 840 : 17
mad world mad k., 201 : 18
may be blessed, 411 : 7
may love treason but traitor hate, 99 : *n* 12
meaner creatures k., 187 : 24
mercy enthroned in hearts of k., 200 : 9
Nature's little k., 251 : 6
nice customs curtsy to great k., 208 : 20
not k. and lords but nations, 449 : 2
on Etruscan cup, 892 : 10
Ozymandias king of k., 466 : 13
peasants born k. of earth, 504 : 12
plucker down of k., 186 : 6
politeness of k., 402 : 2
pretend to watch over economy, 366 : 3
pride of k., 336 : 10, 623 : 8
princes but breath of k., 408 : 18
prophets and k., 43 : 12
right divine of k., 340 : 24
rivers of k., 840 : 5
royal throne of k., 194 : 13
ruin k., 303 : 19
sad stories of death of k., 195 : 2
saddest among k. of earth, 728 : 18
setter up of k., 186 : 6
showers on her k. barbaric pearl, 284 : 3
slave to fate chance k., 254 : 12
spirit of Zeus-fostered k., 57 : 16
sport of k., 328 : 18
sword of justice lay down, 318 : 10
tax heavier than k., 348 : 3
teeming womb of royal k., 194 : 13
they are no k., 318 : 10
tired of k., 494 : 16
triumphing over k. and aces, 818 : 5
tyrants from policy, 373 : 26
until philosophers are k., 84 : 15
vain the ambition of k., 262 : 11
walk with k., 710 : 17
what have k. that privates have not, 208 : 6
would not play at, 377 : 12
Kinquering Congs their titles take, 659 : 10
Kinship with the stars, 600 : 15
Kinsmen, as k. met a night, 605 : 14
Kipling, Rudyards cease from K., 693 : 4
Kirk, below the k., 434 : 7
is this the k., 435 : 4
nearer God more far, 173 : 6
Kiss, ae fond k., 410 : 2
afresh, 266 : 10
after k. comes throttle, 868 : 7
and cling, 614 : *n* 3
and tell, 324 : 12
bee's k. now, 540 : 29
cleanliest shift is to k., 212 : 22
come k. me, 918 : 2
come let us k. and part, 182 : 16
coward does it with k., 676 : 8
fades out from k. to k., 712 : 19
fame treacherous k., 876 : 11
for whole world, 412 : 10
give me a k., 266 : 10
if a body k. a body, 919 : *n* 2
is still a kiss, 830 : 6
Jews k. infidels adore, 334 : 1
keep k. in refrigerator, 837 : 10
last lamenting k., 253 : 14
leave a k. but in the cup, 256 : 8
long as my exile, 242 : 22
make me immortal with a k., 184 : 4
me and be quiet, 341 : 2
me Hardy, 408 : 10
me Kate, 188 : 32
me sweet and twenty, 213 : 23
moth's k. first, 540 : 28
not a k. not look be lost, 868 : 17
not k. your f.ing flag, 829 : 9
of blankets, 796 : 16
of death, 741 : 6
part without k., 618 : 4
place to make well, 449 : 12
rough male k. of blankets, 796 : 16
so k. on, 266 : 10
some that shadows k., 199 : 15
this month is a k., 273 : 13
through a veil, 492 : 3
thy k. would wake dead, 530 : 12
till the cow comes home, 263 : 5
what is a k., 266 : 1
with one long k. my soul, 184 : *n* 3
without single k. or good-bye, 593 : 4
you take is better, 227 : 2
Kissed again with tears, 530 : 23
came to Jesus and k. him, 41 : 15
curtsied when you have and k., 247 : 19
first k. beside thorn, 654 : 17
Good-bye I have k. it, 856 : 10
here hung lips I have k., 224 : 14
in forty years, 817 : 7
Jenny k. me, 454 : 8
lovely grass, 796 : 9
maiden all forlorn, 934 : 9
O sad k. mouth, 632 : 19
pacified Psyche k. her, 527 : 2
righteousness and peace have k. each other, 20 : 9
stones k. by English dead, 827 : 6
them and put them there, 666 : 17
toyed and k., 331 : 20
we have k. away kingdoms, 241 : 8
Kisses, between k. and wine, 721 : 4
bring again bring again, 228 : 28
from female mouth, 460 : 8
give me a thousand k., 101 : 18
I understand thy k., 204 : 17
joy as it flies, 404 : 18
Kisses (*continued*)
many thousand k., 241 : 21
more than k. letters mingle souls, 254 : 4
of enemy deceitful, 25 : 23
played cards for k., 175 : 23
remembered k. after death, 531 : 4
you have forgotten my k., 634 : 3
Kissing don't last cookery do, 600 : 11
fool invented k., 323 : 14
god k. carrion, 220 : 17
had to stop, 543 : 11
hand may feel good, 826 : 5
her down, 863 : 19
no more k. after, 614 : *n* 3
Kit, your old k. bag, 770 : 14
Kitchen, get out of k., 788 : 1
in K. bred, 364 : *n* 1
long and ghastly k., 551 : 15
scrub k. pavement, 712 : 20
set around the k. fire, 665 : 11
Kitchens full of things to be done, 902 : 16
wildcats in your k., 230 : 8
Kite cut from the string, 789 : 15
Kites, chronicle the wars of k., 289 : 12
Kith, one's own kin and k., 855 : 11
Kits cats sacks wives, 930 : 1
Kitten, rather be k. and cry mew, 204 : 13
Kittens, deserve all these k., 760 : 4
soshubble ez baskit er k., 662 : 7
Kitty Fisher found it, 933 : 5
Hawk, 835 : 1
Klopstock questioned, 630 : 18
Klug, und bin so k. als wie zuvor, 396 : *n* 3
Knapsack, marshal's baton in k., 421 : 5
Knave, arrant k., 220 : 2
cat's a cat Rolet a k., 311 : 7
himself a k., 330 : 24
how absolute the k. is, 224 : 12
more k. than fool, 169 : 30, 183 : 14
of Hearts, 931 : 4
playing the k., 309 : 17
rascally yea-forsooth k., 205 : 22
surname epithet for k., 153 : *n* 5
Knavery, religion k. and change, 312 : 13
Knaves all three, 933 : 2
arrant k. all, 221 : 16
called them untaught k., 203 : 8
little better than false k., 209 : 32
thieves and teachers, 233 : 5
Kneaded, a k. clod, 228 : 20
Knee, banjo on my k., 598 : 1
bowed patient k., 458 : 3
her head on her k., 232 : 8
lean in joy upon father's k., 403 : 8
pregnant hinges of the k., 222 : 4
Knee-deep in June, 665 : 12
Kneel before Lord our maker, 20 : 20
down and ask forgiveness, 235 : 12
mother state to thee I k., 639 : 15
Kneeling, lying k. standing, 894 : 10
Kneels, not one k. to another, 574 : 24
Knees, bringing to his k., 823 : 9
brought me down to k., 874 : 17
down on your k., 212 : 16
fell upon k. and blessed God, 265 : 7
first fell on own k., 562 : 14
live on k., 759 : 2, 780 : 14
man-at-arms now serve on k., 177 : 9
no one only she on her k., 912 : 13

Knees (*continued*)
of the gods, 59 : 16
on parent k. newborn child, 394 : 3
they that enter must go on k., 262 : 9
to Thee all k. bent, 614 : 9
work done upon his k., 710 : 22
Knell, by fairy hands k. rung, 364 : 9
curfew tolls k., 361 : 20
of Union, 389 : 14
overpowering k., 461 : 16
strikes like rising k., 457 : 14
that summons, 237 : 16
Knelt down with angry prayers, 732 : 16
Knew, Achilles whom we k., 529 : 13
anguish of marrow, 804 : 22
anybody else I k. as well, 558 : 26
carry all he k., 370 : 11
changed from him they k., 747 : 1
God and I k. once, 630 : 18
he nothing k., 288 : 16
head which all men k., 533 : 3
I k. all her ways, 692 : 5
I k. him Horatio, 224 : 14
I k. him when, 732 : 15
if youth but k. if old age but could, 163 : 11
Johnny I hardly k. ye, 921 : 1
life the old Sabines k., 104 : 7
man who k. more spoke less, 120 : 15
my son was mortal, 83 : 4
never k. so young a body, 200 : 8
not Astrophil, 184 : 12
not Joseph, 9 : 7
phoenix in my youth, 714 : 5
stars flowers birds, 735 : 8
taught me all I k., 710 : 2
they were pilgrims, 265 : 5
things that were and would be, 57 : 6
thy face or name, 252 : 20
we should both forget, 634 : 2
worst too young, 708 : 15
you k. Astrophil, 184 : 12
Knife, cut off tails with k., 929 : 11
hardest k. ill-used, 245 : 7
how cut without k., 930 : 15
I the wound and k., 581 : 1
other men are the carving k., 719 : 9
put a k. to thy throat, 25 : 5
smiler with k., 146 : 24
war even to k., 457 : 3
watering pot pruning k., 536 : 12
when they take k., 604 : 4
wind's like whetted k., 760 : 16
without a blade, 386 : 16
Knight, ail thee k. at arms, 478 : 10
courteoust k. ever bare shield, 149 : 20
dark Care enthroned behind K., 107 : 26
gentle k. pricking on plain, 173 : 8
lean and foolish k., 742 : 10
like young Lochinvar, 430 : 18
never matched of earthly k., 149 : 20
of ghosts and shadows, 918 : 12
of holy spirit, 481 : 10
of the Sorrowful Countenance, 168 : 26
parfit gentil k., 145 : 14
plumed k., 615 : 4
prince can make belted k., 411 : 18
to be their wooer, 927 : 1
Knighthood, grope for evidence of k., 884 : 16
Knighthood (*continued*)
of k. and of freedom flower, 148 : 5
Knightly years were gone, 663 : 13
Knight's bones are dust, 436 : 4
Knights, armorers accomplishing k., 208 : 1
death of most noblest k., 149 : 17
flower of kings and k. destroyed, 149 : 18
ladies dead and lovely k., 245 : 12
let others sing of k., 182 : 6
Knit, come k. hands, 279 : 14
Knits a bolder one, 605 : 8
up raveled sleave of care, 237 : 21
Knitted, from clasp of k. locks, 576 : 18
Knitters in the sun, 214 : 3
Knitting loose train of thy hair, 280 : 3
Knives, hands made before k., 323 : 12
in woodsman's house k. wood, 935 : 14
men with k. in brain, 499 : 6
mishaps like k., 569 : 5
Knock and it shall be opened, 38 : 12
as you please nobody home, 336 : 7
'em out pick round, 915 : 12
heart k. at my ribs, 236 : 11
sounds exceed k. at door, 441 : 23
stand at the door and k., 53 : 6
to wail or k. the breast, 289 : 9
when you k. it never is home, 376 : 5
where k. is open wide, 365 : 8
you but k. breathe shine, 254 : 15
Knockdown argument, 306 : 3, 613 : 16
Knocker, tie up the k., 338 : 5
Knocking around with men, 394 : 15
come k. at my door, 600 : 7
on moonlit door, 739 : 15
the k. when I'm dead, 762 : 1
Knocks, apostolic blows and k., 291 : 5
open locks whoever k., 239 : 7
opportunity k. once, 114 : *n* 4
you down with butt end, 371 : 23
Knolled, bells k. to church, 211 : 12
Knolling departing friend, 205 : 20
Knot, crowned k. of fire, 808 : 18
Gordian k. unloose, 207 : 5
seeking k. in a bulrush, 93 : 10
subtle k. which makes us man, 253 : 7
Knot's tied in public way, 839 : 12
Knots, pokers into true-love k., 436 : 5
Knotted and combined locks part, 219 : 18
Know a subject ourselves, 355 : 17
all ye k. on earth, 477 : 11
allow you do not K., 68 : 11
arrive at what not k., 807 : 18
as I am known, 48 : 25
as if to k. became fatality, 768 : 22
as much as possible, 654 : 7
be still and k. that I am God, 19 : 12
believed what we least k., 164 : 15
best that is in one, 658 : 2
best things not learned, 361 : 5
better be ignorant than half k., 112 : 9
better k. nothing than half-know, 561 : *n* 4
better k. nothing than what ain't so, 561 : 20
blaspheme what they do not k., 300 : 13
both act and k., 296 : 25
by their fruits k. them, 38 : 18
charms slaves never k., 375 : 19
Know (*continued*)
dancer from dance, 715 : 17
determined to k. beans, 560 : 6
different idea of things we k., 735 : 18
disciplines of wars, 207 : 22
disposition of women, 96 : 21
do not k. much about gods, 808 : 1
do you k. me my lord, 220 : 15
doesn't k. what he likes, 831 : 3
don't k. where go better, 747 : 16
dost k. who made thee, 403 : 5
enough of something, 878 : 16
enough who k. how to learn, 635 : 10
every wise man's son k., 213 : 22
everything forgive everything, 417 : *n* 5
for whom bell tolls, 254 : 22
four things wiser to k., 827 : 8
gallanter I k., 604 : 7
go we k. not where, 228 : 20
God with thee k. it not, 425 : 17
greater than we k., 429 : 2
have the gift to k. it, 211 : 9
hawk from handsaw, 220 : 31
heartily k., 494 : 11
how in your darkness k., 733 : 9
how man reacts, 791 : 16
how should I true love k., 223 : 21
how tender 'tis to love babe, 237 : 5
how to grow old, 580 : 10
how to speak falsehoods, 61 : 8
I am but summer, 823 : 4
I am happier than I k., 287 : 5
I k. a bank, 196 : 18
I k. myself a man, 251 : 7
I k. not seems, 218 : 2
I k. not the man, 41 : 18
I k. that is poetry, 608 : 6
I k. thy pride, 12 : 39
I k. what I like, 736 : 2
I k. you all, 203 : 5
I shall meet fate, 713 : 20
if to do as easy as to k., 198 : 9
if you haven't guessed, 709 : 24
if you mean to k. yourself, 386 : 12
if you want to k. yourself, 413 : 1
ignorance toboggans into k., 830 : 3
I'm farther from heaven, 485 : 5
in Boston ask how much k., 625 : 23
in mathematics never k. what about, 737 : 13
in part prophesy in part, 48 : 25
in truth we k. nothing, 79 : 10
it no more, 21 : 7
Jesus loves me this I k., 599 : 4
learn what I wanted to k., 400 : 11
less than all unknown, 260 : 8
less understand more, 781 : 14
let him not k. it, 231 : 10
let not left hand k., 37 : 14
liberty to k., 282 : 4
light falls and fills, 873 : 16
living k. no bounds, 272 : 11
lucky to die and I k. it, 574 : 18
make me to k. mine end, 19 : 1
man not k. of God, 859 : 1
many admire few k., 80 : 11
men k. so little of men, 724 : 16
much say little, 358 : 20
my methods Watson, 689 : 9
my soul hath power to k., 251 : 6
neither shall his place k. him, 15 : 21
never k. how high we are, 607 : 2
never k. what is enough, 404 : 6

Know (*continued*)
never k. when succeeded best, 706 : 13
never prophesy onless k., 568 : 6
never see nor k. nor miss me, 778 : 6
no such liberty, 296 : 2
not enough to k., 87 : 25
not k. I am a woman, 212 : 8
not k. we are dead, 83 : *n* 7
not subtle ways, 495 : 11
not utter what dost not k., 203 : 24
not what they do, 44 : 7
not what they mean, 531 : 3
not what we may be, 223 : 23
not where His islands, 513 : 24
not whether laws be right, 676 : 12
nothing except my ignorance, 79 : 5
one thing I k. is land, 779 : 3
only broken images, 805 : 1
only k. we loved in vain, 456 : 7
only that he nothing knew, 288 : 16
others that we k. not of, 221 : 12
parting all we k. of heaven, 607 : 18
place for first time, 808 : 17
pleasure none but madmen k., 304 : 19
pools I used to k., 691 : 11
power to k. all things, 251 : 6
reason from what we k., 336 : 12
rest who does not k., 113 : 4
safer to k. too little, 620 : 5
said I didn't k., 623 : 7
say not you k. another, 386 : 7
say what I k., 400 : 11
saying all we did not k., 794 : 14
she thinks o' me, 708 : 8
shore of what we k., 900 : 11
something of own country, 360 : 18
strive to grasp what they do not k., 90 : 9
study great deal to k. little, 341 : 11
subject of knowledge is to k., 85 : 19
tell me what you k., 495 : 26
that age to age succeeds, 527 : 22
that I may k. how frail I am, 19 : 1
that man might k. end, 217 : 10
that men are like children, 782 : 10
that my redeemer liveth, 16 : 4
that the Lord is God, 21 : 3
that you do not know, 65 : 5
the best thought and said, 588 : 12
the like no more, 516 : 21
the right moment, 62 : 10
them by their fruits, 38 : 17
they k. and do not k., 806 : 17
this I k. full well, 319 : 19
thought so now I k. it, 332 : 8
thyself, 62 : 4, 337 : 2
till then what love I bore thee, 425 : 6
to k. is nothing, 655 : 5
to k. men thoroughly, 453 : 7
to k. to kill to create, 581 : 8
to k. well involves ignorance, 572 : 9
too much convinced of too little, 809 : 12
trick worth two of that, 203 : 17
want much they do not k., 889 : 6
we are eternal, 309 : 4
we k. the good, 76 : 19
we k. what we are, 223 : 23
well I am not great, 534 : 13
what do I k., 165 : 6
what false heart doth k., 237 : 8
what God and man is, 535 : 10

Know (*continued*)
what I know and write it, 886 : 8
what I like, 736 : 2
what I read in papers, 765 : 15
what is past I k., 34 : 4
what is to come I k. not, 34 : 4
what it is to be child, 694 : 1
what lays afore us, 548 : 1
what no other man can k., 683 : 16
what person thinks by actions, 861 : 13
what should it k. of death, 423 : 3
what should they k. of England, 708 : 16
what 'tis to pity, 211 : 12
what want to prove, 724 : 6
what wood a cudgel's of, 291 : 16
what you don't k. make book, 433 : 13
when one doesn't k. where going, 396 : 1
where'er I go, 426 : 12
who speaks does not k., 64 : 19
who we are enlist again, 907 : 8
whose prayers make whole, 707 : 19
whose woods I think I k., 748 : 5
world unknowable we k., 693 : 16
world without going outdoors, 64 : 17
worst and provide for it, 383 : 1
wot lays afore us, 548 : 1
ye not there is a prince fallen, 13 : 13
ye the land, 459 : 5
you k. we French, 540 : 20
young k. everything, 400 : 12
Knowest, speak less than thou k., 233 : 9
thou k. my downsitting, 22 : 16
thou k. thy estimate, 245 : 1
thou k. 'tis common, 218 : 1
thou the land, 395 : 3
Knoweth, He k. all things, 132 : 13
he k. not who shall gather them, 19 : 3
no man k. of his sepulcher, 11 : 27
sun k. his going down, 21 : 11
Knowhow to nowhere, 876 : 13
Knowing, better friends not be k., 823 : 3
gossip most k. of persons, 114 : 21
I loved my books, 247 : 15
life itself is sheer k., 867 : 12
not k. what they do, 209 : 29
of devil's party without k. it, 403 : 19
secret of happiness freedom, 81 : 5
when to have done, 474 : 9
without author's k. it, 701 : 6
Knowledge, absolute idea of k., 85 : 12
access to k., 861 : 7
acquired under compulsion, 84 : 21
after such k., 804 : 14
all k. and wonder is pleasure, 178 : 18
all k. my province, 178 : 15
and love of God, 56 : 1
and timber seasoned, 519 : 14
apply thine heart unto my k., 24 : 37
birds are kinds of k., 85 : 19
book of k. fair, 285 : 5
born in possession of k., 68 : 22
born to follow k., 141 : 14
brings us nearer ignorance, 806 : 15
but no power, 78 : 21
by suffering, 507 : 1
captivating as new k., 463 : 18
carrier of news and k., 617 : 7
causes to be without k., 63 : 14

Knowledge (*continued*)
chapter of k. very short, 342 : 14
climbing after k. infinite, 183 : 6
collective k. of mankind, 867 : 12
comes wisdom lingers, 530 : 4
conformity of object and intellect, 137 : 8
dawn of k. false dawn, 837 : 13
death is k., 413 : 23
desirable of itself, 490 : 11
desire more love and k., 210 : 18
desire of k. caused man to fall, 180 : 14
desire of k. increases, 360 : 4
diffused k. immortalizes, 416 : 13
diffusion of k. advantageous, 506 : 6
discard k., 90 : 8
do deed without God's k., 71 : 22
doubt grows with k., 397 : 6
dreadful k. of truth, 74 : 2
earth full of k. of Lord, 29 : 19
enormous makes god of me, 478 : 6
essential k., 552 : 11
every sluice of k. opened, 380 : 10
exact k. of the past, 80 : 15
excellent things in counsels and k., 25 : 1
extraordinary collection of k., 891 : 7
faith and k. in medicine, 464 : 4
faith sight and k., 557 : 3
fence against world is k., 308 : 2
follow k. like star, 529 : 10
foundations of k. in mathematics, 139 : 5
furnish means of acquiring k., 418 : 10
great k. of heart, 723 : 12
grow from more to more, 531 : 18
grow virtuously into k., 701 : 13
he that hath k. spareth his words, 24 : 18
he that increaseth k., 26 : 17
help me with k., 546 : 4
her ample page, 362 : 7
highest point not k., 783 : 2
if a little k. dangerous, 596 : 7
improver of natural k., 595 : 10
in traveling carry k., 356 : 6
increase and diffusion of k., 417 : 1
increaseth strength, 25 : 12
is bought in market, 564 : 10
is of two kinds, 355 : 17
is power, 178 : 17, 891 : 6
is proud, 377 : 15
is sufficient to attain, 69 : 15
is the one only good, 79 : 3
island in ocean of non-knowledge, 862 : 5
liberty not preserved without k., 380 : 9
life not k. but action, 596 : 6
light of k. in eyes, 643 : 1
like what we imagine k. to be, 878 : 7
lost in information, 806 : 15
manners must adorn k., 342 : 2
may give weight, 342 : 10
meager and unsatisfactory, 594 : 11
men by nature desire k., 87 : 9
money power, 887 : 8
monk's state transcends k., 73 : 4
more than force, 178 : *n* 10
much k. a curse, 90 : 10
multiplieth words without k., 16 : 25
must come through action, 75 : 6

Knowledge (*continued*)
never learned of schools, 513 : 11
night unto night showeth k., 17 : 27
no k. beyond experience, 307 : 14
no work nor device nor k., 27 : 16
not arrogant because of k., 3 : 4
not infused from without, 89 : 20
not k. but personality, 577 : 2
not true k. but only belief, 132 : 7
objects and k. curious, 576 : 5
of atom through stars, 776 : 10
of God more than burnt offerings, 33 : 11
of Greek thought, 598 : 13
of human nature, 440 : 29, 635 : 1
of itself a treasure, 490 : 11
of nothing, 546 : 9
of other culture appreciate our own, 853 : 13
of our buried life, 585 : 15
of their duty, 81 : 5
of world not in closet, 341 : 17
one thing virtue another, 490 : 12
opinion is k. in making, 282 : 2
out-topping k., 584 : 9
poetry finer spirit of k., 424 : 7
profess not the k., 34 : 28
puffeth up, 48 : 13
quest for k. and progress, 891 : 8
rich storehouse, 179 : 1
science achieve perfect k., 584 : 1
science begets k., 80 : 5
scientific k. from textbooks, 825 : 13
search for k. a passion, 738 : 6
shall any teach God k., 16 : 8
shall be increased, 33 : 6
should be his guide, 84 : 9
show tracks of k., 100 : 16
spirit of k. and fear of the Lord, 29 : 18
subject of k. is to know, 85 : 19
subjective and objective in k., 437 : 10
sun in firmament, 450 : 7
sweetly uttered k., 176 : 10
they have too much k., 65 : 2
this is k., 68 : 11
those enslaved to sects are devoid of k., 125 : 21
to be possessed of all this k., 380 : 6
to the young man k. and discretion, 23 : 1
too high price for k., 325 : *n* 5
too much k. for skeptic, 337 : 2
tree of k. of good and evil, 6 : 20
under difficulties, 444 : 16
virtue harder than k., 307 : 20
wise man has no extensive k., 65 : 10
wise man utter vain k., 15 : 36
you have been given little k., 131 : 8
Knowledgeable of evils, 70 : 21
Knowledges, general k. idiots possess, 405 : 16
Known a better day, 429 : 20
among leaves never k., 476 : 24
and do not want it, 353 : 26
because of all things k., 713 : 12
best k. and thought, 586 : 24
by company he keeps, 77 : *n* 9
cause hidden result well k., 113 : 19
from k. to unknown, 552 : 5
God of fathers k. of old, 709 : 16
have ye not k., 31 : 1
know as I am k., 48 : 25
lady k. as Lou, 752 : 5
Known (*continued*)
letters should not be k., 247 : 26
lightning's hour, 860 : 7
much to be done little k., 353 : 6
searched me and k. me, 22 : 16
the K. fully itself, 902 : 14
too late, 191 : 27
unto whom all desires k., 55 : 15
what do to be forever k., 295 : 1
Know-Nothing, I am not K., 520 : 2
Knows, all this the world well k., 245 : 23
babs k. what and babs k. why, 759 : 15
but world end tonight, 542 : 14
each exercise art he k., 82 : 3
expert k. more about less, 698 : 17
God's mouth k. not falsehood, 71 : 1
greatness k. itself, 204 : 37
happy who k. rural gods, 104 : 6
hope that life k., 916 : 3
how to confess, 347 : 20
it k. not what it is, 715 : 2
man says what he k., 358 : 26
no beast but k. some pity, 187 : 1
no one k. masterpiece, 792 : 17
no one k. till he tries, 112 : 6
not also to unknow, 581 : 13
not draw out more than already k., 658 : 26
not how other half lives, 270 : 21
not how to k., 581 : 13
not what to do, 929 : 10
now God alone k., 630 : 18
reason k. nothing of, 300 : 4
sage k. without going about, 64 : 17
secret sits in middle and k., 749 : 9
sleep that k. not breaking, 431 : 8
tale every schoolboy k., 361 : 7
tell wife all he k., 276 : 16
the less one k., 64 : 17
the universe not himself, 296 : 20
toad beneath harrow k., 707 : 5
what none other k., 717 : 1
what one k. of little moment, 635 : 10
what's what, 546 : 26
who k. does not speak, 64 : 19
who k. himself is enlightened, 64 : 11
who k. one side k. little, 508 : 6
who k. others is wise, 64 : 11
who only England k., 708 : 16
wise father that k. child, 199 : 3
wots' wot, 546 : 26
ye not Heavenly Powers, 395 : 2
Knuckle-end of England, 432 : 18
Ko-ax, brekekekex k. k., 82 : 18
Kodak, It Isn't A K., 829 : 1
Kolyma island of Gulag, 895 : 23
Kosciusko, freedom shrieked as K. fell, 443 : 5
Kosmos, untented K. my abode, 669 : 3
Walt Whitman a k., 574 : 20
with dread abysses, 651 : 3
Kraft durch Freude, 816 : *n* 3
Krapp's last tape, 866 : 15
Kremlin's mountaineer, 819 : 1
Krieg, ernährt den K. 413 : *n* 3
Krishna, splendor of Mighty One K., 94 : 15
Krivchians, the Chuds Slavs and K., 136 : 2
Kronos, son of K., 57 : 12
Kubla Khan, in Xanadu did K., 433 : 21
Kultur, wenn K. höre, 816 : *n* 2
Kunti, son of K. goes, 94 : 14
Kurtz, Mistah K. he dead, 683 : 21
Kyloe, little K. cow, 931 : 7
Kyrie eleison, 54 : 3

L

La Rochefoucauld never lived in Bronx, 859 : 16
Laban said heap of stones a witness, 8 : 23
Labels, men are l. that give name to event, 602 : 3
Labor, a youth of l., 370 : 2
all ye that l., 39 : 8
and capital get together, 725 : 14
and intent study, 281 : 12
and to wait, 509 : 16
and wounds vain, 564 : 16
as another's serf, 60 : 15
at eternal task, 593 : 12
aversion to l., 316 : 13
bad book as much l., 830 : 8
basic hero l., 725 : 10
because they excel, 445 : 17
blossoming or dancing, 715 : 17
bread from mouth of l., 389 : 1
brow of l., 694 : 16
capital fruit of l., 522 : 3
capital solicits aid of l., 450 : 4
capitalists employers of l., 563 : *n* 3
changes l. from burden to honor, 766 : 8
cost is l. to produce thing, 572 : 20
discontinued l. dangerous, 491 : 26
disgraces no man, 590 : 3
exact day l. light denied, 282 : 16
genius intuitive talent for l., 349 : *n* 2
good week's l., 261 : 20
grant me this l., 103 : 22
has natural and market price, 438 : 13
honest l. bears a lovely face, 251 : 10
in all l. there is profit, 24 : 3
in the deep mid-ocean, 528 : 20
in vain, 22 : 8
independent and proud, 450 : 4
independent of l. of hands, 558 : 22
learning without thought is l. lost, 68 : 10
little effect much l., 441 : 3
live by fruit of l., 520 : 8
look after souls in l., 85 : 16
man organized by l., 725 : 10
many must l. for one, 459 : 9
marvels of man's l., 872 : 13
masterpiece not created without l., 727 : 11
men disgrace l., 590 : 3
mountains will be in l., 109 : 25
my l. for my travail, 225 : 33
no sin to l. in vocation, 203 : 3
not ask for reward, 157 : 3
not to be rich, 25 : 6
nothing but l. for pains, 168 : 7
obtain tradition by l., 809 : 2
of an age, 277 : 13
of France poured earnings, 592 : 10
of love, 50 : 16
only relaxation another kind of l., 655 : 8
organization of l., 763 : 8

Labor (*continued*)
prior to capital, 522 : 3
private property fruit of l., 757 : 17
process by which A acquires for B, 647 : 13
product of his l., 523 : 7
pro-l. policies, 775 : 6
property stimulus to l., 758 : 1
reward of l. is life, 618 : 14
say picture shows l., 619 : 5
selling l. power, 563 : *n* 4
six days shalt thou l., 10 : 6, 553 : 17
superior to capital, 522 : 3
take nothing of his l., 27 : 2
that has reference to want, 422 : 16
those who l. in earth, 388 : 2
thou and I waste, 161 : 24
thought l. of intellect, 492 : 1
to his l. until evening, 21 : 11
unemployed l. means want, 811 : 10
union pressure, 775 : 6
unions and inflation, 848 : 4
useless if object useless, 562 : 17
visible and invisible l., 491 : 23
we delight in physics pain, 238 : 4
what profit of all his l., 26 : 11
who have not to l., 515 : 5
why life all l. be, 528 : 16
yet is their strength l. and sorrow, 20 : 13
Laborare, orare est l., 134 : 14
Laboratory, every l. closed ten years, 776 : 4
Labored not for myself only, 36 : 4
nothings, 333 : 5
Laborer finds enemy in middling class, 492 : 20
I am a true l., 212 : 2
right of l. to savings, 621 : 7
son of robust l., 774 : 9
worthy of hire, 43 : 10
Laborer's task o'er, 597 : 15
Laborers, enable l. to subsist, 438 : 13
farmers mechanics and l., 419 : 3
harvest plenteous but l. few, 38 : 32
selling labor power to live, 563 : *n* 4
together with God, 48 : 4
Laboring children can look out, 757 : 5
fine thing needs much l., 713 : 2
sleep of a l. man, 27 : 1
surges of world, 693 : 9
to produce bons mots, 297 : 28
Laborious, consciousness l. achievement, 754 : 3
live l. days, 280 : 15
Labor's, sore l. bath, 237 : 21
Labors, garner fruits of l., 704 : 17
no l. tire, 351 : 18
notice you take of my l., 353 : 26
patient under dangerous l., 617 : 6
rest from their l., 53 : 24
saints who from l. rest, 592 : 1
Labourage et pâturage deux mamelles, 178 : *n* 4
Labyrinth, wandering in dark l., 182 : 20
Labyrinthical, perplexed l. soul, 255 : 4
Labyrinthine ways, 693 : 10
Lace, brace l. latch catch, 656 : 12
Greek is like l., 356 : 15
Lacedemonians not wont to ask how many, 78 : 25
Lacerare, cor l. nequit, 323 : 25
Lacerate, cannot l. his breast, 716 : 6
savage indignation l. heart, 323 : 25
Laces just reveal surge, 604 : 12
Lacessit, nemo me impune l., 134 : 11
Lack, eternal l. of pence, 530 : 16
gall, 221 : 9
good counselors l. no clients, 227 : 25
he that giveth unto the poor shall not l., 25 : 30
if any l. wisdom, 51 : 27
in abundance l., 80 : 1
of many a thing sought, 244 : 11
of money root of evil, 680 : 27
plentiful l. of wit, 220 : 20
shalt not l. any thing, 11 : 14
they l. a sacred poet, 108 : 13
Lacked, being l. and lost, 209 : 31
if I l. anything, 269 : 9
Lackey, card l. to those above, 818 : 5
Lacking, contains all nothing l., 575 : 6
in Nature's inventions nothing l., 152 : 12
little is never l., 101 : 8
lovers l. matter, 212 : 22
neither honor nor lyre, 107 : 13
Lackluster eye, 211 : 5
Lacks, what it l. in length, 749 : 6
Laconic and Olympian, 728 : 18
or sententious type, 730 : 15
Lacrimae, hinc illae l., 96 : *n* 4
rerum, 104 : *n* 13
Lad, blithe Irish l., 443 : 9
born to be king, 688 : 12
come to you my l., 410 : 10
lightfoot l., 691 : 13
of mettle a good boy, 203 : 25
pass me the can l., 691 : 19
up l. when journey's over, 690 : 18
well for sailor l., 530 : 19
when all world young l., 566 : 14
when I was a l., 627 : 14
Ladder always close to schooner, 910 : 7
behold a l., 8 : 19
charity's golden l., 137 : 10
down l. rung by rung, 708 : 15
Jacob's l., 500 : 18, 693 : 19
made death his l., 174 : 14
make a l. of our vices, 129 : 10
of human thought, 690 : 6
of vices frame l., 511 : 22
talk of Jacob's l., 500 : 18
to all high designs, 226 : 1
unto l. turns his back, 215 : 16
young ambition's l., 215 : 16
Ladders, lie down where l. start, 717 : 21
Laddie, your Highland l. gone, 415 : 16
Laden, with rue heart l., 691 : 13
Ladies, Cambridge l., 828 : 14
dust is gentlemen and l., 606 : 7
good fortune to be l., 622 : 21
good night sweet l., 223 : 24
Grecian Urn worth old l., 838 : 13
if l. be but young and fair, 211 : 9
in praise of l. dead, 245 : 12
intellectual, 460 : 11
lion among l., 196 : 24
lords and l. of Byzantium, 715 : 3
novel on tables of l., 488 : 10
of St. James's, 640 : 2
over-offended l., 327 : 17
remember the l., 392 : 7
whose bright eyes, 278 : 5
wild witches noble l., 714 : 4
Ladies', for l. love unfit, 307 : 5
kindling smiles in l. eyes, 486 : 3
pearls in beauteous l. eyes, 190 : 6
Ladies' (*continued*)
rhyme into l. favors, 208 : 18
Ladles, cooks' own l., 541 : 1
Lads, dust was l. and girls, 606 : 7
golden l. and girls, 243 : 27
that die in glory, 691 : 5
though l. far away, 740 : 11
thought no more behind, 246 : 9
Lady be good to me, 835 : 19
Bountiful, 329 : 8
by yonder blessed moon I swear, 192 : 11
colonel's l. an' Judy O'grady, 709 : 11
Disdain, 208 : 27
doth protest too much, 222 : 15
downstairs ran l. O, 920 : 17
enjoyed the L., 404 : 11
faint heart never won fair l., 170 : 10, 629 : 2
fairer l. never seen, 926 : 17
feigning l. by Bazille, 899 : 11
fine l. on horse, 931 : 11
fool called her l. fair, 709 : 14
for secrecy no l. closer, 203 : 24
from Philadelphia, 578 : 8
garmented in light, 468 : 7
he saw a l. bright, 926 : 23
hear l. sing in Welsh, 204 : 18
here comes the l., 193 : 2
here lies beautiful l., 739 : 14
here lies l. of beauty, 810 : 20
History excitable old l., 667 : 6
I asked a lithe l., 404 : 11
if you got to ask, 847 : *n* 2
if you were April's l., 633 : 12
in the case, 331 : 17
Jingly Jones, 551 : 1
Joan as my L., 266 : 9
lent him to a l., 933 : 16
liner she's a l., 709 : 8
longing for that lovely l., 97 : 10
make l. of my own, 424 : 13
many many l. friends, 696 : 3
met l. in meads, 478 : 11
most beautiful l., 739 : 14
my fair l., 929 : 21
my l. sweet arise, 243 : 16
O l. we receive what we give, 435 : 26
of certain age, 461 : 19
of Christ's College, 301 : 5
of my delight, 661 : 11
of Shalott, 528 : 27
old l. from Dubuque, 824 : 2
Old L. of Threadneedle Street, 407 : 12
old l. quoted by Forster, 869 : 9
or the tiger, 618 : 15
Our L. of Guadalupe, 400 : 1
Our L. of Pain, 632 : 12
rather hear L. howl in Irish, 204 : 18
rob l. by marriage, 349 : 23
Seymour's Fat L., 896 : 10
sighed for love of l., 629 : 22
sweet and kind, 918 : 14
talking to hens of Dorking, 551 : 1
that's known as Lou, 752 : 5
that's why l. is tramp, 833 : 18
the brach may stand, 233 : 8
three white leopards, 805 : 22
through whose fragile lips, 829 : 7
weep no more my l., 598 : 5
with Lamp, 512 : 1
you are the cruelest she, 213 : 17
young l. named Bright, 742 : 1

Ladybug fly away home, 930 : 3
Ladylike, birch most l. of trees, 567 : 10
Lady's, brain him with l. fan, 203 : 23
for all l. hire, 933 : 16
get you to l. chamber, 224 : 14
he capers nimbly in l. chamber, 186 : 31
imagination rapid, 440 : 18
in my l. chamber, 931 : 8
in the case, 331 : 17
love learned in l. eyes, 191 : 2
Lady-smocks all silver-white, 191 : 13
Lafayette we are here, 693 : 3
Lag, comfortable time l., 720 : 8
Lag-end of my life, 205 : 1
Lager, give Irishman l., 623 : 12
Laggard in love, 430 : 19
Lags, fiction l. after truth, 372 : 13
superfluous l. veteran, 351 : 21
Laid aside business, 270 : 29
bait l. to make taker mad, 245 : 23
him on the green, 927 : 6
in a manger, 42 : 27
in sad cypress l., 214 : 4
me down with a will, 668 : 20
my heart open to indifference, 882 : 3
on with a trowel, 210 : 14
sun is l. to sleep, 255 : 12
when I am l. in earth, 317 : 3
where wast thou when I l. foundations, 16 : 28
Lain for a century dead, 533 : 25
should I have l. still, 15 : 8
Lair, deep his midnight l. made, 431 : 5
rouse lion from his l., 432 : 11
ruth of l. clings to me, 907 : 22
slugs leave their l., 436 : 9
Laisse un peu de soi-même, 679 : *n* 2
Laissez faire laissez passer, 342 : 20
Laith were gude Scots lords, 926 : 12
Laity, paintings the Bible of l., 137 : 2
Lake, consciousness as bottomless l., 639 : 12
dream life as l. dreams sky, 706 : 5
fire in the l., 5 : 9
goddess of the silver l., 280 : 3
in l. an arm, 149 : 8
Lebarge, 752 : 6
lo the level l., 529 : 1
Pilot of Galilean l., 280 : 19
river l. glimmering pool, 592 : 6
sedge withered from l., 478 : 10
to Rydal L. that lead, 424 : *n* 2
took l. between my legs, 904 : 3
wind over l. image, 5 : 10
Lakes, fish in unruffled l., 868 : 5
genius of placid l., 912 : 3
great l. of North America, 488 : 11
light shakes across l., 530 : 26
Lalah member of ancient profession, 707 : 12
Lama, Eli Eli l. sabachthani, 41 : 27
Lamb at home lion in chase, 423 : 1
blood of the l., 53 : 15
false as fox to l., 226 : 15
go to bed with l., 175 : 17
God will provide himself a l., 8 : 13
he who made L. make thee, 405 : 8
little L. who made thee, 403 : 5
Mary had a little l., 463 : 1
of God, 44 : 23, 54 : 5
pipe song about a L., 403 : 2
quiet as a l., 202 : 4
save one little ewe l., 13 : 19
Lamb (*continued*)
sedulous ape to L., 668 : 23
shall be without blemish, 9 : 23
skin of innocent l. parchment, 185 : 25
tempers wind to shorn l., 163 : 12, 360 : 25
to the slaughter, 31 : 17
was the holy L. of God, 406 : 21
when lion fawns upon l., 186 : 20
will never cease to follow, 186 : 20
wolf shall dwell with the l., 29 : 19
Lambs could not forgive, 548 : 3
gather the l. with his arm, 30 : 35
little hills like l., 21 : 21
poor little l. lost way, 708 : 14
we were as twinned l., 246 : 10
wolves and l. have no concord, 59 : 8
Lame and impotent conclusion, 230 : 12
feet to the l., 16 : 17
little l. balloonman, 828 : 11
live with l. man learn to limp, 120 : 6
man leap as an hart, 30 : 24
wrinkled and slanting-eyed, 58 : 11
Lament, come to dark and l., 749 : 7
do not uselessly l., 702 : 3
for Madame Blaize, 368 : 7
frogs drone their l., 104 : 1
have I not reason to l., 423 : 4
mistakes of good man, 391 : 5
naught other to l., 593 : 4
universal Nature did l., 280 : 14
wild l., 858 : 20
Lamentable, most l. comedy, 196 : 2
that skin of lamb parchment, 185 : 25
Lamentation and praise, 869 : 5
empire's l., 533 : 1
Lamentations, sighs l. and wailings, 140 : 15
Lamenting, last l. kiss, 253 : 14
Lamp, Aladdin's l., 461 : 25, 568 : 20
beside the golden door, 664 : 10
confusing beams from memory's l., 856 : 9
fluttered round l., 614 : 8
God's light like a l., 131 : 16
history with flickering l., 744 : 11
I have but one l., 383 : 2
Lady with L., 512 : 1
of experience, 383 : 2
slaves of the l., 610 : 11
smell of the l., 90 : 12, 730 : 15
stroke beam of my l., 910 : 10
swallowed lighted l., 757 : 6
unlit l. ungirt loin, 543 : 15
unto my feet, 22 : 2
when l. is shattered, 470 : 1
word burned like a l., 36 : 13
writing smelling of l., 730 : 15
Lamps, be l. unto yourselves, 72 : 20
bright l. shone o'er, 457 : 14
expire, 721 : 6
going out over Europe, 699 : 7
golden l. in green light, 297 : 9
heaven's great l. dive, 250 : 3
like hidden l., 376 : 6
lovely l. windows of soul, 167 : 10
not lit in our lifetime, 699 : 7
old l. for new, 919 : 24
poets light but l., 606 : 10
virgins took l., 40 : 28
Lance, never had oar or l., 82 : 2
strong l. of justice, 235 : 3
threw his shining l., 615 : 4
Lancelot mused a space, 528 : 28
Lancelot (*continued*)
sang Sir L., 528 : 26
there thou liest, 149 : 20
through L. war wrought, 149 : 17
Land, after all a poor l., 581 : 3
America my new-found l., 254 : 2
and the pleasant l., 591 : 7
anybody is as their l. is, 752 : 13
appeared at two leagues, 150 : 15
as near by sea as by l., 166 : 13
before ever l. was, 634 : 5
bomb fell it burst it shook l., 777 : 10
bourn bound of l., 247 : 26
bowels of the l., 187 : 23
bringeth thee into a good l., 11 : 13
can be healthy or sick, 875 : 13
can't fly away, 555 : 4
city l. raises taxes, 603 : 14
death's gray l., 795 : 13
Dixie L., 554 : 1
dry and thirsty l., 19 : 29
ethic for tomorrow, 898 : 1
fat of the l., 9 : 1
fenced in piece of l., 358 : 9
flowing with milk and honey, 9 : 13
free l. in beloved home, 578 : 12
go to l. of poetry, 396 : 2
God and native l., 464 : 12
God gave to Cain, 157 : 2
gone into silent l., 608 : 14
good and bad of every l., 555 : 15
grasses in ruined l., 484 : 2
great rock in a weary l., 30 : 21
green and pleasant l., 406 : 21
hail Columbia happy l., 422 : 21
harmony between men and l., 795 : 11
he became a l., 868 : 19
heaven-rescued l., 446 : 2
heroism upon l. and sea, 574 : 6
his hands formed the dry l., 20 : 20
holy l. of Irlonde, 916 : 16
holy l. of Walsinghame, 172 : 8
hour later I saw l., 855 : 9
huge l. will lie revealed, 115 : 13
I will pass through the l., 9 : 25
if by l. one lantern, 382 : 12
ill discoverers think there is no l., 179 : 3
ill fares the l., 369 : 30
imagined l., 767 : 22
in which always afternoon, 528 : 13
Indian l. undefiled, 897 : 19
is bright, 564 : 17
is immortal, 895 : 10
it cometh from a terrible l., 29 : 26
it is promised l., 480 : 16
I've seen promised l., 909 : 17
just the same as on l., 556 : 15
known in any l. or age, 576 : 8
law of the l., 139 : 2
leans against the l., 368 : 20
lie like l. of dreams, 587 : 16
light shines over l. and sea, 745 : 8
lilacs out of dead l., 804 : 26
live deaf to l. beneath us, 819 : 1
long black l., 541 : 13
long l. be bright, 514 : 13
Lord's song in strange l., 22 : 15
loss of native l., 76 : 17
madden round the l., 338 : 6
marching to promised l., 616 : 8
my children leastwise of l., 889 : 7
my l. my father's l., 603 : 1
my native l. good night, 457 : 1

Land (*continued*)
my new-found l., 254 : 2
my own my native l., 430 : 10
never knew piece of l. to run away, 382 : 2
never was on sea or l., 427 : 17
no more l. say fish, 796 : 14
no slave upon our l., 513 : 3
O l. and soil, 831 : 15
o' the leal, 417 : 10
o'er all the pleasant l., 470 : 13
of brown heath, 430 : 11
of Calvin and oatcakes, 432 : 18
of cotton, 554 : 1
of darkness and shadow, 15 : 24
of dead, 839 : 10
of dreams, 587 : 16
of drowsyhead, 345 : 20
of faery, 712 : 10
of Goshen, 9 : 2
of heart's desire, 712 : 11
of hope and glory, 698 : 12
of Just Add Water, 828 : 17
of Lincoln and Pinkham, 828 : 17
of living, 839 : 10
of lost content, 691 : 9
of mountain and flood, 430 : 11
of my dreams, 813 : 7
of nowadays, 729 : 9
of pilgrims' and so forth, 829 : 4
of pilgrims' pride, 514 : 12
of poetry, 396 : 2
of pure delight, 328 : 15
of scholars, 369 : 2
of slaves ne'er mine, 461 : 9
of the Arrow Ide, 828 : 17
of the Cluett Shirt, 828 : 17
of the free, 446 : 1, 815 : 2
of the living, 16 : 13
of unlimited possibilities, 662 : 4
of wheat and barley, 11 : 14
on l. as on the sea, 922 : 11
one if by l., 512 : 7
one thing I know is l., 779 : 3
or cherry isle, 266 : 3
our l. before we her people, 749 : 3
our l. great but no order in it, 136 : 2
ours before we the land's, 749 : 3
owes nothing to l., 359 : 1
Pacific leans on the l., 797 : 12
peace more precious than l., 895 : 16
piece of l. with a garden, 106 : 20
plowed before man, 515 : 11
poet's l., 396 : 2
post o'er l. and ocean, 282 : 17
prepared the dry l., 54 : 17
proclaim liberty throughout l., 10 : 22
Promised L. beyond wilderness, 690 : 8
rats and water rats, 198 : 17
reap the harvest of your l., 10 : 19
rent with civil feuds, 450 : 15
rock in weary l., 30 : 21
salt l. and not inhabited, 32 : 11
scatter plenty o'er smiling l., 362 : 10
search l. of living men, 430 : 15
see l. as community, 795 : 10
seeking l. of Greeks, 395 : 8
seems a moving l., 286 : 30
sees across weary l., 742 : 10
sent to spy out the l., 10 : 24
sing by l. and sea, 708 : 24
six feet of l., 602 : 12
sky and sea and l., 692 : 11

Land (*continued*)
something else than common l., 571 : 8
somewhere in favored l., 704 : 16
spirits of l. and grain, 89 : 28
stone rests on the l., 300 : 19
stranger in a strange l., 9 : 9
stubble l. at harvest home, 203 : 7
supreme law of the l., 391 : 13
sweet l. of liberty, 514 : 12
symbol of her chosen l., 474 : 18
tenure key to Kikuyu life, 818 : 13
that gave you birth, 700 : 6
that I love, 802 : 9
thieves and water thieves, 198 : 17
this l. is your l., 881 : 1
this was charter of l., 345 : 19
thought jump sea and l., 244 : 16
too deep into new l., 432 : 7
turning back without sighting l., 646 : *n* 3
twilight l. no-man's l., 626 : 21
unwillingly I left your l., 105 : 19
various as your l., 840 : 4
verdant l., 570 : 14
violet of native l., 531 : 22
voice of the turtle is heard in our l., 28 : 7
westward look l. bright, 564 : 17
where Bong tree grows, 550 : 8
where cypress and myrtle, 459 : 5
where lemon trees bloom, 395 : 3
where lies the l., 428 : 2, 564 : 13
where my fathers died, 514 : 12
wherein thou shalt eat bread, 11 : 14
which the Lord giveth thee, 10 : 7
woman a foreign l., 593 : 3
wretched he who bound l. to himself, 4 : 1
wrong rules the l., 567 : *n* 1
Landed, Eagle has l., 910 : 13
Landing, fight on l. grounds, 744 : 2
on coast of France, 815 : 12
Landmark, remove not the ancient l., 25 : 3
Landmarks in man's struggle, 841 : 1
set up in Bill of Rights, 836 : 16
Landor, with L. and with Donne, 714 : 2
Land's, land ours before we the l., 749 : 3
sea l. edge also, 808 : 2
Lands and horses part of self, 648 : 17
beyond the sea, 425 : 6
covet no people's l., 824 : 12
envy of less happier l., 194 : 13
faery l. forlorn, 477 : 1
goal of Providence in discovery of l., 154 : 13
God allowed l. to be discovered, 156 : 12
integration of l. and peoples, 912 : 3
longed-for l., 768 : 24
lord of himself not l., 250 : 16
meaning of l. of ancestors, 912 : 5
men in all l., 781 : 8
rulers in all l., 670 : 15
sun in lonely l., 532 : 28
take us l. away, 607 : 4
these l. are ours, 419 : 9
voyager at last, 597 : 15
wait for those who discern their rhythms, 912 : 3
where are Sioux l., 610 : 5

Lands (*continued*)
where Jumblies live, 550 : 11
white men take away l., 418 : 13
Landscape, hands are heart's l., 897 : 8
man shaper of l., 870 : 14
now fades glimmering l., 361 : 21
we are children of our l., 880 : 6
Landscapes drawn in monotones, 794 : 2
of the moon, 734 : 13
Landsmen, we l. build upon, 728 : 11
Lane, boy who lives down l., 930 : 5
in an English l., 542 : 6
lives in Drury L., 933 : 8
long l. knows no turnings, 541 : 4
straight down crooked l., 485 : 10
to land of dead, 868 : 10
Lang, auld l. syne, 410 : 11
Langtry, Mrs. L. and Lady Lonsdale, 914 : *n* 2
Language, American turn of l., 728 : 2
best part of human l., 437 : 21
betrayers of l., 792 : 19
change l. change life, 911 : 2
charged with meaning, 793 : 8
chief merit of l. clearness, 125 : 20
clearness propriety of l., 589 : 6
confound the l. of all earth, 8 : 5
conveyed in best chosen l., 440 : 29
dictionary best book in l., 740 : 18
dies, 703 : 7
dissociate l. from science, 390 : 7
everything in l. perish, 487 : 14
for exchange of information, 904 : 18
force l. into meaning, 809 : 9
gradually varies, 452 : 20
heightened and unlike itself, 657 : 1
high thoughts must have high l., 82 : 20
I love the l., 460 : 8
in her eye, 227 : 3
inherited from Conquistadors, 861 : 1
is archives of history, 498 : 3
learned his great l., 541 : 6
learning me your l., 247 : 18
life is a foreign l., 816 : 10
manners laws customs, 424 : 8
messenger with l. of his folk, 131 : 2
mobilized English l., 742 : *n* 1
money l. nations understand, 312 : 16
music universal l., 509 : 11
mutability of l., 453 : 1
mysterious l. about life, 464 : 7
no l. but a cry, 532 : 10
no l. like Irish, 735 : 6
of Dante common language, 809 : 16
of English poet, 809 : 16
of the heart, 339 : 4
of the living, 808 : 10
of truth language of creation, 735 : 13
often a cheat, 463 : 20
perverters of l., 792 : 19
poetical l., 657 : 1
reduce l. to seven words, 782 : 21
sarcasm l. of devil, 473 : 3
silent l. of peak, 812 : 2
soothing l., 388 : 10
speaks a various l., 471 : 2
that would make hair curl, 629 : 18
things used as l. are attractive, 498 : 16
touched by poetry, 885 : 18
traveleth before he hath l., 180 : 18
universe in l. of mathematics, 182 : 20

Language (*continued*)
universe l. of God, 447 : 17
use any l. you choose, 628 : 26
use in measured l., 531 : 21
vital development in l., 809 : 7
we have l., 884 : 2
we praise thee for perspicuity of l., 136 : 6
Languages, Americans not learn l., 725 : 17
great feast of l., 191 : 7
skilled in works of both l., 108 : 1
Langueur monotone, 659 : *n* 6
Languid patience of thy face, 433 : 18
strings scarcely move, 403 : 1
Languished, smiles and l. air, 402 : 14
Languor, pierce heart with l., 659 : 12
Languors, lilies and l. of virtue, 632 : 11
Lank, bronzed l. man, 765 : 8
long and l. and brown, 434 : 25
poor lean l. face, 520 : 5
Lantern, if by land one l., 382 : 12
Red L. and his undersea folk, 912 : 14
Lanterns, eyes like agate l., 844 : 2
in North Church, 382 : 12
Lanthorn is the moon, 197 : 17
Lap, chestnuts in her l., 236 : 1
dropped in her l., 516 : 12
in l. of the gods, 59 : *n* 3
in thy green l., 362 : 22
me in soft Lydian airs, 278 : 6
of earth, 362 : 17
of legends, 476 : 12
sat Beauty in my l., 674 : 3
see it l. the miles, 605 : 18
Lapel, plucked lint from l., 699 : 14
Lapidary inscriptions, 355 : 18
style, 497 : 31
Lapidem, stilicidi casus l. cavat, 100 : *n* 4
Lapland, lovely as a L. night, 427 : 20
Lapped in lead, 257 : 7
Lapping of water, 874 : 9
water l. of bow, 806 : 8
Lapse, forgotten through l. of Time, 87 : 6
of murmuring streams, 287 : 4
Lapwings, clamorous l., 334 : 16
Larceny, sparkle with l., 757 : 15
Lard their lean books, 258 : 5
Lards lean earth, 203 : 21
Laredo, streets of L., 927 : 14
Large a charter as wind, 211 : 10
and smooth and round, 439 : 11
as life twice as natural, 613 : 17
as store, 268 : 21
cold bottle, 666 : 15
discourse, 223 : 17
divine comfortable words, 534 : 3
I am l. as God, 300 : 18
I am l. contain multitudes, 575 : 2
kingdom for little grave, 195 : 7
limbo l. and broad, 285 : 8
resolute breed of men, 577 : 15
small house and l. garden, 295 : 4
style agrees not with purse, 185 : 8
utterance of gods, 478 : 3
was his bounty, 362 : 18
wealth larger heart, 304 : 14
youth l. lusty loving, 575 : 13
Large-brained woman and large-hearted man, 506 : 13
Larger bill for darker ill, 562 : *n* 2
children of l. growth, 342 : 3
Larger (*continued*)
large wealth l. heart, 304 : 14
Largest and most comprehensive soul, 303 : 5
movements of l. bodies, 397 : 17
those of l. size, 613 : 8
Lark at heaven's gate sings, 243 : 16
busy l. messager of day, 146 : 18
clouds silence then l., 660 : 10
fresh as a l., 428 : 2
hark hark the l., 243 : 16
herald of the morn, 193 : 14
no l. more blithe than he, 382 : 6
now leaves his watery nest, 275 : 30
rise with l., 175 : 17
that soars singing, 142 : 17
when a l. I sang, 874 : 4
Lark's on the wing, 540 : 15
Larks, four l. and wren, 550 : 4
have l. when sky falleth, 159 : 11
mounting l. notes prepare, 334 : 16
Lars Porsena of Clusium, 488 : 13
Lasciva est nobis pagina vita proba, 118 : *n* 15
Lascivious pleasing of a lute, 186 : 31
Lash, blood drawn with l., 524 : 7
I could bear the l., 482 : 17
magic creature, 607 : 7
that beat down Rome, 717 : 4
the l. goes on, 717 : 12
the rascals naked, 232 : 6
Lashed, headstrong liberty l. with woe, 188 : 1
vice but spared name, 322 : 19
Lashes beggar on foot, 717 : 12
Lass, drink to the l., 399 : 1
every l. a queen, 566 : 14
I love a l., 394 : 6
lover and his l., 212 : 33
on Richmond Hill, 399 : 20
penniless l., 417 : 9
unparalleled, 242 : 5
Lasse, tout l., 928 : 3
Lasses a' lilting, 368 : 2
sweetest hours among l. O, 409 : 16
Lassie, I love a l., 731 : 2
Last, a l. a loved a long, 778 : 6
act crowns play, 267 : 18
after l. returns first, 544 : 29
and best of God's works, 287 : 22
arms take your l. embrace, 193 : 28
best hope of earth, 522 : 12
came and last did go, 280 : 19
cobbler stick to your l., 90 : *n* 6
comes at the l., 195 : 3
commonly best, 258 : 6
communion in the haze, 604 : 10
daintiest l. to make end sweet, 193 : 35
death comes at l., 430 : 16
dike of prevarication, 373 : 17
don't be frightened it won't l., 705 : 9
enchantments of Middle Age, 587 : 1
every day passed as if our l., 111 : 29
eyes look your l., 193 : 28
fight till l. gasp, 184 : 16
first and the l., 53 : 33
first l. everlasting day, 252 : 22
first one now later l., 915 : 5
first shall be l., 40 : 8
for more than one century, 101 : 14
framed her l. best work, 410 : 16
free at l., 935 : 22
full measure of devotion, 523 : 4
Last (*continued*)
gasp, 36 : 17, 184 : 16
God's l. Put out the light, 748 : 11
great Englishman low, 533 : 2
have the l. word, 396 : 17
He is the first and the l., 132 : 13
him first him l., 286 : 16
horizon, 852 : 15
Hurrah, 895 : 9
joy our l. not least, 232 : 23
Krapp's l. tape, 866 : 15
laughs best who laughs l., 321 : 6
leaf upon tree, 519 : 19
let every man consider l. day, 74 : 7
looking toward l. things, 650 : 8
love thyself l., 249 : 8
my l. end be like his, 11 : 3
nice guys finish l., 867 : 1
night ah yesternight, 721 : 4
night as I lay on prairie, 927 : 13
no l. or first, 540 : 19
nostalgia, 768 : 4
not judge above his l., 90 : 16
not least in love, 216 : 10
of all the Romans, 217 : 12
of life for which first made, 544 : 8
of red-hot mamas, 788 : *n* 3
on his l. legs, 261 : 14
out night in Russia, 228 : 3
pay for it first or l., 555 : 3
peace at the l., 490 : 10
perform every act as though it were your l., 124 : 6
poor l. I lay upon thy lips, 241 : 21
pure stretch of joy, 875 : 2
rose of summer, 446 : 14
scene of all, 211 : 15
sex to the l., 307 : 7
shall be first, 40 : 8
sleeping at l., 608 : 20
small showers l. long, 194 : 12
syllable of recorded time, 240 : 4
taste of sweets, 194 : 10
think every day your l., 109 : 3
this is the l. of earth, 418 : 11
though l. not least, 174 : 15
till you write your letter, 252 : 3
time I saw Paris, 833 : 9
to lay old aside, 333 : 6
trump, 49 : 7
try fortunes to l. man, 206 : 27
was like the first, 823 : 5
what is it will l., 528 : 17
will not l. the night, 822 : 17
words of Marmion, 431 : 3
world's l. night, 254 : 14
Lasting, just and l. peace, 524 : 7
monument more l. than bronze, 108 : 8
sense of filial duty, 387 : 7
tell if poem l., 749 : 20
Lasts, diamond l. forever, 826 : 5
nothing l. save eternal change, 265 : 3
Latch, crosspatch draw l., 930 : 16
Latched, when present l. postern, 642 : 3
Latchet of whose shoes, 41 : 32
Late and early pray, 250 : 15
and soon, 427 : 29
better l. than never, 110 : 12
born too l., 728 : 20
coffee and oranges, 767 : 2
coming l. try to remember, 907 : 5
falls early or too l., 260 : 17

Late (*continued*)
finds too l. men betray, 369 : 20
getting up l., 463 : 12
good die early bad l., 318 : 12
known too l., 191 : 27
long choosing and beginning l., 287 : 12
love that comes too l., 227 : 22
Miniver born too l., 728 : 20
minute too l., 225 : 18
never too l. to give up prejudices, 559 : 6
not too l. to seek world, 529 : 13
nothing is too l., 512 : 16
riseth l. trot all day, 347 : 22
so l. into the night, 460 : 5
sorrow never comes too l., 361 : 12
toiled so hard and l., 715 : 9
too l. I loved you, 129 : 5
too l. in world too old, 537 : 7
too l. to say anything not said, 315 : 4
too little too l., 816 : 16
Lated, spurs l. traveler apace, 238 : 22
Latent, hard l. value, 653 : 13
Later times more aged than earlier, 178 : *n* 12
to all to each sooner l., 576 : 4
Latest, earliest l. care, 357 : 8
Latet anguis in herba, 103 : *n* 8
Latimer, see L. and Ridley in might of faith, 156 : *n* 5
Latin, all their botany L., 494 : 12
come in L. or in Greek, 276 : 9
he Greek and L. speaks, 290 : *n* 3
imagery of Greek and L., 357 : 19
learn L. as honor, 743 : 8
mouse prevails in L., 365 : 12
small L. and less Greek, 256 : 13
soft bastard L., 460 : 8
speak no word but L., 146 : 14
was no more difficile, 290 : 15
word for three farthings, 190 : 24
Latin-American, not only L. nation, 905 : 19
Latitude, longitude and l. for seine, 623 : 5
send them l. and longitude, 777 : 13
Latter and former rain, 33 : 10
blessed the l. end of Job, 17 : 11
carry off the l., 455 : 2
early and l. rain, 52 : 4
end of a fray, 204 : 36
shall stand at the l. day, 16 : 4
Lattice, cried through the l., 12 : 8
Laud and magnify thy Name, 55 : 18
more l. than gilt o'erdusted, 226 : 21
Laudable things, 281 : 14
Laudamus, te deum l., 54 : 19
Laudator temporis acti, 109 : *n* 14
Laugh and be well, 344 : 14
and grow fat, 210 : *n* 1
and shake, 340 : 14
and world laughs, 670 : 3
anything awful makes me l., 441 : 13
at a play to l. or cry, 322 : 16
at any but fools or foes, 339 : 13
at any mortal thing, 461 : 10
at gilded butterflies, 235 : 12
at them in our turn, 440 : 23
at your friends, 339 : 13
audience never fail to l., 82 : 17
before we are happy, 315 : 7
but smile no more, 526 : 2
dry eyes l. at fall, 542 : 12
Laugh (*continued*)
explode huge l. at feet, 701 : 7
fools l. at men of sense, 315 : 8
for fear of having to cry, 378 : 6
for hope hath place, 562 : 9
if you tickle us do we not l., 199 : 18
in bed l. in bed cry, 290 : 8
lowest type l. heartily, 64 : 14
made a cat l., 480 : 15
make her l. at that, 224 : 14
men that l. and weep, 633 : 20
my bitter l., 518 : 11
myself to death, 248 : 1
never granted before fortieth day, 116 : 8
not l. other men to scorn, 132 : 8
not thing to l. to scorn, 212 : 27
nothing more silly than silly l., 102 : 1
sans intermission, 211 : 7
seas l. when rocks near, 262 : 5
siege to scorn, 240 : 2
that spoke vacant mind, 370 : 4
they l. that win, 231 : 22
thy girlish laughter, 688 : 4
time to l., 26 : 21
to l. proper to man, 157 : 8
to scorn power of man, 239 : 10
too badly hurt to l., 522 : 9
unextinguishable l. in heaven, 275 : 12
watch and l., 617 : 9
we must l. and sing, 716 : 3
when you want a good l., 109 : 3
where we must, 336 : 11
who but must l., 338 : 15
yet all these seem to l., 252 : 25
you may l. the more, 339 : 13
yourselves into stitches, 214 : 20
Laughed consumedly, 329 : 9
day on which not l., 386 : 4
His word to scorn, 376 : 9
in the sun, 796 : 9
like irresponsible foetus, 804 : 9
little dog l., 930 : 17
no man who l. bad, 472 : 20
upright man l. to scorn, 15 : 28
warn't often that we l., 623 : 22
with counterfeited glee, 370 : 10
Laughing Allegra, 512 : 5
at yourselves, 518 : 6
bee on stalk, 908 : 8
fellow rover, 760 : 16
flesh of girls, 899 : 16
he l. said to me, 403 : 2
heard on the hill, 403 : 15
in your sleeve, 398 : 9
leave them l., 759 : 4
quaffing unthinking time, 306 : 27
sets a wise man to l., 60 : 18
shallow dreaming pool, 566 : 13
somewhere men are l., 704 : 16
split sides with l., 169 : 24
sports and plays, 402 : 13
sweetly speaking and softly l., 63 : 5
up her sleeve, 297 : 18
Water, 511 : 17
Laughingstock, make myself l., 170 : 5
Laughs at archer, 580 : 17
at broken hammers, 761 : 17
best who laughs last, 321 : 6
fair l. morn, 363 : 6
joke loses everything when joker l., 412 : 7
Jove l. at lovers' perjuries, 192 : 8
Laughs (*continued*)
Jupiter l. at perjuries of lovers, 113 : 1
laugh and world l., 670 : 3
Laughter, a little time for l., 614 : *n* 3
and ability and sighing, 606 : 7
arose among gods, 57 : 14
beginning of prayer, 823 : 19
better last smile than first l., 321 : *n* 3
edges of l. and anguish, 782 : 4
enjoy l. at right moment, 92 : 18
excessive l., 35 : 33
feast is made for l., 27 : 18
for a month, 203 : 20
gift of l. and sense world mad, 756 : 15
heart is sorrowful even in l., 24 : 1
hidden l., 807 : 8
holding both his sides, 277 : 20
I'll use you for my l., 217 : 1
ill-bred as audible l., 370 : *n* 1
laugh thy girlish l., 688 : 4
love and l., 614 : 17
myriad l. of ocean waves, 70 : 23
no one died of l., 736 : 8
no time for mirth and l., 718 : 12
of children in foliage, 807 : 8
of Gargantua the l., 843 : 17
of her heart, 833 : 9
of the fool, 27 : 5
out of dead bellies, 792 : 15
present l., 213 : 23
running l., 693 : 10
sudden glory maketh l., 264 : 15
take hand part with l., 633 : 15
tinkled among teacups, 804 : 8
tired of tears and l., 633 : 20
under running l., 693 : 10
weeping and the l., 721 : 7
when her lovely l. shows, 250 : 6
wine women mirth l., 460 : 23
with pain fraught, 468 : 14
Launch, joyous we l. out, 576 : 15
Launched, face that l. a thousand ships, 184 : 4
Laundry, dreamed dream called l., 906 : 3
nothing but l., 899 : 13
Laura, grave where L. lay, 172 : 16
if L. Petrarch's wife, 460 : 25
Laurea, concedat l. laudi, 98 : *n* 18
Laurel and myrtle and rose, 395 : 3
burned is Apollo's l. bough, 184 : 11
crown yield to praise, 98 : 27
crowned with l., 823 : 12
for perfect prime, 608 : 18
green for a season, 633 : 6
no l. crown for outrunning burro, 119 : 16
outlives not May, 633 : 6
poison from Caesar's l. crown, 406 : 16
Laurels all are cut, 591 : 6
in chains or in l., 538 : 16
northern l. not change, 378 : 2
worth all your l., 462 : 6
yet once more O ye l., 280 : 6
Lavender in the windows, 271 : 3
Lavender's blue dilly dilly lavender's green, 933 : 13
Laver son linge sale, 420 : *n* 5
Lavish, liar always l. of oaths, 275 : 25
no calamity greater than l. desires, 64 : 16

Lavvy minx or sphinx, 549 : 34
Law admit of no rival, 447 : 18
agin wearin' o' Green, 920 : 21
all things by l. divine, 467 : 24
all's love yet all's l., 543 : 18
and order pay, 644 : 18
and the prophets, 38 : 14, 40 : 16
applications of l., 700 : 2
army of unalterable l., 600 : 28, 804 : 7
ass idiot, 547 : 6
bloody book of l., 229 : 23
blot on escutcheon of Common L., 638 : 8
book of the l., 14 : 30
born under one l. to another bound, 175 : 5
by transgressing kept l., 282 : 7
can only bring freedom, 397 : 1
common l. not omnipresence, 644 : 21
common l. nothing but reason, 171 : 21
common l. of England, 815 : 17
Congress shall make no l., 391 : 14
consistent with liberty, 366 : 2
craving to go to l., 630 : 20
curses in Book of L., 308 : *n* 2
defense is in l. and order, 764 : 4
delight is in l. of the Lord, 17 : 12
despair l. chance hath slain, 254 : 9
do as adversaries in l., 188 : 29
due process of l., 391 : 17, 392 : 4
dusty purlieus of l., 532 : 18
embodies nation's development, 643 : 15
embody the l., 628 : 16
ends tyranny begins, 307 : 17
equal before l., 615 : 1
eternal l., 72 : 16
evolution not cause but l., 637 : 1
extreme l. often extreme injustice, 96 : 12
eye of the l., 615 : 1
faith nor love nor l., 467 : 4
first is l. the last prerogative, 305 : 18
first l. for historian, 98 : 10
for man law for thing, 494 : 8
for rulers and people, 553 : 20
fugitive from l. of averages, 898 : 8
future lays l. of today, 657 : 7
gave l. air of science, 365 : *n* 5
good l. is good order, 88 : 13
good l. would have stood fast, 73 : 5
great cases make bad l., 644 : 9
great l. of culture, 472 : 4
greatest not exempted from l., 175 : 7
has honored us, 451 : 12
hath not been dead, 228 : 8
hatred made l., 864 : 5
having not the l., 46 : 38
head and hoof of l., 709 : 6
higher l., 533 : 7
hint of universal l., 644 : 4
hocus-pocus science, 344 : 20
I my Lords embody l., 628 : 16
ignorance of the l., 263 : 17
in calmness made, 427 : 25
in his l. doth he meditate, 17 : 12
in l. and love same, 556 : 1
in l. as in magic mirror, 643 : 18
in l. what plea so tainted, 199 : 24
in majestic equality, 655 : 14
is a ass a idiot, 547 : 6
is good, 50 : 23

Law (*continued*)
is order, 88 : 13
jealous mistress, 447 : 18
justice the l. my ducats, 199 : 11
lapped in universal l., 530 : 2
last result of wisdom, 353 : 14
lesser breeds without l., 709 : 19
life of l. is experience, 643 : 14
locks up man and woman, 918 : 13
love is fulfilling of l., 47 : 28
love l. to itself, 130 : 4
loving giver of l., 566 : 18
master after my disappearance, 73 : 1
mastered l. in thoughts, 496 : 9
mighty mightier necessity, 396 : 20
mob l., 519 : 23
moral l. within me, 366 : 12
mostly violate l. and custom, 701 : 12
murder by the l., 330 : 1
mysterious l. true source, 286 : 5
natural l. old nonsense, 453 : 14
Nature's kindly l., 337 : 7
nature's l. man made to mourn, 408 : 15
necessity has no l., 129 : 9, 272 : 20
necessity knows no l. except prevail, 111 : 20
never strong without people, 635 : 24
nice sharp quillets of l., 184 : 20
no l. more binding than custom, 688 : 13
no l. of history, 572 : 21
no man above or below l., 687 : 9
no such thing as natural l., 453 : 14
nor l. bade me fight, 714 : 1
not bend to uncertain wishes, 380 : 12
not come to destroy l., 37 : 6
not concerned with trifles, 133 : 18
not l. so much as right, 557 : 22
not make scarecrow of l., 227 : 30
not one jot pass from l., 37 : 7
nothing l. that is not reason, 172 : *n* 1
obedience to l. demanded, 687 : 9
of accumulation free, 621 : 10
of competition, 621 : 6
of God law of good, 583 : 5
of humanity, 373 : 18
of love and law of hate, 671 : 17
of nature and nations, 373 : 18
of our Creator, 373 : 18
of the jungle, 709 : 4
of the land, 139 : 2
of the Medes and Persians, 33 : 2
of the Yukon, 752 : 4
old father antic the l., 202 : 28
old l. sad but not bitter, 758 : 2
one God l. element, 532 : 27
one l. and one truth, 125 : 9
one l. for all, 373 : 18
one with l. majority, 736 : 14
orderly change of l., 644 : 16
ordinance of reason for common good, 140 : 1
others will plead at l., 105 : 24
ought to weed it out, 180 : 3
our reason is our l., 287 : 18
people fight for their l., 70 : 9
people's good the highest l., 99 : 3
people's safety the highest l., 134 : 25
perfection of reason, 171 : 21
poetry not matured by l., 479 : 14
possession eleven points in l., 324 : 25
power politics l. of jungle, 818 : 6

Law (*continued*)
precedents constitute l., 390 : 10
primary l. of every work of art, 590 : 13
principles of l., 700 : 2
professor of Harvard L. School, 777 : 3
protection by l., 419 : 3
public opinion in advance of l., 723 : 4
reason the life of the l., 171 : 21
remoter aspects of l., 644 : 4
rich men rule the l., 369 : 4
rule nations under l., 105 : 24
same l. shapes earth-star and snow-star, 557 : 16
say what l. is, 402 : 3
seat of l. in God, 175 : 7
seven hours to l., 172 : *n* 3
so general a study, 372 : 20
sociability l. of nature, 651 : 7
stable but not stand still, 731 : 10
stands mute in midst of arms, 98 : 5
supreme l. of the land, 391 : 13
sword of war or of l., 389 : 13
tested by higher l., 813 : 10
this is l. I maintain, 920 : 6
to windward of l., 375 : 11
tongue is the l. of kindness, 26 : 9
took to the l., 611 : 10
translating into living l., 794 : 15
true embodiment, 628 : 16
universal l., 366 : 14
unto themselves, 46 : 38
voice of l. harmony, 175 : 7
what I mean by the l., 644 : 2
what others do from fear of l., 87 : 2
where no l. no transgression, 46 : 40
which governs all law, 373 : 18
who to himself is l., 178 : 4
windy side of the l., 209 : *n* 2
world governed by universal l., 566 : 18
write in books of l., 872 : 9
Law-abiding, lawgivers and l., 851 : 16
Lawd, gangway for de L., 814 : 15
Lawful, all things l. for me, 48 : 17
ambitions, 684 : 5
everything is l., 582 : 8
guns aren't l., 827 : 12
is it not l., 40 : 10
without some l. recreation, 169 : 36
Lawfully, if a man use it l., 50 : 23
Lawgiver, stern L., 427 : 15
Lawgivers and law-abiding, 851 : 16
Lawlands, ye Highlands and L., 927 : 6
Lawless attack upon liberty, 365 : 3
discountenance haughty and l., 380 : 6
linsey-woolsey brother, 291 : 15
winged unconfined, 404 : 14
Lawlessness, rush of our l., 582 : 12
world l., 780 : 4
Lawn, rivulets through l., 531 : 13
white as driven snow, 246 : 29
Lawns, like satyrs grazing on the l., 183 : 16
Law's delay, 221 : 12
in l. grave study six, 172 : 6
to take care o' raskills, 565 : 13
Laws, abhor makers and their l. approve, 305 : 26
abounds with l. teems with crimes, 920 : 15
acting around us, 515 : 1

Laws (*continued*)
after desuetude, 631 : 8
and arms foundations of states, 153 : 20
and constitution of country, 391 : 4
and regulations like spider's web, 267 : 3
are like cobwebs, 321 : 15
are sand customs rock, 626 : 6
bad l. bring about worse, 358 : 17
bad or obnoxious l., 589 : 21
base l. of servitude, 303 : 8
best l. teach to trample bad l., 538 : 12
breathing household l., 425 : 15
conflict courts decide, 402 : 3
consequences represent mul- titude of experimental l., 696 : 12
Constitution and l. of U.S., 391 : 13
devise l. for blood, 198 : 10
doing what l. permit, 341 : 8
education in l. of Nature, 595 : 14
end tyranny begins, 351 : 1
equal protection of the l., 392 : 4
flung at head, 819 : 2
for themselves not me, 691 : 22
forms all produced by l., 515 : 1
found state and give it l., 154 : 7
give little Senate l., 338 : 14
God of universal l., 650 : 6
good l. lead to better, 358 : 17
governing use of land, 875 : 13
government free where l. rule, 314 : 10
government of l. not men, 381 : 1
grind the poor, 369 : 4
holier l., 566 : 11
human mind put in nature, 776 : 6
in which we have no voice, 392 : 7
inability to enforce l., 871 : 13
judges of facts not l., 330 : 20
know not whether l. right, 676 : 12
language manners l. customs, 424 : 8
like spiders' webs, 63 : 2
love knoweth no l., 159 : *n* 9
nation territory people l., 522 : 10
Nature and Nature's l. hid, 340 : 6
necessary to preserve order, 763 : 2
not assume physical l. exist, 686 : 9
not care who make l., 317 : 17
not good l. where not armed, 153 : 20
not violate l. of justice, 366 : 8
obedient to their l. we lie, 67 : 19
obey l. respect flag, 725 : 20
of distribution, 621 : 10
of God are forever, 74 : 16
of God laws of man, 691 : 22
of nature and nature's God, 387 : 9
of the jungle, 709 : 6
one by one forging l., 819 : 2
or kings cause or cure, 352 : 21
ought not to remain unaltered, 88 : 2
people make bad l. then suffer, 635 : 24
physical l. and l. of numbers, 610 : 1
physical l. invalid, 762 : 3
power of making l., 401 : 15
right from which l. derive authority, 390 : 14
rules of game l. of nature, 595 : 12
secure equal justice, 80 : 17
self-made l., 581 : 14
sweeps a room as for thy l., 269 : 8
the more l. are made prominent, 64 : 20

Laws (*continued*)
three l. of righteousness, 70 : 22
to execute l. royal office, 374 : 3
true friendship's l., 334 : 23
two l. discrete, 494 : 8
unequal l. to savage race, 529 : 6
useless l. weaken necessary l., 341 : 9
which ran like drinking songs, 81 : 11
Lawsuit machine you go into, 647 : 14
mania, 630 : 20
Lawsuits, win l. and are happy, 81 : 12
Lawyer, deceive not thy l., 269 : 15
draw up the papers l., 660 : 2
has peasant inside, 706 : 9
nor for every quarrel to l., 269 : 28
not what l. tells me, 373 : 1
peasant has l. inside, 706 : 9
prairie l. master of all, 765 : 8
skull of a l., 224 : 10
without history a mechanic, 431 : 21
Lawyers, behave as l. by being l., 645 : 6
charge prepared l. met, 332 : 7
let's kill all the l., 185 : 24
no l. among them, 155 : 4
one hundred and fifty l. do business, 389 : 17
Lay aside long-cherished love, 102 : 15
Cleric before and L. behind, 291 : 15
Doric l., 281 : 5
down in her loveliness, 433 : 31
down life for friends, 45 : 25
down reins of power, 524 : 3
dying in Algiers, 514 : 10
earthly fancies down, 533 : 6
enough to l. up, 331 : 2
field to field, 29 : 4
heart out for my board, 892 : 16
her in the earth, 224 : 17
heroic l. tuneless, 461 : 5
his weary bones among ye, 249 : 10
hold on eternal life, 51 : 3
it on thick, 620 : 12
like folds of bright girdle, 587 : 16
like warrior taking rest, 465 : 8
me down, 915 : 15
me down in peace, 17 : 16
me down to bleed, 926 : *n* 7
me down to sleep, 320 : 12
me on anvil O God, 761 : 10
nature's l. idiot, 253 : 17
no wagers, 370 : *n* 3
not flattering unction, 223 : 7
not up treasures, 37 : 16
on Macduff, 240 : 11
Pelion on Ossa, 60 : *n* 3
proud usurpers low, 411 : 16
simple heartfelt l., 510 : 19
sleeping head my love, 868 : 16
them down in their dens, 21 : 11
till next day there she l., 415 : 6
unpremeditated l., 430 : 1
up treasures in heaven, 37 : 16
upon thy lips, 241 : 21
waste our powers, 427 : 29
Layden, Stuhldreher Miller Crowley L., 773 : 6
Layer upon layer city, 834 : 4
Layers, live in l. not on litter, 864 : 14
Layer-up, ill l. of beauty, 208 : 19
Layeth beams of his chambers, 21 : 8
Lays, constructing tribal l., 708 : 21
eggs for gentlemen, 932 : 14
Laziness, evasion not l., 837 : 20

Laziness (*continued*)
impatience and l., 786 : 6
no l. no procrastination, 593 : *n* 1
Lazy dog, 923 : 2
fokes' stummucks, 662 : 11
geese like snow cloud, 810 : 19
leaden-stepping Hours, 281 : 7
look for something to do, 361 : 4
nonprogressive people, 818 : 12
Scheldt or wandering Po, 368 : 13
Lea, slowly o'er the l., 361 : 20
standing on pleasant l., 428 : 1
sun has left the l., 432 : 9
Lead apes in hell, 188 : 30
bullets made of l., 933 : 12
but not master them, 64 : 4
but to grave, 362 : 3
easy to l., 445 : 1
from death to immortality, 56 : 20
from linotype as from Firearm, 865 : 2
heart of l., 340 : 20
I expect you to l. me, 593 : 17
in traces l. 'em, 568 : 1
kindly Light, 490 : 6
lapped in l., 257 : 7
leader has to l., 788 : 19
little child shall l. them, 29 : 19
me from darkness to light, 56 : 20
me from unreal to real, 56 : 20
me to rock higher than I, 19 : 26
me Zeus and Fate, 92 : 2
my steps aright, 471 : 7
not take l. in all things, 58 : 17
road rail pig l., 760 : 20
sea of l. sky of slate, 711 : 11
sky like l., 868 : 21
tears scald like molten l., 235 : 8
thee to thy grave, 427 : 20
there shall thy hand l. me, 22 : 17
these graces to grave, 213 : 17
those that are with young, 30 : 35
to something else than common land, 571 : 8
us not into temptation, 37 : 15
wild-goose chase, 169 : 3
ye who l. take heed, 728 : 14
Leaden army conquers world, 706 : 23
death, 334 : 16
scepter, 330 : 5
Leaden-eyed despairs, 476 : 24
Leaden-stepping, lazy l. Hours, 281 : 7
Leader and commander to people, 31 : 19
because of not daring to be ahead, 65 : 3
educator wielder of power, 879 : 4
has to lead, 788 : 19
leaves conviction in others, 813 : 12
philosophy you l. of life, 98 : 24
test of l., 813 : 12
that people may require l., 85 : 7
to be l. turn one's back, 689 : 17
who understood terror, 894 : 15
Leaders, ambition of military l., 771 : 2
ambitiously contending, 398 : 2
blind l. of the blind, 39 : 31
lie down till l. have spoken, 709 : 5
Leadership and learning, 892 : 1
new generation of l., 890 : 4
Leadest thou that heifer, 477 : 9
Leadeth me beside still waters, 18 : 7
me in paths of righteousness, 18 : 7

Leads, astronomy l. from this world, 84 : 18
clanging rookery, 529 : 18
heaven that l. men to hell, 245 : 23
highroad l. to England, 354 : 10
on to fortune, 217 : 5
spirit of man who l., 791 : 15
you to believe a lie, 407 : 10
Leaf, abiding l., 875 : 4
are you the l. blossom, 715 : 17
cut a cabbage l., 364 : 5
evening's gold l., 906 : 2
fade as a l., 31 : 27
falling of a l., 571 : 10
falls with l. in October, 260 : 14
flower falling or l., 812 : 3
his l. shall not wither, 17 : 12
I were like the l., 633 : 11
in drawer of sublet room, 910 : 4
in her mouth was an olive l., 7 : 32
last l. upon tree, 519 : 19
let fall no burning l., 822 : 14
lift me as wave l. cloud, 467 : 20
lives on a l., 873 : 11
my days in yellow l., 462 : 18
never tear linnet from l., 714 : 19
November's l., 430 : 13
of grass no less than stars, 574 : 23
olive l. pacific sign, 288 : 2
one red l., 433 : 30
round elm tree bole in tiny l., 541 : 16
sere yellow l., 239 : 31
shall be green, 32 : 11
stone l. unfound door, 852 : 6
turn over a new l., 170 : 15
Leaf-fringed legend, 477 : 4
Leaflet be in you already, 910 : 4
Leaflets advocating euthanasia, 906 : 8
Leafy month of June, 435 : 1
roll up l. Olympus, 103 : 29
streams where cherries, 899 : 16
League, half a l. onward, 533 : 9
in l. with future, 599 : 17
in l. with the stones, 15 : 17
Leagues beyond those leagues, 601 : 19
land appeared at two l., 150 : 15
ten l. beyond world's end, 918 : 12
thousand l. a thousand years, 348 : 10
Leaks, gas l. twenty parts, 699 : 16
Leal, land o' the l., 417 : 10
Lean above me broken-hearted, 787 : 5
and foolish knight, 742 : 10
and hungry look, 215 : 8
and low ability, 214 : 25
and sallow abstinence, 279 : 30
and slippered pantaloon, 211 : 15
as compass needle, 893 : 12
body and visage, 276 : 15
dull privations and l. emptiness, 253 : 1
four l. hounds, 828 : 10
grew l. assailed seasons, 728 : 19
horse l. as is a rake, 145 : 26
I'm l. dog keen dog, 819 : 8
in joy upon father's knee, 403 : 8
lard their l. books, 258 : 5
lards the l. earth, 203 : 21
mother not to l. on, 764 : 6
mournful l. Despair, 402 : 14
on garden urn, 804 : 10
on me, 916 : 9
over too far backward, 831 : 9
people who l., 670 : 1
Pharaoh's l. kine loved, 204 : 6

Lean (*continued*)
poor l. lank face, 520 : 5
rent and beggared, 199 : 6
strong l. upon death, 797 : 17
take fat with l., 549 : 9
unwashed artificer, 202 : 10
we all need someone we can l. on, 916 : 9
wife eat no l., 929 : 16
Lean-faced, Pinch a hungry l. villain, 188 : 15
Leaning across bosom of west, 654 : 15
against the sun, 604 : 15
mother make l. unnecessary, 764 : 6
on reedy shore, 918 : 17
stuffed men l. together, 805 : 15
Leanness, style agrees not with l. of purse, 185 : 8
Leans against the land, 368 : 20
elephant l. or stands, 268 : 20
her cheek upon her hand, 192 : 4
Longing l. and beckons, 569 : 4
Pacific l. on the land, 797 : 12
upon his hoe and gazes, 670 : 14
Leant, on lover's arm l., 530 : 11
Lean-witted, lunatic l. fool, 194 : 16
Leap, giant l. for mankind, 910 : 14
I'll l. up to my God, 184 : 8
in order to stations l., 305 : 9
in the dark, 264 : 21
into thy saddle once more, 569 : 20
lame man l. as an hart, 30 : 24
look before you l., 291 : 23
look ere ye l., 158 : 21
nature does not make l., 652 : *n* 1
nevermore to l. again, 740 : 6
of whale up Niagara, 348 : 4
to pluck bright honor, 203 : 15
to tentative conclusion, 887 : 15
Leaped, in Endymion I l., 479 : 14
into dangerous world I l., 405 : 12
out to wed with thought, 532 : 2
Leaping, brooks too broad for l., 691 : 14
frog l. in, 314 : 7
signs of l. houses, 202 : 23
Leaps, cataract l. in glory, 530 : 26
my heart l. up, 425 : 7
nature not proceed by l., 350 : 6
ship clear she l., 576 : 20
Lear, Hamlet rambles L. rages, 717 : 6
passage in L. haunted me, 478 : *n* 3
pleasant to know Mr. L., 550 : 5
there Hamlet there L., 717 : 5
till I am Timon and L., 717 : 10
Learn about one thing from another, 126 : 18
and propagate best, 586 : 24
as thread plays out, 863 : 19
at no other, 374 : 8
by doing, 87 : 16
by going, 873 : 21
compare collect facts, 665 : 6
craft so long to l., 144 : 8
fools l. in no other, 347 : 23
from having died, 749 : 18
from our enemies, 113 : 20
from those who teach, 74 : 22
gladly he l. and gladly teche, 145 : 28
had to grow old to l., 400 : 11
heart is slow to l., 823 : 7
him or kill him, 623 : 11
how to forget, 267 : 8
how to learn, 898 : 13
in suffering teach in song, 467 : 15

Learn (*continued*)
Irish poets l. trade, 717 : 22
know enough know how to l., 635 : 10
live and l., 321 : 9
man l. nothing without being taught, 116 : 9
neither shall they l. war, 28 : 31
never had time to l., 844 : 16
nor account pang, 544 : 10
not yet so old but she may l., 199 : 29
O voyager to walk, 822 : 5
of nautilus to sail, 337 : 8
of the green world, 793 : 4
read mark l., 56 : 3
sooner than a song, 339 : 26
they l. to be idle, 50 : 32
to bear beams of love, 403 : 7
to behave by being, 645 : 6
to do well, 28 : 30
to hold your own, 681 : 3
to labor and wait, 509 : 16
to read slow, 300 : 16
to teach is to l. twice, 400 : 13
way they eat drink l. and everything, 752 : 13
we were crack-pated, 715 : 8
what life had to teach, 559 : 25
when will they ever l., 896 : 11
wise l. from enemies, 82 : 7
Learned about women from 'er, 709 : 10
all l. all drunk, 377 : 9
although men say he has not l., 68 : 4
and conned by rote, 217 : 4
angling never fully l., 270 : 30
fair and l. and good as she, 265 : 15
fool more foolish, 298 : 15
forgotten everything l., 925 : 5
grew within this l. man, 184 : 11
his great language, 541 : 6
in courtesy have her l., 714 : 17
Jonson's l. sock, 278 : 6
judge should have l. to know evil, 84 : 9
know best things not l., 361 : 5
libraries of the l., 365 : 10
loads of l. lumber, 333 : 19
love first l. in lady's eyes, 191 : 2
love trade you have l., 124 : 21
make the l. smile, 333 : 5
more l. from Dante, 809 : 16
much l. dust, 376 : 26
nothing forgotten nothing, 400 : 16
on earth practice in heaven, 542 : 5
rather able than l., 164 : 13
root of Homer, 257 : *n* 5
thoughts of many men, 59 : 13
to look on nature, 423 : 13
to melt at others' woe, 361 : 14
upright judge l. judge, 200 : 17
we should have l. women, 392 : 11
without sense, 375 : 7
writer shows he is l., 685 : 15
Learning, a' the l. I desire, 409 : 1
abandon l. and no sorrow, 64 : 9
Alcuin my name l. I loved, 135 : 8
angel's wit and singular l., 155 : 11
blundering people live on, 761 : 15
but an adjunct to ourself, 191 : 1
cast into mire, 373 : 27
discourse according to l., 206 : *n* 4
enough l. to misquote, 456 : 14
grammar nonsense and l., 371 : 5
great end of l., 89 : 22
grow old l. many things, 62 : 14

Learning (*continued*)
hath gained most, 276 : 19
how to use eyes, 504 : 17
if I should not be l. now, 93 : 7
inclination towards l. strong, 316 : 4
inflamed with study of l., 281 : 19
labored for them that seek l., 36 : 4
leadership and l., 892 : 1
light liberty l., 502 : 16
little l. dangerous, 332 : 20
love he bore to l., 370 : 10
love of l., 512 : 15
love of slaughter, 792 : 14
much l. make mad, 46 : 33
much l. not teach understanding, 69 : 28
no man wiser for his l., 263 : 18
not attained by chance, 393 : 2
on scraps of l. dote, 329 : 20
pause from l. to be wise, 351 : 17
polite l., 319 : 14
red plague rid you for l. me your language, 247 : 18
royal road to l., 92 : *n* 3
secretary of Nature and all l., 271 : 15
steeped in antique l., 592 : 6
thought without l., 68 : 10
wear l. like watch, 342 : 1
weight of l., 532 : 26
whence is thy l., 331 : 12
who so neglects l. in youth, 77 : 22
wiser without books, 377 : 14
without liberty in vain, 891 : 10
without thought, 68 : 10
Learning's altar vanish, 562 : 10
triumph o'er her foes, 351 : 10
Learns, who l. must suffer, 71 : 5
Lease of my true love, 245 : 13
summer's l. too short, 244 : 5
Leash, slow on the l., 792 : 6
Leashes, collars and l. of vanity, 907 : 24
Leash-men, pallid the l., 792 : 6
Least deserved such a fate, 81 : 9
faithful in l., 43 : 32
I am l. of apostles, 48 : 28
joy last not l., 232 : 23
last not l. in love, 216 : 10
love l. that let men know, 189 : 30
most enjoy contented l., 244 : 9
myself not l. but honored, 529 : 8
not l. in honor or applause, 174 : *n* 3
nothing so l. as truth, 829 : 21
of the evils, 87 : 18
of these my brethren, 41 : 1
of two evils, 58 : *n* 5
promise most given when l. said, 177 : 11
said soonest mended, 169 : *n* 2
though last not l., 174 : 15
unjust in l., 43 : 32
woman who occasions l. talk, 81 : 6
Leather, clothed all in l., 934 : 2
future smells of Russian l., 482 : 4
rest all l. or prunella, 337 : 11
Spanish or neat's l., 291 : 16
trod upon neat's l., 214 : 31
Leathern, flits by on l. wing, 364 : 12
silken or l. purse, 328 : 19
war with reremice for l. wings, 196 : 19
Leave all else to the gods, 107 : 6
all meaner things, 336 : 10
America love or l. it, 925 : 17
at point of bayonets, 397 : 20
Leave (*continued*)
behind bit of ourselves, 679 : 9
bottle on chimleypiece, 547 : 35
by next town drain, 659 : 11
do not need l. your room, 786 : 3
exempt from plunder, 705 : 4
friends and go, 691 : 15
give themselves when you l., 789 : 11
her Johnny leave her, 935 : 2
her to heaven, 219 : 25
I must l. all that, 273 : 8
it unadvertised, 644 : 14
king not l. country, 848 : 2
kiss but in the cup, 256 : 8
light of hope behind, 443 : 8
little lives in air, 334 : 16
living name behind, 262 : 11
long anchorage we l., 576 : 20
low-vaulted past, 519 : 7
man shall l. father and mother, 7 : 4
me a little, 529 : 15
me O Love, 176 : 9
me to repose, 363 : 9
monument behind, 715 : 9
no stone unturned, 77 : 2
not a rack behind, 248 : 13
not a stain, 36 : 5
not l. unless father does, 848 : 2
not l. you comfortless, 45 : 23
off agony leave off style, 661 : 12
off wishing to deserve thanks, 102 : 13
peace I l. with you, 45 : 24
religion to family, 590 : 2
sack and live cleanly, 205 : 17
something to after times, 281 : 12
the rest to heaven, 275 : 19
thee in the storm, 233 : 18
them alone they'll come home 932 : 3
them for the poor and stranger, 10 : 19
them honeyless, 217 : 8
them in midst of his days, 32 : 13
them laughing, 759 : 4
them while looking good, 826 : 4
to l. to die a little, 679 : 9
took l. but was loth to depart, 320 : 21
we Thy servant sleeping, 597 : 16
why did you l. Owen, 552 : 20
wilt thou l. me thus, 161 : 23
world no copy, 213 : 17
your friends and go, 691 : 15
Leaven, a little l., 48 : 9
pain for l., 632 : 9
till lump be l., 542 : 5
Leaveneth the whole lump, 48 : 9
Leaves, air wash l. cover me, 632 : 18
air wild with l., 793 : 16
among l. never known, 476 : 24
birds l. snows, 864 : 2
cane l. swaying, 831 : 14
cover them with l., 917 : 6
cover with l. and flowers, 262 : 3
crisped and sere, 526 : 22
dead driven like ghosts, 467 : 17
drifts of withered l., 588 : 5
easy as l. grow on tree, 711 : 22
fall early, 792 : 9
famous harmony of l., 712 : 7
generation of men like l., 58 : 1
glad green l. like wings, 642 : 3
happier than those he l., 593 : 5
harmony of l., 712 : 7
have drifted from me, 778 : 6
heart-shaped l. of green, 751 : *n* 3
Leaves (*continued*)
lisp of l., 632 : 7
mankind fleet of life like l., 82 : 9
me fifty more, 690 : 17
must walk over the l., 168 : *n* 2
naturally as l. to tree, 479 : 8
no l. no birds, 485 : 12
noiseless noise among l., 474 : 21
oak l. horses' heels, 806 : 12
of any author, 274 : 10
of Grass a person on record, 577 : 11
of Judgment Book unfold, 596 : 16
of life keep falling, 516 : 5
piled against doors, 97 : 10
poplars showed white of l., 627 : 1
private conscience for guide, 305 : 20
raking up l., 641 : 14
sewed fig l. together, 7 : 7
shady l. of destiny, 292 : 8
shatter your l., 280 : 6
stop to rake l. away, 747 : 3
stuck out tongues, 873 : 12
swayed my l. and flowers, 713 : 8
teaches l. to curtsy, 899 : 11
tender l. of hopes, 249 : 3
thick as autumnal l., 283 : 16
though l., are many the root is one, 713 : 8
tomb of green l., 672 : 11
turning in the wind, 766 : 12
unless l. perish, 863 : 14
untroubled about us, 900 : 2
vine l. in hair, 600 : 5
what if my l. falling, 467 : 21
where l. the rose, 516 : 6
wings of seraph, 852 : 14
words are like l., 333 : 4
world to darkness, 361 : 20
yellow l. or none or few, 244 : 27
Leaving all that here win us, 641 : 25
country for country's sake, 329 : *n* 2
love behind, 606 : 9
me never alone, 641 : 22
nothing became him like l., 236 : 14
outgrown shell, 519 : 8
to direct themselves, 825 : 11
to take command of troops, 420 : 12
Leavings, devil's l., 340 : 12
Lebanon, cedars of L., 21 : 10, 759 : 11
grow like a cedar in L., 20 : 18
Lebarge, Lake L., 752 : 6
Lecher, gilded fly does l., 234 : 31
Lecherous goats, 254 : 10
Lecteur, hypocrite l., 580 : *n* 4, 580 : 16
Lecture, if you wish to hold a l., 80 : 2
Lectures, behold I do not give l., 574 : 26
or a little charity, 574 : 26
plant read us l. of ethics, 316 : 8
Led, Bruce has often l., 411 : 15
dumb and silent be l., 379 : 6
neither saint nor sophist l., 585 : 6
regiment from behind, 629 : 25
to believe a lie, 407 : *n* 1
Leda, as L. mother of Helen, 638 : 11
Ledge, rocky l. woods untamed, 696 : 11
Ledlow, farmer L. late at plow, 641 : 10
Lee, between windward and l., 634 : 12
I and my Annabel L., 527 : 8
shore of age, 664 : 1
Leek, by this l., 208 : 14
Leeks, wel loved he garleek oynons l., 146 : 13
Leer, assent with civil l., 338 : 14
Lees, drink life to l., 529 : 7

Lees (*continued*)
mere l. is left, 238 : 7
stirs up l. of things, 570 : 13
wines on the l., 30 : 7
Leeward, soft shower to l., 571 : 8
Leewardings, such lovely l., 571 : 8
unfettered l., 843 : 14
Left booming surge of Aegean, 83 : 6
cannon to l. of them, 533 : 13
country for country's good, 329 : *n* 2
fair Scotland's strand, 410 : 4
for handful of silver l. us, 541 : 5
his garment in her hand, 8 : 30
implacable Charybdis guards l., 200 : *n* 1
in her l. hand riches and honor, 23 : 4
let not l. hand know, 37 : 14
lies on her l. side, 822 : 4
ne'er l. man in mire, 242 : 32
one taken the other l., 40 : 27
the warm precincts, 362 : 14
the web left the loom, 528 : 27
thou hast l. thy first love, 52 : 33
vivid air signed with honor, 876 : 16
Leg, can honor set to l., 205 : 5
caper and shake l., 760 : 5
decreasing l. increasing belly, 205 : 28
justice has wooden l., 722 : 1
never breaks l., 704 : 1
one old timber l., 735 : 3
took him by left l., 931 : 8
Legacies, books l. genius leaves, 326 : 16
Legacy alleviates sorrow, 171 : 7
charm in a good l., 171 : 7
Legal justice art of good and fair, 134 : 8
society without objective l. scale, 895 : 25
super l. aid bureau, 777 : 1
unanimity on l. questions, 700 : 2
Legalizer, time great l., 771 : 17
Legend, lavish extravagance no l. dreamed of, 636 : 15
leaf-fringed l., 477 : 4
of green chapels, 886 : 18
Legend's, qui procul hinc l. writ, 700 : 7
Legends, asleep in lap of l., 476 : 12
fairy tales tone licked clean, 906 : 4
rather believe fables in l., 180 : 16
Leges, silent enim l. inter arma, 98 : *n* 5
Legible, thoughts l. in eye, 184 : 13
Legion, my name is L., 42 : 4
of lost ones, 708 : 13
soldier of the L., 514 : 10
that never was 'listed, 708 : 19
Legiones redde, 110 : *n* 3
Legions, give me back my l., 110 : 5
Legislate, judges do and must l., 644 : 20
Legislation, conquests through l., 483 : 8
deprived of voice in l., 393 : 3
great problem of l., 418 : 9
Legislative, correction through l. action, 678 : 3
every l. body in U.S., 737 : 5
judicial distinct from l., 381 : 11
nominated by executive, 383 : 8
Legislators, poets l. of world, 470 : 7
Legislature, beauty not at call of l., 497 : 30
public opinion stronger than l., 603 : 13
Legitimate, let the end be l., 402 : 6
object of government, 389 : 4
Legs, 'ear 'erse's l., 535 : 7
giving way under me, 602 : 1
his l. bestrid the ocean, 241 : 25
if go high use own l., 657 : 17
not natural to walk on two l., 387 : 1
of iron, 32 : 32
on his last l., 261 : 14
on stilts we walk on our own l., 166 : 9
one pair of English l., 207 : 23
slimy things crawl with l., 434 : 16
that bird never on l., 548 : 14
took lake between my l., 904 : 3
vast trunkless l., 466 : 12
walk under his huge l., 215 : 6
Leibniz, monads of L., 791 : 12
Leicester, farewell L. Square, 753 : 1
Leisure answers leisure, 229 : 8
be doon at l. parfitly, 147 : 25
conversation wants l., 751 : 15
gentleman of l., 685 : 2
means and l. civilizers, 502 : 14
no l. who useth it not, 270 : 20
repent at l., 324 : 5
retired L., 278 : 16
to grow wise, 585 : 17
with dignity, 98 : 8
wooed in haste wed at l., 188 : 34
Leisured class replaced by New Class, 871 : 14
Leisurely, full l. we glide, 611 : 1
say Miserere very l., 273 : 9
Leman, such a l., 927 : 4
Lemon, be with you in squeezing of l., 371 : 6
trees bloom, 395 : 3
twelve miles from a l., 433 : 3
Lemonade, black eyes and l., 447 : 6
weak like your soul, 412 : 6
Lemons, oranges and l., 930 : 7
Lend a hand, 590 : 8
a kind of easiness, 223 : 11
eye a terrible aspect, 207 : 16
eyes the glowworm l. thee, 266 : 14
heaven such grace did l. her, 190 : 4
less than thou owest, 233 : 9
man himself l. a hand, 80 : 13
me leave to come, 174 : 18
me stone strength, 797 : 11
me your ears, 216 : 17
men who borrow men who l., 441 : 17
us thine aid, 452 : 5
you wings of future, 797 : 11
Lender, borrower is servant to the l., 24 : 36
neither borrower nor l., 219 : 2
Lendeth, because it l. light, 174 : 13
unto the Lord, 24 : 26
Lendings, off you l., 234 : 7
Lends hand to honest boldness, 91 : 8
he that l. gives, 270 : 15
soul l. tongue vows, 219 : 6
three things I never l., 500 : 21
Lenero, en casa del l., 935 : 14
Length, concept of l., 776 : 3
drags its slow l. along, 333 : 8
Folly's at full l., 330 : 26
in l. of days understanding, 15 : 30
of days in her right hand, 23 : 4
operations by which l. determined, 776 : 3
what it lacks in l., 749 : 6
words of learned l., 370 : 11
Lengthened sage advices, 411 : 5
Lengthened (*continued*)
shadow of man, 497 : 4
Lengthening, drags l. chain, 368 : 14
Lengthens not a day, 251 : 13
Lenin, Declaration more revolutionary than L., 800 : 8
Lenity, what makes robbers bold but l., 186 : 7
Lenore, lost L., 526 : 12
Lens, each age a l., 606 : 10
Lent him to a lady, 933 : 16
with l. money evil done, 573 : 3
Lente currite noctis equi, 113 : *n* 4, 184 : 8
sois plus l., 464 : *n* 6
Lentiles, gave Esau pottage of l., 8 : 16
Leo, ill policy in L. the Tenth, 379 : 16
Leoline, Sir L. the baron rich, 433 : 28
Leonidas and Washington, 461 : 20
my name L. will echo throughout time, 93 : 2
Leopard change his spots, 32 : 6
cloud that looked like l., 81 : 15
frozen carcass of l., 845 : 8
seeking at that altitude, 845 : 8
shall lie down with the kid, 29 : 19
Leopards, leaping like l. to sky, 604 : 16
three white l., 805 : 22
Leprosy, skin white as l., 434 : 19
Lesbia, let us live and love my L., 101 : 18
my sweetest L., 250 : 3
with her sparrow, 823 : 2
Lesbia's sparrow all alone, 759 : 12
Lesbos, Sappho of L. tenth muse, 63 : *n* 4
Lescaut, story of Manon L., 345 : 1
Less, by hoping more have but l., 189 : 18
can't take l. said Hatter, 611 : 21
fears l. than imaginings, 236 : 11
greater prey upon l., 344 : 13
he spoke more he heard, 660 : 15
how much l. man, 16 : 11
if clod washed away Europe l., 254 : 22
is more, 542 : 24
more and more about l., 698 : 17
more matter with l. art, 220 : 11
never do l. than duty, 509 : 9
nicely calculated l. or more, 429 : 6
no man shall have, 687 : 8
not that I loved Caesar l., 216 : 14
of two evils, 58 : *n* 5
rather than be l. cared not to be, 284 : 5
small Latin and l. Greek, 256 : 13
than kind, 217 : 31
than meets the eye, 857 : 9
the l. one knows, 64 : 17
the little l. what worlds away, 542 : 8
they have the more noise, 340 : 11
weep to make l. depth of grief, 186 : 3
Lessened, one pain l. by another's, 191 : 19
Lessening, little things go l., 544 : 27
Lesser breeds without law, 709 : 19
god made world, 534 : 28
than my name, 195 : 5
woman l. man, 530 : 5
Lesson, draw from others the l., 96 : 8
each reads his own l., 571 : 13
first l. to be learned, 596 : 5

Lesson (*continued*)
  grandest l. On sail on, 646:7
  harder l. how to die, 164:*n* 8
  heart give l. to head, 377:14
  last l. learned thoroughly, 596:5
  on grammar impertinence, 591:10
  seems to carry, 377:24
Lessons of paternalism unlearned, 631:11
  of two such l. forget, 461:7
  three l. I would write, 412:11
Let all her ways be unconfined, 320:17
  another man praise thee, 25:22
  at another l. in the foe, 288:28
  dead bury dead, 38:24
  dearly l. or l. alone, 267:14
  each man exercise art he knows, 82:3
  everything that hath breath praise, 22:25
  face of God shine through, 822:12
  freedom ring, 514:12
  her not walk in the sun, 220:17
  him look to his bond, 199:16
  him never come back, 541:9
  him now speak, 56:7
  him pass for a man, 198:13
  it be, 914:14
  it be forgotten, 787:6
  it be let it pass, 342:*n* 6
  it begin here, 374:19
  joys be as May, 267:20
  justice be done though heaven fall, 133:25
  me die death of righteous, 11:3
  me have no lying, 247:4
  me love, 252:10
  me not to marriage of true minds, 245:18
  me tell the world, 205:7
  my people go, 9:16, 935:21
  never curtain drawn, 748:12
  never l. up for single moment, 788:3
  no bird call, 822:14
  no dog bark, 198:2
  no man's heart fail, 12:40
  no such man be trusted, 201:3
  not heart be troubled, 45:20, 45:24
  not poor Nelly starve, 302:22
  not the sun go down, 49:36
  sleeping dogs lie, 549:5
  slip dogs of war, 216:12
  thame say, 175:4
  the toast pass, 399:1
  the words of my mouth, 18:3
  them eat cake, 359:6
  them have their day, 714:5
  them say, 175:*n* 4
  this cup pass, 41:12
  thy words be few, 26:26
  us all to meditation, 185:19
  us alone, 528:17
  us be backed with God and seas, 186:15
  us be happy as we can, 356:18
  us begin, 890:10
  us go into the house of the Lord, 22:5
  us go singing as far as we go, 103:21
  us go then, 803:9
  us have peace, 589:20
  us have tongs and bones, 197:4
  us live and love, 101:18, 250:3
  us now praise famous men, 36:10
Let (*continued*)
  us reason together, 28:30
  us take it as it comes, 630:4
  us then be up, 509:16
  what will be said or done, 388:10
  who will be clever, 566:12, 773:15
  will not l. thee go, 8:25
  your light shine, 37:6
  Your Mind Alone, 831:7
Lethe, cup that brings sleep of L., 106:24
  go not to L., 477:20
  river of oblivion, 284:22
  rots in ease on L. wharf, 219:19
  time L., 755:6
Lethean, drunken of things L., 633:6
Lethe-wards had sunk, 476:21
Let's call whole thing off, 836:8
  carve him as a dish, 215:20
  choose executors, 195:1
  contend no more love, 541:21
  kill all the lawyers, 185:24
  look at the record, 741:7
  Pretend and we did, 912:14
  talk of graves, 195:1
Lets, make ghost of him that l. me, 219:16
Letter and spirit of constitution, 402:6
  broke spell of dead l., 817:4
  by card by l. by press, 726:12
  killeth, 49:11
  last till you write your l., 252:3
  longer than usual, 299:13
  not l. but spirit, 49:11
  one l. of Richardson's, 355:2
  read in the bitter l., 229:23
  scarlet l. passport, 503:12
  to the world, 605:12
Lettered, locked l. collar, 409:6
Lettering, stripped of l. and gilding, 346:15
Letters by living man, 910:18
  Cadmus gave, 461:7
  fool in four l., 297:17
  in your l. speak of me, 232:20
  man of l., 301:11
  mingle souls, 254:4
  no arts no l. no society, 264:17
  republic of l., 349:25
  should not be known, 247:26
  you bid me burn l., 381:4
Letter-writing, the great art o' l., 546:24
Letting hundred flowers blossom, 826:12
  I dare not, 237:2
Level, boys and girls l. with men, 241:22
  dead l. of mass, 570:12
  in her husband's heart, 214:1
  levelers wish to l. down not up, 354:13
Leveled rule of streaming light, 279:21
  together by Tao, 90:2
Levelers, books true l., 448:5
  wish to level down, 354:13
Leveling, cannot bear l. up, 354:13
  rancorous mind, 716:4
  wind, 715:9
Levels all ranks, 493:5
Lever, mind l. of all things, 450:6
  you can only turn once, 828:4
Leviathan, draw out l. with a hook, 17:4
Leviathan (*continued*)
  hugest of creatures, 286:30
  that crooked serpent, 30:12
  whom thou hast made to play, 21:11
Levity, a little judicious l., 669:11
  say it with utmost l., 680:1
Levy, foreign l., 238:19
Levying war, 391:12
Lewd fellows, 46:14
  the sinful and l., 834:5
Lewdness, though l. court it, 219:22
Lex, de minimis non curat l., 133:18
  salus populi suprema l., 99:*n* 3, 134:25
Lexicographer writer of dictionaries, 352:11
Lexicography, not so lost in l., 352:6
Lexicon of youth, 493:7
Lexington and Bunker Hill, 450:13
Lhude sing cuccu, 916:14
  sing Goddamm, 792:8
Liable, all men are l. to error, 307:16
Liar always lavish of oaths, 275:25
  and the father of it, 45:6
  best l., 620:13
  doubt truth to be l., 220:14
  either l. or madman, 358:19
  makes amount go long way, 620:13
  no one such l. as indignant man, 657:19
  of first magnitude, 324:10
  picturesque l., 624:6
  should have good memory, 117:22
  show me a l., 270:10
  they answered Little l., 730:11
Liars, all men are l., 21:23
  drunkards l. adulterers, 233:5
  when they speak truth, 86:15
Libelous statements about dog, 781:1
Liber, vade salutatem pro me l., 145:*n* 4
Liberal arts study humanizes, 114:2
  education, 319:14
  I am a L., 588:14
  infuses that l. obedience, 373:7
  institutions cease being liberal, 658:12
  little L., 628:23
  luxury of l. government, 553:9
  philosophy, 813:9
  tempered by experience, 588:14
  to love her is l. education, 327:11
Liberalism in politics, 848:12
Liberality in gifts well timed, 315:5
Liberatas, ubi l. ibi patria, 367:11
Liberate men and women—L., 831:19
Liberated, I have l. my soul, 136:10
  the hell out of place, 925:3
Liberates, neither shoots nor l., 560:24
Liberation, madness potential l., 907:1
  of energies of men, 891:5
  of Europe, 815:12
Liberator, shepherd as l., 523:7
Liberavi animam meam, 136:*n* 7
Liberis, pro patria pro l., 102:*n* 15
Libertas, in dubiis l., 294:*n* 6
Libertate, sub l. quietem, 298:*n* 7
Liberté, je suis né pour te nommer L., 832:*n* 1
Liberties, dramatist wants l., 654:1
  liberty above all l., 282:4
  not too strong for l., 524:1
  people never give up l., 373:13

Liberties (*continued*)
preserve l. Americans already had, 800 : 7
Libertine, chartered l., 207 : 5
freedom of l., 762 : 4
puffed and reckless l., 218 : 28
Libertines, self-love makes more l., 358 : 24
Liberty a beloved discipline, 877 : 14
abstract l. not found, 372 : 18
Americans love l., 351 : 3
and glory of his country, 450 : 5
and justice for all, 677 : 10
and tyranny, 523 : 7
and Union, 450 : 16
arduous struggle for l., 383 : 1
as end and means, 677 : 12
assert and maintain l. and virtue, 380 : 6
basis of democratic state is l., 88 : 12
bulwark of continuing l., 780 : 6
bulwark of our l., 520 : 7
bulwarks of l., 367 : 6
by accident got its l., 154 : 8
cannot be preserved without knowledge, 380 : 9
captivity is consciousness so's l., 605 : 9
change from l. to force, 418 : 2
condition on which given l., 397 : 21
contending for l., 379 : 1
corruption symptom of l., 383 : 11
cost of l., 724 : 18
courage secret of l., 677 : 12
cradle of l., 451 : 15
crust of bread and l., 339 : 11
definition of word l., 523 : 7
degradation of idea of l., 882 : 10
democracy seeks equality in l., 506 : 12
deprived of life l. or property, 391 : 17, 392 : 4
divinest l., 435 : 13
doing what laws permit, 341 : 8
doing what one desires, 508 : 15
enjoy delight with l., 174 : 12
enjoy such l., 296 : 4
enjoyment of life and l., 367 : 4
equality fraternity, 928 : 2
establish our real l., 164 : 17
extremism in defense of l., 385 : *n* 2
freedom enfranchisement, 216 : 6
from despotism to l. in featherbed, 388 : 9
give me l. or death, 383 : 5
God who gave life gave l., 387 : 8
greatest dangers to l., 677 : 15
hail L. hail, 484 : 1
Hall, 371 : 8
harder to preserve than obtain, 449 : 11
harmonies of L., 733 : 5
he served human l., 716 : 6
he that commands sea is at l., 181 : 11
headstrong l., 188 : 1
heritage of all men, 520 : 7
highest political end, 615 : 17
history of l. history of safeguards, 776 : 12
history of progress of human l., 556 : 4
I must have l. withal, 211 : 10
if l. found in democracy, 88 : 6
in doubtful things l., 294 : 18
Liberty (*continued*)
in moderate governments, 401 : 13
in mouth of Webster, 495 : 28
in proportion to restraint, 451 : 11
individual l. individual power, 418 : 3
inspire our souls, 325 : *n* 9
interfering with l., 508 : 3
is possibility of doubting, 851 : 4
judiciary safeguard of l., 700 : 1
know no such l., 296 : 2
knows nothing but victories, 538 : 16
law consistent with l., 366 : 2
lawless attack upon l., 365 : 3
life l. pursuit of happiness, 387 : 9
light l. learning, 502 : 16
love of l. God planted, 520 : 7
love of l. love of others, 445 : 15
man establish reign of l., 870 : 13
mocks my loss of l., 402 : 13
most power least l., 303 : 2
mountain nymph sweet l., 277 : 21
must be rationed, 731 : 8
must begin at home, 825 : 10
my heart's at l., 296 : *n* 3
my soul at l., 605 : 8
nation conceived in l., 523 : 4
natural l. establishes itself, 366 : 8
neither in despotism or democracy, 401 : 13
neither l. nor safety, 348 : 2
no pretense of loving l., 520 : 2
not alone to this country, 521 : 8
of a poet, 276 : 1
of conscience, 273 : 11
of individual, 508 : 9
of press, 390 : 11, 506 : 5
of thought life of soul, 344 : 9
only to those who love it, 451 : 3
peace l. and safety, 389 : 2
people so dead to l., 350 : 17
placid repose under l., 298 : 19
plucks justice by nose, 227 : 26
possessions take away l., 704 : 5
power to endanger public l., 380 : 13
precious, 731 : 8
price of l., 397 : *n* 8
proclaim l. throughout land, 10 : 22
property no stamps, 920 : 8
putrid corpse of l., 784 : 2
quick with seed of l., 569 : 9
right to death or l., 593 : 16
sacred fire of l., 379 : 7
secret of happiness, 677 : 12
secure blessings of l., 391 : 10
seeking l. which is so dear, 141 : 18
so loving-jealous of his l., 192 : 18
soul of journey is l., 445 : 11
spirit of l., 372 : 15
survival of l., 890 : 7
sweet land of l., 514 : 12
taken with nature, 636 : 1
that little we do is through L., 546 : 5
this country to preserve l., 390 : 1
this is L. Hall, 371 : 8
to be subserved, 576 : 11
to know, 282 : 4
to think feel do, 445 : 11
trains for liberty, 724 : 19
Tree, 384 : 8
tree of l. refreshed, 388 : 7
tree of l. watered by blood, 401 : 4
we all declare for l., 523 : 7
what crimes in thy name, 400 : 14
where l. there is my country, 367 : 11
Liberty (*continued*)
where slavery is l. cannot be, 539 : 2
without learning is peril, 891 : 10
wrote at l. when of devils, 403 : 19
Liberty's in every blow, 411 : 16
Libraries, have well-furnished l., 258 : 2
I bless God in l., 365 : 10
not made they grow, 666 : 7
science and l. of Europe, 390 : 1
Library, furnished me from mine own l., 247 : 15
public l. affords conviction, 352 : 5
turn over half a l., 355 : 14
was dukedom large enough, 247 : 13
whereon I look, 267 : 4
Libre, l'homme est né l., 358 : *n* 7
Libri, cave ab homine unius l., 133 : 11
Lice tethered, 873 : 11
License, equal l. in bold invention, 109 : 18
innocence never blossom into l., 312 : 10
love not freedom but l., 282 : 12
poetic l., 98 : 11
to see countryside, 894 : 6
Licensing and prohibiting, 282 : 5
Licentiae, poetarum l. liberiora, 98 : *n* 9
Licentious, newspapers the most l., 399 : 5
soldiery, 373 : 12
Lichas, Hercules and L. play at dice, 198 : 30
Lick absurd pomp, 222 : 4
ill cook that cannot l. fingers, 193 : 20
it into form, 117 : *n* 3
the dust, 20 : 1
valleys up, 605 : 18
Licked, admit I'm l., 814 : 17
he l. my wounds, 794 : 5
platter clean, 929 : 16
soup from ladles, 541 : 1
Licker, corn l. stop victim's watch, 757 : 6
talks mighty loud, 662 : 13
Licks, bear l. them into proper shape, 117 : 3
hand raised to shed blood, 336 : 13
pride that l. the dust, 339 : 3
Lid, cat that sits on hot stove l., 625 : 5
earth's l., 792 : 16
penthouse l., 236 : 2
Lids, drops blue-fringed l., 435 : 16
eternal l. apart, 478 : 20
Lie a thought more nigh, 265 : 14
abroad for commonwealth, 251 : 4
all the dead l. down, 605 : 15
all who l. beneath, 710 : 15
asked lady to l. her down, 404 : 11
asks no questions isn't told l., 371 : *n* 2
at proud foot of conqueror, 202 : 19
athwart noses as they l. asleep, 191 : 23
awake in dark weep for sins, 574 : 24
becomes habitual, 388 : 3
before us like land of dreams, 587 : 16
big l., 812 : 17
by emperor's side, 231 : 23
cannot tell a l., 378 : *n* 9
can't pray a l., 624 : 4
children and fools cannot l., 160 : 13
circumstantial, 213 : 4
contrive one noble l., 84 : 11

Lie (*continued*)
countenance cannot l., 184 : 13
credit his own l., 247 : 11
deep buried, 67 : 5
differences between cat and l., 624 : 16
dig grave let me l., 668 : 20
direct, 213 : 4
dost thou l. so low, 216 : 8
down because 'twas night, 252 : 21
down for eon or two, 707 : 21
down in green pastures, 18 : 7
down like tired child, 466 : 15
down till leaders spoken, 709 : 5
down where ladders start, 717 : 21
fain wald l. down, 927 : 8
families l. together, 901 : 13
faults l. gently on him, 249 : 12
for a moment is truth, 582 : 15
give the world the l., 172 : 14
half a truth blackest, 535 : 6
handle which fits all, 519 : 9
has seven endings, 926 : 2
heaven with splendors l., 567 : 11
here let her l., 307 : 10
here obedient to their laws we l., 67 : 19
home to a l., 792 : 14
how l. through centuries, 541 : 20
how still we see thee l., 619 : 16
I can't tell a l., 378 : *n* 9
I l. down alone, 692 : 8
I shall l. in the dust, 59 : 1
I their map l. flat, 254 : 18
if I l. spit in my face, 203 : 30
in cold obstruction, 228 : 20
in cowslip's bell I l., 248 : 16
in Mellstock churchyard now, 641 : 10
in your throat, 205 : 23
inhuman reign of l., 817 : 4
leads you to believe a l., 407 : 10
light lie light, 625 : 20
lightly gentle earth, 263 : 7
like bill on nature's reality, 473 : 12
me down to bleed, 926 : *n* 7
men who will not l., 566 : 3
national l., 625 : 24
nicer to l. in bed, 730 : 19
no worse l. than truth misunderstood, 650 : 5
not a man that he should l., 11 : 4
not know what it is to l., 489 : 1
nothing can need a l., 268 : 4
on knees of the gods, 59 : 16
on Mother's bed, 893 : 3
one daiquiri told the other a l., 884 : 10
permits himself to tell l. 388 : 3
rather l. in woolen, 209 : 4
reclined, 528 : 19
sergeant's widow told l., 518 : 5
sleep will never l., 192 : 21
sleeping dogs l., 549 : 5
so I l. who all day long, 857 : 15
still and slumber, 328 : 8
still ye thief, 204 : 18
stone tell where I l., 332 : 11
summer's l., 830 : 1
sweet compulsion in music l., 277 : 16
sweets compacted l., 268 : 16
talking of fall of man, 560 : 29
tangled in her hair, 296 : 2
thought uttered is l., 500 : 24

Lie (*continued*)
truth in masquerade, 461 : 23
underneath this stone doth l., 256 : 5
unless statistics l., 829 : 11
upon the daisies, 628 : 6
violence intertwined with l., 895 : 22
what is a l., 461 : 23
where'er she l., 292 : 8
which is all a lie, 535 : 6
who loves to l. with me, 211 : 1
with a purpose worst, 721 : 13
with my fathers, 9 : 3
worse thangs than l., 555 : 8
yonder all before us l., 296 : 28
young shall l. down together, 29 : 19
Liebchen with whom should I quarrel, 864 : 11
Lied, said Right as Pippin but l., 730 : 6
those who l. for hire, 792 : 19
Lief not be as be in awe, 215 : 4
Liege of loiterers, 190 : 26
we are men my l., 238 : 14
Lies at last as always, 899 : 17
believe her though she l., 246 : 2
below correct in cypress, 827 : 14
cruelest l. in silence, 667 : 16
dalliance in wardrobe l., 207 : 10
death l. on my tongue, 205 : 10
exposed he l., 306 : 18
fool l. here, 707 : 20
full fathom five thy father l., 247 : 21
great Prince in prison l., 253 : 7
half truth blackest of l., 535 : 6
heaven l. about us, 426 : 14
here food for worms, 346 : 15
here l. a king that ruled, 271 : 18
here l. beautiful lady, 739 : 14
here l. Matthew Prior, 321 : 2
here l. my wife, 307 : 10
here l. one who meant well, 669 : 15
here l. one whose name, 480 : 7
here l. our good Edmund, 371 : 14
here l. truly honest man, 292 : 20
him down the lubber fiend, 278 : 3
historical books with no l., 655 : 3
Hope l. to mortals, 692 : 7
how long a time l. in one word, 194 : 2
in his bed walks with me, 201 : 26
in the rude manger l., 277 : 7
jailed for telling l. to young, 863 : 11
judged according to l., 138 : 8
kindness and l., 859 : 7
long time l. in one word, 194 : 2
Matilda told l., 730 : 9
matters I relate are true l., 818 : 4
music on spirit l., 528 : 14
my captain l., 576 : 7
now l. he there, 216 : 21
old men's l., 792 : 14
on chaliced flowers that l., 243 : 16
on her left side, 822 : 4
poets tell many l., 62 : 13
religion of slaves, 725 : 6
speaking l. in hypocrisy, 50 : 27
steep my speech in l., 71 : 25
subject of all verse, 265 : 15
tells l. without attending, 388 : 3
that made great equals, 892 : 13
that way madness l., 234 : 2
to hide it, 268 : *n* 4
to tell l. not honorable, 75 : 17
truth to cover l., 324 : 9

Lies (*continued*)
uneasy l. head that wears crown, 206 : 19
where he longed to be, 668 : 20
with dogs riseth with fleas, 269 : 31
you can invent, 406 : 12
Life a battle and sojourning, 124 : 10
a bubble, 181 : *n* 7
a fury slinging flame, 532 : 6
a man's real l., 684 : 2
a play of passion, 173 : 1
academic l., 257 : 11
accept Jesus new l., 903 : 7
account of her l. to clod, 209 : 6
actuality of thought is l., 87 : 11
add what we can to l., 664 : 15
admits not of delays, 355 : 24
adore my l. with Bird, 875 : 4
affirmation of l., 756 : 17
after l. is death, 633 : 18
ain't all beer and skittles, 546 : *n* 2
all a man hath will he give for l., 15 : 5
all his l. in the wrong, 315 : 21
all human l. in monkeys and cats, 652 : 8
all I care about is l., 643 : 5
all inclusion and confusion, 653 : 13
all l. is a dream, 273 : 2
all l. is an experiment, 645 : 1
along parabola l. flies, 912 : 10
American l. solvent, 703 : 19
among people who love each other, 504 : 13
and Death and Forever, 566 : 12
and liberty, 367 : 4
and memory of it, 878 : 19
and power of increase, 307 : 12
and power scattered, 450 : 7
and what's a l., 267 : 19
anything for a quiet l., 261 : 19, 546 : 28
art long l. short, 395 : 7
art makes l., 654 : 10
art of drawing conclusions, 620 : 16
as for future l. man judge, 515 : 13
as much as my l. was worth, 360 : 12
as to bed's-feet l. shrunk, 252 : 25
as to breathe were l., 529 : 9
at ease drifts, 601 : 11
at the door of l., 633 : 1
bagatelle of transient experience, 697 : 10
banished from high l., 569 : 19
bankrupt of l., 304 : 1
be not afraid of l., 649 : 15
bear a charmed l., 240 : 8
beautiful or reverse, 689 : 23
becomes rootless plant, 289 : 13
before us lies in daily l., 287 : 3
beg delinquents for l., 893 : 17
begins perpetually, 720 : 6
believe in l., 725 : 3
believe in l. to come, 866 : 14
believeth with l. pain stop, 544 : 18
best part of married l. fights, 839 : 18
best portion of man's l., 423 : 9
best things in l. free, 825 : 7
birth l. and death, 315 : 9
birthday of my l., 608 : 12
bitterness of l., 614 : 6
blameless l., 534 : 1
blot out of book of l., 53 : 4
blow through l., 855 : 17

Life (*continued*)
boat of l. be light, 692 : 15
book of l. begins, 675 : 16
book of l. opened, 53 : 28
books substitute for l., 667 : 21
boredom at core of l., 301 : 10
bread called staff of l., 319 : 8
bread first necessity of l., 666 : 3
bread of l., 44 : 41
bread of l. in mouth, 315 : 1
breath of l., 6 : 17
breathed by Creator, 515 : 3
brief l. our portion, 563 : 12
brisking about the l., 365 : 14
broad margin to my l., 560 : 1
broken l. up for bread, 632 : 21
buried l., 585 : 15
burrs and thorns of l., 475 : 13
but a span, 320 : 11
C Major of this l., 544 : 7
calamity of so long l., 221 : 12
cannot tear out page of l., 504 : 10
can't be wrong whose l. right, 337 : 9
care of l. and happiness, 389 : 4
careless of single l., 532 : 11
care's an enemy to l., 213 : 10
cast a cold eye on l., 718 : 2
casual attitude towards l., 853 : 14
chain of l., 898 : 1
change language change l., 911 : 2
change we think we see in l., 747 : 10
changing scenes of l., 317 : 6
chaos breeds l., 635 : 4
charmed l., 240 : 8
clock stops time come to l., 837 : 16
closed life begins, 576 : 20
closed twice before close, 607 : 18
cold eye on l. on death, 718 : 2
combat between love and hate, 671 : 17
comes before literature, 619 : 17
comes to end in prosperity, 71 : 8
comes to him with love, 857 : 3
communions of death and l., 637 : 17
compared l. to a dream, 165 : 9
compel philosophy to inquire about l., 98 : 25
conduct three-fourths of l., 588 : 23
conscious l. burden, 721 : 1
consciousness of what we can do, 784 : 19
consists with wildness, 560 : 28
contraction of l., 754 : 6
contraries the l. of one another, 274 : 18
controlling circumstances of l., 578 : 6
cool sequestered vale of l., 362 : 12
count l. of battle good, 700 : 6
crowded hour of l., 375 : 1
crowded to the full, 432 : 16
crown of l., 51 : 28, 53 : 1
crown of l. as it closes, 632 : 15
culprit l., 604 : 4
custom guide of human l., 357 : 15
daily beauty in his l., 232 : 11
dancing is l. itself, 690 : 2
dear as light and l., 410 : 18
death after l. does please, 173 : 12
death and l. one, 730 : 2
death makes l. live, 545 : 14
death nor l. nor angels, 47 : 15
death of each day's l., 237 : 21
death part of l., 755 : 8

Life (*continued*)
death side of l. away from us, 756 : 10
defeat my l., 232 : 7
demd horrid grind, 547 : 18
deprive of l. liberty or property, 392 : 4
deprived of l. liberty or property, 391 : 17
desecration against whole of l., 873 : 9
devote his l. in serving his prince, 68 : 4
difficulty in l. is choice, 671 : 6
digressions l. of reading, 360 : 2
dim origins of l., 869 : 13
disease of modern l., 586 : 1
does thy l. destroy, 405 : 5
done their song and dance in your l., 877 : 5
dost thou love l., 347 : 26
doth l. in tendance spend, 174 : 11
doubt he was worthy of l., 903 : 2
dream l. as lake dreams sky, 706 : 5
dream of l., 469 : 11
dreamed l. was beauty, 555 : 23
dreams necessary to l., 858 : 5
dregs of l., 303 : 11
drink l. to lees, 529 : 7
each carries own l. form, 754 : 5
earnest art gay, 413 : 6
ease one l. the aching, 606 : 12
echo undermine hold on l., 764 : 10
education of imaginative l., 654 : 9
education will determine future l., 84 : 13
efflorescence of civilized l., 579 : 11
elevate l. by endeavor, 559 : 24
elysian, 511 : 11
empty dream, 332 : *n* 2, 509 : 13
end in itself, 644 : 6
end of l. cancels bands, 204 : 23
end of l. is to be, 668 : 2
enjoyment of l. and liberty, 367 : 4
enlarge my l., 351 : 20
enough for my l., 35 : 4
entrusts l. to one hole, 93 : 14
envy and wrath shorten l., 36 : 1
essential facts of l., 559 : 25
eternal l. gift of God, 47 : 5
eternal l. in knowledge of God, 55 : 4
everlasting l., 44 : 34
everything in political l., 588 : 20
exempt from public haunt, 210 : 24
exile's l. no l., 93 : 2
expands in proportion to courage, 858 : 9
experience of this sweet l., 142 : 16
fabric of l., 870 : 1
fading fast away, 662 : 22
fall upon thorns of l., 467 : 20
falter l. away, 585 : 22
fancied l. in others' breath, 337 : 12
fashion literature of l., 632 : 1
fear love fear l., 738 : 4
fear of Acheron which troubles l., 100 : 20
feels l. in every limb, 423 : 3
feels like real fight, 649 : 14
felt-l. in producing art, 653 : 11
fever of l. over, 490 : 10
fie upon this quiet l., 203 : 26
for l. and joy and for objects, 576 : 5
for l. six hundred pounds, 339 : 10
for l. to come, 246 : 23

Life (*continued*)
for the living, 616 : 5
for why my l. at end, 926 : 16
force uncomprehended was his l., 602 : 5
fought for l., 876 : 15
free to develop hostile forms as friendly, 631 : 5
friend is medicine of l., 35 : 10
frittered away by detail, 559 : 26
from this cup they drank their l., 929 : 4
front essential facts of l., 559 : 25
fruit she longs to hand you, 864 : 19
fruits of l. and beauty, 404 : 16
fury slinging flame, 532 : 6
gale of l. high, 691 : 7
game is l., 849 : 22
game that must be played, 728 : 16
garment we alter, 839 : 7
gates of new l. to thee, 543 : 23
gave thee l. bid thee feed, 403 : 5
general mist of error, 262 : 7
girls make l. plan, 898 : 5
give as much meaning to l. as possible, 858 : 3
give to eat of the tree of l., 52 : 34
giveth his l. for sheep, 45 : 11
giving l. by death of others, 152 : 2
God gave l. gave liberty, 387 : 8
goes not backward, 782 : 15
goes on forever, 822 : 16
golden tree of l., 396 : 14
good death does honor to whole l., 143 : 4
Good L. waiting for us, 862 : 7
grants nothing without work, 106 : 17
great business of l., 637 : 7
great end of l. is action, 596 : 6
great interpreter of l., 637 : 6
greater price than l., 849 : 1
greatest thing in family l., 750 : 10
Greek thought and l., 598 : 13
Greeks have dreamt dream of l. best, 397 : 12
green l. once lived there, 877 : 15
growth evidence of l., 490 : 7
grunt and sweat under weary l., 221 : 12
half a l. asunder, 612 : 15
half spent before we know, 270 : 22
happy all his l., 270 : 26
harder toward summit, 658 : 16
harmonious and humane l., 589 : 7
has no meaning except responsibility, 823 : 20
have the light of l., 45 : 4
have you found l. distasteful, 545 : 22
he giveth l., 46 : 16
he that findeth l., 39 : 5
he that loveth her loveth l., 35 : 1
he who knows l., 316 : 11
here find l. in death, 438 : 9
high l., 369 : 14, 569 : 19
high l. mistaken path, 463 : 11
his l. a breath of God, 555 : 12
his l. dinner wife, 486 : 4
his l. was gentle, 217 : 14
his l. was in the right, 295 : 19
hollow existence burden, 622 : 11
home l. not natural, 680 : 31
honor dearer than l., 169 : 25
hope for happiness beyond l., 385 : 5
horizon of human l., 498 : 5

Life (*continued*)
horrors of half-known l., 570 : 14
hot for certainties in l., 600 : 20
house to be let for l., 267 : 14
how good man's l., 543 : 16
human l. a large mansion, 479 : 11
human l. a state in which much endured 352 : 17
human l. priceless, 849 : 1
hungry for l. and death, 886 : 8
husks of l., 869 : 13
hymns to glory of l., 801 : 7
I am the bread of l., 44 : 41
I believe in l. everlasting, 55 : 2
I burned my l., 836 : 18
I have painted my l., 801 : 1
I haven't a literary l., 876 : 21
I would like simple l., 908 : 15
if death not tragedy l. is, 687 : 1
if ever I touched a l., 916 : 3
if it be l. to pitch, 716 : 2
if l. bitter pardon, 634 : 13
if not l. what have you had, 653 : 9
if not ready to risk l., 853 : 4
if one had courage l. livable, 600 : 4
if you haven't had l., 653 : 9
ills scholar's l. assail, 351 : 17
imagination master of l., 684 : 6
immortal death has taken mortal l., 101 : 3
in internal environment, 551 : 19
in l. as in football, 687 : 5
in l. courtesy, 718 : 6
in l. did harbor give, 256 : 5
in l. many things draw us aside, 121 : 9
in London all l. can afford, 355 : 26
in middle of journey of l., 140 : 10
in open air condition for happiness, 882 : 12
in our l. nature live, 435 : 26
in sea of l. enisled, 585 : 13
in struggle for l. find love, 820 : 9
in the midst of l. death, 56 : 12
in whom standeth eternal l., 55 : 4
Indian summer of l., 635 : 21
inseparable like l. and consciousness, 790 : 18
intend to lead new l., 55 : 16
interest in death interest in l., 755 : 13
into each l. rain fall, 510 : 11
irremediable poverty of l., 769 : 25
is a circle, 701 : 9
is a copycat, 803 : 2
is a foreign language, 816 : 10
is a jest, 332 : 8
is a wave, 580 : 3
is action and passion, 643 : 16
is all beer and skittles, 546 : *n* 2
is an incurable disease, 295 : 12
is boring, 884 : 9
is but a day, 475 : 10
is but a span, 320 : 11
is creation, 552 : 3
is eternal love immortal, 642 : 10
is fading fast away, 662 : 22
is good, 797 : 10
is its own journey, 867 : 11
is l. a boon, 629 : 23
is l. a thorn, 629 : 24
is l. so dear, 383 : 5
is not l. more than meat, 38 : 2
is only error, 413 : 23

Life (*continued*)
is opening readings secret, 764 : 7
is painting picture, 644 : 13
is real life is earnest, 509 : 13
is short art long, 80 : 9
is supremely easy for men, 59 : 26
is thorny, 434 : 3
is unfair, 891 : 4
is what we make it, 649 : 13
is what you gave, 851 : 1
isn't all beer and skittles, 590 : 10
it takes l. to love l., 728 : 5
it would be l., 605 : 22
itself is sheer knowing, 867 : 12
journey of l., 140 : 10
joy of l. is variety. 352 : 13
jump the l. to come, 236 : 22
jury passing on l., 227 : 31
keep pure both l. and art, 79 : 13
keep way of the tree of l., 7 : 13
lag-end of my l., 205 : 1
large as l. twice as natural, 613 : 17
Last Abode is L., 132 : 1
last hour of my l., 346 : 2
last of l. best, 544 : 8
lasted the rest of my l., 611 : 10
lay down l. for friends, 45 : 25
lay hold on eternal l., 51 : 3
leaves of l. falling, 516 : 5
length of l. leading among inquiries, 124 : 2
let thy l. be sincere, 35 : 6
liberty pursuit of happiness, 387 : 9
light l. pleasure pain, 614 : 17
light love l., 393 : 5
light of l., 45 : 4
light of whole l. dies, 670 : 8
like a dome of many-colored glass, 469 : 16
like a froward child, 302 : 19
like Japanese picture, 645 : 15
like living l. over, 348 : 17
like runners pass on torch of l., 100 : 15
like stroll on beach, 558 : 8
literature war between l. and death, 861 : 18
little l. rounded with sleep, 248 : 13
little needed to make happy l., 125 : 11
live all days of your l., 323 : 16
live l. he has imagined, 560 : 16
live l. not simple, 816 : 18
live l. through is not like crossing field, 934 : 12
live out thy l. as light, 634 : 6
lived forwards, 552 : 10
lived half l. in Paris, 752 : 13
lived in scene it composes, 769 : 15
lived l. talking at street corners, 811 : 7
lived on silver screens, 839 : 3
lively form of death, 177 : 1
London this moment, 781 : 15
long disease my l., 338 : 11
long for another l., 734 : 7
long l. better than figs, 240 : 16
long littleness of l., 795 : 1
looking out from eyes of doe, 823 : 9
lose l. shall find it, 39 : 38
lost in the living, 806 : 15
love an episode in man's l., 417 : 12
love anterior to l., 606 : 11
love l. just the same, 847 : 5
love l. poor as it is, 560 : 18

Life (*continued*)
love of wisdom guide of l., 407 : 17
love only business in l., 453 : 18
love the history of woman's l., 417 : 12
love to woman is l. or death, 670 : 2
loveth her loveth l., 35 : 1
lust for l., 600 : 3
luxuries of l., 519 : 10
making ends meet in l., 776 : 4
man lives l. of epoch, 755 : 7
mankind fleet of l. like leaves, 82 : 9
man's l. cheap as beast's, 233 : 21
many-colored l. he drew, 351 : 10
marble and mud, 503 : 18
married to sea, 741 : 12
married to single l., 292 : 11
material of l., 784 : 22
may perfect be, 256 : 20
meant to be lived, 786 : 14
measured l. with coffee spoons, 803 : 13
medicine for l. which has fled, 65 : 15
memory without pain, 74 : 7
messed up l. for nothing, 809 : 19
mine honor is my l., 193 : 33
miserable mortals flame with l., 59 : 5
money as means to l., 783 : 10
money preserves l., 312 : 22
more abundant l., 779 : 12
more lost than l., 118 : 10
more sweet than painted pomp, 210 : 23
more than he slew in his l., 12 : 21
most loathed worldly l., 228 : 21
most momentous thing in l., 65 : 14
much too far out all my l., 856 : 16
my l. belongs to world, 902 : 7
my l. has gone, 906 : 9
my l. is preserved, 8 : 26
my l. my joy, 168 : 2
my l. poem I would have writ, 558 : 24
my lines and l. are free, 268 : 21
my poems naughty my l. pure, 118 : 21
my way of l. is fallen, 239 : 31
mystery of l., 464 : 7
near bone sweetest, 560 : 19
never know what l. means till you die, 545 : 14
never to have drawn breath of l., 715 : 19
never turn back on l., 786 : 14
new era in l. from book, 559 : 34
new l. begins, 140 : 7
new l. blossoms in ruins, 414 : 2
new l. when sin no more, 552 : 22
nightmare L.-in-Death was she, 434 : 19
no bonds attached him to l., 142 : 23
no life but death, 177 : 1
no l. by others' death, 202 : 8
no l. lives forever, 633 : 22
no l. moves in empty passageways, 74 : 1
no man loses other l. than that he lives, 124 : 7
no man loves l. like old, 75 : 21
no no no l., 235 : 18
no rock bottom to l., 888 : 3
no wealth but l., 572 : 17
nobody write l. of man, 354 : 25
nor love thy l. nor hate, 287 : 30
not cheap but sacred, 499 : 1

Life (*continued*)
not doing a sum, 644 : 13
not get what can from l., 664 : 15
not giving l. but risking l., 870 : 10
not keep advantages of l., 736 : 10
not l. alone makes man, 853 : 9
not L. for which they stand, 618 : 17
not long l. by fire, 696 : 14
not parson teaches conduct, 645 : 6
not take his own l., 83 : 16
not to fancy what were fair in l., 543 : 4
nothing give up l., 873 : 7
nothing in his l., 236 : 14
nothing much to lose, 692 : 9
novel attempt to represent l., 652 : 11
now I live now l. is done, 177 : 10
now is immortal l., 662 : 20
O death in l., 531 : 4
O for l. of sensations, 479 : 3
o' the building, 238 : 5
object of l. something valuable, 422 : 15
observation of human l., 565 : 15
occupations few tranquil l., 124 : 20
ocean of l., 512 : 10
odds l., 320 : 22
o'er ills o' l. victorious, 411 : 7
of humanity may end, 765 : 1
of jealousy, 231 : 2
of law not logic, 643 : 14
of l. he only is deserving, 396 : 25
of man heroic poem, 472 : 9
of man solitary, 264 : 17
of mortal breath, 511 : 11
of peoples and humanity, 602 : 8
of poor man in mean cottage, 35 : 39
of Riley, 922 : *n* 9
of significant soil, 808 : 9
of simplicity independence and magnanimity, 559 : 9
of soul, 344 : 9
of this world, 132 : 7
old age crown of l., 99 : 10
on earth passes away, 4 : 1
on this unavailing star, 711 : 7
one damned thing after another, 756 : 4
one draught of l., 607 : 17
one entrance into l., 34 : 19
one in l. and death are we, 628 : 14
one l. to lose for country, 401 : 9
one long struggle in dark, 100 : 14
only end of l., 668 : 2
only one happiness in l., 504 : 15
ornament l. in fleeting way, 413 : 29
our l. became one, 849 : 9
out of ashes l. again, 660 : 10
out of it are the issues of l., 23 : 9
outlive his l. half a year, 222 : 10
over my long l., 697 : 3
over there behind shelf, 605 : 22
part with l. cheerfully, 124 : 27
perceivers of terror of l., 498 : 21
perfect interpreter of l., 794 : 11
perfected by death, 507 : 1
perfection of l. or work, 716 : 7
philosophy you leader of l., 98 : 24
piece of buffoonery, 723 : 20
poem part of sense of l., 769 : 22
poet gives l. to fictions, 769 : 14
pond's stillness pocked with l., 904 : 7
present l. a diversion and sport, 132 : 1

Life (*continued*)
price l. exacts for peace, 842 : 14
problem with right foot and l., 902 : 5
progress from want to want, 355 : 21
progress to fuller l., 725 : 3
prolong l. only when you shorten miseries, 876 : 6
prose of human l., 508 : 25
protracted is protracted woe, 351 : 20
protracting l. not deduct from death, 101 : 5
psychology connecting with l., 758 : 11
public l. crown of career, 753 : 9
public l. situation of power, 372 : 7
pulse of l. stood still, 330 : 6
pulse of modern l. economic, 763 : 1
pure in l. free from sin, 107 : 11
purpose of human l., 698 : 1
question whether you have enough l., 644 : 6
ran gaily as Thames, 586 : 1
rarely find a happy l., 106 : 13
rationalism renounces l., 784 : 11
reason the l. of the law, 171 : 21
refreshment of inner l., 598 : 14
rejoice in l. mark of Greek spirit, 723 : 14
religion reaction on l., 650 : 3
religious feeling toward l., 728 : 10
relinquish l. for good of country, 420 : 14
rest of his dull l., 263 : 2
resurrection and the l., 45 : 13
resurrection unto eternal l., 56 : 13
reverence for l., 756 : 16
reward of labor is l., 618 : 14
rich for others, 839 : 8
right to dignified l., 774 : 8
rights to a better l., 666 : 22
Roman's l. Roman's arms, 488 : 16
rounded with a sleep, 248 : 13
rover's l., 569 : 20
rule of l. from tonight, 694 : 7
runs on road strange, 569 : 3
sated with banquet of l., 101 : 4
save l. shall lose it, 39 : 38
saw l. steadily saw it whole, 584 : 8
science of l. like hall, 551 : 15
scientific truth woven into l., 509 : 3
scraped l. with fine-tooth comb, 889 : 5
scraping on surface of l., 632 : 1
sea not loved by one whose l. married to it, 741 : 12
seas of l. like wine, 311 : 23
secret l. of belly and bone, 883 : 11
sedentary l. sin, 659 : 1
see into l. of things, 423 : 11
seek not l. of immortals, 71 : 28
self-evolving circle, 501 : *n* 7
sense of what l. means, 650 : 7
set before you l. and death, 11 : 22
set gray l., 529 : 3
set l. at pin's fee, 219 : 13
set my l. on any chance, 238 : 16
set my l. upon cast, 187 : 32
sex pattern of l. process, 689 : 19
shadow of death, 275 : 13, 632 : 9
shall one retrace his l., 721 : 8
shape of l., 784 : 22
sharpened l. commands course, 601 : 11
she is mine for l., 896 : 2

Life (*continued*)
short l. in saddle, 696 : 14
short quiet hours few, 573 : 1
similar to that here below, 734 : 7
sin to prefer l. to honor, 122 : 14
slits the thin-spun l., 280 : 15
smooth road of l., 360 : 24
so short craft so long, 144 : 8
so was it when l. began, 425 : 7
soul the captain of l., 103 : 1
souls with clear vision of l., 704 : 12
sound which tells of l., 441 : *n* 1
space of l. between, 475 : 15
spare all I have take l., 329 : 12
spend l. your own way, 816 : 9
spirit giveth l., 49 : 11
staff of l. bread, 319 : *n* 4
staff of my l., 169 : 12
stands brunt of l., 76 : 20
start l. with good books, 689 : 14
state have possibility of l., 84 : 15
stir within another's l., 901 : 12
story of my l., 229 : 27
stream of subjective l., 648 : 12
strenuous l., 686 : 12
struck on death, 507 : 16
struggle for l., 515 : 2
struggle not warfare, 631 : 4
struggling for l. in the water, 353 : 26
subtle demonisms of l., 570 : 13
succession of preludes, 464 : 17
suicide is about l., 910 : 16
sunny side of l., 775 : 11
sunset of l. gives lore, 443 : 14
sunshine of my l., 916 : 13
superior powers direct l., 673 : 2
surging immensity of l., 518 : 7
sweet courtesies of l., 360 : 24
take honor and my l. is done, 193 : 33
take l. easy, 712 : 1
take l. strivingly, 649 : 5
taken us round obstacle, 734 : 9
taking l. by throat, 750 : 8
taking l. without blood, 701 : 2
tale of human l., 375 : 3
tatty wreckage of my l., 911 : 8
teaches us to be less harsh, 395 : 12
teaching for l., 6 : 1
tedious as twice-told tale, 202 : 1
that breathes with breath, 528 : 2
that dares send challenge, 292 : 9
that they might have l., 45 : 10
that which men call death, 77 : 21
the L. that feeling, 911 : 4
the Lord is the strength of my l., 18 : 11
the old Sabines knew, 104 : 7
the only sanction of l., 703 : 8
the way the truth and the l., 45 : 22
theater of man's l., 179 : 4
theory of poetry theory of l., 768 : 24
therefore choose l., 11 : 22
think l. too long, 316 : 11
thin-spun l., 280 : 15
this alone l. joy empire, 467 : 10
this l. enough, 821 : 3
thought the slave of l., 205 : 10
threatened with suffocation, 834 : 4
three passions governed l., 738 : 6
thrill of l. along keel, 511 : 7
through creatures, 335 : 13
tides and l. of man, 672 : 20
till storm of l. past, 350 : 12
time of l. is short, 205 : 8

Life (*continued*)
time of your l., 875 : 5
time stuff l. made of, 347 : 26
time's fool, 205 : 10
tired of London tired of l., 355 : 26
to beautify l. give it object, 671 : 21
to neighbor's creed lent, 493 : 14
to sovereign power, 528 : 5
today first day of rest of l., 925 : 19
tomorrow's l. is too late, 119 : 1
too short to bore selves, 657 : 25
too short to waste, 494 : 1
too strong for you, 728 : 5
took a man's l. with him, 472 : 13
totality of functions, 429 : 14
tough proposition, 757 : 12
travel by train to see l., 817 : 17
treasured up to l. beyond l., 281 : 24
tree of l. in garden, 6 : 19
Tree of L. middle tree, 285 : 14
tree of our l., 791 : 3
trifles make sum of l., 549 : 10
truth about l., 863 : 3
tugging at perverse l., 873 : 8
twenty years in woman's l., 84 : 14
two things aim at in l., 711 : 4
unbought grace of l., 373 : 23
understand l. at forty, 705 : 11
understood backwards, 552 : 10
unexamined l. not worth living, 83 : 12
ungraspable phantom of l., 570 : 4
use first part of l., 315 : 10
useless l. is early death, 395 : 9
uttered part of man's l., 472 : 12
vagrant gypsy l., 760 : 16
vale of l., 362 : 12
variety's spice of l., 376 : 22
veil those who live call l., 467 : *n* 2
very effective therapist, 789 : 14
vicissitudes of l., 679 : 1
voyage of their l., 217 : 5
warmed hands before fire of l., 443 : 1
water of l., 837 : 11
way that leadeth to l., 38 : 15
we are splendid manifestation of l., 884 : 2
We give l. to everything, 131 : 13
weary pilgrimage, 267 : 19
weathered storms of l., 692 : 17
web of our l., 227 : 16
weight and pain of l., 75 : 14
welcome O l., 777 : 18
well spent is long, 152 : 5
well used happy death, 152 : 4
well-written l. rare, 472 : 3
what am I L., 760 : 21
what gives l. value, 863 : 3
what good the good of your l., 864 : 6
what is l., 581 : 15
what is l. a madness, 273 : 2
what is l. if full of care, 732 : 9
what is l. without love, 413 : 13
what is our l., 173 : 1
what is the prime of l., 84 : 14
what is your l., 52 : 3
what l. is there without Aphrodite, 62 : 3
what makes l. so sweet, 608 : 1
what signifies l. o' man, 409 : 14
what you think of this l., 215 : 4
what's a l., 267 : 19
wheels of weary l., 303 : 16

Life (*continued*)
when I consider l., 303 : 10
when l. is burdensome, 78 : 16
when love and l. fair, 676 : 9
where is l. lost in living, 806 : 15
wherever l. ends it is all there, 164 : 11
while l. there's hope, 96 : 14, 98 : 18
while you do not know l., 68 : 26
who enjoys not l., 274 : 13
whose l., 901 : 12
why l. all labor be, 528 : 16
why should a dog have l., 235 : 18
wine of l. is drawn, 238 : 7
winged l. destroy, 404 : 18
wish l. be pure freedom, 870 : 8
with l. all other passions fly, 440 : 4
with work which bores you l. hell, 725 : 2
without him live no l., 287 : 20
without industry guilt, 573 : 7
woke found l. duty, 555 : 23
wonder of earth and l., 821 : 3
words have longer l. than deeds, 72 : 4
worth living, 703 : 9
write l. with exactness, 354 : *n* 11
wrung l. dry for your lips, 632 : 21
you take my l., 200 : 20
young l. is before us, 134 : 3
Lifeblood, book l. of master spirit, 281 : 24
curiosity l. of civilization, 758 : 3
heresy l. of religions, 726 : 9
of our enterprise, 204 : 28
seemed to sip, 434 : 22
Life-form, each carries own l., 754 : 5
indeterminable, 754 : 5
Life-in-Death, nightmare L. was she, 434 : 19
Life-lie, take l. away take happiness, 600 : 2
Lifeline, throw out the l., 670 : 7
Lifelong toil till lump be leaven, 542 : 5
Life-melody, missing part of l., 573 : 6
Lifepreservers there are none, 829 : 14
Life's a pleasant institution, 630 : 4
a pudding full of plums, 630 : 4
a tough proposition, 757 : 12
brief span forbids us, 107 : 2
business terrible choice, 545 : 12
but a walking shadow, 240 : 4
common way, 425 : 23
dim windows of soul, 407 : 10
dull round, 355 : *n* 8
enchanted cup, 457 : 12
fighting line, 743 : 10
fitful fever, 238 : 19
gymnasium, 577 : 1
here at l. end, 717 : 9
I know my l. a pain, 251 : 7
love o' l. young day, 482 : 13
meaning eluded me, 847 : 5
not a paragraph, 829 : 6
nourisher in l. feast, 237 : 21
old death new, 546 : 4
our l. star, 426 : 14
outcast from l. feast, 777 : 15
page, 457 : 10
pay glad l. arrears, 544 : 22
perhaps the only riddle, 630 : 5
poor play is o'er, 337 : 7
prose, 610 : 8
spirit that on l. rough sea, 178 : 6

Life's (*continued*)
travel on l. common way, 425 : 23
uncertain voyage, 243 : 9
under thy own l. key, 227 : 9
unresting sea, 519 : 8
washed in l. river, 403 : 14
Lifetime burning in every moment, 807 : 23
friendship last a l., 624 : 17
knotting undoing fishnet, 894 : 4
lamps not lit in our l., 699 : 7
live out l. of God, 570 : 6
not l. of one man only, 807 : 23
nothing completed in l., 823 : 21
of happiness hell, 680 : 16
once in a l., 793 : 14
Liffeying waters of, 778 : 5
Lift and loosen old foundations, 761 : 10
every voice and sing, 733 : 5
her with care, 485 : 21
him alive over gullies, 901 : 14
lamp beside golden door, 664 : 10
me as wave leaf cloud, 467 : 20
my soul to heaven, 248 : 25
not painted veil, 467 : *n* 2
people from dust, 494 : 17
people who l., 670 : 1
thou up the light of thy countenance, 17 : 15
unto thee l. hands, 458 : 20
up mine eyes, 22 : 4
up your heads O ye gates, 18 : 9
us as he goes, 600 : 25
waters l. their bosoms, 226 : 2
yesterday almost impossible to l., 878 : 20
your pack, 691 : 15
Lifted, hath not l. his soul unto vanity, 18 : 8
nevermore, 526 : 20
sliding from l. oar, 873 : 16
Lifting, help by l. his heart, 838 : 12
rises by l. others, 615 : 6
Light a glory a fair cloud, 435 : 27
a little warmth a little l., 617 : 3
a little while is l., 45 : 17
afraid of l. all of us, 599 : 15
against after-sunset l., 711 : 11
all the l. I have, 851 : 2
all was l., 340 : 6
and life pleasure pain, 614 : 17
and will aspire, 189 : 8
angel of l., 560 : 26
angels progeny of l., 286 : 22
appareled in celestial l., 426 : 10
armor of l., 47 : 29
around the body, 905 : 16
a-roving by l. of moon, 460 : 5
at end of tunnel, 891 : *n* 2
at night faith in l., 726 : 4
be not darkened, 27 : 24
be the earth, 76 : 4
because it lendeth l., 174 : 13
better to l. one candle, 786 : *n* 4
beyond our lights, 822 : 10
black as if bereaved of l., 403 : 6
body changed to l., 929 : 6
breaks where no sun shines, 886 : 13
bringeth to l. the shadow of death, 15 : 31
broke upon brain, 459 : 23
buried under chains, 842 : 1
burning and shining l., 44 : 37
by her own radiant l., 279 : 22

Light (*continued*)
by l. of moon, 928 : *n* 3
candle and put it under bushel, 37 : 6
candle of understanding, 34 : 6
candle to the sun, 298 : 20
carrying you into fields of l., 76 : 3
certain slant of l., 604 : 18
children of l., 43 : 31, 587 : 3
children of l. and day, 50 : 19
cold l. and hot shade, 405 : 15
colossal figures seeded l., 861 : 2
comes from thine eyes, 918 : 18
commands all l. all influence, 260 : 17
common as l. is love, 467 : 5
consider how l. is spent, 282 : 15
convenient l. switch, 852 : 1
danced by l. of moon, 550 : 10
darkness and l. alike to thee, 22 : 18
dawn's early l., 446 : 1
dear as l. and life, 410 : 18
dies before thy word, 340 : 28
dies suddenly or in glory, 900 : 13
dim religious l., 278 : 26
doth seize my brain, 402 : 15
doth trample on my days, 299 : 8
echo and l. unto eternity, 468 : 23
enough for wot I've to do, 547 : 5
everlasting L., 619 : 16
every hour of l. dark, 576 : 14
exact day labor l. denied, 282 : 16
excelleth darkness, 26 : 18
excess of l., 363 : 2
existence brief crack of l., 846 : 2
fade from eyes, 735 : *n* 1
fade into l. of common day, 426 : 15
fails on winter's afternoon, 808 : 16
faintly muddy l., 796 : 1
falls and fills, 873 : 16
falls the way light fell, 795 : 12
fantastic round, 279 : 14
fantastic toe, 277 : 20
fierce l. beats on throne, 534 : 1
flash of l. cut across sky, 885 : 7
focused by mirrors, 652 : *n* 3
former l. restore, 232 : 14
forward the L. Brigade, 533 : 10
freedom's holy l., 514 : 13
from grave to l., 311 : 2
gains make heavy purses, 177 : 14
garmented in l., 468 : 7
gates of l., 286 : 25
gives a lovely l., 822 : 17
gives l. in darkness, 185 : 12
gladsome l. of jurisprudence 172 : 1
gleams an instant, 866 : 13
gleams and is gone, 587 : 13
God guideth to His l., 131 : 16
God is l., 52 : 19
God l. of heavens and earth, 131 : 16
God shows sufficient l., 545 : 7
God's eldest daughter, 276 : 18
God's first creature l., 285 : *n* 1
gold and silver l., 712 : 15
golden lamps in green l., 297 : 9
gone into world of l., 299 : 7
gospel l. first dawned, 361 : 19
green l., 816 : 11
guide by l. of reason, 678 : 2
hail holy l., 285 : 4
half l. half shade, 529 : 2
half-believers, 585 : 22
have l. of life, 45 : 4
he is angel of l., 560 : 26
heaven to day denies, 459 : 13

Light (*continued*)
heaven's l. forever shines, 469 : 16
here kindled, 265 : 13
Hesperus entreats thy l., 255 : 12
hop l. ladies, 662 : 17
I am l. of the world, 45 : 4
if l. in thee be darkness, 37 : 19
if once we lose this l., 255 : 16
if vital l. inhere, 606 : 10
in despite of l. keep us together, 252 : 21
in minds of others, 769 : 16
in present l. flames, 745 : 8
in ragged luck, 663 : 8
in room by artificial l., 899 : 1
in the dust lies dead, 470 : 1
in this waning of l., 874 : 9
in which freedom lives, 851 : 10
infant crying for l., 532 : 10
inner l. will shine forth, 397 : *n* 6
is all, 873 : 20
is lion comes to drink, 767 : 19
is shadow of God, 275 : 13
it giveth l. unto all, 37 : 6
judged in l. of final issue, 88 : 21
lead kindly L., 490 : 6
lead me from darkness to l., 56 : 20
leading from l. to l., 512 : 12
Let the Big L. in, 831 : 17
let there be l., 6 : 10
let your l. shine, 37 : 6
liberty learning, 502 : 16
lie l. lie l., 625 : 20
life and l. be thine, 540 : 5
lift up the l. of thy countenance, 17 : 15
like gleaming taper's l., 368 : 12
listened, 874 : 12
little drops of l., 276 : 4
little trim little, 629 : 19
live and love in God's l., 155 : 2
live out thy life as l., 634 : 6
lived l. in spring, 585 : 11
long l. shakes, 530 : 26
love in the l., 850 : 10
love life, 393 : 5
made l. of it, 40 : 13
man l. for man, 839 : 6
man like l. kindled and put out, 70 : 7
many hands make l. work, 160 : 31
mass times speed of l. squared, 763 : *n* 2
men of inward l., 291 : 26
mocks at it and sets it l., 194 : 6
more by number than your l., 251 : 1
more l., 397 : 16
my burden is l., 39 : 8
neither heat nor l., 262 : 6
neither joy nor love nor l., 587 : 16
night shadow of l., 632 : 9
no darkness into l. without emotion, 754 : 14
no l. but darkness visible, 283 : 6
noose of l., 516 : 1
not leave my hand without l., 797 : 6
not to wise the l., 671 : 11
of bright world dies, 670 : 8
of fuller day, 566 : 11
of Light, 55 : 3
of light beguile, 190 : 11
of my understanding, 316 : 4
of setting suns, 423 : 13
of step and heart, 739 : 14
of the body, 37 : 18

Light (*continued*)
of the world, 37 : 6, 45 : 4
of things, 423 : 6
of thy sword, 484 : 1
of whole life dies, 670 : 8
old age level l., 822 : 9
on dark theme trace verses of l., 100 : 10
once set is our little l., 250 : 3
one small candle l. a thousand, 265 : 13
out of hell leads to l., 284 : 17
path of America, 729 : 11
people have seen a great l., 29 : 15
people in darkness saw great l., 37 : 2
perturbation of l., 864 : 1
place void of all l., 140 : 21
pleasing dreams slumbers l., 431 : 4
poets l. lamps, 606 : 10
power and l., 902 : 2
prime work of God, 285 : *n* 1
progeny of l., 286 : 22
pure and endless l., 299 : 6
purple l. of Love, 362 : 21
put out the l., 232 : 14, 688 : 2, 748 : 11
radiant l. rests on men, 72 : 2
rage against dying of l., 887 : 4
rather l. candles than curse darkness, 786 : *n* 4
relume, 232 : 14
river of crystal l., 666 : 16
roving by l. of moon, 460 : 5
rule of streaming l., 279 : 21
sadder l. than moon, 513 : 20
seeking light, 190 : 11
servants of l., 610 : 11
shaft of l. in darkness, 891 : 15
she loves, 533 : 21
she treads on it so l., 189 : 15
shines over land and sea, 745 : 8
shineth in darkness, 44 : 18
shower of l. poesy, 475 : 12
shuddering in gloaming l., 626 : 21
so l. a foot, 193 : 2
someday inner l. shine forth, 397 : *n* 6
speed far faster than l., 742 : 1
stand in your own l., 160 : 27
steeps of l., 536 : 3
strikes sultan's turret with l., 515 : 16
strong shadow where much l., 394 : 11
suffusion from that l., 436 : 1
sun gives l. soon as he rises, 348 : 14
suns to l. me rise, 336 : 19
sweetness and l., 321 : 14, 588 : 18
teach l. to counterfeit a gloom, 278 : 20
that cometh from her wisdom, 34 : 20
that is in me, 490 : 19
that let astray 409 : 5
that lies in woman's eyes, 447 : 4
that loses night that wins, 632 : 8
that never was, 427 : 17
that shineth more and more, 23 : 8
the first light of evening, 769 : 2
the Lord is my l., 18 : 11
the true l., 44 : 20
thickens and crow makes wing, 238 : 21
things holy profane grave and l., 264 : 16
those that rebel against the l., 16 : 9

Light (*continued*)
threshold of waking l., 906 : 9
through the word named day, 135 : 2
thy l. is come, 31 : 23
thy l. relume, 232 : 14
time's glory bring truth to l., 189 : 23
to guide, 427 : 13
to lighten Gentiles, 42 : 31
to them in darkness, 42 : 26
to those in darkness, 157 : 4
to whom God assigns no l., 131 : 17
too much l. often blinds, 380 : 4
tracings of eternal l., 412 : 11
travel l., 870 : 2
trifles l. as air, 231 : 7
tripped l. fantastic, 698 : 14
truth not sought for comes to l., 91 : 4
truth will come to l., 148 : *n* 1
truths kindle l. for truths, 100 : 11
two ways of spreading l., 700 : 14
unbarred the gates of l., 286 : 25
unconscious not only dark but l., 754 : 10
unto my path, 22 : 2
unveiled her peerless l., 285 : 25
upon them hath the l. shined, 29 : 15
us down in honor or dishonor, 522 : 12
Vesper now raising his l., 102 : 8
void of l., 283 : 12
waited for the l., 729 : 5
walk while ye have l., 45 : 17
was l. from heaven, 409 : 5
way which opens into l., 512 : *n* 4
we fear in the l., 100 : 22
we shall need no other l., 397 : *n* 6
we sought shining, 587 : 12
what l. is to painting, 670 : 9
what l. through yonder window, 192 : 2
when my l. low, 532 : 5
when our brief l. has set, 101 : 18
which lighteth every man, 44 : 20
white l. of morning, 928 : 14
why rise because 'tis l., 252 : 21
wife make heavy husband, 201 : 7
winning make prize light, 247 : 23
withdrawn which once he wore, 513 : 7
within that's genius, 608 : 8
world rolls into l., 513 : 2
Lighted fools way to dusty death, 240 : 4
Lighten our darkness, 55 : 9
Lightened, thundered and l., 81 : 11
weight of world l., 423 : 10
Lightens, cease to be ere it l., 192 : 13
Lighter than cork danced on waves, 673 : 14
town is l. than vanity, 302 : 5
Lightest, movements of l. atom, 397 : 17
sovereign is the l., 89 : 28
word harrow soul, 219 : 18
Lightfoot, many a l. lad, 691 : 13
Light-hearted, afoot and l., 575 : 9
Lighthouse, below the l. top, 434 : 7
took sitivation at l., 546 : 28
Lighthouses, ocean under pulsation of l., 798 : 13
Lighting a little hour or two, 516 : 9
Lightland, rise in heaven's l., 5 : 4
set in western l., 5 : 5
Lightly draws its breath, 423 : 3
earth rest l. on you, 134 : 28
Lightly (*continued*)
entered into unadvisedly or l., 56 : 6
hid deepest understood, 899 : 11
lie l. gentle earth, 263 : 7
rest, 76 : 4
soul of my youth taken flight, 789 : 15
tread l. she is near, 674 : 14
we esteem too l., 384 : 13
Lightning, bottled l., 547 : 16
countenance like l., 41 : 29
does the work, 626 : 7
done like l., 255 : 8
earthquakes with thunder l., 622 : 19
fateful l., 566 : 4
flashed the living l., 334 : 10
he thence had riven, 462 : 15
in collied night, 195 : 23
in thunder l. or in rain, 235 : 21
makes awful l., 507 : 16
mirth like flash of l., 326 : 21
outstare the l., 241 : 13
pilot, 623 : 9
Satan as l. fall, 43 : 11
scratch head with l., 623 : 5
strikes mountaintop, 107 : 21
Superman the l., 657 : 13
too like the l., 192 : 13
vain to look for defense against l., 112 : 7
zigzag l. stands high, 928 : 18
Lightning's hour, 860 : 7
Lightnings, four l. zigzag from me, 928 : 21
in the splendor of the moon, 528 : 29
veiling l. of song 469 : 8
Light-o'-love lady known as Lou, 752 : 5
Light's, I live in l. extreme, 874 : 5
Lights around the shore, 601 : 23
Father of l., 51 : 29
fled garlands dead, 447 : 8
godfathers of heaven's l., 190 : 12
guttering low, 691 : 15
highest candle l. dark, 769 : 3
love is keeper of warm l., 74 : 23
mansion where we can turn off l., 796 : 2
moon l. up the earth, 63 : 6
Northern L. seen sights, 752 : 6
of the world, 375 : 23
ridicule one of principal l., 325 : 5
see how it is without l., 796 : 2
that do mislead the morn, 228 : 28
turn up l., 699 : 20
water closing over sleepy l., 879 : 9
your l. burning, 43 : 21
Light-winged dryad, 476 : 22
Like a winter my absence, 245 : 8
ape how l. to us, 95 : 3
but oh how different, 427 : 27
doth quit like, 229 : 8
find l. again, 430 : 15
God pairs l. with l., 60 : 21
how do you l. your blueeyed boy, 828 : 13
I don't l. you Sabidius, 119 : 3
I know what I l., 736 : 2
look upon his l. again, 218 : 16
me from heels to head, 668 : 12
more ye see better l. it, 722 : 4
never met man I didn't l., 766 : 6
never met one I didn't l., 766 : 6
not fair terms, 198 : 28
nothing anyone obliged to l., 653 : 4
of each thing, 190 : 13
Like (*continued*)
one that stands on promontory, 186 : 10
people like priest, 33 : 8
poor cat i' the adage, 237 : 2
same things is friendship, 102 : 26
tell me what you l., 573 : 5
those who admire us, 293 : 32
to an hermit poor, 172 : 7
to like, 60 : *n* 9
to see it lap miles, 605 : 18
upon earth there is not his l., 17 : 8
very l. a whale, 222 : 20
very very l. me, 668 : 12
want it most l. it least, 341 : 22
what he loves never l. too much, 256 : 4
will to like, 159 : 10
Liked book the better, 371 : 11
it not and died, 251 : 2
several women, 248 : 3
way it walks, 697 : 1
Likely impossibility preferable, 88 : 19
man in preference to rich, 70 : 16
we are all l. to go astray, 74 : 22
Likeness, devil erected in man's l., 582 : 3
gods in l. of men, 46 : 11
grow into l. of bad men, 86 : 1
in l. not lion, 794 : 5
let us make man after our l., 6 : 13
of filly foal, 196 : 12
very l. of roasted crab, 196 : 12
Likenesses, they are l. of Him, 4 : 3
Likes, doesn't know what he l., 831 : 3
nobody l. man who brings bad news, 74 : 11
Likewise, go and do l., 43 : 15
Liking, all love all l. all delight, 266 : 21
grounds other than l., 565 : 26
happy l. what they do, 361 : 1
saves me trouble of l., 441 : 2
Lilac and brown hair, 806 : 2
bush tall-growing, 751 : *n* 3
heart-leaves of l., 751 : 8
in me, 751 : 8
lost l., 806 : 6
time, 772 : 22
Lilacs last in dooryard bloomed, 576 : 2
out of dead land, 804 : 26
Lilies and languors of virtue, 632 : 11
beauty of the l., 566 : 5
breaking golden l., 507 : 23
crowned with l., 823 : 12
feed among the l., 28 : 11
handfuls of l. to scatter, 105 : 25
of the field, 38 : 4
peacocks and l., 572 : 14
roses and white l. grow, 250 : 5
silent war of l., 189 : 17
that fester, 245 : 6
three l. in her hand, 601 : 13
twisted braids of l., 280 : 3
wheat set about with l., 28 : 19
Lilting house, 886 : 19
I've heard them l., 368 : 2
Lily, how sweet the l. grows, 452 : 6
maid of Astolat, 534 : 11
of the valleys, 28 : 4
on lily o'erlace sea, 543 : 24
paint the l., 202 : 5
poppy or a l., 628 : 7
scarlet l. flamed, 696 : 11
take silver and buy l., 133 : *n* 1

Lily (*continued*)
thick with l. and rose, 618 : 5
trembles to a l., 640 : 2
water l. bloom, 528 : 27
Lily-livered boy, 239 : 30
Lima, curious traveler from L., 363 : 21
Limb, feels life in every l., 423 : 3
neither heat affection l., 228 : 16
of Satan, 623 : 10
sound wind and l., 170 : 23
tail's a l., 830 : 12
Limbecks foul as hell, 245 : 19
Limber, endures l. and firm, 864 : 7
Limbo large and broad, 285 : 8
Limbs, fair l. of the tree, 634 : 5
gentle l. undress, 433 : 31
his l. cold in death, 106 : 7
I the l. and wheel, 581 : 1
lopped l., 873 : 5
melter of l., 61 : 10
of a dismembered poet, 106 : 15
recreant l., 201 : 21
ruddy l. flaming hair, 404 : 16
these l. her provinces, 253 : 11
thy decent l. composed, 335 : 10
young in l. judgment old, 199 : 10
Lime, madeleine soaked in l. flowers, 734 : 1
of love, 266 : 1
tree bower my prison, 433 : 20
Limelight, sit in l., 762 : 7
Limestone quarried near spot, 718 : 2
Limit, fixes solemn l. of Heaven, 76 : 25
horizon l. of sight, 642 : 10
no l. to what novelist attempt, 652 : 13
of becoming mirth, 190 : 21
quiet l. of world, 533 : 28
use me to the l., 687 : 2
what l. to grief for one so dear, 107 : 12
Limitation, civil l. daunts utterance, 601 : 3
of armaments, 778 : 7
Limitations, in l. the master, 397 : 1
no man climb beyond l., 637 : 9
visible and tangible, 636 : 17
Limitless fire and brimstone, 622 : 13
swelling and l. billows, 435 : 18
Limits, hell hath no l., 184 : 1
no l. but sky, 168 : 22
no l. set to thought, 723 : 15
of own field limits of world, 463 : 4
own appointed l. keep, 596 : 18
stony l. cannot hold love, 192 : 7
truth has its l., 166 : 8
Limns on water writes in dust, 181 : 18
Limousine, one perfect l., 827 : 13
Limp and damp as tendrils, 873 : 17
into scalding grave, 735 : 3
live with lame man learn to l., 120 : 6
Limped, hare l. trembling, 476 : 8
Limping with duty, 90 : 7
Limpopo, greasy L. River, 710 : 3
Limps after in base imitation, 194 : 11
Lincoln, beloved of Abraham L., 728 : 7
greatest best moral personality, 577 : 4
I'm a Ford not a L., 882 : 14
in L. something homely, 502 : 5
land of L. and Pinkham, 828 : 17
man to become attached to, 577 : 3
of our literature, 632 : 2
Old Abe L., 519 : *n* 4
shoveled into tombs, 761 : 8
Lincoln's name close to Washington's, 603 : 3
Line, bottom l. is in heaven, 876 : 1
cadence of a rugged l., 304 : 27
cancel half a l., 517 : 2
creep in one dull l., 333 : 7
custom in all l. of order, 225 : 37
draw l. where God has not, 646 : 5
eats dirt in the l., 825 : 3
embroil about fancied l., 311 : 15
far-flung battle l., 709 : 16
fathom l. could never touch, 203 : 15
fight it out on this l., 589 : 17
hit l. hard, 687 : 5
horizontal l. straight, 471 : 14
I had crossed that l., 593 : 15
in the very first l., 371 : 17
in which force impressed, 313 : 14
is gone out through all the earth, 17 : 28
life's fighting l., 743 : 10
Marlowe's mighty l., 256 : 12
met by color l., 556 : 11
most insincere l. written, 803 : 1
no day without a l., 555 : *n* 2
not a day without a l., 90 : 15
of horizon's growing thin, 874 : 20
second l. sublime third bombast, 118 : 15
Shakespeare never blotted l., 256 : 21
stepped across l., 481 : 2
take us hours maybe, 712 : 20
the l. must terminate, 894 : 4
thin red l. of 'eroes, 578 : *n* 4
thin red-l. streak, 578 : 14
three hundred hours in l., 801 : 17
uniform motion in right l., 313 : 13
upon line, 30 : 13
waiting in l. outside prison, 801 : 15
will stretch out, 239 : 14
write a living l., 256 : 16
Linea, nulla dies sine l., 90 : *n* 5, 555 : *n* 2
Lineaments, molded changing l., 638 : 11
of Gospel books, 184 : 13
of gratified desire, 404 : 20
Lined himself with hope, 206 : 6
Linen, airing dirty l. never masterpiece, 911 : 19
all for l. undulation, 850 : 11
not l. wearing out, 485 : 19
old l. wash whitest, 262 : 1
wash dirty l. at home, 420 : 11
Liner she's a lady, 709 : 8
Lines are fallen unto me, 17 : 24
as l. so loves oblique, 297 : 7
desert of a thousand l., 339 : 24
devour own nature, 906 : 14
drawing no unnecessary l., 729 : 7
in nature few sharp l., 905 : 10
just know your l., 852 : 4
let lord once own happy l., 333 : 13
many l. in dial's center, 207 : 8
my l. and life are free, 268 : 21
silken l. silver hooks, 253 : 2
supply l. guarded by navy, 825 : 6
town crier spoke my l., 221 : 23
zones and meridian l., 613 : 22
Linge, laver son l. sale, 420 : *n* 5
Linger, do not live but l., 258 : 20
out a purposed overthrow, 245 : 3
unhappy l. a space, 797 : 13
Lingered under benign sky, 562 : 7
Lingering bays, 351 : 11
dewdrop, 429 : 11
hoping l. flying, 333 : 23
I alone sit l. here, 299 : 7
longing l. look behind, 362 : 14
winter l. chills May, 368 : 18
Lingers, borrowing only l. it out, 206 : 5
find where last rose l., 107 : 17
no falsehood l. to old age, 75 : 20
one who l. behind, 58 : 9
soul that l. sighing, 691 : 12
wisdom l., 530 : 4
Lingo, unless you know l., 485 : 11
Linguistics an ever eerier area, 856 : 14
Lining, look for silver l., 775 : 10
silver l. on the night, 279 : 17
there's a silver l., 740 : 11
Link, I feel the l. of nature, 287 : 23
silver l. silken tie, 430 : 9
Linked analogies, 570 : 15
sweetness long drawn out, 278 : 6
to radiant angel l., 219 : 22
with one virtue, 459 : 10
Links, golf l. lie so near mill, 757 : 5
Linnet, never tear l. from leaf, 714 : 19
Linnets, pipe but as l., 532 : 1
Linotype, lead effective from l., 865 : 2
Linsey-woolsey brother, 291 : 15
brothers, 340 : 21
Lint, invisible strand of l., 699 : 14
Lintel low to keep out pride, 671 : 12
Lion among ladies, 196 : 24
and fatling together, 29 : 19
and lizard keep, 516 : 11
and unicorn, 929 : 19
as l. woos his brides, 366 : 9
at the door, 929 : 9
be l. to frighten wolves, 154 : 1
beard l. in his den, 430 : 23
devil as roaring l., 52 : 16
every l. comes from den, 5 : 6
first beast like a l., 53 : 7
first l. thought last a bore, 438 : 12
fish and swan, 868 : 5
from his claw can tell a l., 133 : 24
he has heart of a l., 132 : 27
honey in the carcass of the l., 12 : 13
hungry l. grievous roar, 438 : 12
in the way, 25 : 19
in thy house, 35 : 3
Indian of l. bearing, 465 : 6
is in the streets, 25 : 19
lamb at home l. in chase, 423 : 1
light is the l. that comes to drink, 767 : 19
living dog better than dead l., 27 : 15
mated by the l., 227 : 11
not l. but pard, 794 : 5
not more fearful wildfowl than l., 196 : 24
not so fierce as they paint him, 269 : 27
on old stone gates, 528 : 9
prince imitate fox and l., 154 : 1
prince must be l., 119 : *n* 13
righteous are bold as a l., 25 : 27
rouse l. from his lair, 432 : 11
rouse l. than start hare, 203 : 14
shall eat straw, 29 : 19
think l. sleeping because he didn't roar, 412 : 8
thou shalt tread upon the l., 20 : 17
thrown into rage like l., 381 : 13
vapor like bear or l., 241 : 17

Lion (*continued*)
well roared L., 197 : 18
when l. fawns upon lamb, 186 : 20
wine, 491 : 22
wrath of l. wisdom of God, 404 : 3
young l. and the dragon, 20 : 17
Lion-eyes, love like l., 889 : 17
Lion's, hardy as Nemean l. nerve, 219 : 15
imperative roar, 867 : 15
patch l. skin with fox's 119 : 24
saw l. shadow ere himself, 200 : 22
there the l. ruddy eyes, 403 : 13
thou wear l. hide, 201 : 21
Lions, cast Daniel into the den of l., 33 : 3
cocks and l. jocund be, 253 : 15
if l. had hands, 67 : 13
my darling from the l., 18 : 22
no compacts between l. and men, 59 : 8
plucks dead l. by beard, 201 : 13
stronger than l., 13 : 9
young l. roar after prey, 21 : 11
Lip, between cup and l., 259 : 11
contempt and anger of l., 214 : 16
coral l. admires, 272 : 1
language in her l., 227 : 3
not l. or eye beauty call, 333 : 1
of hand of foot of l., 245 : 12
reproof on her l., 482 : 9
stiff upper l., 594 : 5
vermeil-tinctured l., 280 : 1
Lips, apply polished l. to ear, 442 : 16
are dumb, 528 : 17
bee stung, 290 : 1
betwixt her l. and mine, 721 : 4
causing l. of those asleep to speak, 28 : 21
closed l. hurt no one, 120 : *n* 2
coral more red than l., 246 : 1
crimson in l. and cheeks, 193 : 27
eternity was in our l., 240 : 18
fitted in thy l., 24 : 37
flattereth with his l., 24 : 32
her l. suck forth my soul, 184 : 4
here hung those l., 224 : 14
his swords are, 177 : 12
keep thy l. from speaking guile, 18 : 21
kiss my soul through my l., 184 : *n* 3
lay upon thy l., 241 : 21
love at the l., 748 : 8
man of unclean l., 29 : 10
name of God upon l., 358 : 19
of a strange woman drop as honeycomb, 23 : 10
of dying men, 586 : 7
open thou my l., 19 : 18
people of unclean l., 29 : 10
persuasion hung upon l., 360 : 1
poverty to the very l., 232 : 2
profound and fragile l., 829 : 7
put l. to it when dispoged, 547 : 35
red l. not so red, 827 : 6
rosy l. and cheeks, 245 : 18
slughorn to my l. I set, 234 : *n* 3
smile on l. tear in eye, 430 : 20
take O take those l. away, 228 : 28
talk of the l. tendeth to penury, 24 : 3
that are for others, 531 : 4
that touch, 811 : 15
that touch liquor, 718 : 7
touch l. part with tears, 633 : 15
Lips (*continued*)
touch sacred fire, 733 : 9
truth from his l., 370 : 8
until moss reached l., 605 : 14
weary l. I close, 363 : 9
were red looks free, 434 : 19
when her l. I touch, 879 : 10
when I ope my l., 198 : 2
where my Julia's l. smile, 266 : 3
whispering with white l., 457 : 18
wrung life dry for your l., 632 : 21
Lipstick, too much l., 856 : 5
Liquefaction of her clothes, 266 : 22
Liquefies drop by drop, 863 : 14
Liquid, bedewed with l. odors, 107 : 3
dew of youth, 218 : 27
fire, 416 : 6
inventing l. wine, 77 : 6
lapse of murmuring streams, 287 : 4
notes close eye of day, 281 : 9
siftings fall, 804 : 25
Liquidation of British Empire, 746 : 2
Liquidity of investment, 783 : 14
Liquor, bumper of good l., 398 : 26
claret the l. for boys, 356 : 11
corn l. stop victim's watch, 757 : 6
drank l. straight, 868 : 18
good l., 371 : 5
is quicker, 855 : 10
lips that touch l., 718 : 7
livelier l. than Muse, 691 : 17
never brewed, 604 : 13
talks mighty loud, 662 : 13
Liquor's out why clink cannikin 541 : 3
Liquors, hot and rebellious l., 210 : 29
Lisp and wear strange suits, 212 : 20
of leaves, 632 : 7
Lisped, I l. in numbers, 338 : 10
somewhat he l., 145 : 24
to me low delicious word, 575 : 18
Lissom clerical printless toe, 796 : 11
List, I've got a little l., 629 : 6
then the l. is done, 605 : 17
thinning l. of single men, 835 : 6
'Listed, legion never was 'l., 708 : 19
Listen all day to such stuff, 611 : 11
and save, 280 : 3
as I am listening now, 468 : 15
awhile ye nations, 475 : 8
do not l. simply wait, 786 : 3
for dear honor's sake, 280 : 3
fur'z you look or l., 568 : 4
go and l. as thou goest, 141 : 24
gods to him particularly l., 57 : 9
good music people don't l., 675 : 20
heath slowly awake and l., 640 : 10
my children, 512 : 6
not l. to reason, 537 : 1
remain sitting and l., 786 : 3
there's a hell of good universe, 829 : 26
to it and do not hear, 64 : 6
to it growling, 878 : 4
to little bird's voice, 82 : 5
to Muse when unhappy, 857 : 2
to the mockingbird, 599 : 5
to the Revolution, 770 : 16
where thou art sitting, 280 : 3
wind is rising, 793 : 16
wise to l. to the Word, 69 : 26
wish him to l., 647 : 9
you hear the grating roar, 587 : 14
Listened and looked sideways up, 434 : 22
Listened (*continued*)
light l., 874 : 12
soul l. intensely, 428 : 15
Listener, speak to unwilling l., 128 : 2
Listening, and to my l. ear, 428 : *n* 5
disease of not l., 205 : 25
mood seemed to stand, 431 : 6
nightly to l. earth, 325 : 9
planets in stations l., 287 : 1
to himself appears, 333 : 19
Listens, he l. well who takes notes, 141 : 12
like three years' child, 434 : 6
Listeth, wind bloweth where it l., 44 : 32
Lit upon gentle sensitive mind, 714 : 7
Literalists of the imagination, 798 : 11
Literary accomplishments in women, 392 : 11
attempt unfortunate, 357 : 18
craftsmanship, 800 : 1
fellow travelers, 770 : 5
German dives into sentence, 624 : 9
I haven't a l. life, 876 : 21
ideals animate my breast, 652 : *n* 3
improved for l. conversation, 258 : *n* 2
indignation at l. wrongs, 437 : 4
intellectuals at one pole, 865 : 17
lock words in l. storehouse, 695 : 5
man has circle, 731 : 9
man write for his public, 731 : 9
men a priesthood, 472 : 6
nature and civilization l. field, 652 : 4
parole of l. men, 356 : 21
performance, 577 : 12
weather l. speciality, 624 : 10
Literature, all else is l., 659 : 18
analysis of character, 861 : 11
best l. become folk l., 866 : 2
Bible l. not dogma, 703 : 18
books not American l., 536 : 10
Borges can weave l., 843 : 7
classicist in l., 809 : 13
clear and cold, 791 : 9
Clemens was Lincoln of l., 632 : 2
complete statement l., 782 : 2
current l. of day, 620 : 19
defect of modern l., 586 : 8
effort to indemnify, 497 : 33
enfant terrible of l., 620 : 22
for l. call back world of shadows, 796 : 2
gives no man sinecure, 792 : 17
good l. must do good, 692 : 13
great l. allegorical, 742 : 5
great l. expression of heart, 723 : 12
had stopped, 817 : 1
ideas to l. what light is to painting, 670 : 9
impurities of l., 782 : 1
in l. read oldest, 493 : 9
investment of genius, 630 : 23
language charged with meaning, 793 : 8
life before l., 619 : 17
little or great l., 664 : 9
masterwork of l., 586 : 19
memory of nation, 895 : 20
modern American l. from one book, 845 : 5
my mistress, 695 : 1
my utopia, 771 : 1
never pursue l. as trade, 437 : 8
news that stays news, 793 : 9
noble sentiments in bad l., 727 : 12

Literature (*continued*)
not abstract science, 702 : 14
or chickens, 846 : 11
out of life, 632 : 1
patronize polite l., 379 : 16
reduced to essence, 735 : 13
reflects spiritual unity, 895 : 21
remarks are not l., 752 : 12
sanity in ancient l., 586 : 8
substitute for experience, 895 : 19
substitute for religion, 809 : 12
the very essence of l., 861 : 18
to produce a little l., 652 : 6
too intellectual becomes sterile, 861 : 18
transmits experience, 895 : 20
we meditate over l., 884 : 6
when l. overly erudite, 861 : 10
with l. as with law, 525 : 8
without charm no l., 711 : 15
written in American way, 728 : 2
Literatures, effort of l. critical 586 : 15
knowledge of different l., 671 : 20
Lithe, I asked a l. lady, 404 : 11
Litigious terms fat contentions, 281 : 18
Litter, live in layers not on l., 864 : 14
Littérature, beaux sentiments de la l., 727 : *n* 8
tout le reste est l., 659 : *n* 12
Little, a l. I can read, 240 : 15
a l. more than kin, 217 : 31
advantages every day, 348 : 20
better is l. with the fear of the Lord, 24 : 7
better than one of wicked, 203 : 2
black sheep, 708 : 14
body with mighty heart, 207 : 11
Bo-peep, 932 : 3
boy blue, 930 : 12
Boy Blue kissed them, 666 : 17
boys made of, 932 : 12
breezes shiver, 528 : 24
but l. at a time, 323 : 1
candle throws beams, 201 : 4
cargo boats, 709 : 8
child shall lead them, 29 : 19
cousins called back, 608 : 7
creature formed of joy, 407 : 3
creatures everywhere, 781 : 11
dear l. Buttercup, 627 : 9
deeds of kindness, 591 : 8
do great right l. wrong, 200 : 10
do l. about infernal fires, 894 : 9
do or can the best of us, 546 : 5
dogs and all, 234 : 15
drops of water, 591 : 7
every l. makes a mickle, 170 : 9
fall by l. and l., 35 : 31
fire quickly trodden out, 186 : 19
fly, 405 : 6
foxes that spoil the vines, 28 : 8
friend of all the world, 709 : 22
gain l. patch of ground, 223 : 16
girl don't cry, 665 : 9
girls made of, 932 : 13
go l. book, 145 : 7, 773 : 15
goodness in l. finger, 323 : 13
great empire and l. minds, 373 : 8
great grace with l. gift, 92 : 16
great ones eat up l. ones, 243 : 13
group of willful men, 682 : 10
happy if say how much, 209 : 11
have and seek no more, 167 : 6
having been a l. chastised, 34 : 13

Little (*continued*)
here a l. and there a l., 30 : 13
here a l. child I stand, 267 : 1
hills like lambs, 21 : 21
hoard l. hearts great, 534 : 6
horse think it queer, 748 : 6
how l. gained, 532 : *n* 5
how l. one knows oneself, 815 : 11
how l. room we take in death, 272 : 11
how l. we think of other, 626 : 15
hunted hares, 732 : 16
if thou have but a l., 34 : 7
infinite riches in l. room, 183 : 12
is never lacking, 101 : 8
Jack Horner, 929 : 20
Johnny Green, 930 : 14
Lamb who made thee, 403 : 5
lame balloonman, 828 : 11
learning dangerous thing, 332 : 20
life rounded with a sleep, 248 : 13
like l. mice stole in and out, 289 : 21
little grave, 195 : 7
love me l. love me long, 266 : 8, 917 : 12
lovely l. flower is free, 429 : 12
lovely moony night, 406 : 6
man had a little gun, 933 : 12
man like l. kingdom, 215 : 18
man wants but l., 330 : 12, 369 : 12
Match Girl, 505 : 9
Miss Muffet, 932 : 15
monstrous l. voice, 196 : 5
more than kin, 217 : 31
more than little is too much, 204 : 20
much drinking l. thinking, 322 : 1
Namby Pamby's l. rhymes, 331 : 4
nameless acts, 423 : 9
Nature's l. kings, 251 : 6
neat l. sweet l. craft, 629 : 19
needed to make happy life, 125 : 11
nothing l. to him that feels it, 354 : 7
nourishment I get, 794 : 3
nut tree, 932 : 1
O thou of l. faith, 39 : 28
O ye of l. faith, 38 : 25
oh the l. more, 542 : 8
old lady from Dubuque, 824 : *n* 2
old New York, 699 : 17
once set is our l. light, 250 : 3
one l. room an everywhere, 251 : 15
one l. word, 194 : 2
one shall become a thousand, 31 : 24
one-horse town, 622 : 10
philosophy inclineth to atheism, 180 : 17
pig went to market, 930 : 11
plans have no magic, 661 : 3
Polly Flinders, 932 : 4
pot and soon hot, 188 : 36
practice l. proceed to greater, 121 : 6
profits that idle king, 529 : 6
put even l. on l., 61 : 20
safer to know too l., 620 : 5
shall I grace my cause, 229 : 25
shrunk to this l. measure, 216 : 8
snug l. island, 429 : 15
so l. done so much to do, 532 : 15, 672 : 18
sorrows sit and weep, 404 : 12
strokes fell great oaks, 347 : 29
sweeten this l. hand, 239 : 27
there is no l. enemy, 347 : 3
things affect little minds, 501 : 20
things go lessening, 544 : 27

Little (*continued*)
think too l., 304 : 9
this l. world, 194 : 13
those who have too l., 780 : 3
though l. I'll work, 919 : 5
though l. she is fierce, 197 : 3
tight l. island, 429 : 15
tin gods on wheels, 707 : 4
tiny boy, 214 : 29
tiny wit, 234 : 1
to earn, 566 : 9
to have l. is to possess, 64 : 10
to leave is to die a l., 679 : 9
Tom Tucker, 930 : 15
Tommy Tittlemouse, 933 : 19
too l. too late, 816 : 16
touch of Harry, 208 : 2
town of Bethlehem, 619 : 16
toy dog covered with dust, 666 : 17
understand how l. we need, 694 : 6
wanton boys that swim on bladders, 249 : 3
we see in nature, 427 : 29
whatever l. seemed great, 488 : 2
when l. fears grow great, 222 : 13
while is the light, 45 : 17
who are a l. wise, 252 : 14
who knows one side knows l., 508 : 6
with a l. pin, 195 : 3
work a little play, 617 : 3
world made cunningly, 254 : 7
world of childhood, 754 : 11
wretched creature, 346 : 4
yield when taken l. by l., 120 : 2
Littleness, assemblage of sloth sleep and l., 381 : 13
long l. of life, 795 : 1
proof of own l, 473 : 23
Littlenesses, disdaining l., 85 : 17
peering l., 534 : 1
Littlepage, Captain L. overset mind, 663 : 16
Little's, Mrs. L. second son, 846 : 14
Liturgy, from poetry l., 861 : 5
Live a barren sister all your life 195 : 20
a little too wise never l. long, 187 : *n* 3
after so many deaths I l., 269 : 5
age youth not l. together, 917 : 11
alive while thy book l., 256 : 11
all days of your life, 323 : 16
all that l. must die, 218 : 1
all you can, 653 : 9
alone in bee-loud glade, 712 : 4
and die all I have to do, 338 : 16
and die in Aristotle's works, 183 : 19
and die in Dixie, 554 : 2
and die r-r-rich, 549 : 35
and die wi' Charlie, 422 : 19
and help live logic, 898 : 1
and learn, 321 : 9
and let live, 919 : 16
and lie reclined, 528 : 19
and love in God's light, 155 : 2
as if eternal, 83 : *n* 7
as if God beheld you, 114 : 16
as long as you please, 164 : 10
as men not ostriches, 781 : 5
as we can, 90 : 17
as you will wish when dying, 360 : 28
at home at ease, 273 : 6
at level of great men, 673 : 5
begins to l. that day, 607 : 3
better l. rich, 356 : 7

Live (*continued*)
better to l. alone, 72 : 18
bid me to l., 266 : 2
by medicine live horribly, 350 : 5
by squeezing from stone, 794 : 3
by yes and no, 650 : 1
can these bones l., 32 : 29
cannot l. without self-control, 862 : 1
can't l. with them or without, 82 : 14
can't l. without or with you, 113 : 8
ceases to l. unreflectively, 756 : 17
content with small means, 536 : 6
converse and l. with ease, 338 : 14
courage to l., 472 : 19
date l. in infamy, 780 : 15
dead l. the living die, 305 : 13
deeds by which we l., 178 : 3
deliberately, 559 : 25
desire to l. again, 658 : 18
desire to l. beyond income, 620 : 17
do not l. but linger, 258 : 20
dying we l., 545 : 24
easy l. quiet die, 432 : 1
eat to l. not l. to eat, 298 : 4, 347 : 1
evil manners l. in brass, 249 : 14
exalt will to l., 756 : 17
for more than one century, 101 : 14
for others not myself, 681 : 8
for what l. but make sport, 440 : 23
for which we bear to l., 337 : 10
Gilpin long l. he, 376 : 16
glad l. and gladly die, 668 : 20
gray dawn, 906 : 9
hair shining and free, 796 : 16
hope without object not l., 436 : 10
How to L. Well on Nothing, 539 : 8
how we l. far from how we ought, 153 : 23
human heart by which we l., 426 : 23
I cannot l. with you, 605 : 22
I cannot l. without books, 389 : 10
I l. I let myself l., 843 : 7
I l. up here, 907 : 6
I still l., 451 : 17
I to die and you to l., 83 : 15
I would not l. alway, 15 : 22
if I l. I will fight, 815 : 9
if I should l. to be, 519 : 19
if l. start to try, 868 : 2
if man die shall he l. again, 15 : 35
ill report while you l., 221 : 4
in any case wilt l. again, 658 : 18
in desire without hope, 704 : 12
in fact or in thought, 900 : 4
in fragments no longer, 764 : 9
in furnished souls, 828 : 14
in him we l., 46 : 17
in house by side of road, 685 : 12
in layers not on litter, 864 : 14
in light's extreme, 874 : 5
in old chaos of sun, 767 : 4
in our life nature l., 435 : 26
in restricted circle, 648 : 3
in small circle as we will, 395 : 23
in this faith I will l. and die, 150 : 8
in world as spectator, 326 : 8
in world good or bad, 558 : 4
Indians know better how to l., 670 : 13
innocently God here, 350 : 9
isn't fit to l., 909 : 6
it all again, 716 : 2
leave sack l. cleanly, 205 : 17
let me l. my own, 338 : 16

Live (*continued*)
let me l. unseen unknown, 332 : 11
let us l. and love, 101 : 18, 250 : 3
life he has imagined, 560 : 16
life through is not like crossing field, 934 : 12
like stoic bird, 793 : 18
like velvet mole, 793 : 19
like wretch and die rich, 258 : 24
live because of sun, 908 : 14
long l. Independence, 400 : 1
long l. our noble king, 331 : 6
long l. the strike, 906 : 17
love wisdom l. accordingly, 559 : 9
loves to l. in the sun, 211 : 3
mad to l. mad to be saved, 901 : 3
make war to l. in peace, 87 : 24
man desires to l. long, 322 : 4
man forgets to l., 315 : 9
martyrdom to l., 275 : 2
marvel how fishes l. in sea, 243 : 13
merrily shall I l. now, 248 : 16
Mirth with thee I mean to l., 278 : 8
more virtue than doth l., 256 : 5
name shall l. behind me, 225 : 1
no evil deed l. on, 647 : 3
no longer l. with honor, 696 : 15
no man shall see me and l., 10 : 14
no one so old he cannot l., 153 : 15
no picture made to l. with, 793 : 1
nobly to l., 73 : 10
not both l. and utter it, 558 : 24
not in myself, 457 : 28
not know how to l., 675 : 22
not l. by bread only, 11 : 12
not l. if England finished, 752 : 2
not l. unto oneself, 91 : 5
not l. with living, 205 : 5
not l. without cooks, 609 : 13
not three good men unhanged, 203 : 28
not to l. but to make war, 876 : 20
now I l. now life is done, 177 : 10
on knees, 759 : 2, 780 : 14
one bare hour to l., 184 : 7
only by risking we l., 649 : 12
or die, 450 : 9
out lifetime of God, 570 : 6
out thy life as light, 634 : 6
past years again, 303 : 11
peaceably, 47 : 23
people who had to l., 624 : 19
pleasurably without living wisely, 91 : 16
plenty to l. on happily, 788 : 2
power to l. and act, 429 : 1
prophets do they l. forever, 33 : 28
proudly, 696 : *n* 2
pure speak true, 534 : 5
rage to l., 335 : 19
rationally for time assigned, 124 : 27
right way to l., 654 : 13
says Death, 106 : 9
sea folk l. to three hundred, 505 : 4
see so much nor l. so long, 235 : 20
shall not l. in vain, 606 : 12
she tried to l. without him, 251 : 2
shown me how to l., 704 : 7
so l. that sinking in last sleep, 394 : 3
so l. that when summons comes, 471 : 6
so long as ye both shall l., 56 : 8
so we'll l. pray sing, 235 : 12
so wise young never l. long, 187 : 13

Live (*continued*)
soil good to l. on, 568 : 26
some l. without wild things, 795 : 8
something that doth l., 426 : 17
take means whereby I l., 200 : 20
taught us how to l., 325 : *n* 5
teach men to l., 164 : 9
teaching nations how to l., 281 : 17
ten times ten, 492 : 6
that nation might l., 523 : 4
that they may eat, 79 : 6
that you desire to l. again, 658 : 18
their wonted fires, 362 : 15
thou hast no more to l., 634 : 13
though dead shall he l., 45 : 13
through time or die by suicide, 519 : 22
till tomorrow, 377 : 21
to be in awe, 215 : 4
to be show and gaze, 240 : 10
to extent they coincide with epoch, 672 : 3
to fight another day, 91 : *n* 7
to itself it l. and die, 245 : 5
to l. is Christ, 50 : 1
to l. is like to love, 621 : 1
to l. is to function, 645 : 12
to l. not simple as to cross field, 816 : 18
to please must please to live, 351 : 14
today, 119 : 1
together in peace, 788 : 20
too beautiful to l., 547 : 10
too much in circle, 501 : 21
true as I l., 261 : 8
truth l. with right and wrong, 829 : 16
turn and l. with animals, 574 : 24
unable to l. in society, 87 : 28
unto the Lord, 47 : 32
upon daily rations, 548 : 15
upon vapor of dungeon, 231 : 6
we die and we l., 132 : 7
we do poorly l., 561 : 1
we how we can, 186 : 21
we l. as we dream alone, 683 : 15
we l. but world passed, 631 : 14
we l. here they l. there, 875 : 8
we must attempt to l., 735 : 12
we must l. as we think, 670 : 10
we only l. only suspire, 808 : 15
we shall l. in his sight, 33 : 9
what thou livest l. well, 287 : 30
while ye may, 285 : 23
who dies if England l., 710 : 24
with but half a heart, 267 : 7
with ease, 338 : 14
with her and live with thee, 277 : 22
with me and be my love, 183 : 8, 253 : 2
with the gods, 125 : 4
with thee and be thy love, 172 : 10
with wolves howl like wolf, 934 : 15
with you love to l., 108 : 2
within no power to l. long, 114 : 18
within reach to l. nobly, 114 : 18
within sense they quicken, 469 : 18
without conscience, 609 : 13
without duties obscene, 500 : 7
without me God cannot l., 300 : 17
without playing knave, 309 : 17
without poetry music art, 609 : 13
world not to l. but to die in, 274 : 21
would you l. forever, 358 : 2
you might as well l., 827 : 12

Live (*continued*)
you will know how to l., 396 : 15
Live-and-help-live logic, 898 : 1
Lived, back above element they l. in, 241 : 25
courage with which men l., 890 : 3
discover I had not l., 559 : 25
end by thinking as we l., 670 : 10
everything l. in me, 595 : 3
for all times, 413 : 5
had we l. tale to tell, 726 : 5
how I have l. unimportant, 800 : 12
I had l. a blessed time, 238 : 7
I have l. long enough, 239 : 31, 633 : 5
I have l. my day, 108 : *n* 7
I have l. today, 305 : 1
I have not l. in vain, 326 : 7
I l. on air, 748 : 8
in cellar damp, 568 : 20
in little house, 933 : 19
in mild magnificent eye, 541 : 6
in Paris as young man, 845 : 14
in practice of every virtue, 81 : 9
in pretty how town, 829 : 18
in tide of times, 216 : 11
judged not to have l., 643 : 16
life l. forwards, 552 : 10
life l. in scene it composes, 769 : 15
life meant to be l., 786 : 14
light in spring, 585 : 11
like foot for thirty years, 911 : 16
long on alms-basket of words, 191 : 7
loved cursed floundered, 654 : 7
men l. like fishes, 243 : *n* 1
moment l. in paradise, 412 : 17
must be l. down, 906 : 5
my father l. his soul, 829 : 21
never to have l. is best, 715 : 19
nightly drank daily, 876 : 8
on River Dee, 382 : 6
she l. unknown, 424 : 12
some l. long l. little, 164 : 11
through this horror, 786 : 13
time not sacred until l., 631 : 2
together in crooked house, 932 : 18
under a hill, 933 : 11
under my woodside, 272 : 21
without disgrace without praise, 140 : 16
Livelier liquor than Muse, 691 : 17
plaything gives youth delight, 337 : 7
Livelihood, anxiety about l., 751 : 11
right l., 73 : 2
Lively, cock with l. din, 277 : 23
from l. to severe, 338 : 1
life l. form of death, 177 : 1
sense of filial duty, 387 : 7
understandable spirit, 873 : 14
Liver, as well speak of female l., 695 : 13
Liverpool, she's the L. packet, 935 : 7
Livers, humble l. in content, 248 : 27
Livery, cunning l. of hell, 228 : 19
in his l. walked crowns, 241 : 25
in sober l. clad, 285 : 24
of burnished sun, 198 : 29
Lives and dies in single blessedness, 195 : 21
and souls dreaming, 571 : 3
at ease that freely lives, 143 : 9
body's beauty l., 767 : 10
brutal l. ugly deaths, 831 : 18
but marches to grave, 509 : *n* 5
Lives (*continued*)
cat has only nine l., 624 : 16
competency l. longer, 198 : 8
cuckold l. in bliss, 230 : 34
do our best and live our l., 863 : 12
evil men do l. after them, 216 : 17
executives know nothing of, 905 : 17
for cap and bells l. pay, 567 : 12
fructify in l. of others, 94 : *n* 9
gave l. that nation live, 523 : 4
gave our l. to save Greece, 67 : 21
God l. not without me, 300 : 17
goodness l. though they are gone, 77 : 18
he l. he wakes, 469 : 13
he l. in bliss, 411 : 22
here or passes night, 786 : 1
history in all men's l., 206 : 21
honest and industrious men's l., 265 : 9
how the other half l., 270 : 21
human creatures' l., 485 : 19
in eternity's sunrise, 404 : 18
in fame died in virtue's cause, 188 : 18
in our alley, 331 : 5
in purer l. service find, 514 : 1
it's men's l. ye're buying, 431 : 22
leave little l. in air, 334 : 16
less conscious actions mold l., 620 : 7
like drunken sailor, 187 : 15
look into l. as into mirror, 97 : 4
loss of l. cannot be valued, 265 : 9
lovely and pleasant in their l., 13 : 9
make our l. sublime, 509 : 15
merry merry l., 696 : 3
more lives than one, 676 : 11
music of men's l., 195 : 16
nine l. like a cat, 160 : 24
noblest l. and dies, 581 : 14
noon and evening of l., 592 : 6
not alone in brain, 191 : 2
not how man dies but l., 354 : 20
not long who battles immortals, 57 : 29
not mounting and unfolding, 754 : 6
of great men, 509 : 15
of quiet desperation, 559 : 4
of shoemaker and peddler, 811 : 8
on a leaf, 873 : 11
on hope die fasting, 347 : 33
one l. but once, 394 : 12
our l. grow together, 633 : 11
our l. in acts exemplary, 178 : 3
our l. our fortunes, 387 : 11
our pilot still, 186 : 23
part as ships, 512 : *n* 3
poet help people live their l., 769 : 16
preaches well that l. well, 170 : 19
public supreme judge of l., 453 : 12
sacrifice l. to preserve virtue, 69 : 10
sacrificed l. and fortunes, 725 : 20
Santa Claus l. forever, 638 : 6
slander l. upon succession, 188 : 8
spend rest of l. in future, 757 : 10
spending l. like serfs, 560 : 7
spoil l. of better people, 669 : 14
talk not of other men's l., 35 : 32
there still, 933 : 11
Thomas Jefferson still l., 382 : 5
those who understand their l., 912 : 4
throbbing between two l., 805 : 7
traced l. of good men, 429 : 4
two l. join oft scar, 542 : 9
Lives (*continued*)
two lives who relives past, 119 : 14
went in jeopardy of their l., 13 : 26
what textures of our l., 875 : 10
while he l. be glad, 633 : 10
who l. everywhere l. nowhere, 119 : 12
who l. unto himself, 267 : 9
who well l. long l., 168 : 1
whose range is small, 619 : 19
woman true and fair, 252 : 2
worry away our l., 884 : 3
ye led were mine, 707 : 3
Livest, be useful where thou l., 268 : 8
Liveth and believeth in me, 45 : 13
I am he that l., 52 : 32
know that my redeemer l., 16 : 4
name l. forevermore, 36 : 12
none l. to himself, 47 : 32
not in fierce desire, 430 : 9
Livia's daughter-sons, 778 : 5
Livid loneliness of fear, 842 : 14
Livin', heap o' l., 774 : 4
not worth l. without inimies 721 : 9
Living, all the l. and the dead, 777 : 16
and dead are same, 70 : 8
and partly living, 806 : 16
as black rock star, 906 : 6
at this hour, 425 : 22
blamed the l. man, 587 : 17
bouquets while I'm l., 762 : 1
brave men l. and dead, 523 : 4
burden of long l., 633 : 17
catch the manners l., 336 : 11
dead govern l., 483 : 13
dead live the l. die, 305 : 13
dead man, 188 : 15
dead not interested in l., 839 : 13
dead think l. worth it, 907 : 8
desire of every l. thing, 22 : 21
difficult chapters in art of l., 580 : 10
dog better than dead lion, 27 : 15
doll can sew cook, 911 : 9
earn l. by sweat, 559 : 14
earned precarious l., 924 : 5
earth belongs to l., 389 : 7
every l. thing of all flesh, 7 : 29
fever called l., 527 : 6
first consideration earning l., 312 : 21
freely and nobly, 738 : 2
from hand to mouth, 167 : 12
glowed with l. sapphires, 285 : 25
God, 39 : 35, 365 : 13
God of l., 43 : 43
habit of l., 275 : 6
half dead a l. death, 288 : 22
heap o' l., 774 : 4
help for l. hope for dead, 615 : 8
Homer begged his bread, 257 : *n* 5
house a machine for l. in, 798 : 4
house appointed for all l., 16 : 18
how good mere l., 543 : 16
I advise you to go on l., 344 : 8
I make war on the l., 161 : 20
in a garret, 364 : 3
in agreement with nature, 91 : 19
in living seasons, 807 : 10
in underground den, 84 : 17
in Yorkshire, 433 : 3
include dying multifold, 606 : 15
it is for us the l., 523 : 4
know no bounds, 272 : 11
know they shall die, 27 : 15
Lady Disdain are you yet l., 208 : 27
land of the l., 16 : 13, 839 : 10

Living (*continued*)
language of the l., 808 : 10
law, 794 : 15
leave a l. name behind, 262 : 11
leave l. to servants, 638 : 1
life for the l., 616 : 5
life lost in the l., 806 : 15
life worth l., 649 : 13, 703 : 9
lightning from her eyes, 334 : 10
like l. in jail, 875 : 8
Lord of l. and dead, 655 : 19
lyre, 362 : 6
mother of all l., 7 : 12
Mother of All L., 833 : 6
motion like l. thing, 424 : 1
my trade and art l., 165 : 1
no l. near her, 209 : 10
no l. with you or without, 119 : 17
no speech for when l., 808 : 10
noble l. and noble dead, 424 : 6
not live with l., 205 : 5
not measured by length but use, 164 : 11
not reverence of dead but envy of l., 264 : 19
not worth l. without enemies, 721 : 9
object in l. to unite, 748 : 18
one thinks to get a l., 359 : 4
pattern of dead and l., 807 : 23
pity for l. envy for dead, 625 : 8
plain l. high thinking, 425 : 15
pleasure the beginning and end of l., 91 : 15
precarious l., 924 : 5
recollection like l. over, 348 : 17
responsibilities to l. things, 912 : 4
riotous l., 43 : 26
round ocean and l. air, 423 : 13
sacrifice, 47 : 18, 55 : 19
scarce able to bury dead, 265 : 10
search land of l. men, 430 : 15
seek l. among dead, 44 : 13
servant of l. God, 365 : 13
shake l. out of Fate, 610 : 7
shall forfeit renown, 430 : 10
something like l. occurs, 906 : 16
Son of the l. God, 39 : 35
sons of the l. God, 33 : 7
sorcery of embraces, 816 : 20
souls departed shadows of l., 275 : 13
summertime and l. easy, 836 : 4
take no notice if he were l., 445 : 8
the l. are not enough, 850 : 3
the l. have never shown me, 704 : 7
theologian born by l., 156 : 8
this life worth l., 649 : 13
this l. hand, 478 : 8
throne, 363 : 2
to one's self, 445 : 5
too much love of l., 633 : 22
translating into l. law, 794 : 15
up to it difficult, 539 : 16
we fret, 545 : 24
well best revenge, 270 : 6
when l. might exceed dead, 274 : 26
whether l. is dying, 82 : 21
which are yet alive, 26 : 22
who l. had no note, 918 : 17
who l. had no roof, 257 : 20
with us even in silence, 395 : 6
write a l. line, 256 : 16
yet we have gone on l., 806 : 16
Living-dead man, 188 : 15
Livings, set to earn l., 690 : 13
Livingstone, Dr. L. I presume, 646 : 15
Livre, je suis moi-même la matière de mon l., 164 : *n* 3
Lizard grasshopper sing together, 637 : 15
lion and l. keep, 516 : 11
seen the good l., 841 : 5
time slips away like l., 756 : 1
Lizzie Borden took ax, 923 : 5
Llorar, quien te quiere te hora l., 935 : 16
Lo footprint is our own, 776 : 7
I am with you always, 41 : 31
the poor Indian, 336 : 16
virtue is at hand, 68 : 23
Load, ass will carry l., 171 : 2
cruelty to l. falling man, 249 : *n* 1
every rift of subject, 480 : 5
of immortality, 479 : 12
would sink a navy, 249 : 5
Loaded, centuries l. fragrant, 499 : 1
Loads of learned lumber in head, 333 : 19
with superfluous burden l. day, 282 : 10
Loaf and invite soul, 574 : 12
better half a l., 160 : 11
of bread and thou, 516 : 7
to every bird, 606 : 6
Loafing around the Throne, 636 : 5
Loan, anything given is on l., 913 : 8
oft loses friend, 219 : 2
Loaning, on ilka green l., 368 : 2
Loath, long and l. at going, 810 : 17
to lay out money on rope, 258 : 23
what maidens l., 477 : 5
Loathe, I l. the country, 324 : 18
sweet tunes, 633 : 3
taste of sweetness, 204 : 20
that I did love, 162 : 5
Loathed Melancholy, 277 : 17
most l. worldly life, 228 : 21
Loathes, all outward l., 252 : 5
Loathing, deepest l. brings, 196 : 23
lost love and l., 858 : 19
Loathsome canker in sweetest bud, 244 : 14
Loaves, five l. and two fishes, 39 : 24
Lobby, in l. in a niche, 897 : 3
Lobotomized, flabby bald l., 893 : 2
Lobster, voice of the L., 612 : 10
Lobster-nights, luxurious l., 334 : 25
Lobsterpot, shattered l., 808 : 2
Lobsters, change l. and dance, 612 : *n* 2
change l. and retire, 612 : 6
thrain l. to fly, 722 : 12
Local cult Christianity, 641 : 18
defense important, 803 : 7
habitation and name, 197 : 12
seemed to be l. dust cloud, 885 : 7
Loch, banks o' L. Lomond, 921 : 9
Lochaber, farewell to L., 331 : 3
Lochinvar, young L., 430 : 17
Lock, cryin' at l., 537 : 6
meant to pick l., 919 : 13
something picked l. slid bolts, 739 : 5
sure l. me up, 810 : 8
Locke sank into swoon, 715 : 15
Locked and frozen in eye, 868 : 13
lettered collar, 409 : 6
naked though l. up in steel, 185 : 17
razor, 892 : 18
'tis in my memory l., 219 : 3
up from mortal eye, 292 : 8
Locket, Lucy L. lost pocket, 933 : 5
Locks are like the snaw, 410 : 7
from clasp of knitted l., 576 : 18
immortal l. fell forward, 57 : 12
knotted and combined l., 219 : 18
open l. whoever knocks, 239 : 7
pluck drowned honor by l., 203 : 15
shake thy gory l. at me, 238 : 25
shaking her invincible l., 282 : 3
time to silver turned, 177 : 8
were like the raven, 410 : 7
which are left are gray, 439 : 15
yellow as gold, 434 : 19
Locksmith, zealous l. died, 919 : 13
Locust, day of the l., 857 : 8
of soul unshelled, 900 : 3
tossed up and down as the l., 21 : 17
Locusts and wild honey, 36 : 27
food as luscious as l., 230 : 4
like in Bible with l., 863 : 6
Lodestone, like needle to l., 570 : 1
Lodge, house to l. friend, 339 : 10
in garden of cucumbers, 28 : 28
in some vast wilderness, 376 : 18
not l. thee by Chaucer, 256 : 11
thorns that in bosom l., 219 : 25
where thou lodgest I will l., 12 : 25
Lodged, love l. in woman's breast, 250 : 13
with me useless, 282 : 15
Lodges, where care l. sleep never lie, 192 : 21
Lodgest, where thou l. I will lodge, 12 : 25
Lodging, grant us safe l., 490 : 10
hard was their l., 318 : 17
my l. is on cold ground, 331 : 11
Phoebus' l., 193 : 8
place of wayfaring men, 32 : 4
Lo'ed, better l. ye canna be, 417 : 5
Loftier race than known, 643 : 1
raise somewhat l. strain, 103 : 13
Loftiest peaks most wrapped, 457 : 22
Loftiness of thought surpassed, 306 : 1
turn lowness into l., 694 : 1
Lofty and sour, 249 : 15
build the l. rhyme, 280 : 7
scene be acted o'er, 216 : 7
sky immeasurably l., 602 : 1
Log hut with simple bench, 609 : 10
Mark Hopkins at end of l., 609 : *n* 3
on l. expiring frog, 546 : 14
roll my l. I roll yours, 115 : 10
tough wedge for tough l., 112 : 2
will never be crocodile, 926 : 8
Logan's, enter L. cabin hungry, 367 : 3
Logic and rhetoric able to contend, 181 : 14
book of female l., 539 : 21
doctrinaire l., 821 : 8
is logic, 519 : 16
of heart absurd, 378 : 13
of mind overtaxed, 519 : 3
page of history worth volume of l., 645 : 4
superb in love and l., 556 : *n* 3
temper l. with wisdom, 821 : 8
that's l., 612 : 24
Logical, built in such l. way, 519 : 15
consequences scarecrows of fools, 596 : 3
Logs, Tom bears l. into the hall, 191 : 14
Loin, ungirt l., 543 : 15
Loins, gird up thy l. like a man, 16 : 27

Loins (*continued*)
he girded up his l., 14:4
let your l. be girded, 43:21
shudder in l., 715:16
with your l. girded, 9:25
Loiterers, liege of all l., 190:26
Loitering, alone and palely l., 478:10
Lolita, immortality you and I share L., 846:5
Loman never made money, 888:2
Lomonosov was our first university, 357:*n*4
London Bridge broken down, 929:21
Bridge falling down, 698:14
broken arch of L. Bridge, 488:7
don't send poet to L., 481:14
flower of cities all, 153:4
fog thirty parts, 699:16
great cesspool, 689:2
hell city much like L., 468:2
in ruins rather than enslaved, 744:5
isn't far from L., 772:22
knowledge of L. extensive, 546:16
Lord Mayor of L., 918:10
loved life L., 781:15
particular a fog, 549:13
sea at best in L., 741:11
this is L., 872:16
tired of L. tired of life, 355:26
to L. to look at queen, 932:8
vast mass of L., 744:5
vilest alleys of L., 689:6
whale-fat of postwar L., 892:12
London's, nursed amid L. noise, 441:9
Lone, a way a l. a last, 778:6
Glenartney's hazel shade, 431:5
lorn creetur, 548:22
not in l. splendor, 478:20
poor l. woman, 206:9
sheiling, 483:20
sky-pointing tree, 587:11
walking by wild l., 710:6
worker makes first advance, 774:2
Loneliness, die of l., 718:5
intense l. and ignorance, 677:3
of fear, 842:14
of spirit, 456:1
of yesterday, 836:17
our l. our love our bodies, 849:12
promise of decade of l., 835:6
Lonely, all the l. people, 914:10
and poor of old, 797:4
and swift like planet, 683:4
consoler of l., 617:7
dark and l. hiding place, 435:16
flowering in l. word, 535:15
God winding l. horn, 712:13
heart l. hunter, 677:5, 894:12
hunts on l. hill, 677:5
I'm l. I'll make world, 733:10
impulse of delight, 714:1
more l. among men, 560:3
people talking to each other, 863:8
rapture on l. shore, 458:24
sea and sky, 760:14
sleep among l. hills, 428:7
so l. 'twas that God, 435:9
sun in l. lands, 532:28
the l. thing, 428:*n*5
thing that shone, 716:15
tramp l. fellow, 812:7
wandered l. as a cloud, 427:7
Lonelyhearts, Miss L., 857:6
Lonesome, be good be l., 624:27
Lonesome (*continued*)
like one that on l. road, 435:3
October, 526:22
place against sky, 671:3
road, 435:3
whippoorwill, 903:1
Lonesomeness, starlight lit l., 640:4
Lonesome's a bad place, 879:15
Long, a loved a l. the, 778:6
anchorage we leave, 576:20
and ghastly kitchen, 551:15
and lank and brown, 434:25
and loath at going, 810:17
and steep is the way, 61:17
and terrible way, 874:23
apprenticehood, 194:4
art l. life short, 395:7
as l. as ever you can, 346:12
as l. as moon rise, 929:5
at l. last able to speak, 832:2
battle rages loud and l., 443:11
be day never so l., 161:7
black land, 541:13
boots hard boots, 761:13
brown path before me, 575:9
calamity of so l. life, 221:12
cool winding saxophones, 761:11
day's journey into night, 810:16
day's task is done, 241:18
deliberate derangement, 674:12
divorce of steel, 248:25
enough and just so long, 829:16
for another life, 734:7
for imperishable quiet, 874:7
for something in yourself, 880:3
from l. to l. in solemn sort, 436:3
Gilpin l. live he, 376:16
gray beard glittering eye, 434:4
groveled here l. enough, 576:16
hair glory to woman, 48:19
happy as heart was l., 887:2
his arm is very l., 78:20
home I l. to be, 671:10
hot summer, 837:15
how l. a time in one word, 194:2
how l. wilt thou forget me, 17:20
I have lived l. enough, 239:31
I loved you once l. ago, 63:7
I speak not loud or l., 174:*n*6
it shan't be l., 342:16
it wont be l. now, 760:6, 760:9
kiss l. as my exile, 242:22
lane knows no turnings, 541:4
life how l. or short, 287:30
life is short art l., 80:9
life well spent is l., 152:5
light shakes, 530:26
littleness of life, 795:1
live Independence, 400:1
live our noble king, 331:6
live the strike, 906:17
long ago, 481:5
long thoughts, 511:25
long trail a-winding, 813:7
long wintry nights, 551:3
Lord how l., 29:12
love me little love me l., 266:8, 917:12
make no l. meals, 370:*n*3
may land be bright, 514:13
mechanic pacings, 529:3
melancholy l. withdrawing roar, 587:16
merry as day is l., 209:5
Long (*continued*)
never make l. visits, 798:16
nor that little l., 330:12, 369:12
not l. life by fire, 696:14
not l. the weeping and the laughter, 721:7
poem does not exist, 527:12
pray that way be l., 702:4
pull strong pull, 549:2
road l. and dusty to grave, 667:14
see so much nor live so l., 235:20
seven l. year, 234:10
short and l. of it, 225:16
short meaning of l. speech, 413:15
small showers last l., 194:12
stubbornly l. or suddenly splendor, 797:10
suits, 818:5
that thy days may be l., 10:7
think life too l., 316:11
thought the travel l., 184:14
three l. mountains, 822:11
time between drinks, 669:12
to talk with lover's ghost, 253:9
trick's over, 760:16
trochee trips from l. to short, 436:3
way l. wind cold, 429:20
way to Tipperary, 753:1
within no power to live l., 114:18
words bother me, 778:12
Long-drawn aisle, 362:4
Longed, lies where l. to be, 668:20
to embrace mother's ghost, 60:8
truly l. for death, 528:2
Longer, impossible takes l., 924:19
letter l. than usual, 299:13
no l. stay with you, 922:13
smile dwells l., 739:7
some days l., 746:14
song had been l., 930:18
stretch him out l., 235:19
words have l. life than deeds, 72:4
Longest fifty-nine minutes, 724:4
journey go, 468:21
journey inwards, 863:4
journey to oblivion, 791:2
nights are l. there, 228:3
part of the journey, 97:11
river in world, 623:2
way round shortest home, 267:*n*6
Longest-lived and shortest-lived die same, 124:9
Longeth, my flesh l. for thee, 19:29
Longfellow's, shown L. grave, 798:16
Long-forgotten peoples rise, 912:5
Long-haired, not these l. men I fear, 99:25
Longing after immortality, 326:3
cast l. eye on offices, 388:14
feeling of sadness and l., 510:18
for stewed prunes, 228:2
for that lovely lady, 97:10
leans and beckons, 569:4
lingering look behind, 362:14
lovers live by l., 873:19
more l. wavering, 214:1
Longings, I have immortal l. in me, 242:2
of insatiate blood, 874:17
Longitude and latitude for seine, 623:5
in l. though scanty, 411:12
send them latitude and l., 777:13
Long-legged fly upon stream, 717:17
Long-leggety beasties, 921:4

Longmans', it's still in L. shop, 424 : *n* 2
Longs, who l. for death, 267 : 2
Longshoreman's union, 722 : 21
Long-stemmed gigantic flowers, 789 : 9
Long-strayed eyes, 252 : 23
Longsuffering and very pitiful, 34 : 23
fruit of Spirit is l., 49 : 30
love is l., 148 : 20
Longue, je n'ai fait celle-ci plus l., 299 : *n* 3
Lonlier, make each other l., 863 : 8
Lonsdale Mrs. Langtry and Lady L., 914 : *n* 2
Loo, oh Miss L., 662 : 17
Look about us and die, 336 : 10
afraid to l. upon God, 9 : 12
after all it is a poor land, 581 : 3
after our people, 726 : 7
after souls in labor, 85 : 16
all world here to l. on me, 196 : 17
and pass on, 140 : 17
angel of backward l., 513 : 23
around choose ground, 462 : 19
as they run l. behind, 361 : 9
ashamed to l. next morning, 271 : 8
astronomy compels soul to l. upwards, 84 : 18
at all the fire-folk, 655 : 21
at record, 741 : 7
at the stars, 655 : 21
at thee with many eyes, 670 : *n* 3
at them long and long, 574 : 24
at things in bloom, 690 : 17
at was to love, 529 : 19
away Dixie Land, 554 : 1
back in anger, 910 : 1
back many times, 770 : 13
backward l. behind assurance, 808 : 5
before time to l. round, 395 : 23
before you leap, 291 : 23
behind the Ranges, 710 : 9
both ways, 776 : 10
clean starved for a l., 244 : 28
direct him where to l. for it, 254 : 5
do it with bitter l., 676 : 8
don't l. back, 867 : 9
don't l. over your shoulder, 856 : 12
down on hate, 457 : 22
ere ye leap, 158 : 21
every l. a dart, 919 : 19
eyes l. your last, 193 : 28
eyes that would not l. on me, 398 : 23
fear in the face, 786 : 13
for me in nurseries, 693 : 8
for me under boot soles, 575 : 4
for truth but not find it, 359 : 13
forty centuries l. down, 420 : 6
forward not back, 590 : 8
forward to posterity, 373 : 20
forward to with hope, 747 : 7
give me a l., 255 : 18
goose l., 239 : 29
her quick l., 873 : 17
her wanton spirits l. out, 227 : 3
homeward Angel, 281 : 3
how floor of heaven, 201 : 1
how others do it, 413 : 1
how ring encompasseth thy finger, 187 : 2
I had fixed my l. on his, 141 : 8
I'll not l. for wine, 256 : 8
immortal l., 544 : 23
in almanac find out moonshine, 196 : 25
Look (*continued*)
in my God's right hand, 936 : 2
in that tone of voice, 660 : 17
in thy heart and write, 176 : 13
into happiness through another's eyes, 212 : 32
into lives as into mirror, 97 : 4
into oneself, 700 : 4
into seeds of time, 236 : 5
into your heart, 413 : 1
last on things lovely, 739 : 17
lean and hungry l., 215 : 8
learned to l. on nature, 423 : 13
let him l. to his bond, 199 : 16
library whereon I l., 267 : 4
like innocent flower, 236 : 20
lingering l. behind, 362 : 14
look up at skies, 655 : 21
love the l. of landscapes, 794 : 2
make man l. sad, 197 : 19
men met with erected l., 305 : 5
morn in russet mantle clad, 217 : 27
my God l. not so fierce, 184 : 9
ne'er l. back, 231 : 18
not down but up, 544 : 13
not thou upon the wine, 25 : 11
of love alarms, 404 : 19
of soft deceit, 404 : 19
on both indifferently, 215 : 3
on my works ye mighty, 466 : 13
on you when last hour comes, 112 : 27
only a l. and voice, 512 : 10
or listen, 568 : 4
out how use proud words, 761 : 13
out not in, 590 : 8
reader l., 256 : 10
round habitable world, 306 : 10
see monument l. around, 309 : 7
soul l. body touch, 717 : 8
take a backward l., 604 : 9
things fairer when we l. back, 569 : 4
through a millstone, 175 : 20
thy last on things lovely, 739 : 17
to essence of a thing, 125 : 13
to it, 522 : 1
turn an envious l., 868 : 6
up at the skies, 655 : 21
up not down, 590 : 8
upon a little child, 350 : 13
upon his like again, 218 : 16
upon world as parish, 346 : 8
upward l. of caution, 749 : 11
we l. before and after, 468 : 14
westward l. land bright, 564 : 17
who comes here, 201 : 24
with favor on bold beginning, 103 : 26
with thine ears, 235 : 2
ye there, 349 : *n* 4
you didn't know where to l., 849 : 14
Looked again found it was, 614 : 6
and sighed again, 306 : 20
as she did love, 478 : 12
before thou leaped, 158 : *n* 15
come when l. for, 552 : 19
down to Camelot, 528 : 27
God l. around and said, 733 : 10
into eye of day, 715 : 19
Lot's wife l. back, 8 : 12
love to eyes which spake, 457 : 14
no sooner l. but loved, 212 : 31
on Beauty bare, 823 : 8
on better days, 211 : 12
out of eye of saint, 716 : 4
over his shoulder, 868 : 21
Looked (*continued*)
she never should have l., 540 : 27
sideways up, 434 : 22
to government for bread, 374 : 11
unutterable things, 345 : 9
with such a wistful eye, 676 : 6
with wild surmise, 475 : 7
Looker-on, patient l., 267 : 18
Lookers-on, only God and angels l., 179 : 4
Looketh, Lord l. on the heart, 12 : 38
on the outward appearance, 12 : 38
well to ways of her household, 26 : 9
Lookin' eastward to sea, 708 : 8
Looking as if alive, 540 : 22
as like as peas, 158 : 12
at self through others, 724 : 17
conscience warns somebody l., 772 : 17
eastward to sea, 708 : 8
even if gods should be l., 60 : 6
for honest man, 86 : 12
for something to do, 361 : 4
fresh as paint, 564 : 1
hand to plow and l. back, 43 : 7
here's l. at you kid, 843 : 4
leave them while l. good, 826 : 4
on happy fields, 531 : 3
one way rowing another, 302 : 7
over harbor and city, 761 : 5
pleasure of l. at each other, 671 : 18
seaman l. for something else, 800 : 5
see without l. through windows, 64 : 17
well can't move her, 289 : 17
Looking Backward was written, 666 : 6
Looking-glass, no use to blame l., 518 : 1
Looking-glasses, women l. reflecting man, 782 : 5
Looks, assurance given by l., 184 : 13
commercing with the skies, 278 : 13
dispatchful l., 286 : 18
everybody's l. of death, 309 : 24
gigantically down, 525 : 13
gods do not give all men good l., 60 : 4
in the clouds, 215 : 16
kindness not beauteous l., 189 : 1
love l. not with eyes, 196 : 1
modes l. cottage adorn, 370 : 17
more elder than thy l., 200 : 12
never l. nor 'eeds, 709 : 8
not deep-searched with saucy l., 190 : 12
old man l. before and after, 57 : 22
on alike, 247 : 1
on tempests, 245 : 18
patron l. with unconcern, 353 : 26
poet l. at world as man at woman, 769 : 23
puts on his pretty l., 201 : 26
quite through deeds of men, 215 : 9
she l. with threatening eye, 202 : 2
she needs good l., 788 : 21
sidelong l. of love, 369 : 29
through Nature up, 337 : 16
toward school with heavy l., 192 : 15
war of l. between them, 189 : 9
were free, 434 : 19
whole world in face, 510 : 8
Loom, I cannot ply the l., 63 : 9
left the web left the l., 528 : 27
Loon, thou cream-faced l., 239 : 29

Loop to hang doubt on, 231 : 13
Looped and windowed raggedness, 234 : 3
Loophole, from her cabined l. peep, 279 : 13
no l. in case drafted, 766 : 3
Loopholes of retreat, 377 : 4
Loose, all hell broke l., 286 : 9
as the wind, 268 : 21
feel his title hang l., 239 : 28
hell's broken l., 178 : 14
imagination, 717 : 9
past free of l. ends, 736 : 9
the bands of Orion, 16 : 33
types of things, 426 : 3
w'en it gits l. fum jug, 662 : 13
Loosed, arrows l. several ways, 207 : 8
blood-dimmed tide l., 714 : 12
fateful lightning, 566 : 4
silver cord be l., 27 : 25
Loosen, old faiths l. and fall, 633 : 6
old foundations, 761 : 10
Loosens fragrant bodice, 476 : 17
Lopped limbs, 873 : 5
tree may grow again, 73 : *n* 9
Loquacious, light griefs l., 115 : 15
Loquacity, poetry checks l., 499 : 20
Lord, all ye works of the L., 36 : 14
am an attendant l., 803 : 17
among wits, 354 : 1
and Father of mankind, 514 : 1
angel of L. came down, 317 : 4
angel of L. came upon them, 42 : 28
anger of L. kindled, 13 : 15
answered Job out of the whirlwind, 16 : 27
be thankit, 411 : 1
be with you, 54 : 1
believing Christians from sky, 151 : 2
better is little with the fear of the L., 24 : 7
bless thee and keep thee, 10 : 23
bless ye the L., 36 : 14
blessed be L. God, 42 : 24
blessed the latter end of Job, 17 : 11
blot out his name, 308 : *n* 2
bringeth thee into good land, 11 : 13
Cain went out from presence of the L., 7 : 20
Christ the L. risen today, 350 : 11
Christ's heart, 495 : 15
climb tree L. to see, 320 : 10
coming of the L., 566 : 4
Dark Maid and her L., 76 : 3
day of the L., 50 : 18
day thou gavest L. is ended, 597 : 17
day which the L. hath made, 21 : 26
dead which die in the L., 53 : 24
died by the hand of the L., 10 : 1
directeth his steps, 24 : 11
disciples of the L., 46 : 4
do if He knew facts, 722 : 9
fear of the L. is beginning of wisdom, 21 : 19
fear of the L. is wisdom, 16 : 15
feast to the L., 9 : 26
for the erring thought, 631 : 15
forbade me to put off my hat, 300 : 21
forgive O L. my jokes, 749 : 15
from winter plague L. deliver us, 250 : 9
gangway for L., 814 : 15
gave and hath taken away, 15 : 4
glory of the L. is risen, 31 : 23

Lord (*continued*)
go and the L. be with thee, 13 : 1
go home to my L. and be free, 936 : 4
God allowed lands to be discovered, 156 : 12
God Almighty, 53 : 7
God caused a deep sleep, 7 : 2
God formed man, 6 : 17
God is subtle, 764 : 1
God made them all, 561 : 8
God of Hosts, 709 : 16
God planted a garden, 6 : 18
God send high wave, 735 : 3
God walking in garden, 7 : 7
good L. deliver us, 55 : 10, 921 : 4
good L. had only ten, 643 : 11
good works better in sight of L., 131 : 11
Gracious L. bomb Germans, 866 : 17
great and dreadful day of the L., 34 : 1
handkerchief of L., 574 : 16
hath chosen thee, 11 : 11
have mercy on us, 54 : 3, 250 : 10
hear me out, 874 : 23
hear word of the L., 32 : 15
help 'em how I pities all, 429 : 19
holy is the L. of hosts, 29 : 9
how discourse is of death, 309 : 24
how long, 29 : 12
how world given to lying, 205 : 16
I am the L. thy God, 10 : 3
I believe, 42 : 10
I heard the voice of the L., 29 : 11
I replied My L., 268 : 23
I want to be in that number, 936 : 8
I were l. in May, 633 : 12
I will sing unto the L., 9 : 32
if you had horse, 790 : 19
in glance of the L., 459 : 16
is a man of war, 9 : 33
is come, 328 : 13
is good, 21 : 3
is in his holy temple, 33 : 27
is in this place, 8 : 20
is it I, 41 : 8
is my helper, 51 : 23
is my light, 18 : 11
is my rock, 13 : 24
is my shepherd, 18 : 7
is my strength and shield, 18 : 13
is my strength and song, 9 : 32
is nigh unto them that call, 22 : 22
is risen, 54 : 10
is risen indeed, 44 : 16
is the strength of my life, 18 : 11
is thy keeper, 22 : 4
is thy shade, 22 : 4
is with thee, 42 : 17
it but a day, 661 : 16
Jehovah Jove or L., 340 : 1
kingdoms of our L., 53 : 18
king's our only l., 182 : 13
know ye that the L. he is God, 21 : 3
land which the L. giveth thee, 10 : 7
lendeth unto the L., 24 : 26
let me shake with purpose, 902 : 6
lift up his countenance, 10 : 23
looketh on the heart, 12 : 38
love is my l. and king, 532 : 25
love the L. with all thine heart, 11 : 9
made all to prosper, 8 : 29
make a joyful noise unto the L., 21 : 3
make his face shine upon thee, 10 : 23

Lord (*continued*)
make me an instrument, 138 : 15
make my enemies ridiculous, 343 : 25
Mayor of London, 918 : 10
mercy on Thy people L., 709 : 20
methought what pain to drown, 187 : 9
more brain O L., 600 : 19
my help cometh from the L., 22 : 4
my L. what a morning, 936 : 1
my soul doth magnify L., 42 : 20
name of the L. in vain, 10 : 5
neat and trimly dressed, 203 : 7
not everyone that saith L., 38 : 19
not in wind earthquake fire, 14 : 5
not tempt the L. your God, 11 : 10
not the weight of an ant escapes the L., 130 : 18
O L. if there is a L., 593 : 9
O L. let her go, 935 : 7
O L. my God I have trusted, 167 : 3
of all Being, 130 : 9
of all yet prey to all, 337 : 2
of far-flung battle line, 709 : 16
of folded arms, 190 : 26
of heaven and earth, 46 : 16
of himself, 250 : 16, 459 : 12
of hosts he is the King of glory, 18 : 10
of living and dead, 655 : 19
of lords, 53 : 26
of the flies, 878 : 22
of the Ocean, 76 : 25
of yourself, 306 : 25
once own happy lines, 333 : 13
our maker, 20 : 20
patient unto coming of L., 52 : 4
peace in our time O L., 56 : 15
praise L. pass ammunition, 871 : 2
pray L. soul to keep, 320 : 12
precious in the sight of the L., 21 : 24
prepare way of L., 30 : 30, 36 : 26
preserve thee, 22 : 4
raise me up I trust, 173 : 5
reason L. makes so many, 523 : 5
reigneth, 21 : 2
replied O L. Thou art, 365 : 6
rib which L. God had taken, 7 : 2
Savior which is Christ the L., 42 : 28
searcheth all hearts, 14 : 24
secret things belong unto the L., 11 : 21
seeth not as man, 12 : 38
servant in love l. in marriage, 147 : 30
servant not above l., 39 : 2
serve the L. with gladness, 21 : 3
set a mark upon Cain, 7 : 19
shall preserve thy going and coming, 22 : 4
short life in saddle L., 696 : 14
showed me so I did see, 300 : 20
sitting upon a throne, 29 : 8
so be it L., 597 : 18
soul is the concern of my L., 131 : 8
Spirit of the L. shall rest upon him, 29 : 18
support us all day long, 490 : 10
sword of the L. and of Gideon, 12 : 10
taste and see that the L. is good, 18 : 20
taught man that he knew not, 132 : 17
through this hour, 924 : 15
thy God is with thee, 11 : 28
thy L. the most generous, 132 : 17
'twant me 'twas the L., 593 : 17

Lord (*continued*)
wait upon the L., 31 : 2
watch between me and thee, 8 : 23
we are as L. made us, 722 : 16
we battle for the L., 687 : 17
went before them, 9 : 30
what fools these mortals be, 197 : 1
what would they say, 714 : 3
where dear L. crucified, 561 : 9
who created man, 132 : 17
whom the L. loveth he chasteneth, 51 : 20
whose hope the L. is, 32 : 11
will wipe away tears, 30 : 8
with me abide, 470 : 23
woman that feareth the L., 26 : 10
won't you buy me a Mercedes-Benz, 916 : 5
word of the L. endureth, 52 : 9
worship the L. in beauty of holiness, 18 : 14
Lordly, butter in a l. dish, 12 : 6
cedar green with boughs, 671 : 3
name is, 526 : 15
Lord's anointed temple, 238 : 5
ask the Lord's b., 918 : 19
earth is the L., 18 : 8, 48 : 18
it is the L. passover, 9 : 25
name is to be praised, 21 : 20
sing the L. song, 22 : 15
who is on the L. side, 10 : 13
Lords and ladies of Byzantium, 715 : 3
and owners of their faces, 245 : 5
but breath of kings, 408 : 18
gude Scots l., 926 : 12
Lord of l., 53 : 26
masters l. and rulers, 670 : 15
neither l. nor shogun, 609 : 7
not kings and l., 449 : 2
o' the creation, 409 : 7
of hell, 532 : 8
of humankind pass by, 369 : 1
of it all, 822 : 3
of ladies intellectual, 460 : 11
princes and l., 369 : 30
Scots l. at his feet, 926 : 13
seemed l. of all, 285 : 17
who lay ye low, 467 : 23
wit among l., 354 : 1
Lordship, plant man's l., 643 : 2
Lordships', dance attendance on l. pleasures, 249 : 16
Lore, admire virtue follow not her l., 288 : 5
Christ's l. and his apostles twelve, 146 : 10
gives me mystical l., 443 : 14
Heaven rejects the l., 429 : 6
poor fool with all my l., 396 : 10
volume of forgotten l., 526 : 10
Lorn, lone l. creetur, 548 : 22
Lorries, monotonously l. sway, 839 : 9
Lose and neglect creeping hours, 211 : 12
comfort or money too, 751 : 20
convictions to win or l., 737 : 7
for everything gain l. something, 497 : 11
freedom if value something more, 751 : 20
gain world l. soul, 39 : 38
good we oft might win, 227 : 29
has no wits to l., 374 : 13
having nothing nothing l., 186 : 13
Lose (*continued*)
he that findeth life shall l. it, 39 : 5
he who doesn't l. wits, 374 : 13
his child's-heart, 89 : 16
I would not l. you, 199 : 21
if once we l. this light, 255 : 16
it in moment you detect, 335 : 13
it that buy it with care, 197 : 27
itself in sky, 544 : 5
knife ill-used l. edge, 245 : 7
lest we l. Edens, 541 : 22
life nothing much to l., 692 : 9
mos people gonna l., 884 : 14
myself in a mystery, 274 : 4
myself in other minds, 442 : 7
name of action, 221 : 12
natural kindness, 714 : 15
never l. touch of the one, 697 : 2
nobly save meanly l., 522 : 12
nor l. common touch, 710 : 17
nothin' left to l., 913 : 10
nothing to l. but chains, 563 : 10
one life to l. for country, 401 : 9
our ventures, 217 : 6
play to win toil to l., 728 : 22
some day l. them all, 551 : 5
some l. their way, 604 : 5
soul's inheritance, 674 : 16
substance by grasping at shadow, 66 : 15
sweets grown common l. delight, 245 : 10
thee lose myself, 287 : 24
this intellectual being, 284 : 9
thy love lose all, 335 : 3
time to l., 26 : 21
tomorrow ground won today, 585 : 22
tragedy to l. heart's desire, 680 : 21
we must l. our loves, 868 : 6
what gives life value, 863 : 3
what he never had, 271 : 9
whatever gained he will l., 69 : 15
whatever you l. no account, 110 : 23
who possesses learn to l., 413 : 29
whosoever l. life shall find it, 39 : 38
win or l. it all, 292 : 3
win war as disastrous as to l., 817 : 18
Loser, I'll show you l., 811 : *n* 1
peace forced upon l., 682 : 9
show me good l., 811 : 3
Losers, both should l. be, 269 : 1
tell me if lovers are l., 761 : 9
Loses both itself and friend, 219 : 2
light that l., 632 : 8
past and dead for future, 77 : 22
what one l. one l., 653 : 9
who l. and who wins, 235 : 12
Loseth, he that l. life shall find it, 39 : 5
Losing, desperateness of l. binds bouquet, 739 : 11
fight when sure of l., 565 : 1
profit by l. our prayers, 240 : 26
stake counter boldly winning or l., 543 : 14
tense for first l., 885 : 2
Loss and possession one, 730 : 2
better to incur l., 93 : 12
black as our l., 801 : 6
grief aggravates l., 917 : 20
increasing store with l., 244 : 22
joys in another's l. of ease, 405 : 4
mocks my l. of liberty, 402 : 13
of all I sing, 906 : 9
of appetite for mediocrities, 651 : 1
Loss (*continued*)
of Eden, 282 : 22
of lives cannot be valued, 265 : 9
of native land, 76 : 17
profit and l., 805 : 9
so overwhelming, 524 : 4
thy so sore l., 693 : 19
unknown no loss, 110 : 18
we note time but from l., 330 : 7
Losses, all l. are restored, 244 : 12
feast of l., 864 : 13
tosses up our l., 808 : 2
wrought by nature, 393 : 7
Lost, all good to me is l., 285 : 13
all is not l., 283 : 8
all l. save honor, 157 : 6
all l. wild America, 840 : 13
all was l., 287 : 19
almost l. that built it, 275 : 8
and by wind grieved ghost, 852 : 8
and waiting for you go, 710 : 9
angel of ruined paradise, 469 : 2
are you l. daddy, 790 : 7
art of getting on together, 776 : 4
become a l. name, 883 : 9
behind the Ranges, 710 : 9
better to have loved and l., 532 : 3
books by which printers have l., 276 : 19
Bo-peep has l. sheep, 932 : 3
but ane twa behin', 411 : 20
causes, 587 : 1, 809 : 14
defaced deflowered, 287 : 22
every other friend, 524 : 3
find what you thought l., 851 : 1
for him I am not l., 94 : 13
for want of nail shoe l., 270 : 4, 347 : 35
found sheep which was l., 43 : 25
France not l. war, 815 : 7
friends I have l. a day, 119 : 20
generation, 752 : 9
haven't l. battle yet, 885 : 2
he is not l. for Me., 94 : 13
heart stiffens, 806 : 6
her honest name, 924 : 10
holding anchor l., 186 : 23
I have l. my reputation, 230 : 23
I once was l. now am found, 367 : 7
in convent's gloom, 334 : 27
in temple l. outright, 517 : 5
in the sweets, 332 : 5
in wandering mazes l., 284 : 19
it with hollaing and singing, 206 : 2
just l. when I was saved, 604 : 11
lacked and l., 209 : 31
lambs who l. way, 708 : 14
land of l. content, 691 : 9
legion of l. ones, 708 : 13
Lenore, 526 : 12
life l. in the living, 806 : 15
love and loathing, 858 : 19
loved and l., 532 : 3
memory of loved and l., 524 : 4
men have l. their reason, 216 : 20
missed it l. it forever, 544 : 24
more l. than life, 118 : 10
more than a friend, 786 : *n* 4
Mule Flat, 840 : 2
never l. as much but twice, 604 : 3
no friend, 336 : 5
no hate l. between us, 261 : 21
no love l., 170 : 22, 255 : 10
not l. but gone before, 114 : 25

Lost (*continued*)
not profited so much as l., 559 : 7
not that you won or l., 773 : 3
not whisper thought kiss l., 868 : 17
nothing except battle l., 421 : 8
nothing l. but money, 871 : 3
old nonchalance of hand, 714 : 7
old simplicity of times, 920 : 15
on roundabouts, 736 : 12
or won game, 489 : 10
pain like l. fire, 874 : 22
people on whom nothing l., 652 : 14
praising what is l., 227 : 20
principles of free constitution l., 383 : 8
race, 852 : 11
reputation, 230 : 23
sea smell, 806 : 6
seek for the l. mind, 89 : 22
sheep of house of Israel, 38 : 33
so fallen so l., 513 : 7
sooner l. and worn, 214 : 1
sun is l. and the earth, 254 : 5
swallowed up and l., 284 : 9
time never found, 347 : 27
to fame, 104 : 4
to love and truth, 708 : 15
violent souls, 805 : 16
virtue l. seldom recovered, 307 : 20
war in time utterly l., 576 : 1
was l. and is found, 43 : 28
what is left when honor l., 110 : 26
what though field be l., 283 : 8
when battle's l. and won, 235 : 21
when faith is l., 513 : 8
when I had l. one shaft, 198 : 6
without deserving, 230 : 24
woman that deliberates l., 325 : 18
woman won or woman l., 715 : 5
wreath has l. rose, 431 : 20
year only l. to me, 268 : 21
yesterday, 480 : 13
Lot, blameless vestal's l., 335 : 4
dwelled in the cities, 8 : 7
is fallen unto me, 17 : *n* 3
no l. is altogether happy, 107 : 24
no man content with l., 106 : 10
of me and all so luscious, 574 : 21
policeman's l., 628 : 3
this l. is bitterest, 72 : 1
Lothario, gay L., 327 : 22
Lot's, remember L. wife, 43 : 37
Lots, cast l. upon my vesture, 18 : 6
Lou, lady known as L., 752 : 5
Loud as the hemlocks, 766 : 12
battle rages l. and long, 443 : 11
could have got l. but hadn't, 878 : 14
had tongue yet never l., 230 : 11
heard the l. bassoon, 434 : 8
helpless naked piping l., 405 : 12
huzzas, 337 : 14
I speak not l. or long, 174 : *n* 6
I'm black and I'm proud, 913 : 1
laugh spoke vacant mind, 370 : 4
licker talks mightty l., 662 : 13
play skillfully with a l. noise, 18 : 19
roared dreadful thunder, 415 : 5
shout out l. and strong, 764 : 12
sing cuckoo, 916 : 14
sing Goddamm, 792 : 8
troublesome insects, 373 : 28
trumpet's l. clangor, 305 : 11
turned in l. fire, 766 : 12
uplifted angel trumpets, 281 : 10
Louder, a little l. but as empty, 337 : 7
cock l. in own farmyard, 555 : 2
he talked of honor, 488 : *n* 1
sing l. around, 403 : 4
Loud-hissing, bubbling and l. urn, 377 : 3
Louis, dear L. of awful cheek, 668 : *n* 4
Loungers of Empire drained, 689 : 2
Loup, comme un complice à pas de l., 581 : *n* 2
Lousy, poor and very l., 348 : 13
unethical and l., 858 : 17
Lovable, Elaine the l., 534 : 11
to be loved be l., 113 : 11
Love, a feeling and a l., 423 : 12
a kind of warfare, 113 : *n* 3
absence cure of l., 169 : 15
absence opens l., 555 : 6
acts of kindness and of l., 423 : 9
ah l. let us be true, 587 : 16
alas how l. can trifle, 190 : 5
all for l. a little for bottle, 393 : 10
all for l. nothing for reward, 173 : 13
all in green went my l. riding, 828 : 9
all l. all liking all delight, 266 : 21
all l. impossible, 903 : 2
all love of other sights controls, 251 : 15
all l. sweet, 467 : 5
all policy's allowed in l., 564 : *n* 1
all she loves is l., 460 : 24
all trust a few, 227 : 9
all we know in l. bitter, 811 : 15
all we know of l., 608 : 5
all's fair in l. and war, 564 : 2
all's l. yet all's law, 543 : 18
almost too much l., 748 : 9
alone capable of uniting beings, 775 : 2
alone give woman full stature, 754 : 1
alters not, 245 : 18
am like to l. three more, 290 : 4
America l. or leave it, 925 : 17
Americans because they love liberty, 351 : 3
and a cough, 269 : 12
and all his pleasures toys, 250 : 7
and be loved by forever, 543 : 23
and be loved by me, 527 : 7
and be wise, 110 : 17
and desire and hate, 721 : 7
and fame to nothingness, 478 : 19
and fear hardly together, 153 : 19
and glory, 830 : 7
and good company, 329 : 11
and have not l., 48 : *n* 5
and I had wit to win, 671 : 4
and laughter, 614 : 17
and man's unconquerable mind, 425 : 21
and scandal, 349 : 16
and shame, 651 : 11
and still to l., 377 : 20
and thanks, 384 : 13
and thought and joy, 425 : 5
and war same thing, 170 : 20
and you must l. him, 424 : 17
anger of lovers renews l., 96 : *n* 6
anterior to life, 606 : 11
archer with low I.Q., 864 : 18
art accomplice of l., 686 : 2
as long as you can love, 536 : 8
ashamed of having been in l., 293 : 11
at first sight, 707 : 7
Love (*continued*)
at the lips, 748 : 8
babe that milks me, 237 : 5
bade me welcome, 269 : 9
ballad in print, 246 : 30
base men being in l., 230 : 15
be but sworn my l., 192 : 5
beareth all things, 48 : 24
beautiful time of young l., 413 : 21
begets love, 874 : 19
believeth all things, 48 : 24
better is thy l. than wine, 28 : 13
between predilection and l., 641 : 2
beyond the world, 314 : 13
bid me take l. easy, 711 : 22
Black l. is B. wealth, 916 : 2
born with pleasure of looking, 671 : 18
bout with l., 67 : 8
boy's l., 234 : 14
breastplate of faith and l., 50 : 20
bridge is l., 839 : 10
brief as woman's l., 222 : 12
bright particular star, 227 : 10
brings bewitching grace, 76 : 22
brook weather that l. not wind, 190 : 28
brotherly l., 47 : 20, 51 : 22
built on beauty, 253 : 16
bumping against obstacles of civilization, 504 : 7
business that we l., 241 : 14
but her love forever, 410 : 3
but I do l. thee, 230 : 30
but you alone, 917 : 4
by heaven I do l., 190 : 31
by l. are driven away, 402 : 14
calls to war, 177 : 12
can come to everyone, 825 : 7
care of discipline is l., 34 : 17
careless l., 893 : 7
carrier of l. and sympathy, 617 : 7
cement glue and lime of l., 266 : 1
chain to bind child to parents, 524 : 12
change old l. for new, 177 : 7
chatter l. and hate, 588 : 7
cherish and obey, 56 : 17
children's gratitude woman's l., 716 : 12
Christ not l. in human way, 856 : 19
clearness of eternal l., 899 : 16
close hand out of l., 657 : 14
clouds of goodness and l., 392 : *n* 1
collaborating in private way of l., 889 : 1
combat between l. and hate, 671 : 17
come unto my l., 174 : 18
comes in at eye, 713 : 7
comforteth like sunshine, 189 : 12
common as light is l., 467 : 5
concluded with impossibility of separation, 671 : 18
conquer l. that run away, 272 : 3
conquers all things, 103 : 24
contend no more l., 541 : 21
converted from thing it was, 244 : 17
could you and I conspire, 517 : 13
countless ties of l., 749 : 5
country support Constitution, 725 : 20
courage l. joy, 332 : 2
course of true l., 195 : 22
covereth all sins, 23 : 23
crime to l. too well, 335 : 8

Love (*continued*)
crown is l. and friendship, 475 : 21
curiosity freckles doubt, 827 : 9
dare l. that and say so too, 252 : 6
dark secret l., 405 : 5
deep as first l., 531 : 4
desire more l. and knowledge, 210 : 18
die for l., 227 : 11
die to what we l., 679 : 9
died before god of l. was born, 253 : 9
dinner of herbs where l. is, 24 : 7
distills desire, 76 : 22
do justly and l. mercy, 33 : 23
do not trifle with l., 537 : 8
do you never my l. repent, 593 : 4
doesn't l. a wall, 747 : 4
dooms of l., 829 : 19
draw as l. with thread, 259 : 18
drew them with bands of l., 33 : 14
dropped like a flower, 101 : 21
dull sublunary lovers' l., 253 : 3
earth's place for l., 747 : 16
ecstasy of l., 220 : 9
end of l. or season, 747 : 2
endureth all things, 48 : 24
envieth not, 48 : 23
episode in man's life, 417 : 12
eyes silent tongues of l., 168 : 16
faith nor l. nor law, 467 : 4
faithful in l., 430 : 18
fall in l. with Athens, 81 : 5
falling out renewing is of l., 96 : *n* 6
false maids in l., 226 : 15
false or true, 712 : 9
fear l. fear life, 738 : 4
fed with necessity of seeing, 671 : 18
few l. to hear sins they act, 243 : 11
fickleness of women I l., 680 : 3
fight no-love every inch, 867 : 14
figure the same for l., 750 : 2
final face of l., 900 : 6
find out way, 919 : 3
first is deep l., 65 : 3
first learned in lady's eyes, 191 : 2
fitter l. for me, 252 : 15
flies out window, 919 : 11
fond l. charmed me, 918 : 9
food of l., 213 : *n* 2, 213 : 7
for ladies' l. unfit, 307 : 5
for l. lead apes in hell, 188 : 30
for l. of Barbara Allen, 926 : 21
for l. sweet l., 576 : 5
for Love's sake, 875 : 4
for sake of being loved, 464 : 19
for what they are, 747 : 15
forbearance l. charity, 383 : 6
force, 727 : 5
forever wilt thou l., 477 : 7
forget l. to friends and
brethren, 34 : 2
forgive us, 476 : 5
forspent with l. and shame, 651 : 11
foundation is l., 909 : 11
freedom hate slavery, 881 : 13
freedom in my l., 296 : 4
freely serve because we freely
l., 286 : 20
friendliness hardiness l., 149 : 5
friendship charity, 226 : 20
from eyelids dripped l., 61 : 11
fruit of Spirit is l., 49 : 30
fruits of l. gone, 462 : 18
fullness even of l., 58 : 16
game beyond prize, 700 : 6

Love (*continued*)
gather rose of l., 173 : 14
gift of fairy tale, 612 : 15
gilds the scene, 398 : 20
give a little l. to child, 573 : 4
give all to l., 494 : 10
give l. not thoughts, 782 : 15
give me more l. or more
disdain, 271 : 22
go l. without the help, 407 : 3
God is l., 52 : 24
God is l. I dare say, 620 : 24
gods l. the obscure, 56 : 23
goes toward love, 192 : 15
gold and l. affairs difficult to
hide, 935 : 17
golden time of first l., 413 : 21
good man's l., 212 : 16
good to l. the unknown, 441 : 24
government filled with l., 903 : 8
great l. grows there, 222 : 13
greater l. hath no man, 45 : 25
greater l. the more false, 868 : 7
greatest is l., 48 : 25
greatness worthy to excite l., 588 : 16
grow from grass I l., 575 : 4
grown old in l., 407 : 4
grows bitter with treason, 633 : 6
gude to be off with old l., 921 : 8
gushed from my heart, 434 : 29
hail wedded l., 286 : 5
half in l. with death, 476 : 28
happiness to l. and be loved, 504 : 15
hardly worth thinking of, 712 : 19
harmony is pure l., 182 : 12
hate foes as far as we soon might l.
them, 73 : 14
hate one and l. other, 38 : 1
hate traitors treason l., 305 : 26
hath an end, 633 : 5
hath so long possessed me, 140 : 8
hatred as well as l., 359 : 5
hatred ceases by l., 72 : 16
he bore to learning, 370 : 10
he was all for l., 393 : 10
he will then l. me, 403 : 8
hearts in l. use own tongues, 209 : 9
heaven is l., 430 : 6
heaven sends l. of her, 4 : 10
hell is to l. no longer, 802 : 14
her till I die, 918 : 15
hid in heart of l., 712 : 6
Highlands forever I l., 410 : 8
him most for enemies, 598 : 11
him who in l. of nature, 471 : 2
his banner over me was l., 28 : 6
hiss of l., 864 : 11
history of woman's life, 417 : 12
hold your tongue and let me
l., 252 : 10
hope nor l. nor friend, 669 : 2
hopeth all things, 48 : 24
how do I l. thee, 507 : 14
how left the ancient l., 403 : 1
how should I true l. know, 223 : 21
how they could l., 923 : 8
how vast a memory has L., 332 : 14
human l. seen at its height, 764 : 9
humanity i l. you, 828 : 15
hunt l. down together, 633 : 13
I am sick of l., 28 : 6
I and my true l., 921 : 9
I both l. and do not l., 67 : 9
I do not l. thee Doctor Fell, 319 : 19

Love (*continued*)
I hate and I l., 102 : 17
I loathe that I did l., 162 : 5
I l. a lass, 394 : 6
I l. a lassie, 731 : 2
I l. broad margin to life, 560 : 1
I l. everything old, 371 : 3
I taught thee to l., 253 : 17
I told my l., 404 : 10
idea of two sexes, 831 : 2
if ever thou shalt l., 213 : 29
if I l. you what business of
yours, 395 : 4
if l. were what rose is, 633 : 11
if music food of l., 213 : 7
if no l. is what feel I so, 144 : 14
if she meant I should not l., 540 : 27
if she will not l., 289 : 18
if thou must l. me, 507 : 10
if world and l. were young, 172 : 10
if you l. you suffer, 817 : 16
in a golden bowl, 403 : 17
in a hut, 476 : 5
in idleness, 196 : 15
in it was l. and desire, 58 : 19
in law and l. same, 556 : 1
in l. and charity with
neighbors, 55 : 16
in l. illusion reaches zenith, 658 : 14
in l. things different, 658 : 14
in l. two solitudes touch, 756 : 6
in l. with American names, 840 : 2
in l. with loving, 129 : 1
in my bosom like a bee, 177 : 4
in others they l. l., 294 : 9
in our will to l. or not, 286 : 20
in sea caves l., 849 : 18
in spite of darkness, 252 : 21
in struggle for life find l., 820 : 9
in summer's wonderland, 772 : 22
in the frost, 886 : 15
inestimable l., 55 : 7
infinite l., 633 : 4
innocence of l., 214 : 3
inspiration l. and freedom, 695 : 3
instill l. of you into world, 4 : 4
irresistible desire, 750 : 7
is a boy, 291 : 19
is a mood to man, 670 : 2
is a sickness full of woes, 182 : 11
is agreement, 182 : 12
is all there is, 608 : 5
is attempt at penetrating
another, 885 : 15
is best, 542 : 4
is blind, 147 : 23, 199 : 7
is dead, 176 : 8
is enough, 618 : 8
is flowerlike, 436 : 8
is fulfilling of law, 47 : 28
is heaven, 430 : 6
is intercourse between tyrants and
slaves, 369 : 25
is kind, 48 : 23
is like measles, 561 : 12
is metaphysical gravity, 833 : 1
is most beautiful among gods, 61 : 10
is most nearly itself, 807 : 24
is my lord and king, 532 : 25
is not all, 823 : 13
is not love which alters, 245 : 18
is only meaning, 839 : 10
is strong as death, 28 : 23
is sweeping the country, 836 : 2

Love (*continued*)
is the soul of genius, 402 : 11
is the whole, 829 : 21
is then our duty, 332 : 4
it and who shall dare, 562 : 11
it would conceal, 436 : 11
itself have rest, 460 : 5
itself slumber on, 469 : 18
jealousy born with l., 294 : 2
joy and l. triumphing, 285 : 6
joy nor l. nor light, 587 : 16
joy of l. too short, 149 : 11
jumps from admiration to l., 440 : 18
keep corner in thing I l., 231 : 6
kelson of creation l., 574 : 14
kill things they do not l., 200 : 4
kill your joys with l., 193 : 30
kindled by virtue, 142 : 5
kindness shall win my l., 189 : 1
King of l. shepherd is, 580 : 15
King without woman I l., 832 : 2
know the l. betwixt us, 295 : 13
knoweth no laws, 159 : *n* 9
knowledge and l. of God, 56 : 1
known l. how bitter, 632 : 20
knows nothing of order, 127 : 11
labor of l.., 50 : 16
laggard in l., 430 : 19
land that I l., 802 : 9
last not least in l., 216 : 10
law to itself, 130 : 4
lay aside long-cherished l., 102 : 15
learn to bear beams of l., 403 : 7
lease of my true l., 245 : 13
least that let men know, 189 : 30
leave me O L., 176 : 9
leaving l. behind, 606 : 9
lest thy l. prove variable, 192 : 11
let l. who never loved, 133 : 14
let me l. river and woodland, 104 : 4
let thy l. be younger, 214 : 2
let us be true, 587 : 16
let us live and l., 101 : 18, 250 : 3
let us surrender to l., 103 : 24
let warm l. in, 477 : 13
life among people who l. each other, 504 : 13
life eternal l. immortal, 642 : 10
life just the same, 847 : 5
light dies when l. done, 670 : 8
light l. life, 393 : 5
like black our black, 889 : 17
like death levels, 493 : 5
like everybody not in l., 734 : 6
like measles, 561 : 12
little words of l., 591 : 8
live and l. in God's light, 155 : 2
live with me and be my l., 183 : 8, 253 : 2
live with thee and be thy l., 172 : 10
lodged in woman's breast, 250 : 13
loneliness l. bodies, 849 : 12
long life better than figs, 240 : 16
long l. doth so, 193 : 1
longing for l. a passion, 738 : 6
look at enemies with l., 309 : 17
look at was to l., 529 : 19
look of l. alarms, 404 : 19
looked as she did l., 478 : 12
looks not with eyes, 196 : 1
Lord with all thy heart, 40 : 16
lose thy l. lose all, 335 : 3
lost l. and loathing, 858 : 19
lost to l. and truth, 708 : 15

Love (*continued*)
love and hate hate, 857 : 1
l. of truth, demanded of genius 397 : 8
lover, 497 : 14
lovers who l. do not write, 655 : 4
lovers' quarrels renewal of l., 96 : 5
lyric l. half angel, 545 : 1
makes world go round, 629 : 2, 928 : 5
makes young, 290 : 6
man in l. endures more, 658 : 14
man in l. with suffering, 581 : 17
man is in l., 715 : 7
mankind except American, 356 : 4
man's l. apart from life, 460 : 19
many waters cannot quench l., 28 : 24
marriage from which l. gone, 859 : 11
marriage without l., 347 : 6
martyrs honor slain, 582 : 9
may perfectly l. thee, 55 : 15
me and keep my commandments, 10 : 5
me in December, 651 : *n* 1
me little love me long, 266 : 8, 917 : 12
me not for grace, 918 : 16
me sure to die, 447 : 14
medicines to make me l. him, 203 : 18
men died but not for l., 212 : 23
Mercy Pity Peace and L., 403 : 10
mercy unto them that l. me, 10 : 5
met you not with my true l., 172 : 8
method is l. and gentleness, 154 : 12
mie l. ys dedde, 399 : 15
mighty pain to l., 295 : 9
ministers of l., 435 : 20
mischievous devil, 620 : 24
mistress to the man I l., 335 : 2
moderately, 193 : 1
money rage and l., 863 : 20
money the sinew of l., 99 : *n* 8
moody food of l., 241 : 3
more libertines than l., 358 : 24
more l. less we flatter, 297 : 29
more than love, 527 : 8
more true than l. to me, 918 : 4
morning and evening star, 791 : 8
most important business, 453 : 18
music food of l., 213 : *n* 2, 241 : 3
music thing I l. most, 310 : 5
my home of l., 245 : 15
my hope my hap my l., 168 : 2
my hope my l., 276 : 6
my lord and king, 532 : 25
my l. and I did meet, 711 : 22
my l. he purloined away, 636 : 12
my l. is come to me, 608 : 12
my l. is dead, 399 : 15
my l. like red red rose, 409 : 22
my l. like the melody, 409 : 22
my l. of a birth as rare, 297 : 6
my whole course of l., 229 : 25
mysterious by this l., 252 : 11
need l. and wish to give it, 914 : 5
needs spirit and spirit love, 754 : 1
ne'er ebb to humble l., 231 : 18
neighbor as thyself, 10 : 21
neighbor well, 646 : 4
neighbor yet pull not down hedge, 269 : 19
never any that could escape l., 127 : 1
never change when l. has found home, 112 : 19

Love (*continued*)
never doubt I l., 220 : 14
never faileth, 48 : 24
never l. stranger, 821 : 2
never l. unless you can, 250 : 4
never see what you l., 735 : *n* 1
never seek to tell thy l., 404 : 10
never seeketh own, 148 : 20
never sick old dead, 172 : 9
never taint my l., 232 : 7
never told her l., 214 : 5
no concern with art, 619 : 8
no creature give orders to l., 504 : 8
no disguise conceal l., 293 : 10
no go my honey l., 870 : 5
no l. but vanity, 454 : 10
no l. lost, 170 : 22, 255 : 10
no more dear l., 531 : 10
no season knows, 252 : 8
noght old as when newe, 147 : 18
none but l. find me out, 172 : 7
none knew thee but to l., 464 : 11
nor grief nor l. enough alone, 889 : 8
nor l. thy life nor hate, 287 : 30
not a gaping pig, 200 : 2
not Death but L., 507 : 8
not enough religion to make us l., 322 : 2
not for l., 212 : 23
not found thing to l., 757 : 4
not freedom but license, 282 : 12
not l. thee dear so much, 296 : 1
not man the less, 458 : 24
not my l. to see, 174 : 13
not Pleasure love God, 473 : 7
not puffed up, 48 : 23
not say all it means, 729 : 1
not to be loved but to l., 138 : 15
not to be purchased, 127 : 8
not to eat not for l., 495 : 21
not to l. when we l., 168 : 31
not wise who buffet against l., 75 : 5
nothing I l. as much as fight, 779 : 5
nothing in l., 239 : 28
nothing we l. overmuch, 714 : 11
nourished without denying l., 898 : 7
now abideth l., 48 : 25
now l. is over, 711 : 10
now warm in l., 334 : 27
now who never loved before, 329 : 16
now with l. now in colde grave, 146 : 28
O human l., 525 : 2
o' life's young day, 482 : 13
O ye that l. mankind, 384 : 12
obedience troops of friends, 239 : 31
of a brute, 526 : 6
of another condition for happiness, 882 : 12
of beauty, 68 : 4
of British people, 373 : 7
of fame vanity, 703 : 12
of flattery, 327 : 16
of gentle woman, 879 : 19
of glory the most ardent, 327 : 14
of God, 49 : 24
of God in Christ, 47 : 15
of home love of country, 547 : 22
of justice simply fear, 293 : 13
of learning, 512 : 15
of liberty, 520 : 7
of money as possession, 783 : 10
of money impulse to effort, 665 : 18
of money the root of evil, 51 : 2

Love (*continued*)
of old for old, 692 : 17
of pleasure, 335 : 21
of praise, 329 : 19
of slaughter, 792 : 14
of spiders, 847 : 3
of sway, 335 : 21
of the turtle, 459 : 5
of the virtuous, 68 : 4
of virtue, 359 : 1
of what is good and just, 881 : 12
of wisdom guide of life, 407 : 17
of you has entrapped me, 4 : 11
of young for young, 692 : 17
offender detest offense, 307 : *n* 2
office and affairs of l., 209 : 9
on l. request for money chilling, 583 : 15
one another, 45 : 19, 47 : 27
one jot of former l. retain, 182 : 16
one maiden only, 534 : 22
only l. sprung from only hate, 191 : 27
only survival, 839 : 10
open rebuke better than secret l., 25 : 23
our hopeless l., 801 : 5
our l. hath no decay, 252 : 22
our occupations, 548 : 15
our principle, 483 : 11
out of l. cheat others, 734 : 8
out of l. with your nativity, 212 : 20
oyster may be crossed in l., 399 : 12
pain to l. in vain, 295 : 9
pains of l. sweeter far, 303 : 7
pangs of disprized l., 221 : 12
pardon to extent we l., 293 : 38
passed muse appeared, 486 : 8
passing the l. of women, 13 : 11
path to deepest mystery path of l., 853 : 8
paths to woman's l., 260 : 20
people and things I l., 876 : 21
people with whom fallen in l., 880 : 1
perfect l. casteth out fear, 52 : 25
perhaps right to dissemble l., 407 : 13
pest of l., 476 : 3
physicians by their l. grown cosmographers, 254 : 18
pitched his mansion, 716 : 18
pity melts mind to l., 260 : *n* 8
pity swells tide of l., 260 : *n* 8
pity's akin to l., 260 : *n* 8
planet of l. on high, 533 : 21
Platonic l., 169 : 20
pleasure and l. are pinions, 395 : 11
pleasure drives l. away, 715 : 13
pleasure of l. in loving, 293 : 30
poets' food l. and fame, 467 : 16
possess heart fall in l., 734 : 2
pray that l. may never come, 76 : 22
prophet of soul, 493 : 16
prosperity's very bond of l., 247 : 3
purlieu of god of l., 253 : 10
purple light of L., 362 : 21
pussy my l., 550 : 7
putting l. away, 607 : 1
quaint figure men l., 765 : 8
quantity of l., 224 : 22
quarrels in concord end, 289 : 4
quench my l. I wonder, 628 : 25
quick-eyed l., 269 : 9
radiant with splendor, 138 : 13
rather than l. than money than fame, 560 : 20

Love (*continued*)
regain l. once possessed, 289 : 3
regent of l. rhymes, 190 : 26
renewed by absence, 352 : 13
repine reason chafe, 495 : 9
resembleth April day, 189 : 32
respect or natural l., 684 : 2
rhymes so rare to l., 657 : 3
right true end of l., 253 : 22
rock know l. better, 811 : 15
rose of our l., 900 : 3
rose yet leave it on stem, 494 : *n* 3
ruined l. when built anew, 245 : 21
rules the court, 430 : 6
rules the gods, 75 : 5
sadder not to be able to l., 706 : 10
sang of l. not of fame, 596 : 17
satisfied, 806 : 1
saved by l., 823 : 21
seals of l., 228 : 28
see how Christians l. one another, 126 : 2
seeketh not self to please, 405 : 3
seeketh self to please, 405 : 4
seem worthy of your l., 424 : 17
seized this man for fair form, 140 : 23
separate us from l. of Christ, 47 : 14
servant in l. lord in marriage, 147 : 30
sets l. task like that, 454 : 10
shackles of old l., 534 : 14
shadow of power, 755 : 2
shall know no quarrels, 107 : 9
she whom I l. hard to catch, 601 : 1
shoot false L., 918 : 3
sidelong looks of l., 369 : 29
sighed for l. of lady, 629 : 22
silence in l. betrays woe, 172 : 13
sin who tell us l. die, 440 : 4
sit down says L., 269 : 10
sleep on my l., 267 : 6
smile of l., 406 : 5
so dear I l. him, 287 : 20
so full in my nature, 543 : 20
so long as we l. we serve, 669 : 13
so many I l. were not yet born, 856 : 7
so sweet l. seemed, 654 : 17
someone to l. and l. you, 692 : 15
something tells me but not l., 199 : 21
sometimes stronger than convictions, 861 : 15
sorrow of l. dureth overlong, 149 : 11
sought is good, 214 : 17
speak low if you speak l., 209 : 8
spirit all compact of fire, 189 : 8
spirit of l., 51 : 6
spirit of l. how quick and fresh, 213 : 8
sports of l., 255 : 16
state of perceptual anesthesia, 772 : 3
steer stars, 914 : 7
stony limits cannot hold l., 192 : 7
strong is your hold O l., 576 : 19
study way to l. each other, 267 : 8
such I believe my l., 154 : 15
suffereth long, 48 : 23
superb in l. and logic, 556 : *n* 3
swears she is made of truth, 246 : 2
sweet as l., 400 : 15
sweet for a day, 633 : 6
sweet is true l., 534 : 15
sweet love, 576 : 5, 898 : 3
sweet lovers l. spring, 212 : 33
sweetest l. I do not go, 252 : 15

Love (*continued*)
take l. away no art, 686 : 2
take l. together to sky, 646 : 11
takes life to l. life, 728 : 5
tale without l., 655 : 16
teach l. of reading, 862 : 9
teach monarch to be wise, 361 : 19
that can be reckoned, 240 : 13
that comes too late, 227 : 22
that endures for breath, 632 : 9
that l. is all is all we know of l., 608 : 5
that moves sun and other stars, 142 : 20
that my l. were in my arms, 917 : 10
that never seen twice, 483 : 6
that never told can be, 404 : 10
that winged seraphs coveted, 527 : 8
that word is l., 75 : 14
the brotherhood, 52 : 11
the good pursue the worst, 113 : *n* 15
the human form divine, 403 : 11
the look of landscapes, 794 : 2
the Lord with all thine heart, 11 : 9
the only priest, 615 : 12
the wild swan, 797 : 20
thee better after death, 507 : 15
thee to the depth, 507 : 14
them as God gives them, 395 : 16
them that love me, 23 : 17
there are those who l. it, 450 : 2
they do not l. that do not show, 189 : 30
they happy are and l., 276 : 8
they l. a train, 223 : *n* 5
things we love for what are, 747 : 15
this bud of l., 192 : 14
this cultured hell, 819 : 4
those I guard I do not l., 713 : 20
those who always loved l. more, 329 : 16
those who l. and create, 672 : 9
those who l. want wisdom, 466 : 17
those who love you, 343 : 17
those who wrong him, 125 : 10
those who yearn for impossible, 396 : 23
thou wast all to me l., 525 : 17
though pressed with ill, 377 : 20
thought l. never change, 654 : 17
through l. come together into one, 75 : 23
through our l. is my lord slain, 149 : 17
throw away l. on conceited, 565 : *n* 2
thy first l., 52 : 33
thy honesty and l., 230 : 22
thy kiss would wake dead, 530 : 12
thy l. to me was wonderful, 13 : 11
thy neighbor, 10 : 21
thy neighbor as thyself, 40 : 16
thy sweet l. remembered, 244 : 10
thyself last, 249 : 8
till I prince of l. beheld, 402 : 12
time to l., 26 : 21
time weakens l., 315 : 6
to be wise and l., 226 : 14
to be worst of company, 321 : 20
to begin journey on Sundays, 323 : 17
to believe in l., 694 : 1
to choose a god of l., 857 : 1
to faults always blind, 404 : 14
to hatred turned, 324 : 16
to have known l. how bitter, 632 : 20

Love (*continued*)
to live is like to l., 621 : 1
to lose myself, 442 : 7
to lose myself in a mystery, 274 : 4
to l. and to cherish, 56 : 9
to l. her a liberal education, 327 : 11
to matrimony in a moment, 440 : 18
to say how much l. is little l., 143 : 5
to see her was to l. her, 410 : 3
to woman life or death, 670 : 2
too much l. of living, 633 : 22
took all my l., 717 : 20
touch of l. and pride, 684 : 1
trade you have learned, 124 : 21
tragedy of l. indifference, 751 : 16
treason but hate traitor, 99 : 16
trembling with L., 721 : 3
true l. a durable fire, 172 : 9
true l. is like ghosts, 293 : 12
true l. kept under, 628 : 25
true l. sits him down, 922 : 12
truth pardon error, 343 : 2
try thinking of l., 870 : 4
tunes shepherd's reed, 430 : 6
turns to thoughts of l., 529 : 16
unconditional l., 909 : 14
unconquerable waster, 74 : 23
unfamiliar Name, 808 : 15
unrelenting foe to l., 345 : 18
unsatisfied, 806 : 1
unsought is better, 214 : 17
up groweth with your age, 145 : 8
vaunteth not, 48 : 23
vegetable l. grow, 296 : 27
vegetable l. not suit me, 628 : 7
very ecstasy of l., 220 : 9
very few to l., 424 : 12
Virtue she alone is free, 280 : 5
waft her l. to Carthage, 200 : 22
we are a small pond, 904 : 5
weathered storms of life, 692 : 17
what a plague is l., 918 : 7
what I l. near at hand, 874 : 10
what is life without l., 413 : 13
what is l., 791 : 8
what is l. 'tis not hereafter, 213 : 23
what l. I bore to thee, 425 : 6
what the world needs now is l., 898 : 3
whatever it was an infection, 908 : 12
when I l. thee not, 230 : 30
when I was in l. with you, 691 : 2
when l. and life fair, 676 : 9
when l. begins to sicken, 216 : 30
when l. is done, 670 : 8
when l. is in excess, 76 : 16
when l. pules and whines, 496 : 24
when L. speaks, 191 : 4
when my l. swears, 246 : 2
when Silence speaks for L., 621 : 14
when we love not, 168 : 31
where I and my l. wont to gae, 927 : 7
where is l. beauty truth, 467 : 13
where l. and need one, 748 : 18
where l. is great, 222 : 13
where l. of man l. of art, 79 : 16
where l. rules no will to power, 755 : 2
where power predominates l. lacking, 755 : 2
where we l. is home, 518 : 16
which graybeards call divine, 186 : 28
white rose breathes of l., 659 : 6

Love (*continued*)
whoever never loved will l., 850 : 10
whom do we l., 874 : 17
whom the gods l., 91 : 1
why am I crying after l., 787 : 7
why is all l. speak, 607 : 10
why L. needs be blind, 196 : *n* 1
wife Belle Aurore, 545 : 15
will creep in service, 160 : *n* 4
will find out way, 919 : 3
wisdom live accordingly, 559 : 9
with all thy faults I l. thee, 375 : *n* 6
with delight discourses, 140 : 9
with streaming hair, 836 : 17
with you l. to live, 108 : 2
without bitterness, 822 : 9
without dissimulation, 47 : 19
without his wings, 456 : 6
without marriage, 347 : 6
without power destroyed, 823 : 16
without the woman I l., 832 : 2
woman more barbarous in l., 657 : 21
women l. lovers, 294 : 9
word l. in mouth of courtesan, 495 : 28
words of l. then spoken, 447 : 7
work is l. made visible, 782 : 17
world in l. with night, 193 : 9
world outlasts l., 584 : 16
worms eaten but not for l., 212 : 23
would be dried up, 581 : 19
wroth with one we l., 434 : 3
wrought new alchemy, 253 : 1
ye do me wrong, 917 : 14
years grow cold to l., 104 : 9
yes I'm in l., 361 : 6
yields to business, 113 : 26
you as New Englanders love pie, 759 : 14
you do not l. me at all, 633 : 9
you for speed of observation, 751 : 7
you for yourself alone, 716 : 5
you in December, 651 : 6
you l. me so much, 790 : 8
you l. the daylight, 76 : 6
you ten years before the Flood, 296 : 27
your enemies, 37 : 11
your eyes that can see, 797 : 20
your life poor as it is, 560 : 18
youth gave l. and roses, 447 : 9
Zeus's bed of l., 76 : 25
Loved, a l. a long, 778 : 6
alas I l. you best, 316 : 7
alas that all we l. of him, 469 : 6
Alcuin my name learning I l., 135 : 8
and cursed and floundered, 654 : 7
and lost, 524 : 4, 532 : 3
and thought himself beloved, 714 : 18
as l. we are indispensable, 669 : 13
at first sight, 183 : 17
at home revered abroad, 408 : 18
betray heart that l. her, 423 : 15
better l. ye canna be, 417 : 5
better to be l. than feared, 153 : 19
better to have l. lost, 532 : 3
burning Sappho l., 461 : 2
conviction we are l., 491 : 15
country as no other man, 590 : 7
did till we l., 251 : 14
each other and were ignorant, 716 : 20
flowers that fade, 654 : 16
for loving's sake, 545 : 13

Loved (*continued*)
God so l. world, 44 : 34
happiness to love and be l., 504 : 15
happy human face, 454 : 1
him because he was he, 164 : 14
him for himself alone, 398 : 24
him like a brother, 411 : 6
him so followed him, 541 : 6
him that l. rose, 693 : 6
him too much not to hate him, 312 : 4
how l. how honored once, 335 : 11
I have l. beauty, 480 : 4
I have l. thee Ocean, 458 : 30
I l. her sometimes she l. me too, 860 : 8
I l. her that she did pity, 229 : 31
I l. Ophelia, 224 : 22
I not honor more, 296 : 1
I saw and l., 384 : 3
if ever man l. by wife, 290 : 12
if I had a friend that l. her, 229 : 31
Jonathan l. him as his own soul, 13 : 5
King Cophetua l. beggarmaid, 192 : 1
know we l. in vain, 456 : 7
knowing I l. my books, 247 : 15
life London this moment, 781 : 15
love and be l. by me, 527 : 7
love now who never l., 329 : 16
love of being l., 641 : 7
mansionry, 236 : 21
me ever so little, 633 : 9
memory of l. and lost, 524 : 4
moments of glad grace, 712 : 9
money with affiction, 722 : 25
Muses l. me, 93 : 2
needs only to be seen, 305 : 16
never l. tree or flower, 447 : 14
never time place l. one, 546 : 3
never to have l., 532 : 3
no man ever l., 245 : 18
no sooner looked but l., 212 : 31
not l. world nor world me, 458 : 3
not that I l. Caesar less, 216 : 14
not wisely but too well, 232 : 20
one blotted from page, 457 : 10
out upon it I have l., 290 : 4
pale hands I l., 707 : 2
passing well, 221 : 1
Pharaoh's lean kine l., 204 : 6
pilgrim soul in you, 712 : 9
produces motion through being l., 87 : 10
remember not only how l., 702 : 5
Rome more, 216 : 14
sad not to be l., 706 : 10
safer to be feared than l., 153 : 19
scenes his fathers l., 857 : 14
scholar travels l. hillside, 587 : 12
see souls we l., 533 : 26
she l. me for dangers, 229 : 31
she l. much, 43 : 4
sighed to many l. one, 456 : 21
so many I l. were not yet dead, 856 : 7
so much cost me so much, 273 : 8
Solomon l. many strange women, 13 : 37
some we l. loveliest, 516 : 14
the man and honor memory, 257 : 1
those who always l. love more, 329 : 16
thou hast not l., 210 : 33
to be l. be lovable, 113 : 11

Loved (*continued*)
to have l. to have thought, 585:11
too late I l. you, 129:5
too much hope of thee l. boy, 256:3
twice or thrice had I l. thee, 252:20
use him as though you l. him, 271:11
we never l. sae kindly, 410:3
when all was young, 566:15
wish I l. human race, 697:1
with more than love, 527:8
woman once l. hateful, 736:3
you once long ago, 63:7
you so I drew tides of men, 810:2
you Wednesday, 507:*n* 1
Love-darting eyes, 280:1
Love-gift of fairy tale, 612:15
Love-in-idleness 196:15
Lovelier flower on earth, 424:13
things mercy shown, 459:3
Loveliest and best, 516:14
despairing songs l., 537:9
of lovely things, 471:9
of trees, 690:16
village of the plain, 369:28
woman born, 714:20
Loveliness exists, 906:10
its l. increases, 475:16
lay down in her l., 433:31
let thy l. fade, 446:11
needs not ornament, 345:14
portion of the l., 469:15
this Adonis in l., 453:22
to believe in l., 694:1
within, 252:5
your l. and my death, 480:3
Lovely, a single l. action, 569:12
all l. things have ending, 811:16
amiable l. death, 201:25
and pleasant in their lives, 13:9
and soothing death, 576:4
apparition sent, 427:3
April of her prime, 244:2
as Lapland night, 427:20
as l. so be various, 833:3
as woman so be l., 833:3
billboard l. as a tree, 855:15
corpse, 547:38
devours all l. things, 823:2
diminutives, 873:15
everything that's l. is, 712:19
faded but still l. woman, 835:12
flowers are l., 436:8
gentleman-like man, 196:9
gives a l. light, 822:17
go l. rose, 276:7, 773:15
he is altogether l., 28:16
honest labor bears as l. face, 251:10
in her bones, 874:1
is the rose, 426:11
ladies dead and l. knights, 245:12
leewardings, 571:8
little flower is free, 429:12
little l. moony night, 406:6
look last on things l., 739:17
loveliness he made more l., 469:15
Mary Morison, 411:3
monster, 863:18
more l. and more temperate, 244:5
more l. than Pandora, 286:3
most l. dead, 525:15
Nature swears l. dears, 409:15
nothing but truth is l., 311:16
poem l. as a tree, 795:6
Richard sweet l. rose, 203:12
Lovely (*continued*)
see cloud appear, 928:15
so l. fair, 232:5
some once l. head, 516:12
Thaïs sits beside thee, 306:19
two l. berries on one stem, 197:2
virtue how l., 286:8
whatsoever things are l., 50:7
when her l. laughter shows, 250:6
wise and the l., 823:12
with me is to be l. still, 377:20
woman stoops to folly, 369:20, 805:8
woods l. dark and deep, 748:7
your eyes, 849:14
you're l. as a flower, 481:8
Lover all as frantic, 197:12
and his lass, 212:33
and sensualist, 663:8
angel appear to l., 329:14
beauty familiar to l., 325:16
cannot having been l., 711:10
dividing l. and l., 632:8
easier to be l. than husband, 484:10
every l. a warrior, 113:5
fond l., 289:17
found my l. on his bed, 4:13
give repentance to her l., 369:21
gold-hatted lover, 835:3
happy as a l., 427:24
high-bouncing l., 835:3
I am l., 757:4
in husband lost, 357:9
it was a l. and his lass, 212:33
Jesus l. of my soul, 350:12
love l., 497:14
lunatic the l. the poet, 197:12
magnetic peripatetic l., 628:9
music sent up by l. and bard, 544:5
no l. and no adventurer, 683:8
of all plagues l. bears, 320:2
of concord, 55:4
of men the sea, 633:2
of populous pavements, 574:3
rooted stays, 495:19
scratch l. find foe, 827:10
sighed as l. obeyed as son, 384:4
sighing like furnace, 211:15
true l. therefore had good end, 149:14
truest l. that ever loved, 149:20
wild Jack for a l., 716:16
without indiscretion no lover, 640:8
woman loves her l., 460:24
woman wailing for demon l., 433:22
Wotton a most dear l., 270:34
you l. of trees, 542:6
Loverly, wouldn't it be l., 894:17
Lover's, act l. or Roman's part, 335:8
death as l. pinch, 242:3
injured l. hell, 286:19
on l. arm leant, 530:11
quarrel with world, 749:8
run into it as to l. bed, 241:19
shall win l. hire, 404:19
slide into l. head, 424:11
some old l. ghost, 253:9
Lovers always talking about themselves, 293:35
among all her l. none to comfort, 32:21
bodies of l. drowned, 770:12
cannot see follies, 199:7
Lovers (*continued*)
falling out of l. renewing of love, 96:*n* 6
fled away into storm, 476:20
for l. touch metamorphosis, 880:2
Frankie and Johnny l., 923:8
free l. free spenders, 726:2
friends l. husbands, 392:10
if any get more than l., 761:9
journeys end in l. meeting, 213:22
lacking matter, 212:22
live by longing, 873:19
lying two and two, 690:19
make two l. happy, 336:8
never tired of each other, 293:35
not of two l. but two loves, 253:23
of beauty without extravagance, 81:1
of virtue, 271:14
of wisdom without unmanliness, 81:1
old l. soundest, 262:1
other l. estranged or dead, 716:20
perjuries of l., 113:1
Romans countrymen and l., 216:13
star-crossed l., 191:17
such as I all true l., 213:29
such end true l. have, 402:14
swear more performance, 226:13
sweet l. love the spring, 212:33
tell me if l. are losers, 761:9
thy l. were all untrue, 307:1
to bed, 197:22
true l. run into strange capers, 210:34
who love do not write, 655:4
woes of hopeless l., 305:12
women love l., 294:9
world will welcome l., 830:7
Lovers', at l. perjuries Jove laughs, 192:8
dull sublunary l. love, 253:3
pure l. souls descend, 253:7
quarrels renewal of love, 96:5
seasons run, 252:7
silver-sweet sound l. tongues, 192:17
sonnets turned psalms, 177:9
Love's architecture is his own, 292:18
but frailty of mind, 324:17
evening star l. harbinger, 287:32
except for l. sake only, 507:10
fires glow longest, 657:6
keen arrow, 212:15
my l. richer than tongue, 232:22
mysteries in souls grow, 253:8
not Time's fool, 245:18
passives, 292:14
pleasure drives love, 715:13
purple with l. wound, 196:15
stricken why, 607:10
such ever l. way, 544:14
true l. the gift, 430:9
young dream, 446:12
Loves, all she l. is love, 460:24
an inner air, 851:10
as lines so l. oblique, 297:7
but their oldest clothes, 252:5
caldron of dissolute l., 128:28
change everything except l., 344:3
cheerly she l. me dearly, 476:4
color l. and skin, 252:5
cowboy that l. you so true, 927:18
cruel mother of sweet l., 108:10
demirep that l., 543:7

Loves (*continued*)
faint in light she l., 533 : 21
fat woman nobody l., 795 : 2
fierce wars and faithful l., 173 : 7
he that l. a rosy cheek, 272 : 1
he that l. sorrow, 251 : 13
heart of woman he l., 734 : 2
him better for faults, 369 : 24
his fellow men, 454 : 6
I have reigned with your l., 164 : 1
if our l. remain, 542 : 6
Jesus l. you Mrs. Robinson, 915 : 14
kills thing he l., 676 : 8
man l. what he is good at, 313 : 22
me best that calls me Tom, 257 : 19
me let him follow me, 143 : 1
mourn ye Graces and L., 101 : 15
muse l. the race of bards, 60 : 7
no man l. life like old, 75 : 21
not his wronger, 230 : 34
of two l. the nests, 253 : 23
seat of pleasures and l., 306 : 6
silence somewhat platonically, 473 : *n* 1
suspects yet soundly l., 230 : 34
to hear himself talk, 192 : 26
to live in the sun, 211 : 3
to sit and hear me sing, 402 : 13
two l. I have, 246 : 3
we must lose our l., 868 : 6
what he l. never like too much, 256 : 4
who l. a garden, 377 : 2, 484 : 6
who l. to lie with me, 211 : 1
whoever really l. you, 935 : 16
world as his body, 64 : 5
Lovesick, twenty l. maidens, 628 : 5
winds were l., 240 : 29
Lovesickness, poem begins as l., 749 : 19
Lovesome, garden l. thing, 603 : 17
wee thing, 410 : 17
Lovest, canst not guide whom thou l., 131 : 19
what thou l. well, 793 : 3
Loveth cheerful giver, 49 : 18
dear God who l. us, 435 : 11
he that l. her l. life, 35 : 1
he that l. not knoweth not God, 52 : 24
him whom my soul l., 28 : 10
prayeth best who l. best, 435 : 11
well both man bird beast, 435 : 10
whom the Lord l. he chasteneth, 51 : 20
Loving, after l. you so much, 894 : 3
can't help l. than man of mine, 833 : 8
children begin l. parents, 675 : 3
die adoring God l. friends, 344 : 12
distance between human beings, 756 : 12
Father surely dwells, 412 : 10
for l. and for saying so, 252 : 13
give a l. heart to thee, 266 : 2
in love with l., 129 : 1
mercy, 385 : 5
never call it l., 507 : 7
night made for l., 460 : 5
pardon for too much l. you, 231 : 3
pleasure of love is in l., 293 : 30
rapid merciless, 893 : 5
shutting away of l. hearts, 823 : 12
so l. to my mother, 218 : 7
take heed of l. me, 253 : 13
Loving (*continued*)
that old armchair, 562 : 11
youth large lusty l., 575 : 13
Loving-jealous of his liberty, 192 : 18
Lovingkindness, goodness and l., 55 : 7
how excellent is thy l., 18 : 23
Low, abatement and l. price, 213 : 8
ambition and pride of kings, 336 : 10
ambition and thirst of praise, 375 : 21
Brer Fox he lay l., 662 : 6
cast one's eyes so l., 234 : 28
death makes equal high and l., 158 : 17
delicious word death, 575 : 18
descending sun, 920 : 12
dost thou lie so l., 216 : 8
exalted them of l. degree, 42 : 22
foreheads villainous l., 248 : 14
gods' custom to bring l. greatness, 78 : 14
high and l. rich and poor, 419 : 4
I'll tak' the l. road, 921 : 9
last great Englishman l., 533 : 2
lean and l. ability, 214 : 25
low breathe and blow, 530 : 25
man adding one to one, 542 : 19
no high no l., 336 : 22
not that I deem them l., 603 : *n* 7
one sang high another l., 920 : 17
speak l., 209 : 8
sweet and l., 530 : 25
swing l. sweet chariot, 935 : 24
swinging l. with sullen roar, 278 : 19
talk L. talk slow, 870 : 7
ten l. words, 333 : 7
too l. for envy, 295 : 2
too l. they build, 330 : 17
valley so l., 920 : 19
voice was gentle and l., 235 : 17
what is l. raise and support, 283 : 2
when my light l., 532 : 5
yellow half-moon large l., 541 : 13
Lowells talk to Cabots, 694 : 14
Lower, a little l. than angels, 17 : 17
brutalizing l. class, 589 : 4
down can fall no l., 291 : 13
middle classes, 628 : 15
night beginning to l., 512 : 3
orders set good example, 675 : 18
part of mankind, 318 : 13
prevent l. from getting more, 88 : 1
see front o' battle l., 411 : 15
take you a buttonhole l., 191 : 10
while there is a l. class, 676 : 18
Lowered, sash l. when night, 748 : 12
Lowest and most dejected thing, 234 : 19
type hear Tao, 64 : 14
Lowing herd wind slowly, 361 : 20
Lowland, between l. and highland, 634 : 12
sails upon l. sea, 935 : 4
Lowlands, ye Highlands and L., 927 : 6
Lowliness, man of l. and affability, 155 : 11
young ambition's ladder, 215 : 16
Lowly air of Seven Dials, 628 : 20
and riding upon an ass, 33 : 32
better to be l. born, 248 : 27
cattle shed, 561 : 10
man bears stamp of l. origin, 515 : 10
meek and l. in heart, 39 : 8
nothing l. in universe, 905 : 9
Lowness, turn l. into loftiness, 694 : 1
Lowry, Malcolm L. of Bowery, 876 : 8
Low-vaulted past, 519 : 7
Loyal and neutral in a moment, 238 : 8
discharging l. service, 299 : 11
nature noble mind, 534 : 21
to a trust, 679 : 10
to club rather than planet, 846 : 12
Loyalties, impossible l., 587 : 1
Loyalty, map of l. in thy face, 185 : 16
oaths and witchhunts, 847 : 4
testing and thought control, 847 : 1
to petrified opinion, 626 : 19
Lps the keys to, 778 : 6
Lubber fiend, 278 : 3
Lubricates, dinner l. business, 393 : 15
Lucan, line in which L. meant to rise, 118 : 15
Lucasta, then my L. might I crave, 296 : 5
Lucent, softly l. as moon, 569 : 2
Lucid, full of l. intervals, 170 : 16
interval, 304 : 25
intervals and happy pauses, 179 : 12
moments, 482 : 6
Lucidity of thought, 589 : 6
sad l. of soul, 584 : 15
Lucifer, he falls like L., 249 : 3
Prince L. uprose, 600 : 27
proud seat of L., 287 : 26
son of the morning, 29 : 22
spirits that fell with L., 183 : 20
Luck, as good l. would have it, 225 : 24
blessed in l. of chase, 929 : 2
counted and cursed his l., 692 : 1
fattenin' hogs ain't in l., 662 : 16
for good l. cast old shoe, 159 : 20
good l. in odd numbers, 225 : 28
had l. met monster, 863 : 18
ill l. seldom alone, 169 : 2
in odd numbers, 225 : 28, 482 : 10
infatuated with efficient, 498 : *n* 6
I've got the L. with me, 630 : 11
light in ragged l., 663 : 8
little bit of l., 894 : 18
nae l. about the house, 382 : 10
not holding best cards, 636 : 7
run to meet ill l., 500 : 17
shallow men believe in l., 498 : 31
spit on us for l., 92 : 13
struck streak of bad l., 630 : 12
watching l. his light-o'-love, 752 : 5
women try l. men risk it, 675 : 5
your l. that is giving way, 702 : 3
Luckiest knows when to go home, 636 : 7
Lucky, book l. or unlucky, 639 : 1
just as l. to die, 574 : 18
not call man happy but l., 62 : 17
sixpence in shoe, 924 : 6
to be alive at great time, 843 : 2
to be born, 574 : 18
to die and I know it, 574 : 18
to have lived in Paris, 845 : 14
Lucre, filthy l., 50 : 26
Lucrece swears he did her wrong, 189 : 27
Lucy, if L. should be dead, 424 : 11
Locket lost her pocket, 933 : 5
when L. ceased to be, 424 : 12
Luddington's my dwelling place, 839 : 11
Luftwaffe, your L. your gobbledygoo, 911 : 17
Lugged, melancholy as l. bear, 202 : 29

Lui, parce que c'était l., 164 : *n* 11
Lui-même, tel qu'en L. l'éternité le change, 651 : *n* 3
Luke beloved physician, 50 : 15
  Matthew Mark L. and John, 294 : 16
Lukewarm, because thou art l., 53 : 5
Lull distant folds, 361 : 21
  no l. in these wars, 572 : 3
Lullaby, dreamy l., 629 : 4
Lulled by slamming of iron, 873 : 12
  in these flowers, 196 : 18
  into half-sleep, 874 : 9
Lumber, dead become l. of world, 315 : 22
  loads of learned l., 333 : 19
Lumbering, creak of l. cart, 712 : 12
Luminous, beating l. wings in vain, 589 : 13
  fair l. cloud, 435 : 27
  island of self, 880 : 4
Lump in throat, 749 : 19
  leaveneth the whole l., 48 : 9
  of same l. make one vessel, 47 : 16
  strange l. of stone, 796 : 1
  till l. be leaven, 542 : 5
  whole thing, 622 : 6
Lunar, held in l. synthesis, 804 : 4
Lunatic asylum in Jerusalem, 690 : 11
  fringe, 687 : 18
  lean-witted fool, 194 : 16
  optimism in l. asylum, 690 : 3
  padded l. asylums, 781 : 16
  the lover the poet, 197 : 12
Lunatics, crowd treat great as l., 115 : *n* 4
Lunch, breakfast dinner l. tea, 730 : 8
Luncheon, Michelangelo for l., 622 : 5
Lune, au clair de l., 928 : 8
Lungs, if l. receive our air, 376 : 20
  my l. began to crow, 211 : 7
Lure it back to cancel, 517 : 2
  of the real in their hearts, 769 : 17
  this tassel-gentle back, 192 : 16
Lurid tricks with memory, 683 : 10
Lurk I in gossip's bowl, 196 : 12
Lurks, foretold that danger l. within, 186 : 18
  politician l. under every stone, 82 : 15
Luscious, food as l. as locusts, 230 : 4
  lot of me and all so l., 574 : 21
  woodbine, 196 : 18
Lust a species of madness, 308 : 22
  and rage, 717 : 13
  for blood and plunder, 745 : 2
  for life, 600 : 3
  for power, 779 : 20
  gold and the l., 834 : 5
  guile and l. of gain, 345 : 21
  in action, 245 : 23
  in youth l., 69 : 20
  into ashes all my l., 297 : 1
  is perjured murderous, 245 : 23
  looketh to l. after her, 37 : 8
  melted him in own grease, 147 : *n* 5
  narrowing l. of gold, 532 : 23
  not after her beauty, 23 : 13
  of goat bounty of God, 404 : 3
  of office, 566 : 3
  power of fright and l., 833 : 6
  sensual l. tempest, 581 : 20
  so l. will sate itself, 219 : 22
  to rage to l. to write to, 253 : 10
Luster, accomplishments give l., 342 : 10
Luster (*continued*)
  ne'er could any l. see, 398 : 23
  shine with such a l., 377 : 18
  shone with preeminent l., 122 : 20
Lustily, swans sing more l., 83 : 18
Lusts, fleshly l., 52 : 10
  not to fulfill l., 47 : 29
Lusty horn, 212 : 27
  month of May, 149 : 13
  my age l. winter, 210 : 30
  sails filled with l. wind, 178 : 6
  stealth of nature, 233 : 3
  yet I am strong and l., 210 : 29
  youth large l. loving, 575 : 13
Lute, heartstrings l., 525 : *n* 3
  lascivious pleasing of a l., 186 : 31
  musical as bright Apollo's l., 191 : 4
  musical as is Apollo's l., 279 : 25
  my l. awake, 161 : 24
  Orpheus with his l., 248 : 29
  rift within l., 534 : 9
  star-studded l. wears black sun, 514 : 9
Lutes, dance to l., 676 : 9
Luve, my l. is like a red red rose, 409 : 22
  my l. is like the melody, 409 : 22
Lux, fiat l., 6 : *n* 14
Luxe calme et volupté, 580 : *n* 8
Luxuries, give us l. of life, 519 : 10
  hindrances, 559 : 8
  two l. in my walks, 480 : 3
Luxurious lobster-nights, 334 : 25
  society as l. as can be, 356 : 2
Luxury and torment of novelist, 652 : 13
  blesses his stars and thinks it l., 325 : 13
  elegance rather than l., 536 : 6
  in self-dispraise, 428 : 14
  it was l. to be, 433 : 19
  morality private costly l., 635 : 12
  more deadly than war, 122 : 10
  of liberal government, 553 : 9
  of one's own opinion, 553 : 13
  of skepticism, 658 : 11
  Persian l. I hate, 107 : 16
  that baneful poison, 392 : 15
  was doing good, 318 : 17
  wealth the parent of l., 84 : 12
  who serves good lord lives in l., 137 : 5
Lycidas, for L. sorrow not dead, 281 : 4
  sunk low but mounted high, 281 : 4
Lydian measures, 306 : 19
  soft L. airs, 278 : 6
Lyeth between bride and bridegroom, 793 : 2
Lying, African moon l. on back, 789 : 10
  awake with headache, 628 : 26
  days of my youth, 713 : 8
  essence of l. not in words, 572 : 12
  History that l., old lady, 667 : 6
  kneeling standing, 894 : 10
  let me have no l., 247 : 4
  lovers l. two and two, 690 : 19
  mighty heart l. still, 425 : 14
  no word to express l., 322 : 14
  not mind l. hate inaccuracy, 621 : 4
  now on his side now on back, 59 : 10
  smallest amount of l., 620 : 13
  till noon, 353 : 7
  vainness drunkenness, 214 : 26
  when asserts contrary is l., 734 : 8
Lying (*continued*)
  world given to l., 205 : 16
Lyonnesse, set out for L., 640 : 4
Lyre, a god has given l. and song, 58 : 17
  bloomin' l., 708 : 24
  idle to play l. for ass, 127 : 17
  lacking neither honor nor l., 107 : 13
  living l., 362 : 6
  make me thy l., 467 : 21
  minstrel's l., 733 : 9
  so long divine, 461 : 5
  tuning l. and handling harp, 70 : 12
  within the sky, 525 : 10
Lyres sound of l. and flutes, 638 : 11
Lyric love half angel, 545 : 1
  name me among l. bards, 106 : 25

M

M, drew everything begins with M., 611 : 22
Mab, Queen M. hath been with you, 191 : 23
Macaroni, called it m., 920 : 9
MacArthur, victory M. had in mind, 788 : 15
Macassar, incomparable oil M., 460 : 10
Macaulay, apostle of Philistines M., 587 : 5
  book in breeches, 433 : 10
  sure of everything, 487 : *n* 1
Macbeth does murder sleep, 237 : 21
  none shall harm M., 239 : 10
  shall never vanquished be, 239 : 12
  shall sleep no more, 237 : 22
Macdonald, wherever M. sits, 496 : 10
Macduff, lay on M., 240 : 11
Mace, sword the m. the crown, 208 : 7
Macedon, Euripides' grave lies in M., 75 : *n* 13
Macedonia, come into M., 46 : 13
MacGregor, my name is M., 431 : 27
  wherever M. sits, 496 : *n* 3
MacGregor's, Mr. M. garden, 719 : 3
Macheath, just a jackknife has M., 840 : 15
Machiavel, every country hath its M., 153 : *n* 5
  much beholden to M., 179 : 5
  Nick M. had ne'er trick, 291 : 28
Machina, deus ex m., 91 : 6
Machinations hollowness treachery, 233 : 4
Machine, air pump or electrical m., 379 : 16
  bathing m., 629 : 1
  beauty of great m., 796 : 16
  created to serve us, 872 : 2
  for living in, 798 : 4
  for turning wine into urine, 789 : 6
  god from the m., 91 : 6
  justice is a m., 723 : 2
  man is a m., 357 : 6
  military m., 745 : 2
  no unnecessary parts, 729 : 7
  not man you're a m., 680 : 13
  pulse of the m., 427 : 5
  slavery of the m., 675 : 25
  time m., 719 : 13
  unreliable as man, 626 : 18
  you're not man you're m., 680 : 13

Machine-à-habiter, 798 : *n* 1
Machinery for reducing amelioration, 640 : 15
of night, 906 : 1
of our intelligence, 703 : 4
Machines, human beings into m., 562 : 18
not whether m. think but men, 862 : 10
slaves not masters, 689 : 27
we only hear m., 839 : 3
Macht, der Wille zur M., 659 : *n* 2
Mächte, ihr himmlischen M., 395 : *n* 2
Machu Picchu Cambridge Mass. Angkor, 884 : 20
Mackerel, stinks like rotten m., 439 : 7
Mackerel-crowded seas, 714 : 22
Mackie's back in town, 840 : 16
Macrocosm, microcosm and m. atoned, 595 : 3
Macte nova virtute puer, 106 : *n* 1
Mad, all poets are m., 258 : 13
am m. and am not m., 67 : 9
and lamentable experiment, 703 : 8
as Bedlam, 548 : 28
as March hare, 152 : *n* 4
bad and dangerous, 454 : 22
born m. some remain so, 866 : 12
cold m. father, 778 : 6
dogs and Englishmen, 843 : 8
don't call a man m., 361 : 2
don't get m. get even, 809 : 21
everyone m. on one point, 707 : 10
face that drove me m., 652 : 3
father and mither gae m., 410 : 10
fitter sane than m., 544 : 29
go m. or unstable, 78 : 9
half m. with beauty, 618 : 3
he first makes m., 78 : 1
heroically m., 304 : 17
Hieronymo's m. againe, 177 : *n* 1
I am not m., 46 : 34
idolatry, 226 : 8
if they behold a cat, 200 : 2
I'm m. as hell, 901 : 10
in pursuit, 245 : 23
laid to make taker m., 245 : 23
makes men m., 232 : 15
man must be a little m., 166 : 4
March days, 760 : 20
March hare, 152 : 19
men God made m., 742 : 4
more deadly than m. dog's tooth, 188 : 13
much learning make m., 46 : 33
naked summer night, 574 : 19
nobly wild not m., 266 : 16
north-northwest, 220 : 31
O fool! I shall go m., 233 : 23
old m. blind despised king, 468 : 4
pleasure in being m., 304 : 19
practice drives m., 917 : 13
prose run m., 338 : 13
provided man not m., 358 : 25
pursuit, 477 : 5
sad and bad and m., 544 : 20
sad m. brother's name, 634 : 11
saint run m., 339 : 31
sense that world m., 756 : 15
that he is m. 'tis true, 220 : 12
that trusts in wolf, 234 : 14
to live mad to be saved, 901 : 3
undevout astronomer is m., 330 : 19
we are m. nationally, 114 : 32
Mad (*continued*)
we have all been m., 707 : *n* 1
went m. and bit the man, 369 : 18
whom God wishes to destroy he makes m., 134 : 21
world, 548 : 28
world mad kings, 201 : 18
Madam is there nothing else, 605 : 20
poetry the supreme fiction m., 766 : 24
Madame Bovary had beauty, 583 : 12
hell M. is to love no longer, 802 : 14
Madden, made mannikin to m. it, 527 : 3
rave recite and m., 338 : 6
to crime, 459 : 5
Maddens, all that most m., 570 : 13
"Trees" m. me, 803 : 1
Madder music stronger wine, 721 : 6
Maddest merriest day, 528 : 12
Madding, far from m. crowd's strife, 362 : 12
Made a rural pen, 403 : 3
and loveth all, 435 : 11
annihilating all that's m., 297 : 3
as he is so was he m., 654 : 19
begotten not m., 55 : 3
by whom all things m., 55 : 3
confusion m. masterpiece, 238 : 5
critics all ready m., 456 : 13
day which the Lord hath m., 21 : 26
did he who m. Lamb, 405 : 8
dost know who m. thee, 403 : 5
fearfully and wonderfully m., 22 : 19
for each other, 432 : 17
friends born not m., 634 : 21
God m. and eaten, 541 : 20
God m. him let him pass for man, 198 : 13
him a little lower than angels, 17 : 17
his pendent bed, 236 : 21
in wisdom hast thou m. all, 21 : 11
incarnate and was m. man, 55 : 3
it is he that hath m. us, 21 : 3
little Lamb who m. thee, 403 : 5
Lord God m. them all, 561 : 8
man was m. to mourn, 408 : 15
marriages m. in heaven, 176 : 3
men and not made them well, 222 : 3
mouths in a glass, 233 : 27
my song a coat, 713 : 14
myself a motley, 245 : 16
of sterner stuff, 216 : 19
poet's m. as well as born, 256 : 17
sea is his and he m. it, 20 : 20
stuff as dreams are m. on, 248 : 13
swears she is m. of truth, 246 : 2
the best of this, 411 : 22
this parting well m., 217 : 9
us with large discourse, 223 : 17
what man has m. of man, 423 : 4
when or you or I are m., 266 : 21
without fear, 17 : 8
world I never m., 691 : 23
world of m. is not world of born, 829 : 25
Madeleine soaked in lime flowers, 734 : 1
upon barroom floor, 652 : 3
Madeline's fair breast, 476 : 16
Mademoiselle from Armenteers, 817 : 7
from St. Nazaire, 817 : 8
Madest, creature that thou m., 692 : 10
Mad-eyed from stating obvious, 900 : 2
Madison, Miss McFlimsey of M., Square, 595 : 4
Madly, stars shot m. from spheres, 196 : 14
twirled fingers m., 551 : 2
Madman, either liar or m., 358 : 19
if he like m. lived, 171 : 8
that is the m., 197 : 12
Madmen, which none but m. know, 304 : 19
worst of m. saint run mad, 339 : 31
Madness, a little m. in spring, 607 : 9
anger a short m., 109 : 2
avarice a piece of m., 308 : *n* 5
despondency and m., 425 : 10, 892 : 15
destroyed by m., 906 : 1
first step towards m., 153 : 13
from breakfast to m., 908 : 8
go you may call it m., 416 : 4
great wits to m. allied, 303 : 20
harmonious m. flow, 468 : 15
in brain, 434 : 3
let us have m. openly, 879 : 7
life is a m., 273 : 2
midsummer m., 214 : 22
mind fill with m., 850 : 12
moon-struck m., 287 : 29
much m. divinest sense, 605 : 11
much of m., 526 : 4
need not be all breakdown, 907 : 1
no genius without touch of m., 115 : 6
of many for gain of few, 334 : 17, 340 : 13
of the Caesars, 555 : 22
risen from hell, 632 : 9
sense starkest m., 605 : 11
species of m., 308 : 22
sudden m. came upon Orpheus, 104 : 12
that fine m., 182 : 19
that way m. lies, 234 : 2
the rest is m. of art, 653 : 5
though this be m., 220 : 21
'tis m. to defer, 330 : 8
to let private enterprise set habits, 826 : 2
to live like wretch, 258 : 24
what m. has caught you, 103 : 9
Madonnas, Rafael of dear M., 544 : 2
Madrigal, woeful stuff this m., 333 : 13
Madrigals, melodious birds sing m., 183 : 9
Madruga, al que m. Dios ayuda, 935 : 9
Madrugar, no por mucho m., 935 : 15
Mads, music m. me, 195 : 18
second m. him, 213 : 16
Maecenas, how comes it M., 106 : 10
Maenad of Massachusetts, 634 : 9
Maggots, breed m. in dead dog, 220 : 17
lie under, 904 : 6
make speech to m., 828 : 8
Maggoty minus, 829 : 20
Magic and traditional ceremonies, 818 : 13
argosies of m. sails, 529 : 24
casements, 477 : 1
lash m. creature, 607 : 7
little plans no m., 661 : 3
no rhymes no m., 724 : 9
numbers, 324 : 15
O m. sleep, 475 : 18
of a face, 272 : 4
of a name, 443 : 6

Magic (continued)
painting form of m., 774 : 11
preservation in books, 473 : 29
scenes shifted like m. on stage of history, 666 : 5
sweet m. brings together, 412 : 9
talking to itself, 908 : 9
tents, 654 : 16
thought and m. sound, 486 : 8
to stir men's blood, 661 : 3
with a m. like thee, 460 : 1
Magical, I am m. mouse, 879 : 14
power imagination, 437 : 16
Magician, Bergson you are m., 688 : n 2
rope-dancer physician m., 122 : 4
Magicians do more by faith, 171 : 16
Magister artis ingenique largitor venter, 117 : n 6
Magisterial or imperative type, 730 : 15
Magistracy is great trust, 374 : 3
Magistrate, by m. equally useful, 383 : 7
grown gray in office, 486 : 11
no name of m., 247 : 26
Magistrates, governed by grave m., 484 : 20
Magna Carta will have no sovereign, 172 : 5
Magna est veritas et praevalet, 34 : n 2
Magnanimity and trust, 559 : 9
in politics, 373 : 8
in victory m., 746 : 11
marks of God in m., 448 : 3
Magnet, by no endeavor can m., 628 : 9
Magnetic nourishing night, 574 : 19
peripatetic lover, 628 : 9
Magnificence, faith condition of intellectual m., 504 : 16
of Hispanic, 357 : 19
pristine m., 480 : 16
Magnificent and awful cause, 376 : 21
blond beast, 658 : 5
but not war, 536 : 5
from work returned m., 287 : 1
mild and m. eye, 541 : 6
most m. movement of all, 380 : 14
Magnificently stern array, 457 : 19
unprepared, 795 : 1
Magnify him, 36 : n 1
laud and m. thy Name, 55 : 18
my soul doth m. Lord, 42 : 20
thy holy Name, 55 : 15
Magnitude, liar of first m., 324 : 10
star of smallest m., 285 : 3
Magnus ab integro saeculorum nascitur ordo, 103 : n 9
inter opes inops, 108 : n 6
Magus Zoroaster my dead child, 466 : 16
Maid, Abyssinian m., 433 : 26
as with m. so with mistress, 30 : 5
be good sweet m., 566 : 12
beggar m. be queen, 530 : 17
chariest m. prodigal, 218 : 27
Dark M. and her Lord, 76 : 3
fair m. dwellin', 926 : 21
lily m. of Astolat, 534 : 11
maiden passion for m., 534 : 23
many a youth and many a m., 278 : 1
my pretty m., 931 : 14
neither m. widow nor wife, 229 : 7
not dead but sleepeth, 38 : 31
nut-brown m., 917 : 4
of Athens, 456 : 19
Maid (continued)
roving with you fair m., 934 : 21
slain by fair cruel m., 214 : 4
sphere-descended m., 364 : 16
still as a m., 404 : 11
was in garden, 931 : 9
way of man with m., 26 : 4, 708 : 22
wedded m. virgin mother, 277 : 6
whom none to praise, 424 : 12
widow or wife, 153 : 3
yonder a m. and wight, 642 : 2
Maiden famous to all time, 108 : 3
fleshed thy m. sword, 205 : 15
I sing of a m., 917 : 3
kissed m. all forlorn, 934 : 9
love one m. only, 534 : 22
meditation fancy-free, 196 : 15
never bold, 229 : 26
of bashful fifteen, 399 : 1
passion for maid, 534 : 23
phoenix ashes new-create, 249 : 17
presence, 219 : 7
rare and radiant m., 526 : 12
rose-lipped m., 691 : 13
simple m. in her flower, 528 : 8
tell me pretty m., 685 : 8
with no other thought, 527 : 7
Maiden-fair poetic soul, 668 : 18
Maidens, all her m. watching, 531 : 8
call it love-in-idleness, 196 : 15
fair m. commonly fortunate, 175 : 19
have not little m. gone, 759 : 12
like moths, 456 : 22
loth, 477 : 5
not human but nymphic, 846 : 3
twenty love-sick m., 628 : 5
young fair m. quiet eyes, 669 : 7
Maid's, sea m. music, 196 : 14
Maids are May when maids, 212 : 25
dance in a ring, 250 : 8
false m. in love, 226 : 15
in modesty say No, 189 : 31
pretty m. in row, 930 : 6
seven m. with seven mops, 613 : 2
that weave with bones, 214 : 3
three little m., 629 : 8
Maidservant, not covet neighbor's m., 10 : 7
Mail from Tunis probably, 607 : 12
on time with southbound m., 731 : n 2
rusty m., 226 : 17
Maimed, dusty cobweb-covered m., 620 : 3
he that wants anger hath m. mind, 277 : 4
poor and m., 43 : 23
Main, arose from out azure m., 345 : 19
beams bemocked sultry m., 434 : 28
chance, 175 : 14, 291 : 23
flooding in the m., 564 : 17
part of the m., 254 : 22
stand to the m. chance, 175 : 14
street on August afternoon, 894 : 14
to cross raging m., 935 : 5
watery m., 244 : 22
Maine, as M. so goes nation, 923 : 3
remember the M., 923 : 7
Mains, dorure en reste aux m., 583 : n 6
Mainstay, workers m. of civilization, 666 : 22
Maintain, fuel to m. his fires, 272 : 1
his argument, 207 : 21
it before whole world, 298 : 11
no ill opinions, 370 : n 3
Maintain (continued)
poet's dignity and ease, 338 : 16
the sublime, 792 : 10
Maintained, boisterously m. as gained, 202 : 3
Maintaining constitutional shield, 794 : 15
independence to this day, 800 : 4
Main-truck higher than kelson low, 570 : 5
Mair, cantie wi' m., 409 : 23
Maître, qui que tu sois voici ton m., 344 : n 4
tel m. tel valet, 163 : n 2
Maize, rose with m. to die, 843 : 20
Majestic free, 425 : 23
instancy, 693 : 11
law in m. equality, 655 : 14
motion, 458 : 7
silence, 377 : n 5
theme, 643 : 18
though in ruin, 284 : 14
Majestical, happy high m., 467 : 13
laid in bed m., 208 : 7
roof, 220 : 28
Majesties deserving in His sight, 156 : 12
purple mountain m., 688 : 5
Majesty, against thy Divine M., 55 : 17
attribute to awe and m., 200 : 9
clad in naked m., 285 : 17
dignity m. sublimity, 380 : 14
moon rising in clouded m., 285 : 25
next in m. surpassed, 306 : 1
of gods is revealed, 59 : n 5
of heaven, 346 : 4
of this world, 869 : 1
rayless m., 330 : 5
ride on in m., 465 : 3
sight so touching in m., 425 : 13
tender m., 605 : 12
thine O Lord is the m., 14 : 25
this earth of m., 194 : 13
Major, model of m. general, 627 : 20
poets read from own works, 846 : 6
Majorities, decision by m. expedient, 517 : 17
not entirely wrong, 579 : 17
Majority, authority not m., 492 : 12
big enough m. in any town, 624 : 3
deprive minority of right, 521 : 10
divine m., 605 : 2
fools big enough m., 624 : 3
he has joined great m., 117 : 12
long since Death had m., 274 : n 11
man with God always in m., 162 : 2
morality what m. like, 698 : 3
never replace man, 812 : 14
not leave right to m., 558 : 3
of one, 558 : 5
one man with courage a m., 419 : 5
one on God's side m., 538 : 14
one with law m., 736 : 14
power in m. of popular assembly, 382 : 4
questions not decided by m., 553 : 6
silent m., 882 : 21
stirred by motives, 724 : 12
'tis m. prevail, 605 : 11
tyranny of m., 616 : 2
when were good and brave in m., 560 : 22
Majors, make m. but not scholars, 259 : 2

Make a joyful noise, 19 : 31, 21 : 3
angels weep, 228 : 10
be and m. new nations, 249 : 18
conscience m. cowards, 221 : 12
content with his fortunes, 234 : 1
fault worse by excuse, 202 : 6
fears m. us traitors, 239 : 16
felicity we m. or find, 352 : 21
ghost of him that lets me, 219 : 16
haste better foot before, 202 : 9
he himself his quietus m., 221 : 12
her laugh at that, 224 : 14
I could not well m. out, 439 : 13
I shall m. reckless choice, 747 : 18
it do or do without, 924 : 4
it over your way, 750 : 11
lady of my own, 424 : 13
life what we m. it, 649 : 13
me a child again, 610 : 10
me a fixed figure, 232 : 3
me a willow cabin, 213 : 18
me immortal with a kiss, 184 : 4
me sick discussing duty, 574 : 24
me that to thee, 335 : 2
me to know mine end, 19 : 1
men m. the city, 81 : 8
mighty ocean, 591 : 7
money by any means, 108 : 18
most of what we yet may spend, 516 : 15
my bed in hell, 22 : 17
my bed soon, 927 : 8
my house your inn, 798 : 17
my seated heart knock, 236 : 11
my small elves coats, 196 : 19
no mistake stranger, 699 : *n* 3
not m. cannot mar, 585 : 1
not m. graven image, 10 : 4
not m. scarecrow of law, 227 : 30
of your prayers one sacrifice, 248 : 25
only God can m. tree, 795 : 7
our lives sublime, 509 : 15
right to m. government, 379 : 10
so much of fragmentary blue, 748 : 1
soul is form and doth body m., 174 : 19
straight a highway for our God, 30 : 30
sudden sally, 533 : 15
the Lord m. his face shine upon thee, 10 : 23
the most of it, 382 : 13
thee an ark, 7 : 28
thee mightier yet, 698 : 12
thick my blood, 236 : 17
unless philosophy m. a Juliet, 193 : 13
up my sum, 224 : 22
us do what we can, 499 : 2
us heirs of all eternity, 190 : 9
war to live in peace, 87 : 24
waves m. towards pebbled shore, 244 : 19
world safe for democracy, 682 : 12
world safe for diversity, 891 : 11
worse appear the better, 81 : 14
yourself do thing you have to, 596 : 5
yourselves another face, 221 : 18
Make-believe, Eve seen through m., 733 : 1
Makeless, maiden that is m., 917 : 3
Maker, flower carries impress of M., 316 : 8
Lord our m., 20 : 20
more pure than his m., 15 : 13
Maker (*continued*)
of Heaven and earth, 55 : 2
reproacheth his M., 24 : 14
rests in lightland, 5 : 6
tool m., 761 : 4
Maker's rage, 767 : 16
Makers, abhor m. and their laws approve, 305 : 26
Makes, another which m., 85 : 8
figure a poem m., 750 : 2
heaven drowsy with harmony, 191 : 4
heretic that m. the fire, 246 : 16
me or fordoes me quite, 232 : 12
me poor indeed, 230 : 33
men mad, 232 : 15
night hideous, 219 : *n* 3
one little room an everywhere, 251 : 15
or mars us, 232 : 9
swanlike end, 199 : 22
sweet music with stones, 189 : 34
them and arts and work, 752 : 13
thinking m. it so, 220 : 25
tongue of him that m. it, 191 : 12
whole world kin, 226 : 20
Makest, thou m. darkness, 21 : 11
what m. thou, 31 : 5
Maketh clouds his chariot, 21 : 8
he m. me to lie down, 18 : 7
the deep to boil, 17 : 7
Making green one red, 238 : 1
many books, 27 : 27, 773 : 14
news better than taking it, 743 : 1
night hideous, 219 : 12
shaping and controlling life, 578 : 6
through creeks and inlets m., 564 : 17
Mal, honi soit qui m. y pense, 143 : 7
Malachite, good speech more hidden than m., 3 : 4
Maladies, soul with all its m., 638 : 10
Maladministration, secured against m., 367 : 5
Malady, greatest m. is poverty, 313 : 4
he smiles it is a m., 101 : 24
medicine worse than m., 111 : *n* 2
of cultivated classes, 580 : 14
of not marking, 205 : 25
Malaria ten parts, 699 : 16
Malcontents, liege of m., 190 : 26
Mars of m., 225 : 11
Male and female created he, 6 : 14
and female equal, 574 : 9
and female fuse into one solid, 80 : 12
cannot tolerate living with equal, 508 : 22
difference of education between m. and female 392 : 12
especially m. of species, 790 : 15
healthy wealthy and dead, 831 : 8
kiss of blankets, 796 : 16
more deadly than m., 710 : 21
Malefactors of great wealth, 687 : 12
Malherbe, at last comes M., 311 : 3
what M. writes will endure, 176 : 19
Malheur, de son âge tout le m., 344 : *n* 3
Malheureux, où nous étions si m., 928 : 4
Malice basest of all instincts, 626 : 10
domestic, 238 : 19
from envy hatred and m., 55 : 10
much m. little wit, 305 : 23
never was his aim, 322 : 19
no m. or ill-will, 418 : 6
Malice (*continued*)
no rampart against m., 297 : 15
no suspicion of m. in his writing, 98 : 10
nor set down aught in m., 232 : 20
only man possesses m., 626 : 10
Pride Envy M., 443 : 2
ridicule without m., 523 : 3
toward none, 524 : 7
treasonous m., 238 : 9
truth with m. in it, 570 : 13
Malices, tiptoe m., 701 : 7
Malicious ferocity, 765 : *n* 1
he is not, 764 : 1
wisdom entereth not in m. mind, 157 : 13
Malignant and turbaned Turk, 232 : 21
so m. so devastating, 821 : 7
Maligner of reputation, 615 : 4
Malignity, motiveless m., 436 : 16
Malitia, ius summum saepe summa est m., 96 : *n* 13
Mallecho, miching m., 222 : 11
Malorum, radix m. est cupiditas, 51 : *n* 2
Malt, ate the m., 934 : 9
does more than Milton can, 691 : 17
Malthus, with M. and Ricardo, 872 : 5
Maltreat, shouldn't m. our idols, 583 : 13
Mama, we've lost good old m., 840 : 18
Mamas, last of red-hot m., 788 : *n* 3
Mammon, cannot serve God and m., 38 : 1
is like fire, 474 : *n* 2
the least erected spirit, 283 : 28
wins his way, 456 : 22
Man, a certain m. went down, 43 : 13
a little mad if not stupid, 166 : 4
a little worse than a m., 198 : 14
a long time coming, 761 : 17
a m. like me, 405 : 6
a m. zealous for nothing, 356 : 10
a social animal, 308 : 20
abandoned on earth, 865 : 11
able m. considers his work, 499 : 25
absolute weapon, 826 : *n* 1
according as m. is must your humor him, 97 : 5
actions show m. we find, 335 : 14
Adam the goodliest m., 285 : 20
after his own heart, 12 : 35
aged m. paltry thing, 715 : 1
ah for m. to arise, 533 : 18
ah when to heart of m., 747 : 2
ain't nothin' but a man, 922 : 8
all pleasant in m., 371 : 16
all that a m. hath will he give, 15 : 5
all that makes m., 534 : 23
all that may become a m., 237 : 3
alone beneath heaven, 430 : 9
alone can enslave man, 876 : 19
always tell Harvard m., 923 : 16
am I not a m. and brother, 375 : 5
ambitious m. have no satisfaction, 255 : 5
and bird and beast, 435 : 10
and brother, 375 : 5
and his fate, 763 : 8
and what he loves have but day, 758 : 2
and woman in garden, 675 : 16
animal not measured by m., 802 : 18
animal which devours own, 388 : 5

Man (*continued*)
animal with primary instincts of survival, 812 : 10
apparel oft proclaims m., 219 : 1
appoints, 148 : *n* 7
arms and the m. 104 : 15, 306 : 11
around m. bend other faces, 443 : 2
art mediatress between nature and m., 437 : 22
as a m. wipeth a dish, 14 : 22
as happy a m. as any, 309 : 21
as M. alone Jesus not saved us, 858 : 1
as m. looks at woman, 769 : 23
as nature made him, 359 : 2
as old as his arteries, 301 : 3
Ascent of M., 870 : 15
assurance of a m., 223 : 3
at thirty m. suspects himself fool, 330 : 10
at wheel taught to feel, 647 : 21
average m., 779 : 13
baker's m., 929 : 18
battlefield heart of m., 582 : 1
be a friend of m., 685 : 12
bear with all the faults of m., 250 : 4
bears stamp of lowly origin, 515 : 10
beautiful thing raises m., 154 : 15
became a living soul, 6 : 17
become ignorant m. again, 768 : 8
before you call him a m., 915 : 2
before you trust a m., 917 : 7
behold m. of flint, 928 : 21
behold the m., 45 : 32
being his own physician, 87 : 5
belief woman made for m., 554 : 7
believe in equality of m., 385 : 5
Benedick the married m., 209 : 3
best m. like water, 64 : 3
best m. worst-natured muse, 315 : 15
better kind of m., 651 : 1
better m. than I Gunga Din, 708 : 6
better spared better m., 205 : 13
beware m. of one book, 133 : 11
beyond m. is universe, 831 : 17
bites dog, 659 : 19
blamed the living m., 587 : 17
blessed m. that spares these stones, 250 : 1
blessings on thee little m., 513 : 10
blood of a British m., 234 : 13
blow the m. down, 934 : 17
bold bad m., 173 : 9, 248 : 26
bold m. first eat oyster, 323 : 10
born dies and does not come again, 925 : 22
boyhood changing into m., 716 : 1
brave m. inattentive to duty, 419 : 1
brave m. struggling, 334 : 13
brave m. with a sword, 676 : 8
breathes there the m., 430 : 10
bronzed lank m., 765 : 8
Brutus is an honorable m., 216 : 18
but be a m., 585 : 6
butterfly dreaming I am a m., 90 : 3
by m. came death, 48 : 29
by m. came resurrection, 48 : 29
by m. shall his blood be shed, 8 : 2
by nature political animal, 87 : 26
Caius is a m., 602 : 11
call Himself a m., 829 : 14
call no m. foe, 821 : 2
came to making of m., 632 : 9
can a m. take fire in his bosom, 23 : 14

Man (*continued*)
can die but once, 206 : 25
can raise thirst, 708 : 10
cannot be deterred, 891 : 8
cannot emerge from himself, 734 : 8
cannot live without self-control, 862 : 1
can't hold m. down without staying, 681 : 26
capable of becoming m., 814 : 8
caverns measureless to m., 433 : 21
cease ye from m., 28 : 33
celebration of m., 887 : 7
cells and gibbets for m., 562 : 12
center of circle, 615 : 2
century of common m., 811 : 11
certainly crazy, 165 : 7
change environment not m., 832 : 12
child conceived, 15 : 7
child father of m., 425 : 7
childhood shows the m., 288 : 12
Christian faithful m., 187 : 8
city is teacher of the m., 67 : 17
civilized m. has habits of house, 557 : 4
civilized m. not live without cooks, 609 : 13
clear cut against last horizon, 852 : 15
clothed with rags, 301 : 20
come forth thou fearful m., 193 : 11
comes with his torment, 413 : 30
common enemies of m., 890 : 11
common m. has triumphed, 658 : 4
composed of all men, 865 : 16
concern for m. himself, 763 : 8
concrete m. has one interest, 648 : 5
condition of m. a condition of war, 264 : 12
conference maketh a ready m., 181 : 13
connection of individual m., 922 : 9
contemporary m. rationalized myths, 885 : 16
control the wind, 585 : 9
count on no one but himself, 865 : 11
country turns out, 499 : 10
coupling of m. and woman, 807 : 10
courage befitting m., 665 : 1
create a fourth a decent m., 702 : 10
create gods who destroy him, 819 : 12
created m. of blood clot, 132 : 17
crime of being young m., 350 : 16
crooked m., 932 : 18
crow sees white m. come, 557 : 18
cruelty to load falling m., 249 : *n* 1
daring young m. on trapeze, 636 : 12
dark as world of m., 801 : 6
dark cloud m., 657 : 13
decides he is not God, 644 : 12
delights not me, 220 : 29
desire for desire of m., 438 : 5
desire of knowledge caused m. to fall, 180 : 14
diapason closing in m., 305 : 9
did not make cannot mar, 585 : 1
dieth and wasteth away, 15 : 34
difference between dog and m., 624 : 24
dignity of m. respected, 787 : 12
dispute it like a m., 239 : 22
divine as myself dead, 576 : 1
does what he must, 890 : 3
doth not live by bread only, 11 : 12
dream past wit of m., 197 : 9

Man (*continued*)
drest in brief authority, 228 : 10
drink takes m., 646 : 12
drove out the m., 7 : 13
dull ear of drowsy m., 202 : 1
dull m. always sure, 772 : 5
each m. act of God, 555 : 12
each m. kills thing he loves, 676 : 8
ear of m. hath not seen, 197 : 10
either m. obsolete or war is, 832 : 13
end of that m. is peace, 18 : 27
endeavoring to turn m. into beast, 853 : 9
errs as long as he strives, 396 : 9
Esau was a m. of the field, 8 : 15
escape from rope and gun, 332 : 5
establish reign of liberty, 870 : 13
even such a m. so faint, 205 : 19
every cry of every m., 405 : 9
every m. a piece of the continent, 254 : 22
every m. architect of his fortune, 103 : 5
every m. at his best state, 19 : 2
every m. for himself, 161 : 14
every m. has his fault, 243 : 3
every m. hath a good and bad angel, 258 : 14
every m. his greatest enemy, 274 : 19
every m. is wanted, 498 : 10
every m. own architect, 545 : 19
every m. satisfied there is truth, 639 : 8
every m. to do duty, 408 : 8
every m. under his vine, 13 : 29
every m. was God or Devil, 304 : 11
exalt m. into a god, 488 : 4
expatiate o'er scene of m., 336 : 10
eye of m. hath not heard, 197 : 10
faced with spiritual, 679 : 5
fallen god, 464 : 16
false m., 317 : 15
false m. does easy, 238 : 10
false to any m., 219 : 2
Family of M., 761 : 16
fashion wears out more than m., 209 : 27
favor with God and m., 42 : 33
favorite of mother, 679 : 6
first m. among these than second in Rome, 99 : 18
first m. takes drink, 646 : 12
first-class fightin' m., 708 : 5
fit night for m. or beast, 770 : 17
foolish fond old m., 235 : 9
foolish passionate m., 717 : 3
foot-in-the-grave young m., 628 : 12
for all seasons, 155 : 11
for m. as for flower beast bird, 790 : 20
for the field, 531 : 7
for the sword, 531 : 7
forgotten as a dead m. out of mind, 18 : 16
forgotten m., 642 : 11, 779 : 6
formed by struggle, 784 : 10
formed for society, 365 : 15
formed m. of dust, 6 : 17
free as Nature made m., 303 : 8
free to do evil as good, 631 : 5
frees himself from bonds, 504 : 9
fresh from natur's mold, 547 : 40
Friday, 318 : 15
frontiers where m. fronts fact, 558 : 17

Man (*continued*)
fury of patient m., 304 : 16
gently scan brother m., 409 : 21
get a new m., 248 : 2
gird up thy loins like a m., 16 : 27
give every m. thy ear, 219 : 1
giveth up the ghost, 15 : 34
glory to M. in highest, 634 : 8
go west young m., 554 : 3
God above or m. below, 336 : 12
God and m. decree, 691 : 22
God became m. devil woman, 491 : 9
god in ruins, 496 : 8
God is not a m., 11 : 4
God's ways to m., 691 : 17
goes riding by, 668 : 11
goeth forth unto his work, 21 : 11
goeth to his long home, 27 : 25
good for a m. that he bear the yoke, 32 : 24
good great m. inherits, 436 : 2
good m. and just, 44 : 12
good m. does not argue, 65 : 10
Good M. pouring from pitcher, 572 : 6
good name in m. and woman, 230 : 33
great m. great ganglion, 644 : 7
great nose great m., 726 : 1
greater m. greater courtesy, 534 : 18
greatest fool is m., 311 : 12
greatest m. ever seen, 372 : *n* 1
greatness of work inside m., 897 : 7
grew within this learned m., 184 : 11
ground colored m. occupies, 556 : 7
grows beyond his work, 857 : 4
grows used to everything, 581 : 18
half part of blessed m., 201 : 16
hand of a mighty m., 22 : 10
hand will be against every m., 8 : 9
happy citizen free, 491 : 25
happy m. be his dole, 159 : *n* 5
happy m. happy dole, 159 : 7
happy m. works ancestral acres, 106 : 23
happy old m., 103 : 8
happy the m. and he alone, 305 : 1
hardly a m. now alive, 512 : 6
harrowing clods, 642 : 2
has Forever, 542 : 17
has two primal passions, 664 : 13
has will woman way, 519 : 4
hath penance done, 435 : 2
having put hand to plow, 43 : 7
he created m., 925 : 22
he was a m., 732 : 6
he was a m. take him for all in all, 218 : 16
he was her m., 923 : 8
heard wise m. say, 690 : 20
heart of m. place devils dwell in, 274 : 15
hearty old m., 439 : 15
height of m. equal to tips of hands, 116 : 14
her wit was more than m., 305 : 8
high abstracted m. alone, 571 : 2
himself lend a hand, 80 : 13
his answer was M., 851 : 3
his greatest enemy, 274 : 19
his own executioner, 274 : 19
honest exceeding poor m., 199 : 1
honest m. appeals to understanding, 391 : 7
honest m. close-buttoned, 377 : 17

Man (*continued*)
honest m. noblest work of God, 337 : 13, 408 : 18
honest m. sent to lie abroad, 251 : 4
horizontal m., 868 : 1
horse noblest conquest of m., 349 : 1
how dieth the wise m., 26 : 20
how many roads m. walk down, 915 : 2
how marvelous is m., 725 : 7
how poor a thing is m., 182 : 10
how proud word M. rings, 725 : 7
howl for flesh of m., 912 : 9
hungry m. not free, 851 : 11
hungry sinner, 461 : 29
I am cease to be, 533 : 18
I am first a m., 341 : 10
I am the m., 574 : 25
I appeal to any white m., 367 : 3
I got my m., 835 : 21
I have been a m., 396 : 3
I know myself a m., 251 : 7
I know thee not old m., 206 : 36
I loved the m. and honor memory, 257 : 1
I must feel it as a m., 239 : 22
I never writ nor no m. loved, 245 : 18
I the m. in the moon, 197 : 17
identifies with his fate, 843 : 6
if a m. die shall he live, 15 : 35
if a m. has talent, 852 : 12
if m. is dust, 886 : 7
if not wedding day is fixed on, 350 : 2
if such a m. there be, 338 : 15
I'll make me a m., 733 : 12
I'm m. of wealth and taste, 916 : 8
improvable reason of m., 482 : 12
in armor slave, 545 : 16
in arms wish to be, 427 : 21
in Brooks Brothers shirt, 881 : 8
in bush God meet, 493 : 13
in every m. two postulations, 581 : 7
in gray flannel suit, 898 : 2
in love endures more, 658 : 14
in love with suffering, 581 : 17
in mind of m. a motion, 423 : 13
in our town, 934 : 7
in soul of m. one Tahiti, 570 : 14
in subjection to white Saxon m., 554 : 6
in unsearchable darkness, 654 : 19
in whose hand cup is found, 8 : 36
in wilderness, 930 : 2
in wit a m., 305 : *n* 2, 336 : 9
incarnate and was made m., 55 : 3
inflicts pain for sport, 626 : 10
ingrateful m., 233 : 24
inner m., 49 : 34
insignificant and aware of it, 738 : 10
intellect of m. choose, 716 : 7
intellectual superiority of m., 626 : 4
interpreter of nature, 471 : 15
intimates eternity to m., 326 : 3
invented m. because disappointed in monkey, 626 : 17
invisible m., 885 : 5
is a machine, 357 : 6
is a prisoner, 83 : 16
is a reasoning animal, 114 : 20
is a thinking reed, 300 : 7
is alone, 865 : 11
is as Heaven made him, 170 : 1
is born for uprightness, 68 : 19
is born free, 358 : 12

Man (*continued*)
is born unto trouble, 15 : 15
is created free, 413 : 2
is God blunder of m., 658 : 10
is his own star, 260 : 17
is man and master, 534 : 7
is m. blunder of God, 658 : 10
is m. no more than this, 234 : 7
is not so good Christian, 669 : 10
is not so great a coward, 669 : 10
is one soul many tongues, 126 : 4
is origin of his action, 87 : 19
is raised above animal, 870 : 10
is singular creature, 870 : 14
is the hunter, 531 : 6
je-ne-sais-quoi young m., 628 : 11
joked about every prominent m., 766 : 6
judge m. by foes, 683 : 9
killed hero in m., 865 : 6
kills thing he loves, 676 : 8
kind m. and died in want, 892 : 13
know myself a m., 251 : 7
know to defy opinion, 417 : 13
know what God and m. is, 535 : 10
knoweth not his time, 27 : 17
known by company he keeps, 77 : *n* 9
lame m. leap as an hart, 30 : 24
large-hearted m., 506 : 13
last strands of m., 656 : 15
laugh to scorn power of m., 239 : 10
law for m., 494 : 8
laws of God beyond m., 74 : 16
laws of God laws of m., 691 : 22
least considerable m., 391 : 4
leave his father and mother, 7 : 4
lengthened shadow of one m., 497 : 4
less no m. have, 687 : 8
let end try the m., 206 : 12
let him pass for a m., 198 : 13
let m. outlive his wealth, 200 : 15
let no such m. be trusted, 201 : 3
let us make m. in our image, 6 : 13
life of m. a circle, 701 : 9
life of m. solitary, 264 : 17
light for man, 839 : 6
lightning out of cloud m., 657 : 13
like light kindled and put out, 70 : 7
little difference between m. and m., 649 : 19
little m. had little gun, 933 : 12
lived with birds and beasts, 90 : 7
lives life of epoch, 755 : 7
living-dead m., 188 : 15
long prepared man of courage, 702 : 3
look no way but down, 302 : 12
looketh on the outward appearance, 12 : 38
looking for honest m., 86 : 12
looks small at wedding, 839 : 12
Lord is a m. of war, 9 : 33
Lord seeth not as m. seeth, 12 : 38
lose what he never had, 271 : 9
lot of m. but once to die, 267 : 17
love is a mood to m., 670 : 2
love not m. the less, 458 : 24
lovely gentleman-like m., 196 : 9
loves what vanishes, 715 : 7
lovin' that m. of mine, 833 : 8
low m. seeks little thing, 542 : 19
made for joy and woe, 406 : 13
made her such a m., 229 : 31
made man can change, 817 : 10
made of ordinary things, 413 : 8

Man (*continued*)
made the town, 376 : 17
made to mourn, 408 : 15
majority never replace m., 812 : 14
makes gods by the dozen, 165 : 7
making deserts of earth, 760 : 6
manners maketh m., 143 : 13
man's inhumanity to m., 408 : 16
man's monument a m., 646 : 10
man's word God in m., 534 : 2
marks earth with ruin, 458 : 25
mass of thawing clay, 560 : 12
master of fate, 534 : 7, 814 : 8
master of himself a happy m., 108 : 7
matures through work, 897 : 9
may fish with worm, 223 : 15
meaning in saying he is a good m., 198 : 16
measure of all things, 78 : 23
mere m., 526 : 6
merely a passage for food, 152 : 2
middle-aged m. build woodshed, 557 : 12
mildest-mannered m., 460 : 26
military m., 207 : 21
mind of m. capable of anything, 683 : 17
mind proper judge of m., 115 : 5
mind's the standard of m., 328 : 1
misfortunes of m. occasioned by m., 116 : 10
mistake young m. for god, 772 : 3
mistakes evil for happiness, 414 : 5
mollusk cheap edition of m., 499 : 19
moral inferiority of m., 626 : 4
moral sensible well-bred m., 376 : 2
more no m. entitled to, 687 : 8
more right than neighbors, 558 : 5
more sinned against, 217 :
mortal m. who hath more joy, 570 : 16
most detestable creature, 626 : 10
muffin m., 933 : 8
must have faults, 117 : 15
my m. Friday, 318 : 15
naked m. in book of moons, 918 : 11
native metal of m., 568 : 17
nature formed one such m., 459 : 20
nature in form of m., 875 : 7
nature removes great m., 498 : 13
nearer atom than star, 776 : 9
necessarily a m., 341 : 10
needs go outside himself, 672 : 7
needs to suffer, 671 : 22
ne'er left m. in mire, 242 : 32
neither angel nor beast, 300 : 8
never bad m. good service, 373 : 14
never is blessed, 336 : 15
never met m. I didn't like, 766 : 6
never saw m. who looked, 676 : 6
new m. raised up in him, 56 : 16
nice m., 322 : 5
no angel, 484 : 14
no benefit in gifts of bad m., 76 : 15
no great m. born too soon, 724 : 13
no indispensable m., 779 : 9
no m. above or below law, 687 : 9
no m. born an angler, 270 : 31
no m. born unto himself, 267 : 9
no m. content with lot, 106 : 10
no m. deserved less at country's hands, 590 : 7
no m. do for your sake, 632 : 21
no m. is an island, 254 : 22
no m. not deserve hanging, 166 : 3

Man (*continued*)
no m. remember me, 640 : 16
no m. see me more, 249 : 1
no m. should marry, 502 : 11
no m. takes wealth with him, 67 : 6
no m. useless who has friend, 669 : 13
no m. worth having true, 321 : 4
no reasonable m. expected, 816 : 1
no sin for m. to labor in vocation, 203 : 3
no such thing as honest m., 330 : 24
noble animal, 275 : 11
noble be m. helpful and good, 394 : 16
noblest work of m., 615 : 10
none more wonderful than m., 74 : 14
not a just m. upon earth, 27 : 9
not a m. but cloud, 826 : 16
not cause of work, 735 : 10
not creature of circumstances, 501 : 7
not fearing any m., 909 : 17
not good that m. be alone, 7 : 1
not happy unless free, 464 : 10
not lifetime of one m. only, 807 : 23
not locked into environment, 870 : 15
not m. you're a machine, 680 : 13
not materials that counts, 826 : 9
not passion's slave, 222 : 6
not sum of what he has, 865 : 8
not take goods with him, 3 : 2
not what kind of paper but m., 558 : 25
nothing come out of artist not in m., 772 : 14
nothing feebler than a m., 60 : 26
nothing more fun than a m., 827 : 15
nothing more wretched than a m., 58 : 29
nothing to do with just m., 41 : 20
nothing wears clothes but M., 268 : 19
O Nature O soul of m., 570 : 15
O that m. might know end, 217 : 10
of action, 815 : 5
of action forced to thought, 723 : 7
of an unbounded stomach, 249 : 13
of cheerful yesterdays, 428 : 18
of comfort no m. speak, 195 : 1
of dust, 6 : 17
of genius had to pay, 736 : 5
of honor regrets discreditable act, 772 : 13
of letters, 301 : 11
of many resources, 59 : 13
of many wiles, 334 : 21
of morals tell me why, 295 : 8
of my kidney, 225 : 25
of my peculiar weakness, 772 : 12
of nasty ideas, 322 : 5
of science at formation of fact, 639 : 14
of sorrows, 31 : 14
of Sorrows, 570 : 16
of sovereign parts, 190 : 20
of strife and contention, 32 : 9
of talent sees two or three, 793 : 10
of unclean lips, 29 : 10
of understanding, 35 : 11
of understanding is of excellent spirit, 24 : 18
of understanding lost nothing, 164 : 16
of virtue, 68 : 20
of words not deeds, 929 : 8
old age in universal m., 178 : *n* 12
old m. broken, 249 : 10

Man (*continued*)
old m. eloquent, 282 : 6
old m. had so much blood, 239 : 25
old m. in dry month, 804 : 13
Old M. River, 833 : 7
old m. to whom old men hearkened, 110 : 10
old m. twice a child, 220 : 32
old m. who will not laugh, 704 : 9
old m. with beard, 550 : 4
old m. with something of young, 99 : 8
old m. wouldn't say prayers, 931 : 8
on horseback, 922 : 6
once to every m. and nation, 567 : 6
one m. among a thousand, 27 : 11
one m. crossing bridge, 766 : 13
one m. one vote, 925 : 8
one m. plays many parts, 211 : 15
one m. with courage a majority 419 : 5
one more wrong to m., 541 : 8
one small step for m., 910 : 14
one upright m., 847 : 7
one-book m., 433 : 8
only animal that blushes, 625 : 11
only feels alone, 885 : 17
only great m. write history, 676 : 5
only great when he acts from passions, 501 : 16
only m. harrowing clods, 642 : 2
only m. is vile, 452 : 9
only one that knows nothing, 116 : 9
only soul m. must save, 841 : 4
organized by labor, 725 : 10
our m. in Havana, 859 : 12
out of me God and m., 634 : 4
out of one m. a race, 286 : 29
outrage a brave m. dead, 73 : 16
outrage when m. destroys nature, 758 : 2
owes not any m., 510 : 8
paint m. as well as features, 619 : 9
Parliament of M., 530 : 1
particularly pure young m., 628 : 7
partly is, 544 : 16
patriot m. and American, 667 : 3
people arose as one m., 12 : 23
perceives it die away, 426 : 15
perhaps this is the m., 896 : 5
picked out of ten thousand, 220 : 16
pig edible to m., 647 : 11
pious m. can't stay in peace, 414 : 3
pious m. not less a m., 297 : 21
place and means for every m., 227 : 17
plain blunt m., 216 : 27
Plato's m., 86 : 10
play is tragedy "M.", 526 : 5
play the m. Master Ridley, 156 : 14
poetry inner calling in m., 861 : 5
poet's privilege to help m. endure, 838 : 12
poor despised old m., 233 : 26
poor m. accustomed to small things, 881 : 7
poor m. being down, 35 : 27
poor m. get out iv Purgatory, 722 : 10
poor m. had nothing, 13 : 19
poor m. is Christ's stamp, 268 : 9
poor m. poor mankind, 838 : 1
poor m. that has loved, 714 : 18
poorest m. in his cottage, 351 : 7
possesses immortality, 866 : 6
power of m. and moment, 586 : 19

Man (*continued*)
powers superior to m., 673 : 2
prayer of righteous m., 52 : 6
preached as dying m., 294 : 17
prejudiced reasonable m., 549 : 12
prentice han' tried on m., 409 : 15
press not falling m., 249 : 2
primitive m. tactile m., 784 : 27
prisoned spirit of m., 739 : 5
projects himself into culture, 865 : 14
proper m. as see in summer's day, 196 : 9
proper study of mankind is m., 337 : 2
proposes God disposes, 148 : 15
prosperity comes to bad m., 67 : 3
proud yet wretched thing, 251 : 7
prudent m. looketh well to his going, 24 : 2
rather be worm than son of m., 798 : 3
reading maketh a full m., 181 : 13
ready money makes the m., 328 : 16
ready to believe what is told, 117 : 13
reasonable m. mythical, 815 : 17
rebuke a wise m., 23 : 19
recovered of the bite, 369 : 19
reduced no m. to atomic elements, 777 : 10
register of God not record of m., 275 : 9
rejoice O young m. in youth, 27 : 23
rejoiceth as a strong m., 17 : 28
republic of m., 852 : 2
rich in things he can let alone, 559 : 21
rich m. beginning to fall, 35 : 27
rich m. enter into kingdom, 40 : 7
rich m. enther Hiven, 722 : 10
richest pleasures cheapest, 557 : 17
rickety poor sort of thing, 626 : 18
righted up falling m., 560 : 21
righteous m. regardeth the life of his beast, 23 : 29
righteous m. to make fall, 173 : 11
rights of m., 373 : 19, 616 : 1
rope between animal and Superman, 657 : 12
round fat oily m. of God, 345 : 22
round m. in square hole, 625 : 22
rousing like strong m., 282 : 3
ruined m., 809 : 18
ruins of the noblest m., 216 : 11
rule will show the m., 62 : 11
sabbath made for m. 41 : 34
said to universe, 732 : 8
savage in m. never eradicated, 557 : 19
says what he knows, 358 : 26
seeks for what is remote, 89 : 11
seems the only growth, 368 : 17
sent from God, 44 : 19
serve time to every trade, 456 : 13
setting m. free from men, 865 : 4
seven women shall take hold of one m., 29 : 2
severe he was, 370 : 10
shall m. be more pure than maker, 15 : 13
shall man no longer crush, 399 : 18
shall mortal m. be more just, 15 : 13
she knows her m., 259 : *n* 8
sight make old m. young, 529 : 2
significance of m., 738 : 10

Man (*continued*)
silliest woman manage m., 707 : 11
singularly deep young m., 628 : 6
slothful m. saith, 25 : 19
small m. may not be entrusted, 69 : 16
smiling destructive m., 317 : 15
smiteth a m. so that he die, 10 : 9
so can any m., 204 : 12
so frail a thing m., 320 : 11
so in way in house, 536 : 14
so is it now I am a m., 425 : 7
so much one m. can do, 296 : 25
so near God to m., 494 : 21
so unto m. woman, 511 : 18
so various, 304 : 10
social friendly honest m., 409 : 2
social world work of m., 324 : 2
something m. will die for, 909 : 6
son of m. that thou visitest him, 17 : 17
sooner kill m. than hawk, 797 : 15
soul of m. imperishable, 85 : 10
soul of m. larger, 480 : 12
spares neither m. nor his works, 383 : 14
speech open m. to m., 310 : *n* 1
sprang to his feet, 540 : 31
stage where every m. play part, 197 : 28
stagger like a drunken m., 21 : 16
state of m. like kingdom, 215 : 18
stole the fruit, 268 : 12
strives for someone to worship, 582 : 6
strong m. digests experiences, 658 : 8
strongest m. stands alone, 599 : 21
style is the m., 349 : 2
subtle knot which makes us m., 253 : 7
successful animal, 686 : 3
such a disagreeable m., 629 : 3
such master such m., 163 : 3
sum of all he has acquired, 360 : 27
superior m. acts before he speaks, 68 : 9
superior m. is modest, 69 : 8
superior m. like heaven, 609 : 6
surest plan to make m., 568 : 11
sweet slumbers of virtuous m., 326 : 4
takes drink drink takes man, 646 : 12
teach you more of m., 423 : 7
tempt not desperate m., 193 : 24
temptation but for m. to master, 545 : 11
that died for men, 636 : 4
that hangs on favors, 249 : 3
that hath his quiver full, 22 : 10
that hath no music, 201 : 3
that hath tongue no man, 190 : 1
that is a worm, 16 : 11
that is born of a woman, 15 : 33
that makes character, 330 : 2
that m. to man the world o'er, 411 : 19
that mocks and sets it light, 194 : 6
that trusteth in man, 32 : 11
that trusteth in the Lord, 32 : 11
that was in evening made, 276 : 4
that's marred, 227 : 15
the third m., 859 : 9
there did meet another m., 353 : 18
there is a m. child conceived, 15 : 7
thin m., 830 : 5
thin m. in every fat m., 857 : 13

Man (*continued*)
think mortal thoughts, 76 : 9
thinking or working is alone, 560 : 3
third beast had a face as a m., 53 : 7
this dust once the m., 576 : 8
this is Plato's m., 86 : 10
this is the state of m., 249 : 3
this m. met rancor, 728 : 18
this m. shall be myself, 359 : 2
this m. this mongrel beast, 794 : 9
this was a m., 217 : 14
thou art the m., 13 : 20
though old m. young gardener, 389 : 6
thought young m. brings forth, 85 : 16
thousandth m., 710 : 20
tills field lies beneath, 533 : 27
time ends in killing m., 580 : 1
time whereof memory of m., 365 : 17
Time you old gypsy m., 732 : 17
tired of being a m., 860 : 9
title from better m. I stole, 668 : 17
to a wise m. ports, 194 : 5
to all country dear, 370 : 5
to be a great m., 581 : 9
to be m. with thy might, 634 : 6
to command, 531 : 7
to every m. a damsel or two, 12 : 9
to every m. according to his work, 19 : 28
to every m. upon earth, 488 : 14
to laugh proper to m., 157 : 8
to match mountains, 671 : 1
to men m. is mind, 647 : 6
to the young m. knowledge and discretion, 23 : 1
tool-using animal, 472 : 22
totality of what he might have, 865 : 8
tree of m. never quiet, 691 : 7
truly be own master, 895 : 14
truly honest m., 292 : 20
trust m. on his oath or bond, 243 : 1
try fortunes to last m., 206 : 27
turns to face snow, 874 : 20
tyranny over mind of m., 388 : 15
unaccommodated m., 234 : 7
unfinished m. and his pain, 716 : 1
until m. fully human, 819 : 12
use every m. after desert, 221 : 5
vain diverse undulating, 164 : 6
various m., 410 : 16
vertical m., 868 : 1
very unclubable m., 354 : 19
victory shifts from m. to m., 58 : 3
vile m. that mourns, 336 : 22
violent m. come down on everyone, 4 : 6
wants but little, 330 : 12, 369 : 12
wars caused by m., 817 : 10
was it God was it m., 634 : 7
was made to mourn, 408 : 15
was there m. dismayed, 533 : 10
wash that m. outa my hair, 833 : 15
way of m. with maid, 26 : 4, 708 : 22
ways of God to m., 336 : 11
We created M., 132 : 10
weak m. better enemy than friend, 561 : 14
wealth even to a wicked m., 67 : 2
well-bred m. knows how to confess, 347 : 20
well-favored m., 209 : 24

Man (*continued*)
went mad and bit the m., 369 : 18
went to bar as very young m., 628 : 22
what a chimera is m., 300 : 11
what a piece of work is m., 220 : 28
what is m. in nature, 299 : 17
what is m. that thou art mindful, 17 : 17
what is m. to live lifetime of God, 570 : 6
what is m. what is he not, 72 : 2
what is m. without beasts, 456 : 1
what is significance of m., 738 : 10
what m. can be he must be, 872 : 15
what m. dare I dare, 238 : 28
what m. has made of m., 423 : 4
what m. may do to himself, 765 : 1
what m. not know of God, 859 : 1
what manner of m., 42 : 2
what may m. within hide, 228 : 27
what mean m. seeks, 69 : 13
what signifies life o' m., 409 : 14
what treaty white m. kept, 610 : 5
when honor dies m. dead, 513 : 8
when I get to be m., 729 : 9
when just m. dies, 869 : 5
when m. marries again, 675 : 5
when m. of rank an author, 356 : 22
when m. of real talent dies, 386 : 19
when right m. rings them, 669 : 6
where love of m. love of art, 79 : 16
whiskey life of m., 934 : 16
white m. warmed before Indians' fire, 374 : 20
white m. will never be alone, 456 : 2
who brings bad news, 74 : 11
who broke bank, 666 : 21
who came to dinner, 813 : 5
who convinces the world, 662 : 3
who craves more is poor, 114 : 14
who expects nothing, 336 : 6
who goes alone start today, 559 : 15
who had been promised, 822 : 8
who has city obedient, 84 : 16
who has found himself out, 694 : 11
who has mind and knows it, 681 : 18
who invented sleep, 556 : 2
who is seen and heard, 705 : 12
who looks part has soul of part, 667 : 4
who never fought pilfers, 82 : 2
who owes nothing to land, 359 : 1
who publishes his letters becomes nudist, 847 : 9
who runs may fight again, 91 : 12
who said one word for woman, 677 : 4
who said This is mine, 358 : 9
who sits facing you, 63 : 5
who sold hyena skin, 746 : 4
who touches this touches m., 576 : 21
who turnips cries, 353 : 12
who used to notice such things, 642 : 3
who was a key a m., 889 : 16
who wasn't there, 756 : 2
who wert once despot, 467 : 9
whole duty of m., 27 : 27
whom Fortune scratched, 227 : 19
whom king delighteth to honor, 14 : 33
who's master who's m., 323 : 22
whose blood is snow-broth, 227 : 28
whose blood warm within, 197 : 29

Man (*continued*)
why can't woman be more like m., 895 : 2
wicked m. Hitler, 744 : 8
will cleave to like, 35 : 26
will no m. say amen, 195 : 10
will not merely endure, 838 : 10
will yet win, 761 : 17
wills us slaves, 385 : 14
wind sweep m. away, 585 : 9
wine a peephole on a m., 62 : 20
wise and moral m., 73 : 3
wise in his own conceit, 25 : 19
wise m. has no extensive knowledge, 65 : 10
wise m. is strong, 25 : 12
wise m. knows himself fool, 212 : 30
wise m. not leave right to chance, 558 : 3
wise m. speaks, 257 : 4
wisest m. does not fancy he is, 311 : 6
with bread on shoulder, 824 : 5
with God always in majority, 162 : 2
with God strive, 458 : 8
with great thing to pursue, 542 : 19
with seven wives, 930 : 1
with the head, 531 : 7
without a flaw, 106 : 16
without a tear, 443 : 20
without imagination, 784 : 26
without money rather than money without man, 70 : 16
witness unto his deeds, 132 : 16
wolf to man, 811 : 9
woman lesser m., 530 : 5
woman more barbarous than m., 657 : 21
woman not depend on protection of m., 578 : 3
woman same needs as m., 914 : 5
woman without m. cannot meet m., 896 : 5
women looking-glasses reflecting m., 782 : 5
wonder and glory of universe, 515 : 7
wonder grandeur woe, 571 : 2
words guard shape of m., 850 : 16
work for m. to mend, 306 : 26
work from sun to sun, 920 : 11
works of present m., 435 : 21
worst cliques one m., 681 : 15
worst use a m. could be put to, 251 : 3
worth makes the m., 337 : 11
wrathful m. stirreth up strife, 24 : 8
writing maketh exact m., 181 : 13
writing master to world, 799 : 6
yes I am fatal m., 539 : 13
you can't face m., 850 : 8
you drop from chamber, 558 : 25
you shall find me grave m., 193 : 5
you'll be a m. my son, 710 : 18
young m. in whom something of old, 99 : 8
young m. married is marred, 227 : 15
young m. there is America, 372 : 12
young m. who has not wept, 704 : 9
you're a good m. Charlie Brown, 901 : 7
you're not a m., 680 : 13
Manacles, mind-forged m., 405 : 9
Manage this matter to a T, 158 : *n* 2
Management of balance of power, 902 : 11

Man-at-arms now serve on knees, 177 : 9
Mandalay, road to M., 708 : 9
Mandamus binds all alike, 398 : 22
Mandarin, my thirty-third m., 582 : *n* 2
Mandragora, give me to drink m., 240 : 20
not poppy nor m., 231 : 8
Mandrake, get with child a m. root, 252 : 1
Mane, laid hand upon thy m., 458 : 31
my bright m. forever, 403 : 14
Manes, whirlwind home in m., 518 : 9
Mangent, qu'ils m. de la brioche, 359 : *n* 2
Manger, cold and not cleanly m., 292 : 17
dog in the m., 66 : 10
for his bed, 561 : 10
in the rude m. lies, 277 : 7
laid in a m., 42 : 27
not live as dogs in m., 781 : 5
One born in a m., 299 : 10
Mangled by the bronze spear, 59 : 6
naked poor m. peace, 208 : 16
Manhattan, of M. the son, 574 : 20
Man-hero not exceptional monster, 768 : 19
Manhood a struggle, 501 : 15
and decrepit age, 267 : 19
bone of m., 372 : 14
conspiracy against m., 496 : 22
do what m. bids thee, 581 : 14
firm against crowd, 531 : 15
grain of m., 288 : 27
honesty m. nor fellowship, 203 : 4
no sounder British m., 472 : 13
of this stone, 900 : 7
Manhood's pondering repose of If, 571 : 4
Mania for maintaining all is well, 343 : 10
lawsuit m., 630 : 20
of owning things, 574 : 24
Maniac scattering dust, 532 : 6
Manic dust of my friends, 864 : 13
statement, 893 : 1
Manifest destiny, 552 : 13
nothing is secret that shall not be m., 43 : 6
plainness, 64 : 8
the m. and the hidden, 132 : 13
work be made m., 48 : 5
Manifestation of unfriendly disposition, 408 : 3
Manifestations, significant m. of life, 867 : 17
Manifesto, this m. more than theory, 645 : 5
Manifold, how m. are thy works, 21 : 11
our m. sins, 55 : 17
sins and wickedness, 54 : 11
Manikin, made m. to madden it, 527 : 3
what an eloquent m., 102 : 6
Manila, admiral down in M. Bay, 647 : 2
Manipulate, science of behavior power to m., 862 : 13
Mankind, all m. done in books, 473 : 29
asses that pull, 462 : 9
at war with rights of m., 388 : 8
by perverse depravity, 316 : 15
by thee less bored, 270 : *n* 7
calamities shared by m., 318 : 13

Mankind (*continued*)
careless of m., 528 : 19
censure injustice, 84 : 7
collective knowledge of m., 867 : 12
composed of two sorts, 672 : 9
crucify m., 694 : 16
custom despot of m., 486 : 5
deserve better of m., 322 : 12
distraction to m., 260 : 16
divided m. into parties, 398 : 2
doings of m. subject of my book, 122 : 1
dwell on heights of m., 413 : 25
entitled to respect of m., 451 : 7
Father of m., 514 : 1
fleet of life like leaves, 82 : 9
fly from not hate m., 457 : 26
furnishing m. with two noblest things, 321 : 14
future of m. waiting, 912 : 4
giant leap for m., 910 : 14
glorious accomplishment of m., 887 : 17
hate m., 243 : 8
heart bettered tradition of m., 667 : 20
hindrances to elevation of m., 559 : 8
if you'd m. degrade, 405 : 15
in charity to all m., 418 : 6
in conscious virtue bold, 334 : 12
in mass duplicates, 571 : 2
inspired made cathedral, 667 : 10
involved in m., 254 : 22
is dream of a shadow, 72 : 2
lay out ourselves in service of m., 392 : 14
let m. agree, 306 : 28
love a lover, 497 : 14
love m. except American, 356 : 4
make science blessing to m., 763 : 8
minus one of one opinion, 508 : 4
mother of m., 283 : 3
no quality more precious has m., 702 : 6
O ye that love m., 384 : 12
of all m. I love but you, 917 : 4
one disillusion was m., 783 : 3
optimistic future of m., 678 : 12
our countrymen m., 505 : 10
plagues with which m. cursed, 318 : 9
poetry mother tongue of m., 374 : 22
poor man poor m., 838 : 1
possesses two blessings, 77 : 6
prepare asylum for m., 384 : 12
proper study of m. is man, 337 : 2
put end to war, 891 : 1
school of m., 374 : 8
serve country and m., 617 : 5
shut gates of mercy on m., 362 : 11
spectator of m., 326 : 8
spiritual unity of m., 895 : 21
surpasses or subdues m., 457 : 22
survey m., 351 : 16
things ride m., 494 : 7
to you and all m., 317 : 5
true nationality m., 720 : 4
war put end to m., 891 : 1
what was meant for m., 371 : 14
wisdom medicine for woes of m., 595 : 15
wisest brightest meanest of m., 337 : 15
Mankind's concern is charity, 337 : 9
epitome, 304 : 10

Mankind's (*continued*)
motto, 296 : 10
Manlier, nobler and m. one, 461 : 7
Manliness, beauty of true m., 609 : 6
native western m., 577 : 3
silent m. of grief, 370 : 18
Manly, avowed erect and m. foe, 422 : 5
deeds womanly words, 270 : *n* 5
his big m. voice, 211 : 15
love is m., 148 : 20
nurse of m. sentiment, 373 : 23
simple modest m. true, 568 : 23
Manna, give us this day m., 141 : 27
it is m., 10 : 2
Mannahatta, dweller in M. my city, 574 : 3
Manner, after m. of men, 47 : 4
after this m. pray ye, 37 : 15
all well all m. of thing well, 808 : 18
ease in Casey's m., 704 : 15
is all in all, 375 : 20
no m. of doubt, 630 : 3
of giving worth more, 275 : 24
pleasant shy m. of mouse, 846 : 14
state in wonted m. keep, 255 : 12
subordinates m. to matter, 437 : 17
to the m. born, 219 : 9
vulgar m., 81 : 13
what m. of man is this, 42 : 2
Mannerly, behave m. at table, 668 : 10
Manners, amiability of m., 589 : 6
are not idle, 534 : 21
as nation no m., 680 : 10
bewrayed by his m., 174 : 4
catch the m. living, 336 : 11
character habits and m., 592 : 7
climates councils, 529 : 8
contact with m. is education, 112 : 18
corrupt good m., 49 : 2
evil m. live in brass, 249 : 14
fine m. need support, 498 : 29
happy ways of doing, 498 : 28
impressions of American m., 449 : 1
language m. laws customs, 424 : 8
maketh man, 143 : 13
mirror which shows portrait, 397 : 9
must adorn knowledge, 342 : 2
not men but m., 349 : 12
of m. gentle, 305 : *n* 2
of undertaker, 726 : 13
old m. books wines, 371 : 3
our nation limps after, 194 : 11
savage men uncouth m., 372 : 12
saw m. in face, 353 : 10
Mannish cowards, 210 : 22
Mano, Dios te tenga en su m., 935 : 18
Manon Lescaut, story of M., 345 : 1
Manor, as if a m. washed away, 254 : 22
Man-o'-war's 'er 'usband, 709 : 8
Man's, a m. worth something, 543 : 9
always been m. world, 870 : 9
any m. death diminishes me, 254 : 22
bad m. refuge, 64 : 22
bedevilment and God's, 691 : 23
best friend is dog, 609 : *n* 1
best portion of m. life, 423 : 9
blind m. ditch, 716 : 2
brown m. burden, 709 : *n* 3
capacity for justice, 823 : 18
capacity to despise self, 703 : 16
character is his fate, 70 : 11
cheer poor m. heart, 430 : 22
cloud like m. hand, 14 : 3
Dead M. Chest, 668 : 4

Man's (*continued*)
deceiver never mine, 692 : 7
desire is for woman, 438 : 5
desiring this m. art, 244 : 9
difference from brutes, 649 : 16
distinctive mark, 544 : 16
efforts to control nature, 814 : 12
every m. Cleopatra, 303 : 13
every old m. eye, 192 : 21
every true m. apparel, 229 : 2
every wise m. son know, 213 : 22
fate, 853 : 6
first disobedience, 282 : 22
fortune in own hand, 181 : 6
good m. feast, 211 : 12
good m. fortune, 233 : 15
good m. love, 212 : 16
good m. sin, 360 : *n* 2
good m. treasure, 64 : 22
gowd for a' that, 411 : 17
great m. memory, 222 : 10
hand not able to taste, 197 : 10
happiness result of man's effort 763 : 3
honest m. aboon his might, 411 : 18
honest m. noblest work, 337 : 13, 408 : 18
idea of sexual rights, 554 : 7
image and his cry, 712 : 7
imagination of m. heart, 7 : 33
imperial race ensnare, 334 : 3
in theater of m. life, 179 : 4
inborn dispositions, 867 : 14
inclination to injustice, 823 : 18
ingratitude, 211 : 16
inhumanity to man, 408 : 16
life allegory, 479 : 19
life cheap as beast's, 233 : 21
looking for m. footprint, 736 : 1
love an episode in m. life, 417 : 12
love of man's life apart, 460 : 19
no m. enemy, 868 : 3
no m. pie is freed, 248 : 20
old m. darling, 161 : 6
old m. eagle mind, 717 : 11
old m. frenzy, 717 : 10
old m. gold, 730 : 18
one m. will all men's misery, 175 : 8
one wise m. verdict, 543 : 6
originality sum of m. thinking, 862 : 6
own resinous heart, 715 : 14
perdition to be safe, 495 : 9
plant m. lordship, 643 : 2
practically inexterminate, 749 : 16
print of m. foot, 318 : 14
proud m. contumely, 221 : 12
reach exceed grasp, 543 : 1
rising to a m. work, 125 : 1
share the good m. smile, 370 : 9
skill built cities, 97 : 14
sorrow not mine but m., 692 : 6
stain my m. cheeks, 233 : 22
strength m. charm, 694 : *n* 2
take each m. censure, 219 : 1
thirty years in m. life, 84 : 14
tilling soil of m. vanity, 750 : 16
truest monument a man, 646 : 10
truly sorry m. dominion, 408 : 13
truth is final resolution, 769 : 18
unconquerable mind, 425 : 21
village his peace of mind, 895 : 11
watch o'er m. mortality, 426 : 23
way to m. heart, 538 : 6
white m. burden, 709 : 21

Man's (*continued*)
word God in man, 534 : 2
work portrait of himself, 620 : 10
young m. fancy, 529 : 16
young m. heart's complaint, 574 : 22
young m. warling, 161 : 6
Manservant, not covet neighbor's m., 10 : 7
Mansion, back to its m. call, 362 : 5
from m. in the sun, 474 : 18
human life a m., 479 : 11
Jove's Court my m., 279 : 2
love has pitched his m., 716 : 18
refuse heavenly m., 716 : 7
where we can turn off lights, 796 : 2
Mansionry, approve by his loved m., 236 : 21
Mansions, green m., 646 : 1
his m. deathless, 59 : 24
in Father's house many m., 45 : 20
in the skies, 328 : 14
Manslaughter, check m. but what of war, 114 : 32
Mantel, morn in russet m. clad, 217 : 27
of wind and chill and rain, 148 : 22
silver m. threw, 285 : 25
twitched his m. blue, 281 : 6
Mantle, green m. of standing pool, 234 : 9
like a standing pond, 198 : 1
of Elijah, 14 : 14
Mantled in mist, 868 : 20
Manual on uses of new metal, 906 : 11
under press of having to write instruction m., 906 : 12
Manufactures, monopoly same as secret in m., 366 : 1
Manunkind, busy monster m., 829 : 24
Manure, natural m., 388 : 7
Manus haec inimica tyrannis, 298 : *n* 7
Manuscript, youth's sweet-scented m., 517 : 12
Many a one for him maks mane, 927 : 5
admire few know, 80 : 11
America one yet m., 885 : 6
and mighty are they, 709 : 6
are called, 40 : 14
as the sand by the sea, 13 : 28
beast with m. heads, 242 : 21
beguile m. beguiled by one, 231 : 21
can brook the weather, 190 : 28
conceive the m. without one, 85 : 14
daughters have done virtuously, 26 : 10
done because we are too m., 641 : 8
exploited by few, 825 : 18
fail one succeeds, 530 : 10
hands make light work, 160 : 31
in hands not of few but m., 80 : 17
in literature the m. force judgment, 493 : 10
inventions, 27 : 12
must labor for one, 459 : 9
mutable rank-scented m., 242 : 17
not how m. enemy are but where, 78 : 25
not m. but much, 134 : 13
one composed of m., 106 : 8
play of the m., 697 : 2
reason Lord makes so m., 523 : 5
receive advice few profit, 110 : 21
safe from the m., 568 : 23
savings of m., 676 : 19
shall run to and fro, 33 : 6
Many (*continued*)
so m. I loved were not yet dead, 856 : 7
so much owed by so m., 744 : 6
sold the m. on the few, 829 : 23
strokes overthrow the oaks, 175 : 13
that are first, 40 : 8
the few and the m., 401 : 12
the few despoilers of the m., 422 : 18
there be which go in thereat, 38 : 15
to keep, 566 : 9
we are m., 42 : 4
what are they among m., 44 : 39
wisdom of m., 921 : 6
Many-colored glass, 469 : 16
life he drew, 351 : 10
Many-fountained Ida, 528 : 4
Many-headed monster of pit, 339 : 28
multitude, 108 : *n* 14, 242 : 14
people a m. beast, 108 : 19
Many-splendored thing, 693 : 18
Many-wintered crow, 529 : 18
Mao, examples from Alexander to M., 800 : 6
Map, I their m., 254 : 18
journey universe in m., 170 : 6
of honor in thy face, 185 : 16
Maple puts corals on in May, 568 : 25
Maple Leaf forever, 608 : 9
Maples, scarlet of m. shake me, 696 : 9
Maps to other world, 251 : 15
Mar, not make cannot m., 585 : 1
striving to better we m., 233 : 12
this fair garden, 600 : 19
your fortunes, 232 : 25
Marathon, Athenians crushed at M. the Medes, 67 : 18
looks on the sea, 461 : 4
patriotism gain force on M., 352 : 22
to Waterloo, 628 : 1
Marble, draw living faces from m., 105 : 24
dwelt in m. halls, 480 : 11
enduring as m. to retain, 171 : 10
forget thyself to m., 278 : 14
head in my hands, 849 : 9
hills full of m., 619 : 17
index of a mind, 424 : 2
left Rome a city of m., 110 : 8
life m. and mud, 503 : 18
nor gilded monuments, 244 : 18
on m. pavement dust grows, 97 : 10
poets that lasting m. seek, 276 : 9
Priapus made of m., 103 : 15
say more than many a braver m., 292 : 20
sleep in dull cold m., 249 : 6
Sunium's m. steep, 461 : 9
sweep through m. halls, 509 : 12
to retain, 460 : 7
wastes statue grows, 154 : 14
well-governed cities, 868 : 21
write evil in m., 155 : 8
Marble-hearted fiend, 233 : 10
Marbles, like m. touching but separate, 637 : 20
Marcellus, joy M. exiled feels, 337 : 14
March, alluvial m. of days, 843 : 19
almost hear breathing as they m., 893 : *n* 2
beware ides of M., 215 : 2
day's m. nearer home, 429 : 17
drought of M. perced to roote, 145 : 12
Hare went on, 611 : 18
March (*continued*)
her m. o'er mountain waves, 443 : 12
Ides of M., 99 : 21, 215 : 2
in ranks of honor, 744 : 11
is outside door, 839 : 1
it is M., 907 : 9
July October May, 162 : *n* 3
mad M. days, 760 : 20
mad M. hare, 152 : 19
men who m. away, 641 : 25
of human mind slow, 373 : 2
of intellect, 440 : 12
of this retreating world, 827 : 7
take winds of M. with beauty, 246 : 26
three Frenchmen, 207 : 23
three hours' m. to dinner, 445 : 12
trees that would m., 765 : 10
truth is on m., 643 : 8
two months back in M., 748 : 17
we must m. my darlings, 575 : 15
worse than sun in M., 204 : 33
Marche, le Congrès ne m. pas, 382 : *n* 6
Marched breast forward, 546 : 7
by a king's name, 822 : 2
on without impediment, 187 : 23
rank on rank, 600 : 28
Märchen aus alten Zeiten, 481 : *n* 7
Marches, Africa m. patiently through time, 867 : 13
army m. on stomach, 421 : 4
funeral m. to grave, 509 : 14
humanitarian, 574 : 5
Marching along, 540 : 25
as to war, 616 : 6
boys are m., 578 : 12
His truth m. on, 566 : 4
single in file, 495 : 5
soul m. on, 619 : 14
through Boston, 893 : 12
through Georgia, 614 : 14
to promised land, 616 : 8
truth m. on, 566 : 4
when saints go m. in, 936 : 8
Marchings, mighty earthly m., 570 : 11
Marchons marchons, 415 : 1
Mare, shoe the m., 934 : 6
Mares eat oats, 933 : 4
Margalo, my name is M., 846 : 15
Margaret are you grieving, 656 : 9
fye na said may M., 926 : 24
you mourn for, 656 : 10
Marge of Lake Lebarge, 752 : 6
Margent, Meander's m. green, 279 : 18
of the world, 693 : 12
Margery Daw, 931 : 2
some went up with M., 868 : 18
Margin, a certain free m., 577 : 8
broad m. to my life, 560 : 1
life not end at m., 645 : 15
meadow of m., 398 : 29
of subsistence, 871 : 16
Margins, outmost m., 797 : 12
Mariana, dejected M., 228 : 24
Marian's nose looks red, 191 : 15
Marigolds, ardent m., 474 : 22
Marijuana, curlicues of m., 893 : 1
Marine, another m. reporting sir, 925 : 1
Mariner, ancient m., 434 : 4
fear thee ancient m., 434 : 25
hath his will, 434 : 6
if Ancient M. called Old Sailor, 621 : 2
monody not wake m., 843 : 13
Mariners of England, 443 : 10

Mariners (*continued*)
rest ye brother m., 528 : 20
Marines, tell that to the m., 432 : 10
that will do for the m., 432 : *n* 3
Marionette, burst from m. show, 904 : 9
Maritime, rebellions of m. provinces, 800 : 11
Mark archer little meant, 431 : 19
as arrows fly to one m., 207 : 8
coming and look brighter, 460 : 16
could man outlook that m., 299 : 9
death loves shining m., 330 : 16
ever-fixed m., 245 : 18
fault of wit to go beyond m., 294 : 4
go m. him well, 430 : 10
God save the m., 203 : 10
God speed the m., 494 : 1
how my fame rings, 647 : 4
how plain tale put you down, 204 : 1
I press toward the m., 50 : 4
man's distinctive m., 544 : 16
Matthew M. Luke and John, 294 : 16
no drowning m. upon him, 247 : 7
of the beast, 53 : 21
on red breast still, 514 : 3
philosophy push beyond m., 532 : 8
read m. learn, 56 : 3
see see their m., 269 : 6
set a m. upon Cain, 7 : 19
some m. of virtue, 199 : 25
the perfect man, 18 : 27
where his carnage, 459 : 7
you his absolute shall, 242 : 18
Mark Antony, woman lost M. the world, 316 : 16
Mark Twain, book by M., 845 : 5
Marked him for her own, 362 : 17
him for his own, 270 : 28
Him in flowering, 534 : 27
I where bolt of Cupid fell, 196 : 15
our hour is m., 420 : 20
Markers, do not move m. on border, 6 : 5
Market competition afford freedom, 790 : 3
do you know considering m., 747 : 19
enemy of m. not idelogy, 872 : 3
existence m. price, 607 : 17
fortune like the m., 180 : 20
keeping m. understocked, 366 : 1
knowledge bought in m., 564 : 10
little pig to m., 930 : 11
of his time, 223 : 17
press at m. maketh deere ware, 147 : 10
price they said, 607 : 17
stock m. a mirror, 871 : 4
to m. to buy fat pig, 933 : 9
truth accepted in m., 645 : 1
Marketplace, bird of night upon m., 215 : 12
idols of the m., 179 : 8
technique of m., 880 : 13
Marking, malady of not m., 205 : 25
Marks, fairer m., 267 : 11
I carry with me, 302 : 15
not won or lost, 773 : 3
of suffering, 835 : 9
our English dead, 709 : 12
Marl, clod of wayward m., 209 : 6
over the burning m., 283 : 15
Marlborough Street, hardly passionate M., 892 : 20
Marlowe's mighty line, 256 : 12
Marmion, last words of M., 431 : 3
Marquis duke and a' that, 411 : 18
Marred, young man m., 227 : 15
Marreth what he makes, 338 : *n* 9
Marriage a necessary evil, 91 : 9
a noose, 170 : 17
accident counts in m., 634 : 16
all thy days as m. day, 267 : 20
an evil most men welcome, 91 : *n* 6
and hanging go by destiny, 159 : *n* 4
as with cages, 165 : 19
community of two slaves, 647 : 15
damnably serious business, 826 : 14
desperate thing, 263 : 23
dirge in m., 217 : 29
disparity in m., 549 : 8
field of battle, 667 : 13
friendships invalidated by m., 620 : 15
from which love gone, 859 : 11
good m. a communion, 156 : 7
good m. each guardian, 756 : 11
has many pains, 352 : 18
has more joy than pain, 75 : 25
hasty m. seldom proveth well, 186 : 14
hearse, 405 : 10
in Cana of Galilee, 44 : *n* 4
in m. husband and wife equal, 471 : 1
in m. room for interpreter, 864 : 12
in m. wish to get out, 498 : 18
is popular, 680 : 24
keep eyes open before m., 347 : 19
love without m., 347 : 6
luxury not necessity, 578 : 6
makes one flesh, 324 : 8
merry as m. bell, 457 : 14
negative feelings about m., 316 : 3
not bed of roses, 667 : 13
O curse of m., 231 : 6
of true minds, 245 : 18
resembles shears, 433 : 9
rob lady of fortune by m., 349 : 23
rush into early m., 898 : 5
school of sincere pretenses, 706 : 2
seldom develop without crises, 754 : 2
servant in love lord in m., 147 : 30
stylish m., 718 : 18
tables, 218 : 14
that's been our m., 599 : 10
triumphal procession air to m., 490 : 2
what Adam and Eve think of m., 798 : 14
what torment not a m. bed, 254 : 23
without love, 347 : 6
Marriages are not escape, 898 : 5
made in heaven, 176 : 3
martini one of happiest m., 837 : 10
Married and that's his plague, 259 : 5
Benedick the m. man, 209 : 3
best part of m. life fights, 839 : 18
happiness in m. estate, 277 : 1
how m. without wife, 930 : 15
I would be m., 292 : 11
imprudently m. barber, 364 : 5
in haste, 324 : 5
man tattered and torn, 934 : 9
mocks m. men, 191 : 13
monagony m. to one person, 815 : *n* 1
most immoderately m., 874 : 13
most m. man I ever saw, 616 : 19
never m. that's his hell, 259 : 5
no taste when you m. me, 398 : 30
Married (*continued*)
not live till I were m., 209 : 19
O let us be m., 550 : 8
on Wednesday, 932 : 11
reader I m. him, 555 : 19
saints rarely m. women, 867 : 5
strange as if m. a great while, 324 : 19
sum m. people owe, 395 : 19
till anes we m. be, 926 : 24
to immortal verse, 278 : 6
to sea, 741 : 12
to single life, 292 : 11
unpleasing to a m. ear, 191 : 13
we will be m. o' Sunday, 188 : 32
well-bred as if not m., 324 : 19
young man m. is marred, 227 : 15
Marries, day one m. her, 67 : 11
doesn't signify whom one m., 416 : 5
times changed with who m., 667 : 14
when man m. again, 675 : 5
when woman m. again, 675 : 5
Marrons, tirer les m. du feu, 297 : *n* 3
Marrow, anguish of m., 804 : 22
dividing joints and m., 51 : 14
fear deep as m., 903 : 2
Puritan m. of my bones, 794 : 2
suck substantific m., 157 : 7
to bestow upon God, 875 : 1
Yankees have the m., 455 : 8
Marrowbone, stole a m., 931 : 3
thinks in a m., 717 : 2
Marrowbones, better down on m., 712 : 20
Marry, advice to persons about to m., 660 : 11
ancient people, 277 : 2
Ann, 680 : 18
as easy to m. rich woman, 539 : 14
better to m. than burn, 48 : 11
boy will you m. it, 911 : 9
certain person at certain time, 489 : 15
error to m. with poets, 884 : 18
every woman should m., 502 : 11
he'll come back and m. me, 934 : 3
is to halve rights double duties, 463 : 2
maiden will you m. me, 628 : 8
may m. whom she likes, 539 : 5
my body to that dust, 267 : 6
on mature basis, 898 : 5
people people m., 696 : 1
prepared to m. again, 628 : 19
proper time to m., 377 : 24
this is miching mallecho, 222 : 11
your son when you will, 269 : 20
Marrying blowing nearly dying, 892 : 12
Mars, an eye like M., 223 : 3
Jupiter aligns with M., 914 : 7
makes us or m. us, 232 : 9
of malcontents, 225 : 11
this seat of M., 194 : 13
Marsh, frogs in the m. mud, 104 : 1
hen secretly builds, 651 : 9
midst of unpeopled m., 488 : *n* 3
space 'twixt m. and skies, 651 : 9
Marshall Plan one of greatest contributions, 788 : 7
Marshal's, French soldier carries m. baton, 421 : 5
truncheon, 228 : 6
Marshes how candid and simple, 651 : 8
of Glynn, 651 : 9

Mart, mighty workings in distant m., 475 : 8
Martha was cumbered with serving, 43 : 16
Martial, airs m. brisk or grave, 377 : 13
airs of England, 451 : 2
cloak around him, 465 : 8
songs be written, 888 : 6
sounds, 283 : 21
swashing and m. outside, 210 : 22
Martin Elginbrodde, 594 : 14
you Doctor M., 908 : 8
Martini, into dry M., 812 : 4
one of happiest marriages on earth, 837 : 10
something about m., 855 : 16
Martin's bells of St. M., 930 : 7
expect Saint M. summer, 184 : 17
Martlet, temple-haunting m., 236 : 21
Martyr, die a m. go to heaven, 144 : 26
saint and m. rule from tomb, 806 : 18
thou fallest a blessed m., 249 : 8
Martyrdom, all have not gift of m., 305 : 21
Negro willing to risk m., 909 : 16
not at all fond of m., 344 : 4
to live, 275 : 2
torches of m., 389 : 5
Martyrdoms have crowned church, 126 : *n* 2
Martyr's, groan of m. woe, 406 : 7
no happiness perfect as m., 699 : 8
Martyrs, blood of m. seed of Church, 126 : *n* 2
create faith, 705 : 18
faith not create m., 705 : 18
love m. honor slain, 582 : 9
noble army of m., 55 : 1
noisy set m. call world, 713 : 1
Martyrs', out of m. bones elegance, 767 : 22
Marvel how fishes live in sea, 243 : 13
more and more, 729 : 15
not Ulysses but Captain M., 911 : 5
Marveling sweetly on her ills, 810 : 20
Marvelous, Chatterton m. boy, 425 : 10
how m. is man, 725 : 7
in all nature something m., 87 : 8
mercies infinite love, 633 : 4
's wonderful 's m., 835 : 20
truth confront us, 902 : 15
unknown taken for m., 123 : 2
what does not first appear m., 116 : 11
what is this m. book, 358 : 23
what m. creatures we are, 746 : 20
Marvels of man's labor, 872 : 13
Marx, Declaration more revolutionary than M., 800 : 8
methods of M., 719 : 10
Marxian socialism portent to historians, 783 : 7
who places trust in M. synthesis, 785 : 3
Marxism, aims and ideals of M., 834 : 7
is a religion, 785 : 1
product of bourgeois mind, 785 : 2
Marx's, strange answer to M. prayer, 785 : 7
Mary at thy window be, 411 : 2
born of the Virgin M., 55 : 2
call cattle home, 566 : 7
had a little lamb, 463 : 1
hath chosen good part, 43 : 17
incarnate of the Virgin M., 55 : 3
Mary (*continued*)
my M., 377 : 20
my sweet Highland M., 410 : 18
no God and M. His Mother, 892 : 14
quite contrary, 930 : 6
Saint Anne mother of M., 638 : 11
was that Mother mild, 561 : 10
young child with M., 36 : 21
Mary-buds, winking M. begin, 243 : 16
Maryland, hills of M., 513 : 17
my Maryland, 639 : 15
Mary's, my M. asleep, 410 : 13
Masai House of God, 845 : 8
Masculine soul a worker, 703 : 13
the usual m. disillusionment, 848 : 9
Mask and antique pageantry, 278 : 6
how recognized under m., 877 : 7
like Castlereagh, 468 : 5
no m. like truth, 324 : 9
off reality remains, 100 : 21
Mason, mere working m., 431 : 21
Masons building roofs of gold, 207 : 7
Masquerade, truth in m., 461 : 23
Masquerades as cream, 627 : 16
Mass and majesty of world, 869 : 1
baby figure of giant m., 226 : 5
blessed mutter of M., 541 : 20
chaos a rough unordered m., 113 : 15
dead level of m., 570 : 12
I am the m., 761 : 3
man m. of thawing clay, 560 : 12
mankind in m. duplicates, 571 : 2
novelty stains ancient m., 650 : 10
of London itself, 744 : 5
of men lead lives of desperation, 559 : 4
of the people, 401 : 12
Paris well worth a M., 174 : 26
particle of general m., 755 : 1
rough unordered m., 113 : 15
skies and earth a solid m., 131 : 13
spirit which goes through m., 755 : 1
the greatest blasphemy, 156 : 6
times speed of light squared, 763 : *n* 2
world terrible in m., 640 : 18
Massachusetts, here's to M., 694 : *n* 3
House of Representatives of M. Bay, 382 : 11
rampant Maenad of M., 634 : 9
there she is, 450 : 13
Massacre, sudden as m. more deadly, 622 : 2
Massa's, old M. gone away, 921 : 14
Masses, back m. against classes, 517 : 23
bow ye m., 628 : 15
cannot write for m., 482 : 2
contradiction between feudalism and m., 826 : 8
huddled m., 664 : 10
little virtue in action of m., 558 : 3
long suits, 818 : 5
Massive, heard her m. sandal, 823 : 8
retaliatory power, 803 : 7
Massy, solid m. hard particles, 313 : 16
two m. keys he bore, 280 : 19
Mast, bends gallant m., 453 : 19
drunken sailor on m., 187 : 15
like drunken sailor on m., 187 : 15
nailed colors to the m., 430 : 14
of some great ammiral, 283 : 15
what though m. blown overboard, 186 : 23
Master, accuse not a servant unto his m., 26 : 2
artist who bids come to heel, 803 : 2
be own m. really exist, 895 : 14
behold m., 344 : 10
blessing of St. Peter's M., 271 : 14
calls no man m., 448 : 7
card m. to those below, 818 : 5
disciple not above m., 39 : 2
everyone can m. grief, 209 : 22
executioner, 65 : 7
fire what a m., 474 : 3
follow the M., 302 : *n* 4
great M. said I see, 511 : 14
has a new m., 248 : 2
hewing wood for m. carpenter, 65 : 7
I am m. of fantasy, 674 : 6
in limitations the m., 397 : 1
into woods M. went, 651 : 11
Jacky have new m., 931 : 2
law m. after my disappearance, 73 : 1
lent his hand, 493 : 20
lifeblood of m. spirit, 281 : 24
loyal service to his m., 299 : 11
man is m. of things, 634 : 8
mistress two slaves, 647 : 15
myth of cold war, 862 : 20
need more to be m., 652 : 4
no more subtle m., 534 : 23
nor master's man, 618 : 10
not be slave not be m., 520 : 6
O worthy M., 511 : 6
of All Good Workmen, 707 : 21
of earth and sea, 711 : 13
of himself, 262 : 19
of himself a happy man, 108 : 7
of his fate, 534 : 7, 814 : 8
of my fate, 663 : 11
of sea master of every country, 181 : *n* 5
of the day of judgment, 130 : 9
of us all, 765 : 8
one for my m., 930 : 5
passion, 626 : 3
recognize Actaeon your m., 113 : 18
severe more harassing m., 768 : 24
Shallow I owe thousand pound, 206 : 37
spirits of this age, 216 : 9
stroke nature's part, 495 : 14
strong enough to be m., 358 : 13
such beauty as you m., 245 : 12
such m. such man, 163 : 3
these forces met m., 779 : 20
thou Virgil art my m. and author, 140 : 12
to lead but not m. them, 64 : 4
unwitting where M. dwells, 760 : 21
which is to be m., 613 : 16
who's m. who's man, 323 : 22
word work, 664 : 17
ye know not when m. cometh, 42 : 14
Mastered any law in thoughts, 496 : 9
Mastering, Thou m. me God, 655 : 19
Masterly, wise and m. inactivity, 416 : 14
Masterpiece, airing dirty linen never m., 911 : 19
appear as flower, 619 : 7
confusion made m., 238 : 5
great m. designed, 410 : 16
joy to artist, 619 : 7
nature's m. writing well, 316 : 5
no one knows m., 792 : 17

Masterpiece (*continued*)
not created without labor, 727 : 11
of nature, 497 : 19
place of m. in mind, 499 : 12
Masterpieces, adventures among m., 655 : 11
not give best at beginning, 734 : 4
Master's, dog starved at m. gate, 406 : 10
lost fiddle stick, 929 : 10
neither master nor m. man, 618 : 10
old M. gone away, 921 : 14
Masters and the slaves, 848 : 3
artist has m. in eye, 504 : *n* 1
ashamed to become disciples, 250 : 11
done away with, 658 : 4
ego serves three harsh m., 678 : 15
free ourselves subdue our m., 392 : 9
lords and rulers, 670 : 15
machines slaves not m., 689 : 27
nails fastened by m., 27 : 26
no man can serve two m., 38 : 1
of our fate, 842 : 12
of their fates, 215 : 6
of things they write, 263 : 20
old m. never wrong, 868 : 9
sleep that m. all, 73 : 13
spread yourselves, 196 : 3
we cannot all be m., 229 : 14
worthy valets, 378 : 5
Masters', crumbs from m. table, 39 : 32
Masterwork, creation of m., 586 : 19
history of m. not failures, 793 : 5
of wisdom, 580 : 10
Mastery, achieve of m. of, 656 : 2
I had m., 827 : 7
mastodon with m., 881 : 11
of desires, 658 : 6
of subject, 755 : 10
strive here for m., 284 : 27
Mast-high, ice m., 434 : 10
Mastiff, toothless m. bitch, 433 : 28
Mastiffs of unmatchable courage, 207 : 25
Mastodon with mastery, 881 : 11
Masts, sailyards tremble m. crack, 178 : 6
though her m. firm, 558 : 9
Match for the devil, 840 : 11
forces of selfishness met m., 779 : 20
I cannot blow out m., 894 : 9
Little M. Girl, 505 : 9
Matched, passions m. with mine, 530 : 5
us with His hour, 797 : 2
with aged wife, 529 : 6
Matches made in heaven, 159 : *n* 4
Matchless deed's achieved, 365 : 9
Matchwood immortal diamond, 656 : 21
Mate, choose not alone proper m., 377 : 24
great artificer made m., 669 : 8
in England I've m., 551 : 2
of Nancy brig, 627 : 7
took unto herself a m., 425 : 19
Mated by the lion, 227 : 11
Mater artium necessitas, 134 : 9
saeva Cupidinum, 108 : *n* 9
Material and obvious things, 311 : 1
computation, 745 : 1
disbranch from her m. sap, 234 : 23
fortune associated with body, 124 : 3
moral spiritual force, 699 : 5
objects of two kinds, 100 : 9
of life, 784 : 22
Material (*continued*)
progress and prosperity, 687 : 15
progress depends on intellectual, 515 : 5
raw m. of opinion, 682 : 2
spiritual stronger than m., 499 : 26
sublime, 438 : 3
surface of things, 583 : 2
welfare of citizens, 687 : 15
wrought in common crude m., 632 : 1
Materialism model for cultures, 903 : 12
Materialistic, far from having m. tendency, 482 : 12
Materializing upper class, 589 : 4
Materially ambitious, 799 : 18
Materials indifferent but not use, 121 : 12
man not m. that counts, 826 : 9
work with m. I am made of, 861 : 4
youth gets together m., 557 : 12
Mates and all intrepid sailors, 575 : 22
moves and m. and slays, 516 : 22
Mathematical, concept of m. beauty, 696 : 5
perfection of m. beauty, 696 : 6
pictures accord with fact, 758 : 9
sciences founded, 610 : 1
Mathematician, Architect of Universe m., 758 : 9
capable of reasoning, 84 : 19
maker of patterns, 758 : 7
reached highest rung, 690 : 6
union of m. with poet, 651 : 4
Mathematicians, people who are merely m., 444 : 10
Mathematics, angling like m., 270 : 30
axioms of book of m., 643 : 15
chemistry m. electronics, 819 : 14
commence in disappointment, 697 : 4
draws necessary conclusions, 525 : 1
eludes our grasp, 697 : 4
foundations of knowledge in m., 139 : 5
fruits of m., 152 : 13
in m. never know what talking about, 737 : 13
in region of necessity, 738 : 1
intuitive calculation transcended m., 756 : 3
mathematicians' short- comings not fault of m., 444 : 10
my sons ought to study m., 381 : 14
poets witty m. subtile, 181 : 14
possesses beauty, 737 : 14
psychology make use of m., 443 : 3
pure m. original creation, 697 : 7
queen of sciences, 444 : 11
universe in language of m., 182 : 20
Mather, Cottons m., 839 : 4
Matilda and house burned, 730 : 11
told dreadful lies, 730 : 9
waltzing M., 705 : 7
Matin, glowworm shows m. near, 219 : 26
Matre pulchra filia pulchrior, 107 : *n* 9
Matrimonial, error of m. union, 641 : 6
Matrimony, critical period in m., 815 : 18
in m. begin with aversion, 398 : 6
jumps from love to m., 440 : 18
road to wealth, 554 : 12
Matrix, freedom of expression m., 730 : 17
Matron's glance reprove, 369 : 29
Matron's (*continued*)
mutine in m. bones, 223 : 5
Matter, atom on m. duplicate in mind, 570 : 15
Berkeley said no m., 461 : 22
carry on m. for own sake, 552 : 15
daily to be shown m., 557 : 21
dirt m. out of place, 638 : 8
for a May morning, 214 : 23
for virtuous deeds, 178 : 3
goes to root of m., 649 : 19
great m. or small, 35 : 7
hear the conclusion of the whole m., 27 : 27
here and now cease to m., 807 : 24
I am full of m., 16 : 22
in his m. and ideas, 586 : 14
indifferent to form, 273 : 10
lovers lacking m., 212 : 22
make a Star Chamber m., 225 : 5
meaning doesn't m., 628 : 6
mince the m., 168 : 6, 230 : 22
mind over m., 482 : 12
more m. with less art, 220 : 11
nervous m., 635 : 5
no m. from the heart, 227 : 6
no m. what he said, 461 : 22
no m. where it's going, 823 : 3
order m. better in France, 360 : 21
poetry does not m., 807 : 12
root of the m. found in me, 16 : 5
solid hard particles, 313 : 16
state of m. at given moment, 594 : 12
subordinates manner to m., 437 : 17
superbly human, 831 : 20
theory of m., 681 : 23
totally different m., 518 : 4
unalterable as quantity of m., 583 : 21
unreal and temporal, 583 : 3
waking no such m., 245 : 2
what is m. never mind, 660 : 13
whether you hate self, 797 : 20
wings shall tell the m., 27 : 19
won't m. whether saved, 815 : 3
Matters I relate are true lies, 818 : 4
read strange m., 236 : 19
to do well is what m., 273 : 3
touch no state m., 370 : *n* 3
what m. what anybody thinks, 498 : *n* 2
Matthew and Waldo guardians, 804 : 7
man named M., 38 : 26
Mark Luke and John, 294 : 16
Mattresses, princess felt pea through m., 505 : 2
Mature, American public more m., 872 : 19
marry on m. basis, 898 : 5
poets steal, 809 : 6
Matures, man m. through work, 897 : 9
Maturing sun, 477 : 17
Maturity of custom, 729 : 11
sacred to ease and relaxation, 665 : 15
Matzoh, only Jew in Danville looking for m., 904 : 10
Maud, come into garden M., 533 : 20
went to college, 889 : 5
Mausolos' tomb, 924 : 3
Maw-crammed beast, 544 : 9
Mawkishness and thousand bitters, 475 : 15
Maxim, act only on that m., 366 : 14
general m. useless, 487 : 12

Maxim (*continued*)
of British people, 743 : 6
old m. in the schools, 322 : 7
only m. of free government, 380 : 13
with Foxey, 547 : 25
Maxima debetur puero
reverentia, 122 : *n* 14
Maxims, little hoard of m., 529 : 22
Maximum temptation maximum
opportunity, 680 : 24
May, April showers M. flowers, 163 : 4
as you do in M., 651 : *n* 1
come what come m., 236 : 13
come what m., 114 : 9, 459 : 4
corals on in M., 568 : 25
darling buds of M., 244 : 5
flowery meads in M., 264 : 23
flush as M., 222 : 27
fresh as month of M., 145 : 15
from M. to December, 802 : 2
full of spirit as month of M., 204 : 30
gather ye rosebuds while ye
m., 266 : 11
he smells April and M., 225 : 20
I were lord in M., 633 : 12
in M. when sea winds, 494 : 4
joys as month of M., 267 : 20
lap of M., 368 : 18
laurel outlives not M., 633 : 6
like snow in M., 269 : 3
love I gave in M., 651 : 6
lusty month of M., 149 : 13
maids M. when maids, 212 : 25
March July October M., 162 : *n* 3
matter for M. morning, 214 : 23
merry month of M., 257 : 6, 926 : 21
month flaps leaves like wings, 642 : 3
nightingale when M. is past, 271 : 20
of April M. of June, 265 : 17
one month on in M., 748 : 17
queen o' the M., 528 : 12
swarm of bees in M., 919 : 10
there's an end of M., 691 : 19
welcome faire fresshe M., 146 : 19
when lusty heart blossom, 149 : 13
when month of M. is comen, 145 : 10
will have no slogardie
anyght, 146 : 16
with thy floures and grene, 146 : 19
Mayakovski's, last years of M.
life, 817 : 1
Maybe, the m. years, 888 : 5
Mayday, more bright than M.
morn, 399 : 20
Mayflower, forefathers not on
M., 766 : 5
including those on M., 781 : 2
Mayor, Lord M. of London, 918 : 10
Maypoles hockcarts wassails, 265 : 17
May's newfangled mirth, 190 : 13
Mays, under blanching m., 692 : 5
Maze, mighty m., 336 : 10
of schools, 332 : 17
Mazes, in wandering m. lost, 284 : 19
Mazy, five miles with m.
motion, 433 : 23
mc², E equals mc², 763 : 5
McClellan's, army is M.
bodyguard, 522 : 4
McFlimsey, Miss M. of Madison
Square, 595 : 4
McGee, cremated Sam M., 752 : 6
McGregor, my name is M., 431 : 27
wherever M. sits, 496 : *n* 3
McGregor's, Mr. M. garden, 719 : 3
McGrew, Dangerous Dan M., 752 : 5
Me, Day got tired of m., 605 : 10
Decade, 911 : 7
does Africa know song of m., 789 : 10
raise stone and find M., 126 : 14
self-subsisting self-seeking
m., 489 : 16
some little talk of m., 516 : 18
this is the real m., 647 : 23
universe is all including m., 833 : 2
who am as a nerve, 467 : 14
who sees M. in all, 94 : 13
woe is m., 29 : 10
ye have not always, 41 : 4
you get no more of m., 182 : 16
Me imperturbe, 573 : 21
Mea culpa, 54 : 2
Mead, by stream and o'er m., 403 : 5
groweth seed bloweth m., 916 : 14
of all flowers in the m., 145 : 11
Meadow, air from faraway m., 571 : 7
flower bloom unfold, 429 : 12
grove and stream, 426 : 10
mother of months in m., 632 : 7
of margin, 398 : 29
ragged m. of my soul, 829 : 7
rivulets overflow, 642 : 6
sheep's in m., 930 : 12
Meadow's, dropped like flower on m.
edge, 101 : 21
Meadows brown and sere, 471 : 10
bypath m. where you linger, 667 : 14
infinite m. of heaven, 511 : 3
paint the m. with delight, 191 : 13
trim with daisies pied, 277 : 25
up from the m., 513 : 16
Meadowsweet, vales of m., 846 : 15
Meads, flowery m. in May, 264 : 23
met lady in m., 478 : 11
Meager knowledge, 594 : 11
shriveled m. hopping, 373 : 28
Meal, barrel of m. wasted not, 13 : 43
handful of m. in a barrel, 13 : 42
in firkin, 496 : 11
morning incense evening m., 400 : 5
without wine, 401 : 8
Meal-drift molded ever, 656 : 6
Meals, make no long m., 370 : *n* 3
Michelangelo between m., 622 : 5
of beef iron steel, 207 : 26
unquiet m. make ill
digestions, 188 : 14
Mealy boys, 547 : 4
Mean actions ascribed to fear, 657 : 9
afterwards I felt m., 873 : 9
between nothing and
everything, 299 : 17
everything I touch m. and
farcical, 600 : 6
few say all they m., 635 : 20
golden m., 107 : 20
I m. what I say, 611 : 18
if conduct m. and paltry, 88 : 23
if they m. to have war, 374 : 19
keep golden m., 107 : *n* 18
know not what they m., 531 : 3
man full of distress, 68 : 24
means what I choose it to m., 613 : 16
never be m., 548 : 29
not careful what they m., 188 : 21
nothing common did or m., 296 : 23
observances of decorum, 432 : 16
or wish to mean, 900 : 3
Mean (*continued*)
poem should not m. but be, 821 : 13
proper m., 343 : 23
stupid public, 445 : 7
suspicion companion of m.
souls, 384 : 10
we speak not what we m., 228 : 12
what I say, 611 : 18
what may this m., 219 : 12
what m. man seeks, 69 : 13
woman of m. understanding, 440 : 17
world is m., 912 : 15
Meander through meadow of
margin, 398 : 29
Meandering with mazy motion, 433 : 23
Meander's margent green, 279 : 18
Meaner, ambition of m. sort, 185 : 3
ask no m. pelf, 557 : 20
beauties of the night, 251 : 1
creatures makes kings, 187 : 24
leave all m. things, 336 : 10
patronizing has m. side, 565 : 7
Meanest flower that blows, 426 : 23
floweret of vale, 362 : 20
honor peereth in m. habit, 189 : 2
wisest brightest m., 337 : 15
Meaning, blunders round m., 338 : 13
deeper m. of Narcissus, 570 : 4
eternal truths have fresh m., 780 : 10
force language into m., 809 : 9
free from all m., 304 : 17
fresh m. for new situation, 780 : 10
give each moment m., 756 : 1
gives new m., 801 : 8
language charged with m., 793 : 8
love is only m., 839 : 10
no m. except responsibility, 823 : 20
novel promises m., 887 : 14
O a meaning, 822 : 10
of lands of ancestors, 912 : 5
of life matches marvels, 872 : 13
poem never lose m., 750 : 4
short m. of long speech, 413 : 15
spirit give life highest m., 754 : 1
that unfolded by surprise, 750 : 4
to faint m. make pretense, 304 : 25
tread upon brink of m., 352 : 26
we each give to life, 858 : 3
what would we know m. of, 496 : 11
year had lost m., 858 : 19
Meanings, hell full of good m., 269 : 23
words and m., 807 : 12
Meanly admires mean things, 539 : 11
child all m. wrapped, 277 : 7
how m. they live, 310 : 11
nobly save m. lose, 522 : 12
Meanness in argument of
conservatism, 497 : 34
poverty the parent of m., 84 : 12
Meannesses, women plunged into
m., 414 : 11
Means, all m. appropriate, 402 : 6
and content, 212 : 1
and leisure civilizers, 502 : 14
appliances and m. to boot, 206 : 18
bad m. and bad men, 384 : 16
by all the m. you can, 346 : 12
by any m. get wealth, 339 : 19
by fair m. if you can, 108 : 18
changes by peaceful m., 700 : 3
content with small m., 536 : 6
dumb sense of what life m., 650 : 7
end must justify the m., 320 : 15
ends and scarce m., 842 : 15

Means (*continued*)
fair m. or foul, 779 : 19
fair up to our means, 543 : 4
find m. of evil, 283 : 11
First Amendment m. what it says, 794 : 19
for every man alive, 227 : 17
game that never m. anything, 836 : 15
give enemies m. of our destruction, 66 : 24
God placed in our power, 383 : 3
heaven finds m. to kill joys, 193 : 30
if all m. permitted to fight evil, 812 : 11
it m. mischief, 222 : 11
justifying m. by the end. 127 : 20
liberty as end and m., 677 : 12
live within m., 616 : 20
love not say all it m., 729 : 1
love of money as m., 783 : 10
make money by any m., 108 : 18
mercy of his m., 887 : 1
not but blunders round meaning, 338 : 13
of destruction hitherto unknown, 787 : 15
requisite to ends, 401 : 17
take m. whereby I live, 200 : 20
thanks for m. of grace, 55 : 7
that wins easiest victory, 812 : 13
to achieve great ends, 815 : 5
to do ill deeds, 202 : 11
to make us one, 253 : 6
war political relations by other m., 448 : 8
what beauty m., 703 : 5
what I choose it to mean, 613 : 16
Meant, more m. than meets ear, 278 : 24
well tried a little, 669 : 15
Measles and if so how many, 616 : 16
Friday died of m., 878 : 18
love is like m., 561 : 12
Measure every wandering planet's course, 183 : 6
fervor with m., 651 : 4
for measure, 229 : 8
last full m. of devotion, 523 : 4
man is m. of all things, 78 : 23
mind's height, 540 : 8
narrow m. spans, 692 : 6
observe due m., 61 : 23
of my days, 19 : 1
of torment measure of youth, 708 : 15
shrunk to this little m., 216 : 8
takes right m. of self, 464 : 1
teach his feet a m., 633 : 13
there is m. in all things, 106 : 12
to a merry m., 469 : 24
what you are speaking about, 594 : 11
with what m. ye mete, 38 : 9
Measured by my soul, 328 : 1
choice word m. phrase, 425 : 11
it shall be m. to you, 38 : 9
language, 531 : 21
motion, 424 : 1
out my life with coffee spoons, 803 : 13
Measureless, caverns m. to man, 433 : 21
rhythms m. and wild, 76 : 22
shut up in m. content, 237 : 12
Measurement, no m. in economics, 775 : 8
Measures, in short m. life perfect be, 256 : 20
Lydian m., 306 : 19
not men, 341 : 15, 369 : 27
not men but m., 372 : 5
Measuring device constructed by observer, 853 : 1
earth and heaven, 85 : 17
Meat, as egg is full of m., 193 : 3
buys opinions like m., 621 : 3
cannot eat but little m., 163 : 9
crazy salad with m., 714 : 16
dined upon cold m., 310 : 4
drink and cloth to us, 158 : 13
flowers in garden m. in hall, 145 : *n* 4
God sends m. Devil sends cooks, 159 : *n* 6
hungered and ye gave m., 40 : 33
hungry and he gave him m., 367 : 3
in due season, 21 : 11
is not life more than m., 38 : 2
made worms' m. of me, 193 : 6
mock m. it feeds on, 230 : 34
not m. but appetite, 290 : 3
not m. nor drink, 823 : 13
on our m. and on us all, 267 : 1
one appointed to buy m., 264 : 7
one man's poison another's m., 101 : *n* 6
out of the eater came m., 12 : 14
outdid the m., 266 : 17
provideth her m. in the summer, 23 : 11
seek their m. from God, 21 : 11
sendeth mouth sendeth m., 159 : 8
sit down and taste my m., 269 : 10
sleep is m. to hungry, 171 : 1
snewed of m. and drynke, 146 : 3
some hae m. canna eat, 411 : 1
strong m. to them of full age, 51 : 15
this dish of m. too good, 271 : 12
upon what m. Caesar feed, 215 : 7
was locusts and wild honey, 36 : 27
we are fish and m., 719 : 9
we hae m. we can eat, 411 : 1
went without the m., 729 : 5
within requisite, 606 : 18
Meatpacker, talent of m., 726 : 13
Meats, funeral baked m., 218 : 14
of all m. soonest cloy, 295 : 3
Meaulnes, Grand M. the wanderer, 795 : 3
le grand m., 795 : 3
Mecca, sacred temple of M., 131 : 5
Mechanic, lawyer without history a m., 431 : 21
long m. pacings, 529 : 3
made poetry m. art, 375 : 22
sad m. exercise, 531 : 21
Mechanical equivalent of heat, 650 : 16
slavery future of world, 675 : 25
Mechanician, visible sage m., 562 : 8
Mechanics, bicycle m. from Dayton, 835 : 1
farmers m. and laborers, 419 : 3
of culture, 725 : 9
paradise of mathematical sciences, 152 : 13
reduced to atomic m., 617 : 11
reduction of nature to m., 594 : 12
Mechanism, battles by m., 473 : 17
Mechanisms, of all escape m., 772 : 15
vital m. have object, 551 : 19
Mechanized armies, 745 : 2
Mechanized (*continued*)
automation, 466 : 7
Med, bloweth m., 916 : 14
Medal, bright hard m., 653 : 15
Med'cinable gum, 232 : 20
Meddle, inclination to m., 445 : 5
not with him that flattereth, 24 : 32
wise men refrain to m., 155 : 5
Meddles with cold iron, 173 : *n* 3
Meddling, every fool will be m., 24 : 28
Mede, of all the floures in the m., 145 : 11
Medea gathered enchanted herbs, 200 : 22
Medes, crushed the gold-bearing M., 67 : 18
law of the M. and Persians, 33 : 2
Mediator, painting m. between world and us, 774 : 11
president mostly a m., 879 : 4
Mediatory, reconciling m. power, 436 : 20
Mediatress, art m. between nature and man, 437 : 22
Medici created and destroyed me, 152 : 16
Medicinable gum, 232 : 20
some griefs are m., 243 : 18
Medicine bundles, 897 : 19
desire to take m. distinguishes man from animals, 664 : 14
doeth good like m., 24 : 17
faith and knowledge in m., 464 : 4
for case like mine, 577 : 7
for life which has fled, 65 : 15
for mental disorders, 833 : 5
for misery, 77 : 6
has to examine disease, 120 : 5
in m. common sense master, 464 : 2
in m. sins of commission mortal, 357 : 11
live by m. live horribly, 350 : 5
most distinguished of arts, 80 : 4
my lawful wife, 695 : 1
no m. but hope, 228 : 13
of life, 35 : 10
thee to sweet sleep, 231 : 8
truth in m. difficult, 463 : 19
worse than malady, 111 : *n* 2
Medicine Hat, war bonnet of M., 840 : 2
Medicines to make me love him, 203 : 18
to make women speak, 655 : 15
Medicos marveling sweetly, 810 : 20
Medieval hand, 628 : 7
Medio tutissimus ibis, 113 : *n* 11
Mediocre, if you are m. and grovel, 378 : 8
minds, 294 : 3
passions, 293 : 31
Mediocrities, loss of appetite for m., 651 : 1
single genius hundred m., 630 : 19
Mediocrity, gratified with m., 417 : 2
history of masterwork not m., 793 : 5
knows nothing higher, 689 : 15
solitude safeguard of m., 498 : 27
Meditate, in his law doth he m., 17 : 12
on blood, 208 : 17
thankless Muse, 280 : 15
Meditating, in path good lizard m., 841 : 5
upon whatsoever state, 94 : 14
Meditation and water wedded, 570 : 4

Meditation (*continued*)
distraction not m., 883 : 7
let us all to m., 185 : 19
maiden m. fancy-free, 196 : 15
of my heart, 18 : 3
where m. neither anxiety nor doubt, 138 : 14
Meditative spleen, 428 : 14
Mediterranean, bagful of blue M., 867 : 13
Mediterraneans see clearly, 784 : 5
Medium, internal m., 551 : 18
is message, 879 : 5
Medusa's, beauty that M. head, 821 : 11
Meed of some melodious tear, 280 : 8
Meek and gentle with these butchers, 216 : 11
blessed are the m., 37 : 4
borne his faculties so m., 236 : 24
gentle Jesus m. and mild, 350 : 13
holy and m. she cries, 404 : 11
I am m. and lowly, 39 : 8
mysteries revealed unto m., 34 : 25
ornament of m. spirit, 52 : 12
safer m. than fierce, 544 : 29
shall inherit the earth, 18 : 24
soft m. patient humble, 251 : 11
Meek-eyed parents, 864 : 15
Meekness, fruit of Spirit is m., 49 : 30
wrath by his m., 403 : 13
Meet, beauteous flower when next we m., 192 : 14
descend to m., 497 : 16
experiment to me is everyone I m., 606 : 18
extremes m., 386 : 2
firm I can m., 422 : 5
him with one tooth, 735 : 3
if we do m. again, 217 : 9
in her aspect and eyes, 459 : 13
in one spirit m. mingle, 467 : 24
it and not see its head, 64 : 7
many ways m. in one town, 207 : 8
methinks they are not m., 162 : 5
Mr. Eliot, 806 : 14
never twain m., 707 : 16
on bridge of time, 581 : 12
political greatness and wisdom m., 84 : 15
shadow rising to m. you, 805 : 1
spirit with spirit m., 535 : 9
thee in that hollow vale, 267 : 6
though infinite never m., 297 : 7
two smiles m., 406 : 5
until we m. again, 636 : 13
we shall m. but miss him, 552 : 18
we three m. again, 235 : 21
when men and mountains m., 407 : 1
where brook and river m., 510 : 13
with champagne and chicken, 341 : 1
with joy in sweet Jerusalem, 186 : 24
your visage here, 844 : 2
Meeter to carry off latter, 455 : 2
Meeting, journeys end in lovers m., 213 : 22
soul may pierce, 278 : 6
Meetings, impossible to prevent such m., 366 : 2
Meets in oppugnancy, 226 : 2
less than m. eye, 857 : 9
more meant than m. ear, 278 : 24
Mehitabel, dance m. dance, 760 : 5
Meilleur, ce m. des monde possibles, 343 : *n* 3
Melancholia of everything completed, 658 : 3
Melancholy and despair, 260 : 2
as battle won, 421 : 8
as gib cat, 202 : 29
bait, 198 : 4
black sun of M., 514 : 9
charm in m., 416 : 4
chord in m., 485 : 7
chronic m. of civilized, 641 : 1
days are come, 471 : 10
divinest M., 278 : 11
dull-eyed m., 243 : 12
fears without cause, 260 : 2
green and yellow m., 214 : 5
House of Usher, 525 : 19
loathed M., 277 : 17
long withdrawing roar, 587 : 16
marked him for her own, 362 : 17
men eat no beans, 258 : 15
men most witty, 259 : 6
mirth has chord in m., 258 : *n* 1
moping m., 287 : 29
most m. of reflections, 597 : 5
most musical most m., 278 : 17
music is good to the m., 308 : 19
naked m. isles, 345 : 15
naught so sweet as m., 258 : 3
never give way to m., 433 : 7
O sweetest m., 261 : 4
ocean's gray m. waste, 471 : 5
of mine own, 212 : 18
pale M. sate retired, 364 : 14
purge m., 247 : 5
rare recipe for m., 441 : 8
rhyme and be m., 190 : 31
shade of m. boughs, 211 : 12
slow, 368 : 13
suck m. out of song, 211 : 2
veiled M., 478 : 1
villainous m., 233 : 6
what charm soothe m., 369 : 20
who dismissed avarice, 386 : 11
Meliorist, not optimist but m., 690 : *n* 1
Mellow, fruit too m. for me, 341 : 4
he who goes to bed m., 260 : *n* 5
rawness of opinions, 692 : 13
Mellowed, fruit that m. long, 303 : 16
to tender light, 459 : 13
Mellowing, delivered upon m. of occasion, 190 : 30
year, 280 : 6
Mellstock, lie in M. churchyard now, 641 : 10
Melodies echoes of that voice, 436 : 1
heard m. sweet, 477 : 6
Melodious birds sing madrigals, 183 : 9
bursts that fill, 528 : 21
meed of some m. tear, 280 : 8
plot, 476 : 22
Melody, blundering kind of m., 304 : 17
could you view the m., 295 : 21
deprived of pitch, 801 : 8
falling in m. back, 435 : 19
life m., 573 : 6
mortal m., 525 : 10
my luve is like the m., 409 : 22
pretty girl like m., 802 : 6
singing and making m., 49 : 37
small foweles maken m., 145 : 13
Melrose, view fair M., 430 : 4
Melt at others' woe, 361 : 14
butter not m. in mouth, 159 : 31
in her own fire, 223 : 5
Melt (*continued*)
let Rome in Tiber m., 240 : 14
too solid flesh would m., 218 : 5
with ruth, 281 : 3
Melted, brown hills m. into spring, 562 : 1
fortune m. to water, 313 : 7
individuals of all nations m. into new race, 382 : 8
into air, 248 : 13
like snow, 459 : 16
Melter of limbs, 61 : 10
Melting airs, 377 : 13
mood, 232 : 20
poem ride on own m., 750 : 4
pot, 706 : 15
snow like teardrops, 801 : 18
sweet music's m. fall, 363 : 13
Melts, grief m. away, 269 : 3
like kisses, 460 : 8
pity m. mind to love, 260 : *n* 8
then m. forever, 411 : 8
Member, club that would accept me as m., 834 : 3
of the earth, 819 : 12
of the rabble, 830 : 16
of the wedding, 894 : 13
Members of human community, 781 : 5
one of another, 49 : 36
that one of thy m. should perish, 37 : 8
Membrane of bright blue sky, 884 : 1
Même, plus a change plus la m., 514 : *n* 3
Mememormee, bussoftlhee m., 778 : 6
Memento, some common m. better, 785 : 9
Memento mori, Death's head or m., 204 : 26
Mémoire, il faut bonne m. après qu'on a menti, 117 : *n* 14
Memoirs, not read Barère's M., 489 : 1
we will write our m., 420 : 17
Memorable, days m. in history, 745 : 7
moments in their lives, 889 : 4
sentences, 609 : 2
Memorandum, make a m. of it, 612 : 16
Memorial, passover shall be for a m., 9 : 26
some have no m., 36 : 11
to soul's eternity, 601 : 17
Memories, dies on wind like m., 770 : 13
encrusted with sublime thoughts, 558 : 13
more m. than if thousand years old, 580 : 21
mother of m., 580 : 19
night of m. and sighs, 442 : 18
of eld, 525 : 16
youth has no long m., 565 : 14
Memory, adduces authority uses m., 152 : 7
archives of m., 730 : 15
be green, 217 : 28
cherish his m., 616 : 22
chords of m., 521 : 14
complains of his m., 293 : 16
dear son of m., 277 : 13
emancipated from time, 437 : 13
exiled from m. of man, 908 : 3
fills m. with natural objects, 395 : 25
flowers of m., 739 : 11
fond m. brings light, 447 : 7
footfalls echo in m., 807 : 2

Memory (*continued*)
Franklin's quiet m., 462 : 15
from false to false, 226 : 15
good m. to keep promises, 657 : 8
green, 217 : 28, 446 : 8
grows fainter relaxes bonds, 734 : 8
hands of m. weave, 636 : 2
he shall have a noble m., 242 : 28
history vitalizes m., 98 : 9
honor his m., 257 : 1
how sweet their m. still, 375 : 15
how vast a m. has Love, 332 : 14
illiterate him from your m., 398 : 5
in book of my m. a rubric, 140 : 7
indebted to m. for jests, 399 : 13
keep m. green, 446 : 8
liar should have good m., 117 : 22
life a m. without pain, 74 : 7
life and m. of it, 878 : 19
literature m. of nation, 895 : 20
mixing m. and desire, 804 : 26
mousetraps moon m. muchness, 611 : 22
my name and m. I leave, 181 : 16
nation's m. and veneration, 761 : 1
nine she-camel hairs aid m., 799 : 13
no force abolish m., 780 : 17
no m. of having starred, 749 : 1
not make philosopher, 490 : 14
not necessary for love, 839 : 10
note you in book of m., 185 : 1
of all he stole, 340 : 17
of all that, 836 : 9
of benefits fades, 73 : 12
of Boatswain a dog, 456 : 9
of loved and lost, 524 : 4
of Paris inexhaustible, 819 : 13
of the just is blessed, 23 : 22
of them is forgotten, 27 : 15
only shield to m., 744 : 11
outlive his life, 222 : 10
painted perfect day, 698 : 16
pluck from m. rooted sorrow, 239 : 32
plucking fruit of m., 684 : 7
poor m. that only works backwards, 613 : 12
pray bring me to men's m., 141 : 6
profitable cherishing m., 616 : 22
proper m. for politician, 637 : 11
proud to have m. graced, 801 : 17
sinner of his m., 247 : 11
some women stay in m., 710 : 11
table of my m., 219 : 27
tablet a gift of M., 85 : 18
their very m. is fair, 299 : 7
thou fond deceiver, 368 : 10
thoughts to m. dear, 431 : 16
throng into my m., 279 : 16
'tis in my m. locked, 219 : 3
vanity tricks m., 683 : 10
ventricle of m., 190 : 30
vibrates in m., 469 : 18
viol of her m., 767 : 11
warder of the brain, 237 : 7
while m. holds a seat, 219 : 27
wit at expense of m., 323 : 26
Memory's, confusing beams from m. lamp, 856 : 9
Mem'ry, cherish his m., 616 : 22
Men, a few honest m., 272 : 16
about me that are fat, 215 : 8
above reach of ordinary m., 425 : 11
adversity test of strong m., 115 : 2
all are m. condemned, 361 : 12

Men (*continued*)
all honorable m., 216 : 18
all m. are liars, 21 : 23
all m. be free, 524 : 8
all m. born distraught, 900 : 4
all m. born free, 282 : 13
all m. created equal, 387 : 9, 523 : 4
all m. liable to error, 307 : 16
all m. make faults, 244 : 14
all m. Noah's sons, 899 : 10
all m. would be tyrants, 318 : 11, 392 : 7
all sorts and conditions of m., 55 : 5
all the king's m., 932 : 2
all the same, 751 : 18
and boys thick as hasty pudding, 920 : *n* 2
and women affirm brotherhood, 870 : 13
and women created equal, 554 : 4
and women merely players, 211 : 15
and women—Liberate, 831 : 19
animals infuse into trunks of m., 200 : 7
April when they woo, 212 : 25
are men, 230 : 21
are m. born to go down like this, 831 : 18
are my teachers, 337 : *n* 2
are products reflections, 672 : 3
are quick to flare up, 60 : 3
are we and must grieve, 425 : 20
are where they are, 560 : 7
arm and burgonet of m., 240 : 22
as in a theater eyes of m., 195 : 15
ask for everything, 896 : 6
aspiring to be angels m. rebel, 336 : 18
at point of death, 193 : 26
at whiles sober, 691 : 21
attend m. and not women, 85 : 16
bad cause bad means bad m., 384 : 16
be read as books too much, 335 : 12
beacons of wise m., 596 : 3
become brothers, 412 : 9
below and saints above, 430 : 6
best m. molded of faults, 229 : 9
best of m., 240 : 28
best of m. that e'er wore earth, 251 : 11
black m. are pearls, 190 : 6
blaspheme what they do not know, 300 : 13
bodies of unburied m., 262 : 3
body of well-instructed m., 515 : 5
books like m., 321 : 10
born under happier stars, 437 : 4
boys and girls level with m., 241 : 22
brave m. and worthy patriots, 281 : 19
brave m. brave from the first, 275 : 17
brave m. lived before Agamemnon, 108 : 13
brave m. living and dead, 523 : 4
busy haunts of m., 470 : 21
busy hum of m., 278 : 4
by nature desire knowledge, 87 : 9
by nature equally free, 367 : 4
call up your m., 432 : 15
cannot learn m. from books, 501 : 3
capable of wickedness, 684 : 4
captain of m. of death, 302 : 17
capture of m. by women, 539 : *n* 2
cause or m. of Emerald Isle, 400 : 10
cheerful ways of m., 285 : 5

Men (*continued*)
children of m. full of wiles, 82 : 8
circumstances rule m., 78 : 17
cities of m. and manners, 529 : 8
condemn m. because few, 560 : 22
Constitution for all m., 553 : 20
countries of m., 850 : 8
creatures that once were m., 725 : 4
creep not walk, 513 : 12
crowd of common m., 272 : 14
cunning m. pass for wise, 180 : 21
darling of m. and gods, 100 : 1
day is for honest m., 77 : 5
dead m. rise up never, 633 : 22
Death that feeds on m., 246 : 5
decay, 369 : 30
deceivers ever, 209 : 16
decent easy m., 384 : 1
descend to meet, 497 : *n* 2
desire the good, 88 : 3
destiny with m. for pieces plays, 516 : 22
determine gods dispose, 259 : *n* 4
die idea does not, 895 : 8
die like m., 20 : 5, 514 : 11
die to make m. free, 566 : 5
died as m. before their bodies died, 869 : 1
died to make m. holy, 566 : 5
difference between m. and women, 853 : 16
difference of forty thousand m., 421 : 9
different from ordinary m., 609 : 5
dine with some m., 753 : 3
disbelief in great m., 473 : 23
disease of old m. avarice, 261 : 11
disgrace labor, 590 : 3
done with roofs and m., 696 : 13
doors for m. to take their exits, 262 : 8
duration of great sentiments makes great m., 657 : 20
dying m., 586 : 7
dying m. enforce attention, 194 : 9
eat hogs, 767 : 8
eat m. like air, 911 : 12
education is making m., 609 : *n* 3
eight or nine elderly m., 706 : 19
elevate condition of m., 522 : 2
England is purgatory of m., 174 : 23
equal right of m. and women, 788 : 20
errors of wise m., 290 : 7
eternal light upon hearts of m., 412 : 11
evil m. do lives after them, 216 : 17
evils draw m. together, 88 : 14
fair women and brave m., 457 : 14
fallible m. governed by bad passions, 387 : 14
fear of little m., 594 : 2
feared witches, 677 : 13
fell out knew not why, 290 : 13
fifteen m. on Dead Man's Chest, 668 : 4
filthy dirty pigs, 751 : 18
finds too late m. betray, 369 : 20
first subjects afterward, 557 : 22
fishers of fish not m., 894 : 2
fishers of m., 37 : 3
flourish only for a moment, 61 : 1
foolery wise m. have, 210 : 13
foolish m. who accuse a woman, 316 : 1

Men (*continued*)
fools laugh at m. of sense, 315 : 8
foot of unfamiliar m., 587 : 6
forty thousand m., 929 : 15
free m. free speech, 922 : 2
gear of foreign dead m., 808 : 2
get there first with most m., 583 : 20
give place to better m., 272 : 19
go armed to seek, 821 : 11
God give us m., 566 : 3
God justifiable to m., 288 : 26
God made mad, 742 : 4
God these old m., 76 : 5
God wrongs not m., 130 : 17
gods fashioned by m., 704 : 6
gods in likeness of m., 46 : 11
goeth on to meet the armed m., 16 : 37
good m. and true, 209 : 23
good m. eat that they may live, 79 : 6
good m. to do nothing, 374 : 12
good will to m., 537 : 16
good will toward m., 42 : 29
goodness of millions of m., 851 : 18
government of laws not m., 381 : 1
great city greatest m., 575 : 12
great m. are not always wise, 16 : 21
great m. can't be ruled, 865 : 5
great m. contending with adversity, 259 : 7
great m. not boasters, 498 : 21
great m. not scholars, 519 : 13
great m. texts of Revelation, 473 : 6
group of willful m., 682 : 10
grow into likeness of bad m., 86 : 1
hanged that horses may not be stolen, 310 : 21
hangin' m. and women, 920 : 22
happy breed of m., 194 : 13
harmony between m. and land, 795 : 11
have died from time to time, 212 : 23
have lost their reason, 216 : 20
have their price, 328 : 21
heard old old m. say, 713 : 3
heart of oak our m., 363 : 16
heaven that leads m. to hell, 245 : 23
His ways with m., 534 : 27
history biography of great m., 473 : 24
hit only what they aim at, 559 : 12
hollow m., 805 : 15, 805 : 16
homely m. charmed women, 699 : 12
honest m. revolutionize, 558 : 2
honest m. shaped conduct, 730 : 14
honor all m., 52 : 11
if all m. were just, 82 : 28
if m. are destroyed, 73 : 8
if m. cease to believe, 819 : 11
if m. like that wise bird, 660 : 15
in catalogue ye go for m., 238 : 14
in m. we various passions find, 335 : 21
infants boys m. Ifs, 571 : 4
inflation few m. remit, 889 : 2
keeping m. off keep them on, 331 : 20
knocking around with m., 394 : 15
know so little of men, 724 : 16
labels that give name to event, 602 : 3
laws not m., 381 : 1
laws of Nature include m., 595 : 14
lead lives of desperation, 559 : 4
let us die like m., 514 : 11
let us praise famous m., 36 : 10

Men (*continued*)
let your light shine before m., 37 : 6
like m. undergo fatigue, 384 : 17
like satyrs grazing, 183 : 16
little group of willful m., 682 : 10
live as m. not ostriches, 781 : 5
live at level of great m., 673 : 5
lived like fishes, 243 : *n* 1
lives of great m. remind us, 509 : 15
lodging place of wayfaring m., 32 : 4
looks quite through deeds of m., 215 : 9
love is waster of rich m., 74 : 23
made m. and not made them well, 222 : 3
made spectacle to m., 48 : 7
make the city, 81 : 8
man that died for m., 636 : 4
masters of their fates, 215 : 6
may come men may go, 533 : 16
may read strange matters, 236 : 19
measures not m., 341 : 15, 369 : 27
melancholy m. eat no beans, 258 : 15
melancholy m. most witty, 259 : 6
men's m., 565 : 28
merriest when from home, 207 : 9
merry m. all, 926 : 16
met with erected look, 305 : 5
mice and m., 408 : 14
mighty m. of valor, 11 : 30
mighty m. which were of old, 7 : 27
mocks married m., 191 : 13
moon m. and barking hounds, 831 : 16
more fortunate than mothers and wives, 665 : 19
more lonely among m., 560 : 3
more m. killed by overwork, 707 : 15
more nearly m. and women, 837 : 11
most m. are like children, 782 : 10
most m. eddy about, 588 : 7
mountains are fountains of m., 637 : 19
must be decided, 89 : 14
must be taught, 333 : 18
must endure their going, 235 : 11
must work women weep, 566 : 9
my m. like satyrs grazing, 183 : 16
nation concerted by real m., 672 : 2
natives of rain rainy m., 766 : 19
naturally in two parties, 390 : 2
need of world of m., 541 : 15
never be beloved by m., 406 : 11
no compacts between lions and m., 59 : 8
no country for old m., 714 : 22
no stander above m. and women, 574 : 20
no two m. cannot be distinguished, 116 : 12
no worse husband than best of m., 240 : 28
nor blame the writings but the m., 333 : 12
not ashamed of age, 898 : 14
not descended from fearful m., 872 : 18
not fit that m. be compared with gods, 102 : 11
not laugh other men to scorn, 132 : 8
not m. but laws, 381 : 1
not m. but manners, 349 : 12
not m. but measures, 372 : 5
not m. you took them for, 209 : 25

Men (*continued*)
not similar are gods and m., 57 : 30
not three good m. unhanged, 203 : 28
nothing great without great m., 815 : 6
O m. in the harbor lane, 93 : 3
O miserable minds of m., 100 : 13
O what m. dare do, 209 : 29
object of making m. happy, 582 : 5
of Athens, 46 : 15
of courtly nurture, 592 : 6
of culture true apostles, 588 : 19
of despised race, 617 : 6
of England wherefore plow, 467 : 23
of few words best, 207 : 20
of good will, 42 : *n* 3, 54 : 4, 814 : 10
of ill judgment ignore good, 73 : 15
of less value than gold, 155 : 3
of like passions, 46 : 12
of my generation, 879 : 7
of other minds, 368 : 20
of philosophic temperament, 697 : 6
of polite learning, 319 : 14
of renown, 7 : 27
of stones, 235 : 16
of the South, 759 : 2
of understanding, 27 : 17
of weak nerves, 837 : 6
old m. are all dead, 642 : 7
old m. are children, 82 : 1
old m. from chimney corner, 176 : 11
old m. garrulous by nature, 99 : 9
old m. have rosy faces, 669 : 7
old m. know young m. fools, 177 : 13
old m. ought to be explorers, 807 : 24
old m. shall dream dreams, 33 : 17
old m. should be explorers, 874 : 8
older m. declare war, 750 : 20
on shore interpreters, 732 : 7
opportunities equal to those of m., 903 : 10
ought to mind business, 616 : 1
our democratic public m., 681 : 12
Oxford m. who went abroad to die, 778 : 10
parole of literary m., 356 : 21
persuade eyes of m. without orator, 189 : 16
place where m. can pray, 742 : 15
port liquor for m., 356 : 11
practical m. absorbed in facts, 697 : 6
practical m. usually slaves, 783 : 16
praise famous m., 36 : 10
preached as to dying m., 294 : 17
princerples nor m., 568 : 3
private m. enjoy, 208 : 6
prize the thing ungained, 225 : 35
proper m. as ever trod, 214 : 31
proud m. in old age, 75 : 2
proud m. of action, 481 : 16
put enemy in their mouths, 230 : 26
quit you like m., 49 : 9
quit yourselves like m., 12 : 31
race of m. rise and take control, 888 : 6
rational spiritual beings, 845 : 15
ready booted and spurred, 298 : 18
reason never failed m., 726 : 12
reject prophets, 582 : 9
rich m. rule the law, 369 : 4
rise on steppingstones, 531 : 19
rivalship of wisest m., 327 : 10
roll of common m., 204 : 11
room for honest m., 384 : 19

Men (*continued*)
sailors but m., 198 : 17
saints aid if m. call, 434 : 2
sandwich m. shuffling, 781 : 15
savage m. uncouth manners, 372 : 12
schemes of mice and m., 408 : 14
school for making first-class m., 577 : 1
search land of living m., 430 : 15
see m. as trees walking, 42 : 9
seek freedom of free m., 915 : 18
seldom make passes, 827 : 11
sensible conscientious m., 354 : *n* 4
sensible m. never tell, 502 : 23
sent not corn for rich m. only, 242 : 8
setting man free from m., 865 : 4
should be what they seem, 230 : 31
shut doors against setting sun, 243 : 2
sing by land an' sea, 708 : 24
sit and hear each other groan, 476 : 24
slain a thousand m. with jawbone, 12 : 17
slave to fate chance desperate m., 254 : 12
sleek-headed m., 215 : 8
small m. afraid of writings, 378 : 10
small things make base m. proud, 185 : 21
so many m. so many opinions, 97 : 2
some m. love not a pig, 200 : 2
some to pleasure take, 335 : 22
sons of m. and angels say, 350 : 11
sons of m. snared in evil time, 27 : 17
speak with tongues of m., 48 : 22
speech given to wise m., 310 : 22
spirit of m. who follow, 791 : 15
spirits of just m., 51 : 21
strange that m. fear, 215 : 26
strength of twenty m., 193 : 22
strong m. shall bow themselves, 27 : 24
subject m. to analysis, 665 : 4
such as sleep o' nights, 215 : 8
such m. are dangerous, 215 : 8
suffer the armed m., 840 : 10
swindled by other men, 871 : 5
take best they can get, 356 : 2
talk of crabbed old m., 101 : 18
talking of fall of man, 560 : 29
text of m. and women, 689 : 18
that are ruined, 374 : 7
that hazard all, 199 : 9
that laugh and weep, 633 : 20
that sow and reap, 633 : 20
that strove with gods, 529 : 12
that were boys when I was a boy, 730 : 3
the cattle of God, 4 : 3
themselves m. wrong, 130 : 17
there before us, 558 : 16
there He makes m., 451 : 16
there is danger from all m., 380 : 13
think all men mortal but themselves, 330 : 11
thoughts of m. decay, 174 : 9
thoughts of m. widened, 530 : 3
thousand m. that fishes gnaw, 187 : 9
tide in affairs of m., 217 : 5
tides of m., 810 : 2
to be leader of m., 689 : 17
to match mountains, 671 : *n* 1
to m. a man is a mind, 647 : 6

Men (*continued*)
tongues of m. and of angels, 48 : 22
touched by heaven's virtue, 312 : 20
traced lives of good m., 429 : 4
tracing upon the hearts of m., 412 : 11
traveled among unknown m., 425 : 6
tread underfoot what feared, 101 : 9
tribe of spirits and of m., 132 : 12
trivial attentions m. pay women, 414 : 10
truest of m. Man of Sorrows, 570 : 16
trust ears less than eyes, 78 : 3
truth on lips of dying m., 586 : 7
truths not for all m., 343 : 15
turn one's back on m., 689 : 17
twelve honest m., 330 : 20
twenty m. crossing bridge, 766 : 13
two m. went up to pray, 43 : 38
two sorts of m., 672 : 9
two strong m. face to face, 707 : 16
uselessness of m. above sixty, 664 : 20
vexes public m., 530 : 16
war between m. and women, 831 : 5
wars planned by old m., 773 : 4
wars won by m., 791 : 15
watch the m. at play, 757 : 5
ways of God to m., 283 : 2
we are m. my liege, 238 : 14
we are the stuffed m., 805 : 15
we petty m., 215 : 6
we will die free m., 393 : 9
were deceivers ever, 209 : 16
we've got the m., 598 : 9
what is it m. in women require, 404 : 20
what m. call treasure, 568 : 18
what mothers made them, 498 : 22
what you and other m. think, 215 : 4
whatever you stuff m. with they bear, 561 : 5
whatsoever ye would m. do, 38 : 14
when bad m. combine, 372 : 4
when force subdues m., 89 : 1
when good m. die, 77 : 18
when m. and mountains meet, 407 : 1
when m. drink they are rich, 81 : 12
when old m. gather, 729 : 9
where dead m. lost bones, 805 : 3
which ordinary m. fit for, 233 : 7
who borrow men who lend, 441 : 17
who can't be bought, 761 : 17
who go through plain are m., 886 : 7
who have a sense of honor, 58 : 24
who know much say little, 358 : 20
who love and those who hate, 672 : 9
who march away, 641 : 25
who possess opinions, 566 : 3
who survive their reputation, 165 : 10
whom lust of office not kill, 566 : 3
whom men condemn as ill, 646 : 5
whose heads do grow beneath their shoulders, 229 : 30
whose visages do cream, 198 : 1
willful m., 682 : 10
willingly believe what they wish, 99 : 15
wise m. cast down rods, 9 : 19
wise m. from the east, 36 : 20
wise m. in great struggle, 383 : 1
wise m. of Gotham, 930 : 18
wise m. profit more from fools, 95 : 10
wise m. refrain to meddle, 155 : 5
wise m. shun mistakes of fools, 95 : 10
wise m. speak fools decide, 63 : 3

Men (*continued*)
wisest m. have erred, 288 : 25
wish m. everywhere free, 522 : 7
with firebrand in hand, 150 : 17
with knives in brains, 499 : 6
with mothers and wives, 485 : 19
with muckrake, 687 : 11
with sisters dear, 485 : 19
women and clergymen, 433 : 2
women better or worse than m., 315 : 11
women foolish to match m., 565 : 12
women try luck m. risk it, 675 : 5
women wiser than m., 781 : 14
won by m. with courage, 81 : 5
wonder m. trust selves with m., 242 : 31
words are women deeds m., 270 : 16
words children of many m., 850 : 15
working m. of all countries unite, 563 : 10
worth a thousand m., 431 : 15
would be angels, 180 : *n* 6, 336 : 18
write what m. do not what they ought, 179 : 5
ye are brothers ye are m., 443 : 17
ye m. of Athens, 46 : 15
ye shall die like m., 20 : 5
years perished to make us m., 631 : 14
you are m. of stones, 235 : 16
young m. all over world, 743 : 10
young m. fitter to invent, 181 : 7
young m. need stiffening, 679 : 10
young m. of new age, 406 : 20
young m. regard elders as senile, 634 : 24
young m. shall see visions, 33 : 17
young m. think it is, 692 : 9
young m. think old m. fools, 177 : 13
youngsters read m. understand, 169 : 39
Menace, atomic energy a m., 763 : 15
Menaces, insolent m. of villains, 382 : 11
Mencken Nathan and God, 775 : 14
Mend, anger and m. not, 339 : 13
fences, 593 : *n* 2
it or be rid on it, 238 : 16
knock breathe seek to m., 254 : 15
never made for man to m., 306 : 26
nor yet too vain to m., 333 : 22
the heart, 334 : 12
we dreamed to m., 715 : 8
your speech a little, 232 : 25
Mendacities, better m., 792 : 13
Mendax, splendide m., 108 : *n* 2
Mended, all is m., 197 : 23
least said soonest m., 169 : *n* 2
my wounds were m., 794 : 5
old houses m., 325 : 1
Mene Tekel Upharsin, 33 : 1
Menny, done because we are too m., 641 : 8
Men's, all m. good, 529 : 5
athwart m. noses as asleep, 191 : 23
business and bosoms, 179 : 21
evil manners live in brass, 249 : 14
faiths wafer-cakes, 207 : 15
fortune and m. eyes, 244 : 8
have grown from sudden fears, 459 : 21
history in all m. lives, 206 : 21
it's m. lives, 431 : 22
judgments parcel of their fortunes, 241 : 10

Men's (*continued*)
men, 565 : 28
music of m. lives, 195 : 16
old m. dream, 304 : 5
old m. heads are bare, 816 : 2
old m. lies, 792 : 14
one man's will all m. misery, 175 : 8
poor m. cottages palaces, 198 : 9
sweat of other m. faces, 524 : 5
talk not of other m. lives, 35 : 32
times that try m. souls, 384 : 13
wives young m. mistresses, 180 : 10
young m. vision, 304 : 5
Mens sana in corpore sano, 122 : *n* 13
Mensch, es irrt der M., 396 : *n* 2
Studium der Menschheit ist der M., 337 : *n* 2
Menschheit, Studium der M. ist der Mensch, 337 : *n* 2
Menschen, alle M. werden Bruder, 412 : *n* 3
Mensonges, choses que je conte sont m., 818 : *n* 1
Mental and corporeal war, 406 : 20
excellence a splendid possession, 102 : 22
fight, 406 : 21
medicine for m. disorders, 833 : 5
most complex m. achievement, 702 : 13
never influences physical, 552 : 7
not have certain m. characteristics, 685 : 7
obesity m. state, 857 : 12
specialists in m. disease, 783 : 10
suffering in Hanover Square, 620 : 9
Mentality, origin of modern m., 847 : 14
Mention, Kremlin's mountaineer get m., 819 : 1
making m. of thee always, 51 : 12
Mentioned, better damned than not m., 385 : 13
Mentioning, keeps m. woman he knew, 135 : 13
Mephistopheles, judges need something of M., 644 : 16
Mer allée avec le soleil, 674 : *n* 1
la m. toujours recommencée, 735 : *n* 3
Mercator's north poles and equators, 613 : 22
Mercedes-Benz, Lord buy me M., 916 : 5
Mercenary, followed m. calling, 692 : 3
slavish m., 379 : 1
Merces, ipsa quidem virtus sibimet pulcherrima m., 270 : *n* 7
Merchandise, not an house of m., 44 : 30
Merchant, mighty M. sneered, 605 : 20
overpolite to customers, 448 : 12
Merchantman, monarchy is a m., 407 : 16
Merchants are princes, 30 : 4
behave as m. by being m., 645 : 6
have no country, 389 : 9
Merci, la belle dame sans m., 478 : 13
Mercies, all occasions invite his m., 255 : 1
marvelous m., 633 : 4
tender m. of the wicked are cruel, 23 : 29
Merciful, a God gracious and m., 14 : 31
and mighty, 452 : 11

Merciful (*continued*)
as constant, 833 : 3
be m. to broken reed, 179 : 11
blessed are the m., 37 : 4
give be m., 56 : 24
God be m. to this drinker, 137 : 11
most m. God, 130 : 9
most m. thing in world, 816 : 8
powers, 237 : 11
to me a fool, 646 : 13
to me a sinner, 43 : 40
Merciless, loving rapid m., 893 : 5
Nature a m. stepmother, 116 : 6
Mercury, station like herald M., 223 : 3
words of M. are harsh, 191 : 16
Mercy and truth are met together, 20 : 9
beauty m. have on me, 607 : 15
betwixt stirrup and ground, 171 : 18
do justly and love m., 33 : 23
doing justice loving m., 385 : 5
full of compassion and m., 34 : 23
God all m. is God unjust, 330 : 13
goodness and m. shall follow me, 18 : 7
ha'e m. o' my soul Lord God, 594 : 14
half so good a grace as m., 228 : 6
hand folks to God's m., 565 : 11
has a human heart, 403 : 11
have m. on us, 54 : 5
his m. endureth for ever, 14 : 23
his m. is everlasting, 21 : 3
how can he m. have, 174 : 3
I asked and found, 171 : 18
I desired m., 33 : 11
I to others show, 340 : 4
is above sceptered sway, 200 : 9
leaving m. to heaven, 349 : 18
Lord have m. on parents, 131 : 6
Lord have m. on us, 54 : 3, 250 : 10
no more could be, 405 : 11
nobility's true badge, 188 : 16
not m. unto others show, 174 : 3
nothing emboldens sin as m., 243 : 4
o' my soul Lord God, 594 : 14
of a rude stream, 249 : 3
of his means, 887 : 1
on my poor people, 166 : 11
on such as we, 708 : 14
on Thy people Lord, 709 : 20
peace on earth m. mild, 350 : 15
Pity Peace and Love, 403 : 10
quality of m. not strained, 200 : 9
render the deeds of m., 200 : 9
seasons justice, 200 : 9
show no m. ourselves, 565 : 11
shown to every failing, 459 : 3
shut gates of m., 362 : 11
so great is his m., 21 : 6
temper justice with m., 287 : 25
tender m. of God, 42 : 26
that m. show to me, 340 : 4
they shall obtain m., 37 : 4
to forgive, 305 : 18
to myself I cried, 424 : 11
unto them that love me, 10 : 5
we do pray for m., 200 : 9
wound with m. round, 656 : 13
Mere, honor a m. scutcheon, 205 : 5
no imagination is m., 639 : 11
Meredith prose Browning, 674 : 18
Merged like the bird, 874 : 13
Meridian, in England under any m., 274 : 17

Meridian (*continued*)
of my glory, 249 : 1
zones and m. lines, 613 : 22
Meridians reel Thy purpose, 843 : 18
Merit, by m. raised to that bad eminence, 284 : 3
handsomely allowed, 356 : 22
makes his cook his m., 297 : 27
makes his way, 248 : 21
of perpetuity, 275 : 7
oft got without m., 230 : 24
patient m. takes, 221 : 12
purchased by m. of wearer, 199 : 14
that which he obtains, 436 : 2
to particularize is m., 405 : 16
truth only m. to history, 616 : 3
unassisted m., 351 : *n* 5
wins the soul, 334 : 11
Merits, careless m., 370 : 6
goodness result of one's own m., 136 : 14
obtain that which he m., 436 : 2
seek his m. to disclose, 362 : 19
Merlin, I am M., 535 : 18
Mermaid on dolphin's back, 196 : 14
Tavern, 477 : 16
what things done at the M., 263 : 2
Mermaids, heard the m. singing, 803 : 19
singing, 252 : 1
singing each to each, 803 : 19
Merrier man never spent talk withal, 190 : 21
the more the m., 161 : 5
Merriest, Christmas told m. tale, 430 : 22
maddest m. day, 528 : 12
when they are from home, 207 : 9
Merrily did we drop, 434 : 7
die all die m., 204 : 34
fly after summer m., 248 : 16
hent the stile-a, 246 : 24
let him drink m., 251 : 13
shall I live now, 248 : 16
Merriment, flashes of m., 224 : 14
innocent m., 629 : 12
Merry, all their wars m., 742 : 4
as cricket, 160 : 3
as day is long, 209 : 5
as marriage bell, 457 : 14
eat drink be m., 27 : 14, 43 : 19
England was m. England, 430 : 22
God rest you m. gentlemen, 919 : 20
good to be m. and wise, 158 : 19
gude to be m. and wise, 921 : 8
guid to be m. and wise, 411 : 24
he that is of a m. heart, 24 : 7
heart doeth good, 24 : 17
heart goes all the day, 246 : 24
heart maketh cheerful countenance, 24 : 6
I am not m., 230 : 10
if to be old and m. be shin, 204 : 6
keep our Christmas m. still, 430 : 21
led m. m. lives, 696 : 3
may'st hear the m. din, 434 : 5
measure, 469 : 24
men all, 926 : 16
men at point of death m., 193 : 26
merry lives, 696 : 3
merry merry roundelay, 177 : 7
monarch scandalous and poor, 315 : 16
month of May, 257 : 6

Merry (*continued*)
never m. when I hear sweet music, 201 : 2
obstinate pliant m. morose, 119 : 17
old soul, 929 : 14
playing of m. organ, 919 : 21
rather have fool make me m., 212 : 19
small cheer makes m. feast, 188 : 5
three m. boys are we, 260 : 15
'tis m. in hall, 163 : 6
turn his m. note, 211 : 1
tu-who a m. note, 191 : 14
very m. dancing drinking, 306 : 27
wanderer of the night, 196 : 12
we were very m., 822 : 19
wine maketh m., 27 : 18
wives may be m., 225 : 27
yarn from fellow rover, 760 : 16
Merryman, Doctor M., 323 : 15
moping mum, 629 : 22
Meshach, Shadrach M. and Abednego, 32 : 33
Meshes, though its m. are wide, 65 : 6
Mess, Benjamin's m., 8 : 33
cleanin' up whole m. of them, 814 : 17
let other people clean up m., 835 : 7
of imprecision of feeling, 807 : 21
Message, knowing how to reply to m., 6 : 1
many a m. from skies, 410 : 15
medium is m., 879 : 5
messenger makes m. clear, 131 : 2
nature's m. into song, 800 : 10
to Garcia, 679 : 10
Messed up life for nothing, 809 : 19
Messenger, busy lark m. of day, 146 : 18
has God sent a mortal as m., 131 : 9
I will send my m., 33 : 37
of sympathy and love, 617 : *n* 3
with language of his folk, 131 : 2
Messengers, bade m. ride forth, 488 : 13
dirty and breathless, 849 : 20
were right, 849 : 21
Messing about in boats, 690 : 14
Met, angels m. it half the way, 305 : 29
day and way we m., 634 : 2
dearest foe in heaven, 218 : 14
guests are m., 434 : 5
hail fellow well m., 323 : 22
lovely monster, 863 : 18
man who wasn't there, 756 : 2
me in evil hour, 409 : 9
men m. with erected look, 305 : 5
mercy and truth are m. together, 20 : 9
never m. man I didn't like, 766 : 6
never m. or never parted, 410 : 3
no sooner m. but looked, 212 : 31
part of all I have m., 457 : *n* 6, 529 : 8
rancor with cryptic mirth, 728 : 18
true when you m. her, 252 : 3
we have m. enemy, 455 : 5
you not with my true love, 172 : 8
Metal, as m. keeps fragrance, 750 : 4
base m. of humanity, 664 : 17
manual on uses of new m., 906 : 11
no use of m., 247 : 26
of man tested, 568 : 17
sonorous m. blowing, 283 : 21
there on shining m., 868 : 21
Metals, keys of m. twain, 280 : 19
Metamorphosis separated me from day before, 739 : 12
Metamorphosis (*continued*)
touch is m., 880 : 2
Metaphor fertile power, 784 : 25
mistaking m. for proof, 735 : 9
motive for m., 768 : 2
Metaphysical impossibility, 472 : 8
love is m. gravity, 833 : 1
Mete and dole laws, 529 : 6
with what measure ye m., 38 : 9
Meteor flag of England, 443 : 13
misled by fancy's m. ray, 409 : 5
of ocean air, 518 : 12
poem is m., 769 : 20
streamed like a m., 283 : *n* 4
streaming to the wind, 283 : 20
Meteors not needed less than mountains, 797 : 10
Meter balladmongers, 204 : 13
prose opposed to m., 436 : 14
Meter-making, not meters but m., 498 : 1
Meters, not m. but meter-making, 498 : 1
Methinks they are not meet, 162 : 5
Method for choosing presidential nominee, 788 : 11
for studying unconscious, 678 : 11
in man's wickedness, 263 : 6
intuitions without m., 703 : 13
invention of m. of invention, 697 : 8
madness yet m. in't, 220 : 21
of drawing up indictment, 372 : 21
of making a fortune, 363 : 11
of scientific investigation, 595 : 8
take m. and try it, 779 : 7
what pragmatic m. means, 650 : 8
which rejects revenge, 909 : 11
Methods, know my m. Watson, 689 : 9
science with greatest number of m., 673 : 9
Methought I heard one calling Child, 268 : 23
I saw the grave, 172 : 16
Methuselah, days of M., 7 : 25
Meticulous, politic cautious and m., 803 : 17
Métier, c'est son m., 482 : 8
mon m. et mon art c'est vivre, 165 : *n* 1
Metternich, Pope Czar M. Guizot, 563 : 2
Mettle enough to kill care, 210 : 7
grasp it like a man of m., 331 : 1
lad of m. a good boy, 203 : 25
Metuant, oderint dum m., 97 : *n* 6
Meurs, je m. de soif en cousté la fontaine, 148 : *n* 10
Meurt, la Garde m. mais ne se rend pas, 421 : *n* 8
Mew, cat m. and dog have day, 224 : 24
kitten and cry m., 204 : 13
Me-wards, to m. your affection's strong, 266 : 8
Mewing her mighty youth, 282 : 3
Mewling and puking, 211 : 15
Mexico, a Virgil at M., 363 : 21
city most wanted to see in M., 906 : 12
God allowed M. to be discovered, 156 : 12
poor M. so far from God so close to U.S., 604 : 2
Mezzotint, an etching a m., 544 : 25
Micawber's favorite expression, 548 : 25
Mice and men, 408 : 14
and rats and such small deer, 234 : 10
cat in gloves catches no m., 347 : 30
desert building about to fall, 117 : 2
fishermen appear like m., 234 : 28
like little m. stole in and out, 289 : 21
schemes of m. and men, 408 : 14
three blind m., 929 : 11
turn m. into horses, 694 : 1
with wings, 873 : 4
Michael and his angels fought, 53 : 19
row the boat ashore, 935 : 25
Michelangelo, Italy from designs by M., 622 : 6
not want M. for dinner, 622 : 5
talking of M., 803 : 10
Miching mallecho, 222 : 11
Mickle, every little makes a m., 170 : 9
Microcosm and macrocosm atoned, 595 : 3
heart sun of their m., 260 : 7
of public school, 501 : 1
Microscope begins where telescope ends, 492 : 2
of thought, 492 : 5
Microscopes of the press, 706 : 19
Microscopy chemistry mathematics, 819 : 14
Midday, kindling eyes at m., beam, 282 : 3
sweat, 267 : 12
Middle age time of improving, 290 : 9
aspirin of m. classes, 854 : 10
beware the m. mind, 794 : 7
class best political community, 88 : 7
class in America the nation, 589 : 8
class the safety of England, 540 : 3
dead vast and m. of night, 218 : 18
enchantments of M. Age, 587 : 1
in politics m. way none at all, 381 : 3
in the m. be sparing, 61 : 21
isthmus of a m. state, 337 : 2
no m. commercial, 873 : 1
of the night, 613 : 1
safest in the m., 113 : 17
son of M. Border, 695 : 12
station fewest disasters, 318 : 13
vulgarizing m. class, 589 : 4
wheel in the m. of a wheel, 32 : 25
whole has beginning m. and end, 88 : 17
wives companions for m. age, 180 : 10
Middle-aged adversity, 842 : 11
build woodshed, 557 : 12
prosperity, 842 : 11
Middle-class blasphemy, 681 : 9
morality, 681 : 8
Middlesex, acre in M., 488 : 5
village and farm, 512 : 7
Middling, worst enemy in m. class, 492 : 20
Midnight bells jangling, 864 : 6
bridge at m., 510 : 16
cease upon the m., 476 : 28
Cerberus and blackest M., 277 : 17
clear, 537 : 16
come again, 874 : 16
deep m. lair made, 431 : 5
dreary, 526 : 10
good morning M. coming home, 605 : 10
gravity out of bed at m., 204 : 2
hags, 239 : 8
heard chimes at m., 206 : 24

Midnight (*continued*)
hour's sleep before m., 270 : 19
into m. galloped, 541 : 12
iron tongue of m., 197 : 22
is noon of thought, 387 : 4
it is m. and time passes, 63 : 8
moan upon m. hours, 477 : 12
mournful m. hours, 395 : 2
ninth-month m., 575 : 17
oil, 267 : 12, 331 : 12
on emperor's pavement, 716 : 9
once upon m. dreary, 526 : 10
owl songs or m. blast, 462 : 1
ride of Paul Revere, 512 : 6
shout and revelry, 279 : 11
strikes and hastens, 692 : 8
through m. streets, 405 : 10
time cease and m. never come, 184 : 7
train whining low, 903 : 1
troubled m. and noon's repose, 804 : 12
year's m., 252 : 24
Midshipmite, bos'un tight and m., 627 : 7
Midst, him first last m., 286 : 16
I am in the m. of them, 40 : 3
in m. of life we are in death, 56 : 12
in the m. of things, 109 : 27
into the m. of the sea upon dry ground, 9 : 31
of eternity, 662 : 20
stood in m. of Jordan, 11 : 29
Midsummer, gorgeous as sun at m., 204 : 30
madness, 214 : 22
Midwife, she is the fairies' m., 191 : 23
Midwifery, my m. like theirs, 85 : 16
Midwinter, bleak m., 608 : 17
Mien, monster of frightful m., 337 : 5
truth has such face and m., 305 : 16
Mieux, je vais de m. en m. 684 : *n* 1
le m. est l'ennemi du bien, 343 : *n* 8
tant pis and tant m., 360 : 23
tout est pour le m., 343 : *n* 3
Might, dear m. of him that walked, 281 : 4
do it with thy m., 27 : 16
exceeds man's m., 226 : 14
half slumbering, 475 : 12
honest man's aboon his m., 411 : 18
is right, 138 : 9
it m. have been, 513 : 14
king's m. greater than human, 78 : 20
Latimer and Ridley in m. of faith, 156 : *n* 5
love the Lord with all thy m., 11 : 9
mighty man not glory in m., 32 : 5
not by m. nor by power, 33 : 30
of gods slow but sure, 77 : 8
of the Gentile, 459 : 16
protect us by thy m., 514 : 13
right makes m., 521 : 5
sadness of her m., 478 : 1
shining with all m., 613 : 1
spend her blood and m., 682 : 13
spirit of counsel and m., 29 : 18
to be man with thy m., 634 : 6
Might-have-been, name is M., 601 : 20
Mightier, cometh one m. than I, 41 : 32
make thee m. yet, 698 : 12
pen m. than sword, 493 : 6
than the noise of many waters, 20 : 19
than they in arms, 286 : 26
Mightiest, Christmas broached m. ale, 430 : 22
in the mightiest, 200 : 9
Julius fell, 217 : 21
Mightily, lay m. in whirl of dust, 58 : 26
pleasing myself m., 310 : 6
strive m. eat as friends, 188 : 29
Mighty above all things, 34 : 3
all proud and m. have, 345 : 3
all that m. heart, 425 : 14
book mighty theme, 571 : 1
Caesar thou art m. yet, 217 : 11
continent hitherto unknown, 151 : 6
dead, 345 : 7
each a m. voice, 428 : 6
eagle mewing her m. youth, 282 : 3
earthly marchings, 570 : 11
fortress is our God, 155 : 15
God who made thee m., 698 : 12
great and m. resolutions, 291 : 10
hand of m. man, 22 : 10
he that is slow to anger is better than the m., 24 : 13
hear the m. crack, 325 : 11
heart is lying still, 425 : 14
how are the m. fallen, 13 : 10
in the Scriptures, 46 : 20
lak' a rose, 685 : 1
law m. mightier necessity, 396 : 20
let m. babe alone, 292 : 18
little body m. heart, 207 : 11
look on my works ye m., 466 : 13
make m. ocean, 591 : 7
man not glory in might, 32 : 5
many and m. are they, 709 : 6
Marlowe's m. line, 256 : 12
maze not without plan, 336 : 10
men of valor, 11 : 30
men which were of old, 7 : 27
Merchant sneered, 605 : 20
merciful and m., 452 : 11
minds of old, 440 : 6
name shall be called the m. God, 29 : 16
O m. Caesar, 216 : 8
pain to love, 295 : 9
poets in misery dead, 425 : 12
put down the m., 42 : 22
scourge of war, 524 : 7
so m. a Redeemer, 54 : 8
some have called thee m., 254 : 11
sound of m. wind, 45 : 38
states characterless, 226 : 15
things from small beginnings grow, 303 : 4
true free Russian speech, 564 : 9
victories of m. generals, 575 : 8
weak and m. Russia, 584 : 3
weak things to confound m., 48 : 1
world of eye and ear, 423 : 14
Mighty One, splendor of M. Krishna, 94 : 15
Migration of the soul, 83 : 13
Migratory, unperplexed like m. birds, 756 : 8
Mild and magnificent eye, 541 : 6
gentle Jesus meek and m., 350 : 13
grateful evening m., 286 : 1
Mary was Mother m., 561 : 10
of affections m., 305 : *n* 2
peace on earth mercy m., 350 : 15
tormenting m. image, 570 : 4
wind mild-looking sky, 571 : 7
Milder fate than tyranny is death, 71 : 10
term to governments, 388 : 5
Mildest-mannered man, 460 : 26
Mildewed day in August, 892 : 6
silo, 757 : 6
Mildness, ethereal m. come, 345 : 10
Mile, crooked m., 932 : 18
every m. two in winter, 270 : 23
miss as good as m., 432 : 13
of warm sea-scented beach, 541 : 14
Mile-a, your sad tires in a m., 246 : 24
Miles around wonder grew, 691 : 2
away in preciousness, 648 : 2
I have many m. to fare, 748 : *n* 2
of fertile ground, 433 : 21
on foot to fare, 748 : *n* 2
river uses up m., 623 : 2
sed m. sed pro patria, 700 : 7
see it lap the m., 605 : 18
Sheridan twenty m. away, 591 : 3
three thousand m. and died, 568 : 14
to go before I sleep, 748 : 7
twelve m. from a lemon, 433 : 3
villain and he many m. asunder, 193 : 16
Milestones, counting m. count on, 518 : 9
into headstones change, 569 : 3
road to Hell without m., 842 : 9
Milieu, le juste m., 343 : *n* 9
un m. entre rien et tout, 299 : *n* 4
Militaristic stairway, 909 : 14
Military, ambition of m. leaders, 771 : 2
civilian control of m., 788 : 14
establishment, 815 : 15
forces are one team, 825 : 3
immense m. establishment, 815 : 15
machine, 745 : 2
man, 207 : 21
mind, 719 : 18
morale in m. unit, 771 : 2
no adequate m. defense, 787 : 15
no difference worth m. encounter, 860 : 4
only one m. organization, 825 : 6
period of m. government, 719 : 8
power and economic output, 871 : 8
unrestrained m. power, 800 : 6
war too serious for m. 401 : 2
Military-industrial complex, 815 : 15
Militia, place dependence upon m., 379 : 4
well-regulated m. necessary, 391 : 15
Milk, adversity's sweet m. philosophy, 193 : 12
and honey blessed, 563 : 13
buys opinions like m., 621 : 3
comes frozen home in pail, 191 : 14
cow of world, 899 : 8
find trout in m., 557 : 14
in pan, 496 : 11
land flowing with m. and honey, 9 : 13
my ewes and weep, 247 : 2
of human kindness, 236 : 16
of Paradise, 433 : 27
skim m. masquerades as cream, 627 : 16
sweet m. of concord, 239 : 19
take m. cheaper than keep cow, 621 : 3
take my m. for gall, 236 : 17
tyrant-hating m., 567 : 9

Milk (*continued*)
white curd of ass's m., 338 : 18
Milked cow with crumpled horn, 934 : 9
Milking, going a-m. sir she said, 931 : 14
lilting at ewe m., 368 : 2
time of m., 807 : 10
Milks, love babe that m. me, 237 : 5
Milk-white, before m. now purple, 196 : 15
hens of Dorking, 551 : 1
Milky, all the m. sky, 712 : 7
baldric of skies, 474 : 18
over Sado the M. Way, 314 : 8
solar walk or m. way, 336 : 16
twinke on m. way, 427 : 8
Milky Way, night sperm of M., 861 : 2
sister in whiteness, 770 : 12
Mill, at the m. with slaves, 288 : 19
cannot grind with water that's past, 269 : 21
does m. make water run, 722 : 6
God's m. grinds slow, 270 : 14
golf links so near m., 757 : 5
John Stuart M., 753 : 4
much water goeth by m., 161 : 2
of the conventional, 652 : 10
of the mind, 717 : 9
of truism, 496 : 13
Milldams o' Binnorie, 927 : 1
Millennium, war usher in m., 813 : 1
Miller, honest m. hath golden thumb, 146 : *n* 3
knoweth not of water, 161 : 2
sees not all the water, 161 : *n* 2
Stuhldreher M. Crowley Layden, 773 : 6
there was a jolly m., 382 : 6
Milliard-headed throng, 335 : *n* 2
Milliner, perfumed like a m., 203 : 7
Million golden birds, 673 : 19
high man aiming at m., 542 : 19
make that thousand up a m., 266 : 10
play pleased not the m., 221 : 3
second m., 358 : 11
Millionaire, power m. has, 844 : 4
right of m. to millions, 621 : 7
ruined m., 807 : 19
trustee of poor, 621 : 10
Millions, be embraced ye m., 412 : 10
fate of unborn m., 379 : 2
for defense, 416 : 12
if m. born m. must die, 798 : 2
of bubbles like us, 516 : 21
of debt, 373 : 10
of mixed shades and shadows, 571 : 3
of spiritual creatures, 286 : 2
of tongues record, 457 : 21
one murder made villain m. a hero, 378 : 3
ready saddled and bridled, 298 : 18
right of millionaire to m., 621 : 7
tear-wrung m., 743 : *n* 2
there's m. in it, 622 : 8
we m. live alone, 585 : 13
with m. under his care, 5 : 2
yearly multiplying m., 552 : 13
yet unborn, 365 : 3
Millionth, encounter for m. time, 777 : 18
Mills, dark Satanic m., 406 : 21
of God grind slowly, 273 : 14
Millstone hanged about neck, 43 : 35
hard as a piece of nether m., 17 : 6
look through a m., 175 : 20
Milquetoast, Caspar M., 793 : 13
Milton aggravated dissociation, 809 : 8
attracts into unity of ideal, 437 : 19
faith hold which M. held, 426 : 1
function as M., 772 : 7
had imaginative mind, 437 : 5
knew too much for poetry, 698 : 11
malt does more than M., 691 : 17
mute inglorious M., 362 : 9
reason M. wrote in fetters, 403 : 19
test of M. to function as M., 772 : 7
thou shouldst be living, 425 : 22
was for us, 541 : 7
Miltonic, balanced and M. style, 656 : 22
Milton's wormwood words, 281 : *n* 4
Miltons, no mute inglorious M., 772 : 7
Miltown, tamed by M., 893 : 3
Mimic motion made cry, 767 : 15
Mimics, we are the m., 768 : 13
Mimsy were borogoves, 612 : 17
Mince, future a m. pie, 846 : 13
not to m. the matter, 168 : 6
this matter, 230 : 22
Mincing poetry, 204 : 14
walking and m. as they go, 29 : 1
Mind, a certain unsoundness of m., 487 : 10
absence of m. we have borne, 442 : 11
accurate m. overtaxed, 519 : 3
acts of m. itself, 437 : 21
all comes from the m., 72 : 15
allus on yer m., 774 : 4
and soul according, 531 : 18
as a dead man out of m., 18 : 16
as m. pitched ear pleased, 377 : 13
aspire to higher things, 176 : 9
atom on matter duplicate in m., 570 : 15
aware of own rectitude, 104 : 28
balloon of the m., 714 : 6
beauty exists in m., 357 : 14
beauty momentary in m., 767 : 10
become aware of itself, 499 : 6
beholding beauty with eye of m., 83 : 10
benevolence is man's m., 89 : 21
best work the human m., 410 : 16
beware the middle m., 794 : 7
blessed man who possesses keen m., 82 : 22
bliss which centers in m., 369 : 5
block of wax, 85 : 18
body filled and vacant m., 208 : 7
bonds only in m., 734 : 8
breaks chains from every m., 404 : 14
capable of anything, 683 : 17
celestial wisdom calms m., 352 : 3
chance favors m. prepared, 591 : 2
changeful m. of mortals, 72 : 13
characteristics of vigorous m., 352 : 4
chaste breast quiet m., 295 : 22
clap padlock on her m., 320 : 17
clear your m. of cant, 356 : 29
clothed and in right m., 42 : 6
cobweb bridge from m., 701 : 7
companion none like unto m., 162 : 4
complicated state of m., 628 : 6
concentrates his m. wonderfully, 355 : 25
conscious m. trained like parrot, 754 : 9
contemplate itself from without, 665 : 4
content, 178 : 11
Mind (*continued*)
corrupt public m., 851 : 14
courage gaiety quiet m., 669 : 17
creation of human m. work of art, 696 : 12
creations of m. be blessing, 763 : 8
cut from nature loses life, 448 : 6
dagger of the m., 237 : 13
daylight in the m., 326 : 21
disdaining littlenesses, 85 : 17
diseased always illusion, 552 : 7
distressed in m. body or estate, 55 : 6
dupe of the heart, 293 : 19
education forms common m., 335 : 15
employ m. to rule, 102 : 21
enabled to number worlds, 482 : 11
essay a loose sally of m., 352 : 8
exercises his m. with suffering, 89 : 25
extract laws from nature, 776 : 6
eye see for hand not m., 558 : 23
face so pleased my m., 918 : 14
face the mirror of the m., 128 : 8
fanatic can't change m., 746 : 15
farewell the tranquil m., 231 : 11
feed this m. of ours, 423 : 5
fiery particle, 461 : 24
fire of the m., 801 : 5
first destroys their m., 78 : *n* 1
first from m. banish understanding, 78 : *n* 1
fool uttereth all his m., 25 : 31
frailty of the m., 324 : 17
free m. guards rights, 448 : 7
free play of m., 586 : 23
freedom of m., 279 : 29, 815 : 3
frugal m., 376 : 14
gentle m. by gentle deeds, 174 : 4
gentle sensitive m., 714 : 7
gentleness of spirit serenity of m., 271 : *n* 1
geometrical m., 318 : 3
golden m. stoops not, 199 : 9
good in which m. at rest, 142 : 4
good m. possesses kingdom, 115 : 14
grateful m. by owing owes not, 285 : 11
great fortitude of m., 353 : 20
greatest powers of m., 440 : 29
grief develops m., 734 : 12
growth of m. widening consciousness, 754 : 3
had such burdens on m., 715 : 9
happy alchemy of m., 344 : 15
has mountains cliffs, 656 : 18
has thousand eyes. 670 : 8
he that wants anger hath maimed m., 277 : 4
heart and m. of America, 869 : 12
heart argues not m., 586 : 13
her m. to be attached like garden, 652 : 9
his eyes are in his m., 196 : *n* 1
his own business, 169 : 8
household in oneness of m., 59 : 28
human m. invents Puss-in-Boots, 853 : 7
I am not in perfect m., 235 : 9
idle m. knows not what it wants, 95 : 5
if m. acts on body, 762 : 3
if no hatred in m., 714 : 19
impatient, 218 : 4
impressions of free m., 718 : 6

Mind (*continued*)
in adversity keep an even m., 107 : 18
in another Zeus puts a good m., 58 : 17
in its purest play, 899 : 15
in m. of man a motion, 423 : 13
in my m. of mankind, 917 : 4
in the m. ever burning, 172 : 9
inability of m. to correlate, 816 : 8
inaction saps vigor of m., 152 : 8
Indian whose untutored m., 336 : 16
is an aviary, 85 : 19
is an enchanting thing, 799 : 11
is its own place, 283 : 13
is like bat, 899 : 15
is peace for m. possible, 138 : 1
is stayed on thee, 30 : 9
it's all in the m., 852 : 9
keep m. steady on keel, 569 : 8
known m. of the Lord, 47 : 17
labyrinthine ways of m., 693 : 10
last infirmity of noble m., 280 : 15
laugh that spoke vacant m., 370 : 4
let dauntless m. still ride, 186 : 11
Let Your M. Alone, 831 : 7
lets go thousand things, 627 : 2
leveling rancorous m., 716 : 4
lever of all things, 450 : 6
like musical instrument, 580 : 4
live on little with contented m., 101 : 8
lives on the heart, 293 : *n* 4
look clean through the m., 175 : 20
love looks with the m., 196 : 1
love Lord with all thy m., 40 : 16
loyal nature noble m., 534 : 21
makes body rich, 189 : 2
man who has m. and knows it, 681 : 18
man's unconquerable m., 425 : 21
marble index of a m., 424 : 2
march of human m. slow, 373 : 2
Marxism product of bourgeois m., 785 : 2
military m., 719 : 18
mill of the m., 717 : 9
mingles with whole frame, 105 : 22
minister to m. diseased, 239 : 32
mirror in every m., 352 : 27
mode of working of human m., 595 : 8
movement so wandering as that of m., 164 : 19
moves upon silence, 717 : 17
music and the step, 920 : 9
my m. forbids to crave, 167 : 5
my m. is troubled, 226 : 22
my m. to me a kingdom, 167 : 5
narrowed his m., 371 : 14
nature of m. mortal, 101 : 2
nature with equal m., 585 : 9
never brought to m., 410 : 11
never m. did m. his grace, 184 : 14
noble m. here o'erthrown, 221 : 19
nobler in m. to suffer, 221 : 12
noblest frailty of m., 313 : 19
nor mouth had no nor m. expressed, 656 : 10
not acquanted with his m., 118 : 18
not body enough to cover m., 432 : 24
not enough to have good m., 272 : 6
not rival save with m., 830 : 12
not set m. for or against, 68 : 15
not sex-typed, 853 : 18

Mind (*continued*)
not to be changed, 283 : 13
not yet of Percy's m., 203 : 26
nothing so irrevocable as m., 703 : 7
of own beauty m. diseased, 458 : 19
of superior man like heaven, 609 : 6
old in body but never m., 99 : 8
old man's eagle m., 717 : 11
one just suited to our m., 443 : 18
only man has nasty m., 626 : 10
open m. free discussion, 737 : 8
openness of m., 589 : 6
opinionated m., 714 : 20
oppressions of body and m., 389 : 12
or body to prefer, 337 : 2
our concern be peace of m., 92 : 13
out of sight out of m., 148 : 18
over matter, 482 : 12
overset m. with reading, 663 : 16
painter's m. with viewer, 483 : 16
palm at end of m., 769 : 11
passion a fever in m., 314 : 17
passion wholly of m., 836 : 18
peace is a state of m., 308 : 3
persecutes the m., 305 : 17
persuaded in his m., 47 : 31
philosophic m., 426 : 22
pity arrests the m., 777 : 17
poem of act of m., 437 : *n* 4
poetry fine-spun from m. at peace, 113 : 27
positive science of m., 733 : 15
power has no bounds, 115 : 19
power lies in m. and body, 102 : 21
presence of m., 96 : 19, 568 : 17
presence of m. in danger, 308 : 15
proper judge of man, 115 : 5
prudent m. can see room, 75 : 4
purify the m., 72 : 17
quiet m. cureth all, 260 : 5
quiet m. richer than crown, 178 : 10
raise and erect the m., 179 : 2
reading an oppression of m., 314 : 19
reading to m. as exercise to body, 327 : 12
reason ignis fatuus of m., 315 : 19
reclothe us in our rightful m., 514 : 1
reeled the m., 854 : 8
regained from nature what it put in, 776 : 7
rest to m. cheerer of spirits, 270 : 34
rocket the m., 900 : 2
seek for the lost m., 89 : 22
serene for contemplation, 326 : *n* 2
sick m. emptying, 850 : 12
sought extended view, 387 : *n* 2
sound m. in sound body, 122 : 17, 307 : 18
sound of body and m., 107 : 13
spirit of a sound m., 51 : 6
steal fire from m., 457 : 12
stops and steps of m., 806 : 2
stress on not changing m., 751 : 9
sublimity the echo of a noble m., 118 : 16
submitting things to desires of m., 179 : 2
subsoil of the m., 688 : 8
Sumner's m. contained itself, 635 : 6
suspicion haunts guilty m., 186 : 27
sweet to let m. unbend, 108 : 15
swift m. beholds, 823 : 7
tact a kind of m. reading, 664 : 3
that can hear music, 797 : 20

Mind (*continued*)
the music and the step, 920 : 9
the music breathing, 295 : *n* 11
time out of m., 168 : 8
to me a kingdom is, 167 : 5
to men man is m., 647 : 6
to mind, 430 : 9
to m. shameful to heart beauty, 582 : 1
torpid in old age, 355 : 27
tranquil m. a m. well ordered, 124 : 13
traversed universe in m., 100 : 3
troubled captain's m., 647 : 21
troubled m. be stranger, 267 : 20
troubled sea of m., 475 : 18
tumors of a troubled m., 288 : 24
tyranny over m. of man, 388 : 15
universal frame without m., 180 : 16
unsuitability of m. and purpose, 549 : 8
untutored m., 336 : 16
vacant is mind distressed, 376 : 8
villain's m., 198 : 28
was still unpledged, 76 : 23
water never formed to m., 767 : 15
weakness of human m., 308 : 9
wet m. and say something clever, 81 : 12
what I am taught, 449 : 15
what is m. no matter, 660 : 13
what pleased to call m., 489 : 14
where is love but in m., 467 : 13
which m. put into nature, 776 : 7
who prop my m., 584 : 7
wisdom entereth not in malicious m., 157 : 13
words are physicians of m. diseased, 70 : 25
your m. and you, 792 : 5
your m. tossing on ocean, 197 : 24
Minded what they were about, 359 : 18
Mind-forged manacles I hear, 405 : 9
Mindful of unhonored dead, 362 : 16
what is man that thou art m., 17 : 17
Mindfulness, right m., 73 : 2
Mindless action, 862 : 21
of its just honors, 429 : 10
Mind-reading, tact a kind of m., 664 : 3
Mind's adventures among masterpieces, 655 : 11
avid substance, 836 : 19
find the m. construction, 236 : 15
in my m. eye Horatio, 218 : 15
measure m. height, 540 : 8
my m. not right, 893 : 7
opaque depths of m. folds, 164 : 19
the standard of man, 328 : 1
Minds, admiration only of weak m., 288 : 7
affect hearts and m., 820 : 14
all to have aspiring m., 183 : 6
are finite, 698 : 1
balm of hurt m., 237 : 21
becks m. to fellowship, 475 : 20
Bentham and Coleridge seminal m., 508 : 2
bore so much as own m., 569 : 7
can heavenly m. yield, 104 : 16
comfortable m., 828 : 14
danger spur of great m., 178 : 7
free to speak our m., 824 : 12
function only when open, 647 : 22
great empire and little m., 373 : 8

Minds (*continued*)
greatest m. capable of greatest vices, 272 : 7
grow in spots, 650 : 10
hearts and m., 56 : 1
hobgoblin of little m., 497 : 2
home in m. of men, 81 : 5
injured by hunger and thirst, 89 : 27
innocent and quiet, 296 : 4
intercourse with superior m., 448 : 5
keep your hearts and m., 50 : 6
let our m. be bold, 678 : 2
lose self in other m., 442 : 7
made better by presence, 564 : 22
marriage of true m., 245 : 18
me o' departed joys, 409 : 24
mediocre m., 294 : 3
men of other m., 368 : 20
mighty m. of old, 440 : 6
naturally affirmative, 631 : 1
not aware of m., 839 : 16
O miserable m. of men, 100 : 13
of different generations, 791 : 12
of few fastidious people, 711 : *n* 1
of gods not changed, 59 : 22
of my generation, 906 : 1
of strongest m. hears least, 428 : 9
reason freed men's m., 115 : 16
record of best m., 470 : 6
refuge of weak m., 342 : 6
religion of feeble m., 374 : 1
small m. never handle great themes, 128 : 11
so many men so many m., 97 : *n* 2
speak m. of thers to speak my own better, 164 : 12
stay our m. be staid, 749 : 14
steadiest m. to waver, 74 : 17
strong m. great hearts, 566 : 3
that have nothing, 429 : 13
themselves our m. impress, 423 : 5
to different m., 495 : 20
we change our m., 884 : 6
weak m. recriminate, 437 : 3
young men's m. are changeable, 57 : 22
Mine, every beast of the forest is m., 19 : 13
eyes have seen glory, 566 : 4
factory dockyard, 745 : 11
fatal words m. and thine, 168 : 15
lives ye led were m., 707 : 3
lovin' that man of m., 833 : 8
mother o' m., 707 : 19
she is m. for life, 896 : 2
she shall be m., 424 : 13
this sun m. and yours, 849 : 19
was always that, 866 : 14
was ever grief like m., 268 : 10
what is yours is m., 93 : 8
what's m. is yours, 229 : 10
why shouldst thou have m., 290 : 2
will defend what's m., 172 : *n* 2
with my heart in it, 248 : 4
Minerals, poisonous m. and that tree, 254 : 10
Mingle blood with blood of children, 486 : 16
in one spirit meet m., 467 : 24
joys with occupation, 350 : 7
letters m. souls, 254 : 4
you that m. may, 261 : 22
Mingled, like kindred drops been m., 376 : 19
Mingled (*continued*)
respect m. with surprise, 431 : 14
yarn good and ill, 227 : 16
Mingles, mind m. with whole frame, 105 : 22
with friendly bowl, 339 : 8
with her cares sweet bitterness, 102 : 10
Mingling, understanding distorts by m., 179 : 9
Miniature thunder where he fled, 748 : 4
Minikin won't set fire to Thames, 364 : 4
Minimum guarantee of First Amendment, 794 : 20
searcher for fecund m., 766 : 18
Mining, titles of m. claims, 840 : 2
Minion, morning's m., 656 : 1
Minions of the moon, 202 : 24
Minister droned monotonously, 622 : 13
king's first m., 746 : 2
patient must m. to himself, 239 : 32
thou flaming m., 232 : 14
to mind diseased, 239 : 32
touch me and no m. so sore, 339 : 7
Ministering angel shall my sister be, 224 : 18
angel thou, 431 : 2
Minister's, poor m. experience, 503 : 14
Ministers, maketh m. flame of fire, 51 : 13
of grace defend us, 219 : 10
of love, 435 : 20
spoke of God as if a monopoly, 560 : 5
you murdering m., 236 : 17
Ministers', my actions are my m., 302 : 21
Ministry, by the m. of the prophets, 33 : 15
frost performs secret m., 435 : 14
Miniver Cheevy, 728 : 19
Minnaloushe creeps through grass, 714 : 8
Minnehaha Laughing Water, 511 : 17
Minnesotan, young M. did heroic thing, 855 : *n* 3
Minnow, whale swims m.-small, 794 : 13
Minnows, swarms of m. show heads, 475 : 1
Triton of the m., 242 : 18
Minnow-small, whale swims m., 794 : 13
Minor pants for twenty-one, 339 : 16
Minorities are qualified individuals, 784 : 17
government controlled by m., 699 : 6
Minority always right, 599 : 19
elite m., 784 : 8
majority deprive m., 521 : 10
most vilified m. in history, 776 : 13
Minstrel Boy to war has gone, 446 : 15
ethereal m., 429 : 8
galleons of fire, 843 : 16
infirm and old, 429 : 20
no m. raptures swell, 430 : 10
wandering m. I, 629 : 4
Minstrel's, power of m. lyre, 733 : 9
Mint, tithe of m., 40 : 18
Minus, maggoty m., 829 : 20
Minuscule, merest m. in gales, 766 : 14
Minute, cage the m., 870 : 6
Minute (*continued*)
Cynthia of this m., 335 : 17
do good in m. particulars, 407 : 6
one m. with him, 786 : 10
speak more in m., 192 : 26
sucker born every m., 536 : 4
too late, 225 : 18
Minutely organized particulars, 407 : 6
Minute's success pays failure, 546 : 6
who buys a m. mirth, 189 : 20
Minutes, a few m. for poetry, 598 : 14
fifteen m. of hell, 660 : 4
five m. with that man, 372 : *n* 1
hasten to their end, 244 : 19
hours and m. dollars and cents, 348 : *n* 1
my thoughts are m., 195 : 17
round earth in forty m., 196 : 16
sixty diamond m., 480 : 13
unless m. capons, 202 : 23
what damned m. tells he, 230 : 34
world-famous for fifteen m., 908 : 1
Minx, don't care whether a M. or Sphinx, 549 : 34
Miracle, cubic inch of space m., 576 : 14
every hour a m., 576 : 14
in veins of man, 850 : 1
man always prays for m., 564 : 8
monstrosity and m. myself, 166 : 5
mystery and authority, 582 : 7
no testimony establish m., 357 : 16
of our age Sir Philip Sidney, 176 : *n* 4
of rare device, 433 : 25
r'ar back pass m., 814 : 16
when you look for m., 850 : 1
Miracles, age of m., 473 : 27
are past, 227 : 14
did Jesus in Cana, 44 : 28
laughed at, 722 : 13
many signal m. on voyage, 151 : 3
propitious accidents, 703 : 17
Miraculous, and that's m., 864 : 10
falsehood more m. than fact, 357 : 16
Mirage of social justice, 844 : 9
works of unbelievers a m., 131 : 17
Mirages, city of m., 908 : 3
Miranda, remember inn M., 730 : 5
Mire, learning cast into m., 373 : 27
ne'er left man in m., 242 : 32
rode him through m., 933 : 16
Mirror, best m. an old friend, 269 : 29
blank page difficult m., 850 : 17
cracked from side to side, 528 : 27
critical m. of culture, 865 : 14
face the m. of the mind, 128 : 8
hold m. up to nature, 222 : 2
in every mind, 352 : 27
in law as magic m., 643 : 18
look into lives as into m., 97 : 4
man's manners a m., 397 : 9
novel a m. that strolls along highway, 453 : 13
of all courtesy, 147 : 5, 248 : 24
speech a m. of soul, 112 : 17
stock market a m., 871 : 4
that reflects candle, 700 : 14
thou glorious m., 458 : 28
understanding is false m., 179 : 9
you who dirty the m., 316 : 2
Mirrored on her sea, 733 : 3
Mirroring, windborne m. soul, 585 : 5
Mirrors, city of m., 908 : 3
light focused by m., 652 : *n* 3
of shadows futurity casts, 470 : 5

Mirrors (*continued*)
should reflect, 818 : 1
upon empty space, 652 : *n* 3
Mirth admit me of thy crew, 277 : 22
and fun fast furious, 411 : 11
as does not make ashamed, 271 : 8
bards of passion and m., 477 : 15
cryptic m., 728 : 18
formed of joy and m., 407 : 3
has chord in melancholy, 258 : *n* 1
he is all m., 209 : 20
home of m. made desolate, 503 : 3
I'll use you for my m., 217 : 1
in funeral, 217 : 29
like flash of lightning, 326 : 21
limit of becoming m., 190 : 21
man of marvelous m. and pastimes, 155 : 11
May's newfangled m., 190 : 13
music of division, 173 : 1
no time for m. and laughter, 718 : 12
present m., 213 : 23
required of us m., 22 : 15
resort of m., 278 : 20
songs of sadness and m., 511 : 13
string attuned to m., 485 : 7
sunburnt m., 476 : 23
that no repenting draws, 282 : 9
tragical m., 197 : 13
vexed with m. ear of night, 456 : 20
who buys a minute's m., 189 : 20
wine women m. laughter, 460 : 23
with thee I mean to live, 278 : 8
Misanthropos, I am M., 243 : 8
Misanthropy and voluptuousness, 487 : 20
Misapplied, virtue turns vice being m., 192 : 20
Misbehaved once at funeral, 441 : 13
Misbeliever, you call me m., 198 : 24
Miscalled, simple truth m. simplicity, 244 : 25
Mischance, ride in triumph over m., 186 : 11
Mischief, draw new m. on, 229 : 33
it means m., 222 : 11
little neglect great m., 347 : 35
mend whatever m., 715 : 8
no return to place which has done m., 114 : 6
O Diamond thou little knowest m., 313 : 18
Satan finds m., 328 : 6
that is past and gone, 229 : 33
virtuous do, 539 : 18
when to m. mortals bend, 334 : 9
Mischiefs, dreadful m. from wine, 316 : 13
Mischievous, gossip is m., 61 : 24
hatched would grow m., 215 : 17
love a m. devil, 620 : 24
Misdeeds, murder and m., 177 : 1
Misdemeanors, high crimes and m., 391 : 11
Misdoings, heartily sorry for m., 55 : 17
Miser, rich honesty like m., 213 : 3
Miserable comforters are ye all, 15 : 37
difficult to make m., 522 : 5
have no other medicine, 228 : 13
I have passed m. night, 187 : 8
if film makes person m., 914 : 1
made neighbors m., 655 : 7
me m., 285 : 12
mercy on us m. offenders, 54 : 14
Miserable (*continued*)
minds of men, 100 : 13
mortals like leaves, 59 : 5
nothing m. but what is thought so, 130 : 2
now made m. by white people, 419 : 12
render last part m., 315 : 10
sharers of the event, 365 : 3
sinners, 56 : 2
to be weak is m., 283 : 10
train, 427 : 22
who longs for death is m., 267 : 2
Miserere 19 : *n* 2
nobis, 54 : 5
say M. leisurely, 273 : 9
Miseries, ambitions climb on m., 684 : 5
bound in shallows and m., 217 : 5
death umpire of men's m., 185 : 2
delivered from perils and m., 265 : 7
equal sharing of m., 746 : 16
extenuate m. of past, 801 : 3
of world are misery, 478 : 21
prolont life only when you shorten m., 876 : 6
to get idea of m., 565 : 21
Miser's, heaps of m. treasure, 279 : 23
Misery acquaints with strange bedfellows, 247 : 30
companions in m., 112 : 13
departure is taken for m., 34 : 13
distant m., 383 : 12
drink and remember m. no more, 26 : 5
gave to m. all he had, 362 : 18
half our m. from foibles, 393 : 13
in m. mindful of happy time, 141 : 2
loves company, 301 : 16
medicine for m., 77 : 6
mighty poets in m. dead, 425 : 12
miseries of world are m., 478 : 21
no friend in m., 257 : 8
one man's will all men's m., 175 : 8
radiant m., 394 : 14
result m., 548 : 27
so full of m., 527 : 19
splendid m., 388 : 13
still delights to trace, 377 : 25
vow eternal m. together, 317 : 1
Misfit, good woman the M. said, 905 : 3
Misfortune, bad neighbor is m., 61 : 18
in other countries poverty m., 493 : 3
it's your m. none of my own, 927 : 10
lose one parent m., 675 : 21
made throne her seat, 327 : 20
never delight in another's m., 111 : 13
of our best friends, 294 : 11
remembrance of former m., 169 : 14
shows who really friends, 88 : 20
to have been happy is most unhappy m., 129 : 22
war national m., 489 : 13
Misfortune's, sour m. book, 193 : 25
Misfortunes, bear another's m. perfectly, 340 : 9
by speaking relieve m., 275 : 23
come from wrong notions, 453 : 7
crimes and m., 343 : 26
endure m. of others, 293 : 2
follies and m. of mankind, 383 : 10
hardest never come, 495 : *n* 3
not unacquainted with m., 60 : 16
of man occasioned by man, 116 : 10
Misgiving, room for m., 75 : 4
Misgivings, not view process with m., 744 : 7
Misgovernment, augur m., 372 : 20
Misguide, blind judgment and m. mind, 332 : 19
Mishaps like knives, 569 : 5
Mislead, lights that m. morn, 228 : 28
Misleading, analogy least m. thing, 620 : 18
generalizations, 825 : 13
Misled by fancy's meteor ray, 409 : 5
simplicity no longer m., 391 : 1
Mislike me not for complexion, 198 : 29
not my speeches you m., 185 : 9
Mismanagement, Great Depression pro- duced by government m., 880 : 14
Misprint, poet not survive m., 674 : 17
Mispronounce, all men m. it, 816 : 10
Misquote, enough learning to m., 456 : 14
Miss as good as mile, 432 : 13
many-splendored thing, 693 : 18
march of retreating world, 827 : 7
McFlimsey of Madison Square, 595 : 4
mine he cannot m., 176 : 7
Nature cannot m., 307 : 4
pain that pain to m., 295 : 9
see nor know nor m. me, 778 : 6
Miss Lonelyhearts priests of twentieth century, 857 : 7
Missed, for everything m. gained something, 497 : 11
I wouldn't have m. it, 856 : 10
it lost it forever, 544 : 24
mr u will not be m., 829 : 23
never would be m., 629 : 6
stars might not have m., 749 : 11
woman much m., 641 : 24
wonder what you've m., 868 : 10
Misses an unit, 542 : 19
Heaven's net m. nothing, 65 : 6
man who m. opportunity, 400 : 19
Missing, nobody is ever m., 884 : 12
part of life melody, 573 : 6
so much and so much, 795 : 2
what m. at the man's heart, 884 : 22
Mission, glorious m. of unions, 666 : 22
Missionary not visited our planet, 570 : 2
stew, 806 : 9
to persuade thousands, 500 : 3
Mississippi, commence travels in M. steamboat, 449 : 1
of falsehood called history, 587 : 4
ran into M. and drowned, 840 : 5
Missouri, 'cross the wide M., 934 : 20
I am from M., 674 : 13
sound of rampaging M., 905 : 18
Misspending time a self-homicide, 310 : 20
Miss T., whatever M. eats, 740 : 4
Mist and cloud turn to rain, 512 : 19
buffalo come out of m., 789 : 7
came both m. and snow, 434 : 10
dispelled when woman appears, 332 : 3
engarlanded, 587 : 11
gray m. on sea's face, 760 : 14
here a m. there a m., 604 : 5
in my face, 544 : 21
life a m. of error, 262 : 7
mantled in m., 868 : 20

Mist (*continued*)
of tears, 693 : 10
only m. is real, 886 : 6
saffron m., 811 : 13
Scotch m., 569 : 13
shouted in m. month ago, 747 : 14
swollen with rank m., 280 : 22
white in blue m. on foam, 553 : 2
wrecked in m. of opium, 589 : 12
Mistake, blue and gold m., 604 : 9
in translation, 321 : 5
is has been shall be no m., 421 : 14
make no m. stranger, 699 : *n* 3
never overlooks m., 595 : 12
not to close eyes, 700 : 4
of enclosing envelope, 790 : 6
pardon Thy M., 866 : 17
pray make no m., 629 : 9
when I make m. it's a beaut, 778 : 9
woman God's second m., 658 : 15
young man for Greek god, 772 : 3
Mistaken, I pronounce m., 294 : *n* 1
intuitive calculation, 756 : 3
overzealous piety, 373 : 15
think that we may be m., 737 : 5
think that ye may be m., 272 : 18, 737 : 5
zeal, 391 : 3
Mistakes, experience name for m., 675 : 12
if you make m. I will protect, 825 : 17
made by writers from ignorance, 95 : 18
man of genius no m., 778 : 3
of good man, 391 : 5
paid in casualties, 815 : 14
Mistaking paradox for discovery, 735 : 9
Mister Death, 828 : 13
Mistress, art a jealous m., 498 : 25
as with maid so with her m., 30 : 5
character of m. from dress of maids, 128 : 7
court a m. she denies you, 256 : 6
in my own, 709 : 15
law a jealous m., 447 : 18
literature my m., 695 : 1
moderately fair, 295 : 5
more fond than m., 335 : 2
my m. the open road, 669 : 3
necessity m. of nature, 152 : 11
no casual m. but wife, 532 : 14
O m. mine, 213 : 21
of herself, 335 : 24
of mistresses, 580 : 19
or a friend, 468 : 21
pensive m., 874 : 21
riches good handmaid worst m., 179 : 14
simplicity deceitful m., 635 : 19
such m. such Nan, 163 : 3
teeming m. barren bride, 335 : 18
to the man I love, 335 : 2
Mistress' eyebrow, 211 : 15
my m. eyes nothing like the sun, 246 : 1
order to perform, 340 : 22
Mistresses, embrace principles or m., 368 : 4
hardly any m., 731 : 14
mistress of m., 580 : 19
others go to bed with m., 672 : 6
wives young men's m., 180 : 10
Mistrust, more ignominious to m., 293 : 15
subordinate who never finds fault, 662 : 2
Mists, errors wanderings m. and tempests, 100 : *n* 7
foul and ugly m., 203 : 5
mothlike in m., 785 : 12
season of m., 477 : 17
the Apennine, 604 : 12
Misty moisty morning, 934 : 2
mountaintops, 193 : 15
out of m. dream, 721 : 7
sheiling of m. island, 483 : 20
Misunderstand, no fate willfully m., 747 : 16
Misunderstanding, culture a m. if not French, 658 : 21
Misunderstands, how often he m. others, 395 : 24
Misunderstood, admired through being m., 818 : 2
to be great to be m., 497 : 3
truth m., 650 : 5
Misuse, oft happeth to m. wit, 148 : 6
Misused, sweet poison of m. wine, 279 : 7
Mite, can't make m. makes gods, 165 : 7
Mites, widow threw in two m., 42 : 13
Mither, father and m. gae mad, 410 : 10
leave to m. dear, 926 : 14
Mithridates, half M., 488 : 12
he died old, 691 : 18
Mitte sectari rosa, 107 : *n* 15
Mixed, elements so m. in him, 217 : 14
in wrong that's all, 810 : 6
Mixing memory and desire, 804 : 26
Mixture give you Nashville drizzle, 699 : 16
good things come in m., 442 : 14
Mizpah, name of it called M., 8 : 23
Moab is my washpot, 19 : 25
Moan, delicious m., 477 : 12
English mother made m., 568 : 14
frosty wind made m., 608 : 17
made sweet m., 478 : 12
of doves in elms, 531 : 13
paid with m., 693 : 7
Moananoaning, moyles of it m., 778 : 6
Moaning, harbor bar m., 566 : 9
no m. of the bar, 535 : 19
now they are m., 368 : 2
Moans, amid no earthly m., 525 : 14
round with many voices, 529 : 13
Moat defensive to a house, 194 : 13
Moated grange, 228 : 24, 527 : 17
Mob, amphibious ill-born m., 318 : 6
asylum among m., 569 : 19
at times m. swayed, 749 : 14
government by m., 687 : 20
honor depends on opinion of m., 308 : 23
I am the m., 761 : 3
is varied and inconstant, 308 : 23
not ask better only different, 155 : 14
of gentlemen, 339 : 23
of unnecessary duplicates, 571 : 2
redress of m. law, 519 : 23
supreme governors the m., 363 : 18
Mobile, donna è m., 105 : *n* 5
Mobilized English language, 742 : *n* 1
when armies are m., 65 : 4
Mobs, best university gauntlet of m., 499 : 14
Moby Dick, evil assailable in M., 570 : 13
Moccasins waiting on silent shelf, 908 : 9
Mock, after I have spoken m. on, 16 : 7
air with idle state, 363 : 4
at the great, 715 : 9
fools make a m. at sin, 23 : 35
meat it feeds on, 230 : 34
mockers after that, 715 : 10
on Voltaire Rousseau, 406 : 3
spirits of wise m. us, 206 : 13
their own presage, 245 : 13
their useful toil, 362 : 2
time with fairest show, 237 : 8
turtle, 612 : 4
Turtle, 612 : 5
your own grinning, 224 : 14
Mocked, as if he m. himself, 215 : 10
God is not m., 49 : 32
my sense is m., 251 : 7
Mocker, wine is a m., 24 : 27
Mockers, mock m. after that, 715 : 10
Mockery king of snow, 195 : 14
monumental m., 226 : 17
of monumental stone, 469 : 10
traffic in m., 715 : 10
unreal m. hence, 238 : 29
world a m., 704 : 3
Mocketh, whoso m. the poor, 24 : 14
Mockingbird, listen to the m., 599 : 5
Mockingbird's, out of m. throat, 575 : 17
Mocks, man that m. and sets it light, 194 : 6
married men, 191 : 13
my loss of liberty, 402 : 13
Moctezuma, America of M., 721 : 3
Mode, it began à la m., 639 : 20
Model, Americans may become m., 368 : 3
British government best m., 401 : 11
of deportment, 549 : 15
of man from natur's mold, 547 : 40
of modern major general, 627 : 20
republican m. of government, 379 : 7
small m. of barren earth, 195 : 2
to thy inward greatness, 207 : 11
Models, ancient m. perpetuated, 129 : 20
nature has all kinds of m., 832 : 9
turn pages of Greek m., 109 : 30
Moderate, give m. alarm, 505 : 12
liberty is in m. governments, 401 : 13
while one with m. haste, 218 : 22
Moderately, a thing m. good, 385 : 4
love m., 193 : 1
mistress m. fair, 295 : 5
rescue wife, 505 : 12
Moderation, astonished at my own m., 367 : 2
counsels of m., 737 : 3
even in excess, 501 : 5
flourishes, 737 : 3
gone no court save, 737 : 3
in all things, 96 : 1
in justice no virtue, 385 : *n* 2
in principle a vice, 385 : 4
in temper a virtue, 385 : 4
keep to m., 118 : 8
not think or write with m., 505 : 12
silken string, 257 : 14
spirit of m., 737 : 3

Moderation (*continued*)
stoutness in m., 628 : 13
urge me not to m., 505 : 12
Moderator of passions, 270 : 34
reasonable m. Death, 274 : 11
Modern, all history m., 769 : 24
American literature from one book, 845 : 5
art is critical, 886 : 11
born empty into m. age, 312 : 20
characteristics of m. spirit, 699 : 4
disease of m. life, 586 : 1
idea antiquated once m., 750 : 14
inconveniences, 623 : 13
life economic, 763 : 1
man invents museum, 834 : 4
old or m. bard, 279 : 6
one must be absolutely m., 674 : 9
origin of m. world, 847 : 14
something for m. stage, 792 : 12
spirit Greek discovery, 723 : 13
wise saws and m. instances, 211 : 15
Moderns only have opinions, 482 : 1
speak of m. without contempt, 341 : 23
Modes, for m. of faith, 337 : 9
Modest and commonly chaste, 463 : 13
coy submission m. pride, 285 : 19
doubt, 226 : 7
front of this small floor, 292 : 20
in speech, 69 : 8
keep m. as giver, 657 : 14
looks cottage adorn, 370 : 17
no more m. than immodest, 574 : 20
quip m., 213 : 4
simple m. manly true, 568 : 23
stillness and humility, 207 : 16
the m. near to virtue, 69 : 4
wee m. crimson-tipped, 409 : 9
woman dressed in finery, 371 : 7
Modesty a species of nobility, 308 : 15
ancient sculpture true m., 455 : 3
and unselfishness, 791 : 13
maids in m. say No., 189 : 31
mine is blushing m., 113 : 3
overstep not m. of nature, 222 : 1
speaks without m., 69 : 7
Modification, bad plan admits no m., 111 : 14
Modified, single substance variously m., 357 : 6
Modify, time to m. shape, 625 : 22
Modifying colors of imagination, 437 : 14
Modo liceat vivere est spes, 96 : *n* 14
Modum, servare m., 118 : *n* 7
Modus, est m. in rebus, 106 : *n* 8
Moi, l'état c'est m., 312 : *n* 1
Moider, I'll m. the bum, 877 : 9
Moi-même, je suis m. la matière de mon livre, 164 : *n* 3
Moist, cold and hot m. and dry 305 : 9
eye dry hand, 205 : 28
hot cold m. and dry, 284 : 27
star upon whose influence, 217 : 22
unpleasant body, 547 : 15
Moisty morning, 934 : 2
Molar to molecular motions, 644 : 20
Mold, fresh from natur's m., 547 : 40
made him and then broke m., 154 : 11
of form, 221 : 20
splashing wintry m., 712 : 12
Molded, best men m. of faults, 229 : 9
changing lineaments, 638 : 11
Molded (*continued*)
heart m. as she pleases, 171 : 10
two berries m. on one stem, 197 : 2
Moldering, a-m. in grave, 619 : 14
Molders hemp and steel, 431 : 24
Molding, wine jar when m. began, 109 : 19
Molds, crack nature's m., 233 : 24
musket m. in his hands, 666 : 17
Mole, live like velvet m., 793 : 19
wilt thou go ask the m., 403 : 17
Molecular motions, 644 : 20
Molecule, propensity to unite even in m., 775 : 1
Molecules, by mathematics m. counted, 697 : 4
simple and indivisible m., 390 : 8
Molehills from mountains made, 829 : 16
Moles, cast his idols to m., 28 : 32
Molle atque facetum, 106 : *n* 14
Mollify it with tears, 743 : *n* 2
Mollusk cheap edition of man, 499 : 19
Molly Stark a widow, 371 : 26
Moloch sceptered king, 284 : 4
Molten, inns of m. blue, 604 : 14
tears scald like m. lead, 235 : 8
Mome raths outgrabe, 612 : 17
Moment, brief shining m. Camelot, 895 : 4
culture m. of clarity, 784 : 6
dissolved in a m., 797 : 13
endurance for m. more, 660 : 8
endures m. or day, 715 : 13
eternity was in that m., 324 : 4
exhaust the little m., 889 : 11
face some awful m., 427 : 24
first m. of atomic age, 885 : 8
force m. to its crisis, 803 : 15
great pith and m., 221 : 12
hide thyself for a little m., 30 : 11
hold every m. sacred, 756 : 1
I cut his throat, 903 : 5
I fall asleep, 850 : 4
in a m. of time, 42 : 34
intense m. isolated, 807 : 23
knew m. to say nothing, 675 : 1
know the right m., 62 : 10
last m. belongs to us, 811 : 8
lifetime burning in m., 807 : 23
lived in paradise, 412 : 17
loyal and neutral in m., 238 : 8
men flourish only for a m., 61 : 1
never let up for single m., 788 : 3
not of action or inaction, 94 : *n* 9
nothing startles beyond m., 479 : 4
of difficulty and danger, 391 : 1
of greatness flicker, 803 : 16
of strength of romance, 683 : 11
of time fleeting by, 638 : 4
once let ripe m. go, 404 : 17
only a m., 683 : 11
only m. here and m. there, 750 : 6
perfection but m., 244 : 4
power of man and m., 586 : 19
precise m. to say nothing, 675 : 1
psychological m., 675 : 1
this m. in June, 781 : 15
this which you deem of no m., 86 : 4
time of death every m., 94 : *n* 9
to decide, 567 : 6
trap m. before ripe, 404 : 17
work of a m., 168 : 13
Momentary, beauty m. in mind, 767 : 10
Moment's monument, 601 : 17
seem a m. thought, 712 : 20
sent to be m. ornament, 427 : 3
Moments, art gives quality to m., 638 : 15
best and happiest m., 470 : 6
hardly dared pass, 848 : 7
history pattern of timeless m., 808 : 16
lucid m., 482 : 6
no two m. the same, 580 : 3
of high exultation, 799 : 20
when everything goes well, 705 : 9
Momentum, psychological m., 675 : *n* 1
Mona Lisa, you're the smile on M., 820 : 4
Monads of Leibniz, 791 : 12
Monagony being married to one person, 815 : *n* 1
Monan's, moon on M. rill, 431 : 5
Monarch, becomes throned m. better than crown, 200 : 9
hears, 306 : 13
love teach m. to be wise, 361 : 19
merry m. scandalous and poor, 315 : 16
morsel for a m., 240 : 24
of all I survey, 376 : 12
of mountains, 460 : 6
of the vine, 241 : 5
richest m. in world, 412 : 18
Monarchs, fate summons m. obey, 304 : 24
perplexes m., 283 : 24
Monarchy is a merchantman, 407 : 16
universal m. of wit, 271 : 18
Monastic aisles, 493 : 16
Monday, born on a M., 932 : 11
going to do on M., 773 : 9
morning press reports, 864 : 17
snatched on M. night, 202 : 25
unromantic as M. morning, 555 : 21
Monday's child fair of face, 932 : 10
Monde, l'amour fait tourner le m., 928 : 5
tard dans m. trop vieux, 537 : *n* 2
Mondes, ce meilleur des m. possibles, 343 : *n* 3
Money, a little wanton m., 155 : 6
alone preserves life, 312 : 22
and goods best references, 549 : 29
answereth all things, 27 : 18
beautiful in laws, 498 : 9
begets money, 301 : 14
bet my m. on bobtail nag, 598 : 2
blessing m. cannot buy, 271 : 13
board m. in ginger jar, 618 : 16
business may bring m., 440 : 28
business other people's m., 594 : 8
by you all the while, 661 : 12
counting out m., 931 : 9
disease called lack of m., 157 : 14
doänt marry for m., 535 : 8
ever tried to buy without m., 855 : 14
fool and his m., 917 : 23
friendship last lifetime if not asked for m., 624 : 17
go where m. is, 535 : 8
government consists in taking m., 343 : 19
hain't the m. but the principle, 725 : 12
having more credit than m., 394 : 15
hired m. didn't they, 736 : 17

Money (*continued*)
honey and plenty of m., 550 : 7
how painful to keep m., 310 : 13
how pleasant to have m., 564 : 15
is like muck 180 : 15
is trash, 251 : 13
keeps m. movin' around, 722 : 15
knowlege m. power, 887 : 8
lack of m. root of evil, 680 : 27
lay out m. on a rope, 258 : 23
let those with m. be without it, 859 : 17
like sixth sense, 751 : 11
lots of things m. won't buy, 855 : 14
love of m. as possession, 783 : 10
love of m. impulse to effort, 665 : 18
love of m. root of evil, 51 : 2
love of m. taken hold, 506 : 2
made m. because loved it, 722 : 25
make m. by any means, 108 : 18
making m. like bee, 73 : 3
making m. slow process, 313 : 8
man without m. rather than m. without man, 70 : 16
may rub off on you, 787 : 2
means and content, 212 : 1
much m. as 'twill bring, 291 : 17
must have m. to use senses, 751 : 11
no m. no change of routine, 859 : 15
no way to make m., 313 : 3
not appreciate m. till spent, 699 : 13
not good unless spread, 180 : 15
not pay for anything, 740 : 17
nothing lost but m., 871 : 3
nothing so demoralizing as m., 74 : 12
old wife old dog ready m., 347 : 17
on love request for m. chilling, 583 : 15
pays m. takes choice, 660 : 12
people who have m., 782 : 9
preoccupation with m., 859 : 17
pretty to see what m. will do, 310 : 9
prose of life, 498 : 9
put m. in thy purse, 230 : 3
put m. in trust, 519 : 5
rage and love, 863 : 20
ready m. Aladdin's lamp, 461 : 25
ready m. makes the man, 328 : 16
reputation more valuable than m., 110 : 19
retreated back into m., 835 : 7
rich have more m., 845 : *n* 1
rich possessed by m., 258 : 22
right to possess m., 537 : 5
seed of money, 358 : 11
sets world in motion, 111 : 30
silk suit cost much m., 309 : 13
sinew of love, 99 : *n* 8
sinews of affairs, 99 : *n* 8
sinews of war, 99 : 11
speaks sense, 312 : 16
store m. in stomachs of needy, 128 : 20
they have more m., 845 : 7
thinking like paper m., 690 : 4
thy m. perish with thee, 46 : 2
time is m., 348 : 1, 491 : *n* 1
times hard m. scarce, 499 : 16
to even get beat with, 766 : 4
touch, 687 : 20
use m. as one pleases, 537 : 5
values comfort or m. more, 751 : 20
voice is full of m., 835 : 5
war begun without m., 157 : 10
waste of public m., 637 : 12

Money (*continued*)
way the m. goes, 922 : 1
we've got the m. too, 598 : 9
what is worth but m., 112 : *n* 2
Willy Loman never made m., 888 : 2
with lent m. evil done, 573 : 3
won't surrender to flirt, 722 : 25
words are m. of fools, 264 : 13
world his who has m., 498 : 24
wrote except for m., 355 : 20
Moneybag, aristocracy of m., 473 : 21
Moneychanger, morals of m., 726 : 13
Moneychangers, tables of the m., 40 : 11
Money-lust before senses, 792 : 19
Moneymaker, not a mere m., 84 : 5
Mongrel best for every day, 681 : 5
I like a bit of a m., 681 : 5
puppy whelp hound, 369 : 17
son and heir of m. bitch, 233 : 13
this m. beast, 794 : 9
Mongrels, Europe continent of m., 706 : 20
Monism thinks all-form only form, 650 : 12
Monitor expressed, 428 : 15
Monk bring to light my toil, 486 : 10
cowl does not make m., 133 : 15
enlightened m. is free, 73 : 4
only connect beast and m., 764 : 9
Spanish m. distraught, 512 : 20
Monkey, as soon be descended from m., 515 : 9
disappointed in m., 626 : 17
heroic little m., 515 : 9
never look long on m., 515 : *n* 1
wine, 491 : 22
Monkeys, cats and m. m. and cats, 652 : 8
New and Old World m., 515 : 7
refrain from speech, 690 : 13
wilderness of m., 199 : 20
Monody not wake mariner, 843 : 13
Monolith, Communist bloc not m., 862 : 20
Monomakh, crown of M., 486 : 12
Monopolies, business m. and inflation, 848 : 4
Monopoly, business m. market power, 848 : 5
collective bargaining bilateral m., 790 : 4
has same effect as trade secret, 366 : 1
no single nation have m., 787 : 15
of God, 560 : 5
Monotonous languor, 659 : 12
nothing so m. as sea, 568 : 16
Monotonously falls the rain, 839 : 9
Monotony, bleats articulate m., 428 : *n* 2
stark m. of stone, 711 : 11
Monroe Doctrine force United States, 687 : 10
will go far, 687 : 6
Monsieur, farewell M. Traveler, 212 : 20
Monster begot upon itself, 231 : 20
faultless m., 289 : *n* 6
green-eyed m., 230 : 34
I had created, 482 : 14
I have lived in the m., 672 : 15
lovely m., 863 : 18
made m. me, 863 : 18
man-hero not exceptional m., 768 : 19
manunkind, 829 : 24

Monster (*continued*)
many-headed m. of pit, 339 : 28
more hideous than sea m., 233 : 10
of wickedness, 745 : 2
queer m. the artist, 654 : 8
see to it not to become m., 657 : 22
simple word destroyed m., 851 : 3
vice m. of frightful mien, 337 : 5
what a m. is man, 300 : 11
with an ache, 881 : 11
with uncounted heads, 205 : 18
Monsters, Imagination abandoned by Reason produces m., 394 : *n* 1
many m. to destroy, 851 : 3
sleep of reason produces m., 394 : 2
whoever fights m., 657 : 22
Monstrosity and miracle myself, 166 : 5
more prodigious than Hydra, 108 : *n* 14
Monstrous anger of guns, 827 : 2
big river, 624 : 2
bottom of m. world, 281 : 2
demonstration, 654 : 11
every fault seeming m., 212 : 12
little voice, 196 : 5
O m., 204 : 9
product of wrongs, 744 : 8
regiment of women, 162 : 1
two evils m. either, 810 : 17
Monstruos, sueño de la razón m., 394 : 2
Mont Blanc monarch of mountains, 460 : 6
Montague, fair M. I am too fond, 192 : 9
Montaigne, book of M. world endorsed, 164 : *n* 4
in his tower, 858 : 20
sedulous ape to M., 668 : 23
Monte Carlo, broke bank at M., 666 : 21
Montes, parturient m. nascetur mus, 109 : *n* 11
Montesquieu, celebrities such as M., 615 : 14
Montezuma, America of M., 721 : 3
halls of M., 922 : 11
who imprisoned M., 488 : 6
Montgomery to Oslo, 909 : 12
Month, April cruelest m., 804 : 26
difference sometimes a m., 671 : 14
follow month with woe, 469 : 7
full of spirit as m. of May, 204 : 30
laughter for a m., 203 : 20
leafy m. of June, 435 : 1
May m. flaps leaves like wings, 642 : 3
merry m. of May, 257 : 6
no trumpets for new m., 755 : 9
old man in dry m., 804 : 13
one m. on in May, 748 : 17
stand to in a m., 192 : 26
this is the m., 277 : 6
this m. is a kiss, 273 : 13
Monthly changes in circled orb, 192 : 11
Months add themselves make years, 534 : 25
mother of m., 632 : 7
nor hours days m., 252 : 8
that have no r, 166 : 12
three m. of cold weather, 590 : 4
travelers of eternity, 313 : 23
two m. after marching, 893 : 12
two m. back in March, 748 : 17
Montreal, O God O M., 620 : 3

Monument, all Greece Euripides' m., 75 : *n* 13
early but enduring m., 469 : 8
leave some m. behind, 715 : 9
like fishbone, 893 : 12
make your m. in love, 3 : 13
man's m. a man, 646 : 10
moment's m., 601 : 17
more lasting than bronze, 108 : 8
Patience on m., 214 : 5
placed where I endured, 801 : 17
sight of such m., 417 : 14
to see m. look around, 309 : 7
vote m. but refuse help, 721 : 10
without a tomb, 256 : 11
Monumental mockery, 226 : 17
smooth as m. alabaster, 232 : 13
Monuments carved from snow, 800 : 10
economic m., 871 : 15
mountains earth's m., 504 : 4
not marble nor gilded m., 244 : 18
of men overgrown with moss, 558 : 13
of safety, 388 : 16
of unaging intellect, 714 : 22
of wit survive monuments of power, 178 : 16
rights over human beings or m., 395 : 21
Monumentum, si m. requiris circumspice, 309 : 7
Mony a one for him, 927 : 5
Monyment, vote m. but refuse help, 721 : 10
Mood apart, 749 : 12
blessed m., 423 : 10
given heart change of m., 748 : 3
in any shape any m., 459 : 22
listening m. seemed to stand, 431 : 6
love is a m. to man, 670 : 2
melting m., 232 : 20
no m. maintained through hours, 755 : 18
puts me in working m., 495 : 13
strain of higher m., 280 : 17
Moody food of love, 241 : 3
Moon, African m. lying on back, 789 : 10
and I, 629 : 9
and I keep this up forever, 773 : 15
and stars thou hast ordained, 17 : 17
appointeth the m. for seasons, 21 : 11
a-roving by light of m., 460 : 5
as long as m. rise, 929 : 5
be not darkened, 27 : 24
be still as bright, 460 : 5
behold the wandering m., 278 : 18
beneath waning m. was haunted, 433 : 22
black dogs bay m., 629 : 20
black m. of highwayman, 841 : 6
body moves like a sliding m., 905 : 16
brilliant m. milky sky, 712 : 7
by light of m., 928 : *n* 3
by yonder blessed m. I swear, 192 : 11
changing m. changing eyes, 714 : 8
close by the m., 285 : 3
cold fruitless m., 195 : 20
come from the dying m., 530 : 25
cow jumped over m., 930 : 17
dance by light of m., 921 : 20
danced by light of m., 550 : 10
daughter of M. Nokomis, 511 : 16
dwelleth in cold of m., 544 : 17
earth barren as m., 760 : 9
Moon (*continued*)
earth viewed from m., 884 : 1
ebb and flow by the m., 235 : 12
eclipses of m. and other experiments, 151 : 7
error of the m., 232 : 15
everyone is a m. has dark side, 625 : 19
fair along Wabash, 732 : 13
fair as the m., 28 : 17
follow changes of the m., 231 : 2
full m. throw shadow, 789 : 10
ghostly galleon, 772 : 23
hang caps on horns of the m., 242 : 9
harvest m., 319 : 1
has set, 63 : 8
hath her eclipse endured, 245 : 13
his head rested on m., 374 : 20
horned m. with one star, 434 : 23
hush with setting m., 533 : 22
I the man in the m., 197 : 17
if m. shine full or no, 291 : 25
in first of the m., 874 : 9
in seventh house, 914 : 7
in silver bag, 716 : 21
inconstant m., 192 : 11
innocent m., 693 : 9
is down, 237 : 9
kneaded by the m., 640 : 11
landscapes of m., 734 : 13
lanthorn is the m., 197 : 17
lies fair upon the straits, 587 : 13
lighting stars comets m., 889 : 14
like a flower, 403 : 12
long glories of winter m., 529 : 1
lucent as rounded m., 569 : 2
lying on the brain, 902 : 6
made of green cheese, 161 : 8
make guilty the m., 233 : 5
minions of the m., 202 : 24
moping owl to m. complain, 361 : 22
Mountains of M., 527 : 5
mousetraps m. memory muchness, 611 : 22
moving m. went up sky, 434 : 27
new m. with auld in arm, 926 : 11
no m. outlives night, 906 : 9
no Moravians in M., 570 : 2
nor the m. by night, 22 : 4
nothing remarkable beneath visiting m., 241 : 22
of Alabama, 840 : 18
of my delight, 517 : 4
on casement wintry m., 476 : 16
on Monan's rill, 431 : 5
on whom pale m. gleams, 659 : 9
one revolving m., 304 : 10
or sun or what you please, 189 : 3
pluck honor from pale-faced m., 203 : 15
poet not been in m., 623 : 16
ragged m., 874 : 16
rather be dog and bay m., 216 : 32
revisitest glimpses of m., 219 : 12
rising in clouded majesty, 285 : 25
roving by light of m., 460 : 5
sadder light than m., 513 : 20
said wind to m., 594 : 13
seventeen times high as m., 932 : 5
shines bright, 200 : 22
shining to quiet m., 435 : 15
shone on Mrs. Porter, 805 : 6
sickle m., 785 : 17
silent as the m., 288 : 21
Moon (*continued*)
silver apples of m., 712 : 14
slowly silently now the m., 739 : 13
stain both m. and sun, 244 : 14
stand still in the valley, 11 : 34
stars about the lovely m., 63 : 6
stars planets fallen on me, 787 : 9
stepping on m. I begin, 864 : 4
subordinated sun and m., 132 : 5
sun and m. in flat sea sunk, 279 : 22
sun and m. should doubt, 406 : 17
swear not by the m., 192 : 11
takes up wondrous tale, 325 : 9
talk by poet, 623 : 16
tell m. to come, 841 : 16
this night of no m., 135 : 10
time for running to m., 874 : 6
tree etched by m., 317 : 16
unmask her beauty to m., 218 : 27
whenever m. and stars set, 668 : 11
white m. beams, 813 : 7
wide awake the m. and I, 629 : 9
will wax wane, 512 : 19
with how sad steps O M., 176 : 14
would have disappeared, 690 : 10
youth build bridge to m., 557 : 12
Moon-calf 248 : 5
Moonlecht, braw brecht m. necht, 730 : 20
Moonless night in small town, 887 : 6
Moonlight, book of m. not written, 766 : 17
come to thee by m., 773 : 1
ghost along m. shade, 335 : 7
how sweet the m. sleeps, 201 : 1
human m., 901 : 14
ill met by m., 196 : 13
incongruous strange m., 819 : 3
one by one in m., 811 : 14
ribbon of m., 772 : 23
softest in Kentucky, 657 : 6
unto sunlight, 530 : 5
visit it by pale m., 430 : 4
white waves in m., 732 : 7
Moonlit door, 739 : 15
Moon's red silver, 901 : 14
Moons, book of m. defend ye, 918 : 11
not hers lie mirrored, 733 : 3
of Saturn, 571 : 2
reason has m., 733 : 3
Moonshine an' snow, 568 : 4
find out m., 196 : 25
glory of war m., 579 : 3
Moon-struck madness, 287 : 29
Moony, little lovely m. night, 406 : 6
Moor bark with two anchors, 110 : 20
never saw a m., 606 : 17
over the purple m., 772 : 23
your daughter and the M., 229 : 20
Moore, before I go Tom M., 460 : 4
Moored, in Downs fleet m., 331 : 9
Moors, mountains m. fens, 735 : 8
Moos, my foos won't m., 778 : 5
Moose, bull m., 687 : 2
Moping melancholy, 287 : 29
merryman m. mum, 629 : 22
owl to moon complain, 361 : 22
Mops, seven m., 613 : 2
Mopsy Cottontail Peter, 719 : 2
Moral, absence of m. revolution, 790 : 1
and material welfare, 687 : 15
and political systems, 763 : 2
attitude in which most alive, 647 : 23
author provided with m., 503 : 16

Moral (*continued*)
authority, 580 : 12
bad m. character, 348 : 13
conquests, 483 : 8
courage physical timidity, 641 : 3
depravity within classes, 794 : 12
difference in m. life, 650 : 4
equivalent of war, 650 : 16
everything's got a m., 612 : 2
flabbiness, 648 : 4
force, 699 : 5
gloom of world, 503 : 3
habits make way into lives, 119 : 25
highly developed m. nature, 597 : 8
immoral thing for m. reasons, 641 : 9
indifference of cultivated, 580 : 14
inferiority of man, 626 : 4
intellectual wants, 649 : 16
law within me, 366 : 12
man and man of honor, 772 : 13
natural and m. forces, 584 : 1
natural philosophy deep m. grave, 181 : 14
no one m. till all m., 579 : 10
of m. evil and of good, 423 : 7
or immoral book, 674 : 22
order needs authority, 774 : 7
perception of beauty m. test, 557 : 11
personality, 577 : 4
persons attempting to find m., 623 : 19
point a m. or adorn tale, 351 : 19
political crises m. crises, 886 : 2
positive m. sense, 634 : 17
prophecies of m. degeneration, 773 : 8
real progress is m. progress, 581 : 6
saintliness a m. procedure, 877 : 12
satire ever m. ever new, 311 : 13
sense of work of art, 653 : 11
sensible well-bred man, 376 : 2
shut in rose, 530 : 14
soil for aesthetic growth, 742 : 3
spark out of stone not m., 631 : 3
stranger m. fervor, 316 : 2
terror overwhelming, 566 : 17
things m. or things evangelical, 302 : 4
truth basis of m. authority, 580 : 12
what is beautiful is m., 583 : 19
what you feel good after, 845 : 1
when uncomfortable, 680 : 20
will ends by settling m., 634 : 17
wise and m. man, 73 : 3
Morale, formula for m. patriotism, 771 : 2
Moralism, American m., 862 : 18
Moralist, statesman cannot afford to be m., 789 : 12
Moralities, never mind m., 625 : 18
Morality, conventionality not m., 555 : 18
courage of making choice, 736 : 10
enliven m. with wit, 326 : 9
foes of popular m., 580 : 14
for morality's sake, 465 : 11
I who dispensed with m., 674 : 8
ignorance of m., 299 : 16
knows nothing of geography, 579 : 9
middle-class m., 681 : 8
never understand politics and m., 637 : 2
not doctrine of how we make ourselves happy, 366 : 13
Morality (*continued*)
of common man, 658 : 4
of his actions, 359 : 1
periodical fits of m., 487 : 19
private costly luxury, 635 : 12
republican m., 452 : 2
taste is the only m., 573 : 5
temper wit with m., 326 : 9
true m. takes no heed of m., 299 : 14
unawares M. expires, 340 : 28
veracity heart of m., 596 : 1
wears m. as garment, 782 : 19
what majority like, 698 : 3
work of m. shaped by geometry, 318 : 3
Moralize my song, 173 : 7
Moralized his song, 173 : *n* 2
Morals, code of modern m., 468 : 21
conventional m., 738 : 3
faith and m. hold, 426 : 1
heedless self-interest bad m., 780 : 1
if m. make you dreary, 669 : 14
man of m. tell me why, 295 : 8
man of rigid m., 313 : 2
obedience to command, 690 : 9
of moneychanger, 726 : 13
time legalizer of m., 771 : 17
Moravians, no M. in Moon, 570 : 2
Morbidity, somewhat disgusting m., 783 : 10
Mordecai rent his clothes, 14 : 32
More and more about less and less, 698 : 17
and more and more, 613 : 4
cannot do m. than duty, 509 : 9
cantie wi' m., 409 : 23
Cawdor shall sleep no m., 237 : 22
celebrities such as M., 615 : 14
come through alive, 58 : 24
easy to take m. than nothing, 611 : 21
giving m. to that which had too much, 210 : 26
grow from m. to m., 531 : 18
how much m. is half than whole, 61 : 14
is man of angel's wit, 155 : 11
know what is m. than enough, 404 : 6
less he spoke m. he heard, 660 : 15
little m. how much, 542 : 8
little m. than kin, 217 : 31
loved Rome m., 216 : 14
Macbeth shall sleep no m., 237 : 22
matter with less art, 220 : 11
meant than meets ear, 278 : 24
nicely calculated less or m., 429 : 6
no man entitled to, 687 : 8
no m. dear love, 531 : 10
no m. of that, 232 : 20
Oliver asked for m., 546 : 30
once m. and no m. after, 633 : 15
say m. than this rich praise, 244 : 29
she yaf awey the more she hadde, 144 : 6
sleep no m., 237 : 21
the m. he uses for others, 65 : 10
the m. the merrier, 161 : 5
there isn't any m., 762 : 6
to be desired than gold, 18 : 1
to say when I am dead, 728 : 21
you see m. in you, 859 : 4
Moremens, onetwo m. more, 778 : 6
Mores, O tempora O m., 98 : 2
Mori, in taberna m., 137 : *n* 1
pro patria m., 107 : *n* 23
Morir, mejor m. a pie, 759 : *n* 2
Morire, come del m., 255 : *n* 4
Morison, lovely Mary M., 411 : 3
Morituri, ave Caesar m. te salutamus, 123 : *n* 12
Morn and cold indifference, 327 : 21
and liquid dew of youth, 218 : 27
approach of even or m., 285 : 5
as yet 'tis early m., 529 : 15
cock trumpet to m., 217 : 24
day's at m., 540 : 15
dewy m. to dewy night, 618 : 5
each m. a thousand roses, 516 : 6
evening follows m., 856 : 7
fair laughs m., 363 : 6
from m. to night my friend, 608 : 10
from m. to noon he fell, 284 : 2
healthy breath of m., 478 : 2
in russet mantle clad, 217 : 27
incense-breathing m., 361 : 24
lark herald of the m., 193 : 14
lights that mislead m., 228 : 28
lived the space of a m., 176 : 17
more bright than Mayday m., 399 : 20
not waking till she sings, 176 : 1
on the Indian steep, 279 : 13
opening eyelids of the m., 280 : 10
peeping in at m., 485 : 4
rays of m. on Shields, 568 : 19
red m. betokened wrack, 189 : 10
rose the morrow m., 435 : 12
rouse the slumbering m., 277 : 23
September m., 513 : 16
sweet is breath of m., 285 : 27
this the happy m., 277 : 6
tresses like the m., 280 : 1
ushers in the m., 349 : 10
waked by circling hours, 286 : 25
Morne plaine, 491 : *n* 7
Mornin', hangin' Danny Deever in m., 708 : 2
nice to get up in m., 730 : 19
top o' the m., 661 : 10
Morning after, 718 : 12
air awash with angels, 899 : 12
all whom m. sends to roam, 692 : 2
almost at odds with m., 239 : 2
already anticipated, 557 : 8
always m. somewhere, 500 : 14
as fed horses in the m., 31 : 33
as m. shows the day, 288 : 12
as the sun the m. dew, 307 : 9
a-walking one m. for pleasure, 927 : 9
bid me good m., 387 : 3
birdsong at m., 669 : 4
breeze of m. moves, 533 : 21
charm to stay m. star, 435 : 22
civilization at m. star, 498 : 8
come in the m., 552 : 19
day perpetual m., 559 : 22
day's disasters in m. face, 370 : 10
Dewey was the m., 647 : 2
dissolutely spent Tuesday m., 202 : 25
early in m., 934 : 18
early in the m. our song, 452 : 11
evening and m. were first day, 6 : 11
fair came forth, 288 : 18
farewell M. Star, 97 : 16
feel like m. star, 619 : 15
forehead of the m. sky, 281 : 4
full many a glorious m., 244 : 13
give him the m. star, 53 : 3
glad confident m., 541 : 9
glorious m. for America, 365 : 4

Morning (*continued*)
glut sorrow on m. rose, 477 : 22
good m. Midnight coming home, 605 : 10
good m. sadness, 832 : 5
hangin' Danny Deever in m., 708 : 2
hear right way in the m., 68 : 14
in bowl of night, 516 : 1
in m. we remember them, 727 : 1
in the m. it flourisheth, 20 : 11
in the m. like grass, 20 : 11
in the m. of the times, 178 : *n* 12
into the m. into the m., 739 : 5
joy cometh in the m., 18 : 15
looketh forth as the m., 28 : 17
love m. and evening star, 791 : 8
magnificent fierce m., 739 : *n* 4
matter for May m., 214 : 23
misty moisty m., 934 : 2
motion of m., 874 : 9
my Lord what a m., 936 : 1
my m. incense, 400 : 5
nice to get up in m., 730 : 19
of the world, 540 : 18
oh what a beautiful m., 833 : 10
our share of m., 604 : 5
penitence next m., 547 : 23
praise at m. blame at night, 333 : 14
quintessence of life, 463 : 12
shadow at m. striding, 805 : 1
shining m. face, 211 : 15
singing each m., 829 : 19
so soft this m., 778 : 6
some m. unaware, 541 : 16
somewhere with m., 761 : 1
son of the m., 29 : 22
sons of the m., 452 : 5
sorrow makes night m., 187 : 11
sow thy seed in the m., 27 : 22
star you shone among living, 468 : *n* 5
stars drift away in invisible m., 907 : 11
stars sang together, 16 : 29
they that watch for m., 22 : 12
think in the m., 404 : 5
this m. came home cloak, 309 : 13
tonight no m. star, 910 : 19
two o'clock in m. courage, 421 : 1
uncertain hour before m., 808 : 13
white light of m., 928 : 14
wings of the m., 22 : 17
woe to them that rise early in m., 29 : 5
womb of m. dew, 173 : 15
would God it were m., 11 : 20
Morning-glory opens blue and cool, 902 : 13
Morning's at seven, 540 : 15
easy m. ride, 607 : 12
minion, 656 : 1
Mornings, forgotten m., 886 : 18
Moron, happy m., 924 : 18
Morose, obstinate pliant merry m., 119 : 17
view of present, 489 : 4
Morrow, a little fun and good m., 617 : 3
cease to ask what m. will bring, 107 : 7
desire of night for the m., 469 : 20
every soul look upon m., 132 : 14
good m. to our waking souls, 251 : 15
good night till it be m., 192 : 19
Morrow (*continued*)
have hope of m., 618 : 12
man's yesterday ne'er like m., 466 : 11
misty m. a myrie someris day, 144 : 22
night urge the m., 469 : 7
put no trust in the m., 107 : 8
rainy m., 245 : 3
rash who reckons on m., 75 : 7
rose the m. morn, 435 : 12
take no thought for m., 38 : 7
Mors, nil igitur m. est ad nos, 101 : *n* 2
ultima ratio, 134 : 10
Morsel for a monarch, 240 : 24
I found you as a m., 241 : 11
under tongue sweet m., 319 : 4
Morsels, tough m. to swallow, 658 : 8
Mort, que la m. me trouve plantant mes choux, 164 : *n* 7
Mortal and may err, 272 : 12
arm and nerve feel, 431 : 24
behind m. bone, 605 : 8
coil, 221 : 12
dreams no m. dared, 526 : 14
element bearable to no m., 878 : 6
every tatter in m. dress, 715 : 1
frame, 435 : 20
genius and m. instruments, 215 : 18
grief itself be m., 469 : 6
grows on m. soil, 280 : 16
has God sent m. as messenger, 131 : 9
here came a m., 584 : 14
I sing with m. voice, 286 : 28
immortal death has taken m. life, 101 : 3
immortal youth to m. maids, 442 : 21
knew my son was m., 83 : 4
laugh at m. thing, 461 : 10
locked up from m. eye, 292 : 8
man who hath more joy, 570 : 16
melody, 525 : 10
millions live alone, 585 : 13
moon eclipse endured, 245 : 13
nature did tremble, 426 : 18
nature of mind m., 101 : 2
no m. could vie with Zeus, 59 : 24
not m. what you desire, 113 : 16
O you m. engines, 231 : 11
or immortal here I die, 570 : 6
purest treasure m. times afford, 193 : 32
put on immortality, 49 : 7
quit this m. frame, 333 : 23
raised a m. to the skies, 306 : 23
reason immortal all else m., 65 : 13
shall m. man be more just, 15 : 13
shuffled off this m. coil, 221 : 12
sins of commission m., 357 : 11
spirit of m. be proud, 463 : 16
splendor, 797 : 10
stakes, 748 : 18
struck a deep m. blow, 71 : 9
sufferest m. griefs, 208 : 6
temples of king, 195 : 2
tend on m. thoughts, 236 : 17
therefore Caius is m., 602 : 11
things doth sway, 174 : 6
think all men m. but themselves, 330 : 11
think m. thoughts, 76 : 9
tree whose m. taste, 282 : 22
what m. heard good of George the Third, 753 : *n* 3
wound is m. and is mine, 830 : 11
Mortalem vitam mors cum immortalis, 101 : *n* 3
Mortality, faint squeak of m., 846 : 9
nothing serious in m., 238 : 7
of inanimate things, 631 : 20
pilgrims of m., 802 : 20
to frail m. trust, 181 : 18
touches the heart, 104 : 26
watch o'er man's m., 426 : 23
weighs on me like sleep, 478 : 7
Mortality's strong hand, 202 : 7
too weak to bear them, 318 : 4
Mortals are blaming the gods, 59 : 15
changeful mind of m., 72 : 13
fellow m. accepted as they are, 565 : 3
happiest of m., 343 : 12
Hope lies to m., 692 : 7
make earth bitter, 473 : 16
miserable m. like leaves, 59 : 5
no ascent too steep for m., 106 : 27
not in m. to command success, 325 : 12
some feelings to m. given, 431 : 10
what all m. may correct, 322 : 19
what fools these m. be, 114 : 13, 197 : 1
when to mischief m. bend, 334 : 9
Mortar, his chest as a m., 570 : 13
Mortgage beats 'em all, 660 : 1
Mortification, live in continual m., 346 : 3
Mortify a wit, 339 : 28
Mortifying reflections, 515 : *n* 1
when woman considers difference of education, 392 : 12
Mortis, timor m. conturbat me, 153 : 6
Mortuis, de m. nil nisi bonum, 62 : *n* 5
Mosaic, glass m. window glass, 715 : 18
religion a father religion, 679 : 4
truth like a laborious m., 858 : 10
Moscas, en boca cerrada no entran m., 935 : 13
Moscow, to M. to M., 695 : 8
what store of riches, 486 : 9
Moses, go down M., 935 : 21
greeted M. from Pisgah, 480 : 16
hid his face, 9 : 12
ridin' on bumblebee, 840 : 8
smote the rock twice, 10 : 26
that which was given to M., 130 : 11
was there forty days, 10 : 15
well has she been called M., 593 : *n* 3
Moses' sepulcher, 11 : 27
Mosquitoes, lets big m. through, 267 : 3
Moss, rolling stone gathers no m., 111 : 17
until m. reached lips, 605 : 14
Moss-covered bucket, 455 : 7
Mosses, addled m. dank, 793 : 7
greenest m. cling, 513 : 6
Mossy cavern, 477 : 16
violet by m. stone, 424 : 12
Most enjoy contented least, 244 : 9
fails where m. it promises, 227 : 13
make the m. of it, 382 : 13
may err grossly as few, 304 : 13
thing they m. do show, 245 : 4
who is it that says m., 244 : 29
Mostest, git thar fustest with m., 583 : *n* 7
hostess with m. on the ball, 802 : 13
Mot, pour ecrire m., 928 : 8
Mote in thy brother's eye, 38 : 9
some m. some eye-flaw, 893 : 13

Motes that people sunbeams, 278 : 10
thick as m. in sonne-beem, 147 : 13
Moth and rust doth corrupt, 37 : 16
blundering by, 874 : 17
both m. and flame, 874 : 17
desire of m. for star, 469 : 20
Mother accursed the night she bore me, 76 : 10
actor pregnant with part, 704 : 14
and lover the sea, 633 : 2
arose a m. in Israel, 12 : 3
as m. so her daughter, 32 : 26
blessed m. of us all, 390 : 5
call me early m., 528 : 12
calls me Willie, 666 : 19
came and caught her, 932 : 4
Charybdis your m., 200 : 1
child to m. sheep to fold, 692 : 2
Church, 126 : 5
cruel m. of sweet loves, 108 : 10
Death m. of Beauty, 767 : 3
despise not thy m., 25 : 10
died today, 882 : 2
diligence m. of good fortune, 170 : 34
earth is my m., 419 : 10
earth no more a m., 116 : *n* 3
English m. made moan, 568 : 14
experience m. of sciences, 169 : 4
fairer daughter of fair m., 107 : 10
father and m. gae mad, 410 : 10
Father-M. God, 583 : 1
first you are wife and m., 599 : 13
foolish son the heaviness of his m., 23 : 21
from one m. both draw breath, 72 : 6
gave m. forty whacks, 923 : 5
give me the sun, 599 : 16
God Father even more M., 881 : 6
God is a M., 810 : 10
great m. of big apples, 879 : 12
happy with such a m., 531 : 14
holy M. Earth, 71 : 2
Holy M. Earth, 928 : 10
honor thy father and thy m., 10 : 7
Ida hearken, 528 : 4
if writer rob m., 838 : 13
ignorance m. of devotion, 259 : 23
in sin did my m. conceive me, 19 : 14
laid her Baby, 561 : 10
leave to m. dear, 926 : 14
make leaning unnecessary, 764 : 6
make my bed soon, 927 : 8
man favorite of m., 679 : 6
man shall leave father and m., 7 : 4
Mary was that M. mild, 561 : 10
may I go out to swim, 924 : 17
Memory m. of Muses, 85 : 18
my m., 449 : 12
my m. bore me, 403 : 6
my m. groaned, 405 : 12
myself commanded by boy's m., 70 : 15
Named is m. of all things, 63 : 12
nature by her m. wit, 174 : 1
nature called m., 483 : 5
Nature tender and benignant m., 152 : 15
necessity m. of invention, 117 : *n* 6, 134 : 9
no God and Mary His M., 892 : 14
no one like one's m. ever lived, 893 : 20
not God for father if not Church for m., 126 : 16
Mother (*continued*)
o' mine, 707 : 19
of Aeneas and his race, 100 : 1
of all living, 7 : 12
of All Living, 833 : 6
of arts and eloquence, 288 : 13
of five sons who died, 524 : 4
of gods and men, 5 : 3
of mankind, 283 : 3
of memories, 580 : 19
of months, 632 : 7
of the free, 698 : 12
old m. Hubbard, 932 : 7
one whom his m. comforteth, 31 : 32
our M. the Earth, 928 : 13
Pembroke's m., 265 : 15
poetry m. tongue of mankind, 374 : 22
raised by perfect m., 574 : 3
Russia, 584 : 3
so loving to my m., 218 : 7
stand by country as m., 590 : 6
sweet m. I cannot ply, 63 : 9
walked with his m., 886 : 18
wedded maid virgin m., 277 : 6
whales lie dreaming, 790 : 22
when my m. died, 403 : 9
who'd give her booby for another, 331 : 13
wit, 174 : 1
worm thou art my m., 15 : 39
Mother Goose, I don't believe in M., 684 : 11
Mother-in-law, go not empty unto thy m., 12 : 27
savage contemplates m., 673 : 4
Motherless, poor m. Eve, 733 : 2
Mother's, botanize upon m. grave, 424 : 15
cannot bear a m. tears, 106 : 2
daughter in m. house, 709 : 15
embrace my dead m. ghost, 60 : 8
great M. train divine, 587 : 11
hang us every m. son, 196 : 7
hardest to forgive, 864 : 19
lie on M. bed, 893 : 3
naked out of my m. womb, 15 : 4
pride father's joy, 431 : 17
sons anchors of m. life, 75 : 18
thou art thy m. glass, 244 : 2
Mothers a bloody brood, 834 : 5
and housewives vacationless, 867 : 8
good m. and fathers, 858 : 15
herd children home to m., 63 : 11
men more fortunate than m., 665 : 19
men what m. made, 498 : 22
men with m. and wives, 485 : 19
talking to you m. and fathers, 780 : 11
Mothers' wombs the tiring houses, 173 : 1
Mothlike in mists, 785 : 12
Moth's kiss first, 540 : 28
Moths among heath and harebells, 562 : 7
fill Ithaca full of m., 242 : 10
like m. caught by glare, 456 : 22
Motion and a spirit, 423 : 13
between acting and first m., 215 : 18
between m. and act, 805 : 17
change of m. proportional, 313 : 14
devoid of sense and m., 284 : 9
endeavor in continual m., 207 : 6
final cause produces m., 87 : 10
gesture without m., 805 : 16
Heat as Mode of M., 580 : 2
Motion (*continued*)
heavens rejoice in m., 253 : 21
her m. blushed at herself, 229 : 26
in one sphere, 205 : 9
meandering with mazy m., 433 : 23
measured m., 424 : 1
mimic m. made cry, 767 : 15
money sets world in m., 111 : 30
no m. has she now, 424 : 14
of hidden fire, 429 : 18
of morning, 874 : 9
of the rising day, 875 : 2
poetry of m., 690 : 15
scoured with perpetual m., 206 : 4
some men forward m. love, 299 : 4
speculators about perpetual m., 152 : 14
this sensible warm m., 228 : 20
uniform m. in right line, 313 : 13
what does awesome m. mean, 518 : 9
with majestic m., 458 : 7
Motionless bronze-lidded sockets, 801 : 18
Motions, molar to molecular m., 644 : 20
skittish in all m., 213 : 29
soul has many m., 874 : 18
stings and m. of sense, 227 : 28
to thy m. lovers' seasons run, 252 : 7
Motive, art framed on single noble m., 590 : 13
every joint and m., 227 : 3
find m. in narrative, 623 : 19
for metaphor, 768 : 2
fruit of action not be m., 94 : 10
hunting, 436 : 16
let not fruits of action be m., 94 : 10
path m. guide, 130 : 3
proportional to m. force, 313 : 14
religion only m. force, 681 : 4
Motiveless malignity, 436 : 16
Motives, anatomizing of m., 499 : 6
idealistic m., 698 : 9
of more fancy, 227 : 23
other than ignoble, 724 : 12
period great if high m., 698 : 9
strongest of economic m., 685 : 3
whereby men work, 307 : 19
Motley fool, 211 : 4
made myself m. to the view, 245 : 16
Motley's the only wear, 211 : 8
Motor cars and omnibuses, 781 : 15
Motors, sound of horns and m., 805 : 6
Mots de la tribu, 808 : *n* 4
Motto, let this be m., 556 : 1
national m. Root hog, 847 : 12
of sundial near Venice, 445 : 14
that is mankind's m., 296 : 10
this be our m., 446 : 2
Mottoes, golden m. in the mouth, 572 : 4
Moulmein, by the old M. pagoda, 708 : 8
Moulting season crisis in lives, 559 : 11
Moults, wing of friendship never m., 547 : 20
Mount all eager and quick, 896 : 13
facing M. Kenya, 818 : 13
mount my soul, 195 : 19
pure and disposed to m. to stars, 142 : 8
rejected Sermon on M., 825 : 1
singing of M. Abora, 433 : 26
to paradise, 494 : 15

Mount (*continued*)
up to the heaven, 21 : 15
up with wings as eagles, 31 : 2
whilst you m. up on high, 195 : 11
Mountain, allowed me to go to m., 909 : 17
and the deep gloomy wood, 423 : 12
as long as shadows touch m. slopes, 104 : 29
Big Blue M. Spirit, 928 : 16
cannot frighten one born on it, 413 : 31
don't care if I see m., 441 : 7
down the m. walls, 717 : 16
flee as a bird to your m., 17 : 19
forked m. or blue promontory, 241 : 17
freedom from m. height, 474 : 18
get thee up into the high m., 30 : 34
huge gap appeared in m., 66 : 13
Kilimanjaro highest m., 845 : 8
land of m. and flood, 430 : 11
like dew on m., 431 : 11
my holy m., 29 : 19
nymph sweet liberty, 277 : 21
poem that took place of m., 769 : 4
purple m. majesties, 688 : 5
Red Hoss M., 666 : 11
robes m. in azure hue, 443 : 4
see one m. and see all, 259 : 4
shall be made low, 30 : 31
sheep are sweeter, 455 : 2
up the airy m., 594 : 2
upon m. height, 428 : *n* 5
woods or steepy m. yields, 183 : 8
Mountaineer, Kremlin's m., 819 : 1
Mountain's, sun over m. rim, 541 : 15
Mountains, across m. across prairies, 745 : 10
Alpine m. cold, 282 : 18
approach over desert, 907 : 14
at distance airy, 443 : *n* 2
beautiful upon the m., 31 : 12
before the m. were brought forth, 20 : 11
by the winter sea, 534 : 29
creep abased below m., 671 : *n* 1
deer walk upon m., 767 : 4
Delectable M., 302 : 9
divide us, 483 : 20
earth's monuments, 504 : 4
England's m. green, 406 : 21
faith that could remove m., 48 : 23
fountains of men, 637 : 19
from m. to prairies, 802 : 10
genius of rugged m., 912 : 3
Greenland's icy m., 452 : 8
high m. a feeling, 457 : 28
hills look down on m., 672 : 12
in primeval sleep, 592 : 6
interposed, 376 : 19
labor mouse brought forth, 109 : 25
look on Marathon, 461 : 4
man to match m., 671 : 1
meteors not needed less than m., 797 : 10
mind has m., 656 : 18
molehills from m. made, 829 : 16
monarch of m., 460 : 6
moors and fens, 735 : 8
New Hampshire m. curl, 747 : 20
not reach m. in height, 131 : 7
of the Moon, 527 : 5
offered this trust to m., 132 : 4
Mountains (*continued*)
on m. is freedom, 413 : 30
one is of the sea one of m., 428 : 6
over m. over waves, 919 : 3
people live in sierras and m., 151 : 9
skipped like rams, 21 : 21
split m. with thunderbolt, 103 : 29
thou deemest m. affixed, 131 : 18
though the m. be carried into the sea, 19 : 10
three long m., 822 : 11
truth bounded by m., 165 : 8
Vermont m. stretch straight, 747 : 20
want to be buried among m., 603 : 1
when men and m. meet, 407 : 1
white man bestrode m., 374 : 20
yonder m. stand upon base, 414 : 1
young hart upon m. of spices, 28 : 25
Mountainside, following plow along m., 425 : 10
from every m., 514 : 12
Mountaintop, lightning strikes m., 107 : 21
standing alone on m., 637 : 21
Mountaintops, stands tiptoe on misty m., 193 : 15
that freeze, 248 : 29
who ascends to m., 457 : 22
Mountebank, mere anatomy a m., 188 : 15
Mounted, beggars m. run horse to death, 186 : 1
better m. than I gives cast, 708 : *n* 3
to his cabin, 731 : 19
Troilus m. Troyan walls, 200 : 22
Mounteth, courage m. with occasion, 201 : 12
Mounting at break of day, 428 : 2
in hot haste, 457 : 17
larks notes prepare, 334 : 16
lives not m. and unfolding, 754 : 6
souls m. to God, 601 : 14
Mounts, in war m. warrior's steed, 430 : 6
Mourir, partir c'est m. un peu, 463 : *n* 3, 679 : *n* 2
Mourn, all beings thou shouldst not m., 94 : 9
blessed are they that m., 37 : 4
can children of bridechamber m., 38 : 29
countless thousands m., 408 : 16
man was made to m., 408 : 15
Margaret you m. for, 656 : 10
mischief past and gone, 229 : 33
mourned and yet shall m., 576 : 2
music bad to those who m., 308 : 19
no longer m. for me, 244 : 26
small gnats m., 477 : 19
the dead, 899 : 7
time to m., 26 : 21
unalterable days, 494 : 23
upon thy bed, 633 : 17
with ever-returning spring, 576 : 2
ye Graces and Loves, 101 : 15
Mourned and yet shall mourn, 576 : 2
at birth not death, 341 : 6
by strangers m., 335 : 10
Mourners go about the streets, 27 : 25
haul up flag you m., 883 : 12
most musical of m., 468 : 24
no m. walk behind me, 640 : 16
Mournful ditty to merry measure, 469 : 24
Mournful (*continued*)
I with m. tread, 576 : 7
lean Despair, 402 : 14
midnight hours, 395 : 2
numbers, 509 : 13
Psyche, 477 : 21
Mourning becomes Electra, 810 : 12
go my way in m., 163 : 7
grief at not wanting to call back, 755 : 17
house of m., 27 : 4
let m. shows be spread, 176 : 8
music in m., 35 : 34
my Lord what a m., 936 : 1
O day of m., 139 : 4
oil of joy for m., 31 : 25
with my m. very handsome, 310 : 10
Mourns his yet unbroken chains, 399 : 18
household of Impulse m., 868 : 15
Nature m. her worshipper, 430 : 8
vile man that m., 336 : 22
Mourra, on m. seul, 300 : *n* 2
Mouse, baby looked like m., 846 : 14
cat watch m., 323 : 19
caught crooked m., 932 : 18
consider the little m., 93 : 14
frightened m. under chair, 932 : 8
I am magical m., 879 : 14
in a trappe if deed or bledde, 145 : 19
like gnawing of m., 822 : 16
lizard sing together, 637 : 15
mountains brought forth m., 109 : 25
not a m. stirring, 217 : 16
not even a m., 446 : 3
pleasant shy manner of m., 846 : 14
prevails in Latin, 365 : 12
ran up clock, 930 : 4
studying to be rat, 757 : 16
that hath one hole, 93 : *n* 11
tiny m. came forth, 66 : 13
town m. country m., 66 : 6
Mousetrap, make better m., 496 : *n* 1
Mousetraps moon memory muchness, 611 : 22
Mousing, by m. owl hawked at, 238 : 11
Moustache, neat m. and Aryan eye, 911 : 17
Moustaches on last Czar, 892 : 17
Mouth, bread from m. of labor, 389 : 1
bread of life in m., 315 : 1
brown hair over m. blown, 806 : 2
butter not melt in m., 159 : 31
cane-lipped scented m., 831 : 16
close m. swallows no flies, 935 : 13
cold hard m. of world, 878 : 7
false witness by their own m., 36 : 15
filled with dust, 255 : 5
filled with gravel, 24 : 31
find m. a rein, 633 : 13
fish dies because he opens m., 935 : 11
fool's m. is his destruction, 24 : 19
from m. flow gentle words, 61 : 9
ginger hot i' the m., 213 : 26
God's m. knows not falsehood, 71 : 1
heart in my m., 117 : 17
her m. is smoother than oil, 23 : 10
his heart's his m., 242 : 20
his m. is most sweet, 28 : 16
in cannon's m., 211 : 15
in her m. was an olive leaf, 7 : 32
ink runs from m., 913 : 4
it as many players do, 221 : 23
kisses from female m., 460 : 8

Mouth (*continued*)
living from hand to m., 167 : 12
made m. to water, 291 : 12
make m. say right thing, 624 : 4
most beautiful m. in world, 342 : 15
my m. shall show forth thy praise, 19 : 18
nay an thou'lt m., 224 : 23
never look gift horse in m., 128 : 22
nor m. had no nor mind expressed, 656 : 10
not that which goeth into m., 39 : 30
not thine own m., 25 : 22
O sad kissed m., 632 : 19
of hell, 533 : 14
of his holy prophets, 42 : 25
of no other country, 822 : 4
of one just dead, 759 : 10
of Plenty's horn, 714 : 20
one's m. is what one becomes, 723 : 9
ope his m. out flew trope, 290 : 18
opened the m. of the ass, 11 : 2
out of the m. of babes, 17 : 17
out of thine own m., 43 : 41
proceedeth out of the m. of the Lord, 11 : 12
pure of m., 4 : 9
purple-stained m., 476 : 23
reasons made m. water, 291 : 12
sendeth m. sendeth meat, 159 : 8
silver spoon in m., 171 : 5
smiling at the good m., 792 : 16
so prim, 806 : 14
speaketh out of abundance, 39 : 11
spew thee out of my m., 53 : 5
that which cometh out of m., 39 : 30
tongue cleave to the roof of my m., 22 : 15
verb in his m., 624 : 9
violence covereth the m. of the wicked, 23 : 22
wear not my dagger in my m., 243 : 26
which dog hath deeper m., 184 : 20
wickedness sweet in his m., 16 : 6
wine comes in at m., 713 : 7
wine near my dying m., 137 : 1
words of his m. were smoother than butter, 19 : 22
words of my m. be acceptable, 18 : 3
Mouth-honor breath, 239 : 31
Mouths, blind m., 280 : 21
enemy in their m., 230 : 26
had I a hundred m., 105 : 20
handful of earth stops m., 482 : 7
have m. but speak not, 21 : 22
made m. in a glass, 233 : 27
not if I had ten m., 57 : 19
Moutons, revenons à nos m., 927 : 20
Movable feast, 845 : 14
feasts, 54 : 9
impenetrable m. particles, 313 : 16
Move, aim of oratory to m., 98 : 16
but if the other do, 253 : 5
but it does m., 183 : 1
doubt that sun doth m., 220 : 14
fantastic century m., 399 : 16
gentle wind does m., 404 : 10
great affair is to m., 667 : 12
I by backward steps m., 299 : 4
I shall m. Hell, 105 : 29
I will m. the earth, 93 : 5
in cloud of ignorance, 839 : 14
languid strings scarcely m., 403 : 1
only in command, 239 : 28
Move (*continued*)
pretty pleasures might me m., 172 : 10
social conscience of nation, 909 : 16
stars m. still time runs, 184 : 8
stones known to m., 239 : 1
stones of Rome to mutiny, 216 : 29
times change and m. continually, 174 : 8
we live and m., 46 : 17
what can I do but m., 900 : 6
when looking well can't m. her, 289 : 17
Moved, I shall not be m., 19 : 27
like a vast shadow m., 299 : 6
more ways than one, 874 : 1
mystery of being m. by words, 887 : 7
not m. with concord, 201 : 3
not suffer thy foot to be m., 22 : 4
she shall not be m., 19 : 11
through dooms of love, 829 : 19
to smile at anything, 215 : 10
virtue never will be m., 219 : 22
we shall not be m., 936 : 7
woman m. like fountain troubled, 189 : 5
Movement, most magnificent m., 380 : 14
no apathy into m. without emotion, 754 : 14
out of dream into codification, 906 : 16
so wandering as that of mind, 164 : 19
symbol of power of m., 790 : 19
Movements, conscious m. reflex, 603 : 5
mass m. and sociology, 858 : 8
of the largest bodies, 397 : 17
Mover, Zeus prime m., 71 : 11
Movers and shakers, 659 : 9
Moves a goddess, 334 : 19
and mates and slays, 516 : 22
cursed be he that m. my bones, 250 : 1
glory of Him who m. everything, 142 : 9
God m. in mysterious way, 375 : 16
laboring surges of world, 693 : 9
love that m. sun and other stars, 142 : 20
no life m. in empty passageways, 74 : 1
she stirs she starts she m., 511 : 7
sits looking then m. on, 761 : 5
to see sad sights m. more, 189 : 25
where I move, 883 : 11
whole creation m., 532 : 27
Movest, great sphere thou m. in, 241 : 20
Movie, happy in even bad m., 889 : 4
Movies, at m. the only modern mystery, 834 : 14
Movin' up and down again, 710 : 10
Moving accidents by flood and field, 229 : 28
always m. as restless spheres, 183 : 6
dead still talk, 908 : 8
finger writes, 517 : 2
forward to greater freedom, 779 : 13
his slow and m. finger, 232 : 3
in m. how express, 220 : 28
into another intensity, 807 : 24
keep m. on, 589 : 15
never stopping, 575 : 16
nightly pitch m. tent, 429 : 17
others themselves as stone, 245 : 4
Moving (*continued*)
push on keep m., 416 : 8
tide as m. seems asleep, 535 : 19
up and down again, 710 : 10
waters at priestlike task, 478 : 20
Mowers sleeping among new-mown hay, 571 : 7
Mown, like rain upon m. grass, 19 : 35
we multiply whenever m. down, 126 : 3
Moyles and moyles of it, 778 : 6
Mozart last chord of European taste, 658 : 1
permitted when M., 906 : 6
some cry up M., 442 : 4
Much, and this is m., 457 : 21
bitter and is not m., 811 : 15
by m. too m., 204 : 20
don't say too m., 870 : 7
drinking little thinking, 322 : 1
enough or too m., 404 : 9
faithful in m., 43 : 32
given much required, 43 : 22, 890 : 6
have I seen and known, 529 : 8
have I traveled, 475 : 6
I do not ask you m., 202 : 18
in few words, 36 : 3
is force of heaven-bred poesy, 190 : 3
know too m. convinced of too little, 809 : 12
lady doth protest too m., 222 : 15
learning doth make thee mad, 46 : 33
learning not teach understanding, 69 : 28
little happy if I could say how m., 209 : 11
little more how m. it is, 542 : 8
missing so m. and so m., 795 : 2
more to that which had too m., 210 : 26
no man wanted m., 498 : 10
not do too m. work, 572 : 13
not many but m., 134 : 13
nothing too m., 62 : 7
of a muchness, 321 : 7, 565 : 28, 611 : 22
of a which of a wind, 830 : 1
of madness, 526 : 4
once that seemed too m., 748 : 8
safer too little than too m., 620 : 5
see so m. nor live so long, 235 : 20
so little time to do so m., 780 : 16
so m. depends upon, 785 : 11
so m. for him, 217 : 30
so m. owed by so many, 744 : 6
so m. to do, 532 : 15, 672 : 18
talk too m., 304 : 9
those who have too m., 780 : 3
too m. of good thing, 168 : 12
unjust in m., 43 : 32
what he loves never like too m., 256 : 4
wrested from sure defeat, 810 : 3
Muchness, much of a m., 321 : 7, 565 : 28, 611 : 22
Muck, all of a m. of sweat, 369 : 13
money is like m., 180 : 15
when stop raking m., 687 : 11
Muckle, twice as m. 's a' that, 411 : 20
Muckrake in his hand, 302 : 12
men with m., 687 : 11
Mud, alive and wagging tail in m., 90 : 11
flies from wings, 892 : 4

Mud (*continued*)
frogs in the marsh m., 104 : 1
garlic and sapphires in m., 807 : 4
in Black M. kingfisher, 892 : 4
in m. eel is, 933 : 4
life marble and m., 503 : 18
searches in m. for bones, 824 : 6
silk stocking filled with m., 421 : 3
silver fountains have m., 244 : 14
Muddied oafs at goals, 709 : 23
Muddle through, 538 : 5
Muddled, he's Don Quixote a m. fool, 170 : 16
state sharpest of realities, 653 : 16
Muddlement, constant force for m., 653 : 16
Muddy ill-seeming thick, 189 : 5
vesture of decay, 201 : 1
Mud-luscious, world is m., 828 : 11
Mudville, no joy in M., 704 : 16
Muffet, little Miss M., 932 : 15
Muffin man, 933 : 8
Muffins, no more inspiration than m., 680 : 18
Muffled and dumb, 495 : 5
oars, 439 : 8
Muffler, Fortune painted blind with m., 181 : *n* 2
Mug's, poetry m. game, 809 : 19
Mugwump educated beyond intellect, 632 : 4
Muhammad, heart of M., 132 : 11
I M. am only a warner, 130 : 14
Multa, non m. sed multum, 134 : 13
Multeity in unity, 436 : 18
Multifold, dying m., 606 : 15
Multiple, register m. perception in art, 793 : 10
Multiplication is vexation, 917 : 13
Multiplied, deviation from truth is m., 87 : 7
entities not m. unnecessarily, 143 : 2
visions, 33 : 15
Multiplieth words without knowledge, 16 : 25
Multiply, be fruitful and m., 6 : 15
survive and m., 515 : 2
thanks to art see world m., 734 : 13
thoughts, 876 : 2
we m. whenever mown down, 126 : 3
Multitude a Hydra, 108 : *n* 14
always in the wrong, 309 : 10
as the sand by the sea in m., 13 : 28
barbarous m., 199 : 13
beast of many heads, 108 : *n* 14
charity creates m. of sins, 676 : 1
charity shall cover m. of sins, 52 : 14
could not name the m., 57 : 19
discordant wavering m., 205 : 18
efforts of busy m., 592 : 5
many-headed m., 108 : *n* 14, 242 : 14
of counselors, 23 : 24
of days, 351 : 20
of friends, 255 : 11
of rulers, 57 : 17
of sins, 52 : 14
of words, 125 : 26
rude m. call afternoon, 191 : 8
swinish m., 373 : 27
that choose by show, 199 : 12
wear another face to m., 503 : 13
Multitudes, against revolted m., 286 : 26
I contain m., 575 : 2

Multitudes (*continued*)
in the valley of decision, 33 : 18
pestilence-stricken m., 467 : 17
vast m. of Russia, 745 : 2
Multitudinous seas incarnadine, 238 : 1
Multiversity, university become m., 879 : 4
Mum, cry m., 170 : *n* 11
merryman moping m., 629 : 22
Mumbo-Jumbo God of the Congo, 765 : 7
Mumbo jumbos, soot-smeared m., 472 : 16
Mummers, grave m., 340 : 21
Mummy, yesterday embryo tomorrow a m., 124 : 27
Mum's the word, 170 : 37, 740 : 2
Munch your good dry oats, 197 : 5
Munched and munched and munched, 236 : 1
Mundi, Stupor M., 892 : 4
Mundus, fiat justitia et pereat m., 133 : *n* 11
Munich, wave M. all thy banners, 443 : 15
Munition, bomb fell on no m. plants, 777 : 10
Munny, doänt marry for m., 535 : 8
goä wheer m. is, 535 : 8
Muove, e pur si m., 183 : *n* 3
Murder and misdeeds, 177 : 1
brother's m., 222 : 25
cannot be hid, 148 : *n* 1
contrived husband's m., 60 : 11
from battle and m., 55 : 12
herein friendship cowardice m., 149 : 5
how easily m. discovered, 148 : *n* 1
I'll m. the bum, 877 : 9
indulges himself in m., 454 : 21
land for private profit, 875 : 13
Macbeth does m. sleep, 237 : 21
met M. on the way, 468 : 5
one m. made a villain, 378 : 3
one to destroy is m., 330 : 1
rage hatred and m., 903 : 2
sacrilegious m., 238 : 5
shrieks out, 148 : *n* 1
speak with miraculous organ, 148 : *n* 1
tell business from m., 722 : 5
thousands, 330 : 1
time to m. and create, 803 : 11
war I call it m., 567 : 20
will out, 148 : 2
woman or child in sleep, 786 : 8
Murdered, all m., 195 : 2
Glamis hath m. sleep, 237 : 22
Murderer, an honorable m., 232 : 19
carcasses bleed at sight of m., 148 : *n* 1
is somebody's old friend, 817 : 13
tender m., 543 : 7
Murdering, you m. ministers, 236 : 17
Murderous innocence of sea, 714 : 14
love come with m. intent, 76 : 22
perjured m. bloody, 245 : 23
water buffaloes even m., 799 : 16
Murders, check m. but what of war, 114 : 32
Mured up in wall of wisdom, 858 : 19
Murmur, ever importunate m., 654 : 2
shallow m. but deep are dumb, 172 : 12

Murmuring, asleep by thy m. stream, 410 : 13
lapse of m. streams, 287 : 4
of innumerable bees, 531 : 13
pines and hemlocks, 510 : 26
surge cannot be heard, 234 : 28
victim without m., 591 : 11
waters m., 278 : 25
Murmurings, crowd and buzz and m., 295 : 3
from within heard m., 428 : 15
Murmurless and shined, 844 : 1
Murmurous haunt of flies, 476 : 27
Murmurs as ocean murmurs, 442 : 16
hear mutual m. sweep, 461 : 9
in hollow m. died, 364 : 15
voice in hollow m., 416 : 11
Murners, no m. walk behind me, 640 : 16
Murray, slain Earl of M., 927 : 6
Murther, tell business from m., 722 : 5
Mus prevails in Latin, 365 : 12
Muscle, brain is like a m., 913 : 3
take m. from bone, 806 : 21
Muscles of brawny arms, 510 : 7
Muscular Christianity, 922 : 3
strength it gave to jaw, 611 : 10
Muse, American M., 840 : 4
be thou the tenth M., 244 : 15
conqueror creates a m., 276 : 2
dear to me the M. and song, 92 : 14
Fool said my m. to me, 176 : 13
has taught them songs, 60 : 7
I was your vassal, 673 : 11
livelier liquor than M., 691 : 17
love passed m. appeared, 486 : 8
meditate the thankless M., 280 : 15
O for a m. of fire, 207 : 1
on dromedary trots, 436 : 5
on nature with poet's eye, 443 : 7
plans credit and the M., 494 : 10
silence m. His praise, 345 : 16
tell me M., 59 : 13, 334 : 21
tenth M. governs press, 554 : 10
Tragic M. trod stage, 334 : 12
why M. speak when unhappy, 857 : 2
worst-natured m., 315 : 15
Mused, many a m. rhyme, 476 : 28
Muses, all charm of all M., 535 : 15
exaltation in chanting of M., 76 : 12
loved me, 93 : 2
Memory mother of M., 85 : 18
of Helicon, 61 : 6
recorded by M. live for ay, 174 : 9
sacrifice to the M., 62 : 16
sage daughters of M., 72 : 3
some say there are nine m., 63 : *n* 4
strength though of M. born, 475 : 13
Muses', I the M. priest sing, 107 : 25
touching all the M. charm, 100 : 10
Museum, British M. of infirmities, 626 : 18
modern man invents m. 834 : 4
Mushroom, supramundane m., 810 : 1
Music above all, 659 : 16
again when light dies, 900 : 13
air in m. wing forsakes, 637 : 15
and sweet poetry agree, 257 : 9
and the step, 920 : 9
and women I give way to, 310 : 2
arose with voluptuous swell, 457 : 14
bad m. people don't talk, 675 : 20
body swayed to m., 715 : 17
brandy of damned, 680 : 19

Music (*continued*)
breathing from her face, 295 : *n* 11
caught in that sensual m., 714 : 22
ceasing of exquisite m., 511 : 2
continuous and stationary m., 417 : 14
crept by me upon waters, 247 : 20
daughters of m. brought low, 27 : 24
deathless m., 728 : 6
die in m., 83 : *n* 1
don't know anything about m., 736 : 2
everyone should hear, 770 : 16
fading in m., 199 : 22
fingers on keys make m., 767 : 9
fled is that m., 477 : 3
food of love, 213 : *n* 2, 241 : 3
from blues American m., 733 : 14
from the spheres, 214 : 13
frozen m., 396 : 6
give children right to study m., 381 : 14
good to the melancholy, 308 : 19
grace and m. of her face, 295 : 21
hampering with ceremonies and m., 90 : 6
has charms to soothe, 324 : 14
heard so deeply, 808 : 8
heard with you more than m., 811 : 12
highest of fine arts, 579 : 15
his voice in all her m., 469 : 14
how potent cheap m. is, 843 : 10
how sour sweet m. is, 195 : 16
I care to hear, 655 : 18
I got m., 835 : 21
I heard with you, 811 : 12
I shall be made thy m., 254 : 17
if m. be the food of love, 213 : 7
in heart I bore, 426 : 6
in its roar, 458 : 24
in mourning, 35 : 34
in space, 396 : *n* 1
intolerable m. falls, 717 : 16
let m. creep in our ears, 201 : 1
like harmony in m., 423 : 18
like m. on the waters, 460 : 1
live without m., 609 : 13
madder m., 721 : 6
mads me, 195 : 18
make m. mute, 534 : 9
make one m. as before, 531 : 18
makes sweet m. with stones, 189 : 34
making of m. in rest, 573 : 6
man that has taste of m., 326 : 12
man that hath no m., 201 : 3
mind that can hear m., 797 : 20
ministers to human welfare, 579 : 15
mirth the m. of division, 173 : 1
moody food, 241 : 3
must investigate discord, 120 : 5
my rampart, 823 : 11
never merry when hear sweet m., 201 : 2
night filled with m., 510 : 22
no m. in a rest Katie, 573 : 6
no m. in nightingale, 190 : 2
noble dissolving m., 864 : 10
not for doctrine but m., 333 : 7
not listen to good m., 675 : 20
of dancing waves, 800 : 10
of flute, 806 : 2
of men's lives, 195 : 16
of poem as well as words, 735 : 7
of the spheres, 214 : *n* 1, 274 : 20

Music (*continued*)
of the Union, 485 : 1
of yonder pine, 92 : 12
oft hath such a charm, 229 : 1
on spirit make m. too, 767 : 9
one chord of m., 596 : 14
painting m. poetry, 579 : 11
poetry painting and m., 407 : 5
prefers live m. to humdrum spheres, 906 : 6
raise and quell, 305 : 10
reasonable good ear in m., 197 : 4
sap is the m., 852 : 14
say it with m., 802 : 7
sent up to God, 544 : 5
setting sun and m. at close, 194 : 10
shall untune the sky, 305 : 13
silence sank like m., 435 : 5
softest m. to attending ears, 192 : 17
soul of m. shed, 446 : 9
sphere-descended maid, 364 : 16
step to the m. he hears, 560 : 17
still sad m. of humanity, 423 : 13
stop da m., 825 : 16
Susanna's m., 767 : 11
sweet compulsion in m. lie, 277 : 16
that deepest reach, 495 : 17
that gentlier lies, 528 : 14
that will melt stars, 583 : 11
thing I love most, 310 : 5
thrush m. went, 749 : 7
to hear m. play, 935 : 5
to hear sea-maid's m., 196 : 14
true m. repeat thought of time, 842 : 3
universal language, 509 : 11
unreality and loud m., 894 : 5
untune the sky, 305 : 13
vibrations of deathless m., 728 : 6
we have m., 884 : 2
we play m., 884 : 6
when soft voices die, 469 : 18
wherever she goes, 931 : 11
wherever there is harmony, 274 : 20
why hearest thou m. sadly, 244 : 3
with silver sound, 917 : 17
yearning like a god, 476 : 10
you are m. while m. lasts, 808 : 8
your m. life you wasted, 850 : 18
Musical as bright Apollo's lute, 191 : 4
as is Apollo's lute, 279 : 25
mind like m. instrument, 580 : 4
most m. most melancholy, 278 : 17
most m. of mourners, 468 : 24
Shakespeare and the m. glasses, 369 : 14
shuttle, 575 : 17
so m. a discord, 197 : 8
Musically, so m. wells, 527 : 11
Musician must make music, 872 : 15
Music-makers, we are the m., 659 : 9
Music's, great m. unforgotten strain, 486 : *n* 1
melting fall, 363 : 13
power obey, 305 : 9
Musing there an hour alone, 461 : 4
while I was m. the fire burned, 18 : 30
Musique, de la m. avant toute chose, 659 : *n* 10
Musk, cankers in m. rose buds, 196 : 19
sweet m. roses and eglantine, 196 : 18
swirls of m., 665 : 7
Musket molds in his hands, 666 : 17
Muslim, I am a M., 904 : 16

Muslin, stretched with m., 835 : 1
Mussel, crow-blue m. shells, 798 : 9
Mussolini, even M. against war, 818 : 16
Must, die we m., 186 : 21
if we can we m., 691 : 20
shoot if you m., 513 : 18
thou m., 494 : 21
to greenwood go, 917 : 5
Mustard, beef without m., 655 : 16
heaven like to m. seed, 39 : 17
Johnson's conversation was m., 386 : 13
Muster many a score, 418 : 7
Mutabile, varium et m. femina, 105 : *n* 5
Mutability, chance death and m., 467 : 7
in large republics, 451 : 18
naught endure but m., 466 : 11
of language, 453 : 1
Mutable cloud, 496 : 17
rank-scented many, 242 : 17
Mute, by and by music m., 534 : 9
hangs as m., 446 : 9
inglorious Milton, 362 : 9
law stands m. in midst of arms, 98 : 5
Nature mourns worshiper, 430 : 8
soon m. however tuneful, 442 : 19
unchanged to hoarse or m., 286 : 28
Mutilate, do not fold spindle or m., 925 : 11
Mutilators of collections, 441 : 18
Mutine in matron's bones, 223 : 5
Mutinous and quarrelsome, 348 : 21
Shannon waves, 777 : 16
Mutiny, move stones of Rome to m., 216 : 29
Mutter, blessed m. of Mass, 541 : 20
unmentionable thoughts, 571 : 11
Mutual aid law of animal life, 651 : 7
and partaken bliss, 279 : 31
bunched in m. glee, 844 : 1
confidence, 737 : 8
envy of the living, 264 : 19
guarantees of independence, 682 : 15
in marriage dependence m., 471 : 1
incomprehension, 865 : 17
inflamed with m. animosity, 398 : 2
meet m. heart, 345 : 18
prevention of m. crime, 88 : 5
succeed if surrender m., 885 : 15
My Lord what a morning, 936 : 1
My-doxy, orthodoxy m., 473 : 19
Myriad laughter of ocean waves, 70 : 23
there died a m., 792 : 16
Myriad-minded Shakespeare, 437 : 20
Myriads of rivulets hurrying, 531 : 13
Myrrh, gold and frankincense and m., 36 : 21
Myrtle and ivy of two-and-twenty, 462 : 6
land where cypress and m., 459 : 5
laurel and m. and rose, 395 : 3
Myrtles brown, 280 : 6
once more ye m., 280 : 6
which a grove of m. made, 257 : 6
Myself, all by m., 149 : 1
am hell, 285 : 12
answer questions about m., 863 : 9
awe of such thing as m., 215 : 4
coming down shift for m., 155 : 9
commanded by boy's mother, 70 : 15
feel it so like m., 882 : 3
first glass for m., 326 : 18

Myself (*continued*)
garden city and m., 865 : 7
hell within m., 274 : 15
his only son m., 366 : 10
I am m. and what is around me, 784 : 4
I celebrate m., 574 : 11
I contradict m., 575 : 2
I live I let m. live, 843 : 7
I live not in m., 457 : 28
I m. am hell, 893 : 7
I owe my fame to m., 275 : 29
I pray for no man but m., 243 : 1
I was at last becoming m., 865 : 13
it is m. I portray, 164 : 5
it is m. I remake, 713 : 4
know all except m., 150 : 11
monstrosity and miracle m., 166 : 5
must I remake, 717 : 10
not disappoint m., 557 : 20
not least honored of all, 529 : 8
not talk so much about m., 558 : 26
quite m. again, 691 : 2
sacred duty to m., 599 : 12
that favorit subject m., 385 : 15
this man shall be m., 359 : 2
understanding of m., 599 : 11
unwitting where Master dwells, 760 : 21
when I give I give m., 574 : 26
when young, 516 : 16
with yesterday's years, 516 : 13
Mysteries are revealed unto the meek, 34 : 25
lie beyond thy dust, 299 : 9
love's m. in souls grow, 253 : 8
mystery of m., 432 : 5
power in m. of thought, 76 : 12
talk of m., 557 : 21
wingy m. in divinity, 274 : 3
Mysterious, beauty m. as well as terrible, 582 : 1
by this love, 252 : 11
God moves in m. way, 375 : 16
God works in m. way, 804 : 20
independent variable, 595 : 18
law true source, 286 : 5
O m. priest, 477 : 9
past of sea, 869 : 13
source of art and science, 763 : 6
thing in soul, 571 : 11
union with native sea, 428 : 15
Mystery, a voice a m., 427 : 2
at movies the only modern m., 834 : 14
beauty is a m., 790 : 17
blessings of Great M., 726 : 8
burthen of the m., 423 : 10
creeds new names for m., 646 : 4
I had m., 827 : 7
I show you a m., 49 : 7
in m. soul abides, 584 : 18
inexplicable m. of sound, 808 : 19
inside enigma, 743 : 17
is that we deny our nothingness, 853 : 3
let others probe m., 875 : 3
lose myself in a m., 274 : 4
miracle m. authority, 582 : 7
no antiquity no m., 504 : 2
now comes the m., 551 : 13
now tongue the m. telling, 139 : *n* 6
of beauty, 711 : 14

Mystery (*continued*)
of having been moved by words, 887 : 7
of life, 464 : 7
of mysteries, 432 : 5
of the atom, 825 : 1
of things, 235 : 12
on bestial floor, 713 : 13
path to deepest m., 853 : 8
pluck out heart of my m., 222 : 18
riddle wrapped in m., 743 : 17
sea wrapped in m., 683 : 14
sense of m., 683 : 3
sweet m. about sea, 571 : 3
threshold of last m., 864 : 7
ultimate m. works sadly, 649 : 10
whole m. of beauty, 711 : 14
you must not touch, 253 : 11
Mystic chords of memory, 521 : 14
fabric sprung, 377 : *n* 5
too full of God, 711 : 16
walk your m. way, 628 : 6
wonderful, 534 : 4
Mystical, gives me m. lore, 443 : 14
Mystics, scientists artists and m., 888 : 1
Mystique, feminine m., 898 : 7
Myth, master m. of cold war, 862 : 20
Mythical, reasonable man m., 815 : 17
Mythologies, embroideries out of old m., 713 : 14
Myths, policies based on m., 862 : 16
rationalized m. not destroyed m., 885 : 16
that actually touched you, 911 : 5

N

Nächte, wer nie die kummervollen N., 395 : *n* 2
Naebody, I care for n., 382 : *n* 4
Nag, bobtail n., 598 : 2
forced gait of shuffling n., 204 : 14
Naiad airs brought me home, 525 : 9
guardian N. of strand, 431 : 6
torn n. from flood, 525 : 7
Naïf, judges n. simple-minded, 644 : 16
Nail, Dick the shepherd blows his n., 191 : 14
fasten him as a n., 30 : 3
for want of n. shoe lost, 270 : 4, 347 : 35
hit n. on head, 161 : 16
Jail smote n. into his temples, 12 : 2
parted from others as n. from flesh, 137 : 4
taller by breadth of n., 322 : 10
Nailed colors to the mast, 430 : 14
for our advantage, 202 : 22
Nails, blind as n. upon Cross, 801 : 6
come near your beauty with n., 185 : 10
fastened by masters, 27 : 26
hard as n., 547 : 1
sellin' tinpinny n., 722 : 5
with broad flat n., 86 : 10
with n. he'll dig them up again, 262 : 4
Naître, la peine de n., 378 : *n* 6
Naive, dare to be n., 832 : 15
domestic Burgundy, 831 : 4
Naked, all are n., 799 : 2

Naked (*continued*)
and he clothed him, 367 : 3
and ye clothed me, 40 : 33
as a worm was she, 144 : 4
bedizened or stark n., 799 : 6
born n. and falls a-whining, 116 : *n* 4
came I out, 15 : 4
cast n. upon n. earth, 116 : 7
clad in n. majesty, 285 : 17
clothe my n. villainy, 187 : 6
enterprise in walking n., 713 : 14
every day he clad, 369 : 16
facts drop cloak stand forth n., 183 : 2
he who wears morality better n., 782 : 19
helpless n. piping loud, 405 : 12
ignorance, 534 : 10
in death on unknown shore, 105 : 13
in n. beauty more adorned, 286 : 3
lash the rascals n., 232 : 6
man in book of moons, 918 : 11
melancholy isles, 345 : 15
newborn child, 394 : 3
outcries call me from n. bed, 176 : 21
pity like n. newborn babe, 236 : 24
poor mangled peace, 208 : 16
poor n. wretches, 234 : 3
print of n. foot, 318 : 14
pure as n. heavens, 425 : 23
shall he return, 27 : 2
shall I return thither, 15 : 4
shingles of the world, 587 : 16
soul cowers n., 791 : 3
soul of Tomlinson, 708 : 17
soul pale stiff and n., 123 : 15
starving hysterical n., 906 : 1
summer night, 574 : 19
they were both n., 7 : 4
though locked in steel, 185 : 17
to go n. best disguise, 324 : 9
to mine enemies, 249 : 9
to naked goes, 717 : 1
truth is I have no shirt, 191 : 11
truths, 478 : 5
wallow n. in December snow, 194 : 7
with n. foot stalking my chamber, 161 : 25
woods, 471 : 10
Nakedness all joys are due to thee, 254 : 3
dance that ends in n., 850 : 9
dogs shame n. of old man, 59 : 6
feeling in all its n., 484 : 13
not in utter n., 426 : 14
of woman work of God, 404 : 3
toil hunger n., 481 : 2
Namby Pamby's little rhymes, 331 : 4
Name, acclaim your glorious n., 829 : 5
age without a n., 375 : 1
at which world grew pale, 351 : 19
become a lost n., 883 : 9
behind hands that wove, 808 : 15
bless his n., 21 : 3
blessed be the n. of the Lord, 15 : 4
blot out his n., 53 : 4
blushes at the n., 592 : 2
breathe not his n., 446 : 7
builds his n., 331 : 16
call his n. Immanuel, 29 : 13
call it by better n., 447 : 11
called his wife's n. Eve, 7 : 12
cannon his n., 601 : 12
cometh in the n. of the Lord, 22 : 1
crimes committed in thy n., 400 : 14

Name (*continued*)
deed without a n., 239 : 9
each heart recalled a n., 596 : 17
established n. an estate, 525 : 8
express my n. my virginity, 164 : 3
faith under another n., 859 : 13
fame nothing but empty n., 375 : 10
filches my good n., 230 : 33
foolish whistling of a n., 295 : 16
forever sad forever dear, 334 : 26
forget my own n., 169 : 22
frailty thy n. is woman, 218 : 9
game in which my n. was, 789 : 10
gathered in thy N., 55 : 8
gathered together in my n., 40 : 3
George Brush is my n., 839 : 11
give each figure living n., 894 : 11
give n. to every fixed star, 190 : 12
glory and nothing of n., 459 : 17
good n. better than precious ointment, 27 : 3
good n. better than riches, 110 : *n* 14
good n. in man and woman, 230 : 33
good n. is rather to be chosen, 24 : 34
good n. like precious ointment, 180 : 11
great in story, 462 : 6
greatness of n. overwhelms son, 257 : 2
hallowed be thy n., 37 : 15
his n. shall endure forever, 20 : 2
holla your n. to hills, 213 : 19
honor and greatness of his n., 249 : 18
hopes no more change n., 427 : 14
how excellent is thy n., 17 : 18
I have forgotten your n., 634 : 3
if there be n. more free, 335 : 2
illustrious and revered, 118 : 12
incompatible things same n., 523 : 7
is Might-have-been, 601 : 20
is on your waters, 465 : 5
is The Invisible Inaudible Subtle, 64 : 6
is Truthful James, 630 : 13
king's n. a tower of strength, 187 : 25
knew thy face or n., 252 : 20
lashed vice spared n., 322 : 19
leave a living n., 262 : 11
led all the rest, 454 : 7
left a n. behind them, 36 : 11
lesser than my n., 195 : 5
liveth forevermore, 36 : 12
local habitation and n., 197 : 12
Lord blot out his n., 308 : *n* 2
Lord's n. is to be praised, 21 : 20
lose the n. of action, 221 : 12
lost her honest n., 924 : 10
love unfamiliar N., 808 : 15
magic of a n., 443 : 6
marched by king's n., 822 : 2
murder takes specious n., 330 : 1
my n. and memory I leave, 181 : 16
my n. endure for eternity, 5 : 1
my n. is Legion, 42 : 4
my n. is MacGregor, 431 : 27
my n. joined to theirs, 113 : 13
my n. survives me, 93 : 2
my 'oss my wife my n., 500 : 21
nature but n. for effect, 377 : 16
no n. of magistrate, 247 : 26
no profit but the n., 223 : 16
not the eternal n., 63 : 12
object take away pleasure of poem, 651 : 16

Name (*continued*)
of friendless n. the friend, 356 : 24
of God upon lips, 358 : 19
of late deceased, 707 : 20
of one was Obstinate, 301 : 21
of scorn, 534 : 25
of the beast, 53 : 21
of the Lord thy God in vain, 10 : 5
of the star is Wormwood, 53 : 17
of the wicked shall rot, 23 : 22
of which echo faint, 442 : 19
our n. not become extinct, 603 : 1
owl calls n. of man to die, 852 : 16
proud his n., 430 : 10
refuse thy n., 192 : 5
right to sign my n., 704 : *n* 2
rose by any n. as sweet, 192 : 6
rouse at n. of Crispian, 208 : 10
Sacco's n. live, 811 : 9
sad bad brother's n., 634 : 11
see n. in print, 456 : 12
shadow of glorious n., 118 : 6
shall be called Wonderful, 29 : 16
shall live behind me, 225 : 1
sing praises to his N., 918 : 19
single nature's double n., 225 : 30
so long shall your n. endure, 104 : 29
something I cannot n., 759 : 13
somewhere a rare n., 82 : 10
Strait forever bear his n., 162 : 11
sun bear no n., 768 : 10
synonym for devil, 153 : *n* 5
teach but to n. tools, 290 : 19
tell one's n. livelong June, 604 : 19
that can be named, 63 : 12
that will not perish, 440 : 7
thy n. shall be Abraham, 8 : 10
to all ages cursed, 303 : 20
weak witness of thy n., 277 : 13
what a wounded n., 225 : 1
what n. Achilles assumed, 275 : 5
what the dickens his n. is, 225 : 19
what thy lordly n. is, 526 : 15
what's in a n., 192 : 6
whispering still her n., 733 : 1
whistling of n., 337 : 15
woman's n. in print twice, 789 : 3
writ in water, 480 : 7
writing is a n. for conversation, 360 : 5
Named, a-tiptoe when day n., 208 : 10
birds without gun, 494 : 14
constitution n. a democracy, 80 : 17
is mother of all things, 63 : 12
thee but to praise, 464 : 11
you n. him not I, 312 : 7
Nameless abyss, 593 : 11
battle overseas, 728 : 13
deed, 416 : 11
the N. is the origin, 63 : 12
unremembered acts, 423 : 9
Name's, for his n. sake, 18 : 7
hated for my n. sake, 39 : 1
Names, American n., 840 : 2
bears greatest n., 289 : 2
call things by right n., 416 : 6
called him soft n., 476 : 28
calleth them all by their n., 22 : 24
commodity of good n., 202 : 30
covered up our n., 605 : 14
different n. after they are produced, 63 : 12
down their chiseled n., 642 : 4
fools' n. like fools' faces, 920 : 5

Names (*continued*)
gossip without real n., 861 : 11
great n. as these, 922 : 10
incompatible n., 523 : 7
judge of authors' n., 333 : 12
listed n. of Kings, 840 : 17
never allow n. mentioned, 440 : 22
new-made honor forget men's n., 201 : 9
not born to die, 464 : 13
of those who fought for life, 876 : 15
old homes old n., 726 : 2
sharp n. never fat, 840 : 2
their botany Latin n., 494 : 12
tongues that syllable men's n., 279 : 16
two most sacred n., 295 : 18
unpopular n. impossible loyalties, 587 : 1
What and Why and When, 710 : 2
whom love of God blessed, 454 : 7
written in letters of gold, 157 : 4
Nan, such mistress such N., 163 : 3
Nancy, mate of N. brig, 627 : 7
Nane sall ken where he is gane, 927 : 5
Nankin, old books old N. blue, 179 : *n* 4
Nantucket, sandhills of N., 571 : 8
Nantucketer, at nightfall the N., 570 : 7
Napoleon, ashes of N. Bonaparte, 421 : 15
celebrities such as N., 615 : 14
mighty somnambulist, 491 : 17
sole obstacle to peace, 420 : 14
without selfishness, 591 : 11
Napping, nodded nearly n., 526 : 10
Narcissus, deeper meaning of N., 570 : 4
Narcotics alcohol and Christianity, 658 : 9
hospital tray of n., 887 : 10
numbing pain, 531 : 21
two great European n., 658 : 9
Narrative as whole untrue, 592 : 7
motive in this n., 623 : 19
Narrator imbue self with the time, 592 : 7
Narrow, across n. beach we flit, 621 : 17
bestride the n. world, 215 : 6
convent's n. room, 427 : 28
creep into n. bed, 588 : 1
dogmatisms, 653 : 4
every bed is n., 823 : 2
fellow in the grass, 606 : 13
honor in strait so n., 226 : 18
in n. cell forever laid, 361 : 23
into its n. shed, 714 : 6
is the way, 38 : 15
measure spans, 692 : 6
track to highest good, 101 : 11
two n. words Hic jacet, 173 : 4
Narrowed his mind, 371 : 14
Narrowing lust of gold, 532 : 23
Narrow-mindedness, superior man will not manifest n., 89 : 3
Narrow-necked bottles, 340 : 11
Narrow-souled people, 340 : 11
Narvous, I have been rather n., 478 : *n* 3
Nascitur, poeta n. non fit, 123 : *n* 15
Nashville drizzle, 699 : 16
Nassau, can Bourbon or N. claim higher, 321 : 2
Nastiest thing in nicest way, 797 : 8
Nastily, live meanly and n., 310 : 11

Nasty brutish and short, 264 : 17
man of n. ideas, 322 : 5
not n. dirty hole, 824 : 3
only man has n. mind, 626 : 10
sin recognized keeps us n., 856 : 18
something n. in woodshed, 854 : 7
Natal, Rome n. neath my consulship, 99 : 2
Natchez, belle of old N., 856 : 2
Nathan, Mencken N. and God, 775 : 14
Nation acts like helpless giant, 882 : 23
America only idealistic n., 682 : 16
America's my n., 839 : 11
as Maine so goes n., 923 : 3
authority n. cannot control, 616 : 1
better one suffer than n. grieve, 304 : 8
blessed above all, 650 : 14
blood of n. never shed, 316 : 14
conceived in liberty, 523 : 4
consider national what is true, 484 : 4
darlings of our n., 229 : 22
diversity of opinion basic to n., 825 : 12
fate of n. in own power, 489 : 12
fate of n. riding, 512 : 8
favors from n. to n., 379 : 14
from single crime know n., 104 : 33
Germany a n. a race, 483 : 18
God hath sifted a n., 307 : 11
greatness of British n., 326 : 22
grown-up n., 860 : 3
guarantees maintenance of citizen, 665 : 17
hardly yet a n., 793 : 11
has government it deserves, 400 : 2
haughty n. proud in arms, 279 : 5
hoop of n., 701 : 8
Horse n., 928 : 12
ignorant and free, 389 : 11
in Japan civilized n., 617 : 8
institutions create n., 502 : 7
is territory people laws, 522 : 10
judged by best not worst, 733 : 8
light shone to whole n., 265 : 13
like pitiful giant 882 : 23
literature memory of n., 895 : 20
look beyond n. and race, 894 : 15
make all ballads of n., 317 : 17
middle class in America the n., 589 : 8
most important element in n., 89 : 28
moving toward two societies, 872 : 14
never abandon fate, 616 : 1
no n. greater than any other, 820 : 10
no n. ruined by trade, 348 : 12
no single n. have monopoly, 787 : 15
not flag only but n., 551 : 11
not only Latin-American n., 905 : 19
of brutes, 683 : *n* 5
of freemen, 519 : 22
of shopkeepers, 359 : *n* 4, 366 : 6
of sovereign states, 725 : 20
once to every man and n., 567 : 6
one n. evermore, 518 : 15
one n. under God, 677 : 10
one-third of a n., 780 : 2
paramount question for n., 556 : 9
perpetually to be conquered, 372 : 16
plant a n., 261 : 23
preserved us a n., 446 : 2
prosperity of n., 687 : 15
publish it to all the n., 320 : 26
puissant n., 282 : 3
Nation (*continued*)
responsible for state, 616 : 1
righteousness exalteth a n., 24 : 4
rise against nation, 40 : 22
secure only while honest, 556 : 13
serve my n. ruin another, 341 : 10
shall not lift up sword, 28 : 31
shopkeeping n., 359 : 9
small one become a strong n., 31 : 24
so conceived so dedicated, 523 : 4
social prosperity means n. great, 491 : 25
spirit part of my n., 790 : 21
stride upward concerted by men, 672 : 2
supports Wall Street, 722 : 13
tardy apish n., 194 : 11
territory not make n., 596 : 4
that that n. might live, 523 : 4
this n. under God, 523 : 4
too great for revenge, 609 : 9
trick of our English n., 206 : 3
truths which can kill n., 777 : 4
values anything more than freedom, 751 : 20
we are here by will of n., 397 : 20
we are n. building, 797 : 7
we are n. of differences, 903 : 11
what it can do for n., 890 : *n* 3
when chips down n. acts helpless, 882 : 23
which enjoys most freedom most powerful, 418 : 3
which keepeth the truth, 30 : 9
will survive, 726 : 12
worthy of mighty n., 836 : 3
National, colossal n. lie, 625 : 24
compass of n. authority, 402 : 1
consciousness, 682 : 4
debt national blessing, 401 : 10, 450 : 12
don't call out N. Guard, 787 : 11
great poetry result of n. spirit, 577 : 13
honor is national property, 407 : 18
injustice national downfall, 517 : 20
lie, 625 : 24
motto Root hog, 847 : 12
nightmare over, 882 : 15
rock of n. resources, 451 : 1
stain washed clean, 815 : 9
there is n. flag, 539 : 3
Nationalism, orthodox in n., 821 : 6
philosophy of black n., 904 : 14
Nationalities, squabbling n., 688 : 1
Nationality, true n. mankind, 720 : 4
Nation's, bind up n. wounds, 524 : 7
freight handler, 761 : 4
hoop, 701 : 9
law embodies n. development, 643 : 15
memory and veneration, 761 : 1
read history in n. eyes, 362 : 10
spirit die of inanition, 586 : 23
ultimate judicial tribunal, 777 : 1
Nations abandon use of force, 781 : 9
advanced n. navigate most, 499 : 8
all n. and kindreds, 53 : 14
all n. gathered, 40 : 32
all n. have left is work, 758 : 1
all n. one blood, 46 : 16
animals are other n., 802 : 18
are as a drop of a bucket, 30 : 36
are destroyed or flourish, 407 : 5
Nations (*continued*)
association of n., 682 : 15
astonishment among all n., 11 : 19
be and make new n., 249 : 18
Becky Sharp's remark application to n., 596 : 2
belong to other n., 627 : 18
books inheritance of n., 559 : 31
breathes of n. saved, 461 : 20
cheap defense of n., 373 : 23
day of small n. past, 627 : 6
dwelling in safety, 781 : 8
eclipsed gaiety of n., 353 : 1
Egypt and Israel, 881 : 15
equal right of n., 788 : 20
Europe prison of n., 766 : 9
father of many n., 8 : 10
fierce contending n., 326 : 5
foreign n. and the next age, 181 : 16
free n. and free men, 891 : 5
general association of n., 682 : 15
get better of other n., 854 : 1
go and teach all n., 41 : 30
great n. not boasters, 498 : 21
great when ideal higher, 586 : 17
happiest n. have no history, 565 : 18
health of n. more important, 789 : 13
individuals of all n. melted into new race, 382 : 8
intercourse with foreign n., 445 : 19
joyful all ye n. rise, 350 : 15
justice toward all n., 379 : 12
kept alive by program, 784 : 7
large and small, 788 : 20
law of nature and n., 373 : 18
like men have infancy, 329 : 3
listen ye n. and be dumb, 475 : 8
make enemies of n., 376 : 19
money language n. understand, 312 : 16
Niobe of n., 458 : 16
not kings but n., 449 : 2
other n. step aside, 518 : 9
ourselves and all n., 524 : 7
peace-loving n., 780 : 4
prison of n., 766 : *n* 3
rights of small n., 682 : 13
rule n. under law, 105 : 24
safeguards acceptable to all n., 787 : 16
science and relations between n., 814 : 13
sea that unitest n., 575 : 22
service fairer than other n., 136 : 3
shall rush like many waters, 29 : 24
some n. increase others diminish, 100 : 15
sovereign n. with power, 763 : 13
stand aside from troika, 582 : 12
sword united n. drew, 457 : 21
teaching n. how to live, 281 : 17
tempted to violate agreements, 780 : 4
touches heart of n., 502 : 5
twilight sheds on half the n., 283 : 24
two n. the rich and poor, 501 : 18
united n., 457 : 21
wake n. underground, 936 : 2
wars and alarums unto n., 174 : 7
which threaten aggression, 781 : 9
world doth two n. bear, 297 : 5
write autobiographies, 573 : 11
Nations' airy navies, 529 : 24
Native, breathe his n. air, 332 : 10

Native (*continued*)
fast by their n. shore, 377 : 19
foot on my n. heath, 431 : 27
goodwill complacency, 703 : 19
his own n. shore, 525 : 9
hue of resolution, 221 : 12
I am a n. in this world, 767 : 18
land good night, 457 : 1
loss of n. land, 76 : 17
metal of man tested, 568 : 17
my own my n. land, 430 : 10
nobility more than is n., 230 : 15
one n. charm, 370 : 15
personality endows man, 577 : 2
strong n. states, 800 : 4
think as n. thinks, 767 : 18
though I am n. here, 219 : 9
true n. of America, 348 : 13
union with n. sea, 428 : 15
violet of n. land, 531 : 22
western manliness, 577 : 3
with n. honor clad, 285 : 17
wood-notes wild, 278 : 6
Natives of rain rainy men, 766 : 19
sovereignty resides in n., 416 : 17
Nativity, in n. chance or death, 225 : 28
out of love with your n., 212 : 20
Natura, divina n. dedit agros, 97 : *n* 10
il fece e poi ruppe la stampa, 154 : *n* 4
non facit saltum, 652 : 1
non facit saltus, 350 : *n* 2
si n. negat facit indignatio versum, 121 : *n* 5
Natural, act against n. equity, 367 : 9
ancient and n. strength, 365 : 16
and moral forces, 584 : 1
and varied abundance, 824 : 12
aristocracy among men, 389 : 8
balance of n. elements, 672 : 14
belief in particular n. law, 856 : 15
bodily form from n. thing, 715 : 3
chapters to n. end, 664 : 8
children kind and n., 207 : 11
desire to appear n., 294 : 8
destroy n. resources, 687 : 14
essential rights, 387 : *n* 4
extinguishes n. candle, 314 : 19
fact symbol of spiritual, 496 : 6
fear increased with tales, 180 : 2
find out n. bent, 85 : 1
hoary establishment beyond n. date, 414 : 16
home life not n., 680 : 31
I do it more n., 213 : 24
improver of n. knowledge, 595 : 10
in n. science nothing petty, 565 : 15
is higher living worth cost in things n., 795 : 9
killing for food not n., 786 : 8
large as life twice as n., 613 : 17
law is old nonsense, 453 : 14
liberty establishes itself, 366 : 8
lose n. kindness, 714 : 15
man has two passions, 664 : 13
manure, 388 : 7
my ordinary n. fashion, 164 : 5
my religion is n. religion, 904 : 16
no such thing as n. law, 453 : 14
order in swampland, 873 : 9
phenomena subject to causation, 617 : 11
philosophy deep moral grave, 181 : 14

Natural (*continued*)
philosophy embodied in mathematical beauty, 696 : 5
piety, 425 : 7
price of labor, 438 : 13
propensities, 374 : 7
revolution n., 538 : 11
right to use pens, 343 : 20
science involves three things, 390 : 7
science knowledge of causes, 465 : 12
sciences never reach aim, 594 : 12
selection, 514 : 14, 579 : 20
simple affecting, 371 : 18
skilled poet through n. gift, 71 : 24
something more than n., 220 : 30
study n. history, 381 : 14
thousand n. shocks, 221 : 12
thus n. thus brief is grief, 812 : 3
to indulge in illusions, 383 : 1
to please, 303 : 18
treating psychology like n. science, 651 : 5
treatise of n. education, 358 : 23
uninstructed in n. history, 595 : 6
wants the n. touch, 239 : 17
wealth and beauty, 890 : 13
what is n. is need, 453 : 14
Naturalist, Goldsmith poet n., 355 : 23
Naturalists, so n. observe a flea, 322 : 21
Naturalized, flag of man n. yesterday, 667 : 2
people n. in U.S., 392 : 4
Naturam, contra n., 793 : 2
Naturamque sequi, 118 : *n* 7
Nature's discipline enjoins mutual help, 848 : 1
Nature a grave, 483 : 5
a kind parent, 116 : 6
a merciless stepmother, 116 : 6
abhors a vacuum, 308 : 4
abhors the old, 497 : 27
above man's aims his n., 610 : 8
accuse not N., 287 : 9
acquisitions by n., 393 : 7
adherence to truth of n., 437 : 14
against process of n., 147 : 31
against the use of n., 236 : 11
agent and patient at once, 87 : 5
all n. seems at work, 436 : 9
all N. wears one grin, 349 : 4
all the powers of n., 497 : 12
allow not n. more, 233 : 21
alter human n., 695 : 14
always does contrive, 628 : 23
always hinting at us, 750 : 5
an experiencing n., 597 : 6
and books belong to eyes, 498 : 4
and civilization literary field, 652 : 4
and Nature's God, 329 : 5
and Nature's laws hid, 340 : 6
art imitates n., 117 : *n* 6
art imitation of n., 114 : 26
art mediatress between n. and man, 437 : 22
assures being-forever, 866 : 6
at ease in n., 573 : 21
be your teacher, 423 : 6
beats in tune, 494 : 6
begins to recognize itself, 875 : 7
beings which compose n., 397 : 17
better angels of our n., 521 : 14
beyond n. of normal man, 312 : 20
binding N. fast in fate, 340 : 2
bit of human n. revolting, 597 : 8

Nature (*continued*)
body N. God soul, 336 : 21
book of N., 168 : *n* 2
book of n., 301 : 11
but name for effect, 377 : 16
by a rule in n. teach, 207 : 6
by her mother wit, 174 : 1
by n. all alike, 259 : 9
by n. men nearly alike, 69 : 18
by n. wise, 262 : 12
by viewing N., 303 : 4
called mother, 483 : 5
cannot miss, 307 : 4
change stamp of n., 223 : 11
child of n., 427 : 18
common goal of n., 884 : 2
compunctious visitings of n., 236 : 17
constant in N. inconstancy, 295 : 6
could no further go, 306 : 1
course of N. art of God, 274 : *n* 3
custom almost second n., 190 : *n* 1
dear Child of N., 427 : 18
death a secret of N., 124 : 15
death one of things N. wills, 125 : 15
death ugly fact n. hides, 609 : 3
description of n., 789 : 2
diseased n. breaks forth, 204 : 10
disguise fair n., 207 : 16
divine n. gave us country, 97 : 14
does not depend on us, 832 : 19
does not make leap, 652 : *n* 1
does nothing uselessly, 87 : 27
drive out N. with a pitchfork, 109 : 4
education in laws of N., 595 : 14
enough till human nature came, 607 : 5
equals stupidity of man, 785 : 14
excelling n., 232 : 14
exposed to method of questioning, 853 : 1
falls into revolt, 206 : 30
fear thy n., 236 : 16
finest spectacles in n., 348 : 4
finest woman in n., 327 : 10
fits all her children, 567 : 19
follow n., 118 : 8
fools of n., 219 : 12
force in n. not increased, 583 : 21
forces by which n. animated, 397 : 17
forces in n., 594 : 12
fortress built by N. for herself, 194 : 13
foster-nurse of n., 234 : 27
frame of N. break, 325 : 11
framed in prodigality of n., 187 : 4
free as N. first made man, 303 : 8
friend masterpiece of n., 497 : 19
fruit your seasons bring N., 124 : 19
full of designs, 650 : 4
full of genius full of divinity, 557 : 15
full of good n. as egg of meat, 193 : *n* 2
generous n. take own way, 372 : 15
good n. agreeable in conversation, 326 : 17
grandest works of N., 776 : 9
habits form second n., 393 : 8
had gone tranquilly on, 732 : 2
happiness depends as N. shows, 375 : 18
happiness of retired n., 326 : 10
happy N. to explore, 337 : 6
has all kinds of models, 832 : 9
has coordinate system, 832 : 9

Nature (*continued*)
hath framed strange fellows, 197 : 26
he is great who is from n., 498 : 12
he of calm and happy n., 84 : 4
heaven and n. sing, 328 : 13
her custom holds, 224 : 4
her masterpiece designed, 410 : 16
highest type of human n., 579 : 21
highly developed moral n., 597 : 8
hints and half-truths, 630 : 24
hold mirror up to n., 222 : 2
human n. changes, 676 : 4
human n. made arrogant by consideration, 81 : 7
human n. not change, 524 : 2
I fear thy n., 236 : 16
I feel the link of n., 287 : 23
I loved, 443 : 1
if n. conquers, 413 : 22
imagination one of forces of n., 769 : 26
impartiality of N. best, 631 : 5
in her inventions, 152 : 12
in love of n. holds, 471 : 2
in n. few sharp lines, 905 : 10
in n. no rewards, 615 : 11
in our life n. live, 435 : 26
in perfect n. no distinction of kind, 90 : 7
in state of war by n., 322 : 20
in terms of cylinder sphere cone, 638 : 3
in you stands on verge, 233 : 19
Indian unconstrained in N., 557 : 4
inexorability of law of n., 562 : 19
insight into universal n., 420 : 3
is but art unknown, 337 : 1
is the art of God, 274 : 7
is there any cause in n., 234 : 16
is wont to hide herself, 69 : 27
kindly bent to ease us, 294 : *n* 4
knowledge of human n., 440 : 29, 635 : 1
knows her business better than we do, 166 : 10
law of n. and nations, 373 : 18
laws of n. and nature's God, 387 : 9
laws which mind put into n., 776 : 6
learned to look on n., 423 : 13
let children walk with n., 637 : 17
liberty taken with n., 636 : 1
lies within something of another n., 902 : 12
like us sometimes caught, 606 : 19
limited n. infinite desires, 464 : 16
link of n., 287 : 23
little we see in n., 427 : 29
living in agreement with n., 91 : 19
living n. not art, 490 : 9
looks through N. up, 337 : 16
losses wrought by n., 393 : 7
lost their original n., 90 : 6
loyal n. noble mind, 534 : 21
lusty stealth of n., 233 : 3
made a pause, 330 : 6
made him then broke mold, 154 : 11
made one with n., 469 : 14
made thee to temper man, 317 : 2
makes fool she means it, 561 : 15
man as n. made him, 359 : 2
man by n. political animal, 87 : 26
man endow n. with soul, 679 : 5
man explorer of n., 870 : 14
man's efforts to control n., 814 : 12

Nature (*continued*)
means God of N. placed in our power, 383 : 3
men by n. desire knowledge, 87 : 9
men by n. equally free, 367 : 4
might stand up and say, 217 : 14
mind cut from n. loses life, 448 : 6
mingling its n. with n. of things, 179 : 9
mistress and guardian of n., 152 : 11
modesty of n., 222 : 1
more than n. needs, 233 : 21
mortal n. did tremble, 426 : 18
mourns her worshipper, 430 : 8
muse on n. with poet's eye, 443 : 7
must obey necessity, 217 : 7
mutable cloud, 496 : 17
my n. is subdued, 245 : 17
my Treatise of Human N., 357 : 18
nearness to n. keeps spirit sensitive, 686 : 8
needed not books to read N., 303 : 6
neutral, 851 : 15
never deceives us, 358 : 22
never did betray, 423 : 15
never makes blunders, 561 : 15
never stale, 861 : 17
never wears mean appearance, 496 : 3
no arrogant wonders of n., 518 : 8
no chance of understanding n., 639 : 13
no part N. has not touched, 125 : 24
no such thing in n., 289 : *n* 6
noble and incapable of deceit, 432 : 12
noble n. poetically gifted, 586 : 16
not from philosophers but n., 260 : 9
not man less but n. more, 458 : 24
not proceed by leaps, 350 : 6
nothing at prompting of n. but weep, 116 : 9
nothing in n. without purpose, 509 : 4
O N. O soul of man, 570 : 15
observer of human n., 546 : 11
of desire not to be satisfied, 88 : 1
of mind mortal, 101 : 2
of the thing, 906 : 9
often hidden, 181 : 4
once out of n., 715 : 3
one and continuous, 558 : 20
one touch of n., 226 : 20
outrage when man destroys n., 758 : 2
owes me another existence, 396 : 5
paints best part, 495 : *n* 2
passing through n. to eternity, 218 : 1
passion could not shake, 231 : 26
pattern of excelling n., 232 : 14
peevish N., 320 : 16
pictures science draws of n., 758 : 9
poets by n. we love, 499 : 21
principles of human n., 453 : 1
progress part of n., 579 : 5
recover hair bald by n., 188 : 3
red in tooth and claw, 532 : 13
reduce problems of n. to numbers, 610 : 1
reduction of n. to mechanics, 594 : 12
remains, 577 : 6
renews annual round untired, 758 : 2
rest in N. not God, 269 : 1
reverence human n., 448 : 3
rich with spoils of n., 274 : 5
rules of game laws of n., 595 : 12

Nature (*continued*)
said lovelier flower, 424 : 13
science of N., 311 : 1
science right interpretation of n., 471 : 15
secret aims of n., 654 : 14
secret of study of n., 504 : 17
secretaries of N., 271 : 16
secretary of N., 271 : 15
seems dead, 237 : 14
sighing through her works, 287 : 19
silent energy of n., 490 : 3
simple n. to his hope given, 336 : 16
simple news n. told, 605 : 12
sloping to southern side, 568 : 24
so priketh n. in hir corages, 145 : 13
sociability law of n., 651 : 7
some made coxcombs n. meant fools, 332 : 17
something marvelous in all n., 87 : 8
soul and n., 703 : 6
speaks in symbols, 513 : 13
such stupidity not in N., 354 : 14
suffers n. of insurrection, 215 : 18
sullenness against N., 281 : 21
superior powers direct n., 673 : 2
supplier of alphabet, 571 : 13
swears lovely dears, 409 : 15
teaches beasts to know friends, 242 : 11
teaches more than preaches, 631 : 3
tendency of man's n. to good, 89 : 18
that framed us, 183 : 6
things rank and gross in n., 218 : 6
think of our life in n., 557 : 21
thou and n. so gently part, 242 : 3
thoughts n. gives way to, 237 : 11
thrust into n. like wedge, 558 : 20
to advantage dressed, 333 : 3
to be commanded must be obeyed, 179 : 10
to him who in love of n., 471 : 2
to read N. he looked inwards, 303 : 6
to white man n. wilderness, 726 : 8
to write and read comes by n., 209 : 24
too noble for world, 242 : 20
trees and all of n., 928 : 10
trying to make us succeed, 832 : 19
unassuming commonplace of n., 426 : 2
understanding distorts n. of things, 179 : 9
universal n. did lament, 280 : 14
universal n. say, 350 : *n* 4
usura sin against n., 793 : 1
vicar of almyghty lorde, 144 : 10
voice of n. cries, 362 : 15, 410 : 15
war of n., 515 : 3
we are ignorant about n., 884 : 5
we fools of n., 219 : 12
we never have enough of n., 560 : 14
what fools call n., 545 : 10
what is man in n., 299 : 17
when n. makes fool she means it, 561 : 15
when n. removes great man, 498 : 13
wherefore thus partial, 152 : 15
which mind put into n., 776 : 7
with equal mind, 585 : 9
without voice or sound, 365 : 6
words like n. half reveal, 531 : 20
works by means of bodies unseen, 100 : 8
world of n. and God, 897 : 19

Nature (*continued*)
write in spite of n., 291 : 9
yet do I fear thy n., 236 : 16
yet remembers, 426 : 17
you've conquered human n., 547 : 8
Nature, qu'est-ce que l'homme dans la n., 299 : *n* 4
Nature-faker 687 : 13
Nature's above art, 234 : 29
artistic skill, 125 : 22
beauty is N. coin, 279 : 31
chief masterpiece, 316 : 5
crack n. molds, 233 : 24
darling, 362 : 22
debt to N. quickly paid, 267 : 15
eye N. walks, 336 : 11
fever is N. instrument, 301 : 1
fresh from n. mold, 547 : 40
fulfills great N. plan, 409 : 2
God, 337 : 16
great n. second course, 237 : 21
handmaid Art, 303 : 4
infinite book of secrecy, 240 : 15
journeymen, 222 : 3
kindly law, 337 : 7
law man made to mourn, 408 : 15
laws hid, 340 : 6
laws of nature and n. God, 387 : 9
lay idiot, 253 : 17
learned breast, 168 : 3
like bill on n. reality, 473 : 12
list to n. teachings, 471 : 3
little kings, 251 : 6
master stroke n., 495 : 14
masterpiece writing well, 316 : 5
message into song, 800 : 10
models are beautiful, 832 : 9
natural bent in accordance with n., 639 : 13
nature and n. God, 329 : 5, 387 : 9
Nature and N. laws hid, 340 : 6
own nobleman, 538 : 3
own sweet cunning hand, 213 : 17
patient sleepless Eremite, 478 : 20
pleasing themes, 345 : 21
single n. double name, 225 : 30
social union, 408 : 13
soft nurse, 206 : 17
spark o' N. fire, 409 : 1
sternest painter, 456 : 18
still is N. priest, 426 : 15
system a real beauty, 832 : 9
tired n. sweet restorer, 330 : 4
trees in N. workshop, 637 : 19
up to N. God, 337 : 16
works to me expunged, 285 : 5
Natures, absolute n. or kinds, 85 : 12
by quiet n. understood, 714 : 20
how call n. forth, 900 : 3
ignominy of our n., 274 : 12
nobility in their n., 230 : 15
train noble n. not to desire more, 88 : 1
Naught but care on ev'ry han', 409 : 14
but vast sorrow there, 739 : 18
by spreading disperse to n., 184 : 18
carry on dread n., 743 : 18
doth Job fear God for n., 15 : 3
enters there, 213 : 8
it is n. saith the buyer, 24 : 30
it will come to n., 46 : 1
let it be for n., 507 : 10
shall make us rue, 202 : 20
so sweet as melancholy, 258 : 3
Naught (*continued*)
stitching and unstitching n., 712 : 20
venture nought have, 160 : 12
Naughtiness of thine heart, 12 : 39
Naughty, good deed in n. world, 201 : 4
my poems n. but life pure, 118 : 21
night to swim in, 234 : 8
Nausea, that's n., 865 : 7
Nauseate, I n. walking, 324 : 18
Nauseous, fee doctor for n. draught, 306 : 26
sham goodfellowship, 681 : 12
Nautilus, learn of n. to sail, 337 : 8
Naval, study n. architecture, 381 : 14
without n. force nothing, 379 : 5
Navarre, helmet of N., 487 : 6
Navee, ruler of Queen's N., 627 : 14
Navies, airy n., 529 : 24
are stranded, 431 : 23
Navigate, advanced nations n. most, 499 : 8
Navigating in sources and ashes, 860 : 9
Navigation commerce agriculture, 381 : 14
freedom of n., 682 : 14
truce to n., 628 : 4
Navigators, winds on side of ablest n., 383 : 13
Navy but rotten timber, 373 : 7
came the n. of Tharshish, 13 : 36
gives you army and n., 373 : 7
load would sink a n., 249 : 5
not reliance against tyranny, 520 : 7
of Charles II, 489 : 7
of England, 365 : 16
Royal N. watchword, 743 : 18
ruler of Queen's N., 627 : 14
supply lines guarded by n., 825 : 6
thoroughly efficient n., 687 : 6
Nay I have done, 182 : 16
say nay for shame, 161 : 23
when he would shall have n., 158 : 23
Nazaire, mademoiselle from St. N., 817 : 8
Nazarene, he shall be called a N., 36 : 24
Nazareth, good thing out of N., 44 : 24
Jesus of N. scientific, 583 : 2
Nazarite, he shall be called a N., 198 : *n* 1
your prophet the N., 198 : 18
Nazi gangsters, 745 : 2
tyranny, 745 : 4, 781 : 8
venom even in thoughts, 865 : 10
Nazism aimed at making you lose soul, 853 : 11
Ne quid nimis, 96 : *n* 2, 134 : *n* 5
Neaera's, tangles of N. hair, 280 : 15
Near, better a neighbor that is n., 25 : 25
duty lies in what is n., 89 : 11
far and n. unite, 384 : 8
I would be n., 875 : 1
peace to him that is n., 31 : 22
slight not what's n., 76 : 14
so n. is God to man, 494 : 21
so n. yet so far, 532 : 20
to heaven by sea, 166 : 13
what I love n. at hand, 874 : 10
who are n. are made happy, 69 : 3
Nearer comes the sun, 790 : 16
little n. or little farther, 849 : 11
my God to thee, 505 : 1
Nearer (*continued*)
not want constellations n., 575 : 11
than hands and feet, 535 : 9
to church further from God, 159 : 19
Nearest and dearest enemy, 204 : 22
catch the n. way, 236 : 16
friends can go, 747 : 9
to gods, 79 : 2
Nearness of rats, 847 : 3
Neat but not gaudy, 319 : 18
little craft, 629 : 19
lord n. and trimly dressed, 203 : 7
rivulet of text, 398 : 29
still to be n., 255 : 17
Neatly, bury for nothing and n., 547 : 37
spreads his claws, 611 : 5
Neatness a duty not sin, 346 : 11
no text condemns n., 346 : 11
plain in thy n., 107 : 3
Neat's, Spanish or n. leather, 291 : 16
trod upon n. leather, 214 : 31
Nebuchadnezzar did eat grass, 32 : 34
we are like N., 496 : 7
Nebulae, path to other n., 770 : 12
Necessaries, dispense with n., 519 : 10
Necessarily, I am n. a man, 341 : 10
it ain't n. so, 836 : 7
Necessary, a little frippery n., 393 : 1
a little kinder than n., 694 : 7
and fundamental principle, 365 : 18
catalogue of things n., 310 : 18
conclusions, 525 : 1
death a n. end, 215 : 26
established inexpugnably in the n., 649 : 16
for triumph of evil, 374 : 12
government a n. evil, 384 : 9
harmless n. cat, 200 : 3
if dhrink evil not n., 722 : 24
if God were not n. Being, 303 : 1
in n. things unity, 294 : 18
Is Sex N., 831 : 6
make yourself n., 499 : 3
marriage a n. evil, 91 : 9
most n. of assumptions, 703 : 9
never say more than n., 398 : 8
no n. evils in government, 419 : 4
rebellion n., 388 : 6
the superfluous is n., 342 : 24, 645 : 8
to burn out false shames, 790 : 14
to dissolve political bands, 387 : 9
to invent him, 344 : 2
to try to think them again, 397 : 10
useless laws weaken n. laws, 341 : 9
war only art n., 153 : 21
Necessitatem in virtutem commutare, 117 : *n* 13
Necessities, art of n. strange, 233 : 30
feigned n. imaginary n., 272 : 20
great n. call out great virtues, 392 : 16
looking away from supposed n., 650 : 8
not my own, 907 : 23
soil of people's n., 698 : 13
Necessity, absolute n. in mathematics, 738 : 1
argument of tyrants, 412 : 4
bread first n. of life, 666 : 3
brings him not pleasure, 141 : 9
calamitous n. of going on, 385 : 6
creed of slaves, 412 : 4
give n. praise of virtue, 117 : 21
has no law, 129 : 9

Necessity (*continued*)
hath no law, 272 : 20
industry a n. not a virtue, 619 : 6
is war biological n., 786 : 8
knows no law except prevail, 111 : 20
law mighty mightier n., 396 : 20
make n. a virtue, 117 : *n* 13
mistress of nature, 152 : 11
mother of invention, 117 : *n* 6, 134 : 9
nature must obey n., 217 : 7
never good bargain, 347 : 9
no virtue like n., 194 : 5
not even gods fight n., 62 : 9
not mother of invention, 817 : 15
of being ready, 522 : 1
of the times, 365 : 3
plea for infringement of liberty, 412 : 4
progress not accident but n., 579 : 5
strives against stress of n., 77 : 11
teach thy n. to reason, 194 : 5
the tyrant's plea, 285 : 21
thy n. greater than mine, 176 : 16
to be what one is, 849 : 5
to glorious gain, 427 : 22
to which world conform, 738 : 1
villains by n., 233 : 5
Necessity's sharp pinch, 233 : 20
Necht, braw brecht moonlecht n., 730 : 20
Neck, chain fastened about own n., 556 : 12
clothed his n. with thunder, 16 : 36
fell upon Benjamin's n., 8 : 37
is as a tower of ivory, 28 : 20
millstone about n., 43 : 35
or nothing, 542 : 18
some chicken some n., 745 : 12
take eloquence wring n., 659 : 17
thrice thrown arms about her n., 105 : 5
would that Roman people had single n., 116 : 1
yield not n. to fortune's yoke, 186 : 11
Neckcurls limp and damp, 873 : 17
Necks, heads erect instead of bowing n., 128 : 12
walk with stretched forth n., 29 : 1
Nectar in a sieve, 436 : 10
of Jove's n. sup, 256 : 8
Nectared, feast of n. sweets, 279 : 25
Need, all men have n. of gods, 59 : 21
all we n. of hell, 607 : 18
all ye n. to know, 477 : 11
and struggle inspire us, 649 : 11
boredom vice and n., 343 : 13
consume according to n., 563 : *n* 1
deserted at utmost n., 306 : 18
disposed to one another by n., 124 : 4
distribution according to n., 45 : 41
England hath n. of thee, 425 : 22
everywhere we have n. of Zeus, 92 : 11
France has more n. of me, 420 : 11
friend in n., 94 : 3
how little we n., 694 : 6
how many things no n. of, 79 : 1
I had most n. of blessing, 237 : 20
in thy n. go by thy side, 917 : 9
na start awa sae hasty, 408 : 12
no n. for tongue, 873 : 2
no n. of valor, 82 : 28
nothing can n. a lie, 268 : 4
of world of men, 541 : 15
Need (*continued*)
only when ceased to n. things, 895 : 14
pray in distress and n., 782 : 18
someone we can lean on, 916 : 9
thy n. greater than mine, 176 : *n* 9
we shall n. no other light, 397 : *n* 6
what is natural is n., 453 : 14
where love and n. one, 748 : 18
Needed, all n. by each, 493 : 14
six feet all he n., 602 : 12
traitor no longer n., 273 : 4
Needful, one thing is n., 43 : 17
Needle, for the n. she, 531 : 7
go through eye of n., 40 : 7
in bottle of hay, 170 : 12
in haystack, 170 : *n* 3
lean as compass n., 893 : 12
like n. to lodestone, 570 : 1
plying n. and thread, 485 : 16
true as n. to pole, 291 : *n* 6
Needle's, see out of n. eye, 547 : 36
Needles, into waves pine n., 314 : 6
Needless Alexandrine ends song, 333 : 8
omit n. words, 729 : 7
show, 605 : 17
to blame things past, 68 : 12
to speak about things done, 68 : 12
Needs, country n. and demands, 779 : 7
fair n. foul I cried, 716 : 17
gives 'er all she n., 709 : 8
go whom devil drive, 161 : 3
more than nature n., 233 : 21
responsible for children's n., 883 : 7
root in human n., 647 : 1
to each according to n., 563 : 1
we must n. die, 13 : 22
Needy hollow-eyed sharp-looking wretch, 188 : 15
I am poor and n., 21 : 17
make not n. eyes to wait, 34 : 29
not for n. but for greedy, 780 : 18
store money in stomachs of n., 128 : 20
strength to the n., 30 : 6
Negate, to define is to n., 784 : 13
Negation, capitalist production begets n., 562 : 19
my art n. of society, 643 : 7
Negative capability, 479 : 5
feelings about marriage, 316 : 3
inversion, 868 : 3
Neglect creeping hours, 211 : 12
easier to mend n. than quicken love, 127 : 10
God and his angels, 255 : 2
heartsease must kings n., 208 : 6
little n. great mischief, 347 : 35
monuments of unaging intellect, 714 : 22
perpetual n. of things, 667 : 22
sweet n. more taketh me, 255 : 18
wise and salutary n., 372 : 15
Neglected, objects of travels n. if under our eye, 123 : 12
Neglectful Nature wherefore thus partial, 152 : 15
Neglects, whoso n. learning in youth, 77 : 22
Negligence, let friendship die by n., 356 : 25
Negligences, noble n., 320 : 23
Negligent, celerity admired by n., 241 : 7
Negligible, discriminate between important and n., 762 : 5
Negotiate, every eye n. for itself, 209 : 9
never fear to n., 890 : 9
never n. out of fear, 890 : 9
Negro blood sure powerful, 855 : 3
boy with curlicues, 893 : 1
cool strong imperturbable, 556 : 10
dehumanizing the N., 520 : 7
duty of younger N. artist, 854 : 11
hate N. see hatred in N., 672 : 13
I am a N., 854 : 13
I am N. and beautiful, 854 : 11
past of rope, 903 : 2
resolve problems that confront N., 900 : 14
schoolchildren, 893 : 15
those who hate N. see hatred in N., 672 : 13
through n. streets, 906 : 1
two-ness an American a N., 724 : 17
what does N. want, 753 : 6
willing to risk martyrdom, 909 : 16
Negroes, abhors oppression of N., 520 : 2
all equal except N., 520 : 2
hear bronze N. breathe, 893 : 12
not women or N. but citizens, 554 : 8
of the Fifty-fourth, 650 : 13
Negro's skin prima facie evidence, 554 : 6
Neiges, où sont les n. d'antan, 150 : *n* 3
Neigh, how joyous his n., 928 : 20
like Boanerges, 605 : 19
Neighbor, bad n. is misfortune, 61 : 18
better a n. that is near, 25 : 25
dagger into back of n., 780 : 9
eye n. as enemy, 737 : 7
false witness against thy n., 10 : 7
good n. policy, 779 : 11
hate your n., 487 : 20
he promised to defend, 488 : 11
helped every one his n., 31 : 3
hungering n. and me, 567 : 14
let n. carve for you, 323 : 1
love n. well, 646 : 4
love n. yet pull not down hedge, 269 : 19
love thy n., 40 : 16
love thy n. as thyself, 10 : 21
not look to see what n. does, 124 : 17
please his evil n., 414 : 3
tyranny of next-door n., 597 : 10
without reproach, 591 : 11
Neighboring communities overlook one another, 65 : 9
cynosure of n. eyes, 277 : 25
Neighbor's, life to n. creed lent, 493 : 14
neighed after his n. wife, 31 : 33
not covet n. wife, 10 : 7
not covet thy n. house, 10 : 7
not move sickle unto n. corn, 11 : 18
your concern when n. wall on fire, 109 : 11
Neighbors, at peace with n., 788 : 2
borrowing everything of n., 310 : 11
call n. in, 930 : 16
first to attack their n., 297 : 16
good fences good n., 747 : 5
innocence of our n., 560 : 13
live as good n., 788 : 20
made n. miserable, 655 : 7
make central empires good n., 783 : 6
make sport for n., 440 : 23

Neighbors (*continued*)
more right than n., 558 : 5
who practices virtue will have n., 68 : 18
will the n. say, 642 : 3
Neighed after his neighbor's wife, 31 : 33
Neighing canyons, 843 : 20
far in haunted air, 811 : 14
farewell the n. steed, 231 : 11
in likeness of filly foal, 196 : 12
Neighs, high and boastful n., 208 : 1
Neither, do two things at once do n., 110 : 16
Nelly, let not poor N. starve, 302 : 22
Nelson touch, 700 : 12
Nemean, hardy as N. lion's nerve, 219 : 15
Nemo me impune lacessit, 134 : 11
repente fuit turpissimus, 122 : *n* 2
Neon Renaissance, 911 : 5
Nephew of my Uncle Sam's, 759 : 6
Neptune, envious siege of watery N., 194 : 14
flatter N. for trident, 242 : 20
floods which N. obey, 919 : 3
intercede with N., 569 : 20
sink ship on even keel, 114 : 28
Neptune's empire stands, 217 : 22
ocean wash this blood, 238 : 1
Neque semper arcum, 107 : *n* 19
Nereids, daughters of sea N., 850 : 10
Nero, tyranny of N., 597 : 10
Nerve, all air and n., 893 : 4
hardy as Nemean lion's n., 219 : 15
iron n., 533 : 4
mortal arm and n. feel, 431 : 24
o'er which do creep, 467 : 14
stretch every n., 346 : 1
Nerves, ganglion in n. of society, 644 : 7
men of weak n., 837 : 6
my firm n. never tremble, 238 : 28
productivity shattered n. punctured stomachs, 889 : 3
strengthens n., 374 : 2
trifles irritate my n., 573 : 15
Nervous, different n. organization, 837 : 9
I have been rather n., 478 : *n* 3
renewal of relations n. matter, 635 : 5
tough but n., 799 : 18
Nessus, shirt of N. upon me, 241 : 16
shirts, 473 : 10
Nest, bird that filleth own n., 153 : 2
builds phoenix' n., 292 : 18
eagle make n. on high, 17 : 1
feathered his n. well, 261 : 10
good to keep n. egg, 170 : 9
help robin to n. again, 606 : 12
jaybird don't rob own n., 662 : 12
no birds in last year's n., 171 : *n* 3
of singing birds, 353 : 21
on greatness of God, 651 : 9
phoenix builds spicy n., 271 : 21
watery n., 275 : 30
Nests, birds in little n. agree, 328 : 4
birds of air have n., 38 : 23
built n. in beard, 550 : 4
of two loves the n., 253 : 23
whatever special n. we make, 637 : 21
Net, all fish that cometh to n., 160 : 14
as fishes taken in evil n., 27 : 17
heaven's n. is vast, 65 : 6
Net (*continued*)
kingdom of heaven like a n., 39 : 19
of gold, 870 : 6
of life and time, 802 : 18
on wall when fish eaten, 894 : 4
to catch us in, 850 : 14
to hold the wind, 262 : *n* 4
Nether, hard as n. millstone, 17 : 6
Nets, heart is snares and n., 27 : 10
kennels taxidermists, 907 : 25
not fall into same n. twice, 128 : 6
tangled in amorous n., 288 : 6
to catch the wind, 262 : 11
Nettings, till n. are legion, 799 : 11
Nettle, out of this n. danger, 203 : 22
tender-handed stroke n., 331 : 1
the world's a n., 331 : *n* 2
Nettlerash, one-armed man with n., 699 : 10
Networks of foam, 798 : 12
Neues, im westen nichts n., 839 : 9
Neurasthenic, water buffaloes n., 799 : 16
Neurotic possessed by fantasy, 865 : 20
Neutral, economics n., 843 : 1
in fact as well as name, 682 : 1
loyal and n. in a moment, 238 : 8
nature is n., 851 : 15
studiously n., 682 : 6
to one n. thing both sexes fit, 252 : 11
Neutrality, armed n., 682 : 11
cold n., 374 : 6
just for a word n., 677 : 11
Neutralize intellectual element, 703 : 19
white not n. black, 545 : 12
Neva, ships sail down flowing N., 801 : 18
Never be mean false cruel, 548 : 29
better late than n., 110 : 12
blows so red, 516 : 12
came back to me, 550 : 12
come back to me, 530 : 20
despair, 107 : 4
do what can put off, 593 : 6
excuse, 197 : 21
forever, 510 : 23
give all the heart, 712 : 19
give in never never, 745 : 6
go to sea, 627 : 15
in field of human conflict, 744 : 6
less idle than wholly idle, 99 : 1
love a stranger, 821 : 2
love unless you can, 250 : 4
man spake like this, 45 : 1
never never never never, 235 : 18
no n. what n., 627 : 11
now or n., 360 : 15
saw wild thing sorry, 790 : 11
seek to tell thy love, 404 : 10
shake thy gory locks, 238 : 25
so little time to do so much, 780 : 16
story of more woe, 193 : 31
thinks of me, 922 : 12
this will n. do, 428 : *n* 3
to be disquieted, 267 : 6
to have lived is best, 715 : 19
to hope again, 249 : 3
too late to give up prejudices, 559 : 6
twain meet, 707 : 16
whispered she, 503 : 11
Never-ending flight of future days, 284 : 12
Never-failing vice of fools, 332 : 19
Nevermore, quoth Raven N., 526 : 18
New, adversity blessing of N. Testament, 180 : 5
all the glad N. Year, 528 : 12
always something n. out of Africa, 117 : 1
and untried, 521 : 4
Aurora, 918 : 1
be and make n. nations, 249 : 18
birth of freedom, 523 : 4
blood of the n. testament, 41 : 10
brave n. world, 248 : 17
build a n. world, 787 : 12
called N. World into existence, 422 : 7
change old love for n., 177 : 7
commandment I give, 45 : 19
cost little less than n., 325 : 1
curse of making things n., 885 : 1
deal for American people, 779 : 8
direction of Time, 790 : 9
draw n. mischief on, 229 : 33
Emperor's N. Clothes, 505 : 5
era in life from reading, 559 : 34
exhausted worlds imagined n., 351 : 10
familiar things made n., 353 : 2
first by whom n. is tried, 333 : 6
force too revolutionary, 787 : 14
fresh woods and pastures n., 281 : 6
friend fit to make old, 664 : 4
friend is as new wine, 35 : 15
Frontier, 890 : 5
generation descends from on high, 103 : 14
generation of Americans, 890 : 7
generation of leadership, 890 : 4
has a n. master get a n. man, 248 : 2
hazard of n. fortunes, 201 : 11
heaven and new earth, 53 : 29
heavens and a new earth, 31 : 30
heraldry hands not hearts, 231 : 19
Homer n. and fresh, 741 : 2
how strange it seems and n., 542 : 13
I strike up for N. World, 574 : 4
Jerusalem, 53 : 29
leisured class replaced by N. Class, 871 : 14
life begins, 140 : 7
life when sin no more, 552 : 22
life's old death n., 546 : 4
love noght oold as whan n., 147 : 18
man raised up in him, 56 : 16
nation conceived in liberty, 523 : 4
no n. acquaintance, 357 : 4
no n. thing under the sun, 26 : 14
not criticize N. Testament, 699 : 1
nothing more perilous than n. order, 153 : 18
nothing quite n. is perfect, 98 : 14
occasions teach new duties, 567 : 8
off with old love before on with n., 921 : 8
off with Old Woman before on with N., 680 : 2
old lamps for n., 919 : 24
old offenses of affections n., 245 : 16
old woes n. wail, 244 : 11
only thing n. in world, 788 : 17
opinions always suspected, 307 : 13
order in Europe, 766 : 9
pain of n. idea, 597 : 3
philosophy calls all in doubt, 254 : 5
piping songs forever n., 477 : 8
plants still awkward, 873 : 15

New (*continued*)
regions we call New World, 152 : 17
reproduction to n. individuals, 393 : 7
ring in the n., 532 : 22
road n. as roads are, 664 : 7
roots better than no roots, 861 : 16
satire ever moral ever n., 311 : 13
scholar replacing older, 769 : 1
sea discoverers to n. worlds, 251 : 15
so various so beautiful so n., 587 : 16
something n., 924 : 6
stand upon threshold of the n., 276 : 12
terms between Old and N. World, 401 : 14
things are made familiar, 353 : 2
things succeed, 266 : 15
time to begin a n., 307 : 1
time was when toy dog n., 666 : 17
to keep good acts refresh with n., 179 : 20
tomorrow a n. day, 170 : 26
too deep into n. land, 432 : 7
turn over a n. leaf, 170 : 15
wail my dear times' waste, 244 : 11
way to pay old debts, 263 : 1
ways to dishonor Sabbath, 624 : 8
what is n. not valuable what valuable not n., 444 : 13
what valuable not n. what is n. not valuable, 451 : 13
wine in old bottles, 38 : 30
word n. with our country, 623 : 3
World favorable to declamation, 683 : 22
world to be won, 890 : 4
world which is the old, 530 : 11
Year's Day in morning, 933 : 3
years ruin and rend, 633 : 6
yielding place to n., 534 : 31
Yorker not edited for old lady, 824 : 2
New England, because I am N., 751 : 8
Brahmin caste of N., 519 : 17
courage of N., 484 : 18
a finished place, 837 : 4
growth of N., 592 : 5
iron N. dark, 838 : 5
lilac all over N., 751 : 8
rum, 705 : 3
underemphasis of N., 803 : 3
weather compels admiration, 622 : 18
weather dazzling uncertainty, 622 : 20
wild N. shore, 470 : 15
New Englanders, as N. love pie, 759 : 14
New England's air, 567 : 9
blustering shore, 558 : 10
New France, expansion of N., 592 : 5
New Hampshire mountains curl in coil, 747 : 20
up in mountains of N., 451 : 16
New Hampshiremen, two N., 840 : 11
New Mexico, in N. he awoke young, 739 : 5
New York, a Xenophon at N., 363 : 21
dawn has mud, 841 : 17
from California to N. island, 881 : 1
governor of N. not acrobat, 741 : 8
homeward bound for N. town, 935 : 1
in N. ask how much worth, 625 : 23
in N. marrying, 892 : 12
little old N., 699 : 17
oh you N. girls, 934 : 23
only credential N. asked, 859 : 20
New York (*continued*)
past lost in N., 699 : 2
present in N. powerful, 699 : 2
she hails from N., 935 : 6
sidewalks of N., 698 : 14
way of taking life, 701 : 2
New York City, I'm in love with N., 864 : 18
New Zealand, traveler from N., 488 : 7
Newborn, glory to n. King, 350 : 15
infant's tear, 405 : 10
on parent knees n. child, 394 : 3
pity like naked n. babe, 236 : 24
Newcastle, carrying coals to N., 106 : *n* 13
Newcomer, blithe n., 427 : 1
New-create another heir, 249 : 17
Newest, oldest sins n. ways, 206 : 33
Newfangled, May's n. mirth, 190 : 13
theories, 502 : 4
Newfangledness, men love n., 147 : 27
New-fledged, tempt its n. offspring, 370 : 7
New-found, America my n. land, 254 : 2
Newgate, condemned cells of N., 620 : 9
New-laid, innocent as n. egg, 627 : 8
New-lighted on heaven-kissing hill, 223 : 3
Newly, bee had stung it n., 290 : 1
New-made clouds, 887 : 2
honor doth forget, 201 : 9
New-mown hay, 732 : 13
New-reaped, chin n., 203 : 7
New-risen, sits as n. from dream, 188 : 38
News, all n. fit to print, 686 : 6
bad n. travels fast, 120 : 14
better making n. than taking it, 743 : 1
bitter n. to hear, 591 : 9
bringer of unwelcome n., 205 : 20
carrier of n., 617 : 7
evil n. fly faster than good, 120 : *n* 5
evil n. rides post, 289 : 7
friend to get n. to you, 625 : 16
git very best o' n., 568 : 12
good n. baits, 289 : 7
good n. from a far country, 25 : 16
hear talk of court n., 235 : 12
if man bites dog that's n., 659 : 19
literature n. that stays n., 793 : 9
man who brings bad n., 74 : 11
much older than their ale, 370 : 12
never good to bring bad n., 241 : 4
no middle commercial on n., 873 : 1
not yet reached my bowels, 907 : 17
of the boat, 496 : 11
office of newspaper gathering n., 661 : 5
print n. and raise hell, 922 : 4
report n. fairly, 820 : 13
simple n. nature told, 605 : 12
suspense in n. is torture, 289 : 8
that's goin' round, 920 : 21
this n. is old enough, 228 : 25
what n. on Rialto, 198 : 18
worthy of acceptation, 319 : 15
New-spangled ore, 281 : 4
Newspaper death, 635 : 11
ghosts between lines of n., 599 : 15
measure of n., 820 : 13
never look into n., 399 : 5
office of n. gathering news, 661 : 5
today's n. old and tired, 741 : 2
Newspaperman, to n. human being is item, 828 : 3
Newspaper's duty to print news, 922 : 4
Newspapers ceaselessly querulous, 772 : 1
government without n., 388 : 4
reads thirty million n., 722 : 13
the most villainous, 399 : 5
without government, 388 : 4
Newt, eye of n. toe of frog, 239 : 5
Newton, a N. at Peru, 363 : 21
God said Let N. be, 340 : 6
with his prism, 424 : 2
Newtonian principle of gravitation, 387 : 13
Newton's, apples on N. head, 750 : 5
peculiar gift, 783 : 12
Newts and blindworms do no wrong, 196 : 21
beetles n. stone-deaf fishes, 873 : 11
Ngaje ngai, 845 : 8
Ngong, eagles of N. look out, 789 : 10
Niagara, leap of whale up N., 348 : 4
never looked on N., 489 : 1
Nibbles in a low voice, 386 : 8
Nibbling, never ceases n., 386 : 8
Nice customs curtsy to great kings, 208 : 20
girl won't give an inch, 119 : 9
guys finish last, 867 : 1
hazard of doubtful hour, 204 : 29
little missionary stew, 806 : 9
makes n. of no vile hold, 202 : 3
man a man of nasty ideas, 322 : 5
new clothes, 932 : 4
sugar spice everything n., 932 : 13
to get up in mornin', 730 : 19
to people on way up, 757 : 13
too n. for a statesman, 371 : 14
Nicean barks of yore, 525 : 9
Nicely calculated less or more, 429 : 6
Nicer to lie in bed, 730 : 19
Nicest, nastiest thing in n. way, 797 : 8
Nicholas, St. N. soon be there, 446 : 3
Nicht, gude n. and joy, 417 : 8
Nichts, im westen n. heues, 839 : 9
Nicias least deserved such fate, 81 : 9
Nicissry, if dhrink evil not n., 722 : 24
Nick, gave name to our Old N., 291 : 28
Nickel, good five-cent n., 673 : *n* 2
Nickname for Providence, 386 : 5
Niece of King Gorboduc, 214 : 27
sister's husband's n., 614 : 7
Niggard earth, 361 : 17
gret fool bothe riche and n., 144 : 7
Nigger saying he would steal his children, 623 : 23
Nigger's, write that n. owner, 624 : 4
Nigh, Athens n. to Euboea, 83 : 6
County Guy hour is n., 432 : 9
Lord is n. unto them that call, 22 : 22
so n. is grandeur, 494 : 21
Nighing his hour, 692 : 1
Night, a little warmth and good n., 617 : 3
accursed the n. she bore me, 76 : 10
acquainted with the n., 748 : 14
admits no ray, 304 : 25
afraid for the terror by n., 20 : 16
after n. I do crowd, 402 : 15
all n. jessamine stirred, 533 : 22
all n. long in dark and wet, 668 : 11
all n. roses heard, 533 : 22
alternation of n. and day, 130 : 16

Night (*continued*)
and day sweet things, 492 : 16
and day you are the one, 820 : 2
and silence who is here, 196 : 22
as darker grows the n., 368 : 12
as I in hoary winter n., 182 : 2
ask of thee beloved N., 469 : 22
at n. faith in light, 726 : 4
at n. hippopotamus hunts, 804 : 20
awake for n. is flying, 176 : 20
azure robe of n., 474 : 18
bare-bosomed n., 574 : 19
be by Silvia in the n., 190 : 2
bed by n. chest of drawers by day, 370 : 13
before Christmas, 446 : 3
beginning to lower, 512 : 3
beneath suffocating n., 691 : 6
beyond n. across day, 530 : 13
bird of dawning singeth all n., 217 : 26
bird of n. did sit, 215 : 12
black bat n., 533 : 20
black hours spent this n., 656 : 19
blasts cold, 742 : 9
blessed candles of n., 201 : 8
borrower of the n., 238 : 12
bowl of n., 516 : 1
braver at n., 908 : 10
braw brecht moonlecht n., 730 : 20
breath of n. wind, 587 : 16
bridegroom all n. through, 690 : 19
broadcast doings of n., 573 : 19
busily all the n., 568 : 15
busy till n., 310 : 6
but daylight sick, 201 : 6
by n. atheist half believes a God, 330 : 14
by n. in a pillar of fire, 9 : 30
by night my life gone, 906 : 9
by n. on my bed I sought him, 28 : 10
calm region where no n., 267 : 5
cap by n. stocking all day, 368 : 8
carried His servant by n., 131 : 5
Chaos and old N., 283 : 21
cheek of n., 191 : 26
city of n. perchance death, 618 : 18
clash by n., 587 : 16
climbing, 822 : 7
closed eyes in endless n., 363 : 2
collied n., 195 : 23
come n. strike hour, 770 : 10
come seeling n., 238 : 21
cometh, 45 : 7
coming tenderly, 854 : 14
councilor ought not sleep whole n., 57 : 15
country astronomy by n., 830 : 17
crown is of n., 634 : 6
Cynthia regent of n., 331 : 8
dark n. of the soul, 167 : 1
day after wedding n., 739 : 12
day and n. shall not cease, 8 : 1
day brought back my n., 282 : 21
dead vast and middle of n., 218 : 18
dear N. world's defeat, 298 : 21
Death and N. wash world, 576 : 1
deep of n. crept, 217 : 7
defend us from dangers of n., 55 : 9
dependency of day and n., 767 : 4
desire of n. for the morrow, 469 : 20
desolation and dim n., 525 : 16
dewy morn to dewy n., 618 : 5
did we lie down because 'twas n., 252 : 21

Night (*continued*)
drawing nigh, 616 : 7
dreaming o'er joys of n., 404 : 12
drooped in sky in n., 576 : 2
drowsy ear of n., 456 : 20
dusky n. rides down sky, 349 : 10
eagle screaming n. away, 928 : 9
empty-vaulted n., 279 : 19
endless n., 266 : 21, 363 : 2, 406 : 19
eternity only a single n., 83 : 13
evening mild silent n., 286 : 1
ever-during n., 250 : 3
filled with music, 510 : 22
firebell in the n., 389 : 14
fit n. for man or beast, 770 : 17
flies in n. in howling storm, 405 : 5
flowing with birds, 874 : 16
follow as n. the day, 219 : 2
for thieves, 77 : 5
forests of the n., 405 : 7
fresh dews of n., 280 : 10
gaudy n., 241 : 12
gentle into that good n., 887 : 4
gets through bad n., 657 : 23
go bump in the n., 921 : 4
God is day n. winter summer, 70 : 2
good-bye n. good-bye, 683 : 11
grew white in single n., 459 : 21
hangs on cheek of n., 191 : 26
Harry in the n., 208 : 2
has a thousand eyes, 670 : 8
hath a thousand eyes, 176 : 2
hear this passing n., 477 : 1
hoary winter n., 182 : 2
horses of the n., 113 : 6, 184 : *n* 4
hung aloft the n., 478 : 20
I could have danced all n., 894 : 21
I have passed miserable n., 187 : 8
I saw Eternity the other n., 299 : 6
I who am in n., 171 : 12
ignorant armies clash by n., 587 : 16
in her silence, 585 : 12
in lonesome October, 526 : 22
in n. imagining some fear, 197 : 12
in the day in the n., 576 : 4
in the forests of the n., 405 : 7
in Valparaiso, 861 : 2
in winter get up at n., 668 : 9
infant crying in n., 532 : 10
infinite day excludes n., 328 : 15
interminable n., 808 : 13
into the n. go one and all, 663 : 9
is a fiction, 897 : 5
is dark, 490 : 6, 925 : 2
is drawing nigh, 616 : 7
is far spent, 47 : 29
is growing gray, 641 : 25
is starry bright, 860 : 8
is thine, 721 : 6
it will not last the n., 822 : 17
joint-laborer with day, 217 : 20
joys of n., 404 : 12
kingdom of perpetual n., 187 : 10
last n. ah yesternight, 721 : 4
last n. among fellow roughs, 536 : 7
last out n. in Russia, 228 : 3
late in n. fires are out, 668 : 11
lies upon the deep, 104 : 18
like firebell in the n., 389 : 14
like fountain n. and day, 535 : 1
little lovely moony n., 406 : 6
lives here or passes n., 786 : 1
long day's journey into n., 810 : 16
lovely as a Lapland n., 427 : 20

Night (*continued*)
lovers' tongues by n., 192 : 17
machinery of n., 906 : 1
mad naked summer n., 574 : 19
made for loving, 460 : 5
magnetic nourishing n., 574 : 19
makes n. seep into day, 132 : 5
makes no difference, 266 : 9
making n. hideous, 219 : 12
many a watchful n., 206 : 29
meaner beauties of the n., 251 : 1
meditate day and n., 17 : 12
merry wanderer of the n., 196 : 12
middle of the n., 613 : 1
moonless n. in small town, 887 : 6
morning and noontide night, 187 : 11
mother of day, 513 : 6
motions of spirit dull as n., 201 : 3
Nature's laws hid in n., 340 : 6
naughty n. to swim in, 234 : 8
night my ho head halls, 778 : 5
no moon outlives n., 906 : 9
nodding n., 574 : 19
not n. that kills, 705 : 21
not only a n. an age, 748 : 11
not snow nor rain nor heat nor n., 78 : 19
not spend another such n., 187 : 8
nothing but the n., 691 : 16
now tell me elm, 778 : 5
nurse through n. ethereal spark, 883 : 8
of cloudless climes, 459 : 13
of dark intent, 748 : 11
of doubt and sorrow, 616 : 8
of large few stars, 574 : 19
of memories and sighs, 442 : 18
of south winds, 574 : 19
of the soul, 835 : 11
of time surpasseth day, 275 : 10
oft in the stilly n., 447 : 7
on a starred n., 600 : 27
on marge of Lake Lebarge, 752 : 6
one blue dew, 875 : 11
one calm summer n., 729 : 5
out of n. that covers me, 663 : 10
perpetual n., 101 : 18, 187 : 10, 255 : 16
plunges lower than n., 785 : 14
portals alternate n. and day, 516 : 10
praise at morning blame at n., 333 : 14
primeval cosmic n., 754 : 13
proof through the n., 446 : 1
read and drive n. away, 143 : 17
resonance recedes, 716 : 8
returned home previous n., 742 : 1
revelry by n., 457 : 14
round me too the n., 587 : 10
run slowly horses of n., 113 : 6, 184 : *n* 4
sable goddess, 330 : 5
sash lowered when n., 748 : 12
say to n. Pass slowly, 464 : 15
sea half-held by n., 574 : 19
shadow of light, 632 : 9
shadow of n. comes on, 822 : 1
shadows of n., 513 : 2
ships that pass in n., 512 : 10
show dangerous brow by n., 215 : 19
shrouds remote antiquity, 324 : 2
silent n. holy n., 466 : 2
silver lining on the n., 279 : 17
singeth all n. long, 217 : 26
sits and smiles on the n., 403 : 12

Night (*continued*)
sleep in the n., 404 : 5
sleep neither n. nor day, 236 : 2
sleep of perpetual n., 101 : 18
sleep one ever-during n., 250 : 3
snatched on Monday n., 202 : 25
soft stillness and the n., 201 : 1
some born to endless n., 406 : 19
soon comes the n., 489 : 10
sorrow makes n. morning, 187 : 11
specter n. and day, 406 : 1
sperm of Milky Way, 861 : 2
spirit of n., 469 : 21
stars from field of n., 515 : 16
stars of summer n., 510 : 15
starshine at n., 669 : 4
stilly n., 447 : 7
storms hunger ridicule, 574 : 1
such a n. as this, 200 : 22
such n. in England, 488 : 3
suffocating n., 691 : 6
sweat with terror, 715 : 6
tell me elm n. n., 778 : 5
tender and growing n., 574 : 19
tender is the n., 476 : 25
that hides things from us, 142 : 18
that makes or fordoes me, 232 : 12
that n. that year, 656 : 16
that wins, 632 : 8
then it's n. once more, 866 : 13
there shall be no n., 53 : 31
thief in the n., 50 : 18
this n. of no moon, 135 : 10
those who dream at n., 526 : 3
thou makest darkness and it is n., 21 : 11
thy tempests fell all n., 269 : 5
tire the n. in thought, 267 : 12
tired with one spend n. with other, 695 : 1
to remember, 892 : 3
toiling upward in n., 511 : 23
tore the azure robe of n., 474 : 18
trailing garments of N., 509 : 12
tranced summer n., 478 : 4
troubled n. depart, 443 : 13
turn by n. or day, 426 : 10
unto night showeth knowledge, 17 : 27
unwept in eternal n., 108 : 13
urge the morrow, 469 : 7
walks n. in silver shoon, 739 : 13
wampum of the n., 604 : 8
wanderer of the n., 196 : 12
war's annals cloud into n., 642 : 2
watch in the n., 20 : 11
watch that ends n., 328 : 11
watches of n., 512 : 21
watchman tell us of n., 465 : 10
we are not of the n., 50 : 19
weepeth sore in the n., 32 : 21
weeping may endure for a n., 18 : 15
what hath n. to do with sleep, 279 : 12
what is the n., 239 : 2
what of the n., 30 : 1
whatever flames upon n., 715 : 14
when kings ride elephants, 879 : 20
when no man can work, 45 : 7
when she deserts the n., 288 : 21
whispered me through n., 575 : 18
who art dark as n., 246 : 7
windy n. rainy morrow, 245 : 3
wings of N., 510 : 17
witching time of n., 222 : 23

Night (*continued*)
with great gift of sleep, 663 : 12
with n. we banish sorrow, 257 : 18
with n. will go, 402 : 15
with train of stars, 663 : 12
womb of uncreated n., 284 : 9
world in love with n., 193 : 9
world's last n., 254 : 14
year plunges into n., 785 : 14
year turn on hinge that n., 864 : 1
yield day to n., 184 : 15
Nightcap decked his brows, 368 : 8
every wave had n., 667 : 8
Nightfall, at n. the Nantucketer, 570 : 7
Nightingale, brown bright n. amorous, 632 : 7
Chinese n., 765 : 9
hark ah the n., 586 : 5
no music in n., 190 : 2
roar you as any n., 196 : 8
sing like a n., 121 : 5
sing of hope, 505 : 7
sings round it, 447 : 12
tawny-throated, 586 : 5
that on yon bloomy spray, 281 : 8
tongueless n., 476 : 15
wakeful n., 285 : 25
when May is past, 271 : 20
Nightingales are singing near Convent, 804 : 25
silent when eggs hatched, 277 : 1
the n. the n., 507 : 25
thy N. awake, 591 : 9
where n. singing, 813 : 7
Nightly on deep Galilee, 459 : 14
owl that n. hoots, 196 : 20
pitch moving tent, 429 : 17
shore, 526 : 15
sings the staring owl, 191 : 14
to listening earth, 325 : 9
Nightmare from which trying to awake, 778 : 1
in n. of the dark, 868 : 12
Life-in-Death, 434 : 19
national n. over, 882 : 15
vexed to nightmare, 714 : 13
Nightmares of other islands, 878 : 17
Night's black arch the keystane, 411 : 9
candles are burnt out, 193 : 15
o'er n. brim day, 540 : 14
owl n. herald, 189 : 11
piercing n. dull ear, 208 : 1
Plutonian shore, 526 : 15
rung n. yawning peal, 238 : 20
starred face, 478 : 18
sweet bird, 469 : 14
trust not one n. ice, 270 : 3
Nights all white an' still, 568 : 4
and feasts of gods, 106 : 21
are longest there, 228 : 3
are very damp, 614 : 8
are wholesome, 217 : 26
checkerboard of n. and days, 516 : 22
chill thy dreaming n., 478 : 8
days and n. to Addison, 352 : 23
delights as short as n., 261 : 4
fasted forty days and n., 37 : 1
fled Him down the n., 693 : 10
forty days and forty n., 7 : 30
in bottomless n. you sleep, 673 : 19
long wintry n., 551 : 3
luxurious lobster-n., 334 : 25
men such as sleep o' n., 215 : 8

Nights (*continued*)
Moses was there forty days and forty n., 10 : 15
no more profit of shining n., 190 : 12
of waking, 431 : 8
revels long o' n., 216 : 1
shorten tedious n., 250 : 7
two n. to every day, 268 : 18
waste n. in discontent, 174 : 10
Nighttime, dog did nothing in n., 689 : 8
Night-walkers' song, 716 : 8
Nihil est ab omni parte beatum, 107 : *n* 21
nimis, 134 : 12
nos haec novimus esse n., 119 : *n* 9
Nihilist man who does not bow, 564 : 3
spring abhorrent to n., 766 : 18
Nil desperandum, 107 : *n* 4
habet infelix paupertas, 122 : *n* 4
humani n. a me alienum puto, 96 : *n* 8
igitur mors est ad nos, 101 : *n* 2
posse creari de nilo, 100 : *n* 3
tam difficile est, 96 : *n* 11
terribile nisi ipse timor, 179 : *n* 3
Nile, allegory on banks of N., 398 : 12
dogs drink running at the N., 114 : 7
outvenoms worms of N., 243 : 21
serpent of old N., 240 : 23
waters of the N., 611 : 5
you're the N., 820 : 4
Nimble airy servitors, 281 : 15
in calling of selling, 791 : 5
Jack be n., 932 : 17
thought can jump, 244 : 16
with n. feet dance on air, 676 : 9
words so n., 263 : 2
Nimbly and sweetly, 236 : 21
he capers n. in lady's chamber, 186 : 31
Nimis, ne quid n., 96 : *n* 2, 134 : *n* 5
Nimrod the mighty hunter, 8 : 4
Nine and fifty swans, 713 : 15
and sixty ways, 708 : 21
bean rows have there, 712 : 4
by N. Gods he swore, 488 : 13
days old, 931 : 18
lives like a cat, 160 : 24
she-camel hairs aid memory, 799 : 13
some say there are n. muses, 63 : *n* 4
stitch in time saves n., 117 : *n* 7
then there were n., 933 : 22
Ninety and nine went not astray, 40 : 2
Ninety-eight, who fears to speak of N., 592 : 2
Ninety-nine percent of people fools, 839 : 17
Ninety-two, the glorious N., 382 : 11
Nineveh, one with N. and Tyre, 709 : 18
quinquireme of N., 760 : 19
Ninny, compared to Handel's a n., 341 : 13
Ninth beatitude, 336 : 6
part of a hair, 204 : 15
what is N. Symphony, 751 : 4
Ninth-month midnight, 575 : 17
Niobe, like N. all tears, 218 : 10
of nations, 458 : 16
Nipped, blood is n. and ways foul, 191 : 14
my flower sae early, 410 : 19
Nipping, winter with wrathful n. cold, 185 : 14

Nipple, plucked n. from his gums, 237 : 5
Nips his root then he falls, 249 : 3
Nix, sticks n. hicks pix, 741 : 5
Nixon, won't have N. to kick, 882 : 17
No comment is splendid expression, 746 : 8
continuing city, 51 : 25
cross no crown, 267 : 10
discharge in that war, 27 : 13
effects, 473 : 12
everlasting n., 472 : 23
evil deed live on, 647 : 3
forces one to repeat n., 659 : 2
go not to Lethe, 477 : 20
hard gifts, 797 : 13
I was out for stars, 749 : 7
in him is n. darkness, 52 : 19
let me taste the whole, 544 : 22
lot is altogether happy, 107 : 24
love lost, 170 : 22
maids in modesty say n., 189 : 31
mainly hears the n., 395 : 10
man content with lot, 106 : 10
man is an island, 254 : 22
man see me more, 249 : 1
more parades, 740 : 10
more trusting in women, 60 : 14
new thing under the sun, 26 : 14
nice girl won't say n., 119 : 9
no no I dare not, 917 : 16
no no life, 235 : 18
one means all he says, 635 : 20
one so accursed by fate, 510 : 10
others said n., 301 : 18
person who could not say n., 875 : 14
remembrance of former things, 26 : 15
saying N. to authority, 851 : 4
this morning sir I say, 507 : 5
time like present, 319 : 21
to everything bad, 650 : 1
to think is say n., 724 : 5
No passarán, 833 : 21
No one can return from there, 3 : 1
cares for me, 382 : 7
conquers who doesn't fight, 150 : 4
goes and comes back, 3 : 2
should judge own case, 111 : 19
Noah begat Shem Ham Japheth, 7 : 26
God gave N. rainbow sign, 903 : 3
often said to wife, 742 : 16
same to N. as to me, 571 : 8
Noah's, all men N. sons, 899 : 10
into N. ark, 376 : 10
Nobilitas sola est atque unica virtus, 122 : *n* 9
Nobility, betwixt wind and his n., 203 : 8
idleness an appendix to n., 258 : 18
in their natures, 230 : 15
of style, 453 : 17
species of n., 308 : 15
the only virtue, 122 : 13
true n. exempt from fear, 185 : 22
war alone brings n., 784 : 1
Nobility's, mercy is n. true badge, 188 : 16
Nobis pereunt et imputantur, 119 : *n* 3
Noble and incapable of deceit, 432 : 12
and most sovereign reason, 221 : 21
and puissant nation, 282 : 3
army of Martyrs, 55 : 1
be man helpful and good, 394 : 16
Noble (*continued*)
bright gleam of n. deeds, 72 : 7
British sentence n. thing, 743 : 8
contrive one n. lie, 84 : 11
cookery a n. science, 258 : 16
do n. things, 566 : 12
dust of Alexander, 224 : 15
efforts in last war, 351 : 3
eightfold path, 73 : 2
eminently n., 586 : 14
false idol or n. true birth, 85 : 16
happy human beings, 572 : 19
he shall have a n. memory, 242 : 28
hearts of the n. may be turned, 58 : 22
horsemanship, 204 : 32
in reason, 220 : 28
invention, 387 : 1
is he no more, 73 : 12
last infirmity of n. mind, 280 : 15
living and noble dead, 424 : 6
long live our n. king, 331 : 6
man a n. animal, 275 : 11
mind here o'ethrown, 221 : 19
nature passion not shake, 231 : 26
nature poetically gifted, 586 : 16
nature too n. for world, 242 : 20
negligences teach, 320 : 23
never alone accompanied with n. thoughts, 176 : 5
not one altogether n., 720 : 3
not rebellion which is n., 882 : 7
not think n., 863 : 12
now cracks a n. heart, 225 : 3
person attracts noble people, 395 : 14
productivity of Victorians n., 889 : 3
quiet us in death so n., 289 : 9
repressed their n. rage, 362 : 7
savage, 303 : 8
sentiments, 727 : 12
shame, 567 : 1
silence n. till end, 632 : 10
silent part of n. work, 573 : 13
society exists for n. actions, 88 : 5
spirit raises itself in disaster, 120 : 3
steed, 462 : 5
to be good, 528 : 11
train n. natures, 88 : 1
truth of sorrow, 72 : 23
type of good, 512 : 1
work is alone n., 474 : 4
work of n. note, 529 : 12
Nobleman, interest equal to n., 391 : 4
nature's own n., 538 : 3
underrated n., 630 : 1
when n. writes book, 356 : *n* 5
Noblemen, worth sweat of n., 367 : 1
Nobleness, no security in n. of another, 738 : 13
Nobler and manlier one, 461 : 7
in mind to suffer, 221 : 12
things brought America into being, 729 : 11
two of far n. shape, 285 : 17
yet in his own worth, 304 : 15
Nobles and heralds by your leave, 321 : 2
by earlier creation, 487 : 7
Noblesse oblige, 416 : 7
Noblest deed will die if unsung, 72 : 10
frailty of mind, 313 : 19
function of object, 706 : 7
horse n. conquest of man, 349 : 1
lives and noblest dies, 581 : 14
of sailing vessels, 800 : 10
Noblest (*continued*)
prospect a Scotchman sees, 354 : 10
Roman of them all, 217 : 13
ruins of the n. man, 216 : 11
Thames n. river, 326 : 22
time's n. offspring, 330 : 25
two n. of things, 321 : 14
work of God, 337 : 13, 408 : 18
work of man, 615 : 10
work she classes O, 409 : 15
Nobly born must nobly meet fate, 77 : 16
Cape St. Vincent, 541 : 18
deeds die however n. done, 174 : 9
O let us n. die, 819 : 6
perfect woman n. planned, 427 : 6
possession prevents living n., 738 : 2
save or meanly lose, 522 : 12
to be n. born now crime, 262 : 20
to die, 73 : 10
to live, 73 : 10
too difficult to think n., 359 : 4
wild not mad, 266 : 16
within reach to live n., 114 : 18
work they so n. advanced, 523 : 4
Nobodaddy, old N. aloft, 404 : 22
Nobody, are you n. too, 604 : 19
asked you, 931 : 16
cares for me, 382 : *n* 4
come because nobody does, 641 : 5
expected me to be President, 520 : 5
fat white woman n. loves, 795 : 2
gets old and crafty, 712 : 10
give a war and n. come, 761 : 14
house with n. in it, 620 : *n* 2
I care for n., 382 : 7
I hate n., 323 : 5
I'm n. who are you, 604 : 19
knock as you please n. home, 336 : 7
knows trouble I've seen, 935 : 19
likes man who brings bad news, 74 : 11
more space where n. than anybody, 752 : 14
never made me, 539 : 1
not even the rain, 829 : 13
praises everybody praises n., 385 : 16
shoots at Santa Claus, 741 : 9
tells me anything, 723 : 1
who does not rise early, 353 : 7
Nobody's enemy but own, 548 : 34
everybody's business n. business, 271 : 2
funeral, 807 : 17
here, 893 : 7
Noche oscura del alma, 167 : *n* 1
Noctes, O n. cenaeque deum, 106 : *n* 17
Noctis, lente currite n. equi, 113 : *n* 4, 184 : 8
Nocturne, double n. in serge, 841 : 14
Nod, affects to n., 306 : 13
Cain dwelt in land of N., 7 : 20
ready with every n. to tumble, 187 : 15
Wynken Blynken and N., 666 : 16
Nodded nearly napping, 526 : 10
Nodding o'er yellow plain, 345 : 13
still n. night, 574 : 19
violet grows, 196 : 18
Nodding-places, rests and n. in writer, 326 : 15
Nods a little that's all, 329 : 6
and becks, 277 : 19
even good old Homer n., 110 : 2

Nods (*continued*)
nor is it Homer n., 332 : 18
old horse stumbles and n., 642 : 2
Nohow 612 : 23
Noir, A n. E blanc, 673 : *n* 13
comme le diable, 400 : *n* 3
Noise, above n. and danger, 299 : 10
and whip of whirlwind, 889 : 20
boys that fear no n., 371 : 10
crowds beloved smoke, 441 : 9
dangerous who make no n., 296 : 19
dreadful n. of waters, 187 : 9
folly n. and sin, 542 : 4
govern most make least n., 264 : 1
he who sleeps in n., 631 : 17
impertinent interruption, 463 : 7
in the beast's belly, 149 : 7
inexplicable dumbshows and n., 221 : 23
like of hidden brook, 435 : 1
make a joyful n., 19 : 31, 20 : 20, 21 : 3
makes no n. over good deed, 125 : 2
narrow-souled people make n., 340 : 11
neglect God for n. of a fly, 255 : 2
noiseless n. among leaves, 474 : 21
nursed amid n., 441 : 9
of folly, 278 : 17
of many waters, 20 : 19
of tongues and deeds, 527 : 22
picked sparingly without n. 575 : 22
play skillfully with a loud n., 18 : 19
those who make the n., 373 : 28
what n. soever ye hear, 184 : 6
Noised, fame n. throughout country, 11 : 32
Noiseless current strong obscure, 588 : 22
foot of time, 227 : 21
noise among leaves, 474 : 21
tenor of their way, 362 : 12
Noises in a swound, 434 : 11
isle is full of n., 248 : 10
of the northern sea, 528 : 29
Noisome pestilence, 20 : 16
unsightly n. things, 493 : 15
Noisy bells be dumb, 691 : 4
keys, 596 : 13
thought idler by n. set, 713 : 1
world hears least, 428 : 9
Nokomis, wigwam of N. 511 : 16
Noli me tangere, 45 : *n* 5
Noll, for shortness called N., 363 : 17
No-love, love fight n. every inch, 867 : 14
Nom, needed a n. de guerre, 621 : *n* 2
No-man-fathomed, cliffs frightful n., 656 : 18
No-man's land, 626 : 21
No-man's-years between the wars, 827 : 20
Nominated, if n. not run, 579 : *n* 3
so n. in the bond, 200 : 13
Nominative, her n. case, 394 : 6
Nominee, choosing presidential n., 788 : 11
Nommé, c'est toi qui l'a n., 312 : *n* 4
No-more, also called N., 601 : 20
Non dulce non et decor, 792 : 14
effugies meos iambos, 102 : *n* 8
omnia possumus omnes, 103 : *n* 11
omnis moriar, 108 : *n* 8
semper ea sunt quae videntur, 114 : *n* 3
Non (*continued*)
sum qualis eram, 108 : *n* 9
Non-action, ruler takes n. as his way, 97 : 8
Nonaggression, treaty of strict n., 878 : 1
Nonbeing, being comes from n., 64 : 13
let there always be n., 63 : 12
penetrates no space, 64 : 15
Nonchalance, lost n. of hand, 714 : 7
Noncommunication, communication strengthen n., 885 : 19
Nonconformist, be man be n., 496 : 23
Nonconformity mark of disaffection, 737 : 7
None but brave deserves fair, 306 : 12
dare call it treason, 181 : 21
go just alike, 332 : 15
I in twelve thousand n., 195 : 10
I think there embrace, 297 : 1
I'll n. of it, 205 : 5
is born wise, 3 : 3
is safe, 799 : 2
knew thee but to love thee, 464 : 11
lives unto himself lives to n., 267 : 9
liveth to himself, 47 : 32
malice toward n., 524 : 7
of these so lonely, 797 : 4
of woman born, 239 : 10
one world or n., 828 : 2
other but the house of God, 8 : 21
power to hurt and will do n., 245 : 4
sall ken where he is gane, 927 : 5
should see salvation, 200 : 9
so poor to do him reverence, 216 : 21
there was n. with me, 31 : 26
this little pig had n., 930 : 11
trust n., 207 : 15
usurp this height, 478 : 21
who dares do more is n., 237 : 3
yellow leaves or n. or few, 244 : 27
Nonentity, disembodied emotion n., 649 : 8
Nones, the N. the seventh, 162 : *n* 3
two days less for N. and Ides, 162 : *n* 3
Nonino, hey n., 212 : 33
Non-knowledge, ocean of n., 862 : 5
Nonprogressive, lazy n. people, 818 : 12
Nonrepeatable historical case, 775 : 9
Nonselfness, thought of n. terrifying, 884 : 4
Nonsense and beauty close connections, 764 : 8
corner of n., 438 : 7
firm anchor in n., 871 : 7
grammar n. and learning, 371 : 5
through sense and n., 304 : 17
Nonviolence and truth inseparable, 727 : 6
first article of faith, 727 : 4
is the answer, 909 : 11
where King could have lived and preached n., 915 : 18
Nonviolent action supplement change, 909 : 15
resistance paralyzed, 909 : 16
Nook, a privacy an obscure n., 540 : 10
book and shady n., 643 : 3
Nooks, sequestered n., 512 : 15
Noon, act in the n., 404 : 5
and evening of lives, 592 : 6
athwart the n., 435 : 16
dark amid blaze of n., 288 : 20
Noon (*continued*)
far from fiery n., 478 : 2
from morn to n. he fell, 284 : 2
from n. to dewy eve, 284 : 2
lying till n., 353 : 7
midnight is n. of thought, 387 : 4
now you come at n., 933 : 14
qhosts' high n., 629 : 20
riding near her highest n., 278 : 18
sun at n., 255 : 1
under the palmtree at n., 806 : 13
weight of primary n., 768 : 2
whirling hands at n., 863 : 16
Noonday, age clearer than n., 15 : 26
bird of night at n., 215 : 12
destruction that wasteth at n., 20 : 16
Noon's, troubled midnight and n. repose, 804 : 12
Noontide, night morning and n. night, 187 : 11
Noose, a n. a question, 893 : 13
marriage a n., 170 : 17
of light, 516 : 1
very best o' n., 568 : 12
Noosed, strapped n. nighing hour, 692 : 1
Nooses give, 827 : 12
Nor'east to sou'west winds, 622 : 19
Norm, constraining n. shaping, 685 : 4
Normal, beyond nature of n. man, 312 : 20
rate of growth, 620 : 20
situation n. fouled up, 924 : 21
Norman blood, 528 : 11
Norman's, reef of N. Woe, 510 : 6
Noroway o'er the faem, 926 : 10
North, Ariosto of the N., 458 : 9
awake O n. wind, 28 : 14
Countree hard countree, 834 : 5
elevation of the n. star, 151 : 7
fair weather cometh out of the n., 16 : 26
farewell to the n., 410 : 8
fifty n. forty west, 709 : 24
guilt on N. equally with South, 577 : 16
Hotspur of the N., 203 : 26
infect to n. star, 209 : 10
iron door of n., 864 : 2
lanterns in N. Church, 382 : 12
next gale from n., 383 : 5
no N. no East no West, 444 : 6
poles and equators, 613 : 22
ship came from n. country, 935 : 4
unripened beauties of n., 325 : 15
wind doth blow, 932 : 6
without sharp n., 251 : 16
North America, native warrior of N., 463 : 13
North American civilization engulfed world, 903 : 12
North Americans use reality, 885 : 14
North Carolina, said to governor of N.C., 669 : 12
Northeast, heel of N. Trade, 708 : 22
to sou'west winds, 622 : 19
Northern charm southern efficiency, 892 : 2
constant as n. star, 216 : 3
kind and n. face, 843 : 17
laurels not change, 378 : 2
Lights seen queer sights, 752 : 6
ocean in vast whirls, 345 : 15
states muddle through, 538 : 5

Northern (*continued*)
thought slow durable, 542 : 20
Northland, skoal to the N., 510 : 3
soul, 834 : 5
North-northeast, wind always n., 729 : 2
North-northwest, but mad n., 220 : 31
Northwest, Chicago at n. gates, 728 : 12
Passage to intellectual world, 360 : 16
to n. died away, 541 : 18
Norval, my name is N., 366 : 10
Norwegian, pine hewn on N. hills, 283 : 15
Nor'wester's, strong n. blowing Bill, 429 : 19
Nose, any n. ravage rose, 540 : 13
as n. on man's face, 189 : 33
as sharp as pen, 207 : 13
assert n. on face his own, 376 : 1
blackbird snipped off n., 931 : 9
Cleopatra's n., 300 : 1
entuned in hir n. ful semely, 145 : 18
European n., 900 : 5
gave pouncet box his n., 203 : 7
great n. great man, 726 : 1
innocent n., 210 : 25
jolly red n., 268 : 1
liberty plucks justice by n., 227 : 26
makes chimney of your n., 401 : 3
Marian's n. looks red, 191 : 15
nose nose nose, 268 : 1
often wipe bloody n., 331 : 15
paying through n., 923 : 19
plain as n. in face, 158 : 9
red n. makes me ashamed, 310 : 12
ring at end of n., 550 : 8
that's his precious n., 485 : 15
thirty inches from n., 869 : 6
which direction to point n., 869 : 8
with spectacles on n., 211 : 15
Nosegay of culled flowers, 166 : 6
Noses, athwart n. as asleep, 191 : 23
hold n. to grindstone, 159 : 15
Nostalgia for living existence, 850 : 2
last n., 768 : 4
Nostrils, blast of thy n., 9 : 35
breathed into his n., 6 : 17
whose breath is in his n., 28 : 33
Not an Attic grace, 792 : 12
as I will but thou, 41 : 12
as the world giveth, 45 : 24
for love, 212 : 23
I not I, 790 : 9
in vain, 746 : 5
lost but gone before, 114 : 25
my will but thine, 44 : 4
so wild a dream, 503 : 6
that I loved Caesar less, 216 : 14
thus not thus, 56 : 21
to eat not for love, 495 : 21
what we give but share, 567 : 14
Notary's, in n. heart remains of poet, 583 : 14
Note and enjoy noting, 654 : 8
bolder n. than this, 525 : 10
deed of dreadful n., 238 : 20
dreadful n. of preparation, 208 : 1
eternal n. of sadness, 587 : 14
fain would change n., 918 : 9
it in a book, 30 : 17
living had no n., 918 : 17
silent n. Cupid strikes, 274 : 20
take a n. of that, 489 : 14
take n. O world, 231 : 15
that swells gale, 362 : 20
Note (*continued*)
to which love charmed, 918 : 9
tu-who a merry n., 191 : 14
when found make n., 548 : 18
work of noble n., 529 : 12
world little n., 523 : 4
wrapped in five-pound n., 550 : 7
you in book of memory, 185 : 1
Notebook, set in a n., 217 : 4
Notes are few, 403 : 1
as warbled to the string, 278 : 22
by distance made sweet, 364 : 14
chield's amang you takin' n., 410 : 20
curls done up with bank n., 554 : 11
flute in dying n., 305 : 12
he listens well who takes n., 141 : 12
liquid n. close day, 281 : 9
of gladness, 443 : 21
range of n., 580 : 4
rough n. and dead bodies, 726 : 5
thrill deepest n. of woe, 410 : 1
thrills thick-warbled n., 288 : 14
through all compass of n., 305 : 9
with many a winding bout, 278 : 6
write N. from Olympus, 783 : 5
Nothing, a man zealous for n. 356 : 10
a worm a mere n., 346 : 4
a Year, 539 : 8
ain't heard n. yet, 795 : 4
ain't worth nothin' but it's free, 913 : 10
airy n., 197 : 12
all for love n. for reward, 173 : 13
all or n., 599 : 6
and it was n. more, 423 : 16
becomes him ill, 190 : 20
before and nothing behind, 435 : 18
begins and nothing ends, 693 : 7
begot of n. but vain fantasy 191 : 24
beside remains, 466 : 13
better know useless things than n., 114 : 30
blessed man who expects n., 336 : 6
book's a book though n. in 't, 456 : 12
both new and valuable, 451 : 13
bring peace but yourself, 497 : 9
brought n. into world, 51 : 1
burden of n. to do, 311 : 17
but hath been said, 258 : 6
but pack of cards, 612 : 14
but talk of his horse, 198 : 11
but the night, 691 : 16
but the truth, 169 : 29
call our own but death, 195 : 2
can be accomplished alone, 823 : 21
can be created from nothing, 100 : 5
can be done hastily and prudently, 111 : 21
can bring back hour, 426 : 21
can help you, 838 : 3
can need a lie, 268 : 4
can rescue me, 184 : 6
can touch him further, 238 : 19
cannot create when n. to say, 853 : 5
certain but death and taxes, 348 : 16
come out of artist not in man, 772 : 14
comes amiss so money comes, 188 : 28
comes from nothing, 885 : 9
comes out, 496 : 13
comes without cause, 346 : 5
common law n. but reason, 171 : 21
constant but inconstancy, 321 : 16
contains all n. lacking, 575 : 6
created something of n., 277 : 3
Nothing (*continued*)
dancer kneeling on n., 899 : 4
death in itself is n., 303 : 9
death is n. to us, 91 : 14, 101 : 2
deed everything glory n., 396 : 24
did n. in particular, 628 : 24
do much harm, 830 : 18
do n. be a gentleman, 177 : 15
done merely for beauty, 925 : 4
done while anything remained, 118 : 9
dusty n., 226 : 15
easier than self-deceit, 88 : 22
easy in war, 815 : 14
easy to take more than n., 611 : 21
either good or bad, 220 : 25
else is, 252 : 9
emboldens sin as mercy, 243 : 4
endures but change, 69 : 25
esteem everything esteem n., 297 : 25
everything in relation to n., 299 : 17
except battle lost, 421 : 8
exists without some effect, 308 : 6
expect something for n., 671 : 16
extenuate, 232 : 20
eyes n. like the sun, 246 : 1
fair alone, 493 : 14
fame created something of n., 277 : 3
fear God n. else, 553 : 16
fear n. you carry Caesar, 99 : 20
Flaubert write novel about n., 897 : 14
for which no standard, 602 : 6
give your services for n., 79 : 16
given nothing required, 349 : 11
glory and n. of a name, 459 : 17
good men to do n., 374 : 12
good that ignores individuals, 576 : 9
grated to dusty n., 226 : 15
great without chimeras, 593 : 13
great without enthusiasm, 497 : 28
great without great men, 815 : 6
greater than one's self, 574 : 27
griefs that fuel n., 889 : 21
had n. can't take more, 611 : 21
half so sweet in life, 446 : 12
happened to us at all, 623 : 22
happens unless first dream, 761 : 12
happens which he is not fitted to bear, 125 : 3
has n. give n., 863 : 5
has value, 764 : 10
have value but object of utility, 562 : 17
having n. n. can he lose, 186 : 13
having n. possessing all, 49 : 17
having n. to say, 565 : 30
he could not bring alone, 769 : 7
he wants n. you want, 590 : 11
he who believes n., 387 : 12
heaven says n., 312 : 20
heaven's net misses n., 65 : 6
her wishes and ways be as n., 640 : 13
human is alien, 96 : 7
I am n., 48 : 23
I am n. I see all, 496 : 4
I ask n. want n., 138 : 3
I can add to songs, 759 : 3
I do n. upon myself, 254 : 20
I had seen n. sacred, 844 : 14
I have everything yet n., 96 : 16
I know these are n., 119 : 19
I love as good fight, 779 : 5
I n. lack if I am his, 580 : 15

Nothing (*continued*)
if not critical, 230 : 9
in excess, 134 : 12
in his life, 236 : 14
in love only on command, 239 : 28
in Nature's inventions n. lacking, 152 : 12
in n. else so happy, 194 : 19
in relation to infinite, 299 : 17
in Stupidity Street, 733 : 4
in the pot, 737 : 2
in truth we know n., 79 : 10
in world single, 467 : 24
indolent but agreeable doing n., 123 : 11
infinite deal of n., 198 : 5
is had for nothing, 564 : 11
is here for tears, 289 : 9
is it n. to you, 32 : 22
is secret, 43 : 6
is too late, 512 : 16
it profiteth me n., 48 : 23
knew moment to say n., 675 : 1
know n., 561 : 20
know n. except my ignorance, 79 : 5
know only that he n. knew, 288 : 16
lasts save eternal change, 265 : 3
law that is not reason, 172 : *n* 1
learned n. forgotten n., 400 : 16
left remarkable, 241 : 22
left to lose, 913 : 10
less will content me, 372 : 17
life grants n. without work, 106 : 17
like a dame, 833 : 16
like the sun, 246 : 1
little to him that feels it, 354 : 7
lost but money, 871 : 3
love shows by excusing n., 297 : 29
lowly in universe, 905 : 9
man n. before We created him, 131 : 12
mean between n. and everything, 299 : 17
miserable but what is thought so, 130 : 2
more beautiful than death, 574 : 10
more fun than a man, 827 : 15
more indisputable than our senses, 363 : 14
more perilous than new order 153 : 18
more silly than silly laugh, 102 : 1
more terrible than ignorance, 397 : 11
more than n., 611 : 21
more wretched than a man, 58 : 29
neck or n., 542 : 18
nothing at all, 821 : 12
of him that doth fade, 247 : 21
of n. am I in want, 96 : 16
off time you spend dead, 164 : 10
people on whom n. lost, 652 : 14
perfect and entire wanting n., 51 : 27
plenty of n., 836 : 6
poor man had n., 13 : 19
quite new is perfect, 98 : 14
quite so least as truth, 829 : 21
real except humanity, 483 : 12
real till experienced, 479 : 20
refuse, 494 : 10
reputed wise for saying n., 198 : 3
sacred, 844 : 14
said that has not been said, 96 : 15
say n. in dangerous times, 264 : 4
seen n. yet, 169 : 18

Nothing (*continued*)
senseless N., 517 : 6
serious in mortality, 238 : 7
shall be impossible, 42 : 18
she speaks yet says n., 192 : 3
signifying n., 240 : 4
situate under heaven's eye, 188 : 1
sleep in that cellar, 873 : 6
so demoralizing as money, 74 : 12
so good as beforehand, 565 : 19
so irrevocable as mind, 703 : 7
so ridiculous but philosopher said it, 98 : 22
sole or whole, 716 : 18
soul takes n. with her, 84 : 3
stranger ever happened, 878 : 13
stronger than habit, 113 : 12
succeeds like success, 491 : 6
success n. to long for, 914 : 6
sure in sea fight, 408 : 6
take n. of his labor, 27 : 2
take n. on looks, 549 : 28
telling n. in great harangue, 297 : 26
terrible except fear itself, 179 : 13
thank you for n., 168 : 21
that is can pause, 512 : 19
there is n. hid from the heat, 17 : 28
they that starve with n., 198 : 7
think n. done, 416 : 1
'tis something n., 230 : 33
to be feared as fear, 557 : 9
to be thus is n., 238 : 13
to confer, 429 : 13
to do with case, 629 : 15
to do with just man, 41 : 20
to have yet think enow, 257 : 11
to it n. uncertain, 397 : 17
to look backward to, 747 : 7
to lose but chains, 563 : 10
to offer but blood, 743 : 19
to say say nothing, 448 : 9
to wear, 595 : 4
to write about, 123 : 7
too much, 62 : 7
true writer n. to say, 901 : 5
trust that man in n., 360 : 8
turn n. into everything, 694 : 1
useless is or low, 511 : 12
venture nothing win, 629 : 2
want something for n., 681 : 17
war settles n., 817 : 18
we can carry n. out, 51 : 1
we do is wiped out, 648 : 11
we love overmuch, 714 : 11
wears clothes but Man, 268 : 19
whatsoever to do, 894 : 14
when from past n., 733 : 17
will come of nothing, 232 : 24
will help, 830 : 18
will remain, 691 : 2
worth doing completed, 823 : 21
would give up life, 873 : 7
yields n. but discontent, 372 : 8
you couldn't actually say, 793 : 7
Nothingness, created from n., 768 : 24
death a state of n., 83 : 13
death irruption of n., 583 : 16
pass into n., 475 : 16
quintessence even from n., 253 : 1
to n. do sink, 478 : 19
we deny our n., 853 : 3
Nothingnesses of human beings, 85 : 17
Nothing's plenty for me, 836 : 6

Nothing's (*continued*)
so hard but search will find it out, 266 : 18
Nothings, labored n., 333 : 5
Nothing-withholding and free, 651 : 8
Notice, man who used to n. such things, 642 : 3
would they take n., 445 : 8
you take of my labors, 353 : 26
Notion, an' foolish n., 409 : 8
of absolute beauty, 83 : 9
of good life, 869 : 10
Notions about things that happen to us, 453 : 7
call old n. fudge, 569 : 1
fair practices to fair n., 83 : 9
Notorious, rather be n. for calamities, 118 : 20
Notre Dame, Four Horsemen of N., 773 : *n* 4
Nourish, praise doth n. agues, 204 : 33
show contain and n. all world, 191 : 5
Nourished, both male and female n. in both, 80 : 12
how begot how n., 199 : 23
in womb of pia mater, 190 : 30
to its rot, 863 : 14
without denying love, 898 : 7
Nourisher, chief n. in life's feast, 237 : 21
Nourishes, spirit within n., 105 : 22
war n. war, 413 : 16
Nourishing, magnetic n. night, 574 : 19
Nourishment, Demeter gave n. of grain, 77 : 6
little n. I get, 794 : 3
which is called supper, 190 : 14
Nous avons changé tout cela, 297 : *n* 6
Novel a mirror that strolls along highway, 453 : 13
about nothing, 897 : 14
anything that happens subject of n., 136 : 1
attempt to represent life, 652 : 11
balanced between true and false, 887 : 14
best French n. in language, 892 : 11
boom in petroleum but not n., 886 : 10
happens because storyteller moved to passion, 135 : 14
only a n., 440 : 29
only obligation of n. to be interesting, 652 : 12
passion spent its n. force, 529 : 17
supersede fashionable n., 488 : 10
Novelist, no limit to what n. attempt, 652 : 13
Novels, more entertaining than half the n., 751 : 19
which do not die at once, 555 : 9
Novelties, world full of untold n., 595 : 11
Novelty and freshness with familiar, 437 : 17
interest of n., 437 : 14
stains ancient mass, 650 : 10
what a n. is man, 300 : 11
November 485 : 12
fifth of N., 919 : 12
now in N. nearer comes, 790 : 16
thirty days hath N., 162 : 7
what is late N. doing, 807 : 11
November's leaf, 430 : 13
sky chill and drear, 430 : 13

Novus ordo saeclorum, 103 : *n* 9
Now, an everlasting n., 295 : *n* 1
  children need one n., 883 : 7
  eternal n., 295 : 11
  he is dead should I fast, 13 : 21
  here and n. cease to matter, 807 : 24
  history is n. and England, 808 : 16
  if n. 'tis not to come, 224 : 28
  is eternity, 662 : 20
  is immortal life, 662 : 20
  is the accepted time, 49 : 15
  is the winter of our discontent, 186 : 29
  is time for drinking, 107 : 15
  laborer's task o'er, 597 : 15
  leave N. for dogs, 542 : 17
  now cried the Queen, 612 : 20
  or never, 360 : 15
  the day is over, 616 : 7
  the n. years, 888 : 5
  there is merely silence, 794 : 14
  time on either side of n., 904 : 12
  what man wants he wants n., 886 : 3
Nowadays, land of n., 729 : 9
Nowhere did abide, 434 : 27
  dressed up n. to go, 726 : 11
  Eclipse first the rest n., 364 : 6
  knowhow to n., 876 : 13
  to go but out, 684 : 15
  who lives everywhere lives n., 119 : 12
Now's the day, 411 : 15
Nox est perpetua una dormienda, 101 : *n* 15
Noxiae poena, 99 : *n* 5
Nozzle, hold n. agin bank, 636 : 3
Nuclear control, 891 : 15
  disaster engulf all, 891 : 1
  giants ethical infants, 825 : 2
  hell of n. destruction, 909 : 14
Nudgers, numb n., 873 : 11
Nudist, man who publishes his letters becomes n., 847 : 9
Nudnik who believes he's profound, 861 : 12
Nuffin' in de pot, 737 : 2
Nuisance, guest a n. after three days, 94 : 1
  not be n. to others, 508 : 9
  relating exploits a n., 308 : 14
  universal n., 308 : 12
  violetflavored n., 829 : 3
Nuit, je dis à cette n., 464 : *n* 6
  vienne n. sonne l'heure, 770 : *n* 4
Null, splendidly n., 533 : 17
Nullifies, amendment n. discrimination, 776 : 11
Numb nudgers, 873 : 11
Number, god delights in odd n., 117 : *n* 5
  greatest happiness of greatest n., 342 : *n* 5
  harmony manifest in n., 696 : 5
  he telleth the n. of the stars, 22 : 24
  if I called wrong n., 831 : 1
  Lord I want to be in that n., 936 : 8
  more by your n. than light, 251 : 1
  profitable things without n., 150 : 18
  synergetics identifies energy with n., 832 : 16
  teach us to n. our days, 20 : 14
  the clouds in wisdom, 16 : 35
  wealth arithmetic cannot n., 262 : 21
  wealth n. and happiness, 373 : 9
Numbered, God hath n. thy kingdom, 33 : 1
  hairs of head n., 39 : 3
  that which is wanting cannot be n., 26 : 16
Numbering, time made me n. clock, 195 : 17
Numberless are world's wonders, 74 : 14
  infinities of souls, 254 : 8
  shadows n., 476 : 22
Numbers, a few honest men better than n., 272 : 16
  beautiful whole n., 832 : 9
  came, 338 : 10
  determination of quantities by n., 610 : 1
  divinity in odd n., 225 : 28
  express it in n., 594 : 11
  good luck in odd n., 225 : 28
  greatest happiness for greatest n., 342 : 19
  I lisped in n., 338 : 10
  if opposed n. pluck hearts, 208 : 8
  in n. warmly pure, 364 : 10
  long n. rocket mind, 900 : 2
  luck in odd n., 482 : 10
  magic n., 324 : 15
  makes small n. formidable, 378 : 14
  mournful n., 509 : 13
  odd n. most effectual, 117 : 7
  physical laws and laws of n., 610 : 1
  slight acquaintance with n., 417 : 3
  vast n. of disinherited, 694 : 3
  wise words taught in n., 174 : 9
Numbing, narcotics n. pain, 531 : 21
Numbness diffuses my senses, 106 : 24
  drowsy n. pains, 476 : 21
Numerical precision soul of science, 696 : 4
Numerous free active individuals, 586 : 17
  writers become more n., 368 : 6
Numismate, pro tali n. tales merces, 150 : *n* 1
Nun, between two doors sits n., 897 : 3
  holy time quiet as n., 425 : 16
  I became a n., 316 : 3
Nunnery, get thee to a n., 221 : 15
  of thy chaste breast, 295 : 22
Nuns fret not, 427 : 28
Nurse, Athens n. of men, 75 : 12
  best n. Contemplation, 279 : 22
  habit is his n., 413 : 8
  if ye had a good n., 721 : 11
  into greatness, 85 : 5
  meet n. for poetic child, 430 : 11
  Nature's soft n., 206 : 17
  of arms, 369 : 2
  of full-grown souls, 567 : 5
  of manly sentiment, 373 : 23
  old husky n., 575 : 22
  Peace dear n. of arts, 208 : 16
  sucks the n. asleep, 242 : 4
  this n. this teeming womb, 194 : 13
  through night ethereal spark, 883 : 8
  time that aged n., 475 : 19
Nursed dear gazelle, 447 : 14
Nurseries of heaven, 693 : 8
  schools n. of vice, 349 : 14
Nurse's, mewling in n. arms, 211 : 15
Nurses, wives old men's n., 180 : 10
Nursing unconquerable hope, 586 : 2
  wrath to keep it warm, 411 : 4
Nursling of the sky, 468 : 10
Nurslings of immortality, 467 : 3
Nurture, courtly n., 592 : 6
Nurtured by Ramadans, 570 : 9
  secretly n. in cellar, 800 : 7
Nurturing Venus, 100 : 1
Nut, figure of a n., 606 : 18
  little n. tree, 932 : 1
Nut-brown maid, 917 : 4
  spicy n. ale, 278 : 2
Nutmeg, silver n., 932 : 1
Nutmegs ginger cinnamon cloves, 268 : 1
Nutrition, to draw n., 337 : 3
Nutritive truth, 653 : 11
Nuts, we's all poor n., 810 : 6
Nutshell, bounded in a n., 220 : 26
Nymph, haste thee N., 277 : 19
  in thy orisons, 221 : 13
  mountain n. sweet liberty, 277 : 21
  sweet Echo sweetest n., 279 : 18
Nympha pudica Deum vidit, 292 : *n* 3
Nymphets, creatures I designate n., 846 : 3
Nymphic, maidens not human but n., 846 : 3
Nymph's, twitch n. garment off, 541 : 19
Nymphs and satyrs, 717 : 16
  blush not he, 601 : 3
  tell me n., 436 : 13

O

O Altitudo, 274 : 4
  Altitudo in bloodstream, 812 : 1
  blue O, 673 : 20
  cropped out with teeth, 804 : 17
  fortunatam natam me consule Romam, 99 : *n* 2
  my prophetic soul, 219 : 20
  O O O Shakespeherian Rag, 805 : 4
  quanta qualia sunt illa sabbata, 136 : *n* 4
  tempora O mores, 98 : 2
  terque quaterque beati, 104 : *n* 10
  wooden O, 207 : 2
Oafs, muddied o. at goals 709 : 23
Oak and ash and thorn, 710 : 12, 926 : 20
  bend knotted o., 324 : 14
  grass blade's no easier than o., 567 : 15
  heart of o. our ships, 363 : 16
  hearts of o., 158 : 10
  hollow o. our palace, 453 : 20
  in o. none is, 933 : 4
  in the driving keel, 572 : 1
  inherent as o. in acorn, 813 : 13
  many strokes fell the o., 175 : *n* 6
  owl lived in o., 660 : 15
  revolution growth natural as o., 538 : 11
  shadow of British o., 373 : 28
  under o. in stormy weather, 323 : 2
Oak-cleaving thunderbolts, 233 : 24
Oaken, old o. bucket, 455 : 7
Oakhurst, body of John O., 630 : 12
Oakleaves, stone steel stone o., 806 : 12
Oaks branch-charmed, 478 : 4
  fell great o., 347 : 29
  from little acorns, 134 : 15
  many strokes overthrow o., 175 : 13

Oar, broken o. and gear of dead, 808 : 2
forsake, 494 : 6
never had o. or lance, 82 : 2
no better companion than o., 592 : 8
put in her o., 170 : 7
sliding from lifted o., 873 : 16
spread the thin o., 337 : 8
water in music o. forsakes, 637 : 15
wind and wave and o., 528 : 20
Oars, both o. with little skill, 611 : 1
falling o. kept time, 297 : 10
keep time, 446 : 5
muffled o., 439 : 8
were silver, 240 : 29
Oasis in air of lost connections, 893 : 2
Oatcakes, Calvin o. and sulphur, 432 : 18
Oaten, if aught of o. stop, 364 : 11
Oath, blushed as he gave o., 360 : 17
break o. he never made, 291 : 22
Cophetua sware o., 530 : 17
good mouth-filling o., 204 : 19
he that imposes o., 291 : 22
in lapidary inscriptions not upon o., 355 : 18
punishment if one swears false o., 59 : 3
swore full great o., 926 : 20
this o. and this indenture, 79 : 13
trust man on o. or bond, 243 : 1
whore's o., 234 : 14
Oaths are but words, 291 : 20
are straws, 207 : 15
false as dicers' o., 223 : 1
God not take you to task for o., 130 : 13
liar always lavish of o., 275 : 25
strange o., 211 : 15
Oats, definition of o. meant to vex, 352 : *n* 3
grain given to horses, 352 : 12
mares eat o., 933 : 4
munch your good dry o., 197 : 5
Obadias, young O., 320 : 6
Obdured, arm the o. breast, 284 : 21
Obedience bane of genius, 466 : 7
blind o., 690 : 9
enforced o., 233 : 5
fear keeps men in o., 259 : 24
flies to best fitted, 570 : 1
go beyond o. and respect, 701 : 12
infuses that liberal o., 373 : 7
love o. troops of friends, 239 : 31
makes slaves of men, 466 : 7
morals o. to command, 690 : 9
principle of rule or o., 381 : 2
rebellion o. to God, 920 : 14
to God, 920 : 13
to law demanded, 687 : 9
to which is fixed o., 207 : 6
transforms o. into duty, 358 : 13
Obedient, city o. to his will, 84 : 16
compulsion to become o., 791 : 7
to their laws we lie, 67 : 19
to truth, 580 : 7
to whomsoever in authority, 80 : 17
Obelisk, strong upright like o., 683 : 12
Obelisks, these two great o., 5 : 1
Obermann, sedulous ape to O., 668 : 23
Oberon, I jest to O., 196 : 12
my O. what visions, 197 : 7
Obese, solitude grew o., 905 : 1
Obesity mental state, 857 : 12
Obey, Anna whom three realms o., 334 : 4
drift wait and o., 711 : 3
fate summons monarchs o., 304 : 24
haunch and hump is O., 709 : 6
I but o. urge of song, 749 : 18
in silence tyrannous word, 598 : 15
music's power o., 305 : 9
my duty to o. orders, 594 : 9
nature must o. necessity, 217 : 7
thy heart, 494 : 10
to love cherish and o., 56 : 17
voice at eve, 495 : 8
weight of time o., 235 : 20
woman to o., 531 : 7
young blood not o. old decree, 190 : 33
Obeyed at prime, 495 : 8
customs have to be o., 626 : 5
nature to be commanded must be o., 179 : 10
parents insist on being o., 414 : 14
sighed as lover o. as son, 384 : 4
sun and moon o. him, 348 : 11
Truth o. his call, 717 : 10
what wind had taught, 800 : 10
Obeys, bends him but o. him, 511 : 18
has humor when she o., 335 : 23
whoever o. the gods, 57 : 9
Object all sublime, 629 : 11
conformity of o. and intellect, 137 : 8
consideration of public o., 80 : 16
hope without o., 436 : 10
in living to unite, 748 : 18
in possession seldom retains charm, 123 : 8
legitimate o. of government, 389 : 4
let our o. be our country, 450 : 8
noblest function of o., 706 : 7
obligation to o. possessed, 600 : 24
of British government, 401 : 11
of war is peace, 579 : 2
only of war honorable, 384 : 20
paramount o. save Union, 522 : 6
perceived harmony of o., 436 : 19
see o. as it is, 586 : 15
something valuable as o., 422 : 15
strange and high, 297 : 6
suggests vast conditions, 565 : 15
to beautify life give it o., 671 : 21
when gold becomes her o., 206 : 30
Objective and subjective united, 437 : 10
church and state demand, 779 : 12
correlative, 809 : 5
of poet to achieve poetry, 769 : 19
Objectives, liberalism defined in terms of o., 848 : 12
Objectivity and again objectivity, 793 : 7
subjectivity and o., 834 : 13
Objects, all o. of all thought, 423 : 13
and knowledge curious, 576 : 5
classified, 395 : 25
earnest about these o., 791 : 6
extended in space, 769 : 15
extracted from many o., 212 : 18
in an airy height, 320 : 14
material o. are of two kinds, 100 : 9
Oblations, bring no more vain o., 28 : 29
Obligation, haste in paying o., 293 : 28
not created sense of o., 732 : 8
only o. of novel to be interesting, 652 : 12
opportunity implies o., 752 : 3
Obligation (*continued*)
to John owed o., 320 : 26
to object possessed, 600 : 24
under least o. to like, 653 : 4
Obligations, in marriage o. reciprocal, 471 : 1
just o. of government, 631 : 9
rank has its o., 416 : 7
with us in darkness as light, 450 : 20
Oblige, noblesse o., 416 : 7
Obliged, so obliging he ne'er o., 338 : 14
to be a citizen, 584 : 2
to struggle with world, 414 : 4
wealthy and relieved poor, 57 : *n* 8
whatever a body is o. to do, 622 : 12
Obliging, so o. he ne'er obliged, 338 : 14
Oblique, as lines so loves o., 297 : 7
Obliterate, allowing rejection to o. sky, 858 : 11
Obliteration, potential for o., 898 : 12
Oblivion, alms for o., 226 : 16
blind o. swallowed cities, 226 : 15
blindly scattereth poppy, 275 : 7
commend to cold o., 468 : 21
diffuses senses with o., 106 : 24
formless ruin of o., 227 : 4
Lethe the river of o., 284 : 22
longest journey to o., 791 : 2
my o. is a very Antony, 240 : 19
not to be hired, 275 : 9
of a day, 600 : 16
razure of o., 229 : 5
river of o., 593 : 11
sacred to o., 258 : 1
second childishness and o., 211 : 15
six months' o., 635 : 11
voyage of o., 791 : 4
wall of o., 838 : 14
Oblivioni sacrum, 258 : 1
Oblivious, sweet o. antidote, 239 : 32
Oblomovism 550 : 1
Obnoxious, bad or o. laws, 589 : 21
Obscene, abstract words o., 844 : 14
live without duties o., 500 : 7
sailing on o. wings, 435 : 16
things holy profane clean o., 264 : 16
Obscure, cloud o. science, 390 : 1
destiny o., 362 : 2
gods love the o., 56 : 23
hermit poor in place o., 172 : 7
little grave an o. grave, 195 : 7
regions of philosophy, 357 : 17
the palpable o., 284 : 16
when brief I become o., 109 : 20
Obscured, excess of glory o., 283 : 23
Obscurely, body to be buried o., 181 : 16
Obscures show of evil, 199 : 24
Obscurity, no defense but o., 326 : 13
origin involved in o., 452 : 12
Obsequies, celebrates his o., 430 : 8
come to these sorrowful o., 102 : 18
solemnized their o., 275 : 1
Obsequious and conciliating abroad, 452 : 16
Obsequiousness begets friends, 96 : 2
Obsequium amicos parit, 96 : *n* 3
Observance, more honored in breach than o., 219 : 9
Observances of paltry decorum, 432 : 16
Observation, bearings of this o., 548 : 20
devotion to exact o., 762 : 5
know evil from long o., 84 : 9
let o. observe, 351 : *n* 6
man's own o. best physic, 181 : 2

Observation (*continued*)
of human life, 565 : 15
passive science, 551 : 14
speed of o., 751 : 7
with extensive view, 351 : 16
Observations of predecessors, 762 : 5
return to soundness of o., 311 : 1
thickets of erroneous o., 825 : 13
which ourselves we make, 335 : 12
Observe degree priority and place, 225 : 37
due measure, 61 : 23
our different religions, 824 : 12
phenomena we o., 758 : 10
physician with diligence, 254 : 19
pretty in amber to o., 338 : 12
so naturalists o. a flea, 322 : 21
the opportunity, 35 : 2
what we w. not nature itself, 853 : 1
Observed, all his faults o., 217 : 4
of all observers, 221 : 20
single carrot freshly o., 638 : 5
Observer, he is a great o., 215 : 9
measuring device constructed by o., 853 : 1
of human nature, 546 : 11
Observer's, partial for o. sake, 335 : 12
Observers, observed of all o., 221 : 20
Observes, artist o. selects guesses, 695 : 4
Observeth, he that o. the wind, 27 : 21
Observing, quick-eyed Love o. me, 269 : 9
wrongdoing and righteousness, 60 : 25
Obsession, in sorrow's o., 167 : 3
Obsolescence, planned o. of people, 881 : 10
Obsolete, either man o. or war, 832 : 13
not o. language for poetry, 657 : 1
Obstacle, life taken us round o., 734 : 9
Napoleon sole o. to peace, 420 : 14
to every o. oppose patience, 388 : 10
Obstacles, combat o. to get repose, 635 : 18
knows what o. there, 899 : 15
of civilization, 504 : 7
ride over o. win race, 549 : 1
Obstinacy in bad cause, 274 : 8, 359 : 24
Obstinate condolement, 218 : 4
fished by o. isles, 792 : 11
name of one was O., 301 : 21
pliant merry morose, 119 : 17
virtue, 298 : 3
Obstruction, lie in cold o., 228 : 20
Obtain, any man o. that which merits, 436 : 2
Revolution not to o. freedom, 800 : 7
they shall o. mercy, 37 : 4
Obtained, with great sum o. freedom, 46 : 26
Obtaining, pursuing and o. happiness, 367 : 4
Obtains, merit that which he o., 436 : 2
Obvious, education in the o., 644 : 16
gods hate the o., 56 : 23
grand and impressive to mistrust o., 125 : 23
mad-eyed from o., 900 : 2
material and o. things, 311 : 1
Occasion, bent on evil never want o., 111 : 12
courage mounteth with o., 201 : 12
Occasion (*continued*)
delivered upon mellowing of o., 190 : 30
ecstasy affords o., 798 : 15
ill ne'er wants o., 269 : 16
rise with o., 522 : 12
rough torrent of o., 206 : 26
to true o. true, 533 : 4
Occasionem cognosce, 62 : *n* 7
Occasions, all o. invite his mercies, 255 : 1
and causes why, 208 : 13
await o., 536 : 6
do inform against me, 223 : 17
new o. teach new duties, 567 : 8
woman who o. least talk, 81 : 6
Occupation, absence of o. not rest, 376 : 8
idleness and lack of o., 80 : 7
mingle joys with o., 350 : 7
no o. all men idle, 247 : 26
pleasant o. for Chancellor, 628 : 18
pride in his o., 623 : 8
serious o., 422 : 16
Occupation's, Othello's o. gone, 231 : 11
Occupations, let us love o., 548 : 15
let your o. be few, 124 : 20
pause in the day's o., 512 : 3
Occupied territories, 745 : 4
Occupy, face to o. age with dream of, 544 : 26
Occur, accidents o. in best-regulated families, 548 : 35
as they occur, 767 : 21
waiting for something to o., 750 : 12
Occurred, ought never have o., 753 : 5
Ocean, abandon the o., 444 : 2
all we do touched with o., 900 : 11
appalling o., 570 : 14
biddest mighty o. deep, 596 : 18
blue as cornflower, 505 : 3
caves of o. bear, 362 : 8
Cybele fresh from o., 458 : 7
dark secrets of o., 482 : 11
darkened o. booms, 767 : 13
for his fame the o. sea, 257 : 5
grossest iridescence of o., 768 : 12
his legs bestrid the o., 241 : 25
hungry o. gain, 244 : 22
I have loved thee O., 458 : 30
is ever sending gusts, 59 : 26
isn't God upon o., 556 : 15
laughter of o. waves, 70 : 23
loose chains of things, 115 : 13
Lord of the O., 76 : 25
make mighty o., 591 : 7
men want o. without roar, 556 : 4
meteor of o. air, 518 : 12
mind is tossing on the o., 197 : 24
more than o. water broken, 748 : 11
Neptune's o. wash blood, 238 : 1
Northern o. in vast whirls, 345 : 15
nothing but sky and the o., 435 : 18
of hills and hollows, 93 : 3
of life, 512 : 10
of non-knowledge, 862 : 5
of truth undiscovered, 313 : 17
old o. chosen by thee, 575 : 22
painted o., 434 : 14
pores of o. and shores, 468 : 10
post o'er land and o., 282 : 17
roll on thou deep and dark blue o., 458 : 25
round o. and living, air, 423 : 13
Ocean (*continued*)
serpent in o., 907 : 3
shell murmurs as o., 442 : 16
sinks daystar in o. bed, 281 : 4
song of o. seemed to sing, 428 : *n* 5
soul fall into the o., 184 : 9
source of all, 58 : 21
speed over great o. routes, 800 : 10
title to the o., 163 : 13
tomorrow we sail the O. Sea, 107 : 5
under pulsation of lighthouses, 798 : 13
vast and furious o., 265 : 7
veritable o., 767 : 15
where broad o. leans, 368 : 20
wherein the whale, 794 : 13
Ocean's, ancient as o. hills, 907 : 2
as near o. edge as can, 558 : 8
gray melancholy waste, 471 : 5
in o. bosom unespied, 297 : 8
Oceans drowned, 830 : 2
fight on seas and o., 744 : 2
same image in o., 570 : 4
white with foam, 802 : 10
wilderness o., 592 : 6
Oceanus the ocean river, 869 : 13
O'clock, it's now ten o., 537 : 6
says wisely it is ten o., 211 : 5
two o. in morning courage, 421 : 1
October, falls with leaf in O., 260 : 14
lonesome O., 526 : 22
March July O. May, 162 : *n* 3
now for O. eves, 793 : 16
something in O., 696 : 10
October's bright blue weather, 609 : 11
Octopus, adopt character of o., 67 : 4
Octosyllabic verse, 459 : 8
Ocular, give me o. proof, 231 : 12
O'Day, grave of Mike O., 925 : 10
Odd, and this was o., 613 : 1
as can be, 740 : 4
divinity in o. numbers, 225 : 28
good luck in o. numbers, 225 : 28
he never leaves doorway, 567 : 16
luck in o. numbers, 482 : 10
numbers are most effectual, 117 : 7
old ends stolen of holy writ, 187 : 6
people's voice o., 339 : 21
this was scarcely o., 613 : 9
volumes, 441 : 18
Odd-eyed, seld-shaven o., 441 : 6
Oddness, my poetry on side of o., 656 : 22
Odds, all Caesar's and what o., 292 : 12
almost at o. with morning, 239 : 2
facing fearful o., 488 : 14
is gone, 241 : 22
life, 320 : 22
of man's bedevilment, 691 : 23
things at o. when thinker loose, 723 : 16
what is the o., 547 : 20
Ode, I intended an o., 639 : 20
Oderint dum metuant, 97 : *n* 6
Odes, quoted o. and jewels, 530 : 24
rather make o. than beds, 867 : 2
Odi et amo, 102 : *n* 6
et profanum vulgus, 295 : *n* 5
Odious, comparisons are o., 149 : 3
she and comparisons o., 253 : 19
something o. in government leagues off, 381 : 5
vermin, 322 : 11
Odium of success, 670 : 11

Odor, dry aromatic o., 739 : 5
no o. so bad as goodness tainted, 559 : 18
of honeysuckle, 699 : 16
stealing and giving o., 213 : 7
Odorous, amber scent of o. perfume, 288 : 30
Odors, bedewed with liquid o., 107 : 3
crushed sweeter still, 180 : *n* 2
of ointments more durable, 180 : 11
virtue like precious o., 180 : 8
when violets sicken, 469 : 18
Odysseus, soon as he had seen O., 60 : 24
Odyssey, thunder of the O., 657 : 4
Oedipus, I am Davos not O., 96 : 4
met Sphinx, 851 : 3
solved riddle of Sphinx, 74 : 6
O'ercast, sun's o. with blood, 201 : 22
O'erdoing Termagant, 221 : 23
O'erdusted, more laud than gilt o., 226 : 21
O'erfraught heart, 239 : 20
O'er-informed tenement of clay, 303 : 20
O'erleaps, ambition which o. itself, 236 : 24
O'erthrown, noble mind here o., 221 : 19
O'ertrip, fearfully o. the dew, 200 : 22
O'erwhelm, though all earth o. them, 218 : 26
Off agin on agin, 727 : 13
let's call whole thing o., 836 : 8
on bus or o. bus, 913 : 7
with her head, 612 : 1
with his head, 187 : 14, 324 : 27
with Old Woman, 680 : 2
with you where you want to go, 145 : *n* 4
you lendings, 234 : 7
Offend, averse to flatter or o., 333 : 22
if thy right hand o. thee, 37 : 8
not o. you by speaking truth, 154 : 4
Offended, brother o. is harder to be won, 24 : 21
Deity o., 409 : 13
devils being o., 230 : 8
him have I o., 216 : 16
if we shadows have o., 197 : 23
this hath not o. king, 155 : 10
with his estate, 130 : 1
Offender, hugged o. forgave offense, 307 : 7
love o. detest offense, 307 : *n* 2
never pardons, 115 : *n* 3
Offenders, mercy on us miserable o., 54 : 14
society o., 629 : 6
Offending Adam, 207 : 3
most o. soul alive, 208 : 9
Offends me to the soul, 221 : 23
no law is king indeed, 178 : 4
Offense, conscience void of o., 46 : 30
dire o. from amorous causes, 333 : 24
giving and receiving o., 472 : 10
hugged offender forgave o., 307 : 7
let punishment match o., 99 : 5
love offender detest o., 307 : *n* 2
my o. is rank, 222 : 25
pardon one o. encourage many, 112 : 3
real o. was having mind, 652 : 9
rock of o., 29 : 14
scorn to take o., 333 : 10
would appear o. in us, 215 : 14
Offenses, book wherein written our o., 260 : 4
enemies for small o., 258 : 9
old o. of affections new, 245 : 16
Offer he can't refuse, 897 : 18
I o. hunger thirst battles, 509 : 7
instantly close with o., 595 : 16
itself to be unmasked, 786 : 3
not o. to people but ask, 890 : 5
nothing to o. but blood, 743 : 19
yourselves to sea, 651 : 8
Offered, I o. Being for it, 605 : 20
Offering, a lamb for a burnt o., 8 : 13
too little asking too much, 422 : 6
Offerings, knowledge of God more than burnt o., 33 : 11
pale Hecate's o., 237 : 14
Office and affairs of love, 209 : 9
and custom, 225 : 37
boy to attorney's firm, 627 : 14
Circumlocution O., 549 : 19
have only o. no opinion, 413 : 9
heaven about to confer great o., 89 : 25
I shall return to the o., 327 : 7
insolence of o., 221 : 12
lust of o., 566 : 3
never ask refuse resign o., 348 : 19
public o. public trust, 539 : 4, 631 : *n* 1
serves it in o. of a wall, 194 : 13
so act toward o. so toward wealth, 121 : 20
so clear in his great o., 236 : 24
spoils of o., 566 : 3
to execute laws royal o., 374 : 3
to o. and so to bed, 773 : 11
unfit to hold an o., 93 : 6
vice-presidency most insignificant o., 381 : 16
which false man does easy, 238 : 10
Officeholder, president is o., 879 : 4
Officer, drunken o. of British rule, 911 : 1
fear each bush an o., 186 : 27
Officers, behind o. government people, 590 : 6
civil o. removed on impeachment, 391 : 11
her o. march with armies, 539 : 15
make o. but not scholars, 259 : 2
public o. servants, 631 : 6
white o. cast lot, 617 : 6
Offices acceptable as elsewhere, 388 : 14
cast longing eye on o., 388 : 14
estates degrees and o., 199 : 14
female sex excluded from honors and o., 393 : 3
imperfect o. of prayer, 428 : 10
people I cannot win with o., 300 : 23
post o. and cabinet appointments, 520 : *n* 3
Official, no o. high or petty, 821 : 6
Officious fool worse than foe, 420 : 5
innocent sincere, 356 : 24
Officiously to keep alive, 564 : 19
Offspring of heaven firstborn, 285 : 4
of idle hour, 636 : 10
tempt its new-fledged o., 370 : 7
terrible from camps, 864 : 15
time's noblest o., 330 : 25
true source of human o., 286 : 5
we are also his o., 46 : 17, 92 : 11
Offspring (*continued*)
we are your o., 92 : 1
Oft in the stilly night, 447 : 7
Often, hit o., 777 : 12
strike o. as you can, 589 : 15
Ogalala Iroquois, 874 : 8
O'Grady, colonel's lady an' Judy O., 709 : 11
Oh what a beautiful mornin', 833 : 10
Oil, everything soothed by o., 116 : 5
for its own wheels, 376 : 7
her mouth is smoother than o., 23 : 10
incomparable o. Macassar, 460 : 10
land of o. olive, 11 : 14
little o. in a cruse, 13 : 42
midnight o., 267 : 12, 331 : 12
no use of o., 247 : 26
of joy for mourning, 31 : 25
pouring o. on the sea, 116 : *n* 2
thou anointest my head with o., 18 : 7
vinegar sugar, 371 : 13
wasted o. unprofitably burns, 376 : 6
wisdom out of midnight o., 715 : 17
words were softer than o., 19 : 22
Oilrinsed circles of ecstasy, 844 : 1
Oily, glib and o. art, 232 : 29
round fat o. man of God, 345 : 22
Ointment, at three hundred pence o. prize, 268 : 11
better than precious o., 27 : 3
box of precious o., 41 : 2
good name like precious o., 180 : 11
not sold for three hundred pence, 45 : 16
Ointments, odors of o. more durable, 180 : 11
O.K. 921 : 19
OK, I'm O. you're O., 877 : 13
Okie means scum, 857 : 5
Oklahoma, Okie mean from O., 857 : 5
Olaf glad and big, 829 : 8
Old Abe Lincoln, 519 : *n* 4
abusing of God's patience, 225 : 12
accompany o. age, 239 : 31
acquaintance be forgot, 410 : 11
Adam, 56 : 16
age a regret, 501 : 15
Age and Experience, 315 : 21
age coming bolt door, 133 : 2
age crown of life, 99 : 10
age, education best provision for o., 87 : 4
age ill layer up of beauty, 208 : 19
age, in a good o., 8 : 8
age in universal man, 178 : *n* 12
age is an island, 614 : 10
age is women's hell, 296 : 6
age lacking neither honor nor lyre, 107 : 13
age level light, 822 : 9
age may come after you, 575 : 13
age most unexpected, 770 : 7
age play's last act, 99 : 10
age should burn, 887 : 4
age the harbor of all ills, 92 : 5
age the only disease, 497 : 27
age time of spending, 290 : 9
all times o. are good, 462 : 13
always wanted to be o., 884 : 24
and bitter of tongue, 712 : 10
and crafty and wise, 712 : 10
and foolish king, 26 : 25
and godly and grave, 712 : 10

Old (*continued*)
and gray full of sleep, 712 : 8
and gray-headed error, 274 : 25
and haughty nation, 279 : 5
and old sad and old, 778 : 6
and stricken in years, 11 : 35
and tried, 521 : 4
and young on last cruise, 667 : 17
Apple Tree, 753 : 2
armchair, 562 : 11
as I am for love unfit, 307 : 5
as the hills, 432 : 4, 740 : 17
as we left grow o., 727 : 1
as yonder elm, 778 : 5
ash on o. man's sleeve, 808 : 11
ask for the o. paths, 31 : 37
at evening candlelit, 162 : 12
authors to read, 179 : 18
bald cheater Time, 255 : 13
ball game, 765 : 14
bawd is dead, 717 : 18
beats off louring O. Age, 153 : 8
beauty making beautiful o. rhyme, 245 : 12
before we grow o. and die, 713 : 7
bellows full of angry wind, 714 : 20
bells of O. Bailey, 930 : 7
bitch gone in teeth, 792 : 16
Black Joe, 598 : 7
black ram tupping ewe, 229 : 18
books manners times wines, 371 : 3
books old Nankin blue, 179 : *n* 4
born o. and ugly, 547 : 28
busy o. fool unruly Sun, 252 : 7
cast me not off in the time of o. age, 19 : 34
Cervantes, 570 : 11
change o. love for new, 177 : 7
chaos of sun, 767 : 4
chilly and grown o., 543 : 12
chip of o. block, 373 : 11
conservatism adherence to o., 521 : 4
custom made life sweet, 210 : 23
dance attention on o. age, 717 : 13
dance in o. dame yet, 760 : 1
darling I am growing o., 662 : 22
despise not thy mother when she is o., 25 : 10
disease of o. men avarice, 261 : 11
dog barks backward, 749 : 2
dog Tray, 443 : *n* 4
dogs shame nakedness of o. man, 59 : 6
ends stolen of holy writ, 187 : 6
England to adorn, 710 : 12
England's winding sheet, 406 : 18
every o. man's eye, 192 : 21
experience do attain, 279 : 1
faiths loosen and fall, 633 : 6
familiar faces, 441 : 5
fashions please best, 188 : 33
father antic the law, 202 : 28
father old artificer, 777 : 18
Father William, 439 : 15, 611 : 9
few know how to be o., 294 : 7
foolish fond o. man, 235 : 9
former things grow o., 266 : 15
forsake not o. friend, 35 : 15
forsaken bough, 519 : 19
fortify thy name against o. age, 182 : 7
friends are best, 179 : *n* 4
friends times manners, 371 : 3
friends to trust, 179 : 18

Old (*continued*)
gang, 663 : 4
glorious song of o., 537 : 16
Glory, 493 : 11
glory of o. story is forever, 105 : 30
Glory on broomstick, 699 : 13
God of our fathers known of o., 709 : 16
God these o. men, 76 : 5
gratitude soon grows o., 86 : 17
green o. age, 303 : 15
grew o. between fires of Troy, 850 : 13
grow o. along with me, 544 : 8
grow o. in body but never mind, 99 : 8
grow o. learning many things, 62 : 14
grow o. without visiting, 65 : 9
grow virtuous in o. age, 340 : 12
growing o. in drawing nothing, 376 : 27
grown o. before my time, 608 : 18
grown o. in love, 407 : 4
had to grow o. to learn, 400 : 11
half as o. as Time, 416 : 3, 552 : 9
half-witted sheep, 428 : *n* 2
happy o. man, 103 : 8
he will make us o., 787 : 6
heads on young shoulders, 896 : 1
heard o. o. men say, 713 : 3
hearts not grown o., 713 : 16
hermit of Prague, 214 : 27
homes old names old splendors, 726 : 2
hot time in o. town, 705 : 1
houses mended, 325 : 1
how did I get o. so quick, 856 : 9
how o. is Ann, 924 : 2
husky nurse, 575 : 22
I an o. woman now, 641 : 14
I grow o. I grow o., 803 : 18
I have been young and now am o., 18 : 25
I know thee not o. man, 206 : 36
I love everything o., 371 : 3
if Ancient Mariner called O. Sailor, 621 : 2
if to be o. and merry be sin, 204 : 6
if youth but knew if o. age but could, 163 : 11
in o. age intent upon our interests, 97 : 6
in o. age learn to be wise, 75 : 2
in story, 530 : 26
in the glint o. gold, 742 : 9
Kentucky home, 598 : 5
kept thy truth so pure of o., 282 : 18
King Cole, 929 : 14
kit bag, 770 : 14
know how to grow o., 580 : 10
lads that will never be o., 691 : 5
lady from Dubuque, 824 : 2
Lady of Threadneedle Street, 407 : 12
lamps for new, 919 : 24
last to lay o. aside, 333 : 6
life's o. death new, 546 : 4
like him that's growing o., 75 : 21
like to give good advice, 293 : 17
linen wash whitest, 262 : 1
little o. New York, 699 : 17
loosen o. foundations, 761 : 10
love never sick o. dead, 172 : 9
love noght o. as whan newe, 147 : 18
love of o. for o., 692 : 17
lovers soundest, 262 : 1

Old (*continued*)
mad blind despised king, 468 : 4
man as o. as his arteries, 301 : 3
man broken, 249 : 10
man eloquent, 282 : 6
man had so much blood, 239 : 25
man in dry month, 804 : 13
man looks before and after, 57 : 22
man to whom old men hearkened, 110 : 10
man twice a child, 220 : 32
man weds tyrant, 77 : 19
man who will not laugh, 704 : 9
man who wouldn't say prayers, 931 : 8
man with beard, 550 : 4
man with something of young, 99 : 8
man young gardener, 389 : 6
manners books wines, 371 : 3
man's darling, 161 : 6
man's eagle mind, 717 : 11
man's frenzy, 717 : 10
man's gold, 730 : 18
men are children, 82 : 1
men from chimney corner, 176 : 11
men garrulous by nature, 99 : 9
men have rosy faces, 669 : 7
men know young men fools, 177 : 13
men ought to be explorers, 807 : 24
men shall dream dreams, 33 : 17
men should be explorers, 874 : 8
men's dream, 304 : 5
men's heads bare, 816 : 2
men's lies, 792 : 14
mighty men of o., 7 : 27
Minstrel infirm and o., 429 : 20
Mithridates he died o., 691 : 18
moon in her arm, 926 : 11
mother Hubbard, 932 : 7
my body now o. tree, 314 : 2
Nankin blue, 179 : *n* 4
nature abhors the o., 497 : 27
new friend fit to make o., 664 : 4
new way to pay o. debts, 263 : 1
new wine in o. bottles, 38 : 30
New World redress balance of O., 422 : 7
new world which is o., 530 : 11
no country for o. men, 714 : 22
no falsehood lingers to o. age, 75 : 20
no fool like o. fool, 160 : 21
no man would be o., 322 : 4
no o. age only sorrow, 701 : 4
no one so o. he cannot live, 153 : 15
no time like o. time, 519 : 1
not criticize O. Testament, 699 : 1
not O. Brown any longer, 560 : 26
not one continued faithful until o. age, 86 : 5
not so o. not so plain, 628 : 19
not to be tuneless in o. age, 107 : *n* 11
not yet so o. but she may learn, 199 : 29
nothing o. about country, 623 : 3
now my o. bawd dead, 717 : 18
oaken bucket, 455 : 7
ocean chosen by thee, 575 : 22
ocean's gray melancholy, 471 : 5
off with O. Woman, 680 : 2
offenses of affections new, 245 : 16
one is fat and grows o., 203 : 28
or modern bard, 279 : 6
order changeth, 534 : 31
pardon o. fathers, 713 : 10

Old (*continued*)
peaceful as o. age, 543 : 2
penny in o. man's hat, 921 : 3
people in o. times had convictions, 482 : 1
pippins toothsomest, 262 : 1
poetics in my alchemy, 674 : 7
poets comfort to man, 663 : 17
poor despised o. man, 233 : 26
Pretender, 812 : 12
prosperity blessing of O. Testament, 180 : 5
pry loose o. walls, 761 : 10
religious facitons, 374 : 5
ring out the o., 532 : 22
roast beef of O. England, 349 : *n* 3
rugged cross, 738 : 11
save o. worth saving, 723 : 11
say I'm growing o., 454 : 8
saying wise and o., 173 : *n* 8
sea captains young or o., 575 : 22
seem though I die o., 717 : 3
sepulchral urns, 376 : 6
shade of O. Apple Tree, 753 : 2
ships sail like swans, 785 : 16
shoes easiest for feet, 179 : *n* 4
sight make o. man young, 529 : 2
sight yet somehow young, 571 : 8
sign of o. age, 433 : 16
so be it when I grow o., 425 : 7
so young body with so o. head, 200 : 8
soakers, 309 : 23
soldiers never die, 771 : 7, 924 : 9
soldiers surest, 262 : 1
some o. lover's ghost, 253 : 9
something o. something new, 924 : 6
speak truth more as I grow o., 165 : 16
stones that cannot be deciphered, 807 : 23
studies a delight to the o., 98 : 7
sublime in o. sense, 792 : 10
surgeon to o. shoes, 214 : 30
sweetheart of mine, 665 : 10
talk of crabbed o. men, 101 : 18
tedious o. fools, 220 : 22
tell o. tales and laugh, 235 : 12
terms between O. and New World, 401 : 14
tested to extreme o. age, 584 : 8
text is o. orator green, 189 : 13
they shall not grow o., 727 : 1
things worn out and o., 712 : 12
think he is growing o., 453 : 4
this news is o. enough, 228 : 25
though I look o. I am strong, 210 : 29
thousand wars of o., 532 : 23
till stars o., 596 : 16
time as he grows o., 70 : 26
Time is still a-flying, 266 : 11
Time makes these decay, 272 : 1
time to be o., 495 : 7
Time you o. gypsy man, 732 : 17
times manners books wines, 371 : 3
times not forgotten, 554 : 1
'tis well o. age is out, 307 : 1
today's newspaper o., 741 : 2
too revolutionary for o. ideas, 787 : 14
unhappy far-off things, 426 : 5
universal truths, 838 : 8
veracity with o. age, 294 : 6
very o. most selfish, 539 : 23
vigor in man not yet o., 116 : 2

Old (*continued*)
Virginia, 596 : 12
wars planned by o. men, 773 : 4
we knew thee of o., 484 : 1
weary and o. with service, 249 : 3
weeping philosopher when o., 198 : 12
what men of o. sought, 314 : 4
when he is o. he will not depart, 24 : 35
when he's o. cashiered, 229 : 15
when o. age crept over, 696 : 3
when o. men gather, 729 : 9
when thou art o. and rich, 228 : 16
when time is o., 226 : 15
wine to drink, 179 : 18
wine wholesomest, 262 : 1
wines, 371 : 3
winter hangs on till o., 739 : 2
with o. woes new wail, 244 : 11
wives' fables, 50 : 29
wives' tale, 720 : 13
woman lived in shoe, 931 : 10
woman lived under hill, 933 : 11
woman tossed in blanket, 932 : 5
women should not be perfumed, 62 : 1
wood burn brightest, 262 : 1
wood to burn, 179 : 18
words when short best, 746 : 17
world not grow o. at all, 310 : 7
World overrun with oppression, 384 : 12
world too o., 537 : 7
you never can be o., 245 : 11
young and o. come forth to play, 278 : 1
young and o. the same, 70 : 8
young blood not obey o. decree, 190 : 33
young in limbs judgment o., 199 : 10
young men think o. men fools, 177 : 13
Older men declare war, 750 : 20
news o. than ale, 370 : 12
place than Eden, 742 : 11
she is o. every minute, 647 : 19
than the rocks, 638 : 11
they hurt me I grow o., 792 : 9
we grow o. world stranger, 807 : 23
Oldest hath borne most, 235 : 20
loves but their o. clothes, 252 : 5
sins newest ways, 206 : 33
two o. professions, 801 : 9
Old-fashioned house we dwell in, 607 : 16
poetry choicely good, 271 : 7
Old-time conceptions of sovereignty, 837 : 14
that o. religion, 921 : 15
Old-timers, we are o., 892 : 18
'Ole, if you knows of better 'o., 796 : 3
O'Leary, with O. in grave, 713 : 11
Oligarchical, power in o. junto, 382 : 4
Oligarchy government resting on property, 85 : 2
Oliphant, Roland sonnez de votre o., 136 : *n* 9
Olive grove of Academe, 288 : 14
in her mouth was an o. leaf, 7 : 32
land of oil o., 11 : 14
leaf pacific sign, 288 : 2
vines and o. trees, 868 : 21
Oliver, a Roland for an O., 136 : *n* 10
Roland valorous O. wise, 136 : 13

Oliver (*continued*)
Twist asked for more, 546 : 30
Olives, girl goes gathering o., 841 : 7
of endless age, 245 : 13
Olivia, cry out O., 213 : 19
Olympian bards, 494 : 9
in wrath the O. Pericles, 81 : 11
is a difficult foe, 57 : 13
laconic and O., 728 : 18
Olympic, victor in O. games or announcer, 70 : 20
Olympus ever unchanging, 59 : 27
made O. tremble, 57 : 12, 60 : *n* 3
Notes from O., 783 : 5
pile Ossa on O., 60 : 9
roll up leafy O., 103 : 29
shady O., 60 : *n* 3
Om 57 : 1
Omar, diver O. plucked from bed, 569 : 2
inclined to agree with O., 856 : 12
Omega, I am Alpha and O., 53 : 33
Omelet, can't make o. without breaking eggs, 928 : 6
Omen, may it not be an o., 133 : 4
Omens, barbaric o., 798 : 1
sits watching for o., 82 : 12
'Omer smote bloomin' lyre, 708 : 24
Omission, sins of o. venial, 357 : 11
Omissions are not accidents, 798 : *n* 3
Omit needless words, 729 : 7
Omitted all voyage of their life, 217 : 5
Omne ignotum pro magnifico est, 123 : *n* 2
Omnes eodem cogimur, 107 : *n* 17
eodem patre nati, 259 : 9
Omnia vincit amor, 103 : *n* 13
Omnibuses, carriages and o., 781 : 15
Omnipotence, sea creation of O., 741 : 12
Omnipotent but friendless to reign, 467 : 4
defy the O. to arms, 283 : 4
docile and o., 605 : 19
Father with his thunder, 60 : *n* 3
Omnipresence, brooding o. in sky, 644 : 21
Omnipresent, government o. teacher, 678 : 1
process of sex, 689 : 19
Omnis cellula a cellula, 584 : 5
Omnivorous, I am o., 861 : 4
with feelings beings events, 861 : 4
On bus or off bus, 913 : 7
off agin o. agin, 727 : 13
Stanley on, 431 : 3
with New Woman, 680 : 2
with the dance, 457 : 15
ye brave, 443 : 15
Once I was beautiful, 908 : 9
in a lifetime, 793 : 14
man can die but o., 206 : 25
more unto the breach, 207 : 16
more upon waters, 457 : 11
one lives but o., 394 : 12
to every man and nation, 567 : 6
to have died o. enough, 106 : 1
Ondoyant, l'homme vain divers et o., 164 : *n* 5
One a penny, 931 : 17
acquainted with night, 748 : 14
all for o., 189 : 19, 491 : 5
all o. a hundred years hence, 498 : 17
all things are o., 69 : 26

One (*continued*)
alone I am with him, 126 : 14
America o. yet many, 885 : 6
among a thousand, 16 : 23
and inseparable, 450 : 16
and one with shadowy third, 542 : 9
and the same thing, 308 : 19
be strong be also o., 597 : 2
bell strikes o., 330 : 7
born in a manager, 299 : 10
by one in moonlight, 811 : 14
by one two by two, 468 : 6
clear call for me, 535 : 19
composed of many, 106 : 8
conceive many without the o., 85 : 14
country one constitution, 451 : 4
crowded hour, 375 : 1
damned thing after another, 756 : 4
dead deathless hour, 601 : 17
each hath o. and is o., 251 : 15
ear herde at tothir out, 144 : 25
enemy is too much, 270 : 7
eternity and I are o., 631 : 16
fair daughter and no more, 221 : 1
fall o. by o., 372 : 4
far-off divine event, 532 : 27
fire burns out another's, 191 : 19
fish ball, 592 : 4
flag one land one heart, 518 : 15
flew over cuckoo's nest, 933 : 15
food to o. poison to others, 101 : 6
foot in sea one on shore, 209 : 16
for all, 189 : 19, 491 : 5
for my master, 930 : 5
for o. sweet grape vine
destroy, 189 : 20
found truth in all but o., 195 : 10
from all, 126 : 19
from all things o. and from o. all
things, 70 : 5
god greatest among gods, 67 : 14
God law element, 532 : 27
good knowledge, 79 : 3
good turn deserves another, 117 : 14
grand sweet song, 566 : 12
hearts that beat as o., 508 : 1
hundred years of solitude, 908 : 3
I am only o., 590 : 5
I am party of o., 846 : 17
if by land, 512 : 7
if ever two were o., 290 : 12
illness one cure, 380 : 5
in life and death, 628 : 14
is fat and grows old, 203 : 28
is or is not, 85 : 15
just o. of those things, 820 : 5
less than tenth part of o., 226 : 13
life to lose, 401 : 9
little o. shall become a
thousand, 31 : 24
live as two, 806 : 11
lost but o. twa behin', 411 : 20
low man adding o. to o., 542 : 19
majority of o., 558 : 5
man among a thousand, 27 : 11
man of o. book, 133 : 11
man one vote, 925 : 8
man's meat another's
poison, 101 : *n* 6
man's will all men's misery, 175 : 8
minute with him, 786 : 10
more river, 936 : 3
more unfortunate, 485 : 21
my little o. pretty o., 530 : 25

One (*continued*)
nation evermore, 518 : 15
nation indivisible, 677 : 10
nature o. and continuous, 558 : 20
near one too far, 542 : 9
never lose touch of the o., 697 : 2
not o. for putting off proof, 748 : 15
on God's side majority, 538 : 14
only o. military organization, 825 : 6
our life became o., 849 : 9
our two souls which are o., 253 : 4
pain lessened by another's, 191 : 19
parted between twelve and o., 207 : 13
pay for o. by o., 708 : 18
people arose as o. man, 12 : 23
perfect limousine, 827 : 13
perfect rose, 827 : 13
road up and road down o. and
same, 70 : 6
shock of recognition, 569 : 18
small o. a strong nation, 31 : 24
small step for man, 910 : 14
Spirit that is O., 657 : 5
spot where I made O., 517 : 14
striking at root of evil, 559 : 19
swallow not a summer, 87 : 15
sweet sacrifice, 248 : 25
sweetly solemn thought, 594 : 6
that loved not wisely, 232 : 20
the o. and the many, 85 : 11
the other will contain, 605 : 21
thinks of all the hands, 804 : 3
third of a nation, 780 : 2
this o. thing I do, 50 : 4
three centuries removed, 857 : 14
to succeed possible only o.
way, 87 : 17
touch of nature, 226 : 20
touch of Venus, 861 : 8
two and third in your bosom, 192 : 23
two moremens more, 778 : 6
two one two, 612 : 18
two three strikes you're out, 765 : 14
twothreefourfive pigeons, 828 : 13
we are o. flesh, 287 : 24
who died for truth, 605 : 13
with law a majority, 736 : 14
word frees us, 75 : 14
world or none, 828 : 2
world's life and mine o., 595 : 3
One-and-twenty, when I was o., 690 : 20
One-armed man pasting
wallpaper, 699 : 10
One-book man, 433 : 8
One-horse town, 622 : 10
One-hoss shay, 519 : 15
Oneness, household in o. of
mind, 59 : 28
One's, nothing greater than o.
self, 574 : 27
Ones, great o. eat up little o., 243 : 13
Oneself, belong to o., 164 : 18
desire to think well of o., 809 : 10
entirely honest with o., 678 : 5
hell is o., 809 : 1
idea of o. as cause, 308 : 13
little one knows o., 815 : 11
look better into o., 700 : 4
mistaking o. for oracle, 735 : 9
more difficult to judge o., 849 : 3
not live unto o., 91 : 5
stranger to o. estranged from
others, 867 : 7
to be saint for o. 581 : 9

One-third of a nation, 780 : 2
One-upmanship 848 : 14
Onion atoms lurk in bowl, 433 : 11
let first o. flourish, 668 : 18
thumb instead of o., 911 : 13
will do well for such shift, 188 : 24
Onions, eat no o. nor garlic, 197 : 11
wel loved he garleek o. lekes, 146 : 13
Onlie begetter of insuing
sonnets, 243 : *n* 4
Only love sprung from only
hate, 191 : 27
that it is your o. one, 87 : 29
Onset, stand aside from enemy's
o., 81 : 5
with eternity, 604 : 11
word of o. gave, 426 : 9
Ontogenesis recapitulation of
phylogenesis, 617 : 10
Ontogeny recapitulates
phylogeny, 617 : *n* 5
Onward Christian soldiers, 616 : 6
goes pilgrim band, 616 : 8
half a league o., 533 : 9
sailors cry, 688 : 12
steer right o., 282 : 19
upward still and o., 567 : 8
Ootah, Eskimo O. had
explanation, 679 : 12
Oozing out at palm of my
hands, 398 : 18
Oozy weeds about me twist, 572 : 7
Opal, cloudy flaming o. ring, 711 : 12
Ope his mouth out flew trope, 290 : 18
their golden eyes, 243 : 16
when I o. my lips, 198 : 2
Open afresh starry folds, 474 : 22
and friendly in private, 80 : 17
covenants of peace, 682 : 14
door, 636 : 8
doors of his face, 17 : 5
ear the o. vowels tire, 333 : 7
ever-o. door, 57 : *n* 8
eyes o. before marriage, 347 : 19
face facts with both eyes o., 154 : 10
free and o. encounter, 282 : 5
locks whoever knocks, 239 : 7
mind free discussion, 737 : 8
my heart, 542 : 7
my mistress the o. road, 669 : 3
no right to o. door, 83 : 16
one door closes another o., 153 : 17
page of book carelessly o., 908 : 12
ports of slumber o., 206 : 29
rebuke better than secret love, 25 : 23
road, 575 : 9, 669 : 3
sentence is for o. war, 284 : 6
sesame, 920 : 1
sesame to every portal, 664 : 17
society, 861 : 7
speech o. man to man, 310 : *n* 1
take to o. road, 575 : 9
thou my lips, 19 : 18
Time and let him pass, 696 : 13
unto whom all hearts are o., 55 : 15
war, 284 : 6
where knock is o. wide, 365 : 8
wounds shrunk sometimes, 835 : 9
ye everlasting gates, 287 : 1
ye the gates, 30 : 9
Opened, door we never o., 807 : 2
he o. us, 889 : 16
knock and it shall be o., 38 : 12
Lord o. mouth of the ass, 11 : 2

Opened (*continued*)
my heart new o., 249 : 3
your eyes shall be o., 7 : 6
Openest, thou o. thine hand, 22 : 21
Open-eyed Conspiracy, 247 : 28
Opening eyelids of the morn, 280 : 10
of a door, 608 : 4
Open-minded impartial adjustment, 682 : 14
Opens into a world, 406 : 6
Operation, our Constitution in o., 348 : 16
preparing us for fatal o., 887 : 10
Operations by which length determined, 776 : 3
we perform without thinking, 697 : 5
Ophelia, I loved O., 224 : 22
Ophir, distant O., 760 : 19
Opiate, emptied dull o., 476 : 21
religion o. of people, 706 : 6
Opinion, backed o. with quotations, 320 : 19
basis of government o., 388 : 4
custom supported by popular o., 688 : 13
determined by feelings, 579 : 8
difference of o., 273 : 16, 624 : 26
diversity of o. basic to nation, 825 : 12
error of o. tolerated, 388 : 16
government is organized o., 751 : 2
governs world, 682 : 2
gross and scope of my o., 217 : 18
have only office no o., 413 : 9
having no o. at all, 386 : 17
historians of o., 783 : 7
hold o. with Pythagoras, 200 : 7
honor depends on o. of mob, 308 : 23
inconsistencies of o., 451 : 10
individual given freedom of o., 778 : 11
intelligence of public o., 617 : 4
is knowledge in making, 282 : 2
is of his own o. still, 291 : 30
is truth filtered, 538 : 17
is uniformity of o. attainable, 387 : 15
live after world's o., 497 : 1
luxury of own o., 553 : 13
man know to defy o., 417 : 13
no o. but their own, 682 : 10
no very exalted o., 372 : 10
of Pythagoras concerning wildfowl, 200 : *n* 3
of strongest always best, 296 : 9
only one of contrary o., 508 : 4
orthodox in o., 821 : 6
petrified o., 626 : 19
public o. everything, 521 : 2
public o. exacts obedience, 597 : 10
public o. in advance of law, 723 : 4
public o. in reverence, 626 : 13
public o. stronger than legislature, 603 : 13
public o. variable, 595 : 18
public o. weak tyrant, 559 : 2
public o. welcomes talent, 80 : 17
raw material of o., 682 : 2
researchers into public o., 869 : 2
sacrifices it to your o., 372 : 9
science and o., 80 : 5
stifling o. is evil, 508 : 8
subject o. to coercion, 387 : 14
that there are no gods, 86 : 5
the more unpopular an o., 620 : 20
think last o. right, 333 : 14

Opinion (*continued*)
this fool-gudgeon this o., 198 : 4
unanimity of o., 700 : 2
vagrant o. without support, 647 : 16
we endeavor to stifle, 508 : 8
whole climate of o., 868 : 14
woman's soon estranged o., 470 : 10
Opinionated mind, 714 : 20
Opinions and a will, 566 : 3
are accursed, 714 : 20
bought golden o., 237 : 1
buys o. like meat, 621 : 3
common o. uncommon abilities, 597 : 9
decent respect to o., 387 : 9
forever testing new o., 638 : 14
have rate of growth, 620 : 20
how long halt ye between two o., 14 : 1
I have my own o., 564 : 5
learning and infused o., 206 : *n* 4
maintain no ill o., 370 : *n* 3
moderns only have o., 482 : 1
much writing many o., 282 : 2
never two o. alike, 165 : 14
new o. always suspected, 307 : 13
not survive without fight, 755 : 12
proper o. for time, 869 : 2
rawness of personal o., 692 : 13
share no man's o., 564 : 5
so many men so many o., 97 : 2
State takes no notice of o., 272 : 17
stiff in o., 304 : 10
tell you what his o. is, 626 : 12
time will change your o., 86 : 3
turned from one's course by o., 93 : 6
zeal for different o., 398 : 2
Opium, Coleridge wrecked in o., 589 : 12
let us give them o., 706 : 6
Opponent, malign o. glorify himself, 502 : 20
never corner o., 834 : 1
of children of light, 587 : 3
weaned from error, 727 : 5
Opponents of innovation die out, 686 : 11
Opporchunity, home of o., 722 : 23
Opportunities, new problems new o., 890 : 4
provide women with economic o., 903 : 10
woman with fair o., 539 : 5
Opportunity, age o. no less than youth, 512 : 17
fleeting, 80 : 9
freedom not safety but o., 789 : 5
healing also matter of o., 79 : 14
home of o., 722 : 23
implies obligation, 752 : 3
is great bawd, 347 : 11
is that wherein is no time, 79 : 15
Jupiter not bring back o., 114 : 12
knocks only once, 114 : *n* 4
man who forces o., 400 : 19
maximum of o., 680 : 24
misses o., 400 : 19
neglected o. comes not back, 109 : *n* 5
observe the o., 35 : 2
replace despair with o., 872 : 10
stop to think and miss o., 110 : 22
time is that wherein is o., 79 : 15
to make dreams true, 824 : 12
transient, 395 : 7

Opportunity (*continued*)
wealth o. for achievement, 81 : 1
woman's time of o. short, 82 : 12
Oppose not only tyranny but tyrant, 384 : 12
Olympian difficult to o., 57 : 13
Opposed by watchful men, 846 : 17
new opinions usually o., 307 : 13
numbers pluck hearts, 208 : 8
that o. may beware thee, 219 : 1
two o. ideas at same time, 835 : 10
Opposeth, truth as o. no profit, 264 : 20
Opposing, by o. end them, 221 : 12
one superstition to another, 357 : 17
Opposite, equal to a god sitting o. you, 102 : 5
is beneficial, 70 : 4
shadows on o. wall of cave, 84 : 17
shore will be, 512 : 7
to do o. is form of imitation, 386 : 18
Opposites are cure for opposites, 80 : 3
Opposition, don't say in power what say in o., 723 : 8
most excited when position uncertain, 755 : 4
sweet, 565 : 2
that has convictions, 480 : 9
to idea, 755 : 4
Oppress, conspiracy to o. rob degrade, 556 : 14
doleful dumps mind o., 917 : 17
of toll, 607 : 4
vex and o. each other, 398 : 2
Oppressed and powerful Russia, 584 : 3
by world o., 715 : 11
foal of an o. race, 433 : 18
heart and voice o., 563 : 13
not submit to be o., 390 : 12
protection to the o., 80 : 17
relieve the o., 28 : 30
with two weak evils, 211 : 14
Oppresses like the heft, 604 : 18
this that o. soul, 614 : 3
Oppression, abhors o. of Negroes, 520 : 2
but behold o., 29 : 4
force and o. made wrecks, 726 : 12
free in prison's o., 167 : 3
make o. bitter, 221 : 9
Old World overrun with o., 384 : 12
overcome o. without o., 909 : 11
power in behalf of o., 904 : 17
reading an o. of mind, 314 : 19
rumor of o. and deceit, 376 : 18
we're anti-o., 904 : 13
Oppressions, else unfelt o. of earth, 467 : 14
tyranny and o. vanish, 389 : 12
Oppressive, old forms of government o., 579 : 14
Oppressively, clouds o. low, 525 : 19
Oppressor and oppressed in opposition, 563 : 3
commit brutality openly, 909 : 16
on o.'s head break chain, 418 : 4
Oppressor's wrong, 221 : 12
Oppressors, southern o. tremble, 505 : 11
Oppugnancy, mere o., 226 : 2
Optics, wont to turn o. in, 291 : 26
Optima dies prima fugit, 104 : *n* 3
Optimism, complacency thoughtlessness and o., 703 : 19
in lunatic asylum, 690 : 3

Optimism (*continued*)
is a mania, 343 : 10
perceive evil where exists is o., 867 : 10
pessimism agreeable as o., 720 : 15
religious vision ground for o., 697 : 10
Optimist, difference between o. and pessimist, 758 : 12
never had much experience, 760 : 3
not o. but meliorist, 690 : *n* 1
proclaims we live in best of all worlds, 762 : 10
sees doughnut, 758 : 12
Optimistic about future of mankind, 678 : 12
Options, explore all o., 862 : 21
Opulence, defense of more importance than o., 366 : 5
private o., 871 : 11
Opus, finis coronat o., 133 : 26
Oracle, I am Sir O., 198 : 2
inspired o. pronounced, 288 : 15
mistaking oneself for o., 735 : 9
Oracles are dumb, 277 : 10
Oracular, use of my o. tongue, 398 : 11
Orange bright like lamps, 297 : 9
gold o. glows, 395 : 3
squeeze o. throw away skin, 343 : 6
Oranges and lemons, 930 : 7
coffee and o. in chair, 767 : 2
stench of stale o., 792 : 19
Orare est laborare, 134 : 14
Orator good man skilled in speaking, 95 : 14
no o. as Brutus is, 216 : 27
persuade eyes of men without o., 189 : 16
text is old o. too green, 189 : 13
thy tongue thy shame's o., 188 : 9
with flood of words, 347 : 13
Orator's, poet's and o. help, 650 : 13
Orators, Demosthenes first of o., 353 : *n* 4
dumb when beauty pleadeth, 189 : 22
swords play o. for us, 183 : 3
when out will spit, 212 : 22
Oratory, aim of forensic o., 98 : 16
Orb, foolery walk about o. like sun, 214 : 11
like angel sings, 201 : 1
monthly changes in circled o., 192 : 11
quail and shake the o., 241 : 25
Orbed, securely o., 794 : 4
Orbi, urbi et o., 134 : 33
Orbit and sum of Shakespeare, 494 : 22
Orbs, ice-blue o. shivering above, 860 : 8
of royal blue, 647 : 2
Orchard, all Russia our o., 695 : 9
for a dome, 605 : 4
in o. enough to eat, 331 : 2
keep cold young o., 748 : 10
sings on o. bough, 541 : 16
what o. yields, 854 : 2
Ordain and establish Constitution, 391 : 10
Ordained, hast thou o. strength, 17 : 17
moon and stars thou hast o., 17 : 17
Ordains bee to be, 768 : 15
mild Heaven a time o., 282 : 10
Order and disorder, 344 : 19
best words in best o., 438 : 4
blessed rage for o., 767 : 16
breeds habit, 635 : 4
Order (*continued*)
custom in all line of o., 225 : 37
decently and in o., 48 : 27
defense is in law and o., 764 : 4
equilibrium from within, 784 : 14
first step to mastery, 755 : 10
follow well in o., 575 : 14
go for refuge to the O., 73 : 6
God is an "in o. to," 706 : 4
great disorder is o., 767 : 20
half one o. half another, 291 : 15
in o. to stations leap, 305 : 9
in variety we see, 334 : 15
is rapidly fadin', 915 : 5
law is o., 88 : 13
laws and o. made prominent, 64 : 20
love knows nothing of o., 127 : 11
matter better in France, 360 : 21
more than usual o., 437 : 17
music wherever there is o., 274 : 20
new o. in Europe, 766 : 9
nothing more perilous than new o., 153 : 18
of things satisfy, 496 : 2
of your going, 238 : 30
old o. changeth, 534 : 31
our foundations, 483 : 11
our land great but no o. in it, 136 : 2
populations forth, 864 : 2
races brought to good o., 154 : 12
rarely overthrown, 813 : 14
reigns in Warsaw, 439 : *n* 1
security and peace, 774 : 6
set thine house in o., 14 : 21
severity not path to o., 637 : 14
sitting well in o. smite, 529 : 13
social o. and thirsty aspiration, 875 : 9
to peopled kingdom, 207 : 6
true o. of going, 83 : 9
violent o. disorder, 767 : 20
words of sea, 767 : 16
Ordering, hints for better o. of universe, 139 : 6
Orders, Almighty's o. to perform, 325 : 7
duty to obey o., 594 : 9
execute o., 374 : 3
friar of o. gray, 188 : 37, 917 : 19
in his hand, 731 : 19
lower o. set example, 675 : 18
Ordinance, bounds of o., 648 : 7
Ordinances, profane no divine o., 370 : *n* 3
recognizing o. of heaven, 69 : 21
reimpressed by external o., 352 : 24
unwritten o., 80 : 17
Ordinary actions ascribed to habit, 657 : 9
all that is o. in life, 565 : 23
different from o. men, 609 : 5
I am but an o. man, 381 : 13
ideal higher than o., 586 : 17
man made of o. things, 413 : 8
men are fit for, 233 : 7
most o. most terrible, 602 : 10
my simple o. fashion, 164 : 5
reach of o. men, 425 : 11
Ordine, ancient o. retrogrado, 178 : 21
Ordo, magnus ab integro saeclorum nascitur o., 103 : *n* 9
novus o. seclorum, 103 : *n* 9
Ordre règne à Varsovie, 439 : *n* 1
Ore, load subject with o., 480 : 5
Ore (*continued*)
new-spangled o., 281 : 4
of body into purity, 790 : 14
Oreilles ventre affamé n'a point d'o., 296 : *n* 8
Oremus, bibi-mus vivi-mus o., 365 : 12
Organ, frequent use of any o., 393 : 7
let the pealing o. blow, 278 : 26
playing of merry o., 919 : 21
seated one day at o., 596 : 13
such as handle harp and o., 7 : 22
Organic, each o. being striving to increase, 515 : 2
part of human race, 790 : 21
Organically incapable of tune, 441 : 21
Organization and discipline of war, 153 : 21
juridical-political o., 774 : 8
only one military o., 825 : 6
shape economic society, 872 : 1
trouble with peace is no o., 840 : 19
Organize, give it something to o., 900 : 13
Organized charity scrimped and iced, 659 : 8
common peace, 682 : 8
conspiracies, 862 : 20
had society been well o., 414 : 18
minutely o. particulars, 407 : 6
opinion, 751 : 2
politeness o. indifference, 735 : 19
rivalries, 682 : 8
Organizer a woman, 104 : 23
Organizing flux of senses, 436 : 20
Organs, barrel o., 781 : 15
hath not a Jew o., 199 : 17
praise him with o., 22 : 25
Orgies, emotional o., 703 : 1
Orgulous, princes o., 461 : *n* 1
Orient, beauty's o. deep, 271 : 19
corn was o., 311 : 21
of o. pearl a double row, 250 : 6
Orientation, pragmatic method attitude of o., 650 : 8
Oriflamme, be your o. today, 487 : 6
Origin, families of doubtful o., 452 : 12
indelible stamp of lowly o., 515 : 10
man is o. of his action, 87 : 19
of modern world, 847 : 14
Original, depravity and o. sin, 569 : 16
diminution of o. sin, 581 : 10
great and o. writer, 428 : 8
great O. proclaim, 325 : 8
guide o. and end, 130 : 3
lost their o. nature, 90 : 6
more o. than originals, 500 : 1
most o. creation of spirit, 697 : 7
not lost o. brightness, 283 : 23
sin of man, 323 : 28
spare strange, 656 : 5
though uttered hundred times, 519 : 2
true o. native of America, 348 : 13
writer one nobody can imitate, 419 : 7
Originality, good things fruits of o., 508 : 10
merits first consideration, 138 : 4
sum of man's thinking, 862 : 6
Originals, more original than o., 500 : 1
Originate, death not o. in God, 583 : 4
Originated, no matter where thing o., 422 : 17

Originator, next to o. first
quoter, 499 : 27
Origins, dim o. of life, 869 : 13
of ourselves and our o., 767 : 16
Orion, loose the bands of O., 16 : 33
plunges prone, 692 : 8
Orisons, nymph in thy o., 221 : 13
patter out hasty o., 827 : 2
Ormus and of Ind, 284 : 3
Ornament, foreign aid of o., 345 : 14
greatest defense and o., 365 : 16
is but the guiled shore, 199 : 26
life in fleeting way, 413 : 29
of her sex, 547 : 21
of house friends, 499 : 15
of meek and quiet spirit, 52 : 12
sent to be moment's o., 427 : 3
studies an o. in prosperity, 98 : 7
Ornate rhetoric of rule of Plato, 281 : 20
so bedecked o. and gay, 288 : 30
Oro, el o. y amores malos de
encubrir, 935 : 17
O'Rourke, me and Mamie O., 698 : 14
Orphan, care for widow and o., 524 : 7
defeat is an o., 857 : 11
Orphans, listenest to sighs of o., 454 : 18
Orpheus, bid soul of O. sing, 278 : 22
sudden madness came upon
O., 104 : 12
they are in you now forever, 877 : 5
with his lute, 248 : 29
Orpheus' voice and poetry, 76 : 3
Orthodox in politics or religion, 821 : 6
prove their doctrine o., 291 : 5
Orthodoxy chokes dissent, 737 : 7
my doxy, 345 : 2, 473 : 19
what I call o., 809 : 20
Oscar, you will O. you will, 619 : 12
Oscura, noche o. del alma, 167 : *n* 1
Oslo, from Montgomery to O., 909 : 12
'Oss, my 'o. my wife my name, 500 : 21
Ossa, from O. hurled Pelion, 60 : *n* 3
pile O. on Olympus, 60 : 9
pile O. on Pelion, 103 : 29
Ossete, every killing is treat for
O., 819 : 2
Ostentatious, elegant but not o., 352 : 23
Ostrich, America cannot be o., 682 : 7
imagination wings of o., 487 : 15
with head in sand, 682 : 7
Ostriches, live as men not o., 781 : 5
Othello's occupation's gone, 231 : 11
Other America, 908 : 5
gatherer of o. men's stuff, 166 : *n* 6
hear o. side, 129 : 7
heard o. side, 77 : 1
hell is o. people, 865 : 12
how o. half lives, 270 : 21
I can do no o., 155 : 13
I was becoming that O., 865 : 13
made for each o., 432 : 17
man only being searching for
O., 885 : 17
not as o. men are, 43 : 39
one ends o. begins, 526 : 7
she can do no o., 682 : 13
talk not of o. men's lives, 35 : 32
turn the o. cheek, 37 : 10
voices other rooms, 903 : 4
Others abide our question, 584 : 9
bring peace to o., 148 : 19
cannot make o. as you wish, 148 : 14
do not do to o., 69 : 14
draw from o. lesson, 96 : 8
Others (*continued*)
food to one poison to o., 101 : 6
forsaking all o., 56 : 8
from o. take example, 97 : 4
fructify in lives of o., 94 : *n* 9
grudge o. what themselves cannot
enjoy, 66 : 10
how often he misunderstands
o., 395 : 24
how shall I rule over o., 157 : 11
live for o. not self, 681 : 8
look a needless show, 605 : 17
never again move to rhythms of
o., 883 : 5
not been as o. were, 525 : 5
not false to o., 180 : 22
not mercy unto o. show, 174 : 3
profit by folly of o., 117 : 5
see ourselves as o. see us, 409 : 8
the more he uses for o., 65 : 10
to encourage the o., 343 : 11
want to understand o., 413 : 1
what then are the o., 343 : 9
who were before us, 795 : 12
work better with bronze, 105 : 24
Others', authority from o.
books, 190 : 12
women place o. needs first, 883 : 6
Otherwise, beguile by seeming
o., 230 : 10
gods thought o., 105 : 4
I cannot do o., 155 : *n* 6
so and no o., 710 : 8
some weatherwise some o., 347 : 14
Otii, ignobilis o., 104 : *n* 6
Otium cum dignitate, 98 : *n* 7
Oublié, dieu a donc o., 312 : *n* 2
rien appris ni rien o., 400 : *n* 4
Ou-boum 764 : 10
Ought, enjoy things we o., 87 : 22
every day to hear song, 395 : 5
how we live far from how we
o., 153 : 23
not what we o. to say, 235 : 20
Sophocles drew men as they o. to
be, 73 : *n* 10
tell me I o. to do, 373 : 1
vigor in what they o. to do., 89 : 14
what we o. not we do, 585 : 8
write not what they o. to do, 179 : 5
Oughtness, incapable of reaching for
o., 909 : 13
Ounce, give me an o. of civet, 235 : 1
grow by inch or o., 717 : 6
trouble's an o., 718 : 17
Our man in Havana, 859 : 12
Ours, country no longer o. nor
yours, 849 : 11
little in nature that is o., 427 : 29
self not mine but o., 905 : 13
Oursels, see o. as others see us, 409 : 8
Ourselves and immortality, 606 : 4
and of our origins, 767 : 16
author and finisher, 519 : 22
devils to o., 227 : 1
fault not in stars but in o., 215 : 6
griefs we cause o., 74 : 4
how much we think of o., 626 : 15
if it be o. or others, 795 : 12
in o. triumph and defeat, 512 : 18
in seas and o. safety lies, 186 : 15
it is he and not we o., 21 : 3
lay out o. in service of
mankind, 392 : 14
Ourselves (*continued*)
leave behind bit of o., 679 : 9
less harsh with o. and others, 395 : 12
more satisfied with o., 580 : 13
not die before we have explained
o., 382 : 3
not talk about o. at all, 293 : 22
see o. as others see us, 409 : 8
we deceive o., 52 : 20, 358 : 22
we in o. rejoice, 436 : 1
when is death not within o., 70 : 8
with Barbarians left out, 588 : 13
Out at heels, 225 : 10
Betsey and I are o., 660 : 2
candles are all o., 237 : 10
damned spot, 239 : 23
include me o., 777 : 6
look o. not in, 590 : 8
no way o. for me, 817 : 6
nowhere to go but o., 684 : 15
of all whooping, 212 : 6
of date, 792 : 10
of Egypt have I called my son, 36 : 22
of God's blessing into sun, 160 : 32
of key with his time, 792 : 10
of sight out of mind, 148 : 18
of suits with fortune, 210 : 16
of the cradle, 575 : 17
of the depths have I cried, 22 : 11
of the eater came meat, 12 : 14
of the mouth of babes, 17 : 17
of the night, 663 : 10
of the strong came sweetness, 12 : 14
of thine own mouth, 43 : 41
one two three strikes you're
o., 765 : 14
out brief candle, 240 : 4
rancor will o., 185 : 9
soul is all but o. of me, 822 : 14
those o. wish to get in, 165 : 19,
498 : 18
upon it I have loved, 290 : 4
vile jelly, 234 : 18
when age in wit o., 209 : 28
where handclasp's stronger, 739 : 7
who's in who's o., 235 : 12
Out-babying Wordsworth, 493 : 8
Outcast, beweep my o. state, 244 : 8
from life's feast, 777 : 15
Outcome of the war in our
hands, 58 : 25
of words is in the council, 58 : 25
Outcries call me from naked
bed, 176 : 21
Outdid the meat, 266 : 17
Outdistance advanced
countries, 731 : 5
Outdo, fruits o. what flowers
promised, 176 : 18
Outdoor, in and o. schooling, 749 : 17
Outdoors, man o. who cherishes
thought, 558 : 22
Outer darkness, 40 : 31, 614 : 17
your head concerned with o., 748 : 13
Out-glittering Keats, 493 : 8
Outgrabe, mome raths o., 612 : 17
Outgrown shell, 519 : 8
Out-herods Herod, 221 : 23
Outjump any frog, 621 : 18
Outlasts, world o. aversion love
effort, 584 : 16
Outlawed, corporations cannot be
o., 172 : 4
Outleaps, word o. world, 873 : 20

Outlet, Dead Sea has no o., 759 : 11
Outline, dowager's a demd o., 547 : 14
Outlines, countesses had no o., 547 : 14
Outlive, desire o. performance, 206 : 16
his life half a year, 222 : 10
let man o. his wealth, 200 : 15
this powerful rhyme, 244 : 18
Outlived the doctor's pill, 332 : 5
Outlives, he that o. this day, 208 : 10
in fame the pious fool, 275 : *n* 1
Outlook, could man o. that mark, 299 : 9
Outmost margins, 797 : 12
Outnumber, busy thoughts o., 466 : 10
Outnumbered, so o. we attack, 782 : 13
Out-paramoured the Turk, 234 : 6
Outrage brave man dead, 73 : 16
of the poor, 494 : 16
when man destroys nature, 758 : 2
Outrageous fortune, 221 : 12
Outrageously virtuous, 327 : 17
Outride, beggar will o. the Devil, 186 : *n* 1
Outrider, torchbearing o., 653 : 3
Outruns, desire that o. delight, 632 : 14
Outshone the wealth of Ormus, 284 : 3
Outside, goodly o. falsehood hath, 198 : 23
on o. grows furside, 733 : 16
swashing and martial o., 210 : 22
Outskirts of hope, 872 : 10
Outsoared shadow of night, 469 : 12
Outspeak and has its reasons, 906 : 10
Outstare the lightning, 241 : 13
Outstretched, with his arms o., 226 : 19
Out-topping knowledge, 584 : 9
Outvenoms worms of Nile, 243 : 21
Outward, Americans must look o., 642 : 9
and inward man at one, 83 : 7
and visible sign, 56 : 5
angel on o. side, 228 : 27
hang banners on o. walls, 240 : 2
looketh on the o. appearance, 12 : 38
showing an o. pity, 195 : 13
things o. draw inward quality, 241 : 10
'tis my o. soul, 253 : 11
virtue on o. parts, 199 : 25
Outweighs all the fools', 543 : 6
one hour years o., 337 : 14
surging sea o., 495 : 19
wisdom o. wealth, 75 : 1
Outworn buried age, 244 : 21
creed o., 428 : 1
creeds o., 467 : 2
winter weeds o., 468 : 17
Oval O cropped with teeth, 804 : 17
Oven, day that shall burn as o., 33 : 38
in o. for baby and me, 929 : 18
Over, game isn't o. till it's o., 903 : 14
head and heels, 101 : 22
hill over dale, 764 : 11
June bustin' out all o., 833 : 12
me bright April, 787 : 5
over there, 759 : 8
prologues are o., 768 : 1
seven times o. and o., 578 : 9
the river, 490 : 20
Overboard, what though mast blown o., 186 : 23
Overcame, I came saw and o., 206 : 28
Over-canopied with luscious woodbine, 196 : 18
Overcoat, Gogol's O., 582 : 16
put on your o., 568 : 27
Overcome, art where resistance o., 727 : 11
be not o. of evil, 47 : 25
but half his foe, 283 : 27
difficulty to be o., 68 : 20
evil with good, 47 : 25
finitude is o., 703 : 15
I have o. the world, 45 : 29
nature sometimes o., 181 : 4
oppression without oppression, 909 : 11
softest things o. hardest, 64 : 15
strong by what we o., 631 : 5
terror at own finitude, 703 : 15
we shall o., 925 : 9
Overcomes, who o. by force, 283 : 27
Overcometh, to him that o., 52 : 34
Overexpecting happiness in married estate, 277 : 1
Overfed, horses and poets not o., 171 : 17
Overflow, meadow rivulets o., 642 : 6
of powerful feelings, 424 : 9
Overflows, the fountain o., 404 : 4
Overgrow, suffer them and they'll o. garden, 185 : 15
Overhanging, brave o. firmament, 220 : 28
Overhear cry of pain, 878 : 14
Overlook, communities o. one another, 65 : 9
knowing what to o., 649 : 6
Overmastered with piece of dust, 209 : 6
Over-offended ladies, 327 : 17
Overpast, until the indignation be o., 30 : 11
Overpowering knell, 461 : 16
Overpraised season, 620 : 8
Overrefines argument brings self to grief, 143 : 3
Overruled, court o. earlier decisions, 678 : 3
Overrun, country unjustly o., 558 : 2
Overseas, nameless battle o., 728 : 13
Overseer, no guide o. or ruler, 23 : 11
Over-serious, reindeer seem o., 799 : 16
Overset mind with reading, 663 : 16
Overstep not modesty of nature, 222 : 1
Overt, two witnesses to o. act, 391 : 12
Overtake, I thy fate shall o., 267 : 6
Overthrew the tables of moneychangers, 40 : 11
Overthrow, forcible o. of social conditions, 563 : 10
linger out a purposed o., 245 : 3
of institutions by force, 700 : 3
revolutionary right to o., 521 : 11
whom thou thinkest thou o., 254 : 11
ye cannot o. it, 46 : 1
Overthrown by revolution, 813 : 14
Overtime, works o. all his life, 773 : 8
Overuse, use and o. word new, 623 : 3
Overweathered ribs, 199 : 6
Overwhelm myself in poesy, 475 : 11
Overwhelming, let it be o., 748 : 15
loss so o., 524 : 4
Overwhelms, greatness of name o. son, 257 : 2
Overwise in doing thy business, 35 : 19
keep talk from getting o., 748 : 15
Overwork, killed by o., 707 : 15
Overworked, neither idle nor o., 618 : 10
Overzealous, mistaken o. piety, 373 : 15
Ovid, Venus clerk O., 144 : 1
Ovo, ab o., 109 : *n* 12
Owe, duty we o. Creator, 383 : 6
fame only to myself, 275 : 29
God a death, 206 : 25
I o. a cock, 79 : 8
if I can't pay I can o., 158 : 17
it to posterity, 390 : 13
me five farthings, 930 : 7
no man anything, 47 : 27
no man hate, 212 : 2
Shallow I o. thousand pound, 206 : 37
sum married people o., 395 : 19
to this place I o. everything, 521 : 6
Owed, so much o. by so many, 744 : 6
throw away dearest thing he o., 236 : 14
Owedst, sleep which thou o., 231 : 8
Owen, why did you leave us O., 552 : 20
Owes, by owing o. not, 285 : 11
duty subject o. prince, 189 : 6
me another existence, 396 : 5
no homage unto sun, 274 : 22
not any man, 510 : 8
nothing to land, 359 : 1
your representative o. you, 372 : 9
Owest, lend less than thou o., 233 : 9
worm no silk, 234 : 7
Owing, by o. owes not, 285 : 11
Owl and pussycat, 550 : 7
by mousing o. hawked at, 238 : 11
calls name of man to die, 852 : 16
clamorous o., 196 : 20
Creek Bridge, 647 : 5
for all his feathers, 476 : 8
in Douglas fir turn head, 905 : 18
lived in an oak, 660 : 15
nightly sings the staring o., 191 : 14
night's herald, 189 : 11
pussy said to o., 550 : 8
sadder than o. songs, 462 : 1
that shrieked, 237 : 17
to moon complain, 361 : 22
Owlet Atheism, 435 : 16
whoops to wolf below, 435 : 6
Owls, bringing o. to Athens, 82 : 6
companion to o., 16 : 19
couch when o. do cry, 248 : 16
court for o., 30 : 22
no o. in whole island, 356 : *n* 1
two o. and hen, 550 : 4
Own a bit of ground, 603 : 7
everyone to his o., 300 : 19
he forgets not his o., 918 : 19
how feel to be on your o., 915 : 6
if any provide not for his o., 50 : 31
ill-favored thing but mine o., 213 : 2
my o. my native land, 430 : 10
my o. shall come to me, 630 : 21
no superior, 576 : 12
of thine o. have we given, 14 : 26
only soul his o., 841 : 4
poor thing but mine o., 213 : *n* 1
the soft impeachment, 398 : 19
thing that is your o., 87 : 29
Owned, dearest thing he o., 236 : 14
I was o. of thee, 606 : 16
Owner of the sphere, 495 : 15
ox knoweth his o., 28 : 26
write that nigger's o., 624 : 4

Owner's, blanch without o. crime, 428 : 23
Owners, lords and o. of their faces, 245 : 5
Ownership, woman proclaim o., 699 : 14
Owning, mania of o. things, 574 : 24
Ox, as an o. goeth to the slaughter, 23 : 16
eateth grass as an o., 17 : 3
eating grass like o., 496 : 7
knoweth his owner, 28 : 26
lion eat straw like the o., 29 : 19
makes difference whose o. gored, 156 : 11
not covet neighbor's o., 10 : 7
of the wrongdoer, 4 : 3
stalled o. and hatred therewith, 24 : 7
stands on my tongue, 71 : 4
tired o. treads with firmer step, 128 : 15
Oxen, draw more than hundred pair of o., 259 : *n* 8
of his own breeding, 106 : 23
who drives fat o., 356 : 30
years like great black o., 712 : 2
Oxford, from O. up pathway strays, 587 : 6
leave O. by town drain, 659 : 11
spires of O., 778 : 10
Street stony-hearted, 454 : 18
Oxlips and nodding violet grows, 196 : 18
Oyster, bold man first eat o., 323 : 10
may be crossed in love, 399 : 12
not eat o. in months with no r, 166 : 12
pearl in your foul o., 213 : 3
solitary as o., 548 : 4
world's mine o., 225 : 15
Oyster-bank, shelving in o., 499 : 19
Oysters come walk with us, 613 : 3
wait a bit the o. cried, 613 : 6
Oz, feel like I'm in O., 856 : 14
road to O., 677 : 8
wizard of O., 677 : 7
Ozymandias king of kings, 466 : 13

P

Pace, creeps in this petty p., 240 : 4
from deep to deep varies p., 728 : 11
keeps p. with sun, 559 : 22
not keep p. with companions, 560 : 17
of change, 814 : 5
requiescat in p., 134 : 22
thoughts with violent p., 231 : 18
traveling all same p., 517 : 15
unperturbed p., 693 : 11
Paced into the hall, 434 : 9
Pacem, desiderat p. praeparet bellum, 128 : *n* 10
in terris, 774 : 6
Paces about room again alone, 805 : 8
three p. through room, 528 : 27
time travels in divers p., 212 : 11
Pacific, frontier from Atlantic to P., 743 : 16
in his name to great P., 765 : 10
leans on the land, 797 : 12
olive leaf p. sign, 288 : 2
stared at the P., 475 : 7
Pacified Psyche and kissed her, 527 : 2
Pacify touchy tribe of poets, 109 : 17
Pacis, nunc patimur longae p. mala, 122 : *n* 7
Pack, as huntsman his p., 371 : 19
clouds away, 257 : 18
hear baying of p., 817 : 6
lift p. leave friends, 691 : 15
meets with pack in jungle, 709 : 5
murderous cowardly p., 819 : 7
nothing but p. of cards, 612 : 14
relations a tedious p., 675 : 22
up your troubles, 770 : 14
when it begins to rain, 233 : 18
Packet, flash of p. fame, 935 : 6
Liverpool p., 935 : 7
Packs and sets of great ones, 235 : 12
Padded lunatic asylums, 781 : 16
Paddle, dip p. in lake, 494 : 6
in cold streams, 713 : 16
own canoe, 112 : *n* 11, 466 : 1
Paddling palms and pinching fingers, 246 : 11
Paddocks, cold as p., 267 : 1
Paddy dear did ye hear, 920 : 21
Padlock, clap p. on her mind, 320 : 17
Pagan, Christian p. spoiled, 706 : 14
poor p. planet of ours, 570 : 2
suckled in creed outworn, 428 : 1
who defends religion, 732 : 5
Page, beautiful quarto p., 398 : 29
blank p. difficult mirror, 850 : 17
cannot tear out p. of life, 504 : 10
excels at title p., 368 : 5
history's purchased p., 457 : 24
knowledge her ample p., 362 : 7
life's p., 457 : 10
new p. in public expenditures, 449 : 6
of book carelessly open, 908 : 12
of prancing poetry, 607 : 4
pictures for p. atone, 340 : 18
refine her sterling p., 311 : 13
shone not on poet's p., 108 : *n* 11
this void the blank p., 851 : 1
Pageant, insubstantial p. faded, 248 : 13
Pageantry, mask and antique p., 278 : 6
of a king, 391 : 2
Pages, turn p. of Greek models, 109 : 30
Pagoda, old Moulmein p., 708 : 8
Pagus, private p. or demense, 869 : 6
Paid, attention must be p., 888 : 2
debt to Nature's quickly p., 267 : 15
delusion to be p. before work, 171 : *n* 2
in his own coin, 168 : 25
tell you what I p., 607 : 17
well p. that is satisfied, 200 : 21
with moan, 693 : 7
with sighs aplenty, 690 : 21
Paige, inclined to agree with Satchel P., 856 : 12
Pail, milk comes frozen home in p., 191 : 14
Pain a thing glad forgotten, 797 : 13
after great p. formal feeling, 605 : 6
and anguish wring brow, 431 : 2
and boredom foes of happiness, 463 : 8
and evil in life of worms, 595 : 5
and pleasure rudders, 307 : *n* 8
aromatic p., 336 : 20
as readily blisses as p., 640 : 3
assuage unforgotten p., 601 : 21
beauty pierce like p., 755 : 5
believeth with life p. stop, 544 : 18
Pain (*continued*)
bitterest p. among men, 78 : 21
born in other's p., 693 : 7
clings cruelly to us, 476 : 2
comes from darkness, 885 : 9
cool one p., 606 : 12
cry of p. that could have got worse, 878 : 14
cure not worth the p., 111 : *n* 2
cures me of my p., 919 : 19
darkness and cold, 544 : 22
dashed with p., 748 : 9
death puts end to p., 534 : 15
die of rose in aromatic p., 336 : 20
disposed to one another by p., 124 : 4
doomed to company with p., 427 : 22
doubt hesitation and p., 541 : 9
draw thy breath in p., 225 : 1
envy calumny hate p., 469 : 12
equal ease unto my p., 271 : 22
eternal p., 586 : 6
feast of joy a dish of p., 177 : 10
for leaven, 632 : 9
for sport, 626 : 10
full of p. this intellectual being, 284 : 9
happiness episode in drama of p., 640 : 17
has element of blank, 606 : 2
heart rapture then p., 660 : 10
history of wound beguiles p., 360 : 3
I know my life's a p., 251 : 7
inflicts p. for sport, 626 : 10
it is p., 885 : 9
joys three parts p., 544 : 10
king of p., 633 : 13
labor we delight in physics in p., 238 : 4
laughter with p. fraught, 468 : 14
life a memory without p., 74 : 7
light life pleasure p., 614 : 17
man dies in p., 315 : 9
marriage has more joy than p., 75 : 25
memory-wounding p., 850 : 7
mighty p. to love, 295 : 9
narcotics numbing p., 531 : 21
neither any more p., 53 : 30
never p. to tell thy love, 404 : *n* 1
no consciousness without p., 754 : 2
no p. as great as being alive, 721 : 1
not akin to p., 510 : 18
occasional enjoyments lighting p., 697 : 10
of a new idea, 597 : 3
of finite hearts, 542 : 10
oh the p. the bliss, 333 : 23
older connotation of p., 871 : 14
one p. lessened by another's, 191 : 19
Our Lady of P., 632 : 12
painful pleasure to pleasing p., 173 : 19
peace nor help for p., 587 : 16
pleasure is intermission of p., 264 : 5
pleasure so exquisite almost p., 454 : 11
pleasures banish p., 328 : 15
positive eternity of p., 619 : 1
poverty full of p., 485 : 24
purchase p., 335 : 19
records of heart in p., 486 : 2
sense of pity beauty p., 683 : 3
short joy eternal, 413 : 27
somebody's p. and wrong, 653 : 15
sudden cry of p., 781 : 10

Pain (*continued*)
sweet pleasure after p., 306 : 16
tender for another's p., 361 : 12
that cannot forget, 71 : 5
time cancels young p., 76 : 13
'tis p. that p. to miss, 295 : 9
to the bear, 489 : 6
tongueless vigil and all the p., 632 : 7
travaileth in p., 47 : 9
turns with ceaseless p., 368 : 14
understand p. in all meanings, 464 : 6
unfinished man and his p., 716 : 1
wanders through bones, 874 : 22
weight and p. of life, 75 : 14
what p. it was to drown, 187 : 9
who is fortunate learn p., 413 : 29
with frantic p., 402 : 15
with no p. cease upon midnight, 476 : 28
with p. purchased inherit p., 190 : 10
words of p. tones of anger, 140 : 15
world p., 415 : *n* 7
yearning like god in p., 476 : 10
you purchase p., 335 : 19
Paineth, what p. thee, 513 : 9
Painful, consciousness p. achievement, 754 : 3
good honest p. sermon, 309 : 16
how glorious and p., 537 : 10
how p. to keep money, 310 : 13
inch to gain, 564 : 17
it's p. and difficult, 850 : 3
pensive poets p. vigils, 340 : 16
pleasure to pleasing pain, 173 : 19
to excess, 798 : 1
truth, 383 : 1
warrior famoused for fight, 244 : 7
Pains, capacity for taking p., 630 : 17
died in bitter p., 609 : 12
disciplined state of pleasures and p., 307 : *n* 8
marriage has many p., 352 : 18
members partake of p., 169 : 38
nothing but labor for p., 168 : 7
nothing without p., 168 : *n* 5
numbness p. sense, 476 : 21
of all p. the greatest, 295 : 9
of love be sweeter far, 303 : 7
she gave me for my p., 229 : 31
stings you for your p., 331 : 1
Paint an inch thick, 224 : 14
capture reality in p., 638 : 4
does he p., 543 : 31
fresh as p., 564 : 1
good-bye Old P., 927 : 11
he best can p. them, 335 : 6
here was something to p., 843 : 2
hire idiots to p., 405 : 15
in public's face, 619 : *n* 1
lily, 202 : 5
lion not so fierce as they p. him, 269 : 27
man as well as features, 619 : 9
me bold rocks, 804 : 16
meadows with delight, 191 : 13
my picture truly like me, 272 : 22
vices and follies, 324 : 6
what will be seen, 735 : 15
Painted, angels are p. fair, 317 : 2
child of dirt, 338 : 19
Duchess p. on wall, 540 : 22
earth's last picture p., 707 : 21
fears a p. devil, 237 : 23
I have p. my life, 801 : 1
Painted (*continued*)
love things we see p., 543 : 29
memory p. perfect day, 698 : 16
not so black as p., 177 : 5
not so young as p., 735 : 21
panel statuary, 715 : 18
players and p. stage, 717 : 20
pomp, 210 : 23
ship upon painted ocean, 434 : 14
to the eyes, 640 : 2
veil called life, 467 : *n* 2
winged Cupid p. blind, 196 : 1
Painter maker of patterns, 758 : 7
Nature's sternest p., 456 : 18
not paint what he sees, 735 : 15
some great p. dips pencil, 466 : 14
trainer soothsayer, 122 : 4
Painter's brush consumes dreams, 715 : 13
mind with that of viewer, 483 : 16
Painters and poets have equal license, 109 : 18
boldest p. cannot trace, 328 : 17
Painting, as in p. so in poetry, 110 : 3
bridge linking painter's mind, 483 : 16
dramatic action, 774 : 10
feast for eyes, 483 : 15
give children right to study p., 381 : 14
gives form to terrors, 774 : 11
is silent poetry, 68 : 1
man that has taste of p., 326 : 12
mediator between world and us, 774 : 11
music poetry, 579 : 11
poetry is p. that speaks, 68 : 1
poetry p. and music, 407 : 5
six essentials in p., 135 : 11
that lends joyousness, 646 : 8
what light is to p., 670 : 9
Paintings Bible of the laity, 137 : 2
farewell dear p., 273 : 8
heard of your p., 221 : 18
Pair, no burial this pretty p., 917 : 6
nor build nor sing, 436 : 9
of ragged claws, 803 : 14
of sparkling eyes, 630 : 7
of star-crossed lovers, 191 : 17
of very strange beasts, 213 : 1
one p. of English legs, 207 : 23
then there's a p. of us, 604 : 19
yet happy p., 285 : 23
Paired butterflies yellow, 792 : 9
Paisley, cutty sark o' P. harn, 411 : 12
Pajamas fresh from washer, 892 : 20
I in p. for heat, 790 : 12
Palace and prison on each hand, 458 : 5
Beautiful, 302 : 1
built upon sand, 822 : 18
cypress in p. walk, 531 : 11
fair and stately p., 526 : 1
give p. for hermitage, 195 : 6
golden mean avoids envy of p., 107 : 20
hollow oak our p., 453 : 20
more than a house, 438 : 6
of Cyrus, 924 : 3
of Eternity, 279 : 4
of the soul, 276 : 10, 457 : 6
Palaces, cottages princes' p., 198 : 9
Death beats at p. of kings, 107 : 1
gorgeous p., 248 : 13
'mid pleasures and p., 465 : 4
Palaces (*continued*)
my body parks and p., 668 : 21
not so arched as princes' p., 262 : 9
prosperity within thy p., 22 : 6
Paladin, starry p., 540 : 11
Paladins, knights and p. aged accents, 182 : 6
Palate, against p., fine, 478 : 1
Pale and specter-thin, 476 : 24
Anguish keeps gate, 676 : 13
bond which keeps me p., 238 : 21
brambles p. with mist, 587 : 11
cast of thought, 221 : 12
cygnet to this p. swan, 202 : 16
death on his p. horse, 287 : 28
Death with impartial tread, 107 : 1
death's p. flag, 193 : 27
Ebenezer, 730 : 12
edged with poplar p., 277 : 11
fear p. and hungry-looking men, 99 : 25
Galilean, 633 : 6
hands I loved, 707 : 2
Hecate's offerings, 237 : 14
his uneffectual fire, 219 : 26
horse, 53 : 11, 287 : 28
in saffron mist, 811 : 13
leaves yellow black p., 467 : 17
lies shadow of tomb, 600 : 17
make p. my cheeks with care, 264 : 23
Melancholy sate retired, 364 : 14
name at which world grew p., 351 : 19
neither p. nor bright, 899 : 14
over park over p., 196 : 10
poetic pearl, 570 : 11
Ramón, 767 : 16
rest at p. evening, 854 : 14
so thin so p. yet gold, 400 : 9
student glued to desk, 592 : 8
turn not p. beloved snail, 612 : 9
unripened beauties, 325 : 15
visit it by p. moonlight, 430 : 4
why so p. and wan, 289 : 17
with breath of cloister, 592 : 6
Pale-faced, pluck honor from p. moon, 203 : 15
Palely loitering, 478 : 10
Paleness of symbolic expression, 610 : 2
Paleozoic time, 688 : 3
Paler than grass, 63 : 5
Palestine, sunny P., 760 : 19
Palfrey, his p. brown as is a berye, 145 : 21
Pall, black p. of nothing, 821 : 12
in sceptered p. sweeping by, 278 : 21
Palladium of rights, 390 : 11
Pallas, pallid bust of P., 526 : 19
Pallid and emasculate scholarship, 592 : 8
angels all p. and wan, 526 : 5
bust of Pallas, 526 : 19
the leash-men, 792 : 6
Palls, everything p., 928 : 3, 928 : 3
upon the sense, 325 : 16
Palm at end of mind, 769 : 11
dominion over p. and pine, 709 : 16
hold infinity in p. of hand, 406 : 8
hold them in your p., 849 : 18
itching p., 216 : 31
like some tall p., 377 : *n* 5
oozing out at p. of hands, 398 : 18
righteous flourish like the p. tree, 20 : 18
strife with the p., 585 : 12

Palm (*continued*)
under p. tree at noon, 806:13
wind is in p. trees, 708:8
Palmer's weed, 279:15
Palms before my feet, 742:17
fronded p. in air, 513:24
more palmy than p., 571:8
on the staircase, 866:16
other p. are won, 426:23
paddling p. and pinching fingers, 246:11
Palmy, high and p. state of Rome, 217:21
more p. than palms, 571:8
prosperity, 471:13
Palmyra, editions of Balbec and P., 363:21
Palo, cuchillo de p., 935:14
Palpable Elysium, 793:3
obscure, 284:16
roll of world p., 640:6
then thus the p., 793:3
Palpitate, heart cease to p., 512:16
Palsied, beg alms of p. eld, 228:16
crippled p. slain, 752:4
Palsy, brought p. to bed, 793:2
shakes gray hairs, 476:24
Palsy-stricken churchyard thing, 476:14
Palter with us in double sense, 240:9
Paltry, aged man p. thing, 715:1
compensations of mankind, 526:9
decorum, 432:16
friendship of man, 526:6
if conduct mean and p., 88:23
Paly flames, 208:1
Pan, beloved P., 83:7
great god P., 507:23
great god P. is dead, 120:19
milk in p., 496:11
out of frying p. into fire, 126:10
twitch nymph's garment off, 541:19
Panacea, I swear by P., 79:13
Panaceas, tobacco goes beyond all p., 259:15
Panache, white p. rallying point, 175:1
Panama with its poverty, 481:2
Pancakes, as flat as p., 261:12
Pandemonium city and proud seat, 287:26
Panders, reason p. will, 223:5
Pandion, King P. he is dead, 257:7
Pandora, more lovely than P., 286:3
Panegyric, practitioner in p., 399:7
Panem et circenses, 122:*n* 11
Pang, feel beautiful incentive as p., 653:12
finds p. as great, 228:17
ghastly p., 434:24
learn nor account p., 544:10
preceding death, 368:11
Pange lingua gloriosi, 139:*n* 6
Pangolins hornbills pitchers catchers, 799:17
Pangs, in sweet p. remember me, 213:29
more p. and fears, 249:3
more p. wilder wring, 656:17
of disprized love, 221:12
Panic, cowardice distinguished from p., 845:10
hair stand up in p. fear, 75:15
idiocy during p., 871:3
shouting fire causing p., 644:23
Panic's in thy breastie, 408:12
Panics have their uses, 384:14
Panjandrum, grand P., 364:5
Pan's cavern, 717:16
Pansies for thoughts, 224:1
Pant Time up Time up, 856:6
Pantaloon, lean and slippered p., 211:15
Panteth, as hart p. after water brooks, 19:5
Pantheism atheism in disguise, 705:14
Panthers, administering to p., 889:14
Panting, chase p. syllable, 376:10
Time toiled after him, 351:10
Pants, as p. the hart, 317:7
Trousers, cloud in t., 826:16
Pants, neither vest nor p., 620:4
Panza, God's blessing said Sancho P., 171:*n* 1
so Sancho P. said, 556:2, 773:14
Panzer-man panzer-man you, 911:17
Papa, as P. used to say, 548:24
potatoes poultry, 549:20
Papacy ghost of Roman Empire, 264:18
Paper, bread dry as p., 793:1
bullets of the brain, 209:19
contrary to king built p. mill, 185:28
dry dust and stray p., 792:19
hand that signed the p., 886:14
he hath not eat p., 190:27
make dust our p., 195:1
name never in p., 888:2
not what kind of p. but man, 558:25
not worth p. witten on, 509:1
receipt of little bit of p., 571:10
scrap of p., 677:11
unpleasantest words that blotted p., 199:30
virtue of p. government, 372:10
you drop in ballot box, 558:25
Paper-mill, contrary to king built p., 185:28
Papers don't purtend to print, 568:12
draw up the p. lawyer, 660:2
in each hand, 338:6
know what I read in p., 765:15
turns over your p., 386:9
Papists Jews Turks in one ship, 273:11
or Protestants, 354:9
Paquin pull down, 793:4
Par, below p. to extent of two whiskies, 723:17
Parable, God coined a p., 131:3
Parables, God setteth forth p., 131:16
of sunlight, 886:18
Parabola, along p. life flies, 912:10
Parachutes, minds like p., 647:22
Parade, Files on P., 708:1
solemnized with pomp and p., 381:7
Parades, no more p., 740:10
turkey-cock p., 899:14
Paradigm, green barbarism turning p., 766:15
Paradise, drunk milk of P., 433:27
England a p. for women, 259:22
England the p. of women, 174:23
fool's p., 497:7, 917:8
gaze toward p., 843:16
heavenly p. is that place, 250:5
if p. on face of earth, 919:1
is where I am, 342:23
Italy p. for horses, 259:22
itself were dim, 447:16
Paradise (*continued*)
let woman into P., 934:10
lost angel of ruined p., 469:2
mechanics p. of mathematical sciences, 152:13
moment lived in p., 412:17
mount to p., 494:15
not only in my eyes is P., 142:14
of bureaucratic apparatus, 775:7
of exiles Italy, 467:12
of Fools to few unknown, 285:8
on earth, 724:10
same old glimpse of P., 693:1
stood formed in her yen, 145:2
they paved p., 916:6
thought would destroy p., 361:12
to him are opening p., 362:20
to what we fear of death, 228:21
transport heart of man into p., 782:22
wilderness were p., 516:7
with me in p., 44:9
Paradox, challenging p., 811:10
glorious Epicurean p., 519:10
love p. without losing wit, 497:32
mistaking p. for discovery, 735:9
not p. but truism, 85:11
Paragon, earthly p., 243:24
Paragraph, life's not a p., 829:6
no unnecessary sentences, 729:7
Parallax, as p. a flame, 607:5
Parallel, none but himself his p., 115:*n* 5
ours so truly p., 297:7
Parallelism, friendship needs p., 635:9
Parallels in beauty's brow, 244:20
Paralyze, campaigns p. cerebration, 703:1
Paralyzed force, 805:16
power structures, 909:16
Parameters, slip through p. of skies, 132:12
Paramount object to save Union, 522:6
question for nation, 556:9
Parapets, Europe of ancient p., 673:18
Paraphrase, classics in p., 792:13
Parasite, like any p., 293:*n* 4
Parcel of boilers and vats, 356:20
of their fortunes, 241:10
of vain strivings, 557:2
Parcels of dreadful past, 528:17
Parched, inhabit the p. places, 32:11
Parchment, from p. shaking dust, 486:10
should undo a man, 185:25
skin of innocent lamb p., 185:25
Parchments, everything written on p. unrepeatable, 908:3
Parcus deorum cultor et infrequens, 107:*n* 12
Pard, bearded like the p., 211:15
false as p. to hind, 226:15
not lion but p., 794:5
Pardlike spirit, 469:9
Pardon, a God ready to p., 14:31
beg death's p. now, 899:7
cannot beg for p., 870:6
cannot help nor p., 868:8
for too much loving you, 231:3
if life bitter to thee p., 634:13
love truth p. error, 343:2
me thou bleeding piece of earth, 216:11
old fathers 713:10

Pardon (*continued*)
one offense encourage many, 112 : 3
pity though not p., 187 : 34
remorseful p., 227 : 22
to spirit of liberty, 372 : 15
virtue of vice p. beg, 223 : 9
we p. to extent we love, 293 : 38
Pardonable, to speak dishonorably is p., 75 : 17
Pardoned all except her face, 461 : 17
her iniquity is p., 30 : 30
Pardoning, in p. we are pardoned, 138 : 15
Pardonner, tout comprendre tout p., 417 : *n* 5
Pardonnera, bien sûr, il me p., 482 : 8
Pardons, never p. those he injures, 115 : *n* 3
Pared and wintered by, 886 : 15
Paree, after they've seen P., 801 : 12
Parent, lose one p. misfortune, 675 : 21
Nature a kind p., 116 : 6
of bills of rights, 367 : *n* 4
of good, 286 : 15
on p. knees newborn child, 394 : 3
poverty is p. of meanness, 84 : 12
wealth is p. of luxury, 84 : 12
Parental, mild p. sway, 592 : 6
Parenthesis, death i think no p., 829 : 6
small p. in eternity, 275 : 15
Parents and child at window, 906 : 2
bones on which children sharpen teeth, 898 : 14
bore their children, 681 : 6
children begin loving p., 675 : 3
girl needs good p., 788 : 21
honor thy p., 564 : 19
if in serving his p., 68 : 4
in peace children inter p., 78 : 5
in Philadelphia ask who p., 625 : 23
insist on being obeyed, 414 : 14
lose both p. carelessness, 675 : 21
meek-eyed p., 864 : 15
reverence for p., 70 : 22
show kindness to p., 131 : 6
was the same, 924 : 10
were Lord knows who, 318 : 7
who weighed measured priced, 549 : 18
Parents, le sort fait les p., 385 : *n* 6
Pares, primus inter p., 134 : 19
Parfums, les p. les couleurs, 580 : *n* 6
Paris, after they've seen P., 801 : 12
Americans die go to P., 675 : 14
artist no home save P., 658 : 23
from P. to Japan, 311 : 12
I will die in P., 824 : 4
is P. burning, 813 : 2
is well worth a Mass, 174 : 26
last time I saw P., 833 : 9
last time I see P., 819 : 13
lived half life in P., 752 : 13
mighty P. when he found, 716 : 19
movable feast, 845 : 14
my home town, 752 : 13
no good speech save in P., 150 : 9
our black classic, 892 : 10
some love P. some Purdue, 864 : 18
Paris, il n'est bon bec que de P., 150 : *n* 4
vaut bien une messe, 174 : *n* 8
Parish, look upon world as p., 346 : 8
plain as way to p. church, 211 : 11
Paris's back Achilles' heel, 907 : 13
Park, over p. over pale, 196 : 10
Parking, paved paradise put up p. lot, 916 : 6
Parks, my body p. and palaces, 668 : 21
Parley, no truce or p., 745 : 3
Parley-voo, hinky dinky p., 817 : 7
Parliament, coach through act of P., 920 : 2
of Man, 530 : 1
Parliamentary, Rupert of p. discussion, 501 : 13
Parliaments, kings and p., 348 : 3
Parliment, Three Estates in P., 472 : *n* 2
Parlor, queen in p., 931 : 9
read in p. kitchen nursery, 538 : *n* 6
walk into p., 485 : 23
Parlors, bells in your p., 230 : 8
Parlous boy, 187 : 12
Parmgianino did it, 906 : 15
Parochial, worse than provincial p., 652 : 7
Parodies most penetrating, 830 : 10
Parole, classical quotation p. of literary men, 356 : 21
Parole humaine comme chaudron fêlé, 583 : *n* 5
Parrot, conscious mind trained like p., 754 : 9
Parsimony not economy, 374 : 9
requires no providence, 374 : 10
Parsnips, words butter no p., 432 : 2
Parson, if p. lost senses, 732 : 16
in arguing p. owned skill, 370 : 11
Parson's, coughing drowns p. saw, 191 : 15
Part, act lover's or Roman's p., 335 : 8
art too precise in every p., 266 : 7
beginning most important p., 84 : 8
better p. of valor, 205 : 14
book and heart never p., 320 : 5
choosest not better p., 703 : 3
come between bid us p., 345 : 18
come let us kiss and p., 182 : 16
death p. of life, 755 : 8
each play p. in memorable days, 745 : 7
every man must play a p., 197 : 28
from yours will not p., 290 : 2
half p. of blessed man, 201 : 16
his blessed p. to heaven, 249 : 11
I am p. of all met, 457 : *n* 6, 529 : 8
I am p. of earth, 790 : 21
I am p. of my family, 790 : 21
I am p. of the sun, 790 : 21
immortal p. of myself, 230 : 23
know in p., 48 : 25
looks p. has soul of p., 667 : 4
love's passives his activest p., 292 : 14
maid of Athens ere we p., 456 : 19
Mary hath chosen good p., 43 : 17
my garments among them, 18 : 6
my hair behind, 803 : 19
Nature hath done her p., 287 : 9
ninth p. of a hair, 204 : 15
none shall p. us, 628 : 14
of solution or part of problem, 913 : 5
of the human race, 790 : 21
of wisdom, 377 : 8
prophesy in p., 48 : 25
read p. all through, 777 : 8
some p. of day I had rued, 748 : 3
take my own p., 492 : 17
that which is in p., 48 : 25
thou and nature so gently p., 242 : 3
Part (*continued*)
till death us do p., 56 : 9
to p. is die a little, 463 : *n* 3
touch lips p. with tears, 633 : 15
we sadly in troublous world, 186 : 24
which laws or kings cause, 352 : 21
without kiss, 618 : 4
you and I must p., 918 : 18
Partake gale, 338 : 2
sacred emblems to p., 604 : 10
Partaken, banquet p. in anxiety, 66 : 6
mutual and p. bliss, 279 : 31
Parted are those singing today, 627 : 5
between twelve and one, 207 : 13
by hurrying world, 424 : 3
fool and money p., 917 : 23
from others as nail from flesh, 137 : 4
never be p. bliss or woe, 287 : 23
never met or never p., 410 : 3
remember way we p., 634 : 2
when we two p., 456 : 8
Partes, Gallia est omnis divisa in p. tres, 99 : *n* 10
Parteth the hoof, 10 : 16
Parthenon, earth proudly wears P., 493 : 19
these were our P., 800 : 10
Parthenope nourished me, 104 : 13
Partial evil universal good, 337 : 1
for observer's sake, 335 : 12
Nature wherefore thus p., 152 : 15
Partiality, no p. in his writing, 98 : 10
Participate in America's growth, 875 : 10
Participation, deny them p. of freedom, 373 : 6
Particle, each of us p. of mass, 755 : 1
mind very fiery p., 461 : 24
Particles, impenetrable movable p., 313 : 16
not composed of same p., 580 : 3
spatial motions of material p., 636 : 17
straining at p. of light, 480 : 1
Particular, each p. hair to stand, 219 : 18
London p. a fog, 549 : 13
love a bright p. star, 227 : 10
Particularize, to p. is merit, 405 : 16
Particulars, do good in minute p., 407 : 6
flies from p. to axioms, 179 : 7
minutely organized p., 407 : 6
Parties, divided mankind into p., 398 : 2
good temper between p., 650 : 14
men naturally in two p., 390 : 2
Parting all we know of heaven, 607 : 18
foretaste of death, 463 : 5
genius with sighing sent, 277 : 11
if not this p. well made, 217 : 9
is such sweet sorrow, 192 : 19
king stood at p. of way, 32 : 27
shakes p. guest by hand, 226 : 19
speed the p. guest, 334 : 23, 715 : 11
Partir c'est mourir un peu, 463 : *n* 3, 679 : *n* 2
Partisan cares nothing about rights, 84 : 1
of truth alone, 260 : 10
Partisans, rabid p. or empty quacks, 650 : 14
Partition, union in p., 197 : 2
Partitions, thin p., 303 : 20

Partners, our property subject to control of p., 393 : 3
set to p. change lobsters, 612 : 6
Partridge sitteth on eggs, 32 : 13
Parts, affliction enamored of thy p., 193 : 11
Gaul divided into three p., 99 : 14
here the p. shift, 543 : 20
if p. allure thee, 337 : 15
machine no unnecessary p., 729 : 7
man of sovereign p., 190 : 20
of good natural p., 169 : 7
of it are excellent, 660 : 18
one man plays many p., 211 : 15
only Christian come to these p., 151 : 1
remembers me his gracious p., 201 : 26
uttermost p. of the sea, 22 : 17
virtue on outward p., 199 : 25
Parturient montes nascetur mus, 109 : *n* 11
Party, come to aid of p., 923 : 1
comes from grass roots, 698 : 13
fire tolerable third p., 557 : 13
I am p. of one, 846 : 17
injured p., 630 : 20
is madness of many, 340 : 13
of revolution civilization, 492 : 7
offices not for p., 449 : 8
platforms are contracts, 788 : 8
print strongest weapon of p., 766 : 7
serves p. best, 590 : 9
spirit at best madness, 334 : 17
spirit of p., 379 : 11
test of political p., 851 : 8
that succeeds in elections, 616 : 2
that works both sides of street, 781 : 3
to p. gave up, 371 : 14
tribe or clan, 922 : 9
true poet and of Devil's p., 403 : 19
unshackled by p., 429 : 16
what that p. has done for women, 578 : 4
Parvis e glandibus quercus, 134 : 15
Pas, premier p. qui coûte, 344 : *n* 6
Pasarán, no p., 833 : 21
Pascal, celebrities such as P., 615 : 14
Pasqueflower, chance to find p., 795 : 9
Pass, all which will not p. away, 457 : 21
all ye that p. by, 32 : 22
ammunition, 871 : 2
and turn again, 495 : 11
by me as idle wind, 217 : 2
by sight so touching, 425 : 13
gates of Hades, 67 : 5
he brings to p. every word, 71 : 1
heaven and earth p., 37 : 7
heaven and earth p. away, 430 : 12
horseman p. by, 718 : 2
I p. a willful stranger, 669 : 3
in angels say, 494 : 15
into nothingness, 475 : 16
it on, 639 : 17
joy to p. to world below, 105 : 12
let him p. for a man, 198 : 13
let it be let it p., 342 : *n* 6
let the toast p., 399 : 1
loveliest soonest p. away, 471 : 9
me the can lad, 691 : 19
my words not p. away, 40 : 26
not away, 8 : 11

Pass (*continued*)
not p. save with My authority, 132 : 12
not p. this way again, 439 : 2
O let him p., 235 : 19
o'er green cornfield did p., 212 : 33
on let us pass, 770 : 13
onward though dynasties p., 642 : 2
open Time let him p., 696 : 13
ships that p. in night, 512 : 10
strangely p., 244 : 17
stronger peoples p. us by, 687 : 4
these things come to p., 40 : 22
they shall not p., 679 : 13, 833 : 21
this too shall p. away, 521 : 3
through grass behind bush, 778 : 6
through land of Egypt, 9 : 25
virtues men praise and p. by, 791 : 13
we p. the gate, 721 : 7
world, 852 : 15
Passage broad to Hell, 92 : *n* 5
fret p. through it, 276 : 15
immediate p., 576 : 16
man merely p. for food, 152 : 2
Northwest P. to intellectual world, 360 : 16
of angel's tear, 475 : 5
shortest p. to riches, 391 : 9
to remorse, 236 : 17
we did not take, 807 : 2
you think particularly fine, 355 : 8
Passages, apprenticehood to foreign p., 194 : 4
history has cunning p., 804 : 14
which seem confidences, 499 : 17
Passageways, no life moves in empty p., 74 : 1
Passé, hiverné dans mon p., 770 : *n* 5
Passe, on ne p. pas, 679 : *n* 4
tout p., 928 : 3
Passed away glory from earth, 426 : 12
below horizon of homing, 808 : 13
clean over Jordan, 11 : 29
even shade is p. away, 425 : 20
for dangers I had p., 229 : 31
fortunes that I have p., 229 : 27
over on dry ground, 11 : 29
so he p. over, 302 : 16
Passenger e'er pukes in, 461 : 14
Passengers are just that distance from death, 63 : 1
ask conductor, 761 : 6
Passer deliciae meae puellae, 101 : *n* 12
laissez faire laissez p., 342 : 20
ne les laisserez pas p., 679 : *n* 4
Passeront, ils ne p. pas, 679 : *n* 4
Passes, all p., 640 : 1
among the impure, 86 : *n* 7
bright youth p. swiftly, 67 : 7
every hour that p. O, 409 : 14
everything p. art eternal, 538 : 7
everything p. perishes palls, 928 : 3
men seldom make p., 827 : 11
now fancy p. by, 691 : 2
rise to feet as He p., 707 : 23
Passest, tell Spartans thou who p. by, 67 : 19
Passeth, fashion of world p., 48 : 12
one generation p. away, 26 : 11
peace which p. understanding, 50 : 6, 57 : *n* 2
that within which p. show, 218 : 3
wind p. over it, 21 : 7
Passing, all is p., 770 : 13

Passing (*continued*)
bells for these who die, 827 : 2
could not wait their p., 587 : 8
longest part of journey p. of gate, 97 : 11
out O bitter ending, 778 : 6
past or p. or to come, 715 : 3
power p. from the earth, 428 : 5
see her p. by, 918 : 14
speak each other in p., 512 : 10
the love of women, 13 : 11
through nature to eternity, 218 : 1
tribute of a sigh, 362 : 13
wind is p. by, 608 : 19
Passio, hysterica p., 233 : 17
Passion, all p. spent, 289 : 11
and death of a friend, 197 : 19
bards of p., 477 : 15
by p. driven, 409 : 5
caprice and lifelong p., 675 : 2
chaos of thought and p., 337 : 2
choleric who subdued p., 386 : 11
connect prose and p., 764 : 9
cows my p., 548 : 19
crushed in winepress of p., 150 : 2
drug which takes away p., 59 : 25
eternal p. eternal pain, 586 : 6
fever in mind, 314 : 17
for a scarlet coat, 322 : 16
for anonymity, 762 : 9
for hunting something, 547 : 2
for righteousness, 799 : 18
for truth, 685 : 5
gratification of every p., 583 : 9
greatest width of p., 809 : 17
happier in p. we feel, 293 : 30
haunted me like a p., 423 : 12
hopeless p., 539 : 13
I must speak in p., 204 : 4
ignorance and p. foes of morality, 580 : 14
impulse of p. or interest, 398 : 1
in first p. woman loves lover, 460 : 24
in first p. women love lovers, 294 : 9
infinite p. and pain, 542 : 10
intellectual p. drives out sensuality, 152 : 3
interpret story of P., 859 : 10
justice forever in p., 539 : 21
kindle p. of former days, 744 : 11
life a play of p., 173 : 1
life action and p., 643 : 16
maiden p. for maid, 534 : 23
master p. hunger for self-approval, 626 : 3
master p. in breast, 337 : 4
ne'er like angels till p. dies, 251 : 12
no longer a p. hidden, 312 : 8
nor p. wild, 584 : 8
nothing great without p., 422 : 13
novel happens because storyteller moved to p., 135 : 14
of resentment, 658 : 20
one p. expel another, 177 : 18
our p. is our task, 653 : 5
poet binds together by p., 424 : 8
poetry not purpose but p., 526 : 9
rebirth brings delight and p., 72 : 23
red rose whispers of p., 659 : 6
ruling p. be it what will, 336 : 2
ruling p. conquers reason, 336 : 2
self-centered p., 839 : 14
shocks of p. prepare, 428 : 23
sick of an old p., 721 : 4

Passion (*continued*)
slept, 351 : 12
spent its novel force, 529 : 17
strain bonds of affection, 521 : 14
strongly rooted as envy, 399 : 4
talking is p. of woman, 323 : 30
tear a p. to tatters, 221 : 23
that left ground, 544 : 5
their fury and my p., 247 : 20
utmost p. of her heart, 503 : 10
what p. cannot music raise, 305 : 10
which maketh laughter, 264 : 15
whirlwind of p., 221 : 23
wholly of mind, 836 : 18
whom p. could not shake, 231 : 26
with correctness, 651 : 4
without tenderness, 895 : 6
worst sin p. commit, 827 : 22
Passionate, beautiful p. body, 632 : 13
beyond the will, 836 : 19
fantastical imagination, 715 : 4
foolish p. man, 717 : 3
full of p. intensity, 714 : 12
hardly p. Marlborough Street, 892 : 20
intuition, 428 : 16
make p. my hearing, 190 : 23
repeated with p. love, 442 : 19
simple sensuous and p., 281 : 20
women, 712 : 19
Passionflower at gate, 533 : 24
Passion's slave, 222 : 6
Passions, all other p. fly, 440 : 4
all p. all delights, 435 : 20
cannot alter facts, 380 : 11
capable of boundless p., 583 : 14
expand time, 734 : 5
exquisite p., 638 : 10
govern my p., 302 : 24
hath not a Jew p., 199 : 17
held in reverence, 526 : 9
infusing p., 437 : 22
like floods and streams, 172 : 12
malice most hateful of p., 626 : 10
man only great when he acts from p., 501 : 16
matched with mine, 530 : 5
mediocre p., 293 : 31
men governed by bad p., 387 : 14
men of like p., 46 : 12
moderator of p., 270 : 34
most transient of p., 681 : 1
natural man has two p., 664 : 13
never let angry p. rise, 328 : 3
not conform to reason, 401 : 16
of base p. fear most accursed, 185 : 5
other p. fleet to air, 199 : 28
sculptor well p. read, 466 : 12
spin the plot, 600 : 18
three p. governed life, 738 : 6
various ruling p. find, 335 : 21
without justice, 703 : 13
Passive Master lent hand, 493 : 20
observation p. science, 551 : 14
resistance, 727 : 5
Passiveness, wise p., 423 : 5
Passives, love's p., 292 : 14
Passivity, divest himself of p., 909 : 15
Passons passons tout passe, 770 : *n* 7
Passover, Christ our P., 48 : 10
for a memorial, 9 : 26
it is the Lord's p., 9 : 25
Past, all p. in mind of man, 683 : 17
all the p. is his, 74 : 18
Past (*continued*)
and to come seem best, 206 : 8
articulate voice of p., 473 : 28
as yesterday when it is p., 20 : 11
beginning of beginning, 719 : 14
best of prophets is the p., 462 : 8
born back into p., 835 : 8
bucket of ashes, 761 : 7
changes constantly, 816 : 4
condemned to repeat p., 703 : 11
correctly informed as to p., 489 : 4
cure I am, 246 : 6
democracy shuts p. opens future, 506 : 8
died to keep P. upon throne, 568 : 14
dogmas of quiet p., 522 : 12
dream p. the wit of man, 197 : 9
every advantage in p. judged, 88 : 21
exact knowledge of the p., 80 : 15
extenuate miseries of p., 801 : 3
extolling p., 433 : 16
free of irrelevancies, 736 : 9
Ghost of Christmas P., 548 : 7
gone and p. help, 246 : 18
grieve not for what p., 917 : 20
hallowed quiets of p., 568 : 22
help should be past grief, 246 : 18
here lies my p., 856 : 10
hibernated in my p., 770 : 11
history stumbles trail of p., 744 : 11
hope past cure past help, 193 : 19
in p. our light flickered, 745 : 8
inaccessible tower of p., 569 : 4
indemnity for the p., 351 : *n* 3
judging future but by p., 383 : 2
kept house the p. and I, 641 : 22
lives two lives relives p., 119 : 14
long distant p., 733 : 17
look not mournfully to p., 510 : 2
loses p. and dead for future, 77 : 22
lost in New York, 699 : 2
low-vaulted p., 519 : 7
miracles are p., 227 : 14
mischief p. and gone, 229 : 33
more than things long p., 194 : 10
my days are p., 15 : 38
mysterious p. of sea, 869 : 13
needless to blame things p., 68 : 12
never past redeeming, 899 : 7
never plan future by p., 374 : 4
nightingale when May is p., 271 : 20
nothing worthy in p. departs, 472 : 14
or passing or to come, 715 : 3
our dancing days, 191 : 25
parcels of dreadful p., 528 : 17
pay debt to p., 753 : 8
poor old P. the Future's slave, 572 : 2
power to undo the p., 82 : 27
praiser of p. time, 109 : 28
present contains p., 688 : 9
Present P. Future sees, 405 : 1
problems have roots in p., 788 : 6
psychology long p. short history, 666 : 10
quarrel between p. and present, 744 : 3
reason hunted, 245 : 23
Reason is p. care, 246 : 6
remembrance of things p., 244 : 11
rememoring of cursed p., 811 : 9
repeat p., 703 : 11
repent what's p., 223 : 8
revolution comes from p., 538 : 11
sediment of long Chinese p., 796 : 1
Past (*continued*)
stone strength of p., 797 : 11
the p. a foreign country, 833 : 20
these things are p. and gone, 101 : 17
things p. or things to come, 302 : 4
time present and time p., 807 : 1
times preserve themselves, 834 : 4
trail of the p., 744 : 11
upon the p. has power, 305 : 2
vanished like dream, 473 : 28
what calls back p., 513 : 4
what is p. I know, 34 : 4
what's p. and what's to come, 227 : 4
what's p. is prologue, 247 : 27
when from p. nothing subsists, 733 : 17
when June is p. the fading rose, 271 : 19
when our perils are p., 421 : 22
where all p. years are, 252 : 1
with its pleasures rewards, 863 : 13
work of art, 736 : 9
your p. Scrooge, 548 : 7
Paste and cover to our bones, 195 : 2
Pasted, sun p. in sky, 732 : 4
Pastepot, shears and p., 730 : 15
Pastime and our happiness, 428 : 4
poetry universal p., 509 : 11
Pastimes, man of mirth and p., 155 : 11
Pastoral, oaten stop or p. song, 364 : 11
Pastors, as some ungracious p., 218 : 28
Pasture, clean p. spring, 747 : 3
sheep of his p., 21 : 3
we are the people of his p., 20 : 20
Pastures deep in fern, 846 : 15
England's pleasant p., 406 : 21
fresh woods and p. new, 281 : 6
green p., 18 : 7
pipe me to p. still, 655 : 18
sea p., 571 : 3
Pat he comes, 233 : 6
it and prick it, 929 : 18
now might I do it p., 222 : 26
Pat-a-cake baker's man, 929 : 18
Patch and tinker more than renew, 650 : 10
gain little p. of ground, 223 : 16
griefs with proverbs, 210 : 3
lion's skin with fox's, 119 : 24
matchwood immortal diamond, 656 : 21
Patched, peeled p. and piebald, 340 : 21
Patches, king of shreds and p., 223 : 6
thing of shreds and p., 629 : 4
Patchez, garments in p., 856 : 2
Pate, breaks by p. across, 221 : 8
you beat your p., 336 : 7
Patent leather souls, 841 : 12
Paternal, a few p. acres bound, 332 : 10
Paternalism, lessons of p. unlearned, 631 : 11
Pates, fat paunches have lean p., 128 : *n* 1
Path, direct us in the right p., 130 : 9
easy p. not p. of virtue, 165 : 2
eightfold p., 72 : 23, 73 : 2
emerges then closes, 721 : 7
every p. we tread, 377 : 18
follow p. of action, 68 : 25
genius disdains p., 519 : 24
light p. of America, 729 : 11
light unto my p., 22 : 2
long brown p. before me, 575 : 9

Path (*continued*)
maketh a p. to shine after him, 907 : *n* 1
motive guide, 130 : 3
no quick p. to light switch, 852 : 1
nor p. to follow, 576 : 17
of duty in what is near, 89 : 11
of duty way to glory, 533 : 5
of gold for him, 541 : 15
of rain wind ruin, 850 : 2
of the just is as shining light, 23 : 8
pity straightest p. to love, 260 : 20
primrose p. of dalliance, 218 : 28
righteousness his straight p., 89 : 10
righteousness is man's p., 89 : 21
song that found p., 477 : 1
subtle spirit my p. attended, 794 : 5
through blood of slaughtered, 733 : 6
to deepest mystery path of love, 853 : 8
world make p. to door, 496 : *n* 1
Pathetic, everything human is p., 625 : 4
fallacy, 572 : 10
Pathless, heaven's wide p. way, 278 : 18
woods, 458 : 24
Pathological generation, 584 : 5
lack of balance into p., 755 : 3
Pathos piety courage, 764 : 10
Paths, all her p. are peace, 23 : 5
all p. lead to same goal, 860 : 13
ask for the old p., 31 : 37
leadeth me in p. of righteousness, 18 : 7
make his p. straight, 36 : 26
of all p. to woman's love, 260 : 20
of glory lead to grave, 362 : 3
of peevish Nature, 320 : 16
praise those who follow other p., 106 : 10
so many p. that wind and wind, 670 : 4
Pathway to ballot box, 554 : 8
Patience a blending, 641 : 3
abusing of God's p., 225 : 12
and shuffle cards, 170 : 24
and sympathy, 727 : 5
bear with p. injustice, 298 : 1
best remedy for trouble, 93 : 13
everywhere like fog, 859 : 11
flower of wyfly p., 147 : 19
genius aptitude for p., 349 : 3
genius is p., 349 : *n* 2
habits of peace and p., 270 : 34
have her perfect work, 51 : 27
have unlimited p., 834 : 1
how long Catiline abuse our p., 98 : 1
how poor that have not p., 230 : 29
husbandman hath long p., 52 : 4
ingredient of genius, 349 : *n* 2
is an heigh vertu, 147 : 29
is good, 3 : 13
kingdom and p. of Jesus Christ, 52 : 27
languid p. of thy face, 433 : 18
may compass anything, 158 : 6
means self-suffering, 727 : 5
my p. are exhausted, 778 : 2
no p. wear hunger out, 683 : 18
no wedded man assaille wyves p., 147 : 21
of Job, 52 : 5
on a monument, 214 : 5
pattern of all p., 233 : 28
Patience (*continued*)
perseverance and soothing, 388 : 10
possess soul in p., 44 : 1
possess soul with p., 305 : 28
preached up p., 320 : 19
rocked me to p., 475 : 19
run with p., 51 : 19
Russia homeland of p., 500 : 26
stubborn p. as with triple steel, 284 : 21
thou cherubin, 232 : 4
Time and P. strongest of warriors, 602 : 4
where p. neither anger nor vexation, 138 : 14
you tread upon my p., 203 : 6
Patient, be p. therefore, 52 : 4
cure disease kill p., 180 : 25
etherized upon table, 803 : 9
fates have given a p. soul, 59 : 11
fury of p. man, 304 : 16
in tribulation, 890 : 11
inattention, 601 : 9
looker-on, 267 : 18
love is p., 148 : 20
merit takes, 221 : 12
must minister to himself, 239 : 32
Nature agent and p. at once, 87 : 5
or out of sorts, 864 : 17
play fair just and p., 595 : 12
poor as Job but not p., 205 : 26
sail upon her p. breast, 225 : 36
sleepless Eremite, 478 : 20
soft meek p. humble, 251 : 11
some p. force, 531 : 15
sons before me stand, 368 : 20
Patientia, quo usque Catilina abutere p., 98 : *n* 2
Patines of bright gold, 201 : 1
Patio heaven's watercourse, 843 : 5
Patmos, isle that is called P., 52 : 27
Patre, omnes eodem p. nati, 259 : 9
Patrem, non deum p. ecclesiam non matrem, 126 : *n* 12
Patria, died some pro p., 792 : 14
pro p. mori, 107 : *n* 23
pro p. pro liberis, 102 : *n* 15
sed miles sed pro p., 700 : 7
ubi bene ibi p., 134 : 32
ubi libertas ibi p., 367 : 11
Patriarch to command of God, 580 : 7
Patriarch's, like p. angel, 513 : 5
Patriarchs, had she lived to age of P., 392 : *n* 1
Patrician plebeian lord and serf, 563 : 3
Patrick, guide Sir P. Spens, 926 : 13
Patrick's, Saint P. day, 920 : 21
Patrie, enfants de la p., 415 : 1
Patrimony, that was his only p., 756 : 15
Patriot a fool in every age, 339 : 12
battlefield and p. grave, 521 : 14
devotion of p. soldier, 617 : 6
great p. man American, 667 : 3
no p. on empty stomach, 421 : *n* 3
steady p. of world alone, 422 : 3
sunshine p., 384 : 13
Patriotic control in hard times, 471 : 13
deep p. devotion, 853 : 17
Patriotism gain force on Marathon, 352 : 22
in female most disinterested of virtues, 393 : 3
in military unit, 771 : 2
is not enough, 706 : 17
Patriotism (*continued*)
last refuge of scoundrel, 355 : 15
no concern with art, 619 : 8
politicians not necessary to p., 764 : 15
protection and p., 449 : 7
Patriot's, cowards mock p. fate, 592 : 2
such is the p. boast, 368 : 15
Patriots, American p. sacrificed, 725 : 20
blood of p. and tyrants, 388 : 7
brave men and worthy p., 281 : 19
last effort of p., 380 : 14
seeds of p. and heroes, 367 : *n* 8
so to be p., 372 : 6
Patris, Filius P., 54 : 5
Patroclus, unwept unburied P., 59 : 9
Patron and the jail, 351 : 17
is not a p. my lord, 353 : 26
Patronize polite literature, 379 : 16
Patronizing has meaner side, 565 : 7
Patrons, best of all p., 102 : 4
Pattable, if she p., 856 : 4
Patte, la p. du chat, 297 : *n* 3
Patter of little feet, 512 : 4
our hasty orisons, 827 : 2
Pattern called war, 751 : 6
cunning'st p. of nature, 232 : 14
is imposing a p. on experience, 698 : 5
judge piece by p., 652 : 14
made him our p., 541 : 6
more complicated of dead and living, 807 : 23
of all patience, 233 : 28
of celestial peace, 185 : 7
of dead and living, 807 : 23
to live and to die, 541 : 6
which controls phenomena, 758 : 10
Patterns, Christ what are p. for, 751 : 6
extended to display its p., 70 : 18
made with ideas, 758 : 7
mathematician maker of p., 758 : 7
Paul, by the apostle P., 187 : 29
good for P. and Silas, 921 : 16
Great P. great pail of sound, 899 : 3
I P. a Jew of Tarsus, 46 : 24
I P. a Pharisee, 46 : 29
leave Saint P. nothing, 160 : *n* 2
rob Peter pay P., 160 : 4
said But I was free born, 46 : 26
Saul becomes P., 686 : 11
thou art beside thyself, 46 : 33
Paulo maiora canamus, 103 : *n* 9
Paul's, designing Saint P., 753 : 3
ruins of St. P., 363 : 21
Paumanok, fish-shape P., 574 : 3
Paunch, fat p. never breeds fine thoughts, 128 : 1
Paunches, fat p. have lean pates, 128 : *n* 1
Pauper in midst of wealth, 108 : 6
whom nobody owns, 486 : 1
Paupered arm of old Cervantes, 570 : 11
Pause for a reply, 216 : 16
from learning to be wise, 351 : 17
in day's occupation, 512 : 3
must give us p., 221 : 12
Nature made a p., 330 : 6
no work p. for death, 545 : 5
to p. to make end, 529 : 9
Pauses, lucid intervals and happy p., 179 : 12
Pausing upon yellow flutterings, 475 : 2

Paved, hell p. with good
intentions, 136 : *n* 8, 269 : *n* 2
they p. paradise, 916 : 6
Pavement, emperor's p., 716 : 9
on marble p. dust grows, 97 : 10
riches of heaven's p., 283 : 28
scrub kitchen p., 712 : 20
stand on highest p., 804 : 10
Pavements, lover of populous p., 574 : 3
Pavilioned in splendor, 445 : 21
Pavilions, pale p., 848 : 7
Paving, horses' heels over p., 806 : 12
Paw, cat's p., 297 : 11
grim wolf with privy p., 280 : 22
Paweth, he p. in the valley, 16 : 37
Pawn your intelligence, 828 : 15
Pawnbrokers, glorified p., 687 : 20
Pax, in terra p., 54 : 4
Pay, business in life is p., 642 : 11
devil to p., 169 : 31
double debt to p., 370 : 13
equal p. for equal work, 578 : 2
every debt, 495 : 3
for all we take we p., 707 : 17
for all you have, 729 : 3
for it first or last, 555 : 3
for one by one, 708 : 18
for what gods given him, 736 : 5
forgotten man p. for all, 642 : 11
get what you p. for, 150 : 5
glad life's arrears, 544 : 22
great deal too dear, 246 : 8
I p. thy poverty not thy will, 193 : 21
I will p. you in grave, 470 : 4
if I can't p. I can owe, 158 : 17
in erg and atom exact p., 839 : 3
just man will p. more tax, 84 : 6
law and order p., 644 : 18
make me able to p. for it, 309 : 13
man of genius had to p., 736 : 5
money not p. for anything, 740 : 17
new way to p. old debts, 263 : 1
no worship to garish sun, 193 : 9
not p. honor with tears, 95 : 2
only things we can p., 675 : 7
our lives we p., 567 : 12
piper, 324 : 11
remember to p. the debt, 79 : 8
rob Peter p. Paul, 160 : 4
served without p., 617 : 6
taxes p. for civilized society, 644 : 8
the rent of seem, 829 : 16
vow and not p., 26 : 27
we must anguish p., 604 : 6
we shall p. any price, 890 : 7
when will you p. me, 930 : 7
with a deadly blow, 71 : 16
with all you are, 729 : 3
with ratiocination, 290 : 17
words p. no debts, 226 : 11
you ought to p. you know, 612 : 23
Paying, enrage those p. your
annuities, 344 : 8
through nose, 923 : 19
Pays, he that dies p. all debts, 248 : 9
he who p. piper, 324 : *n* 5
him in own coin, 323 : 20
money takes choice, 660 : 12
to advertise, 923 : 10
us with age and dust, 173 : 5
Pays, du p. qu'on enchaine, 928 : 7
fameux dans les chansons, 581 : *n* 3
Pea, like as one p. to other, 158 : 12
Pea (*continued*)
princess felt p. through
mattresses, 505 : 2
tearing up p. patch, 831 : 11
Peace, abides a p. of thine, 585 : 1
above all earthly dignities, 249 : 4
adventure art p., 697 : 14
age in which p. preserved, 891 : 2
all her paths are p., 23 : 5
and rest can never dwell, 283 : 7
and tranquility to earth, 882 : 20
angels lead in p., 899 : 16
armed p., 273 : 12
as a river, 31 : 7
at last, 765 : 9
at p. with himself, 872 : 15
at p. with neighbors, 788 : 2
at the last, 490 : 10
author of p., 55 : 4
be American without threatening
p., 796 : 8
be at p. henceforward, 511 : 15
be within thy walls, 22 : 6
beasts shall be at p. with thee, 15 : 17
between effect and it, 236 : 17
between equals, 682 : 9
beyond voices p., 534 : 26
bodies are buried in p., 36 : 12
bring p. to others, 148 : 19
calm P. and Quiet, 278 : 15
calm world and long p., 204 : 35
cannot live alone at p., 781 : 5
carry gentle p., 249 : 8
cease not to advocate p., 348 : *n* 2
commerce honest friendship, 389 : 2
Constitution law in war and
p., 553 : 20
contributions to p. of world, 788 : 7
corrupt, 288 : 1
crimes against p., 821 : 7
crowned with smiles, 299 : 10
crust eaten in p., 66 : 6
cultivate p. and harmony, 379 : 12
dangerous to p. and safety, 408 : 3
deep dream of p., 454 : 4
depart in p., 455 : 13
end of that man is p., 18 : 27
endeavors to preserve p., 780 : 4
enemies called for p., 731 : 16
enemies in war in p. friends, 387 : 10
first in war first in p., 402 : 10
follow after p., 47 : 33
fool when he holdeth p., 24 : 18
for our time, 727 : 2
forced upon loser, 682 : 9
fruit of Spirit is p., 49 : 30
gentlemen may cry P., 383 : 5
give p. a chance, 914 : 13
give to all nations p., 55 : 13
go in p., 43 : 5, 134 : 34
go sleep with Turks, 195 : 9
god has brought this p., 103 : 6
God is war p. surfeit hunger, 70 : 2
great war petty p., 720 : 1
guide planets, 914 : 7
habits of p. and patience, 270 : 34
hard and bitter p., 890 : 7
hath her victories, 282 : 14
hope to see p. established, 781 : 8
I am for p., 22 : 3
I give unto you, 45 : 24
I leave with you, 45 : 24
if p. not with honor, 727 : *n* 1
if you want p., 568 : 9
Peace (*continued*)
ignoble p., 687 : 4
imperishable p., 692 : 11
in His will is our p., 142 : 11
in our time, 56 : 15
in p. children inter parents, 78 : 5
in p. goodwill, 746 : 11
in p. just generous, 463 : 13
in p. love tunes, 430 : 6
in p. nothing so becomes man, 207 : 16
in p. provided for war, 128 : *n* 10
in p. thinks of war, 259 : 13
in p. ye critics dwell, 334 : 24
in what p. a Christian can die, 327 : 5
indivisibility of p., 757 : *n* 2
indivisible, 757 : 11
inglorious arts of p., 296 : 22
into poet as flour into bread, 861 : 3
is in grave, 467 : 1
is not absence of war, 308 : 3
is p. so sweet, 383 : 5
is poor reading, 641 : 20
is what I seek, 586 : 12
its ten thousands, 378 : 4
it's wonderful, 776 : 5
just and lasting p., 524 : 7
justice made for sake of p., 156 : 2
justice p. and sobriety, 273 : 11
keep him in perfect p., 30 : 9
keep p. within yourself, 148 : 19
lay me down in p., 17 : 16
let us have p., 589 : 20
liberty and safety, 389 : 2
live together in p., 788 : 20
make a desert call it p., 123 : 3
make war to live in p., 87 : 24
makes solitude calls it p., 459 : 7
man's village his p. of mind, 895 : 11
may he rest in p., 134 : 22
means of preserving p., 379 : 9
Mercy Pity P. and Love, 403 : 10
more important than justice, 156 : 2
more precious than land, 895 : 16
my p. is gone, 396 : 18
my preservation of p., 164 : 3
naked poor mangled p., 208 : 16
Napoleon sole obstacle to p., 420 : 14
never good war or bad p., 348 : 6
no p. unto the wicked, 31 : 8
nor help for pain, 587 : 16
nor shall this p. sleep with
her, 249 : 17
not made for justice, 156 : 2
not p. but a sword, 39 : 4
nothing bring p. but self, 497 : 9
nothing contributes more to p. of
soul, 386 : 17
object of war p., 579 : 2
of all countries connected, 774 : 6
of God which passeth all
understanding, 56 : 1
of p. there shall be no end, 29 : 16
on earth mercy mild, 350 : 15
on earth p. and good will, 42 : 29
on the earth, 537 : 16
order security and p., 774 : 6
organized common p., 682 : 8
our concern be p. of mind, 92 : 13
our p. in His will, 806 : 7
our p. our innocence, 425 : 15
passes into anesthesia, 697 : 15
pattern of celestial p., 185 : 7
perfectionism may obstruct p., 781 : 4
perpetual p., 277 : 6

Peace (*continued*)
pious man can't stay in p., 414 : 3
poetry act of p., 861 : 3
poetry fine-spun from mind at p., 113 : 27
price life exacts for p., 842 : 14
Prince of P., 29 : 16
proclaims olives of age, 245 : 13
promoter of p. and goodwill, 617 : 7
publisheth p., 31 : 12
reigns in Warsaw, 439 : 1
rest in soft p., 256 : 4
righteousness and p. have kissed each other, 20 : 9
running wild all over, 840 : 19
seek p. and pursue it, 18 : 21
separate p., 844 : 11
servant depart in p., 42 : 30
sinews of p., 746 : 10
slept in p., 249 : 11
snow said p., 811 : 17
soft phrase of p., 229 : 24
speak or forever hold his p., 56 : 7
spoke I think of p., 765 : 9
star of p. return, 443 : 13
suffering evils of long p., 122 : 10
Tahiti full of p. joy, 570 : 14
take chances for p., 803 : 8
thank God for p., 738 : 12
the human dress, 403 : 11
there is no p., 383 : 5
they are in p., 34 : 13
thousand years of p., 532 : 23
time of p., 26 : 21
to bitter bones, 863 : 19
to him that is far off, 31 : 22
to men of good will, 42 : *n* 3, 54 : 4
to this house, 43 : 9
United States declare p., 818 : 8
universal p., 529 : 5
unjust p. before just war, 348 : *n* 2
until I come in p., 14 : 11
unto you, 882 : 1
uproar the universal p., 239 : 19
vision of eternal p., 881 : 14
we now to p. and darkness, 692 : 10
we shall find p., 695 : 7
weak piping time of p., 186 : 32
what hast thou to do with p., 14 : 17
when there is no peace, 31 : 36
when there was p. he was for p., 869 : 2
where p. neither anxiety nor doubt, 138 : 14
which passeth understanding, 50 : 6, 57 : *n* 2
who desires p. prepare for war, 128 : 25
will for p., 780 : 4
with disgrace, 95 : 16
with honor, 502 : 18, 727 : 2
with justice and honor, 95 : 16
without honor not peace, 466 : 3
without victory, 682 : 9
work us a perpetual p., 277 : 6
world p. or destruction, 729 : 12
Peaceably along highway, 359 : 20
if we can, 438 : *n* 1
live p., 47 : 23
to assemble, 391 : 14
Peaceful abodes of the gods, 59 : *n* 5
as old age tonight, 543 : 2
changes by p. means, 700 : 3
coexistence, 862 : 17
Peaceful (*continued*)
flowering of man, 852 : 2
generous just, 522 : 12
lead p. people into war, 682 : 13
revolution, 891 : 3
sloth, 284 : 13
welcome p. evening in, 377 : 3
what p. hours enjoyed, 375 : 15
Peace-loving nations, 780 : 4
Peacemaker, "if" is the only p., 213 : 5
title of p., 882 : 19
Peacemakers, blessed are the p., 37 : 4, 185 : 11
Peach, asked thief to steal me p., 404 : 11
dare to eat a p., 803 : 19
had a p. from the tree, 404 : 11
once bitter almond, 624 : 14
ripest p. highest, 665 : 8
Peaches, tree that bears bitter p., 314 : 2
Peacock pie, 740 : 1
pride of p. glory of God, 404 : 3
Peacocks and lilies, 572 : 14
heard them cry the p., 766 : 12
ivory apes and p., 13 : 36, 760 : 19
turning as tails of p., 766 : 12
Pea-green boat, 550 : 7
Peak, dwindle p. and pine, 236 : 3
frozen p., 748 : 17
ice silent language of p., 812 : 2
in Darien, 475 : 7
Peaks most wrapped in clouds, 457 : 22
Peal, rung night's yawning p., 238 : 20
wildest p. for years, 732 : 16
Pealing anthem swells, 362 : 4
let the p. organ blow, 278 : 26
Peanuts, buy p. and cracker-jack, 765 : 13
Pear, go to p. tree for pears, 111 : 31
golden p., 932 : 1
Pearl and crystal shining bright, 406 : 6
barbaric p. and gold, 284 : 3
chain of all virtues, 257 : 14
for carnal swine, 291 : 21
hang p. in cowslip's ear, 196 : 11
in bosom of sea, 257 : 13
in your foul oyster, 213 : 3
of great price, 39 : 18
of orient p. a double row, 250 : 6
pale poetic p., 570 : 11
quarelets of p., 266 : 5
robe of gold and p., 208 : 7
tankards scooped in p., 604 : 13
threw a p. away, 232 : 20
Pearls and vermin, 489 : 8
asked how p. did grow, 266 : 5
black men are p., 190 : 6
cast p. before swine, 38 : 11
of thought, 569 : 2
string of p. to me, 700 : 13
string p. strung on, 653 : 7
that were his eyes, 247 : 21
Pearly monotones, 794 : 2
shells of p. hue, 442 : 16
Pears, go to pear tree for p., 111 : 31
Peas, tame pigeons p., 290 : *n* 3
Peasant has lawyer inside, 706 : 9
have chicken in pot, 174 : 25
lawyer has p. inside, 706 : 9
rogue and p. slave, 221 : 6
toe of p., 224 : 13
told by p. gospeler, 715 : 18
Peasantry, bold p., 369 : 30
Peasants born kings of earth, 504 : 12
carry honor in their hands, 264 : 8
Pease-porridge hot, 931 : 18
Pebble, finding smoother p., 313 : 17
Pebbled, waves make towards p. shore, 244 : 19
Pebbles, grating roar of p., 587 : 14
of holy streams, 886 : 21
pick Jackson from p., 570 : 11
unnumbered idle p., 234 : 28
Peccata, qui tollis p. mundi, 54 : 5
Péché c'est obscurcit l'âme, 727 : *n* 7
Peck, for daws to p. at, 229 : 17
of pickled peppers, 932 : 9
of troubles, 153 : 10
truly a p. of provender, 197 : 5
Pecks, three p. of barley meal, 934 : 1
Pecksniff, said Mr. P. tenderly, 547 : 31
Pecksniffian, Philadelphia p., 772 : 4
Pectus est enim quod disertos facit, 118 : *n* 1
Peculiar, an air and p. grace, 328 : 17
deposit for virtue, 388 : 2
doctrine right to interfere, 560 : 23
extensive and p., 546 : 16
God's p. light, 155 : 2
plant on p. spot, 337 : 3
Pedagogues, clouds are p., 768 : 13
Pedal, poverty soft p. on activity, 771 : 16
Pedantical, figures p., 191 : 9
Pedants, dilettantes and p., 705 : 20
learned p. much affect, 290 : 20
Peddler, lives of shoemaker and fish p., 811 : 8
Pede, ex p. Herculem, 78 : *n* 6
Pedestaled in triumph, 545 : 11
Pedigree as far as Deluge, 539 : 20
lass wi' lang p., 417 : 9
of honey, 607 : 13
Peeking into her own clasped hands, 912 : 13
Peel, d'ye ken John P., 474 : 19
me a grape, 824 : 9
Peeled patched and piebald, 340 : 21
Peep about to find graves, 215 : 6
and botanize, 424 : 15
at such a world, 377 : 4
critic p., 494 : 1
from her cabined loophole p., 279 : 13
heaven p. through blanket, 236 : 18
nevermore to p. again, 740 : 6
treason can but p., 223 : 27
Peephole, wine is a p., 62 : 20
Peeping in at morn, 485 : 4
Peeps over glass's edge, 543 : 3
primrose p. beneath thorn, 370 : 17
Peer, do not p. too far, 71 : 23
King Stephen worthy p., 917 : 21
many a p. of England brews, 691 : 17
Peereth, honor p. in meanest habit, 189 : 2
Peering, into darkness p., 526 : 14
littlenesses, 534 : 1
Peerless, unveiled her p. light, 285 : 25
Peers, among p. happy warrior, 427 : *n* 2
battle with my p., 529 : 8
heroes of old, 544 : 22
House of P. throughout war, 628 : 24
judgment of his p., 139 : 2
powerful amidst p., 656 : 8
Peevish Nature, 320 : 16
Peg, square p. in round hole, 432 : *n* 5

Pegasus, gallop P. to death, 339:15
turn and wind a fiery P., 204:32
Peignoir, complacencies of p., 767:2
Peine, la p. de naître, 378:*n* 6
Peinture, la lumière à p., 670:*n* 4
Pejorist, not pessimist but p., 690:*n* 1
Peking, improved relations with P., 882:22
Peleus', wrath of P. son, 57:3, 334:18
Pelf, ask no meaner p., 557:20
I crave no p., 243:1
in scramble for p., 556:1
titles power and p., 430:10
Pelican jee, 551:7
Lord Jesu blessed P., 139:13
wonderful bird is p., 765:12
Pelicans all of sudden came p., 888:13
Pelion, from Ossa hurled P., 60:*n* 3
pile Ossa on P., 103:29
with its leafy forests, 60:9
Pellinore followed questing beast, 149:7
Pellucid in azure depths, 577:7
Peloponnesians, war between P. and Athenians, 80:14
Pelops', Thebes or P. line, 278:21
Pelting of pitiless storm, 234:3
Pembroke's mother, 265:15
Pen, and I made a rural p., 403:3
antique p. would have expressed, 245:12
breathing revenge, 561:2
cold words of tongue or p., 732:15
excellent instrument, 380:7
feather whence p. shaped, 429:4
galley slave to p., 484:11
gleaned teeming brain, 478:17
in hand, 356:16
in his hand a torpedo, 353:22
lend me your p., 928:*n* 3
make famous by my p., 292:*n* 2
make glorious by my p., 292:4
mightier than sword, 493:6
my tongue is the p. of a ready writer, 19:8
never saw p. and ink, 214:27
nose as sharp as p., 207:13
poet's p. turns to shapes, 197:12
preferable to sword, 169:34
sad words of tongue or p., 513:14
taught man by the p., 132:17
through every other word, 433:14
wherewith thou heavenly sing, 429:*n* 1
whether chisel p. brush, 714:7
with such acts fill a p., 182:15
words as with burning p., 412:11
worse than the sword, 259:3
write p. for I am volumes, 190:18
written with a p. of iron, 32:10
Penal, chains and p. fire, 283:4
Penalty, greatest p. of evildoing, 86:1
paying p. for no idealism, 698:9
Penance, hath p. done, 435:2
more will do, 435:2
sit doing p., 489:2
Pence, eternal lack of p., 530:16
eternal want of p., 157:*n* 15
for thirty p. my death, 268:11
take care of p., 341:21
three hundred p., 45:16
Pendent, blown about p. world, 228:20
made his p. bed, 236:21

Pendent (*continued*)
towered citadel p. rock, 241:17
world as a star, 285:3
Pends-toi brave Crillon, 175:*n* 2
Penelope, constant as P., 918:8
cretonnes of P., 769:6
faithful P., 61:5
true P. was Flaubert, 792:11
Penetrable to shower of gold, 473:13
Penetrates eternal justice as eye into sea, 142:15
nonbeing p. no space, 64:15
sun p. privies, 86:13
Penetrating, fault of p. wit, 294:4
love is attempt at p. another, 885:15
parodies p. criticisms, 830:10
Peniel, called the place P., 8:26
Penitence holidays awaken, 547:23
vague kind of p., 547:23
Penknife in your heart, 929:9
Penniless, forgive man for being p., 484:13
lass wi' lang pedigree, 417:9
Penny, beg p. by and by, 811:16
for your thought, 160:25
in for p. in for pound, 629:2
in old man's hat, 921:3
Jacky have p. a day, 931:2
not a p. in it, 933:5
one a p. two a p., 931:17
plain and twopence colored, 669:1
postage stamp, 614:8
wise pound foolish, 258:10
Pens, if trees in earth were p., 132:3
louder than thunder, 169:*n* 3
natural right to use p., 343:20
of diplomats not ruin, 386:15
quirks of blazoning p., 230:7
skewered with office p., 549:6
Pensant, un roseau p., 300:*n* 4
Pense, honi soit qui mal y p., 143:7
il faut vivre comme on p., 670:*n* 5
je p. donc je suis, 272:10
Pensée, la p. à littérature que la lumière à peinture, 670:*n* 4
Pensées, mes p. sont mes catins, 359:*n* 6
Pension never enriched young man, 270:5
Pensions and family gratuities, 449:6
Pensive Eve, 364:11
mistress, 874:21
poets painful vigils, 340:16
soul, 364:14
Pent, here in the body p., 429:17
long in city p., 475:4
long in populous city p., 287:17
Pentameter, in p. aye falling, 435:19
Penthouse, hang upon his p. lid, 236:2
Pent-up love of my heart, 661:10
Penuries, to fill all p., 255:1
Penury, age ache p., 228:21
chill p., 362:7
talk tendeth only to p., 24:3
People, a few fastidious p., 711:*n* 1
a stiffnecked p., 10:12
after p. are dead, 733:17
all exulting, 576:6
all p. and tongues, 53:14
all sorts of p., 237:1
all the lonely p., 914:10
all with one accord, 368:7
are calling each other, 902:3
are like water, 826:11

People (*continued*)
arose as one man, 12:23
attentive unto book of law, 14:30
be nice to p. on way up, 757:13
beat my p. to pieces, 28:35
beautiful p., 914:*n* 2
because we hate no p., 824:12
behind p. the country, 590:6
believe these p. from sky, 151:5
black p. unite, 914:15
bludgeoning of p. by p. for p., 675:24
brave new world that has such p., 248:17
British p. like to be told worst, 744:15
came to their senses, 732:16
capable of becoming happier, 814:8
cautious p. never bring reform, 577:17
census treats p. as units, 879:17
change what is in themselves, 131:1
cheerfully support government, 631:11
chief business of American p., 736:16
chosen p. of God, 388:2
colored p. understand white p., 733:7
come to church good p., 691:4
come ye thankful p., 536:2
comfort ye my p., 30:29
common denominator of progress, 871:15
common p. of the skies, 251:1
common sense of our p., 841:3
common-looking p. best, 523:5
complained of long voyage, 150:14
conceited p. carry comfort, 565:17
confidence in justice of p., 521:12
considered by p. equally true, 383:7
contracts with the p., 788:8
cooperation of free p., 682:17
country belongs to p., 521:11
dangerous who make no noise, 296:19
descend to meet, 497:16
difference between rich and other p., 845:*n* 1
difficult to govern, 65:2
easily becomes prey, 154:8
economics as if p. mattered, 879:16
enslaved by things they want, 895:12
experiment of American p., 379:7
eyes of all p. upon us, 264:22
fear and distrust the p., 390:2
few p. who write know anything, 597:7
find p. have good sense, 294:1
fool some p., 524:10
former p., 725:4
freedom light, 817:6
given over in troops to disease and death, 101:12
glory of thy p. Israel, 42:31
God save the p., 449:3
good tidings to all p., 42:28
governed by magistrates, 484:20
government for benefit of p., 444:3
government for the p., 450:14
government not support p., 631:11
government of all the p., 505:19
government of by for p., 523:4, 537:15, 725:20

People (*continued*)
government of p., 505 : 19
grown-up p., 690 : 12
grudge what they cannot enjoy, 66 : 10
happiness except where p., 722 : 14
happy p. die whole, 797 : 13
have always some champion, 85 : 5
have right to knowledge, 380 : 9
hell is other p., 865 : 12
his p. are free, 447 : 10
his p. were his temple, 300 : 20
hoop unbroken p. flourished, 701 : 8
how you are to govern p., 372 : 8
I am the p., 761 : 3
if you love your p., 881 : 13
imagine a vain thing, 17 : 13
in arms, 483 : 9
in front get the jar, 758 : 5
in glass houses, 269 : *n* 3
in hotels strike no roots, 725 : 18
in old times had convictions, 482 : 1
included in We the p., 913 : 9
indictment against whole p., 372 : 21
indomitable p. of Vermont, 736 : 19
is a great beast, 108 : *n* 14
Jewish p. gave New World vision, 881 : 14
judging p. by appearances, 296 : 16
land of Russian p., 500 : 26
law for rulers and p., 553 : 20
lazy nonprogressive p., 818 : 12
lazy p. look for something to do, 361 : 4
leader and commander to the p., 31 : 19
least sure most dogmatic, 871 : 6
let go hold of p., 839 : 13
let my p. go, 9 : 16, 935 : 21
lift p. from dust, 494 : 17
like p. like priest, 33 : 8
living deeply no fear of death, 858 : 4
lonely p. talking to each other, 863 : 8
look after our p., 726 : 7
love of British p., 373 : 7
made the Constitution, 402 : 8
maintain control of government, 780 : 6
make bad laws then suffer, 635 : 24
many-headed beast, 108 : 19
marry ancient p., 277 : 2
masses of p. not qualified, 784 : 17
may be made to follow path, 68 : 25
may grow old without visiting, 65 : 9
mercy on my poor p., 166 : 11
mercy on Thy p. Lord, 709 : 20
more than half p. right, 846 : 16
most important element, 89 : 28
motes that p. sunbeams, 278 : 10
multitude of the gross p., 108 : *n* 14
my p. are Americans, 842 : 3
my p. lending their strength, 888 : 5
my p. would increase, 603 : 1
narrow-souled p., 340 : 11
nation territory p. laws, 522 : 10
never give up liberties, 373 : 13
never learned from history, 422 : 9
new deal for American p., 779 : 8
ninety-nine percent of p. fools, 839 : 17
no doubt but ye are the p., 15 : 27
no more give the p. straw, 9 : 17
not always what seem, 374 : 15

People (*continued*)
numerous and warlike, 151 : 9
O my p. what have I done to thee, 806 : 4
O stormy p., 147 : 20
oats supports p., 352 : 12
of his pasture, 20 : 20
of p. by p. for p., 523 : 4, 537 : 15, 725 : 20
of unclean lips, 29 : 10
of Western Europe, 815 : 12
old trees used to p., 840 : 6
on whom nothing lost, 652 : 14
on world not in it, 637 : 20
one man die for p., 45 : 15
one of beautiful p., 914 : 12
one should like to drop, 356 : 19
one thing besides p. I know, 779 : 3
only p. for me mad, 901 : 3
our land before we her p., 749 : 3
our p. covered the land, 455 : 14
our sovereign the p., 450 : *n* 8
people have for friends, 696 : 1
people marry, 696 : 1
planned obsolescence of p., 881 : 10
poet help p. live their lives, 769 : 16
poor p. know poor p., 859 : 16
power from the p., 501 : 6
protection of p., 367 : 5
public officers servants of p., 631 : 6
really good at heart, 909 : 5
relation between white and colored p., 556 : 9
relationship waits for p., 877 : 4
religion opiate of p., 706 : 6
representatives of p., 464 : 20
resemble wild beast, 154 : 8
retain virtue and vigilance, 521 : 13
right of p. to make government, 379 : 10
right of trampling on p., 490 : 17
right p. in right jobs, 553 : 14
Sacco's name in hearts of p., 811 : 9
safe depository of powers, 389 : 15
seldom judge right, 401 : 12
sensed by p. expressed by p., 593 : 10
should be beautiful, 695 : 6
should fight for their law, 70 : 9
shouted with a great shout, 11 : 31
show my head to the p., 412 : 3
showed thy p. hard things, 19 : 24
signs for a god-fearing p., 130 : 16
small country with few p., 65 : 9
so dead to liberty, 350 : 17
so in need of help, 889 : 6
special p. unto himself, 11 : 11
spoil lives of better p., 669 : 14
still in the gristle, 372 : 14
such tongue to great p., 564 : 9
sum married p. owe, 395 : 19
superintending industry of private p., 366 : 8
talebearer among thy p., 10 : 20
talk sense to American p., 851 : 9
that once bestowed commands, 122 : 15
that p. may require leader, 85 : 7
the p. will live on, 761 : 15
there is a p. risen, 300 : 23
this Bible for government by p., 143 : 12
thy p. shall be my p., 12 : 25
to all the p. you can, 346 : 12
to these p. I owe everything, 521 : 6

People (*continued*)
tricked and sold, 761 : 15
turn to benevolent rule, 89 : 9
two kinds of p., 670 : 1, 855 : 17
two p. shaken by dizziness, 886 : 5
two thirds of p. killed, 763 : 14
tyranny enter if p. lose spirit, 577 : 15
under violent passion, 681 : 1
unimproved p., 871 : 15
visited and redeemed his p., 42 : 24
voice of p. is voice of God, 135 : 6
watch over economy of private p., 366 : 3
we are his p., 21 : 3
we the p., 391 : 10
welfare of p. object of government, 687 : 15
were passed clean over Jordan, 11 : 29
what is the city but p., 242 : 19
what kind of p. do they think we are, 745 : 9
what p. are like here, 394 : 13
what p. say behind back, 671 : 15
what p. say of us true, 711 : 5
where no vision the p. perish, 25 : 32
which sat in darkness, 37 : 2
who blow through life, 855 : 17
who eat the earth, 863 : 6
who have had to live, 624 : 19
who have money, 782 : 9
who know little, 358 : 20
who lean, 670 : 1
who lift, 670 : 1
who love each other, 504 : 13
win friends influence p., 803 : 4
wish p. to think well of you, 299 : 15
wishes of p. concerned, 781 : 7
with no weaknesses, 655 : 9
with rights in hands, 505 : 19
with whom we have just fallen in love, 880 : 1
without history, 808 : 16, 928 : 11
witness to the p., 31 : 19
would that Roman p. had single neck, 116 : 1
Peopled, earthly ball a p. garden, 395 : 6
teach order to p. kingdom, 207 : 6
world must be p., 209 : 19
People's, covet no p. lands, 824 : 12
good is highest law, 99 : 3
in p. eyes life, 781 : 15
nor p. judgment always true, 304 : 13
not sit on other p. backs, 657 : 17
other p. money, 594 : 8
prayer, 304 : 5
reforming other p. habits, 624 : 22
safety is highest law, 134 : 25
sits high in p. hearts, 215 : 14
soil of p. necessities, 698 : 13
state worst of all states, 275 : 21
sustenance in taxation, 631 : 9
this is a p. contest, 522 : 2
voice odd, 339 : 21
Peoples, bolder and stronger p., 687 : 4
concert of free p., 682 : 13
English-speaking p., 672 : 16
happiness of p., 655 : 7
history life of p., 602 : 8
of United Nations, 788 : 20
sink or swim together, 730 : 16
who have courage to face war, 784 : 1

Peopling earth waters and sky, 311 : 12
the void air, 585 : 10
Peor and Baalim, 277 : 12
Peoria, it'll play in P., 904 : 1
Poet in command of fantasy, 865 : 20
Peppercorn, I am a p., 204 : 24
Peppered highest, 371 : 20
two of them, 203 : 30
Peppermint, big p. hotels, 888 : 9
Peppers, peck of pickled p., 932 : 9
Per caputque pedesque, 101 : *n* 16
Perceive, find little to p., 429 : 13
here a divided duty, 229 : 32
what they half create and what p., 423 : 14
world as men p. it, 862 : 15
ye are too superstitious, 46 : 15
yourself sole heir of world, 311 : 20
Perceived harmony of object, 436 : 19
Perceivers of terror of life, 498 : 21
Perceives, artist p. more than fellows, 736 : 22
it die away, 426 : 15
Perceiving, conscious that we are p., 87 : 21
genius p. in unhabitual way, 649 : 4
Percents, elegant simplicity of three p., 394 : 1
Perception and attempt, 720 : 8
conscience p. of rejection, 678 : 7
imagination agent of p., 437 : 11
internal p. of rejection, 678 : 7
of beauty moral test, 557 : 11
pale colorless, 649 : 7
register multiple p. in art, 793 : 10
Perceptual, love is p. anesthesia, 772 : 3
Perch, custom make it their p., 227 : 30
where eagles dare not p., 187 : 5
Perches in the soul, 604 : 17
Perchings, flights and p., 648 : 13
Percy, old song of P. and Douglas, 176 : 12
Percy's, not yet of P. mind, 203 : 26
Perdition, bottomless p., 283 : 4
catch my soul, 230 : 30
to be safe, 495 : 9
Perdu, tout p. fors l'honneur, 157 : *n* 8
Pereant qui nostra ante nos dixerunt, 134 : 16
Pereat, fiat justitia et p. mundus, 133 : *n* 11
Peremptory, would not with p. tone, 376 : 1
Perennial pleasures plants, 484 : 6
spring of prodigality, 373 : 10
Perfect and entire, 51 : 27
as p. in vile man, 336 : 22
be ye therefore p., 37 : 13
circle and vicious circle, 881 : 2
end of p. day, 698 : 15
every p. gift, 51 : 29
form a more p. Union, 391 : 10
glory be the p. one, 606 : 5
happiness p. as martyr's, 699 : 8
his work is p., 11 : 23
honest and p. man, 260 : 17
I am not in p. mind, 235 : 9
in bud as in bloom, 619 : 7
in heaven p. round, 544 : 4
in p. nature no distinction of kind, 90 : 7
interpreter of life, 794 : 11
it was p. it was rounded, 623 : 18
keep him in p. peace, 30 : 9
Perfect (*continued*)
let patience have her p. work, 51 : 27
life may p. be, 256 : 20
love casteth out fear, 52 : 25
made p. in weakness, 49 : 23
man in future more p., 515 : 15
mark the p. man, 18 : 27
move in p. phalanx, 283 : 22
nothing quite new is p., 98 : 14
one p. limousine, 827 : 13
practice makes p., 111 : *n* 8
produce p. circles, 89 : 7
shineth unto the p. day, 23 : 8
spirits of just men made p., 51 : 21
then if ever p. days, 567 : 13
visit p. in being too short, 440 : 26
when that which is p., 48 : 25
woman nobly planned, 427 : 6
world p. everywhere, 413 : 30
Perfectest, silence p. herald of joy, 209 : 11
Perfectibility of man, 506 : 6
Perfection as culture conceives it, 588 : 17
culture study of p., 588 : 15
dead p., 533 : 17
discovers p. in beloved, 453 : 8
fullness of p. in him, 201 : 16
holds in p. but moment, 244 : 4
law is p. of reason, 171 : 21
little concerned with p., 643 : 5
never built empire, 815 : 5
of life or of work, 716 : 7
of mathematical beauty, 696 : 6
of mathematics, 737 : 14
pink of p., 371 : 4
rides upon p. of his officials, 97 : 8
right praise true p., 201 : 5
stern p. as greatest art, 737 : 14
through art realize p., 674 : 19
unattainable p., 711 : 7
vowing p. of ten, 226 : 13
what's come to p. perishes, 542 : 5
Perfectionism may obstruct peace, 781 : 4
Perfections, sweet p. caught, 184 : 14
Perfidious Albion, 421 : 6
fatal and p. bark, 280 : 18
Perform, ability they never p., 226 : 13
Almighty's orders to p., 325 : 7
every act as though it were your last, 124 : 6
His wonders to p., 375 : 16
never promise more than p., 111 : 18
Performance, desire outlive p., 206 : 16
literary p., 577 : 12
lovers swear more p., 226 : 13
takes away the p., 238 : 3
Performed, look for deed soul p., 132 : 14
to a T, 158 : 5
Performs, man p. engenders, 838 : 2
Perfume, amber scent of odorous p., 288 : 30
owest cat no p., 234 : 7
puss-gentleman all p., 376 : 4
throw p. on violet, 202 : 5
Perfumed like milliner, 203 : 7
old women should not be p., 62 : 1
sea, 525 : 9
so p. that winds lovesick, 240 : 29
Perfumes, all the p. of Arabia, 239 : 27
colors sounds echo, 580 : 18
Perhaps, seek a grand p., 158 : 14
Pericles calls quality lucidity, 589 : 6
in wrath the Olympian P., 81 : 11
Periclum ex aliis facito, 96 : *n* 9
Periculum in mora, 175 : *n* 5
Periit, qui ante diem p., 700 : 7
Peril, in p. mask is off, 100 : 21
those in p. on sea, 596 : 18
use our pens at our p., 343 : 20
woods more free from p., 210 : 23
Perilous, cleanse bosom of p. stuff, 239 : 32
dewdrop on p. way, 475 : 10
fight, 446 : 1
nothing more p. than new order, 153 : 18
seas in faery lands forlorn, 477 : 1
thought without learning is p., 68 : 10
turns to p. waters, 140 : 11
unsifted in p. circumstance, 219 : 4
Perils, avoid p. by united forces, 308 : 21
bring fraternity, 492 : 4
defend us from all p., 55 : 9
how many p. do enfold, 173 : 11
of actual existence, 674 : 19
of camp march and battle, 617 : 6
spoke I think of p. past, 765 : 9
when our p. are past, 421 : 22
Period at the right moment, 828 : 5
immersed in place and p., 800 : 3
of effectiveness of generation, 784 : 20
Periodic, success to p. sentence, 834 : 9
Periodization of European history, 847 : 14
Peripatetic lover, 628 : 9
Periphrastic study, 807 : 12
Perish, city to p. if it finds buyer, 103 : 3
drink unto him that is ready to p., 26 : 5
fame of her excellence will never p., 61 : 5
hero p. or sparrow fall, 336 : 14
if it had to p. twice, 748 : 2
if we must p. in fight, 514 : 11
in our own, 693 : 7
in their infancy, 918 : 18
in this wilderness, 265 : 8
let justice be done though world p., 133 : *n* 11
let the day p., 15 : 7
may they p. who used our words, 134 : 16
name not p. in dust, 440 : 7
or catch up, 731 : 5
plan civilization or p., 826 : 1
shall not p. from earth, 523 : 4
should not p., 44 : 34
so p. all who do the like, 334 : 22
spirit of moderation p., 737 : 3
surely weak p., 752 : 4
survive or p., 450 : 9
that one of thy members should p., 37 : 8
the thought, 324 : 28
their goodness does not p., 77 : 18
thy money p., 46 : 2
truths wake to p. never, 426 : 19
twice, 748 : 2
unless leaves p. tree not renewed, 863 : 14
weakly p. at another moment, 59 : 5
where no vision the people p., 25 : 32
with the sword, 41 : 16

Perishable stuff, 863 : 14
Perished as they had never been, 36 : 11
by own follies they p., 59 : 14
in his pride, 425 : 10
the weapons of war p., 13 : 11
who p. being innocent, 15 : 10
years p. to make us men, 631 : 14
Perishes, come to perfection p., 542 : 5
everything p., 928 : 3
Perishing, shine p. republic, 797 : 10
Periuria ridet amantum Iupiter, 113 : *n* 1
Periwig, new p. make a great show, 310 : 10
Periwig-pated, robustious p. fellow, 221 : 23
Perjured, gloriously p., 108 : 3
murderous bloody, 245 : 23
Perjuries, at lovers' p. Jove laughs, 192 : 8
of lovers, 113 : 1
Perjury, Jove laughs at lovers' p., 192 : *n* 3
Perked up in glistering grief, 248 : 27
Permanence sea cannot claim, 640 : 11
Permanent alliances, 379 : 13
and certain characteristics, 352 : 4
and the same, 585 : 19
contract on temporary feeling, 641 : 6
disuse of any organ, 393 : 7
feelings p. and the same, 585 : 19
grandeur of States, 574 : 8
interests of community, 398 : 1
more p. than fish or weeds, 910 : 10
nothing ought to be p., 506 : 6
share in government, 401 : 12
system of security, 781 : 9
Permission, nobody without Count's p., 786 : 1
to go out from household, 73 : 5
Permit base contagious clouds, 203 : 5
child to join, 604 : 10
doing what laws p., 341 : 8
how long p. to Heaven, 287 : 30
if you p. evil, 864 : 6
Permitte divis cetera, 107 : *n* 6
Permitted, not forbidden is p., 413 : 7
to shuffle in slippers, 706 : 19
Pernicious consequences, 553 : 20
love of flattery, 327 : 16
race of odious vermin, 322 : 11
weed, 376 : 3
Perpetual, court in p. session, 786 : 5
desire a p. rack, 258 : 21
devotion to business, 667 : 22
feast of nectared sweets, 279 : 25
kingdom of p. night, 187 : 10
neglect of other things, 667 : 22
night, 101 : 18, 187 : 10, 255 : 16
our interests eternal and p., 454 : 12
scoured with p. motion, 206 : 4
sleep of p. night, 101 : 18
speculators about p. motion, 152 : 14
work us a p. peace, 277 : 6
Perpetually, life begins p., 720 : 6
nation p. to be conquered, 372 : 16
one hour then damned p., 184 : 7
saves itself p., 878 : 2
Perpetuated, ancient models p., 129 : 20
through hereditary dyspepsias, 570 : 9
Perpetuity, merit of p., 275 : 7
Perplexed in the extreme, 232 : 20
labyrinthical soul, 255 : 4
Perplexed (*continued*)
to have plenty is to be p., 64 : 10
Perplexes and affronts, 883 : 11
monarchs, 283 : 24
Perplexity of radical evil, 866 : 10
Persecute, despitefully use and p. you, 37 : 11
you for my sake, 37 : 4
Persecuted church of God, 48 : 28
for righteousness' sake, 37 : 4
most p. minority, 776 : 13
Persecutes the mind, 305 : 17
Persecutest, why p. thou me, 46 : 5
Persecution bad way to plant religion, 274 : 9
gives p. no assistance, 379 : 8
opposition christened p., 565 : 2
religious p. shield itself, 373 : 15
Persecutions have made Church grow, 126 : *n* 2
Persephone, down the way P. goes, 791 : 1
even where P. goes, 791 : 1
Persepolis, ride in triumph through P., 183 : 5
Persever in obstinate condolement, 218 : 4
Perseverance and soothing language, 388 : 10
fortitude and p., 365 : 3
in good cause, 359 : 24
keeps honor bright, 226 : 17
more prevailing than violence, 120 : 2
Persevere, forbear and p., 669 : 17
if we all p., 891 : 2
Persia, past first sleep in P., 275 : 14
Persian, how can anyone be P., 341 : 5
luxury I hate, 107 : 16
pearls of thought in P. gulfs bred, 569 : 2
Persian's heaven easily made, 447 : 6
Persians accustomed to deliberate when drunk, 78 : 6
law of the Medes and P., 33 : 2
old P. hold sea holy, 570 : 4
taught three things, 462 : 4
Persicos odi puer apparatus, 107 : *n* 14
Persistence of the unforeseen, 640 : 17
Persistent, unsubstantial p. faithful, 733 : 17
Person, aging p. give attention to self, 754 : 6
agreeable p. agrees, 502 : 13
arts outside p., 690 : 1
arts that express in p., 690 : 1
attention must be paid to p., 888 : 2
beggared all description, 240 : 29
blood of this just p., 41 : 22
dignity and worth of p., 788 : 20
dignity of p. acknowledged, 774 : 8
don't believe no sich p., 548 : 2
France a p., 483 : 18
freedom of p., 389 : 2
frontier of my P., 869 : 6
Leaves of Grass a p. on record, 577 : 11
no more a p. but climate of opinion, 868 : 14
no p. must have to, 374 : 14
no sich p., 548 : 2
noble p. attracts noble, 395 : 14
of contrary opinion, 508 : 4
of its head root of family, 89 : 8
portrayed and portrait, 784 : 23
Person (*continued*)
produce the p., 134 : 4
really hope no white p., 916 : 2
sacrificed to individual, 778 : 11
show you hungry p., 916 : 1
very 'humble p., 548 : 30
we are not p. involved, 624 : 18
who seizes two things, 926 : 1
with care p. adorning, 466 : 5
with no social armor, 778 : 11
young p. occupied with self, 754 : 6
Personages, high p. of household against me, 151 : 3
Personal considerations in public duty, 590 : 1
inner p. experiences, 650 : 9
knowledge not p. experience, 84 : 9
space invisible boundaries, 910 : 12
Personalities, meeting of p. chemical contact, 754 : 4
trivial p. decomposing, 781 : 17
Personality, actions from total p., 688 : 7
artist's extinction of p., 809 : 3
cult of p., 830 : 13
fitness of p., 702 : 13
Lincoln greatest best moral p., 577 : 4
moral p., 577 : 4
native p. endows man, 577 : 2
needs a good p., 788 : 21
poetry escape from p., 809 : 4
taint of p., 600 : 26
Personalizing, magic feat of p. by totalizing, 775 : 2
Personified, evil to Ahab p., 570 : 13
Personne, celui que p. ne peut imiter, 419 : *n* 2
Persons about to write history, 615 : 16
advice to p. about to marry, 660 : 11
all p. born in U.S. citizens, 392 : 4
all p. share in government, 88 : 6
divers paces with divers p., 212 : 11
God in three P., 452 : 11
God no respecter of p., 46 : 10
great p. great kindnesses, 170 : 28
neither p. nor property safe, 556 : 14
respect of place p. time, 213 : 25
without respect of p., 52 : 8
Perspective, cylinder sphere cone in p., 638 : 3
Perspicuity, we praise thee for p. of language, 136 : 6
Perspiration, ninety-nine percent p., 661 : 9
Persuade, beauty doth of itself p., 189 : 16
even if you p. me, 82 : 25
if possible the rulers, 84 : 11
tongue to p., 289 : 16
Persuaded, burnt each other quite p., 460 : 14
in his own mind, 47 : 31
none could advise thou p., 173 : 4
Persuader, president is p., 879 : 4
Persuades, truth p. by teaching, 126 : 6
when speaking fails, 246 : 15
Persuadest, almost p. me to be a Christian, 46 : 36
Persuading, by p. others convince ourselves, 391 : 3
fair-spoken and p., 249 : 15
Persuasion and belief, 428 : 16
companion's words of p., 58 : 12
hung upon his lips, 360 : 1

Persuasion (*continued*)
in it was blandishing p., 58 : 19
two gods P. and Compulsion, 70 : 17
whatever race creed or p., 794 : 15
Persuasions, winged P., 469 : 3
Persuasive, demonstrative or p. type, 730 : 15
sound, 324 : 15
Persuasiveness, literature depends on p., 702 : 14
Pert as schoolgirl can be, 629 : 8
Perturbation of the light, 864 : 1
polished p., 206 : 29
Perturbed, rest p. spirit, 220 : 5
Peru, a Newton at P., 363 : 21
mankind from China to P., 351 : 16
there lies P., 481 : 2
Peruse conquered fame of heroes, 575 : 8
Perverse, art selfish and p., 421 : 20
imp of the p., 526 : 21
mankind by p. depravity, 316 : 15
tugging at p. life, 873 : 8
widows most p. creatures, 326 : 20
Perverseness primitive impulse, 526 : *n* 1
Perversion, Christianity enormous p., 658 : 17
Perverted, woman's cold p. will, 470 : 10
Perverters of language, 792 : 19
Perverts who set money-lust before pleasures, 792 : 19
Pessimism agreeable as optimism, 720 : 15
name given to wisdom, 837 : 6
Pessimist, difference between optimist and p., 758 : 12
fears this is true, 762 : 10
I am not p., 867 : 10
not p. but pejorist, 690 : *n* 1
sees hole, 758 : 12
Pessimistic utterances in Bible, 649 : 11
Pest that fairest joys give unrest, 476 : 3
Pestered with a popinjay, 203 : 9
Pestilence, Famine P. Destruction Death, 773 : 6
noisome p., 20 : 16
power like desolating p., 466 : 7
that walketh in darkness, 20 : 16
winter plague and p., 250 : 9
Pestilence-stricken multitudes, 467 : 17
Pestilent, foul and p., 220 : 28
Petal, now sleeps crimson p., 531 : 11
Petals on wet black bough, 792 : 7
Petar, hoist with his own p., 223 : 13
Peter and Wendy, 694 : 13
denied Lord and cried, 320 : 7
Flopsy Mopsy Cottontail P., 719 : 2
give not Saint P. so much, 160 : *n* 2
jealous Judas cowardly P., 859 : 10
Piper picked peck, 932 : 9
Pumpkin-Eater, 932 : 16
remembered word of Jesus, 41 : 18
rob P. pay Paul, 160 : 4
thou art P., 39 : 36
wept bitterly, 41 : 18
Peterkin, quoth little P., 439 : 14
Peter's, blessing of St. P. Master, 271 : 14
dome, 493 : 18
Petersburg most theoretical town, 581 : 16
window on Europe, 486 : *n* 6
Petite, oh my P., 893 : 4
Petition government for redress, 391 : 14
Petitions, desires and p. of thy servants, 55 : 8
Petrarch's, if Laura P. wife, 460 : 25
Petrel, waters of p. and porpoise, 807 : 24
Petrified opinion, 626 : 19
truth, 621 : *n* 2
Petrifies the feeling, 409 : 12
Petticoat, feet beneath her p., 289 : 21
government, 452 : 13
tempestuous p., 266 : 7
turned out of realm in my p., 163 : 16
Petty, creeps in this p. pace, 240 : 4
makes each p. artery, 219 : 15
never be p., 883 : 3
official high or p., 821 : 6
we p. men, 215 : 6
Peuple, pitié de mon pauvre p., 166 : *n* 8
Peur, de p. d'en pleurer, 378 : *n* 5
le plus de p. que la p., 164 : *n* 6
Peut-être, chercher un grand p., 158 : *n* 9
Pewter, no p. no pub, 811 : 1
Pez muere por la boca, 935 : 11
Phalanx, move in perfect p., 283 : 22
where is Pyrrhic p., 461 : 7
wrinkles progress in p., 798 : 12
Phantasma, like p. or hideous dream, 215 : 18
Phantom deer arise, 840 : 13
of delight, 427 : 3
of hungry poor, 621 : 16
of ourselves, 587 : 17
ungraspable p. of life, 570 : 4
Pharaoh, one more plague upon P., 9 : 22
tell old P., 935 : 21
tomb that swallowed P., 569 : 20
Pharaoh's, he hardened P. heart, 9 : 19
lean kine loved, 204 : 6
wise men cast down rods, 9 : 19
Pharaohs of Egypt, 924 : 3
Pharisee, one a P. the other a publican, 43 : 38
the son of a P., 46 : 29
Pharisees, scribes and P., 40 : 18
Pharisees', drowns in P. hypocrisy, 816 : 18
Pharos of Egypt, 924 : 3
Phenomena, concepts call p. to mind, 390 : 7
hypothesis not deduced from p., 313 : 11
natural p. subject to causation, 617 : 11
new p. lead to bombs, 763 : 12
not disclose essence of p., 789 : 2
pattern which controls p., 758 : 10
predict p., 472 : 1
same circumstances same p., 324 : 1
sequence of p., 390 : 7
Phenomenon, felicitous p., 799 : 14
infant p., 547 : 12
portray p. concept needed, 390 : 7
Phidias, by P. done, 924 : 3
Jove young P. brought, 493 : 17
unable to reach all the material, 125 : 24
Philadelphia, I'd rather be in P., 770 : 19
Philadelphia (*continued*)
in P. ask who were parents, 625 : 23
lady from P., 578 : 8
pecksniffian, 772 : 4
Philanthropist, masterpiece delusion to p., 619 : 7
Philanthropy of Captain Brown, 560 : 24
only virtue appreciated, 559 : 20
which forgives, 448 : 3
which neither shoots nor liberates, 560 : 24
Philippine, our forces on P. soil, 771 : 4
Philistia triumph thou because of me, 19 : 25
Philistine, American P. livelier, 589 : 9
David prevailed over the P., 13 : 3
strong dogged unenlightened, 587 : 3
what is called a P., 463 : 9
Philistines, apostle of P. Macaulay, 587 : 5
avenged of P., 12 : 20
Barbarians P. Populace, 588 : 13
be upon thee, 12 : 18
put out Samson's eyes, 12 : 19
Philologists who chase syllable, 376 : 10
Philosopher, anything implausible already said by p., 272 : 9
definition of p., 610 : 9
doesn't think in vacuum, 698 : 6
endure toothache, 210 : 5
great poet profound p., 437 : 18
guide p. and friend, 338 : 3, 773 : 14
I have tried too to be p., 357 : 12
memory not make p., 490 : 14
not aloof to gain reputation, 85 : 17
nothing so ridiculous but p. said it, 98 : 22
scold jester raconteur, 847 : 10
thinks like a p., 359 : 8
to be p. to love wisdom, 559 : 9
was a p. yet hadde but litel gold, 145 : 27
weeping p. when old, 198 : 12
what are sinews of p., 121 : 13
worship considered by p., 383 : 7
Philosopher's stones, 259 : 15
work p. stone, 664 : 17
Philosophers come down from mountains, 637 : 19
discovered unconscious, 678 : 11
God of Abraham not p., 300 : 15
have died of gout, 301 : 2
heroes statesmen p., 392 : 11
illusion of p., 837 : 18
not from p. but nature, 260 : 9
quotidian saps p., 766 : 22
truth not always object of p., 662 : 1
until p. are kings, 84 : 15
verses and sayings of p., 291 : 14
Philosophia biou kybernetes, 407 : *n* 5
O vitae p. dux, 98 : *n* 16
Philosophic ideals alters to unknown gods, 648 : 6
men of p. temperament, 697 : 6
poetry more p., 88 : 18
years bring p. mind, 426 : 22
Philosophical, European p. tradition footnotes to Plato, 697 : 12
speculators of common sort, 166 : 15
Philosophies of one age aburdities of next, 664 : 12
Philosophize, to ridicule philosophy is to p., 300 : 10

Philosophy, adversity's sweet milk
p., 193 : 12
aim of Platonic p., 488 : 4
bladders of p., 315 : 20
call p. down from heavens, 98 : 25
clip angel's wings, 476 : 6
Comte's p., 595 : 13
depth in p. bringeth to
religion, 180 : 17
divine p., 279 : 25, 532 : 8
dreamed of in any p., 821 : 5
dreamed of in your p., 220 : 3
experimental p., 313 : 11
false p., 284 : 20
gained this by p., 87 : 2
goal in p., 690 : 5
good horse in stable, 369 : 22
guide of life, 407 : 17
handmaid to religion, 179 : 6
hang up p., 193 : 13
hast any p. in thee, 211 : 19
history is p. learned from
examples, 112 : 18
I have no p. myself, 821 : 5
if p. could find it out, 220 : 30
in p. experts differ, 700 : 2
is for the few, 166 : 14
liberal p., 813 : 9
little p. inclineth to atheism, 180 : 17
make a Juliet, 193 : 13
microscope of thought, 492 : 5
my sons ought to study p., 381 : 14
natural p. deep moral grave, 181 : 14
natural p. embodied in
mathematical beauty, 696 : 5
new p. calls all in doubt, 254 : 5
new p. proceeds from world, 250 : 12
not faith but mere p., 274 : 14
not pretend to doubt in p., 639 : 9
not technical matter, 650 : 7
nothing but discretion, 263 : 22
obscure regions of p., 357 : 17
pieced thoughts into p., 715 : 6
sense of what life means, 650 : 7
spirit and power of p., 84 : 15
to get rid of self-conceit, 121 : 14
to ridicule p., 300 : 10
triumphs over past evils, 293 : 3
truth object of p., 662 : 1
will not reform, 699 : 3
written in universe, 182 : 20
you leader of life, 98 : 24
Phlebas the Phoenician, 805 : 9
Phlegmatic, deliver me from p.
preachers, 392 : 10
emerged from indolence, 386 : 11
Phobias, tell us your p., 812 : 5
Phoebus 'gins arise, 243 : 16
sent Plato, 83 : *n* 3
Phoebus', hindmost wheels of P.
wain, 279 : 15
lodging, 193 : 8
Phoenician, Phlebas the P., 805 : 9
Phoenix builds phoenix' nest, 292 : 18
builds spicy nest, 271 : 21
her ashes new-create, 249 : 17
knew p. in youth, 714 : 5
riddle hath more wit, 252 : 11
Phone off the hook, 908 : 12
why did you answer p., 831 : 1
Phosphorescence word to lift hat
to, 608 : 8
Photograph, give each figure in p.
name, 894 : 11
Photograph (*continued*)
shows Hiroshima, 893 : 14
Phrase, a fico for the p., 225 : 9
ancient Saxon p., 510 : 12
art for art's sake empty p., 504 : 18
choice word measured p., 425 : 11
for significant manifestations of
life, 867 : 17
good and bad at same time, 828 : 4
portentous p., 462 : 1
proverbed with grandsire p., 191 : 21
soft p. of peace, 229 : 24
string of gems, 362 : *n* 4
sudden unintelligible p., 593 : 4
Phrases, discourse in novel p., 628 : 6
hackneyed p., 685 : 14
I detest, 693 : 5
learned by rote, 322 : 16
retailer of p., 324 : 20
taffeta p., 191 : 9
your p. in my verse, 724 : 9
Phyllida my Phyllida, 640 : 2
Phyllis is my only joy, 312 : 12
Phylogenesis, ontogenesis
recapitulation of p., 617 : 10
Phylogeny, ontogeny recapitulates
p., 617 : *n* 5
Physic, gold in p. is a cordial, 146 : 6
jostled by quacks, 463 : 17
man's own observation best p., 181 : 2
take p. pomp, 234 : 4
throw p. to the dogs, 239 : 32
what p. relieve conscience, 260 : 5
wisdom beyond rules of p., 181 : 2
Physical concepts free
creations, 763 : 10
events reduced to spatial
motions, 636 : 17
laws and laws of numbers, 610 : 1
laws are invalid, 762 : 3
mental never influences p., 552 : 7
moral aesthetic wants, 649 : 16
not assume p. laws exist, 686 : 9
not to live in p. world, 768 : 5
pleasures lightly called p., 739 : 9
reduction of p. processes, 636 : 16
science not console me, 299 : 16
vivid p. illustration, 610 : 2
Physician, beloved p., 50 : 15
deceive not thy p., 269 : 15
died last night of my p., 320 : 20
go not for every grief to p., 269 : 28
good cheer is best p., 72 : 3
hath favorite disease, 349 : 17
heal thyself, 43 : 2
honor a p., 36 : 7
I swear by Apollo P., 79 : 13
kill thy p., 232 : 28
man being his own p., 87 : 5
no p. considers own good, 84 : 5
observe p. with diligence, 254 : 19
of Iron Age, 585 : 3
read book of Nature, 168 : *n* 2
recover through contentment with
p., 79 : 16
rope-dancer p. magician, 122 : 4
whole need not p., 38 : 27
Physicians, best of all p., 666 : 13
by their love grown
cosmographers 254 : 18
evil conscience beyond p., 517 : 19
magicians do more than p., 171 : 16
use three p., 323 : *n* 3
words are p. of mind diseased, 70 : 25
Physicist, survey minutest with
p., 776 : 9
Physicists have known sin, 861 : 6
Physics experience arranged, 636 : 14
great theories of p., 696 : 12
labor we delight in p. pain, 238 : 4
not change nature of world, 862 : 13
tries to discover pattern, 758 : 10
Physiological experiment, 515 : 12
Pia mater of mine, 274 : 3
womb of p. mater, 190 : 30
Pianist, do not shoot p., 675 : 6
Piano, pounding of old p., 711 : 7
Piccadilly, good-bye P., 753 : 1
walk down P., 628 : 7
Pick about the gravel, 479 : 4
knock out p. round, 915 : 12
no quarrels, 370 : *n* 3
not p. one, 822 : 15
not scruple to p. pocket, 318 : 1
Pickaxe shovel spade, 455 : 8
Picked, age grown so p., 224 : 13
from leaves of any author, 274 : 10
man p. out of ten thousand, 220 : 16
peck of pickled peppers, 932 : 9
sparingly without noise, 575 : 22
up broken point, 815 : 8
Pickerel, sidelong p. smile, 873 : 17
Pickest and cullest the race, 575 : 22
Picket's off duty forever, 598 : *n* 3
Pickety, hickety p., 932 : 14
Picking men of genius, 825 : 11
Pickle, put you in this p., 168 : 11
Picks flowers of memory, 739 : 11
Pickwickian sense, 546 : 10
Picnic, hard-boiled as p. egg, 834 : 6
Picninnies and the Joblillies, 364 : 5
Pictura, ut p. poesis, 110 : *n* 2
Picture condensation of
sensations, 728 : 9
earth's last p. painted, 707 : 21
fain paint p., 543 : 31
life is painting p., 644 : 13
no p. made to endure, 793 : 1
not at his p. but his book, 256 : 10
one p. worth more than ten
thousand words, 132 : 24
placed the busts between, 330 : 26
say p. shows labor, 619 : 5
see a fine p., 395 : 5
shows what dozens of pages
expound, 564 : 7
true p. of ancestors, 489 : 5
truly like me, 272 : 22
Pictures, apples of gold in p. of
silver, 25 : 14
cutting all p. out, 729 : 14
for page atone, 340 : 18
in our eyes to get, 253 : 6
mathematical p. accord with
fact, 758 : 9
out of doors, 230 : 8
science draws of nature, 758 : 9
sleeping are but as p., 237 : 23
statues p. verse grand, 618 : 17
without p. or conversations, 611 : 2
you furnish p. I furnish war, 702 : 12
Picturesque and gloomy wrong, 504 : 2
liar, 624 : 6
Pie, apple p. and cheese best
physician, 666 : 13
as New Englanders love p., 759 : 14
ate umble p., 549 : 4
baked in a p., 931 : 9

Pie (*continued*)
calico p., 550 : 12
Christmas p., 929 : 20
finger in every p., 168 : 29
future a mince p., 846 : 13
humble p., 549 : 4
in the sky, 764 : 13
no man's p. is freed, 248 : 20
peacock p., 740 : 1
rich pumpkin p., 513 : 4
violence American as cherry p., 915 : 16
when p. opened, 931 : 9
Piebald linsey-woolsey brothers, 340 : 21
Piece, all of a p. throughout, 307 : 1
bleeding p. of earth, 216 : 11
equal p. of justice Death, 274 : 11
faultless p. to see, 333 : 2
fenced in p. of land, 358 : 9
irregular indigested p., 352 : 8
of the continent, 254 : 22
what a p. of work is man, 220 : 28
Piecemeal, heart break p., 557 : 1
our bodies are dying, 791 : 3
Pieces, all in p. all coherence gone, 254 : 5
beat my people to p., 28 : 35
chess p. phenomena of universe, 595 : 12
dashed in p. the enemy, 9 : 34
of eight, 668 : 7
tear to p. that great bond, 238 : 21
thirty p. of silver, 33 : 34, 41 : 5
Pied, daisies p. shallow brooks, 277 : 25
daisies p. violets blue, 191 : 13
Pieman, met a p., 930 : 13
Pierce, beauty p. like pain, 755 : 5
meeting soul may p., 278 : 6
neither graze nor p., 231 : 26
pigmy's straw does p. it, 235 : 3
sun p. thickest cloud, 544 : 29
Pierced, how sharp it p. and stung, 646 : 14
Pierces, deep surmise p., 558 : 21
Piercing night's dull ear, 208 : 1
Pierian spring, 332 : 20
Pierre, découvrir saint P. pour couvrir saint Paul, 160 : *n* 2
Pierrot, eyes of P., 843 : 17
my friend P., 928 : *n* 3
Pierrot, mon ami P., 928 : 8
Piety, all your p. nor wit, 517 : 2
bound by natural p., 425 : 7
filial p. is root of man, 289 : 13
first show p. at home, 50 : 30
grant this in return for p., 102 : 16
grow warmer in Iona, 352 : 22
mistaken overzealous p., 373 : 15
pathos p. courage, 764 : 10
requires to honor truth, 87 : 14
towards universe, 704 : 6
Pig, buy a fat p., 933 : 9
dear p. are you willing, 550 : 9
eat Tom beat, 931 : 13
i only guinea p. I have, 832 : 14
in a poke, 161 : 15
in as p. out as sausage, 647 : 14
little p. to market, 930 : 11
love not a gaping p., 200 : 2
rather a handsome p., 611 : 16
road rail p. lead, 760 : 20
satisfied, 508 : 19
snake edible to p., 647 : 11
Pig (*continued*)
solitude obese like p., 905 : 1
Pigeon, finality of wild p., 800 : 10
Pigeon-livered, I am p., 221 : 9
Pigeons, casual flocks of p., 767 : 4
on grass alas, 752 : 10
onetwothreefourfive p., 828 : 13
tame p. peas, 290 : *n* 3
Piggy, said p. I will, 550 : 9
Pigmei gigantum humeris impositi, 118 : *n* 6
Pigments, secret of durable p., 846 : 5
Pigmy's straw does pierce it, 235 : 3
Pigs, fell out over p., 781 : 13
men filthy p., 751 : 18
speak Greek naturally as p. squeak, 290 : 15
whether p. have wings, 613 : 5
Pike, holy text of p. and gun, 291 : 4
Pilate saith what is truth, 45 : 30
suffered under Pontius P., 55 : 2
washed his hands, 41 : 22
what is truth said jesting P., 179 : 22
with P. wash your hands, 195 : 13
Pile bodies at Austerlitz, 761 : 6
on brown man's burden, 709 : *n* 3
Ossa on Olympus, 60 : 9
Ossa on Pelion, 103 : 29
Piled, labor of an age in p. stones, 277 : 13
Pilfer, contrive our fees to p., 82 : 2
Pilgrim band, 616 : 8
came forth with p. steps, 288 : 18
gray, 364 : 9
intent to be a p., 302 : 14
my first p. has shown his face, 145 : *n* 4
of Eternity, 469 : 8
of the sky, 429 : 8
soul in you, 712 : 9
Pilgrimage, blisses about my p., 640 : 3
comforts of weary p., 356 : 25
Goethe done p., 585 : 3
life a weary p., 267 : 19
succeed me in my p., 302 : 15
thus I'll take my p., 172 : 15
to new Jerusalems, 864 : 4
Pilgrimages, longen folk to goon on p., 145 : 13
Rome and other p., 152 : 1
Pilgrim's, for alms a p. wallet, 314 : 2
Progress about man left his family, 623 : 24
Pilgrims, greatness of P., 590 : 4
of mortality, 802 : 20
they knew they were p., 265 : 5
we p. passing to and fro, 146 : 29
Pilgrims', land of p. and so forth, 829 : 4
land of p. pride, 514 : 12
Pill, outlived doctor's p., 332 : 5
sugarcoat the p., 298 : 6
Pillage, slaughter p. devastation, 745 : 2
Pillaged, houses and farms p., 379 : 2
Pillar of cloud by day, 9 : 30
of fire by night, 9 : 30
of salt, 8 : 12
of state, 284 : 14
triple p. of the world, 240 : 12
twig and a p., 90 : 2
Pillared dark, 749 : 7
Pillars of society, 599 : 8
Pillars (*continued*)
wisdom hath hewn out her seven p., 23 : 18
Pillicock sat on Pillicock-hill, 234 : 5
Pillow, my bended arm for p., 68 : 21
sloth finds down p. hard, 243 : 23
something whispered on p., 739 : 5
stone better p. than visions, 797 : 16
under p. rush walruses, 570 : 7
warmth of sun on her p., 769 : 8
Pilot cares about nothing but river, 623 : 8
daring p. in extremity, 303 : 20
great p. sail with canvas rent, 114 : 19
in calm sea every man p., 301 : 12
lightning p., 623 : 9
lives our p. still, 186 : 23
no chance to p. Union, 521 : 7
of the Galilean lake, 280 : 19
see P. face to face, 535 : 21
that weathered storm, 421 : 22
unstable p. steers leaking ship, 127 : 13
Pilots of purple twilight, 529 : 24
Pimples warts and everything, 272 : 22
Pin, with a little p., 195 : 3
Pinafore, captain of the P., 627 : 10
Pinch, death as lover's p., 242 : 3
East and West will p. heart, 822 : 12
hungry lean-faced villain, 188 : 15
necessity's sharp p., 233 : 20
Pinches, none tell where shoe p. me, 119 : 23
shoe fits one p. another, 754 : 5
Pinching, paddling palms and p. fingers, 246 : 11
Pindar, flying abroad as P. says, 85 : 17
Pine, against blue a p. tree, 317 : 16
because they lost virtue, 117 : 10
dwindle peak and p., 236 : 3
for what is not, 468 : 14
for which soul did p., 525 : 17
into waves p. needles, 314 : 6
palm and p., 709 : 16
scent of p. and woodthrush, 806 : 8
shadows of p. boughs, 319 : 1
shall I ever sigh and p., 268 : 21
tall p. of the forest, 408 : 11
tallest p., 283 : 15
with fear and sorrow, 174 : 10
yonder p. that sings, 92 : 12
Pineapple of politeness, 398 : 10
Pined and wanted food, 423 : 2
she p. in thought, 214 : 5
Pines, cones under his p., 747 : 5
keep shape of wind, 850 : 16
murmuring p. hemlocks, 510 : 26
profligate of p., 831 : 15
roar in the p., 728 : 4
watching p. shore and stars, 849 : 6
Pining pining, 656 : 7
Pinions, drift of p., 693 : 17
of great deeds, 395 : 11
'Pinions tell you what his 'p. is, 626 : 12
Pink, Bacchus with p. eyne, 241 : 5
of courtesy, 170 : 14, 192 : 25
of perfection, 371 : 4
twenty-nine when p. shades, 675 : 13
Pinkham land of Lydia E. P., 828 : 17
Pinks that grow, 229 : *n* 1
Pinnace like fluttered bird, 535 : 11
Pinnacle, imagined p. and steep, 478 : 7
Pinnacled dim in inane, 467 : 7
Pin's, set life at p. fee, 219 : 13

Pint, come within p. of wine, 327 : 8
of sweat save blood, 792 : 4
people to goal, 568 : 1
Pioneer, died in boots like p., 839 : 19
Pioneers O pioneers, 575 : 14
Pious action sugar o'er, 221 : 11
all were p., 320 : 6
Eleazer Wheelock p., 705 : 3
feeling of gratitude, 450 : 5
fool that raised it, 275 : *n* 1
fraud as with bad action, 385 : 6
frauds of friendship, 350 : 1
impiety of p., 579 : 18
love is p., 148 : 20
man can't stay in peace, 414 : 3
man not less a man, 297 : 21
not p. longer than rod behind, 156 : 1
ones of Plymouth, 562 : 14
thoughts as harbingers, 276 : 14
times ere priestcraft, 303 : 17
Pipe but as linnets, 532 : 1
called for p., 929 : 14
cat dog p. or two, 692 : 15
easier played on than p., 222 : 19
for fortune's finger, 222 : 6
me to pastures still, 655 : 18
piped silly p., 479 : 14
rumor is a p., 205 : 18
song about a Lamb, 403 : 2
Piped silly pipe, 479 : 14
with merry cheer, 403 : 2
Piper, followed the P., 541 : 2
he who pays p., 324 : *n* 5
pay the p., 324 : 11
Peter P. picked peck, 932 : 9
pipe songs again, 403 : 2
Piper's son, 931 : 13
Pipers, wi' a hundred p. an' a', 417 : 7
Pipes and timbrels, 477 : 5
and whistles in his sound, 211 : 15
Piping, cicadas pour out their p. voices, 57 : 23
down valleys wild, 403 : 2
helpless naked p. loud, 405 : 12
songs forever new, 477 : 8
songs of pleasant glee, 403 : 2
took troubled sound, 587 : 8
weak p. time of peace, 186 : 32
Pippin, right as Ribstone P., 730 : 6
Pippins, old p. toothsomest, 262 : 1
Piracee, vary p., 628 : 4
Piracies not sullied with stealing, 622 : 14
Piracy, let's vary p., 628 : 4
Pirate king, 627 : 19
Pirates, wonder at cruelty of p., 568 : 16
Pire qu'un crime c'est une faute, 415 : 3
Pis, tant p. and tant mieux, 360 : 23
Pisa, you're the Tower of P., 820 : 4
Piscem natare doces, 134 : 17
Pisgah, greeted Moses from P., 480 : 16
Pistol, if his p. misses fire, 371 : 23
pun a p. not feather, 442 : 12
Pistols, astronomy of shapeless p., 841 : 13
fire p. for new century, 755 : 9
have you your p., 575 : 14
put on p. went riding, 811 : 2
Pit, black as the p., 663 : 10
eagle know what is in p., 403 : 17
many-headed monster of p., 339 : 28
ponies, 732 : 16
whoso diggeth a p., 25 : 20
Pitch and fall of earth, 822 : 5
Pitch (*continued*)
daubed with slime and p., 9 : 8
he that toucheth p., 35 : 24
into frog-spawn, 716 : 2
melody deprived of p., 801 : 8
nightly p. moving tent, 429 : 17
pitched past p. of grief, 656 : 17
they that touch p. defiled, 209 : 26
what validity and p., 213 : 8
which hawks flies higher p., 184 : 20
Pitch-black, night p. upon the deep, 104 : 18
Pitched, as mind p. ear pleased, 377 : 13
betwixt heaven and Charing Cross, 693 : 19
his tent toward Sodom, 8 : 7
love p. mansion, 716 : 18
past pitch of grief, 656 : 17
Pitcher, as wheel runs why water p., 109 : 19
broken at the fountain, 27 : 25
Good Man pouring from p., 572 : 6
Pitchers, small p. wide ears, 160 : 30
Pitchfork, clothes thrown on with p., 323 : 9
drive out Nature with p., 109 : 4
Piteous, coursed down in p. chase, 210 : 25
thing among wretched mortals, 59 : 6
Pitfalls, snares traps gins p., 539 : *n* 2
Pith, enterprises of great p., 221 : 12
Pitiable, world p. in units, 640 : 18
Pitied, better envied than p., 78 : 10
how they p. Eve, 733 : 2
lost respect and p. it, 558 : 7
pity and be p., 211 : 12
Pities, Lord help 'em how I p. all, 429 : 19
plumage, 385 : 1
Pitiful helpless giant, 882 : 23
longsuffering and very p., 34 : 23
selfish Public, 445 : 7
tender eye of p. day, 238 : 21
'twas wondrous p., 229 : 31
Pitiless, pelting of p. storm, 234 : 3
Pitt, celebrities such as P., 615 : 14
Pity a human face, 403 : 11
akin to love, 260 : *n* 8
beyond all telling, 712 : 6
deserveth double p., 172 : 13
feeling which arrests mind, 777 : 17
for living envy for dead, 625 : 8
for suffering mankind, 738 : 6
for who looks on inward sphinx, 721 : 2
from blust'ring wind, 296 : 5
gave ere charity began, 370 : 6
hid in heart of love, 712 : 6
his ignorance, 547 : 11
know what 'tis to p., 211 : 12
knows not wrath nor p., 486 : 11
like naked newborn babe, 236 : 24
loved her that she did p., 229 : 31
me that heart is slow, 823 : 7
melts mind to love, 260 : *n* 8
Mercy P. Peace and Love, 403 : 10
my simplicity, 350 : 13
no beast but knows touch of p., 187 : 1
no concern with art, 619 : 8
no p. sitting in clouds, 193 : 18
of it Iago, 231 : 25
of War, 827 : 1
peace refuge for all, 626 : 16
Pity (*continued*)
Poetry is in the p., 827 : 1
runneth soone in gentil herte, 146 : 22
seas of p. lie, 868 : 13
sense of p. beauty pain, 683 : 3
she's a whore, 264 : 10
showing an outward p., 195 : 13
stands before door, 406 : 4
straightest path to love, 260 : 20
swells tide of love, 260 : *n* 8
their want of faith, 385 : 9
then embrace, 337 : 5
this busy monster, 829 : 24
thou never come for p., 469 : 24
'tis 'tis true, 220 : 12
upon the poor, 24 : 26
we may p. though not pardon, 187 : 34
what are p. conscience fear, 816 : 20
would be no more, 405 : 11
Pitying the tender cries, 403 : 13
Pity-pat, heart goin' p., 568 : 5
Pity's akin to love, 260 : *n* 8
straightest of paths, 260 : 20
Pity-Zekle, hern went p., 568 : 5
Pix, sticks nix hicks p., 741 : 5
Pixy, time slips away like p. wife, 756 : 1
Pizarro traced line with sword, 481 : 2
Place, all other things give p., 331 : 17
and means for every man, 227 : 17
authority and p. try tempers of men, 120 : 4
bounds of p. and time, 363 : 2
called Armageddon, 53 : 25
called Calvary, 44 : 6
called Golgotha, 41 : 24
candle in holy p., 773 : 16
degree priority and p., 225 : 37
dwelleth in the secret p., 20 : 16
for everything, 627 : 3
get wealth and p., 339 : 19
give p. to better men, 272 : 19
grave's fine private p., 297 : 1
he that stands on slippery p., 202 : 3
heavenly paradise is that p., 250 : 5
hiding p. from the wind, 30 : 21
his p. is everywhere, 295 : 10
home p. they have to take you, 747 : 8
hope hath happy p., 562 : 9
I go to prepare a p., 45 : 20
if man aspires to highest p., 98 : 12
immersed in p. and period, 800 : 3
in the sun, 663 : 2
know p. for first time, 808 : 17
lodging p. of wayfaring men, 32 : 4
lonesome p. against sky, 671 : 3
lonesome's a bad p., 879 : 15
look down on world from high p., 120 : 3
many are in high p., 34 : 25
me on Sunium's steep, 461 : 9
mind is its own p., 283 : 13
neither shall his p. know him, 15 : 21
nor time nor p., 237 : 4
nor to one p. trusted, 197 : 25
not circumscribed in one self p., 184 : 1
not safe unless degree preserved, 112 : 14
of a skull, 41 : 24
of excrement, 716 : 18
of skulls, 457 : 13

Place (*continued*)
older p. than Eden, 742 : 11
out of p. as Presbyterian in hell, 626 : 8
philosophy in cities, 98 : 25
prayed to genius of the p., 105 : 27
rain upon p. beneath, 200 : 9
remote and islanded, 664 : 5
respect of p. persons time, 213 : 25
resting p. for those who gave lives, 523 : 4
risk of losing p., 502 : 25
rivers of water in a dry p., 30 : 21
running to keep in p., 612 : 21
savage p. holy enchanted, 433 : 22
shall know it no more, 15 : *n* 3
stand in his holy p., 18 : 8
sunshine in the shady p., 173 : 10
the Lord is in this p., 8 : 20
thereof shall know it no more, 21 : 7
this is the p., 490 : 16
thou hast been our dwelling p., 20 : 11
till there be no p., 29 : 4
time p. loved one, 546 : 3
to be happy is here, 615 : 12
to this p. I owe everything, 521 : 6
towering in pride of p., 238 : 11
truth in first p. or second, 814 : 4
was cool and pleasant, 885 : 7
waters and watering p., 749 : 10
what p. is this, 761 : 6
where is the p. of understanding, 16 : 12
where men can pray, 742 : 15
where mind own business, 616 : *n* 4
where they have gone, 3 : 1
whereon thou standest is holy, 9 : 11
wrong war at wrong p., 825 : 5
you'll not find another p., 702 : 2
Placed jar in Tennessee, 767 : 7
Places, all p. airs one country, 274 : 17
all p. alike to cat, 710 : 5
angels keep ancient p., 693 : 18
change p. handy-dandy, 235 : 2
deep p. of the earth, 20 : 20
eye of heaven visits, 194 : 5
follow in their proper p., 300 : 16
in all the p. you can, 346 : 12
in dry p. husk remains, 877 : 15
in highlands in country p., 669 : 7
in life's fighting line, 743 : 10
inhabit parched p., 32 : 11
lines fallen unto me in pleasant p., 17 : 24
moveth us in sundry p., 54 : 11
often seen in public p., 920 : 5
people I cannot win with p., 300 : 23
proper words in proper p., 322 : 8
rough p. made plain, 30 : 31
shadows and windy p., 632 : 7
spiritual wickedness in high p., 49 : 39
which built desolate p., 15 : 8
Placid and self-contained, 574 : 24
Plagiarè, borrowing accounted P., 282 : 11
Plagiarism, steal from one author p., 757 : 14
Plague, everyone hath his particular p., 62 : 6
fiends that p. thee, 434 : 12
instruments to p. us, 235 : 14
married and that's his p., 259 : 5
my wife is my p., 62 : 6
Plague (*continued*)
not such a p. when young, 717 : 13
o' both your houses, 193 : 6
of all cowards, 203 : 27
of sighing and grief, 204 : 3
one more p. upon Pharaoh, 9 : 22
pleasing p. stole on me, 361 : 6
red p. rid you, 247 : 18
'tis the strumpet's p., 231 : 21
upon such backing, 203 : 29
what a p. is love, 918 : 7
winter p. and pestilence, 250 : 9
Plagues and dotages of human-kind, 258 : 25
blights with p., 405 : 10
O death I will be thy p., 33 : 16
of all p. good Heaven, 422 : 5
of all p. lover bears, 320 : 2
with which mankind cursed, 318 : 9
Plaid, beneath tartan p., 551 : 9
Plain, a few p. rules, 428 : 19
air over the p. quiver, 789 : 10
and simple faith, 216 : 30
as nose in face, 158 : 9
as way to parish church, 211 : 11
Autumn o'er yellow p., 345 : 13
blood bedewed endless p., 743 : *n* 2
blunt man, 216 : 27
cities of the plain., 8 : 7
common sense p. dealing, 497 : 29
darkling p., 587 : 16
divine p. face, 441 : 15
doctrines p. and clear, 291 : 27
dust and drought of p., 852 : 14
eminently p. and direct, 586 : 14
fruited p., 688 : 5
gentle knight pricking on p., 173 : 8
gentle p. just resolute, 576 : 8
great Gromboolian p., 551 : 3
hev it p. an' flat, 567 : 20
hills vales woodland p., 334 : 15
in dress sober in diet, 341 : 2
in meadow or p., 632 : 7
in thy neatness, 107 : 3
Jacob was a p. man, 8 : 15
living high thinking, 425 : 15
loveliest village of p., 369 : 28
not so old not so p., 628 : 19
peaceful generous just, 522 : 12
penny p., 669 : 1
rich stone best p. set, 181 : 8
send you to Elysian p., 59 : 26
snow on dark central p., 777 : 16
so easy and so p. a stop, 205 : 18
speak p. and to purpose, 209 : 15
tale shall put you down, 204 : 1
true p. hearts, 251 : 16
vanish from the p., 562 : 10
Waterloo dismal p., 491 : 12
way so p. we may lose way, 742 : 15
who go through p. are men, 886 : 7
will of the Yukon p., 752 : 4
Plainly, tale speeds best p. told, 187 : 19
to deal p., 235 : 9
very p. before daybreak, 575 : 18
Plainness and soundness of observations, 311 : 1
manifest p., 64 : 8
of speech, 49 : 12
Plains, great grass p. or sagebrush, 739 : 5
of windy Troy, 529 : 8
Plaisir, tel est notre bon p., 154 : *n* 2
Plan, bad p. admits no modification, 111 : 14
civilization or perish, 826 : 1
evil p. most harmful to planner, 61 : 16
eye intent on wondrous p., 410 : 16
fulfills great Nature's p., 409 : 2
if true to p., 607 : 2
maze not without p., 336 : 10
my ways, 490 : 9
never p. future by past, 374 : 4
of Zeus, 57 : 4
reforms p., 330 : 10
sufficeth simple p., 426 : 7
surest p. to make Man, 568 : 11
Plancus, my youth when P. was consul, 108 : 5
Planes, no sound of p., 885 : 7
Planet, destroy p. several times, 898 : 12
every man on p. has right to road, 659 : 7
flesh from living p., 873 : 9
life on this p. may end, 765 : 1
lifetime on this p., 890 : 10
loyal to club rather than p., 846 : 12
of love on high, 533 : 21
poor pagan p. of ours, 570 : 2
protection of whole p., 853 : 17
rhyming p., 210 : 8
ship like small p., 683 : 4
sojourners on p., 482 : 11
swiftly tilting p., 811 : 13
when new p. swims, 475 : 7
Planetary influence, 233 : 5
not disturbed by p. war, 794 : 4
Planet's, wandering p. course, 183 : 6
Planets and the firmament, 254 : 5
come to me, 711 : 13
had fallen on me, 787 : 9
in stations listening, 287 : 1
in their turn, 325 : 9
observe degree, 225 : 37
peace guide p., 914 : 7
then no p. strike, 217 : 26
Planned obsolescence of people, 881 : 10
perfect woman nobly p., 427 : 6
shield deliberately p., 794 : 15
soul o'er him p., 493 : 20
Planner, evil plan most harmful to p., 61 : 16
Planners difficult to find, 719 : 11
Planning, competition means decentralized p., 844 : 5
Plans, all men's p. to fulfillment, 59 : 2
credit and Muse, 494 : 10
lay p. as if immortal, 650 : 4
make no little p., 661 : 3
that build from bottom up, 779 : 6
what are p., 413 : 28
your life p. despair, 702 : 3
Plant a nation, 261 : 23
can read us lectures, 316 : 8
error hardy p., 537 : 17
fixed like a p., 337 : 3
grow yet be embryo, 900 : 8
helped to p. wound, 456 : 17
if tree dies p. another, 350 : 10
land set out to p. wood, 339 : 10
life becomes rootless p., 289 : 13
no roses at my head, 608 : 13
persecution bad way to p. religion, 274 : 9
sensitive p. grew, 468 : 8
this thorn this canker, 203 : 12

Plant (*continued*)
time to p., 26 : 21
vineyards and eat the fruit, 31 : 31
we have become feeble p., 408 : 11
whose virtues not discovered, 500 : 6
writer like bean p., 846 : 10
Planted England with stubborn trust, 840 : 5
God first p. a garden, 181 : 10
I have p., 48 : 3
tree p. by rivers of water, 17 : 12
tree p. by the waters, 32 : 11
Planting trees that would march, 765 : 10
wheat for this p., 307 : *n* 4
Plants, as aromatic p. bestow, 180 : *n* 2
beyond p. are animals, 831 : 17
fruits of life and beauty, 404 : 16
he that p. trees loves others, 95 : *n* 10
his footsteps in the sea, 375 : 16
perennial pleasures p., 484 : 6
scatter leaflets, 906 : 8
sickly p. niggard earth, 361 : 17
still awkward in soil, 873 : 15
trees to benefit another generation, 95 : 15
Plastic, pure p. act secondary, 774 : 10
Plat of rising ground, 278 : 19
Plata, priente de p., 935 : 8
Plate, enjoy ice cream while it's on p., 839 : 15
life fruit ripe on p., 864 : 19
make ourselves recording p., 638 : 4
sin with gold, 235 : 3
Plateaus, history knows no p., 902 : 10
Plates, break china p. of others, 694 : 5
dropped from his pocket, 241 : 25
Platform, stand upon p. pretty well, 451 : 13
Platforms contracts with the people, 788 : 8
Plato and truth are dear, 87 : 14
Aristotle Socrates secretaries of Nature, 271 : 16
dear to me truth dearer, 87 : *n* 6
European philosophical tradition footnotes to P., 697 : 12
having defined man, 86 : 10
healer of the soul, 83 : *n* 3
rather be wrong with P., 98 : 23
rhetoric of rule of P., 281 : 20
thou reasonest well, 326 : 3
Platonic, aim of P. philosophy, 488 : 4
love, 169 : 20
tolerance vain, 715 : 12
Platonically, loves silence p., 473 : *n* 1
Plato's brain, 495 : 15
retirement, 288 : 14
this is P. man, 86 : 10
Platter, licked p. clean, 929 : 16
Platters, unwashed p. ride, 844 : 2
Plaudits, shouts and p., 512 : 18
Plausibly, nut upon tree equally p., 606 : 18
Play, a little work a little p., 617 : 3
all her sons at p., 585 : 9
all work and no p., 271 : 17
anything possible except fair p., 640 : 12
at a p. to laugh or cry, 322 : 16
at Christmas p., 163 : 2
equity and fair p., 737 : 3
fair just and patient, 595 : 12
father author of p., 704 : 14
Play (*continued*)
few boys late at p., 588 : 5
fool with the foolish, 91 : 2
fools with the time, 206 : 13
for mortal stakes, 748 : 18
foul p., 218 : 25
free p. of mind, 586 : 23
game, 700 : 11
good p. audience pleased, 741 : 14
hart ungalled p., 222 : 17
I doubt some foul p., 218 : 25
if music food of love p. on, 213 : 7
is over, 133 : 5
it again Sam, 913 : 11
it Sam, 913 : *n* 3
it'll p. in Peoria, 904 : 1
judge not p. before p. done, 267 : 18
kings would not p. at, 377 : 12
last act crowns p., 267 : 18
leviathan whom thou hast made to p., 21 : 11
life's poor p., 337 : 7
little victims p., 361 : 10
mind in its purest p., 899 : 15
needs no excuse, 197 : 21
no harp so cheerily p., 443 : 9
not let my p. run, 318 : 2
on fiddle in Dooney, 712 : 17
out the play, 204 : 8
perform tragic p., 717 : 5
played out, 539 : 10
pleased not the million, 221 : 3
pleasure when I p. not, 167 : 7
rather thy discourse than p., 259 : 16
see that interesting p., 730 : 10
seem saint when most p. devil, 187 : 6
shouts with sister at play, 530 : 19
sit and p. with similes, 426 : 3
skillfully with a loud noise, 18 : 19
stage where every man p. part, 197 : 28
stake counter boldly if you p., 543 : 14
tale which holdeth children from p., 176 : 11
that fails a bad play, 741 : 14
the fool, 442 : 22
the man Master Ridley, 156 : 14
the Roman fool, 240 : 7
the swan and die in music, 83 : *n* 1
the villain, 230 : 28
theories of a good p., 741 : 14
thy summer's p., 405 : 6
time let me p., 887 : 1
to win or toil to lose, 728 : 22
to you death to us, 294 : 20
tragedy "Man", 526 : 5
tune he could p., 931 : 12
up and play the game, 700 : 11
watch men at p., 757 : 5
whatever body not obliged to do, 622 : 12
when I p. with cat, 165 : 3
wise enough to p. fool, 214 : 12
with flowers and smile, 207 : 13
with towns you built of blocks, 839 : 20
young and old come forth to p., 278 : 1
Playboy of Western world, 735 : 4
Played, as if they p. at bo-peep, 266 : 13
before the Lord on instruments, 13 : 14
easier p. on than pipe, 222 : 19
farce is p., 158 : 14
Played (*continued*)
game that must be p., 728 : 16
how you p. game, 773 : 3
I have p. the fool, 13 : 7
on dulcimer p., 433 : 26
play p. out, 539 : 10
sedulous ape, 668 : 23
sweetly p. in tune, 409 : 22
whether p. black or white, 489 : 10
with and humored, 302 : 19
Player on other side hidden, 595 : 12
strutting p., 226 : 4
that struts and frets, 240 : 4
with railroads, 761 : 4
Player's, tiger's heart in p. hide, 178 : 12
Players and painted stage, 717 : 20
in your housewifery, 230 : 8
men and women merely p., 211 : 15
mouth it as many p. do, 221 : 23
though the most be p., 257 : 3
Playful, when I'm p., 623 : 5
Playing fields of Eton, 421 : 16
Idiot's Delight, 836 : 15
if year p. holidays, 203 : 5
of merry organ, 919 : 21
seal p. in sun like me, 929 : 7
ugly Yahoo tricks, 765 : 4
without p. no creative work, 753 : 11
Playmates, I have had p., 441 : 5
Playroom, our house a p., 599 : 10
Play's, old age p. last act, 99 : 10
the thing, 221 : 10
Plays, destiny with men p., 516 : 22
eats drinks and p., 705 : 12
God p. dice with world, 763 : 16
like actors in ancient p., 673 : 17
one man p. many parts, 211 : 15
sports and p. with me, 402 : 13
such fantastic tricks, 228 : 10
tune enchantress p., 692 : 5
Plaything, livelier p., 337 : 7
no book but p., 455 : 4
Plaza, Duke of P. Toro, 630 : 1
Plea, general good is p. of scoundrel, 407 : 6
in law what p. so tainted, 199 : 24
necessity is the p., 412 : 4
necessity tyrant's p., 285 : 21
though justice be thy p., 200 : 9
Plead for the widow, 28 : 30
virtues p. like angels, 236 : 24
Pleadeth, orators dumb when beauty p., 189 : 22
Pleasance here all vainglory, 153 : 7
joy p. revel, 230 : 26
youth full of p., 917 : 11
Pleasant, all p. in man, 371 : 16
and the p. land, 591 : 7
bread eaten in secret is p., 23 : 20
castle hath p. seat, 236 : 21
country's earth, 195 : 8
eat his p. fruits, 28 : 14
England's p. pastures, 406 : 21
few think him p. enough, 550 : 5
from p. to severe, 311 : 2
green and p. land, 406 : 21
how good and how p., 22 : 14
how p. to have money, 564 : 15
lines fallen unto me in p. places, 17 : 24
love is p., 148 : 20
lovely and p. in their lives, 13 : 9
piping songs of p. glee, 403 : 2
place was cool and p., 885 : 7

Pleasant (*continued*)
sitting in a p. shade, 257:6
standing on p. lea, 428:1
thing if thou keep them within thee, 24:37
thrilling glorious hours, 560:18
through loopholes of retreat, 377:4
to gaze upon another's tribulation, 100:12
to know Mr. Lear, 550:5
to make thy riches p., 228:16
to perceive from what ills you are free, 100:12
to remember even this, 104:22
to see name in print, 456:12
vices make instruments, 235:14
walk pleasant talk, 613:3
wherein all p. fruits flow, 250:5
year's p. king, 250:8
Pleasanter than tie of host and guest, 71:17
Pleasantness, her ways are ways of p., 23:5
Please again to be himself, 203:5
allow me to introduce myself, 916:8
art to p., 338:14
cannot p. himself, 311:8
death after life does p., 173:12
do not shoot pianist, 675:6
each art to p., 338:14
genius p. the talentgang, 829:16
hard to p. everybody, 112:1
his evil neighbor, 414:3
hurry up p. its time, 805:5
if rich whenever you p., 86:11
in choice of horse p. himself, 584:6
live to p. must p. to live, 351:14
love seeketh not self to p., 405:3
love seeketh self to p., 405:4
natural to p., 303:18
ne'er believe do what you p., 406:17
old fashions p. best, 188:33
peppered highest surest to p., 371:20
she never fails to p., 312:12
sound what stop she p., 222:6
studious to p., 351:15
takes things that p. us, 355:24
they p. are pleased, 368:19
to call it rush candle, 189:3
to put penny, 921:3
towered cities p. us then, 278:4
try to p. and p. not, 835:13
uncertain coy hard to p., 431:2
woman says what will p., 358:26
Pleased, all seemed well p., 286:23
Almighty's orders to perform, 325:7
as mind pitched ear p., 377:13
daughter of Herodias p. Herod, 39:22
disposition to be p., 355:24
God to visit us with death, 265:10
good play audience p., 741:14
in whom I am well p., 36:31
play p. not the million, 221:3
seemed p. but were not all, 286:23
still p. to praise, 333:22
they please are p., 368:19
to the last, 336:13
with a rattle, 337:7
with danger, 303:20
with this bauble still, 337:7
with what he gets, 211:3
Pleases, right to say what one p., 794:20
Pleases (*continued*)
world cannot please himself, 311:8
Pleasing anxious being, 362:14
dreadful thought, 326:3
dreams slumbers light, 431:4
every p. prudent part, 335:20
eye or face, 918:16
imagine himself p. to all, 308:12
land of drowsyhead, 345:20
lascivious p. of a lute, 186:31
love quarrels in p. concord end, 289:4
myself mightily, 310:6
nature's p. themes, 345:21
painful pleasure to p. pain, 173:19
plague stole on me, 361:6
punishment women bear, 187:33
serpents there's no p. them, 611:12
ware is half sold, 269:13
whence this p. hope, 326:3
Pleasurable and genial feeling, 438:8
Pleasurably, live p. without living wisely, 91:16
Pleasure, all knowledge and wonder is p., 178:18
and love are pinions, 395:11
as great of being cheated, 291:24
at the helm, 363:6
beginning and end of living, 91:15
blind with tears, 469:3
built soul p. house, 528:6
created for thy p., 53:8
dispensation of p., 453:2
disposed to one another by p., 124:4
dissipation without p., 384:5
dome, 433:21, 433:25
drink it with p., 35:15
forget p. during getting estate, 310:3
friend of P., 364:16
good p. ease content, 337:10
harmless p., 353:1
have much to teach him, 701:13
I have no p. in them, 27:24
if you were queen of p., 633:13
imprint of the Eternal P., 142:17
in faults of others, 293:5
in pathless woods, 458:24
in trim gardens takes his p., 278:16
in what yet remain, 303:11
indulge more in p., 310:3
intermission of pain, 264:5
light life p. pain, 614:17
little p. in the house, 382:10
little p. of the game, 320:14
love not P., 473:7
love of p., 335:21
love's p. drives love, 715:13
necessity brings him not p., 141:9
never is at home, 477:14
no p. unseasoned by variety, 111:9
no profit where no p., 188:25
not great p. to bring death, 74:15
of believing what we see, 467:11
of itself not vice, 356:5
of love is in loving, 293:30
of poem is guessing, 651:16
of poem itself, 750:2
of talking, 323:30
oft a visitant, 476:2
only p. I have left, 344:8
pain and p. rudders, 307:*n* 8
painful p. to pleasing pain, 173:19
poetry communication of p., 436:14
pride is therefore p., 308:11
Pleasure (*continued*)
rich gets p., 924:11
Riches Fame and P., 309:6
richness quietness and p., 580:20
so exquisite almost pain, 454:11
some to p. take, 335:22
stately p. dome decree, 433:21
studies a p. for us at home, 98:7
sunny p. dome, 433:25
sure in being mad, 304:19
sweet is p. after pain, 306:16
thou wilt come for p., 469:24
though on p. she was bent, 376:14
to be drunk, 349:5
to deceive deceiver, 296:13
to do good by stealth, 442:15
to do of his good p., 50:3
to spectators, 489:6
to stand upon the shore, 100:*n* 7
truth as opposeth no p., 264:20
turn to p. all they find, 344:15
unholy p., 729:14
variety soul of p., 312:14
vibrate sweetest p., 410:1
when a woman is a p., 67:11
when I play not, 167:7
when p. can be had, 355:24
wince at p., 893:12
with pain for leaven, 632:9
without joy hollow, 895:6
worldly ease or p., 346:3
youth and p. meet, 457:15
youth of p. wasteful, 545:22
Pleasure-house, built soul p., 528:6
Pleasure's a sin, 460:18
Pleasures, after such p., 253:15
and toils, 432:12
banish pain, 328:15
cannot understand p. of other, 440:25
celibacy has no p., 352:18
conversation one of greatest p., 751:15
dance attendance on lordships' p., 249:16
disciplined state of p. and pains, 307:*n* 8
every age has its p., 311:5
go look at their p., 565:21
homely home simple p., 692:15
let go hold of p., 839:13
lightly called physical, 739:9
like poppies spread, 411:8
love and all his p. toys, 250:7
man richest p. cheapest, 557:17
'mid p. and palaces, 465:4
money-lust before p., 792:19
newly found, 425:9
of heroic poesy, 276:1
of its p. tired, 424:3
of youth, 327:15
perennial p. plants, 484:6
pretty p. might me move, 172:10
seat of p. and of loves, 306:6
some new p. prove, 253:2
soothed soul to p., 306:19
sucked on country p., 251:14
than all other p. are, 303:7
the past with its p., 863:13
too refined to please, 335:19
unreproved p. free, 277:22
we will all the p. prove, 183:8
Pledge allegiance to flag, 677:10
our lives our fortunes, 387:11

Pledge (*continued*)
to each other our lives, 387 : 11
with mine, 256 : 8
you I pledge myself, 779 : 8
Pleiades, moon has set and the P., 63 : 8
sweet influences of P., 16 : 33
Pleiads, rainy P. wester, 692 : 8
Plenteous, harvest is p., 38 : 32
Plenties, nurse of arts p., 208 : 16
Plentiful lack of wit, 220 : 20
Plentitude of plan not suffice, 889 : 8
Plenty, here is God's p., 307 : 3
heroes were p., 922 : 16
in delay no p., 213 : 23
just had p., 409 : 17
laurels though ever so p., 462 : 6
of nothing, 836 : 6
of the kind, 527 : 21
reasons as p. as blackberries, 203 : 31
rich happy in p., 337 : 6
scatter p. o'er smiling land, 362 : 10
to have p. is to be perplexed, 64 : 10
to live on happily, 788 : 2
want in midst of p., 811 : 10
Plenty's, mouth of P. horn, 714 : 20
Pleure dans mon coeur, 659 : *n* 7
Pleuré, j'ai p. et j'ai cru, 419 : *n* 1
Pleurer, de peur d'en p., 378 : *n* 5
Pleut, comme il p. sur la ville, 659 : *n* 7
doucement sur la ville, 674 : *n* 3
Pliable, name of other was p., 301 : 21
Pliant instrument of Executive, 439 : 4
obstinate p. merry morose, 119 : 17
Plied, by little arms p., 611 : 1
myself to fruitless poetry, 177 : 3
Plighted, what p. cunning hides, 233 : 1
Pliny, is it Aristotle P. Buffon, 358 : 23
Plodders, dull tramp of p., 569 : 20
small have p. won, 190 : 12
Plodding from cradles to graves, 569 : 20
Plods, plowman homeward p., 361 : 20
Ploffskin Pluffskin Pelican jee, 551 : 7
Plot, blessed p. this earth, 194 : 13
gunpowder treason and p., 919 : 12
horror soul of p., 526 : 4
melodious p., 476 : 22
passions spin p., 600 : 18
persons attempting to find p., 623 : 19
souls that cringe and p., 567 : 11
thickens, 302 : 20
time someone invented p., 782 : 7
women guide the p., 398 : 20
Plots true or false necessary, 303 : 19
Plotted, foul deed which she p., 60 : 11
Plow ancient and valuable, 515 : 11
farmer Ledlow late at p., 641 : 10
following p. along mountainside, 425 : 10
for lords who lay ye low, 467 : 23
friends who p. sea, 628 : 4
having put hand to p., 43 : 7
sow reap mow, 919 : 5
speed his p., 178 : 2
what avail p. or sail, 495 : 10
Plowed, dashed to earth p. under, 929 : 1
I have p. and planted, 482 : 17
if ye had not p. with my heifer, 12 : 15
land p. before man, 515 : 11
sea, 452 : 3
wickedness, 33 : 13
Plowing, men want crops without p., 556 : 4
Plowman, heavy steps of p., 712 : 12
homeward plods, 361 : 20
Plowman's story is of bulls, 112 : 20
Plows, drinks water her keel p. air, 178 : 6
in the fields, 789 : 10
my grandmothers followed p., 888 : 7
the sand, 794 : 9
Plowshare, drives p. o'er creation, 330 : 18
put not p. too deep, 432 : 7
stern Ruin's p., 409 : 10
Plowshares, beat swords into p., 28 : 31
Pluck a crow together, 188 : 7
bright honor from moon, 203 : 15
from memory rooted sorrow, 239 : 32
I come to p. your berries, 280 : 6
it out and cast it from thee, 37 : 8
love not flower they p., 494 : 12
out heart of my mystery, 222 : 18
out his flying feather, 633 : 13
stoop p. posy, 545 : 23
sworn to weed and p. away, 194 : 22
their hearts from them, 208 : 8
this flower safety, 203 : 22
till time and times done, 712 : 14
time to p. up, 26 : 21
up drowned honor, 203 : 15
you out of crannies, 535 : 10
Plucked, an olive leaf p. off, 7 : 32
Diogenes p. a cock, 86 : 10
fruit she p. she eat, 287 : 19
his gown, 370 : 9
lint from lapel, 699 : 14
my nipple from his gums, 237 : 5
violets p., 260 : 19
Plucker down of kings, 186 : 6
Plucking fruit of memory, 684 : 7
Plucks dead lions by beard, 201 : 13
liberty p. justice, 227 : 26
off my beard, 221 : 8
with a thread p. it back, 192 : 18
Plum, pulled out p., 929 : 20
some gave p. cake, 929 : 19
survives its poems, 766 : 20
Plumage, pities p., 385 : 1
Plumbing, portable p., 816 : 12
shadows of p. left of city, 907 : 18
Plume, blast-beruffled p., 641 : 12
helmet and the p., 528 : 27
prête-moi ta p., 928 : 8
white p. shine, 487 : 6
Plumed, farewell p. troop, 231 : 11
helmets gleamed in forests, 592 : 6
knight, 615 : 4
war bonnet, 840 : 2
Plumes, borrowed p., 66 : 7
feathered with eagle's p., 66 : 24
her feathers, 279 : 22
Plummet, deeper than p. sound, 248 : 15
Plummet's, heavy p. pace, 281 : 7
Plummets to dust of hope, 74 : 3
Plump, banish p. Jack, 204 : 7
Plumpskin Ploshkin Pelican jill, 551 : 7
Plumpy Bacchus with pink eyne, 241 : 5
Plums, life's a pudding full of p., 630 : 4
Plunder, capitalism in ascendancy p., 562 : 20
exempt from p., 705 : 4
lust for blood and p., 745 : 2
public p., 449 : *n* 3
Plunder (*continued*)
years p. one thing after another, 109 : 16
Plunge hands in water, 868 : 10
Plunges into scientific questions, 596 : 11
lower than night, 785 : 14
Orion p. prone, 692 : 8
year p. into night, 785 : 14
Plural, unity is p., 832 : 17
Pluralism lets exist in each-form, 650 : 12
Plus est quam vita salusque, 118 : *n* 9
Plus a change plus la même, 514 : *n* 3
Pluto, won the ear of P., 278 : 8
Plutocracy, government by p., 687 : 20
Plutonian shore, 526 : 15
Pluto's, iron tears down P. cheek, 278 : 22
Ply, I cannot p. the loom, 63 : 9
the sampler, 280 : 1
Plyin' boats a-p. up and down, 709 : 8
Plying needle and thread, 485 : 16
Plymouth, pious ones of P., 562 : 14
Pneumatic bliss, 804 : 23
Po, wandering P., 368 : 13
Pobble who has no toes, 551 : 5
Pobbles happier without toes, 551 : 6
Pocket full of rye, 931 : 9
holding p. handkerchief, 613 : 8
learning in private p., 342 : 1
Lucy Locket lost p., 933 : 5
never alone with poet in p., 381 : 15
not scruple to pick p., 318 : 1
plates dropped from his p., 241 : 25
put me in your p., 790 : 8
save their own p., 80 : 16
Pod, seeds in dry p. tick, 728 : 4
Poe and four conditions for happiness, 882 : 12
with his raven, 567 : 18
Poem a poem and nothing more, 527 : 13
bathed in p. of sea, 673 : 16
begins as lump in throat, 749 : 19
day is a p., 798 : 1
dignity in writing p., 681 : 25
does p. not merely says p., 474 : 10
don't make p. with ideas, 651 : 17
fain write p., 543 : 31
feeling for single good p., 395 : 25
figure p. makes, 750 : 2
finds the thought, 749 : 19
for poem's sake, 527 : 13
heroic p. a biography, 472 : 9
illuminated reader is p., 741 : 13
inhabits p., 869 : 10
is a meteor, 769 : 20
language touched by poetry is p., 885 : 18
lovely as a tree, 795 : 6
marred by superfluous verse, 512 : 23
meter-making argument makes p., 498 : 1
music of p. in translation, 735 : 7
my life p. I would have writ, 558 : 24
of the act of the mind, 437 : *n* 4
of world, 859 : 1
ought himself to be true p., 281 : 14
part of sense of life, 769 : 22
phrase long p. contradiction, 527 : 12
pleasure of p. guessing, 651 : 16
pleasure of p. itself, 750 : 2
poetry subject of p., 767 : 17

Poem (*continued*)
pretty p. Mr. Pope, 319 : 3
questions when reading p., 869 : 10
read a good p., 395 : 5
ride on own melting, 750 : 4
right reader of good p., 749 : 20
rooted in awe, 869 : 11
should not mean, 821 : 13
something not in p. creep in, 887 : 7
suggestibility of p., 718 : 4
tear p. apart, 887 : 7
tell how it can, 750 : 2
that took place of mountain, 769 : 4
to which we return, 437 : 1
true p. an invocation, 833 : 6
United States greatest p., 573 : 19
way to tell if p. lasting, 749 : 20
what guy inhabits p., 869 : 10
who wants to understand p., 396 : 2
write p. for money, 863 : 20
write saddest p. tonight, 860 : 8
Poème, baigné dans le P., 673 : *n* 9
supprimer la jouissance du p., 651 : *n* 5
Poem's, poem for p. sake, 527 : 13
Poems by water-drinkers, 109 : 12
dictionaries and temporary p., 352 : 10
hymns of praise to life, 801 : 7
I will put in my p., 574 : 6
laying p. away in long box, 908 : 15
made by fools like me, 795 : 7
more p. produced, 747 : 19
my p. naughty but life pure, 118 : 21
plum survives its p., 766 : 20
take old p. as teachers, 138 : 5
that's how book of p. made, 119 : 2
ye are living p., 512 : 2
Poena, noxiae p., 99 : *n* 5
Poesis, ut pictura p., 110 : *n* 2
Poesy, force of heaven-bred p., 190 : 3
heavenly gift of p., 305 : 7
in p. participation of divineness, 179 : 2
overwhelm myself in p., 475 : 11
pleasures of heroic p., 276 : 1
should be friend, 475 : 13
shower of light is p., 475 : 12
Poet a void, 850 : 2
all p. can do is warn, 827 : 1
and saint to thee alone, 295 : 18
beneath this sod p. lies, 438 : 9
binds together by passion, 424 : 8
blood of a p., 818 : 3
born not made, 123 : *n* 15
brings soul into activity, 437 : 16
buffoon and p., 663 : 8
Chaucer broad famous p., 261 : 15
Coleridge p. and philosopher, 589 : 12
comic p. paint follies, 324 : 6
could not but be gay, 427 : 10
creates world, 769 : 14
don't send p. to London 481 : 14
every p. in his kind, 322 : 21
find more than p. expressed, 504 : 3
flourished here disheveled, 912 : 8
force language into meaning, 809 : 9
gives life to fictions, 769 : 14
Goldsmith p. naturalist, 355 : 23
great p. writes his time, 809 : 11
had no p. and died, 339 : 32
he was a true p., 403 : 19
he was p. and hated approximate, 756 : 5
Poet (*continued*)
I the p. still do Thank God, 912 : 14
if p. interprets poem, 718 : 4
is barometer but also part of weather, 866 : 4
language of English p., 809 : 16
like prince of clouds, 580 : 17
limbs of a dismembered p., 106 : 15
looks at world, 769 : 23
lunatic the lover the p., 197 : 12
make his imagination the people's, 769 : 16
maker of patterns, 758 : 7
makes himself seer, 674 : 12
man that lies in Bedlam, 878 : 11
moon talk by p., 623 : 16
most unpoetical, 479 : 18
must have sensuous eye, 500 : 10
must write, 872 : 15
mystic communion p. feels, 812 : 9
never alone with p. in pocket, 381 : 15
never sure of value, 809 : 19
no p. without unsoundness, 487 : 10
not every year a p. born, 123 : 17
not have to be p., 584 : 2
not survive misprint, 674 : 17
objective of p. achieve poetry, 769 : 19
our ever-living p., 243 : *n* 4
peace into p. as flour into bread, 861 : 3
potent figure, 769 : 14
priest soldier p., 581 : 8
profound philosopher, 437 : 18
proof of a p., 573 : 20
read from some humbler p., 510 : 21
skilled p. through natural gift, 71 : 24
so great a p. and friend, 306 : 24
soaring in high reason, 281 : 11
take away liberty of p., 276 : 1
they lack a sacred p., 108 : 13
this truth p. sings, 529 : 20
to make a p. excellent, 292 : 2
to p. nothing useless, 352 : 16
union of mathematician with p., 651 : 4
was ever p. so trusted, 355 : 11
wasted time for nothing, 809 : 19
whatever p. writes with enthusiasm, 79 : 9
when the P. dies, 430 : 8
who dares doubt p. wise, 275 : 31
who wishes to understand p., 396 : 2
whole race is a p., 768 : 7
with so many felicities, 423 : *n* 1
without love impossibility, 472 : 8
worst tragedy for p., 818 : 2
worthy name of p., 474 : 10
you explain nothing p., 724 : 8
Poeta nascitur non fit, 123 : *n* 15
Poetarum licentiae liberiora, 98 : *n* 9
Poète semblable au prince, 580 : *n* 5
Poetic faith, 437 : 15
fields encompass me, 325 : 6
Justice, 340 : 15
license, 98 : 11
meet nurse for p. child, 430 : 11
no p. raptures feel, 399 : 16
pale p. pearl, 570 : 11
wine-scented and p. soul, 668 : 18
Poetical character, 479 : 17
language should be current, 657 : 1
worn-out p. fashion, 807 : 12
would gods made thee p., 212 : 14
Poetically, noble nature p. gifted, 586 : 16
Poetics, never indulge in p., 94 : 17
old p. in my alchemy, 674 : 7
Poetry act of peace, 861 : 3
actual is rarest p., 558 : 18
aim at inscape in p., 656 : 22
all p. difficult, 545 : 4
antithesis to science, 436 : 14
as in painting so in p., 110 : 3
Ben Jonson his best p., 256 : 4
best p. a power, 589 : 11
best words in best order, 438 : 4
book not concerned with P., 827 : 1
boom in petroleum but not p., 886 : 10
breath of knowledge, 424 : 7
checks loquacity, 499 : 20
civilization advances p. declines, 487 : 9
cleanses, 891 : 16
communicate before understood, 809 : 15
communication of pleasure, 436 : 14
dead art of p., 792 : 10
do a hundred things, 869 : 11
does not matter, 807 : 12
drops into p., 549 : 30
efflorescence of civilized life, 579 : 11
emptied of its p., 868 : 11
escape from emotion, 809 : 4
essential p., 437 : 1
fettered fetters race, 407 : 5
fine-spun from mind at peace, 113 : 27
fleshly school of p., 643 : 10
for p. idea everything, 589 : 5
from p. liturgy psalms religions, 861 : 5
gaudiness of p., 769 : 12
genius behind p., 608 : 8
genius of p., 479 : 14
give children right to study p., 381 : 14
grain of p. season a century, 672 : 4
grand style in p., 586 : 16
great and unobtrusive, 479 : 6
great p. result of national spirit, 577 : 13
hate p. with design on us, 479 : 6
heart subject of Japanese p., 344 : 19
homely definitions of p., 438 : 4
I have been eating p., 913 : 4
I know that is p., 608 : 6
I too dislike p., 798 : 10
if this is p. very easy, 618 : 2
in unconscious fastidiousness, 799 : 1
inner calling in man, 861 : 5
is in the pity, 827 : 1
is painting that speaks, 68 : 1
is poetry, 769 : 19
journey to unknown, 826 : 17
joy and function of p., 887 : 7
knew well how to write p., 92 : 18
language is fossil p., 498 : 3
language touched by p., 885 : 18
learned about p. from Dante, 809 : 16
less subtle and fine, 281 : 20
like stove in summer, 314 : 3
literature reduced to essence, 735 : 13
live without p., 609 : 13
made p. mechanic art, 375 : 22
medium for writing in prose, 674 : 18
mincing p., 204 : 14

Poetry (*continued*)
more philosophic than history, 88 : 18
most beautiful mode, 587 : 2
mother tongue of mankind, 374 : 22
music and p. agree, 257 : 9
must be good sense, 438 : 6
must be new and old, 495 : 25
must be well written as prose, 793 : 6
must go to land of p., 396 : 2
my p. errs on oddness, 656 : 22
no man ever talked p., 546 : 23
not antithesis to prose, 436 : 14
not p. but prose run mad, 338 : 13
not purpose but passion, 526 : 9
objective of poet achieve p., 769 : 19
of earth never dead, 475 : 9
of motion, 690 : 15
of Natural Philosophy, 696 : 5
of speech, 458 : 13
old-fashioned p. choicely good, 271 : 7
one who knows p., 344 : 19
Orpheus' voice and p., 76 : 3
painting and music, 407 : 5
painting is silent p., 68 : 1
plied myself to fruitless p., 177 : 3
praise for being, 869 : 11
prancing p., 607 : 4
prophecy and religion, 572 : 11
purged of idols, 735 : 13
purging of world's poverty, 769 : 25
record of best moments, 470 : 6
refreshment with p., 598 : 14
religion unconscious p., 589 : 5
reminds of limitations, 891 : 16
rhythmical creation, 527 : 14
romance and p. need ruin, 504 : 2
search for inexplicable, 770 : 3
Shakespeare wrote better p., 698 : 11
she that with p. is won, 291 : 18
simple and passionate, 281 : 20
skin bristles at p., 692 : 14
spontaneous overflow, 424 : 9
subject matter of p. life, 769 : 15
subject of poem, 767 : 17
supreme fiction, 766 : 24
surprise by excess, 479 : 7
sympathy with the p., 437 : 17
taking life by throat, 750 : 8
teaches force of words, 499 : 20
theory of p. theory of life, 768 : 24
thinking a kind of p., 690 : 4
tuned to p. life's prose, 610 : 8
two cardinal points of p., 437 : 14
universal pastime, 509 : 11
vein of p. in all men, 473 : 26
way of taking life by throat, 750 : 8
we all scribble p., 109 : 24
we read p., 884 : 6
when p. ceased to exist, 817 : 1
whining p., 252 : 13
wit flock to aid, 496 : 13
work of bard and people, 672 : 8
Poetry's unnat'ral, 546 : 23
Poet's and orator's help, 650 : 13
dignity and ease, 338 : 16
dream, 427 : 17
eye, 443 : 7
eye in fine frenzy, 197 : 12
feverish blood, 585 : 18
flattery lost on p. ear, 430 : 7
inward pride, 860 : 7
joy conceals despair, 757 : 7
made as well as born, 256 : 17
Poet's (*continued*)
must go to the p. land, 396 : 2
pen turns to shapes, 197 : 12
possess a p. brain, 182 : 19
privilege to help man endure, 838 : 12
shone not on p. page, 108 : *n* 11
Poets, among English p. after death, 479 : 16
among us can be literalists, 798 : 11
architects like p., 800 : 10
are mad, 258 : 13
as we to brutes p. to us, 601 : 8
avoid citations from p., 80 : 2
begin in gladness, 425 : 10
by education and practice, 499 : 21
by nature, 499 : 21
by their sufferings grow, 292 : 2
Catullus worst of all p., 102 : 4
clever young p., 438 : 4
come down from mountains, 637 : 19
creatures most absurd, 339 : 29
die of loneliness, 718 : 5
discovered unconscious, 678 : 11
error to marry with p., 884 : 18
first p. then sun, 605 : 17
great p. great audiences, 577 : 9
great p. never yet read, 559 : 32
hallucinations of p., 772 : 7
haven't all been p., 622 : 21
hierophants, 470 : 5
Homer first of heroic p., 353 : *n* 4
horses and p. not overfed, 171 : 17
I write p. all, 605 : 17
immature p. imitate, 809 : 6
Irish p. learn trade, 717 : 22
legislators of world, 470 : 7
light but lamps, 606 : 10
lose half the praise, 276 : 11
major p. read from own works, 846 : 6
mature p. steal, 809 : 6
mighty p. in misery dead, 425 : 12
mirrors of gigantic shadows, 470 : 5
must be difficult, 809 : 9
not yet priests, 672 : 1
old p. comfort to man, 663 : 17
only great p. can read great p., 559 : 32
pacify touchy tribe of p., 109 : 17
painters and p. have equal license, 109 : 18
pensive p. painful vigils, 340 : 16
puff p. of other days, 119 : 13
reviewers would have been p., 436 : 15
room for p. in world, 507 : 20
sometimes seem businesslike, 747 : 19
souls of p. dead and gone, 477 : 16
steal from Homer, 258 : 6
tell many lies, 62 : 13
that lasting marble seek, 276 : 9
there were p. before Homer, 98 : 15
things the first p. had, 182 : 18
three p. in three ages, 306 : 1
two classes of p., 499 : 21
we p. in youth, 425 : 10, 892 : 15
what company good p. are, 671 : 19
witty mathematics subtile, 181 : 14
your p. have said, 46 : 17
youthful p. dream, 278 : 6
Poets' food love and fame, 467 : 16
wares harder to get rid of, 747 : 19
Point, by falling in make p., 888 : 14
Point (*continued*)
choice of p. of view, 784 : 12
everyone mad on one p., 707 : 10
except for p. no dance, 807 : 6
highest p. not knowledge, 783 : 2
highest p. of my greatness, 249 : 1
men at p. of death, 193 : 26
moral or adorn tale, 351 : 19
of a diamond, 32 : 10
on which soul fix eye, 482 : 15
people to the goal, 568 : 1
picked up broken p., 815 : 8
put too fine a p., 171 : 9
slow and moving finger, 232 : 3
still p. of world, 806 : 13
where tooth p. goes, 707 : 5
Pointed firs, 664 : 2
Points, armed at p. exactly, 218 : 19
beaten at all p., 81 : 10
possession eleven p., 324 : 25
silent finger p. to heaven, 428 : 17
to yonder glade, 335 : 7
true to kindred p., 429 : 9
Poirot tapped his forehead, 817 : 12
Poised like souls to remind us, 733 : 17
Poisened with blood of both, 911 : 1
Poison, all men possess p., 116 : 13
deeds like p. weeds, 676 : 13
England at roots, 741 : 16
food to one p. to others, 101 : 6
from Caesar's laurel crown, 406 : 16
if you p. us do we not die, 199 : 18
instead of dirt and p., 321 : 14
luxury that baneful p., 392 : 15
more deadly than mad dog's tooth, 188 : 13
one man's meat another man's p., 101 : *n* 6
one man's p., 101 : *n* 6
ounce of p. in pocket, 488 : 12
steel nor p., 238 : 19
sweet p. for age's tooth, 201 : 10
sweet p. of misused wine, 279 : 7
Poisoned, brims the p. well, 572 : 6
rat in hole, 322 : 18
some p. by their wives, 195 : 2
Poisoning, slow process of p., 775 : 13
Poisonous dart not pugnacity, 786 : 8
minerals and that tree, 254 : 10
Nessus shirts, 473 : 10
wolf's-bane for p. wine, 477 : 20
Poke, drew dial from his p., 211 : 5
pig in a p., 161 : 15
Pokers into true-love knots, 436 : 5
Pole, beloved from p. to p., 434 : 30
black as pit from p. to p., 663 : 10
embrace P. as Frenchman, 166 : 2
from Indus to P., 335 : 1
heavens from p. to p., 407 : 10
intellectuals at one p., 865 : 17
so tall to reach p., 328 : 1
soldier's p. is fallen, 241 : 22
top of greasy p., 502 : 9
true as needle to p., 291 : *n* 6
truth from p. to p., 325 : 9
Poles, north p. and equators, 613 : 22
Police, international p. power, 687 : 10
those who arrest you, 908 : 6
Policeman's lot not happy one, 628 : 3
Policemen, not enough p. to control thoughts, 876 : 2
Policies based on myths, 862 : 16
Policy, Fabian p., 95 : *n* 1
foreign relations p., 813 : 11

Policy (*continued*)
honesty best p., 170 : 29
ill p. in Leo the Tenth, 379 : 16
kings tyrants from p., 373 : 26
of letting flowers blossom, 826 : 12
of the good neighbor, 779 : 11
stare decisis wise p., 678 : 3
theory of matter a p., 681 : 23
turn him to cause of p., 207 : 5
Policy's, all p. allowed in war and love, 564 : *n* 1
Polish, fitter to bruise than p., 290 : 10
Polished handle of big front door, 627 : 14
idleness, 416 : 15
perturbation, 206 : 29
satire like p. razor, 341 : 3
Polisher, comedy the civilizer the p., 600 : 22
Polite, compulsion to become p., 791 : 7
costs nothing to be p., 746 : 13
learning, 319 : 14
patronize p. literature, 379 : 16
Politeness organized indifference, 735 : 19
out of p. cheat others, 734 : 8
pineapple of p., 398 : 10
punctuality p. of kings, 402 : 2
Politesse, l'exactitude la p. des rois, 402 : *n* 1
l'indifférence organisée, 735 : *n* 5
Politic, body p. like human body, 358 : 16
cautious and meticulous, 803 : 17
Political affairs, 517 : 24
and cultural freedom, 757 : 17
appeasement, 778 : 7
beginning and end of p. education, 635 : 1
best p. community, 88 : 7
campaigns emotional orgies, 703 : 1
creed of our p. faith, 389 : 2
crises moral crises, 886 : 2
democracy training school, 577 : 1
dissolve p. bands, 387 : 9
economic freedom means to p. freedom, 880 : 11
everything in p. life, 588 : 20
executive magistracy, 374 : 3
free p. discussion, 700 : 3
freedom business of government, 779 : 16
fundamental article of p. creed, 382 : 4
give me p. economist, 566 : 6
good carried to extreme, 414 : 15
greatness and wisdom meet, 84 : 15
happy warrior of p. battlefield, 741 : *n* 3
ideas and imagination, 866 : 1
institutions superstructure, 731 : 3
liberty highest p. end, 615 : 17
like to see p. reaction, 830 : 15
man a p. animal, 87 : 26
mode of half world, 852 : 2
moral and p. systems, 763 : 2
philosophy of black nationalism, 904 : 14
power out of barrel of gun, 826 : 7
Principles of P. Economy, 753 : 4
rather p. than religious, 354 : 9
rebellion in p. world, 388 : 6
society exists for noble actions, 88 : 5
test of p. party, 851 : 8
Political (*continued*)
thicket, 776 : 14
try to score p. points, 898 : 12
tutelage, 719 : 8
tyranny of p. assemblies, 506 : 3
understanding to run government, 788 : 10
variable of p. calculation, 595 : 18
volcanic p. instinct, 681 : 21
Politician, characteristics of popular p., 81 : 13
coffee makes p. wise, 334 : 8
I am not a p., 616 : 13
is an arse, 829 : 22
proper memory for p., 637 : 11
scurvy p., 235 : 4
under every stone lurks p., 82 : 15
would circumvent God, 224 : 9
Politicians, control p. in own community, 904 : 14
friends lovers husbands, 392 : 10
God and p., 818 : 8
not necessary to patriotism, 764 : 15
one rule for p., 723 : 8
tinhorn p., 726 : 10
whole race of p., 322 : 12
Politics almost exciting as war, 743 : 7
applesauce, 765 : 16
art of happiness, 706 : 21
art of possible, 553 : *n* 3
Cobbett a fourth estate in p., 445 : 3
control p. in own community, 904 : 14
customs p. and tongue, 593 : 3
difference of p., 538 : 18
education part of p., 483 : 19
expensive, 766 : 4
greatest adventure, 753 : 9
I must study p. and war, 381 : 14
in p. middle way none at all, 381 : 3
killed many times in p., 743 : 7
liberalism in p., 848 : 12
like ours profess, 344 : 13
like religion, 389 : 5
magnanimity in p., 373 : 8
makes strange bedfellows, 603 : 11
my p. like my religion, 616 : 10
never understand p. and morality, 637 : 2
no more with gallantry than p., 398 : 27
not engaged in domestic p., 797 : 7
not exact science, 553 : 7
of accommodatin' character, 616 : 10
of joy, 879 : 1
orthodox in p., 821 : 6
power p. law of jungle, 818 : 6
power p. obstruct peace, 781 : 4
practical p., 517 : 21, 635 : 13
purification of p., 615 : 3
royalist in p., 809 : 13
ruins character, 553 : 15
saturates p. with thought, 586 : 22
struggle of forces, 635 : 17
thermonuclear war not continuation of p., 448 : *n* 4
war not separated from p., 826 : 10
who gets what when how, 855 : 6
work of p. shaped by geometry, 318 : 3
world of power p., 818 : 5
Polity, ideal p., 84 : 16
Polka, can't you dance p., 934 : 23
Poll, talked like poor P., 363 : 17
Pollertics of accommodatin' character, 616 : 10
Polliwogs, frogs' eggs turning into p., 878 : 17
Polluted, not p. though it passes among impure, 86 : *n* 7
shun the p. flock, 793 : 18
sun not p. by privies, 86 : 13
Pollutes whate'er it touches, 466 : 7
Pollution, no frontiers against p., 853 : 17
tide of cultural p., 903 : 13
Pollutions, sun remains pure through p., 86 : *n* 7
Polly, little P. Flinders, 932 : 4
put kettle on, 933 : 17
you might have toyed, 331 : 20
Polygamy, before p. was made a sin, 303 : 17
well held in dread, 461 : 18
Polyp would be conceptual, 649 : 2
Pomegranate, from Browning some P., 506 : 14
sweet p. wine, 4 : 12
Pomegranates, land of p., 11 : 14
Pomp and circumstance, 231 : 11
and feast and revelry, 278 : 6
and glory of this world, 249 : 3
and pride, 671 : 12
blot out p. check impulse, 125 : 17
bright p. ascended, 287 : 1
came in slow p., 469 : 3
happiness enemy to p., 326 : 10
in lowly p. ride on, 465 : 3
lick absurd p., 222 : 4
lintel low to keep out p., 671 : 12
lo p. of yesterday, 709 : 18
of death, 899 : 14
of emperors ridiculous, 496 : 5
of power, 362 : 3
painted p., 210 : 23
puts all p. to flight, 335 : 5
solemnized with p. and parade, 381 : 7
sultan after sultan with p., 516 : 10
take physic p., 234 : 4
tide of p. that beats, 208 : 7
vain p. and glory, 56 : 4
what is p. rule reign, 186 : 21
Pompous in the grave, 275 : 11
no lover of p. title, 164 : 3
Pond, an old p., 314 : 7
fish have their stream and p., 796 : 13
four ducks on p., 594 : 3
love we are a small p., 904 : 5
mantle like a standing p., 198 : 1
Ponder, first p. then dare, 489 : 11
Ponderable to our touch, 714 : 11
Pondered weak and weary, 526 : 10
Pondering repose of If, 571 : 4
Ponderous, no p. axes rung, 377 : *n* 5
Pond's stillness rippled, 904 : 7
Ponds, some p. thought bottomless, 560 : 11
Pone, whar man gits corn p., 626 : 12
Poniards, she speaks p., 209 : 10
Ponies, wretched blind pit p., 732 : 16
Pons asinorum, 92 : *n* 2
Pontic, like to the P. sea, 231 : 18
Pontius Pilate, suffered under P., 55 : 2
Pony, had a little p., 933 : 16
won't stand, 927 : 11
Yankee Doodle on p., 920 : 9
Pool, dreaming p., 566 : 13

Pool (*continued*)
green mantle of standing p., 234 : 9
river lake glimmering p., 592 : 6
Pools I used to know, 691 : 11
where it offers to curiosity, 808 : 2
Poop was beaten gold, 240 : 29
Poop-poop, O bliss O p., 690 : 15
Poor agent despised, 227 : 8
alas p. Yorick, 224 : 14
and content is rich, 231 : 1
and maimed, 43 : 23
and often very lousy, 348 : 13
and unhappy brains, 230 : 17
annals of the p., 362 : 2
apt the p. to be proud, 214 : 14
as dirt don't get rhythm, 912 : 15
as Job, 205 : 26
bare forked animal, 234 : 7
beetle we tread upon, 228 : 17
being p. have only dreams, 712 : 16
benighted 'eathen, 708 : 5
better is a p. and wise child, 26 : 25
blessed are p. in spirit, 37 : 4
brains for drinking, 230 : 17
brotherhood bind rich and p., 621 : 5
but honest friends, 227 : 12
but she was honest, 924 : 10
cannot help many who are p., 890 : 8
care of the p., 309 : 1
cat i' the adage, 237 : 2
cheer p. man's heart, 430 : 22
compassion to p., 289 : 14
contents him, 337 : 6
cried Caesar wept, 216 : 19
dear God, 836 : 15
Death beats at p. man's door, 107 : 1
decent provision for p., 354 : 23
deer thou makest testament, 210 : 26
defraud not the p., 34 : 29
degenerate from ape, 830 : 12
die not p. death, 254 : 11
dog Tray, 443 : 9
exchequer of the p., 194 : 20
few save p. feel for p., 492 : 8
fools decoyed, 310 : 1
for urban p. police arrest, 908 : 6
foundest p. and keepest so, 371 : 1
freedom to rich or p., 824 : 10
get poorer, 795 : 5
gets the blame, 924 : 11
give me your tired your p., 664 : 10
give to the p., 40 : 6
giveth unto the p., 25 : 30
gout kills more rich than p., 301 : 2
grind the faces of the p., 28 : 35
grow p. staying in one place, 137 : 6
hear p. rogues talk of news, 235 : 12
heart would fain deny, 239 : 31
high and low rich and p., 419 : 4
honest exceeding p. man, 199 : 1
how p. a thing is man, 182 : 10
hungry p., 621 : 16
I am even p. in thanks, 220 : 27
I am p. and needy, 21 : 17
I am p. once more, 604 : 3
if p. whenever you can, 86 : 11
if we not make somebody p., 405 : 11
in behalf of despised p., 486 : 16
infirm weak old man, 233 : 26
intricated soul, 255 : 4
Jim Jay, 740 : 3
Kiltartan's p., 713 : 20
last I lay upon thy lips, 241 : 21
law forbids rich as well as p., 655 : 14

Poor (*continued*)
laws catch the weak and p., 63 : 2
laws grind the p., 369 : 4
lean lank face, 520 : 5
leave them for the p. and stranger, 10 : 19
little lambs lost way, 708 : 14
little one-horse town, 622 : 10
lo the p. Indian, 336 : 16
lone woman, 206 : 9
lonely and p. of old, 797 : 4
love country and be p., 340 : 7
love life p. as it is, 560 : 18
makes me p. indeed, 230 : 33
making rich not p., 336 : 3
man accustomed to small things, 881 : 7
man being down, 35 : 27
man deprived of power, 85 : 2
man get out iv Purgatory, 722 : 10
man had nothing, 13 : 19
man is Christ's stamp, 268 : 9
man poor mankind, 838 : 1
man that hangs on favors, 249 : 3
man who craves more is p., 114 : 14
many a p. man that loved, 714 : 18
many good men are p., 62 : 12
men's cottages palaces, 198 : 9
my children who are p., 889 : 7
my p. fool is hanged, 235 : 18
my wife p. wretch, 309 : 19
naked p. mangled peace, 208 : 16
naked wretches, 234 : 3
neither rich nor p., 618 : 10
no disgrace to be p., 725 : 11
no p. person be deprived, 903 : 6
none so p. to do him reverence, 216 : 21
not p. who has enough to use, 109 : 6
obliged wealthy and relieved p., 57 : *n* 8
outrage of p., 494 : 16
pagan planet of ours, 570 : 2
people know poor people, 859 : 16
pity upon the p., 24 : 26
player that struts, 240 : 4
poorer, 814 : 7
prey of rich on p., 388 : 5
problem of rich and p., 621 : 10
purses proud garments p., 189 : 2
relation irrelevant, 442 : 6
rich gifts wax p., 221 : 14
rich honesty in p. house, 213 : 3
rich rob p., 483 : 2
rob not the p., 25 : 2
rob one another, 483 : 2
scandalous and p., 315 : 16
scandals of the p., 722 : 2
shall never cease, 11 : 17
slipping out of consciousness, 908 : 5
so p. he could not keep a dog, 127 : 2
sold the p. for a pair of shoes, 33 : 19
solitary p. nasty, 264 : 17
sort of memory, 613 : 12
soul sat sighing, 232 : 8
soul the center, 246 : 4
splendid wings, 634 : 10
strength to the p., 30 : 6
that have not patience, 230 : 29
thing but mine own, 213 : *n* 1
Tom's a-cold, 234 : 12
too p. for bribe, 363 : 11
two nations the rich and p., 501 : 18
weak palsy-stricken, 476 : 14

Poor (*continued*)
what will p. robin do, 932 : 6
when anything to eat, 86 : *n* 5
whoso mocketh the p., 24 : 14
why not given to p., 45 : 16
with hunger rich and p. as one, 77 : 3
world said I, 292 : 17
wot gets blame, 924 : 11
ye have p. always, 41 : 4
Poorer, for richer for p., 56 : 9
poor p., 814 : 7
Poorest he that is in England, 264 : 11
in p. thing superfluous, 233 : 21
man in his cottage, 351 : 7
nor p. receive contentment, 255 : 5
this traverse p. take, 607 : 4
Poorhouse, glorious hours even in p., 560 : 18
over hill to p., 660 : 5
Poorly satisfy our eyes, 251 : 1
Pop goes the weasel, 922 : 1
Pope and emperor, 491 : 8
better err with P., 456 : 16
Czar Metternich Guizot, 563 : 2
pretty poem Mr. P., 319 : 3
Popery, inclines a man to P., 180 : *n* 7
Popinjay, pestered with a p., 203 : 9
Popinjays, reverences gilt p., 472 : 16
Pop'lar, dead always p., 721 : 10
Poplar, edged with p. pale, 277 : 11
Poplars showed white of leaves, 627 : 1
stand and tremble, 691 : 11
Poppet, no go my p., 870 : 5
Poppies, fume of p., 477 : 18
in Flanders p. blow, 737 : 9
pleasures like p. spread, 411 : 8
Poppy, not p. nor mandragora, 231 : 8
oblivion blindly scattereth p., 275 : 7
or a lily, 628 : 7
Populace, Barbarians Philistines P., 588 : 13
law deaf to clamors of p., 380 : 12
man to whom p. is entrusted, 57 : 15
Popular, addressing p. audiences, 88 : 15
art never try to be p., 676 : 3
characteristics of p. politician, 81 : 13
conscience, 777 : 2
custom supported by p. opinion, 688 : 13
dead always p., 721 : 10
morality, 580 : 14
power in majority of p. assembly, 382 : 4
President cannot always be p., 788 : 9
propaganda has to be p., 812 : 16
runs against p. tastes, 314 : 3
spirit and form of p. government, 398 : 3
truth not so p. as fiction, 462 : *n* 1
war will cease to be p., 674 : 20
when Fortune on our side, 110 : 29
Popularity glory's small change, 491 : 10
is a crime, 310 : 19
Populate, to govern is to p., 737 : 11
Population, hungry and squalid p., 596 : 2
unchecked increases, 417 : 3
Populations, order p. forth, 864 : 2
Populi, salus p. suprema lex, 99 : *n* 3, 134 : 25
vox p. vox Dei, 135 : 6
Populous and smoky city, 468 : 2

Populous (*continued*)
long in p. city pent, 287 : 17
lover of p. pavements, 574 : 3
Porcelain clay of humankind, 306 : 2
give children right to study p., 381 : 14
Porches of mine ears, 219 : 23
Porcupine, quills upon fretful p., 219 : 18
Pore benighted 'eathen, 708 : 5
Pores of ocean and shores, 468 : 10
Porgy and Bess, 836 : *n* 2
Pork, yes to smell p., 198 : 18
Porpentine, quills upon fretful p., 219 : 18
Porphyry font, 531 : 11
Porpoise close behind us, 612 : 7
waters of petrel and p., 807 : 24
Porridge, comfort like cold p., 247 : 25
pease p. hot, 931 : 18
spare breath to cool p., 62 : *n* 3
Porsches, my friends all drive P., 916 : 5
Porsena, Lars P. of Clusium, 488 : 13
Port after stormy seas, 173 : 12
bomb might destroy whole p., 763 : 12
liquor for men, 356 : 11
near bells I hear, 576 : 6
pride in their p., 369 : 1
quilt p. o' heaven, 700 : 8
Scylla to p., 200 : *n* 1
Portable, get hold of p. property, 549 : 27
plumbing, 816 : 12
Portal, fitful tracing of p., 767 : 10
opens to receive me, 416 : 11
we call death, 511 : 11
Portals alternate night day, 516 : 10
errors p. of discovery, 778 : 3
fragrant p. dimly starred, 767 : 16
of church and school, 737 : 5
Portas, Hannibal ad p., 134 : 5
Portent of fate of Nazi tyranny, 745 : 4
of new atomic age, 729 : 12
Portentous phrase I told you so, 462 : 1
sight, 435 : 16
Porter, all p. and skittles, 546 : 27
Mrs. P. in the spring, 805 : 6
Portion, best p. of man's life, 423 : 9
brief life our p., 563 : 12
dedicate p. of field, 523 : 4
equal p. for who lingers, 58 : 9
he wales a p., 408 : 17
no p. in us after, 721 : 7
of that around me, 457 : 28
worst p. in this life, 874 : 21
Portions and parcels of past, 528 : 17
Portrait, Hero of Our Time a p., 553 : 1
manners mirror which shows p., 397 : 9
man's work p. of himself, 620 : 10
no man loth to sit for p., 736 : 6
of person one knows, 395 : 20
of vices of generation, 553 : 1
person portrayed and p., 784 : 23
two styles of p. painting, 547 : 9
Portray, it is myself I p., 164 : 5
Portrayed, person p. and portrait, 784 : 23
Ports and happy havens, 194 : 5
of slumber open, 206 : 29
Portugal, like bay of P., 212 : 26
Posies, thousand fragrant p., 183 : 10
Position, in highest p. least freedom, 102 : 27
not a good p. I'm in, 884 : 11
not certain of own p., 755 : 4
Positive economics can be objective, 880 : 7
endeavors to preserve peace, 780 : 4
power of p. thinking, 842 : 13
Possess, find lose but never p., 863 : 3
general knowledges idiots p., 405 : 16
heart fall in love, 734 : 2
let us p. one world, 251 : 15
only who strive mightily p., 728 : 8
right to p. property, 537 : 3
soul with patience, 305 : 28
souls in patience, 44 : 1
that they p. they scatter, 189 : 18
them not with fear, 208 : 8
things rank and gross p. it, 218 : 6
to have little is to p., 64 : 10
Possessed, I die but have p., 459 : 4
object p., 600 : 24
of no value p., 316 : 15
regain love once p., 289 : 3
rich p. by money, 258 : 22
two evils p. me, 810 : 17
Webster p. by death, 804 : 21
Possesses, he is above everything he p., 343 : 12
more he gives more he p., 65 : 10
virtue in abundance, 64 : 18
who p. learn to lose, 413 : 29
Possessing, acquiring and p. property, 367 : 4
for thy sure p., 513 : 5
having nothing p. all, 49 : 17
heart of woman, 734 : 2
too dear for my p., 245 : 1
Possession, best p. is sympathetic wife, 77 : 17
cheapens, 631 : 18
composed to be everlasting p., 80 : 15
eleven points in law, 324 : 25
fie on p., 147 : 28
housed where it gets p., 188 : 8
implies duty, 752 : 3
loads us with weariness, 573 : 8
loss and p., 730 : 2
love of money as p., 783 : 10
mad in pursuit and in p., 245 : 23
object in p. seldom retains charm, 123 : 8
of truth as of a city, 274 : 2
one p. outvalues others, 625 : 15
prevents living freely, 738 : 2
put him in p. of truth, 307 : 15
take intellectual p., 653 : 17
use of riches better than p., 153 : 12
virtue that p. would not show, 209 : 31
without obligation, 600 : 24
Possessions, covetous of others' p., 102 : 23
give of p. give little, 782 : 16
his p. are deathless, 59 : 24
jealous p. of happiness, 727 : 7
take away liberty, 704 : 5
Possibilities, automation has unbounded p., 831 : 23
believe only p., 274 : 14
land of unlimited p. 662 : 4
minds finite p. infinite, 698 : 1
seven hundred pounds and p., 225 : 7
Possibility, even p. can transform us, 658 : 19
Possibility (*continued*)
preferable to unconvincing p., 88 : 19
State have p. of life, 84 : 15
Possible, anything p. except fair play, 640 : 12
best of all p. worlds, 762 : 10
best of p. worlds, 343 : 8
Christ that it were p., 533 : 26
Father if it be p., 41 : 12
made last step p., 762 : 5
make p. things not so held, 246 : 12
no p. doubt whatever, 630 : 3
O God that it were p., 257 : 17
politics art of p., 553 : *n* 3
shadow of doubt, 630 : 3
thing humanly p. is within reach, 125 : 7
to fail in many ways, 87 : 17
you may be mistaken, 272 : 18
Post o'er land and ocean, 282 : 17
offices and cabinet appointments, 520 : *n* 3
Post equitem sedet atra cura, 107 : *n* 22
hoc ergo propter hoc, 134 : 18
Posteriors of this day, 191 : 8
Posterity bear witness to his mind, 418 : 5
Constitution for p., 444 : 7
contemplate forefathers and p., 365 : 3
deprive or divest p., 367 : 4
do something for us, 327 : 4
evoke one's p., 828 : 8
look forward to p., 373 : 20
of work of art, 734 : 3
of yet unborn, 326 : 16
ourselves and our p., 391 : 10
owe it to p., 390 : 13
plant tree for p., 95 : *n* 10
say of Washington, 348 : 10
think of p., 123 : 4
to be without p., 89 : *n* 2
to have no p., 89 : 13
to p. world without end, 378 : 1
unlimited undefined, 444 : 7
weaves no garlands, 413 : 4
when we are planning for p., 384 : 11
Postern, when present latched p., 642 : 3
Posthumously, some born p., 658 : 25
Posting, breath rides on p. winds, 243 : 21
Postponed power, 644 : 1
Posts, up men to your p., 596 : 12
Postulations, two simultaneous p., 581 : 7
Postumus, alas P. fleeting years slip by, 107 : 23
Posture of a whore, 241 : 27
Posy, stoop pluck p., 545 : 23
Pot calls kettle black, 170 : 36
chicken in p. every Sunday, 174 : 25
crackling of thorns under a p., 27 : 5
death in the p., 14 : 15
fame for p. of ale, 207 : 19
go to p., 371 : 25
greasy Joan doth keel p., 191 : 14
kettle and earthen p., 35 : 25
little p. and soon hot, 188 : 36
maketh the deep boil like a p., 17 : 7
melting p., 706 : 15
nor for every thirst to p., 269 : 28
nuffin' in de p., 737 : 2
of paint in public's face, 619 : *n* 1

Pot (*continued*)
pease-porridge in p., 931 : 18
put on p. says Greedy-gut, 931 : 6
who is potter who p., 517 : 9
Potable gold, 259 : 15
Potations pottle deep, 230 : 18
Potatoes, small p., 603 : 12
Potency, presuming on changeful p., 227 : 1
symbol of surging p., 790 : 19
Potent, government p. teacher, 678 : 1
how p. cheap music is, 843 : 10
make p. more powerful, 419 : 3
poet p. figure, 769 : 14
Potentates blazing in the heavens, 71 : 3
Potential, circle of p. being, 648 : 3
short p. stir, 607 : 8
Potentialities, gamut of human p., 853 : 15
Potions, what p. have I drunk, 245 : 19
Potiphar's wife, 8 : 30
Potius sero quam numquam, 110 : *n* 7
Potomac, all quiet along P., 598 : 10
Army of the P., 522 : 4
Pots, take size of p. of ale, 290 : 21
Potsherd, Jack joke poor p., 656 : 21
Pottage, gave Esau bread and p., 8 : 16
kept breath to cool his p., 62 : 5
Potter bears grudge against potter, 61 : 13
did hand of p. shake, 517 : 8
hath not p. power, 47 : 16
thumping his wet clay, 516 : 20
who is p. who pot, 517 : 9
Potter's field, 41 : 19
Potters' fields of four continents, 571 : 3
Pottle, potations p. deep, 230 : 18
Pouch, with p. on side, 211 : 15
Poultice, silence like p., 518 : 13
Pounces unerringly on human core, 651 : 2
Pouncet box, 203 : 7
Pound, cannot live on twenty p., 268 : 6
in for penny in for p., 629 : 2
penny wise p. foolish, 258 : 10
right half the time, 845 : 6
Shallow I owe thousand p., 206 : 37
Pounding of old piano, 711 : 7
Pounds, crowns p. and guineas, 690 : 20
for life six hundred p., 339 : 10
handsome in three hundred p., 225 : 21
rich with forty p. a year, 370 : 5
seven hundred p. and possibilities, 225 : 7
seven p. tenpence a man, 371 : 26
take care of themselves, 341 : 21
two hundred p. a year, 291 : 27
Pour, cicadas p. out their piping voices, 57 : 23
millions like us and will p., 516 : 21
sweet milk of concord, 239 : 19
waters of Nile, 611 : 5
Poured, best yuh ever p. yuh, 840 : 1
forth unpremeditated strain, 345 : 21
through mellow horn, 364 : 14
Pourest thy full heart, 468 : 11
Pouring forth soul abroad, 476 : 28
more noise they make p. out, 340 : 11
Pours among stormy Hebrides, 345 : 15
Poverty a weary thing, 485 : 24
all men know p., 724 : 16
anarchy of p., 785 : 13

Poverty (*continued*)
anticipate charity by preventing p., 137 : 10
better is p. in hand of god, 6 : 6
bitter p. makes men ridiculous, 122 : 5
blindness about p., 908 : 5
boredom keynote of p., 859 : 15
brings greatest distress, 313 : 4
but not my will consents, 193 : 21
change evil death, 769 : 25
China suffering from p., 719 : 10
come as one that traveleth, 23 : 12
comes in door, 919 : 11
degradation not to overcome p., 81 : 1
drink and forget p., 26 : 5
drove me to verses, 109 : 15
drunkard and glutton come to p., 25 : 9
golden mean avoids p., 107 : 20
greatest of evils, 680 : 28
humble and sweet p., 899 : 16
I pay thy p. not thy will, 193 : 21
irremediable p. of life, 769 : 25
is great reality, 858 : 7
is no sin, 270 : 17
keeps homes together, 731 : 15
knows how to endure p., 108 : 14
less work more p., 602 : 13
neither p. nor riches, 26 : 1
no disgrace to acknowledge p., 81 : 1
of the incapable, 579 : 7
oppressed with pride and p., 315 : 17
Panama with its p., 481 : 2
parent of meanness, 84 : 12
parts good company, 432 : 8
qualities thwarted by p., 122 : 6
reproach to government, 314 : 12
rich in p., 171 : 13
riches p. and use of service, 247 : 26
rising from affluence to p., 624 : 7
sister of beggary, 82 : 24
soft pedal on activity, 771 : 16
some because of p., 872 : 10
stepmother of genius, 561 : 18
the America of p., 908 : 5
the greatest p., 768 : 5
to the very lips, 232 : 2
tyranny p. disease war, 890 : 11
view age of p., 200 : 15
we live in ambitious p., 122 : 7
where p. and joy, 138 : 14
where p. enforced, 556 : 14
with us p. a crime, 493 : 3
worth by p. depressed, 351 : 9
Poverty's catching, 312 : 15
Pow, blessings on your frosty p., 410 : 7
Powder, keep p. dry, 444 : 12
Powder's runnin' low, 700 : 8
Power a trust, 501 : 6
absolute p. corrupts absolutely, 615 : 15
absolute p. in majority, 382 : 4
absolute p. over wives, 392 : 9
accord women equal p., 578 : 6
action nor p. of speech, 216 : 28
adjudication in terms of p., 790 : 4
and beauty of lyre, 733 : 9
and light, 902 : 2
and publicity, 634 : 23
and the glory, 14 : 25
arrogance of p., 863 : 1
balance of p., 328 : 20, 682 : 8, 902 : 11
beauty hath strange p., 289 : 3
believe source of p. is sky, 151 : 5

Power (*continued*)
black p., 914 : *n* 2, 914 : 15
by Thy p. no foot slide, 924 : 15
certainty of p., 860 : 7
commitments and p. balance, 813 : 11
community of p., 682 : 8
corridors of p., 865 : 19
corrupts poetry cleanses, 891 : 16
critical p. creative p., 586 : 20
deep p. of joy, 423 : 11
desire of p. in excess, 180 : 14
destroy p. of reasoning, 85 : 13
disjoins remorse from p., 215 : 15
don't say in p. what say in opposition, 723 : 8
earthly p. then likest God's, 200 : 9
educator wielder of p., 879 : 4
effect of p. on men, 634 : 23
empire p. in trust, 304 : 7
encroachments of those in p., 398 : 4
everything includes itself in p., 226 : 3
extent of beauty and p., 487 : 14
eye made quiet by p., 423 : 11
fate in own p., 489 : 12
fewer laws less p., 498 : 7
force from which sun draws p., 787 : 13
force of temporal p., 200 : 9
forces of lust for p., 779 : 20
friend in p. friend lost, 634 : 22
from the people, 501 : 6
good want p., 466 : 17
goodness armed with p., 823 : 16
great P. make me think true, 595 : 16
greater than people, 449 : 9
hardly in a body's p., 409 : 4
hath not potter p., 47 : 16
have joy or p., 495 : 23
have seen the wicked in great p., 18 : 26
hope of pride and p., 525 : 4
human p. cannot remove, 808 : 15
if women submit to p., 414 : 8
imagination reconciling p., 436 : 20
immensity of first p., 417 : 3
in defense of freedom, 904 : 17
in government sovereign, 401 : 17
in hands of friends, 635 : 16
in mysteries of thought, 76 : 12
in p. of no calamity, 657 : *n* 7
in p. unpleased, 303 : 20
in spite of variety and p., 586 : 8
in struggle for p., 556 : 1
includes right to means, 401 : 17
individual liberty individual p., 418 : 3
influence of sea p., 642 : 8
into will, 226 : 3
Jove for his p. to thunder, 242 : 20
judicial p. distinct from legislative, 381 : 11
just cause overwhelming p., 689 : 1
knowledge but no p., 78 : 21
knowledge is p., 178 : 17, 891 : 6
knowledge money p., 887 : 8
laugh to scorn p. of man, 239 : 10
lay down reins of p., 524 : 3
lead life to p., 528 : 5
lies in mind and body, 102 : 21
like pestilence pollutes, 466 : 7
living p. prime agent, 437 : 11
love of p. love of selves, 445 : 15
love without p. destroyed, 823 : 16
man wrested p. from nature, 851 : 15

Power (*continued*)
massive retaliatory p., 803 : 7
metaphor fertile p., 784 : 25
millionaire has, 844 : 4
misplaced p., 815 : 15
monuments of wit survive monuments of p., 178 : 16
more real than commands army, 644 : 1
most p. least liberty, 303 : 2
Music's p. obey, 305 : 9
my fanatical will p., 812 : 19
nations that have sea p. have freedom, 800 : 6
nations with great p., 763 : 13
no one fit to be trusted with p., 865 : 18
no war won without sea p., 800 : 11
nonviolence paralyzed p. structures, 909 : 16
not by might nor by p., 33 : 30
not now in fortune's p., 291 : 13
obtained by weakness, 414 : 11
of beauty I remember yet, 307 : 5
of fright and lust, 833 : 6
of grace, 443 : 6
of making laws, 401 : 15
of man and moment, 586 : 19
of one fair face, 155 : 1
of positive thinking, 842 : 13
of public plunder, 449 : *n* 3
of surplus in banks, 449 : 9
of sustaining and delighting, 589 : 11
of the atom, 764 : 3
of visible is invisible, 799 : 3
of world works in circles, 701 : 8
only prize of powerful p., 644 : 15
over the clay, 47 : 16
passing from the earth, 428 : 5
poesy supreme of p., 475 : 12
police p., 687 : 10
political p. out of barrel of gun, 826 : 7
politics law of jungle, 818 : 6
politics obstruct peace, 781 : 4
pomp of p., 362 : 3
possesses the genuine p., 437 : 1
preeminence and p., 398 : 2
pride of p. sink, 372 : 15
proud Edward's p., 411 : 15
public life situation of p., 372 : 7
ransom them from the p. of the grave, 33 : 16
rapture of postponed p., 644 : 1
rather in p. than use, 227 : 9
relentless p., 361 : 13
rich have p. and poor deprived, 85 : 2
riches and p. gifts of fate, 136 : 14
right hand is glorious in p., 9 : 34
rise of misplaced p., 815 : 15
same in all countries, 444 : 4
science increases p., 552 : 2
sea p. never led to despotism, 800 : 6
seals of p. and place, 418 : 8
shadow of love, 755 : 2
shadow of unseen P., 466 : 8
some p. giftie gie us, 409 : 8
sorrow hath less p. to bite, 194 : 6
spare thee past my p., 409 : 9
spirit of p., 51 : 6
star revolve by invisible p., 571 : 5
surpassed others but had no more p., 110 : 9
symbol of p. of Heaven, 799 : 14

Power (*continued*)
symbol of p. of movement, 790 : 19
take who have the p., 426 : 7
tends to corrupt, 615 : 15
the great aphrodisiac, 902 : 9
thine is the p., 37 : 15
thought because we had p., 840 : 9
titles p. and pelf, 430 : 10
to add or detract, 523 : 4
to be silent, 308 : 10
to build black institutions, 914 : *n* 2
to cancel his captivity, 215 : 13
to chasten and subdue, 423 : 13
to declare Act of Congress void, 644 : 17
to do me ill, 249 : *n* 4
to drink or rise, 455 : 1
to hurt and will do none, 245 : 4
to know all things, 251 : 6
to live and act, 429 : 1
to say Behold, 195 : 23
to tax not power to destroy, 645 : 9
to tax power to destroy, 402 : 7
to undo the past, 82 : 27
to which Rome not compared, 451 : 2
transfiguring p., 658 : 14
trust no man with p. to endanger liberty 380 : 13
twilight of p., 852 : 1
unemployed purchasing p., 811 : 10
unlimited p. corrupt, 351 : 1
unlimited p. into hands of husbands, 392 : 7
unrestrained military p., 800 : 6
upon the past has p., 305 : 2
villains in p., 382 : 11
waits upon him who earns it, 631 : 5
we here hold the p., 522 : 12
weird p. in spoken word, 683 : 7
what p. divine, 436 : 13
whence come thy lasting p., 636 : 10
where love rules no will to p., 755 : 2
where p. predominates love lacking, 755 : 2
which men call Chance, 279 : 28
while death in our p., 657 : *n* 7
who has purse has p., 553 : 12
wielded by abnormal energy, 635 : 15
will and p., 226 : 3
will to p., 659 : 3
wisdom goodness, 319 : 22
witch hath p. to charm, 217 : 26
with p. and glory, 44 : 2
without abusing it, 488 : 18
witty beauty a p., 601 : 4
Powerful amidst peers, 656 : 8
black p., 855 : 3
boy is most p. of Hellenes, 70 : 15
from walls of p. house, 576 : 18
goodness want, 466 : 17
has power over self, 157 : *n* 13
humblest peer of most p., 615 : 1
impulse to punish p., 657 : 15
make potent more p., 419 : 3
nation which enjoys most freedom most p., 418 : 3
only prize of p. power, 644 : 15
oppressed and p. Russia, 584 : 3
outlive this p. rhyme, 244 : 18
overflow of p. feelings, 424 : 9
sisterhood is p., 915 : 8
word of God is p., 51 : 14
Powerless to be born, 586 : 10

Powerlessness, to have no cash means p., 504 : 14
Powers, against principalities and p., 49 : 39
colonizations by European p., 408 : 1
cultivation of her p., 471 : 1
deem that there are p., 423 : 5
deny us for our good, 240 : 26
depository of ultimate p., 389 : 15
desires dreams and p., 633 : 20
draw p. into higher classes, 390 : 2
equal to tasks, 619 : 18
evils avoided p. exercised, 121 : 13
fear of divine and supreme p., 259 : 24
in touch with unseen p., 686 : 8
just p. from consent, 387 : 9, 725 : 20
knows ye not Heavenly P., 395 : 2
lay waste our p., 427 : 29
merciful p., 237 : 11
never two continental p., 812 : 18
of augury, 57 : 20
of combination, 374 : 10
Princedoms Virtues P., 286 : 22
principalities nor p. 47 : 15
scorn not your p., 115 : 19
specified p., 402 : 1
superior to man, 673 : 2
tempt frailty of our p., 227 : 1
that be, 47 : 26
vacant p., 813 : 14
wars of European p., 408 : 2
Pox, die on gallows or of p., 368 : 4
Practical men absorbed in facts, 697 : 6
men usually slaves, 783 : 16
politics, 517 : 21
politics ignoring facts, 635 : 13
Practice and thought forge art, 103 : 28
best of instructors, 111 : 11
by p. get to be wide apart, 69 : 18
childish ways, 59 : 17
Christian forbearance, 383 : 6
constituted for p. of good, 89 : 19
doctrine or p. or interpretation, 125 : 13
drives me mad, 917 : 13
five things, 69 : 19
good p. to verify references, 402 : 9
helping men p. virtue, 89 : 2
humility all preach none p., 263 : 14
in heaven, 542 : 5
is everything, 111 : *n* 8
little proceed to greater, 121 : 6
lived in p. of every virtue, 81 : 9
makes perfect, 111 : *n* 8
prudence never to p. either, 625 : 9
success in p., 640 : 7
they diligently p. Tao, 64 : 14
this without me, 399 : 10
to deceive, 431 : 1
what you would make habitual, 121 : 15
what you preach, 94 : 6, 127 : 21
world of p., 586 : 21
Practicer, frequent p. of angling, 270 : 34
Practices, fair p. to fair notions, 83 : 9
of American people, 862 : 19
who p. virtue will have neighbors, 68 : 18
Practitioner in panegyric, 399 : 7
Praetors, our consuls and our p., 701 : 15
Praevalet, magna est veritas et p., 34 : *n* 2

Pragmatic method attitude of orientation, 650 : 8
Prague, as old hermit of P. said, 214 : 27
Prairie, bury me not on lone p., 927 : 16, 927 : 16
bury me out on p., 927 : 17
last night as I lay on p., 927 : 13
lawyer master of all, 765 : 8
lone p. where coyotes howl, 927 : 16
to make a p., 608 : 3
Prairies for which speech no name, 471 : 11
from mountains to p., 802 : 10
wide-rolling watery p., 571 : 3
Praise a little more, 774 : 5
ask criticism want p., 751 : 10
at morning blame at night, 333 : 14
be to God, 130 : 9
best diet for us, 433 : 4
boldness certain to win p., 112 : 22
book people p. don't read, 625 : 10
bury Caesar not p. him, 216 : 17
damn with faint p., 338 : 14
dispraised no small p., 288 : 9
famous men, 36 : 10
for being and happening, 869 : 11
forced p. on our part, 541 : 9
forms no part of beauty, 124 : 18
from Sir Hubert Stanley, 416 : 9
garment of p., 31 : 25
girded with p., 445 : 21
God from whom all blessings flow, 311 : 19
guests p. it not cooks, 181 : 22
he fathers-forth p. him, 656 : 5
her own works p. her, 26 : 10
him and exalt him, 36 : 14
I p. the Frenchman, 376 : 11
if there be any p., 50 : 7
in country you p. city, 106 : 22
in deeper reverence p., 514 : 1
in p. of ladies dead, 245 : 12
into his courts with p., 21 : 3
kind of strife man might p., 61 : 12
lamentation and p., 869 : 5
laurel crown yield to p., 98 : 27
let another man p. thee, 25 : 22
let every thing p. the Lord, 22 : 25
lived without disgrace without p., 140 : 16
Lord pass ammunition, 871 : 2
love of p., 329 : 19
low ambition and thirst of p., 375 : 21
maid whom none to p., 424 : 12
my mouth shall show forth thy p., 19 : 18
named thee but to p., 464 : 11
never p. sister to sister, 707 : 8
nor blame the writings, 333 : 12
nourish agues, 204 : 33
of ancient authors, 264 : 19
only to be praised, 293 : 23
or blame momentary, 479 : 13
or blame too far, 749 : 14
pleased to p., 333 : 22
poets lose half the p., 276 : 11
praise praise for death, 576 : 5
prayer and p., 428 : 10
right p. and true perfection, 201 : 5
sacrament of p., 767 : 11
say more than this rich p., 244 : 29
scarce could p., 351 : 11
sea on shore remain, 174 : 24
see how man receives p., 114 : 23
Praise (*continued*)
sent us back to p., 305 : 29
shall sanctify our rest, 597 : 17
silence muse His p., 345 : 16
sing thee a song in thy p., 410 : 13
solid pudding empty p., 340 : 15
still pleased to p., 333 : 22
swells note of p., 362 : 4
that will never die, 81 : 5
thirst of p., 375 : 21
those who follow other paths, 106 : 10
those who spoke her p., 368 : 7
to give, 256 : 11
to glory of life, 801 : 7
verses but read something else, 119 : 8
virtues men p. and pass by, 791 : 13
we p. thee for perspicuity of language, 136 : 6
we p. thee O God, 54 : 19
we scarcely can p. it, 371 : 14
what is p. or pride, 900 : 1
your p. not worth dying for, 119 : 13
Praise-all, Blame-all and P. blockheads, 347 : 5
Praised be fathomless universe, 576 : 5
honesty is p. and starves, 121 : 23
Lord's name is to be p., 21 : 20
praise only to be p., 293 : 23
the dead already dead, 26 : 22
woman that feareth the Lord shall be p., 26 : 10
Praiser of past time, 109 : 28
Praises, earth with voices p. God, 435 : 23
everybody praises nobody, 385 : 16
faintly then he p., 338 : *n* 9
might be reported, 36 : 11
sing p. to his Name, 918 : 19
so long shall your p. endure, 104 : 29
with enthusiastic tone, 629 : 7
Praising, advantage of p. oneself, 620 : 12
lean and sallow abstinence, 279 : 30
most dispraises, 338 : *n* 9
what is lost, 227 : 20
Prances, far back in soul horse p., 790 : 19
Prancing poetry, 607 : 4
Prate, hear him p., 601 : 9
stones p. of whereabout, 237 : 15
Prates, all she p. has nothing in it, 322 : 16
Prattle, nor do children p. about his knees, 57 : 29
thinking his p. tedious, 195 : 15
Praxed, Saint P. in a glory, 541 : 19
Praxiteles unable to reach all the material, 125 : 24
Pray, after this manner p. ye, 37 : 15
all p. in their distress, 403 : 10
as if to die tomorrow, 347 : 31
can't p. a lie, 624 : 4
farmers p. that summers be wet, 103 : 27
for me and come not, 184 : 6
for no man but myself, 243 : 1
for them which despitefully use you, 37 : 11
for wisdom yet, 597 : 1
God absolve us all, 150 : 10
God to keep me from being proud, 309 : 12
goes to bed and does not p., 268 : 18
Pray (*continued*)
heaven holds place for those who p., 915 : 14
how they p. for death, 76 : 5
I p. you in your letters, 232 : 20
in distress and need, 782 : 18
in fullness of joy, 782 : 18
late and early p., 250 : 15
Lord soul to keep, 320 : 12
make able to pay for it, 309 : 13
make no mistake, 629 : 9
never learned to p., 864 : 9
one to watch one to p., 294 : 16
place men can p., 742 : 15
remained to p., 370 : 8
so we'll live p. sing, 235 : 12
that love may never come, 76 : 22
that the way be long, 702 : 4
to be stronger, 619 : 18
to praise who came to p., 305 : 29
to p. is to work, 134 : 14
two went to p., 292 : 6
watch and p., 41 : 13
we do p. for mercy, 200 : 9
will not p. with you, 198 : 18
without ceasing, 50 : 21
work and p. live on hay, 764 : 13
you now forget, 235 : 10
you undo this button, 235 : 18
Prayable, barely p. prayer, 808 : 4
Prayed, caught God's skirts p., 540 : 31
of course I p., 605 : 7
to genius of the place, 105 : 27
Prayer and praise, 428 : 10
barely prayable p., 808 : 4
be sure p. will be granted, 661 : 2
Christ's progress and His p. time, 298 : 21
comes round again, 717 : 3
effectual fervent p., 52 : 6
every p. reduces to this, 564 : 8
fool there was made p., 709 : 14
for all who lie beneath, 710 : 15
for S.T.C., 438 : 9
four spend in p., 172 : 6
from heart's deep core, 736 : 23
God erects house of p., 318 : 5
grant before conclude p., 305 : 29
indeed good, 80 : 13
laughter beginning of p., 823 : 19
more wrought by p., 535 : 1
my house a house of p., 40 : 12
never made but one p., 343 : 25
of hawk not get chicken, 926 : 5
of the one Annunciation, 808 : 4
rises better p. answered, 600 : 9
same p. doth teach us all, 200 : 9
soul's sincere desire, 429 : 18
the people's p., 304 : 5
which rises from heart in grace, 141 : 22
Wing and P., 866 : 5
Prayerbooks, beads and p., 337 : 7
Prayers, among p. a piece of land, 106 : 20
angry p., 732 : 16
are daughters of Zeus, 58 : 11
fall to thy p., 206 : 36
for a pretense make p., 42 : 12
God answers sharp some p., 507 : 18
hate enough to hear your p., 66 : *n* 8
make of your p. one sacrifice, 248 : 25
mention of thee in my p., 51 : 12
profit by losing our p., 240 : 26

Prayers (*continued*)
to preserve travel, 323 : 17
to punish they answer p., 66 : *n* 8
which are age his alms, 177 : 9
whose p. make me whole, 707 : 19
wouldn't say p., 931 : 8
Prayeth best who loveth best, 435 : 11
well who loveth well, 435 : 10
Praying, now he is p., 222 : 26
Prays, thus the suppliant p., 351 : 20
Preach gospel to every creature, 42 : 16
humility a virtue all p., 263 : 14
practice what you p., 94 : 6, 127 : 21
preached as never p. again, 294 : 17
Preached as never to preach again, 294 : 17
I have p. the truth, 72 : 19
law that I have p., 73 : 1
up patience, 320 : 19
Preacher, I remember I heard p., 575 : 23
vanity of vanities saith the P., 26 : 11
Preachers, deliver from phlegmatic p., 392 : 10
say Do as I say, 264 : 6
Preaches contentment to toad, 707 : 5
nature teaches more than p., 631 : 3
well that lives well, 170 : 19
Preaching down daughter's heart, 529 : 22
silent church better than p., 497 : 5
woman p., 354 : 15
word for dull conversation, 432 : 19
Preamble, beauty and cogency of p., 800 : 8
Precarious living, 924 : 5
Precautions against disease of writing, 136 : 8
Precedence, England not forget p., 281 : 17
Precedent embalms principle, 502 : 1
not unsettled overnight, 730 : 14
one p. creates another, 390 : 10
solitary p. not conclusive, 444 : 5
supported by precedents will become p., 122 : 22
without p. and imitator, 359 : 2
Precedents accumulate become law, 390 : 10
accumulation of old p., 813 : 10
established by wise, 444 : 5
supported by p. will become precedent, 122 : 22
Preceding, pang p. death, 368 : 11
Precept, example more efficacious than p., 352 : 19
first p. never to accept thing as true, 272 : 8
must be upon precept, 30 : 13
no humbling of reality to p., 905 : 11
poetry not by p., 479 : 14
true business p., 547 : 33
Precepts backed by authority, 679 : 1
'Preciate things left behind, 774 : 4
Precincts, warm p. of cheerful day, 362 : 14
Preciosity or euphuism, 730 : 15
Precious, adds p. seeing to the eye, 191 : 3
all things from friends, 92 : 16
bane, 284 : 1
bearing p. seed, 22 : 7
better than p. ointment, 27 : 3
box of p. ointment, 41 : 2
Precious (*continued*)
days spend with you, 802 : 3
Europe a p. graveyard, 582 : 2
gift though small is p., 60 : 1
glory p. forever, 77 : 9
good name like p. ointment, 180 : 11
half so p. as they sell, 517 : 11
husbandman waiteth for p. fruit, 52 : 4
in the sight of the Lord, 21 : 24
jewel in his head, 210 : 24
liberty p., 731 : 8
make vile things p., 233 : 30
more p. than rubies, 16 : *n* 2
most p. thing, 359 : 1
no quality more p. has mankind, 702 : 6
nothing so p. as time, 91 : *n* 9
ointment, 41 : 2
possession cheapens p., 631 : 18
stone set in silver sea, 194 : 13
things most p. to me, 239 : 22
truth is p. and divine, 291 : 21
unspeakably p. things, 625 : 9
virtue like p. odors, 180 : 8
Preciousness, miles away in p., 648 : 2
Precipice, close to edge of p., 835 : 15
Precise, art too p. in every part, 266 : 7
silken terms p., 191 : 9
Precisely, thinking too p. on event, 223 : 18
Precision, numerical p. soul of science, 696 : 4
Precocity, for p. price demanded, 536 : 11
to laugh a miracle of p., 116 : 8
Preconceived, waiting in vain for p., 654 : 13
Predatory human hands, 690 : 10
Predecessor, illustrious p., 350 : *n* 1
Predecessors, illustrious p., 350 : 4
scientist takes off from p., 762 : 5
Predestinate, he also did p., 47 : 11
Predestined elect thinned down, 622 : 13
from all eternity, 602 : 3
intimates p., 635 : 3
what fate p., 420 : 20
Predict, economics p. consequences of changes, 880 : 9
phenomena, 472 : 1
Prediction, rage when p. went awry, 862 : 8
Predicts ruin of the state, 406 : 10
Predilection, between p. and love, 641 : 2
I have p. for painting, 646 : 8
Predominance, teachers by spherical p., 233 : 5
Preeminence, contending for p., 398 : 2
Preeminent, to be bravest and p., 58 : 2
Pre-existing, cells from p. cells, 584 : *n* 2
Prefer geniality to grammar, 685 : 13
gentlemen p. blondes, 826 : 3
mind or body to p., 337 : 2
Preferable, most p. of evils, 58 : 28
Preference, disposed to one another by p., 124 : 4
systems of p. or restraint, 366 : 8
Preferment, riches and p., 391 : 9
Preferreth all countries before his own, 262 : 13
Prefigure, signs should p. events, 98 : 21
Pregnant, actor p. with part, 704 : 14
Pregnant (*continued*)
hinges of the knee, 222 : 4
Prejudice against color, 554 : 6
emancipation of woman from p., 842 : *n* 5
fought against p., 788 : 12
freedom from p., 589 : 6
in favor of two eyes, 547 : 7
not adjust to p., 898 : 6
ran against a p., 695 : 16
skilled appeals to p., 596 : 11
that cut off view, 695 : 16
this pretension itself p., 655 : 6
unconscious p., 825 : 13
vagrant opinion, 647 : 16
Prejudices, beliefs and p. of past, 719 : 16
bombs shook men out of p., 719 : 16
man without p., 655 : 6
never too late to give up p., 559 : 6
of true Englishman, 326 : 22
overcome and conquer p., 666 : 22
traced back to intestines, 659 : 1
we keep old p., 650 : 10
Prelate, religion without p., 484 : *n* 6
Preluded melodious bursts, 528 : 21
Preludes, life succession of p., 464 : 17
Premature arrival of future, 909 : *n* 1
Premise, articulate major p., 644 : 11
Premises, insufficient p., 620 : 16
Prent, faith he'll p. it, 410 : 20
Prentice hand she tried on man, 409 : 15
Preoccupation, constant p. with money, 859 : 17
with possession, 738 : 2
Preordained, whatever may befall was p., 125 : 19
Preparation, dreadful note of p., 208 : 1
Prepare asylum for mankind, 384 : 12
every heart p. room, 328 : 13
good God p. me, 310 : 17
I go to p. a place, 45 : 20
shocks of passion p., 428 : 23
the way before me, 33 : 37
thrifty to p. today, 66 : 11
to shed them now, 216 : 22
way of the Lord, 30 : 30, 36 : 26
who desires peace p. for war, 128 : 25
Prepared for rage, 748 : 11
for war, 379 : 9
holy city p. as bride, 53 : 29
to extend freedom, 824 : 10
Preparest, thou p. a table before me, 18 : 7
Preponderant sea power, 800 : 11
Prerogative, first is law the last p., 305 : 18
Près de l' église loin de Dieu, 159 : *n* 10
Presage, mock their own p., 245 : 13
Presbyterian in hell, 626 : 8
true blue, 291 : 3
Prescribe orthodox, 821 : 6
Presence, absence involves p., 906 : 14
come before his p. with singing, 21 : 3
equal in p. of death, 110 : 14
flee from thy p., 22 : 17
how many ships my p. worth, 88 : 25
minds made better by p., 564 : 22
of body in question, 442 : 11
of mind, 96 : 19
of mind in danger, 308 : 15
of mind in emergencies, 568 : 17
of mine enemies, 18 : 7

Presence (*continued*)
scanter of your maiden p., 219 : 7
that disturbs me, 423 : 13
'tis my p. that doth trouble, 185 : 9
world force not p., 770 : 2
Present, a very p. help in trouble, 19 : 10
absent in body p. in spirit, 48 : 8
arrest p. moment, 649 : 3
at your funeral, 830 : *n* 2
clear and p. danger, 644 : 23
contains past, 688 : 9
evils triumph, 293 : 3
except the p. company, 394 : 7
extolling past at expense of p., 433 : 16
falls away, 875 : 2
fears less than imaginings, 236 : 11
Ghost of Christmas P., 548 : 9
gone in becoming, 649 : 3
happiness in p. hour, 479 : 4
house for future prison for p., 886 : 3
in p. light flames, 745 : 8
in time future, 807 : 1
is all thou hast, 513 : 5
is thine, 510 : 2
it is p. that matters, 828 : 8
joys more to flesh and blood, 305 : 25
latched its postern, 642 : 3
mirth hath present laughter, 213 : 23
morose view of p., 489 : 4
no time like the p., 319 : 21
Past Future sees, 405 : 1
previous benefaction or p. satisfaction, 79 : 16
quarrel between past and p., 744 : 3
quiet past stormy p., 522 : 12
submit to the p. evil, 114 : 3
the P. teaches in vain, 737 : 1
things p. nor things to come, 47 : 15
things p. worst, 206 : 8
time p. and time past, 807 : 1
to divine majority p. no more, 605 : 2
to whom p. my new book, 101 : 13
unbirthday p., 613 : 15
unto thee O Lord our selves, 55 : 19
what if p. were world's last night, 254 : 14
when p. latched postern, 642 : 3
works of present man, 435 : 21
Presentation copy does not sell, 442 : 13
Presented with a universal blank, 285 : 5
Presents endear absents, 441 : 25
not Christmas without p., 610 : 6
Preservation, in wildness p. of world, 560 : 27
magic p. in books, 473 : 29
of species, 414 : 20
ruin rather than p., 153 : 23
we bless thee for our p., 55 : 7
Preserve as chiefest treasure, 729 : 14
constitutional rights, 700 : 3
entire those rights, 390 : 13
he shall p. thy soul, 22 : 4
liberties Americans already had, 800 : 7
liberty harder to p., 449 : 11
life liberty happiness, 800 : 7
me from a tyrant, 255 : 14
me from unseasonable sleep, 353 : 4
prayers to p. travel, 323 : 17
reform that you may p., 487 : 21
sacrifice lives to p. virtue, 69 : 10
stars from wrong, 427 : 16
Preserve (*continued*)
the Lord shall p. thee, 22 : 4
this country to p. liberty, 390 : 1
thy going out and coming in, 22 : 4
unity of empire, 373 : 6
wants energy to p. itself, 388 : 17
what we give and p., 522 : 12
within wild sanctuary, 750 : 15
your sangfroid, 388 : 10
Preserved, atoms p. by solidity, 100 : 9
bee p. in amber, 119 : 7
by delaying he p. state, 95 : 1
by reproduction, 393 : 7
his gore O, 630 : 2
liberty not p. without knowledge, 380 : 9
my life is p., 8 : 26
reputation not p. dies, 308 : 23
that long p. virginity, 297 : 1
to yield is to be p., 64 : 10
Union must be p., 419 : 2
unless degree p. place not safe, 112 : 14
us a nation, 446 : 2
Preserver, Creator and P., 55 : 5
destroyer and p. hear, 467 : 18
time destroyer time p., 808 : 6
Preserves, money p. life, 312 : 22
us not for specialists, 906 : 10
Preserving conditions of life, 551 : 19
peace, 379 : 9
sweetness of proportion, 256 : 2
Preside over liquidation of Empire, 746 : 2
Presided, Angel that p. o'er birth, 407 : 3
Presidency has followed change, 879 : 4
President be removed on impeachment, 391 : 11
cannot always be popular, 788 : 9
constantly on top of events, 788 : 3
had a dream, 523 : 5
if p. trouble happens to you, 760 : 12
needs political understanding, 788 : 10
nobody expected me to be P., 520 : 5
of multiversity, 879 : 4
of the Immortals, 641 : 4
ordains bee to be, 768 : 15
rather be right than P., 444 : 8
telling off p., 893 : 1
understand what it is to be P., 788 : 4
when P. does it not illegal, 883 : 4
Wintergreen for P., 836 : 1
Presidential, choosing p. nominee, 788 : 11
Presidents, stand before p. with aplomb, 577 : 2
Press acknowledges accountability to no one, 789 : 4
close bare-bosomed night, 574 : 19
corporation of p., 539 : 15
enable p. to serve communication, 789 : 5
fell dead-born from p., 357 : 18
free p. good or bad, 882 : 11
free p. necessity, 814 : 1
free speech p. assembly, 700 : 3
freedom of p., 389 : 2
freedom of p. bulwark of liberty, 367 : 6
freedom of p. has suffered most, 882 : 10
freedom of speech or of p., 391 : 14
Press (*continued*)
inform p. home Christmas, 724 : 4
liberty of p., 390 : 11, 506 : 5
microscopes and telescopes of p., 706 : 19
Monday p. reports, 864 : 17
my last p. conference, 882 : 17
not falling man, 249 : 2
not p. upon brow of labor, 694 : 16
sort of wild animal, 789 : 4
tenth Muse governs p., 554 : 10
toward the mark, 50 : 4
where ye see plume, 487 : 6
with vigor on, 346 : 1
Pressed into service out of shape, 747 : 12
love though p. with ill, 377 : 20
Presses, clatter of p., 792 : 19
Presseth, thy hand p. me sore, 18 : 28
Pressmen, so we be named p., 610 : 11
Press's, gret P. freedom, 568 : 1
Pressure, form and p., 222 : 2
grace under p., 844 : 18
hardly feel p. of age, 84 : 4
of cosmos, 650 : 7
opening first p. off second, 750 : 9
Prestige, convenience comfort p., 925 : 4
Presume Dr. Livingstone I p., 646 : 15
not God to scan, 337 : 2
yourself ignorant, 437 : 9
Presuming on changeful potency, 227 : 1
Presumption, amused by its p., 831 : 4
in kings and ministers, 366 : 3
in wisdom, 372 : 15
Presumptions, art flies in face of p., 652 : 15
Pretend, let us not p. to doubt, 639 : 9
Let's P. and we did, 912 : 14
to know when you do not, 65 : 5
Pretender, God bless the P., 341 : 12
had she known p. he was, 733 : 1
James I James II and Old P., 812 : 12
who P. or who King, 341 : 12
Pretense, for a p. make prayers, 42 : 12
no p. of liberty, 520 : 2
to faint meaning make p., 304 : 25
undivulged p., 238 : 9
Pretenses to break known rules by, 272 : 20
which are sincere, 706 : 2
Pretension, this p. a prejudice, 655 : 6
Pretensions, government draw into p., 617 : 9
Pretentiousness, correcting of p., 600 : 22
Prêtre guerrier poète, 581 : *n* 5
Prettier, pebble or p. shell, 313 : 17
Pretty, all my p. ones, 239 : 21
Babe all burning bright, 182 : 2
birds do sing, 250 : 8
Bobby Shaftoe, 934 : 3
but is it art, 708 : 11
drink p. creature, 425 : 3
everything that p. is, 243 : 16
Fanny's way, 329 : 15
feet like snails, 266 : 13
follies themselves commit, 199 : 7
how town, 829 : 18
how-de-do, 629 : 10
in amber to observe, 338 : 12
it is a p. world, 879 : 12
kettle of fish, 628 : 21

Pretty (*continued*)
little toes, 932 : 4
maids all in row, 930 : 6
my p. maid, 931 : 14
no burial this p. pair, 917 : 6
only p. ring time, 212 : 33
pleasures might me move, 172 : 10
poem Mr. Pope, 319 : 3
puts on his p. looks, 201 : 26
state of things, 629 : 10
tell me p. maiden, 685 : 8
to see what money will do, 310 : 9
to think so, 844 : 13
what do for p. girls, 717 : 18
young wards, 628 : 17
Preudunt course steadied, 568 : 3
Prevail, conditions dat p., 825 : 15
evening shades p., 325 : 9
fair words p., 709 : 5
gates of hell not p., 39 : 36
God who is able to p., 270 : 28
his rising fogs p., 304 : 25
make best ideas p., 586 : 20
man will p., 838 : 10
necessity knows no law except p., 111 : 20
'tis the majority p., 605 : 11
truth shall p., 34 : *n* 2
will looking ill p., 289 : 17
Prevailed, David p. over the Philistine, 13 : 3
the dragon p. not, 53 : 19
with double sway, 370 : 8
Prevails, when vice p., 326 : 2
where commerce long p., 368 : 16
Prevalent, religion most p., 372 : 19
Prevarication, last dike of p., 373 : 17
Prevent, enjoy religion p. others, 616 : 17
faults it has not strength to p., 369 : 15
lower from getting more, 88 : 1
me from carrying you up, 76 : 3
surest way to p. war, 439 : 6
Preventing angels met it, 305 : 29
Prevention, anthology used for p., 833 : 5
of mutual crime, 88 : 5
Prevents our being natural, 294 : 8
Previous, calling to mind p. benefaction, 79 : 16
returned home p. night, 742 : 1
Prey, animals and athletes not p., 799 : 17
at fortune, 231 : 4
beast of p. in aristocratic races, 658 : 5
eagle seeketh p., 17 : 1
expects his evening p., 363 : 6
fear birds of p., 227 : 30
great lord yet p. to all, 337 : 2
greater p. upon less, 344 : 13
have they not divided the p., 12 : 9
of fear, 799 : 8
of rich on poor, 388 : 5
on garbage, 219 : 22
people easily becomes p., 154 : 8
smaller fleas on him p., 322 : 21
to dumb forgetfulness a p., 362 : 14
to hastening ills a p., 369 : 30
universal p., 226 : 3
Venus fastened to p., 312 : 8
where eagles dare not perch, 187 : 5
young lions roar after p., 21 : 11
Priam's curtain, 205 : 19
Priapus, it is I P. crying, 93 : 3
made of marble, 103 : 15
Price, abatement and low p., 213 : 8
cruel high, 707 : 17
existence market p., 607 : 17
for precocity p. demanded, 536 : 11
freedom with great p., 814 : 20
great p. for wisdom, 600 : 15
greater p. than life, 849 : 1
greet cheep holde at litel p., 147 : 10
heaven put p. on goods, 384 : 13
is far above rubies, 26 : 6
is labor in exchange for thing, 572 : 20
life exacts for peace, 842 : 14
market p. they said, 607 : 17
men have their p., 328 : 21
natural and market p., 438 : 13
of everything, 675 : 11
of justice eternal publicity, 720 : 16
of liberty, 397 : *n* 8
of thousand horses, 735 : 1
of wisdom is above rubies, 16 : 14
pay any p., 890 : 7
pearl of great p., 39 : 18
sell above natural p., 366 : 1
system mechanism for communicating, 844 : 6
too high p. for harmony, 582 : 4
weighed for my p., 33 : 34
what p. glory, 802 : 4
will fall, 180 : 20
Priced, weighed measured p. everything, 549 : 18
Priceless, human life p., 849 : 1
Prices, contrivance to raise p., 366 : 2
vicious spiral of rising p., 762 : 8
Prick and sting her, 219 : 25
if you p. us do we not bleed, 199 : 18
it mark it with B., 929 : 18
sides of my intent, 236 : 24
Pricking, gentle knight p. on plain, 173 : 8
gonfalon bubble, 773 : 12
of my thumbs, 239 : 7
Pricks, honor p. me on, 205 : 5
kick against the p., 46 : 6, 71 : 12
to subsequent volumes, 226 : 5
Pride, age that will p. deflower, 173 : 14
aiming at blessed abodes, 336 : 18
aiming at blest abodes, 180 : *n* 6
all the p. cruelty and ambition, 173 : 4
and conceit original sin, 323 : 28
and courage of patriot, 617 : 6
as if p. not humble, 545 : 26
bear affection without p., 665 : 1
bold peasantry country's p., 369 : 30
chastening in hour of p., 521 : 3
coy submission modest p., 285 : 19
death would be his p., 759 : 12
Envy Avarice three sparks, 141 : 5
Envy Malice, 443 : 2
fell with my fortunes, 210 : 17
from p. vainglory and hypocrisy, 55 : 10
goeth before destruction, 24 : 12
he that is low no p., 302 : 13
I know thy p., 12 : 39
idleness and p., 348 : 3
in Casey's bearing, 704 : 15
in occupation, 623 : 8
in p. in reasoning p., 336 : 18
in their port, 369 : 1
Pride (*continued*)
is hateful before God, 35 : 16
is his own glass, 226 : 9
is therefore pleasure, 308 : 11
king over children of p., 17 : 9
land of Pilgrims' p., 514 : 12
lintel low to keep out p., 671 : 12
look backward with p., 747 : 7
mother's p. father's joy, 431 : 17
my high-blown p. broke under me, 249 : 3
never-failing vice of fools, 332 : 19
of country, 539 : 3
of kings, 336 : 10, 623 : 8
of peacock glory of God, 404 : 3
of power sink, 372 : 15
of those who survived, 746 : 5
oppressed with p., 315 : 17
perished in his p., 425 : 10
plume here buckle, 656 : 3
poet's inward p., 860 : 7
pomp and circumstance, 231 : 11
pomp and p., 671 : 12
praise or p., 900 : 1
rank p., 325 : 14
reasoning p., 336 : 18
rid earth of him in my p., 728 : 15
science lowers p., 552 : 2
shall bring him low, 25 : 33
soldier's p., 540 : 21
solemn p. yours, 524 : 4
speak with p. of our doings, 798 : 6
stoic's p., 337 : 2
strong dose of p., 815 : 5
surpasses p. of kings, 623 : 8
tasted all the summer's p., 402 : 12
that apes humility, 435 : 17, 440 : 15
that licks the dust, 339 : 3
that puts country down, 917 : 22
they lost their p., 869 : 1
to relieve wretched his p., 370 : 6
touch of love and p., 684 : 1
touched to quick, 540 : 21
towering in p. of place, 238 : 11
tyrant is child of P., 74 : 3
vain the sage's p., 339 : 32
was not made for men, 35 : 18
will have a fall, 74 : *n* 3
Priest all shaven and shorn, 934 : 9
free me from turbulent p., 137 : 9
God's high p., 46 : 28
I the Muses' p. sing, 107 : 25
like people like p., 33 : 8
love the only p., 615 : 12
no difference 'twixt P. and Clerk, 266 : 9
O mysterious p., 477 : 9
of most authentic creed, 615 : 7
soldier poet, 581 : 8
still is Nature's p., 426 : 15
the true God's p., 271 : 18
well ought p. example give, 218 : *n* 5
while runnin' for p., 786 : 10
Priestcraft, pious times ere p., 303 : 17
Priesthood, literary men a p., 472 : 6
Priestlike, waters at p. task, 478 : 20
Priestly vestments in dens, 592 : 6
Priests bless her when she is riggish, 241 : 1
by mightier hand, 487 : 7
my ancestors p. in temple, 501 : 9
not merit praise of poets, 672 : 1
not necessary to religion, 764 : 15
poets not yet p., 672 : 1

Priests (*continued*)
stood firm on dry ground, 11 : 29
tapers temples, 335 : 5
Priests', hell paved with p. skulls, 128 : 23
Priez Dieu que tous nous veuille absoudre, 150 : *n* 5
Prim little craft, 629 : 19
mouth so p., 806 : 14
Primal eldest curse, 222 : 25
Primary, great p. human affections, 585 : 19
imagination, 437 : 11
noon, 768 : 2
Prime, buried him before p., 927 : 4
gather rose whilst p., 173 : 14
give him always of p., 323 : 1
laurel for perfect p., 608 : 18
light the p. work of God, 285 : *n* 1
lovely April of her p., 244 : 2
minister returned, 727 : 2
obeyed at p., 495 : 8
of youth a frost of cares, 177 : 10
one's p. elusive, 896 : 3
rose up in his p., 811 : 2
what is the p. of life, 84 : 14
wisdom, 287 : 3
Zeus p. mover, 71 : 11
Prime Minister, what war said P.M., 858 : 16
Primer, armed with his p., 444 : 14
Primeval cosmic night, 754 : 13
forest p., 510 : 26
sleep, 592 : 6
Primitive impulses of heart, 526 : *n* 1
man tactile man, 784 : 27
North America, 847 : 12
people not waken sleeper, 673 : 3
terror, 808 : 5
unattached state, 755 : 6
Primitives, attack from p., 815 : 3
Primitivism, America was p., 784 : 16
Primordial images of collective unconscious, 753 : 12
Primrose, bring the rathe p., 281 : 1
by river's brim, 423 : 16
path of dalliance treads, 218 : 28
sweet as the p., 370 : 17
way, 238 : 2
Primus inter pares, 134 : 19
Prince, advise the p., 803 : 17
can make belted knight, 411 : 18
duty subject owes p., 189 : 6
first servant of state, 358 : 3
good night sweet p., 225 : 3
great P. in prison lies, 253 : 7
have no study but war, 153 : 21
I am not P. Hamlet, 803 : 17
I warn you, 864 : 16
imitate fox and lion, 154 : 1
in serving his p., 68 : 4
keeps tortoise enclosed, 90 : 11
Lucifer uprose, 600 : 27
must be lion, 119 : *n* 13
my p. you'd soon forget, 325 : 15
not propose it to my p., 341 : 10
of apple towns, 886 : 20
of Aquitaine, 514 : 9
of clouds haunts tempest, 580 : 17
of darkness a gentleman, 234 : 11
of Peace, 29 : 16
Rasselas P. of Abyssinia, 352 : 15
semblable au p. des nuées, 580 : *n* 5
subject Father Son, 254 : 5
Prince (*continued*)
there is a p. fallen, 13 : 13
till I p. of love beheld, 402 : 12
who relies on words ruined, 153 : 24
Princedoms Virtues Powers, 286 : 22
Princely counsel in his face, 284 : 14
Princerple, don't believe in p., 568 : 2
Princerples, ain't by p. or men, 568 : 3
Princes, all p. I, 252 : 9
and lords may flourish, 369 : 30
blaze forth death of p., 215 : 25
but breath of kings, 408 : 18
contentment in being equal to p., 255 : 5
fall like one of the p., 20 : 5
find few real friends, 357 : 7
gilded monuments of p., 244 : 18
God's true p., 570 : 12
hate traitor but love treason, 99 : *n* 12
kings and p. have philosophy, 84 : 15
like to heavenly bodies, 180 : 19
orgulous, 461 : *n* 1
put not your trust in p., 22 : 23
sweet aspect of p., 249 : 3
whose merchants are p., 30 : 4
Princes', cottages p. palaces, 198 : 9
hangs on p. favors, 249 : 3
not so arched as p. palaces, 262 : 9
Princess descended of kings, 242 : 6
felt pea through mattresses, 505 : 2
thoughtless saying of p., 359 : 6
three days afterward p. buried, 602 : 2
Principal translators between dream and reality, 801 : 8
wisdom is the p. thing, 23 : 7
Principalities, against p. and powers, 49 : 39
never known to exist, 153 : 23
nor powers, 47 : 15
Principality in Utopia, 488 : 5
Principle, active p. of literature, 735 : 13
but a cold p., 270 : *n* 7
divine P., 583 : 5
don't believe in p., 568 : 2
every word a p., 865 : 10
general p. gives no help, 422 : 10
Greatest Happiness P., 508 : 18
hain't money but p., 725 : 12
inconsistencies in p., 640 : 7
love our p., 483 : 11
moderation in p. a vice, 385 : 4
necessary and fundamental p., 365 : 18
nihilist takes no p. on trust, 564 : 3
o' the thing, 725 : 12
of conservation of force, 583 : 21
old but true as fate, 99 : *n* 12
on which society not founded, 361 : 1
one God one p. of being, 125 : 9
one p. make universe single creature, 126 : 19
precedent embalms p., 502 : 1
rebels from p., 373 : 26
same tyrannical p., 520 : 8
Principles, absorbed in general p., 697 : 6
ain't by p. or men, 568 : 3
elements or p. of bodies, 390 : 8
embrace p. or mistresses, 368 : 4
facts alarm more than p., 391 : 6
faithfulness and sincerity as first p., 68 : 5
Principles (*continued*)
first p. take deepest root, 392 : 11
fools say man has or has not p., 484 : 14
fundamental p. of equity, 737 : 3
guide his life by true p., 101 : 8
important p. inflexible, 524 : 9
less than chaff, 683 : 18
looking away from p., 650 : 8
might p. swaller, 567 : 23
moral p., 862 : 19
never defeated, 505 : 17
of Political Economy, 753 : 4
of resistance, 372 : 19
renounce his p., 391 : 5
restless unfixed in p., 303 : 20
serve as counsels, 737 : 3
that gave America birth, 682 : 13
to effect safety, 387 : 9
unchanging p. of human nature, 453 : 1
weaving of general p., 697 : 6
Print, all I own is a p., 544 : 25
all news fit to p., 686 : 6
eternity of p., 781 : 17
faith he'll p. it, 410 : 20
gentle-hearted in p., 441 : 6
I love a ballad in p., 246 : 30
news and raise hell, 922 : 4
of a man's naked foot, 318 : 14
on'y wut Guv'ment choose, 568 : 12
s' death I'll p. it, 338 : 7
see name in p., 456 : 12
sharpest weapon, 766 : 7
some said John p. it, 301 : 18
woman's name in p. twice, 789 : 3
Printed, that they were p. in a book, 16 : 3
Printer, Benjamin Franklin P., 346 : 15
Printers, books by which p. have lost, 276 : 19
Printing and Protestant religion, 472 : 5
and the Reformation, 755 : 14
caused p. to be used, 185 : 28
invented art of p., 472 : 21
Printing-house, hen-yard in p., 792 : 19
Printless toe, 796 : 11
Prior, what was Matthew P., 321 : 2
work of past centuries, 673 : 10
Priority, degree p. and place, 225 : 37
Prism and silent face, 424 : 2
prunes and p., 549 : 20
Prison, beast brought up in p., 154 : 8
bloom in p. air, 676 : 13
civilized man's house p., 557 : 4
come let's away to p., 235 : 12
dove coo over and over, 801 : 18
each confirms a p., 805 : 13
each in his p., 805 : 13
Europe p. of nations, 766 : 9
for color of his hair, 692 : 12
great Prince in p. lies, 253 : 7
grind in the p. house, 12 : 19
house for future p. for present, 886 : 3
in p. and ye came unto me, 40 : 33
lime tree bower my p., 433 : 20
of nations, 766 : *n* 3
only house in slave state, 558 : 6
open door of p. and run away, 83 : 16
outside p. in Leningrad, 801 : 15
palace and p., 458 : 5
Russia is p., 464 : 9
self only p., 671 : 13

Prison (*continued*)
soul in p. I am not free, 676 : 18
stone walls do not p. make, 296 : 4
taking him to p. for hair, 692 : 12
tongue astray led me to p., 894 : 10
true place for just man, 558 : 6
wake up and find myself in p., 273 : 5
walls cannot control, 296 : *n* 3
wear out in a walled p., 235 : 12
Prisoned spirit of man, 739 : 5
Prisoner in his twisted gyves, 192 : 18
man is a p., 83 : 16
stone walls a p. make, 296 : *n* 2
takes the reason p., 236 : 8
to white man, 418 : 12
Prisoner's, jailer envious of p. dreams, 514 : 8
jury passing on p. life, 227 : 31
Prisoners call the sky, 676 : 6
images p. tattoo, 850 : 6
inexorable to cries of p., 380 : 12
of hope, 33 : 33
of Shall and Will, 875 : 3
of starvation, 555 : 24
Prison-house, shades of the p., 426 : 14
Prison-pent, forever p., 852 : 7
Prisons, reform schools and little reform needed in p., 572 : 18
Pristine magnificence, 480 : 16
Prithee pretty maiden, 628 : 8
Privacy, a p. an obscure nook, 540 : 10
American has no p., 681 : 20
civilization progress toward p., 865 : 4
goldfish for p. I got, 731 : 13
no p. in America, 681 : 20
suffocate for p., 893 : 12
tumultuous p. of storm, 493 : 22
Private, abolition of p. property, 563 : 7
beneficence inadequate, 694 : 3
conscience for guide, 305 : 20
consumption, 871 : 11
dog to gain p. ends, 369 : 18
enterprise not yet tried, 780 : 7
enterprise set habits of age, 826 : 2
equal justice in p. disputes, 80 : 17
game of p. theatricals, 649 : 14
grave's a fine p. place, 297 : 1
griefs, 216 : 26
in p. life watch and laugh, 617 : 9
judgment, 365 : 5
men enjoy, 208 : 6
men governed by p. reasons, 387 : 14
morality p. luxury, 635 : 12
nor public flame nor p., 340 : 28
of the Buffs, 536 : 7
open and friendly in p., 80 : 17
opulence public squalor, 871 : 11
pagus or demesne, 869 : 6
post of honor is p. station, 326 : 2
property economy, 848 : 12
property fruit of labor, 757 : 17
public good and p. rights, 398 : 3
served no p. end, 336 : 5
sets p. friendship above public, 74 : 10
sin in p. not sin, 297 : 22
sin not so prejudicial, 170 : 21
superintending industry of p. people, 366 : 8
system of p. property, 844 : 3
takes no p. road, 337 : 16
wealth I decline, 704 : 5
wipe out p. initiative, 775 : 7
Privates, what have kings that p. have not, 208 : 6
Privation, scientist ready to bear p., 828 : 1
Privations, cheerful amid p., 617 : 6
dull p. and lean emptiness, 253 : 1
Privies, sun penetrates p., 86 : 13
Privilege, ague's p., 194 : 16
let others enjoy p. too, 344 : *n* 5
of absurdity, 264 : 14
poet's p. to help man endure, 838 : 12
writer's p. to help, 838 : 12
Privileges do not make common law, 128 : 21
if we mean to preserve p., 383 : 4
laws add exclusive p., 419 : 3
or immunities of citizens, 392 : 4
sharing p. of government, 519 : 21
Privilegia paucorum non faciunt legem, 128 : *n* 7
Privilieges because of sex, 898 : 6
Privy, grim wolf with p. paw, 280 : 22
to do gentil dedes, 147 : 15
Prize above my dukedom, 247 : 15
at three hundred pence ointment p., 268 : 11
decline the Pulitzer P., 791 : 7
freedom is the p., 418 : 4
humble hen we p., 923 : 10
in war no second p., 825 : 4
light winning make p. light, 247 : 23
love game beyond p., 700 : 6
men p. the thing ungained, 225 : 35
of general is command, 644 : 15
of powerful is power, 644 : 15
one receiveth p., 48 : 15
rain influence and judge the p., 278 : 5
ribbon or throne, 556 : 1
we sought won, 576 : 6
what we have we p. not, 209 : 31
Prized beyond sculptured flower, 471 : 9
something he p., 785 : 9
Pro aris atque focis, 102 : *n* 15
bono publico, 134 : 20
patria mori, 107 : *n* 23
patria pro liberis, 102 : *n* 15
tali numismate tales merces, 150 : *n* 1
Probabilities, judge between p., 515 : 13
theory of p., 397 : 18
Probable, no warrants but upon p. cause, 391 : 16
possible shadow of doubt, 630 : 3
the supernatural is p., 704 : 11
war regarded as inevitable p., 860 : 5
Probe, let others p. mystery, 875 : 3
Probing through you toward me, 844 : 2
Probitas laudatur et alget, 121 : *n* 4
Problem, common p. yours mine everyone's, 543 : 4
economic factor in ultimate p., 790 : 2
exquisite p. of artist, 653 : 10
holding mental p. in mind, 783 : 12
not whether machines think, 862 : 10
of age administration of wealth, 621 : 5
of artist to draw circle, 653 : 10
of rich and poor, 621 : 10
of twentieth century is color line, 724 : 15
part of solution or of p., 913 : 5
race and color p., 800 : 9
Problem (*continued*)
wholeness of human p., 755 : 21
Problems, great p. of life, 753 : 12
have roots in past, 788 : 6
resolve p. that confront Negro, 900 : 14
world's p., 813 : 8
Procedural, history of p. safeguards, 776 : 12
Proceed ad infinitum, 322 : 21
nature not p. by leaps, 350 : 6
so they resolved to p., 265 : 6
Proceedeth, every word that p., 11 : 12
wickedness p. from the wicked, 13 : 6
Proceeding from heat-oppressed brain, 237 : 13
Proceedings interested him no more, 630 : 14
Proceeds from known to unknown, 552 : 5
Process, cosmic and ethical p., 596 : 10
due p. of law, 391 : 17, 392 : 4
evolution a p., 637 : 1
golden p., 732 : 2
in creative p. father mother child, 704 : 14
inexorable inner p. contraction of life, 754 : 6
not view p. with misgivings, 744 : 7
of the suns, 530 : 3
verity is a p., 650 : 11
Processes, reduction of physical p., 636 : 16
Procession, stay with p., 718 : 9
systematic p. of universe, 154 : 10
Proclaim, friends his truth p., 304 : 6
great Original p., 325 : 8
liberty throughout land, 10 : 22
no shame, 223 : 5
they will p. me heretic, 153 : 9
with angelic host p., 350 : 15
Proclaiming peace and good will to men, 392 : 9
Proclaims, apparel oft p. the man, 219 : 1
peace p. olives of age, 245 : 13
Proconsuls, each year new p., 123 : 17
Procrastination, incivility and p., 454 : 21
is thief of time, 330 : 9
keeping up with yesterday, 760 : 2
no idleness no p., 593 : *n* 1
Procreant cradle, 236 : 21
urge of world, 574 : 13
Procul hinc procul este severi, 113 : *n* 5
Procurer of contentedness, 270 : 34
Procuress to lords of hell, 532 : 8
Prodigal, Catiline p. of own possessions, 102 : 23
chariest maid p. enough, 218 : 27
enemy be p., 868 : 3
how like the p. return, 199 : 6
how p. the soul, 219 : 6
O my P., 843 : 15
of ease, 304 : 1
son, 43 : 26
younker or p., 199 : 6
Prodigality, framed in p. of nature, 187 : 4
spring of p., 373 : 10
Prodigies, all Africa and her p., 274 : 6
Prodigy, what a p. is man, 300 : 11
Produce according to aptitudes, 563 : *n* 1

Produce (*continued*)
but not take possession, 64 : 4
eating p. of the land, 59 : 5
laboring to p. bons mots, 297 : 28
perfect circles and squares, 89 : 7
the person, 134 : 4
things and to rear them, 64 : 4
Produced, after they are p., 63 : 12
intellectual product judged from age p., 638 : 9
Producer organization market power, 848 : 5
promoting interest of p., 366 : 7
Produces, final cause p. motion, 87 : 10
what community p., 871 : 9
Producing, consume happiness or wealth without p., 680 : 8
Product, byproduct more than p., 689 : 25
happiness nor spontaneous p., 763 : 3
monstrous p. of wrongs, 744 : 8
of others' labor, 523 : 7
Production, capitalist p. begets negation, 562 : 19
consumption sole end of p., 366 : 7
entrepreneur contributes to p., 784 : 28
improvement of instruments of p., 563 : 5
means of social p., 563 : *n* 3
principle of economic p., 763 : 1
utility or cost of p., 652 : 2
Productivity, raging p. of Victorians, 889 : 3
Profanation to keep in, 266 : 20
Profane and old wives' fables, 50 : 29
and vain babblings, 51 : 5
for me to p. it, 469 : 19
hence ye p., 295 : 15
no divine ordinances, 370 : *n* 3
things holy p. clean obscene, 264 : 16
things sacred or things p., 302 : 4
Profaned heavenly gift of poesy, 305 : 7
one word too often p., 469 : 19
Profess not the knowledge, 34 : 28
politics like ours p., 344 : 13
Profession, hold up Adam's p., 224 : 5
is to disguise, 155 : 4
most ancient p., 707 : 12
Professional, between amateur and p., 837 : 9
Professionally declines and falls, 549 : 30
Professions, one of p. which are full, 559 : 17
satisfied to have two p., 695 : 1
Professor of art of puffing, 399 : 7
of Harvard Law School, 777 : 3
profit p. naught, 177 : 3
Professors like literature dead, 791 : 9
of dismal science, 474 : 11
Proffer, fawning greyhound did p., 203 : 16
Profferer, have p. construe Aye, 189 : 31
Profit, and the p. and loss, 805 : 9
between p. and the loss, 806 : 5
by folly of others, 117 : 5
by losing our prayers, 240 : 26
by their example, 382 : 13
emoluments in wages or p., 366 : 1
engine of enterprise, 783 : 8
entrepreneurial p., 784 : 28
few p. by advice, 110 : 21
Profit (*continued*)
in all labor there is p., 24 : 3
murder land for p., 875 : 13
no more p. of shining nights, 190 : 12
no p. but the name, 223 : 16
no p. where no pleasure, 188 : 25
private enterprise for p., 780 : 7
professor naught, 177 : 3
title and p. I resign, 326 : *n* 2
truth as opposeth no p., 264 : 20
what p. of all his labor, 26 : 11
winds blow p., 870 : 5
wise men p. more from fools, 95 : 10
without p. no development, 784 : 29
Profitable, lie with purpose most p., 721 : 13
things without number, 150 : 18
Profited, age not p. so much as lost, 559 : 7
never p. from public service, 883 : 2
what is a man p., 39 : 38
Profits, keeping p. up by keeping wages down, 438 : 14
little p. that idle king, 529 : 6
Profound and fragile lips, 829 : 7
both may be called p., 63 : 12
I, 824 : 6
in his view, 380 : *n* 2
man thinks woman p., 658 : *n* 2
subtle and p. female, 64 : 2
talked with looks p., 370 : 12
Profuse strains of unpremeditated art, 468 : 11
Progeny, angels p. of light, 286 : 22
give world corrupt p., 107 : 30
of learning, 398 : 7
soul whose p. they are, 281 : 22
Prognostics not always prophecies, 364 : 1
Program, computer no better than its p., 876 : 12
for tomorrow, 784 : 7
of revolution, 719 : 8
Progress and prosperity, 687 : 15
based on universal desire, 620 : 17
call p. tomorrow, 491 : 19
Christ's p. and His prayer time, 298 : 21
comfortable disease, 829 : 24
common denominator of p., 871 : 15
competition essential to p., 621 : 6
depends on intellectual work, 515 : 5
from want to want, 355 : 21
history p. of freedom, 422 : 12
in economic world slow, 652 : 1
in human virtue, 414 : 7
industrial p. available, 787 : 17
man's mark, 544 : 16
more general than retrogression, 515 : 6
most p. most failure, 543 : 27
no p. except individual, 581 : 6
no steady unretracing p., 571 : 4
no struggle no p., 556 : 4
not accident but necessity, 579 : 5
not real not permanent, 638 : 7
of all countries connected, 774 : 6
of artist self-sacrifice, 809 : 3
opinion and social p., 617 : 4
our goal, 483 : 11
part of nature, 579 : 5
promote p. of science, 826 : 12
Rake's P., 539 : 12
scientific thought human p., 660 : 6
Progress (*continued*)
separate yet one in p., 681 : 24
social p. checking of cosmic process, 596 : 10
social p. of each country, 774 : 6
swell a p., 803 : 17
test of our p., 780 : 3
to fuller life, 725 : 3
Progressive, scientific activity p., 787 : 4
Prohibited, means which are not p., 402 : 6
Prohibiting free exercise thereof, 391 : 14
licensing and p., 282 : 5
Prohibitions, meant p. to be absolutes, 794 : 17
Proie, à sa p. attachée, 312 : *n* 5
Project for extracting sunbeams, 322 : 13
for the sun, 768 : 10
Projections, other figures p., 809 : 1
Projects, fitter for new p., 181 : 7
Pro-labor policies of governments, 775 : 6
Proletarian state, 725 : 9
Proletarians have nothing to lose, 563 : 10
Proletariat class of wage laborers, 563 : *n* 4
dictatorship of p., 719 : 10
Italian p., 783 : 18
product of industry, 563 : 6
revolutionary class, 563 : 6
state is p., 731 : 7
Proliferation or accident in weapons race, 860 : 6
Prologue, excuse came p., 287 : 21
make a long p., 36 : 16
what's past is p., 247 : 27
Prologues, happy p. to swelling act, 236 : 10
over, 768 : 1
Prolongeth, joyfulness p. his days, 35 : 41
Promethean heat, 232 : 14
sparkle right P. fire, 191 : 5
Prominent, the more laws are made p., 64 : 20
Promise, broke no p., 336 : 5
eating air on p. of supply, 206 : 6
keep word of p. to our ear, 240 : 9
made debt unpaid, 752 : 7
most given when least said, 177 : 11
never p. more than perform, 111 : 18
none relies on, 315 : 14
not to do a thing, 622 : 15
of decade of loneliness, 835 : 6
of pneumatic bliss, 804 : 23
oh p. me, 646 : 11
only to do our best, 863 : 12
self-hatred waste of unfulfilled p., 859 : 18
what signs of p. are, 465 : 10
years of p. rapidly roll round, 418 : 4
Promise-crammed, I eat the air p., 222 : 8
Promised, fruits outdo what flowers p., 176 : 18
I've seen p. land, 909 : 17
land, 480 : 16, 616 : 8
Land beyond wilderness, 690 : 8
Man who had been p., 822 : 8
shalt be what thou art p., 236 : 16

Promises, age perform p. of youth, 352 : 15
America was p., 822 : 8
fails where most it p., 227 : 13
good memory to keep p., 657 : 8
to keep, 748 : 7
Promontory, as if a p. washed away, 254 : 22
blue p. with trees, 241 : 17
like one that stands on p., 186 : 10
once I sat upon p., 196 : 14
see one p. and see all, 259 : 4
seems to me sterile p., 220 : 28
stretched like a p., 286 : 30
Promote commerce not betray it, 310 : *n* 1
flourishing of arts, 826 : 12
general welfare, 391 : 10
public interest, 366 : 4
Promoter of mutual acquaintance, 617 : 7
Promoting, not by destroying but p., 373 : 9
Promotion, none sweat but for p., 210 : 31
Prompt, apology too p., 287 : 21
electrically p., 626 : 2
in attack, 372 : 20
Prompter, dreamer is p., 754 : 12
Prompters, how many p., 442 : 22
Promptly found out, 783 : 13
gives twice who gives p., 133 : 10
gratified to answer p., 623 : 7
Prompts tongue to deal in fiction, 331 : 14
Prone to introspection, 799 : 18
Prongs, therrble p., 778 : 6
Pronoun, that relative p., 686 : 1
Pronounce, foreigners spell better than p., 622 : 4
Pronounced, speak as I p. it to you, 221 : 23
Pronouncement, faith of p., 730 : 14
Pronouns, wise in use of p., 636 : 6
Proof, bliss in p., 245 : 23
dost thou ask p., 587 : 12
give me ocular p., 231 : 12
history p. of theories, 616 : 4
mistaking metaphor for p., 735 : 9
not one for putting off p., 748 : 15
of a poet, 573 : 20
of insufficient work, 619 : 6
of pudding in eating, 169 : 33
subtler more urgent p., 768 : 24
through the night, 446 : 1
undying p., 617 : 6
Proofs, how I would correct p., 470 : 12
of holy writ, 231 : 7
to test man p. shift, 544 : 15
Proosian, French or Turk or P., 627 : 18
Prop, my very p., 199 : 2
that doth sustain house, 200 : 20
who p. thou askst, 584 : 7
Propaganda has to be popular, 812 : 16
no frontiers against p., 853 : 17
Propagate and rot, 337 : 3
learn and p. best, 586 : 24
Propagated, Revolution p. downwards, 593 : 1
Propagates character by sword, 391 : 7
Propagation, all our p., 253 : 6
Propensities, excess of subjective p., 649 : 16
excite my amorous p., 353 : 23
Propensities (*continued*)
natural p., 374 : 7
semi-criminal p., 783 : 10
Propensity for emulation, 685 : 3
internal p. to unite, 775 : 1
to forego, 647 : 20
Proper, circumstance and p. timing, 83 : 1
fitting and p., 523 : 4
gardener's work, 710 : 22
in our own p. entrails, 217 : 11
man as see in summer's day, 196 : 9
mate, 377 : 24
mean, 343 : 23
memory for politician, 637 : 11
men as ever trod, 214 : 31
opinions for time of year, 869 : 2
price upon goods, 384 : 13
silence give p. grace to women, 73 : 9
stations, 548 : 15
study of mankind is man, 337 : 2
time to marry, 377 : 24
union of gin and vermouth, 837 : 10
words in proper places, 322 : 8
Propertied as all tuned spheres, 241 : 25
Property, a very handsome p., 603 : 8
abolition of private p., 563 : 7
acquiring and possessing p., 367 : 4
common judges of p., 352 : 9
contempt for equality of p., 506 : 2
deprive of life liberty p., 392 : 4
deprived of life liberty or p., 391 : 17
get hold of portable p., 549 : 27
government resting on p., 85 : 2
has duties, 501 : 19
is theft, 527 : 15
judiciary safeguard of p., 700 : 1
liberty p. no stamps, 920 : 8
national honor national p., 407 : 18
natural stimulus to work, 758 : 1
neither persons nor p. safe, 556 : 14
neither p. nor honor touched, 154 : 2
of easiness, 224 : 8
our p. subject to control and disposal, 393 : 3
owns them, 615 : 9
private p. fruit of labor, 757 : 17
proputty proputty, 535 : 7
right to possess p., 537 : 3
sacredness of p., 621 : 7
subject to community, 687 : 16
system of private p., 844 : 3
they can call their own, 379 : 2
unequal distribution of p., 398 : 2
was thus appalled, 225 : 30
Prophecies of what courts will do, 644 : 2
prognostics not always p., 364 : 1
Prophecy, experience p. of wise men, 464 : 18
gratuitous error, 565 : 22
poetry p. and religion, 572 : 11
re-created from Bible, 903 : 3
spirit of p. in me, 83 : 18
that may sound peculiar, 603 : 3
trumpet of p. O Wind, 467 : 22
Prophesy, don't never p., 568 : 6
in part, 48 : 25
O I could p., 205 : 10
Prophesying war, 433 : 24
Prophet, ask us p., 900 : 3
Elijah the p., 34 : 1
historian p. in reverse, 438 : 15
not without honor, 39 : 21
Prophet (*continued*)
of the soul, 493 : 16
said I, 526 : 17
sons of the p., 922 : 15
under judgment he preaches, 823 : 17
your p. the Nazarite, 198 : 18
Prophetic, awful pause p. of end, 330 : 6
O my p. soul, 219 : 20
soul of the wide world, 245 : 13
strain, 279 : 1
Prophets and kings, 43 : 12
best of p. is the past, 462 : 8
beware false p., 38 : 16
come down from mountains, 637 : 19
do they live forever, 33 : 28
is Saul among the p., 12 : 33
Jerusalem that killest p., 40 : 21
law and the p., 38 : 14, 40 : 16
men reject p., 582 : 9
ministry of the p., 33 : 15
mouth of holy p., 42 : 25
not destroy law or p., 37 : 6
that which was given to the P., 130 : 11
wisest p. make sure, 364 : 1
Prophets', see fulfilled p. warning, 139 : 4
Propitiation, he is p. for our sins, 52 : 21
religion p. of powers, 673 : 2
Propitiatory bird, 863 : 19
Propitious hours, 464 : 14
miracles p. accidents, 703 : 17
Propontic and Hellespont, 231 : 18
Proportion, insisture course p., 225 : 37
music wherever there is p., 274 : 20
preserving sweetness of p., 256 : 2
proper dignity and p., 124 : 22
some strangeness in p., 181 : 9
when no p. kept, 195 : 16
Proportional, acceleration p. to applied force, 313 : *n* 5
to motive force, 313 : 14
Proportioned, freight p. to groove, 608 : 5
to human constitution, 330 : 22
Proportions, in small p. beauties see, 256 : 20
Propose to fight it out, 589 : 17
Proposed, before a joy p., 245 : 23
Proposes, man p. God disposes, 148 : 15
Proposition, life tough p., 757 : 12
no general p. worth damn, 645 : 2
that all men equal, 523 : 4
Propositions, general p. concrete cases, 644 : 11
man to frame general p., 645 : 2
Propriété c'est le vol, 527 : 15
Propriety, frights isle from her p., 230 : 20
not infused from without, 89 : 20
rules of p., 69 : 22
Propter vitam vivendi perdere causas, 122 : *n* 10
Proputty proputty proputty, 535 : 7
Prorsus credibile est quia ineptum est, 126 : *n* 5
Pro's, from p. and con's they fell, 169 : 16
Prose, all not p. is verse, 298 : 9
Browning used poetry for writing in p., 674 : 18
connect p. and passion, 764 : 9
his p. was flowery, 876 : 8

Prose (*continued*)
homely definitions of p., 438 : 4
life's p., 610 : 8
Meredith p. Browning, 674 : 18
money p. of life, 498 : 9
of human life, 508 : 25
opposed to meter, 436 : 14
poetry must be as well written as p., 793 : 6
run mad, 338 : 13
speaking p. without knowing it, 298 : 8
unattempted yet in p. or rhyme, 283 : 1
verse will seem p., 316 : 6
what others say in p., 339 : 25
words in best order, 438 : 4
Prosecuted, find motive be p., 623 : 19
help p. and victim, 820 : 9
Prospect, dull p. of distant good, 305 : 25
every p. pleases, 452 : 9
no p. of an end, 367 : 12
noblest p. Scotchman sees, 354 : 10
not within p. of belief, 236 : 6
Prospects, all his p. brightening, 370 : 3
more pleasing than fruition, 123 : *n* 7
shining p. rise, 325 : 6
Prosper, evil deeds do not p., 60 : 5
made all to p. in his hand, 8 : 29
state will p., 726 : 12
treason doth never p., 181 : 21
whatsoever he doeth shall p., 17 : 12
wolf that keep it p., 709 : 4
Prospered, honor friend who p., 71 : 7
Prosperity and salvation in union, 730 : 16
arrived at in lifetime, 620 : 6
ascend hill of p., 625 : 14
been in p. and it remembren, 144 : 24
best discover vice, 180 : 7
blessing of Old Testament, 180 : 5
comes to bad man, 67 : 3
dormant in p., 452 : 15
doth bewitch men, 262 : 5
friend not known in p., 35 : 23
good things which belong to p., 180 : 4
in day of p. be joyful, 27 : 7
in p. easy to find friend, 88 : *n* 4
in the day of p., 35 : 21
jest's p. lies in ear, 191 : 12
life comes to end in p., 71 : 8
makes friends, 112 : 10
middle-aged p., 842 : 11
more supportable than p., 620 : 6
not favorable to public virtue, 471 : 13
not without fears, 180 : 6
one man who can stand p., 474 : 1
remembrance of p., 35 : 21
social p. means man happy, 491 : 25
studies are an ornament in p., 98 : 7
thy p. exceedeth the fame, 13 : 35
tries souls even of wise, 102 : 25
undermining the very p., 687 : 14
with more taste, 323 : 29
within thy palaces, 22 : 6
would not be so welcome, 290 : 11
Prosperity's very bond of love, 247 : 3
Prosperous, make dog p. will not bite, 624 : 24
remorse sleeps in p. period, 359 : 3
Prospers, homeland is wherever he p., 82 : 26
Prospers (*continued*)
turns ashes or p., 516 : 9
who p. one day suffer reverse, 75 : 4
Prostitute, I puff the p. away, 305 : 3
Protect, heaven p. working girl, 684 : 17
I will p. you, 825 : 17
I'll p. it now, 492 : 10
two solitudes p. each other, 756 : 6
us by thy might, 514 : 13
what it advertises, 906 : 15
whom he could not p., 903 : 2
woman taught to p. herself, 578 : 3
Protection and patriotism reciprocal, 449 : 7
and security of people, 367 : 5
equal p. of the laws, 392 : 4
equally entitled to p., 419 : 3
of economic weak, 848 : 12
return for p. of society, 508 : 12
to the oppressed, 80 : 17
Protector when he first appears, 85 : 5
Protects lingering dewdrop, 429 : 11
Protest, lady doth p. too much, 222 : 15
openly discrimination slander, 753 : 7
voice of p. needed, 598 : 15
Protestant, because I was P., 824 : 1
gunpowder and P. religion, 472 : 5
protestantism of P. religion, 372 : 19
thy P. to be, 266 : 2
Protestantism of Protestant religion, 372 : 19
Protestants Jews Turks in one ship, 273 : 11
Papists or P., 354 : 9
Protesting, dignity of truth lost with p., 255 : 19
Proteus of fire and flood, 437 : 19
rising from sea, 428 : 1
Protracted, life p. is p. woe, 351 : 20
Protracting life not deduct from death, 101 : 5
Proud, all p. and mighty have, 345 : 3
and angry dust, 691 : 20
and chivalrous spirit, 88 : 23
apt the poor to be p., 214 : 14
arrogancy of the p., 29 : 21
befits p. birth, 73 : 10
captain of thine own fate, 103 : *n* 1
clergyman, 350 : 3
death be not p., 254 : 11
eats up himself, 226 : 9
Edward's power, 411 : 15
ever fair and never p., 230 : 11
every cock p. on own dunghill, 111 : *n* 3
exultation of discoverer, 799 : 20
fashions in p. Italy, 194 : 11
foot of conqueror, 202 : 19
gods and commodores of earth, 570 : 5
grief is p., 201 : 20
here shall thy p. waves be stayed, 16 : 30
his name, 430 : 10
how p. word Man rings, 725 : 7
how you use p. words, 761 : 13
I'm black and I'm p., 913 : 1
in arms, 279 : 5
in humility, 259 : 1
inconstant childish p., 475 : 3
instruct sorrows to be p., 201 : 20
is spirit of Zeus-fostered kings, 57 : 16
knowledge is p., 377 : 15
Proud (*continued*)
lay p. usurpers low, 411 : 16
make death p. to take us, 241 : 23
man drest in authority, 228 : 10
man's contumely, 221 : 12
me no prouds, 193 : 17
men in old age, 75 : 2
men of action, 481 : 16
mistress' order to perform, 340 : 22
O p. death, 225 : 4
of ancient heritage, 890 : 7
our purses shall be p., 189 : 2
pray God to keep me from being p., 309 : 12
radio was rather p., 873 : 1
Rose sad Rose, 712 : 3
scattered the p., 42 : 22
Science, 336 : 16
seat of Lucifer, 287 : 26
setter up and puller down of kings, 186 : *n* 3
sleepy and p., 810 : 19
small things make base men p., 185 : 21
spirit of mortal be p., 463 : 16
taken in by flattery, 309 : 2
that he learned so much, 377 : 15
that they are not proud, 259 : 1
'tis all the p. shall be, 335 : 11
too p. for a wit, 371 : 14
too p. for relief, 749 : 13
too p. to beg, 922 : 14
too p. to fight, 682 : 3
too p. to importune, 363 : 11
tower in the town, 525 : 13
towers, 458 : 7
uncertain balance of p. time, 178 : 13
vain man may become p., 308 : 12
wear it like banner for p., 854 : 16
world said I, 292 : 18
yet not p. to know, 333 : 21
yet wretched thing, 251 : 7
Proudest of his works, 383 : 14
Proudly, bearing birthrights p., 201 : 11
die p. if not live p., 696 : *n* 2
what so p. we hailed, 446 : 1
Proud-pied April, 245 : 9
Prouds, proud me no p., 193 : 17
Prove a beauteous flower, 192 : 14
all things, 50 : 22
believing where cannot p., 531 : 16
came to p. him with hard questions, 13 : 34
cannot p. an aspiration, 637 : 3
fairy gold and 'twill p., 246 : 20
go to p. my soul, 540 : 6
him first, 35 : 8
if I do p. her haggard, 231 : 4
I'll p. more true, 192 : 10
mysterious by this love, 252 : 11
show doubt p. faith, 543 : 8
simplest matter of fact, 464 : 8
so fond, 243 : 1
some new pleasures p., 253 : 2
warrant she'll p. an excuse, 399 : 1
we p. what we want to p., 724 : 6
we will all the pleasures p., 183 : 8
when givers p. unkind, 221 : 14
Proved a very woe, 245 : 23
believe one who has p. it, 106 : 6
error and upon me p., 245 : 18
them and found them worthy, 34 : 13
Provençal song, 476 : 23
Provence, in P. New York, 892 : 12

Provender, truly a peck of p., 197 : 5
Proverb, a p. and a byword, 13 : 33
flashes through head, 530 : 10
hare of whom p. goes, 201 : 13
thou shalt become a p., 11 : 19
till life illustrated p., 479 : 20
Proverbed with grandsire phrase, 191 : 21
Proverbs, books like p., 302 : 18
contradict each other, 876 : 3
King Solomon wrote P., 696 : 3
of Solomon, 548 : 18
patch griefs with p., 210 : 3
Solomon spake three thousand p., 13 : 30
Proveth, hasty marriage seldom p. well, 186 : 14
Provide, foes will p. with arms, 105 : 3
for common defense, 391 : 10
for human wants, 373 : 21
for those with too little, 780 : 3
God will p. himself a lamb, 8 : 13
good the gods p. thee, 306 : 19
if any p. not for his own, 50 : 31
in peace need in war, 128 : *n* 10
know worst and p. for it, 383 : 1
provide, 749 : 1
Provided, right that wants be p., 373 : 21
Providence, behind frowning p., 375 : 17
behold now another p., 265 : 12
fashioned us holler, 567 : 23
grand scene and design in p., 380 : 8
main goal of divine P., 154 : 13
may assert eternal P., 283 : 2
nickname for P., 386 : 5
on side of last reserve, 294 : *n* 9
one thing in creation to demonstrate P., 121 : 4
parsimony requires no p., 374 : 10
place p. found you, 496 : 21
reasoned high of P., 284 : 19
reliance on divine p., 387 : 11
rubs which P. sends, 369 : 8
special p., 224 : 28
their guide, 288 : 4
trust in P., 271 : 14
Provident, women p. instead, 836 : 20
Providently caters for sparrow, 210 : 28
Provider, essential p. of elements, 586 : 23
Provides, fury p. arms, 104 : 20
Provideth her meat in the summer, 23 : 11
Province, all knowledge my p., 178 : 15
send clerk to distant p., 313 : 2
Provinces, kissed away kingdoms and p., 241 : 8
rebellions of maritime p., 800 : 11
these limbs her p., 253 : 11
Provincial, worse than p. parochial, 652 : 7
Proving absurd all written, 543 : 25
Provision, decent p. for poor, 354 : 23
education best p. for old age, 87 : 4
make not p. for flesh, 47 : 29
society make collective p., 773 : 8
Provisions not suspended in exigencies, 553 : 20
Provoke conscious Something, 517 : 6
good p. to harm, 229 : 1
not children to anger, 50 : 13
silent dust, 362 : 5
Provokes desire, 238 : 3
no one p. me with impunity, 134 : 11
Provoketh, beauty p. thieves, 210 : 21
Provoking most justly thy wrath, 55 : 17
Prow, youth on the p., 363 : 6
Prowler, cop both p. and father, 910 : 11
Prows, water from sharp p., 785 : 12
Proximity, exaltation from p. of disaster, 743 : 3
Proximus ardet Ucalegon, 104 : *n* 17
Proxumus sum egomet mihi, 96 : *n* 7
Prudence, forced into p. in youth, 441 : 1
never to practice either, 625 : 9
Prudent course is steadied, 568 : 3
every pleasing p. part, 335 : 20
love is p., 148 : 20
man looketh well to his going, 24 : 2
mind can see room, 75 : 4
pushes his p. purpose, 330 : 10
virtue and p. act, 373 : 4
Prudery a kind of avarice, 453 : 11
Prudes, stay far hence you p., 113 : 7
Prunella, rest all leather or p., 337 : 11
Prunes and prisms, 549 : 20
longing for stewed p., 228 : 2
Pruninghooks, spears into p., 28 : 31
Pruritus, disputanti p. ecclesiarum scabies, 251 : *n* 3
Prussia hurried to the field, 399 : *n* 7
in Germany forward, 663 : 3
make moral conquests, 483 : 8
part of Germany, 480 : 10
Prussian army people in arms, 483 : 9
French or Turk or P., 627 : 18
Pry, animals and athletes not p., 799 : 17
loose old walls, 761 : 10
never p. lest lose Edens, 541 : 22
Psalmist, sweet p. of Israel, 13 : 25
Psalms, from poetry p., 861 : 5
King David wrote P., 696 : 3
lovers' sonnets turned p., 177 : 9
make joyful noise with p., 20 : 20
show selves glad with p., 54 : 16
speaking to yourselves in p., 49 : 37
Psalteries, played before the Lord on p., 13 : 14
Psaltery, praise him with p., 22 : 25
Psara, blackened spine of P., 484 : 2
Pseudonym of God, 655 : 13
Psyche, mournful P., 477 : 21
my soul, 527 : 1
Psychiatrist, anybody who goes to a p., 777 : 9
Psychic development of individual, 678 : 9
gods as p. factors, 754 : 7
powers part of man's self, 648 : 17
Psychical acts develop by reflex, 603 : 5
Psychoanalysis not the only way, 789 : 14
Psychological moment, 675 : 1
momentum or factor, 675 : *n* 1
reason, 653 : 1
Psychologists claim to science of mind, 733 : 15
Psychology based on self-observation, 614 : 15
cannot experiment with men, 443 : 3
connecting with life, 758 : 11
help p. become natural science, 651 : 5
Psychology (*continued*)
knife cuts both ways, 582 : 14
long past short history, 666 : 10
of adultery, 738 : 3
purpose of p. different idea, 735 : 18
results of experimental p., 702 : 13
treating p. like natural science, 651 : 5
Ptolemy, authority and researches of P., 151 : 7
Pub, no pewter no p., 811 : 1
Public, American p. more reasonable, 872 : 19
be damned, 584 : 4
British p. in fit of morality, 487 : 19
buys opinions like meat, 621 : 3
calm, 586 : 12
care, 284 : 14
common good and p. authority, 774 : 7
consideration of p. object, 80 : 16
conspiracy against the p., 366 : 2
corrupt p. mind, 851 : 14
debt public blessing, 401 : *n* 6
demands certainties, 771 : 18
entertainer who understood his time, 774 : 12
excitement runs high, 836 : 16
exempt from p. haunt, 210 : 24
fit for p. authority, 74 : 19
for the p. good, 134 : 20
friend to p. amusements, 355 : 1
good and private rights, 398 : 3
government bad if no p. opinion, 751 : 2
has crude ideas, 453 : 12
in field of p. education, 820 : 14
indifferent to p. welfare, 393 : 3
intelligence of p. opinion, 617 : 4
interest, 814 : 3
knot's tied in p., 839 : 12
life crown of career, 753 : 9
life situation of power, 372 : 7
like a frog, 604 : 19
literary man write for his p., 731 : 9
make itself artistic, 676 : 3
make the p. stare, 461 : 1
mean animal, 445 : 7
men nor cheering crowds, 714 : 1
men slop over, 616 : 14
microcosm of p. school, 501 : 1
moral habits induced by p. practices, 119 : 25
must and will be served, 314 : 18
no personal considerations in p. duty, 590 : 1
no strike against p. safety, 736 : 13
nor p. flame nor private, 340 : 28
odium and public hatred, 444 : 4
office public trust, 539 : 4, 631 : *n* 1
officer without vices, 591 : 11
officers servants of people, 631 : 6
offices p. trusts, 449 : 8
opinion everything, 521 : 2
opinion exacts obedience, 597 : 10
opinion held in reverence, 626 : 13
opinion in advance of law, 723 : 4
opinion stronger than legislature, 603 : 13
opinion variable, 595 : 18
opinion weak tyrant, 559 : 2
opinion welcomes talent, 80 : 17
power to endanger p. liberty, 380 : 13
prejudicial as p. indecency, 170 : 21

Public (*continued*)
private as well as p. reasons, 387 : 14
promote p. interest, 366 : 4
reproached me in p., 420 : 11
researchers into p. opinion, 869 : 2
say what one pleases about p. affairs, 794 : 20
scandal is wicked, 297 : 22
schools nurseries of vice, 349 : 14
seldom forgive twice, 386 : 10
servants serve you right, 851 : 13
services failed, 871 : 11
sets friendship above p. welfare, 74 : 10
sound of p. scorn, 287 : 27
speedy and p. trial, 392 : 1
squalor, 871 : 11
steal from p. purse, 851 : 14
strength individual security, 401 : 11
trusts in hands of fit, 319 : 16
tune vulgar if p. hums it, 662 : 18
unite for p. safety, 420 : 15
vexes p. men, 530 : 16
want of pence vexes p. men, 157 : *n* 15
waste of p. money, 637 : 12
welfare, 687 : 16
world-wide p. authorities, 774 : 7
Publican, fawning p., 198 : 19
the other a p., 43 : 38
Publicans and sinners, 39 : 7
Publicity, effect of p. on men, 634 : 23
price of justice p., 720 : 16
withhold finding from p., 396 : 7
Publish and be damned, 421 : 17
it not in the streets, 13 : 8
it to all the nation, 320 : 26
right or wrong, 456 : 11
yourselves to sky, 651 : 8
Published, what should not be p. abroad, 79 : 13
Publisher, Barabbas a p., 462 : 20
Publisheth peace, 31 : 12
Puck, streak of P., 663 : 8
Pudding, hasty p., 920 : *n* 2
life's a p., 630 : 4
proof of p. in eating, 169 : 33
solid p. empty praise, 340 : 15
sweets of hasty p., 400 : 5
to make bag p., 934 : 1
Pudding-bag string, 934 : 5
Puddle, stepped in a p., 933 : 10
world is p.-wonderful, 828 : 12
Puddles, novel reflects mud p. underfoot, 453 : 13
Puddle-wonderful, world is p., 828 : 12
Puff the prostitute away, 305 : 3
Puffed and reckless libertine, 218 : 28
charity not p. up, 48 : 23
love not p. up, 48 : 23
with pomp of death, 899 : 14
Puffeth, knowledge p. up, 48 : 13
Puffing, professor of art of p., 399 : 7
Puffins razorbills guillemots and kittiwakes, 419 : *n* 5
Pugnacity, murder in sleep not p., 786 : 8
Puissant nation rousing herself, 282 : 3
Pukes, sea passenger p. in, 461 : 14
Puking, mewling and p., 211 : 15
Pules and whines, 496 : 24
Pulitzer, decline the P. Prize, 791 : 7
Pull all together, 549 : 2
chestnuts out of fire, 297 : 11

Pull (*continued*)
door called p., 923 : 9
down thy vanity, 793 : 4
long p. strong p., 549 : 2
not down your hedge, 269 : 19
Paquin p. down, 793 : 4
weight, 687 : 7
Puller down of kings, 186 : *n* 3
Pulleth sword out of stone, 149 : 6
Pulleys, cry of p., 899 : 12
Pullin', you do de p. Sis Cow, 662 : 9
Pullman, ten years on P. cars, 810 : 7
Pulls, who p. me down, 184 : 8
Pulpit drum ecclesiastic, 290 : 14
Pulpits, some to common p., 216 : 6
Pulse, let me feel your p., 188 : 12
of life stood still, 330 : 6
of modern life economic, 763 : 1
of the machine, 427 : 5
poll feeling p., 745 : 5
Pulses, axioms proved on p., 479 : 10
give world other p., 475 : 8
Pulsing in our spirits and blood, 888 : 6
Pumice, smoothed with dry p. stone, 101 : 13
Pump, president is p., 879 : 4
tremble even at air p., 379 : 16
Pumpkin, frost is on p., 665 : 14
put her in p. shell, 932 : 16
rich p. pie, 513 : 4
Pumpkins, coaches that change into p., 853 : 7
turn p. into coaches, 694 : 1
where early p. blow, 550 : 16
Pun, good p. may be admitted, 386 : 1
make so vile a p., 318 : 1
pistol not feather, 442 : 12
Punch bowl's brink, 646 : 12
brothers, 614 : 16
in presence of passenjare, 614 : 16
Puncheon floor in summertime, 623 : 25
Punctilious envoys Thine and Mine, 311 : 15
in conventionalities, 620 : 20
Punctual as a star, 605 : 19
rape of every day, 899 : 13
Punctuality politeness of kings, 402 : 2
Pundit devil's advocate enthusiast, 847 : 10
Punic faith, 103 : 4
Punica fide, 103 : *n* 3
Punish, distrust impulse to p., 657 : 15
the world for evil, 29 : 21
to p. they answer prayers, 66 : *n* 8
Punished as enemy of country, 418 : 14
big words always p., 75 : 2
in the sight of men, 34 : 13
Punishing anyone between them, 433 : 9
beware of p. wrongfully, 4 : 2
Punishment, broad effects of p. 658 : 6
could not name all types of p., 105 : 20
cruel and unusual p., 392 : 3
Erinyes exact p. underground, 59 : 3
fit the crime, 629 : 11
good evil reward p., 307 : 19
is greater than I can bear, 7 : 18
let p. match offense, 99 : 5
no p. prevent crimes, 866 : 8
not make man better, 658 : 6
pleasing p. women bear, 187 : 33
servitude p. of guilt, 397 : 21
tames man, 658 : 6
worthy of reward not p., 486 : 15

Punishments, for great wrongdoing great p., 78 : 8
in nature no p., 615 : 11
rewards and p. in cards, 818 : 5
the past with its p., 863 : 13
Punkin, frost is on p., 665 : 14
Punt, slow p. swings round, 585 : 21
Pup, in dust with Hector's p., 856 : 6
remember when he was p., 749 : 2
since Hector was p., 921 : 18
Pupil, encouraging clever p., 350 : 8
Pupils, my p. crème de la crème, 896 : 1
Puppets best and worst are we, 540 : 19
shut up box and p., 539 : 10
Puppies, greyhound p., 518 : 4
Puppy dogs' tails, 932 : 12
happiness is warm p., 901 : 6
mongrel p. whelp hound, 369 : 17
Puppyism, dogmatism p. at full growth, 500 : 15
Pur comme un ange, 400 : *n* 3
Purblind doomsters, 640 : 3
wimpled whining p., 190 : 26
Purchase, unless abroad p. alliance, 186 : 12
you p. pain, 335 : 19
Purchased at price of chains, 383 : 5
by merit of the wearer, 199 : 14
history's p. page, 457 : 24
love is not to be p., 127 : 8
with pain p. inherit pain, 190 : 10
Purchaser, worth what p. will pay, 112 : 8
Purchasing, unemployed p. power, 811 : 10
Purdue, some love Paris some P., 864 : 18
Pure aimlessness pursued, 874 : 17
and complete sorrow impossible, 602 : 7
and disposed to mount to stars, 142 : 8
and eloquent blood, 254 : 6
and endless light, 299 : 6
as an angel, 400 : 15
as naked heavens, 425 : 23
as snow, 221 : 17
beauty of mathematics, 737 : 14
blessed are the p. in heart, 37 : 4
clean hands and a p. heart, 18 : 8
clear as crystal, 550 : 1
fool, 552 : 17
harmony is p. love, 182 : 12
hearts as p. and fair, 628 : 20
I will keep p. and holy, 79 : 13
I would be p., 785 : 8
immortals cannot escape, 74 : 23
in life free from sin, 107 : 11
in numbers warmly p., 364 : 10
land of p. delight, 328 : 15
literature p. and dead, 791 : 9
live p. speak true, 534 : 5
love without power, 823 : 16
lovers' souls descend, 253 : 7
mathematics original, 697 : 7
more p. as tempted more, 427 : 23
motion of rising day, 875 : 2
my heart is p., 530 : 15
my poems naughty my life p., 118 : 21
of mouth pure of hands, 4 : 9
particularly p. young man, 628 : 7
religion breathing laws, 425 : 15

Pure (*continued*)
religion would have lasted long, 73 : 5
shall man be more p. than maker, 15 : 13
silence of p. innocence, 246 : 15
Simon P., 321 : 8
sleep from p. digestion bred, 286 : 12
so p. and fair to see, 481 : 8
soul unto captain Christ, 195 : 8
stars are not p. in his sight, 16 : 11
stretch of joy, 875 : 2
substantial world p. and good, 428 : 4
summon vision declare it p., 873 : 19
thy truth so p. of old, 282 : 18
unclouded brow, 612 : 15
unto p. all things p., 51 : 11
whatsoever things are p., 50 : 7
whether his work be p., 24 : 29
women innocent and p., 247 : 26
young man, 628 : 7
Purer science holier laws, 566 : 11
than purest gold, 256 : 1
Purest, frost from p. snow, 242 : 23
heartiest tenderness, 577 : 3
purer than p. gold, 256 : 1
ray serene, 362 : 8
treasure mortal times afford, 193 : 32
Purgatory, England is p. of men, 174 : 23
poor man get out iv P., 722 : 10
Purge and leave sack, 205 : 17
me with hyssop, 19 : 15
melancholy, 247 : 5
Purging, poetry p. of world's poverty, 769 : 25
Purification of politics, 615 : 3
Purified, every creature p., 184 : 2
Purify dialect of tribe, 808 : 14
the mind, 72 : 17
whatever corrupt in republic, 452 : 2
Puritan born in France by mistake, 597 : 12
hated bear-baiting, 489 : 6
marrow of my bones, 794 : 2
Puritanism laid egg of democracy, 569 : 9
Puritans founded to give thanks, 722 : 3
gave world action, 538 : 13
great artists never p., 772 : 2
nobly fled, 616 : 17
thanks we are presarved fr'm P., 722 : 3
Purity ability to contemplate difilement, 876 : 18
of race not exist, 706 : 20
ore of body into p., 790 : 14
Purlieu of god of love, 253 : 10
Purlieus, dusty p. of law, 532 : 18
Purloined, my love he p. away, 636 : 12
Purple, abbots p. as their wines, 340 : 26
all the ground, 281 : 1
beggar in p., 708 : 23
beyond utmost p. rim, 530 : 13
blossom in p. and red, 533 : 25
cow, 718 : 15
first from out the p. grape, 279 : 7
gleaming in p. and gold, 459 : 14
light of Love, 362 : 21
mountain majesties, 688 : 5
pilots of p. twilight, 529 : 24
quenching in p., 604 : 16
restore to whiteness wool dyed p., 128 : 14
Purple (*continued*)
riot, 476 : 13
rustling of p. curtain, 526 : 13
stars in p. dusk, 811 : 13
testament of bleeding war, 195 : 4
the sails, 240 : 29
waves with long p. forms, 673 : 17
with love's wound, 196 : 15
Purple-stained mouth, 476 : 23
Purpose a horse of that color, 213 : 27
bait on p. laid, 245 : 23
cite Scripture for his p., 198 : 22
end in one p., 207 : 8
infirm of p., 237 : 23
inherent in art so in nature, 87 : 5
let me shake with p., 902 : 6
lie with p. worst, 721 : 13
my p. holds, 529 : 13
nothing in nature without p., 509 : 4
of human life, 698 : 1
one increasing p. runs, 530 : 3
poetry not p. but passion, 526 : 9
pushes his prudent p., 330 : 10
shake my fell p., 236 : 17
speak plain and to p., 209 : 15
steady p. tranquilize mind, 482 : 15
tenacious of p. in rightful cause, 107 : 28
time to every p., 26 : 21
to speak and p. not, 232 : 29
to what p. this waste, 41 : 3
true joy being used for p., 680 : 15
unconquerable p. realized, 441 : 12
with p. of its own, 424 : 1
Purposed, linger out a p. overthrow, 245 : 3
Purposes, Almighty has own p., 524 : 6
search out p. of gods, 72 : 8
Purr myself to sleep, 623 : 5
Purrs and never shows tooth, 794 : 7
Purse, consumption of the p., 206 : 5
costly as p. can buy, 219 : 1
it drains your p., 401 : 3
large style agrees not with p., 185 : 8
money burned out his p., 155 : 6
of gold resolutely snatched, 202 : 25
public p., 851 : 14
put money in thy p., 230 : 3
silken or leathern p., 328 : 19
so little in his p., 257 : 10
who has p. has power, 553 : 12
who steals my p. steals trash, 230 : 33
Purses, light gains make heavy p., 177 : 14
our p. shall be proud, 189 : 2
Pursue culture in bands, 700 : 15
flies when I p. it, 163 : 14
free to p. truth, 779 : 15
know good or knowing it p., 306 : 10
love good p. the worst, 113 : *n* 15
man with great thing to p., 542 : 19
my reason to O altitudo, 274 : 4
phantoms of hope, 352 : 15
seek peace and p. it, 18 : 21
seem to fly it it will p., 256 : 6
the unknown end, 645 : 3
triumph partake gale, 338 : 2
vain war with heaven, 284 : 3
Pursued, exit p. by a bear, 246 : 19
habits well p. betimes, 393 : 14
it with forks and hope, 614 : 4
pure aimlessness p., 874 : 17
villain still p. her, 661 : 13
Pursues fame at risk of losing self, 90 : 5
Pursueth, wicked flee when no man p., 25 : 27
Pursuing and obtaining happiness, 367 : 4
he is talking or he is p., 14 : 2
still achieving still p., 509 : 16
Pursuit, clear paths of laudable p., 522 : 2
culture a p. of perfection, 588 : 12
indefatigable p., 711 : 7
mad in p., 245 : 23
of happiness, 387 : 9
of knowledge, 444 : 16
vain p. of human glory, 271 : 23
what mad p., 477 : 5
Pursy, fatness of these p. times, 223 : 9
Push and pressure of cosmos, 650 : 7
back into shadows, 796 : 2
door called p., 923 : 9
heart can p. sea and land, 822 : 12
in their tides, 886 : 13
off, 529 : 13
on keep moving, 416 : 8
Pushed just so far, 724 : 3
Pushes prudent purpose to resolve, 330 : 10
Pushing their bones, 908 : 8
Puss-gentleman all perfume, 376 : 4
Puss-in-Boots, human mind invents P., 853 : 7
Pussy, I like little p., 449 : 14
O lovely p., 550 : 7
Pussycat, owl and p., 550 : 7
where have you been, 932 : 8
Pussy's in well, 930 : 14
Put a tongue in every wound, 216 : 29
antic disposition on, 220 : 4
away childish things, 860 : 3
blessed to p. cares away, 101 : 23
bullet through his head, 729 : 5
candle shall never be p. out, 156 : 14
candle which shall not be p. out, 34 : 6
down Richard, 203 : 12
down what really happened, 845 : 2
eggs in one basket, 624 : 23
enemy in their mouths, 230 : 26
forward best foot, 202 : *n* 4
Germany in saddle, 553 : 10
God in his statements, 575 : 23
her in pumpkin shell, 932 : 16
I p. away childish things, 48 : 25
in her oar, 170 : 7
me in a cage, 810 : 8
me in your pocket, 790 : 8
money in thy purse, 230 : 3
never do what can p. off, 593 : 6
not your trust in princes, 22 : 23
off thy shoes, 9 : 11
on armor of light, 47 : 29
on good behavior, 461 : 15
on Lord Jesus Christ, 47 : 29
on pistols went riding, 811 : 2
on whole armor of God, 49 : 38
out the light, 232 : 14, 688 : 2, 748 : 11
plain tale p. you down, 204 : 1
shall be surely p. to death, 10 : 9
shoulder to the wheel, 66 : 19
too fine a point, 171 : 9, 549 : 14
up your caravan, 732 : 17
when I p. out to sea, 535 : 19

Put (*continued*)
worst use a man could be p. to, 251 : 3
yourself in his shoes, 834 : 1
Putrefy, most swiftly p., 245 : *n* 1
Putrid corpse of liberty, 784 : 2
Puts all heaven in a rage, 406 : 9
forth tender leaves of hopes, 249 : 3
he who p. armor off, 512 : 13
record on gramophone, 805 : 8
Putting, dispatch in p. end to it, 89 : 6
love away, 607 : 1
off the proof, 748 : 15
on breastplate of faith, 50 : 20
us to ignorance, 543 : 25
Puzzle, rule of three p., 917 : 13
schoolmasters p. brain, 371 : 5
to botanist, 619 : 7
Puzzles the will, 221 : 12
Puzzling, though p. not beyond conjecture, 275 : 5
Pye, shine with P., 456 : 16
Pygmies on shoulders of giants, 118 : 7
Pygmy body, 303 : 20
Pyramid, bottom of economic p., 779 : 6
star-y-pointing p., 277 : 13
Pyramids first, 924 : 3
from summit of p., 420 : 6
Pyramus and Thisby, 196 : 2
cruel death of P., 196 : 2
Pyre, ghost escapes from vanquished p., 112 : 26
Pyrrha for whom bindest thou thy hair, 107 : 3
Pyrrhic victory, 92 : *n* 8
you have P. dance, 461 : 7
Pythagoras, hold opinion with P., 200 : 7
opinion of P. concerning wildfowl, 200 : *n* 3
said to his scholars, 258 : 15
Pythagoreans, rather wrong with Plato than right with P., 98 : 23

Q

Q.E.D. 92 : 3
Quacks, empty q., 650 : 14
on one side science on other, 463 : 17
Quadrangular, spots q. of diamond form, 377 : 6
Quadrant and sextant, 843 : 13
Quadrille, leaves curtsy and q., 899 : 11
Quadruped, hairy q. with tail, 515 : 8
Quae est domestica sede iucundior, 98 : *n* 13
Quaffed, jested q. and swore, 536 : 7
Quaffing, laughing q. unthinking time, 306 : 27
Quail and shake the orb, 241 : 25
when footpads q., 629 : 20
whistle about us, 767 : 4
Quails, he brought q., 21 : 12
Quaint and curious volume, 526 : 10
and curious war is, 641 : 15
enameled eyes, 281 : 1
great figure, 765 : 8
honor turn to dust, 297 : 1
wonders at q. spirits, 196 : 20
Quake, earth did q., 41 : 28
Quakers, first called us Q., 300 : 22
Qualifications, adverbs only q. I respect, 654 : 6
Qualified, I am q., 233 : 7
masses are not q., 784 : 17
Qualify, my flame to q., 245 : 14
Qualis artifex pereo, 118 : *n* 3
Qualities, chose on various q., 734 : 6
such q. as would wear, 369 : 7
Quality, composition and fierce q., 233 : 3
draw inward q. after, 241 : 10
greatness not size but q. 619 : 19
hate counsels not in such a q., 199 : 21
intimate q. of handmade, 739 : 4
let not q. escape thee, 125 : 5
not quantity but q., 134 : *n* 6
of mercy not strained, 200 : 9
rather than quantity, 114 : 22
royal banner and all q., 231 : 11
taste of your q., 221 : 2
true-fixed and resting q., 216 : 3
vital q. self-confidence, 792 : 1
Qualms, many many q., 696 : 3
Quanch my heart trobling, 811 : 9
Quangle Wangle, 550 : 15
Quantities, determination of q. by numbers, 610 : 1
ghosts of departed q., 330 : 21
such q. of sand, 613 : 2
Quantity, not q. but quality, 134 : *n* 6
of force in nature eternal, 583 : 21
of love, 224 : 22
of matter unalterable, 583 : 21
quality rather than q., 114 : 22
Quantum, waive q. o' the sin, 409 : 12
Quarantine aggressors, 780 : *n* 1
to protect community, 780 : 4
Quarelets of pearl, 266 : 5
Quarles saved, 340 : 18
Quarrel between past and present, 744 : 3
beware entrance to q., 219 : 1
find q. in a straw, 223 : 19
how they behave in q., 680 : 4
lover's q. with world, 749 : 8
no q. with Viet Cong, 915 : 13
nor for every q. to lawyer, 269 : 28
or reprimand, 494 : 1
over water, 787 : 11
pretty q. as it stands, 398 : 17
sudden and quick in q., 211 : 15
thrice armed that hath q. just, 185 : 17
with bread and butter, 323 : 7
with whom should I q., 864 : 11
Quarreling, chickens quit q. over food, 760 : 10
set them a-q., 357 : 17
Quarrels, dove loves when it q., 129 : 12
full of q. as egg of meat, 193 : 3
love know no sundering q., 107 : 9
love q. in concord end, 289 : 4
lovers' q. renewal of love, 96 : 5
pick no q., 370 : *n* 3
religion breeds q., 538 : 18
who in q. interpose, 331 : 15
wine cause of q., 316 : 13
would not last long, 294 : 10
Quarrelsome, countercheck q., 213 : 4
mutinous and q., 348 : 21
Quarrelsomeness, when strong guard against q., 69 : 20
Quarried, limestone q. near spot, 718 : 2
Quarries of Sicily, 850 : 13
Quarry, go not like q. slave, 471 : 6
mine blessed am I, 929 : 2
Quartering, love hanging and drawing and q., 404 : 22
Quarterly, I says the Q., 462 : 11
Quarters, steeple sprinkle q., 691 : 24
Quarto, beautiful q. page, 398 : 29
Que sais-je, 165 : *n* 3
Queen and huntress, 255 : 12
be drunk as we, 349 : 5
beggar maid my q., 530 : 17
British warrior q., 377 : 22
come not near our fairy q., 196 : 21
every lass a q., 566 : 14
feminine soul a q., 703 : 13
flaunting extravagant q., 399 : 1
grace a summer's q., 431 : 18
I am your anointed Q., 163 : 16
I would not be a q., 248 : 28
it no inch further, 247 : 2
Mab hath been with you, 191 : 23
mathematics q. of sciences, 444 : 11
moves a goddess looks a q., 334 : 19
now now cried the Q., 612 : 20
o' the May, 528 : 12
of all my sins, 908 : 9
of Hearts, 931 : 4
of pleasure, 633 : 13
of Sheba heard of Solomon, 13 : 34
of this summer hotel, 908 : 8
poor memory the Q. remarked, 613 : 12
rose of rosebud garden, 533 : 23
tell 'em Q. Anne's dead, 415 : 7
to London to look at q., 932 : 8
turned crimson with fury, 612 : 1
unveiled peerless light, 285 : 25
upon a card, 535 : 4
was in parlor, 931 : 9
you shall be q., 933 : 13
you will though Q. said, 612 : 16
Queen's, ruler of Q. Navee, 627 : 14
Queens, dreamed of Oriental q., 583 : 14
have died young and fair, 250 : 10
Queequeg, in one word Q., 570 : 9
Queer, all q. save me and thee, 923 : 14
horse must think it q., 748 : 6
how strange and q., 542 : *n* 3
ill-tempered and q., 550 : 5
inimitable gracefulness, 789 : 9
monster the artist, 654 : 8
Northern Lights seen q. sights, 752 : 6
thee a little q., 923 : 14
you look so q., 921 : 1
Queerer, universe q. than we suppose, 821 : 5
Queerest folk of all, 696 : 1
they ever did see, 752 : 6
Quell, music raise and q., 305 : 10
Quelle est cette île triste et noire, 581 : *n* 3
Quem deus vult perdere, 134 : 21
Quench, fire rivers cannot q., 186 : 19
if I q. thee, 232 : 14
many waters cannot q. love, 28 : 24
my great love I wonder, 628 : 25
smoking flax shall he not q., 31 : 4
Quenched in most cold repose, 469 : 5
Quenching in purple, 604 : 16
Querulous, newspapers q. and bellicose, 772 : 1
usual q. serenity, 440 : 21

Quest for superfluous, 649 : 16
go Soul the body's q., 172 : 14
in q. to have extreme, 245 : 23
ultimate ideal yet hopeless q., 697 : 9
whither and what thy q., 654 : 15
Questing, Pellinore followed q. beast, 149 : 7
snail, 875 : 4
Question, a noose a q., 893 : 13
beautiful q., 829 : 15
greatest q. ever debated, 381 : 6
he would not ask any q., 639 : 8
if his glory, 606 : 5
ignorance never settles q., 502 : 6
important q. what you think, 586 : 18
in that case what is the q., 752 : 15
interrupt with silly q., 359 : 19
is absurd, 869 : 3
is which is to be master, 613 : 16
let history answer q., 388 : 18
momentous q. like firebell, 389 : 14
most momentous q. on continent, 592 : 9
no q. ever settled, 670 : 5
not been able to answer, 679 : 7
not every q. deserves answer, 111 : 25
not harm nor q. much, 253 : 11
now of final belief, 768 : 1
others abide our q., 584 : 9
remains How, 481 : 9
settle q. discuss it, 487 : 16
that is the q., 221 : 12
two sides to every q., 78 : 24
what q. you desire to answer, 740 : 15
young embarrassed to q. older, 59 : 20
Questionable, comest in such q. shape, 219 : 11
erotic instinct q., 755 : 3
superfluity small beer, 185 : *n* 6
Questioned me story of my life, 229 : 27
Questioning, drew nearer sweetly q., 269 : 9
nature exposed to method of q., 853 : 1
needs no q. before he speaks, 77 : 14
warned prior to q., 820 : 15
Questions, answer q. about myself, 863 : 9
answer q. intelligently, 615 : 7
answered three q., 611 : 11
ask me no q., 371 : 12
attempt to answer q., 740 : 15
better to know some q., 831 : 12
came to prove him with hard q., 13 : 34
looks upon inward sphinx and q., 721 : 2
no q. unanswerable, 496 : 2
them that asks no q., 371 : *n* 2
though puzzling q. not beyond conjecture, 275 : 5
unanimity on legal q., 700 : 2
Quhat say thai, 175 : 4
Qui ante diem periit, 700 : 7
procul hinc legend's writ, 700 : 7
Qui s'excuse s'accuse, 163 : *n* 5
Quibbles, in q. angel and archangel, 339 : 22
Quick and dead, 55 : 2
brown fox, 923 : 2
even in death, 171 : 13
eyes gone, 792 : 16
feeling q. and transient, 542 : 20
her q. look, 873 : 17
Quick (*continued*)
how did I get old so q., 856 : 9
how q. and fresh art thou, 213 : 8
Jack be q., 932 : 17
now here now always, 807 : 8
path to light switch, 852 : 1
so q. bright things come to confusion, 195 : 23
sudden and q. in quarrel, 211 : 15
sunrise come, 855 : 5
to arm, 792 : 14
to flare up, 60 : 3
true apothecary thy drugs q., 193 : 29
word of God is q., 51 : 14
Quicken, live within sense they q., 469 : 18
Quickened, not q. except it die, 49 : 3
Quickeneth, spirit that q., 44 : 42
Quickens to rebel, 806 : 6
Quicker, end a contest q., 398 : 26
liquor is q., 855 : 10
Quick-eyed Love observing me, 269 : 9
Quickly, behold I come q., 53 : 32
bring me beaker of wine, 81 : 12
do q. that thou doest, 45 : 18
doubly benefits who gives q., 110 : 15
little fire q. trodden, 186 : 19
nature falls into revolt, 206 : 30
to pass gates of Hades, 67 : 5
turn away, 715 : 19
'twere well it were done q., 236 : 22
well done is q. done, 110 : 7
Quickness to hear move see, 705 : 4
too much q. to be taught, 335 : 19
Quicksands, soundings q. rocks, 479 : 14
Quid datur a divis felici optatius hora, 102 : *n* 4
si nunc caelum ruat, 96 : *n* 12
Quiddities, quips and q., 202 : 26
where be his q. now, 224 : 10
Quiddity, entity and q., 291 : 2
Quien bien te quiere, 935 : 16
Quiet, all q. along Potomac, 598 : 10
all q. on Western front, 839 : 9
anything for a q. life, 261 : 19
as a lamb, 202 : 4
as a stone, 478 : 2
be q. and go a-angling, 271 : 14
bower q. for us, 475 : 16
breath, 476 : 28
by q. natures understood, 714 : 20
calm Peace and Q., 278 : 15
calm q. innocent recreation, 271 : 10
chaste breast and q. mind, 295 : 22
conscience stands brunt of life, 76 : 20
consummation have, 243 : 28
courage gaiety q. mind, 669 : 17
crisis q. but urgent, 898 : *n* 1
desperation, 559 : 4
Doctor Q., 323 : 15
easy live q. die, 432 : 1
enforced from q. sphere, 206 : 26
entertain lag-end with q. hours, 205 : 1
eye made q. by power, 423 : 11
fie upon this q. life, 203 : 26
harvest of a q. eye, 424 : 18
here where world q., 633 : 19
holy time q. as nun, 425 : 16
hours few, 573 : 1
imperishable q., 874 : 7
in q. she reposes, 586 : 3
inability to stay q., 597 : 4
Quiet (*continued*)
interchange of sentiments, 355 : 16
kiss me and be q., 341 : 2
lain still and been q., 15 : 8
limit of world, 533 : 28
mind cureth all, 260 : 5
mind richer than crown, 178 : 10
minds innocent and q., 296 : 4
my temptation q., 717 : 9
o'er hilltops is q. now, 397 : 3
ornament of q. spirit, 52 : 12
retirement rural q. friendship, 345 : 12
rich q. and infamous, 488 : 9
richness q. and pleasure, 580 : 20
scallop shell of q., 172 : 15
shining to the q. moon, 435 : 15
singeth a q. tune, 435 : 1
sleep when the long trick's over, 760 : 16
sleepers in q. earth, 562 : 7
spirit so still and q., 229 : 26
still and q. conscience, 249 : 4
study to be q., 50 : 17
tree of man never q., 691 : 7
truth hath a q. breast, 194 : 1
wise and good, 469 : 25
young maidens q. eyes, 669 : 7
Quiet-colored end of evening, 542 : 3
Quieting, soothing and q., 735 : 6
Quietly shining to quiet moon, 435 : 15
Quietness, bride of q., 477 : 4
handful with q., 26 : 23
richness q. and pleasure, 580 : 20
Quietness', king made for q. sake, 264 : 7
Quiets, hallowed q. of past, 568 : 22
Quietus, he himself his q. make, 221 : 12
Quill, condor's q., 571 : 1
from angel's wing, 429 : *n* 1
Quillets, his q. his cases, 224 : 10
nice sharp q. of law, 184 : 20
Quills, stops of various q., 281 : 5
upon fretful porpentine, 219 : 18
Quince, slices of q., 550 : 10
Quinquireme of Nineveh, 760 : 19
Quintessence even from nothingness, 253 : 1
morning q. of life, 463 : 12
of dust, 220 : 29
Quintilian, made Q. stare and gasp, 282 : 8
Quintilius give me back my legions, 110 : 5
Quip modest, 213 : 4
Quippe secundae res sapientium animos fatigant, 102 : *n* 12
Quips and cranks, 277 : 19
and quiddities, 202 : 26
shall q. and sentences awe, 209 : 19
Quire of bad verses, 488 : 12
Quiring to young-eyed cherubins, 201 : 1
Quirks of blazoning pens, 230 : 7
Quis custodiet ipsos custodes, 122 : *n* 8
Quislings, vile race of q., 744 : 16
Quit certainty for uncertainty, 352 : 14
John and I are q., 320 : 26
oh quit this mortal frame, 333 : 23
port o' heaven, 700 : 8
quit for shame, 289 : 18
rats have q. it, 247 : 14
you can't q., 879 : 3
you like men, 49 : 9

Quit (*continued*)
yourselves like men, 12 : 31
Quitter, if faut q. tout cela, 273 : *n* 3
Quiver, air q. with a color, 789 : 10
aspens q., 528 : 24
happy is the man that hath his q. full, 22 : 10
inward q. of some kind, 648 : 2
Quivered in his heart, 456 : 17
Quivering, light q. aspen, 431 : 2
ratio, 604 : 6
Quiver's choice, 462 : 3
Quixote, Don Q. a muddled fool, 170 : 16
Quixote's, youngsters read Don Q. story, 169 : 39
Quixotic sense of honorable, 527 : 4
Quo usque Catilina abutere patientia, 98 : *n* 2
vadis, 45 : *n* 3
Quod erat demonstrandum, 92 : 3
semper quod ubique quod ab omnibus, 129 : *n* 6
Quos deus vult perdere, 134 : 21
Quot homines tot sententiae, 97 : *n* 2
Quotation, classical q., 356 : 21
good if writer goes my way, 708 : *n* 3
Quotations, backed opinion with q., 320 : 19
Bartlett's Familiar Q., 743 : 9
book furnishes no q., 455 : 4
give meaning better, 685 : 15
good to read books of q., 743 : 9
I hate q., 495 : 26
pretentious q. tedium, 685 : 15
some q. ill-advised, 685 : 15
wrapped himself in q., 708 : 23
Quote fights historical, 628 : 1
grow immortal as they q., 329 : 20
kill you if you q. it, 718 : 16
we all q., 500 : 2
wise reader q. wisely, 484 : 7
Quoted, famous remarks seldom q. correctly, 770 : 4
odes and jewels, 530 : 24
Quoter, first q. next to originator, 499 : 27
Quoth, give me q. I, 236 : 1
Raven Nevermore, 526 : 18
Quotidian saps philosophers, 766 : 22

R

R, months that have no r, 166 : 12
Southerner no use for r, 623 : 14
Rabbit in a snare, 781 : 10
ole man R. say scoot, 662 : 10
skin to wrap baby, 931 : 5
thoughts of r. are rabbits, 500 : 11
Rabbits, four little r., 719 : 2
thoughts of rabbit are r., 500 : 11
Rabble, army would be base r., 373 : 7
member of the r., 830 : 16
Rabelais' easy chair, 340 : 14
Rabid partisans, 650 : 14
Race, a simple r., 430 : 7
all run in r., 48 : 15
and color problem, 800 : 9
another r. hath been, 426 : 23
appointed for my second r., 299 : 2
arms r., 897 : 10
barred on account of r., 891 : 13

Race (*continued*)
between education and catastrophe, 720 : 5
Californians a r., 699 : 15
competition best for r., 621 : 6
conscience of my r., 777 : 18
credit to human r., 877 : 8
culture not function of r., 796 : 6
death of the r., 900 : 2
despised r., 617 : 6
distinctions of r., 579 : 9
dusky r., 530 : 6
every man honor his r., 667 : 1
fair chance in r. of life, 522 : 2
feelings permanently in r., 585 : 19
flower of all his r., 423 : 1
foal of an oppressed r., 433 : 18
friend to human r., 57 : *n* 8
future of human r., 758 : 8
Germany a r., 483 : 18
giant r. before the flood, 306 : 7
happiness of human r., 373 : 9
heavenly r. demands zeal, 346 : 1
here lived another r., 465 : 6
history of our r., 745 : 7
human r. born to fly upward, 142 : 2
human r. has means for annihilating itself, 775 : 13
human r. never have rest from evils, 84 : 15
in conversation see capacities of r., 784 : 9
individual development repetition of r., 678 : 9
individuals of all nations melted into new r., 382 : 8
is to the swift, 684 : 13
judged by best not worst, 733 : 8
laborers perpetuate r., 438 : 13
laws unto savage r., 529 : 6
loftier r. than known, 643 : 1
lost r., 852 : 11
man's imperial r. ensnare, 334 : 3
mother of Aeneas and his r., 100 : 1
my lot bound up with human r., 448 : 3
no matter what r., 824 : 10
no r. monopoly on virtue, 900 : 15
no special right to one r., 672 : 10
not similar are r. of gods and men, 57 : 30
not superior by r., 615 : 5
not to the swift, 27 : 17
not to the swift the r., 671 : 11
of ancient r. by birth, 304 : 15
of glory run, 288 : 29
of shame, 288 : 29
once they were happy r., 419 : 12
our r. may be accident, 746 : 20
out of one man a r., 286 : 29
over work never done, 645 : 12
part of the human r., 790 : 21
pernicious r. of vermin, 322 : 11
pickest and cullest r., 575 : 22
poetry fettered fetters r., 407 : 5
purity of r. not exist, 706 : 20
rage and hate of r., 570 : 13
rejoiceth as a strong man to run a r., 17 : 28
ride over obstacles win r., 549 : 1
right to vote not denied on account of r., 392 : 5
run r. set before us, 51 : 19
same with human r., 760 : 10

Race (*continued*)
sceptered r., 442 : 17
slaughters of r. writ, 641 : 19
slow and steady wins the r., 66 : 3
stars of human r., 375 : 23
suffering human r., 585 : 3
the earth the human r., 641 : 16
there is one r. humanity, 671 : 5
to separate because of r., 820 : 14
type of all her r., 536 : 7
vanishing r., 836 : 14
vile r. of quislings, 744 : 16
whatever r. creed or persuasion, 794 : 15
where immortal garland, 282 : 1
whole r. is a poet, 768 : 7
whole r. of politicians, 322 : 12
win r. runs by himself, 707 : *n* 2
winding-sheet of Edward's r., 363 : 5
wish I loved human r., 697 : 1
world the r. the soul, 576 : 22
worn out quite, 461 : 21
you-all means r., 922 : 9
young men not lost r., 852 : 11
Racehorse, breed r. in few generations, 646 : 9
Races, beast of prey in aristocratic r., 658 : 5
brought to good order, 154 : 12
condemned to one hundred years of solitude, 908 : 3
difference of opinion makes horse r., 624 : 26
horse dominated mind of early r., 790 : 19
preservation of favored r., 579 : 20
quick to flare up we r. of men, 60 : 3
we the youthful sinewy r., 575 : 15
Rachel, Jacob served seven years for R., 8 : 22
weeping for her children, 36 : 23
Racial, not by r. affiliation but ancestry, 685 : 6
Racine, facts about life of R., 735 : 10
will go out of style, 301 : 8
Racine's, art of R. verse, 735 : 10
Racism is dogma, 796 : 7
move beyond r., 901 : 1
my religion makes me against r., 904 : 16
still accused of r., 916 : 11
Racist, reject r. institutions and values, 914 : 15
Rack, desire a perpetual r., 258 : 21
leave not a r. behind, 248 : 13
no r. torture me, 605 : 8
of this tough world, 235 : 19
ship weathered every r., 576 : 6
then we r. the value, 209 : 31
Racked with deep despair, 283 : 9
Racket, would I were r. pressed, 866 : 19
Radiance, grief terrible r., 491 : 16
of eternity, 469 : 16
of love, 413 : 13
of thousand suns, 94 : 15
white r. stretches above it, 59 : 27
Radiant, among r. venturing on, 761 : 1
by her own r. light, 279 : 22
light rests on men, 72 : 2
misery, 394 : 14
palace reared its head, 526 : 1
rare and r. maiden, 526 : 12
squalors, 899 : 14

Radiant (*continued*)
to r. angel linked, 219 : 22
Radical chic, 911 : 6
Radio, car r. bleats, 893 : 7
when r. was proud alert and fast, 873 : 1
Radix malorum est cupiditas, 51 : *n* 2
Rafael made century of sonnets, 543 : 30
Raffiniert ist der Herr Gott, 764 : *n* 1
Raft, feel mighty free on a r., 624 : 1
no home like a r., 624 : 1
republic a r., 407 : 16
Rag and bone and hank of hair, 709 : 14
consuming r. and bone, 717 : 9
Shakespeherian R., 805 : 4
Rag-and-bone shop of heart, 717 : 21
Rage against dying of light, 887 : 4
and hate from Adam down, 570 : 13
blessed r. for order, 767 : 16
crack your cheeks r. blow, 233 : 24
for fame, 385 : 13
hard-favored r., 207 : 16
hatred and murder, 903 : 2
heaven has no r., 324 : 16
hence r. and tears, 96 : *n* 4
in their r. whirl asunder, 201 : 22
jealousy is the r. of a man, 23 : 15
let storm r. stronger, 725 : 5
lust and r., 717 : 13
maker's r., 767 : 16
minds yield to such r., 104 : 16
money r. and love, 863 : 20
much did I r. when young, 715 : 11
no r. like love to hatred turned, 324 : 16
not die here in r., 322 : 18
of the vulture, 459 : 5
outside happy ground, 587 : 8
prepared for r., 748 : 11
puts all heaven in r., 406 : 9
repressed their noble r., 362 : 7
strong without r., 294 : 19
sum of general r., 570 : 13
swalloweth the ground with r., 16 : 38
swell the soul to r., 306 : 22
thrown into r. like lion, 381 : 13
to live, 335 : 19
to r. to lust to write to, 253 : 10
when r. is on one side, 469 : 26
why do the heathen r., 17 : 13
Rages, battle r. loud and long, 443 : 11
dog-star r., 338 : 5
furious winter's r., 243 : 27
Lear r., 717 : 6
Ragged, drunken dog r. head, 441 : 6
light in r. luck, 663 : 8
meadow of my soul, 829 : 7
moon, 874 : 16
overweathered ribs r. sails, 199 : 6
pair of r. claws, 803 : 14
Raggedness, looped and windowed r., 234 : 3
Raging in the dark, 716 : 7
strong drink is r., 24 : 27
waves of the sea, 52 : 26
Rags, arm it in r., 235 : 3
bread ever more of stale r., 793 : 1
clothe man with r., 25 : 9
into r. rend ye, 918 : 11
man clothed with r., 301 : 20
of time, 252 : 8
righteousnesses as filthy r., 31 : 27
some in r., 933 : 21
Rags (*continued*)
tear a passion to very r., 221 : 23
unwomanly r., 485 : 16
virtue though in r., 305 : 4
Raid on inarticulate, 807 : 21
Rail against other folks, 349 : 15
let them r., 427 : 18
road r. pig lead, 760 : 20
run till she leaves r., 731 : *n* 2
Raillery, placing r. in railing, 322 : 17
subject not bear r., 325 : *n* 3
Railroad, I've been working on r., 921 : 17
once I built r., 842 : 5
rides upon us, 559 : 27
spinning-jenny and r., 566 : 6
Railroads, player with r., 761 : 4
Rails upon yon thief, 235 : 2
Railway, threatened with r. share, 614 : 4
Raiment, is not body more than r., 38 : 2
no black r. when I am gone, 95 : *n* 2
sparkling r. bright, 536 : 3
stain all my r., 31 : 26
white as snow, 41 : 29
Rain a deluge showered, 415 : 5
cats and dogs, 919 : 23
cloud turn to r., 512 : 19
clouds return after the r., 27 : 24
collect on roof, 583 : 10
come in out of r., 155 : *n* 2
comforteth like sunshine after r., 189 : 12
dark r. sniveling continuously, 896 : 4
droppeth as gentle r., 200 : 9
dull roots with r., 804 : 26
early and latter r., 52 : 4
fringes be falling r., 928 : 14
go away, 929 : 17
go out of the r., 155 : 5
great houses r. down, 74 : 20
hard dirty r., 824 : 4
hath the r. a father, 16 : 32
he shall come unto us as r., 33 : 10
hey ho wind and r., 214 : 29, 234 : 1
in dust on her shoulders, 822 : 4
in Spain stays in plain, 894 : 19
in thunder lightning r., 235 : 21
influence, 278 : 5
into each life some r., 510 : 11
is over and gone, 28 : 7
it raineth every day, 214 : 29, 234 : 1
knew it would r., 627 : 1
latter and former r., 33 : 10
like r. upon mown grass, 19 : 35
Lord this is huge r., 144 : 20
lovely see r. draw near, 928 : 15
makes not fresh again, 260 : 19
mantle of wind and chill and r., 148 : 22
men want r. without thunder, 556 : 4
monotonously falls r., 839 : 9
naked in dark r., 791 : 3
natives of r. rainy men, 766 : 19
no r. left in heaven, 578 : 9
nobody not even the r., 829 : 13
nor ever wet with r., 59 : 27
nor winter storm nor r., 59 : 26
not raining r. to me, 705 : 5
number the drops of r., 34 : 21
on corn a sad thing, 103 : 11
out o' cold and r., 709 : 1
Rain (*continued*)
pack when it begins to r., 233 : 18
people daily wet with r., 155 : 5
rain go away, 929 : 17
ripple of r., 632 : 7
roof against the r., 823 : 13
sendeth r. on just and unjust, 37 : 12
shower of commanded tears, 188 : 24
silver hosannas of r., 852 : 14
small r. down can r., 917 : 10
smell dew and r., 269 : 5
snow hail and drought, 622 : 19
snow nor r. nor heat, 78 : 19
softly under snow or r., 742 : 15
some r. must fall, 510 : 11
still falls the r., 801 : 6
sunshine after r., 189 : 12
thirsty earth soaks up r., 295 : 7
useful trouble of r., 534 : 8
waiting for r., 804 : 13
walked to hotel in r., 844 : 17
was upon the earth, 7 : 30
weeping like r. on city, 659 : 13
wind storm r. may enter, 351 : 7
with silver flail, 794 : 13
Rainbow, add hue to r., 202 : 5
border be standing r., 928 : 14
comes and goes, 426 : 11
curled around shoulder, 733 : 11
God gave Noah r. sign, 903 : 3
in the sky, 425 : 7
now and then on r., 912 : 10
rainbow rainbow, 878 : 5
somewhere over r., 842 : 6
Rainbow's glory shed, 470 : 1
Rain-drenched hair, 787 : 5
Raindrop, down names r. plows, 642 : 4
Rained ghastly dew, 529 : 24
Raineth drop staineth slop, 792 : 8
rain it r. every day, 214 : 29, 234 : 1
Rainfall, West begins where r. drops, 837 : 5
Rain-giver, Jove the R., 113 : 2
Raining daffodils, 705 : 5
violets, 705 : 6
Rain's, hard r. a-gonna fall, 915 : 4
out of wind's and r. way, 774 : 1
Rains, long r. were falling, 135 : 9
return in rivers, 869 : 13
softly on the town, 674 : 11
winter's r. and ruins, 632 : 8
Rainstorms, inspector of r., 557 : 7
Rain-washed, white as r. bone, 708 : 17
Rainwater, glazed with r., 785 : 11
Rainy evening to read this discourse, 270 : 32
eyes, 195 : 1
morrow, 245 : 3
natives of rain r. men, 766 : 19
Pleiads wester, 692 : 8
weary of wench guest weather r., 347 : 2
Raise commonwealths, 303 : 19
Death old captain r. anchor, 581 : 4
hue and cry, 169 : 10
joys and triumphs high, 350 : 11
Lord shall r. me up I trust, 173 : 5
man can r. a thirst, 708 : 10
music r. and quell, 305 : 10
print news and r. hell, 922 : 4
somewhat loftier strain, 103 : 13
song of harvest home, 536 : 2
stone and find me, 671 : 9
stone cleave wood, 126 : 14

Raise (*continued*)
the genius, 334 : 12
what is low r. and support 283 : 2
Raised a mortal to the skies, 306 : 23
dead shall be r., 49 : 7
in incorruption, 49 : 5
new man r. up in him, 56 : 16
not a stone, 465 : 9
Raisin in the sun, 855 : 2
Raising dingy shades, 804 : 3
empire for r. customers, 366 : 6
Raisons, le coeur a ses r., 300 : *n* 3
Rake among scholars, 488 : 19
every woman at heart r., 335 : 22
horse lean as is a r., 145 : 26
stop to r. leaves away, 747 : 3
Rake's Progress, 539 : 12
Rakes, scholar among r., 488 : 19
Raking up leaves, 641 : 14
when stop r. muck, 687 : 11
Rale, rehearsing with strangled r., 899 : 14
Ralliez-vous à mon panache blanc, 175 : *n* 1
Rally once again, 578 : 13
round the flag boys, 578 : 13
Rallying, white panache r. point, 175 : 1
Ram, black r. tupping your ewe, 229 : 18
caught in a thicket, 8 : 14
how wind doth r., 792 : 8
Ramadans, nurtured by R., 570 : 9
Rambles, Hamlet r., 717 : 6
Rambling, be not r. in thought, 125 : 14
Ramm, how wind doth r., 792 : 8
Ramón, pale R., 767 : 16
Rampallian, away you r., 206 : 10
Rampant for spoil and victory, 658 : 5
maenad of Massachusetts, 634 : 9
Rampart, corse to r. we hurried, 465 : 7
music my r., 823 : 11
no r. against malice, 297 : 15
Ramparts we watched, 446 : 1
Ramps, hasten down r., 864 : 15
Rams, mountains skipped like r., 21 : 21
Ran a hundred years to a day, 519 : 15
before Ahab, 14 : 4
dismayed away, 200 : 22
grief with glass that r., 632 : 9
my heedless ways, 887 : 2
neighing canyons, 843 : 20
on ten winters more, 303 : 16
sunset r. one glorious blood-red, 541 : 18
Rancor, met r. with mirth, 728 : 18
outpouring of inferiority, 784 : 3
will out, 185 : 9
Rancorous rational mind, 716 : 4
Randal, Felix R. the farrier, 656 : 7
Lord R. my son, 927 : 8
Randolph thy wreath has lost rose, 431 : 20
Random grim forge, 656 : 8
I am writing at r., 480 : 1
shaft at r. sent, 431 : 19
we thrown down here at r., 853 : 3
Rang, gongs r. loudly, 767 : 13
sabbath r. slowly, 886 : 21
Range, certain r. of notes, 580 : 4
Cupid doth r., 918 : 15
lives whose r. is small, 619 : 19
weapons their force and r., 900 : 2
with humble liver, 248 : 27
Ranged his tropes, 320 : 19
if I have r., 245 : 15
Ranged (*continued*)
wide arch of r. empire fall, 240 : 14
Ranges, something lost behind the r., 710 : 9
Rank, battle of the first r., 491 : 18
black r. and file, 617 : 6
but guinea's stamp, 411 : 17
great beautifier, 493 : 4
has its obligations, 416 : 7
keep no r. nor station, 892 : 19
marched r. on r., 600 : 28
me with barbarous multitude, 199 : 13
my offense is r., 222 : 25
swollen with r. mist, 280 : 22
things r. and gross, 218 : 6
when man of r. an author, 356 : 22
Rankers, gentlemen r., 708 : 14
Ranks, close r., 915 : 1
for adoration all the r., 365 : 7
of honor, 744 : 11
of Tuscany, 488 : 17
the same with God, 540 : 19
Rank-scented many, 242 : 17
Ransom captive Israel, 563 : 14
them from the power of the grave, 33 : 16
Rant, I'll r. as well as thou, 224 : 23
when you r. and swear, 259 : *n* 8
Rapacious and licentious soldiery, 373 : 12
Rape, castration infanticide r., 903 : 2
of every day, 899 : 13
Raphael made a century of sonnets, 543 : 30
Raphaels, talked of their R., 371 : 21
Rapid, drive the r. car, 377 : 26
Homer eminently r., 586 : 14
lady's imagination r., 440 : 18
Rapidly, works done least r., 542 : 5
Rapping at chamber door, 526 : 10
Rapt seraph adores and burns, 336 : 22
ship run on side so low, 178 : 6
soul sitting in thine eyes, 278 : 13
Rapture, each gay turn thy r. move, 333 : 11
first fine careless r., 541 : 17
of postponed power, 644 : 1
on lonely shore, 458 : 24
then a pain, 660 : 10
Raptures and roses of vice, 632 : 11
illustrious acts high r. infuse, 276 : 2
no minstrel r. swell, 430 : 10
no poetic r. feel, 399 : 16
Rapture-smitten frame, 443 : 6
R'ar back an' pass a miracle, 814 : 16
Rara avis in terris, 122 : *n* 5
Rare and bloodless week of repose, 82 : *n* 6
and radiant maiden, 526 : 12
are solitary woes, 223 : *n* 5
as day in June, 567 : 13
Beaumont, 265 : 14
Ben Jonson, 255 : *n* 3
bird on earth, 122 : 8
delicate and r., 676 : 9
excellent things r., 309 : 5
few rid selves of friendship, 619 : 4
my love of birth as r., 297 : 6
neither rich nor r., 338 : 12
somewhere a r. name, 82 : 10
to meet man outdoors, 558 : 22
tobacco divine r., 259 : 15
Rarely rarely comest thou, 469 : 23
Rarer gifts than gold, 797 : 4
Rarity of Christian charity, 485 : 22
Rascal, biggest r. that walks, 123 : 6
if r. had not given medicines, 203 : 18
Rascally yea-forsooth knave, 205 : 22
Rascals in coach, 567 : *n* 1
lash the r. naked, 232 : 6
law's to take care o' r., 565 : 13
would you live forever, 358 : 2
Rase, slowly r. she up, 926 : 22
Rash, different from being r., 791 : 17
hand in evil hour, 287 : 19
not splenetive and r., 224 : 21
too r. too unadvised, 192 : 13
who reckons on morrow, 75 : 7
Rash-embraced despair, 199 : 28
Rashes, green grow the r. O, 409 : 16
Rashly charged troops of error, 274 : 1
importunate, 485 : 21
Rashness, beware of r., 523 : 1
Raskills, law's to take care o' r., 565 : 13
Rasselas Prince of Abyssinia, 352 : 15
Rast ich so rost ich, 919 : 17
Rat, a dog a horse a r., 235 : 18
begin to smell a r., 169 : 32
how now a r., 222 : 29
killed the r., 934 : 9
mouse studying to be r., 757 : 16
poisoned r. in hole, 322 : 18
Rathe, bring the r. primrose, 281 : 1
Raths, mome r. outgrabe, 612 : 17
Ratify my little halves, 889 : 8
Ratio, increases in geometrical r., 417 : 3
keen and quivering r., 604 : 6
subsistence in arithmetical r., 417 : 3
Ratiocination, pay with r., 290 : 17
Rational ethics, 703 : 14
I am r. therefore sing hymns, 121 : 5
men r. beings, 845 : 15
one r. voice dumb, 868 : 15
rancorous r. mind, 716 : 4
to r. being irrational unendurable, 121 : 1
world presents r. aspect, 422 : 11
Rationalism adventure in clarification of thought, 697 : 11
renounces life, 784 : 11
Rationalist whose reason not sufficient, 844 : 8
Rationalized, contemporary man r. myths, 885 : 16
Rationally, him who looks on world r., 422 : 11
live r. for time assigned, 124 : 27
till women more r. educated, 414 : 7
Rationed, so precious must be r., 731 : 8
Rations, live upon daily r., 548 : 15
Ratisbon, stormed R., 540 : 20
Rats came tumbling, 541 : 2
desert sinking ship, 117 : *n* 2
have quit it, 247 : 14
houses destroyed by r., 312 : 25
land r. and water r., 198 : 17
mice r. and such small deer, 234 : 10
nearness of r., 847 : 3
they fought dogs, 541 : 1
Rats' alley, 805 : 3
Rattle his bones over stones, 486 : 1
pleased with a r., 337 : 7
rifles' rapid r., 827 : 2
Rattling good history, 641 : 20
he was as r. thunder, 241 : 25
o'er stony street, 457 : 15

Rattling (*continued*)
of a coach, 255 : 2
Ravages, irreparable r. of time, 312 : 11
Rave at close of day, 887 : 4
no more 'gainst time, 630 : 21
recite and madden, 338 : 6
Raved, but as I r., 268 : 23
Raveled sleave of care, 237 : 21
Raven, censure pardons r., 122 : 2
grim and ancient R., 526 : 15
himself is hoarse, 236 : 17
locks were like the r., 410 : 7
never flitting, 526 : 19
Poe with his r., 567 : 18
smoothing the r. down, 279 : 19
Ravening, inwardly are r. wolves, 38 : 16
Ravens brought him bread, 13 : 41
He that doth r. feed, 210 : 28
three r. on a tree, 927 : 2
Raving skies opened to voyager, 673 : 19
Ravished ears, 306 : 13
eyes, 325 : 6
with whistling of name, 337 : 15
Ravishing, what dear r. thing, 312 : 19
Raw inclement summers, 322 : 13
Marian's nose red and r., 191 : 15
material of opinion, 682 : 2
Rawness of personal opinions, 692 : 13
Ray, emits a brighter r., 368 : 12
misled by fancy's meteor r., 409 : 5
on ray split the shroud, 545 : 25
purest r. serene, 362 : 8
Shadwell's night admits no r., 304 : 25
Rayformer, called r. remains at large, 722 : 12
Rayless majesty, 330 : 5
Raypublican party broke ye, 721 : 15
Rays, artists send special r., 734 : 13
hide your diminished r., 285 : *n* 3
like ice beneath sun's r., 313 : 7
of morn on Shields, 568 : 19
your r. in midst of sea, 5 : 7
Raze out troubles of brain, 239 : 32
Razed, from books of honor r., 244 : 7
Nature's works to me r., 285 : 5
Razón, sueño de la r. monstruos, 394 : 2
Razor, each holds locked r., 892 : 18
satire like polished r., 341 : 3
Razor's, fate hung on r. edge, 67 : 21
Razors to my wounded heart, 188 : 17
Razure of oblivion, 229 : 5
Reach, above r. of ordinary men, 425 : 11
apple pickers not r. it, 63 : 10
dignity of crimes, 393 : 14
enjoy resources within thy r., 71 : 28
fool to follow what is out of r., 120 : 12
I cannot r. it, 299 : 5
man's r. exceed grasp, 543 : 1
me a gentian, 791 : 1
not condescending to anything within r., 85 : 17
of wisdom and of r., 220 : 7
thing humanly possible is within r., 125 : 7
unreachable star, 890 : 1
until we r. ripest fruit, 183 : 6
wishes for that beyond r., 316 : 15
Reached, heaven not r. at bound, 566 : 2
Reaches five hundred thousand readers, 635 : 7
Reaches (*continued*)
of the street, 804 : 4
thoughts beyond r. of souls, 219 : 12
Reaching forth unto things before, 50 : 4
irritable r. after fact, 479 : 5
Reaction, attack is the r., 355 : 12
if any r. both transformed, 754 : 4
like to see political r., 830 : 15
relation of r. to world, 665 : 3
religion r. on life, 650 : 3
to every action equal r., 313 : 15
Reactionary, I am a r., 830 : 15
Reacts, critic valuable as he r., 653 : 3
know how man r., 791 : 16
Read a good poem, 395 : 5
a little I can r., 240 : 15
and drive night away, 143 : 17
as deliberately as written, 559 : 29
as inclination leads, 354 : 11
aught I could ever r., 195 : 22
best company when you r., 433 : 6
better neither r. nor write, 445 : 4
blockheads r. what blockheads write, 342 : 11
book of fate, 206 : 20
book people praise don't r., 625 : 10
both r. the Bible, 407 : 9
but not distinguish what worth it, 758 : 4
chosen few who r. him, 731 : 9
damn authors they never r., 375 : 12
dare to r. think speak write, 380 : 10
each wound each weakness, 585 : 3
from own works, 846 : 6
from some humbler poet, 510 : 21
haven't r. that for years, 884 : 24
he that runs may r., 377 : 18
history in nation's eyes, 362 : 10
Homer once, 316 : 6
I have r. all the books, 651 : 13
in the bitter letter, 229 : 23
know what I r. in papers, 765 : 15
learn to r. slow, 300 : 16
mark learn, 56 : 3
my title clear, 328 : 14
never r. book not year old, 499 : 5
not poem we have r., 437 : 1
not that I ever r. them, 399 : 5
old authors to r., 179 : 18
only books that wound us, 786 : 4
part all through, 777 : 8
poetry difficult to r., 545 : 4
resolved once more to r. him, 309 : 22
see friends and r. books, 338 : 16
sins scarlet books r., 730 : 13
strange matters, 236 : 19
take up r., 129 : 4
that day r. no more, 454 : 2
that day we r. no farther, 141 : 3
timetable sooner than nothing, 751 : 19
to by a boy, 804 : 13
to doubt or read to scorn, 432 : 6
to r. comes by nature, 209 : 24
very few to r., 424 : *n* 2
what do you r. my lord, 220 : 19
whoso that kan r. hem as they write, 144 : 13
wits to r., 256 : 11
youngsters r. men understand, 169 : 39
Readable, book chief need is be r., 555 : 11
Reader, arouse illusion in r., 652 : *n* 3
delighting and instructing r., 110 : 1
delights r. instructs too, 311 : 13
exciting sympathy of r., 437 : 14
good r. makes good book, 499 : 17
hypocrite r., 580 : 16
I married him, 555 : 19
illuminated is the poem, 741 : 13
last r. reads no more, 518 : 14
look, 256 : 10
no tears in r., 750 : 3
right r. of good poem, 749 : 20
take them not for mine, 145 : *n* 4
what conceal from r., 869 : 10
wise r. quote wisely, 484 : 7
Reader's consciousness, 739 : 3
Readers and hearers like my books, 181 : 22
become more indolent, 368 : 6
five hundred thousand r., 635 : 7
not all books dull as r., 559 : 33
of Boston Evening Transcript, 804 : 6
should be critical of historians, 95 : 18
sleepless to give r. sleep, 340 : 16
Readest, thou r. black, 407 : 9
Readeth, he may run that r. it, 33 : 25
Readiness is all, 224 : 28
Reading, affect you agreeably in r., 386 : 12
after r. your work, 343 : 16
contemplation more than r., 301 : 4
cursed hard r., 399 : 11
digressions sunshine of r., 360 : 2
English dictionary best r., 740 : 18
it with perfect contempt, 798 : 10
maketh a full man, 181 : 13
new era in life from r., 559 : 34
no accident in choice of r., 791 : 11
no r. more fascinating than catalogue, 655 : 2
oppression of mind, 314 : 19
overset mind with r., 663 : 16
peace makes poor r., 641 : 20
sheer casual r. matter, 740 : 18
such r. as never read, 340 : 25
tact a kind of mind r., 664 : 3
teach love of r., 862 : 9
theologian not born by r., 156 : 8
to mind as exercise to body, 327 : 12
tyrannical habit of r., 569 : 7
valueless books, 573 : 1
write things worthy r., 347 : 18
Readings, our r. secret, 764 : 7
Reads, all he r. assails, 333 : 19
as task, 354 : 11
but one book, 270 : 27
he r. much great observer, 215 : 9
Ready, a God r. to pardon, 14 : 31
completely r. state, 553 : 9
conference maketh a r. man, 181 : 13
fire when r. Gridley, 631 : 13
for war way to avoid it, 316 : 12
get weapons r., 575 : 14
in defense, 372 : 20
minds to fellowship, 475 : 20
money Aladdin's lamp, 461 : 25
money makes the man, 328 : 16
my tongue is the pen of a r. writer, 19 : 8
necessity of being r., 522 : 1
no r. way to virtue, 274 : 16
old wife old dog r. money, 347 : 17
rough sir but r., 548 : 21

Ready (*continued*)
to perish in wilderness, 265 : 8
to ride spread alarm, 512 : 7
to try our fortunes, 206 : 27
we always are r., 363 : 16
when sorrow came, 665 : 1
with every nod to tumble, 187 : 15
with you be r. to die, 108 : 2
Real, a man's r. life, 684 : 2
and permanent grandeur, 574 : 8
coming back to r., 768 : 23
dark night of soul, 835 : 11
lead me from unreal to r., 56 : 20
life r. life earnest, 509 : 13
lure of the r., 769 : 17
nothing r. but humanity, 483 : 12
nothing r. till experienced, 479 : 20
only mist is r., 886 : 6
Simon Pure, 321 : 8
something r. yet to be realized, 697 : 9
spirit r. and eternal, 583 : 3
that is moral, 581 : 6
thing that made emotion, 845 : 2
this is the r. me, 647 : 23
war never in books, 577 : 5
what is r. is reasonable, 422 : 8
Realism, Dostoevski's r., 784 : 22
Realities and creators, 496 : 22
less dangerous than fancies, 738 : 9
muddled state sharpest of r., 653 : 16
not images of beauty but r., 83 : 10
Reality, afraid of word R., 776 : 8
appearance never attain r., 413 : 22
attained only be detached, 876 : 17
between idea and r., 805 : 17
capture r. in paint, 638 : 4
fantasy have base in r., 736 : 4
fantasy should have base in r., 736 : 4
final word in r., 909 : 14
flee from r., 784 : 24
give r. to illusion, 757 : 9
history illumines r., 98 : 9
history small part of r., 587 : *n* 2
human kind nor bear much r., 806 : 20
in r. atoms and space, 79 : 11
is things as they are, 769 : 15
mask off r. remains, 100 : 21
no humbling of r. to precept, 905 : 11
of distress, 385 : 1
of experience, 777 : 18
poverty is great r., 858 : 7
regulate imagination by r., 353 : 15
split apart in painting, 774 : 10
the more threatening r. appears, 775 : 3
three mirror same r., 390 : 7
translators between dream and r., 801 : 8
use r. rather than know it, 885 : 14
when criticism parts with r., 744 : 12
your own r. for yourself, 683 : 16
Realize bitterness of life, 614 : 6
I'd been happy, 882 : 3
you don't need aid, 838 : 3
Realized, design of all his words r., 768 : 25
Realm, invade borders of my r., 163 : 15
mysterious r., 471 : 6
riding o'er azure r., 363 : 6
this r. this England, 194 : 13
Realm (*continued*)
turned out of r. in my petticoat, 163 : 16
Realms above, 434 : 3
and islands as plates, 241 : 25
Anna whom three r. obey, 334 : 4
of gold, 475 : 6
whatever r. to see, 368 : 14
Reap an act, 922 : 18
as you sow ye r., 291 : 23
blessings of freedom, 384 : 17
harvest of your land, 10 : 19
he that regardeth the clouds shall not r., 27 : 21
in joy, 22 : 7
men that sow and r., 633 : 20
not wholly r. the corners, 10 : 19
sow not neither r., 38 : 2
that shall he also r., 49 : 32
the whirlwind, 33 : 12
we r. our sowing, 617 : 3
Reaped, all the harvest I r., 516 : 17
iniquity, 33 : 13
wheat never r. nor sown, 311 : 21
Reaper whose name is Death, 510 : 1
Reaping, autumn that grew by r., 241 : 25
Reappraisal, agonizing r., 893 : 2
Reaps bearded grain at breath, 510 : 1
wholesome harvests r., 484 : 6
Rear my dusky race, 530 : 6
tender thought, 345 : 11
to produce and to r. them, 64 : 4
Reared arm crested the world, 241 : 25
hills r. in vain, 562 : 10
himself a throne, 525 : 11
Rearward of a conquered woe, 245 : 3
Reason against it instinct for it, 621 : 1
and experiment have been indulged, 387 : 13
and will of God prevail, 588 : 18
argument needs no r., 65 : 16
art has r. for being, 499 : 11
asked one another the r., 212 : 31
beast that wants discourse of r., 218 : 11
but from what we know, 336 : 12
by r. of strength, 20 : 13
capability and godlike r., 223 : 17
chafe, 495 : 9
common law nothing but r., 171 : 21
customs not concerned with r., 626 : 5
destroys book kills r., 281 : 23
dethroned bereft of r., 496 : 7
discourse of r., 218 : 11
feast of r. flow of soul, 339 : 8
flood of words drop of r., 347 : 13
freed men's minds, 115 : 16
give r. on compulsion, 203 : 31
God's crowning gift, 74 : 21
greatest enemy faith has, 156 : 9
guide by light of r., 678 : 2
has moons, 733 : 3
have I not r. to lament, 423 : 4
human r. is fate, 755 : 11
humanity r. and justice, 373 : 1
ignis fatuus of mind, 315 : 19
Imagination abandoned by R., 394 : *n* 1
immortal all else mortal, 65 : 13
improvable r. of, 482 : 12
in images of sense, 436 : 20
in itself confounded, 225 : 31
in man like God in world, 140 : 3
Reason (*continued*)
is of no use to us, 379 : 6
is past care, 246 : 6
keep r. under control, 125 : 17
know truth not only by r., 300 : 5
knows nothing of, 300 : 4
law is perfection of r., 171 : 21
law ordinance of r. for common good, 140 : 1
left free to combat error, 388 : 16
left free to combat it, 389 : 16
let my will take place of r., 122 : 9
let us r. together, 28 : 30, 872 : 6
lies between spur and bridle, 270 : 12
life of the law, 171 : 21
limitations of conscious r., 844 : 8
losing one's r., 853 : 11
make worse appear better r., 81 : 14
men have lost their r., 216 : 20
Milton wrote in fetters, 403 : 19
most sovereign r., 221 : 21
never failed men, 726 : 12
no other but woman's r., 189 : 29
noble in r., 220 : 28
not listen to r., 537 : 1
not yet guided by r., 732 : 10
nothing law that is not r., 172 : *n* 1
of this thusness, 616 : 18
or any other r. why, 315 : 13
our r. is our law, 287 : 18
panders will, 223 : 5
passions not conform to r., 401 : 16
past r. hunted, 245 : 23
psychological r., 653 : 1
pursue my r. to O altitudo, 274 : 4
rather to f. than r., 414 : 11
rhyme nor r., 174 : 22
right deed for wrong r., 806 : 19
ruling passion conquers r., 336 : 2
salvation of freedom, 851 : 17
sanctity of r., 286 : 31
shall enforce her sway, 399 : 18
sleep of r. produces monsters, 394 : 2
still keeps its throne, 329 : 6
takes the r. prisoner, 236 : 8
teach thy necessity to r., 194 : 5
tell me the r. I pray, 439 : 15
theirs not to r. why, 533 : 12
themselves out again, 208 : 18
to rule mercy to forgive, 305 : 18
victory over r., 812 : 13
we bicker creates war, 165 : 4
we r. deeply when we feel, 414 : 19
what someone else has to say, 537 : 1
where faith in r. timid, 737 : 7
why I cannot tell, 319 : 19
with reasonable men, 505 : 15
worse appear better r., 284 : 8
yield with grace to r., 747 : 2
Reasonable, American public more r., 872 : 19
good ear in music, 197 : 4
holy and living sacrifice, 55 : 19
man mythical, 815 : 17
moderator Death, 274 : 11
no r. man expected, 816 : 1
nothing r. from pure reason, 742 : 3
speak a few r. words, 395 : 5
what is real is r., 422 : 8
wrong way more r., 671 : 7
Reasonableness, will and well-meaning r., 754 : 5
Reasonably, speaking writing voting r., 650 : 14

Reasoned errors, 596 : 8
Reasonest, Plato thou r. well, 326 : 3
Reasoning but to err, 337 : 2
cowards in r., 325 : 4
destroy power of r., 85 : 13
in pride in r. pride, 336 : 18
man is a r. animal, 114 : 20
mathematician capable of r., 84 : 19
self-sufficing thing, 424 : 16
Reasonings, versed in r. of men, 76 : 12
Reason's icy intimations, 486 : 2
in erring r. spite, 337 : 1
words clothed in r. garb, 284 : 13
Reasons, and he had r., 728 : 19
as two grains of wheat, 198 : 5
find of settled gravity, 244 : 17
for scarcity of capital, 783 : 15
governing order and disorder, 344 : 19
heart has its r., 300 : 4
heroism never r., 497 : 24
immoral thing for moral r., 641 : 9
made his mouth water, 291 : 12
plenty as blackberries, 203 : 31
private as well as public r., 387 : 14
Reassures, science r., 776 : 1
Rebecks, jocund r. sound, 278 : 1
Rebeginnings on the frightful task, 883 : 8
Re-begot, ruined me and I am r., 253 : 1
Rebel and revolutionize, 558 : 2
aspiring to angels men r., 180 : *n* 6
aspiring to be angels men r., 336 : 18
good old r., 632 : 5
heretic r. thing to flout, 671 : 4
I'm a good old r., 632 : 5
in act and deed, 704 : 17
quickens to r., 806 : 6
those that r. against the light, 16 : 9
Rebellion, a little r. a good thing, 388 : 6
against United States, 522 : 8
century and half without r., 388 : 7
demands r. makes upon us, 882 : 7
determined to foment r., 392 : 7
lay in his way, 205 : 2
not r. which is noble, 882 : 7
now and then good, 388 : 6
rude eye of r., 202 : 14
rum Romanism r., 546 : 8
to tyrants, 920 : 14
Rebellions of maritime provinces, 800 : 11
Rebellious hell, 223 : 5
hot and r. liquors, 210 : 29
revolting and r. heart, 31 : 35
storms it wooeth, 553 : 3
stubborn and r. generation, 20 : 3
Rebels from principle, 373 : 26
our countrymen again, 589 : 19
Rebirth, craving leads to r., 72 : 23
of Union, 682 : 4
Rebounds, hit hard it r., 355 : 12
Rebuff, welcome each r., 544 : 10
Rebuilding of backward countries, 813 : 15
Rebuke a wise man, 23 : 19
is better than secret love, 25 : 23
recoils, 746 : 18
Rebus, est modus in r., 106 : *n* 8
Recalled, each r. different name, 596 : 17
word cannot be r., 109 : 10
Recant, if I do not r., 153 : 9
Recapitulation, ontogenesis r. of phylogenesis, 617 : 10
Recapture, never could r., 541 : 17
Recede, heard r. disappointed tide, 604 : 11
unpurged images r., 716 : 8
Receipt of little bit of paper, 571 : 10
sitting at r. of custom, 38 : 26
Receive, ask and ye shall r., 45 : 28
Christ r. him, 533 : 6
from dregs of life r., 303 : 11
hand stretched out to r., 35 : 3
if lungs r. our air, 376 : 20
more blessed to give than r., 46 : 23
my soul at last, 350 : 12
our skill to r., 702 : 14
the fugitive, 384 : 12
thy own, 794 : 9
wax to r., 460 : 7
we r. but what we give, 435 : 26
Received, freely ye have r., 38 : 34
Receives comfort like cold porridge, 247 : 25
reproach of being, 245 : 22
Receiveth, one r. prize, 48 : 15
Recht, yer a' r. that's a', 730 : 20
Recipe for making Delacroix, 646 : 9
rare r. for melancholy, 441 : 8
Reciprocal enforceable safeguards, 787 : 16
in marriage obligations r., 471 : 1
Recitative, rude brief r., 575 : 21
Recite In the name of thy Lord, 132 : 17
rave r. and madden, 338 : 6
Reck the rede, 218 : *n* 5
Reckless, make r. choice, 747 : 18
puffed and r. libertine, 218 : 28
what I do to spite world, 238 : 15
Reckon ill who leave me out, 495 : 12
when I count at all, 605 : 17
Reckoned, love that can be r., 240 : 13
Reckoners without host reckon twice, 159 : 17
Reckoning, day of great r., 4 : 9
God swift at the r., 131 : 17
honor a trim r., 205 : 5
no r. made, 219 : 24
sense of r., 208 : 8
truth to the end of r., 229 : 6
Reckons, rash who r. on morrow, 75 : 7
up by dozens, 627 : 13
Recks not his own rede, 218 : 28
Reclined, all on a rock r., 331 : 7
on hills together, 528 : 19
Reclothe us in rightful mind, 514 : 1
Recognition of evil, 63 : 13
of ugliness, 63 : 13
shock of r., 569 : 18
Recognize a wise man, 67 : 15
gods' hand, 863 : 20
good but be barred, 72 : 1
same experience again, 649 : 2
Recognizes, man r. himself in culture, 865 : 14
my book in me, 165 : 20
which God God r., 864 : 17
Recoiled, warmest heart r. at war, 829 : 8
Recoils, rebuke r., 746 : 18
Recollect, cannot r. ignorance in which born, 360 : 26
cannot r. when it begun, 606 : 2
that Almighty gave dog, 432 : 12
Recollected, emotion r. in tranquillity, 424 : 9
Recollection, fond r. presents them, 455 : 6
like living life over, 348 : 17
structure of r., 733 : 17
Recommencée, la mer toujours r., 735 : *n* 3
Recommendation, fair exterior a silent r., 110 : 27
Recommended, no one style r., 900 : 10
Recommends, nimbly and sweetly r. itself, 236 : 21
Recompense as largely send, 362 : 18
injury with justice, 69 : 9
no evil for evil, 47 : 22
service beyond all r., 275 : 28
Reconciled, God and sinners r., 350 : 15
Reconciles, custom r. to everything, 372 : 1
discordant elements, 423 : 18
forgotten wars, 807 : 4
good dinner r., 309 : 25
Reconciliation, covenant of r., 565 : 29
of opposite qualities, 437 : 17
Reconciling mediatory power, 436 : 20
Reconstructed, won't be r., 632 : 6
Reconstructing creature that made footprint, 776 : 7
Reconstruction, demand in R. suffrage, 554 : 8
Record, dreadful r. of sin, 689 : 6
look at the r., 741 : 7
one more the final r., 486 : 10
puts r. on gramophone, 805 : 8
register of God not r. of man, 275 : 9
weep to r., 360 : *n* 2
Recorded, assurance of r. history, 808 : 5
by Muses live for ay, 174 : 9
last syllable of r. time, 240 : 4
Recorders, flutes and soft r., 283 : 22
Recording Angel dropped a tear, 360 : 17
make ourselves r. plate, 638 : 4
man shaving, 860 : 1
Records that defy tooth of time, 330 : 3
trivial fond r., 219 : 27
Recount, such bickerings to r., 289 : 12
Recover and prove an ass, 197 : 20
hair that grows bald, 188 : 3
health through contentment, 79 : 16
that I may r. strength, 19 : 4
Recovered, character easier kept than r., 384 : 21
innocence, 560 : 13
man r. of the bite, 369 : 19
virtue if lost seldom r., 307 : 20
Recovery, I do not believe in r., 863 : 13
Recreant limbs, 201 : 21
Recreation, calm quiet innocent r., 271 : 10
second necessity of life, 666 : 3
without some lawful r., 169 : 36
Recriminate first defense of weak, 437 : 3
Recruit, body of little r., 839 : 9
Rectifies, winds up and r. his own, 289 : 19
Rectitude and sincerity of actions, 744 : 11
marks of God in r., 448 : 3
mind aware of own r., 104 : 28
Rector's, in garden the r. wife, 896 : 15

Recure, woes time cannot r., 172 : 7
Recurrent end of unending, 808 : 13
Red animal war, 732 : 1
as a rose is she, 434 : 9
as stones kissed by dead, 827 : 6
badge of courage, 732 : 3
beauty whose r. and white, 213 : 17
beholding myself rosy r., 726 : 3
blossom in purple and r., 533 : 25
China not seeking to dominate world, 825 : 5
coat r. breeches blue, 440 : 14
coral is far more r., 246 : 1
cow all r. and white, 668 : 13
fair weather for sky is r., 39 : 33
fortunes of my r. people, 419 : 11
hammer of r. and blue, 768 : 2
her lips were r., 434 : 19
herrings, 930 : 2
Hoss Mountain, 666 : 11
I green U blue O, 673 : 20
in coats of r., 740 : 5
in him the r. earth, 671 : 2
in tooth and claw, 532 : 13
jolly r. nose, 268 : 1
Lantern and his undersea folk, 912 : 14
leaf r. and sear, 430 : 13
life stream again, 478 : 8
lips not so red, 827 : 6
lips r. and one was thin, 290 : 1
making the green one r., 238 : 1
Marian's nose looks r., 191 : 15
mark on r. breast still, 514 : 3
men scalped each other, 488 : 11
morn that betokened, 189 : 10
my luve like a r. r. rose, 409 : 22
my sin is r., 315 : 3
my skin is r., 610 : 5
nose makes me ashamed, 310 : 12
pale and hectic r., 467 : 17
plague rid you, 247 : 18
remember R. River Valley, 927 : 18
right hand, 284 : 10
rise with my r. hair, 911 : 12
rose is a falcon, 659 : 6
Rose proud Rose, 712 : 3
rose whispers of passion, 659 : 6
roses r. and violets blew, 173 : 16
sap make cherry r., 799 : 9
shadow under r. rock, 805 : 1
slayer, 495 : 11
so r. the rose, 516 : 12
soldier r. with rust, 666 : 17
spirits and gray, 261 : 22
still and awful r., 434 : 28
sun pasted in sky, 732 : 4
swift r. flesh, 843 : 20
tape, 549 : 6
thin r. 'eroes, 708 : 3
thin r. line of 'eroes, 578 : *n* 4
thin r. line streak, 578 : 14
thoughts were r. thoughts, 731 : 16
tigers in r. weather, 767 : 1
wheelbarrow, 785 : 11
wine when it is r., 25 : 11
Redbreast, robin r. in cage, 406 : 9
Robin R. piously, 917 : 6
Reddens, as an apple r., 63 : 10
where apple r., 541 : 22
Rede, reck the r., 218 : *n* 5
recks not his own r., 218 : 28
Redeem the time, 806 : 3
them from death, 33 : 16
Redeem (*continued*)
these hours, 257 : 17
unread vision, 806 : 3
us from virtue, 632 : 16
Redeemed of the Lord shall return, 31 : 9
visited and r., 42 : 24
Redeemer in hospital gown, 884 : 21
know that my r. liveth, 16 : 4
my strength and my r., 18 : 3
so mighty a R., 54 : 8
Redeeming, past never past r., 899 : 7
Redemption, condemned into everlasting r., 210 : 1
from above did bring, 277 : 6
inestimable love in r., 55 : 7
Redemptive, suffering is r., 909 : 8
Redemptorem, tantum meruit habere R., 54 : 8
Red-handed 134 : 1
Red-hot, last of r. mamas, 788 : *n* 3
Rediscover gods as psychic factors, 754 : 7
Red-leaved table of my heart, 257 : 15
Red-letter day, 170 : *n* 4
days, 441 : 16
Red-line streak, 578 : 14
Redoubling efforts, 703 : 10
Redress balance of the Old, 422 : 7
music send r., 917 : 17
no r. by mob law, 519 : 23
of grievances, 391 : 14
procure r. of wrongs, 380 : 6
things past r. now past care, 194 : 23
Reduce language to seven words, 782 : 21
selfishness, 64 : 8
Reduction of physical processes, 636 : 16
Redundant, summer r., 546 : 1
Redwood, from r. forest to Gulf Stream waters, 881 : 1
Reed, be merciful to broken r., 179 : 11
bruised r. shall he not break, 31 : 4
love tunes shepherd's r., 430 : 6
man is a thinking r., 300 : 7
staff of this broken r., 30 : 26
Reeds, bending r. again and again, 905 : 18
down in r. by river, 507 : 23
Reedy shore, 918 : 17
Reef of Norman's Woe, 510 : 6
Reek, dust and r. of towns, 569 : 20
Reeking herd, 793 : 18
into Cadiz Bay, 541 : 18
Reel, about in r. and rout, 434 : 17
to and fro, 21 : 16
Reeled mind, 854 : 8
sagged and r., 765 : 5
Reeling, send me r. in, 607 : 14
through summer days, 604 : 14
Reference to one consent, 207 : 8
References, money and goods best r., 549 : 29
verify your r., 402 : 9
Refine, cannot r. war, 578 : 15
if good sense r. her page, 311 : 13
it ne'er so much, 256 : 1
Refined, gild r. gold, 202 : 5
or artificial type, 730 : 15
pleasures too r., 335 : 19
thee but not with silver, 31 : 6
Refinement of everyday thinking, 763 : 9
Refinement (*continued*)
on resistance, 372 : 19
rather than fashion, 536 : 6
Refines, how the style r., 333 : 13
Refining, still went on r., 371 : 14
Reflect before throwing images, 818 : 1
how awful to r., 711 : 5
how you are to govern, 372 : 8
Reflected, in law r. lives of men, 643 : 18
Reflecting man twice natural size, 782 : 5
Reflection, adornment is r. of heart, 782 : 12
dispense with necessity of r., 673 : 7
Liberal tempered by r., 588 : 14
on acts of mind, 437 : 21
remembrance and r. allied, 303 : *n* 1
you may come tomorrow, 470 : 4
Reflections, except r. escapades of death, 768 : 18
mortifying r., 515 : *n* 1
Reflects novel reflects blue of skies, 453 : 13
on this fantasia, 769 : 1
who r. too much, 413 : 32
Reflex, conscious movements r., 603 : 5
Reform carried to excess needs reforming, 437 : 2
cautious people never bring r., 577 : 17
is not to equalize property, 88 : 1
let us r. schools, 572 : 18
responsibility step to r., 635 : 24
taking bone from dog, 699 : 3
that you may preserve, 487 : 21
Reformation mere episode, 847 : 14
printing and the R., 755 : 14
revolution and r., 389 : 2
Reformer, no fidget no r., 696 : 8
remains at large, 722 : 12
Reformers of error, 389 : 5
Reforming other people's habits, 624 : 22
reform carried to excess needs r., 437 : 2
Reforms, at forty r. plan, 330 : 10
Refrain from setting yourself judge, 86 : 3
from unholy pleasure, 729 : 14
time to r. from embracing, 26 : 21
tonight, 223 : 11
Refrains, when God sends cheerful hour r., 282 : 10
Refresh, to keep good acts r. with new, 179 : 20
Refreshed, tree of liberty r., 388 : 7
Refreshes, presence of wildness r., 560 : 28
Refreshment, fill full of r., 511 : 4
Refrigerator called England, 711 : 2
keep martini in r., 837 : 10
Refuge, bad man's r., 64 : 22
be r. unto yourselves, 72 : 20
death become sought-after r., 78 : 16
death r. for all, 626 : 16
eternal God is thy r., 11 : 26
go for r. to Buddha, 73 : 6
God is our r. and strength, 19 : 10
God the Everlasting R., 132 : 19
he is my r. and fortress, 20 : 16
home is safest r., 172 : *n* 2
hotel r. from home life, 680 : 11
idleness r. of weak minds, 342 : 6

Refuge (*continued*)
patriotism last r. of scoundrel, 355 : 15
studies a r. in adversity, 98 : 7
Refugium, domus tutissimum r., 172 : 2
Refuse, creeds that r., 632 : 16
heavenly mansion, 716 : 7
make offer he can't r., 897 : 18
never ask r. resign office, 348 : 19
not r. the something I can, 590 : 5
nothing r., 494 : 10
profane fables, 50 : 29
thy name, 192 : 5
till conversion of Jews, 296 : 27
wretched r. of shore, 664 : 10
Refused, stone which the builders r., 21 : 25
Refuses to defend rights, 418 : 14
what one r. in a minute, 412 : 13
Refusing, all remedies r., 182 : 11
caution in r. benefits, 308 : 24
says a lot in vain r., 395 : 10
Refutable, charm of theory r., 657 : 18
Refute, attempts to r. natural law, 856 : 15
who can r. a sneer, 390 : 9
Regain it if you wish, 850 : 18
love once possessed, 289 : 3
Regard, strict r. to conscience, 382 : 11
two qualities inspire r., 87 : 29
without remedy without r., 238 : 17
Regarded, heard not r., 204 : 21
Regardeth, he that r. the clouds, 27 : 21
Regardez c'est un pauvre terre, 581 : *n* 3
Regardless, alas r. of their doom, 361 : 10
Regards to Broadway, 759 : 5
what is before his feet, 95 : 4
Regeneration, suffering may be r., 565 : 10
Regent, Cynthia r. of night, 331 : 8
of love rhymes, 190 : 26
Regent's, Dewey were R. eyes, 647 : 2
Regime collapses of weakness, 813 : 14
gentlemen of old r., 789 : 3
no r. ever loved great writers, 895 : 18
Regiment, half the r. dead, 893 : 12
learned in r. and class, 644 : 14
led r. from behind, 629 : 25
monstrous r. of women, 162 : 1
warring within for r., 183 : 6
Regio, cuius r. eius religio, 133 : 16
Region, calm r. where no night, 267 : 5
thrilling r. of ice, 228 : 20
walk toward unknown r., 576 : 17
Regions, genius seeks r. unexplored, 519 : 24
in soft r. born soft men, 78 : 22
obscure r. of philosophy, 357 : 17
of sorrow doleful shades, 283 : 7
these external r., 768 : 18
Register, history r. of crimes, 383 : 10
multiple perception in art, 793 : 10
of God, 275 : 9
Reg'lar, so awful r. can't stand it, 622 : 16
Regret can die, 532 : 16
die in evening without r., 68 : 14
I have but one life, 401 : 9
my seedtime, 893 : 1
O last r., 532 : 16
old age a r., 501 : 15
Regret (*continued*)
only r. leaving the sky, 142 : 23
or secret happiness, 664 : 5
possibilities I didn't embrace, 654 : 7
remember and r., 492 : 9
trifling education of females, 392 : 13
vain desire vain r., 601 : 21
wild with all r., 531 : 4
Regrets, congratulatory r., 502 : 19
past r. future fears, 516 : 13
that resemble hopes, 564 : 4
wild r. bloody sweats, 676 : 11
Regrette l'Europe aux anciens parapets, 673 : *n* 11
Regretted speech never silence, 112 : 16
Regrow, dragons r. their parts, 885 : 3
Regular, icily r., 533 : 17
most r. most excellent, 696 : 6
so awful r. can't stand it, 622 : 16
Regulate, free to r. industry, 389 : 1
imagination by reality, 353 : 15
my room, 353 : 3
use of property, 687 : 16
Rehearse as ny as evere he kan, 146 : 15
truth within mind r., 527 : 20
Rehearsing his latest breath, 899 : 14
Reign, awful darkness r., 551 : 3
come to r. over us, 136 : 2
existence saw him spurn r., 351 : 10
in hell, 283 : 14
king shall r. in righteousness, 30 : 20
of the good Cinara, 108 : 10
to r. is worth ambition, 283 : 14
to r. to be omnipotent but friendless, 467 : 4
wealth and freedom r., 368 : 16
what is pomp rule r., 186 : 21
where saints immortal r., 328 : 15
Reigned, I have r. with your loves, 164 : 1
Reigneth, the Lord r., 21 : 2
Reigns but does not govern, 167 : 4
God r. government lives, 609 : 8
if censorship r., 378 : 10
no crude surfeit r., 279 : 25
of terror, 579 : 14
Reilly, is that Mr. R., 922 : 17
Reimbursed my store, 604 : 3
Reimpressed by external ordinances, 352 : 24
Rein, find his mouth a r., 633 : 13
not give dalliance r., 248 : 12
rung upon r., 656 : 1
so hold und schön und r., 481 : *n* 8
Reindeer seem over-serious, 799 : 16
Reins, gae his bridle r. a shake, 410 : 6
of power, 524 : 3
Reject, fired that house r. him, 338 : 7
ignoring all you r., 500 : 8
men r. prophets, 582 : 9
that they r. is wrong, 634 : 17
Rejected, despised and r. of men, 31 : 14
Sermon on Mount, 825 : 1
Rejection, allowing r. to obliterate sky, 858 : 11
of particular wish, 678 : 7
Rejects, consciousness r. object, 648 : 15
Heaven r. the lore, 429 : 6
Rejoice at birth grieve at funeral, 624 : 18
desert shall r., 30 : 23
for I have found sheep, 43 : 25
hear thee and r., 427 : 1
heavens r. in motion, 253 : 21
Rejoice (*continued*)
in ancestral Jove Troy's sons r., 105 : 28
in life mark of Greek spirit, 723 : 14
in thy youth, 27 : 23
let James r., 365 : 11
let the earth r., 21 : 2
not over thy enemy, 35 : 13
we are victorious, 71 : 19
we in ourselves r., 436 : 1
Rejoices in the lost lilac, 806 : 6
Rejoiceth as a strong man, 17 : 28
in his strength, 16 : 37
more of that sheep, 40 : 2
Rejoicing, come again with r., 22 : 7
in hope, 890 : 11
see riches partake in r., 281 : 21
Relate and embellish adventures, 385 : 10
these unlucky deeds r., 232 : 20
Related, to whom r. by whom begot, 335 : 11
Relation, all just supply and all r., 254 : 5
poor r. irrevelant, 442 : 6
Relations between aspects of experience, 789 : 2
candor and amicable r., 408 : 3
foreign r., 813 : 11
human r. perfectly exhibited, 89 : 7
in economics no constant r., 775 : 8
renewal of r. nervous, 635 : 5
squire and his r., 548 : 15
stop nowhere, 653 : 10
tedious pack of people, 675 : 22
with intellect only collateral r., 527 : 14
women's training in human r., 853 : 19
Relationship, essential r. to existence, 552 : 11
friendly and charming r., 156 : 7
of author to works, 683 : 6
pervading mystery, 877 : 4
social and family r., 689 : 23
Relative, set out in r. way, 742 : 1
that r. pronoun, 686 : 1
Relatives, fate chooses our r., 385 : 12
vagaries of unattached r., 826 : 15
Relaxation, allowed himself fun and r., 78 : 9
maturity sacred to r., 665 : 15
only r. from labor, 655 : 8
Release, deadly forfeit should r., 277 : 6
ensured r., 692 : 11
from little things, 842 : 14
of atomic energy, 787 : 14
Released prisoned spirit of man, 739 : 5
Relent, shall make him once r., 302 : 14
Relenting fool, 187 : 21
Relentless, Hades is r., 58 : 7
power, 361 : 13
war r., 731 : 5
Relents, my rigor r., 372 : 15
Reliability, shifts of Fortune test r. of friends, 99 : 6
Reliable reporting, 814 : 2
Reliance against tyranny, 520 : 7
brave r. on free discussion, 737 : 8
on divine providence, 387 : 11
self-reliance r. on God, 498 : 19
Relic of departed worth, 457 : 7
Relics, hallowed r. should be hid, 277 : 13

Relics (*continued*)
make music out of fife and drum, 864 : 10
these r. on display, 864 : 10
unhonored his r. laid, 446 : 7
Relief, cricket no r., 805 : 1
for greedy, 780 : 18
for this r. much thanks, 217 : 15
hold out r. coming, 579 : *n* 1
not seek for kind r., 403 : 16
too proud for r., 749 : 13
Relies, on hope wretch r., 368 : 11
Relieve misfortunes by speaking, 275 : 23
the oppressed, 28 : 30
to r. wretched his pride, 370 : 6
what wealth r. conscience, 260 : 5
Relieved, by desperate appliance r., 223 : 14
obliged wealthy and r. poor, 57 : *n* 8
Religio, tantum r. potuit suadere malorum, 100 : *n* 2
Religion a force in itself, 912 : 3
airy subtleties in r., 274 : 3
and not atheism, 373 : 3
Anglo-Catholic in r., 809 : 13
any r. keeping masses satisfied, 814 : 8
behold clear r., 475 : 20
blunderbuss against r., 354 : 2
blushing veils fires, 340 : 28
breathing household laws, 425 : 15
breeds quarrels, 538 : 18
but a childish toy, 183 : 11
Christianity a son r., 679 : 4
depth in philosophy bringeth to r., 180 : 17
different opinions on r., 398 : 2
doubt part of all r., 862 : 3
duty we owe Creator, 383 : 6
enjoy r. prevent others, 616 : 17
enough r. to make us hate, 322 : 2
enterprise for glory of Christian r., 151 : 1
essence of r., 508 : 26
establishment of r., 391 : 14
evil deeds r. prompt, 100 : 4
excess reproach to r., 314 : 12
falls in with our desires, 679 : 3
feelings in solitude, 650 : 2
for religion's sake, 465 : 11
free exercise of r., 383 : 6
free for r., 821 : 10
freedom of r., 389 : 2
full grandeur of r., 679 : 1
get at man through his r., 681 : 4
good that teaches good, 385 : 3
grandeur of States r., 574 : 8
he who controls area controls r., 133 : 16
in r. so uneven, 318 : 8
inconsistent with Christian r., 364 : 7
is an illusion, 679 : 3
knavery and change, 312 : 13
leave r. to family, 590 : 2
lies r. of slaves, 725 : 6
literature substitute for r., 809 : 12
made honest woman, 870 : 3
Marxism is a r., 785 : 1
Mosaic r. a father r., 679 : 4
most prevalent in colonies, 372 : 19
my r. is to do good, 385 : 2
my r. makes me against racism, 904 : 16
Religion (*continued*)
no heresies in dead r., 726 : 9
no part of r. to compel r., 126 : 12
not popular error, 593 : 10
of feeble minds, 374 : 1
of Humanity, 508 : 26
of inequality, 589 : 3
of well-doing and daring, 354 : *n* 4
of which rewards distant, 352 : 24
one r. hundred versions, 680 : 12
one r. true as another, 260 : 1
one's r. neither harms nor helps another, 126 : 11
opiate of people, 706 : 6
opium of people, 562 : 15
orthodox in r., 821 : 6
pagan who defends r., 732 : 5
persecution bad way to plant r., 274 : 9
philosophy handmaid to r., 179 : 6
politics like r., 389 : 5
poverty a reproach to r., 314 : 12
powerless to bestow, 499 : 23
priests not necessary to r., 764 : 15
printing and Protestant r., 472 : 5
propitiation of powers, 673 : 2
protestantism of Protestant r., 372 : 19
restores man to dignity, 704 : 10
rum and true r., 460 : 20
self-righteousness not r., 555 : 18
sensible men of same r., 502 : 23
severed unknowable from r., 853 : 12
slovenliness no part of r., 346 : 11
stands on tiptoe, 269 : 11
substitute for r., 809 : 12
superstition incongruous r., 580 : 8
talk r. to hungry man, 680 : 29
that old-time r., 921 : 15
to control sensory world, 679 : 2
total reaction on life, 650 : 3
vision of something beyond behind within, 697 : 9
we too have our r., 615 : 8
what r. undertakes to do, 679 : 1
when r. becomes frantic, 570 : 8
will not last so long, 73 : 5
without prelate, 484 : *n* 6
wonders of Christian r., 319 : 22
your r. is success, 694 : 12
Religion's, earth and stars for r. sake, 574 : 7
Religions, from poetry r., 861 : 5
heresy lifeblood of r., 726 : 9
necessary to preserve order, 763 : 2
observe our different r., 824 : 12
thirty-two r. one dish, 400 : 18
vicissitude of sects and r., 181 : 15
Religious, appeals to r. prejudice, 596 : 11
dim r. light, 278 : 26
do evil from r. conviction, 300 : 14
duties consist in justice, 385 : 5
feeling a verity, 580 : 9
feeling toward life, 728 : 10
freedom, 757 : 17
limited r. nature, 597 : 8
old r. factions, 374 : 5
people suspicious, 707 : 9
persecution, 373 : 15
ranks of devoutly r. men, 763 : 7
rather political than r., 354 : 9
seed of r. liberty, 569 : 9
suspended r. inquiries, 384 : 2
Religious (*continued*)
thinkers doubters, 862 : 3
vision our ground for optimism, 697 : 10
waves of r. emotion, 799 : 18
way to think of death, 755 : 8
Religious-good, good but not r., 640 : 5
Religiousness, center of true r., 763 : 7
Relinquish, time does not r. rights, 395 : 21
Relish for better kind of man, 651 : 1
him more in soldier, 230 : 13
imaginary r. is so sweet, 226 : 10
no r. of those arts, 326 : 12
of saltness of time, 205 : 24
versing, 269 : 5
Relished, taste by which r., 428 : 8
Reluctance and wrath, 856 : 1
Reluctant feet, 510 : 13
independence r. last resort, 800 : 7
sweet r. amorous delay, 285 : 19
Reluctantly, difficult when you do it r., 96 : 13
Relume, Promethean heat thy light r., 232 : 14
Rely on yourself, 556 : 1
Rem tene verba sequentur, 95 : *n* 9
Remain, as things have been they r., 564 : 16
if our loves r., 542 : 6
laws ought not to r. unaltered, 88 : 2
my thoughts r. below, 222 : 28
nothing will r., 691 : 2
securely orbed, 794 : 4
shall France r. here, 592 : 9
sitting at your table, 786 : 3
smell and taste r., 733 : 17
until death do part, 681 : 1
wished to r. immortally, 734 : 7
with unavenged suffering, 582 : 4
Remained to pray, 370 : 8
Remaineth, while the earth r., 8 : 1
Remains, be kind to my r., 306 : 9
heap of dust alone r., 335 : 11
nature r., 577 : 6
nothing done while aught r., 416 : 1
the One r., 469 : 16
what r. is bestial, 230 : 23
what r. Nature r., 577 : 6
what thou lovest well r., 793 : 3
Remake, it is myself I r., 713 : 4
myself must I r., 717 : 10
Remark, Frenchman's r. shrewd, 376 : 11
Remarkable, nothing r. beneath moon, 241 : 22
Remarks are not literature, 752 : 12
seldom quoted correctly, 770 : 4
Rembrandt, not Velasquez never R., 884 : 23
whether R. or Vermeer, 734 : 13
Remedies, all r. refusing, 182 : 11
die of r. not illnesses, 298 : 17
he that will not apply new r., 180 : 24
worse than disease, 111 : 4
Remedy against consumption of purse, 206 : 5
cannot r. folly of people, 155 : 5
force not r., 538 : 4
Fortune leaves door to r., 168 : 20
found out the r., 228 : 7
God wounds r. follow, 153 : 16
is to inform discretion, 389 : 15
patience best r. for trouble, 93 : 13

Remedy (*continued*)
sought the r., 212 : 31
things without all r., 238 : 17
tobacco sovereign r., 259 : 15
too strong for disease, 75 : 16
true r. for superstition, 373 : 3
worse than disease, 111 : *n* 2
Remember Alamo, 506 : 1
all it is about to r., 899 : 13
and be sad, 608 : 15
and regret, 492 : 9
and understand, 542 : 2
branches ne'er r., 478 : 14
bygone days, 856 : 7
calmness to r., 597 : 1
can't r. how they go, 603 : *n* 7
Christ our Savior, 919 : 20
die on day I now r., 824 : 4
distinctly I r., 526 : 11
fifth of November, 919 : 12
for years r. with tears, 594 : 3
forget that I r., 633 : 16
gentlemen r. blondes, 826 : 3
God and history r., 820 : 10
half r. human words, 735 : 8
house where I was born, 485 : 4
I heard preacher, 575 : 23
if I do not r. thee, 22 : 15
if thou wilt r., 608 : 13
in sweet pangs r. me, 213 : 29
in your narrowing hours, 837 : 3
inn Miranda, 730 : 5
lists of birds, 893 : 8
little note nor r., 523 : 4
Lot's wife, 43 : 37
me to Herald Square, 759 : 5
me when I am gone, 608 : 14
me when in thy kingdom, 44 : 8
night to r., 892 : 3
no man r. me, 640 : 16
not only how much loved, 702 : 5
not r. what I must be, 195 : 5
now thy Creator, 27 : 24
oh still r. me, 446 : 6
only this, 801 : 5
pleasant to r. even this, 104 : 22
politician knows what to r., 637 : 11
Red River Valley, 927 : 18
such a one I r., 529 : 19
sweet Alice Ben Bolt, 566 : 1
that We created man, 131 : 12
that we die all, 35 : 13
the end, 35 : 12
the ladies, 392 : 7
the Maine, 923 : 7
the neckcurls, 873 : 17
the sabbath day, 10 : 6
thee, 219 : 27
things that were precious, 239 : 22
this day in which ye came out, 9 : 29
time to r., 683 : 11
to pay the debt, 79 : 8
us if at all not as lost, 805 : 16
way we parted, 634 : 2
we will r. them, 727 : 1
what I almost heard, 907 : 5
what is imprinted, 85 : 18
what we say here, 523 : 4
who commended yellow
stockings, 214 : 10
who will r. unheroic dead, 795 : 16
who you are, 612 : 22
Remembered, be all my sins r., 221 : 13
blue r. hills, 691 : 9
Remembered (*continued*)
dead r. footsteps, 728 : 17
he shall be no more r., 16 : 10
how often you and I, 591 : 9
I was owned of thee, 606 : 16
in spite of ourselves, 522 : 12
kisses after death, 531 : 4
knolling departing friend, 205 : 20
my God, 439 : 16
no books undeservedly r., 869 : 7
not r. in thy epitaph, 205 : 12
poor Julian, 845 : 7
thy sweet love r., 244 : 10
time r., 632 : 8
when we r. Zion, 22 : 15
would have made self r., 480 : 4
Rememberest not slightest
folly, 210 : 33
Remembering happier things, 529 : 20
soul r. my good friends, 194 : 19
this he wept bitterly, 59 : 10
with twinklings and twinges, 889 : 12
Remembers all that he wrought, 60 : 20
its august abodes, 442 : 16
me his gracious parts, 201 : 26
nature yet r., 426 : 17
who r. famous day, 512 : 6
Remembrance, absence doth breed
continual r., 148 : *n* 8
and reflection allied, 303 : *n* 1
bids r. rise, 368 : 9
do this in r. of me, 48 : 20
fallen from heaven, 632 : 9
fortunate he who has good r., 4 : 1
Jamaicas of r., 607 : 14
let his r. rest, 36 : 8
makes r. dear, 227 : 20
of a guest, 34 : 16
of former things, 26 : 15
of precedent sins, 260 : 4
of prosperity, 35 : 21
of them is grievous, 55 : 17
of things past, 244 : 11
of things to come, 26 : 15
poetry almost r., 479 : 7
rosemary for r., 224 : 1
this do in r. of me, 44 : 3
writ in r., 194 : 10
Remembrances, burden our r., 248 : 18
Rememoring, false god dim r., 811 : 9
Remind him of glory of country, 450 : 5
lives of great men r. us, 509 : 15
things poised to r. us, 733 : 17
to r. me of Lff, 778 : 6
Reminiscence, most dramatic r., 577 : 4
Remission, shed for r. of sins, 41 : 10
without shedding of blood no
r., 51 : 17
Remnant of Spartan dead, 461 : 6
show r. of their fires, 311 : 11
Remnants, deal in r. of r., 324 : 20
Remold it nearer to heart's
desire, 517 : 13
R-e-m-o-r-s-e 718 : 12
Remorse, access and passage to
r., 236 : 17
disjoins r. from power, 215 : 15
farewell r., 285 : 13
sleeps, 359 : 3
such as I cast r., 716 : 3
Remorseful, gaudy blabbing r.
day, 185 : 20
pardon, 227 : 22
Remote, do in that r. spot, 420 : 17
Remote (*continued*)
from the happy, 868 : 20
from wrangling world, 384 : 15
is virtue a thing r., 68 : 23
man seeks for what is r., 89 : 11
place r. and islanded, 664 : 5
something r. yet present, 697 : 9
sound of thunder heard r., 284 : 18
unfriended melancholy, 368 : 13
where r. Bermudas ride, 297 : 8
Remoteness, snow said r., 811 : 17
Remoter aspects of law, 644 : 4
no need of r. charm, 423 : 12
Remove ancient curse, 404 : 21
bends with remover to r., 245 : 18
no one has right to r. us, 419 : 9
not the ancient landmark, 25 : 3
shirt human power not r., 808 : 15
the joint, 613 : 20
things which elemented it, 253 : 3
till Birnam wood r., 239 : *n* 2
Removed, though the earth be r., 19 : 10
three centuries r., 857 : 14
Remover, bends with r. to
remove, 245 : 18
Removes, three r. as bad as
fire, 347 : 34
Remuneration Latin word for three
farthings, 190 : 24
Remus knew this life, 104 : 7
Renaissance mere episode, 847 : 14
Neon R., 911 : 5
Rend, new years ruin and r., 633 : 6
the affrighted skies, 334 : 10
time to r., 26 : 21
turn and r. you, 520 : 7
words divide and r., 632 : 10
Rend, la Garde meurt mais ne se r.
pas, 421 : *n* 8
Rended, forests are r., 431 : 23
Render back from breast, 461 : 6
deeds of mercy, 200 : 9
praise and favor, 507 : 4
to all their dues, 47 : 27
unto Caesar, 40 : 15
Renderest, thou r. to every man
according to his work, 19 : 28
Rendezvous, shall not fail r., 811 : 6
with Death, 811 : 5
with destiny, 779 : 17
Renew a right spirit within me, 19 : 16
herbs that did r. Aeson, 200 : 22
their strength, 31 : 2
tinker more than r., 650 : 10
unspeakable sorrow you bid me
r., 104 : 31
Renewal, flowering of holiness and
r., 881 : 5
lovers' quarrels r. of love, 96 : 5
of relations nervous, 635 : 5
plant seeds watch r., 603 : 7
Renewed, cycle of the ages r., 103 : 14
sum of things ever being r., 100 : 15
to be worn out is to be r., 64 : 10
tree not r., 863 : 14
Renewing, falling out of friends r.
is, 96 : *n* 6
Renounce, guilty of corruption and r.
defense, 179 : 11
the devil, 56 : 4
Renouncement, Liberal tempered by
r., 588 : 14
Renown and grace is dead, 238 : 7
end is the r., 227 : 18

Renown (*continued*)
forfeit fair r., 430 : 10
in high place and of r., 34 : 25
let me win noble r., 59 : 1
men of r., 7 : 27
naught but breath of wind, 142 : 1
oh thou unknown r., 607 : 8
purchased not by violence, 453 : 2
set cause above r., 700 : 6
some for r., 329 : 20
speak no more of his r., 533 : 6
win high r., 59 : 28
Renowned be thy grave, 243 : 28
farewell r. Eretria, 83 : 6
Spenser, 265 : 14
Rent, blood and sweat for r., 743 : *n* 2
envious Casca made, 216 : 23
is sorrow income tears, 267 : 14
lean r. and beggared, 199 : 6
Mordecai r. his clothes, 14 : 32
nothing whole that has not been r., 716 : 18
pay the r. of seem, 829 : 16
spontaneous joy, 713 : 6
the rocks r., 41 : 28
veil of temple r., 41 : 28
Rents, what are thy r., 208 : 6
Reorganized upon the floor, 804 : 24
Repair, Freedom shall awhile r., 364 : 9
keep friendship in r., 354 : 4
some to church r., 333 : 7
Repairs, man always undergoing r., 626 : 18
Reparation for rights at home, 351 : 4
Repay, I will r., 47 : 24
shut when thou shouldest r., 35 : 3
tomorrow will r., 303 : 10
Repeal of obnoxious laws, 589 : 21
Repeat, condemned to r. past, 703 : 11
don't say anything won't have to r. it, 736 : 20
no again and again, 659 : 2
no grievances, 370 : *n* 3
past, 703 : 11
Repeateth, he that r. a matter, 24 : 15
Repeating, oft r. they believe 'em, 320 : 24
Repeats his words, 201 : 26
Repent at leisure, 324 : 5
never my love r., 593 : 4
restore should I r. me, 232 : 14
we do earnestly r., 55 : 17
what's past, 223 : 8
ye kingdom is at hand, 36 : 25
ye who do truly and earnestly r., 55 : 16
you will r. by jingo, 485 : 11
Repentance, call sinners to r., 38 : 28
decline to buy r., 88 : 24
fear of consequence, 293 : 24
garment of r., 516 : 4
give r. to her lover, 369 : 21
on a Sunday, 773 : 9
tears of r. you'll wipe, 404 : 17
Repented, strove and much r., 460 : 15
Repenting, mirth that no r. draws, 282 : 9
Repetition, of r. most master, 768 : 19
Repine, do not r. my friends, 547 : 31
love r., 495 : 9
Replace despair with opportunity, 872 : 10
no one could r. Franklin, 346 : *n* 5
Replenish the earth, 6 : 15
Replication of your sounds, 215 : 1
Replied Fish fiddle de-dee, 551 : 5
O Lord Thou art, 365 : 6
shade r., 527 : 5
with chuckle r., 774 : 3
Replies, heart r., 377 : 13
Reply churlish, 213 : 4
pause for a r., 216 : 16
reply, 199 : 23
sing ye heavens earth r., 350 : 11
theirs not to r., 533 : 12
Report, by evil r. and good r., 49 : 16
fully accurately fairly, 820 : 13
heroism from American view, 574 : 6
ill r. while you live, 221 : 4
me and cause aright, 224 : 31
nor heart to r., 197 : 10
of fashions in proud Italy, 194 : 11
true r. to him who sent you, 25 : *n* 1
vexation only to understand the r., 30 : 15
whatsoever things are of good r., 50 : 7
who knows how he may r., 289 : 6
Reported, their praises might be r., 36 : 11
Reporters' Gallery fourth estate, 472 : *n* 2
Reporting, intelligent r., 814 : 2
Reports of my death exaggerated, 625 : 21
Repose, as well for defense as r., 172 : 3
earned night's r., 510 : 9
foster-nurse of nature is r., 234 : 27
hushed in grim r., 363 : 6
in r. distinct, 902 : 12
in trembling hope r., 362 : 19
leave me to r., 363 : 9
long for a r., 427 : 14
not destiny of man, 644 : 3
placid r. under liberty, 298 : 19
pondering r. of If, 571 : 4
quenched in cold r., 469 : 5
rare and bloodless week of r., 82 : *n* 6
spirit of r., 490 : 3
tabooed by anxiety, 628 : 26
that ever is the same, 427 : 14
thoughts nature gives way to in r., 237 : 11
when got r. insupportable, 635 : 18
worship but no r., 468 : 16
Reposes, in quiet she r., 586 : 3
Reposing, sorrow breaks r. hours, 187 : 11
Repository of hatred, 744 : 8
Reprehend, if I r. anything in world, 398 : 11
Represent, effort to see and r., 653 : 16
Muhammad did not falsely r., 132 : 11
Representation, laws in which we have no r., 392 : 7
taxation without r., 367 : 10
Representative, individual with r., 437 : 17
of highest spiritual authority, 774 : 9
owes you, 372 : 9
proper office of r. assembly, 508 : 17
Representatives, conscience of r., 777 : 2
House of R., 382 : 11
more I see r. of people, 464 : 20
women ought to have r., 414 : 13
Repressed their noble rage, 362 : 7
Repression, price of r., 724 : 18
Reprimand, quarrel or r., 494 : 1
Reproach, cheerfully bear r., 489 : 5
curse astonishment hissing and r., 32 : 16
everything that is a r. among men, 67 : 12
mine ways without r., 113 : 3
neighbor without r., 591 : 11
no defense against r., 326 : 13
receives r. of being, 245 : 22
Reproached me in public, 420 : 11
Reproacheth his Maker, 24 : 14
Reproaching, without r. brethren, 448 : 1
Reprobate, who such r. as I, 640 : 14
Reprobation, fall to r., 232 : 17
Reproduction, preserved by r., 393 : 7
Reproof on her lip, 482 : 9
valiant, 213 : 4
Reprove, check erring and r., 427 : 13
matron's glance r., 369 : 29
not a scorner, 23 : 19
sager sort our deeds r., 250 : 3
Reproved each dull delay, 370 : 7
Republic a raft, 407 : 16
democracy in a r., 725 : 20
for which it stands, 677 : 10
give to r. fourth power, 452 : 2
if you can keep it. 348 : 15
is a dream, 761 : 12
jewel in crown of Social R., 638 : 8
not established by cowards, 814 : 19
of letters, 349 : 25
of man, 852 : 2
security of R., 700 : 3
shine perishing r., 797 : 10
they died to save, 524 : 4
Republican, eternal importance like R. Party, 791 : 6
forming a r. government, 401 : 13
highest government, 579 : 21
model of government, 379 : 7
morality, 452 : 2
only form of government, 388 : 8
party broke ye, 721 : 15
work for R. party, 578 : 4
Republicans, we are all R., 388 : 16
we are R., 546 : 8
Republics, destiny of r. settled, 569 : 10
envy vice of r., 511 : 1
in small r. is stability, 451 : 18
never known to exist, 153 : 23
Repudiate support of communism, 779 : 19
Repudiation, inflation is r., 736 : 15
Repulses, science r. indefinite, 551 : 16
Repulsive, free speech in r. form, 746 : 6
Reputation an idle imposition, 230 : 24
at every word r. dies, 334 : 5
better than my r., 413 : 24
bubble r., 211 : 15
for kindness enters deeply, 89 : 26
gain forever r. among men, 79 : 13
I have lost my r., 230 : 23
maligner of r., 615 : 4
men who survive their r., 165 : 10
more valuable than money, 110 : 19
not aloof in order to gain r., 85 : 17
not carefully preserved, 308 : 23
part of man's self, 648 : 17
reputation reputation, 230 : 23
sold r. for song, 517 : 10
spotless r., 193 : 32

Reputation (*continued*)
written out of r., 319 : 2
Repute, sink present r. for freedom, 567 : 17
Reputed wise for saying nothing, 198 : 3
Request deed in silence, 141 : 13
Requiem, to thy high r., 476 : 28
Requiems, arointing dreams with r., 766 : 21
Requiescat in pace, 134 : 22
Require, that people may r. leader, 85 : 7
thought 'e might r., 708 : 24
what is it men in women r., 404 : 20
Required, much given much r., 43 : 22, 890 : 6
nothing given nothing r., 349 : 11
of us a song, 22 : 15
of us mirth, 22 : 15
this night soul shall be r., 43 : 20
Requires, all human frame r., 730 : 8
for my behove, 162 : 5
Requisite, first r. of good citizen, 687 : 7
meat r. to squirrels, 606 : 18
right to r. means, 401 : 17
Reread classic, 859 : 4
Reremice, some war with r., 196 : 19
Re-resolves then dies, 330 : 10
Rerum, sunt lacrimae r., 104 : *n* 13
Res iudicata pro veritate habetur, 134 : 23
Rescind, voted not to r., 382 : 11
Rescue me protect me, 4 : 9
my soul from their destructions, 18 : 22
nothing can r. me, 184 : 6
trump of r. sound, 494 : 17
Research contribution to ideas, 887 : 17
to steal from many authors is r., 757 : 14
Researchers into public opinion, 869 : 2
Resemblance neglects spirit of objects, 135 : 12
showy r. of distress, 385 : 1
Resemble, actions r. personality, 688 : 7
these donkeys, 899 : 16
Resembled my father as he slept, 237 : 19
Resembles, the most r. God, 409 : 19
Resembleth, love r. April day, 189 : 32
Resent, do not r. criticism, 744 : 12
yoke, 517 : 6
Resentful, when r. it thunders, 609 : 6
Resentment consumes a man, 658 : 20
whim envy or r., 375 : 12
Reserve back shop all our own, 164 : 17
side of last r., 294 : *n* 9
thy judgment, 219 : 1
Reservedly, read books as r. as written, 559 : 29
Réserver une arrière boutique toute notre, 164 : *n* 13
Reside at Table Mountain, 630 : 13
in thrilling region, 228 : 20
Residence, forted r., 229 : 5
Residences, inns not r., 798 : 17
Resides, fire that in heart r., 584 : 18
Resign, never ask refuse r. office, 348 : 19
title and profit I r., 326 : *n* 2
Resignation gently slopes the way, 370 : 3
Resigned, I am not r., 823 : 12
Resigned (*continued*)
pleasing being e'er r., 362 : 14
to shutting away, 823 : 12
trees more r. than other things, 738 : 16
Resinous heart has fed, 715 : 14
Resist beginnings, 113 : 25
boots not to r. wind and tide, 186 : 16
easier to r. at beginning, 152 : 10
everything except temptation, 675 : 8
functions which r. death, 429 : 14
not evil, 37 : 10
strength not adequate to r., 89 : 1
the devil, 52 : 2
Resistance, art begins with r., 727 : 11
effort supposes r., 639 : 7
nonviolent r. paralyzed, 909 : 16
or abject submission, 379 : 2
passive r., 727 : 5
principles of r., 372 : 19
spirit of r., 390 : 12
Resistances, breaking down half-hearted r., 583 : 9
Resisted, rejoice that America r., 350 : 17
Resolute, be bloody bold and r., 239 : 10
breed of men, 577 : 15
gentle plain just r., 576 : 8
haughty vigilant r., 488 : 12
think beforehand that actions be r., 89 : 15
Resolutely, purse most r. snatched, 202 : 25
Resolution, in war r., 746 : 11
man's truth final r., 769 : 18
native hue of r., 221 : 12
never tell r. beforehand, 264 : 3
passed without dissenting, 381 : 6
road to r., 267 : 16
Resolutions, careful r. unerring decisions, 121 : 13
great and mighty r., 291 : 10
keep r., 353 : 5
Resolve is not to seem but be, 71 : 18
itself into a dew, 218 : 5
not only way to r. conflicts, 789 : 14
not shaken from his firm r., 107 : 28
pushes his purpose to r., 330 : 10
to conquer or die, 379 : 2
we here highly r., 523 : 4
Resolved, Catullus be r. and firm, 101 : 20
is once to be r., 231 : 2
once more to read him, 309 : 22
so they r. to proceed, 265 : 6
to be irresolute, 743 : 12
to die in last dike, 373 : 17
to live a fool, 263 : 2
to ruin or rule state, 304 : 3
to take Fate by throat, 610 : 7
Resolves and re-resolves, 330 : 10
Resonance of emerald, 607 : 12
sinister r., 683 : *n* 3
Resort, independence reluctant last r., 800 : 7
of mirth, 278 : 20
Resound in another street, 886 : 6
not r. on earth again, 486 : *n* 1
where word r., 806 : 4
Resources, enjoy r. within thy reach, 71 : 28
full of r., 372 : 20
greater than we supposed, 648 : 3
Resources (*continued*)
man of many r., 59 : 13
of civilization not exhausted, 517 : 22
oneness of r., 898 : 1
rock of national r., 451 : 1
small portion of soul's r., 648 : 3
waste natural r., 687 : 14
Respect, but you lose their r., 154 : 4
decent r. to opinions, 387 : 9
have his son r. him, 308 : 1
idle wind which I r. not, 217 : 2
mingled with surprise, 431 : 14
neighborly r., 743 : 16
no r. of persons with God, 46 : *n* 2
not law so much as right, 557 : 22
of place persons time, 213 : 25
or natural love, 684 : 2
some scholars' stutters, 899 : 5
strength without fearing, 388 : 12
that makes calamity of life, 221 : 12
those equal in any r., 88 : 8
three worthy of r., 581 : 8
too much r. upon world, 197 : 27
woman takes off claim to r., 78 : 4
you in my r. are world, 196 : 17
Respectable, be worthy not r., 536 : 6
great artists seldom r., 772 : 2
hell, 724 : 10
highly r. tribe, 922 : 14
more ashamed more r., 680 : 17
not one r. or unhappy, 574 : 24
professors of dismal science, 474 : 11
since when genius r., 507 : 21
turkey a more r. bird, 348 : 13
Respectables, n'existe que trois êtres r., 581 : *n* 5
Respected, dignity of man r., 787 : 12
Respecter, God no r. of persons, 46 : 10, 486 : 16
Respectful to his elders, 68 : 3
Respectfully return Him ticket, 582 : 4
Respite from long year's watch, 71 : 3
to be dead, 606 : 15
Resplendent, most r. hair, 428 : 23
Responds, some heart r., 510 : 10
Responsibilities, accept your r., 743 : 10
in dreams begin r., 713 : *n* 1
infinite r. of man, 865 : 11
to all living things, 912 : 4
who has many r., 57 : 15
Responsibility, at summit r. increases, 658 : 16
aware under r., 839 : 16
chain of r., 788 : 4
first step in responsibility, 724 : 19
first step to reform, 635 : 24
in dreams begins r., 713 : 9
intellectual r., 818 : 10
no meaning except r., 823 : 20
no one who has not had r., 788 : 4
of great states, 787 : 10
right implies r., 752 : 3
without woman I love, 832 : 2
writer's only r., 838 : 13
Responsible, Chicago r. for Tribune, 801 : 11
for children's needs, 883 : 7
for what we are, 865 : 9
journalism, 814 : 3
no snowflake in avalanche feels r., 876 : 4
not r. for dreams, 754 : 9
through time and eternity, 522 : 11

Responsive, government r. to people, 700 : 3
Rest, absence of occupation not r., 376 : 8
and be thankful, 921 : 5
and faith we need it, 707 : 21
and will not let me r., 481 : 7
body continues in state of r., 313 : 13
cannot r. for seeing countries, 926 : 19
choose ground and take r., 462 : 19
choose their place of r., 288 : 4
cities never have r. from evils, 84 : 15
die or r. at last, 468 : 18
dove found no r., 7 : 31
embrace r. that knows no care, 101 : 4
even fountain have r., 561 : 4
failing that the r. of the city, 84 : 11
far far better r., 549 : 24
for the dead, 616 : 5
from their labors, 53 : 24
furls sails lays him to r., 570 : 7
gets him to r., 208 : 7
God r. you merry, 919 : 20
gone to eternal r., 525 : 11
good in which mind at r., 142 : 4
grant us holy r., 490 : 10
hearts do in the faces r., 251 : 16
her soul she's dead, 224 : 11
here set up my everlasting r., 193 : 28
I will give you r., 39 : 8
if England r. but true, 202 : 20
I'll r. but thou walk, 926 : 19
in doubt to act or r., 337 : 2
in Nature not God, 269 : 1
in soft peace, 256 : 4
is dross, 793 : 3
is silence, 225 : 2
lay me down and take my r., 17 : *n* 2
let his remembrance r., 36 : 8
light rest light, 625 : *n* 3
lightly r., 76 : 4
long long ago at r., 591 : 9
long r. or death, 528 : 18
may he r. in peace, 134 : 22
miseries not let them r., 478 : 21
much veneration but no r., 180 : 19
my heart is at r., 403 : 15
no music in r. Katie, 573 : 6
not our business, 807 : 22
peace and r. never dwell, 283 : 7
perturbed spirit, 220 : 5
profound as grave, 635 : 11
shall shortly be at r., 288 : 29
she's at r. and so am I, 307 : 10
sing thee to thy r., 225 : 3
so may he r., 249 : 12
soldier r., 431 : 8
Swift sailed into his r., 716 : 6
then had I been at r., 15 : 8
then would I fly away and be at r., 19 : 20
there the weary be at r., 15 : 9
thou too shalt r., 397 : 3
thy praise sanctify our r., 597 : 17
to mind cheerer of spirits, 270 : 34
toil and not seek r., 157 : 3
under the trees, 594 : 10
unto your souls, 39 : 8
water rush to r. in air, 837 : 1
wear ourselves and never r., 183 : 6
when I r. I rust, 919 : 17
where peace and r. can never dwell, 283 : 7
who does not know, 113 : 4

Rest (*continued*)
who sink to r., 364 : 8
will not let me r., 567 : 9
William Yeats laid to r., 868 : 11
without haste but without r., 397 : 15
ye brother mariners, 528 : 20
you told them r. first, 849 : 20
Reste, j'y suis j'y r., 514 : *n* 4
Restful, for r. death I cry, 244 : 23
Resting, history knows no r. places, 902 : 10
not a having and r., 588 : 17
place for those who gave lives, 523 : 4
true-fixed and r. quality, 216 : 3
Restless, blown with r. violence, 228 : 20
press r. gigantic, 789 : 4
tenacious but r., 799 : 18
unfixed in principles, 303 : 20
Restlessness, waves made by their r., 571 : 3
Restore, thy former light r., 232 : 14
to earth and thee r., 692 : 10
Restored, all losses are r., 244 : 12
chaos is r., 340 : 28
civilization could be r., 763 : 14
O divinely r., 484 : 1
Restorer, tired nature's sweet r., 330 : 4
Restoreth, he r. my soul, 18 : 7
Restrain, creeds that r., 632 : 16
in me cursed thoughts, 237 : 11
men from injuring, 389 : 1
Restrained, American public more r., 872 : 19
Restraint, acknowledge r. of reverence, 80 : 17
not silence but r., 798 : 17
socialism seeks equality in r., 506 : 12
systems of preference or r., 366 : 8
what r. to grief for one so dear, 107 : 12
wholesome r., 451 : 11
Zeus grant grave r., 71 : 27
Restricted circle of potential, 648 : 3
Restrictions, ascend above r. of world, 621 : 15
Rests and nodding-places, 326 : 15
forgotten that no one r., 849 : 20
here r. his head, 362 : 17
Resty sloth finds down pillow hard, 243 : 23
Result, cause hidden r. well known, 113 : 19
faith in r. makes r., 649 : 12
firm ground of r., 742 : 18
full r. of all, 333 : 1
happiness, 548 : 27
misery, 548 : 27
shot at without r., 743 : 2
Results, science with least r., 673 : 9
Resurrection and the life, 45 : 13
by man came r., 48 : 29
foretaste of r., 463 : 5
in doubt as to the R., 131 : 14
newspaper r. rare, 635 : 11
of dry sticks, 873 : 5
of the body, 55 : 2
of the dead, 48 : 29
unto eternal life, 56 : 13
Resuscitate dead art, 792 : 10
Retail, God who does wholesale not r., 650 : 6
Retailer of phrases, 324 : 20
Retain ability to function, 835 : 10
enduring as marble to r., 171 : 10

Retain (*continued*)
marble to r., 460 : 7
not r. all rare works, 734 : 4
Retaliatory, massive r. power, 803 : 7
Retire like guest sated, 101 : 4
like satisfied guest, 106 : 13
then must art r., 413 : 22
Retired, happiness of r. nature, 326 : 10
Leisure, 278 : 16
pale Melancholy sate r., 364 : 14
sweet r. solitude, 279 : 22
Retirement, Plato's r., 288 : 14
rural quiet friendship, 345 : 12
urges sweet return, 287 : 15
Retiring at high speed toward Japanese, 777 : 14
in r. draw hearts after, 288 : 6
ne'er feels r. ebb, 231 : 18
Retort courteous, 213 : 4
Retrace, shall one r. life, 721 : 8
Retreat, friend in my r., 376 : 11
honorable r., 212 : 5
loopholes of r., 377 : 4
my soul's calm r., 298 : 21
not r. a single inch, 505 : 13
sinner's last r., 892 : 7
Retreated back into money, 835 : 7
Retreating to the breath, 587 : 16
world, 827 : 7
Retrograde if not advance, 383 : 15
Retrogression, progress more general than r., 515 : 6
Retrouvée, l'Éternité r., 674 : *n* 1
Return, all things r. to you Nature, 124 : 19
bid time r., 194 : 27
departed never to r., 409 : 24
dust shall r. to earth, 27 : 25
gone and never must r., 280 : 11
he shall not r. to me, 13 : 21
I ask to be allowed to r., 603 : 1
I shall r., 771 : 3
like him that travels I r., 245 : 15
like prodigal doth she r., 199 : 6
may r. if dissatisfied, 749 : 18
naked shall he r., 27 : 2
naked shall I r. thither, 15 : 4
no eternity will r., 412 : 13
no more to his house, 15 : 21
no one r. from there, 3 : 1
O Shulamite, 28 : 18
once dead never r., 516 : 19
only dead who do not r., 401 : 5
redeemed of the Lord shall r., 31 : 9
retirement urges sweet r., 287 : 15
snatch me not to r., 747 : 16
spirit shall r. unto God, 27 : 25
their thankfulness, 403 : 10
till thou r. unto the ground, 7 : 12
unto dust r., 7 : 12
way whence shall not r., 15 : *n* 3
with the greatest pleasure, 437 : 1
with the year seasons r., 285 : 5
ye children of men, 20 : 11
Returned home previous night, 742 : 1
I have r., 771 : 4
when her aunt r., 730 : 11
Returneth, dog r. to his vomit, 25 : 19
fool r. to his folly, 25 : 19
to dust again, 614 : 17
Returning as tedious as go o'er, 239 : 3
Returns, all r. to sea, 869 : 13
earth's r., 542 : 4
home to find needs, 671 : 8

Returns (*continued*)
justice r., 103 : 14
no traveler r., 221 : 12
not to me r. day, 285 : 5
road whence no one r., 101 : 16
the Golden Age, 103 : 14
Reuben, Tranter R. Farmer Ledlow, 641 : 10
Réussit, rien ne r. comme le succès, 491 : *n* 3
Rêve, un peu de r., 617 : *n* 1
Reveal, full heart r., 436 : 11
half r. half conceal, 531 : 20
joy r. itself when transformed in us, 756 : 9
no secrets, 370 : *n* 3
Revealed by fire, 48 : 5
hath root of wisdom been r., 34 : 22
majesty of gods is r., 59 : *n* 5
things holy r. only to men holy, 80 : 6
unto the meek, 34 : 25
walk r. her as true goddess, 104 : 24
Reveals, time r. all, 115 : *n* 2
to man own folly, 837 : 18
Revel, joy pleasance r., 230 : 26
Revelation, bogus r., 771 : 14
great men texts of R., 473 : 6
in text of men and women, 689 : 18
Revelations, ends with R., 675 : 16
Revelry by night, 457 : 14
midnight shout and r., 279 : 11
mistaken path to happiness, 463 : 11
pomp and feast and r., 278 : 6
Revels long o' nights, 216 : 1
now are ended, 248 : 13
Revenge a wild justice, 180 : 3
breathing r., 561 : 2
by this leek horribly r., 208 : 14
capable and wide r., 231 : 18
Christianity instinct of r., 658 : 17
delight of mean spirit, 122 : 18
envy and r., 283 : 3
if not victory is yet r., 284 : 7
if you wrong us shall we not r., 199 : 18
little R. ran on, 535 : 14
living well best r., 270 : 6
method which rejects r., 909 : 11
nation too great for r., 609 : 9
pen breathing r., 561 : 2
spur my dull r., 223 : 17
study of r. immortal hate, 283 : 8
sweet as my r., 242 : 22
sweet is r., 460 : 17
woman has r. ready, 297 : 19
woman more barbarous in r. 657 : 21
Revenged, so I am r., 222 : 26
Revengeful, in peace hospitable r., 463 : 13
Revenges, time brings in r., 214 : 28
Revenons à nos moutons, 927 : 20
Revenue, individual labors to render r., 366 : 4
scheme yields no r., 372 : 8
streams of r. gushed, 451 : 1
tax where no r. found, 372 : 8
Reverberate hills, 213 : 19
Revere, ride of Paul R., 512 : 6
the unfathomable, 397 : 7
Revered, loved at home r. abroad, 408 : 18
name illustrious and r., 118 : 12
Reverence, acknowledge restraint of r., 80 : 17
Reverence (*continued*)
bards have share of r., 60 : 7
due tradition increases, 657 : 10
for life, 756 : 16
for life-giving earth, 897 : 19
for parents, 70 : 22
great r. for his son, 308 : 1
greatest r. due the young, 122 : 19
Hell do it r., 525 : 14
human nature, 448 : 3
humility sense of r., 77 : 10
in deeper r. praise, 514 : 1
kill r. you've killed hero, 865 : 6
more of r. in us, 531 : 18
none so poor to do him r., 216 : 21
not r. of dead but envy of living, 264 : 19
passions held in r., 526 : 9
some r. for laws, 531 : 15
Reverences gilt popinjays, 472 : 16
Reverend vice, 204 : 5
Reverently, entered into r., 56 : 6
Reverie, excited r., 714 : 14
pleasure of intellect, 492 : 1
Reveries, dreams somnambulisms r., 571 : 3
fantastic r., 638 : 10
so airy, 376 : 27
valley of r., 750 : 15
Reverse, time will r. your opinions, 86 : 3
who prospers one day suffer r., 75 : 4
Reversion is the action of Tao, 64 : 13
no bright r. in sky, 335 : 8
temporal r., 808 : 9
Revery alone will do, 608 : 3
clover bee and r., 608 : 3
not meet cork without r., 607 : 14
Review, can't write can r., 567 : 19
Reviewed, book r. after thirty years, 637 : 10
Reviewers stupid and malignant, 436 : *n* 1
would have been poets, 436 : 15
Reviewing not criticism, 653 : 2
Revile and persecute you, 37 : 4
Revilest God's high priest, 46 : 28
Revised and corrected by author, 346 : 15
Revisit in dreams the dear dead, 76 : 2
Revisitest thus glimpses of moon, 219 : 12
Revisits, gladden him who r. it, 450 : 5
Revive, after two days will he r. us, 33 : 9
lamps straight again r., 250 : 3
Reviving old desires, 516 : 2
Revolt, art r. against fate, 853 : 6
inferiors r. to be equal, 88 : 9
is it a r., 394 : 5
nature falls into r., 206 : 30
Revolted, against r. multitudes, 286 : 26
Revolting and rebellious heart, 31 : 35
bit of human nature r., 597 : 8
Revolution, absence of moral r., 790 : 1
and more cannon shot, 717 : 12
and reformation, 389 : 2
call r. progress, 491 : 19
carrot in painting set off r., 638 : 5
civilization crust over r., 689 : 26
deprive minority justify r., 521 : 10
done away with short of r., 644 : 16
eats own children, 552 : 8
emancipation through r., 866 : 9
Revolution (*continued*)
fellow travelers of r., 770 : 5
French R. began at top, 593 : 1
hurrah for r., 717 : 12
image of r., 5 : 9
in three stages, 719 : 8
inward and outward r., 448 : 4
is natural, 538 : 11
lasts fifteen years, 784 : 20
leaders of social r., 706 : 6
like Saturn, 552 : 8
listen to the R., 770 : 16
not same as inviting to dinner, 826 : 6
not make r. with silk gloves, 766 : 10
not to obtain freedom, 800 : 7
of Rising Expectations, 894 : 16
party of r. civilization, 492 : 7
peaceful r., 891 : 3
produced Declaration of Independence, 800 : 8
scientific r., 847 : 14
served r. plowed sea, 452 : 3
sire it is a r., 394 : 5
stop r. at beginning, 851 : 12
touching is the true r., 916 : 3
tremble at Communist r., 563 : 10
true r. would succeed, 797 : 9
Revolutionary, atomic energy r. force, 787 : 14
bourgeoisie historically r., 563 : 4
either r. or not, 914 : 4
higher ideals r., 649 : 17
if not r. be artist, 914 : 4
in r. times, 816 : 5
movement enters ruins, 813 : 14
proletariat alone r., 563 : 6
reconstitution of society, 563 : 3
right to overthrow, 521 : 11
Revolutionize, not too soon to r., 558 : 2
Revolutions, collapse of r. of 1848, 703 : 2
frequency of r., 871 : 13
in r. great interests at stake, 88 : 10
never go backward, 538 : 19
not made they come, 538 : 11
of China, 826 : 8
state which creates r., 88 : 9
Revolver, hear word culture reach for my r., 816 : 6
Revolving, grief with r. year, 469 : 4
in course of one r. moon, 304 : 10
with a r. wheel, 607 : 12
Reward according to his works, 51 : 10
all for love nothing for r., 173 : 13
angling r. to itself, 270 : 34
good evil r. punishment, 307 : 19
if thou not thine own r., 270 : *n* 7
labor not ask for r., 157 : 3
neither have they any more a r., 27 : 15
no r. offered, 480 : 13
not punishment, 486 : 15
of knowing we do Thy will, 157 : 3
of labor is life, 618 : 14
of thing to have done it, 498 : 11
of virtue is virtue, 497 : 21
success its own r., 670 : 11
virtue is her own r., 270 : *n* 7
waived all r., 545 : 13
Washington without r., 591 : 11
Rewarded evil for good, 8 : 34
for that which ye have done, 132 : 6
they shall be greatly r., 34 : 13

Rewarder, who now will be my r., 302 : 15
Rewardeth evil for good, 24 : 16
Rewards and fairies, 262 : 14
and punishments in cards, 818 : 5
fortune's buffets and r., 222 : 5
in nature no r., 615 : 11
religion of which r. distant, 352 : 24
the past with its r., 863 : 13
Rewrite, don't r. what moving finger writ, 856 : 12
Rex, ego sum r., 298 : *n* 6
Rhadamanthys, fair-haired R., 59 : 26
Rhapsody in blue, 842 : 2
of words, 223 : 2
Rhein, die Wacht am R., 573 : *n* 2
Rhetoric able to contend, 181 : 14
for r. he could not ope, 290 : 18
heavenly r. of thine eye, 190 : 32
in the study, 559 : 30
obscure by aimless r., 596 : 11
of rule of Plato, 281 : 20
wit and gay r., 280 : 2
Rhetorician, grammarian r. geometrician, 122 : 4
sophisticated r., 502 : 20
Rhetorician's rules, 290 : 19
Rheumatics, unless down with r., 94 : 17
Rhine frontier of England, 720 : 11
German's river, 420 : 2
wash city of Cologne, 436 : 13
watch along the R., 573 : 12
wide and winding R., 457 : 25
Rhinoceros, armed r., 238 : 28
Rhodes, Colossus of R., 924 : 3
Rhodopè, no voices O R., 442 : 19
Rhodora, fresh r. in woods, 494 : 4
Rhone, arrowy R., 457 : 27
Rhyme, beauty making beautiful old r., 245 : 12
into ladies' favors, 208 : 18
it hath taught me to r., 190 : 31
lofty r., 280 : 7
many a mused r., 476 : 28
more sweetly than r., 477 : 4
nor reason, 174 : 22
outlive this powerful r., 244 : 18
rounds with r. rune, 494 : 6
rudder of verses, 291 : 8
Runic r., 527 : 11
sudden thought careless r., 636 : 11
told them in r., 440 : 8
unattempted yet in prose or r., 283 : 1
Rhymed doggerel, 148 : 3
Rhymes as suggest freedom, 495 : 22
Namby Pamby's little r., 331 : 4
no r. in my verse, 724 : 9
of r. I had store, 440 : 8
regent of love r., 190 : 26
ripples in r., 494 : 6
so rare to love, 657 : 3
Rhyming, bad r. a disease, 339 : 30
planet, 210 : 8
Rhythm, disturbed some r., 873 : 9
essential in painting, 135 : 11
find absolute r., 783 : 1
I got r., 835 : 21
keeping r. in dancing, 807 : 10
melody deprived of pitch, 801 : 8
one of principal translators, 801 : 8
poor as dirt don't get r., 912 : 15
Rhythm (*continued*)
to world of sound what light is, 801 : 8
Rhythmical creation of beauty, 527 : 14
Rhythms measureless and wild, 76 : 22
those who discern r. of lands, 912 : 3
we tap crude r. for bears, 583 : 11
Rialto, what news on R., 198 : 18
Rib, smote him under the fifth r., 13 : 12
which Lord God had taken, 7 : 2
Riband in cap of youth, 224 : 3
to stick in coat, 541 : 5
Ribbed sea sand, 434 : 25
Ribbon, a r. at a time, 605 : 3
in cap of youth, 224 : 3
prize r. or throne, 556 : 1
road r. of moonlight, 772 : 23
round it, 933 : 5
Ribs down rolling, 822 : 7
he took one of his r., 7 : 2
heart knock at my r., 236 : 11
of Death, 279 : 27
overweathered r., 199 : 6
Ribstone Pippin, 730 : 6
Ricardo, with Malthus and R., 872 : 5
Rice, not stir r. though it sticks, 170 : 32
same old r., 693 : 1
with coarse r. to eat, 68 : 21
Rich abode, 560 : 18
abundance of the r., 27 : 1
and poor all as one, 77 : 3
and poor loved and unloved, 626 : 16
and rare were gems, 446 : 10
as easy to marry r. woman, 539 : 14
attire creeps rustling, 476 : 17
be wealthy not r., 536 : 6
beauty too r. for use, 191 : 26
better live r. than die r., 356 : 7
beyond dreams of avarice, 356 : 20, 358 : 8
blow bugles over r. dead, 797 : 4
brotherhood bind r. and poor 621 : 5
choose likely man in preference to r., 70 : 16
company of just men better than r. estate, 77 : 12
dies r. dies disgraced, 621 : 11
difference between r. and other people, 845 : *n* 1
different from you and me, 845 : 7
dull and drank, 845 : 7
favor to r., 289 : 14
few are r. and wellborn, 401 : 12
few r. own property, 615 : 9
flames and hired tears, 275 : 1
folk ride on camels, 547 : 36
for others if r. for you, 839 : 8
freedom to r. or poor, 824 : 10
get rich, 795 : 5
gets the pleasure, 924 : 11
gifts wax poor, 221 : 14
God who made us r., 507 : 12
gout kills more r. than poor, 301 : 2
gret fool both r. and nygard, 144 : 7
had I interfered for r., 486 : 15
happy in plenty, 337 : 6
have more money, 845 : *n* 1
have power and poor deprived, 85 : 2
high and low r. and poor, 419 : 4
honesty dwells like miser, 213 : 3
hues marriage made, 654 : 16
if r. gets foolish, 722 : 15
if r. whenever you please, 86 : 11
in good works, 51 : 4
Rich (*continued*)
in loss of all I sing, 906 : 9
in poverty, 171 : 13
in things he can let alone, 559 : 21
is better, 789 : 1
jewel in Ethiop's ear, 191 : 26
joys fall not to r. alone, 109 : 8
knowledge a r. storehouse, 179 : 1
labor not to be r., 25 : 6
law forbids r. as well as poor, 655 : 14
laws broken by mighty and r., 63 : 2
let him be r. and weary, 269 : 2
live and die in r-r-r., 549 : 35
live like a wretch and die r., 258 : 24
make r. richer, 419 : 3
maketh haste to be r., 25 : 28
man beginning to fall, 35 : 27
man enther Hiven, 722 : 10
man not glory in riches, 32 : 5
man to enter into kingdom, 40 : 7
many evil men are r., 62 : 12
men rule the law, 369 : 4
moral soil, 742 : 3
neither r. nor poor, 618 : 10
neither r. nor rare, 338 : 12
nor r. at forty, 269 : 32
not gaudy, 219 : 1
people know rich people, 859 : 16
people most afraid, 816 : 5
people who are r., 782 : 9
poor and content is r., 231 : 1
possessed by money, 258 : 22
problem of r. and poor, 621 : 10
pumpkin pie, 513 : 4
quiet and infamous, 488 : 9
richer poor poorer, 814 : 7
riches not make one r., 153 : 14
rob poor, 483 : 2
save few who are r., 890 : 8
say more than this r. praise, 244 : 29
seems it r. to die, 476 : 28
sent empty away, 42 : 23
sent not corn for r. men only, 242 : 8
snow year a r. year, 269 : 17
society productivity and income, 871 : 16
soil for aesthetic growth, 742 : 3
something r. and strange, 247 : 21
stone best plain set, 181 : 8
tempts by making r., 336 : 3
the treasure, 306 : 16
'tis mind makes body r., 189 : 2
to hear wooden dialogue, 226 : 4
too r. a pearl for swine, 291 : 21
two nations the r. and poor, 501 : 18
waster of r. men, 74 : 23
when he is hungry, 86 : *n* 5
when men drink they are r., 81 : 12
when thou art old and r., 228 : 16
with corn, 513 : 16
with forty pounds a year, 370 : 5
with spoils of nature, 274 : 5
with spoils of time, 362 : 7
wot gets pleasure, 924 : 11
Richard Cory one summer night, 729 : 5
Sir R. Grenville lay, 535 : 11
sweet lovely rose, 203 : 12
Richardson, if you read R. for story, 355 : 3
one letter of R.'s, 355 : 2
Richer, bankers are r., 855 : 18
for r. for poorer, 56 : 9
love's r. than my tongue, 232 : 22

Richer (*continued*)
make rich r., 419 : 3
man held to be holier, 127 : 12
quiet mind r. than crown, 178 : 10
rich r. poor poorer, 814 : 7
than all his tribe, 232 : 20
Riches and honors by unrighteousness, 68 : 21
and power gifts of fate, 136 : 14
are for spending, 181 : 1
are ready snares, 150 : 1
best r. ignorance of wealth, 370 : 1
by theft will not stay, 6 : 7
cover multitude of woes, 90 : 18
deceitfulness of r., 39 : 16
earth is full of thy r., 21 : 11
embarrassment of r., 344 : 5
fame and pleasure, 309 : 6
feverish preoccupation with r., 773 : 7
full of days r. and honor, 14 : 28
good handmaid worst mistress, 179 : 14
good name better than r., 110 : *n* 14
good name rather than r., 24 : 34
grow in hell, 284 : 1
have wings, 377 : 1
he heapeth up r., 19 : 3
he that getteth r. not by right, 32 : 13
he that trusteth in his r., 23 : 26
house field and wife great r. 347 : 8
if r. valuable to heaven, 322 : 9
in her left hand r. and honor, 23 : 4
infinite r. in little room, 183 : 12
make themselves wings, 25 : 7
means by which r. acquired, 773 : 7
Moscow store of r., 486 : 9
neglect objects of r., 773 : 7
neither poverty nor r., 26 : 1
no r. above a sound body, 35 : 40
nor r. to men of understanding, 27 : 17
not exchange our excellence for r., 62 : 12
not make one rich, 153 : 14
not profit the sluggish, 3 : 6
of heaven's pavement, 283 : 28
Peru with its r., 481 : 2
poverty and use of service, 247 : 26
renown which r. or beauty confer, 102 : 22
rich man not glory in r., 32 : 5
see her r. partake in rejoicing, 281 : 21
to make gifts to friends, 77 : 3
to make thy r. pleasant, 228 : 16
to such a scoundrel, 322 : 9
use of r. better than possession, 153 : 12
virtue and r. seldom in one man, 259 : 8
watching for r., 36 : 2
Richesses, l'embarras des r., 344 : *n* 2
Richest alchemy, 215 : 14
country r. with happy people, 572 : 19
East with r. hand, 284 : 3
man r. pleasures cheapest, 557 : 17
monarch in Christian world, 412 : 18
Spain is become r. of countries, 151 : 9
Richly, storied windows r. dight, 278 : 26
Richmond, broad-streeted R., 840 : 6
on R. Hill a lass, 399 : 20
Richmonds, six R. in the field, 187 : 32
Richness, much r. in little space, 183 : *n* 9
of soul, 86 : 14
quietness and pleasure, 580 : 20
something in r. I hate, 794 : 2
Rich-proud cost of outworn age, 244 : 21
Rich-wrought, Aphrodite on your r. throne, 63 : 4
Rickety, man r. poor sort of thing, 626 : 18
Rid, can't r. myself of spirits I summoned, 395 : 17
earth of him in my pride, 728 : 15
mend it or be r. on it, 238 : 16
never r. of rest of her, 321 : 3
of friendship of the many, 619 : 4
of temptations by yielding, 484 : 15
of things by writing them, 845 : 3
poets' wares harder to get r., 747 : 19
red plague r. you, 247 : 18
to have got r. of folly, 108 : 17
Ridden, millions ready to be r., 298 : 18
should nonetheless have r., 156 : 10
Riddle, glory jest and r., 337 : 2
had not found out my r., 12 : 15
life's the only r., 630 : 5
of China trade, 799 : 19
of destiny, 442 : 3
of the Sphinx, 74 : 6, 74 : *n* 5
Phoenix r. hath more wit, 252 : 11
redundant, 546 : *n* 1
Sphinx asked Oedipus r., 851 : 3
we shrink from giving up, 630 : 5
wrapped in mystery, 743 : 17
Riddles, God sets nothing but r. 581 : 20
Riddling perplexed soul, 255 : 4
Ride, a few to r. millions, 298 : 18
and spread alarm, 512 : 7
beggar will r. a gallop, 186 : *n* 1
beggars might r., 301 : 13
boldly ride, 527 : 5
cockhorse, 931 : 11
draw bow r. and speak truth, 462 : 4
easy morning's r., 607 : 12
for me I r., 542 : 15
Germany knows how to r., 553 : 10
Haggards r. no more, 693 : 4
in triumph over mischance, 186 : 11
in triumph through Persepolis, 183 : 5
like unwashed platters r., 844 : 2
mankind, 494 : 7
midnight r. of Paul Revere, 512 : 6
next doth r. abroad, 376 : 16
not free horse to death, 171 : 2
of the Valkyries, 552 : 16
on in majesty, 465 : 3
poem r. on own melting, 750 : 4
remote Bermudas r., 297 : 8
roughshod, 549 : 1
to r. to run, 174 : 11
together forever ride, 542 : 16
under water r., 919 : 8
watersmooth-silver stallion, 828 : 13
we do not r. railroad, 559 : 27
Rider, ego to id as r. to horse, 678 : 14
for want of horse r. lost, 270 : 4, 347 : 35
horse and his r. hath he thrown, 9 : 32
steed that knows r., 457 : 11
that breaks youth, 270 : 9
whither your dead r., 841 : 6
Riders of darkness pass, 880 : 4
Rides back to shave again, 846 : 8
breath r. on posting winds, 243 : 21
dusky night r. down sky, 349 : 10
evil news r. post, 289 : 7
forever r. in vain, 742 : 10
hobbyhorse peaceably, 359 : 20
in whirlwind, 325 : 7, 340 : 22
narrow fellow occasionally r., 606 : 13
railroad r. upon us, 559 : 27
tiger afraid to dismount, 743 : *n* 2
upon perfection of his officials, 97 : 8
upon the storm, 375 : 16
Ridicule accidents rebuffs, 574 : 1
best test of truth, 342 : 12
kindness not free from r., 523 : 3
test of r., 325 : 4
to r. philosophy, 300 : 10
without much malice, 523 : 3
Ridiculous, at times almost r., 803 : 17
bitter poverty makes men r., 122 : 5
contemptible animal, 350 : 3
don't make me r., 441 : 6
excess, 202 : 5
from sublime to r., 420 : 9
made arms r., 288 : 23
make my enemies r., 343 : 25
mouse will be brought forth, 109 : 25
no spectacle so r., 487 : 19
nothing so r. but philosopher said it, 98 : 22
pomp of emperors r., 496 : 5
sublime borders on r., 385 : 7
waste sad time, 807 : 8
Riding, cowpuncher a-r. along, 927 : 9
down by Eildon Tree, 926 : 23
eyes through your side, 844 : 2
fate of nation r., 512 : 8
highwayman came r., 772 : 23
in his r. of rolling level, 656 : 1
man goes r. by, 668 : 11
near her highest noon, 278 : 18
o'er azure realm, 363 : 6
on smile and shoeshine, 888 : 3
put on pistols went r., 811 : 2
to and from wife, 846 : 8
upon an ass, 33 : 32
went my love r., 828 : 9
Riding's a joy, 542 : 15
Ridley, Latimer and R. in might of faith, 156 : *n* 5
play the man Master R., 156 : 14
Rien appris ni rien oublié, 400 : *n* 4
de plus, 378 : *n* 6
milieu entre r. et tout, 299 : *n* 4
ne réussit comme le succès, 491 : *n* 3
Rifle, no better companion than r., 592 : 8
Rifles' rapid rattle, 827 : 2
Rift, every r. of subject, 480 : 5
within lute, 534 : 9
Rigged with curses dark, 280 : 18
Rigging, winds whistling in r., 800 : 10
Riggish, bless her when she is r., 241 : 1
Right against unreasonable searches and seizures, 391 : 16
all's r. with the world, 540 : 15
always do r., 626 : 1
are and of r. ought to be, 378 : 12
as a trivet, 546 : 29
as much r. to the road, 659 : 7
as Ribstone Pippin, 730 : 6
aspirations, 73 : 2
be sure r. go ahead, 455 : 9
born to set it r., 220 : 6

Right (*continued*)
cannon to r., 533 : 13
can't be wrong whose life r., 337 : 9
chiefly with the strong, 311 : 15
child of my r. hand, 256 : 3
common r. of humanity, 520 : 8
conduct, 73 : 2
conduct r. argument wrong, 371 : 15
constitutional r. of amending, 521 : 11
contemplation, 73 : 2
customs not concerned with r., 626 : 5
deed for wrong reason, 806 : 19
defend r. to say it, 344 : 11
did that which was r. in his own eyes, 12 : 24
divine of kings, 340 : 24
divine r. of kings, 520 : 8
do great r. little wrong, 200 : 10
dwelling much on r., 311 : 15
effort, 73 : 2
every r. implies responsibility, 752 : 3
every single one is r., 708 : 21
Ezra r. half the time, 845 : 6
firmness in the r., 524 : 7
fool now and then r., 375 : 25
frightening when convinced they are r., 867 : 16
Gertrude always r., 845 : 6
give Rus r. of way, 518 : 9
God defend the r., 185 : 13
great Power make me do r., 595 : 16
hand forget her cunning, 22 : 15
hand is become glorious, 9 : 34
hand offend thee, 37 : 8
hands of fellowship, 49 : 25
he who maintains he's r., 396 : 17
hew to line of r., 602 : 15
his life was in the r., 295 : 19
how forcible are r. words, 15 : 19
idea of the gods, 86 : 4
if r. to vote denied, 578 : 5
if thy r. eye offend, 37 : 8
in r. with two or three, 567 : 4
It must be r., 400 : 6
judge judges wrong, 74 : 13
kind of victory, 788 : 15
know not whether laws r., 676 : 12
length of days in her r. hand, 23 : 4
little island, 429 : 15
livelihood, 73 : 2
makes might, 521 : 5
man knows r. from wrong, 626 : 4
man more r. than neighbors, 558 : 5
may country be always r., 417 : 17
may she always be r., 445 : 19
men should be r. by instinct, 74 : 22
might is r., 138 : 9
mindfulness, 73 : 2
minority always r., 599 : 19
more precious than peace, 682 : 13
more than half people r., 846 : 16
most valued by civilized, 677 : 14
my mind's not r., 893 : 7
my r. none to dispute, 376 : 12
natural r. to use pens, 343 : 20
no r. to bliss, 585 : 7
no r. to open door, 83 : 16
not law so much as r., 557 : 22
not leave r. to chance, 558 : 3
not leave r. to majority, 558 : 3
obedience to law r. not favor, 687 : 9
of conquest, 358 : 14
of laborer to savings, 621 : 7
of millionaire to millions, 621 : 7

Right (*continued*)
of people to assemble, 391 : 14
of way, 925 : 10
on r. hand of God, 55 : 2
original r. of the people, 390 : 14
our country r. or wrong, 445 : 19, 603 : 4
people have r. to knowledge, 380 : 9
people in right jobs, 553 : 14
perhaps r. to dissemble love, 407 : 13
praise and true perfection, 201 : 5
procure advancement of r., 380 : 6
rather be r. than President, 444 : 8
rather wrong with Plato than r. with these, 98 : 23
reader of good poem, 749 : 20
red r. hand, 284 : 10
revolutionary r. to overthrow, 521 : 11
rule of r. and wrong, 602 : 6
rule of r. fitness of things, 349 : 19
sacred r. of elective franchise, 554 : 5
Scylla guards r. side, 200 : *n* 1
simply does what is r., 89 : 15
somebody's r. and ease, 653 : 15
sparkle r. Promethean fire, 191 : 5
speech, 73 : 2
speech after silence r., 716 : 20
struggle between r. and wrong, 520 : 8
that which they will is r., 634 : 17
thing happens to happy, 875 : 3
think at your age r., 611 : 9
those who died with thee for r., 737 : 1
though r. worsted, 546 : 7
thy r. hand shall hold me, 22 : 17
to be let alone, 677 : 14
to be r. is art of arts, 648 : 5
to dignified life, 774 : 8
to keep and bear arms, 391 : 15
to make government, 379 : 10
to possess property, 537 : 3
to remain silent, 820 : 15
to requisite means, 401 : 17
to say what one pleases, 794 : 20
to speedy and public trial, 392 : 1
to strike, 736 : 13
to trial by jury, 392 : 2
to vote not abridged on account of sex, 392 : 6
to vote not denied or abridged, 392 : 5
to write badly, 828 : 7
transforms strength into r., 358 : 13
tried so hard to do r., 631 : 12
true end of love, 253 : 22
truth live with r. and wrong, 829 : 16
until question settled r., 670 : 5
views, 73 : 2
wars for r. thing, 788 : 15
what is r. he will follow, 68 : 15
what thy r. hand doeth, 37 : 14
whatever is is r., 337 : 1
what's r. and fair, 590 : 11
when r. man rings them, 669 : 6
when r. to be kept r., 603 : 4
with strikers r. or wrong, 765 : 11
word powerful agent, 626 : 2
wrong follow king, 534 : 5
ye're a' r. that's a', 730 : 20
you are, 723 : 18
Righted up falling man, 560 : 21
Righteous are bold as a lion, 25 : 27

Righteous (*continued*)
armor of r. cause, 694 : 15
be not r. over much, 27 : 8
company of just and r., 77 : 12
die the death of the r., 11 : 3
flourish like palm, 20 : 18
have not seen the r. forsaken, 18 : 25
I am not come to call r., 38 : 28
judgments of Lord r., 18 : 1, 524 : 7
let him be r. still, 53 : 32
man regardeth the life of his beast, 23 : 29
man to make fall, 173 : 11
nation which keepeth the truth, 30 : 9
not to r. grace, 671 : 11
prayer of r. man, 52 : 6
sold the r. for silver, 33 : 19
souls of the r. are in hand of God, 34 : 13
where were the r. cut off, 15 : 10
Righteousness and peace have kissed, 20 : 9
as waves of sea, 31 : 7
exalteth a nation, 24 : 4
force of r., 727 : 5
found in the way of r., 24 : 13
he looked for r., 29 : 4
his straight path, 89 : 10
hunger and thirst after r., 37 : 4
in view of gain thinks of r., 69 : 6
is man's path, 89 : 21
king shall reign in r., 30 : 20
leadeth me in paths of r., 18 : 7
not infused from without, 89 : 20
not r. to outrage man dead, 73 : 16
three laws of r., 70 : 22
wrath worketh not r., 51 : 30
wrongdoing and r. of men, 60 : 25
Righteousness', persecuted for r. sake, 37 : 4
Righteousnesses are as filthy rags, 31 : 27
Rightful, tenacious of purpose in r. cause, 107 : 28
Rightly to be great, 223 : 19
Rights, ABC of woman's r., 577 : 18
at war with r. of mankind, 388 : 8
become accumulated wrong, 704 : 17
Bill of R. into suicide pact, 821 : 8
certain unalienable r., 387 : 9
civil r. citizens equal, 615 : 1
Declaration of Human R., 774 : 8
essential unalienable r., 387 : *n* 4
fighting for human r., 904 : 15
fundamental human r., 788 : 20
God-given r., 505 : 18
halve r. double duties, 463 : 2
individual given equality of r., 778 : 11
inextinguishable r. of human nature, 418 : 1
inherent in human being, 505 : 18
inherent r., 367 : 4
make real the Bill of R., 753 : 6
man's idea of sexual r., 554 : 7
never exceed your r., 358 : 10
of all human beings, 904 : 16
of children not respected, 796 : 5
of Englishman, 390 : 11
of man, 373 : 19, 616 : 1
of small nations, 682 : 13
parent of American bills of r., 367 : *n* 4

Rights (*continued*)
partisan cares nothing about r., 84 : 1
preserve constitutional r., 700 : 3
preserve entire r., 390 : 13
public good and private r., 398 : 3
reparation for r. at home, 351 : 4
share our r., 824 : 12
slow undoing of human r., 890 : 7
squatter's r. of heart, 848 : 8
talked long enough about equal r., 872 : 9
time does not relinquish its r., 395 : 21
to secure these r., 387 : 9
trample on r. of others, 520 : 7
wilderness bill of r., 841 : 2
women have as much r. as man, 483 : 1
word man defines all r., 672 : 10
Rightwise king of England, 149 : 6
Rigid, man of r. morals, 313 : 2
Rigor, my r. relents, 372 : 15
of the game, 441 : 19
Rigorous teachers seized my youth, 586 : 9
Riley, life of R., 922 : *n* 9
Rill, cool Siloam's shady r., 452 : 6
moon on Monan's r., 431 : 5
Rim, beyond utmost purple r., 530 : 13
sun over mountain's r., 541 : 15
sun's r. dips, 434 : 21
Rima wild solitary girl, 646 : 2
Rime was on the spray, 640 : 4
Rimini miminy piminy, 628 : 11
Rimless floods, 843 : 14
Ring at end of nose, 550 : 8
at last r. to evensong, 161 : 7
becomes thin by wearing, 100 : 7
bells of heaven, 732 : 16
bright gold r. on wand, 446 : 10
bright the r. of words, 669 : 6
circle of wedding r., 325 : 2
cloudy flaming opal r., 711 : 12
curfew not r. tonight, 669 : 19
dance in r. and suppose, 749 : 9
impression as from seal of r., 85 : 18
let freedom r., 514 : 12
maids dance in a r., 250 : 8
my r. encompasseth thy finger, 187 : 2
O bells, 576 : 7
of pure and endless light, 299 : 6
only pretty r. time, 212 : 33
out the old, 532 : 22
out wild bells, 532 : 21
out your bells, 176 : 8
the r. so worn, 400 : 9
what shall we do for r., 550 : 8
with harmonies of Liberty, 733 : 5
with importunate chink, 373 : 28
with this r. I thee wed, 56 : 10
woods answer and Echo r., 174 : 17
Ring-a-rosie, tots sang R., 698 : 14
Ringed with azure world, 532 : 28
Ringing grooves of change, 530 : 8
plains of Troy, 529 : 8
Rings, in airy r. skim heath, 334 : 16
tumbling in twenty r., 733 : 1
when right man r. them, 669 : 6
Rintrah roars, 403 : 18
Rio, rolling down to R., 710 : 4
Riot, purple r., 476 : 13
spent waves' r., 633 : 19
woods in r., 691 : 7
Rioting, not in r. and drunkenness, 47 : 29
Riotous living, 43 : 26
Riotously, flung roses r., 721 : 5
Ripe and good scholar, 249 : 15
cherry r. I cry, 266 : 3
crops are r., 740 : 1
field of r. corn, 804 : 6
from hour to hour we r., 211 : 6
hour r., 206 : 32
once let r. moment go, 404 : 17
trap moment before it's r., 404 : 17
what shelter to grow r., 585 : 17
Ripeness is all, 235 : 11
Ripening his greatness is a-r., 249 : 3
summer's r. breath, 192 : 14
Riper, amuse his r. stage, 337 : 7
Ripest fruit first falls, 194 : 17
fruit of all, 183 : 6
peach highest, 665 : 8
Ripple of rain, 632 : 7
Ripples in rhymes, 494 : 6
Rippling, folds r. in breeze, 539 : 3
Rire de tout, 378 : *n* 5
est le propre de l'homme, 157 : *n* 10
Rise alone and drink more, 455 : 1
and fight again, 926 : *n* 7
and shine give God glory, 935 : 26
and take control, 888 : 6
and walk with him, 76 : 5
at six dine at ten, 492 : 6
bids remembrance r., 368 : 9
by sin, 228 : 1
caused himself to r., 338 : 14
constellations when they r., 71 : 3
created half to r., 337 : 2
early to r., 347 : 12, 831 : 8
evening is come r. up, 102 : 8
expectation r., 368 : 11
foul deeds will r., 218 : 26
from flesh to spirit, 873 : 20
happy those whose walls already r., 104 : 25
I caused sun to r., 726 : 3
in heaven's lightland, 5 : 4
in the heart, 531 : 3
joyful all ye nations r., 350 : 15
kings r. and set, 468 : 16
let a new earth r., 888 : 6
light to r. by and I r., 545 : 7
like fountain for me, 535 : 1
maketh sun r. on evil and good, 37 : 12
move stones of Rome to r., 216 : 29
my Shakespeare r., 256 : 11
not r. early never do good, 353 : 7
out of ash I r., 911 : 12
out of wreck r., 546 : 2
stoop to r., 262 : 18
sun sets to r. again, 545 : 22
suns that set may r. again, 255 : 16
then we shall r., 267 : 5
though war should r. against me, 18 : 12
till we are called to r., 607 : 2
to feet as He passes by, 707 : 23
to r. love stoops, 544 : 14
tomorrow's sun may never r., 324 : 23
truth crushed will r. again, 471 : 12
up at the voice of the bird, 27 : 24
up my love, 28 : 7
up so early in morn, 921 : 17
we die and r. the same, 252 : 11
we fall to r., 546 : 7
Rise (*continued*)
what are you when sun shall r., 251 : 1
why r. because 'tis light, 252 : 21
wilt thou therefore r. from me, 252 : 21
with lark, 175 : 17
with occasion, 522 : 12
woe unto them that r. up early, 29 : 5
Risen, Christ r. from dead, 48 : 29
Christ the Lord r. today, 350 : 11
He is r., 42 : 15
he is r., 54 : 10
Jesus Christ r. today, 317 : 8
Lord is r. indeed, 44 : 16
the Lord is r., 54 : 10
there is a people r., 300 : 23
Riser, dawn comes no sooner for early r., 935 : 15
Rises by lifting others, 615 : 6
from prayer better, 600 : 9
hidden laughter, 807 : 8
hooray up she r., 934 : 19
howls hoo and r., 768 : 12
my gorge r. at it, 224 : 14
soul that r. with us, 426 : 14
sun gives light soon as he r., 348 : 14
unspeakable desire, 585 : 15
Riseth from feast with keen appetite, 199 : 5
late trot all day, 347 : 22
with fleas, 269 : 31
Rising, beating way for r. sun, 854 : 3
before the r. sun, 328 : 11
earth a meaning to us, 822 : 10
every land rejoices at his r., 5 : 3
Expectations, 894 : 16
fogs prevail upon day, 304 : 25
from affluence to poverty, 624 : 7
from r. of the sun unto going down, 21 : 20
I see them r., 778 : 6
let others hail r. sun, 363 : 15
listen the wind is r., 793 : 16
more worship r. than setting sun, 99 : 12
motion of r. day, 875 : 2
of the sun, 919 : 21
or falling's all one, 874 : 20
plat of r. ground, 278 : 19
Proteus r. from sea, 428 : 1
Revolution of R. Expectations, 894 : 16
shadow r. to meet you, 805 : 1
through change and storm, 465 : 2
vicious spiral of r. prices, 762 : 8
warm cheek and r. bosom, 362 : 21
wind is r., 735 : 12
Risk, art unthinkable without r., 816 : 17
conquer without r., 275 : 16
flatterer r. everything, 323 : 27
I had to take and took, 749 : 11
if not ready to r. life, 853 : 4
of reigns of terror, 579 : 14
t'other half for freedom, 567 : 17
Risking, not giving life but r. life, 870 : 10
only by r. we live, 649 : 12
Risks, great deeds wrought at great r., 78 : 18
take calculated r., 791 : 17
Rival, cannot r. for one hour, 609 : 11
know I may not r. him, 830 : 12

Rival (*continued*)
law admit of no r., 447 : 18
remains to r. what they have done, 81 : 5
Rivalries, organized r., 682 : 8
Rivalry of aim, 635 : 9
Rivals are the worst, 320 : 2
jealousy of r. near throne, 392 : 12
Rivalship of wisest men, 327 : 10
River, Alph the sacred r., 433 : 21
among r. sallows, 477 : 19
at my garden's end, 339 : 10
away you rolling r., 934 : 20
crookedest r. in world, 623 : 2
cross r. rest under trees, 594 : 10
down in reeds by r., 507 : 23
drifting down big r., 623 : 22
Eliza across r., 538 : 21
genius of each r. valley, 912 : 3
Germany's r. but not border, 420 : 2
ghastly rapid r., 526 : 2
glideth at own sweet will, 425 : 14
great r. and sea which is fresh, 151 : 6
great r. take me to main, 531 : 10
lake glimmering pool, 592 : 6
let me love r. and woodland, 104 : 4
Lethe the r. of oblivion, 284 : 22
like foam on r., 431 : 11
like snow falls in r., 411 : 8
lived on R. Dee, 382 : 6
longest r. in world, 623 : 2
monstrous big r., 624 : 2
not step twice into same r. 70 : 3
Oceanus the ocean r., 869 : 13
of crystal light, 666 : 16
of oblivion, 284 : 22, 593 : 11
on a tree by a r., 629 : 16
one more r. to cross, 936 : 3
over r. through wood, 490 : 20
peace as a r., 31 : 7
pilot cares about nothing but r., 623 : 8
Rhine wash city of Cologne, 436 : 13
see one r. and see all, 259 : 4
she's fading down r., 700 : 10
spreadeth out her roots by the r., 32 : 11
strong brown god, 808 : 1
swap horses crossing r., 523 : 8
Thames noblest r., 326 : 22
there is a r., 19 : 11
time a r. of strong current, 124 : 25
time r. without banks, 925 : 6
tirra lirra by r., 528 : 26
washed in life's r., 403 : 14
water of r. never the same, 137 : 13
way-hay you rolling r., 934 : 20
weariest r., 633 : 22
where brook and r. meet, 510 : 13
will reach sea, 633 : *n* 3
Rivering, beside r. waters of, 778 : 5
River's, primrose by r. brim, 423 : 16
Rivers, as brooks make r., 307 : 2
as long as r. flow, 929 : 5
as long as r. shall run, 104 : 29
at their source, 793 : 19
by shallow r. birds sing, 183 : 9
by the r. of Babylon, 22 : 15
deepest r. least sound, 172 : *n* 7
fire r. cannot quench, 186 : 19
I've known r., 854 : 12
my soul deep like r., 854 : 12
no r. no wells no springs, 849 : 12

Rivers (*continued*)
not step twice into same r., 70 : 3
of the kings, 840 : 5
of water in a dry place, 30 : 21
rains return in r., 869 : 13
run into the sea, 26 : 12
run to seas, 307 : 2
same image in r., 570 : 4
shallow brooks and r. wide, 277 : 25
tree planted by r., 17 : 12
Rivets, busy hammers closing r., 208 : 1
on bands of gold, 888 : 11
Rivulet, neat r. of text, 398 : 29
Rivulets hurrying through lawn, 531 : 13
meadow r. overflow, 642 : 6
Road, 'ammer along 'ard 'igh r., 660 : 14
as much right to the r., 659 : 7
below me, 669 : 2
broad hard-beaten r., 495 : 29
but one r. leads to Corinth, 109 : *n* 4
butterfly upon r., 707 : 5
by r. his ever-open door, 57 : *n* 8
dark r. whence no one returns, 101 : 16
devils in twists of r., 735 : 3
does r. wind uphill, 608 : 10
endless r. you tread, 691 : 15
free as the r., 268 : 21
from Montgomery, 909 : 12
from which whole earth call, 899 : 9
grows strange, 569 : 3
heaven above r. below, 669 : 2
house by side of r., 57 : 32, 685 : 12
is smooth, 61 : 17
lonesome r., 435 : 3
long and dusty to grave, 667 : 14
matrimony r. to wealth, 554 : 12
new to me as always, 664 : 7
no r. or ready way to virtue, 274 : 16
no royal r. to accommodations, 737 : 4
no royal r. to geometry, 92 : 4
open r., 575 : 9, 669 : 3
poor slaves tread, 468 : 21
rail pig lead, 760 : 20
ribbon of moonlight, 772 : 23
right r. to Ireland, 855 : 9
rough r. leads to greatness, 114 : 27
royal r. to Thebes, 863 : 18
smooth r. of life, 360 : 24
straggling r. in Spain, 742 : 10
take to open r., 575 : 9
takes no private r., 337 : 16
to Hades easy to travel, 92 : 7
to hell gradual, 842 : 9
to resolution, 267 : 16
to stars through atom, 776 : 10
Tobacco R., 857 : 10
up and down City R., 922 : 1
up and road down one and same, 70 : 6
virtue demands thorny r., 165 : 2
which leads to peace, 389 : 2
will be less tedious, 103 : 21
wind uphill all the way, 608 : 10
winding r. before me, 445 : 12
with bread and wine walk r., 935 : 10
ye'll take the high r., 921 : 9
Yellow Brick R., 677 : 8
Roads, Backward Glance o'er Traveled R., 577 : 10
crooked r. are of genius, 404 : 7
how many r. man walk down, 915 : 2

Roads (*continued*)
improvement makes straight r., 404 : 7
open when you rise, 5 : 7
road new as r. are, 664 : 7
two r. diverged, 747 : 13
Roadway, cry of child by r., 712 : 12
Roam, absent from Him I r., 429 : 17
all morning sends to r., 692 : 2
dunce sent to r., 375 : 24
ever let fancy r., 477 : 14
everywhere I r., 598 : 4
faithful Gêlert r., 423 : 1
home where buffalo r., 927 : 19
long wont to r., 525 : 9
not their hearts that r., 709 : 7
on light shining still, 587 : 12
soar but never r., 429 : 9
though we may r., 465 : 4
where'er I r., 368 : 14
wish to r. farther, 396 : 28
Roamed, how sweet I r., 402 : 12
with my soul, 527 : 1
Roamin' in the gloamin', 731 : 1
Roaming, after r. many lands, 574 : 3
ceaseless thoughts of r., 313 : 23
in the gloamin', 731 : 1
mistress mine where r., 213 : 21
storm r. sky uneasily, 878 : 4
Roar, cannon's opening r., 457 : 16
grating r. of pebbles, 587 : 14
grievous r., 438 : 12
grumble rumble r., 591 : 3
hear it r. now, 429 : 19
hiss now becoming r., 811 : 17
Homer and Whitman r., 728 : 4
lion's imperative r., 867 : 15
melancholy long withdrawing r., 587 : 16
men want ocean without roar, 556 : 4
music in its r., 458 : 24
of only beast in arena, 720 : 17
other side of silence, 565 : 23
set table on a r., 224 : 14
swinging low with sullen r., 278 : 19
Terror in house does r., 406 : 4
think lion sleeping because he didn't r., 412 : 8
thundering cannons r., 371 : 10
welkin r., 206 : 15
you as any nightingale, 196 : 8
you gently as sucking dove, 196 : 8
young lions r. after prey, 21 : 11
Roared, cracked growled r. howled, 434 : 11
Declamation r., 351 : 12
loud r. dreadful thunder, 415 : 5
well r. Lion, 197 : 18
Roaring Bill who killed him, 730 : 12
devil as r. lion, 52 : 16
empty tigers or r. sea, 193 : 23
with hollow blasts, 331 : 7
words of my r., 18 : 5
Roars it through the hall, 592 : 4
Rintrah r., 403 : 18
Roast beef of England, 349 : 7
beef of old England, 349 : *n* 3
in hell r. you like herrin, 411 : 14
rules the r., 152 : *n* 5
set house on fire to r. eggs, 180 : 23
with fire, 9 : 24
Roasted crabs hiss in bowl, 191 : 15
very likeness of r. crab, 196 : 12
Rob, if writer r. mother, 838 : 13

Rob (*continued*)
jaybird don't r. own nes', 662 : 12
lady by marriage, 349 : 23
neighbor he promised to defend, 488 : 11
not the poor, 25 : 2
Peter pay Paul, 160 : 4
rich r. poor, 483 : 2
starve ere I'll r. further, 203 : 19
us of our joys, 920 : 4
words r. Hybla bees, 217 : 8
Robbed, he's not r. at all, 231 : 10
not wanting what stolen, 231 : 10
that smiles, 230 : 1
we was r., 836 : 11
Robber, Barabbas a r., 45 : 31
Robbers, the more r. there will be., 64 : 20
what makes r. bold but lenity, 186 : 7
Robbing, live by sharping and r., 348 : 13
think little of r., 454 : 21
Robe, giant's r., 239 : 28
intertissued r. of gold, 208 : 7
judge's r., 228 : 6
of clouds, 460 : 6
Robert, believe R. who has tried it, 106 : *n* 4
Robes and furred gowns, 235 : 3
embroidered scarlet r., 701 : 15
garland and singing r., 281 : 11
loosely flowing, 255 : 18
mountain in azure hue, 443 : 4
riche or fithele, 145 : 27
sky r. spun of Iris' woof, 279 : 8
washed r. in blood, 53 : 15
Robespierre, Declaration more revolutionary than R., 800 : 8
sea-green Incorruptible, 473 : 20
Robin, call for r. redbreast, 262 : 3
fainting r., 606 : 12
redbreast in a cage, 406 : 9
redbreast piously, 917 : 6
what will poor r. do., 932 : 6
who killed Cock R., 930 : 9
Robin Hood, old wives' tales of R., 720 : *n* 3
Robinson Crusoe, 318 : 13, 358 : 23
here's to you Mrs. R., 915 : 14
Robot, waited upon by r. slaves, 832 : 1
Robots, Rossum's Universal R., 814 : 14
Robs me of that which not enriches him, 230 : 33
Robust and vivid illustration, 610 : 2
Robustious periwig-pated fellow, 221 : 23
Rock, all on a r. reclined, 331 : 7
ay this is the famed r., 639 : 16
cradle will r., 660 : 19
crag of the r., 17 : 1
dwell on r. or in cell, 172 : 17
eagle dwelleth on r., 17 : 1
eagle of the r., 793 : 18
founded upon r., 38 : 20
hard r. feels nothing, 721 : 1
he is the R., 11 : 23
he only is my r., 19 : 27
it is the Inchcape R., 440 : 1
knew the perilous r., 439 : 17
laws sand customs r., 626 : 6
lean upon death as on r., 797 : 17
living as black r. star, 906 : 6
Lord is my r., 13 : 24
meeting rock know love, 811 : 15
Rock (*continued*)
Moses smote r. twice, 10 : 26
no water only r., 805 : 10
of Ages, 386 : 3
of offense, 29 : 14
of our salvation, 20 : 20
on which Freedom stumped toe, 855 : 4
poetry old as r., 495 : 25
safe upon solid r., 822 : 18
sails well but strike r., 407 : 16
shadow under red r., 805 : 1
shadows of a great r. in a weary land, 30 : 21
small r. holds back great wave, 59 : 23
takes on appearance of nearby r., 67 : 4
that is higher than I, 19 : 26
the tall r. the mountain, 423 : 12
this r. shall fly, 431 : 13
towered citadel pendant r., 241 : 17
upon this r. I will build, 39 : 36
way of a serpent upon a r., 26 : 4
which Hercules bequeathed, 639 : 16
will split, 790 : 10
with motion of morning, 874 : 9
Rockabye baby, 660 : 19
Rockbound, stern and r. coast, 470 : 14
Rocked in cradle of deep, 456 : 5
me to patience, 475 : 19
to sleep between billows, 570 : 7
Rocket, life like r. flies, 912 : 10
numbers r. mind, 900 : 2
Rockets' red glare, 446 : 1
Rockies, ghost train in R. buried in snow, 905 : 18
Rocking, cradle endlessly r., 575 : 17
cradles now r. in land, 623 : 1
Rock-ribbed, hills r., 471 : 4
Rocks and stones and trees, 424 : 14
bold anfractuous r., 804 : 16
cries of cicadas sink into r., 314 : 1
even among these r., 806 : 7
hand that r. cradle, 573 : 18
nor can sap be in r., 101 : 1
older than r., 638 : 11
over r. wood and water, 490 : 3
seas laugh when r. near, 262 : 5
soften r. or bend oak, 324 : 14
soundings quicksands r., 479 : 14
that are steepest, 919 : 3
the r. rent, 41 : 28
throne of r., 460 : 6
trees wind, 557 : 21
walled round with r., 634 : 12
what gray r., 806 : 8
whereon greatest men wrecked, 288 : 8
Rocky ledge woods untamed, 696 : 11
shore beats back siege, 194 : 14
Rod, a chief a r., 337 : 13
Aaron's r., 9 : 19
and blows not much good, 156 : 1
beaten with his own r., 158 : 20
cast thy r. before Pharaoh, 9 : 18
creed is a r., 634 : 6
criticism r. of divination, 711 : 17
Father chiefly known by r., 570 : 6
he that spareth his r., 23 : 34
Jonathan put forth the r., 12 : 37
lo with a little r., 674 : 16
not pious longer than r., 156 : 1
of empire, 362 : 6
Rod (*continued*)
of iron, 53 : 2
out of the stem of Jesse, 29 : 18
spare r. and spoil child, 91 : *n* 3, 291 : 19
spare r. spile child, 722 : 22
thy r. and thy staff, 18 : 7
to check the erring, 427 : 13
wisdom be put in silver r., 403 : 17
Rode by witches, 623 : 21
him through mire, 933 : 16
horses up to bed, 740 : 5
off in all directions, 728 : 1
the six hundred, 533 : 9
upon a cherub, 17 : 26
Roderick, where was R. then, 431 : 15
Roderick Dhu, Saxon I am R., 431 : 12
Rodillas, mejor morir que vivir en r., 759 : *n* 2
Rodless Walton of brooks, 685 : 10
Rods, bleeding from Roman r., 377 : 22
Roe, be thou like to a r., 28 : 25
following the r., 410 : 9
Roes, breasts like two young r., 28 : 11
Roger, Sir R. made reflections, 326 : 22
Rogue and peasant slave, 221 : 6
every inch not fool is r., 304 : 18
joined this r. and whore, 323 : 2
Rogues, hear r. talk of court news, 235 : 12
Roguish, equity is a r. thing, 263 : 13
Roi, plus royaliste que le r., 927 : 21
Rois, l'exactitude la politesse des r., 402 : *n* 1
Roland, a R. for an Oliver, 136 : *n* 10
Child R. to dark tower, 234 : *n* 3
sound your horn, 136 : 12
valorous Oliver wise, 136 : 13
Roland est preux et Oliver est sage, 136 : *n* 10
Role, child r. to be born, 704 : 14
Roles, self-interest plays all r., 293 : 7
Rolet, cat's a cat R. a knave, 311 : 7
Roll, centuries r. back to age of gold, 108 : 11
confirm tidings as they r., 325 : 9
darkling down torrent, 352 : 1
'em up, 921 : 12
eyes begin to r., 340 : 17
from soul to soul, 531 : 2
in ecstasy at your feet, 786 : 3
me over fair, 572 : 7
my log I roll yours, 115 : 10
of common men, 204 : 11
of world eastward palpable, 640 : 6
on from yonder tower, 773 : 15
on thou deep and dark blue ocean, 458 : 25
out of me years r., 634 : 4
seas r. to waft me, 336 : 19
up leafy Olympus, 103 : 29
walk the r. of earth, 822 : 5
Rolled as five thousand years ago, 571 : 9
round in earth's diurnal, 424 : 14
two gentlemen r. into one, 415 : 9
wear bottoms of trousers r., 803 : 18
Rollest, thou r. now, 458 : 27
Rolleth a stone, 25 : 20
Rolling Dakotas under hull, 822 : 7
down to Rio, 710 : 4
eye in fine frenzy r., 197 : 12
like a r. stone, 915 : 6
no more through r. clouds, 456 : 17

Rolling (*continued*)
over r. waters go, 530 : 25
stone gathers no moss, 111 : 17
time hath pressed, 516 : 14
Rolls, blue wave r. nightly, 459 : 14
it under his tongue, 319 : 4
through all things, 423 : 13
Roma locuta est causa finita est, 129 : *n* 5
Romam, O fortunatam natam me consule R., 99 : *n* 2
Roman, all Greek all R. fame, 339 : 20
bleeding from R. rods, 377 : 22
candles exploding, 901 : 3
Catholic Church still exist, 488 : 7
concern to rule under law, 105 : 24
ghost of deceased R. Empire, 264 : 18
gibber in R. streets, 217 : 21
high R. fashion, 241 : 23
historian of R. Empire, 384 : 6
holiday, 458 : 21
Holy R. Empire, 343 : 7
I am a R. citizen, 98 : 4
I am the R. king, 298 : *n* 6
I'm a R. for that, 329 : 10
more antique R. than Dane, 224 : 32
neither R. nor an empire, 343 : 7
noblest R. of them all, 217 : 13
play the R. fool, 240 : 7
rather be a dog than such a R., 216 : 32
senate long debate, 325 : 17
struggle to found R. state, 104 : 17
sweet R. hand, 214 : 21
then R. now I, 691 : 7
thought hath struck him, 240 : 17
wherever R. conquers he dwells, 115 : 8
world is falling, 128 : 12
would that R. people had single neck, 116 : 1
Romance, absence of r. in my history, 80 : 15
and poetry need ruin, 504 : 2
learned r. as she grew older, 441 : 1
moment of strength of r., 683 : 11
symbols of high r., 478 : 18
touch honey of r., 674 : 16
Romanism, rum R. rebellion, 546 : 8
Roman's, act lover's or R. part, 335 : 8
life Roman's arms, 488 : 16
Romans call it stoicism, 325 : 14
countrymen and lovers, 216 : 13
established friendly relations, 81 : *n* 1
friends R. countrymen, 216 : 17
last of all the R., 217 : 12
to whom R. pray, 488 : 16
when in Rome do as R. do, 127 : *n* 5
Romantic character in art, 639 : 4
Ireland's dead and gone, 713 : 11
ruin that's r., 629 : 17
Romanus, civis R. sum, 98 : *n* 4
orbis ruit, 128 : *n* 4
Rome, aisles of Christian R., 493 : 18
and other pilgrimages, 152 : 1
city of the soul, 458 : 15
found R. a city of bricks, 110 : 8
from R. to Iceland, 311 : 12
grandeur that was R., 525 : 9
has spoken case closed, 129 : 13
high and palmy state of R., 217 : 21
hook-nosed fellow of R., 206 : 28
idea of writing decline and fall of R., 384 : 7
Rome (*continued*)
if built at all, 893 : 18
in R. you long for country, 106 : 22
lash that beat down R., 717 : 4
let R. in Tiber melt, 240 : 14
loved R. more, 216 : 14
move stones of R., 216 : 29
my country, 458 : 15
natal neath my consulship, 99 : 2
not built in one day, 160 : 8
since the founding of R., 133 : 3
taller town than R., 742 : 11
time doubt of R., 461 : 12
when in R. live in Roman style, 127 : 6
when R. falls the world, 458 : 22
Romeo come forth, 193 : 11
Juliet and her R., 193 : 31
wherefore art thou R., 192 : 5
Romuli, in R. faece, 98 : *n* 11
Romulus, dregs of R., 98 : 17
Ronsard writ praise for me, 162 : 12
Ronyon, rump-fed r. cries, 236 : 1
Rood, no r. has not star, 494 : 2
terrace walk and half r., 339 : 10
Roof against the rain, 823 : 13
burning r. and tower, 715 : 16
cat on hot tin r., 301 : *n* 3
cat on tin r., 887 : 11
Cinderella fulfilling beneath r., 768 : 18
fretted with golden fire, 220 : 28
may be frail r. shake, 351 : 7
no r. to shroud his head, 257 : 20
rain collect on r., 583 : 10
rule under this r., 382 : 1
starry firmament for r., 637 : 21
tongue cleave to the r. of my mouth, 22 : 15
Roofs, done with r. and men, 696 : 13
of gold, 207 : 7
of the world, 575 : 3
Rooftops, purple dusk above r., 811 : 13
Rookery, leads clanging r. home, 529 : 18
Rooks in families homeward go, 642 : 6
Rooky, makes wing to r. wood, 238 : 21
Room, ample r. and verge enough, 363 : 5
city r. of Transcript, 846 : 1
civet in the r., 376 : 4
cleanly r. lavender in windows, 271 : 3
coming to that holy r., 254 : 17
convent's narrow r., 427 : 28
do not need leave your r., 786 : 3
Elysium as far as nearest r., 608 : 4
fifty springs little r., 690 : 17
flung himself from r., 728 : 1
for many a more, 936 : 5
for misgiving, 75 : 4
for Shakespeare in your tomb, 265 : 14
from which faith gone, 859 : 11
glowing embers through the r., 278 : 20
heart prepare Him r., 328 : 13
her empty r. is cold, 97 : 10
here in little lonely r., 711 : 13
how little r. we take in death, 272 : 11
in r. friend await, 608 : 4
in the r. women come and go, 803 : 10
infinite riches in little r., 183 : 12
lain in adjoining r., 605 : 13
Room (*continued*)
my heart keeps empty, 267 : 6
no r. in the inn, 42 : 27
no r. now for dilettante, 745 : 11
not r. for Death, 562 : 5
not r. to swing cat, 365 : 2
ocean sea not sufficient r., 257 : 5
of absent child, 201 : 26
on earth for honest men, 384 : 19
one little r. an everywhere, 251 : 15
paces about r. alone, 805 : 8
regulate my r., 353 : 3
sea r. to tell truth in, 569 : 17
smoke-filled r., 695 : 11
soul hath elbow r., 202 : 17
struggle for r. and food, 514 : *n* 7
tiptoed to daughter's r., 912 : 13
unable to sit still in a r., 299 : 20
who sweeps a r., 269 : 8
wine-barrel r., 765 : 5
world house of one r., 637 : 21
world in one small r., 713 : 17
Rooms, been in r. we cannot die in, 902 : 4
boys in the back r., 762 : 7
other voices other r., 903 : 4
talked between the r., 605 : 14
thousand furnished r., 804 : 3
Roosevelt, answer I will give R., 744 : 13
died in harness, 746 : 7
Roosian, might have been R., 627 : 18
Roost, come home to r., 440 : 3
ruleth all the r., 152 : 20
Rooster, hongry r. don't cackle, 662 : 14
Rooster-heeled in all weather, 902 : 1
Root and all in hand, 535 : 10
ax laid unto the r., 36 : 29
filial piety r. of man, 289 : 13
free down to r., 429 : 12
from which tyrant springs, 85 : 5
get with child a mandrake r., 252 : 1
government never take r., 420 : 8
hog or die, 847 : 12
insane r., 236 : 8
lack of money r. of evil, 680 : 27
learned r. of Homer, 257 : *n* 5
leaves many r. one, 713 : 8
love of money r. of evil, 51 : 2
nips his r. then he falls, 249 : 3
of heaven and earth, 64 : 2
of honesty in good education, 120 : 7
of the kingdom, 89 : 8
of the matter, 16 : 5, 649 : 19
of wisdom, 34 : 22
one striking at r. of evil, 559 : 19
tree whose r. is firmly fixed, 131 : 3
what you are r. and all, 535 : 10
withered because no r., 39 : 14
Rooted, great r. blossomer, 715 : 17
honor r. in dishonor, 534 : 14
lover r. stays, 495 : 19
shakes r. folly of age, 311 : 13
sorrow, 239 : 32
strongly r. as envy, 399 : 4
weeds are shallow-r., 185 : 15
Rootholds, go back to earth for r., 761 : 15
Rootless, life becomes r. plant, 289 : 13
Root's, buds sleep in r. white core, 478 : 9
white core, 478 : 9
Roots, branch shall grow out of his r., 29 : 18

Roots (*continued*)
discover your r., 861 : 16
grass r., 698 : 13
marsh grass sends in sod, 651 : 9
new r. better than no r., 861 : 16
no r. in hotels, 725 : 18
of lilac under soil, 751 : 8
poison England at r., 741 : 16
problems have r. in past, 788 : 6
rose among r., 668 : 18
spreadeth out her r. by the river, 32 : 11
stirring dull r., 804 : 26
Rope between animal and Superman, 657 : 12
draw sin with a cart r., 29 : 6
enough till haltered themselves, 158 : *n* 7
escape from r. and gun, 332 : 5
just above ground, 786 : 2
lay out money on a r., 258 : 23
Negro past of r., 903 : 2
to hang yourselves, 158 : 11
Rope-dancer physician magician, 122 : 4
Ropes, all its r. relent, 749 : 4
blunders like r., 491 : 21
Rory O'More, says R., 482 : 10
Rosa, sub r., 274 : *n* 10
Rosalind, heavenly R., 210 : 19
no jewel like R., 212 : 3
Rosary, couple o' guns and R. beads, 786 : 11
my r. my r., 700 : 13
Rose again the third day, 55 : 2
among thorns, 127 : 4
and put down Yellow Book, 866 : 16
autumn r. more exquisite, 171 : 20
Aylmer whom these wakeful eyes, 442 : 18
beauty's r. might never die, 243 : 31
bestows the fading r., 271 : 19
breast that gives r., 600 : 21
bud of thought wants to be r., 720 : 19
by any other name as sweet, 192 : 6
cankers in musk r. buds, 196 : 19
cheerless over hills, 513 : 20
crossed the road, 639 : 20
desert shall blossom as the r., 30 : 23
die of a r., 336 : 20
earthlier happy is r. distilled, 195 : 21
fairest when budding, 175 : *n* 9
familiar as r. in spring, 124 : 26
find where last r. lingers, 107 : 17
fire and r. are one, 808 : 18
gather r. whilst prime, 173 : 14
glut sorrow on r., 477 : 22
go lovely r., 276 : 7, 773 : 15
gone with all his r., 516 : 3
him that loved r., 693 : 6
if love were what r. is, 633 : 11
immortal Shakespeare r., 351 : 10
in deeps of my heart, 712 : 12
in gutter, 812 : 9
into the r. garden, 807 : 2
is a rose is a rose, 752 : 8
killing as canker to r., 280 : 13
last r. of summer, 446 : 14
laurel and myrtle and r., 395 : 3
leaves when r. dead, 469 : 18
love r. leave on stem, 494 : *n* 3
loved wood r., 494 : 14
lovely is the r., 426 : 11
mighty lak' a r., 685 : 1
moral shut in r., 530 : 14
Rose (*continued*)
my luve like a red red r., 409 : 22
no more desire r., 190 : 13
O R. thou art sick, 405 : 5
of our love, 900 : 3
of Sharon, 28 : 4
of yesterday, 516 : 6
of youth, 241 : 9
on such lopped limbs, 873 : 5
one perfect r., 827 : 13
onion r. among roots, 668 : 18
queen r. of garden, 533 : 23
ravage r., 540 : 13
red as a r. is she, 434 : 9
red r. a falcon, 659 : 6
red r. proud r. sad r., 712 : 3
red r. whispers of passion, 659 : 6
Richard sweet lovely r., 203 : 12
said r. of love, 900 : 3
she lived as roses do, 176 : 17
slowly r. she up, 926 : 22
so red the r., 516 : 12
spring vanish with r., 517 : 12
sweeter in bud, 175 : 22
tell the crooked r., 886 : 12
tell you how sun r., 605 : 3
that lives little hour, 471 : 9, 773 : 15
the morrow morn, 435 : 12
thick with lily and red r., 618 : 5
Thistle Shamrock R. entwine, 608 : 9
thought like full-blown r., 476 : 13
threatening to bloom, 897 : 6
under the r., 274 : 24
up in his prime, 811 : 2
vernal bloom or summer's r., 285 : 5
wavers to a r., 640 : 2
white r. a dove, 659 : 6
white r. breathes of love, 659 : 6
without a thorn, 399 : 20
without thorn the r., 285 : 16
wreath has lost r., 431 : 20
Roseau, un r. pensant, 300 : *n* 4
Rosebud garden of girls, 533 : 23
set with willful thorns, 530 : 22
Rosebuds, crown ourselves with r., 34 : 11
filled with snow, 250 : 6
gather ye r., 266 : 11
Rose-lipped maiden, 691 : 13
young and r. cherubin, 232 : 4
Rosemary and rue, 246 : 25
for remembrance, 224 : 1
Rose-red city half old as time, 552 : 9
Rose's scent bitterness, 693 : 6
Roses, all night r. heard, 533 : 22
and white lilies grow, 250 : 5
ash burnt r. leave, 808 : 11
bein' Gawd ain't bed of r., 814 : 18
by Bendemeer's stream, 447 : 12
courts thee on r., 107 : 3
days of wine and r., 721 : 7
each morn thousand r., 516 : 6
flung r. riotously, 721 : 5
for flush of youth, 608 : 18
gather r. of life today, 162 : 13
have thorns fountains mud, 244 : 14
love and r., 447 : 9
make thee beds of r., 183 : 10
marriage not bed of r., 667 : 13
money beautiful as r., 498 : 9
never friends with r., 633 : 3
no r. at my head, 608 : 13
not on bed of r., 721 : 3
raptures and r. of vice, 632 : 11
Roses (*continued*)
red and violets blew, 173 : 16
rose she lived as r. do, 176 : 17
all the way, 541 : 10
scent of r. hang still, 447 : 2
seek r. in December, 456 : 15
Sergeant Cuff fondness to r., 594 : 7
silent war of lilies and r., 189 : 17
strew on her r., 586 : 3
sweet days and r., 268 : 16
sweet musk r. and eglantine, 196 : 18
virgins soft as r., 459 : 6
women are as r., 214 : 2
Rossum's Universal Robots, 814 : 14
Rost, rast ich so r. ich, 919 : 17
Rosy, 'cause another's r. are, 264 : 23
hands in steam, 899 : 13
he that loves a r. cheek, 272 : 1
lips and cheeks, 245 : 18
not gray but r., 545 : 23
old men have r. faces, 669 : 7
wreath, 256 : 9
Rosy-fingered dawn, 57 : 11
Rot, deep did r., 434 : 16
enough to r. upon ground, 331 : 2
from hour to hour we r., 211 : 6
inwardly, 280 : 22
lie in cold obstruction and r., 228 : 20
name of the wicked shall r., 23 : 22
nourished to its r., 863 : 14
propagate and r., 337 : 3
water and fire r., 808 : 12
Rote, learned and conned by r., 217 : 4
phrases learned by r., 322 : 16
sarcastikul, 616 : 11
Rots in ease on Lethe wharf, 219 : 19
Rotten, apple r. at the heart, 198 : 23
dead and r., 347 : 18
mackerel by moonlight, 439 : 7
small choice in r. apples, 188 : 26
something r. in state of Denmark, 219 : 17
timber, 373 : 7
Rottenness begins in conduct, 388 : 14
Rotting grave ne'er get out, 406 : 15
Rotundity, thick r. o' the world, 233 : 24
Rough, being father can be r., 610 : 12
but ready, 548 : 21
diamond knowledge, 342 : 2
island story, 533 : 5
male kiss of blankets, 796 : 16
notes and our dead bodies, 726 : 5
oil smooths what is r., 116 : 5
paths of peevish Nature, 320 : 16
places made plain, 30 : 31
rude sea, 194 : 26
spirit that on life's r. sea, 178 : 6
steep the way and r. at first, 61 : 17
torrent of occasion, 206 : 26
turns smoothness r., 544 : 10
unordered mass, 113 : 15
what r. beast, 714 : 13
winds do shake, 244 : 5
winter and r. weather, 211 : 1
Roughest, runs through r. day, 236 : 13
Rough-hew them how we will, 224 : 25
Roughly, speak r. to little boy, 611 : 15
visit her face too r., 218 : 7
Roughness and spirit of defiance, 577 : 15
Roughnesses pimples and everything, 272 : 22
Roughs, among his fellow r., 536 : 7
Roughshod, ride r., 549 : 1

Round, attains upmost r., 215 : 16
earth's imagined corners, 254 : 8
everything tries to be r., 701 : 8
fat oily man of God, 345 : 22
giddy thinks world turns r., 189 : 4
I pick r., 915 : 12
in heaven perfect r., 544 : 4
justice in fair r. belly, 211 : 15
large and smooth and r., 439 : 11
life's dull r., 355 : *n* 8
light fantastic r., 279 : 14
longest way r. shortest home, 267 : *n* 6
man in square hole, 625 : 22
nature renews r. untired, 758 : 2
ocean and living air, 423 : 13
square person in r. hole, 432 : 17
stones prepared r. ready, 905 : 14
turned r. and r. in world, 571 : 5
unvarnished tale deliver, 229 : 25
world away, 566 : 14
Roundabouts, lost on r., 736 : 12
Rounded, it was perfect it was r., 623 : 18
Peter's dome, 493 : 18
with a sleep, 248 : 13
Roundelay, merry merry merry r., 177 : 7
Rounders, come all you r., 731 : *n* 2
Round-heads and Wooden-shoes, 326 : 6
Rounds, completion of their appointed r., 78 : *n* 8
with rhyme every rune, 494 : 6
Rouse, at dismal treatise r., 240 : 3
at name of Crispian, 208 : 10
lion from his lair, 432 : 11
lion than start hare, 203 : 14
the slumbering morn, 277 : 23
up O young men, 406 : 20
Roused, demon r. will rend you, 520 : 7
Rousing like a strong man, 282 : 3
Rousseau asks the reader, 582 : *n* 2
mock on R., 406 : 3
not ask Jean Jacques R., 377 : 23
Rout, about in reel and r., 434 : 17
ruin upon ruin r. on r., 285 : 2
Route of evanescence, 607 : 12
Routes, speed over ocean r., 800 : 10
Routine work large part of life, 639 : 3
Rove, wherever I r., 410 : 8
Rover, blood's a r., 690 : 18
laughing fellow r., 760 : 16
whither away fair r., 654 : 15
Rover's life, 569 : 20
Roving, go no more a-r., 460 : 5
I'll go no more a-r., 934 : 21
Roving's been my ruin, 934 : 21
Row, crosses r. on r., 737 : 9
devil knows how to r., 435 : 7
of moccasins, 908 : 9
of orient pearl a double r., 250 : 6
one way look another, 120 : *n* 8
seraphim in burning r., 281 : 10
uninterrupted central tail r., 799 : 5
where strikers shot, 765 : 11
Rowed with muffled oars, 439 : 8
Rower, head up while r. breathes, 873 : 16
Rowers who advance backward, 120 : *n* 8
Rowing home to haven, 760 : 19
looking one way r. another, 302 : 7
Rowland, child R. to dark tower, 234 : 13
Rowley, sing heigh-ho says R., 929 : 13
Rows, nine bean r. have, 712 : 4
Royal banner and all quality, 231 : 11
David's city, 561 : 10
descended of so many r. kings, 242 : 6
game of goose, 370 : 14
Navy watchword, 743 : 18
no r. road to accommodations, 737 : 4
road to geometry, 92 : 4
road to Thebes, 863 : 18
sware a r. oath, 530 : 17
teeming womb of r. kings, 194 : 13
throne of kings, 194 : 13
throne of r. state, 284 : 3
to execute laws r. office, 374 : 3
Royalist in politics, 809 : 13
more r. than king, 927 : 21
Royaliste, plus r. que le roi, 927 : 21
Royalists, economic r., 779 : 16
of economic order, 779 : 16
Ruach smoke, 679 : 5
Ruant, fiat justitia r. coeli, 133 : *n* 11
Ruat coelum fiat voluntas tua, 134 : 24
fiat justitia r. coelum, 133 : 25
Rub, always r. against money, 787 : 2
let the world r., 169 : 5
there's the r., 221 : 12
Rub-a-dub-dub 933 : 2
Rubente dextera, 284 : *n* 2
Rubies, her price is above r., 26 : 6
price of wisdom is above r., 16 : 14
Rubric in book of my memory, 140 : 7
Rubs, little r. which Providence sends, 369 : 8
Ruby, lack brightness of r., 796 : 1
Rudder, rhyme r. of verses, 291 : 8
steer my r. true, 114 : *n* 9
Rudders, pain and pleasure r., 307 : *n* 8
Ruddy drop of manly blood, 495 : 19
drops that visit heart, 215 : 23
limbs flaming hair, 404 : 16
temper the hammer, 768 : 2
there the lion's r. eyes, 403 : 13
Rude am I in my speech, 229 : 24
brief recitative, 575 : 21
by r. bridge, 494 : 13
dust the r. wind blows, 234 : 22
engines whose r. throats, 231 : 11
eye of rebellion, 202 : 14
forefathers of the hamlet, 361 : 23
in speech, 49 : 19
in the r. manger lies, 277 : 7
mercy of a r. stream, 249 : 3
multitude call afternoon, 191 : 8
no r. hand deface it, 425 : 4
races r. barbarous gross, 154 : 12
rough r. sea, 194 : 26
savage extreme r. cruel, 245 : 23
sea grew civil at her song, 196 : 14
with forced fingers r., 280 : 6
witty to be r., 322 : 17
Rudely great, 337 : 2
speak he never so r., 146 : 15
Rudge, like Barnaby R., 567 : 18
Rudis indigestaque moles, 113 : *n* 10
Rudyards cease from Kipling, 693 : 4
Rue, naught shall make us r., 202 : 20
rosemary and r., 246 : 25
sold for endless r., 690 : 21
wear r. with a difference, 224 : 2
with r. heart laden, 691 : 13
Rued, day I had r., 748 : 3
Ruerent, cur imbres r., 115 : *n* 12
Ruffian, father r., 204 : 5
Ruffle of drums, 676 : *n* 5
Ruffles, giving pair of laced r., 319 : 20
like sending them r., 371 : 22
Rufus, Curtius R. descended from himself, 86 : *n* 1
Rug, snug as bug in r., 348 : 5
Rugged and without a beach, 311 : 14
cadence of a r. line, 304 : 27
individualism, 750 : 17
old r. cross, 738 : 11
Russian bear, 238 : 28
Ruh', meine R. ist hin, 396 : *n* 6
Ruin and combustion, 283 : 4
around the dear r., 446 : 11
bad herdsmen r. flocks, 60 : 22
dyspepsy r. of most things, 454 : 20
exaltation from disaster and r., 743 : 3
final R. fiercely drives, 330 : 18
formless r. of oblivion, 227 : 4
he that tastes woman r. meets, 332 : 5
here meets rain wind r., 850 : 2
in r. and confusion hurled, 325 : 11
into r. hurled, 336 : 14
kings, 303 : 19
majestic though in r., 284 : 14
man marks earth with r., 458 : 25
my country's r., 316 : 9
new years r. and rend, 633 : 6
of our sex, 365 : 1
pens of diplomats not r., 386 : 15
predicts r. of the state, 406 : 10
princes and their r., 249 : 3
rather than preservation, 153 : 23
romance and poetry need r., 504 : 2
science without conscience r. of soul, 157 : 13
seize thee ruthless king, 363 : 4
serve my nation r. another, 341 : 10
since roving's been my r., 934 : 21
spreading r. scattering ban, 507 : 23
that was my r. 396 : 19
that's romantic, 629 : 17
to make them grow, 504 : 2
upon ruin rout on rout, 285 : 2
when truth entails r., 75 : 17
whom God to r. has designed, 78 : *n* 1
Ruined, archangel r., 283 : 23
bare r. choirs, 244 : 27
by amateurs, 801 : 9
Jim most r. for servant, 623 : 21
love when built anew, 245 : 21
me and I am re-begot, 253 : 1
men that are r., 374 : 7
millionaire, 807 : 19
no nation r. by trade, 348 : 12
prince who relies on words r., 153 : 24
seldom r. but by himself, 354 : 8
spend wealth at once you are r., 484 : 13
threshold of r. tenement, 351 : 7
to be r. man a vocation, 809 : 18
Ruinous, all r. disorders, 233 : 4
Ruin's, stern R. plowshare, 409 : 10
Ruins, fragments shored against r., 805 : 14
Germany r. culture, 658 : 22
in r. rather than enslaved, 744 : 5
man is a god in r., 496 : 8
musing amidst r. of Capitol, 384 : 7
new life blossoms in r., 414 : 2

Ruins (*continued*)
of another's fame, 331 : 16
of St. Paul's, 363 : 21, 488 : 7
of the noblest man, 216 : 11
politics r. character, 553 : 15
revolutionary movement enters r., 813 : 14
the very r. destroyed, 118 : 14
winter's rains and r., 632 : 8
Rule, a little r. a little sway, 345 : 3
authors established it as r., 326 : 15
Britannia, 345 : 19
but one r. to be clear, 453 : 15
by r. in nature teach, 207 : 6
capable of r. if he had not ruled, 122 : 25
circumstances r. men, 78 : 17
divide and r., 133 : 21
done by the r., 241 : 2
employ mind to r., 102 : 21
exception proves r., 258 : *n* 10
from tomb, 806 : 18
given by Christ, 602 : 6
Golden R., 38 : *n* 1
golden r. is no golden r., 680 : 22
golden r. to fit everybody, 618 : 9
golden r. toward patients, 665 : 1
good old r. sufficeth, 426 : 7
government free where laws r., 314 : 10
gran'ther's r. safer, 568 : 6
his own house, 50 : 25
Homer's r. best, 339 : 9
ill can he r. the great, 174 : 2
inch r. of taste, 635 : 2
leveled r. of streaming light, 279 : 21
my heart, 490 : 9
never look into newspaper, 399 : 5
new r. from tonight, 694 : 7
no r. admits not exception, 258 : 17
of joy and duty one, 644 : 5
of right, 349 : 19
of right and wrong, 602 : 6
of three puzzle me, 917 : 13
of universal harmony, 583 : 5
one r. for politicians, 723 : 8
over all the departed dead, 60 : 15
people turn to benevolent r., 89 : 9
reason to r., 305 : 18
rich men r. the law, 369 : 4
ruin or r. state, 304 : 3
sage Homer's r. best, 339 : 9
should r. who r. best, 88 : 4
silent r. of heaven, 312 : 20
the roost, 152 : *n* 5
them with rod of iron, 53 : 2
thoughts r. world, 499 : 26
too fond to r. alone, 338 : 14
under law your proper skill, 105 : 24
under this roof, 382 : 1
well thyself, 148 : 10
what is pomp r. reign, 186 : 21
will show the man, 62 : 11
Ruled as he thought fit, 271 : 18
genius for not being r., 489 : 19
great men can't be r., 865 : 5
man willingly r. ruleth safely, 148 : 17
roast, 452 : 13
rulers and r., 851 : 16
with little understanding world r., 157 : 1
Ruler, convention is r. of all, 72 : 12
having human body as subject, 84 : 5
let there be one r., 57 : 17
Ruler (*continued*)
no guide overseer or r., 23 : 11
no longer r. of own spirit, 418 : 2
of Queen's Navee, 627 : 14
of the waters, 458 : 7
soul the r. of life, 103 : 1
takes non-action as his way, 97 : 8
winter r. of inverted year, 377 : 5
Rulers and ruled, 851 : 16
in all lands, 670 : 15
knowledge of characters and conduct of r., 380 : 9
law for r. and people, 553 : 20
multitude of r., 57 : 17
of the darkness, 49 : 39
persuade if possible the r., 84 : 11
Rules, a few plain r., 428 : 19
community evolved, 751 : 14
gods have their own r., 113 : 22
habit r. unreflecting herd, 429 : 3
love r. the gods, 75 : 5
never shows she r., 335 : 23
of game laws of nature, 595 : 12
of propriety, 69 : 22
pretenses to break r. by, 272 : 20
rhetorician's r., 290 : 19
rocks cradle r. world, 573 : 18
threw you in told you r., 844 : 16
twelve good r., 370 : 14
where love r. no will to power, 755 : 2
Ruleth all the roost, 152 : 20
he that r. his spirit, 24 : 13
Ruling ideas of age, 563 : 9
ideas of r. class, 563 : 9
like cooking small fish, 64 : 21
no dominant r. class here, 615 : 1
passion be it what will, 336 : 2
passion conquers reason, 336 : 2
various r. passions find, 335 : 21
Rum and true religion, 460 : 20
curriculum was r., 705 : 3
five hundred gallons of r., 705 : 3
Romanism rebellion, 546 : 8
yo-ho-ho and bottle of r., 668 : 4
Rumble of distant drum, 516 : 8
Rumbling, wild dark times r. toward us, 482 : 3
Ruminate, as thou dost r., 230 : 32
Ruminating, learn r. from kine, 657 : 16
Rumination, by often r., 212 : 18
Rumor flies, 105 : 7
history distillation of r., 473 : 18
in place of inquiry, 737 : 6
is a pipe, 205 : 18
of oppression and deceit, 376 : 18
Rumors, wars and r. of wars, 40 : 22
Rump-fed ronyon cries, 236 : 1
Rum-tumming, drums r. everywhere, 759 : 7
Run and not be weary, 31 : 2
beggars mounted r. horse to death, 186 : 1
bow to that whose course r., 363 : 15
Congress doesn't r. it waltzes, 382 : 9
do not choose to r., 736 : 18
don't choose to r., 766 : 3
gwine to r. all night, 598 : 2
he may r. that readeth it, 33 : 25
hold with hare r. with hound, 159 : 26
I can fly or I can r., 280 : 4
if nominated I will not r., 579 : *n* 3
into it as to lover's bed, 241 : 19
lovers' seasons r., 252 : 7
Run (*continued*)
many shall r. to and fro, 33 : 6
never knew piece of land to r. away, 382 : 2
open door of prison and r. away, 83 : 16
political understanding to r. government, 788 : 10
rejoiceth as a strong man to r. a race, 17 : 28
saints to windows r., 604 : 15
see how they r., 929 : 11
slowly horses of night, 113 : 6, 184 : *n* 4
still as they r., 361 : 9
stream of time doth r., 206 : 26
stumble that r. fast, 192 : 22
sweet Thames r. softly, 174 : 21
tailors, 931 : 7
they conquer love that r. away, 272 : 3
though not soar, 487 : 15
through fire and water, 225 : 22
till she leaves rail, 731 : *n* 2
time will r. back, 277 : 9
to ride to r., 174 : 11
true love never did r. smooth, 195 : 22
wit enough to r. away, 292 : 1
with patience, 51 : 19
yet we will make him r., 297 : 2
Runcible hat, 550 : 6
spoon, 550 : 10
Rune, rounds with rhyme r., 494 : 6
Rung, by fairy hands knell r., 364 : 9
down ladder r. by r., 708 : 15
how grandly it had r., 646 : 14
night's yawning peal, 238 : 20
on ladder of thought, 690 : 6
Rungs, iron r. of growing up, 894 : 5
Runic rhyme, 527 : 11
Runners, like r. pass on torch of life, 100 : 15
Runner-up, in war no prize for r., 825 : 4
Runneth, my cup r. over, 18 : 7
not to the contrary, 365 : 17
Runnin' away and fightin', 722 : 17
for priest an' doctor, 786 : 10
Running all over the sea, 683 : 13
away and fightin', 722 : 17
books in r. brooks, 210 : 24
call of r. tide, 760 : 15
farced title r. 'fore king, 208 : 7
first sprightly r., 303 : 11
it never runs from us, 252 : 22
laughter, 693 : 10
of the deer, 919 : 21
off upon instinct, 901 : 14
to keep in same place, 612 : 21
trouble r. any country, 760 : 12
under r. laughter, 693 : 10
under r. water, 806 : 13
water walk, 779 : 1
written in r. water, 102 : 12
Runs, he that r. may read, 377 : 18
he that r. well r. twice, 119 : *n* 5
heart r. away with head, 415 : 12
man who r. may fight again, 91 : 12
running it never r. from us, 252 : 22
so r. world away, 222 : 17
through roughest day, 236 : 13
time r. the clock will strike, 184 : 8
win race r. by himself, 707 : *n* 2
with intrepid shorebirds, 874 : 9

Rupert of parliamentary discussion, 501 : 13
Rural, and I made a r. pen, 403 : 3
happy who knows r. gods, 104 : 6
honor taken refuge in r. setting, 264 : 8
no r. person be deprived, 903 : 6
quiet friendship, 345 : 12
Rus I see you, 518 : 8
said to people of R., 136 : 2
similar to troika, 518 : 9
Rus in urbe, 119 : *n* 8
Rush, fools r. in, 333 : 20
herds of walruses and whales, 570 : 7
into the skies, 336 : 18
my only into your arms, 778 : 6
nations shall r. like many waters, 29 : 24
of cochineal, 607 : 12
please to call it r. candle, 189 : 3
rushed along with r., 750 : 12
to glory or grave, 443 : 15
Rushed along with the rush, 750 : 12
to meet insulting foe, 399 : 17
Rushing of many waters, 29 : 24
sound of r. wind, 45 : 38
Russet, morn in r. mantle clad, 217 : 27
Russia, all R. our orchard, 695 : 9
been over into R., 719 : 7
heart of R. not forget, 500 : 25
homeland of patience, 500 : 26
how sad our R., 518 : 10
is a prison, 464 : 9
last out night in R., 228 : 3
looks through window, 486 : *n* 6
Mother R., 584 : 3
not forecast action of R., 743 : 17
prison of nations, 766 : *n* 3
seen R. content anywhere else, 464 : 10
vast multitudes of R., 745 : 2
Russian, communism R. autocracy upside down, 550 : 2
future smells of R. leather, 482 : 4
great R. allies, 815 : 12
great R. word, 802 : 1
I am true R., 912 : 11
might have been R., 627 : 18
mighty R. speech, 564 : 9
one sound for R. hearts, 486 : 9
people make sorrow diversion, 725 : 8
refusal to accept defeat, 771 : 9
rugged R. bear, 238 : 28
tongue to converse with all, 357 : 19
Russians dashed towards line, 578 : 14
Russians' joy to drink, 136 : 4
Russia's chondria for short, 486 : 6
future a danger, 550 : 3
Rust, better to wear out than r. out, 303 : 3
dew will r. them, 229 : 21
eaten to death with r., 206 : 4
his sword r., 436 : 4
if gold r. what shal iren do, 146 : 9
military machine r., 745 : 2
moth and r. doth corrupt, 37 : 16
strong men r., 834 : 5
that which never taketh r., 176 : 9
time r. sharpest sword, 431 : 24
to the harrow, 740 : 1
toy soldier red with r., 666 : 17
unburnished, 529 : 9
when I rest I r., 919 : 17
Rustics, amazed gazing r., 370 : 11
Rustled, stars in sky r. softly, 673 : 12
Rustling of purple curtain, 526 : 13
spring with r. shade, 811 : 5
to her knees, 476 : 17
Rusts, iron r. from disuse, 152 : 8
Rusty, cane leaves r. with talk, 831 : 14
for want of fighting r., 291 : 7
mail, 226 : 17
Ruth, melt with r., 281 : 3
of approval, 907 : 25
of kindness, 907 : 23
of lair clings to me, 907 : 22
of prepared comforts, 907 : 24
sad heart of R., 477 : 1
Ruthless extortion, 631 : 9
good writer r., 838 : 13
in war cunning r., 463 : 13
nor any wildcat so r., 82 : 13
ruin seize thee r. king, 363 : 4
Ruthlessly pricking bubble, 773 : 12
Rutledge, I am Anne R., 728 : 7
Rydal, to R. Lake that lead, 424 : *n* 2
Rye, catcher in the r., 896 : 9
coming through r., 919 : 18
pocket full of r., 931 : 9

S

'S death I'll print it, 338 : 7
Sabachthani, Eli Eli lama s., 41 : 27
Sabato, iddio non paga s., 545 : *n* 3
Sabbath, abhor and detest S., 624 : 8
child born on S., 932 : 10
eternal S. of his rest, 304 : 23
keep S. going to church, 605 : 4
made for man, 41 : 34
rang slowly, 886 : 21
remember the s. day, 10 : 6
Sabbath-breaking, drinking and S., 454 : 21
Sabbaths, endless s. blessed ones see, 136 : 7
Sabidius, I don't like you S., 119 : 3
Sabina has thousand charms, 919 : 19
Sabine, bounded by S., 535 : 22
Sabines, life the old S. knew, 104 : 7
Sable cloud, 279 : 17
it was a s. silvered, 218 : 23
night s. goddess, 330 : 5
Sleep son of s. Night, 182 : 4
underneath this s. hearse, 265 : 15
Sables, suit of s., 222 : 9
Sabrina fair, 280 : 3
Sacco's name will live, 811 : 9
Sack, each s. had seven cats, 930 : 1
if s. and sugar be fault, 204 : 6
intolerable deal of s., 204 : 9
leave s. live cleanly, 205 : 17
unless hours cups of s., 202 : 23
Sackcloth, put on s. with ashes, 14 : 32
Sacked the holy citadel of Troy, 59 : 13
Sacks, seven s., 930 : 1
Sacrament of praise, 767 : 11
of summer days, 604 : 10
virtue of s. like light, 86 : *n* 7
Sacred, Alph the s. river, 433 : 21
Awe, 783 : 2
cod, 694 : *n* 3
drama heaved, 717 : 4
duty to myself, 599 : 12
facts are s., 661 : 5
Sacred (*continued*)
feed his s. flame, 435 : 20
fire, 733 : 9
fire of liberty, 379 : 7
hair dissever, 334 : 10
head now wounded, 276 : 13
head of thine, 280 : 18
history a s. thing, 169 : 40
hold every moment s., 756 : 1
hoop of the nation, 701 : 8
human body s., 575 : 5
let there be s. silence, 107 : 25
life not cheap but s., 499 : 1
lips touch s. fire, 733 : 9
nothing s., 844 : 14
our s. honor, 387 : 11
preserve cradles as s., 623 : 1
sane and s. death, 576 : 3
source of sympathetic tears, 363 : 1
they lack a s. poet, 108 : 13
things s. or things profane, 302 : 4
time not s. until lived, 631 : 2
to departed spirit, 133 : 20
to oblivion, 258 : 1
two most s. names, 295 : 18
veils her s. fires, 340 : 28
Sacredness of property, 621 : 7
Sacrifice acceptable to God, 47 : 18
coming to s., 477 : 9
living s., 47 : 18, 55 : 19
make one sweet s., 248 : 25
mercy and not s., 33 : 11
of devil's leavings, 340 : 12
too long a s., 714 : 10
you make for sentiment, 723 : 5
Sacrificed, Christ our Passover s., 48 : 10
person s. to individual, 778 : 11
Sacrifices it to your opinion, 372 : 9
like stockyards, 844 : 14
of friends, 815 : 13
of friendship, 731 : 17
such s. my Cordelia, 235 : 13
win world by s., 745 : 11
with such s. God is pleased, 51 : 26
Sacrilegious murder hath broke ope, 238 : 5
Sacrum, oblivioni s., 258 : 1
Sad, a little sunny a little s., 635 : 21
all their songs s., 742 : 4
all world s. dreary, 598 : 4
and bad and mad, 544 : 20
and weary I go back, 778 : 6
as angels, 360 : *n* 2
augurs mock own presage, 245 : 13
bad brother's name, 634 : 11
be beautiful and be s., 581 : 5
brooding on country's fate, 564 : 9
companion dull-eyed melancholy, 243 : 12
created you while s., 702 : 7
cypress, 214 : 4
experience make me s., 212 : 19
flesh is s. alas, 651 : 13
heart foams at stern, 673 : 13
heart of Ruth, 477 : 1
how s. our Russia, 518 : 10
is Eros builder of cities, 868 : 15
kissed mouth, 632 : 19
last gray hairs, 476 : 24
lucidity of soul, 584 : 15
make man look s., 197 : 19
mechanic exercise, 531 : 21
mine a s. one, 197 : 28

Sad (*continued*)
my verse s. no wonder, 692 : 6
name forever s., 334 : 26
no s. songs for me, 608 : 13
not to be loved, 706 : 10
of itself, 317 : 10
old law s. not bitter, 758 : 2
or singing weather, 633 : 11
remember and be s., 608 : 15
rose of all my days, 712 : 3
say I'm s., 454 : 8
soul s. glance glum, 629 : 22
sound of horn, 483 : 4
still s. music of humanity, 423 : 13
stories of death of kings, 195 : 2
sullen and s., 345 : 4
tale's best for winter, 246 : 14
thing s. of itself, 317 : 10
tires in a mile-a, 246 : 24
to see s. sights moves, 189 : 25
'twas s. by fits, 364 : 13
uncertain rustling, 526 : 13
vicissitude of things, 359 : 17
visit my s. heart, 215 : 23
votarist in palmer's weed, 279 : 15
weight of this s. time, 235 : 20
when one says it is s., 317 : 10
words of tongue or pen, 513 : 14
Sadder and wiser man, 435 : 12
light than waning moon, 513 : 20
not to be able to love, 706 : 10
than owl songs, 462 : 1
those who hear s. than I, 616 : 15
Saddest among kings of earth, 728 : 18
are these, 513 : 14
of the year, 471 : 10
story ever heard, 740 : 8
sweetest songs s. thought, 468 : 14
when I sing, 616 : *n* 3, 616 : 15
Saddle, boot s. to horse, 540 : 26
come s. your horses, 432 : 15
leap into thy s. once more, 569 : 20
no better place than s., 592 : 8
put Germany in s., 553 : 10
short life in s., 696 : 14
things are in s., 494 : 7
Saddled, millions s. and bridled, 298 : 18
Sadie stayed home, 889 : 5
Thompson answer, 751 : 18
Sadly descends autumn, 588 : 5
part we s. in troublous world, 186 : 24
why hearest thou music s., 244 : 3
Sadness, begin in s., 892 : 15
diverter of s., 270 : 34
eternal note of s., 587 : 14
farewell s., 832 : 5
feeling of s. longing, 510 : 18
humorous s., 212 : 18
I cannot explain the s., 481 : 7
I look at you and s., 481 : 8
more prevailing s., 443 : 21
of a vale, 478 : 2
of conviction, 643 : 19
of her might, 478 : 1
songs of s. and mirth, 511 : 13
sweet though in s., 467 : 21
unmannerly s. in youth, 198 : 12
where s. let me sow joy, 138 : 15
wraps me in humorous s., 212 : 18
Sado, over S. the Milky Way, 314 : 8
Safe and sane Fourth, 719 : 1
believe soldiers nothing s., 609 : 1
bind safe find, 159 : *n* 2
compulsion to become s., 791 : 7
Safe (*continued*)
depository of public interests, 390 : 2
direct and honest not s., 231 : 15
for democracy, 703 : 2
for hypocrisy, 852 : 10
from the many, 568 : 23
he that's secure is not s., 347 : 28
hold me but s., 544 : 23
none is s., 799 : 2
perdition to be s., 495 : 9
run into a s. harbor, 62 : 21
see me s. up, 155 : 9
shall wooden wall continue, 70 : *n* 3
upon solid rock, 822 : 18
weariest river s. to sea, 633 : 22
wish him s. at home, 415 : 16
world s. for democracy, 682 : 12
world s. for diversity, 891 : 11
Safeguard, judiciary s. of liberty, 700 : 1
of the west, 425 : 18
Safeguarding community from incitements, 700 : 3
Safeguards acceptable to all nations, 787 : 16
history of procedural s., 776 : 12
Safely, but to be s. thus, 238 : 13
Judah and Israel dwelt s., 13 : 29
ship of state s. to harbor, 74 : 9
toddle s. home, 795 : 15
Safer being meek than fierce, 544 : 29
to be feared than loved, 153 : 19
Safest, home is s. refuge, 172 : *n* 2
in the middle, 113 : 17
just when s. sunset touch, 543 : 5
road to hell, 842 : 9
Safety, as if s. in stupidity, 560 : 15
concern for s. in face of dangers, 902 : 8
dangerous to peace and s., 408 : 3
enlightenment civilization, 582 : 12
fame for ale and s., 207 : 19
for my son brother shipmates, 151 : 10
freedom not s. but opportunity, 789 : 5
greatest degree of s., 367 : 5
in multitude of counselors, 23 : 24
in s. within boundaries, 781 : 8
in seas and ourselves s. lies, 186 : 15
in skating s. speed, 497 : 23
neither liberty nor s., 348 : 2
no s. here below, 156 : 1
no strike against public s., 736 : 13
obtaining happiness and s., 367 : 4
peace liberty and s., 389 : 2
people's s. is highest law, 134 : 25
pluck this flower s., 203 : 22
principles to effect s., 387 : 9
to hope not safety, 105 : 2
unite for public s., 420 : 15
with which error tolerated, 388 : 16
Saffron mist, 811 : 13
Sagacious bluestocking, 488 : 12
bold and turbulent of wit, 303 : 20
how s. the mouse, 93 : 14
Sagacity, no s. no powers, 374 : 10
Sage, by saint by savage by s., 340 : 1
daughters of Muses, 72 : 3
does not accumulate, 65 : 10
government of the s., 63 : 14
hoary s. replied, 353 : 11
hold tongue pass for s., 112 : 11
Homer's rule best, 339 : 9
Sage (*continued*)
knows without going about, 64 : 17
lengthened s. advices, 411 : 5
mechanician, 562 : 8
Milton's wormwood words, 281 : *n* 4
never strives for the great, 64 : 12
Way of s. is to act, 65 : 10
Sage, que m'importe que tu sois s., 581 : *n* 4
Sagebrush desert, 739 : 5
Sager sort our deeds reprove, 250 : 3
Sage's, vain the s. pride, 339 : 32
Sages appeared crawling for charity, 90 : 7
by s. perfectly exhibited, 89 : 7
error of the S., 90 : 7
have seen in thy face, 376 : 13
holy s. once did sing, 277 : 6
superior only in cleverness, 375 : 2
than all the s. can, 423 : 7
wisdom of our s., 389 : 2
Sagged and reeled, 765 : 5
Sahara dies, 607 : 6
Said, by and by easily s., 222 : 22
fool hath s. in his heart, 17 : 21
he himself has s. it, 627 : 17
he was against sin, 736 : 21
I didn't know, 623 : 7
I kept my word he s., 739 : 16
I s. in my haste, 21 : 23
I to myself said I, 628 : 22
in grief or pride, 823 : 10
inadvertently s. some evil thing, 86 : 7
least s. soonest mended, 169 : *n* 2
let what will be s., 388 : 10
little s. soon amended, 169 : 17
much s. on both sides, 326 : 14
never to himself hath s., 430 : 10
no sooner s. than done, 94 : 16
nothing s. that has not been s., 96 : 15
so Sancho Panza s., 556 : 2, 773 : 14
the best thought and s., 588 : 12
thing that is s. is s., 148 : 8
thing which was not, 322 : 14
'tis well s. again, 248 : 31
to my soul be still, 807 : 17
too late to say anything not s., 315 : 4
way of saying above thing s., 771 : 15
well as if I had s. it, 323 : 11
who s. Peacock pie, 740 : 1
without one word s., 404 : 11
word dead when s., 607 : 3
Sail, all s. no anchor, 489 : 9
at break of day, 783 : 17
bark attendant s., 338 : 2
beyond sunset and stars, 529 : 13
cried A s. a s., 434 : 18
even with canvas rent, 114 : 19
hoist s. while gale, 159 : *n* 1
learn of nautilus to s., 337 : 8
like swans asleep, 785 : 16
more s. than ballast, 314 : 16
on, 646 : 7
on O Ship of State, 511 : 8
out on your trades again, 93 : 3
sea-mark of my utmost s., 232 : 18
shake out every s., 576 : 16
shallow bauble boats dare s., 225 : 36
solitary s. that rises, 553 : 2
soul s. leagues beyond, 601 : 19
time to take in s., 495 : 7
tomorrow s. the Ocean Sea, 107 : 5
tomorrow soul sets s., 850 : 5

Sail (*continued*)
two lofty ships set s., 935 : 3
we must s. not drift, 519 : 6
wet seas roun', 709 : 8
what avail plow or s., 495 : 10
white and rustling s., 453 : 19
with unshut eye, 584 : 13
Sailed away year and day, 550 : 8
off in wooden shoe, 666 : 16
Swift s. into rest, 716 : 6
Sailing celestial spaces, 637 : 21
denies voyager further s., 76 : 25
great whales s. by, 584 : 13
like a stately ship, 288 : 30
noblest of s. vessels, 800 : 10
on obscene wings, 435 : 16
ship a-s. with the wind, 933 : 7
ships s. the seas, 575 : 21
Sailor, drunken s. on mast, 187 : 15
here and there old s., 767 : 1
home is the s., 668 : 20
if Ancient Mariner called Old S., 621 : 2
lives like drunken s., 187 : 15
soldier an' s. too, 709 : 13
staring s. that shakes watch, 878 : 11
well for s. lad, 530 : 19
what shall we do with drunken s., 934 : 18
Sailor's wife had chestnuts, 236 : 1
Sailors but men, 198 : 17
half our s. swallowed, 186 : 23
images s. tattoo, 850 : 6
intrepid s., 575 : 22
onward s. cry, 688 : 12
say weather a great bluffer, 847 : 8
soldiers s. airmen, 746 : 7
won't believe it, 432 : 10
Sail's shaking, 760 : 14
Sails, argosies of magic s., 529 : 24
biased by full s., 843 : 18
broad bellying s., 785 : 12
filled streamers waving, 288 : 30
filled with lusty wind, 178 : 6
from windless kingdom, 907 : 14
furls s. lays him to rest, 570 : 7
handed all s. and set treo, 150 : 15
overweathered ribs ragged s., 199 : 6
purple the s., 240 : 29
set of s. not gales, 669 : 21
spread fox wings, 901 : 14
swell full, 492 : 14
thy white s. crowding, 654 : 15
vessel of my genius now hoists s., 141 : 17
well but strike rock, 407 : 16
white s. fly seaward, 806 : 6
Sail-yards tremble masts crack, 178 : 6
Saint and martyr rule from tomb, 806 : 18
by s. by savage by sage, 340 : 1
corrupt a s., 203 : 1
dead sinner, 647 : 17
doctor and s., 516 : 16
for oneself, 581 : 9
if God does not exist, 882 : 8
looked out of eye of s., 716 : 4
neither s. nor sophist led, 585 : 6
old s. in forest, 657 : 11
poet and s. to thee alone, 295 : 18
run mad, 339 : 31
saw my late espoused s., 282 : 20
seem s. when most play devil, 187 : 6
strained so much, 873 : 5
Saint (*continued*)
such injury vex a s., 188 : 35
threadbare s., 251 : 9
to be a s. for oneself, 581 : 9
Saint Agnes' Eve , 476 : 8
Saint Anne mother of Mary, 638 : 11
yes by S., 213 : 26
Saint Augustine thanked God, 754 : 9
well said, 511 : 22
Saint Clement's, bells of S., 930 : 7
Saint George, England and S., 207 : 18
for England, 742 : 14
that swinged dragon, 201 : 15
Saint George's Hanover Square, 620 : 9
Saint Ives, going to S., 930 : 1
Saint James's, ladies of S., 640 : 2
Saint John, awake my S., 336 : 10
ancient animal symbols of S., 482 : 3
buried Evangelist S., 571 : 3
there S. mingles, 339 : 8
Saint John's, whether bounded by the S., 535 : 22
Saint Martin's, expect S. summer, 184 : 17
Saint Nazaire, mademoiselle from S., 817 : 8
Saint Nicholas soon would be there, 446 : 3
Saint Paul's, designing S., 753 : 3
ruins of S., 363 : 21, 488 : 7
Saint Peter's, blessing of S. Master, 271 : 14
Saint Stephen's choir, 892 : 4
Saint Theresa in wild lament, 858 : 20
Saint Vincent, nobly Cape S., 541 : 18
Sainted, thing enskyed and s., 227 : 27
Sainte-Terrer, there goes a S., 557 : *n* 2
Saintliness not a state, 877 : 12
Saintly, woman't normal occupations counter s. life, 867 : 5
Saints aid if men call, 434 : 2
choir of s., 254 : 17
Communion of S., 55 : 2
for all the s., 592 : 1
heroes if we will, 584 : 10
in your injuries, 230 : 8
men below and s. above, 430 : 6
precious is the death of his s., 21 : 24
rarely married women, 867 : 5
slaughtered s., 282 : 18
soul with s. I trust, 436 : 4
sweetly sing, 314 : 21
take your s. and virgins, 566 : 6
to windows run, 604 : 15
when s. go marching in, 936 : 8
where s. immortal reign, 328 : 15
Saint-seducing gold, 191 : 18
Saintship of an anchorite, 456 : 23
Sairey, oh S. S. little do we know, 548 : 1
Sais, que s.-je, 165 : *n* 3
Saisons, O s. O châteaux, 674 : *n* 2
Saith, he s. among the trumpets, 16 : 38
Sake, for bellies' s. creep, 280 : 20
for God's s. sit upon ground, 195 : 2
for his name's s., 18 : 7
good friend for Jesus' s., 250 : 1
hated for my name's s., 39 : 1
love for Love's s., 875 : 4
persecute you for my s., 37 : 4
poem for poem's s., 527 : 13
wine for thy stomach's s., 50 : 33
Sakes, heaven and future's s., 748 : 18
Saki, eternal S. from bowl poured, 516 : 21
O S. you pass, 517 : 14
Salaam, shalom s. forever, 882 : 1
Salad, capacious s. bowl, 668 : 18
crazy s. with meat, 714 : 16
days, 240 : 25
Garrick's a s., 371 : 13
Salads, ho 'tis time of s., 360 : 19
Salaputtium disertum, 102 : *n* 3
Salary, draw s. before spending, 718 : 10
Sale, base s. of chapmen's tongues, 190 : 19
city for s., 103 : 3
Salesman, Willy was a s., 888 : 3
Saliva makes serpents take flight, 116 : 13
Salley, down by s. gardens, 711 : 22
Sallied flesh, 218 : *n* 1
Sallow, lean and s. abstinence, 279 : 30
Sallows, among river s., 477 : 19
Sally in our alley, 331 : 5
loose s. of mind, 352 : 8
make a sudden s., 533 : 15
none like pretty S., 331 : 5
Salmon falls, 714 : 22
wasn't wine was s., 546 : 12
Salome danced, 39 : 22
Salt, became a pillar of s., 8 : 12
eat peck of s. with him, 917 : 7
eaten your bread and s., 707 : 3
forever inheriting s. kingdom, 864 : 7
furrowing s. acres, 907 : 2
how s. is another's bread, 142 : 13
if s. have lost savor, 37 : 5
land and not inhabited, 32 : 11
no joy but lacks s., 748 : 9
not worth his s., 117 : 16
of the earth, 37 : 5
one s. sea, 207 : 8
sea waves, 745 : 11
seasoned with Attic s., 298 : 14
speech seasoned with s., 50 : 14
thing of watery s., 760 : 21
tides seawards flow, 584 : 11
upon their tails, 321 : 12
water unbounded, 710 : 7
with a grain of s., 117 : 6
Salt-caked smokestack, 760 : 20
Salted, wherewith shall it be s., 37 : 5
Saltness of time, 205 : 24
sugar and s. agree, 371 : 13
Saltsick, seasilt s., 778 : 6
Saltum, natura non facit s., 652 : 1
Saltus, natura non facit s., 350 : *n* 2
Salus extra ecclesiam non est, 126 : *n* 13
populi suprema lex, 99 : *n* 3, 134 : 25
Salutary influence of example, 352 : 24
wise and s. neglect, 372 : 15
Salute, we about to die s. you, 123 : 14
Saluted, long inveterate foes s., 305 : 5
Salutes everyone in early days, 85 : 6
Salvage of our civilization, 771 : 9
Salvaged, ships s. and retiring, 777 : 14
Salvation, concern temporal s., 383 : 1
for helmet the hope of s., 50 : 20
for him there is s., 396 : 26
for our s. came down, 55 : 3
genius work out s., 479 : 14
he is become my s., 9 : 32, 29 : 20
he only is my rock and s., 19 : 27
in union, 730 : 16
my bottle of s., 172 : 15
my light and my s., 18 : 11

Salvation (*continued*)
no s. outside Church, 126 : 17
none shall see s., 200 : 9
rock of our s., 20 : 20
three things necessary for s., 139 : 14
waited for thy s., 9 : 5
work out own s., 50 : 2
work out s. with diligence, 72 : 22
Sam, play it again S., 913 : 11
play it S., 913 : *n* 3
Samaria, woman of S., 44 : 35
Samaritan had compassion, 43 : 14
Samarra, appointment in S., 751 : 17
Same, always and never s., 496 : 17
descent to Hades is s., 72 : 14
ever the s., 164 : 2
men all the s., 751 : 18
not be then the s., 489 : 10
permanent and the s., 585 : 19
repose that ever is the s., 427 : 14
self was not the s., 225 : 30
the more they remain s., 514 : 5
the s. as everywhere, 394 : 13
to Noah as to me, 571 : 8
whole world over, 924 : 11
yesterday today and forever, 51 : 24
Sameness of sheep, 847 : 3
precise s. is terrifying, 884 : 4
self has continuity and s., 854 : 5
with difference, 437 : 17
Sames of am, 829 : 19
Samian wine, 461 : 8
Samite, arm clothed in white s., 149 : 8
clothed in white s. mystic, 534 : 4
Samoa attitude towards life, 853 : 14
Samphire, one that gathers s., 234 : 28
Sample, by s. we judge whole, 168 : 10
Sampler, serve to ply the s., 280 : 1
Sam's, nephew of my Uncle S., 759 : 6
Samson, Philistines be upon thee S., 12 : 18
Philistines brought S. to Gaza, 12 : 19
Samurai, business of the s., 299 : 11
San Francisco is West as all hell, 699 : *n* 3
West is S., 699 : 15
San Salvador, island called S., 150 : 15
Sancho Panza, God's blessing said S., 171 : *n* 1
so S. said so say I, 556 : 2, 773 : 14
Sanctify, thy praise s. our rest, 597 : 17
Sanction, gives bigotry no s., 379 : 8
happiness the only s. of life, 703 : 8
laws with s., 401 : 15
ultimate s. of exploitation, 825 : 18
Sanctity of reason, 286 : 31
Sanctuary, of s. and choir, 808 : 12
wild s., 750 : 15
Sanctum of the soul, 754 : 13
Sand, abstinence sows s. all over, 404 : 16
as the s. by the sea, 13 : 28
blood of Ignacio on s., 841 : 16
build on fortune build on s., 265 : 4
handful of s., 838 : 16
he plows the s., 794 : 9
heap of loose s., 719 : 9
house built on s., 38 : 21
laws are s. customs rock, 626 : 6
little grains of s., 591 : 7
number the s. of the sea, 34 : 21
on edge of s., 550 : 10
ostrich with head in s., 682 : 7
ribbed sea s., 434 : 25
Sand (*continued*)
roll down golden s., 452 : 8
see world in grain of s., 406 : 8
shining palace upon s., 822 : 18
such quantities of s., 613 : 2
sun s. wild uproar, 493 : 15
throw s. against the wind, 406 : 3
weaving s., 500 : 9
Sandal, battering s., 656 : 8
heard her massive s., 823 : 8
shoon, 223 : 21
Sandalwood cedarwood, 760 : 19
Sanded, nicely s. floor, 370 : 13
Sandhills of Nantucket, 571 : 8
Sandpiper, cries of s., 874 : 9
one little s. and I, 621 : 17
Sands and shores, 279 : 16
come unto these yellow s., 247 : 19
crucified the George S., 554 : 9
footprints on s. of time, 509 : 15
ghosts countless as s., 599 : 15
golden s. crystal brooks, 253 : 2
lone level s. stretch, 466 : 13
of Dee, 566 : 7
of time, 509 : 15
steer too nigh s., 303 : 20
suffice, 607 : 6
Sand-strewn caverns, 584 : 12
Sandwich men shuffling, 781 : 15
Sandy, false as s. earth, 226 : 15
gray-green s. grass, 711 : 11
swift s. glass, 257 : 17
Sane and had to fly, 902 : 8
and sacred death, 576 : 3
assent you are s., 605 : 11
fitter s. than mad, 544 : 29
safe and s. Fourth, 719 : 1
Saner to be rebel, 704 : 17
Sang, all s. Annie Laurie, 596 : 17
all we said or s., 717 : 14
beyond genius of sea, 767 : 15
bonny bonny Biscay O, 920 : 17
from morn till night, 382 : 6
full weel s. service dyvyne, 145 : 18
his didn't, 829 : 18
in my chains like sea, 887 : 3
morning stars s. together, 16 : 29
of love not of fame, 596 : 17
perhaps it may turn out s., 409 : 11
Sir Lancelot, 528 : 26
summer s. in me, 823 : 6
tilly-loo, 550 : 12
to small guitar, 550 : 7
what song the Sirens s., 275 : 5
when a lark I s., 874 : 4
where late sweet birds s., 244 : 27
Willow titwillow, 629 : 16
within bloody wood, 804 : 25
Sang, qu'un s. impur, 415 : 1
Sangfroid, preserve your s., 388 : 10
Sanglots longs des violons, 659 : *n* 6
Sangreal, noble history of S., 149 : 4
Sanguine who checked volatility, 386 : 11
Sanguinis, hic est enim Calix S. mei, 54 : 7
Sanitary, give me s. reformer, 566 : 6
Sanity virtue of ancient literature, 586 : 8
Sank my boat, 890 : 2
sighted sub s. same, 882 : 16
Sans wine song singer, 516 : 15
teeth eyes everything, 211 : 15
Santa Claus, no S., 638 : 6
Santa Claus (*continued*)
nobody shoots at S., 741 : 9
things in dark besides S., 750 : 19
yes Virginia there is S., 638 : *n* 4
Sap, dried s. out of veins, 713 : 6
is the music, 852 : 14
make cherry red, 799 : 9
material s., 234 : 23
nor can s. be in rocks, 101 : 1
world's whole s. is sunk, 252 : 25
Sapless, earth s. as bone, 760 : 9
Sapphire bracelet lasts forever, 826 : 5
the s. blaze, 363 : 2
Sapphires, garlic and s., 807 : 4
glowed with living s., 285 : 25
Sappho, burning S., 461 : 2
of Lesbos tenth muse, 63 : *n* 4
would speak openly, 751 : 7
Sapping solemn creed, 458 : 1
Sarcasm language of devil, 473 : 3
Sarcastikul, this is rote s., 616 : 11
Sargasso, your mind and you S. Sea, 792 : 5
Sash lowered night comes, 748 : 12
Sat among the cinders, 932 : 4
at good man's feast, 211 : 12
by the fleshpots, 10 : 1
like a cormorant, 285 : 14
like Patience on monument, 214 : 5
on a tuffet, 932 : 15
on Pillicock hill, 234 : 5
Satan exalted s., 284 : 3
so Tiberius might have s., 588 : 4
upon which everyone has s., 829 : 22
Satan as lightning fall, 43 : 11
came also, 15 : 1
exalted sat, 284 : 3
finds mischief, 328 : 6
get thee behind me S., 39 : 37
interview with S., 690 : 11
limb of S., 623 : 10
now wiser than of yore, 336 : 3
old serpent called S., 53 : 20
that waiteth to bigile, 147 : 7
towards God the other towards S., 581 : 7
Satanic, dark S. mills, 406 : 21
school, 440 : 10
Satchel, whining schoolboy with s., 211 : 15
Sate itself in celestial bed, 219 : 22
Sated with banquet of life, 101 : 4
Satire a sort of glass, 321 : 13
be my song, 456 : 11
ever moral ever new, 311 : 13
like polished razor, 341 : 3
or sense can Sporus feel, 338 : 18
points at no defect, 322 : 19
what closes Saturday, 813 : 3
Satire's my weapon, 339 : 6
Satisfaction, ambitious man have no s., 255 : 5
in making it possible for others, 883 : 6
previous benefaction or present s., 79 : 16
that I have not lived in vain, 326 : 7
work brings, 725 : 2
Satisfactory, plant seeds most s., 603 : 7
Satisfied, charm makes us more s., 580 : 13
greatest fools oft most s., 311 : 10
I can't be s., 854 : 15
love s. greater torment, 806 : 1

Satisfied (*continued*)
nature of desire not to be s., 88 : 1
pig s., 508 : 19
retire like s. guest, 106 : 13
superior man s. and composed, 68 : 24
to live in hunger, 814 : 8
well paid that is well s., 200 : 21
Satisfies, makes hungry where most s., 241 : 1
Satisfiest desire of every living thing, 22 : 21
Satisfy, poorly s. our eyes, 251 : 1
what will s. soul, 576 : 12
your greed, 709 : *n* 3
Satisfying curiosity of young, 655 : 10
full and s. life, 862 : 7
Saturates politics with thought, 586 : 22
Saturday, died on S., 932 : 11
God's time not S., 545 : 17
mornings we listened to Red Lantern, 912 : 14
satire closes S., 813 : 3
what he did on S., 773 : 9
Saturday's child, 932 : 10
Saturdays, God not pay S., 545 : *n* 3
Saturn, gray-haired S., 478 : 2
moons of S., 571 : 2
Revolution like S., 552 : 8
Saturnians through life's Tempe led, 572 : 4
Satya truth, 727 : 6
Satyagraha, term S. coined by me, 727 : 5
Satyr, forty till fifty man s., 677 : 2
Hyperion to a s., 218 : 7
Satyrs, men like s. grazing, 183 : 16
nymphs and s., 717 : 16
Sauce, bread s. of happy ending, 653 : 6
cloyless s., 240 : 27
good crier of green s., 158 : 2
no s. like hunger, 170 : 2
Saucy doubts and fears, 238 : 23
not deep-searched with s. looks, 190 : 12
Saul and Jonathan were lovely and pleasant, 13 : 9
becomes Paul, 686 : 11
hath slain his thousands, 13 : 4
is S. among the prophets, 12 : 33
why persecutest thou me, 46 : 5
yet breathing slaughter, 46 : 4
Saunders, a bed Clerk S. said, 926 : 24
Saunter, great art to s., 557 : 5
Sauntered Europe round, 340 : 27
Sauntering from à la Sainte Terre, 557 : *n* 2
Sausage, in as pig out as s., 647 : 14
Sausages, men are like s., 561 : 5
Savage and Tartarly, 462 : 11
breast, 324 : 14
bull bear the yoke, 209 : 2
by saint by s. by sage, 340 : 1
contemplates mother-in-law, 673 : 4
dole laws to s. race, 529 : 6
extreme rude cruel, 245 : 23
half s. country, 792 : 10
in man never eradicated, 557 : 19
indignation, 323 : 25, 716 : 6
is he who saves himself, 152 : 9
men and uncouth manners, 372 : 12
noble s., 303 : 8
place as holy and enchanted, 433 : 22
ruled s. hordes, 592 : 6
servility slides by, 893 : 16
Savage (*continued*)
soothe a s. breast, 324 : 14
take some s. woman, 530 : 6
wilderness into empire, 373 : 9
young man who not wept s., 704 : 9
Savage-creating fellow, 82 : 19
Savageness, sing s. out of a bear, 231 : 24
Savages, grow like s., 208 : 17
in unknown island, 501 : 9
Savage-wild, time and intents are s., 193 : 23
Savannas, dweller in Mannahatta or southern s., 574 : 3
Save, assist him to s. face, 834 : 1
came to s. sinners, 50 : 24
conquer but to s., 443 : 17
destroy town to s. it, 925 : 18
died to s. us all, 561 : 9
eternal Father strong to s., 596 : 18
God s. the king, 12 : 34, 195 : 10, 331 : 6
God s. the mark, 203 : 10
himself he cannot s., 41 : 26
listen and s., 280 : 3
many to s. with thyself, 588 : 8
me from candid friend, 422 : 5
me from therrble prongs, 778 : 6
my soul if I have soul, 593 : 9
myself by work and faith, 865 : 15
nobly s. or meanly lose, 522 : 12
not s. it it not s. me, 784 : 4
old worth saving, 723 : 11
one drop would s. my soul, 184 : 8
only soul man must s., 841 : 4
squadron honor France, 545 : 15
thee Ancient Mariner, 434 : 12
what is around me, 784 : 4
whosoever s. life shall lose it, 39 : 38
wish to s. their own pocket, 80 : 16
with ample income can s., 871 : 16
Saved by faith, 823 : 21
by hope, 823 : 21
by love, 823 : 21
country s. from itself, 689 : 22
harvest is past and we are not s., 32 : 2
he s. others, 41 : 26
I have s. myself, 61 : 25
lost when I was s., 604 : 11
part of day rued, 748 : 3
there be souls must be s., 230 : 19
Union of these States, 576 : 8
won't matter whether s., 815 : 3
youthful hose well s., 211 : 15
Saves, humor s. a few steps, 799 : 7
itself perpetually, 878 : 2
savage he who s. himself, 152 : 9
soul in new French books, 543 : 7
who helps others s. himself, 138 : 6
Saving, company hardly worth s., 622 : 13
not s. but selection, 374 : 10
property stimulus to s., 758 : 1
save old worth s., 723 : 11
Western civilization worth s., 815 : 3
whiskey the s. of him, 623 : 12
Savings, not by s. and capital, 872 : 4
of many in hands of one, 676 : 19
Savior at his sermon on mount, 541 : 19
Christ our S., 919 : 20
of 'is country, 708 : 4
which is Christ, 42 : 28
Savior's birth celebrated, 217 : 26
Savior's (*continued*)
sing tongue the S. glory, 139 : 9
Savoir être à soi, 164 : *n* 14
tuer et creer, 581 : *n* 5
Savor, filths s. but themselves, 234 : 24
fleeting delights, 464 : 14
if salt have lost s., 37 : 5
seeming and s. all winter, 246 : 25
thoughts that s. of content, 178 : 10
Saw, all at once I s. a crowd, 427 : 7
best minds of generation, 906 : 1
coughing drowns parson's s., 191 : 15
do not s. the air, 221 : 23
first one another s., 252 : 22
heavens fill, 529 : 24
him with my own eyes, 297 : 23
I at a glance, 427 : 9
I came I s. I conquered, 99 : 23
I came s. and overcame, 206 : 28
I s. and loved, 384 : 3
last time I s. Paris, 833 : 9
life steadily saw it whole, 584 : 8
man clothed with rags, 301 : 20
manners in face, 353 : 10
ne'er s. I never felt, 425 : 14
never s. a man who looked, 676 : 6
never s. a moor, 606 : 17
never s. purple cow, 718 : 15
no sound of s., 377 : 11
not seen as others s., 525 : 5
on a cloud I s. a child, 403 : 2
skull beneath skin, 804 : 21
spiders marching, 892 : 6
spires of Oxford, 778 : 10
then I s. the Congo, 765 : 6
three ships, 933 : 3
water lily bloom, 528 : 27
young Harry with beaver on, 204 : 31
Sawdust Caesar, 817 : 9
Saws, full of wise s., 211 : 15
Sawyer, Adventures of Tom S., 623 : 20
Saxa, in spatio pertundere s., 100 : *n* 4
Saxon, ancient S. phrase, 510 : 12
eyes barbarous souls, 721 : 3
I am Roderick Dhu, 431 : 12
in subjection to white S. man, 554 : 6
Saxophones, long cool winding s., 761 : 11
Say a thing straight, 652 : *n* 3
cannot create when nothing to s., 853 : 5
canst not s. I did it, 238 : 25
can't s. anything good, 786 : 7
defend right to s. it, 344 : 11
disapprove of what you s., 344 : 11
do as I s. not as I do, 264 : 6
do not s. things, 499 : 24
don't s. anything, 736 : 20
don't s. too much, 870 : 7
everything interestingly, 667 : 5
find right thing to s., 680 : 1
first of God above, 336 : 12
good deed to s. well, 248 : 31
good night till it be morrow, 192 : 19
I s. it's spinach, 846 : 7
I shall have less to s., 747 : 18
it ain't so Joe, 924 : 13
it as you understand it, 413 : 18
it loud I'm black and proud, 913 : 1
it with utmost levity, 680 : 1
know much s. little, 358 : 20
light stream of what we s., 588 : 22
Lord what would they s., 714 : 3
love not s. all it means, 729 : 1

Say (*continued*)
more to s. when dead, 728 : 21
nastiest thing in nicest way, 797 : 8
need to be young to s., 400 : 11
never s. I was false 245 : 14
never s. more than necessary, 398 : 8
not of Beauty, 793 : 20
not struggle naught availeth, 564 : 16
not what we ought to s., 235 : 20
not what you s. but how, 609 : 2
nothin' without compelled, 568 : 13
nothin' you can be held to, 568 : 13
nothing but what said, 258 : 6
nothing to s., 565 : 30
nothing to s. s. nothing, 448 : 9
nothing you couldn't actually s., 793 : 7
one may s. what one thinks, 122 : 24
person who could not s. no, 875 : 14
remember what we s. here, 523 : 4
right to s. what one pleases, 794 : 20
secure within can s., 305 : 1
see what I s., 869 : 9
shall my little bark, 338 : 2
shame s. what it will, 224 : 4
shudder to s. it, 104 : 34
Silence has much to s., 621 : 14
so long as we can s., 234 : 20
some s. world end in fire, 748 : 2
style of what man has to s., 588 : 9
tale as said to me, 430 : 5
temple bells they s., 708 : 8
that's all I s., 519 : 16
there is no more to s., 227 : 7
they s. my verse sad, 692 : 6
things I did not do or s., 716 : 13
this with presence of mind, 96 : 19
though I s. it that should not, 263 : 11
to all the world, 217 : 14
to the fleet, 408 : *n* 5
too late to s. anything not said, 315 : 4
way they s. it, 857 : 5
wet mind and s. something clever, 81 : 12
what else to s. but everything, 889 : 15
what everyone else does not s., 658 : 13
what law is, 402 : 3
what more is there to s., 715 : 7
what others s. of them, 299 : 18
what people s. behind back, 671 : 15
what s. they let them s., 175 : *n* 4
what will Mrs. Grundy s., 416 : 10
what you mean, 611 : 18
what you would be, 121 : 19
which can s. more, 244 : 29
which grain will grow, 236 : 5
will it not be the same, 489 : 10
wouldn't s. so till tried, 774 : 3
Saying all we did not know, 794 : 14
for loving and for s. so, 252 : 13
good-bye to statue, 844 : 17
is one thing, 165 : 13
mode of s., 587 : 2
reputed wise for s. nothing, 198 : 3
sea what is it s., 548 : 17
thoughtless s. of princess, 359 : 6
way of s. above thing said, 771 : 15
what are wild waves s., 548 : *n* 1
wise and old, 173 : *n* 8
Wrath by his meekness, 403 : 13
Sayings full of knowledge and advice, 25 : *n* 1
Says a lot in vain refusing, 395 : 10
First Amendment means what it s., 794 : 19
no one means all he s., 635 : 20
she speaks yet s. nothing, 192 : 3
what he s. least important, 637 : 13
who is it that s. most, 244 : 29
who s. it what he s., 637 : 13
Scab of churches, 251 : 5
Scabbard, sword of justice has no s., 400 : 3
sword within the s. keep, 306 : 28
Scabby, hated with s. hatred, 912 : 11
Scabies, disputandi pruritus ecclesiarum s., 251 : *n* 3
Scaffold sways the future, 567 : 7
truth forever on s., 567 : 7
Scaffoldage, 'twixt footing and s., 226 : 4
Scald, tears s. like molten lead, 235 : 8
Scalding grave, 735 : 3
Scale, every golden s., 611 : 5
he by geometric s., 290 : 21
in equal s. weighing, 217 : 29
Justice with lifted s., 340 : 15
lapping scale with regularity, 799 : 5
so shall you s. the stars, 106 : 3
society without objective legal s., 895 : 25
Scaled invention or artistry, 793 : 4
Scales are his pride, 17 : 5
father held out golden s., 59 : 7
fell from his eyes, 46 : 8
put Hannibal in the s., 122 : 16
waves as formal as s. on fish, 798 : 8
Scallop shell of quiet, 172 : 15
Scalped each other, 488 : 11
Scan, faults to s., 370 : 6
gently s. brother man, 409 : 21
presume not God to s., 337 : 2
Scandal, dreaded s. more than disease, 701 : 2
greatest s. waits on greatest state, 189 : 24
love and s., 349 : 16
public s. is wicked, 297 : 22
tea and s., 324 : 7
Scandalous and poor, 315 : 16
Scandals of the poor, 722 : 2
short and simple s., 722 : 2
Scant, if store of crowns be s., 257 : 8
Scanted, what s. in hair given in wit, 188 : 4
Scanter of your maiden presence, 219 : 7
Scanty, in longitude though s., 411 : 12
'Scape who should 's. whipping, 221 : 5
'Scaped, heart s. this sorrow, 245 : 3
Scapegoat, let him go for a s., 10 : 18
'Scapes hair-breadth 's., 229 : 28
Scar, two lives join oft s., 542 : 9
virtue or vice leaves s., 648 : 11
wound heals s. disappears, 558 : 20
Scarce, ends and s. means, 842 : 15
Scarcely greet me with that sun, 244 : 17
Scarceness, eat bread without s., 11 : 14
Scarcity, on first s. will turn, 374 : 11
reasons for s. of capital, 783 : 15
Scare, don't let them s. you, 815 : 1
nor shall you s. with talk, 900 : 2
white clouds on, 747 : 18
Scarecrow, not make s. of law, 227 : 30
Scarecrows of fools, 596 : 3
Scared, always been s. of you, 911 : 17
to go to brink, 803 : 8
Scarf up tender eye of day, 238 : 21
Scarfed bark puts from her bay, 199 : 6
Scarfs garters gold, 337 : 7
Scarlet, got up in embroidered s., 701 : 15
in S. town, 926 : 21
letter her passport, 503 : 12
lily flamed, 696 : 11
of maples shake me, 696 : 9
passion for a s. coat, 322 : 16
sins s. books read, 730 : 13
though your sins be as s., 28 : 30
Scars, belong to what s., 863 : 19
he jests at s., 192 : 2
I carry with me, 302 : 15
inveterate s., 807 : 4
of others teach caution, 128 : 9
writes of s. healed, 835 : 9
Scat, w'en Miss Rabbit say s., 662 : 10
Scatted, Miss Rabbit say they s., 662 : 10
Scatter and unloose it from bond, 189 : 18
plenty o'er smiling land, 362 : 10
Scattered, after things s., 733 : 17
driftwood bleached and dry, 621 : 17
he hath s. the proud, 42 : 22
Israel s. upon the hills, 14 : 10
to the wind, 527 : 21
when cloud s., 470 : 1
Scattering, all's a s., 874 : 9
maniac s. dust, 532 : 6
Scatters, anarchy s. armies, 74 : 20
deep surmise s., 558 : 21
rear of darkness thin, 277 : 23
Scene, dreamer is dream s., 754 : 12
gay and festive s., 549 : 32
last s. of all, 211 : 15
live o'er each s., 334 : 12
lofty s. be acted o'er, 216 : 7
love gilds the s., 398 : 20
not ask to see distant s., 490 : 6
speaks a new s., 267 : 18
start a s. or two, 803 : 17
Scenery essential in painting, 135 : 11
fine human nature finer, 479 : 9
Vermont s. and climate, 736 : 19
Scenes, changing s. of life, 317 : 6
from s. like these, 408 : 18
gay gilded s., 325 : 6
his fathers loved, 857 : 14
ill-bred s., 701 : 2
lent heart to such s., 441 : 9
no more behind your s. David, 353 : 23
of my childhood, 455 : 6
shifted on stage of history, 666 : 5
Scent, amber s. of perfume, 288 : 30
of her hair, 822 : 4
of pine and woodthrush, 806 : 8
of roses hang round it, 447 : 2
rose's s. bitterness, 693 : 6
survives their close, 693 : 6
the fair annoys, 376 : 3
which pays the best, 568 : 3
Scents, sweet unmemoried s., 654 : 16
Scepter, balm s. and ball, 208 : 7
leaden s., 330 : 5
nor crown nor s. would I ask, 418 : 8
shows force of power, 200 : 9
snatched with unruly hand, 202 : 3

Sceptered, in s. pall sweeping by, 278 : 21
isle, 194 : 13
mercy above s. sway, 200 : 9
Moloch s. king, 284 : 4
what avails the s. race, 442 : 17
Scheldt, lazy S. or wandering Po, 368 : 13
Scheme, for breakfast a s., 329 : 23
of weal and woe, 544 : 6
sorry s. of things, 517 : 13
yields no revenue, 372 : 8
Schemes, best-laid s., 408 : 14
Schiller has material sublime, 438 : 3
Schlachthof meant slaughterhouse, 901 : *n* 2
Scholar among rakes, 488 : 19
determined s. and man of virtue, 69 : 10
he was a s., 249 : 15
if s. have not faith, 89 : 24
more in soldier than s., 230 : 13
new s. replacing older, 769 : 1
showed him gentleman an' s., 409 : 6
ten o'clock s., 933 : 14
thou art a s., 217 : 17
travels loved hillside, 587 : 12
who cherishes love of comfort, 69 : 5
who pursues fame not s., 90 : 5
Scholar's, courtier's soldier's s., 221 : 19
ills s. life assail, 351 : 17
Scholars and gentlemen, 424 : 4
dispute and case still before courts, 109 : 21
God of Abraham not s., 300 : 15
land of s., 369 : 2
make majors but not s., 259 : 2
not great men, 519 : 13
Pythagoras said to his s., 258 : 15
senseless s., 314 : 19
Scholars', some s. stutters, 899 : 5
Scholarship, history of s., 700 : 2
pallid emasculate s., 592 : 8
record of disagreements, 700 : 2
Schön, so hold und s. und rein, 481 : *n* 8
war ich auch, 396 : *n* 7
School, corrupted youth in erecting s., 185 : 28
creeping like snail to s., 211 : 15
elongated-yellow-fruit s. of writing, 846 : 1
experience keeps dear s., 347 : 23
fleshly s. of poetry, 643 : 10
for making first-class men, 577 : 1
free common s. system, 851 : 5
God the Father a s. divine, 339 : 22
high s. closer to core of experience, 901 : 9
in joyful s. days, 441 : 5
in my s. days, 198 : 6
in which nothing harsh, 129 : 21
leave religion to private s., 590 : 2
microcosm of public s., 501 : 1
of mankind, 374 : 8
of Stratford atte Bowe, 145 : 18
Satanic s., 440 : 10
stealthy s. of criticism, 601 : 22
tales out of s., 159 : 25
threadbare saint in wisdom's s., 251 : 9
three little maids from s., 629 : 8
time the s. in which we learn, 883 : 10
to s. not to travel, 180 : 18
toward s. with heavy looks, 192 : 15
School (*continued*)
we left s., 889 : 13
Schoolboy, every s. knows, 488 : 6
every s. knows it, 294 : 13
tale every s. knows, 361 : 7
whining s. with satchel, 211 : 15
Schoolboy's tale, 457 : 5
Schoolboys, as s. from books, 192 : 15
Schoolchildren, Negro s., 893 : 15
School-days, in joyful s., 441 : 5
Schoolgirl, pert as s. can be, 629 : 8
Schooling, government provides poor s., 880 : 18
in and outdoor s., 749 : 17
Schoolman's subtle art, 339 : 4
Schoolmaster is abroad, 444 : 14
Schoolmasters, bankers s. clergymen, 713 : 1
father more than hundred s., 270 : 11
let s. puzzle brain, 371 : 5
Schoolrooms, better s. than cells, 562 : 12
Schools, jargon of the s., 320 : 13
knowledge never learned of s., 513 : 11
let us reform s., 572 : 18
maze of s., 332 : 17
nurseries of vice, 349 : 14
old maxim in the s., 322 : 7
Schooner Hesperus, 510 : 4
ladder close to s., 910 : 7
Schweigen ist golden, 473 : 9
Science, ABC of s., 665 : 5
achieve perfect knowledge, 584 : 1
active field of s. like anthill, 883 : 15
admits no exceptions, 551 : 17
advance of s. an evolution, 673 : 10
advancement of pure s., 825 : 11
aim of exact s., 610 : 1
and applications together, 591 : 1
and opinion, 80 : 5
and relations between nations, 814 : 13
and technology unite humanity, 904 : 18
and the humanities, 871 : 1
applied s. not exist, 591 : 1
art and s. in particulars, 407 : 6
art is I s. is we, 552 : 4
be blessing and not curse, 763 : 8
built with facts, 673 : 8
cannot exist on treaty, 878 : 1
cemetery of dead ideas, 705 : 15
challenge of rootless s., 842 : 1
Christian Scientists some s., 721 : 11
cloud obscure s., 390 : 1
collection of facts not s., 673 : 8
common sense antipodes of s., 724 : 2
communication of truth, 436 : 14
cookery a noble s., 258 : 16
countenance of all s., 424 : 7
defense not in s., 764 : 4
dismal s., 474 : 11
dissociate language from s., 390 : 7
economics dismal s., 872 : 5
education for citizenship, 684 : 16
endless frontier, 814 : 9
enfant terrible of s., 620 : 22
experimentation active s., 551 : 14
fair S. frowned not, 362 : 17
falsely so called, 51 : 5
first-rate furniture, 519 : 18
frees us, 566 : 17
Science (*continued*)
from ancient subject newest s., 666 : 9
God whom s. recognizes, 650 : 6
guide of action, 660 : 6
his s. and his only art, 703 : 3
how define Christian S., 583 : 5
impersonality of s., 552 : 4
important part of culture, 814 : 13
in natural s. nothing petty, 565 : 15
in s. credit to man who convinces world, 662 : 3
in s. experts differ, 700 : 2
in s. read newest, 493 : 9
in s. truth only end, 471 : 16
increases power lowers pride, 552 : 2
is a habit, 260 : 11
knowledge of many, 465 : 12
law a hocus-pocus s., 344 : 20
literature not abstract s., 702 : 14
man of s. devoting life to truth, 639 : 14
most significant contribution of twentieth-century s., 884 : 5
mysterious is source of art and s., 763 : 6
natural s. involves three things, 390 : 7
no category of s. applied, 591 : 1
not safe for S. to divulge causes, 251 : 8
numerical precision soul of s., 696 : 4
object of s. truth, 436 : 14
observation passive s., 551 : 14
of behavior power to manipulate, 862 : 13
of conduct and behavior, 733 : 15
of consciousness, 733 : 15
of life superb hall, 551 : 15
of Nature, 311 : 1
out of olde bokes newe s., 144 : 9
physical s. not console me, 299 : 16
pictures s. draws of nature, 758 : 9
poetry antithesis to s., 436 : 14
politics not exact s., 553 : 7
progress of s., 812 : 10
promote progress of s., 826 : 12
proud S., 336 : 16
purer s. holier laws, 566 : 11
pursuit of s., 584 : 1
quacks one side s. other, 463 : 17
reassures, 776 : 1
refinement of everyday thinking, 763 : 9
repulses indefinite, 551 : 16
right interpretation of nature, 471 : 15
scarcely advanced to s., 594 : 11
search for truth, 854 : 1
spirit of s. in international affairs, 854 : 1
teaches doubt, 552 : 1
temple of s., 686 : 10
theologians at cradle of s., 595 : 7
though no s. worth seven, 336 : 4
thought to aim at some good, 87 : 13
treasures in laps of all, 636 : 15
treating psychology like natural s., 651 : 5
true s. teaches doubt, 705 : 16
waves of s. beat in vain, 580 : 9
where s. progressed farthest, 776 : 7
which draws conclusions, 525 : 1
with least results, 673 : 9

Science (*continued*)
without conscience ruin, 157 : 13
Sciences, books must follow s., 181 : 20
experience mother of s., 169 : 4
mathematical s. founded, 610 : 1
mathematics queen of s., 444 : 11
mechanics paradise of mathematical s., 152 : 13
natural s. aim never reach, 594 : 12
Scientia potestas est, 178 : 17
Scientiam, de subjecto vetustissimo novissimam s., 666 : *n* 3
Scientific, Abraham of s. men, 580 : 7
activity cumulative, 787 : 4
advances available, 787 : 17
discovery and sovereignty, 837 : 14
ideals altars to unknown gods, 648 : 6
innovation rarely converts opponents, 686 : 11
Jesus most s. man, 583 : 2
knowledge from textbooks, 825 : 13
knowledge transform world, 814 : 13
method for studying, 678 : 11
method of s. investigation, 595 : 8
plunges into s. questions, 596 : 11
revolution, 847 : 14
thought is human progress, 660 : 6
truth in different forms, 610 : 2
truth property of few, 509 : 3
Scientist cannot dispense with faith, 686 : 10
independent s., 831 : 24
ready to bear privation, 828 : 1
takes off from predecessors, 762 : 5
values research, 887 : 17
wiser not to withhold, 396 : 7
Scientists at other pole, 865 : 17
collectors classifiers tidiers-up, 888 : 1
Scintillant in cloudless days, 785 : 12
Scissors, two halves of pair of s., 433 : *n* 2
upper or under blade of s., 652 : 2
Scoff, fools who came to s., 370 : 8
Scold jester raconteur confidant, 847 : 10
Scolded, nobody ever s. him, 719 : 5
Scones, buttered s. and crumpets, 804 : 19
Scooped, seas s. in vain, 562 : 10
tankards s. in pearl, 604 : 13
Scoot, old man Rabbit say s., 662 : 10
Scooted, w'en Rabbit say they s., 662 : 10
Scope had not been so short, 249 : *n* 4
of my opinion, 217 : 18
this man's art that man's s., 244 : 9
within s. of Constitution, 402 : 6
Scorch, fires that s., 514 : 3
Score, from seventy springs a s., 690 : 17
give me a kiss and to that a s., 266 : 10
muster many a s., 418 : 7
no books but s. and tally, 185 : 28
Scored, our days are s. against us, 119 : 10
Scorer, One Great S., 773 : 3
Scorn, bright creature s. not one, 429 : 11
child of s., 728 : 19
dangers make us s., 411 : 10
delights, 280 : 15
figure for time of s., 232 : 3
Scorn (*continued*)
foul s. that prince invade, 163 : 15
her own image, 222 : 2
laugh a siege to s., 240 : 2
laugh to s. power of man, 239 : 10
laughed His word to s., 376 : 9
looks beautiful, 214 : 16
mine ever name of s., 534 : 25
not all free who s. chains, 374 : 17
not laugh other men to s., 132 : 8
not the sonnet, 429 : 10
not thing to laugh to s., 212 : 27
not your powers, 115 : 19
of mankind down centuries, 744 : 16
read to s., 432 : 6
silence expression of s., 681 : 14
sound of public s., 287 : 27
the codfish, 923 : 10
to change state with kings, 244 : 10
to take offense, 333 : 10
under solemn fillet saw s., 495 : 6
upright man laughed to s., 15 : 28
Scorned his spirit, 215 : 10
woman s., 324 : 16
Scorner, reprove not a s., 23 : 19
Scornful, most bitter is s. jest, 351 : 8
sitteth in the seat of the s., 17 : 12
yet jealous eyes, 338 : 14
Scorning base degrees, 215 : 16
our blank in s., 604 : 5
Scorns, whips and s. of time, 221 : 12
Scorpion, heart of s. set, 850 : 10
under every stone a s., 82 : *n* 9
Scorpions, ants centipedes and s., 760 : 6
I will chastise with s., 13 : 38
Scotch mist, 569 : 13
Scotched, we have s. the snake, 238 : 18
Scotchman, beggarly S., 354 : 2
if caught young, 355 : 5
noblest prospect S. sees, 354 : 10
Scotia's grandeur springs, 408 : 18
Scotland, in S. before ye, 921 : 9
in S. supports people, 352 : 12
Scotland's, left fair S. strand, 410 : 4
Scots dispersed over whole earth, 177 : 16
gude S. lords, 926 : 12
kills six or seven dozen S., 203 : 26
lords at his feet, 926 : 13
only a few industrious S., 177 : 16
wha hae wi' Wallace bled, 411 : 15
Scott hand in Southern character, 623 : 17
Scoundrel, A is a s., 772 : 16
and coward, 354 : 2
hypocrite flatterer, 407 : 6
man the s., 581 : 18
patriotism last refuge of s., 355 : 15
Scoundrels, healthy hatred of s., 474 : 13
pack of s. Order of State, 864 : 8
talk about future are s., 828 : 8
Scoured with perpetual motion, 206 : 4
Scourge, faith is her own s., 118 : *n* 9
iron s., 361 : 13
laid upon your hate, 193 : 30
mighty s. of war, 524 : 7
of God, 183 : 7
of small cords, 44 : 29
of war, 788 : 20
Scourged to his dungeon, 471 : 6
Scout, blabbing eastern s., 279 : 13
flout 'em and s. 'em, 248 : 8
Scowl of cloud, 545 : 25
Scramble, great s. and big divide, 642 : 11
Scrambling to the shore, 613 : 4
Scrap of paper, 677 : 11
worn out before on s. heap, 680 : 15
Scrape cable, 553 : 17
Scraping, Death's ironic s., 767 : 11
Scraps, on s. of learning dote, 329 : 20
stolen the s., 191 : 7
Scratch Christian find pagan, 706 : 14
head with lightning, 623 : 5
it with a hoe, 603 : 7
lover find foe, 827 : 10
on wall of oblivion, 838 : 14
Scratched, expect to be s., 169 : 9
head kept thinking, 728 : 20
man whom Fortune s., 227 : 19
out both eyes, 934 : 7
Scratchez, Ah itchez Ah s., 856 : 2
Scratching at the floor, 695 : 17
Scrawls, few hundred s., 786 : 11
Scrawny cry a chorister, 769 : 10
Scream, not a shriek not a s., 614 : 2
Screaming, eagle s. night away, 928 : 9
over yawning gulf, 571 : 9
Screams of horror rend, 334 : 10
Screen, world vast s. of snow, 811 : 17
Screens, life lived on silver s., 839 : 3
Screw your courage, 237 : 6
Scribblative, babblative and s., 440 : 11
Scribble scribble scribble, 387 : 6
we all s. poetry, 109 : 24
Scribbled, parchment s. o'er undo a man, 185 : 25
Scribe worthy to be courtier, 6 : 9
Scribes and Pharisees, 40 : 18
Scrimped, charity s. and iced, 659 : 8
Scrip and scrippage, 212 : 5
nor s. nor shoes, 43 : 8
of joy immortal diet, 172 : 15
Scrippage, scrip and s., 212 : 5
Scripture, devil can cite S., 198 : 22
moveth us, 54 : 11
Scriptures, bounds of sermons and s., 912 : 3
let us look at the s., 263 : 12
mighty in S., 46 : 20
search S., 44 : 38
Scrooge, Bah said S. Humbug, 548 : 5
covetous old sinner, 548 : 4
Ghost of Christmas Yet to Come said S., 548 : 12
Scrub kitchen pavement, 712 : 20
Scrunch or be scrunched, 549 : 36
Scrunched, scrunch or be s., 549 : 36
Scruple, not s. to pick pocket, 318 : 1
some craven s., 223 : 18
Scruples, annotator has s. too, 766 : 16
Scrutamini scripturas, 263 : 12
Scullion, away you s., 206 : 10
Sculptor well those passions read, 466 : 12
Sculpture painting music, 579 : 11
Scum of the earth, 421 : 11
Okie means s., 857 : 5
Scurvy politician, 235 : 4
Scutcheon, blot in thy s., 170 : 31
honor a mere s., 205 : 5
Scuttled ship or cut throat, 460 : 26
Scuttlefish, disputants like s., 327 : 1
rejoice with s., 365 : 11
Scuttling across floors of seas, 803 : 14
Scylla guards right side, 200 : *n* 1

Scylla (*continued*)
to port, 200 : *n* 1
when I shun S., 200 : 1
Scythe, work the s. of time, 420 : 17
Scythian, Barbarian S. bond nor free, 50 : 12
Sea, all our s. our own, 276 : 3
all returns to s., 869 : 13
all the rivers run into the s. 26 : 12
alone dwell kings of s., 584 : 14
alone on wide wide s., 434 : 26
and air common to all, 163 : 13
and heaven rolled as one, 767 : 14
as long as rivers run to s., 104 : 29
as near by s. as by land, 166 : 13
as on s. as on fields, 902 : 6
as the sand by the s., 13 : 28
Atlanta to the s., 614 : 14
bark is on s., 460 : 4
bathed in poem of s., 673 : 16
beetles o'er base into s., 219 : 14
before ever the s., 634 : 5
being smooth, 225 : 36
best in chair before fire, 741 : 11
better cast into s., 43 : 35
beyond genius of s., 767 : 15
beyond leagues more s., 601 : 19
blue fresh ever free, 456 : 3
bodies thrown into s., 850 : 11
born across the s., 566 : 5
bound with triumphant s., 194 : 14
bred to the s., 465 : 15
bristling s. coasts, 520 : 7
by the deep s., 458 : 24
calm tonight, 587 : 13
captains young or old, 575 : 22
changed Egdon remained, 640 : 11
cold gray stones O s., 530 : 19
creation of Omnipotence, 741 : 12
crept into bosom of the s., 185 : 20
dance like wave of s., 712 : 17
daughters of s., 850 : 10
deep s. swell, 805 : 9
delaying not hurrying not, 575 : 18
delicate algae and s. anemone, 808 : 2
demons down under s., 527 : 9
depths congealed in heart of s., 9 : 35
desert of the s., 29 : 26
discoverers, 251 : 15
do you not hear s., 478 : *n* 3
dolphin-torn s., 716 : 11
down there s. folk live, 505 : 3
down's edge, 634 : 12
dragon that is in the s., 30 : 12
dwellers by the s., 672 : 20
earth and fire and s. and air, 643 : 2
eastward to the s., 708 : 8
Egypt's dark s., 447 : 10
empty tigers or roaring s., 193 : 23
espouse everlasting s., 425 : 19
ever-renewing s., 735 : 11
far from the s., 428 : *n* 5
far-heard whisper o'er the s., 434 : 21
Father of Waters unvexed to s., 523 : 2
feel thee again old s., 569 : 20
firm-footed by s., 486 : 14
fishes of the s. shall declare, 15 : 29
forbid it s. gods, 569 : 20
fright he is, 907 : 3
from s. to shining s., 688 : 5
frozen s. inside us, 786 : 4
ghost of garden fronts s., 634 : 12
glitter of s., 911 : 15

Sea (*continued*)
go down to the s. in ships, 21 : 14
God a s. of infinite substance, 135 : 5
gods forbid it, 569 : 20
goes to s. for nothing, 253 : 22
gone with the sun, 674 : 1
grasped eastern and western s., 374 : 20
gray s. long black land, 541 : 13
great and wide s., 21 : 11
great river and s. which is fresh, 151 : 6
green isle in s., 525 : 17
grew civil at her song, 196 : 14
guiled shore to dangerous s., 199 : 26
half-held by night, 574 : 19
has many voices, 808 : 2
hast thou entered into the springs of the s., 16 : 31
hates a coward, 810 : 13
he that commands s. is at liberty, 181 : 11
herd ran into s., 42 : 5
heroism upon land and s., 574 : 6
hold helm when s. calm, 111 : 6
houses all gone under s., 807 : 14
how many strawberries in s., 930 : 2
hurt not the s., 53 : 13
in calm s. every man pilot, 301 : 12
in flat s. sunk, 279 : 22
in gentle autumnal season, 782 : 22
in peril on the s., 596 : 18
in s. caves a thirst, 849 : 18
in s. toils traveling, 907 : 2
influence of s. power, 642 : 8
into the s. upon dry ground, 9 : 31
is calm tonight, 587 : 13
is his and he made it, 20 : 20
is not full, 26 : 12
isles that o'erlace s., 543 : 24
itself floweth in veins, 311 : 20
kingdom by s., 527 : 8
land's edge also, 808 : 2
lands beyond the s., 425 : 6
lies all around us, 869 : 13
life's unresting s., 519 : 8
light over land and s., 745 : 8
like stars on the s., 459 : 14
like to drink whole s., 861 : 4
lonely s. and sky, 760 : 14
lost s. smell, 806 : 6
lost s. voices, 806 : 6
love it you cannot, 741 : 12
lover of men the s., 633 : 2
made for his tomb, 257 : 5
maid's music, 196 : 14
man not afraid of s., 735 : 5
man to match the s., 671 : 1
Marathon looks on s., 461 : 4
marvel how fishes live in s., 243 : 13
master of earth and s., 711 : 13
master of s. master of every country, 181 : *n* 5
mirrored on her s., 733 : 3
monotonous as s., 568 : 16
more hideous than s. monster, 233 : 10
mountains by the winter s., 534 : 29
murderous innocence of s., 714 : 14
my blood part of the s., 790 : 21
nations that have s. power have freedom, 800 : 6
never changes, 683 : 14

Sea (*continued*)
never loved by anyone married to it, 741 : 12
never never sick at s., 627 : 11
never saw the s., 606 : 17
never trust s. when calm, 100 : 18
never was on s. or land, 427 : 17
no land when see but s., 179 : 3
no war won without s. power, 800 : 11
not all water in rough rude s., 194 : 26
nothing but hath bound in s., 188 : 1
nothing sure in s. fight, 408 : 6
number the sand of the s., 34 : 21
ocean s. not sufficient room, 257 : 5
of cause and theory, 742 : 18
of dew, 666 : 16
of faith, 587 : 16
of Galilee and Dead Sea, 759 : 11
of illiteracy, 871 : 15
of lead sky of slate, 711 : 11
of Tranquillity, 864 : 4
of troubles, 221 : 12
of upturned faces, 431 : 25
of words, 782 : 3
offer yourselves to s., 651 : 8
ole davil s., 810 : 5
on land as on the s., 922 : 11
once made England secure 752 : 1
one foot in s. one on shore, 209 : 16
one is of the s., 428 : 6
one salt s., 207 : 8
or fire, 217 : 25
order words of s., 767 : 16
our heritage the s., 453 : 20
over great s. winds trouble waters, 100 : 12
over s. to Skye, 688 : 12
passenger e'er pukes in, 461 : 14
pastures, 571 : 3
pearl in bosom of s., 257 : 13
people know salt of s., 761 : 16
perfumed s., 525 : 9
Persians hold s. holy, 570 : 4
plants footsteps in s., 375 : 16
plow the s., 628 : 4
Pontic s., 231 : 18
pouring oil on the s., 116 : *n* 2
power never led to despotism, 800 : 6
praise s. on shore remain, 174 : 24
precious stone set in silver s., 194 : 13
Proteus rising from s., 428 : 1
raging waves of the s., 52 : 26
righteousness as waves of s., 31 : 7
rising nor sky clouding, 654 : 15
river will reach s., 633 : *n* 3
round cape sudden came s., 541 : 15
running all over s., 683 : 13
rustles in and out of seaweed, 798 : 12
sailed wintry s., 510 : 4
sailor home from s., 668 : 20
sails upon lowland s., 935 : 4
sang in my chains like s., 887 : 3
see one s. and see all, 259 : 4
sepulcher there by s., 527 : 10
served revolution plowed s., 452 : 3
shadow only s. keeps, 843 : 13
shadows upon a s. obscure, 131 : 17
Sherman's buzzin' to s., 840 : 8
ship's way on s., 708 : 22
ships of war at s., 535 : 11
shows false alluring smile, 100 : 18
shroud of s., 571 : 9
sight of immortal s., 426 : 20
silent s., 434 : 13

Sea (*continued*)
sing by land and s., 708 : 24
singing over the wine-dark s., 59 : 19
sinks to another s., 562 : 9
sky and s. and land, 692 : 11
slimy s., 434 : 16
snuff thee up s. breeze, 569 : 20
spirit that on life's rough s., 178 : 6
summers in a s. of glory, 249 : 3
sun was shining on s., 613 : 1
sunless s., 433 : 21
surging s. outweighs, 495 : 19
sweet mystery about s., 571 : 3
swimming in this s. and that s., 849 : 11
swing of the s., 655 : 17
syllabub s., 550 : 13
talk from S. of Tranquility, 882 : 20
that pickest and cullest, 575 : 22
the s. is his, 54 : 17
the sea the open sea, 456 : 3
the s. the s., 83 : 3
there was no more s., 53 : 29
though the mountains be carried into the s., 19 : 10
thought jump s. and land, 244 : 16
thousand furlongs of s., 247 : 8
to sea through your expanse, 518 : 8
to s. to s., 492 : 14
tomb by side of s., 527 : *n* 3
tomb by sounding s., 527 : 10
tomorrow we sail the Ocean S., 107 : 5
troubled s. of mind, 475 : 18
trunk spouts out a s., 286 : 30
two if by s., 512 : 7
unicorns come down to s., 811 : 14
union with native s., 428 : 15
unplumbed estranging s., 585 : 14
uttermost parts of the s., 22 : 17
voice whose sound like s., 425 : 23
walking on the s., 39 : 26
waters cover the s., 29 : 19
waves of wind-ruffled s., 455 : 14
way of a ship in the s., 26 : 4
weariest river winds to s., 633 : 22
we'll o'er the s., 422 : 19
went to sea in sieve, 550 : 11
wet sheet flowing s., 453 : 19
whales in waves of s., 790 : 22
what is it saying, 548 : 17
when I put out to s., 535 : 19
where Drake sleeps in s., 569 : 20
whether in s. or fire, 217 : 25
white s. widening, 875 : 2
who can say s. is old, 640 : 11
who commands the s. has command, 70 : 19
who hath desired s., 710 : 7
who run across s. do not change disposition, 109 : 5
why s. boiling hot, 613 : 5
wind nor tide nor s., 630 : 21
wind of western s. 530 : 25
winds pierced solitudes, 494 : 4
wish you a wave of the s., 246 : 28
work in land or s., 494 : 6
wrapped in mystery, 683 : 14
wrinkled s. beneath, 532 : 28
you'll not find another s., 702 : 2
your mind and you Sargasso S. 792 : 5
Sea-room to tell truth in, 569 : 17
Sea-banks, upon the wild s., 200 : 22
Sea-born treasures, 493 : 15
Sea-change, suffer a s., 247 : 21
Sea-down's edge, 634 : 12
Seafarers, hour that turns back longing of s., 141 : 26
Seafaring man on desert of waters, 603 : 2
Sea-green incorruptible, 473 : 20
Seagulls, as I watched s., 783 : 1
Seal, god seem to set his s., 223 : 3
impression as from s. of ring, 85 : 18
playing in sun like me, 929 : 7
scales shut together as with close s., 17 : 5
sense in deathly slumber, 739 : 17
set me as a s., 28 : 23
slumber did my spirit s., 424 : 14
to such a bond, 198 : 26
up avenues of ill, 495 : 3
upon thine arm, 28 : 23
Sealed, at birth our death s., 115 : 18
bag of ducats, 199 : 11
in vain, 228 : 28
thy fate and mine s., 531 : 10
with seven seals, 53 : 9
Sealing, come s. night, 238 : 21
shoes ships s. wax, 613 : 5
snapped off like s. wax, 548 : 14
Seal's wide spindrift gaze, 843 : 16
Seals, I want s. of power and place, 418 : 8
of love sealed in vain, 228 : 28
sealed with seven s., 53 : 9
to fish and to s., 878 : 6
Seam, sew a fine s., 931 : 19
without s. without joining, 5 : 1
Sea-maid's music, 196 : 14
Seaman, betokened wrack to s., 189 : 10
delight as only s. may know, 799 : 20
looking for something else, 800 : 5
Seaman's story is of tempest, 112 : 20
Sea-mark of my utmost sail, 232 : 18
Seamen, all her s. know, 564 : 13
forty singing s., 772 : 21
thus with s., 569 : 21
were not gentlemen, 489 : 7
Sear, leaf red and s., 430 : 13
Search for inexplicable, 770 : 3
happy man who could s. out causes, 104 : 5
land of living men, 430 : 15
not worth the s., 198 : 5
out purposes of gods, 72 : 8
so painful and so long, 315 : 21
the scriptures, 44 : 38
their own glory, 25 : 17
thine own heart, 513 : 9
things above thy strength, 34 : 26
took day to s. for God, 696 : 11
vain my weary s. to find, 369 : 5
walked in the s. of the depth, 16 : 31
will find it out, 266 : 18
Searched me and known me, 22 : 16
Searcher for fecund minimum, 766 : 18
obedient to truth, 580 : 7
Searches, tent that s., 226 : 7
unreasonable s. and seizures, 391 : 16
Searcheth, Lord s. all hearts, 14 : 24
Searching, by s. find out God, 15 : 25
to rediscover first seed, 849 : 7
Seared and blighted heart, 525 : 4
conscience s. with hot iron, 50 : 27
Sears Northland soul, 834 : 5
Sea's face and gray dawn, 760 : 14
Sea's (*continued*)
great s. voice, 732 : 7
green crying towers a-sway, 843 : 18
thoughts with s. boundlessness, 850 : 2
Seas, backed with God and s., 186 : 15
colder than Hebrides, 785 : 15
dangers of the s., 273 : 6
desperate s. long wont, 525 : 9
diver in deep s., 638 : 11
down to s. again, 760 : 14
faithless as winds or s., 312 : 12
fight on s. and oceans, 744 : 2
floors of silent s., 803 : 14
freedom of s., 682 : 14
from the s. and streams, 468 : 9
guard our native s., 443 : 10
half s. over, 323 : 6
he hath founded it upon the s., 18 : 8
I must down to s., 760 : 14, 760 : 15, 760 : 16
incarnadine, 238 : 1
laugh when rocks near, 262 : 5
launch on trackless s., 576 : 15
mackerel-crowded s., 714 : 22
of life like wine, 311 : 23
of pity lie, 868 : 13
of space and time, 802 : 20
perilous s., 477 : 1
port after stormy s., 173 : 12
rivers run to s., 307 : 2
roaring with blasts, 331 : 7
roll to waft me, 336 : 19
sail wet s. roun', 709 : 8
scooped in vain, 562 : 10
seven s. of ink, 132 : 3
ships sailing the s., 575 : 21
shoreless s., 646 : 6
sink her in Indian s., 558 : 10
snarled and yelping s., 804 : 16
strange s. of thought, 424 : 2
tossed upon cloudy s., 772 : 23
unsuspected isle in s., 540 : 17
wandering over many s. to these obsequies, 102 : 18
waste of s., 483 : 20
what s. what shores, 806 : 8
wine-dark s., 868 : 21
Sea-scented beach, 541 : 14
Seashore, like boy playing on s., 313 : 17
Seaside stroll a gallery, 595 : 6
Seasilt saltsick, 778 : 6
Season, a convenient s., 46 : 31
be instant in s. 51 : 8
bringeth forth his fruit in s., 17 : 12
each thing that in s. grows, 190 : 13
end of love or s., 747 : 2
ever 'gainst that s., 217 : 26
for wild oats, 701 : 1
grain of poetry s. century, 672 : 4
little s. of love laughter, 614 : 17
love no s. knows, 252 : 8
meat in due s., 21 : 11
moulting s. crisis, 559 : 11
my scope had not this s., 249 : *n* 4
no s. such delight can bring, 265 : 16
of love and laughter, 614 : 17
of mists, 477 : 17
of ships is here, 93 : 3
of snows and sin, 632 : 8
overpraised s., 620 : 8
proportion s. form, 225 : 37
shock of corn cometh in s., 15 : 18
tale out of s., 35 : 34

Season (*continued*)
things by s. seasoned, 201 : 5
to come and go, 339 : 29
to every thing there is a s., 26 : 21
word spoken in due s., 24 : 9
your admiration, 218 : 17
youth's s. for joys, 332 : 4
Seasoned, speech s. with salt, 50 : 14
things by season s., 201 : 5
timber never gives, 268 : 17
with a gracious voice, 199 : 24
with Attic salt, 298 : 14
Seasoning of all enjoyments, 298 : 2
sharp s. of truth, 127 : 18
Seasons, afford costly s., 906 : 10
all s. thine O Death, 470 : 20
all times are his s., 255 : 1
appointeth moon for s., 21 : 11
as swift s. roll, 519 : 7
assailed the s., 728 : 19
defend you from s., 234 : 3
form great circle, 701 : 9
he makes the s., 5 : 3
joys abound as s. fleet, 185 : 14
lovers' s. run, 252 : 7
man for all s., 155 : 11
mercy s. justice, 200 : 9
not the full four s., 823 : 4
O s. clear, 843 : 16
O s. O châteaux, 674 : 2
sorrow breaks s., 187 : 11
time of s. and constellations, 807 : 10
vernal s. of year, 281 : 21
with the year s. return, 285 : 5
yin and yang became four s., 97 : 7
Seat, castle hath pleasant s., 236 : 21
God's great Judgment S., 707 : 16
of desolation, 283 : 12
of Mars, 194 : 13
of pleasures and loves, 306 : 6
of sensation stomach, 692 : 14
proud s. of Lucifer, 287 : 26
sitteth in the s. of the scornful, 17 : 12
sitting in catbird s., 831 : 11
thy s. is up on high, 195 : 19
thyself sultanically, 571 : 2
upon intellectual throne, 585 : 23
while memory holds a s., 219 : 27
wild sequestered s., 364 : 14
Seated, all s. on the ground, 317 : 4
grace s. on this brow, 223 : 3
heart knock at my ribs, 236 : 11
in thy silver chair, 255 : 12
one day at organ, 596 : 13
Seatown, years around s. corner, 887 : 5
Seats, put down mighty from s., 42 : 22
Seaward flying unbroken wings, 806 : 6
from the town, 453 : 23
looked s. among islands, 664 : 2
trees seemed to march s., 664 : 2
Seawards, salt tides s. flow, 584 : 11
Seaweed, sea rustles in and out of s., 798 : 12
Secluded chapel, 808 : 16
eternally from God, 254 : 23
Second, appointed for my s. race, 299 : 2
best to go back quickly, 75 : 13
best's gay goodnight, 715 : 19
childishness, 211 : 15
children for s. time, 82 : 1
class citizens, 824 : 11
custom almost s. nature, 190 : *n* 1
Second (*continued*)
Daniel, 200 : 19
first among these than s. in Rome, 99 : 18
friend is a s. self, 99 : 7
great nature's s. course, 237 : 21
in war no s. prize, 825 : 4
is frugality, 65 : 3
mads him, 213 : 16
Mrs. Tanqueray, 730 : 10
nature, 393 : 8
no dishonor to halt at s. place, 98 : 12
office of government easy, 388 : 13
Theseus a s. Hercules, 119 : 22
thoughts are best, 76 : 21
what's on s., 832 : 3
wife hateful to children, 76 : 1
Secondary imagination, 437 : 12
Seconded with will and power, 226 : 3
Secrecy and free government, 788 : 18
for s. no lady closer, 203 : 24
nature's infinite book of s., 240 : 15
the human dress, 405 : 14
Secret aims of nature, 654 : 14
and his dark s. love, 405 : 5
anniversaries of heart, 512 : 22
as grave, 170 : 38
be s. and exult, 713 : 12
black midnight hags, 239 : 8
book with s. reference, 504 : *n* 1
bread eaten in s., 23 : 20
cleanse me from s. faults, 18 : 2
courage s. of liberty, 677 : 12
death a s. of Nature, 124 : 15
dwelleth in s. place, 20 : 16
every creature s. to other, 549 : 23
extort s. lose curiosity, 496 : 3
guilt by silence betrayed, 305 : 27
inwardly in s. great, 568 : 23
isolated joy of thinker, 644 : 1
keeps s. well as child, 491 : 24
liberty s. of happiness, 677 : 12
life of belly and bone, 883 : 11
locked within them, 852 : 11
ministry, 435 : 14
not secret if confided, 561 : 11
nothing is s., 43 : 6
of being a bore, 343 : 1
of freedom a brave heart, 81 : 5
of happiness freedom, 81 : 5
of my success, 645 : 13
of study of nature, 504 : 17
of success constancy, 502 : 15
of their own discovery, 852 : 11
only s. is Immortality, 608 : 2
open rebuke better than s. love, 25 : 23
our readings s., 764 : 7
powers of atom, 720 : 6
self-contained solitary, 548 : 4
single s. will still be man, 830 : 2
sits in middle and knows, 749 : 9
source of humor, 625 : 4
sympathy, 430 : 9
tell you a great s., 882 : 9
things belong unto the Lord, 11 : 21
though s. it rolls, 446 : 8
thoughts run over all things, 264 : 16
three keep s. if two dead, 347 : 10
trade s., 366 : 1
treasures in s. kept, 555 : 17
Vereker's s., 653 : 7
waters, 834 : 11
whence this s. dread, 326 : 3
Secret (*continued*)
whispers of other's watch, 208 : 1
with every s. thing, 27 : 27
Secretaries of Nature, 271 : 16
Secretary of Nature, 271 : 15
Secretly, how swift how s., 822 : 1
nurtured in cellar, 800 : 7
Secret's safe 'twixt you and me, 545 : 20
Secrets cry aloud, 873 : 2
dark s. of ocean, 482 : 11
everybody guesses, 680 : 6
from whom no s. are hid, 55 : 15
holding such things to be holy s., 79 : 13
learned s. of grave, 638 : 11
reveal no s., 370 : *n* 3
shake s. from my bones, 874 : 6
trust not him with s., 386 : 9
Sect, know neither s. nor idolatry, 151 : 5
never attached to that s., 468 : 21
slave to no s., 337 : 16
Section, you-all means s., 922 : 9
Sects, enslaved to s., 125 : 21
vicissitude of s. and religions, 181 : 15
Seculo, alteri s., 95 : *n* 10
Secure a few minutes for poetry, 598 : 14
amidst falling world, 325 : 11
and now never mourn, 469 : 12
approval if try hard, 625 : 6
blessings of liberty, 391 : 10
friends by doing favors, 81 : 3
from change, 568 : 19
he that's s. is not safe, 347 : 28
he who s. within can say, 305 : 1
repeal of bad laws, 589 : 21
strong just weak s., 891 : 2
you count many friends, 113 : 28
Secured against maladministration, 367 : 5
Securely founded, 395 : 18
orbed, 794 : 4
Security, absolute s., 860 : 3
against future violations, 351 : 4
culture moment of s., 784 : 6
for average man, 779 : 13
for the future, 351 : *n* 3
how little s. we have, 445 : 6
in old book, 569 : 6
militia necessary to s. of free State, 391 : 15
no s. in nobleness of another, 738 : 13
of all countries connected, 774 : 6
of future, 609 : 9
of people, 367 : 5
of the Republic, 700 : 3
order s. and peace, 774 : 6
public strength individual s., 401 : 11
system of general s., 781 : 9
to democracies against despots, 397 : *n* 8
took a tumble, 847 : 1
Sed haec prius fuere, 101 : *n* 13
Sedate, ignorance s., 352 : 1
Sedentary life sin, 659 : 1
Sedge withered from lake, 478 : 10
Sediment of long Chinese past, 796 : 1
Sedition, wine cause of s., 316 : 13
Sedulous ape, 668 : 23
Sedulously cultivate free speech, 746 : 6
See a fine picture, 395 : 5
all we s. or seem, 525 : 3

See (*continued*)
and be seen, 113 : 9
anyone coming, 919 : 22
author has nothing to s., 597 : 7
bachelor of threescore again, 209 : 1
best not to s. beams of sun, 67 : 5
blind as will not s., 319 : 11
blind now I s., 45 : 8
bosom I must not s., 297 : 20
can I s. another's woe, 403 : 16
cannot s. forest for trees, 380 : 4
change we think we s., 747 : 10
cherry hung with snow, 690 : 17
Christ stand, 543 : 23
church by daylight, 209 : 7
clear day s. forever, 895 : 5
come up and s. me, 824 : 8
dagger I s. before me, 237 : 13
deep difficulty braved, 653 : 12
direction which thou canst not s., 337 : 1
dwarf on giant s. farther, 258 : 7
eye begins to s., 874 : 15
eye to eye, 31 : 13
eyes and s. not, 31 : 34
eyes have they but s. not, 21 : 22
eyes that can s., 797 : 20
eyes weep but never s., 442 : 18
from where I stood, 822 : 11
full plain I s., 435 : 7
girl I like to s., 866 : 18
God made and eaten, 541 : 20
God whom we s. not is, 634 : 15
gold that I never s., 691 : 8
happy moron, 924 : 18
have thee not yet s. thee still, 237 : 13
heaven's glories shine, 562 : 4
here it is, 478 : 8
here shall he s. no enemy, 211 : 1
higher than himself, 537 : 13
how she leans her cheek, 192 : 4
how they run, 929 : 11
how world goes, 235 : 2
how world wags, 211 : 5
how yond justice rails, 235 : 2
how you would do, 407 : 2
I don't s. said Caterpillar, 611 : 8
I s. not feel how beautiful, 435 : 25
I s. what I eat, 611 : 18
I'll s. you again, 843 : 9
image of what we actually s., 638 : 4
in all things thee to s., 269 : 7
in my flesh shall I s. God, 16 : 4
in small proportions beauties s., 256 : 20
into life of things, 423 : 11
it clearly in the idea, 768 : 8
it lap the miles, 605 : 18
it shining plain, 691 : 9
it yet remains to s., 607 : 18
kings have desired to s., 43 : 12
let mine eyes not s., 213 : 9
little tippler, 604 : 15
lovers cannot s. follies, 199 : 7
may I be there to s., 376 : 16
me safe up, 155 : 9
Mediterraneans s. clearly, 784 : 5
meet and not s. its head, 64 : 7
more people s. than weigh, 342 : 10
more ye s. better like it, 722 : 4
my shining palace, 822 : 18
my way as birds, 540 : 6
never s. nor know nor miss me, 778 : 6

See (*continued*)
never s. tree at all, 855 : 15
no evil, 919 : 2
no man s. me more, 249 : 1
none should s. salvation, 200 : 9
none so blind as not s., 319 : 11
not my love to s., 174 : 13
not s. me stopping here, 748 : 5
not s. more clearly for whistling, 678 : 10
not the bottom of it, 226 : 22
not worth going to s., 356 : 12
object as it really is, 586 : 15
Oh can't you s. it, 831 : 13
oh say can you s., 446 : 1
old flagpole stands, 771 : 5
one mountain and see all, 259 : 4
one-third of nation ill-housed, 780 : 2
only their own shadows, 84 : 17
only with heart one can s., 849 : 4
other whole against sky, 756 : 12
oursels as others see us, 409 : 8
pygmies s. more than giants, 118 : 7
really do not s. signal, 408 : 5
sad sights moves, 189 : 25
see their mark, 269 : 6
seem to s. things thou dost not, 235 : 4
she stirs, 511 : 7
Shelley plain, 542 : 13
shut my eyes to s., 875 : 1
smile his work to s., 405 : 8
so far as one may, 644 : 14
so much nor live so long, 235 : 20
so sadly to s., 690 : 12
sons what things you are, 206 : 30
sun with ignorant eye, 768 : 8
taste and s. that the Lord is good, 18 : 20
ten things where ordinary man sees one, 793 : 10
the conquering hero, 346 : 7
the Way of Heaven, 64 : 17
there shall no man s. me, 10 : 14
they bark at me, 234 : 15
they shall s. God, 37 : 4
things as they are, 353 : 15
things bare to the buff, 669 : 5
things seen I s. no more, 426 : 10
things through his eyes, 834 : 1
think I shall never s., 795 : 6, 855 : 15
those things ye see, 43 : 12
thou canst not s. my face, 10 : 14
through glass darkly, 48 : 25
to s. clearly is poetry, 572 : 11
to s. her was to love her, 410 : 3
under press of having to write manual, 906 : 12
veil through which not s., 516 : 18
Venus let me never s., 321 : 1
was blind but now I s., 367 : 7
we are as much as we s., 557 : 3
what a rent, 216 : 23
what I say, 869 : 9
what I see, 221 : 22
what s. elsewhere not here, 148 : 16
whatever you s. is Jupiter, 118 : 13
whatsoever I shall s. or hear, 79 : 13
where Christ's blood streams, 184 : 8
where it flies, 184 : 4
where she comes appareled like spring, 243 : 10
Winter comes, 345 : 4

See (*continued*)
with half an eye, 170 : 27
with not through the eye, 407 : 10
world in grain of sand, 406 : 8
you s. more in you, 859 : 4
you s. things, and say Why, 681 : 11
young men shall s. visions, 33 : 17
your good works, 37 : 6
Seed, bearing precious s., 22 : 7
blood of Christians is s., 126 : 3
blood of martyrs s. of Church, 126 : *n* 2
broadcast catch somewhere, 537 : 11
de beginnin, 837 : 17
de first en last, 837 : 17
enmity between thy s. and her s., 7 : 10
ground more malign with bad s., 142 : 7
groweth s., 916 : 14
heaven like to mustard s., 39 : 17
money the s. of money, 358 : 11
nor his s. begging bread, 18 : 25
of religious liberty, 569 : 9
searching to rediscover first s., 849 : 7
sow thy s. in the morning, 27 : 22
sows himself for s., 794 : 9
they moved through fields sowing s., 888 : 7
wonder the s. of knowledge, 178 : 18
work is s. sown, 472 : 18
Seeds, fruitful error full of s., 662 : 21
in dry pod tick, 728 : 4
of despotism at doors, 520 : 7
of godlike power, 584 : 10
of patriots and heroes, 367 : *n* 8
of time, 236 : 5
plant s. watch renewal, 603 : 7
some s. fell by wayside, 39 : 13
treason sows secret s., 138 : 9
Seedtime and harvest, 8 : 1
fair s. had my soul, 423 : 17
regret my s., 893 : 1
Seeing, adds precious s. to the eye, 191 : 3
eye is not satisfied with s., 26 : 13
eyes made for s., 494 : 5
fatality of s. too well, 768 : 22
hearing ear s. eye, 24 : 29
individual way of s., 650 : 7
my head is worth s., 412 : 3
necessity of s. each other, 671 : 18
the root of the matter, 16 : 5
understands without s., 64 : 17
worth s. not going to see, 356 : 12
Seek all day ere you find them, 198 : 5
and ye shall find, 38 : 12
armed to s. and sever, 821 : 11
beauteous eye of heaven to garnish, 202 : 5
by trophies and dead things, 262 : 11
carry with us wonders we s., 274 : 6
empty world again, 562 : 2
flee from me that did me s., 161 : 25
for Eldorado, 527 : 5
for the lost mind, 89 : 22
for truth in groves of Academe, 109 : 14
fortunes further than home, 188 : 27
going to s. grand perhaps, 158 : 14
Heaven itself in our folly, 106 : 27
how s. empty world again, 562 : 2
I s. a form, 720 : 19

Seek (*continued*)
it in My arms, 693 : 15
judgment, 28 : 30
knock breathe and s. to mend, 254 : 15
labored for them that s. learning, 36 : 4
never s. to tell thy love, 404 : 10
newer world, 529 : 13
no farther s. his merits, 362 : 19
not life of immortals, 71 : 28
not out things that are too hard, 34 : 26
not s. for kind relief, 403 : 16
not s. support of communism 779 : 19
not to make them like you 782 : 15
out soldier's grave, 462 : 19
peace and pursue it, 18 : 21
peace what I s., 586 : 12
poets that lasting marble s., 276 : 9
seek shall I seek, 561 : 1
so sadly to s., 690 : 12
some dewdrops here, 196 : 11
their meat from God, 21 : 11
they s. a sign, 43 : 18
those that s. me early, 23 : 17
to bring largest good, 649 : 18
to strive s. find, 529 : 14
we s. no wider war, 872 : 12
we s. the truth, 793 : 12
what men of old sought, 314 : 4
where s. is find, 365 : 8
why s. living among dead, 44 : 13
with fear and trembling, 649 : 18
world was not to s. me, 356 : 27
ye first the kingdom of God, 38 : 6
Seekest thou great things, 32 : 19
Seeketh, love never s. own, 148 : 20
love s. not self to please, 405 : 3
love s. self to please, 405 : 4
Seeking bubble reputation, 211 : 15
find what we are s., 823 : 1
knot in a bulrush, 93 : 10
leopard s. at that altitude, 845 : 8
light s. light, 190 : 11
may be found by s., 96 : 10
new ways to use strength, 789 : 4
the food he eats, 211 : 3
unperplexed s. find Him, 542 : 19
whom he may devour, 52 : 16
with the soul, 395 : 8
Seeks abroad may find, 477 : 18
human that can be accounted for, 769 : 1
man s. for what is remote, 89 : 11
serves and s. for gain, 233 : 18
Wisdom's self oft s., 279 : 22
with the sword repose, 298 : 19
Seeling, come s. night, 238 : 21
Seem a saint when most play devil, 187 : 6
all uses of this world, 218 : 5
all we see or s., 525 : 3
earth to me did s., 426 : 10
finale of s., 766 : 25
grow to what they s., 368 : 19
here no inch to gain, 564 : 17
men should be what they s., 230 : 31
not always what they s., 374 : 15
not to s. but be best, 71 : 18
pay the rent of s., 829 : 16
things not always what they s., 114 : 10
things not what they s., 509 : 13
Seem (*continued*)
things seldom what s., 627 : 16
though I die old, 717 : 3
to fly it, 256 : 6
to see things thou dost not, 235 : 4
Seemed, absence s. my flame to qualify, 245 : 14
all s. but were not all, 286 : 23
but a few days, 8 : 22
scarce s. there to be, 435 : 9
that which once s. he, 438 : 9
they s. to die, 34 : 13
to me like king, 790 : 13
Seeming and savor all winter, 246 : 25
beguile by s. otherwise, 230 : 10
of s. arms make essay, 307 : 8
Seemly for young man to lie mangled, 59 : 6
Seems, I know not s., 218 : 2
madam Nay it is, 218 : 2
no bigger than his head, 234 : 28
part of wisdom 377 : 8
she hangs on cheek of night, 191 : 26
such s. your beauty still, 245 : 11
to shake the spheres, 306 : 13
Seen, after they've s. Paree, 801 : 12
artist records more than s., 736 : 22
atoms, 818 : 9
best of our time, 233 : 4
better days, 211 : 13, 243 : 6
better days who has not, 462 : 12
duty and done it, 923 : 17
ear of man hath not s., 197 : 10
ere I had s. that day, 218 : 14
evidence of things not s., 51 : 18
eye hath not s., 48 : 2
first came the s., 793 : 3
further than Descartes, 313 : 10
glory of coming of Lord, 566 : 4
guess unseen from s., 652 : 14
I have s. better faces, 233 : 14
I have s. God face to face, 8 : 26
I have s. the sunset, 673 : 17
I have s. the wicked in great power, 18 : 26
loved needs only be s., 305 : 16
man s. and heard, 705 : 12
moment of greatness flicker, 803 : 16
no man hath s. God, 44 : 22
not s. as others saw, 525 : 5
not s. the righteous forsaken, 18 : 25
not s. yet believed, 45 : 37
nothing sacred, 844 : 14
nothing yet, 169 : 18
our sports shall be s., 403 : 4
paint what will be s., 735 : 15
pearl in sea never s., 257 : 13
pin faith in things not s., 125 : 23
starry archipelagoes, 673 : 19
thee oft amid store, 477 : 18
things not s. eternal, 49 : 13
things s. are temporal, 49 : 13
through make-believe, 733 : 1
to be hated needs but be s., 337 : 5
too early s. unknown, 191 : 27
touch scarcely felt or s., 341 : 3
war hate war, 779 : 18
what I have seen, 221 : 22
Seer, Baudelaire foremost s., 580 : *n* 3
one must make self a s., 674 : 12
poet makes himself a s., 674 : 12
Sees all her sons at play, 585 : 9
care not who s. your back, 203 : 29
doubts from what he s., 406 : 17
Sees (*continued*)
God who made him s., 710 : 22
into bottom of my grief, 193 : 18
it and does it, 542 : 19
man control wind, 585 : 9
Me in all, 94 : 13
neither hears nor s., 424 : 14
never s. a whole, 585 : 5
not paint what he s., 735 : 15
Present Past Future s., 405 : 1
some morning unaware, 541 : 16
sun which s. all things, 57 : 26
things as they are, 647 : 10
what he foresaw, 427 : 25
Seesaw Margery Daw, 931 : 2
Seest, what thou s. write, 52 : 28
Seeth, Lord s. not as man s., 12 : 38
now mine eye s. thee, 17 : 10
Seevility, a little s., 922 : 7
Sei personaggi in cerca d'autore, 723 : 19
Seine, longitude and latitude for s., 623 : 5
torn s. shattered lobsterpot, 808 : 2
Seize fate by the throat, 421 : 18
good fortune, 396 : 28
light doth s. my brain, 402 : 15
ruin s. thee, 363 : 4
the day, 107 : 8
the flower, 411 : 8
what hand dare s. fire, 405 : 7
Seized, love s. me so strongly, 140 : 23
Seizures, unreasonable searches and s., 391 : 16
Seldom he smiles, 215 : 10
how s. friend, 436 : 2
Seld-shaven odd-eyed, 441 : 6
Selecting, assimilating educating s., 737 : 11
Selection, art discrimination and s., 653 : 13
natural s., 514 : 14, 579 : 20
not saving but s., 374 : 10
Selects, artist observes s. guesses, 695 : 4
soul s. her own society, 605 : 2
Self, applause from none but s., 581 : 14
concentered all in s., 430 : 10
enough of s. undamaged, 883 : 8
Entity greater than s., 895 : 13
experience s. with continuity, 854 : 5
eyes of your creature s., 864 : 7
for my single s., 215 : 4
friend is a second s., 99 : 7
his own inexorable s., 570 : 5
is hateful, 300 : 12
is honey of all beings, 56 : 22
love seeketh s. to please, 405 : 4
luminous island of s., 880 : 4
not mine but ours, 905 : 13
nothing greater than one's s., 574 : 27
only prison, 671 : 13
Sidney's s., 540 : 11
swear by thy gracious s., 192 : 12
through eyes of others, 724 : 17
to thine own s. be true, 219 : 2
toll me back from thee to my sole s., 477 : 2
total of all he can call his, 648 : 17
try to speak hidden s., 585 : 16
was not the same, 225 : 30
what jailer inexorable as s., 503 : 19
Self-affrighting, learns it is s., 714 : 21
Self-appeasing, learns it is s., 714 : 21

Self-appointed inspector of snowstorms, 557 : 7
Self-approval, hunger for s., 626 : 3
Self-approving hour, 337 : 14
Self-balanced, O to be s. for contingencies, 574 : 1
Self-blinding, nothing so s., 834 : 1
Self-canceling, democracy s., 473 : 22
Self-centered passion, 839 : 14
sovereign state s., 860 : 2
Self-circling energies, 436 : 20
Self-complacency is pleasure, 308 : 13
Self-conceit may lead to self-destruction, 66 : 9
philosophy to get rid of s., 121 : 14
Self-confidence complete and bumptious, 792 : 1
in military unit, 771 : 2
Self-conscious, not make us s., 799 : 17
Self-contained, placid and s., 574 : 24
Self-control, cannot live without s., 862 : 1
self-knowledge s., 528 : 5
Self-deceit, nothing easier than s., 88 : 22
Self-delighting, learns it is s., 714 : 21
Self-denial indulgence, 647 : 20
Self-denying, in war ruthless s., 463 : 13
Self-destruction, capitalist tendency toward s., 785 : 5
self-conceit may lead to s., 66 : 9
Self-devoted, in war s., 463 : 13
Self-disparagement, inward s., 428 : 14
Self-dispraise, luxury in s., 428 : 14
Self-dissection introversion, 499 : 6
Self-esteem grounded on right, 287 : 10
Self-evident, hold these truths s., 554 : 4
hold truths to be s., 387 : 9
Self-feeling depends on ourselves, 649 : 1
Self-government, democracy direct s., 537 : *n* 4
Self-hatred is waste, 859 : 18
Self-help root of growth, 551 : 8
Self-homicide, misspending time a s., 310 : 20
Self-idealization childish, 860 : 3
Self-interest, heedless s. bad economics, 780 : 1
of immediate auditor, 783 : 4
speaks all tongues, 293 : 7
Selfish, art s. and perverse, 421 : 20
being all my life, 440 : 24
feverish s. little clod, 680 : 15
in practice not principle, 440 : 24
spiteful Public, 445 : 7
very old most s., 539 : 23
Selfishness curse of race, 517 : 25
forces of s. met match, 779 : 20
Napoleon without s., 591 : 11
reduce s., 64 : 8
systems perverted by s., 775 : 4
Self-knowledge, more skillful in s., 427 : 23
self-control, 528 : 5
Self-love and social be made the same, 418 : 9
and social the same, 338 : 4
greatest of flatterers, 293 : 1
in jealousy more s., 293 : 36
makes more libertines, 358 : 24
strike at s., 599 : 3
Self-made from elements, 878 : 3
Self-made (*continued*)
laws, 581 : 14
Selfness essential fact of life, 884 : 4
Self-observation, psychology based on s., 614 : 15
Self-pity, in God's name s., 900 : 2
Self-possession, courtesy and s., 718 : 6
Self-preservation, first law of nature s., 904 : 16
instinct of s., 685 : 3
Self-protection sole end for interfering, 508 : 3
Self-reliance aversion to society, 496 : 22
discontent want of s., 497 : 6
reliance on God, 498 : 19
Self-respect, draw breath of s., 851 : 10
in military unit, 771 : 2
never break word or lose s., 124 : 12
not manifest want of s., 89 : 3
Self-revelation, terrible fluidity of s., 654 : 4
Self-reverence self-knowledge, 528 : 5
Self-righteousness, avoid s., 834 : 1
not religion, 555 : 18
Self-sacrifice, progress of artist s., 809 : 3
risk and spiritual s., 816 : 17
vocation demands s., 831 : 24
Self-sacrificing love of brute, 526 : 6
Selfsame, shot fellow s. way, 198 : 6
song that found path, 477 : 1
sun that shines upon court, 247 : 1
winds that blow, 669 : 21
Self-slaughter, his canon 'gainst s., 218 : 5
Self-subsisting self-seeking me, 489 : 16
Self-suffering, patience means s., 727 : 5
Self-sufficing, reasoning s. thing, 424 : 16
Self-trust, teacher inspires s., 484 : 5
Sell a country, 419 : 13
buy with you s. with you, 198 : 18
did s. himself to work wickedness, 14 : 9
don't s. America short, 924 : 14
for a shilling, 550 : 9
go and s. that thou hast, 40 : 6
made to s. and s. quickly, 793 : 1
no branch over wine that will s., 112 : 12
no man might buy or s., 53 : 21
not here to s. boilers, 356 : 20
precious as stuff they s., 517 : 11
to none s. right or justice, 139 : 3
Seller needs not one eye, 270 : 1
Selling, buying and s. spending lives, 560 : 7
is antisocial, 665 : 16
nimble in s. houses, 791 : 5
short your lies, 892 : 13
writers are always s. you out, 913 : 2
Sells eternity to get toy, 189 : 20
Selves, beautiful in thoughts in s., 695 : 6
better s., 424 : 3
our s. our souls and bodies, 55 : 19
Semblable au prince des nuées, 580 : *n* 5
hypocrite lecteur mon s., 580 : 16
mon s. mon frère, 580 : *n* 4
Semblance in another's case, 377 : 25
Semel emissum volat irrevocabile verbum, 109 : *n* 5
Semel (*continued*)
insanivimus omnes, 707 : *n* 1
Semen est sanguis christianorum, 126 : *n* 2
Semi-criminal semi-pathological, 783 : 10
Semihuman and demonic, 754 : 10
Seminal, Bentham and Coleridge s. minds, 508 : 2
Semi-pathological propensities, 783 : 10
Semper eadem, 164 : 2
fidelis, 134 : 26
Sempronius, we'll do more S., 325 : 12
Senate admiring its members, 634 : 20
Caesar with s. at heels, 337 : 14
enforce rules of S., 722 : 21
Roman s. long debate, 325 : 17
Senator, I am United States s., 872 : 7
seldom proclaims inferiority, 634 : 20
Senators of mighty woods, 478 : 4
Send an Angel before thee, 10 : 11
choice grain into his wilderness, 307 : 11
fortune will s. it, 251 : 13
here am I s. me, 29 : 11
home my long-strayed eyes, 252 : 23
homeless tempest-tossed, 664 : 10
me reeling in, 607 : 14
more grace than gifts to s., 250 : 15
never s. to know for whom bell tolls, 254 : 22
recompense as largely s., 362 : 18
spy enemy could s., 606 : 3
them latitude and longitude, 777 : 13
them that s. unto thee, 25 : 1
whom shall I s., 29 : 11
Senex, fortunate s., 103 : *n* 6
Senile, regarding elders as s., 634 : 24
Senior-junior giant-dwarf, 190 : 26
Sennacherib king of Assyria departed, 14 : 20
Sens, donner un s. plus pur, 808 : *n* 4
Sensation instinct intelligence, 482 : 12
Sensational event changing from brown suit, 791 : 6
something s. to read, 675 : 23
Sensations, condensation of s., 728 : 9
rather than thoughts, 479 : 3
sweet felt in blood, 423 : 8
Sense aches at thee, 232 : 5
common s. appall, 696 : 1
common s. hasty superficial, 558 : 18
common s. not so common, 343 : 18
common s. of our people, 841 : 3
common s. on ground floor, 519 : 18
common s. plain dealing, 497 : 29
common s. reduced to calculus, 397 : 18
common s. without genius, 813 : 12
devoid of s. and motion, 284 : 9
dictate of common s., 346 : 6
divinest s., 605 : 11
enchants my s., 226 : 10
find people have good s., 294 : 1
fools laugh at men of s., 315 : 8
from thought divide, 303 : *n* 1
fruit of s. beneath, 333 : 4
genius s. and wit, 375 : 20
good s. equally distributed, 272 : 5
good s. gift of Heaven, 336 : 4
good s. in country, 390 : 12
good s. of Americans, 506 : 4
good s. refine her page, 311 : 13
humility s. of reverence, 77 : 10

Sense (*continued*)
in larger s. cannot dedicate, 523 : 4
learned without s., 375 : 7
lively s. of filial duty, 387 : 7
men of s. approve, 333 : 11
money like sixth s., 751 : 11
money speaks s., 312 : 16
moral s. of work of art, 653 : 11
much s. starkest madness, 605 : 11
my s. is mocked, 251 : 7
no s. of ills to come, 361 : 10
not s. enough to come in, 155 : *n* 2
nothing good makes complete s., 823 : 21
of death in apprehension, 228 : 17
of future favors, 293 : *n* 6
of honor in action, 81 : 5
of it is anyhow, 545 : 4
of life, 769 : 22
of obligation, 732 : 8
of reckoning, 208 : 8
of what life means, 650 : 7
one has s. of humor, 799 : 7
one that has another s., 326 : 12
palls upon the s., 325 : 16
palter with us in double s., 240 : 9
Pickwickian s., 546 : 10
poem part of s. of life, 769 : 22
poetry more than good s., 438 : 6
rich grape juice of good s., 128 : 17
rich in common s., 533 : 3
satire or s., 338 : 18
seal s. in slumber, 739 : 17
Shadwell never deviates into s., 304 : 25
silent when you doubt s., 333 : 17
sound an echo to s., 333 : 9
stings and motions of s., 227 : 28
sublime, 423 : 13
sublime in old s., 792 : 10
take care of s., 612 : 3
talk s. to a fool, 77 : 7
talk s. to American people, 851 : 9
that world was mad, 756 : 15
through s. and nonsense, 304 : 17
want of decency want of s., 309 : 9
who can spot, 546 : *n* 1
whose soul is s., 253 : 3
Senseless, abhorred that s. tribe, 322 : 19
kind of s. wit, 899 : 15
Nothing to provoke, 517 : 6
scholars, 314 : 19
Senses, barrier of s., 771 : 1
connects intellect with s., 436 : 17
derangement of all s., 674 : 12
diffuses s. with oblivion, 106 : 24
five and country s., 886 : 15
flies from s. and particulars to axioms, 179 : 7
forever in joy, 543 : 16
hath not a Jew s., 199 : 17
if parson lost s., 732 : 16
indisputable existence of s., 363 : 14
money-lust before s., 792 : 19
not apprehended by s., 679 : 5
not available to ordinary men, 783 : 4
our gentle s., 236 : 21
so long as I keep my s., 490 : 1
steep s. in forgetfulness, 206 : 17
Sensibility, dissociation of s., 809 : 8
feels it with great s., 354 : 7
inexhaustible s., 654 : 8
soil of subject, 653 : 11
Sensible affections of flesh, 274 : 13
and conscientious men, 354 : *n* 4
banished from high life, 569 : 19
fish swims down, 686 : *n* 4
impressions of free mind, 718 : 6
men never tell, 502 : 23
moral s. well-bred man, 376 : 2
this s. warm motion, 228 : 20
to feeling as to sight, 237 : 13
Sensibly refrain from speech, 690 : 13
Sensitive, gentle s. mind, 714 : 7
plant in garden grew, 468 : 8
Sensory, control s. world, 679 : 2
external s. stimulation, 603 : 6
Sensual, caught in s. music, 714 : 22
lust a tempest, 581 : 20
this wisdom is s., 52 : 1
turbulent fleshy s., 574 : 20
Sensualist, lover and s., 663 : 8
Sensuality, intellectual passion drives out s., 152 : 3
Sensuous, simple s. and passionate, 281 : 20
Sent, him that s. me, 45 : 7
parting genius with sighing s., 277 : 11
thee late a rosy wreath, 256 : 9
to my account, 219 : 24
to spy out the land, 10 : 24
Sentence, death s. of Versailles, 812 : 19
every s. victory, 129 : 17
first verdict afterwards, 612 : 12
full of high s., 803 : 17
German dives into s., 624 : 9
hungry judges s. sign, 334 : 6
I catch every s., 695 : 5
my s. is for open war, 284 : 6
no unnecessary words, 729 : 7
not understand words apart from s., 602 : 5
originator of good s., 499 : 27
structure of British s., 743 : 8
success to periodic s., 834 : 9
true in all times, 521 : 3
waiting s. in bullpen, 893 : 1
Sentences, backward ran s., 854 : 8
memorable s., 609 : 2
paragraph no unnecessary s., 729 : 7
say in ten s. what others in book, 658 : 13
shall quips and s. awe, 209 : 19
that stir bile, 693 : 5
Sententiae, quot homines tot s., 97 : *n* 2
Sententious, laconic or s. type, 730 : 15
Sentest, thou s. forth thy wrath, 9 : 35
Sentient, critic s. and restless, 653 : 3
tree happy scarcely s., 721 : 1
Sentiment and alliteration, 619 : 7
domestic s. of mankind, 502 : 5
fungus crop of s., 631 : 19
in s. public crude, 453 : 12
living s. and dying s., 450 : 10
nurse of manly s., 373 : 23
read Richardson for s., 355 : 3
sacrifice you make for s., 723 : 5
Sentimental, body for s. value, 870 : 2
value, 870 : 2
Sentimentalist, no s., 574 : 20
Sentimentality failure of feeling, 769 : 21
Sentimentally disposed to harmony, 441 : 21
Sentiments, duration of great s., 657 : 20
Sentiments (*continued*)
embodied in Declaration, 521 : 8
grandest of human s., 454 : 17
noble s. in bad literature, 727 : 12
precluded from offering s., 379 : 6
quiet interchange of s., 355 : 16
them's my s., 539 : 6
to which bosom echo, 352 : 27
weigh less than action, 569 : 12
Sentinel, scarce worth the s., 369 : 10
Sentinels almost receive, 208 : 1
Sentry are you there, 572 : 7
at this door England s., 639 : 16
stands a winged s., 299 : 10
Senzala, casa grande e s., 848 : 3
Separate and equal station, 387 : 9
and unequal, 872 : 14
but equal, 820 : 14
church and state s., 590 : 2
dying ember, 526 : 11
facilities unequal, 820 : 14
from what forces one to repeat No, 659 : 2
he shall s. them, 40 : 32
like marbles touching but s., 637 : 20
peace, 844 : 11
people s. rigidly alone, 637 : 20
quite quite s., 602 : 11
to s. because of race, 820 : 14
us from love of Christ, 47 : 14
Separated, war not s. from politics, 826 : 10
Separately, hang together or hang s., 348 : 8
Separateness of all things, 873 : 15
Separateth, he that repeateth a matter s. friends, 24 : 15
Separation, causes which impel s., 387 : 9
not fighting for s., 904 : 15
prepare definitely for s., 438 : 11
yield who will to s., 748 : 18
September, aftermaths of soft S., 692 : 5
from frosted S. to dark, 791 : 1
frosted S., 791 : 1
morn, 513 : 16
thirty days hath S., 162 : 7
when you reach S., 802 : 2
within bosom S., 917 : 24
Sepulcher, night dome of vast s., 467 : 19
no man knoweth of his s., 11 : 27
there by the sea, 527 : 10
whole earth s. of famous men, 81 : 5
Sepulchers, grandest of all s., 81 : 5
shrouds and s. delight, 475 : 13
whited s., 40 : 20
Sepulchral, old s. urns, 376 : 6
Sequel, unto God is the s., 132 : 2
Sequence, natural s. of unnatural beginning, 441 : 1
of phenomena, 390 : 7
Sequent, nor s. centuries hit, 494 : 22
Sequestered, her wild s. seat, 364 : 14
nooks, 512 : 15
vale of life, 362 : 12
Seraph I shape, 852 : 14
rapt s. adores and burns, 336 : 22
Seraphically, song s. free, 600 : 26
Seraphim, bright s. in burning row, 281 : 10
Seraphims, above it stood the s., 29 : 8
Seraphs swing snowy hats, 604 : 15
where s. might despair, 456 : 22

Seraphs (*continued*)
winged s. of heaven, 527 : 8
Sere, fallen into the s., 239 : 31
leaf red and s., 430 : 13
leaves crisped and s., 526 : 22
meadows brown and s., 471 : 10
with ivy never s., 280 : 6
Serene before direst death, 592 : 6
count only hours s., 445 : *n* 3
I fold my hands, 630 : 21
mind s. for contemplation, 326 : *n* 2
old age s. and bright, 427 : 20
purest ray s., 362 : 8
see with eye s., 427 : 5
true friendship never s., 301 : 7
Serenely arriving arriving, 576 : 4
full epicure would say, 433 : 12
Serenity, gentleness of spirit s. of mind, 271 : *n* 1
give us outside sleep s., 849 : 13
steady and perpetual s., 326 : 21
sweet s. of books, 512 : 15
to accept with s., 823 : 15
usual querulous s., 440 : 21
Serf, labor as another's s., 60 : 15
patrician plebeian lord and s., 563 : 3
Serfdom, abolish s. from above, 561 : 7
Serfs, spending lives like s., 560 : 7
vassals and s., 480 : 11
Sergeant, back to army again s., 709 : 1
Color S. said, 708 : 1
this fell s. death, 224 : 30
Sergeant Cuff, the roses get it says S., 594 : 7
Sergeant's widow told lie, 518 : 5
Serious and alarming consequences, 379 : 6
and the smirk, 547 : 9
audience takes him s., 766 : 2
Cervantes' s. air, 340 : 14
comedian takes himself s., 766 : 2
companions few in s. business, 67 : 1
I never was more s., 441 : 6
imitation of action that is s., 88 : 16
insisted always on being s., 78 : 9
marriage damnably s. business, 826 : 14
no human thing of s. importance, 85 : 9
nothing s. in mortality, 238 : 7
one who is s. all day, 3 : 10
strenuous and s., 810 : 4
war too s. for military, 401 : 2
Sermon, calls it a s., 432 : 19
everyone has one s., 923 : 15
good honest painful s., 309 : 16
perhaps turn out a s., 409 : 11
rejected S. on Mount, 825 : 1
verse find who s. flies, 268 : 2
whole of her s., 764 : 9
Sermons and soda water, 460 : 23
bounds of s. and scriptures, 912 : 3
bricks and s., 625 : 24
in stones, 210 : 24
lie to throw s. at, 625 : 24
no s. in stones, 631 : 3
Serpent, be the s. under it, 236 : 20
beguiled me, 7 : 9
biteth like a s., 25 : 11
curling s. in ocean, 907 : 3
infernal s. whose guile, 283 : 3
Leviathan that crooked s., 30 : 12
like Aaron's s., 337 : 4
more s. than dove, 183 : 14
Serpent (*continued*)
of old Nile, 240 : 23
old s. called Devil, 53 : 20
rod shall become a s., 9 : 18
sharpened their tongues like a s., 22 : 20
sting thee twice, 200 : 5
subtlest beast, 287 : 14
trail of s. over all, 447 : 13
was more subtile, 7 : 5
way of a s. upon a rock, 26 : 4
wise as s., 38 : *n* 3
Serpent's egg, 215 : 17
sharper than s. tooth, 233 : 11
word, 863 : 19
Serpents, all the s. bite, 5 : 6
be wise as s., 38 : 36
envious, 254 : 10
rods became s., 9 : 19
saliva makes s. take flight, 116 : 13
there's no pleasing them, 611 : 12
Servant, accuse not a s. unto his master, 26 : 2
borrower is s. to the lender, 24 : 36
carried His s. by night, 131 : 5
good and faithful s., 40 : 29
he shall be my s., 8 : 36
hear what s. girls said, 735 : 2
in love lord in marriage, 147 : 30
individual make state his s., 848 : 12
is thy s. a dog, 14 : 16
Jim most ruined for s., 623 : 21
lettest thy s. depart, 42 : 30
not above lord, 39 : 2
of God well done, 286 : 26
of living God, 365 : 13
of scattered family, 617 : 7
prince first s. of state, 358 : 3
thy s. heareth, 12 : 30
Thy s. sleeping, 597 : 16
unprofitable s., 40 : 31
virtues expected of s., 378 : 5
with this clause, 269 : 8
Servants, desires and petitions of thy s., 55 : 8
fire best of s., 474 : 3
frantic among thy s., 35 : 3
gods s. of human interest, 704 : 6
leave living to s., 638 : 1
of light, 610 : 11
of the machine, 872 : 2
public officers s., 631 : 6
public s. serve you right, 851 : 13
Servants', never equality in s. hall, 694 : 8
Servare modum, 118 : *n* 7
Serve, also s. who only stand, 282 : 17
and not dominate world, 787 : 10
as Thou deservest, 157 : 3
as we love we s., 669 : 13
because we freely love, 286 : 20
cannot s. God and mammon, 38 : 1
country and mankind, 617 : 5
employ body to s., 102 : 21
faithfully to s. State, 272 : 17
future hour, 429 : 1
if elected I will not s., 579 : *n* 3
in heaven, 283 : 14
knives that s. or cut, 569 : 5
long apprenticehood, 194 : 4
my nation ruin another, 341 : 10
no man can s. two masters, 38 : 1
not s. God if devil bid, 229 : 19
the Lord with gladness, 21 : 3
Serve (*continued*)
they also s., 282 : 17
'tis enough 'twill s., 193 : 5
while not able to s. men, 68 : 26
whom should we s., 392 : 14
you right, 851 : 13
Served, first come first s., 138 : *n* 8
God with half zeal, 249 : 9
human liberty, 716 : 6
my time in hell, 925 : 1
no private end, 336 : 5
public will be s., 314 : 18
youth will be s., 492 : 18
Serves it in office of a wall, 194 : 13
party best serves country best, 590 : 9
sir which s. and seeks for gain, 233 : 18
take current when it s., 217 : 6
Serveth not another's will, 250 : 14
Service, all s. same with God, 540 : 19
best s. for country, 644 : 14
beyond all recompense, 275 : 28
desert in s., 226 : 20
discharging loyal s., 299 : 11
do a friend s., 73 : 14
done the state some s., 232 : 20
essential s. to country, 322 : 12
fairer than other nations, 136 : 3
full weel soong s. dyvyne, 145 : 18
greater than the god, 226 : 8
greatest s. or greatest injury, 84 : 3
high and anthems clear, 278 : 26
in purer lives s., 514 : 1
injustice sometimes public s., 391 : 6
is perfect freedom, 55 : 4
lay out ourselves in s. of mankind, 392 : 14
never bad man good s., 373 : 14
pressed into s., 747 : 12
riches poverty and use of s., 247 : 26
shrink from s. of country, 384 : 13
small s. is true s., 429 : 11
strong for s. still, 376 : 23
weary and old with s., 249 : 3
yeoman's s., 224 : 27
Serviceable, fool be made s., 684 : 3
Services, Europe's s. to humanity, 755 : 14
failure to maintain essential s., 871 : 13
give your s. for nothing, 79 : 16
goods and s. paid with goods and s., 740 : 17
printing and Reformation s., 755 : 14
public s. failed, 871 : 11
Servile fetters breaks, 919 : 19
inciters of s. insurrection, 617 : 6
to all skyey influences, 228 : 15
Servility, savage s. slides by, 893 : 16
Serving, betrays instead of s., 372 : 9
cumbered with s., 43 : 16
duly and daily s. him, 365 : 13
Servingmen, six honest s., 710 : 2
Servitors, airy s., 281 : 15
Servitude, base laws of s. began, 303 : 8
beast brought up in s., 154 : 8
consequence of crime, 397 : 21
freedom and not s., 373 : 3
previous condition of s., 392 : 5
socialism seeks equality in s., 506 : 12
Sesame, open s., 920 : 1
work open s., 664 : 17
Sesquipedalia verba, 109 : *n* 9

Session, court in perpetual s., 786 : 5
Sessions of sweet silent
thought, 244 : 11
Sestos and Abydos of her
breasts, 253 : 23
Set about with fever trees, 710 : 3
born to s. it right, 220 : 6
candle in the sun, 259 : 19
cause above renown, 700 : 6
children's teeth s. on edge, 32 : 17
do not s. eyes on things far
off, 71 : *n* 9
down aught in malice, 232 : 20
exact wealth of states, 204 : 29
forth for somewhere, 747 : 18
god seem to s. his seal, 223 : 3
gray life, 529 : 3
have s. before you life and
death, 11 : 22
he s. a tabernacle for the sun, 17 : 28
hen has right to s., 616 : 21
himself doggedly to it, 353 : 24
honor in one eye, 215 : 3
I'd s. my ten commandments in
face, 185 : 10
in a notebook, 217 : 4
in western lightland, 5 : 5
is our little light, 250 : 3
kings rise and s., 468 : 16
life at pin's fee, 219 : 13
me as a seal, 28 : 23
minutely s. ingenious
machine, 789 : 6
moon has s., 63 : 8
my life on any chance, 238 : 16
my life upon a cast, 187 : 32
my poor heart free, 229 : *n* 1
noisy s., 713 : 1
of sails tells the way, 669 : 21
out one day, 742 : 1
precious stone s. in silver sea, 194 : 13
rich stone best plain s., 181 : 8
slughorn to my lips I s., 234 : *n* 3
sun has right to s., 616 : 21
sun must s., 464 : 21
suns that s. may rise again, 255 : 16
table on a roar, 224 : 14
thine house in order, 14 : 21
today on flesh of hare, 912 : 9
when our brief light has s., 101 : 18
wild echoes flying, 530 : 26
Setebos Setebos and Setebos, 544 : 17
Sets, packs and s. of great ones, 235 : 12
sun in dominions never s., 412 : 18
sun never s. on empire, 412 : *n* 6
sun s. to rise again, 545 : 22
Setter up of kings, 186 : 6
Setteth the solitary in families, 19 : 33
Setting endeavor in continual
motion, 207 : 6
gather round s. sun, 426 : 23
had elsewhere its s., 426 : 14
haste now to my s., 249 : 1
hush with s. moon, 533 : 22
it up to fear birds, 227 : 30
light of s. suns, 423 : 13
more worship rising than s.
sun, 99 : 12
shut doors against s. sun, 243 : 2
sun and music at close, 194 : 10
with the s. sun, 284 : 2
yourself up as judge, 86 : 3
Settle, though there he s.
young, 593 : 3
Settled, applicable rule of law s., 678 : 3
by precedent, 730 : 14
gravity, 244 : 17
no q. settled until right, 670 : 5
Settlement, consider s. of America
with reverence, 380 : 8
in Asia, 813 : 15
Settlers, children like s., 868 : 19
Settles, public opinion s.
everything, 626 : 13
Seul, on mourra s., 300 : *n* 2
Seven ages, 211 : 15
churches in Asia, 52 : 28
cities warred, 257 : 20
days shall ye eat unleavened
bread, 9 : 27
Dials, 628 : 20
empty ears, 8 : 31
everything left at six and s., 144 : *n* 11
fairly worth the s., 336 : 4
fourscore and s. years, 523 : 4
from s. till s. times s., 407 : 4
gates of Thebes, 840 : 17
golden candlesticks, 52 : 29
good kine, 8 : 31
hours to law, 172 : *n* 3
hundred pounds and
possibilities, 225 : 7
Jacob served s. years, 8 : 22
keep thing s. years, 432 : 14
lie has s. endings, 926 : 2
long year, 234 : 10
maids with seven mops, 613 : 2
morning's at s., 540 : 15
pounds tenpence a man, 371 : 26
sealed with s. seals, 53 : 9
sette world on six and s., 144 : 26
seventy times s., 40 : 4
sleepers' den, 251 : 14
stars in hair s., 601 : 13
thin kine, 8 : 31
times one are seven, 578 : 9
times over and over, 578 : 9
wisdom hath hewn out her s.
pillars, 23 : 18
years of famine, 8 : 31
Seven-pillared, freedom s. house, 810 : 2
Seventeen times high as moon, 932 : 5
Seventeenth century
dissociation, 809 : 8
Seventh day thou shalt not work, 10 : 6
men of S. Regiment, 650 : 13
on s. holystone decks, 553 : 17
Seventy, oh to be s. again, 645 : 14
times seven, 40 : 4
Sever, and then we s., 410 : 2
armed to seek and s., 821 : 11
he our good will s., 255 : 16
to s. for years, 456 : 8
Several, for s. virtues s. women, 248 : 3
sometimes think I'm s., 874 : 5
Severe, as holy as s., 228 : 26
critic on own works, 479 : 13
eyes s. and beard, 211 : 15
from lively to s., 338 : 1
from pleasant to s., 311 : 2
man s. he was, 370 : 10
merely just is s., 343 : 3
or if s. in aught, 370 : 10
truth s., 363 : 8
Severed, our state cannot be s., 287 : 24
Severity not path to order, 637 : 14
treats subject with s., 586 : 16
Seville, dogs of S., 535 : 13
Sew a fine seam, 931 : 19
time to s., 26 : 21
Sex, amoebas started s., 732 : 14
and beauty inseparable, 790 : 18
and the dead, 718 : 3
brain not organ of s., 695 : 13
conceal its s., 855 : 12
fair s., 170 : 8
fair s. your department, 689 : 13
female of s. it seems, 288 : 30
Is S. Necessary, 831 : 6
Italian for converse with feminine
s., 357 : 19
no other difference than s., 414 : 21
no stronger than my s., 215 : 24
omnipresent process of s., 689 : 19
ornament of her s., 547 : 21
prejudice against color against
s., 554 : 6
privileges because of s., 898 : 6
right to vote not abridged on
account of s., 392 : 6
ruin of our s., 365 : 1
spirits either s. assume, 283 : 18
superiority to s. that kills, 870 : 10
to the last, 307 : 7
whose presence civilizes, 376 : 3
woman's s. prima facie
evidence, 554 : 6
Sexes, love idea of two s., 831 : 2
there are three s., 433 : 2
to one neutral thing both s. fit, 252 : 11
Sex's, your s. earliest care, 357 : 8
Sextant, compass quadrant and
s., 843 : 13
Sexton, no s. to toll bell, 640 : 16
tolled the bell, 485 : 3
went and told s., 485 : 3
Sex-typed, mind not s., 853 : 18
Sexual, eliminate s.
discrimination, 903 : 10
man's idea of s. rights, 554 : 7
Sexually atrophied, 703 : 13
Seymour's Fat Lady, 896 : 10
Shabby corner, 640 : 19
equipment deteriorating, 807 : 21
Genteel, 922 : 14
tamed and s. tigers, 732 : 16
winter hangs on till s., 739 : 2
Shackles accidents, 241 : 24
of a historian, 276 : 1
of an old love, 534 : 14
touch our country s. fall, 376 : 20
Shade, admiring in gloomy s., 276 : 4
boundless contiguity of s., 376 : 18
checkered s., 278 : 1
cold light and hot s., 405 : 15
cone of self-thrown s., 897 : 5
difference matter of a s., 648 : 2
fable song or fleeting s., 266 : 21
gentlemen of the s., 202 : 24
ghost along moonlight s., 335 : 7
green thought in green s., 297 : 3
I'll s. him from heat, 403 : 8
inviolable s., 586 : 2
let it sleep in the s., 446 : 7
lone Glenartney's hazel s., 431 : 5
measure by s. it casts, 540 : 8
no s. no shine, 485 : 12
of melancholy boughs, 211 : 12
of Old Apple Tree, 753 : 2
of that once great, 425 : 20
replied, 527 : 5
round me night weaves s., 587 : 10

Shade (*continued*)
sitting in a pleasant s., 257 : 6
sport with Amaryllis in the s., 280 : 15
spring with rustling s., 811 : 5
the Lord is thy s., 22 : 4
trees crowd into a s., 332 : 12
variable as the s., 431 : 2
without color, 805 : 16
Shaded, no s. stream, 399 : 16
Shades, crowns in s. like these, 370 : 2
doleful s., 283 : 7
evening s. prevail, 325 : 9
mixed s. and shadows, 571 : 3
of the prison-house, 426 : 14
raising dingy s., 804 : 3
spirit fled indignant to s., 106 : 7
twenty-nine when pink s., 675 : 13
Shadow, abide under the s. of the Almighty, 20 : 16
at evening rising, 805 : 1
at morning striding, 805 : 1
bringeth to light the s. of death, 15 : 31
by grasping at the s., 66 : 15
cruciform s., 817 : 3
daisy by s. it casts, 429 : 11
darkness and s. of death, 15 : 24, 21 : 13, 42 : 26
days are as a s., 14 : 27
doubt is truth's s., 532 : *n* 6
every s. of authority, 373 : 10
fabulous s., 843 : 13
falls the S., 805 : 17
falls thy s. Cynara, 721 : 6
fell thy s. Cynara, 721 : 4
fleeth as a s., 15 : 33
follow a s., 256 : 6
God within s., 567 : 7
hanging over me, 914 : 9
hence horrible s., 238 : 29
henceforward in thy s., 507 : 9
hope beyond s. of dream, 476 : 1
how slow s. creeps, 730 : 1
I am gone like the s., 21 : 17
I have a little s., 668 : 12
if earth be s. of heaven, 286 : 21
kills the growth, 257 : 2
land of darkness and s. of death, 15 : 24
land of the s. of death, 29 : 15
lengthened s. of man, 497 : 4
life is a s., 273 : 2
life is little s., 581 : 15
life s. of death, 275 : 13, 632 : 9
life's but a walking s., 240 : 4
light is s. of God, 275 : 13
like a s. like a dream, 60 : 8
like a vast s. moved, 299 : 6
mankind is dream of a s., 72 : 2
meanwhile cast one s., 904 : 8
my care like my s., 163 : 14
night is s. of light, 632 : 9
no s. no antiquity, 504 : 2
no s. of doubt, 630 : 3
no s. where no sun, 730 : 2
of British oak, 373 : 28
of glorious name, 118 : 6
of night comes on, 822 : 1
of the Glen, 735 : 2
of the tomb, 600 : 17
of turning, 51 : 29
of unseen power, 466 : 8
only sea keeps, 843 : 13
over gravel of drive, 789 : 10

Shadow (*continued*)
saw lion's s. ere himself, 200 : 22
ship's huge s., 434 : 28
sit in s. of death, 21 : 13, 42 : 26
soul from out s., 526 : 20
strong s. where much light, 394 : 11
swift as a s., 195 : 23
swollen s., 883 : 11
that goes in and out, 668 : 12
then a spark, 660 : 10
time is a very s., 34 : 10
under red rock, 805 : 1
under s. of thy wings, 17 : 25
under the earth, 907 : 3
Valley of s., 527 : 5
valley of s. of death, 18 : 7
we are but dust and s., 108 : 12
word s. of deed, 79 : 12
Shadowed livery of burnished sun, 198 : 29
Shadowless like silence, 485 : 9
Shadow's bliss, 199 : 15
Shadows and windy places, 632 : 7
as long as s. touch mountain slopes, 104 : 29
beckoning s. dire, 279 : 16
best are but s., 197 : 15
call back world of s., 796 : 2
cast s. before, 443 : 14
come like s. so depart, 239 : 13
earth's s. fly, 469 : 16
fatal s. walk by us, 260 : 17
flee away, 28 : 9
from s. into truth, 490 : 15
futurity casts on present, 470 : 5
how fast s. fall, 730 : 1
if we s. have offended, 197 : 23
illustrate all s., 255 : 1
knight of ghosts and s., 918 : 12
mixed shades and s., 571 : 3
not substantial things, 272 : 15
numberless, 476 : 22
of a great rock, 30 : 21
of living, 275 : 13
of pine boughs, 319 : 1
of plumbing left of city, 907 : 18
of the evening, 616 : 7
out of s. of night, 513 : 2
see only their own s., 84 : 17
some that s. kiss, 199 : 15
substance of grief hath twenty s., 194 : 18
through s. face of death, 721 : 8
titles are s., 318 : 10
tonight have struck terror, 187 : 29
unsubstantial as s., 82 : 9
until s. lengthen, 490 : 10
upon a sea obscure, 131 : 17
Shadowy, boundaries s. and vague, 526 : 7
third, 542 : 9
Shadrach Meshach and Abednego, 32 : 33
Shadwell never deviates into sense, 304 : 25
Shadwell's genuine night, 304 : 25
Shady, but cloud and like s. grove, 403 : 7
cypress tree, 608 : 13
leaves of destiny, 292 : 8
o'er s. groves they hover, 262 : 3
Olympus, 60 : *n* 3
sadness of vale, 478 : 2
sunshine in s. place, 173 : 10

Shaft at random sent, 431 : 19
of light across land, 529 : 5
that quivered in heart, 456 : 17
when I had lost one s., 198 : 6
Shaftoe's, Bobby S. gone to sea, 934 : 3
Shafts remain, 873 : 3
spend s. spare not, 918 : 3
Shaggy, brown heath and s. wood, 430 : 11
Shake, boughs which s. against cold, 244 : 27
caper and s. leg, 760 : 5
darling buds of May, 244 : 5
did hand of potter s., 517 : 8
gae his bridle reins a s., 410 : 6
hands forever, 182 : 16
laugh and s., 340 : 14
living out of Fate, 610 : 7
man that did s. kingdoms, 29 : 23
my fell purpose, 236 : 17
never s. thy gory locks, 238 : 25
of poor little head, 629 : 16
of the hand, 804 : 11
off dust of your feet, 38 : 35
off this downy sleep, 238 : 6
one and it awakens, 442 : 16
our disposition, 219 : 12
out every sail, 576 : 16
quail and s. the orb, 241 : 25
saintship of anchorite, 456 : 23
seems to s. the spheres, 306 : 13
this war s. world, 813 : 1
whom passion could not s., 231 : 26
yoke of inauspicious stars, 193 : 28
Shaked, when degree is s., 226 : 1
Shaken, looks on tempests never s., 245 : 18
neither s. by winds nor wet, 59 : 27
not s. from his firm resolve, 107 : 28
so s. as we are, 202 : 21
to be well s., 415 : 10
Shakers, movers and s., 659 : 9
Shakes across the lakes, 530 : 26
hacks spits blood, 824 : 6
his dewy wings, 275 : 30
out rain-drenched hair, 787 : 5
parting guest by hand, 226 : 19
roars and s. his fires, 403 : 18
rooted folly of age, 311 : 13
wings and will not stay, 305 : 3
Shake-scene, only S. in country, 178 : 12
Shakespeare and the musical glasses, 369 : 14
better not knowing much, 698 : 11
born at Stratford, 301 : 6
darts himself forth, 437 : 19
debts to authors, 500 : 1
Fancy's child, 278 : 6
first of dramatists, 353 : *n* 4
greatest width of passion, 809 : 17
had largest soul, 303 : 5
immortal S. rose, 351 : 10
Jew that S. drew, 340 : 8
life of allegory, 479 : 19
my S. rise, 256 : 11
myriad-minded S., 437 : 20
never blotted line, 256 : 21
not our poet, 442 : 24
room for S. in your tomb, 265 : 14
tongue S. spake, 426 : 1
unlocked heart, 429 : 10
was naturally learned, 303 : 6
was of us, 541 : 7
what needs my S., 277 : 13

Shakespeare's strain, 495 : 15
wit, 494 : 22
Shakespeherian Rag, 805 : 4
Shaking, fall without s., 341 : 4
her invincible locks, 282 : 3
sail's s., 760 : 14
Shalimar, pale hands beside S., 707 : 2
Shall, all that is and s. be, 74 : 18
mark you his absolute s., 242 : 18
prisoners of S., 875 : 3
Shallow bauble boats, 225 : 36
brooks and rivers wide, 277 : 25
by s. rivers birds sing, 183 : 9
changing woman, 187 : 21
draughts intoxicate, 332 : 20
I owe thousand pound, 206 : 37
in himself, 288 : 17
laughing s. dreaming pool, 566 : 13
men believe in luck, 498 : 31
murmur but deep are dumb, 172 : 12
spirit of judgment, 184 : 20
streams run dimpling, 339 : 1
surface stream s. light, 588 : 22
vain or s. thought, 493 : 17
weeds are s.-rooted, 185 : 15
woman not even s., 658 : *n* 2
Shallows, bound in s. and miseries, 217 : 5
Shalom salaam forever, 882 : 1
Shalott, Lady of S., 528 : 27
Sham, Fourth of July celebration a s., 556 : 5
nauseous s. goodfellowship, 681 : 12
Shame, ain't it bloomin' s., 924 : 11
all worst could wish, 869 : 1
Allen with awkward s., 339 : 14
avoid s. but not seek glory, 432 : 20
beneath feet deed of s., 511 : 22
bloomin' s., 924 : 11
cast s. when cast off smock, 147 : 12
cometh behind, 74 : *n* 3
despair her teachers, 503 : 12
doff it for s., 201 : 21
erring sister's s., 459 : 3
everything that is a s. among men, 67 : 12
forspent with love and s., 651 : 11
glory and s. of universe, 300 : 11
he was not born to s., 193 : 10
hide s. from every eye, 369 : 21
is ashamed to sit, 193 : 10
nay say nay for s., 161 : 23
noble s., 567 : 1
on herself and all women, 60 : 12
print it and s. fools, 338 : 7
proclaim no s., 223 : 5
product of wrongs and s., 744 : 8
put him to open s., 51 : 16
quit quit for s., 289 : 18
race of s., 288 : 29
say what it will, 224 : 4
secret thoughts without s., 264 : 16
speak truth and s. Devil, 158 : 8
them derides, 233 : 1
transgression brings admitted s., 80 : 17
waste of s., 245 : 23
waves foaming out their s., 52 : 26
where is thy blush, 223 : 5
who hangs head for s., 592 : 2
whose glory is in their s., 50 : 5
with grief and s. bowed down, 276 : 13
Shameful conquest of itself, 194 : 15
to mind s. to heart beauty, 582 : 1
Shameless, nothing more s., 60 : 11
nothing worse than s. woman, 82 : 16
Shame's, thy tongue thy s. orator, 188 : 9
Shames, burn out false s., 790 : 14
hold candle to my s., 199 : 8
Shamest to show dangerous brow, 215 : 19
Shamrock by law forbid, 920 : 21
Thistle S. Rose entwine, 608 : 9
Shams inequalities unfairnesses, 625 : 24
Shangri-La, serenity of S., 848 : 7
Shank, shrunk s., 211 : 15
Shannon, green banks of S., 443 : 9
mutinous S. waves, 777 : 16
Shanti 57 : 2
Shanty of consul in foreign town, 699 : 13
Shape, Attic s., 477 : 10
bear licks them into proper s., 117 : 3
borrow every changing s., 804 : 2
cloud in s. of a camel, 222 : 20
contemplate my flaccid s., 830 : 12
court it in s. of heaven, 219 : 22
execrable s., 284 : 25
grim s. towered up, 424 : 1
haunts about thy s., 477 : 4
if s. it might be called, 284 : 24
in any s. any mood, 459 : 22
it as he would, 534 : 28
know not said second s., 626 : 21
let it keep one s., 227 : 30
may be summoning itself, 905 : 13
neither s. of danger dismay, 427 : 26
no bigger than agate stone, 191 : 23
of life, 784 : 22
of things to come, 720 : 9
pressed out of s., 747 : 12
questionable s., 219 : 11
seraph I s., 852 : 14
take any s. but that, 238 : 28
two of far nobler s., 285 : 17
without form, 805 : 16
words guard s. of man, 850 : 16
Shaped, feather whence pen was s., 429 : 4
Shapen, I was s. in iniquity, 19 : 14
Shapes and gives new meaning, 801 : 8
bright container can contain, 874 : 1
calling s. and beckoning shadows, 279 : 16
divinity that s. our ends, 224 : 25
full of s. is fancy, 213 : 8
horrid s. and shrieks, 277 : 17
of foul disease, 532 : 23
poet's pen turns to s., 197 : 12
ring out old s., 532 : 23
shirts who coming to breathe s., 907 : 21
two s. face to face, 626 : 21
Shaping, deliberate s. of things, 718 : 6
Shard-borne beetle, 238 : 20
Share action and passion of time, 643 : 16
all persons s. in government, 88 : 6
bear own s. with courage, 595 : 5
friends s. all things, 65 : 11
good man's smile, 370 : 9
no man's opinions, 564 : 5
not what give but s., 567 : 14
our rights, 824 : 12
our s. of night to bear, 604 : 5
they invite person to s., 151 : 4
Share (*continued*)
threatened with railway s., 614 : 4
Shared experiences, 420 : 8
goods not s. not goods, 153 : 11
joyless if not s. with him, 447 : 16
Sharer of action he describes, 592 : 7
Sharers, full s. in abundance, 666 : 22
miserable s. of the event, 365 : 3
Shares the darkness, 823 : 2
Sharing, equal s. of miseries, 746 : 16
privileges of government, 519 : 21
unequal s. of blessings, 746 : 16
Shark teeth pearly white, 840 : 15
Sharon, rose of S., 28 : 4
Sharp as a two-edged sword, 23 : 10
flash, 768 : 2
how s. it pierced, 646 : 14
in nature few s. lines, 905 : 10
names never get fat, 840 : 2
necessity's s. pinch, 233 : 20
nice s. quillets of law, 184 : 20
nose as s. as pen, 207 : 13
without s. north, 251 : 16
wood has a s. ear, 146 : *n* 5
Sharp-edged axes, 575 : 14
Sharpen with cloyless sauce his appetite, 240 : 27
Sharpened life commands course, 601 : 11
their tongues like a serpent, 22 : 20
Sharpeneth, iron s. iron, 25 : 26
Sharpens skill, 374 : 2
Sharper, slander whose edge s. than sword, 243 : 21
than a serpent's tooth, 233 : 11
than two-edged sword, 51 : 14
Sharpest, time rush s. sword, 431 : 24
Sharping, live by s. and robbing, 348 : 13
Sharp-looking, hollow-eyed s. wretch, 188 : 15
Sharp's, Becky S. acute remark, 596 : 2
Sharp-sighted, fear is s., 168 : 28
Shatter it to bits and then, 517 : 13
possibility can s. us, 658 : 19
vase if you will, 447 : 2
your leaves, 280 : 6
Shattered lobsterpot, 808 : 2
visage lies, 466 : 12
when lamp is s., 470 : 1
Shaun, tale of S. or Shem, 778 : 5
Shave, haircut and a s., 816 : 2
rides back to s. again, 846 : 8
Shaven, all s. and shorn, 934 : 9
Shavers, two of a thousand s., 116 : *n* 9
Shaves and takes train, 846 : 8
Shaving, man s. at window, 860 : 1
Shaw, courage of Robert S., 650 : 13
O Captain S., 628 : 25
Shawl, famous top-hat plain s., 765 : 8
Shawnee, I am a S., 419 : 11
Shay, one-hoss s., 519 : 15
Shays, General S. has sneaked off, 407 : 14
She and comparisons are odious, 253 : 19
cruelest s. alive, 213 : 17
fair chaste unexpressive s., 211 : 18
finished by such a s., 201 : 16
for God in him, 285 : 18
forget the he and s., 252 : 6
that not impossible s., 292 : 7
Shea, Kelly Burke and S., 661 : 4
Sheaf, brushwood s., 541 : 16

Sheaf (*continued*)
sickle and wheaten s., 345 : 13
Shears, abhorred s., 280 : 15
and pastepot, 730 : 15
marriage resembles s., 433 : 9
Sheath, one sword keeps another in s., 270 : 13
sets sword back in s., 742 : 10
sword outwears s., 460 : 5
Sheathed swords for lack of argument, 207 : 17
Sheaves, after the reapers among the s., 12 : 26
bringing his s. with him, 22 : 7
God comes as s. in harvest, 255 : 1
Sheba, queen of S. heard of Solomon, 13 : 34
She-bear pops head into shop, 364 : 5
Shed, balloon of mind in s., 714 : 6
bitter tear, 613 : 2
bitter tears to s., 591 : 9
blood of nation never s., 316 : 14
by man shall his blood be s., 8 : 2
for many for remission, 41 : 10
for this all blood s., 713 : 11
hand raised to s. blood, 336 : 13
its bloom is s., 411 : 8
lowly cattle s., 561 : 10
O s. no tear, 478 : 9
prepare to s. them now, 216 : 22
Sheddeth, whoso s. man's blood, 8 : 2
Shedding, without s. of blood, 51 : 17
Sheds, disastrous twilight s., 283 : 24
he that s. blood with me, 208 : 11
Sheelah, when S. was nigh, 443 : 9
Sheen of their spears, 459 : 14
Sheep, Abel was keeper of s., 7 : 14
and wolf not agreed, 523 : 7
as s. that have not a shepherd, 14 : 10
baa baa black s., 930 : 5
Bo-peep has lost s., 932 : 3
boy looks after s., 930 : 12
bringing thy s. in thy hand, 588 : 8
divideth s. from goats, 40 : 32
drives wolf from s., 523 : 7
found s. which was lost, 43 : 25
giveth life for s., 45 : 11
glad to have kept s., 272 : 21
hungry s. look up, 280 : 22
like s. to slaughter, 379 : 6
little black s., 708 : 14
lost s. of house of Israel, 38 : 33
men again led like s., 582 : 7
mountain s. sweeter, 455 : 2
noble ensample to his s., 146 : 8
of his hand, 20 : 20
of his pasture, 21 : 3
old half-witted s., 428 : *n* 2
other s. I have, 45 : 12
owest s. no wool, 234 : 7
rejoiceth more of that s., 40 : 2
return to our s., 927 : 20
sameness of s., 847 : 3
shepherd tells tale of s., 112 : 20
shepherdess of s., 661 : 11
shepherding s. below holy Helicon, 61 : 7
strayed like lost s., 54 : 12
to fold, 692 : 2
unintelligent, 799 : 16
valley s. fatter, 455 : 2
we like s. have gone astray, 31 : 16
which went not astray, 40 : 2
wine, 491 : 22
Sheep (*continued*)
without shepherd, 552 : 20
without shepherd s. not flock, 934 : 14
you herd s., 63 : 11
Sheephook, know how to hold a s., 280 : 21
Sheepish calm, 893 : 2
Sheep's, casts a s. eye, 170 : 3
come in s. clothing, 38 : 16
in the meadow, 930 : 12
wolf in s. clothing, 65 : 17
Sheer, frightful s. no-man-fathomed, 656 : 18
here a s. hulk, 393 : 11
into heart of foe, 535 : 14
Sheet, burnt hole in s., 897 : 6
old England's winding s., 406 : 18
seemed a s. of sun, 885 : 7
waters his winding s., 257 : 5
wet s. flowing sea, 453 : 19
who ever got out of winding s., 255 : 3
Sheeted dead, 217 : 21
Sheets, cool kindliness of s., 796 : 16
fumble with the s., 207 : 13
three s. in wind, 553 : *n* 4, 553 : 18
Sheiling, lone s., 483 : 20
Shelf, dust of upper s., 487 : 8
life over there behind s., 605 : 22
Shell, hot heart's s., 570 : 13
I found a s., 428 : *n* 5
kill him in the s., 215 : 17
leaving outgrown s., 519 : 8
pebble or prettier s., 313 : 17
scallop s. of quiet, 172 : 15
smooth-lipped s., 428 : 15
snail which has lost s., 314 : 2
unseen within thy airy s., 279 : 18
Shelley, Burns S. were with us, 541 : 7
ineffectual angel, 589 : 13
of my age, 892 : 16
see S. plain, 542 : 13
Shells, all hard like s., 849 : 18
crow-blue mussel s., 798 : 9
of pearly hue, 442 : 16
Shelter, dead tree no s., 805 : 1
from the stormy blast, 328 : 10
what s. to grow ripe, 585 : 17
where storm drives I s., 108 : 16
Sheltered, in youth it s., 492 : 10
Shelters, happy house s. friend, 497 : 17
Shelves, symmetry of s., 441 : 18
upon the glazen s., 804 : 7
Shem, Noah begat S., 7 : 26
tale of Shaun or S., 778 : 5
Shenandoah I long to hear you, 934 : 20
Shepherd, any philosophy in thee s., 211 : 19
as sheep that have not a s., 14 : 10
as s. divideth sheep, 40 : 32
call you S. from hill, 585 : 20
Dick the s. blows his nail, 191 : 14
drives wolf from sheep, 523 : 7
every s. tells his tale, 277 : 24
faithful s. bringing sheep, 588 : 8
feed his flock like a s., 30 : 35
giveth his life, 45 : 11
hears their thundering, 57 : 28
I am the good s., 45 : 11
King of love my s. is, 580 : 15
Lord is my s., 18 : 7
sheep without s., 552 : 20
star that bids s. fold, 279 : 9
tells his tale of sheep, 112 : 20
Shepherd (*continued*)
valiant s. who drives flock, 5 : 3
weather s. shuns, 642 : 5
without s. sheep not flock, 934 : 14
Shepherdess O Eiffel Tower, 770 : 9
of sheep, 661 : 11
Shepherding below holy Helicon, 61 : 7
Shepherd's, homely slighted s. trade, 280 : 15
lays s. crook, 493 : 5
love tunes s. reed, 430 : 6
truth in s. tongue, 172 : 10
Shepherds abiding in field, 42 : 28
watched flocks by night, 317 : 4
Shepherds', I who once played s. songs, 104 : 14
Sherbet-eaters, frightened s. off terrace, 897 : 13
Sheridan, broke die molding S., 459 : 20
twenty miles away, 591 : 3
Sherlock Holmes, 689 : 7
Sherman's buzzin' to de sea, 840 : 8
Sherry, cocktail and s. cobbler, 452 : 14
is dull, 354 : 14
Sherwood, in S. about break of day, 773 : 2
She-wolf's, eats s. young, 435 : 6
Shibboleth, say now S., 12 : 12
Shield and defender Ancient of Days, 445 : 21
art s. from existence, 674 : 19
constancy and valor s., 744 : 9
Constitution a s., 553 : 20
constitutional s., 794 : 15
for defenseless, 615 : 6
God s. us, 196 : 24
his truth shall be thy s., 20 : 16
idle spear and s., 277 : 8
Lord is my strength and my s., 18 : 13
of its protection, 553 : 20
of rectitude, 744 : 11
only s. to memory, 744 : 11
persecution s. itself, 373 : 15
took spear but left s., 399 : 17
what care I for that s., 61 : 25
with s. march in honor, 744 : 11
Shielding men from effects of folly, 579 : 22
Shields of Expectation, 568 : 19
Shift, cleanliest s. is to kiss, 212 : 22
here the parts s., 543 : 20
I can s. for myself, 155 : 9
onion will do well for such s., 188 : 24
thus times do s., 266 : 15
Shifted his trumpet, 371 : 21
Shifts of Fortune test friends, 99 : 6
to escape thinking, 569 : 7
victory s. from man to man, 58 : 3
Shilling, sell for s. ring, 550 : 9
Splendid S., 328 : 19
Shillings, ducks and drakes with s., 177 : 15
rather than forty s., 225 : 8
Shine, all thou dost s. upon, 466 : 9
by side of path we tread, 377 : 18
continuous as stars that s., 427 : 8
face of God s. through, 822 : 12
for thy light is come, 31 : 23
forever singing as they s., 325 : 10
forth upon clouded hills, 406 : 21
full alchemized and free, 475 : 20
glories afar s. bright, 262 : 6
heaven's glories s., 562 : 4
holy glimmers of goodbyes, 827 : 4

Shine (*continued*)
if moon s. at full or no, 291 : 25
inner light will s. forth, 397 : *n* 6
let your light s., 37 : 6
make his face s. upon thee, 10 : 23
make sun s. for you, 775 : 10
moon nothing does but s., 693 : 9
nor public flame dares s., 340 : 28
not to s. in use, 529 : 9
perishing republic, 797 : 10
rise and s. give God glory, 935 : 26
shall s. like the gold, 403 : 14
singing as they s., 325 : 10
someday inner light s. forth, 397 : *n* 6
traffic of Jacob's ladder, 693 : 19
upon my brow today, 662 : 22
vessels oft handled brightly s., 183 : 18
where bright sun shall s., 249 : 18
wind's feet s. along sea, 632 : 18
wit will s., 304 : 27
with Pye, 456 : 16
you but knock breathe s., 254 : 15
Shined, although not s. upon, 291 : 29
eye of heaven s. bright, 173 : 10
in my angel infancy, 299 : 2
murmurless and s., 844 : 1
think how Bacon s., 337 : 15
upon them hath the light s., 29 : 15
Shines and stinks, 439 : 7
faith s. equal arming me, 562 : 4
foolery s. everywhere, 214 : 11
gold s. like fire, 71 : 20
good deed, 201 : 4
incongruous moonlight s., 819 : 3
light where no sun s., 886 : 13
moon s. bright, 200 : 22
simile that solitary s., 339 : 24
upon court and cottage, 247 : 1
whether s. in spotlight, 825 : 3
wise moral m. s. like fire, 73 : 3
wit s. at expense of memory, 323 : 26
Shineth everlasting Light, 619 : 16
light s. in darkness, 44 : 18
light that s. unto perfect day, 23 : 8
when sun s. make hay, 159 : 2
Shingles, naked s. of world, 587 : 16
Shining, a scattering a s., 874 : 9
Big-Sea-Water, 511 : 16
burning and s. light, 44 : 37
death loves s. mark, 330 : 16
eyes s. for me, 810 : 2
improve each s. hour, 328 : 5
improve s. tail, 611 : 5
light s. still, 587 : 12
live hair s. and free, 796 : 16
look s. at architecture, 868 : 4
morning face, 211 : 15
no more profit of s. nights, 190 : 12
nowhere but in the dark, 299 : 9
of the stars, 534 : 27
on broken fragments, 450 : 15
on the sea, 613 : 1
only one s. in sky, 424 : 12, 773 : 14
palace upon sand, 822 : 18
path of the just is as s. light, 23 : 8
pearl and crystal s. bright, 406 : 6
prospects rise, 325 : 6
sea to s. sea, 688 : 5
see it s. plain, 691 : 9
shade evades the s., 897 : 5
spangled heavens s. frame, 325 : 8
state of his s., 864 : 7
through dark cloud s., 740 : 11
Shining (*continued*)
to the quiet moon, 435 : 15
with all his might, 613 : 1
Shins, break s. against wit, 210 : 36
Ship aboard the ship, 575 : 20
an isle a sickle moon, 785 : 17
anchor heaves s. swings free, 492 : 14
and I took off suddenly, 855 : 8
being in s. is being in jail, 354 : 6
build s. of death, 791 : 2
build your s. of death, 791 : 4
came from north country, 935 : 4
capital s. for ocean trip, 647 : 21
clear at last, 576 : 20
comes into the harbor, 265 : 12
community like s., 599 : 18
don't give up the s., 449 : *n* 1
flag or s. signal, 575 : 21
fragment from earth, 683 : 4
goes wop with wiggle, 709 : 24
idle as painted s., 434 : 14
immortal ship, 575 : 20
land to which s. must go, 428 : 2
me east of Suez, 708 : 10
name of s. Golden Vanity, 935 : 4
never sink except on even keel, 114 : 28
of state, 62 : *n* 13, 74 : 9
of State, 511 : 8
of the body, 575 : 20
of the soul, 575 : 20
of Union, 521 : 7
one s. drives east, 669 : 21
only one s. seeking us, 901 : 4
Papists Protestants Jews Turks in one s., 273 : 11
place s. alongside enemy, 408 : 7
rapt s. run on side so low, 178 : 6
rats desert sinking s., 117 : *n* 2
sailing like a stately s., 288 : 30
scuttled s. or cut throat, 460 : 26
tall s. and star to steer, 760 : 14
trip on Government s., 935 : 5
unstable pilot steers leaking s., 127 : 13
was cheered, 434 : 7
way of a s. in the sea, 26 : 4
we too take s. O soul, 576 : 15
weathered every rack, 576 : 6
whither O splendid s., 654 : 15
whose weal and woe is common, 273 : 11
Shipmate, joy s. joy, 576 : 20
Shipmates, but oh s., 570 : 5
safety for my s., 151 : 10
Ship's, aboard at s. helm, 575 : 19
huge shadow, 434 : 28
way on the sea, 708 : 22
Ships are but boards, 198 : 17
are only hulls, 74 : 1
are swift as a bird, 60 : 2
believe these s. from sky, 151 : 5
board the well-benched s., 62 : 18
by s. lies a dead man, 59 : 9
clipper s. of 1850's, 800 : 10
dim-discovered, 345 : 8
distant storm-beaten s., 642 : 8
face that launched a thousand s., 184 : 4
fare north, fare south, 5 : 7
go down to the sea in s., 21 : 14
great gray s. come in, 738 : 12
guarded with s., 276 : 3
heart of oak our s., 363 : 16
Ships (*continued*)
how many s. my presence worth, 88 : 25
land to which s. go, 564 : 13
like s. steer courses, 291 : 8
of war at sea, 535 : 11
on decks of decayed s., 849 : 10
sail like swans asleep, 785 : 16
sail softly down Neva, 801 : 18
sailing the seas, 575 : 21
salvaged and retiring, 777 : 14
season of s. is here, 93 : 3
shoes s. sealing wax, 613 : 5
stately s. go on, 530 : 19
that pass in night, 512 : 10
there go the s., 21 : 11
there were two lofty s., 935 : 3
Thracian s. foreign faces, 632 : 7
three s. come sailing, 933 : 3
upon wine-dark seas, 868 : 21
we've got the s., 598 : 9
wooden wall is your s. 70 : 13
Shipshape and Bristol fashion, 553 : 19
Ship-signal, special flag or s., 575 : 21
Shipwreck, delivered from s. of blood, 842 : 1
Shipwrecked before I got aboard, 114 : 29
Shiraz, wine of S. into urine, 789 : 6
Shirker, no room for s., 745 : 11
Shirt, essayist can pull on any s., 847 : 10
happy man's without s., 158 : 16
land of the Cluett S., 828 : 17
man in Brooks Brothers s., 881 : 8
naked truth is I have no s., 191 : 11
never s. on back, 319 : 20
of flame, 808 : 15
of Nessus upon me, 241 : 16
song of the s., 485 : 17
tortured by my own s., 849 : 16
when wanting a s., 371 : 22
Shirtless, sleeveless some s. others, 340 : 21
Shirts, Nessus s., 473 : 10
white s. who coming to breathe shapes, 907 : 21
Shirtsleeves, three generations s. to s., 621 : 13
Shirttails Into Drawers, 829 : 1
Shiver, breezes dusk and s., 528 : 24
runs down spine, 833 : 6
sunset breezes s., 700 : 10
Shivering bicycle mechanics, 835 : 1
stood s. in snow, 182 : 2
Shivering-sweet to touch, 795 : 2
Shoal, bank and s. of time, 236 : 22
Shock disturbing delicate balance, 875 : 9
fodder's in the s., 665 : 14
future s., 909 : 1
like s. of corn cometh, 15 : 18
of recognition, 569 : 18
strikes with shivering s., 440 : 1
we shall s. them, 202 : 20
you must s. bourgeois, 581 : 11
Shocked by violent death of slaveholder, 560 : 23
Shocks of passion prepare, 428 : 23
thousand natural s., 221 : 12
Shod, worse s. than shoemaker's wife, 160 : 15
Shoe, cannot put s. on every foot, 111 : 28

Shoe (*continued*)
dame has lost s., 929:10
fits one pinches another, 754:5
for want of nail s. lost, 270:4, 347:35
none tell where s. pinches me, 119:23
not do anymore black s., 911:16
old s. for good luck, 159:20
old woman lived in s., 931:10
one s. off one s. on, 933:1
over Edom will I cast out my s., 19:25
sailed in wooden s., 666:16
shoemakers hang out s., 451:16
sixpence in her s., 262:15, 924:6
the horse, 934:6
whether s. be Spanish, 291:16
Shoemaker, lives of s. and peddler, 811:8
Shoemaker's, worse shod than s. wife, 160:15
Shoemakers hang out shoe, 451:16
Shoes and ships and sealing wax, 613:5
east soles offen s., 840:1
him that makes s. go barefoot, 160:*n* 10
latchet of whose s., 41:32
nor scrip nor s., 43:8
old s. easiest for feet, 179:*n* 4
put off thy s., 9:11
put yourself in his s., 834:1
sold the poor for a pair of s., 33:19
surgeon to old s., 214:30
walk in velvet s., 793:17
with your s. on your feet, 9:25
Shoeshine, riding on smile and s., 888:3
Shoestring, careless s. in whose tie, 266:7
Shogun, neither lords nor s., 609:7
Shone, eyes that s. now dimmed, 447:7
far off his coming s., 286:27
glory s. around, 317:4
glory s. round about them, 42:28
light here kindled s. unto many, 265:13
like meteor streaming, 283:20
moon s. on Mrs. Porter, 805:6
princely counsel s., 284:14
they s. not on poet's page, 108:*n* 11
with preeminent luster, 122:20
Shoo fly, 619:15
Shook all our coffins, 642:1
softening chalk of bones, 873:12
ten days that s. world, 801:4
Shoon, cork-heeled s., 926:12
sandal s., 223:21
silver s., 739:13
Shoot, do not s. pianist, 675:6
don't s. Colonel, 455:10
false love, 918:3
fellow down, 641:15
first inquire afterwards, 825:17
folly as it flies, 336:11
guns begin to s., 708:4
her every minute, 905:3
if you must, 513:18
not s. with butter, 838:15
teach young idea to s., 345:11
Shootin', what's all s. for, 759:9
Shooting, glory like a s. star, 194:24
stars attend thee, 266:14
Shoots, boy that s. so trim, 917:18
his wit, 213:6
neither s. nor liberates, 560:24
nobody s. at Santa Claus, 741:9
of everlastingness, 299:3
Shop, back s. our own free, 164:17
closed for other business, 524:11
keep s. and s. keep thee, 177:14
said you were coming from s., 614:12
she-bear pops head into s., 364:5
Shopkeeper, what is true of s., 359:9
Shopkeepers, government influenced by s., 366:6
nation of s., 359:*n* 4, 366:6
Shopkeeping nation, 359:9
Shops, in s. nothing to eat, 733:4
Shore, Afric's burning s., 438:12
beats back envious siege, 194:14
boat is on s., 460:4
breast on reedy s., 918:17
by what s. tarriest, 588:6
fast by their native s., 377:19
gaze from s. on another's tribulation, 100:12
guiled s. to dangerous sea, 199:26
hang it by the s., 700:8
high s. of world, 208:7
his own native s., 525:9
I on opposite s., 512:7
kingdom of the s., 244:22
lee s. of age, 664:1
left beauty on s., 493:15
lights around s., 601:23
man's control stops at s., 458:25
men on s. interpreters, 732:7
naked in death on unknown s., 105:13
never reach the s., 659:4
New England's blustering s., 558:10
nightly s., 526:15
no earthly s., 843:16
ocean's wave-beat s., 552:22
of what we know, 900:11
one foot in sea one on s., 209:16
one s. beyond desire, 843:18
Plutonian s., 526:15
praise sea on s. remain, 174:24
rapture on lonely s., 458:24
refuse of teeming s., 664:10
roar echoed along s., 438:12
round earth's s., 587:16
scrambling to the s., 613:4
sees sea bottom from s., 142:15
spies a far-off s., 186:10
stayed upon green s., 479:14
sunshine on strange s., 683:11
swiftly courses from s., 576:20
then on s. of world, 478:19
unhappy folks on s. now, 429:19
unknown and silent s., 441:10
upon farther s., 597:15
upon the Irish s., 410:6
varying s. of the world, 241:20
voiceless s., 461:5
watery s., 405:2
waves make towards pebbled s., 244:19
wide-watered s., 278:19
wild New England s., 470:15
Shorebirds, intrepid s., 874:9
Shoreditch, bells of S., 930:7
Shoreless, before only s. seas, 646:6
watery wild, 585:13
Shores and desert wildernesses, 279:16
concave s., 215:1
exult O s., 576:7
fearless for unknown s., 576:15
look beyond own s., 891:2
not ghost of s., 646:6
of Gitche Gumee, 511:16
of Tripoli, 922:11
pores of ocean and s., 468:10
pure ablution round s., 478:20
what seas what s., 806:8
whisperings round desolate s., 478:16
Shoreward, small boat drifts s., 873:16
Shorewards, great winds s. blow, 584:11
Shorn, tempers wind to s. lamb, 163:12
Short and long of it, 225:16
and simple annals, 362:2
and simple scandals, 722:2
angels' visits s. and bright, 318:4
arm to reach heaven, 693:20
art long life s., 395:7
as any dream, 195:23
as watch that ends night, 328:11
as wrong as to fall s., 68:27
cut to everything, 353:8
duration of panics s., 384:14
full description of happy state, 307:18
in s. I was afraid, 803:16
in s. measures life perfect be, 256:20
in the story itself, 36:16
joy of love too s., 149:11
July's day s. as December, 246:13
lack time to make it s., 299:13
let thy speech be s., 36:3
life how long or s., 287:30
life in saddle Lord, 696:14
life is s. art long, 80:9
life s. quiet hours few, 573:1
life too s. to bore ourselves, 657:25
meaning of long speech, 413:15
my scope had not been so s., 249:*n* 4
nasty brutish and s., 264:17
nearest comes so far s., 747:9
not make sentences s., 729:7
of seeming arms s. essay, 307:8
one ready for my own, 749:8
one s. sleep past, 254:13
pain s. joy eternal, 413:27
perfect in being too s., 440:26
potential stir, 607:8
shrill shriek, 364:12
sighs s. and infrequent, 805:2
sudden storms are s., 194:12
summer's lease too s., 244:5
time of life is s., 205:8
trips from long to s., 436:3
woman's time of opportunity s., 82:12
words are best, 746:17
Shortcomings in exclusive occupations, 444:10
Shorten, envy and wrath s. life, 36:1
stature of my soul, 600:16
tedious nights, 250:7
Shorter, Cleopatra's nose s., 300:1
make you s. by the head, 163:17
your epigrams are s., 119:5
Shorter-Catechist, something of S., 663:8

Shortest, longest way round s. home, 267 : *n* 6
Shortest-lived, longest-lived and s. die same, 124 : 9
Short-lived, good fortune may be s., 265 : 4
Shortly, near to be thought so s., 209 : 32
Shortness, spend that s. basely, 205 : 8
Shot arrow into air, 510 : 24
at without result, 743 : 2
delivered straighter to heart, 606 : 9
find plot in narrative s., 623 : 19
good at long s., 455 : 12
he that s. so trim, 192 : 1
heard round world, 494 : 13
I s. his fellow, 198 : 6
it through the head, 933 : 12
more cannon s., 717 : 12
not fired s. cry for blood, 579 : 3
of accident, 231 : 26
off s. the specter bark, 434 : 21
stars s. madly from spheres, 196 : 14
the albatross, 434 : 12
war just a s. away, 916 : 10
when stars s. and fell, 749 : 11
Should, nae better than he s. be, 409 : 3
no better than s. be, 168 : 30
no the thing I s. be, 411 : 21
of stood in bed, 836 : 12
Shoulder, any s. that I see, 233 : 14
backward half-look over s., 808 : 5
belly s. bum, 717 : 16
don't look over your s., 856 : 12
good women s. to s., 839 : 12
government shall be upon his s., 29 : 16
loaf of bread on s., 824 : 5
put your s. to the wheel, 66 : 19
rainbow around s., 733 : 11
she looked over his s., 868 : 21
sky drink ale, 691 : 20
to shoulder, 618 : 13
Shoulder-clapper, back-friend a s., 188 : 11
Shoulders, city of big s., 761 : 4
dwarf on s. of giant, 258 : 7
heads grow beneath s., 229 : 30
old heads on young s., 896 : 1
pygmies on s. of giants, 118 : 7
rain in dust on her s., 822 : 4
square s. lift pack, 691 : 15
standing on s. of giants, 313 : 10
Shout about my ears, 742 : 17
as loud as fifty men, 57 : 31
battle s., 518 : 12
golden shouts, 600 : 10
great s. upon hills, 671 : 3
made universal s., 215 : 1
midnight s. and revelry, 279 : 11
out your numbers, 764 : 11
people shouted with a great s., 11 : 31
silent hardly a s., 588 : 5
somewhere children s., 704 : 16
that tore hell's concave, 283 : 21
Shouted in mist month ago, 747 : 14
sons of God s. for joy, 16 : 29
Shouting battle cry of freedom, 578 : 13
heavens fill with s., 529 : 24
not substitute for thinking, 851 : 17
society evolves not by s., 884 : 6
their emulation, 242 : 9
thunder of the captains and the s., 16 : 38
Shouting (*continued*)
tumult and s. dies, 709 : 17
Shouts and plaudits of throng, 512 : 18
shout golden s., 600 : 10
with sister at play, 530 : 19
Shoved, idealism s. aside, 698 : 9
Shovel, pickaxe s. spade, 455 : 8
under let me work, 761 : 6
Shoveled into the tombs, 761 : 8
Show an unfelt sorrow, 238 : 10
and gaze o' the time, 240 : 10
authority and s. of truth, 209 : 30
contain and nourish all world, 191 : 5
dangerous brow by night, 215 : 19
doubt prove faith, 543 : 8
every man walketh in vain s., 19 : 3
freely your worst trait, 503 : 14
his eyes, 239 : 13
I s. you doubt, 543 : 8
judges all ranged a terrible s., 332 : 7
look a needless s., 605 : 17
man as nature made him, 359 : 2
man who keeps his house, 74 : 19
me a greater evil, 74 : 20
me a hero, 835 : 14
me a liar, 270 : 10
me but thy worth, 208 : 6
me dear Christ Thy spouse, 254 : 16
me good loser, 811 : 3
me steep and thorny way, 218 : 28
mock time with fairest s., 237 : 8
more fair, 425 : 13
multitude that choose by s., 199 : 12
my head to the people, 412 : 3
my mouth shall s. forth thy praise, 19 : 18
near approach bed may s., 290 : 8
new periwig make great s., 310 : 10
no business like s. business, 802 : 12
not love that do not s. love, 189 : 30
nothing else we can s. today, 605 : 20
obscures the s. of evil, 199 : 24
of inconvenience, 785 : 10
something different from either, 805 : 1
that mercy s. to me, 340 : 4
that within which passeth s., 218 : 3
thing they most do s., 245 : 4
vilely to desire small beer, 185 : *n* 6
virtue her own feature, 222 : 2
virtue that possession would not s., 209 : 31
what thy short visit meant, 442 : 3
whole world a freeman, 379 : 1
you have got to s. me, 674 : 13
you have one, 342 : 1
Showed him gentleman an' scholar, 409 : 6
Lord s. me so I did see, 300 : 20
more s. than men understand, 34 : 27
Shower, arrowy s., 363 : 10
breath of vernal s., 363 : 13
drainless s. of light, 475 : 12
favors alike, 419 : 4
grew in sun and s., 424 : 13
of curates, 555 : 20
of gold, 473 : 13
rain s. of commanded tears, 188 : 24
soft s. to leeward, 571 : 8
Showered, rain a deluge s., 415 : 5
Showers and dewdrops wet, 608 : 13
April s. May flowers, 163 : 4
April with his s. soote, 145 : 12
as s. that water the earth, 19 : 35
Showers (*continued*)
barbaric pearl, 284 : 3
bring fresh s., 468 : 9
drying after bracing s., 834 : 8
for thirsting flowers, 468 : 9
nor clouds soak with s., 59 : *n* 5
of sweet discourse, 292 : 10
Sidnaeian s., 292 : 10
small s. last long, 194 : 12
suck the honeyed s., 281 : 1
Showest, have more than thou s., 233 : 9
Showeth, firmament s. his handiwork, 17 : 27
night unto night s. knowledge, 17 : 27
Showing, truth s. face undisguised, 72 : 5
Shown, worlds on worlds have s., 251 : 15
Showpiece, not s. of an hour, 80 : 15
Shows games sports guns, 381 : 7
let mourning s. be spread, 176 : 8
purrs and never s. tooth, 794 : 7
scepter s. force of power, 200 : 9
when her lovely laughter s., 250 : 6
Shreds, king of s. and patches, 223 : 6
thing of s. and patches, 629 : 4
Shrew, tame a s., 259 : 14
Shrewd, Frenchman's remark s., 376 : 11
guess valuable, 887 : 15
Shrewdly, air bites s., 219 : 8
Shrews, under s. at home, 452 : 16
Shriek, not a s. not a scream, 614 : 2
short shrill s., 364 : 12
solitary s., 460 : 21
Shrieked, it was the owl that s., 237 : 17
Shrieking, hooting and s., 215 : 12
Shrieks and groans of wounded, 579 : 3
horrid shapes and s., 277 : 17
Shrieve me holy man, 435 : 8
Shrill, farewell the s. trump, 231 : 11
hear thy s. delight, 468 : 13
short s. shriek, 364 : 12
Shrimp of an author, 363 : 12
Shrine, fountain and s., 525 : 17
goddess to thy s. we come, 412 : 9
melancholy has sovran s., 478 : 1
sought faith's pure s., 561 : 1
temple's inner s., 425 : 17
Shrink from service of country, 384 : 13
not because they s. from it, 84 : 7
Shrinking from weight of noon, 768 : 2
Shrinks, why s. the soul, 326 : 3
Shrive me holy man, 435 : 8
Shriveled heart recovered greenness, 269 : 4
meager hopping, 373 : 28
Shroud, great s. of sea, 571 : 9
no roof to s. his head, 257 : 20
of thoughts, 458 : 4
ray on ray split s., 545 : 25
stiff dishonored s., 804 : 25
wear it like banner not s., 854 : 16
whoever comes to s. me, 253 : 11
Shrouds, darkness worms and s., 475 : 13
Shrunk, as to bed's-feet life s., 252 : 25
shank, 211 : 15
those s. strangely in our lives, 850 : 2
to this little measure, 216 : 8
vanished and s. away, 182 : 3
Shudder, hands over with s., 783 : 10
in loins, 715 : 16

Shudder (*continued*)
to say it, 104 : 34
Shuddering fear green-eyed jealousy, 199 : 28
I with s. fall, 600 : 21
in gloaming light, 626 : 21
Shuffle, patience and s. cards, 170 : 24
permitted to s. in slippers, 706 : 19
Shuffled off this mortal coil, 221 : 12
Shuffling, forced gait of s. nag, 204 : 14
sandwich men s., 781 : 15
Shulamite, return O S., 28 : 18
Shun, dews of evening s., 342 : 17
father and mother, 496 : 24
frumious Bandersnatch, 612 : 17
heaven that leads men to hell, 245 : 23
let me s. that, 234 : 2
polluted flock, 793 : 18
studies in which work dies with worker, 152 : 6
when I s. Scylla, 200 : 1
who doth ambition s., 211 : 3
wise men s. mistakes of fools, 95 : 10
Shuns, weather shepherd s., 642 : 5
Shut doors against setting sun, 243 : 2
doors s. in the streets, 27 : 24
drew circle s. me out, 671 : 4
eyes against painful truth, 383 : 1
fountain s., 561 : 4
gates of mercy, 362 : 11
in from world without, 513 : 21
moral s. in rose, 530 : 14
my eyes to see, 875 : 1
no door is s., 697 : 2
of evening flowers, 287 : 16
shut the door, 338 : 5
them in with their triumphs, 542 : 4
up box and puppets, 539 : 10
up he explained, 790 : 7
up in measureless content, 237 : 12
when thou shouldest repay, 35 : 3
Shut-in homes closed doors, 727 : 7
Shuts up story of our days, 173 : 5
Shutter, camera with s. open, 860 : 1
it may be in the s., 557 : 6
Shutters, close s. fast, 377 : 3
Shutteth up bowels of compassion, 52 : 23
Shutting away of loving hearts, 823 : 12
Shuttle, musical s., 575 : 17
swifter than weaver's s., 15 : 20
Shy, birch most s. of trees, 567 : 10
we are not s., 629 : 9
Sibboleth, he said S., 12 : 12
Sic semper tyrannis, 134 : 27, 635 : 23
sic iuvat ire sub umbras, 105 : *n* 6
transit gloria mundi, 148 : 13
Sicilian, so ended S. expedition, 81 : 10
Sicily, quarries of S., 850 : 13
Sick almost to doomsday, 217 : 22
and full of burning, 892 : 7
and ye visited me, 40 : 33
at heart, 217 : 15
danger for the healthy, 658 : 7
enterprise is s., 226 : 1
for home, 477 : 1
get s. of what men do, 847 : 2
hope deferred maketh heart s., 23 : 31
I am s. at heart, 217 : 15
I am s. I must die, 250 : 10
I am s. of both, 355 : 22
in fortune, 233 : 5
love never s. old dead, 172 : 9
Sick (*continued*)
make me s. discussing duty, 574 : 24
mind emptying, 850 : 12
need physician, 38 : 27
never never s. at sea, 627 : 11
night but daylight s., 201 : 6
nothing but to make him s., 253 : 22
O Rose thou art s., 405 : 5
of an old passion, 721 : 4
of its business, 424 : 3
of love, 28 : 6
of terra firma toils, 569 : 20
say I'm s. I'm dead, 338 : 5
superintend s., 79 : 16
that surfeit with too much, 198 : 7
think we're s., 852 : 9
too much culture s. animal, 755 : 3
use treatment to help s., 79 : 13
whole head is s., 28 : 27
with desire, 715 : 2
Sicken, appetite may s. and die, 213 : 7
when love begins to s., 216 : 30
Sickle, could not make s. yield, 404 : 15
crowned with the s., 345 : 13
in fruitful field, 404 : 15
moon, 785 : 17
never thrust s. in another's corn, 111 : 27
not move s. unto neighbor's corn, 11 : 18
Sickle's, bending s. compass, 245 : 18
Sicklied o'er with thought, 221 : 12
Sickly plants niggard earth, 361 : 17
smile, 630 : 14
Sickness, age or grief or s., 267 : 6
and troubled mind, 267 : 20
by his health s., 403 : 13
enlarges dimension of self, 442 : 10
in s. and in health, 56 : 9
love a s. full of woes, 182 : 11
sin and death, 583 : 4
trublit now with gret s., 153 : 6
universal s. implies idea of health, 866 : 3
Sickness-broken body, 276 : 14
Side, a thousand shall fall at thy s., 20 : 16
angel on outward s., 228 : 27
back and s. go bare, 163 : 10
cracked from s. to s., 528 : 27
curse angel from his s., 232 : 17
East S. West S., 698 : 14
everyone moon with dark s., 625 : 19
God on s. of big squadrons, 294 : 21
good or evil s., 567 : 6
hear other s., 129 : 7
heard other s., 77 : 1
history is on our s., 830 : 14
house by s. of road, 57 : 32, 685 : 12
lies on her left s., 822 : 4
on that s. toil hunger, 481 : 2
spinning-jenny out of s., 715 : 15
stands out on either s., 822 : 12
trumpets on other s., 302 : 16
which s. that I must g., 201 : 22
who is on the Lord's s., 10 : 13
windy s. of care, 209 : 12
windy s. of law, 209 : *n* 2
with pouch on s., 211 : 15
wrong s. of thirty, 323 : 8
Sideaways, trot s., 856 : 1
Sidelong looks of love, 369 : 29
pickerel smile, 873 : 17
Sides, god would have three s., 341 : 7
Sides (*continued*)
Laughter holding both his s., 277 : 20
much said on both s., 326 : 14
prick s. of my intent, 236 : 24
split s. with laughing, 169 : 24
thorns in your s., 12 : 1
two s. to every question, 78 : 24
unfed s., 234 : 3
Sidewalk, Tom appeared on s., 622 : 11
Sidewalks of New York, 698 : 14
Sideways, listened and looked s. up, 434 : 22
Sidnaeian showers, 292 : 10
Sidney, friend to Sir Philip S., 175 : 6
I shall meet Sir Philip S., 804 : 18
miracle of our age, 176 : *n* 4
Sidney's self, 540 : 11
sister Pembroke's mother, 265 : 15
Siege, envious s. of watery Neptune, 194 : 14
laugh a s. to scorn, 240 : 2
of city of Gaunt, 926 : 18
Sieges, battles s. fortunes, 229 : 27
Sienta, el que s. en la perta, 935 : 12
Sierras, crossed the S., 822 : 2
people who live in s., 151 : 9
Siesta, allowed-for as Spanish s., 835 : 17
Sieve, nectar in a s., 436 : 10
to sea in s., 550 : 11
water through a s., 613 : 18
Sifted, God hath s. a nation, 307 : *n* 4
Siftings, liquid s. fall, 804 : 25
Sigh back at them, 874 : 1
is just a sigh, 830 : 6
lack of many a thing, 244 : 11
like Tom o' Bedlam, 233 : 6
no more ladies, 209 : 16
passing tribute of s., 362 : 13
prompts eternal s., 337 : 10
shall I ever s. and pine, 268 : 21
some a light s., 492 : 15
sword of Angel King, 406 : 7
telling this with s., 747 : 13
that silence heaves, 474 : 21
time for a s., 683 : 11
to those who love me, 460 : 4
took her with a s., 404 : *n* 2
very beadle to humorous s., 190 : 25
weep no more nor s., 260 : 19
Sighed and looked and sighed again, 306 : 20
and looked unutterable things, 345 : 9
as lover obeyed as son, 384 : 4
for Agnes' dreams, 476 : 11
for love of lady, 629 : 22
for such a one, 182 : 5
Launcelot wept not greatly but s., 149 : 19
no sooner loved but s., 212 : 31
soul toward Grecian tents, 200 : 22
to many though he loved one, 456 : 21
when small birds s., 874 : 1
Sighing by a sycamore tree, 232 : 8
farewell goes out s., 226 : 19
laughter ability s., 606 : 7
lover s. like furnace, 211 : 15
more singing less s., 739 : 8
parting genius with s. sent, 277 : 11
plague of s. and grief, 204 : 3
shall flee away, 30 : 25
soul that lingers s., 691 : 12
sound lights around shore, 601 : 23

Sighing (*continued*)
that Nature formed but one, 459 : 20
through all her works, 287 : 19
with s. and crying, 167 : 3
Sighs, before my s. did dry it, 268 : 21
Bridge of S., 458 : 5
his alarms, 177 : 12
lamentations and wailings, 140 : 15
most s. edited, 876 : 7
night of memories and s., 442 : 18
paid with s. aplenty, 690 : 21
short and infrequent, 805 : 2
Sorrow with family of S., 469 : 3
sovereign of s. and groans, 190 : 26
still breathed in s., 334 : 26
world of s., 229 : 31
Sight, be acceptable in thy s., 18 : 3
charms strike the s., 334 : 11
earth and every common s., 426 : 10
faith s. and knowledge, 557 : 3
falling in love at first s., 707 : 7
field has s., 146 : *n* 5
for sore eyes, 323 : *n* 1
found favor in thy s., 8 : 11
gleamed upon my s., 427 : 3
glorious stirring s., 690 : 15
half so fine a s., 289 : 21
hide us from each other's s., 267 : 5
horizon limit of s., 642 : 10
idea with sense of s., 698 : 7
keen discriminating s., 422 : 4
lecher in my s., 234 : 31
let it be in s. of thee, 607 : 15
loved at first s., 183 : 17
near s. of mere size of him, 778 : 6
of means to do ill deeds, 202 : 11
of Proteus rising, 428 : 1
of salt water unbounded, 710 : 7
old s. yet somehow young, 571 : 8
out of s. out of mind, 148 : 18
portentous s., 435 : 16
precious in the s. of the Lord, 21 : 24
secluded from s. of God, 254 : 23
see such s. in life, 929 : 11
sensible to feeling as s., 237 : 13
so touching in majesty, 425 : 13
spare my aching s., 363 : 7
spotted s. or sound, 793 : 19
stars not pure in his s., 16 : 11
to dream of not to tell, 434 : 1
to make old man young, 529 : 2
two eyes one in s., 748 : 18
visionary anger cleansing s., 910 : 5
walk by faith not s., 49 : 14
we shall live in his s., 33 : 9
Sighted fifty-three, 535 : 11
Sightless couriers of the air, 236 : 24
realm where darkness awake, 791 : 1
Sights as youthful poets dream, 278 : 6
love of other s. controls, 251 : 15
night full of ugly s., 187 : 8
Northern Lights seen s., 752 : 6
shrieks and s. unholy, 277 : 17
to see sad s. moves, 189 : 25
troublous s. and sounds, 721 : 8
what ugly s. of death, 187 : 9
Sign brings customers, 296 : 18
divine s. indicates future, 79 : 4
God didn't want to s., 655 : 13
he dies and makes no s., 185 : 18
hungry judges sentence s., 334 : 6
in this s. conquer, 127 : 3
nay but I have s., 604 : 1
of old age, 433 : 16
Sign (*continued*)
olive leaf pacific s., 288 : 2
outward and visible s., 56 : 5
they seek a s., 43 : 18
to know gentle blood, 174 : 20
V s. symbol, 745 : 4
you must not touch, 253 : 11
Signal, death loves s. blow, 330 : 16
only a s. shown, 512 : 10
really do not see s., 408 : 5
special flag or ship s., 575 : 21
Signals, hackneyed phrases danger s., 685 : 14
neither seen or understood, 408 : 7
recognize s. of ancient flame, 142 : 6
unless they call s., 825 : 3
Signed, hand that s. the paper, 886 : 14
with their honor, 876 : 16
Significance, death gives life s., 545 : 14
no personal s. spare us, 522 : 12
of man, 738 : 10
what is s. of man, 738 : 10
Significant, life of s. soil, 808 : 9
Signifies, what s. life o' man, 409 : 14
Signify, doesn't s. whom one marries, 416 : 5
Signifying nothing, 240 : 4
Signposts, without s., 842 : 9
Signs, all things full of s., 126 : 18
in what God has created, 130 : 16
men hang out s., 451 : 16
merely conventional s., 613 : 22
of the times, 39 : 34
should prefigure events, 98 : 21
speaks in symbols and s., 513 : 13
Silas, good for Paul and S., 921 : 16
Silence, all s. an' glisten, 568 : 4
alone great, 483 : 7
and damn little of that, 922 : *n* 5
and desolation, 525 : 16
and slow time, 477 : 4
baring tatty wreckage of my life, 911 : 8
be checked for s., 227 : 9
birdless s., 901 : 4
calumnies answered best with s., 255 : 15
craters of s., 864 : 4
cruelest lies told in s., 667 : 16
darkness again and s., 512 : 10
deep and white, 568 : 15
deep as death, 443 : 16
deep as eternity, 473 : *n* 1
deepest feeling in s., 798 : 17
die by negligence and s., 356 : 25
dust and s. of shelf, 487 : 8
elected s. sing to me, 655 : 18
envious tongues, 249 : 8
expressive s., 345 : 16
fall like dews, 793 : 17
fell with waking bird, 533 : 22
float upon wings of s., 279 : 19
genre of s., 828 : 6
gives consent, 369 : 26
gives proper grace to women, 73 : 9
golden, 473 : 9
great souls suffer in s., 412 : 16
guard careful s., 751 : 7
guilt by s. betrayed, 305 : 27
hath more eloquence, 538 : 1
horse in s. champed, 739 : 15
icy s. of tomb, 478 : 8
impostor imposes s., 391 : 7
in love bewrays woe, 172 : 13
Silence (*continued*)
in s. and tears, 456 : 8
in s. hushed his very soul, 428 : 15
in s. preserve integrity, 140 : 4
infinitude of s., 580 : 4
is best tactic, 293 : 14
is contempt, 504 : 6
is expression of scorn, 681 : 14
isolates, 755 : 15
kept by ourselves in s., 512 : 22
learned s. from talkative, 782 : 20
let all the earth keep s., 33 : 27
let there be sacred s., 107 : 25
like poultice comes, 518 : 13
listening to s., 485 : 9
living with us even in s., 395 : 6
loves s. platonically, 473 : *n* 1
majestic s., 377 : *n* 5
mind moves upon s., 717 : 17
Mrs. Browning guard s., 751 : 7
my gracious s. hail, 242 : 13
night and s. who is here, 196 : 22
night in her s., 585 : 12
no medicines to make women keep s., 655 : 15
no worse than cheers, 691 : 3
noble till the end, 632 : 10
not here not enough s., 806 : 4
not s. but restraint, 798 : 17
now there is merely s., 794 : 14
occasional flashes of s., 433 : 10
of infinite spaces, 300 : 2
often of pure innocence, 246 : 15
perfectest herald of joy, 209 : 11
regretted speech never s., 112 : 16
request deed in s., 141 : 13
rest is s., 225 : 2
roar other side of s., 565 : 23
rushed me to sleep, 911 : 8
sank like music, 435 : 5
sigh that s. heaves, 474 : 21
small things and s., 881 : 7
speech after long s., 716 : 20
speech small change of S., 600 : 12
stand in her s., 822 : 10
supreme, 614 : 2
that dreadful bell, 230 : 20
that is in starry sky, 428 : 7
then a lark, 660 : 10
thunders of white s., 507 : 6
time to keep s., 26 : 21
treasures in s. sealed, 555 : 17
wakened by s., 631 : 17
was pleased, 285 : 25
well-timed s., 538 : 1
when s. speaks for love, 621 : 14
when S. speaks for Love, 621 : 14
white s. below, 793 : 17
widening slowly s. all, 534 : 9
wings of s., 279 : 19
wisest thing to heed, 72 : 5
woman hold to keeping s., 504 : 9
wrapped in beard and s., 840 : 7
your eyes have their s., 829 : 12
Silenced man not converted, 637 : 5
Silences, three s. there are, 512 : 20
time of hidden s., 883 : 8
Silencing, not justified in s. one, 508 : 4
Silent and amazed, 575 : 23
as the moon, 288 : 21
be s. as to his works, 356 : 9
be s. that you may hear, 216 : 13
center of s. Word, 806 : 4
chew cud and are s., 373 : 28

Silent (*continued*)
church, 497 : 5
cities and villages are s., 456 : 2
colossal national lie, 625 : 24
counsel of the Unseen and S., 474 : 7
dumb and s. be led, 379 : 6
dust, 362 : 5
duty not to be s., 598 : 15
enim leges inter arma, 98 : *n* 5
evening mild s. night, 286 : 1
fair exterior a s. recommendation, 110 : 27
finger points to heaven, 428 : 17
flock in wooly fold, 476 : 8
flooding in the main, 564 : 17
floors of s. seas, 803 : 14
gone into s. land, 608 : 14
gradual and s. encroachments, 398 : 4
halls of death, 471 : 6
hardly a shout, 588 : 5
haunches, 761 : 5
icicles, 435 : 15
impossible to be s., 373 : 16
in the dark and s. grave, 173 : 5
into the s. funeral, 807 : 17
language of peak, 812 : 2
lark that soars singing then s., 142 : 17
long and s. street, 674 : 15
majority, 882 : 21
manliness of grief, 370 : 18
my tongue falls s., 63 : 5
night holy night, 466 : 2
note Cupid strikes, 274 : 20
painting is s. poetry, 68 : 1
part is best, 573 : 13
power in men to be s., 308 : 10
prism and s. face, 424 : 2
right to remain s., 820 : 15
sea, 434 : 13
slow and s. stream Lethe, 284 : 22
spectator of scene, 445 : 5
splendid s. sun, 575 : 24
spring, 870 : 1
stars go by, 619 : 16
sweet s. thought, 244 : 11
tents are spread, 578 : 10
the truly s. who keeps apart, 6 : 4
these three s. things, 759 : 10
till you see whites of eyes, 368 : *n* 1
to be s. better than to speak, 120 : 10
unknown and s. shore, 441 : 10
upon peak in Darien, 475 : 7
war of lilies, 189 : 17
when eggs hatched, 277 : 1
when you doubt sense, 333 : 17
why art s. and invisible, 404 : 13
why art thou s., 487 : 3
with s. delight, 403 : 12
wound deep in her breast, 105 : 9
Silently as a dream, 377 : 11
falls through ether s., 475 : 5
how s. with how wan face, 176 : 14
invisibly, 404 : 10
now the moon, 739 : 13
one by one, 511 : 3
steal away, 510 : 22
Silk, delicate-filmed as s., 642 : 3
not make revolution with s. gloves, 766 : 10
owest worm no s., 234 : 7
soft as s. remains, 331 : 1
sound of her s. skirt, 97 : 10
Silk (*continued*)
stocking filled with mud, 421 : 3
stockings and white bosoms, 353 : 23
suffering behind golden s., 849 : 19
suit which cost me much, 309 : 13
that thing of s., 338 : 18
Silken dalliance, 207 : 10
flanks, 477 : 9
in field s. tent, 749 : 4
lines silver hooks, 253 : 2
moderation s. string, 257 : 14
or in leathern purse, 328 : 19
sad uncertain, 526 : 13
terms precise, 191 : 9
tie, 430 : 9
ties of love, 749 : 5
white s. turbans wreathed, 288 : 11
Silks, in s. my Julia goes, 266 : 22
my s. and fine array, 402 : 14
Silk-sack clouds, 656 : 6
Silkworm size or immense, 799 : 14
Silliest woman manage clever man, 707 : 11
Sillons, abreuve nos s., 415 : 1
Silly, envy slayeth the s., 15 : 14
joy at silly things, 370 : *n* 1
loved its s. face, 697 : 1
men as s. and wise, 524 : 2
nothing more s. than s. laugh, 102 : 1
question, 359 : 19
sooth, 214 : 3
Silo, mildewed s., 757 : 6
Siloam's shady rill, 452 : 6
Silver and gold have I none, 45 : 40
apples of gold in pictures of s., 25 : 14
apples of moon, 712 : 14
bells cockleshells, 930 : 6
buckles on knee, 934 : 3
churn, 628 : 9
companions cut s. strings, 850 : 4
cord be loosed, 27 : 25
for handful of s. he left, 541 : 5
fountains have mud, 244 : 14
give him s. bridge, 935 : 8
goddess of the s. lake, 280 : 3
gold and s. ivory and apes, 13 : 36
gold and s. light, 712 : 15
hooks, 253 : 2
hosannas of rain, 852 : 14
if you have two pieces of s., 133 : *n* 1
into s. dawn, 828 : 9
life lived on s. screens, 839 : 3
light on foliage, 841 : 11
lining on the night, 279 : 17
lining through cloud, 740 : 11
link, 430 : 9
look for s. lining, 775 : 10
mantle threw, 285 : 25
moon in s. bag, 716 : 21
moon's red s., 901 : 14
nutmeg, 932 : 1
oars were s., 240 : 29
picking up gold and s., 921 : 2
precious stone set in s. sea, 194 : 13
rain with s. flail, 794 : 13
refined thee but not with s., 31 : 6
seated in thy s. chair, 255 : 12
shoon, 739 : 13
sixpence in shoe, 924 : *n* 2
snarling trumpets, 476 : 9
sold the righteous for s., 33 : 19
speak s. reply gold, 926 : 4
speech is s., 473 : 9
spoon in mouth, 171 : 5
Silver (*continued*)
stroke his s. hair, 403 : 8
swan who living, 918 : 17
thirty pieces of s., 33 : 34, 41 : 5
threads among gold, 662 : 22
tips with s. fruit-tree tops, 192 : 11
wisdom be put in s. rod, 403 : 17
Silvered, completely s. o'er, 376 : 23
it was a sable s., 218 : 23
Silver-footed ironies, 701 : 7
Silver-sandaled, dawn with s. feet, 674 : 15
Silver-sweet sound lovers' tongues, 192 : 17
Silver-white, lady-smocks all s., 191 : 13
Silvia, be by S. in the night, 190 : 2
who is S. what is she, 190 : 4
Simia quam similis nobis, 95 : *n* 3
Simiadae branched off, 515 : 7
Simians, true fairy story of s., 746 : 20
Similar, not s. are race of gods, 57 : 30
sons s. to their fathers, 59 : 18
to mortals neither in shape nor thought, 67 : 14
Simile a like perfection, 899 : 15
that solitary shines, 339 : 24
Similes, sit and play with s., 426 : 3
Similitudes, I have used s., 33 : 15
Simon Pure, 321 : 8
simple S., 930 : 13
Simple, a s. child, 423 : 3
and faithless as smile, 804 : 11
and heartfelt lay, 510 : 19
as false dawn, 899 : 12
facts in naked s. beauty, 183 : 2
faith than Norman blood, 528 : 11
gout kills more wise than s., 301 : 2
great swindles s., 699 : 9
how s. and frugal is happiness, 782 : 23
I would like s. life, 908 : 15
Ivan Ilych's life most s., 602 : 10
maiden in her flower, 528 : 8
modest manly true, 568 : 23
my s. natural fashion, 164 : 5
natural s. affecting, 371 : 18
no vice so s., 199 : 25
ordinary therefore terrible, 602 : 10
plain and s. faith, 216 : 30
race, 430 : 7
rails upon yon s. thief, 235 : 2
sensuous and passionate, 281 : 20
short and s. annals, 362 : 2
Simon, 930 : 13
sufficeth them the s. plan, 426 : 7
the s. are near to virtue, 69 : 4
to give subtilty to the s., 23 : 1
too s. to admire it, 487 : 18
truth his utmost skill, 250 : 14
truth miscalled simplicity, 244 : 25
Simple-minded, judges naïf s., 644 : 16
modes of discrimination, 776 : 11
Simpler, better and s. people, 669 : 14
Simples, compounded of many s., 212 : 18
Simplest note that swells gale, 362 : 20
Simplicitas, O sancta s., 148 : *n* 5
Simplicity, ancient s. is gone, 312 : 24
and charm, 106 : 19
complete s., 808 : 18
deceitful mistress, 635 : 19
embrace s., 64 : 8
in s. a child, 305 : *n* 2
in s. sublime, 533 : 3

Simplicity (*continued*)
in wit man s. child, 336 : 9
independence magnanimity, 559 : 9
makes s. a grace, 255 : 18
makes uneducated effective, 88 : 15
mine is unadorned s., 113 : 3
no greatness where no s., 602 : 6
no hindrance to subtlety, 637 : 8
no longer misled, 391 : 1
O holy s., 148 : 12
of three percents, 394 : 1
old s. of times, 920 : 15
pity my s., 350 : 13
simple truth miscalled s., 244 : 25
Spartan s., 925 : 4
treats with s. or severity, 586 : 16
Simplification first step to mastery of subject, 755 : 10
Simplify, art should s., 739 : 3
simplify, 559 : 26
Simply, want to speak s., 850 : 5
Simulacrum, sun the dark s. of God, 275 : 13
Simulate, no disguise can s. love, 293 : 10
Sin, Adam's sons conceived in s., 259 : 9
against Holy Ghost, 637 : 12, 659 : 1
against s., 736 : 21
and blot, 646 : 5
be ye angry and s. not, 49 : 36
before polygamy made a s., 303 : 17
blossoms of my s., 219 : 24
born of a little S., 822 : 20
by that s. fell the angels, 249 : 7
choose one s., 555 : 8
cunning s. cover itself, 209 : 30
darling s., 435 : 17
depravity and original s., 569 : 16
draw s. with cart rope, 29 : 6
dreadful record of s., 689 : 6
feared no danger knew no s., 305 : 14
fight with death and s., 536 : 3
folly noise and s., 542 : 4
fools make a mock at s., 23 : 35
go and s. no more, 45 : 3
good man's s., 360 : *n* 2
guilty of dust and s., 269 : 9
has many tools, 519 : 9
he that is without s., 45 : 2
herein hate virtue s., 149 : 5
his favorite s., 440 : 15
hold it half a s., 531 : 20
human sympathy for s., 503 : 2
hypocrite falls into s., 128 : 18
I impute to frustrate ghost, 543 : 15
if old and merry be s., 204 : 6
ignorance not innocence but s., 545 : 21
in private not sin, 297 : 22
in s. did my mother conceive me, 19 : 14
in this be free from s., 480 : 1
learned s. to fly, 320 : 8
much of madness more of s., 526 : 4
my s. is red, 315 : 3
neatness a duty not s., 346 : 11
no s. but ignorance, 183 : 11
no s. except stupidity, 674 : 21
no s. to labor in vocation, 203 : 3
not only as s. but bore, 461 : 18
nothing emboldens s. as mercy, 243 : 4
of Judah, 32 : 10
only deadly s. cynicism, 724 : 1

Sin (*continued*)
original s., 581 : 10
original s. of man, 323 : 28
physicists have known s., 861 : 6
plate s. with gold, 235 : 3
pleasure's a s., 460 : 18
poverty is no s., 270 : 17
private s. not so prejudicial, 170 : 21
pure in life free from s., 107 : 11
recognized keep us humble, 856 : 18
sedentary life s., 659 : 1
shall be no more, 552 : 22
sickness s. death, 583 : 4
some rise by s., 228 : 1
sure your s. will find you out, 11 : 7
taketh away s. of world, 44 : 23
that I s. not with my tongue, 18 : 29
their conception, 262 : 7
'tis s. nay profanation, 266 : 20
to covet honor, 208 : 9
to prefer life to honor, 122 : 14
usura s. against nature, 793 : 1
wages of s. is death, 47 : 5
waive quantum o' the s., 409 : 12
was too much hope, 256 : 3
weeps incessantly for my s., 406 : 1
what is unpardonable s., 503 : 4
whatever obscures soul, 727 : 9
where s. abounded, 47 : 2
who tell us love can die, 440 : 4
without s., without guilt, 4 : 9
worst s. passion can commit, 827 : 22
worst s. to fellow creatures, 680 : 14
ye do by two and two, 708 : 18
Sinai, Wilson write Notes from S., 783 : 5
Sinais, we S. climb, 567 : 11
Sincere flattery, 378 : 10
friend person with whom s., 497 : 18
his soul s., 362 : 18
if his words are s., 68 : 4
let thy life be s., 35 : 6
love is s., 148 : 20
men always s., 718 : 14
not s. even when saying not s., 705 : 10
of soul s., 336 : 5
officious innocent s., 356 : 24
prayer soul's s. desire, 429 : 18
pretenses which are s., 706 : 2
think beforehand that words be s., 89 : 15
work give reality to illusion, 757 : 9
Sincerely from author's soul, 830 : 8
Sincerest, our s. laughter, 468 : 14
Sincérité, changent de s., 718 : *n* 3
Sincerities, men change s., 718 : 14
Sincerity, hold faithfulness and s., 68 : 5
panics touchstone of s., 384 : 14
shield of s., 744 : 11
tell young men with great s., 353 : 7
to practice s., 69 : 19
way of heaven, 89 : 12
wrought in sad s., 493 : 18
Sinecure, gives no man a s., 792 : 17
Sinew, money the s. of love, 99 : *n* 8
Sinews abolished will, 892 : 7
coin is s. of war, 157 : 10
cracks s. cakes brain, 570 : 13
exercises s. with toil, 89 : 25
money s. of war, 99 : 11
of peace, 746 : 10
of soul, 277 : 4

Sinews (*continued*)
of virtue, 271 : 4
stiffen s. summon blood, 207 : 16
wealth the s. of affairs, 92 : 6
what are s. of philosopher, 121 : 13
Sinewy, we the youthful s. races, 575 : 15
Sinful, center of my s. earth, 246 : 4
desires of the flesh, 56 : 4
games, 630 : 13
greedy the s. and lewd, 834 : 5
Sing, a little time to s., 614 : *n* 3
all a green willow, 232 : 8
ancient ways, 712 : 3
and build the lofty rhyme, 280 : 7
and louder sing, 715 : 1
another song, 614 : 13
arms and the man I s., 104 : 15, 306 : 11
at her flowery work doth s., 278 : 25
awake and s., 30 : 10
Bah to you, 628 : 10
because I must, 532 : 1
bid soul of Orpheus s., 278 : 22
bow themselves when he did s., 248 : 29
by land and sea, 708 : 24
cannot s. old songs, 603 : 16
caused the widow's heart to s., 16 : 16
celebrate myself s. myself, 574 : 11
charmingly sweet you s., 550 : 8
dance and drink and s., 405 : 6
do not think they s. to me, 803 : 19
eagle suffers little birds to s., 188 : 21
elected silence s. to me, 655 : 18
for Horse nation, 928 : 12
Grecian woes goddess s., 334 : 18
hark the herald angels s., 350 : 15
hear angels s., 537 : 16
hear lady s. in Welsh, 204 : 18
heaven and nature s., 328 : 13
heavenly s., 429 : *n* 1
heigh-ho says Rowley, 929 : 12
Hey to you, 628 : 10
holy sages once did s., 277 : 6
I can't s., 616 : 15
I s. as bird sings, 395 : 1
I s. of brooks, 265 : 17
I s. on one breath, 759 : 3
I s. with mortal voice, 286 : 28
I will s. unto the Lord, 9 : 32
in a hempen string, 260 : 15
in my brain I s. it, 544 : 2
let others s. of knights, 182 : 6
lhude s. cuccu, 916 : 14
Lhude s. Goddamm, 792 : 8
lift every voice and s., 733 : 5
like birds i' the cage, 235 : 12
Long live king, 376 : 16
loss of all I s., 906 : 9
louder around, 403 : 4
me your song O, 629 : 21
mouse lizard grasshopper s. together, 637 : 15
myself, 574 : 11
nightingale came to s., 505 : 7
no birds s., 478 : 10
no sad songs for me, 608 : 13
of a maiden, 917 : 3
of days that are gone, 636 : 9
of everything and anything, 781 : 12
of Olaf glad and big, 829 : 8
of thee I s., 514 : 12
of thee I s. baby, 836 : 3

Sing (*continued*)
of you i s., 828 : 17
one of the songs of Zion, 22 : 15
or cease to sing, 339 : 29
our sorrowful song, 860 : 13
pair nor build nor s., 436 : 9
pipe as linnets s., 532 : 1
praises to his Name, 918 : 19
pretty birds do s., 250 : 8
riding's a joy, 542 : 15
saddest when I s., 616 : *n* 3, 616 : 15
saints sweetly s., 314 : 21
savageness out of a bear, 231 : 24
set upon bough to s., 715 : 3
sit and hear me s., 402 : 13
so we'll live pray s., 235 : 12
so wildly well, 525 : 10
song of cheer again, 824 : 13
song of ocean seemed to s., 428 : *n* 5
song of sixpence, 931 : 9
songs not heard before, 107 : 25
still wouldst thou s., 476 : 28
strange that death should s., 202 : 16
swanlike s. and die, 461 : 9
the Lord's song, 22 : 15
thee a song in thy praise, 410 : 13
thee to thy rest, 225 : 3
tongue of the dumb shall s., 30 : 24
tongue the Savior's glory, 139 : 9
unto him a new song, 18 : 19
unto the Lord a new song, 21 : 1
we must laugh and s., 716 : 3
we'll s. another song, 614 : 13
what shall I s., 934 : 5
whatever well made, 717 : 22
when birds do s., 212 : 33
willow willow willow, 232 : 8
wrath of Achilles, 57 : 3
ye heavens earth reply, 350 : 11
Singe, flame that cannot s. sleeve, 716 : 10
ich s. wie der Vogel singt, 395 : *n* 1
my white head, 233 : 24
so hot that it s. yourself, 248 : 22
Singer accompany the king, 413 : 25
he the s. passes, 601 : 10
idle s. of empty day, 618 : 6
none hear beside the s., 442 : 23
sans wine song s., 516 : 15
song after death of s., 577 : 14
thou s. I song, 628 : 14
Singers, God sent s. on earth, 511 : 13
Singest of summer, 476 : 22
soaring ever s., 468 : 12
Singeth all night long, 217 : 26
quiet tune, 435 : 1
Singing and making melody, 49 : 37
as they shine, 325 : 10
come before his presence with s., 21 : 3
come with s. unto Zion, 31 : 9
comes deer to my s., 929 : 2
commercials not allowed, 873 : 1
delight in s., 442 : 23
each morning, 829 : 19
forty s. seamen, 772 : 21
garland and s. robes, 281 : 11
go s. as far as we go, 103 : 21
gold, 787 : 6
hear America s., 574 : 2
hear mermaids s., 252 : 1
heard the mermaids s., 803 : 19
heart like s. bird, 608 : 11
hollaing and s. of anthems, 206 : 2
Singing (*continued*)
in the choir, 919 : 21
in the wilderness, 516 : 7
locust of soul, 900 : 3
masons building roofs, 207 : 7
more s. less sighing, 739 : 8
of Mount Abora, 433 : 26
out of empty cisterns, 805 : 12
perhaps s. bird come, 132 : 25
sad or s. weather, 633 : 11
sets even a wise man s., 60 : 18
solitary s. in the West, 574 : 4
songs of expectation, 616 : 8
still dost soar, 468 : 12
those who are s. today, 627 : 5
till his heaven fills, 600 : 25
time of the s. of birds, 28 : 7
we are nest of s. birds, 353 : 21
where nightingales s., 813 : 7
where weeping willows, 599 : 5
with muses of Helicon begin s., 61 : 6
woodthrush s. through fog, 806 : 8
your s. is the thing, 667 : 7
Singist, as s. not success, 616 : 15
Single, beauty draws with s. hair, 334 : 3
best augury is to fight, 58 : 14
blessedness, 195 : 21
dram of heaven, 607 : 17
draw you with s. hair, 259 : *n* 8
eternity only a s. night, 83 : 13
every s. one is right, 708 : 21
existence is illusion, 887 : 14
for my s. self, 215 : 4
from s. crime know nation, 104 : 33
hound, 606 : 8
man in possession of fortune, 440 : 16
married to s. life, 292 : 11
must begin with a s. step, 65 : 1
nature's double name, 225 : 30
no s. nation have monopoly, 787 : 15
no such creature as s. individual, 883 : 14
not a s. kind of strife, 61 : 12
nothing in world s., 467 : 24
secret will be man, 830 : 2
soul in two bodies, 87 : 1
spies, 223 : 25
thinning list of s. men, 835 : 6
Single-minded like migratory birds, 756 : 8
Sings a solitary song, 424 : 20
at grave-making, 224 : 7
below inveterate scars, 807 : 4
each song twice, 541 : 17
for his supper, 930 : 15
he that s. lasting song, 717 : 2
in boat on bay, 530 : 19
know why caged bird s., 736 : 23
lark at heaven's gate s., 243 : 16
like an angel s., 201 : 1
morn not waking till she s., 176 : 1
nightingale s. all day, 447 : 12
nightly s. the staring owl, 191 : 14
on orchard bough, 541 : 16
this truth poet s., 529 : 20
thus s. he Cuckoo, 191 : 13
tune without the words, 604 : 17
yonder pine that s., 92 : 12
Singulars, statements of history are s., 88 : 18
Sinister resonance, 683 : *n* 3
spring-laden breeze s., 728 : 13
urge to kill s., 912 : 9
Sinit, enforce rules iv S., 722 : 21
Sink downward to darkness, 767 : 4
dropped thing s., 798 : 13
heart and voice oppressed, 563 : 13
her in Indian seas, 558 : 10
hold you as I s., 112 : 27
I'd die down over feet, 778 : 6
load would s. a navy, 249 : 5
Neptune s. ship on even keel, 114 : 28
not gross to s. but light, 189 : 8
of uncertainty and error, 300 : 11
or swim, 203 : 13
or swim live or die, 450 : 9
or swim together, 730 : 16
present repute for freedom, 567 : 17
pride of power s., 372 : 15
raft which will never s., 407 : 16
to nothingness do s., 478 : 19
tosses but doesn't s., 134 : 2
who s. to rest, 364 : 8
Sinking in thy last long sleep, 394 : 3
into inferiority, 449 : 10
kind of alacrity in s., 225 : 23
knowledge like s. star, 529 : 10
rats desert s. ship, 117 : *n* 2
someone s. today, 670 : 7
Sinks and I am ready to depart, 443 : 1
daystar in ocean bed, 281 : 4
gross flesh s. downward, 195 : 19
honor s., 368 : 16
if my bark s., 562 : 9
whoever raises great stones, 849 : 16
with bubbling groan, 458 : 26
Sinn, das kommt mir nicht aus dem S., 481 : *n* 7
Sinned against my brother the ass, 139 : 1
in Adam's fall s., 320 : 4
more s. against than sinning, 217 :
we have s. against thee, 32 : 7
Sinner, dead s. revised and edited, 647 : 17
desireth not death of s., 54 : 15
forgive some s., 772 : 6
merciful to me a s., 43 : 40
of his memory, 247 : 11
too weak to be a s., 242 : 32
whether he be s., 45 : 8
who write with no dinner, 811 : 1
Sinner's last retreat, 892 : 7
Sinners, call s. to repentance, 38 : 28
came to save s., 50 : 24
God and s. reconciled, 350 : 15
if s. entice thee, 23 : 2
in hands of God, 892 : *n* 1
miserable s., 56 : 2
publicans and s., 39 : 7
Son of man betrayed to s., 41 : 14
standeth in the way of s., 17 : 12
we are s. all, 185 : 19
Sinning, more sinned against than s., 217 :
Sin's, sometimes s. a pleasure, 460 : 18
Sins, acknowledge our manifold s., 55 : 17
be all my s. remembered, 221 : 13
charity creates s., 676 : 1
double for all her s., 30 : 30
few love to hear s. they act, 243 : 11
forgiveness of s., 54 : 7
Forgiveness of s., 55 : 2
forgiveth s. and saveth, 34 : 23
her s. which are many, 43 : 4
lie in dark weep for s., 574 : 24

Sins (*continued*)
love covereth all s., 23 : 23
manifold s. and wickedness, 54 : 11
multitude of s., 52 : 14
of commission mortal, 357 : 11
of fathers upon children, 77 : 23
of omission venial, 357 : 11
of whole world, 52 : 21
oldest s. newest ways, 206 : 33
other s. only speak, 148 : *n* 1
queen of all my s., 908 : 9
remembrance of precedent s., 260 : 4
scarlet books read, 730 : 13
shed for remission of s., 41 : 10
snows and s., 632 : 8
takest away s. of the world, 54 : 5
they are inclined to, 291 : 6
they love to act, 243 : 11
though your s. be as scarlet, 28 : 30
two cardinal s., 786 : 6
Sinuous shells of pearly hue, 442 : 16
Sion, never climbed Mount S., 893 : 9
wept when we remembered S., 22 : *n* 5
Sioux owned the world, 610 : 5
Sip, can't be tasted in s., 547 : 24
lifeblood seemed to s., 434 : 22
twitter and feathers sleek, 475 : 2
Sipped no sup, 629 : 22
Sir Oracle, 198 : 2
Sired by hurricane, 623 : 4
Siren, listen to song of s., 383 : 1
song of s. nor voice of hyena, 177 : 17
tears, 245 : 19
Sirens, what song the S. sang, 275 : 5
Sires, heroic s., 311 : 11
Sires' age worse than grandsires', 107 : 30
Sirius, kingly brilliance of S., 640 : 6
Siroccos, felt s. crawl, 605 : 16
Sisera, mother of S. looked out window, 12 : 8
stars fought against S., 12 : 5
Sister Anne do you see, 919 : 21
art my mother and my s., 15 : 39
calls me Will, 666 : 19
Caroline, 733 : 13
Jerusalem thy s. calls, 407 : 7
live a barren s. all your life, 195 : 20
Milky Way s. in whiteness, 770 : 12
ministering angel my s., 224 : 18
never praise s. to s., 707 : 8
no friend like s., 608 : 16
poverty is s. of beggary, 82 : 24
shouts with s., 530 : 19
Sidney's s. Pembroke's mother, 265 : 15
still gentler s. woman, 409 : 21
the whole day long, 548 : *n* 1
Sisterhood is powerful, 915 : 8
Sister's, erring s. shame, 459 : 3
husband's niece, 614 : 7
Sisters, all s. virtuous, 919 : 14
brothers and s. beware, 710 : 14
cousins and aunts, 627 : 13
Death and Night, 576 : 1
depart in peace, 455 : 13
twa s. in bour, 927 : 1
under skins, 709 : 11
wayward s. depart, 455 : 13
weird s., 239 : 15
Sisyphus, believe S. happy, 882 : 6
Sit alone with conscience, 660 : 9
and drink with me, 730 : 3
Sit (*continued*)
and hear me sing, 402 : 13
and play with similes, 426 : 3
beside lonely fire, 597 : 1
bird of night did s., 215 : 12
dickybird why do you s., 629 : 16
doing penance, 489 : 2
down says Love, 269 : 10
here will we s., 201 : 1
in a barn, 932 : 6
in darkness, 42 : 26, 284 : 15
Jessica look, 201 : 1
let us s. upon the ground, 195 : 2
like grandsire in alabaster, 197 : 29
little sorrows s. and weep, 404 : 12
nor s. nor stand but go, 544 : 10
not fit that you s. here longer, 272 : 19
not s. on throne of bayonets, 696 : 2
on a cushion, 931 : 19
on our own bottom, 166 : 9
openly to weather, 785 : 10
right here by me, 786 : 7
shame is ashamed to s., 193 : 10
so I did s. and eat, 269 : 10
such as s. in darkness, 21 : 13
teach us to s. still, 805 : 21
thee down sorrow, 190 : 17
their strength is to s. still, 30 : 17
them that s. in darkness, 42 : 26
thou a patient looker-on, 267 : 18
though I s. down now, 501 : 11
tibi terra levis, 134 : 28
trees where you s., 332 : 12
unable to s. still, 299 : 20, 884 : 3
Sits and smiles on the night, 403 : 12
as one new-risen from dream, 188 : 38
high in people's hearts, 215 : 14
looking over harbor, 761 : 5
on horse at hostess' door, 201 : 15
secret s. in middle, 749 : 9
truth s. on lips of dying, 586 : 7
watching for omens, 82 : 12
wind in that corner, 209 : 17
with keen appetite he s. down, 199 : 5
Sittest throned in glory, 614 : 9
Sitteth in the seat of the scornful, 17 : 12
Sitting, as cheap s. as standing, 323 : 4
by desolate streams, 659 : 9
careless on floor, 477 : 18
equal to a god s. opposite you, 102 : 5
in a pleasant shade, 257 : 6
in catbird seat, 831 : 11
in the sun, 439 : 10
listen where thou art s., 280 : 3
no pity s. in clouds, 193 : 18
remain s. at your table, 786 : 3
still is s., 526 : 19
well in order smite, 529 : 13
Situation excellent I am attacking, 670 : 6
fresh meaning for new s., 780 : 10
inwardness of s., 650 : 16
normal all fouled up, 924 : 21
Six characters in search of author, 723 : 19
days shalt thou labor, 10 : 6, 553 : 17
essentials in painting, 135 : 11
everything left at s. and seven, 144 : *n* 11
feet of land, 602 : 12
honest servingmen, 710 : 2
hours in sleep, 172 : 6
hundred pounds a year, 339 : 10
Six (*continued*)
impossible things before breakfast, 613 : 14
of one half-dozen other, 465 : 16
or seven dozen Scots, 203 : 26
Richmonds in the field, 187 : 32
rode the s. hundred, 533 : 9
sette world on s. and sevene, 144 : 26
snowed for s. days and s. nights, 887 : 5
weeks to frost, 816 : 14
Sixes, things go at s. and sevens, 144 : *n* 11
Sixpence, found crooked s., 932 : 18
I give thee s., 422 : 1
in her shoe, 262 : 15, 924 : 6
not a s. sir, 416 : *n* 6
song of s., 931 : 9
Sixteen hours ago Hiroshima, 787 : 13
Sixth of population slaves, 558 : 2
Sixty minutes an hour, 842 : 10
Sixtyfold, brought forth fruit s., 39 : 15
Size, near sight of mere s. of him, 778 : 6
no virtue with s., 494 : 20
not grandeur, 596 : 4
not s. but spirit, 820 : 13
silkworm s. or immense, 799 : 14
take s. of pots of ale, 290 : 21
those of largest s., 613 : 8
Skating, in s. safety is speed, 497 : 23
Skeleton, ague of s., 804 : 22
found s. and clothed it, 365 : *n* 5
Skeptic, too much knowledge for s., 337 : 2
Skepticism highest of duties, 595 : 10
luxury of s., 658 : 11
more clearly understood, 165 : 6
profound s. faborable to conventions, 704 : 8
then s. then disbelief, 571 : 4
wise s. is good critic, 569 : 15
Skeptics' way of speaking, 165 : 5
Sketch ruins of St. Paul's, 488 : 7
Skevar, Ivan Petrofski S., 922 : 16
Skewered with office pens, 549 : 6
Skies above clear again, 824 : 13
and earth a solid mass, 131 : 13
are hanged, 830 : 2
as long as s. are blue, 469 : 7
ashen and sober, 526 : 22
change s. above them, 709 : 7
cloudless climes starry s., 459 : 13
common people of the s., 251 : 1
common sun air s., 362 : 20
distant deeps or s., 405 : 7
faith deciphered in s., 703 : 3
fear can see more in s., 168 : 28
forehead of frowning s., 167 : 8
heifer lowing at s., 477 : 9
islands whose raving s. opened, 673 : 19
join triumph of the s., 350 : 15
ladder to s., 174 : 14
look up at s., 655 : 21
looks commercing with the s., 278 : 13
mansions in the s., 328 : 14
many a message from s., 410 : 15
molded and melted across s., 656 : 6
moon climbest s., 176 : 14
my canopy the s., 336 : 19
not cloudy all day, 927 : 19
parameters of s. and earth, 132 : 12
raised mortal to the s., 306 : 23

Skies (*continued*)
rend the affrighted s., 334 : 10
resume sophistries of June, 604 : 9
rush into the s., 336 : 18
spacious s., 688 : 5
statures touch s., 607 : 2
suns s. clouds of June, 609 : 11
tempt offspring to s., 370 : 7
watcher of the s., 475 : 7
wings across canceled s., 821 : 12
Skill, a little s. in antiquity, 180 : *n* 7
author's s. to give, 702 : 14
force has no place for s., 78 : 12
honor hath no s. in surgery, 205 : 5
man's s. built cities, 97 : 14
nature's artistic s., 125 : 22
nor favor to men of s., 27 : 17
oars plied with little s., 611 : 1
pass days in that where s. greatest, 112 : 21
product of tendencies and training, 752 : 18
sharpens s., 374 : 2
simple truth his utmost s., 250 : 14
'tis God gives s., 564 : 21
to conceal skill, 293 : 29
to him that can get it, 302 : 15
Skilled in works of both languages, 108 : 1
orator a good man s. in speaking, 95 : 14
poet through natural gift, 71 : 24
Skillful, all s. in the wars, 299 : 10
be s. in speech, 3 : 12
man a different integration, 837 : 9
more s. in self-knowledge, 427 : 23
Skillfulest arithmetician, 562 : 8
Skillfully, play s. with a loud noise, 18 : 19
Skim, in airy rings s. heath, 334 : 16
milk masquerades, 627 : 16
Skimble-skamble stuff, 204 : 16
Skin, after my s. worms destroy, 16 : 4
beauty's but s. deep, 250 : 2
because my s. is red, 610 : 5
calf's s. on recreant limbs, 201 : 21
can the Ethiopian change his s., 32 : 6
chameleon's tuning s., 899 : 6
color loves and s., 252 : 5
come into world with thick s., 482 : 4
come off with whole s., 168 : 27
deep, 250 : *n* 1
for skin, 15 : 5
free from judging by color of s., 904 : 16
item with s. wrapped around, 828 : 3
like dusk on horizon, 831 : 13
man who sold hyena s., 746 : 4
Negro's s. prima facie evidence, 554 : 6
no matter color of s., 824 : 10
not judged by color of s., 909 : 10
of innocent lamb parchment, 185 : 25
patch lion's s. with fox's, 119 : 24
rip off s., 923 : *n* 5
skull beneath the s., 804 : 21
snake throws enameled s., 196 : 18
squeeze orange throw away s., 343 : 6
take s. from arm, 806 : 21
white as leprosy, 434 : 19
with the s. of my teeth, 16 : 2
worth not related to color of s., 900 : 15
Skinny, fear thy s. hand, 434 : 25
Skins not colored like your own, 556 : 6
sisters under s., 709 : 11
Skinside is inside, 733 : 16
Skipped, mountains s. like rams, 21 : 21
Skipper had taken daughter, 510 : 4
Skirmish of wit, 208 : 24
Skirt, sound of her silk s., 97 : 10
Skirts, God's s., 540 : 31
Skittish, unstaid and s. in motions, 213 : 29
Skittles, beer and s., 546 : *n* 2, 590 : 10
porter and s., 546 : 27
Skoal to the Northland, 510 : 3
Skugg, here S. lies, 348 : 5
Skull beneath the skin, 804 : 21
of a lawyer, 224 : 10
place of s., 41 : 24
some poor fellow's s., 439 : 12
Skulls, hell paved with priests' s., 128 : 23
leaden they don't weep, 841 : 12
place of s., 457 : 13
Sky, above the vaulted s., 470 : 9
above world stretched the s., 822 : 12
admitted to that equal s., 336 : 17
against pearl-gray s., 778 : 10
all the milky s., 712 : 7
allowing rejection to obliterate s., 858 : 11
and sea and land, 692 : 11
anybody as s. low or high, 752 : 13
banners flout the s., 235 : 23
beautiful as the s., 576 : 1
believe power and goodness in s., 151 : 5
believe these ships from s., 151 : 5
bird is in the s., 300 : 19
blue ethereal s., 325 : 8
blue s. bends over all, 434 : 2
blue s. of spring, 594 : 3
blue s. over my head, 445 : 12
bluebird carries s., 557 : 10
brain wider than s., 605 : 21
bridal of earth and s., 268 : 15
bright reversion in s., 335 : 8
buffalo under copper s., 789 : 7
change she earth or s., 918 : 15
changes when wives, 212 : 25
clean s., 806 : 21
daffodil s., 533 : 21
daily bread of eyes, 495 : 24
descending black and white, 892 : 9
dusky night rides down s., 349 : 10
eagle looking at s., 478 : 7
earth and all stars in s., 574 : 7
equal s., 336 : 17
ethereal s., 283 : 4
fair weather for s. is red, 39 : 33
flash of color beneath s., 676 : *n* 5
flows into house, 843 : 5
forehead of morning s., 281 : 4
go forth under open s., 471 : 3
goal the s., 924 : 16
guides through s. thy flight, 471 : 7
immeasurably lofty, 602 : 1
inverted bowl we call s., 517 : 3
isolation of s., 767 : 4
like lead, 868 : 21
lingered under benign s., 562 : 7
living air and blue s., 423 : 13
lonely sea and s., 760 : 14
lonesome place against s., 671 : 3
Sky (*continued*)
lord believing Christians from s., 151 : 2
lose itself in s., 544 : 5
lyre within s., 525 : 10
measure pathways of s., 105 : 24
membrane of bright blue s., 884 : 1
moving moon went up s., 434 : 27
music shall untune s., 305 : 13
no bright reversion in s., 335 : 8
no foreign s. protected me, 801 : 14
no limits but s., 168 : 22
nothing but hath bound in s., 188 : 1
nothing but s. and the ocean, 435 : 18
November's s., 430 : 13
nurlsing of the s., 468 : 10
of adults over kids, 911 : 20
of slate, 711 : 11
old and true as s., 709 : 4
only one shining in s., 424 : 12, 773 : 14
only regret leaving the s., 142 : 23
our Father the S., 928 : 13
peopling earth waters s., 311 : 12
pie in s., 764 : 13
pilgrim of the s., 429 : 8
prisoners call the s., 676 : 6
publish yourselves to s., 651 : 8
pulling blanket off eastern s., 928 : 9
rain from dirty s., 896 : 4
rainbow in the s., 425 : 7
ring out to wild s., 532 : 21
robes spun of Iris' woof, 279 : 8
sea rising nor s. clouding, 654 : 15
sent him down the s., 591 : 9
shoulder s. drink ale, 691 : 20
showcase of spurs, 841 : 14
silence in starry s., 428 : 7
sings about the s., 461 : 13
snow sheets out s., 552 : 20
somewhere s. touches Earth, 925 : 23
soul larger than s., 480 : 12
sparkling with diamonds, 695 : 7
split the s. in two, 822 : 12
spread out against s., 803 : 9
squired glacier woman down s., 843 : 20
stand at Judgment Seat, 707 : 16
star that burns forever in s., 929 : 6
stars look cold about s., 748 : *n* 2
steal across the s., 616 : 7
storm roaming s., 878 : 4
sweep cobwebs from s., 932 : 5
take love together to s., 646 : 11
tears of s., 342 : 17
teatray in the s., 611 : 20
tree cannot grow in s., 101 : 1
under wide and starry s., 668 : 20
wanderer in her s., 822 : 10
went out under s. Muse, 673 : 11
western s. in night, 576 : 2
what a scowl, 545 : 25
what if s. were to fall, 96 : 11
while s. and sea stand, 692 : 11
wide s. above me, 839 : 19
will cave in on him, 822 : 12
wrote across s. in stars, 810 : 2
Skye, over sea to S., 688 : 12
Skyey, servile to s. influences, 228 : 15
Sky-hawk pecking at flag, 571 : 9
Sky-pointing tree, 587 : 11
Sky's the limit, 168 : *n* 14
whatever s. above me, 460 : 4
Skyscrapers, send s. toppling, 875 : 9

Slack, observing me grow s., 269 : 9
Slain a thousand men with jawbone, 12 : 17
all whom war hath s., 254 : 9
brothers sons kindred s., 338 : *n* 8
by fair cruel maid, 214 : 4
crippled palsied s., 752 : 4
death ere thou s. another, 265 : 15
Earl of Murray, 927 : 6
from graves of our s., 484 : 1
frosts are s., 632 : 8
her own eyes see him s., 618 : 4
honor those they have s., 582 : 9
if s. thinks he is s., 56 : 25
Jabberwock, 612 : 18
more come through alive than are s., 58 : 24
my will, 875 : 1
Saul hath s. his thousands, 13 : 4
some s. in war, 195 : 2
think he is slain, 495 : 11
thrice he slew the s., 306 : 17
through our love is my lord s., 149 : 17
where s. are there is she, 17 : 1
with him beauty s., 189 : 14
wounded but not s., 926 : *n* 7
Slam, set doors ajar and s. them, 751 : 7
Slamming, lulled by s. of iron, 873 : 12
Slander, do not repeat s., 3 : 9
enemy to s. you, 625 : 16
give lie to s., 455 : 12
lives upon succession, 188 : 8
protest discrimination and s., 753 : 7
that gradually soaks into mind, 69 : 1
vindication against s., 523 : 9
whose edge sharper than sword, 243 : 21
Slanderous, death by s. tongues, 210 : 10
Slant, certain s. of light, 604 : 18
Slanting, Greek accent s. wrong, 560 : 21
Slanting-eyed, lame wrinkled and s., 58 : 11
Slashed, she s. him, 933 : 16
Slaughter, as an ox goeth to the s., 23 : 16
as lamb to the s., 31 : 17
like sheep to s., 379 : 6
love of s., 792 : 14
pillage devastation, 745 : 2
threatenings and s., 46 : 4
through s. to throne, 362 : 11
Slaughtered, blood of s., 733 : 6
saints, 282 : 18
this s. age, 879 : 7
Slaughterhouse Five, 901 : *n* 2
Slaughtering, as well as war and s., 404 : 22
Slaughters of race writ, 641 : 19
Slave, be no s. have no s., 521 : 1
before I'd be a s., 936 : 4
believing s. better than idolater 130 : 12
commonly called s. trade, 346 : 9
deserves to be a s., 418 : 14
fingering s., 424 : 15
freeman s. patrician plebeian, 563 : 3
frees her s. again, 919 : 19
galley s. to pen, 484 : 11
God commands s. to rise, 418 : 4
half s. half free, 520 : 4
I am a czar a s., 387 : 5
Slave (*continued*)
I speak for the s., 560 : 24
in some degree a s., 379 : 12
man in armor s., 545 : 16
man once despot and s., 467 : 9
no s. on our land, 513 : 3
not be s. not be master, 520 : 6
not like quarry s., 471 : 6
of words, 472 : 24
passion's s., 222 : 6
prison only house in s. state, 558 : 6
prisoner but not s., 296 : *n* 2
rogue and peasant s., 221 : 6
save Union without freeing s., 522 : 6
sleep soundly as wretched s., 208 : 7
spirit below, 794 : 12
think ye meant for s., 461 : 7
this s. country, 486 : 16
thought the s. of life, 205 : 10
to animosity or affection, 379 : 12
to fate, 254 : 12
to no sect, 337 : 16
to thousands, 230 : 33
trade, 346 : 9
what to s. your Fourth of July, 556 : 5
you were a Christian s., 663 : 13
Slaveholder, interfere by force with s., 560 : 23
violent death of s., 560 : 23
Slaveholders, men and women of North s., 577 : 16
Slavekeeping inconsistent, 364 : 7
Slaveowners, men and women of South s., 577 : 16
sons of former s., 909 : 9
Slavery, advocates of s. push it, 520 : 4
but one aspect of problem, 800 : 9
chains and s., 383 : 5, 411 : 15
children given into s., 152 : 15
children sold into s., 482 : 17
continually shocked by s., 560 : 23
economic s. nobody's business, 779 : 16
elections end s. begins, 381 : 10
every tone testimony against s., 556 : 3
great fortune great s., 115 : 7
hear anyone arguing for s., 524 : 8
ignorance only s., 615 : 12
intellectuals deserve s., 764 : 2
love freedom hate s., 881 : 13
mechanical s., 675 : 25
of half of humanity, 870 : 12
of the machine, 675 : 25
opponents of s. arrest spread, 520 : 4
or death, 325 : 17
price of chains and s., 383 : 5
they can have anywhere, 373 : 5
when s. comes upon him, 60 : 23
where s. is liberty cannot be, 539 : 2
wrecks of s., 631 : 19
writing instrument of s., 364 : 7
wrong and demoralizing, 675 : 25
Slavery's, hatred s. aftermath, 672 : 5
Slave's, death is s. freedom, 915 : 18
Slaves, all persons held as s., 522 : 8
Americans freemen or s., 379 : 2
at the mill with s., 288 : 19
Britons never will be s., 345 : 19
cannot breathe in England, 376 : 20
civilization requires s., 675 : 25
creed of s., 412 : 4
fit instruments to make s., 350 : 17
Slaves (*continued*)
fought for freedom, 490 : 18
howe'er contented, 375 : 19
if any should be s., 524 : 8
land of s. ne'er mine, 461 : 9
lies religion of s., 725 : 6
machines s. not masters, 689 : 27
man wills us s., 385 : 14
masters ans the s., 848 : 3
necessity the creed of s., 412 : 4
of defunct economist, 783 : 16
of the lamp, 610 : 11
our new mechanized s., 832 : 1
save Union by freeing s., 522 : 6
sixth of population s., 558 : 2
songs of s. testimony, 556 : 3
sons of former s., 909 : 9
tired of ruling over s., 358 : 5
to do ugly horrible work, 675 : 25
tyrants and s., 369 : 25
who fear to speak, 567 : 3
Slavish, emancipation of s. part of mankind, 380 : 8
imitators you s. herd, 109 : 13
mercenary, 379 : 1
Slavs, Chuds S. and Krivchians, 136 : 2
Slay, reject prophets s. them, 582 : 9
though he s. me yet will I trust, 15 : 32
Slayer, if s. thinks he slays, 56 : 25
red s., 495 : 11
Slayeth child in womb, 793 : 2
envy s. the silly, 15 : 14
Slays, envy s. itself by own arrows, 132 : 21
if slayer thinks he s., 56 : 25
moves mates s., 516 : 22
slayer think he s., 495 : 11
war its thousands s., 378 : 4
war never s. bad man, 75 : 8
Sleave, raveled s. of care, 237 : 21
Sledge drops in vain, 873 : 3
Sleek as laughing flesh, 899 : 16
fat and s. a true hog, 109 : 3
Sleek-headed men, 215 : 8
Sleekit, wee s. cow'rin', 408 : 12
Sleep a wink, 339 : 5
abundance will not suffer him to s., 27 : 1
after toil, 173 : 12
among lonely hills, 428 : 7
an act or two, 249 : 19
an after-dinner's s., 228 : 16
and a forgetting, 426 : 14
and feed, 223 : 17
and if life was bitter, 634 : 13
as they sleep even so, 633 : 7
ask not whom s. beside, 690 : 19
at ten, 492 : 6
azure-lidded s., 476 : 18
balmy s., 330 : 4
be in bed and s. not, 835 : 13
beneath these weeds, 728 : 7
big s., 803 : 5
blessings on him who invented s., 171 : 1
brother of d., 58 : 20
brother to death, 182 : 4
by a s. to say we end, 221 : 12
cannot break his s., 516 : 11
care driveth away s., 36 : 2
care-charmer s., 182 : 4
centuries of stony s., 714 : 13
cheap pleasure, 171 : 1

Sleep (*continued*)
Church s. and feed at once, 804 : 20
councilor ought not s. whole night, 57 : 15
covers man like cloak, 171 : 1
cup that brings s. of Lethe, 106 : 24
curtained s., 237 : 14
death an eternal s., 415 : 17
Death and brother S., 466 : 6
death is a s., 633 : 8
death like s. steal, 466 : 15
Death's brother S., 105 : 17
death's counterfeit, 238 : 6
death's twin brother, 58 : *n* 3
deep and dreamless s., 619 : 16
dewy-feathered s., 278 : 25
do I wake or s., 477 : 3
downy s., 238 : 6
even in our s. pain, 71 : 5
exposition of s. upon me, 197 : 6
first sweet s. of night, 468 : 1
flowers as in causes s., 271 : 19
folding of the hands to s., 23 : 12
freed from everlasting s., 275 : 14
friend of woe, 440 : 5
full of sweet dreams, 475 : 16
fullness even of s., 58 : 16
gates of S., 105 : 26
gentle s., 206 : 17
give us s. serenity, 849 : 13
Glamis hath murdered s., 237 : 22
go home and get s., 727 : 2
God bless man who invented s., 171 : *n* 1
great gift of s., 663 : 12
he giveth his beloved s., 22 : 9
Homer may s., 110 : *n* 1
hour's s. before midnight, 270 : 19
how s. the brave, 364 : 8
I always s. upon ale, 329 : 7
I s. alone, 63 : 8
I will not give s. to mine eyes, 22 : 13
ignominy s. with thee, 205 : 12
in Abraham's bosom, 187 : 17
in dull cold marble, 249 : 6
in exile, 673 : 19
in s. a king, 245 : 2
in soot I s., 403 : 9
in the night, 404 : 5
in the shade, 446 : 7
in thy s. little sorrows, 404 : 12
innocent s., 237 : 21
invented s., 556 : 2
is a death, 274 : 23
is drink to thirsty, 171 : 1
is meat to hungry, 171 : 1
it is a gentle thing, 434 : 30
itself must end, 275 : 14
kind assassin S., 900 : 12
lay me down in peace and s., 17 : 16
lay me down to s., 320 : 12
Lord God caused a deep s., 7 : 2
Macbeth does murder s., 237 : 21
Macbeth shall s. no more, 237 : 22
man who invented s., 556 : 2
medicine thee to sweet s., 231 : 8
men such as s. o' nights, 215 : 8
miles to go before s., 748 : 7
most gentle s., 206 : *n* 2
most things s. lying, 268 : 20
mountains in primeval s., 592 : 6
murder in s. not pugnacity, 786 : 8
Nature's soft nurse, 206 : 17
neither night nor day, 236 : 2

Sleep (*continued*)
neither slumber nor s., 22 : 4
nevermore to s. again, 740 : 6
nice quiet s., 727 : 2
no more, 237 : 21
no s. till morn, 457 : 15
nor shall this peace s. with her, 249 : 17
not dream not, 561 : 21
not hypocrites in s., 445 : 18
not my design to s., 273 : 1
nothing s. in that cellar, 873 : 6
O magic s., 475 : 18
of a laboring man, 27 : 1
of death, 221 : 12
of Lethe, 106 : 24
of perpetual night, 101 : 18
of reason produces monsters, 394 : 2
old and gray full of s., 712 : 8
on my love in thy cold bed, 267 : 6
one ever-during night, 250 : 3
one short s. past, 254 : 13
only s., 541 : 21
opium so they can s., 706 : 6
out the thought of it, 246 : 23
out this great gap, 240 : 20
past first s. in Persia, 275 : 14
perchance to dream, 221 : 12
primeval s., 592 : 6
purr to s. with thunder, 623 : 5
quiet s. when trick's over, 760 : 16
rocked to s. between billows, 570 : 7
rounded with a s., 248 : 13
rude forefathers s., 361 : 23
sets fool and wise even, 171 : 1
shake off this downy s., 238 : 6
shall our gratitude s., 421 : 22
shall we s. after all, 633 : 6
silence rushed me to s., 911 : 8
sinking in thy last long s., 394 : 3
six hours in s., 172 : 6
sleep beauty bright, 404 : 12
sleeping wake and waking s., 165 : 9
sleepless to give readers s., 340 : 16
snow said s., 811 : 17
soft smiling, 875 : 12
softly eagle forgotten, 765 : 3
some must watch some s., 222 : 17
son of sable Night, 182 : 4
sooner over sooner to s., 566 : 10
soundly as wretched slave, 208 : 7
spirited from s., 899 : 12
strong man after s., 282 : 3
sun is laid to s., 255 : 12
sword s. in my hand, 406 : 21
task done we must s., 241 : 18
that knits up raveled sleave, 237 : 21
that knows not breaking, 431 : 8
that masters all, 73 : 13
the brother of death, 58 : 20
the sleep of death, 407 : 7
they are as a s., 20 : 11
they s. and it is lifted, 467 : 6
time enough to s., 690 : 18
time for s., 60 : 10
timely dew of s., 285 : 26
to die to s., 221 : 12
to s. perchance to dream, 221 : 12
to wake, 546 : 7
turned aside to s., 252 : 17
two gates of s., 105 : 26
under bridges beg and steal, 655 : 14
unseasonable immoderate s., 353 : 4
upon golden bed, 716 : 19

Sleep (*continued*)
visit soul in s., 466 : 10
voices that make me s. again, 248 : 10
wake to s., 873 : 21
waked after long s., 248 : 10
was airy light, 286 : 12
we shall not all s., 49 : 7
weary of everything but s., 633 : 20
weighs like unwilling s., 478 : 7
well-spent day happy s., 152 : 4
what hath night to do with s., 279 : 12
why wilt thou s., 407 : 7
will never lie, 192 : 21
with golden Aphrodite, 60 : 6
with Turks and infidels, 195 : 9
without wink of s., 168 : 19
ye harlots s. at ease, 334 : 24
yet a little s., 23 : 12
Sleeper, primitives not waken s., 673 : 3
soul of s. away, 673 : 3
Sleepers in that quiet earth, 562 : 7
numb nudgers, 873 : 11
Sleepers', seven s. den, 251 : 14
Sleepeth, not dead but s., 38 : 31
peradventure he s., 14 : 2
Sleepin' there below, 700 : 9
Sleepiness, took swim to keep off s., 623 : 22
Sleeping, all all s. on hill, 728 : 3
among new-mown hay, 571 : 7
and the dead as pictures, 237 : 23
at last, 608 : 20
candle burning while s., 258 : 2
dogs lie, 549 : 5
he find you s., 42 : 14
is a wool blanket, 82 : 21
mourn upon thy bed, 633 : 17
one nightwalking one, 902 : 7
some s. killed, 195 : 2
think lion s. because he didn't roar, 412 : 8
Thy servant s., 597 : 16
tree growing when ye're s., 431 : 28
try by s. what it is to die, 274 : 23
wake and waking sleep, 165 : 9
wakened us from s., 797 : 2
woods all night, 435 : 1
Sleepless Eremite, 478 : 20
soul that perished, 425 : 10
to give readers sleep, 340 : 16
vigilance, 523 : 1
watches of night, 512 : 21
Sleeps, after life's fever s., 238 : 19
creation s., 330 : 6
Goethe in Weimar s., 585 : 2
great engine never s., 539 : 15
happy warrior s., 427 : *n* 2
in continual noise, 631 : 17
moonlight s. upon this bank, 201 : 1
now s. crimson petal, 531 : 11
on watch, 372 : 7
remorse s., 359 : 3
there s. Titania, 196 : 18
thinks and wills, 705 : 12
till tired he s., 337 : 7
where Drake s. in sea, 569 : 20
while my little one s., 530 : 25
Sleepy and proud, 810 : 19
I am s. and weeds twist, 572 : 7
Sleepyhead, to bed says S., 931 : 6
Sleet, iron s., 363 : 10
Sleeve, ash on old man's s., 808 : 11
flame that cannot singe s., 716 : 10

Sleeve (*continued*)
laughing in your s., 398 : 9
laughing up her s., 297 : 18
raveled s. of care, 237 : 21
wear heart upon my s., 229 : 17
Sleeveless errand, 159 : 16
some shortless others, 340 : 21
Sleeves, fluttering empty s., 767 : 15
Sleigh, carry the s., 490 : 20
Sleighbells, ghost of s., 747 : 14
Sleight, tricks by s. of hand, 324 : 13
Slender, as cedar tall and s., 394 : 6
debt to Nature, 267 : 15
thy s. stem, 409 : 9
waist confined, 276 : 5
Slenderly, fashioned so s., 485 : 21
Slept azure-lidded sleep, 476 : 18
dreamed life beauty, 555 : 23
George Washington s. here, 813 : 6
I should have s., 15 : 8
in peace, 249 : 11
law not dead though it s., 228 : 8
one wink, 243 : 22
Passion s., 351 : 12
resembled my father as he s., 237 : 19
touched him and he s., 532 : 17
while companions s., 511 : 23
Slew, as ambitious I s. him, 216 : 15
dead which he s. at his death, 12 : 21
Death s. not him, 174 : 14
enemy nearly s. ye, 921 : 1
on tree they s. Him, 651 : 12
thrice he s. the slain, 306 : 17
Slice, no matter how thin s., 741 : 10
Slices of quince, 550 : 10
Slide into lover's head, 424 : 11
Kelly slide, 923 : 4
let world s., 158 : 17
no foot shall s., 924 : 15
Sliding from lifted oar, 873 : 16
Slight little light little, 629 : 19
nor Fame I s., 332 : 13
not what's near, 76 : 14
Slightest, rememberest not s. folly, 210 : 33
Slightly shakes parting guest, 226 : 19
Slime, daubed with s. and pitch, 9 : 8
in grains of State, 864 : 5
Slimy things did crawl with legs, 434 : 16
Sling, my s. the s. of David, 672 : 15
prevailed with a s. and with a stone, 13 : 3
Slinging, fury s. flame, 532 : 6
Slings and arrows of fortune, 221 : 12
Slinks out of race, 282 : 1
Slip away before they're up, 778 : 6
given them the s., 319 : 12
giving enemies s., 359 : 22
let it s. useless away, 474 : 16
let s. dogs of war, 216 : 12
'twixt cup and lip, 259 : *n* 4
Slipped, thrice it s. through my hands, 60 : 8
Slippered, lean and s. pantaloon, 211 : 15
Slippers, same old s., 693 : 1
shuffle about in s., 706 : 19
Slippery, he that stands on s. place, 202 : 3
words s. thought viscous, 635 : 20
Slippy-sloppy, water s. in larder, 719 : 5
Slips, greyhounds in s., 207 : 18
seizes two things one s., 926 : 1
Slit, tongue be s., 929 : 22
Slithy toves, 612 : 17
Slits the thin-spun life, 280 : 15
Sliver and disbranch, 234 : 23
Slop over, 616 : 14
staineth s., 792 : 8
Slope through darkness to God, 532 : 12
Slopes, gently s. the way, 370 : 3
Sloping to southern side, 568 : 24
Sloppy Joe's, 868 : 18
Sloth and cowardice that clings, 742 : 12
assemblage of s. sleep and littleness, 381 : 13
egotism s. idleness, 452 : 2
finds down pillow hard, 243 : 23
peaceful s., 284 : 13
Slothful ease, 687 : 4
man saith, 25 : 19
Slouches toward Bethlehem, 714 : 13
Slough was Despond, 301 : 22
Slovenliness is no part of religion, 346 : 11
Slovenly unhandsome corpse, 203 : 8
wilderness, 767 : 7
Slow, a God s. to anger, 14 : 31
and moving finger, 232 : 3
and silent stream Lethe, 284 : 22
and steady wins, 66 : 3
as tardy as too s., 193 : 1
be s. to speak s. to wrath, 51 : 30
but sure, 270 : 14
but sure moves might, 77 : 8
cold and to temptation s., 245 : 4
come he s., 430 : 16
confidence plant of s. growth, 350 : 18
drag of days, 76 : 5
drag the s. barge, 377 : 26
drags its s. length along, 333 : 8
drip over stones, 873 : 12
free to go very s., 750 : 12
he that is s. to anger, 24 : 8
heart is s. to learn, 823 : 7
how s. shadow creeps, 730 : 1
I am s. of speech, 9 : 15
I am s. of study, 196 : 6
in assembling, 80 : 16
learn to read s., 300 : 16
man catches up with swift, 60 : 5
march of human mind s., 373 : 2
Meander's margent green, 279 : 18
melancholy s., 368 : 13
northern thought s. durable, 542 : 20
of a s. tongue, 9 : 15
on the leash, 792 : 6
progress in economic world s., 652 : 1
punt swings round, 585 : 21
rises worth, 351 : 9
silent walk, 642 : 2
sort of country, 612 : 21
spondee stalks, 436 : 3
sun climbs s. how slowly, 564 : 17
swift s. sweet sour, 656 : 5
talk low talk s., 870 : 7
tarry awhile says S., 931 : 6
tremulous cadence s., 587 : 14
unreckoning hearts, 900 : 2
vaster than empires and more s., 296 : 27
walk it s. where you go, 912 : 15
wisely and s., 192 : 22
Slow-breathing unconscious Kosmos, 651 : 3
Slowest, haste of fool s. thing, 313 : 20
Slowly, art appreciated only s., 740 : 14
Slowly (*continued*)
ever forward but s., 386 : 14
follies of town crept s., 371 : 2
lowing herd wind s., 361 : 20
mills of God grind s., 273 : 14
night pass more s., 464 : 15
rase she up, 926 : 22
run s. horses of night, 113 : 6, 184 : *n* 4
silently now moon, 739 : 13
spring comes s., 433 : 29
sun climbs slow how s., 564 : 17
twist s. in wind, 904 : 2
Slug-a-bed, sweet s., 266 : 19
Sluggard, go to the ant thou s., 23 : 11
no room for s., 745 : 11
voice of the s., 328 : 9
Sluggardy, May wol have no s. anyght, 146 : 16
Slughorn to my lips I set, 234 : *n* 3
Slugs leave their lair, 436 : 9
Sluice, every s. of knowledge opened, 380 : 10
Slumber, death is s., 466 : 10
did my spirit seal, 424 : 14
he that keepeth thee will not s., 22 : 4
honey-heavy dew of s., 215 : 22
I must s. again, 328 : 9
kindly earth s., 530 : 2
lie still and s., 328 : 8
love itself s. on, 469 : 18
more sweet than toil, 528 : 20
neither s. nor sleep, 22 : 4
nor s. nor a roof, 823 : 13
ports of s. open, 206 : 29
seal sense in s., 739 : 17
to mine eyelids, 22 : 13
to soothing s. seven, 172 : *n* 3
where s. abbots, 340 : 26
yet a little s., 23 : 12
Slumbered, you have but s. here, 197 : 23
Slumberers, tossing like s. in beds, 571 : 3
Slumbering in open air, 436 : 9
might half s., 475 : 12
rouse the s. morn, 277 : 23
scepter o'er s. world, 330 : 5
thoughts, 275 : 14
Slumber's chain bound me, 447 : 7
Slumbers, fire extinguished often s., 275 : 26
how imagine unquiet s., 562 : 7
pleasing dreams s. light, 431 : 4
soul dead that s., 509 : 13
sweet s. of virtuous, 326 : 4
what s. in background, 412 : 14
Sly, tough and devilish s., 548 : 16
Smack and tang of elemental things, 671 : 2
my life s. sweet, 545 : 22
of age in you, 205 : 24
Small, air thoroughly s. and dry, 805 : 21
all things how s. soever, 307 : 12
and could not hope, 869 : 1
and great beasts, 21 : 11
buoy too s. for sight, 234 : 28
but sullen horn, 364 : 12
cabin build there, 712 : 4
candle light a thousand, 265 : 13
cannot reach the s., 174 : 2
choice in rotten apples, 188 : 26
chronicle s. beer, 230 : 12

Small (*continued*)
compare great things with s., 103 : 7, 285 : 1
country with few people, 65 : 9
creatures great and s., 561 : 8
daily task beat labors of Hercules, 555 : 10
day of s. nations past, 627 : 6
day of s. things, 33 : 31
felony to drink s. beer, 185 : 23
frizzled stale and s., 892 : 19
gnats mourn, 477 : 19
God s. as I, 300 : 18
graceful the s. before danger, 874 : 9
gray coffeepot, 793 : 15
great matter or s., 35 : 7
grind exceeding s., 273 : 14
have plodders won, 190 : 12
home where s. experience grows, 188 : 27
hot bird, 666 : 15
house and large garden, 295 : 4
how s. of all hearts endure, 352 : 21
in s. proportions beauties see, 256 : 20
is beautiful, 879 : 16
is it so s. a thing, 585 : 11
Latin and less Greek, 256 : 13
make my s. elves coats, 196 : 19
man may not be entrusted, 69 : 16
manye s. maken a greet, 148 : 9
men afraid of writings, 378 : 10
mice and such s. deer, 234 : 10
mighty things from s. beginnings grow, 303 : 4
model of barren earth, 195 : 2
my house though s., 270 : 2
no great no s., 336 : 22
nobody has such s. hands, 829 : 13
one a strong nation, 31 : 24
out of s. beginnings, 265 : 13
potatoes, 603 : 12
questionable superfluity s. beer, 185 : *n* 6
rain down can rain, 917 : 10
rights of s. nations, 682 : 13
rock holds back great wave, 59 : 23
service is true service, 429 : 11
showers last long, 194 : 12
speaks s. like a woman, 225 : 6
still s. voice, 14 : 5
still s. voice of gratitude, 363 : 13
sweet courtesies of life, 360 : 24
sweet s. clumsy feet, 829 : 7
thing analogy of great things, 100 : 16
things and silence, 881 : 7
things both great and s., 435 : 11
things make base men proud, 185 : 21
vices do appear, 235 : 3
whale swims minnow-s, 794 : 13
Smaller and dryer than will, 805 : 21
fleas that on him prey, 322 : 21
made s. with art, 840 : 4
Smallest orb like angel sings, 201 : 1
star of s. magnitude, 285 : 3
Small-knowing, unlettered s. soul, 190 : 15
Smallness of the mind, 115 : 19
Smart, girls that are so s., 331 : 5
little craft, 629 : 19
shall s. for it, 23 : 24
some will s. for it, 210 : 6
Smarts so little as fool, 338 : 8
Smash, why s. the chairs, 518 : 2
Smashed up things, 835 : 7
Smattering of everything, 546 : 9
Smell, ancient and fishlike s., 247 : 29
and taste of things, 733 : 17
begin to s. a rat, 169 : 32
blood of British man, 234 : 13
blood of Englishman, 934 : 4
dew and rain, 269 : 5
far worse than weeds, 245 : 6
fire whose gown burns, 269 : 18
lilies that fester s. worse, 245 : 6
lost sea s., 806 : 6
of burning fills air, 729 : 16
of old clothes, 796 : 16
of the lamp, 90 : 12, 730 : 15
rose by any name s. as sweet, 192 : 6
stop and s. flowers, 821 : 4
sweet and blossom in dust, 272 : 13
sweet keen s., 601 : 23
yes to s. pork, 198 : 18
Smellest so sweet, 232 : 5
Smelleth the battle afar off, 16 : 38
Smelling of the lamp, 730 : 15
Smells, gas s. awful, 827 : 12
he s. April and May, 225 : 20
heaven's breath s. wooingly, 236 : 21
like gangrene, 757 : 6
not of itself but thee, 256 : 9
to heaven, 222 : 25
Smelt heaviest ore of body, 790 : 14
Smile, affliction s. again, 190 : 17
and be a villain, 220 : 1
and get work to do, 856 : 17
as I do now, 519 : 19
at claims of descent, 528 : 10
better last s., 321 : *n* 3
calm thou mayst s., 394 : 3
did he s. work to see, 405 : 8
disdainful s., 362 : 2
dwells longer, 739 : 7
faithless as a s., 804 : 11
forget and s., 608 : 15
gleam of her own dying s., 469 : 3
horror unbend and s. at us, 775 : 3
if we meet we shall s., 217 : 9
in her eye, 482 : 9
jest to Oberon make him s., 196 : 12
kind of sickly s., 630 : 14
laugh bur s. no more, 526 : 2
loving s. surely hail, 612 : 15
make the learned s., 333 : 5
of deceit, 406 : 5
of love, 406 : 5
of smiles, 406 : 5
on Casey's face, 704 : 15
on lips tear in eye, 430 : 20
on the Mona Lisa, 820 : 4
once more turn thy wheel, 233 : 16
one vast substantial s., 548 : 8
riding on s. and shoeshine, 888 : 3
sea shows false alluring s., 100 : 18
share the good man's s., 370 : 9
sidelong pickerel s., 873 : 17
smile smile, 770 : 14
social s., 361 : 18
sweet s. at his father, 102 : 7
there is s. of love, 406 : 5
thrust close your s., 902 : 16
to those who hate, 460 : 4
too wicked for a s., 435 : 21
upon fingers' ends, 207 : 13
vain tribute of a s., 430 : 7
vehicle for ambiguities, 571 : 12
we would aspire to, 249 : 3
when only dead could s., 801 : 16
Smile (*continued*)
when you call me that s., 696 : 7
where my Julia's lips s., 266 : 3
world seems to s. upon me, 309 : 21
Smiled, all around thee s., 394 : 3
all sat back and s., 695 : 14
at the dame, 404 : 11
God s. again, 733 : 11
he never s. again, 470 : 22
kind of sickly smile, 630 : 14
of darkness till it s., 279 : 19
Spain's chivalry away, 461 : 26
Smiler with knyf, 146 : 24
Smiles, all s. stopped together, 540 : 24
and languished air, 402 : 14
and soap, 614 : 4
as if he mocked himself, 215 : 10
down from height at me, 866 : 18
dying lives and unborn s., 880 : 4
eternal s., 339 : 1
full of s. in early days, 85 : 6
he s. it is a malady, 101 : 24
in which two s. meet, 406 : 5
kindling s. in ladies' eyes, 486 : 3
Peace crowned with s., 299 : 10
quiet-colored evening s., 542 : 3
same flower that s. today, 266 : 11
seldom he s., 215 : 10
sits and s. on the night, 403 : 12
sweet strains pensive s., 493 : 16
tears of boyhood's years, 447 : 7
the robbed that s., 230 : 1
there is a smile of s., 406 : 5
welcome ever s., 226 : 19
wreathed s., 277 : 19
Smilest and art still, 584 : 9
Smiling and beautiful countryside, 689 : 6
at grief, 214 : 5
at the good mouth, 792 : 16
damned villain, 220 : 1
destructive man, 317 : 15
from world's snare, 241 : 15
gently s. jaws, 611 : 5
hides s. face, 375 : 17
in my face, 237 : 5
I've seen the s., 359 : 10
not s. back is earthquake, 888 : 3
scatter plenty o'er s. land, 362 : 10
sleep soft s., 875 : 12
the boy fell dead, 540 : 21
through tears, 58 : 5
Smirk, serious and the s., 547 : 9
Smite all the firstborn, 9 : 25
baseness we will s., 728 : 14
God shall s. thee, 46 : 27
once and smite no more, 280 : 22
sounding furrows, 529 : 13
the sun shall not s. thee, 22 : 4
thee on thy right cheek, 37 : 10
without hands to s., 632 : 9
Smiteth so that he die, 10 : 9
Smith mighty man, 510 : 7
Smithsonian, to found S. Institution, 417 : 1
Smithy of soul, 777 : 18
village s. stands, 510 : 7
Smitten, illness with which s., 486 : 6
with our own feathers, 66 : *n* 10
Smock, cast shame when cast off s., 147 : 12
Smoke and stir of this dim spot, 279 : 3
consume own s., 473 : 31, 664 : 18
days are consumed like s., 21 : 4

Smoke (*continued*)
days gone up in s., 693 : 14
gets in your eyes, 740 : 13
good cigar is a s., 707 : 6
good strong incense s., 541 : 20
herbs to drink s. thereof, 150 : 17
no fire without s., 160 : 33
noise crowds beloved s., 441 : 9
ruach means s., 679 : 5
thin s. without flame, 642 : 2
w'at do wid de s., 662 : 15
Smoke-filled room, 695 : 11
Smokes, wretcheder one s. more, 617 : 1
Smokestack, salt-caked s., 760 : 20
Smoking flax shall he not quench, 31 : 4
Smoky, populous and s. city, 468 : 2
Smooth as monumental alabaster, 232 : 13
away trouble, 796 : 16
billows s. and bright, 613 : 1
block s. and well fitting, 792 : 20
chose him five s. stones, 13 : 2
easy inoffensive down to Hell, 92 : *n* 5
large and s. and round, 439 : 11
road is s., 61 : 17
road of life, 360 : 24
runs water where brook deep, 172 : *n* 7
sea being s., 225 : 36
the ice, 202 : 5
till it is hushed and s., 475 : 18
true love never did run s., 195 : 22
Smoothed his wrinkled front, 186 : 30
Smoother, finding s. pebble, 313 : 17
her mouth is s. than oil, 23 : 10
words were s. than butter, 19 : 22
Smoothest, stream s. water deepest, 172 : *n* 7
Smooth-faced gentleman Commodity, 201 : 19
Smoothing the raven down, 279 : 19
Smooth-lipped, convolutions of s., shell, 428 : 15
Smoothly, my task is s. done, 280 : 4
Smoothness, temperance may give it s., 221 : 23
turns s. rough, 544 : 10
Smooths hair with automatic hand, 805 : 8
oil s. what is rough, 116 : 5
Smooth-shaven, dry s. green, 278 : 18
Smote him thus, 232 : 21
him under the fifth rib, 13 : 12
Jael s. the nail into his temples, 12 : 2
'Omer s. bloomin' lyre, 708 : 24
them hip and thigh, 12 : 16
Smother up his beauty, 203 : 5
Smothered, I should die there s., 790 : 8
Smothery, cramped up and s., 624 : 1
Snafu 924 : 21
Snail, creeping like s. to school, 211 : 15
glister me forward, 873 : 12
questing S., 875 : 4
turn not pale beloved s., 612 : 9
went to kill s., 931 : 7
which has lost shell, 314 : 2
whiting to a s., 612 : 7
Snail's on the thorn, 540 : 15
Snails, like s. leave faint thread, 912 : 1
pretty feet like s., 266 : 13
snips and s., 932 : 12
Snake came to water trough, 790 : 12
eagle or s., 708 : 22

Snake (*continued*)
earth like s. renew, 468 : 17
in the grass, 103 : 12
like a wounded s., 333 : 8
stood up for evil, 747 : 21
throws enameled skin, 196 : 18
toad edible to s., 647 : 11
we have scotched the s., 238 : 18
Snakes eat frogs, 767 : 8
gliding up hollow, 495 : 21
hogs eat s., 767 : 8
no s. to be met with, 356 : 1
spotted s. with double tongue, 196 : 21
strangled s. beside Hercules, 595 : 7
Snakeskin titles of claims, 840 : 2
Snap like vixens at truth, 794 : 7
Snapper-up of unconsidered trifles, 246 : 22
Snaps, vow s. itself, 534 : 19
Snare of the fowler, 20 : 16
rabbit in a s., 781 : 10
trial by jury a s., 445 : 20
world's great s., 241 : 15
Snares, heart is s. and nets, 27 : 10
riches are ready s., 150 : 1
traps gins pitfalls, 539 : *n* 2
Snark was a Boojum, 614 : 5
Snarled and yelping seas, 804 : 16
Snarling, silver s. trumpets, 476 : 9
Snatch a fearful joy, 361 : 9
me away not to return, 747 : 16
Snatched, purse most resolutely s., 202 : 25
scepter s. with unruly hand, 202 : 3
spear but left shield, 399 : *n* 7
Snatches, ballads songs s., 629 : 4
Snatching victuals from table, 743 : 15
Snaw, locks are like the s., 410 : 7
Sneaked, General Shays has s. off, 407 : 14
Sneaking, valor is s. off, 398 : 18
Sneer at me for leaning, 517 : 8
of cold command, 466 : 12
sapping creed with s., 458 : 1
who can refute a s., 390 : 9
without sneering teach to s., 338 : 14
Sneered, Mighty Merchant s., 605 : 20
Sneering, born s., 629 : 5
without s. teach to sneer, 338 : 14
Sneezed, not to be s. at, 415 : 8
Sneezes, beat him when he s., 611 : 15
Snicker, eternal Footman s., 803 : 16
Snicker-snack, blade went s., 612 : 18
Snickersnee, I drew my s., 629 : 14
Sniff, let me s. sea breeze, 569 : 20
Sniffed baited fingers, 907 : 23
Sniffs round the mass as dog, 653 : 13
Snips and snails, 932 : 12
Snob admires mean things, 539 : 11
Snobbish, camels are s., 799 : 16
Snobs, majority of English s., 681 : 2
Snodgrass, murmured Mr. S., 546 : 12
Snore, weariness s. upon flint, 243 : 23
Snorted we in seven sleepers' den, 251 : 14
Snout, jewel of gold in a swine's s., 23 : 25
Snow, a little s. starting to fall, 885 : 13
arrives the s., 493 : 21
bells across the s., 532 : 22
birds sit brooding in s., 191 : 15
black evening white s., 770 : 15
buck in the s., 823 : 9
came both mist and s., 434 : 10

Snow (*continued*)
chaste as unsunned s., 243 : 17
cherry hung with s., 690 : 17
diadem of s., 460 : 6
dripping s. on grass, 810 : 19
dust of s., 748 : 3
face oncoming s., 874 : 20
fallen s. on s., 608 : 17
falling faintly through universe, 777 : 16
falling s. silent, 759 : 10
farewell s. of ferne yere, 145 : 5
fleece white as s., 463 : 1
frolic architecture of s., 493 : 23
frost from purest s., 242 : 23
geese like s. cloud, 810 : 19
general over Ireland, 777 : 16
ghost of s., 747 : 14
had begun in gloaming, 568 : 15
hide hills of s., 229 : *n* 1
I shall be whiter than s., 19 : 15
if s. be white, 246 : 1
lay round about, 563 : 11
like s. falls in river, 411 : 8
like s. in May, 269 : 3
like s. on desert's face, 516 : 9
locks are like s., 410 : 7
melted like s., 459 : 16
melting s. like teardrops, 801 : 18
mockery king of s., 195 : 14
monuments carved from s., 800 : 10
moonshine an' s., 568 : 4
no s. is there, 59 : 26
nor does s. come near it, 59 : 27
not s. nor rain nor heat, 78 : 19
pure as s., 221 : 17
raiment white as s., 41 : 29
rain s. hail and drought, 622 : 19
rosebuds filled with s., 250 : 6
said peace cold sleep, 811 : 17
she is near under s., 674 : 14
shuts out sky, 552 : 20
sins shall be white as s., 28 : 30
something crabwise across s., 904 : 4
step softly under s., 742 : 15
stood shivering in s., 182 : 2
swept world end to end, 817 : 2
swooned as he heard s., 777 : 16
try s. of heaven, 830 : 18
wallow naked in December s., 194 : 7
we shall have s., 932 : 6
white and drifted s., 490 : 20
white as driven s., 246 : 29
wish s. in May's mirth, 190 : 13
woods fill with s., 748 : 5
world vast screen of s., 811 : 17
wrapped in clouds and s., 457 : 22
year rich year, 269 : 17
Snow-broth, man whose blood is s., 227 : 28
Snowed for six days and six nights, 887 : 5
it s. of mete amd drynke, 146 : 3
whole world over, 817 : 2
Snowflake in avalanche, 876 : 4
not a s. escapes fashioning hand, 557 : 15
Snowflakes, words like winter s., 57 : 25
Snows and sins, 632 : 8
birds leaves s., 864 : 2
of the year 1941, 912 : 7
where are s. of yesteryear, 150 : 7
where s. of yesteryear, 601 : 16
Snow-star, earth-star and s. 557 : 16

Snowstorms, inspector of s., 557 : 7
Snow-white, little s. feet, 711 : 22
Snowy, seraphs swing s. hats, 604 : 15
summits old in story, 530 : 26
Snub, hard to s. beautiful woman, 746 : 18
Snuff approach of tyranny, 372 : 20
let me s. sea breeze, 569 : 20
shifted his trumpet took s., 371 : 21
Snuffbox, fill his s., 319 : 20
Snuffed out by article, 461 : 24
Snug as bug in rug, 348 : 5
little farm the world, 440 : 13
little island, 429 : 15
So and no otherwise, 710 : 8
can any man, 204 : 12
if it was s. it might be, 612 : 24
if she be not s. to me, 264 : 23
it has been, 823 : 12
much for him, 217 : 30
runs world away, 222 : 17
Soakers, old s., 309 : 23
Soaking in comfortable baths, 834 : 8
Soap and education deadly, 622 : 2
invisible s., 485 : 13
smiles and s., 614 : 4
what no s., 364 : 5
Soar, angels alone that s. above, 296 : 4
but never roam, 429 : 9
flitter dip and s., 899 : 15
in action s. as high, 557 : 20
into air above dunes, 835 : 1
not too high to fall, 262 : 18
run though not s., 487 : 15
singing still dost s., 468 : 12
Soaring ever singest, 468 : 12
in high reason of fancies, 281 : 11
Soars, if he s. with own wings, 404 : 2
no bird s. too high, 404 : 2
Sob as you spin, 868 : 20
heavy world, 868 : 20
on the saxophones, 761 : 11
Sober as a hymn, 663 : 7
as a judge, 349 : 8
be s. be vigilant, 52 : 16
certainty of waking bliss, 279 : 20
creeping thing in s. way, 562 : 8
healthful and with his wits, 294 : 15
in s. livery clad, 285 : 24
men at whiles s., 691 : 21
plain in dress s. in diet, 341 : 2
skies ashen and s., 526 : 22
steadfast and demure, 278 : 12
studious days, 334 : 25
take s. coloring from eye, 426 : 23
to bed go s., 260 : 14
Soberly, entered into s., 56 : 6
Soberness, speak truth and s., 46 : 34
Sobers, drinking s. again, 332 : 20
Sobriety a species of courage, 308 : 15
justice peace and s., 273 : 11
property stimulus to s., 758 : 1
something said for s., 884 : 13
Sobs of violins of autumn, 659 : 12
with s. and tears sorted out, 613 : 8
Sociability law of nature, 651 : 7
Sociable ez baskit er kittens, 662 : 7
no comfort to one not s., 243 : 25
Social and family relationship, 689 : 23
armor, 778 : 11
Capitalism creates s. unrest, 785 : 4
conscience of nation, 909 : 16
friendly honest man, 409 : 2
imbalance reflects itself, 871 : 13
Social (*continued*)
in things s. separate yet one in progress, 681 : 24
jewel in crown of S. Republic, 638 : 8
laws which advance s. justice, 871 : 13
less arbitrary s. fabric, 853 : 15
lived in s. intercourse, 354 : 25
man is a s. animal, 308 : 20
mirage of s. justice, 844 : 9
nature's s. union, 408 : 13
order and thirsty aspiration, 875 : 9
our s. arrangements unsatisfactory, 813 : 15
overthrow of s. conditions, 563 : 10
progress a checking of cosmic process, 596 : 10
progress of each country, 774 : 6
prosperity, 491 : 25
self-love and s. be made the same, 418 : 9
self-love and s. the same, 338 : 4
smile, 361 : 18
state natural to man, 508 : 20
Statics, 644 : 10
struggle not reduced, 790 : 1
world work of man. 324 : 2
Socialism, concern for unfortunate not s., 879 : 2
democracy and s. have word equality, 506 : 12
in authoritarian terms, 834 : 7
inherent virtue of s., 746 : 16
Marxian s. portent to historians, 783 : 7
means to end, 814 : 6
present fascist features, 785 : 7
what I mean by s., 618 : 10
Socialist competition, 766 : 8
culture to thrive, 826 : 12
democracy may be sham, 785 : 6
Socializing, conversation s. instrument, 784 : 9
Socially invisible, 908 : 5
Societies, two s. one clack one white, 872 : 14
Society, before group enter open s., 915 : 1
build a Great S., 872 : 13
care of poor incumbent on s., 309 : 1
cling together in one s., 423 : 18
communication in free s., 789 : 5
conflicting interests of s., 737 : 4
conspiracy against manhood, 496 : 22
create open s., 901 : 1
democratic s. like ours, 777 : 2
distributes itself, 588 : 13
established s., 859 : 13
evolves not by shouting, 884 : 6
exists for noble actions, 88 : 5
great s. here at home, 813 : 15
great s. on earth, 424 : 6
had s. been well organized, 414 : 18
happiness of s. end of government, 381 : 8
human combination or s., 273 : 11
human s. a great bluffer like weather, 847 : 8
humanizing body of s., 589 : 7
humble members of s., 419 : 3
if free s. cannot help poor it cannot save rich, 890 : 8
in this factitious s., 504 : 14
individual not accountable to s., 508 : 13
Society (*continued*)
individual promotes interest of s., 366 : 4
is a blessing, 384 : 9
is no comfort, 243 : 25
keep happiness in store in s., 763 : 4
make collective provision for needs, 773 : 8
man was formed for s., 365 : 15
my art negation of s., 643 : 7
my glittering bride, 428 : 13
nerves of s., 644 : 7
no arts no letters no s., 264 : 17
no one would talk much in s., 395 : 24
no s. bring kingdom of God, 775 : 4
of neither rich nor poor, 618 : 10
offenders, 629 : 6
one polished horde, 461 : 28
open s., 861 : 7
pillars of s., 599 : 8
principle on which s. not founded, 361 : 1
protection of s., 508 : 12
reduce s. to one level, 537 : 4
revolutionary reconstitution of s., 563 : 3
rich s. productivity and income, 871 : 16
shape economic s., 872 : 1
so riven that moderation gone, 737 : 3
solitude best s., 287 : 15
soul selects her s., 605 : 2
state not a mere s., 88 : 5
such s. as is quiet, 469 : 25
suspicion bane of good s., 384 : 10
taxes what we pay for s., 644 : 8
three chairs for s., 560 : 4
till s. is differently constituted, 414 : 14
to be in s. a bore, 675 : 17
to be out of s. tragedy, 675 : 17
true change in future s., 504 : 11
true founder of civil s., 358 : 9
unable to live in s., 87 : 28
urban s., 814 : 1
vanilla of s., 433 : 1
vast empire of human s., 424 : 8
where none intrudes, 458 : 24
which acts as family, 895 : 15
wholesome for character, 569 : 14
without aristocracy not society, 784 : 8
without objective legal scale, 895 : 25
Society's chief joys, 376 : 3
Sociologists astrologers, 706 : 11
Sociology science with greatest number of methods, 673 : 9
understanding of s., 858 : 8
Sock, Jonson's learned s., 278 : 6
Socket, burn to the s., 428 : 11
Sockets, motionless bronze-lidded s., 801 : 18
Socrates and two great disciples, 703 : 14
corrupts the youth, 83 : 11
dissatisfied, 508 : 19
first to call philosophy down, 98 : 25
is a doer of evil, 83 : 11
not because S. said so, 166 : 2
Plato Aristotle S. secretaries of Nature, 271 : 16
wisest of men, 288 : 15
Sod, beneath s. poet lies, 438 : 9

Sod (*continued*)
builds on watery s., 651 : 9
Ephesian s., 571 : 3
lay s. over me, 927 : 15
roots grass sends in s., 651 : 9
saw His footprint in s., 696 : 11
that was in the s., 604 : 3
to thy requiem a s., 476 : 28
Soda, sermons and s. water, 460 : 23
wash feet in s. water, 805 : 6
water the day after, 460 : 23
Sodom, is there beauty in S., 582 : 1
pitched his tent toward S., 8 : 7
Soeur, Voie Lactée ô s. lumineuse, 770 : *n* 6
Sofa, wheel s. round, 377 : 3
Soft answer turneth away wrath, 24 : 5
as breast of doves, 795 : 2
bastard Latin, 460 : 8
complaining flute, 305 : 12
eyes looked love, 457 : 14
face of a girl, 74 : 23
flutes and s. recorders, 283 : 22
her voice was ever s., 235 : 17
in s. regions born s. men, 78 : 22
look of s. deceit, 404 : 19
Lydian airs, 278 : 6
meek patient humble, 251 : 11
Nature's s. nurse, 206 : 17
own the s. impeachment, 398 : 19
phrase of peace, 229 : 24
rest in s. peace, 256 : 4
shower to leeward, 571 : 8
so s. this morning, 778 : 6
stillness and the night, 201 : 1
summer air, 598 : 6
summer season when s. was sun, 143 : 14
time make s. iron wood, 823 : 14
underbelly of Axis, 746 : 3
voice of intellect s., 678 : 12
what s. incense, 476 : 26
zephyr blows, 363 : 6
Soften rocks or bend oak, 324 : 14
to us our enemies, 669 : 17
Softened, cultivation of taste s. me, 877 : 11
Softening chalk of my bones, 873 : 12
Softer, words were s. than oil, 19 : 22
Softest clothing wooly bright, 403 : 5
music to attending ears, 192 : 17
overcome the hardest, 64 : 15
Softheartedness will ruin him, 313 : 9
Soft-lifted by winnowing wind, 477 : 18
Softly, fair and s. goes far, 144 : *n* 12
go s. all my years, 30 : 28
she was going up, 434 : 27
sleep s. eagle forgotten, 765 : 3
speak s. carry big stick, 687 : 6
step s. under snow, 742 : 15
sweet in Lydian measures, 306 : 19
sweet Thames run s., 174 : 21
sweetly speaking and s. laughing, 63 : 5
tread s. on dreams, 712 : 16
wash again and again, 576 : 1
Softness of indifference, 614 : 11
she for s. formed, 285 : 18
Soft-sigh me home, 873 : 12
Soil, awkward in their s., 873 : 15
belongs to unborn generations, 779 : 2
contact with s., 717 : 14
deserve precious bane, 284 : 1
Soil (*continued*)
difference of s. and climate, 424 : 8
for aesthetic growth, 742 : 3
free s. free men, 922 : 2
good to be born on, 568 : 26
grows on mortal s., 280 : 16
life of significant s., 808 : 9
lilac under s. of New England, 751 : 8
not every s. can bear all, 104 : 2
of man's vanity, 750 : 16
of people's necessities, 698 : 13
of which such men made, 568 : 26
our forces on Philippine s., 771 : 4
red s. and sweet-gum tree, 831 : 15
saving s. and water, 779 : 2
subsistence out of s., 590 : 4
weed that grows in every s., 373 : 5
where first they trod, 470 : 16
win of watery main, 244 : 22
wounded by my s., 849 : 16
Soiled and pure rich and poor, 626 : 16
poor wings so s., 634 : 10
softly wash s. world, 576 : 1
truth impossible to be s., 86 : *n* 7
Soi-même, on laisse un peu de s., 679 : *n* 2
si l'homme a s., 164 : *n* 12
Soir, voice le s. charmant, 581 : *n* 2
Sojers, ack like s., 898 : 10
Sojourner as all my fathers were, 19 : 4
Sojourners, we are s. on planet, 482 : 11
Sojourning, life a battle and s., 124 : 10
Solace, freedom all s. to man gives, 143 : 9
Solar, hub of s. system, 519 : 11
walk or milky way, 336 : 16
Sold cheap what is most dear, 245 : 16
Dickon thy master s., 173 : *n* 8
Esau s. his birthright, 8 : 16
even to cloak I wore, 151 : 11
for endless rue, 690 : 21
for old man's gold, 730 : 18
goodness s. itself, 926 : 3
my father s. me, 403 : 9
pleasing ware is half s., 269 : 13
reputation for song, 517 : 10
righteous for silver, 33 : 19
the many on the few, 829 : 23
virtue now is s., 256 : 7
Soldier, a s. and afeard, 239 : 24
an' sailor too, 709 : 13
as s. for his country, 700 : *n* 1
come back British s., 708 : 8
devotion of patriot s., 617 : 6
first king fortunate s., 343 : 4
French s. carries marshal's baton, 421 : 5
full of strange oaths, 211 : 15
gallant old s., 439 : *n* 3
he would himself have been s., 203 : 11
in full military array, 444 : 14
in s. is flat blasphemy, 228 : 11
no s. in gallant band, 630 : 2
priest s. poet, 581 : 8
red with rust, 666 : 17
relish him more in s., 230 : 13
rest, 431 : 8
stool pigeon when cannot be s., 583 : 8
summer s. sunshine patriot, 384 : 13
tells his wounds, 112 : 20
to be successful s., 791 : 16
toy s. red with rust, 666 : 17
Soldier (*continued*)
vital quality s. can possess, 792 : 1
without cruelty, 591 : 11
Soldier's, ambition s. virtue, 241 : 6
courtier's s. scholar's, 221 : 19
grave best, 462 : 19
history of s. wound, 360 : 3
pole is fallen, 241 : 22
pride touched to quick, 540 : 21
sound of white s. axe, 591 : 4
Soldiers, act like s., 898 : 10
are dreamers, 795 : 14
behave as s. by being s., 645 : 6
believe s. nothing safe, 609 : 1
bore dead bodies by, 203 : 8
by two and by three, 926 : 18
Christian s., 616 : 6
citizens of death's land, 795 : 13
envious of wounded s., 732 : 3
French s. with artilleryman, 602 : 1
grow like savages as s. will, 208 : 17
Ireland gives England s., 601 : 7
morale of s., 771 : 2
of Christ arise, 350 : 14
old s. never die, 771 : 7, 924 : 9
old s. surest, 262 : 1
sailors and airmen, 746 : 7
substance of ten thousand s., 187 : 29
Soldiers', steel my s. hearts, 208 : 8
Soldiery, emperor's drunken s., 716 : 8
licentious s., 373 : 12
Sole arbiter is taste, 527 : 14
crown of head to s., 209 : 20
go it s. alone, 749 : 13
God beside whom is none, 5 : 8
rest for the s. of her foot, 7 : 31
unbusy thing, 436 : 9
Soleil bas taché d'horreurs mystique, 673 : *n* 10
Solemn drifting down river, 623 : 22
fillet, 495 : 6
gorgeous palaces s. temples, 248 : 13
he says with s. air, 408 : 17
one sweetly s. thought, 594 : 6
pride yours, 524 : 4
sapping s. creed, 458 : 1
stillness lay, 537 : 16
suits of s. black, 218 : 2
this her s. bird, 286 : 1
world a s. place, 884 : 17
Solemnities, feasts and high s., 280 : 1
Solemnized their obsequies, 275 : 1
with pomp and parade, 381 : 7
Soles, eats s. offen shoes, 840 : 1
look for me under boot s., 575 : 4
Soliciting, still s. eye, 232 : 30
Solicitious, not s. what men think, 289 : 15
Solid angularity of facts, 496 : 15
earth actual world, 557 : 21
for fluidity, 743 : 12
heaven presents s. hue, 748 : 1
massy hard particles, 313 : 16
nothing s. is its s. self, 768 : 6
pudding empty praise, 340 : 15
safe upon s. rock, 822 : 18
sop of all this s. globe, 226 : 2
this too too s. flesh, 218 : 5
virtue, 231 : 26
Solidarity, family and clan s., 719 : 9
independent of differences, 904 : 18
Solidity, atoms preserved by absolute s., 100 : 9
Solitary and cannot impart it, 353 : 26

Solitary (*continued*)
as oyster, 548 : 4
be not s. be not idle, 260 : 6
convent's s. gloom, 334 : 27
God setteth the s. in families, 19 : 33
how doth the city sit s., 32 : 20
if idle be not s. if s. be not idle, 356 : 13
love all s. places, 467 : 11
men know friendship, 739 : 6
poor nasty brutish, 264 : 17
precedent not conclusive, 444 : 5
quite still and s., 786 : 3
rare are s. woes, 223 : *n* 5
sail that rises, 553 : 2
shriek, 460 : 21
simile that s. shines, 339 : 24
singing in the West, 574 : 4
sings a s. song, 424 : 20
stirred by s. cloud, 313 : 23
thinkers, 616 : 1
took their s. way, 288 : 4
Solitude, acquire everything but character in s., 453 : 10
at depth of human condition, 885 : 17
bliss of s., 427 : 11
companion so feel s. more, 735 : 17
companionable as s., 560 : 3
drives poet to s., 585 : 18
each guardian of other's s., 756 : 11
friend to genius, 498 : 27
grew more obese, 905 : 1
how benign is s., 424 : 3
how sweet is s., 376 : 11
I love tranquil s., 469 : 25
independence of s., 497 : 1
is sweet, 376 : 11
island s. unsponsored, 767 : 4
makes s. calls it peace, 459 : 7
needful to imagination, 569 : 14
not exchange s. for anything, 883 : 5
nurse of souls s., 567 : 5
O S. where are charms, 376 : 13
of his own heart, 506 : 9
one chair for s., 560 : 4
one hundred years of s., 908 : 3
pass through s. and difficulty, 860 : 13
religion experiences in s., 650 : 2
safeguard to mediocrity, 498 : 27
sometimes best society, 287 : 15
soul to s. retires, 516 : 2
sweet retired s., 279 : 22
teach us to die, 458 : 8
unsponsored free, 767 : 4
Solitudes, in love two s. touch, 756 : 6
pierced our s., 494 : 4
Solo game, 752 : 5
Solomon, behold a greater than S., 39 : 12
curtains of S., 28 : 2
Grundy, 932 : 11
in all his glory, 38 : 5
King David and King S., 696 : 3
loved many strange women, 13 : 37
man in thousand S. says, 710 : 19
priests in temple of S., 501 : 9
Proverbs of S., 548 : 18
wisdom of S., 13 : 31
Solomon's glory, 649 : 11
song of songs which is S., 28 : 1
truest of books S., 570 : 16
Solon was under a delusion, 84 : 20
Solution, dissatisfaction with other s., 496 : 1
Solution (*continued*)
for world peace, 771 : 10
of conflict without and within, 723 : 12
of international problems, 854 : 1
part of s. ot of problem, 913 : 5
they would have been a kind of s., 702 : 1
waste elocution on s., 630 : 4
Solutions, convenient s. to doubt or believe everything, 673 : 7
Solvency a matter of temperament, 711 : 6
Solvent, American life powerful s., 703 : 19
Somber, I am the s. one, 514 : 9
Some are born great, 214 : 9
born posthumously, 658 : 25
come to take their ease, 249 : 19
for adventure, 792 : 14
gave white bread, 929 : 19
must watch some sleep, 222 : 17
of you with Pilate, 195 : 13
quick to arm, 792 : 14
said John print it, 301 : 18
say world will end in fire, 748 : 2
talk of Alexander, 922 : 10
that shadows kiss, 199 : 15
to kill cankers, 196 : 19
war with reremice, 196 : 19
will smart for it, 210 : 6
Somebody, how dreary to be s., 604 : 19
may be looking, 772 : 17
necessary to s., 499 : 3
said it couldn't be done, 774 : 3
to hew and hack, 291 : 7
when everyone is s., 630 : 8
Somebody's always throwing bricks, 765 : 4
even I be in S. hand, 640 : 14
pain and wrong, 653 : 15
Someday I must go into that, 749 : 16
inner light shine forth, 397 : *n* 6
to prove our foe, 73 : 14
Someone better be prepared, 748 : 11
find next morning it was s. else, 416 : 5
gently rapping, 526 : 10
had blundered, 533 : 11
is sinking today, 670 : 7
not be something but s., 782 : 8
someone else begat, 749 : 16
somewhere sings, 461 : 13
to love and someone to love you, 692 : 15
we can lean on, 916 : 9
Something about a martini, 855 : 16
amiss or out of place, 873 : 4
attempted something done, 510 : 9
bright and alien, 855 : *n* 3
crabwise across snow, 904 : 4
dead in each of us, 676 : 10
ere the end, 529 : 12
everything good for s., 304 : 22
expect s. for nothing, 671 : 16
fame created s. of nothing, 277 : 3
far more interfused, 423 : 13
for modern stage, 792 : 12
freedom for s., 789 : 5
gaining on you, 867 : 9
good and bad of every land, 555 : 15
have in me s. dangerous, 224 : 21
he prized and is known by, 785 : 9
hidden behind things, 764 : 5
Something (*continued*)
hidden go and find it, 710 : 9
I cannot name, 759 : 13
in her gizzard, 310 : 14
in richness I hate, 794 : 2
in the wind, 188 : 6
in this more than natural, 220 : 30
in us never dies, 410 : 15
know enough of s., 878 : 16
like a star, 749 : 14
lost behind Ranges, 710 : 9
must be left to chance, 408 : 6
nasty in woodshed, 854 : 7
no reasonable man expected, 816 : 1
not be s. but someone, 782 : 8
of Shorter-Catechist, 663 : 8
old something new, 924 : 6
one must be s. to do s., 396 : 4
religion vision of s. beyond, 697 : 9
rich and strange, 247 : 21
rotten in state of Denmark, 219 : 17
soft wild and free, 739 : 5
still I can do s., 590 : 5
tells me but not love, 199 : 21
that doesn't love a wall, 747 : 4
that doth live, 426 : 17
that had greater price than life, 849 : 1
there is s. in a face, 328 : 17
time for a little s., 778 : 13
'tis s. nothing, 230 : 33
to do, 567 : 19
to resent yoke, 517 : 6
too much of this, 222 : 6
very like Him, 564 : 14
want s. for nothing, 681 : 17
what is that s., 849 : 1
would turn up, 501 : 25
wrong something human, 885 : 10
you do s. to me, 820 : 1
Sometime did me seek, 161 : 25
woman a s. thing, 836 : 5
Somewhat, I have s. against thee, 52 : 33
Somewhere ages hence, 747 : 13
beyond the curtain, 716 : 15
east of Suez, 708 : 10
in desolate space, 626 : 21
in favored land, 704 : 16
over the rainbow, 842 : 6
people Freedom light, 817 : 6
set forth for s., 747 : 18
what with all these clouds, 82 : 10
with morning, 761 : 1
Somewheres east of Suez, 708 : 10
Somnambulisms, dreams s. reveries, 571 : 3
Somnambulist of vanished dream, 491 : 17
Son, Absalom my s. my s., 13 : 23
and heir of mongrel bitch, 233 : 13
antichrist denieth Father and S., 52 : 22
as every s. longed to do, 679 : 4
be a man my s., 710 : 18
bring forth a s., 36 : 19
brought forth firstborn s., 42 : 27
crucify S. of God afresh, 51 : 16
David the s. of Jesse, 13 : 25
dear s. of memory, 277 : 13
every wise man's s. doth know, 213 : 22
false as stepdame to s., 226 : 15

Son (*continued*)
Father S. and Holy Ghost, 41 : 30, 311 : 19
foolish s. calamity of father, 24 : 25
foolish s. the heaviness of his mother, 23 : 21
glory be to the S., 54 : 18
greatness in father overwhelms s., 257 : 2
grim Death my s. and foe, 284 : 26
hang us every mother's s., 196 : 7
have his s. respect him, 308 : 1
his only s. myself, 366 : 10
if s. ask bread, 38 : 13
in father's stead, 679 : 4
knew my s. was mortal, 83 : 4
Lord Randal my s., 927 : 8
man is s. of own works, 103 : *n* 5
marry s. when you will, 269 : 20
my beloved S., 36 : 31
of a Pharisee, 46 : 29
of Atreus, 57 : 27
of Bharata, 94 : 9
of first fish ashore, 907 : 17
of God goes forth to war, 452 : 7
of Heaven's eternal king, 277 : 6
of humble laborer, 774 : 9
of Kronos, 57 : 12
of man came eating and drinking, 39 : 7
of man coming in cloud, 44 : 2
of man is betrayed, 41 : 14
of man nowhere to lay head, 38 : 23
of man that thou visitest him, 17 : 17
of man which is a worm, 16 : 11
of Manhattan the s., 574 : 20
of the living God, 39 : 35
of the Middle Border, 695 : 12
of the morning, 29 : 22
of the Sun, 88 : 26
only begotten S., 44 : 34
out of Egypt called my s., 36 : 22
prince subject Father S., 254 : 5
prodigal s., 43 : 26
rather be worm than s. of man, 798 : 3
reverence for his s., 308 : 1
safety for my s. brother shipmates, 151 : 10
seek father who need s., 888 : 8
sighed as lover obeyed as s., 384 : 4
struck father when s. swore, 259 : 21
the carpenter's s., 39 : 20
this is my s. Telemachus, 529 : 11
this my s. was dead, 43 : 28
thou art ever with me, 43 : 29
thou art the S. of God, 39 : 29
till he gets wife, 597 : 14
to her s. she ches, 917 : 3
Tom the piper's s., 931 : 13
unfeathered thing a s., 304 : 2
unto us a s. is given, 29 : 16
virgin shall bear a s., 29 : 13
where one s. only, 735 : 1
wise s. maketh a glad father, 23 : 21
woman behold thy s., 45 : 33
wrath of Peleus' s., 334 : 18
you are young my s., 86 : 3
Song, a god has given the lyre and s., 58 : 17
art and s., 716 : 20
burden of his s., 382 : 7
burden of my s., 917 : 12
dance and Provençal s., 476 : 23

Song (*continued*)
does Africa know s. of me, 789 : 10
echo of mournful s., 518 : 8
fable s. or fleeting shade, 266 : 21
famed in s. famous Athens, 72 : 9
filled thicket with honeyed s., 82 : 5
fishers of s., 685 : 11
from beginning to end, 510 : 25
full lasting is s., 601 : 10
gentlemen singing this s., 540 : 25
give us s. to cheer, 618 : 1
glorious s. of old, 537 : 16
good s. ringing clear, 705 : 2
great s. after death of singer, 577 : 14
had been longer, 930 : 18
hear a little s., 395 : 5
heel on throat of my s., 826 : 19
in England's s. forever, 700 : 10
in thy praise, 410 : 13
Jehovah is my s., 29 : 20
lasting singer passes, 601 : 10
learn sooner than a s., 339 : 26
learn suffering teach in s., 467 : 15
let satire be my s., 456 : 11
let them take it, 713 : 14
listen to s. of siren, 383 : 1
Lord is my strength and s., 9 : 32
made s. a coat, 713 : 14
moralize my s., 173 : 7
nature's message into s., 800 : 10
needless Alexandrine ends s., 333 : 8
never heard in tale or s., 279 : 6
new unhallowed s., 684 : 13
night-walkers' s., 716 : 8
oaten stop or pastoral s., 364 : 11
of a merryman, 629 : 22
of Africa, 789 : 10
of faithful Penelope, 61 : 5
of harvest home, 536 : 2
of night's sweet bird, 469 : 14
of ocean seemed to sing, 428 : *n* 5
of siren nor voice of hyena, 177 : 17
of sixpence, 931 : 9
of songs, 28 : 1
of the shirt, 485 : 17
on the wings of s., 481 : 13
one grand sweet s., 566 : 12
one immortal s., 304 : 4
perhaps it may turn out s., 409 : 11
perhaps self-same s., 477 : 1
pipe s. about a Lamb, 403 : 2
read s. not sermon, 268 : *n* 2
remake a s., 713 : 4
required of us a s., 22 : 15
sea grew civil at her s., 196 : 14
seraphically free, 600 : 26
shall rise to Thee, 452 : 11
sing another s., 614 : 13
sing one s. for old Kentucky home, 598 : 5
sing our sorrowful s., 860 : 13
sing the Lord's s., 22 : 15
sing unto him a new s., 18 : 19
sing unto the Lord a new s., 21 : 1
sings a solitary s., 424 : 20
sings lasting s., 717 : 2
sings s. twice over, 541 : 17
sold reputation for a s., 517 : 10
sounded by Death, 464 : 17
spur me into s., 717 : 13
suck melancholy out of s., 211 : 2
swear to truth of s., 320 : 22
sweetest s. ever heard, 459 : 23
sword sung s. of death, 404 : 15

Song (*continued*)
taught Hesiod beauteous s., 61 : 7
thou singer I s., 628 : 14
till I end my s., 174 : 21
time an endless s., 712 : 11
to sing O, 629 : 21
unlike subject frame s., 342 : 16
urge of a s., 749 : 18
want no sound except s., 857 : 15
what s. the Sirens sang, 275 : 5
when this s. sung and past, 161 : 24
whose note sounded by death, 464 : 17
wind's s. sail's shaking, 760 : 14
wine women and s., 399 : 14
wrote one s., 544 : 2
Songe, la vie apparié a un s., 165 : *n* 5
Songs, all their s. sad, 742 : 4
and I wrote my happy s., 403 : 3
angelic s. swelling, 552 : 22
ballads s. snatches, 629 : 4
because my s. brief, 759 : 3
Book of S. and Sonnets, 225 : 8
cannot sing old s., 603 : 16
composed of tears, 537 : 9
despairing s. loveliest, 537 : 9
folk s. from soul sounds, 831 : 16
forever new, 477 : 8
harsh after s. of Apollo, 191 : 16
his s. were a thousand and five, 13 : 30
I who once played shepherds' s., 104 : 14
laws which ran like drinking s., 81 : 11
leave to sing own s., 704 : 17
make and well endyte, 145 : 16
muse has taught them s., 60 : 7
my s. draw Daphnis home, 103 : 17
no sad s. for me, 608 : 13
of expectation, 616 : 8
of our children's children, 802 : 1
of pleasant glee, 403 : 2
of sadness and mirth, 511 : 13
of slaves testimony, 556 : 3
of Zion, 22 : 15
out of woe, 481 : 6
psalms hymns and spiritual s., 49 : 37
sage daughters of Muses, 72 : 3
sing s. not heard before, 107 : 25
song of s., 28 : 1
spared nothing in my s., 759 : 3
strongest s. yet to be sung, 577 : 13
sweetest s. saddest thought, 468 : 14
without words best, 617 : 2
would you have s. endure, 540 : 12
your gambols your s., 224 : 14
Sonitum ventis concessit, 115 : *n* 12
Sonnet a moment's monument, 601 : 17
it turned to a s., 639 : 20
scorn not the s., 429 : 10
Sonneteer, starved hackney s., 333 : 13
Sonnets, Book of Songs and S., 225 : 8
century of s., 543 : 30
lovers' s. turned psalms, 177 : 9
onlie begetter of insuing s., 243 : *n* 4
prophetic s., 846 : 5
written s. all his life, 460 : 25
Sonorous metal blowing, 283 : 21
Son's son till he gets wife, 597 : 14
Sons acclaim your glorious name, 829 : 5
Adam's s. conceived in sin, 259 : 9
all her s. at play, 585 : 9

Sons (*continued*)
all men Noah's s., 899 : 10
anchors of mother's life, 75 : 18
bears all its s. away, 328 : 12
brothers s. kindred slain, 338 : *n* 8
degenerate s. and daughters, 728 : 5
earth's heedless s., 834 : 11
five s. died gloriously, 524 : 4
forward s. of France, 415 : *n* 1
give them to your s., 931 : 17
guide Arcturus with his s., 16 : 34
happy to be father to many s., 186 : 9
her patient s., 368 : 20
more worthless than sires, 107 : 30
of Atreus, 701 : 10
of Belial, 283 : 19
of dark and bloody ground, 578 : 11
of Edward sleep, 187 : 17
of former slaves, 909 : 9
of God shouted for joy, 16 : 29
of men and angels say, 350 : 11
of the living God, 33 : 7
of the morning, 452 : 5
of the prophet, 922 : 15
of toil, 592 : 6
see s. what things you are, 206 : 30
similar to their fathers, 59 : 18
that my s. may have liberty to study, 381 : 14
things are s. of heaven, 352 : 6
to thy jubilee throng, 465 : 1
what I sowed brother's s. gathering, 854 : 2
who Shem and Shaun s. of, 778 : 5
Soon as once set is our little light, 250 : 3
better three hours too s., 225 : 18
late and s., 427 : 29
little pot and s. hot, 188 : 36
said to eve Be s., 693 : 13
shall thy arm, 377 : 26
Sooner it's over sooner to sleep, 566 : 10
kill man than hawk, 797 : 15
stay awhile end the s., 179 : 17
to all to each s. later, 576 : 4
Soonest, least said s. mended, 169 : *n* 2
Soot, dust and s. of complaints, 664 : 18
in s. I sleep, 403 : 9
Sooth, dream dream this also s., 711 : 21
silly s., 214 : 3
Soothe a savage breast, 324 : 14
cares lift thoughts, 475 : 13
flattery s. ear of death, 362 : 5
or wound heart, 431 : 19
songs s. with their touch, 72 : 3
thine ear, 364 : 11
what charm s. melancholy, 369 : 20
Soothed by unfaltering trust, 471 : 6
soul to pleasures, 306 : 19
Soothing, Irish language for s., 735 : 6
language, 388 : 10
lovely and s. death, 576 : 4
Soothsayer, painter trainer s., 122 : 4
Soothsayers make better living than truthsayers, 386 : 20
Sop, give s. to Cerberus 132 : 22
of all this solid globe, 226 : 2
Sophist, saint nor s. led, 585 : 6
Sophisters, age of s., 373 : 22
Sophisticated modes of discrimination, 776 : 11
three on 's are s., 234 : 7
Sophistries, old old s. of June, 604 : 9
Sophistry, destroy fib or s., 338 : 9
Sophocles drew men as they ought to be, 73 : *n* 10, 75 : *n* 13
long ago, 587 : 15
Sophonisba, O S. S. O, 345 : 17
Sorbonne, straight one day at S., 768 : 20
Sorcerer, I who fashioned myself s., 674 : 8
Sorcery of hot embraces, 816 : 20
Sordello, can but be one S., 792 : 18
Sordid boon, 427 : 29
covetous s. fellow, 341 : 21
perils of actual existence, 674 : 19
Sore, good for s. eyes, 323 : 3
if your friends are s., 339 : 13
labor's bath, 237 : 21
task, 217 : 19
thy hand presseth me s., 18 : 28
thy so s. loss, 693 : 19
Sore-eyed, he's dropsical she s., 663 : *n* 1
Sorrow, a little fun to match s., 617 : 3
abandon learning and no s., 64 : 9
and joy are one, 869 : 5
and sighing shall flee away, 30 : 25
bee has no time for s., 404 : 1
bitterest cup of s., 735 : *n* 1
bread in s. ate, 395 : 2
breaks seasons, 187 : 11
bring forth children in s., 7 : 11
by s. of the heart the spirit is broken, 24 : 6
calls no time that's gone, 260 : 19
death and s. our companions, 744 : 9
disorder and early s., 755 : 20
down thou climbing s., 233 : 17
drink today and drown s., 260 : 13
enough to disarm, 511 : 19
ere s. comes with years, 507 : 2
excursion same for s. as joy, 877 : 2
find s. near at hand, 69 : 11
for angels, 541 : 8
for his women, 903 : 2
for lost Lenore, 526 : 12
for Lycidas s. not dead, 281 : 4
for the dead, 453 : 3
frowsy couch in s. steep, 411 : 23
give s. words, 239 : 20
glut s. on rose, 477 : 22
hang s. care'll kill cat, 210 : *n* 1
happy in s., 171 : 13
hath less power to bite, 194 : 6
he that increaseth knowledge increaseth s., 26 : 17
he that loves s., 251 : 13
I had a little S., 822 : 20
I have known s., 104 : 30
idleness s. friend foe, 827 : 8
keep thy s. to thyself, 34 : 5
legacy alleviates s., 171 : 7
more in s. than anger, 218 : 21
more of joy than s., 570 : 16
nae s. there John, 417 : 11
naught but vast s. there, 739 : 18
never comes too late, 361 : 12
night of doubt and s., 616 : 8
no more s., 53 : 30
no old age only s., 701 : 4
noble truth of s., 72 : 23
not be in s. too, 403 : 16
not mine but man's, 692 : 6
now melt into s., 459 : 5
of human existence, 375 : 3
of love dureth overlong, 149 : 11
Sorrow (*continued*)
parting is such sweet s., 192 : 19
pine with fear and s., 174 : 10
pure and complete s. impossible, 602 : 7
regions of s., 283 : 7
rent is s. income tears, 267 : 14
rooted s., 239 : 32
Russian people make s. a diversion, 725 : 8
see if there be s. like unto my s., 32 : 22
sickness and troubled mind, 267 : 20
sing away s., 169 : 6
sit by fireside with s., 470 : 4
sit thee down s., 190 : 17
sorrow's crown of s., 529 : 20
source of humor, 625 : 4
sphere of our s., 469 : 20
stranger to s., 76 : 11
sweet that teaches, 900 : 6
to s. bade good-morrow, 476 : 4
to think full of s., 476 : 24
unfelt s., 238 : 10
unspeakable s. you bid me renew, 104 : 31
veiling song in s., 469 : 8
we are not sure of s., 633 : 21
wear a golden s., 248 : 27
when my heart 'scaped this s., 245 : 3
where s. there holy ground, 676 : 15
why should s. last, 917 : 20
wilt thou live with me, 532 : 14
with family of Sighs, 469 : 3
with night we banish s., 257 : 18
with s. to the grave, 8 : 32
write s. on bosom of the earth, 195 : 1
year wake year to s., 469 : 7
yet is their strength labor and s., 20 : 13
Sorrowful, even in laughter the heart is s., 24 : 1
O sad kissed mouth how s., 632 : 19
soul s. unto death, 41 : 11
they were exceeding s., 41 : 8
Sorrowing goeth a-s., 163 : 5
Sorrow's crown of sorrow, 529 : 20
Sorrows, carried our s., 31 : 15
come not single spies, 223 : 25
disease or s. strike him, 564 : 14
instruct s. to be proud, 201 : 20
little s. sit and weep, 404 : 12
losses restored and s. end, 244 : 12
man of s., 31 : 14
Man of S., 570 : 16
of your changing face, 712 : 9
when gods bring s., 60 : 26
when s. have end, 918 : 5
women plunged into s., 414 : 11
Sorry, cheeks of s. grain, 280 : 1
feel s. because we cry, 649 : 7
heartily s. for misdoings, 55 : 17
if our wishes were gratified, 66 : 21
man who is s. will win, 65 : 4
now I wrote it, 718 : 16
scheme of things, 517 : 13
truly s. man's dominion, 408 : 13
union of very s. men, 58 : 15
wild thing s. for itself, 790 : 11
Sort, ambition of meaner s., 185 : 3
le s. fait les parents, 385 : *n* 6
sager s. our deeds reprove, 250 : 3
two of every s., 7 : 29
Sorted out largest size, 613 : 8

Sorts, all s. and conditions of
men, 55 : 5
all s. of people, 237 : 1
of things and weather, 494 : 3
Soshubble ez baskit er kittens, 662 : 7
So-so is good, 212 : 29
some good some s., 119 : 2
Soudan, home in the S., 708 : 5
Sought, by night on my bed I s.
him, 28 : 10
he s. the storms, 303 : 20
I never s. world, 356 : 27
it with thimbles, 614 : 4
less often s. than found, 462 : 19
light we s. shining, 587 : 12
love s. is good, 214 : 17
many a thing I s., 244 : 11
not s. support of communism, 779 : 19
out many inventions, 27 : 12
popularity crime when s., 310 : 19
prize we s. won, 576 : 6
seek what men of old s., 314 : 4
the remedy, 212 : 31
to men that s. him sweet, 249 : 15
truth not s. for, 91 : 4
unknowing what he s., 307 : 6
what s. they thus afar, 561 : 1
Soul above buttons, 415 : 15
adventure most unto itself s., 606 : 8
America save s. rather than
face, 787 : 8
amortization of heart and s., 826 : 18
and in my s. am free, 296 : 4
and nature, 703 : 6
architect expends s., 395 : 22
art in life of s., 697 : 13
art work of body and s., 572 : 15
astounded s., 899 : 12
astronomy compels s. to look
upwards, 84 : 18
awake my s., 311 : 18, 346 : 1
away O s., 576 : 16
be not disturbed, 794 : 4
beat s. of enemy man, 791 : 16
beauty in inward s., 83 : 7
belongs to the idea, 639 : 6
bequeath my s. to God, 181 : 16
beyond ego reach, 754 : 13
bitterness of my s., 30 : 28
body brevity wit s., 435 : 24
body Nature is and God the
s., 336 : 21
brevity the s. of wit, 220 : 10
bright incalculable s., 828 : 16
built s. a pleasure-house, 528 : 6
call upon my s., 213 : 18
calm S. of all things, 585 : 1
can split sky in two, 822 : 12
captain of his s., 814 : 8
captain of life, 103 : 1
captain of my s., 663 : 11
chainless s., 562 : 3
charge not s. save to its
ability, 131 : 15
chariot that bears human s., 607 : 4
circumnavigator of s., 711 : 18
clap hands and sing, 715 : 1
cold waters to a thirsty s., 25 : 16
condemned to be, 606 : 8
cowers naked, 791 : 3
crowd not on my s., 363 : 7
damned of body and s., 707 : 19
dare call s. my own, 507 : 17
darest thou now O s., 576 : 17

Soul (*continued*)
dark night of the s., 167 : 1
dead that slumbers, 509 : 13
deck s. with gladness, 295 : 20
digressions s. of reading, 360 : 2
dim windows of the s., 407 : 10
discipline s. of army, 378 : 14
dissever my s. from s. of Annabel
Lee, 527 : 9
dividing s. and spirit, 51 : 14
dream is hidden door of the
s., 754 : 13
dull would he be of s., 425 : 13
dusty answer gets s., 600 : 20
eager s. biting for anger, 276 : 15
eat eat me s., 315 : 1
echoes roll from s. to s., 531 : 2
engineers of s., 725 : 9
eternally unslayable, 94 : 9
even-balanced s., 584 : 8
extinguish hope from s., 674 : 4
extinguished his s., 520 : 7
fair seedtime had my s., 423 : 17
fairy godmother in s., 694 : 1
false words infect the s., 84 : 2
fame consumes house of s., 876 : 10
far back in s. horse prances, 790 : 19
fates have given a patient s., 59 : 11
feminine s. a queen, 703 : 13
fiery s., 303 : 20
find beautiful human s., 393 : 4
flow of s., 339 : 8
folk songs from s. sounds, 831 : 16
for which s. did pine, 525 : 17
force, 727 : 5
forces which threaten s., 778 : 11
freedom of the s., 296 : *n* 3
from out that shadow, 526 : 20
gain world lose s., 39 : 38
genial current of s., 362 : 7
gives heart and s. away, 691 : 1
go S. the body's quest, 172 : 14
go to prove my s., 540 : 6
God changes I am the s., 634 : 4
grapple them to thy s., 218 : 30
grave unto a s., 201 : 24
half conceal s. within, 531 : 20
half of my own s., 106 : 26
hang like fruit my s., 243 : 30
hark hark my s., 552 : 22
harrow up thy s., 219 : 18
has fled, 513 : 8
has many motions, 874 : 18
has to itself decreed, 475 : 11
hath been alone, 435 : 9
hath elbow room, 202 : 17
hath not lifted his s. unto
vanity, 18 : 8
hath power to know all things, 251 : 6
haughtiness of s., 325 : 14
he restoreth my s., 18 : 7
he shall preserve thy s., 22 : 4
he whose s. is flat, 822 : 12
heart and s. and senses
forever, 543 : 16
heaven take my s., 202 : 12
height my s. can reach, 507 : 14
her lips suck forth my s., 184 : 4
hidden s. beneath, 571 : 3
hidden s. of harmony, 278 : 7
him whom my s. loveth, 28 : 10
his s. sincere, 362 : 18
honor belongs to s., 124 : 3
horror s. of plot, 526 : 4

Soul (*continued*)
human s. take wing, 459 : 22
hyacinths to feed s., 133 : *n* 1
I have liberated my s., 136 : 10
I was and thy s. in me, 634 : 5
icebergs behoove the s., 878 : 3
idea does not belong to s., 639 : 6
if you would keep s., 793 : 19
immortal because has s., 838 : 11
impropriety s. of wit, 751 : 13
in bliss, 235 : 8
in body and in s. bind, 430 : 9
in mystery s. abides, 584 : 18
in prison I am not free, 676 : 18
in s. of man one Tahiti, 570 : 14
in the s. in the clod, 543 : 19
ingenuity developed first s.
afterwards, 812 : 10
intercourse from s. to s., 335 : 1
into boughs does glide, 297 : 4
invite my s., 574 : 12
iron entered into his s., 56 : 14
is all but out of me, 822 : 14
is form and doth body make, 174 : 19
is his own, 208 : 5
is immortal or perishes, 83 : *n* 7
is in a ferment, 475 : 15
is marching on, 619 : 14
is the concern of my Lord, 131 : 8
jaundice of the s., 305 : 24
Jesus lover of my s., 350 : 12
Jonathan loved him as his own
s., 13 : 5
joy's s. lies in doing, 225 : 34
kindled at conwiviality, 547 : 20
kiss my whole s., 184 : *n* 3
knows no release, 842 : 14
larger than sky, 480 : 12
largest and most comprehensive
s., 303 : 5
lay not unction to s., 223 : 7
lemonade weak like your s., 412 : 6
lends tongue vows, 219 : 6
life of s., 344 : 9
lift my s. to heaven, 248 : 25
like cloudy opal ring, 711 : 12
listened intensely, 428 : 15
little s. wandering guest, 123 : 15
locust of s. unshelled, 900 : 3
look and body touch, 717 : 8
look for deed s. performed, 132 : 14
looks part has s. of part, 667 : 4
love is the s. of genius, 402 : 11
love the Lord with all thy s., 11 : 9
made up of wants, 565 : 14
man became a living s., 6 : 17
man endow nature with s., 679 : 5
many a man's s. and faith, 916 : 8
marching on, 619 : 14
masculine s. a worker, 703 : 13
measured by my s., 328 : 1
meeting s. may pierce, 278 : 6
merit wins the s., 334 : 11
merry old s., 929 : 14
migration of the s., 83 : 13
mind and s. according, 531 : 18
mirroring s., 585 : 5
more stately mansions O s., 519 : 7
most offending s. alive, 208 : 9
mount mount my s., 195 : 19
my father lived his s., 829 : 21
my own s. bright green, 558 : 11
my prophetic s., 219 : 20
my s. at liberty, 605 : 8

Soul (*continued*)
my s. deep like rivers, 854 : 12
my s. doth magnify the Lord, 42 : 20
my s. there is a country, 299 : 10
my s. thirsteth for thee, 19 : 29
my s. waiteth for the Lord, 22 : 12
my unconquerable s., 663 : 10
mysterious thing in s., 571 : 11
naked s. of Tomlinson, 708 : 17
Nazism aimed at making you lose s., 853 : 11
never broke chain freed s., 626 : 19
never taught to stray, 336 : 16
new depths broken in s., 448 : 4
no coward s. mine, 562 : 4
no higher than s. high, 822 : 12
Northland s., 834 : 5
not bruised to pleasure s., 715 : 17
not disappoint hoping s., 412 : 19
not more than body, 574 : 27
not spoken of the s., 509 : 13
nothing contributes more to peace of s., 386 : 17
numerical precision s. of science, 696 : 4
O my prophetic s., 219 : 20
O my s. is white, 403 : 6
O Nature O s. of man, 570 : 15
O s. be changed to waterdrops, 184 : 9
of Adonais like star, 469 : 17
of business, 342 : 9
of fire, 351 : 18
of friend we've made, 698 : 16
of goodness in things evil, 208 : 3
of grandam inhabit a bird, 200 : *n* 3
of man immortal, 85 : 10
of music shed, 446 : 9
of my youth, 789 : 15
of sleeper away, 673 : 3
of s. sincere, 336 : 5
of the age, 256 : 11
of the plot, 526 : 4
of truth in things erroneous, 579 : 16
of wit, 220 : 10, 751 : 13
offends me to the s., 221 : 23
on that day no s. wronged, 132 : 6
one s. though many tongues, 126 : 4
only s. man must save, 841 : 4
organic part of human race, 790 : 21
palace of the s., 276 : 10, 457 : 6
pensive s., 364 : 14
perches in the s., 604 : 17
perdition catch my s., 230 : 30
pilgrim s. in you, 712 : 9
Plato healer of s., 83 : *n* 3
poet brings s. into activity, 437 : 16
poor intricated s., 255 : 4
poor s. sat sighing, 232 : 8
poor s. the center, 246 : 4
possess s. with patience, 305 : 28
pouring forth s., 476 : 28
poverty keepeth down s., 485 : 24
pray Lord my s. keep, 320 : 12
prison that can bind s., 671 : 13
prophet of the s., 493 : 16
prophetic s. of world, 245 : 13
Psyche my s., 527 : 1
pure and clear as crystal, 550 : 1
ragged meadow of my s., 829 : 7
rapt s. in thine eyes, 278 : 13
receive my s. at last, 350 : 12
recovers radical innocence, 714 : 21
rejoices in truth uttered, 554 : 7

Soul (*continued*)
remembering my good friends, 194 : 19
rescue my s. from their destructions, 18 : 22
research into feminine s., 679 : 7
rest her s. she's dead, 224 : 11
richness of s., 86 : 14
riddling perplexed s., 255 : 4
roamed with my s., 527 : 1
sad glance glum, 629 : 22
sad lucidity of s., 584 : 15
said to s. be still, 807 : 17
sail leagues and leagues, 601 : 19
same in all creatures, 80 : 12
sanctum of the s., 754 : 13
save my s. if I have s., 593 : 9
saves s. in new French books, 543 : 7
science without conscience ruin of s., 157 : 13
seeking with s. land of Greeks, 395 : 8
selects her society, 605 : 2
shall be required of thee, 43 : 20
ship of the s., 575 : 20
shorten stature of s., 600 : 16
shrinks from all to remember, 899 : 13
sighed s. toward Grecian tents, 200 : 22
sin whatever obscures s., 727 : 9
sincerely from author's s., 830 : 8
sinews of s., 277 : 4
single s. in two bodies, 87 : 1
sleepless s. that perished, 425 : 10
smithy of s., 777 : 18
so dead, 430 : 10
so panteth my s. after thee, 19 : 5
soothed s. to pleasures, 306 : 19
sorrowful unto death, 41 : 11
speech a mirror of s., 112 : 17
spiritual principle, 679 : 5
stirred s. to inmost depths, 490 : 3
strains that might create a s., 279 : 27
strong is the s., 584 : 10
strong s. by what shore, 588 : 6
subject's s. his own, 208 : 5
sun steadies my s., 799 : 8
sweet and virtuous s., 268 : 17
swell the s. to rage, 306 : 22
swims without gills, 759 : 3
swooned slowly, 777 : 16
takes nothing with her, 84 : 3
taste sadness of might, 478 : 1
that can be honest, 260 : 18
that lingers sighing, 691 : 12
that maketh all, 336 : *n* 8
that o'er him planned, 493 : 20
that rises with us, 426 : 14
the hungry s., 25 : 24
the timid s., 793 : 13
thirst that from s. doth rise, 256 : 8
thirsteth for God, 19 : 5
this that oppresses s., 614 : 3
thou hast much goods, 43 : 19
thoughtful s. to solitude, 516 : 2
thy s. the fixed foot, 253 : 5
time the s. of this world, 120 : 22
'tis my outward s., 253 : 11
to bear my s. away, 294 : 16
to dare, 431 : 7
tocsin of s., 461 : 16
tomorrow s. sets sail, 850 : 5
tumult of the s., 428 : 21

Soul (*continued*)
unconquerable s., 663 : 10
unlettered small-knowing s., 190 : 15
unto captain Christ, 195 : 8
unto self imperial friend, 606 : 3
upon my s. between kisses, 721 : 4
variety s. of pleasure, 312 : 14
wake s. by tender strokes, 334 : 12
was like a star, 425 : 23
we take ship O s., 576 : 15
wears out breast, 460 : 5
weddings of the s., 767 : 21
what fortitude s. contains, 608 : 4
what of s. left I wonder, 543 : 11
what s. without flaw, 674 : 2
what will satisfy s., 576 : 12
whispereth within him, 132 : 10
whose progeny they are, 281 : 22
whose s. is sense, 253 : 3
why art thou cast down O my s., 19 : 6
why castest thou off my s., 20 : 10
why shrinks the s., 326 : 3
windows of my s. open, 513 : 15
windows of the s., 167 : 10, 407 : 10
wine-scented poetic s., 668 : 18
winning s. to good or evil, 65 : 14
with all its maladies, 638 : 10
with all thy heart and s., 40 : 16
with my whole s., 32 : 18
with saints I trust, 436 : 4
witness of s. naturally Christian, 126 : 1
world the race the s., 576 : 22
yet my s. drew back, 269 : 9
Soul-destroying hatred, 744 : 8
Soul-hungry, worse to be s., 923 : 22
Soul-making, vale of s., 480 : 2
Soul's arrest, 742 : 12
dark cottage, 276 : 12
for s. good do things disliked, 751 : 12
invincible surmise, 703 : 3
must I lose s. inheritance, 674 : 16
my s. calm retreat, 298 : 21
prayer s. sincere desire, 429 : 18
whole s. tasking, 567 : 12
Souls, all s. were forfeit, 228 : 7
are in the hand of God, 34 : 13
awkward to play with s., 543 : 13
beams of wit on other s., 304 : 25
beyond reaches of our s., 219 : 12
boundless as we wish our s., 467 : 11
conscience grinds our s., 260 : 4
corporations have no s., 172 : 4
damp s. of housemaids, 804 : 5
departed shadows of living, 275 : 13
dwell in house of tomorrow, 782 : 15
evil only in men's s., 851 : 15
flame of freedom in s., 643 : 1
great s. suffer in silence, 412 : 16
have sight of sea, 426 : 20
immediate jewel of their s., 230 : 33
in s. sympathy with sounds, 377 : 13
jealous s. not answered, 231 : 20
left your s. on earth, 477 : 15
letters mingle s., 254 : 4
liberty inspire our s., 325 : *n* 9
live in furnished s., 828 : 14
lives and s. dreaming, 571 : 3
look after s. in labor, 85 : 16
love's mysteries in s. grow, 253 : 8
many valiant s. of heroes, 57 : 3
memory green in our s., 446 : 8
miserable state wretched s., 140 : 16

Souls (*continued*)
mounting up to God, 601 : 14
must not be saved, 230 : 19
numberless infinities of s., 254 : 8
nurse of full-grown s., 567 : 5
of animals infuse themselves, 200 : 7
of blood, 792 : 6
of emperors and cobblers, 165 : 4
of poets dead, 477 : 16
our selves our s. and bodies, 55 : 19
our s. survive death, 112 : *n* 13
our two s. which are one, 253 : 4
patent leather s., 841 : 12
poised like s. to remind, 733 : 17
possess s. in patience, 44 : 1
prosperity tries s. even of wise, 102 : 25
pure lovers' s. descend, 253 : 7
Saxon eyes barbarous s., 721 : 3
see s. we loved, 533 : 26
sit close and silently, 167 : *n* 9
such harmony in immortal s., 201 : 1
sucks two s., 253 : 14
suspicion companion of mean s., 384 : 10
that cringe and plot, 567 : 11
there be s. must be saved, 230 : 19
through such s. God shows light, 545 : 7
times that try men's s., 384 : 13
to believing s. gives light, 185 : 12
two s. alas, 396 : 12
two s. dwell in my breast, 396 : 12
two s. erect and strong, 507 : 11
two s. with single thought, 508 : 1
unbodied, 254 : 3
violent s., 805 : 16
waking s., 251 : 15
what are they after our s., 849 : 10
wounded by such things, 297 : 20
Sound as of rushing wind, 45 : 38
believeth it is s. of trumpet, 16 : 38
bells s. on Bredon, 691 : 4
came o'er my ear like sweet s., 213 : 7
come back s., 170 : 23
deeper than plummet s., 248 : 15
drum's discordant s., 375 : 4
empty vessel greatest s., 208 : 12
far-off curfew s., 278 : 19
full of s. and fury, 240 : 4
Great Paul great pail of s., 899 : 3
hammer the hard s. 768 : 2
heal blows of s., 518 : 13
hearest the s. thereof, 44 : 32
heart s. as bell, 209 : 21
idea with sense of s., 698 : 7
is forced, 403 : 1
let it s. no more, 195 : 18
let s. of it flee, 384 : 8
mind in sound body, 122 : 17, 307 : 18
music with silver s., 917 : 17
must seem echo to sense, 333 : 9
my barbaric yawp, 575 : 3
mystery of s., 808 : 19
nature without voice or s., 365 : 6
no riches above s. body, 35 : 40
no s. dissonant, 441 : *n* 1
no s. of hammer, 377 : 11
no s. of planes, 885 : 7
no s. of water, 805 : 1
no s. save rush of river, 598 : *n* 3
no war or battle's s., 277 : 8
not fourth s. but star, 544 : 3
nought but eyr ybroken, 143 : 18
Sound (*continued*)
of body and mind, 107 : 13
of great Amen, 596 : 14
of her silk skirt, 97 : 10
of horn at night, 483 : 3
of horns and motors, 805 : 6
of public scorn, 287 : 27
of revelry by night, 457 : 14
of the grinding is low, 27 : 24
of thunder heard remote, 284 : 18
of voice that is still, 530 : 19
one s. for Russian hearts, 486 : 9
persuasive s., 324 : 15
piping took troubled s., 587 : 8
rhythm to world of s., 801 : 8
silver-sweet s. lovers' tongues, 192 : 17
slight s. at evening, 557 : 6
stagnant hollow s., 849 : 12
sweet is every s., 531 : 13
the loud timbrel, 447 : 10
thought and magic s., 486 : 8
thundering s., 370 : 11
to bells' cheerful s., 403 : 4
too full for s., 535 : 19
trump of rescue s., 494 : 17
trumpet beat drums, 346 : 7
trumpet give uncertain s., 48 : 26
trumpet shall s., 49 : 7
trumpets beat drums, 306 : 14
upon bugle horn, 529 : 15
voice as s. of many waters, 52 : 30
voice whose s. like sea, 425 : 23
what stop she please, 222 : 6
wooden dialogue and s., 226 : 4
Sounded, trumpets s. for him, 302 : 16
Soundest, old lovers s., 262 : 1
Sounding brass or tinkling cymbal, 48 : 22
cataract haunted me, 423 : 12
Soundings, acquainted with s., 479 : 14
Soundless day in autumn, 525 : 19
footsteps on grass, 723 : 3
Soundly, sleep s. as wretched slave, 208 : 7
suspects yet s. loves, 230 : 34
Soundness of observation, 311 : 1
Sounds and sweet airs, 248 : 10
army stilly s., 208 : 1
articulate sweet s., 713 : 1
concord of sweet s., 201 : 3
exceed knock at door, 441 : 23
ghostlier demarcations keener s., 767 : 16
let s. of music creep, 201 : 1
martial s., 283 : 21
of nameless battle, 728 : 13
out of three s. frame, 544 : 3
perfumes colors s. echo, 580 : 18
replication of your s., 215 : 1
selfsame s. on spirit, 767 : 9
sympathy with s., 377 : 13
take care of themselves, 612 : 3
that echo still, 528 : 21
three great elemental s., 802 : 19
troublous sights and s., 721 : 8
Soup, beautiful s., 612 : 11
bouillabaisse sort of s., 539 : 19
licked s. from ladles, 541 : 1
of the evening, 612 : 11
steward into s. tureen, 709 : 24
Sour, conscience made him s., 530 : 18
eaten a s. grape, 32 : 17
every sweet has s., 497 : 10
Sour (*continued*)
grapes are s., 66 : 1
how s. sweet music is, 195 : 16
keep at times frae being s., 409 : 4
lofty and s., 249 : 15
misfortune's book, 193 : 25
prove in digestion s., 194 : 3
Source, forget s. that keeps it filled, 601 : 2
little water in stream fault of s., 127 : 15
mysterious law true s., 286 : 5
mysterious s. of art and science, 763 : 6
ocean the s. of all, 58 : 21
of all my bliss, 371 : 1
of innocent merriment, 629 : 12
of sympathetic tears, 363 : 1
Sources, all our s. related, 791 : 11
water of s. and ashes, 860 : 9
Soured milk of human kindness, 236 : *n* 1
South, come thou s. wind, 28 : 14
full of the warm S., 476 : 23
guilt on North equally with S., 577 : 16
in S. war what A.D. elsewhere, 623 : 15
is avenged, 635 : 23
know no S. no North, 444 : 6
men of the S., 759 : 2
night of s. winds, 574 : 19
some genius of S., 831 : 16
swallow flying s., 531 : 5
'twixt s. and southwest, 290 : 16
why do you hate the S., 838 : 5
South Africa, interracial groups in S., 916 : 11
South Carolina, governor of S.C. said, 669 : 12
Southard, varying to s. and westard, 622 : 19
Southbound mail, 731 : *n* 2
Southerly, when wind s. know hawk, 220 : 31
Southern, boon s. country, 587 : 11
bore me in s. wild, 403 : 6
change to s. willows, 378 : 2
culture fostered imagination, 905 : 5
efficiency, 892 : 2
nature to s. side, 568 : 24
Scott hand in S. character, 623 : 17
wind blow softly, 625 : 20
writer adept at recognizing grotesque 905 : 4
Southern Cross, noiseless chariot of S., 861 : 2
Southerner has no use for "r," 623 : 14
Southey's, four first rhymes are S., 145 : *n* 4
Southwest, 'twixt south and s. side, 290 : 16
Sovereign, common law voice of s., 644 : 21
discharged from duty of superintending, 366 : 8
five s. fingers, 886 : 14
is the lightest, 89 : 28
life to s. power, 528 : 5
lord the king, 315 : 14
Magna Carta will have no s., 172 : 5
man of s. parts, 190 : 20
nation of s. states, 725 : 20
nations with great power, 763 : 13

Sovereign (*continued*)
noble and most s. reason, 221 : 21
of sighs and groans, 190 : 26
our s. the people, 450 : *n* 8
power in government s., 401 : 17
powers brutal lives ugly deaths, 831 : 18
press, 789 : 4
state self-centered, 860 : 2
states perfect union, 725 : 20
Sovereignty, nonsense of conceptions of s., 837 : 14
top of s., 478 : 5
unlimited s. in majority of popular assembly, 382 : 4
women desire s., 147 : 14
Soviet Union, no difference between S. and U.S. worth military encounter, 860 : 4
run by dictatorship, 780 : 8
Sow a thought, 922 : 18
as you s. ye reap, 291 : 23
he that observeth wind not s., 27 : 21
men that s. and reap, 633 : 20
they s. not, 38 : 2
they that s. in tears, 22 : 7
thy seed in the morning, 27 : 22
wrong s. by ear, 161 : 10
Sowed dragon's teeth, 840 : 10
what I s. what orchard yields, 854 : 2
Sowest, that which thou s., 49 : 3
Soweth, whatsoever a man s., 49 : 32
Sowing, farmer s. the corn, 934 : 9
Sown, flower on earth never s., 424 : 13
in corruption, 49 : 5
never reaped nor was s., 311 : 21
the wind, 33 : 12
wild oats not s. more than once, 701 : 1
Sows, abstinence s. sand all over, 404 : 16
himself for seed, 794 : 9
Space, alchemized and free of s., 475 : 20
and time are stupidity, 784 : 18
annihilate s. and time, 336 : 8
awful majesty of outer s., 852 : 3
chained to point in s., 482 : 11
civilize a s., 889 : 10
desolate windswept s., 626 : 21
duty beyond s. and time, 745 : 1
engenders forgetfulness, 755 : 6
every inch of s. a miracle, 576 : 14
eye vanquished by s., 171 : 14
God stepped on s., 733 : 10
here is my s., 240 : 14
in reality atoms and s., 79 : 11
in s. and time universes, 576 : 22
king of infinite s., 220 : 26
memory emancipated from s., 437 : 13
much richness in little s., 183 : *n* 9
music in s., 396 : *n* 1
nonbeing penetrates no s., 64 : 15
objects extended in s., 769 : 15
out of S. out of Time, 526 : 8
personal s. invisible boundaries, 910 : 12
put on earth a little s., 403 : 7
seas of s. and time, 802 : 20
unhappy linger a s., 797 : 13
Spaces in togetherness, 782 : 14
sailing celestial s., 637 : 21
silence of infinite s., 300 : 2
Spaces (*continued*)
vacant interstellar s., 807 : 16
Spaceship, automated S. Earth, 832 : 8
Spacious firmament on high, 325 : 8
skies, 688 : 5
times of Elizabeth, 528 : 21
Spade, call s. a s., 91 : 7
part Sam S. liked, 830 : 4
poet bow not but to s., 912 : 8
Spaded, delicately gelded or s., 829 : 2
Spades, darkly auspicious as ace of s., 899 : 14
emblems of graves, 377 : 6
let s. be trumps, 334 : 7
Spaghetti, ticker tape ain't s., 778 : 8
Spain, building castles in S., 149 : 1
comes forth, 860 : 11
devildoms of S., 535 : 12
from each hollow of S., 860 : 11
is become richest of countries, 151 : 9
long live sister S., 416 : 18
look at broken S., 860 : 10
not ruler of America, 416 : 18
rain in S., 894 : 19
result in less evil to S., 599 : 1
Spain's, king of S. daughter, 932 : 1
Spake as a child, 48 : 25
never man s. like this, 45 : 1
of disastrous chances, 229 : 28
so s. the Fiend, 285 : 21
Solomon s. three thousand proverbs, 13 : 30
upon this hint I s., 229 : 31
Span, eternity shut in a s., 292 : 19
Eve s., 917 : 1
life is but s., 320 : 11
life less than s., 181 : 17
life's brief s. forbids us, 107 : 2
life's but a s., 251 : 7
Spangled heavens a shining frame, 325 : 8
Spangles of heaven's floor, 557 : 16
Spaniard, I am a S., 784 : 26
man without imagination, 784 : 26
Spaniards, emotions of S., 480 : 16
Spaniel, ghost may s. it, 797 : 13
Spanish, Catholic America S. America, 721 : 3
I speak S. to God, 143 : 16
monk distraught, 512 : 20
or neat's leather, 291 : 16
ships of war at sea, 535 : 11
sun never sets in S. dominions, 412 : *n* 6
Spans, narrow measure s., 692 : 6
Spar to men that sink, 823 : 13
Spare all I have take my life, 329 : 12
brother can you s. dime, 842 : 5
establish peace s. conquered, 105 : 24
Fast, 278 : 15
he will not s. in day of vengeance, 23 : 15
me that I may recover strength, 19 : 4
my aching sight, 363 : 7
rod and spoil child, 91 : *n* 3, 291 : 19
spend shafts s. not, 918 : 3
thee past my power, 409 : 9
to us our friends, 669 : 17
us word of weapons, 900 : 2
women for Thy Sake, 866 : 17
woodman s. beechen tree, 443 : 19
woodman s. that tree, 492 : 10
your country's flag, 513 : 18
Spared, better s. better man, 205 : 13
lashed vice s. name, 322 : 19
nothing in my songs, 759 : 3
Spares, blessed man that s. these stones, 250 : 1
neither man nor his works, 383 : 14
war s. not the brave, 67 : 10
Spareth, he that s. his rod, 23 : 34
Sparing, in the middle be s., 61 : 21
Sparingly, picked s. without noise, 575 : 22
Spark, dusk shadow then s., 660 : 10
from heaven, 585 : 22
from heaven immortal, 412 : 9
gie me ae s., 409 : 1
great flame follows little s., 142 : 10
my little s. of courage, 925 : 2
nor human s. is left, 340 : 28
nurse through night ethereal s., 883 : 8
of heavenly fire, 452 : 15
of that ancient flame, 105 : 8
out of stone not moral, 631 : 3
vital s. of heavenly flame, 333 : 23
Sparkle, on forefinger of time s., 530 : 24
out among fern, 533 : 15
still right Promethean fire, 191 : 5
with larceny, 757 : 15
Sparkles near the brim, 457 : 12
Sparkling cross she wore, 334 : 1
fount more s. than glass, 108 : 4
pair of s. eyes, 630 : 7
Sparks, as the s. fly upward, 15 : 15
like s. of fire befriend thee, 266 : 14
Sparrergrass, hit look lak s., 662 : 5
Sparrow, brawling of s., 712 : 7
caters for s., 210 : 28
come before window, 479 : 4
hero perish or s. fall, 336 : 14
I said the s., 930 : 9
I watch and am as a s., 21 : 5
Lesbia with her s., 823 : 2
Lesbia's s. all alone, 759 : 12
my lady's s. is dead, 101 : 15
old king to s., 740 : 1
providence in fall of s., 224 : 28
Sparrows, as boys do s., 321 : 12
two s. sold for farthing, 39 : 3
Spartan, remnant of S. dead, 461 : 6
simplicity, 925 : 4
Spartans, go tell the S., 67 : 19
Spasmodic Hercules, 555 : 10
Spatial motions of material particles, 636 : 17
Speak a few reasonable words, 395 : 5
after manner of men, 47 : 4
all that love can s., 607 : 10
arrows which s. to the wise, 71 : 24
at long last s., 832 : 2
by the card, 224 : 12
causing lips of those asleep to s., 28 : 21
comfortably to Jerusalem, 30 : 30
daggers to her, 222 : 24
dare to read think s. write, 380 : 10
did he stop s. to you, 542 : 13
don't s. well of self, 299 : 15
each other in passing, 512 : 10
for yourself John, 511 : 21
free to s. our minds, 824 : 12
free to think s. write, 390 : 2
freedom to s., 567 : 17
friends absent s., 254 : 4

Speak (*continued*)
gently she can hear, 674 : 14
grief that does not s., 239 : 20
hands for me, 216 : 4
have mouths but s. not, 21 : 22
how to s. true things, 61 : 8
I must s. in passion, 204 : 4
I only s. right on, 216 : 28
I want to s. simply, 850 : 5
I will s. to thee, 219 : 11
if any s., 216 : 16
ill of the dead, 62 : 8
in monstrous little voice, 196 : 5
in whatever way given, 726 : 12
less than thou knowest, 233 : 9
let no one s. ill of absent, 112 : 23
let not God s. with us, 10 : 8
let us not s. of them, 140 : 17
liars when they s. truth, 86 : 15
live pure s. true, 534 : 5
Lord for thy servant heareth, 12 : 30
low if you speak love, 209 : 8
masters of things they s., 263 : 20
minds of others to speak my own better, 164 : 12
more in minute, 192 : 26
needless to s. about things done, 68 : 12
no evil, 919 : 2
no man s. to him, 308 : *n* 2
no more of his renown, 533 : 6
no one left to s. up, 824 : 1
not loud or long, 174 : *n* 6
of Bolívar from mountain, 451 : *n* 7
of comfort no man s., 195 : 1
of me as I am, 232 : 20
of moderns without contempt, 341 : 23
of one that loved, 232 : 20
one to s. another hear, 558 : 12
or forever hold his peace, 56 : 7
power to s., 308 : 10
rather of sterner days, 745 : 7
rather s. ill of selves, 293 : 22
Reilly they s. of so highly, 922 : 17
roughly to little boy, 611 : 15
Sappho would s. openly, 751 : 7
silver reply gold, 926 : 4
slaves who fear to s., 567 : 3
slow to s., 51 : 30
softly carry big stick, 687 : 6
Spanish to God, 143 : 16
suffer me that I may s., 16 : 7
tears that s., 295 : 17
the affirmative, 500 : 8
the speech I pray you, 221 : 23
time to s., 26 : 21
to be silent better than to s., 120 : 10
to God as if men listening, 114 : 16
to him again, 542 : 13
to Him for He hears, 535 : 9
to it Horatio, 217 : 17
to me as to thy thinkings, 230 : 32
to me not of me, 540 : 16
to s. and purpose not, 232 : 29
to s. and s. well are two things, 257 : 4
to s. dishonorably is pardonable, 75 : 17
to the earth, 15 : 29
to whom can I s. today, 4 : 5, 4 : 6, 4 : 7
to your silent ashes, 102 : 18
too full of God to s., 711 : 16

Speak (*continued*)
trees known to s., 239 : 1
truth and shame Devil, 158 : 8
truth more as I grow old, 165 : 16
we s. not what we mean, 228 : 12
what we feel, 235 : 20
what you think today, 497 : 2
when I s. they are for war, 22 : 3
when I think I s., 212 : 8
when spoken to, 668 : 10
who knows does not s., 64 : 19
with pride of our doings, 798 : 6
with tongues of men, 48 : 22
woe when men s. well, 43 : 3
write s. associate, 872 : 18
you s. like a green girl, 219 : 4
Speakest, think before thou s., 169 : 27
wiser than thou art ware, 210 : 35
Speaketh, out of abundance of the heart mouth s., 39 : 11
Speaking, distant s. of voices, 887 : 5
hears you nearby sweetly s., 63 : 5
idle biologically s., 823 : 1
in s. for myself, 229 : 25
keep thy lips from s. guile, 18 : 21
lies in hypocrisy, 50 : 27
measure what s. about, 594 : 11
orator a good man skilled in s., 95 : 14
persuades when s. fails, 246 : 15
prose without knowing it, 298 : 8
terms with itself, 721 : 14
things which they ought not, 50 : 32
writing voting reasonably, 650 : 14
Speaks a new scene, 267 : 18
according to his actions, 68 : 9
acts before he s., 68 : 9
as man s. so is he, 112 : 17
for Family of Man, 761 : 16
heart thinks tongue s., 209 : 21
her foot s., 227 : 3
hides one thing and s. another, 58 : 8
holiday, 225 : 20
infinite deal of nothing, 198 : 5
money s. sense, 312 : 16
needs no questioning before he s., 77 : 14
poetry is painting that s., 68 : 1
she s. poniards, 209 : 10
she s. yet says nothing, 192 : 3
small like a woman, 225 : 6
subject he s. or writes upon, 342 : 8
when he s. air is still, 207 : 5
when Love s., 191 : 4
who s. does not know, 64 : 19
wise man s., 257 : 4
without modesty, 69 : 7
Spear, bring me my s., 406 : 21
burning s. horse of air, 918 : 12
idle s. and shield, 277 : 8
mangled by the bronze s., 59 : 6
to equal tallest pine, 283 : 15
to thrust club to strike, 157 : 5
took s. but left shield, 399 : 17
Spearmint Girl, 828 : 17
Spears into pruninghooks, 28 : 31
sheen of their s., 459 : 14
stars threw down s., 405 : 8
Special flag or ship signal, 575 : 21
people unto himself, 11 : 11
providence, 224 : 28
Specialists in mental disease, 783 : 10
preserves us not for s., 906 : 10
Specialty, weather literary s., 624 : 10
Species, especially male of s., 790 : 15

Species (*continued*)
female of s., 710 : 21
not individual but s., 349 : 12
one s. of superstition, 357 : 17
preservation of s., 414 : 20
Specious, murder takes s. name, 330 : 1
Speckled band, 689 : 5
Spectacle unto the world, 48 : 7
Spectacles, finest s. in nature, 348 : 4
grandest of earthly s., 454 : 17
of books, 303 : 6
on nose pouch on side, 211 : 15
Spectator, blood and disposition of s., 538 : 17
live in world as s., 326 : 8
of action he describes, 592 : 7
of mankind, 326 : 8
of mighty scene, 445 : 5
Spectators, pleasure to s., 489 : 6
some must be s., 257 : 3
Spectatum veniunt veniunt spectentur, 113 : *n* 7
Specter bark, 434 : 21
haunting Europe, 563 : 2
my s. around me, 406 : 1
Specter-gray, when frost was s., 641 : 11
Specters' holiday, 629 : 20
Specter-thin, pale and s., 476 : 24
Speculating, theologian not born by s., 156 : 8
Speculation, everybody watches s., 547 : 34
Speculators about perpetual motion, 152 : 14
philosophical s., 166 : 15
Speech, abridging freedom of s., 391 : 14
after long silence, 716 : 20
be alway with grace, 50 : 14
be skillful in s., 3 : 12
cordial s., 495 : 17
day unto day uttereth s., 17 : 27
dead had no s. for, 808 : 10
ere thought wed with s., 532 : 2
finely framed, 36 : 18
first silence of s., 512 : 20
free men from bondage, 677 : 13
free s. Frémont, 922 : 2
free s. in repulsive form, 746 : 6
free s. press assembly, 700 : 3
freedom of s., 625 : 9
freedom of s. and expression, 780 : 13
freedom of s. means, 794 : 18
freedom of s. taken, 379 : 6
from him never real s., 474 : 7
from the deep quiet well, 899 : 3
given to communicate, 310 : 22
good s. more hidden than malachite, 3 : 4
great s. impassioned, 90 : 1
I am slow of s., 9 : 15
I wrote in a garret, 350 : *n* 5
impelled us, 808 : 14
in substance ys but air, 143 : 18
is civilization, 755 : 15
is image of actions, 62 : 15
is like tapestries, 70 : 18
is small change of Silence, 600 : 12
let thy s. be short, 36 : 3
like cracked kettle, 583 : 11
make s. to maggots, 828 : 8
many harmed by s., 162 : 4
mend your s. a little, 232 : 25
mighty Russian s., 564 : 9

Speech (*continued*)
mirror of soul, 112 : 17
modest in s., 69 : 8
monkeys refrain from s., 690 : 13
never taxed for s., 227 : 9
no good s. save in Paris, 150 : 9
not to express but conceal, 310 : *n* 1
nowhere is s. freer, 746 : 6
on him no s., 442 : 24
our concern was s., 808 : 14
plainness of s., 49 : 12
poetry of s., 458 : 13
protection of free s., 644 : 23
regretted s. never silence, 112 : 16
right s., 73 : 2
rude am I in my s., 229 : 24
rude in s., 49 : 19
shallow as time, 473 : *n* 1
short meaning of long s., 413 : 15
silence golden s. silver, 473 : 9
small s. cantankerous, 90 : 1
speak the s. I pray you, 221 : 23
steep my s. in lies, 71 : 25
subtle s. delights us, 98 : 13
suppression of free s., 677 : 13
sweeter than honey, 57 : 10
Tennysonianness of s., 793 : 7
thy s. bewrayeth thee, 41 : 17
to conceal thoughts, 343 : 24
to stir men's blood, 216 : 28
took all heart for s., 713 : 19
what s. escaped your teeth, 57 : 27
Speeches, men's charitable s., 181 : 16
no one hears our s., 819 : 1
not my s. you mislike, 185 : 9
questions not decided by s., 553 : 6
Speed, all deliberate s., 820 : *n* 4
be wise with s., 329 : 21
bonny boat, 688 : 12
candles held to s. them, 827 : 4
deliberate s., 693 : 11
ease and s. not give work beauty, 147 : *n* 11
far faster than light, 742 : 1
full s. ahead, 490 : 4
good s. to your youthful valor, 106 : 3
his plow, 178 : 2
in skating safety s., 497 : 23
is but plummet's pace, 281 : 7
mass times s. of light squared, 763 : *n* 2
more haste less s., 110 : 6
of my desire, 596 : 15
of observation, 751 : 7
over great ocean routes, 800 : 10
retiring at high s. toward Japanese, 777 : 14
the going guest, 339 : 9
the parting guest, 334 : 23
the plow, 178 : *n* 2
the soft intercourse, 335 : 1
thousands at his bidding s., 282 : 17
through the antiseptic tunnel, 908 : 8
today put back tomorrow, 174 : 10
wrong to s. a guest, 60 : 19
Speeding, Rus whither are you s., 518 : 9
Speeds, dawn s. a man, 61 : 22
parting guest, 715 : 11
tale s. best plainly told, 187 : 19
wit s. too fast, 190 : 22
Speedy and public trial, 392 : 1
Spell, foreigners s. better than pronounce, 622 : 4
Spell (*continued*)
infancy's unconscious s., 571 : 4
soon fades the s., 489 : 10
Spencer, expression used by S., 514 : 15
Spencer's, Mr. S. Social Statics, 644 : 10
Spend, doth life in tendance s., 174 : 11
he that will s. it, 251 : 13
life your own way, 816 : 9
mind business s. less, 309 : 20
must s. to exist, 871 : 16
ne'er s. fury on child, 186 : 25
not s. another such night, 187 : 8
not then his gifts in vain, 255 : 16
shafts and spare not, 918 : 3
sweetest hours e'er I s., 409 : 16
that shortness basely, 205 : 8
time most valuable thing man can s., 91 : 17
to s. to give to want, 174 : 11
we s. our years as a tale that is told, 20 : 12
wealth at once you are ruined, 484 : 13
what we yet may s., 516 : 15
whatever you have s. less, 356 : 26
wherewith to s., 257 : 8
Spenders, free lovers free s., 726 : 2
Spending, cut taxes by cutting government s., 880 : 16
draw salary before s., 718 : 10
getting and s., 427 : 29
lives like serfs, 560 : 7
old age time of s., 290 : 9
riches are for s., 181 : 1
youth now bravely s., 811 : 16
Spendthrift trusts no place in Common Law, 638 : *n* 5
Spendthrifts, kings and ministers greatest s., 366 : 3
Spens, guide Sir Patrick S., 926 : 13
Spenser, not lodge thee by S., 256 : 11
renowned S., 265 : 14
Spent, all passion s., 289 : 11
confess this world's s., 254 : 5
consider how light is s., 282 : 15
days are s. without hope, 15 : 20
dissolutely s. Tuesday morning, 202 : 25
hours s. with thee, 700 : 13
life half s. before we know, 270 : 22
life well s. is long, 152 : 5
never s. hour's talk withal, 190 : 21
under belly, 261 : 7
waves' riot, 633 : 19
Sperm, created you of s. drop, 131 : 14
night s. of Milky Way, 861 : 2
Spes, dum anima est s. est, 98 : *n* 12
modo liceat vivere est s., 96 : *n* 14
Spew thee out of my mouth, 53 : 5
Sphere, all quit their s., 336 : 18
enforced from quiet s., 206 : 26
great s. thou movest in, 241 : 20
make up year and s., 494 : 3
motion in one s., 205 : 9
nature in terms of s., 638 : 3
owner of s., 495 : 15
storm-troubled s., 562 : 4
Sphere-descended, Music s., maid, 364 : 16
Spheres, driven by the s., 299 : 6
ever-moving s. of heaven, 184 : 7
moving as the restless s., 183 : 6
music from the s., 214 : 13
music of the s., 274 : 20
Spheres (*continued*)
prefers live music to humdrum s., 906 : 6
seems to shake the s., 306 : 13
stars shot madly from their s., 196 : 14
start from their s., 219 : 18
tuned s., 241 : 25
Spherical, body perfectly s., 550 : 6
predominance, 233 : 5
read that world was s., 151 : 7
Sphery chime, 280 : 5
Sphinx, don't care whether a Minx or S., 549 : 34
inward s., 721 : 2
Oedipus met S., 851 : 3
riddle of S., 74 : *n* 5
riddle of the S., 74 : 6
Spice, sugar and s., 932 : 13
variety's s. of life, 376 : 22
Spices thereof may flow out, 28 : 14
young hart upon mountains of s., 28 : 25
Spicy grove cinnamon tree, 857 : 14
no s. fragrance while they grow, 180 : *n* 2
nut-brown ale, 278 : 2
Phoenix builds s. nest, 271 : 21
Spider, almost like a s., 167 : 11
along came a s., 932 : 15
confined in web's center, 167 : 11
saw s. die, 892 : 7
subtle s. web, 167 : *n* 9
to fly, 485 : 23
Spider-like we feel the touch, 167 : *n* 9
Spider's, laws compared to s. web, 267 : 3
touch how fine, 167 : *n* 9
Spiders crying together, 893 : 10
I see what s. do, 847 : 2
like s. across stars, 901 : 3
love of s., 847 : 3
marching through air, 892 : 6
preserved in amber, 119 : *n* 2
Spiders', laws like s. webs, 63 : 2
Spies a far-off shore, 186 : 10
God's s., 235 : 12
single s., 223 : 25
Spile rod and child, 722 : 22
Spill, all germens s. at once, 233 : 24
my bright incalculable soul, 828 : 16
Spilled, as water s. on the ground, 13 : 22
fearing to be s., 223 : 20
Spills in fearing to be spilt, 223 : 20
Spin, great world s. forever, 530 : 8
set by fire and s., 930 : 16
sob as you s., 868 : 20
toil not neither s., 38 : 4
webs from entrails s., 167 : *n* 9
Spinach and the hell with it, 846 : 7
gammon and s., 548 : 33, 929 : 13
Spindle, do not fold s. or mutilate, 925 : 11
Spindrift gaze toward paradise, 843 : 16
Spinning our own fates, 648 : 11
Spinning-jenny and railroad, 566 : 6
out of his side, 715 : 15
Spinning-wheel, make me O Lord Thy s., 314 : 22
Spinoza, atheism like that of S., 704 : 6
Spins, hither and thither s., 585 : 5

Spinsters and knitters in the sun, 214 : 3
Spiral down militaristic stairway, 909 : 14
Spires, dreaming s., 587 : 7
of Oxford, 778 : 10
what s. what farms, 691 : 9
whose silent finger, 428 : 17
ye distant s., 361 : 8
Spirit, absent in body present in s., 48 : 8
Accusing S., 360 : 17
actions must be his s., 88 : 23
against flesh, 49 : 29
all compact of fire, 189 : 8
all save s. of man divine, 459 : 6
alone give highest meaning, 754 : 1
and instinct in harmony, 755 : 3
and with your s., 54 : 1
animating universe, 482 : 11
be thou s. fierce, 467 : 21
Big Blue Mountain S., 928 : 16
blessed are poor in s., 37 : 4
blithe s., 468 : 11
bloweth and is still, 584 : 18
body and s. twins, 634 : 14
body without s. is dead, 51 : 33
born of the S., 44 : 32
borrows name from wind, 679 : 5
by my s. saith the Lord, 33 : 30
by sorrow s. broken, 24 : 6
capable of compassion, 838 : 11
Chinese national s., 719 : 9
collective body and common s., 895 : 21
Creator drew his s., 307 : 9
decides issue, 771 : 12
delighted s., 228 : 20
descending like dove, 36 : 30
dividing soul and s., 51 : 14
erring s., 217 : 25
essential in painting, 135 : 11
everything that emancipates s., 397 : 13
expense of s. in waste of shame, 245 : 23
fled indignant to the shades, 106 : 7
follow your s., 207 : 18
fruit of the S., 49 : 30
full of s. as month of May, 204 : 30
gentleness of s. serenity of mind, 271 : *n* 1
gentlier on s. lies, 528 : 14
given on earth, 525 : 2
giveth life, 49 : 11
gods created of human s., 819 : 10
great poetry from national s., 577 : 13
haughty s. before a fall, 24 : 12
he that ruleth his s., 24 : 13
Hellenism s. of consciousness, 588 : 21
holiday-rejoicing s., 442 : 2
humble in s., 25 : 33
humble tranquil s., 251 : 11
I commend my s., 44 : 10
ill s. have so fair a house, 247 : 24
immortal s. grows, 423 : 18
in God's hand, 300 : 19
in one s. meet mingle, 467 : 24
in s. and truth, 44 : 36
in touch with unseen powers, 686 : 8
in which gift offered, 668 : 3
invisible s. of wine, 230 : 25
is departed, 36 : 8

Spirit (*continued*)
is willing, 41 : 13
knight of holy s., 481 : 10
letter and s. of constitution, 402 : 6
lifeblood of master s., 281 : 24
lively understandable s., 873 : 14
loneliness of s., 456 : 1
love needs s. and s. love, 754 : 1
Mammon least erected s., 283 : 28
man of understanding is of excellent s., 24 : 18
mark of Greek s., 723 : 14
meek and quiet s., 52 : 12
modern s. Greek discovery, 723 : 13
motion and a s., 423 : 13
motions of his s. dull, 201 : 3
my s. too weak, 478 : 7
nation's s. die of inanition, 586 : 23
naught so much s. calms, 460 : 20
no longer ruler of own s., 418 : 2
no s. can walk abroad, 217 : 26
noble s. raises itself in disaster, 120 : 3
not letter but s., 49 : 11
not size but s., 820 : 13
of age, 344 : 7
of Beauty that dost consecrate, 466 : 9
of counsel and might, 29 : 18
of defiance, 577 : 15
of Delight, 469 : 23
of divinest Liberty, 435 : 13
of fear, 51 : 6
of God moved upon face of the waters, 6 : 10
of government spirit of country, 672 : 14
of his own epoch, 755 : 1
of knowledge and fear of the Lord, 29 : 18
of liberty, 372 : 15
of love how quick and fresh, 213 : 8
of men who follow, 791 : 15
of moderation, 737 : 3
of night, 469 : 21
of party, 379 : 11
of popular government, 398 : 3
of prophecy in me, 83 : 18
of repose, 490 : 3
of science, 854 : 1
of suspicion and distrust, 737 : 6
of the time, 592 : 7
of the valley never dies, 64 : 2
of wisdom and understanding, 29 : 18
of youth in everything, 245 : 9
of Zeus-fostered kings, 57 : 16
original creation of s., 697 : 7
pardlike beautiful swift, 469 : 9
part of my nation, 790 : 21
party s. at best madness, 334 : 17
passed before my face, 15 : 12
perturbed s., 220 : 5
poetry finer s. of knowlege, 424 : 7
prisoned s. of man, 739 : 5
proud and chivalrous s., 88 : 23
real and eternal, 583 : 3
renew a right s. within me, 19 : 16
resemblance neglects s. of objects, 135 : 12
revenge delight of mean s., 122 : 18
rise from flesh to s., 873 : 20
rises with rising wind, 874 : 6
runs in and out of waves, 874 : 9
sacred to departed s., 133 : 20

Spirit (*continued*)
scorned his s., 215 : 10
selfsame sounds on s., 767 : 9
sensitive to impressions, 686 : 8
shall rest upon him, 29 : 18
shall return unto God, 27 : 25
shallow s. of judgment, 184 : 20
slave s. below, 794 : 12
slumber did my s. seal, 424 : 14
so still and quiet, 229 : 26
spur the clear s. doth raise, 280 : 15
straight in strength of s., 634 : 6
streaming from baptism, 694 : 1
strongest and fiercest s., 284 : 4
subtle s. my path attended, 794 : 5
that always denies, 396 : 13
that is One, 657 : 5
that on life's rough sea, 178 : 6
that quickeneth, 44 : 42
that stands by naked man, 918 : 11
thy s. walks abroad, 217 : 11
too much s. to be at ease, 335 : 19
tool carries s. by which created, 852 : 17
travail and vexation of s., 26 : 23
truth shows s. and substance, 135 : 12
tyranny enter if people lose s., 577 : 15
vanity and vexation of s., 26 : 16
vital s., 688 : 11
weak s. quickens, 806 : 6
whatever anguish of s., 383 : 1
which goes through mass, 755 : 1
whither shall I go from thy s., 22 : 17
who longs to strengthen s., 701 : 12
why s. of mortal proud, 463 : 16
wild s. moving everywhere, 467 : 18
with more s. chased, 199 : 6
with spirit can meet, 535 : 9
within me constraineth me, 16 : 22
within nourishes, 105 : 22
wounded s. who can bear, 24 : 20
yearning in desire, 529 : 10
yet woman too, 427 : 4
Spiriting, do my s. gently, 247 : 17
Spiritless, man so faint so s., 205 : 19
Spirit's, clown of s. motive, 883 : 11
Spirits, all s. and melted into air, 248 : 13
apothecary never out of s., 398 : 21
be free all worthy s., 178 : 5
black s. and white, 261 : 22
blast drives wicked s., 140 : 22
by our own s. defied, 425 : 10
call s. from vasty deep, 204 : 12
can either sex assume, 283 : 18
cheerer of s., 270 : 34
day of s., 298 : 21
good s. when well dressed, 547 : 29
her wanton s. look out, 227 : 3
how can you serve s., 68 : 26
I summoned up, 395 : 17
insult to s. of ancestors, 591 : 4
like two s. suggest me, 246 : 3
maketh his angels s., 51 : 13
master s. of this age, 216 : 9
not finely touched, 227 : 24
not jump with common s., 199 : 13
of great events, 443 : *n* 6
of just men, 51 : 21
of land and grain, 89 : 28
of wise mock us, 206 : 13
other s. there stand apart, 475 : 8
pulsing in our s., 888 : 6

Spirits (*continued*)
red s. and gray, 261 : 22
stories from land of s., 436 : 2
that fell with Lucifer, 183 : 20
that tend thoughts, 236 : 17
tribe of s. and of men, 132 : 12
unclean s. entered swine, 42 : 5
unhappy s. fell with Lucifer, 183 : 20
vanish like evil s., 389 : 12
we are s. not animals, 745 : 1
who live in twilight, 686 : 13
with morning as such s. will, 761 : 1
wonders at quaint s., 196 : 20
Spirit-stirring drum, 231 : 11
Spiritu, et cum s. tuo, 54 : 1
Spiritual, erotic instinct s., 755 : 3
excitement, 588 : 9
forces, 679 : 5
found s. cause, 583 : 2
highest s. authority, 774 : 9
inward and s. grace, 56 : 5
material moral s. force, 699 : 5
men s. beings, 845 : 15
millions of s. creatures, 286 : 2
natural fact symbol of s., 496 : 6
poverty and s. activity, 771 : 16
psalms hymns and s. songs, 49 : 37
risk and s. self-sacrifice, 816 : 17
stronger than material, 499 : 26
superhuman s. and divine, 754 : 10
unbidden unconscious, 536 : 6
values such as taste, 782 : 11
wickedness in high places, 49 : 39
Spirituality, air image of s., 679 : 5
Spiritus, animus s., 679 : 5
Spirochete, without little s., 900 : 5
Spit, if I lie s. in my face, 203 : 30
no gun but I can s., 869 : 6
on us for luck, 92 : 13
orators when out will s., 212 : 22
upon my Jewish gaberdine, 198 : 24
Spite, death aims with fouler s., 267 : 11
force in s. of Nature, 291 : 9
in erring reason's s., 337 : 1
O cursed s., 220 : 6
of cormorant devouring Time, 190 : 8
the world, 238 : 15
Spiteful envious animal the Public, 445 : 7
Splashing wintry mold, 712 : 12
Spleen, in a s. unfolds heaven and earth, 195 : 23
meditative s., 428 : 14
that scourge of Britain, 486 : 6
Splendid a star, 545 : 25
abilities utterly corrupt, 439 : 7
and sterile Dolores, 632 : 12
by the vision s., 426 : 15
eloquence, 342 : 8
few but how s. stars, 785 : 17
in ashes, 275 : 11
misery, 388 : 13
poor s. wings, 634 : 10
shilling, 328 : 19
silent sun, 575 : 24
tear, 533 : 24
you rise, 5 : 4
Splendide mendax, 108 : *n* 2
Splendidly null, 533 : 17
Splendor and travail of earth, 802 : 18
falls on castle walls, 530 : 26
guilty s., 376 : 24
in the grass, 426 : 21
mortal s., 797 : 10
Splendor (*continued*)
not in lone s., 478 : 20
of the Mighty One Krishna, 94 : 15
on earth no such s., 136 : 3
pavilioned in s., 445 : 21
your s. like heaven's s., 5 : 2
Splendors and glooms, 469 : 3
heaven with s. lie, 567 : 11
old homes old s., 726 : 2
one of radiant s. of France, 504 : *n* 4
Splenetive and rash, 224 : 21
Split ears of groundlings, 221 : 23
mountains with thunderbolt, 103 : 29
reality s. in painting, 774 : 10
sides with laughing, 169 : 24
the sky in two, 822 : 12
Splits, who s. wood warms twice, 560 : *n* 2
Splitting, warmed while s. stumps, 560 : 9
Spoil it by trying to explain, 398 : 17
little foxes that s. the vines, 28 : 8
lives of better people, 669 : 14
no more s. upon my face, 208 : 19
rampant for s. and victory, 658 : 5
rod and child, 722 : 22
spare rod and s. child, 91 : *n* 3, 291 : 19
villainous company s. of me, 204 : 25
Spoiled, Christian a pagan s., 706 : 14
Spoiling nice new clothes, 932 : 4
Spoils, conquests glories triumphs s., 216 : 8
of time, 362 : 7
rich with s. of nature, 274 : 5
to victor belong s., 455 : 11
treasons stratagems and s., 201 : 3
victor belongs to s., 835 : 2
Spoke I think of perils past, 765 : 9
man who knew more s. less, 120 : 15
more he heard less he s., 660 : 15
never s. with God, 606 : 17
of disastrous chances, 229 : 28
town crier s. my lines, 221 : 23
without one word s., 404 : *n* 3
Spoken, glorious things of thee s., 367 : 8
God's last Put out light s., 748 : 11
lie down till leaders s., 709 : 5
not s. of soul, 509 : 13
Rome has s. case closed, 129 : 13
speak when s. to, 668 : 10
weird power in s. word, 683 : 7
word at random s., 431 : 19
Spondee, slow s. stalks, 436 : 3
Spontaneity, studied s. of Horace, 117 : 19
Spontaneous cooperation of free people, 682 : 17
happiness not s. product, 763 : 3
joy and natural content, 713 : 6
overflow of feelings, 424 : 9
Spoon, dish ran away with s., 930 : 17
hire long s. eat with feend, 147 : 26
runcible s., 550 : 10
silver s. in mouth, 171 : 5
Spoons, faster counted s., 488 : *n* 1
guard our s., 488 : 1
let us count our s., 354 : 12
measured life with coffee s., 803 : 13
woman with silver s., 558 : 7
Sport, boys throw stones in s., 92 : 9
ended his s. with Tess, 641 : 4
inflicts pain for s., 626 : 10
Sport (*continued*)
make s. for neighbors, 440 : 23
no s. in hate, 469 : 26
of kings, 328 : 18
pain for s., 626 : 10
present life a diversion and s., 132 : 1
that wrinkled Care derides, 277 : 20
they kill us for their s., 234 : 21
to have enginer hoist, 223 : 13
with Amaryllis, 280 : 15
would be tedious, 203 : 5
Sported on the green, 439 : 10
Sports and plays with me, 402 : 13
Christmas brought s. again, 430 : 22
joy of youthful s., 458 : 30
of love, 255 : 16
our s. shall be seen, 403 : 4
shows games s. guns, 381 : 7
Sportsman, bloodless s. I, 685 : 10
Sporus, let S. tremble, 338 : 18
Spot, black s. to keep concealed, 599 : 7
certain am I of s., 606 : 17
dim s. men call earth, 279 : 3
do in that remote s., 420 : 17
earth one mighty blood s., 503 : 2
one small s. a continent, 610 : 8
out damned s., 239 : 23
plant on peculiar s., 337 : 3
stand on right s., 395 : 18
there is no s. in thee, 28 : 12
what is Black S., 668 : 6
Spotless reputation, 193 : 32
Spotlight of the backfield, 825 : 3
Spots, leopard change his s., 32 : 6
minds grow in s., 650 : 10
quadrangular of diamond form, 377 : 6
Spotted sight or sound, 793 : 19
snakes with double tongue, 196 : 21
Spouse so bright and clear, 254 : 16
Spout till you have drenched, 233 : 24
Spouted arms, 843 : 20
Spouts, trunk s. out a sea, 286 : 30
Sprang to the stirrup, 541 : 11
Sprat, Jack S. eat no fat, 929 : 16
Spray, never a s. of yew, 586 : 3
nightingale on bloomy s., 281 : 8
rime was on the s., 640 : 4
toss in the s., 584 : 11
whinny in thy s., 569 : 20
Spread alarm, 512 : 7
dreams under your feet, 712 : 16
masters s. yourselves, 196 : 3
money not good unless s., 180 : 15
out against sky, 803 : 9
silent tents s., 578 : 10
the thin oar, 337 : 8
truth from pole to pole, 325 : 9
Spreading, by broad s. disperse, 184 : 18
chestnut tree, 510 : 7
himself like a green bay tree, 18 : 26
Spreads, wrath s. through hearts of men, 58 : 30
Sprechen ist silbern, 473 : 9
Spree, gentlemen rankers on s., 708 : 14
Sprial of rising prices, 762 : 8
Sprightliness of French tongue, 357 : 19
Sprightly, first s. running, 303 : 11
tossing heads in s. dance, 427 : 9
Spring, a little madness in s., 607 : 9
abhorrent to nihilist, 766 : 18
absent in the s., 245 : 9
appareled like the s., 243 : 10
blossom by blossom s. begins, 632 : 8

Spring (*continued*)
blue sky of s., 594 : 3
breaks through again, 843 : 9
brings back balmy warmth, 102 : 3
brown hills melted into s., 562 : 1
came on forever, 765 : 9
can s. be far behind, 467 : 22
clean pasture s., 747 : 3
come gentle S., 345 : 10
comes slowly up this way, 433 : 29
comes with rustling shade, 811 : 5
direful s., 334 : 18
disturbance of the s., 807 : 11
ever-returning s., 576 : 2
first day of s. one thing first s. day another, 671 : 14
flowers that bloom in s., 629 : 15
from her may violets s., 224 : 17
full of sweet days, 268 : 16
haunted s. and dale, 277 : 11
hounds of s., 632 : 7
in Just-s., 828 : 11
in s. young man's fancy, 529 : 16
in the fire of s., 516 : 4
infants of s., 218 : 27
last leaf in s., 519 : 19
lived light in s., 585 : 11
makest a s. to gush forth, 131 : 9
melted into s., 562 : 1
Mrs. Porter in s., 805 : 6
no season such delight as s., 265 : 16
no s. nor summer beauty, 253 : 20
not as in bud of s., 255 : 1
of ever-flowing water, 106 : 20
of love gushed from heart, 434 : 29
of love resembleth April day, 189 : 32
of prodigality, 373 : 10
Pierian s., 332 : 20
ran canyons all s., 843 : 20
season of s. comes on, 58 : 1
silent s., 870 : 1
starless and bible-black, 887 : 6
stirring roots with s. rain, 804 : 26
summer autumn winter, 829 : 18
sweet lovers love the s., 212 : 33
targeted trod like s., 716 : 15
this young s., 859 : 2
'tis s. and weeds shallow-rooted, 185 : 15
vanish with rose, 517 : 12
weather gets through more in s., 622 : 18
winter mother of s., 513 : 6
would not be so pleasant, 290 : 11
year's at s., 540 : 15
year's pleasant king, 250 : 8
youth like s. overpraised, 620 : 8
Springes to catch woodcocks, 219 : 5
Spring-laden breeze sinister, 728 : 13
Springs, beside the s. of Dove, 424 : 12
entered into s. of sea, 16 : 31
every thought that s., 429 : 7
fifty s. little room, 690 : 17
from seventy s. a score, 690 : 17
hope s. eternal, 336 : 15
joy's delicious s., 457 : 2
of behavior hidden, 741 : 12
root from which tyrant s., 85 : 5
Scotia's grandeur s., 408 : 18
steeds to water at those s., 243 : 16
we have no s., 849 : 12
Springth the wude nu, 916 : 14
Springtime, birds warble sweet in s., 672 : 19
Springtime (*continued*)
deceives, 641 : 14
fragrance of all s., 888 : 4
in s. every day growth, 565 : 20
never yet was s., 637 : 22
only pretty ring time, 212 : 33
younger than s., 833 : 14
Sprinkle quarters on town, 691 : 24
Sprinkled, blood s. upon my garments, 31 : 26
isles, 543 : 24
Sprite, angelic s., 254 : 7
Sprites and goblins, 246 : 14
Sprouting despondently at gates, 804 : 5
no cabbages s. out, 520 : 5
Spruce affectation, 191 : 9
cone regularity, 799 : 5
Sprung, vile dust whence he s., 430 : 10
Spun, gods have s. the thread, 59 : 12
of Iris' woof, 279 : 8
yarn s. in Ulysses' absence, 242 : 10
Spur, avarice s. of industry, 357 : 13
between s. and bridle, 270 : 12
fame is the s., 280 : 15
me into song, 717 : 13
my dull revenge, 223 : 17
no s. to my intent, 236 : 24
not unbroken horse, 432 : 7
reward and punishment s., 307 : 19
studies a s. to young, 98 : 7
Spurn, existence saw him s. reign, 351 : 10
had he power to s., 607 : 8
Spurned, youth s. in vain, 177 : 8
Spurns that patient merit takes, 221 : 12
Spurred boldly on and dashed, 304 : 17
ready booted and s., 298 : 18
Spurs, let boy win his s., 143 : 8
now s. lated traveler, 238 : 22
sky showcase of s., 841 : 14
Spy, most agonizing s., 606 : 3
seize what she could s., 856 : 6
sent to s. out the land, 10 : 24
who came in from cold, 911 : 3
Squabbling nationalities, 688 : 1
Squadron, save s. honor France, 545 : 15
Squadrons, God on side of big s., 294 : 21
Squads, undisciplined s. of emotion, 807 : 21
Squalid cash interpretation, 648 : 4
hungry s. population, 596 : 2
Squall of time, 822 : 7
Squalor, public s., 871 : 11
Squalors, radiant s., 899 : 14
Squander, do not s. time, 347 : 26
faith treasure we must not s. 504 : 16
gather and s., 588 : 7
Square, all around the s., 485 : 10
damned thick s. book, 387 : 6
deal, 687 : 8
everything upon the s., 170 : 4
gathered on public square, 701 : 14
I have not kept my s., 241 : 2
person in round hole, 432 : 17
produces perfect squares, 89 : 7
round man in s. hole, 625 : 22
triangular person in s. hole, 432 : 17
Squared, mass times speed of light s., 763 : *n* 2
Squares, produce perfect s., 89 : 7
why streets and s. emptying, 702 : 1
Squash blossom dies, 905 : 15
Squat like toad at ear of Eve, 286 : 6
Squatter's rights of heart, 848 : 8
Squeak and gibber, 217 : 21
faint s. of mortality, 846 : 9
speak Greek naturally as pigs s., 290 : 15
Squeaking Cleopatra, 241 : 27
Squeaks, wheel that s. gets grease, 561 : 19
Squealing of wry-necked fife, 199 : 4
Squeeze orange throw away skin, 343 : 6
Squeezing, be with you in s. of lemon, 371 : 6
from a stone, 794 : 3
Squire and Lady Susan, 641 : 10
that s. of dames, 173 : 18
Squired glacier woman, 843 : 20
Squirmers in bogs, 873 : 11
Squirrel, like coffeepot sits s., 793 : 15
Squirrel's heart beat, 565 : 23
Squirrels, requisite to s. and to me, 606 : 18
Sredni Vashtar went forth, 731 : 16
St. Johns, wall of S. in the city, 896 : 15
Stability in small republics, 451 : 18
of internal medium, 551 : 18
Stabilization of aggregate demand, 871 : 16
Stable earth proper element, 265 : 7
ensure s. economy, 903 : 9
good horse in s., 369 : 22
its own s. door, 605 : 19
law s. but not stand still, 731 : 10
steed stolen shut s. door, 159 : 30
within s. economy, 903 : 10
Stabs, every word s., 209 : 10
intention s. the center, 246 : 12
Stack or the barn door, 277 : 23
Stacker of wheat, 761 : 4
Staff, bread called s. of life, 319 : 8
cockle hat and s., 223 : 21
I'll break my s., 248 : 15
not wave s. in air, 494 : 6
of faith to walk upon, 172 : 15
of life bread, 319 : *n* 4
of life ease of burdens, 169 : 12
of this broken reed, 30 : 26
resting upon broken s., 379 : 4
stay and the s., 28 : 34
thy rod and thy s., 18 : 7
very s. of my age, 199 : 2
with your s. in your hand, 9 : 25
Stag at eve, 431 : 5
Stage, all the world's a s., 211 : 15
daily s. of duty run, 311 : 18
dreamer is s. manager, 754 : 12
earth a s., 211 : *n* 3
frets his hour upon s., 240 : 4
glory in one day doth fill s., 267 : 19
great s. of fools, 235 : 5
lags the veteran on s., 351 : 21
last s. of all, 587 : 17
meet disease at first s., 117 : 11
of history, 666 : 5
on the s. he was natural, 371 : 18
players and painted s., 717 : 20
something for modern s., 792 : 12
Tragic Muse trod s., 334 : 12
well-graced actor leaves s., 195 : 15
well-trod s., 278 : 6
where every man play part, 197 : 28
wonder of our s., 256 : 11
world's a s., 211 : *n* 3

Stagecoach, travel faster than s., 371 : 2
Stages, hundred thousand s., 717 : 6
Stagger but not with strong drink, 30 : 16
like a drunken man, 21 : 16
Staggered and terrible-eyed, 866 : 16
Stagnant, fen of s. waters, 425 : 22
water loses purity, 152 : 8
Staid, stay our minds be s., 749 : 14
very s. head, 200 : *n* 4
Stain all my raiment, 31 : 26
both moon and sun, 244 : 14
crave s. of tears, 748 : 9
felt s. like wound, 373 : 24
in thine honor, 36 : 5
my man's cheeks, 233 : 22
stiff dishonored shroud, 804 : 25
world's slow s., 469 : 12
Stained, and I s. the water clear, 403 : 3
sunset s. with horrors, 673 : 17
with mystic horrors, 673 : 17
Staineth slop, 792 : 8
Stainless, conscience upright and s., 141 : 19
Stains white radiance of eternity, 469 : 16
Stair, as I was going up s., 756 : 2
climbing the third s., 806 : 2
Staircase, palms on s., 866 : 16
wit, 359 : 14
Stairs, darker and darker s., 791 : 1
down darker and darker s., 791 : 1
how hard the way up another's s., 142 : 13
of concepts, 857 : 4
threw him down the s., 931 : 8
Stairway leads to dark gulf, 743 : 14
militaristic s., 909 : 14
of surprise, 494 : 15
Stake counter boldly, 543 : 14
great interests at s., 88 : 10
I am tied to the s., 234 : 17
in glorious institution, 373 : 7
that appeared on green cloth, 625 : 25
when honor's at the s., 223 : 19
Stakes, mortal s., 748 : 18
were thrones, 462 : 14
Stale, bread ever more s. rags, 793 : 1
dull s. tired bed, 233 : 3
frizzled s. and small, 892 : 19
how weary s. flat. 218 : 5
nature never s., 861 : 17
nor custom s., 241 : 1
stench of s. oranges, 792 : 19
winter hangs on till s., 739 : 2
Stalk, corn ear on tip of s., 928 : 15
gathering s. and root, 854 : 2
half asleep as they s., 642 : 2
left it on s., 494 : 14
of death, 908 : 8
Stalking, with naked foot s. my chamber, 161 : 25
Stalking-horse, uses folly like s., 213 : 6
Stalks, slow spondee s., 436 : 3
Stalled ox and hatred therewith, 24 : 7
Stallion, like a s. on the track, 4 : 10
shod with fire, 596 : 15
watersmooth-silver s., 828 : 13
Stalls above like elephant, 893 : 6
Stamp and esteem of ages, 302 : 18
change s. of nature, 223 : 11
man bears s. of lowly origin, 515 : 10
of human condition, 165 : 18
Stamp (*continued*)
penny postage s., 614 : 8
poor man is Christ's s., 268 : 9
rank but guinea's s., 411 : 17
Stamped foot cried Give me, 605 : 7
Stamps, liberty property no s., 920 : 8
wrinkle deeper, 457 : 10
Stand a little out of my sun, 86 : 9
alone and think, 478 : 19
and look at them long, 574 : 24
and stare all's blue, 545 : 23
and wait, 282 : 17
at the door and knock, 53 : 6
a-tiptoe when day named, 208 : 10
bade each other s., 626 : 21
by the fire and stink, 233 : 8
by to crash, 821 : 1
by uniting we s., 378 : 11
darkling s. varying shore, 241 : 20
earth's foundations s., 692 : 11
fast in faith, 49 : 9
give me where to s., 93 : 5
hair s. up, 75 : 15
hair to s. an end, 219 : 18
having done all to s., 49 : 39
hazard of the die, 187 : 32
he shall s. at the latter day, 16 : 4
henceforward in thy shadow, 507 : 9
here a little child I s., 267 : 1
here I and you s., 641 : 21
here I s., 155 : 13
house divided cannot s., 41 : 35
how beautiful they s., 470 : 13
I must s. the course, 234 : 17
if you can't s. heat, 788 : 1
in great hand of God I s., 238 : 9
in his holy place, 18 : 8
in your own light, 160 : 27
incessantly s. on head, 611 : 9
law not s. still, 731 : 10
learn to s. alone, 599 : 11
like an anvil, 269 : *n* 5
like Druids of old, 510 : 26
like greyhounds in slips, 207 : 18
me now in good stead, 777 : 18
Nature s. up and say, 217 : 14
never s. to doubt, 266 : 18
no time to s. and stare, 732 : 9
nor sit nor s. but go, 544 : 10
not idly s. aside, 81 : 5
not upon order of going, 238 : 30
on highest pavement, 804 : 10
on right spot, 395 : 18
on terrible threshold, 863 : 15
on your own ground, 555 : 4
poplars s. and tremble, 691 : 11
still ever-moving spheres, 184 : 7
sun s. still upon Gibeon, 11 : 34
then I'll s. and stroke, 403 : 8
to in a month, 192 : 26
to the main chance, 175 : 14
too near one another, 257 : 2
undisturbed as monuments, 388 : 16
united we s. divided we fall, 378 : *n* 7
up and take war, 710 : 23
up stand up for Jesus, 562 : 13
up straight, 879 : 19
upon threshold of the new, 276 : 12
virtue not left to s. alone, 68 : 18
who only s. and wait, 282 : 17
with us now, 815 : 12
word of our God shall s., 30 : 33
ye in the ways, 31 : 37
your ground, 374 : 19
Standard, is higher s. of living worth cost, 795 : 9
mind's the s. of man, 328 : 1
nothing for which no s., 602 : 6
unfurled s. to air, 474 : 18
Standards, compel philosophy to inquire about s., 98 : 25
Standest, place whereon thou s. is holy, 9 : 11
Standeth God within shadow, 567 : 7
in the way of sinners, 17 : 12
Standing apart from it, 800 : 3
as cheap sitting as s., 323 : 4
at ease in nature, 573 : 21
given gladly not to be s. here, 872 : 8
green mantle of s. pool, 234 : 9
in the community, 671 : 15
jokes, 326 : 6
mantle like a s. pond, 198 : 1
on pleasant lea, 428 : 1
things s. thus unknown, 225 : 1
upon shoulders of giants, 313 : 10
with reluctant feet, 510 : 13
Stands, as the case s., 261 : 13
bigly under unruly scrutiny, 889 : 19
brunt of life, 76 : 20
by naked man, 918 : 11
church clock at ten to three, 796 : 12
elephant leans or s., 268 : 20
great ox s. on my tongue, 71 : 4
he that s. it now, 384 : 13
in Elgin's place, 536 : 7
like one that s. on promontory, 186 : 10
Massachusetts there she s., 450 : *n* 7
nature s. on very verge, 233 : 19
Neptune's empire s., 217 : 22
on slippery place, 202 : 3
Pity s. before the door, 406 : 4
republic for which it s., 677 : 10
ringed with world he s., 532 : 28
there she s. childless, 458 : 16
tiptoe on misty mountaintops, 193 : 15
what s. if freedom fall, 710 : 24
while s. the Coliseum, 458 : 22
who Time s. still withal, 212 : 11
world s. out on either side, 822 : 12
Stanley, approbation from Sir Hubert S., 416 : 9
on S. on, 431 : 3
Staple, finer than s. of his argument, 191 : 6
Star, Adonais like a s., 469 : 17
as a beauty I'm not a s., 758 : 5
boy finding s. in haymow, 879 : 11
bright particular s., 227 : 10
bright s. would I were steadfast, 478 : 20
captains glow, 785 : 15
catch a falling s., 252 : 1
Chamber matter, 225 : 5
charm to stay morning s., 435 : 22
civilization at morning s., 498 : 8
compared to north polar s., 68 : 8
constant as northern s., 216 : 3
danced, 209 : 13
dark cooling s., 746 : 20
desire of moth for s., 469 : 20
dropped like falling s., 284 : 2
elevation of North S. north to south, 151 : 7
emigrated to another s., 609 : 12
evening s. love's harbinger, 287 : 32

Star (*continued*)
evening s. you shine on dead, 468 : *n* 5
eve's one s., 478 : 2
fair as a s., 424 : 12
farewell Morning S., 97 : 16
feel like morning s., 619 : 15
fixed s. in constitutional constellation, 821 : 6
for every state, 536 : 1
for which evening waits, 729 : 6
give him the morning s., 53 : 3
give name to every fixed s., 190 : 12
glory like a shooting s., 194 : 24
gracious evening s., 552 : 14
great s. early drooped, 576 : 2
here a s. there a s., 604 : 5
high s. of Truth, 586 : 9
hitch your wagon to a s., 499 : 9
if thou follow thy s., 141 : 10
in the east, 36 : 20
infect to north s., 209 : 10
knowledge like sinking s., 529 : 10
living as black rock s., 906 : 6
loftiest s. of heaven, 467 : 7
looks down at me, 641 : 21
love morning and evening s., 791 : 8
man is his own s., 260 : 17
man nearer atom than s., 776 : 9
moist s., 217 : 22
moon with one bright s., 434 : 23
morning s. you shone among living, 468 : *n* 5
my only s. is dead, 514 : 9
name of the s. is Wormwood, 53 : 17
no rood has not s., 494 : 2
not fourth sound but s., 544 : 3
of empire, 330 : *n* 9
of fate declined, 460 : 3
of peace return, 443 : 13
of smallest magnitude, 285 : 3
on stars thou gazest my s., 176 : *n* 2
one s. differeth, 49 : 4
or two beside, 434 : 27
orbed in this contracted s., 794 : 4
our life's s., 426 : 14
punctual as a s., 605 : 19
quickly come as the Evening S., 97 : 16
reach unreachable s., 890 : 1
shining s. and inspiration, 836 : 3
silent language of s., 812 : 2
something like a s., 749 : 14
soul was like s., 425 : 23
splendid a s., 545 : 25
stone flesh soul, 543 : 19
sunset and evening s., 535 : 19
that bids shepherd fold, 279 : 9
that burns forever in sky, 929 : 6
to every wandering bark, 245 : 18
to stay our minds on, 749 : 14
to steer her by, 760 : 14
tonight no morning s., 910 : 19
twinkle little s., 449 : 13
unavailing s., 711 : 7
varying s. of the world, 241 : *n* 4
westward the s. of empire, 330 : *n* 9
your aim the s., 924 : 16
Starboard hand of every woe, 570 : 5
on s. beam Charybdis, 200 : *n* 1
Star-crossed lovers, 191 : 17
Stardust, we are s., 916 : 7
Stare and sting forever, 821 : 11
decisis is wise policy, 678 : 3
Stare (*continued*)
eyes that s., 811 : 15
make the public s., 461 : 1
Quintilian s. and gasp, 282 : 8
stand and s., 732 : 9
stand and s. all's blue, 545 : 23
stare in basin, 868 : 10
stony British s., 533 : 19
super vias antiquas, 31 : *n* 4
Stared at the Pacific, 475 : 7
Starers, stupid s. and loud huzzas, 337 : 14
Starfish hermit crab whale's backbone, 808 : 2
Staring, nightly sings the s. owl, 191 : 14
Stark insensibility, 353 : 20
Molly S. a widow, 371 : 26
monotony of stone, 711 : 11
Starkest madness, 605 : 11
Starless and bible-black, 887 : 6
Starlight and dewdrop waiting, 598 : 8
lit my lonesomeness, 640 : 4
Starlike, from s. eyes seek, 272 : 1
Starlit fences, 691 : 12
Starred, memory of having s., 749 : 1
night's s. face, 478 : 18
on a s. night, 600 : 27
portals dimly s., 767 : 16
Starry archipelagoes, 673 : 19
dynamo, 906 : 1
entertain s. stranger, 292 : 17
firmament for roof, 637 : 21
flag, 578 : 12
floor, 405 : 2
Galileo, 458 : 12
heavens above me, 366 : 12
Hesperus led s. host, 285 : 25
paladin, 540 : 11
round of s. folds, 474 : 22
silence that is in s. sky, 428 : 7
threshold of Jove's Court, 279 : 2
train, 286 : 1
wide and s. sky, 668 : 20
Stars about the lovely moon, 63 : 6
above us govern, 234 : 26
and planets fallen on me, 787 : 9
are dead, 868 : 8
as long as s. graze, 104 : 29
as many farewells as s., 226 : 24
baths of western s., 529 : 13
be not darkened, 27 : 24
between me and the s., 424 : 1
between profusion of matter and s., 853 : 3
blesses s. and thinks it luxury, 325 : 13
blossomed lovely s., 511 : 3
branch-charmed by s., 478 : 4
broad stripes bright s., 446 : 1
brothers above arch of s., 412 : 10
build beneath s., 330 : 17
by mathematics s. weighed, 697 : 4
came forth to see again s., 141 : 16
clad in beauty of thousand s., 184 : 5
conclave of all the night's s., 71 : 3
continuous as s. that shine, 427 : 8
country far beyond s., 299 : 10
crossway of s., 843 : 5
crowned with s., 311 : 20
cut him out in little s., 193 : 9
doubt thou s. are fire, 220 : 14
drift away in invisible morning, 907 : 11
earth and all s. in sky, 574 : 7
Stars (*continued*)
earth Danaë to s., 531 : 12
fault is not in our s., 215 : 6
few but how splendid s., 785 : 17
fleet of s. anchored, 785 : 15
from field of night, 515 : 16
gateways of s., 693 : 12
gave the first delight, 276 : 4
he telleth the number of the s., 22 : 24
hide diminished heads, 285 : 10
husk of young s., 886 : 15
ideals like s., 603 : 2
in her hair were seven, 601 : 13
in purple dusk, 811 : 13
in sky rustled softly, 673 : 12
in spite of Nature and s., 291 : 9
in s. writen deeth of every man, 147 : 6
in their calm, 585 : 12
in their courses fought, 12 : 5
inauspicious s., 193 : 28
intelligence of s., 864 : 4
islanded in stream of s., 802 : 20
it is the s., 234 : 26
journeywork of s., 574 : 23
kings are like s., 468 : 16
kinship with s., 600 : 15
knew s. flowers birds, 735 : 8
knowledge of atom through s., 776 : 10
lighting s. comets moon, 889 : 14
like s. on the sea, 459 : 14
like s. start from spheres, 219 : 18
listen to s. and birds, 536 : 6
little s. hide your diminished rays, 285 : *n* 3
look at the s., 655 : 21
look cold about sky, 748 : *n* 2
looked at s. in sky, 927 : 13
love steer s., 914 : 7
love that moves sun and other s., 142 : 20
make guilty the s., 233 : 5
men born under happier s., 437 : 4
might not have missed me, 749 : 11
moon and s. thou hast ordained, 17 : 17
morning s. sang together, 16 : 29
move still time runs, 184 : 8
music that will melt s., 583 : 11
night of large few s., 574 : 19
night with train of s., 663 : 12
no I was out for s., 749 : 7
not fire nor s., 76 : 22
not pure in his sight, 16 : 11
nothing the matter with the s., 907 : 11
of human race, 375 : 23
of summer night, 510 : 15
of thy fate, 413 : 17
on backs looking at s., 623 : 22
on s. thou gazest my star, 176 : *n* 2
others forecast the rising s., 105 : 24
owl looked up to s., 550 : 7
preserve s. from wrong, 427 : 16
pure and disposed to mount to s., 142 : 8
puts s. to flight, 516 : 1
realm amidst s., 720 : 6
rush out, 434 : 21
seven s. solar year, 495 : 15
shining of the s., 534 : 27
shooting s. attend thee, 266 : 14
shot madly from spheres, 196 : 14

Stars (*continued*)
silent s. go by, 619 : 16
sing with morning s., 637 : 15
so shall you scale the s., 106 : 3
some of us looking at s., 675 : 9
strike s. with my exalted head, 106 : 25
strives to touch the s., 173 : 6
swings across trees s., 822 : 5
that round her burn, 325 : 9
till s. are old, 596 : 16
to s. through hardships, 133 : 7
true movements of s., 875 : 7
two s. keep not motion, 205 : 9
wandering s., 52 : 26
we all gaze at s., 95 : 4
when s. begin to fall, 936 : 1, 936 : 2
when s. shining bright, 468 : 1
when s. threw down, 405 : 8
whenever moon and s. set, 668 : 11
women's eyes for s., 918 : 6
would have disappeared, 690 : 10
wrote across sky in s., 810 : 2
Starshine at night, 669 : 4
Star-spangled banner, 446 : 1
Start from their spheres, 219 : 18
rouse lion than s. hare, 203 : 14
straining upon the s., 207 : 18
world all over at, 749 : 16
wrong from the s., 792 : 10
Started, arrive where we s., 808 : 17
jumps in after train s., 704 : 1
like a guilty thing, 217 : 23
Startle or amaze with subject, 479 : 6
statements that s. like a wound, 69 : 1
Starts, by s. 'twas wild, 364 : 13
direction in which education s., 84 : 13
everything by s., 304 : 10
home is where one s., 807 : 23
she s. she moves, 511 : 7
think by fits and s., 691 : 21
Starvation of the idle, 579 : 7
prisoners of s., 555 : 24
scientist ready to bear s., 828 : 1
Starve, bargain catch cold and s., 243 : 14
ere I'll rob further, 203 : 19
for want of wonder, 742 : 8
let not poor Nelly s., 302 : 22
neither s. nor stuff, 323 : 1
never s. for wonders, 742 : 8
numerous train below, 315 : 17
they that s. with nothing, 198 : 7
Starved at master's gate, 406 : 10
clean s. for a look, 244 : 28
hackney sonneteer, 333 : 13
Starves her generous birth, 361 : 17
honesty is praised and s., 121 : 23
Starving hysterical naked, 906 : 1
make s. dog prosperous, 624 : 24
Star-y-pointing pyramid, 277 : 13
Stat magni nominis umbra, 118 : *n* 5
State, basis of democratic s., 88 : 12
beweep my outcast s., 244 : 8
body continues in s. of rest, 313 : 13
by delaying preserved s., 95 : 1
change my s. with kings, 244 : 10
church and s. demand for country, 779 : 12
church and s. separate, 590 : 2
coercive power of s., 844 : 4
compelled to change s., 313 : 13

State (*continued*)
completely ready s., 553 : 9
damned vacillating s., 527 : 16
death a s. of nothingness, 83 : 13
done the s. some service, 232 : 20
every man at his best s. is vanity, 19 : 2
faithfully to serve s., 272 : 17
falling with falling s., 334 : 13
for every star, 536 : 1
found s. and give it laws, 154 : 7
free men to develop faculties, 677 : 12
glories of our blood and s., 272 : 15
gods of the s., 83 : 11
have possibility of life, 84 : 15
high and palmy s. ofRome, 217 : 21
his s. is kingly, 282 : 17
I am the s., 312 : 1, 420 : 11
in whatsoever s. to be content, 50 : 8
in wonted manner keep, 255 : 12
independent of everybody but s., 379 : 3
individual make s. his servant, 848 : 12
initiation into new s., 565 : 10
is proletariat, 731 : 7
isthmus of a middle s., 337 : 2
managing affairs of bourgeoisie, 563 : 4
mock air with idle s., 363 : 4
my glories and s. depose, 195 : 12
my mother s., 639 : 15
nation responsible for s., 616 : 1
no fetters in Bay S., 513 : 3
no S. abridge privileges or immunities, 392 : 4
not a mere society, 88 : 5
of chassis, 786 : 9
of Denmark, 219 : 17
of man inconstancy, 299 : 19
of man like kingdom, 215 : 18
pack of scoundrels Order of S., 864 : 8
peace is a s. of mind, 308 : 3
people's s., 275 : 21
pillar of s., 284 : 14
predicts ruin of the s., 406 : 10
primitive unattached s., 755 : 6
prince first servant of s., 358 : 3
proletarian s., 725 : 9
renders service to s., 322 : *n* 3
root of kingdom the s., 89 : 8
ruin or rule s., 304 : 3
saintliness not a s., 877 : 12
saw that s. was half-witted, 558 : 7
scandal waits on greatest s., 189 : 24
ship of s., 62 : *n* 13, 74 : 9
Ship of S., 511 : 8
slime in grains of S., 864 : 5
social s. natural to man, 508 : 20
something rotten in s., 219 : 17
sovereign s. self-centered, 860 : 2
storms of s., 249 : 10
strange eruption to our s., 217 : 18
struggle to found Roman s., 104 : 17
such is s. of America, 372 : 8
takes no notice of opinions, 272 : 17
taking-over by the s., 834 : 7
this is the s. of man, 249 : 3
touch no s. matters, 370 : *n* 3
traduced the s., 232 : 21
wall between church and s., 794 : 16
will prosper, 726 : 12
without king, 484 : 20

State (*continued*)
world or church or s., 568 : 23
world s. inherent in U.N., 813 : 13
worth of s. is individuals, 508 : 14
Statecraft, German s., 553 : 8
Stated calls to worship, 352 : 24
Statehouse, Boston S. the hub, 519 : 11
Stately homes of England, 470 : 13, 781 : 16
pleasure dome decree, 433 : 21
sailing like a s. ship, 288 : 30
ships go on, 530 : 19
Statement, complete s. which is literature, 782 : 2
manic s., 893 : 1
Statements interesting but tough, 623 : 24
of poetry are universals, 88 : 18
put God in his s., 575 : 23
States, all s. work together, 852 : 2
dissevered discordant, 450 : 15
foundations of s. laws and arms, 153 : 20
free and independent s., 378 : 12, 381 : 6
goodly s. and kingdoms, 475 : 6
indestructible S., 514 : 4
laws of the several s., 644 : 17
mighty s. characterless, 226 : 15
responsibility of great s., 787 : 10
saved Union of these S., 576 : 8
set exact wealth of s., 204 : 29
she is all s., 252 : 9
sink or swim together, 730 : 16
sovereign s., 725 : 20
strong native s., 800 : 4
thirteen s. bound together, 401 : 14
unborn and accents yet unknown, 216 : 7
worst of all s. is people's state, 275 : 21
Statesman cannot afford to be moralist, 789 : 12
chemist s. and buffoon, 304 : 10
constitutional s., 597 : 9
too nice for a s., 371 : 14
yet friend to truth, 336 : 5
Statesmanship, in s. get formalities right, 625 : 18
Statesmen, adored by little s., 497 : 2
haven't all been s., 622 : 21
heroes s. philosophers, 392 : 11
village s. talked, 370 : 12
Station like herald Mercury, 223 : 3
middle s. fewest disasters, 318 : 13
no rank nor s., 892 : 19
post of honor is private s., 326 : 2
reflecting on s. in life, 299 : 11
separate and equal s., 387 : 9
take another s., 628 : 4
Stationary, continuous and s. music, 417 : 14
Stations, in order to s. leap, 305 : 9
know our proper s., 548 : 15
planets in s. listening, 287 : 1
Statistic, million deaths s., 766 : 11
Statistical, cautious s. Christ, 659 : 8
figures historical data, 775 : 9
Statistics, unless s. lie, 829 : 11
Statists, hold it as our s. do, 224 : 26
Statuary, give children right to study s., 381 : 14
painted panel s., 715 : 18
Statue, ask why I have no s., 95 : 11
embraced the cold s., 365 : *n* 5

Statue (*continued*)
Jupiter's s., 924 : 3
like good-bye to s., 844 : 17
marble wastes s. grows, 154 : 14
son of France lack s., 725 : 16
stood of Newton, 424 : 2
sum of all it has acquired, 360 : 27
Statues pictures verse grand, 618 : 17
two gross broken s., 792 : 16
world blooms with s., 619 : 17
Stature, add one cubit to s., 38 : 3
full s. of their kind, 900 : 7
increased in wisdom and s., 42 : 33
love give woman full s., 754 : 1
shorten s. of soul, 600 : 16
what s. is she of, 212 : 10
Statures touch the skies, 607 : 2
Status, human s. not depend on economics, 775 : 5
inferiority as to s., 820 : 14
Staunch strong goodly vessel, 511 : 6
sturdy and s. he stands, 666 : 17
Staunchless, time s. flows, 830 : 11
Stay a little the price will fall, 180 : 20
and cooperate, 818 : 15
and the staff, 28 : 34
awhile end the sooner, 179 : 17
behind my tremulous s., 642 : 3
easier s. out than get out, 625 : 7
far hence you prudes, 113 : 7
here I am here s., 514 : 6
I wish he'd s. away, 756 : 2
I'm contented you should s., 560 : 30
longer in hour than week, 632 : 3
me with flagons, 28 : 6
neither have hearts to s., 292 : 1
no longer s. with you, 922 : 13
O sweet, 918 : 18
of water, 28 : 34
shakes wings and not s., 305 : 3
star to s. our minds on, 749 : 14
that's why I'll always s. around, 916 : 13
the bottles of heaven, 16 : 35
whole s. of bread, 28 : 34
will you not s., 732 : 17
with me God, 925 : 2
with thee to go is to s., 288 : 3
Stayed, here shall thy proud waves be s., 16 : 30
joyous time not be s., 174 : 16
should we have s. at home, 878 : 9
Stayeth young man's courting, 793 : 2
Stays, lover rooted s., 495 : 19
S.T.C., prayer for S., 438 : 9
Stead, stand me ever in good s., 777 : 18
Steadfast as thou art, 478 : 20
bears sorrows with s. spirit, 60 : 26
place landsmen build upon, 728 : 11
sober s. and demure, 278 : 12
Steadfastness courage hope, 771 : 13
Steadied, preudunt course s., 568 : 3
Steadiest minds to waver, 74 : 17
Steadily, saw life s., 584 : 8
Steady boys steady, 363 : 16
candle flame, 541 : 20
of heart, 430 : 3
patriot of world alone, 422 : 3
slow and s. wins, 66 : 3
storm of correspondences, 874 : 16
the Buffs, 707 : 13
Steak, to tavern to eat s., 327 : 7
tough as a s., 834 : 6
Steal a few hours from night, 447 : 1
Steal (*continued*)
across the sky, 616 : 7
asked thief to s. me peach, 404 : 11
away their brains, 230 : 26
cannot s. from you, 875 : 6
come not to s. away hearts, 216 : 27
fire from mind, 457 : 12
foh a fico for phrase, 225 : 9
from many is research, 757 : 14
from one author plagiarism, 757 : 14
from public purse, 851 : 14
mature poets s., 809 : 6
my Basil-pot, 476 : 7
my thunder, 318 : 2
our poets s. from Homer, 258 : 6
silently s. away, 510 : 22
sleep under bridges beg and s., 655 : 14
thou shalt not s., 10 : 7
too honest to s., 922 : 14
where thieves break through and s., 37 : 16
Stealin', big s. makes you emperor, 810 : 7
little s. gets you in jail, 810 : 7
Stealing and giving odor, 213 : 7
big s. makes you emperor, 810 : 7
command against s. in Bible, 622 : 14
I feel it s. now, 572 : 7
little s. gets you in jail, 810 : 7
piracies not sullied with s., 622 : 14
plain simple s., 622 : 14
sadness comes s. over me. 481 : 8
will continue s., 569 : 1
Steals goose from common, 918 : 13
mind even of the wise, 58 : 19
something from the thief, 230 : 1
who s. my purse s. trash, 230 : 33
Stealth, do good by s., 339 : 14
good action by s., 442 : 15
lusty s. of nature, 233 : 3
Stealthy school of criticism, 601 : 22
Steam drill beat me down Lord, 922 : 8
engine in trousers, 433 : 5
gas s. or table turning, 581 : 10
rosy hands in s., 899 : 13
thy arm unconquered s., 377 : 26
Steamboat, commence travels in Mississippi s., 449 : 1
Steamer from Harwich, 629 : 1
Steams out footprints that led us, 894 : 1
Steamy, throws up a s. column, 377 : 3
Steed, farewell the neighing s., 231 : 11
in war mounts warrior's s., 430 : 6
noble s., 462 : 5
that knows his rider, 457 : 11
threatens steed, 208 : 1
was the best, 430 : 17
Steeds, fiery-footed s., 193 : 8
strange s., 518 : 9
to water at those springs, 243 : 16
Steel, again in complete s., 219 : 12
against intimation, 768 : 2
age employed in edging s., 399 : 16
clad in complete s., 279 : 24
foeman bares s. tarantara, 628 : 2
foemen worthy of s., 431 : 14
grapple with hoops of s., 218 : 30
long divorce of s., 248 : 25
meals of beef iron s., 207 : 26
molders hemp and s., 431 : 24
my soldiers' hearts, 208 : 8
naked though locked up in s., 185 : 17
Steel (*continued*)
no s. pierce heart so chillingly, 828 : 5
nor poison, 238 : 19
nor s. has lit, 716 : 9
stone bronze stone s., 806 : 12
tipped with line of s., 578 : 14
triple s., 284 : 21
true as s., 145 : 3
Steel-true and blade-straight, 669 : 8
Steep and thorny way to heaven, 218 : 28
Atlantic stream, 279 : 10
frowsy couch in sorrow s., 411 : 23
long and s. is the way, 61 : 17
morn on the Indian s., 279 : 13
my speech in lies, 71 : 25
no ascent too s. for mortals, 106 : 27
of godlike hardship, 478 : 7
senses in forgetfulness, 206 : 17
stay star in his s. course, 435 : 22
Sunium's marble s., 461 : 9
Steeped me in poverty to lips, 232 : 2
Steeple, deep and quiet s. well, 899 : 3
stood and heard s., 691 : 24
unseen as weathercock on s., 189 : 33
Steeples, drenched our s., 233 : 24
still s. hum, 691 : 4
Steeps, azure s., 843 : 13
Steepy, woods or s. mountain yields, 183 : 8
Steer clear of permanent alliances, 379 : 13
from grave to gay, 338 : 1
honest course to success, 312 : 20
in verse s. from grave to light, 311 : 2
right onward, 282 : 19
star to s. her by, 760 : 14
too nigh sands, 303 : 20
Steered, boats that are not s., 243 : 29
Steering, young steersman s., 575 : 19
Steersman, Cybernetics from Greek s., 831 : 22
young s. steering, 575 : 19
Stein, Gertrude S. always right, 845 : 6
on table, 705 : 2
Stem is the flute, 852 : 14
love rose leave it on s., 494 : *n* 3
or stone, 778 : 5
rod out of the s. of Jesse, 29 : 18
thy slender s., 409 : 9
two berries on one s., 197 : 2
Stemming with hearts of controversy, 215 : 5
Stems, cut s. struggling, 873 : 5
Stench of stale oranges, 792 : 19
Stenches, two and seventy s., 436 : 12
Stentor, great-hearted S., 57 : 31
Step, fanaticism to barbarism one s., 359 : 15
first s. is hardest, 344 : 18
from sublime to ridiculous, 420 : 9
highest s. of charity's golden ladder, 137 : 10
keep s. obey in silence, 598 : 15
light of s. and heart, 739 : 14
made last s. possible, 762 : 5
mind music and s., 920 : 9
must begin with single s., 65 : 1
not s. twice into same rivers, 70 : 3
one small s. for man, 910 : 14
one s. enough for me, 490 : 6
softly under snow, 742 : 15
to music he hears, 560 : 17
to s. aside is human, 409 : 21

Stepdame, false as s. to son, 226 : 15
Stephen, feast of S., 563 : 11
King S. worthy peer, 917 : 21
Stephen's, St. S. choir, 892 : 4
Stepmother, Nature a merciless s., 116 : 6
Nature cruel and ruthless s., 152 : 15
poverty s. of genius, 561 : 18
stony-hearted s., 454 : 18
Stepped down to the Four, 783 : 5
in a puddle, 933 : 10
in blood s. in so far, 239 : 3
out of their clothes, 717 : 1
Stepping westward, 426 : 4
Steppingstones of dead selves, 531 : 19
to understanding, 762 : 5
Steps, age with stealing s., 162 : 6
beware of desperate s., 377 : 21
by due s. aspire, 279 : 4
came forth with pilgrim s., 288 : 18
foot wear s. of his door, 35 : 11
hear not my s., 237 : 15
heavy s. of plowman, 712 : 12
humor saves a few s., 799 : 7
I by backward s. move, 299 : 4
invites my s. and points, 335 : 7
lead my s. aright, 471 : 7
Lord directeth his s., 24 : 11
my s. along this street, 886 : 6
same s. as author, 479 : 10
stops and s. of mind, 806 : 2
wandering s. and slow, 288 : 4
were higher that they took, 305 : 5
with how sad s. O Moon, 176 : 14
Sterile, compulsion to become s., 791 : 7
earth seems a s. promontory, 220 : 28
splendid and s. Dolores, 632 : 12
truth for yourself, 662 : 21
Sterility in economic monuments, 871 : 15
Sterling, refine her s. page, 311 : 13
Stern, a s. a true-born Englishman, 194 : *n* 2
and rockbound coast, 470 : 14
battle's s. array, 457 : 19
Caledonia s. and wild, 430 : 11
custom spreads afar, 412 : 9
daughter of voice of God, 427 : 12
joy warriors feel, 431 : 14
Lawgiver, 427 : 15
man s. to view, 370 : 10
my sad heart foams at s., 673 : 13
Ruin's plowshare, 409 : 10
Sterner, ambition of s. stuff, 216 : 19
days not darker days, 745 : 7
Sternest, gives s. good-night, 237 : 17
knight to foe, 149 : 20
Nature's s. painter, 456 : 18
Stew, convert you into s., 806 : 9
missionary s., 806 : 9
w'en s. smokin' hot, 737 : 2
Steward falls into soup tureen, 709 : 24
Stewards of their excellence, 245 : 5
Stewed, longing for s. prunes, 228 : 2
Stick across your back, 929 : 9
carry a big s., 687 : 6
coat upon a s., 715 : 1
hips s., 856 : 5
I am a burr I shall s., 229 : 3
more close than brother, 710 : 19
there I'll s., 169 : 5
thine arrows s. fast in me, 18 : 28
to s. the heart of falsehood, 226 : 15
to your last, 90 : *n* 6
Stick (*continued*)
with fist instead of s., 290 : 14
Sticketh closer than a brother, 24 : 23
Sticking, ay s. in a tree, 431 : 28
Sticking-place, screw your courage to s., 237 : 6
Sticks nix hicks pix, 741 : 5
resurrection of dry s., 873 : 5
Sticky, gilded and s., 794 : 8
Stiff dishonored shroud, 804 : 25
flags straining, 742 : 9
in opinions, 304 : 10
twin compasses, 253 : 5
upper lip, 594 : 5
Stiffen sinews summon blood, 207 : 16
Stiffening of vertebrae, 679 : 10
Stiffens, heart s. and rejoices, 806 : 6
Stiffish cocktail, 544 : 28
Stiffnecked, a s. people, 10 : 12
Stiffness and soul's arrest, 742 : 12
freedom from s., 589 : 6
Stifle, opinion we endeavor to s., 508 : 8
Stile, over hedge before s., 168 : 24
Stile-a, merrily hent the s., 246 : 24
Still and awful red, 434 : 28
and quiet conscience, 249 : 4
as a maid, 404 : 11
be s. and know that I am God, 19 : 12
be s. Hanging Gardens a dream, 752 : 16
be s. wait, 873 : 14
beside the s. waters, 18 : 7
everything else is s., 403 : 15
falls the rain, 801 : 6
heart is lying s., 425 : 14
how s. we see thee lie, 619 : 16
lute be s. I have done, 161 : 24
mightest s. the enemy, 17 : 17
point of turning workd, 806 : 13
quite s. and solitary, 786 : 3
sad music of humanity, 423 : 13
should I have lain s., 15 : 8
small voice, 14 : 5
small voice of gratitude, 363 : 13
sound of voice that is s., 530 : 19
spirit bloweth and is s., 584 : 18
spirit so s. and quiet, 229 : 26
take heed of s. waters, 172 : *n* 7
to be neat, 255 : 17
we must be s. and s. moving, 807 : 24
when all woods are s., 281 : 8
when sun out wind s., 748 : 17
Stille Nacht Heilige Nacht, 466 : *n* 1
Stillness, air solemn s. holds, 361 : 21
modest s. and humility, 207 : 16
soft s. and the night, 201 : 1
solemn s. lay, 537 : 16
such s., 314 : 1
talent formed in s., 395 : 15
Still-vexed Bermoothes, 247 : 16
Stilly, army s. sounds, 208 : 1
Stilts, on s. we walk on our own legs, 166 : 9
Stilus virum arguit, 258 : 8
Stimulate and direct experiment, 681 : 23
wicks they s., 606 : 10
Stimulation, initial cause of action s., 603 : 6
Stimulus, property is s. to work, 758 : 1
Sting, cold doth not s., 250 : 8
death where is thy s., 49 : 8
each s. that bids, 544 : 10
how bitter a s. a little fault, 141 : 19
Sting (*continued*)
prick and s. her, 219 : 25
serpent s. thee twice, 200 : 5
stare and s. forever, 821 : 11
with a little s., 794 : 8
Stinger, 'tis a s., 261 : 16
Stingeth like an adder, 25 : 11
Stingless, death s. indeed, 637 : 17
Stings, dust of friends s. face, 864 : 13
stinks and s., 338 : 19
wanton s. of sense, 227 : 28
what s. is justice, 772 : 9
you for your pains, 331 : 1
Stink, fish and visitors s., 94 : *n* 1
stand by the fire and s., 233 : 8
Stinks and stings, 338 : 19
like rotten mackerel, 439 : 7
several s., 436 : 12
Stint, if you s. them now, 562 : *n* 2
Stir, all hell s. for this, 208 : 15
at dismal treatise rouse and s., 240 : 3
crown me without my s., 236 : 12
dream all night without s., 478 : 4
each make but once, 607 : 8
Jamaicas of remembrance s., 607 : 14
men's blood, 216 : 28
not s. rice though it sticks, 170 : 32
now s. the fire, 377 : 3
of the great Babel, 377 : 4
smoke and s. of this dim spot, 279 : 3
without great argument, 223 : 19
Stirred by solitary cloud, 313 : 23
casement jessamine s., 533 : 22
heart of Englishman, 726 : 5
troubled like fountain s., 226 : 22
up with envy and revenge, 283 : 3
up with high hopes, 281 : 19
Stirring, always s. up some war, 85 : 7
dull roots, 804 : 26
not a creature s., 446 : 3
not a mouse s., 217 : 16
Stirrings, gently awful s., 571 : 3
Stirrup, betwixt s. and ground, 171 : 18
foot in s., 927 : 11, 927 : 12
sprang to s., 541 : 11
Stirs, blood more s. to rouse lion, 203 : 14
culprit life, 604 : 4
divinity that s. within, 326 : 3
of discontented strife, 257 : 11
see she s., 511 : 7
this mortal frame, 435 : 20
up lees of things, 570 : 13
Stitch in time saves nine, 117 : *n* 7
stitch stitch, 485 : 16
Stitches, laugh yourselves into s., 214 : 20
Stitching and unstitching naught, 712 : 20
Stithy, foul as Vulcan's s., 222 : 7
Stock market a mirror, 871 : 4
of Barabbas, 200 : 16
see how his s. went on, 440 : 13
words once my s. wanting, 306 : 24
Stocking all the day, 368 : 8
silk s. filled with mud, 421 : 3
yawns and draws s. up, 804 : 24
Stockings, commended yellow s., 214 : 10
hung by chimney, 446 : 3
silk s. and white bosoms, 353 : 23
to bed with s. on, 933 : 1
Stocks, worshiped s. and stones, 282 : 18
Stockyards, sacrifices like s., 844 : 14

Stoic, every s. was a s., 497 : 8
from forty till fifty man is s., 677 : 2
live like s. bird, 793 : 18
of the woods, 443 : 20
Stoicism, Romans call it s., 325 : 14
Stoic's pride, 337 : 2
Stole, like little mice s. in and out, 289 : 21
man s. the fruit, 268 : 12
memory of all he s., 340 : 17
pig and away run, 931 : 13
tarts and took them away, 931 : 4
thence life o' building, 238 : 5
title from better man I s., 668 : 17
Stolen, better had I s. whole, 668 : 17
ducats s. by my daughter, 199 : 11
enough to be s., 331 : 2
many a man's soul and faith, 916 : 8
men hanged that horses not be s., 310 : 21
my three-and-twentieth year, 277 : 14
not wanting what is s., 231 : 10
odd old ends s. of holy writ, 187 : 6
steed s. shut stable door, 159 : 30
sweets are best, 325 : 3
the scraps, 191 : 7
waters are sweet, 23 : 20
Stomach, army marches on s., 421 : 4
dispenser of invention, 117 : 8
full talk of fasting easy, 128 : 10
goes much against my s., 211 : 19
good-humored s., 115 : 1
hungry s. cannot hear, 296 : 21
is not good, 163 : 9
loathing to s. brings, 196 : 23
man of an unbounded s., 249 : 13
no patriot on empty s., 421 : *n* 3
seat of sensation s., 692 : 14
teacher of arts, 117 : 8
thought depends on s., 344 : 1
way to heart through s., 538 : 6
Stomachaches, tuned like fifty s., 548 : 8
Stomach's, wine for thy s. sake, 50 : 33
Stomachs, lazy folks' s., 662 : 11
store money in s. of needy, 128 : 20
who have best s. not best thinkers, 344 : 1
Stone, ask bread and give s., 38 : 13
at his heels a s., 223 : 22
better pillow than visions, 797 : 16
bows to wood and s., 452 : 10
bronze stone steel, 806 : 12
cold as any s., 207 : 14
conscious s. to beauty, 493 : 18
dash foot against s., 43 : 1
dash thy foot against a s., 20 : 17
dripping water hollows s., 100 : 7
dry s. no water, 805 : 1
fling s. giant dies, 344 : 14
flung s. puts stars to flight, 516 : 1
got to become like s., 850 : 1
he that rolleth a s., 25 : 20
head s. of the corner, 21 : 25
heart firm as s., 17 : 6
heart harder than s., 61 : 4
heart turned to s., 231 : 23
heavy as yonder s., 778 : 5
house of good s., 792 : 20
if any have s. to throw, 794 : 6
in one hand a s., 93 : 11
Jackson like s. wall, 594 : 4
leaf unfound door, 852 : 6
leave no s. unturned, 77 : 2
Stone (*continued*)
legs of s., 466 : 12
let him first cast s., 45 : 2
like a rolling s., 915 : 6
live by squeezing from s., 794 : 3
look on stone's face, 900 : 2
make s. of heart, 714 : 10
manhood of this s., 900 : 7
mark with white or black s., 170 : 13
mockery of monumental s., 469 : 10
moving others themselves as s., 245 : 4
no bigger than agate s., 191 : 23
not to conclude against s., 899 : 15
not with club nor s., 607 : 7
of stumbling, 29 : 14
one stark monotony of s., 711 : 11
precious s. set in silver sea, 194 : 13
pulleth sword out of s., 149 : 6
quiet as s., 478 : 2
raise s. and find me, 671 : 9
raise s. cleave wood, 126 : 14, 671 : 9
rests on the land, 300 : 19
rich s. best plain set, 181 : 8
rich s. in bowels of earth, 257 : 13
rolling s. gathers no moss, 111 : 17
shall cry out of wall, 33 : 26
sleep softly eagle under s., 765 : 3
spark out of s. not moral, 631 : 3
stem or s., 778 : 5
strange lump of s., 796 : 1
strength of past, 797 : 11
take s. from s., 806 : 21
tell where I lie, 332 : 11
that puts stars to flight, 516 : 1
thought not crush to s., 873 : 3
to beauty grew, 493 : 18
turn s. start wing, 693 : 18
under every s. a politician, 82 : 15
underneath this s. lie, 256 : 5
violet by mossy s., 424 : 12
walls do not prison make, 296 : 4
water like a s., 608 : 17
we raised not a s., 465 : 9
which the builders refused, 21 : 25
without gout or s., 302 : 24
work philosopher's s., 664 : 17
written of me on my s., 749 : 8
youth s. dead, 795 : 15
Stone Age, bomb into S., 867 : 3
Stone-deaf fishes, 873 : 11
Stonefence sherry cobbler, 452 : 14
Stone's, stone look on s. face, 900 : 2
within a s. throw, 169 : 13
Stones are iron, 11 : 14
blessed man that spares these s., 250 : 1
boys throw s. at frogs, 92 : 9
chose him five smooth s., 13 : 2
cold gray s. O sea, 530 : 19
cry out, 43 : 42
don't throw s. if your windows glass, 347 : 16
have been known to move, 239 : 1
heap of s. a witness, 8 : 23
heap of s. not house, 673 : 8
his look drained s., 873 : 13
house glass not throw s., 269 : 25
in league with s. of field, 15 : 17
kissed by English dead, 827 : 6
labor of an age in piled s., 277 : 13
makes music with enameled s., 189 : 34
men of s., 235 : 16
Stones (*continued*)
move s. of home, 216 : 29
no sermons in s., 631 : 3
not decked with Indian s., 186 : 8
of Troy, 226 : 15
philosopher's s., 259 : 15
prate of my whereabout, 237 : 15
prepared round ready, 905 : 14
rocks and s. and trees, 424 : 14
roots of trees and s., 793 : 19
scrub pavement or break s., 712 : 20
sermons in s., 210 : 24
shows that wood s. are one, 85 : 11
slow drip over s., 873 : 12
that cannot be deciphered, 807 : 23
time to cast away s., 26 : 21
trees and s. will teach you, 136 : 9
whoever raises great s., 849 : 16
worshiped stocks and s., 282 : 18
you are men of s., 235 : 16
Stonest them sent unto thee, 40 : 21
Stonewall, want you to s. it, 883 : 1
Stony British stare, 533 : 19
limits cannot hold love out, 192 : 7
Stony-hearted stepmother, 454 : 18
Stood against world, 216 : 21
among them not of them, 458 : 4
and heard steeple, 691 : 24
apart studiously neutral, 682 : 6
aside been indifferent, 859 : 13
for country's glory, 430 : 14
from everlasting to everlasting, 311 : 21
graves s. tenantless, 217 : 21
hair of my flesh s. up, 15 : 12
here like trees in ground, 576 : 16
in tears amid corn, 477 : 1
in whirling summer, 858 : 20
long I s. there, 526 : 14
not death for I s. up, 605 : 15
on bridge at midnight, 510 : 16
see from where I s., 822 : 11
should of s. in bed, 836 : 12
snake s. up for evil, 747 : 21
that night against fire, 235 : 7
where none before hath s., 261 : 23
Stool pigeon when cannot be soldier, 583 : 8
Stools, between two s., 158 : 22
Stoop as you go through it, 320 : 1
do I s. I pluck a posy, 545 : 23
grief makes owner s., 201 : 20
heaven itself s. to her, 280 : 5
to action, 638 : 2
to become friend, 711 : 10
to rise, 262 : 18
Stooping shows sufficient of His light, 545 : 7
through a fleecy cloud, 278 : 18
Stoops, golden mind s. not, 199 : 9
grass s. not, 189 : 15
to folly, 369 : 20, 805 : 8
to rise love s., 544 : 14
Stop and smell the flowers, 821 : 4
better never to begin than to s., 135 : 4
da music, 825 : 16
did he s. speak to you, 542 : 13
docile and omnipotent, 605 : 19
gangsters will s., 90 : 8
go to end then s., 612 : 13
hole to keep wind away, 224 : 16
if aught of oaten s., 364 : 11
kissing had to s., 543 : 11

Stop (*continued*)
not s. for death, 606 : 4
one heart from breaking, 606 : 12
revolution at beginning, 851 : 12
so easy and so plain a s., 205 : 18
sound what s. she please, 222 : 6
the s. to busy fools, 298 : 21
up access and passage, 236 : 17
where are we to s., 414 : 8
without farmhouse near, 748 : 6
Stopped, he kindly s. for me, 606 : 4
Stoppest, wherefore s. thou me, 434 : 4
Stoppeth, deaf adder that s. her ear, 19 : 23
one of three, 434 : 4
Stopping a bunghole, 224 : 15
moving never s., 575 : 16
noble truth of s. of sorrow, 72 : 23
not see me s. here, 748 : 5
tricking and s., 810 : 19
Stops and steps of mind, 806 : 2
buck s. here, 788 : 16
never s. at all, 604 : 17
of various quills, 281 : 5
Storage, heat in little s., 810 : 18
put it in cold s., 698 : 10
Store, increasing s. with loss, 244 : 22
large as s., 268 : 21
oft amid thy s., 477 : 18
Stored, grapes of wrath s., 566 : 4
with books, 258 : 2
Storehouse, knowledge a rich s., 179 : 1
lock words in literary s., 695 : 5
Tao is s. of all things, 64 : 22
Storied urn or animated bust, 362 : 5
windows richly dight, 278 : 26
Stories, amuse you with s., 372 : 12
from land of spirits, 436 : 2
how much believe my s., 453 : 5
human s. repeat themselves, 738 : 14
only two or three human s., 738 : 14
sad s. of death of kings, 195 : 2
Storm, after s. calm, 319 : 13, 830 : 18
and stress, 399 : 19
bar foul s. out, 715 : 10
brows like gathering s., 411 : 4
calm rising through s., 465 : 2
clouds brood on heights, 551 : 4
death a hideous s. of terror, 262 : 7
directs the s., 325 : 7, 340 : 22
every cloud engenders not s., 186 : 22
flies in night in howling s., 405 : 5
in a teapot, 99 : 4
leave thee in the s., 233 : 18
let s. rage stronger, 725 : 5
like wagon crossing bridge, 877 : 1
lovers fled into s., 476 : 20
nor ever heavy winter s., 59 : 26
of correspondences, 874 : 16
on that side s. desertion death, 481 : 2
pelting of pitiless s., 234 : 3
pilot that weathered s., 421 : 22
rides upon the s., 375 : 16
roaming sky uneasily, 878 : 4
storms formed behind s. we feel, 572 : 1
till s. of life past, 350 : 12
try s., 830 : 18
tumultuous privacy of s., 493 : 22
where s. drives I shelter, 108 : 16
wind s. rain may enter, 351 : 7
Stormed Ratisbon, 540 : 20
Storms, as if s. give repose, 553 : 3
Storms (*continued*)
asked to be where no s., 655 : 17
ere winter s. begin, 536 : 2
he sought the s., 303 : 20
necessary as s., 388 : 6
of state, 249 : 10
outside happy ground, 587 : 8
struggling in s. of fate, 334 : 13
sudden s. are short, 194 : 12
where no s. come, 655 : 17
Storm-troubled sphere, 562 : 4
Stormy blast, 328 : 10
calm or s. weather, 608 : 16
Hebrides, 281 : 2, 345 : 15
husky brawling, 761 : 4
O s. people, 147 : 20
patient out of sorts, 864 : 17
quiet past s. present, 522 : 12
weather, 323 : 2
winds do blow, 273 : 7, 443 : 11
Story and byword through world, 264 : 22
ephemeral and doomed, 838 : 8
epitaph to be my s., 749 : 8
ere their s. die, 642 : 2
fairy s. of simians, 746 : 20
hole in the s., 845 : 13
honor the subject of my s., 215 : 4
if you read Richardson for s., 355 : 3
illusion shadow s., 273 : 2
inventing s. with grass, 901 : 11
my s. being done, 229 : 31
never was a s. of more woe, 193 : 31
not that s. need be long, 299 : *n* 3
of Cambuscan bold, 278 : 23
of my life, 229 : 27
place where s. ended, 808 : 11
repeats s. of her birth, 325 : 9
rough island s., 533 : 5
saddest s. ever heard, 740 : 8
seaman's s. is of tempest, 112 : 20
short in the s. itself, 36 : 16
shuts up s. of our days, 173 : 5
some pretty s. tell, 449 : 12
still same old s., 830 : 7
summits old in s., 530 : 26
teach him to tell my s., 229 : 31
tell my s., 225 : 1
that's another s., 360 : 7
will never go down, 349 : 9
Story-dressers do as much, 258 : 6
Story's about you, 106 : 11
Storyteller, novel happens because s. moved to passion, 135 : 14
Stoure, crush amang the s., 409 : 9
Stout of hand, 430 : 3
so s. a gentleman, 205 : 11
Stoutly struts his dames before, 277 : 23
Stoutness in moderation, 628 : 13
Stove, grandmother sings to s., 878 : 10
ice on hot s., 750 : 4
poetry like s. in summer, 314 : 3
Stowed away in Montreal, 620 : 3
Straddled adjectives, 793 : 7
Stradivari's violins, 564 : 21
Stradivarius, effort to reproduce S., 819 : 14
Straggling road in Spain, 742 : 10
Straight, avoid naming it s., 652 : *n* 3
branch that might have grown s., 184 : 11
build me s., 511 : 6
course to highest good, 101 : 11
crooked cannot be made s., 26 : 16
Straight (*continued*)
crooked shall be made s., 30 : 31
despised s., 245 : 23
down crooked lane, 485 : 10
I called unto mind, 182 : 3
improvement makes s. roads, 404 : 7
in strength of spirit, 634 : 6
line accurately s., 471 : 14
make his paths s., 36 : 26
make s. a highway for our God, 30 : 30
never able to make others s., 89 : 5
one day at Sorbonne, 768 : 20
righteousness his s. path, 89 : 10
road long and s. to grave, 667 : 14
say thing s., 652 : *n* 3
set crooked s., 618 : 7
teach crab to walk s., 82 : 4
to be bent is to become s., 64 : 10
Vermont mountains s., 747 : 20
walketh upright in a s. way, 132 : 15
was path of gold, 541 : 15
Straightest, pity's the s., 260 : 20
Straightforward man more acceptable, 4 : 3
Straightway, he goeth after her s., 23 : 16
Strain at a gnat, 40 : 19
continuous unbroken s., 451 : 2
great music's unforgotten s., 486 : *n* 1
great s. on affections, 565 : 27
guardian angels sung this s., 345 : 19
hold cheap the s., 544 : 10
I heard of higher mood, 280 : 17
prophetic s., 279 : 1
raise somewhat loftier s., 103 : 13
Shakespeare's s., 495 : 15
that s. again, 213 : 7
that s. once more, 368 : 9
unpremeditated s., 345 : 21
Strained, quality of mercy not s., 200 : 9
Straining at particles of light, 480 : 1
in night blasts cold, 742 : 9
upon the start, 207 : 18
Strains as would have won the ear, 278 : 8
blessed s. telling, 552 : 22
of unpremeditated art, 468 : 11
sweet s. pensive smiles, 493 : 16
that might create a soul, 279 : 27
Strait, honor in s. so narrow, 226 : 18
is the gate, 38 : 15
shall forever bear his name, 162 : 11
Straitjacket or club, 676 : 16
Straits, moon fair upon s., 587 : 13
stranger in financial s., 79 : 16
Strand, guardian Naiad of s., 431 : 6
India's coral s., 452 : 8
left fair Scotland's s., 410 : 4
pass to American s., 269 : 11
walked along the S., 353 : 18
wandering on foreign s., 430 : 10
waves fling pebbles up high s., 587 : 14
world's s., 655 : 19
Stranded, navies are s., 431 : 23
Strands, last s. of man, 656 : 15
there he is crossing s., 735 : 3
Strange already said by philosopher, 272 : 9
and well-bred, 324 : 19
art of necessities s., 233 : 30
bedfellows, 247 : 30, 603 : 11
but true, 462 : 2

Strange (*continued*)
capers, 210 : 34
crossroads lie, 839 : 6
dark interludes, 810 : 11
disease of modern life, 586 : 1
eruption to our state, 217 : 18
eruptions, 204 : 10
eventful history, 211 : 15
fear what is too s., 900 : 2
force in s. steeds, 518 : 9
how s. it seems and new, 542 : 13
interlude, 810 : 11
interludes, 810 : 11
lips of a s. woman drop as honeycomb, 23 : 10
lisp and wear s. suits, 212 : 20
Lord's song in s. land, 22 : 15
lump of stone, 796 : 1
more cunning to be s., 192 : 10
most s. that men fear, 215 : 26
Nature hath framed s. fellows, 197 : 26
nothing so s. as truth, 450 : 18
object s. and high, 297 : 6
pair of very s. beasts, 213 : 1
read s. matters, 236 : 19
road grows s., 569 : 3
seas of thought, 424 : 2
so strangely sweet not s., 654 : 17
soldier full of s. oaths, 211 : 15
Solomon loved many s. women, 13 : 37
something rich and s., 247 : 21
stranger in a s. country, 75 : 9
stranger in a s. land, 9 : 9
terrible world war, 745 : 11
that death should sing, 202 : 16
that desire outlive performance, 206 : 16
things come out, 413 : 19
throne in s. city, 525 : 11
truth always s., 462 : 2
'twas passing s., 229 : 31
world is a s. affair, 297 : 14
Strangely pass, 244 : 17
so s. sweet not strange, 654 : 17
Strangeness, addition of s. to beauty, 639 : 4
some s. in proportion, 181 : 9
Stranger across crowded room, 833 : 13
and afraid, 691 : 23
and alone, 852 : 7
and ye took me in, 40 : 33
as we grow older world s., 807 : 23
danger not from s., 897 : 17
doth not intermeddle, 23 : 36
entertain this starry s., 292 : 17
Europe regards her as s., 384 : 12
gray s. in dream, 897 : 16
he that is surety for a s., 23 : 24
I am a s. with thee, 19 : 4
I pass a willful s., 669 : 3
I was s. on earth, 864 : 4
in a strange country, 75 : 9
in a strange land, 9 : 9
in financial straits, 79 : 16
leave them for poor and s., 10 : 19
make no mistake s., 699 : *n* 3
never love a s., 821 : 2
nothing s. ever happened, 878 : 13
than fiction, 462 : 2
to oneself estranged from others, 867 : 7
to sorrow, 76 : 11

Stranger (*continued*)
troubled mind be s., 267 : 20
unless with bedroom eyes, 869 : 6
wiles of s., 855 : 11
Strangers and beggars are from Zeus, 60 : 1
by s. honored, 335 : 10
desire we may be better s., 212 : 9
entertain s., 51 : 22
gods likening themselves to s., 60 : 25
gracious and courteous to s., 180 : 13
Strangest, fate of architect s., 395 : 22
Strangle, vapors seem to s. him, 203 : 5
Strangled Atahualpa, 488 : 6
snakes beside Hercules, 595 : 7
Strapped noosed nighing hour, 692 : 1
Straps, hang in their own s., 213 : 11
Stratagem, take tea without a s., 329 : 23
Stratagems, treasons s. and spoils, 201 : 3
which errors seem, 332 : 18
Strategy involve us in wrong war, 825 : 5
Stratford, Shakespeare was born at S., 301 : 6
Stratosphere of icy certainty, 700 : 2
Straw dogs, 64 : 1
find quarrel in a s., 223 : 19
headpiece filled with s., 805 : 15
I don't care one s., 96 : 18
lion shall eat s., 29 : 19
no more s. to make brick, 9 : 17
pigmy's s. does pierce it, 235 : 3
see which way wind is, 263 : 21
stumbles at a s., 173 : 6
tickled with a s., 337 : 7
turkey in the s., 921 : 12
vote, 699 : 18
Strawberries, feed upon s., 931 : 19
great s. at mouth of pot, 179 : 16
how many s. in sea, 930 : 2
melts on vine, 665 : 12
of angling as of s., 271 : 10
Strawberry, like s. wives, 179 : 16
Straws, as s. that blow, 663 : 9
hairs or s. or dirt, 338 : 12
oaths are s., 207 : 15
Stray, dry dust and s. paper, 792 : 19
empty house like s. dog, 620 : 14
if with me fondly s., 332 : 1
never taught to s., 336 : 16
wishes never learned to s., 362 : 12
Strayed like lost sheep, 54 : 12
Streak, red-line s., 578 : 14
Streakings of morning light, 474 : 18
Stream, bashful s. hath seen God, 292 : *n* 3
by thy murmuring s., 410 : 13
ever-rolling s., 328 : 12
fish have their s., 796 : 13
islanded in s. of stars, 802 : 20
meadow grove and s., 426 : 10
mercy of a rude s., 249 : 3
no shaded s., 399 : 16
no striving against s., 169 : 35
of consciousness, 648 : 13
of his body, 901 : 14
of time run, 206 : 26
of what we feel indeed, 588 : 22
of what we say and feel, 588 : 22
red life s. again, 478 : 8
roses by Bendemeer's s., 447 : 12
slow and silent s. Lethe, 284 : 22

Stream (*continued*)
smoothest water deepest, 172 : *n* 7
steep Atlantic s., 279 : 10
strove against s. in vain, 531 : 10
summer eves be haunted s., 278 : 6
surface s. shallow light, 588 : 22
time s. I go a-fishing in, 559 : 28
trailing in cool s., 585 : 21
Streamed like a meteor to air, 283 : *n* 4
Streamer of the northern morn, 528 : 29
Streamers, sails filled s. waving, 288 : 30
Streaming, before his s. eyes, 613 : 8
from waters of baptism, 694 : 1
light, 279 : 21
Love with s. hair, 836 : 17
meteor s. to the wind, 283 : 20
Streams and woods belong, 685 : 11
cold companionable s., 713 : 16
cooling s., 317 : 7
flow with ambrosia, 76 : 25
lapse of murmuring s., 287 : 4
like thunderstorm, 458 : 17
may valley s. content me, 104 : 4
meet in one salt sea, 207 : 8
passions like floods and s., 172 : 12
pebbles of holy s., 886 : 21
shallow s. run dimpling, 339 : 1
showers from seas and s., 468 : 9
sitting by desolate s., 659 : 9
wavy bodies 'gainst s., 475 : 1
what eternal s., 525 : 18
where cherries tremble, 899 : 16
whereof make glad city of God, 19 : 11
Street, along s. comes blare of bugles, 676 : *n* 5
ballad in s., 496 : 11
car rattling o'er s., 457 : 15
clamor of crowded s., 512 : 18
crossing s. saw parents and child, 906 : 2
don't do it in street, 706 : 16
down long and silent s., 674 : 15
fought s. by s., 744 : 5
harlot's cry from s. to s., 406 : 18
main s. on August afternoon, 894 : 14
my steps along s., 886 : 6
not done by jostling in s., 407 : 1
Old Lady of Threadneedle S., 407 : 12
once walked down s., 710 : 11
reaches of the s., 804 : 4
Wall S. lays egg, 741 : 4
works both sides of s., 781 : 3
Streetcar named Desire, 887 : 9
Streets and squares all emptying, 702 : 1
doors shut in the s., 27 : 24
fight in fields and s., 744 : 2
gibber in Roman s., 217 : 21
grass grow in s., 750 : 18
in thy dark s. shineth, 619 : 16
lion is in the s., 25 : 19
mourners go about the s., 27 : 25
of Laredo, 927 : 14
of our city, 900 : 2
publish it not in the s. of Askelon, 13 : 8
through midnight s., 405 : 10
through negro s., 906 : 1
world's most crowded s., 585 : 15
Strength, all your s. in union, 511 : 15
all your s. is weakness, 74 : 16
alone of muses born, 475 : 13
ancient and natural s., 365 : 16

Strength (*continued*)
and honor are her clothing, 26 : 8
as s. wears away, 302 : 24
as thy days so thy s., 11 : 25
barbarous s. within her, 769 : 9
beyond hope and despair, 806 : 2
by experience with fear, 786 : 13
castle's s. will laugh, 240 : 2
charm woman's s., 694 : *n* 2
collected s. and struck, 692 : 1
credulity child's s., 441 : 22
culture moment of s., 784 : 6
different source of s., 903 : 11
disease gained s. by delays, 113 : 25
dogged s., 724 : 17
enough to do work, 710 : 13
exert his utmost s., 68 : 4
faults it has not s. to prevent, 369 : 15
feeling his cold s., 797 : 12
fight beyond your s., 58 : 18
for the weak, 615 : 6
forsake me not when my s. faileth, 19 : 34
giant's s., 228 : 9
God is our refuge and s., 19 : 10
growing s. in air, 744 : 2
hast thou given the horse s., 16 : 36
hast thou ordained s., 17 : 17
he flourishes in his s., 60 : 26
he rejoiceth in his s., 16 : 37
his hairy s., 278 : 3
if by reason of s. they be fourscore, 20 : 13
if democracy keeps s., 814 : 11
in union even of sorry men, 58 : 15
is a man's charm, 694 : *n* 2
is as strength of ten, 530 : 15
is to sit still, 30 : 17
Jehovah is my s., 29 : 20
justice without s., 300 : 6
king's name a tower of s., 187 : 25
knowledge increaseth s., 25 : 12
lies in attack, 812 : 15
Lord is my s. and my shield, 18 : 13
Lord is my s. and song, 9 : 32
Lord is the s. of my life, 18 : 11
moment of s. of romance, 683 : 11
muscular s. to jaw, 611 : 10
my people lending their s., 888 : 5
my s. and my redeemer, 18 : 3
new ways to use s., 789 : 4
no s. exerted on heat, 892 : 7
not given s. to be artist, 695 : 2
not s. of sentiment but duration, 657 : 20
of final clenching, 888 : 6
of the ancient giants, 60 : *n* 3
of the hills is his, 20 : 20, 54 : 17
of twenty men, 193 : 22
perfect in weakness, 49 : 23
public s. individual security, 401 : 11
renew their s., 31 : 2
respect s. without fearing, 388 : 12
search things above thy s., 34 : 26
stone s. of past, 797 : 11
submit because s. not adequate, 89 : 1
that I may recover s., 19 : 4
they go from s. to s., 20 : 7
through joy, 816 : 7
to forbear and persevere, 669 : 17
to force the moment, 803 : 15
to the needy, 30 : 6
to the poor, 30 : 6
tower of s., 533 : 4

Strength (*continued*)
transforms s. into right, 358 : 13
union gives s., 66 : 22
unity makes s., 597 : 2
what though s. fails, 112 : 22
without boasting, 388 : 12
without hands to smite, 632 : 9
without insolence, 456 : 9
without justice, 300 : 6
Strengthen, charm s. and teach, 511 : 14
me only this once, 12 : 20
who longs to s. spirit, 701 : 12
Strengthens, bread s. man's heart, 319 : 8
nerves, 374 : 2
time s. friendship, 315 : 6
Strenuous life, 686 : 12
sounds s. and serious, 810 : 4
tongue, 478 : 1
Stress and disorientation, 909 : 1
on not changing mind, 751 : 9
storm and s., 399 : 19
strives against s. of necessity, 77 : 11
Stretch every nerve, 346 : 1
far as coin would s., 202 : 27
him out longer, 235 : 19
last pure s. of joy, 875 : 2
nor does Apollo always s. bow, 107 : 22
will line s. out, 239 : 14
yourselves for greatness, 178 : 5
Stretched, above world s. the sky, 822 : 12
forefinger of time, 530 : 24
out chimney's length, 278 : 3
pia mater of mine, 274 : 3
thickest cloud s., 544 : 29
'twixt his s. footing, 226 : 4
walk with s. forth necks, 29 : 1
with muslin, 835 : 1
Stretches of pure delight, 799 : 20
out feet and dies, 892 : 7
out my golden wing, 402 : 13
Stretching before and after, 807 : 8
Strew, flowers to s. Thy way, 268 : 13
on her roses, 586 : 3
Strewed thy grave, 224 : 20
with husks, 227 : 4
Stricken deer go weep, 222 : 17
I was a s. deer, 376 : 25
love's s. why, 607 : 10
old and s. in years, 11 : 35
Strict, death s. in his arrest, 224 : 30
regard to conscience, 382 : 11
Strictly held by none, 749 : 5
meditate thankless Muse, 280 : 15
vow binds too s., 534 : 19
Strictness, Hebraism s. of conscience, 588 : 21
Stride, at one s. comes dark, 434 : 21
nation s. upward concerted by men, 672 : 2
right in middle of s., 900 : 12
Striding high there how he rung, 656 : 1
shadow s. behind you, 805 : 1
the blast, 236 : 24
Strife, age of discord and continual s., 185 : 7
all things born through s., 70 : 4
and envying, 47 : 29
appeaseth s., 24 : 8
clubs typical of s., 377 : 6
din of s., 585 : 15

Strife (*continued*)
from the s. of tongues, 18 : 18
honor for a man to cease from s., 24 : 28
ignoble s., 362 : 12
man of s. and contention, 32 : 9
no s. between me and thee, 8 : 6
none worth my s., 443 : 1
not a single kind of s., 61 : 12
of love, 113 : *n* 3
of Truth with Falsehood, 567 : 6
stirs of discontented s., 257 : 11
with the palm, 585 : 12
wrathful man stirreth up s., 24 : 8
Strifes, hatred stirreth up s., 23 : 23
Strike, afraid to s., 338 : 14
against public safety, 736 : 13
angry because we s., 649 : 7
as hard as you can, 589 : 15
at self-love, 599 : 3
awe into beholders, 322 : 10
but hear me, 70 : 14
clock doth s. by algebra, 291 : 1
clock will s. Devil will come, 184 : 8
disease or sorrows s. him, 564 : 14
flat thick rotundity, 233 : 24
for altars and fires, 464 : 12
honor foe while you s., 700 : 6
it and it hurts my hand, 231 : 23
it when powder's low, 700 : 8
long live the s., 906 : 17
mine eyes but not my heart, 255 : 18
my hearts s. twelve, 863 : 16
out fine passage, 355 : 8
right to s., 736 : 13
sails well but s. rock, 407 : 16
spear to thrust club to s., 157 : 5
stars with my exalted head, 106 : 25
take care you s. in anger, 680 : 25
the tent, 509 : 10
then no planets s., 217 : 26
truth may s. out his teeth, 173 : 3
when a hammer s., 269 : 30
when iron is hot, 110 : *n* 16
when you s. at king kill him, 500 : 12
Strikers, with s. right or wrong, 765 : 11
Strikes, lightning s. mountaintop, 107 : 21
like rising knell, 457 : 14
midnight s. and hastens, 692 : 8
one two three s. you're out, 765 : 14
silent note Cupid s., 274 : 20
Striking blow for freedom, 798 : 6
clocks were s. hour, 510 : 16
so s. and grotesque, 488 : 12
sometimes a friend, 268 : 7
String attuned to mirth, 485 : 7
chewing bits of s., 730 : 7
eyes upon double s., 253 : 6
harp not on that s., 187 : 20
kite cut from s., 789 : 15
moderation is silken s., 257 : 14
notes as warbled to the s., 278 : 22
of pearls to me, 700 : 13
pearls strung on, 653 : 7
pudding-bag s., 934 : 5
sing in a hempen s., 260 : 15
untune that s., 226 : 2
Stringbean, little girl my s., 908 : 13
Stringencies, dead hands dead s., 911 : 14
Stringent execution of bad laws, 589 : 21
protection of free speech, 644 : 23

Strings, bawdy s. of elders, 767 : 11
better not wibrated, 547 : 27
languid s. scarcely move, 403 : 1
leaving tangle of s., 904 : 9
like untuned s. women are, 183 : 18
many s. to bow, 160 : 9
Stringy, has his day then gets s., 846 : 10
Strip away useless decoration, 796 : 2
Stripes, broad s. and bright stars, 446 : 1
cut his s. away, 708 : 2
forty s. save one, 49 : 21
Stripling Thames, 585 : 21
Strive, alone man with God s., 458 : 8
and hold cheap the strain, 544 : 10
earth and water s. again, 334 : 15
here for mastery, 284 : 27
mightily eat as friends, 188 : 29
nor weep, 541 : 21
not possible to fight even if you s., 58 : 18
officiously to keep alive, 564 : 19
on to finish work, 524 : 7
seven cities s. for Homer, 257 : *n* 5
to be like them, 782 : 15
to grasp what they do not know, 90 : 9
to set crooked straight, 618 : 7
to s. to seek to find, 529 : 14
who s. mightily possess, 728 : 8
Striven to be Thine more than world's, 570 : 6
Strives against stress of necessity, 77 : 11
man errs as long as he s., 396 : 9
sage never s. for the great, 64 : 12
to touch the stars, 173 : 6
who s. always to utmost, 396 : 26
Striving, my s. eye dazzles, 299 : 5
no s. against stream, 169 : 35
to better oft we mar, 233 : 12
to grasp continent, 592 : 5
Strivingly, take life s., 649 : 5
Strivings, parcel of vain s., 557 : 2
two unreconciled s., 724 : 17
Strode after me, 424 : 1
Stroke, constitution produced at single s., 517 : 24
his silver hair, 403 : 8
master s. nature's, 495 : 14
of death as lover's pinch, 242 : 3
tender-handed s. nettle, 331 : 1
tune of flutes kept s., 240 : 29
Strokes, amorous of their s., 240 : 29
calumnious s., 218 : 27
little s. fell great oaks, 347 : 29
many s. overthrow the oaks, 175 : 13
tender s. of art, 334 : 12
Stroll, country s. is a gallery, 595 : 6
life like s. on beach, 558 : 8
Strong, a few s. instincts, 428 : 19
and diverse heart, 840 : 4
Anteus-like grew s., 717 : 14
armed so s. in honesty, 217 : 2
as a bull moose, 687 : 2
as flesh and blood, 428 : 4
as iron bands, 510 : 7
as proofs of holy writ, 231 : 7
battle is to the s., 684 : 13
battle not to the s., 27 : 17, 383 : 3
be s. and of good courage, 11 : 28
be s. and quit yourselves, 12 : 31
be s. be also one, 597 : 2
Strong (*continued*)
be s. stand fast on faith, 49 : 9
brown god, 808 : 1
cause s. or weak, 567 : 17
corruption inhabits blood, 214 : 26
devised to keep s. in awe, 187 : 30
devouring of weak by s., 579 : 19
dogged opponent of light, 587 : 3
drink is raging, 24 : 27
enough to be master, 358 : 13
fifty score s., 540 : 25
follow s. drink, 29 : 5
for much to suffer, 785 : 8
for service still, 376 : 23
founded s., 691 : 10
friend is a s. defense, 35 : 9
gentleness my s. enforcement, 211 : 12
give s. drink unto him that is ready to perish, 26 : 5
God make me s., 925 : 2
gongs groaning, 742 : 9
harder to be won than a s. city, 24 : 21
harm to s. from weakest, 658 : 7
heavens fresh and s., 427 : 16
I am s. I am woman, 915 : 9
is the soul, 584 : 10
is your hold O mortal flesh, 576 : 19
just weak secure, 891 : 2
keep s. if possible, 834 : 1
know the wall is s., 676 : 12
lance of justice, 235 : 3
lean upon death, 797 : 17
life too s. for you, 728 : 5
long pull and s. pull, 549 : 2
love built anew more s., 245 : 21
love is s., 148 : 20
made what is s. just, 300 : 6
man digests experiences, 658 : 8
meat to them of full age, 51 : 15
men rust, 834 : 5
men shall bow themselves, 27 : 24
mortality's s. hand, 202 : 7
most exquisite and s., 318 : 4
native states, 800 : 4
Negro cool s. imperturbable, 556 : 10
nor s. at thirty, 269 : 32
nor'wester's blowing Bill, 429 : 19
not to s. the fight, 671 : 11
O s. soul, 588 : 6
obscure and deep, 588 : 22
only s. thrive, 752 : 4
out of the s. came sweetness, 12 : 14
pull, 549 : 2
pure and sweetly s., 364 : 10
rejoiceth as a s. man, 17 : 28
remedy too s. for disease, 75 : 16
right chiefly with the s., 311 : 15
rousing like s. man, 282 : 3
shadow where much light, 394 : 11
shoulderings aside of weak by s., 579 : 7
small one become a s. nation, 31 : 24
some circumstantial evidence s., 557 : 14
stagger but not with s. drink, 30 : 16
they shall be gentle brave s., 643 : 2
thick stupefying incense, 541 : 20
to me-wards your affection's s., 266 : 8
to save, 596 : 18
toil of grace, 242 : 7
tricks hath s. imagination, 197 : 12
two s. men face to face, 707 : 16
we that are s., 47 : 34
Strong (*continued*)
wise man is s., 25 : 12
without rage, 294 : 19
yet I am s. and lusty, 210 : 29
Stronger, America would have been s., 875 : 10
by weakness, 276 : 12
Fate s. than anything, 76 : 12
gods are on side of s., 123 : 1
handclasp's s., 739 : 7
if bowl had been s., 930 : 18
let storm rage s., 725 : 5
madder music s. wine, 721 : 6
more doubt s. faith, 543 : 8
Negroes s. than we are, 837 : 20
no s. than my sex, 215 : 24
nothing s. than habit, 113 : 12
pray to be s., 619 : 18
than all afterthoughts, 76 : 18
than hosts of error, 694 : 15
than lions, 13 : 9
what s. breastplate, 185 : 17
win because we are s., 761 : 2
Strongest and the fiercest spirit, 284 : 4
God with s. battalions, 358 : 4
man stands alone, 599 : 21
never strong enough, 358 : 13
not from s. harm comes, 658 : 7
opinion of s. always best, 296 : 9
poison ever known, 406 : 16
right of s., 358 : 14
songs yet to be sung, 577 : 13
time consume s. cord, 431 : 24
tower of delight, 571 : 10
tribalism is s. force in world, 912 : 2
Strongly it bears us along, 435 : 18
Strove, a little still she s., 460 : 15
against stream, 531 : 10
to resuscitate dead art, 792 : 10
with none, 443 : 1
Strow brooks in Vallombrosa, 283 : 16
Struck all of a heap, 398 : 25
collected strength and s., 692 : 1
father when son swore, 259 : 21
finger on the place, 585 : 3
I am s. a deep mortal blow, 71 : 9
mighty Casey s. out, 704 : 16
one chord of music, 596 : 14
so the s. eagle, 456 : 17
streak of bad luck, 630 : 12
the board, 268 : 21
Structure of British sentence, 743 : 8
of recollection, 733 : 17
Structures, inquisitor of s., 768 : 25
Struggle against limitations of our intelligence, 832 : 1
all I care about is s., 643 : 5
and flight, 587 : 16
and horror past, 608 : 20
arduous s. for liberty, 383 : 1
Byron's s. cease, 585 : 2
contemptible s., 372 : 4
eternal s. between principles, 520 : 8
eternal s. of soul with pain, 836 : 13
for adaptation, 753 : 12
for existence, 514 : 16, 753 : 12
for life, 515 : 2
for maintaining government, 522 : 2
for power scramble for pelf, 556 : 1
for room and food, 514 : *n* 7
fulfill heart of man, 882 : 6
in s. for life find love, 820 : 9
life one long s. in dark, 100 : 14
life s. not warfare, 631 : 4

Struggle (*continued*)
long twilight s., 890 : 11
man formed by s., 784 : 10
manhood a s., 501 : 15
naught availeth, 564 : 16
need and s. inspire us, 649 : 11
no long s. no desire, 892 : 7
no s. no progress, 556 : 4
not basely abandon noble s., 383 : 4
not of men but forces, 635 : 17
sociability as natural as s., 651 : 7
social s. not reduced, 790 : 1
to reach top, 882 : 6
vast s. to found Roman state, 104 : 17
what s. to escape, 477 : 5
with exterior forces, 784 : 10
with world calls forth faculties, 414 : 4
Struggled, men who s. here, 523 : 4
Struggles, class s., 563 : 3
to idealize and unify, 437 : 12
Struggling for life in the water, 353 : 26
in storms of fate, 334 : 13
to put down feet, 873 : 5
Strumpet wind, 199 : 6
Strumpet's, 'tis the s. plague, 231 : 21
transformed into s. fool, 240 : 12
Strung high to notes of gladness, 443 : 21
lute s. with his hair, 191 : 4
on English thread, 569 : 2
Struts his dames before, 277 : 23
player that s. and frets, 240 : 4
there s. Hamlet, 717 : 5
Strutting player, 226 : 4
Stubble, consumed them as s., 9 : 35
land at harvest home, 203 : 7
Stubborn and rebellious generation, 20 : 3
facts are s. things, 323 : 31, 380 : 11
heart shall fare evil, 34 : 28
patience as with triple steel, 284 : 21
Stubbornly long or suddenly a splendor, 797 : 10
Stubbornness, course of impious s., 218 : 4
Stubborn-pulling fellow, 82 : 19
Stuck, Amen s. in my throat, 237 : 20
fast in yesterday, 740 : 3
suspicion s. full of eyes, 205 : 6
Student dassn't doze, 839 : 5
for the s. the saddle, 592 : 8
glued to desk, 592 : 8
Studied in my foolish youth, 150 : 6
method by which unconscious s., 678 : 11
one s. in his death, 236 : 14
with me at the U, 422 : 2
Studies, air of delightful s., 281 : 13
in which work dies with worker, 152 : 6
spur to the young, 98 : 7
Studious, sober s. days, 334 : 25
there s. let me sit, 345 : 7
to please, 351 : 15
Studiously neutral, 682 : 6
Studium, eigentliche S. der Menschheit, 337 : *n* 2
Study a great deal to know little, 341 : 11
but litel on the Bible, 146 : 5
commonwealth affairs his s., 207 : 4
culture s. of perfection, 588 : 15
events in their bearings, 592 : 7

Study (*continued*)
give children right to s. painting, 381 : 14
hard think quietly, 536 : 6
I am slow of s., 196 : 6
in brown s., 175 : 12
in law's grave s. six, 172 : 6
labor and intent s., 281 : 12
law so general a s., 372 : 20
like heaven's glorious sun, 190 : 12
lives on a leaf, 873 : 11
much s. is a weariness, 27 : 27
my sons ought to s. mathematics, 381 : 14
of revenge immortal hate, 283 : 8
periphrastic s., 807 : 12
politics and war, 381 : 14
prince have no s. but war, 153 : 21
rhetoric in the s., 559 : 30
secret of s. of nature, 504 : 17
to be quiet, 50 : 17
we that did nothing s., 267 : 8
what you most affect, 188 : 25
Stuff, ale's the s. to drink, 691 : 17
all our perishable s., 863 : 14
ambition of sterner s., 216 : 19
as dreams are made on, 248 : 13
Correggios and s., 371 : 21
everything made of one s., 497 : 12
he is writing bad s., 685 : 14
listen all day to such s., 611 : 11
neither starve nor s., 323 : 1
of various s. various man, 410 : 16
precious as s. they sell, 517 : 11
right American s., 632 : 1
skimble-skamble s., 204 : 16
stuffed bosom of perilous s., 239 : 32
the head with reading, 340 : 25
whatever you s. men with they bear, 561 : 5
written volumes of s., 550 : 5
youth's a s. will not endure, 213 : 23
Stuffed bosom of perilous stuff, 239 : 32
men, 805 : 15, 805 : 16
with epithets of war, 229 : 11
Stuffs out vacant garments, 201 : 26
Stuhldreher Miller Crowley Layden, 773 : 6
Stultitia, tanta s. mortalium est, 114 : *n* 6
Stumble, designed to make people s., 786 : 2
men that s. at threshold, 186 : 18
that run fast, 192 : 22
Stumbles at a straw, 173 : 6
old horse s. and nods, 642 : 2
Stumbling, stone of s., 29 : 14
Stumped and paupered arm of Cervantes, 570 : 11
Stung, bee had s. it newly, 290 : 1
pierced and s., 646 : 14
Stupefaction, death releases aura of s., 583 : 16
Stupefying incense smoke, 541 : 20
Stupendous, parts of one s. whole, 336 : 21
Stupid, be as s. as one wants, 735 : 14
believe to be truthful is easy, 738 : 18
clown of spirit's motive, 883 : 11
dastardly Public, 445 : 7
moments when only s., 482 : 6
starers and loud huzzas, 337 : 14
what wise or s. thing, 396 : 22

Stupidity, against s. gods contend, 413 : 26
as if safety in s., 560 : 15
nature equals s. of man, 785 : 14
no sin except s., 674 : 21
of the universe, 784 : 18
space and time are s., 784 : 18
such excess of s., 354 : 14
with s. man may front much, 473 : 4
Stupor Mundi, 892 : 4
Sturdiness of German tongue, 357 : 19
Sturdy and staunch he stands, 666 : 17
Sturm und Drang, 399 : 19
Stuttering or other epithet, 441 : 6
rifles' rapid rattle, 827 : 2
Stutters, some scholars' s., 899 : 5
Stygian cave forlorn, 277 : 17
Style agrees not with purse, 185 : 8
betrays us, 258 : 8
Celts certainly have s., 588 : 10
Cobbett s. stuns readers, 445 : 3
definition of s., 322 : 8
dress of thought, 319 : 18
dress of thoughts, 342 : 7
familiar but not coarse, 352 : 23
grand s., 586 : 16
honorable s. of Christian, 273 : 15
how the s. refines, 333 : 13
in the arts s., 718 : 6
is a recasting and heightening, 588 : 9
is the man, 349 : 2
killed calf in high s., 301 : 6
labored nothings in strange s., 333 : 5
lapidary s., 497 : 31
leave off s., 661 : 12
no one s. recommended, 900 : 10
Racine will go out of s., 301 : 8
steep minds in old s., 138 : 5
tell me in good old s., 123 : 7
vigor it will give s., 433 : 14
will make writers unreadable, 453 : 17
Styles develop freely, 826 : 12
Stylization makes art, 317 : 11
Styx by which gods take oath, 105 : 18
Suades, facias ipse quod faciamus s., 94 : *n* 4
Suage, words have power to s., 288 : 24
Sub rosa, 274 : *n* 10
sighted s. sank same, 882 : 16
Subdue appetites my dears, 547 : 8
force may s. for moment, 372 : 16
free ourselves s. our masters, 392 : 9
power to chasten and s., 423 : 13
replenish the earth and s. it, 6 : 15
Subdued, be s., 56 : 24
eyes, 232 : 20
my nature is s., 245 : 17
Subdues, surpasses or s. mankind, 457 : 22
when one by force s., 89 : 1
Subduing, necessity of s. again, 372 : 16
Subhuman, live by s. means, 313 : 6
Subject, any s. taught to any child, 887 : 16
duty s. owes prince, 189 : 6
everything is a s., 483 : 14
fanatic won't change s., 746 : 15
from ancient s. newest science, 666 : 9
grant artist his s., 652 : 15
grasp s. words will follow, 95 : 13
honor the s. of my story, 215 : 4

Subject (*continued*)
idea donnée, 652 : 15
know a s. ourselves, 355 : 17
matter of poetry life, 769 : 15
not bear raillery, 325 : *n* 3
of all verse, 265 : 15
of it is War, 827 : 1
of knowledge is to know, 85 : 19
poetry s. of poem, 767 : 17
prince s. Father Son, 254 : 5
ruler having human body as s., 84 : 5
sensibility soil of s., 653 : 11
that favorite s. myself, 385 : 15
treats serious s. with simplicity, 586 : 16
unlike s. I frame song, 342 : 16
Subjection to white Saxon man, 554 : 6
Subjective, creation s., 754 : 12
excess of s. propensities, 649 : 16
objective and s. united, 437 : 10
stream of s. life, 648 : 12
Subjectivity and objectivity, 834 : 13
Subject's duty is king's, 208 : 5
Subjects always right, 862 : 8
fit s. of tyrant, 520 : 7
free and loyal s., 920 : 8
good of s. end of kings, 318 : 10
men first s. afterward, 557 : 22
of which soul speaks same everywhere, 126 : 4
rebels from principle, 373 : 26
were their s. wise, 377 : 12
Subjugation, foreign conquest and s., 451 : 2
Sublime, aim at something more s., 414 : 22
bards s., 510 : 20
boundless endless and s., 458 : 29
dashed to pieces, 438 : 7
from s. to ridiculous, 420 : 9
in simplicity s., 533 : 3
lieth s., 526 : 8
maintain the s., 792 : 10
make our lives s., 509 : 15
material s., 438 : 3
object all s., 629 : 11
second line s. third bombast, 118 : 15
sense s., 423 : 13
tobacco, 462 : 16
when authors talk of s., 385 : 7
Sublimely, fustian's so s. bad, 338 : 13
Sublimity echo of a noble mind, 118 : 16
in effort of patriots, 380 : 14
Sublunary lovers' love, 253 : 3
Submission, bear his share with s., 595 : 5
lower the wing of s., 131 : 6
no wisdom but in s., 75 : 2
resistance or abject s., 379 : 2
yielded with coy s., 285 : 19
Submit because strength not adequate, 89 : 1
courage never to s., 283 : 8
I s. let it be done, 486 : 16
to be oppressed, 390 : 12
woman know to s. to opinion, 417 : 13
Submits, in love s. to everything, 658 : 14
Submitting, by s. sways, 335 : 23
Subordinate who never finds fault, 662 : 2
Subordinates art to nature, 437 : 17
Subsequent, pricks to s. volumes, 226 : 5
proceedings, 630 : 14
Subserved, liberty to be s., 576 : 11
Subsidize people not to work, 880 : 15
Subsist, beg leave to s., 704 : 17
Subsistence in arithmetical ratio, 417 : 3
margin of s., 871 : 16
mere s. out of soil, 590 : 4
Subsoil of the mind, 688 : 8
Substance, direct in s. of thought, 586 : 14
each s. of a grief, 194 : 18
God a sea of infinite s., 135 : 5
lose s. by grasping at shadow, 66 : 15
mind's avid s., 836 : 19
of ten thousand soldiers, 187 : 29
of things hoped for, 51 : 18
one s. with the Father, 55 : 3
single s. variously modified, 357 : 6
truth shows spirit and s., 135 : 12
wasted his s., 43 : 26
Substances not able to decompose, 390 : 8
Substantial and genuine virtue, 388 : 2
shadows not s. things, 272 : 15
world pure and good, 428 : 4
Substitute, bloodless s. for life, 667 : 21
drunken dog, 441 : 6
for experience is art, 895 : 19
manner is s. for genius, 375 : 20
no s. for hard work, 661 : 8
no s. for talent, 830 : 9
no s. for victory, 771 : 6
Subterranean weeds, 873 : 11
Subtle and profound female, 64 : 2
but malicious he is not, 764 : 1
demonisms of life, 570 : 13
its name is The S., 64 : 6
knot which makes us man, 253 : 7
know not s. ways, 495 : 11
Lord God is s., 764 : 1
manner of speech delights us, 98 : 13
no more s. master, 534 : 23
poetry less s. and fine, 281 : 20
poets witty mathematics s., 181 : 14
rapture of postponed power, 644 : 1
schoolman's s. art, 339 : 4
serpent was more s., 7 : 5
spirit my path attended, 794 : 5
thief of youth, 277 : 14
words full of s. flame, 263 : 2
wreath of hair, 253 : 11
Subtlest, serpent s. beast, 287 : 14
Subtleties, airy s. in religion, 274 : 3
door of all s., 63 : 12
of American joke, 622 : 7
Subtlety, brother came with s., 8 : 18
simplicity no hindrance to s., 637 : 8
to give s. to the simple, 23 : 1
Subtract work of men above forty, 664 : 19
Subtraction, mend a wrong s., 565 : 4
Suburb of life elysian, 511 : 11
Suburbs, asylum in s. of Jerusalem, 690 : 11
through s. sleepless people, 842 : 1
Subversion, reason is not s., 851 : 17
Subversive, disloyal or s., 863 : 9
Subway Bagdad-on-the-S., 699 : 11
Succeed, but for fools rest of us could not s., 625 : 12
I s. him not replace, 346 : *n* 5
if mediocre you s., 378 : 8
nature trying to make us s., 832 : 19
new things s., 266 : 15
Succeed (*continued*)
other means may s., 522 : 12
to s. add water to wine, 705 : 8
to s. in the world appear successful, 293 : 9
to s. possible only one way, 87 : 17
Succeeded in using whole talent, 852 : 12
never know when s. best, 706 : 13
Succeeds, age to age s., 527 : 22
by force or fraud, 616 : 2
many fail one s., 530 : 10
nothing s. like success, 491 : 6
Success, as long as gods give s., 60 : 26
as singist not a s., 616 : 15
bear s. with humility, 665 : 1
beauty that comes from s., 583 : 12
bitch-goddess S., 648 : 4
can change human mechanism, 859 : 19
cannot ask of heaven s., 417 : 17
cash interpretation of s., 648 : 4
catch with surcease s., 236 : 22
command s., 325 : 12
confidence of s., 679 : 6
depends on three things, 637 : 13
deserve s. in war, 746 : 12
four flights, 724 : 4
heaven's s. or earth's failure, 542 : 18
its own reward, 670 : 11
like horrible disaster, 876 : 9
makes s. only subsequent, 68 : 20
no honor in sure s., 810 : 3
not guarantee s. in war, 746 : 12
nothing succeeds like s., 491 : 6
nothing to long for, 914 : 6
only one s., 816 : 9
owes s. to inconsistencies, 640 : 7
people judge men by s., 293 : 26
secret of my s., 645 : 13
secret of s. constancy, 502 : 15
sense of s. in work, 572 : 13
steer honest course to s., 312 : 20
things ill got had bad s., 186 : 5
to periodic sentence, 834 : 9
to the weak, 378 : 14
unexpected in common hours, 560 : 16
vulgarizes what it touches, 670 : 11
writer not want s., 838 : 14
your religion is s., 694 : 12
Successful, everything to appear s., 293 : 9
man s. animal, 686 : 3
may country be s., 417 : 17
men cause neighbors envy, 116 : 3
runs back to s. soldier, 343 : *n* 1
to be s. soldier, 791 : 16
unsuccessful or s. war, 376 : 18
when men drink they are s., 81 : 12
Successfully executed, 395 : 18
if delicately gelded, 829 : 2
Succession, contract s. bourn, 247 : 26
slander lives upon s., 188 : 8
Successor, no s. for great man, 498 : 13
Successors of Charles the Fifth, 383 : 16
Successors', our s. victory, 809 : 14
Such as sit in darkness, 21 : 13
men are dangerous, 215 : 8
of s. is kingdom of God, 42 : 11
seems your beauty still, 245 : 11
Suck, doth s. his sweet, 177 : 4
her lips s. forth my soul, 184 : 4
honeyed showers, 281 : 1

Suck (*continued*)
I have given s. and know, 237 : 5
melancholy out of song, 211 : 2
Sucked, bit arm s. blood, 434 : 18
on country pleasures, 251 : 14
tyrant-hating milk, 567 : 9
Sucker born every minute, 536 : 4
hello s., 785 : 18
never give s. even break, 683 : 1
Sucking green from ferns, 822 : 7
roar you gently as s. dove, 196 : 8
Suckle fools, 230 : 12
Suckled by thee old nurse, 575 : 22
in creed outworn, 428 : 1
Suckling child shall play, 29 : 19
whale-tender young, 790 : 22
Sucklings, out of the mouth of babes and s., 17 : 17
Sucks, as weasel s. eggs, 211 : 2
the nurse asleep, 242 : 4
two souls, 253 : 14
where the bee s., 248 : 16
Sudan, home in the S., 708 : 5
Sudden and quick in quarrel, 211 : 15
be not afraid of s. fear, 23 : 6
death best, 99 : 22
farewells be s., 462 : 7
from s. death, 55 : 12
from wine s. friendship, 331 : 19
glory maketh laughter, 264 : 15
if thing comes in his head, 186 : 26
in shaft of sunlight, 807 : 8
in s. blackness the pall, 821 : 12
make s. sally, 533 : 15
said to dawn Be s., 693 : 13
storms are short, 194 : 12
this s. Diomede, 145 : 4
too unadvised too s., 192 : 13
unintelligible phrase, 593 : 4
violent and s. usurpations, 398 : 4
Suddenly, lest coming s., 42 : 14
mortal splendor, 797 : 10
Sue, we were not born to s., 193 : 34
Sueño de la razón monstruos, 394 : 2
toda la vida es s., 273 : *n* 1
Sueños sueños son, 273 : *n* 1
Suez, east of S., 708 : 10
Suffer, act or s., 806 : 17
all alike, 241 : 10
armed men, 840 : 10
better to s. than die, 296 : 10
detraction will not s. it, 205 : 5
don't s. more for us, 885 : 12
fools gladly, 49 : 20
for such a woman they s., 57 : 24
great souls s. in silence, 412 : 16
hell I s. seems a heaven, 285 : 12
him who has done deed to s., 71 : 16
if you love you s., 817 : 16
little children, 42 : 11
man needs to s., 671 : 22
me that I may speak, 16 : 7
me to come, 350 : 13
neither enjoy nor s., 686 : 13
never s. evil in future, 60 : 26
nobler in mind to s., 221 : 12
one s. than nation grieve, 304 : 8
rivalship of wisest men, 327 : 10
sea-change, 247 : 21
tamely lawless attack, 365 : 3
than one innocent s., 365 : 19
them and they'll overgrow garden, 185 : 15
there is much to s., 785 : 8
Suffer (*continued*)
though guiltless must s., 77 : *n* 12
thy foot to be moved, 22 : 4
who aim at great deeds must s., 97 : 15
who learns must s., 71 : 5
Sufferance badge of all our tribe, 198 : 24
in corporal s., 228 : 17
Suffered, enjoyed and s., 654 : 7
entire city has s., 61 : 15
fire s. rivers cannot quench, 186 : 19
I s. I was there, 574 : 25
in his heart many woes, 59 : 13
one who has most s., 585 : 23
under Pontius Pilate, 55 : 2
you have s. worse things, 104 : 21
Sufferer, best of men was a s., 251 : 11
each s. his say, 544 : 6
unites with human s., 777 : 17
Sufferest more of mortal griefs, 208 : 6
Suffereth, charity s. long, 48 : 23
love s. long, 48 : 23
Sufferin', injye other people's s., 722 : 18
Suffering, about s. never wrong, 868 : 9
acting is s., 806 : 17
auxiliary of creation, 661 : 1
behind golden silk, 849 : 19
Christian principle of s., 504 : 9
comparable to loss of finger, 835 : 9
enjoy other people's s., 722 : 18
exercises his mind with s., 89 : 25
great s. on Greece, 850 : 11
healed of s. by experiencing it, 734 : 11
human race, 585 : 3
implants responsibility, 635 : 24
is redemptive, 909 : 8
knowledge by s., 507 : 1
learn s. teach song, 467 : 15
man consume own smoke, 473 : 31
man in love with s., 581 : 17
may be called baptism, 565 : 10
medicine for s. is wisdom, 595 : 15
miserable doing or s., 283 : 10
more exposed to s., 427 : 23
more mental s. in St. George's 620 : 9
pity for s. a passion, 738 : 6
truth by s., 727 : 5
unavenged s., 582 : 4
Sufferings, grave in human s., 777 : 17
poets by their s. grow, 292 : 2
to each his s., 361 : 12
Suffers, eagle s. little birds to sing, 188 : 21
man born s. dies, 705 : 12
then nature of insurrection, 215 : 18
Suffice for those who belong, 575 : 11
ice also would s., 748 : 2
O when may it s., 714 : 10
sands s., 607 : 6
Sufficeth, God s. me, 130 : 15
good old rule s., 426 : 7
Sufficiency, elegant s., 345 : 12
Sufficient, be s. unto oneself, 164 : 18
beauty s. end, 714 : 15
earth is s., 575 : 11
ocean sea not s. room, 257 : 5
understand that he is s., 198 : 16
unto the day is evil thereof, 38 : 7
virtue s. of herself, 270 : *n* 7
whether s. to finish, 43 : 24
Sufficiently decayed, 629 : 17
Suffocate for privacy, 893 : 12
Suffocating night, 691 : 6
Suffocation, life threatened with s., 834 : 4
Suffrage for all citizens, 554 : 8
individual given universal s., 778 : 11
Suffuses all with blackness of death, 100 : 20
Suffusion from that light, 436 : 1
Sugar and spice, 932 : 13
heaven's s. cake, 314 : 23
if sack and s. be fault, 204 : 6
in the gourd, 921 : 13
my hair, 612 : 10
not made of s. candy, 745 : 10
oil vinegar s., 371 : 13
pious action s. o'er, 221 : 11
Sugarcoat the pill, 298 : 6
Sugarplums, decorating with s., 685 : 14
Suggest, like two spirits s. me, 246 : 3
to s. is ideal of poem, 651 : 16
Suggestibility, limits poem's s., 718 : 4
Suggestion, yield to that s., 236 : 11
Suicide, Bill of Rights into s. pact, 821 : 8
committing s. by working, 706 : 5
despair and s., 514 : 7
is about life, 910 : 16
is confession, 450 : 17
live through time or die by s., 519 : 22
means to universal s., 448 : *n* 4
then he may commit s., 857 : 3
thought of s. consolation, 657 : 23
Suicides and other conjecturally damned, 640 : 19
Suis, j'y s. j'y reste, 514 : *n* 4
Suit action to the word, 222 : 1
bring s. in Supreme Court, 787 : 11
certainly not s. me, 628 : 7
changing from brown s. to gray, 791 : 6
face creator in this s., 894 : 2
man in gray flannel s., 898 : 2
of ancient black, 765 : 8
of sables, 222 : 9
shall I be still in s., 268 : 21
silk s. which cost much, 309 : 13
Suitors, widows destroyed by s., 312 : 25
Suits, long s., 818 : 5
of solemn black, 218 : 2
out of s. with fortune, 210 : 16
these but s. of woe, 218 : 3
wear strange s., 212 : 20
Sukey take it off again, 933 : 18
Sulky, our s. sullen dame, 411 : 4
Sullen and sad, 345 : 4
beetle winds s. horn, 364 : 12
hear the surly s. bell, 244 : 26
our sulky s. dame, 411 : 4
swinging low with s. roar, 278 : 19
tongue sounds as s. bell, 205 : 20
untamed intractable, 808 : 1
white surf, 571 : 9
winter hangs on till s., 739 : 2
Sullenness against Nature, 281 : 21
Sullied flesh, 218 : *n* 1
with crime of stealing, 622 : 14
Sulphur, Calvin oatcakes and s., 432 : 18
Sulphurous and thought-executing 233 : 24
Sultan after sultan with his pomp, 516 : 10

Sultanically among moons of Saturn, 571 : 2
Sultan's turret, 515 : 16
Sultry, common where climate's s., 460 : 13
gray-fly winds her s. horn, 280 : 10
main, 434 : 28
Sum, giving thy s. of more, 210 : 26
life not doing s., 644 : 13
make up my s., 224 : 22
man not s. of what he has, 865 : 8
married people owe, 395 : 19
of all villainies, 346 : 9
of earthly bliss, 287 : 7
of good government, 389 : 1
of human achievement, 664 : 19
of human happiness, 776 : 4
of things ever being renewed, 100 : 15
statue s. of all it acquired, 360 : 27
trifles s. of human things, 393 : 13
with a great s. obtained freedom, 46 : 26
Sumer is icumen in, 916 : 14
Summary court in perpetual session, 786 : 5
Summer, after many a s. dies the swan, 533 : 27
after s. barren winter, 185 : 14
afternoon most beautiful words, 654 : 12
and winter shall not cease, 8 : 1
capriciousness of s. air, 749 : 5
commend all s. long, 714 : 22
days oftest in Kentucky, 657 : 6
dream beneath tamarind, 525 : 7
embraced s. dawn, 674 : 10
ends now, 656 : 6
eternal s. gilds them, 461 : 3
eves by haunted stream, 278 : 6
expect Saint Martin's s., 184 : 17
fight if it takes all s., 589 : 17
flies on s. eves, 476 : 27
fly after s. merrily, 248 : 16
God is day night winter s., 70 : 2
hath its joys, 250 : 7
hearts dry as s. dust, 428 : 11
in s. the other way, 668 : 9
Indian s. of life, 635 : 21
invincible s., 882 : 13
is ended, 32 : 2
is icumen in, 916 : 14
it was a s. evening, 439 : 10
last rose of s., 446 : 14
long hot s., 837 : 15
mad naked s. night, 574 : 19
made s. by sun of York, 186 : 29
my father paints s., 899 : 1
no season such delight as s., 265 : 16
no spring nor s. beauty, 253 : 20
now s. came to pass, 138 : 7
one swallow makes a s., 87 : *n* 7
one swallow not a s., 87 : 15
poetry like stove in s., 314 : 3
provideth her meat in the s., 23 : 11
redundant, 546 : 1
reeling through s. days, 604 : 14
sacrament of s. days, 604 : 10
sang in me, 823 : 6
season when soft was the sun, 143 : 14
singest of s., 476 : 22
soldier sunshine patriot, 384 : 13
summer summer, 723 : 3
summer's flower to s. sweet, 245 : 5
sun and s. gale, 362 : 22
Summer (*continued*)
sun shine friendly, 625 : *n* 3
sun shine kindly, 625 : 20
sweet as s., 249 : 15
that I was ten, 896 : 16
then s. then heaven of God, 605 : 17
this guest of s., 236 : 21
thy eternal s. not fade, 244 : 6
to your heart, 823 : 4
tranced s. night, 478 : 4
we have had s. evenings, 793 : 16
welcome s. with sonne softe, 144 : 12
whirling s., 858 : 20
with flowers that fell, 632 : 9
words in winter articulated next s., 120 : 16
Summer's, all on s. day, 931 : 4
compare thee to s. day, 244 : 5
day and with setting sun, 284 : 2
fantastic s. heat, 194 : 7
flower to summer sweet, 245 : 5
grace a s. queen, 431 : 18
lease too short, 244 : 5
lie, 830 : 1
proper man as see in s. day, 196 : 9
ripening breath, 192 : 14
tasted all the s. pride, 402 : 12
thy s. play, 405 : 6
vernal bloom or s. rose, 285 : 5
wonderland, 772 : 22
Summers, farmers pray that s. be wet, 103 : 27
in a sea of glory, 249 : 3
raw inclement s., 322 : 13
Summertime and livin' easy, 836 : 4
Summit, dewdrop from tree's s., 475 : 10
dreadful s. of the cliff, 219 : 14
from s. of pyramids, 420 : 6
life harder toward s., 658 : 16
Summits, snowy s. old in story, 530 : 26
Summon his array, 488 : 13
up remembrance of things past, 244 : 11
up the blood, 207 : 16
Summoned am to tourney, 918 : 12
by bells, 866 : 20
spirits I s. up, 395 : 17
Summons, black Hecate's s., 238 : 20
Black Spot a s., 668 : 6
fate s. monarchs obey, 304 : 24
fearful s., 217 : 23
thee to heaven or hell, 237 : 16
to greatness, 882 : 19
when s. comes to join, 471 : 6
Summum bonum, 98 : *n* 17, 101 : *n* 9
ius summa iniuria, 134 : 29
Sumner's mind contained itself, 635 : 6
Sumptuous variety about weather, 622 : 18
Sun, again the s., 799 : 8
all except s. is set, 461 : 3
also ariseth, 26 : 11
and all we can become, 874 : 6
and moon in flat sea sunk, 279 : 22
and moon should doubt, 406 : 17
and with the setting s., 284 : 2
ariseth they gather themselves, 21 : 11
as if s. blackamoor, 767 : 6
as long as s. shine, 929 : 5
as s. the morning dew, 307 : 9
at going down of s., 727 : 1
at noon, 255 : 1
Sun (*continued*)
awake my soul and with s., 311 : 18
aweary of the s., 240 : 5
be not darkened, 27 : 24
beating way for rising s., 854 : 3
before the rising s., 328 : 11
best not to see beams of s., 67 : 5
black with strong s., 822 : 4
born dies comes again, 925 : 21
born of the s., 876 : 16
born over and over, 887 : 2
breaks through darkest clouds, 189 : 2
Brother S. who brings us day, 138 : 12
burn the great sphere, 241 : 20
cast in brass to s., 924 : 3
chaos of the s., 767 : 4
clear as the s., 28 : 17
climbs slow how slowly, 564 : 17
common s. air skies, 362 : 20
countries of s., 850 : 8
dark simulacrum of God, 275 : 13
day past and yet I saw no s., 177 : 10
die with face to s., 672 : 11
distilled by the s., 640 : 11
doubt that s. doth move, 220 : 14
dry s. dry wind, 159 : *n* 2
errand boy, 571 : 5
evenin' s. go down, 740 : 12
eyes behold s. last time, 450 : 15
face downward in s., 822 : 1
fame s. of dead, 484 : 12
far from the s., 362 : 22
fear no more heat o' the s., 243 : 27
first poets then s., 605 : 17
foolery about orb like s., 214 : 11
force from which s. draws power, 787 : 13
frisk i' the s., 246 : 10
from rising of the s. unto going down, 21 : 20
fruit I bore was the s., 120 : *n* 10
gather round setting s., 426 : 23
gives light soon as he rises, 348 : 14
gladdest thing under s., 822 : 15
glorious s. in heaven, 435 : 16
go out in midday s., 843 : 8
golden apples of s., 712 : 14
gorgeous as s. at midsummer, 204 : 30
greater none beneath s., 710 : 12
grew in s. and shower, 424 : 13
has left the lea, 432 : 9
he set a tabernacle for the s., 17 : 28
heap o' s. and shadder, 774 : 4
heart s. of their micrososm, 260 : 7
himself at center of universe, 154 : 10
himself fair hot wench, 202 : 23
his own animal s., 901 : 14
hold farthing candle to s., 259 : *n* 9
hold glimmering tapers to s., 259 : *n* 9
hope s. will pierce, 544 : 29
I am part of the s., 790 : 21
I myself caused s. to rise, 726 : 3
I saw under the s., 27 : 17
if s. breed maggots, 220 : 17
images where s. beats, 805 : 1
imitate the s., 203 : 5
in bowling alley bowled s., 314 : 20
in dim eclipse, 283 : 24
in dominions never sets, 412 : 18
in golden cup, 716 : 21
in lonely lands, 532 : 28
inconceivable idea of s., 768 : 8
into the warm s., 160 : 32

Sun (*continued*)
is gone down while it was day, 32 : 8
is laid to sleep, 255 : 12
is lost and the earth, 254 : 5
it was ours this s., 849 : 20
itself which makes times, 252 : 22
Juliet is the s., 192 : 2
keeps pace with s., 559 : 22
knitters in s., 214 : 3
knoweth his going down, 21 : 11
knowledge is great s., 450 : 7
laughed in the s., 796 : 9
leaning against s., 604 : 15
leaves and flowers in s., 713 : 8
let not the s. go down, 49 : 36
let others hail rising s., 363 : 15
light candle to the s., 298 : 20
light dies with dying s., 670 : 8
light where no s. shines, 886 : 13
like ball of fire, 418 : 12
like Joshua commanded s., 348 : 11
liken Homer to setting s., 118 : 17
little window where s., 485 : 4
live because of s., 908 : 14
livery of burnished s., 198 : 29
looked over mountain's rim, 541 : 15
loss of s., 342 : 17
Love that moves s. and other stars, 142 : 20
loves to live in the s., 211 : 3
low descending s., 920 : 12
made summer by s. of York, 186 : 29
make guilty the s., 233 : 5
make our s. stand still, 297 : 2
maketh s. rise on evil and good, 37 : 12
man work s. to s., 920 : 11
maturing s., 477 : 17
mere fire, 900 : 2
moon or s. or what you please, 189 : 3
moon stars sweet, 492 : 16
more worship rising than setting s., 99 : 12
mother give me s., 599 : 16
must bear no name, 768 : 10
my mistress' eyes nothing like the s., 246 : 1
nearer comes the s., 790 : 16
neither shall s. light on them, 53 : 16
never sets on empire, 412 : *n* 6
no better thing under the s., 27 : 14
no matter how fair s., 464 : 21
no new thing under the s., 26 : 14
no shadow where no s., 730 : 2
no s. its day, 906 : 9
no s. upon an Easter day, 289 : 21
not move of himself, 571 : 5
not till s. excludes you, 576 : 13
of righteousness arise, 33 : 39
on green, 859 : 2
our America daughter of S., 721 : 3
out of God's blessing into s., 160 : 32
owes no homage unto s., 274 : 22
part of the colossal s., 769 : 10
pasted in sky, 732 : 4
pay no worship to garish s., 193 : 9
penetrates privies, 86 : 13
place in the s., 663 : 2
project for the s., 768 : 10
protects dewdrop from s., 429 : 11
question if his glory, 606 : 5
raisin in the s., 855 : 2
ran s. down with talk, 93 : 1

Sun (*continued*)
reflected from almshouse, 560 : 18
remains pure through pollutions, 86 : *n* 7
risen to hear him crow, 565 : 9
rising of the s., 919 : 21
rose and set on Sioux land, 610 : 5
sand and wild uproar, 493 : 15
sea gone with s., 674 : 1
see s. with different eyes, 850 : 9
see s. with ignorant eye, 768 : 8
seemed a sheet of s., 885 : 7
self-same s. on court and cottage, 247 : 1
set a candle in the s., 259 : 19
sets to rise again, 545 : 22
setting s. and music at close, 194 : 10
setting s. set to rights, 479 : 4
shall not smite thee, 22 : 4
shine friendly here, 625 : *n* 3
shine kindly here, 625 : 20
shineth upon dunghill, 86 : *n* 7
shut doors against setting s., 243 : 2
sitting in the s., 439 : 10
somewhere s. is shining, 704 : 16, 775 : 10
son of the S., 88 : 26
splendid silent s., 575 : 24
stain both moon and s., 244 : 14
stand a little out of my s., 86 : 9
stand still upon Gibeon, 11 : 34
steadies my soul, 799 : 8
study like heaven's glorious s., 190 : 12
subordinated s. and moon, 132 : 5
summer season when soft was s., 143 : 14
summer whan softe was s., 143 : 14
tell you how s. rose, 605 : 3
thank heavens s. gone in, 711 : 9
that brief December day, 513 : 20
that is young once only, 887 : 1
that s. thine eye, 244 : 17
this s. mine and yours, 849 : 19
till s. grows cold, 596 : 16
tired s. with talking, 591 : 9
to have enjoyed s., 585 : 11
to me is dark, 288 : 21
tomorrow's s. may never rise, 324 : 23
traveled short while towards s., 876 : 16
true as dial to s., 291 : 29
unruly S., 252 : 7
walk in the s., 220 : 17
warmth of s. on her pillow, 769 : 8
was shining on the sea, 613 : 1
was warm wind chill, 748 : 17
what are you when s. shall rise, 251 : 1
when s. goes down, 831 : 13
when s. out wind still, 748 : 17
when s. shineth make hay, 159 : 2
wherever bright s. of heaven, 249 : 18
which sees all things, 57 : 26
who drives horses of s., 661 : 16
who scattered into flight, 515 : 16
wide open to the s., 513 : 15
wing subdivided by s., 799 : 11
wishes lengthen as our s. declines, 330 : 15
with golden ball, 794 : 13
works done under the s., 26 : 16
worse than s. in March, 204 : 33
would have disappeared, 690 : 10

Sun (*continued*)
yesternight s. went hence, 252 : 16
you can't face s., 850 : 8
you kept all of s., 849 : 21
Sunbeam impossible to be soiled, 86 : *n* 7
in winter's day, 345 : 3
thick as motes in s., 147 : 13
Sunbeams, chances like s. pass, 347 : *n* 5
gay motes that people s., 278 : 10
out of cucumbers, 322 : 13
stream forward, 928 : 17
Sunburnt by glare of life, 507 : 19
mirth, 476 : 23
this s. face, 403 : 7
Sunday, buried on S., 932 : 11
chicken in pot every S., 174 : 25
grand flights S. baths, 767 : 21
heard preacher every S., 575 : 23
not divide S. from week, 217 : 19
put on his S. clothes, 466 : 5
repentance on a S., 773 : 9
we will be married o' S., 188 : 32
Sundays, begin journey on S., 323 : 17
Sundered, as if birth s., 558 : 20
Sundering, love know no s. quarrels, 107 : 9
Sundial, motto of s., 445 : 14
Sundown, elected between s. and sunup, 766 : 1
Sundry contemplation of my travels, 212 : 18
moveth us in s. places, 54 : 11
Sung by barbaric birds, 857 : 15
by forms unseen dirge s., 364 : 9
guardian angels s. this strain, 345 : 19
her amorous descant s., 285 : 25
her first and last, 918 : 17
no more, 918 : 17
Sappho loved and s., 461 : 2
strongest songs yet to be s., 577 : 13
sword s. on barren heath, 404 : 15
sword s. song of death, 404 : 15
Sunium's marble steep, 461 : 9
Sunk, all s. beneath waves, 377 : 19
beneath watery floor, 281 : 4
in flat sea s., 279 : 22
Lethe-wards had s., 476 : 21
so low that sacred head, 280 : 18
world's whole sap is s., 252 : 25
Sunless sea, 433 : 21
Sunlight, dustbin with s., 812 : 9
golden s. glows, 553 : 3
moonlight unto s., 530 : 5
never heard of trees, 905 : 8
on garden, 870 : 6
parables of s., 886 : 18
sudden in shaft of s., 807 : 8
swings s. up wall, 822 : 5
weave s. in hair, 804 : 10
Sunlit arch, 748 : 17
Sunnier side of doubt, 535 : 16
Sunny, a little s. a little sad, 635 : 21
count only s. hours, 445 : *n* 3
in s. beams did glide, 402 : 12
Palestine, 760 : 19
pleasure dome, 433 : 25
side of life, 775 : 11
side up, 825 : 8
web of s. air, 555 : 16
Sunrise, dewdrops gathered at s., 699 : 16

Sunrise (*continued*)
lives in eternity's s., 404 : 18
lost between s. and sunset, 480 : 13
out of Africa, 855 : 5
Sun's, like ice beneath s. rays, 313 : 7
o'ercast with blood, 201 : 22
rim dips, 434 : 21
Suns, inhere as do s., 606 : 10
light of setting s., 423 : 13
process of the s., 530 : 3
radiance of a thousand s., 94 : 15
skies clouds of June, 609 : 11
systemed s. globed and lit, 641 : 19
that set may rise again, 255 : 16
to light me rise, 336 : 19
Sunset and evening star, 535 : 19
at s. folds wings, 570 : 7
between sunrise and s., 480 : 13
breezes shiver, 700 : 10
come to the s. tree, 470 : 19
I have seen s., 673 : 17
life little shadow in s., 581 : 15
of life gives me lore, 443 : 14
ran one glorious blood-red, 541 : 18
sail beyond the s., 529 : 13
stained with horrors, 673 : 17
touch, 543 : 5
Sunsets, I eat s. and trees, 879 : 14
Sunshine and good water, 670 : 13
comforteth like s. after rain, 189 : 12
digressions s. of reading, 360 : 2
eternity about me in s., 662 : 20
fill sky with cloudless s., 108 : 7
glorious birth, 426 : 12
holiday, 278 : 1
in s. blank pages, 503 : 15
in the shady place, 173 : 10
like day without s., 401 : 8
of my life, 916 : 13
on strange shore, 683 : 11
patriot, 384 : 13
Sunt lacrimae rerum, 104 : *n* 13
Sun-treader life be thine, 540 : 5
Sunup, elected between sundown and s., 766 : 1
Sup at six sleep at ten, 492 : 6
before we go, 931 : 6
of Jove's nectar s., 256 : 8
sipped no s., 629 : 22
Super legal aid bureau, 777 : 1
Superannuated idol, 326 : 11
Supercilious hypocrisy of bishop, 391 : 2
Superego, world s. and id, 678 : 15
Superexcellent, tobacco divine rare s., 259 : 15
Superficial, common sense hasty s., 558 : 18
Superfluities, happiness in s., 519 : *n* 3
Superfluity, barren s. of words, 318 : 16
questionable s. small beer, 185 : *n* 6
sooner white hairs, 198 : 8
Superfluous, in Nature's inventions nothing s., 152 : 12
in poorest thing s., 233 : 21
lags the veteran on stage, 351 : 21
quest for the s., 649 : 16
to demand time of day, 202 : 23
to many the s. is necessary, 645 : 8
to point out this is war, 509 : 2
verse, 512 : 23
very necessary thing, 342 : 24
with s. burden loads day, 282 : 10
Superhighway of justice, 909 : 12
Superhuman spiritual and divine, 754 : 10
Superintend sick, 79 : 16
Superintending industry of private people, 366 : 8
Superior, educated men s., 86 : 19
equals revolt to be s., 88 : 9
intelligence, 758 : 10
man, 69 : 16
man acts before he speaks, 68 : 9
man distressed by want of ability, 69 : 12
man is modest in speech, 69 : 8
man mind like heaven, 609 : 6
man satisfied and composed, 68 : 24
man will not manifest narrowmindedness, 89 : 3
never finds fault with s., 662 : 2
no attribute of s. man greater, 89 : 2
not s. by reason of race, 615 : 5
own no s., 576 : 12
people never make long visits, 798 : 16
powers s. to man, 673 : 2
providence of inferior, 615 : 6
sages s. only in cleverness, 375 : 2
three things s. man guards against, 69 : 20
to slavish mercenary, 379 : 1
what s. man seeks, 69 : 13
Superiority, dogma of ethnic s., 796 : 7
feeling of s., 772 : 12
intellectual s. of man, 626 : 4
not admit assumptions of s., 89 : 17
of their women, 506 : 10
over dead level, 570 : 12
Senate s. invisible, 634 : 20
to sex that kills, 870 : 10
Superiors, between s. and inferiors, 69 : 2
Superlatives, lifts me to all my s., 739 : *n* 2
Superman lightning out of dark cloud, 657 : 13
not Hercules but S., 911 : 5
rope between animal and S., 657 : 12
Supermen, democracy not saved by s., 851 : 18
Supernatural, existence of s. probable, 704 : 11
honest woman of s., 870 : 3
nothing impossible in s., 704 : 11
Superpowers able to destroy planet, 898 : 12
Supersede last fashionable novel, 488 : 10
Superseded, life-form not s., 754 : 5
Superstition constructive religion, 580 : 8
die detesting s., 344 : 12
fear source of s., 738 : 5
has ample wages, 156 : 4
infamous thing, 343 : 17
less than chaff, 683 : 18
opposing one s. to another, 357 : 17
religion of feeble minds, 374 : 1
true remedy for s., 373 : 3
Superstitions, haunted by grossest s., 515 : 9
truths end as s., 596 : 9
Superstitious atheist, 543 : 7
in all things too s., 46 : 15
modest chaste, 463 : 13
valuation of Europe, 652 : 5
Superstructure on economic foundation, 731 : 3
Supinely enjoyed gifts of founder, 384 : 1
fools s. stay, 400 : 7
Supped full with horrors, 240 : 3
Supper, hope good breakfast bad s., 179 : 15
Michelangelo for s., 622 : 5
nourishment which is called s., 190 : 14
sings for his s., 930 : 15
when s. things is done, 665 : 11
Suppers, more killed by s., 269 : 26
Supplement not replace change, 909 : 15
Suppliant, thus the s. prays, 351 : 20
Supplied, can never be s., 369 : 30
charm by thought s., 423 : 12
Supply, all just s. and all relation, 254 : 5
eating air on promise of s., 206 : 6
lines guarded by navy, 825 : 6
no man will s. thy want, 257 : 8
of truth in excess of demand, 561 : 17
Supplying, never fully s. demand, 366 : 1
Support Caledonia's cause, 411 : 24
it will s. itself, 602 : *n* 4
that renders independent, 379 : 3
to s. him after, 242 : 29
visible means of s., 647 : 16
what is low raise and s., 283 : 2
Supporting, fatigue of s. freedom, 384 : 17
stop s. that crowd, 602 : *n* 4
Suppose, dance in ring and s., 749 : 9
do you s. Walrus said, 613 : 2
less than most s., 375 : 18
my daughters I s., 864 : 16
they gave a war nobody came, 761 : *n* 3
universe queerer than we s., 821 : 5
Supposed as forfeit to confined doom, 245 : 13
Supposes, effort s. resistance, 639 : 7
Suppress nothing that is true, 98 : 10
Suppressed, all one has s. in reader's consciousness, 739 : 3
neither world to be s., 586 : 21
no innocent wit s., 386 : 1
Suppressing, French for s. one, 586 : 21
Suppression of free speech, 677 : 13
Supramundane mushroom, 810 : 1
Suprema, salus populi s. est lex, 99 : *n* 3, 134 : 25
Supremacy, faith in s. of good, 703 : 6
Supreme, bring suit in S. Court, 787 : 11
Coort follows iliction, 721 : 12
governors the mob, 363 : 18
heart's s. ambition, 357 : 8
law of the land, 391 : 13
poetry s. fiction, 766 : 24
self-sacrifice, 831 : 24
silence s., 614 : 2
theme of art and song, 716 : 20
triumph to be most alive, 790 : 20
Surcease, catch with his s. success, 236 : 22
Surcingles, gilt s., 607 : 11
Sure and firm-set earth, 237 : 15
as death, 255 : *n* 4, 255 : 6
be s. give ocular proof, 231 : 12
be s. your sin will find you out, 11 : 7

Sure (*continued*)
clear conscience is s. card, 175 : 16
delight, 570 : 5
he's a s. card, 304 : 21
it may be so in Denmark, 220 : 1
joy was never s., 633 : 21
least s. most dogmatic, 871 : 6
make assurance double s., 239 : 11
man always dull, 772 : 5
more s. of all I thought, 747 : 1
no s. foundation on blood, 202 : 8
nothing s. in sea fight, 408 : 6
slow but s., 270 : 14
slow but s. moves might, 77 : 8
sweet cement of love, 266 : 1
this Jesus will not do, 407 : 11
what man has he's s. of, 170 : 35
Sure-enwinding arms of death, 576 : 5
Surely every man walketh in a vain show, 19 : 3
goodness and mercy shall follow me, 18 : 7
Surest, old soldiers s., 262 : 1
way to get a thing, 489 : 20
Surety, he that is s. for a stranger, 23 : 24
Surf, sullen white s., 571 : 9
Surface and shadow, 796 : 1
below s. stream, 588 : 22
fine glossy s., 369 : 7
go where we will on s., 558 : 16
look beneath the s., 125 : 5
material s. of things, 583 : 2
setting right s. of things, 490 : 13
Surfeit begets insolence, 67 : 3
God is war peace s. hunger, 70 : 2
no crude s. reigns, 279 : 25
of our own behavior, 233 : 5
sick that s. with too much, 198 : 7
when the daffodil, 606 : 5
Surfeited with honey, 204 : 20
Surfeiting appetite may sicken, 213 : 7
Surge and thunder of Odyssey, 657 : 4
booming s. of Aegean, 83 : 6
laces just reveal s., 604 : 12
murmuring s., 234 : 28
Thule and Atlantic s., 345 : 15
Surgeon, licked my heel like s., 902 : 5
to old shoes, 214 : 30
with help of s. recover, 197 : 20
Surgeons must be careful, 604 : 4
Surgery, honor hath no skill in s., 205 : 5
Surges, laboring s. of world, 693 : 9
Surging immensity of life, 518 : 7
sea outweighs, 495 : 19
symbol of s. potency, 790 : 19
Surly, hear the s. sullen bell, 244 : 26
Surmise, deep s. pierces, 558 : 21
soul's invincible s., 703 : 3
wild s., 475 : 7
Surmises jealousies conjectures, 205 : 18
Surname, his s. epithet for knave, 153 : *n* 5
Surpass, charms other maids' s., 399 : 20
nothing earthly s. her, 460 : 10
Surpassed, loftiness of thought s., 306 : 1
others but had no more power, 110 : 9
Surpasses, not to be born s. thought, 75 : 13
or subdues mankind, 457 : 22
Surpasseth, night of time s. day, 275 : 10
Surplus, democracy appropriate for economic s., 877 : 16
power of s. in banks, 449 : 9
wealth sacred trust, 621 : 8
Surprise, come as welcome s., 109 : 3
meaning unfolded by s., 750 : 4
respect mingled with s., 431 : 14
stairway of s., 494 : 15
unfolded by s., 750 : 4
you with ingenuity, 792 : 2
Surprised by joy, 428 : 20
guilty thing s., 426 : 18
sore s. them all, 409 : 18
to find it done at all, 354 : 15
was I with sudden heat, 182 : 2
Surrender, break out rather than s., 746 : *n* 2
explaining instead of acting, 741 : 1
fear hate s. defiance, 913 : 6
Guards die never s., 421 : 21
let us s. to love, 103 : 24
man may be forced to s., 274 : 2
not s. freedom for security, 820 : 12
of life nothing, 449 : 10
succeed if s. mutual, 885 : 15
to Him we s., 130 : 11
unconditional s., 589 : 16
we shall never s., 744 : 2
Surrenders, whosoever s. his face to God, 132 : 2
Surrounds, ever-during dark s. me, 285 : 5
Survey mankind, 351 : 16
monarch of all I s., 376 : 12
time takes s. of world, 205 : 10
Survival, assure s. of liberty, 890 : 7
love only s., 839 : 10
not choose s. it chooses us, 862 : 11
of fittest, 514 : 15, 579 : 20, 621 : 6
of wildlife in Africa, 898 : 11
without victory no s., 744 : 1
Survive and multiply, 515 : 2
monuments of wit s. monuments of power, 178 : 16
nation will s., 726 : 12
not s. wrongs repeated, 821 : 7
only the fit s., 752 : 4
opinions not s. without fight, 755 : 12
or perish, 450 : 9
our souls s. death, 112 : *n* 13
we shall not s. war, 817 : 18
Survived, don't see how Henry s., 884 : 8
I s., 394 : 9
pride of those who s., 746 : 5
Survives, plum s. its poems, 766 : 20
Thomas Jefferson s., 382 : 5
Survivor of that time that place, 801 : 14
Survivors', dying more s. affair, 755 : 16
Susanna, O S., 598 : 1
Susanna's music, 767 : 11
Suspect everybody, 547 : 25
once s. Caspian fact, 607 : 6
thoughts of others, 198 : 27
Suspected, new opinions always s., 307 : 13
wished wife not so much as s., 99 : 17
Suspecting, without s. our abode, 607 : 16
Suspects himself of virtues, 835 : 4
yet soundly loves, 230 : 34
Suspend functioning of imagination, 845 : 10
I s. my judgment, 165 : 5
men cannot s. fate, 318 : 12
Suspended, I s. religious inquiries, 384 : 2
'twixt heaven and earth s., 669 : 20
Suspense in news is torture, 289 : 8
Suspension of disbelief, 437 : 15
Suspicion always haunts guilty mind, 186 : 27
Caesar's wife must be above s., 99 : *n* 13
companion of mean souls, 384 : 10
general s. and distrust, 737 : 6
jealousy feeds upon s., 293 : 6
more than half right, 846 : 16
no s. of partiality in his writing, 98 : 10
stuck full of eyes, 205 : 6
Suspicions, fresh s., 231 : 2
Suspicious friend, 338 : 14
of blessings of civilization, 625 : 25
religious people s., 707 : 9
Suspire, we only live only s., 808 : 15
Sustain, prop that doth s. house, 200 : 20
Sustenance, people's s. in taxation, 631 : 9
white s. despair, 606 : 1
Swabs, doctors is all s., 668 : 5
Swag, clouds s. on the deep, 403 : 18
Swaggering underemphasis, 803 : 3
Swagman, jolly s., 705 : 7
Swain, frugal s., 366 : 10
Swains, that all our s. commend her, 190 : 4
Swaller, principles s., 567 : 23
Swallow a camel, 40 : 19
blow and s. at same moment, 94 : 5
come before s. dares, 246 : 26
flying south, 531 : 5
gudgeons ere they're catch'd, 65 : *n* 10
more beliefs than digest, 690 : 7
one s. makes a summer, 87 : *n* 7
one s. not a summer, 87 : 15
principles s., 567 : 23
revenge s. them up, 231 : 18
swallow flying, 531 : 5
up death in victory, 30 : 8
Swallowed, Aaron's rod s. their rods, 9 : 19
as a s. bait, 245 : 23
death s. up, 49 : 8
easier s. than flap-dragon, 191 : 7
grog they dreamed s., 772 : 21
half our sailors s., 186 : 23
lighted kerosene lamp, 757 : 6
oblivion s. cities up, 226 : 15
other books to be s., 181 : 12
up and lost, 284 : 9
up in death, 83 : 17
Swalloweth the ground with fierceness, 16 : 38
Swallowing, pity from s. wave, 296 : 5
Swallow's, hope flies with s. wings, 187 : 24
Swallows up the rest, 337 : 4
west wind and the s., 93 : 3
Swam in a gondola, 212 : 20
little fish s., 550 : 13
Swamp of Styx by which gods take oath, 105 : 18

Swamped, atoms cannot be s. by force, 100 : 9
Swampland, natural order in s., 873 : 9
Swan, black s. rare bird, 122 : 8
cygnet to pale faint s., 202 : 16
dies the s., 533 : 27
every goose s. lad, 566 : 14
he himself was s., 505 : 8
impenetrable like felt s., 860 : 9
love the wild s., 797 : 20
of Avon, 256 : 18
play the s. and die in music, 83 : *n* 1
silver s. who living, 918 : 17
song, 83 : 18
think thy s. a crow, 191 : 20
were I s. sing like s., 121 : 5
Swanee, way down upon S. River, 598 : 3
Swanlike, makes a s. end, 199 : 22
sing and die, 461 : 9
Swans, all his geese are s., 364 : 2
all our geese are s., 258 : 26
as much spirit of prophecy as s., 83 : 18
geese s. s. geese, 588 : 2
in winter air, 868 : 5
more geese than s., 918 : 17
nine-and-fifty s., 713 : 15
of others are geese, 364 : 2
sail like s. asleep, 785 : 16
sing more lustily, 83 : 18
Swap, botch trying to s., 523 : 8
horses crossing river, 523 : 8
Swarm, Europe really a s., 784 : 15
not good for s. not good for bee, 125 : 8
of bees and honey in the carcass, 12 : 13
of bees in May, 919 : 10
Swart convict Bunyan, 570 : 11
Swashing and martial outside, 210 : 22
Swat, Akond of S., 550 : 14
Swath, spares next s., 477 : 18
Sway, a little rule a little s., 345 : 3
govern my passions with absolute s., 302 : 24
in wind like corn, 804 : 6
love of s., 335 : 21
mercy above sceptered s., 200 : 9
mild parental s., 592 : 6
mortal things doth s., 174 : 6
of the sea, 655 : 19
prevailed with double s., 370 : 8
sweeping whirlwind's s., 363 : 6
till all creatures own thy s., 597 : 18
Swayed, at times mob s., 749 : 14
body s. to music, 715 : 17
leaves and flowers in sun, 713 : 8
rod of empire might have s., 362 : 6
Sways, by submitting s., 335 : 23
gently s. at ease, 749 : 4
so s. she level, 214 : 1
Swear an eternal friendship, 298 : 10
began to curse and s., 41 : 18
by Apollo Physician, 79 : 13
by thy gracious self, 192 : 12
by yonder blessed moon I s., 192 : 11
do not s. at all, 192 : 12
lovers s. more performance, 226 : 13
make deacon s., 568 : 7
not at all, 37 : 9
not bound to s. allegiance, 108 : 16
not by the moon, 192 : 11
nowhere woman true and fair, 252 : 2
Swear (*continued*)
to truth of song, 320 : 22
when very angry s., 624 : 20
when you rant and s., 259 : *n* 8
Sweareth to his own hurt, 17 : 23
Swearin', judicious s. keeps temper, 722 : 17
Swears, Lucrece s. he did her wrong, 189 : 27
Nature s. lovely dears, 409 : 15
punishment if one s. false oath, 59 : 3
she is made of truth, 246 : 2
Sweat, all of a muck of s., 369 : 13
and whine, 574 : 24
athlete crowned in s. of brow, 127 : 14
blood toil tears s., 743 : 19
cold s. bathes me, 63 : 5
drop of s. on drill ground, 792 : *n* 2
earned with s. of brows, 168 : 9
gods put s. in front of excellence, 61 : 17
grunt and s., 221 : 12
midday s., 267 : 12
night s. with terror, 715 : 6
none s. but for promotion, 210 : 31
of his brow, 559 : 14
of other men's faces, 524 : 5
of thy face, 7 : 12
save gallon of blood, 792 : 4
tears s. or blood, 743 : *n* 2
wet with honest s., 510 : 8
who casts to write must s., 256 : 16
worth s. of noblemen, 367 : 1
Sweating, harbors I by s. blood won, 151 : 10
Sweats, bloody s., 676 : 11
easier than I do, 559 : 14
Falstaff s. to death, 203 : 21
Sweaty faces of coffee-pickers, 789 : 10
head on s. bolster, 899 : 17
this s. haste, 217 : 20
Swede, strike terror in S., 486 : 14
Sweeney to Mrs. Porter, 805 : 6
Sweep clouds no more, 518 : 12
cobwebs from sky, 932 : 5
on you citizens, 210 : 27
over thee in vain, 458 : 25
wind s. man away, 585 : 9
your chimneys I s., 403 : 9
Sweepers, as chimney s. come to dust, 243 : 27
Sweeping, in sceptered pall s. by, 278 : 21
love s. the country, 836 : 2
of heaven's floor, 557 : 16
up the heart, 607 : 1
us into nameless abyss, 593 : 11
whirlwind's sway, 363 : 6
Sweeps a room as for thy laws, 269 : 8
next gale that s. from north, 383 : 5
Sweet, adversity's s. milk philosophy, 193 : 12
air coming into house, 798 : 8
Alice Ben Bolt, 566 : 1
all love is s., 467 : 5
allaying both with its s. air, 247 : 20
amazing grace how s. the sound, 367 : 7
and bitter fancy, 212 : 28
and honorable to die for country, 107 : 27
and low, 530 : 25
and musical as Apollo's lute, 191 : 4
and twenty, 213 : 23
Sweet (*continued*)
and virtuous soul, 268 : 17
approach of even or morn, 285 : 5
are uses of adversity, 210 : 24
as by fancy feigned, 531 : 4
as English air, 530 : 22
as I could bear, 748 : 8
as love, 400 : 15
as my revenge, 242 : 22
as summer, 249 : 15
as the primrose, 370 : 17
aspect of princes, 249 : 3
attractive grace, 285 : 18
attractive kind of grace, 184 : 13
Auburn, 369 : 28
be good s. maid, 566 : 12
bells jangled, 221 : 21
bird that shunnest noise, 278 : 17
bird's throat, 211 : 1
bitter all utterly things s., 829 : 20
bitter conduce to s., 900 : 5
blazon of s. beauty's best, 245 : 12
blown hair s., 806 : 2
bread of deceit is s., 24 : 31
bye-and-bye, 927 : 13
came o'er my ear like s. sound, 213 : 7
cement of love, 266 : 1
chariot, 935 : 24
cheat gone, 739 : 18
childish days, 425 : 8
city dreaming spires, 587 : 7
coming my own my s., 533 : 25
compulsion in music lie, 277 : 16
concord of s. sounds, 201 : 3
courtesies of life, 360 : 24
cowslip's grace, 394 : 6
day so cool so calm, 268 : 15
disorder in the dress, 266 : 6
dividing throat, 271 : 20
doth suck his s., 177 : 4
dream when trick's over, 760 : 16
Echo sweetest nymph, 279 : 18
every bitter thing is s., 25 : 24
every s. has sour, 497 : 10
experience of this s. life, 142 : 16
fierce hour and s., 742 : 17
flow gently s. Afton, 410 : 13
food of knowledge, 176 : 10
for love s. love, 576 : 5
for s. grape vine destroy, 189 : 20
for thy more s. understanding, 190 : 16
fountain of s. tears, 425 : 5
Genevieve, 636 : 2
girl graduates, 530 : 21, 595 : 9
glideth at own s. will, 425 : 14
good amiable or s., 287 : 22
good night s. prince, 225 : 3
great s. mother, 633 : 2
guess each s., 476 : 26
he makes s. music with stones, 189 : 34
heard melodies s., 477 : 6
Helen make me immortal, 184 : 4
his mouth is most s., 28 : 16
how monie counsels s., 411 : 5
how sour s. music is, 195 : 16
how s. and fair she seems, 276 : 7
how s. I roamed, 402 : 12
how s. is solitude, 376 : 11
how s. their memory still, 375 : 15
if life s. give thanks, 634 : 13
imaginary relish is so s., 226 : 10

Sweet (*continued*)
in s. pangs remember me, 213 : 29
influences of Pleiades, 16 : 33
is breath of vernal shower, 363 : 13
is death, 534 : 15
is every sound, 531 : 13
is peace so s., 383 : 5
is pleasure after pain, 306 : 16
is revenge, 460 : 17
is the breath of morn, 285 : 27
is the whispering music, 92 : 12
is true love, 534 : 15
keen smell, 601 : 23
lady s. and kind, 918 : 14
land of liberty, 514 : 12
life s. brother, 492 : 16
little craft, 629 : 19
loathe s. tunes, 633 : 3
look s. upon seat, 718 : 18
love s. for a day, 633 : 6
lovers love the spring, 212 : 33
made s. moan, 478 : 12
magic brings together, 412 : 9
medicine thee to s. sleep, 231 : 8
meet in s. Jerusalem, 186 : 24
mercy nobility's badge, 188 : 16
milk of concord, 239 : 19
mingles s. bitterness with her cares, 102 : 10
more s. than painted pomp, 210 : 23
mountain nymph s. liberty, 277 : 21
music's melting fall, 363 : 13
musk roses and eglantine, 196 : 18
my Adonis hath a s. tooth, 175 : 21
my home s. home, 802 : 10
my lady s. arise, 243 : 16
my life smack s., 545 : 22
my s. Highland Mary, 410 : 18
mystery about sea, 571 : 3
nature's s. cunning hand, 213 : 17
naught so s. as melancholy, 258 : 3
neglect more taketh me, 255 : 18
never merry when hear s. music, 201 : 2
none the less s. for wisdom, 595 : 9
not s. to dance on air, 676 : 9
notes by distance made s., 364 : 14
o' the year, 246 : 21
oblivious antidote, 239 : 32
of bitter bark, 748 : 9
one grand s. song, 566 : 12
one s. sacrifice, 248 : 25
Parthenope nourished me, 104 : 13
parting is such s. sorrow, 192 : 19
Peace is crowned, 299 : 10
perfections caught, 184 : 14
pleasures newly found s., 425 : 9
poison for age's tooth, 201 : 10
poison of misused wine, 279 : 7
pour s. dew on his tongue, 61 : 9
psalmist of Israel, 13 : 25
reluctant amorous delay, 285 : 19
retired solitude, 279 : 22
retirement urges s. return, 287 : 15
Richard s. lovely rose, 203 : 12
Roman hand, 214 : 21
rose by any name as s., 192 : 6
sensations s., 423 : 8
serenity of books, 512 : 15
showers of s. discourse, 292 : 10
silent thought, 244 : 11
singing in the choir, 919 : 21
sleep of laboring man s., 27 : 1
slug-a-bed, 266 : 19

Sweet (*continued*)
slumbers of virtuous, 326 : 4
small clumsy feet, 829 : 7
smell s. and blossom in dust, 272 : 13
smellest so s., 232 : 5
so strangely s. not strange, 654 : 17
softly s. in Lydian measures, 306 : 19
solitude is s., 376 : 11
some born to s. delight, 406 : 19
sounds and s. airs, 248 : 10
sounds together, 713 : 1
spring full of s. days, 268 : 16
spring year's pleasant king, 250 : 8
stay O s., 918 : 18
stolen waters are s., 23 : 20
such fleet things s., 634 : 1
such s. thunder, 197 : 8
summer's flower to summer s., 245 : 5
swan of Avon, 256 : 18
sweets to the s., 224 : 19
sweets with s. war not, 244 : 3
tell not s. I am unkind, 295 : 22
Thames run softly, 174 : 21
the coming on of evening, 286 : 1
the moonlight sleeps, 201 : 1
then how it was s., 544 : 20
thing to revisit in dreams, 76 : 2
things s. to taste prove sour, 194 : 3
though in sadness, 467 : 21
though wickedness be s., 16 : 6
thoughts that savor of content, 178 : 10
thy s. love remembered, 244 : 10
to dance to violins, 676 : 9
to know eye will mark, 460 : 16
to let mind unbend, 108 : 15
to look into fair, 475 : 4
to make the end most s., 193 : 35
took s. counsel together, 19 : 21
touches of s. harmony, 201 : 1
two-and-twenty, 462 : 6
unmemoried scents, 654 : 16
utter s. breath, 197 : 11
wee wife o' mine, 410 : 17
what makes life so s., 608 : 1
where late s. birds sang, 244 : 27
white wine, 760 : 19
world not s. in end, 633 : 6
your most s. voices, 242 : 16
youth that I thought s., 162 : 5
Zeus grant s. delight, 71 : 27
Sweeten my imagination, 235 : 1
this little hand, 239 : 27
Sweeteners of tea, 349 : 16
Sweeter air where it was made, 799 : 10
mountain sheep s., 455 : 2
odors crushed s. still, 180 : *n* 2
pains of love be s. far, 303 : 7
rose is s. in bud, 175 : 22
speech s. than honey, 57 : 10
than apples to children, 673 : 15
than honey and the honeycomb, 18 : 1
than sound of instrument, 274 : 20
world hath not a s. creature, 231 : 23
wrath s. than honeycomb, 58 : 30
yet is gratitude, 363 : 13
Sweetes' li'l' feller, 685 : 1
Sweetest, canker lives in s. bud, 244 : 14
girl I know, 753 : 1
hours e'er I spend, 409 : 16
last taste s. last, 194 : 10
Lesbia, 250 : 3
life near bone s., 560 : 19

Sweetest (*continued*)
little feller, 685 : 1
love I do not go, 252 : 15
melancholy, 261 : 4
rain makes not fresh, 260 : 19
Shakespeare Fancy's child, 278 : 6
song ear ever heard 459 : 23
songs saddest thought, 468 : 14
songs yet to be sung, 577 : 13
surfeit of the s. things, 196 : 23
sweet Echo s. nymph, 279 : 18
thing that ever grew, 424 : 19
vibrate s. pleasure, 410 : 1
voice of God's creatures, 525 : *n* 3
way to me, 708 : 22
Sweet-gum, red soil and s. tree, 831 : 15
Sweetheart good night, 625 : *n* 3
stay my s. never go, 647 : 6
that old s. of mine, 665 : 10
Tray Blanch and S., 234 : 15
Sweetly, hears you nearby s. speaking, 63 : 5
how s. did they float, 279 : 19
marveling s. on ills, 810 : 20
methinks how s. flows, 266 : 22
more s. than rhyme, 477 : 4
nimbly and s. recommends, 236 : 21
one s. solemn thought, 594 : 6
played in tune, 409 : 22
pure and s. strong, 364 : 10
so s. were forsworn, 228 : 28
worm feed s. upon me, 255 : 5
worm shall feed s. on him, 16 : 10
Sweetmeats, taking s. only hooking, 622 : 14
Sweetness and light, 321 : 14, 588 : 18
by convention s., 79 : 11
flows into breast, 716 : 3
keeps with perfect s., 497 : 1
linked s. long drawn out, 278 : 6
loathe taste of s., 204 : 20
of proportion, 256 : 2
out of the strong came s., 12 : 14
through mine ear, 278 : 26
waste s. on desert air, 362 : 8
Sweets, brought'st Thy s. along, 268 : 13
compacted lie, 268 : 16
diffuse balmy s. around, 180 : *n* 2
feast of nectared s., 279 : 25
grown common lose delight, 245 : 10
into your list, 454 : 8
last taste of s., 194 : 10
lost in the s., 332 : 5
of hasty pudding, 400 : 5
stolen s. are best, 325 : 3
to the sweet, 224 : 19
wilderness of s., 286 : 17
with sweet war not, 244 : 3
Sweet-scented manuscript close, 517 : 12
Swell a progress, 803 : 17
bosom with thy fraught, 231 : 17
deep sea s., 805 : 9
from lyre within sky, 525 : 10
green s. in havens dumb, 655 : 17
music with voluptuous s., 457 : 14
no minstrel raptures s., 430 : 10
soul to rage, 306 : 22
throat in vain, 476 : 15
Swelling and limitless billows, 435 : 18
angelic songs s., 552 : 22
prologues to the s. act, 236 : 10
Swells, note that s. gale, 362 : 20
pealing anthem s., 362 : 4

Swells (*continued*)
pity s. tide of love, 260 : *n* 8
Swept, be not s. off feet by impression, 121 : 16
cleaned windows s. floor, 627 : 14
it for half a year, 613 : 2
with confused alarms, 587 : 16
Swerve a hair from truth, 226 : 15
Swift as a bird or thought, 60 : 2
as a shadow, 195 : 23
be approaching flight, 469 : 22
has sailed into rest, 716 : 6
how s. how secretly, 822 : 1
lonely and s. like planet, 683 : 4
love is s., 148 : 20
mind beholds, 823 : 7
not to s. the race, 671 : 11
O time too s., 177 : 8
race is not to the s., 27 : 17
race is to the s., 684 : 13
red flesh, 843 : 20
sandy glass, 257 : 17
slow man catches up with s., 60 : 5
slow sweet sour, 656 : 5
spirit beautiful and s., 469 : 9
terrible s. sword, 566 : 4
to harry, 792 : 6
to hear, 51 : 30
too s. arrives as tardy, 193 : 1
true hope is s., 187 : 24
Swifter than eagles, 13 : 9
than weaver's shuttle, 15 : 20
Swiftest traveler goes afoot, 559 : 13
Swiftly, bright youth passes s., 67 : 7
courses from shore, 576 : 20
flowing cups pass s. round, 296 : 3
happiness too s. flies, 361 : 12
most s. fester or putrefy, 245 : *n* 1
tilting planet, 811 : 13
walk over wave, 469 : 21
Swiftness, O s. never ceasing, 177 : 8
Swig, absorb deep s. of it, 757 : 6
Swim before my sight, 335 : 5
creep s. or fly, 311 : 12
mother may I s., 924 : 17
naughty night to s. in, 234 : 8
sink or s., 203 : 13
sink or s. live or die, 450 : 9
sink or s. together, 730 : 16
teaching a fish to s., 134 : 17
took s. now and then, 623 : 22
wanton boys that s. on bladders, 249 : 3
wherever wood can s., 420 : 16
with bladders of philosophy, 315 : 20
Swimmer, strong s. in agony, 460 : 21
Swimmin', old s. hole, 665 : 13
Swimming from tree to tree, 892 : 6
in this sea and that sea, 849 : 11
under water, 835 : 18
Swims, Altitudo in bloodstream s., 812 : 1
into his ken, 475 : 7
only gamefish s. upstream, 686 : 5
sensible fish s. down, 686 : *n* 4
soul s. without gills, 759 : 3
whale s. minnow-small, 794 : 13
Swindled, men s. by other men, 871 : 5
Swindles, great s. simple, 699 : 9
without compeer among s., 623 : 18
Swindling, men s. themselves, 871 : 5
Swine, cast pearls before s., 38 : 11
is unclean, 10 : 17
nor feed the s., 931 : 19
Swine (*continued*)
pearl for carnal s., 291 : 21
unclean spirits entered s., 42 : 5
wine, 491 : 22
Swine's, jewel of gold in a s. snout, 23 : 25
Swing dat yaller gal, 662 : 17
low sweet chariot, 935 : 24
of the sea, 655 : 17
seraphs s. snowy hats, 604 : 15
that fellow's got to s., 676 : 7
tramp and trudge, 781 : 15
Swinged, Saint George that s. dragon, 201 : 15
Swinger of birches, 747 : 17
Swinging low with sullen roar, 278 : 19
Swings, lost on roundabouts pulls up on s., 736 : 12
slow punt s. round, 585 : 21
Swinish, hoofs of s. multitude, 373 : 27
Swirls of musk, 665 : 7
Switch, hazel s. for discovery, 711 : 17
quick path to light s., 852 : 1
Swiveller, here's a state cried S., 547 : 24
Swollen shadow, 883 : 11
slothful ease, 687 : 4
Swoon, Locke sank into s., 715 : 15
Swooned nor uttered cry, 531 : 8
soul s. slowly, 777 : 16
Swoop, at one fell s., 239 : 21
Sword, another drawn with s., 524 : 7
arm held fair s., 149 : 8
axis of world, 815 : 4
brave man with s., 676 : 8
deputed s., 228 : 6
die on mine own s., 240 : 7
every man's s. was against his fellow, 12 : 36
eye tongue s., 221 : 19
fallen by edge of the s., 35 : 38
famous by my s., 292 : 4
father's s. girded on, 446 : 15
flaming s. which turned, 7 : 13
fleshed thy maiden s., 205 : 15
glorious by my s., 292 : *n* 2
I with s. will open, 225 : 15
is the s. unswayed, 187 : 22
kindest that ever struck with s., 149 : 20
let s. of France fall, 815 : 8
light of thy s., 484 : 1
man for the s., 531 : 7
nation shall not lift s., 28 : 31
nor shall my s., 406 : 21
nor s. nor age destroy, 113 : 24
not peace but a s., 39 : 4
of heaven will bear, 228 : 26
of justice has no scabbard, 400 : 3
of justice lay down, 318 : 10
of the Lord and of Gideon, 12 : 10
of war or of law, 389 : 13
one s. keeps another in sheath, 270 : 13
outwears its sheath, 460 : 5
pen mightier than s., 493 : 6
pen preferable to s., 169 : 34
pen worse than s., 259 : 3
Pizarro traced line with s., 481 : 2
propagates character by s., 391 : 7
pulleth s. out of stone, 149 : 6
rust, 436 : 4
seeks with the s. repose, 298 : 19
sets s. back in sheath, 742 : 10
Sword (*continued*)
shall be against his brother, 32 : 31
sharp as a two-edged s., 23 : 10
sharper than two-edged s., 51 : 14
sigh s. of Angel King, 406 : 7
slander whose edge sharper than s., 243 : 21
sleep in my hand, 406 : 21
sung on barren heath, 404 : 15
sung song of death, 404 : 15
take the s. perish with s., 41 : 16
terrible swift s., 566 : 4
the mace the crown, 208 : 7
time rust sharpest s., 431 : 24
to him that succeed me, 302 : 15
turning word forgiveness to s., 893 : 19
united nations drew, 457 : 21
unsmote by s., 459 : 16
within the scabbard keep, 306 : 28
Swords into plowshares, 28 : 31
keep up your bright s., 229 : 21
lips his s. are, 177 : 12
little after draw out s., 34 : 2
play orators for us, 183 : 3
sheathed s. for lack of argument, 207 : 17
walks and turns our s., 217 : 11
yet were they drawn s., 19 : 22
Swore, armies s. in Flanders, 360 : 10
full great oath, 926 : 20
in faith 'twas strange, 229 : 31
jested quaffed and s., 536 : 7
my tongue s., 76 : 23
struck father when son s., 259 : 21
to be true to each other, 923 : 8
Sworn, be but s. my love, 192 : 5
had I so s. as you, 237 : 5
hostility against tyranny, 388 : 15
I have s. thee fair, 246 : 7
in s. twelve have thief, 227 : 31
to weed and pluck away, 194 : 22
who hath not s. deceitfully, 18 : 8
Swound, noises in a s., 434 : 11
Swung, out she s. far out, 669 : 20
tired of dominion s. fiend, 600 : 27
Sycamore, sighing by a s. tree, 232 : 8
Sycamores, through s. lights, 732 : 13
Syllable, built of just s., 607 : 10
chase panting s., 376 : 10
last s. of recorded time, 240 : 4
men's names, 279 : 16
Syllables, equal s. require, 333 : 7
govern the world, 264 : 2
Syllabub sea, 550 : 13
Syllogism from Kiezewetter's Logic, 602 : 11
Syllogisms, army of six hundred s., 153 : 9
Sylvan historian, 477 : 4
Sylvia, be by S. in the night, 190 : 2
who is S. what is she, 190 : 4
Symbol, concrete and living s., 905 : 5
good s. best argument, 500 : 3
idea conveyed but by s., 437 : 6
of her chosen land, 474 : 18
of power of Heaven, 799 : 14
of surging potency, 790 : 19
Symbolic expression, 610 : 2
Symbolism, impoverishment in s., 754 : 7
Symbols, ancient animal s. of St. John, 482 : 3
discourses to us by s., 438 : 1

Symbols (*continued*)
from s. into truth, 490 : 15
harmonious in themselves, 436 : 20
nature speaks in s., 513 : 13
of high romance, 478 : 18
we are s. and inhabit s., 498 : 2
Symmetrical complete colossal, 623 : 18
Symmetry, frame thy fearful s., 405 : 7
of shelves, 441 : 18
Sympathetic, sacred source of s. tears, 363 : 1
tear, 361 : 18
wife best possession, 77 : 17
Sympathies, culture lives by s., 651 : 2
tumor kills s., 634 : 23
Sympathize, I deeply s., 613 : 8
Sympathy, carrier of love and s., 617 : 7
cold to distant misery, 383 : 12
exciting s. of reader, 437 : 14
no conscious s. or relationship, 637 : 20
patience and s., 727 : 5
secret s., 430 : 9
with sounds, 377 : 13
Symphony, this is my s., 536 : 6
what is Ninth S., 751 : 4
Syne, auld lang s., 410 : 11, 410 : 12
Synergetics energetic geometry, 832 : 16
Synergy behavior of whole systems, 832 : 10
Synge, John S. and Augusta Gregory, 717 : 14
Syntax, both in s. and words, 586 : 14
Synthesis, held in lunar s., 804 : 4
Synthesizes, artist selects guesses s., 695 : 4
Synthetic magical power imagination, 437 : 16
Syracusans, eight victories over S., 78 : 2
Syria, the three equally bad for S., 702 : 9
Syrups, drowsy s. of world, 231 : 8
System, convention s. has faults, 788 : 11
extend s. to this hemisphere, 408 : 3
federal s. too perfect, 452 : 1
individuals adjusted to s., 502 : 25
liable to convulsions, 666 : 4
nature's s. a real beauty, 832 : 9
of general security, 781 : 9
two-party s., 862 : 19
Systematic procession of universe, 154 : 10
Systemed suns globed and lit, 641 : 19
Systems and creeds, 527 : 22
atoms or s., 336 : 14
moral and political s., 763 : 2
of preference or restraint, 366 : 8
our little s. have day, 531 : 17
perverted by selfishness, 775 : 4
synergy behavior of whole s., 832 : 10
that make black man foreigner, 916 : 12
Szilard, work by Fermi and S., 763 : 11

T

T, fitted him to a T, 158 : *n* 2
performed to a T, 158 : 5
Tabble, Casey's t. dote, 666 : 11
Taberna, in t. mori, 137 : *n* 1
Tabernacle, cloudy t. parted, 480 : 16
he set a t. for the sun, 17 : 28
who shall abide in thy t., 17 : 22
Tabernacles, how amiable are thy t., 20 : 6
how goodly thy t., 11 : 6
of the most High, 19 : 11
Table, arose from t. sober, 294 : 15
behave mannerly at t., 668 : 10
candle burned on t., 817 : 2
Casey's t. d'hôte, 666 : 11
crumbs from masters' t., 39 : 32
earth dice human bones, 462 : 14
etherized upon a t., 803 : 9
gas steam or t. turning, 581 : 10
general joy of whole t., 238 : 27
of my memory, 219 : 27
red-leaved t. of my heart, 257 : 15
remain sitting at your t., 786 : 3
reside at T. Mountain, 630 : 13
set t. on a roar, 224 : 14
snatching from t., 743 : 15
there is head of t., 496 : 10
thou preparest a t. before me, 18 : 7
with a stein on t., 705 : 2
write it before them in a t., 30 : 17
Tableaux, adieu chers t., 273 : *n* 3
Tables, he wrote upon t. words of covenant, 10 : 15
make it plain upon t., 33 : 25
marriage t., 218 : 14
near t. wanted food, 423 : 2
of moneychangers, 40 : 11
Tablet gift of Memory, 85 : 18
Tabooed by anxiety, 628 : 26
Taciturnity, cultivate t., 664 : 18
Tackle, bravery on and t. trim, 288 : 30
Tackling, difficulty most worth t., 653 : 12
Tacks, come to brass t., 806 : 10
Tact a kind of mind reading, 664 : 3
Tactic, silence is best t., 293 : 14
Tactics, adopting European war t., 800 : 4
triumph over weapons and t., 756 : 3
Tactile, primitive man t. man, 784 : 27
Taddy, carry me along t., 778 : 6
Tadpole, when you t. and I fish, 688 : 3
Taffeta, fair hot wench in t., 202 : 23
phrases, 191 : 9
Taffy was a Welshman, 931 : 3
Tags, some in t., 933 : 21
Tahiti, in soul of man one T., 570 : 14
insular T. full of peace, 570 : 14
Tail, Aesop's fox when he lost his t., 258 : 12
alive and wagging t. in mud, 90 : 11
and pointed ears, 515 : 8
bear your blazing t., 767 : 6
beginning with end of t., 611 : 17
durst not touch t., 931 : 7
hangs down behind, 709 : 3
hole where t. came through, 440 : 14
improve shining t., 611 : 5
my t. go to ground, 158 : 22
such little t. behind, 729 : 15
tied to me as to dog's t., 715 : 4
tips of his beautiful t., 928 : 17
treading on my t., 612 : 7
uninterrupted central t. row, 799 : 5
waving wild t., 710 : 6
Tailor, enter t. shops movie houses, 860 : 9
Tailors, four and twenty t., 931 : 7
Tail's a limb, 830 : 12
Tails behind them, 932 : 3
cut off t., 929 : 11
puppy dogs' t., 932 : 12
salt upon their t., 321 : 12
turning as t. of peacocks, 766 : 12
Taint, any t. of vice, 214 : 26
I cannot t. with fear, 239 : *n* 2
never t. my love, 232 : 7
of personality, 600 : 26
Tainted, goodness t., 559 : 18
tyranny in t. breeze, 372 : 20
what plea so t., 199 : 24
Take a bond of fate, 239 : 11
advantage get advantage, 565 : 8
another station, 628 : 4
any shape but that, 238 : 28
arms against sea of troubles, 221 : 12
arms t. your last embrace, 193 : 28
away art of writing, 419 : 8
beak from out heart, 526 : 18
bread from mouth of labor, 389 : 1
but degree away, 226 : 2
calculated risks, 791 : 17
can't t. it with you, 813 : 4
can't t. that away from me, 836 : 9
care of the sense, 612 : 3
chances for peace, 803 : 8
each man's censure, 219 : 1
eat this is my body, 41 : 10
for all we t. we pay, 707 : 17
form from off my door, 526 : 18
from seventy springs score, 690 : 17
from them sense of reckoning, 208 : 8
give an inch t. an ell, 161 : *n* 6
give me today t. tomorrow, 132 : 23
good the gods provide, 306 : 19
hand part with laughter, 633 : 15
heaven t. my soul, 202 : 12
heed of loving me, 253 : 13
her up tenderly, 485 : 21
him and cut him in stars, 193 : 9
him for all in all, 218 : 16
honor from me and life done, 193 : 33
how did you t. it, 718 : 17
I believe and t. it, 164 : 4
into air my breath, 476 : 28
it as it comes, 630 : 4
it from me, 699 : 19
it from me kiddo, 828 : 17
kiss you t. is better, 227 : 2
knows also how to t., 689 : 24
life easy, 712 : 1
love together to sky, 646 : 11
mankind in mass, 571 : 2
my drum to England, 700 : 8
my milk for gall, 236 : 17
my waking slow, 873 : 21
my yoke, 39 : 8
no thought for morrow, 38 : 7
not able to t. the lead, 58 : 17
not t. his own life, 83 : 16
not t. it any more, 901 : 10
not thy holy spirit from me, 19 : 17
note O world, 231 : 15
nothing of his labor, 27 : 2
nothing on looks, 549 : 28
O take those lips away, 228 : 28
of English earth, 710 : 15
of London fog thirty parts, 699 : 16
pair of sparkling eyes, 630 : 7
passage we did not t., 807 : 2
physic pomp, 234 : 4

Take (*continued*)
pray Lord soul t., 320 : 12
risk I had to t. and took, 749 : 11
some come to t. their ease, 249 : 19
the wings of the morning, 22 : 17
thee with her eyelids, 23 : 13
them he cannot t., 591 : 9
thine ease, 43 : 19
thine old cloak about thee, 917 : 22
this cadence from Yeats, 873 : 18
this cannot t. her, 289 : 18
this child to myself t., 424 : 13
thy rod, 9 : 18
to open road, 575 : 9
triple ways to t., 708 : 22
up read, 129 : 4
up thy bed, 41 : 33
upon's mystery of things, 235 : 12
we must t. the current, 217 : 6
what course others may t., 383 : 5
what is given, 750 : 11
what sweet hour yields, 470 : 4
what there is and use it, 654 : 13
who have the power, 426 : 7
will for the deed, 158 : 7
winds of March, 246 : 26
you a buttonhole lower, 191 : 10
you t. my house, 200 : 20
you would not t. it, 822 : 6
Taken, anything given can be t. away, 913 : 8
ark of God is t., 12 : 32
at the flood, 217 : 5
away that which he hath, 40 : 30
fun where found it, 709 : 9
hath t. away thy blessing, 8 : 18
home gone and t. thy wages, 243 : 27
no profit where no pleasure t., 188 : 25
one t. the other left, 40 : 27
the Lord hath t. away, 15 : 4
to drink, 729 : 8
when t. to be shaken, 415 : 10
worth's unknown though height t., 245 : 18
Taker, laid to make t. mad, 245 : 23
Takes away the performance, 238 : 3
blesseth him that t., 200 : 9
no fairy t., 217 : 26
no man t. wealth with him, 67 : 6
no private road, 337 : 16
soul t. nothing with her, 84 : 3
the reason prisoner, 236 : 8
time t. all gives all, 171 : 11
Takest, bringing in secret whom thou t. away, 97 : 16
whatsoever thou t. in hand, 35 : 12
Taketh away sin of world, 44 : 23
he t. wise in craftiness, 15 : 16
sweet neglect more t. me, 255 : 18
Taking, brief as the t., 812 : 3
from one class to give to other, 343 : 19
in hand a city, 70 : 12
in one another's washing, 924 : 5
Taking-over by the state, 834 : 7
Talcum always walcum, 855 : 13
Tale, as a t. that is told, 20 : 12
Christmas told merriest t., 430 : 22
every schoolboy knows, 361 : 7
every t. condemns me, 187 : 28
every tongue brings in t., 187 : 28
fair t. of a tub, 155 : 7
flowery t. more sweetly, 477 : 4
Tale (*continued*)
hear by t. or history, 195 : 22
I could a t. unfold, 219 : 18
love-gift of fairy t., 612 : 15
moon takes up wondrous t., 325 : 9
never heard in t. or song, 279 : 6
of hardihood endurance, 726 : 5
of human life, 375 : 3
of ocean seemed to tell, 428 : *n* 5
of Shaun or Shem, 778 : 5
of Troy divine, 278 : 21
old wives' t., 720 : 13
out of season, 35 : 34
plain t. put you down, 204 : 1
point moral or adorn t., 351 : 19
round unvarnished t., 229 : 25
say t. as said to me, 430 : 5
schoolboy's t., 457 : 5
shepherd tells his t., 277 : 24
speeds best plainly told, 187 : 19
tell a t. after a man, 146 : 15
tell t. tit, 929 : 22
that I relate, 377 : 24
thereby hangs a t., 211 : 6
thus the t. ended, 510 : 3
told by an idiot, 240 : 4
Truth hero of my t., 601 : 24
twice-told t., 202 : 1
which holdeth children from play, 176 : 11
without love, 655 : 16
would cure deafness, 247 : 12
yet often told a t., 443 : 21
Talebearer, go up and down as a t., 10 : 20
Talebearers as bad as talemakers, 398 : 28
Talemakers, talebearers as bad as t., 398 : 28
Talent, blessed who have no t., 495 : 27
blessed with each t., 338 : 14
contribution according to t., 563 : *n* 1
discover I had no t., 812 : 6
does what it can, 609 : 14
extraordinary collection of t., 891 : 7
formed in stillness, 395 : 15
grieved when man of t. dies, 386 : 19
happy possessor of t., 865 : 15
has t. cannot use it, 852 : 12
honors t. in every branch, 80 : 17
inspiration love, 695 : 3
is in a man's power, 569 : 11
man of t. sees two or three, 793 : 10
no substitute for t., 830 : 9
no t. but character, 482 : 5
of meatpacker, 726 : 13
recognizes genius, 689 : 15
succeeded using whole t., 852 : 12
to see what under nose, 869 : 8
which is death to hide, 282 : 15
Talentgang, genius please the t., 829 : 16
Talents equal to business, 122 : 21
grounds are virtue and t., 389 : 8
la carrière ouverte aux t., 420 : 19
let fools use t., 213 : 15
reviewers tried t. failed, 436 : 15
Tale's, sad t. best for winter, 246 : 14
Tales already plainly told, 60 : 17
natural fear increased with t., 180 : 2
of an old wife, 720 : *n* 3
out of school, 159 : 25
tell old t. and laugh, 235 : 12
to me so dear, 481 : 5
Tales (*continued*)
witch t. Annie tells, 665 : 11
words as idle t., 44 : 14
Talk a little wild, 248 : 23
about the rest of us, 646 : *n* 2
after-dinner t., 528 : 3
always t. who never think, 256 : *n* 6
and never think, 256 : 19
bad music people don't t., 675 : 20
Cabots t. only to God, 694 : 14
cane leaves rusty with t., 831 : 14
cannot t. with civet in room, 376 : 4
come after me let people t., 141 : 23
create do not t., 397 : 2
fishes t. like whales, 371 : 24
fool may t. wise man speaks, 257 : 4
from getting overwise, 748 : 15
froze me to hear such t., 623 : 23
gently act frankly, 536 : 6
good gods how he will t., 317 : 12
hear t. of court news, 235 : 12
innocent of t. or action, 863 : 9
is of bullocks, 36 : 9
let's t. of graves, 195 : 1
let's t. of wills, 195 : 1
living doll can t. t. t., 911 : 9
loves to hear himself t., 192 : 26
low talk slow, 870 : 7
moon t. by poet, 623 : 16
never spent hour's t. withal, 190 : 21
night crept upon our t., 217 : 7
no one would t. much in society, 395 : 24
not of other men's lives, 35 : 32
not of wasted affection, 511 : 4
not to me of name, 462 : 6
nothing but t. of his horse, 198 : 11
of crabbed old men, 101 : 18
of death of race, 900 : 2
of degeneracy and decay, 489 : 4
of many things, 613 : 5
of mysteries, 557 : 21
of nothing but business, 150 : 12
of pushing their bones, 908 : 8
of things heavenly, 302 : 4
only to conceal the mind, 310 : *n* 1
our dark t. last night, 900 : 9
pleasant walk pleasant t., 613 : 3
ran sun down with t., 93 : 1
save us, 778 : 5
sense to a fool, 77 : 7
sense to American people, 851 : 9
small t. dies in agonies, 468 : 3
so much about myself, 558 : 26
some little t. awhile, 516 : 18
some t. of Alexander, 922 : 10
telephone really able to t., 610 : 3
tendeth only to penury, 24 : 3
'tisn't beauty nor good t., 710 : 11
to him of Jacob's ladder, 500 : 18
tongues have their t., 168 : *n* 12
too much, 304 : 9
true I t. of dreams, 191 : 24
two t. one hear, 497 : 20
war t. by men, 623 : 16
what common t. of town is, 309 : 18
with crowds keep virtue, 710 : 17
with lover's ghost, 253 : 9
with you walk with you, 198 : 18
woman who occasions least t., 81 : 6
Talkative, learned silence from t., 782 : 20
Talked between the rooms, 605 : 14
catched fish and t., 623 : 22

Talked (*continued*)
I believe they t. of me, 329 : 9
like poor Poll, 363 : 17
long enough about rights, 872 : 9
of their Raphaels, 371 : 21
with looks profound, 370 : 12
worse than being t. about, 674 : 24
Talker, time is a t., 77 : 14
Talkers, know little great t., 358 : 20
no good doers, 187 : 7
Talking and eloquence not same, 257 : 4
best about themselves, 655 : 12
Frenchman always t., 356 : 14
he is t. or is pursuing, 14 : 2
he will be t., 209 : 28
hydrant in yard, 750 : 9
in mathematics never know what t., 737 : 13
is passion of woman, 323 : 30
know what we are t. about, 654 : 7
lived life t. at street corners, 811 : 7
lonely people t. to each other, 863 : 8
magic t. to itself, 908 : 9
of axes, 611 : 14
of fall of man, 560 : 29
of Michelangelo, 803 : 10
tired sun with t., 591 : 9
to hens of Dorking, 551 : 1
Talks, don't care how much man t., 561 : 16
wish I liked way it t., 697 : 1
Tall, as cedar t. and slender, 394 : 6
divinely t., 528 : 22
like some t. palm, 377 : *n* 5
oaks branch-charmed, 478 : 4
ship and star to steer, 760 : 14
to reach the pole, 328 : 1
yond t. anchoring bark, 234 : 28
Taller by breadth of nail, 322 : 10
town than Rome, 742 : 11
Tallest pine, 283 : 15
Tall-growing, lilac bush t., 751 : *n* 3
Tally, no books but score and t., 185 : 28
Talmud, rather believe fables in T., 180 : 16
Tam, ah T. thou'll get thy fairin, 411 : 14
lo'ed him like brither, 411 : 6
was glorious, 411 : 7
Tamarind, dream beneath t. tree, 525 : 7
Tamburlaine must die, 183 : 7
the Scourge of God, 183 : 7
Tame a shrew, 259 : 14
glass thou canst not t., 268 : 3
heyday in the blood is t., 223 : 4
of all t. a flatterer, 255 : 14
tongue can no man t., 51 : 35
Tamed and shabby tigers, 732 : 16
by Miltown, 893 : 3
countries t. and made to bear, 739 : 5
Tamely, suffer t. lawless attack, 365 : 3
Tameness, trusts in t. of a wolf, 234 : 14
Tamer of human breast, 361 : 13
Tames, punishment t. man, 658 : 6
Tammie, as T. glowered, 411 : 11
Tan, caftan of t., 767 : 5
cheek of t., 513 : 10
Tan-faced children, 575 : 14
Tangere, noli me t., 45 : *n* 5
Tangible, limitations of visible and t., 636 : 17
Tangle of squabbling nationalities, 688 : 1
Tangled in amorous nets, 288 : 6
Tangled (*continued*)
lie t. in her hair, 296 : 2
web we weave, 431 : 1
Tangles of Neaera's hair, 280 : 15
Tankards scooped in pearl, 604 : 13
Tanqueray, Second Mrs. T., 730 : 10
Tant pis and tant mieux, 360 : 23
Tantum religio potuit suadere malorum, 100 : *n* 2
Tao, action of T., 64 : 13
destruction of T. and virtue, 90 : 7
function of T., 64 : 13
is storehouse of all things, 64 : 22
leveled together by T., 90 : 2
look at T. and do not see it, 64 : 6
takes no action, 64 : 13
that can be told of, 63 : 12
when average hear T., 64 : 14
when highest hear T., 64 : 14
when lowest hear T., 64 : 14
why it is so near to T., 64 : 3
Tape, Krapp's last t., 866 : 15
red t., 549 : 6
ticker t. ain't spaghetti, 778 : 8
Taper of conwiviality, 547 : 20
Taper-light, with t. garnish heaven, 202 : 5
Taper's, like gleaming t. light, 368 : 12
Tapers, hold glimmering t. to sun, 259 : *n* 9
priests t. temples, 335 : 5
Tapestries, speech like embroidered t., 70 : 18
Tapestry, give children right to study t., 381 : 14
on this side of t., 897 : 15
Tappertit, strings said Mr. T., 547 : 27
Tapping, suddenly there came t., 526 : 10
Tar baby ain't sayin' nuthin', 662 : 6
in fir t. is, 933 : 4
water proportioned, 330 : 22
Tarantara tarantara, 628 : 2
Ta-ra-ra-boom-de-ay 719 : 6
Tara's halls, 446 : 9
Tarbaby ain't sayin' nuthin', 662 : 6
Tard dans un monde trop vieux, 537 : *n* 2
Tardy apish nation, 194 : 11
as t. as too slow, 193 : 1
Tarentum, far from my native T., 93 : 2
Tares, crop of corn a field of t., 177 : 10
of mine own brain, 274 : 10
Targeted trod like spring, 716 : 15
Tarn, dank t. of Auber, 526 : 23
Tarnish late on Wenlock Edge, 691 : 8
Tarquin, great house of T., 488 : 13
viewed in her face's field, 189 : 17
Tarried, too long we t., 550 : 8
Tarries with yesterday, 782 : 15
Tarriest, by what shore t., 588 : 6
Tarrieth, guest that t. but a day, 34 : 16
tide t. no man, 159 : 3
time nor tide t., 159 : *n* 1
Tarry at Jericho until beards be grown, 13 : 17
awhile says Slow, 931 : 6
we cannot t. here, 575 : 15
why t. the wheels of his chariots, 12 : 8
Tar's labor or Turkman's rest, 462 : 16
Tarsus, a Jew of T., 46 : 24
stately ship of T., 288 : 30
Tart, to eat with apple t., 668 : 13
Tartan, beneath the t. plaid, 551 : 9
Tartarly, savage and T., 462 : 11
Tarts, made some t., 931 : 4
Tarzan of the Apes, 753 : 10
Tashtego, bird incommoding T., 571 : 9
Task, by day by night to ply t., 418 : 8
delightful t., 345 : 11
labor at eternal t., 593 : 12
laborer's t. o'er, 597 : 15
long day's t. is done, 241 : 18
my t. is smoothly done, 280 : 4
of pure ablution, 478 : 20
of twentieth century to explore unconscious, 688 : 8
rebeginnings on frightful t., 883 : 8
remaining before us, 523 : 4
small daily t. beat labors of Hercules, 555 : 10
sore t., 217 : 19
there's the rub the t., 105 : 15
though hard be t., 594 : 5
uncompleted t., 648 : 1
what he reads as t., 354 : 11
worldly t. hast done, 243 : 27
Tasking, whole soul's t., 567 : 12
Taskmaster's, my great T. eye, 277 : 15
Taskmasters, lies religion of t., 725 : 6
Tasks, highest to humblest t., 745 : 11
not t. equal to powers, 619 : 18
Tassel-gentle, lure this t. back, 192 : 16
Taste, all ashes to the t., 457 : 20
and see that the Lord is good, 18 : 20
arbiter of t., 122 : 23
by which relished, 428 : 8
connects active with passive, 436 : 17
dull were all we t., 829 : 20
forbade myself to have t., 877 : 11
from fountain wells up bitter t., 101 : 7
good strong thick smoke, 541 : 20
inch rule of t., 635 : 2
is the only morality, 573 : 5
last t. of sweets, 194 : 10
liquor never brewed, 604 : 13
loathe t. of sweetness, 204 : 20
man of wealth and t., 916 : 8
man's hand not able to t., 197 : 10
never t. who always drink, 256 : *n* 6
no t. when you married me, 398 : 30
not Pierian spring, 332 : 20
of American people, 772 : 20
of death but once, 215 : 26
of your quality, 221 : 2
prosperity with more t., 323 : 29
questions of t. and feeling, 635 : 2
sans t. sans everything, 211 : 15
sit down and t. my meat, 269 : 10
smell and t. of things, 733 : 17
sole arbiter is t., 527 : 14
spiritual values such as t., 782 : 11
things sweet to t. prove sour, 194 : 3
touch not t. not, 50 : 10
tree whose mortal t., 282 : 22
whole joys, 254 : 3
whole of it, 544 : 22
wild vicissitudes of t., 351 : 13
wretched t., 417 : 2
your ware, 930 : 13
Tasted all the summer's pride, 402 : 12
can't be t. in sip, 547 : 24
eternal joys of Heaven, 183 : 21
I t. careless then, 605 : 1
of desire, 748 : 2
some books to be t., 181 : 12

Tasted (*continued*)
two worms, 659 : 11
Tasteless, this age how t., 102 : 2
Tastes like wrath to come, 757 : 6
no accounting for t., 133 : 17
runs against popular t., 314 : 3
wit ne'er t., 338 : 19
woman ruin meets, 332 : 5
Tasting of Flora and country, 476 : 23
Tat, tit for t., 160 : 28
Taters, corn and t. grow, 672 : 19
Tathagata has no closed fist, 72 : 19
Tathagatas, few and far between are T., 72 : 21
Tatter in mortal dress, 715 : 1
Tattered coat upon stick, 715 : 1
married man t. and torn, 934 : 9
through t. clothes, 235 : 3
Tatters, tear a passion to t., 221 : 23
Tattlers and busybodies, 50 : 32
Tattoo, images prisoners t., 850 : 6
Tatty wreckage of my life, 911 : 8
Taught as if you taught them not, 333 : 18
character t. learned, 588 : 11
dream t. me this wisdom, 273 : 5
first he wroghte afterward t., 146 : 8
folly's all they t. me, 447 : 5
genius never can be t., 306 : 8
happy is he born and t., 250 : 14
her dazzling fence, 280 : 2
I t. thee to love, 253 : 17
it hath t. me to rhyme, 190 : 31
man never flogged never t., 91 : 3
man that he knew not, 132 : 17
me all I knew, 710 : 2
me serpent's world, 863 : 19
mind what I am t., 449 : 15
obeyed what wind had t., 800 : 10
rather be t. than teach, 150 : 3
three useful things, 462 : 4
tortoise because he t. us, 612 : 4
us how to live, 325 : *n* 5
what heart t. me I t. world, 545 : 13
wise words t. in numbers, 174 : 9
you t. me language, 247 : 18
Taut, by going slightly t., 749 : 5
Tautness, greyhound's gentle t., 893 : 12
Tavern, happiness produced by t., 355 : 19
I am come to t. alone, 327 : 7
in the town, 922 : 12
intend to die in t., 137 : 11
let me die in a t., 137 : 1
Mermaid T., 477 : 16
my t. the Big Bear, 673 : 12
one flash in t. caught, 517 : 5
opened t. for friends, 724 : 14
Taverns, knew t. wel in every toun, 145 : 23
Tawny, gray rats t. rats, 541 : 2
Tawny-throated, nightingale t., 586 : 5
Tax for being eminent, 322 : 3
heavier than kings, 348 : 3
I t. you not you elements, 233 : 25
just man will pay more income t., 84 : 6
not t. bill but t. relief bill, 780 : 18
power to t. not power to destroy, 645 : 9
power to t. power to destroy, 402 : 7
where no revenue found, 372 : 8
Taxation, more t. than necessary, 631 : 9
without representation, 367 : 10
Taxed, never t. for speech, 227 : 9
without consent, 367 : *n* 9
Taxes, cut t. by cutting government spending, 880 : 16
death and t., 348 : 16
death t. childbirth, 848 : 10
generally raised on city land, 603 : 14
pay for civilized society, 644 : 8
true as t., 548 : 32
war certain to increase t., 384 : 22
Taxi throbbing waiting, 805 : 7
Taxidermists, nets kennels t., 907 : 25
Te deum laudamus, 54 : 19
spectem te teneam, 112 : *n* 14
Te Deum before battle begun, 490 : 2
Tea, after t. and cakes and ices, 803 : 15
and comfortable advice, 479 : 14
and scandal, 324 : 7
and sometimes t., 334 : 4
breakfast dinner lunch t., 730 : 8
breakfasts at five-o'clock t., 614 : 1
clever beings at t. with me, 914 : *n* 2
destruction of t. so bold, 380 : 14
glad not born before t., 433 : 15
honey still for t., 796 : 12
hot water remain upon t., 273 : 9
Michelangelo for t., 622 : 5
sweeteners of t., 349 : 16
take some more t., 611 : 21
thank God for t., 433 : 15
without stratagem, 329 : 23
Teach act of order to kingdom, 207 : 6
aim of oratory to t., 98 : 16
beasts shall t. thee, 15 : 29
charm strengthen and t., 511 : 14
child to doubt, 406 : 15
crab to walk straight, 82 : 4
eggs do not t. hen, 934 : 13
gladly lerne and gladly t., 145 : 28
go and t. all nations, 41 : 30
he who shall t. child, 406 : 15
high thought, 534 : 23
him to tell my story, 229 : 31
him what said in past, 3 : 3
himself to be afraid, 838 : 8
his feet a measure, 633 : 13
learn from those who can t., 74 : 22
learn suffering t. in song, 467 : 15
learn what it had to t., 559 : 25
let such t. others, 332 : 16
love of reading, 862 : 9
me half the gladness, 468 : 15
me my God and King, 269 : 7
me to feel another's woe, 340 : 4
me to hear mermaids singing, 252 : 1
men sense of existence, 657 : 13
new occasions t. duties, 567 : 8
noble negligences t., 320 : 23
nothing but to name tools, 290 : 19
order to peopled kingdom, 207 : 6
pleased to t., 333 : 21
rather be taught than t., 150 : 3
same prayer doth t. us all, 200 : 9
shall any t. God, 16 : 8
still pleased to t., 333 : 21
the earth shall t. thee, 15 : 29
them diligently unto thy children, 11 : 9
thy necessity to reason, 194 : 5
to t. is to learn twice, 400 : 13
trees and stones will t. you, 136 : 9
Teach (*continued*)
unforgetful to forget, 601 : 21
us good Lord to serve Thee, 157 : 3
us how to die, 458 : 8
us to care, 805 : 21
us to have aspiring minds, 183 : 6
us to number our days, 20 : 14
us to sit still, 805 : 21
villainy you t. me, 199 : 19
without sneering t. to sneer, 338 : 14
ye how to climb, 280 : 5
you more of man, 423 : 7
young idea to shoot, 345 : 11
Teacher affects eternity, 635 : 8
city is t. of the man, 67 : 17
closed fist of t., 72 : 19
government potent t., 444 : *n* 1, 678 : 1
Nature be your t., 423 : 6
true t. has no disciple, 484 : 5
value of true t., 609 : 10
who can arouse feeling, 395 : 25
Teachers by spherical predominance, 233 : 5
men are my t., 337 : *n* 2
seized my youth, 586 : 9
shame despair her t., 503 : 12
ungrateful to those t., 782 : 20
Teaches, experience t., 548 : *n* 2
grief t. to waver, 74 : 17
hard dealing t. them suspect, 198 : 27
he who cannot t., 680 : 23
leaves to curtsy, 899 : 11
life t. us to be less harsh, 395 : 12
nature t. beasts to know friends, 242 : 11
nature t. more than preaches, 631 : 3
religion good that t. good, 385 : 3
standing on toes, 839 : 5
such beauty as woman's eye, 191 : 1
time t. all things, 70 : 26
us to see, 900 : 6
Teaching a fish to swim, 134 : 17
for life, 6 : 1
hold fast to t. as a lamp, 72 : 20
is awakening curiosity, 655 : 10
nations how to live, 281 : 17
only t. on Tuesdays, 892 : 20
thank thee Jew for t. word, 200 : 19
truth persuades by t., 126 : 6
what t. is and was, 839 : 5
Teachings, nature's t., 471 : 3
Teacup, crack in t. opens, 868 : 10
Teacups, tinkled among t., 804 : 8
Team and driver drowned, 897 : 13
military forces are one t., 825 : 3
of little atomies, 191 : 23
Teapot, storm in a t., 99 : 4
Tear a passion to tatters, 221 : 23
all he had a t., 362 : 18
angel's t., 475 : 5
cannot t. out page of life, 504 : 10
each other's eyes, 328 : 3
every t. from every eye, 406 : 14
from eyelids wiped t., 211 : 12
heart to dog to t., 710 : 14
intellectual thing, 406 : 7
man without a t., 443 : 20
melodious t., 280 : 8
never t. linnet from leaf, 714 : 19
newborn infant's t., 405 : 10
O shed no t., 478 : 9
poem apart, 887 : 7

Tear (*continued*)
Recording Angel dropped a t., 360 : 17
shed bitter t., 613 : 2
shed one English t., 489 : 3
smile on lips t. in eye, 430 : 20
splendid t., 533 : 24
still ushered with t., 334 : 26
sympathetic t., 361 : 18
tattered ensign, 518 : 12
to pieces that great bond, 238 : 21
too foolish for t., 435 : 21
we shed though secret, 446 : 8
Teardrops, melting snow like t., 801 : 18
Tearing up pea patch, 831 : 11
Tears, angry t. gone, 714 : 4
are on her cheeks, 32 : 21
before my t. did drown it, 268 : 21
big round t. coursed down, 210 : 25
bitter t. to shed, 591 : 9
blood toil t. sweat, 743 : 19
blotted all over with t., 539 : 21
broomsticks and t., 714 : 4
bucket full of t. am I., 195 : 11
but without t., 893 : 10
cannot bear a mother's t., 106 : 2
crave stain of t., 748 : 9
crocodile t., 177 : *n* 6
dark with torment and t., 561 : 21
drop t. as fast, 232 : 20
fight from eyes t., 811 : 9
flow with t. of gold, 403 : 13
fountain of sweet t., 425 : 5
fountains fraught with t., 177 : 1
from wrath-bearing tree, 804 : 15
girlish t., 688 : 4
hence these t., 96 : 3
here are the t. of things, 104 : 26
hired t., 275 : 1
idle tears, 531 : 3
if you have t., 216 : 22
in silence and t., 456 : 8
in t. amid corn, 477 : 1
iron t. down Pluto's cheek, 278 : 22
kissed again with t., 530 : 23
like Niobe all t., 218 : 10
Lord God will wipe away t., 30 : 8
mine own t. do scald, 235 : 8
mist of t., 693 : 10
never wipe off t. of woe, 404 : 17
no t. in writer no t. in reader, 750 : 3
nor all your t. wash out, 517 : 2
not pay honor with t., 95 : 2
nothing is here for t., 289 : 9
now am full of t., 712 : 1
of eternity, 692 : 6
of one tiny creature, 582 : 5
of repentance you'll wipe, 404 : 17
of sky for loss of sun, 342 : 17
of things, 104 : 26
rain shower of commanded t., 188 : 24
remember with t., 594 : 3
rent is sorrow income t., 267 : 14
shall drown the wind, 236 : 24
siren t., 245 : 19
smiles t. of boyhood's years, 447 : 7
smiling through t., 58 : 5
songs composed of t., 537 : 9
such as angels weep, 283 : 26
sweat or blood, 743 : *n* 2
sympathetic t., 363 : 1
that speak, 295 : 17
thaw not frost, 468 : 22
they that sow in t., 22 : 7

Tears (*continued*)
thoughts too deep for t., 426 : 23
time to plant t., 878 : 10
time with gift of t., 632 : 9
tired of t. and laughter, 633 : 20
touch lips part with t., 633 : 15
unseen and unknown, 518 : 7
waste not fresh t., 77 : 15
watered heaven with t., 405 : 8
way with t. watered, 733 : 6
weep barren t., 466 : 17
wipe away all t., 53 : 30
with sobs and t. sorted, 613 : 8
young foolish full of t., 712 : 1
your death brought me t., 93 : 1
Tear-wrung millions, 743 : *n* 2
Teas, twine wine and China t., 558 : 10
where small talk dies, 468 : 3
Tease, fools no more I'll t., 334 : 24
the housewife's wool, 280 : 1
Teases, he knows it t., 611 : 15
mind over for years, 664 : 9
Teatray, like t. in sky, 611 : 20
Techniques to create full life, 862 : 7
Technological world, 861 : 7
Technologies with vast power to manipulate, 862 : 13
Technology, alienation result of t., 885 : 19
knack of arranging world, 878 : 21
shape economic society, 872 : 1
Tecum vivere amem tecum obeam libens, 108 : *n* 1
Tedious as twice-told tale, 202 : 1
historical books t., 655 : 3
old fools, 220 : 22
relations t. pack, 675 : 22
returning as t. as go o'er, 239 : 3
road will be less t., 103 : 21
shorten t. nights, 250 : 7
sport would be t., 203 : 5
thinking his prattle t., 195 : 15
to tell tales already told, 60 : 17
Tedium, pretentious quotations t., 685 : 15
Teeming brain, 478 : 17
mistress barren bride, 335 : 18
refuse of t. shore, 664 : 10
womb of kings, 194 : 13
Teenage, American T. Drive-In Life, 911 : 4
Teeth, bid them keep t. clean, 242 : 15
bitch gone in the t., 792 : 16
children's t. set on edge, 32 : 17
dragon's t., 840 : 10
O cropped out with t., 804 : 17
red thoughts t. white, 731 : 16
sans t. sans eyes, 211 : 15
shark has pretty t., 840 : 15
terrible round about, 17 : 5
truth may strike out his t., 173 : 3
weeping and gnashing of t., 38 : 22
what speech escaped your t., 57 : 27
who made t. shall give bread, 159 : *n* 6
with the skin of my t., 16 : 2
Teetotaler, beer t. not champagne t., 680 : 9
Tehee quod she, 146 : 32
Tekel, Mene Mene T. Upharsin, 33 : 1
Telegraph, Cunard's liners and t., 566 : 6
Telemachus, mine own T., 529 : 11
Teleology is theology, 706 : 4

Telepathic instinct, 783 : 4
Telephant, elephant tried to use t., 667 : 9
Telephone, elephone tried to use t., 667 : 9
humble appearance of t., 610 : 3
Telescope ends microscope begins, 492 : 2
Telescopes of the press, 706 : 19
Television, crouch to t. set, 893 : 15
geese more important than t., 795 : 9
if t. no further advanced, 776 : 4
Tell, a bore to t. everything, 343 : 1
aloud greatest failing, 322 : 17
can t. you being dead, 808 : 10
can't t. him much, 923 : 16
don't t. they'd advertise, 604 : 19
dream of not t., 434 : 1
'em Queen Anne's dead, 415 : 7
every word t., 729 : 7
feat of T. the archer, 414 : 1
fowls shall t. thee, 15 : 29
her one thing and keep another, 60 : 13
her that wastes her time, 276 : 7
her what I tell to thee, 531 : 5
him he hates flatterers, 215 : 21
him to go to hell, 454 : 15
how it really was, 480 : 8
if one but t. a thing well, 72 : 7
I'll t. you no fibs, 371 : 12
it like it is, 856 : *n* 4
it like it was, 856 : 14
it not in Gath, 13 : 8
kiss and t., 324 : 12
me I ought to do, 373 : 1
me if lovers are losers, 761 : 9
me Muse, 59 : 13, 334 : 21
me not here, 692 : 5
me not in mournful numbers, 509 : 13
me not sweet I am unkind, 295 : 22
me of John or Shaun, 778 : 5
me pretty maiden, 685 : 8
me tales to me dear, 481 : 5
me tell me elm, 778 : 5
me thy company, 170 : 25
me whar man gits corn pone, 626 : 12
me what thy name is, 526 : 15
me what you eat, 401 : 6
me what you know, 495 : 26
me what you like, 573 : 5
me where all past years are, 252 : 1
me where fancy bred, 199 : 23
my story, 225 : 1
never seek to t. thy love, 404 : 10
never t. how to do things, 792 : 2
never t. resolution beforehand, 264 : 3
not ever t. me who I am, 875 : 12
old tales and laugh, 235 : 12
sad stories of death of kings, 195 : 2
tale of ocean seemed to t., 428 : *n* 5
tale tit, 929 : 22
tales already told, 60 : 17
teach him to t. my story, 229 : 31
that I cannot t. said he, 439 : 14
that to the marines, 432 : 10
the crooked rose, 886 : 12
the world, 205 : *n* 1, 205 : 7
them I Am, 365 : 6
them I came, 739 : 16
them what to do, 792 : 2
those who sent you, 397 : 20
truth and shame devil, 158 : *n* 4

Tell (*continued*)
truth or trump, 624 : 11
us your phobias, 812 : 5
what and where they be, 533 : 26
what thou art, 170 : 25
wife all he knows, 276 : 16
with moderate haste t., 218 : 22
you a great secret, 882 : 9
you my drift, 209 : 14
you what you are, 401 : 6, 573 : 5
young men, 353 : 7
Teller, truth never hurts t., 545 : 18
Telleth number of the stars, 22 : 24
Telling battle on once more, 591 : 3
blessed strains t., 552 : 22
I am not arguing I am t., 619 : 11
nothing in great harangue, 297 : 26
off state and president, 893 : 1
pity beyond all t., 712 : 6
this with sigh, 747 : 13
Tells lies without attending, 388 : 3
nobody t. me anything, 723 : 1
of a nameless deed, 416 : 11
when too much lipstick, 856 : 5
Telltale tit, 929 : 22
Telmetale of stem or stone, 778 : 5
Téméraire, Fighting T., 700 : 10
Tempe, through life's T. led, 572 : 4
Temper doctrinaire logic, 821 : 8
enforce with t., 358 : 6
hot t. leaps over, 198 : 10
judicious swearin' keeps t., 722 : 17
justice with mercy, 287 : 25
made thee to t. man, 317 : 2
moderation in t. a virtue, 385 : 4
ruddy t. the hammer, 768 : 2
slander result of hot t., 3 : 9
unless I mistake its t., 779 : 7
which blades bears better t., 184 : 20
wit with morality, 326 : 9
woman of uncertain t., 440 : 17
Temperament, corner of creation seen through t., 643 : 6
harmony of t. and circumstances, 583 : 12
men of philosophic t., 697 : 6
solvency matter of t., 711 : 6
Temperamental atmosphere of Gallup Poll, 745 : 5
Temperance a species of courage, 308 : 15
acquire and beget a t., 221 : 23
as easy as t. difficult, 353 : 19
fruit of Spirit is t., 49 : 30
Temperate affords me none, 271 : 22
more lovely and more t., 244 : 5
wise amazed t. furious, 238 : 8
Temperature, poll taking t., 745 : 5
Tempered, absolutism t. by assassination, 417 : 4
by war, 890 : 7
Tempers, authority and place try t. of men, 120 : 4
wanton t., 380 : 12
wind to shorn lamb, 163 : 12, 360 : 25
Tempest, betokened t. to field, 189 : 10
covert from the t., 30 : 21
haunts t., 580 : 17
in a teapot, 99 : *n* 4
in the very torrent t., 221 : 23
no more hear t. howling, 393 : 11
on me t. falls, 71 : 2
seaman's story is of t., 112 : 20
sensual lust t., 581 : 20
Tempest (*continued*)
still is high, 350 : 12
terrible t. separated vessels, 151 : 10
Tempests, errors wanderings mists and t., 100 : *n* 7
fell all night, 269 : 5
glasses itself in t., 458 : 28
looks on t., 245 : 18
Tempest-tossed, send t. to me, 664 : 10
Tempestuous petticoat, 266 : 7
Temple bells they say, 708 : 8
better than in t. lost, 517 : 5
burned t. of Diana, 275 : 8
drove out of t., 44 : 29
hangs on Dian's t., 242 : 23
his people were his t., 300 : 20
his train filled the t., 29 : 8
Lord is in his holy t., 33 : 27
Lord's anointed t., 238 : 5
many a t. half as old, 416 : 3
no sooner t. built to God, 156 : *n* 2
nothing ill in such t., 247 : 24
of delight, 478 : 1
of Dian, 924 : 3
of fame, 391 : 9
of God is holy, 48 : 6
of Jerusalem, 131 : 5
of science, 686 : 10
sacred t. of Mecca, 131 : 5
singing vespers in T. of Jupiter, 384 : 7
two went into t. to pray, 43 : 38
veil of t. rent, 41 : 28
Temple-haunting martlet, 236 : 21
Temple's inner shrine, 425 : 17
Temples, builds glorious t., 567 : 16
forsake their t. dim, 277 : 12
God's first t., 471 : 8
gorgeous palaces solemn t., 248 : 13
made with hands, 46 : 16
mortal t. of king, 195 : 2
of his gods, 488 : 14
priests tapers t., 335 : 5
shall my joyful t. bind, 276 : 5
smote the nail into his t., 12 : 2
which men had commanded, 300 : 20
Tempora mutantur nos et mutamur, 134 : 30
O t. O mores, 98 : 2
Temporal, concern t. salvation, 383 : 1
everything t. be subordinated, 154 : 13
force of t. power, 200 : 9
matter unreal and t., 583 : 3
reversion, 808 : 9
things seen are t., 49 : 13
Temporary, dictionaries and t. poems, 352 : 10
obtain a little t. safety, 348 : 2
permanent contract on t. feeling, 641 : 6
use of force but t., 372 : 16
Temps, ah les bons vieux t., 928 : 4
au t. de ma jeunesse folle, 150 : *n* 2
le t. a laissé son manteau, 148 : *n* 11
ô t. suspends vol, 464 : *n* 5
Tempt frailty of our powers, 227 : 1
its new-fledged offspring, 370 : 7
me no more, 860 : 7
not desperate man, 193 : 24
shall not t. the Lord, 11 : 10
upper classes, 684 : 17
Temptation, blessed the man that endureth t., 51 : 28
Temptation (*continued*)
cold and to t. slow, 245 : 4
comes in fine gay colors, 250 : *n* 1
enter not into t., 41 : 13
last t. greatest treason, 806 : 19
lead us not into t., 37 : 15
maximum of t., 680 : 24
my t. is quiet, 717 : 9
resist everything except t., 675 : 8
to get rid of t. yield, 674 : 27
to the editor, 790 : 6
white fever of t., 817 : 3
why t. but for man to meet, 545 : 11
ye're aiblins nae t., 409 : 20
Temptations, cowardice protection against t., 625 : 13
not good to be without t., 597 : 11
rid of t. by yielding, 484 : 15
to belong to other nations, 627 : 18
Tempted her out of gloom, 527 : 2
more pure as t. more, 427 : 23
Tempts by making rich, 336 : 3
Tempus edax rerum, 113 : *n* 17
omnia t. revelat, 115 : *n* 2
Ten, and David his t. thousands, 13 : 4
aren't no T. Commandments, 708 : 10
better t. guilty escape, 365 : 19
Commandments not budge, 569 : 1
Council of T., 783 : 5
days that shook world, 801 : 4
death hath t. thousand doors, 262 : 8
good Lord had only t., 643 : 11
it's now t. o'clock, 537 : 6
jokes a hundred enemies, 359 : 21
little Indians, 933 : 22
live t. times t., 492 : 6
low words, 333 : 7
men who haven't and don't, 681 : 18
not if I had t. tongues, 57 : 19
o'clock scholar, 933 : 14
public opinion and T. Commandments, 603 : 13
set my t. commandments in your face, 185 : 10
strength as strength of t., 530 : 15
thousand miles away, 935 : 5
thousand saw I at a glance, 427 : 9
thousand times ten thousand, 536 : 3
thousand to go out of it, 321 : 10
to the world allot, 172 : *n* 3
vowing perfection of t., 226 : 13
was there only one summer I was t., 896 : 16
when angry count t., 390 : 4
wrote words of t. commandments, 10 : 15
years ago split air, 856 : 6
Tenacious but restless, 799 : 18
of purpose in rightful cause, 107 : 28
Tenanted, by good angels t., 526 : 1
Tenantless, graves stood t., 217 : 21
save to wind, 457 : 23
Tend, great God to thee we t., 130 : 3
on mortal thoughts, 236 : 17
Tendance, doth life in t. spend, 174 : 11
Tendencies, original t. and training, 752 : 18
Tendency to good like water, 89 : 18
Tender and growing night, 574 : 19
and true, 597 : 13
eye of pitiful day, 238 : 21
for another's pain, 361 : 12
grace of day dead, 530 : 20
happiness betray, 427 : 26

Tender (*continued*)
  irreproachably t., 826:16
  is the night, 476:25
  know how t. 'tis, 237:5
  leaves of hopes, 249:3
  majesty, 605:12
  mercies of the wicked are cruel, 23:29
  murderer, 543:7
  pitying the t. cries, 403:13
  rear t. thought, 345:11
  stops of various quills, 281:5
  strokes of art, 334:12
  the t. mercy of God, 42:26
  too t. or too firm heart, 335:8
  yearning sweet hoping, 413:21
Tender-handed stroke a nettle, 331:1
Tenderly, at the last t., 576:18
  be not impatient, 576:19
  night coming t., 854:14
Tenderness its joys and fears, 426:23
  of Italian tongue, 357:19
  passion without t., 895:6
  purest heartiest t., 577:3
  shape of t., 850:2
  thanks to its t., 426:23
Tendrils, limp and damp as t., 873:17
  strong, 428:4
Ténébreux, je suis le t., 514:*n*5
Tenement of clay, 303:20
  threshold of ruined t., 351:7
  upon clothes behind t., 819:3
Teneriff or Atlas unremoved, 286:10
Tenets, faith in some nice t., 295:19
Tennessee, placed jar in T., 767:7
Tennis anyone, 843:3
  world place with room for t., 884:17
Tennyson not Tennysonian, 654:11
Tennysonianness of speech, 793:7
Tenor, noiseless t. of their way, 362:12
Tenpence, seven pounds t. a man, 371:26
Tenpenny, sellin' t. nails, 722:5
Tense for first losing, 885:2
Tent, Alexander in his t., 858:20
  I rede you t. it, 410:20
  in field silken t., 749:4
  little t. of blue, 676:6
  low green t., 513:22
  nightly pitch moving t., 429:17
  outside t. whirling drift, 726:7
  pitched his t. toward Sodom, 8:7
  prize of general not t., 644:15
  strike the t., 509:10
  that searches bottom of worst, 226:7
Tenth, be thou the t. Muse, 244:15
  less than t. part of one, 226:13
  Muse governs press, 554:10
Tenting tonight, 618:1
Tents, dwell in the t. of wickedness, 20:8
  dwelling in t., 8:15
  fold t. like Arabs, 510:22
  how goodly are thy t., 11:6
  magic t., 654:16
  of Kedar, 28:2
  sighed soul toward Grecian t., 200:22
  silent t. spread, 578:10
  such as dwell in t., 7:21
  to your t. O Israel, 13:39
Tenuity of symbolic expression, 610:2
Tenure, land t. key to Kikuyu life, 818:13
Tenures, his t. and his tricks, 224:10
Tepee warm in winter cool in summer, 670:13
Tepees round like nests of birds, 701:9
Term, served a t., 627:14
Termagant, whipped for overdoing T., 221:23
Terminate torment, 806:1
Termination, no government provides for its own t., 521:9
Terminations, terrible as her t., 209:10
Terminological inexactitude, 743:5
Terms between Old and New World, 401:14
  fair t. and villain's mind, 198:28
  litigious t., 281:18
  of armistice with fate, 837:7
  silken t. precise, 191:9
  too deep for me, 628:6
  unconditional surrender, 589:16
  unfamiliar t., 125:20
Terra firma of accomplished discovery, 762:5
  in t. pax, 54:4
  sick of t. firma toils and cares, 569:20
Terrace walk and half rood, 339:10
Terre, c'est un pauvre t., 581:*n*3
  Dieu donna à Caïn, 157:*n*2
Terrestrial ball, 856:3
  written on t. things, 641:13
Terrible as an army with banners, 28:17
  as her terminations, 209:10
  beauty born, 714:9
  beauty t. and awful, 581:20
  burden of nothing to do, 311:17
  children, 502:24
  enfant t. of literature, 620:22
  fluidity of self-revelation, 654:4
  from a t. land, 29:26
  from camps, 864:15
  gift lifted from hearts, 582:7
  grumble rumble roar, 591:3
  haughtiness of the t., 29:21
  humanity may come to t. end, 765:1
  invent new beasts so t., 482:3
  judges all ranged a t. show, 332:7
  lend the eye t. aspect, 207:16
  life ordinary life t., 602:10
  long and t. way, 874:23
  no accuser so t., 95:19
  not death but dying is t., 349:26
  nothing more t. than ignorance, 397:11
  nothing t. except fear itself, 179:13
  prongs, 778:6
  sociologists, 706:11
  strange t. world war, 745:11
  swift sword, 566:4
  tempest separated vessels, 151:10
  thing happening to him, 888:2
  threshold, 863:15
  times, 672:1
  years of Yezhov terror, 801:15
Terrible-eyed, staggered and t., 866:16
Terribles, enfants t., 502:24
Terribly, armies swore t., 360:10
Terrified, bored and t., 888:12
Terrifies, silence of spaces t. me, 300:2
Terrify, heart they ought to t., 414:17
Territorial aggrandizement, 781:7
  integrity, 682:15
  no t. changes, 781:7
Territories, occupied t., 745:4
Territory, comes with the t., 888:3
Territory (*continued*)
  nation t. people laws, 522:10
  not make nation, 596:4
  only of certain durability, 522:10
Terror, afraid for the t. by night, 20:16
  and force, 812:13
  at own finitude, 703:15
  bodily t., 566:17
  death a hideous storm of t., 262:7
  human form divine, 405:14
  in happiness, 894:7
  in house does roar, 406:4
  night sweat with t., 715:6
  no t. Cassius, 217:2
  perceivers of t. of life, 498:21
  perch and not t., 227:30
  primitive t., 808:5
  reigns of t., 579:14
  shadows struck t. to Richard, 187:29
  strike t. in Swede, 486:14
  thermonuclear t., 871:8
  towards primitive t., 808:5
  understood t. and hope, 894:15
  victory in spite of t., 744:1
  wins easiest victory, 812:13
Terrors, dare deadly t. clasp, 405:8
  king of t., 16:1
  painting gives form to t., 774:11
Tertullian, every word of T. a sentence, 129:17
Tess, ended his sport with T., 641:4
Test, acid final t., 851:8
  facts t. all theories, 509:5
  faith force we cannot t., 665:2
  habit with him t. of truth, 400:6
  humor only t. of gravity, 325:*n*3
  lies in action, 71:25
  no t. which is not fanciful, 75:6
  of first-rate intelligence, 835:10
  of leader, 813:12
  of man's or woman's breeding, 680:4
  of political party, 851:8
  of ridicule, 325:4
  of true theories to predict, 472:1
  perception of beauty moral t., 557:11
  ridicule best t. of truth, 342:12
  to t. man proofs shift, 544:15
  true t. of civilization, 354:23, 499:10
  untrained to stand t., 648:9
Testament, blood of the new t., 41:10
  new t. in my blood, 48:21
  prosperity blessing of Old T., 180:5
  purple t. of bleeding war, 195:4
  than my T. fer that, 567:20
  thou makest t. as worldlings, 210:26
Tested, metal of man t., 568:17
  to extreme old age, 584:8
Testify, bricks alive to t., 185:27
  intellectual refuse to t., 764:2
Testimony, every tone t. against slavery, 556:3
  no t. establish miracle, 357:16
  of Jesus Christ, 52:27
Testing, forever t. new opinions, 638:14
  whether nation endure, 523:4
Testis unus testis nullus, 134:31
Tests, accuracy tried by severe t., 80:15
Testyment, than my T. fer that, 567:20
Tetchy and wayward thy infancy, 187:18

Tête, plutôt la t. bien faite que bien pleine, 164 : *n* 10
Tether, end of my t., 407 : 15
time or tide, 159 : *n* 1
Tethered, lice t., 873 : 11
Text, holy t. of pike and gun, 291 : 4
is old orator green, 189 : 13
neat rivulet of t., 398 : 29
of civil instruction, 389 : 2
of men and women, 689 : 18
Textbooks, scientific knowledge from t., 825 : 13
Thai half said, 175 : 4
Thaïs, lovely T. beside thee, 306 : 19
where is T., 601 : 16
Thalatta 83 : *n* 1
Thames and rivers of kings, 840 : 5
at Bablock-hithe, 585 : 21
life ran gaily as T., 586 : 1
no allaying T., 296 : 3
noblest river, 326 : 22
set fire to T., 364 : 4
sweet T. run softly, 174 : 21
Thane, I am T. of Cawdor, 236 : 11
of Fife had a wife, 239 : 26
Thank God Almighty, 935 : 22
God for peace, 738 : 12
God for tea, 433 : 15
God I also am American, 451 : 8
heaven fasting, 212 : 16
heavens sun gone in, 711 : 9
me no thankings, 193 : 17
thee I am not as other men, 43 : 39
thee Jew for word, 200 : 19
whatever gods may be, 633 : 22, 663 : 10
with brief thanksgiving, 633 : 22
you for nothing, 168 : 21
you for your voices, 242 : 16
Thanked, God be t., 797 : 2
she t. me, 229 : 31
when I'm not t., 349 : 6
Thankful, be t. unto him, 21 : 3
come ye t. people, 536 : 2
for fools, 625 : 12
rest and be t., 921 : 5
Thankfulness, return their t., 403 : 10
Thankings, thank me no t., 193 : 17
Thankless arrant, 172 : 14
child, 233 : 11
meditate the t. Muse, 280 : 15
Thanks, angels yield eternal t., 365 : 7
exchequer of poor, 194 : 20
for this relief much t., 217 : 15
his my special t., 584 : 8
humble and hearty t., 55 : 7
I am even poor in t., 220 : 27
if life sweet give t., 634 : 13
leave off wishing to deserve t., 102 : 13
of man and woman, 384 : 13
of Republic, 524 : 4
Puritans founded to give t., 722 : 3
taken with equal t., 222 : 5
to give t. is good, 634 : 13
to the human heart, 426 : 23
we are presarved fr'm Puritans, 722 : 3
words are empty t., 324 : 26
Thanksgiving, come before his presence with t., 20 : 20, 54 : 16
enter into his gates with t., 21 : 3
our t. accept, 631 : 15
received with t., 50 : 28
thank with brief t., 633 : 22
Tharshish, came the navy of T., 13 : 36
That and which, 686 : 1
for a' t., 411 : 19, 411 : 20
relative pronoun, 686 : 1
that is is, 214 : 27
thou art t., 56 : 19
thou doest do quickly, 45 : 18
which is grows, 125 : 25
which is not becomes, 125 : 25
Thatch, weeded and worn ancient t., 527 : 17
That's all there is, 762 : 6
the way it is, 888 : 15
Thaw and resolve itself in dew, 218 : 5
Thawing, man mass of t. clay, 560 : 12
tunes came out by t., 385 : 8
Theater, as in a t. eyes of men, 195 : 15
aspirin, 854 : 10
aunt was off to t., 730 : 10
can flourish in barbarism, 654 : 5
coughing in t. criticism, 895 : 7
dream is a t., 754 : 12
how wide t. expands, 442 : 22
idols of the t., 179 : 8
in t. of man's life, 179 : 4
shouting fire in t., 644 : 23
world's a t., 211 : *n* 3
Theatricals, game of private t., 649 : 14
Thebes or Pelops' line, 278 : 21
road to T., 851 : 3, 863 : 18
seven gates of T., 840 : 17
Thee, I to t. thou to me, 628 : 14
no more of t. and me, 516 : 18
of t. I sing, 514 : 12
of t. I sing baby, 836 : 3
through t. and me kings destroyed, 149 : 18
Thee's, from me to T. long way, 874 : 23
Theft, Christ forgave t., 545 : 3
property is t., 527 : 15
riches by t. will not stay, 6 : 7
Theirs but to do and die, 533 : 12
Theme, act of the imperial t., 236 : 10
fools are my t., 456 : 11
glad diviner's t., 304 : 5
majestic t., 643 : 18
mighty book mighty t., 571 : 1
of art and song, 716 : 20
on dark t. trace verses of light, 100 : 10
saluting felicitously every t., 486 : 3
Themes, nature's pleasing t., 345 : 21
no t. so human as those, 653 : 15
small minds never handle great t., 128 : 11
Them's my sentiments, 539 : 6
Themselves, hear good of t., 319 : 9
help them that help t., 66 : 20
judging for t., 399 : 8
law unto t., 46 : 38
must strike the blow, 457 : 8
our minds impress, 423 : 5
subject people talk best about, 655 : 12
think all men mortal but t., 330 : 11
Theologian born by living, 156 : 8
not born by thinking, 156 : 8
Theologians, believe t. nothing innocent, 609 : 1
extinguished t., 595 : 7
Theology, in t. experts differ, 700 : 2
teleology is t., 706 : 4
Theoretic and visionary fear, 388 : 17
Theoretical, Petersburg most t. town, 581 : 16
Theoric, bookish t., 229 : 13
Theories, catastrophist constructs t., 471 : 17
facts test all t., 509 : 5
great t. of physics, 696 : 12
newfangled t., 502 : 4
test of true t. to predict, 472 : 1
Theory, all t. is gray, 396 : 14
helps us bear ignorance, 703 : 4
of description matters most, 768 : 6
of physics work of art, 696 : 12
of poetry theory of life, 768 : 24
of probabilities, 397 : 18
sea of cause and t., 742 : 18
that does not affect life, 758 : 11
whole t. of universe, 576 : 10
Therapist, life an effective t., 789 : 14
There a little, 30 : 13
because it is t., 710 : *n* 1
gone here and t., 245 : 16
I suffered I was t., 574 : 25
over over t., 759 : 8
tell gang I will be t., 759 : 5
there is nothing but grace, 580 : 20
Thereby hangs a tale, 211 : 6
There's the rub, 221 : 12
Theresa, Saint T. in wild lament, 858 : 20
Thermonuclear terror, 871 : 8
war means to universal suicide, 448 : *n* 4
Thermopylae, make a new T., 461 : 6
Therrble prongs, 778 : 6
Thersites was the ugliest man, 57 : 18
These are the arks, 182 : 7
desolate dark weeks, 785 : 14
Theseus a second Hercules, 119 : 22
Thick and fast came at last, 613 : 4
another damned t. book, 387 : 6
as autumnal leaves, 283 : 16
as hasty pudding, 920 : *n* 2
blood t. water's thin, 629 : 2
blushing honors t. upon him, 249 : 3
butter's spread too t., 613 : 7
dashed through t. and thin, 304 : 17
inlaid with patines, 201 : 1
lay it on t., 620 : 12
make t. my blood, 236 : 17
muddy ill-seeming t., 189 : 5
paint an inch t., 224 : 14
rotundity o' the world, 233 : 24
stupefying incense smoke, 541 : 20
through t. and thenne, 147 : 3
Thickens, light t. and crow makes wing, 238 : 21
plot t., 302 : 20
Thicker, blood t. than water, 301 : 15
Thicket, filled t. with honeyed song, 82 : 5
in t. ahead danger or treasure, 896 : 13
political t., 776 : 14
ram caught in a t., 8 : 14
Thicket's, deep t. gloom, 395 : 3
Thickets of erroneous observations, 825 : 13
Thick-ribbed ice, 228 : 20
Thicks man's blood with cold, 434 : 19
Thick-sighted, ambition t., 475 : 15
Thick-warbled, trills her t. notes, 288 : 14

Thief, asked t. to steal me peach, 404 : 11
bankrupt t., 436 : *n* 1
doth fear each bush, 186 : 27
dwarfish t., 239 : 28
fits your t., 229 : 2
give to a t., 875 : 6
he winked at the t., 404 : 11
honest t. tender murderer, 543 : 7
I'll show thee a t., 270 : 10
in the night, 50 : 18
in twelve have t. or two, 227 : 31
lie still ye t., 204 : 18
no longer a t., 875 : 6
procrastination t. of time, 330 : 9
rails upon yon simple t., 235 : 2
said last kind word, 545 : 3
steals something from t., 230 : 1
Taffy was t., 931 : 3
Time subtle t. of youth, 277 : 14
time you t., 454 : 8
which is the t., 235 : 2
you cannot banish, 864 : 16
Thief-taker, thief turns t., 436 : *n* 1
Thieves, beauty provoketh t., 210 : 21
fell among t., 43 : 13
knaves t. and teachers, 233 : 5
land t. and water t., 198 : 17
made it a den of t., 40 : 12
night is for t., 77 : 5
the more t. there will be, 64 : 20
where t. break through, 37 : 16
Thieving Time take what must, 705 : 4
Thigh, bee with honeyed t., 278 : 25
smote them hip and t., 12 : 16
Thimbles, sought it with t., 614 : 4
Thin air, 248 : 13
horizon's growing t., 874 : 20
lips red and one was t., 290 : 1
man, 830 : 5
man in every fat one, 857 : 13
my wit is t., 147 : 24
no matter how t. slice, 741 : 10
partitions, 303 : 20
red 'eroes, 708 : 3
red line of 'eroes, 578 : *n* 4
red line streak, 578 : 14
ring becomes t. by wearing, 100 : 7
seven t. kine, 8 : 31
smoke without flame, 642 : 2
so t. so pale yet gold, 400 : 9
spread the t. oar, 337 : 8
through thick and t., 304 : 17
through thikke and t., 147 : 3
water's t., 629 : 2
Thine, fatal words mine and t., 168 : 15
is the kingdom, 14 : 25
not my will but t., 44 : 4
wear both for both are t., 187 : 2
Thing, a little learning is a dangerous t., 332 : 20
a tear an intellectual t., 406 : 7
acting of dreadful t., 215 : 18
aged man paltry t., 715 : 1
asked no other t., 605 : 20
awe of such t. as myself, 215 : 4
brood on Christian t., 863 : 14
crush the infamous t., 343 : 17
dejected t. of fortune, 234 : 19
do not do t. they most do show, 245 : 4
doing is another t., 165 : 13
each t. his turn does hold, 266 : 15
each t. in its entity, 905 : 7
Thing (*continued*)
enskyed and sainted, 227 : 27
every bitter t. is sweet, 25 : 24
excellent t. in woman, 235 : 17
far far better t., 549 : 24
fine t. needs laboring, 713 : 2
foolish t. but a toy, 214 : 29
funny t. happened, 908 : 4
good t. out of Nazareth, 44 : 24
guilty t. surprised, 426 : 18
hates t. he would not kill, 200 : 4
having seen one t., 633 : 5
hedgehog knows one great t., 62 : 2
how divine a t. woman, 427 : 19
how poor a t. is man, 182 : 10
I am every dead t., 253 : 1
I do my t. you your ., 827 : 19
I have done one braver t., 252 : 4
I was born to do, 182 : 9
ill-favored t. but mine own, 213 : 2
important if think it important, 649 : 9
is it so small a t., 585 : 11
keep corner in t. I love, 231 : 6
kills t. he loves, 676 : 8
law for t., 494 : 8
learn about one t. from another, 126 : 18
little learning dangerous t., 332 : 20
make good t. too common, 206 : 3
many a t. sought, 244 : 11
many-splendored t., 693 : 18
mastery of the t., 656 : 2
men prize the t. ungained, 225 : 35
moderately good, 385 : 4
motion like living t., 424 : 1
must be sad of itself, 317 : 10
necessary for triumph of evil, 374 : 12
never beheld so fair a t., 150 : 16
never said a foolish t., 315 : 14
no bird but invisible t., 427 : 2
no new t. under the sun, 26 : 14
no such cold t., 269 : 3
no the t. I should be, 411 : 21
not done in a corner, 46 : 35
not t. to laugh to scorn, 212 : 27
of beauty joy forever, 475 : 16
of evil, 526 : 17
of shreds and patches, 629 : 4
of watery salt, 760 : 21
one damned t. after another, 756 : 4
only t. to fear is fear, 779 : 10
pleasant t. if thou keep them within thee, 24 : 37
poor t. but mine own, 213 : *n* 1
quite another t., 341 : 12
reasoning self-sufficing t., 424 : 16
reward of t. to have done it, 498 : 11
right t. and clean t., 624 : 4
said t. which was not, 322 : 14
same t. good bad indifferent, 308 : 19
saying is one t., 165 : 13
sleep it is a gentle t., 434 : 30
small t. analogy of great things, 100 : 16
so neatly you never feel t., 900 : 12
started like a guilty t., 217 : 23
sudden if t. comes in his head, 186 : 26
surest way to get a t., 489 : 20
sweetest t. that ever grew, 424 : 19
that eats the heart, 864 : 3
that ends all other deeds, 241 : 24
that hath been is that which shall be, 26 : 14
Thing (*continued*)
that is your own, 87 : 29
the play's the t., 221 : 10
thou art the t. itself, 234 : 7
throw away dearest t. owed, 236 : 14
time least t. we have of, 845 : 11
to every t. there is a season, 26 : 21
to love, 757 : 4
too much of good t., 168 : 12
unfeathered two-legged t., 304 : 2
very odd t., 740 : 4
want to do that very t., 622 : 15
we may nat lightly have, 147 : 9
what their joining t., 889 : 14
what t. of sea or land, 288 : 30
which has been, 619 : 2
winning is only t., 925 : 15
winsome wee t., 410 : 17
with feathers, 604 : 17
your singing is the t., 667 : 7
Things added to things, 498 : 16
after t. broken, 733 : 17
age best in four t., 179 : 18
all these t. added unto you, 38 : 6
all t. all day long, 534 : 10
all t. are artificial, 274 : 7
all t. are as they were, 125 : 18
all t. are momentary, 125 : 18
all t. are one, 69 : 26
all t. be brought, 900 : 7
all t. born through strife, 70 : 4
all t. bright beautiful, 561 : 8
all t. by law divine, 467 : 24
all t. come of thee, 14 : 26
all t. great and small, 435 : 11
all t. how small soever, 307 : 12
all t. taken from us, 528 : 17
all t. to all men, 48 : 14
all thinking t., 423 : 13
always best in beginning, 299 : 12
and weather, 494 : 3
are in saddle, 494 : 7
are not what they seem, 509 : 13
are sons of heaven, 352 : 6
as language attractive, 498 : 16
as they are, 769 : 15
as t. have been they remain, 564 : 16
at home are crossways, 660 : 2
at odds when thinker loose, 723 : 16
beautiful and good, 467 : 1
beginnings of t. not distinguished by eye, 100 : 6
behind gold and silk, 849 : 21
best t. confused with ill, 466 : 17
best t. in life free, 825 : 7
bitterness of t., 429 : 7
both great and small, 435 : 11
by season seasoned, 201 : 5
by whom all t. were made, 55 : 3
calm Soul of all t., 585 : 1
compare great t. with small, 103 : 7, 285 : 1
counter original spare, 656 : 5
dappled t., 656 : 4
day of small t., 33 : 31
desired and timely t., 692 : 2
discern t. outside of self, 784 : 10
do noble t., 566 : 12
does away with ideas of t., 85 : 13
done a thousand dreadful t., 188 : 22
dreaming on t. to come, 245 : 13
drift of t., 747 : 2
elemental t., 671 : 2
equal to all t., 371 : 14

Things (*continued*)
eternal fitness of t., 349 : 19
evidence of t. not seen, 51 : 18
excellent t. in counsels, 25 : 1
facts are stubborn t., 323 : 31, 380 : 11
fair and flagrant t., 292 : 13
fairer when we look back, 569 : 4
fall apart, 714 : 12
feed brain with better t., 742 : 12
for all t. unfit, 371 : 14
forms of t. unknown, 197 : 12
four t. come not back, 109 : *n* 5
friends share all t., 65 : 11
from all t. one and from one all t., 70 : 5
fundamental t. apply, 830 : 6
glorious t. of thee spoken, 367 : 8
good t. strive to dwell, 247 : 24
good t. which belong to prosperity, 180 : 4
great t. are done, 407 : 1
great t. made of little, 544 : 27
greatest vicissitude of t., 181 : 15
he can afford to let alone, 559 : 21
he is before all t., 50 : 9
here are the tears of t., 104 : 26
holy profane clean obscene, 264 : 16
holy revealed only to men holy, 80 : 6
how can these t. be, 44 : 33
how many t. I have no need of, 79 : 1
human t. subject to decay, 304 : 24
I did not do or say, 716 : 13
impossible t., 613 : 14
in all t. thee to see, 269 : 7
in books' clothing, 442 : 9
in the midst of t., 109 : 27
interested in big t., 701 : 5
judge of all t., 300 : 11
just one of those t., 820 : 5
kill t. they do not love, 200 : 4
lack of elemental t., 802 : 17
learned on earth, 542 : 5
leave all meaner t., 336 : 10
looked unutterable t., 345 : 9
love conquers all t., 103 : 24
loveliest t. soonest pass, 471 : 9
made by human hand, 739 : 4
make vile t. precious, 233 : 30
mania of owning t., 574 : 24
material surface of t., 583 : 2
measure in all t., 106 : 12
met with by the way, 690 : 5
mind lets go thousand t., 627 : 2
moderation in all t., 96 : 1
more than t. long past, 194 : 10
more t. in heaven and earth, 220 : 3, 821 : 5
more t. wrought by prayer, 535 : 1
most beautiful t. most useless, 572 : 14
moving at equal rate, 100 : 17
mystery of t., 235 : 12
nature of t., 324 : 1
no remembrance of former t., 26 : 15
not always go your way, 664 : 18
not always what they seem, 114 : 10
not seen are eternal, 49 : 13
old unhappy far-off t., 426 : 5
order of t. satisfy, 496 : 2
out of small beginnings greater t., 265 : 13
outward draw inward quality, 241 : 10

Things (*continued*)
past redress now past care, 194 : 23
penetrable to shower of gold, 473 : 13
present nor things to come, 47 : 15
pretty state of t., 629 : 10
prove all t., 50 : 22
remembrance of t. past, 244 : 11
remembrance of t. to come, 26 : 15
responsibilities to living t., 912 : 4
rise to higher t., 531 : 19
rolls through all t., 423 : 13
sad vicissitude of t., 359 : 17
said or done long years ago, 716 : 13
see into life of t., 423 : 11
see sons what t. you are, 206 : 30
see t. bare to buff, 669 : 5
seekest thou great t., 32 : 19
seem to see t. thou dost not, 235 : 4
seen and unseen, 768 : 24
seen are temporal, 49 : 13
seen I see no more, 426 : 10
seizes two t. one slips, 926 : 1
seldom what they seem, 627 : 16
sensible t., 569 : 19
set affection on t. above, 50 : 11
shape anew in Milton, 437 : 19
shape of t. to come, 720 : 9
silently gone out of mind, 424 : 8
slimy t. crawl, 434 : 16
small t. make base men proud, 185 : 21
smell and taste of t., 733 : 17
snob admires mean t., 539 : 11
some live without wild t., 795 : 8
sorry scheme of t., 517 : 13
standing thus unknown, 225 : 1
submitting shows of t. to desires of mind, 179 : 2
substance of t. hoped for, 51 : 18
such t. to be, 532 : 15
sum of human t., 393 : 13
surfeit of sweetest t., 196 : 23
talk of many t., 613 : 5
tears of t., 104 : 26
that are more excellent, 46 : 39
that are too hard for thee, 34 : 26
that cannot be changed, 823 : 15
that feed mind, 654 : 9
that go bump in night, 921 : 4
that help with things that hurt, 653 : 15
that in each other included whole, 768 : 17
that ne'er were nor are, 289 : 20
that should be changed, 823 : 15
that were and would be, 57 : 6
that would astonish you, 628 : 23
the more t. change, 514 : 5
these t. are past and gone, 101 : 17
these t. come to pass, 40 : 22
these t. shall be, 643 : 1
think on these t., 50 : 7
thou art to me all t., 288 : 3
three silent t., 759 : 10
three t. in building, 395 : 18
three t. unfilial, 89 : 13
three t. which are too wonderful, 26 : 4
time bears away all t., 103 : 20
time eases all t., 74 : 5
to be done, 260 : 11
to be known, 260 : 11
to come, 226 : 5
to vilest t. am thrall, 251 : 6

Things (*continued*)
truth in t. erroneous, 579 : 16
two t. believed of any man, 729 : 8
two t. fill mind with wonder, 366 : 12
unattempted yet, 283 : 1
uncomely and broken, 712 : 12
unknown proposed, 333 : 18
used to notice such t., 642 : 3
vicissitudes in all t., 96 : 17
vilest t. become themselves, 241 : 1
we ought to have done, 54 : 13
we passed a hundred times, 543 : 29
which are Caesar's, 40 : 15
which are not, 253 : 1
who mind earthly t., 50 : 5
who receives small t. greatly, 130 : 6
without all remedy, 238 : 17
won are done, 225 : 34
work contrariously, 207 : 8
world full of number of t., 668 : 14
you do not hope happen, 94 : 4
Thing-um-a-jig, especially t., 613 : 21
Thingumbob, hello t. again, 649 : 2
Think aloud, 497 : 18
always talk who never t., 256 : *n* 6
anew act anew, 522 : 12
as native thinks, 767 : 18
before thou speakest, 169 : 27
better than you dare t., 511 : 5
books t. for me, 442 : 8
by fits and starts, 691 : 21
comedy to those that t., 363 : 22
continually of truly great, 876 : 15
dare to read t. speak write, 380 : 10
death i t. no parenthesis, 829 : 6
do thing you t. you cannot, 786 : 13
every day your last, 109 : 3
fellows it hurts to t., 691 : 17
fool doth t. he is wise, 212 : 30
for yourselves, 344 : *n* 5
free to t. speak write, 390 : 2
freedom to t., 567 : 17, 859 : 3
greatly t. or bravely die, 335 : 8
haply I t. on thee, 244 : 9
he can't t. without hat, 866 : 11
him as serpent's egg, 215 : 17
him so, 568 : 11
him so because think him so, 189 : 29
himself act of God, 555 : 12
horse t. it queer, 748 : 6
how Bacon shined, 337 : 15
how know what I t., 869 : 9
how much we t. of selves, 626 : 15
I t. therefore I am, 272 : 10
important question what you t., 586 : 18
in battered caravanserai, 516 : 10
in it as native, 767 : 18
in the morning, 404 : 5
it possible you may be mistaken, 272 : 18
mortal thoughts, 76 : 9
necessary to try to t. them again, 397 : 10
never blows so red the Rose, 516 : 12
not God at all, 288 : 26
not king did banish thee, 194 : 5
not t. beforehand of his words, 89 : 15
not t. clearly, 784 : 5
not whether machines t. but men, 862 : 10
nothing done, 416 : 1
of firelit homes, 795 : 14
of posterity, 123 : 4

Think (*continued*)
of the storm roaming, 878 : 4
on thee dear friend, 244 : 12
on these things, 50 : 7
one may t. what one likes, 122 : 24
only this of me, 797 : 1
quietly talk gently, 536 : 6
right if you t. you are, 723 : 18
so then thought so still, 551 : 7
solicitous what men t., 289 : 15
speak what you t. today, 497 : 2
stand alone and t., 478 : 19
stop to t. miss opportunity, 110 : 22
talk and never t., 256 : 19
that day lost, 920 : *n* 3
that I shall never see, 795 : 6
that ye may be mistaken, 737 : 5
the world imagined good, 769 : 2
those that t. must govern, 369 : 3
thy swan a crow, 191 : 20
to t. is full of sorrow, 476 : 24
to t. is say no, 724 : 5
too difficult to t. nobly, 359 : 4
too little talk too much, 304 : 9
twice and follow lead, 313 : 3
unthinkable, 862 : 21
we are in rats' alley, 805 : 3
we have enow, 257 : 11
we must live as we t., 670 : 10
what kind of people t. we are, 745 : 9
what will Mrs. Grundy t., 416 : 10
what you and other men t., 215 : 4
when I t. I speak, 212 : 8
where man's glory, 717 : 15
whose woods I t. I know, 748 : 5
you I am no stronger, 215 : 24
young men t. it is, 692 : 9
Thinker, beware when t. loose, 497 : 25
secret joy of t., 644 : 1
things at odds when t. loose, 723 : 16
valuable coin of t., 887 : 15
Thinkers, solitary t., 616 : 1
who have best stomachs not best t., 344 : 1
Thinketh, as he t. in his heart, 25 : 8
Thinking a kind of poetry, 690 : 4
all t. things, 423 : 13
and then to t., 445 : 12
atom changed everything save t., 764 : 3
blood around heart is t., 75 : 24
bourgeois t. vulgar, 583 : 18
comparable to paper money, 690 : 4
conscious that we are t., 87 : 21
curtsy while t., 612 : 19
drinking pause from t., 462 : 17
effort of t. troublesome, 635 : 25
end by t. as we lived, 670 : 10
fatal to leave off t., 508 : 7
form and frame from t., 768 : 25
God does t. not I, 571 : 5
greatest happiness for t. man, 397 : 7
high t., 425 : 15
human t. closer to laws of world, 875 : 7
is dismissal of irrelevancies, 832 : 11
is experimental dealing, 678 : 17
it ain't t. about it, 555 : 5
love hardly seem worth t., 712 : 19
makes it so, 220 : 25
man t. or working is alone, 560 : 3
much drinking little t., 322 : 1
of the key, 805 : 13
on fantastic summer's heat, 194 : 7
Thinking (*continued*)
on frosty Caucasus, 194 : 7
on thinking, 87 : 12
operations we perform without t., 697 : 5
originality sum of man's t., 862 : 6
power of positive t., 842 : 13
reed, 300 : 7
refinement of everyday t., 763 : 9
scratched head kept t., 728 : 20
shifts to escape t., 569 : 7
stops action mindless, 862 : 21
theologian not born by t., 156 : 8
through t. few or none harmed, 162 : 4
too highly of himself, 308 : 11
too much t. to have common thought, 335 : 19
too precisely on event, 223 : 18
Thinkings, speak as to thy t., 230 : 32
Thinks better of gilded fool, 251 : 9
divine thought t. of itself, 87 : 12
evil to him who evil t., 143 : 7
he t. too much, 215 : 8
heart t. tongue speaks, 209 : 21
himself wise is great fool, 344 : 6
in a marrowbone, 717 : 2
know she t. o' me, 708 : 8
know what person t. by actions, 861 : 13
like a philosopher, 359 : 8
never t. of me, 922 : 12
not look to see what neighbor t., 124 : 17
of all the hands, 804 : 3
sleeps t. and wills, 705 : 12
think as native t., 767 : 18
to get a living, 359 : 4
too little or too much, 337 : 2
what a man t. of himself, 559 : 2
Thinned down predestined elect, 622 : 13
Thinness, gold to airy t. beat, 253 : 4
Thinning briefcase of enthusiasm, 835 : 6
list of single men, 835 : 6
Thin-spun, slits the t. life, 280 : 15
Third and fourth generation of them that hate me, 10 : 5
day comes a frost, 249 : 3
day he will raise us up, 33 : 9
drink not the t. glass, 268 : 3
drowns him, 213 : 16
fire tolerable t. party, 557 : 13
I don't know is on t., 832 : 3
in your bosom, 192 : 23
is not to dare to be ahead, 65 : 3
shadowy t., 542 : 9
the t. man, 859 : 9
to make t. she joined former two, 306 : 1
who walks beside you, 805 : 11
Thirst, a t. love ecstasy, 849 : 18
after happiness, 359 : 7
dangerous thing, 692 : 15
die of t. at fountainside, 900 : 4
drank without t., 322 : 15
dying of t. by the fountain, 148 : 21
fame t. of youth, 458 : 2
goes away with drinking, 157 : 9
he that believeth in me shall never t., 44 : 41
hunger and t. after righteousness, 37 : 4
Thirst (*continued*)
low ambition and t. of praise, 375 : 21
man can raise t., 708 : 10
mouth and belly injured by t., 89 : 27
neither t. any more, 53 : 16
no wine wonderful as t., 823 : 5
nor for every t. to pot, 269 : 28
of praise, 375 : 21
that from soul doth rise, 256 : 8
this t. blister easier, 605 : 1
Thirsteth, everyone that t., 31 : 18
my soul t. for God, 19 : 5
my soul t. for thee, 19 : 29
Thirsty and ye gave drink, 40 : 33
busy curious t. fly, 344 : 16
cold waters to a t. soul, 25 : 16
earth soaks up the rain, 295 : 7
if thine enemy be t., 25 : 15
in a dry and t. land, 19 : 29
let the t. think, 646 : 12
sleep is drink to t., 171 : 1
Thirteen, clock striking t., 858 : 13
Thirties, in t. want friends, 835 : 16
Thirty, at t. man suspects himself fool, 330 : 10
days hath November, 162 : 7
feel like t. cents, 718 : 11
for t. pence my death, 268 : 11
live enough before t., 722 : 7
look to these t. chapters, 6 : 8
never admitted I am more than t., 675 : 13
nor strong at t., 269 : 32
on the wrong side of t., 323 : 8
once t. already old, 396 : 21
pieces of silver, 33 : 34, 41 : 5
promise of loneliness, 835 : 6
sayings full of knowledge, 25 : *n* 1
years in man's life, 84 : 14
Thirty-five, from t. to fifty-five, 788 : 21
Thirtyfold, brought forth fruit t., 39 : 15
Thirty-four, this day t. years old, 310 : 8
Thirty-one, all the rest have t., 162 : 7
This above all, 219 : 2
after t. therefore because of t., 134 : 18
do in remembrance of me, 44 : 3
hath not offended king, 155 : 10
is London, 872 : 16
is my beloved, 28 : 16
is my beloved Son, 36 : 31
is my body, 41 : 10
is my friend, 28 : 16
is my own my native land, 430 : 10
is our gracious will, 154 : 9
is the real me, 647 : 23
is the way, 30 : 19
is the worst, 234 : 20
it is t. oh it is t., 919 : 1
that it should come to t., 218 : 6
was a man, 217 : 14
Thisbe fearfully o'ertrip dew, 200 : 22
Thisby, Pyramus and T., 196 : 2
Thistle Shamrock Rose entwine, 608 : 9
Thistles, figs of t., 38 : 17, 534 : 17
Thither, hither and t. spins, 585 : 5
Thomas, saith he to T., 45 : 36
true T., 926 : 23
Thompson, Sadie T. answer, 751 : 18
Thor, da stehe ich nun ich armer T., 396 : *n* 3
Thoreau, living like T., 712 : *n* 1
unperfect unfinished, 652 : 7

Thoreau's, no question of T. genius, 652 : 7
Thorn, first kissed beside t., 654 : 17
in the flesh, 49 : 22
is life a t., 629 : 24
no harvest but a t., 268 : 21
oak and ash and t., 710 : 12, 926 : 20
other world like t., 905 : 17
plant this t. this canker, 203 : 12
primrose peeps beneath t., 370 : 17
rose without a t., 399 : 20
snail's on t., 540 : 15
wantons through flowering t., 409 : 24
withering on virgin t., 195 : 21
without t. the rose, 285 : 16
Thornbush, this t. my t., 197 : 17
Thorns and dangers of this world, 202 : 13
burrs and t. of life, 475 : 13
crown of t. on labor, 694 : 16
fall upon t. of life, 467 : 20
grapes of t., 38 : 17
in your sides, 12 : 1
little willful t., 530 : 22
noble crown is of t., 474 : 5
rose among t., 127 : 4
rosebud set with t., 530 : 22
roses have t. fountains mud, 244 : 14
snow on barren t., 777 : 16
that in bosom lodge, 219 : 25
thy only crown, 276 : 13
under a pot, 27 : 5
Thorny hedgehogs, 196 : 21
life is t., 434 : 3
undertaking to follow mind, 164 : 19
virtue demands t. road, 165 : 2
way to heaven, 218 : 28
Thou art that, 56 : 19
art the man, 13 : 20
beside me singing, 516 : 7
duty whispers t. must, 494 : 21
holier than t., 31 : 29
Though an host should encamp, 18 : 12
Thought, actuality of t. is life, 87 : 11
adorns nature with new thing, 498 : 1
adventure in clarification of t., 697 : 11
agents of men of t., 481 : 16
all I t. was true, 747 : 1
all objects of all t., 423 : 13
American cast of t., 728 : 2
armor is his honest t., 250 : 14
as a child, 48 : 25
because we had power, 840 : 9
believe own t. genius, 496 : 19
beneath slight film, 604 : 12
best known and t., 586 : 24
beyond utmost bound of t., 529 : 10
brightest t. incomplete, 580 : 5
bud of t. wants to be rose, 720 : 19
by t. word and deed, 55 : 17
chaos of t. and passion, 337 : 2
charm by t. supplied, 423 : 12
child of action, 501 : 3
community of t., 635 : 9
consciously directed t., 844 : 7
control, 847 : 1
depends on stomach, 344 : 1
divine t. thinks of itself, 87 : 12
divorced from eye, 836 : 18
does not crush, 873 : 3
dome of t., 457 : 6
elastic and vigorous t., 559 : 22
Thought (*continued*)
energy of t., 490 : 8
erring t., 631 : 15
essential in painting, 135 : 11
even t. can shatter us, 658 : 19
every t. a conquest, 865 : 10
every t. that springs, 429 : 7
evolution of t., 586 : 14
feathered wakeful t., 557 : 8
finds the words, 749 : 19
flashes in world of t., 580 : 5
flies to bo-tree, 874 : 13
free t., 645 : 11
freedom for t. we hate, 645 : 11
freedom of t., 365 : 5
God t. and t., 733 : 12
gods t. otherwise, 105 : 4
Greek t. and life, 598 : 13
green t. in green shade, 297 : 3
her body t., 254 : 6
high t. amiable words, 534 : 23
his mind a t. of God, 555 : 12
his who says it best, 568 : 21
human t. or form, 466 : 9
impose on creations of t., 636 : 17
in t. as in action, 872 : 2
in you boundless t. born, 518 : 8
independent of labor, 558 : 22
indolent vacuity of t., 377 : 7
is free, 248 : 8
kept beating like heart, 769 : 8
ladder of human t., 690 : 6
lean upon the t., 585 : 8
leaped to wed with thought, 532 : 2
learning without t., 68 : 10
liberty of t. life of soul, 344 : 9
like full-blown rose, 476 : 13
live in fact or t., 900 : 4
lived with no other t., 527 : 7
loftiness of t. surpassed, 306 : 1
love and t. and joy, 425 : 5
lucidity of t., 589 : 6
man of action forced to t., 723 : 7
microscope of t., 492 : 5
midnight is noon of t., 387 : 4
near to be t. so shortly, 209 : 32
nimble t. can jump, 244 : 16
no freedom of t. without doubt, 859 : 3
no limits set to t., 723 : 15
nor t. of leveling wind, 715 : 9
northern t. slow, 542 : 20
not a t. be lost, 868 : 17
not from vain shallow t., 493 : 17
not t. but action, 538 : 13
not t. death undone so many, 805 : 2
not t. of own in head, 683 : 12
not utilize t., 818 : 12
of China and Greece, 858 : 20
of kindnesses done, 102 : 14
often original, 519 : 2
old man had so much blood, 239 : 25
one t. in breast another on tongue, 102 : 24
one t. of thee, 335 : 5
pale cast of t., 221 : 12
passes swiftly as a t., 67 : 7
pearls of t., 569 : 2
penny for your t., 160 : 25
perish the t., 324 : 28
pleasing dreadful t., 326 : 3
plunged into sea of words, 782 : 3
power in mysteries of t., 76 : 12
practice and t. forge art, 103 : 28
Thought (*continued*)
principle of free t., 645 : 11
process by which human ends answered, 450 : 6
rear tender t., 345 : 11
Roman t. hath struck him, 240 : 17
saturates politics with t., 586 : 22
scientific t. human progress, 660 : 6
seem a moment's t., 712 : 20
sense from t. divide, 303 : *n* 1
she pined in t., 214 : 5
slave of life, 205 : 10
sleep out the t. of it, 246 : 23
sleeps in book, 499 : 17
sow a t., 922 : 18
strange seas of t., 424 : 2
stream of t., 648 : 12
style dress of t., 319 : 18
subtle demonisms of t., 570 : 13
sudden t. careless rhyme, 636 : 11
sweet silent t., 244 : 11
sweetest songs saddest t., 468 : 14
sweetly solemn t., 594 : 6
swift as a bird or t., 60 : 2
take no t. about what is distant, 69 : 11
take no t. for morrow, 38 : 7
taking t. add one cubit, 38 : 3
the best t. and said, 588 : 12
thee bright, 246 : 7
think so then t. so still, 551 : 7
third silence of t., 512 : 20
tire the night in t., 267 : 12
to have loved t. done, 585 : 11
to justify wrongdoings, 343 : 24
to t. added will, 495 : 13
too much thinking to have common t., 335 : 19
too much to stoop to action, 638 : 2
traversed universe in t., 100 : 3
troubled seas of t., 871 : 7
two souls with single t., 508 : 1
uffish t., 612 : 18
understandest my t. afar off, 22 : 16
unmeaning thing they call a t., 333 : 8
uttered a lie, 500 : 24
vitality of t., 697 : 17
want of t. and heart, 485 : 8
weave emotion t. sound, 486 : 8
wed with thought, 532 : 2
What jolly fun, 697 : 1
what oft was t., 333 : 3
what thing not t. of ages long ago, 396 : 22
when t. takes breath away, 591 : 10
whistled for want of t., 307 : 6
wish father to t., 206 : 31
without learning, 68 : 10
without stimulation t. inconceivable, 603 : 6
words slippery t. viscous, 635 : 20
would destroy paradise, 361 : 12
young man brings forth, 85 : 16
Thought-executing fires, 233 : 24
Thoughtless, hour of t. youth, 423 : 13
my t. hand, 405 : 6
saying of great princess, 359 : 6
Thoughtlessness and optimism, 703 : 19
Thought's slave of life, 205 : 10
Thoughts according to inclination, 206 : *n* 4
all intelligent t. already thought, 397 : 10

Thoughts (*continued*)
all t. all passions, 435 : 20
and intents of heart, 51 : 14
assault of t. on unthinking, 783 : 11
beautiful in t., 695 : 6
beyond reaches of souls, 219 : 12
calmer of t., 270 : 34
ceaseless t. of roaming, 313 : 23
discerner of the t., 51 : 14
doubtful t., 199 : 28
fat paunch never breeds fine t., 128 : 1
fly in twinkling of eye, 919 : 7
fond and wayward t., 424 : 11
fresh t. along shores, 536 : 10
give thy t. no tongue, 218 : 29
give thy worst of t., 230 : 32
go blowing through them, 796 : 15
gored mine own t., 245 : 16
great t. come from heart, 361 : 3
high t. must have high language, 82 : 20
high-erected t. in heart of courtesy, 176 : 4
holy profane clean obscene, 264 : 16
in these t. myself despising, 244 : 9
joy of elevated t., 423 : 13
leave to think own t., 704 : 17
legible in the eye, 184 : 13
less conscious t. mold lives, 620 : 7
live in t. not breaths, 555 : 13
long long t., 511 : 25
multiply t., 876 : 2
my bloody t., 231 : 18
my sad t. doth clear, 299 : 7
my t. are minutes, 195 : 17
my t. my trollops, 359 : 12
my t. not your t., 31 : 21
Nazi venom in t., 865 : 10
never alone accompanied with noble t., 176 : 5
never spoken or written, 490 : 1
of a turtle turtles, 500 : 11
of earthly men, 60 : 26
of men decay, 174 : 9
of men widened, 530 : 3
of other men, 684 : 2
of youth long, 511 : 25
on hospitable t. intent, 286 : 18
ought to control t., 515 : 4
pansies for t., 224 : 1
pieced t. into philosophy, 715 : 6
pious t. as harbingers, 276 : 14
quotations give good t., 743 : 9
remain below, 222 : 28
rule the world, 499 : 26
second t. are best, 76 : 21
secret t. run over all things, 264 : 16
sensations rather than t., 479 : 3
shroud of t., 458 : 4
slumbering t., 275 : 14
so thy t. when thou gone, 469 : 18
soothe cares lift t., 475 : 13
speech to conceal t., 343 : 24
style the dress of t., 342 : 7
suspect the t. of others, 198 : 27
tend on mortal t., 236 : 17
that arise in me, 530 : 19
that breathe, 363 : 3
that nature gives way to, 237 : 11
that savor of content, 178 : 10
they have own t., 782 : 15
think mortal t., 76 : 9
think other men's t., 597 : 10

Thoughts (*continued*)
to memory dear, 431 : 16
to think great t. be heroes, 643 : 19
too deep for tears, 426 : 23
turns to t. of love, 529 : 16
understandeth all imaginations of the t., 14 : 24
unexpressed fall dead, 109 : *n* 5
unmentionable t., 571 : 11
unrighteous man forsake his t., 31 : 20
unthinkable t., 862 : 21
uplifting t. in baths, 834 : 8
wander through eternity, 284 : 9
were always downward bent, 283 : 28
were red thoughts, 731 : 16
what sweet t. what longing, 141 : 1
which were not their thoughts, 458 : 4
with sea's boundlessness, 850 : 2
words without t., 222 : 28
wrapped in my t., 149 : 1
Thousand, a t. shall fall at thy side, 20 : 16
actions once afoot, 207 : 8
after t. victories foiled, 244 : 7
ages in Thy sight, 328 : 11
cattle upon t. hills, 19 : 13
conscience hath t. tongues, 187 : 28
day in thy courts better than a t., 20 : 8
days, 890 : 10
death hath ten t. doors, 262 : 8
difference of forty t. men, 421 : 9
done a t. dreadful things, 188 : 22
doors that lead to death, 262 : *n* 2
earth with t. voices, 435 : 23
few t. battered books, 792 : 16
forty t. brothers, 224 : 22
fragrant posies, 183 : 10
freedom has a t. charms, 375 : 19
furlongs of sea, 247 : 8
furnished rooms, 804 : 3
give me a t. kisses, 101 : 18
hacking at branches of evil, 559 : 19
hearts beat happily, 457 : 14
Hell rising from t. thrones, 525 : 14
his songs were a t. and five, 13 : 30
homeless near t. homes, 423 : 2
hundred t. trained men, 786 : 11
I in twelve t. none, 195 : 10
journey of a t. miles, 65 : 1
leagues a thousand years, 348 : 10
little one shall become a t., 31 : 24
man in a t., 710 : 19
man picked out of ten t., 220 : 16
men that fishes gnaw, 187 : 9
more memories than if a t., 580 : 21
natural shocks, 221 : 12
near a t. tables, 423 : 2
night has t. eyes, 670 : 8
night hath a t. eyes, 176 : 2
of t. kisses the poor last, 241 : 21
one among a t., 16 : 23
one man among a t., 27 : 11
one small candle light a t., 265 : 13
peering littlenesses, 534 : 1
radiance of a t. suns, 94 : 15
saw a t. fearful wracks, 187 : 9
Shallow I owe t. pound, 206 : 37
slain a t. men with jawbone, 12 : 17
Solomon spake three t. proverbs, 13 : 30
ten t. saw I at a glance, 427 : 9

Thousand (*continued*)
ten t. times ten t., 536 : 3
ten t. to go out of it, 321 : 10
three hundred t. more, 537 : 2
to that hundred, 266 : 10
torture word ten t. ways, 304 : 26
twangling instruments, 248 : 10
wars of old, 532 : 23
worth a t. men, 431 : 15
would he had blotted a t., 256 : 21
years are as yesterday, 20 : 11
years of peace, 532 : 23
Thousands, and David his ten t., 13 : 4
at his bidding speed, 282 : 17
countless t. mourn, 408 : 16
equally were meant, 322 : 19
mercy unto t. that love me, 10 : 5
murder t., 330 : 1
peace its ten t., 378 : 4
Saul hath slain his t., 13 : 4
slave to t., 230 : 33
war its t. slays, 378 : 4
Thousandth man, 710 : 20
Thousendsthee, till t., 778 : 6
Thracian ships and foreign faces, 632 : 7
Thrained, hundhred thousand t. men, 786 : 11
Thrall, free though t., 171 : 13
thee hath in t., 478 : 13
to least and vilest things am t., 251 : 6
Thread, as t. plays out, 863 : 19
draw as love with t., 259 : 18
feels at each t., 167 : *n* 9
like snails leave faint t., 912 : 1
nothing my own but the t., 166 : 6
of his verbosity, 191 : 6
our eyes upon double string, 253 : 6
spun the t. for wretched mortals, 59 : 12
strung on English t., 569 : 2
strung on golden t., 362 : *n* 4
that ties them together, 166 : 6
touch the utmost t., 167 : *n* 9
weave their t. with bones, 214 : 3
with a t. plucks it back, 192 : 18
Threadbare juggler fortuneteller, 188 : 15
saint, 251 : 9
Threadneedle, Old Lady of T. Street, 407 : 12
Threads, silver t. among gold, 662 : 22
Threat to justice everywhere, 909 : 7
Threaten aggression, 781 : 9
and command, 223 : 3
life of soul, 778 : 11
Threatened life with railway share, 614 : 4
Threatening, looks with t. eye, 202 : 2
tyrant's t. countenance, 107 : 28
Threatenings and slaughter, 46 : 4
Threatens, steed t. steed, 208 : 1
Threats, no terror in your t., 217 : 2
of halter, 393 : 9
Three, after t. days weary of guest, 347 : 2
always t. o'clock, 835 : 11
arts with all things, 85 : 8
at t. hundred pence ointment prize, 268 : 11
bags full, 930 : 5
beings worthy of respect, 581 : 8
better t. hours too soon, 225 : 18

Three (*continued*)
blind mice, 929 : 11
come t. corners of world, 202 : 20
fiddlers t., 929 : 14
fifths of him genius, 567 : 18
for t. years out of key, 792 : 10
galloped all t., 541 : 11
Gaul divided into t. parts, 99 : 14
generations of imbeciles, 645 : 7
generations shirtsleeves, 621 : 13
god would have t. sides, 341 : 7
great elemental sounds, 802 : 19
hour's sleep before midnight worth t. after, 270 : 19
hundred hours in line, 801 : 17
I have t. treasures, 65 : 3
in right with two or t., 567 : 4
jolly gentlemen, 740 : 5
jolly huntsmen, 933 : 6
jovial, huntsmen, 349 : *n* 4
keep counsel if two away, 160 : 29
keep secret if two dead, 347 : 10
Latin word for t. farthings, 190 : 24
laws of righteousness, 70 : 22
little maids from school, 629 : 8
long mountains, 822 : 11
men in a tub, 933 : 2
merry boys are we, 260 : 15
no guest welcome after t. days, 94 : 1
not t. good men unhanged, 203 : 28
o'clock in morning courage, 421 : *n* 1
on 's are sophisticated, 234 : 7
one of the t. will want me, 702 : 9
pecks of barley meal, 934 : 1
poets in three ages born, 306 : 1
ravens on a tree, 927 : 2
removes as bad as fire, 347 : 34
rule of t., 917 : 13
sheets in the wind, 553 : 18
sheets in wind, 553 : *n* 4
ships come sailing, 933 : 3
silent things, 759 : 10
stink in t. days, 94 : *n* 1
stoppeth one of t., 434 : 4
these t. alone lead life, 528 : 5
things in building, 395 : 18
things to be happy in work, 572 : 13
things unfilial, 89 : 13
things which are too wonderful, 26 : 4
two live as t., 806 : 11
we t. meet again, 235 : 21
whine of amateur for t., 619 : 3
white leopards, 805 : 22
who gives self feeds t., 567 : 14
whole days together, 290 : 4
wise men of Gotham, 930 : 18
without t. good friends, 212 : 1
woodspurge has cup of t., 601 : 15
years she grew, 424 : 13
years we waited for herald, 849 : 6
Three-and-twentieth year, 277 : 14
Threefold cord not quickly broken, 26 : 24
fourfold tomb, 265 : 14
Three-fourths, conduct t. of life, 588 : 23
Three-personed God, 254 : 15
Three-piled hyperboles, 191 : 9
Threescore, of my t. years and ten, 690 : 17
our years are t. and ten, 20 : 13
see bachelor of t., 209 : 1
Threshold high to turn deceit, 671 : 12
men that stumble at t., 186 : 18
of Jove's Court, 279 : 2

Threshold (*continued*)
of ruined tenement, 351 : 7
of the last mystery, 864 : 7
of waking light, 906 : 9
stand upon t. of the new, 276 : 12
terrible t., 863 : 15
whining at t., 695 : 17
Threw down their spears, 405 : 8
him downstairs, 931 : 8
pearl away, 232 : 20
their caps, 242 : 9
warm gules, 476 : 16
you in told you rules, 844 : 16
Thrice and four times blessed, 104 : 19
and four times happy, 158 : 4
armed that hath quarrel just, 185 : 17
deny me t., 41 : 18
gorgeous ceremony, 208 : 7
he assayed, 283 : 26
he slew the slain, 306 : 17
tried to clasp her image, 60 : 8
Thrift may follow fawning, 222 : 4
thrift Horatio, 218 : 14
Thrifty, here's to housewife that's t., 399 : 1
never stale in t. mind, 159 : *n* 2
to prepare today, 66 : 11
Thrill deepest notes of woe, 410 : 1
joy the t. the whirl, 569 : 20
new t., 491 : 14
of life along keel, 511 : 7
that comes once in lifetime, 793 : 14
Thrilling glorious hours, 560 : 18
region of ice, 228 : 20
Thrive, let copulation t., 234 : 31
only strong t., 752 : 4
Throat, Amen stuck in my t., 237 : 20
as if my hand at t., 893 : 7
brazen t. of war, 287 : 33
chokin' in my t., 666 : 11
coat from heel to t., 713 : 14
constricted, 833 : 6
fishbone in city's t., 893 : 12
fog in t. mist in face, 544 : 21
heel on t. of my song, 826 : 19
lie in your t., 205 : 23
moment I cut his t., 903 : 5
out of mockingbird's t., 575 : 17
poem begins as lump in t., 749 : 19
put a knife to thy t., 25 : 5
scuttled ship or cut t., 460 : 26
seize fate by the t., 421 : 18
sweet bird's t., 211 : 1
swell t. in vain, 476 : 15
taking life by t., 750 : 8
took by t. circumcised dog, 232 : 21
unlocked silent t., 918 : 17
your sweet dividing t., 271 : 20
Throats, engines whose rude t., 231 : 11
Throbbed, war drum t. no longer, 530 : 1
Throbbing between two lives, 805 : 7
taxi t. waiting, 805 : 7
Throe, dare never grudge t., 544 : 10
Throne, Aphrodite on your rich-wrought t., 63 : 4
barge like burnished t., 240 : 29
bust outlasts t., 640 : 1
Death reared t., 525 : 11
died to keep Past upon t., 568 : 14
down to Gehenna up to t., 707 : 14
ebon t. in rayless majesty, 330 : 5
for King George upon t., 415 : 16
give t. would be easy, 89 : 4

Throne (*continued*)
God's footstool may be t., 746 : 20
heaven is God's t., 37 : 9
heaven to t. in, 242 : 24
intellectual t., 585 : 23
jealousy of rivals near t., 392 : 12
light beats on t., 534 : 1
loafing around the T., 636 : 5
Lord sitting upon a t., 29 : 8
Misfortune made t. seat, 327 : 20
name t. in possession, 525 : 8
no brother near t., 338 : 14
nor tide of pomp, 208 : 7
of bayonets, 696 : 2
of rocks, 460 : 6
of royal state, 284 : 3
on highest t. we sit on our own bottom, 166 : 9
prize ribbon or t., 556 : 1
ready to descend t., 420 : 14
reason keeps its t., 329 : 6
royal t. of kings, 194 : 13
something behind t., 351 : 2
the living t., 363 : 2
through slaughter to t., 362 : 11
thunder him higher than t., 570 : 11
thy t. never pass away, 597 : 18
what is the t., 420 : 11
wrong forever on t., 567 : 7
Throned, becomes t. monarch better, 200 : 9
in glory, 614 : 9
on hundred isles, 458 : 6
Thrones Dominations Princedoms, 286 : 22
Hell rising from thousand t., 525 : 14
not t. and crowns, 449 : 2
stakes were t., 462 : 14
Throng, flung roses with t., 721 : 5
hideous t. rush out, 526 : 2
into my memory, 279 : 16
plaudits of t., 512 : 18
thou idol I t., 628 : 14
Throops, go out alone come with t., 722 : 14
Throttle, after kiss comes t., 868 : 7
Through, best way out is t., 747 : 11
muddle t., 538 : 5
Through-and-through universe, 651 : 3
Throw away dearest thing owed, 236 : 14
bricks and sermons, 625 : 24
do not t. book about, 729 : 14
gods themselves t. incense, 235 : 13
greater t. from weaker hand, 198 : 30
if any have stone to t., 794 : 6
myself down in my chamber, 255 : 2
of dice not abolish chance, 651 : 15
out the lifeline, 670 : 7
people in glass houses shouldn't t. stones, 347 : 16
physic to the dogs, 239 : 32
quaint enameled eyes, 281 : 1
sand against the wind, 406 : 3
time t. dart at thee, 265 : 15
torch hold it high, 737 : 10
whole book in fire, 504 : 10
within a stone's t., 169 : 13
yourself into coach, 799 : *n* 1
Thrown, discretion should be t. aside, 91 : 2
Throws himself on God, 542 : 19
little candle t. beams, 201 : 4
shadows which fire t., 84 : 17

Throws (*continued*)
snake t. enameled skin, 196 : 18
up a steamy column, 377 : 3
Thrush, deception of t., 807 : 3
frail gaunt small, 641 : 12
music went, 749 : 7
that's the wise t., 541 : 17
Thrust, greatness t. upon them, 214 : 9
into nature like wedge, 558 : 20
ivrybody but cut cards, 722 : 11
man who knows when to t., 157 : 5
of cure, 908 : 8
spear to t. club to strike, 157 : 5
Thrusts thing we prayed for, 507 : 18
Thucydides, a T. at Boston, 363 : 21
wrote history of war, 80 : 14
Thule, farthest T., 103 : 25, 345 : 15
ultima T., 103 : *n* 14, 115 : *n* 9
Thumb, he who has t. on purse, 553 : 12
instead of onion, 911 : 13
miller hath golden t., 146 : *n* 3
O Tom T., 192 : *n* 2
of gold, 146 : 11
put in his t., 929 : 20
Thumbs, forget green t., 886 : 15
pricking of my t., 239 : 7
Thunder, clothed his neck with t., 16 : 36
comb me all to t., 622 : 16
crawl flash or t. in, 887 : 7
dawn comes up like t., 708 : 9
earthquakes t. lightning, 622 : 19
he was as rattling t., 241 : 25
he who rules t., 323 : 2
him higher than throne, 570 : 11
impressive, 626 : 7
is good, 626 : 7
Jove for his power to t., 242 : 20
lightning or in rain, 235 : 21
loud roared dreadful t., 415 : 5
men want rain without t., 556 : 4
miniature t. where fled, 748 : 4
moan of t. to song, 469 : 14
of the captains, 16 : 38
of the Odyssey, 657 : 4
of the wings, 797 : 20
of your words, 236 : *n* 1
omnipotent Father with his t., 60 : *n* 3
pens louder than t., 169 : *n* 3
purr to sleep with t., 623 : 5
sound of t. heard remote, 284 : 18
steal my t., 318 : 2
such sweet t., 197 : 8
thou all-shaking t., 233 : 24
wresting from Jupiter his t., 115 : 16
Thunderbolt, like t. he falls, 532 : 28
split mountains with t., 103 : 29
Thunderbolts and tyrants, 346 : *n* 5
oak-cleaving t., 233 : 24
Thundered and lightened, 81 : 11
before Franklin took hint, 750 : 5
volleyed and t., 533 : 13
Thundering Aeschylus, 256 : 14
cannons roar, 371 : 10
shepherd hears their t., 57 : 28
sound, 370 : 11
Thunders condemnation, 555 : 24
indignation, 609 : 6
of white silence, 507 : 6
what you are t., 499 : 24
Thunderstorm, no t. for new year, 755 : 9
streams like t., 458 : 17
Thursday come and week gone, 270 : 8
do not love you T., 507 : *n* 1
like today in autumn, 824 : 4
took ill on T., 932 : 11
Thursday's child, 932 : 10
Thus joy to pass to world below, 105 : 12
to be t. is nothing, 238 : 13
why is this t., 616 : 18
Thusness, reason of this t., 616 : 18
Thwackum was for doing justice, 349 : 18
Thy-doxy, heterodoxy t., 473 : 19
Thyme, bank whereon wild t. blows, 196 : 18
Thyrsis and I, 587 : 6
hear it O T., 587 : 11
still had T. then, 587 : 6
Thyself, know then t., 337 : 2
love thy neighbor as t., 10 : 21
love t. last, 249 : 8
only gift portion of t., 498 : 6
rule well t., 148 : 10
so true to t., 180 : 22
Tiara of proud towers, 458 : 7
Tiber, Father T., 488 : 16
let Rome in T. melt, 240 : 14
not a drop of allaying T., 242 : 12
trembled underneath banks, 215 : 1
Tiberius, coin outlasts T., 640 : 1
had T. been cat, 588 : 4
tyranny of T., 597 : 10
Tick, seeds in dry pod t., 728 : 4
what makes it technically t., 887 : 7
Ticker tape ain't spaghetti, 778 : 8
Ticket, respectfully return Him t., 582 : 4
Tickle, if you t. us do we not laugh, 199 : 18
one's vanity, 583 : 9
your catastrophe, 206 : 10
Tickled with a straw, 337 : 7
Tickling, trout caught with t., 214 : 7
what gnawing of worm not t., 254 : 23
Tid, yes t. there's where, 778 : 6
Tiddler's, Tom T. ground, 921 : 2
Tide, a-going out with t., 549 : 3
blood-dimmed t. loosed, 714 : 12
boots not to resist wind and t., 186 : 16
call of running t., 760 : 15
deaths at ebb t., 672 : 20
dire gorge of salt sea t., 200 : *n* 1
disappointed t., 604 : 11
drinks incoming t., 837 : 2
full moon lies fair, 587 : 13
in affairs of men, 217 : 5
is coming in, 487 : 17
of pomp that beats, 208 : 7
of times, 216 : 11
rode t. to Ararat, 899 : 10
such t. as seems asleep, 535 : 19
tarrieth no man, 159 : 3
time nor t. tarrieth, 159 : *n* 1
turning o' the t., 207 : 13
under the whelming t., 281 : 2
unheard beyond ocean t., 568 : 14
when just cause reaches flood t., 689 : 1
wind nor t. nor sea, 630 : 21
Tides and life of man, 672 : 20
contrive no farther t., 843 : 13
dread abysses unknown t., 651 : 3
of grass foam of flowers, 632 : 18
of men into my hands, 810 : 2
push in their t., 886 : 13
Tides (*continued*)
salt t. seawards flow, 584 : 11
Tidiers-up, scientists t., 888 : 1
Tidings, bringer of good t., 130 : 14
confirm t. as they roll, 325 : 9
dismal t. when he frowned, 370 : 10
glad t. of great joy, 317 : 5
good t. of great joy, 42 : 28
him that bringeth good t., 31 : 12
Tie, careless shoestring in whose t., 266 : 7
educational relations strongest t., 672 : 17
of host and guest, 71 : 17
silken t., 430 : 9
stand before glass t. my t., 811 : 13
untwisting chains that t., 278 : 7
up the knocker, 338 : 5
up thy fears, 268 : 22
Tied by chance bond together, 557 : 2
I am t. to the stake, 234 : 17
to me as to dog's tail, 715 : 4
Tiger, Hyrcan t., 238 : 28
imitate action of the t., 207 : 16
lady or t., 618 : 15
rides t. afraid to dismount, 743 : *n* 2
Tiger burning bright, 405 : 7
Tiger's heart in player's hide, 178 : 12
heart in woman's hide, 186 : 2
sinks into my throat t. tooth, 819 : 4
Tigers, catches t. in red weather, 767 : 1
empty t. or roaring sea, 193 : 23
getting hungry, 743 : 13
in the wood, 899 : 11
not daughters, 234 : 25
shabby t., 732 : 16
they dare not dismount, 743 : 13
Tight hot cell, 836 : 20
little island, 429 : 15
little slight little, 629 : 19
Tighter, without t. breathing, 606 : 14
Tightfisted hand at the grindstone, 548 : 4
Tight-rooted, wolf's-bane t., 477 : 20
Tiles, as many devils in Worms as t., 156 : 10
Tillage begins other arts follow, 451 : 6
Tilled, little field well t., 347 : 8
Tiller, Cain was t. of ground, 7 : 14
Tilling and grazing feed France, 178 : 9
dignity in t. field, 681 : 25
soil of vanity, 750 : 16
Tills, man t. field lies beneath, 533 : 27
Tilly-loo, sang T., 550 : 12
Tilt at all I meet, 339 : 6
Tilth vineyard none, 247 : 26
Tilting at windmills, 168 : *n* 9
planet, 811 : 13
Tim, Tiny T. last of all, 548 : 11
Timber, crazy as hauling t. into woods, 106 : 18
knowledge and t. seasoned, 519 : 14
one old t. leg, 735 : 3
rotten t., 373 : 7
seasoned t. never gives, 268 : 17
Timbrel is stilled, 836 : 17
praise him with t., 22 : 25
sound the loud t., 447 : 10
Timbrels, pipes and t., 477 : 5
played before the Lord on t., 13 : 14
Time, a little t. for laughter, 614 : *n* 3
a t. when it was not, 606 : 2
abysm of t., 247 : 10

Time (*continued*)
Africa marches patiently through t., 867 : 13
age and body of the t., 222 : 2
almighty t. disquiets, 75 : 11
an endless song, 712 : 11
and chance happeneth to all, 27 : 17
and intents are savage-wild, 193 : 23
and Patience strongest of warriors, 602 : 4
and the hour, 236 : 13
and world ever in flight, 712 : 13
annihilate space and t., 336 : 8
arrest your flight, 464 : 14
art long t. fleeting, 509 : 14
art's long though t. short, 80 : *n* 2
as needed, 883 : 8
as one born out of t., 48 : 28
as t. goes by, 830 : 6, 830 : 7
ask for anything except t., 420 : 7
at hands of T. and Chance, 640 : 12
at same t. good bad indifferent, 308 : 19
author of authors, 178 : 19
ay fleeth t., 147 : 17
backward turn backward t., 610 : 10
bank and shoal of t., 236 : 22
bears away all things, 103 : 20
beautiful t. of young love, 413 : 21
bid t. return, 194 : 27
bind us in t., 843 : 16
bird of t. has little way, 516 : 4
books of all t., 573 : 2
born out of my due t., 618 : 7
bounds of place and t., 363 : 2
bridge of t., 581 : 12
brief chronicles of the t., 221 : 4
but little at a t., 323 : 1
cancels young pain, 76 : 13
captive of t., 816 : 19
cease and midnight never come, 184 : 7
chinks that T. has made, 276 : 12
chronicle of wasted t., 245 : 12
come t. and haste day, 399 : 18
comfortable t. lag, 720 : 8
condemned to kill t., 886 : 1
consume strongest cord, 431 : 24
convinced of imbecility by t., 353 : 5
cools time clarifies, 755 : 18
cormorant devouring t., 190 : 8
corridors of t., 510 : 20
could have had damned good t., 844 : 13
cracks in furious flower, 889 : 18
creeping hours of t., 211 : 12
criticized for us, 569 : 6
crumbles things, 87 : 6
daughters of t., 495 : 5
Death old captain it is t., 581 : 4
defy tooth of t., 330 : 3
destroyer time preserver, 808 : 6
devourer of all things, 113 : 23
die for such a long t., 297 : 12
died far away before his t., 700 : *n* 1
discovers truth, 115 : 3
dissipates to ether, 496 : 15
do not squander t., 347 : 26
does not relinquish its rights, 395 : 21
done his best for his t., 413 : 5
doth transfix flourish, 244 : 20
driveth onward fast, 528 : 17
duty beyond space and t., 745 : 1
eases all things, 74 : 5

Time (*continued*)
enchanted isle of t., 846 : 4
engenders forgetfulness, 755 : 6
enough for sleep, 690 : 18
enough for that, 247 : 6
entertainer who understood his t., 774 : 12
envious and calumniating t., 226 : 20
everflowing stream of t., 869 : 13
every day is elastic, 734 : 5
falling oars kept t., 297 : 10
feet in ancient t., 406 : 21
fire in which we burn, 883 : 10
fleet the t. carelessly, 210 : 11
flying never to return, 104 : 10
fool some people all the t., 524 : 10
footprints on sands of t., 509 : 15
for a change, 854 : 4
for a little something, 778 : 13
for all good men, 923 : 1
for many words, 60 : 10
for sleep, 60 : 10
for such a word, 240 : 4
for us to leave her, 935 : 2
foremost files of t., 530 : 7
future in time past, 807 : 1
goes you say, 639 : 19
good t. coming, 431 : 26, 553 : 4
great legalizer, 771 : 17
great poet writes his t., 809 : 11
grown old before my t., 608 : 18
habit fills up t., 734 : 5
half as old as T., 416 : 3, 552 : 9
happiest t. of New Year, 528 : 12
has come Walrus said, 613 : 5
has no divisions, 755 : 9
hath taming hand, 490 : 5
hath to silver turned, 177 : 8
hath wallet at his back, 226 : 16
haven't t. to take our t., 881 : 3
healing a matter of t., 79 : 14
heals all wounds, 96 : *n* 10
held me green and dying, 887 : 3
his t. is forever, 295 : 10
history the witness to passing t., 98 : 9
history triumphed over t., 173 : 2
hold fast the t., 756 : 1
holy t. quiet as nun, 425 : 16
hot t. in old town, 705 : 1
how long a t. in one word, 194 : 2
hurry up please its t., 805 : 5
I had lived a blessed t., 238 : 7
idea whose t. come, 491 : 11
image of eternity, 125 : 27
in a moment of t., 42 : 34
in his good t., 540 : 7
in hours days years, 299 : 6
in space and t. universes, 576 : 22
in t. we know not fate begin, 633 : 14
in your flight, 610 : 10
irreparable ravages of t., 312 : 11
is a kind friend, 787 : 6
is a very shadow, 34 : 10
is dead, 837 : 16
is man's angel, 413 : 14
is money, 348 : 1, 491 : *n* 1
is of essence, 923 : 13
is on our side, 517 : 18
is out of joint, 220 : 6
is still a-flying, 266 : 11
is that wherein is opportunity, 79 : 15
it doesn't take much t., 850 : 12
it is t. to choose, 768 : 1

Time (*continued*)
joyous t. not be stayed, 174 : 16
keeping t., 807 : 10
kill t. injuring eternity, 559 : 3
killing t. essence of comedy, 706 : 3
lack t. to make it short, 299 : 13
lag, 720 : 8
laid hand on my heart, 512 : 11
last syllable of recorded t., 240 : 4
last t. I see Paris, 819 : 13
least thing we have of, 845 : 11
let me play, 887 : 1
Lethe, 755 : 6
life and spirit of t., 592 : 7
like ever-rolling stream, 328 : 12
like fashionable host, 226 : 19
lilac t., 772 : 22
long t. between drinks, 669 : 12
lost may nought recovered be, 144 : 27
lost t. never found, 347 : 27
lucky to be alive at great t., 843 : 2
machine, 719 : 13
made me his numbering clock, 195 : 17
make soft iron wood, 823 : 14
makes ancient good uncouth, 567 : 8
makes possible Day of Judgment, 786 : 5
makes these decay, 272 : 1
man knoweth not his t., 27 : 17
maniac scattering dust, 532 : 6
market of his t., 223 : 17
memory emancipated from t., 437 : 13
mild Heaven a t. ordains, 282 : 10
misspending t. a kind of self-homicide, 310 : 20
mock t. with fairest show, 237 : 8
moment of t. fleeting by, 638 : 4
more than half the t., 846 : 16
most valuable thing, 91 : 17
must have stop, 205 : 10
my t. is at hand, 41 : 6
my t. is today, 842 : 3
my t. not come either, 658 : 25
never t. and place, 546 : 3
new direction of T., 790 : 9
night of t. surpasseth day, 275 : 10
no t. for sorrow, 404 : 1
no t. like old t., 519 : 1
no t. like present, 319 : 21
no t. to speak of hopes, 745 : 11
noiseless foot of t., 227 : 21
nor tide tarrieth, 159 : *n* 1
nor t. nor place, 237 : 4
not of an age but for all t., 256 : 15
not sacred until lived, 631 : 2
not yet by t. silvered, 376 : 23
nothing destroys us but t., 132 : 7
nothing so precious as t., 91 : *n* 9
now is accepted t., 49 : 15
now is t. for drinking, 107 : 15
now near at hand, 379 : 2
nyl no man abide, 147 : 17
O t. too swift, 177 : 8
of death every moment, 94 : *n* 9
of life is short, 205 : 8
of milking time of harvest, 807 : 10
of peace, 26 : 21
of scorn, 232 : 3
of the singing of birds, 28 : 7
of war, 26 : 21
of your life, 875 : 5

Time (*continued*)
old bald cheater T., 255 : 13
old common arbitrator T., 227 : 5
on either side of now, 904 : 12
one is so lucky as to have, 653 : 9
only pretty ring t., 212 : 33
open T. let him pass, 696 : 13
opportunity is that wherein is no t., 79 : 15
out of key with his t., 792 : 10
out of mind, 168 : 8, 823 : 12
out of Space out of T., 526 : 8
Paleozoic t., 688 : 3
pant T. up T. up, 856 : 6
panting T. toiled after him, 351 : 10
pass the t. away, 921 : 17
passions expand t., 734 : 5
past comes not back, 109 : *n* 5
peace for our t., 727 : 2
peace in our t. O Lord, 56 : 15
people not redeemed from t., 808 : 16
play the fools with t., 206 : 13
preparing us for fatal operation, 887 : 10
present and time past, 807 : 1
procrastination thief of t., 330 : 9
proper t. to marry, 377 : 24
rags of t., 252 : 8
rave no more 'gainst t., 630 : 21
redeem the t., 806 : 3
remembered, 632 : 8
removes distress, 96 : 9
respect of place persons t., 213 : 25
reveals all, 115 : *n* 2
rider that breaks youth, 270 : 9
ripe for running to moon, 874 : 6
river of strong current, 124 : 25
river without banks, 925 : 6
rolling t. hath pressed, 516 : 14
runs on cried she, 916 : *n* 3
runs the clock will strike, 184 : 8
rust sharpest sword, 431 : 24
saltness of t., 205 : 24
sands of time, 509 : 15
school in which we learn, 883 : 10
seas of space and t., 802 : 20
seeds of t., 236 : 5
seen the best of our t., 233 : 4
served my t. in hell, 925 : 1
shall throw a dart at thee, 265 : 15
shall unfold, 233 : 1
show and gaze o' the t., 240 : 10
silence and slow t., 477 : 4
so gracious is the t., 217 : 26
so little t. to do so much, 780 : 16
sons of men snared in evil t., 27 : 17
soul of this world, 120 : 22
space and t. are stupidity, 784 : 18
spend and waste t., 839 : 14
spoils of t., 362 : 7
squall of t., 822 : 7
staunchless flows, 830 : 11
stays we go, 639 : 19
stream I go a-fishing in, 559 : 28
stream of t. run, 206 : 26
strengthens friendship, 315 : 6
subtle thief of youth, 277 : 14
sun and moon journey toward preordained t., 132 : 5
superfluous to demand t. of day, 202 : 23
take no note of t., 330 : 7
take t. by the forelock, 174 : *n* 4
takes all gives all, 171 : 11

Time (*continued*)
teaches all things, 70 : 26
that aged nurse, 475 : 19
that may not sojourne, 144 : 3
that takes in trust, 173 : 5
that takes survey of world, 205 : 10
that t. of year in me behold, 244 : 27
that which man trying to kill, 580 : 1
the avenger, 458 : 20
the greatest innovator, 180 : 24
thief you cannot banish, 864 : 16
thieving T., 705 : 4
this day T. winds, 410 : 14
this great gap of t., 240 : 20
this is my hard t., 873 : 12
though t. be fleet, 612 : 15
through t. t. conquered, 807 : 7
till t. and times done, 712 : 14
time time, 527 : 11
'tis almost fairy t., 197 : 22
to be born, 26 : 21
to break down, 26 : 21
to build up, 26 : 21
to cast away, 26 : 21
to cast away stones, 26 : 21
to dance, 26 : 21
to die, 26 : 21
to embrace, 26 : 21
to every purpose, 26 : 21
to gather stones together, 26 : 21
to get, 26 : 21
to hate, 26 : 21
to heal, 26 : 21
to keep, 26 : 21
to keep silence, 26 : 21
to kill, 26 : 21
to laugh, 26 : 21
to lose, 26 : 21
to lose t. displeasing, 141 : 20
to love, 26 : 21
to mourn, 26 : 21
to murder and create, 803 : 11
to plant, 26 : 21
to plant tears, 878 : 10
to pluck up, 26 : 21
to refrain from embracing, 26 : 21
to remember, 683 : 11
to rend, 26 : 21
to sew, 26 : 21
to speak, 26 : 21
to stand and stare, 732 : 9
to stop revolution, 851 : 12
to weep, 26 : 21
to wonder Do I dare, 803 : 12
too much change too short t., 909 : 1
tooth of t., 229 : 5
transported, 920 : 4
travels in divers paces, 212 : 11
turn up his glass, 257 : 17
uncertain balance of proud t., 178 : 13
unconscionable t. dying, 302 : 23
unimaginable touch of t., 429 : 5
unthinking t., 306 : 27
upset fighting faiths, 645 : 1
vague crepuscular t., 564 : 4
was when toy dog new, 666 : 17
waste sad t., 807 : 8
wasted t. now doth t. waste me, 195 : 17
wastes her t. and me, 276 : 7
wasting of t. an abomination, 3 : 6
we don't have t., 849 : 21
weak piping t. of peace, 186 : 32
weakens love, 315 : 6

Time (*continued*)
weight of this sad t., 235 : 20
what's t., 542 : 17
when meadow grove stream, 426 : 10
when only dead smile, 801 : 16
when t. is broke, 195 : 16
when t. is old, 226 : 15
whereof memory of man, 365 : 17
which antiquates antiquities, 275 : 4
whips and scorns of t., 221 : 12
whirligig of t., 214 : 28
whole earth and all t., 424 : 8
will change your opinions, 86 : 3
will come you will hear me, 501 : 11
will doubt of Rome, 461 : 12
will explain all, 77 : 14
will not be ours forever, 255 : 16
will run back, 277 : 9
wings of T. grief flies, 296 : 17
wisest of counselors T., 73 : 7
witching t. of night, 222 : 23
with gift of tears, 632 : 9
with thee I forget all t., 285 : 27
woes t. cannot recure, 172 : 7
woman's t. of opportunity short, 82 : 12
work expands to fill t., 876 : 14
work the scythe of t., 420 : 17
world enough and t., 296 : 26
worn out with eating t., 303 : 16
wounds all heels, 862 : 14
wrecks of t., 636 : 11
writes no wrinkle, 458 : 27
wrong war at wrong t., 825 : 5
you have to spend dead, 164 : 10
you old gypsy man, 732 : 17
you thief, 454 : 8
youth 'gainst t. and age, 177 : 8
youth the t. for toil, 84 : 20
Timed, gifts well t., 315 : 5
Time-harried prisoners, 875 : 3
Time-honored bread sauce, 653 : 6
Timeless, pattern of t. moments, 808 : 16
Timely, desired and t. things, 692 : 2
dew of sleep, 285 : 26
gain t. inn, 238 : 22
Timeo Danaos et dona ferentis, 104 : *n* 15
Time's fell hand, 244 : 21
fin hoof wing fang, 879 : 8
flies, 243 : 5
glory calm contending kings, 189 : 23
life t. fool, 205 : 10
love's not T. fool, 245 : 18
noblest offspring, 330 : 25
toppling wave, 868 : 5
winged chariot, 296 : 28
Times, all classes t. circumstances, 553 : 20
all old t. good, 462 : 13
all t. are his seasons, 255 : 1
are in his hand, 544 : 8
at all the t. you can, 346 : 12
at t. almost ridiculous, 803 : 17
background of the t., 412 : 14
before you, 274 : 26
best of t. worst of t., 549 : 22
brisk and giddy-paced t., 213 : 28
change and move continually, 174 : 8
change and new life blossoms, 414 : 2
change and we change with them, 134 : 30

Times (*continued*)
changed with him who marries, 667 : 14
cowards die many t., 215 : 26
fashion of these t., 210 : 31
glory of their t., 36 : 11
go by turns, 182 : 1
good old t., 519 : *n* 1
good old t. when unhappy, 928 : 4
hard and wages low, 935 : 2
hard doubtful t., 471 : 13
hard money scarce, 499 : 16
illusion that t. were better, 538 : 9
in the morning of the t., 178 : *n* 12
in which a genius would live, 392 : 16
later t. more aged than earlier, 178 : *n* 12
lived for all t., 413 : 5
my t. are in thy hand, 18 : 17
necessity of the t., 365 : 3
O what fine t., 342 : 22
of great Elizabeth, 528 : 21
oh the t. the customs, 98 : 2
old simplicity of t., 920 : 15
old t. manners books, 371 : 3
old t. not forgotten, 554 : 1
past t. preserve themselves, 834 : 4
people in old t. had convictions, 482 : 1
purest treasure mortal t. afford, 193 : 32
pursy t., 223 : 9
seven t. over and over, 578 : 9
signs of the t., 39 : 34
sun itself which makes t., 252 : 22
terrible t., 672 : 1
that try men's souls, 384 : 13
these t. are ancient t., 178 : 21
these unhappy t., 779 : 6
they are a-changin', 915 : 5
thus t. do shift, 266 : 15
tide of t., 216 : 11
till time and t. done, 712 : 14
truth which cunning t. put on, 199 : 27
truths not for all t., 343 : 15
wild dark t. rumbling toward us, 482 : 3
Times', my dear t. waste, 244 : 11
Timetable, read t. sooner than nothing, 751 : 19
Timid soul, 793 : 13
state t. as lone woman, 558 : 7
Timidity, whistles and disavows t., 678 : 10
Timing, circumstance and proper t., 83 : 1
is most important factor, 61 : 23
Timon, till I am T. and Lear, 717 : 10
Timor mortis conturbat me, 153 : 6
nil terribile nisi ipse t., 179 : *n* 3
Timorous beastie, 408 : 12
foe, 338 : 14
Timothy learned sin to fly, 320 : 8
O T. keep thy trust, 51 : 5
Tim'rous beastie, 408 : 12
Tin, cat on hot t. roof, 301 : *n* 3
cat on t. roof, 887 : 11
cheap t. trays, 760 : 20
in t. factory human being crushed, 885 : 8
little t. gods, 707 : 4
Tin Pan Alley hit, 751 : 4
Tincture, best virtue has t. of vice, 165 : 12
Tinged by what absorbs it, 650 : 10
eyelids and hands, 638 : 11
Tinhorn politicians, 726 : 10
Tinker more than renew, 650 : 10
to Evers to Chance, 773 : 12
Tinkled among teacups, 804 : 8
Tinkling, chime of words t., 711 : *n* 1
with their feet, 29 : 1
Tinklings, drowsy t. lull, 361 : 21
Tinpinny, sellin' t. nails, 722 : 5
Tintinnabulation musically wells, 527 : 11
Tiny, little t. boy, 214 : 29
little t. wit, 234 : 1
round bole in t. leaf, 541 : 16
Tim last of all, 548 : 11
violetflavored nuisance, 829 : 3
Tiphys disclose new worlds, 115 : 13
Tippecanoe and Tyler too, 439 : *n* 3
iron-armed soldier of T., 439 : *n* 3
Tipped with line of steel, 578 : 14
Tippenny, wi' t. fear nae evil, 411 : 10
Tipperary, long way to T., 753 : 1
Tippled drink more fine, 477 : 16
Tippler, little t. leaning, 604 : 15
Tips with silver fruit-tree tops, 192 : 11
Tipsy dance and jollity, 279 : 11
Tiptoe malices, 701 : 7
on misty mountaintops, 193 : 15
religion stands on t., 269 : 11
stand a-t. when day named, 208 : 10
upon a little hill, 474 : 20
Tiptoed to daughter's room, 912 : 13
Tirade, your old-fashioned t., 893 : 5
Tire day in toil, 267 : 12
ear the open vowels t., 333 : 7
night in thought, 267 : 12
of all creation, 519 : 11
speeds too fast 'twill t., 190 : 22
Tired, dull stale t. bed, 233 : 3
eyelids upon tired eyes, 528 : 14
give me your t. your poor, 664 : 10
nature's sweet restorer, 330 : 4
no time to be t., 483 : 10
of being a man, 860 : 9
of his dark dominion, 600 : 27
of honest things, 823 : 10
of its pleasures t., 424 : 3
of kings, 494 : 16
of London tired of life, 355 : 26
of my turmoil, 893 : 11
of ruling over slaves, 358 : 5
of tears and laughter, 633 : 20
on day of victory no one t., 132 : 26
Sister Caroline t., 733 : 13
stummucks don't git t., 662 : 11
sun with talking, 591 : 9
till t. he sleeps, 337 : 7
today's newspaper t., 741 : 2
waves vainly breaking, 564 : 17
we were very t., 822 : 19
with all these, 244 : 23
Tirer les marrons du feu, 297 : *n* 3
Tires, sad t. in a mile-a, 246 : 24
unchartered freedom t., 427 : 14
Tiresias, I T. though blind, 805 : 7
Tiresome verse-reciter Care, 470 : 4
Tiring, mothers' wombs the t. houses, 173 : 1
Tirlin' at the window, 537 : 6
Tirra lirra by the river, 528 : 26
Tit for tat, 160 : 28
Tit (*continued*)
tell tale t., 929 : 22
Titania, ill met by moonlight proud T., 196 : 13
there sleeps T., 196 : 18
Titanic, alley t., 527 : 1
Tithe of mint and anise, 40 : 18
Title and profit I resign, 326 : *n* 2
excels at t. page, 368 : 5
farced t. 'fore king, 208 : 7
feel his t. hang loose, 239 : 28
from better man I stole, 668 : 17
gained no t., 336 : 5
like t. for it not mine, 668 : 17
neither can t. to ocean belong, 163 : 13
no lover of pompous t., 164 : 3
no t. I deem more honorable, 777 : 3
ready my t. clear, 328 : 14
Titles are shadows, 318 : 10
gratuities privileges, 419 : 3
high though his t., 430 : 10
kinquering congs t. take, 659 : 10
of mining claims, 840 : 2
power and pelf, 430 : 10
such as Indispensable, 701 : 11
Titter w'en stew smokin' hot, 737 : 2
Tittle, jot or t., 37 : 7
Tittlemouse, Tommy T., 933 : 19
Tityrus, once sang of you T., 104 : 14
To, going t. and fro in earth, 15 : 2
many shall run t. and fro, 33 : 6
reel t. and fro, 21 : 16
the unknown god, 46 : 15
Toad beneath harrow knows, 707 : 5
glorious sight murmured T., 690 : 15
I had rather be a t., 231 : 6
like t. at ear of Eve, 286 : 6
like t. ugly and venomous, 210 : 24
preaches contentment to t., 707 : 5
without which no garden complete, 603 : 10
worm to a t., 647 : 11
Toads brooding in wells, 873 : 12
imaginary gardens with real t., 798 : 11
Toast attributed to one of naval heroes, 417 : 17
golden for its beauty, 625 : 14
let the t. pass, 399 : 1
works down to babies, 622 : 21
Toasted, dreamed of t. cheese, 668 : 8
Toasts of the young men, 394 : 8
Tobacco crumbs vases fringes, 889 : 12
devilish and damned t., 259 : 15
divine rare, 259 : 15
for thy sake T., 442 : 5
is a filthy weed, 401 : 3
nothing compared with t., 462 : *n* 6
Road, 857 : 10
sublime t., 462 : 16
this night leave off t., 441 : 12
Tobacco's fragrance greet, 900 : 5
Toboggans, ignorance t. into know, 830 : 3
Toby, my uncle T., 360 : 10
Toccatas, sat and played t., 543 : 10
Tocsin of the soul, 461 : 16
Today a king, 35 : 17
be good and happy t., 433 : 17
be wise t., 330 : 8
beneath foeman's frown, 536 : 7
call t. his own, 305 : 1
describe world of t., 840 : 20

Today (*continued*)
first day of rest of life, 925 : 19
flower that smiles t., 266 : 11
future lays law of t., 657 : 7
give me t. take tomorrow, 132 : 23
he puts forth tender leaves, 249 : 3
here t. gone tomorrow, 312 : 18
here t. next week tomorrow, 690 : 15
I have dined t., 433 : 12
I have lived t., 305 : 1
in t. walks tomorrow, 443 : *n* 6
isn't any other day, 613 : 11
live t., 119 : 1
lose ground won t., 585 : 22
Mother died t., 882 : 2
never do t. what you can put off, 593 : 6
never jam t., 613 : 11
nor care beyond t., 361 : 10
nothing else show t., 605 : 20
our pleasure to be drunk, 349 : 5
rude brief recitative, 575 : 21
same yesterday t. and forever, 51 : 24
shalt thou be with me, 44 : 9
speak what you think t., 497 : 2
speed t. put back tomorrow, 174 : 10
such a day tomorrow as t., 246 : 9
thrifty to prepare t., 66 : 11
Today's t., 76 : 8
tomorrow be t., 512 : 19
tomorrow is not until t. past, 75 : 7
voice of t., 706 : 23
wasn't there again t., 756 : 2
weep no more t., 598 : 5
what he is doing t., 496 : 14
what you can do t., 593 : *n* 1
wiser t. than yesterday, 340 : 10
yesterday to t. so lightly, 878 : 20
Today's achievement tomorrow's confusion, 631 : 18
newspaper old, 741 : 2
today, 76 : 8
Toddle safely home, 795 : 15
Toe, eye of newt t. of frog, 239 : 5
fill me from crown to t., 236 : 17
Freedom stumped t., 855 : 4
light fantastic t., 277 : 20
lissom clerical printless t., 796 : 11
of peasant, 224 : 13
Toes, bells on her t., 931 : 11
frozen t., 729 : 2
Pobble who has no t., 551 : 5
Pobbles happier without t., 551 : 6
pretty little t., 932 : 4
teaches on t., 839 : 5
turn out your t., 612 : 22
Toga, let arms yield to t., 98 : 27
Together achieve victory, 815 : 12
articulate sweet sounds t., 713 : 1
bring us t. again, 882 : 18
damned good time t., 844 : 13
evils draw men t., 88 : 14
for brethren to dwell t., 22 : 14
gathered t. in my name, 40 : 3
gathered t. on public square, 701 : 14
getting on t., 776 : 4
good fellows get t., 705 : 2
hang t. or hang separately, 348 : 8
let us reason t., 28 : 30, 872 : 6
pull all t., 549 : 2
ride t. forever, 542 : 16
time place loved one t., 546 : 3
took sweet counsel t., 19 : 21
vow an eternal misery t., 317 : 1

Together (*continued*)
we gather t., 918 : 19
we'll pluck crow t., 188 : 7
Togetherness, spaces in t., 782 : 14
Toil and not seek rest, 157 : 3
and trouble caldron bubble, 239 : 4
blood t. tears sweat, 743 : 19
consumed midnight oil, 331 : 12
envy want, 351 : 17
exercises sinews and bones with t., 89 : 25
govern those that t., 369 : 3
her strong t. of grace, 242 : 7
horny hands of t., 567 : 2
hunger nakedness, 481 : 2
mock their useful t., 362 : 2
my grandmothers bent to t., 888 : 7
not neither spin, 38 : 4
of breath, 438 : 9
of growing up, 716 : 1
play to win t. to lose, 728 : 22
sleep after t., 173 : 12
slumber more sweet than t., 528 : 20
sons of t., 592 : 6
spasmodic not constant t., 883 : 7
till lump be leaven, 542 : 5
tire the day in t., 267 : 12
unrequited t., 524 : 7
war is t. and trouble, 306 : 19
waste their t., 430 : 7
youth the time for extraordinary t., 84 : 20
zealous nameless t., 486 : 10
Toiled, forgot for which he t., 244 : 7
so hard and late, 715 : 9
Toiling upward in night, 511 : 23
Toils, backward goes who t. most, 141 : 27
despair to reach, 320 : 23
easier to get into enemy's t., 66 : 23
pleasures and t., 432 : 12
terra firma t., 569 : 20
Toilsome way into upper air, 480 : 16
Toilsomely, can we follow t., 770 : 12
Token of a covenant, 8 : 3
Tokens, show him of Our t., 131 : 5
Told, as a tale that is t., 20 : 12
but he never t. anybody, 710 : 6
Christmas t. merriest tale, 430 : 22
hath it not been t. you, 31 : 1
I t. her all my heart, 404 : 10
I t. it not, 405 : 13
I t. my love, 404 : 10
I t. you so, 462 : 1, 512 : 9
I would have t. you, 45 : 20
love that never t. can be, 404 : 10
me Heraclitus, 591 : 9
my wrath, 405 : 13
never t. her love, 214 : 5
tale speeds best plainly t., 187 : 19
tale t. by an idiot, 240 : 4
tales already plainly t., 60 : 17
Toledo trusty, 291 : 7
Tolerable accommodation, 737 : 4
fire most t. third party, 557 : 13
Tolerance, Platonic t. vain, 715 : 12
practice t., 788 : 20
work for t. for justice, 811 : 7
Tolerant, understand everything makes t., 417 : 15
Tolerate, not afraid to t. error, 389 : 16
Tolerated, error of opinion t., 388 : 16
not only t. but encouraged, 439 : 5

Toleration, learned t. from intolerant, 782 : 20
Toll for the brave, 377 : 19
me back from thee, 477 : 2
oppress of t., 607 : 4
Tolle lege tolle lege, 129 : *n* 1
Tolled, sexton t. bell, 485 : 3
Tolls, curfew t. knell, 361 : 20
faintly t. evening chime, 446 : 5
for whom the bell t., 254 : 22
it t. for thee, 254 : 22
Tolstoi stands unshaken, 601 : *n* 2
Tom, Adventures of T. Sawyer, 623 : 20
appeared on sidewalk, 622 : 11
bears logs into the hall, 191 : 14
before I go T. Moore, 460 : 4
Fool's errand, 359 : 23
Jones will outlive Escurial, 383 : 16
little T. Tucker, 930 : 15
loves me best that calls me T., 257 : 19
o' Bedlam, 233 : 6
O T. Thumb, 192 : *n* 2
poor T. Bowling, 393 : 11
Tom piper's son, 931 : 13
Tom Jones, more knowledge of heart than in all T., 355 : 2
Tomb, Achilles' t., 461 : 12
adjusted in the t., 605 : 13
by side of sea, 527 : *n* 3
by sounding sea, 527 : 10
distant shadow of t., 600 : 17
earth t. of rest, 761 : 16
e'en from t. nature cries, 362 : 15
icy silence of t., 478 : 8
man t. for other animals, 152 : 2
Mausolos' t., 924 : 3
monument without a t., 256 : 11
of Battiades, 92 : 18
of Callimachus, 92 : 18
of green leaves, 672 : 11
Prince Andrey went to t., 602 : 2
room for Shakespeare in your t., 265 : 14
room my heart keeps in thy t., 267 : 6
rule from t., 806 : 18
saint and martyr rule from t., 806 : 18
sea was made for his t., 257 : 5
that swallowed Pharaoh, 569 : 20
threefold fourfold t., 265 : 14
Tombs, half-acre t., 252 : 12
in dust in cool t., 761 : 8
shoveled into the t., 761 : 8
Tombstone, end of fight t. white, 707 : 20
Tomlinson, naked soul of T., 708 : 17
Tommy this and Tommy that, 708 : 4
Tittlemouse, 933 : 19
Tomorrow, and t. and t., 240 : 4
ask for me t., 193 : 5
be today, 512 : 19
blossoms, 249 : 3
boast not thyself of t., 25 : 21
call progress t., 491 : 19
do thy worst, 305 : 1
eat drink t. we die, 30 : 2
fair adventure of t., 202 : 15
feather duster, 740 : 7
fill sky with clouds, 108 : 7
give me today take t., 132 : 23
gone down drain of eternity, 76 : 8
happiest time, 528 : 12
herald of t., 706 : 23
here today gone t., 312 : 18
here today next week t., 690 : 15

Tomorrow (*continued*)
house of t., 782 : 15
I am going to do that t., 131 : 10
I purpose to regulate room, 353 : 3
in today walks t., 443 : *n* 6
is not, 75 : 7
jam t. jam yesterday, 613 : 11
king t. shall die, 35 : 17
know nothing of t., 433 : 17
land ethic for t., 898 : 1
last chance, 726 : 6
let him love, 133 : 14
let us do or die, 261 : *n* 1
live till t., 377 : 21
lose t. ground won today, 585 : 22
never put off till t., 593 : *n* 1
new day, 170 : 26
no t. nor yesterday, 252 : 22
nor can buy t., 251 : 13
not bother about t., 665 : 1
not worry about t., 655 : 1
once again sail Ocean Sea, 107 : 5
one who comes t., 495 : 16
perhaps not do't t., 260 : 13
prepare for wants of t., 66 : 11
program for t., 784 : 7
put off till t., 593 : 6
soul sets sail, 850 : 5
speak what tomorrow thinks, 497 : 2
speed today be put back t., 174 : 10
such day t. as today, 246 : 9
to fresh woods, 281 : 6
unborn t. dead yesterday, 517 : 1
wait not till t., 162 : 13
why t. I may be, 516 : 13
will be dying, 266 : 11
will repay, 303 : 10
wisdom of t., 664 : 12
Tomorrow's falser than former day, 303 : 10
life is too late, 119 : 1
sun may never rise, 324 : 23
today's achievement t. confusion, 631 : 18
Tomorrows, confident t., 428 : 18
Tom's food for seven long year, 234 : 10
poor T. a-cold, 234 : 12
Tomtit, little t., 629 : 16
Ton, trouble's a t., 718 : 17
Tone, antediluvian t., 614 : 2
deep autumnal t., 467 : 21
licked clean over centuries, 906 : 4
peremptory t., 376 : 1
Robert Emmet and Wolfe T., 713 : 11
take t. of company, 341 : 20
testimony against slavery, 556 : 3
withers takes grass's t., 711 : 11
Tongs, let us have t. and bones, 197 : 4
Tongue, all-obliterated t., 516 : 20
at will yet never loud, 230 : 11
can no man tame, 51 : 35
candied t. lick pomp, 222 : 4
cleave to the roof of my mouth, 22 : 15
cold words of t. or pen, 732 : 15
confuted by conscience, 276 : 17
could scarcely cry, 403 : 9
customs politics and t., 593 : 3
death lies on my t., 205 : 10
dove with flickering t., 808 : 13
every t. brings in tale, 187 : 28
eye t. sword, 221 : 19
fair words never hurt t., 159 : 22
fallen by the t., 35 : 38
falls silent, 63 : 5

Tongue (*continued*)
falsehood of the t., 388 : 3
fellows of infinite t., 208 : 18
flattering t. speeds guest, 715 : 11
fool hold t. and pass for sage, 112 : 11
from his t. flowed speech, 57 : 10
give thy thoughts no t., 218 : 29
great ox stands on my t., 71 : 4
heart thinks t. speaks, 209 : 21
her t. fetters breaks, 919 : 19
his t. dropped manna, 284 : 8
his t. must vent, 242 : 20
hold your t. and let me love, 252 : 10
I am the t. of war, 912 : 7
insupportable trespassing t., 894 : 10
iron t. of midnight, 197 : 22
is the clapper, 209 : 21
is the law of kindness, 26 : 9
keep good t. in head, 248 : 7
keep thy t. from evil, 18 : 21
keep t. and keep freend, 148 : 7
live t. all dispelled, 900 : 3
love's richer than my t., 232 : 22
man that hath t. no man, 190 : 1
murder though no t. speak, 148 : *n* 1
my t. is the pen of a ready writer, 19 : 8
my t. swore, 76 : 23
never ear did hear that t., 184 : 14
never hold t. a minute, 322 : 16
never in t. that makes it, 191 : 12
no need for t., 873 : 2
no t. to wound us, 447 : 3
nor speak with double t., 494 : 19
not able to conceive, 197 : 10
not far from Kilmer cheek, 803 : 1
now t. the mystery telling, 139 : *n* 6
of a slow t., 9 : 15
of the dumb shall sing, 30 : 24
old and bitter of t., 712 : 10
on his t. they pour sweet dew, 61 : 9
one thought in breast another on t., 102 : 24
outvenoms all worms of Nile, 243 : 21
poetry mother t. of mankind, 374 : 22
put a t. in every wound, 216 : 29
rolls it under his t., 319 : 4
Russian t. to converse with all, 357 : 19
sad words of t., 513 : 14
Shakespeare spake, 426 : 1
shall be slit, 929 : 22
sharp t. grows keener, 452 : 17
sing t. the Savior's glory, 139 : 9
snakes with double t., 196 : 21
so varied in discourse, 442 : 24
soul lends t. vows, 219 : 6
sounds as sullen bell, 205 : 20
strenuous t., 478 : 1
such t. to great people, 564 : 9
that I sin not with my t., 18 : 29
though he hide it under his t., 16 : 6
thy own shame's orator, 188 : 9
to deal in fiction, 331 : 14
to persuade, 289 : 16
trippingly on the t., 221 : 23
truth in shepherd's t., 172 : 10
understanding but no t., 218 : 24
use of my oracular t., 398 : 11
use our t. at our peril, 343 : 20
wery good thing, 546 : 15
when my t. blabs, 213 : 9
wherever German t. heard, 420 : 1
with his t. win a woman, 190 : 1

Tongue (*continued*)
with own t. edifies ears, 333 : 19
wool of bat t. of dog, 239 : 5
would t. utter, 530 : 19
Tongued with fire beyond living, 808 : 10
Tongueless nightingale, 476 : 15
vigil, 632 : 7
Tongues, all people and t., 53 : 14
and deeds, 527 : 22
aspics' t., 231 : 17
bray of bragging t., 74 : 8
clocks the t. of bawds, 202 : 23
conscience hath thousand t., 187 : 28
evil days and evil t., 286 : 28
eyes silent t. of love, 168 : 16
from the strife of t., 18 : 18
gift of t., 396 : 17
govern t. with difficulty, 308 : 10
had I a hundred t., 105 : 20
had I your t. and eyes, 235 : 16
have their talk, 168 : *n* 12
hearts in love use own t., 209 : 9
in all t. called fools, 213 : 1
in trees, 210 : 24
leaves stuck out t., 873 : 12
millions of t. record, 457 : 21
not if I had ten t., 57 : 19
not uttered by chapmen's t., 190 : 19
of Douglas and myself, 520 : 8
of dying men, 194 : 9
of fire, 45 : 39
of flame infolded, 808 : 18
of men and angels, 48 : 22
one soul though many t., 126 : 4
self-interest speaks all t., 293 : 7
sharpened their t. like a serpent, 22 : 20
silence envious t., 249 : 8
silver-sweet sound lovers' t., 192 : 17
slanderous t., 210 : 10
speak with other t., 45 : 39
that syllable men's names, 279 : 16
woods have t., 146 : *n* 5
word pure on t. and free, 802 : 1
Tongue-tied by authority, 244 : 24
Tonic, we need t. of wildness, 560 : 14
Tonight, child again just for t., 610 : 10
curfew not ring t., 669 : 19
from Oxford strays, 587 : 6
hot time in old town t., 705 : 1
met in thee t., 619 : 16
refrain t., 223 : 11
tenting t. on campground, 618 : 1
tonight won't be just any night, 910 : 19
world may end t., 542 : 14
Tonnage, damp t., 843 : 19
Tonsorial or agglutinative type, 730 : 15
Too little too late, 816 : 16
Took all heart for speech, 713 : 19
all which I t. from thee, 693 : 15
by throat circumcised dog, 232 : 21
circle that t. him in, 671 : 4
her with a sigh, 404 : *n* 2
him by left leg, 931 : 8
might vantage best have t., 228 : 7
not men you t. them for, 209 : 25
one draught of life, 607 : 17
one less traveled by, 747 : 13
suffering human race, 585 : 3
to my heels, 96 : 22
to the law, 611 : 10

Took (*continued*)
wages and are dead, 692 : 3
went and t. same as me, 708 : 24
Tool carries spirit by which created, 852 : 17
grows keener with use, 452 : 17
maker, 761 : 4
nor any t. of iron, 13 : 32
Too-late, also called T., 601 : 20
Tools, give us the t., 744 : 13
no jesting with edge t., 261 : 2
sin has many t., 519 : 9
teach but to name t., 290 : 19
to make tools, 688 : 10
to who can handle them, 420 : *n* 6
with t. he is all, 472 : 22
Tool-using animal, 472 : 22
Tooth, defy t. of time, 330 : 3
for tooth, 10 : 10
had alwey coltes t., 147 : 11
more deadly than mad dog's t., 188 : 13
my Adonis hath a sweet t., 175 : 21
of the ego, 881 : 11
of time, 229 : 5
one t. and it aching, 735 : 3
poison for age's t., 201 : 10
purrs and never shows t., 794 : 7
red in t. and claw, 532 : 13
sharper than serpent's t., 233 : 11
sinks into throat tiger's t., 819 : 4
where each t. point goes, 707 : 5
Toothache, philosopher endure t., 210 : 5
Toothless mastiff bitch, 433 : 28
Toothpaste and dandruff ads, 844 : 2
Toothsomest, old pippins t., 262 : 1
Tootings at weddings of soul, 767 : 21
Top, die at the t., 323 : 23
events soon on t. of him, 788 : 3
fool me to t. of my bent, 222 : 21
get to the t. everybody cheers, 911 : 20
He which is t. of judgment, 228 : 7
higher t. of delight, 570 : 5
o' the mornin', 661 : 10
of head taken off, 608 : 6
of sovereignty, 478 : 5
President on t. of events, 788 : 3
Revolution began at t., 593 : 1
struggle to reach t., 882 : 6
you're the t., 820 : 4
Top-hat, famous high t., 765 : 8
Topics, only two serious t., 718 : 3
other fashionable t., 369 : 14
two t. yourself and me, 355 : 22
while serious t. disputing, 486 : 3
Topless towers of Ilium, 184 : 4
Toppling, send skyscrapers t., 875 : 9
Tops, tips with silver fruit-tree t., 192 : 11
Torch, bright t. and casement, 477 : 13
give me a t., 791 : 1
like runners pass on t. of life, 100 : 15
of a flower, 791 : 1
passed to new generation, 890 : 7
throw t. hold it high, 737 : 10
truth is t., 360 : 29
Torchbearing outrider, 653 : 3
Torches of martyrdom, 389 : 5
Torchlight crimson on kettledrums, 742 : 9
Tore, shout t. hell's concave, 283 : 21
Torment, dark with t. and tears, 561 : 21
delicious t., 497 : 15

Torment (*continued*)
I feel it and am in t., 102 : 17
is my joy, 874 : 19
luxury and t. of novelist, 652 : 13
man comes with his t., 413 : 30
measure of our t., 708 : 15
of love unsatisfied, 806 : 1
there shall no t. touch them, 34 : 13
what t. not a marriage bed, 254 : 23
when religion positive t., 570 : 8
who devised the t., 808 : 15
Tormented with ten thousand hells, 183 : 21
Tormenting, cant of criticism most t., 360 : 11
mild image in fountain, 570 : 4
Torments in wedding ring, 325 : 2
most maddens and t., 570 : 13
of grief endured, 495 : 18
Torn and beaten out he lies, 470 : 11
between passion for righteousness, 799 : 18
by dreams, 768 : 7
frayed soiled and t., 634 : 10
naiad from flood, 525 : 7
persons with t. bodies happy, 732 : 3
seine shattered lobsterpot, 808 : 2
to pieces by dogs, 850 : 14
Torpedo, pen in his hand a t., 353 : 22
Torpedoes, damn the t., 490 : 4
Torpid, mind t. in old age, 355 : 27
Torquatus stretching his baby hands, 102 : 7
Torrent, character formed in world's t., 395 : 15
in the very t. tempest, 221 : 23
of his fate, 352 : 1
rough t. of occasion, 206 : 26
wind t. of darkness, 772 : 23
Torrents, blood in t. pour, 684 : 14
down the gorges go, 572 : 1
Torrid or frozen zone, 271 : 22
Tortoise because he taught us, 612 : 4
hare and t., 66 : 3
prince keeps t. enclosed, 90 : 11
Tortuous road from Montomery, 909 : 12
Torture, hum of cities t., 457 : 28
Negro past of t., 903 : 2
no rack t. me, 605 : 8
one poor word, 304 : 26
one tiny creature, 582 : 5
suspense in news is t., 289 : 8
touch him not t. not again, 469 : 12
Tortured brilliant bold, 481 : *n* 5
by my own shirt, 849 : 16
millions of innocent t., 387 : 15
with history, 843 : 19
Torturing hour, 361 : 13
Toss in the spray, 584 : 11
weariness t. him to my breast, 269 : 2
Tossed, I am t. up and down, 21 : 17
old woman t. in blanket, 932 : 5
the dog, 934 : 9
them human hearts, 468 : 6
Tosses but doesn't sink, 134 : 2
hints of earlier creation, 808 : 2
up our losses, 808 : 2
Tossing aloft invisible, 683 : 5
crossing Channel t., 629 : 1
green water, 785 : 12
heads in sprightly dance, 427 : 9
mind is t. on the ocean, 197 : 24
sea of cause and theory, 742 : 18

Tossing (*continued*)
so as to scare clouds, 747 : 18
Total grandeur of total edifice, 768 : 25
irrecoverably dark t. eclipse, 288 : 20
isolationism no answer, 852 : 1
Totalitarianism threaten free nations, 882 : 23
Totality of functions, 429 : 14
of what he might have, 865 : 8
Totalizing, personalizing by t., 775 : 2
Tots sang Ring-a-rosie, 698 : 14
Totter into vogue, 363 : 20
Touch a hundred flowers, 822 : 15
at t. I yield, 531 : 10
common t., 710 : 17
fear not to t. the best, 172 : 14
furs to t., 796 : 16
great death, 732 : 6
Happy Isles, 529 : 13
harps of gold, 537 : 16
he wants the natural t., 239 : 17
hills whose heads t. heaven, 229 : 29
honey of romance, 674 : 16
is metamorphosis, 880 : 2
it and do not find, 64 : 6
keep the Nelson t., 700 : 12
lips part with tears, 633 : 15
lips that t., 811 : 15
lips t. sacred fire, 733 : 9
little t. of Harry, 208 : 2
me afresh, 655 : 19
me and no minister so sore, 339 : 7
me not, 45 : 35
money t., 687 : 20
must have t. of earth, 534 : 12
natural t., 239 : 17
never lose t. of the one, 697 : 2
no beast but knows t. of pity, 187 : 1
no state matters, 370 : *n* 3
not taste not, 50 : 10
nothing can t. him further, 238 : 19
O for t. of hand, 530 : 19
of earthly years, 424 : 14
of greatness, 534 : 13
of Harry in night, 208 : 2
of love and pride, 684 : 1
of vanished hand, 530 : 19
one t. of nature, 226 : 20
one t. of Venus, 861 : 8
our country shackles fall, 376 : 20
ponderable to t., 714 : 11
puts it not unto t., 292 : 3
scarcely felt or seen, 341 : 3
shivering-sweet to t., 795 : 2
soul look body t., 717 : 8
spider's t. how fine, 167 : *n* 9
strives to t. the stars, 173 : 6
sweet as I could bear, 748 : 8
that I might t. that cheek, 192 : 4
they that t. pitch defiled, 209 : 26
truth needs no other t., 256 : 1
two solitudes t. each other, 756 : 6
unimaginable t. of time, 429 : 5
whatever you t. is Jupiter, 118 : 13
when safest sunset t., 543 : 5
world intangible we t., 693 : 16
you must not t., 253 : 11
Touched, chord in unison t., 377 : 13
God's finger t. him, 532 : 17
nothing he did not adorn, 355 : 23
spirits not finely t., 227 : 24
to the quick, 540 : 21
with fire, 643 : 17
with moon's red silver, 901 : 14

Toucher, il ne faut pas t. aux idoles, 583 : *n* 6
Touches, mortality t. the heart, 104 : 26
of sweet harmony, 201 : 1
who t. this t. a man, 576 : 21
Toucheth, he that t. pitch, 35 : 24
Touching is the true revolution, 916 : 3
like marbles t. but separate, 637 : 20
not succeed in t. ideals, 603 : 2
sight so t. in majesty, 425 : 13
Touchstone by which we try services, 389 : 2
calamity man's true t., 263 : 10
panics t. of sincerity, 384 : 14
Touchstones, dreams t. of characters, 558 : 15
Touchy, pacify t. tribe of poets, 109 : 17
Tough and devilish sly, 548 : 16
and final growth, 863 : 14
as a steak, 834 : 6
but nervous, 799 : 18
customer, 547 : 26
interesting but t., 623 : 24
life t. proposition, 757 : 12
rack of this t. world, 235 : 19
wedge for tough log, 112 : 2
worm in little inside, 629 : 16
Toughness, subtlety and emotional t., 870 : 15
Toujours gai, 760 : 1
Tourney, summoned am to t., 918 : 12
Tout, comprendre t. pardonner, 417 : *n* 5
est pour le mieux, 343 : *n* 3
milieu entre rien et t., 299 : *n* 4
passe, 538 : *n* 2
passe casse lasse, 928 : 3
perdu fors l'honneur, 157 : *n* 8
rire de t., 378 : *n* 5
Toves, slithy t., 612 : 17
Tower, burning roof and t., 715 : 16
clock collected in t., 692 : 1
cries as from lighted t., 779 : *n* 2
inaccessible t. of past, 569 : 4
intending to build t., 43 : 24
ivory t., 504 : 5
ivory t. of cultural, 755 : 21
ivy-mantled t., 361 : 22, 773 : 15
king's name a t. of strength, 187 : 25
Montaigne in his t., 858 : 20
neck is as a t. of ivory, 28 : 20
of ivory, 504 : 5
of strength, 533 : 4
Prince of Aquitaine whose t. destroyed, 514 : 9
proud t., 525 : 13
stand like a firm t., 141 : 23
strongest t. of delight, 571 : 10
to dark t. came, 234 : 13
Trojans sitting on the t., 57 : 23
yonder ivy-mantled t., 361 : 22
Towered citadel pendant rock, 241 : 17
cities please us then, 278 : 4
grim shape t. up, 424 : 1
Towering confidence of twenty-one, 354 : 5
hopes like t. falcons, 320 : 14
in her pride of place, 238 : 11
Towers and battlements it sees, 277 : 25
cloud-capped t., 248 : 13
elephants endorsed with t., 288 : 10
higher t. heavier fall, 78 : *n* 7
no t. along the steep, 443 : 12
proud t., 458 : 7

Towers (*continued*)
sea's green crying t., 843 : 18
topless t. of Ilium, 184 : 4
walls and t. girdled round, 433 : 21
whispering from her t., 587 : 1
wind suitor of t., 841 : 7
ye antique t., 361 : 8
Town, all around the t., 698 : 14
all round t., 929 : 19
another hill t., 888 : 10
atheist, 847 : 13
bear witness to his munificence, 418 : 5
consul in foreign t., 699 : 13
country in t., 119 : 18
crier spoke my lines, 221 : 23
dear damned distracting t., 334 : 24
defend village t. city, 744 : 5
destroy t. to save it, 925 : 18
distressed and forsaken, 309 : 24
down that t. settle hence, 525 : 14
drunkard, 847 : 13
Dürer in a t. like this, 798 : 7
follies of t. crept slowly, 371 : 2
hot time in old t., 705 : 1
in Scarlet t., 926 : 21
is lighter than vanity, 302 : 5
it rains softly on t., 674 : 11
leave by t. drain, 659 : 11
little t. of Bethlehem, 619 : 16
Mackie's back in t., 840 : 16
man in our t., 934 : 7
man made the t., 376 : 17
many ways meet in one t., 207 : 8
one-horse t., 622 : 10
Paris my home t., 752 : 13
Petersburg theoretical intentional t., 581 : 16
pretty how t., 829 : 18
proud tower in t., 525 : 13
sent them out of t., 929 : 19
sprinkle quarters on t., 691 : 24
taller t. than Rome, 742 : 11
tavern in the t., 922 : 12
what common talk of t. is, 309 : 18
woods go seaward from t., 453 : 23
Yankee Doodle came to t., 920 : 9
Towns, away away from t., 470 : 3
dust and reek of t., 569 : 20
empty but not uninhabited, 877 : 15
prince of apple t., 886 : 20
seven t. contend for Homer, 257 : *n* 5
taken t. with words, 259 : *n* 2
winter too long in country t., 739 : 2
you built of blocks, 839 : 20
Toy dog covered with dust, 666 : 17
foolish thing but a t., 214 : 29
had not friend nor t., 568 : 20
like through t. fair, 778 : 6
religion but a childish t., 183 : 11
sells eternity to get t., 189 : 20
soldier red with rust, 666 : 17
truth her painted t., 711 : 19
Toyed and kissed, 331 : 20
Toys, all is but t., 238 : 7
brooches and t. for delight, 669 : 4
enemies for t., 258 : 9
for your delight, 669 : 4
love and all his pleasures t., 250 : 7
of age, 337 : 7
Trace, boding tremblers learned to t., 370 : 10
characters of hell to t., 363 : 5
misery still delights to t., 377 : 25

Trace (*continued*)
noble dust of Alexander, 224 : 15
on dark theme t. verses of light, 100 : 10
painters cannot t., 328 : 17
Traced lives of good men, 429 : 4
Traces, in the t. lead 'em, 568 : 1
of original sin, 581 : 10
winter's t., 632 : 7
Tracing, fitful t. of portal, 767 : 10
Tracings of eternal light, 412 : 11
Track, around ancient t., 600 : 28
down relations of aspects of experience, 789 : 2
golden t. 765 : 6
narrow t. to highest good, 101 : 11
Trackless, launch on t. seas, 576 : 15
way, 540 : 6
Tracks, die in our t., 726 : 6
show t. of knowledge, 100 : 16
Tract of inland ground, 428 : 15
Trade, came for t. unionists, 824 : 1
commonly called slave t., 346 : 9
dreadful t., 234 : 28
food of us that t. in love, 241 : 3
free t., 487 : 5
free t. in ideas, 645 : 1
free t. not principle, 501 : 12
heel of Northeast T., 708 : 22
homely slighted shepherd's t., 280 : 15
instrument of t., 617 : 7
Irish poets learn t., 717 : 22
love t. you have learned, 124 : 21
mission of t. unions, 666 : 22
my t. and art is living, 165 : 1
never pursue literature as t., 437 : 8
no nation ruined by t., 348 : 12
nothing to do but t., 384 : 15
of blood and guile, 435 : 21
people of the same t., 366 : 2
riddle of China t., 799 : 19
secret, 366 : 1
serve time to every t., 456 : 13
slave t., 346 : 9
those who affected to t. for public good, 366 : 4
two of a t. never agree, 331 : 18, 600 : 14
Trades, critic most degraded of t., 626 : 11
sail out on your t. again, 93 : 3
Tradesmen, bow ye t., 628 : 15
lying becomes none but t., 247 : 4
Trading company, monopoly granted to t., 366 : 1
Tradition becomes holy, 657 : 10
cannot be inherited, 809 : 2
desert t., 496 : 13
finally inspires awe, 657 : 10
for three hundred years, 675 : 15
grows more venerable, 657 : 10
heart bettered t. of mankind, 667 : 20
not enough, 809 : 20
reverence due t. increases, 657 : 10
youth of America oldest t., 675 : 15
Traditions, what pattern of our t., 875 : 10
Traduced the state, 232 : 21
Traffic, green t. light, 816 : 11
in mockery, 715 : 10
no kind of t., 247 : 26
of Jacob's ladder, 693 : 19
Trafficked for strange webs, 638 : 11

Tragedies, only two t. in world, 675 : 10
two t. in life, 680 : 21
Tragedy, American t., 732 : 12
death always t., 687 : 1
go litel bok litel myn t., 145 : 7
gorgeous t., 278 : 21
herein t. of age, 724 : 16
imitation of action, 88 : 16
killing eternity essence of t., 706 : 3
of love indifference, 751 : 16
play is the t. "Man," 526 : 5
to be out of society a t., 675 : 17
world is a t., 363 : 22
worst t. for poet, 818 : 2
write you a t., 835 : 14
wrought to uttermost, 717 : 6
Tragic house with nobody in it, 620 : *n* 2
in t. life no villains, 600 : 18
Muse first trod stage, 334 : 12
perform t. play, 717 : 5
Tragical mirth, 197 : 13
Trahison des clercs, 720 : 12
Trail, ever t. held true, 707 : 22
long long t., 813 : 7
neither go from t., 709 : 5
of serpent over all, 447 : 13
out of it is dark cloud, 928 : 18
Trailing clouds of glory, 426 : 14
garments of Night, 509 : 12
in stream fingers wet, 585 : 21
Train filled the temple, 29 : 8
follows in His t., 452 : 7
great Mother's t. divine, 587 : 11
isn't t. I wouldn't take, 823 : 3
jumps in after t. started, 704 : 1
midnight t. whining low, 903 : 1
miserable t., 427 : 22
noble natures not to desire more, 88 : 1
off on morning t., 935 : 5
sensational to read in t., 675 : 23
shaves and takes t., 846 : 8
starry t., 286 : 1
starve numerous t. below, 315 : 17
they love a t., 223 : *n* 5
travel by t. to see life, 817 : 17
trees that would t., 765 : 10
up child in way he should go, 24 : 35
war t. of circumstances, 384 : 22
world and all her t., 299 : 6
Trained, conscious mind t. like parrot, 754 : 9
hundred thousand t. men, 786 : 11
Trainer, painter t. soothsayer, 122 : 4
Training, difficult to get on-the-job t., 880 : 18
genius will live without t., 536 : 12
is everything, 624 : 14
original tendencies and t., 752 : 18
rather than birth counts, 312 : 23
Train's, Gospel t. a-comin', 936 : 6
Trains are wonderful, 817 : 17
Trait whereby worst inferred, 503 : 14
Traitor, brazen forehead of t., 615 : 4
love treason but hate t., 99 : 16
no longer needed, 273 : 4
not die like t. in dark, 672 : 11
Traitorously corrupted youth, 185 : 28
Traitors escape detection, 737 : 6
fears make us t., 239 : 16
hate t. and treason love, 305 : 26
our doubts are t., 227 : 29
Trammel up the consequence, 236 : 22
Tramp, dull t. of plodders, 569 : 20
gentleman poet dreamer, 812 : 7
swing t. and trudge, 781 : 15
that's why lady is t., 833 : 18
tramp tramp, 578 : 12
Trample bad laws under feet, 538 : 12
light doth t. on my days, 299 : 8
on rights of others, 520 : 7
them in my fury, 31 : 26
vices underfoot, 129 : 10
whose rights I t., 615 : 5
young lion and dragon shalt thou t., 20 : 17
Trampling on feelings, 839 : 14
out the vintage, 566 : 4
right of t. on people, 490 : 17
tall defiant grass, 857 : 15
Tramplings of three conquests, 275 : 3
Tranced summer night, 478 : 4
Trances, days are t., 525 : 18
Tränen, er nie sein Brod mit T. ass, 395 : *n* 2
Tranquil, benevolence t. habitation, 89 : 10
cliffs vast in t. bay, 587 : 13
farewell the t. mind, 231 : 11
humble t. spirit, 251 : 11
mind a mind well ordered, 124 : 13
occupations few t. life, 124 : 20
solitude, 469 : 25
Tranquility Base here, 910 : 13
talk from Sea of T., 882 : 20
Tranquilize, steady purpose t. mind, 482 : 15
Tranquilized Fifties, 893 : 1
Tranquillité règne à Varsovie, 439 : 1
Tranquillity, emotion recollected in t., 424 : 9
feeling of inward t., 499 : 23
insure domestic t., 391 : 10
Sea of T., 864 : 4
unbroken t. in adult stage, 640 : 17
Tranquilly, nature gone t. on, 732 : 2
Transatlantic, control of t. force, 401 : 14
Transcendental kind, 628 : 6
Transcends, monk's state t. expression, 73 : 4
Transcribe my chronicles, 486 : 10
Transcribed without acknowledgment, 116 : 4
Transcript, Boston Evening T., 804 : 6
Transfigured, come t. back, 568 : 19
Transfigures wretched, 491 : 16
you and me, 566 : 5
Transfiguring power, 658 : 14
Transfigurings of freshest blue, 767 : 14
Transfix flourish set on youth, 244 : 20
Transform, even a thought can t. us, 658 : 19
future t. self in us, 756 : 7
hope to effective desire, 639 : 3
ourselves into beasts, 230 : 26
world ideas were to t., 616 : 1
Transformations, book of t., 864 : 14
strange and monstrous t., 90 : 2
Transformed, if any reaction both t., 754 : 4
into strumpet's fool, 240 : 12
joy t. in us, 756 : 9
whole of you t. into feeling, 702 : 7
Transforming, no t. without emotion, 754 : 14
Transforms strength into right, 358 : 13
Transgress, if I t. and forswear, 79 : 13
Transgressed custom brings punishment, 626 : 6
Transgressing, by t. truly kept law, 282 : 7
Transgression brings admitted shame, 80 : 17
no law no t., 46 : 40
Transgressors, way of t. is hard, 23 : 32
Transient, early bright t. chaste, 307 : *n* 3
human life t., 697 : 10
most t. of passions, 681 : 1
opportunity t., 395 : 7
quick and t., 542 : 20
Transit where dreams cross, 806 : 5
Transition, what seems death is t., 511 : 11
Transitory, false world but t., 153 : 7
Translated, Bottom thou art t., 196 : 26
from despotism to liberty, 388 : 9
Translating into living law, 794 : 15
Montaigne into all tongues, 164 : *n* 4
Translation give music as well as words, 735 : 7
mistake in t., 321 : 5
Translator of Homer, 586 : 14
Translators between dream and reality, 801 : 8
Translucent, glassy cool t. wave, 280 : 3
Translunary, those brave t. things, 182 : 18
Transparent, I become t. eyeball, 496 : 4
pure t. freedom, 870 : 8
Transport stem to victory, 743 : 4
Transported, Time t., 920 : 4
Trap moment before ripe, 404 : 17
Trapeze, young man on flying t., 636 : 12
Trappings, these but t. of woe, 218 : 3
Traps, be fox to recognize t., 154 : 1
not fall into same t. twice, 128 : 6
snares t. gins pitfalls, 539 : *n* 2
Trash, money is t., 251 : 13
steals my purse steals t., 230 : 33
Traurig, dass ich so t. bin, 481 : *n* 7
ich so t. bin, 481 : *n* 7
Travail and vexation of spirit, 26 : 23
great t. so gladly spent, 161 : 22
mine the t. thyn the glorie, 146 : 26
my labor for my t., 225 : 33
Travaileth, groaneth and t., 47 : 9
Travel faster than stagecoach, 371 : 2
for travel's sake, 667 : 12
from Dan to Beersheba, 360 : 22
hopefully better than arrive, 668 : 1
light, 870 : 2
never t. without diary, 675 : 23
not to go anywhere, 667 : 12
on life's common way, 425 : 23
part of education, 180 : 18
prayers to preserve t., 323 : 17
real only way to t., 690 : 15
road to Hades easy to t., 92 : 7
thought the t. long, 184 : 14
to go, 667 : 12
to home among dead, 468 : 21
to school not to t., 180 : 18
wherever I t. Greece wounds me, 849 : 17
youth who from east t., 426 : 15
Traveled a good deal in Concord, 559 : 1

Traveled (*continued*)
among unknown men, 425 : 6
Backward Glance o'er T. Roads, 577 : 10
much have I t., 475 : 6
short while towards sun, 876 : 16
somewhere i have never t., 829 : 12
took one less t. by, 747 : 13
whoe'er has t., 355 : *n* 8
Traveler, a t. came by, 404 : 10
anybody there said T., 739 : 15
farewell Monsieur T., 212 : 20
from antique land, 466 : 12
from cradle to grave, 467 : 9
from New Zealand, 488 : 7
has right to embellish, 385 : 10
hour that pierces new t. with love, 141 : 26
no t. returns, 221 : 12
spurs lated t. apace, 238 : 22
swiftest t. afoot, 559 : 13
world-besotted t., 716 : 6
Traveler's, I have eaten t. fare, 314 : 2
Travelers, fellow t. of revolution, 770 : 5
must be content, 210 : 32
never met in single files, 907 : 12
of eternity, 313 : 23
Traveleth before he hath language, 180 : 18
poverty come as one that t., 23 : 12
Traveling all same pace, 517 : 15
consider my t. expenses, 826 : 17
fool's paradise, 497 : 7
in t. carry knowledge, 356 : 6
on decks of decayed ships, 849 : 10
through dense forest, 789 : 8
to regulate imagination, 353 : 15
without fatigue of t., 170 : 6
Travel's, travel for t. sake, 667 : 12
Travels, bad news t. fast, 120 : 14
commence t. in Mississippi steamboat, 449 : 1
fastest travels alone, 707 : 14
he who t. with another, 559 : 15
in search of needs, 671 : 8
in strait so narrow, 226 : 18
like him that t., 245 : 15
objects of t. neglected if under our eye, 123 : 12
scholar t. loved hillside, 587 : 12
sundry contemplation of my t., 212 : 18
time t. in divers paces, 212 : 11
Traverse, this t. poorest take, 607 : 4
Tray Blanch and Sweetheart, 234 : 15
dog T., 443 : 9
Trays, cheap tin t., 760 : 20
Treacherous, dog never t., 609 : 4
experience t., 80 : 9
generals, 860 : 10
kiss, 876 : 11
Treachery, friend without t., 591 : 11
machinations hollowness t., 233 : 4
wedlock t., 289 : 4
Treacle, fly that sips t., 332 : 5
Tread, close behind him t., 435 : 3
Death with impartial t., 107 : 1
don't t. on me, 920 : 13
each deed of shame, 511 : 22
each other's heel, 223 : *n* 5
endless road you t., 691 : 16
ever so airy t., 533 : 25

Tread (*continued*)
far-off shore where he would t., 186 : 10
hungry generations t., 477 : 1
I with mournful t., 576 : 7
lightly she is near, 674 : 14
men t. underfoot what feared, 101 : 9
on classic ground, 325 : 6
poor beetle we t. upon, 228 : 17
shine by side of path we t., 377 : 18
softly t. on dreams, 712 : 16
them in mine anger, 31 : 26
thou shalt t. upon the lion, 20 : 17
upon another's heel, 223 : *n* 5
upon brink of meaning, 352 : 26
upon my patience, 203 : 6
where angels fear to t., 333 : 20
where'er we t. haunted, 457 : 9
where'er you t., 332 : 12
years like oxen t. world, 712 : 2
Treadeth winepress of wrath, 53 : 27
Treading course of virtue, 69 : 17
on my tail, 612 : 7
Treads, one who t. alone, 447 : 8
primrose path of dalliance t., 218 : 28
she t. on it so light, 189 : 15
Treason against the United States, 391 : 12
bloody t. flourished, 216 : 25
bribery or other high crimes, 391 : 11
but trusted like fox, 205 : 6
can but peep, 223 : 27
corporations cannot commit t., 172 : 4
cried the Speaker, 382 : 13
doth never prosper, 181 : 21
ever less than t., 747 : 2
gunpowder t. and plot, 919 : 12
has done his worst, 238 : 19
hate traitors and t. love, 305 : 26
if this be t., 382 : 13
last temptation greatest t., 806 : 19
love bitter with t., 633 : 6
love t. but hate traitor, 99 : 16
none dare call it t., 181 : 21
of the intellectuals, 720 : 12
sows secret seeds, 138 : 9
Treasonous malice, 238 : 9
Treasons stratagems and spoils, 201 : 3
Treasure, buried t. of his books, 653 : 7
chiefest t., 729 : 14
considers impartiality as his t., 97 : 8
danger or t., 896 : 13
discovery of buried t., 711 : 17
good man's t., 64 : 22
great t. and trouble, 24 : 7
hath found a t., 35 : 9
heaps of miser's t., 279 : 23
purest t. mortal times afford, 193 : 32
rich the t., 306 : 16
thou shalt have t., 40 : 6
what men call t., 568 : 18
where your t. is, 37 : 17
witty woman a t., 601 : 4
Treasured, embalmed and t. up, 281 : 24
Treasures, bee's collected t., 363 : 13
heart has hidden t., 555 : 17
I have three t., 65 : 3
lay not up t., 37 : 16
lay up t. in heaven, 37 : 16
science t. in laps of all, 636 : 15
sea-born t., 493 : 15
see t. that prevail, 910 : 9
Treasury, our heart is a t., 484 : 13
Treat as dogs do the Nile, 114 : *n* 2

Treat (*continued*)
friend as if he might become enemy, 111 : 8
killing t. for Ossete, 819 : 2
nature as cylinder, 638 : 3
two impostors same, 710 : 16
you'd t. if met where bar, 641 : 15
Treated as wish to be treated, 891 : 12
I t. him God cured him, 162 : 9
Treaties, thirty years life of t., 706 : *n* 3
under authority of U.S., 391 : 13
Treatise, at dismal t. rouse, 240 : 3
my T. of Human Nature, 357 : 18
of natural education, 358 : 23
Treatment, dark world present t., 725 : 1
fair t. and appreciation, 771 : 2
stomach endure rough t., 115 : 1
use t. to help sick, 79 : 13
Treatments, for extreme illnesses extreme t., 80 : 10
Treaty, if t. serves ten years, 706 : 18
of strict nonaggression, 878 : 1
what t. white man kept, 610 : 5
Treble, childish t., 211 : 15
Tree, against blue a pine t., 317 : 16
almond t. shall flourish, 27 : 25
apple t. among the trees, 28 : 5
as twig bent t. inclined, 335 : 15
at my window, 748 : 12
beneath the tamarind t., 525 : 7
billboard lovely as t., 855 : 15
Bong t. grows, 550 : 8
boughs off many a t., 268 : 13
but I must climb the t., 268 : 12
cannot grow in sky, 101 : 1
cinnamon t., 857 : 14
coolibar t., 705 : 7
crumpetty t., 550 : 15
cut the cherry t., 378 : *n* 9
dead t. no shelter, 805 : 1
dew bespangling herb and t., 266 : 19
do these things in green t., 44 : 5
down to calico t., 550 : 12
easy as leaves grow on t., 711 : 22
elm t. bole, 541 : 16
fair limbs of the t., 634 : 5
fleet of life like t. leaves, 82 : 9
forbidden t. whose mortal taste, 282 : 22
friendship a sheltering t., 436 : 8
give me my hollow t., 339 : 11
give to eat of the t. of life, 52 : 34
go to pear t. for pears, 111 : 31
golden t. of life, 396 : 14
good word like good t., 131 : 3
greenwood t., 211 : 1
growing when ye're sleeping, 431 : 28
had a peach from the t., 404 : 11
hang harp on willow t., 922 : 13
hang there till t. die, 243 : 30
happy scarcely sentient, 721 : 1
hate the t., 129 : 11
I shall be like t., 323 : 23
if t. dies plant another, 350 : 10
is hewn down, 36 : 29
is known by fruit, 39 : 10
keep green t. in heart. 132 : 25
keep way of the t. of life, 7 : 13
last leaf upon t., 519 : 19
leopards under juniper t., 805 : 22
Liberty T., 384 : 8
lighted from a blessed t., 131 : 16
like a t. planted by rivers, 17 : 12

Tree (*continued*)
like t. grown in meadow, 6 : 4
like t. standing by water, 936 : 7
lime t. bower my prison, 433 : 20
little nut t., 932 : 1
lone sky-pointing t., 587 : 11
lopped t. may grow again, 73 : *n* 9
loved t. or flower, 447 : 14
man plants t. for posterity, 95 : *n* 10
my body now an old t., 314 : 2
never see t. at all, 855 : 15
not renewed, 863 : 14
not too far from yew t., 808 : 9
O chestnut t., 715 : 17
of knowledge of good and evil, 6 : 20
of liberty refreshed, 388 : 7
of liberty watered by blood, 401 : 4
of life, 6 : 19, 285 : 14
of man never quiet, 691 : 7
of our life, 791 : 3
Old Apple T., 753 : 2
on a t. by a river, 629 : 16
on t. they slew Him, 651 : 12
only God can make t., 795 : 7
our t. crowns hill, 587 : 12
planted by the waters, 32 : 11
poem lovely as a t., 795 : 6
poisonous minerals and that t., 254 : 10
presents upon a t., 606 : 18
riding by Eildon T., 926 : 23
righteous like palm t., 20 : 18
rolls deep where grew the t., 532 : 24
shady cypress t., 608 : 13
she gave me of the t., 7 : 8
sighing by a sycamore t., 232 : 8
snow from hemlock t., 748 : 3
spreading chestnut t., 510 : 7
spreading himself like a green bay t., 18 : 26
still our t. there, 587 : 11
swimming from t. to t., 892 : 6
tall slim t., 854 : 14
thou t. I flower, 628 : 14
too happy happy t., 478 : 14
tree dry and green, 841 : 7
under the bamboo t., 806 : 11
under the gallows t., 260 : 15
under the greenwood t., 211 : 1
which did not know, 295 : 13
window t., 748 : 12
with ease from t. to t., 329 : 13
woodman spare beechen t., 443 : 19
woodman spare that t., 492 : 10
wrath-bearing t., 804 : 15
yet crowns the hill, 587 : 12
you have grown to be a mighty t., 408 : 11
Zaccheus climb t., 320 : 10
Tree's, as twig bent t. inclined, 335 : 15
Trees, all the t. green, 566 : 14
amidst tall ancestral t., 470 : 13
among gusty t., 772 : 23
and all of nature, 928 : 10
and fields tell nothing, 337 : *n* 2
and stones will teach you, 136 : 9
Arabian t. their med'cinable gum, 232 : 20
ax laid unto root of the t., 36 : 29
beautiful and different, 150 : 16
birch most shy of t., 567 : 10
birds are asleep in t., 397 : 3
birds in the t., 714 : 22
blasts roots of t., 886 : 12
Trees (*continued*)
blue promontory with t., 241 : 17
bosomed high in tufted t., 277 : 25
brotherhood of venerable t., 426 : 8
cannot see forest for t., 380 : 4
cannot see wood for t., 160 : 26
cross river rest under t., 594 : 10
dryad of the t., 476 : 22
family t. remember name, 840 : 6
flowers watercraft, 577 : 8
grow up again quickly, 73 : 8
grown strong with forest t., 637 : 19
he that plants t. loves others, 95 : *n* 10
herbs and t. flourish in May, 149 : 13
herbs are sprouting, 5 : 7
hurt not the t., 53 : 13
if t. in earth were pens, 132 : 3
known to speak, 239 : 1
land of vines and fig t., 11 : 14
lemon t. bloom, 395 : 3
loveliest of t., 690 : 16
maddens me, 803 : 1
men as t. walking, 42 : 9
more resigned, 738 : 16
my apple t. never eat cones, 747 : 5
of all t. so fair, 710 : 12
old t. used to people, 840 : 6
Orpheus with lute made t., 248 : 29
rest under the t., 594 : 10
rocks and stones and t., 424 : 14
roots of t. and stones, 793 : 19
seemed to march seaward, 664 : 2
set about with fever t., 710 : 3
shall be my books, 211 : 17
stood like t. in ground, 576 : 16
sunlight never heard of t., 905 : 8
sunsets and tops of t., 879 : 14
swings across t. stars, 822 : 5
that grow so fair, 710 : 12
that would march, 765 : 10
those dying generations, 714 : 22
to benefit another generation, 95 : 15
tongues in t., 210 : 24
turn bare, 906 : 10
uptorn, 475 : 13
vines and olive t., 868 : 21
walked among ancient t., 405 : 1
when t. bow down heads, 608 : 19
where you sit, 332 : 12
wind in t. a sad thing, 103 : 11
wind is in palm t., 708 : 8
you lover of t., 542 : 6
Treetop, baby on t., 660 : 19
Treetops, in all t. hardly a breath, 397 : 3
Trelawny, shall T. die, 500 : 13
Tremble, afraid because we t., 649 : 7
at word of Lord, 300 : 22
enemies of blacks t., 505 : 11
even at air pump, 379 : 16
I t. for my country, 388 : 1
keepers of the house shall t., 27 : 24
let Sporus t., 338 : 18
like guilty thing surprised, 426 : 18
made the earth to t., 29 : 23
my firm nerves never t., 238 : 28
poplars stand and t., 691 : 11
Quakers because I bid them t., 300 : 22
sail-yards t. masts crack, 178 : 6
under her feet, 533 : 25
while they gaze, 363 : 2
Trembled, Tiber t. underneath banks, 215 : 1
Trembler, no t. in world's sphere, 562 : 4
Tremblers, boding t., 370 : 10
Trembles before your glory, 74 : 23
in the breast, 429 : 18
to be so understood, 768 : 22
Trembling cold in ghastly fears, 404 : 10
cup of t., 31 : 10
fear came upon me and t., 15 : 11
for you in voices, 702 : 5
hare limped t., 476 : 8
hoping lingering, 333 : 23
in t. hope repose, 362 : 19
seizes me all over, 63 : 5
work out salvation with fear and t., 50 : 2
Tremendous object of creation, 371 : 7
pace of change, 814 : 5
Tremulous cadence slow, 587 : 14
stay, 642 : 3
Trench confessions, 792 : 15
Trenchant blade Toledo trusty, 291 : 7
Trencher, dead Caesar's T., 241 : 11
Trencher-friends 243 : 5
Trencherman, valiant t., 208 : 23
Trenches in beauty's field, 244 : 1
Treo, handed all sails and set t., 150 : 15
Trespass, those who t. against us, 37 : *n* 5
Trespasses against duty, 372 : 7
forgive us all our t., 781 : 11
forgive us our t., 37 : *n* 5
Tresses, fair t. race ensnare, 334 : 3
like the morn, 280 : 1
withered cheek t. gray, 429 : 20
Trial and error, 678 : 3
by juries, 389 : 2
by jury, 392 : 2
by jury a security, 445 : 20
democracy still upon t., 650 : 15
fiery t. which we pass, 522 : 12
for crimes against peace, 821 : 7
future great national t., 524 : 2
man on t. in good fortune, 599 : 2
right to speedy and public t., 392 : 1
truth the t. of itself, 256 : 1
Trials, when you ask God to send t., 661 : 2
Triangles and other geometrical figures, 182 : 20
if t. had god, 341 : 7
Triangular person in square hole, 432 : 17
Tribal, constructing t. lays, 708 : 21
Tribalism strongest force in world, 912 : 2
Tribe, abhorred senseless t., 322 : 19
and all that t., 106 : 14
cursed be my t., 198 : 21
family party t. clan, 922 : 9
highly respectable t., 922 : 14
his t. were God Almighty's gentlemen, 304 : 12
idols of the t., 179 : 8
may his t. increase, 454 : 4
of spirits and of men, 132 : 12
pacify touchy t. of poets, 109 : 17
phylogenesis development of t., 617 : 10
purify dialect of t., 808 : 14
richer than all his t., 232 : 20
whole t. of fops, 233 : 3

Tribes, all t. of birds sang, 138 : 7
barbaric t. brought to faith, 156 : 12
goal of Providence in discovery of t., 154 : 13
greatness of t. now a memory, 455 : 14
that which has been sent down on the T., 130 : 11
two mighty t., 461 : 28
Tribu, mots de la t., 808 : *n* 4
Tribulation, brother and companion in t., 52 : 27
came out of great t., 53 : 15
gaze from shore on another's t., 100 : 12
patient in t., 890 : 11
youth inherit t. of war, 750 : 20
Tribunal, nation's ultimate judicial t., 777 : 1
Tribune, Chicago responsible for T., 801 : 11
Tribute, not one cent for t., 416 : 12
passing t. of a sigh, 362 : 13
to whom t. due, 47 : 27
vain t. of a smile, 430 : 7
Trice, change in a t., 632 : 11
Triche pour le beau, 757 : *n* 1
Trick, get the t., 624 : 11
Machiavel had ne'er t., 291 : 28
of our English nation, 206 : 3
when in doubt win t., 327 : 6
worth two of that, 203 : 17
Tricking and stopping, 810 : 19
Trickled through my head, 613 : 18
Trick's, long t. over, 760 : 16
Tricks by sleight of hand, 324 : 13
fox has many t., 62 : *n* 1
his tenures and his t., 224 : 10
no t. in faith, 216 : 30
plays such fantastic t., 228 : 10
such t. hath strong imagination, 197 : 12
vanity plays lurid t., 683 : 10
Yahoo t., 765 : 4
Trident, flatter Neptune for t., 242 : 20
Tried a little failed much, 669 : 15
accuracy t. by severe tests, 80 : 15
and found wanting, 742 : 2
first by whom new t., 333 : 6
he t. each art, 370 : 7
old and t., 521 : 4
private enterprise not yet t., 780 : 7
so hard to do right, 631 : 12
their adoption t., 218 : 30
thou that hast not t., 174 : 10
to hustle the East, 707 : 20
to live without him, 251 : 2
wouldn't say so till t., 774 : 3
Tries everything before arms, 96 : 20
no one knows till he t., 112 : 6
Trifle, at t. scorn to take offense, 333 : 10
careless t., 236 : 14
do not t. with love, 537 : 8
dying is a t., 606 : 15
how love can t. with itself, 190 : 5
Trifled, freedom not t. with, 820 : 12
Trifles, dispense with t., 225 : 13
irritate my nerves, 573 : 15
law not concerned with t., 133 : 18
light as air, 231 : 7
make sum of life, 549 : 10
sum of human things, 393 : 13
think my t. worth something, 101 : 13
Trifles (*continued*)
unconsidered t., 246 : 22
win us with honest t., 236 : 9
Trifling, mere imagination would be mere t., 639 : 11
narrow education of females, 392 : 13
Trigger, draw t. at his death, 354 : 2
Trilling wire in blood, 807 : 4
Trills her thick-warbled notes, 288 : 14
Trilobite, eye of t., 509 : 4
Trim, April dressed in all his t., 245 : 9
array, 428 : 2
boy that shook t., 917 : 18
bravery on and tackle t., 288 : 30
gardens, 278 : 16
he that shot so t., 192 : 1
honor a t. reckoning, 205 : 5
in gallant t. vessel goes, 363 : 6
little prim little craft, 629 : 19
meadows t. with daisies pied, 277 : 25
Trinity, blessed T., 452 : 11
unscriptural doctrine, 448 : 1
Trip, fearful t. done, 576 : 6
it as you go, 277 : 20
taking t. on Government ship, 935 : 5
Triple, arm as with t. steel, 284 : 21
pillar of the world, 240 : 12
ways to take, 708 : 22
Tripoli, shores of T., 922 : 11
Tripped light fantastic, 698 : 14
Trippingly on the tongue, 221 : 23
Trissotin, half T., 488 : 12
Triste, la chair t. hélas, 651 : *n* 2
sois belle et sois t., 581 : *n* 4
Tristesse, adieu t. bonjour t., 832 : *n* 2
Triton, hear old T., 428 : 1
of the minnows, 242 : 18
Triumph and disaster, 710 : 16
and the jingle, 781 : 15
brings void, 649 : 11
Chief who in t. advances, 431 : 9
few men know, 852 : 12
in ourselves t. and defeat, 512 : 18
join the t. of skies, 350 : 15
keep alive rather than t., 809 : 14
learning's t. o'er foes, 351 : 10
necessary for t. of evil, 374 : 12
of hope over experience, 354 : 22
one more devils' t., 541 : 8
over scientific weapons, 756 : 3
pedestaled in t., 545 : 11
Philistia t. thou because of me, 19 : 25
pursue t. partake gale, 338 : 2
ride in t. over mischance, 186 : 11
ride in t. through Persepolis, 183 : 5
right worsted wrong t., 546 : 7
supreme t. to be most alive, 790 : 20
that agony our t., 811 : 8
the more glorious the t., 384 : 13
this is our career our t., 811 : 7
without glory, 275 : 16
Triumphal procession air to marriage, 490 : 2
Triumphant, bound in with t. sea, 194 : 14
o'er our fears, 511 : 9
Triumphed, he hath t. gloriously, 9 : 32
history t. over time, 173 : 2
Jehovah has t., 447 : 10
morality of common man t., 658 : 4
nothing but eternity t., 173 : 2
Triumphing over kings and aces, 818 : 5
with Joy and Love t., 285 : 6
Triumphs, conquests glories t. spoils, 216 : 8
raise joys and t. high, 350 : 11
shut them in with their t., 542 : 4
Trivet, right as t., 546 : 29
Trivial and political, 354 : 9
attentions men think manly, 414 : 10
personalities decomposing, 781 : 17
rise from t. things, 333 : 24
wipe away t. fond records, 219 : 27
Triviality, above insolence and t., 798 : 11
Trochee trips from long to short, 436 : 3
Trod by rocky ledge, 696 : 11
in footsteps of calf, 685 : 9
soil where first t., 470 : 16
still by faith he t., 765 : 2
upon neat's leather, 214 : 31
Trodden gold, 283 : 28
little fire quickly t. out, 186 : 19
the winepress alone, 31 : 26
under hoofs of multitude, 373 : 27
worm will turn being t. on, 186 : 4
Troika, fatal t. dashes on, 582 : 12
Rus similar to nimble t., 518 : 9
winged t. who invented you, 518 : 9
Troilus mounted Troyan walls, 200 : 22
Trojan gestes as they felle, 144 : 13
no distinction between T. and Tyrian, 104 : 27
Trojans, no reason to blame T., 57 : 24
we have been T., 105 : 1
were sitting on the tower, 57 : 23
Trollops, my thoughts my t., 359 : 12
Trône, au plus élevé t. assis sur notre cul, 166 : *n* 7
Troop, farewell plumed t., 231 : 11
foreign t. in my country, 351 : 5
Troops, charged t. of error, 274 : 1
go out alone come with t., 722 : 14
hoist colors to peak, 771 : 5
led by the Czar, 922 : 16
of Allied Expeditionary Force, 815 : 12
of friends, 239 : 31
pass through seek gold, 591 : 4
sense any blunder, 815 : 14
take command of t., 420 : 12
what t. he considered best, 421 : 2
wherever enemy goes t. go, 589 : 18
Trope, out flew a t., 290 : 18
Tropes, ranged his t., 320 : 19
Trophies, all their t. pass away, 636 : 11
and dead things, 262 : 11
cloudy t., 478 : 1
these are the arks the t., 182 : 7
unto enemies of truth, 274 : 1
Tropic for your balm, 830 : 18
Tropics zones and meridian lines, 613 : 22
Trot, riseth late t. all day, 347 : 22
sideaways, 856 : 1
Troth, I wonder by my t., 251 : 14
Trots, who Time t. withal, 212 : 11
Trouble, a very present help in t., 19 : 10
and turmoil over, 608 : 20
comforting thought when not our t., 760 : 13
days begin with t., 320 : 11
deaf heaven, 244 : 8
dishonor will not t. me, 76 : 7
double toil and t., 239 : 4

Trouble (*continued*)
genius capacity for getting into t., 620 : 21
genius capacity for taking t., 349 : *n* 2, 474 : 14
great treasure and t., 24 : 7
happens to others, 760 : 12
happens to you, 760 : 12
here where all t. seems, 633 : 19
in t. and in joy, 317 : 6
is what you make it, 718 : 17
man is born unto t., 15 : 15
my presence that doth t. ye, 185 : 9
nobody know t. I've seen, 935 : 19
not bring t. to people, 863 : 9
of few days and full of t., 15 : 33
of the rain, 534 : 8
running any country, 760 : 12
smooth away t., 796 : 16
take utmost t., 680 : 1
time of t. not our t., 760 : 13
toil and t. caldron bubble, 239 : 4
useful t. of rain, 534 : 8
war is toil and t., 306 : 19
went to t. to be born, 378 : 9
with peace is no organization, 840 : 19
words weighty with t., 773 : 12
Troubled air, 283 : *n* 4
be not t., 40 : 22
bridge over t. water, 915 : 15
by this beauty, 638 : 10
captain's mind, 647 : 21
fish in t. waters, 319 : 7
gold gateways of stars, 693 : 12
I am t., 799 : 4
let not heart be t., 45 : 20, 45 : 24
mind, 267 : 20
my mind is t., 226 : 22
piping took t. sound, 587 : 8
see that ye be not t., 40 : 22
tumors of a t. mind, 288 : 24
woman moved like fountain t., 189 : 5
Trouble's a ton or ounce, 718 : 17
Troubles, fear of Acheron which t. life, 100 : 20
of proud and angry dust, 691 : 20
pack up your t., 770 : 14
peck of t., 153 : 10
sea of t., 221 : 12
written t. of the brain, 239 : 32
Troublesome disguises which we wear, 286 : 4
effort of thinking t., 635 : 25
loud and t. insects, 373 : 28
ways to dishonor Sabbath, 624 : 8
Troubling, the wicked cease from t., 15 : 9
Troublous, part we sadly in t. world, 186 : 24
sights and sounds, 721 : 8
Trough, snake came to water t., 790 : 12
Trousers, not best t. to fight, 599 : 20
steam engine in t., 433 : 5
wear bottoms of t. rolled, 803 : 18
wear white flannel t., 803 : 19
Trout, find t. in milk, 557 : 14
here comes the t., 214 : 7
Trovato, se non è vero è ben t., 387 : *n* 1
Trowel, laid on with a t., 210 : 14
Troy, did not go to citadel of T., 62 : 18
fields of corn where T. was, 113 : 14
fired another T., 306 : 21
Troy (*continued*)
fires of T., 850 : 13
half his T. was burned, 205 : 19
has been, 105 : 1
heard T. doubted, 461 : 12
sacked the holy citadel of T., 59 : 13
tale of T. divine, 278 : 21
walls famed in battle, 104 : 35
was there another T., 713 : 5
what care I for T. town, 558 : 19
why Grecians sacked T., 184 : *n* 2
windy T., 529 : 8
woman laid T. in ashes, 316 : 16
worn the stones of T., 226 : 15
Troyan, Troilus mounted T. walls, 200 : 22
Truant disposition, 218 : 13
every t. knew, 370 : 10
Truce, never t. between virtue and vice, 560 : 8
no t. or parley with Hitler, 745 : 3
to navigation, 628 : 4
Truckin', keep on t., 915 : 17
Trudge, swing tramp and t., 781 : 15
Trudged unknowing what he sought, 307 : 6
Trudges up to ignorance, 830 : 3
Trudgin' my weary way, 660 : 5
True, advanced t. friends, 585 : 11
all I thought was t., 747 : 1
and honorable wife, 215 : 23
and righteous altogether, 524 : 7
apothecary thy drugs quick, 193 : 29
art for sake of t., 504 : 18
as dial to sun, 291 : 29
as I live, 261 : 8
as needle to pole, 291 : *n* 6
as stars above, 923 : 8
as stiel, 145 : 3
as taxes, 548 : 32
as turnips, 548 : 32
be t. be t., 503 : 14
beautiful words are not t., 65 : 10
beggar true king, 374 : 16
beginning of our end, 197 : 14
best not expected to go t., 353 : 16
blue, 291 : 3
both t. both wise, 295 : 4
child always say what's t., 668 : 10
children and fools speak t., 160 : *n* 8
considered by people equally t., 383 : 7
course of t. love, 195 : 22
dare to be t., 268 : 4
definition of style, 322 : 8
democracy never existed, 358 : 15
distinguish t. from false, 308 : 7
ease in writing, 333 : 9
eloquent but 'tis not t., 585 : 16
every t. man's apparel, 229 : 2
everyone's t. worship, 83 : 2
face of death, 721 : 8
false idol or noble t. birth, 85 : 16
falsely t., 534 : 14
first t. gentleman, 251 : 11
for you true for all, 496 : 19
founder of civil society, 358 : 9
free Russian speech, 564 : 9
friendship never serene, 301 : 7
generous t. and fierce, 743 : 11
good men and t., 209 : 23
great Power make me think t., 595 : 16
gude to be honest and t., 921 : 8
True (*continued*)
guid to be honest and t., 411 : 24
happiness not in multitude of friends, 255 : 11
he was a t. poet, 403 : 19
how should I t. love know, 223 : 21
how to speak t. things, 61 : 8
I am a t. laborer, 212 : 2
I am t. Russian, 912 : 11
I and my t. love, 921 : 9
I have gone here and there, 245 : 16
I talk of dreams, 191 : 24
I to my pledged word t., 811 : 6
I would be t., 785 : 8
idea of what t. and false, 308 : 7
if England rest but t., 202 : 20
if not t. a happy invention, 387 : *n* 1
if we are t. to plan, 607 : 2
I'll prove more t., 192 : 10
in mathematics never know what t., 737 : 13
in print sure they are t., 246 : 30
is it t. in and for itself, 422 : 17
judgments of Lord t., 18 : 1, 524 : 7
lease of my t. love, 245 : 13
live pure speak t., 534 : 5
love a durable fire, 172 : 9
love is like ghosts, 293 : 12
love kept under, 628 : 25
love sits him down, 922 : 12
lovers run into strange capers, 210 : 34
make dreams come t., 824 : 12
making dream come t., 775 : 15
marriage of t. minds, 245 : 18
matter decided considered t., 134 : 23
matters I relate are t. lies, 818 : 4
more t. than love to me, 918 : 4
music repeat thought of people, 842 : 3
mysterious law t. source, 286 : 5
nation consider national what is t., 484 : 4
never accept thing as t., 272 : 8
no man worth having t., 321 : 4
nobility exempt from fear, 185 : 22
not too good to be t., 319 : 15
not t. or undeveloped, 570 : 16
nothing t. makes complete sense, 823 : 21
nothing t. that may not seem false, 165 : 5
novel t. and false, 887 : 14
oh 'tis t. 'tis t., 690 : 21
one religion t. as another, 260 : 1
order of going, 83 : 9
Penelope was Flaubert, 792 : 11
people's judgment t., 304 : 13
pessimist fears this is t., 762 : 10
pity 'tis 'tis t., 220 : 12
plain hearts, 251 : 16
plots t. or false necessary, 303 : 19
poem an invocation, 833 : 6
proved t. before prove false, 291 : 27
right praise t. perfection, 201 : 5
right t. end of love, 253 : 22
ring in the t., 532 : 22
simple modest manly t., 568 : 23
small service is t. service, 429 : 11
so t. so brave, 423 : 1
so t. to thyself, 180 : 22
so young my lord and t., 232 : 26
strange but t., 462 : 2
such as I all t. lovers, 213 : 29

True (*continued*)
tender and t., 597 : 13
that he is mad 'tis t., 220 : 12
the blushful Hippocrene, 476 : 23
the t. light, 44 : 20
theory of t. civilization, 581 : 10
think of companions t., 422 : 2
Thomas, 926 : 23
'tis t. 'tis day, 252 : 21
'tis t., 'tis pity, 220 : 12
to kindred points, 429 : 9
to thee till death, 552 : 21
to thine own self be t., 219 : 2
to t. occasion t., 533 : 4
to you in my fashion, 820 : 8
trail held t., 707 : 22
trusty dusky vivid t., 669 : 8
way but yet untried, 179 : 7
way goes over rope, 786 : 2
what each wishes he believes t., 88 : 22
what is t. of shopkeeper, 359 : 9
what people say of us t., 711 : 5
whatsoever things are t., 50 : 7
when you met her, 252 : 3
who would distinguish t., 308 : 7
wit nature to advantage, 333 : 3
woman t. and fair, 252 : 2
wood yew wood, 689 : 16
words are not beautiful, 65 : 10
worshipers shall worship, 44 : 36
writ your annals t., 242 : 26
writes thing not t., 317 : 9
you are not t., 899 : 8
True-begotten father, 198 : 31
True-born Englishman, 194 : 8
True-fixed and resting quality, 216 : 3
True-love, my t. hath my heart, 176 : 7
pokers into t. knots, 436 : 5
Truer to be rebel, 704 : 17
Truest of books Solomon's, 570 : 16
of men Man of Sorrows, 570 : 16
Truism, not paradox but t., 85 : 11
Truly a peck of provender, 197 : 5
here lies t. honest man, 292 : 20
those who were t. great, 876 : 15
Trump, farewell the shrill t., 231 : 11
last t., 49 : 7
of rescue sound, 494 : 17
tell truth or t., 624 : 11
Trumpet, believeth that it is sound of the t., 16 : 38
blow t. to arms, 384 : 8
cock the t. to the morn, 217 : 24
first blast of the t., 162 : 1
give uncertain sound, 48 : 26
great sound of a t., 40 : 25
hear t. sound, 936 : 2
heart moved more than with t., 176 : 12
of his own virtues, 210 : 9
of prophecy O Wind, 467 : 22
praise him with t., 22 : 25
pride his own t., 226 : 9
shall be heard on high, 305 : 13
shall sound, 49 : 7
shifted his t., 371 : 21
sound t. beat drums, 346 : 7
summons again, 890 : 11
when people heard sound of t., 11 : 31
Trumpet's loud clangor, 305 : 11
Trumpets, blow your t. angels, 254 : 8
he saith among the t., 16 : 38
loud uplifted angel t., 281 : 10
Trumpets (*continued*)
no t. for new year, 755 : 9
of the sky, 493 : 21
silver snarling t., 476 : 9
sound t. beat drums, 306 : 14
sounded for him, 302 : 16
tuckets then t., 742 : 9
Trumpet-tongued, angels t., 236 : 24
Trumps, let spades be t., 334 : 7
they were, 334 : 7
Truncheon, marshall's t., 228 : 6
Trunk, clean t. of death, 863 : 14
joy up t. needles tingle, 901 : 12
so large a t. before, 729 : 15
spouts out a sea, 286 : 30
Trunkless legs of stone, 466 : 12
Trunks, animals infuse into t. of men, 200 : 7
Trust, a little t., 617 : 3
all t. impossible, 903 : 2
before you t. a man, 917 : 7
blessings-of-civilization t., 625 : 25
brains t., 853 : 2
built absolute t., 236 : 15
did not t. own impressions, 80 : 15
ears less than eyes, 78 : 3
empire power in t., 304 : 7
everybody but cut cards, 722 : 11
follow it with absolute t., 783 : 1
government is a t., 444 : 3
husband doth safely t. in her, 26 : 6
in God hope for best, 432 : 21
in God is our t., 446 : 2
in God keep powder dry, 444 : 12
in Him I put my t., 130 : 15
in him will I t., 20 : 16
in Providence, 271 : 14
life of magnanimity and t., 559 : 9
Lord shall raise me up I t., 173 : 5
love all t. a few, 227 : 9
magistracy is great t., 374 : 3
make man trustworthy t. him, 723 : 22
man bore this t., 132 : 4
man on his oath or bond, 243 : 1
no agent, 209 : 9
no man with power to endanger liberty, 380 : 13
none, 207 : 15
not him with secrets, 386 : 9
not one night's ice, 270 : 3
not t. in money, 519 : 5
old friends to t., 179 : 18
power a t., 501 : 6
public office public t., 539 : 4, 631 : *n* 1
put no t. in the morrow, 107 : 8
put not your t. in princes, 22 : 23
put their t. in him, 34 : 14
rude cruel not to t., 245 : 23
soothed by unfaltering t., 471 : 6
soul's invincible surmise, 703 : 3
surplus wealth sacred t., 621 : 8
that man in nothing, 360 : 8
that somehow good, 532 : 9
thee gentle Kate, 203 : 24
there are those who t. me, 785 : 8
they that put their t. in him, 17 : 14
though he slay me yet will I t., 15 : 32
time that takes in t., 173 : 5
to frail mortality t., 181 : 18
tomorrow will repay, 303 : 10
try to t. one another, 818 : 15
Trust (*continued*)
tyranny's disease to t. no friends, 70 : 24
under his wings shalt thou t., 20 : 16
wonder men t. selves with men, 242 : 31
yourself, 396 : 15
Trusted, I have t. in thee, 167 : 3
let no such man be t., 201 : 3
not in one bottom t., 197 : 25
to thy billows, 458 : 31
treason but t. like fox, 205 : 6
was ever poet so t., 355 : 11
with government of others, 388 : 18
Trustee, millionaire t. of poor, 621 : 10
Trustees, officers of government t., 444 : 3
Trustest in staff of this broken reed, 30 : 26
Trusteth, he that t. in his riches, 23 : 26
in his own heart, 25 : 29
in man, 32 : 11
in the Lord, 32 : 11
Trusting, calls his t. benevolence, 369 : 23
no more t. in women, 60 : 14
Trusts, foolish man who t. woman, 105 : *n* 5
in tameness of wolf, 234 : 14
offices public t., 449 : 8
public t. in hands of fit, 319 : 16
spendthrift t. no place in Common Law, 638 : *n* 5
Trustworthy, make man t. trust him, 723 : 22
not one altogether t., 720 : 3
Trusty, ancient t. drouthy crony, 411 : 6
dusky vivid true, 669 : 8
Toledo t., 291 : 7
Truth about life, 863 : 3
absurd is the first t., 882 : 5
accepted in market, 645 : 1
adherence to t. of nature, 437 : 14
affirm what seems to be t., 85 : 15
all we know for t., 713 : 7
always bitter, 127 : 19
always strange, 462 : 2
and all that makes man, 534 : 23
and nonviolence inseparable, 727 : 6
as opposeth no profit, 264 : 20
authority and show of t., 209 : 30
awoke and found it t., 479 : 2
basis of moral authority, 580 : 12
be in the field, 282 : 5
beauty, 477 : 11
beauty adventure, 697 : 14
beauty must be t., 479 : 1
begets hatred, 96 : 2
being truth tell it, 158 : *n* 4
between us, 498 : 30
blessed strains telling, 552 : 22
bright countenance of t., 281 : 13
bring t. to light, 189 : 23
by instant illumination, 858 : 10
call upon him in t., 22 : 22
can live with right and wrong, 829 : 16
capsule of t., 846 : 9
carp of t., 220 : 7
certainty of the words of t., 25 : 1
comes like bastard, 281 : 16
crushed to earth, 471 : 12
cry of all game of few, 330 : 23
depository of t., 300 : 11

Truth (*continued*)
deviation from t. is multiplied, 87 : 7
dignity of t. lost with protesting, 255 : 19
disagreeable t., 386 : 8
does not blush, 126 : 7
doubt t. to be liar, 220 : 14
draw bow ride and speak t., 462 : 4
dreadful knowledge of t., 74 : 2
enemies of t., 274 : 1
error more dangerous the more t., 580 : 11
every man satisfied there is t., 639 : 8
evidence of t. but only evidence, 444 : 5
exists falsehood invented, 776 : 2
faithfulness to t. of history, 592 : 7
fiction lags after t., 372 : 13
follow t. too near heels, 173 : 3
follow t. wherever it may lead, 389 : 16
for a moment lie is t., 582 : 15
for t. ought to die, 495 : 9
for truth's sake, 685 : 5
forever absolute, 538 : 17
forever on scaffold, 567 : 7
found t. in all but one, 195 : 10
found when men free, 779 : 15
fragment by fragment, 858 : 10
free movement in search of t., 774 : 8
free to pursue t., 779 : 15
friend to t., 336 : 5
friends his t. proclaim, 304 : 6
from his lips prevailed, 370 : 8
from shadows into t., 490 : 15
full of grace and t., 44 : 21
gate of horn for t., 105 : 26
God of t., 11 : 23
goes a-begging, 156 : 4
good and t. to borrow, 495 : 16
great is t., 34 : 3
great is t. and shall prevail, 34 : *n* 2
habit with him test of t., 400 : 6
half t. blackest lie, 535 : 6
half-t. or t. and a half, 751 : 5
happens to idea, 650 : 11
has limits, 166 : 8
has such face and mien, 305 : 16
hath a quiet breast, 194 : 1
heart fed upon t., 438 : 2
hero of my tale, 601 : 24
high star of T., 586 : 9
highest thyng men kepe, 147 : 32
Him who is T. itself, 319 : 22
his t. endureth, 21 : 3
His t. marching on, 566 : 4
his t. shall be thy shield, 20 : 16
holding on to t., 727 : 5
honor t. above friends, 87 : 14
hour of t. now, 757 : 1
how sweet the t., 552 : 22
I am very fond of t., 344 : 4
I have preached the t., 72 : 19
I will be harsh as t., 505 : 12
if life be t., 273 : 3
ill-timed t., 646 : 14
image of inner t., 5 : 10
impossible to be soiled, 86 : *n* 7
in different forms, 610 : 2
in first place or second, 814 : 4
in masquerade, 461 : 23
in medicine most difficult, 463 : 19
in peril t. drawn from heart, 100 : 21
in science t. only end, 471 : 16

Truth (*continued*)
in shepherd's tongue, 172 : 10
in spirit and t., 44 : 36
in the end t. will conquer, 143 : 10
in t. we know nothing, 79 : 10
in wine is t., 62 : *n* 12, 134 : 6
is great and endures, 3 : 5
is marching on, 566 : 4
is not in us, 52 : 20
is on the march, 643 : 8
is precious and divine, 291 : 21
is there in t. no beauty, 268 : 14
is torch, 360 : 29
is truth to the end, 229 : 6
judgment of intellect half t., 753 : 13
justice t. in action, 502 : 2
keep abreast of t., 567 : 8
kept strict regard for t., 730 : 9
language of t., 735 : 13
liars when they speak t., 86 : 15
lie which is half t., 535 : 6
lies in the depth, 79 : 10
light between t. and intellect, 141 : 25
like bastard comes into world, 281 : *n* 4
look for t. not find it, 359 : 13
lost to love and t., 708 : 15
love of t., demanded of genius, 397 : 8
love t. pardon error, 343 : 2
maintained cause of t., 286 : 26
make the t. known, 717 : 9
man's t. is final resolution, 769 : 18
map of t. in thy face, 185 : 16
marvelous t. confront us, 902 : 15
mathematics possesses t., 737 : 14
may strike out his teeth, 173 : 3
mercy and t. are met together, 20 : 9
misunderstood, 650 : 5
more by faith than t., 171 : 16
most valuable thing, 625 : 2
naked t. is I have no shirt, 191 : 11
nation which keepeth the t., 30 : 9
never fell dead in streets, 537 : 11
never hurts teller, 545 : 18
never is undone, 873 : 3
never understood and not believed, 404 : 8
no concern with duty or t., 527 : 14
no eternal t., 818 : 10
no god higher than t., 727 : 6
no greatness where no t., 602 : 6
no special time of own, 757 : 1
no t. dies, 472 : 14
no t. in him, 45 : 6
no t. to be discovered, 772 : 8
noble t. of sorrow, 72 : 23
not always object of philosophers, 662 : 1
not better for showing face, 72 : 5
not conceal t. knowingly, 130 : 10
nor grave nor bed denied, 716 : 17
not offend you by speaking t., 154 : 4
not only by reason, 300 : 5
not sought for, 91 : 4
not veil t. with falsehood, 130 : 10
nothing but the t., 169 : 29
nothing but t. is lovely, 311 : 16
nothing more damaging to new t., 397 : 5
nothing so least as t., 829 : 21
nothing so strange as t., 450 : 18
now her painted toy, 711 : 19
nutritive or suggestive t., 653 : 11

Truth (*continued*)
obedience bane of t., 466 : 7
obeyed his call, 717 : 10
object of philosophy, 662 : 1
object of science t., 436 : 14
ocean of t. undiscovered, 313 : 17
of history, 592 : 7
of imagination, 479 : 1
on march nothing can stop, 643 : 8
on one side Ease on other, 537 : 12
one law and one t., 125 : 9
one t. is clear, 337 : 1
one who died for t., 605 : 13
only in imagination, 684 : 6
only merit to history, 616 : 3
only two ways of discovering t., 179 : 7
opinion is t. filtered, 538 : 17
painful t., 383 : 1
partisan of t. alone, 260 : 10
peeps over glass's edge, 543 : 3
persuades by teaching, 126 : 6
petrified t., 621 : *n* 2
pick way from t. to t., 464 : 5
Plato and t. are dear, 87 : 14
Plato dear t. dearer, 87 : *n* 6
poet sings, 529 : 20
possession of t. as city, 274 : 2
put in possession of t., 307 : 15
put to the worse, 282 : 5
rather than love give me t., 560 : 20
receives t. as angel, 448 : 7
religion instinctive t., 593 : 10
ridicule best test of t., 342 : 12
Satya t., 727 : 6
science search for t., 854 : 1
scientific t. property of few, 509 : 3
sea room to tell t. in, 569 : 17
searcher obedient to t., 580 : 7
secret of eloquence, 580 : 12
seek t. in groves of Academe, 109 : 14
severe, 363 : 8
shall be thy warrant, 172 : 14
shall make you free, 45 : 5
shall prevail, 34 : *n* 2
sharp seasoning of t., 127 : 18
shows spirit and substance, 135 : 12
simple t. his utmost skill, 250 : 14
simple t. miscalled simplicity, 244 : 25
sits on lips of dying, 586 : 7
snap like vixens at t., 794 : 7
sole judge of t., 337 : 2
sometimes improbable, 462 : *n* 1
soul of t. in things erroneous, 579 : 16
soul rejoices in t. uttered, 554 : 7
speak t. and shame Devil, 158 : 8
speak t. and soberness, 46 : 34
speak t. as much as I dare, 165 : 16
spirit of t. and freedom, 599 : 8
spread t. from pole to pole, 325 : 9
sterile t., 662 : 21
stranger than fiction, 462 : *n* 1
strife of T. Falsehood, 567 : 6
suffers by heat of defenders, 314 : 11
supply of t. in excess of demand, 561 : 17
swear to t. of song, 320 : 22
swears she is made of t., 246 : 2
swerve a hair from t., 226 : 15
takes two to speak t., 558 : 12
tell how t. may be, 430 : 5
tell t. or trump, 624 : 11
tells disagreeable t. boldly, 386 : 8
the t. and the life, 45 : 22

Truth (*continued*)
thee shal delivere, 148 : 10
they shall understand the t., 34 : 14
thought I knew t., 874 : 17
thy t. so pure of old, 282 : 18
time discovers t., 115 : 3
to cover lies, 324 : 9
to one error to other, 727 : 5
to save t. renounces life, 784 : 11
told with bad intent, 406 : 12
trial of itself, 256 : 1
trouble to build up t., 464 : 3
Twain told t. mainly, 623 : 20
unarmed t., 909 : 14
universally acknowledged, 440 : 16
vantage ground of t., 100 : *n* 7, 180 : 1
veracity in intention of t., 437 : 7
vindication against slander, 523 : 9
vindication of t. by suffering, 727 : 5
we seek the t., 793 : 12
weep for me who has t., 152 : 1
well of true wit t., 601 : 6
what is t., 45 : 30
what is t. said jesting Pilate, 179 : 22
what of t. boundered by mountains, 165 : 8
what remains must be t., 689 : 3
when in doubt tell t., 625 : 1
when no help in t., 74 : 2
when t. entails ruin, 75 : 17
where doubt there t., 532 : *n* 6
where is t. we seek, 467 : 13
which cunning times put on, 199 : 27
will come to light, 148 : *n* 1
willing to know whole t., 383 : 1
wine dear boy and t., 62 : 19
wit has t. in it, 827 : 18
with gold she weighs, 340 : 15
with malice in it, 570 : 13
wither into t., 713 : 8
within little compass, 329 : 2
within mind rehearse, 527 : 20
without error, 139 : 5
woman reveals by causing to suffer 734 : 10
Truthful James, 630 : 13
stupid believe easy to be t., 738 : 18
Truthfulness, artistic growth refining of t., 738 : 18
Truth's a dog must to kennel, 233 : 8
thy country's thy God's and t., 249 : 8
truth for t. sake, 685 : 5
Truths, all t. half-truths, 697 : 16
art establishes t., 891 : 16
bear all naked t., 478 : 5
begin as blasphemies, 681 : 10
begin as heresies, 596 : 9
discovery of divine t., 329 : 5
doubts more cruel than t., 297 : 30
end as superstitions, 596 : 9
eternal t. have fresh meaning, 780 : 10
Freud and larger t., 698 : 4
in and out of favor, 747 : 10
in flag government and t., 551 : 11
instruments of darkness tell us t., 236 : 9
irrationally held t., 596 : 8
kindle light for truths, 100 : 11
kindness and lies worth thousand t., 859 : 7
mistaking verbiage for t., 735 : 9
not for all men nor times, 343 : 15
of the heart, 838 : 8
Truths (*continued*)
old universal t., 838 : 8
symbols conductors of t., 436 : 20
treating half-truths as whole t., 697 : 16
wake to perish never, 426 : 19
we hold these t., 387 : 9
we hold these t. self-evident, 554 : 4
which can kill nation, 777 : 4
Truthsayers, soothsayers make better living than t., 386 : 20
Try, above all t. something, 779 : 7
axe's edge did t., 296 : 23
fair adventure of tomorrow, 202 : 15
first thyself, 66 : *n* 7
fortunes to last man, 206 : 27
guiltier than him they t., 227 : 31
if live start to t., 868 : 2
let end t. the man, 206 : 12
might as well not t., 747 : 9
one white foot t. him, 923 : 11
then worms shall t., 297 : 1
times that t. men's souls, 384 : 13
to be one on whom nothing lost, 652 : 14
tropic for your balm, 830 : 18
whole cause condemn you, 611 : 6
with all my might to mind, 449 : 15
Trying, because we have gone on t., 808 : 9
for us there is only t., 807 : 22
makes friends without t., 739 : 8
Trysted, the wished the t. hour, 411 : 2
Trysting, named a t. day, 488 : 13
Tu, et t. Brute, 99 : *n* 17, 216 : 5
Tub, every t. stand upon bottom, 301 : *n* 4
fair tale of a t., 155 : 7
three men in a t., 933 : 2
Tubal-cain artificer in brass and iron, 7 : 23
Tubes twisted and dried, 707 : 21
Tuckahaw, high t., 921 : 12
Tucker, little Tom T., 930 : 15
Tuckets, then t. then trumpets, 742 : 9
Tucson and Deadwood, 840 : 2
Tuesday, christened on T., 932 : 11
dissolutely spent T. morning, 202 : 25
Tuesday's child full of grace, 932 : 10
Tuesdays, only teaching on T., 892 : 20
Tuffet, sat on a t., 932 : 15
Tufted, bosomed high in t. trees, 277 : 25
Tug, then was the t. of war, 317 : 13
Tugged with fortune, 238 : 16
Tugging all day at perverse life, 873 : 8
Tugs, each t. in different way, 462 : 9
Tulgey wood, 612 : 18
Tumble, anarchy why cities t., 74 : 20
another t., 485 : 15
ready with every nod to t., 187 : 15
Tumbler, clean t. corkscrew, 547 : 16
Tumbling in twenty rings, 733 : 1
Jill t. after, 931 : 1
Tumor that kills victim's sympathies, 634 : 23
Tumors of a troubled mind, 288 : 24
Tumult and shouting dies, 709 : 17
in the clouds, 714 : 1
of mighty harmonies, 467 : 21
of the soul, 428 : 21
whirling through air forever dark, 140 : 15
Tumultuous privacy of storm, 493 : 22
Tune, all t. he could play, 931 : 12
enchantress plays, 692 : 5
he who pays piper calls t., 324 : *n* 5
hurdygurdies make t. their own, 662 : 18
incapable of t., 441 : 21
instrument here at the door, 254 : 17
of flutes kept stroke, 240 : 29
out of t. and harsh, 221 : 21
singeth a quiet t., 435 : 1
sings t. without words, 604 : 17
sweetly played in t., 409 : 22
turn on t. in drop out, 897 : 11
voices keep t. oars time, 446 : 5
vulgar if public hums, 662 : 18
what t. enchantress plays, 692 : 5
Tuned like fifty stomachaches, 548 : 8
spheres, 241 : 25
to poetry life's prose, 610 : 8
Tuneful, soon mute however t., 442 : 19
Tuneless, heroic lay t., 461 : 5
not to be t. in old age, 107 : *n* 11
Tunes, cathedral t., 604 : 18
devil have all good t., 393 : 6
frozen up in horn, 385 : 8
loathe sweet t., 633 : 3
love t. shepherd's reed, 430 : 6
Tuning lyre and handling harp, 70 : 12
Tunis, mail from T. probably, 607 : 12
Tunnel, antiseptic t., 908 : 8
end of t., 891 : 9
Tupping your white ewe, 229 : 18
Turbaned, malignant and t. Turk, 232 : 21
Turbans, white silken t. wreathed, 288 : 11
Turbulence, dejected manner to t., 766 : 14
Turbulent fleshy sensual, 574 : 20
free me from t. priest, 137 : 9
people t. and changing, 401 : 12
sagacious and t. of wit, 303 : 20
Turc, la galère d'un T., 298 : *n* 5
Tureen, steward falls into t., 709 : 24
Turf, bless t. that wraps clay, 364 : 9
dappled t. at ease, 426 : 3
grass-green t., 223 : 22
green be t. above thee, 464 : 11
green t. beneath feet, 445 : 12
on green t. suck showers, 281 : 1
Turk, bear like the T., 338 : 14
malignant and turbaned T., 232 : 21
or Proosian, 627 : 18
out-paramoured the T., 234 : 6
work hard as T., 919 : 5
Turkey a more respectable bird, 348 : 13
black t. gobbler, 928 : 17
in the straw, 921 : 12
it was a t., 548 : 14
Turkey-cock parades, 899 : 14
Turkish, be taken by T. enemy, 935 : 4
English not T. court, 206 : 35
Turkman's rest, 462 : 16
Turk's, on board a T. galley, 298 : *n* 5
Turks, Papists Protestants Jews T. in one ship, 273 : 11
sleep with T. and infidels, 195 : 9
Turlock, sing together on T. sands, 637 : 15
Turmoil, tired of my t., 893 : 11
Turn again Whittington, 918 : 10
and live with animals, 574 : 24
away no more, 405 : 2

Turn (*continued*)
backward O time, 610 : 10
by fortune from weaker, 198 : 30
currents t. awry, 221 : 12
dark cloud inside out, 740 : 11
death because chose to t., 801 : 13
do not hope to t., 805 : 20
do not t. back at goal, 111 : 24
down empty glass, 517 : 14
each thing his t. does hold, 266 : 15
good t. asketh another, 160 : 16
him to cause of policy, 207 : 5
his merry note, 211 : 1
hope to t. again, 805 : 20
I t. my back to the east, 402 : 15
in door once turn once only, 805 : 13
Lordship t. it over, 489 : 14
never t. back on life, 786 : 14
now t. different hue, 67 : 4
on hinge that night, 864 : 1
on tune in drop out, 897 : 11
one good t. deserves another, 117 : 14
out your toes, 612 : 22
over a new leaf, 170 : 15
over half a library, 355 : 14
pass and t. again, 495 : 11
quickly t. away, 715 : 19
smile once more t. thy wheel, 233 : 16
something t. up, 501 : 25
stone start a wing, 693 : 18
the other cheek, 37 : 10
thee behind me, 14 : 17
to t. you out t. you out, 708 : 1
up the lights, 699 : 20
where shall I t., 911 : 1
wheresoe'er I may, 426 : 10
why wilt thou t. away, 405 : 2
worm will t., 186 : 4
yet I t. I t., 864 : 13
Your Shirttails Into Drawers, 829 : 1
Turned aside to sleep, 252 : 17
dead and t. to clay, 224 : 16
face with ghastly pang, 434 : 24
from one's course by opinions, 93 : 6
having once t. walks on, 435 : 3
he t. up his eyes, 404 : 11
heart is t. to stone, 231 : 23
him right and round about, 410 : 6
home his footsteps t., 430 : 10
in case anything t. up, 548 : 25
like yonder windlass, 571 : 5
one who never t. back, 546 : 7
round and round in world, 571 : 5
suddenly cried and t. away, 796 : 10
sword which t. every way, 7 : 13
them inside outside, 733 : *n* 1
world t. upside down, 258 : 11
Turnest, thou t. man to destruction, 20 : 11
Turning as flames in fire, 766 : 12
condones, 863 : 19
from itself never t., 172 : 9
gas steam or table t., 581 : 10
in widening gyre, 714 : 12
neither shadow of t., 51 : 29
o' the tide, 207 : 13
still point of t. world, 806 : 13
to gold all it touches, 600 : 13
wine into urine, 789 : 6
Turnings, long lane knows no t., 541 : 4
Turnip, rather have t. than father, 353 : 12
Turnips, man who t. cries, 353 : 12
true as t., 548 : 32
Turns again home, 535 : 19
climber upward t. face, 215 : 16
earth's smoothness rough, 544 : 10
giddy thinks world t. round, 189 : 4
his necessity to gain, 427 : 22
into Miss T., 740 : 4
lightly t. to love, 529 : 16
no more his head, 435 : 3
over your papers, 386 : 9
poet's pen t. to shapes, 197 : 12
times go by t., 182 : 1
to face on-coming snow, 874 : 20
to thoughts of love, 529 : 16
uneasily from fire, 839 : 1
unto ladder t. his back, 215 : 16
with ceaseless pain, 368 : 14
Turpissima bestia, 95 : *n* 3
Turquoise Horse of Johano-ai, 928 : 20
Turret, sultan's t. with light, 515 : 16
Turtle, clever of t., 855 : 12
lives 'twixt decks, 855 : 12
love of the t., 459 : 5
mock t., 612 : 4
Mock T., 612 : 5
thoughts of t. turtles, 500 : 11
voice of the t. is heard, 28 : 7
Turtledove, voice of the t., 4 : 13
Turtle's breast, 806 : 13
Tuscany, ranks of T., 488 : 17
Tut child said Duchess, 612 : 2
done thousand dreadful things, 188 : 22
Tutelage, period of political t., 719 : 8
Tu-whit tu-who, 191 : 14
Twa, lost but ane t. behin', 411 : 20
sisters in bour, 927 : 1
Twain, book made by Mr. Mark T., 623 : 20
from one book by Mark T., 845 : 5
never t. meet, 707 : 16
Twangling, thousand t. instruments, 248 : 10
Tweedledee, Contrariwise continued T., 612 : 24
Tweedledum and Tweedledee, 341 : 13
Twelve, all my hearts strike t., 863 : 16
good men, 444 : 15
good rules, 370 : 14
honest men, 330 : 20
I in t. thousand none, 195 : 10
in sworn t. have thief, 227 : 31
in t. found truth in all but one, 195 : 10
iron tongue hath told t., 197 : 22
o'clock, 804 : 4
parted between t. and one, 207 : 13
snowed for t. days and t. nights, 887 : 5
Twelvemonth's, run t. length again, 410 : 14
Twentieth, party make t. century, 492 : 7
Twentieth-Century blues, 843 : 11
Twentieth-century, most significant contribution of t. science, 884 : 5
Twenty ballads stuck about wall, 271 : 3
cannot live on t. pound, 268 : 6
love-sick maidens, 628 : 5
men crossing bridge, 766 : 13
not handsome at t., 269 : 32
strength of t. men, 193 : 22
substance of grief hath t. shadows, 194 : 18
sweet and t., 213 : 23
Twenty (*continued*)
to that t. add hundred more, 266 : 10
to twenty-five the years, 743 : 10
understand life at t., 705 : 11
will not come again, 690 : 17
years in woman's life, 84 : 14
Twenty-eight, came to serve at t., 151 : 11
Twenty-five, between t. and forty, 664 : 19
first t. years worth all, 492 : 19
Twenty-nine, she had a long t., 675 : *n* 5
when there are pink shades, 675 : 13
Twenty-one, brisk minor pants for t., 339 : 16
confidence of t., 354 : 5
Twenty-seven, woman of t., 835 : 12
Twice as muckle 's a' that, 411 : 20
blessed, 200 : 9
life closed t. before close, 607 : 18
never lost as much but t., 604 : 3
not step t. into same rivers, 70 : 3
old man t. a child, 220 : 32
or thrice had I loved thee, 252 : 20
serpent sting thee t., 200 : 5
to teach is to learn t., 400 : 13
who splits wood warms t., 560 : *n* 2
woman's name in print t., 789 : 3
wood stumps warmed me t., 560 : 9
Twice-told tale, 202 : 1
Twig and a pillar, 90 : 2
as t. bent tree's inclined, 335 : 15
birch t. for castigation, 711 : 17
Twilight and evening bell, 535 : 20
between birth and dying, 806 : 5
brown t. atmosphere, 503 : 15
disastrous t. sheds, 283 : 24
dreamcrossed t., 806 : 5
glimmer of t., 541 : 9
hour of breath, 721 : 8
land no-man's land, 626 : 21
live in gray t., 686 : 13
of power, 852 : 1
of things that began, 634 : 7
past is t. of dawn, 719 : 14
pilots of purple t., 529 : 24
still evening and t. gray, 285 : 24
struggle, 890 : 11
was it cry against t., 766 : 12
Twilight's last gleaming, 446 : 1
Twin, stiff t. compasses, 253 : 5
Twine, soft as roses they t., 459 : 6
wine and China teas, 558 : 10
Twined flowers, 477 : 18
Twinkle little bat, 611 : 20
little star, 449 : 13
on milky way, 427 : 8
Twinkling of an eye, 49 : 7
Twinklings, remembering with t. and twinges, 889 : 12
Twinned, we were as t. lambs, 246 : 10
Twins, body and spirit t., 634 : 14
two young roes that are t., 28 : 11
Twirled, Brazil he t. button, 605 : 20
fingers madly, 551 : 2
Twist 'em up, 921 : 12
neither with volition nor consciousness, 798 : 13
no more t., 719 : 4
Oliver T. asked for more, 546 : 30
oozy weeds about me t., 572 : 7
secret lies in invisible t., 828 : 4
wolf's-bane, 477 : 20
Twisted braids of lilies, 280 : 3

Twisted (*continued*)
cue, 629 : 13
our eye-beams t., 253 : 6
prisoner in his t. gyves, 192 : 18
tubes t. and dried, 707 : 21
Twisting, character of t. octopus, 67 : 4
Twitched his mantle blue, 281 : 6
Twitches, death t. my ear, 106 : 9
Twitter and feathers sleek, 475 : 2
Two and one are three, 428 : *n* 2
and two make four, 619 : 3
as stiff twin compasses, 253 : 5
bicycle built for t., 718 : 18
blackbirds, 934 : 8
by two in ark of ache, 902 : 17
can t. walk together, 33 : 20
cardinal sins, 786 : 6
do t. things do neither, 110 : 16
fifths sheer fudge, 567 : 18
gods Persuasion and Compulsion, 70 : 17
grains of wheat in chaff, 198 : 5
grant that twice t. not four, 564 : 8
gross of broken statues, 792 : 16
I am t. fools I know, 252 : 13
if by sea, 512 : 7
if ever t. were one, 290 : 12
in right with t. or three, 567 : 4
irons in the fire, 263 : 3
kinds of people, 670 : 1, 855 : 17
lads that thought no more behind, 246 : 9
lanterns in North Church, 382 : 12
live as one, 806 : 11
lost but are t. behin', 411 : 20
love idea of t. sexes, 831 : 2
lovely berries on one stem, 197 : 2
loves I have, 246 : 3
may keep counsel, 160 : *n* 17
may talk one hear, 497 : 20
more onetwo moremens more, 778 : 6
not without God, 126 : 14
o'clock in morning courage, 421 : 1
of every sort, 7 : 29
of far nobler shape, 285 : 17
of trade never agree, 331 : 18, 600 : 14
oldest professions, 801 : 9
one t. and third in your bosom, 192 : 23
or three gathered together, 40 : 3
our t. souls which are one, 253 : 4
roads diverged in wood, 747 : 13
seizes t. things one slips, 926 : 1
sides to every question, 78 : 24
sin ye do by t. and t., 708 : 18
single soul in t. bodies, 87 : 1
sisters sat in a bour, 927 : 1
sleep an act or t., 249 : 19
souls dwell in my breast, 396 : 12
stars keep not motion, 205 : 9
strings to bow, 160 : *n* 6
supreme blessings, 77 : 6
takes t. to speak truth, 558 : 12
things believed of any man, 729 : 8
unity at minimum is t., 832 : 17
voices are there, 428 : 6
we t. alone will sing, 235 : 12
went to pray, 292 : 6
Two Lands are in festivity, 5 : 6
Two-and-twenty, I am t., 690 : 21
sweet t., 462 : 6
Two-edged, sharp as a t. sword, 23 : 10
Two-edged (*continued*)
sharper than t. sword, 51 : 14
Two-handed engine, 280 : 22
Two-legged, unfeathered t. thing, 304 : 2
Two-ness an American a Negro, 724 : 17
Two-party system, 862 : 19
Twopence a week and jam, 613 : 10
colored, 669 : 1
Twopenny, don't care t. damn, 421 : 15
wi' t. fear nae evil, 411 : 10
Tyler, Tippecanoe and T., 439 : *n* 3
Tyne, cargo of T. coal, 760 : 20
Type, highest t. nowhere existing, 579 : 21
I am t., 706 : 23
of all her race, 536 : 7
of the wise, 429 : 9
of true love kept under, 628 : 25
so careful of t., 532 : 11
Types, loose t. of things, 426 : 3
movable t., 472 : 21
of judicial writing, 730 : 15
Typhus, cholera t. ignorance, 773 : 8
Typical, clubs t. of strife, 377 : 6
Tyrannical, grow t. fighting tyranny, 847 : 4
habit of reading, 569 : 7
strength without justice is t., 300 : 6
Tyrannies, of all t. on humankind, 305 : 17
shams inequalities, 625 : 24
war dearth age agues t., 254 : 9
Tyrannis, sic semper t., 635 : 23
Tyrannous to use it like giant, 228 : 9
word of command, 598 : 15
Tyranny and oppressions vanish, 389 : 12
death a milder fate than t., 71 : 10
destruction of Nazi t., 781 : 8
discourage and abolish t. and vice, 380 : 6
economic t. above, 794 : 12
enter if people lose spirit, 577 : 15
fate awaiting Nazi t., 745 : 4
fortune's wayward t., 73 : 11
Frederick without t., 591 : 11
freedom versus t., 866 : 9
government transformed to t., 451 : 18
grow tyrannical fighting t., 847 : 4
Law ends T. begins, 307 : 17
laws end t. begins, 351 : 1
liberty and t., 523 : 7
like hell not easily conquered, 384 : 13
not only t. but tyrant, 384 : 12
of majority, 616 : 2
of Mrs. Grundy, 579 : 13
of next-door neighbor, 597 : 10
of one literature, 671 : 20
only bar against t., 577 : 15
over mind of man, 388 : 15
poverty disease war, 890 : 11
power in behalf of t., 904 : 17
reliance against t., 520 : 7
snuff approach of t., 372 : 20
struggle to be free of t., 841 : 1
taxation without representation t., 367 : 10
Tyranny's disease, 70 : 24
ecclesiastic t. worst, 318 : 9
Tyrant, any excuse will serve t., 66 : 14
conform to t. custom, 167 : 14
Tyrant (*continued*)
first cunning t., 520 : 7
if t. trouble happens to others, 760 : 12
in man fled, 850 : 10
is child of Pride, 74 : 3
little t. of fields, 362 : 9
not only tyranny but t., 384 : 12
old man weds t., 77 : 19
preserve me from a t., 255 : 14
public opinion weak t., 559 : 2
root from which t. springs, 85 : 5
when t. has disposed of enemies, 85 : 7
Tyrant-hating milk, 567 : 9
Tyrant's, Ercles' vein a t. vein, 196 : 4
necessity the t. plea, 285 : 21
threatening countenance, 107 : 28
Tyrants, all men would be t., 318 : 11, 392 : 7
and slaves, 369 : 25
argument of t., 412 : 4
blood of patriots and t., 388 : 7
controlled by t. or by ourselves, 862 : 12
fall in every foe, 411 : 16
fear reigns with t., 511 : 1
hand unfriendly to t., 298 : 19
how can t. govern home, 186 : 12
kings t. from policy, 373 : 26
rebellion to t., 920 : 14
their t. their historians, 490 : 18
three t. of ego, 678 : 15
thunderbolts and t., 346 : *n* 5
thus always to t., 134 : 27, 635 : *n* 4
to t. no quarter, 505 : 15
watered by blood of t., 401 : 4
Tyre, one with Nineveh and T., 709 : 18
Tyrian, no distinction between Trojan and T., 104 : 27

U

U, green U blue O, 673 : 20
will not be missed, 829 : 23
Ubi bene ibi patria, 134 : 32
libertas ibi patria, 367 : 11
saeva indignatio, 323 : 25
Ubiquitous, her envoys u., 539 : 15
man u. animal, 870 : 14
Ucalegon's afire next door, 104 : 36
Uffish thought, 612 : 18
Ugliest man who came to Ilium, 57 : 18
North American civilization one of u., 903 : 12
Uglification and derision, 612 : 5
Ugliness, one's beauty another's u., 497 : 26
recognition of u., 63 : 13
Ugly America, 898 : 1
born old and u., 547 : 28
dirty bird u. and offensive, 505 : 8
fact nature hides, 609 : 3
foul and u. mists, 203 : 5
houses stand, 822 : 18
like toad u. and venomous, 210 : 24
night full of u. sights, 187 : 8
what u. sights of death in eyes, 187 : 9
woman not u., 342 : 4
women indisputably u., 342 : 4
Yahoo tricks, 765 : 4

Ukelele, died playing u., 876 : 8
Ultima Thule, 103 : *n* 14, 115 : *n* 9
Ultimate, depository of u. powers, 389 : 15
ideal yet hopeless quest, 697 : 9
mystery works sadly, 649 : 10
power u. aphrodisiac, 902 : *n* 1
sanction of exploitation, 825 : 18
Ulysses, admitted to U.S., 759 : 1
but was it U., 769 : 8
is it U. that approaches, 769 : 5
Joyce technique in U., 758 : 13
like U. made glorious voyage, 162 : 10
Ulysses' absence, 242 : 10
Umbered, sees other's u. face, 208 : 1
'Umble very 'u. person, 548 : 30
Umbrella against Scotch mist, 569 : 13
Umbris, ex u. in veritatem, 490 : 15
Umpire, death u. of men's miseries, 185 : 2
Unable to live in society, 87 : 28
to sit still in a room, 299 : 20
Unaccommodated man, 234 : 7
Unaccustomed to fear, 922 : 15
Unacquainted, not u. with misfortunes, 60 : 16
Unadorned, beauty u., 312 : 17
when u. adorned most, 345 : 14
Unadvertised, leave it u., 644 : 14
Unadvised, too rash too u., 192 : 13
Unadvisedly, entered into u., 56 : 6
Unaffected, affecting to seem u., 324 : 22
Unafraid, gentlemen u., 707 : 23
of change, 701 : 5
Unaging intellect, 714 : 22
Unalienable, certain u. rights, 387 : 9
essential and u. rights, 387 : *n* 4
Unalterable, army of u. law, 600 : 28, 804 : 7
days, 494 : 23
quantity of force u., 583 : 21
Unaltered, laws ought not to remain u., 88 : 2
Unaneled, unhouseled disappointed u., 219 : 24
Unanimity, feel way toward u., 706 : 19
on legal questions, 700 : 2
Unapproachable in White House, 783 : 5
Unarm Eros, 241 : 18
Unarmed, being u. be despised, 153 : 22
truth, 909 : 14
Unashamed, brawling judgments u., 534 : 10
Unassisted merit advances slowly, 351 : *n* 5
Unassuming commonplace of Nature, 426 : 2
Unattached, vagaries of u. relatives, 826 : 15
Unattainable perfection, 711 : 7
Unattained, how vast the u., 532 : *n* 5
Unattempted yet in prose or rhyme, 283 : 1
Unavailing star, 711 : 7
Unavenged, insults u., 428 : 12
suffering, 582 : 4
Unaware, blessed them u., 434 : 29
hope he knew and I u., 641 : 13
some morning u., 541 : 16
Unawares, entertained angels u., 51 : 22
Unbarred gates of light, 286 : 25
Unbeautiful and have comfortable minds, 828 : 14
Unbecoming, not u. men that strove, 529 : 12
Unbelief, fearful u. in yourself, 473 : 5
help thou mine u., 42 : 10
Unbelievers, do not the u. see, 131 : 13
works of u. a mirage, 131 : 17
Unbelieving came home, 792 : 14
Unbend, sweet to let mind u., 108 : 15
universal horror u., 775 : 3
Unbidden guests welcomest when gone, 184 : 19
Unbirthday present, 613 : 15
Unblighted unredeemed wilderness, 637 : 16
Unbodied, souls u., 254 : 3
Unborn, fate of u. millions, 379 : 2
generations, 779 : 2
millions yet u., 365 : 3
posterity of those u., 326 : 16
states u., 216 : 7
ye u. ages, 363 : 7
Unborrowed, interest u. from the eye, 423 : 12
Unbought grace of life, 373 : 23
health u., 306 : 26
Unbound, so are ye u., 494 : 17
Unbounded, man of an u. stomach, 249 : 13
salt water u., 710 : 7
Unbowed, head bloody but u., 663 : 10
Unbreathed, virtue unexercised and u., 282 : 1
Unbroken, seaward flying u. wings, 806 : 6
spur not u. horse, 432 : 7
Unburied, bodies of u. men, 262 : 3
unwept u. Patroclus, 59 : 9
Unburnished, rust u., 529 : 9
Unbusy, sole u. thing, 436 : 9
Unbutton, come u. here, 234 : 7
Uncaught, from world's snare u., 241 : 15
Uncertain balance of proud time, 178 : 13
coy hard to please, 431 : 2
glory of April day, 189 : 32
hour before morning, 808 : 13
life's u. voyage, 243 : 9
rustling of curtain, 526 : 13
to it nothing u., 397 : 17
trumpet give u. sound, 48 : 26
world u. comes, 495 : 19
Uncertainties, capable of u., 479 : 5
Uncertainty, New England weather dazzling u., 622 : 20
quit certainty for u., 352 : 14
sink of u. and error, 300 : 11
Unchanging, no u. truth, 818 : 10
Olympus ever u., 59 : 27
Uncharitable to ourselves, 274 : 19
Uncharitableness, from all u. deliver, 55 : 10
Unchartered freedom tires, 427 : 14
Unchecked, capitalist society u., 814 : 7
population u. increases, 417 : 3
Unchristened, Homer and his u. heart, 716 : 14
Uncircumcision, neither circumcision nor u., 50 : 12
Uncivilized Eastern instincts, 707 : 7
Unclasps her warmed jewels, 476 : 17
Uncle, I have good eye u., 209 : 7
me no uncle, 194 : 21
my prophetic soul my u., 219 : 20
Uncle (*continued*)
nephew of my U. Sam's, 759 : 6
Unclean, man of u. lips, 29 : 10
people of u. lips, 29 : 10
spirits entered swine, 42 : 5
swine is u., 10 : 17
Unclothed, bodies u. must be, 254 : 3
Unclouded, pure u. brow, 612 : 15
weather, 528 : 25
Unclubable, very u. man, 354 : 19
Uncoffined and unknown, 458 : 26
Uncomely, things u. and broken, 712 : 12
Uncomfortable feel tarantara, 628 : 2
inn to lodge in, 570 : 8
moral when u., 680 : 20
Uncommon, common opinions u. abilities, 597 : 9
valor common virtue, 791 : 14
Uncompleted, hanging on of u. task, 648 : 1
Uncompromising as justice, 505 : 12
hostility, 860 : 2
Unconcern, patron looks with u., 353 : 26
Unconcerned hear mighty crack, 325 : 11
Unconditional and immediate surrender, 589 : 16
love, 909 : 14
right to say what one pleases, 794 : 20
war, 891 : 1
Unconfined, lawless winged u., 404 : 14
let all her ways be u., 320 : 17
let joy be u., 457 : 15
Unconquerable, love u. waster, 74 : 23
man's u. mind, 425 : 21
nursing u.hope, 586 : 2
soul, 663 : 10
will, 283 : 8, 745 : 4
Unconquered, thy arm u. steam, 377 : 26
Unconscionable time dying, 302 : 23
Unconscious, all greatness u., 472 : 11
archetypes of u., 754 : 7
collective u., 753 : 12
discovered u. before me, 678 : 11
explore u., 688 : 8
fastidiousness, 799 : 1
God and U. are one, 906 : 7
humor, 620 : 19
infancy's u. spell, 571 : 4
Kosmos, 651 : 3
not only evil by nature, 754 : 10
part of man's life, 472 : 12
poetry, 589 : 5
prejudice, 825 : 13
spiritual unbidden u., 536 : 6
studied, 678 : 11
the source of good, 754 : 10
without having to go, 856 : 17
work, 632 : 1
Unconsidered, decisive actions often u., 727 : 10
snapper-up of u. trifles, 246 : 22
Unconsoled widower, 514 : 9
Unconstitutional, power to pronounce u., 506 : 3
Uncontrollable laughter, 57 : 14
mystery, 713 : 13
Unconvincing, preferable to u. possibility, 88 : 19
Uncornered animal's, 901 : 14
Uncorseted her friendly bust, 804 : 23

Uncounted, monster with u. heads, 205 : 18
Uncouth, ancient good u., 567 : 8
savage men u. manners, 372 : 12
Uncreated conscience of race, 777 : 18
wide womb of u. night, 284 : 9
Uncreating word, 340 : 28
Uncrowned in the underworld, 790 : 13
Unction, flattering u., 223 : 7
Uncumbered with a wife, 306 : 25
Uncut hair of graves, 574 : 17
Undaunted by villains in power, 382 : 11
daughter of desires, 292 : 15
we must be u., 744 : 9
Undazzled, kindling her u. eyes, 282 : 3
Undecided, decided only to be u., 743 : 12
Undefeated because we have gone on trying, 808 : 9
Undefiled, well of English u., 173 : 22
Under blossom that hangs on bough, 248 : 16
every stone a politician, 82 : 15
the greenwood tree, 211 : 1
Underbelly, soft u. of Axis, 746 : 3
Underdeveloped, growth of u. areas, 787 : 17
Underemphasis, swaggering u., 803 : 3
Underestimating intelligence of American people, 772 : 20
Underfoot, men tread u. what feared, 101 : 9
Undergraduates limited to four, 740 : 16
Underground, defense not in going u., 764 : 4
go burrow u., 793 : 19
her alchemy, 494 : 6
living in u. den, 84 : 17
might well be u., 629 : 6
wake nations u., 936 : 2
Underjaw, most things move u., 268 : 20
Underlings, that we are u., 215 : 6
Undermine, echo u. her hold on life, 764 : 10
Undermining prosperity, 687 : 14
Underneath all individuals, 576 : 9
are the everlasting arms, 11 : 26
in uplifting get u., 718 : 8
this sable hearse, 265 : 15
this stone doth lie, 256 : 5
Undernourishment, extinction from u., 845 : 16
Underrated nobleman, 630 : 1
Understand and control nature, 814 : 12
at last to u., 768 : 22
Black love is Black wealth, 916 : 2
both these do not u. 56 : 25
everything makes tolerant, 417 : 15
fury in your words, 232 : 1
Gettysburg you can't u., 838 : 4
go on explaining cease to u., 782 : *n* 5
how little we need, 694 : 6
I u. thy kisses, 204 : 17
if I could u., 535 : 10
individual part he can never u., 844 : 7
know less u. more, 781 : 14
life at forty, 705 : 11
may not be made to u. it, 68 : 25
men and women u. each other, 689 : 21
ne'er quite u. customs, 593 : 3
never u. folks they hate, 568 : 8
Understand (*continued*)
no human being u. another, 859 : 8
not to be understood but to u., 138 : 15
not u. only by intellect, 753 : 13
remember and u., 542 : 2
say it as you u. it, 413 : 18
so many tried to u., 840 : 4
that he is sufficient, 198 : 16
that he should u., 768 : 4
they that trust in him shall u., 34 : 14
to admire we should not u., 324 : 13
vexation only to u. the report, 30 : 15
want to u. others, 413 : 1, 810 : 4
what it is to be President, 788 : 4
write for those who u., 731 : 9
writer's ignorance, 437 : 9
youngsters read men u., 169 : 39
Understandable spirit, 873 : 14
Understandest my thought afar off, 22 : 16
Understandeth, Lord u. all the imaginations, 14 : 24
Understanding action of forces, 584 : 1
begged Him to take away my u., 316 : 4
candle of u., 34 : 6
declare if thou hast u., 16 : 28
first from mind banish u., 78 : *n* 1
foolish people without u., 31 : 34
for thy more sweet u., 190 : 16
give it an u., 218 : 24
gone a-woolgathering, 261 : *n* 6
ignorant of his u., 437 : 9
in length of days u., 15 : 30
is false mirror, 179 : 9
is joyous, 913 : 3
man of u. is of excellent spirit, 24 : 18
man of u., 35 : 11
man of u. lost nothing, 164 : 16
men of u., 27 : 17
much learning not teach u., 69 : 28
myself, 810 : 4
no full u. of own epoch, 755 : 1
not hand but u., 169 : 37
not obliged to find u., 357 : 1
of mass movements, 858 : 8
of myself and things around me, 599 : 11
Peace of God passeth all u., 56 : 1
peace which passeth u., 50 : 6, 57 : *n* 2
political u. to run government, 788 : 10
spirit of wisdom and u., 29 : 18
steppingstones to u., 762 : 5
to depart from evil is u., 16 : 15
to direct, 391 : 4
we reach u., 884 : 6
well-meaning but without u., 677 : 15
where is the place of u., 16 : 12
wife, 262 : 12
wise and u. heart, 13 : 27
with all thy getting get u., 23 : 7
with little u. world ruled, 157 : 1
woman of mean u., 440 : 17
Understandings, best flattered upon u., 342 : 4
Understands, not as he u. but as he not yet u., 639 : 14
relentlessly she u. you, 864 : 19
without seeing, 64 : 17
Understood as a child, 48 : 25
by quiet natures u., 714 : 20
harmony not u., 337 : 1
Understood (*continued*)
his time, 774 : 12
life u. backwards, 552 : 10
lightly hid deepest u., 899 : 11
poetry communicate before u., 809 : 15
trembles to be so u., 768 : 22
truth never u. and not believed, 404 : 8
Undertake executions for master executuoner, 65 : 7
Undertaken, work we have u., 264 : 22
Undertaker, manners of u., 726 : 13
Undertaking, thorny u. to follow movement of mind, 164 : 19
Underwear, never heard of u., 817 : 8
Underwood, green u. and cover, 632 : 8
Underworld, uncrowned in the u., 790 : 13
Undescribable, describe u., 458 : 11
Undeserved, wear u. dignity, 199 : 14
Undeservedly forgotten, 869 : 7
Undeveloped, not true or u., 570 : 16
Undevout astronomer is mad, 330 : 19
Undigested apple dumpling, 570 : 9
Undiminished natural wealth, 890 : 13
Undisciplined squads of emotion, 807 : 21
Undiscovered, bring light otherwise u., 384 : 14
country from whose bourn, 221 : 12
ocean of truth lay all u., 313 : 17
Undisguised, truth showing face u., 72 : 5
Undismayed unintimidated inquiry, 737 : 6
Undisturbed, stand u. as monuments, 388 : 16
Undivulged pretense, 238 : 9
Undo, equivocation will u. us, 224 : 12
me so, 641 : 23
parchment scribbled o'er u. a man, 185 : 25
power to u. the past, 82 : 27
pray you u. this button, 235 : 18
so much of either may u. thee, 262 : 16
things done, 257 : 17
Undone, another such victory and we are u., 92 : 10
death u. so many, 805 : 2
I am u., 29 : 10
John Donne Anne Donne U., 251 : *n* 7
left u. those things, 54 : 13
truth never is u., 873 : 3
wish estate of world u., 240 : 5
wrongdoer often left something u., 125 : 16
yet is nothing left u., 64 : 13
Undreamed, wait the u. of, 904 : 6
Undress, gentle limbs u., 433 : 31
Undulate round the world, 576 : 4
Undulating, man vain diverse u., 164 : 6
Undulations, ambiguous u., 767 : 4
of Ephesian sod, 571 : 3
Unearned increment, 508 : 16
suffering, 909 : 8
Uneasy lies head that wears crown, 206 : 19
Uneducated, educated superior to u., 86 : 19
simplicity makes u. effective 88 : 15
Uneffectual, pale his u. fire, 219 : 26
Unemployed labor means want, 811 : 10

Unemployed (*continued*)
purchasing power, 811 : 10
Unemployment, inflation makes u. inevitable, 844 : 10
outcome of pro-labor policies, 775 : 6
solution to high u., 880 : 15
Unencompassable, encompass u., 561 : 3
Unending, end of the u., 808 : 13
Unenlightened, strong dogged u., 587 : 3
Unequal distribution of property, 398 : 2
laws unto savage race, 529 : 6
separate and u., 872 : 14
separate inherently u., 820 : 14
sharing of blessings, 746 : 16
Unequals, equals and u. alike, 85 : 3
Unerringly, sniffs u. as dog, 653 : 13
to you, 576 : 10
Unespied, in ocean's bosom u., 297 : 8
Unethical and lousy, 858 : 17
Unexamined, life which is u., 83 : 12
Unexercised, virtue u. and unbreathed, 282 : 1
Unexpected, absurd not the u., 552 : 12
always happens, 94 : *n* 3
old age most u., 770 : 7
Unexplored, genius seeks regions u., 519 : 24
Unexpressed, uttered or u., 429 : 18
volumes of the u., 912 : 1
Unexpressive, fair chaste u. she, 211 : 18
Unextinguishable laugh in heaven, 275 : 12
Unfair, life is u., 891 : 4
Unfairnesses that afflict peoples, 625 : 24
Unfaithful, faith u., 534 : 14
to what we have been, 734 : 7
Unfamiliar, black-sailed u., 901 : 4
foot of u. men, 587 : 6
love u. Name, 808 : 15
nothing detracts so much as u. terms, 125 : 20
Unfathomable, revere the u., 397 : 7
Unfathomed center, 480 : 12
dark u. caves, 362 : 8
Unfeathered two-legged thing, 304 : 2
Unfed sides, 234 : 3
Unfeeling, the u. for his own, 361 : 12
Unfelt, show an u. sorrow, 238 : 10
Unfettered, afford all u. start, 522 : 2
beat earth with u. foot, 107 : 15
leewardings, 843 : 14
Unfilial, three things u., 89 : 13
Unfinished man and his pain, 716 : 1
work they nobly advanced, 523 : 4
Unfirm, fancies more giddy and u., 214 : 1
Unfit, for a calm u., 303 : 20
for all things u., 371 : 14
for ladies' love u., 307 : 5
for nation of shopkeepers, 366 : 6
picture u. for view, 619 : 5
to hold an office, 93 : 6
Unfix, horrid image doth u. hair, 236 : 11
Unfixed in principles, 303 : 20
Unfold, I could a tale u., 219 : 18
leaves of Judgment Book u., 596 : 16
meadow flower bloom u., 429 : 12
O clouds u., 406 : 21
such companions thou'dst u., 232 : 6
Unfold (*continued*)
what cunning hides, 233 : 1
Unfolded by surprise, 750 : 4
Unfolds both heaven and earth, 195 : 23
Unforeseen, absurd not the u., 552 : 12
persistence of u., 640 : 17
Unforgetful, teach u. to forget, 601 : 21
Unforgiving, an u. eye, 399 : 2
Unfortified, heart u., 218 : 4
Unfortunate, literary attempt u., 357 : 18
Miss Bailey, 415 : 13
one more u., 485 : 21
Unfound door, 852 : 6
Unfriended, remote u. melancholy, 368 : 13
Unfriendly, disposition toward U.S., 408 : 3
this hand u. to tyrants, 298 : 19
to society's chief joys, 376 : 3
Unfruitful, invention is u., 372 : 13
Unfurled o'er all world, 535 : *n* 4
to April's breeze u., 494 : 13
Ungained, men prize the thing u., 225 : 35
Ungalled, hart u. play, 222 : 17
Ungartered and down-gyved to ankle, 220 : 8
Ungenial climate, 590 : 4
Ungirt loin, 543 : 15
Ungodly are like chaff, 17 : 12
hope of the u., 34 : 16
walketh not in counsel of u., 17 : 12
Ungracious, as some u. pastors, 218 : 28
Ungraspable phantom of life, 570 : 4
Ungrateful, dog never u., 609 : 4
man less to blame, 293 : 18
public, 445 : 7
to those teachers, 782 : 20
Ungue, ex u. leonem, 133 : 24
Unhabitual, genius perceiving in u. way, 649 : 4
Unhallowed, uplift a new u. song, 684 : 13
Unhand me gentlemen, 219 : 16
Unhandsome, slovenly u. corpse, 203 : 8
Unhanged, not three good men u., 203 : 28
Unhappiness comes of greatness, 472 : 26
of his age has the u., 344 : 7
of person who could not say no, 875 : 14
Unhappy as we imagine, 293 : 8
brains for drinking, 230 : 17
clergymen's households generally u., 620 : 11
family u. in own way, 602 : 9
folks on shore now, 429 : 19
good old times when u., 928 : 4
hates, 586 : 12
how much more u. he might be, 327 : 3
linger a space, 797 : 13
lot finds no enemies, 111 : 15
none u. but great, 327 : 20
not one respectable or u., 574 : 24
old u. far-off things, 426 : 5
these u. times, 779 : 6
to have been happy u. misfortune, 129 : 22
why Muse speak when u., 857 : 2
wight, 174 : 11
Unhatched egg greatest challenge, 847 : 6
Unheard beyond ocean tide, 568 : 14
those u. sweeter, 477 : 6
Unhelped by any wind, 435 : 14
Unheroic dead who fed guns, 795 : 16
Unhinged brains of better heads, 274 : 3
Unholy pleasure, 729 : 14
shrieks and sights u., 277 : 17
Unhonored, mindful of u. dead, 362 : 16
unwept u. unsung, 430 : 10
Unhounded by sordid cares, 772 : 12
Unhouseled disappointed unaneled, 219 : 24
Unhurrying chase, 693 : 11
Unicorn, lion and u., 929 : 19
Unicorns come down to sea, 811 : 14
jeweled u., 806 : 3
Un-ideaed, wretched u. girls, 353 : 25
Uniform motion in right line, 313 : 13
Uniformitarian demolishes theories, 471 : 17
Uniformity, is u. of opinion attainable, 387 : 15
not lightly sacrificed, 730 : 14
Unify, imagination struggles to u., 437 : 12
Unimaginable touch of time, 429 : 5
Unimpaired, strong and u., 376 : 23
Unimportant, interesting because u., 817 : 14
situation that was intolerable becomes u., 734 : 9
where I was born u., 800 : 12
Unimproved people, 871 : 15
Unintelligent, sheep u., 799 : 16
Unintelligible, find explanation u., 758 : 10
sudden u. phrase, 593 : 4
weight of u. world, 423 : 10
Unintimidated inquiry, 737 : 6
Union be imperiled, 644 : 17
bonds of u. dissolved, 438 : 11
cause, 617 : 6
Civil War rebirth of U., 682 : 4
common cause to save U., 521 : 7
flag of our u., 492 : 11
form a more perfect U., 391 : 10
further u. deeper communion, 807 : 24
gives strength, 66 : 22
in partition, 197 : 2
is my country, 444 : 6
join u. and say equal pay, 578 : 2
keep step to music of U., 485 : 1
knell of U., 389 : 14
labor u. pressure, 775 : 6
longshoreman's u., 722 : 21
nature's social u., 408 : 13
not expect the U. to be dissolved, 520 : 4
now and forever, 450 : 16
object to save U., 522 : 6
of English-speaking peoples, 672 : 16
of gin and vermouth, 837 : 10
of hands and hearts, 294 : 14
of mathematician with poet, 651 : 4
of very sorry men, 58 : 15
once glorious U., 450 : 15
one and inseparable, 725 : 20
our Federal U., 419 : 2
salvation in u., 730 : 16
save U. by freeing slaves, 522 : 6
saved U. of these States, 576 : 8

Union (*continued*)
ship of U., 521 : 7
strength in u., 511 : 15
strict and indissoluble U., 401 : 14
strong and great, 511 : 8
swell chorus of U., 521 : 14
we say we are for U., 522 : 12
wish to dissolve U., 388 : 16
with native sea, 428 : 15
Unionist, I wasn't a trade u., 824 : 1
Unions, glorious mission of u., 666 : 22
labor u. and inflation, 848 : 4
power and discipline which u. have, 848 : 5
Unique, greatness of art to find u., 861 : 14
someone else u. and great, 701 : 11
Unison, chord in u. is touched, 377 : 13
in u. strike twelve, 863 : 16
Unit, collective u. form, 650 : 12
misses u., 542 : 19
morale in military u., 771 : 2
Unitas, in necessarius u., 294 : *n* 6
Unite avocation and vocation, 748 : 18
black people u., 914 : 15
bonds that u. only in mind, 734 : 8
far and near u., 384 : 8
for public safety, 420 : 15
internal propensity to u., 775 : 1
workers of the world u., 563 : *n* 5
United, avoid perils by u. forces, 308 : 21
faction u. by common impulse, 398 : 1
nations, 457 : 21
States and Europe, 408 : 3
States of Europe, 492 : 7
States of World, 492 : 7
sword u. nations drew, 457 : 21
we must be u., 744 : 9
we stand divided we fall, 378 : *n* 7
United Nations, lost courage in U.N., 895 : 24
peoples of U.N., 788 : 20
plan for liberation, 815 : 12
world state inherent in U.N., 813 : 13
United States, all people born in U.S. citizens, 392 : 4
American without threatening peace, 796 : 8
bounded on north, 535 : *n* 6
British Empire and U.S., 744 : 7
Constitution and laws of U.S., 391 : 13
Constitution for U.S., 391 : 10
Constitution of U.S. shield, 553 : 20
declare peace, 818 : 8
deliberately attacked, 780 : 15
flag of U.S., 677 : 10
fools drunkards and U.S., 924 : 7
gives bigotry no sanction, 379 : 8
greatest potential force, 699 : 5
has thirty-two religions, 400 : 18
I believe in U.S., 725 : 20
in U.S. more space, 752 : 14
incarnation of utilitarianism, 737 : 12
join U.S., 748 : 16
land of free speech, 746 : 6
monster the U.S., 672 : 15
neutral in fact, 682 : 1
not end if we declare Act of Congress void, 644 : 17
not proclaimed democracy, 741 : 15
poor Mexico so close to the U.S., 604 : 2
rendered U.S. helpless, 682 : 10
United States (*continued*)
result in evil to U.S., 599 : 1
so happy as in U.S., 772 : 12
students from U.S., 672 : 16
themselves greatest poem, 573 : 19
treason against the U.S., 391 : 12
Ulysses admitted into U.S., 759 : 1
unfriendly towards U.S., 408 : 3
warning to the world, 491 : 2
we the people of the U.S., 391 : 10
Unites, happy whom unbroken bond u., 107 : 9
Unitest nations, 575 : 22
Unities sir are a completeness, 547 : 13
Uniting, by u. we stand, 378 : 11
Unity, confound all u. on earth, 239 : 19
doth enchant me, 171 : 13
dwell together in u., 22 : 14
give to all nations u., 55 : 13
in necessary things u., 294 : 18
is plural, 832 : 17
lands and peoples in u., 912 : 3
makes strength, 597 : 2
multeity in u., 436 : 18
of death and life, 637 : 17
of German nation, 812 : 19
of humanity in word, 755 : 21
preserve u. of empire, 373 : 6
Universal and common bond, 166 : 2
appetite an u. wolf, 226 : 3
blank, 285 : 5
books of u. appeal, 740 : 9
cock, 767 : 6
currents of U. Being, 496 : 4
darkness buries all, 340 : 28
Declaration of Human Rights, 774 : 8
dismal u. hiss, 287 : 27
dovetailedness, 547 : 13
frame without mind, 180 : 16
God of u. laws, 650 : 6
grin, 349 : 4
harmony, 583 : 5
horror unbend, 775 : 3
insight into u. nature, 420 : 3
lapped in u. law, 530 : 2
law, 366 : 14
made u. shout, 215 : 1
monarchy of wit, 271 : 18
Nature did lament, 280 : 14
nature say, 350 : *n* 4
nuisance, 308 : 12
old age in u. man, 178 : *n* 12
partial evil u. good, 337 : 1
peace like light, 529 : 5
prey, 226 : 3
quality is diversity, 165 : 14
Rossum's U. Robots, 814 : 14
sickness implies idea of health, 866 : 3
this u. frame began, 305 : 9
truths, 838 : 8
uproar the u. peace, 239 : 19
world governed by u. law, 566 : 18
Universally relations stop nowhere, 653 : 10
Universals, statements of poetry are u., 88 : 18
Universe, accident in meaningless u., 746 : 20
aggregate of humanity's experiences, 832 : 18
allegorical of u., 742 : 5
anthology of u., 838 : 16
benign indifference of u., 882 : 3
Universe (*continued*)
beyond man is u., 831 : 17
born for the u., 371 : 14
chess pieces phenomena of u., 595 : 12
concentration camp u., 881 : 9
connect subject with u., 644 : 4
Creator of u., 307 : 12
each is a u., 879 : 17
emptiness produced the u., 97 : 7
fathomless u., 576 : 5
glory and shame of u., 300 : 11
glory of the u., 515 : 7
Great Architect of U., 758 : 9
Great Spirit that rules this u., 419 : 11
harmony for you my U., 124 : 19
hell of a good u., 829 : 26
hints for better ordering of u., 139 : 6
I accept the u., 536 : 13
in boundless u., 527 : 20
in harmony with u., 566 : 6
in u. neither center nor circumference, 171 : 15
information about u., 679 : 1
is all including me, 833 : 2
is change, 124 : 14
know another's view of u., 734 : 13
knows the u. not himself, 296 : 20
language of God, 447 : 17
largest u. of good, 649 : 18
man said to u., 732 : 8
meets own destruction, 774 : 10
never say u. accident, 862 : 4
not hostile nor friendly, 764 : 16
nothing lowly in u., 905 : 9
one u. made up of all that is, 125 : 9
open to our gaze, 182 : 20
piety towards u., 704 : 6
queerer than we suppose, 821 : 5
single complex living creature, 126 : 19
snow falling faintly through u., 777 : 16
something gained for u., 649 : 14
spirit animating u., 482 : 11
sun himself at center of u., 154 : 10
systematic procession of u., 154 : 10
this grand book the u., 182 : 20
through-and-through u., 651 : 3
traversed boundless u. in thought, 100 : 3
true piety towards u., 704 : 6
way into u. through forest, 637 : 18
whole theory of u., 576 : 10
Universes, in space and time u., 576 : 22
University become multiversity, 879 : 4
best u. gauntlet of mobs, 499 : 14
collection of books, 473 : 30
diversity of opinion basic to u., 825 : 12
he who enters u., 825 : 9
hirelings in u., 406 : 20
Lomonosov our first u., 357 : *n* 4
place of light, 502 : 16
Unjust, God all mercy is God u., 330 : 13
in least unjust in much, 43 : 32
let him be u. still, 53 : 32
peace before just war, 348 : *n* 2
sendeth rain on just and u., 37 : 12
war protracted, 573 : 3
will pay less tax, 84 : 6
Unkind, learned kindness from u., 782 : 20
tell me not I am u., 295 : 22

Unkind (*continued*)
thou art not so u., 211 : 16
when givers prove u., 221 : 14
Unkindest cut of all, 216 : 24
Unkindness, I tax you not with u., 233 : 25
may defeat my life, 232 : 7
may do much, 232 : 7
Unkissed, unknown u. and lost, 144 : 17
Unknelled uncoffined, 458 : 26
Unknow, knows not also to u., 581 : 13
Unknowable, awareness of u., 853 : 12
world u. we know, 693 : 16
Unknown, accents yet u., 216 : 7
affection hath u. bottom, 212 : 26
altars to u. gods, 648 : 6
and silent shore, 441 : 10
behind dim u., 567 : 7
black and u. bards, 733 : 9
critics shouting He's u., 647 : 4
enemy is the u., 755 : 10
fearless for u. shores, 576 : 15
footprint on shores of u., 776 : 7
forms of things u., 197 : 12
from known to u., 552 : 5
good to love the u., 441 : 24
hardships we suffered, 822 : 2
know less than all u., 260 : 8
let me live unseen u., 332 : 11
like a complete u., 915 : 6
loss no loss, 110 : 18
means of destruction hitherto u., 787 : 15
mighty continent hitherto u., 151 : 6
naked in death on u. shore, 105 : 13
nature is but art u., 337 : 1
not lived ill who passed u., 109 : 8
not to know me argues yourselves u., 286 : 7
out of me unworthy u., 728 : 6
poetry journey to u., 826 : 17
region, 576 : 17
renown, 607 : 8
she lived u., 424 : 12
taken for marvelous, 123 : 2
things standing thus u., 225 : 1
things u. proposed, 333 : 18
to fortune and fame u., 362 : 17
to the u. god, 46 : 15
too early seen u., 191 : 27
traveled among u. men, 425 : 6
unkissed and lost, 144 : 17
unknelled uncoffined u., 458 : 26
worth's u. though height taken, 245 : 18
Unlamented let me die, 332 : 11
Unlearned, amaze the u., 333 : 5
lessons of paternalism u., 631 : 11
Unleashed power of the atom, 764 : 3
Unleavened bread and bitter herbs, 9 : 24
seven days shall ye eat u. bread, 9 : 27
Unleaving, Goldengrove u., 656 : 9
Unless statistics lie, 829 : 11
Unlessoned girl unschooled, 199 : 29
Unlettered small-knowing soul, 190 : 15
Unlimited, land of U. possibilities, 662 : 4
power apt to corrupt, 351 : 1
rights will become u., 358 : 10
Unlit lamp ungirt loin, 543 : 15
Unlocked, Shakespeare u. heart, 429 : 10
Unlocked (*continued*)
silent throat, 918 : 17
Unloose, Gordian knot u., 207 : 5
not worthy to u., 41 : 32
scatter and u. it from bond, 189 : 18
Unloved year, 864 : 1
Unlovely, keep u. things afar, 92 : 13
Unlucky, book lucky or u., 639 : 1
these u. deeds relate, 232 : 20
Unmake, people can u. Constitution, 402 : 8
Unmanageable, most u. of all animals, 86 : 2
Unmanliness, wisdom without u., 81 : 1
Unmanly, 'tis u. grief, 218 : 4
Unmannerly, called them untaught u., 203 : 8
sadness in youth, 198 : 12
Unmask her beauty to moon, 218 : 27
time's glory to u. falsehood, 189 : 23
Unmasked, offer itself to be u., 786 : 3
Unmatchable, mastiffs of u. courage, 207 : 25
Unmeaning thing they call a thought, 333 : 8
Unmentionable thoughts, 571 : 11
Unmerciful disaster, 526 : 16
Unmoor no more, 571 : 4
Unmotived herd, 223 : *n* 3
Unmoved cold and to temptation slow, 245 : 4
see thee dying, 546 : 14
Unmysterious flesh, 836 : 19
Unnat'ral, poetry's u., 546 : 23
Unnatural, nothing u. that is not impossible, 399 : 9
something u. in government leagues off, 381 : 5
vices fathered by heroism, 804 : 15
Unnecessarily, entities not multiplied u., 143 : 2
Unnecessary, curious in u. matters, 34 : 27
heroic in u. points, 648 : 9
mob of u. duplicates, 571 : 2
sentence no u. words, 729 : 7
wants, 649 : 16
Unnerved and untrained, 648 : 9
Unnoticed, rather attacked than u., 356 : 9
Unnumbered idle pebbles, 234 : 28
Unobtrusive, poetry should be u., 479 : 6
Unordered, Chaos a rough u. mass, 113 : 15
Unpaid, promise made is debt u., 752 : 7
you with u. bill, 470 : 4
Unparalleled catastrophes, 764 : 3
in thought u., 445 : 14
lass u., 242 : 5
Unpardonable, what is u. sin, 503 : 4
Unpassioned beauty of great machine, 796 : 16
Unpeel, white Godiva I u., 911 : 14
Unperceived decay, 370 : 3
Unperiphrastic 82 : 19
Unperplexed like migratory birds, 756 : 8
seeking find Him, 542 : 19
Unperturbed pace, 693 : 11
Unpitied sacrifice, 372 : 4
unrespited u. unreprieved, 284 : 11
Unpleasant, demd u. body, 547 : 15
Unpleasant (*continued*)
to meet Mr. Eliot, 806 : 14
Unpleasantest words that blotted paper, 199 : 30
Unpleased, in power u., 303 : 20
Unpleasing to a married ear, 191 : 13
Unpledged, mind was still u., 76 : 23
Unplumbed salt estranging sea, 585 : 14
Unpoetical, poet u., 479 : 18
Unpolluted, fair and u. flesh, 224 : 17
Unpopular, free trade u., 487 : 5
names impossible loyalties, 587 : 1
the more u. an opinion, 620 : 20
Unpossessed, is empire u., 187 : 22
Unpracticed, unlessoned girl u., 199 : 29
Unpremeditated art, 468 : 11
lay, 430 : 1
strain, 345 : 21
verse, 287 : 11
Unprepared courage, 421 : 1
magnificently u., 795 : 1
Unprincipled for good of unprincipled, 69 : 2
Unprofitable, how weary stale flat u., 218 : 5
servant, 40 : 31
Unprofitably, wasted oil u. burns, 376 : 6
Unpurged images of day, 716 : 8
Unqualified blessing, 419 : 4
Unquenchable, gleam of noble deeds ever u., 72 : 7
Unquiet, hate to be u. at home, 310 : 16
heart and brain, 531 : 21
how imagine u. slumbers, 562 : 7
meals make ill digestions, 188 : 14
slumbers, 562 : 7
Unravished bride of quietness, 477 : 4
Unread his works, 424 : *n* 2
vision, 806 : 3
Unreadable forty years from now, 453 : 17
Unreal, lead me from u. to real, 56 : 20
matter u. and temporal, 583 : 3
mockery hence, 238 : 29
Unreality and loud music, 894 : 5
Unreason, age of u., 872 : 18
and anti-intellectualism, 851 : 17
world's God full of u., 797 : 14
Unreckoning hearts, 900 : 2
Unredeemed, unblighted u. wilderness, 637 : 16
Unredressed, wrongs u., 428 : 12
Unreflecting herd, 429 : 3
Unreflectively, ceases to live u., 756 : 17
Unregarded time slips away, 756 : 1
Unregenerate, more about iniquity than u., 707 : 9
Unrelenting foe to love, 345 : 18
haughty Juno's u. hate, 306 : 11
our cruel and u. enemy, 379 : 2
Unremembered, nameless u. acts, 423 : 9
Unreprieved, unrespited unpitied u., 284 : 11
Unreproved pleasures free, 277 : 22
Unrequited toil, 524 : 7
Unrespited unpitied unreprieved, 284 : 11
Unrest, attacks on Court expression of u., 644 : 18
Capitalism creates social u., 785 : 4
fairest joys give u., 476 : 3

Unrest (*continued*)
frantic-mad with evermore u., 246 : 6
men miscall delight, 469 : 12
secret u. tortured, 481 : *n* 5
Unresting cells, 760 : 21
Unrestrained military power, 800 : 6
Unrestricted access to knowledge, 861 : 7
Unretracing, steady u. progress, 571 : 4
Unrighteous, if you know a thing is u., 89 : 6
man forsake his thoughts, 31 : 20
Unrighteousness, riches and honors by u., 68 : 21
Unripened beauties of north, 325 : 15
Unroll, page did ne'er u., 362 : 7
Unromantic as Monday morning, 555 : 21
Unruly, scepter snatched with u. hand, 202 : 3
Sun, 252 : 7
tongue an u. evil, 51 : 35
wit's an u. engine, 268 : 7
Unsafe, democracy u., 703 : 2
Unsaid, something u., 908 : 12
Unsatisfied indignation, 582 : 4
love u., 806 : 1
Unscathed, come through struggle u., 678 : 6
Unschooled, unlessoned girl u., 199 : 29
Unscottified, most u. of your countrymen, 355 : 9
Unsearchable dispose, 289 : 10
secret aims of nature, 654 : 14
Unseasonable and immoderate sleep, 353 : 4
Unseasoned telling found in legends, 906 : 4
Unseemly, not u. to die in defense, 58 : 23
Unseen, born to blush u., 362 : 8
by forms u. dirge sung, 364 : 9
counsel of the U. and Silent, 474 : 7
down u. full of water, 195 : 11
guess u. from seen, 652 : 14
I walk u., 278 : 18
ill habits by u. degrees, 307 : 2
in touch with u. powers, 686 : 8
jest u. inscrutable, 189 : 33
let me live u. unknown, 332 : 11
nature works by bodies u., 100 : 8
thou art u. yet I hear, 468 : 13
walk the earth u., 286 : 2
within thy airy shell, 279 : 18
Unselfish, absolutely u. friend is dog, 609 : 4
love of brute, 526 : 6
Unselfishness, modesty and u., 791 : 13
Unsettled, precedent not u. overnight, 730 : 14
Unsex me here, 236 : 17
Unshackled by party, 429 : 16
exercise of every faculty, 491 : 3
Unshaken, Tolstoi stands u., 601 : *n* 2
Unshorn fields boundless beautiful, 471 : 11
Unshut eye, 584 : 13
Unsifted in perilous circumstance, 219 : 4
Unsightly noisome things, 493 : 15
Unslayable, soul eternally u., 94 : 9
Unsmote by the sword, 459 : 16
Unsought, love u. is better, 214 : 17
Unsoundness of mind, 487 : 10
Unspeakable desire, 585 : 15
is sorrow you bid me renew, 104 : 31
Unspoken, words which were better u., 60 : 18
Unsponsored, solitude u. free, 767 : 4
Unspotted from the world, 51 : 32
Unstable as water, 9 : 4
become u. without knowing it, 78 : 9
feet u., 765 : 5
society unstable world, 736 : 11
woman always fickle u. thing, 105 : 10
Unstaid and skittish in motions, 213 : 29
Unstained, left u. what there found, 470 : 16
Unsteadiness of second class, 401 : 12
Unstilled world whirled, 806 : 4
Unsubstantial as shadows, 82 : 9
persistent faithful, 733 : 17
Unsuccessful or successful war, 376 : 18
Unsung noblest deed will die, 72 : 10
unwept unhonored u., 430 : 10
Unsunned, chaste as u. snow, 243 : 17
heaps of miser's treasure, 279 : 23
Unsure, habitation giddy and u., 206 : 7
what's to come still u., 213 : 23
Unsuspected isle in far-off seas, 540 : 17
Unswayed, is the sword u., 187 : 22
Untainted, what stronger breastplate than heart u., 185 : 17
Untamed continent, 592 : 6
indomitable u. as thee, 575 : 22
sullen u. intractable, 808 : 1
voice still heard, 557 : 18
woods u., 696 : 11
Untaught, called them u. knaves, 203 : 8
Untell the days, 257 : 17
Untender, so young and so u., 232 : 26
Untented Kosmos my abode, 669 : 3
Unthinkable, if u. thinking stops, 862 : 21
Unthinking, assault of thoughts on u., 783 : 11
time, 306 : 27
Unthread rude eye of rebellion, 202 : 14
Untidy, beginnings and endings u., 723 : 10
Until the day break, 28 : 9
Untilled air between, 869 : 6
Untimely grave, 271 : 23
graves, 377 : 6
'Unting, ain't 'u. as 'urts 'un, 660 : 14
Untitled aristocracy, 519 : 17
Untouched, strings u. will harshly jar, 183 : 18
Untrained hand, 624 : 10
to stand test, 648 : 9
Untraveled, gleams u. world, 529 : 8
heart u. turns to thee, 368 : 14
Untried, Christian ideal u., 742 : 2
difficult and left u., 742 : 2
emergencies, 568 : 17
new and u., 521 : 4
Untrodden, dwelt among u. ways, 424 : 12
Untroubling and untroubled where I lie, 470 : 9
Untrue, cloth u. twisted cue, 629 : 13
might telle his tale u., 146 : 15
narrative as a whole u., 592 : 7
thy lovers were all u., 307 : 1
unsad and evere u., 147 : 20
Untrustworthy, make man u. distrust, 723 : 22
Untruth, never dare utter u., 98 : 10
Untune, music shall u. the sky, 305 : 13
that string, 226 : 2
Untuned, like u. strings women are, 183 : 18
Untutored, Indian whose u. mind, 336 : 16
Untwist last strands of man, 656 : 15
Untwisting all the chains that tie, 278 : 7
Unum, E pluribus u., 106 : *n* 5
Unus, E pluribus u., 106 : *n* 5
Unused, fust in us u., 223 : 17
to the melting mood, 232 : 20
Unusual, cruel and u. punishment, 392 : 3
Unutterable, looked u. things, 345 : 9
Unuttered part of man's life, 472 : 12
Unvanquished, I u. and unyielding, 782 : 6
Unvarnished, round u. tale deliver, 229 : 25
Unveil, immortality u. third event, 607 : 18
Unveiled her peerless light, 285 : 25
Unveiling, uprising u. affirm, 526 : 5
Unvexed to the sea, 523 : 2
Unvictorious, conscripted u. ones, 795 : 16
Unwashed, great u., 445 : 2
lean u. artificer, 202 : 10
platters ride, 844 : 2
Unwastefully, manage affairs u., 618 : 10
Unwearied still lover by lover, 713 : 16
Unwelcome, bringer of u. news, 205 : 20
Unwept in eternal night, 108 : 13
unburied Patroclus, 59 : 9
unhonored unsung, 430 : 10
Unwholesome to eat oyster in months with no r, 166 : 12
Unwillingly I left your land, 105 : 19
to school, 211 : 15
Unwise to be heedless while giving advice, 114 : 5
Unwitting where Master dwells, 760 : 21
Unwomanly rags, 485 : 16
Unworthy, merit of the u. takes, 221 : 12
out of me u. unknown, 728 : 6
Unwritten ordinances, 80 : 17
written and u. law, 125 : 28
Unwrung, our withers are u., 222 : 16
Unyielding, Hades is u., 58 : 7
I unvanquished and u., 782 : 6
Unyoked humor of idleness, 203 : 5
Up and down City Road, 922 : 1
boots movin' u. and down again, 710 : 10
cannot bear leveling u., 354 : 13
game is u., 243 : 20
go u. and down as a talebearer, 10 : 20
lad when journey's over, 690 : 18
look not down but u., 544 : 13
look u. not down, 590 : 8
men to your posts, 596 : 12
mind thine aim, 494 : 1
nice to people on way u., 757 : 13
road u. and road down one and same, 70 : 6
rose sonne and Emelye, 146 : 25
Satan walking u. and down, 15 : 2
so floating many bells, 829 : 18
sunny side u., 825 : 8

Up (*continued*)
you've got to get u., 802 : 5
Upbraid my falsehood, 226 : 15
Upbringing, children look after own u., 909 : 4
Upharsin, Mene Mene Tekel U., 33 : 1
Uphill, road u. all the way, 608 : 10
Upholds, giant Atlas u., 76 : 25
Upland dim, 587 : 11
Uplifted, from despair thus high u., 284 : 3
loud u. angel trumpets, 281 : 10
Uplifting, in u. get underneath, 718 : 8
thoughts in baths, 834 : 8
Upmost, attains u. round, 215 : 16
Upon me soul Reilly, 922 : 17
Upper crust, 463 : 15, 481 : 3
materializing u. class, 589 : 4
part of mankind, 318 : 13
stiff u. lip, 594 : 5
Upraised, eyes u. as inspired, 364 : 14
Upright, as long as there is one u. man, 847 : 7
behold the u., 18 : 27
God hath made man u., 27 : 12
judge learned judge, 200 : 17
man is laughed to scorn, 15 : 28
man should be u. not kept u., 124 : 11
these set our flesh u., 254 : 1
walketh u. in a straight way, 132 : 15
Uprightness, man is born for u., 68 : 19
Uprising, my downsitting and mine u., 22 : 16
unveiling affirm, 526 : 5
Uproar, in bellow and u., 781 : 15
sand and wild u., 493 : 15
universal peace, 239 : 19
Uprose, Prince Lucifer u., 600 : 27
Upset calculations, 313 : 1
Upsets, art u., 776 : 1
Upside, world turned u. down, 258 : 11
Upstairs and downstairs, 537 : 6
equal u., 694 : 8
Upstart crow beautified with our feathers, 178 : 12
Upstream, only gamefish swims u., 686 : 5
Upswept angel wings, 817 : 3
Upturned, sea of u. faces, 431 : 25
Upward and inward delight, 570 : 5
as the sparks fly u., 15 : 15
climber u. turns face, 215 : 16
human race born to fly u., 142 : 2
look of caution, 749 : 11
still and onward, 567 : 8
toiling u. in night, 511 : 23
Upwards, astronomy compels soul to look u., 84 : 18
Uranium new source of energy, 763 : 11
Uranus, it may be in U., 557 : 6
Urban, complicated u. society, 814 : 1
crisis stems from failure, 900 : 14
for u. poor police arrest, 908 : 6
Urbi et orbi, 134 : 33
Urge and urge and urge, 574 : 13
no healths, 370 : *n* 3
of a song, 749 : 18
procreant u. of world, 574 : 13
to kill, 912 : 9
wrestle resurrection, 873 : 5
Uriah, set ye U. in forefront of battle, 13 : 18
Urine, turning wine into u., 789 : 6
Urn, bubbling loud-hissing u., 377 : 3
Urn (*continued*)
fills blue u. with fire, 494 : 18
Grecian U. worth old ladies, 838 : 13
lean on garden u., 804 : 10
storied u., 362 : 5
well-wrought u. becomes greatest ashes, 252 : 12
Urns, old sepulchral u., 376 : 6
Us, met enemy and it is u., 455 : *n* 1
then Finn again, 778 : 6
'Usband, man-o'-war's 'er 'u., 709 : 8
Use a little wine for stomach's sake, 50 : 33
again until eternity, 607 : 1
against the u. of nature, 236 : 11
all gently, 221 : 23
almost change nature, 223 : 11
and overuse word new, 623 : 3
any language you choose, 628 : 26
beauty too rich for u., 191 : 26
cannot u. talent, 852 : 12
come to deadly u., 234 : 23
doth breed habit, 190 : 7
every man after desert, 221 : 5
find but seldom u. them, 497 : 22
frequent u. of any organ, 393 : 7
glad to be of u., 803 : 17
God made for u. of men, 303 : 1
harms beauty, 706 : 7
him as though loved him, 271 : 11
I'll u. you for my mirth, 217 : 1
in measured language, 531 : 21
it and never wear it out, 64 : 2
it up wear it out, 924 : 4
know not how to u. victory, 94 : 7
living measured by u., 164 : 11
main thing is u. it well, 272 : 6
make proper u. of victories, 95 : 17
many books and never u. them, 258 : 2
materials indifferent but not u., 121 : 12
me to the limit, 687 : 2
no u. of metal, 247 : 26
not poor who has enough to u., 109 : 6
not to shine in u., 529 : 9
of force but temporary, 372 : 16
of him more than I see, 668 : 12
of riches better than possession, 153 : 12
public u. and custom, 163 : 13
rather in power than u., 227 : 9
ring worn thin by u., 100 : *n* 4
speak daggers but u. none, 222 : 24
sure to find u. for it, 432 : 14
treatment to help sick, 79 : 13
try to have and u. it, 87 : 25
tyrannous to u. it like giant, 228 : 9
want of u. mind torpid, 355 : 27
what's the u., 740 : 7
worship he found in u., 83 : 2
worst u. a man could be put to, 251 : 3
Used, I am u. to it, 523 : 3
I have u. similitudes, 33 : 15
key always bright, 347 : 24
knowledge not u. till seasoned, 519 : 14
man grows u. to everything, 581 : 18
my credit, 202 : 27
only witchcraft I have u., 229 : 31
wine good if well u., 230 : 27
Useful, be u. where thou livest, 268 : 8
Useful (*continued*)
books you may carry most u., 353 : 17
by magistrate equally u., 383 : 7
I'll try to be u. to country, 702 : 8
lesson to head, 377 : 14
mock their u. toil, 362 : 2
most beautiful most u., 696 : 6
nothing in house not u., 618 : 9
trouble of rain, 534 : 8
villain would have been u., 414 : 18
Usefulness common goal of nature, 884 : 2
Useless, art quite u., 674 : 23
better know u. things than nothing, 114 : 30
each without other, 511 : 18
general maxim u., 487 : 12
gold in itself u., 155 : 3
if object u. labor u., 562 : 17
laws weaken necessary laws, 341 : 9
life is early death, 395 : 9
lodged with me u., 282 : 15
most beautiful most u., 572 : 14
no man u. who has friend, 669 : 13
nothing u. is, 511 : 12
other virtues would be u., 298 : 1
second good third u., 154 : 3
slip u. away, 474 : 16
to excel, 357 : 10
to poet nothing u., 352 : 16
Uselessly, nature does nothing u., 87 : 27
Uselessness of men above sixty, 664 : 20
Uses, corner for others' u., 231 : 6
one art which u. things, 85 : 8
panics have u., 384 : 14
seem all u. of this world, 218 : 5
sweet are u. of adversity, 210 : 24
the more he u. for others, 65 : 10
to what base u. return, 224 : 15
Usher, House of U., 525 : 19
Ushered, still u. with tear, 334 : 26
Ushers in the morn, 349 : 10
Usquebae, wi' u. face the devil, 411 : 10
Usura sin against nature, 793 : 1
slayeth child in womb, 793 : 2
with U., 792 : 20
Usurpations, violent and sudden u., 398 : 4
Usurpers, lay proud u. low, 411 : 16
Usury, from all u. free, 106 : 23
lent heart with u., 441 : 9
Utilitarianism word of English spirit, 737 : 12
Utility, in science not seek immediate u., 584 : 1
nothing value but object of u., 562 : 17
of futility, 90 : 4
of useful things, 90 : 4
or cost of production, 652 : 2
the Greatest Happiness Principle, 508 : 18
Utmost bound of human thought, 529 : 10
bound of the everlasting hills, 9 : 6
Thule, 103 : 25
Utopia, literature is my U., 771 : 1
principality in U., 488 : 5
Utter, feel it cannot u. it, 852 : 11
liberty to u., 282 : 4
not both live and u. it, 558 : 24
not in u. nakedness, 426 : 14
not u. what do not know, 203 : 24

Utter (*continued*)
nothing for which not responsible, 522 : 11
sweet breath, 197 : 11
wise man u. vain knowledge, 15 : 36
would tongue u., 530 : 19
Utterance, action nor u., 216 : 28
civil limitation daunts u., 601 : 3
divine u., 601 : 8
of early gods, 478 : 3
Uttered, not u. by chapmen's tongues, 190 : 19
or unexpressed, 429 : 18
part of man's life, 472 : 12
Uttereth, day unto day u. speech, 17 : 27
fool u. all his mind, 25 : 31
wisdom u. her voice, 23 : 3
Uttering such dulcet breath, 196 : 14
Utterly destroy power of reasoning, 85 : 13
things sweet, 829 : 20
Uttermost parts of the sea, 22 : 17
Uzzah put forth his hand, 13 : 15

V

V sign is symbol and portent, 745 : 4
Vacancy, gloomy calm of idle v., 354 : 18
Vacant, body filled and v. mind, 208 : 7
chair, 511 : 10, 552 : 18
heart hand eye, 432 : 1
interlunar cave, 288 : 21
interstellar spaces, 807 : 16
laugh that spoke v. mind, 370 : 4
mind distressed, 376 : 8
powers, 813 : 14
stuffs out v. garments, 201 : 26
the v. go into the v., 807 : 16
Vacationless, mothers and housewives v., 867 : 8
Vacillating, damned v. state, 527 : 16
Vacuity, indolent v. of thought, 377 : 7
Vacuous, keeps their hearts v., 63 : 14
Vacuum, author's life a v., 597 : 7
nature abhors a v., 308 : 4
think in v., 698 : 6
Vade in pace, 134 : 34
salutatem pro me liber, 145 : *n* 4
Vae victis, 134 : 35
Vagabond shalt thou be, 7 : 17
Vagaries of unattached relatives, 826 : 15
Vague, boundaries shadowy and v., 526 : 7
crepuscular time, 564 : 4
evolution from v. to definite, 639 : 10
The V. and Elusive, 64 : 7
Vagueness perhaps ignorance, 577 : 8
Vain, a' is done in v., 410 : 5
ah v. English fields, 587 : 11
all delights are v., 190 : 10
ambition of kings, 262 : 11
beauty is v., 26 : 10
begot of v. fantasy, 191 : 24
behold thee flippant v., 475 : 3
blood pour in v., 684 : 14
bring no more v. oblations, 28 : 29
call it not v., 430 : 8
citadels not walled, 827 : 7
deluding Joys, 278 : 9
Vain (*continued*)
denial v. and coy excuse, 280 : 9
desire vain regret, 601 : 21
Doric discipline, 715 : 12
dream of joy all but in v., 149 : *n* 1
every man walketh in a v. show, 19 : 3
fools make such v. keeping, 262 : 7
hatching v. empires, 284 : 15
hence all you v. delights, 261 : 4
I have not lived in v., 326 : 7
ignobly v., 334 : 14
ill-natured Englishman, 318 : 6
in v. always in v., 684 : 14
in v. to wish for death, 75 : 3
king grew v., 306 : 17
know we loved in v., 456 : 7
labor and wounds v., 564 : 16
man may become proud, 308 : 12
man pleased with effect on people, 736 : 7
man v. diverse undulating, 164 : 6
mock on 'tis all in v., 406 : 3
most v. most generous, 663 : 8
my weary search to find, 369 : 5
name of the Lord in v., 10 : 5
nor yet too v. to mend, 333 : 22
not in v., 746 : 5
oblations, 28 : 29
pain to love in v., 295 : 9
parcel of v. strivings, 557 : 2
people imagine a v. thing, 17 : 13
pomp and glory, 56 : 4, 249 : 3
profane and v. babblings, 51 : 5
pursuit of human glory, 271 : 23
says a lot in v. refusing, 395 : 10
sealed in v., 228 : 28
shallow thought, 493 : 17
spend not then his gifts in v., 255 : 16
the Present teaches in v., 737 : 1
they are disquieted in v., 19 : 3
they labor in v., 22 : 8
to look for defense against lightning, 112 : 7
tribute of a smile, 430 : 7
war with heaven, 284 : 3
was the chief's pride, 339 : 32
watchman waketh but in v., 22 : 8
wisdom all, 284 : 20
wise man utter v. knowledge, 15 : 36
words in your oaths, 130 : 13
youth is v., 434 : 3
Vaincrons parce que plus forts, 761 : *n* 2
Vaine, la vie est v., 617 : *n* 1
Vainglory, from pride v. and hypocrisy, 55 : 10
humble through v., 165 : 11
pleasance here all v., 153 : 7
Vainness, lying v. drunkenness, 214 : 26
Vale, ave atque v., 102 : *n* 7
depart this v., 772 : 6
far sunken, 478 : 2
meanest floweret of v., 362 : 20
meet thee in hollow v., 267 : 6
of soul-making, 480 : 2
of years, 231 : 5
sequestered v. of life, 362 : 12
violet-embroidered v., 279 : 18
Valentine, heart shaped like v., 888 : 4
Vales, hills v. woodland plain, 334 : 15
o'er v. and hills, 427 : 7
of meadowsweet, 846 : 15
Valet, hero to his v., 88 : *n* 8
not aware of this, 88 : 26
Valets, masters worthy v., 378 : 5
Valiant, as v. I honor him, 216 : 15
be v. not too venturous, 175 : 9
brothers v., 919 : 14
dust, 209 : 6
England breeds v. creatures, 207 : 25
he who would v. be, 302 : *n* 4
if you are very v., 57 : 7
in velvet, 663 : 8
never taste of death but once, 215 : 26
reproof v., 213 : 4
souls of heroes, 57 : 3
trencherman, 208 : 23
Validation, validity process of v., 650 : 11
Validity process of validation, 650 : 11
what v. and pitch, 213 : 8
Valkyries, ride of the V., 552 : 16
Valley, all in the v. of death, 533 : 9
bicker down v., 533 : 15
darker grows the v., 601 : 2
down in the v., 920 : 19
every v. shall be exalted, 30 : 31
he paweth in the v., 16 : 37
hill becomes the v., 875 : 3
his golden cup, 600 : 25
may v. streams content me, 104 : 4
of Ajalon, 11 : 34
of decision, 33 : 18
of dry bones, 32 : 28
of Humiliation, 302 : 2
of reveries, 750 : 15
of Shadow, 527 : 5
of shadow of death, 18 : 7
sheep fatter, 455 : 2
spirit of the v. never dies, 64 : 2
take me to green v., 927 : 15
Valleys, greenest of our v., 526 : 1
groves hills fields, 183 : 8
hills and v. dales and fields, 183 : *n* 5
lick v. up, 605 : 18
lily of the v., 28 : 4
of Hall, 651 : 10
piping down v. wild, 403 : 2
Vallombrosa, strow the brooks in V., 283 : 16
Valor, as well as v. may, 534 : 20
better part of v. discretion, 205 : 14
birthplace of v., 410 : 8
brute beauty and v., 656 : 3
constancy and v. our shield, 744 : 9
courtesy wins as v., 534 : 20
deed whereat v. will weep, 242 : 27
God's help and their v., 420 : 12
good speed to your youthful v., 106 : 3
he for v. formed, 285 : 18
mighty men of v., 11 : 30
my v. is certainly going, 398 : 18
no need of v., 82 : 28
plucks dead lions, 201 : 13
thy v. prevail, 484 : 1
to which monuments reared, 650 : 13
uncommon v. common virtue, 791 : 14
who would true v. see, 302 : 14
Valorous, Roland v. Oliver wise, 136 : 13
Valparaiso, night in V., 861 : 2
Valuable, byproduct more v., 689 : 25
coin of thinker, 887 : 15
if riches v. to heaven, 322 : 9
reputation more v. than money, 110 : 19

Valuable (*continued*)
something v. as object, 422 : 15
time most v. thing, 91 : 17
truth most v. thing, 625 : 2
what v. not new, 444 : 13, 451 : 13
Valuation, government resting on v. of property, 85 : 2
superstitious v. of Europe, 652 : 5
Value at a penny talk of old men, 101 : 18
book counts more than v., 639 : 1
carry body for its sentimental v., 870 : 2
cynic knows v. of nothing, 675 : 11
dearness only gives v., 384 : 13
easier discover deficiency than see v., 422 : 14
from stamp of ages, 302 : 18
governed by utility or cost of production, 652 : 2
hard latent v., 653 : 13
is life-giving power of thing, 572 : 20
it next to good conscience, 271 : 13
Jews generally give v., 681 : 17
men of less v. than gold, 155 : 3
no v. when possessed, 316 : 15
none but horizontal, 868 : 1
nothing has v., 764 : 10
nothing v. but object of utility, 562 : 17
of sentiment is sacrifice, 723 : 5
of what entrepreneur contributes, 784 : 28
of what poet has written, 809 : 19
rubs enhance v. of favors, 369 : 8
supreme v. not future but present, 886 : 3
survival as a v., 862 : 11
then we rack the v., 209 : 31
what gives life v., 863 : 3
Valued, loss of lives cannot be v., 265 : 9
Valueless, reading v. books, 573 : 1
Values anything more than freedom, 751 : 20
Vampire, like v. dead many times, 638 : 11
Vanessa extraordinary woman, 322 : *n* 2
Vanilla of society, 433 : 1
Vanish from the plain, 562 : 10
like evil spirits, 389 : 12
where did children v., 864 : 16
with the rose, 517 : 12
Vanished and shrunk away, 182 : 3
Cheshire Cat v. slowly, 611 : 17
past v. like dream, 473 : 28
touch of v. hand, 530 : 19
Vanishes, man loves what v., 715 : 7
Vanisheth, life a vapor that v., 52 : 3
Vanishing, keep beauty from v., 656 : 12
never there already v., 907 : 4
race, 836 : 14
Vanitas vanitatum, 539 : 10
Vanities, guides us by v., 804 : 14
man of my v., 772 : 12
Vanity, all is v., 26 : 11
all others but v., 440 : 4
and vexation of spirit, 26 : 16
beauty without v., 456 : 9
collars and leashes of v., 907 : 24
conscience or v. appalled, 716 : 13
cords of v., 29 : 6
Vanity (*continued*)
cry out v. of world, 309 : 3
cured of every folly but v., 358 : 25
dispel v. with v., 126 : 13
every man at his best state is v., 19 : 2
extreme actions ascribed to v., 657 : 9
Fair, 302 : 5, 539 : 7
give no hollow aid, 458 : 8
Golden V., 935 : 4
hath not lifted his soul unto v., 18 : 8
highest v. love of fame, 703 : 12
in years, 204 : 5
my days are v., 15 : 22
no competition no v., 355 : 16
no love but v., 454 : 10
of human hopes, 352 : 5
of immediate auditor, 783 : 4
of vanities, 26 : 11
plays tricks with memory, 683 : 10
pull down thy v., 793 : 4
repeyreth hom fro worldly v., 145 : 8
tickle one's v., 583 : 9
tilling soil of v., 750 : 16
town is lighter than v., 302 : 5
Vanquished by desire, 63 : 9
had Cato, 118 : 5
Macbeth never v. be, 239 : 12
one safety to v., 105 : 2
though v. argue still, 370 : 11
victor's terms on v., 682 : 9
Vans, omnibuses and v., 781 : 15
to beat the air, 805 : 21
Vantage, coign of v., 236 : 21
might v. best have took, 228 : 7
Vantage-ground of truth, 100 : *n* 7
Vapor, floating like v. on air, 598 : 6
life a v. that vanisheth, 52 : 3
like bear or lion, 241 : 17
live upon v. of dungeon, 231 : 6
Vaporized no public buildings, 777 : 10
Vapors both away, 253 : 14
congregation of v., 220 : 28
strangle him, 203 : 5
weep their burthen, 533 : 27
Variable as the shade, 431 : 2
lest thy love prove v., 192 : 11
mysterious independent v., 595 : 18
Variableness, with whom is no v., 51 : 29
Variation if useful preserved, 514 : 14
Varied, mob is v. and inconstant, 308 : 23
natural and v. abundance, 824 : 12
rule the v. year, 345 : 4
Variety, abjure my so much loved v., 253 : 21
about New England weather, 622 : 18
democracy full of v., 85 : 3
in spite of v. and power, 586 : 8
infinite v., 241 : 1
joy of life is v., 352 : 13
mother of enjoyment, 501 : 4
no pleasure unseasoned by v., 111 : 9
order in v. we see, 334 : 15
soul of pleasure, 312 : 14
Variety's spice of life, 376 : 22
Various, a man so v., 304 : 10
as lovely so be v., 833 : 3
as your land, 840 : 4
constant as v., 833 : 3
distribution of property, 398 : 2
gift to each, 511 : 14
of v. stuff the v. man, 410 : 16
Various (*continued*)
so v. so beautiful so new, 587 : 16
speaks a v. language, 471 : 2
stops of v. quills, 281 : 5
Varium et mutabile femina, 105 : *n* 5
Varnished clock, 370 : 13
Varsovie, l'ordre règne a V., 439 : *n* 1
Varying shore of the world, 241 : 20
Vase, shatter v. if you will, 447 : 2
Vases, beads dolls cloths v., 889 : 12
Vassal, God how fine a v., 137 : 3
Muse I was your v., 673 : 11
Vassals and serfs at side, 480 : 11
Vast and furious ocean, 265 : 7
complex technological world, 861 : 7
conspiracy against law, 908 : 6
dead v. and middle of night, 218 : 18
deserts of v. eternity, 296 : 28
edges drear, 587 : 16
heaven's net is v., 65 : 6
how v. a memory has Love, 332 : 14
how v. unattained, 532 : *n* 5
intelligence were v. enough, 397 : 17
like a v. shadow moved, 299 : 6
lodge in v. wilderness, 376 : 18
mass of London itself, 744 : 5
more devils than v. hell, 197 : 12
single object suggests v. conditions, 565 : 15
slow-breathing unconscious, 651 : 3
soul o'er him planned, 493 : 20
structure of recollection, 733 : 17
struggle to found Roman state, 104 : 17
wings across skies, 821 : 12
Vaster, grow v. than empires, 296 : 27
Vastness and age and memories, 525 : 16
Vasty, call spirits from v. deep, 204 : 12
hall of death, 586 : 4
Vat, every v. stand upon bottom, 301 : 23
Vater werden ist nicht schwer, 610 : *n* 5
Vaterland, lieb V. magst ruhig sein, 573 : *n* 2
Vats, cheeses out of v., 541 : 1
parcel of boilers and v., 356 : 20
Vault, fretted v., 362 : 4
left this v. to brag of, 238 : 7
Vaulter in sunny grass, 454 : 3
Vaulting ambition, 236 : 24
Vaults, heaven's v. should crack, 235 : 16
Vaunt-couriers to thunderbolts, 233 : 24
Vaunted works of art, 495 : 14
Vaunteth, charity v. of not, 48 : 23
Vauntie, her best and she was v., 411 : 12
Vaunting aloud, 283 : 9
Vaward of our youth, 205 : 27
Vécu, j'ai v., 394 : 9
rose a v. ce que vivent les roses, 176 : *n* 11
Vegetable, halfmoon's v. eye, 886 : 15
love not suit me, 628 : 7
my v. love should grow, 296 : 27
Vegetate like the country, 445 : 10
Vegetative gracefulness, 789 : 9
Vehicle, idea is to make v., 897 : 2
Veil, my v. no mortal ever took up, 120 : 20
of temple rent, 41 : 28
painted v. called life, 467 : *n* 2
through which not see, 516 : 18

Veiled jokes tiptoe malices, 701 : 7
melancholy, 478 : 1
Veiling lightnings of song, 469 : 8
Veillons dormants et veillants dormons, 165 : *n* 5
Veils, religion v. her fires, 340 : 28
Vein, divided to the v., 911 : 1
Ercles' v. a tyrant's v., 196 : 4
King Cambyses' v., 204 : 4
not in giving v. today, 187 : 16
Veined humanity, 506 : 14
Veins, blood burns in v., 576 : 16
bound bones and v. in me, 655 : 19
dried sap out of v., 713 : 6
in my v. red life, 478 : 8
man's v. net gods made, 850 : 14
miracle in v. of man, 850 : 1
sea itself floweth in v., 311 : 20
Velasquez, not V. never Rembrandt, 884 : 23
why drag in V., 619 : 13
Velocities of evanescent increments, 330 : 21
Velvet, gilded and covered with v., 420 : 11
iron hand in v. glove, 161 : 19
live like v. mole, 793 : 19
some in v. gowns, 933 : 21
valiant in v., 663 : 8
walk in v. shoes, 793 : 17
Venenum, ali cibus aliis v., 101 : *n* 6
Venerable, brotherhood of v. trees, 426 : 8
every tradition grows v., 657 : 10
parts of constitution, 373 : 10
Venerably dull, 375 : 7
Venerate four characters, 386 : 11
Veneration, much v. but no rest, 180 : 19
nation's memory and v., 761 : 1
Venetian, Turk beat a V., 232 : 21
Vengeance, blood v. desolation, 579 : 3
for v. do nothing, 609 : 9
in the day of v., 23 : 15
is mine, 47 : 24
just my v. complete, 540 : 31
nor one feeling of v., 400 : 10
of history terrible, 770 : 8
Veni vidi vici, 99 : *n* 16
Venial, sins of omission v., 357 : 11
Venice, at V. gave his body, 195 : 8
death in V., 755 : 19
in commonwealth of V. this inscription, 259 : 13
more than any man in V., 198 : 5
on Bridge of Sighs, 458 : 5
sate in state, 458 : 6
Venienti occurrite morbo, 117 : *n* 7
Venizelos observed, 745 : 13
Venom, bubbling v. flings, 457 : 2
clamors of jealous woman, 188 : 13
Nazi v., 865 : 10
Venomous, like toad ugly and v., 210 : 24
no means too v., 658 : 17
Vent, his tongue must v., 242 : 20
le v. se lève, 735 : *n* 4
Ventre affamé, 296 : *n* 8
Ventricle of memory, 190 : 30
Venture, each v. new beginning, 807 : 21
naught v. naught have, 160 : 12
nothing v. nothing win, 629 : 2
to call himself architect, 431 : 21
Ventured like wanton boys, 249 : 3
neck or nothing, 542 : 18
Ventures, lose our v., 217 : 6
not in one bottom trusted, 197 : 25
Venturing, among radiant v. on, 761 : 1
Venturous, be valiant not too v., 175 : 9
Venus grown fat, 454 : 9
here choose dwelling, 306 : 6
herself fastened to prey, 312 : 8
mingles sweet bitterness with cares, 102 : 10
nurturing V., 100 : 1
one touch of V., 861 : 8
take my votive glass, 321 : 1
Vénus toute entière, 312 : *n* 5
Veracity, entertain doubt of my v., 385 : 9
heart of morality, 596 : 1
not in saying truth, 437 : 7
which increases with age, 294 : 6
Verb, emerges with v. in mouth, 624 : 9
God is a v., 832 : 7
Verba, rem tene v. sequentur, 95 : *n* 9
Verbal, poem a v. contraption, 869 : 10
Verbiage, mistaking v. for truths, 735 : 9
Verbosity, thread of his v., 191 : 6
Verdant land, 570 : 14
Verdantly, entwine itself v., 446 : 11
Verderben, und das war mein V., 396 : *n* 7
Verdict afterwards, 612 : 12
one wise man's v., 543 : 6
Verdun, Ypres and V., 761 : 6
Verdure, vast forest v., 592 : 6
Vereker's secret, 653 : 7
Verge, ability to get to v., 803 : 8
ample room and v. enough, 363 : 5
on very v. of her confine, 233 : 19
Verification, verity process of v., 650 : 11
Verify your references, 402 : 9
Véritable Amphitryon, 298 : *n* 2
Veritable ocean, 767 : 15
Veritas, amicus Plato sed magis amica v., 87 : *n* 6
in vino v., 62 : *n* 12, 134 : 6
magna est v., 34 : *n* 2
non erubescit, 126 : *n* 4
odium parit, 96 : *n* 3
Veritatem dies aperit, 115 : *n* 2
Vérité que ces montagnes, 165 : *n* 5
Verities and truths of heart, 838 : 8
Verity is an event, 650 : 11
religious feeling a v., 580 : 9
verifying itself, 650 : 11
which drags me to ground, 380 : 3
Vermeer, whether Rembrandt or V., 734 : 13
Vermeil-tinctured lip, 280 : 1
Vermin, pearls and v., 489 : 8
race of odious v., 322 : 11
Vermont, as Maine so goes V., 923 : *n* 2
indomitable people of V., 736 : 19
mountains stretch straight, 747 : 20
Vermouth, not the v., 855 : 16
union of gin and v., 837 : 10
Vernal, breath of v. shower, 363 : 13
flowers, 281 : 1
one impulse from v. wood, 423 : 7
seasons of the year, 281 : 21
sight of v. bloom, 285 : 5
Verneint, der Geist der stets v., 396 : *n* 4
Vero, se non è v. è ben trovato, 387 : *n* 1
Versailles, death sentence of V., 812 : 19
was a gulf, 592 : 10
Verse, able to bumbast out blank v., 178 : 12
all not prose is v., 298 : 9
art of Racine's v., 735 : 10
brings to his v. cadence, 311 : 3
cheered with ends of v., 291 : 14
cursed be the v., 338 : 17
find him who sermon flies, 268 : 2
give up v. my boy, 792 : 17
gives immortal youth, 442 : 21
happy who in v. steer, 311 : 2
immortal v. becomes hieroglyphic, 703 : 7
make the first v. well, 297 : 13
married to immortal v., 278 : 6
my v. sad no wonder, 692 : 6
no rhymes in my v., 724 : 9
octosyllabic v., 459 : 8
of all my v. like not, 668 : 17
read out my v., 162 : 12
says in v. what others say in prose, 339 : 25
statues pictures v. grand, 618 : 17
subject of all v., 265 : 15
superfluous v., 512 : 23
this v. grave for me, 668 : 20
unpremeditated v., 287 : 11
whatever I tried to write was v., 113 : 29
will seem prose, 316 : 6
yet write v. badly, 297 : 31
Versed, deep v. in books, 288 : 17
in reasonings of men, 76 : 12
Verse-reciter, tiresome v. Care, 470 : 4
Verses, Appius says in v., 103 : 5
as literary performance, 577 : 12
doctrine hidden under strange v., 141 : 7
false gallop of v., 212 : 4
I hate my v., 797 : 19
indignation will produce v., 121 : 24
no one ever get at my v., 577 : 12
on dark theme trace v. of light, 100 : 10
poverty drove me to writing v., 109 : 15
praise v. but read something else, 119 : 8
quire of bad v., 488 : 12
rhyme rudder of v., 291 : 8
stop abusing my v. or publish, 119 : 4
underneath the bough, 516 : 7
writes v. speaks holiday, 225 : 20
Versing, relish v., 269 : 5
Versions, one religion hundred v., 680 : 12
Vertebrae, stiffening of v., 679 : 10
Vertical man, 868 : 1
Very beadle to humorous sigh, 190 : 25
God of very God, 55 : 3
Vesper now raising his light, 102 : 8
Vespers, barefoot friars singing v., 384 : 7
Vessel, a chosen v., 46 : 7
empty v. greatest sound, 208 : 12
gilded v. goes, 363 : 6
goodly v., 511 : 6
he that v. made, 517 : 7
I am like a broken v., 18 : 16
of more ungainly make, 517 : 8

Vessel (*continued*)
of my genius now hoists sails, 141 : 17
one v. unto honor, 47 : 16
strikes with shivering shock, 440 : 1
though masts be firm, 558 : 9
wife the weaker v., 52 : 13
Vessels, noblest of sailing v., 800 : 10
oft handled brightly shine, 183 : 18
terrible tempest separated v., 151 : 10
Vest, casting the body's v., 297 : 4
neither v. nor pants, 620 : 4
Vestal's, blameless v. lot, 335 : 4
Vestige, no v. of a beginning, 367 : 12
Vestigia, agnosco veteris v. flammae, 105 : *n* 4
Vestments, priestly v. in dens, 592 : 6
Vesture, cast lots upon my v., 18 : 6
muddy v. of decay, 201 : 1
Vesuvius' crater for inkstand, 571 : 1
Veteran, lags the v. on stage, 351 : 21
Veuf, le v. l'inconsolé, 514 : *n* 5
Vex and oppress each other, 398 : 2
definition of oats meant to v., 352 : *n* 3
not his ghost, 235 : 19
such injury v. a saint, 188 : 35
Vexation, multiplication is v., 917 : 13
only to understand the report, 30 : 15
travail and v. of spirit, 26 : 23
vanity and v. of spirit, 26 : 16
Vexed with mirth ear of night, 456 : 20
Vexes public men, 530 : 16
Vexing dull ear of drowsy man, 202 : 1
Viands, what v. he preferred, 666 : 15
Vias, stare super v. antiquas, 31 : *n* 4
Vibrate sweetest pleasure, 410 : 1
Vibrates in memory, 469 : 18
Vibration, brave v. each way free, 266 : 22
Vibrations, deaden its v., 512 : 11
of deathless music, 728 : 6
Vicar, justice judge or v., 398 : 26
of Bray, 920 : 6
Vicars, God as revealed to v., 864 : 17
Vice, abolish v. destroy virtue, 274 : 18
accommodating v., 298 : 3
amusements keep people from v., 355 : 1
any taint of v., 214 : 26
avarice not so much a v., 308 : *n* 5
best virtue has tincture of v., 165 : 12
boredom v. and need, 343 : 13
bullied out of v., 500 : 22
by action dignified, 192 : 20
creature of heejous mien, 722 : 4
discourage and abolish tyranny and v., 380 : 6
distinction between virtue and v., 354 : 12
dreary morals like v., 669 : 14
encourage no v., 370 : *n* 3
extremism in defense of liberty no v., 385 : *n* 2
gathered every v., 340 : 27
good old-gentlemanly v., 261 : *n* 8
homage v. pays to virtue, 293 : 27
hypocrisy v. of vices, 866 : 10
inherent v. of capitalism, 746 : 16
lashed v. spared name, 322 : 19
lost half its evil, 373 : 25
moderation in principle a v., 385 : 4
monster of frightful mien, 337 : 5
no v. so simple, 199 : 25
pleasure of itself not v., 356 : 5
Vice (*continued*)
pride v. of fools, 332 : 19
prosperity best discover v., 180 : 7
raptures and roses of v., 632 : 11
reverend v., 204 : 5
schools nurseries of v., 349 : 14
to be intent upon our interests, 97 : 6
to flee v. beginning of virtue, 108 : 17
truce between virtue and v., 560 : 8
virtue is not desiring v., 680 : 26
virtue itself turns v., 192 : 20
virtue of v. pardon beg, 223 : 9
virtue or v. leaves scar, 648 : 11
virtue sold and almost every v., 256 : 7
when v. prevails, 326 : 2
Vice-presidency most insignificant office ever contrived, 381 : 16
Vice-President be removed on impeachment, 391 : 11
Viceroy, outward soul v., 253 : 11
Vices, all v. of our generation, 553 : 1
and follies of humankind, 324 : 6
aped from white men, 837 : 20
capable of greatest v., 272 : 7
committed genteelly, 355 : 13
fathered by heroism, 804 : 15
good to be without v., 597 : 11
make a ladder of our v., 129 : 10
may be of use, 391 : 8
of v. frame ladder, 511 : 22
our pleasant v., 235 : 14
public officer without v., 591 : 11
small v. do appear, 235 : 3
virtues of man without v., 456 : 9
virtues v. in disguise, 292 : 21
Vici, veni vidi v., 99 : *n* 16
Vicious circle, 617 : 1
display their v. nature, 154 : 7
perfect circle and v. circle, 881 : 2
Viciousness, poverty the parent of v., 84 : 12
Vicissitude, greatest v. of things, 181 : 15
of sects and religions, 181 : 15
sad v. of things, 359 : 17
Vicissitudes, changing v. of life, 679 : 1
in all things, 96 : 17
of fortune, 383 : 14
wild v. of taste, 351 : 13
Vicisti Galilaee, 127 : *n* 4
Victim, I v. and executioner, 581 : 1
must be found, 629 : 6
o' cunnubiality, 546 : 19
O saving V. opening wide, 139 : 12
power marks its v., 444 : 4
without murmuring, 591 : 11
Victim's, tumor kills v. sympathies, 634 : 23
Victims, little v. play, 361 : 10
priests altars v., 335 : *n* 1
Victis, vae v., 134 : 35
Victor belongs to spoils, 835 : 2
can go it alone, 556 : 1
eventual v., 767 : 22
had gods vanquished had Cato, 118 : 5
or announcer of the victor, 70 : 20
to v. belong spoils, 455 : 11
Victoria uti nescis, 94 : *n* 5
Victorians, raging productivity of V., 889 : 3
turned admiration into hero worship, 663 : 6
Victories, after thousand v. foiled, 244 : 7
eight v. over Syracusans, 78 : 2
go forward give us v., 523 : 1
Liberty knows nothing but v., 538 : 16
make proper use of v., 95 : 17
of mighty generals, 575 : 8
peace hath her v., 282 : 14
worse than defeat, 565 : 1
Victorious, hold your hand v., 77 : 9
o'er ills o' life v., 411 : 7
rejoice we are v., 71 : 19
renowned expedition, 702 : 11
those which are v., 421 : 2
Victor's terms on vanquished, 682 : 9
Victors, let v. in, 536 : 3
let v. when they come, 588 : 3
most glorious to v., 81 : 10
Victory, another such v. and we are undone, 92 : 10
at all costs, 744 : 1
beautiful bright-colored flower, 743 : 4
best kind of v., 171 : 4
blessed with v. and peace, 446 : 2
by bombing Chinese cities, 788 : 15
by expanding conflict, 788 : 15
Cadmean v., 78 : 7
death swallowed in v., 49 : 8
defeat preface to v., 809 : 14
dishonest v. at Chaeronea, 282 : 6
fell in the great v., 439 : 12
for humanity, 480 : 14
God of Clotilda grant v., 129 : 19
gory bed or to v., 411 : 15
grave has no v., 637 : 17
grave where is thy v., 49 : 8
highest point not v., 783 : 2
hundred fathers, 857 : 11
if not v. is yet revenge, 284 : 7
illusion of philosophers, 837 : 18
in spite of terror, 744 : 1
in v. magnanimity, 746 : 11
know how to win v. Hannibal, 94 : 7
MacArthur had in mind, 788 : 15
morale wins v., 771 : 12
no substitute for v., 771 : 6
not v. nor defeat, 686 : 13
on day of v. no one tired, 132 : 26
over reason, 812 : 13
peace without v., 682 : 9
Pyrrhic v., 92 : *n* 8
rampant for spoil and v., 658 : 5
right and wrong kind of v., 788 : 15
shifts from man to man, 58 : 3
spirit that gains v., 791 : 15
swallow up death in v., 30 : 8
terror wins easiest v., 812 : 13
thine O Lord is the v., 14 : 25
this alone life and v., 467 : 10
together achieve v., 815 : 12
'twas a famous v., 439 : 14
Westminster Abbey or v., 408 : 4
without v. no survival, 744 : 1
world beyond v., 745 : 11
Victrix deis victa Catoni, 118 : *n* 4
Victuals, not difficult to please about v., 546 : *n* 2
served v. course by course, 743 : 15
Vida, toda la v. es sueño, 273 : *n* 1
Vidders, be careful o' v., 546 : 18
Video meliora deteriora sequor, 113 : *n* 15

Vidi, veni v. vici, 99 : *n* 16
Vie apparié à un songe, 165 : *n* 5
la v. est un songe, 165 : *n* 5
la v. est vaine, 617 : *n* 1
with Zeus, 59 : 24
Vieille, quand vous serez bien v., 162 : *n* 8
Vieillesse est l'enfer des femmes, 296 : *n* 4
si v. pouvait, 163 : 11
Viet Cong, no quarrel with V., 915 : 13
Vietnam, on war in V., 915 : 13
Vieux, aussi v. que le journal d'aujourdhui, 741 : *n* 1
bons v. temps, 928 : 4
View, American point of v., 574 : 6
beast in v., 307 : 1
both worlds at once they v., 276 : 12
choice of point of v., 784 : 12
demon in my v., 525 : 6
eye like mind sought extended v., 387 : *n* 2
fair Melrose, 430 : 4
gloomy v. of future, 758 : 8
keep end in v., 118 : 8
made myself motley to the v., 245 : 16
man stern to v., 370 : 10
observation with extensive v., 351 : 16
ourselves with clearer eyes, 267 : 5
prejudice cut off v., 695 : 16
recollection presents to v., 455 : 6
which has grander v., 492 : 2
with hollow eye, 200 : 15
world invisible we v., 693 : 16
worm's-eye v., 848 : 15
Viewed his own feather, 456 : 17
in her face's field, 189 : 17
View-halloo, Peel's v., 474 : 19
Viewing, by v. Nature, 303 : 4
verses as literary performance, 577 : 12
Viewless, imprisoned in v. winds, 228 : 20
Views, adopt new v. if true v., 522 : 7
not do something to people for v. they express, 794 : 18
right v., 73 : 2
take short v., 432 : 21
Vigil in soft face of girl, 74 : 23
tongueless v., 632 : 7
Vigilance, energy and sleepless v., 523 : 1
eternal v., 397 : 21, 814 : 20
while people retain v., 521 : 13
wrenlike v., 893 : 12
Vigilant, be sober be v., 52 : 16
haughty v. resolute, 488 : 12
to the v. active brave, 383 : 3
Vigils, pensive poets pensive v., 340 : 16
Vigny more secret, 504 : 5
Vigor, exist in undiminished v., 488 : 7
flows like tides, 819 : 4
from the limb, 457 : 12
in man not yet old, 116 : 2
in what they ought to do, 89 : 14
inaction saps v. of mind, 152 : 8
O future V., 673 : 19
of bone, 226 : 20
press with v. on, 346 : 1
takes v. from arms, 373 : 10
what v. it will give style, 433 : 14
Vigorous, characteristics of v. mind, 352 : 4
Vigorous (*continued*)
elastic and v. thought, 559 : 22
survive and multiply, 515 : 2
writing concise, 729 : 7
Vigueur, ô future V., 673 : *n* 12
Vile antithesis, 339 : 2
behold I am v., 17 : 2
better v. than v. esteemed, 245 : 22
blows and buffets, 238 : 15
durance v., 411 : 23
dust whence he sprung, 430 : 10
fled from this v. world, 244 : 26
George the First v., 753 : *n* 3
guns, 203 : 11
ill-favored faults, 225 : 21
insect that has risen up, 346 : 4
make so v. a pun, 318 : 1
make v. things precious, 233 : 30
makes nice of no v. hold, 202 : 3
man that mourns, 336 : 22
not one altogether v., 720 : 3
only man is v., 452 : 9
out v. jelly, 234 : 18
phrase beyond others v., 693 : 5
race of quislings, 744 : 16
squealing of wry-necked fife, 199 : 4
wisdom and goodness to v., 234 : 24
Vilely, show v. to desire small beer, 185 : *n* 6
Vileness, if one had spoken v., 764 : 10
Viler George the Second, 753 : *n* 3
Vilest, ape v. of beasts, 95 : 3
deeds like poison weeds, 676 : 13
things become themselves, 241 : 1
to v. things am thrall, 251 : 6
with v. worms to dwell, 244 : 26
Vilified, most v. minority, 776 : 13
Villa submit to idea of revolution, 797 : 9
Village all declared how much he knew, 370 : 10
any well-established v., 847 : 13
belongs to Castle, 786 : 1
crossing bridge into v., 766 : 13
defend v. town city, 744 : 5
every Middlesex v., 512 : 7
global v., 879 : 6
his house in v. though, 748 : 5
Indian knows his v., 852 : 16
loveliest v. of the plain, 369 : 28
man's v. his peace of mind, 895 : 11
of Howling, 854 : 6
smithy stands, 510 : 7
some v. Hampden, 362 : 9
statesmen talked, 370 : 12
Villages, dollar no devotees in v., 453 : 6
skipped towns jumped, 690 : 15
when you think v. deserted, 456 : 2
Villain and he be many miles asunder, 193 : 16
every tale condemns me for v., 187 : 28
ne'er v. in Denmark, 220 : 2
no v. need be, 600 : 18
one murder made a v., 378 : 3
Pinch a hungry lean-faced v., 188 : 15
play the v., 230 : 28
smile and be a v., 220 : 1
smiling damned v., 220 : 1
some v. hath done me wrong, 189 : *n* 3
still pursued her, 661 : 13
who calls me v., 221 : 8
Villain (*continued*)
would have been useful, 414 : 18
Villainies, execrable sum of all v., 346 : 9
Villainous company spoil of me, 204 : 25
demitasses, 684 : 17
foreheads v. low, 248 : 14
my cue v. melancholy, 233 : 6
newspapers the most v., 399 : 5
Villain's mind, 198 : 28
Villains by necessity, 233 : 5
in power, 382 : 11
Villainy, clothe my naked v., 187 : 6
natural expression of v., 622 : 9
you teach me, 199 : 19
Ville, comme il pleut sur la v., 659 : *n* 7
il pleut doucement sur la v., 674 : *n* 3
Villon our sad bad brother's name, 634 : 11
Vincent nobly Cape St. V., 541 : 18
Vincere scis Hannibal, 94 : *n* 5
Vinchy, spell Vinci pronounce V., 622 : 4
Vinci pronounce Vinchy, 622 : 4
Vindicate ways of God to man, 336 : 11
Vindication of truth, 727 : 5
truth v. against slander, 523 : 9
Vindictively, Deity ever v., 527 : 3
Vine, every man under his v., 13 : 29
for one grape v. destroy, 189 : 20
fruit of the v., 41 : 10
gadding v., 280 : 12
I drank at every v., 823 : 5
leaves in his hair, 600 : 5
thou monarch of the v., 241 : 5
viol violet and v., 525 : 12
Vinegar, oil v. sugar, 371 : 13
Vines and olive trees, 868 : 21
bosomed deep in v., 340 : 26
land of v. and fig trees, 11 : 14
little foxes that spoil the v., 28 : 8
Vineyard, bound of land tilth v., 247 : 26
my wellbeloved hath a v., 29 : 3
not glean thy v., 10 : 19
Vineyards, plant v. and eat the fruit, 31 : 31
Vino, con pan y v., 935 : 10
in v. veritas, 62 : *n* 12, 134 : 6
Vintage, better than the v. of Abiezer, 12 : 11
bitter v. of race problem, 800 : 9
draught of v., 476 : 23
from v. time pressed, 516 : 14
trampling out v., 566 : 4
Vintners, wonder often what v. buy, 517 : 11
Viol of her memory, 767 : 11
violet and vine, 525 : 12
Violate agreements, 780 : 4
mostly v. law and custom, 701 : 12
Violations, security against future v., 351 : 4
Violence American as cherry pie, 915 : 16
blown with restless v., 228 : 20
covereth the mouth of the wicked, 23 : 22
dictatorship maintained by v., 770 : 6
intertwined with the lie, 895 : 22
nation at mercy of v., 813 : 9
never by v. constrained, 163 : 16
not by force or v., 383 : 6
overcome v. without v., 909 : 11

Violence (*continued*)
perseverance more prevailing than v., 120 : 2
returns on him who began, 101 : 10
revolution act of v., 826 : 6
truth not permit v., 727 : 5
Violent and sudden usurpations, 398 : 4
death of slaveholder, 560 : 23
delights have violent ends, 192 : 27
fear and danger of v. death, 264 : 17
fires soon burn out, 194 : 12
inclination towards learning, 316 : 4
lost v. souls, 805 : 16
man come down on everyone, 4 : 6
most v. of passions, 681 : 1
order is disorder, 767 : 20
population v. and gross, 596 : 2
so over v. or over civil, 304 : 11
thoughts with v. pace, 231 : 18
Violently if they must, 438 : 11
things v. destroyed, 424 : 8
Violet by mossy stone, 424 : 12
hour, 805 : 7
nodding v. grows, 196 : 18
of his native land, 531 : 22
throw perfume on v., 202 : 5
viol v. and vine, 525 : 12
what v. has camellia not, 694 : *n* 2
Violet-crowned, bright and v., 72 : 9
Violet-embroidered vale, 279 : 18
Violetflavored nuisance, 829 : 3
Violets are dark too, 103 : 23
breathes upon bank of v., 213 : 7
daisies pied and v. blue, 191 : 13
from her may v. spring, 224 : 17
I would give you some v., 224 : 2
plucked, 260 : 19
raining v., 705 : 6
roses red and v. blew, 173 : 16
when sweet v. sicken, 469 : 18
Violin, effort to reproduce v. of Stradivarius, 819 : 14
flute v. bassoon, 533 : 22
wherein play v. with grace, 889 : 10
Violins, sobs of v., 659 : 12
Stradivari's v., 564 : 21
sweet to dance to v., 676 : 9
Violoncello young man's complaint, 574 : 22
Violons de l'automne, 659 : *n* 6
Viper not more hateful, 76 : 1
Vipers, generation of v., 36 : 28
Virgil, a V. at Mexico, 363 : 21
said the master V., 141 : 23
thou V. art my master, 140 : 12
Virgin, born of V. Mary, 55 : 2
incarnate of the V. Mary, 55 : 3
shall be with child, 36 : 19
shall conceive, 29 : 13
wedded maid v. mother, 277 : 6
withering on v. thorn, 195 : 21
Virginia, first families in V., 840 : 14
yes V. there is a Santa Claus, 638 : *n* 4
you are from Old V., 596 : 12
Virginia Woolf, who's afraid of V., 908 : 2
Virginian, not V. but American, 382 : 14
Virginity, express my name my v., 164 : 3
that long preserved v., 297 : 1
Virginny, old V., 672 : 19
Virgin's sidelong looks, 369 : 29
Virgins, foolish v., 40 : 28
Virgins (*continued*)
soft as roses they twine, 459 : 6
take your saints and v., 566 : 6
wise v., 40 : 28
Virile, intellectual v. courageous, 726 : 1
Virtue, abolish vice destroy v., 274 : 18
admire v. follow not her lore, 288 : 5
adversity best discover v., 180 : 7
ambition the soldier's v., 241 : 6
and conscience of her worth, 287 : 6
and prudent act, 373 : 4
and riches seldom in one man, 259 : 8
and worthiness, 215 : 14
as it never will be moved, 219 : 22
assert and maintain liberty and v., 380 : 6
assume a v., 223 : 10
assumes some mark of v., 199 : 25
at expense of injuring their v., 69 : 10
beauty and v. rarely together, 143 : 6
best v. has tincture of vice, 165 : 12
born to follow v., 141 : 14
cloistered v., 282 : 1
constitutes perfect v., 69 : 19
could see to do what Virtue would, 279 : 22
crime like v. has degrees, 312 : 10
debases in justifying, 342 : 21
demands thorny road, 165 : 2
destruction of Tao and v., 90 : 7
discretion better part of v., 856 : 13
distinction between v. and vice, 354 : 12
dwelling place of God in v., 118 : 13
economy distributive v., 374 : 10
escapes not calumnious strokes, 218 : 27
extends our days, 119 : 14
flattered into v., 500 : 22
forbearance ceases to be v., 372 : 2
friendship with his v., 89 : 17
germ of all v., 567 : 1
government by means of his v., 68 : 8
grounds are v. and talents, 389 : 8
had gone out of him, 42 : 8
harder than knowledge, 307 : 20
has heroes too, 413 : 10
helping men practice v., 89 : 2
herein be seen hate v. sin, 149 : 5
highest point not v., 783 : 2
highest proof of v., 488 : 18
homage vice pays to v., 293 : 27
humility most difficult v., 809 : 10
if lost seldom recovered, 307 : 20
if there be any v., 50 : 7
if V. feeble were, 280 : 5
in conscious v. bold, 334 : 12
in her shape how lovely, 286 : 8
infinite v., 241 : 15
inherent v. of socialism, 746 : 16
is at hand, 68 : 23
is bold, 228 : 23
is her own reward, 270 : *n* 7
is not desiring vice, 680 : 26
is not hereditary, 384 : 11
is v. a thing remote, 68 : 23
itself turns vice, 192 : 20
knowledge one thing v. another, 490 : 12
learning flock to aid, 496 : 13
like a rich stone, 181 : 8
like precious odors, 180 : 8
lilies and languors of v., 632 : 11
Virtue (*continued*)
lived in practice of every v., 81 : 9
lo v. is at hand, 68 : 23
love of v., 359 : 1
love V. she alone is free, 280 : 5
lovers of v., 271 : 14
make ambition v., 231 : 11
man of v., 68 : 20
men touched by heaven's v., 312 : 20
moderation in justice no v., 385 : *n* 2
moderation in temper a v., 385 : 4
more to man than water, 69 : 17
more v. than doth live, 256 : 5
much v. in If, 213 : 5
near to v. are firm simple modest, 69 : 4
no empty echo, 413 : 3
no road or ready way to v., 274 : 16
no v. like necessity, 194 : 5
no v. with size, 494 : 20
nobility the only v., 122 : 13
not always amiable, 381 : 12
not left to stand alone, 68 : 18
not sufficient to hold, 69 : 15
now is sold, 256 : 7
obedience bane of v., 466 : 7
obstinate v., 298 : 3
of ancient literature, 586 : 8
of paper government, 372 : 10
of vice must pardon beg, 223 : 9
one v. thousand crimes, 459 : 10
only flourish amongst equals, 414 : 6
or vice leaves scar, 648 : 11
patriotic v. in female sex, 393 : 3
peace is a v., 308 : 3
person who loved v., 68 : 13
philanthropy only v. appreciated, 559 : 20
pine because they lost v., 117 : 10
possesses v. in abundance, 64 : 18
profound and secret v., 64 : 4
progress in human v., 414 : 7
prosperity not favorable to public v., 471 : 13
redeem us from v., 632 : 16
reward of v. is v., 497 : 21
seldom associated with true v., 68 : 2
show v. her own feature, 222 : 2
sinews of v., 271 : 4
solid v., 231 : 26
some by v. fall, 228 : 1
some mark of v., 199 : 25
substantial and genuine v., 388 : 2
sufficient of herself, 270 : *n* 7
talk with crowds keep v., 710 : 17
that possession would not show, 209 : 31
though in rags, 305 : 4
to die honorably greatest v., 67 : 20
to flaming youth v. wax, 223 : 5
to flee vice beginning of v., 108 : 17
to make necessity a v., 117 : *n* 13
treading the course of v., 69 : 17
truce between v. and vice, 560 : 8
truth secret of v., 580 : 12
uncommon valor common v., 791 : 14
unexercised unbreathed, 282 : 1
vice assumes some v., 199 : 25
vice pays homage to v., 293 : 27
which requires to be guarded, 369 : 10
while people retain v., 521 : 13
wickedness easier than v., 353 : 8
Virtue's, died in v. cause, 188 : 18

Virtue's (*continued*)
failings leaned to V. side, 370 : 6
Virtues, average of all v., 630 : 16
be to her v. very kind, 320 : 17
curse on his v., 325 : 19
expected of servant, 378 : 5
for several v. several women, 248 : 3
forced upon us by crimes, 804 : 15
great necessities call out great v., 392 : 16
greatest vices as well as v., 272 : 7
if individuals no v., 391 : 8
in v. nothing surpass her, 460 : 10
men praise and pass by, 791 : 13
of man without his vices, 456 : 9
of no avail, 830 : 9
other v. would be useless, 298 : 1
pearl chain of all v., 257 : 14
Princedoms V. Powers, 286 : 22
suspects himself of v., 835 : 4
these v. of delight, 403 : 10
to sustain good fortune, 293 : 4
trumpet of his own v., 210 : 9
vices in disguise, 292 : 21
we write in water, 249 : 14
will plead like angels, 236 : 24
world to hide v. in, 213 : 14
Virtuous, because v. no more cakes and ale, 213 : 26
grow v. in old age, 340 : 12
hated what was not v., 68 : 13
I wish to be v., 68 : 23
love of the v., 68 : 4
matter for v. deeds, 178 : 3
mischief v. do, 539 : 18
nation secure only while v., 556 : 13
on ten thousand a year, 596 : 2
outrageously v., 327 : 17
sisters v., 919 : 14
sweet and v. soul, 268 : 17
sweet slumbers of v., 326 : 4
who can find a v. woman, 26 : 6
who most v. alway, 147 : 15
woman is a crown, 23 : 28
wrongdoing v. for good cause, 110 : 24
Virtuousest discreetest best, 287 : 8
Virtuously, many daughters have done v., 26 : 10
Virulence of appetite for revelation, 771 : 14
Virum, stilus v. arguit, 258 : 8
Visage, hides not v. from cottage, 247 : 1
Launcelot saw her v., 149 : 19
lean body and v., 276 : 15
meet your v. here, 844 : 2
shattered v. lies, 466 : 12
with devotion's v., 221 : 11
Visages cream and mantle, 198 : 1
Viscous, words slippery thought v., 635 : 20
Visibility, from him never real v., 474 : 7
Visible, all things v. and invisible, 50 : 9
communion with v. forms, 471 : 2
elements least v., 878 : 3
labor, 491 : 23
limitations of v. and tangible, 636 : 17
no light but darkness v., 283 : 6
outward and v. sign, 56 : 5
poem of world, 859 : 1
power of v. is invisible, 799 : 3
sage mechanician, 562 : 8
work is love made v., 782 : 17

Vision, abortion of great v., 819 : 12
art of seeing invisible, 322 : 6
baseless fabric of this v., 248 : 13
beatific, 283 : 28
boundless v. grows upon us, 592 : 6
by the v. splendid, 426 : 15
fatal v., 237 : 13
I saw in v., 733 : 4
in v. once I saw, 433 : 26
inward v., 703 : 3
of all that is ordinary, 565 : 23
of Christ thou dost see, 407 : 8
of the world, 529 : 24
on inward v. close eyes, 703 : 3
or waking dream, 477 : 3
perfect blessedness v. of God, 140 : 2
religion v. of something beyond, 697 : 9
religious v. ground for optimism, 697 : 10
summon v. declare it pure, 873 : 19
unread v. in higher dream, 806 : 3
where there is no v., 25 : 32
who have clearest v., 81 : 2
write the v., 33 : 25
young men's v., 304 : 5
Visionary anger cleansing sight, 910 : 5
gleam, 426 : 13
theoretic and v. fear, 388 : 17
Vision's, my v. greatest enemy, 407 : 8
Visions, I have multiplied v., 33 : 15
of glory, 363 : 7
stone better pillow than v., 797 : 16
what v. have I seen, 197 : 7
while these v. did appear, 197 : 23
young men shall see v., 33 : 17
Visit, delightful v. too short, 440 : 26
drops that v. heart, 215 : 23
her face too roughly, 218 : 7
it by pale moonlight, 430 : 4
not v. house of tomorrow, 782 : 15
only here for short v., 821 : 4
sins of fathers upon children, 77 : 23
us with death, 265 : 10
what thy short v. meant, 442 : 3
Visitant, pleasure oft a v., 476 : 2
Visited, dayspring hath v. us, 42 : 26
he hath v. and redeemed, 42 : 24
nor v. in heaven, 606 : 17
sick and ye v. me, 40 : 33
Visitest, son of man that thou v. him, 17 : 17
Visiting acquaintance, 398 : 14
nothing remarkable beneath v. moon, 241 : 22
the iniquity of the fathers, 10 : 5
Visitings, compunctious v. of nature, 236 : 17
Visits, angel v., 443 : 8
angels' v., 318 : 4
his dinners not him, 297 : 27
never make long v., 798 : 16
places eye of heaven v., 194 : 5
Vita brevis est, 80 : *n* 2
incipit v. nova, 140 : 7
Vitae, cursores v. lampada tradunt, 100 : *n* 9
philosophia dux, 98 : *n* 16
summa brevis spem vetat, 107 : *n* 2
Vital arrogant X, 768 : 2
élan v., 688 : 11
if v. light inhere, 606 : 10
imagination essentially v., 437 : 12
measure of newspaper, 820 : 13

Vital (*continued*)
mechanisms one object, 551 : 19
quality self-confidence, 792 : 1
resources, 648 : 3
spark of heavenly flame, 333 : 23
spirit, 688 : 11
Vitality, fragile but with more v., 733 : 17
of thought in adventure, 697 : 17
Vitalizes, history v. memory, 98 : 9
Vitalizing work between twenty-five and forty, 664 : 19
Viva la huelga, 906 : 17
Vivamus atque amemus, 101 : *n* 15
Vivere, nec sine te nec tecum v. possum, 113 : *n* 6
Vivez n'attendez à demain, 162 : *n* 9
Vivid air signed with honor, 876 : 16
physical illustration, 610 : 2
trusty dusky v. true, 669 : 8
Vivi-mus, bibi-mus v. oremus, 365 : 12
Vivre, il faut tenter de v., 735 : *n* 4
il faut v. comme on pense, 670 : *n* 5
Vixens, snap like v. at truth, 794 : 7
Vixi, ille potens sui dixisse V., 108 : *n* 7
Vocation, avocation and v., 748 : 18
demands self-sacrifice, 831 : 24
no sin to labor in v., 203 : 3
'tis my v. Hal, 203 : 3
to be ruined man is a v., 809 : 18
whole v. endless imitation, 426 : 16
without v. existence meaningless, 895 : 13
Vogel, ich singe wie der V. singt, 395 : *n* 1
Vogue, totter into v., 363 : 20
Voice, a v. a mystery, 427 : 2
all with one v., 46 : 22
arrow like sweet v., 462 : 3
as sound of many waters, 52 : 30
audible v. of past, 473 : 28
beat and a V. beat, 693 : 11
behind me whispered low, 676 : 7
bird or wandering v., 427 : 1
bird shall carry the v., 27 : 19
by v. by posted card, 726 : 12
can honor's v. provoke, 362 : 5
cannon his v., 601 : 12
cry Sleep no more, 237 : 21
crying in the wilderness, 36 : 26
distant v. in darkness, 512 : 10
each a mighty v., 428 : 6
give but few thy v., 219 : 1
great sea's v., 732 : 7
hear v. in every wind, 361 : 9
hear v. of the bard, 405 : 1
heard the v. of the Lord, 29 : 11
hearing of a v., 571 : 10
heart and v. oppressed, 563 : 13
her v. was ever soft, 235 : 17
his big manly v., 211 : 15
his v. in all her music, 469 : 14
his v. was propertied, 241 : 25
horrible v. a politician, 81 : 13
I hear this night, 477 : 1
I sing with mortal v., 286 : 28
I will aggravate my v., 196 : 8
in every v. every ban, 405 : 9
in hollow murmurs, 416 : 11
in v. and tossing, 747 : 18
is and is not voice of God, 339 : 21
is full of money, 835 : 5
is Jacob's voice, 8 : 17
joy is the sweet v., 436 : 1

Voice (*continued*)
joy's the v., 829 : 17
laws in which we have no v., 392 : 7
lift every v. and sing, 733 : 5
look in that tone of v., 660 : 17
love's v. wearies not, 467 : 5
melodies echoes of that v., 436 : 1
monstrous little v., 196 : 5
my v. fails me, 372 : 8
my v. I have lost it, 206 : 2
my v. is still for war, 325 : 17
nature without v. or sound, 365 : 6
no v. but of the silence, 435 : 5
not because has inexhaustible v., 838 : 11
O for a falconer's v., 192 : 16
obey v. at eve, 495 : 8
of charmers charming, 19 : 23
of fate, 413 : 20
of gods makes heaven drowsy, 191 : 4
of him that crieth in the wilderness, 30 : 30
of intellect soft, 678 : 12
of iron, 105 : 20
of law harmony, 175 : 7
of many waters, 53 : 22
of my heart, 487 : 3
of nature cries, 362 : 15
of Nature loudly cries, 410 : 15
of people is voice of God, 135 : 6
of protest warning appeal, 598 : 15
of the bard, 405 : 1
of the Lobster, 612 : 10
of the Lord God walking in garden, 7 : 7
of the sluggard, 328 : 9
of the turtle is heard, 28 : 7
of the turtledove, 4 : 13
of the wild goose, 4 : 11
of thy brother's blood, 7 : 16
of today herald of tomorrow, 706 : 23
one rational v. dumb, 868 : 15
only a look and a v., 512 : 10
Orpheus' v. and poetry, 76 : 3
people's v. odd, 339 : 21
rise like fountain, 535 : 1
rise up at the v. of the bird, 27 : 24
said Cry, 30 : 32
said I ant I want, 887 : 12
seasoned with gracious v., 199 : 24
selfsame toothless v., 899 : 2
so charming left his v., 287 : 2
sole daughter of his v., 287 : 18
song of siren nor v. of hyena, 177 : 17
Stentor with brazen v., 57 : 31
stern daughter of v. of God, 427 : 12
still small v., 14 : 5, 527 : 19
still small v. of gratitude, 363 : 13
sweeter thy v., 531 : 13
sweetest v. has Israfel, 525 : *n* 3
that breathed o'er Eden, 465 : 13
that is still, 530 : 19
think public opinion v. of God, 626 : 13
thy sweet v. to me, 460 : 1
untamed v. still heard above forge, 557 : 18
unwearying, 57 : 19
watchdog's v., 370 : 4
water never formed to v., 767 : 15
what inner v. says, 412 : 19
wherefore let thy v., 535 : 1
which I uttered was crying, 34 : 18
whose sound like sea, 425 : 23

Voice (*continued*)
wisdom uttereth her v., 23 : 3
without reply, 495 : 9
Voiceless shore, 461 : 5
wailing, 808 : 3
Voices, ancestral v. prophesying war, 433 : 24
cicadas pour out their piping v., 57 : 23
deep moans with many v., 529 : 13
distant speaking of v., 887 : 5
earth with thousand v., 435 : 23
gentle v. calling, 598 : 7
human v. wake us, 804 : 1
I thank you for your v., 242 : 16
keep tune oars time, 446 : 5
lost sea v., 806 : 6
music when soft v. die, 469 : 18
no v. O Rhodopè, 442 : 19
of dissent, 862 : 21
other v. other rooms, 903 : 4
sea has many v., 808 : 2
singing out of cisterns, 805 : 12
still thy pleasant v., 591 : 9
that make me sleep again, 248 : 10
to Thee all v. pray, 614 : 9
trembling for you in v., 702 : 5
two v. are there, 428 : 6
we shall never hear, 802 : 18
when v. of children, 403 : 15
where beyond v. peace, 534 : 26
Voici des fruits des fleurs, 659 : *n* 8
Void, act against Constitution v., 367 : 9
act against natural equity v., 367 : 9
conscience v. of offense, 46 : 30
declare Act of Congress v., 644 : 17
if you do not trust v., 851 : 1
is what you gave, 851 : 1
it has long stood v., 267 : 14
of envy guile lust, 345 : 21
of light, 283 : 12
they have left aching v., 375 : 15
triumph brings v., 649 : 11
without form and v., 6 : 10
Voie Lactée ô soeur lumineuse, 770 : *n* 6
Vol, la propriété c'est le v., 527 : 15
Volatility, sanguine who checked v., 386 : 11
Volcanic political instinct, 681 : 21
Volcano, dancing on v., 472 : 2
of revolution, 689 : 26
Volcanoes, old factions are v., 374 : 5
Volenti non fit iniuria, 135 : 1
Volition, neither with v. nor consciousness, 798 : 13
Volitional and portals of discovery, 778 : 3
Volleyed and thundered, 533 : 13
Volscians, fluttered your V., 242 : 26
Voltage, chattering v., 816 : 14
Voltaire invented history, 344 : 17
mock on V., 406 : 3
Volts, weeping with a hundred thousand v., 902 : 3
Volume of forgotten lore, 526 : 10
within awful v. lies, 432 : 5
within v. of my brain, 219 : 28
Volumes, creators of odd v., 441 : 18
dry v. of ethics, 387 : 7
I prize above dukedom, 247 : 15
might be written, 579 : 18
of Addison, 352 : 23

Volumes (*continued*)
of the unexpressed, 912 : 1
pricks to subsequent v., 226 : 5
whole v. in folio, 190 : 18
Voluminous writer, 326 : 15
Voluntas, ruat coelum fiat v. tua, 134 : 24
Voluntatis, hominibus bonae v., 54 : 4
Volunteered when disaster clouded, 617 : 6
Volupté, luxe calme et v., 580 : *n* 8
Voluptuous, music with v. swell, 457 : 14
Voluptuousness, misanthropy and v., 487 : 20
Vomit, dog returneth to his v., 25 : 19
dog turned to his own v., 52 : 18
Vorpal blade, 612 : 18
Vortex of our grave, 843 : 16
Votaress, imperial v. passed on, 196 : 15
Votaries, hatred renders v. credulous, 359 : 5
Votarist, sad v. in palmer's weed, 279 : 15
Vote and act to bring good, 649 : 18
early vote often, 590 : 12
give hand and heart to v., 450 : 9
if right to v. denied, 578 : 5
monyment refuse to help fam'ly, 721 : 10
not live to see women v., 491 : 1
one man one v., 925 : 8
right to v. not abridged on account of sex, 392 : 6
right to v. not denied or abridged, 392 : 5
straw v., 699 : 18
supporting church and school, 642 : 11
Voted not to rescind, 382 : 11
Voter exercises public trust, 631 : 7
Voters, commitments v. don't know can't hurt you, 856 : 13
Votes, as long as I count v., 594 : 1
Voting, speaking v. reasonably, 650 : 14
Votive, Venus take my v. glass, 321 : 1
Voulu, vous l'avez v. Georges Dandin, 298 : *n* 3
Vow, better that thou not v., 26 : 27
eternal misery together, 317 : 1
it shall be so for me, 189 : 3
that binds too strictly, 534 : 19
Vowels, colors for v., 673 : 20
ear the open v. tire, 333 : 7
I recount your births, 673 : 20
only consonants and v., 811 : 1
Vowing more than perfection, 226 : 13
Vows, cancel all our v., 182 : 16
made in wine, 212 : 17
our v. are heard betimes, 305 : 29
soul lends tongue v., 219 : 6
write woman's v. upon wave, 75 : 22
Vox populi vox Dei, 135 : 6
Voyage, all v. of their life, 217 : 5
finish of a v., 723 : 10
I am about to take last v., 264 : 21
life's uncertain v., 243 : 9
like Ulysses made glorious v., 162 : 10
many signal miracles on v., 151 : 3
not for gain honor wealth, 152 : 1
of oblivion, 791 : 4
people complained of long v., 150 : 14
save ship of Union on v., 521 : 7
to Ithaca, 702 : 4

Voyager, denies v. further sailing, 76 : 25
lands v. at last, 597 : 15
learn O v. to walk, 822 : 5
raving skies opened to v., 673 : 19
Voyagers, fare forward v., 808 : 7
years are v., 313 : 23
Voyages, selecting v. you never make, 741 : 11
Voyaging through strange seas, 424 : 2
voyaging voyaging, 575 : 20
Voyelles je dirais vos naissances, 673 : n 13
Vulcan's, foul as V. stithy, 222 : 7
Vulgar, both great v. and small, 295 : 15
bourgeois thinking v., 583 : 18
buildeth on v. heart, 206 : 7
Discobolus, 620 : 4
familiar but by no means v., 218 : 30
manner popular politician, 81 : 13
tune v. if public hums it, 662 : 18
war looked on as v., 674 : 20
worse than wicked it's v., 660 : 16
Vulgarize day of judgment, 500 : 16
Vulgarizes, success v., 670 : 11
Vulgarizing middle class, 589 : 4
Vulture, rage of the v., 459 : 5
Vuoi, come tu mi v., 723 : 21

W

Wabash, banks of W., 732 : 13
Wabe, gimble in the w., 612 : 17
Wacht am Rhein, 573 : n 2
die W. am Rhein, 573 : n 2
Wade, should I w. no more, 239 : 3
through slaughter to throne, 362 : 11
Wading up to eyes in blood, 372 : 8
Wafer, sun pasted like w., 732 : 4
Wafer-cakes, man's faiths w., 207 : 15
Waft her love to Carthage, 200 : 22
seas roll to w. me, 336 : 19
sigh from Indus to Pole, 335 : 1
Wafted, let me be w., 576 : 18
Wag, let world w., 159 : 14
where beards w. all, 163 : 6
Wage, harm by minimum w. law, 880 : 18
laborers having no means of production, 563 : n 4
Wägen, erst w. dann wagen, 489 : n 3
Wagers, lay no w., 370 : n 3
Wages are value expression, 784 : 28
bargaining for w., 762 : 8
emoluments in w. or profits, 366 : 1
home gone and ta'en thy w., 243 : 27
keeping profits up by keeping w. down, 438 : 14
of sin is death, 47 : 5
times hard and w. low, 935 : 2
took w. and are dead, 692 : 3
world looks for w., 545 : 17
Wagging, alive and w. tail in mud, 90 : 11
Wagon, hitch w. to star, 499 : 9
storm like w. crossing bridge, 877 : 1
water w. place for me, 718 : 12
Wagons, honored among w., 886 : 20
Wags, see how world w., 211 : 5
so w. the world, 211 : n 1
Wail, new w. times' waste, 244 : 11
night bird's w., 629 : 20
Wail (*continued*)
or knock the breast, 289 : 9
to w. such woes, 172 : 7
who buys mirth to w. a week, 189 : 20
Wailful choir, 477 : 19
Wailing, voiceless w., 808 : 3
winds naked woods, 471 : 10
woman w. for demon-lover, 433 : 22
Wailings, sighs lamentations and w., 140 : 15
Wain, wheels of Phoebus' w., 279 : 15
Waist, round w. felt it fold, 530 : 11
slender w. confined, 276 : 5
Wait a bit oysters cried, 613 : 6
a man should w., 83 : 16
all things come to who w., 496 : n 4
be still w., 873 : 14
could not w. their passing, 587 : 8
digestion w. on appetite, 238 : 24
do not listen simply w., 786 : 3
do not w. be still, 786 : 3
do not w. for last judgment, 882 : 9
drift w. and obey, 711 : 3
everything comes if man w., 501 : 26
fold hands and w., 630 : 21
for wisest of counselors, 73 : 7
I almost had to w., 312 : 3
labor and to w., 509 : 16
O we can w. no longer, 576 : 15
stand and w., 282 : 17
the undreamed of, 904 : 6
these w. all upon thee, 21 : 11
till other is ready, 559 : 15
times we can't w. for somebody, 913 : 7
to fawn to crouch to w., 174 : 11
to watch water clear, 747 : 3
upon I would, 237 : 2
upon the Lord, 31 : 2
who only stand and w., 282 : 17
why w. until next year, 89 : 6
Waited, death past so he w., 543 : 17
for billy-boil, 705 : 7
for the light, 729 : 5
for thy salvation, 9 : 5
three years w. for herald, 849 : 6
Waiter roars it through hall, 592 : 4
Waitest for spark from heaven, 585 : 22
Waiteth, my soul w. for the Lord, 22 : 12
Waiting for invasion so are fishes, 744 : 10
for rain, 804 : 13
for something to occur, 750 : 12
taxi throbbing w., 805 : 7
what are we all w. for, 701 : 14
worse things w. than death, 633 : 1
Waits, destiny w. alike, 71 : 15
human engine w., 805 : 7
star for which evening w., 729 : 6
woman w. for me, 575 : 6
Waive quantum o' the sin, 409 : 12
Wake and call me early, 528 : 12
and feel fell of dark, 656 : 19
awake for night is flying, 176 : 20
die before I w., 320 : 12
do I w. or sleep, 477 : 3
empire followed in w., 799 : 19
eternally, 254 : 13
for the sun, 515 : 16
him no not I, 930 : 12
hoary shoulders spouting, 907 : 2
human voices w. us, 804 : 1
in durance vile I w., 411 : 23
nations underground, 936 : 2
Wake (*continued*)
remember and understand, 542 : 2
sleep to w., 546 : 7
sleeping w. and waking sleep, 165 : 9
thou wilt not w., 267 : 6
thy kiss would w. the dead, 530 : 12
to sleep, 873 : 21
truths w. to perish never, 426 : 19
unto me, 598 : 8
you will w. and remember, 542 : 2
Waked after long sleep, 248 : 10
by the circling hours, 286 : 25
I w. she fled, 282 : 21
priest all shaven, 934 : 9
to ecstasy living lyre, 362 : 6
you have w. me too soon, 328 : 9
Wakeful, feathered w. thought, 557 : 8
nightingale, 285 : 25
Wakefulness, wit and w., 899 : 11
Waken, primitives not w. sleeper, 673 : 3
thou with me, 531 : 11
Wakened by silence, 631 : 17
us from sleeping, 797 : 2
Wakens, firefly w., 531 : 11
Wakes, maypoles hockcarts wassails w., 265 : 17
whoever w. in England, 541 : 16
Waketh, watchman w. but in vain, 22 : 8
Waking bliss, 279 : 20
hope a w. dream, 86 : 16
morn not w. till she sings, 176 : 1
nights of w., 431 : 8
no such matter, 245 : 2
silence with w. bird, 533 : 22
sleeping wake and w. sleep, 165 : 9
souls, 251 : 15
take my w. slow, 873 : 21
thou shalt fear w., 633 : 17
threshold of w. light, 906 : 9
vision or w. dream, 477 : 3
Walcum, talcum always w., 855 : 13
Walden only book I own, 558 : n 1
Waldo, Matthew and W. guardians, 804 : 7
Walk a little faster, 612 : 7
amidst beautiful things, 704 : 5
and not faint, 31 : 2
and wot not what they are, 190 : 12
ask for old paths and w. therein, 31 : 37
before they dance, 339 : 17
by faith, 49 : 14
can two w. together, 33 : 20
Catullus w. that way, 714 : 3
closer w. with God, 375 : 14
crust where I must w., 893 : 9
cypresss in palace w., 531 : 11
deck my Captain lies, 576 : 7
down Piccadilly, 628 : 7
fatal shadows w. by us, 260 : 17
fishermen that w. beach, 234 : 28
foolery does w. about, 214 : 11
free, 576 : 12
from breakfast to madness, 908 : 8
happily may I w., 928 : 19
how many roads man w. down, 915 : 2
humbly with thy God, 33 : 23
I w. unseen, 278 : 18
I'll rest but thou w., 926 : 19
in fear and dread, 435 : 3
in velvet shoes, 793 : 17

Walk (*continued*)
into my parlor, 485 : 23
it slow where you go, 912 : 15
learn O voyager to w., 822 : 5
let her not w. in the sun, 220 : 17
let us w. honestly, 47 : 29
make running water w., 779 : 1
no spirit can w. abroad, 217 : 26
not natural to w. on two legs, 387 : 1
not on earth exultantly, 131 : 7
on eggs, 257 : 16
out toward unknown region, 576 : 17
oysters come w. with us, 613 : 3
pleasant w. pleasant talk, 613 : 3
race of men who w. upon earth, 57 : 30
revealed her as true goddess, 104 : 24
rise and w. with him, 76 : 5
shall not w. in darkness, 45 : 4
slow silent w., 642 : 2
solar w. or milky way, 336 : 16
take up bed and w., 41 : 33
talk with you w. with you, 198 : 18
teach crab to w. straight, 82 : 4
the earth unseen, 286 : 2
through fields in gloves, 795 : 2
through valley of shadow, 18 : 7
through volumes of unexpressed, 912 : 1
under water men w., 919 : 8
upon England's mountains, 406 : 21
upon the beach, 803 : 19
where'er you w., 332 : 12
which way they w., 237 : 15
while ye have light, 45 : 17
with kings, 710 : 17
with stretched forth necks, 29 : 1
ye in it, 30 : 19
your ghost will w., 542 : 6
your mystic way, 628 : 6
Walked along the Strand, 353 : 18
among ancient trees, 405 : 1
as he forth w. on way, 188 : 37
cat w. by himself, 710 : 5
crowns and crownets, 241 : 25
Enoch w. with God, 7 : 24
eye-deep in hell, 792 : 14
glittered when he w., 729 : 4
him that w. the waves, 281 : 4
in glory and in joy, 425 : 10
in the search of the depth, 16 : 31
people that w. in darkness, 29 : 15
straight out of ark, 432 : 22
through wilderness of world, 301 : 19
to hotel in rain, 844 : 17
with his mother, 886 : 18
without upward look, 749 : 11
Walketh, devil w. about, 52 : 16
every man w. in a vain show, 19 : 3
he who w. upright, 132 : 15
not in counsel of ungodly, 17 : 12
pestilence that w. in darkness, 20 : 16
upon the wings of the wind, 21 : 8
Walking and mincing as they go, 29 : 1
as I was a-w., 927 : 9
by wild lone, 710 : 6
close at hand, 613 : 2
Devil is gone a-w., 440 : 13
dog's w., 354 : 15
enterprise in w. naked, 713 : 14
giant wings prevent w., 580 : 17
have ye not seen us w., 295 : 13
I nauseate w., 324 : 18
in an air of glory, 299 : 8
Walking (*continued*)
life's but a w. shadow, 240 : 4
like two angels white, 654 : 18
men as trees w., 42 : 9
on the sea, 39 : 26
round the fold, 403 : 13
up and down in it, 15 : 2
Walks, a man w. by, 824 : 5
at noon upon two feet, 74 : *n* 5
biggest rascal that w., 123 : 6
eye Nature's w., 336 : 11
God w. in mine, 604 : 1
having once turned w. on, 435 : 3
in beauty, 459 : 13
in w. it seems to me, 730 : 4
lards lean earth as he w., 203 : 21
night in silver shoon, 739 : 13
o'er dew on eastern hill, 217 : 27
on hallowed ground, 825 : 9
she w. lady of delight, 661 : 11
third who w. beside you, 805 : 11
thy spirit w. abroad, 217 : 11
two luxuries in w., 480 : 3
up and down with me, 201 : 26
up stairs of concepts, 857 : 4
wish I liked way it w., 697 : 1
with tender growing night, 574 : 19
Wall, ballads stuck about w., 271 : 3
before I built a w., 747 : 6
between church and state, 794 : 16
Blake beat upon w., 717 : 10
bores through his castle w., 195 : 3
broken w. burning tower, 715 : 16
close w. up with English dead, 207 : 16
confronting apparition, 582 : 12
crannied w., 535 : 10
doesn't love a w., 747 : 4
even w. fell down, 816 : 13
faces turned to w., 595 : 6
fell down flat, 11 : 31
fight for law as for w., 70 : 9
find the body by w., 588 : 3
Humpty Dumpty sat on w., 932 : 2
Jackson like stone w., 594 : 4
know the w. is strong, 676 : 12
must be kept high, 794 : 16
not conclude against w. of stone, 899 : 15
of oblivion, 838 : 14
of wisdom, 858 : 19
painting lends joy to w., 646 : 8
pressed to w., 819 : 7
serves it in office of a w., 194 : 13
shadows on opposite w. of cave, 84 : 17
stone shall cry out of w., 33 : 26
they which builded on w., 14 : 29
thou whited w., 46 : 27
wainscot and mouse, 808 : 11
waters were a w., 9 : 31
weakest goes to w., 169 : 35
when icicles hang by the w., 191 : 14
whitewashed w., 370 : 13
wit is the only w., 831 : 21
without a city w., 561 : 9
wooden w. is your ships, 70 : 13
your concern when neighbor's w. on fire, 109 : 11
Wall Street, economy reflected in W., 871 : 4
lays egg, 741 : 4
nation that supports W., 722 : 13
Wallace, wi' W. bled, 411 : 15
Walled round with rocks, 634 : 12
vain citadels not w., 827 : 7
wear out in a w. prison, 235 : 12
Wallet at his back, 226 : 16
for alms a pilgrim's w., 314 : 2
Walling in or walling out, 747 : 6
Walloping Window Blind, 647 : 21
Wallow naked in December snow, 194 : 7
Wallpaper, one-armed man pasting w., 699 : 10
Walls and towers girdled round, 433 : 21
are nothing, 74 : 1
close her from ancient w., 407 : 7
come tumblin' down, 935 : 20
down the mountain w., 717 : 16
falls on castle w., 530 : 26
hang banners on outward w., 240 : 2
happy those whose w. already rise, 104 : 25
have ears, 146 : *n* 5
peace be within thy w., 22 : 6
prison w. cannot control, 296 : *n* 3
pry loose old w., 761 : 10
stone w. not prison make, 296 : 4
Troilus mounted Troyan w., 200 : 22
Troy w. famed in battle, 104 : 35
watches from mountain w., 532 : 28
Walnut, here beneath w. bough, 558 : 19
Walnuts and wine, 528 : 3
Walrus and the Carpenter, 613 : 2
weep for you W. said, 613 : 8
Walruses, herds of w. and whales, 570 : 7
Walsinghame, holy land of W., 172 : 8
Walt Whitman a kosmos, 574 : 20
Walter, Sir W. responsible for war, 623 : 17
Walton, rodless W., 685 : 10
Waltzes, Congress doesn't run it w., 382 : 9
Waltzing Matilda, 705 : 7
such w. not easy, 873 : 10
Waly waly up the bank, 927 : 7
Wampum of the night, 604 : 8
Wan, angels pallid and w., 526 : 5
how silently with how w. face, 176 : 14
so w. with care, 202 : 21
why so pale and w., 289 : 17
Wander, children shall w. in the wilderness, 10 : 25
forth sons of Belial, 283 : 19
hand in hand, 772 : 22
if I might, 618 : 5
thoughts that w. through eternity, 284 : 9
we will not w. more, 528 : 20
where'er I w. boast of this, 194 : 8
wherever I w. wherever I rove, 410 : 8
whither shall I w., 931 : 8
Wandered east wandered west, 482 : 13
fingers w. idly, 596 : 13
I have w. in a face, 905 : 16
lonely as cloud, 427 : 7
till I died, 587 : 12
Wanderer, ah do not we w., 585 : 22
Grand Meaulnes the w., 795 : 3
halts and hears, 691 : 12
in her sky, 822 : 10
merry w. of the night, 196 : 12

Wanderer (*continued*)
the w., 795 : 3
weary wayworn w., 525 : 9
Wandering about from house to house, 50 : 32
between two worlds, 586 : 10
bird or w. voice, 427 : 1
by lone sea breakers, 659 : 9
from nightly shore, 526 : 15
in w. mazes lost, 284 : 19
Jew, 926 : 19
lazy Scheldt or w. Po, 368 : 13
minstrel I, 629 : 4
moon, 278 : 18
movement so w. as that of mind, 164 : 19
on foreign strand, 430 : 10
planet's course, 183 : 6
star to every w. bark, 245 : 18
stars, 52 : 26
steps and slow, 288 : 4
through many countries, 102 : 18
to nest from w. wide, 692 : 2
with great Mother's train, 587 : 11
Wanderings, errors w. mists and tempests, 100 : *n* 7
to guide, 611 : 1
Wane, constellations when they w., 71 : 3
moon who knowest no w., 517 : 4
moon will wax w., 512 : 19
Waneth, youth w. by increasing, 177 : 8
Wangle, quangle w., 550 : 15
Waning, beneath w. moon haunted, 433 : 22
in this w. of light, 874 : 9
sadder than w. moon, 513 : 20
Want, buy what you do not w., 390 : 3
climacteric of his w., 893 : 6
covetous man ever in w., 109 : 1
died in w., 892 : 13
enslaved by things they w., 895 : 12
for one who comes not, 835 : 13
for w. of nail shoe lost, 270 : 4, 347 : 35
freedom from w., 780 : 13, 781 : 8
get what you w., 711 : 4
House of W., 638 : 7
I shall not w., 18 : 7
I w. I w. I w., 887 : 12
if you w. me again, 575 : 4
in midst of plenty, 811 : 10
it most like it least, 341 : 22
labor with reference to w., 422 : 16
no cash means frightful w., 504 : 14
no man will supply thy w., 257 : 8
nothing you w., 590 : 11
of coincidence between accounts, 80 : 15
of decency want of sense, 309 : 9
only w. and discontent, 292 : 2
progress from w. to w., 355 : 21
prove what we w. to prove, 724 : 6
this to be yours, 910 : 4
thy w. as an armed man, 23 : 12
to be alone, 863 : 2
to be forgotten, 540 : 10
to be masters of fate, 842 : 12
to spend to give to w., 174 : 11
toil envy w., 351 : 17
we do not do what we w., 865 : 9
woeful w., 450 : 1
Wanted, every man is w., 498 : 10
never w. a good word, 368 : 7
Wanted (*continued*)
nothing he could not bring alone, 769 : 7
one immortal song, 304 : 4
when discovered not w., 800 : 5
Wanting is what, 546 : 1
not w. what is stolen, 231 : 10
perfect and entire w. nothing, 51 : 27
that which is w. cannot be numbered, 26 : 16
tried and found w., 742 : 2
weighed in the balances and found w., 33 : 1
words once my stock w., 306 : 24
Wanton, as flies to w. boys, 234 : 21
boys that swim on bladders, 249 : 3
freak, 475 : 2
friar ther was w. and merye, 145 : 22
gods that w. in the air, 296 : 2
her w. spirits look out, 227 : 3
imaginations and w. tempers, 380 : 12
stings of sense, 227 : 28
stretched forth necks and w. eyes, 29 : 1
wiles, 277 : 19
Wantoned with thy breakers, 458 : 30
Wantonness, chambering and w., 47 : 29
kindles in clothes a w., 266 : 6
Wanton's, no further than w. bird, 192 : 18
Wantons thro' flowering thorn, 409 : 24
Wants, everything he w., 590 : 11
fantastic unnecessary w., 649 : 16
getting what one w., 675 : 10
has more than he w., 327 : 3
having fewest w., 79 : 2
man w. but little, 330 : 12, 369 : 12
my w. are many, 418 : 7
nor w. that little long, 330 : 12, 369 : 12
not getting what one w., 675 : 10
nothing but eternity, 242 : 24
provide for human w., 373 : 21
speech not to express w., 310 : *n* 1
the natural touch, 239 : 17
to make flesh creep, 546 : 13
what man w. he w. now, 886 : 3
what other Americans want, 753 : 6
War, a god has given deeds of w., 58 : 17
a just w., 348 : *n* 2, 384 : 20
abolishing teaching of w., 881 : 14
adopting European w. tactics, 800 : 4
aftermath of w., 750 : 20
all policy's allowed in w., 564 : *n* 1
all's fair in love and w., 564 : 2
alone brings nobility, 784 : 1
always stirring up some w., 85 : 7
amidst ranks of w., 487 : 6
an invention, 784 : 21
and carnage be lost, 576 : 1
annihilating itself in big w., 775 : 13
annihilation through w., 866 : 9
art of w. simple, 589 : 15
as much and as little of w., 181 : 11
as well as w. and slaughtering, 404 : 22
battlefield of that w., 523 : 4
begun without money, 157 : 10
between life and death, 861 : 18
Between Men and Women, 831 : 5
blast of w. in ears, 207 : 16
blessing compared with reign of lie, 817 : 4
War (*continued*)
blood-swollen god, 732 : 1
brazen throat of w., 287 : 33
breeds war again, 684 : 14
chance of w., 225 : 32
check murders but what of w., 114 : 32
circumstance of glorious w., 231 : 11
class w. destroy inequalities, 719 : 10
coin is sinews of w., 157 : 10
cold w. getting warmer, 729 : 13
concealed throughout w., 630 : 2
condition of man condition of w., 264 : 12
conquer us, 818 : 7
Constitution is law in w. and peace, 553 : 20
contagion, 780 : 5
continuation of political relations, 448 : 8
dastard in w., 430 : 19
dauntless in w., 430 : 18
dearth age agues, 254 : 9
delays dangerous in w., 175 : *n* 5
deserve success in w., 746 : 12
disease and w. itself, 890 : 11
dogs of w., 216 : 12
Don John going to w., 742 : 9
drum throbbed no longer, 530 : 1
each w. creation of preceding w., 757 : *n* 2
ease after w., 173 : 12
economic interest as cause of w., 790 : 5
either man obsolete or w., 832 : 13
enemies in w. in peace friends, 387 : 10
engaged in great civil w., 523 : 4
epithets of w., 229 : 11
even to the knife, 457 : 3
everybody against w., 818 : 16
fever famine and w., 664 : 16
first in w. first in peace, 402 : 10
first invented w., 183 : 4
fought with atomic bomb, 763 : 14
France has not lost w., 815 : 7
garland of the w., 241 : 22
generation shorn by w., 743 : 10
generator of wars, 757 : *n* 2
give a w. nobody come, 761 : 14
God is w. peace surfeit hunger, 70 : 2
Great Britain going to w., 677 : 11
great w. petty peace, 720 : 1
grow too fond of w., 509 : 8
has actually begun, 383 : 5
hath smoothed his front, 186 : 30
how much w. seen, 898 : 9
I am for w., 591 : 4
I am the tongue of w., 912 : 7
I call it murder, 567 : 20
I have seen w. I hate w., 779 : 18
I make w. on the living, 161 : 20
if they mean to have w., 374 : 19
I'll furnish the w., 702 : 12
image of w. without guilt, 328 : 18
in heaven, 53 : 19
in his heart, 19 : 22
in peace provided for w., 128 : *n* 10
in peace thinks of w., 259 : 13
in state of w. by nature, 322 : 20
in this w. books weapons, 780 : 17
in w. daring boastful, 463 : 13
in w. mounts warrior's steed, 430 : 6
in w. no second prize, 825 : 4

War (*continued*)
in w. no substitute for victory, 771 : 6
in w. nothing impossible, 792 : 3
in w. parents inter children, 78 : 5
in w. resolution, 746 : 11
in Zurich during the w., 914 : 4
inevitable, 763 : 13
infection and hand of w., 194 : 13
is a contagion, 780 : 5
is a game, 377 : 12
is at best barbarism, 579 : 3
is cruelty, 578 : 15
is glorious art, 330 : 1
is hell, 579 : 3
is just a shot away, 916 : 10
is still the cry, 457 : 3
is toil and trouble, 306 : 19
is w. biological necessity, 786 : 8
its thousands slays, 378 : 4
killed only once in w., 743 : 7
lead peaceful into w., 682 : 13
let slip dogs of w., 216 : 12
let there be no more w., 895 : 17
levying w., 391 : 12
liberty to begin and end w., 181 : *n* 5
lived peacefully without w., 419 : *n* 5
Lord is a man of w., 9 : 33
love and w. same thing, 170 : 20
love calls to w., 177 : 12
love of w. for itself, 484 : 18
luxury more deadly than w., 122 : 10
magnificent but not w., 536 : 5
make w. for scrap of paper, 677 : 11
make w. to live in peace, 87 : 24
makes rattling good history, 641 : 20
mankind put end to w., 891 : 1
marching as to w., 616 : 6
master myth of cold w., 862 : 20
men unproved in w., 617 : 6
mental and corporeal w., 406 : 20
money sinews of w., 99 : 11
moral equivalent of w., 650 : 16
my voice is still for w., 325 : 17
national misfortune, 489 : 13
neither shall they learn w., 28 : 31
never good w. or bad peace, 348 : 6
never slays bad man, 75 : 8
no discharge in w., 27 : 13, 710 : 10
no great w. come again, 814 : 11
no modern w. won without sea
power, 800 : 11
no w. or battle's sound, 277 : 8
no will to win w., 771 : 8
noble efforts in last w., 351 : 3
not an instinct, 784 : 21
not disturbed by planetary w., 794 : 4
not separated from politics, 826 : 10
not to live but to make w., 876 : 20
nothing easy in w., 815 : 14
nourishes war, 413 : 16
object of w. peace, 579 : 2
object only of w. honorable, 384 : 20
of everyone against
everyone, 264 : 12
of looks between them, 189 : 9
of nature, 515 : 3
older men declare w., 750 : 20
on w. in Vietnam, 915 : 13
only art necessary, 153 : 21
open or secret w., 388 : 8
outcome of the w. in our
hands, 58 : 25
pattern called w., 751 : 6

War (*continued*)
peace better than most just
w., 348 : *n* 2
peace corrupt w. waste, 288 : 1
peace not absence of w., 308 : 3
political relations by other
means, 448 : 8
politics almost exciting as w., 743 : 7
prepared for w., 379 : 9
prince have no study but w., 153 : 21
prophesying w., 433 : 24
purple testament of bleeding
w., 195 : 4
put end to mankind, 891 : 1
quaint and curious w. is, 641 : 15
ready for w. to avoid it, 316 : 12
real w. never in books, 577 : 5
reason we bicker creates w., 165 : 4
red animal, 732 : 1
regarded as inevitable
probable, 860 : 5
regarded as wicked, 674 : 20
relentless, 731 : 5
result of mistaken calculation, 756 : 3
Scott responsible for w., 623 : 17
scourge of w., 524 : 7, 788 : 20
seek no wider w., 872 : 12
seldom enters but where wealth
allures, 305 : 22
sentence is for open w., 284 : 6
settles nothing, 817 : 18
silent w. of lilies, 189 : 17
sinews of w., 99 : 11, 157 : 10
some slain in w., 195 : 2
Son of God goes forth to w., 452 : 7
Spanish ships of w., 535 : 11
spares not the brave, 67 : 10
stand up and take w., 710 : 23
strange terrible world w., 745 : 11
study politics and w., 381 : 14
subject of it is W., 827 : 1
suppose they gave a w., 761 : *n* 3
sweets with sweet w. not, 244 : 3
sword of w. or of law, 389 : 13
talk by men who have been in
war, 623 : 16
tempered by w., 890 : 7
that will end war, 719 : 17
the w. is over, 589 : 19
there was w. in heaven, 53 : 19
thermonuclear w. not continuation
of politics, 448 : *n* 4
they could do with good w., 840 : 19
this is w., 509 : 2
this w. elemental conflict, 813 : 1
those who brought w. to Far
East, 787 : 13
though w. should rise against
me, 18 : 12
Thucydides wrote history of
w., 80 : 14
time of w. time of peace, 26 : 21
to make world safe, 703 : 2
to prevent w. not fear it, 439 : 6
to w. and arms I fly, 295 : 22
tongue of w., 912 : 7
too serious for military, 401 : 2
train of circumstances, 384 : 22
ultimate sanction of
exploitation, 825 : 18
unconditional w., 891 : 1
unjust peace before just w., 348 : *n* 2
unjust w. protracted, 573 : 3
unsuccessful or successful w., 376 : 18

War (*continued*)
vain w. with heaven, 284 : 3
vast aloof absentee, 914 : 2
want an end to w., 781 : 6
warmest heart recoiled at w., 829 : 8
wealth of seas spoils of w., 561 : *n* 1
weapons important in w., 826 : 9
weapons of w. perished, 13 : 11
well that w. so terrible, 509 : 8
what A.D. is elsewhere, 623 : 15
what w. said Prime Minister, 858 : 16
when aggressions require w., 389 : 3
when I speak they are for w., 22 : 3
when w. he went, 869 : 2
when w. is done, 795 : 15
who desires peace prepare for
w., 128 : 25
will to win w., 771 : 8
win w. as disastrous as to
lose, 817 : 18
win w. rise bloody, 889 : 10
with reremice, 196 : 19
with rights of mankind, 388 : 8
woman cause of ten years' w., 316 : 16
wrong w. at wrong time, 825 : 5
youth I love gone to w., 929 : 3
War bonnet of Medicine Hat, 840 : 2
Warble child, 190 : 23
native wood-notes wild, 278 : 6
sweet in springtime, 672 : 19
Warbled to the string, 278 : 22
Warbler, Dan Chaucer first w., 528 : 21
mysterious w. followed me, 646 : 2
Warblest at eve, 281 : 8
Warbling his Doric lay, 281 : 5
thou w. bird, 409 : 24
Warder is Despair, 676 : 13
memory the w. of brain, 237 : 7
Wardrobe, dalliance in w. lies, 207 : 10
Wards in Chancery, 628 : 17
pretty young w., 628 : 17
Ware, ill w. is never cheap, 269 : 13
pleasing w. is half sold, 269 : 13
taste your w., 930 : 13
that will not keep, 690 : 18
wiser than thou art w., 210 : 35
Wares harder to get rid of, 747 : 19
Warfare is accomplished, 30 : 30
life struggle not w., 631 : 4
love a kind of w., 113 : *n* 3
mutual help as often as w., 848 : 1
thy w. o'er, 431 : 8
Warhorse, hurl Jackson on w., 570 : 11
Warlike, people numerous and
w., 151 : 9
Warling, young man's w., 161 : 6
Warm and capable of grasping, 478 : 8
cheek and rising bosom, 362 : 21
heart within, 377 : 17
her coat is so w., 449 : 14
into the w. sun, 160 : 32
keeper of w. lights, 74 : 23
keeps w. her note, 271 : 20
let out to w. air, 322 : 13
man whose blood is w., 197 : 29
now w. in love, 334 : 27
nursing wrath to keep it w., 411 : 4
precincts of cheerful day, 362 : 14
ruddy drops that w. heart, 215 : *n* 5
sea-scented beach, 541 : 14
so cold no fire w., 608 : 6
summer sun shine friendly, 625 : *n* 3
summer sun shine kindly, 625 : 20
sun was w. wind chill, 748 : 17

Warm (*continued*)
this sensible w. motion, 228 : 20
virtue keep me w., 305 : 4
weather in bed, 321 : 17
wind the west wind, 760 : 17
with friends I make, 823 : 3
without heating, 330 : 22
Warm-blooded animals from one filament, 378 : 1
Warmed, glow has w. the world, 786 : *n* 4
hands before fire of life, 443 : 1
unclasps w. jewels, 476 : 17
wood stumps w. me twice, 560 : 9
Warmest heart recoiled at war, 829 : 8
welcome at an inn, 355 : *n* 8
Warming pretty little toes, 932 : 4
Warmly, in numbers w. pure, 364 : 10
Warms, who splits wood w. twice, 560 : *n* 2
Warmth, a little w. a little light, 617 : 3
about my heart, 479 : 12
no w. no cheerfulness, 485 : 12
of heart increase with years, 826 : 15
spring brings back balmy w., 102 : 3
warmth more warmth, 705 : 21
Warn, all poet can do is w., 827 : 1
to comfort and command, 427 : 6
Warned, friends be w. by me, 730 : 8
in a dream, 36 : 21
prior to questioning, 820 : 15
Warner, I am only a w., 130 : 14
Warning, come without w., 552 : 19
give w. to world, 244 : 26
voice of w. needed, 598 : 15
Warp, may w. be light of morning, 928 : 14
weave the w., 363 : 5
Warped, our ideas w. on death, 637 : 17
Warrant him heart-whole, 212 : 21
she'll prove an excuse, 399 : 1
truth shall be thy w., 172 : 14
Warrants, no w. but upon probable cause, 391 : 16
Warred for Homer dead, 257 : 20
Warring within breasts, 183 : 6
Warrior, better thing exists not for w., 94 : 9
British w. queen, 377 : 22
every lover a w., 113 : 5
happy w. of politics, 741 : *n* 3
happy w. sleeps, 427 : *n* 2
home brought her w., 531 : 8
lay like w. taking rest, 465 : 8
like an armed w., 615 : 4
of North America, 463 : 13
painful w. famoused for fight, 244 : 7
who is the happy W., 427 : 21
Warrior's, in war mounts w. steed, 430 : 6
Warriors, female w., 343 : 22
in this circle O w., 701 : *n* 4
stern joy w. feel, 431 : 14
Time and Patience strongest of w., 602 : 4
where are Sioux w., 610 : 5
War's a game, 377 : 12
annals cloud into night, 642 : 2
disciplinary functions, 650 : 16
glorious art, 330 : 1
Wars, all skillful in the w., 299 : 10
all their w. merry, 742 : 4
and alarums unto nations, 174 : 7
and rumors of wars, 40 : 22
Wars (*continued*)
boys not sent into foreign w., 780 : 11
brought nothing about, 307 : 1
caused by man, 817 : 10
chronicle the w. of kites, 289 : 12
dates of w., 627 : 2
disciplines of w., 207 : 22
end to beginnings of w., 781 : 6
fierce w. and faithful loves, 173 : 7
for right thing, 788 : 15
forgotten w., 807 : 4
fought by babies, 901 : 8
more pangs than w. or women, 249 : 3
most terrible of all w., 682 : 13
no lull in these w., 572 : 3
no more w., 882 : 1
not acts of God, 817 : 10
of European powers, 408 : 2
of interest and intrigue, 418 : 2
part in developing man, 631 : 5
planned by old men, 773 : 4
that make ambition virtue, 231 : 11
thousand w. of old, 532 : 23
won by men, 791 : 15
wrong from every standpoint, 788 : 15
Warsaw, order reigns in W., 439 : *n* 1
Warts and all, 272 : *n* 7
pimples w. and everything, 272 : 22
Was, he is or w. or has to be, 344 : 10
I am not what I w., 321 : 1
tell it like it w., 856 : 14
which w. and is and is to come, 53 : 7
Wash, air w. leaves cover me, 632 : 18
and wash our own, 900 : 7
balm from anointed king, 194 : 26
bid them w. their faces, 242 : 15
dirty linen at home, 420 : 11
feet in soda water, 805 : 6
gulfs w. us down, 529 : 13
incessantly softly w., 576 : 1
me and I shall be whiter than snow, 19 : 15
old linen w. whitest, 262 : 1
she makes me w., 622 : 16
that man outa my hair, 833 : 15
the river Rhine, 436 : 13
the wind, 806 : 21
this blood from my hand, 238 : 1
what art w. guilt away, 369 : 20
with Pilate w. your hands, 195 : 13
ye may not w. name out, 465 : 5
Washed, if clod w. away, 254 : 22
in life's river, 403 : 14
Pilate w. hands, 41 : 22
robes in blood, 53 : 15
Washing hands with invisible soap, 485 : 13
home and being w. day, 310 : 4
one another's w., 924 : 5
Washington, America furnished W., 451 : 7
bequeathed name of W., 459 : 11
city of southern efficiency, 892 : 2
George W. slept here, 813 : 6
government at W. lives, 609 : 8
in clear upper sky, 450 : 11
inflation made in W., 880 : 17
Leonidas and W., 461 : 20
like Joshua of old, 348 : 11
never slopt over, 616 : 14
task greater than W., 521 : 6
what posterity say of W., 348 : 10
Washington (*continued*)
without reward, 591 : 11
Washington's a watchword, 462 : 15
Lincoln's name close to W., 603 : 3
Washpot, Moab is my w., 19 : 25
Washup, die down only to w., 778 : 6
Waspish, when you are w., 217 : 1
Wasps and hornets break through, 321 : 15
Wassails, maypoles hockcarts w., 265 : 17
Waste and solitary places, 467 : 11
haste maketh w., 158 : 18
his flames must w. away, 272 : 1
lay w. our powers, 427 : 29
my dear times' w., 244 : 11
natural resources, 687 : 14
nights in discontent, 174 : 10
not fresh tears, 77 : 15
now doth time w. me, 195 : 17
of public money, 637 : 12
of seas, 483 : 20
of shame, 245 : 23
peace corrupt war w., 288 : 1
sad time, 807 : 8
self-hatred w. of unfulfilled promise, 859 : 18
sweetness on desert air, 362 : 8
their toil, 430 : 7
to what purpose this w., 41 : 3
wherefore w. elocution, 630 : 4
willful w. woeful want, 450 : 1
Wasted, affection never w., 511 : 4
barrel of meal w. not, 13 : 43
chronicle of w. time, 245 : 12
his substance, 43 : 26
most w. day of all, 386 : 4
no act of kindness ever w., 66 : 2
oil unprofitably burns, 376 : 6
they that w. us, 22 : 15
time now doth time waste me, 195 : 17
your music life you w., 850 : 18
Wasteful and ridiculous excess, 202 : 5
youth of pleasure w., 545 : 22
Wastefulness, conspicuous w., 685 : 4
Waster of rich men, 74 : 23
Wastes and withers there, 676 : 13
gray-green crashing, 907 : 2
her time and me, 276 : 7
marble w. statue grows, 154 : 14
more of future, 760 : 8
Wasteth, destruction that w. at noonday, 20 : 16
man dieth and w. away, 15 : 34
Wasting, shall I w. in despair, 264 : 23
Watch along the Rhine, 573 : 12
and laugh, 617 : 9
and pray, 41 : 13
authentic w. is shown, 289 : 19
care keeps his w., 192 : 21
cat w. mouse, 323 : 19
corn licker stop victim's w., 757 : 6
could ye not w., 41 : 13
ef you don't w. out, 665 : 11
from their graves, 541 : 7
I could w. I could w., 873 : 15
I w. and am as a sparrow, 21 : 5
in the night, 20 : 11
keeping w. above own, 567 : 7
keeping w. over their flock, 42 : 28
kept w. Matthew and Waldo, 804 : 7
Lord w. between thee and me, 8 : 23
men at play, 757 : 5

Watch (*continued*)
not one another out of fear, 251 : 15
o'er man's mortality, 426 : 23
one to w. one to pray, 294 : 16
out w'en gittin' all you want, 662 : 16
secret whispers of other's w., 208 : 1
sleeps upon w., 372 : 7
some must w. some sleep, 222 : 17
tells time of poet, 878 : 11
that basket, 624 : 23
that ends night, 328 : 11
they that w. for the morning, 22 : 12
this long year's w., 71 : 3
wear learning like w., 342 : 1
woods fill with snow, 748 : 5
ye stand fast, 49 : 9
ye therefore, 42 : 14
Watchdog's honest bark, 460 : 16
voice, 370 : 4
Watched, deaths ye died w. beside, 707 : 3
ramparts we w., 446 : 1
you with light and darkness, 851 : 2
Watcher of the skies, 475 : 7
Watches, dictionaries are like w., 353 : 16
of night, 512 : 21
with judgments as w., 332 : 15
Watchful, many a w. night, 206 : 29
place of w. intentness, 640 : 10
stubbornly opposed by w. men, 846 : 17
Watching, all her maidens w., 531 : 8
Big Brother w., 858 : 14
for riches, 36 : 2
pines shore and stars, 849 : 6
sits w. for omens, 82 : 12
with eternal lids apart, 478 : 20
Watchman tell us of night, 465 : 10
waketh but in vain, 22 : 8
what of the night, 30 : 1
Watchmen on the heights are crying, 176 : 20
Watchword, Royal Navy w., 743 : 18
Washington's a w., 462 : 15
Water and a crust, 476 : 5
and fire shall rot, 808 : 12
as showers that w. the earth, 19 : 35
as the hart panteth after w. brooks, 19 : 5
as w. flows downwards, 89 : 9
as w. split on the ground, 13 : 22
as w. unto wine, 530 : 5
as wheel runs why w. pitcher, 109 : 19
benefit written in w., 155 : *n* 4
benison of hot w., 796 : 16
best man like w., 64 : 3
better deeds in w. writ, 155 : *n* 4
blood is thick w. thin, 629 : 2
blood thicker than w., 301 : 15
bridge over troubled w., 915 : 15
brief as w. falling, 812 : 3
brimming w. among stones, 713 : 15
bring w. bring wine, 67 : 8
buffaloes neurasthenic, 799 : 16
burn everything or throw into w., 156 : 13
burned on the w., 240 : 29
but the desert, 458 : 18
by w. We give life, 131 : 13
came out abundantly, 10 : 26
cast shadow in air or w., 904 : 8
charmed w. burnt alway, 434 : 28
Christ walks on black w., 892 : 4

Water (*continued*)
conscious w. saw its God, 292 : 5
dark fingers of w., 879 : 9
daughter of Earth and W., 468 : 10
death of w. and fire, 808 : 12
does mill make w. run, 722 : 6
don't care where w. goes, 742 : 16
don't go near w., 924 : 17
down unseen full of w., 195 : 11
drawers of w., 11 : 33
drink no longer w., 50 : 33
drinks w. her keel plows air, 178 : 6
dripping w. hollows stone, 100 : 7
drunk your w. and wine, 707 : 3
dry and thirsty land where no w. is, 19 : 29
dry stone no w., 805 : 1
earth and w. strive again, 334 : 15
earth hath bubbles as w., 236 : 7
etched with waves, 798 : 8
everywhere, 434 : 15
false as w., 226 : 15, 232 : 16
feet are always in w., 407 : 16
fetch pail of w., 931 : 1
fire and w., 225 : 22
fish out of w., 313 : 21
flows clear from Lebanon, 759 : 11
fortune melted to w., 313 : 7
give thine enemy w., 25 : 15
glory like circle in w., 184 : 18
green w. through my hull, 673 : 15
grind with w. that's past, 269 : 21
hears thy faintest word, 292 : *n* 3
heaven as near by w., 166 : *n* 10
honest w., 242 : 32
hot w. to remain upon tea, 273 : 9
I came like w., 516 : 17
if British went by w., 382 : 12
imperceptible w., 485 : 13
in Arkansas River, 787 : 11
in music oar forsakes, 637 : 15
in w. lives the fish, 300 : 19
is best, 71 : 20
is good, 64 : 3
is my will, 874 : 9
Just Add Hot W., 828 : 17
know worth of w., 347 : 25
land rats and w. rats, 198 : 17
land thieves and w. thieves, 198 : 17
Laughing W., 511 : 17
leave log in w., 926 : 8
like a stone, 608 : 17
lily bloom, 528 : 27
limns on w. writes in dust, 181 : 18
little drops of w., 591 : 7
little w. in stream fault of source, 127 : 15
meditation and w. wedded, 570 : 4
more than ocean w. broken, 748 : 11
more w. glideth by mill, 161 : *n* 2
most encourage flame, 829 : 16
much w. goeth by mill, 161 : 2
name writ in w., 480 : 7
never formed to mind, 767 : 15
never hold w., 324 : 29
never miss w. till well dry, 347 : *n* 5
no more w., 903 : 3
no sound of w., 805 : 1
no w. only rock, 805 : 10
not all w. in rough rude sea, 194 : 26
o'er the w. to Charlie, 422 : 19
of affliction, 14 : 11, 30 : 18
of life given to us, 837 : 11
of river never the same, 137 : 13

Water (*continued*)
of sources and ashes, 860 : 9
on hands like Pilate, 859 : 13
over cliff w. drops, 894 : 1
over rocks wood and w., 490 : 3
people are like w., 826 : 11
plunge hands in w., 868 : 10
quarrel over w., 787 : 11
reasons made mouth w., 291 : 12
reflects images, 635 : 6
rivers of w. in a dry place, 30 : 21
run through fire and w., 225 : 22
running w. walk, 779 : 1
rush to rest in air, 837 : 1
salt w. unbounded, 710 : 7
saving soil and w., 779 : 2
send down w. on earth, 131 : 14
skuttle fish blackens w., 327 : 1
slippy-sloppy in larder, 719 : 5
snake came to w. trough, 790 : 12
sound of w., 314 : 7
spring of ever-flowing w., 106 : 20
stagnant w. loses purity, 152 : 8
stained the w. clear, 403 : 3
steeds to w. at those springs, 243 : 16
stream smoothest w. deepest, 172 : *n* 7
street before the w. gate, 14 : 30
struggling for life in the w., 353 : 26
sunshine and good w., 670 : 13
supposes mirage to be w., 131 : 17
tar w. so mild and benign, 330 : 22
through a sieve, 613 : 18
through fire and through w., 19 : 32
to succeed add w. to wine, 705 : 8
tossing green w., 785 : 12
tree planted by rivers of w., 17 : 12
under running w., 806 : 13
under w. men walk, 919 : 8
unstable as w., 9 : 4
until desert knows w., 607 : 6
virtue more than w. or fire, 69 : 17
virtues we write in w., 249 : 14
wagon place for me, 718 : 12
wait to watch w. clear, 747 : 3
was made wine, 44 : 27
wash feet in soda w., 805 : 6
welling from earth, 802 : 17
what w. lapping bow, 806 : 8
which they beat, 240 : 29
whole stay of w., 28 : 34
wide w. inescapable, 767 : 4
with w. to drink, 68 : 21
without a flaw, 837 : 1
written in running w., 102 : 12
Watercolors to impaint his cause, 205 : 3
Watercourse, patio heaven's w., 843 : 5
Watercraft, not be precise about w., 577 : 8
Water-drinkers, no poems by w. please for long, 109 : 12
Waterdrops, soul be changed to w., 184 : 9
women's weapons w., 233 : 22
worn stones of Troy, 226 : 15
Watered, Apollos w., 48 : 3
by blood of tyrants, 401 : 4
heaven with tears, 405 : 8
our horses in Helicon, 178 : 8
with tears w., 733 : 6
Waterfall, from w. named her, 511 : 17
Watering last year's crops, 565 : 5
pot and pruning knife, 536 : 12

Watering (*continued*)
your waters and w. place, 749 : 10
Waterloo, Austerlitz and W., 761 : 6
battle of first rank, 491 : 18
dismal plain, 491 : 12
every man meets W., 538 : 15
from Marathon to W., 628 : 1
thou fatal W., 457 : 21
won on playing fields, 421 : 16
Waterman, great-grandfather was but a w., 302 : 7
Watermen look astern row ahead, 120 : 18
Water's my will, 874 : 9
thin, 629 : 2
Waters and their powers, 458 : 7
at their priestlike task, 478 : 20
beams of his chambers in w., 21 : 8
beautiful drifts like w., 713 : 3
beside the still w., 18 : 7
cannot quench love, 28 : 24
cast thy bread upon the w., 27 : 20
cold w. to a thirsty soul, 25 : 16
come ye to the w., 31 : 18
cover the sea, 29 : 19
desert of w., 603 : 2
do business in great w., 21 : 14
dreadful noise of w., 187 : 9
Father of W. unvexed to sea, 523 : 2
fen of stagnant w., 425 : 22
fish in troubled w., 319 : 7
here are your w., 749 : 10
hitherandthithering w., 778 : 5
liffeying w., 778 : 5
like music on w., 460 : 1
murmuring, 278 : 25
music crept by upon w., 247 : 20
nearer roll, 350 : 12
no w. breed or break, 901 : 4
noise of many w., 20 : 19
of beginning and end, 790 : 22
of petrel and porpoise, 807 : 24
of the heart, 886 : 13
once more upon w., 457 : 11
over great sea winds trouble w., 100 : 12
over rolling w. go, 530 : 25
peopling earth w. and sky, 311 : 12
pour w. of Nile, 611 : 5
returning to springs, 511 : 4
rivering w., 778 : 5
rushing of many w., 29 : 24
secret w., 834 : 11
should lift their bosoms, 226 : 2
shout golden shouts, 600 : 10
Spirit of God moved upon w., 6 : 10
stilled at even, 601 : 13
stolen w. are sweet, 23 : 20
take heed of still w., 172 : *n* 7
their name is on your w., 465 : 5
tree planted by the w., 32 : 11
turns to perilous w., 140 : 11
vast w. of petrel, 807 : 24
voice as sound of many w., 52 : 30
voice of many w., 53 : 22
were a wall, 9 : 31
were gathered together, 9 : 35
were his winding sheet, 257 : 5
what West has thrown on w., 903 : 13
wonderful w. round you, 593 : 7
words writ in w., 155 : *n* 4
your divine w., 899 : 16
Watersmooth-silver stallion, 828 : 13
Watery, crown the w. glade, 361 : 8
Watery (*continued*)
envious siege of w. Neptune, 194 : 14
main, 244 : 22
nest, 275 : 30
shore, 405 : 2
sunk beneath w. floor, 281 : 4
thing of w. salt, 760 : 21
wide-rolling w. prairies, 571 : 3
Watson, know my methods W., 689 : 9
Mr. W. come here, 661 : 7
Wattle, ever hear of Captain W., 393 : 10
Wattles, of clay and w. made, 712 : 4
Wave, all sunk beneath the w., 377 : 19
as w. succeeds w., 223 : *n* 5
blue w. rolls nightly, 459 : 14
cry wind cry vast waters, 807 : 24
dance like w. of sea, 712 : 17
every w. had nightcap, 667 : 8
glassy cool translucent w., 280 : 3
life is a w., 580 : 3
lift me as w. leaf cloud, 467 : 20
never w. of all waves, 709 : 12
obeyed what w. had taught, 800 : 10
of the future, 867 : 4, 891 : 5
small rock holds back great w., 59 : 23
star-spangled banner w., 446 : 1
swiftly walk over w., 469 : 21
Time's toppling w., 868 : 5
to wash him from world, 735 : 3
whose arm bind restless w., 596 : 18
wind or swallowing w., 296 : 5
winning w. deserving note, 266 : 7
wish you a w. of the sea, 246 : 28
wrack ancient as ocean's hills, 907 : 2
write woman's vows upon w., 75 : 22
Wave-beat shore, 552 : 22
Waved her lily hand, 331 : 10
long has it w. on high, 518 : 12
Waver, steadiest minds to w., 74 : 17
Wavering between profit and loss, 806 : 5
discordant w. multitude, 205 : 18
more longing w., 214 : 1
Waves, amber w. of grain, 688 : 5
bound as steed, 457 : 11
breaking w. dashed, 470 : 14
Britannia rule the w., 345 : 19
come as the w. come, 431 : 23
cypress in palace walk, 531 : 11
ever-rolling w. made by restlessness, 571 : 3
formal as scales on fish, 798 : 8
here shall thy proud w. be stayed, 16 : 30
him that walked the w., 281 : 4
hopping through frothy w., 613 : 4
I danced on the w., 673 : 14
into w. pine needles, 314 : 6
laughter of ocean w., 70 : 23
make towards pebbled shore, 244 : 19
march o'er mountain w., 443 : 12
music of dancing w., 800 : 10
mutinous Shannon w., 777 : 16
never wave of all w., 709 : 12
nothing but w. and I, 461 : 9
of religious emotion, 799 : 18
of science beat in vain, 580 : 9
on side of ablest navigators, 383 : 13
over mountains over w., 919 : 3
paced to and fro, 732 : 7
pebbles which w. fling, 587 : 14
raging w. of the sea, 52 : 26
remained shadow of w., 850 : 2
Waves (*continued*)
righteousness as w. of sea, 31 : 7
rise and fall unceasingly, 571 : 3
salt sea w., 745 : 11
sunset illumine w., 673 : 17
tired w. vainly breaking, 564 : 17
whales in w. of sea, 790 : 22
what are wild w. saying, 548 : *n* 1
when w. went high, 303 : 20
which only He may walk, 829 : 14
white w. paced to and fro, 732 : 7
wild w. whist, 247 : 19
Waves', spent w. riot, 633 : 19
Waving, not w. but drowning, 856 : 16
sails filled streamers w., 288 : 30
wild tail, 710 : 6
Wax and Bristles three sheets in wind, 553 : *n* 4
fill hives with honey and w., 321 : 14
mind a block of w., 85 : 18
moon will w. wane, 512 : 19
my heart is w., 171 : 10
rich gifts w. poor, 221 : 14
shoes ships sealing w., 613 : 5
snapped like sealing w., 548 : 14
to flaming youth virtue w., 223 : 5
to receive, 460 : 7
Waxed, Jeshurun w. fat, 11 : 24
Waxworks, if we're w. you pay, 612 : 23
Way, a w. a lone a last, 778 : 6
abode hour and went his w., 516 : 10
all the w. home, 930 : 11
best w. out is through, 747 : 11
birds their trackless w., 540 : 6
broad is the w., 38 : 15
carnivorous W. of these lines, 906 : 14
catch the nearest w., 236 : 16
come all the w. for this, 618 : 4
crow shook snow, 748 : 3
died maintaining right of w., 925 : 10
down upon Swanee River, 598 : 3
every day in every w., 684 : 9
every one his own w., 97 : 2
every w. makes my gain, 232 : 10
everything's going my w., 833 : 10
go not into every w., 35 : 5
God moves in mysterious w., 375 : 16
going the w. of all the earth, 11 : 36
Great White W., 696 : 16
he says it, 901 : 5
he should go, 24 : 35
hear right w. in the morning, 68 : 14
heaven's wide pathless w., 278 : 18
home's the farthest way, 267 : 16
in dark wood where straight w. lost, 140 : 10
in whatsoever w. any come to Me, 94 : 12
is plain peaceful just, 522 : 12
I've a long w. to go, 864 : 9
jog on the footpath w., 246 : 24
Karamozov w., 582 : 8
king stood at parting of w., 32 : 27
lambs who lost w., 708 : 14
let each go his own w., 112 : 24
let the wicked forsake his w., 31 : 20
life's common w., 425 : 23
like wild beast guards w., 406 : 1
long and steep is the w., 61 : 17
long is the w. and hard, 284 : 17
long w. to Tipperary, 753 : 1
long wind cold, 429 : 20
longest w. round shortest home, 267 : *n* 6

Way (*continued*)
love find w., 919 : 3
make it over your w., 750 : 11
many a weary w., 482 : 13
merit makes his w., 248 : 21
met you not my love by the w., 172 : 8
my w. of life is fallen, 239 : 31
narrow is the w., 38 : 15
new w. to pay old debts, 263 : 1
no ready w. to virtue, 274 : 16
no w. out for me, 817 : 6
noiseless tenor of their w., 362 : 12
not pass this w. again, 439 : 2
of a fool, 23 : 30
of a man with a maid, 26 : 4
of a serpent upon a rock, 26 : 4
of a ship in the sea, 26 : 4
of all flesh, 262 : 2
of an eagle in the air, 26 : 4
of coming into world, 321 : 10
of Heaven has no favorites, 65 : 8
of Heaven to benefit others, 65 : 10
of ignorance, 807 : 18
of man with maid, 708 : 22
of sage is to act, 65 : 10
of saying above thing said, 771 : 15
of the tree of life, 7 : 13
of transgressors is hard, 23 : 32
old paths where is the good w., 31 : 37
out of hell leads up, 284 : 17
out of wind's and rain's w., 774 : 1
plods his weary w., 361 : 20
prepare the w. before me, 33 : 37
prepare the w. of the Lord, 30 : 30, 36 : 26
pretty Fanny's w., 329 : 15
primrose w., 238 : 2
rebellion lay in his w., 205 : 2
roses all the w., 541 : 10
see the W. of Heaven, 64 : 17
set out in relative w., 742 : 1
ship's w. on sea, 708 : 22
so plain we may lose way, 742 : 15
solar walk or milky w., 336 : 16
such ever love's w., 544 : 14
sweetest w. to me, 708 : 22
tells us the w. to go, 669 : 21
that can be told of, 63 : 12
that w. madness lies, 234 : 2
that with tears watered, 733 : 6
that's my w. sir, 565 : 1
that's the w. it is, 888 : 15
that's the w. to do it, 454 : 13
the money goes, 922 : 1
the truth and the life, 45 : 22
there is a lion in the w., 25 : 19
they eat drink learn and everything, 752 : 13
they say it, 857 : 5
this is w. world ends, 805 : 18
this the w. walk ye in it, 30 : 19
thorny w. to heaven, 218 : 28
though hell bar w., 773 : 1
thoughts nature gives w. to, 237 : 11
to be immortal is die daily, 274 : 13
to bliss, 267 : 10
to draw new mischief, 229 : 33
to dusty death, 240 : 4
to keep thee in the w., 10 : 11
to man's heart, 538 : 6
to tell if poem lasting, 749 : 20
took their solitary w., 288 : 4
trudgin' weary w., 660 : 5

Way (*continued*)
true w. but yet untried, 179 : 7
true w. goes over rope, 786 : 2
twinkle on milky w., 427 : 8
unlikely to be undone, 820 : 14
which is the w., 874 : 20
win my w. to the coast, 76 : 25
wisdom finds a w., 400 : 7
world ends, 805 : 18
wrong w. more reasonable, 671 : 7
Wayfarer, when w. whistles in dark, 678 : 10
world-renowned, 135 : 7
Wayfaring, lodging place of w. men, 32 : 4
Way-hay you rolling river, 934 : 20
Ways, amend your w., 32 : 1
blood nipped and w. be foul, 191 : 14
consider her w. and be wise, 23 : 11
dazzled by w. of God, 765 : 2
dwelt among untrodden w., 424 : 12
from cheerful w. of men, 285 : 5
God's w. to man, 691 : 17
her w. are w. of pleasantness, 23 : 5
high-hearted w., 568 : 19
his w. are judgment, 11 : 23
I knew all her w., 692 : 5
I will take heed to my w., 18 : 29
in all the w. you can, 346 : 12
in His w. found Him not, 534 : 27
just are the w. of God, 288 : 26
keep thee in all thy w., 20 : 17
labyrinthine w., 693 : 10
many w. meet in one town, 207 : 8
nine and sixty w., 708 : 21
of God justifiable, 288 : 26
of God to man, 336 : 11
of God to men, 283 : 2
oldest sins newest w., 206 : 33
possible to fail in many w., 87 : 17
practice childish w., 59 : 17
sing ancient w., 712 : 3
stand ye in the w., 31 : 37
to lengthen our days, 447 : 1
to make thy w. known, 55 : 5
triple w. to take, 708 : 22
your w. are not my w., 31 : 21
Wayside, seeds fell by w., 39 : 13
Wayward, clod of w. marl, 209 : 6
fond and w. thoughts, 424 : 11
fortune's w. tyranny, 73 : 11
purblind w. boy, 190 : 26
sisters depart, 455 : 13
tetchy and w. thy infancy, 187 : 18
Wayworn, weary w. wanderer, 525 : 9
We about to die salute you, 123 : 14
are ancients of the earth, 178 : *n* 12
are as much as we see, 557 : 3
are his offspring, 46 : 17, 92 : 11
are his people, 21 : 3
are many, 42 : 4
are not amused, 573 : 17
are the hollow men, 805 : 15
art is I science is w., 552 : 4
be brethren, 8 : 6
content at the last, 808 : 9
gather together, 918 : 19
happy few, 208 : 11
must needs die, 13 : 22
my ship and I., 855 : 8
real cool, 889 : 13
shall not be moved, 936 : 7
that had loved him so, 541 : 6

We (*continued*)
the peoples of United Nations, 788 : 20
thought we would try, 855 : 8
were very tired, 822 : 19
would and would not, 229 : 4
Weak and beggarly elements, 49 : 26
and fruitless words, 524 : 4
and mighty Russia, 584 : 3
concessions of the w., 372 : 11
creatures of clay, 82 : 9
defense of w. is recriminate, 437 : 3
devouring of w. by strong, 579 : 19
differences don't make us w., 903 : 11
evils age and hunger, 211 : 14
fear to appear w., 301 : 9
flesh is w., 41 : 13
God hath chosen w., 48 : 1
grow w. keeping on guard, 658 : 24
head with strongest bias, 332 : 19
infirmities of w., 47 : 34
lemonade w. like your soul, 412 : 6
man better enemy than friend, 561 : 14
men as w. and strong, 524 : 2
men not change mind, 751 : 9
my spirit too w., 478 : 7
no w. person be deprived, 903 : 6
not w. if we use means, 383 : 3
ones that cry for help, 820 : 9
piping time of peace, 186 : 32
pondered w. and weary, 526 : 10
poor infirm w. old man, 233 : 26
poor w. palsy-stricken, 476 : 14
refuge of w. minds, 342 : 6
shoulderings aside of w., 579 : 7
speak for fallen and w., 567 : 3
spirit quickens to rebel, 806 : 6
strength for w., 615 : 6
strong just w. secure, 891 : 2
success to the w., 378 : 14
surely w. perish, 752 : 4
to be w. is miserable, 283 : 10
too w. to be a sinner, 242 : 32
too w. to bear them long, 318 : 4
without justice courage w., 347 : 4
witness of thy name, 277 : 13
Weaken, to convince is to w., 739 : 10
Weakening eye of day, 641 : 11
Weakens, time w. love, 315 : 6
Weaker, may turn from w. hand, 198 : 30
we are getting w. of course, 726 : 7
wife the w. vessel, 52 : 13
Weakest fruit drops earliest, 200 : 6
goes to wall, 169 : 35
harm to strong from w., 658 : 7
Weak-eyed bat, 364 : 12
Weakling, no room for w., 745 : 11
Weakly perish at another moment, 59 : 5
Weakness, all else is w., 483 : 7
all your strength is w., 74 : 16
amiable w., 349 : 22
carp at w. of human mind, 308 : 9
credulity man's w., 441 : 22
fear of w., 792 : 14
is function of Tao, 64 : 13
is it w. of intellect, 629 : 16
made perfect in w., 49 : 23
man of my w., 772 : 12
no w. no contempt, 289 : 9
of children's limbs innocent, 128 : 27
of most public men, 616 : 14

Weakness (*continued*)
power obtained by w., 414 : 11
read each wound each w., 585 : 3
regime collapses of w., 813 : 14
stronger by w., 276 : 12
too much w. for stoic's pride, 337 : 2
you saw his w., 413 : 33
Weaknesses, people with no w. terrible, 655 : 9
Weal and woe is common, 273 : 11
come w. come woe, 422 : 19
scheme of w. and woe, 544 : 6
Wealth, administer w. for good, 621 : 8
all that w. e'er gave, 362 : 3
and children adornment of life, 131 : 11
and freedom reign, 368 : 16
arithmetic cannot number, 262 : 21
best riches ignorance of w., 370 : 1
Black love is Black w., 916 : 2
boundless his w., 430 : 10
build up great fortunes, 638 : 7
by any means get w., 339 : 19
cause of covetousness, 183 : 13
company of just men better than w., 77 : 12
consume w. without producing it, 680 : 8
equal w. and opportunities, 666 : 2
even to wicked man, 67 : 2
governments confiscate w., 783 : 9
greater w. thicker dirt, 871 : 10
health and w. missed me, 454 : 8
health more important than w., 789 : 13
honor or w., 436 : 2
I ask not, 669 : 2
if you spend w. at once, 484 : 13
large w. larger heart, 304 : 14
let man outlive his w., 200 : 15
loss of w. loss of dirt, 158 : 16
love of w. in all that Americans do, 506 : 11
love remembered such w. brings, 244 : 10
maketh many friends, 24 : 24
malefactors of great w., 687 : 12
man of w. and taste, 916 : 8
matrimony road to w., 554 : 12
no man takes w. to Hades, 67 : 6
no w. but life, 572 : 17
nor too much w. nor wit, 262 : 16
not set heart on w., 6 : 7
number and happiness, 373 : 9
of Indies, 356 : 6
of kings can give nothing more, 109 : 6
of Ormus and of Ind, 284 : 3
of seas spoils of war, 561 : *n* 1
opportunity for achievement, 81 : 1
parent of luxury, 84 : 12
pauper in midst of w., 108 : 6
pernicious influence of w., 451 : 5
piled by unrequited toil, 524 : 7
private w. I decline, 704 : 5
proper administration of w., 621 : 5
set exact w. of states, 204 : 29
sinews of affairs, 92 : 6
small aid is w., 77 : 3
so act toward office so toward w., 121 : 20
such great w. can be drawn, 151 : 8
surplus w. sacred trust, 621 : 8
than w. in storehouse, 6 : 6

Wealth (*continued*)
to live on little with contented mind, 101 : 8
true gospel concerning w., 621 : 12
undiminished natural w., 890 : 13
unequal distribution of w., 719 : 10
voyage not for gain honor w., 152 : 1
war where w. allures, 305 : 22
where w. accumulates, 369 : 30
which all men desire, 157 : 4
wisdom outweighs w., 75 : 1
wisdom to use w., 872 : 11
without profit no w., 784 : 29
Wealthy, be w. not rich, 536 : 6
curled darlings, 229 : 22
healthy w. and dead, 831 : 8
healthy w. and wise, 347 : 12
man and kindly, 57 : 32
obliged w. and relieved poor, 57 : *n* 8
reckon wise w., 83 : 7
Weaned away from earth, 839 : 13
child shall put hand on cockatrice' den, 29 : 19
from error, 727 : 5
heart from low desires, 155 : 1
were we not w. till then, 251 : 14
Weans, are w. in bed, 537 : 6
Weapon, every experiment like w., 157 : 5
his w. wit, 627 : *n* 2
man absolute w., 826 : *n* 1
print is strongest w., 766 : 7
satire's my w., 339 : 6
with other hand held w., 14 : 29
Weaponless himself, 288 : 23
Weapons, books are w., 780 : 17
change but not man, 791 : 16
get your w. ready, 575 : 14
important in war, 826 : 9
of war perished, 13 : 11
race get out of hand, 860 : 6
spare us word of w., 900 : 2
to win beat man not w., 791 : 16
triumph over w. and tactics, 756 : 3
women's w. waterdrops, 233 : 22
Wear an undeserved dignity, 199 : 14
both for both are thine, 187 : 2
bottoms of trousers rolled, 803 : 18
day out before it comes, 664 : 6
disguises which we w., 286 : 4
golden sorrow, 248 : 27
hat not worse for w., 376 : 15
heart upon my sleeve, 229 : 17
him in my heart's core, 222 : 6
I get that I w., 212 : 2
let the devil w. black, 222 : 9
long boots, 761 : 13
motley's the only w., 211 : 8
ne'er w. out everlasting flint, 193 : 2
not my dagger in my mouth, 243 : 26
nothing to w., 595 : 4
ourselves and never rest, 183 : 6
out better than rust, 303 : 3
out in a walled prison, 235 : 12
such qualities as would w., 369 : 7
the gold hat, 835 : 3
thou w. lion's hide, 201 : 21
use and never w. it out, 64 : 2
use it up w. it out, 924 : 4
weeds of Athens he doth w., 196 : 22
white flannel trousers, 803 : 19
women w. the breeches, 258 : 11
your rue with a difference, 224 : 2

Wearer, honor purchased by merit of w., 199 : 14
Weariest and most loathed life, 228 : 21
river, 633 : 22
Wearin' o' the Green, 920 : 21, 920 : 22
Weariness and fault, 748 : 9
can snore upon flint, 243 : 23
fever and the fret, 476 : 24
may toss him to my breast, 269 : 2
much study a w., 27 : 27
of thee, 252 : 15
possession loads us with w., 573 : 8
Wearing, not linen you're w. out, 485 : 19
o' the Green, 920 : 21
ring becomes thin by w., 100 : 7
weight of learning, 532 : 26
Wearing-stone or open eye, 748 : 1
Wearisome condition of humanity, 175 : 5
Wears faith as fashion of hat, 208 : 25
head that w. a crown, 206 : 19
his wit in his belly, 226 : 6
morality as best garment, 782 : 19
on smiling face dream, 436 : 9
rose of youth, 241 : 9
so w. she to him, 214 : 1
those that April w., 229 : *n* 1
Weary, across a w. land, 742 : 10
after three days men grow w., 347 : 2
age not w. them, 727 : 1
and ill at ease, 596 : 13
and old with service, 249 : 3
Blues, 854 : 15
comforts of w. pilgrimage, 356 : 25
eyelids a little w., 638 : 10
fingers w. and worn, 485 : 16
great rock in a w. land, 30 : 21
grunt and sweat under w. life, 221 : 12
how my heart grows w., 598 : 4
how w. stale flat, 218 : 5
I sae w. fu' o' care, 409 : 24
I w. for thee, 167 : 3
in well-doing, 49 : 33
lay his w. bones among ye, 249 : 10
let him be rich and w., 269 : 2
life a w. pilgrimage, 267 : 19
lips I close, 363 : 9
lonely for me he longs, 929 : 3
most w. cry I can no more, 656 : 15
of breath, 485 : 21
of days and hours, 633 : 20
of existing government, 521 : 11
plods his w. way, 361 : 20
pondered weak and w., 526 : 10
run and not be w., 31 : 2
sad and w. I go back, 778 : 6
say I'm w., 454 : 8
she's w. go down Death, 733 : 13
there the w. be at rest, 15 : 9
trudgin' w. way, 660 : 5
vain my w. search to find, 369 : 5
wayworn wanderer, 525 : 9
weight of world, 423 : 10
wheels of w. life, 303 : 16
wi' hunting, 927 : 8
with disasters, 238 : 16
world w. of past, 468 : 18
Wearyin', jest a-w. fer you, 684 : 18
Weasel, as w. sucks eggs, 211 : 2
methinks it is like a w., 222 : 20
pop goes the w., 922 : 1
Weasels fighting in a hole, 715 : 6
Weather a great bluffer, 847 : 8

Weather (*continued*)
all sorts of things and w., 494 : 3
always doing something, 622 : 18
always fair w., 705 : 2
appeared when w. cleared, 647 : 21
blue unclouded w., 528 : 25
born with anxiety about w., 630 : 22
calm or stormy w., 608 : 16
clear w. spreads cloudless, 59 : 27
cloudy was the w., 934 : 2
come wind come w., 302 : 14
everybody talks about w., 603 : 15
excellent campaigning w., 842 : 11
fair w. cometh out of the north, 16 : 26
fine w. heavier on depressed, 896 : 4
get behind w., 683 : 13
I see what w. does, 847 : 2
if it prove fair w., 290 : 4
inner w., 748 : 13
it will be fair w., 39 : 33
literary speciality, 624 : 10
many can brook the w., 190 : 28
mighty good w. as general thing, 623 : 22
mine with inner w., 748 : 13
New England w., 622 : 18
New England w. dazzling uncertainty, 622 : 20
nobody does anything about w., 603 : 15
October's bright blue w., 609 : 11
one hundred thirty-six kinds of w., 622 : 18
poet barometer but also w., 866 : 4
rooster-heeled in all w., 902 : 1
sad or singing w., 633 : 11
shepherd shuns, 642 : 5
things and w., 494 : 3
this w. for to slepen inne, 144 : 20
three months of cold w., 590 : 4
tigers in red w., 767 : 1
to w. as to grief, 785 : 10
trying to get behind w., 683 : 13
under oak in stormy w., 323 : 2
warm w. in bed, 321 : 17
weary of wench guest w. rainy, 347 : 2
wind or w., 436 : 7
winter and rough w., 211 : 1
won't hold up the w., 870 : 5
Weathercock, unseen as w. on steeple, 189 : 33
Weathered, love w. storms of life, 692 : 17
pilot that w. storm, 421 : 22
ship w. every rack, 576 : 6
Weatherman, you don't need a w., 915 : 7
Weatherwise, some w. some otherwise, 347 : 14
Weave circle round him thrice, 433 : 27
flitter dip and soar, 899 : 15
garment of brightness, 928 : 14
hands of memory w., 636 : 2
nets to catch wind, 262 : 11
old England's winding sheet, 406 : 18
sunlight in your hair, 804 : 10
tangled web we w., 431 : 1
the warp, 363 : 5
their thread with bones, 214 : 3
Weaver's, swifter than w. shuttle, 15 : 20
Weaving sand, 500 : 9
Weaving (*continued*)
web of days, 633 : 14
Web, invisible w. you wove, 808 : 19
laws compared to spider's w., 267 : 3
left the w. left the loom, 528 : 27
of our life, 227 : 16
of sunny air, 555 : 16
out flew the w., 528 : 27
subtle spider w., 167 : *n* 9
tangled w. we weave, 431 : 1
weaving w. of days, 633 : 14
Web's, spider in w. center, 167 : 11
Webs from entrails spin, 167 : *n* 9
laws are like spiders' w., 63 : 2
trafficked for strange w., 638 : 11
Webster, Daniel W. steam engine, 433 : 5
eloquence of Mr. W., 840 : 12
liberty in mouth of W., 495 : 28
much possessed by death, 804 : 21
Wed, December when they w., 212 : 25
fair Ellen, 430 : 19
love star and think to w. it, 227 : 10
thought w. with thought, 532 : 2
with this ring I thee w., 56 : 10
wooed in haste w. at leisure, 188 : 34
Wedded, hail w. love, 286 : 5
maid virgin mother, 277 : 6
man assaille wyves pacience, 147 : 21
meditation and water w., 570 : 4
to calamity, 193 : 11
Wedding, chose wife as she her w. gown, 369 : 7
circle of w. ring, 325 : 2
dance barefoot on w. day, 188 : 30
day absolutely fixed, 350 : 2
day after w. night, 739 : 12
earliest w. day, 465 : 13
Guest stood still, 434 : 6
is destiny, 159 : 6
man looks small at w., 839 : 12
member of w., 894 : 13
O w. Guest, 435 : 9
saw a w. in the church, 310 : 1
Weddings of the soul, 767 : 21
Wede, flowers of the forest a' w. away, 368 : 2
Wedge, hard like tip of w., 790 : 10
thrust into nature like w., 558 : 20
tough w. for tough log, 112 : 2
Wedlock forced a hell, 185 : 7
treachery, 289 : 4
Wednesday, he that died o' W., 205 : 5
if I loved you W., 507 : *n* 1
married on W., 932 : 11
Wednesday's child, 932 : 10
Weds, old man w. tyrant, 77 : 19
Wee doch-an'-dorris, 730 : 20
modest crimson-tipped flower, 409 : 9
sleekit cow'rin beastie, 408 : 12
sweet w. wife o' mine, 410 : 17
wee wee, 930 : 11
Willie Winkie, 537 : 6
winsome w. thing, 410 : 17
Weed, anger is a w., 129 : 11
duller than fat w., 219 : 19
flower in disguise, 500 : *n* 1
ill w. groweth fast, 159 : 32
ill w. grows apace, 159 : *n* 16
in wild w. a citizen, 889 : 19
is unloved flower, 500 : *n* 1
law ought to w. it out, 180 : 3
O thou w., 232 : 5
palmer's w., 279 : 15
Weed (*continued*)
pernicious w., 376 : 3
sworn to w. and pluck away, 194 : 22
that grows in every soil, 373 : 5
tobacco a filthy w., 401 : 3
what is a w., 500 : 6
wide to wrap a fairy, 196 : 18
Weeded and worn the ancient thatch, 527 : 17
Weeds and foam, 493 : 15
are shallow-rooted, 185 : 15
deeds like poison w., 676 : 13
garden full of w., 929 : 8
great w. grow apace, 159 : *n* 16
of Athens he doth wear, 196 : 22
of mine own brain, 274 : 10
oozy w. about me twist, 572 : 7
sleep beneath these w., 728 : 7
smell far worse than w., 245 : 6
subterranean w., 873 : 11
winter w. outworn, 468 : 17
Week, argument for a w., 203 : 20
eighth day of w., 863 : 17
in beak enough for w., 765 : 12
longer in hour than w., 632 : 3
not divide Sunday from w., 217 : 19
rare and bloodless w. of repose, 82 : *n* 6
Thursday come and w. gone, 270 : 8
who buys mirth to wail a w., 189 : 20
Week's, good w. labor, 261 : 20
Weeks, desolate dark w., 785 : 14
his brief hours and w., 245 : 18
to months, 534 : 25
Weel done Cutty Sark, 411 : 13
Weep a people inurned, 488 : *n* 3
all around thee w., 394 : 3
and you weep alone, 670 : 3
at joy, 208 : 22
away life of care, 466 : 15
but never see, 442 : 18
deed whereat valor will w., 242 : 27
do not w. it's chronic, 547 : 31
for Adonais, 468 : 22
for me who has charity, 152 : 1
for you the Walrus said, 613 : 8
heart break e'er I'll w., 233 : 23
I w. for what I'm like alone, 874 : 2
if she saugh mous kaught, 145 : 19
if you wish me to w., 109 : 23
in durance vile I w., 411 : 23
laugh that I may not w., 461 : 10
lie in dark w. for sins, 574 : 24
little sorrows sit and w., 404 : 12
make the angels w., 228 : 10
men that laugh and w., 633 : 20
men work women w., 566 : 9
milk my ewes and w., 247 : 2
mourners w. again, 468 : 24
no more my lady, 598 : 5
no more nor sigh, 260 : 19
no more O weep no more, 478 : 9
quanch heart to not w., 811 : 9
scarcely cry w., 403 : 9
she must w. or she will die, 531 : 8
stricken deer go w., 222 : 17
strive nor w., 541 : 21
tears such as angels w., 283 : 26
thy girlish tears, 688 : 4
time to w., 26 : 21
to record, 360 : *n* 2
to see you haste away so soon, 266 : 12
to w. is to make less depth, 186 : 3
vapors w. their burthen, 533 : 27

Weep (*continued*)
what's Hecuba that he should w., 221 : 7
who would not w., 338 : 15
words that w., 295 : 17
you are Emperor yet w., 312 : 5
Weeper, calm the w., 4 : 2
Weepeth, goeth forth and w., 22 : 7
sore in the night, 32 : 21
Weeping anarchic Aphrodite, 868 : 15
and gnashing of teeth, 38 : 22
and the laughter, 721 : 7
do ye hear children w., 507 : 2
dwell a w. hermit there, 364 : 9
full cause of w., 233 : 23
in my heart, 659 : 13
joy at w., 208 : 22
may endure for a night, 18 : 15
not celebrate funeral with w., 95 : 2
philosopher when old, 198 : 12
Rachel w. for her children, 36 : 23
their birth w., 262 : 7
thou sat'st, 394 : 3
upon his bed has sate, 395 : 2
weeping multitudes, 804 : 19
wipe my w. eyes, 328 : 14
without cease, 659 : 15
Weeps incessantly for my sin, 406 : 1
Weft, may w. be red light of evening, 928 : 14
Weib, Wein W. und Gesang, 399 : *n* 3
Weigh eyelids down, 206 : 17
faith the force we cannot w., 665 : 2
let us not w. them, 250 : 3
more people see than w., 342 : 10
things w. me down, 716 : 13
Weighed in the balances, 33 : 1
me dust by dust, 607 : 17
measured priced everything, 549 : 18
stars w. molecules counted, 697 : 4
thirty pieces of silver, 33 : 34
Weighing delight and dole, 217 : 29
Weighs, always w. the same, 869 : 1
mortality w. like sleep, 478 : 7
stuff which w. upon heart, 239 : 32
truth with gold she w., 340 : 15
Weight, all that carries w., 869 : 1
and pain of life, 75 : 14
bear w. of Antony, 240 : 21
force without wisdom falls of own w., 107 : 29
knowledge may give w., 342 : 10
nothing left but the w., 850 : 2
of another's burthen, 270 : 18
of centuries, 670 : 14
of chance desires, 427 : 14
of learning, 532 : 26
of primary noon, 768 : 2
of this sad time, 235 : 20
of unintelligible world, 423 : 10
pull his w. 687 : 7
Weights, equal rate with unequal w., 100 : 17
lift artificial w. from shoulders, 522 : 2
lifted from men, 521 : 8
Weimar, Goethe in W. sleeps, 585 : 2
Wein Weib und Gesang, 399 : *n* 3
Weir, woodland of W., 526 : 23
Weird power in spoken word, 683 : 7
sisters, 239 : 15
wild w. clime, 526 : 8
Weirs, glimmering w., 691 : 12
grass grows on w., 712 : 1
Weiss, ich w. nicht, 481 : *n* 7
Welcome adoo, 616 : 9
advice is seldom w., 341 : 22
all wonders, 292 : 19
be thou faire fresshe May, 146 : 19
come as w. surprise, 109 : 3
coming guest, 334 : 23, 339 : 9
deep-mouthed w., 460 : 16
dog first to w., 456 : 10
each rebuff, 544 : 10
ever smiles, 226 : 19
great w. makes merry feast, 188 : 5
home discarded faith, 202 : 14
kindred glooms, 345 : 5
love bade me w., 269 : 9
make w. the present guest, 60 : 19
marriage an evil most men w., 91 : *n* 6
O life, 777 : 18
pack clouds away and w. day, 257 : 18
peaceful evening in, 377 : 3
say W. friend, 292 : 9
such truth to all men, w., 264 : 20
to your gory bed, 411 : 15
warmest w. at an inn, 355 : *n* 8
Welcomes, consciousness w. object, 648 : 15
little fishes in, 611 : 5
Welcomest, unbidden guests w. when gone, 184 : 19
Welded, ice and iron not w., 669 : 16
Welfare, indifferent to public w., 393 : 3
moral and material w., 687 : 15
music ministers to human w., 579 : 15
of people object of government, 687 : 15
promote general w., 391 : 10
property use subject to public w., 687 : 16
sets friendship above public w., 74 : 10
Welkin, hark how w. rings, 350 : *n* 4
let the w. roar, 206 : 15
Well, all is not w., 218 : 25
all is w. I feel happy, 810 : 4
all w. that ends w., 159 : 28
all's w. that ends w., 227 : 18
bedtime Hal and all w., 205 : 4
begun is half done, 88 : 11
brims the poisoned w., 572 : 6
bucket which hung in w., 455 : 7
Chaucer w. of English, 173 : 22
content to entertain lag-end of my life, 205 : 1
day is a poem, 798 : 1
done and fitting for a princess, 242 : 6
done Cutty Sark, 411 : 13
done good and faithful servant, 40 : 29
done is quickly done, 110 : 7
don't speak w. of self, 299 : 15
fitted in arts, 190 : 20
foolish thing w. done, 355 : 6
for fisherman's boy, 530 : 19
God is and all w. 514 : 2
golden crown like a deep w., 195 : 11
good deed to say w., 248 : 31
hope all will yet be w., 521 : 6
it were done quickly, 236 : 22
kiss place to make w., 449 : 12
laugh and be w., 344 : 14
learn to do w., 28 : 30
mania for maintaining all is w., 343 : 10
Well (*continued*)
moments when everything goes w., 705 : 9
not so deep as a w., 193 : 5
not wisely but too w., 232 : 20
nothing becomes ill that he would w., 190 : 20
of true wit truth, 601 : 6
paid that is satisfied, 200 : 21
poetry must be w. written as prose, 793 : 6
preaches w. that lives w., 170 : 19
pussy's in w., 930 : 14
roared Lion, 197 : 18
servant of God w. done, 286 : 26
sing so wildly w., 525 : 10
till the w. runs dry, 347 : *n* 5
to do w. is what matters, 273 : 3
worth doing is worth doing w., 341 : 16
Well-a-way, youth cry W., 926 : 21
Well-begotten raised by perfect mother, 574 : 3
Well-being dependent on wellbeing of others, 781 : 5
goal of Providence w. of souls, 154 : 13
instructions for, 6 : 1
Well-beloved in that home, 875 : 12
my w. hath a vineyard, 29 : 3
Well-benched, board the w. ships, 62 : 18
Wellborn, few are rich and w., 401 : 12
Well-bred man knows how to confess, 347 : 20
moral sensible w. man, 376 : 2
very strange and w., 324 : 19
Well-chosen anthology, 833 : 5
book or friend, 250 : 15
Well-doing, be not weary in w., 49 : 33
religion of w. and daring, 354 : *n* 4
Well-dressed, sense of being perfectly w., 499 : 23
Well-equipped American bathrooms, 834 : 8
Weller's knowledge of London, 546 : 16
Well-favored man, 209 : 24
Well-fed, not these w. men I fear, 99 : 25
Well-filled, well-made rather than w. head, 164 : 13
Well-furnished libraries, 258 : 2
Well-governed, marble w. cities, 868 : 21
Well-graced actor leaves, 195 : 15
Well-greaved Achaeans, 57 : 24
Wellington's army, 359 : *n* 4
Well-instructed, body of w. men, 515 : 5
Well-made rather than well-filled head, 164 : 13
Well-meaning but without understanding, 677 : 15
Well-read, writer shows he is w., 685 : 15
Well's, when the w. dry, 347 : 25
Wells, buckets into empty w., 376 : 27, 432 : 25
exhausted w., 805 : 12
toads brooding in w., 873 : 12
we have no w., 849 : 12
Well-spent, rare as w. life, 472 : 3
Wellspring, bubbling w., 601 : 2
Well-trod stage, 278 : 6
Well-wishing adventurer, 243 : *n* 4
Well-written life rare, 472 : 3

Well-wrought urn becomes greatest ashes, 252 : 12
Welsh, hear lady sing in W., 204 : 18
Welshman, Taffy was a W., 931 : 3
Weltering in his blood, 306 : 18
Weltgeschichte ist das Weltgericht, 412 : *n* 5
Weltschmerz 1763ricj20 415 : 18
Wenceslas, good King W., 563 : 11
Wench, besides the w. is dead, 183 : 15
  fair hot w. in taffeta, 202 : 23
  one w. in the house, 263 : *n* 2
  weary of w. guest weather, 347 : 2
Wendy, Peter and W., 694 : 13
Wenlock, tarnish late on W. Edge, 691 : 8
Went in jeopardy of their lives, 13 : 26
  Lord w. before them, 9 : 30
  ne'er w. up again, 929 : 15
  same door wherein I w., 516 : 16
  to bed with stockings on, 933 : 1
  to woods to live deliberately, 559 : 25
Wept as I remembered, 591 : 9
  he w. to hear, 403 : 2
  I w. and I believed, 419 : 6
  Jesus w., 45 : 14
  Launcelot w. not greatly but sighed, 149 : 19
  like anything to see, 613 : 2
  my father w., 405 : 12
  not one but has w., 720 : 3
  Peter w. bitterly, 41 : 18
  remembering he w. bitterly, 59 : 10
  that he was born, 728 : 19
  when the poor cried Caesar w., 216 : 19
  when we remembered Zion, 22 : 15
  young man who has not w., 704 : 9
Were, blank page gives back what you w., 850 : 17
  Euripides drew men as they w., 73 : *n* 10
  now you are not as you w., 641 : 24
Werewolf's painful change, 899 : 17
West begins where rainfall drops, 837 : 5
  bosom of urgent w., 654 : 15
  Cincinnatus of W., 459 : 11
  East and W. will pinch heart, 822 : 12
  East is East W. W., 707 : 16
  east or w. Phoenix builds, 271 : 21
  East Side W. Side, 698 : 14
  far down among dim W., 525 : 11
  fifty north forty w., 709 : 24
  go w. young man, 554 : 3
  imaginative genius of w., 577 : 13
  Lochinvar out of the w., 430 : 17
  most beautiful lady in W. Country, 739 : 14
  new Judea between East and W., 565 : 29
  of these out to seas, 785 : 15
  one flew w., 933 : 15
  one ship east another w., 669 : 21
  open the W. Port, 432 : 15
  out of the gladdening w., 728 : 13
  safeguard of w., 425 : 18
  San Francisco W. as all hell, 699 : *n* 3
  solitary singing in the W., 574 : 4
  spirit of w. Greek discovery, 723 : 13
  that's where W. begins, 739 : 7
  the achieved W., 837 : 8
  turn to great w., 538 : 8
West (*continued*)
  what W. has thrown on waters, 903 : 13
  where W. begins, 739 : 7
  Wicked Witch of W., 677 : 9
  Wild W. began, 726 : 8
  wild w. wind, 467 : 17
  wind and the swallows, 93 : 3
  wind full of cries, 760 : 17
  without declining w., 251 : 16
Westard eastard points between, 622 : 19
Westen, im W. nichts neues, 839 : 9
Wester, rainy Pleiads w., 692 : 8
Western, all quiet on W. front, 839 : 9
  brookland, 691 : 11
  civilization be feminized, 886 : 9
  civilization not know contenment, 818 : 11
  civilization worth saving, 815 : 3
  custom of one wife, 731 : 14
  equipped as W. world, 617 : 8
  from east to w. Ind, 212 : 3
  little w. flower, 196 : 15
  many w. islands, 475 : 6
  native w. manliness, 577 : 3
  playboy of W. world, 735 : 4
  walk over w. wave, 469 : 21
  wind blow kindly, 625 : *n* 3
  wind of w. sea, 530 : 25
  wind when wilt thou blow, 917 : 10
  world lost civil courage, 895 : 24
Westerners, Greeks first w., 723 : 13
Westminster Abbey or victory, 408 : 4
Westward eastward points between, 622 : 19
  ho, 214 : 15
  look the land is bright, 564 : 17
  stepping w., 426 : 4
  the course of empire, 330 : 25
Wet, all dirty and w., 323 : 22
  all night in dark and w., 668 : 11
  black bough, 792 : 7
  eye manes dhry heart, 722 : 8
  farmers pray that summers be w., 103 : 27
  liked getting feet w., 719 : 5
  my mind and say something clever, 81 : 12
  nor ever w. with rain, 59 : 27
  not nasty dirty w. hole, 824 : 3
  out of w. clothes, 812 : 4
  sail w. seas roun', 709 : 8
  sheet and flowing sea, 453 : 19
  wild woods, 710 : 6
  would not w. her feet, 160 : 7
Whacks, forty w., 923 : 5
Whale eyes wide open in waters, 790 : 22
  leap of w. up Niagara, 348 : 4
  swims minnow-small, 794 : 13
  very like a w., 222 : 20
Whalebone, all that w. from whales, 897 : 12
Whale-fat of postwar London, 892 : 12
Whale's backbone, 808 : 2
  white hump, 570 : 13
Whales, all that whalebone from w., 897 : 12
  drag Atlantic for w., 623 : 5
  great w. sailing by, 584 : 13
  herds of walruses and w., 570 : 7
  in mid-ocean, 790 : 22
  talk like w., 371 : 24
Whaleship my Yale and Harvard, 570 : 10
Wharf, rots in ease on Lethe w., 219 : 19
What ain't so, 561 : 20
  am I Life, 760 : 21
  and Why and When, 710 : 2
  are they among many, 44 : 39
  are you when sun shall rise, 251 : 1
  art thou idol ceremony, 208 : 6
  can I do for her, 890 : *n* 3
  could she have done being what she is, 713 : 5
  did hand of potter shake, 517 : 8
  do I know, 165 : 6
  does a woman want, 679 : 7
  God hath joined, 40 : 5
  hath God wrought, 11 : 5
  have I done unto thee, 11 : 2
  have I to do with thee, 44 : 26
  I am so shall thou be, 135 : 7
  I have done with where I have been, 800 : 12
  is a man profited, 39 : 38
  is Africa to me, 857 : 14
  is city but people, 242 : 19
  is left when honor lost, 110 : 26
  is love 'tis not hereafter, 213 : 23
  is man, 789 : 6
  is our life, 173 : 1
  is so rare as day in June, 567 : 13
  is that something, 849 : 1
  is the grass, 574 : 15
  is the night, 239 : 2
  is this quintessence of dust, 220 : 29
  is truth, 45 : 30
  is truth said jesting Pilate, 179 : 22
  is your life, 52 : 3
  is yours is mine, 93 : 8
  know wot's w., 546 : 26
  makest thou, 31 : 5
  needs my Shakespeare, 277 : 13
  news on the Rialto, 198 : 18
  no soap, 364 : 5
  of the night, 30 : 1
  price glory, 802 : 4
  say they let them say, 175 : *n* 4
  shall I cry, 30 : 32
  tell them w. to do, 792 : 2
  the anvil, 405 : 8
  the devil was he doing in that galley, 298 : 12
  the hammer, 405 : 8
  thou seest write, 52 : 28
  we did after we arrived, 903 : 11
  who why which w., 550 : 14
  world needs now is love, 898 : 3
  you cannot as you would achieve, 188 : 20
  you have let it suffice, 6 : 7
Whatever begotten born and dies, 714 : 22
  best administered is best, 337 : 9
  comes with years, 633 : 15
  gods may be, 633 : 22, 663 : 10
  I tried to write was verse, 113 : 29
  is fickle freckled, 656 : 5
  is in its causes just, 303 : 14
  is is right, 337 : 1
  Miss T. eats, 740 : 4
  stirs this mortal frame, 435 : 20
  you have spend less, 356 : 26
  you lose reckon no account, 110 : 23
Whatever's, hold own with w. going, 750 : 11

What's come to perfection, 542:5
done is done, 238:17
gone and what's past help, 246:18
Hecuba to him, 221:7
her history, 214:5
in a name, 192:6
past and what's to come, 227:4
past is prologue, 247:27
the shootin' for, 759:9
use of worrying, 770:14
Whatsoever, in w. way any come to Me, 94:12
ye would men do, 38:14
What-was-his-name 613:21
What-you-may-call-um 613:21
Wheat, belly is like a heap of w., 28:19
fields tall with w., 846:15
foam to w. glitter of seas, 911:15
for this planting, 307:*n* 4
gasoline more cause of conflict than w., 876:20
hid in two bushels of chaff, 198:5
immortal w., 311:21
land of w. and barley, 11:14
lifted as w. of our bodies, 831:20
stacker of w., 761:4
worm in the w., 733:4
Wheaten, sickle and w. sheaf, 345:13
Wheel, as w. runs why water pitcher, 109:19
bound upon w. of fire, 235:8
breaks butterfly upon w., 338:18
broken at the cistern, 27:25
ever-whirling w., 174:6
I the limbs and w., 581:1
in the middle of a wheel, 32:25
is come full circle, 235:15
man at w. taught to feel, 647:21
no place for fifth w., 138:10
shoulder to the w., 66:19
smile once more turn thy w., 233:16
sofa round, 377:3
that squeaks gets grease, 561:19
with a revolving w., 607:12
Wheelbarrow, red w. glazed with rain, 785:11
Wheelock, Eleazer W. pious man, 705:3
Wheel's kick and winds' song, 760:14
Wheels, beetle w. droning flight, 361:21
clicked off by little w., 837:16
little tin gods on w., 707:4
of Phoebus' wain, 279:15
of weary life, 303:16
oil for its own w., 376:7
why tarry the w. of his chariots, 12:8
Whelming, under the w. tide, 281:2
Whelp, mongrel puppy w. hound, 369:17
When, I knew him w., 732:15
men drink they are rich, 81:12
not w. but why families came, 903:11
or how I cannot tell, 601:23
shall we three meet again, 235:21
that I was little tiny boy, 214:29
What and Why and W., 710:2
what never has been may have w., 619:2
will they ever learn, 896:11
Whence and what art thou, 284:25
comest thou, 15:2
cradle asks w., 615:7
Whence (*continued*)
had they come, 717:4
Whenever, if poor w. you can if rich w. you please, 86:11
Whensoever called to make exit, 393:9
Where and oh where, 415:16
are snows of yesteryear, 150:7
are they where art thou, 461:5
are we now, 761:6
are you going to, 931:14
cries out W. is it, 435:16
fear to be we know not w., 303:9
go without my mount, 896:13
have all the flowers gone, 896:11
hell is there must we be, 184:1
How and W. and Who, 710:2
I am there ye may be, 45:21
is fancy bred, 199:23
is it now the glory, 426:13
is she now, 239:26
not how many but w. they are, 78:25
was Roderick then, 431:15
wast thou when I laid the foundations, 16:28
we are is hell, 184:1
who are we w. are we, 557:21
your treasure is, 37:17
Whereabout, stones prate of my w., 237:15
Whereas I was blind, 45:8
Where'er she lie, 292:8
you walk, 332:12
Wherefore are these things hid, 213:13
art thou Romeo, 192:5
causes why and w., 208:13
every why hath a w., 188:2
stopp'st thou me, 434:4
Wherein lies happiness, 475:20
Where's my serpent of old Nile, 240:23
Wheresoever called to make exit, 393:9
Wherever, home w. that may be, 878:9
they burn books, 481:11
Whetstone, finest edge with blunt w., 175:10
of wits, 210:12
Whetted, wind's like w. knife, 760:16
Whey, curds and w., 932:15
Which, at odds with morning w. is w., 239:2
God only knows w. is w., 634:14
is the justice, 235:2
much of a w. of a wind, 830:1
of us has known brother, 852:7
that and w., 686:1
who why w. what, 550:14
Whiff of grapeshot, 473:15
Whiffling through tulgey wood, 612:18
Whiggery, what is W., 716:4
Whigs, caught the W. bathing, 501:22
While there's life there's hope, 96:14, 98:18
Whim envy or resentment, 375:12
just as the w. bites, 442:4
Whimper, not bang but w., 805:18
Whine, sweat and w., 574:24
Whines, pules and w., 496:24
Whining at the threshold, 695:17
born naked and falls a-w., 116:*n* 4
of a door, 255:2
poetry, 252:13
schoolboy with satchel, 211:15
wimpled w. purblind, 190:26
Whinny in thy spray, 569:20
Whip all hell yet, 579:*n* 1
fear of hell's a hangman's w., 259:*n* 11
in every honest hand a w., 232:6
so small you could not see, 607:7
weight in wildcats, 666:12
Whipped for overdoing Termagant, 221:23
he must be w. out, 233:8
her little daughter, 932:4
offending Adam, 207:3
she w. him, 933:16
them all soundly, 931:10
Whipping, future smells of w., 482:4
who should 'scape w., 221:5
Whippoorwill, hear that lonesome w., 903:1
Whips and scorns of time, 221:12
my father chastised you with w., 13:38
Whirl asunder and dismember me, 201:22
joy the thrill the w., 569:20
lay mightily in w. of dust, 58:26
Whirled, unstilled world w., 806:4
Whirligig of time, 214:28
Whirling hands at noon, 863:16
summer, 858:20
Whirls, expectation w. me round, 226:10
Northern ocean in vast w., 345:15
Whirlwind, Elijah went up by a w., 14:12
home in your manes, 518:9
Lord answered Job out of the w., 16:27
noise and whip of w., 889:20
of passion, 221:23
reap the w., 33:12
rides in the w., 325:7, 340:22
Whirlwind's, sweeping w. sway, 363:6
Whirlwinds in the south, 29:26
Whiskers, oh my fur and w., 611:7
Whiskey for my Johnny, 934:16
good old w. drink it down, 630:15
is the saving of him, 623:12
must have w. you know why, 840:18
on your breath, 873:10
polishes copper, 623:12
say boys another w., 652:3
Whiskies, born two w. below par, 723:17
Whisper, breathed the husky w., 669:19
busy w. circling round, 370:10
elves w. in ear, 694:1
far-heard w. o'er the sea, 434:21
in ear Not true, 899:8
not a w. be lost, 868:17
Whispered, Devil w. behind leaves, 708:11
little daughter w., 556:15
me through night, 575:18
to ear on pillow, 739:5
voice behind me w. low, 676:7
Whispereth, soul w. within him, 132:10
Whispering ambitions, 804:14
bayed the w. wind, 370:4
from her towers, 587:1
humbleness, 198:25
I will ne'er consent, 460:15
maid and wight w. by, 642:2
music of yonder pine, 92:12

Whispering (*continued*)
still her name, 733 : 1
with white lips, 457 : 18
Whisperings, keeps eternal w., 478 : 16
Whispers, duty w. low, 494 : 21
listen to w. of fancy, 352 : 15
o'erfraught heart, 239 : 20
of each other's watch, 208 : 1
what good author w., 711 : 8
Whist, wild waves w., 247 : 19
Whistle and I'll come to you, 410 : 10
and she'll come to you, 263 : 9
blackbird 'tis to w., 290 : 15
clear as a w., 341 : 14
don't you hear w. blowing, 921 : 17
go w. for the rest, 169 : 1
her joly w. wel ywet, 147 : 4
I love to w., 846 : 15
I'd w. her off, 231 : 4
let it w. as it will, 430 : 21
on a brick, 892 : 7
pay too much for w., 348 : 9
quail w. about us, 767 : 4
them back, 371 : 19
Whistled for want of thought, 307 : 6
Whistles far and wee, 828 : 11
in the dark, 678 : 10
in the wind, 424 : 20
pipes in w. in his sound, 211 : 15
thrice, 434 : 20
Whistling, blackbird w. or just after, 767 : 12
foolish w. of a name, 295 : 16
ravished with w. of name, 337 : 15
to bear courage up, 306 : *n* 2
to keep from being afraid, 306 : 4
winds w. in rigging, 800 : 10
White, a moment w., 411 : 8
all w. like a doll, 878 : 12
and drifted snow, 490 : 20
angels w. flaming w., 850 : 1
as angel English child, 403 : 6
as driven snow, 246 : 29
as leprosy, 434 : 19
as rain-washed bone, 708 : 17
beard decreasing leg, 205 : 28
beautiful when it helps, 900 : 15
beauty whose red and w., 213 : 17
black evening w. snow, 770 : 15
Black Hawk fought against w. men, 418 : 13
black spirits and w., 261 : 22
black where I read w., 407 : 9
bosoms of actresses, 353 : 23
bread and butter, 930 : 15
candle in holy place, 773 : 16
chickens, 785 : 11
chrysanthemum remains immaculate, 314 : 5
cliffs of Dover, 752 : 1
clothed in w. samite, 149 : 8, 534 : 4
clouds on wing, 594 : 3
colored people understand w. people, 733 : 7
cow all red and w., 668 : 13
crimson petal now w., 531 : 11
crow sees w. man come, 557 : 18
degrading w. people, 520 : 2
doesn't mean we're anti-w., 904 : 13
dreaming of w. Christmas, 802 : 11
end of fight tombstone w., 707 : 20
fall on w. silence below, 793 : 17
fat w. woman, 795 : 2
fever of temptation, 817 : 3
White (*continued*)
fleece w. but 'tis too cold, 173 : *n* 8
flower of blameless life, 534 : 1
foam flew, 434 : 13
Goddess, 833 : 6
Godiva I unpeel, 911 : 14
Great W. Way, 696 : 16
hair become very w., 611 : 9
hair not w. in single night, 459 : 21
hatred for w. men, 903 : 2
how ill w. hairs become fool, 206 : 36
I appeal to any w. man, 367 : 3
if snow be w., 246 : 1
in subjection to w. Saxon man, 554 : 6
in w. black and green, 919 : 8
is their color, 269 : 6
little missionary stew, 806 : 9
long hotel acutely w., 711 : 11
made w. in blood, 53 : 15
man warmed before Indians' fire, 374 : 20
man will never be alone, 456 : 2
man's burden, 709 : 21
moon beams, 813 : 7
nights all w. an' still, 568 : 4
nor w. so very w., 422 : 4
not neutralize black, 545 : 12
O my soul is w., 403 : 6
o'er his w. banes, 927 : 5
officers cast lot, 617 : 6
one w. foot try him, 923 : 11
or colored signs, 891 : 13
panache rallying point, 175 : 1
played black or w., 489 : 10
prisoner to w. man, 418 : 12
radiance of Eternity, 469 : 16
radiance stretches above it, 59 : 27
raiment w. as snow, 41 : 29
really hope no w. person, 916 : 2
red thoughts teeth w., 731 : 16
relation between w. and colored people, 556 : 9
rose breathes of love, 659 : 6
rose is a dove, 659 : 6
roses and w. lilies grow, 250 : 5
sails still fly seaward, 806 : 6
samite, 149 : 8, 534 : 4
scare w. clouds on, 747 : 18
sea widening, 875 : 2
seas show w. when rocks near, 262 : 5
Shields of Expectation, 568 : 19
silence, 507 : 6, 793 : 17
silence deep and w., 568 : 15
silken turbans wreathed, 288 : 11
singe my w. head, 233 : 24
sins shall be w. as snow, 28 : 30
sound of w. soldier's axe, 591 : 4
striped pure celestial w., 474 : 18
sullen w. surf, 571 : 9
superfluity comes by w. hairs, 198 : 8
sustenance despair, 606 : 1
sweet w. wine, 760 : 19
three w. leopards, 805 : 22
thunders of w. silence, 507 : 6
to w. man nature wilderness, 726 : 8
tupping your w. ewe, 229 : 18
two societies one black one w., 872 : 14
ugly when oppresses blacks, 900 : 15
vlack and w. separate as fingers, 681 : 24
we black and they w., 875 : 8
wear w. flannel trousers, 803 : 19
White (*continued*)
whale's w. hump, 570 : 13
what treaty w. man kept, 610 : 5
why should I want to be w., 854 : 11
wild w. horses play, 584 : 11
wings one black other w., 289 : 2
White House, unapproachable in W., 783 : 5
White-chokered and clean-shaven, 651 : 3
Whited sepulchers, 40 : 20
thou w. wall, 46 : 27
Whiten, willows w., 528 : 24
Whiteness came back after footstep, 907 : 12
Milky Way sister in w., 770 : 12
restore to w. wool dyed purple, 128 : 14
Whiter, I shall be w. than snow, 19 : 15
Whites human not superior, 916 : 11
move beyond racism, 901 : 1
of their eyes, 358 : 1, 368 : 1
Whitespread wings, 778 : 6
Whitest, old linen wash w., 262 : 1
Whitewash and a long-handled brush, 622 : 11
Whitewashed wall, 370 : 13
Whither, advice not to inquire why or w., 839 : 15
away fair rover, 654 : 15
coffin asks w., 615 : 7
fled visionary gleam, 426 : 13
goest thou, 45 : 27
shall I go from thy spirit, 22 : 17
so high, 932 : 5
thou goest I will go, 12 : 25
Whithersoever, with thee w. thou goest, 11 : 28
Whiting to a snail, 612 : 7
Whitman, Homer and W. roar in pines, 728 : 4
Walt W. a kosmos, 574 : 20
Whittington, turn again W., 918 : 10
Whittled out of hickory, 835 : 1
Who are these coming, 477 : 9
are we where are we, 557 : 21
are you cried one agape, 626 : 21
can hold fire in his hand, 194 : 7
doesn't desire father's death, 582 : 11
doth ambition shun, 211 : 3
ever got out of winding sheet, 255 : 3
ever loved not at first sight, 183 : 17
fears to speak of Ninety-eight, 592 : 2
follows in His train, 452 : 7
gets what when how, 855 : 6
has seen the wind, 608 : 19
hath desired sea, 710 : 7
hath known mind of Lord, 47 : 17
How and Where and W., 710 : 2
I'm nobody w. are you, 604 : 19
is in who's out, 235 : 12
is master who's man, 323 : 22
is Silvia what is she, 190 : 4
is the happy Warrior, 427 : 21
is the third, 805 : 11
is this King of glory, 18 : 10
killed Cock Robin, 930 : 9
killed John Keats, 462 : 11
knows but world may end, 542 : 14
loses and who wins, 235 : 12
night and silence w. is here, 196 : 22
ran to help me, 449 : 12
said Peacock pie, 740 : 1

Who (*continued*)
shall ascend into the hill of the Lord, 18 : 8
shall bell cat, 66 : 16
shall deliver me, 47 : 7
shall stand in his holy place, 18 : 8
should 'scape whipping, 221 : 5
then devised torment, 808 : 15
to himself law no law doth need, 178 : 4
touches a hair, 513 : 19
why which what, 550 : 14
will bell cat, 143 : 15
would have thought so much blood, 239 : 25
Whoe'er has traveled, 355 : *n* 8
she be, 292 : 7
thou art behold master, 344 : 10
Whoever really loves you, 935 : 16
wishes to attain English style, 352 : 23
you are behold your master, 344 : 10
Whole America nothing less, 372 : 17
armor of God, 49 : 38
beautiful w. numbers, 832 : 9
better had I stolen w., 668 : 17
by sample we judge w., 168 : 10
climate of opinion, 868 : 14
complicate amassing harmony, 768 : 17
drink and be w. again, 749 : 10
duty of man, 27 : 27
earth for religion's sake, 574 : 7
earth is sepulcher of famous men, 81 : 5
earth our hospital, 807 : 19
first comprehend w., 605 : 17
general joy of w. table, 238 : 27
happy people die w., 797 : 13
has beginning middle and end, 88 : 17
how much more is half than w., 61 : 14
I am equal and w., 634 : 4
indictment against w. people, 372 : 21
individual representative of w., 858 : 8
love is the w., 829 : 21
makes w. world kin, 226 : 20
man composed of all men, 865 : 16
my w. course of love, 229 : 25
need not physician, 38 : 27
never sees a w., 585 : 5
nothing sole or w., 716 : 18
one stupendous w., 336 : 21
prayers make me w., 707 : 19
saw life w., 584 : 8
soul's tasking, 567 : 12
taste w. of it, 544 : 22
tribe of fops, 233 : 3
volumes in folio, 190 : 18
wide sky above me, 839 : 19
willing to know w. truth, 383 : 1
Wholeness of human problem, 755 : 21
Wholes, couples are w. and not w., 70 : 5
Wholesale, God who does w. business, 650 : 6
Wholesome, believe doctors nothing w., 609 : 1
even for king, 607 : 9
harvests reaps, 484 : 6
nights are w., 217 : 26
Wholesomest, old wine w., 262 : 1
Wholly, I shall not w. die, 108 : 9
Whom shall I fear, 18 : 11
they fear they hate, 95 : 6
Whoopee ti yi yo git along little dogies, 927 : 10
Whooping, out of all w., 212 : 6
Whoops, devil w., 708 : 12
owlet w. to wolf below, 435 : 6
Whore, joined this rogue and w., 323 : 2
pity she's a w., 264 : 10
posture of a w., 241 : 27
the woman's a w., 355 : 10
Whore's oath, 234 : 14
Whores, till all w. burned alive, 320 : 18
Whorled ear, 655 : 18
Who's afraid of Virginia Woolf, 908 : 2
in who's out, 235 : 12
master who's man, 323 : 22
on first, 832 : 3
to doom, 571 : 6
Whose, to w. advantage, 98 : 6
world or mine or theirs, 793 : 3
Why, causes w. and wherefore, 208 : 13
don't you speak for yourself, 511 : 21
every w. hath a wherefore, 188 : 2
I can't say w. I don't like you, 119 : 3
I can't think w., 629 : 3
I dream and say W. not, 681 : 11
is plain as way to church, 211 : 11
is this thus, 616 : 18
love's stricken w., 607 : 10
man of morals tell me w., 295 : 8
men fell out knew not w., 290 : 13
not inquire w. or whither, 839 : 15
not when but w. families came, 903 : 11
persecutest thou me, 46 : 5
then oh why can't I, 842 : 6
though I could never tell w., 627 : 9
What and W. and When, 710 : 2
who w. which what, 550 : 14
you see things and say W., 681 : 11
Wibrated, strings better not w., 547 : 27
Wicked are wicked no doubt, 539 : 18
deceitful and desperately w., 32 : 12
dreams abuse sleep, 237 : 14
flee when no man pursueth, 25 : 27
forsake his way, 31 : 20
God help the w., 204 : 6
I have seen the w. in great power, 18 : 26
intents w. or charitable, 219 : 11
little better than one of w., 203 : 2
man Hitler, 744 : 8
men are w. who is good, 724 : 16
name of the w. shall rot, 23 : 22
no peace unto the w., 31 : 8
public scandal is w., 297 : 22
punish w. for their iniquity, 29 : 21
something w. this way comes, 239 : 7
tender mercies of the w. are cruel, 23 : 29
the w. cease from troubling, 15 : 9
the w. oppressing, 918 : 19
too w. for smile, 435 : 21
violence covereth the mouth of the w., 23 : 22
war regarded as w., 674 : 20
wealth even to a w. man, 67 : 2
wickedness proceedeth from the w., 13 : 6
will betrayed still, 631 : 15
Witch of West, 677 : 9
work your w. will, 745 : 3
worse than w. it's vulgar, 660 : 16
Wickedness, did sell himself to work w., 14 : 9
dwell in the tents of w., 20 : 8
easier than virtue, 353 : 8
far be it from God that he should do w., 16 : 24
flower of w., 545 : 9
follies and w., 865 : 18
Hitler monster of W., 745 : 2
manifold sins and w., 54 : 11, 55 : 17
men capable of every w., 684 : 4
method in man's w., 263 : 6
of a woman, 35 : 36
or folly, 521 : 13
plowed w. reaped iniquity, 33 : 13
proceedeth from the wicked, 13 : 6
spiritual w. in high places, 49 : 39
though w. be sweet, 16 : 6
turn from w. and live, 54 : 15
Wicket, flanneled fools at w., 709 : 23
Wicklow, chink in old W. house, 735 : 2
Wicks they simulate, 606 : 10
Wictim o' connubiality, 546 : 19
Widder eats by a bell, 622 : 16
Wide and starry sky, 668 : 20
and winding Rhine, 457 : 25
arch of ranged empire fall, 240 : 14
capable and w. revenge, 231 : 18
dark world and w., 282 : 15
enough to wrap a fairy, 196 : 18
ever the w. world over, 707 : 22
gates of dark Death stand w., 105 : 15
great and w. sea, 21 : 11
great w. beautiful world, 593 : 7
heaven's w. pathless way, 278 : 18
is the gate, 38 : 15
no wider than heart w., 822 : 12
nor so w. as church door, 193 : 5
shallow brooks and rivers w., 277 : 25
sky above me, 839 : 19
spindrift gaze, 843 : 16
though its meshes are w., 65 : 6
too w. for shrunk shank, 211 : 15
water inescapable, 767 : 4
wide sea, 434 : 26
womb of uncreated night, 284 : 9
world dreaming on things to come, 245 : 13
world w. enough to hold both, 360 : 6
Widely, doors are w. flung, 873 : 2
Widened, thoughts of men w., 530 : 3
Widening, ever w. slowly silence, 534 : 9
on farther shore, 875 : 2
turning in w. gyre, 714 : 12
Wider and permanent system, 781 : 9
no w. than heart wide, 822 : 12
seek no w. war, 872 : 12
still and wider, 698 : 12
Wide-rolling watery prairies, 571 : 3
Wide-sounding Zeus, 58 : 17, 60 : 23
Wide-watered shore, 278 : 19
Wide-waving wings, 377 : 26
Widow, a certain poor w., 42 : 13
at Windsor, 708 : 7
Black W. death, 892 : 8
care for w. and orphan, 524 : 7
do not oppress w., 4 : 2
eats by a bell, 622 : 16
here's to the w. of fifty, 399 : 1
how is she become as a w., 32 : 20
maid w. not wife, 229 : 7
maid w. or wife, 153 : 3
Molly Stark a w., 371 : 26

Widower, unconsoled w., 514 : 9
Widow's, caused the w. heart to sing, 16 : 16
Widows destroyed by suitors, 312 : 25
most perverse creatures, 326 : 20
very careful o' w., 546 : 18
when w. against second marriages, 350 : 2
Widows', devour w. houses, 42 : 12
Wie es eigentlich gewesen, 480 : *n* 2
Wife, adored first w., 675 : 5
all world and his w., 323 : 21
and children are impediments, 180 : 9
and children part of self, 648 : 17
and children stand afraid, 274 : 12
and hardly any mistresses, 731 : 14
argued each case with w., 611 : 10
be your w. gladly, 551 : 2
Caesar's w. must be above suspicion, 99 : *n* 13
choice of horse and w., 584 : 6
chose w. as she wedding gown, 369 : 7
cleave unto his w., 7 : 4
contentions of a w., 24 : 25
covet thy neighbor's w., 10 : 7
damned in a fair w., 229 : 12
debauch friend's w. gentelly, 355 : 13
devil has trouble with w., 679 : 12
don't be gentle to your w., 60 : 13
eat no lean, 929 : 16
enough for a' that, 411 : 20
expect of friend's w., 441 : 11
first you are w. and mother, 599 : 13
gardener Adam and w., 528 : 10
giving honor unto the w., 52 : 13
had seven sacks, 930 : 1
had w. couldn't keep her, 932 : 16
here lies my w., 307 : 10
his life dinner w., 486 : 4
husband and w. keep household in oneness, 59 : 28
husband frae w. despises, 411 : 5
I'd have no w., 292 : 11
if ever man loved by w., 290 : 12
if ever w. happy in man, 290 : 12
kill w. with kindness, 188 : 39
letter from his w., 614 : 6
light w. make heavy husband, 201 : 7
little w. well willed, 347 : 8
Lot's w. looked back, 8 : 12
love neighbor's w., 487 : 20
love w. Belle Aurore, 545 : 15
maid widow or w., 153 : 3
make w. happy while you are alive, 3 : 8
matched with aged w., 529 : 6
medicine my lawful w., 695 : 1
must be in want of w., 440 : 16
my child w., 549 : 7
my 'oss my w. my name, 500 : 21
my w. hath something in her gizzard, 310 : 14
my w. is my plague, 62 : 6
my w. poor wretch, 309 : 19
neighed after his neighbor's w., 31 : 33
neither maid widow nor w., 229 : 7
no casual mistress but w., 532 : 14
no man worth having true to w., 321 : 4
not appreciate w. till she joins club, 699 : 13
of thy bosom, 11 : 16
Wife (*continued*)
old flame my w., 893 : 8
old w. old dog ready money, 347 : 17
pixy w., 756 : 1
Potiphar's w., 8 : 30
ran after farmer's w., 929 : 11
remember Lot's w., 43 : 37
riding to and from w., 846 : 8
ruled roast, 452 : 13
sailor's w. had chestnuts, 236 : 1
says to w. Fie upon quiet life, 203 : 26
second w. hateful to children, 76 : 1
shun w. and brother, 496 : 24
so act toward children so toward w., 121 : 20
son till he gets w., 597 : 14
sweet wee w. o' mine, 410 : 17
sympathetic w. best possession, 77 : 17
take w. or cowl, 168 : *n* 12
tales of old w., 720 : *n* 3
tell w. all he knows, 276 : 16
Thane of Fife had a w., 239 : 26
true and honorable w., 215 : 23
uncumbered with a w., 306 : 25
understanding w., 262 : 12
unspoken contract of w. and her works, 889 : 2
we fell out my w. and I, 530 : 23
weds tyrant not w., 77 : 19
whoso findeth a w., 24 : 22
wished w. not so much as suspected, 99 : 17
without e'er a w., 930 : 15
worse shod than shoemaker's w., 160 : 15
yelping w., 874 : 21
Wig, fritter my w., 613 : 21
Wiggle, ship goes wop with w., 709 : 24
Wight, bless hous from wikked w., 146 : 30
maid and her w., 642 : 2
unhappy w., 174 : 11
Wights, descriptions of fairest w., 245 : 12
Wigwam of Nokomis, 511 : 16
Wilbur, best place thought W., 847 : 3
Wild, air w. with leaves, 793 : 16
anarchy of drink, 256 : 19
and dreamlike trade, 435 : 21
and fair, 431 : 18
ass stamp o'er his head, 516 : 11
bank whereon w. thyme blows, 196 : 18
birds rounding hill, 899 : 9
bore me in southern w., 403 : 6
by starts 'twas w., 364 : 13
Caledonia stern and w., 430 : 11
call and clear call, 760 : 15
cataract leaps, 530 : 26
civility, 266 : 7
creatures and places are natural resources, 898 : 11
dark times rumbling toward us, 482 : 3
Decembers, 562 : 1
dog and alone, 819 : 8
ducks plunging to bottom, 600 : 1
echoes flying, 530 : 26
ecstasy, 477 : 5
geese spread gray wing, 713 : 11
goose chase, 169 : 3
grew more fierce and w., 268 : 23
harp slung behind him, 446 : 15
Wild (*continued*)
heaven in w. flower, 406 : 8
her eyes were w., 478 : 11
home of w. mirth, 503 : 3
in woods noble savage ran, 303 : 8
it was the winter w., 277 : 7
Jack for a lover, 716 : 16
lament, 858 : 20
lead a w.-goose chase, 169 : 3
like w. beast guards way, 406 : 1
locusts and w. honey, 36 : 27
longings of blood, 874 : 17
love the w. swan, 797 : 20
native wood-notes w., 278 : 6
New England shore, 470 : 15
nobly w. not mad, 266 : 16
nor passion w., 584 : 8
not so w. a dream, 503 : 6
oats not sown more than once, 701 : 1
of all w. beasts preserve me from tyrant, 255 : 14
piping down valleys w., 403 : 2
press a w. animal, 789 : 4
regrets bloody sweats, 676 : 11
revenge a w. justice, 180 : 3
rhythms measureless and w., 76 : 22
ring out w. bells, 532 : 21
sanctuary, 750 : 15
sequestered seat, 364 : 14
some live without w. things, 795 : 8
something soft w. free, 739 : 5
spiders crying, 893 : 10
surmise, 475 : 7
talk a little w., 248 : 23
thing sorry for itself, 790 : 11
upon the w. sea-banks, 200 : 22
vicissitudes of taste, 351 : 13
walking by w. lone, 710 : 6
waves whist, 247 : 19
waving w. tail, 710 : 6
weird clime, 526 : 8
West began, 726 : 8
west wind, 467 : 17
wet w. woods, 710 : 6
what are w. waves saying, 548 : *n* 1
white horses play, 584 : 11
witches noble ladies, 714 : 4
with all regret, 531 : 4
wonder and w. desire, 545 : 1
words ought to be w., 783 : 11
worm in w. apple, 798 : 3
Wildcat, nor w. so ruthless, 82 : 13
Wildcats in your kitchens, 230 : 8
whip weight in w., 666 : 12
Wilder willful-wavier meal-drift, 656 : 6
Wilderness, a scapegoat into the w., 10 : 18
artificial w., 868 : 21
beasts fly to w., 89 : 9
bill of rights, 841 : 2
choice grain into this w., 307 : 11
first flower of w., 465 : 2
great fresh unredeemed w., 637 : 16
in the w. a lodging place, 32 : 4
Indian w., 319 : 22
inhabit parched places in w., 32 : 11
into empire, 373 : 9
into w. to teach Indian, 705 : 3
Lincoln came out of w., 519 : *n* 4
lodge in vast w., 376 : 18
man in w., 930 : 2
oceans mingling with sky, 592 : 6
of monkeys, 199 : 20

Wilderness (*continued*)
of sweets, 286 : 17
of this world, 301 : 19
Promised Land beyond w., 690 : 8
ready to perish in w., 265 : 8
slovenly w., 767 : 7
sweet berries in w., 767 : 4
though in w. never alone, 121 : *n* 2
to white man nature w., 726 : 8
to w. I wander, 918 : 12
voice crying in the w., 36 : 26
voice that crieth in the w., 30 : 30
wander in the w. forty years, 10 : 25
way into universe through w., 637 : 18
were paradise enow, 516 : 7
women have no w., 836 : 20
Wildernesses, desert w., 279 : 16
Wildest peal for years, 732 : 16
rhymes suggest w. freedom, 495 : 22
Wildfowl, not a more fearful w., 196 : 24
opinion of Pythagoras concerning w., 200 : *n* 3
Wild-goose, lead a w. chase, 169 : 3
Wildlife, survival of our w. in Africa, 898 : 11
Wildly, sing so w. well, 525 : 10
striking sometimes a friend, 268 : 7
Wildness, in God's w. hope of world, 637 : 16
in w. is preservation of world, 560 : 27
life consists with w., 560 : 28
need tonic of w., 560 : 14
Wile, with endearing w., 370 : 9
Wiles, full of w. full of guile, 82 : 8
man of many w., 334 : 21
of stranger, 855 : 11
wanton w., 277 : 19
Wilhelmine, little grandchild W., 439 : 10
Will, abolished w., 892 : 7
act according to w. of another, 414 : 8
and Intellect the same, 308 : 8
appetite w. and power, 226 : 3
be there a w., 400 : 7
boy's w. wind's w., 511 : 25
built against w. of gods, 58 : 13
city obedient to his w., 84 : 16
committed to w. of God, 265 : 6
complies against his w., 291 : 30
conscious w. and reasonableness, 754 : 5
creature of people's w., 402 : 8
decisions more of instincts than w., 754 : 5
doeth w. of my Father, 38 : 19
dread puzzles the w., 221 : 12
enchains us to ill, 467 : 13
fixed fate free w., 284 : 19
for peace, 780 : 4
forget not because we w., 586 : 11
free the human w., 340 : 2
free w. not free at all, 602 : 3
free w. not one but many wills, 905 : 2
God's w. be done, 385 : 14
good or ill lies in own w., 121 : 8
good w. to men, 537 : 16
good w. toward men, 42 : 29
greatest gift freedom of w., 142 : 12
here by w. of nation, 397 : 20
his w. to make known, 918 : 19
I pay thy poverty not thy w., 193 : 21
I w. as God wills, 385 : 14

Will (*continued*)
if God w., 131 : 10
Immanent W. and its designs, 641 : 17
in His w. is our peace, 142 : 11
infirmity of w., 497 : 6
into appetite, 226 : 3
its one w. flow, 843 : 19
killing by simply exerting w., 582 : *n* 2
laid me down with a w., 668 : 20
let my w. take place of reason, 122 : 9
living lies in your w., 164 : 11
love-sick against w., 628 : 5
man has w. woman way, 519 : 4
Mariner hath his w., 434 : 6
men of good w., 42 : *n* 3, 54 : 4, 814 : 10
mighty effort of w., 753 : 4
more strongly than fate, 755 : 11
most incorrect to heaven, 218 : 4
my fanatical w. power, 812 : 19
my poverty but not my w. consents, 193 : 21
not as I w. but thou, 41 : 12
not my w. but thine, 44 : 4
not when he may, 158 : 23
nothing good or evil save in w., 121 : 18
of God prevail, 588 : 18
of the Yukon, 752 : 4
one man's w. all men's misery, 175 : 8
opinions and a w., 566 : 3
our peace in His w., 806 : 7
own sweet w., 425 : 14
own w. heaven's w., 714 : 21
passionate beyond the w., 836 : 19
power into w., 226 : 3
prisoners of W., 875 : 3
Providence w. and fate, 284 : 19
reason panders w., 223 : 5
serveth not another's w., 250 : 14
sister calls me W., 666 : 19
slain my w., 875 : 1
smaller and dryer than w., 805 : 21
take away our free w. and glory, 154 : 6
that it become universal law, 366 : 14
this is our gracious w., 154 : 9
though heaven fall thy w. be done, 134 : 24
Thy w. be done, 37 : 15
thy w. my power to believe, 543 : 21
to do, 431 : 7
to grace as horse to rider, 128 : 26
to live, 756 : 17
to power, 659 : 3
to thought added w., 495 : 13
to w. and to do his pleasure, 50 : 3
to win, 771 : 8
triumph by mystic w., 756 : 3
unconquerable w., 283 : 8, 745 : 4
undisappointed, 121 : 13
want to do God's w., 909 : 17
water's my w., 874 : 9
what women w. is right, 634 : 17
when you w. they won't, 96 : 21
wicked w. baffled still, 631 : 15
woman's cold perverted w., 470 : 10
woman's w., 201 : 14
word to a thing when We w. it, 131 : 4
work your wicked w., 745 : 3
wrote w. across sky, 810 : 2
you w. Oscar you w., 619 : 12

Will (*continued*)
you won't you, 612 : 8
Willas cather, 839 : 4
Wille zur Macht, 659 : *n* 2
Willed, if forgetting could be w., 601 : 2
little wife well w., 347 : 8
never felt nor clearly w., 585 : 22
Willful, gigantic w. young, 728 : 12
group of w. men, 682 : 10
little w. thorns, 530 : 22
stranger, 669 : 3
waste woeful want, 450 : 1
who for my w. crime, 288 : 3
Willful-wavier meal-drift, 656 : 6
William, Father calls me W., 666 : 19
old Father W., 439 : 15, 611 : 9
Willie, Mother calls me W., 666 : 19
wee W. Winkie, 537 : 6
Willin', Barkis is w., 548 : 23
Willing, able and w. to pull weight, 687 : 7
faithfully to serve State, 272 : 17
spirit is w., 41 : 13
suspension of disbelief, 437 : 15
to wound, 338 : 14
Willingly as one would kill fly, 188 : 22
Willingness, where great w. difficulties not great, 154 : 5
Willow, all a green w., 158 : 15, 232 : 8
all under the w. tree, 399 : 15
cabin at gate, 213 : 18
Dido with w. in her hand, 200 : 22
hang harp on w. tree, 922 : 13
sing all a green w., 232 : 8
titwillow, 629 : 16
willow waly, 628 : 8
willow willow, 232 : 8
Willows, change to southern w., 378 : 2
hanged harps upon w., 22 : 15
weeping w. wave, 599 : 5
whiten, 528 : 24
Wills, God w. it, 133 : 19
God w. us free, 385 : 14
let's talk of w., 195 : 1
many w. in one man, 905 : 2
our w. are gardeners, 230 : 2
Wilson could write from Sinai, 783 : 5
unable to start, 726 : 6
Wilt, do what thou w., 157 : 12
flowers that do not w., 799 : 13
Wimpled whining purblind, 190 : 26
Wimpling wing, 656 : 1
Win at cost of infinite loss, 599 : 1
at hazard of lives, 687 : 4
because we are stronger, 761 : 2
convictions to w. or lose, 737 : 7
for Gipper, 811 : 4
friends and influence people, 803 : 4
here win everywhere, 845 : 9
in the game to w., 825 : 3
kindness shall w. my love, 189 : 1
know how to w. victory Hannibal, 94 : 7
lawsuits and are happy, 81 : 12
lose good we oft might w., 227 : 29
love and I had wit to w., 671 : 4
man who is sorry will w., 65 : 4
man will yet w., 761 : 17
my way to the coast, 76 : 25
noble renown, 59 : 1
nothing venture nothing w., 629 : 2
or lose it all, 292 : 3
play to w. toil to lose, 728 : 22
race runs by himself, 707 : *n* 2

Win (*continued*)
shall w. lover's hire, 404 : 19
soil w. of watery main, 244 : 22
they laugh that w., 231 : 22
those who hate you don't w., 883 : 3
those who know how to w., 95 : 17
us to our harm, 236 : 9
us with honest trifles, 236 : 9
wanting to w. is everything, 925 : *n* 6
war as disastrous as to lose, 817 : 18
war rise bloody, 889 : 10
when in doubt w. trick, 327 : 6
will to w., 771 : 8
with his tongue w. a woman, 190 : 1
world to w., 563 : 10
world which lies beyond struggles, 745 : 11
Wince, let galled jade w., 222 : 16
Winced, not w. nor cried aloud, 663 : 10
Wind a fiery Pegasus, 204 : 32
all aloud w. doth blow, 191 : 15
always north-northeast, 729 : 2
and clouds now here, 470 : 10
and wave and oar, 528 : 20
anybody as w. or no w., 752 : 13
argument with east w., 568 : 27
as large a charter as w., 211 : 10
a-sailing with the w., 933 : 7
assault and battery of w., 714 : 19
at a little w. dost thou fall, 142 : 2
awake O north w., 28 : 14
bayed the whispering w., 370 : 4
bellies and drags in w., 714 : 6
bellows full of angry w., 714 : 20
between w. and the grass, 69 : 2
betwixt w. and his nobility, 203 : 8
blasted with the east w., 8 : 31
blow kindly here, 625 : *n* 3
blow softly here, 625 : 20
blow thou winter w., 211 : 16
blow w. come wrack, 240 : 6
bloweth where it listeth, 44 : 32
blowin' in the w., 915 : 3
blowing at my door, 139 : 8
blowing new direction, 790 : 9
blows cradle rock, 660 : 19
blows it back again, 406 : 3
blustering w. or swallowing wave, 296 : 5
breath of night w., 587 : 16
brook weather that love not w., 190 : 28
care for w. nor tide, 630 : 21
chaff which w. driveth away, 17 : 12
changes and I stir, 901 : 12
come w. come weather, 302 : 14
comes off frozen peak, 748 : 17
crannying w., 457 : 23
cruel w. blows, 864 : 2
doth ramm, 792 : 8
dry sun dry w., 159 : *n* 2
dust blown away with the w., 34 : 16
dust the rude w. blows, 234 : 22
east w. never blow, 270 : 32
eight points of w., 850 : 1
every w. of doctrine, 49 : 35
fair stood w. for France, 182 : 14
false as w., 226 : 15
fate seemed to w. him up, 303 : 16
feather for each w., 246 : 17
fill belly with east w., 15 : 36
flights against w., 724 : 4
fly upon the wings of the w., 17 : 26
forgot to w. clock, 359 : 19
Wind (*continued*)
fresh west w., 59 : 19
friends who go with the w., 139 : 8
frosty w. made moan, 608 : 17
full of birds' cries, 760 : 17
gentle w. does move, 404 : 10
going down the w., 309 : 15
gone with the w., 721 : 5
green w. green branches, 841 : 8
gusts of clear-blowing west w., 59 : 26
he that observeth the w., 27 : 21
hear voice in every w., 361 : 9
hear w. blow, 920 : 19
hears him in the w., 336 : 16
hey ho w. and rain, 214 : 29, 234 : 1
hiding place from the w., 30 : 21
hollow blasts of w., 331 : 7
hymns that fall out of w., 768 : 23
ill w. blows no man good, 161 : 11
impatient as the w., 428 : 20
in a rising w., 864 : 13
in trees a sad thing, 103 : 11
inherit w., 23 : 27
is chill, 430 : 21
is in palm trees, 708 : 8
is in the cane, 831 : 14
is passing by, 608 : 19
leaves turning in w., 766 : 12
let her down the w., 231 : 4
leveling w., 715 : 9
like whetted knife, 760 : 16
like w. I go, 516 : 17
listen the w. is rising, 793 : 16
looks for grief it belongs to, 907 : 20
loose as the w., 268 : 21
Lord was not in the w., 14 : 5
lost and by w. grieved, 852 : 8
man control w., 585 : 9
mantle of w. and chill and rain, 148 : 22
meteor streaming to w., 283 : 20
mild w. mild-looking sky, 571 : 7
much of a which of a w., 830 : 1
net to hold the w., 262 : *n* 4
nets to catch the w., 262 : 11
no 'twas but the w., 457 : 15
nor tide nor sea, 630 : 21
north w. doth blow, 932 : 6
O w. weder gynneth clere, 144 : 18
obeyed what w. had taught, 800 : 10
of criticism, 357 : 2
of doctrine, 49 : 35
of western sea, 530 : 25
on buffalo grass, 928 : 11
or weather, 436 : 7
over lake inner truth, 5 : 10
pass by me as idle w., 217 : 2
passeth over it, 21 : 7
paths that w. and w., 670 : 4
pines keep shape of w., 850 : 16
renown but breath of w., 142 : 1
restless w. of inlets, 837 : 2
rising attempt to live, 735 : 12
said w. to moon, 594 : 13
said You know I'm result, 905 : 6
sails filled with lusty w., 178 : 6
sall blaw for evermair, 927 : 5
scattered to w., 527 : 21
scatters some leaves, 58 : 1
sits w. in that corner, 209 : 17
something in the w., 188 : 6
sound of rushing w., 45 : 38
sound w. and limb, 170 : 23
southern w. blow softly, 625 : 20
Wind (*continued*)
sown the w., 33 : 12
spirit borrows name from w., 679 : 5
spirit rises with rising w., 874 : 6
stop hole to keep w. away, 224 : 16
storm rain may enter, 351 : 7
straw see which way w. is, 263 : 21
strumpet w., 199 : 6
suitor of towers, 841 : 7
sun was warm w. chill, 748 : 17
sway in w. like corn, 804 : 6
sweep man away, 585 : 9
swollen with w. and mist, 280 : 22
tears shall drown the w., 236 : 24
tempers w. to shorn lamb, 163 : 12, 360 : 25
that blows through me, 790 : 9
that follows fast, 453 : 19
three sheets in w., 553 : *n* 4, 553 : 18
through woods in riot, 691 : 7
throw sand against w., 406 : 3
thunderstorm against w., 458 : 17
to know which way w. blows, 915 : 7
torrent of darkness, 772 : 23
twist slowly in w., 904 : 2
unhelped by any w., 435 : 14
warm w. the west w., 760 : 17
wash w., 806 : 21
wave cry w. cry, 807 : 24
way long w. cold, 429 : 20
west w. and the swallows, 93 : 3
western w. when wilt thou blow, 917 : 10
what is w. in that door, 149 : 10
what woman says written in w., 102 : 12
when she dances in the w., 305 : 3
when sun out w. still, 748 : 17
when w. southerly know hawk, 220 : 31
whenever w. is high, 668 : 11
where a w. ever soft, 395 : 3
whistles in the w., 424 : 20
who has seen w., 608 : 19
wild west w., 467 : 17
wings of the w., 17 : 26, 21 : 8
winnow not with every w., 35 : 5
winnowing w., 477 : 18
wiped out by w., 908 : 3
words are but w., 291 : 20
words are easy like the w., 257 : 8
Windborne mirroring soul, 585 : 5
Winding, God w. lonely horn, 712 : 13
long cool w. saxophones, 761 : 11
long trail a-w., 813 : 7
notes with many a w. bout, 278 : 6
Winding-sheet of Edward's race, 363 : 5
old England's w., 406 : 18
waters were his w., 257 : 5
who ever got out of w., 255 : 3
Windlass, turned like yonder w., 571 : 5
Windlasses and assays of bias, 220 : 7
Windless, sails from w. kingdom, 907 : 14
Windmills, tilting at w., 168 : *n* 9
Window, clapped the w. to, 146 : 32
habit not flung out w., 624 : 15
Jezebel looked out at a w., 14 : 19
light through yonder w., 192 : 2
little w. where sun, 485 : 4
love flies out w., 919 : 11
Mary at thy w. be, 411 : 2
on Europe, 486 : 14
parents and child at w., 906 : 2

Window (*continued*)
sit looking out of w., 906 : 11
tirlin' at w., 537 : 6
tree, 748 : 12
Walloping W. Blind, 647 : 21
Windowed, looped and w. raggedness, 234 : 3
Windows be darkened, 27 : 24
cleaned w. swept floor, 627 : 14
dim w. of the soul, 407 : 10
factory w. always broken, 765 : 4
if your w. are glass, 347 : 16
lavender in the w., 271 : 3
lovely lamps w. of soul, 167 : 10
of my soul, 513 : 15
saints to w. run, 604 : 15
see without looking through w., 64 : 17
storied w. richly dight, 278 : 26
sun reflected from w. of almshouse, 560 : 18
through w. call on us, 252 : 7
Wind's feet shine along sea, 632 : 18
like whetted knife, 760 : 16
out of w. and rain's way, 774 : 1
will, 511 : 25
Winds are left behind, 596 : 15
ascribing to w. the noise, 115 : 16
at height of madness w. pause, 572 : 3
beetle w. sullen horn, 364 : 12
beteem w. of heaven, 218 : 7
blow profit, 870 : 5
blow w. crack your cheeks, 233 : 24
blow ye w. heigh ho, 935 : 5
breath rides on posting w., 243 : 21
come as the w. come, 431 : 23
courted by all the w., 288 : 30
cradled in sea, 869 : 13
faithless as w. or seas, 312 : 12
flask of w. empties, 850 : 4
four w. of the heaven, 33 : 29
four-square to w., 533 : 4
gray-fly w. sultry horn, 280 : 10
great w. shorewards blow, 584 : 11
huntsman w. his horn, 349 : 10
imprisoned in viewless w., 228 : 20
lashing corners of earth, 761 : 16
neither shaken by w. nor wet, 59 : 27
night of south w., 574 : 19
nor'east to sou'west w., 622 : 19
of doctrine, 282 : 5
of heaven in our land, 813 : 8
on side of ablest navigators, 383 : 13
over great sea w. trouble waters, 100 : 12
rough w. do shake, 244 : 5
sea w. pierced solitudes, 494 : 4
selfsame w. that blow, 669 : 21
somewhere safe to sea, 633 : 22
stormy w. do blow, 273 : 7, 443 : 11
take w. of March with beauty, 246 : 26
time w. th' exhausted chain, 410 : 14
up and rectifies his own, 289 : 19
wailing w. naked woods, 471 : 10
were lovesick, 240 : 29
when w. breathing low, 468 : 1
where w. are all asleep, 584 : 12
whistling in rigging, 800 : 10
Winds' and spent waves' riot, 633 : 19
Windsor, on W. Marsh saw spider die, 892 : 7
Widow at W., 708 : 7
Windswept, desolate w. space, 626 : 21
Wind-walks, what w., 656 : 6
Windward, between w. and lee, 634 : 12
to w. of law, 375 : 11
Windy booms hoo-hooed it, 767 : 13
flung us on w. hill, 796 : 9
night rainy morrow, 245 : 3
shadows and w. places, 632 : 7
side of care, 209 : 12
side of law, 209 : *n* 2
Troy, 529 : 8
Wine, age leaves friends and w., 447 : 9
and women go together, 258 : 25
and women mirth laughter, 460 : 23
as water unto w., 530 : 5
best w. that goeth down sweetly, 28 : 21
better is thy love than w., 28 : 13
between kisses and w., 721 : 4
blood fizz like w., 760 : 5
blushes into w., 292 : *n* 3
bored with good w., 501 : 17
bring me beaker of w., 81 : 12
bring water bring w., 67 : 8
came upon no w., 823 : 5
Canary w., 477 : 16
come within pint of w., 327 : 8
comes in at mouth, 713 : 7
days of w. and roses, 721 : 7
dear boy and truth, 62 : 19
did not know the w., 605 : 1
drinking blude-red w., 926 : 9
drinks w. with laughter, 922 : 12
drunk your water and w., 707 : 3
drunken but not with w., 30 : 16
enjoy laughter over the w., 92 : 18
for thy stomach's sake, 50 : 33
frolic w., 266 : 17
from w. sudden friendship, 331 : 19
glass of w. happiness, 782 : 23
good w. a friend or being dry, 315 : 13
good w. a good creature, 230 : 27
good w. needs no bush, 112 : *n* 5
hard to hide ignorance over w., 70 : 10
Helen threw into w. a drug, 59 : 25
if it doesn't get into w., 742 : 16
I'll not look for w., 256 : 8
immortal w., 604 : 10
in w. is truth, 62 : *n* 12, 134 : 6
insolence and w., 283 : 19
inspires us and fires us, 332 : 2
inventing liquid w., 77 : 6
invisible spirit of w., 230 : 25
is a mocker, 24 : 27
is a peephole, 62 : 20
jar when molding began, 109 : 19
jug of w. loaf of bread, 516 : 7
leaving drinking of w., 309 : 20
lion w., 491 : 22
madder music stronger w., 721 : 6
maketh merry, 27 : 18
meal without w., 401 : 8
mischiefs from w., 316 : 13
monkey w., 491 : 22
murmured Snodgrass, 546 : 12
near my dying mouth, 137 : 1
new friend as new w., 35 : 15
new w. in old bottles, 38 : 30
no use of metal corn or w., 247 : 26
not hang branch over w., 112 : 12
of astonishment, 19 : 24
of life is drawn, 238 : 7
old w. to drink, 179 : 18
Wine (*continued*)
old w. wholesomest, 262 : 1
placed near my dying mouth, 137 : 11
poisonous w., 477 : 20
Samian w., 461 : 8
sans w. song singer, 516 : 15
seas of life like w., 311 : 23
sheep w., 491 : 22
should not refuse a little w., 142 : 21
strong w. reed as blood, 146 : 13
sure there was w., 268 : 21
sweet poison of misused w., 279 : 7
sweet pomegranate w., 4 : 12
sweet white w., 760 : 19
swine w., 491 : 22
that maketh glad the heart, 21 : 9
thine immortal w., 604 : 10
to succeed add water to w., 705 : 8
turning w. into urine, 789 : 6
unto those of heavy hearts, 26 : 5
urges me on, 60 : 18
vows made in w., 212 : 17
walnuts and w., 528 : 3
water made w., 44 : 27
when it is red, 25 : 11
when the w. goes in, 413 : 19
which over flows, 600 : 25
with bread and w. walk road, 935 : 10
with not a drop of Tiber, 242 : 12
women and song, 399 : 14
women and w., 332 : 2
wonderful as thirst, 823 : 5
Wine-barrel room, 765 : 5
Winebibber, gluttonous and a w., 39 : 7
Wine-dark seas, 868 : 21
singing over the w. sea, 59 : 19
Winepress, crushed in w. of passion, 150 : 2
fill w. of eloquence, 128 : 17
of fierceness and wrath, 53 : 27
trodden the w. alone, 31 : 26
Wines, abbots purple as their w., 340 : 26
feast of w. on the lees, 30 : 7
old w. times manners, 371 : 3
willingly drinks their w., 396 : 16
Wine-scented poetic soul, 668 : 18
Wing, air in music w. forsakes, 637 : 15
and a Prayer, 866 : 5
bird is on the w., 516 : 4
Conquest's crimson w., 363 : 4
crows that w. midway air, 234 : 28
damp my intended w., 287 : 13
dropped from angel's w., 429 : 4
flits by on leathern w., 364 : 12
gray w. upon tide, 713 : 11
hidden under dove's w., 806 : 13
hide head under his w., 932 : 6
inconstant w. as winds, 466 : 8
lark's on w., 540 : 15
makes w. to rooky wood, 238 : 21
of friendship never moults, 547 : 20
of submission, 131 : 6
quill from angel's w., 429 : *n* 1
see soul take w., 459 : 22
shall brush my w., 405 : 6
speed like bird on w., 688 : 12
stretches out my golden w., 402 : 13
though w. closely bound, 296 : *n* 3
turn stone start w., 693 : 18
wimpling w., 656 : 1
Wing-beats, where happy w. are, 412 : 9
Winged, change me to w. bird, 76 : 24
Cupid painted blind, 196 : 1

Winged (*continued*)
Cupid w. doth range, 918 : 15
does w. life destroy, 404 : 18
he addressed her w. words, 57 : 8
hours of bliss, 443 : 8
lawless w. unconfined, 404 : 14
seraphs of heaven, 527 : 8
shaft quivered in heart, 456 : 17
stands a w. sentry, 299 : 10
Time's w. chariot, 296 : 28
Winging, ever w. up and up, 600 : 25
Wings across canceled skies, 821 : 12
angel w. cast shadow, 817 : 3
at heaven's gates claps w., 176 : 1
beating luminous w. in vain, 589 : 13
bug with gilded w., 338 : 19
cannot fly like eagle with w. of wren, 646 : 3
disastrous beating of w., 732 : 11
downward beat thy w., 100 : *n* 8
downward on extended w., 767 : 4
each had six w., 29 : 8
fly upon the w. of the wind, 17 : 26
folds w. and is rocked, 570 : 7
four beasts had each six w., 53 : 7
fox w. lift him alive, 901 : 14
giant w. prevent walking, 580 : 17
golden hours on angel w., 410 : 18
green leaves like w., 642 : 3
healing in his w., 33 : 39
hear sound of w., 842 : 14
hope flies with swallow's w., 187 : 24
horse with w., 243 : 19
I am the w., 495 : 12
if he soars with own w., 404 : 2
leaves w. of seraph, 852 : 14
lets grow her w., 279 : 22
love without his w., 456 : 6
mice with w., 873 : 4
mount up with w. as eagles, 31 : 2
no longer wings to fly, 805 : 21
O for a horse with w., 243 : 19
obscene w., 435 : 16
of borrowed wit, 265 : 2
of night, 510 : 17
of silence, 279 : 19
of the dove, 459 : 18
of the future, 797 : 11
of the morning, 22 : 17
of the wind, 17 : 26, 21 : 8
on the w. of song, 481 : 13
on what w. dare he aspire, 405 : 7
on w. of Time grief flies, 296 : 17
one black other white, 289 : 2
philosophy clip angel's w., 476 : 6
poor splendid w., 634 : 10
riches have w., 377 : 1
riches make themselves w., 25 : 7
shakes his dewy w., 275 : 30
shakes w. and not stay, 305 : 3
shall tell the matter, 27 : 19
show black and golden w., 475 : 2
spread w. on the blast, 459 : 15
that I had w. like a dove, 19 : 20
thunder of the w., 797 : 20
unbroken w., 806 : 6
under his w. shalt thou trust, 20 : 16
under the shadow of thy w., 17 : 25
war with reremice for leathern w., 196 : 19
were blue, 550 : 12
whether pigs have w., 613 : 5
whitespread w., 778 : 6
wide-waving w., 377 : 26
Wingy mysteries in divinity, 274 : 3
Wink at homely girl, 772 : 6
not changed a w., 571 : 8
of eternity, 843 : 14
sleep a w., 339 : 5
slept one w., 243 : 22
without w. of sleep, 168 : 19
Winked, he w. at the thief, 404 : 11
Winkie, wee Willie W., 537 : 6
Winking at the brim, 476 : 23
Mary-buds begin, 243 : 16
Winks, nor w. the gold fin, 531 : 11
Winning, crown sullied in the w., 413 : 11
fight when sure of w., 565 : 1
games without cheating, 848 : 13
glory of w. were she won, 601 : 1
governing more important than w., 851 : 8
if world be worth thy w., 306 : 19
isn't everything, 925 : 15
light w. make prize light, 247 : 23
not worth wooing not worth w., 511 : 20
soul to good or evil, 65 : 14
stake counter boldly w. or losing, 543 : 14
wave deserving note, 266 : 7
Winnow not with every wind, 35 : 5
Winnowing wind, 477 : 18
Wins, Britain w. last battle, 745 : 13
corruption w. not more than honesty, 249 : 8
night that w., 632 : 8
slow and steady w., 66 : 3
who loses and who w., 235 : 12
Winsome wee thing, 410 : 17
Winter afternoons, 604 : 18
and rough weather, 211 : 1
blow thou w. wind, 211 : 16
come and gone, 469 : 4
comes to rule varied year, 345 : 4
ending in July 461 : 27
every mile is two in w., 270 : 23
furious w. blowing, 810 : 17
garment of repentance, 516 : 4
glories of w. moon, 529 : 1
God is day night w. summer, 70 : 2
hath his delights, 250 : 7
hoary w. night, 182 : 2
if we had no w., 290 : 11
if w. comes, 467 : 22
in w. get up at night, 668 : 9
is icumen in, 792 : 8
it was the w. wild, 277 : 7
king, 843 : 20
like a w. my absence, 245 : 8
lingering chills May, 368 : 18
lo the w. is past, 28 : 7
mother of spring, 513 : 6
mountains by w. sea, 534 : 29
moving isles of w., 528 : 29
my age lusty w., 210 : 30
nine months of w., 590 : 4
no season such delight as w., 265 : 16
nor ever heavy w. storm, 59 : 26
now winds of w. blow, 715 : 8
of our discontent, 186 : 29
plague and pestilence, 250 : 9
ruler of inverted year, 377 : 5
sad tale's best for w., 246 : 14
savor all the w. long, 246 : 25
slumbering in open air, 436 : 9
spend w. in refrigerator, 711 : 2
Winter (*continued*)
summer and w. shall not cease, 8 : 1
there was no w. in 't, 241 : 25
too long in country towns, 739 : 2
weeds outworn, 468 : 17
with his wrathful nipping cold, 185 : 14
words in w. articulated next summer, 120 : 16
words like w. snowflakes, 57 : 25
Wintered, pared and w. by, 886 : 15
Wintergreen for President, 836 : 1
Winter's afternoon in chapel, 808 : 16
crown old W. head, 292 : 10
dregs made desolate, 641 : 11
furious w. rages, 243 : 27
rains and ruins over, 632 : 8
sunbeam in w. day, 345 : 3
traces, 632 : 7
Winters and keeps warm her note, 271 : 20
forty w. besiege brow, 244 : 1
ran he on ten w. more, 303 : 16
summers wet and w. clear, 103 : 27
Wintertime, life breath of buffalo in w., 581 : 15
wooed her in w., 921 : 11
Wintry, gray and w. glens, 735 : 8
in w. age feel no chill, 377 : 20
long w. nights, 551 : 3
on casement w. moon, 476 : 16
splashing w. mold, 712 : 12
youth bent by w. fever, 886 : 12
Wipe away all tears, 53 : 30
away tears from all faces, 30 : 8
away trivial fond records, 219 : 27
Jerusalem as a dish, 14 : 22
my weeping eyes, 328 : 14
never w. off tears of woe, 404 : 17
often w. bloody nose, 331 : 15
out Eastern instincts, 707 : 7
tears of repentance you'll w., 404 : 17
Wiped away weeds and foam, 493 : 15
from eyelids w. tear, 211 : 12
nothing we do is w. out, 648 : 11
Wipeth, as a man w. a dish, 14 : 22
Wire, chattering like broken w., 816 : 14
trilling w. in blood, 807 : 4
Wireless, if w. no further advanced, 776 : 4
Wires grow on her head, 246 : 1
Wiretapping dirty business, 645 : 10
Wisdom, all men's w., 921 : *n* 1
and deliberation follow chance, 166 : 1
and goodness seem vile, 234 : 24
and Wit are little seen, 330 : 26
apply our hearts unto w., 20 : 14
authority without w., 290 : 10
automatism but also w., 837 : 9
banish w., 90 : 8
be put in silver rod, 403 : 17
beauty and w. rarely conjoined, 117 : 18
beginning of her w., 34 : 17
beginning of w., 21 : 19, 108 : 17, 583 : 17, 738 : 5
beyond rules of physic, 181 : 2
blear-eyed w., 715 : 17
bodily decrepitude w., 716 : 20
by awful grace of God, 71 : 5
cease from thine own w., 25 : 6
celestial w. calms mind, 352 : 3

Wisdom (*continued*)
conquer fear beginning of w., 738 : 5
contrivance of human w., 373 : 21
crieth without, 23 : 3
dispose of highest W., 289 : 10
distrust that age brings w., 772 : 10
dream taught me this w., 273 : 5
ends in w., 750 : 2
enter to grow in w., 617 : 5
entereth not in malicious mind, 157 : 13
exalteth her children, 35 : 1
excelleth folly, 26 : 18
fear of the Lord beginning of w., 21 : 19
fear of the Lord is w., 16 : 15
finds a way, 400 : 7
force without w. falls of own weight, 107 : 29
get from experience only w. in it, 625 : 5
give them w. that have it, 213 : 15
great w. generous, 90 : 1
hath builded her house, 23 : 18
hatred of bourgeois beginning of w., 583 : 17
how can he get w., 36 : 9
if any lack w., 51 : 27
in despair comes w., 71 : 5
in much w. is much grief, 26 : 17
in w. hast thou made all, 21 : 11
in women, 796 : 15
is humble, 377 : 15
is not bought, 926 : 6
is the principal thing, 23 : 7
Jesus increased in w., 42 : 33
joy is w., 712 : 11
justified of her children, 39 : 7
law last result of w., 353 : 14
light that cometh from her w., 34 : 20
lingers, 530 : 4
lost in knowledge, 806 : 15
love of w. guide of life, 407 : 17
love w. live accordingly, 559 : 9
married to immortal verse, 278 : *n* 1
masterwork of w., 580 : 10
medicine for woes of mankind, 595 : 15
never comes when gold, 600 : 15
never dear if genuine, 538 : 10
no happiness where no w., 75 : 2
no w. but in submission, 75 : 2
no w. can calculate end, 384 : 22
no w. in the grave, 27 : 16
none the less sweet for w., 595 : 9
not by age is w. acquired, 93 : 9
not to do desperate things, 559 : 5
not white hair that engenders w., 91 : 10
not w. to be only wise, 703 : 3
number the clouds in w., 16 : 35
of a just content, 610 : 8
of head and of heart, 549 : 17
of humility, 807 : 13
of many, 921 : 6
of our ancestors, 372 : 3
of our sages, 389 : 2
of Solomon, 13 : 31
of the ancients, 372 : *n* 3
of tomorrow, 664 : 12
one's w. another's folly, 497 : 26
only w. hope to acquire, 807 : 13
outweighs wealth, 75 : 1
pain comes we call it w., 885 : 9

Wisdom (*continued*)
part of w., 377 : 8
pessimism name given to w., 837 : 6
petty w. contentious, 90 : 1
political greatness and w. meet, 84 : 15
power w. goodness, 319 : 22
pray for w. yet, 597 : 1
presumption in w., 372 : 15
price of w. is above rubies, 16 : 14
prime w., 287 : 3
quite shut out, 285 : 5
rid of folly beginning of w., 108 : 17
root of w., 34 : 22
shall die with you, 15 : 27
spirit of w. and understanding, 29 : 18
takes w. from councils, 373 : 10
temper logic with w., 821 : 8
this w. not from above, 52 : 1
those who love want w., 466 : 17
thought we had w., 840 : 9
thus do we of w., 220 : 7
thy w. exceedeth the fame, 13 : 35
to believe heart, 703 : 3
to dare highest w., 448 : 4
to distinguish one from other, 823 : 15
to use wealth, 872 : 11
unerring w. never below, 311 : 9
use blessings with w., 108 : 14
vain w. all, 284 : 20
wall of w., 858 : 19
was mine, 827 : 7
what is w., 77 : 9
what w. greater than kindness, 358 : 21
where shall w. be found, 16 : 12
where w. neither fear nor ignorance, 138 : 14
wise man not glory in w., 32 : 5
wit and w. born with man, 263 : 19
with how little w. world governed, 263 : *n* 10
with the ancient is w., 15 : 30
without unmanliness, 81 : 1
wrath of lion w. of God, 404 : 3
Wisdom's aid, 364 : 16
self oft seeks, 279 : 22
threadbare saint in w. school, 251 : 9
Wise, a little too w. never live long, 187 : *n* 3
and beautiful, 584 : 10
and frugal government, 389 : 1
and masterly inactivity, 416 : 14
and moral man, 73 : 3
and salutary neglect, 372 : 15
and the lovely, 823 : 12
and understanding heart, 13 : 27
and wonderful, 561 : 8
arrows which speak to the w., 71 : 24
art of being w., 649 : 6
be w. as serpents, 38 : 36
be w. today, 330 : 8
be w. with speed, 329 : 21
beacon of the w., 226 : 7
beacons of w. men, 596 : 3
better is a poor and w. child, 26 : 25
both true both w., 295 : 4
by nature w., 262 : 12
coffee makes politician w., 334 : 8
consider her ways and be w., 23 : 11
consider w. what they cleave to, 124 : 24
country never so w., 689 : 22
cunning men pass for w., 180 : 21

Wise (*continued*)
dare to be w., 108 : 20
darkly w., 337 : 2
days that make us w., 760 : 18
defer not to be w., 324 : 23
enough to play fool, 214 : 12
errors of w. men, 290 : 7
every w. man's son know, 213 : 22
exceeding w. fair-spoken, 249 : 15
father that knows child, 199 : 3
folly to be w., 361 : 12
fool counted w., 24 : 18
fool doth think he is w., 212 : 30
fool talks w. man speaks, 257 : 4
foolery w. men have, 210 : 13
foolish things to confound w., 48 : 1
fools have always mocked w., 138 : 8
full of w. saws, 211 : 15
good to be merry and w., 158 : 19, 411 : 24
gout kills more w. than simple, 301 : 2
government knows how to enforce, 358 : 6
great men are not always w., 16 : 21
gude to be merry and w., 921 : 8
he that kan hymselven knowe, 148 : 4
he was wondrous w., 934 : 7
healthy wealthy w., 347 : 12
hear the words of the w., 24 : 37
heard w. man say, 690 : 20
histories make men w., 181 : 14
holy fair and w. is she, 190 : 4
honest and w. men rule, 382 : 1
how dieth the w. man, 26 : 20
if w. gets rich, 722 : 15
in his own conceit, 25 : 19
in old age learn to be w., 75 : 2
in use of pronouns, 636 : 6
in your own conceits, 47 : 22
learn from enemies, 82 : 7
leisure to grow w., 585 : 17
like w. one died, 171 : 8
love and be w., 110 : 17
love teach monarch to be w., 361 : 19
love that's w., 729 : 1
madness to think oneself w., 153 : 13
man has no extensive knowledge, 65 : 10
man is a school for magnates, 3 : 12
man is strong, 25 : 12
man knows himself fool, 212 : 30
man not glory in wisdom, 32 : 5
man not leave right to chance, 558 : 3
man utter vain knowledge, 15 : 36
man's verdict outweighs, 543 : 6
men from the East, 36 : 20
men in great struggle, 383 : 1
men of Gotham, 930 : 18
men profit more from fools, 95 : 10
men refrain to meddle, 155 : 5
men shun mistakes of fools, 95 : 10
men speak fools decide, 63 : 3
more fools than w., 918 : 17
more w. master simpler work, 140 : 5
neither yet bread to w., 27 : 17
no man w. by himself, 94 : 2
none is born w., 3 : 3
nor ever did a w. one, 315 : 14
nor w. at fifty, 269 : 32
not even God is w. enough, 926 : 7
not to the w. the light, 671 : 11

Wise (*continued*)
not wisdom to be only w., 703 : 3
not w. who buffet against love, 75 : 5
not worldly w., 267 : 13
old and crafty and w., 712 : 10
on exercise depend, 306 : 26
passiveness, 423 : 5
pause from learning to be w., 351 : 17
penny w. pound foolish, 258 : 10
powers deny us for our good, 240 : 26
precedents established by w., 444 : 5
prosperity tries souls even of w., 102 : 25
quiet w. and good, 469 : 25
rebuke a w. man, 23 : 19
reputed w. for saying nothing, 198 : 3
Roland valorous Oliver w., 136 : 13
saying w. and old, 173 : *n* 8
skepticism of critic, 569 : 15
so w. so young, 187 : 13
son maketh a glad father, 23 : 21
speech given to w. men, 310 : 22
spirits of w. mock us, 206 : 13
steals mind even of the w., 58 : 19
takes w. man to recognize w., man, 67 : 15
taketh the w. in craftiness, 15 : 16
thinks himself w. is great fool, 344 : 6
thrush, 541 : 17
to be w. and love, 226 : 14
to listen to the Word, 69 : 26
to w. man are ports and havens, 194 : 5
type of the w., 429 : 9
virgins, 40 : 28
want love, 466 : 17
wealthy, 83 : 7
were their subjects w., 377 : 12
what w. or stupid thing, 396 : 22
when he had pen in hand, 356 : 16
who are a little w., 252 : 14
who can be w. amazed, 238 : 8
who dares doubt poet w., 275 : 31
who knows others is w., 64 : 11
who tries everything before arms, 96 : 20
wine sets w. man singing, 60 : 18
wish to appear w. among fools, 118 : 3
without folly not so w., 293 : 25
woman never yields, 453 : 9
word to w. enough, 170 : 33, 347 : 32
words are w. men's counters, 264 : 13
words of the w. are as goads, 27 : 26
words taught in numbers, 174 : 9
wretch, 335 : 19
Wisecracking calisthenics with words, 827 : 18
Wisely, ability capacity to act w., 697 : 18
and slow, 192 : 22
charming never so w., 19 : 23
fair and softe, 144 : 28
live pleasurably without living w., 91 : 16
loved not w. but too well, 232 : 20
worldly, 267 : 13
Wiser being good than bad, 544 : 29
four things w. to know, 827 : 8
grow w. and better, 302 : 24
learn but not w. grow, 321 : 9
no man w. for his learning, 263 : 18
no w. than a daw, 184 : 20
no w. than before, 396 : 10
Wiser (*continued*)
sadder and w. man, 435 : 12
Satan w. than of yore, 336 : 3
scientist w. not to withhold, 396 : 7
than children of light, 43 : 31
than our ordinary selves, 588 : 20
than their own, 796 : 15
than thou art ware of, 210 : 35
today than yesterday, 340 : 10
without books, 377 : 14
women w. than men, 781 : 14
Wisest ask no more of Fate, 568 : 23
brightest meanest, 337 : 15
days to come are w. witnesses, 71 : 21
fool in Christendom, 175 : 3
man does not fancy he is, 311 : 6
men have erred, 288 : 25
of counselors Time, 73 : 7
of mankind enjoy life, 711 : 4
prophets make sure, 364 : 1
rivalship of w. men, 327 : 10
seeming truth to entrap w., 199 : 27
silence w. thing to heed, 72 : 5
Socrates w. of men, 288 : 15
these are w. 77 : 10
virtuousest discreetest, 287 : 8
Wish all men everywhere free, 522 : 7
believe we what we w., 303 : 14
control by w. world, 679 : 2
each w. of my heart, 446 : 11
every man in arms w. to be, 427 : 21
father to thought, 206 : 31
half grant what I w., 747 : 16
happy whose w. and care, 332 : 10
heart dry of blood, 478 : 8
Heaven of all their w., 796 : 14
him safe at home, 415 : 16
I liked way it talks, 697 : 1
I loved human race, 697 : 1
I thought What jolly fun, 697 : 1
I was in land of cotton, 554 : 1
I were a moron, 924 : 18
I w. he'd stay away, 756 : 2
I'd said that, 619 : 12
in vain to w. for death, 75 : 3
men believe what they w., 99 : 15
my days to be, 425 : 7
of some is to avenge, 80 : 16
rejection of particular w., 678 : 7
snow in May's mirth, 190 : 13
to be virtuous, 68 : 23
to save their own pocket, 80 : 16
what is it gentlemen w., 383 : 5
you a wave of the sea, 246 : 28
Wished heaven made her such a man, 229 : 31
I oft w. for Hell, 407 : 4
she had not heard it, 229 : 31
the w. the trysted hour, 411 : 2
to remain immortally, 734 : 7
to see thee cross-gartered, 214 : 10
Wishes, by country's w. blessed, 364 : 8
cannot alter facts, 380 : 11
expressed w. of people, 781 : 7
for that beyond reach, 316 : 15
her w. and ways be as nothing, 640 : 13
if w. were horses, 301 : 13
in idle w. fools stay, 400 : 7
law not bend to w., 380 : 12
lengthen as our sun declines, 330 : 15
never learned to stray, 362 : 12
soon as granted fly, 430 : 9
sorry if w. were gratified, 66 : 21
Wishes (*continued*)
what each w. he believes, 88 : 22
whom God w. to destroy, 78 : 1
Wishing his foot equal with eye, 186 : 10
Wishings, hell full of good w., 269 : 23
Wish-world control of sensory world, 679 : 2
Wist ye not, 42 : 32
Wistful, such a w. eye, 676 : 6
Wit, a w. is a feather, 337 : 13
all your piety nor w., 517 : 2
among lords, 354 : 1
and wakefulness, 899 : 11
and wisdom born with man, 263 : 19
as a w. if not first, 371 : 17
beams of w. on other souls, 304 : 25
beauty w. high birth, 226 : 20
boast his w., 303 : 20
bold and turbulent of w., 303 : 20
borrowed w., 265 : 2
brevity the soul of w., 220 : 10
cause w. in other men, 205 : 21
craves a kind of w., 214 : 12
cries up to be w., 309 : 22
devise w. write pen, 190 : 18
does harm to my w., 213 : 12
dream past the w. of man, 197 : 9
drink goes in w. goes out, 269 : 24
drunkenness is sepulture of w., 148 : 1
enjoy your dear w., 280 : 2
enliven morality with w., 326 : 9
enough to run away, 292 : 1
every age has its w., 311 : 5
false w., 325 : *n* 3
fancy w. will come, 336 : 7
fault of penetrating w., 294 : 4
genius sense and w., 375 : 20
good nature more agreeable than w., 326 : 17
half the w. credited, 417 : 16
has truth in it, 827 : 18
her w. was more than man, 305 : 8
his weapon w., 627 : *n* 2
his w. invites you, 336 : *n* 2
hope flock to aid, 496 : 13
how the w. brightens, 333 : 13
impropriety soul of w., 751 : 13
in w. a man, 305 : *n* 2, 336 : 9
invites you by his looks to come, 376 : 5
is an unruly engine, 268 : 7
is the noblest frailty, 313 : 19
is wall between us and dark, 831 : 21
kind of senseless w., 899 : 15
lasts two centuries, 453 : 16
levels all distinctions, 500 : 4
little tiny w., 234 : 1
liveliest effusions of w., 440 : 29
love and I had w. to win, 671 : 4
love paradox without losing w., 497 : 32
makes its own welcome, 500 : 4
men of w., 322 : 7
monuments of w. survive monuments of power, 178 : 16
mortify a w., 339 : 28
much malice little w., 305 : 23
my w. is thynne, 147 : 24
nature by her mother w., 174 : 1
ne'er tastes, 338 : 19
no innocent w. suppressed, 386 : 1
no man's w. can well direct him, 254 : 5

Wit (*continued*)
nor too much wealth nor w., 262 : 16
nor words nor worth, 216 : 28
of one wisdom of many, 921 : 6
one man's w., 921 : *n* 1
Phoenix riddle hath more w., 252 : 11
plentiful lack of w., 220 : 20
put his whole w. in a jest, 263 : 2
Shakespeare's w., 494 : 22
shines at expense of memory, 323 : 26
shoots his w., 213 : 6
skirmish of w., 208 : 24
soul of epigram, 435 : 24
soul of w., 220 : 10, 751 : 13
staircase w., 359 : 14
temper w. with morality, 326 : 9
that can creep, 339 : 3
too proud for a w., 371 : 14
true w. is nature to advantage dressed, 333 : 3
universal monarchy of w., 271 : 18
ware of mine own w., 210 : 36
wears his w. in his belly, 226 : 6
well of true w. truth, 601 : 6
what scanted in hair given in w., 188 : 4
when age in w. out, 209 : 28
when man hath over-greet a w., 148 : 6
will shine, 304 : 27
Wisdom and W., 330 : 26
with dunces, 340 : 23
your w. is too hot, 190 : 22
Witch, aroint thee w., 236 : 1
hath power to charm, 217 : 26
I have gone out a w., 908 : 10
tales Annie tells about, 665 : 11
Wicked W. of West, 677 : 9
world with noble horsemanship, 204 : 32
Witchcraft celebrates, 237 : 14
only w. I have used, 229 : 31
Witches, been rode by w., 623 : 21
feared w. burned women, 677 : 13
wild w. noble ladies, 714 : 4
Witchhunts, loyalty oaths and w., 847 : 4
Witching time of night, 222 : 23
Withal, money comes w., 188 : 28
Withdrawing, melancholy long w., roar, 587 : 16
Withdrawn, he has departed w., gone away, 98 : 3
Wither, age cannot w. her, 241 : 1
and come to deadly use, 234 : 23
his leaf shall not w., 17 : 12
into the truth, 713 : 8
your beauty will w., 163 : 1
Withered as if stained zucchini, 905 : 15
because no root, 39 : 14
before they be w., 34 : 11
cheek tresses gray, 429 : 20
drifts of w. leaves, 588 : 5
flowers of forest w. away, 359 : 11
flowers w. while I spent my days, 135 : 9
hand capped w. heart, 858 : 20
impenetrable like felt swan, 860 : 9
is garland of the war, 241 : 22
sedge w. from lake, 478 : 10
there it could not w. be, 256 : 9
when my father died, 224 : 2
withering of w. flowers, 808 : 3
Withereth, grass w., 30 : 33, 52 : 9
Withering, leaves w. and sere, 526 : 22
now w. in my bloom, 334 : 27
of withered flowers, 808 : 3
on virgin thorn, 195 : 21
Withers gray-green, 711 : 11
our w. are unwrung, 222 : 16
wastes and w. there, 676 : 13
Withhold not thine hand in the evening, 27 : 22
scientist wiser not to w., 396 : 7
Within, birds w. despair, 165 : 19
consecration from w. himself, 831 : 24
foretold that danger lurks w., 186 : 18
I have that w., 218 : 3
Without, birds w. despair to get in, 165 : 19
can't live with them or w., 82 : 14
can't live w. or with you, 113 : 8
four things better w., 827 : 9
me God cannot live, 300 : 17
mind contemplate itself from w., 665 : 4
prepared for doing w., 489 : 20
Withstand in the evil day, 49 : 39
Withstood, little tyrant of fields w., 362 : 9
Witness against himself, 391 : 17
call heaven and earth to w., 11 : 8
call the gods to w., 242 : 30
false w. by their own mouth, 36 : 15
for me that I have fought, 302 : 15
God appointed me w., 486 : 10
heap of stones a w., 8 : 23
heaven and earth to w., 11 : 8
history the w. to passing time, 98 : 9
I stand w. to common lot, 801 : 14
man w. unto his deeds, 132 : 16
no w. so dreadful, 95 : 19
of soul naturally Christian, 126 : 1
shalt not bear false w., 10 : 7
single w. is no w., 134 : 31
to the people, 31 : 19
weak w. of thy name, 277 : 13
without w. against me, 4 : 9
your eyes my w., 260 : 12
Witnesses, cloud of w., 51 : 19
days to come are wisest w., 71 : 21
to same overt act, 391 : 12
trees and all of nature w., 928 : 10
Wit's, a w. a feather, 337 : 13
an unruly engine, 268 : 7
at their w. end, 21 : 16
the noblest frailty, 313 : 19
your w. too hot, 190 : 22
Wits, dunce with w., 340 : 23
from table with his w., 294 : 15
good w. jump, 170 : 33
great w. to madness allied, 303 : 20
has no w. to lose, 374 : 13
he who doesn't lose w., 374 : 13
home-keeping youth homely w., 189 : 28
honors beauties w., 252 : 22
lord among w., 354 : 1
so many heads so many w., 97 : *n* 2
summoned w. from woolgathering, 261 : 9
to read, 256 : 11
were fresh and clear, 586 : 1
whetstone of w., 210 : 12
Witticism, to fail in w. is worst, 442 : 20
Wittily, old hermit very w. said, 214 : 27
Witty beauty a power, 601 : 4
buzz w. and fair annoys, 338 : 19
Witty (*continued*)
difficult to be w. every day, 484 : 10
it shall be w., 342 : 16
melancholy men most w., 259 : 6
not only w. in myself, 205 : 21
poets w. mathematics subtile, 181 : 14
to be rude, 322 : 17
woman a treasure, 601 : 4
words though ne'er so w., 172 : 13
Wives, absolute power over w., 392 : 9
gifted energetic w. of writers, 889 : 1
girls turn w., 906 : 10
if women had w. to keep house, 914 : 3
like strawberry w., 179 : 16
man with seven w., 930 : 1
many many w., 696 : 3
may be merry, 225 : 27
men more fortunate than w., 665 : 19
sky changes when w., 212 : 25
some poisoned by their w., 195 : 2
think of homes and w., 795 : 14
to be paid in consideration, 889 : 2
young men's mistresses, 180 : 10
Wives', old w. fables, 50 : 29
old w. tale, 720 : 13
Wiving, hanging and w. go by destiny, 159 : *n* 4
Wizard of Oz, 677 : 7
Woe, all my bliss and w., 371 : 1
bottom of w. deep, 570 : 5
can I see another's w., 403 : 16
cavalry of w., 604 : 7
come weal come w., 422 : 19
conquered w., 245 : 3
Ecclesiastes steel of w., 570 : 16
every w. a tear claim, 459 : 3
feel another's w., 340 : 4
fig for w., 158 : 17
great w. to their enemies, 59 : 28
groan of martyr's w., 406 : 7
heritage of w., 459 : 12
hideous notes of w., 462 : 1
Ho told story of w., 614 : 2
howling w., 402 : 15
if love good wheenes cometh w., 144 : 14
is me for I am undone, 29 : 10
is me to have seen, 221 : 22
is me Winter come, 469 : 4
liberty lashed with w., 188 : 1
man made for joy and w., 406 : 13
melt at others' w., 361 : 14
month follow month with w., 469 : 7
never parted bliss or w., 287 : 23
never was a story of more w., 193 : 31
never wipe off tears of w., 404 : 17
none save exiles feel, 551 : 10
of human bliss to w., 290 : 8
one w. tread upon another's heel, 223 : *n* 5
out of w. make songs, 481 : 6
protracted w., 351 : 20
proved a very w., 245 : 23
reef of Norman's W., 510 : 6
scheme of weal and w., 544 : 6
silence in love bewrays w., 172 : 13
sleep friend of w., 440 : 5
starboard hand of w., 570 : 5
succeeds a woe, 223 : *n* 5
suits of w., 218 : 3
thrill deepest notes of w., 410 : 1
to him that reads but one book, 270 : 27

Woe (*continued*)
to the conquered, 134 : 35
unto them that call evil good, 29 : 7
unto them that draw iniquity, 29 : 6
unto them that join house to house, 29 : 4
unto them that rise up early, 29 : 5
unto you scribes and Pharisees, 40 : 18
unto you when men speak well, 43 : 3
unutterable w., 551 : 10
voiceless w., 458 : 16
weal and w. is common, 273 : 11
with loss of Eden, 282 : 22
wonder grandeur w., 571 : 2
world but thoroughfare of w., 146 : 29
Woebegone, so dead in look so w., 205 : 19
Woeful ballad, 211 : 15
stuff this madrigal, 333 : 13
want, 450 : 1
Woes as time cannot recure, 172 : 7
beyond their share, 59 : 15
cluster, 223 : *n* 5
for such a woman they suffer w., 57 : 24
Grecian w., 334 : 18
he suffered in his heart many w., 59 : 13
love a sickness full of w., 182 : 11
of hopeless lovers, 305 : 12
rare are solitary w., 223 : *n* 5
riches cover multitude of w., 90 : 18
spring of w. unnumbered, 334 : *n* 4
starry Galileo with w., 458 : 12
upon Achaeans myriad w., 57 : 3
what is worst of w., 457 : 10
with old w. new wail, 244 : 11
Wohnet, der in den Zweigen w., 395 : *n* 1
Woke and found life was duty, 555 : 23
Wolf, appetite an universal w., 226 : 3
at door, 695 : 17
boy cried W., 66 : 5
by the ears, 97 : 3
cloud that looked like w., 81 : 15
denounces shepherd, 523 : 7
false as w. to heifer's calf, 226 : 15
from door, 153 : 1
grim w. with privy paw, 280 : 22
hates when it flatters, 129 : 12
in fold sad thing, 103 : 11
in sheep's clothing, 65 : 17
keep the w. far thence, 262 : 4
like w. on the fold, 459 : 14
live with wolves howl like w., 934 : 15
man w. to man, 811 : 9
neither yield to howling of w., 177 : 17
owlet whoops to w. below, 435 : 6
shall dwell with lamb, 29 : 19
sheep and w. not agreed, 523 : 7
that keep it prosper, 709 : 4
that's foe to men, 262 : 4
trusts in tameness of w., 234 : 14
who's afraid of big bad w., 908 : *n* 1
Wolfe, Robert Emmet and W. Tone, 713 : 11
Wolf's-bane tight-rooted, 477 : 20
Wollstonecrafts, crucified the Mary W., 554 : 9
Wolves and lambs have no concord, 59 : 8
eat like w. fight like devils, 207 : 26
Wolves (*continued*)
inwardly ravening w., 38 : 16
live with w. howl like wolf, 934 : 15
Woman a foreign land, 593 : 3
a good-natured w., 441 : 11
a sometime thing, 836 : 5
adores Fascist, 911 : 18
always fickle thing, 105 : 10
always the w. to Sherlock Holmes, 689 : 7
aren't I a w., 482 : 17
as easy to marry rich w., 539 : 14
as man looks at w., 769 : 23
as you are w., 833 : 3
beautiful w. with one eye, 401 : 7
behold thy son, 45 : 33
being w. hard beset, 794 : 3
belief w. made for man, 554 : 7
believe w. or epitaph, 456 : 15
body of weak and feeble w., 163 : 15
brawling w. in a wide house, 24 : 33
caparisons don't become young w., 398 : 15
cast shame away, 147 : 12
causes us to suffer, 734 : 10
Christ came from God and w., 483 : 1
clever w. manage fool, 707 : 11
compete not as w. but as human being, 898 : 6
constant but yet a w., 203 : 24
coupling of man and w., 807 : 10
courtesy wins w., 534 : 20
created w. boredom ceased, 658 : 15
destructive damnable w., 316 : 16
devil became w., 491 : 9
did ever w. since creation, 359 : 19
die because a w. is fair, 264 : 23
disillusionment that w. has brain, 848 : 9
dissimulation innate in w., 463 : 6
emancipation of w., 842 : *n* 5
enjoy being w., 898 : 4
enmity between thee and w., 7 : 10
every w. gift of world to me, 481 : 12
every w. should marry, 502 : 11
excellent thing in w., 235 : 17
faded but still lovely w., 835 : 12
fair w. without discretion, 23 : 25
fat white w., 795 : 2
finest w. in nature, 327 : 10
first loves lover, 460 : 24
foolish men who accuse w., 316 : 1
for such a w. they suffer, 57 : 24
for the hearth, 531 : 7
for thy understanding a w., 190 : 16
frailty thy name is w., 218 : 9
fury of disappointed w., 324 : *n* 7
gained by flattery, 342 : 13
glacier w., 843 : 20
God's second mistake, 658 : 15
good name in man and w., 230 : 33
good w. if five thousand a year, 539 : 9
good w. the Misfit said, 905 : 3
hard to snub beautiful w., 746 : 18
has her way, 519 : 4
has revenge ready, 297 : 19
hate a dumpy w., 460 : 12
have I not found, 27 : 11
he that tastes w. ruin meets, 332 : 5
heart of w. he loves, 734 : 2
how divine a thing w., 427 : 19
I am a w. first, 858 : 2
I am w., 915 : 9
Woman (*continued*)
I an old w. now, 641 : 14
I love, 832 : 2
in argument with men a w. worse, 289 : 1
in hours of ease, 431 : 2
in kimono, 860 : 1
in this humor wooed, 187 : 3
is a contradiction, 335 : 25
is a dish for gods, 242 : 1
is at heart a rake, 335 : 22
is his game, 531 : 6
is one of greatest institooshuns, 616 : 12
is only a woman, 707 : 6
keeps mentioning w. he knew, 135 : 13
know to submit, 417 : 13
large-brained w., 506 : 13
last thing civilized, 600 : 8
lesser man, 530 : 5
let w. into Paradise, 934 : 10
let w. then go on, 471 : 1
like that not woman quite, 908 : 11
lips of a strange w. drop as honeycomb, 23 : 10
little girl my stringbean my lovely w., 908 : 13
lived in shoe, 931 : 10
lone w. with silver spoons, 558 : 7
long hair glory to w., 48 : 19
look for the w., 491 : 7
love alone give w. full stature, 754 : 1
love improves a w., 329 : 11
love to w. life or death, 670 : 2
loveliest w. born, 714 : 20
lovely in her bones, 874 : 1
lovely w. stoops to folly, 369 : 20, 805 : 8
made he a w., 7 : 2
made mouths in a glass, 233 : 27
man and w. in garden, 675 : 16
man that is born of a w., 15 : 33
man's desire for w., 438 : 5
mighty ills done by w., 316 : 16
mist dispelled when w. appears, 332 : 3
mistake young w. for goddess, 772 : 3
modest w. in finery, 371 : 7
more barbarous than man, 657 : 21
more charming if not fall into hands, 647 : 18
mortifying when w. considers difference of education, 392 : 12
moved like fountain troubled, 189 : 5
much missed, 641 : 24
nakedness of w. work of God, 404 : 3
no animal more invincible than w., 82 : 13
no w. so precious as truths, 734 : 10
none of w. born, 239 : 10
not born w. becomes one, 870 : 11
not even shallow, 658 : *n* 2
not kill w. who wronged you, 647 : 19
not know I am a w., 212 : 8
not ugly thinks herself handsome, 342 : 4
nothing worse than shameless w., 82 : 16
O w. lovely w., 317 : 2
O w. perfect w., 260 : 16
of mean understanding, 440 : 17
of Samaria, 44 : 35
off with old w. before new, 680 : 2

Woman (*continued*)
often changes, 105 : *n* 5
old w. lived under hill, 933 : 11
old w. tossed in blanket, 932 : 5
once loved hateful, 736 : 3
once w. has given heart, 321 : 3
one compassionate w., 847 : 7
one that was a w. sir, 224 : 11
one word for w., 677 : 4
one would bury for nothing, 547 : 37
organizer a w., 104 : 23
overmastered with dust, 209 : 6
oweth duty to husband, 189 : 6
perfect w. nobly planned, 427 : 6
poor lone w., 206 : 9
preaching, 354 : 15
proclaim ownership, 699 : 14
rejoices in revenge, 122 : 18
reveals truths by causing to suffer, 734 : 10
same needs as man, 914 : 5
sat in unwomanly rags, 485 : 16
says what will please, 358 : 26
scorned, 324 : 16
shallow changing w., 187 : 21
silliest w. manage man, 707 : 11
so hard on woman, 531 : 9
so unto man is w., 511 : 18
sort of bloom on w., 694 : 10
speaks small like a w., 225 : 6
spirit yet w. too, 427 : 4
still be a w. to you, 329 : 14
still gentler sister w., 409 : 21
stock rising in market, 491 : 1
stoops to folly, 369 : 20, 805 : 8
take elder than herself, 214 : 1
take some savage w., 530 : 6
takes off claim to respect, 78 : 4
talking passion of w., 323 : 30
taught to protect herself, 578 : 3
that deliberates is lost, 325 : 18
that feareth the Lord, 26 : 10
the w. is a whore, 355 : 10
therefore to be won, 185 : 6
to be w. and writer, 867 : 2
to obey, 531 : 7
tremble to win w., 503 : 10
true and fair, 252 : 2
understanding harmful in w., 316 : 4
Vanessa extraordinary w., 322 : *n* 2
venom clamors of jealous w., 188 : 13
virtuous w. is a crown, 23 : 28
wailing for demon-lover, 433 : 22
waits for me, 575 : 6
what a w. thinks of women, 601 : 5
what does a w. want, 679 : 7
what have I to do, 44 : 26
what w. says written in wind, 102 : 12
when a w. is a pleasure, 67 : 11
when I behold thee, 475 : 3
when w. marries again, 675 : 5
who can find a virtuous w., 26 : 6
who did not care, 709 : 14
who grieve for this w., 801 : 13
who has wronged you, 647 : 19
who occasions least talk, 81 : 6
who plans such deeds, 60 : 11
whom thou gavest, 7 : 8
whose heart is snares, 27 : 10
whosoever looketh on a w., 37 : 8
why can't w. be more like man, 895 : 2
wickedness of a w., 35 : 36
with fair opportunities, 539 : 5

Woman (*continued*)
with his tongue win a w., 190 : 1
with the heart, 531 : 7
with whom be stupid, 735 : 14
without man cannot meet man, 896 : 5
without w. I love, 832 : 2
witty w. a treasure, 601 : 4
woman's body is the w., 647 : 6
won or woman lost, 715 : 5
worthy w. al hir lyve, 146 : 7
would run through fire, 225 : 22
Woman-chaser, sorriest little w., 583 : 14
Womanhood and childhood fleet, 510 : 13
heroic w., 512 : 1
Womankind, faith in w., 531 : 14
Womanly, manly deeds w. words, 270 : *n* 5
Woman's a contradiction, 335 : 25
Abolitionists yet to learn w. rights, 577 : 18
body is the woman, 647 : 6
brief as w. love, 222 : 12
charm w. strength, 694 : *n* 2
children's gratitude w. love, 716 : 12
cold preverted will, 470 : 10
come to my w. breasts, 236 : 17
desire for desire of man, 438 : 5
die because a w. fair, 264 : 23
gift to rain tears, 188 : 24
life history of affections, 452 : 19
light lies in w. eyes, 447 : 4
love lodged in w. breast, 250 : 13
love of being loved, 641 : 7
love the history of w. life, 417 : 12
love w. whole existence, 460 : 19
name in print twice, 789 : 3
no other but w. reason, 189 : 29
normal occupations, 867 : 5
old age is w. hell, 296 : 6
only books w. looks, 447 : 5
paths to w. love, 260 : 20
sex prima facie evidence, 554 : 6
spark in w. heart, 452 : 15
such beauty as w. eye, 191 : 1
the w. a whore, 355 : 10
tiger's heart in w. hide, 186 : 2
time of opportunity short, 82 : 12
tongue good when an't w., 546 : 15
twenty years in w. life, 84 : 14
vows write upon wave, 75 : 22
wife joined w. club, 699 : 13
will, 201 : 14
work never done, 920 : 11
Womb, came forth of mother's w., 27 : 2
cold in the w., 907 : 16
fruit of thy w., 42 : 19
naked out of my mother's w., 15 : 4
of morning dew, 173 : 15
of pia mater, 190 : 30
of uncreated night, 284 : 9
shall forget him, 16 : 10
since black w. held, 883 : 11
slayeth child in w., 793 : 2
teeming w. of royal kings, 194 : 13
Wombs, mothers' w. the tiring houses, 173 : 1
Women, accord w. equal power, 578 : 6
and children first, 921 : 21
and elephants, 731 : 12
and wine, 332 : 2
are angels wooing, 225 : 34

Women (*continued*)
are as roses, 214 : 2
are like tricks, 324 : 13
are seldom inventors, 343 : 22
as workers not as w., 578 : 1
attend men and not w., 85 : 16
better or worse than men, 315 : 11
bevy of fair w., 287 : 31
blessed among w., 42 : 17
brought shame on all w., 60 : 12
by bad w. been deceived, 288 : 25
capture of men by w., 539 : *n* 2
children of larger growth, 342 : 3
come and go, 803 : 10
compare with me ye w., 290 : 12
dear dead w., 543 : 12
degraded by trivial attentions, 414 : 10
desire sovereynetee, 147 : 14
die of loneliness but for w., 718 : 5
difference between men and w., 853 : 16
duty of w. to secure francise 554 : 5
economic equality for w., 903 : 9
educated for dependence, 414 : 8
England a paradise for w., 259 : 22
England is paradise of w., 174 : 23
equal right of men and w., 788 : 20
especially to w., 460 : 17
fair w. and brave men, 457 : 14
fairest among w., 28 : 3
faithful w. alike, 777 : 5
feared witches burned w., 677 : 13
fickleness of w. I love, 680 : 3
find few real friends, 357 : 7
fine w. eat crazy salad, 714 : 16
foolish to match men, 565 : 12
framed to make w. false, 230 : 5
friends to talk about w. with, 718 : 5
gave what other w. gave, 717 : 1
Germans are like w., 658 : 27
getting along with w., 394 : 15
given deplorable education, 504 : 9
good w. shoulder to shoulder, 839 : 12
great city greatest w., 575 : 12
growing honester,695 : 14
guide the plot, 398 : 20
hangin' men and w., 920 : 22
happiest w. no history, 565 : 18
hate all w. when thou gone, 252 : 19
have as much rights as man, 483 : 1
have no characters, 335 : 16
have no depths, 658 : 27
have no wilderness, 836 : 20
have positive moral sense, 634 : 17
hid himself among w., 275 : 5
homely men charmed w., 699 : 12
how hard for w. to keep counsel, 216 : 2
I know disposition of w., 96 : 21
if w. had not received permission, 73 : 5
if w. had wives to keep house, 914 : 3
in w. two divide, 335 : 21
indisputably beautiful, 342 : 4
innocent and pure, 247 : 26
Italy hell for w., 259 : 22
kindness in w. not looks, 189 : 1
know jealous readiest to forgive, 582 : 10
know less than men, 781 : 14
knowledge of w. of his own family, 508 : 21
learned about w. from 'er, 709 : 10

Women (*continued*)
let w. into your life, 681 : 7
like to be conquered, 539 : 22
like untuned golden strings, 183 : 18
liked several w., 248 : 3
literary accomplishments in w., 392 : 11
looking glasses reflecting man, 782 : 5
love lovers, 294 : 9
make public judge, 453 : 12
men and w. affirm brotherhood, 870 : 13
men and w. created equal, 554 : 4
men and w. merely players, 211 : 15
men and w.—Liberate, 831 : 19
men w. and clergymen, 433 : 2
men work w. weep, 566 : 9
monstrous regiment of w., 162 : 1
more nearly men and w., 837 : 11
more pangs than wars or w., 249 : 3
music and w. give way to, 310 : 2
no medicines to make w. keep silence, 655 : 15
no more trusting in w., 60 : 14
not so young as painted, 735 : 21
not w. or Negroes but citizens, 554 : 8
old w. should not be perfumed, 62 : 1
other w. cloy appetites, 241 : 1
ought to have representatives, 414 : 13
passing the love of w., 13 : 11
passionate w., 712 : 19
pleasing punishment w. bear, 187 : 33
plunged into cares and sorrows, 414 : 11
possibilities for expansion by w., 914 : 3
provide w. with economic opportunities, 903 : 10
pursuit of loose w., 583 : 9
run to extremes, 315 : 11
saints rarely married w., 867 : 5
seven w. take hold of one man, 29 : 2
silence gives grace to w., 73 : 9
Solomon loved many strange w., 13 : 37
some w. charm all, 694 : 10
some w. handsome without adornment, 98 : 13
some w. stay in memory, 710 : 11
sorrow for his w., 903 : 2
spare w. for Thy sake, 866 : 17
special contribution awareness, 853 : 19
superiority of their w., 506 : 10
text of men and w., 689 : 18
that's the nature of w., 168 : 31
these impossible w., 82 : 14
thou fairest among w., 28 : 3
till w. more rationally educated, 414 : 7
trained to place others' needs first, 883 : 6
try luck men risk it, 675 : 5
understand more than men, 781 : 14
upset everything, 681 : 7
war between men and w., 831 : 5
we should have learned w., 392 : 11
wear the breeches, 258 : 11
what a woman thinks of w., 601 : 5
what is it men in w. require, 404 : 20
what that party promises w., 578 : 4

Women (*continued*)
when candles out all w. fair, 120 : 17
who are not beautiful, 751 : 3
who knows what w. can be, 898 : 7
wine and w. go together, 258 : 25
wine w. and song, 399 : 14
wine w. mirth laughter, 460 : 23
wisdom in w., 796 : 15
with w. heart argues, 586 : 13
words are w. deeds men, 270 : 16
Women's eyes for stars, 918 : 6
from w. eyes this doctrine, 191 : 5
intelligence nourished, 898 : 7
sooner lost than w., 214 : 1
weapons waterdrops, 233 : 22
Won by captain of second rank, 491 : 18
by men with courage, 81 : 5
game is done I've w., 434 : 20
glory of winning were she w., 601 : 1
harbors I by sweating blood w., 151 : 10
lose ground w. today, 585 : 22
lost or w. game, 489 : 10
new world to be w., 890 : 4
not that you w. or lost, 773 : 3
on playing fields of Eton, 421 : 16
other palms are w., 426 : 23
prize we sought w., 576 : 6
she that with poetry w., 291 : 18
small have plodders w., 190 : 12
so melancholy as battle w., 421 : 8
the ear of Pluto, 278 : 8
things w. are done, 225 : 34
wars w. by men, 791 : 15
was woman in this humor w., 187 : 3
when battle's lost and w., 235 : 21
woman therefore to be w., 185 : 6
woman w. or woman lost, 715 : 5
wooed and not unsought be w., 287 : 6
world made to be w. by youth, 743 : 11
Wonder, all knowledge and w. is pleasure, 178 : 18
all w. that would be, 529 : 24
and glory of universe, 515 : 7
and wild desire, 545 : 1
at so grotesque a blunder, 753 : 5
at the workmanship, 280 : 1
basis of worship, 473 : 1
bird of w. dies, 249 : 17
capacity for w., 683 : 3
do I dare, 803 : 12
dreaming eyes of w., 612 : 15
ever-increasing w. and awe, 366 : 12
grandeur woe, 571 : 2
how I w. what you're at, 611 : 20
how the devil, 338 : 12
I am come to her w., 879 : 11
I w. by my troth, 251 : 14
if not same with human race, 760 : 10
men trust themselves, 242 : 31
miles around w. grew, 691 : 2
my curiosity my w., 705 : 4
my verse sad no w., 692 : 6
of an hour, 457 : 5
of earth and life, 821 : 3
of our stage, 256 : 11
past reach of wonder, 822 : 10
quench my love I w., 628 : 25
starve for want of w., 742 : 8
still the w. grew, 370 : 11
what I was begun for, 919 : 15
what you are, 449 : 13

Wonder (*continued*)
what you're at, 611 : 20
what you've missed, 868 : 10
Wonderful, all things wise and w., 561 : 8
bird is pelican, 765 : 12
days a-coming, 618 : 11
grass on breast, 593 : 7
mystic w., 534 : 4
name shall be called W., 29 : 16
no wine w. as thirst, 823 : 5
none more w. than man, 74 : 14
one-hoss shay, 519 : 15
peace it's w., 776 : 5
's w. 's marvelous, 835 : 20
seasoning of enjoyments, 298 : 2
three things which are too w., 26 : 4
thy love to me was w., 13 : 11
wide beautiful w. world, 593 : 7
wizard of Oz, 677 : 7
wonderful most wonderful, 212 : 6
Wonderfully, fearfully and w. made, 22 : 19
Wondering fearing doubting dreaming, 526 : 14
Wonderland, summer's w., 772 : 22
Wonders, America land of w., 506 : 7
at our quaint spirits, 196 : 20
carry with us w. we seek, 274 : 6
His w. to perform, 375 : 16
never cease, 393 : 12
numberless are world's w., 74 : 14
of all w. I have heard, 215 : 26
of Christian religion, 319 : 22
welcome all w., 292 : 19
world not starve for w., 742 : 8
Wonder-working earth puts forth sweet flowers, 100 : 2
Wondrous architecture of world, 183 : 6
days have been w. free, 329 : 13
eye intent on w. plan, 410 : 16
he was w. wise, 934 : 7
it grew w. cold, 434 : 10
moon takes up w. tale, 325 : 9
'twas w. pitiful, 229 : 31
Wont, more near earth than w., 232 : 15
Won't, when you will they w., 96 : 21
will you w. you, 612 : 8
Wonted, live their w. fires, 362 : 15
Woo her as lion, 366 : 9
men April when they w., 212 : 25
that would w. her, 229 : 31
Wood, an ark of gopher w., 7 : 28
beyond these a bit of w., 106 : 20
Birnam w. to Dunsinane, 239 : 12, 765 : 10
bows to w. and stone, 452 : 10
brown heath and shaggy w., 430 : 11
burgeoning w. brings forth, 58 : 1
cannot see w. for trees, 160 : 26
children in the w., 917 : 6
cleave w. there am I, 126 : 14, 671 : 9
correct in cypress w., 827 : 14
crow makes wing to rooky w., 238 : 21
dark w. where straight way lost, 140 : 10
deep and gloomy w., 423 : 12
field hath eyen w. eres, 146 : 20
grainy w., 796 : 16
has a sharp ear, 146 : *n* 5
heap on more w., 430 : 21
hewers of w., 11 : 33
hewing w. for master carpenter, 65 : 7

Wood (*continued*)
in w. a piggy-wig, 550 : 8
in w. furious winter blowing, 810 : 17
in woodsman's house knives w., 935 : 14
know what w. cudgel's of, 291 : 16
land set out to plant w., 339 : 10
loved w. rose, 494 : 14
of English bows, 689 : 16
old w. burn brightest, 262 : 1
old w. to burn, 179 : 18
one impulse from vernal w., 423 : 7
over river through w., 490 : 20
red herrings in w., 930 : 2
sang within bloody w., 804 : 25
stumps warmed me twice, 560 : 9
throne is bit of w. gilded, 420 : 11
tigers in the w., 899 : 11
time make soft iron w., 823 : 14
to wild w. and downs, 470 : 3
true w. yew w., 689 : 16
tulgey w., 612 : 18
two roads diverged in w., 747 : 13
wherever w. can swim, 420 : 16
who splits w. warms twice, 560 : *n* 2
Woodbine, luscious w., 196 : 18
Woodcocks, springes to catch w., 219 : 5
Wooden dialogue and sound, 226 : 4
float easy as w. boat, 919 : 9
justice has w. leg, 722 : 1
O, 207 : 2
wall is your ships, 70 : 13
water through my w. hull, 673 : 15
Wooden-shoes, Round-heads and W., 326 : 6
Woodland, hills vales w. plain, 334 : 15
let me love river and w., 104 : 4
of Weir, 526 : 23
Woodlands, about w. I will go, 690 : 17
Woodlawn, at W. heard dead cry, 873 : 12
Woodman spare beechen tree, 443 : 19
spare that tree, 492 : 10
Wood-notes, native w. wild, 278 : 6
Woods against stormy sky, 470 : 14
are full of them, 921 : 10
are the w. for me, 834 : 10
crazy as hauling timber into w., 106 : 18
culture no better than its w., 869 : 4
decay and fall, 533 : 27
enter enchanted w., 600 : 29
fierce and accustomed to w., 154 : 8
fill up with snow, 748 : 5
for hunters of dreams, 685 : 11
fresh w. and pastures new, 281 : 6
Greta w. are green, 431 : 18
have ears, 146 : *n* 5
have tongues, 146 : *n* 5
horn in depths of w., 483 : 3
I am for the w., 834 : 10
in riot, 691 : 7
in w. Yonghy-Bonghy-Bo, 550 : 16
into w. Master went, 651 : 11
light w. go seaward, 453 : 23
lovely dark deep, 748 : 7
more free from peril, 210 : 23
more in w. than in books, 136 : 9
naked w., 471 : 10
of Arcady dead, 711 : 19
or steepy mountain yields, 183 : 8
out of w. He came, 651 : 12
pleasure in pathless w., 458 : 24
rhodora in the w., 494 : 4

Woods (*continued*)
senators of mighty w., 478 : 4
shall to me answer, 174 : 17
stoic of w., 443 : 20
streams and w. belong, 685 : 11
to sleeping w. singeth, 435 : 1
to w. to live deliberately, 559 : 25
untamed, 696 : 11
we'll to w. no more, 591 : 6
wet wild w., 710 : 6
when all w. are still, 281 : 8
whose w. these are, 748 : 5
wild in w. noble savage, 303 : 8
wind through w. in riot, 691 : 7
Woodshed, middle-aged build w., 557 : 12
something nasty in w., 854 : 7
Woodside, lived under my w., 272 : 21
Woodsman's, in w. house knives wood, 935 : 14
Woodspurge has cup of three, 601 : 15
Woodthrush singing through fog, 806 : 8
Wooed and not unsought be won, 287 : 6
beautiful therefore to be w., 185 : 6
fortune too w. is farther off, 161 : 18
I w. her in wintertime, 921 : 11
in haste wed at leisure, 188 : 34
woman in this humor w., 187 : 3
world made to be w. by youth, 743 : 11
Wooer, knight to be their w., 927 : 1
Woof, Iris' w., 279 : 8
weave the w., 363 : 5
Wooing, if I am not worth w., 511 : 20
in my boys, 920 : 4
women are angels w., 225 : 34
Wooingly, heaven's breath smells w., 236 : 21
Wool, bending to your w., 162 : 12
have you any w., 930 : 5
much cry and no w., 149 : 2
of bat tongue of dog, 239 : 5
owest sheep no w., 234 : 7
restore to whiteness w. dyed purple, 128 : 14
sleeping is a w. blanket, 82 : 21
tease the housewife's w., 280 : 1
Woolen, rather lie in w., 209 : 4
Woolf, who's afraid of Virginia W., 908 : 2
Woolgathering, summoned wits from w., 261 : 9
Wooly, flock in w. fold, 476 : 8
softest clothing w. bright, 403 : 5
Woos, as lion w. his brides, 366 : 9
Word a lamp unto my feet, 22 : 2
accident erased from dictionary, 862 : 4
against W. unstilled world, 806 : 4
alchemy of the w., 674 : 7
allowing w. to obliterate sky, 858 : 11
and a blow, 193 : 4
answer me in one w., 212 : 7
as good as bond, 170 : 30
at random spoken, 431 : 19
better than a gift, 35 : 29
blotted w. out forever, 360 : 17
bring to light kindly w., 762 : 1
brings to pass every w., 71 : 1
burned like a lamp, 36 : 13
but a w. and a blow, 306 : 3
but yet the w., 863 : 19

Word (*continued*)
by His firm W., 131 : 3
by thought w. and deed, 55 : 17
cannot be recalled, 109 : 10
center of silent W., 806 : 4
choice w. measured phrase, 425 : 11
choleric w., 228 : 11
conscience but w. cowards use, 187 : 30
corrupt w., like corrupt tree, 131 : 3
dead when it is said, 607 : 3
deals destruction, 683 : 7
define life in a w., 552 : 3
definition of w. liberty, 523 : 7
doers of the w., 51 : 31
done for least w. said, 632 : 21
ears have heard Holy W., 405 : 1
eaten thee for a w., 191 : 7
effect of right w. physical, 626 : 2
every w. a principle, 865 : 10
every w. a sentence, 129 : 17
every w. stabs, 209 : 10
every w. tell, 729 : 7
every w. that proceedeth, 11 : 12
fashion's w. is out, 717 : 3
fitly spoken, 25 : 14
flowering in lonely w., 535 : 15
frantic boast foolish w., 709 : 20
freedom indivisible w., 824 : 10
God in works and in w., 329 : 5
God the w. spake it, 164 : 4
good w. like good tree, 131 : 3
great Russian w., 802 : 1
Greeks had w. for it, 794 : 10
have last w., 396 : 17
hear the w. of the Lord, 32 : 15
hesitating so long at a w., 392 : 8
his w. was Fie foh fum, 234 : 13
how proud w. Man rings, 725 : 7
I catch every w., 695 : 5
I kept my w. he said, 739 : 16
I to my pledged w. true, 811 : 6
ill deeds doubled with evil w., 188 : 10
impossible not French, 420 : 10
in beginning the W., 44 : 17
in w. unity of humanity, 755 : 21
keep w. of promise to our ear, 240 : 9
Latin w. for three farthings, 190 : 24
laughed His w. to scorn, 376 : 9
let w. go forth, 890 : 7
lightest w. harrow soul, 219 : 18
like a bell, 477 : 2
love which graybeards call divine, 186 : 28
low delicious w. death, 575 : 18
making of a world, 768 : 6
man defines all rights, 672 : 10
man's w. God in man, 534 : 2
master w. work, 664 : 17
mightier than they in arms, 286 : 26
mum's the w., 170 : 37, 740 : 2
needed for concept, 390 : 7
never break w. or lose self-respect, 124 : 12
never wanted a good w., 368 : 7
O w. of fear, 191 : 13
of Caesar stood, 216 : 21
of earth in ears of world, 634 : 7
of gentleman and Christian, 169 : 26
of God is quick, 51 : 14
of onset gave, 426 : 9
of our God shall stand, 30 : 33
of the Lord endureth, 52 : 9
one little w., 194 : 2

Word (*continued*)
one w. for woman, 677 : 4
one w. frees us, 75 : 14
one w. too often profaned, 469 : 19
outleaps world, 873 : 20
over all, 576 : 1
pen through every other w., 433 : 14
preserves contact, 755 : 15
right w. powerful agent, 626 : 2
searches for perfect w., 771 : 15
seldom heard discouraging w., 927 : 19
serpent's w., 863 : 19
shadow of deed, 79 : 12
single irradiating w., 609 : 2
some with flattering w., 676 : 8
spoken comes not back, 109 : *n* 5
spoken in due season, 24 : 9
struggles against divine W., 156 : 9
suit action to the w., 222 : 1
thank thee Jew for teaching me that w., 200 : 19
theory of the w., 768 : 6
there it was w. for w., 769 : 4
thief said last kind w., 545 : 3
thou speakest shalt thou hear, 132 : 20
time for such a w., 240 : 4
to a thing when We will it, 131 : 4
to lift hat to, 608 : 8
to wise is enough, 170 : 33, 347 : 32
to write a w., 928 : *n* 3
torture one poor w., 304 : 26
tremble at w. of Lord, 300 : 22
uncreating w., 340 : 28
was God, 44 : 17
was made flesh, 44 : 21
was with God, 44 : 17
wash out a w. of it, 517 : 2
water hears faintest w., 292 : *n* 3
we had not sense to say, 646 : 14
we pass w. around, 884 : 6
weird power in spoken w., 683 : 7
what is honor a w., 205 : 5
what w. did make it, 164 : 4
when I use w., 613 : 16
where w. be found, 806 : 4
without father's w., 470 : 18
without one w. spoke, 404 : *n* 3
written can be destroyed, 109 : *n* 5
Word-coining genius, 782 : 3
Words, abstains from w., 565 : 30
addressed her winged w., 57 : 8
aged accents untimely w., 182 : 6
alms-basket of w., 191 : 7
alone certain good, 711 : 20
amiable w., 534 : 23
and meanings, 807 : 12
apt w. have power, 288 : 24
are daughters of earth, 352 : 6
are empty thanks, 324 : 26
are like leaves, 333 : 4
are no deeds, 248 : 31
are women deeds men, 270 : 16
as idle tales, 44 : 14
at long last say w. of my own, 832 : 2
barren superfluity of w., 318 : 16
be not slave of w., 472 : 24
beautiful w. are not true, 65 : 10
bethumped with w., 201 : 17
big w. always punished, 75 : 2
both in syntax and w., 586 : 14
braver than fighting, 3 : 12
bright the ring of w., 669 : 6

Words (*continued*)
butter no parsnips, 432 : 2
by his command w. cut, 718 : 2
calisthenics with w., 827 : 18
certainty of the w. of truth, 25 : 1
charm agony with w., 210 : 4
children of many men, 850 : 15
chime of w. tinkling, 711 : *n* 1
clothed in reason's garb, 284 : 13
cold w. of tongue or pen, 732 : 15
comfortable w., 534 : 3
companion's w. of persuasion, 58 : 12
Conquistadors left us w., 861 : 1
design of all his w., 768 : 25
divide and rend, 632 : 10
do make difference, 650 : 4
easy like the wind, 257 : 8
endure in writing, 3 : 13
enormous force of few w., 499 : 20
everyday w. yet not same, 724 : 9
fair w. prevail, 709 : 5
false w. infect the soul, 84 : 2
far from the w. of my roaring, 18 : 5
feign thyng or fynde w. new, 146 : 15
fine w. and insinuating appearance, 68 : 2
flood of w. drop of reason, 347 : 13
foot and a half long w., 109 : 22
for want of w. no doubt, 289 : 1
force of w., 69 : 23
from mouth flow gentle w., 61 : 9
fury in your w., 232 : 1
give sorrow w., 239 : 20
good w. worth much, 269 : 22
grasp subject w. will follow, 95 : 13
guard shape of man, 850 : 16
half remember human w., 735 : 8
hasty w. fly abroad, 473 : 14
have longer life than deeds, 72 : 4
he that hath knowledge spareth his w., 24 : 18
hear the w. of the wise, 24 : 37
hoarded w., 759 : 3
honest w. suffered corruption, 261 : 17
honeyed w. like bees, 794 : 8
how forcible are right w., 15 : 19
how you use proud w., 761 : 13
hurteth not to give fair w., 159 : 22
I use are everyday, 724 : 9
ideas that can be expressed in w., 688 : 6
if he says it in few w., 561 : 16
if his w. are sincere, 68 : 4
immodest w. admit no defense, 309 : 9
in two w. im-possible, 777 : 7
in which concepts expressed, 390 : 7
in winter articulated next summer, 120 : 16
intensely right w., 626 : 2
kindly w. do not enter so deeply, 89 : 26
last w. of Marmion, 431 : 3
let the w. of my mouth, 18 : 3
let thy w. be few, 26 : 26
like nature half reveal, 531 : 20
like nimble airy servitors, 281 : 15
like winter snowflakes, 57 : 25
little w. of love, 591 : 8
long w. bother me, 778 : 12
love soft w. hate iniquity, 699 : 3
man of w. not deeds, 929 : 8
men of few w. best, 207 : 20

Words (*continued*)
Milton's wormwood w., 281 : *n* 4
much in few w., 36 : 3
multiplieth w. without knowledge, 16 : 25
multitude of w., 125 : 26
my w. are my own, 302 : 21
my w. fly up, 222 : 28
my w. shall not pass away, 40 : 26
mystery of being moved by w., 887 : 7
no more w., 836 : 17
not do something to people for w., 794 : 18
not let deeds belie w., 127 : 21
not think beforehand of his w., 89 : 15
oaths but w. and w. wind, 291 : 20
of all sad w., 513 : 14
of fragrant portals, 767 : 16
of God not be exhausted, 132 : 3
of learned length, 370 : 11
of love spoken, 447 : 7
of Mercury are harsh, 191 : 16
of the convenant, 10 : 15
of the wise are as goads, 27 : 26
of truth and soberness, 46 : 34
old short w. best of all, 746 : 17
omit needless w., 729 : 7
once my stock are wanting, 306 : 24
order w. of sea, 767 : 16
ought to be wild, 783 : 11
our w. lives pains, 811 : 8
outcome of w. is in the council, 58 : 25
pay no debts, 226 : 11
physicians of mind diseased, 70 : 25
picture worth more than ten thousand w., 132 : 24
poem w. not ideas, 651 : 17
prince who relies on w. ruined, 153 : 24
proper w. in proper places, 322 : 8
prose w. in best order, 438 : 4
put in w. grief I feel, 531 : 20
razors to wounded heart, 188 : 17
reduce language to seven w., 782 : 21
rhapsody of w., 223 : 2
sea of w., 782 : 3
sentence no unnecessary w., 729 : 7
shall be in thine heart, 11 : 9
short w. are best, 746 : 17
should be old ones, 138 : 4
slippery thought viscous, 635 : 20
small coin of empty w., 504 : 16
smoother than butter, 19 : 22
so nimble, 263 : 2
softer than oil, 19 : 22
songs without w., 617 : 2
speak a few reasonable w., 395 : 5
speak other men's w., 597 : 10
speak what you think in hard w., 497 : 2
speaker of w. and doer, 58 : 10
stuttering unintelligible w., 849 : 20
such as glory obscene, 844 : 14
taken towns with w., 259 : *n* 2
ten low w., 333 : 7
that burn, 363 : 3
that my w. were written, 16 : 3
that weep tears that speak, 295 : 17
the worst of w., 230 : 32
they rob Hybla bees, 217 : 8
though ne'er so witty, 172 : 13
thought finds the w., 749 : 19
three w. as with burning pen, 412 : 11

Words (*continued*)
three w. for human race, 677 : 4
thunder of your w., 236 : *n* 1
time for many w., 60 : 10
time to say our few w., 850 : 5
to say it flow with ease, 311 : 4
to the end of the world, 17 : 28
true w. are not beautiful, 65 : 10
tune without w., 604 : 17
two narrow w. Hic jacet, 173 : 4
two w. for man, 677 : 4
two w. have undone world, 263 : 12
understand fury but not w., 232 : 1
unpleasantest w. that blotted paper, 199 : 30
vain w. in your oaths, 130 : 13
weak and fruitless w., 524 : 4
which were better unspoken, 60 : 18
why good w. ne'er said, 660 : 7
wise men's counters, 264 : 13
wise w. taught in numbers, 174 : 9
wit nor w. nor worth, 216 : 28
without thoughts, 222 : 28
won't fill bushel, 347 : 32
words mere words, 227 : 6
words words, 220 : 19
world of w., 769 : 26
worms are the w., 829 : 17
wormwood w., 281 : *n* 4
writ in waters, 155 : *n* 4
wrote w. of the covenant, 10 : 15
Wordsworth both art thine, 428 : *n* 2
out-babying W., 493 : 8
sedulous ape to W., 668 : 23
Wore at their hearts, 876 : 15
it in world's eyes, 713 : 14
Work, a little w. a little play, 617 : 3
according to light in me, 490 : 19
advantageous sharing of w., 904 : 18
after reading your w., 343 : 16
all aglow is the w., 104 : 11
all great w. of world, 761 : 3
all in day's w., 920 : 10
all nature seems at w., 436 : 9
all w. and no play, 271 : 17
all w. noble, 474 : 4
and pray live on hay, 764 : 13
artist keep w. to himself, 396 : 7
as hard as Turk, 919 : 5
as if to live hundred years, 347 : 31
at her flowery w., 278 : 25
at his dirty w. again, 338 : 9
bad w. follers ye, 568 : 10
be fit for w., 572 : 13
be made manifest, 48 : 5
beginning most important part of w., 84 : 8
best w. the human mind, 410 : 16
between twenty-five and forty, 664 : 19
bring every w. into judgment, 27 : 27
by w. one knows workman, 296 : 11
cells w. they know not why, 760 : 21
Central Park single w. of art, 590 : 13
contrariously, 207 : 8
dawn speeds him in his w., 61 : 22
day's wages for day's w., 474 : 2
delusion to be paid before w., 171 : *n* 2
dictate direction w. must take, 828 : 1
did sell himself to w. wickedness, 14 : 9
dirty w. at crossroads, 922 : 5
do day's w. well, 665 : 1
Work (*continued*)
efface footsteps of work, 619 : 6
end crowns the w., 133 : 26
enjoy idling if w. to do, 692 : 16
enough w. to do, 710 : 13
entire land sets to w., 5 : 7
equal pay for equal w., 578 : 2
establish the w. of our hands, 20 : 15
every person who wants to w., 903 : 9
evils of idleness shaken off by w., 114 : 24
expands to fill time, 876 : 14
extra draught of hard w., 664 : 18
frivolous w., 416 : 15
from sun to sun, 920 : 11
good day's w., 348 : 21
great equalizer, 664 : 17
greatness of w. inside man, 897 : 7
grows beyond his w., 857 : 4
half proper gardener's w., 710 : 22
hammer out solid w., 644 : 14
hands from day to day, 870 : 5
hands that w. on us, 756 : 13
harder yet thought idler, 713 : 1
he can w. no faster, 931 : 2
he who has found w., 474 : 6
his six days' w. a world, 287 : 1
his w. is perfect, 11 : 23
how the hell can I w., 924 : 8
I am rising to a man's w., 125 : 1
I don't like w., 683 : 16
I like what is in w., 683 : 16
I want w., 203 : 26
if this w. be of men, 46 : 1
incessantly to the last, 396 : 5
is seed sown, 472 : 18
judgeth according to w., 52 : 8
Kaspar's w. was done, 439 : 10
keeps us from three evils, 343 : 13
labor and do all thy w., 10 : 6
leave w. sit at temple, 782 : 17
less w. more poverty, 602 : 13
let patience have her perfect w., 51 : 27
light prime w. of God, 285 : *n* 1
lightning does the w., 626 : 7
like madness in brain, 434 : 3
like other men do, 924 : 8
love made visible, 782 : 17
lovely dears her noblest w., 409 : 15
man goeth forth unto his w., 21 : 11
man matures through w., 897 : 9
many hands make light w., 160 : 31
men w. women weep, 566 : 9
more wise master simpler w., 140 : 5
nakedness of woman w. of God, 404 : 3
never made w. for man to mend, 306 : 26
night when no man can w., 45 : 7
no immortal w. behind me, 480 : 4
no substitute for hard w., 661 : 8
no w. begun shall pause, 545 : 5
no w. nor device nor knowledge, 27 : 16
no w. to do, 924 : 8
no workman may w. wel and hastily, 147 : 25
noblest w. of God, 337 : 13, 408 : 18
noblest w. of man, 615 : 10
noblest w. she classes, 409 : 15
none of older connotation of pain, 871 : 14
nor fire nor age shall destroy, 113 : 24
Work (*continued*)
not do too much w., 572 : 13
nothing without hard w., 106 : 17
of a moment, 168 : 13
of art corner of creation, 643 : 6
of Henry James, 812 : 12
of noble note, 529 : 12
of thy hand, 31 : 28
on seventh day God ended his w., 6 : 16
others w. better with bronze, 105 : 24
out own salvation, 50 : 2
partly done, 799 : 8
perfection of life or w., 716 : 7
philosopher's stone, 664 : 17
play for mortal stakes, 748 : 18
portrait of self, 620 : 10
posterity of w. of art, 734 : 3
prior w. of past centuries, 673 : 10
property stimulus to w., 758 : 1
put us to w. anew, 707 : 21
race over w. never done, 645 : 12
routine w. large part of life, 639 : 3
save myself by w. and faith, 865 : 15
scythe of time, 420 : 17
sense of success in w., 572 : 13
seventh day thou shalt not w., 10 : 6
shall not be lost, 346 : 15
short of what it should be, 499 : 25
shovel under let me w., 761 : 6
silent part of noble w., 573 : 13
sincere w. give reality to illusion, 757 : 9
slaves to do ugly w., 675 : 25
smile and get w. to do, 856 : 17
smile his w. to see, 405 : 8
so w. the honeybees, 207 : 6
social world w. of man, 324 : 2
soon as your day's w. done, 614 : 12
sport tedious as a w., 203 : 5
spur whereby mankind w., 307 : 19
stops expenses run on, 95 : 8
strive on to finish w., 524 : 7
studies in which w. dies with worker, 152 : 6
subsidize prople not to w., 880 : 15
that aspires to art, 683 : 2
those who w. with joy, 782 : 17
three things needed in w., 572 : 13
to be happy in w., 572 : 13
to every man according to his w., 19 : 28
to pray is to w., 134 : 14
to w. wolf at door, 695 : 17
together for good, 47 : 10
unfinished w. they advanced, 523 : 4
until our w. done, 490 : 10
us a perpetual peace, 277 : 6
we are w. of thy hand, 31 : 28
we have corrected Thy w., 582 : 7
we have undertaken, 264 : 22
we w. in the dark, 653 : 5
what a piece of w. is man, 220 : 28
whatever body obliged to do, 622 : 12
whether his w. be pure, 24 : 29
which bores you, 725 : 2
who first invented w., 442 : 2
why don't you w., 924 : 8
with materials I have, 861 : 4
with one hand wrought in w., 14 : 29
with so fine a brush, 441 : 3
without hope, 436 : 10
woman's w. never done, 920 : 11
work work, 485 : 18

Work (*continued*)
works of him that sent me, 45 : 7
world's need of w., 725 : 2
your wicked will, 745 : 3
your w. that has failed, 702 : 3
Worked and sang, 382 : 6
and waited for light, 729 : 5
Worker, lone w. makes first advance, 774 : 2
masculine soul a w., 703 : 13
studies in which work dies with w., 152 : 6
to w. God lends aid, 66 : *n* 7
value of what w. produces, 784 : 28
Workers, as w. not as women, 578 : 1
brainsick brain w., 618 : 10
freedom for all poor w., 820 : 9
heartsick hand w., 618 : 10
mainstay of civilization, 666 : 22
of world unite, 563 : *n* 5
Park to supply w. God's handiwork, 590 : 14
Worketh, wrath w. not righteousness, 51 : 30
Workhouse, Christmas Day in w., 661 : 14
Working, advanced guard of w. class, 731 : 7
committing suicide by w., 706 : 5
for dead horse, 171 : 3
heaven protect w. girl, 684 : 17
man thinking or w. is alone, 560 : 3
men of all countries unite, 563 : 10
mere w. mason, 431 : 21
mood, 495 : 13
necessary mode of w. of mind, 595 : 8
on the railroad, 921 : 17
Working-day world, 210 : 20
Workings, hum of mighty w., 475 : 8
Workman, by work one knows w., 296 : 11
common sense master w., 464 : 2
no w. may werke wel and hastily, 147 : 25
that needeth not to be ashamed, 51 : 7
Workmanship, dark inscrutable w., 423 : 18
most may wonder at w., 280 : 1
Workmen, Master of all good w., 707 : 21
Works, all ye w. of the Lord, 36 : 14
authors' names not w., 333 : 12
be silent as to his w., 356 : 9
been into future it w., 719 : 7
best of all God's w., 287 : 22
both sides of street, 781 : 3
done least rapidly, 542 : 5
done under the sun, 26 : 16
faith without w., 51 : 33
fat of others' w., 258 : 5
for sweetness and light, 588 : 18
God in w. and in word, 329 : 5
good w. better in sight of Lord, 131 : 11
her own w. praise her, 26 : 10
how manifold are thy w., 21 : 11
I know thy w., 53 : 5
live and die in Aristotle's w., 183 : 19
look on my w. ye mighty, 466 : 13
man is son of own w., 103 : *n* 5
move immediately upon your w., 589 : 16
Nature's w. expunged, 285 : 5

Works (*continued*)
not retain rare w., 734 : 4
of art products of danger, 756 : 14
of darkness, 47 : 29
of him that sent me, 45 : 7
of unbelievers a mirage, 131 : 17
our w. do not ennoble us, 140 : 6
part of man's self, 648 : 17
poets reading from own w., 846 : 6
present w. of present man, 435 : 21
relationship of author to w., 683 : 6
renounce the devil and his w., 56 : 4
reward according to his w., 51 : 10
rich in good w., 51 : 4
see your good w., 37 : 6
sighing through all her w., 287 : 19
skilled in w. of both languages, 108 : 1
spares man nor his w., 383 : 14
subdued to what it w. in, 245 : 17
these are thy glorious w., 286 : 15
unread his w., 424 : *n* 2
Workshop, best business father's w., 538 : 8
of serious inquirer, 636 : 16
trees in Nature's w., 637 : 19
World a little overgrown, 507 : 20
a solemn place, 884 : 17
abounds with laws, 920 : 15
above w. stretched the sky, 822 : 12
absolutes in w. affairs, 860 : 3
age of antiquity youth of w., 178 : *n* 11
all kingdoms of the w., 42 : 34
all the w. and his wife, 323 : 21
all this sad w. needs, 670 : 4
all this the w. well knows, 245 : 23
all w. here to look on me, 196 : 17
all w. sad and dreary, 598 : 4
all's right with w., 540 : 15
altitude pressed w. on heart, 892 : 12
always been man's w., 870 : 9
Americans hope of w., 368 : 3
and all her train, 299 : 6
and my being were one, 595 : 3
and they that dwell therein, 18 : 8
another and better w., 415 : 3
another w. be born, 888 : 6
appears like great family, 315 : 17
applaud hollow ghost, 587 : 17
appointment at end of w., 789 : 8
Arahat Buddhas who appear in w., 72 : 21
as fresh as at first day, 595 : 11
as God made it beauty, 540 : 30
as good out of w., 324 : 24
as men perceive it, 862 : 15
attracts envy of w., 372 : 12
banish Jack banish all w., 204 : 7
beautifully dressed, 593 : 7
being by w. oppressed, 715 : 11
being kind all w. needs, 670 : 4
belie all corners of w., 243 : 21
best known and thought in w., 586 : 24
bestride the narrow w., 215 : 6
better w. than this, 210 : 18
beyond struggles and victory, 745 : 11
bigger w. of adult life, 754 : 11
black green red yellow, 912 : 15
blood of the w., 830 : 11
blooms with statues, 619 : 17
blows and buffets of w., 238 : 15

World (*continued*)
book of Montaigne w. endorsed, 164 : *n* 4
books wealth of w., 559 : 31
bottom of monstrous w., 281 : 2
brave new w., 248 : 17
brave w. sir, 312 : 13
breaks everyone, 844 : 15
breathes contagion to this w., 222 : 23
bright edges of w., 739 : 5
bring w. under rule, 715 : 6
broad highway of w., 468 : 21
brothers in w. too, 757 : 2
brought death into w., 282 : 22
build a new w., 787 : 12
bundle of hay, 462 : 9
busy w. and I ne'er agree, 295 : 3
but thoroughfare of woe, 146 : 29
by meeting friend new w. born, 858 : 6
call w. if you please, 480 : 2
came death into the w., 34 : 12
came once a w., 605 : 1
cankers of calm w., 204 : 35
cannot hold thee close enough, 822 : 13
canted in this canting w., 360 : 11
canvas to imaginations, 558 : 14
capable of alteration, 840 : 20
care of this w., 39 : 16
caricature of itself, 704 : 3
changed by two people, 886 : 5
charged with grandeur of God, 655 : 20
chess board the w., 595 : 12
children of w. wiser, 43 : 31
citizen of the w., 79 : 7, 180 : 13
citizens of the w., 781 : 5
cognition of modern w., 756 : 3
cold accretion called w., 640 : 18
cold hard mouth of w., 878 : 7
Columbus found a w., 703 : 3
come round to him, 496 : 12
come three corners of w., 202 : 20
Commodity bias of the w., 201 : 19
community, 774 : 8
concepts not uniquely determined by w., 763 : 10
conquest of w. by creed, 891 : 5
content with setting surface right, 490 : 13
contributions to peace of w., 788 : 7
count as naught in w., 568 : 23
crumbles to nothing, 453 : 15
cry out vanity of w., 309 : 3
dark as w. of man, 801 : 6
dark w. and wide, 282 : 15
dark w. present treatment, 725 : 1
dead become lumber of w., 315 : 22
dear Agnes is strange, 297 : 14
death is but crossing w., 314 : 13
destruction of w. not dreadful, 515 : 15
determination for better w., 699 : 4
dissatisfaction with w., 699 : 4
do not grow old at all, 310 : 7
domination of w., 687 : 4
don't live in w. alone, 757 : 2
doth two nations bear, 297 : 5
dragon w., 793 : 4
dreaming on things to come, 245 : 13
dreams books each a w., 428 : 4
drives poet to w., 585 : 18
drowsy syrups of w., 231 : 8

World (*continued*)
end in fire, 748 : 2
ends of w. are come, 638 : 10
enough and time, 296 : 26
enough in w. for everyone, 788 : 2
even unto end of w., 41 : 31
ever the wide w. over, 707 : 22
every force maintaining w., 581 : 19
every woman gift of w. to me, 481 : 12
everybody in w. down on me, 916 : 4
everyone in w. is Christ, 757 : 3
false w. but transitory, 153 : 7
fashion of w. passeth, 48 : 12
fate of w. in hands, 865 : 1
Federation of the w., 530 : 1
fill w. with fools, 579 : 22
find w. beautiful and
delightful, 723 : 14
fine place worth fighting for, 845 : 9
fled from this vile w., 244 : 26
foolery governs w., 263 : 24
foppery of the w., 233 : 5
forgetting by world forgot, 335 : 4
founded on four freedoms, 780 : 13
freedom everywhere in w., 780 : 13
friends make your w., 649 : 20
frippery necessary for looking like
rest of w., 393 : 1
from all deceits of the w., 55 : 11
full of number of things 668 : 14
full of untold novelties, 595 : 11
gain whole w., 39 : 38
gained w. gave w. lesson, 646 : 7
gave his honors to the w., 249 : 11
Germany in w. forward, 663 : 3
getting on in w., 738 : 8
ghosts all over w., 599 : 15
giddy thinks w. turns round, 189 : 4
give the w. the lie, 172 : 14
give warning to w., 244 : 26
give w. another heart, 475 : 8
give w. assurance of a man, 223 : 3
given to lying, 205 : 16
gleams of remotor w., 466 : 10
gleams untraveled w., 529 : 8
global village, 879 : 6
glow has warmed the w., 786 : *n* 4
go into the w., 42 : 16
go well with thee, 922 : 13
God made w., 46 : 16
God plays dice with w., 763 : 16
God so loved w., 44 : 34
golden w., 210 : 11
good deed in naughty w., 201 : 4
good w. to live in, 746 : 20
good-bye proud w., 493 : 12
governed by universal law, 566 : 18
great wonderful w., 593 : 7
great w. spin forever, 530 : 8
green fruits of w., 766 : 23
grown gray, 633 : 6
half brother of w., 555 : 15
half w. knows not how other
lives, 270 : 21
half w. not understand pleasures of
other, 440 : 25
hanging around in w., 750 : 12
harbor gives to w., 663 : 15
harmoniously confused, 334 : 15
harmony of w. form and
number, 696 : 5
has joked incessantly, 630 : 9
hath not a sweeter creature, 231 : 23
healthy free w. before me, 575 : 9

World (*continued*)
heaven commences ere w.
past, 370 : 3
high shore of this w., 208 : 7
his six days' work a w., 287 : 1
his who has money to go, 498 : 24
history is world's court, 412 : 12
history of w. biography, 473 : 24
history of w. progress of
freedom, 422 : 12
hog butcher for w., 761 : 4
hold w. but as w., 197 : 28
honest as w. goes, 220 : 16
hope to w. for future, 521 : 8
house with firmament for
roof, 637 : 21
how w. originated, 509 : 6
huge w. come to him, 496 : 12
I am in charity with w., 323 : 5
I am light of w., 45 : 4
I have overcome w., 45 : 29
I never made, 691 : 23
I never sought w., 356 : 27
I strike up for New W., 574 : 4
ideas were to transform, 616 : 1
if there's another w., 411 : 22
if w. and love were young, 172 : 10
if w. be worth winning, 306 : 19
I'll make me a w., 733 : 10
imagined ultimate good, 769 : 2
in arms, 488 : 12
in faith and hope w. disagree, 337 : 9
in love with night, 193 : 9
in one small room, 713 : 17
in part constructed by men, 862 : 12
in solemn stillness, 537 : 16
in this harsh w., 225 : 1
in wildness preservation of
w., 560 : 27
in w. not of it, 445 : 5
incessantly wash w., 576 : 1
intangible we touch, 693 : 16
intellectual w. divided, 705 : 20
into dangerous w. leaped, 405 : 12
into our first w., 807 : 3
invisible we view, 693 : 16
is a bubble, 181 : 17
is a comedy, 363 : 22
is a fine place, 845 : 9
is a force not presence, 770 : 2
is a king, 421 : 20
is a nettle, 331 : *n* 2
is all aleak, 829 : 14
is but small parenthesis, 275 : 15
is ever-living fire, 70 : 1
is grown so bad, 187 : 5
is in state of chassis, 786 : 9
is mean, 912 : 15
is mine oyster, 225 : 15
is so faithless, 163 : 7
it is a pretty w., 879 : 12
it is a w. to see, 175 : 15
joy to pass to w. below, 105 : 12
joy to the w., 328 : 13
just felt w. go by, 604 : 11
justice is wanting in w., 414 : 12
kiss for whole w., 412 : 10
knowledge of w. acquired in
w., 341 : 17
laboring surges of w., 693 : 9
lash rascals through w., 232 : 6
laugh and w. laughs, 670 : 3
lawlessness, 780 : 4

World (*continued*)
leaden army that conquers
w., 706 : 23
learn of green w., 793 : 4
leave the w. no copy, 213 : 17
leave w. by natural door, 672 : 11
leaves w. to darkness, 361 : 20
lesser god made w., 534 : 28
let justice be done though w.
perish, 133 : *n* 11
let the w. mind him, 542 : 19
let us possess one w., 251 : 15
let w. slide, 158 : 17
let w. wag., 159 : 14
letter to w., 605 : 12
life of this w., 132 : 7
light of bright w. dies, 670 : 8
light of the w., 37 : 6, 45 : 4
lights of the w., 375 : 23
limits of vision limits of w., 463 : 4
listen then as I now, 468 : 15
little friend of all w., 709 : 22
little note nor long remember, 523 : 4
little w. made cunningly, 254 : 7
little w. of childhood, 754 : 11
live in w. as spectator, 326 : 8
look round habitable w., 306 : 10
look upon w. as parish, 346 : 8
looks for wages, 545 : 17
looks on w. rationally, 422 : 11
looks whole w. in face, 510 : 8
losers and world forsakers, 659 : 9
love beyond w., 314 : 13
love makes w. go round, 629 : 2,
928 : 5
lover's quarrel with w., 749 : 8
loves w. as his body, 64 : 5
mad as Bedlam, 548 : 28
mad w. mad kings, 201 : 18
made in six days, 420 : 7
made safe for democracy, 682 : 12
made safe for differences, 796 : 8
made to be won by youth, 743 : 11
maintain before whole w., 298 : 11
make w. a desert, 851 : 15
make w. safe for democracy, 703 : 2
makes whole w. kin, 226 : 20
margent of w., 693 : 12
mass and majesty of w., 869 : 1
mass of public wrongs, 177 : 1
may end tonight, 542 : 14
mere anarchy loosed on w., 714 : 12
mighty w. of eye and ear, 423 : 14
milk cow of w., 899 : 8
money sets w. in motion, 111 : 30
more overwork than w.
justifies, 707 : 15
morning of the w., 540 : 18
most people on w. not in it, 637 : 20
movers and shakers of w., 659 : 9
mud-luscious, 828 : 11
must be peopled, 209 : 19
must conform to necessity, 738 : 1
my all the w., 168 : *n* 1
my country is the w., 385 : 2
my life belongs to w., 902 : 7
naked shingles of w., 587 : 16
native in this w., 767 : 18
nature too noble for w., 242 : 20
needs men of real talent, 386 : 19
never enjoy w. aright, 311 : 20
never starve for wonders, 742 : 8
New W. favorable to
declamation, 683 : 22

World (*continued*)
new w. to be won, 890 : 4
new w. which is old, 530 : 11
next w. as closely apprehended, 275 : 2
no government stable in unstable w., 736 : 11
no local defense contain Communist w., 803 : 7
no world but wrongs, 177 : 1
noisy set martyrs call w., 713 : 1
Northwest Passage to intellectual w., 360 : 16
not as w. giveth, 45 : 24
not be queen for all w., 248 : 28
not inn but hospital, 274 : 21
not live at level of great, 673 : 5
not lose sight of conventions of w., 621 : 15
not loved w. nor w. me, 458 : 3
not sweet in the end, 633 : 6
not to live but die in, 274 : 21
not to live in physical w., 768 : 5
now bubble burst now w., 336 : 14
O w. intangible, 693 : 16
O w. invisible, 693 : 16
O w. thou choosest not, 703 : 3
O w. unknowable, 693 : 16
O world world world, 227 : 8
of adult life, 754 : 11
of cards, 818 : 5
of compensation, 521 : 1
of eye and ear, 423 : 14
of fashion birth intellect, 593 : 1
of future a struggle, 832 : 1
of happy days, 187 : 8
of human community, 861 : 7
of ideas, 586 : 21
of light, 299 : 7
of made, 829 : 25
of men for me, 541 : 15
of nature and God, 897 : 19
of nuclear giants, 825 : 2
of sighs, 229 : 31
of vile faults, 225 : 21
of words, 769 : 26
on back burden of w., 670 : 14
on dreaming fed, 711 : 19
on w. to turn thine eyes, 351 : 17
one custom corrupt w., 534 : 31
one w. or none, 828 : 2
only fence against the w., 308 : 2
only thing new in w., 788 : 17
opinion governs w., 682 : 2
organization of w. community, 774 : 8
origin of modern w., 847 : 14
other w. by which faith advanced, 151 : 8
our country the w., 505 : 10
outlasts aversion outlasts love, 584 : 16
over w. and under w., 707 : 22
pain, 415 : 18
part we sadly in troublous w., 186 : 24
parted by hurrying w., 424 : 3
pass through w. once, 439 : 2
pass w., 852 : 15
peace or world destruction, 729 : 12
peace reversal of record, 771 : 10
peep at such a w., 377 : 4
pendant w., 228 : 20, 285 : 3
perfect everywhere, 413 : 30

World (*continued*)
place where I do not care to be, 884 : 15
playboy of Western w., 735 : 4
please w. and father, 296 : 14
pleases w. cannot please himself, 311 : 8
poet creates w., 769 : 14
poet looks at w., 769 : 23
poets legislators of w., 470 : 7
poor w. said I, 292 : 17
power of w. works in circles, 701 : 8
presents rational aspect, 422 : 11
procreant urge of w., 574 : 13
puddle-wonderful, 828 : 12
queer save me and thee, 923 : 14
quiet limit of w., 533 : 28
race soul all going somewhere, 576 : 22
rack of this tough w., 235 : 19
read that w. was spherical, 151 : 7
reared arm crested the w., 241 : 25
rebellion in political w., 388 : 6
regions we call New W., 152 : 17
relation of reaction to w., 665 : 3
remote from wrangling w., 384 : 15
retire from w. satisfied, 106 : 13
retreating w., 827 : 7
rhythm to w. of sound, 801 : 8
richest monarch in w., 412 : 18
riddle of the w., 337 : 2
ringed with azure w., 532 : 28
rivers ancient as w., 854 : 12
rocks cradle rules w., 573 : 18
roll of w. palpable, 640 : 6
rolls into light, 513 : 2
roofs of w., 575 : 3
round w. forever and aye, 584 : 13
sad and dreary, 598 : 4
safe for democracy, 682 : 12, 703 : 2
safe for diversity, 891 : 11
safe for hypocrisy, 852 : 10
same whole w. over, 924 : 11
same w. a hell a heaven, 495 : 20
say to all the w., 217 : 14
scientific knowledge transform w., 814 : 13
secure amidst falling w., 325 : 11
see how w. goes, 235 : 2
see w. in grain of sand, 406 : 8
seek a newer w., 529 : 13
seek empty w. again, 562 : 2
seem all uses of this w., 218 : 5
seems to smile upon me, 309 : 21
sense that w. mad, 756 : 15
sensory w. and wish w., 679 : 2
serpent deceiveth whole w., 53 : 20
serve and not dominate w., 787 : 10
shaketh, 618 : 13
shore of the wide w., 478 : 19
shot heard round w., 494 : 13
should he need next w., 542 : 19
show contain and nourish all w., 191 : 5
shut in from w. without, 513 : 21
sins of whole w., 52 : 21
slumbering w., 330 : 5
smother up beauty from w., 203 : 5
snow swept w. end to end, 817 : 2
snowed whole w. over, 817 : 2
snug little farm the W., 440 : 13
so passes glory of w., 148 : 13
so runs w. away, 222 : 17
so wags the w., 211 : *n* 1

World (*continued*)
sob heavy w., 868 : 20
social w. work of man, 324 : 2
solid earth actual w., 557 : 21
solution of conflict without and within, 723 : 12
spectacle unto w., 48 : 7
stands out, 822 : 12
start w. all over at, 749 : 16
starve for want of wonder, 742 : 8
state inherent in U.N., 813 : 13
steady patriot of w. alone, 422 : 3
still point of turning w., 806 : 13, 807 : 5
stood against w., 216 : 21
story and byword through w., 264 : 22
strange terrible w. war, 745 : 11
struggle with w. calls forth faculties, 414 : 4
such w. I fashioned not, 641 : 16
superego and id are harsh masters, 678 : 15
sword axis of w., 815 : 4
syllables govern the w., 264 : 2
take note O w., 231 : 15
taketh away sin of w., 44 : 23
technological w., 861 : 7
technology knack of arranging w., 878 : 21
tell the w., 205 : *n* 1, 205 : 7
ten days that shook w., 801 : 4
ten hours to w. allot, 172 : *n* 3
terms between Old and New W., 401 : 14
terrible in mass, 640 : 18
that few is all the w., 182 : 8
the w. the book of God, 250 : 12
their words to end of w., 17 : 28
thick rotundity o' the w., 233 : 24
thinks Go, 816 : 11
thirsts for love and truth, 881 : 5
this little w., 194 : 13
this war shake w., 813 : 1
thorns and dangers of w., 202 : 13
thoughts rule w., 499 : 26
through all w. she followed him, 530 : 13
through art w. multiply, 734 : 13
thus one goes through w., 394 : 15
time and w. in flight, 712 : 13
time takes survey of w., 205 : 10
time the soul of this w., 120 : 22
to hide virtues in, 213 : 14
to succeed in the w., 293 : 9
to the city and the w., 134 : 33
to win, 563 : 10
today sick, 802 : 17
too beautiful this year, 822 : 14
too much respect upon w., 197 : 27
too much with us, 427 : 29
too old, 537 : 7
too wide for shrunk shank, 211 : 15
transform w. into bureau, 775 : 7
triple pillar of the w., 240 : 12
troublous w., 186 : 24
true and human w., 876 : 21
turned round and round in w., 571 : 5
turned upside down, 258 : 11
uncertain comes, 495 : 19
undulate round w., 576 : 4
United States of W., 492 : 7
unknowable we know, 693 : 16
unspotted from the w., 51 : 32
unstilled w. whirled, 806 : 4

World (*continued*)
untraveled w., 529 : 8
up above w. fly, 611 : 20
up above w. so high, 449 : 13
varying shore of the w., 241 : 20
vast screen of snow, 811 : 17
visible poem of w., 859 : 1
vision of the w., 529 : 24
visits his dinners not him, 297 : 27
void the w. can never fill, 375 : 15
wags, 211 : 5
wants to be deceived, 152 : 18
was all before them, 288 : 4
was all forgot, 454 : 2
was always yours, 822 : 6
was not to seek me, 356 : 27
wave to wash him from w., 735 : 3
way of coming into w., 321 : 10
way w. ends, 805 : 18
weary of past, 468 : 18
weight of unintelligible w., 423 : 10
what an age what a w., 309 : 17
what I do to spite w., 238 : 15
what is this w., 146 : 28
what shall w. do with children, 905 : 17
what thrown on waters of w., 903 : 13
what w. needs now is love, 898 : 3
when all the w. dissolves, 184 : 2
when all w. young lad, 566 : 14
when Rome falls the w., 458 : 22
where alienation awaits, 906 : 18
where England dead, 752 : 2
where is any author in w., 191 : 1
where much to be done, 353 : 6
where nothing for nothing, 564 : 11
which seems before us, 587 : 16
whole face of w. changed, 300 : 1
whole w. kin, 226 : 20
whom w. flattered thou despised, 173 : 4
whose w. or mine or theirs, 793 : 3
wide enough to hold both, 360 : 6
wilderness of this w., 301 : 19
will freely offer itself, 786 : 3
will welcome lovers, 830 : 7
win w. which lies beyond struggles, 745 : 11
wish estate of w. undone, 240 : 5
with old w. to the grave, 663 : 13
within it opens into w., 406 : 6
without end, 54 : 18, 378 : 1
wondrous architecture of w., 183 : 6
word making of a w., 768 : 6
word of earth in ears of w., 634 : 7
word outleap w., 873 : 20
work of w. done through me, 761 : 3
workers of w. unite, 563 : *n* 5
working-day w., 210 : 20
worth fighting for, 845 : 9
would go round faster, 611 : 13
wrangling w., 384 : 15
writing master to this w., 799 : 6
years like oxen tread w., 712 : 2
you in my respect are w., 196 : 17
yourself sole heir of w., 311 : 20
World-besotted traveler, 716 : 6
World-famous for fifteen minutes, 908 : 1
Worldliness mistaken path to happiness, 463 : 11
Worldlings, testament as w. do, 210 : 26
Worldly, all his w. goods, 550 : 16
hope men set hearts upon, 516 : 9

Worldly (*continued*)
most loathed w. life, 228 : 21
never desire w. ease, 346 : 3
task hast done, 243 : 27
wisely w., 267 : 13
with all my w. goods, 56 : 18
Worldly-Wise-Man, Mr. W., 301 : 24
World-mothering air, 656 : 14
World-renowned, wayfarer w., 135 : 7
World's a bubble, 181 : 17
a nettle, 331 : *n* 2
a stage, 211 : *n* 3
all the w. a stage, 211 : 15
better w. in birth, 555 : 24
brave heroes, 922 : 10
character formed in w. torrent, 395 : 15
confess this w. spent, 254 : 5
God is treacherous, 797 : 14
government w. best hope, 388 : 17
great age begins anew, 468 : 17
great snare, 241 : 15
great w. altar-stairs, 532 : 12
hath this w. good, 52 : 23
hustings, 570 : 12
involved in w. problems, 813 : 8
last night, 254 : 14
live after w. opinion, 497 : 1
mine oyster, 225 : 15
most crowded streets, 585 : 15
Night this w. defeat, 298 : 21
numberless are w. wonders, 74 : 14
Shakespeare w. poet, 442 : 24
she that was w. delight, 632 : 17
slow stain, 469 : 12
storm-troubled sphere, 562 : 4
strand, 655 : 19
what all w. alarms, 716 : 19
whole sap is sunk, 252 : 25
wore it in w. eyes, 713 : 14
world history is w. court, 412 : 12
Worlds, allured to brighter w., 370 : 7
as many w. as artists, 734 : 13
best of possible w., 343 : 8, 762 : 10
beyond ken of eye, 482 : 11
both w. at once they view, 276 : 12
death destroyer of w., 861 : *n* 2
exhausted w. imagined new, 351 : 10
little less w. away, 542 : 8
not w. undone, 461 : 20
on worlds have shown, 251 : 15
sea discoverers to new w., 251 : 15
so many w., 532 : 15
Tiphys disclose new w., 115 : 13
wandering between two w., 586 : 10
World-transforming Charlemagne, 717 : 4
World-wearied flesh, 193 : 28
Worldwide public authorities, 774 : 7
Worm, a w. a mere nothing, 346 : 4
be with me, 873 : 12
canker and grief, 462 : 18
catch Christ with w., 892 : 5
conqueror W., 526 : 5
fish that hath fed of w., 223 : 15
her hulk shall bore, 558 : 10
I am a w. a god, 387 : 5
in the bud, 214 : 5
in the wheat, 733 : 4
invisible w., 405 : 5
man edible to w., 647 : 11
man that is a w., 16 : 11
naked as a w. was she, 144 : 4
no god dare wrong w., 495 : 1

Worm (*continued*)
or beetle, 660 : 1
owest w. no silk, 234 : 7
rather be w. in apple, 798 : 3
rooster don't cackle w'en find w., 662 : 14
shall feed sweetly on him, 16 : 10
shall feed sweetly upon me, 255 : 5
that hath eat of a king, 223 : 15
to a toad, 647 : 11
to the w. thou art my mother, 15 : 39
tough w. in your inside, 629 : 16
vessel bears w., 558 : 9
want to be a w., 695 : 15
what gnawing of w., 254 : 23
when I was a w., 874 : 4
will turn, 186 : 4
Worms are the words, 829 : 17
as many devils in W. as tiles, 156 : 10
darkness w. and shrouds, 475 : 13
destroy this body, 16 : 4
dirt or grubs or w., 338 : 12
entertains exclusive w., 827 : 14
filled with ends of w., 824 : 3
flies w. and flowers, 328 : 7
food for w., 346 : 15
graves w. and epitaphs, 195 : 1
have eaten them, 212 : 23
nor w. forget, 548 : 3
outvenoms w. of Nile, 243 : 21
pain woven in life of w., 595 : 5
tasted two w., 659 : 11
then w. shall try, 297 : 1
they will surely become w., 819 : 11
with vilest w. to dwell, 244 : 26
Worms', made w. meat of me, 193 : 6
Worm's-eye point of view, 848 : 15
Wormwood and the gall, 32 : 23
feed them with w., 32 : *n* 3
her end is bitter as w., 23 : 10
Milton's w. words, 281 : *n* 4
name of the star is W., 53 : 17
wormwood, 222 : 14
Worn, all things w. out and old, 712 : 12
out before on scrap heap, 680 : 15
out with eating time, 303 : 16
sooner lost and w., 214 : 1
the ring so w., 400 : 9
to be w. out is to be renewed, 64 : 10
weeded and w. ancient thatch, 527 : 17
Worn-out poetical fashion, 807 : 12
Worried the cat, 934 : 9
Worry away our lives, 884 : 3
did not w. about it after, 788 : 5
don't hurry don't w., 821 : 4
i should w. and fret, 760 : 1
two days about which not w., 655 : 1
Worrying, we are w. animal, 884 : 3
what's use of w., 770 : 14
Worse, a little w. than a man, 198 : 14
approve better but follow w., 113 : 21
as heaven made him and sometimes w., 170 : 1
bad laws bring about w., 358 : 17
bark w. than bite, 270 : 25
better day w. deed, 261 : *n* 3
enslavement certainty of w., 882 : 11
fault w. by excuse, 202 : 6
for better for w., 56 : 9
gives greater feeling to the w., 194 : 7
hat not w. for wear, 376 : 15
make w. appear the better, 81 : 14
medicine w. than malady, 111 : *n* 2

Worse (*continued*)
most are w. than their fathers, 59 : 18
no w. a husband than best, 240 : 28
nothing w. than shameless woman, 82 : 16
on Friday, 932 : 11
pen w. than the sword, 259 : 3
pray gods they change for w., 177 : 7
remedies w. than disease, 111 : 4
than an infidel, 50 : 31
than be swinger of birches, 747 : 17
than crime it is blunder, 415 : 3
than sun in March, 204 : 33
than wicked it's vulgar, 660 : 16
things than lie, 555 : 8
things waiting than death, 633 : 1
to fear worst cures w., 226 : 12
you have suffered w. things, 104 : 21
Worship bitch-goddess Success, 648 : 4
by golden deeds, 534 : 22
come to w. him, 36 : 20
compelled from their w., 273 : 11
everyone's true w., 83 : 2
Father in spirit, 44 : 36
freedom of w., 780 : 13
freedom to w. God, 470 : 16
hero w., 663 : 6
in Roman world, 383 : 7
justice the only w., 615 : 12
let us w. and bow down, 20 : 20
let us w. God, 408 : 17
man strives for someone to w., 582 : 6
more w. rising than setting sun, 99 : 12
none save Him, 131 : 6
of world but no repose, 468 : 16
pay no w. to garish sun, 193 : 9
stated calls to w., 352 : 24
the Lord in beauty of holiness, 18 : 14
Thee do we w., 130 : 9
true worshipers shall w., 44 : 36
what thou hast burned, 129 : 18
with what deep w., 435 : 13
wonder basis of w., 473 : 1
Worshiped, fell down and w. him, 36 : 21
neither w. with hands, 46 : 16
stocks and stones, 282 : 18
Worshiper, grudging w. of the gods, 107 : 14
Nature mourns her w., 430 : 8
Worshipers, sufferest more than thy w., 208 : 6
true w. shall worship, 44 : 36
Worshipped, burn what thou hast w., 129 : 18
no graven images w., 564 : 18
Worst and best inclined to snap, 794 : 7
are full of passionate intensity, 714 : 12
began best can't end w., 544 : 29
best and w. of this is, 634 : 3
bottom of the w., 226 : 7
British like to be told w., 744 : 15
Catullus w. of all poets, 102 : 4
cliques are one man, 681 : 15
comes to the worst, 261 : 6
death not the w., 75 : 3
do your w. we our best, 745 : 3
ecclesiastic tyranny's w., 318 : 9
friend and enemy Death, 797 : 3
give thy w. of thoughts, 230 : 32
good bad w. best, 525 : 11
his face the w. thing, 228 : 4
intellectual hatred w., 714 : 20

Worst (*continued*)
is better than none, 353 : 16
is death, 194 : 28
is not, 234 : 20
is yet to come, 535 : 5
knew w. too young, 708 : 15
know w. and provide for it, 383 : 1
love good pursue the w., 113 : *n* 15
no w. there is none, 656 : 17
of all states, 275 : 21
of madmen is saint run mad, 339 : 31
of the company, 321 : 20
of words, 230 : 32
persecutes the mind, 305 : 17
portion in this life, 874 : 21
race and nation judged by best not w., 733 : 8
rivals are the w., 320 : 2
so much good in w., 646 : *n* 2
things present w., 206 : 8
this is the w., 234 : 20
to fear w. cures worse, 226 : 12
tomorrow do thy w., 305 : 1
tragedy for poet, 818 : 2
treason has done his w., 238 : 19
use a man could be put to, 251 : 3
when w. little better than beast, 198 : 14
where best like w., 708 : 10
yet to come, 535 : 5
Worsted, though right w., 546 : 7
Worst-natured muse, 315 : 15
Worth a thousand men, 431 : 15
an age without a name, 375 : 1
as much as my life was w., 360 : 12
conscience of her w., 287 : 6
country of w., 410 : 8
dignity and w., 788 : 20
doing is worth doing well, 341 : 16
good words w. much, 269 : 22
how many ships my presence w., 88 : 25
hundred coats-of-arms, 528 : 8
in New York ask how much w., 625 : 23
in the w. and choice, 255 : 11
little more than coward, 419 : 1
makes the man, 337 : 11
man w. as he esteems himself, 158 : 1
my being's w., 607 : 17
never knew w. of him, 728 : 15
nobler yet in his own w., 304 : 15
not w. going to see, 356 : 12
not w. his salt, 117 : 16
not w. paper written on, 509 : 1
not w. the search, 198 : 5
not w. wooing not w. winning, 511 : 20
nothing w. doing completed, 823 : 21
of state worth of individuals, 508 : 14
on foot rascals in coach, 567 : *n* 1
Paris well w. a Mass, 174 : 26
show me but thy w., 208 : 6
slow rises w., 351 : 9
sweat of noblemen, 367 : 1
trick w. two of that, 203 : 17
what is w. but money, 112 : *n* 2
what is w. in anything, 291 : 17
what purchaser will pay, 112 : 8
when we see men of w., 68 : 16
wit nor words nor w., 216 : 28
with all his w. and pains, 436 : 2
you are not w. the dust, 234 : 22
Zeus takes away half a man's w., 60 : 23

Worthies, than all the W. did, 252 : 4
Worthily, write w. of American things, 652 : 4
Worthiness, change to virtue and w., 215 : 14
love in excess brings nor w., 76 : 16
Worthless, sons more w. than sires, 107 : 30
Worth's unknown though height taken, 245 : 18
Worthwhile, worrying never w., 770 : 14
Worthy, be w. not respectable, 536 : 6
brave men and w. patriots, 281 : 19
doubt he was w. of life, 903 : 2
formen w. of steel, 431 : 14
I am not w. to unloose, 41 : 32
laborer w. of hire, 43 : 10
no w. action done, 920 : 12
nothing w. departs, 472 : 14
of self kindred to God, 522 : 5
proved them and found them w., 34 : 13
seem w. of your love, 424 : 17
taketh not cross is not w., 39 : 5
valets, 378 : 5
Wot, knows wot's w., 546 : 26
walk and w. not what they are, 190 : 12
Wotton a most dear lover, 270 : 34
Would God I had died for thee, 13 : 23
God it were even, 11 : 20
God it were morning, 11 : 20
he had blotted a thousand, 256 : 21
that I did too, 586 : 3
thou hadst ne'er been born, 232 : 5
wait upon I w., 237 : 2
we w. and we w. not, 229 : 4
when he w. shall have nay, 158 : 23
Wound, earth felt the w., 287 : 19
felt stain like w., 373 : 24
he will never get over, 749 : 20
heal by degrees, 230 : 29
heals scar disappears, 558 : 20
history of soldier's w., 360 : 3
honor take away grief of w., 205 : 5
I the w. and knife, 581 : 1
immortal w., 749 : 20
is mortal and is mine, 830 : 11
jests that never felt w., 192 : 2
much too big for hip, 839 : 9
purple with love's w., 196 : 15
put a tongue in every w., 216 : 29
read each w. each weakness, 585 : 3
read only books that w. us, 786 : 4
red badge of courage, 732 : 3
silent w. deep in her breast, 105 : 9
soothe or w. heart, 431 : 19
startle like a w., 69 : 1
that laid thee low, 456 : 17
up every morning, 595 : 16
what missing so he does not w., 884 : 22
willing to w., 338 : 14
with mercy round, 656 : 13
with thee in thee isled, 656 : 14
with touch scarcely felt, 341 : 3
Wounded but not slain, 926 : *n* 7
by my soil, 849 : 16
envious of w. soldiers, 732 : 3
in house of my friends, 33 : 35
is the wounding heart, 292 : 14
like a w. snake, 333 : 8
my heart is w. within me, 21 : 17

Wounded (*continued*)
O sacred head now w., 276 : 13
razors to my w. heart, 188 : 17
shrieks and groans of w., 579 : 3
souls w. by such things, 297 : 20
spirit who can bear, 24 : 20
what a w. name, 225 : 1
you're w., 540 : 21
Wounded Knee, bury heart at W., 840 : 3
Wounding, wounded is the w., heart, 292 : 14
Wounds, bind up my w., 187 : 26
bind up nation's w., 524 : 7
faithful are w. of friend, 25 : 23
fight and not heed w., 157 : 3
Greece w. me, 849 : 17
he licked my w., 794 : 5
in thine hands, 33 : 35
invisible, 212 : 15
labor and w. vain, 564 : 16
my w. were mended, 794 : 5
open w. shrunk sometimes, 835 : 9
soldier tells his w., 112 : 20
time heals all w., 96 : *n* 10
time w. all heels, 862 : 14
when God w. from on high, 153 : 16
Wove, delicate web you w., 808 : 19
shirt of flame, 808 : 15
your doom Faustine, 633 : 14
Wrack, betokened w. to seaman, 189 : 10
blow wind come w., 240 : 6
Wracks, thousand fearful w., 187 : 9
Wraggle- taggle gypsies O, 920 : 18
Wrang, may gang a kennin w., 409 : 21
Wrangling, remote from w. world, 384 : 15
Wrap baby bunting in, 931 : 5
wide enough to w. a fairy, 196 : 18
Wrapped, child all meanly w., 277 : 7
himself in quotations, 708 : 23
in clouds and snow, 457 : 22
in five-pound note, 550 : 7
in swaddling clothes, 42 : 27
tiger's heart w. in woman's hide, 186 : 2
Wrappings, under all misleading w., 651 : 2
Wraps me in humorous sadness, 212 : 18
Wrath, Achilles' w., 334 : *n* 4
between dragon and w., 232 : 27
by his meekness, 403 : 13
day of w. dreadful day, 430 : 12
day of w. O day of mourning, 139 : 4
did grow, 405 : 13
envy and w. shorten life, 36 : 1
flee from w. to come, 36 : 28
grapes of w., 566 : 4
grapes of w. not yielded all, 800 : 9
I told my w., 405 : 13
in w. the Olympian Pericles, 81 : 11
infinite w. and despair, 285 : 12
killeth the foolish man, 15 : 14
knows not w. nor pity, 486 : 11
let not sun go down on w., 49 : 36
my w. did end, 405 : 13
neither w. of love nor fire, 113 : 24
nursing w., 411 : 4
of Almighty God, 53 : 27
of lion wisdom of God, 404 : 3
of Peleus' son, 57 : 3, 334 : 18
provoking most justly thy w., 55 : 17
reluctance and w., 856 : 1
Wrath (*continued*)
sentest forth thy w., 9 : 35
slow to w., 51 : 30
soft answer turneth away w., 24 : 5
surely not in w. destroy, 517 : 7
sweeter than honeycomb, 58 : 30
tastes like w. to come, 757 : 6
winepress of w., 53 : 27
worketh not righteousness, 51 : 30
Wrath-bearing, tears from w. tree, 804 : 15
Wrathful man stirreth up strife, 24 : 8
winter with w. nipping cold, 185 : 14
Wreath, Don John home with w., 742 : 10
has lost rose, 431 : 20
rosy w., 256 : 9
subtle w. of hair, 253 : 11
Wreathe iron pokers into knots, 436 : 5
Wreathed, blow w. horn, 428 : 1
smiles, 277 : 19
with fairy fruits, 525 : 17
Wreaths, bindest in w. thy golden hair, 107 : 3
no w. please, 785 : 9
Wreck, came to explore w., 910 : 8
decay of colossal w., 466 : 13
out of the w. I rise, 546 : 2
Wreckage, tatty w. of my life, 911 : 8
Wrecked, greatest men oftest w., 288 : 8
in mist of opium, 589 : 12
on lee shore of age, 664 : 1
Wrecks, force made w. in world, 726 : 12
of slavery, 631 : 19
of time, 636 : 11
Wren, cannot fly like eagle with wings of w., 646 : 3
four larks and w., 550 : 4
goes to it, 234 : 31
hurt the little w., 406 : 11
robin redbreast and w., 262 : 3
Sir Christopher W., 753 : 3
Wrenlike vigilance, 893 : 12
Wrens make prey where eagles dare not, 187 : 5
Wrested from sure defeat, 810 : 3
power from nature, 851 : 15
Wresting from Jupiter his thunder, 115 : 16
Wrestle, this urge w. resurrection, 873 : 5
we w. not against flesh, 49 : 39
with demons in breast, 678 : 6
with the angel Art, 572 : 5
with words and meanings, 807 : 12
Wrestled as angel with Jacob, 270 : 28
until breaking of day, 8 : 24
Wrestles, he that w. with us, 374 : 2
Wrestling for world axeth a fal, 148 : 11
with my God my God, 656 : 16
Wretch, beware of robbing w., 6 : 3
concentered all in self, 430 : 10
excellent w., 230 : 30
hollow-eyed sharp-looking w., 188 : 15
I beheld the w., 482 : 14
I w. lay wrestling, 656 : 16
live like a w., 258 : 24
my wife poor w., 309 : 19
on hope w. relies, 368 : 11
saved a w., like me, 367 : 7
treat poor w., 319 : 20
whip to haud w. in order, 259 : *n* 11
wise w., 335 : 19
Wretched and abundant Russia, 584 : 3
blind pit ponies, 732 : 16
child expires, 730 : 8
companions consolation to w., 112 : 13
despicable creature, 346 : 4
grief transfigures w., 491 : 16
have no friends, 303 : 12
is he who bound land to himself, 4 : 1
learned to aid w., 104 : 30
man outlive wealth, 200 : 15
man w. whom no man pleases, 119 : 11
men cradled into poetry, 467 : 15
nothing more w. than a man, 58 : 29
of the earth, 555 : 24
poor man that hangs on princes' favors, 249 : 3
proud yet w. thing, 251 : 7
refuse of teeming shore, 664 : 10
sleep soundly as w. slave, 208 : 7
taste gratified with mediocrity, 417 : 2
to relieve w. his pride, 370 : 6
un-ideaed girls, 353 : 25
Wretcheder one is the more one smokes, 617 : 1
Wretchedness, consigned to state of w., 379 : 2
that glory brings, 243 : 7
Wretches, feel what w. feel, 234 : 4
hang that jurymen dine, 334 : 6
hired, 352 : 9
poor naked w., 234 : 3
who never were alive, 140 : 18
Wrights, crucified the Fanny W., 554 : 9
Wrigley, Spearmint Girl With W. Eyes, 828 : 17
Wring his bosom, 369 : 21
pain and anguish w. brow, 431 : 2
pangs wilder w., 656 : 17
Wringing bread from sweat, 524 : 5
Wrinkle, no w. on azure brow, 458 : 27
stamps w. deeper, 457 : 10
Wrinkled Care derides, 277 : 20
lame w. and slanting-eyed, 58 : 11
sea, 532 : 28
smoothed his w. front, 186 : 30
view with w. brow, 200 : 15
Wrinkles, eyes mid many w., 717 : 7
progress in phalanx, 798 : 12
Wrist, ease darbies at w., 572 : 7
hands in up to w., 868 : 10
Wristwatch taken from wrist, 894 : 7
Writ, having w. moves on, 517 : 2
I never w., 245 : 18
in remembrance, 194 : 10
name w. in water, 480 : 7
odd old ends stolen of Holy W., 187 : 6
proofs of holy w., 231 : 7
slaughters of race w., 641 : 19
with me in misfortune's book, 193 : 25
your annals true, 242 : 26
Write about it Goddess, 340 : 25
about things you know best, 861 : 16
after that about infinite, 824 : 6
after that about my double, 824 : 5
baseness to w. fair, 224 : 26
better neither read nor w., 445 : 4
blockheads read what blockheads w., 342 : 11
born to w., 338 : 14
can't w. can review, 567 : 19
casts to w. living line, 256 : 16
dare to read think speak w., 380 : 10

Write (*continued*)
devise wit w. pen, 190 : 18
does he w., 543 : 31
evil in marble, 155 : 8
few who w. know anything, 597 : 7
finely upon broomstick, 322 : *n* 2
for those who understand, 731 : 9
free to think speak w., 390 : 2
from worm's-eye view, 848 : 15
good in dust, 155 : 8
history don't, 615 : 16
I detest what you w., 344 : *n* 5
I do not think I can w. more, 726 : 7
I live and w., 269 : 5
I w. nothing other than images, 850 : 6
I w. poets all, 605 : 17
I w. wonders of religion, 319 : 22
in books of law, 872 : 9
in de blotter I was born, 810 : 8
in spite of Nature, 291 : 9
in youth men w. wisely, 504 : 1
instruction manual, 906 : 11
know what I know and w. it, 886 : 8
knowingly w. what is false, 95 : 18
last till you w. your letter, 252 : 3
literary man w. for his public, 731 : 9
look in thy heart and w., 176 : 13
man may w. at any time, 353 : 24
masters of things they w., 263 : 20
me as one that loves, 454 : 6
me down an ass, 210 : 2
not Died in pains, 609 : 12
not w. down happiness, 655 : 4
nothing to w. about, 123 : 7
on principle of iceberg, 845 : 13
only great man w. history, 676 : 5
poem for money, 863 : 20
poetry very easy to w., 618 : 2
right to w. badly, 828 : 7
saddest poem tonight, 860 : 8
sorrow on bosom of the earth, 195 : 1
speak associate, 872 : 18
the next chapter, 872 : 9
the vision, 33 : 25
things worthy reading, 347 : 18
three lessons I would w., 412 : 11
to rage to lust to w. to, 253 : 10
to w. and read comes by nature, 209 : 24
'twas certain he could w., 370 : 10
virtues we w. in water, 249 : 14
well in laudable things, 281 : 14
well of American things, 652 : 4
whatever I tried to w. was verse, 113 : 29
with ease to show breeding, 399 : 11
with no dinner, 811 : 1
woman's vows upon wave, 75 : 22
yet w. verse badly, 297 : 31
you a tragedy, 835 : 14
Writer, character of w. in writings, 472 : 7
concealed beauties of w., 326 : 19
doesn't want success, 838 : 14
dream anguishes w., 838 : 13
excels at title page, 368 : 5
give that you're a w., 845 : 4
great and original w., 428 : 8
great w. second government, 895 : 18
if w. omits something, 845 : 13
like bean plant, 846 : 10
moment here and there w. has, 750 : 6
Writer (*continued*)
my tongue is the pen of a ready w., 19 : 8
no tears in w. no tears in reader, 750 : 3
nodding-places in w., 326 : 15
of dictionaries, 352 : 11
original w. one nobody can imitate, 419 : 7
Southern w. adept at recognizing grotesque, 905 : 4
teach himself to be afraid, 838 : 8
to be woman and w., 867 : 2
true w. nothing to say, 901 : 5
when w. becomes nudnik, 861 : 12
Writer's privilege to help man endure, 838 : 12
responsibility to art, 838 : 13
understand w. ignorance, 437 : 9
Writers, ancient w. say, 715 : 19
are always selling you out, 913 : 2
become more numerous, 368 : 6
compulsion put upon w., 791 : 7
forgotten for want of w., 108 : *n* 11
gifted energetic wives of w., 889 : 1
habit of accurate w., 616 : 4
make mistake of enclosing envelope, 790 : 6
mistakes made by w. out of ignorance, 95 : 18
of small histories, 352 : 10
some w. cannot them digest, 181 : 22
transcribed from former works, 116 : 4
Writes, great poet w. his time, 809 : 11
limns on water w. in dust, 181 : 18
moving finger w., 517 : 2
of scars healed, 835 : 9
subject he speaks or writes upon, 342 : 8
verses speaks holiday, 225 : 20
very well for a gentleman, 328 : *n* 4
whatever poet w. with enthusiasm, 79 : 9
Writhed not at passing joy, 478 : 15
Writing a name for conversation, 360 : 5
denied full w. life, 883 : 8
do things worth the w., 347 : 18
easy w. is hard reading, 399 : 11
elongated-yellow-fruit school of w., 846 : 1
faucet upstairs, 750 : 9
get w., 800 : 1
in book of gold, 454 : 5
in w. himself writes his time, 809 : 11
in w. joy of discovery, 771 : 15
incurable itch for w., 122 : 12
joruri, 317 : 9
judicial w., 730 : 15
maketh an exact man, 181 : 13
master to this world, 799 : 6
much w. many opinions, 282 : 2
nature's masterpiece w. well, 316 : 5
no partiality in his w., 98 : 10
not give up w. too famous, 812 : 6
not obliged to like particular w., 653 : 4
precautions against disease of w., 136 : 8
putting it down in w., 348 : 17
rid of things by w. them, 845 : 3
swimming under water, 835 : 18
take away art of w., 419 : 8
Writing (*continued*)
that was written, 33 : 1
true ease in w., 333 : 9
vigorous w. concise, 729 : 7
voting reasonably, 650 : 14
Writing's, easy w. cursed hard reading, 399 : 11
Writings, character of writer in w., 472 : 7
praise nor blame w., 333 : 12
small men afraid of w., 378 : 10
Written, absurd all w. hitherto, 543 : 25
and unwritten law, 125 : 28
as it is w., 48 : 2
books well or badly w., 674 : 22
censure who have w. well, 332 : 16
everything w. as good as dramatic, 750 : 1
most insincere line w., 803 : 1
next chapter already w., 864 : 14
of me on my stone, 749 : 8
out of reputation, 319 : 2
poetry well w. as prose, 793 : 6
read books as deliberately as w., 559 : 29
sonnets all his life, 460 : 25
that mine adversary had w. a book, 16 : 20
that my words were w., 16 : 3
troubles of the brain, 239 : 32
volumes might be w., 579 : 18
what woman says w. in wind, 102 : 12
Wrong, accumulated w., 704 : 17
all his life in the w., 315 : 21
always in the w., 304 : 10
can't be w. whose life right, 337 : 9
citizens clamoring for what is w., 107 : 28
conduct right argument w., 371 : 15
cradled into poetry by w., 467 : 15
customs not concerned with w., 626 : 5
divinely in the w., 329 : 22
do great right little w., 200 : 10
do w. to none, 227 : 9
done my credit w., 517 : 10
dreary morals w., 669 : 14
dwelling much on w., 311 : 15
fact that man can do w., 626 : 4
faith in nice tenets w., 295 : 19
fashioning characters w. way, 648 : 10
forever on throne, 567 : 7
Frenchmen can't be w., 924 : 12
friends have it I do w., 713 : 4
from the start, 792 : 10
gloomy w., 504 : 2
had anything been w., 869 : 3
he done her w., 923 : 8
he who believes what is w., 387 : 12
I know I've done wrong, 927 : 15
if end brings me out w., 524 : 11
if I called w. number, 831 : 1
if you w. us not revenge, 199 : 18
just as dead as if w., 925 : 10
kind of victory, 788 : 15
king can do no w., 365 : 18
Lucrece swears he did her w., 189 : 27
majorities not entirely w., 579 : 17
may gang a kennin w., 409 : 21
mixed in w. that's all, 810 : 6
multitude always in w., 309 : 10
ne'er pardon who have done w., 115 : *n* 3

Wrong (*continued*)
never ashamed to own w., 340 : 10
never dreamed w. triumph, 546 : 7
never w. old masters, 868 : 9
newts and blindworms do no w., 196 : 21
no end to w., 4 : 7
no harm in being w., 783 : 13
no one harm man who does self no w., 128 : 24
one idea and that w., 354 : 21
one more w. to man, 541 : 8
oppressor's w., 221 : 12
our country right or w., 445 : 19, 603 : 4
poem begins as sense of w., 749 : 19
preserve stars from w., 427 : 16
rather be w. with Plato, 98 : 23
right judge judges w., 74 : 13
right of kings to govern w., 340 : 24
right w. follow king, 534 : 5
rule of right and w., 602 : 6
rules the land, 567 : *n* 1
side of thirty, 323 : 8
some villain hath done me w., 189 : *n* 3
somebody's pain and w., 653 : 15
something w. something human, 885 : 10
sow by ear, 161 : 10
struggle between and right w., 520 : 8
suffer w. no more, 488 : 13
that they reject is w., 634 : 17
themselves men w., 130 : 17
those not present w., 329 : 17
to speed a guest, 60 : 19
truth live with right and w., 829 : 16
unavenged suffering w., 582 : 4
unless w. I but obey, 749 : 18
war at wrong time, 825 : 5
wars w. from every standpoint, 788 : 15
way seems more reasonable, 671 : 7
when w. Ezra so w., 845 : 6
when w. to be put right, 603 : 4
whether laws w., 676 : 12
which roams earth, 4 : 7
with strikers right or w., 765 : 11
wrongest in Kentucky, 657 : 6
ye do me w., 917 : 14
Wrongdoer often left something undone, 125 : 16
ox of w., 4 : 3
Wrongdoing, abstain from intentional w., 79 : 13
and righteousness of men, 60 : 25
for great w. great punishments, 78 : 8
never with view to w., 79 : 13
of one generation, 503 : 16
or impotence, 687 : 10
virtuous for good cause, 110 : 24
Wrongdoings, thought to justify w., 343 : 24
Wronged, I am w., 71 : 2
on that day no soul w., 132 : 6
woman who has w. you, 647 : 19
Wronger, loves not his w., 230 : 34
Wronging your image that blossoms, 712 : 12
Wrongs, arise avenger of w., 105 : 11
God w. not men, 130 : 17
mass of public w., 177 : 1
monstrous product of w., 744 : 8
procure redress of w., 380 : 6
Wrongs (*continued*)
unredressed, 428 : 12
we seek to condemn, 821 : 7
Wrote, and I w. my happy songs, 403 : 3
ever w. except for money, 355 : 20
gentlemen who w. with ease, 339 : 23
like an angel, 363 : 17
one song, 544 : 2
Purple Cow, 718 : 16
reason Milton w. in fetters, 403 : 19
sarcastikul, 616 : 11
that never w. to me, 605 : 12
Thucydides w. history of war, 80 : 14
upon tables words of covenant, 10 : 15
will across sky, 810 : 2
Wroth with one we love, 434 : 3
Wrought, being w. perplexed, 232 : 20
first he w. afterward taughte, 146 : 8
ghost upon floor, 526 : 11
in sad sincerity, 493 : 18
love w. new alchemy, 253 : 1
more w. by prayer, 535 : 1
not into evil w., 631 : 15
remembers all that he w., 60 : 20
so distinctly w., 254 : 6
what hath God w., 11 : 5
wore as though they w. it, 713 : 14
Wrung life dry for your lips, 632 : 21
Wry-necked fife, 199 : 4
Wum, rooster don't cackle w'en fine w., 662 : 14
Wyllowe-tree, al under the w., 399 : 15
Wynken Blynken and Nod, 666 : 16
Wyoming will be your new home, 927 : 10

X

X, dominant X, 768 : 2
Xanadu, in X. did Kubla Khan, 433 : 21
Xenophon, a X. at New York, 363 : 21
Xerxes did die, 320 : 9

Y

Yacht and bank account man's self, 648 : 17
annual upkeep of y., 923 : *n* 8
Yahoo tricks, 765 : 4
Yale, whaleship my Y. College, 570 : 10
Yang, yin and y., 97 : 7
Yankee Doodle, 920 : 9
I'm a Y. Doodle dandy, 759 : 6
in Eden would alter it, 561 : 13
Yankees have the marrow, 455 : 8
tough but nervous, 799 : 18
Yanks are coming, 759 : 7
Yarn, merry y. from rover, 760 : 16
mingled y. good and ill, 227 : 16
spun in Ulysses' absence, 242 : 10
Yawn, churchyards y., 222 : 23
never y. or say commonplace, 901 : 3
yawning make another y., 258 : 19
Yawning make another yawn, 258 : 19
rung night's y. peal, 238 : 20
Yawns and draws stocking up, 804 : 24
Yawp, barbaric y., 575 : 3
Yea, everlasting y., 472 : 25
Yea-forsooth, rascally y. knave, 205 : 22
Year and a day, 550 : 8
circle of golden y., 529 : 5
dirge of dying y., 467 : 19
every y. passed day, 907 : 10
famous day and y., 512 : 6
farewell snow of ferne y., 145 : 5
fiftieth y. jubilee, 10 : 22
firstling of the infant y., 272 : 2
flower bloom another y., 478 : 9
food for seven long y., 234 : 10
grief with revolving y., 469 : 4
had lost meaning, 858 : 19
heaven's eternal y., 305 : 6
if y. playing holidays, 203 : 5
in y. of his age, 133 : 9
is at the spring, 540 : 15
is going let him go, 532 : 22
live well on nothing a y., 539 : 8
make up y. and sphere, 494 : 3
mellowing y., 280 : 6
most immemorial y., 526 : 22
new y. reviving desires, 516 : 2
no trumpets for new y., 755 : 9
not every y. a king or poet born, 123 : 17
only lost to me, 268 : 21
outlive his life half a y., 222 : 10
plunges into night, 785 : 14
proper opinions for time of y., 869 : 2
rich with forty pounds a y., 370 : 5
ruler of inverted y., 377 : 5
saddest of the y., 471 : 10
sailed away y. and a day, 550 : 8
seven stars solar y., 495 : 15
six hundred pounds a y., 339 : 10
snow y. a rich y., 269 : 17
sun is elder by a y., 252 : 22
sweet o' the y., 246 : 21
that night that y. of now, 656 : 16
that time of y. in me behold, 244 : 27
thou crownest the y. with thy goodness, 19 : 30
three hundred pounds a y., 225 : 21
three-and-twentieth y., 277 : 14
twenty pound a y., 268 : 6
two hundred pounds a y., 291 : 27
unloved y., 864 : 1
varied y., 345 : 4
wake year to sorrow, 469 : 7
whose days are long, 676 : 12
Yearn, believe in God y. for God, 705 : 17
finite hearts that y., 542 : 10
love those who y. for impossible, 396 : 23
Yearned for telling found in legends, 906 : 4
Yearning like god in pain, 476 : 10
spirit y. in desire, 529 : 10
tender y. sweet hoping, 413 : 21
to breathe free, 664 : 10
while hearts y., 740 : 11
Yearnings for equal division, 449 : 4
Year's at the spring, 540 : 15
midnight, 252 : 24
no birds in last y. nest, 171 : *n* 3
pleasant king, 250 : 8
watering last y. crops, 565 : 5
Years, age not numbered by y., 168 : 1
ah no the y. O, 642 : 4
all hopes of future y., 511 : 8
all one hundred y. hence, 498 : 17
are still a burden, 76 : 5
are threescore and ten, 20 : 13

Years (*continued*)
are voyagers, 313 : 23
around sea-town corner, 887 : 5
been around for long long y., 916 : 8
beginning of y., 632 : 9, 634 : 7
bliss bought by y., 561 : 21
damp my intended wing, 287 : 13
disingenuousness of y., 489 : 2
fifty y. of Europe, 530 : 9
first hundred y. hardest, 757 : 12
first twenty-five y., 492 : 19
fleet away with wings, 459 : 18
fleeting y. slip by, 107 : 23
for three y. out of key, 792 : 10
forty y. on, 627 : 5
fourscore and seven y., 523 : 4
fourteen hundred y. ago were nailed, 202 : 22
glass of y. is brittle, 633 : 7
God's instant men call y., 545 : 6
golden y. return, 468 : 17
gone y. now y. maybe y., 888 : 5
grow cold to love, 104 : 9
hair gray but not with y., 459 : 21
house to be let for life or y., 267 : 14
humor saves y., 799 : 7
imagining future y. come, 714 : 14
Jacob served seven y., 8 : 22
knightly y. were gone, 663 : 13
like great black oxen, 712 : 2
live past y. again, 303 : 11
long dull middle-aged y., 842 : 11
may be for y., 487 : 3
middle-aged y., 842 : 11
months add selves make y., 534 : 25
more memories than if thousand y. old, 580 : 21
new y. ruin and rend, 633 : 6
no-man's-y., 827 : 20
nor the y. draw nigh, 27 : 24
nor y. condemn, 727 : 1
not count man's y., 499 : 18
O for ten y., 475 : 11
old and stricken in y., 11 : 35
our hope for y. to come, 328 : 10
out of me y. roll, 634 : 4
outweighs whole y., 337 : 14
perished to make us men, 631 : 14
plunder one thing after another, 109 : 16
ran a hundred y. to a day, 519 : 15
roll into centuries, 534 : 25
sea folk live to three hundred y., 505 : 4
seven y. of famine, 8 : 31
short space of four y., 521 : 13
sorrow comes with y., 507 : 2
spend our y. as a tale that is told, 20 : 12
spend this little span of y., 100 : 13
steal fire from mind, 457 : 12
survive two thousand million y., 758 : 8
ten y. on Pullman cars, 810 : 7
that bring philosophic mind, 426 : 22
thousand leagues a thousand y., 348 : 10
thousand y. are as yesterday, 20 : 11
thousand y. of peace, 532 : 23
three y. she grew, 424 : 13
threescore y. and ten, 20 : 13, 690 : 17
Time in hours days y., 299 : 6
touch of earthly y., 424 : 14

Years (*continued*)
twenty y. in woman's life, 84 : 14
two y. ten y., 761 : 6
vale of y., 231 : 5
vanity in y., 204 : 5
wander in the wilderness forty y., 10 : 25
whatever comes with y., 633 : 15
where all past y. are, 252 : 1
wind him for fourscore y., 303 : 16
work as if to live hundred y., 347 : 31
yesterday's seven thousand y., 516 : 13
Yeats, cadence from man named Y., 873 : 18
in churchyard Y. laid, 718 : 1
William Y. laid to rest, 868 : 11
Yell, gave y. for y. to gale, 683 : 5
Yelled, flew down y. at craft, 855 : 9
Yellow, all looks y., 333 : 16
black pale hectic red, 467 : 17
Brick Road, 677 : 8
cheek white beard, 205 : 28
come unto these y. sands, 247 : 19
commended y. stockings, 214 : 10
cuckoo-buds of y. hue, 191 : 13
dawn becomes y., 928 : 17
drifts of withered leaves, 588 : 5
flutterings, 475 : 2
green and y. melancholy, 214 : 5
half-moon large low, 541 : 13
leaves or none or few, 244 : 27
locks y. as gold, 434 : 19
my days in y. leaf, 462 : 18
nodding o'er y. plain, 345 : 13
not your y. hair, 716 : 5
primrose was to him, 423 : 16
put down The Y. Book, 866 : 16
roman candles exploding, 901 : 3
the sere the y. leaf, 239 : 31
with August, 792 : 9
Yellow-colored objects appear gold, 137 : *n* 8
Yelping seas, 804 : 16
wife, 874 : 21
Yeoman's service, 224 : 27
Yes by Saint Anne, 213 : 26
I answered last night, 507 : 5
I said yes I will yes, 778 : 4
my darling daughter, 924 : 17
tid there's where, 778 : 6
to everything good, 650 : 1
to the very end, 608 : 10
Virginia there is a Santa Claus, 638 : *n* 4
Yesterday bird of night did sit, 215 : 12
call back y., 194 : 27, 257 : 17
came suddenly, 914 : 9
egg tomorrow duster, 740 : 7
fact today doctrine, 390 : 10
foolishness of y., 664 : 12
great families of y., 318 : 7
jam tomorrow jam y., 613 : 11
keeping up with y., 760 : 2
loneliness of y., 836 : 17
man's y. ne'er like morrow, 466 : 11
maybe it was y., 882 : 2
no tomorrow nor y., 252 : 22
not worry about y., 655 : 1
pomp of y., 709 : 18
rose of y., 516 : 6
same y. today and forever, 51 : 24
sleep which thou owedst y., 231 : 8
stuck fast in y., 740 : 3

Yesterday (*continued*)
tarries with y., 782 : 15
thousand years are as y., 20 : 11
to today so lightly, 878 : 20
unborn tomorrow dead y., 517 : 1
who has seen y., 462 : 12
wiser today than y., 340 : 10
word of Caesar stood, 216 : 21
Yesterday's seven thousand years, 516 : 13
Yesterdays have lighted fools, 240 : 4
man of cheerful y., 428 : 18
Yesternight, last night ah y., 721 : 4
the sun went hence, 252 : 16
Yesteryear, where are snows of y., 150 : 7
where snows of y., 601 : 16
Yet a little while, 45 : 17
forget not y., 161 : 22
the end is not y., 40 : 22
Yew, never spray of y., 586 : 3
not too far from y., 808 : 9
to deck my grave, 402 : 14
true wood y. wood, 689 : 16
Yezhov, terrible years of Y., 801 : 15
Yield, and not to y., 529 : 14
at touch I y., 531 : 10
could not make sickle y., 404 : 15
courage never to y., 283 : 8
historian y. self to subject, 800 : 3
neither y. to song of siren, 177 : 17
not neck to fortune's yoke, 186 : 11
not to evils, 105 : 14
to get rid of temptation, 674 : 27
to that suggestion, 236 : 11
to y. is to be preserved, 64 : 10
who will to separation, 748 : 18
with grace to reason, 747 : 2
Yielded bitter vintage, 800 : 9
with coy submission, 285 : 19
Yielding place to new, 534 : 31
to temptations, 484 : 15
Yields nothing but discontent, 372 : 8
what sweet hour y., 470 : 4
woods or steepy mountain y., 183 : 8
Yin and yang, 97 : 7
Yo-ho-ho and bottle of rum, 668 : 4
Yoke, bear his mild y., 282 : 17
bear the y. in his youth, 32 : 24
my y. is easy, 39 : 8
resent y., 517 : 6
savage bull bear y., 209 : 2
shake y. of inauspicious stars 193 : 28
take my y., 39 : 8
yield not neck to fortune's y., 186 : 11
Yoknapatawpha County, 838 : 6
Yolk, heaven like egg earth like y., 123 : 16
Yonder all before us lie, 296 : 28
Yonghy-Bonghy-Bo, lived Y., 550 : 16
Yore, not now as of y., 426 : 10
Yorick, alas poor Y., 224 : 14
York, made summer by sun of Y., 186 : 29
Yorkshire, living in Y., 433 : 3
You ain't heard nothing yet, 795 : 4
alone are you, 244 : 29
also Brutus, 99 : 24
and I past dancing days, 191 : 25
are you and I am I, 827 : 19
are young my son, 86 : 3
as y. are woman, 833 : 3
asses made to bear so are y., 188 : 31
can't go home again, 852 : 13

You (*continued*)
do something to me, 820 : 1
do your thing, 827 : 19
Doctor Martin, 908 : 8
have conquered Galilean, 127 : 5
have named him, 312 : 7
I and y. and all of us, 216 : 25
I get a kick out of y., 820 : 3
I to die and y. to live, 83 : 15
land made for y. and me, 881 : 1
one single individual Y., 576 : 10
story's about y., 106 : 11
two are bookmen, 190 : 29
utter y. twenty times, 636 : 6
while I am I y. are y., 542 : 11
would not take it, 822 : 6
your mind and y., 792 : 5
You-all means race or section, 922 : 9
Young Adam Cupid, 192 : 1
affections run to waste, 458 : 18
ambition's ladder, 215 : 16
and easy, 886 : 19
and foolish, 711 : 22
and have world before you, 320 : 1
and old come forth to play, 278 : 1
and old the same, 70 : 8
and rose-lipped cherubin, 232 : 4
and so fair, 485 : 21
ask the y., 400 : 12
Bacchus ever fair and y., 306 : 15
beautiful time of y. love, 413 : 21
blood have course, 566 : 14
blood not obey old decree, 190 : 33
bloom of y. desire, 362 : 21
boys and girls level, 241 : 22
buds sleep in root, 478 : 9
caparisons don't become y. woman, 398 : 15
child with Mary, 36 : 21
compliment on looking y., 453 : 4
crime of being y. man, 350 : 16
daring y. man, 636 : 12
deep y. man, 628 : 6
discretion in man not too y., 116 : 2
eats the she-wolf's y., 435 : 6
fair maidens quiet eyes, 669 : 7
find us y. keep us so, 494 : 9
foot-in-the-grave y. man, 628 : 12
freeze thy y. blood, 219 : 18
gigantic willful y., 728 : 12
go west y. man, 554 : 3
great with y., 927 : 3
greatest reverence due y., 122 : 19
Harry with beaver on, 204 : 31
how y. America is, 729 : 11
I am too y. to understand, 486 : 16
I being y. and foolish, 711 : 22
I have been y. and now am old, 18 : 25
I was very y., 403 : 9
I would be y. as any, 894 : 5
if ladies but y. and fair, 211 : 9
if world and love were y., 172 : 10
in limbs judgment old, 199 : 10
in New Mexico he awoke y., 739 : 5
in one another's arms, 714 : 22
jailed for telling lies to y., 863 : 11
je-ne-sais-quoi y. man, 628 : 11
judge should not be y., 84 : 9
keep cold y. orchard, 748 : 10
knew worst too y., 708 : 15
lady named Bright, 742 : 1
lead those that are with y., 30 : 35
lion and fatling together, 29 : 19
lion and the dragon, 20 : 17

Young (*continued*)
lions roar after prey, 21 : 11
Lochinvar, 430 : 17
look y. till forty, 394 : *n* 3
love of y. for y., 692 : 17
loved when all was y., 566 : 15
love's y. dream, 446 : 12
man embarrassed to question, 59 : 20
man in whom something of old, 99 : 8
man married is marred, 227 : 15
man there is America, 372 : 12
man to lie mangled, 59 : 6
man who has not wept, 704 : 9
man you're dyin', 926 : 22
man's fancy turns, 529 : 16
man's heart's complaint, 574 : 22
men all over world, 743 : 10
men fitter to invent, 181 : 7
men need stiffening, 679 : 10
men not lost race, 852 : 11
men of new age, 406 : 20
men shall see visions, 33 : 17
men think it is, 692 : 9
men think old men fools, 177 : 13
men's minds changeable, 57 : 22
men's vision, 304 : 5
myself when y., 516 : 16
need to be y. to say, 400 : 11
no one so y. he cannot die, 153 : 15
not so y. as painted, 735 : 21
not such plague when y., 717 : 13
O y. fresshe folkes, 145 : 8
old men know y. men fools, 177 : 13
old sight yet somehow y., 571 : 8
ones suck up blood, 17 : 1
person occupied with himself, 754 : 6
pure y. man, 628 : 7
queens have died y. and fair, 250 : 10
rage when y., 715 : 11
regard elders as senile, 634 : 24
rejoice O y. man in youth, 27 : 23
Scotchman if caught y., 355 : 5
sea captains y. or old, 575 : 22
shall lie down together, 29 : 19
she died so y., 525 : *n* 5
she died y., 262 : 10
sight to make old man y., 529 : 2
so wise so y., 187 : 13
so y. and so untender, 232 : 26
so y. body with so old head, 200 : 8
so y. my lord and true, 232 : 26
spring, 859 : 2
star captains glow, 785 : 15
stayeth y. man's courting, 793 : 2
steersman steering, 575 : 19
studies are a spur to y., 98 : 7
sun y. once only, 887 : 1
teach y. idea to shoot, 345 : 11
that ever died so y., 525 : 15
the y. need old men, 898 : 14
though old man y. gardener, 389 : 6
thought y. man brings forth, 85 : 16
time cancels y. pain, 76 : 13
time of y. love, 413 : 21
to bar as very y. man, 628 : 22
to be y. was very heaven, 424 : 5
to y. man knowledge and discretion, 23 : 1
very y. most selfish, 539 : 23
we loved each other, 716 : 20
we that are y., 235 : 20
when all world y. lad, 566 : 14
when you and I were y., 519 : 1, 636 : 9

Young (*continued*)
whom age doth chill, 290 : 6
whom gods love dies y., 91 : 1
whom he finds y. keeps y., 290 : 6
wives y. men's mistresses, 180 : 10
you are y. my son, 86 : 3
Younger generation, 600 : 7
love be y. than thyself, 214 : 2
than springtime, 833 : 14
Youngest critic died, 707 : 21
Young-eyed cherubins, 201 : 1
Youngster, heart of an old y., 877 : 7
Youngsters read men understand, 169 : 39
Younker, how like a y., 199 : 6
You're the top, 820 : 4
Yours, what is y. is mine, 93 : 8
what's mine is y., 229 : 10
world was always y., 822 : 6
Yourself, cannot make y. as you wish, 148 : 14
don't speak well of y., 299 : 15
first keep peace in y., 148 : 19
give of y. truly give, 782 : 16
if you can take y. away, 560 : 30
if you want to know y., 413 : 1
keep y. to y., 546 : 22
long for something in y., 880 : 3
love you for y. alone, 716 : 5
rely on y., 556 : 1
so hot that it singe y., 248 : 22
speak for y. John, 511 : 21
your subject is y., 483 : 14
Yourselves, be lamps unto y., 72 : 20
quit y. like men, 12 : 31
Youth a blunder, 501 : 15
a stuff will not endure, 213 : 23
age not so well qualified as y., 559 : 7
age of antiquity y. of world, 178 : *n* 11
age perform promises of y., 352 : 15
age preferable to y., 327 : 15
and age equally a burden, 84 : 4
and I lived in 't together, 436 : 7
bear the yoke in his y., 32 : 24
beauty for confiding y., 428 : 23
becomes as aged, 228 : 16
bedewed with liquid odors, 107 : 3
bent by wintry fever, 886 : 12
bourgeois in ferment of y., 583 : 14
bright y. passes swiftly, 67 : 7
build bridge to moon, 557 : 12
caught our y., 797 : 2
crabbed age and y., 917 : 11
dew of y., 21 : 18, 218 : 27
don't regret excess of y., 654 : 7
eyes of y., 225 : 20
face to lose y. for, 544 : 26
fame thirst of y., 458 : 2
fight and die, 750 : 20
flaming y., 223 : 5
flourish set on y., 244 : 20
flowering y. sinking age, 851 : 1
follies cease with y., 350 : 16
foundation laid in y., 689 : 21
freakish y., 376 : 23
friends of my y. where are they, 132 : 28
from y. to extreme old age, 584 : 8
full of grace, 575 : 13
full of pleasance, 917 : 11
'gainst time and age, 177 : 8
gather gather your y., 163 : 1
gave love and roses, 447 : 9
gives y. delight, 337 : 7

Youth (*continued*)
glass wherein y. dress, 206 : 14
grows pale, 476 : 24
heart is evil from his y., 7 : 33
hell that tests my y., 819 : 4
home-keeping y. homely wits, 189 : 28
hour of thoughtless y., 423 : 13
I love gone to war, 929 : 3
if y. but knew if old age but could, 163 : 11
if y. season of hope, 565 : 24
immortal y. to mortal maids, 442 : 21
in my hot y., 108 : 5
in my y. said his father, 611 : 10
in the days of my y., 439 : 16
in y. begin in sadness, 892 : 15
in y. hearts touched with fire, 643 : 17
in y. it sheltered me, 492 : 10
in y. men write wisely, 504 : 1
is given, 897 : 1
is vain, 434 : 3
I've done it from my y., 400 : 6
knew phoenix in y., 714 : 5
large lusty loving, 575 : 13
lexicon of y., 493 : 7
like spring overpraised, 620 : 8
liquid dew of y., 218 : 27
lying days of y., 713 : 8
many a y. and many a maid, 278 : 1
measure of our y., 708 : 15
mewing her mighty y., 282 : 3
moment of glamor of y., 683 : 11
much depends upon education of y., 392 : 11
now bravely spending, 811 : 16
of America tradition, 675 : 15
of England are on fire, 207 : 10
of labor, 370 : 2
of pleasure wasteful, 545 : 22
on the prow, 363 : 6
our y. our joys our all, 173 : 5
passed age not arrived, 564 : 4
poets in y. begin, 425 : 10
prime of y. a frost of cares, 177 : 10
rejoice O young man in y., 27 : 23
remember thy Creator in days of thy y., 27 : 24
replies I can, 494 : 21
riband in cap of y., 224 : 3
rider that breaks y., 270 : 9
rose of y., 241 : 9
roses for flush of y., 608 : 18
sacred to education, 665 : 15
season for enjoyment, 492 : 19
season made for joys, 332 : 4
season of credulity, 350 : 18
should be filial, 68 : 3
so are children of the y., 22 : 10

Youth (*continued*)
Socrates corrupts the y., 83 : 11
soul of my y., 789 : 15
spirit of y. in everything, 245 : 9
stone dead, 795 : 15
studied in my foolish y., 150 : 6
that fired Ephesian dome, 275 : *n* 1
that I thought sweet, 162 : 5
thou hast nor y. nor age, 228 : 16
thoughts of y. long, 511 : 25
time for extraordinary toil, 84 : 20
time of getting, 290 : 9
Time subtle thief of y., 277 : 14
to fortune and fame unknown, 362 : 17
to whom given so much, 425 : 1
traitorously corrupted y., 185 : 28
unmannerly sadness in y., 198 : 12
vaward of our y., 205 : 27
waneth by increasing, 177 : 8
what done with your y., 659 : 15
when y. and pleasure meet, 457 : 15
who daily farther travel, 426 : 15
wholly experimental, 669 : 18
will be served, 492 : 18
world made to be won by y., 743 : 11
Youthful, days when we y., 519 : *n* 1
harlot's curse, 405 : 10
hose well saved, 211 : 15
jest and y. jollity, 277 : 19
sights as y. poets dream, 278 : 6
sinewy races, 575 : 15
Youth's a stuff will not endure, 213 : 23
heritage, 544 : 12
sweet-scented manuscript, 517 : 12
the season made for joys, 332 : 4
You've got to get up, 802 : 5
Ypres, pile them high at Y., 761 : 6
Yukon Jake, 834 : 6
law of the Y., 752 : 4
will of the Y., 752 : 4

Z

Zaccheus he did climb tree, 320 : 10
Zarathustra said to his heart, 657 : 11
Zeal, all z. Mr. Easy, 465 : 14
confidence z. loyalty, 771 : 13
for different opinions, 398 : 2
half the z. I served my king, 249 : 9
heavenly race demands z., 346 : 1
mistaken z., 391 : 3
Zealots, let graceless z. fight, 337 : 9
Zealous, a man z. for nothing, 356 : 10
locksmith died, 919 : 13
Zealously affected in good thing, 49 : 27
Zeiten, ein Märchen aus alten Z., 481 : *n* 7
Zek, country inhabited by Z. people, 895 : 23
Zekle, hern went pity-Z., 568 : 5
Zèle, pas de z., 401 : *n* 1
Zenith, dropped from the z., 284 : 2
illusion reaches its z., 658 : 14
Zephyr, soft z. blows, 363 : 6
Zero at the bone, 606 : 14
Zeus accomplisher, 71 : 27
all strangers and beggars are from Z., 60 : 1
divine bird of Z., 71 : 24
does not bring all plans to fulfillment, 59 : 2
drag Z. from heaven to earth, 58 : 6
dream too is from Z., 57 : 5
first cause, 71 : 11
from Z. let us begin, 92 : 11
god of council loves them, 57 : 16
lead me Z. and Fate, 92 : 2
might change me to bird, 76 : 24
no mortal could vie with Z., 59 : 24
plan of Z., 57 : 4
prayers are daughters of Z., 58 : 11
takes half a man's worth, 60 : 23
two jars on floor of Z., 59 : 12
wide-sounding Z., 58 : 17, 60 : 23
Zeus-fostered, proud is spirit of Z. kings, 57 : 16
Zeus's bed of love, 76 : 25
Eros Z. child, 76 : 22
Zigzag, four lightnings z. from me, 928 : 21
lightning stands high, 928 : 18
Zion, at ease in Z., 33 : 21, 772 : 12
city of our God, 367 : 8
come with singing unto Z., 31 : 9
songs of Z., 22 : 15
wept when we remembered Z., 22 : 15
Zodiac, handfull z., 886 : 15
Zone, best gem on her z., 493 : 19
He who from z. to z., 471 : 7
torrid or frozen z., 271 : 22
Zones and meridian lines, 613 : 22
Zoologic types develop ceaselessly, 673 : 10
Zoroaster, holy prophet Z. said, 159 : *n* 6
Magus Z. my dead child, 466 : 16
Zounds never so bethumped, 201 : 17
Zucchini, withered as if stained z., 905 : 15
Zuleika on desert island, 736 : 1
Zurich, learned three things in Z., 914 : 4
Zweigen, der in den Z. wohnet, 395 : *n* 1